The BBQ Queens' Big Book of Barbecue

Enjoy!
Karen Adler
&
Judith Fertig

The BBQ Queens' Big Book of Barbecue

Karen Adler and Judith Fertig

The Harvard Common Press · Boston, Massachusetts

The Harvard Common Press
535 Albany Street
Boston, Massachusetts 02118
www.harvardcommonpress.com

Printed in the United States of America

LIBRARY OF CONGRESS CATALOGING-IN-PUBLICATION DATA

Adler, Karen.
The bbq queens' big book of barbecue / Karen Adler and Judith M. Fertig.
p. cm.
Includes index.
ISBN 1-55832-296-5 (hc : alk. paper) — ISBN 1-55832-297-3 (pbk : alk. paper)
1. Barbecue cookery. I. Fertig, Judith M. II. Title.
TX840.B3A32 2005
641.5'784—dc22

2004029897

Special bulk-order discounts are available on this and other Harvard Common Press books. Companies and organizations may purchase books for premiums or resale, or may arrange a custom edition, by contacting the Marketing Director at the address above.

Cover and interior design by Richard Oriolo
Illustrations by Laura Tedeschi
Grill photograph courtesy of Bob Lyon
Cover photography by Terri Voyles with Omni Images

10 9 8 7 6 5 4 3 2 1

To our families,

especially Karen's husband, Dick,

and Judith's children, Sarah and Nick,

who are always ready to praise and encourage us

and to taste a tender morsel or two and say,

"That's not bad!"

Contents

ACKNOWLEDGMENTS ▪ ix

Meet the BBQ Queens ▪ xiii

The BBQ Queens on the Basics ▪ 1

Sprinkle, Slather, Soak, and Drizzle:
Rubs, Marinades, Vinaigrettes, and Sauces ▪ 45

An A to Z of Grilled and Smoked Veggies, Cheeses, and Pizza ▪ 113

Taking Wing: Poultry and Game Birds ▪ 187

In the Swim: Fish and Shellfish ▪ 251

Here's the Beef ▪ 299

Bringing Home the Bacon: Pork ▪ 361

A Little Lamb ▪ 417

RESOURCE GUIDE ▪ 443
MEASUREMENT EQUIVALENTS ▪ 448
INDEX ▪ 449

Acknowledgments

We love to cook outdoors because it's relaxing and a great way to share techniques, recipes, great food, and cool drinks. Whether it's schmoozing with friends and family on a deck or patio, conversing over a smoker at a barbecue competition, or shootin' the bull at a tailgate, count us in! Although this book is a salute to women who sizzle and smoke, we also owe a lot to the men in our lives. Karen's son-in-law Brian Young's experimentation with smoking wild game has been inspiring. Her other son-in-law, Jimmy Donnici, is also an ace at the grill and has shared many recipes with her. Good friend Don Coffey is an exceptional cook and outdoor smoker who has a special way with wild duck.

Judith's father, Jack Merkle, learned the meat trade from his generations-old family business and has taught her a lot.

We want to thank the staff of the many cooking schools where we have enjoyed teaching and meeting new food friends, including Larry Oates, owner of KitchenArt in West Lafayette, Indiana; Priscilla Barnes, owner of Cook's Nook in McPherson, Kansas; Deb Lackey at Dorothy Lane School of Cooking in Dayton, Ohio; Viking Culinary Centers all across the country; Carol Tabone at Jungle Jim's Cooking School in Fairfield, Ohio; Marilyn Markel at A Southern Season in Chapel Hill, North Carolina; Kitchen Conservatory and Dierberg's in St. Louis; Kathleen Craig and the great staff at Cooks of Crocus Hill in Minneapolis and St. Paul; Byerly's in Minneapolis and St. Paul; Chef's Gallery in Stillwater, Minnesota; Marshall Field's Culinary Studio in Chicago; Debbie Meyer at Market Street in Dallas; Central Market's Cooking School at various locations in Texas; Cooks Warehouse in Atlanta; Sur La Table Cooking Schools throughout the United States; Hall's Crown Center in Kansas City, Missouri; Culinary Center of Kansas City in Overland Park, Kansas; Rebecca Miller at Whole Foods Market in Overland Park, Kansas; and Denise Manu at Roth Concept Center in Lenexa, Kansas.

Special venues where we have met great people while we cooked up a royal feast include the Seattle Grillfest in Seattle and Charlie Trotter's To Go in Chicago. Special people include Cheryl Parker at the American Royal Barbecue Cooking Stage in Kansas City, Missouri, and Mark Dressler and Matt Sutherland, who supported and promoted the BBQ Queens at the First Annual Traverse Epicurean Festival in Traverse City, Michigan.

The Kansas City Barbeque Society, under the guidance of cofounder and executive director Carolyn Wells, has guided so many of us toward true slow-smoked American barbecue. The society promotes good food with good friends and emphasizes "having fun while doing so!" We hope that we live up to the honors that have been bestowed on us by our friend Ardie Davis, a.k.a. Remus Powers, Ph.B.: Karen's Master of Barbecue from Greasehouse University and Judith's place in the Order of the Magic Mop.

We thank all of our friends and colleagues in Les Dames d'Escoffier International and charter members of the Kansas City chapter for their encouragement and support. Our involvement with the International Association of Culinary Professionals has helped steer our culinary careers to new vistas. We have enjoyed all the good people from our Slow Foods Convivium in Kansas City, led by Jasper Mirabile Jr. Our involvement with the American Barbecue Hall of Fame and Museum is in its infancy, but we hope that the vision of our chairman, George Vesel, has us cooking at a venue solely dedicated to barbecue in the near future.

We're grateful for the wonderful recipes submitted by our friends the BBQ Babes and the Grill Gals: Carolyn Wells, Cheryl Alters Jamison, Diane Phillips, Dotty Griffith, Paula Lambert, Karen Putman, Candy Weaver, Janeyce Michel-Cupito, Beckie Baker, Julie Fox, Kathy Smith, Celina Tio, Bonnie Tandy Leblang, Rozane Miceli Prather, Latifa Raoufi, Debbie Moose, and Lisa Readie Mayer. Additional barbecue friends and companies that have helped us include Donna Myers, Paul Kirk, Dennis Hayes, Steve Raichlen, Nick Nicholas, Jim Eber, Dave Eckert, KitchenAid, Traeger, and Cookshack.

Special thanks goes to our many "foodie" friends, including the Kansas City Cookbook Club (Dee Barwick, Liz Benson, Vicki Johnson, Gayle Parnow, Mary Pfeifer, Kathy Smith, and Roxanne Wyss) and all the 'Que Queens (Beckie Baker, Dee Barwick, Janeyce Michel-Cupito, Cathy Jones, Ronna Keck, Kathy Smith, Jean Tamburello, Lou Jane Temple, Bunny Tuttle, and Carolyn Wells).

Of course, we want to thank everyone at The Harvard Common Press, from publisher Bruce Shaw to editors Pam Hoenig and Valerie Cimino to P.R. experts Skye Stewart and Liza Beth—and everyone else there. Special recognition goes to our agent, Lisa Ekus, and her able staff—and to the radio DJ who said that women couldn't barbecue!

Last, we would be remiss to leave out two women—our mentors—whose wacky partnership keeps on inspiring us: Lucy Ricardo and Ethel Mertz.

Thanks, everybody!

BBQ-2

Meet the BBQ Queens

Some women wear false eyelashes. Some women wear purple. The BBQ Queens wear tiaras and beauty queen sashes, lots of jewelry, and sometimes even big hair. It's all for a good cause, though—getting people excited about the thrill of the grill and the art of slow smoking. We, Karen Adler and Judith Fertig, the BBQ Queens, are cookbook authors, culinary instructors, and members of an all-girl barbecue team that was formed when a local Kansas City DJ infamously proclaimed, "Women can't barbecue!" Those were fightin' words to us. In response, we didn't burn our bras or wring our hands. We stepped up to the grill and smoker and let the power of sizzle and smoke do our talking at the legendary Battle of the Sexes Barbecue Contest in Kansas City.

We had so much fun and so much success that we felt like royalty. We decided we should be BBQ Queens and that was that.

From our first flimsy dime store glitter tiaras, we've moved up the royal chain to real rhinestones and even a working tiara that doubles as a sun visor. Someday, we're gonna have tiaras bedecked with cubic zirconias (but only if lots of people buy this book, so spread the word). Believe us, everything looks and tastes better when you're wearing a tiara.

So the tiara-totin' BBQ Queens are here to tell you that women *can* barbecue. They can also grill, smoke, rotisserie cook, plank, stir-grill, and yadda, yadda, yadda. From sea to shining sea, we've met lots of Grill Gals, BBQ Babes, and even a Silver Queen Corn Queen who all reinforce that idea, and you'll meet them in the pages of this book.

We're here to share our expertise at the grill and smoker with you. We'll even tell you how to do the four queen waves (see page 224), a life skill you definitely should have. Who else is gonna show you that? After all, you never know when sudden fame could be thrust upon you and somehow you have to cope. We know all about that. We sleep much better at night knowing that we know how to wave like the really royal people we are. You will, too.

And for those who say they can never figure women out, here's how we explain ourselves.

The BBQ Queen Philosophy

1. We grill and smoke like girls. Is there a gender difference in the way people approach grilling and smoking? You bet.

Like the best-selling self-help series states, men *are* from Mars, even at the grill and smoker. They might single-mindedly grill or smoke part of the meal, sitting outside with a frosty beer, watching the world go by as they wait for their barbecued brisket or ribs or grilled chicken wings to get done. Our dads grilled fabulous steaks and burgers over charcoal when we were growing up. Karen's husband, Dick, grills thick and juicy strip steaks to perfection. Judith's dad grills a wonderful beef tenderloin that has become the centerpiece of family celebrations. And Judith's son, Nick, grills a mean hamburger stuffed with blue cheese as well as a moist and delicious beer can chicken.

Women, on the other hand, are from Venus, and they usually plan the menu, shop, prepare the food for the grill or smoker, cook it, serve it, and clean up. No wonder we deserve tiaras!

When we say we grill and smoke like girls, we mean that we like to grill or smoke more than one thing at a time and think about the big picture—the whole meal—not just one part. We can grill great steaks and burgers and smoke divinely delicious ribs or briskets. But we also think about the rest of the meal—and actually prepare it. Oooh, a sauce would be good with this. Which side dish? How about dessert?

The instructions we give for each master recipe sometimes encourage you to add something else to the grill or smoker to make the most of your time and streamline dinner preparation. We suggest some "crowning glories" to finish off the dish or serve on the side. We also encourage cooking for leftovers, as you'll see in many recipes, and urge you to grill or smoke foods to use as condiments, saving you time down the road.

Besides thinking about the total menu rather than one component, women exhibit other differences at the grill and smoker. According to our informal backyard research, women tend to be more experimental in what they grill or smoke at home. Women are more likely to grill fish or vegetables or pizza, for instance, or to try smoked goat cheese. Men tend to rely on that old saw "If it ain't broke, don't fix it" and stick to the things they do well, such as great grilled steak or smoked brisket. *Vive la différence!*

Woman also tend to want things neat and tidy, even in the backyard. That's why women are more likely to flip on the switch to a gas grill rather than take the time to build a charcoal fire. (See page 8 for how to build a charcoal fire using a charcoal chimney. It's really easy.) The BBQ Queens love the convenience of gas grills, but a hot hardwood lump charcoal fire is hard to beat for searing and charring with lots of extra flavor.

And last, time is of the essence to the fairer sex. Unless women are competing in a barbecue contest, they're not likely to baby-sit a smoking brisket for 12 hours, as a lot of guys do. Although the BBQ Queens do traditional slow-smoked brisket, we offer choices such as smoking in an electric water smoker or smoke-roasting meats using the smoker and the oven to produce delicious results in only 5 hours. Likewise, we show how to use the indoor stovetop smoker pan that literally flies off the shelves every time we talk about it in a class. (We wish we had stock in that company.)

2. Grilling and smoking are meant to be fun. As our culinary school students have heard us say time and time again, relax and have fun at the grill or smoker. This is not rocket science.

You don't need calipers or a stopwatch to cook a great meal on the grill or smoker. (An instant-read meat thermometer is sure handy, though.) You just need to pay attention to your food. If you know what to look for (and each of our recipes will tell you), you'll know when your food is done. The more you grill or smoke, the more relaxed you'll be.

3. Make "rustic" part of your food vocabulary. Your food doesn't have to be absolutely perfect to be really good. That's why "rustic" is our favorite word. If your burgers aren't exactly the same size and shape, so what? That's rustic. If your grilled food doesn't look as if a chef towered it into heights of glory, so what? That's rustic, and that's charming, we think. Rustic food looks like it's homemade, and that's very appealing. Casually arranged on a plate or platter, garnished simply with fresh herbs or other natural ingredients, grilled or smoked food can look great as well as taste great.

The rustic approach can shorten prep time in the kitchen, too. Instead of fine mincing, simple chopping saves time with the same taste results.

4. A recipe is a general blueprint. Another key component to our relaxed philosophy is that every recipe is a blueprint, not an immutable law carved in stone. (We guess that means we're type B people at heart.) Just as you probably wouldn't build a new house without changing at least one thing in the architect's plans—more closet space, please!—you should feel free to change these recipes to suit your own taste. We encourage you to experiment.

We always cringe when we read recipes for "perfectly grilled" steak (or perfectly grilled anything). Perfect according to whom? A perfect steak, to us, means a little char on the exterior and medium-rare on the inside. To others, it might mean less char, more smoke flavor, and medium on the inside. It's all a matter of personal taste.

That's why we start you off with a master recipe, then suggest ways that you could modify it if you like your food done a different way.

5. Start simple, then get frilly. After you feel comfortable with the master grilled or smoked recipe, it's time to branch out with other versions or riffs on leftovers. Basically, we start you off with a simple recipe, then jazz it up as we go along. No matter which food you want to grill or smoke, you'll find lots of ways to enjoy it.

For instance, you'll find Grilled Asparagus on page 117, a master recipe. When you've grilled asparagus simply and find you want a new twist, then you can try Grilled Asparagus with Shaved Parmigiano-Reggiano or even Asian-Style Asparagus with Peanut Butter Dipping Sauce. If you have leftovers, you can make our Grilled Asparagus Frittata.

So put on your imaginary tiara and get grilling and smoking with the BBQ Queens!

The BBQ Queens on the Basics

Checking out at the grocery store should be simple, right? But no, it's a litany of questions: Paper or plastic? Credit or debit? Drive up or carry out? This chapter is about answering those kinds of questions for cooking with fire. What kind of grill or smoker do you have or do you want? How do you want to cook—grill, smoke, rotisserie, plank, or stir-grill? What type of fire do you need to prepare? How do you get the temperature you need? How long do you grill or smoke something? How do you know when your food is done?

The Difference Between Grilling and Smoking

Is grilling from Mars, smoking from Venus? Nah. Although grilling and smoking seem to be very opposite cooking techniques, they're actually similar. Just like going from white to black involves ever-darkening shades of gray, going from grilling to smoking involves ever-cooling degrees of temperature, moving foods from directly over the fire to farther away from it.

Grilled foods cook fast over a medium to hot fire (300 to 500°F or more) to char them slightly and give them a robust flavor. Because the foods cook fast, you usually grill foods that are already fairly tender, such as chicken breasts, pork chops, pork tenderloin, steaks, fish fillets, shellfish, and vegetables.

Slow-smoked foods, also known as true barbecue, cook slowly and indirectly—next to (not over) a low fire, perhaps with fragrant wood added. For that reason, smoked foods take on a heavier wood smoke flavor. Because the foods cook low (200 to 250°F) and slow, you usually smoke foods that need a longer cooking time, such as beef brisket, pork loin, spareribs, and pork shoulder or butt. The great thing about smoking, however, is that you can also smoke foods that you normally grill.

In between simple grilling and simple smoking are all kinds of specialty techniques, such as stir-grilling, planking, rotisserie cooking, and stovetop smoking, all of which we will cover later on in this chapter.

Which Grill Is Right for You?

People always ask us whether we grill with charcoal or gas, to which we answer yes—we swing both ways, as they say. The majority of American households have at least one outdoor grill, which, more often than not, is gas rather than charcoal. Although Grill Gals are more likely to use a gas grill, there are those among us who swear by charcoal. As far as we're concerned, to get great flavor and char, charcoal is the way to go—in particular, hardwood lump charcoal, which burns really hot for a terrific sear. But there are pluses to gas grilling as well, not the least of which is you just flip a switch and it's on. You can add wood smoke to a gas grill, too, as we'll show you later on. Just make sure you buy a unit with enough BTUs for hot surface searing.

Barbecue expert Donna Myers is president of DHM Group, a public relations company specializing in the barbecue industry. In the 1990s, she conducted biannual surveys with the Barbecue Industry Association (now the Hearth, Patio, and Barbecue Association). One of those surveys reported that the average American household owns 1.6 grills. In fact, 20 million households own two grills and 9.8 million households own three or more grills.

The BBQ Queens have eleven different kinds of outdoor grills and smokers. Karen has large and small kettle charcoal grills, a gas grill, a kamado-style ceramic grill, and an electric smoker oven; all her equipment can also be used for slow smoking. Her husband, Dick, owns a portable gas grill. Judith has a medium-size gas grill with one burner (for grilling only), as well as a charcoal grill and an electric-fired wood pellet–fueled grill, both of which can be used for smoking and grilling. We both have electric bullet-shaped water smokers. Plus, for indoor use, we have Camerons Stovetop Smokers and an assortment of grill pans and electric grills/griddles.

The kind of grill *you* choose should be determined by the space you have, the kind of fuel you want to use, the amount of cooking surface you need, the look of the grill (hey, it should look as good as you do!), and how much money you want to spend.

In addition to the grills and smokers we own and cook on, we have also cooked on a whole assortment of others, including various models made by Cookshack, Traeger, BeefEater, Big Green Egg, Grill Dome, Weber, Viking, KitchenAid, Wolf, Char-Broil, Sunshine, Fire Magic, Sunbeam, Ducane, Hasty-Bake, Napoleon, Brinkmann, and Charmglow—and we'll be adding more to this list. Check out our guide to grilling and smoking equipment on pages 3–5 and 18–21.

Gas Grills

So many choices abound in this category that we can't begin to list them all here. But go to our resource guide for a detailed look at gas grill manufacturers. The biggest decision to make is whether you want to buy a unit that uses propane fuel or natural gas. Most propane grills are movable, unless you have them built in. A movable grill means that if it is a windy or rainy day, you can pick up your grill and drag it to a place of shelter (but never indoors or in the garage, unless you want to leave this life prematurely). Natural gas units must be hooked up to your gas line, which will make the grill stationary.

Once you've decided which kind of gas you want, the next step is to go shopping at your local grill store. Most grill retailers go to trade shows, where they must choose from hundreds of gas grill models, trying to purchase a variety of grills from reputable manufacturers that will satisfy their customers' needs. Our best advice is make friends with your local grill retailer and find out how he (or she) stands behind his products, whether he makes service calls, and whether the grills have warranties. Another big plus is buying from a store that will preassemble and deliver the grill. But you need to ask!

You want to buy a gas grill with at least two separate burners so you can turn off one of the burners to cook indirectly and smoke on the grill. The burners need to heat the entire surface, so if you have a fairly large cooking surface, you will need four or more burners. If you don't have enough burners, there may not be enough heat coverage, and you will have hot and cold spots on your grill. Go for more burners if you can afford it, because the more burners you have, the more temperature selections you have, allowing you to grill several items that may need different levels of heat at the same time.

If you can afford it, buy a grill that is rust-resistant (or get a cover for it) and on which you can crank up the heat level to at least 36,000 BTUs. Make sure the cooking surface is large enough for your needs. (Manufacturers often include the warming rack and side burners in their total cooking surface dimensions, so you need to make sure how much of that space is actual cooking surface.)

Charcoal Grills

Charcoal grills come in all sizes and shapes, with or without lids. The big choices with a charcoal grill are the amount of cooking surface on the grill rack, how far the grill grates are from the fire, and whether you have a lid or not. Also, check for sturdy legs and heavy metal construction. Cheaper grills are often not the bargain they seem to be. Many of the kettle-shaped grills of lesser quality are imitating the popular Weber kettle grills first introduced to Americans by George Stephen in 1951. Both of the BBQ Queens own Webers. Karen recently replaced her Weber after more than 15 years of use. Her investment added up to about $5 a year. Now *that's* a bargain!

If you grill a lot or entertain and grill, you may want a large cooking surface. If you're in a small apartment (make sure the fire codes allow you to operate an outdoor grill on your balcony), opt for a hibachi. With charcoal, no matter the size of your grill, you get great flavor in your food, especially if you burn hardwood lump charcoal, which is irregularly shaped and made only from hardwoods, unlike charcoal briquettes, which have a uniform shape and are made from several different materials.

Electric Grills

Electric grills are available for indoor and outdoor use. The heat level of these grills is usually not high enough for great searing. Some outdoor models are ideal for homes and apartments with small patios that might not allow for gas or charcoal grills. One of the most popular indoor electric grills is the George Foreman. It has heating elements on both sides of the grill, which cooks foods extremely fast and eliminates the need to turn them.

Wood Pellet Grills

Wood pellet grills combine the ease of an electric starter with the flavor of compressed wood pellets. These grills need to be plugged into an electrical outlet. Wood pellets are added to the hopper, which feeds the pellets down a chute to burn and smoke. Because the pellets are compressed, they take up much less storage space than charcoal, while still imparting a wonderful wood flavor to foods. You can buy different flavors of pellets and mix and match them for your own custom wood taste. The leader in making this kind of grill is Traeger.

Kamado Grills

Kamado porcelain cookers are Asian-style cookers shaped like an egg, similar to ancient clay vessels such as the tandoor. Kamados are very heavy and usually sold on either a metal base with wheels or a heavy-duty wooden cart with wheels. When the lid is clamped shut, the kamado cooks like a pressure cooker, quicker than a regular smoker. With the lid open, it works well as a grill, nice and hot. Big Green Egg offers a lifetime guarantee on their grills that can't be beat.

Water Smokers

The bullet-shaped water smoker is about 18 inches in diameter and 3 to 4 feet tall. The unit is relatively small but has enough cooking space to smoke two big hams or a couple of turkeys at once. The choices for fuel are charcoal, electricity, and gas. Prices range

Utensils for Grilling and Smoking

Several basic tools make grilling and smoking easier. Kitchen shops, hardware stores, restaurant supply stores, and barbecue and grill retailers are good sources for the items listed below. Professional utensils are superior in quality and durability and worth the extra money. Long handles are preferable on everything, to keep you a safe distance from the fire.

- A *stiff wire brush* with a scraper makes cleaning the grill easy. Tackle this while the grill is still warm.
- One *natural-bristle basting brush* can be used to apply oil to the grill and a second to baste food during grilling or smoking.
- *Grate Chef Grill Wipes* are small pads saturated with high-temperature cooking oil. You can use them for oiling the grill grates prior to cooking, then turn them over to clean the grill when you're finished cooking. The high-temperature oil doesn't smoke, and it doesn't drip from the pads, which prevents flare-ups.
- *Perforated grill racks* are placed on top of the grill grates to accommodate small or delicate food items, such as chicken wings, fish fillets, shellfish, and vegetables, which might fall through the grates. Always oil the grill rack before using so that the food won't stick.
- *Hinged grill baskets* hold food in place and make turning easy.
- *Grill woks and metal baskets* with perforated holes let in smoky flavor while sitting directly on top of the grill. Stir-grill fish, chicken, shellfish, or vegetables by tossing them with long-handled wooden paddles.
- *Heat-resistant oven or grill mitts* offer the best hand protection, especially when you need to touch any hot metal, such as skewers, during the grilling process.
- *Long-handled, spring-loaded tongs* are easier to use than the scissors type. They are great for turning shellfish, sliced vegetables, and skewers. Buy two sets of tongs—one for raw meats and the other for cooked meats.

- ***Long-handled offset spatulas*** **with extra-long spatula surfaces are great for turning large pieces of food.**

- **A *long, wooden-handled offset fish spatula* with a 5- to 6-inch blade is essential for turning fish fillets. Oil it well to avoid sticking.**

- **Keep a *spray bottle or pan filled with water* handy to douse flare-ups. A garden hose within easy reach can substitute, but make sure the water is turned on!**

- ***Skewers*** **—wooden or metal—allow smaller items to be threaded loosely together and then placed on the grill to cook. Wooden or bamboo skewers should be soaked for at least 30 minutes before using so that the ends won't char during grilling. Flat wooden or metal skewers are preferred, so that cubed food doesn't spin while turning. Or use double skewers to keep cubed food from spinning.**

- ***Disposable aluminum pans*** **hold meats or vegetables and their natural juices or sauces for basting. Place small vegetables, shellfish, or cheese in them to smoke. The pans can be bent and shaped to fit in a small grill or smoker. Or use one as a tent to create a mini oven for thick meats that need a longer cooking time.**

- **We suggest using two *professional baking sheets,* double-stacked, to carry foods to and from the grill. Place the raw food on the top sheet and carry it out to the grill. Use the clean sheet to receive the cooked food off the grill.**

- **We like to have an *instant-read meat thermometer* handy by the grill. A *heatproof meat thermometer* is great to place in a leg of lamb, a whole chicken, a pork loin, or another roast before putting it on the rotisserie. For smoking on a charcoal or gas grill, a *grill thermometer* inserted through a small hole (you may have to drill the hole yourself) in the dome of the grill will tell you the internal temperature; 225 to 250°F is the optimum temperature for slow smoking.**

- **A *charcoal chimney or electric fire starter* is key for starting a charcoal fire.**

- **A good-quality *chef's knife* is essential for slicing meat.**

from $50 to $250, with charcoal smokers being the least expensive and gas the most expensive. A water smoker is a vertical smoker with two or three chambers. The bottom holds the heating unit, whether it's the fire grate for charcoal, the electric coil, or the gas burners. This is where you add your wood chunks or pellets for smoking. The next cylinder holds the water pan, with either one or two racks above it. The water pan shields the food you are cooking from the fire. Manufacturers claim that you can use these units as grills by placing one of the grill grates over the fire grate. However, many of the electric and gas units can reach only about 250°F—perfect for smoking but not hot enough for grilling. Charcoal units are better for grilling. That being said, the BBQ Queens prefer to use this small but mighty piece of equipment as a smoker, with electricity as our choice of fuel. Electric smokers cost just a bit more than charcoal units, but all you have to do is plug them in and add the wood. You'll save oodles in operating expenses, too.

Grilling 101

Lighting the Fire

In each grilling recipe in this book, we tell you to "prepare a (medium to hot) fire in a grill." This means "direct heat," with the flames under the food you're cooking. Preparing a direct-heat fire is done differently depending on the type of equipment you have.

CHARCOAL GRILLS

A charcoal fire can be started in any of several safe, ecologically sound ways. We prefer using real hardwood lump charcoal instead of compressed charcoal briquettes. Hardwood lump charcoal gives a better flavor and is an all-natural product without chemical additives. Hardwood lump charcoal is labeled as such. It is readily available at most barbecue and grill shops, hardware stores with large grill departments, and some grocery stores. Start your hardwood lump charcoal in a metal charcoal chimney with an electric fire starter, or with solid fire starters made with paraffin, also available at hardware, discount, and home improvement stores. Start a charcoal grill about 30 minutes before you're ready to grill.

Lighting the fire with a charcoal chimney With a charcoal grill, you'll want to buy a charcoal chimney, which lets you start a fire using only a match, newspaper, and charcoal. The chimney is an upright cylindrical metal canister, like a large metal coffee can with a handle. Fill it with 15 to 20 pieces of hardwood lump charcoal, then place it on a nonflammable surface, such as concrete or the grill rack. Slightly tip the chimney over and stuff one or two crumpled sheets of newspaper in the convex-shaped bottom. Light the paper with a match. After about 15 minutes, the coals will be hot and starting to ash over, signaling that you can get a hot fire going. Be sure to check it after the first 5 minutes to make sure the charcoal has caught fire, or you may need to light another piece of newspaper.

Making fire with electricity An electric fire starter is another easy way to start a fire in a charcoal grill. You'll need an outdoor electrical outlet or extension cord. Place the coil on the lower rack of the grill and stack charcoal on top of it. Plug it in and the fire will start in 10 to 15 minutes. Remove the coil and let the starter cool on a nonflammable surface, out of the reach of children and pets.

Lighting the fire with solid starters Solid starters are compressed wood blocks or sticks treated with a flammable substance such as paraffin. They are easy to ignite and don't give off a chemical odor. Solid starters are great to have on hand if you absolutely must start a fire regardless of the weather. Competition barbecuers always have these in their toolboxes, at the ready in case of inclement weather. Two or three will easily light the charcoal; set them on top of or beside the charcoal and ignite.

GAS GRILLS

Follow the manufacturer's directions for starting your gas grill. You'll need at least 36,000 combined BTUs (which measure the maximum heat output of a burner) to sear a steak, burger, or chop effectively. That means if each gas burner has a maximum of 25,000 BTUs, you'll need to turn both burners to medium-high or high and close the grill lid to let the grill reach 50,000 BTUs. Then open the lid and immediately place the food to sear on the hot grate. Again, check with the manufacturer or grill store retailer for heating information. The manufacturer's directions will tell you how long your grill takes to reach the temperature you want. Newer grills have inset thermometers that register the temperature inside the grill.

ELECTRIC GRILLS, WOOD PELLET GRILLS, SMOKER OVENS, AND WATER SMOKERS

Electric grills need to be plugged into an electrical outlet. Electric units vary in the kinds of temperature controls they have, so read the manufacturer's directions.

An electric-fired wood pellet grill is as easy to use as a gas grill, but prevention is worth a pound of cure, as the saying goes. If wood pellets get damp, they turn to mush, which can clog the ignition and keep the grill from lighting. If this happens, remove the grill grate. Remove the sliding barrier tray and cover with aluminum foil. Check to make sure that nothing is clogging the electric ignition in the bottom of the grill. Make sure the wood pellets in the hopper are dry. Replace the barrier tray and grill grate. Plug the grill into an outdoor electrical outlet and turn on the grill. Hold your hand over the grill rack to make sure the grill is heating up, then set the desired temperature.

Electric smoker ovens and water smokers need to be plugged into an outlet. Then you add the kind of wood you want and follow the manufacturer's directions for direct and indirect cooking.

KAMADO GRILLS

Kamado grills have a ceramic firebox for the charcoal at the grill's inner base. The charcoal can be started by placing two or three crumpled pieces of newspaper on the bottom and placing enough charcoal on top so that when the paper burns and the charcoal settles, it is just below the air holes in the firebox. You may use an electric fire starter for this kind of grill, but never use lighter fluid.

Fueling the Fire: Direct Versus Indirect Heat

Okay, you have your fire lit. Now what?

It's time to build the fire to the desired temperature, and for that you need fuel. In a charcoal grill, that means more charcoal. In a gas grill, it means propane or natural gas. In an electric grill, it means electricity. And in an electric-fired wood pellet grill, it means wood pellets.

You also have to decide which type of fire you need to make a particular recipe. Your choices are direct or indirect.

Knowing how to cook over direct and indirect heat will allow you to get the most flavor out of your food. Direct heat means that you're cooking directly over the heat source, whether it be coals in a charcoal grill or lit burners in a gas grill. Indirect heat means that you're cooking away from the source of heat, whether your food is off to the side of the heat source, in the center of the grill with the fire banked on both sides, or at a distance above the fire. If you own or cook on a pit barbecue, the indirect fire is in an offset firebox.

Here's how to prepare direct and indirect fires in both charcoal and gas grills.

CHARCOAL GRILLS

Direct Fire First, make sure the bottom vents of the grill are open, because fire needs oxygen. Next, start a fire in a charcoal chimney using hardwood lump charcoal and newspaper. Or use an electric fire starter or solid starters. Place more hardwood charcoal in the bottom of the grill. Your fire should extend out about 2 inches beyond the space you will need for the food you plan to grill. When the coals are hot in the charcoal chimney, dump them on top of the charcoal in the bottom of the grill and wait for all the coals to catch fire and ash over. When they've just begun to ash over and turn a whitish gray, replace the grill grate. When you put the food on the grate, it will be directly over the coals.

Indirect Fire Prepare a direct fire first. Once your hot coals are in the bottom of the grill, there are two ways you can create an indirect fire. First, using a long-handled grill spatula, push the coals over to one side of the grill to provide direct heat there. The other side of the grill will now have indirect heat. Second, bank the coals on both sides of the grill. The center of the grill will then be the indirect cooking area. For smoking, carefully place a disposable aluminum pan filled with water on the indirect side, next to the hot coals on the bottom of the grill or smoker. (Smoking is longer and slower, so you need the extra moisture from the water.) Place the hardwood chunks, chips, or pellets (for wood smoke flavoring) on top of the coals. Replace the grill grate. With an indirect fire, you can grill directly over the hot coals while you smoke over the indirect side. When cooking indirectly, close the grill lid and use the vents on the top and bottom of the grill to adjust the fire temperature. Open vents allow more oxygen in and make the fire hotter, partially closed vents lower the heat, and closed vents extinguish the fire.

GAS GRILLS

Direct Fire Turn on the burners. Place the food on the grill grate directly over the hot burner, and that is direct heat. To cook this way, ideally leave the grill lid up. When it is raining or snowing, however, closing the lid is preferable. This will essentially turn the hot grill into a hot oven, meaning you'll actually be grill-roasting. Also, because you can't see the food, it is easier to overcook it with the lid down.

Grill with the Lid Open or Shut?

Traditionally, grilling was done over an open fire or flame. Think about Wild West cattle drives and big Texas barbecue parties. Steaks were grilled on open brazier grills, while whole goats and quarters or sides of beef were smoked by digging a hole or pit in the ground. Thus, many grillers believe that *true* grilling is with the lid open.

If you are using hardwood lump charcoal and if you add wood chips or pellets to your fire (gas or charcoal), you will probably get more smokiness if you grill with the lid closed. Also, a thicker piece of meat will cook to the desired doneness faster with the lid closed. And if it is very cold, windy, rainy, or snowy, closing the lid makes good sense.

So should you grill with the lid open or shut? It's your choice.

Indirect Fire Your grill must have at least two burners for indirect grilling. Fire up the burner on one half of the grill only. The side of the grill with the burner off is for indirect cooking. For smoking, add water-soaked wood chips or dry compressed wood pellets to a smoker box or in an aluminum foil packet pierced with holes. Also, place a disposable aluminum pan filled with water over the direct heat. To cook this way, close the grill lid. If you have three or more burners, you may also set up your grill with the two outer burners on and the center of your grill used for indirect cooking. Adjust the burners to regulate the level of heat.

WOOD PELLET GRILLS

Wood pellet grills are constructed so that they provide only indirect fire, although you can adjust the temperature from low smoking at 250°F to indirect grilling at 500°F.

KAMADO GRILLS

Follow the manufacturer's directions, which usually recommend using hardwood lump charcoal placed just below the air holes in the firebox. The temperature is regulated by the amount of air allowed to flow in. More air means a hotter fire. The lid clamps down and seals tightly for smoking. With the lid open, you can grill directly. Smoking in a kamado is more like roasting in an oven. A water pan is not used.

WATER SMOKERS

Bullet-shaped water smokers fueled with charcoal work best for grilling. Place the grill rack over the hot fire in the firebox and grill. Remember that the grill rack is very close to the fire, so it grills hot and fast. The gas and electric models don't get hot enough for grilling. All the models use a vertical indirect grilling setup. For smoking, three or four chunks of water-soaked wood or a foil packet of wood pellets is placed in the firebox at the base. Next, the cylinder that holds the water pan is set on top, followed by the grill rack. The water pan separates the grill rack from the fire; thus the fire is indirect. The lid closes loosely, and now you're smoking.

ELECTRIC OVENS

This is similar in concept to the water smoker. The BBQ Queens are most familiar with the Cookshack Smokette, which Karen has. The oven box is a bit smaller than bullet-shaped water smokers and can smoke about 22 pounds of meat. The tight construction of this unit allows the food to smoke without a water pan, if you like. Because it is electric and the construction is tight, meaning the smoke does not escape, this unit is very popular with restaurant kitchens. The ease of these electrical units is that they use wood for the wood smoke flavor, but the fire is controlled by a thermostat. You can time your food (45 to 60 minutes per pound in the smoker) and do other things while the food is smoking.

Grilling Temperature

Most food is grilled directly over a medium-hot to hot fire, depending on the distance your grill rack sits from the fire and the heat of the fire itself.

In a charcoal grill, the fire is ready when the flames have subsided and the coals are glowing red and just beginning to ash over. This is a hot fire. You can recognize a medium-hot fire when the coals are no longer red but instead are ashen.

For a gas grill, read the manufacturer's directions for the time it takes the grill to reach the desired temperature. Or use the hand method (see box, right) or a grill thermometer to judge the grill's temperature.

The Hand Method for Judging a Grill's Temperature

Hold your hand 5 inches above the heat source. If you can hold it there for about 2 seconds, your fire is hot (about 500°F or more) and perfect for grilling. Being able to hold your hand there for 3 seconds indicates a medium-hot fire (about 400°F), good for grilling; 4 seconds indicates a medium fire (about 350°F), for grilling or higher-heat indirect cooking; and 5 to 6 seconds indicates a low fire (200 to 250°F), ideal for slow smoking.

ADJUSTING YOUR GRILL'S TEMPERATURE

On a charcoal grill, always begin the fire with the bottom or side vents open. Lower the temperature by partially closing the vents, and raise the temperature by opening the vents or by adding more charcoal to ratchet up the fire. More air means the fire will burn faster and hotter; less air makes for a slower and lower fire.

On a gas grill, adjust the heat by turning the heat control knobs to the desired level. Most heat control knobs are marked "high," "medium," and "low," although some are marked only "high" and "low." On some models, you can control the temperature by turning the temperature dial.

On a wood pellet grill, you just turn the dial to the temperature you want. Other electric units may produce only one temperature or have a temperature dial for adjusting the temperature.

Gas Grilling with a Kiss of Smoke

A gas grill is very easy to use but does not impart the flavor that hardwood charcoal or wood pellets do. To get more wood smoke flavor on a gas grill, moisten the wood chips or place dry wood pellets in an aluminum foil packet. Poke holes in the packet and place on the grill rack directly over the heat. The wood chips or pellets will smolder rather than burn, adding smoky flavor. Do not put chips or pellets directly on the lava rock, metal flame guard, or ceramic plates in the bottom of the grill, because the residue could block the holes in the gas burners. This is definitely *not* a good thing.

Getting Ready to Grill

The grill should be clean and the grill rack lightly oiled prior to starting the fire. We like to use Grate Chef Grill Wipes, premoistened towelettes for oiling and cleaning the grill.

Have all your equipment handy.

Decide whether you are going to cook with the grill lid closed, which will allow you to cook your food faster and conserve fuel, or with the lid open, which will require a hot fire to sear the food you are grilling.

Preparing Food for Grilling

Preparing food for grilling can be as simple as brushing it with olive oil and seasoning it with salt and pepper or applying a marinade, sauce, or rub beforehand. Preparing food in these ways will help it stay juicier and more flavorful when grilled. Avoid rubs, marinades, or sauces with a high sugar content, because the sugar will burn as it grills. Also, remove any excess marinade or sauce that might drip onto the heat source and flare up.

How to Grill

Once your grill is at the proper temperature, place the food on the hot grill grate. Let it sear and char before turning it with grill tongs or a grill spatula. We prefer not to use a grill fork, because it pokes holes in the food and causes the juices to escape. Avoid turning the food unless the recipe says to do so. The food needs to sit undisturbed for a time to get those lovely grill marks.

BASTING

Some foods that tend to dry out with the hot, fast searing of the grill—such as boneless, skinless chicken breasts; thin, butterflied pork chops; and fish or shellfish—might benefit from the moisture and flavor of basting. A baste can be any liquid that will provide moisture, from fruit juice to a vinaigrette to a melted butter– or olive oil–based sauce. A baste also adds flavor to food. Use a basting brush to coat food during grilling. Always make sure that the basting sauce is cooked off—meaning that if you baste the top of the chicken breast, for example, you turn it to cook the baste, which may have come in contact with the raw meat when it was first placed on the grill.

An eye-catching way to baste is to use an herb brush. Gather together a small bouquet of fresh mint, lavender, rosemary, thyme, or other herb. Tie the stems together tightly with kitchen twine or a twist tie. Dip your brush into the basting liquid and baste as described above. Mint brushes are delicious with lamb; rosemary brushes work well with pork and poultry.

GLAZING

A glaze usually contains sugar, which will burn if left too long over a hot fire. To avoid scorching your food, apply the glaze during the last 5 to 10 minutes of grilling.

Sweet tomato-based barbecue sauce is probably the most popular glaze used in American backyard grilling. Barbecue sauce gives food a pretty sheen and color. Jams, jellies, and preserves, which are heated to melt them before they are applied, add a sheen and sweet flavor to grilled poultry and pork. A grilled ham steak glazed with apricot preserves or chicken paillards glazed with cherry preserves are both pretty and delicious.

Grilling Times

Estimated grilling times are just that—estimates, not hard and fast rules. In every recipe, we give you an estimate of how long something will take to grill, but we also give you a doneness signal—an internal temperature or appearance—that will let you know when the food is done. When you cook outdoors, the weather is a big factor in cooking time. Things grill faster on hot days than on cold ones.

People in our cooking classes always seem to worry that foods won't be cooked properly on a grill. Don't worry about undercooking food. If you want to fret about something, fret about overcooking it. Undercooked food can always be put back on the grill, or you can finish cooking it by zapping it in the microwave for a few seconds or putting it in the oven. If food is undercooked, you can always rescue it. If food is overcooked, you've got nowhere to go but the grilling doghouse.

GRILLING TIMETABLE

People usually grill small, thin cuts of meat. For these, we prefer a hot fire, around 500°F, because we like a little char. If you don't, cook over a medium to medium-hot fire and increase the cooking time by 2 to 3 minutes. We recommend turning meat or fish once, halfway through the total cooking time.

Beefsteak	**1 inch thick**	**8 minutes for rare**
Burger	**1/2 inch thick**	**8 minutes for rare**
Chicken breast paillard	**1/2 inch thick**	**4 minutes for done**
Chicken leg or thigh	**5 to 8 ounces each**	**8 to 12 minutes for done**
Fish fillet or steak	**5 to 8 ounces each**	**10 minutes per inch of thickness**
Lamb chop	**1 inch thick**	**8 minutes for rare**
Pork loin or rib chop	**1 inch thick**	**8 minutes for rare**
Pork steak or blade	**1 inch thick**	**8 minutes for rare**
Pork tenderloin	**2 inches thick**	**12 to 15 minutes for rare**

WHEN TO PULL FOOD OFF THE GRILL

We recommend that if you're just starting to grill, you use an instant-read meat thermometer to test the doneness of grilled chicken, pork, beef, veal, lamb, and game. Insert the thermometer in the thickest part of the meat and read the temperature. After a while, you'll be able to tell the doneness of grilled meats by touch alone. When you touch a pork tenderloin with tongs and it's soft and wiggly, it's too rare. When the tenderloin begins to offer some resistance, it's rare to medium-rare. When it just begins to firm up, it's medium. When it feels solid, it's well done. You can also tell how red meat is cooked by its color. When the internal temperature of red meat is under 140°F, it is red; from 140 to 160°F, the color ranges from red to pink; at 175°F, the meat is brown or gray and very well done.

Fish doneness is best judged by appearance. Fish is done when it begins to flake when tested with a fork in the thickest part. Shellfish is done when it is opaque and somewhat firm to the touch. Vegetables are done when they look done and are cooked to your preferred degree of tenderness. Breads are done when they have risen and browned.

Foods continue to cook for a few minutes after they're taken off the grill, raising the internal temperature another 5 to 10°F. Use our doneness chart (see page 17) as a guideline in helping you choose the desired degree of doneness you prefer. Take the internal temperature of meat while it is on the grill and consider that the temperature will continue to rise off the grill. If a pork loin registers an internal temperature of 145°F on the grill, it will go up to 150 to 155°F while resting for 10 to 15 minutes before slicing. If you leave the pork loin on the grill or smoker until it reaches 155°F, it will be 160 to 165°F once it has rested. By the time meat reaches 175°F, it is too well done, making it dry and less appetizing. For more information about safe meat temperatures, call the USDA Meat and Poultry Hotline at (888) 674-6854.

Burgers can be made from beef, chicken, lamb, pork, or even tuna. Because they're all ground and have a similar texture and volume, they follow the same doneness guidelines. The Centers for Disease Control and Prevention does not recommend eating undercooked (pink) ground beef, but hey, you're the grill mistress; you make the call.

DONENESS CHART FOR GRILLING

Personal preferences run the gamut from very rare to very well done. Use this chart as a guideline for your outdoor grilling.

Beefsteak	**125°F for rare, 140°F for medium, 160°F for well done**
Burger	**140°F for medium, 160°F for well done**
Chicken breast	**160°F**
Chicken leg or thigh	**165°F**
Fish fillet or steak	**Begins to flake when tested with a fork in thickest part**
Lamb chop	**125°F for rare, 140°F for medium**
Pork loin or rib chop	**140°F for medium**
Pork tenderloin	**140°F for medium, 160°F for well done**
Shellfish	**Opaque and somewhat firm to the touch**
Turkey breast	**165°F**
Turkey leg or thigh	**175 to 180°F**
Veal chop	**125°F for rare, 140°F for medium, 160°F for well done**
Vegetables	**Cooked to your liking**

Smoking 101

With most types of grills or smokers—including gas grills—you can slow smoke almost any food for delicious barbecue in your own backyard. Most grills can be set up to function as a smoker, as long as they have a lid that can be closed. Some smokers can function as a grill, too, while others can function only as a smoker. Be aware of this and ask the right questions for the kind of grilling or smoking you want to do.

People who sell smoking equipment will ask whether you're a "backyarder," meaning that you barbecue only in your own backyard for friends and family, or a "competitor," meaning that you participate in barbecue contests. Backyarders can use just about any kind of smoker, including those that run on electricity, but competitors rely mainly on the charcoal type.

The Best Smoker for You

The kind of smoker you choose is determined by the space you have, the kind of fuel you want to use, the amount of cooking surface you need, and how much money you want to spend. The fuel choices are gas, electric, charcoal, and hardwood. Some of the most popular units for home use are Weber kettle-shaped charcoal grills, the charcoal Weber Smokey Mountain Cooker, and the Brinkmann, Weber, and Char-Broil bullet-shaped water smokers, which are variously fueled by charcoal, electricity, or gas. These units are moderately priced, ranging from under $50 to $250, and can be used for grilling and smoking. Backyarders also can use wood pellet grills, ceramic smokers, smoker ovens, and gas grills with two or more burners for smoking. Some gas grills can even be adapted to cook with charcoal or charcoal and gas at the same time. Passionate backyarders may even use medium to large smoking rigs or pit smokers with a firebox on the side.

Competition barbecuers usually start out small with a Weber charcoal grill or a Weber Smokey Mountain Cooker, then graduate to bigger smoking rigs. Our barbecue buddy Paul Kirk has a special rig costing around $18,000 that he hauls on a trailer to barbecue events. This type of smoker uses both charcoal and "sticks," or pieces of hardwood cut to fit the width of the firebox.

Preparing Your "Pit," Equipment, and Utensils

Your grill or smoker should be clean, and your fuel should be handy. Wood chips should be soaked in water for at least 30 minutes before smoking. Wood chunks need to be soaked for at least an hour. If you're using flavored wood pellets, use them dry; when wet, wood pellets turn to mush. If you prepare your food and have all your equipment ready, your smoking experience will be relaxing and enjoyable.

Lighting and Fueling the Fire

You light the fire for the smoker in the same way you do for grilling, whether you're using a charcoal, gas, wood pellet, electric, or kamado grill or a big smoker rig. The difference is that you prepare an indirect fire and keep the temperature lower, around 200 to 250°F.

CHARCOAL GRILLS

Use a charcoal chimney, electric fire starter, or solid starters to light the hardwood lump charcoal. When the coals have ashed over, position the coals on one or both sides of the grill, so that the other side of the grill or the center section is indirect. Place a metal or disposable aluminum pan of water beside the coals. Place the grill rack over the top. The section(s) with the coals is direct heat; the section with the water is indirect heat. Use grill thermometers to monitor the temperature in both sections. Ideally, smoking is done at a temperature (measured in the indirect section) of 200 to 250°F.

CHARCOAL WATER SMOKERS

Start your charcoal in a charcoal chimney. Place the coals in the bottom third of the smoker (the firebox). Place wood chunks or chips or aluminum foil packets of wood pellets on the coals for optimum smoke flavor. Fill the water pan and place it in the second chamber of the smoker. The grill racks (usually two) fit directly above the water pan. Close the lid and monitor the fire until it is about 275°F. (*Note:* The lid on this type of smoker does not fit tightly, allowing for air and smoke to circulate.) When the food is placed in the smoker, it will probably lower the temperature to the desired 200 to 250°F. You can grill on a charcoal water smoker by placing the grill rack directly over the charcoal fire in the firebox. You do not use the other chambers for grilling.

ELECTRIC AND GAS WATER SMOKERS

Like a charcoal water smoker, electric and gas smokers are usually built in three sections. In an electric model, the bottom section is a bed of lava rock on which an electric coil rests. Gas smokers have a covered gas flame unit. Add an aluminum foil packet of water-soaked wood chips or dry wood pellets near but not touching the heating elements. The next section of the smoker contains the water pan and the smoker racks, on which you place the food to be smoked. The third portion of the smoker is the lid. Cover the smoker, plug it in or turn on the gas, and set the thermostat (if it has one) to 200 to 250°F. Then leave it alone. Resist the urge to lift the lid and keep checking the meat or food you are smoking. The more you lift the lid, the longer the food will take to smoke. The temperature should remain at a fairly constant 200 to 250°F.

These are the BBQ Queens' favorite smokers. We call them outdoor slow cookers. You turn them on and almost forget about them, which frees you to make the rest of the meal (or do your nails, read a book, whatever).

COMPETITION-STYLE SMOKERS

A big smoker rig usually has a large cooking chamber with a firebox attached to the side. This offset firebox is where the charcoal fire is built. The food smokes in the main chamber from the indirect heat produced in the firebox. The firebox has its own door, so you can add more charcoal or wood when necessary, without having to open the door to the large smoking chamber. A venting system with dampers between the firebox and the main chamber helps control the heat and the amount of smoke flowing into the main chamber. Smaller models can use charcoal or wood chunks. Larger models might rely on hickory, oak, cherry, or apple logs for both heat and smoke. The food is smoked on racks in the larger chamber.

GAS GRILLS

To prepare an indirect fire on a gas grill, you need one with two or more burners. Turn one burner on and leave the other one off. The side with the burner on is direct heat; the side with the burner off is indirect heat. You may place a water pan in the back of the grill on the direct side. Add water-soaked wood chips or dry wood pellets to the direct side of the grill above the fire by placing the wood in a metal smoker box or in an aluminum foil packet that has been poked with holes. The presoaked wood chips or dry wood pellets will smolder and smoke and give the food a luscious smoky flavor. Some gas grills have a built-in smoker box, to which you can add water-soaked wood chips or dry wood pellets and even regulate the heat.

WOOD PELLET GRILLS

Wood pellet grills are designed for indirect cooking only. The ignition and flame are about a foot below the grill rack where the food is placed. To turn this type of grill into a smoker, set the temperature at 200 to 250°F and close the lid. Wood pellets are available in more than a dozen different flavors, from alder and mesquite to mulberry and sassafras.

KAMADO GRILLS

Kamado smokers have a ceramic firebox for the charcoal at the inner base. The charcoal can be started by placing two or three crumpled pieces of newspaper on the bottom and placing enough charcoal on top so that when the paper burns and the charcoal settles, it is just below the air holes in the firebox. You may use an electric fire starter, but never use lighter fluid for this kind of grill. The kamado does not need very much charcoal, so start with a small amount as you learn to regulate the heat a small fire can produce. Again, aim for a temperature of 200 to 250°F for slow smoking.

ADDING WOOD FOR SMOKE FLAVOR

When you're slow smoking at a low temperature, the flavor comes from smoldering aromatic woods—hickory, cherry, oak, mesquite, pecan, and others—that are placed on or near the fire. But beware: most slow smokers agree that there is nothing worse than too much smoke. When the BBQ Queens were learning how to barbecue, we both made the mistake of thinking, "If three chunks of wood are good, maybe five are better," and ended up with inedibly bitter food. Err on the side of too little smoke. You can always put the food back in for more smoking, but oversmoked food can't be rescued.

You may use several different types of woods, depending on the type of smoking equipment you have.

Fine wood chips: For the stovetop smoker. These chips are a little bigger than sawdust. You use them dry and in small amounts—1 to 2 tablespoons placed in the middle of the bottom of the smoker. When you place the smoker over a heat source, these fine chips smolder and burn, giving off aromatic smoke. Medium-high heat is used for stovetop smoking, which means that the food cooks quite fast. The smoke is able to penetrate the food well because the unit itself is very small and the smoke quite intense.

Shredded wood chips: For charcoal and gas grills or smokers. These small pieces of wood should be soaked in water for at least 30 minutes before using. You want them to smolder, not burn. Use about 1 cup at a time and replenish them every hour or so. In a charcoal grill or smoker, scatter them directly on the coals. In a gas grill or in an electric bullet

Great Smoke Flavors

WOOD FLAVORS

Whether you use logs, sticks, chunks, pellets, shreds, sawdust, vines, or chips, hardwoods can infuse foods with great smoke flavor. From common hardwoods such as hickory and oak to grapevines and sassafras, the variety of woods for smoking is wide and delicious. Many woods are synonymous with regional barbecuing, such as hickory smoke from the South, where hickory trees are plentiful, mesquite smoke from the Southwest, and alder from the Northwest. A word of caution: do not use resinous or sappy softwoods such as pine, or your food will be inedible.

- *Alder:* Gives a light, aromatic flavor. Alder and seafood are a match made in heaven.
- *Apple:* Provides a sweeter, aromatic flavor that is good with chicken or pork. It's also used in combination with hickory and oak by competition barbecuers.
- *Black walnut:* Lends a strong smoke flavor that is delicious with game, pork, and beef.
- *Cedar:* Provides a strong flavor that is good with salmon, chicken, and shrimp. Usually used as planks for wood planking.
- *Cherry:* Lends a deeper, sweeter note to smoked foods. Cherry is delicious with beef tenderloin, pork, chicken, and lamb.
- *Citrus:* Gives a moderate fruit flavor that is great with fish, seafood, poultry, and fruit.
- *Grapevines:* Provides a medium fruit flavor that pairs well with game, lamb, and poultry.
- *Hickory:* Gives a strong, hearty smoke flavor that is perfect for beef, pork, and chicken.
- *Maple:* Lends a mild flavor to ham, pork, and poultry.
- *Mesquite:* Provides the strongest, smokiest flavor and is best suited to beef, especially brisket. Make sure you don't use too much, or your food will taste acrid.
- *Mulberry:* Gives a flavor similar to grapevine smoke and works nicely with pork, poultry, ham, and game birds.
- *Oak:* Provides a medium smoke flavor without being bitter and goes well with any food.

- *Oak barrel wood:* **Provides a unique smoke flavor similar to "oaky" wines, such as some Chardonnays. These wood chunks and chips are made from oak barrels used to age wine.**
- *Orange:* **Gives a moderate fruit flavor that is great with fish, seafood, poultry, and fruit.**
- *Peach:* **Lends a moderate fruit flavor to fish, seafood, poultry, and fruit.**
- *Pear:* **Provides a moderate fruit flavor that's nice with fish, seafood, poultry, and fruit.**
- *Pecan:* **Creates a medium smoke flavor that is less pronounced than hickory but more pronounced than oak. Pecan is great to use for grilling fish, poultry, and pork with a kiss of smoke.**
- *Sassafras:* **Lends a musky flavor that is good with lamb, pork, and poultry.**

OTHER SMOKE FLAVORS

Smoke flavor also comes from a variety of other flora. Fresh herbs on the fire emit a fragrant scent. When herb leaves die off in the fall, those woody stems (from lavender, rosemary, thyme, or lemon balm) are perfect for adding smoky flavor. We like the flavor of mint stalks and lemon balm thrown on the fire. Try branches of rosemary while grilling or smoking lamb. Dried corncobs, ground up or not, can be thrown on a hot fire to create a sweet smokiness. Cornhusks add a smoky flavor as well. A little bit of hay can make a sweet, smoky difference (see Prairie-Style Hay-Smoked Steak on page 326). The shells of pecans, peanuts, almonds, walnuts, and other nuts add flavor, too. Even fruit tree leaves can be used on a fire for an interesting smoke flavor. And if you live by the coast, seaweed may be your ticket to a tempting smoky meal.

The BBQ Queens agree that slow smoking enhances meats and vegetables with a deeper smoke flavor than grilling. However, we have a theory about adding various woods, herbs, and the like to a hot grill fire. Although this smoke may not have enough time to penetrate the meat, the smoke does permeate the air around you, your clothes, and your skin. So when you throw aromatics on the fire, even for just a short time, the aroma will be part of the sensual experience as you devour your grilled foods.

smoker, place them in an aluminum foil packet, poke holes in the packet, and place it on the grill rack over the heat (in a gas grill) or near the electric coil (in an electric smoker). You also may use a metal smoker box instead of a foil packet.

Wood pellets: For charcoal, gas, electric, and wood pellet grills or smokers. These are basically pellet-shaped bits of compressed sawdust used in wood pellet grills for fuel and wood smoke flavor. You can also use them with other grills or smokers. Wood pellets must be used dry; if you moisten them, they turn into a mushy sawdust. Because you don't have to soak them, they are always ready to go. Plus, because they are compressed, they take up less space than other wood products. For smoking, use 1/3 cup at a time. For a charcoal grill or smoker, place the pellets in an aluminum foil packet, poke holes in the packet, and place it directly on the coals. For a gas grill or an electric bullet smoker, place the packet on the grill rack over the heat (in a gas grill) or near the electric coil (in an electric smoker). A metal smoker box may be used instead of the foil packets. Wood pellets must be replenished about every hour (the wood pellet grill does this automatically).

Wood chunks: For charcoal and electric smokers. These are bigger pieces of aromatic wood, 3 to 4 inches long and wide. You need to soak them for at least 1 hour before using. Wood chunks are most often placed directly on hot coals or near but not touching the electric coil. We don't recommend using wood chunks with a gas grill because they're not as effective as wood pellets or chips. Three or four wood chunks will last 2 to 3 hours when you're slow smoking.

Wood "sticks" or logs: For big smoker rigs. These are even bigger pieces of wood, cut to fit the diameter of the firebox and placed right on the hot coals. Use three sticks to start and replenish them as necessary.

Getting Ready to Smoke

The smoker should be clean and the rack(s) lightly oiled. Have all your equipment handy. If you are using charcoal, have plenty on hand. If you are using gas, make sure your tanks are full. Soak wood chips or chunks in water (at least 30 minutes for chips, an hour for chunks) or have dry wood pellets handy.

Place the wood of your choice on or near the heat source, according to the kind of smoker you have, and follow the manufacturer's directions. The directions may or may not tell you the amount of wood to use. Our recommendation is to use wood during the first 2 to 3 hours of cooking. Different smokers burn wood at different rates, so you will have to check the smoker and replenish the wood as necessary. For foods that take longer to smoke, such as brisket or pork butt, check to see whether the food has a good smoky aroma before adding more wood during the longer cooking time. It may not need more smoke flavor.

Smoke with the lid or hood closed. This will trap the heat and smoke, allowing greater circulation and a steadier temperature.

The Hand Method for Judging a Smoker's Temperature

If your unit has a temperature gauge, set the temperature to 200 to 250°F. If it does not, hold your hand 5 inches above the indirect section of a grill or over the rack in a smoker. If you can hold it there for only 5 to 6 seconds, the fire is ideal for slow smoking.

Adjusting Your Smoker's Temperature

On a charcoal grill, lower the temperature by closing the vents; raise the temperature by opening the vents or adding more charcoal. Keeping the lid on the smoker closed will also help maintain a steady temperature.

On a gas grill, adjust the heat by turning the control knobs to the desired level. For smoking, adjust the heat control on one burner while leaving the other burner(s) off. Some models allow you to control the temperature by turning a temperature dial. You can also crack the lid slightly to lower the temperature.

On an electric grill, turn the temperature dial to 200 to 250°F.

Preparing Food for Smoking

Preparing food for smoking can be as simple as brushing it with olive oil and seasoning it with salt and pepper. Foods for the smoker stay more juicy and flavorful when marinated, slathered, or rubbed beforehand. Even delicate foods such as cheese need to be brushed or sprayed with olive oil, or they may develop an unappetizing bronze "skin."

How to Smoke

When your smoker is at the proper temperature of 200 to 250°F, place the food on the grill racks or in a disposable aluminum pan, set in the smoker, and close the lid. Let the food cook and smoke for about half of the total cooking time before checking it. Remember, the more you open the smoker, the more the temperature will drop, the more smoke you will lose, and the longer your food will take to get done.

When the BBQ Queens smoke on an electric bullet-shaped water smoker, which registers a constant 225°F, this is how we figure our cooking time. In moderate, calm weather with an outside temperature of 60 to 75°F, we estimate our smoking time at 20 to 30 minutes per pound, with at least 3 to 4 pounds of food on the smoker. For instance, a 12-pound whole turkey will take 4 to 6 hours to smoke. For a turkey, we stoke the smoker with three to five chunks of wood, fill the water pan, close the lid, and smoke for 2 to 3 hours without lifting the lid. If you have a charcoal smoker, you may have to check on the food sooner to add more fuel to the fire.

BASTING

Some foods, such as ribs, brisket, and pork butt, which take several hours to smoke, can benefit from basting. A baste can be any liquid that will provide moisture, from black coffee, cider vinegar, or apple juice to flavorful mixtures such as Rosemary, Garlic, and Lemon Baste (page 68), Homemade Teriyaki Marinade (page 69), and Lemon Butter Drizzle (page 87). A baste adds moisture and flavor to smoked foods. Traditionally, fatty foods such as pork butt or brisket get a bracing, somewhat acidic baste with coffee, vinegar, or apple juice to help cut the fat. Nonfatty foods such as fish or shellfish are more likely to get a moistening baste of butter or olive oil.

Thin basting mixtures, especially those with some sugar in them, also can add a sheen to foods. Homemade Teriyaki Marinade (page 69) is terrific for adding a "lacquered" finish to grilled or smoked foods.

Let the food smoke for an hour or so before basting. Remember to allow more cooking time when basting because opening the lid for basting will lower the temperature inside.

GLAZING

Glazing is done during the last 30 to 60 minutes of smoking. This process also adds a sheen to smoked or grilled foods. Glazing is usually done with barbecue sauce, which contains some sugar or corn syrup and thus creates a burnished, satin finish. Fruit preserves and glazes made with preserves are popular for pork, poultry, and ham.

To glaze foods such as ribs or chicken, turn them bottom side up and brush with barbecue sauce or another glaze. Cover the smoker and let the sauce set for 15 to 30 minutes. Then turn the food over, brush with glaze, close the lid, and let the sauce set for another 15 to 30 minutes. Serve more sauce at the table.

Smoking Times

Smoking times vary based on the heat of the fire, the temperature outdoors, and whether the day is windy, sunny, overcast, or rainy. The better you can control the temperature of your smoker, the easier it is to estimate the cooking time and the better your barbecue will be.

Exact time is less crucial with smoking than with grilling, because smoking is a gentler cooking process. But smoking foods too long will give them a bitter flavor. Use the suggested cooking time given in each recipe as a guide, but also watch your food while it's smoking and use an instant-read meat thermometer inserted in the thickest part to gauge doneness. To be on the safe side, we recommend allowing about an hour extra when smoking any food.

SMOKING TIMETABLE

This chart provides some idea of how long foods will take to smoke at 200 to 250°F. The better you can control your fire, and thus the temperature, the more reliable these cooking times will be.

Beef brisket (trimmed)	**10 to 12 lbs.**	**12 to 15 hours**
Chicken (whole)	**4 to 5 lbs.**	**2½ to 3 hours**
Chicken breast (bone-in)	**4 lbs.**	**1½ to 2½ hours**
Lamb (leg)	**6 to 8 lbs.**	**3 to 4½ hours**
Pork (Boston) butt	**6 to 7 lbs.**	**8 to 12 hours**
Pork loin roast	**4 to 5 lbs.**	**3 to 3½ hours**
Pork ribs (2 slabs at a time)		
Baby back	**3 to 4 lbs.**	**3½ to 4 hours**
Spareribs	**5 to 6 lbs.**	**4 to 6 hours**
Pork sausage	**1½ to 2½ in. diam.**	**1 to 3 hours**
Turkey (whole)	**10 to 12 lbs.**	**5 to 6 hours**
Turkey breast (boneless)	**3 lbs.**	**1½ to 2 hours**

DONENESS CHART FOR SMOKING

Knowing at what temperature your smoked food is done is crucial. You want succulent, moist, tender barbecue—not dried-out jerky. For ribs, the doneness test is visual—when the rib meat has pulled back about an inch from the bones. The BBQ Queens use both heat-safe meat thermometers (inserted in brisket or pork butt and left in during smoking) and instant-read meat thermometers (quickly inserted in foods and then removed).

Beef brisket (trimmed)	**10 to 12 lbs.**	**160°F**
Chicken (whole)	**4 to 5 lbs.**	**175°F**
Chicken breast (bone-in)	**4 lbs.**	**165°F**
Lamb (leg)	**6 to 8 lbs.**	**140 to 145°F**
Pork (Boston) butt	**6 to 7 lbs.**	**160°F**
Pork loin roast	**4 to 5 lbs.**	**145 to 155°F**
Pork ribs (2 slabs at a time)		
Baby back	**3 to 4 lbs.**	**Meat pulls back from bone**
Spareribs	**5 to 6 lbs.**	**Meat pulls back from bone**
Pork sausage	**1 1/2 to 2 1/2 in. diam.**	**150 to 155°F**
Turkey (whole)	**10 to 12 lbs.**	**175 to 180°F**
Turkey breast (boneless)	**3 lbs.**	**170 to 175°F**

Now Let's Have Some Fun!

Want to add even more pizzazz to your outdoor cooking repertoire? We like to wow family, friends, and other foodies with skewers of all kinds, wok baskets made specifically for the grill, stovetop smoking, rotisserie meat preparation, and wood plank cooking.

Skewering on all kinds of sticks, from traditional wooden skewers to herb stalks and even sugar cane, is fun indeed. A whole meal prepared in a grill wok is simplicity at its best. (Try shrimp with seasonal fresh vegetables for a winner every time.) Similarly, a stovetop smoker can give you great smoke flavor all year-round in any kind of weather. Move over rotisserie chicken! A pork loin roast or beef tenderloin is succulent when spit roasted. And there's nothing prettier than a salmon fillet planked on cedar. The combination of pink salmon and burnished wood looks great and tastes even better.

The Art of the Skewer

Sometimes BBQ Queens just wanna have fun. We always have fun out at the grill or smoker, where everyone seems to gather. When we want to have even more fun, we grill something a little unexpected. Our new fun favorite is arranging food on skewers, in unusual, eye-catching ways. Think "stick" in its many forms: fresh rosemary or lavender branches, sugar cane, lemongrass, bamboo, or the old campfire standard, the twig. Or how about round skewers? Those new coiled metal skewers produced by Charcoal Companion look snazzy served on dinner plates.

SKEWERING 101

The first decision is the skewer itself, and you have lots of choices here.

Wooden skewers, which come in packages at the grocery store, need to be soaked in water for at least 30 minutes before threading them with food and grilling. After grilling, you just throw the charred skewers away.

Reusable metal skewers, some with prongs on both ends, or the new metal coil skewers can be easily cleaned with soapy water after grilling , then towel-dried so they don't get water spots. We generally prefer flat metal skewers to wooden ones (see page 32).

Kabob baskets—some long and cylindrical, others wide and flat to hold several metal skewers at a time—are a good choice if you like to grill skewers a lot and want more control when grilling. You need to spray or brush the baskets with oil before grilling so the food doesn't stick. When you're ready to turn the skewers, you just flip the entire basket.

Finally, there are natural skewers, such as herb stalks. Fresh rosemary and lavender branches, bamboo, lemongrass, sugar cane, and twigs from the yard are all safe for food to touch. Before you branch out into the unknown, however, check to make sure that natural skewers are safe to use. Poisoning your barbecue guests with mystery skewers is not a queenly thing to do.

We've found that the best way to make sure all the food gets done at the same time is to avoid those 1950s-style kabobs, with meat or chicken and vegetables all on one stick. We think it's better to have all vegetables, meat, fish, or fruit on one skewer so that every-

Herb Grilling

In an old nursery rhyme and children's song, the king was in his countinghouse, counting all his money. The queen was in the parlor, eating bread and honey. In real time, the men in our lives watch the daily rise and fall of the stock market (more rise than fall, we hope). And we, the BBQ Queens, would rather putter around in our herb gardens than eat bread and honey.

A few years ago, Karen laid out four formal raised beds in her backyard, where a profusion of herbs (basil, Italian parsley, lemon balm, tarragon, and oregano) grows along with her beloved heirloom tomatoes. Judith practices container gardening for herbs that can't withstand the extremes of Kansas weather—bay, scented geranium (Rober's Lemon Rose is her favorite), lemon verbena, and lemongrass.

We wish we could say that we summon various vassals to do the transplanting, weeding, and watering, but not so. We're hands-on queens, so we put on our working tiaras (black sun visors with a glittery tiara design—very chic) and head outdoors.

We both love the fresh scent and taste of herbs and use them whenever we can. Fresh or dried, herbs can really enhance the flavor of foods before, during, or even after grilling. Here's how you do it.

Before grilling: Slather Rosemary Pesto (page 62) on beef or pork tenderloin or boneless chicken breasts, then grill over medium heat. Infuse fish and shellfish with aromatic Lemongrass Marinade (page 74). Use marinades with lots of herbs, such as Amogio (page 72), Chimichurri Sauce (page 346), and Aromatic Lemon-Herb Marinade (page 68), for fish, poultry, and pork.

Use fresh herb stalks as skewers for grilled foods of all kinds. Thread shrimp or scallops on slender but sturdy stalks of lemongrass or lemon verbena. Thread chunks of

thing cooks evenly and you don't have a charred cherry tomato next to a bloody chunk of beef. Leave about 1/8 inch of space between foods on a skewer. If the pieces are squashed together, the inside surfaces where they touch will not cook as fast as the outside surfaces. And goodness knows you don't want chicken sushi on a stick.

beef, pork, or parboiled new potatoes on fresh rosemary stalks. Thread fresh peach or nectarine halves on sturdy lavender stalks. Sandwich fresh scented geranium leaves between nectarine or peach halves or large, pitted sweet cherries on a metal or presoaked wooden skewer.

During grilling: **Stir-grill cherry tomatoes with fresh basil and mint in a grill wok. Grill chicken breasts or portobello mushrooms on a hinged grill rack with fresh herb branches sandwiched inside. Or try our favorite Silver Queen Corn Queen's Rosemary-Scented Grilled Butterflied Chicken (page 205), grilled over a bed of fresh rosemary.**

Thinly slice potatoes lengthwise, then sandwich a fresh sage leaf between two potato slices, brush with olive oil, and grill. Use fresh herb branches to baste foods during grilling. When you cut back your woody herbs in the fall, save the trimmings and place them on a charcoal fire for grilling fish, chicken, or a boneless leg of lamb—in the Provençal way. Wrap fingers of bread dough in large leafy herbs, brush with olive oil, and grill, as in Grilled Leaf-Wrapped Bread Sticks (page 181). Simmer apple jelly or a mild honey with fresh or dried herbs to use as a glaze during the last minutes of grilling chicken breasts, pork tenderloin, or lamb chops.

After grilling: **Serve Rustic Béarnaise Sauce (page 98) with grilled shrimp, salmon, or chicken. Make a simple Gremolata (page 274) with freshly grated lemon zest, Italian parsley, and garlic. Swirl together butter, tomato *concassé*, fresh basil, and fresh lemon juice for an aromatically wonderful finishing touch over grilled veggies, chicken, or fish. Or serve Thousand-Herb Sauce (page 192) over grilled chicken, fish, shellfish, pork, or lamb.**

When you grill skewers, try to arrange them so that they are not in danger of falling through the grill grate. If we can, we place them horizontally and turn them with grill tongs. If you're really worried about your food falling though the grate, use a kabob basket or place the skewers on a perforated grill rack, then on the grate.

The Double-Skewer Approach

We prefer flat metal skewers because the flat blade keeps the chunks of food from spinning around and the metal can't catch on fire. However, if you're cooking for a crowd, it's less expensive to invest in wooden skewers. To keep the food from spinning, thread it onto two parallel skewers.

Food on a skewer will take anywhere from 20 seconds to 10 minutes to grill, so grilling skewers is fast, fast, fast—perfect for Grill Gals on the move.

Wok on the Wild Side

Stir-grilling foods over a hot fire is a great way to make lowfat, one-dish meals on the grill—and no mess in the kitchen! You can, if you wish, serve stir-grilled dishes with steamed rice, soba noodles, pasta ribbons, or couscous, but they're also terrific on their own. Stir-grilled meals add lots of big flavor but few calories to any healthy eating plan.

STIR-GRILLING 101

To stir-grill, you need a grill wok, a hexagonal metal wok with perforations (they usually cost less than $30), along with wooden spoons, paddles, or long-handled spatulas. The perforations in the wok allow for more of the wood and charcoal flavors to penetrate the food. The standard wok is 12 inches, but some manufacturers also make a 15-inch wok. The BBQ Queens prefer a bigger wok because more space means potentially more char and more room for a larger quantity of food. We like to use long-handled wooden paddles or spoons to toss the food in a grill wok. We call this technique "stir-grilling," a similar but healthier alternative to stir-frying.

To stir-grill, first marinate the food—sometimes overnight, sometimes just for 30 minutes—in a sealable plastic bag in the refrigerator. Then prepare a hot fire in the grill and coat the inside of the grill wok with nonstick cooking spray. Place the prepared wok in the sink and dump the bag of marinated food into the wok. The marinade will drain away. Place the wok on a baking sheet and take it outside to the grill. Place the wok over direct heat and stir-grill the food, using wooden paddles or long-handled spoons or metal grill spatulas, until done.

When choosing what to stir-grill, think like a gal—fresh, colorful vegetables cut into interesting sizes and shapes and tender cuts of meat, such as chicken breasts and pork or beef tenderloin. The finished dish will have great eye appeal, as well as being healthy and delicious.

Burnin' Ring of Fire: Rotisserie Cooking

Rotisserie cooking, or spit roasting, is habit-forming. Once you do it, you're hooked. Just ask Diane Phillips, a BBQ Babe (see page 434) whose specialty is rotisserie cooking. Check out her book *The Ultimate Rotisserie Cookbook* (The Harvard Common Press, 2002).

What hooks you with rotisserie cooking is the flavor. As the spit constantly turns, the food bastes in its own juices, producing an exceptionally tender and moist result. (And don't you know, the BBQ Queens love tender!) Whole birds; beef, lamb, veal, and pork roasts; and ribs are all excellent candidates for the outdoor rotisserie. (See the box on page 40 for information about rotisserie cooking fish and vegetables.) This is certainly a nice alternative to have in your culinary arsenal.

THE RIGHT ROTISSERIE FOR THE JOB

When you buy an electric rotisserie for your grill, make sure the motor has adequate power to turn the size and weight of food you want to cook. The manufacturer's directions should make this clear for a whole turkey (10 to 12 pounds), a boneless prime rib roast (9 to 14 pounds), a whole pork loin roast (5 to 6 pounds), and a whole chicken (4 to 5 pounds).

ROTISSERIE COOKING 101

First, set up your rotisserie on the grill. On charcoal grills, the rotisserie unit is often an add-on product that needs to be clamped to the sides of the grill. We recommend that you follow the manufacturer's directions for doing this and for placing the drip pan beneath the meat. On some gas grills, the cooking grate(s) must be removed and the lava rock moved aside so a drip pan can be placed on the rock grate directly beneath where the meat will sit on the spit. In either case, the drip pan should contain about an inch of liquid—a marinade, vinegar, juice, beer, wine, or just plain water. This liquid will steam up into the meat, adding moisture and a wonderful aroma as the meat turns and cooks.

Do not skewer the meat and place it on a lit grill until you are certain that everything is set up properly. With the grill off or unlit, measure the meat over the drip pan. The pan will prevent flare-ups, so make sure the meat is not larger than the drip pan you plan to use. If it is, use either a larger pan or two pans. For easy cleanup, the BBQ Queens prefer to use a disposable aluminum pan.

Trim the meat, then season it. Use pliers to tighten the thumbscrews on the spit forks to prevent loosening during the rotisserie process. Slide the meat onto the spit rod and push it into the secured spit fork so that it is held firmly by the fork's tines. Slide the

Smoking in the Fast Lane

When Karen first heard about the stovetop smoker, she scoffed. After all, she is from Missouri, the Show Me State. How good could food that received only a short shot of smoke really be? Show me the smoke!

Well, Karen tried this gadget, then Judith tried it, and the BBQ Queens now decree: The stovetop smoker is great! Long live the stovetop smoker!

With the stovetop smoker, you can get great smoke flavor under certain conditions and with certain foods. It certainly doesn't replace the art of slow-smoked barbecue, but it does have a place in our fast-paced, sometimes even frenetic, kitchens.

Basically, the stovetop smoker (which usually costs less than $50), looks like an old-fashioned popcorn popper—the kind folks used to hold over a flame and shake to keep the kernels from burning. Of course, we use the smoker in our own inimitable way, as we'll explain.

STOVETOP SMOKING 101

Made of stainless steel, the stovetop smoker is designed to trap and smolder tiny wood particles away from the food so the resulting smoke permeates the food but doesn't make your kitchen smoke alarm go crazy.

To use it, place about 1 tablespoon of very fine wood chips in the center of the base of the smoker. These chips are available in many different varieties, including alder, apple, cherry, corncob, hickory, maple, mesquite, oak, and pecan. Make sure the chips are dry when you put them in the smoker so that they will smolder effectively.

A metal drip tray fits snugly on top of the chips, then a coated, footed wire rack is placed on the tray. Coat or brush whatever food you're smoking with olive oil, then season it with salt and pepper. If you wish, you can marinate the food first and pat it dry, or sprinkle on a rub, before smoking. You can also use up to 1/4 cup of a slather, but that's as fancy as we get. We don't use any concoctions that may drip and burn, affecting the taste of the food. Arrange your food in a single layer on the rack, so you have the most surface area exposed to the smoke. (If you want to double our recipes, smoke the food in two batches.) Slide the metal lid closed, extend the handles, and place the smoker over one burner. Gas or electric coil burners work just fine, but flat ceramic burners require 20 percent more cooking time.

Turn the burner to medium (375°F), medium-high (400°F), or high (450°F-plus) heat. Although the instructions enclosed with the smoker say to keep the heat on medium, we don't. We mainly use medium-high or high heat so that the food gets cooked fast and doesn't dry out. Your stovetop smoker won't be in perfect alignment after placing it over high heat, but who cares? Ours still work just fine.

Start keeping track of the cooking time when you see the first hint of smoke escaping from the smoker.

Although the instruction booklet enclosed with the smoker says that you can smoke a whole turkey, brisket, or rack of spareribs by tenting foil over the smoker (without the metal lid), we prefer smoking already-tender foods with shorter cooking times. Fish and shellfish, chicken, pork and beef tenderloin, soft and semisoft cheeses, and vegetables work well. We think that cuts of meat such as brisket, pork butt, and pork loin roast, which need long, slow cooking to tenderize, taste better cooked in a "real" smoker, on a rotisserie, or over indirect heat on a grill.

It's easy to tell when your food is done. Fish and shellfish should have a bronzish cast and be opaque all the way through. Chicken, beef, and pork also will have a bronzish color and can be checked for doneness with an instant-read meat thermometer. Vegetables and cheeses are done when they have the amount of smoky taste you desire.

We start meats such as pork or beef tenderloin on an outdoor grill or in an indoor grill pan, then finish them in the stovetop smoker. That way, we get a slight caramelization and grill marks on the exterior and a smoky and juicy interior. Perfect!

After you've finished smoking (you can check your food periodically by sliding the lid back), remove the smoker from the heat. Be careful: the smoker will be very hot. Let it sit for a minute or two, then remove the food and let the smoker cool. After the charred

wood chips have cooled completely, rinse them down the drain (so you don't start a fire in your wastebasket).

The stovetop smoker can be cleaned with hot soapy water or placed in the dishwasher. The bottom of the smoker will become discolored after the first use because of the direct heat, but you didn't want to display your smoker in your china cabinet anyway, did you?

Try some of the following recipes, and you'll be a stovetop smoker convert in no time flat. Smoke a variety of foods, then accompany them with any of the "crowning glories" in other smoked recipes that suit your fancy.

Stovetop Smoked Soft Cheese

Smoked soft cheese—such as cream cheese or fresh goat cheese—is one of our favorite goodies, delicious in spreads, crumbled over grilled vegetable salads, or sitting atop a simply dressed salad of baby greens. The crimped foil "tray" keeps the cheese from melting on the rack, because the stovetop smoker cooks food at a higher temperature than an outdoor smoker does. SERVES 4

SUGGESTED WOOD: Apple, cherry, hickory, or pecan

One 8-ounce package cream cheese or one 6- to 9-ounce piece fresh goat cheese

Olive oil

1. Remove the cheese from the package, brush or spray with olive oil, and place on a double thickness of aluminum foil. Crimp the edges to make a "tray" and place on the smoker pan rack. Secure the lid.

2. Place the smoker over one burner on the stove, set at medium heat. When a wisp of smoke escapes from the smoker, start the timer for 10 minutes. Slide open the lid to check for doneness. When the cheese has a smoky aroma and a bronzed appearance, remove the smoker from the heat but keep the lid closed for another minute. Serve hot, at room temperature, or cold.

Stovetop Smoked Shrimp

This has become the BBQ Queens' favorite appetizer to serve at home or bring to a gathering. In about 8 minutes, you have a fabulously smoky dish. How easy is that? Serve the shrimp with your favorite cocktail sauce. The same amount of large sea scallops will smoke in the same amount of time. SERVES 12 AS AN APPETIZER

SUGGESTED WOOD: Hickory or pecan

1 pound large shrimp, peeled and deveined
Olive oil
Fine kosher or sea salt and freshly ground black pepper to taste

1. Rinse the shrimp under cold running water, drain, and pat dry with paper towels. Arrange on the smoker pan rack, drizzle with olive oil, and sprinkle with salt and pepper. Close the lid.

2. Place the smoker over one burner on the stove, set at high heat. When a wisp of smoke escapes from the smoker, start the timer for 6 minutes. Slide open the lid to check for doneness. When the shrimp are bronzish pink, opaque, and somewhat firm to the touch, remove the smoker from the heat but keep the lid closed for another 2 minutes. Serve hot, at room temperature, or cold.

Stovetop Smoked Tomatoes

You can use either large beefsteak or smaller Roma tomatoes, whichever you have on hand. Add them to sauces or the sublime Smoked Tomato Grits (page 164). SERVES 4

SUGGESTED WOOD: Hickory or pecan

4 large beefsteak tomatoes, cored, or 12 Roma tomatoes, cut in half
Olive oil
Fine kosher or sea salt and freshly ground black pepper to taste

1. Arrange the tomatoes on the smoker pan rack, cut sides up. Drizzle with olive oil and sprinkle with salt and pepper. Close the lid.

2. Place the smoker over one burner on the stove, set at medium-high heat. When a wisp of smoke escapes from the smoker, start the timer for 8 to 10 minutes. Slide open the lid to check for doneness. When the tomatoes have cracked skins and are soft to the touch, remove the smoker from the heat but keep the lid closed for another minute. Serve hot, at room temperature, or cold.

Stovetop Double-Smoked Ham

When Judith lived in Vermont, she and her family enjoyed the local corncob-smoked cheddar and ham. Now you can do the same at home. The smoked ham is delicious sliced and served as an entrée. But, oh my, what wonderful grilled smoked ham and cheese sandwiches, smoked ham club sandwiches, and diced smoked ham and bean soup this makes. SERVES 12

SUGGESTED WOOD: Apple, cherry, or oak with a pinch (about 1/2 teaspoon) of corncob; or use plain hickory

1 spiral-sliced or whole boneless ham

1. Place the ham on the smoker pan rack and tent with a double thickness of aluminum foil, securing it tightly around the rim of the smoker.

2. Place the smoker over one burner on the stove, set at medium heat. When a wisp of smoke escapes from the smoker, start the timer for 30 minutes. When the ham has a smoky aroma, remove the smoker from the heat but keep the lid closed for another minute. Serve hot, at room temperature, or cold.

Stovetop Smoked Pork Tenderloin

We like to lay some grill marks on the tenderloin first, then smoke it to medium doneness. We slice the pork and serve it with a variety of dipping sauces, such as Cilantro-Peanut Dipping Sauce (page 389), Spicy Lemon-Soy Sauce (page 312), and Picadillo Olive Salsa (page 192). Sliced smoked pork tenderloin is great platter food to serve at a party. SERVES 6 TO 8

SUGGESTED WOOD: Apple, cherry, or oak

Two 1½-pound pork tenderloins

Olive oil

Fine kosher or sea salt and freshly ground black pepper to taste

1. Brush or spray the pork tenderloin with olive oil. Heat an indoor grill pan over high heat and sear the meat on all sides, 2 to 3 minutes per side. Season with salt and pepper, then place the seared tenderloins on the smoker pan rack. Secure the lid.

2. Place the smoker over one burner on the stove, set at high heat. When a wisp of smoke escapes from the smoker, start the timer for 8 to 10 minutes. Slide open the lid to check for doneness. When an instant-read meat thermometer inserted in the center registers 145°F for medium, remove the smoker from the heat but keep the lid closed for another minute. Serve hot, at room temperature, or cold.

Stovetop Smoked Beef Tenderloin

Get fancy with Tricolored Peppercorn Rub (page 62) instead of plain salt and pepper, then accompany with Peppercorn Beurre Blanc (page 102) or Smoked Chile Beurre Blanc (page 99) for heavenly eating. SERVES 8

SUGGESTED WOOD: **Hickory or mesquite**

One 4-pound beef tenderloin, trimmed of any fat and silverskin

Olive oil

Fine kosher or sea salt and freshly ground black pepper to taste

1. Brush or spray the tenderloin with olive oil. Heat an indoor grill pan over high heat and sear the meat on all sides until you have good grill marks, about 5 minutes per side. Season with salt and pepper, then place the seared tenderloin on the smoker pan rack. Secure the lid.

2. Place the smoker over one burner on the stove, set at high heat. When a wisp of smoke escapes from the smoker, start the timer for 15 minutes. Slide open the lid to check for doneness. When an instant-read meat thermometer inserted in the center registers 135°F for rare, remove the smoker from the heat but keep the lid closed for another minute. Serve hot, at room temperature, or cold.

A Tisket, a Tasket, Put Your Fish (or Veggies) in a Basket

Whole fish, such as trout and char, and large fish fillets, such as salmon and halibut, are delicious cooked on a rotisserie, but to do so, you need a special fish basket. This hinged wire basket prevents the fish from falling off the spit. Simply oil the interior of the basket and place the fish inside. Follow your rotisserie manufacturer's directions for attaching the basket to the spit.

You can also use this basket for vegetables, including cut squash, torpedo onions (large bulb or spring onions), and root vegetables.

other fork onto the spit so that it also holds the meat securely and tighten its thumbscrew with the pliers.

It's very important to balance the meat on the spit so it can turn easily. If the meat is not balanced, it could shorten the life of your rotisserie. To balance the rod, hold it so that the ends lay across the palms of your hands. Position the meat on the rod so that there is no heavy side; otherwise, the heavy side will rotate down. Tie any loose bits to the body of the meat with kitchen twine. Insert a heatproof meat thermometer in the thickest part of the meat, away from any bone(s) and positioned so that it will turn freely with the meat and you can read it. Place the spit on the rotisserie. Start the rotisserie, letting it rotate enough times until you're sure the meat turns easily.

Check to make sure the grill's lid will close while the rotisserie is on. If necessary, you can prop the grill lid open a bit with bricks or metal cans.

Now prepare a medium-hot fire in your grill. You want to cook the meat at 300 to 350°F, which is measured at a distance above the coals, so the actual fire has to be a little hotter.

Cover and cook, checking the meat, the fire, and the drip pan at least every hour. Sometimes the thumbscrews will loosen, or the meat may shrink and the forks may need to be adjusted, so keep a clean pair of pliers handy. Keep checking the meat thermometer so that you know when the meat is done. During the last hour of cooking, apply any finishing sauce or glaze every 30 minutes.

When the meat is done, remove it from the spit and let it rest for at least 15 minutes before slicing.

Now you've got some mighty fine eatin', and your guests will sing your praises. Brush up on the four queen waves (see page 224) so that you're ready for the accolades.

Serving It Up on a Shingle

As BBQ Queens, we certainly get a lot of attention when we wear our tiaras out in public. But at home, it's another story.

Tooling Around with the BBQ Queens

We both have our own BBQ toolboxes—small plastic storage boxes for all our grill necessities. That way, we can take everything outside at once—or to a TV station to do an on-air demo.

Here's some of the stuff we won't leave home without.

Needle-nose pliers: Useful for pulling the membrane off the back of a slab of ribs or to fine-tune the apparatus on a rotisserie.

Instant-read meat thermometer: A must for checking the doneness of meat and poultry.

Grill utensils: Long-handled grill tongs, a grill spatula, a wide-bladed fish spatula, and a wire grill brush.

Newspaper and long matches: For starting the charcoal chimney.

Aluminum foil: For lining the bottom of a charcoal grill; wrapping up packets of wood chips or pellets; and protecting food from the heat of a grill, smoker, or rotisserie.

Kitchen twine: For tying up roasts or whole birds for the grill, smoker, or rotisserie.

Disposable aluminum pans: Buy these in several sizes for grilling or smoking; they make for easy cleanup.

Paper towels: For cleaning up.

Empty spray bottles: You may want two, one filled with water to douse excessive flare-ups (remember—we like char) and the other filled with a marinade you can just spritz on.

Brushes and dish mops: Indispensable for basting and slathering.

Grate Chef Grill Wipes: Great for oiling the grill grates without having excessive oil drip onto the flames.

Flavored wood pellets: We love the herb-, mulberry-, and orange-flavored wood pellets available from BBQr's Delight (sold in small packages, perfect for our toolboxes).

Extra tiaras: Just in case!

You know how you hate it when you get a new haircut or hair color and no one in your family notices? Or when you ask your partner or children to do something and they just don't seem to hear you? (Judith swears that she has a voice with a frequency that only dogs can hear. Karen knows that her husband, Dick, would hear just fine if she asked him to build a duck blind in their backyard, but somehow he misses her request to take out the trash or mow the lawn.) Well, say goodbye to their "see no evil, hear no evil" ways. We guarantee that if you serve your friends and family dinner on a wooden plank, they *will* notice.

Plank cooking is an ancient culinary art originating with Native Americans on both coasts. When the shad ran in New England rivers and the salmon in Pacific Northwest waters, these fish were caught, then pegged to maple or alder planks, which were placed upright around a bonfire to cook. Planking is currently experiencing a revival as Americans explore all the possibilities of cooking on the backyard grill. Once your guests see—and taste—your planked entrées, they'll understand why. The secret to great flavor is to keep the food on the plank in one layer—the more food touching the plank, the more aromatic the taste.

Everything from tuna to tenderloin has a certain "wow" factor when it's cooked and served on a plank. Whereas grilled foods slightly char to take on a robust flavor, and smoked foods have a heavier wood smoke taste, planked foods absorb the gentle aroma and flavor of the wood they are cooked on.

PLANKING 101

Plank cooking is easy. We suggest that you buy untreated hardwood planks. The most important consideration in choosing a plank is to make sure it fits inside your grill. Planks are commonly 15 to 16 inches long, 6 to 7 inches wide, and 1/4 to 1/2 inch thick. The BBQ Queens also use those 2- to 3-inch-thick reinforced cedar baking planks, which are available at gourmet or barbecue and grill shops. They last a long time and are slightly hollowed out, keeping any sauce on the plank. You can also buy commercial-grade 1- to 2-inch-thick untreated hardwood planks at the lumberyard and cut them to fit your grill rack. Food cooks the same on thinner or thicker planks, but thicker planks last longer. Planks can be reused until they're either too charred or too brittle to hold food.

Although planking on cedar is the universal favorite because it gives the best aromatic flavor, any regional hardwood—such as alder, hickory, maple, oak, or pecan—available in barbecue and grill shops will produce great-tasting planked food, too.

Submerge the plank in water for at least 1 hour before using. A deep sink or a large rectangular container that you can fill with water works well. Use a heavy can to weight down the plank. A water-soaked plank produces maximum smoke flavor and is more resistant to charring on the grill.

Prepare an indirect fire in a grill, with a hot fire on one side and a medium fire on the other. You can do this in a gas grill with dual burners or in a charcoal grill by massing two-thirds of the hot coals on the "hot" side and one-third on the "medium" side.

Now here's where Karen and Judith agree to disagree. Judith prefers to season the presoaked plank over hot coals. She places the plank over high heat for about 5 minutes. When the plank starts to char and pop, she turns it over so the charred side is up, then arranges the food in a single layer on that side. Karen doesn't like to season her planks. Both produce great-tasting food. You decide which method you prefer.

Don't crowd the food on the plank. Arrange it in a single layer to ensure the best flavor. Use two planks, if necessary.

Place the plank(s) on the grill grate and close the lid. Cook for 12 to 20 minutes, depending on the amount of food. (Each of our recipes tells you how long.) Stay close by, in case of flare-ups, for which you should keep a spray bottle filled with water handy.

For a rustic and restaurant-style effect, serve the food right on the plank, like a platter. After you've cooked and served on the plank, cleanup couldn't be easier—a little hot soapy water and a good rinse. Eighty-grit sandpaper may be used to spruce up the plank, too.

Common Hardwood Flavors for Planking

- **ALDER:** Gives a light, aromatic flavor. Alder and seafood are a match made in heaven.
- **CEDAR:** Probably the most aromatic wood, it lends a deep but gentle flavor to planked food of all kinds.
- **HICKORY:** Supplies a strong, hearty wood flavor that is wonderful with beef, pork, and chicken.
- **MAPLE:** Smolders to a sweet, mild flavor that pairs well with chicken, vegetables, and fish.
- **OAK:** Provides a medium woodsy aroma without being bitter. It goes well with any food.

Greasehouse University and the Order of the Magic Mop: The Kansas City Barbeque Society

Although Karen is the more certified barbecue cook—she has attained an M.B. (Master of Barbecue) at the esteemed and fictional Greasehouse University, but she hasn't yet taken her oral exams for the Ph.B. (Doctor of Barbecue Philosophy)—it was Judith who was inducted into the Order of the Magic Mop.

The honor could have been awarded for her service to the barbecue world in helping Paul Kirk whip his manuscript into shape for his gargantuan *Paul Kirk's Championship Barbecue* (The Harvard Common Press, 2004); her work as coauthor with Karen of *Fish & Shellfish, Grilled & Smoked* (The Harvard Common Press, 2002) and *Easy Grilling & Simple Smoking with the BBQ Queens* (Pig Out Publications, 1997); her how-to barbecue classes that she teaches with Karen; or because she's friends with Ardie Davis, a.k.a. Remus Powers, Ph.B., in the colorful world of competition barbecue. Ardie is the bestower of the mop.

The barbecue ritual involves the lowly dish mop, that wood-handled, yarn-headed tool used to clean dishes and "mop" basting liquid on slow-smoking meats. Ardie's dish mop, however, is a special kind that he buys only at Piggly Wiggly grocery stores in the Memphis area for $1.49. "It's got a plain wood handle, no glue at all, just fastened together with a wire and a nail. The top is Egyptian cotton," Ardie says.

Ardie uses his mop to "bless" barbecue rigs or induct barbecuers into the Order of the Magic Mop by the simple gift of a new mop, autographed by Remus Powers himself. He flicks the mop over your rig, your food, and you, while intoning, "In the name of the steer and the hog and the holy smoke, you are now a member of the Order of the Magic Mop."

Like Tinker Bell's pixie dust, it's magic if you think it is. The BBQ Queens believe!

Sprinkle, Slather, Soak, and Drizzle: Rubs, Marinades, Vinaigrettes, and Sauces

Adding another flavor element to foods that are grilled or smoked can be done at two different times—before or after cooking. Foods cooked on the grill or in the smoker will already be getting a slightly charred, caramelized, or wood smoke flavor. The addition of citrus, garlic, fresh or dried herbs, spices, wine, or aromatic vegetables can further enhance the flavor. Think of basic grilled or smoked foods as clear polish on your nails—classic and in good taste. Rubs, pastes, slathers, and marinades applied before cooking, and vinaigrettes, drizzles, and sauces used after cooking, are more like a French manicure—a lot more sophisticated and quietly wow-y. You can't go wrong with either.

The BBQ Queens promise that you won't find recipe versions of iridescent, grunge-blue polish painted on talon-like nails here. After all, we don't wear real rhinestone tiaras for our health. We wear them because we have good taste. So you can trust us, girlfriend. You won't catch us in bright blue eye shadow. Nnnuh-uh.

Dry Rubs, Pastes, and Slathers

In cosmetic makeup terms, olive oil, salt, and pepper function as the flavor foundation for grilled foods of all kinds. Sure you could go without them and be totally plain-Jane, but we don't recommend it. Beyond the basic olive oil, salt, and pepper are dry rubs, pastes, and slathers.

Dry rubs are dry herb and spice mixtures that are sprinkled on the surface of fish, poultry, meat, or vegetables before grilling or smoking. Like Tinker Bell's fairy dust, you sprinkle on a rub for some culinary magic.

Rubs can be as simple as salt and pepper or as complex as a mixture of 12 ingredients. The key is that everything going into a rub should be dry, so that the rub stays in suspension. If you even think about adding fresh garlic or herbs, then you no longer have a dry rub. (Not that there's anything wrong with that—it's just not a rub and it will keep refrigerated for only a few days.) Rubs are used on both grilled and smoked foods.

Wow-factor pastes, such as those with fresh garlic or smoke-roasted red bell peppers, add a big burst of flavor to food destined for the grill. They're like all-in-one cosmetics—a foundation that's also a bronzer, a lipstick that's also a balm. You get the picture: no need for a separate foundation of olive oil, salt, and pepper when you use a paste because they're already in the paste. Pastes need to be brushed on the surface of food, then left to sit for about 30 minutes before cooking to let the flavors develop.

The idea for slathers comes from our Kansas City barbecue buddy Paul Kirk, author of *Paul Kirk's Championship Barbecue* (The Harvard Common Press, 2004). Basically, a slather is a mustard-based mixture—or just plain American or Dijon mustard—spread over a food before slow smoking or planking. The slather is then sprinkled with a rub and left to sit until it gets tacky to the touch, about 15 minutes. The combination of the slather and the rub makes a kind of savory bark on the food, keeping it moist and flavorful. We use slathers on slow-smoked pork loin roasts, pork butts, and planked salmon fillets.

BBQ Queens' All-Purpose Rub 49
Memphis Blue-Ribbon Rib Rub 49
Prizewinning Rib Rub 50
Fair for Fowl Rub 51
Spicy Orange Rub 51
Zesty Sugar and Spice Rub 52
Spicy Red-Hot Lemon Pepper Rub 53

SALTS OF THE EARTH
Lavender Salt 55
Rosemary Salt 56
Fennel Salt 56
Spicy, Savory Seasoned Salt 56
Smoked Hickory Salt 57

Cajun Steak Rub 58
BBQ Queens' Photo Op Barbecue Rub 58
Texas Two-Steppin' Mesquite Rub 59
Fireworks Rub 60
Ole Hickory Rub 60
Dukka 61
Tricolored Peppercorn Rub 62
Rosemary Pesto 62
Chive Pesto 64
Five-Spice Asian Paste 64
Porcini Paste 65
Mustard-Mayo Slather 66
- Mustard-Mayo-Dill Slather 66
- Mustard-Mayo-Orange Slather 66
- Mustard-Mayo-Tarragon Slather 66

Rosemary, Garlic, and Lemon Baste 68
Aromatic Lemon-Herb Marinade 68
Homemade Teriyaki Marinade 69
Garlic-Citrus Marinade 70
Provençal Red Wine Marinade 70
Rosemary-Mustard Marinade 71
Amogio 72
Fennel and Orange Marinade 72
- Fennel and Orange Drizzling Sauce 73

Tequila-Lime Marinade 73
Lemongrass Marinade 74
Tandoori Marinade 74
Lemon-Tarragon Vinaigrette 75
Saffron Vinaigrette 76
Wheat Beer Vinaigrette 77

THEY DUBBED IT . . . COLESLAW
Blue Cheese Coleslaw 79
Crunchy Broccoli Slaw with Thai Chile-Peanut Dressing 80
Layered Vinegar Slaw 80
Mediterranean Summer Squash Slaw 81
Frozen Asset Slaw 82
Red Cabbage and Apple Slaw 83

Citrus Caesar Vinaigrette 84
Balsamic-Thyme Vinaigrette 84
Fresh Basil Vinaigrette 85
Hot Shallot Vinaigrette 85
Chipotle Vinaigrette 86
Lemon Butter Drizzle 87
Vietnamese Drizzle 87
Honey-Almond Grilling Glaze 88
BBQ Queens' Love Potion for the Swine 89
The Doctor Is In Apricot-Bourbon Barbecue Sauce 90
Simply Delicious Bordelaise Sauce 91
Mango-Lemon Sauce 92
Raspberry and Blood Orange Sauce 92
Poblano Cream Sauce 93
Smoked Garlic and Cilantro Cream Sauce 93
Roasted Red Pepper Sauce 94
Tomato-Fennel Sauce 95
Pistachio-Pomegranate Sauce 96
Food Processor or Blender Hollandaise 97
Rustic Béarnaise Sauce 98
Smoked Chile Beurre Blanc 99
Mustard-Cornichon Beurre Blanc 100
Raspberry Beurre Blanc 101
Peppercorn Beurre Blanc 102

Kimizu 103

Lemon-Garlic Mayonnaise 103

Rustic Aioli 104

White Truffle Aioli 105

BAKED OR BARBECUED BEANS

Texas-Style Pinto Beans 106

BBQ Queens' Barbecued Beans 107

Jazzy Java Baked Beans 108

Easy Southern-Style Baked Beans 109

The Doctor Is In Easy Aioli 110

Creamy Blue Cheese Dressing 111

Tzatziki 112

Zapatos
Shoes

BBQ Queens' All-Purpose Rub

As the title of this recipe suggests, you can use this on just about anything you grill or smoke—from flatbreads and cheese to veggies, fish, chicken, and meats. This spice mixture provides a sweet (from the celery seeds) and hot (from the black pepper) one-two punch with a savory underlayer (from the garlic powder and onion salt). MAKES ABOUT 2 CUPS

1/2 cup freshly ground black pepper
1/2 cup sweet Hungarian paprika
1/4 cup garlic powder
1/4 cup onion salt
3 tablespoons dry mustard
3 tablespoons celery seeds
3 tablespoons chili powder

Combine all the ingredients in a large glass jar with a tight-fitting lid. Secure the lid and shake to blend. This rub will keep in the cupboard for several months.

Memphis Blue-Ribbon Rib Rub

This is delicious on pork ribs, pork butt, pork loin, pork chops, and pork steaks. We sound like that shrimp character in *Forrest Gump*, don't we? MAKES ABOUT 3 CUPS

1 cup sweet Hungarian paprika
1/2 cup lemon pepper seasoning
1/2 cup freshly ground black pepper
1/4 cup garlic salt
1/4 cup chili powder
1/2 cup firmly packed light or dark brown sugar, spread on a baking sheet and left to dry for 1 hour

Combine all the ingredients in a large glass jar with a tight-fitting lid. Secure the lid and shake to blend. This rub will keep in the cupboard for several months.

Prizewinning Rib Rub

The celery salt in this seasoning adds a slightly sweet flavor that's perfect with pork, chicken, and fish. MAKES ABOUT 3/4 CUP

- 1/4 cup sugar
- 2 tablespoons garlic salt
- 2 tablespoons freshly ground black pepper
- 2 tablespoons sweet Hungarian paprika
- 2 tablespoons celery salt

Combine all the ingredients in a small glass jar with a tight-fitting lid. Secure the lid and shake to blend. This rub will keep in the cupboard for several months.

BBQ Queens' Rub Pantry

A rub is always made with dry ingredients, so the following spices, seasonings, and herbs are all dried. The list can be endless, so decide on the number of seasonings you like best and enjoy!

THE BASICS

- Brown sugar, light and dark
- Celery seeds or salt
- Chili powder
- Garlic powder
- Mustard, dry
- Onion powder
- Paprika, sweet Hungarian
- Pepper: freshly ground black, lemon, seasoned
- Red pepper flakes
- Salt: kosher or sea salt, garlic salt, onion salt

BBQ QUEENS' FANCY RUB PANTRY

- Anise seeds
- Basil
- Cayenne pepper
- Citrus peel, ground dried
- Coriander, ground or seeds
- Cumin, ground or seeds
- Fennel seeds
- Garlic, granulated
- Lavender
- Onion, granulated
- Rosemary
- Tarragon
- Thyme
- White pepper, ground

Fair for Fowl Rub

A former chef at Kansas City's Peppercorn Duck Club developed this rub, which he used on a hickory-smoked duck he entered in the American Royal Barbecue Contest. It's not limited to duck, of course. Try it if you want on rotisserie or slow-smoked fowl of any kind, from chicken and turkey to Cornish game hens and duck. This recipe makes enough to rub one 4-pound chicken or duck. Multiply it about three times to use on a turkey. MAKES ABOUT 2/3 CUP

1/2 cup coarse kosher or sea salt
1 teaspoon dried rosemary
1 teaspoon fennel seeds
1 teaspoon anise seeds
1 teaspoon garlic powder
1 teaspoon ground white pepper
1 teaspoon sweet Hungarian paprika

Combine all the ingredients in a small glass jar with a tight-fitting lid. Secure the lid and shake to blend. This rub will keep in the cupboard for several months.

Spicy Orange Rub

Savory, spicy, and zesty, this is great on grilled fish, chicken, duck, turkey, or pork. Pair this pretty orange rub with a darker one, such as Fireworks Rub (page 60), sprinkling alternating 1-inch stripes of the rubs on a raw fish fillet. It's beautiful and tasty, too. MAKES ABOUT 1/3 CUP

3 tablespoons ground dried orange peel
1 tablespoon onion powder
1 1/2 teaspoons ground ginger
1 tablespoon red pepper flakes

Combine all the ingredients in a glass jar with a tight-fitting lid. Secure the lid and shake to blend. This rub will keep in the cupboard for several months.

Zesty Sugar and Spice Rub

Five-spice powder, available at better grocery stores and Asian markets, sets the tone here, joined by allspice, coriander, cinnamon, sugar, and dried orange peel to make a heady and aromatic rub that is fabulous on duck, turkey, game birds, and pork. We also like it sprinkled on fresh apple or pear slices used raw in a salad or sautéed in butter for a side dish. MAKES ABOUT 2/3 CUP

2 teaspoons five-spice powder
2 teaspoons ground allspice
2 teaspoons ground coriander
2 teaspoons ground cinnamon
2 tablespoons sugar
2 tablespoons ground dried orange peel

Combine all the ingredients in a glass jar with a tight-fitting lid. Secure the lid and shake to blend. This rub will keep in the cupboard for several months.

Spicy Red-Hot Lemon Pepper Rub

This hot and lemony rub is very versatile. Try it on poultry, pork, fish, and vegetables. MAKES ABOUT 1 CUP

- **1/2 cup lemon pepper seasoning**
- **2 tablespoons chili powder**
- **2 tablespoons ground cumin**
- **2 tablespoons ground coriander**
- **1 tablespoon firmly packed light or dark brown sugar**
- **1 1/2 teaspoons fine kosher or sea salt**
- **1 1/2 teaspoons red pepper flakes**
- **1 tablespoon freshly ground black pepper**

Combine all the ingredients in a small jar with a tight-fitting lid. Secure the lid and shake to blend. This rub will keep in the cupboard for several months.

Salts of the Earth

Chefs—as well as avid backyard cooks and competition barbecuers—are always after that signature flavor, that certain something you can't quite put your finger on that elevates a dish to fantastic. In this quest, they're rediscovering, of all things, salt.

Not just any salt, of course, but specialty salts, either naturally flavorful or helped along with the addition of smoke, herbs, or other seasonings. As an article in the *New York Times Magazine* recently related, "A sprinkle of these rare, natural salts from the sea brings out the best (flavor, that is) in just about any food—even sweets." (Note that all salt is sea salt. Even if it is found inland, it was created from long-ago seas.)

A few of these "new" old salts have been harvested since around the eighth century B.C. The most basic is *fleur de sel*, or "flower of the sea." This salt is made when sun and wind conditions are ideal on the coasts of Normandy and Brittany, France, where it is hand-harvested from salt ponds. Douglas Rodriguez, author of *Latin Flavors on the Grill* (Ten Speed Press, 2000), sprinkles *fleur de sel* over cantaloupe seared in caramelized sugar. Petrossian, the caviar emporium and specialty bakery, serves it on chocolate cake.

Another specialty salt is Hawaiian red alae salt. After drying, it is combined with Hawaiian red clay for added minerals and a somewhat flinty taste. Tom Colicchio of New York City's Gramercy Tavern uses it over grilled turbot.

Peruvian pink sea salt comes from an ancient ocean trapped underground. The salt dissolves into a spring located high in the Andes, and the spring water is collected in terraced ponds in the Sacred Valley of the Incas. According to chef Michael Mischan of Aspen, Colorado, this salt's mineral quality is "unbelievable on sliced ripe tomatoes."

In *Saveur* magazine, editor Colman Andrews has raved about Danish smoked salt, an ancient Viking seasoning (needed, we guess, to make all the wind-dried cod more palatable after months of eating it). Seawater is boiled in a cauldron over a fire of cherry, elm, juniper, beech, and oak until the water evaporates, and the resulting salt "tastes like a bonfire," Andrews says. This salt gives an instant rich, smoky flavor to any food.

Rosemary and lavender salts are produced by Eatwell Farm, an organic farm in northern California that grows organic herbs and mixes them with gray French sea salt.

Eatwell Farm products are available from the Cooking School of Aspen (www.salt-traders.com or 800-641-7258).

In most recipes in this book, we recommend "kosher or sea salt." According to Robert Wolke in his book *What Einstein Told His Cooks* (W. W. Norton, 2002), kosher salt is distinguished by its coarse, irregular crystals and the rabbinical supervision of its manufacture. Kosher salt is pure and clean with no additives (except that Morton Coarse Kosher Salt lists a trace amount of anticaking agent). Its coarse crystals are well suited to adhering to foods.

Using one or more of these salts can elevate your food to the celestial—nothing to sneeze at if you're working on the title of culinary goddess. Hawaiian red alae salt, Peruvian pink sea salt, and other more arcane salts, such as South African sea salt, Japanese nazuna, Hawaiian black lava salt, and Mexican *benequenes,* are available from the Cooking School of Aspen (see above). Danish smoked salt is carried by several different spice emporiums, or you can make your own Smoked Hickory Salt (below). It's also very easy to make your own lavender, rosemary, or fennel salt or a special seasoned salt, as described below.

Lavender Salt

This coarse salt blend is meant to be sprinkled on lamb, beef, and pork before grilling. Use unsprayed lavender buds from your garden, as Judith does, or buy organic lavender buds from a health food store. For the best flavor, rub the salt mixture between your hands before sprinkling it on food to release the natural oils in the lavender.

MAKES ABOUT 1/4 CUP

2 tablespoons dried lavender buds

2 tablespoons best-quality coarse sea salt, preferably *fleur de sel*

Combine the ingredients in a small glass jar with a tight-fitting lid. Cover and shake to blend. This salt will keep in the cupboard for up to 1 year.

Rosemary Salt

Sprinkle this salt on lamb, beef, and pork before grilling. It's also great over vegetables, grilled fish, or steak. For the best flavor, rub the salt mixture between your hands before sprinkling it on food to release the natural oils in the rosemary. MAKES ABOUT 1/4 CUP

2 tablespoons dried rosemary

2 tablespoons best-quality coarse sea salt, preferably *fleur de sel*

Combine the ingredients in a small glass jar with a tight-fitting lid. Cover and shake to blend. This salt will keep in the cupboard for several months.

Fennel Salt

Use this salt on lamb, fish, or pork before grilling, then finish the dish with Fennel and Orange Drizzling Sauce (page 73). For the best flavor, rub the salt mixture between your hands before sprinkling it on food to release the natural oils in the fennel seeds. MAKES ABOUT 1/4 CUP

2 tablespoons fennel seeds

2 tablespoons best-quality coarse sea salt, preferably *fleur de sel*

Combine the ingredients in a small glass jar with a tight-fitting lid. Cover and shake to blend. This salt will keep in the cupboard for several months.

Spicy, Savory Seasoned Salt

This all-purpose salt and spice blend can go on anything before grilling or smoking. MAKES ABOUT 3/4 CUP

1/2 cup fine sea salt

2 tablespoons sweet Hungarian paprika

1 tablespoon dry mustard

1 teaspoon crumbled dried thyme

1 teaspoon crumbled dried marjoram

1 teaspoon garlic powder

1 teaspoon ground celery seeds

1 teaspoon onion powder

1 teaspoon dillweed

Combine all the ingredients in a small glass jar with a tight-fitting lid. Cover and shake to blend. This salt will keep in the cupboard for several months.

Smoked Hickory Salt

The BBQ Queens have been intrigued by all the fancy salts from around the world. The smoked salts really caught our eye but distressed our pocketbooks. Not willing to spend $10 to $20 for a few ounces, we thought we could smoke our own and put the money we saved into dazzling cubic zirconia tiaras. And so we did. This recipe was tested in a Camerons Stovetop Smoker. You can also use other woods, such as mesquite, pecan, or oak. Heavier smoke flavors work best. MAKES ABOUT 1 CUP

2 tablespoons hickory wood chips made for a stovetop smoker

1 cup coarse kosher salt

1. Place the wood chips in the center of the smoker pan. Place the drip pan and rack in the pan.

2. Spread the salt evenly in a Pyrex baking dish that fits in the smoker pan. The layer of salt should be about $^1/_8$ inch thick, so that the smoke can penetrate it easily. Place the dish on top of the rack and close the lid. (If the dish is too deep to allow the lid to slide closed, cover the pan with a sheet of heavy-duty aluminum foil crimped tightly around the pan.) Place the smoker over medium-high heat and smoke the salt for 15 to 20 minutes.

3. Turn off the heat and let the smoke dissipate before opening the lid, 10 to 15 minutes. The salt will be lightly browned and taste of hickory. Store in a glass jar with a tight-fitting lid. It will keep indefinitely in the cupboard.

Cajun Steak Rub

This rub is great on steaks, hamburgers, pork tenderloin, chops, even chicken breasts. Spray or brush light olive or vegetable oil evenly on the surface of the food, then sprinkle it with the rub before grilling. MAKES ABOUT 1/4 CUP

1 tablespoon garlic powder
1 tablespoon freshly ground black pepper
1 tablespoon sweet Hungarian paprika
1 1/2 teaspoons cayenne pepper
1 teaspoon fine kosher or sea salt
1/2 teaspoon ground white pepper

Combine all the ingredients in a small glass jar with a tight-fitting lid. Secure the lid and shake to blend. This rub will keep in the cupboard for several months.

BBQ Queens' Photo Op Barbecue Rub

While photographing gadgets, grills, and spices for this book, we arranged different-colored dried herbs and spices on a white plate. We thought, "Wonder what it would taste like if we combined them all in a rub?" We did, and it was pretty darn good. Try this on chicken, pork, or even fish, then smile for the camera. MAKES ABOUT 1 CUP

3 tablespoons firmly packed dark brown sugar
2 tablespoons chili powder
2 tablespoons ground ancho chile (see box on page 59)
2 tablespoons ground chipotle chile (see box on page 59)
2 tablespoons lemon pepper seasoning
2 tablespoons sweet Hungarian paprika

2 tablespoons dillweed

2 tablespoons granulated onion

2 tablespoons celery seeds

Combine all the ingredients in a large glass jar with a tight-fitting lid. Secure the lid and shake to blend. This rub will keep in the cupboard for several months.

Texas Two-Steppin' Mesquite Rub

Try this rub on brisket. It makes lots—remember, we're talkin' Texas. MAKES ABOUT 2 CUPS

1/2 cup coarse kosher salt

1/4 cup garlic powder

1/4 cup lemon pepper seasoning

1/4 cup firmly packed light or dark brown sugar

3 tablespoons ground chipotle or ancho chile (see box)

3 tablespoons mesquite seasoning (see box)

3 tablespoons dried thyme

3 tablespoons ground cumin

Combine all the ingredients in a large glass jar with a tight-fitting lid. Secure the lid and shake to blend. This rub will keep in the cupboard for several months.

McCormick Seasonings

If you want to add some great ready-made rubs to your pantry, we recommend McCormick Grill Mates. Flavors include Barbecue Seasoning, Mesquite Seasoning, Montreal Steak Seasoning, and Spicy Montreal Steak Seasoning. For your "fancy" rub pantry, try McCormick Chipotle Chile Pepper and Ancho Chile Pepper. They are fine alone, but we like to doctor them up, too.

Fireworks Rub

The spiciness and heat of this rub makes it a good seasoning for just about anything. We use it on grilled fish for fish tacos, smoked brisket, grilled chicken wings, and even grilled pork tenderloin. If you like really hot stuff, double the amount of red pepper flakes. MAKES ABOUT 1 CUP

1/4 cup chili powder
1/4 cup ground cumin
1/4 cup ground coriander
2 tablespoons firmly packed light or dark brown sugar
2 tablespoons red pepper flakes
2 tablespoons freshly ground black pepper
1 tablespoon coarse kosher salt

Combine all the ingredients in a large glass jar with a tight-fitting lid. Secure the lid and shake to blend. This rub will keep in the cupboard for several months.

Ole Hickory Rub

This southern-style rub has hickory salt as the key ingredient. It is delicious on pork—shoulder, butt, ribs, chops, and tenderloin. MAKES ABOUT 2 CUPS

1/2 cup store-bought hickory salt or Smoked Hickory Salt (page 57)
1/4 cup garlic powder or granulated garlic
1/4 cup onion powder
1/4 cup chili powder
3 tablespoons sweet Hungarian paprika
3 tablespoons firmly packed light or dark brown sugar

3 tablespoons dry mustard

1 1/2 tablespoons ground ginger

1 1/2 tablespoons red pepper flakes

Combine all the ingredients in a large glass jar with a tight-fitting lid. Secure the lid and shake to blend. This rub will keep in the cupboard for several months.

Dukka

Adapted from a recipe by the late Laurie Colwin (see box on page 63), this Egyptian nut and spice powder is addictive. We've kicked up the heat by adding red pepper flakes to the original recipe. Sprinkle it on food before slow smoking, or sprinkle it on simply grilled food after cooking. We love it on grilled vegetables, grilled or smoked chicken, or grilled flatbreads that have been brushed with olive oil. MAKES ABOUT 3/4 CUP

1/2 cup walnut pieces

1/4 cup sesame seeds

2 tablespoons coriander seeds

1 1/2 tablespoons cumin seeds

1 1/2 teaspoons black peppercorns

1 1/2 teaspoons coarse kosher or sea salt

1 teaspoon ground cinnamon

1 teaspoon ground allspice

1/2 teaspoon red pepper flakes

1. In a small skillet over medium-high heat, toast all the ingredients, stirring constantly, until the walnuts have turned a deeper brown, about 5 minutes. Let cool slightly.

2. In a food processor or blender, or by hand in a mortar with a pestle, grind the mixture into a fine powder. Spoon into a small glass jar with a tight-fitting lid. Secure the lid and shake to blend. This powder will keep in the cupboard for several months.

Tricolored Peppercorn Rub

You'll need a mortar and pestle to crack but not completely grind the toasted peppercorns. But once you taste this rub on a grilled filet mignon, strip steak, or tuna steak, or on a smoked brisket or rib roast, you'll be glad for the effort. For an even greater hit of peppercorn, serve grilled beef, salmon, or tuna steaks with this rub, accompanied by Peppercorn Beurre Blanc (page 102). Wow! MAKES ABOUT 1/3 CUP

2 tablespoons Szechuan or white peppercorns

2 tablespoons black peppercorns

1 tablespoon dried green peppercorns

1 tablespoon coarse kosher or sea salt

1. Place all the ingredients in a small cast-iron skillet over medium-high heat and toast, stirring frequently, until the spices become aromatic, about 2 minutes.

2. Scrape the mixture into a mortar and grind them with a pestle until crushed and still somewhat coarse. Use right away.

Rosemary Pesto

Bold, gutsy, and Ethel Merman–like, this version of pesto has a "nothing like a dame" flavor. We like to slather it on pork tenderloin or pork chops, lamb steaks or rack of lamb, or beef tenderloin before grilling over a medium-hot fire (so the pesto doesn't char too much) on a well-oiled grill rack. Turn the meat only once and very carefully, using two grill spatulas. Rosemary pesto is also great on grilled bread or tossed with grilled zucchini and summer squash coins. MAKES ABOUT 1 CUP

1/2 cup fresh rosemary leaves

8 cloves garlic, peeled

1/2 cup pine nuts

1/2 cup olive oil

1 tablespoon fine kosher or sea salt

1 teaspoon freshly ground black pepper

In a food processor, process the rosemary, garlic, and pine nuts together until you have a smooth paste. With the processor running, drizzle in the olive oil in a slow, steady stream until the pesto solidifies. Add the salt and pepper and pulse to combine. Use immediately or spoon into a small jar with a tight-fitting lid. This pesto will keep in the refrigerator for up to 3 days or in the freezer for up to 6 months.

In Laurie Colwin's Pantry

In *More Home Cooking: A Writer Returns to the Kitchen* (HarperCollins, 1993), Laurie Colwin waxes rhapsodic on her favorite condiments. They're some of our favorites, too.

"I myself am hipped on a number of condiments without which I would not dream of cooking," Colwin wrote. "This shows me to be a politically correct and multicultural person. After all, to cook without stepping out of your own country is boring, the sort of culinary equivalent of reading only what are now called DWEMs—dead white European males."

Here's a sampling of Colwin's favorite condiments—and how we use them.

- ***Lime pickle* (Colwin favored Bedekar's Lime Chilli Pickle) mixed with yogurt to accompany grilled chicken**
- ***Fermented black beans* sprinkled over olive-oil-and-garlic-marinated grilled vegetables or on top of grilled focaccia**
- ***Capers* in browned butter served with simply grilled fish**
- ***Thai red curry paste* mixed with canned unsweetened coconut milk as a dipping sauce for grilled shrimp**
- ***Gomashio,* a Japanese condiment of toasted sesame seeds and salt, sprinkled over simply grilled foods**
- ***Dukka,* an Egyptian spice powder (page 61), sprinkled over anything**

Chive Pesto

Karen's vegetable and herb garden consists of four raised beds. One of the beds is bordered with onion chives and another with garlic chives. "That's a lot of chives!" Judith wisecracked, until Karen made this pesto at a class they taught at KitchenArt in West Lafayette, Indiana. "Put this in our BBQ Queen book, please," Judith urged. "It would be a fabulous condiment on a great grilled burger or chicken breast." 'Nuf said. MAKES ABOUT 1 CUP

2 cups chopped fresh garlic or onion chives
1/2 cup pine nuts
1 clove garlic, crushed or roughly chopped
3/4 cup regular or extra virgin olive oil
1/2 cup freshly grated Parmesan or Romano cheese
Kosher or sea salt and freshly ground black pepper to taste

In a food processor, process the chives, pine nuts, and garlic until they form a smooth paste. With the processor running, drizzle in the olive oil in a slow, steady stream until the pesto solidifies. Add the Parmesan, season with salt and pepper, and pulse just to combine. Use immediately or spoon into a small jar with a tight-fitting lid. This pesto will keep in the refrigerator for 4 to 5 days or in the freezer for up to 6 months.

Five-Spice Asian Paste

Spread this paste over duck before grilling or smoking for a fusion feast of Asian barbecue. We also love it on salmon fillets, pork tenderloin, or even oysters before grilling or smoking. Five-spice powder, with its hit of anise, is available at better grocery stores and Asian markets. MAKES ABOUT 1 1/4 CUPS

1 cup firmly packed light brown sugar
2 tablespoons soy sauce

2 tablespoons vegetable oil

1 tablespoon five-spice powder

2 cloves garlic, minced

In a small bowl, combine all the ingredients until you have a paste. Use immediately or spoon into a small jar with a tight-fitting lid. This paste will keep in the refrigerator for up to 1 week.

Porcini Paste

Dried porcini mushrooms, available in the produce section of better grocery stores, can make a very savory addition to the spice cupboard. Simply grind them into a powder in a clean coffee grinder or blender, then use them in delicious concoctions like this one. Slather this paste on a big, thick steak, on smaller filets mignons, on a pork tenderloin, or on a whole chicken destined for the rotisserie. Let marinate for at least 30 minutes, then cook. This paste gives foods a deep, complex, somewhat garlicky, decidedly luscious flavor. We adapted this recipe from one by our barbecue buddy Paul Kirk.

MAKES ABOUT 3/4 CUP

2 tablespoons sugar

1 tablespoon kosher salt

5 large cloves garlic, minced

1 tablespoon red pepper flakes

1 tablespoon freshly ground black pepper

1/4 cup dried porcini mushrooms, ground to a powder in a coffee grinder

1/4 cup extra virgin olive oil

In a small bowl, combine all the ingredients until you have a paste. Use immediately or spoon into a small jar with a tight-fitting lid. This paste will keep in the refrigerator for up to 1 week.

Mustard-Mayo Slather

Short of buying a jar of Hellmann's Dijonnaise, this couldn't get any easier. Use a brush to slather it over ribs, pork loin roast, pork tenderloin, a whole chicken, chicken breasts, or a leg of lamb before smoking, or on salmon, char, trout, catfish, or halibut fillets before planking. **MAKES ABOUT 1 CUP**

1/2 cup Dijon mustard

1/2 cup mayonnaise (lowfat is okay)

Whisk the ingredients together in a bowl. Use immediately.

Mustard-Mayo-Dill Slather: Add 1 teaspoon dillweed, 1 teaspoon granulated garlic, and the juice of 1/2 lemon. This is especially good on fish or chicken. **MAKES ABOUT 1 CUP**

Mustard-Mayo-Orange Slather: Add 1 tablespoon Spicy Orange Rub (page 51). Primo on chicken and pork. **MAKES ABOUT 1 CUP**

Mustard-Mayo-Tarragon Slather: Add 2 teaspoons dried tarragon, 1 teaspoon ground white pepper, and the juice of 1/2 lemon. A winner on chicken, pork, and fish. **MAKES ABOUT 1 CUP**

Soak or Drizzle: Marinades Versus Vinaigrettes

What's the difference between a marinade and a vinaigrette? Both usually have similar ingredients—a vegetable oil, either acidic lemon juice or vinegar, and seasonings. If you know the difference between a facial toner (higher in alcohol or acid) and a moisturizer (higher in oil), this will be a snap. The crucial difference is in the ratio of vegetable oil to vinegar. In marinades, the ratio is in favor of vinegar, sometimes as much as three parts vinegar to one part oil. That's why more acidic marinades are used to imbue foods with flavor before cooking. A vinaigrette has more oil, sometimes half vinegar and half oil, sometimes two or three parts oil to one part vinegar. Vinaigrettes are more often used as a "crowning glory"—as a finishing "sauce" poured over a salad or drizzled on grilled foods—because there's not as much of an acidic punch and the higher oil content helps them coat better. You *can* use a vinaigrette as a marinade (and a lot of Grill Gals use bottled Italian-style vinaigrette as an easy marinade), but it's a good idea to pat the food dry before grilling to avoid flare-ups.

The trick with marinades is to know when and how long to use them. A marinade is used to flavor, not tenderize, but it does help leaner meats and poultry, such as flank steak and turkey, stay moist during grilling or smoking and perks up their somewhat bland flavor. If you keep meat, fish, or vegetables in a marinade too long, they will become mushy, as the higher acidic content will start to break down the proteins.

Most fish and shellfish should marinate for only 30 minutes. The acid in a marinade could cook the fish, and you'll end with ceviche, not grilled or smoked fish.

Sturdy vegetables such as onions, carrots, and bell peppers can marinate for several hours. Tomatoes, zucchini, eggplant, and mushrooms are delicate and need only an hour or so. They will become waterlogged if marinated too long.

Cuts of beef, pork, chicken, and lamb can marinate for 8 to 12 hours or overnight, as long as the marinade is not too acidic or intensely flavored.

For the best flavor, make the marinade right before you want to use it. Most marinades will keep in the refrigerator for up to a week, but they will deteriorate in flavor.

In every recipe here, the BBQ Queens decree how each marinade or vinaigrette is best used and for what foods.

Rosemary, Garlic, and Lemon Baste

Looser than a paste, this is a wonderfully aromatic baste to use on beef steaks, pork chops, pork tenderloin, chicken breasts, or leg of lamb before and during grilling. We also love this brushed on the cut sides of Italian bread sliced lengthwise, then wrapped in foil and put on the grill to warm. Or try brushing it on pizza dough, then sprinkle the dough with shredded mozzarella and grill. Or slather it on fish, chicken, pork, or lamb cubes threaded on skewers. For the best texture, use a mortar and pestle. You also may use a food processor. MAKES ABOUT 1/2 CUP

1 tablespoon finely chopped fresh rosemary
1/2 teaspoon fine kosher or sea salt
2 cloves garlic, minced
1/2 cup olive oil
Juice of 1 lemon
Freshly ground black pepper to taste

1. If using a mortar and pestle, combine the rosemary, salt, and garlic in the mortar and grind into a fine paste with the pestle. Drizzle in the olive oil and grind again. Add the lemon juice, grind, and taste. Add more salt, if desired, and season with pepper.

   If using a food processor, follow the directions above while pulsing the processor on and off to avoid overprocessing.
2. The baste will keep in the refrigerator for up to 1 week.

Aromatic Lemon-Herb Marinade

Fresh herbs, lemon juice, and garlic combine to make this fabulously aromatic marinade. It's great on everything from vegetables to duck, lamb, fish, and shellfish. We also love it as a marinade for rotisserie chicken or pork. MAKES ABOUT 3 CUPS

1 cup olive oil
1/2 cup fresh lemon juice (3 to 4 lemons)
1/2 cup dry white wine

5 cloves garlic, minced
2 tablespoons chopped fresh basil
2 tablespoons chopped fresh mint
2 tablespoons chopped fresh oregano
2 tablespoons chopped fresh rosemary
2 tablespoons chopped fresh Italian parsley
2 teaspoons celery salt

Whisk together all the ingredients in a medium-size bowl. Use immediately or pour into a large jar with a tight-fitting lid. This marinade will keep in the refrigerator for up to 3 days. Let come to room temperature before using.

Homemade Teriyaki Marinade

Teriyaki is one of those formerly "foreign" dishes—like salsa and bruschetta—that have now gone mainstream in American cuisine. We think we know what it is. After all, you can find bottled teriyaki sauce at the grocery store and teriyaki-grilled foods on just about every casual restaurant menu. But we've only scratched the surface. The word "teriyaki" is a combination of the Japanese words *teri*, meaning "glaze," and *yaki*, meaning "to broil." In a teriyaki dish, ingredients are cooked over high heat after being marinated in or basted with teriyaki sauce, which gives luster or shine to the food. The key ingredient in teriyaki sauce is mirin, a pale gold, sweet Japanese wine made from fermented rice (look for the Takara Shuzo brand). Mirin is very good at masking any slight fishy smell, so it's a wonderful ingredient in fish marinades (see Japanese-Style Grilled Fish, page 258). Use this as a marinade, baste, or sauce for just about anything you want to grill. MAKES ABOUT 1 CUP

1/2 cup soy sauce
1/2 cup mirin (see headnote)
2 tablespoons sugar

Combine all the ingredients in a small saucepan over medium heat and bring to a simmer. Cook, stirring, until the sugar has completely dissolved and the flavors have blended. Let cool. Use immediately or pour into a small jar with a tight-fitting lid. This marinade will keep in the refrigerator indefinitely.

Garlic-Citrus Marinade

This is a delicious way to marinate skirt, sirloin, or flank steak, but it's also good with chicken, pork, lamb, fish, or vegetables. Guess we like this with everything! MAKES ABOUT 3/4 CUP

1/4 cup fresh lime juice (4 to 5 limes)
1/4 cup fresh orange juice (1 to 2 oranges)
2 cloves garlic, minced
2 tablespoons olive oil
2 tablespoons red wine vinegar
2 tablespoons chopped fresh Italian parsley
1 teaspoon dried oregano

Place all the ingredients in a small jar with a tight-fitting lid. Cover and shake to blend. This marinade will keep in the refrigerator for up to 1 week.

Provençal Red Wine Marinade

Use this heady blend as a marinade for lamb, beef, or chicken destined for the rotisserie or the grill. It's also good as a finishing touch to grilled vegetables, especially portobello mushrooms. If you want to transform this into a vinaigrette—wonderful over any of our seafood salads—whisk in 3/4 cup more olive oil and add a squeeze of lemon juice. MAKES ABOUT 1 1/2 CUPS

1 cup dry red wine
1/4 cup olive oil
4 cloves garlic, minced
1 tablespoon dried herbes de Provence
2 teaspoons fine kosher or sea salt
1 teaspoon freshly ground black pepper

Combine all the ingredients in a medium-size jar with a tight-fitting lid. Cover and shake to blend. This marinade will keep in the refrigerator for up to 1 week.

Rosemary-Mustard Marinade

This marinade is fabulous as a pretreatment for grilled butterflied leg of lamb, lamb chops, lamb shanks, lamb anything. We also like it with pork tenderloin and pork chops. If you want to transform it into a vinaigrette (great over grilled vegetables or smoked goat cheese), whisk in 1/2 cup more olive oil and add a squeeze of lemon juice. MAKES ABOUT 2 CUPS

3/4 cup dry red wine
1/2 cup olive oil
1/3 cup Dijon mustard
1/4 cup red wine vinegar
1/4 cup fresh rosemary leaves
2 tablespoons green peppercorns in brine, drained
1 tablespoon dried oregano
2 large cloves garlic, minced

Place all the ingredients in a food processor and process until the rosemary leaves are completely ground. Use the day you make it.

BBQ QUEEN
BBQ QUEEN

Amogio

Amogio is a Sicilian marinade composed of lemon juice and/or white wine, olive oil, garlic, and herbs—the exact recipe varies from household to household. It's used as both a soak and a drizzle, so remember to keep about 1/2 cup reserved for drizzling on food that has been grilled or smoked. Marinate chicken, pork, lamb, or beef for up to 24 hours. Amogio is especially good on grilled chicken skewers. MAKES ABOUT 1 3/4 CUPS

3 tablespoons minced garlic
1/2 cup olive oil
1/2 cup dry white wine
1/2 cup fresh lemon juice (3 to 4 lemons)
1/4 cup chopped fresh Italian parsley
1 tablespoon chopped fresh mint
1/4 teaspoon red pepper flakes

1. Combine all the ingredients in a medium-size bowl.
2. To use, reserve 1/2 cup of the marinade in the refrigerator and use the rest to marinate the food for at least 1 hour or overnight. Grill or smoke the food, then drizzle with the reserved marinade right before serving.

Fennel and Orange Marinade

Sweet and fragrant, this marinade is great with pork, chicken, or lamb. We especially like it with rotisserie or slow-smoked pork loin. MAKES ABOUT 3 CUPS

1 cup cider vinegar
1/2 cup olive oil
1/4 cup clover or other medium-colored honey
1/2 cup dry white wine

Juice and grated zest of 2 oranges

3 large cloves garlic, minced

2 shallots, minced

3 tablespoons fennel seeds

1 teaspoon freshly ground black pepper

1/2 teaspoon fine kosher or sea salt

In a medium-size bowl, whisk together all the ingredients. Use the same day.

Fennel and Orange Drizzling Sauce: To make this into a drizzling sauce, use half the recipe to marinate the food and reserve the other half in the refrigerator. Bring to room temperature right before serving and whisk in an additional 1/2 cup olive oil. **MAKES ABOUT 3 1/2 CUPS TOTAL**

Tequila-Lime Marinade

Sort of like a margarita, but more savory. We love this as a marinade for grilled fish or shellfish, chicken, zucchini or yellow summer squash, and ears of fresh corn. After grilling or smoking fish or shellfish—especially shrimp or scallops—drizzle some of this on top. MAKES ABOUT 3/4 CUP

1/4 cup tequila

1/4 cup fresh lime juice (4 to 5 limes)

1/4 cup olive oil

2 cloves garlic, minced

1 tablespoon minced shallot

1/2 teaspoon kosher salt

1/2 teaspoon red pepper flakes

Combine all the ingredients in a small jar with a tight-fitting lid. Cover and shake to blend. The marinade will keep in the refrigerator for up to 1 week.

Lemongrass Marinade

A little bit of this flavorful and aromatic marinade goes a surprisingly long way. Use it to flavor fish, chicken, or vegetables before grilling. This contemporary take on a marinade is somewhere between a traditional liquid marinade and a paste. MAKES ABOUT 2/3 CUP

1 tablespoon thinly sliced fresh lemongrass (available at Asian markets)
1 clove garlic, minced
1 tablespoon grated fresh ginger (if using a microplane, you don't need to peel)
1 small red Thai chile, trimmed, seeded, and finely chopped
1 teaspoon Asian fish sauce
1 teaspoon rice vinegar
2 teaspoons cornstarch
1 tablespoon peanut oil or other vegetable oil
1/2 cup chicken or vegetable broth
1 teaspoon soy sauce
1 teaspoon toasted sesame oil
Kosher or sea salt and freshly ground white pepper to taste

In a medium-size bowl, mix all the ingredients together. This marinade will keep, covered, in the refrigerator for up to 3 days.

Tandoori Marinade

Cooling with yogurt and warm with spices, this marinade helps keep foods such as chicken, lamb, fish, and vegetables moist during indirect grilling and rotisserie cooking at a medium temperature (tandoori marinade is not meant for high-heat grilling). Traditionally a technique from northern India, "tandoori" refers to cooking over coals in a clay vessel, or tandoor. A covered grill works about the same way, as Grill Gal and cookbook author Smita Chandra points out in *Indian Grill: The Art of Tandoori Cooking at Home* (Ecco Press, 1999). In this recipe, adapted from one by Chandra, the saffron turns the marinade—and the food—a wonderful pale gold. Marinate food for up to 24 hours in the refrigerator before grilling. There is no need to baste, as tandoori food self-bastes. MAKES ABOUT 1 1/4 CUPS

1 cup plain yogurt (don't use reduced fat)

¼ teaspoon saffron threads

Juice of ½ lemon

4 cloves garlic, minced

One 1-inch piece fresh ginger, grated (if using a microplane, you don't need to peel)

1 tablespoon finely chopped fresh cilantro

1 tablespoon vegetable oil

1 teaspoon ground coriander

1 teaspoon ground cumin

In a medium-size bowl, whisk the yogurt until smooth. Whisk in the saffron, then the remaining ingredients. Use the day you make it.

Lemon-Tarragon Vinaigrette

The BBQ Queens love the combination of lemon and tarragon. So when we saw this recipe created by California wine country chef and cookbook author John Ash, we knew we had to adapt it for our book. Fresh tarragon has a pronounced anise flavor, compared to dried tarragon, which tastes and smells more like new-mown hay. Ash uses fresh, but we prefer dried in our version, which can also serve as a marinade. (If you want to use fresh, substitute 2 tablespoons finely minced fresh tarragon for the dried.) This is dynamite with chicken, fish, or shellfish. We also recommend using it to dress grilled vegetables. MAKES ABOUT 2 CUPS

½ cup fresh lemon juice (3 to 4 lemons)

1 teaspoon grated lemon zest

2 tablespoons tarragon vinegar

1 tablespoon finely minced shallot

2 teaspoons dried tarragon

2 teaspoons honey, or to taste

½ cup olive oil

¼ cup chicken broth

Fine kosher or sea salt and ground white pepper to taste

In a medium-size bowl, combine the lemon juice, zest, vinegar, shallot, tarragon, and honey and mix with a hand blender. Whisk in the olive oil and broth and season with salt and white pepper. The vinaigrette will not emulsify. Use immediately or pour into a medium-size jar with a tight-fitting lid. It will keep in the refrigerator for up to 3 days.

Saffron Vinaigrette

We prefer this gorgeously sunny dressing as a finishing sauce for grilled fish, shellfish, chicken, or vegetables. It's wonderful over still-warm new potatoes that have been steamed or grilled, or as the dressing for a grilled fish or shellfish salad. In our view, saffron is too expensive to be relegated to a mere marinade. It needs to be shown off after cooking, not before. In this recipe, you first infuse the olive oil with the saffron, then whisk the oil into the remaining ingredients for the vinaigrette. MAKES ABOUT 1 1/2 CUPS

1 cup olive oil
1/4 teaspoon saffron threads
1/2 cup white wine vinegar or sherry vinegar
2 teaspoons Dijon mustard
Fine kosher or sea salt and freshly ground black pepper to taste

1. Pour the olive oil into a small saucepan over low heat. Stir in the saffron and heat until warm, about 10 minutes. Remove from the heat and let the mixture infuse for 10 to 15 minutes.

2. In a small bowl, whisk the vinegar and mustard together. Slowly pour in the warm saffron oil and whisk to blend. Season with salt and pepper and whisk again. Use immediately.

Wheat Beer Vinaigrette

On the days before Carry Nation, Kansas—where "prairie girl" Judith lives—had more than 80 mom-and-pop breweries. Outdoor beer gardens shaded by hop vines provided a cool place to sip a frothy mug on a hot day. Today, microbreweries dot the Great Plains. And what better beer to drink than a wheat beer—made from wheat grown and harvested a few miles down the road—brightened with a little lemon? Wheat beer gives this vinaigrette a mellow flavor that is delicious as a salad dressing or a marinade for grilled asparagus or meat, especially flank steak. You could also simmer this vinaigrette, whisk in 2 tablespoons of unsalted butter just before taking it off the heat, and have a delicious sauce for steak. MAKES ABOUT 1 1/2 CUPS

1 cup wheat beer
1/3 cup olive oil
Juice of 1 lemon
2 cloves garlic, minced
1 tablespoon wildflower, clover, or other medium-colored honey
1 tablespoon Dijon mustard
1 teaspoon ground white pepper

Whisk all the ingredients together in a medium-size bowl. Use the day you make it.

They Dubbed It . . . Coleslaw

Go to any casual restaurant or barbecue joint, and coleslaw will be on the menu, usually as part of a "platter" offering of a sandwich or entrée with French fries. From the Dutch *kool* for cabbage and *sla* for salad, coleslaw existed in our culinary melting pot long before the term was finally attached to the basic recipe. Cabbage, though not native to the Americas, arrived in seed form with the first Pilgrims and Puritans. Greens such as cabbage, raw or cooked and simply dressed with vinegar and oil, were so common that few seventeenth-century recipes exist. Why write it down when it was easy enough to remember?

Other European immigrants with a fondness for pickled or sweet-and-sour cabbage paved the way for the many varieties of coleslaw that we enjoy today. Compilers of the 1875 *Presbyterian Cook Book* from Dayton, Ohio, were very fond of coleslaw. They included three recipes and actually called the dish "cole-slaw." One is made with chopped celery and hard-boiled eggs, another with celery seeds, and all three with a boiled dressing. When North Carolinians got together for a pig-pickin' in the lean days after the Civil War, they had to have vinegar-dressed slaw as an accompaniment.

As BBQ Queens, we love all kinds of slaws because they do double duty as vegetable and salad, can be made ahead before you go out to the grill or smoker, and give you lots of bang for your culinary buck.

Blue Cheese Coleslaw

This has become Judith's family's favorite coleslaw, great with grilled burgers and steaks or slow-smoked ribs. She prefers to use Maytag blue cheese from Iowa for its mellow, creamy blue cheese bite. SERVES 8

SLAW

2 pounds Napa cabbage, cored and shredded

8 ounces blue cheese, crumbled

1/4 cup chopped green onions

DRESSING

3/4 cup vegetable oil

1/3 cup cider vinegar

2 tablespoons sugar

1 teaspoon celery seeds

1/2 teaspoon kosher or sea salt

1/2 teaspoon ground white pepper

1/4 teaspoon dry mustard

2 cloves garlic, minced

1. To make the slaw, toss the cabbage, blue cheese, and green onions together in a large salad bowl. Set aside or keep covered and refrigerated for up to 24 hours.

2. To make the dressing, right before serving whisk all the ingredients together in a small bowl. Pour over the slaw and toss to coat evenly. The slaw will wilt after it is tossed with the dressing, so serve right away.

Crunchy Broccoli Slaw with Thai Chile-Peanut Dressing

This is a great way to get kids to eat their broccoli. We could make a meal of this alone—and sometimes do. SERVES 8

SLAW

One 16-ounce package broccoli slaw (shredded raw broccoli with red cabbage and carrot)

One 8-ounce can sliced water chestnuts, drained

1 large red bell pepper, seeded and very thinly sliced

THAI CHILE-PEANUT DRESSING

One 12-ounce bottle Thai sweet chili sauce

1/2 cup salted roasted peanuts (dry-roasted is fine)

2 tablespoons toasted sesame oil

1/2 cup water

1. To make the slaw, combine the broccoli slaw, water chestnuts, and bell pepper in a large bowl and set aside.

2. To make the dressing, in a food processor, process the chili sauce, peanuts, and sesame oil together until the peanuts are chopped fine. Add the water and pulse several times to combine. Pour the dressing over the slaw and toss to blend. Serve right away.

Layered Vinegar Slaw

Traditionally served with barbecued pork of all kinds, this slaw is best made the night before, then stirred together right before serving. There's nothing better on a pulled pork sandwich. SERVES 8

SLAW

1 medium-size head cabbage, cored and shredded

1 cup shredded carrot

1 large onion, diced

3/4 cup sugar

DRESSING

3/4 cup vegetable oil

1 cup distilled white vinegar or cider vinegar

1 tablespoon dry mustard

1 tablespoon celery seeds

1 tablespoon fine sea salt

1. To make the slaw, in a large serving bowl, layer, in order, the cabbage, carrot, onion, and sugar.

2. To make the dressing, combine all the ingredients in a medium-size saucepan and bring to a boil. Immediately pour over the cabbage mixture but do not stir. Allow to cool, then cover and refrigerate overnight.

3. Stir together right before serving.

Mediterranean Summer Squash Slaw

Adapted from a recipe by cookbook author Janet Hazen, this "slaw"—heady with the flavor of fresh basil—will keep for up to 3 days, covered, in the refrigerator (without the basil), and it's great with grilled foods of all kinds. We use a mandoline to cut the squash. SERVES 6

6 small zucchini, ends trimmed and cut into matchstick-size pieces

6 small yellow summer squash, ends trimmed and cut into matchstick-size pieces

6 medium-size ripe tomatoes, finely chopped

1 clove garlic, minced

2 tablespoons extra virgin olive oil

Kosher or sea salt and freshly ground black pepper to taste

1 cup finely chopped fresh basil

1. In a large serving bowl, combine the squash, tomatoes, and garlic. Drizzle with the olive oil, then season with salt and pepper.

2. Just before serving, stir in the basil.

Frozen Asset Slaw

This unusual slaw is crisp when defrosted. The large amount of sugar keeps it that way, but the vinegar cuts the sweetness. This is not for the low-carb crowd, but it is a great make-ahead side dish for everyone else. SERVES 10

1 medium-size head cabbage, cored and chopped
1 teaspoon fine sea salt
4 stalks celery, thinly sliced
1/2 large green bell pepper, seeded and chopped
1/2 large red bell pepper, seeded and chopped
1 cup distilled white vinegar
2 cups sugar
1 teaspoon celery seeds
1 teaspoon mustard seeds

1. Place the cabbage in a large bowl and sprinkle with the salt. Let stand for 1 hour.
2. Combine the celery and peppers in another large bowl and set aside.
3. In a medium-size saucepan, combine the vinegar, sugar, celery seeds, and mustard seeds. Bring to a boil, let boil for 1 minute, and let cool to lukewarm, about 15 minutes.
4. Squeeze and drain the cabbage. Add the cabbage to the celery and peppers and mix well. Pour the cooled vinegar mixture over the salad and stir to combine. Transfer the slaw to a freezer container and freeze for at least 24 hours or up to 3 months.
5. Before serving, defrost the slaw for 10 to 20 minutes at room temperature (the amount of time will vary depending on the size of the container). When you can stir the slaw with a fork, it's ready to serve.

Red Cabbage and Apple Slaw

To make this slaw up to a day ahead, combine the dressing ingredients and store in the refrigerator. If you wish, you can also shred the cabbage and place in a plastic bag in the refrigerator. Then all you have to do is prepare the apples before serving and assemble everything else instantly. The pretty green and red colors of this slaw are perfect for a holiday buffet. SERVES 4 TO 6

SLAW

2 Granny Smith apples, cored and diced

4 cups cored and coarsely shredded red cabbage

DRESSING

1/4 cup cider vinegar

1/4 cup vegetable oil

2 tablespoons sugar

1/2 teaspoon ground cumin

1/2 teaspoon fine sea salt

Freshly ground black pepper to taste

1. To make the slaw, combine the apples and cabbage in a large serving bowl.
2. To make the dressing, combine all the ingredients in a measuring cup. Taste for salt and pepper. Pour over the cabbage mixture and stir to blend. Refrigerate for up to 1 hour before serving.

Citrus Caesar Vinaigrette

This has more citrus and less garlic than the traditional Caesar dressing and is wonderful on salads or on vegetables, fish, shellfish, chicken, or pork—before or after grilling. Anchovy paste is available in metal tubes at better grocery stores and gourmet shops. Or buy canned anchovies and mash them with a fork. MAKES ABOUT 1 CUP

2/3 cup extra virgin olive oil
3 tablespoons fresh lemon juice
2 tablespoons anchovy paste
1 tablespoon white wine vinegar
1 tablespoon grated lemon zest
1 clove garlic, minced

Combine all the ingredients in a small jar with a tight-fitting lid. Cover and shake to blend. Store in the refrigerator for up to 1 week.

Balsamic-Thyme Vinaigrette

Hearty, savory, and delicious on grilled vegetables—especially mushrooms and eggplant—or a goat cheese salad, this vinaigrette is also great for marinating flank steak or pork. MAKES ABOUT 1 CUP

1/4 cup balsamic vinegar
3/4 cup extra virgin olive oil
2 teaspoons fresh thyme leaves
Fine kosher or sea salt and freshly ground black pepper to taste

Combine all the ingredients in a small jar with a tight-fitting lid. Cover and shake to blend. This vinaigrette will keep in the refrigerator for up to 1 week.

Fresh Basil Vinaigrette

When fresh basil is luxuriant and aromatic in your garden (the BBQ Queens grow their own) or at the farmers' market, use it to make this addictive vinaigrette. You'll need a very large bunch (or three to four packages from the grocery store) to make 1 cup chopped basil, but this luscious vinaigrette is worth it. Because basil can discolor quickly, make this right before serving. MAKES ABOUT 2 CUPS

1 1/2 cups extra virgin olive oil
1/2 cup fresh lemon juice (3 to 4 lemons)
2 cloves garlic, minced
1 tablespoon Dijon mustard
1 cup finely chopped fresh basil
Fine kosher or sea salt and freshly ground black pepper to taste

Combine all the ingredients in a medium-size jar with a tight-fitting lid. Cover and shake to blend. Use as soon as you make it.

Hot Shallot Vinaigrette

Drizzle this vinaigrette over grilled fish fillets, fish steaks, or oysters for a fabulous finish. It's also good over grilled vegetables or a finely shredded cabbage salad. MAKES ABOUT 1 CUP

8 shallots, minced
1/2 cup minced fresh Italian parsley
1/2 cup olive oil
1/4 cup fresh lemon juice (about 2 lemons)
2 tablespoons balsamic vinegar
Kosher or sea salt and freshly ground black pepper to taste

1. Whisk together the shallots, parsley, olive oil, lemon juice, and vinegar in a medium-size saucepan. Season with salt and pepper.

2. Right before serving, bring to a boil over high heat. Reduce the heat to low and simmer until the shallots are translucent, about 4 minutes. Use immediately.

Chipotle Vinaigrette

We demonstrated this vinaigrette for the editors at Meredith Corporation (the home of *Better Homes and Gardens, Country Home, Traditional Home, Ladies' Home Journal, Midwest Living,* and *More* magazines) to rave reviews. It can go on just about anything, from salads to grilled or smoked foods. We adapted the recipe from one by the late, great food writer Michael McLaughlin and used it in our book *Fish & Shellfish, Grilled & Smoked* (The Harvard Common Press, 2002). But it's too good to limit to seafood alone, so here it is again. MAKES ABOUT 1 CUP

3 tablespoons sherry vinegar

1 tablespoon balsamic vinegar

2 cloves garlic, peeled

2 canned chipotle chiles in adobo sauce (or more to taste), chopped, plus 2 tablespoons adobo sauce

1/2 teaspoon fine kosher or sea salt

2/3 cup olive oil

Freshly ground black pepper to taste

In a food processor or blender, combine the vinegars, garlic, chipotles, adobo sauce, and salt and process until smooth. With the motor running, add the olive oil in a slow, steady stream through the feed tube until incorporated. Season with pepper and pulse to blend. Use immediately or pour into a small jar with a tight-fitting lid. This vinaigrette will keep in the refrigerator for up to 3 days.

Lemon Butter Drizzle

When you want a very easy yet ingenious baste, marinade, or finishing sauce, this is it. We love it on everything from steak to asparagus, salmon to tomatoes, shellfish to mushrooms, chicken to eggplant. MAKES ABOUT 1/2 CUP

1/2 cup (1 stick) unsalted butter, melted

Juice and grated zest of 1 lemon

2 tablespoons chopped fresh herbs, such as Italian parsley, chives, tarragon, and/or basil

In a small bowl, combine the melted butter and lemon juice and zest. Add the herbs right before basting or serving. Keep warm so the butter stays melted.

Vietnamese Drizzle

There is lots of aromatic, sour pizzazz in this recipe, adapted from one by food writer Nigella Lawson. It's wonderful on grilled foods of all kinds, especially shrimp or asparagus, or on Rotisserie Chicken (page 217). It's perfect for Atkins or South Beach Diet aficionados—just use sugar substitute. Bottled fish sauce is available in the Asian section of most supermarkets. And if you want to sneak in a few drops of toasted sesame oil, who are we to argue? MAKES ABOUT 3/4 CUP

One 1-inch piece fresh ginger, grated (if using a microplane, you don't need to peel)

2 cloves garlic, minced

2 small red serrano or Thai chiles, finely chopped (with or without seeds)

1/4 cup Asian fish sauce

2 tablespoons fresh lime juice

1/4 cup water

2 tablespoons sugar

In a small bowl, whisk together all the ingredients. Use the day you make it.

Honey-Almond Grilling Glaze

A glaze usually has a higher concentration of sugar than does a drizzle, marinade, or vinaigrette. The sugar is what provides the sheen when you brush the glaze on food during the last minutes of grilling. This sweetly aromatic glaze is excellent on grilled seafood, chicken, or pork. Brush it on 1 minute before your food is ready to come off the grill. Don't brush it on too soon, or the sugar will char. Don't turn or glaze the other side—just let the heat of the grill set the glaze on top. This is also yummy as a finishing sauce. MAKES ABOUT 2 1/2 CUPS

1/2 cup (1 stick) plus 3 tablespoons unsalted butter

2 tablespoons all-purpose flour

1 cup slivered almonds

2 tablespoons Cajun Steak Rub (page 58) or Cajun seasoning

1 cup chopped celery

1 cup clover or other medium-colored honey

1 cup chicken broth

1 teaspoon grated lemon zest

1/8 teaspoon freshly grated nutmeg

1. In a small saucepan over medium heat, melt 3 tablespoons of the butter. Whisk in the flour until smooth and cook until the mixture smells slightly nutty, 1 to 2 minutes; set aside.

2. In a 10-inch skillet over medium-high heat, melt the remaining 1/2 cup butter. When it begins to sizzle, add the almonds, Cajun rub, and celery and cook, stirring frequently, until the almonds are browned. Stir in the honey, broth, lemon zest, and nutmeg and cook, stirring occasionally, to let the flavors blend, about 3 minutes. Whisk in the flour and butter mixture until the sauce has slightly thickened, 30 to 60 seconds. Remove from the heat.

3. Brush the glaze on top of the grilled food about 1 minute before it's done. Reserve any unused glaze. Close the grill lid so the glaze can set. Pass the reserved glaze at the table. The glaze will keep in the refrigerator for up to 1 week.

BBQ Queens' Love Potion for the Swine

This is our version of the luscious, thick sauce that our barbecue team has used to win the Battle of the Sexes Barbecue Contest and also has sold for charity. We always tell people that this sauce has aphrodisiac properties so we sell more bottles! You can judge for yourself whether any of these ingredients have romantic potential. If you are a chile head, add 1 to 2 tablespoons more dry mustard and red pepper flakes. If you like to use barbecue sauce as a mop when you're slow smoking, add an extra 1/4 to 1/2 cup vinegar to thin it. This all-purpose sauce tastes great on barbecued chicken or brisket, but it's really kickin' with ribs. Give a bottle of homemade sauce to family and friends—or that special someone. MAKES ABOUT 6 CUPS

One 24-ounce bottle ketchup
One 12-ounce bottle chili sauce
1/2 cup firmly packed dark brown sugar
1/2 cup honey
1/2 cup cider vinegar
1/2 cup molasses
1/4 cup dry mustard
2 tablespoons red pepper flakes
1 tablespoon celery seeds
1 tablespoon garlic salt
1 tablespoon Worcestershire sauce
1 tablespoon liquid smoke flavoring
1 teaspoon onion salt
1/4 cup water

In a large saucepan, combine all the ingredients and simmer over medium-low heat for 45 to 60 minutes. After you pour the ketchup and chili sauce into the saucepan, turn the almost-empty bottles upside down and add the rest to the mixture. Use immediately, or store, covered, in the refrigerator for several months.

The Doctor Is In
Apricot-Bourbon Barbecue Sauce

Some people doctor up cake mixes. The BBQ Queens doctor up barbecue sauce. That's because it's hard, at home, to duplicate the silky smoothness of the manufactured products when you make barbecue sauce from scratch. So find a tomato-based barbecue sauce you like and experiment. This version is great with lamb, pork, or chicken on the grill, rotisserie, or smoker. MAKES ABOUT 2 CUPS

1 cup tomato-based barbecue sauce of your choice
3/4 cup apricot nectar
1/4 cup bourbon
Fresh lemon juice to taste, if needed

In a medium-size bowl, whisk together the barbecue sauce, nectar, and bourbon. Taste, then add lemon juice, if necessary, to sharpen the flavor. Use immediately, or pour into a covered container and store in the refrigerator indefinitely.

Tiara-Worthy Variations: To your favorite 14-ounce bottle of tomato-based barbecue sauce, add one of the following:

- **2 tablespoons of your favorite rub mixture to make Spicy Barbecue Sauce**
- **2 teaspoons liquid smoke flavoring to make Smoky Barbecue Sauce**
- **1 cup seedless raspberry jam and 3 tablespoons seeded and finely chopped jalapeños for Raspberry-Jalapeño Barbecue Sauce**
- **1/2 cup clover or other medium-colored honey for Honeyed Barbecue Sauce (especially good with a mustard-based barbecue sauce)**
- **2 tablespoons soy sauce and 2 teaspoons toasted sesame oil for Asian Barbecue Sauce**
- **1 chopped canned chipotle chile in adobo sauce, plus 1 tablespoon adobo sauce, for Chipotle Barbecue Sauce**

Simply Delicious Bordelaise Sauce

It doesn't get much easier or more delicious than this shortcut sauce. (The classic French recipe uses homemade beef stock that has reduced for hours.) We love this sauce with everything from gourmet grilled hamburgers to rib-eye and filet mignon steaks. Bordelaise is best with beef, although it can be mighty tasty on grilled pork or lamb chops—or a leg of lamb, for that matter. MAKES ABOUT 2 1/2 CUPS

One 10.5-ounce can beef broth
1 beef broth can dry red wine
1 bay leaf
1 teaspoon dried thyme
2 cloves garlic, minced
2 green onions
1/4 cup (1/2 stick) unsalted butter, cubed
Juice of 1/2 lemon, or to taste
Freshly ground black pepper to taste

1. In a small saucepan over medium-high heat, bring the beef broth, wine, bay leaf, thyme, garlic, and green onions to a boil. Reduce the heat to medium-low and simmer until reduced by half, about 12 minutes.

2. Strain the solids out of the mixture and return the liquid to the pan over medium-low heat. Whisk in the butter, one cube at a time, until the butter is suspended in the mixture. Remove from the heat and stir in the lemon juice. Season with pepper. Keep warm in the top of a double boiler or transfer to a stainless steel bowl and set over a pan of hot, not boiling, water until ready to serve.

Mango-Lemon Sauce

Sublimely simple and superbly delicious, this sauce is especially fabulous with grilled or smoked shellfish. If you can't find mango puree (look in the freezer section), buy a ripe mango and peel, seed, chop, and puree it in a food processor. Lime juice is also delicious in place of the lemon. MAKES ABOUT 1 CUP

1 cup mango puree

1 tablespoon fresh lemon juice

1/2 teaspoon ground cumin

1/4 teaspoon cayenne pepper

Kosher salt to taste

In a small bowl, whisk all the ingredients together. Use the day you make it.

Raspberry and Blood Orange Sauce

We love this on grilled chicken breasts, fish fillets or steaks, lamb chops, or pork tenderloin. Blood orange juice is sometimes available bottled at health food stores. MAKES ABOUT 1/2 CUP

2/3 cup fresh blood orange juice (10 to 12 blood oranges) or a combination of fresh orange juice and fresh lemon juice (6 to 7 oranges and 2 lemons)

1/3 cup raspberry vinegar

1/4 cup (1/2 stick) unsalted butter, cut into small pieces

Fine kosher or sea salt and ground white pepper to taste

1. In a small, heavy saucepan over high heat, bring the orange juice and vinegar to a boil. Continue to boil until reduced to a syrupy liquid, about 8 minutes.

2. Quickly whisk in the butter until melted. Remove from the heat and season with salt and white pepper. Use immediately.

Poblano Cream Sauce

This fabulously easy sauce is great with grilled skirt steak, chicken, or pork tenderloin. If you can't find a fresh poblano, substitute a jalapeño. MAKES ABOUT 1 1/2 CUPS

1 poblano chile, smoked (see page 140)
2 cups heavy cream or evaporated milk
1/2 cup (1 stick) unsalted butter, cut into pieces
Kosher or sea salt and freshly ground black pepper to taste

1. Combine the poblano and cream in a medium-size, heavy saucepan and simmer over medium heat until reduced to 1 cup, about 15 minutes.

2. Strain the mixture, discard the chile, and return the cream to the pan over low heat. Whisk in the butter, one piece at a time, until you have a smooth sauce. Season with salt and pepper and serve immediately.

Smoked Garlic and Cilantro Cream Sauce

Just reading that recipe title makes our mouths water! We adapted this fabulous sauce from one by fellow Grill Gal Blanca Aldaco, a chef in San Antonio, Texas. Aldaco likes to serve it over grilled chicken breast, pork tenderloin, or shellfish that has been marinated for an hour in a combination of 6 tablespoons olive oil, 3 tablespoons fresh lime juice, and garlic salt to taste. This is enough sauce for six grilled boneless, skinless chicken breasts. If you don't want to use smoked garlic, substitute two minced garlic cloves for a sharper but still delicious flavor. MAKES ABOUT 2 1/2 CUPS

2 cups heavy cream
1/2 cup fresh cilantro leaves, plus more for garnish
3 tablespoons fresh lime juice
1/2 teaspoon kosher or sea salt
6 cloves garlic, smoked (see page 140) and peeled

1. In a blender or food processor, combine all the ingredients and process until smooth.

2. Transfer the puree to a medium-size saucepan over medium-high heat and cook until the sauce begins to bubble. Serve immediately.

Roasted Red Pepper Sauce

We love grill-roasted or smoked red bell peppers, but we also know that not everybody has them on hand all the time. The BBQ Queens' cupboards always contain jars of roasted red peppers that we can use as a high-flavor convenience food to add snap to any sauce or dressing. We love this sauce on anything grilled, and it goes exceptionally well with foods that have been slathered with Rosemary Pesto (page 62) before grilling. MAKES ABOUT 2 CUPS

2 grill-roasted large red bell peppers (see page 145) or one 12-ounce jar roasted red peppers, drained

20 oil- or brine-cured Kalamata or Niçoise olives, pitted

1/2 cup fresh lemon juice (3 to 4 lemons)

2 tablespoons balsamic vinegar

2 teaspoons capers, drained

2 teaspoons anchovy paste

3 tablespoons olive oil

Fine kosher or sea salt and freshly ground black pepper to taste

Combine the red peppers, olives, lemon juice, vinegar, capers, and anchovy paste in a food processor and process until fairly smooth. With the machine running, drizzle the olive oil through the feed tube in a steady stream until the sauce solidifies. Season with salt and pepper. Use immediately or spoon into a medium-size jar with a tight-fitting lid. This sauce will keep in the refrigerator for up to 3 days or in the freezer for up to 6 months.

Tomato-Fennel Sauce

The sunny flavors in this colorful, chunky sauce go well with grilled fish, chicken, shellfish, eggplant, or lamb. Fennel looks somewhat like celery, but with a broader base and delicate frond-like leaves. It has a mild, sweet, licorice-like flavor that blends well with sharp, sassy tomato. Use vegetable broth in place of chicken for a vegetarian sauce. **MAKES ABOUT 4 CUPS**

5 tablespoons olive oil

1 shallot, finely chopped

1 clove garlic, minced

1/4 cup roughly chopped carrot

1/4 cup roughly chopped celery

1/2 cup roughly chopped fennel stalks

1/2 cup Pernod, anisette, ouzo, or other anise-flavored liqueur

One 28-ounce can chopped tomatoes (we prefer Muir Glen fire-roasted tomatoes), with their juice

1 cup chicken broth

Kosher or sea salt and freshly ground black pepper to taste

1. In a medium-size saucepan, heat 2 tablespoons of the oil over medium-high heat. Add the shallot, garlic, carrot, celery, and fennel and cook, stirring, until tender, about 5 minutes. Stir in the Pernod and cook until it is almost evaporated, 5 to 7 minutes. Stir in the tomatoes and broth and cook, stirring occasionally, until thickened, about 30 minutes.

2. When ready to serve, season with salt and pepper and stir in the remaining 3 tablespoons olive oil.

Pistachio-Pomegranate Sauce

We wish we could reach out from the pages of this book and give you a taste of this sauce, but you'll have to make it yourself (or come to one of our cooking classes) to sample it. We *looooooove* this on grilled, rotisserie, or smoked lamb—especially rack of lamb. It's also good with grilled pork, duck, or chicken. In the Kansas City area, we find pomegranate molasses at Asian and Indian markets, bottled pomegranate juice at Whole Foods Market or health food stores, and grenadine at the liquor store. **MAKES ABOUT 2 CUPS**

1 cup shelled unsalted pistachios
1/4 cup water
1/4 cup (1/2 stick) unsalted butter
1 1/2 teaspoons firmly packed light brown sugar
1 teaspoon honey
2 tablespoons port or dry sherry
1/4 cup pomegranate molasses
1/4 cup pomegranate juice
Juice of 1/2 lemon
Grenadine
Fine kosher or sea salt and freshly ground black pepper to taste
Chopped unsalted pistachios for garnish

1. Divide the shelled pistachios in half. Grind half in a food processor and set aside. Combine the remaining whole pistachios and the water in a small saucepan and bring to a boil. Remove from the heat, cover, and set aside.

2. Melt the butter in a medium-size saucepan over medium-high heat and stir in the brown sugar, honey, port, pomegranate molasses, and pomegranate juice. Cook for 2 minutes, stirring, then add the lemon juice and blend in the ground pistachios. Drain the whole pistachios and stir into the sauce. Add a few drops of grenadine until you have a pleasing rosy color. Season with salt and pepper.

3. To serve, nap the food with the sauce and garnish with chopped pistachios.

Food Processor or Blender Hollandaise

Serve this wonderful all-purpose sauce on grilled vegetables, fish, chicken, or that breakfast classic—eggs Benedict. MAKES ABOUT 1 1/2 CUPS

- **6 large egg yolks**
- **2 tablespoons fresh lemon juice**
- **1 teaspoon dry mustard**
- **1 cup (2 sticks) unsalted butter, melted and still hot**
- **1/4 teaspoon cayenne pepper, or to taste**
- **Fine kosher or sea salt to taste**

Place the egg yolks, lemon juice, and mustard in a food processor or blender and process until smooth. Drizzle in the hot melted butter, pulsing the food processor or with the blender on low speed, until the sauce thickens. Add the cayenne and season with salt. Keep warm in the top of a double boiler or transfer to a stainless steel bowl and set over a pan of hot, not boiling, water until ready to serve.

Emulsion Sauces

As we developed more as cooks, we began to experiment with emulsion sauces—those sauces made with an acidic base of white wine, vinegar, or lemon juice to which egg yolks and/or butter are added to make a sauce similar to a thin but still rich mayonnaise. Emulsion sauces such as hollandaise, Béarnaise, and *beurre blanc* are fantastic with grilled foods of all kinds. If you've never attempted them, now's the time to start.

Our suggestion is to begin with Food Processor or Blender Hollandaise (above), then move on to Rustic Béarnaise Sauce (page 98) and the *beurre blanc* recipes (pages 99–102). You do have to stay close by when you make these sauces—not talk on the phone or put in a load of laundry. Emulsion sauces require your undivided attention.

If—*quelle horreur!*—your emulsion sauce breaks (that is, the butter begins to leach out of the sauce instead of staying suspended), no problem. Just whisk an ice cube or two into the broken sauce to bring it back to its beauteous emulsified state. If your sauce does break, it's because you've kept it on the heat too long, so be mindful next time.

Rustic Béarnaise Sauce

This sauce is a staple at Judith's house, an accompaniment she has been making since the 1970s (when she was a very precocious elementary school student). Chunkier and zippier than the classic smooth and mild Béarnaise, this version goes with anything grilled. **MAKES ABOUT 1 CUP**

1/3 cup dry white wine

1/4 cup tarragon vinegar

1 tablespoon finely chopped shallot

1 teaspoon dried tarragon

1/4 teaspoon fine kosher or sea salt

1/2 cup (1 stick) plus 3 tablespoons unsalted butter, cubed

3 large egg yolks, lightly beaten

Cayenne pepper to taste

In a small saucepan, bring the wine, vinegar, shallot, tarragon, and salt to a boil. Continue to boil until reduced to 2 tablespoons, about 8 minutes. Reduce the heat to low and whisk in the butter, one cube at a time. When the butter has almost melted, whisk in the egg yolks and keep whisking to blend the yolks and butter. Remove from the heat when slightly thickened, 4 to 5 minutes. Taste for tarragon and season with cayenne. Serve immediately.

Smoked Chile Beurre Blanc

When we saw this recipe on the Cookshack Web site, we knew we had to have it in our book. So we fooled around with it and came up with the BBQ Queens' version. If you smoke food ahead for leftovers, as we're always preaching, and have smoked bell peppers, jalapeños or other chiles, and garlic already frozen (see page 140), making this sauce is a snap. We love it on anything. **MAKES ABOUT 4 CUPS**

2 cups dry white wine
1/2 cup white wine vinegar
1/4 cup finely chopped green onions
2 tablespoons heavy cream
1 red bell pepper, smoked, seeded, and chopped (about 3/4 cup)
1 yellow bell pepper, smoked, seeded, and chopped (about 3/4 cup)
1 green bell pepper, smoked, seeded, and chopped (about 3/4 cup)
2 jalapeños, smoked, seeded, and chopped (about 1/4 cup)
2 shallots, smoked, peeled, and chopped (about 2 tablespoons)
2 large cloves garlic, smoked and peeled (about 2 teaspoons)
3/4 cup (1 1/2 sticks) unsalted butter, at room temperature, cubed
Coarse kosher or sea salt and freshly ground black pepper to taste

1. In a large saucepan, combine the wine, vinegar, and green onions and bring to a boil. Continue to boil until reduced by half, about 10 minutes. Whisk in the cream and smoked vegetables and cook until the vegetables are warm, about 5 minutes. Remove from the heat.

2. Whisk in the butter, one cube at a time, until melted into the sauce but not separated. Season with salt and pepper and serve immediately.

Mustard-Cornichon Beurre Blanc

Somewhere between the classic, piquant *sauce Gribiche* and the mellower Béarnaise, this easy sauce offers a jolt of flavor that is perfect with grilled steak, lamb, or fish. Cornichons, small 2-inch-long pickles usually served with pâtés, are available in small jars at better grocery stores. They add wonderful texture and taste. This is adapted from a recipe by Stuart Cameron, chef at the Napa Valley Grille in Providence, Rhode Island. MAKES ABOUT 1½ CUPS

½ cup (1 stick) unsalted butter, softened
⅓ cup Dijon mustard
1 cup dry white wine
⅓ cup tarragon vinegar or white wine vinegar
1 shallot, minced
2 tablespoons minced fresh tarragon or 2 teaspoons dried tarragon
12 cornichons, finely chopped
⅓ cup heavy cream
Fine kosher or sea salt and freshly ground black pepper to taste

1. In a small bowl, mix the softened butter and mustard together. Cover and refrigerate for 15 minutes.

2. Combine the wine, vinegar, and shallot in a small saucepan and bring to a boil. Continue to boil until reduced to ½ cup, about 10 minutes.

3. Reduce the heat to low and whisk in the butter mixture, 1 tablespoon at a time. Continue whisking until the butter has been incorporated into the sauce. Whisk in the tarragon, cornichons, and heavy cream. Season with salt and pepper and serve immediately.

Raspberry Beurre Blanc

The BBQ Queens love raspberries in general, but in this sauce, they're divine. Serve it with grilled zucchini or yellow summer squash, duck or turkey breast, chicken, pork tenderloin, salmon, or scallops. MAKES ABOUT 1 1/2 CUPS

1 tablespoon minced shallot

1/4 cup fresh lemon juice (about 2 lemons)

1 cup dry white wine

1 cup fresh or individually frozen raspberries (no need to defrost)

1 small clove garlic, minced

1/4 cup sugar

1 cup heavy cream

1/4 cup (1/2 stick) cold unsalted butter, cubed

1. In a small saucepan over medium-high heat, combine the shallot, lemon juice, wine, raspberries, garlic, and sugar and bring to a boil. Continue to boil until reduced to about 1/4 cup, about 5 minutes. (If you don't want raspberry seeds in your sauce, strain the mixture, discard the solids, and return the liquid to the pan.)

2. Pour in the cream, return to a boil, and continue to boil until reduced by half, about 5 minutes.

3. Remove from the heat and whisk in the butter, one cube at a time, until the sauce glistens and thickens. Keep warm in the top of a double boiler or transfer to a stainless steel bowl and set over a pan of hot, not boiling, water until ready to serve.

Peppercorn Beurre Blanc

Sprinkle foods destined for the grill or smoker with Tricolored Peppercorn Rub (page 62), then serve this sauce as an accompaniment for a welcome culinary hot flash. **MAKES ABOUT 1 CUP**

2 teaspoons Szechuan or white peppercorns

1 teaspoon black peppercorns

1 teaspoon dried green peppercorns

3/4 cup dry white wine

1 tablespoon minced shallot

1 cup (2 sticks) cold unsalted butter, cubed

1/4 teaspoon fine kosher or sea salt

1. Place all the peppercorns in a small cast-iron skillet over medium-high heat and toast, stirring frequently, until aromatic, about 2 minutes. Scrape into a mortar and grind with a pestle until crushed but still somewhat coarse.

2. In a small saucepan, bring the crushed peppercorns, wine, and shallot to a boil. Continue to boil until reduced to 2 tablespoons, 10 to 15 minutes. Remove the pan from the heat and turn the heat to low. Whisk in 2 cubes of butter, then return the pan to the heat. Whisk until the butter has almost melted into the liquid. Continue whisking in the butter, one cube at a time, until all the butter has been emulsified into the sauce and the sauce has thickened. Remove from the heat immediately and whisk in the salt. Keep warm in the top of a double boiler or transfer to a stainless steel bowl and set over a pan of hot, not boiling, water until ready to serve.

Kimizu

This Japanese-style emulsion sauce uses cornstarch instead of butter as an extra thickening agent. Watch this sauce carefully, as it cooks over low heat. If it begins to boil, it will curdle (and an ice cube whisked in won't help, because the sauce contains no butter). This delicately flavored sauce, adapted from a recipe by Mary Evely at Simi Winery in California, goes very well with any grilled mild-flavored fish, such as tilapia, John Dory, farm-raised catfish, halibut, haddock, walleye, or Alaskan cod. It's also great with lightly smoked shrimp or scallops. MAKES ABOUT 3/4 CUP

3 large egg yolks
3/4 cup water
3 tablespoons rice vinegar
1 tablespoon sugar
1 tablespoon cornstarch
1 teaspoon wasabi paste or powder (available at Asian markets)

1. Place all the ingredients in a food processor or blender and process until smooth.

2. Transfer to a small saucepan over low heat. Cook, stirring constantly, until the sauce thickens, about 15 minutes. Keep warm in the top of a double boiler or transfer to a stainless steel bowl and set over a pan of hot, not boiling, water until ready to serve.

Lemon-Garlic Mayonnaise

Spoon this creamy mayonnaise over your favorite grilled fish, shellfish, vegetables, or poultry. It has the flavor of aioli, without the preparation. MAKES ABOUT 1 CUP

1 cup mayonnaise (lowfat is okay)
Juice of 2 lemons
1 clove garlic, minced
1 teaspoon ground white pepper

Combine all the ingredients in a small bowl, whisking to blend. This mayonnaise will keep, covered, in the refrigerator for up to 2 weeks.

Rustic Aioli

Traditional aioli, a garlicky emulsion sauce from the south of France, is made with a mortar and pestle or a bowl and whisk. Arguments fly as to whether traditional aioli can really be made in the food processor. We've tried making aioli by hand and with a machine, and believe it or not, both take the same amount of time. The texture is more emulsified in the processor version, however. Here is the handmade version, made even zestier by the judicious addition of anchovies and basil. For the food processor technique, see White Truffle Aioli (recipe follows). We love aioli as an accompaniment to grilled foods of all kinds. MAKES ABOUT 1 CUP

2 large egg yolks, preferably organic

2 anchovy fillets, minced, or 1 tablespoon anchovy paste

2 cloves garlic, minced

2 tablespoons chopped fresh basil or 1 teaspoon dried basil

1/2 teaspoon Worcestershire sauce

1/2 teaspoon red wine vinegar

1 tablespoon fresh lemon juice

1 cup olive oil

Fine kosher or sea salt and hot pepper sauce to taste

Place the egg yolks in a medium-size glass bowl and microwave for 15 to 20 seconds on high. Whisk them together and add the anchovies, garlic, basil, Worcestershire, vinegar, and lemon juice. Slowly whisk in the olive oil. If the mixture gets too thick, thin with a little warm water. Season with salt and hot sauce. Mix thoroughly, cover, and refrigerate until ready to serve. This sauce will keep, covered, in the refrigerator for up to 3 days.

White Truffle Aioli

The BBQ Queens are quite fond of aioli, that mayonnaise-like sauce that can take on many different flavorings. This version takes on the heady, earthy perfume of the white truffle, its essence captured in vegetable oil. Our suggestion is to add just half of the white truffle oil at first, taste and see whether you like it, and then add the rest, if desired. White truffle oil can be overpowering if you use too much. You can buy small bottles of white truffle oil at gourmet shops or order it online. (Try adding a few drops to mashed potatoes or risotto. Delicious!) We love this aioli with grilled or smoked beef tenderloin, grilled potatoes, or grilled tuna. It's dynamite on grilled chicken or steak sandwiches, too. We adapted this from a recipe by Richard Chamberlain of the restaurant at the Little Nell in Aspen, Colorado. MAKES ABOUT 1 1/2 CUPS

2 large egg yolks
1 teaspoon fresh lemon juice
1 large clove garlic, minced
1/4 teaspoon kosher or sea salt
1/4 teaspoon ground white pepper
1 cup olive oil
2 tablespoons white truffle oil, or to taste

Place the egg yolks in a medium-size bowl and microwave for 15 to 20 seconds on high. Whisk them together and add the lemon juice, garlic, salt, and white pepper. Whisk until smooth. Slowly whisk in the olive oil and truffle oil until the sauce thickens. Use immediately, or spoon into a small jar with a tight-fitting lid and store in the refrigerator for up to 3 days.

Baked or Barbecued Beans

Anyone who has ever gnawed on a rib bone knows that the three real, true American side dishes for a slow-smokin' barbecue are barbecued or baked beans, coleslaw, and potato salad. That being said, the recipes vary as much as the topography of the land and the style of barbecue practiced on it.

For beans, the differences are in the variety of beans used and whether they're in a spicy or sweet sauce, cooked with or without meat, and cooked indoors or out on the smoker. We prefer to put these right on the smoker along with whatever else we're smoking—ribs, pork butt, brisket—or rotisserie cooking. Here are some recipes that any BBQ Babe would be proud to serve.

Texas-Style Pinto Beans

We adapted this recipe from Paris Permenter and John Bigley's *Texas Barbecue* (Pig Out Publications, 1994). They're delicious with Texas-style barbecued brisket, chicken, ribs, or pork butt. Pinto beans have a creamy, velvety texture when they're done. SERVES 12

1 pound dried pinto beans
Three 10-ounce cans Ro-Tel diced tomatoes with green chiles, with their juice
8 ounces sliced bacon, chopped
1 medium-size white onion, chopped
2 jalapeños, seeded and chopped
1/2 teaspoon ground cumin
1/2 teaspoon cayenne pepper
1/2 teaspoon chili powder
1/2 teaspoon fine kosher or sea salt
1/2 teaspoon freshly ground black pepper
Chopped green onions for garnish (optional)

1. Pick over the beans, rinse, place in a large bowl, and add enough cold water to cover. Let stand at room temperature for several hours or overnight.

2. Drain the beans, rinse well, and transfer to a large pot. Add the remaining ingredients and enough hot water to cover.

3. To cook outdoors, prepare an indirect fire in a smoker. Smoke the beans, with the lid closed, until tender, 5 to 6 hours. To cook indoors, bring the beans to a boil, cover, and simmer on the stovetop until tender, 3 to 4 hours.

BBQ Queens' Barbecued Beans

Here's a Kansas City–style barbecued bean recipe. Most competition barbecuers use canned pork and beans, but you can use 3 cups dried navy beans if you want to be a purist. Simply soak them in water overnight, then drain and cook them in a pot with enough water to cover until tender, about 40 minutes. We recommend BBQ Queens' Love Potion for the Swine (page 89) barbecue sauce for this recipe. SERVES 12

8 cups canned pork and beans
1 cup firmly packed light or dark brown sugar
1 large onion, finely chopped
1/2 cup ketchup
2 cups smoky, spicy barbecue sauce of your choice
1/4 cup Dijon mustard
2 cups chopped smoked meats, such as beef, pork, sausage, or turkey
Kosher or sea salt and freshly ground black pepper to taste

1. Combine all the ingredients in a large, heavy casserole dish or disposable aluminum pan.

2. To cook outdoors, prepare an indirect fire in a smoker. Smoke the beans, with the lid closed, at 225 to 250°F until smoky and bubbling, about 3 hours. To cook indoors, preheat the oven to 350°F and bake, uncovered, until thickened, browned, and bubbling, about 1 1/2 hours.

Jazzy Java Baked Beans

A traditional baked bean recipe enlivened with a jolt of java! Coffee is sometimes used as a mop or basting mixture for slow-smoked brisket and pork butt, so it's a natural in any bean dish you would serve with them. SERVES 12

1 pound dried navy beans
8 ounces sliced bacon, diced
1 medium-size onion, diced
4 cloves garlic, minced
1/4 cup lightly packed dark brown sugar
1 tablespoon molasses
2 tablespoons brown mustard
2 cups water
1 cup strong black coffee
1 cup barbecue sauce of your choice
1 teaspoon hot pepper sauce
Fine kosher or sea salt and freshly ground black pepper to taste

1. Pick over the beans, rinse, and place in a large bowl. Cover with water and let stand for several hours or overnight.

2. Drain the beans, rinse well, and transfer to a large Dutch oven. Add the remaining ingredients and stir to combine.

3. To cook indoors, preheat the oven to 300°F. Bake, stirring once an hour, until the beans are soft and the liquid syrupy, about 4 hours. To cook outdoors, prepare an indirect fire in a smoker and smoke the beans with the lid closed at 225 to 250°F until smoky and bubbling, 4 to 5 hours.

Easy Southern-Style Baked Beans

Here's a sweeter-style baked bean recipe that bakes lower and slower. These beans could also be put in the smoker to smoke-cook for 3 hours. SERVES 8

Three 15-ounce cans pork and beans
1 cup firmly packed light brown sugar
3/4 cup ketchup
3/4 cup cola
1 medium-size onion, diced
2 teaspoons dry mustard
6 to 8 slices bacon

1. Preheat the oven to 300°F.

2. In a large bowl, combine the beans, brown sugar, ketchup, cola, onion, and mustard. Spread the beans in a 13 x 9-inch baking dish and lay the bacon slices over the top. Bake until the beans are bubbling and the bacon is thoroughly cooked, about 1 1/2 hours.

BBQ-2

The Doctor Is In Easy Aioli

The BBQ Queens like big flavor, and aioli fits the ticket. Shortcut aioli can be pretty good when you use a good-quality store-bought mayonnaise. We are particularly fond of a canola-based mayonnaise that is the house brand at Whole Foods Market. The product is creamy and makes for a more authentic "doctored" aioli. However, any good-quality mayonnaise you like will taste fine—just don't use salad dressing. MAKES ABOUT 1 CUP

1 cup good-quality mayonnaise
2 tablespoons fresh lemon juice
2 teaspoons grated lemon zest
2 cloves garlic, minced
Fine kosher or sea salt to taste

In a medium-size bowl, whisk all the ingredients together. This sauce will keep, covered, in the refrigerator for 7 to 10 days.

Tiara-Worthy Variations: Here are more easy ways to doctor up aioli, whether it's a shortcut or entirely homemade. To 1 cup The Doctor Is In Easy Aioli, add one of the following:

- **2 tablespoons prepared horseradish to make Horseradish Aioli (great on steak or smoked or rotisserie beef sandwiches)**
- **1/2 cup finely chopped roasted red peppers (homemade, see page 145, or from a jar) to make Roasted Red Pepper Aioli**
- **1 smoked tomato (see page 161), peeled, seeded, and chopped, to make Smoked Tomato Aioli**
- **1/2 cup finely chopped fresh herbs to make Fresh Herb Aioli**
- **2 tablespoons homemade or prepared pesto to make Pesto Aioli**

Creamy Blue Cheese Dressing

This wonderfully pungent blue cheese dressing from Judith's *Prairie Home Cooking* (The Harvard Common Press, 1999) makes a great dipping sauce for chicken wings or raw or grilled vegetables. It's also superb served over a crisp wedge of iceberg lettuce. If you like a thinner consistency, add 2 to 3 more tablespoons of vinegar. MAKES ABOUT 4 CUPS

2 cups sour cream

8 ounces good-quality blue cheese, such as Maytag, crumbled

2/3 cup mayonnaise

3 tablespoons cider vinegar

1 teaspoon red pepper flakes

Onion salt, celery salt, and Worcestershire sauce to taste

Combine all the ingredients in a medium-size bowl, whisking to blend. For the best results, cover and let the flavors develop in the refrigerator for 24 hours before serving chilled. This dressing will keep, covered, in the refrigerator for up to 2 weeks.

BBQ QUEEN
1

Tzatziki

Fresh pita bread, brushed with olive oil and grilled, or grilled or rotisserie lamb, tastes even more fabulous when served with this Greek yogurt sauce, enlivened with garlic, cucumber, and dillweed. It's easy to make, but allow enough time to drain the yogurt. Do this by lining a colander with cheesecloth, a double thickness of sturdy paper towels, or a very thin tea towel. Place the colander in a bowl and spoon the yogurt into the colander. Wait for the excess liquid to drain away, which takes about 2 hours at room temperature. You'll end up with about 1 cup of drained liquid to discard. If you can find real Greek yogurt, you can skip the draining. MAKES 3 GENEROUS CUPS

4 cups plain yogurt (don't use reduced fat), drained (see headnote)
1 medium-size cucumber, peeled, seeded, and finely shredded
4 large cloves garlic, minced
2 tablespoons olive oil
1/2 teaspoon dillweed
Fine kosher or sea salt and freshly ground black pepper to taste

Transfer the drained yogurt to a medium-size bowl. Blot the shredded cucumber with paper towels to remove as much moisture as possible. Stir the cucumber, garlic, olive oil, and dillweed into the yogurt. Season with salt and pepper. Use immediately, or spoon into a covered container and store in the refrigerator for up to 3 days.

An A to Z of Grilled and Smoked Veggies, Cheeses, and Pizza

Charred or smoked vegetables fresh from the grocer, farmers' market, or your own backyard get an extra depth of flavor from fire and smoke. Cheese is served well by a kiss of smoke, whether through traditional smoking or sitting atop an aromatic wood plank. We like pizza on the grill, charred crisp on one side, then flipped and layered with thinly sliced vegetables and charred crisp again. Even a loaf of bread, slathered with something good, then tightly wrapped in foil and placed above the flames, gets a crusty burnish that is yummy. Fresh thick or thin spears of asparagus or slices of zucchini are drizzled with a bit of olive oil and grilled until charred a caramel brown or smoked with aromatic woods that make the freshest vegetables taste incredible. And oh my, what you can do with those charred and smoked veggies—from Grilled Gazpacho (page 155) to Smoked Tomato and Basil Butter (page 177).

Say cheese, please, and make mine smoked—from a wheel of Brie to a crock of goat cheese. Pizza and bread on the grill put their indoor oven counterparts to absolute shame. And best yet, all this outdoor cooking keeps the kitchen cool in the summer and neat and tidy in the winter.

Grilled Asparagus 117

Grilled Asparagus with Shaved Parmigiano-Reggiano 118

Asian-Style Asparagus with Peanut Butter Dipping Sauce 118

Grilled Asparagus Frittata 118

Grilled Corn 119

Southwestern-Style Grilled Corn Relish 120

Grilled Corn and Smoked Vegetable Pudding 120

Grilled Corn Layered Salad 120

Smoked Corn in the Husks 121

Smoked Corn, Sliced Tomato, and Slivered Red Onion Salad 122

Smoky Chipotle Corn Pudding 122

Smoked Corn, Ham, and Hominy Casserole 123

Grilled Eggplant 123

Grilled Eggplant, Peppers, and Goat Cheese with Balsamic-Thyme Vinaigrette 124

Sonoma Farmers' Market Eggplant Spread 124

Warm Asian Eggplant Salad 125

Grilled Eggplant Roll-Ups with Feta-Olive-Lemon Filling 126

Fettuccine with Grilled Eggplant–Garlic Sauce 126

Grilled Greens 126

Grilled Radicchio and Red Cabbage with Herbed Caesar Dressing 127

Grilled Romaine Caesar Salad 127

Grilled Romaine and Green Onions with Lemon and Olives 127

Fennel and Feta Salad 128

Grilled Cheese in a Sarong 128

GRILLED VEGETABLES ON PARADE

Grilled Vegetable Platter with Fresh Basil Vinaigrette 129

Grilled Vegetable and Goat Cheese Terrine 130

Grilled Mushrooms 132

Grilled Portobellos with Garlic, Pine Nuts, Basil, and Goat Cheese 133

Grilled Portobello Mushroom "Burgers" 133

Smoked Mushrooms 134

Smoked Stuffed Mushrooms 135

Smoked PLT 136

Smoked Mushroom Bisque 136

Grilled Onions 137

Grilled Green Onions and Red Onion Slices 138

Grilled Onion Soufflé 138

Grilled Onions with Thyme and Garlic Cream 138

Smoked Onions 139

Honey-Basted Smoked Onions 141

Smoked (or Grilled) Onion Marmalade 141

Smoked Onion Tart 141

Pickled Brewpub Smoked Onions 142

Grilled Peppers 142

Cheesy Grilled Pepper Boats 143

Grilled Chiles Rellenos with Baby Shrimp 143

BBQ QUEENS' GRILLED ANTIPASTO PLATTER

Queen-Size Spiced Olives 145

Grill-Roasted Peppers 145

Pick a Peck of Grilled Peppers Sauce 145

Grilled Potatoes 147

Grilled Whole Potatoes 148

Rustic Grill-Roasted Potato Salad 148

Grilled Red Potato and Fennel Salad 148

Grilled Vegetable Tart 149

Skewered Potatoes (and Other Vegetables) 149

THE UNGRILLED POTATO SALAD

Creamy Dijon Potato Salad for a Crowd 151

Grilled Antipasto Skewers 151

Grilled Sweet Potato and Red Onion Skewers 151

Smoked Potatoes 152

Smoked Potato and Aioli Gratin 152

BBQ Queens' Smoked Potato Casserole 153

Smoked Potato Soup 153

Smoked New or Fingerling Potato Platter 154

Grilled Summer Squash 154

Grilled Gazpacho 155

Char-Grilled Baby Summer Squash 155

GRILLED VEGETABLES ON PARADE

Vegetable Ribbon Skewers 156

Smoked Squash 157
Smoked Vegetable Confit 158
Smoked Vegetable Confit on Country Bread with Tapenade and Goat Cheese 158
Linguine with Smoked Butternut Squash, Fresh Sage, and Morel Cream Sauce 158
Smoked Spicy Acorn Squash 159

Grilled Tomatoes 159
Grilled Tomato "Burgers" with Herbed Cream Cheese 160
Grilled Goat Cheese Tomatoes 160
Grilled Roma Tomatoes with Anchovy, Garlic, and Parsley 160
Grilled Tomatoes Provençal 160
Indoor Grilled Tomatoes Provençal 161

Smoked Tomatoes 161

TWO SMOKIN' SALSAS
Charred Tomato-Chipotle Salsa 162
Grilled Tomatillo Salsa 163

Smoked Tomato Grits 164
Smoked Greek Stuffed Tomatoes 164
Fettuccine with Smoked Garlic and Tomatoes 165
Smoked Tomato with Tuna, Lemon, and Herbs 165

Stir-Grilled Vegetables 166
Thai-Style Stir-Grilled Vegetables in Lemongrass Marinade 167
Stir-Grilled Balsamic-Thyme Vegetables 167
Stir-Grilled Summer Squash with Fresh Herbs 167
Mediterranean-Style Stir-Grilled Mushrooms and Olives 168
Stir-Grilled Red Bell Peppers with Garlic and Thyme 168
Stir-Grilled Asian Lettuce Wraps 168

Smoked Soft Cheese 169
Crunchy Smoked Cheese Dip 170
Smoked Goat Cheese Salad 170
Smoked Cheesy Smashed Potatoes 170
Homemade Vegetable Crisps with Smoky Cheese Dip 170
Smoky Beef and Asparagus Saddlebags 171

Smoked Semisoft Cheese 172
Smoky Grilled Cheese Sandwich 173
Smoked Mozzarella, Tomato, and Fresh Basil Salad 173
Smoked Gouda and Tomato Pasta Salad 173

Planked Semisoft Cheese 174
Maple-Planked Cheese with Tricolored Peppers 175
Hickory-Planked Cheese with Dried Cranberry Relish 175

SAVORY BREADS ON THE GRILL
Wood-Grilled Flatbreads 176
Cheesy Italian Pesto Bread 177
Rustic Bread with Smoked Tomato and Basil Butter 177
Fiesta Bread 178

Grilled Pizza 179
Garlic-Herb Pizza Dough 180
Grilled Pizza with Fire-Roasted Tomato and Olive Topping 180
Grilled Pizza with Caramelized Onions and Brie 180
Grilled Leaf-Wrapped Bread Sticks 181
Bolani (Afghani Flatbreads with Fresh Herb Filling) 182

GRILL GALS: SHE GRILLS FAST AND FABULOUS ONE-DISH MEALS MENU
Super Sicilian Sandwich 184
Grilled Artichoke Pizza on Parmesan-Herb Crust 185

Grilled Asparagus

Asparagus on the grill is as good as it gets. In Kansas City, our outlying pick-your-own asparagus farms gear up for business as early as late April and go into June. Anything you do to fresh-picked asparagus tastes delicious. But grilled asparagus aficionados fall into two camps—those who prefer the very slender baby stalks and those who like the fatter more mature spears.

Obviously, it's easier to grill the fatter stalks, as they take the heat better and are less likely to fall through the grill grate. Look for the freshest asparagus with tight buds and avoid those with woody stalks. If your asparagus is a bit old (you can tell by looking at the bottom, or cut part, of the stalk—if it looks old, it is), we recommend blanching it in boiling water for 2 minutes, plunging it into a bowl of ice water, patting it dry, and brushing it with olive oil. Then grill for about 6 minutes over a hot fire.

If you prefer the skinniest asparagus spears you can find, a grill wok or grill rack is your best friend. Toss the spears with a little olive oil and grill over a hot fire.

To avoid losing medium or large spears through the grill grate, you can either skewer the spears together using the double-skewer approach (see page 32) or place the spears on a grill rack. On a gas grill, it is easiest to place the spears perpendicular to the openings in the grill grate.

Oh, and the easiest way to trim the woody bottoms off asparagus is to simply hold an end of a spear in each hand and snap. The asparagus will automatically snap off at the best place, leaving the tough end to discard and the tender end to eat.

Grill asparagus right alongside chicken breasts, pork tenderloin, steaks, or burgers. Leftovers will keep in a covered container in the refrigerator for 3 to 4 days. **SERVES 6 TO 8**

2 pounds fresh asparagus, bottoms trimmed
Olive oil
Fine kosher or sea salt to taste

1. Prepare a hot fire in a grill.

2. Lay the asparagus spears in a deep baking dish and drizzle with olive oil to coat lightly. Sprinkle with salt.

3. Place the spears perpendicular to the openings in the grill grate so they don't fall through. Grill until crisp-tender and slightly charred, 8 to 10 minutes for thick stalks and 6 to 7 minutes for thin ones. Serve hot or at room temperature.

Crowning Glories

Grilled asparagus is delicious all by itself or with a sauce such as:

Food Processor or Blender Hollandaise *(page 97)*

Rustic Aioli *(page 104)*

White Truffle Aioli *(page 105)*

Grilled Asparagus with Shaved Parmigiano-Reggiano: Top your grilled asparagus with shavings of Parmigiano-Reggiano (or Pecorino Romano) cheese. Other crumbled cheeses of choice would be feta cheese, goat cheese, blue cheese, or *ricotta salata*. **SERVES 6 TO 8**

Asian-Style Asparagus with Peanut Butter Dipping Sauce: Serve this as an appetizer or side dish. The marinade used here is great with other vegetables, pork, chicken, fish, and even beef. We always have a large quantity of it on hand because it keeps in the refrigerator for a couple of weeks. Also, it is the base for the peanut butter dipping sauce, which is very addictive and also excellent served with grilled lamb or pork or as a dressing for Asian noodles. In a medium-size bowl, combine 1/2 cup soy sauce, 1/2 cup rice vinegar, 2 tablespoons toasted sesame oil, 2 tablespoons clover or other medium-colored honey, 1 teaspoon minced fresh ginger (if using a microplane, you don't need to peel), 2 minced garlic cloves and 1/2 teaspoon lemon pepper seasoning and use to marinate the asparagus for 30 to 60 minutes before grilling as instructed above. Reserve the marinade. For the dipping sauce, in a small bowl whisk together 1/2 cup smooth or crunchy peanut butter and 2 to 4 tablespoons of the reserved marinade. Add more marinade if you want the dipping sauce to be thinner. Serve on the side with the asparagus. **SERVES 6 TO 8**

Grilled Asparagus Frittata: Use this recipe as a blueprint frittata recipe for any leftover grilled or smoked vegetables you may have in the fridge. Leftover grilled or smoked meat would make a tasty addition, too. Turn on the oven broiler. Grate about 3/4 cup Parmesan or Pecorino Romano cheese and set aside. In a large 10- to 12-inch ovenproof sauté pan, heat 1 tablespoon olive oil. Add 1/2 sliced medium-size onion and cook, stirring, until tender. Add 2 cups chopped grilled asparagus and cook, stirring a few times, until hot, 3 to 4 minutes. Turn off the heat and let the pan sit. In a medium-size bowl, beat 6 large eggs with about half the cheese, then season with fine kosher or sea salt to taste and 1/2 teaspoon red pepper flakes. Pour into the sauté pan on top of the veggies. Do not stir. Sprinkle the remaining cheese over the top. Place the pan under the broiler until the frittata is light and puffy and just beginning to brown, 3 to 4 minutes. Remove from the oven and cut into wedges. **SERVES 4 TO 6**

Grilled Corn

Really good fresh sweet corn is in season for so short a time that we've all learned to gorge on it while the gorgin' is good. After you've had it boiled and served with a smear of unsalted butter, it's time to branch out a bit.

Sweet corn varieties such as Silver Queen, Purdue Super Sweet, Country Gentleman, and Peaches and Cream are mighty fine on the grill. Fresh picked is best, so go to your farmers' market in the morning or pick from your own garden, then keep the corn cool until you're ready to grill the same day; that will deter the natural sugars from converting to starch.

We think it's a great idea to grill a lot of corn at one time. Invite friends and family over for a cookout, allowing extra ears for those who will eat more than one, or grill for leftovers. If you do have leftovers, cut the kernels off the cob and refrigerate them in a covered container for 3 to 4 days.

Our grilled corn is great just as it comes off the grill, but if you're feeling decadent, by all means slather on the butter or drizzle on a flavored oil. SERVES 8 TO 10

12 ears corn, in the husks
1/2 cup olive oil
Fine kosher or sea salt and freshly ground black pepper to taste

1. Pull back the husks from each ear and remove the corn silk. Pull the husks back over the corn, put in a large bucket of cold water, and soak for 30 minutes while you prepare your fire.

2. Prepare a hot fire in a grill.

3. When ready to grill, remove the corn from the water and drain. Pull a long piece of husk off each ear of corn, then pull back the husks and tie them together with the long piece. Drizzle the kernels on each ear with olive oil and sprinkle with salt and pepper. Place the corn on the grill, with the husk "handles" off the fire. Grill for 2 to 4 minutes total, turning by hand with the husk handles or with grill tongs every 30 seconds or so. You want a slight browning or charring of the kernels, not blackened corn. Serve hot.

It Keeps Going and Going and . . .

You can recycle a marinade that has been used only for vegetables. If the marinade has been used for fish, meat, or poultry, however, dispose of it.

Crowning Glories

Grilled corn is delicious all by itself or slathered with:

Smoked Tomato and Basil Butter ***(page 177)***

Chive Pesto ***(page 64)***

Southwestern-Style Grilled Corn Relish: Make this when you have 2 leftover ears of grilled corn, then serve it with grilled fish or chicken and Poblano Cream Sauce (page 93) or Smoked Garlic and Cilantro Cream Sauce (page 93) for a fabulous meal in minutes. It's also good in a grilled chicken burrito. Cut the kernels off the corn. In a medium-size bowl, combine the corn; 1 peeled, seeded, and diced medium-size ripe tomato; 1 seeded and finely chopped jalapeño; the juice of 1 lime; 1/2 teaspoon kosher or sea salt; and 1 tablespoon olive oil. Cover and refrigerate until ready to serve. Stir before serving. **MAKES ABOUT 2 CUPS**

Grilled Corn and Smoked Vegetable Pudding: Here's the classic updated with a bit of char and a kiss of smoke. Preheat the oven to 350°F. In a greased baking dish, combine 2 cups grilled corn kernels (about 4 ears) and 2 cups mixed smoked vegetables, such as tomatoes, bell peppers, onions, and garlic (see page 140). Top with 1 minced garlic clove and 8 ounces finely shredded sharp cheddar cheese. In a medium-size bowl, whisk together 2 cups milk, 4 large eggs, 1 teaspoon kosher or sea salt, and 1/4 teaspoon cayenne pepper, then pour over the corn mixture. Bake until bubbling and set, 50 to 60 minutes. Serve hot. **SERVES 6 TO 8**

Grilled Corn Layered Salad: Our first encounters with layered salads came in the early 1970s, when we started attending and giving wedding showers and needed luncheon dishes that required minimal expense and culinary skill. The layered salad filled the bill. Here is one adapted from many that gets rave reviews. Prepare it in a glass bowl to show off the layers. In a large 3-quart salad bowl, spread 3 cups chopped fresh spinach. Sprinkle with 1/4 teaspoon kosher or sea salt, 1/4 teaspoon freshly ground black pepper, and 1 teaspoon sugar. Have ready 1 pound crumbled crisp-cooked sliced bacon, 6 peeled and sliced hard-boiled large eggs, 1 cup thinly sliced celery, 2 cups grilled corn kernels (about 4 ears), and 1/2 cup sliced green onions. Layer beginning with the crumbled bacon, then the eggs, celery, corn, and green onions. In a small bowl, combine 1 package dry ranch dressing, 1 cup lowfat sour cream, and 1 cup mayonnaise. Spread over the salad to seal. Sprinkle 1 1/2 cups freshly grated Parmesan or Romano cheese over that. Cover tightly with plastic wrap and refrigerate overnight. Toss just before serving. **SERVES 8 TO 12**

Smoked Corn in the Husks

Many people have read the works of Garrison Keillor (of *A Prairie Home Companion* fame and as Mr. Blue, the former advice columnist on Salon.com) or have heard him on National Public Radio. But he's also a fresh corn fanatic. The proof? Our favorite Keillor quote from his book *Leaving Home* (Penguin, 1987): "Sweet corn was so delicious, what could have produced it except sex? . . . People have wanted sex to be as good as sweet corn and have worked hard to improve it, and afterward they lay together in the dark and said . . . 'That was so wonderful . . . but it wasn't as good as fresh sweet corn.'"

Here in Kansas City, where the climate can be really dry in the summer, we usually get the Peaches and Cream variety of sweet corn. But Judith still longs for the tender and sweet Silver Queen variety she used to enjoy in Ohio. Silver Queen corn is so good that it has inspired another kind of royalty—the Silver Queen Corn Queens in Raleigh, North Carolina. Fellow Harvard Common Press author Debbie Moose (*Deviled Eggs: 50 Recipes from Simple to Sassy*, 2004) is one of them, and she says that because her group of Silver Queen Corn Queens is so fine, you have to say "queen" twice. They *are* mighty fine.

And sweet corn is mighty fine, too. Fresh-picked, pale yellow corn in season is the best, of course, for the following recipes. Smoked corn stays moist but takes on a smoky aroma. As always, we like to smoke with leftovers in mind—in this case, for use in soups and salads, or to make a smoked corn relish.

You can also smoke frozen shoepeg corn that has been defrosted. Place it in a disposable aluminum pan, anoint it with oil and seasonings, and smoke it for 30 to 45 minutes. SERVES 12

**SUGGESTED WOOD: Apple, cherry, oak, or pecan;
avoid mesquite or even hickory, which can be too heavy**

12 ears corn, in the husks
1/2 cup olive oil
Kosher salt and freshly ground black pepper to taste

1. Pull back the husks from each ear and remove the corn silk. Pull the husks back over the corn and put it in a large bowl or bucket of cold water. Soak for 1 to 2 hours.

2. Prepare a fire in a smoker.

3. When ready to smoke, remove the corn from the water and drain. Pull back half of the husks and drizzle each ear with olive oil and sprinkle with salt and pepper. Smoke over indirect heat at 225 to 250°F for 1 to 1 1/2 hours, until the corn is tender.

4. To serve, pull a long piece of husk off each ear of corn, then pull back the husks and tie them together with the long piece.

Crowning Glories

Smoked corn is delicious with similar finger-lickin' dishes, such as Smoked Pork Butt (page 409) and Smoked Wings and Things (page 212).

Also try it slathered or sprinkled with:

Lemon Butter Drizzle *(page 87)*

Chive Pesto *(page 64)*

Spicy Red-Hot Lemon Pepper Rub *(page 53)*

Smoked Corn, Sliced Tomato, and Slivered Red Onion Salad: Consider this a basic blueprint for a tasty summer salad, or enhance it with myriad other ingredients, such as grilled peppers, squash, or green onions; olives and artichoke hearts; or smoked peppers and onions. Jazz up the dressing with additional herbs and a bit of spicy mustard, if you like. Arrange 2 or 3 peeled and sliced garden-ripe tomatoes on a large platter and scatter 12 slivered fresh basil leaves over them. Cut the kernels from 4 ears smoked corn. Combine with 1/2 cup slivered red onion, drizzle with 1/4 cup extra virgin olive oil and 2 tablespoons balsamic vinegar, and season with coarse kosher or sea salt and freshly ground black pepper to taste. Toss gently, then spoon over the tomato slices and serve. **SERVES 4**

Smoky Chipotle Corn Pudding: Leftover smoked corn never tasted so good as in this piquant corn pudding. This is a delicious side dish to serve at Thanksgiving, too. Turn up the heat by adding more chipotles, but be careful. The remaining chipotles can be stored in individual sealable plastic bags. Label, date, and place in the freezer, where they will keep for several months. Preheat the oven to 350°F. Grease a 1-quart baking dish. In a large bowl, combine 2 cups smoked corn kernels (about 4 ears), 1 chopped canned chipotle chile in adobo sauce plus 1 tablespoon adobo sauce, 1/4 cup chopped green onions, 1 1/2 tablespoons all-purpose flour, 2 teaspoons sugar, 1/4 teaspoon kosher salt, and 1/4 teaspoon cornstarch. In a small bowl, beat 2 large eggs and stir in 1 cup heavy cream. Pour into the corn mixture and mix well, then spoon into the prepared baking dish. Place the dish in a larger, shallow pan and add water to a depth of 1 inch. Place both pans in the oven and bake until a knife inserted in the center comes out clean, about 1 hour. **SERVES 6 TO 8**

Smoked Corn, Ham, and Hominy Casserole: Use either white or yellow hominy for this unique casserole, which can be made with or without the ham. By all means, use leftover Double-Smoked Ham (page 411) if you have it. Preheat the oven to 350°F. Grease a large baking dish. In a large bowl, combine 2 cups smoked corn kernels (about 4 ears); 2 cups canned hominy, drained well on paper towels; 1 cup cubed or shredded smoked ham; 2 minced garlic cloves; and 1 cup finely shredded sharp cheddar cheese. In a small bowl, beat 2 cups whole milk and 4 large eggs together. Whisk in 1 teaspoon kosher or sea salt, 1/4 teaspoon cayenne pepper, and 1/4 teaspoon ground cumin and pour over the corn mixture. Bake until set and the top is bubbling, 50 to 60 minutes. Remove from the oven and let rest for 5 to 10 minutes before serving. **SERVES 6 TO 8**

Grilled Eggplant

The BBQ Queens love the regal purplish hue of eggplant, but eggplant, quite frankly, is a very bland-tasting vegetable—kind of a vegetable version of tofu. The upside to this blandness is that eggplant is the perfect vehicle for rubs, bastes, slathers, marinades, and sauces. So get thee to the rubs and marinades chapter to liven up thy eggplant.

When you grill eggplant, you get a smoky char that adds a deeper, richer flavor to this hot-weather Mediterranean vegetable—without the extra fat of the traditional fried or roasted eggplant common in Italian cuisine. Use any kind of eggplant you want—the large, elongated purple (Agora), the more slender Japanese (Asian Bride or Farmer's Long), the small, oval white (Easter Egg), or the Italian heirlooms (Violette di Firenze or Rosa Bianca) with their rosy lavender and white globe fruits. White varieties of eggplant have a milder, fuller flavor than those of purple varieties, but we encourage you to try many different varieties from your farmers' market or grocery store.

Whether sliced into long, thin pieces or cut into rounds, eggplant doesn't need to be salted or peeled before grilling. Either a charcoal or a gas grill works well. You can also use a grill pan indoors on the stovetop. Eggplant slices are sturdy enough to be placed directly on the grill grate, but if you're

nervous, use an oiled perforated grill rack. Grill eggplant at the same time you're grilling a leg of lamb or lamb chops for a Middle Eastern–inspired meal. SERVES 4

$2^1/_2$ pounds eggplants, ends trimmed and cut lengthwise into $^1/_2$-inch-thick slices

Olive oil

Fine kosher or sea salt and freshly ground black pepper to taste

1. Prepare a hot fire in a grill.
2. Brush or spray the eggplant slices on both sides with a light coating of olive oil. Grill for 3 to 4 minutes per side, turning once (or three times if you want good grill marks). Season with salt and pepper. Serve hot.

Crowning Glories

Grilled eggplant is delicious dressed with:

Citrus Caesar Vinaigrette *(page 84)*

Roasted Red Pepper Aioli *(page 110)*

Tzatziki *(page 112)*

Grilled Eggplant, Peppers, and Goat Cheese with Balsamic-Thyme Vinaigrette: Greet your vegetarian pals with this entrée, and they'll love you to death. As a side dish, it goes well with grilled steak or fish. While you're grilling the eggplant, also put a whole medium-size red and a whole medium-size yellow bell pepper on to char on all sides. Remove the peppers from the grill and place them, hot, in a plastic bag to steam for a few minutes. Let cool slightly, then remove the skin and seeds with a paring knife and discard. Slice the peppers into long, thin strips. Slice a small red onion into thin rings. Arrange the grilled eggplant on a rectangular platter and top with the roasted pepper strips, then layer on the onion rings. Scatter about 4 ounces crumbled fresh goat cheese on top, drizzle everything with $^1/_2$ cup Balsamic-Thyme Vinaigrette (page 84), and garnish with chopped fresh Italian parsley. SERVES 6

Sonoma Farmers' Market Eggplant Spread: A graphic designer friend of Judith's, Mary Carroll, created this recipe when she lived in California. No matter where you live, this will have you California dreamin'. Grill the eggplant so it is well browned on both sides. Place the entire recipe of hot-off-the-grill slices in a food processor and add 1 tablespoon sea salt, 4 minced garlic cloves, 1 teaspoon dried tarragon, $^1/_4$ teaspoon freshly ground black pepper, and 1 teaspoon sugar. Process until smooth and well blended. With the machine running, drizzle in 1/2 cup olive oil through the feed tube to make a smooth spread. Serve on flatbread or crackers. This will keep, covered, in the refrigerator for up to 2 days. **SERVES 8**

Warm Asian Eggplant Salad: Here's a different twist on grilled eggplant. Arrange the grilled eggplant slices on a platter. In a small bowl, whisk together 2 tablespoons warm water, 2 tablespoons mirin (a sweet Japanese wine), 1 tablespoon soy sauce, 1/4 teaspoon toasted sesame oil, 3 finely chopped green onions, and freshly ground black pepper to taste. Drizzle over the eggplant, then sprinkle with 2 tablespoons each chopped fresh mint and cilantro. The Asian drizzle is also good on other grilled vegetables, fish, chicken, or pork. **SERVES 4**

An Obento Box Lunch

The BBQ Queens attended the James Beard Foundation Awards ceremony in New York City when Judith's cookbook *Prairie Home Cooking* (The Harvard Common Press, 1999) was nominated. They had a terrific time taking part in all the festivities. They even splashed out on an obento box lunch at Takashimaya, that minimalist luxury goods store on Fifth Avenue. An obento box is a tray with compartments containing small portions of several dishes, each with a different flavor, color, and texture. In its simplest form, an obento box is basically a sack lunch, Japanese style, but one prepared with great artistry. This isn't something you could do for a crowd, but if you're grilling for up to four people, you can give each person a tray with little dishes serving the following courses. Accompany with the best green tea you can find.

Warm Asian Eggplant Salad *(above)*

Chopstix Chicken with Gingered Teriyaki Glaze *(page 196)*

Batayaki Beef *(page 312)*

Steamed rice

Grilled Eggplant Roll-Ups with Feta-Olive-Lemon Filling: Pretend that you can see us doing the four queen waves to Nigella Lawson, our favorite Grill Gal. This is our take on an appetizer recipe in her wonderful cookbook *Forever Summer* (Hyperion, 2003). Before you go out to the grill, make the filling. In a medium-size bowl, mix together 8 ounces crumbled feta cheese; 1 tablespoon olive oil; 1/2 cup pitted, drained, and finely chopped oil- or brine-cured Kalamata or Niçoise olives; 2 tablespoons finely chopped green onions; and 1 teaspoon grated lemon zest. Get good grill marks on the eggplant slices. While they're still warm from the grill, place about 2 teaspoons of the feta filling on the end third of a grilled eggplant slice and roll it up. If you're nervous, secure each roll with a toothpick. Arrange the roll-ups on a platter. Serve warm or at room temperature. **SERVES 4 TO 6**

Fettuccine with Grilled Eggplant–Garlic Sauce: Fabulous! This sauce is also good over grilled vegetables of any kind, as well as grilled chicken, salmon, or pork tenderloin. Puree the entire recipe of grilled eggplant slices in a food processor along with 4 garlic cloves, 1/2 cup whole-grain or Dijon mustard, 1 cup heavy cream, and 1/2 cup chicken broth. Transfer to a medium-size saucepan and bring to a boil. Reduce the heat to medium-low and simmer until thickened, about 10 minutes. Season with kosher or sea salt and freshly ground black pepper to taste. **MAKES ENOUGH FOR 1 POUND COOKED FETTUCCINE**

Grilled Greens

Why not grill salad greens? As with any other food, grilling adds a touch of caramelization, which means *flavor*. You get some char on the outside leaves, while the inside leaves remain tender and crisp. The BBQ Queens choose sturdy greens for the grill: quartered heads of romaine, radicchio, red or green cabbage, or quartered fennel bulbs. We also like to wrap small rounds of cheese in "sarongs" of Swiss chard or spinach leaves that have been blanched, then brush the packets with vinaigrette and grill until the cheese softens and melts.

The trick to grilling and not burning the greens is a medium temperature and vigilance. Most greens take only 8 to 10 minutes to grill, but it's best to watch them carefully so they don't burn. Grill greens before or after you grill chicken breasts or steaks. You can slice the cooked chicken or steak and toss it with the greens for a grilled salad. SERVES 6 TO 8

1 small head radicchio, quartered lengthwise

1 small head red cabbage, quartered lengthwise and cored

2 large heads romaine lettuce, quartered lengthwise

Olive oil

Fine kosher or sea salt and freshly ground black pepper to taste

1. Prepare a medium-hot fire in a grill.

2. Brush the radicchio, cabbage, and romaine with olive oil and season with salt and pepper. Grill on the flat cut sides, turning once, until browned and sizzled on the outside and warm in the middle, 8 to 10 minutes total. Serve warm or at room temperature, as is or cut up as you prefer.

Crowning Glories

Grilled greens are delicious topped with:

Crumbled crisp-cooked bacon, finely chopped red or Spanish onion, and

Creamy Blue Cheese Dressing *(page 111)*

Garlic-Citrus Marinade *(page 70)*

Chipotle Vinaigrette *(page 86)*

Grilled Radicchio and Red Cabbage with Herbed Caesar Dressing: In a small bowl, whisk together 1 teaspoon anchovy paste or mashed anchovies, 1 tablespoon Dijon mustard, the juice of 1/2 lemon, 1 minced garlic clove, 1 teaspoon chopped fresh rosemary, 1 tablespoon minced fresh Italian parsley, and 6 tablespoons olive oil. Grill 1 small head radicchio and 1 small head red cabbage, both quartered lengthwise, as directed above. Drizzle the dressing over the grilled greens and serve. **SERVES 4**

Grilled Romaine Caesar Salad: Grill 2 large heads romaine lettuce, quartered lengthwise, as directed above. Place each grilled wedge on a salad plate and drizzle with Herbed Caesar Dressing (above), Citrus Caesar Vinaigrette (page 84), or your own favorite Caesar dressing. With a vegetable peeler, shave some Parmigiano-Reggiano cheese over each salad and serve. **SERVES 8**

Grilled Romaine and Green Onions with Lemon and Olives: Think old-fashioned wilted lettuce salad, but with a new, light twist. You can also try this using Belgian endive or Napa cabbage; double the grill time. Improvise and add grilled shrimp or scallops to make a complete meal. Grill 2 large heads romaine lettuce, quartered lengthwise, as directed above. Also throw 16 green onions onto the grill, cooking them until charred on all sides. In a small bowl, combine 1 tablespoon drained capers, 2 tablespoons chopped red bell pepper, the juice and grated zest of 1 lemon, 1/4 cup extra virgin olive oil, 1/4 teaspoon kosher or sea salt, and 1/4 teaspoon freshly ground black pepper. Plate each wedge of romaine and divide equally 1/4 cup pitted and drained oil- or brine-cured black olives and the green onions among the plates. Drizzle with the dressing and serve warm. **SERVES 8**

Fennel and Feta Salad: If you want to serve 1/4 fennel bulb to each guest, trim them of their fronds and grill as directed above until tender, 12 to 15 minutes. If your company grows, chop the fennel after it is grilled. In a large bowl, combine 2 to 3 tablespoons olive oil and 1 tablespoon fresh lemon juice. Season with kosher or sea salt and freshly ground black pepper to taste. Add 4 cups mixed greens, such as spinach and arugula, and toss to coat. Divide the greens among 4 serving plates. Top with the grilled fennel and sprinkle with 1/4 cup crumbled feta cheese. Serve immediately. **SERVES 4**

Grilled Cheese in a Sarong: Grilled cheese a new way! You know how helpful a good sarong wrap is for the dreaded bathing suit parade to the beach or pool. Swiss chard does the job here. Choose large, sturdy Swiss chard or spinach leaves to wrap any semisoft cheese you like, such as fontina, mozzarella, goat cheese, or Camembert. To blanch the leaves, bring a pot of water to a boil and plunge in 8 leaves until they wilt, about 1 minute. Transfer to a bowl of ice water to cool. Pat dry with paper towels and lay each leaf on a flat surface. Place a 1-inch-thick round or square of cheese in the center of each leaf, wrapping the ends to enclose the filling. Secure with a toothpick. Place each packet on a baking sheet and take to the grill. Coat a perforated grill rack with nonstick cooking spray and place on the hot grill. Brush each packet with Citrus Caesar Vinaigrette (page 84) and grill, turning once and basting with the vinaigrette, for 8 to 10 minutes total. Serve at the table, drizzled with the remaining vinaigrette. **SERVES 4**

Grilled Vegetables on Parade

Fresh vegetables are so naturally colorful and delicious, they don't need tiaras or beauty queen sashes to stand out. (Ouch, that hurts!)

We love these two grilled vegetable dishes because they taste wonderful, they're good for you, and they have a definite wow factor. There's also a distinct likelihood—for all of us—that at least one of our friends or relatives has become a vegetarian. Why discreetly slip a veggie burger onto someone's plate when you can please all your diners with one of these dazzling dishes?

Grilled Vegetable Platter with Fresh Basil Vinaigrette

Easy to prepare and assemble, this vegetarian appetizer, salad, or main dish platter has a rustic appearance and a vibrant flavor. It can be prepared hours ahead and kept at room temperature. It can also be doubled or tripled easily. Accompaniments include crusty bread and fresh goat cheese. SERVES 8 TO 10

2 pounds fresh asparagus
8 baby eggplants
4 large red bell peppers
2 pounds baby yellow pattypan squash
Olive oil
Fine kosher or sea salt and freshly ground black pepper to taste
2 pints cherry tomatoes
Fresh basil sprigs for garnish
Fresh Basil Vinaigrette (page 85)

1. Prepare a hot fire in a grill. Coat two perforated grill racks or hinged grill baskets and a grill wok with nonstick cooking spray and set aside.

2. Prepare the vegetables. Snap off the tough ends of the asparagus. Trim the ends of the eggplants and cut each lengthwise into 1/2-inch-thick slices. Seed the red bell peppers and cut each lengthwise into 1/2-inch strips. Place the asparagus, eggplant slices, and bell

pepper strips on the prepared grill racks. Place the squash in the prepared grill wok. Spray the vegetables with olive oil and season with salt and pepper.

3. Have a large bowl ready near the grill. Toss the squash in the grill wok, using wooden grill paddles or a grill spatula, until tender, about 10 minutes. Meanwhile, grill the vegetables on the grill racks, turning with grill tongs, until tender and slightly charred, 4 to 5 minutes per side. When the squash are done, transfer to the bowl and add the cherry tomatoes to the grill wok. Grill until the skins just begin to crack, about 5 minutes. When the asparagus, eggplant, and bell peppers are done, transfer to the bowl. Add the tomatoes and set aside to cool slightly.

4. Arrange the vegetables on a large platter in a pleasing pattern or just a jumble, your preference. Garnish with the basil. Drizzle the vinaigrette over everything. Serve immediately, or cover with plastic wrap and let sit at room temperature for up to 2 hours.

Grilled Vegetable and Goat Cheese Terrine

We like this as the main dish for a fancy-schmancy ladies lunch or as a drop-dead-gorgeous dish you can bring to a gathering. Another redeeming feature is that it can be made up to 2 days ahead and kept covered in the refrigerator. Serve as is, drizzled with a little vinaigrette, or with crusty bread. SERVES 8

2 large red bell peppers

1 large eggplant, ends trimmed and cut lengthwise into 1/2-inch-thick slices

2 large zucchini, ends trimmed and cut lengthwise into 1/4-inch-thick slices

Olive oil

Fine kosher or sea salt and freshly ground black pepper to taste

FILLING

One 11-ounce package soft, mild goat cheese, such as Montrachet, at room temperature

3 tablespoons olive oil

2 tablespoons chopped fresh thyme

Fine kosher or sea salt and freshly ground black pepper to taste

1/2 cup pitted oil- or brine-cured olives, such as Kalamata or Niçoise, drained and chopped

1 large bunch arugula, chopped

1 cup fresh arugula or other salad or herb leaves for garnish

1. Prepare a hot fire in a grill.

2. Brush or spray the peppers, eggplant, and zucchini slices with olive oil and season with salt and pepper.

3. Have a baking sheet and a paper bag ready near the grill. Grill the vegetables, turning with grill tongs, until tender and slightly charred, 4 to 5 minutes per side. Transfer the peppers to the bag, close, and let steam for 15 minutes. Transfer the eggplant and zucchini to the baking sheet and let cool.

4. With a paring knife, remove the charred skin, membranes, and seeds from the grilled peppers.

5. To make the filling, place the goat cheese in a food processor and puree. With the machine running, drizzle the olive oil through the feed tube. Add the grilled peppers and pulse until the peppers are coarsely chopped and the cheese mixture begins to color. Pulse in the thyme. Season with salt and pepper.

6. To make the terrine, line a 9 x 5-inch loaf pan with plastic wrap, leaving a 4-inch overhang all around. Place a single layer of grilled zucchini in the bottom, completely covering the bottom and trimming the slices to fit. Spread one-third of the cheese filling on top of the zucchini. Sprinkle with one-third of the chopped olives and arugula. Cover with a single layer of eggplant, trimming the slices to fit. Spread half of the remaining cheese mixture over the eggplant and sprinkle with half of the chopped olives and arugula. Finish with a single layer of eggplant, trimming to fit. Spread the remaining cheese mixture on top and sprinkle with the remaining chopped olives and arugula. Completely cover with the plastic wrap and refrigerate until firm, at least 6 hours or up to 24 hours.

7. Remove the terrine from the refrigerator 30 minutes before you plan to serve it. To serve, arrange arugula leaves on a platter. Open the plastic wrap on top of the terrine. Unmold the terrine onto the platter, removing and discarding the plastic. Cut into slices and serve.

Grilled Mushrooms

Now that more and more mushroom varieties are hitting our grocery store shelves and farmers' market stalls, it's more fun than ever to grill these goodies. From the regular button mushrooms, you can branch out to sample cremini, chanterelle, shiitake, oyster, or portobello mushrooms. Look for fresh mushrooms that are firm and plump, with no discoloration around the edges and a fresh clean smell.

Mushrooms like a little drizzle of butter or olive oil and a sprinkling of salt when you grill them over a hot fire alongside whatever you're cooking for dinner. That way, they sizzle and brown instead of steam. Small mushrooms that may fall through the grill grate may be grilled on skewers or stir-grilled in an oiled and preheated grill wok. SERVES 4

1 1/2 pounds fresh mushrooms

3 to 4 tablespoons olive oil, as needed

Fine kosher or sea salt to taste

2 tablespoons balsamic vinegar (optional)

2 tablespoons chopped fresh herbs, such as Italian parsley, chives, rosemary, thyme, and/or oregano (optional)

1 loaf crusty bread (optional), sliced

1. Prepare a hot fire in a grill. Place an oiled grill wok, iron skillet, or grill rack directly over the fire. Heat the cooking vessel until very hot.

2. Brush any dirt off the mushrooms with a paper towel. Trim off any dry or ragged ends. Remove the stems from portobello or shiitake mushrooms. If necessary, cut the mushrooms so that they are a uniform size, place in a large bowl, add the olive oil, and toss to coat. Season with salt.

3. Transfer the mushrooms to the cooking vessel over the hot fire. Cook for about 8 minutes, tossing them several times so they do not burn. Remove from the grill. If you wish, toss them with the vinegar and herbs, then serve hot and sizzling with the sliced bread, if using.

Crowning Glories

Grilled mushrooms are delicious alone or topped or tossed with:

Simply Delicious Bordelaise Sauce *(page 91)*

Pesto Aioli *(page 110)*

Grated Parmesan cheese and chopped fresh herbs

Citrus Caesar Vinaigrette *(page 84)*

Grilled Portobellos with Garlic, Pine Nuts, Basil, and Goat Cheese: Often the BBQ Queens disagree on how to prepare something. We guess it's our way of "dueling" without the swords. Bottom line is that the disagreements are simply personal preferences about how to prepare something. For this dish, Judith likes to grill the gill side of the mushrooms with the grill lid open, then turn them, add the goodies, and finish grilling with the lid closed. Karen likes to fill the caps with all the goodies and grill the bottom side only with the grill lid closed. So pick your favorite way. Remove the stems from 4 large portobello mushrooms, then brush both sides with 1/4 cup extra virgin olive oil. In a small bowl, combine 4 minced garlic cloves; 8 ounces crumbled or cubed goat cheese (or feta cheese, Boursin, Gorgonzola, or Brie); 2 tablespoons toasted pine nuts; and 8 to 10 chopped fresh basil leaves. *Karen's version:* Place one-fourth of the mixture inside each mushroom cap. Season with kosher or sea salt to taste. Place the mushroom caps directly over the hot fire and grill with the lid down until the mushrooms are soft, 8 to 10 minutes. *Judith's version:* Grill the mushrooms gill side down for about 4 minutes with the grill lid open. Turn the mushrooms, fill them with the goodies, and season with salt. Close the lid and grill for another 4 minutes. Serve hot. **SERVES 4 AS A MAIN DISH**

Grilled Portobello Mushroom "Burgers": We love these vegetarian burgers, especially with melted mozzarella and pizza sauce as a condiment. Blend 2 tablespoons olive oil and 1 minced garlic clove together in a small bowl. Remove the stems from 4 large portobello mushrooms and brush with the garlic oil. Grill over a hot fire for about 4 minutes per side, until the mushrooms are soft. Place on French bread or sesame seed hamburger buns and serve with mayonnaise, lettuce, and tomato slices, if desired. **SERVES 4**

Smoked Mushrooms

From button mushrooms to portobellos, smoking enhances this earthy vegetable as nothing else can. The simplest way to smoke is to leave the mushrooms whole, but they may be sliced, if you like.

When we embellish the mushrooms—or get decked out in our gaudy costume jewelry for a royal culinary appearance—it's hard to stop. Mushrooms can take on any number of flavors, from savory cheese and garlic to sweet bell pepper and herbs to mellow cream. They're also wonderful as "burgers" or as a burger topping, pickled, sliced on a salad, in a soup or sauce, on a pizza, with pasta, or stuffed.

But sometimes the BBQ Queens disagree on their preparation. Judith likes to remove the gills of the portobellos before smoking them for a cleaner presentation when they are sliced. If the mushrooms are very fresh, Karen prefers to leave the gills on—one less chore for this royal gal. You decide which method you prefer.

Experiment with the smoke flavor by adding water-soaked ground pecan shells, corncobs, grapevine, or woody herb stalks to the fire. **SERVES 4**

SUGGESTED WOOD: Fruitwood, hickory, maple, mesquite, or oak

1 pound button, cremini, or portobello mushrooms
2 tablespoons olive oil
Coarse kosher or sea salt to taste

1. Prepare an indirect fire in a smoker.

2. Trim the mushroom stems, removing them completely if using portobellos. Place the mushrooms in a disposable aluminum pan. Drizzle with the olive oil and toss to coat. Place in the smoker, cover, and smoke at 225 to 250°F until the mushrooms are supple to the touch, golden brown, and fragrant. The smaller button-size mushrooms will take 30 to 40 minutes, portobellos about 1 hour.

3. Remove from the smoker and season with salt. If there are juices in the pan, you may drizzle them over the mushrooms or reserve for another use. Serve immediately.

Crowning Glories

Smoked mushrooms pair well with smoked or rotisserie main dishes and sauces such as:

Simply Delicious Bordelaise Sauce *(page 91)*

Chile–Ginger–Green Onion Sauce *(page 318)*

Fresh Basil Vinaigrette *(page 85)*

An Aioli Platter

Presenting beautifully grilled food on a large platter is a great way to entertain. Whenever we do this dish for our cooking classes, people rave. The aioli platter is an updated version of the French classic dish of boiled salt cod with a garlicky mayonnaise, which was usually served as part of the Christmas festivities. But who wants boiled salt cod when you can have a succulent grilled salmon fillet? We love to surround the salmon with seasonal vegetables chosen for their color as well as flavor, although really good oil- or brine-cured black olives and artichokes hearts are always welcome.

In summer, we might place mounds of steamed *haricots verts* or freshly grated carrot tossed with a dressing around the salmon. In winter, we use roasted fingerling potatoes and steamed baby carrots. Anything, of course, tastes good with aioli.

Grilled salmon fillets *(page 257)*

Rustic Aioli *(page 104)*

Haricots Verts Salad with Mustard-Shallot Vinaigrette *(page 327)*

Bistro Grated Carrot Salad *(page 329)*

Celery Root Rémoulade *(page 328)*

Grilled Mushrooms *(page 132)*

Grilled Potatoes *(page 147)*

Oil- or brine-cured Kalamata or Gaeta olives

Artichoke hearts

Smoked Stuffed Mushrooms: Whether these treats are served with dinner or passed as an appetizer, they are divine. Everyone will proclaim you a BBQ Babe! Clean and stem 24 large mushrooms; chop the stems finely. Heat 2 tablespoons olive oil in a medium-size skillet over medium heat. Add the mushroom stems and 1 chopped medium-size onion. Cook, stirring, until the onion is transparent, about 5 minutes. Set aside. In a food processor, combine one 8-ounce package softened cream cheese, 1/2 cup grated Pecorino Romano cheese, 2 teaspoons snipped fresh chives, 2 tablespoons chopped fresh Italian parsley, the sautéed onion and mushrooms, and fine kosher or sea salt and freshly ground black pepper to taste. Blend until smooth. Stuff the mushroom caps evenly with the cheese mixture. Arrange the mushrooms on a perforated grill rack or in a disposable aluminum pan and place in the smoker. Cover and smoke at 225 to 250°F for 1 hour. **SERVES 12 AS AN APPETIZER OR 8 AS A SIDE DISH**

Smoked PLT: Portobello mushroom, lettuce, and tomato on rustic Asiago bread or a bun is a delight whether you're vegetarian or not. The flavorful heft of the mushroom makes meat unnecessary, but if you'd like to add a slice or two of crisp-cooked apple-smoked bacon, be our guest. If you're serving a crowd, make this sandwich on a split loaf of Italian bread and, depending on the size of the loaf, triple or quadruple the ingredients. Slice into 6 to 8 sandwiches and serve the gang. For 1 sandwich, begin with a bun slathered with aioli (see pages 104–105 and 110) or store-bought mayonnaise. Place a smoked portobello mushroom on the bun and add a slice of beefsteak tomato and a crunchy lettuce leaf. Season with coarse kosher or sea salt and freshly ground black pepper to taste and enjoy.

Smoked Mushroom Bisque: Rich, creamy bisques are elegant, yet homey and comfortable, too. This simple from-scratch soup forbids you to think of the canned version. Melt 2 tablespoons unsalted butter in a large saucepan over medium heat. Add 1/2 cup chopped onion (use grilled or smoked onion if you have it) and cook, stirring, until softened, about 5 minutes. Stir in 2 tablespoons all-purpose flour to make a roux and cook for 2 minutes. Add 2 tablespoons sun-dried tomato paste or finely chopped oil-packed sun-dried tomatoes and blend. Slowly add 1 1/2 cups heavy cream or evaporated milk and stir until thickened. Add 1/4 cup brandy and 1 pound fresh mushrooms that have been smoked as described above and chopped, plus any mushroom juice from the pan. Heat to warm through. Season with kosher salt and freshly ground black pepper. If the soup is too thick (remember that a bisque usually is creamy and thick), thin it by adding 1/4 to 1/2 cup beef or vegetable broth. **SERVES 4**

Grilled Onions

Grilling onions is a snap. It's so simple, in fact, that you might have some resident doubters try to steer you toward a more complex method. But don't listen to them!

The first time Karen tried to grill her garden onions (bulbs, green stems, and all), her husband, Dick, thought she was nuts. Karen harvested her first cultivated onion crop (it was all of three onions), brushed off the dirt, and put the unpeeled onions directly over the hot fire in their charcoal grill. Dick, of course, told her they wouldn't be any good this way. He wanted to remove the skins, but Karen insisted that they stay on the grill until charred well on the outside. The outer skins were charred enough that it was easy to remove them. The finished onions were lightly caramelized and so, so sweet.

Use any kind of onion you want—paper-skinned keeping onions such as yellow, white, Spanish, or red; sweet varieties such as Walla Walla, Maui, or Vidalia; or bulb onions with green shoots such as torpedoes or garden onions. We don't recommend grilling other members of the onion family—shallots and garlic—because they're fiddly to grill and taste better slow smoked. If you're determined to grill shallots and garlic, then thread whole shallots and individual garlic cloves onto a skewer, brush them with olive oil, and grill over a hot fire, turning frequently, for about 5 minutes, until browned and softened.

This is a great campfire recipe, too. Simply place the whole onions with their skins into the embers of the fire and roast until the skins are charred and the onions are tender when pierced with a fork.

You don't need to brush the onions with olive oil if you leave the skins on during grilling. That means lower fat, and we like that! Just remember to be gentle when rubbing the skins off after they're done. Grilled onions are a knockout side dish with steak or burgers. SERVES 3 TO 6

3 medium-size white, yellow, or red onions (about 1½ pounds), or 12 bulb or green onions (the white bulbs are larger—2 to 3 inches in diameter—than the smaller green onions)

1. Prepare a hot fire in a grill.

2. Place the onions, with the skins on, directly over the fire. Grill, turning so that the entire outside gets well charred, at least 25 minutes.

3. When cool enough to handle, gently rub the charred outer skin off the onions. Serve whole or cut in half.

Crowning Glories

Grilled onions are delicious alone or topped with:

Smoked Hickory Salt *(page 57)*

Kimizu *(page 103)*

BBQ Queens' Love Potion for the Swine *(page 89)*

Grilled Green Onions and Red Onion Slices: Even easier and faster, try grilling green onions to serve as a side dish or garnish. They are especially pretty served on a platter of mixed vegetables or an aioli platter. The green onions may be skewered with either toothpicks or wooden skewers so they don't fall through the grill grates. This makes them easier to turn, too. Slice the red onions 3/4 to 1 inch thick. You can also try this with sweet white or yellow onions. Clean and rinse 2 bunches of green onions (about 20 onions). Trim the tops and bottoms and pat dry. Lightly coat the green onions and 2 sliced red onions with 2 tablespoons olive oil. Using a hot fire, place the green onions directly over the fire and perpendicular to the openings in the grill grate so they will not fall through. Set the red onion slices directly over the fire or stick a skewer through them to keep the rings intact. Grill the green onions for 6 to 7 minutes, turning to char evenly. Grill the onion slices for 10 to 12 minutes (or more), turning once halfway through the cooking time. Serve hot or at room temperature. **SERVES 6 TO 8**

Grilled Onion Soufflé: If the title is too fancy for you, just call this onion pie. It is an upscale way to use onions, whether you grill them fresh or use leftovers from the grill or sauté pan. Preheat the oven to 350°F. Coat a large soufflé dish with nonstick cooking spray. In a large bowl, combine 3 pounds peeled and chopped grilled onions (about 6 large), 1/2 cup freshly grated Parmesan or Pecorino Romano cheese, 1/2 cup finely shredded Gruyère or sharp cheddar cheese, 3 lightly beaten large eggs, 1 tablespoon Dijon mustard, 1 teaspoon Worcestershire sauce, and 1/4 teaspoon red pepper flakes. Blend well. Pour into the prepared dish and bake until puffed and golden brown, about 45 minutes. Serve hot. **SERVES 6**

Grilled Onions with Thyme and Garlic Cream: We changed our grilling method a bit to accommodate this recipe, which is fabulous. We love these sumptuous guy-in-your-life-pleasing grilled onions served with grilled steaks or pork tenderloin. You'll want a hot fire to grill the steaks, but more of a medium heat to do the onions. The trick is to find a place on your grill where the heat is not as intense. Just feel around with your hand to find a relatively cool spot. We've found that placing the onions along the edge of the grill grate or even up on a rack several inches above the grate will work. In a small bowl, whisk together 2 minced garlic cloves, 1/2 teaspoon dried thyme, 1/2 teaspoon freshly ground black pepper, 1/2 teaspoon coarse kosher or sea salt, and 1 cup heavy cream. Slice about 1/2 inch off the top and bottom of 6 to 8 small peeled yellow onions (about 3 inches in diameter). Brush the bottom of each with olive oil. With a grapefruit spoon or paring knife, cut out a small, 1-inch-deep core from the top of each onion. Spoon in about 1 tablespoon of the garlic cream, letting some drizzle down the sides. Place the onions around the perimeter of a hot fire in your grill. Cover and grill for about 20 minutes without turning (although you should twirl the onions around if they get scorched on one side), until the onions have browned and softened (you can grill the steaks at the same time over the hot fire). Serve with the remaining cream spooned over the top. **SERVES 4 TO 6**

Smoked Onions

Big girls do cry when onions are in the picture. But we cry for joy because the flavor is so luscious when this most common of root vegetables is kissed with smoke. Once smoked, they can be placed in labeled and dated sealable plastic bags and frozen for a couple of months—but only if you don't have time to put them to good use right then and there.

We like to smoke onions for a couple of hours, until they are very soft. The extra time allows for more caramelization, too—remember, brown is the color of taste. We smoke with wood for the first hour, then let them cook for another hour without adding more wood. Three chunks of water-soaked wood is our mantra if you're using an electric smoker. For a charcoal smoker, if you're using hardwood lump charcoal, three chunks will do as well.

Smoked onions may be pickled; put into soup, sauce, or pasta; placed on a pizza or tart; or stuffed. SERVES 4

SUGGESTED WOOD: Alder, fruitwood, mesquite, oak, or pecan

1 pound onions of your choice
2 tablespoons olive oil
Coarse kosher or sea salt and freshly ground black pepper to taste

1. Prepare an indirect fire in a smoker.

2. Remove the outer papery skins of the onions and cut off the tops and bottoms. The onions may be sliced or left whole. Place in a disposable aluminum pan, drizzle with the

Smoking for Compliments, er, We Mean Condiments

Like most women, we prefer to do two or three things at once, so while we're smoking ribs or chicken, we also smoke bell peppers, garlic, shallots, and/or chiles.

Smoking softens and bronzes, but doesn't char, these vegetables. They take on a smoky aroma and flavor that is luscious in sauces, soups, stews, casseroles—you name it.

Preparing these vegetables can be as easy as drizzling them with olive oil and placing them whole in disposable aluminum pans. Or you can prepare them in the following ways:

Bell peppers: We like to smoke red, green, and yellow bell peppers for color and flavor. Simply remove the stems, then cut the peppers in half and remove the seeds. Place the halves in a disposable aluminum pan and drizzle with olive oil.

Chiles: You can smoke any fresh chile, such as Anaheim, jalapeño, serrano, or even Hatch chiles from New Mexico (we especially love those!). Remove the stems and seeds, then place in a disposable aluminum pan and drizzle with olive oil.

Garlic: To smoke a whole head of garlic, use a paring knife to slice off about 1/2 inch of the pointed top to reveal the individual cloves. Trim the bottom of the bulb, if necessary, so that it sits evenly. Set the head in a special garlic smoker or disposable aluminum pan and drizzle with olive oil. To smoke individual cloves of garlic, choose the biggest ones. Peel, then thread onto wooden skewers (no need to soak first) and drizzle with olive oil. Place the skewers right on the smoker grate over indirect heat.

Shallots: To smoke a whole shallot bulb, use a paring knife to slice off about 1/2 inch of the pointed top. Trim the bottom of the bulb so that it sits evenly. Set the shallot in a garlic smoker or disposable aluminum pan and drizzle with olive oil.

SUGGESTED WOOD: Hickory, maple, mesquite, or oak

Smoke the vegetables at 225 to 250°F until soft and aromatic, 1 to 1 1/2 hours. Obviously, a whole bulb of garlic will take longer to smoke and soften than individual cloves, so keep checking after 1 hour in the smoker. Don't smoke these veggies for more than 1 1/2 hours. Too much smoke can result in a bitter flavor.

Let the vegetables cool, roughly chop, and place in labeled sealable plastic bags. They will keep in the freezer for up to 6 months. Then it's time to do another batch.

olive oil, and toss to coat. Season with salt and pepper and place in the smoker. Cover and smoke at 225 to 250°F until supple to the touch, golden brown, and fragrant. Sliced onions will take 30 to 40 minutes, whole onions about 1 hour (or more).

3. Remove from the smoker. If there are juices in the pan, drizzle them over the onions or reserve for another use. Serve immediately.

Crowning Glories

Smoked onions pair well with:

Smoked Pork Loin *(page 404)*

Smoked Leg of Lamb *(page 438)*

Smoked Brisket *(page 356)*

Honey-Basted Smoked Onions: This steps up the caramelization process of the onions and is very pretty. Cut 4 sweet onions in half. Remove the outer papery skins and trim off the tops and bottoms. Place the onions cut side up in a disposable aluminum pan and smoke as directed above. Meanwhile, in a small saucepan, combine 2 tablespoons each honey, unsalted butter, and balsamic vinegar and cook over low heat until the butter melts and everything is blended together. Begin liberally basting the onions with the mixture every 15 minutes. Smoke for about 1 hour total. When done, the onions will be a burnished color and perfect to serve on a platter with the main dish of your choice. **SERVES 8**

Smoked (or Grilled) Onion Marmalade: In a word, divine! This simple marmalade is a must to make if you plan on smoking or grilling onions. Spread it over a butterflied pork loin roast, roll up the pork, and then roast in the oven, rotisserie cook, or smoke for a signature dish. The marmalade is also good spooned over a block of cream cheese for an easy, but again signature, appetizer to serve with crackers. Roughly chop 2 smoked or grilled medium-size onions and place in a medium-size bowl. Add 2 tablespoons each balsamic vinegar and honey. Season with coarse kosher or sea salt and freshly ground black pepper to taste. **MAKES ABOUT 2 CUPS**

Smoked Onion Tart: Let's make this so easy that your 10-year-old princess-in-training could make it. Begin with a base crust, which can be defrosted frozen puff pastry placed on a cookie sheet or a store-bought Boboli. Spread 4 ounces softened Boursin or crumbled goat cheese over the crust. Thinly slice 2 grilled or smoked medium-size onions and scatter over the cheese. Bake in a preheated 350°F oven until the crust is crisp, 20 to 25 minutes. Then decide whether you want to invite three people to share this with you or not. **SERVES 1 TO 4**

Pickled Brewpub Smoked Onions: Great with a pub lunch of crusty bread, sweet butter, aged cheddar cheese, and a glass of microbrewed beer, this recipe works with either grilled or smoked onions, but they need to be very small. Peel (which is the hardest part) about 2 pounds small white boiling or creamer onions about 1 inch in diameter. Place in a disposable aluminum pan and toss or spray with 2 tablespoons olive oil. Smoke as directed above until tender. While the onions are smoking, combine 5 cups malt vinegar, 1/2 cup sugar, 2 tablespoons pickling spices, 5 whole cloves, and 10 to 12 black peppercorns in a large saucepan. Bring to a boil, then continue to boil for 5 minutes. Set aside to cool. Combine the smoked onions and pickling liquid in a plastic tub or a large glass jar with a tight-fitting lid. Let steep in the refrigerator for at least 3 weeks before using. These onions will keep in the refrigerator for up to 6 months. **SERVES 4 TO 6**

Grilled Peppers

During the 1980s, the world of peppers exploded for many Americans. Most of us had grown up thinking a pepper meant green bell pepper, the immature vegetable that, if left on the plant, would mature and turn red, yellow, or orange. All of a sudden, there were jalapeños and even hotter poblano, serrano, and Thai chiles. What a revelation. People were having hot flashes all over the place and loving it.

Both sweet bell peppers and hot chiles taste great on the grill. However, bell peppers are treated more as a vegetable dish, while chiles are used more as a flavoring or part of a dish. Both are easy to grill.

To grill the smaller chiles, pierce them lengthwise with a double set of skewers to keep them from spinning as you turn them. **SERVES 6**

2 red bell peppers, seeded and cut lengthwise into 1-inch wedges
2 green bell peppers, seeded and cut lengthwise into 1-inch wedges
2 yellow or orange bell peppers, seeded and cut lengthwise into 1-inch wedges
1/4 cup olive oil
Fine kosher or sea salt and freshly ground black pepper to taste

1. Prepare a hot fire in a grill. Place an oiled perforated rack directly over the fire.

2. In a large bowl, combine all the ingredients and toss well to coat the peppers. Place the peppers on the grill rack and grill until scorched and blackened underneath, about 5 minutes. Turn and grill for another 3 to 4 minutes, until blackened.

3. Transfer to a platter, taste for salt and pepper, and serve hot or at room temperature.

Crowning Glories

Grilled peppers can be tossed into hot pasta with more olive oil and minced garlic or served with:

Rustic Aioli *(page 104)*

Bacon-Wrapped Turkey Fillets *(page 223)*

Grilled Italian sausage *(page 365)*

Cheesy Grilled Pepper Boats: This fanciful recipe is a great vegetarian appetizer to make when you can find good-quality fresh bell peppers in different colors. (If you grow your own, experiment with what you have on hand.) Stem, seed, and quarter 4 bell peppers. Place the pepper "boats" skin side down on a baking sheet. In a medium-size bowl, combine one and a half 8-ounce packages softened cream cheese; 1/2 cup chopped fresh basil; 1/2 cup chopped fresh Italian parsley; 1/2 cup pitted, drained, and chopped oil- or brine-cured Kalamata olives; and freshly ground black pepper to taste. Dollop a big spoonful of the cream cheese mixture into each boat. Sprinkle 1 tablespoon freshly grated Parmesan or Pecorino Romano cheese on top. Transfer the boats to an oiled grill grate, cover, and grill until the bottoms are scorched and the cheese has melted, 4 to 5 minutes. Serve hot.

SERVES 8

Grilled Chiles Rellenos with Baby Shrimp: We love these grilled with a kiss of smoke (see page 13), but they're delicious just simply grilled. Cut a slit lengthwise in each of 6 poblano chiles. Remove the seeds and ribs, taking care not to tear the peppers. In a medium-size bowl, combine one 15-ounce can drained and rinsed Great Northern or cannellini beans, 1 pound peeled and deveined baby shrimp, one 8-ounce package cubed Boursin or other herb and garlic cream cheese, 1/4 cup salsa, 1 teaspoon chili powder, and 1 teaspoon ground cumin. Gently spoon the filling into the peppers. Use toothpicks across the opening of each pepper so they don't gape open during cooking. Place the stuffed peppers on an oiled perforated grill rack and brush with olive oil. Place the rack

BBQ Queens' Grilled Antipasto Platter

For a big backyard do, nothing beats a platter of antipasto. Let color and shape be your guide in selecting a variety of our grilled vegetables. One of the timesaving benefits to this kind of appetizer is that some of the foods can be from the pantry. We particularly like artichoke hearts, an assortment of oil- or brine-cured olives, capers, sardines, anchovies, tapenade (black olive paste), and pickled vegetables.

For even more effortless entertaining—so you don't chip a nail or frizz or flatten your hairdo as your guests are arriving—grill everything the day before, let the foods bathe in the olive oil overnight in the refrigerator, and assemble everything right before your party. For presentation, a rectangular platter is very pretty with rows of each item. An oval or round platter looks great with the items arranged in wedge shapes. SERVES 10 TO 12

3 cups Queen-Size Spiced Olives (right)

3 cups grill-roasted red bell peppers cut into strips (3 or 4 peppers; see right)

3 cups canned fire-roasted whole tomatoes (we like the Muir Glen brand), drained

3 cups mixed grilled seasonal vegetables

Extra virgin olive oil

4 ounces Pecorino Romano cheese

Crusty bread, sliced

On a large platter, arrange a row of each vegetable. Drizzle lightly with olive oil, then shave the cheese evenly over the top. Serve with the bread.

in the grill, cover, and cook over a hot fire for 2 minutes. Turn, using grill tongs, grill for another 2 minutes, and turn again. Keep turning and cooking until the peppers are soft and slightly charred on all sides. Serve hot, passing extra salsa at the table. **SERVES 6 AS AN APPETIZER OR LIGHT LUNCH**

Queen-Size Spiced Olives

Of course we use queen-size olives for a royal antipasto platter. "The olives are dandy in martinis or Manhattans, too," says Karen's King Richard. MAKES ABOUT 5 CUPS

One 42-ounce jar pimento-stuffed queen-size green olives, undrained
40 whole cloves
16 large cloves garlic, sliced
3 tablespoons distilled white vinegar
4 teaspoons red pepper flakes
4 teaspoons dillweed

In a large saucepan, combine all the ingredients and bring just to a boil. Remove from the heat. Using a canning funnel, divvy up the olives, juice, and flavorings into clean sterile jars or return to the original jar. Let cool, then tighten the lid(s). Refrigerate for at least 2 weeks to let the flavors blend. They will keep in the refrigerator for 2 to 3 months.

Grill-Roasted Peppers

To grill-roast peppers, place them on an oiled perforated grill rack. Set the rack directly over a hot fire, turning the peppers until they blister and burn on all sides, 15 to 20 minutes. Place the peppers in a paper bag to steam. When cool, remove the skins, seeds, and membranes with a paring knife.

Pick a Peck of Grilled Peppers Sauce: When garden-fresh peppers of all varieties dominate your garden or farmers' market, turn them into this satisfying sauce. Grilling and caramelizing the peppers and onions deepens and enriches their natural sweetness. Use 1/2 to 3/4 cup of this sauce over 1 pound cooked penne and garnish with chopped fresh

Italian parsley and freshly grated Parmesan cheese, spread it over a wheel of warm Brie for an appetizer, or enjoy it on a grilled chicken sandwich. Brush with olive oil 6 seeded and sliced bell peppers, 6 seeded and sliced chiles (any variety), and 3 sliced onions. Grill as directed above until scorched and softened. Process together in a food processor, in batches if necessary, until roughly chopped. Heat 1/2 cup olive oil in a large saucepan over medium-high heat. Add 1/4 cup chopped garlic and cook, stirring, for 1 minute. Add the chopped grilled vegetables and cook, stirring, until much of the liquid from the vegetables has cooked away and they are just beginning to brown, about 10 minutes. Serve hot or let cool, then transfer to a covered container and refrigerate until ready to serve. This sauce will keep in the refrigerator for up to 2 weeks and in the freezer for up to 6 months. **MAKES ABOUT 2 CUPS**

Grilled Potatoes

It's amazing now to think that people had to be persuaded even to try the lowly potato. Indigenous to South America, the earliest potatoes were very small and multicolored: purple, yellow, orange, red, russet, and brown. Like other plant varieties from the New World, the potato was brought back to Europe by the 1550s but didn't really catch on at first. It took the efforts of an ill-fated queen to make it happen.

In the mid-1700s, Antoine-Auguste Parmentier, courtier to Marie Antoinette, decided that the potato was the plant that would ease the famine that still plagued rural France. However, the wily Parmentier didn't start an educational campaign to promote the potato. He didn't tell people the potato was good for them. Instead, he posted guards around his potato fields, which encouraged people to steal this apparently precious vegetables and try cooking them at home. He encouraged Marie Antoinette to wear potato flowers in her hair, the "milk mustache" ploy of the eighteenth century.

So we're taking a tip from Parmentier and we're telling you not to try any of these recipes. No matter which varieties you *don't* try—russet, red, sweet, Yukon Gold, fingerling, or new—potatoes are superb grilled.

Use small new or fingerling potatoes, or cut larger potatoes into wedges, for faster grilling. Just make sure the wedges or whole potatoes are uniform in size. If not, you'll need to adjust the cooking time to accommodate the different sizes. Crusty charred potato wedges taste wonderful unadorned, or you can fancy them up with a dipping sauce on the side. SERVES 6

2 large russet potatoes, scrubbed and cut lengthwise into 1/2-inch wedges

2 large red potatoes, scrubbed and cut lengthwise into 1/2-inch wedges

2 large sweet potatoes, scrubbed and cut lengthwise into 1/2-inch wedges

1/4 cup olive oil

1 tablespoon seasoned salt

1 tablespoon seasoned pepper

1. Prepare a hot fire in a grill. Place an oiled grill rack directly over the fire.

2. In a large bowl, combine all the ingredients and toss well to coat the potatoes. Place the potatoes on the grill rack. Because of the olive oil, there may be flare-ups, so close the grill lid quickly. After a minute or so, open the lid. Cook for about 40 minutes total, turning the potatoes with long-handled spatulas about every 10 minutes so they brown evenly. Serve hot or at room temperature.

Crowning Glories

Grilled potatoes are delicious alone or dolloped with:

Rustic Aioli *(page 104)*

Ranch dressing, sour cream, or caviar

Smoked Tomato and Basil Butter *(page 177)*

Grilled Whole Potatoes: Scrub 6 potatoes, rub each with 1/2 teaspoon olive oil, and sprinkle lightly with garlic salt. Place the potatoes directly over a medium-hot fire, close the lid, and grill-roast for about 45 minutes, turning halfway through the cooking time. The potatoes should be browned and fork tender. If your fire is too hot and the potatoes are burning instead of browning, move them to the indirect side of the grill and close the lid. Continue cooking until done. Serve like a baked potato. **SERVES 6**

Rustic Grill-Roasted Potato Salad: Here we offer a potato salad that may be served hot or at room temperature. Add ingredients such as roasted red peppers, chopped celery, hard-boiled eggs, capers, or artichoke hearts, and it goes from simple and satisfying to sublime. Place 6 whole grill-roasted potatoes, sliced or chunked, skins on or off, in a large bowl. Sprinkle with 3 tablespoons tarragon vinegar. Add 1 sliced small red onion, 1 minced garlic clove, 1/4 cup chopped fresh Italian parsley or chervil, and 3 tablespoons olive oil. Season with kosher or sea salt and freshly ground black pepper to taste. Lightly toss to blend. Serve hot. If refrigerated, let the salad come to room temperature before serving. **SERVES 8 TO 10**

Grilled Red Potato and Fennel Salad: Slightly charred from the grill, sweet from the fennel, and salty from the olives, this potato salad is great to take on a tailgate picnic—or snarf down as a one-dish meal. In a large bowl, toss together 2 pounds quartered small red potatoes; 2 trimmed, quartered, cored, and thinly sliced medium-size fennel bulbs; and 1/4 cup olive oil. Season lightly with kosher or sea salt and freshly ground black pepper. Grill as directed above, turning often, until blistered, slightly blackened, and tender, about 15 minutes. Transfer to a bowl and toss with another 1/4 cup olive oil; 1/4 cup red wine vinegar; 1/3 cup pitted, drained, and chopped oil- or brine-cured Niçoise olives; and 1/3 cup chopped green onions. Taste for salt and pepper. This salad can be made several hours ahead and kept at room temperature or a day ahead and refrigerated, tightly covered. Let come to room temperature before serving. **SERVES 4 TO 6**

Grilled Vegetable Tart: This is an elegant yet easy dish to make for company. Serve it with your favorite green salad for lunch or a light supper. No one will suspect that you've used leftovers. This tart can be made ahead and frozen, then rebaked at 350°F for 30 to 45 minutes. Preheat the oven to 400°F. Unfold 1 defrosted sheet frozen puff pastry and roll out to a 15 x 12-inch rectangle on a sheet of waxed paper. Transfer to an 11 x 8-inch tart pan with a removable bottom, allowing the excess pastry to flop over the edges. Fold the excess pastry inside so that it is even with the rim of the pan. Press the pastry against the side of the pan, then, using a sharp knife, trim the pastry even with the edge of the pan except at the corners. Pinch the pastry at the corners so that it extends 1/4 inch above the pan. Spread 6 cups mixed grilled or smoked vegetables (such as 2 cups each chopped or sliced potatoes, onions, and mushrooms) over the pastry. Drizzle 1 tablespoon olive oil over the vegetables. Season with kosher salt and freshly ground black pepper to taste. Bake for 15 minutes. Remove from the oven and top with 6 crumbled slices crisp-cooked bacon and 1 cup shredded Gouda cheese. Return to the oven and bake until the top is browned and the pastry is cooked through, 15 to 20 minutes more. Cut the tart into 6 or 8 pieces and serve hot or warm. SERVES 6 TO 8

Skewered Potatoes (and Other Vegetables)

This is the BBQ Queens' take on the classic Italian dish of roasted potatoes with olive oil and rosemary. Use sturdy, fresh rosemary branches (from the produce section of the grocery store, a nursery, or your own garden) as skewers for small new potatoes. This recipe also works with coins of zucchini and yellow summer squash; peeled and deveined large shrimp; or chunks of chicken, beef, lamb, or pork (all uncooked before grilling). SERVES 4 TO 6

12 fresh rosemary branches, about 8 inches long
12 small new potatoes, cooked in boiling water for 5 minutes and drained
Rosemary, Garlic, and Lemon Baste (page 68)

1. With your fingers or a paring knife, remove the leaves from the bottom two-thirds of each rosemary branch. Save some of the leaves to make the baste. Thread 3 potatoes on each branch. Brush with the baste and place each skewer on a tray to rest for 30 minutes. Reserve the remaining baste.

The Ungrilled Potato Salad

As accompaniments to grilled or smoked foods, potatoes add a mellow note—a transition from the smoky, caramelized, carbon flavors of meats to the sharp, bitter flavors of vegetables and the sour taste of vinaigrette on salads. Atkins diet or no, potatoes give the palate a little rest—comfort food for the overwhelmed.

One of our favorite ways to eat potatoes with grilled or smoked foods is in potato salad, and one of our *favorite* favorites is Tapas-Style Potato Salad from our book *Fish & Shellfish, Grilled & Smoked* (The Harvard Common Press, 2002). It's just potatoes, mayonnaise, minced garlic, and chopped Italian parsley, but oh how good! You also can't go wrong with the simple combination of cooked russet or Idaho potatoes, mayonnaise, chopped green onions, salt, and ground white pepper.

We like to dress our salads while the potatoes are still warm, making them absorb more of the dressing. We agree with food writer Laurie Colwin's comment that, "It is always wise to make too much potato salad. Even if you are cooking for two, make enough for five."

Here's one of our *new* favorite potato salads.

2. Prepare a hot fire in a grill.

3. Grill the skewers for 4 to 5 minutes per side, brushing a few times with the baste, until the potatoes get grill marks and are tender all the way through. Serve hot or at room temperature.

Crowning Glories

These potatoes are delicious dipped into:

Food Processor or Blender Hollandaise *(page 97)*

Roasted Red Pepper Aioli *(page 110)*

Extra virgin olive oil

Creamy Dijon Potato Salad for a Crowd

When you have lots of hungry folks to feed, this is the potato salad to do it. With just a slight mustard flavor, it is rich and oh so satisfying. **SERVES 14 TO 16**

9 medium-size russet potatoes
4 hard-boiled large eggs, peeled and roughly chopped
1/2 cup thinly sliced celery
1/3 cup chopped onion
2 cups mayonnaise
1/4 cup Dijon mustard
2 teaspoons fine kosher or sea salt
2 teaspoons freshly ground black pepper
1 teaspoon sweet Hungarian paprika

1. In a large pot with enough water to cover, boil the potatoes until tender, about 30 minutes. Drain and let cool slightly. When cool enough to handle, peel and cube to yield 9 cups. Place in a large bowl and stir in the eggs, celery, and onion.

2. In a medium-size bowl, whisk the mayonnaise, mustard, salt, pepper, and paprika together until smooth. Add to the potato mixture, tossing gently. Serve slightly warm, or cover and refrigerate until ready to serve. It will keep in the refrigerator for up to 1 week.

Grilled Antipasto Skewers: Alternate parboiled new potatoes with chunks of haloumi or fontina cheese, pitted and drained oil- or brine-cured Kalamata or Niçoise olives, and wedges of roasted red peppers from a jar on rosemary skewers. Brush with the baste and grill for 4 to 5 minutes per side. Serve hot or at room temperature, on a platter. **SERVES 4 TO 6**

Grilled Sweet Potato and Red Onion Skewers: This is a colorful appetizer. Peel 2 medium-size sweet potatoes and cut into 1 1/2- to 2-inch chunks. Parboil for 7 to 8 minutes, until just able to pierce with a fork. Cut 2 medium-size red onions into wedges. Alternate sweet potato chunks and onion wedges on the rosemary skewers. Brush with the baste and grill for 4 to 5 minutes per side. Serve hot or at room temperature, on a platter. **SERVES 4**

Smoked Potatoes

When our working tiaras get a little dingy from barbecue smoke, sometimes we think about getting away from all that fire and becoming one of those outrageous and sexy Sweet Potato Queens. That's when we throw a couple of sweet potatoes on the smoker.

But don't limit yourself to sweet potatoes. You can also smoke new, red, russet, Idaho, fingerling, or Yukon Gold potatoes as a stand-alone side dish or in place of boiled or baked potatoes in all kinds of salads, casseroles, and soups. SERVES 4

SUGGESTED WOOD: **Apple, cherry, hickory, or pecan**

1 pound potatoes of your choice, scrubbed
Olive oil
Coarse kosher salt and freshly ground black pepper to taste

1. Prepare an indirect fire in a smoker.

2. Prick the potatoes all over with a fork or paring knife. Rub with olive oil and season with salt and pepper. Smoke the potatoes until tender, about 1 hour for fingerling potatoes, $1^{1}/_{2}$ hours for medium-size potatoes, and 2 hours for large potatoes. Serve just like baked or roasted potatoes.

Crowning Glories

Smoked potatoes pair well with smoked or rotisserie main dishes such as:

Smoked turkey *(page 226 or 230)*
French Tarragon Rotisserie Chicken *(page 218)*
Rotisserie Leg of Lamb *(page 431)*

Smoked Potato and Aioli Gratin: We used to get weak in the knees when we thought about Harrison Ford (Judith) or Sean Connery (Karen). Now we feel a sinking spell coming on when we taste this dish in our imaginations—or even better, in real life. Whoooeee! If you love smoke and you love garlic, this is just the thing to serve with a grilled, smoked, or rotisserie leg of lamb. Smoke 6 medium-size potatoes until almost tender, about $1^{1}/_{2}$ hours. Peel, slice as thinly as you can, and place in a bowl. Gently fold in Rustic Aioli (page 104) if you're feeling gutsy or White Truffle Aioli (page 105) if you're feeling flush until well blended. Transfer to a greased casserole dish and bake at 400°F until golden, about 15 minutes. **SERVES 6 TO 8**

BBQ Queens' Smoked Potato Casserole: We made up this recipe after we had traveled to do a cooking class and discovered we had forgotten to bring shredded hash browns for our Absolutely Decadent Potatoes (which cookbook author and food scientist Shirley Corriher loves). We did have leftover potatoes we had smoked for the previous class, so voilà!—a new recipe was born. And it's durn good. We think Shirley, the Queen of Culinary Questions, will approve. Preheat the oven to 300°F. Coat a 2-quart baking dish with nonstick cooking spray. Slice 1 1/2 pounds smoked potatoes (you can peel them if you wish, but it's not necessary) and place half in the prepared dish. Drizzle with 2 tablespoons melted unsalted butter and 1/3 cup heavy cream. Sprinkle with 1 tablespoon minced fresh chives, 1/2 teaspoon garlic powder and fine kosher or sea salt and freshly ground black pepper to taste. Repeat the layering one more time. Bake until browned and bubbling, about 2 hours. Ahhh. **SERVES 6 TO 8**

Smoked Potato Soup: Comfort food from the hearth. Smoke 4 large russet or Idaho potatoes. Cut in half and scoop out the flesh; discard the skins. In a medium-size saucepan, melt 1/2 cup (1 stick) unsalted butter over medium-high heat. Add 1/2 cup finely chopped onion and 1/2 cup all-purpose flour and cook until the onion is transparent, about 3 minutes. Whisk in 4 cups whole milk and cook until smooth and thickened. Add the potato pulp and season with kosher salt and freshly ground black pepper to taste. Stir in 6 slices crumbled crisp-cooked bacon, 4 chopped green onions, and 1 cup finely shredded sharp cheddar cheese. Cook over medium heat until heated through, 6 to 8 minutes. Stir in one 8-ounce container sour cream (lowfat is okay) and heat for 1 minute. Serve garnished with more crumbled bacon, chopped green onions, and shredded cheese, if desired. **SERVES 8 TO 10**

Smoked New or Fingerling Potato Platter: This is a great no-brainer appetizer. You can smoke the potatoes ahead of time, then warm them up in the oven before serving. For tailgating, put the hot potatoes in an empty beverage cooler to keep them warm. Smoke 2 to 3 pounds small new or fingerling potatoes as directed above and arrange them on a platter. Accompany with bowls of sour cream, tapenade (black olive paste), chopped red or green onions, crumbled crisp-cooked bacon, or whatever tickles your fancy. Guests pick up a small potato and dip. **SERVES 8 TO 12**

Grilled Summer Squash

A hot fire, a brush of olive oil, a sprinkling of fresh herbs, a bit of salt, and careful attention add up to great grilled summer squash. Zucchini or yellow summer squash are a great choice when you're in a hurry because they cook so fast and can take on many different flavorings almost instantly. If you have squash in your garden, this is a handy recipe to have on hand. One day you have tiny baby squash in your garden, and the next day they're big old torpedoes. If you garden, pick 'em when they're little. If you're buying them, get the smallest ones you can find.

Don't be afraid to get a good char on summer squash, similar to caramelizing in a sauté pan, but don't cook them so long that they get mushy. If you want to cut the squash into rounds or large chunks, you may want to use a grill wok instead. SERVES 4

4 small to medium-size zucchini or yellow summer squash
1/4 cup olive oil
1/2 cup chopped fresh herbs, such as Italian parsley, chives, and/or tarragon
Fine kosher or sea salt and freshly ground black pepper to taste

1. Prepare a hot grill.

2. Trim the tops and bottoms of the squash. Slice about 1 inch thick on the diagonal or lengthwise. Place in a bowl or sealable plastic bag, add the oil, and toss until well coated.

3. Place on the grill (or a perforated grill rack) and cook for 7 to 10 minutes, turning every 2 to 3 minutes. The squash are done when they're charred and slightly soft but not mushy.

4. Transfer to a bowl and toss with the fresh herbs. Season with salt and pepper and serve.

Crowning Glories

Grilled summer squash is delicious all by itself or topped with or added to:

Smoked Tomato and Basil Butter *(page 177)*
Grilled Asparagus Frittata *(page 118)*
Grilled Pizza with Caramelized Onions and Brie *(page 180)*

Grilled Gazpacho: This is the ultimate gazpacho, with flavors to hit every one of your taste buds. Use leftover grilled vegetables or grill everything fresh. Smoked vegetables will fare well in this soup, too. Place 2 large onions cut into 1/2-inch-thick slices, 2 medium-size zucchini trimmed and cut lengthwise into 1/4-inch-thick strips, and 1 large red and 1 large green bell pepper cut in half and seeded on an oiled perforated grill rack, skin side down. Brush the vegetables with a little olive oil on both sides. Grill over a hot fire, turning once, until slightly charred and caramelized, about 5 minutes per side. Remove from the grill and set aside to cool. When cool enough to handle, peel most of the blistered skins from the peppers. Place the grilled onions, zucchini, and peppers in a food processor and pulse several times until coarsely chopped. Transfer to a large bowl and add 8 seeded and diced large ripe tomatoes; 3 peeled, seeded, and diced medium-size cucumbers; 8 minced garlic cloves; 1/2 cup fresh sourdough bread crumbs; 1/2 cup red wine vinegar; and 2 cups tomato juice. Stir with a wooden spoon. Add 2/3 cup olive oil, stir, and season with fine kosher or sea salt and freshly ground black pepper to taste. Cover and refrigerate for 4 to 5 hours. To serve, ladle into 6 shallow soup bowls and garnish with 1/2 cup lowfat sour cream and a mixture of 1/4 cup chopped green onions; 2 tablespoons finely diced red onion; and 1/4 cup peeled, seeded, and chopped cucumber. **SERVES 6**

Char-Grilled Baby Summer Squash: Judi and Bill Walker are great friends of the Adlers. Karen was introduced to this simple and scrumptious platter of grilled baby squash while vacationing at the Walkers' Michigan summerhouse. Oil a perforated grill rack and set aside. In a large bowl, place 2 pounds mixed baby summer squash (pattypan, zucchini, yellow, or whatever is small and fresh from the market). Drizzle with 2 to 3 tablespoons olive oil and season with 1 teaspoon coarse kosher or sea salt and 1 teaspoon lemon pepper seasoning. Place the vegetables on the rack and grill, turning several times, until they are softened and have grill marks, 15 to 20 minutes. **SERVES 6 TO 8**

Vegetable Ribbon Skewers

This is really a girly-girl recipe, with ruffles and ribbons and the need for a gentle touch. If you have a mandoline, this is the time to get it out. If not, slice the veggies as thinly as humanly possible; otherwise, the slices will crack as you try to thread them onto the skewers. Try carrot, zucchini, and yellow squash ribbons for a wow-y effect on a platter. Use medium to large, evenly shaped vegetables to get the best-looking slices. These veggies are very appealing to kids, but you might have to help them slide the veggies off the skewers. SERVES 4

2 large, thick carrots, peeled
1 medium-size zucchini, ends trimmed
1 medium-size yellow summer squash, ends trimmed
12 wooden skewers, soaked in water for at least 30 minutes before grilling
1 recipe Lemon Butter Drizzle (page 87)
Chopped fresh herbs, such as basil, Italian parsley, and/or cilantro, for garnish

1. Using a very sharp knife or mandoline, cut the vegetables lengthwise into paper-thin slices. Immediately (so the slices don't dry out and crack), gently gather each slice into a large ruffle and thread it onto a skewer, 3 slices per skewer. Place carrots on one, zucchini on another, and so on, so that every person will have three different vegetable skewers. Place the skewers on a baking sheet and brush with the drizzle.

2. Prepare a hot fire in a grill.

3. Grill the skewers for 3 to 4 minutes per side, turning once, until grill marks appear. Brush with more of the drizzle, garnish with the chopped herbs, and serve hot or at room temperature.

Smoked Squash

Both winter and summer squash get the royal treatment from slow smoking. Winter squash taste great in its own right from the smoker, but summer squash is better combined with onions, eggplants, and tomatoes.

We prefer to par-cook winter squash until it's almost tender before throwing it in the smoker. We leave small acorn squash whole but cut larger squash such as butternut into big pieces. Then we place the squash cut side down on a baking sheet lined with aluminum foil or parchment paper and bake in a preheated 350°F oven for 30 to 45 minutes before putting it in the smoker. Alternatively, you can microwave it, cut side down, in a glass baking dish for about 10 minutes on high before smoking.

Summer squash can just be cut into rounds or cut in half lengthwise before going in the smoker.

Sometimes we like to sprinkle a rub on squash—BBQ Queens' All-Purpose Rub (page 49), Spicy Orange Rub (page 51), and Zesty Sugar and Spice Rub (page 52) are good—before smoking. And as we keep saying, we like to smoke with leftovers in mind. SERVES 4

SUGGESTED WOOD: **Apple, cherry, hickory, or pecan**

4 medium-size zucchini or yellow summer squash, ends trimmed and sliced into rounds or cut in half lengthwise; 1 large butternut, hubbard, delicata, or sweet dumpling squash, peeled, seeded, cut into pieces, and par-cooked (see headnote); or 4 small acorn squash, left whole and par-cooked

Olive oil or other vegetable oil

Kosher or sea salt and freshly ground black pepper to taste

1. Prepare an indirect fire in a smoker.

2. Arrange the squash cut side up in a disposable aluminum pan. Drizzle with oil and season with salt and pepper. Cover and smoke at 225 to 250°F until tender, about 1 hour. Serve hot.

Crowning Glories

Smoked squash pairs well with smoked or rotisserie main dishes such as:

Smoked turkey *(page 226 or 230)*

Rosemary-Scented Grilled Butterflied Chicken *(page 205)*

Smoked Leg of Lamb *(page 438)*

Smoked Vegetable Confit: Also called a *bayaldi* of vegetables, this is a casserole of sliced summer squash, tomatoes, and onions that is slow smoked to perfection. It's a great dish to put on with something else you're smoking. Or make two confits, one to serve, the other to make wonderful sandwiches (see below). In a square disposable aluminum pan, arrange 1 thinly sliced red or Spanish onion on the bottom and scatter 2 chopped garlic cloves and 1 teaspoon each chopped fresh thyme and rosemary over the onion. Slice the following vegetables 1/4 inch thick, then alternate them in the pan in rows, so that the slices are standing up: 2 small yellow summer squash, 2 small zucchini, 4 yellow pear tomatoes, 4 Roma tomatoes, and 2 Japanese eggplants. Drizzle with olive oil, then sprinkle with coarse kosher or sea salt and ground white pepper to taste. Cover and smoke at 225 to 250°F, basting with olive oil every 30 minutes, until the vegetables are tender, 2 1/2 to 3 hours. **SERVES 6**

Smoked Vegetable Confit on Country Bread with Tapenade and Goat Cheese: This open-faced sandwich is the biggest reason we make Smoked Vegetable Confit (above). If you're a low-carb person, you can skip the country bread and just enjoy the confit topped with a slice of goat cheese and a dollop of tapenade (black olive paste). On a slice of toasted artisanal or country bread, spread 1 tablespoon tapenade. Top with confit and a 1/4-inch-thick slice fresh goat cheese. Place on a baking sheet and toast in a preheated 450°F oven until the cheese begins to melt, 3 to 4 minutes. Eat with a knife and fork. **SERVES 1**

Linguine with Smoked Butternut Squash, Fresh Sage, and Morel Cream Sauce: Smoke an extra butternut squash to use in this recipe. With its autumnal colors and hint of wood smoke, this is one great dish. Dried morels are much more readily available in the produce section of grocery stores than ever before. Soak 1/4 cup dried morels in warmed brandy to cover for 15 minutes. Cook 1 pound linguine according to the package directions. While the pasta is cooking, melt 2 tablespoons unsalted butter in a large skillet over medium-high heat and cook 12 fresh sage leaves for 1 minute. Remove from the pan and set aside. Add 4 green onions cut on the diagonal into 1-inch pieces to the pan. Cook, stirring, until tender, about 3 minutes. Stir in the morels and brandy and cook for 1 minute, then stir in 1 cup heavy cream. Cut the smoked squash into bite-size pieces and stir into the cream sauce. When the linguine is done, drain the pasta and add it to the skillet, tossing to blend the pasta and sauce. Serve garnished with sage leaves. **SERVES 6 TO 8**

Smoked Spicy Acorn Squash: Here's a great side dish to serve with smoked turkey for Thanksgiving. Cut 3 medium-size acorn squash in half horizontally and remove the seeds. Brush the cut sides with vegetable oil, then cover with aluminum foil. Poke a few holes in the foil to let the smoke permeate the flesh. Place cut side (foil side) down on the smoker rack and smoke at 225 to 250°F until tender, about 2 hours. When ready to serve, melt 6 tablespoons (3/4 stick) unsalted butter in a small skillet and stir in 1 teaspoon ground cinnamon, 1/4 cup firmly packed dark brown sugar, and 1/2 teaspoon chili powder. Drizzle over the cut surfaces of the squash and serve. (Alternatively, remove the squash flesh from the skin and place in a large bowl. Combine the butter mixture with the squash. Place in a shallow baking dish and bake at 350°F until heated through, about 30 minutes.) **SERVES 6**

Grilled Tomatoes

Summer and tomatoes are synonymous. In Missouri and Kansas, we keep our fingers crossed that a couple of our garden tomatoes are ripe by the Fourth of July. To grill the first tomatoes of the season would be sacrilegious. The peasant comes out in us, and we want plain and simple sliced tomatoes, sprinkled only with a bit of kosher or sea salt and freshly ground black pepper. However, by the time August rolls around and the vines are laden with the bright red love fruit, we are ready to give tomatoes the royal barbecue treatment.

Hearty beefsteak, Better Boy, Better Girl (our favorite!), and other meaty tomato varieties are best for the heat of the grill. Overripe tomatoes will get too mushy, so stay with ripe but firm tomatoes for the best results. SERVES 4

2 large ripe but firm beefsteak tomatoes
Extra virgin olive oil
Fine kosher or sea salt and freshly ground pepper to taste

1. Prepare a hot grill.

2. Remove the stemmed cap from the tomatoes. Cut them into 3/4-inch-thick slices and lightly coat with olive oil to keep them from sticking to the grill grate. Place directly over the heat and cook for 2 to 3 minutes per side. Transfer to a platter and season with salt and pepper. Serve immediately.

Crowning Glories

Grilled tomatoes are delicious served with:

Citrus Caesar Vinaigrette ***(page 84)***

Roasted Red Pepper Aioli ***(page 110)***

Grilled Green Onions and Red Onion Slices ***(page 138)***

Grilled Tomato "Burgers" with Herbed Cream Cheese: Here's a creative take on the common burger. Combine one 8-ounce package softened cream cheese, 1 minced garlic clove, 2 tablespoons chopped fresh basil, and 1 tablespoon snipped fresh chives in a small bowl. Slice open 4 kaiser rolls and grill until warm. Spread the inside of each roll with the herbed cream cheese mixture. Place 2 grilled tomato slices on each bun and serve. **SERVES 4**

Grilled Goat Cheese Tomatoes: This recipe is in our book *Fish & Shellfish, Grilled & Smoked* (The Harvard Common Press, 2002). It is simply divine and must be included again. Because you don't flip the tomatoes to grill on both sides, a thinner slice works well here. Drizzle eight 1/2-inch-thick slices beefsteak tomatoes with olive oil and seasoned with kosher or sea salt and freshly ground black pepper to taste. Top each tomato with 1 ounce crumbled fresh goat cheese. (You may also use crumbled feta cheese or blue cheese or cubed Boursin, herbed cream cheese, or mozzarella.) Sprinkle with chopped fresh herbs, if you like. Grill directly over a hot fire or on a grill rack until the tomatoes are warmed through and the cheese has melted, 6 to 8 minutes. Serve hot. **SERVES 4**

Grilled Roma Tomatoes with Anchovy, Garlic, and Parsley: This is an easy appetizer served with grilled country bread or as part of an antipasto platter. You need 1 1/2 pounds Roma tomatoes. Cut each tomato lengthwise into 6 wedges and arrange in a disposable aluminum pan. In a small bowl, whisk together 1 tablespoon anchovy paste, 2 minced garlic cloves, 1/4 teaspoon red pepper flakes, 1/4 cup chopped fresh Italian parsley, and 1/2 cup olive oil. Drizzle over the tomatoes and toss to blend. Place the pan on the grill, cover, and cook, turning once, until the tomatoes are tender, wrinkled, and slightly browned, 20 to 30 minutes. Serve warm or at room temperature. **SERVES 6**

Grilled Tomatoes Provençal: This is a terrific recipe for tomatoes that are not quite at their peak. If using vine-ripened fruits, make sure they are not too ripe. Core 4 large tomatoes, then cut in half lengthwise. Lightly coat the cut sides with olive oil and set aside. Combine 4 to 6 minced garlic cloves, 1/2 cup fresh bread crumbs, 1/4 cup chopped fresh

Italian parsley, and 2 to 3 tablespoons freshly grated Pecorino Romano cheese in a small bowl. Set aside. Grill the tomatoes as directed above, cut side down, for 2 to 3 minutes. Transfer to a serving platter. Sprinkle with the crumb mixture and drizzle with olive oil. Serve warm or at room temperature. **SERVES 4**

Indoor Grilled Tomatoes Provençal: Heat 1 tablespoon olive oil in a large skillet over high heat. Place the tomatoes cut side down in the skillet and cook for 2 to 3 minutes. Sprinkle with the crumb mixture and drizzle with olive oil. **SERVES 4**

Smoked Tomatoes

Smoking fresh tomatoes is simplicity itself. It's one of those fairly effortless ways to ratchet up the flavor in your food—without fat grams or carbs. And we love that! Smoking tomatoes leaves you plenty of time for other important tasks—such as retouching your makeup, getting a pedicure, or making a hair appointment (or, let's get real here, baking the dessert, setting the table, cleaning the house, carpooling, etc.).

The BBQ Queens love to smoke several tomatoes at once, then peel, seed, and dice them for immediate use, as in the addictive Smoked Tomato and Basil Butter (page 177), and for later on. Because they're already cooked, they freeze well for up to 3 months. You can eat them plain with just a drizzle of olive oil and a sprinkling of sea salt, stuff and smoke them, or smoke and chop them for use in other recipes. If you have vegetarian guests, this is a great barbecue dish that you can serve in place of smoked meat, as in Smoked Greek Stuffed Tomatoes (page 164).

We don't recommend smoking smaller cherry-type tomatoes, because they smoke to mush and are fiddly to eat. We also don't recommend heirloom tomatoes, whose different and delicate flavors, colors, and textures would be overpowered by the smoke. SERVES 4

SUGGESTED WOOD: Apple, hickory, pecan, or a combination

4 large beefsteak tomatoes, cored, or 12 Roma tomatoes, cut in half lengthwise

1. Prepare an indirect fire in a smoker.
2. Place the tomatoes cut side up in a disposable aluminum pan. Cover and smoke at 225 to 250°F until the tomatoes have softened and the skins begin to crack, 1 to 1½ hours. Serve immediately.

Two Smokin' Salsas

Salsa is the number-one-selling condiment in the United States. Why? Because it tastes so good! It's best when chunky and more like a relish. The BBQ Queens offer two of their favorites here: a southwestern-flavored salsa and an authentic Mexican one.

Charred Tomato-Chipotle Salsa

Adapted from a recipe by Paul Kirk, author of *Paul Kirk's Championship Barbecue* (The Harvard Common Press, 2004), this is big-flavor, lowfat, low-carb cooking at its finest. We love it with grilled fish steaks, such as salmon, swordfish, tuna, or halibut. MAKES ABOUT 1 1/2 CUPS

1 cup wood chips or chunks, mesquite or flavor of your choice
3 dried arbol or cayenne chiles
1 cup boiling water
1 large ripe tomato
1/2 medium-size onion, peeled
1 large clove garlic, peeled
2 canned chipotle chiles in adobo sauce, plus 2 teaspoons adobo sauce
2 tablespoons chopped fresh cilantro
2 teaspoons fresh lime juice
Fine kosher or sea salt and freshly ground black pepper to taste

1. Soak the wood chips or chunks in water for at least 30 minutes. (If you're using chunks, soak for at least 1 hour.) Place the dried chiles in a heatproof bowl, pour the boiling water over them, and let stand for 30 minutes. Drain the chiles. Discard the stems and seeds and finely chop the chiles.

2. Prepare a medium-hot fire in a grill. Lightly brush the grill grate with vegetable oil. When the coals have ashed over, add the wood chips. Place the tomato stem side down in the center of the grill. Cover and cook, turning occasionally, until softened and charred all over, about 10 minutes. Meanwhile, thread the onion and garlic clove onto a skewer.

Place the skewer at the edge of the fire, where it is cooler. Cook, turning occasionally, until lightly browned and just softened, about 8 minutes.

3. Core, peel, and seed the tomato. In a blender or food processor, combine the tomato pulp with the chopped chiles, smoked garlic and onion, chipotles and adobo sauce, cilantro, and lime juice. Process until just a little chunky. Season with salt and pepper. Serve immediately, or cover and refrigerate for up to 1 week.

Grilled Tomatillo Salsa

Complex and smoky, this green salsa goes well with grilled fish and chicken. You can also use it as a dip for tortilla chips or a chunky dressing for a taco salad. **MAKES ABOUT 1 1/2 CUPS**

8 tomatillos
1 small onion, peeled
4 cloves garlic
2 Anaheim chiles
1/2 bunch fresh cilantro
1/4 teaspoon sugar
2 tablespoons olive oil

1. Prepare a medium-hot fire in a grill.

2. On an oiled perforated grill rack, grill the tomatillos, onion, garlic, and chiles, turning occasionally, until softened and charred in places, 8 to 10 minutes. Let cool briefly. When cool enough to handle, husk the tomatillos and peel the garlic. Stem and seed the chiles.

3. Place the grilled vegetables in a food processor along with the cilantro, sugar, and olive oil and process until just a little chunky. Use immediately or spoon into a small jar with a tight-fitting lid. This salsa will keep in the refrigerator for up to 3 days.

Crowning Glories

Smoked tomatoes are delicious served with:

Smoked Leg of Lamb *(page 438)*

Grilled Eggplant Roll-Ups with Feta-Olive-Lemon Filling *(page 126)*

Smoked Corn, Ham, and Hominy Casserole *(page 123)*

Smoked Tomato Grits: When we saw this recipe from Atlanta chef Doug Turbush in the *Atlanta Journal-Constitution*, we knew we had to try it. These are grits to the max! And their wonderful flavor comes from pureed hickory-smoked tomatoes, jalapeños, onion, and garlic. Turbush uses a stovetop smoker (see page 34). We've adapted his recipe as follows. Using hickory, smoke as directed above 4 ripe Roma tomatoes cut in half lengthwise, 4 peeled garlic cloves, 1 thickly sliced white onion, and 2 stemmed jalapeños. Puree the vegetables in a blender or food processor. In a large pot, whisk together 1 cup half-and-half, 1 cup heavy cream, 3 tablespoons tomato paste, and the smoked puree and bring to a boil. Wearing oven mitts, gradually whisk in 3/4 cup yellow stone-ground grits, reduce the heat to low, and simmer, stirring frequently with a wooden spoon, until the mixture thickens, about 10 minutes. Season with kosher salt and freshly ground black pepper to taste. If you like, divide the grits among 4 plates and top with grilled scallops (see page 289). **SERVES 4**

Smoked Greek Stuffed Tomatoes: This is a great main dish for a hot summer day. Use textured vegetable protein (TVP) or crumbled firm tofu in place of ground lamb or beef for a vegetarian entrée. Core 8 large beefsteak tomatoes, scoop out most of the pulp with a grapefruit spoon, transfer the pulp to a food processor, and puree. Heat 2 tablespoons olive oil in a large skillet over medium-high heat. Add 2 minced garlic cloves, 1 pound ground lamb or beef, and the tomato puree and cook until the meat is no longer pink, 8 to 10 minutes. Transfer to a bowl and stir in 1/4 cup dry white wine, 1/4 cup dry bread crumbs, 1 lightly beaten large egg, 2 teaspoons dried oregano, 1/2 cup crumbled feta cheese, and 2 tablespoons finely chopped fresh Italian parsley. Place the tomato shells in a disposable aluminum pan and spoon in the filling. Cover and smoke at 225 to 250°F until warmed through, about 1 hour. Drizzle with a little olive oil and serve warm or at room temperature. Or cover and refrigerate and serve cold. **SERVES 8**

Fettuccine with Smoked Garlic and Tomatoes: Here's another great way to use smoked tomatoes and 1 whole smoked garlic clove. Cook 1 pound fettuccine according to the package directions. Peel, seed, and chop 4 large smoked tomatoes and place in a large bowl. Squeeze the softened smoked garlic clove out of its skin into the bowl. Add 1/4 cup extra virgin olive oil. When the pasta is done, drain and toss with the garlic and tomato mixture. Sprinkle 1/4 cup shredded fresh basil leaves on top, toss again, and season with coarse kosher or sea salt and freshly ground black pepper to taste. **SERVES 4 TO 6**

Smoked Tomato with Tuna, Lemon, and Herbs: Smoke for leftovers, we always say. With a tomato you've already smoked, make the best tuna salad you've ever had. Combine 1 peeled, seeded, and chopped smoked tomato and one 6.5-ounce can drained water-packed tuna in a medium-size bowl. Stir in the grated zest of 1 lemon, 2 tablespoons fresh lemon juice, 1/2 teaspoon dried oregano, 1 minced garlic clove, and 1/4 cup extra virgin olive oil and gently combine. Spread on toasted slices of baguette or use to make a yummy tuna salad sandwich. **MAKES ABOUT 1 CUP**

If You Can't Grill with the Equipment You Love, Love the Equipment You Grill With

I have grilled under just about every circumstance imaginable, including a fancy country inn where there was no kitchen, only a fireplace in the room. I went down to the local grocery, bought all the foods I could find that could be cooked on a grill-type arrangement, hurried back to my room to put papers down in front of the fireplace, and cooked right there. It was wonderful to have something delicious to eat when the dining accommodations could not provide it: grilled tortillas; tomatoes, sliced and grilled; red peppers, red onions, and chicken pieces, all cooked over the aromatic open fire.

—Alice Waters, *Chez Panisse Menu Cookbook* (Random House, 1982)

Stir-Grilled Vegetables

Stir-grilling vegetables is simplicity itself. You need veggies cut into small pieces, a sealable plastic bag, a marinade of some kind, a grill wok, wooden stir-grilling paddles or grill spatulas, and a grill.

Basically, you marinate the veggies in the bag, then pour the contents of the bag into the grill wok, which is placed over the sink or in the grass outside (no mess). Then you cook the veggies on the grill, stirring with the paddles or spatulas, until the food is done to your liking. For more information on this technique, see Stir-Grilling 101 (page 32).

You'll be amazed at the extra flavor stir-grilling can impart to the most basic of foods. Once you've tried this recipe, get creative and try other tender vegetables, such as zucchini, yellow summer squash, cherry or grape tomatoes, onions of all kinds, sugar snap peas, and more.

Do not slice the vegetables too thinly, or they may fall through the holes in the grill wok. The only other mistake is to put too much in the wok. Fill it only halfway so you have room to stir and turn the vegetables with the paddles. You don't want any of those delicious veggies to escape, now, do you?

Serve stir-grilled veggies with any grilled food, such as chicken breasts, Italian sausage, fish fillets or steaks, lamb or pork chops, beefsteaks, fajitas, or pork tenderloin. SERVES 4

1 large red bell pepper, seeded and sliced
1 large green bell pepper, seeded and sliced
1 large red onion, sliced
1/4 cup olive oil
Garlic salt and freshly ground black pepper to taste

1. Place the vegetables in a large sealable plastic bag and drizzle with the olive oil. Seal the bag and turn to blend. (This recipe can be prepared to this point up to 24 hours ahead and refrigerated.)

2. Prepare a hot fire in a grill and spray a grill wok lightly with olive oil.

3. Turn the bag of marinated vegetables into the prepared grill wok so the extra oil drains away. Place the wok on a baking sheet and take it out to the grill. Place the wok over direct heat and stir-grill, tossing the mixture with wooden paddles or grill spatulas, until all the vegetables have browned and the onions are tender and caramelized, 10 to 15 minutes. Transfer to a bowl, season with salt and pepper, and bring to the table to serve with other grilled fare.

Crowning Glories

Stir-grilled veggies are delicious topped with:

Freshly grated Parmesan or Asiago cheese

Chopped fresh herbs

Crumbled feta or fresh goat cheese

Thai-Style Stir-Grilled Vegetables in Lemongrass Marinade: It's amazing how much flavor you get from the very lowfat, aromatic Lemongrass Marinade (page 74). The tofu takes on the flavor of the marinade and adds body to this dish, so don't leave it out. Serve this with Texas pecan rice or the more fragrant jasmine rice. As a finishing touch, use Vietnamese Drizzle (page 87) over all. In a sealable plastic bag, place 8 ounces firm tofu cut into 1-inch pieces, 4 ounces sliced fresh mushrooms, 1 pint grape or cherry tomatoes, one 8-ounce can drained sliced water chestnuts, 1/2 cup green onions cut on the diagonal into 1-inch pieces, and 1 cup cored and chopped Napa cabbage. Pour the marinade over everything, seal the bag, and toss to coat. Marinate in the refrigerator for 30 minutes, then drain and stir-grill as directed above until everything is lightly browned, about 15 minutes. Serve over rice, garnished with toasted sesame seeds. **SERVES 4**

Stir-Grilled Balsamic-Thyme Vegetables: This is a wonderful side dish to serve with steak for a hearty meal or with an omelet for a light supper. Place 1 pint cherry tomatoes, 2 sliced small zucchini, 2 sliced small yellow summer squash, 1 cup sliced red onion, and 1 cup seeded and sliced red bell pepper in a sealable plastic bag. Pour 1 recipe Balsamic-Thyme Vinaigrette (page 84) or 1 cup bottled balsamic vinaigrette over everything. Seal the bag and toss to cost. Marinate at room temperature or in the refrigerator for at least 30 minutes or up to 2 hours. Drain and stir-grill as directed above until everything is lightly browned, about 15 minutes. Serve hot as a side dish or tossed with hot pasta, then sprinkled with freshly grated Parmesan cheese or crumbled feta cheese. **SERVES 6**

Stir-Grilled Summer Squash with Fresh Herbs: This stir-grilled dish is as delicately flavored as it is colored, with the pale yellows and greens of fresh summer squash and zucchini. The BBQ Queens love it with grilled, rotisserie, or smoked chicken or fish during the dog days of summer. Place 4 sliced small zucchini, 4 sliced small yellow summer squash, 1 bunch green onions cut on the diagonal into 1-inch pieces, and 1/2 cup olive oil in a sealable plastic bag. Seal the bag and toss to coat. Refrigerate, if you wish, until ready to grill, up to 12 hours. Drain and stir-grill as directed above until everything is lightly browned, about 15 minutes. Transfer the vegetables to a large serving bowl and toss with 1/2 cup mixed chopped fresh herbs, such as tarragon, chives, and basil. Season with fine kosher or sea salt and freshly ground black pepper to taste. Serve hot or at room temperature. **SERVES 6**

Mediterranean-Style Stir-Grilled Mushrooms and Olives: Mushrooms are made for vegetable medleys. Use this recipe as a blueprint for adding your favorite Mediterranean flavors, such as lemon zest, artichoke hearts, red bell peppers, and even a bit of anchovy. Scent it with your favorite herbs. If you have any leftovers, use them as a topping for pizza. In a large bowl, combine 1 pound trimmed fresh mushrooms (such as cremini or portobellos), 1 slivered red onion, 3 minced garlic cloves, 1/2 cup pitted and drained oil- or brine-cured olives (such as Kalamata), 2 tablespoons chopped fresh Italian parsley, 1 teaspoon chopped fresh rosemary, 2 tablespoons olive oil, 1 tablespoon fresh lemon juice, and coarse kosher or sea salt and freshly ground black pepper to taste. Toss to blend evenly. Drain (reserving any remaining liquid) and stir-grill as directed above for about 10 minutes, tossing the vegetables two or three times during the grilling. Just as the vegetables are almost done, close the grill lid for a minute or two to heat thoroughly. Transfer to a platter, drizzle with the reserved liquid, and serve hot or at room temperature. This is also wonderful with 1 to 2 cups grilled shrimp (see page 289) or shredded grilled chicken (see page 191) added and served over pasta or rice. **SERVES 4 TO 6**

Stir-Grilled Red Bell Peppers with Garlic and Thyme: This dish is adapted from a recipe by famed Parisian chef Joël Robuchon, who has so many shining Michelin stars he has to wear shades. We love it paired with smoked goat cheese. Combine 4 seeded and sliced red bell peppers, 5 minced large garlic cloves, 2 teaspoons chopped fresh thyme, 3 tablespoons olive oil, and 1 tablespoon sherry vinegar in a sealable plastic bag and marinate in the refrigerator for 30 minutes or up to 24 hours. Drain and stir-grill as directed above until the peppers are tender and caramelized, 15 to 20 minutes. Serve hot, at room temperature, or cold. **SERVES 4**

Stir-Grilled Asian Lettuce Wraps: Once you get the hang of stir-grilling, you can really get creative. In this update of a sophisticated Chinese, Thai, or Vietnamese restaurant classic, most of the filling is grilled, then wrapped in lettuce leaves. These are "tacos" for a new generation! This recipe is adapted from one by Rebecca Miller, marketing director for our beloved Whole Foods Market in Overland Park, Kansas. In a large bowl, mix together 1 pound firm tofu cut into pieces or 1 pound ground turkey or chicken, 1 tablespoon toasted sesame oil, 4 minced garlic cloves, 2 tablespoons finely minced fresh ginger (if using a microplane, you don't need to peel), 2/3 cup teriyaki sauce, and 1 bunch green onions cut on the diagonal into 1/2-inch pieces. Cover and refrigerate until ready to cook, up to 8 hours. Arrange Boston lettuce leaves on a platter. Place 1 cup shredded carrot, 1 cup peeled and seeded cucumber cut into matchsticks, and 1 cup daikon (Oriental radish) cut into matchsticks on the platter. Drain the tofu mixture and stir-grill as directed above for 15 to 20 minutes, until the tofu is browned (or the ground meat is cooked through) and the green onions are tender and caramelized. Transfer to a serving bowl and serve with the platter of toppings and a small bowl of hoisin sauce. To make a wrap, spoon some of the cooked filling into the center of a lettuce leaf, sprinkle on the toppings of your choice, and dip the wrap in hoisin sauce. **SERVES 4**

Smoked Soft Cheese

Smoked soft cheese—such as fresh goat cheese, Boursin, or cow's milk cream cheese—is a revelation. The first time we tried smoking cheese was for a cooking class in St. Louis. Our smoked goat cheese was such a hit that we've been making it ever since.

At first we worried that the soft cheese might melt in the process, but we were wrong! At 225 to 250°F, even a soft cheese stays firm and gets deliciously smoky. From trial and error, we have found that it's essential to spray or brush the cheese with olive oil before smoking; if you don't, an unappetizingly dry brown skin will form on the cheese. And you want sort of a blank-slate mild cheese, not one that's assertively flavored. After all, the smoky flavor will dominate.

We recommend cutting either fresh goat cheese or full-fat or lowfat cream cheese into smaller pieces before smoking: the more surface area, the more smoke flavor.

And let us nag you yet again: smoke for leftovers! Use smoked soft cheese as a sandwich spread or dip, or as the basis for unique pasta dishes or green salads. Try blending a combination of cheeses together, such as feta and cream cheese, or grated Romano and cream cheese—get the picture? SERVES 8

SUGGESTED WOOD: Hickory or pecan

1/4 cup olive oil
1/4 cup seasoned dry bread crumbs
1/4 teaspoon kosher salt
1/4 teaspoon freshly ground black pepper
8 ounces fresh goat cheese or cream cheese, cut into 8 pieces

1. Prepare an indirect fire in a smoker.

2. Pour the olive oil into a small shallow bowl. Combine the bread crumbs, salt, and pepper in another shallow bowl. Dip each piece of cheese into the olive oil, then into the crumb mixture to coat completely. Place the cheese in a disposable aluminum pan, put the pan in the smoker, and close the lid. Smoke at 225 to 250°F for 1 hour. Serve warm. Smoked soft cheese will keep in the refrigerator for up to 1 week.

Crowning Glories

Smoked soft cheese is delicious served atop a vinaigrette-dressed salad or as a topping for or part of:

Grilled Pizza *(page 179)*

Savory Breads on the Grill *(pages 176–178)*

Grilled Vegetable Platter with Fresh Basil Vinaigrette *(page 129)*

Crunchy Smoked Cheese Dip: Spread the cheese evenly in an 8-inch square disposable aluminum pan. Drizzle with olive oil to cover. Combine 1/4 cup seasoned dry bread crumbs, 1/4 teaspoon kosher salt, and 1/4 teaspoon freshly ground black pepper and sprinkle over the cheese. Smoke for 1 hour, then serve in a bowl, with pita chips for dipping. **MAKES ABOUT 1 CUP**

Smoked Goat Cheese Salad: This is our favorite way to enjoy smoked goat cheese. Rinse and pat dry 4 cups salad greens and place in a large bowl. Whisk together 1 tablespoon Dijon mustard, 1 minced garlic clove, 1/4 cup white wine vinegar, 1/2 cup olive oil, and coarse kosher or sea salt and freshly ground pepper to taste. Drizzle over the greens and toss. Arrange the greens on 4 salad plates and top each salad with a round of smoked cheese. **SERVES 4**

Smoked Cheesy Smashed Potatoes: See why we say to smoke for leftovers? In a medium-size saucepan, bring 4 peeled and diced large baking potatoes and enough water to cover to a boil. Continue to boil until the potatoes are tender, about 15 minutes. Drain and transfer to a serving bowl. With a potato masher or fork, smash the potatoes with 6 to 8 ounces smoked cream cheese. Add some finely chopped green onions if you wish. Season with sea salt and freshly ground black pepper to taste. Serve hot. **SERVES 4 TO 6**

Homemade Vegetable Crisps with Smoky Cheese Dip: Technicolor chips and a smoky cheese dip will banish the thought of regular chip-and-dip offerings. Use a mandoline to slice these vegetables paper-thin: 1 peeled large baking potato, 1 peeled large sweet potato, 1 peeled large beet. Place on paper towels and pat dry. Heat about 2 inches of vegetable oil in a high-sided skillet, electric skillet, or deep fryer to 350°F. Fry the vegetables in batches until golden. Remove from the oil with a slotted spoon and drain on paper towels. Immediately season with coarse kosher or sea salt and freshly ground black pepper to taste. Make the dip by mashing together 8 ounces smoked goat or cream cheese, 1 cup sour cream, and fine kosher or sea salt and freshly ground black pepper to taste. Serve the crisps on a platter, nestled around a bowl of the dip. **SERVES 4**

Smoky Beef and Asparagus Saddlebags: Here's a great make-ahead appetizer for when the check really is in the mail. In a medium-size bowl, mix together 8 ounces softened

There Is Nothing Like a Dame Royal Feast

On a fall night in a Chicago suburb, the BBQ Queens were summoned to provide a sumptuous grilled and smoked dinner for 50 members and guests of the Windy City's chapter of Les Dames d'Escoffier. We had been invited to do our BBQ Queen gig—complete with the four queen waves—at the behest of our good friend Dame Rose Kallas, who always thinks BIG. Dame Betty Hughes from Weber-Stephen provided a couple of charcoal water smokers for the smoking, and Rose had a huge outdoor grill—as well as a large lower-level catering kitchen. We arrived in Chicago a day ahead to get started. We knew we better be good because the partygoers included top chefs, cookbook authors, and culinary corporate gurus. We were up to the challenge and received rave reviews for our dinner. Rose hired a kicky bluegrass band, and everyone enjoyed the evening in her wonderful garden, twinkling with votives.

Grilled Pizza with Caramelized Onions and Brie *(page 180)*

Smoked Goat Cheese Salad *(page 170)*

Apple-Smoked Turkey *(page 233)*

Smoked Pork Ribs *(page 384)*

Blue Cheese Coleslaw *(page 79)*

A Platter of Fresh Tomatoes *(page 206)*

Dessert bar

smoked cream cheese, 2 tablespoons prepared horseradish, 1/4 cup crumbled crisp-cooked bacon, and 2 tablespoons finely chopped fresh Italian parsley. Plunge 24 long chive stems into boiling water to blanch for 10 seconds, then remove with a slotted spoon and let cool on paper towels. Cook 24 thin asparagus spears in the boiling water just until crisp-tender, drain, and set aside. Slice a cooled 2-pound Grilled Beef Tenderloin (page 336) into 24 thin slices. Lay the slices out on a sheet of waxed or parchment paper. Spread each slice with about 1 tablespoon of the cream cheese mixture. Place an asparagus spear in the center of each slice and roll up. Tie each roll together with a chive stem. Place on a tray, cover, and refrigerate until ready to serve, up to 24 hours. **SERVES 6 TO 8**

Smoked Semisoft Cheese

Once you've got the hang of Smoked Soft Cheese (page 169), it's time to spread your wings a bit. There's a whole semisoft cheese world of mozzarella, Edam, Gouda, Brie, Monterey Jack, and even pepper Jack out there waiting to be smoked.

Serve one of your home-smoked cheeses as part of a cheese platter, use it to make incredible grilled cheese sandwiches, or blend it into a gourmet pasta salad. And notice how smoked mozzarella really jazzes up that classic salad of tomato, mozzarella, and fresh basil.

Don't worry about the cheese melting in the smoker. At 225 to 250°F, even a soft cheese stays firm and gets deliciously smoky. Just make sure you spray or brush the cheese with olive oil before smoking; if you don't, an unappetizingly dry brown skin will form. And again, go for a cheese with a milder flavor. There's no point in overpowering the rich nuttiness of a wonderful Gruyère by laying on the smoke, but bring on those shy, self-effacing Goudas and Edams for a smoky makeover.

We recommend using small rounds or blocks of semisoft cheese. Cut larger portions of cheese into smaller wedges before smoking. The more surface area that's exposed, the more smoke flavor the cheese will have. SERVES 4

SUGGESTED WOOD: Hickory or pecan

1/4 cup olive oil

Four 3-ounce wedges semisoft cheese, such as mozzarella, Gouda, Edam, or Monterey Jack

1. Prepare an indirect fire in a smoker.

2. Pour the olive oil into a small bowl. Dip each cheese wedge into the olive oil to coat completely. Place in a disposable aluminum pan and smoke at 225 to 250°F for 1 hour.

Crowning Glories

Smoked semisoft cheese is delicious served atop a baked potato, stirred into a vegetable soup, or served with:

Grilled Onions *(page 137)*

Grilled Tomatoes *(page 159)*

Grilled Boneless, Skinless Chicken Breasts *(page 191)*

Smoky Grilled Cheese Sandwich: Let your smoked cheese cool, then thinly slice or shred it to use in grilled cheese sandwiches like this one. Butter one side of each of 2 slices of good-quality rustic bread. Place 1 slice buttered side down in a skillet. Add the smoked semisoft cheese and 1 tablespoon each smoked shallot, bell pepper, and garlic (see page 140) or jarred roasted red peppers and pitted, drained, and sliced oil- or brine-cured Kalamata olives. Place the remaining bread slice on top, buttered side up. Cook over medium-high heat for 3 to 4 minutes per side, turning when the bread is a deep golden brown. **SERVES 1**

Smoked Mozzarella, Tomato, and Fresh Basil Salad: *Insalata Caprese*, look out! Here comes the new kid on the block. Slice 2 large ripe tomatoes and 2 small rounds of smoked mozzarella. Alternate the tomato and mozzarella slices on a small platter or 2 individual salad plates. Drizzle with your favorite vinaigrette and garnish with chopped fresh basil. **SERVES 2**

Smoked Gouda and Tomato Pasta Salad: We love a salad similar to this that you can get at Whole Foods Market. Have ready 8 ounces finely shredded smoked Gouda and 2 chopped smoked tomatoes (see page 161). Cook 1 pound penne pasta according to the package directions. Drain, saving some of the pasta water, and return to the pot. Drizzle with about 2 tablespoons olive oil and quickly toss. Sprinkle on the shredded Gouda and toss again until the cheese melts into the pasta. Stir in the tomatoes and 1 teaspoon dried basil. Season with coarse kosher or sea salt and freshly ground black pepper to taste. If the pasta is too dry, add about 1/4 cup of the reserved pasta water to the mixture to moisten it. Serve immediately. **SERVES 6 TO 8**

Planked Semisoft Cheese

Besides 8-minute shrimp from the stovetop smoker (see page 37), this is our other favorite appetizer. First of all, it has a colorful, rustic appeal. Second, it's easy to do. And third, the gently aromatic flavor breathes a little life into that somewhat tired (but still yummy) appetizer of baked Brie.

You can use any semisoft cheese you like, from Brie to Camembert to Gouda. But we don't recommend giving this treatment to a really fine cheese, which is best savored in its natural state.

You can use any type of untreated wood plank. Because we live in Kansas City, a grilling and smoking mecca, we can get all kinds of planks, including alder, cedar, pecan, hickory, and maple. The aromatic flavor you get from a plank is mild, so be assured that whatever kind of wood you use, you will get very tasty results.

There are two tricks to planking. The first is to make sure you soak your plank in water for at least 1 hour before using. The second trick is to use a dual-heat fire—a hot fire on one side of the grill and a medium fire on the other. See Planking 101 (page 42) for the whole process. You also have to be able to close the lid for your food to cook, so a grill without a lid is not an option. (You can plank in the oven, however.)

We love to accompany this appetizer with cocktail crackers of all kinds, sliced baguettes, or sliced artisanal breads. SERVES 12

One 12 x 10 x 1-inch plank, maple or wood of your choice, soaked in water for at least 1 hour before grilling

One 1-pound wheel of Brie, about 8 inches in diameter

1/2 cup lingonberry preserves or chutney

1. Prepare a dual-heat fire in a grill (see headnote).

2. Place the plank on the grill rack over the hot fire until it begins to char and pop. Turn the plank over and move to the medium fire. Carefully place the Brie on the charred side of the plank. Cover and cook until the Brie begins to soften and melt, about 10 minutes.

3. Serve on the plank, with lingonberry preserves spooned on top of the cheese.

Crowning Glories

This is also delicious topped with:

Smoked Tomato and Grilled Red Onion Relish ***(page 324)***

Charred Tomato-Chipotle Salsa ***(page 162)***

Southwestern-Style Grilled Corn Relish ***(page 120)***

Maple-Planked Cheese with Tricolored Peppers: This is a colorful and flavorful appetizer, perfect for casual entertaining. In a large sealable plastic bag, toss 1 cup each yellow, green, and red bell pepper strips with 1/4 cup olive oil. Transfer to a large grill wok or disposable aluminum pan. Prepare a dual-heat fire (see headnote). Grill the pepper strips on the hot side of the grill, turning, until softened and slightly charred, about 10 minutes. Set aside. Using a maple plank, plank a 1-pound wheel of Brie, Camembert, or Gouda as directed above. Arrange the peppers over and around the cheese and serve hot with assorted crackers and breads. **SERVES 12**

Hickory-Planked Cheese with Dried Cranberry Relish: This is great cold-weather fare to nibble when you're sitting by the fire. Serve as an accompaniment to a simmering soup or stew, or serve during the holidays with oven-toasted slices of *panettone*, the Italian holiday sweet bread. Make up a batch of relish by combining 1/3 cup chopped onion, 1/3 cup seeded and chopped jalapeños, 1/3 cup seeded and chopped green bell peppers, 1/3 cup sweetened dried cranberries, and 1/3 cup canned cranberry relish. Add fresh lemon juice to taste. Using a hickory plank, plank a 1-pound wheel of Brie, Camembert, or Gouda as directed above. Spoon the relish on top of the cheese and serve hot with assorted breads and crackers. **SERVES 12**

Savory Breads on the Grill

As an accompaniment to any grilled or smoked food, a savory bread satisfies like nothing else. A loaf-type sandwich cooked on the grill puts a fresh and delicious new spin on a casual dinner—with minimal cleanup and no hot oven to heat up your kitchen. Wrap these breads in aluminum foil and place on the grill (or in the oven) while your other food is cooking. If you have a hot fire, place the breads as far away from the heat source as possible (off to the side away from the coals in a charcoal grill or on a shelf in a gas grill) or turn them frequently to prevent scorching.

Wood-Grilled Flatbreads

Even packaged pita bread tastes better when you grill it with a kiss of smoke. You want a heavier smoke from hickory, pecan, or mesquite, because these breads hit the grill for only a few minutes. SERVES 8

8 pita breads, 1 long loaf Afghan bread, 8 flour tortillas, or other wheat-based flatbreads

Olive oil

1. Prepare a hot fire in a grill and set up for grilling with a kiss of smoke (see page 13), using hickory, pecan, or mesquite.

2. Brush the breads on both sides with olive oil and place on a baking sheet to take outside. Have a sheet of aluminum foil ready to cover the baking tray full of warm breads.

3. Grill each flatbread until grill marks appear on both sides, about 2 minutes per side, turning with grill tongs. Place the grilled breads on the baking sheet and cover with foil to keep warm. Serve warm.

Cheesy Italian Pesto Bread

This is a delicious alternative to garlic bread and wonderful served with any kind of salad topped with grilled chicken, beef, or seafood. SERVES 8

1 large loaf Italian or French bread
Olive oil
Two 4-ounce jars prepared pesto
1 cup freshly grated Parmesan or Asiago cheese

1. Prepare a medium-hot fire in a grill or preheat the oven to 350°F.

2. Slice the bread in half lengthwise. Brush olive oil on the cut surfaces. Spread the pesto on the bottom half of the loaf and sprinkle the cheese over the pesto. Replace the top half of the loaf and brush the top with olive oil. Wrap in aluminum foil and grill or bake until warmed through, 10 to 15 minutes.

Rustic Bread with Smoked Tomato and Basil Butter

We love this flavored butter on just about anything, but slathered on a crusty loaf of bread and warmed on the grill is the best. SERVES 4 TO 6

1 large loaf Italian or French bread

SMOKED TOMATO AND BASIL BUTTER

2 large smoked tomatoes (see page 161), peeled, seeded, and chopped
1 cup (2 sticks) unsalted butter, softened
1/2 cup chopped fresh basil
Kosher or sea salt and freshly ground black pepper to taste

Olive oil

1. Prepare a medium-hot fire in a grill or preheat the oven to 350°F.

2. Slice the loaf in half lengthwise.

3. To make the butter, mash together the tomatoes, butter, and basil in a medium-size bowl. Season with salt and pepper. Spread the butter on the cut surfaces of the bread and reform into a loaf. Brush the top with olive oil. Wrap in aluminum foil and grill or bake until warmed through, 10 to 15 minutes.

Fiesta Bread

Grill Gal Judi Walker says people go crazy over this bread, so you might want to make a double batch. We agree! SERVES 6 TO 8

3/4 cup (1 1/2 sticks) unsalted butter, softened
2 teaspoons Dijon mustard
2 teaspoons onion flakes
2 teaspoons fresh lemon juice
1 teaspoon beau monde seasoning
1 tablespoon poppy seeds
1 large loaf Italian or French bread
12 to 16 slices Swiss, Monterey Jack, pepper Jack, or provolone cheese

1. Prepare a medium-hot fire in a grill or preheat the oven to 350°F.

2. In a small bowl, combine all the ingredients except the bread and cheese. Cut the bread into 1-inch-thick slices, but do not cut all the way through. Spread the butter mixture on the cut sides of the bread. Place a slice of cheese in each slit. Wrap in aluminum foil and grill or bake until warmed through and the cheese has melted, about 25 minutes.

Grilled Pizza

When the moon in the sky's like a big pizza pie, that's *amore* (or something like that). Yes, the BBQ Queens love pizza on the grill.

Although you get a better smoke flavor by using hardwood charcoal in a kettle grill, this recipe also works with a gas grill. The technique is to grill one side of the pizza first over direct heat, flip it over onto a baking sheet and add the toppings, and then carefully slide the pizza onto the grill over indirect heat to finish cooking. With a frosty glass of wheat beer served up with a wedge of lemon and a fresh fruit dessert, you can beat the heat in style. MAKES TWO 12- TO 15-INCH PIZZAS OR FOUR 8-INCH PIZZAS

FOOD PROCESSOR PIZZA DOUGH

3 1/4 cups all-purpose flour

1/4 cup semolina or cornmeal

2 tablespoons instant yeast

1 cup warm water (about 110°F)

3 tablespoons olive oil, plus more for brushing

1 tablespoon honey

1/2 teaspoon kosher or sea salt

Toppings of your choice

1. To make the dough, combine the flour, semolina, and yeast in a food processor. Combine the water, olive oil, honey, and salt in a measuring cup and stir to blend. With the machine running, pour the liquid mixture through the feed tube in a steady stream. Process until the dough forms a mass and pulls away from the side of the bowl.

2. Turn the dough out onto a floured work surface and knead by hand until smooth and elastic, about 5 minutes. Place in a large oiled bowl, turn to coat, and cover with plastic wrap. (The dough can be refrigerated for up to 3 days at this point. After that, it will taste bitter. Let the dough come to room temperature, then let it rise the final time before continuing.) Let rise in a warm place until doubled in bulk, 1 to 1 1/2 hours.

3. Divide the dough in half and press or roll each half into the desired size pizza.

4. Prepare an indirect fire in a grill (a medium-hot fire on one side and no fire on the other).

5. To grill using a pizza stone, place the pizza stone on a grill rack over medium-high heat, cover, and let preheat for 10 minutes. Sprinkle cornmeal on 2 large baking sheets and place a round of dough on each sheet. Have olive oil for brushing and the toppings ready and bring everything out to the grill. Slide a round of pizza dough onto the preheated stone. Brush with olive oil and arrange the toppings on the dough. Cover and grill until the dough is golden brown and the toppings are hot, 10 to 15 minutes.

To grill directly on the grill grate, sprinkle cornmeal on 2 large baking sheets and place a round of dough on each sheet. Have olive oil and the toppings ready and bring everything out to the grill. Brush one side of the pizza dough with olive oil and place, oiled side down, on the grill grate. Grill for 1 to 2 minutes, until you see the dough start to bubble. Brush the top side with olive oil and flip the dough, using tongs, back onto the baking sheet. Arrange the toppings on the pizza. Use a grill spatula to place it on the indirect side of the grill. Cover and grill until the toppings are hot, about 5 minutes.

Garlic-Herb Pizza Dough: Heat 2 tablespoons olive oil in a small skillet over medium heat. Add 1 tablespoon minced garlic, 1/4 teaspoon dried oregano, 1/4 teaspoon dried basil, and 1 teaspoon freshly ground black pepper. Cook, stirring, until the garlic softens, about 2 minutes. Remove from the heat, let cool, and add to the flour along with the honey mixture in step 1 above. **MAKES TWO 12- TO 15-INCH PIZZAS OR FOUR 8-INCH PIZZAS**

Grilled Pizza with Fire-Roasted Tomato and Olive Topping: This zesty, savory topping is well suited to the smoky flavor of the pizza. Chop 1 recipe Grilled Tomatoes (page 159) or one 28-ounce can drained Muir Glen fire-roasted tomatoes. Transfer to a bowl and add 1 large grill-roasted red bell pepper (see page 145) or 1/2 cup jarred roasted red peppers cut into strips; 2 tablespoons drained capers; 12 chopped small green olives; and 12 drained, pitted, and chopped oil- or brine-cured Kalamata olives. Have 1 cup finely shredded fontina cheese ready. Prepare the pizza dough as described above. Spoon the topping over the dough, spreading it evenly, then sprinkle evenly with the cheese. Grill as described above. **MAKES TWO 12- TO 15-INCH PIZZAS OR FOUR 8-INCH PIZZAS**

Grilled Pizza with Caramelized Onions and Brie: This sophisticated pizza is wonderful served as an appetizer. While the pizza dough is rising, melt 2 tablespoons unsalted butter in a large skillet over medium-low heat. Add 2 thinly sliced large onions and cook until translucent and very soft, about 15 minutes. Sprinkle with 1/2 teaspoon sugar and drizzle with 2 tablespoons port. Turn the heat to medium-high and cook, stirring, until the onions turn golden brown all over. Remove from the heat and set aside to cool. (You can make the caramelized onions up to 1 week in advance. Store them, covered, in the refrigerator.) When you're ready to grill, have 8 ounces Brie cut into small pieces ready. When the pizzas are ready for topping, use a fork to spread the caramelized onions over the dough and top with the Brie. Grill as described above. **MAKES TWO 12- TO 15-INCH PIZZAS OR FOUR 8-INCH PIZZAS**

Grilled Leaf-Wrapped Bread Sticks: Judith created a similar recipe in *Prairie Home Breads* (The Harvard Common Press, 2001) and for *Cooking Light* magazine. Somehow the combination of bread dough, beet leaf, and coarse salt tastes like black olives. Serve the bread sticks on a large earthenware platter surrounding a bowl of sour cream or extra virgin olive oil for dipping. While the pizza dough is rising, oil a perforated grill rack and set

Pizza Party with Pizzazz

Kids of all ages—and that includes our adult cooking school students—love making their own pizzas. Talk about fun! This party offers a personalized pizza for each guest. Set up a table with mounds of pizza dough and plenty of flour and allow your guests to have a hands-on cooking experience.

The pizza toppings can come from the pantry—jarred roasted red pepper strips, artichoke hearts, black beans, salsa, fire-roasted tomatoes, capers, anchovies, chutney, and tapenade (black olive paste)—and the grocery store deli or salad bar—pregrilled or smoked meats, olives, and assorted veggies. Of course, you can try some of our recipes if you'd like to offer grilled sausage, smoked onions, or even smoked mozzarella. Start with our homemade pizza dough, fire up the grill, and go from there.

Food Processor Pizza Dough *(page 179)*
Grilled Peppers *(page 145)*
Grilled Summer Squash *(page 154)*
Grilled or smoked sausage *(page 365–368)*
Fire-Roasted Tomato and Olive Topping *(page 180)*
Caramelized Onions and Brie *(page 180)*
Smoked Onions *(page 139)*
Smoked mozzarella *(page 172)*

aside. Rinse and pat dry 24 fresh beet or chard leaves, 6 to 8 inches long. After the dough has gone through its first rise, roll it out on a floured work surface to make a 12-inch square. With a serrated knife or pizza wheel, cut into twelve 1-inch-wide strips. Cut each strip in half horizontally and place each strip on the prepared grill rack. Carefully wrap a beet leaf around the middle of each strip, tucking the ends underneath the dough. Brush the strips with olive oil and sprinkle with coarse kosher or sea salt to taste. Cover with plastic wrap and let rise in a warm place until doubled in bulk, about 45 minutes. Remove the plastic wrap. Place the grill rack over a medium-hot fire, cover, and grill for 5 minutes. Brush with olive oil again and carefully turn the bread sticks if the bottoms are getting too browned. Grill for another 5 minutes, until the bread sticks are puffed and browned. Serve warm. **MAKES TWENTY-FOUR 6-INCH-LONG BREAD STICKS**

Bolani (Afghani Flatbreads with Fresh Herb Filling): These savory flatbreads, from a recipe by Latifa Raoufi (see page 332), are usually served on a platter. Instead of making the dough, Raoufi says that you can also use prepared pizza dough or defrosted frozen bread dough. While the pizza dough is rising, make the filling. In a medium-size bowl, combine 1 cup finely chopped green onions, 1 cup finely chopped fresh cilantro, 1 seeded and finely chopped small hot green chile (such as Thai or jalapeño), and 1/4 teaspoon fine kosher or sea salt. Transfer to a sieve placed over a small bowl and let drain for about 15 minutes. Discard the liquid and return the herb mixture to the bowl. Stir in 1 tablespoon vegetable oil and set aside. Punch down the dough and turn out onto a floured work surface. Using a serrated knife, cut the dough into four pieces. Roll each piece into a 12 x 8-inch oval. Place one-quarter of the filling on the top half of each oval, leaving a 1-inch border. Brush water along the border and fold the bottom half of the oval over the filling. Press the edges of the dough together. Brush each bolani with vegetable oil and grill over a hot fire until grill marks appear, 2 to 3 minutes per side. Cut each bolani in half and serve warm or at room temperature. **SERVES 4**

Grill Gals

She Grills Fast and Fabulous One-Dish Meals Menu

Super Sicilian Sandwich

Grilled Artichoke Pizza on Parmesan-Herb Crust

Blond and trim thirty-something Rozane Miceli Prather jokes that she "doesn't eat in order to run, but runs in order to eat." During the week, Rozane limits herself to short runs of just a few miles. On weekends, she tries to get in a long run of at least 10 miles. When training for a race or a marathon, she runs 25 to 30 miles a week. Rozane's teenage children, Paul and Jenna, and her husband, Dean, sometimes run along with her.

Because Rozane works from her Kansas City home as a freelance writer of travel guidebooks, she can usually start something for dinner in the afternoon. And she loves to grill. "I like to do the whole meal on the grill, if I can," she says. "The flavor is so wonderful, and you don't have to have a lot of fat to get the flavor." Her Super Sicilian Sandwich and Grilled Artichoke Pizza on Parmesan-Herb Crust are good examples of delicious foods that are low in fat, high in flavor, and easy to do. And no guilt, whether you run or not!

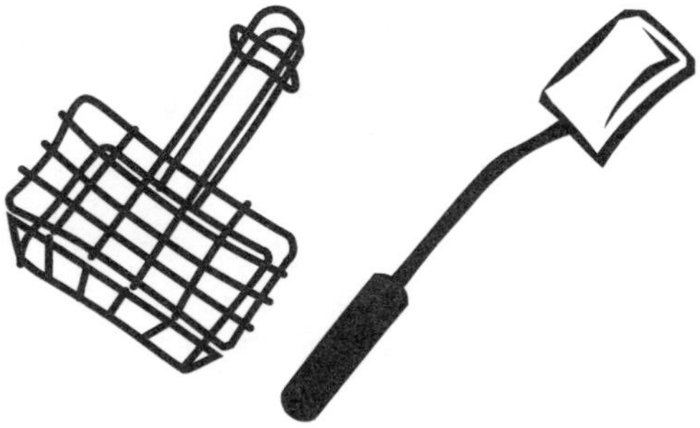

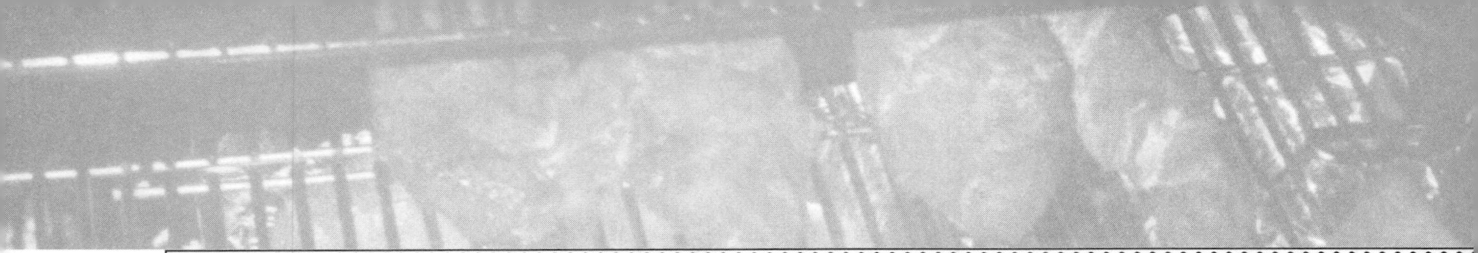

Super Sicilian Sandwich

You can assemble the sandwich hours ahead, wrap it in aluminum foil or plastic wrap, and refrigerate it so you're ready to put it on the grill as soon as you get home from a busy day. Rozane likes to serve this with potato salad and fresh fruit. SERVES 4 TO 6

1 loaf Italian or French bread
1/3 cup chopped fresh basil
2 tablespoons olive oil
1 tablespoon balsamic vinegar
6 ounces mozzarella, thinly sliced
8 ounces thinly sliced lean deli roast beef
2 Roma tomatoes, thinly sliced lengthwise
1/2 cup seeded mild banana peppers cut into rings or thin strips
Freshly ground black pepper to taste

1. Cut the bread in half lengthwise. With your fingers or a fork, hollow out about a third of the top half of the loaf.

2. In a small bowl, combine the basil, oil, and vinegar. Layer half the cheese, and all of the meat, tomatoes, and banana peppers on the bottom half of the loaf. Drizzle with the basil mixture and season with black pepper. Top with the remaining cheese and the hollowed-out top. Wrap well in heavy-duty aluminum foil.

3. When ready to serve, prepare a medium fire in a grill.

4. Grill the foil-wrapped sandwich, turning once, until heated through, 20 to 25 minutes. Slice and serve hot.

Grilled Artichoke Pizza on Parmesan-Herb Crust

Here's a good reason to make pizza at home—fabulous flavor. Get your kids or grandkids involved in making the dough, putting on the toppings, and grilling the pizza. This is great as a main dish or appetizer. MAKES ONE 14-INCH PIZZA OR FOUR 7-INCH PIZZAS

CRUST

3 to $3\frac{1}{2}$ cups all-purpose flour

1 package instant or bread machine yeast

$\frac{3}{4}$ teaspoon kosher or sea salt

2 cloves garlic, minced

$\frac{1}{2}$ cup freshly grated Parmesan cheese

$\frac{1}{2}$ teaspoon cracked black peppercorns

2 teaspoons dried basil, oregano, or rosemary

1 cup warm water (about 110°F)

2 tablespoons extra virgin olive oil

TOPPINGS

One 14-ounce can artichoke hearts, drained and thinly sliced

1 cup red onions sliced into thin wedges

$1\frac{1}{2}$ cups sliced fresh mushrooms

8 ounces mozzarella, shredded

2 tablespoons extra virgin olive oil

1. To make the crust, combine 2 cups of the flour, the yeast, salt, garlic, Parmesan, peppercorns, and basil in a large bowl. Stir in the water, olive oil, and enough of the remaining flour to make a soft dough. Knead lightly on a floured work surface until smooth, about 5 minutes. Cover and let rest for 10 minutes.

2. Prepare a medium-hot fire in a grill. Lightly oil a heavy-duty baking sheet or a perforated grill rack.

3. Roll out the dough to fit the pan and transfer to the pan.

4. To top the pizza, arrange the artichokes, onions, and mushrooms on the dough. Place the baking sheet on the grill, close the lid, and grill for 20 to 30 minutes, sprinkling on the shredded mozzarella during the last 10 minutes of grilling. The pizza is done when the crust has browned on the edges and the cheese has melted. Just before serving, drizzle with the olive oil.

Taking Wing: Poultry and Game Birds

If you take an informal poll of what people like best to grill, hamburgers and hot dogs would probably be first, followed by steak. But running a close third is chicken. If you also take a similar poll of what people like best to slow smoke, brisket and ribs would be first, followed by chicken or turkey. Happily, you're in good hands with the BBQ Queens, because we can do it all and are delighted to show you how. If you've tried to grill a boneless, skinless chicken breast and it ended up either like chicken sushi or dry shoe leather, we have an easy new technique that guarantees moist, tasty results every time. Plus, if you've ever thought "chicken—again?" we have lots of new ways for you to give it a lick of flame or a kiss of smoke—skewered, stir-grilled, planked, rotisserie cooked, or smoked on the stovetop. For those on a low-carb or high-protein diet, these new ways with chicken add big flavor without extra calories.

When chicken goes on sale, buy it in quantity, then grill or smoke for leftovers, as the BBQ Queens are always saying to do. That way, you'll have time another day to give yourself a pedicure for those strappy summer sandals.

Turkey is fast becoming the new "in" thing to grill or smoke, because it's moist, delicious, economical, and high in protein. Because turkey tenderloins and breasts are bigger than those from chicken, we offer special grilling techniques for them. And if you've ever considered slow smoking or rotisserie cooking a whole turkey, now's your chance.

Domestic duck and Cornish game hens are also fabulous on the grill or in the smoker, and we have lots of yummy recipes for them. We find that serving grilled duck or Cornish game hens makes a meal seem more festive. We're also including game birds (see more about them on page 245), because these are more available than they used to be and because Karen is such an expert at cooking them—grilling, smoking, and every other way imaginable. (That's what happens when your husband is an avid hunter.) Judith benefits by being the beneficiary of the Adlers' wild bounty.

Grilled Boneless, Skinless Chicken Breasts 191

Grilled Chicken Lemonata 192

Cubano Grilled Chicken with Picadillo Olive Salsa 192

Grilled Chicken with Thousand-Herb Sauce 192

One-Dish-Meal Grilled Chicken Sicilian 192

Chicken Breasts Grilled Indoors 192

Planked Boneless, Skinless Chicken Breasts 193

Planked Chicken Breasts with Pecorino Romano–Artichoke Glaze 194

Planked Balsamic-Thyme Chicken with Peppers and Onions 194

Grilled Chicken Skewers 195

Chopstix Chicken with Gingered Teriyaki Glaze 196

Grilled Chicken Satay 196

Curlicue Chicken Caesar Salad 196

Stir-Grilled Chicken and Vegetables 198

Stir-Grilled Chicken with Asparagus and Shaved Parmigiano-Reggiano 199

Stir-Grilled Chicken and Summer Vegetable Pasta with Fresh Basil Vinaigrette 199

Stir-Grilled Tequila-Lime Chicken 199

Grilled Bone-In, Skin-On Chicken Breasts 199

Grilled Cheese-Stuffed Bone-In Chicken Breasts 200

Pesto Chicken Sandwich with Cranberry Preserves 201

Fresh Greens and Grilled Chicken Salad 201

Grilled Half a Chicken 201

GRILL GALS: THE SILVER QUEEN CORN QUEEN GRILLS MENU

Fresh Corn and Tomato Salad 203

Beelzebub's Bloody Marys 204

Rosemary-Scented Grilled Butterflied Chicken 205

YOU SAY TO-MAH-TO, THE BBQ QUEENS SAY TOMATO

A Platter of Fresh Tomatoes 206

Italian Roma Tomato Salad 207

Roasted Cherry Tomatoes with Frizzled Herbs 208

Late-Harvest Tomato Tart 209

Grilled Wings and Things 210

Sizzling Wings and Things with Sage Butter and Romano Cheese 211

Grilled Chicken Wings Amogio 211

Grilled Drumsticks or Thighs Stuffed with Herbed Goat Cheese or Boursin 211

Smoked Wings and Things 212

Chopped Smoked Chicken Salad 213

Pulled Smoked Chicken Salad with Basil Mayonnaise 213

Barbecued Chicken on Fire 213

BBQ BABES: SHE'LL SMOKE FOR SOUP MENU

Smoked Chicken Breasts with Southwest Heat 215

Green Chile and Smoked Chicken Soup 216

Rotisserie Chicken 217

French Tarragon Rotisserie Chicken 218

Puerto Rican–Style Rotisserie Chicken 218

Karen's Famous Rotisserie Chicken Sandwich 218

Smoked Whole Chicken 219

Italian Barbecued Chicken 220

Rosemary-Garlic Smoked Chicken 220

Smoked Sesame-Soy Marinated Chicken 221

Smoked Chicken and Vegetable Lasagna 221

Grilled Turkey Breast Tenderloin Steaks 222

Tarragon Grilled Turkey Breast 223

Turkey Steaks with Spicy Horseradish Sauce 223

Bacon-Wrapped Turkey Fillets 223

Smoked Boneless Turkey Breast 226

Smoked Turkey with Cranberry-Orange Salsa 227

Penne with Smoked Turkey, Goat Cheese Cream Sauce, and Sun-Dried Tomatoes 227

Brie and Basil–Stuffed Turkey Breast 227

Rotisserie Turkey 228

Traditional Rotisserie Turkey Gravy 229

Day-After Rotisserie Turkey Sandwich 229

Smoked Whole Turkey 230

Smoked Turkey and Monterey Jack Club Sandwiches 231

Smoked Turkey Hash 231

BBQ BABES: SHE'S SMOKIN' AND TALKIN' TURKEY MENU

Apple-Smoked Turkey 233

Rosemary-Apple Salsa 234

Grilled Duck Paillards 235

Grilled Duck Paillards with Dried Sweet Cherry–Port Sauce 237

Grilled Duck Breast Salad 237

Smoked Whole Duck 238

Smoked Duck and Wild Rice Soup 239

Smoked Duck Breasts 239

Smoked Duckling with Five-Spice Asian Paste 239

Duck on a Beer Can 239

BBQ BABES: SHE'S WILD FOR SMOKE MENU

Apricot and Cognac–Glazed Duck 241

Drunk Elk or Venison 242

Durn Good Rice 243

Grilled Stuffed Apples 244

Grilled Game Birds 245

Cornish Game Hens with Orange-Honey Baste 246

Grilled Cornish Game Hens à la Chez Panisse 246

Warm Grilled Quail Salad with Spiced Pears and Mushrooms 246

Smoked Small Game Birds 247

Bacon-Wrapped Smoked Quail and Pheasant 248

Smoked Game Bird Salad 248

Smoked Game Birds and Pasta 249

Smoked Pheasant Breasts 249

Sangria! 250

Grilled Boneless, Skinless Chicken Breasts

Sometimes the seemingly simplest things to grill can be the most difficult. Take the boneless, skinless chicken breast, for example. Julia Child popularized this cut during the late 1960s and early 1970s on her groundbreaking PBS cooking program *The French Chef*. In those days, you had to bone and skin the chicken breast yourself. Now you can pick up a package of boneless, skinless breasts in any grocery store.

When you look at a chicken breast, you'll see that it's very thin at the ends and thick in the middle. How do you grill it so that every part stays tender and juicy? By turning it into a *paillard*, a French term for a boneless piece of meat that has been flattened to an equal thickness. The easiest way we've found to do this with chicken is to use the rim of a saucer. Simply pound the chicken breast, starting in the middle and working your way out to the sides, until the chicken is of an even 1/4- to 1/2-inch thickness. This technique—and these recipes—also works for veal paillards (also known as scallops, or *scaloppine* in Italian), usually cut from the leg and pounded thin.

On a hot grill or in a grill pan over high heat, a chicken or veal paillard will take a total cooking time of 10 minutes per inch of thickness. Grill a 1/2-inch-thick paillard for 2 1/2 minutes per side, or 5 minutes total. A 1/4-inch-thick paillard will take about only 1 1/4 minutes per side, so it makes sense to serve it with equally fast side dishes, such as Haricots Verts with Lemon, Garlic, and Parsley (page 274).

SERVES 4

4 boneless, skinless chicken breast halves, pounded to a 1/2-inch thickness
Olive oil
Fine kosher or sea salt and freshly ground black pepper to taste

1. Prepare a hot fire in a grill.
2. Brush or spray the paillards on both sides with olive oil. Grill for 2 1/2 minutes per side, turning once. Season with salt and pepper and serve.

Crowning Glories

Try serving your grilled chicken breasts with a baked potato, a green salad, and lemon wedges or a splash or dollop of:

Citrus Caesar Vinaigrette *(page 84)*

Roasted Red Pepper Aioli *(page 110)*

Chicken Breasts Grilled Indoors

Use a grill pan indoors when you don't want to fire up the grill. Brush each chicken paillard with a mixture of olive oil, crushed garlic, and lemon juice and let sit at room temperature for 15 minutes. Then heat the grill pan over high heat until you can hold your hand about 2 inches above the pan for only 4 to 5 seconds. Right before cooking, sprinkle the chicken with sea salt and freshly ground black pepper to taste, or with Lavender Salt (page 55), Fennel Salt (page 56), or Rosemary Salt (page 56) to taste. A 1/2-inch-thick paillard will cook in about 2 1/2 minutes per side.

Grilled Chicken Lemonata: Usually served with veal scaloppine, this easy sauce is a wonderful last-minute glaze for grilled chicken paillards as well. In a small saucepan over medium-high heat, warm 2 tablespoons fresh lemon juice for about 30 seconds, then swirl in 2 tablespoons cut-up unsalted butter and 2 tablespoons finely chopped fresh Italian parsley until the butter has melted. Grill the chicken as described above. Spoon a little sauce over each grilled paillard and serve. **SERVES 4**

Cubano Grilled Chicken with Picadillo Olive Salsa: After applying the olive oil to each paillard, dust or sprinkle both sides with your favorite Caribbean or jerk seasoning, then grill as directed above. For the salsa, in a medium-size bowl combine 1 chopped medium-size onion, 1 seeded and chopped large red bell pepper, one 10-ounce can Ro-Tel diced tomatoes with green chiles (with their juice), 3/4 cup drained and chopped pimento-stuffed green olives, 1/2 cup golden raisins, 1 tablespoon drained capers, and 1 tablespoon Worcestershire sauce. Grill the chicken as described above. Serve each grilled paillard with a topping of salsa. **SERVES 4**

Grilled Chicken with Thousand-Herb Sauce: Okay, so there really aren't a thousand herbs in this sauce. The fresh flavor only *suggests* a thousand. The sauce brings out the best in the chicken breasts, as well as grilled vegetables such as asparagus or zucchini. Like Chimichurri Sauce (page 346), this sauce is more like a vinaigrette. In a small bowl, combine 3 tablespoons extra virgin olive oil, 1 cup finely minced mixed fresh herbs (we like tarragon, Italian parsley, basil, and chives), and 2 tablespoons tarragon vinegar. Season with fine kosher or sea salt and freshly ground black pepper to taste. Grill the chicken as described above. Spoon a little sauce over each grilled paillard and serve. **SERVES 4**

One-Dish-Meal Grilled Chicken Sicilian: When the summer vegetable and herb gardens are at their peak, this is a delicious and healthy recipe to prepare. If you like, you can substitute grilled polenta for the linguine, or steamed white rice seasoned with additional rub. Drizzle the paillards with 2 tablespoons olive oil and sprinkle with 1/4 cup Spicy Red-Hot Lemon Pepper Rub (page 53), then grill as directed above. Transfer to a plate. Heat 1/4 cup olive oil in a large skillet over medium heat. Add 2 chopped large garlic cloves, 1 slivered

red onion, and 2 red bell and 2 green bell peppers seeded and cut into matchsticks. Cook, stirring, until crisp-tender. Add 2 to 3 chopped Roma tomatoes, 1 cup pitted and drained oil- or brine-cured Kalamata or Niçoise olives, and 2 tablespoons each chopped fresh thyme and basil. Cook, stirring a few times, until hot. Pour into a bowl and set aside until ready to serve. In the same pan, pour in 1 cup chicken broth and add 1 pound cooked linguine. Heat thoroughly over medium-high heat. Divide the linguine equally among 4 plates. Place a paillard on top of the pasta in each plate. Divide the vegetables equally over the paillards and serve. **SERVES 4**

Planked Boneless, Skinless Chicken Breasts

Planking boneless, skinless chicken breasts is yet another way to do something deliciously different with a common ingredient. Cooking on a plank produces chicken that is tender and juicy, with the slight woodsy aroma of the plank. With a dual-heat fire, one side hot and the other side at medium heat, you can plank cook more quickly. (See page 42 for complete directions on how to plank.) Just make sure you soak your plank for at least 1 hour before you put it on the grill.

The BBQ Queens' way is to start simple, then get fancy, so we begin with a plainer version of planked chicken, then jazz it up below. Feel free to use whatever planks are available in your area—alder, cedar, hickory, maple, even pecan. Each wood imparts a different yet gentle aroma to the food as it cooks.

One caveat: Keep a spray bottle of water by the grill just in case your plank catches fire and you need to douse the flames. That has never happened to us, but if you have a gas grill with a grate very near the heat source, it's best to be prepared.

For a side dish, you could plank asparagus, sliced bell peppers and onions, or thinly sliced zucchini. Use the same treatment as in the master recipe and cook it along with the chicken until done to your liking. Of course, a yummy potato salad never goes amiss, either. SERVES 4

4 boneless, skinless chicken breasts

Olive oil

Lemon pepper seasoning to taste

One 16 x 6 x 1/2-inch cedar or oak plank, soaked in water for at least 1 hour before grilling

1. Prepare a dual-heat fire, with a hot fire on one side and a medium fire on the other.

2. Place the chicken on a baking sheet, brush or spray with olive oil, and season with lemon pepper seasoning. Bring the chicken and plank outside.

3. Place the plank over the hot fire until it begins to smoke and pop, 4 to 5 minutes. Turn the plank over and move to the medium-heat side. Carefully place the chicken breasts on the charred side of the plank. Cover and cook until an instant-read meat thermometer inserted in the thickest part of the meat registers 160 to 165°F, 12 to 15 minutes. Serve hot.

Crowning Glories

Planked chicken is delicious topped with:

Chive Pesto *(page 64)*

Rustic Aioli *(page 104)*

Tomato-Fennel Sauce *(page 95)*

Planked Chicken Breasts with Pecorino Romano–Artichoke Glaze: A simple topping—in this case, a version of the tried-and-true artichoke dip—complements the aromatic wood flavor of the chicken. Make the topping from scratch or use a jar of prepared artichoke pesto. For other topping variations, try tapenade (black olive paste), Rosemary Pesto (page 62), Rosemary, Garlic, and Lemon Baste (page 68), or Mustard-Mayo-Dill Slather (page 66). Make the glaze by placing one 8-ounce can drained artichoke hearts in a food processor and pulse to chop roughly. Add 8 ounces freshly grated Pecorino Romano (or Asiago) cheese and 1 cup mayonnaise (lowfat is okay). Pulse to blend. (Use immediately or spoon into a glass jar with a tight-fitting lid. The glaze will keep, covered, in the refrigerator for up to 3 days.) Season the chicken breasts with lemon pepper seasoning, spread with the artichoke glaze, and plank as directed above. **SERVES 4**

Planked Balsamic-Thyme Chicken with Peppers and Onions: In this recipe, we soak 2 planks and cook chicken and vegetables on each. Make 1 recipe Balsamic-Thyme Vinaigrette (page 84). Cut 1 seeded medium-size green bell pepper into strips and 1 medium-size red onion into slivers. Place the chicken breasts and vegetables in a sealable plastic bag and pour in half the vinaigrette. Let marinate in the refrigerator for 30 minutes or up to overnight. Remove the chicken and vegetables from the marinade, place on a baking sheet, and take outside. Prepare the planks as described above. Arrange 2 chicken breasts and half the vegetable mixture on each plank. Cook as directed above. Serve the chicken and vegetables drizzled with the remaining vinaigrette. **SERVES 4**

Grilled Chicken Skewers

When you want to add a little creativity to plain old chicken on the grill, think skewer (see The Art of the Skewer, page 29).

If you're using wooden skewers, make sure you soak them in water for at least 30 minutes before grilling to keep them from singeing. You could also expand your idea of "skewer" to include fresh rosemary branches from your garden, the new metal spiral skewers that you can serve right on a dinner plate, or even fresh spikes of sugar cane (available at Hispanic markets).

The BBQ Queens don't recommend combining chicken with vegetables or fruits on the same skewer. The different ingredients have different cooking times, and you'll end up with either overdone vegetables or underdone chicken. But it is fun to serve grilled new potatoes on rosemary branches or grilled vegetable kabobs as an easy side dish that you can cook before, after, or while you're grilling the chicken.

We like to bring all the chicken skewers out to the grill on two baking sheets, one stacked on top of the other. The top one is for the raw chicken, the bottom one is for the cooked chicken, and never the twain shall meet for food safety reasons. **SERVES 4 TO 6**

2 pounds boneless, skinless chicken breasts or thighs, cut into 36 pieces or 18 strips

1 cup bottled Italian-style vinaigrette

2 tablespoons soy sauce

Juice and grated zest of 1 lemon

1. Rinse the chicken and place in a large sealable plastic bag. Pour the vinaigrette over the chicken and add the soy sauce and lemon juice and zest. Seal the bag and turn several times to coat the chicken. Marinate in the refrigerator at least 20 minutes or up to 2 hours.

2. Prepare a hot fire in a grill.

3. Remove the chicken from the bag and thread 3 pieces or a strip of chicken on each skewer. Grill until the chicken is firm and opaque all the way through, 2 to 3 minutes per side. Serve hot.

Crowning Glories

Skewered chicken is delicious served with dipping sauces such as:

Picadillo Olive Salsa ***(page 192)***

Ancho Mayonnaise ***(page 311)***

Thai Green Curry Sauce ***(page 290)***

Chopstix Chicken with Gingered Teriyaki Glaze: Ho-hum chicken gets an Asian-style makeover, skewered on fresh bamboo shoots, which you can cut off a bamboo plant (making sure, of course, that it hasn't been treated with anything). Or use traditional wooden skewers, also cut from bamboo. Bamboo is the new darling of kitchenware aficionados for cutting boards and serving pieces, because it is a renewable resource and looks great, too. The teriyaki glaze adds flavor and a burnished sheen to this dish. Make the glaze by combining 1 teaspoon peeled and finely minced fresh ginger, 1/4 cup homemade (see page 69) or prepared teriyaki sauce, and 2 tablespoons vegetable oil in a small bowl. Have ready 12 fresh bamboo shoots or 12 wooden skewers, about 8 inches long, soaked in water for at least 30 minutes before grilling. Cut the chicken into 36 pieces and thread 3 pieces onto each bamboo shoot, piercing the chicken first with a wooden skewer if necessary. Brush the chicken with the glaze, place the skewers on a baking sheet, and refrigerate for 30 minutes. Reserve the remaining glaze. Grill the skewers, brushing with the glaze, as directed above. Serve hot. **SERVES 4 TO 6**

Grilled Chicken Satay: For more of a satay look and taste to your chicken skewers, cut the meat into 12 to 18 strips. Place them in a sealable plastic bag. Prepare 1 recipe Cilantro-Peanut Dipping Sauce (page 389) and pour half of it over the chicken. Seal the bag and refrigerate for 30 minutes. Reserve the remaining sauce in a small bowl. Have ready 12 to 18 wooden skewers or fresh sugar cane spikes, about 8 inches long, soaked in water for at least 30 minutes before grilling. Thread 1 chicken strip onto each skewer. Grill the skewers as described above. Serve hot with the remaining dipping sauce. **SERVES 4 TO 6**

Curlicue Chicken Caesar Salad: Have fun grilling and serving chicken pieces on spiral metal skewers in this new take on grilled chicken Caesar salad. Make 1 recipe Citrus Caesar Vinaigrette (page 84). Cut the chicken into 36 pieces. Place the chicken and half the vinaigrette in a sealable plastic bag and refrigerate for 1 hour, turning several times. Right before you're ready to grill, divide one 8-ounce package Caesar salad greens among 6 plates. Have ready 6 spiral metal skewers (or 12 wooden skewers, about 8 inches long, soaked in water for at least 30 minutes before grilling). Thread 6 pieces of chicken on each metal skewer (3 on each wooden skewer). Grill the skewers as described above. Serve each curlicue skewer (or 2 wooden skewers) on a plate of greens, drizzled with the remaining vinaigrette. **SERVES 6**

BBQ Queens

An (Almost) All-Female Barbecue Team

Before the 'Que Queens barbecue team (to which Karen and Judith, the BBQ Queens, belong), there was Boss Hawg, a Memphis-based team of four women—Linda Thomason, Mabel Thomason (Linda's mother), Judy Braswell, and Virginia Smith—and one man, Virginia's husband, Randy. (Head cook Linda's only complaint about Randy is that he won't shave his legs, but because Virginia doesn't seem to mind, Linda doesn't make an issue of it.)

Hairy legs or not, Boss Hawg has been competing in barbecue contests since 1981 and has come away with top honors in many. In 1987, the team placed third in Ribs in the prestigious Memphis in May contest.

Breaking into a traditionally all-male realm was not too difficult, Linda says. "At first, the male teams were stunned at an 'all-female' cooking team on the barbecue circuit. We have turned around the perception a bit. Barbecuers are not a sexist bunch and kinda look out for us."

Karen and Judith's competition barbecue team, the 'Que Queens, had a similar experience in a Battle of the Sexes Barbecue Contest, a fun for-charity contest that pits a women's team against a men's team. The guys have looked out for the 'Que Queens, too. Sorta. "I got to the cooking site at 6:30 A.M. before the rest of our team," Karen recalls. "The guys offered me coffee, so I took a sip and almost fell over from all the booze in it. Next they offered me a bloody mary. By 9:00 A.M., they were on to beer."

By the time the judges were assembled to taste barbecued ribs from the men's and women's teams at 11:00 A.M., guess which team was well on its way to losing?

Stir-Grilled Chicken and Vegetables

How easy is this for a weeknight meal? Cut boneless, skinless chicken breasts or thighs into small pieces along with the vegetables of your choice, marinate everything in a sealable plastic bag, and stir-grill it all together in a grill wok. As you toss the food over the hot fire with wooden paddles or grill spatulas, you can look forward to minimal kitchen cleanup.

For instructions on how to stir-grill, see page 32. Serve stir-grilled dishes as is or accompany them with steamed rice, soba noodles, or pasta. SERVES 4

1 1/2 pounds boneless, skinless chicken breasts, cut into 2-inch pieces

2 cups fresh or defrosted frozen snow peas or 2 cups zucchini cut into small pieces

1 bunch green onions, cut on the diagonal into 1-inch pieces

1 pint yellow teardrop tomatoes or 2 cups chunked yellow (or other color) tomatoes

3/4 cup bottled balsamic vinaigrette

1 clove garlic, minced

1. Place the chicken and vegetables in a sealable plastic bag and add the balsamic vinaigrette and garlic. Seal the bag and toss to coat the chicken and vegetables with the marinade. Let marinate in the refrigerator for 30 minutes.

2. Prepare a hot fire in a grill. When ready to grill, add fruitwood such as cherry, apple, or pear for a kiss of smoke (see page 13).

3. Coat a grill wok with nonstick cooking spray and place over the sink or outside on the grass. Pour the marinated chicken and vegetables into the wok, allowing the excess marinade to drain away. Place the grill wok over direct heat and stir-grill, tossing the food with wooden paddles or grill spatulas, until everything is lightly browned, 12 to 15 minutes. Close the lid for 2 to 3 minutes to heat thoroughly, then serve.

Crowning Glories

Stir-grilled chicken is delicious topped with a garnish of:

Chopped fresh herbs

Gremolata ***(page 274)***

Crumbled smoked goat cheese ***(page 169)***

Stir-Grilled Chicken with Asparagus and Shaved Parmigiano-Reggiano: For a different flavor, marinate the chicken and 1 pound trimmed asparagus cut on the diagonal into 2-inch pieces in your favorite Italian-style vinaigrette or Amogio (page 72). Grill as directed above. Shave Parmigiano-Reggiano cheese over each serving. **SERVES 4**

Stir-Grilled Chicken and Summer Vegetable Pasta with Fresh Basil Vinaigrette: So many ways to stir-grill chicken, so little time! Make 1 recipe Fresh Basil Vinaigrette (page 85). Marinate the chicken along with 1 small zucchini cut into rounds, 1 small yellow summer squash cut into rounds, and 1 cup grape or cherry tomatoes in half of the vinaigrette. Grill as directed above. Serve over 1 pound cooked pasta, drizzled with the remaining vinaigrette. **SERVES 4**

Stir-Grilled Tequila-Lime Chicken: This is definitely a recipe for margarita lovers (count us in). Make 1 recipe Tequila-Lime Marinade (page 73). Marinate the chicken along with 1 small zucchini cut into rounds, 1 small yellow summer squash cut into rounds, and 1 cup grape or cherry tomatoes in the marinade. Grill as directed above and serve with lime wedges. **SERVES 4**

Grilled Bone-In, Skin-On Chicken Breasts

Many people prefer bone-in chicken, claiming that it has more flavor than boneless, skinless breasts. We like chicken any way you grill it. Here's how to tackle the breast of the bird with the bone in.

To start with, bone-in chicken breasts take longer to grill (all meat takes longer with the bone in). So the trick is to cook them longer without drying them out. To do this, you must have the skin on and turn them several times (every 5 to 10 minutes for about 30 minutes) over a medium-hot fire. For this, long-handled hinged tongs are a necessity, and you may want to wear long heat-resistant gloves as well. *Important:* The chicken breasts should be set out at room temperature for 20 to 30 minutes before grilling. This allows the seasoning to impart more flavor and results in a breast that is hot and juicy all the way through.

Is the extra effort worth it? You bet! The skin gets charred and caramelized and is delicious. The skin also gives you a little "pouch" that can be stuffed with cheese, pesto, flavored butter, herbs, prosciutto, or anything else that sounds appealing to you. And having the bone in and skin on keeps the meat juicier and hotter for a longer period of time after it comes off the grill. Such a deal!

The BBQ Queens offer a very simple treatment for the master recipe. Once you get the hang of that, sprinkle on Spicy Red-Hot Lemon Pepper Rub (page 53) or BBQ Queens' Photo Op Barbecue Rub (page 58), or soak the chicken in Fennel and Orange Marinade (page 72), before grilling.

While you're grilling the chicken, why not grill some vegetables, too? We like Grilled Asparagus (page 117) or Grilled Romaine and Green Onions with Lemon and Olives (page 127). Or serve the chicken with sliced fresh tomatoes and warmed rustic bread. SERVES 4

4 bone-in, skin-on chicken breast halves
Olive oil
Kosher or sea salt and seasoned pepper of your choice to taste
2 lemons, cut in half

1. Prepare a medium-hot fire in a grill.

2. Brush the chicken on both sides with olive oil and sprinkle with salt and seasoned pepper. Lightly brush the cut sides of the lemons with oil, too.

3. Place the chicken skin side down over the fire. Grill with the lid open for about 30 minutes, turning the chicken every 5 to 10 minutes. Baste with olive oil, if you wish. Grill the lemons cut side down for 5 to 7 minutes during the last 10 minutes of cooking. The chicken is done when an instant-read meat thermometer inserted in the thickest part of the breast registers 170 to 175°F. Serve with the grilled lemons on the side.

Crowning Glories

Grilled chicken breasts are delicious anointed with:

Pesto Aioli *(page 110)*

Mango-Lemon Sauce *(page 92)*

Poblano Cream Sauce *(page 93)*

Grilled Cheese-Stuffed Bone-In Chicken Breasts: Stuffing is an extra step that can be done several hours ahead or even the day before. Gently loosen part of the skin without tearing it. Stuff each breast with a 1/4-inch-thick slice of pepper Jack cheese or 1 tablespoon pimento cream cheese. Lightly coat the chicken with olive oil and season with kosher or sea salt and freshly ground black pepper to taste. Grill as directed above and serve. **SERVES 4**

Pesto Chicken Sandwich with Cranberry Preserves: Slice any leftover chicken for a sandwich. Spread 1 tablespoon Chive Pesto (page 64) on a slice of bread. Spread another slice of bread with cranberry preserves (or chutney). Pile on the chicken, close the sandwich, and eat. **SERVES 1**

Fresh Greens and Grilled Chicken Salad: Arrange 1 cup greens on each of 4 salad plates. Top each plate of greens with 3 or 4 oil- or brine-cured olives, 2 tablespoons crumbled feta cheese, 4 or 5 halved cherry tomatoes, and several strips of grilled chicken breast. Drizzle with Lemon-Tarragon Vinaigrette (page 75) and serve. **SERVES 4**

Grilled Half a Chicken

Once you master grilling bone-in, skin-on chicken breasts (see page 199), grilling half a chicken is a snap. Half a chicken is a handsome piece of meat, and this is about as large a piece of chicken as you'll want to grill over direct heat. (For a whole chicken, it's best to smoke it slow or grill it on the indirect side of a medium-hot grill. Slow smoking at 225 to 250°F will take about 30 minutes per pound of chicken, or 2 to 2½ hours for a 4-pound bird. Indirect grilling at a higher temperature of 350°F will take about 1½ hours for the same size bird.)

Place 2 chicken halves that weigh about 2 pounds each in a sealable plastic bag. Place the bags upright in the sink. Pour 1 cup of your favorite marinade—try Homemade Teriyaki Marinade (page 69) or Hot Shallot Vinaigrette (page 85)—over each half and close the bag. Reserve ½ cup marinade for basting. Marinate in the refrigerator for at least 1 hour or up to 12 hours.

When ready to grill, take the chicken out of the refrigerator and let sit at room temperature for about 30 minutes. Prepare a medium-hot fire in a grill. Grill the chicken for 35 to 40 minutes over direct heat, turning every 5 to 10 minutes and basting with the reserved marinade. The chicken is done when an instant-read meat thermometer inserted in the thigh registers 170 to 175°F. **SERVES 4**

Grill Gals

The Silver Queen Corn Queen Grills Menu

Fresh Corn and Tomato Salad

Beelzebub's Bloody Marys

Rosemary-Scented Grilled Butterflied Chicken

Judith met Debbie Moose, a Silver Queen Corn Queen, when Judith was giving cooking classes at A Southern Season in Chapel Hill, North Carolina. Debbie was easy to spot because she was the only person—other than Judith—wearing a tiara, and a very dainty one at that.

Now an award-winning freelance food writer, Debbie used to be the food editor for the *News & Observer* in nearby Raleigh. Along the way, she has cooked up some pretty good stuff—and become a Silver Queen Corn Queen, part of a group of women who get together for coffee every Saturday and for regular margarita gatherings at one member's pool during warm weather. "We are registered with the Sweet Potato Queens as a bona fide chapter—or one member was supposed to make us legal, and I assume she did," Debbie says. "We picked the name out of our love of summer sweet corn, and because we're so queenly, we had to say it twice!"

Debbie believes that "charcoal is The One True Grilling Method." Her variations on the classic deviled egg are collected in her first cookbook, *Deviled Eggs: 50 Recipes from Simple to Sassy* (The Harvard Common Press, 2004). She is a cook after our own hearts—someone who is inspired to throw things together first, then figure out just what she did later.

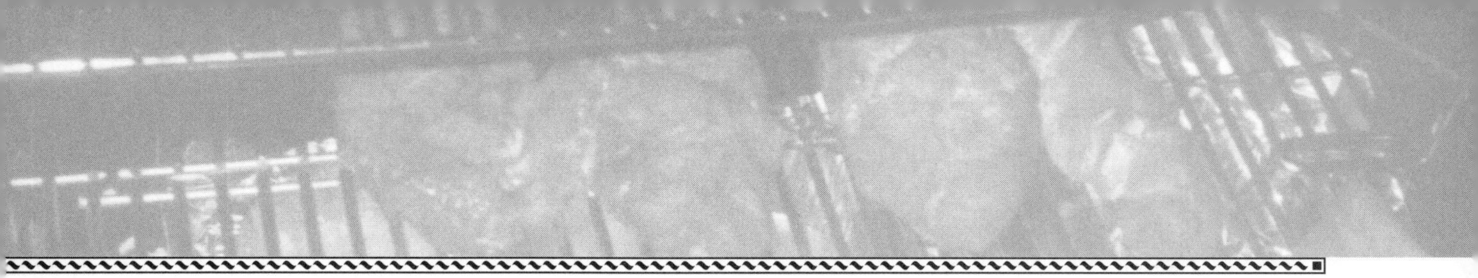

Fresh Corn and Tomato Salad

"I tossed this together to use up a summer bounty of fresh vegetables from my local farmers' market," Debbie says. "The dressing will soften the corn somewhat, but because it isn't cooked, be sure to use only the freshest, most tender summer corn for this salad. You could turn this from a side dish to a main dish by adding a cup of cooked black beans." SERVES 6

1/2 cup white wine vinegar

1 cup olive oil

Kosher or sea salt and freshly ground black pepper to taste

1 clove garlic, crushed

3 cups fresh sweet corn kernels, such as Silver Queen, Peaches and Cream, or Country Gentleman (about 6 ears)

2 medium-size ripe tomatoes, peeled, seeded, and chopped

1 medium-size green bell pepper, seeded and chopped

1 medium-size Vidalia or other sweet onion, chopped

1. In a small bowl, combine the vinegar and olive oil. Season with salt and pepper, add the garlic, and set aside for a few minutes.

2. In a large bowl, stir together all the remaining ingredients. Remove the garlic from the vinaigrette and pour over the vegetables. Stir to combine. Taste for salt and pepper. Cover with plastic wrap and refrigerate for 4 to 6 hours before serving.

Beelzebub's Bloody Marys

This one is adapted from Debbie's book, *Deviled Eggs*. "Add as much Tabasco as you can stand," she says. Puree the sun-dried tomatoes in the food processor for the best texture. One of her tasters called these "the naughtiest deviled eggs ever." MAKES 6

3 hard-boiled large eggs, peeled and cut in half lengthwise
2 tablespoons mayonnaise
$1\frac{3}{4}$ teaspoons pureed oil-packed sun-dried tomatoes
$1\frac{1}{2}$ teaspoons prepared horseradish
$\frac{1}{4}$ teaspoon Tabasco sauce, or more to taste
$\frac{1}{4}$ teaspoon vodka (optional)
$\frac{1}{2}$ teaspoon Worcestershire sauce
$1\frac{1}{2}$ teaspoons finely chopped celery with leaves, plus more for garnish
$\frac{1}{4}$ teaspoon Dijon mustard
$\frac{1}{4}$ teaspoon celery seeds
Kosher or sea salt and freshly ground black pepper to taste

1. In a small bowl, mash the egg yolks. Add the mayonnaise and combine. Stir in the tomato puree, horseradish, Tabasco, vodka (if using), Worcestershire, celery, mustard, and celery seeds. Season with salt and pepper.

2. Fill the egg whites with the mixture and garnish with chopped celery. Refrigerate for several hours or overnight for the flavors to blend. Serve cold.

Rosemary-Scented Grilled Butterflied Chicken

Debbie adapted this recipe from one by Jeanne Voltz, the late great Grill Gal, in *Barbecued Ribs, Smoked Butts and Other Great Feeds* (Alfred A. Knopf, 1996). **SERVES 4**

One $3\frac{1}{2}$- to 4-pound chicken
Olive oil
2 lemons, cut in half
2 cloves garlic, cut into slivers
Kosher or sea salt and freshly ground black pepper to taste
5 or 6 fresh rosemary branches, 6 to 8 inches long

1. Butterfly the chicken by cutting vertically through the backbone with a pair of kitchen shears. Press the chicken firmly to flatten it out as much as possible. Place the chicken in a large bowl and rub it all over with olive oil. Squeeze both lemons over the chicken, rubbing in the juice. Sprinkle with the garlic and season with salt and pepper. Marinate in the refrigerator for 2 to 3 hours.

2. Soak the rosemary branches in water to cover for at least 10 minutes (a little longer won't hurt). Weight them down with a saucer, if necessary, to keep the herbs submerged. Meanwhile, prepare a hot fire in a covered charcoal or gas grill.

3. When ready to grill, remove the chicken from the marinade. Remove the rosemary branches from the water and shake off the excess water. Place the branches on the hot grill in such a way that they won't fall through. Brush the underside of the chicken with a bit of olive oil and place skin side up on top of the branches. Cover and cook for 10 to 15 minutes. Brush the chicken with olive oil and turn over so the skin side is against the rosemary. Cover and cook for another 10 to 15 minutes. If the chicken begins to turn too dark, pull it to the side of the grill briefly. If the rosemary begins to flame, remove it or spritz lightly with water. Continue to check and turn the chicken, brushing with more oil, if necessary, every 10 minutes or so until an instant-read meat thermometer inserted in the thickest part registers 170 to 175°F, about 40 minutes total. Serve hot.

You Say To-mah-to, the BBQ Queens Say Tomato

You may be familiar with the late Duchess of Windsor and her famous alleged remark, "One can never be too rich or too thin." Because she was from the United States, we think she might have wanted to add, "And one can never have too many tomatoes!" (even though the duchess banished any chef who had the audacity to serve tomatoes with their seeds).

We also sympathize with Imelda Marcos (a dethroned "queen," sort of) who *almost* said, "One can never have too many shoes—or too many tomatoes."

Karen and her husband, Dick, always grow tomatoes in their backyard garden. Dick's favorites are the beefsteak-style tomatoes that are perfect for slicing. Karen likes to grow cherry, Roma, teardrop, and heirloom varieties. Karen never refrigerates her tomatoes. If she has too many, she shares them with friends (such as Judith!).

Fresh tomatoes add a bit of acidity to a grilled meal, which rounds out the slight bitterness from the exterior char and the sweet interior of grilled foods. They add color and pop to a platter or table, and they're easy to prepare. What more could you want?

A Platter of Fresh Tomatoes

When making a platter of tomatoes, think color and shape. Slice some of the tomatoes and quarter others; keep some of the cherry or grape tomatoes whole and cut others in half. Then add any of the following items:

Cheese: Crumbled blue cheese, goat cheese, or feta cheese, or sliced fresh mozzarella

Onions: Slivers of red onion or rings of Maui or Vidalia onions

Peppers: Rings of green, yellow, or red bell peppers; diced or sliced chiles such as banana or jalapeño chiles

Olives: Green or black

Savories: Anchovy fillets, capers, sliced hearts of palm, or quartered artichoke hearts

Mayonnaise: Doctor up 1 cup mayonnaise with 1 tablespoon fresh citrus juice of your choice, 1 chopped garlic clove, and 1 1/2 teaspoons of your favorite chopped fresh herb

Vinegar or vinaigrette: Drizzle with balsamic vinegar or other vinegar or vinaigrette, bottled or homemade

Italian Roma Tomato Salad

In our book, "rustic" means easy to prepare, tasty, and pretty—in a rough-and-ready kind of way. SERVES 6

- 9 Roma tomatoes, cut in half
- 1/2 cup pitted oil- or brine-cured olives, such as Kalamata or Niçoise, drained
- 2 ounces fresh mozzarella, cubed
- 2 ounces feta cheese, crumbled
- 1/4 cup packed fresh basil leaves, torn
- 2 tablespoons extra virgin olive oil
- Sea salt and freshly ground black pepper to taste

Place the tomatoes, olives, cheeses, and basil in a large bowl. Drizzle with the olive oil, season with salt and pepper, toss lightly, and serve right away.

Roasted Cherry Tomatoes with Frizzled Herbs

Karen's friend Maureen Hasseltine first served this while Karen was visiting her in Cabo San Lucas, Mexico. Maureen loves to use fresh basil from her garden, and lots of it, with a shaved hard cheese such as Parmesan. When Karen returned home to her winter garden in Kansas City, she had only fresh oregano available. It worked like a charm, too. So now we say experiment and use what is fresh from your garden. SERVES 6 TO 8

2 pints cherry or grape tomatoes
10 to 12 fresh herb sprigs, such as basil, oregano, and/or dill, to your taste
1/2 cup shaved hard goat cheese
1 tablespoon olive oil
Fine kosher or sea salt and freshly ground black pepper to taste (optional)

1. Preheat the oven to 350°F.

2. Place the tomatoes in a shallow 1-quart baking dish and bake until some of them have burst their skins, about 15 minutes.

3. Remove from the oven and quickly tuck the herbs around the tomatoes. Sprinkle with the cheese and drizzle with the olive oil. Return to the oven for 10 minutes. The herbs will be very crisp and the cheese will have melted. Season with salt and pepper, if you like, but the flavor is quite luscious without them. Serve hot.

Late-Harvest Tomato Tart

Inspired by Susan Herrmann Loomis's tomato tart recipe in her *Farmhouse Cookbook* (Workman, 1991), this dish is great when you have a big bowl of assorted cherry-type tomatoes. MAKES ONE 9-INCH TART; SERVES 6 TO 8

1 sheet frozen puff pastry, defrosted
1 cup heavy cream
2 large eggs
1 tablespoon chopped fresh thyme or tarragon or 1 teaspoon dried thyme or tarragon
2 small cloves garlic, minced
Fine kosher or sea salt and freshly ground black pepper to taste
12 ounces Swiss cheese, cubed
5 pounds mixed ripe tomatoes, such as cherry, grape, and teardrop

1. Preheat the oven to 425°F.

2. Roll out the puff pastry to an 11-inch square. Line a 9-inch tart pan with the pastry, trim the edges, and prick with a fork. Place in the freezer for 5 minutes, then bake until golden, about 10 minutes. Remove from the oven.

3. In a large bowl, whisk together the cream and eggs. Blend in the thyme and garlic, then season with salt and pepper.

4. Arrange the cheese cubes evenly in the crust. Cut the larger tomatoes in half and leave the smaller ones whole. Scatter the tomatoes over the cheese. They will mound slightly in the center of the pan, which is fine.

5. Pour the cream mixture into the crust. Place the tart on a baking sheet and bake for 10 minutes, then reduce the oven temperature to 350°F and continue to bake until the custard is set and the pie is golden on top, 45 to 55 minutes. Let cool for at least 10 minutes before serving warm or at room temperature.

Grilled Wings and Things

If your royal budget is a concern, get thee to the market and buy chicken wings. Buy legs and thighs, too, which are sometimes sold very cheaply as chicken quarters. Make no bones about it, chicken wings, legs, and thighs are some of the tastiest parts of the bird. The flavor comes from the rich, succulent meat close to the bone. Invite your family and friends over to eat, drink, and be merry. You might be on a budget, but they'll never know.

You can add flavor in two ways. Brush the parts with olive oil, then sprinkle on a rub, such as the Middle Eastern za'atar (sumac, sesame, salt, and dried thyme) or another herb and spice mixture, and grill. Or flavor dem bones by marinating or basting with a hot vinegar sauce, an Asian-style sauce with soy sauce as a component, Amogio (page 72), or good old American barbecue sauce. Just remember that anything with sugar in it will burn faster than other marinades, so be prepared to move the chicken to the indirect side of the fire to quell any flare-ups (or have a spray bottle handy to douse them with water).

Grilling with a kiss of smoke (see page 13) makes wings and things fit for a queen (or king). For a smoky flavor, add a handful of water-soaked wood chips to a hot charcoal fire or make up an aluminum foil package of water-soaked wood chips or dry wood pellets for a gas grill. We especially like apple, cherry, hickory, and pecan with chicken.

Leaving the chicken wings whole is the simplest and fastest way to prepare them. If you like to serve them as drummies, place the wings on a cutting board and split them at the joints with a sharp knife, then discard the tips. Also use a chef's knife to split the drumsticks from the thighs for easier eating and smaller portions. SERVES 4

2 pounds chicken wings, drumsticks, and/or thighs
1 cup bottled Italian-style vinaigrette
Juice and grated zest of 1 lemon

1. Rinse the chicken and place in a large sealable plastic bag. Pour in the vinaigrette and add the lemon juice and zest. Seal the bag and mix by turning it several times. Marinate in the refrigerator for at least 20 minutes or up to 2 hours.

2. Prepare a hot fire in a grill.

3. Remove the chicken from the bag and place directly over the fire. Pour the marinade into a container and use to baste the chicken every 5 minutes for the first 15 minutes, then discard. Continue to grill, turning, until nicely browned and crisp all over and

the meat begins to shrink at the base of the bone. Total cooking time is about 20 minutes for wings, 30 minutes for thighs or drumsticks. Serve hot.

Crowning Glories

Wings and things are great served with a dipping sauce such as:

Creamy Blue Cheese Dressing *(page 111)*

Spicy Lemon-Soy Sauce *(page 312)*

Peanut Butter Dipping Sauce *(page 118)*

Season or marinate the chicken pieces with any of these:

Spicy Orange Rub *(page 51)*

BBQ Queens' All-Purpose Rub *(page 49)*

Vietnamese Drizzle *(page 87)*

Sizzling Wings and Things with Sage Butter and Romano Cheese: This one goes together quick—the hot crispy chicken being topped with the butter and cheese as soon as it comes off the grill. Cook the chicken as described above. Meanwhile, in a small saucepan over medium heat, melt 1/2 cup (1 stick) unsalted butter and add 3 or 4 fresh sage leaves. Cook until the butter browns and is infused with the sage flavor, about 20 minutes. When the chicken is done, transfer to a platter, drizzle with the hot sage butter, sprinkle with 1/3 cup freshly grated Romano cheese, and serve. Yum! **SERVES 4**

Grilled Chicken Wings Amogio: Judith prepared these for a cooking class she did at A Southern Season in Chapel Hill, North Carolina. Arrange the wings on a brightly colored platter for instant pizzazz as a finger-lickin'-good appetizer or casual main dish. If the bars on your grill grate are far apart, place the wings on a perforated grill rack and grill them in batches. Make 1 recipe of Amogio (page 72), reserving 1/2 cup for drizzling. Place 3 pounds chicken wings in a large sealable plastic bag. Pour in the remaining amogio, seal the bag, and marinate in the refrigerator for at least 1 hour or overnight. Remove the chicken, discarding the marinade. Grill as instructed above. Drizzle a little of the reserved amogio over each wing and serve. **SERVES 4**

Grilled Drumsticks or Thighs Stuffed with Herbed Goat Cheese or Boursin: When we were kids, our dads told us that wings were scrawny and not very good. So that left the drumsticks to vie for. Now you can buy packages of just drumsticks, wings, or thighs, making family life a bit more civilized. Prepare 2 legs or thighs for each person. (On second thought, you may want to double this recipe for leftovers.) Begin with 8 chicken drumsticks or thighs that have been rinsed and patted dry. Loosen the skin from each chicken piece and stuff $1\frac{1}{2}$ teaspoons herbed fresh goat cheese or Boursin under the skin ($\frac{1}{4}$ cup total). Smear $\frac{1}{2}$ teaspoon Dijon mustard (4 teaspoons total) over each chicken piece, then season with a spice rub or kosher or sea salt and freshly ground black pepper to taste. Finish with 8 slices hickory-smoked bacon, 1 slice wrapped around each chicken piece and secured with a toothpick. Grill over a medium-hot fire for about 30 minutes, turning to brown all over. Now go eat—and no fighting allowed! **SERVES 4**

Smoked Wings and Things

By now we think you've caught on to the fact that smoking time depends on how much food is in the smoker—it's a per pound thing, for the most part. So let's have fun with all these chicken pieces, and remember that you can use these recipes with different chicken parts as well. Mix and match your favorite marinades, rubs, pastes, and drizzles to have slightly different smoked wings and things every time you go out to the smoker. Try Tequila-Lime Marinade (page 73) or Tricolored Peppercorn Rub (page 62) for something a little different, or even bottled Italian-style vinaigrette if that's what you have on hand. SERVES 8 TO 10

SUGGESTED WOOD: Apple, oak, maple, mesquite, or hickory

Two 3-pound fryers, cut into serving-size pieces, or about 5 pounds chicken parts

2 cups Tandoori Marinade (page 74)

1. Rinse the chicken and place in a shallow dish. Pour 1 cup of the marinade over the chicken. Let sit at room temperature in a cool kitchen for about 30 minutes, turning the pieces to coat well and flavor.

2. Prepare an indirect fire in a smoker.

3. Place the chicken on the smoker, cover, and smoke at 225 to 250°F. After 2 hours, start basting with the remaining 1 cup marinade every 30 minutes for another 1 to 2 hours. The chicken is done when an instant-read meat thermometer inserted in the thickest part of the meat registers 170 to 175°F. The wings and breasts will get done sooner than the thighs and legs. Serve hot.

Crowning Glories

Smoked chicken parts are delicious served with potato or pasta salad, baked beans, or A Platter of Fresh Tomatoes (page 206), along with your favorite barbecue sauce or a dipping sauces, such as:

Creamy Blue Cheese Dressing ***(page 111)***

Chipotle Barbecue Sauce ***(page 90)***

Chopped Smoked Chicken Salad: A fave that gets raves! Chop 1 head iceberg lettuce and arrange on a platter. In columns, place 3 peeled and chopped hard-boiled large eggs; 1 cup chopped artichoke hearts; 1 cup pitted, drained, and sliced oil- or brine-cured black olives; 2 cups chopped smoked (or grilled or rotisserie) chicken down the center of the plate; 1 cup chopped red tomatoes; 8 slices crumbled crisp-cooked bacon; and 4 ounces crumbled blue cheese or feta cheese. Drizzle with your favorite dressing and serve. **SERVES 6 TO 8**

Pulled Smoked Chicken Salad with Basil Mayonnaise: Using the meat from 4 smoked (or grilled) chicken breast halves, pull the meat off the bones into strips. To make the mayonnaise, in a small bowl whisk together 2 cups good-quality mayonnaise, 1/2 teaspoon dry mustard, the juice and grated zest of 1 lemon, and 1/4 cup chopped fresh basil. Wash 1 medium-size head butter lettuce and arrange the leaves on a large platter. Place a bowl in the center of the platter and transfer the mayonnaise to it. Arrange the pulled chicken around the bowl. Crumble 4 ounces feta cheese over the chicken. Place cherry or grape tomatoes and assorted olives around the rim of the platter and serve. **SERVES 6**

Barbecued Chicken on Fire: This smoked chicken is a little faster to cook because you use more heat and boneless, skinless chicken breasts. Combine 1 cup spicy barbecue sauce, 2/3 cup orange marmalade, 1 tablespoon Worcestershire sauce, and 2 teaspoons prepared horseradish in a medium-size bowl. Reserve 1 cup of the sauce in a small bowl for serving on the side. The remaining sauce is for basting. Rinse and pat dry 6 pounds boneless, skinless chicken breast halves (about 12), then season with kosher salt and freshly ground black pepper to taste. Grill over a hot fire for about 2 minutes per side to sear and mark, basting with the sauce. Move the chicken to the indirect side of the grill and add 1 cup wood chips soaked in water for at least 30 minutes. Cover and maintain a medium-hot fire. Baste the chicken every 10 minutes until done, about 45 minutes. An instant-read meat thermometer inserted in the thickest part of the meat should register 160 to 165°F. Serve with the reserved sauce. **SERVES 10 TO 12**

BBQ Babes

She'll Smoke for Soup Menu

Smoked Chicken Breasts with Southwest Heat
Green Chile and Smoked Chicken Soup

The Jamisons, Bill and Cheryl, blazed the barbecue trail with their phenomenally successful *Smoke & Spice* (The Harvard Common Press, 1994 and 2003), which won both International Association of Culinary Professionals (IACP) and James Beard Foundation awards. Cheryl sent us these terrific recipes, which we adapted.

Like the BBQ Queens, Cheryl often makes extra smoked foods to have leftovers for other dishes at her home in Santa Fe, New Mexico. She likes to smoke even lower and slower than we do, at about 200 to 220°F (we like to keep it at 225 to 250°F). Try chicken smoked at both temperatures and see which you prefer.

The soulful Green Chile and Smoked Chicken Soup is one of the couple's favorite leftover chicken treats. It's so good you'll be tempted to fire up your smoker and make it from scratch. You can easily cook the chicken a day or two ahead of when you want to prepare the soup.

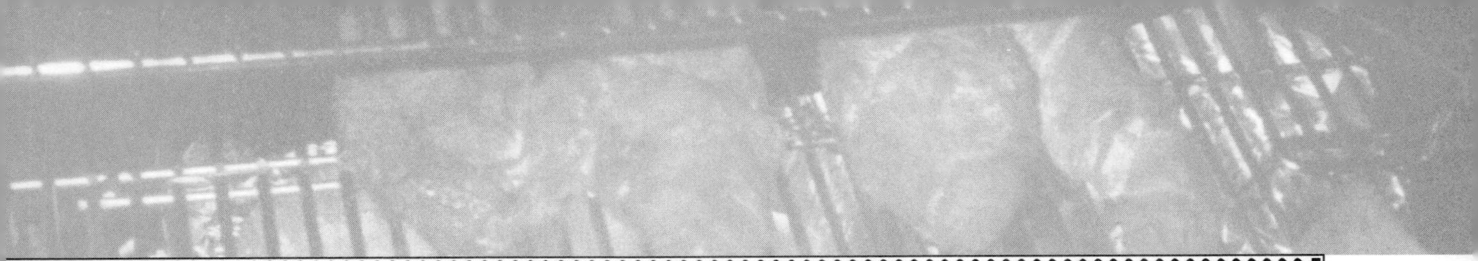

Smoked Chicken Breasts with Southwest Heat

Earthy and pungent with heat hitting the back of your throat is what you get with this delicious smoked chicken. Serve it with a side of Rustic Bread with Smoked Tomato and Basil Butter (page 177). SERVES 4

SUGGESTED WOOD: Apple or a combination of apple and hickory

SOUTHWEST HEAT

2 tablespoons ground Hatch chile (see page 140)
2 tablespoons ground ancho chile (see page 59)
2 teaspoons coarse kosher or sea salt
2 teaspoons ground cumin
1/4 teaspoon dried oregano, preferably Mexican

4 or 5 bone-in, skin-on chicken breast halves (7 to 8 ounces each)

1. At least 2 hours before you plan to barbecue, or up to the night before, make the heat by combining all the ingredients in a small bowl. With your fingers, loosen the skin of the breasts and massage the chicken with the spice mixture, rubbing over and under the skin. Place the breasts in a sealable plastic bag and refrigerate for at least 1 1/2 hours or up to 12 hours.

2. Prepare an indirect fire in a smoker. Remove the chicken from the refrigerator and let sit at room temperature for about 20 minutes.

3. Transfer the chicken pieces to the smoker, skin side up. Cover and cook at 200 to 220°F until cooked through and the juices run clear when a skewer is inserted in the thickest part, 50 to 60 minutes. Enjoy right away, or let cool for making the following soup.

Green Chile and Smoked Chicken Soup

This is spicy and addictive. If you can find Hatch chiles (from Hatch, New Mexico), use them. SERVES 8

2 tablespoons vegetable oil

1 medium-size onion, chopped

2 large carrots, chopped

2 to 3 cloves garlic, to your taste, minced

8 cups chicken broth

One 14-ounce can stewed tomatoes, preferably a Mexican-flavored variety, with their juice

1 cup chopped roasted mild green chiles, such as Hatch or poblano, preferably fresh or defrosted frozen chiles

2 cups grilled or smoked fresh corn kernels (about 2 ears) or defrosted frozen kernels

1 1/4 teaspoons dried oregano

Coarse kosher or sea salt to taste

1 recipe Smoked Chicken Breasts with Southwest Heat (page 215)

Minced fresh cilantro and finely shredded Monterey Jack cheese for garnish

1. Warm the oil in a large pot over high heat. Stir in the onion, carrots, and garlic and cook, stirring, until the onion is softened and browned on the edges. Frequently scrape up the vegetables from the bottom of the pan. Pour in the broth and add the tomatoes, chiles, corn, oregano, and salt. Bring to a boil, then reduce the heat to a simmer and cook until all the vegetables are tender, 25 to 30 minutes. (The broth can be prepared a day or two ahead to this point and refrigerated. Bring back to a simmer before adding the chicken.)

2. When the chicken is cool enough to handle, shred the meat into bite-size chunks, discarding the skin and bones or saving them to make smoky chicken stock later. Stir the chicken into the broth and continue to simmer for about 10 minutes. Ladle the soup into bowls, garnish with cilantro and cheese, and serve hot.

Rotisserie Chicken

In the last decade or so, rotisserie chicken has gone from a rare treat to a staple of weeknight family dinners. It seems as if every larger-scale grocery store, deli, or takeout restaurant offers rotisserie chicken in some way, shape, or form. But if you like rotisserie chicken that you buy, you'll *love* rotisserie chicken you make yourself.

You'll want a good-quality chicken to start with—preferably free-range, meaning the chicken was free to roam and search for its own food, not raised in close quarters in a huge chicken house. Because the flavor of the bird itself stands out when you rotisserie it, quality does matter. You'll want a younger chicken in the fryer range—3 to 4 pounds at the most. Remember to check both cavities of the bird for those little bundles of neck and giblets and remove them.

Check the maximum weight your rotisserie motor can handle, then buy your chicken. Rotisserie 2 or 3 chickens at a time and plan for delicious leftovers. (Karen makes the absolute best rotisserie chicken sandwiches; she packs them for when the BBQ Queens hit the road to give cooking classes or perform at other royal engagements.) This is our essential rotisserie chicken recipe. You could also marinate the chicken in Aromatic Lemon-Herb Marinade (page 68) or sprinkle on a rub after marinating the chicken; try Fair for Fowl Rub (page 51), Spicy Orange Rub (page 51), or Zesty Sugar and Spice Rub (page 52). The flavor of this chicken is so good and its texture so tender that we regard it as a stand-alone dish—no sauce needed. SERVES 6 TO 8

1/2 cup chopped fresh Italian parsley
6 cloves garlic, minced
Juice of 2 lemons
1/4 cup olive oil
Two 3- to 4-pound free-range chickens, giblets and necks removed
Kosher or sea salt and freshly ground black pepper to taste

1. In a small bowl, stir the parsley, garlic, lemon juice, and olive oil together. With a brush, slather the mixture all over the chickens, inside and out. Cover the chickens with plastic wrap and refrigerate for at least 1 hour or overnight.

2. Set up your grill for rotisserie cooking (see page 33). Prepare a medium fire (around 350°F).

3. Season the chickens with salt and pepper inside and out. Tie the legs together with kitchen twine. Attach a clamp to one end of each chicken. Push the rotisserie rod

through one clamp and the center of the chicken so the bird is balanced. Place the other chicken, clamp side out, on the rod, then push the rod through the second clamp. Attach the clamps to the spit and place a drip pan under the chickens. Cover and cook until an instant-read meat thermometer inserted in the thigh registers 170 to 175°F and a skewer inserted in the thickest part of a leg produces clear juices, about 1 1/2 hours.

4. Transfer the chickens to serving platters and tent with aluminum foil to keep warm. Let rest for 15 minutes before carving and serving.

Crowning Glories

Rotisserie chicken is delicious served family style with potato salad, sliced tomatoes, and other accompaniments that reflect the best of the farmers' market, such as:

Mediterranean Salad with Lemon-Sumac Vinaigrette *(page 279)*

Grilled Romaine Caesar Salad *(page 127)*

Grilled Corn *(page 119)*

French Tarragon Rotisserie Chicken: Instead of the herb and garlic slather, mix together 1/2 cup (1 stick) softened unsalted butter, 1 small bunch chopped fresh tarragon, and the juice of 1 lemon. Slather each chicken with this mixture inside and out, then sprinkle with kosher or sea salt and ground white pepper to taste. Marinate and cook as directed above. **SERVES 6 TO 8**

Puerto Rican–Style Rotisserie Chicken: Here's another intensely aromatic way of doing a whole chicken. Instead of the herb and garlic slather, in a mortar with a pestle crush together 8 black peppercorns, 1 tablespoon sea salt, and 4 garlic cloves until the peppercorns are at least cracked and you have a somewhat smooth paste. Using the pestle, stir in 1 tablespoon dried oregano, the juice of 2 limes, and 2 tablespoons olive oil until well blended. Slather each chicken with this mixture inside and out. Marinate and cook as directed above. **SERVES 6 TO 8**

Karen's Famous Rotisserie Chicken Sandwich: No boring airline food or typical burger fast food for the BBQ Queens when we travel! Karen packs two of these sandwiches in a cooler for the road. (They are so big, we eat only half at a time.) Even if we're driving in rain or get stuck driving around and around a country town (which we did once), these melt-in-your-mouth sandwiches sustain us. The surprising secret? Still-warm hard-boiled eggs that seem to vanish into the mayonnaise. Place 2 large eggs in a saucepan with water to cover, then bring to a boil over medium heat. Cook for 5 minutes, take off the heat to finish cooking gradually, then somewhat cool for about 8 minutes. Peel the eggs, then cut into very small pieces while still warm. Combine with 1 tablespoon chopped shallot, 1 tablespoon finely chopped celery, 1 cup chopped leftover rotisserie chicken, and $^1/_4$ to $^1/_2$ cup mayonnaise. Season with kosher or sea salt and freshly ground black pepper to taste. Spread the chicken salad between 2 slices of good-quality sourdough bread slathered with Dijon mustard. Add lettuce, if you like. **SERVES 1**

Smoked Whole Chicken

Smoked chicken is a versatile dish. You can never have too much of it on hand. Add it to salads, pasta dishes, chowders, or soups; use it to top a pizza; or combine it with crisp-cooked bacon for a club sandwich at lunch. If you love roast chicken, you'll also want to try it smoked. The difference is simply exchanging your hot oven for a slow smoker and allowing the extra time it takes for chicken to cook. It's sublime, queen's honor.

A whole chicken weighs anywhere from 3 to 6 pounds, with the 3- to 4-pound size being the most common. Use a good-quality bird, preferably free-range.

The smoking process is very similar to that for rotisserie cooking (see page 33). So if you don't have a rotisserie, you'll be smokin' your birds this way. The skin browns to a glistening mahogany color, and the meat is juicy and smoky. As with smoked pork butt, you can either slice or pull apart the meat of a slow-smoked chicken.

With all of the wonderful dishes you can make, the BBQ Queens recommend smoking two or three chickens at a time. (You can always throw one of the smoked chickens in the freezer for later—well wrapped, of course.) Smoking will take 45 to 60 minutes per pound of bird at 225 to 250°F. (Remember, the weather affects your smoking time, so allow more time for cold and windy weather and less time on a hot, still day.) Basically, a 4-pound chicken needs to smoke for about 3 hours, until the leg joint moves easily.

Don't forget to check the chicken's cavities for the giblets and neck, then anoint it with oil and season to taste. The fancier treatment is to sprinkle the bird with a rub (see pages 49–62), coat it with a slather (see page 66), or place it in a marinade (see pages 67–75) before smoking. Chicken is mild and adaptable to many different flavors, so we give you the royal okay to experiment. SERVES 4 TO 6

SUGGESTED WOOD: Fruitwood, grapevines, oak, mesquite, or hickory, or a combination

Two 3- to 4-pound chickens, giblets and necks removed

2 tablespoons olive oil

Fine kosher or sea salt and freshly ground black pepper to taste

1. Prepare an indirect fire in a smoker.

2. Rinse the birds thoroughly and pat dry. Rub 1 tablespoon olive oil over each and rub with salt and pepper. Place the birds in the smoker, close the lid, and smoke at 225 to 250°F. The chickens are done when a leg joint moves easily and the meat is no longer pink, about 2½ hours. An instant-read meat thermometer inserted in the thigh should register 170 to 175°F. Serve hot, or let cool to room temperature and place in the refrigerator. When cold, wrap in aluminum foil or plastic to keep for a couple of days chilled—perfect for raiding the icebox on a hot summer night.

Crowning Glories

Smoked whole chicken is delicious marinated in, prepared with, or served with:

Provençal Red Wine Marinade *(page 70)*

Fair for Fowl Rub *(page 51)*

Mustard-Mayo-Tarragon Slather *(page 66)*

Lemon Butter Drizzle *(page 87)*

Italian Barbecued Chicken: One of the members of the 'Que Queens, our competition barbecue team, owned her own barbecue restaurant. Jean Tamburello's Italian fusion barbecue at Marty's Bar-B-Que made the pages of *Saveur* magazine and was the toast of the town in Kansas City for years, until she retired and closed the restaurant. Her Italian fusion barbecue secret? Marinate a whole chicken in Amogio (page 72), smoke it, and then serve the smoked chicken with fresh amogio at the table. Simply delicious! **SERVES 4**

Rosemary-Garlic Smoked Chicken: This is from Karen's *Best Little Barbecue Cookbook* (Celestial Arts, 2000). It is as good as, if not better than, any store-bought rotisserie garlic chicken. Plus, when you prepare it yourself, you have braggin' rights. Coat each chicken with 1 tablespoon olive oil and sprinkle with 1 tablespoon chopped fresh rosemary. Cut about ½ inch off the top of 2 heads of garlic and place 1 head in the cavity of each chicken. Smoke as directed above and discard the garlic before serving. **SERVES 4 TO 6**

Smoked Sesame-Soy Marinated Chicken: A terrific marinade can make all the difference in the world. Combine 3/4 cup soy sauce, 2 tablespoons toasted sesame oil, 2 tablespoons dark honey, and 2 minced garlic cloves in a small bowl. Place each chicken in a sealable plastic bag and pour half of the marinade into each bag. Seal the bags and marinate in the refrigerator for at least 2 hours or up to 12 hours. Remove the chickens, discarding the marinade, and smoke as directed above. This Asian-style recipe also turns the smoky chicken into a perfect shredded meat to serve on a salad drizzled with Citrus Caesar Vinaigrette (page 84) that you spike with an additional 1 to 2 tablespoons soy sauce. **SERVES 4 TO 6**

Smoked Chicken and Vegetable Lasagna: Sometimes making lasagna can be a real mess, and we don't like that. Here is a recipe you can prepare in make-ahead steps. Preheat the oven to 350°F. In a large bowl, combine one 16-ounce container ricotta cheese, 1 cup freshly grated Pecorino Romano cheese, 2 cups whole milk, and 1 teaspoon garlic salt. (The sauce can be made several days ahead and refrigerated.) Pour 1 cup of the sauce in a greased 13 x 9 x 2-inch baking pan. Lay 3 no-cook lasagna noodles over the sauce. Top with 1 1/2 cups sliced grilled or smoked portobello mushrooms (see page 132 or 134) and 1 cup sauce. Lay 3 more lasagna noodles over the mushrooms. Top with 2 to 3 cups shredded smoked chicken (or duck) and 1 cup sauce. Repeat with the last layer of noodles, topped with more mushrooms or sliced grill-roasted bell peppers (see page 145) and the remaining 1 cup sauce. Sprinkle with 1 cup freshly grated Pecorino Romano cheese. (The lasagna can be refrigerated for up to 1 day.) Bake until browned and bubbling, 35 to 40 minutes. Remove from the oven and let sit for 15 minutes, then serve hot. **SERVES 10 TO 12**

BBQ QUEEN

Grilled Turkey Breast Tenderloin Steaks

Turkey is the real lean and mean deal for all of you high-protein, low-carb aficionados. Because turkey is mild, you can rub, slather, or sauce it any way you like. Haven't tried turkey on the grill yet? There is no trick, really, just common sense. The most difficult part is which cut to choose, because turkey comes in all sizes and shapes: whole, legs, turkey breast bone-in and boneless, cutlets, chops, tenderloin, tenderloin steaks, and ground.

Turkey makes for a light and easy summertime feast. Our Tarragon Grilled Turkey Breast (next page) comes out moist and delicious—fit for a queen! An easy chutney, store-bought or homemade (which is also good over cream cheese), is a delicious partner to turkey or chicken, hot or cold. Cool side dishes, such as coleslaw, pasta salad, or sliced tomatoes, complement the tasty bird and take you far from the roasted Thanksgiving turkey.

Let's focus on the easiest part to grill, turkey breast tenderloin steaks cut 1/2 inch thick. Yeah, we know the grocery store has those thick-cut turkey steaks with bacon wrapped around them, but they're about 1 1/2 inches thick and take longer to cook, plus it takes time to get the bacon crisp (and they end up tasting like bacon). We prefer thinner steaks for our simple version here.

We recommend a medium to medium-hot fire for turkey, because you don't want the meat to dry out before it's cooked all the way through. For some of these recipes, you'll need to prepare an indirect fire, which means you'll have a medium-hot fire on one side and no fire on the other side. Cook boneless turkey cuts to an internal temperature of 160 to 165°F and bone-in cuts to 170 to 175°F. Serve your grilled turkey with Grilled Red Potato and Fennel Salad (page 148) or Warm Asian Eggplant Salad (page 125). SERVES 4

Four 4- to 6-ounce turkey breast tenderloin steaks, 1/2 inch thick
Olive oil
Fine kosher or sea salt and freshly ground black pepper to taste

1. Prepare a medium to medium-hot fire in a grill.

2. Rub the steaks with olive oil and season with salt and pepper. Place directly over the fire until no longer pink, turning once after the first 6 or 7 minutes, for a total of 12 to 15 minutes. Boneless turkey is done when an instant-read meat thermometer inserted in the meatiest part registers 160 to 165°F. Serve hot.

Crowning Glories

Grilled turkey is delicious served with:

Bourbon-Mustard Cream Sauce ***(page 377)***

Chimichurri Sauce ***(page 346)***

Grilled Tomatillo Salsa ***(page 163)***

Tarragon Grilled Turkey Breast: This is a recipe for grilling half a bone-in turkey breast. It requires a much longer cooking time and needs to be constantly turned and basted while on the grill. The vinegar marinade gives the turkey a wonderful, tangy Carolina barbecue flavor. Rinse the split breast halves of 1 whole bone-in turkey breast and place in a sealable plastic bag. In a small bowl, combine 1/2 cup tarragon vinegar, 1/3 cup olive oil, 1 1/2 teaspoons poultry seasoning, 1 teaspoon dried tarragon, 2 minced garlic cloves, 1 1/2 teaspoons freshly ground black pepper, 2 teaspoons fine kosher or sea salt, 1 teaspoon hot pepper sauce, and 1 teaspoon fresh lemon or lime juice. Pour over the turkey, seal the bag, and marinate in the refrigerator for at least 1 hour or overnight. Remove from the marinade. Transfer the reserved marinade to a small saucepan, bring to a boil, and continue to boil for about 5 minutes. Cook the turkey directly over a medium-hot fire for about 1 hour, turning and basting with the reserved marinade every 5 minutes. The turkey is done when an instant-read meat thermometer inserted in the meatiest part registers 170 to 175°F. Serve hot. **SERVES 6 TO 8**

Turkey Steaks with Spicy Horseradish Sauce: The pungent flavors of this concoction complement plain meat, fish, and especially turkey. This is from Karen's *Best Little BBQ Sauces Cookbook* (Celestial Arts, 2000). In a small bowl, combine 1 cup lowfat sour cream, 1/4 cup prepared horseradish, 2 tablespoons chopped pimento, 1 tablespoon sweet Hungarian paprika, 1 teaspoon ground cumin, 1 teaspoon ground allspice, 1/2 teaspoon ground coriander, and 1/2 teaspoon red pepper flakes. Chill for at least 1 hour or up to 3 days before serving with the grilled turkey steaks. **SERVES 4**

Bacon-Wrapped Turkey Fillets: Yes, these are the grocery store treats that everyone buys. Lightly coat 4 turkey fillets with olive oil and season with kosher salt and freshly ground black pepper to taste. Roll each fillet into a cylinder. Wrap a slice of bacon around the middle of the cylinder, then wrap another slice around the cylinder lengthwise and secure with toothpicks. Grill the fillets for about 8 minutes, turning when the bacon begins to brown. Sear for 3 to 4 minutes, then move the fillets to the indirect side of the grill and close the lid. Cook until the center of a fillet registers 160 to 165°F on an instant-read meat thermometer, about 10 minutes. Serve with the condiments of your choice. **SERVES 4**

BBQ Queens

The Queen Waves

Whenever we do a cooking class or a demonstration, we always start out by teaching this important life skill.

Yes, knowing the four queen waves is a life skill. You never know when you're going to be homecoming queen, salesperson or employee of the year, mayor of your town, or the celebrity in a ticker-tape parade. That sort of thing can creep up on you unawares. It's best to be prepared for every eventuality. That's why most of us all have insurance. This is your celebrity insurance.

We have this information on good authority—from former Miss America Debbye Turner, who taught us these waves during a BBQ Queen television appearance in St. Louis.

It's hard to describe the waves in print; it's better to see them done in person. But we think you've probably seen enough beauty queen contests to get the general drift. So here are the four queen waves, from most rigorous (when your arm is fresh) to easier (when your arm is flagging, halfway through the parade) to the intimate wave when you're heading onstage to receive your award, your crown, your commendation, your key to the city, your accolade.

Screwing in the light bulb: With this wave, you just raise your arm so your upper arm is parallel to the ground, your elbow is bent, and your lower arm is straight up. Cup your hand and revolve your wrist a half turn and back, as if you were screwing in a light bulb. As Karen always says, this is Queen Elizabeth's favorite wave, although she does it differently because she's never had to screw in a light bulb.

Wiping the windshield: When your wrist starts to hurt, change to this wave. Again, raise your arm so your upper arm is parallel to the ground, your elbow is bent, and your lower arm is straight up. Open your hand so that your palm faces outward and wipe the windshield.

Fluttering the air: **Okay, so now your wrist *really* hurts. Change to a wave that will take the kinks out. This is a limper wave, so be less rigid. Raise your arm so your upper arm is parallel to the ground, your elbow is bent, and your lower arm is straight up. Bend your wrist up and down as you flutter your fingers. Bend and flutter, bend and flutter. (This is also good for carpal tunnel prevention, so you could do this at your desk at work.)**

The intimate wave: **All right. You have walked onstage. You've won! Now it's time to thank all those little people, seated in the audience, who have helped you get where you are today. Look out at each one. Point your arm straight out at them and pat in the air. A squeal of glee (think boo-boo-be-doo—oooo!) usually accompanies this gesture. Do this as many times as necessary, but once is not enough.**

BBQ-2

Smoked Boneless Turkey Breast

Half a smoked boneless, skinless turkey breast makes four 6-ounce servings. (A turkey tenderloin, which is much smaller, serves only two.) If you want leftovers for sandwiches, you'd better smoke two halves. Because the turkey is skinless, it needs to be covered. You can wrap it in leaves, cornhusks (facing each other and tied together), or prosciutto or bacon. We like to think of it as a pretty package that keeps the turkey meat moist while it is being anointed with luscious smoke.

The turkey breast can be slathered with mustard, flavored mayonnaise, chutney, or preserves, then wrapped in its protective coat. Also, season the breast meat with the herbs and spices of your choice. Or get a little adventurous and try Spicy, Savory Seasoned Salt (page 56) or Porcini Paste (page 65).

Turkey breast (or tenderloin) can be butterflied and pounded thin to make beautiful roulades. Even easier than roulades is to make turkey pockets by slitting the turkey breast in half lengthwise, but not cutting it all the way through, then stuffing with herbs, cheese, bread or fruit stuffing, or vegetables before smoking.

In addition to smoking domestic turkey, you can also go wild. Karen's husband, Dick, hunts wild turkeys, and she's had good luck—and lots of practice—with cooking wild turkey breasts in the smoker. (The legs are too tough, and she usually cuts them off.) Prepare and smoke a wild turkey breast like its domestic long-lost cousin.

Turkey smokes best at 225 to 250°F. Cooking time is 30 to 40 minutes per pound, so 3 pounds of boneless turkey will take 1½ to 2 hours to smoke. SERVES 4

SUGGESTED WOOD: Fruitwood, grapevines, pecan, oak, or maple

2 boneless, skinless turkey breast halves (about 3 pounds)
1 tablespoon olive oil
4 ounces thinly sliced prosciutto

1. Prepare an indirect fire in a smoker.

2. Rinse the turkey and pat dry. Lightly coat both breasts with the olive oil. Wrap each breast with half of the prosciutto. Place the turkey in the smoker, cover, and smoke at 225 to 250°F, until an instant-read meat thermometer inserted in the thickest part of the breast registers 160 to 165°F, 1½ to 2 hours. The turkey will have a hint of pink. Let rest for about 10 minutes before cutting into 3/8-inch-thick slices. Serve warm or chilled.

Crowning Glories

Smoked turkey is delicious served with all the traditional Thanksgiving trimmings.
But why not try something new, such as:
Grilled Portobellos with Garlic, Pine Nuts, Basil, and Goat Cheese *(page 133)*
Grilled Vegetable Platter with Fresh Basil Vinaigrette *(page 129)*
Summer Tomato, Pine Nut, and Caper Relish *(page 425)*

Smoked Turkey with Cranberry-Orange Salsa: Smoke the turkey breasts as described above, then make this salsa to serve with them. Over a medium-size bowl, grate the zest of 2 navel oranges. Peel the remaining white membrane from the oranges, discarding it. Chop the oranges and add to the bowl. Rinse and pick over 2 1/2 cups fresh cranberries, place in a food processor, and coarsely chop. Add to the oranges along with 1 seeded and diced jalapeño and 3/4 cup sugar. Toss to mix. (This salsa will keep in the refrigerator for several weeks or in the freezer for several months.) Serve with the smoked turkey. **SERVES 4**

Penne with Smoked Turkey, Goat Cheese Cream Sauce, and Sun-Dried Tomatoes: Cook 1 pound penne according to the package directions. Drain (reserving 1 cup of the pasta water) and set aside. In a large skillet, heat 2 tablespoons olive oil over medium heat. Add 2 minced garlic cloves and cook, stirring, for 1 to 2 minutes. Add 3/4 cup dry white wine and 1 bay leaf and bring to a boil, then reduce the heat to low and simmer for 10 minutes. Add 3 cups heavy cream and bring to a boil again. Reduce the heat to medium-low and simmer until thickened, about 4 minutes. Reduce the heat to low, whisk in 8 ounces crumbled fresh goat cheese, and simmer for about 5 minutes. (Be careful not to scorch.) Add the cooked pasta and gently warm, separating the penne. Stir in 1 1/2 to 2 cups chopped smoked turkey. If the sauce is too thick, add 2 or 3 tablespoons of the reserved pasta water at a time until the sauce is a medium-thick consistency. Using kitchen shears, cut 8 oil-packed sun-dried tomatoes into thin slivers and stir into the pasta. Serve hot. **SERVES 6**

Brie and Basil–Stuffed Turkey Breast: We were both awestruck looking at the oven- and grill-ready meats at the gourmet Dorothy Lane Markets in Dayton, Ohio. The Brie and basil–stuffed turkey breast was memorable, and we share our rendition here. Make a pocket slit in one 1 1/2-pound boneless, skinless turkey breast. Place 3 or 4 thin slices of Brie evenly inside the slit. Tuck 4 or 5 fresh basil leaves evenly on top of the cheese. Wrap the breast with about 2 ounces thinly sliced prosciutto. Smoke as directed above, which will take about 1 hour. **SERVES 2**

Rotisserie Turkey

Every year, magazine and newspaper food editors ask the same question: what can we do differently with the holiday bird for our readers?

The BBQ Queens have the answer: rotisserie that turkey! You'll free up your oven, give a rambunctious or annoying relative something to do (keep an eye on the turkey outside), and serve a bronzed, delicious, juicy entrée worthy of being the centerpiece of your feast. Our only reservation is that most rotisserie units are not placed high enough above the grill grate to allow you to twirl around a big bird, although you can probably manage a 10- to 12-pound whole turkey or a turkey breast or two. Be sure to check the manufacturer's instructions before you head to the store.

Also check the maximum weight your rotisserie motor can handle *before* you buy your turkey. Our recipe gives directions for a traditional rotisserie setup with an electric motor over a gas grill. If you have a fancy-schmancy setup with infrared technology, refer to the manufacturer's instructions for cooking times, as your turkey will take less time.

Our essential rotisserie turkey recipe is similar to the one for chicken on page 217—slathered with a paste made from fresh tarragon, garlic, lemon juice, and olive oil, then grilled rotisserie style. (Remember to check both cavities of the turkey to remove the giblets and neck.)

Instead of gravy, try this with our scrumptious The Doctor Is In Apricot-Bourbon Barbecue Sauce (page 90). However, if you add water, the giblets and neck, a bay leaf, and an onion to the drip pan—and keep it full of hot water—you *can* make that traditional turkey gravy (see right).

Rotisserie turkey is wonderful served with Autumn Roasted Red Pepper and Cannellini Bean Relish (page 426) if you want to go contemporary, or with mashed potatoes, green bean casserole, cranberry relish, and all the traditional trimmings for a holiday meal. **SERVES 8 TO 10**

1 cup chopped fresh tarragon
6 cloves garlic, minced
Juice of 4 lemons
1 cup olive oil
One 10- to 12-pound turkey, giblets and neck removed
Kosher and sea salt and freshly ground black pepper to taste

1. In a medium-size bowl, combine the tarragon, garlic, lemon juice, and olive oil. With a brush, slather the mixture all over the turkey, inside and out. Cover with plastic wrap and refrigerate for at least 1 hour or overnight.

2. Set up your grill for rotisserie cooking (see page 33). Prepare a medium fire (around 350°F).

3. Season the turkey with salt and pepper, inside and out. Tie the legs together with kitchen twine. Attach a clamp to each end of the turkey. Push the rotisserie rod through the clamps and the center of the turkey so the bird is balanced. Attach the clamps to the spit and place a drip pan under the turkey. Cover and cook until an instant-read meat thermometer inserted in the thickest part of a thigh registers 170 to 175°F or a skewer inserted in the thickest part of a leg produces clear juices, about 4 hours.

4. Transfer the turkey to a serving platter and tent with aluminum foil to keep warm. Let rest for 15 minutes before carving and serving.

Crowning Glories

Rotisserie turkey is delicious anointed with one of these during the last 1½ hours of cooking:

Honeyed Barbecue Sauce *(page 90)*

Raspberry-Jalapeño Barbecue Sauce *(page 90)*

Pistachio-Pomegranate Sauce *(page 96)*

Traditional Rotisserie Turkey Gravy: When you set up your drip pan under the turkey, place 1 halved large onion, the giblets and neck, and a bay leaf in it. Add 2 cups water and keep replenishing the water during the time the turkey cooks. You want the onion and giblets to brown some but not dry out. When the turkey is done, bring the drip pan indoors and discard the giblets, neck, bay leaf, and onion. Transfer the liquid to a saucepan. Try to scrape as many of the browned bits into the pan as you can. You should have about 2 cups liquid. (If not, add canned chicken broth to make 2 cups.) In a jar with a tight-fitting lid, place 2 tablespoons all-purpose flour and 1 cup cold water. Secure the lid and shake to blend well. Place the saucepan over medium-high heat and bring to a boil. Slowly pour in the flour mixture, whisking constantly, until the gravy thickens. Season with kosher or sea salt and freshly ground black pepper to taste and serve hot. **MAKES ABOUT 3 CUPS**

Day-After Rotisserie Turkey Sandwich: The day after your rotisserie turkey feast, you can relax and enjoy this tasty sandwich made with leftovers. Between 2 slices of good-quality sourdough bread, pile slices of leftover turkey, a dollop of Roasted Red Pepper Aioli (page 110), and lettuce if you like. Ahhh. **SERVES 1**

Smoked Whole Turkey

Traditionally, people smoke turkeys only for Thanksgiving. But when you fall in love with the exquisite kiss of smoke, how can you wait another year for moist and succulent smoked turkey?

When the Chicago chapter of Les Dames d'Escoffier invited us to do our BBQ Queen gig at a big party hosted by our good friend Dame Rose Kallas, three apple-smoked turkeys were on our menu (see page 171 for the rest). So the next time you need an entrée to serve a crowd, think smoked turkey!

Turkey smokes best at 225 to 250°F. The cooking time is about 30 minutes per pound, or until an instant-read meat thermometer inserted in the meatiest part of the thigh registers 175 to 180°F. Apply these guidelines whether you are smoking a whole turkey or a whole turkey breast with the bone in.

The turkey can be slathered with mustard, chutney, or preserves, or seasoned or marinated with Rosemary Salt (page 56) or Wheat Beer Vinaigrette (page 77). It adapts well to many flavors, so sprinkle with just about any rub you like. Our recipe is foolproof and produces a luscious and juicy bird.

SERVES 8 TO 10

SUGGESTED WOOD: Apple, oak, maple, mesquite, or hickory

One 10- to 12-pound turkey, giblets and neck removed
2 to 3 tablespoons olive oil, as needed
3 tablespoons sweet Hungarian paprika
2 tablespoons fine sea salt
2 tablespoons lemon pepper seasoning

1. Rinse the bird and pat dry. Place in a disposable aluminum pan and coat lightly with oil.

2. In a glass jar with a tight-fitting lid, combine the paprika, salt, and lemon pepper. Shake to blend, then sprinkle on the turkey inside and out. Set the bird aside for about 20 minutes.

3. Prepare an indirect fire in a smoker.

4. Place the turkey in the smoker, cover, and smoke at 225 to 250°F until an instant-read meat thermometer inserted in the thigh registers 170 to 175°F, 4 to 5 hours. The smoked turkey will be golden brown on the outside and the meat will have a slightly pinkish color. Serve hot.

Crowning Glories

Smoked turkey is delicious served with all the traditional Thanksgiving trimmings, or with oven-roasted potatoes and butternut squash wedges seasoned with olive oil and fresh rosemary. In the summer, serve it with your favorite barbecue side dishes, such as:

Smoked Tomato Grits ***(page 164)***

Warm Asian Eggplant Salad ***(page 125)***

Savory Breads on the Grill ***(pages 176–178)***

Smoky Chipotle Corn Pudding ***(page 122)***

Smoked Turkey and Monterey Jack Club Sandwiches: Don't you want one right now? Spread 4 slices of sourdough bread (toasted if you wish) with mayonnaise or Dijon mustard. For each sandwich, on 1 slice of bread layer a couple of slices of smoked turkey, 1 or 2 slices of Monterey Jack cheese, 2 or 3 slices of crisp-cooked bacon, and some sliced ripe avocado. Add a thin slice of tomato or slivers of oil-packed sun-dried tomatoes. Top with the other bread slice and feast. **SERVES 2**

Smoked Turkey Hash: You either like hash or you don't. Karen and Dick both love it, corned beef or turkey, made into a patty, sautéed until browned and crisp, and served with a soft fried or poached egg on top. This recipe makes it soufflé style in a lightly greased 13 x 9 x 2-inch pan. Preheat the oven to 375°F. In a food processor, coarsely chop enough smoked turkey to yield 3 cups and place in a large bowl. Add 1 finely chopped large onion, 3 cups chopped cooked potatoes or stuffing, 1 cup leftover or defrosted frozen corn (optional), 1/2 cup freshly grated Pecorino Romano cheese, 2 minced garlic cloves, and 2 tablespoons chopped fresh Italian parsley and mix well. Season with kosher salt and freshly ground black pepper to taste. In a medium-size bowl, beat together 3 large eggs and 1 cup half-and-half. Add to the turkey mixture, mix well, and spoon into the prepared pan. In a small bowl, combine 1/2 cup freshly grated Pecorino Romano cheese and 1/4 cup seasoned dry bread crumbs and sprinkle on top. Bake for 30 minutes, then turn on the broiler and brown the top. Serve with a mixed greens and frisée salad, with a poached egg atop either the hash or the salad. Very continental! **SERVES 10 TO 12**

BBQ Babes

She's Smokin' and Talkin' Turkey Menu

Apple-Smoked Turkey

Rosemary-Apple Salsa

BBQ Babe Carolyn Wells is the cofounder and executive director of the Kansas City Barbeque Society. During competition barbecue season from spring to fall, she's out and about every weekend, traveling all over the country as an ambassador for barbecue. She's at her busiest during the first weekend in October, when the gargantuan American Royal Barbecue Contest is in full swing in Kansas City.

Although she's a great judge of barbecue, Carolyn is also a pretty mean cook herself. She dished out this memorable smoked turkey and salsa to members of the food media in New York City at Tavern on the Green in the early 1990s to rave reviews. Try it as a fresh and delicious change of pace for Thanksgiving.

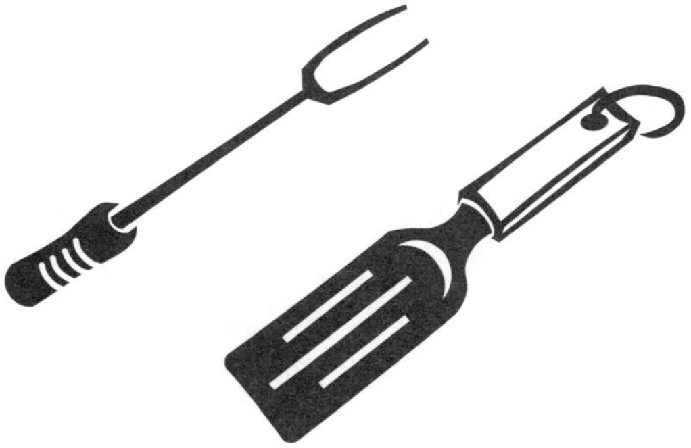

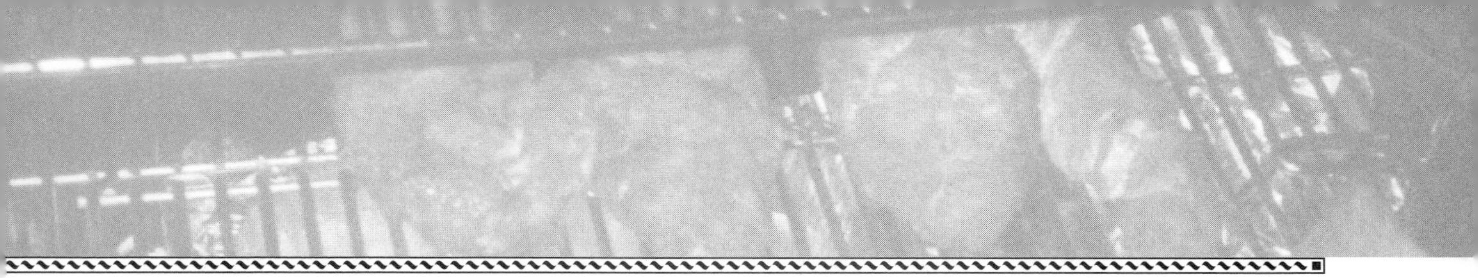

Apple-Smoked Turkey

The interior of a smoked turkey is a pinkish color, the exterior dark bronze. The best way to make sure it's done is to use an instant-read meat thermometer inserted in the thickest part of the thigh. When it registers 170 to 175°F, your bird is the word. You definitely won't mind these smoked turkey leftovers. They make terrific sandwiches.
SERVES 8

SUGGESTED WOOD: Apple or a combination of apple and hickory

One 10-pound turkey or 2 whole bone-in turkey breasts
1 cup balsamic vinegar
1/4 cup water
3 tablespoons sweet Hungarian paprika
2 tablespoons coarse sea salt
2 tablespoons lemon pepper seasoning
1/4 teaspoon dried marjoram

1. Remove the giblets and neck from the whole turkey, if using. Rinse the whole turkey or turkey breasts. Place in a large plastic bag and set in the kitchen sink.

2. Combine the vinegar, water, paprika, salt, lemon pepper, and marjoram in a glass jar with a tight-fitting lid. Cover and shake to blend. Pour the marinade into the bag and seal with a twist tie. Keeping the bag upright so it won't leak, let the turkey marinate in the refrigerator for at least 1 hour, preferably overnight. If the turkey is too large to fit in your refrigerator, put it in an iced cooler. Make sure it stays cold.

3. Prepare an indirect fire in a smoker.

4. Remove the turkey from the marinade and place in the smoker. Cover and smoke at 225 to 250°F until an instant-read meat thermometer inserted in the thickest part of the thigh registers 170 to 175°F, 4 to 5 hours. When the turkey is smoked, the meat will have a pale pink color. Serve hot.

Rosemary-Apple Salsa

The fresh crispness and tang of rosemary in this salsa pairs well with both poultry and pork. MAKES ABOUT 4 CUPS

1 large yellow bell pepper, seeded and chopped
1 Granny Smith apple, cored and chopped
1 large Jonathan apple, cored and chopped
8 green onions
1/3 cup diced dried apricots
3 tablespoons fresh lemon juice
1 cup extra virgin olive oil
2 teaspoons finely chopped fresh rosemary
1/2 teaspoon sea salt
Freshly ground black pepper to taste

In a large bowl, combine all the ingredients. Cover and refrigerate for at least 1 hour before serving. This salsa will keep, covered, in the refrigerator for 3 to 4 days.

Grilled Duck Paillards

Karen and Dick like their wild mallard duck breast grilled or pan-seared to medium-rare (a medium temperature is also acceptable); medium-well to well done produces a dry, unappetizing dish. If that's the way you prefer your meat, perhaps duck is not for you. For a larger Muscovy duck breast, score the skin by using a sharp knife and cutting diagonal slashes through it (but do not cut into the duck meat). This allows the fat to cook off and the skin to crisp. Grill the larger breasts over medium-hot heat until an instant-read meat thermometer inserted in the thickest part registers 140 to 145°F for medium-rare, about 7 minutes.

Here's a lesson on making duck (or other wild game bird) breasts into a *paillard,* a French term for a boneless piece of meat that has been flattened to a uniform thickness. The easiest way we've found to do this is to use the rim of a saucer. Simply pound the breast, starting in the middle and working your way out to the sides, until the meat is an even 1/2 to 1 inch thick. In a hot grill or in a grill pan over high heat, cook the paillard for 10 minutes per inch of thickness. For example, grill a 1/2-inch-thick paillard for 2 1/2 minutes per side, or 5 minutes total. If the skin is on the breast meat, cook the skin side an additional 1 to 2 minutes to get it nice and crispy.

While you're grilling duck, try these sides on the grill, too: Grilled Green Onions and Red Onion Slices (page 138), Char-Grilled Baby Summer Squash (page 155), and Grilled Tomatoes (page 159).

SERVES 4

Four 4- to 5-ounce boneless, skinless wild or domestic duck breasts, flattened to about 1/2 inch thick (see headnote)

1/2 cup red wine

8 juniper berries

4 sprigs each fresh thyme and oregano

1 tablespoon olive oil

Kosher salt and freshly ground black pepper to taste

1. Place the duck breasts in a sealable plastic bag and add the wine, juniper berries, and herb sprigs. Seal the bag and marinate in the refrigerator for 1 to 2 hours.

2. Prepare a medium-hot fire in a grill.

3. Remove the duck from the bag and dispose of the marinade. Pat the duck dry, lightly coat with the olive oil, and season with salt and pepper. Place on the grill directly over the fire. Grill for 2 1/2 to 3 minutes per side for medium-rare, or until an instant-read meat thermometer inserted in the thickest part registers 140 to 145°F.

Duck, Duck, Goose

Karen is the queen of game cooking. Her husband, Dick, is an avid hunter of upland game birds, waterfowl, and wild turkeys. Karen hunts a little, but her time is more successfully spent cooking the quarry. Upland game birds from the Midwest are plentiful and tasty, too, because the birds feed on the rich farmland crops and natural prairie grasses of the region. Elsewhere in the United States, ducks and other waterfowl may be referred to as gamy or fishy because their main food intake is fish.

Wild ducks and other game birds are very tasty when grilled. Sizes for dressed birds range from the smaller, 1-pound ducks such as teals and wood ducks, to midsize widgeons at $1\frac{1}{2}$ pounds, to the prized mallards at about 2 pounds (farm-raised mallards are available, too). Canvasbacks and black ducks are a bit larger, at 3 pounds, and they are followed by geese, at 6 to 10 pounds. The differences between wild and farm-raised birds are the taste and the fat content, which is uniformly higher on farm-raised birds. The amount of fat on wild ducks and geese depends on what time of year they are killed. Early in the fall, the birds are leaner, and by winter, they are fattier.

The domestic ducks most readily available include the Pekin duck, also referred to as the Long Island duck, which is a big, plump white duck with a mild taste; the Muscovy duck, a flavorful and musky bird that is much larger than the Long Island duck; and Moulard duck, a cross of Muscovy and Pekin and prized for its delicious *foie gras*. Then there are upland game birds, which vary in size from the small quail (8 ounces) to the grouse, chukar, and prairie chicken (1 to 3 pounds) to the pheasant (4 to 6 pounds).

The point of all this for the cook is that when a recipe calls for duck or other game bird breasts, there are many variables: whether you are using wild or domestic, whether the skin is on or off, whether the breast is fatty or lean. The way we are going to address this huge variable is to prepare the breasts as paillards of a uniform thickness.

Grilling whole ducks or other birds is best over an indirect fire, which is more like smoking than grilling. The whole bird roasts in the closed grill over an indirect fire, with the temperature at 350°F. Domestic game birds will most likely have the skin on. Wild game birds are often field dressed by skinning them. Preparing these skinless birds on the grill requires care not to dry them out. One way to do this is by wrapping them in lettuce leaves, cornhusks, prosciutto, or bacon. Wild birds have little fat, so preparing them like a boneless, skinless chicken paillard (see page 191) is also an option.

Crowning Glories

Try a nice sauce to serve on the side or to pool on the plate with your duck breasts:

Raspberry and Blood Orange Sauce *(page 92)*

Mustard-Cornichon Beurre Blanc *(page 100)*

Pistachio-Pomegranate Sauce *(page 96)*

Grilled Duck Paillards with Dried Sweet Cherry–Port Sauce: Score the skin of 4 boneless, skinless duck breasts pounded into 1-inch-thick paillards and sprinkle each with 1 tablespoon Spicy Red-Hot Lemon Pepper Rub (page 53). In a small saucepan, combine 1 cup beef broth, 1/4 cup port, 1/2 cup dried sweet cherries, 1 tablespoon soy sauce, and 2 tablespoons packed dark brown sugar. Bring to a boil and reduce by half, stirring often. Remove from the heat and add 1 tablespoon cornstarch dissolved in 2 tablespoons cold water. Whisk and return to medium heat to thicken slightly, continuing to stir, about 5 minutes. Set aside. Prepare a medium-hot fire in a grill. Grill the duck breasts skin side down until the skin is browned, about 7 minutes. Turn and grill for 5 minutes more. For medium-rare, the duck should register 140 to 145°F on an instant-read meat thermometer inserted in the thickest part of the breast. Slice on the diagonal, spoon the warm sauce over the meat, and serve. **SERVES 4**

Grilled Duck Breast Salad: This is a favorite at the Adlers' house. In a large bowl, combine 1 cup shredded cooked duck, 1 cup fresh fruit (such as orange wedges or berries), 1/2 cup crumbled Maytag blue cheese, 2 tablespoons slivered red onion, 3 cups lettuce, and 2 to 3 tablespoons of a sweet and tangy dressing such as Balsamic-Thyme Vinaigrette (page 84) or a homemade or bottled poppy seed dressing. Toss lightly to coat everything with the dressing. Serve with crusty bread (or a duck sandwich on the side). **SERVES 2**

Smoked Whole Duck

Karen is always tweaking her duck recipes and has found a couple of favorite ways to smoke duck. Shortcut versions of smoking include using store-bought spice blends. She says any kind of herb or pepper blend is quite nice. You can take the grocery store route and pick up a couple of McCormick spice blends (such as chipotle chile; see page 59) or buy an exotic blend online from Penzeys Spices or Vanns Spices (see Resource Guide, page 446). SERVES 6

SUGGESTED WOOD: Fruitwood, black walnut, pecan, or grapevines

3 wild or domestic ducks, such as mallards (about 6 pounds total)

1 tablespoon olive oil

3 tablespoons pepper blend

1 tablespoon fine kosher or sea salt

1/2 cup barbecue sauce of your choice, thinned with 2 tablespoons fresh lemon juice

1. Rinse the ducks well and make sure all the pinfeathers and shot have been removed. Singe the hairs off the birds. Pat dry. Place in a shallow disposable aluminum pan, rub with the olive oil, and sprinkle all over (including the cavities) with the pepper blend and salt.

2. Prepare a smoker for an indirect fire with a water pan filled with hot water. Add 3 or 4 chunks of water-soaked wood to the fire.

3. Smoke the ducks at 225°F for 20 to 30 minutes per pound, basting with the barbecue sauce 2 or 3 times during cooking. Three ducks weighing 6 pounds total will take 2 to 3 hours. The ducks are done when an instant-read meat thermometer inserted in a thigh registers 170 to 175°F. Serve hot.

Crowning Glories

Serve your smoked duck with:

Classic Creamed Spinach *(page 319)*

Decadent Garlic Mashed Potatoes *(page 321)*

Smoked Tomato and Basil Butter *(page 177)*

Smoked Duck and Wild Rice Soup: This is a hearty soup fit for company. It works well if you have just a little leftover smoked duck or a lot. Heat 2 to 3 tablespoons olive oil in a large Dutch oven over medium-high heat. Add 1 chopped onion, 2 chopped carrots, and 2 chopped celery stalks and sauté for about 5 minutes, until softened. Turn the heat to medium-low, add 2 tablespoons all-purpose flour, and stir to make a roux. Increase the heat to medium and add two 10-ounce cans beef consommé. Cook, stirring, until thickened, about 10 minutes. Add 4 cups cooked wild rice and 1 to 2 cups chopped smoked duck meat. Add 1 to 2 cups water, enough just to cover all the food. Continue cooking until heated through. Serve hot, with 1 ounce feta cheese crumbled over each bowl. **SERVES 4 TO 6**

Smoked Duck Breasts: Wild duck breasts are usually skinless, but domestic duck breasts usually have the skin on. The skin and its layers of fat help keep the breasts from drying out. Lightly coat 4 duck breasts with olive oil and season with coarse kosher salt and freshly ground black pepper to taste. If using wild duck, wrap the breasts in bacon or prosciutto to keep the meat moist. Prepare a smoker as directed above. Place the breasts in the smoker and cook for 20 to 30 minutes per pound. Serve warm, or refrigerate and toss lightly with mayonnaise and chopped fresh herbs to make a simple duck salad. **SERVES 4**

Smoked Duckling with Five-Spice Asian Paste: This is Asian fusion cooking at its best. Rub the interior and exterior of a Long Island duck or two 8- to 10-ounce bone-in Muscovy duck breasts with Five-Spice Asian Paste (page 64). Place in a disposable aluminum pan, cover, and smoke as directed above. **SERVES 2**

Duck on a Beer Can: Try this one, my little ducky! Prepare a 3- to 4-pound duck by soaking it in a marinade or applying a dry rub of your choice. Place the duck cavity side down on a can of beer (or other liquid such as fruit juice or apple cider). Make an indirect fire in a smoker as described above. Close the lid and smoke at 300°F until an instant-read meat thermometer inserted in the thigh registers 160 to 170°F, about 1 hour. **SERVES 2**

BBQ Babes

She's Wild for Smoke Menu

Apricot and Cognac–Glazed Duck

Drunk Elk or Venison

Durn Good Rice

Grilled Stuffed Apples

BBQ Babe Candy Weaver's family-owned business BBQr's Delight manufactures flavored wood pellets for smoking. Yep, you got it, she makes her own smoke. And the flavors she creates are sublime, from the more unusual orange, mulberry, sassafras, black walnut, and savory herb to hickory, pecan, mesquite, oak, and more, totaling 12 flavors and growing. These all-natural wood pellets do not have to be presoaked, so they are ready to use at a moment's notice. You just wrap 1/3 cup of pellets in aluminum foil, poke holes in the packet, place it over the smoker's heat source, and get ready for some tasty eating. (See Resource Guide, page 447, for more information about this product.)

Candy is a country girl from Arkansas and proud of it. Here are some of her delectable recipes featuring game, which is plentiful in her neck of the woods. If game is not your thing, substitute chicken or turkey for the duck, and beef for the elk or venison. These recipes come from Candy's cookbook, *Smoking with Wood Pellets* (available from BBQr's Delight).

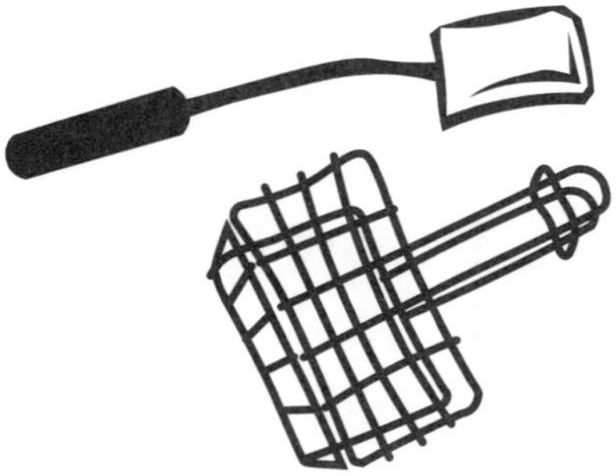

Apricot and Cognac–Glazed Duck

This glaze is also delicious on pork, ham, and other poultry. Two or three wild mallard ducks can be substituted for one larger duck. SERVES 4

APRICOT AND COGNAC GLAZE

8 ounces dried apricots, chopped, or 1/4 cup apricot jam

1 cup cognac or brandy

1 1/2 cups water

One 5-pound duck (or chicken, turkey, or goose)

1. To make the glaze, place the apricots and cognac in a small saucepan and cook over low heat until the apricots dissolve, 10 to 15 minutes. Add the water and simmer over medium heat until it just begins to boil. Turn the heat down and continue to simmer until the mixture is thick, about 10 minutes.

2. Prepare a medium-hot indirect fire in a grill. Put a mixture of pecan, black walnut, and sassafras pellets in an aluminum foil pouch or smoke box and set over the fire.

3. When the smoke starts, put the duck on the indirect side of the grill. If you have a rotisserie, you may use it (see page 33). Close the lid and cook the duck, turning every 20 minutes, for 1 1/2 hours. Baste with the glaze for the last 20 to 30 minutes of cooking time. The duck is done when an instant-read meat thermometer inserted in the thigh and breast registers 180°F.

Drunk Elk or Venison

Because elk and venison are so lean, injecting the buttery cheese mixture is very important to keep the meat moist during cooking. **SERVES 6 TO 8**

One 3- to 4-pound elk or venison tenderloin or roast

INJECTION

2 cups beef broth
1/4 cup (1/2 stick) butter
8 ounces Merkts sharp cheddar cheese spread or other cheese spread
2 tablespoons granulated garlic
2 tablespoons Tiger Sauce or other hot pepper sauce
2 tablespoons soy sauce
2 tablespoons Worcestershire sauce
1/2 cup whiskey

MARINADE

1/2 cup olive oil
1/2 cup soy sauce
1/3 cup fresh lemon juice
2 tablespoons red wine vinegar
2 to 4 cloves garlic, to your taste, chopped

1. Bring the meat to room temperature.

2. To make the injection, combine all the ingredients in a small saucepan over low heat and stir until dissolved. Remove from the heat and let cool briefly, then pour into the injector and inject the meat in 8 to 10 places. Place the meat in a large sealable plastic bag.

3. To make the marinade, combine all the ingredients in a small bowl. Pour into the bag, seal, and refrigerate for 12 to 24 hours.

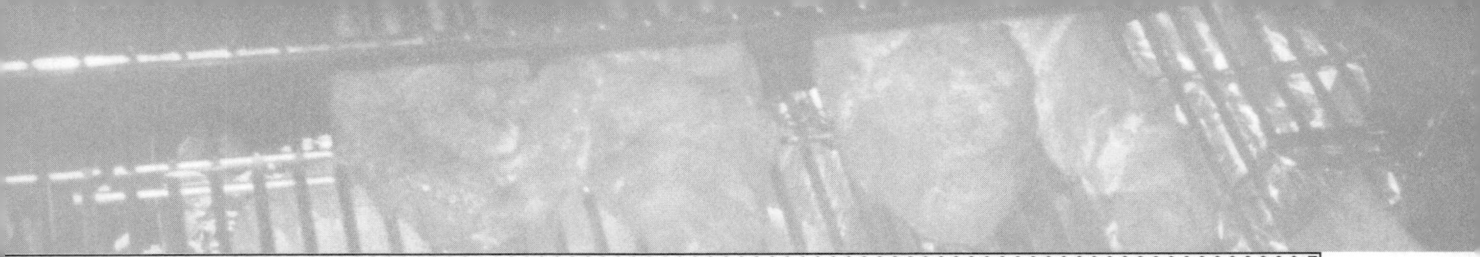

4. When ready to smoke, prepare an indirect fire in a grill. Place a packet of Jack Daniel's wood pellets (available from BBQr's Delight) over the fire.

5. When the fire reaches 250°F, remove the meat from the marinade and place it on the indirect side of the grill. Discard the marinade. Close the lid and cook until an instant-read meat thermometer inserted in the thickest part registers 130 to 140°F, 1 to $1\frac{1}{2}$ hours.

Durn Good Rice

This recipe works with wild rice, too, which is a nice accompaniment to game. If you like, substitute 3 cups precooked wild rice for the raw rice. The beauty of this is that it's smoking right along with the meat. SERVES 4 TO 6

1 cup long-grain white or brown rice
1 small onion, finely chopped
$\frac{1}{4}$ large red bell pepper, seeded and finely chopped
1 stalk celery, finely chopped
1 tablespoon unsalted butter
$\frac{1}{4}$ teaspoon garlic powder
1 tablespoon Worcestershire sauce
$2\frac{1}{2}$ cups chicken broth or water
1 green onion, chopped, for garnish
2 tablespoons chopped fresh Italian parsley or cilantro for garnish (optional)

1. Place all the ingredients except the green onion and parsley in a heatproof baking dish or disposable aluminum pan and stir to combine. Cook on the indirect side of the grill (alongside the meat you are cooking) until all the liquid is evaporated and the rice is tender, 1 to 2 hours.

2. Remove the rice from the grill and garnish with the green onion and parsley before serving.

Grilled Stuffed Apples

Any flavor of smoke works well here. **SERVES 4**

4 Rome or Granny Smith apples

1 teaspoon ground cinnamon

4 teaspoons raisins

4 teaspoons chopped nuts (optional)

2 teaspoons honey

Cut the top off each apple (looks like a cap) and save. Core the apples. Sprinkle the inside of each with 1/4 teaspoon cinnamon. Combine the raisins and nuts (if using) in a cup, then pack the center of each apple evenly with the mixture. Drizzle the stuffing with 1/2 teaspoon honey. Put the tops back on the apples. Place in a baking dish or disposable aluminum pan. Smoke for about 1 hour on the indirect side of the grill (alongside the meat you are cooking). Serve warm.

Grilled Game Birds

After the hazy heat of August on the prairie, the crisp blue skies of September herald the beginning of autumn and game bird hunting season. Pheasant, quail, ruffed and sharp-tailed grouse, and prairie chicken thrive in the tall prairie grasses, where they make their nests and raise their young. To stalk these upland game birds, hunters—including Karen's husband, Dick—walk through fields with their dogs, hoping to startle the birds into flight. Upland game birds—mainly quail and pheasant—are also farm-raised in Illinois and Indiana, supplying the restaurant trade as well as upscale butcher shops and gourmet markets (such as Whole Foods Market, Central Market, and Dean & Deluca).

Smaller birds, such as quail and woodcock, may be grilled, roasted, or baked. Cornish game hens, which are usually available frozen, are great substitutes for quail. Pheasant do better with lower, slower smoking. A marinade or baste containing butter or oil is used to keep the meat from drying out during hot and fast grilling.

Our basic recipe for grilled quail, woodcock, or Cornish game hens is based on one found in Karen's *Best Little Grilling Book* (Celestial Arts, 2000). Adding a handful of water-soaked apple, cherry, or grape wood chips to the fire will give these birds a pleasant, smoky flavor. To accompany grilled game birds, try Decadent Garlic Mashed Potatoes (page 321), Olive Oil Smashed Potatoes (page 320), or Crunchy Broccoli Slaw with Thai Chile-Peanut Dressing (page 80). SERVES 4

8 quail or woodcock, or 4 Cornish game hens, split in half

Handful of apple, cherry, or grape wood chips (optional), soaked in water for at least 30 minutes before grilling

1 cup (2 sticks) unsalted butter, melted

2 teaspoons chopped fresh tarragon

Fine kosher or sea salt and freshly ground black pepper to taste

1. Rinse the quail under cold running water, then pat dry.

2. Prepare a medium-hot fire in a grill. Add the wood chips, if desired.

3. In a medium-size bowl, stir together the melted butter and tarragon and take to the grill. Dip the quail in the mixture, then place on the grill. Grill for 3 to 4 minutes, turn, baste with the butter mixture, and grill for 3 to 4 minutes more. The quail breast meat will turn opaque and the underside will be pale pink. (The Cornish game hens will take 10 to 15 minutes per side. An instant-read meat thermometer inserted in the thickest part of the thigh should register 170 to 175°F. The meat should not be at all pink. Turn the hens every 5 minutes and baste while grilling.) Season with salt and pepper and serve hot.

Crowning Glories

Try slathering your game birds with:

Honeyed Barbecue Sauce *(page 90)*

Raspberry-Jalapeño Barbecue Sauce *(page 90)*

Asian Barbecue Sauce *(page 90)*

Cornish Game Hens with Orange-Honey Baste: You can slow smoke these game hens at 250°F for 1 1/2 to 2 hours or grill them over a medium-hot fire (see above) for 25 to 30 minutes—it's your choice. A combination of mesquite and pecan wood chunks for smoking or wood chips for grilling adds another flavor component. (Soak the chunks in water for at least 1 hour before using. Soak the chips for at least 30 minutes.) Rinse and pat dry 4 Cornish game hens. Mix together 1 cup orange juice, 3 tablespoons Cointreau or other orange-flavored liqueur, 1/2 cup honey, and 1/4 cup (1/2 stick) melted unsalted butter. Place the hens and marinade in an extra-large sealable plastic bag, seal, and marinate in the refrigerator for at least 4 hours or overnight, turning several times. Remove from the marinade and smoke or grill. **SERVES 4**

Grilled Cornish Game Hens à la Chez Panisse: This recipe is adapted from a grilled quail recipe by Alice Waters at Chez Panisse in Berkeley, California. In a small bowl, combine 1 cup dry white wine, 3/4 cup olive oil, 3 sliced shallots, 6 minced garlic cloves, 10 juniper berries, and 3 bay leaves. Place 4 Cornish game hens (or woodcock or quail) in an extra-large sealable plastic bag, add the marinade, seal, and marinate in the refrigerator for several hours or overnight. Grill as directed above and serve simply garnished with Italian parsley sprigs and lemon wedges. **SERVES 4**

Warm Grilled Quail Salad with Spiced Pears and Mushrooms: Served in the fall or winter, this wonderful salad is both comforting and exotically aromatic. Use fresh shiitake mushrooms if you can find them; if not, sliced button mushrooms will do just fine. Arrange a handful of mixed greens (such as escarole, frisée, romaine lettuce, and baby spinach) on 4 salad plates. Right after you grill the quail (see above), tent them with aluminum foil to keep warm. Then peel, core, and slice 4 ripe but firm pears. Dust the slices with Zesty Sugar and Spice Rub (page 52). Melt 2 tablespoons unsalted butter in a large skillet over medium-high heat. Add the pear slices and cook, turning once, until tender, about 8 minutes. Remove from the pan and arrange over the salad greens. In the same pan over medium-high heat, cook 4 ounces stemmed and quartered shiitake mushrooms, stirring, until softened, about 5 minutes. Place on top of the pears. Place a grilled quail on top of each salad. Deglaze the pan over high heat with a mixture of 2 tablespoons cider vinegar, 1 tablespoon Dijon mustard, and 1 tablespoon olive oil, scraping up any browned bits from the pan. Boil for 30 seconds, stir, and drizzle over the salads. Serve warm. **SERVES 4**

Smoked Small Game Birds

Smoked game birds such as quail, chukar, and roughed grouse, all weighing in at 1 to 3 pounds, are perfect for the smoker. If you purchase the birds from a supplier, they will most likely be dressed out, with the skin on. If they come from a hunter, often they will be dressed without the skin. Skinless birds need to be wrapped with bacon or prosciutto so the meat doesn't dry out. Cornish game hens can be substituted in these recipes.

For other sizes of game birds, follow the directions for poultry weighing about the same. For instance, whole pheasant can be smoked using any of the poultry recipes. (Simply smoke for 20 to 30 minutes per pound.) Remember that game birds are often leaner than domestic birds and so tend to dry out faster, so shorten the cooking time.

When ready, the skin of smoked game birds is a glistening mahogany color and the meat is juicy and smoky. Just like smoked pork butt, you can either slice or pull apart the meat. Because these are smaller game birds, we recommend smoking four or more birds at a time. (One quail serves a dainty appetite. Two quail are a regular serving for dinner, but if you have more, smoke them—they will disappear quickly.) In place of the olive oil and salt and pepper, experiment with rubs (pages 49–62), slathers (page 66), or marinades (pages 67–75) prior to smoking. SERVES 4

SUGGESTED WOOD: Fruitwood, grapevines, oak, mesquite, or hickory, or a combination

8 quail or other small game birds (about 4 pounds total), skinned and cleaned
3 tablespoons olive oil
Fine kosher or sea salt and freshly ground black pepper to taste

1. Rinse the quail thoroughly and pat dry. Rub about 1 teaspoon olive oil over each quail, then rub with salt and pepper.
2. Prepare an indirect fire in a smoker.

3. Place the birds side by side in the smoker and close the lid. Smoke at 225°F. The quail are done when a leg joint moves easily and the meat is no longer pink, about 2 hours. An instant-read meat thermometer inserted in the meatiest portion of the bird but not touching the bone should register 170°F. Serve hot, or let cool to room temperature and refrigerate. When cold, wrap in aluminum foil or plastic and store in the refrigerator for up to 2 days.

Crowning Glories

Marinate, baste, or serve these birds up with:

Homemade Teriyaki Marinade *(page 69)*

Rosemary, Garlic, and Lemon Baste *(page 68)*

Hot Shallot Vinaigrette *(page 85)*

Bacon-Wrapped Smoked Quail and Pheasant: This recipe comes from Karen's *Best Little Barbecue Cookbook* (Celestial Arts, 2000). You need 8 skinned and cleaned quail, 1 skinned and cleaned pheasant cut in half, and 10 slices of bacon or prosciutto. In a large container, combine 1/2 cup soy sauce, 1/4 cup olive oil, 1/4 cup Marsala wine, the juice and grated zest of 1 orange, and 2 minced garlic cloves. Add the birds, cover, and refrigerate for 4 to 12 hours. Prepare a hot fire on one side of a grill. Remove the birds from the marinade and wrap each quail and pheasant half with a slice of bacon or prosciutto. Over the hot fire, sear the pheasant halves for about 3 minutes per side and quail for about 2 minutes per side. Place the pheasant halves bone side down on the indirect side of grill, then stack the quail on top of the pheasant. Close the lid and cook at 300°F for 30 to 45 minutes, until the leg joints move easily. (Wild pheasant legs can be very tough, sometimes even inedible, depending on the age of the bird.) The quail and pheasant should be done at the same time. If not, remove the quail and keep warm. Continue cooking the pheasant until an instant-read meat thermometer inserted in the thickest part of the breast registers 170°F. Serve immediately. **SERVES 8**

Smoked Game Bird Salad: This is the perfect way to use leftover poultry of any kind. Begin with 1 cup mixed greens or baby spinach. Garnish with pomegranate seeds; 1/2 teaspoon grated orange zest; 1/4 cup chopped fresh herbs; and 1 to 2 tablespoons toasted pine nuts, chopped pecans, or chopped walnuts. Drizzle with the vinaigrette of your choice. (Fresh Basil Vinaigrette, page 85, is nice.) **SERVES 1**

Smoked Game Birds and Pasta: This is a favorite summer recipe. Start with about 2 cups of game bird meat pulled off the bone. Place the meat and thinly sliced wedges of 2 or 3 ripe tomatoes in the bottom of a serving bowl. Cook 1/2 pound orzo according to the package directions in a pot of boiling water until *al dente*. Drain, then spoon over the meat and tomatoes. (The heat from the pasta will warm them.) Add 1 cup crumbled feta cheese and 1/4 cup snipped fresh chives. Toss, season with kosher salt and freshly ground black pepper to taste, and serve with grilled bread (see pages 176–178). **SERVES 4**

Z
Zapatos
Shoes
Z

Smoked Pheasant Breasts

A boneless, skinless pheasant breast half weighs about 1 pound and has a lovely, sweet taste. Smoking a pheasant breast without having it dry out is a challenge. Try this easy recipe for 2 pheasant breast halves. Lightly oil the meat and sprinkle with Fair for Fowl Rub (page 51) or the seasoning of your choice. Wrap each breast with 2 or 3 thin slices of pancetta or prosciutto, securing the slices with a toothpick if necessary. Prepare a smoker with 3 or 4 cherry wood chunks (soaked in water for at least 1 hour before smoking). Place a water pan in the smoker and place the pheasant breasts on a rack above the pan. Smoke at 225°F until an instant-read meat thermometer inserted in the thickest part registers 155 to 160°F, 45 to 60 minutes. Let the meat sit for about 5 minutes, then slice and serve with Smoked Corn in the Husks (page 121) and a leafy green salad. SERVES 4

Sangria!

When Judith did a grilled and smoked tapas class at A Southern Season in Chapel Hill, North Carolina, the students slurped down a refreshing sangria with the little bites. Marilyn Markel, the director of the school, was gracious enough to let us have her recipe, which can be made with either red or white wine. SERVES 4

1/2 cup sugar
1/2 cup water
1 orange, washed and very thinly sliced
1 lemon, washed and very thinly sliced
1 lime, washed and very thinly sliced
One 750 ml bottle dry red or white wine
2 cups club soda or sparkling water

1. Make a simple syrup by combining the sugar and water in a small saucepan over high heat. Bring to a boil and cook until the sugar has completely dissolved, about 1 minute. Remove from the heat and let cool.

2. Place the sliced fruit in a 2-quart pitcher and pour the simple syrup over it. Using a stainless steel spoon, mash the fruit and syrup together. Allow to stand for 5 minutes, then mash it some more. Pour the wine over the fruit, stir, and refrigerate until cold, stirring occasionally.

3. To serve, pour the sparkling water into the pitcher, stir gently, and serve.

In the Swim: Fish and Shellfish

If there is one food that most people are afraid to cook, it's probably fish. In our book *Fish & Shellfish, Grilled & Smoked* (The Harvard Common Press, 2002), we took our readers step by step through the process of grilling and smoking the luscious and tender denizens of lakes, streams, and oceans. We've demonstrated how to grill, smoke, plank, stir-grill, skewer, and rotisserie cook fish and shellfish in countless classes around the country. So you can believe us when we tell you that cooking fish and shellfish is a lot easier than it seems. You'll want to use the freshest fish and shellfish you can find, and sometimes that might mean IQF (individually quick frozen) or FAS (frozen at sea). Go to a reputable fishmonger or market where there is a high turnover of product.

We're also including a fish substitution chart (see pages 254–255), so you can always be prepared to use the best fish possible. For example, if you want to grill bluefish but it's not available at the market, you can substitute a similar fish in flavor and texture. If you had your heart set on salmon but it's not available, you can use char or halibut. If all of the fresh fish looks past its prime, go with frozen from the freezer case, not frozen and thawed in the store (who knows how long the fish has been there?). As always, fresh fish and shellfish should smell briny, like the sea, not like ammonia, and be somewhat firm to the touch. Whole fish should have clear eyes.

Even when the skin has been removed from a fish fillet, you can still see where it used to be. So when you're grilling fish and we tell you to start with the flesh side down, you'll know which side that is (the interior side along the backbone, which never had skin on it). Grilling fish flesh side down first makes it easier for you to keep the fillet together after you turn it on the grill.

BBQ QUEEN
BBQ QUEEN

Grilled Fish Fillets 257
Herb-Grilled Fish 258
Grilled Fish Veracruzano 258
Grilled Fish with Basil Oil Mashed Potatoes and Warm Citrus Garnish 258
Japanese-Style Grilled Fish 258

Grilled Fish or Shellfish Skewers 259
Thai-Style Halibut on Lemongrass Skewers 260
Caribbean Grouper on Sugar Cane Skewers 260
Aussie Shrimp on the Barbie with Orange-Ginger Baste 261
Orange and Tarragon–Glazed Scallop Skewers 261

PASSING THE BAR
S'mores 262
Chocolate-Coconut-Macadamia Bars 262
Pecan Pie Bars 263
Almond Cookie Brittle 264
Rice Krispies Treats 265

GRILL GALS: SHE SIZZLES SEASHELLS BY THE SEASHORE MENU
Oyster, Prosciutto, and Bay Leaf Skewers 267
Grilled Clams with Lemon Butter Drizzle 268
Tequila-Lime Scallop Skewers 269
Zucchini-Stuffed Tomatoes with Basil 270

Grilled Fish Steaks 271
Down Under Grilled Fish Steaks with Lime-Ginger Marinade 271
Lime-Grilled Swordfish with Charred Tomato-Chipotle Salsa 272
Seared Rare Tuna Steaks with Toasted Sesame Oil 272

GREAT VEGETABLE SIDE DISHES
Haricots Verts with Lemon, Garlic, and Parsley 274
Baby Carrots Braised in Late-Harvest Riesling 275
Sautéed Baby Spinach with Olive Oil and Garlic 275

Smoked Fish Fillets 272
Smoked Fish with Sauce Verte 273
Smoked Trout Benedict with Confetti Hash 273
Smoked Fish Pâté with Dill and Lemon 276

Planked Fish or Shellfish 277
Oak-Planked Peppercorn Tuna Steaks with Orange Mayonnaise 278
Cedar-Planked Shrimp Chimichurri 278

SENSATIONAL SALADS
Mediterranean Salad with Lemon-Sumac Vinaigrette 279
Moroccan Orange, Fennel, and Olive Salad 280
Kath's Cucumbers 281
Elaborate Yet Easy Cucumbers in Poppy Seed Dressing 282
Cauliflower, Roasted Red Pepper, and Cured Olive Salad 282
Hearts of Palm Salad 283
Italian Bean Salad 284

Smoked Whole Fish 285
Happy, Happy, Happy Hour Salmon 286
Happy, Happy, Happy Hour Salmon Spread 286
Apple Cider–Smoked Trout with Horseradish Cream 286

Grilled Oysters, Clams, or Mussels in the Shell 287
Grilled Oysters in Pesto 288
Grilled Littleneck Clams with Pernod Butter 288
Black Fettuccine with Grilled Mussels, Garlic, and Parsley 288

Italian-Style Grilled Lobster 288

Grilled Shrimp, Scallops, or Squid 289
Grilled Shrimp or Scallops in Thai Green Curry Sauce 290
Grilled Shrimp with Nuevo Latino Cocktail Sauce 290
Grilled Scallops with Fennel, Red Pepper, and Lemon-Tarragon Vinaigrette 291
Grilled Stuffed Calamari with Thousand-Herb Sauce 291

GRILL GALS: SHE SPENDS SUMMERS OFF AT THE JERSEY SHORE MENU
Grilled Prosciutto and Basil–Wrapped Shrimp with Garlic Dipping Sauce 293
Grilled Bruschetta with Jersey Tomatoes 294
Grilled Lobster 294
Blueberry-Peach Tart with Macaroon Crust 295

Stir-Grilled Shellfish 297
"Wonton"-Wrapped Stir-Grilled Shellfish 298
Grilled Squid Linguine with Amogio 298
Stir-Grilled Scallop Po'boy Sandwiches 298

FISH SUBSTITUTION GUIDE FOR THE GRILL

Use this guide to help you select the freshest fish at the market. If your fish choice is not available, substitute another fish from the same category, or one category over. Some recipes will work with almost any kind of fish, so experiment, if you like.

This guide will help you choose your fish by flavor—mild to pronounced—and by texture—firm to delicate. If you want to grill a delicate-texture fish, we recommend using a perforated grill rack, disposable aluminum pan, NordicWare fish boat, or heavy-duty aluminum foil. This is so the fish doesn't flake and fall through the grill grate onto the fire. Keep this in mind when choosing from the delicate texture category.

Names of fish can be confusing. There's the fish family name; the local or regional name; and possibly a Hawaiian, Spanish, or French name commonly used. The most common usage is included to aid you in your fish shopping.

FIRMNESS	MILD FLAVOR	MODERATE FLAVOR	FULL FLAVOR
FIRM TEXTURE	Blackfish	Black Drum	Bigeye Tuna/Ahi
	Halibut	Clams	Chilean Sea Bass
	John Dory/St. Peter's Fish	Cobia/Sargentfish	Cuttlefish
	Kinklip	Drum/White Sea Bass	Escolar
	Lingcod/Greenling	Moonfish/Opah	Garfish/Needlefish
	Lobster	Salmon	Marlin/A'u
	Monkfish	Shark	Mussels
	Oreo Dory	Shortbill Spearfish/Hebi	Octopus
	Prawns	Skate	Oysters
	Red Drum/Redfish	Striped Marlin/Nairagi	Sailfish
	Sea Bass/Loup de Mer	Sturgeon	Squid
	Sea Robin	Swordfish	Triggerfish
	Shrimp	Yellowfin Tuna	Tuna
	Soft-Shell Crab		

FIRMNESS	MILD FLAVOR	MODERATE FLAVOR	FULL FLAVOR
MODERATELY FIRM TEXTURE	Canary Rockfish/ Pacific Red Snapper Catfish Grouper Haddock Ocean Perch/Rockfish/Redfish Orange Roughy Pompano Porgy Scup/Porgy Sea Scallops Sheepshead/Convictfish Snapper Striped Bass Tilefish Walleye Whitefish Wolffish	Arctic Char Barracuda Bonito Mahi-mahi/Dorado Sablefish/Black Cod Sea Bream/Daurade Sea Trout/Weakfish Tilapia Trout	Amberjack Kingfish King Mackerel Mackerel Mullet Permit Yellowtail Jack/ Hamachi Yellowtail Snap Wahoo/Ono
DELICATE TEXTURE	Bass (Freshwater) Cod Crayfish Flounder Fluke Hake/Whiting Hoki/Blue Hake Pink Snapper/Opakapaka Red Snapper Sand Dab Turbot	Butterfish Herring Pomfret/Dollar Fish Shad Smelts/Whitebait	Anchovies Bluefish Buffalofish Sardines

Maybe the Next Grill Generation Will Be Initiated by Their Mothers

The appeal of a charcoal grill is a mysterious combination of its warmth, the sight of the fire, the aromas, and the smoky taste of the foods cooked over it. The primeval appeal of cooking over an open fire first made itself known to me when I watched my father barbecue steaks; I was entranced.

—Alice Waters, *Chez Panisse Menu Cookbook* (Random House, 1982)

Rules for Grilling and Smoking Fish and Shellfish

Preparing fish and shellfish for the grill or smoker is a snap: a brush of olive oil, a sprinkling of seasoning, or a marinade. Just don't marinate fish and shellfish for more than 30 minutes (as a general rule), or you could "cook" the delicate flesh into ceviche, which is delicious, but not what you want here. The only exception would be a very oily fish with a mildly acidic marinade, as in Japanese-Style Grilled Fish (page 258).

The rule of thumb for most fish is to grill it for 10 minutes per inch of thickness over a hot fire. That means if you have a typical 3/4-inch-thick fish fillet, measured at the thickest part, you should grill it for 3 1/2 to 4 minutes on the flesh side, turn the fillet, and grill it for 3 to 4 minutes more.

The exceptions to that rule are meaty fish such as tuna, swordfish, and shark, which many people like to eat rare to medium, and shellfish. These types of fish and shellfish will be well done over a hot fire in 6 to 7 minutes per inch of thickness. If you want a rare tuna steak, grill it for 1 to 2 minutes per side over a hot fire.

For smoking, which is done at 225 to 250°F, the timing is, of course, longer. As a rule, you want to smoke fish for 20 to 25 minutes per pound. A typical salmon fillet or steak will take 45 to 60 minutes to slow smoke, a whole fish 1 to 1 1/2 hours.

The general rules for grilling fish are:

1. Buy the freshest fish available, which sometimes will be frozen!
2. Marinate for only 30 minutes.
3. Grill for 10 minutes per inch of thickness.

The general rules for smoking fish are:

1. Buy the freshest fish available, which sometimes will be frozen!
2. Marinate for only 30 minutes.
3. Smoke for 20 to 25 minutes per pound.

Grilled Fish Fillets

Fish fillets are delicious, good for you, and quick to grill, yet many people still have qualms about cooking them.

In our book *Fish & Shellfish, Grilled & Smoked* (The Harvard Common Press, 2002), we began to spread the word that grilled fish is simple, easy, and fast. There are two key factors in grilling great fish fillets. The first is your choice of a fish fillet. If you're a beginner, start with farm-raised catfish because it's mild-flavored yet fairly firm in texture, so it stays together well on the grill. Then move on to salmon, halibut, and the whole big world of fish. When starting out, avoid very delicate and flat fish fillets, such as Dover sole or turbot. Once you get the hang of grilling fish, try these more delicate varieties. Just use an oiled perforated grill rack and two big fish spatulas to turn the fillets one time.

The second factor in grilling fish involves heat and timing. Grill fish fillets for 10 minutes per inch of thickness (judged by the thickest part of the fillet) over a hot fire. A catfish fillet, for example, is usually about 3/4 inch thick in the thickest part. That means you should grill the fillet for about 7 minutes total, turning once halfway through. A very thin Dover sole fillet, maybe 1/2 inch thick, will take 5 minutes total, turning once.

Marinate most fish for only 30 minutes maximum. Any longer, and an acidic marinade (one made with citrus juice, vinegar, or wine) could "cook" the fish into ceviche, which is delicious, but not what you want here. **SERVES 4**

4 fish fillets, skin removed, if necessary

Olive oil

Fine kosher or sea salt and freshly ground black pepper to taste

1. Prepare a hot fire in a grill. Oil the grill grate or a perforated grill rack.

2. Brush or spray the fillets on both sides with olive oil. Place the fish flesh side down on the grill rack and grill for 10 minutes per inch of thickness, turning once halfway through. A fish fillet is done when it begins to flake when tested with a fork in the thickest part. Remove from the grill, season with salt and pepper, and serve hot.

Crowning Glories

These fillets are scrumptious topped with a spoonful of:

Citrus Caesar Vinaigrette *(page 84)*

Roasted Red Pepper Aioli *(page 110)*

Poblano Cream Sauce *(page 93)*

Herb-Grilled Fish: Grilling fish over fresh herb leaves and woody stalks is an aromatic tradition from the south of France. The best "woody" herbs (meaning the plants develop woody stalks) for this are thyme, rosemary, and lavender. If you're using charcoal, prepare a hot fire and, right before grilling, place 6 large fresh or dried thyme, rosemary, or lavender branches on the fire. If you're using a gas grill, wrap the herbs in aluminum foil, poke holes in the top of the packet, and place on the coals. Brush 4 fish fillets with olive oil, season with one of our herb salts (see pages 55–57), and grill as directed above. **SERVES 4**

Grilled Fish Veracruzano: Before you grill your fish, make this zesty Spanish-inspired tomato sauce. We like to use fire-roasted canned tomatoes (Muir Glen brand) for a hit of smoky flavor. Heat 2 tablespoons olive oil in a medium-size saucepan over medium-high heat. Add 1 thinly sliced onion and 4 minced garlic cloves and cook, stirring a few times, until golden, about 5 minutes. Add 2 tablespoons chopped pickled jalapeño and one 28-ounce can fire-roasted tomatoes, undrained and chopped. (Use kitchen shears inserted in the open can to chop the tomatoes if they're not chopped already.) Cook, stirring, until almost all the liquid has evaporated, about 15 minutes. Stir in 1 tablespoon fresh oregano leaves or 1 teaspoon dried oregano and 1/2 cup chopped green olives. Brush 4 fish fillets of your choice (we recommend fish from the Gulf of Mexico, such as red snapper, redfish, and grouper) with olive oil and grill as described above. Top with the sauce and serve with lime wedges. **SERVES 4**

Grilled Fish with Basil Oil Mashed Potatoes and Warm Citrus Garnish: Use a warm-water ocean fish such as red snapper, grouper, mahi-mahi, bonito, pompano, or tilapia for this aromatic and flavorful dish (see our fish substitution chart on pages 254–255). Peel and section 2 navel oranges and 2 limes. Heat 2 tablespoons olive oil in a large skillet over medium heat. Add the orange and lime sections and cook, stirring a few times, until lightly browned; keep warm. Bring 2 1/2 pounds peeled and chopped red potatoes and water to cover to a boil and continue to boil until tender, about 15 minutes. Drain and keep covered. In a food processor, puree 30 fresh basil leaves and 3/4 cup olive oil. Mash the potatoes with 1/2 cup of the basil oil and season with kosher or sea salt and freshly ground black pepper to taste. Brush 4 fish fillets with the remaining basil oil, sprinkle with salt and pepper, and grill as directed above. Garnish each fillet with warm citrus and fresh basil leaves and serve with the potatoes. **SERVES 4**

Japanese-Style Grilled Fish: The marinade provides a robust flavor. To make sure it doesn't overpower the fish, we suggest using a strong-flavored, oily fish such as amberjack, bluefish, salmon, mackerel, marlin, mullet, or even our old standby, farm-raised catfish, which can take on any flavor. In a small saucepan, combine 1/4 cup soy sauce, 1/4 cup sake or dry white wine, 1/4 cup mirin (a sweet Japanese wine), 2 tablespoons sugar, and 2 tablespoons peeled and finely chopped fresh ginger. Bring to a boil over medium-high heat, then immediately remove from the heat. Cover and let cool to room temperature. Arrange 4 fish fillets in a deep baking dish and pour the marinade over. Cover and refrigerate for 4 hours or overnight (this is okay with an oily fish and a mildly acidic marinade), turning the fish occasionally. Remove the fish from the marinade and pat dry. Brush with vegetable oil and grill as directed above. Serve each fillet garnished with paper-thin slices of lemon. **SERVES 4**

Grilled Fish or Shellfish Skewers

If you want to make sure your family is eating healthy food but they're getting tired of fish or shellfish, try grilling it on skewers.

Marinate the fish or shellfish while you start the grill, and have some helpers thread the pieces onto skewers. That's the only tricky part.

If you have bought fish steaks, just make sure all the skin is off, then cut the fish into cubes. If you have bought fish fillets, again make sure the skin is off. Cut the fish lengthwise into 2-inch-wide strips. If you have peeled and deveined shrimp or whole scallops, just rinse and pat them dry. When you thread the fish or shellfish onto skewers, make sure to leave a little breathing room between the pieces.

For skewers, we'll start you out with plain old wooden skewers, then get fancier as we go along with fresh stalks of lemongrass and spikes of sugar cane. Grill the skewers over a hot fire until the fish is opaque all the way through, a matter of minutes. Then serve with your favorite dipping sauce, maybe some of the reserved and unused marinade.

Grill some vegetables along with the fish skewers, serve a salad on the side, and you've got dinner!

If you're a beginner, we recommend that you start with farm-raised catfish. It's available year-round, is mild-flavored, can take any kind of seasoning or marinade, and is easy to work with. SERVES 4

4 farm-raised catfish fillets, skin removed

1/2 cup bottled Italian-style vinaigrette

16 wooden skewers, soaked in water for at least 30 minutes before grilling

1. Prepare a hot fire in a grill.

2. Lay the fillets so the grain of the fish is horizontal. Using a pizza wheel or chef's knife, cut the fillets into 2-inch-wide strips. Place in a bowl and pour the vinaigrette over. Cover and refrigerate for 30 minutes.

3. Thread the fish pieces onto the skewers, leaving space between them. Grill for 2 to 3 minutes per side, turning once. Serve hot.

Crowning Glories

Top these beauties with:

More vinaigrette

Chopped fresh herbs

Finely chopped green onions, bell peppers, and tomatoes

Thai-Style Halibut on Lemongrass Skewers: Fresh lemongrass skewers add a fragrant citrus note to the halibut. If you use the packaged lemongrass stalks available in the produce section of most grocery stores, cut them lengthwise into 4 more slender stalks to use as skewers. You can also buy lemongrass plants at better plant nurseries. Green curry paste, fish sauce, and toasted sesame oil are available in the Asian section of grocery stores. Salmon would also taste wonderful prepared this way. Combine 1 tablespoon green curry paste, 1 minced garlic clove, 1 tablespoon grated fresh ginger (if using a microplane, you don't need to peel), 1 teaspoon Asian fish sauce, 1 tablespoon rice vinegar, 2 tablespoons vegetable oil, and 1 teaspoon toasted sesame oil in a small bowl. Spread the paste on 1 1/2 pounds skinned halibut steaks, then cut into 1-inch pieces. Cover and refrigerate for 30 minutes. Have ready 12 fresh lemongrass stalks, about 1/4 inch in diameter and 6 inches long. Thread the halibut onto the stalks, 3 to 4 pieces per skewer. If necessary, pierce the fish with a wooden skewer first, then insert the lemongrass stalk. Do not crowd the pieces on the skewer. Grill as directed above, about 5 minutes per side. Serve hot or at room temperature. **SERVES 4**

Caribbean Grouper on Sugar Cane Skewers: If you love Caribbean rum drinks, you'll love this. You could substitute 18 sea scallops or large shrimp for the grouper. Cut 1 1/2 pounds skinned grouper fillets into 2-inch-wide strips as directed above. Place the strips in a baking dish. Combine 1/4 cup light rum, 1/4 cup fresh lime juice (4 to 5 limes), 1/4 cup olive oil, 2 minced garlic cloves, and 1 tablespoon minced shallot in a bowl and pour half the marinade over the fish. Cover and refrigerate for 30 minutes. Reserve the remaining marinade in a small bowl. Have ready 6 slender spikes of sugar cane (at least 6 inches long; available at Hispanic markets, better grocery stores, and sometimes Target). Thread the fish onto the sugar cane, leaving space between the pieces. Place the reserved marinade by the grill. Set the skewers on the grill grate and brush each with a little marinade. Cover and grill for 2 to 3 minutes. When the fish is opaque on the bottom, turn the skewers and brush with the remaining marinade. Cover and cook for 2 to 3 minutes, until the fish is opaque all the way through. Serve hot. **SERVES 4**

Aussie Shrimp on the Barbie with Orange-Ginger Baste: The northern coast of Australia is replete with crustaceans of all kinds, including Moreton Bay "bugs," which are really large, crayfish-like shellfish. For this recipe, use the largest shrimp you can find—or even lobster tails out of the shell. Start with 12 to 24 peeled and deveined large shrimp. Soak 12 to 24 long wooden skewers in water for at least 30 minutes before grilling, then push the skewers through the shrimp lengthwise, from head to tail, with only 1 shrimp to a skewer. In a medium-size bowl, whisk together 1/4 cup (1/2 stick) melted unsalted butter, 1 cup orange juice, 2 tablespoons sherry or rum, 1 teaspoon grated orange zest; 2 finely chopped green onions, and 1 teaspoon grated fresh ginger (if using a microplane, you don't need to peel). Reserve half of the sauce in a small serving bowl. Dip the skewered shrimp in the remaining sauce and place the skewers on an oiled perforated grill rack about 4 inches above the heat. Baste liberally with the sauce and grill for 2 to 4 minutes, turn, and grill for 2 to 4 minutes more, until pink and cooked through. Serve hot. Pass the reserved sauce at the table. **SERVES 6**

Orange and Tarragon–Glazed Scallop Skewers: A glaze, which has a higher sugar content than a marinade or baste, can both flavor and add a mouthwatering sheen to grilled foods. Orange and tarragon gently infuse these grilled scallops. This recipe also works well with shrimp. Make the glaze by mixing together 2 tablespoons olive oil, 1 teaspoon dried tarragon, 1 teaspoon grated orange zest, the juice of 1 orange, and 2 tablespoons clover or other medium-colored honey in a small bowl. Place 18 sea scallops, rinsed and patted dry, in a large sealable plastic bag and pour 1/2 cup of the glaze over them. Seal the bag and refrigerate for 30 minutes. Reserve the remaining glaze in the bowl. Have ready 6 wooden skewers, soaked in water for at least 30 minutes before grilling. Thread 3 scallops on each skewer, leaving space between them. Place the reserved glaze by the grill. Set the skewers on the grill grate and use a spoon to drizzle each skewer with a little glaze. Cover and grill for 4 to 5 minutes, until the scallops are opaque on the bottom, then turn the skewers and brush with the remaining glaze. Cover and cook for 3 to 4 minutes, until the scallops are shiny yet opaque all the way through. Serve on a platter, over a bed of thinly sliced oranges and cucumbers. **SERVES 6**

Passing the Bar

Both Karen and Judith are dessert lovers. For barbecues, we're partial to bar cookies that can be made ahead and frozen. They're a perfect ending to a simple outdoor meal, and, like the biblical loaves and fishes, they can be portioned to feed any size crowd. We've chosen our easiest and very best to share with you.

S'mores

Kind of a stretch of the definition of bar cookies, but who cares when they're this good? If you've never shared this treat with your kids, it's time to get to it. For each s'more, you need 2 whole (double-section) graham crackers and a piece of milk chocolate about the same size. Place the chocolate on one cracker. Roast a marshmallow over the fire. When it is hot, place it on top of the chocolate and place the other cracker on top to make a sandwich. Let cool a little, then gobble it up.

Chocolate-Coconut-Macadamia Bars

Karen first came across a recipe similar to this while judging a holiday cooking contest. The saltines add just the right amount of salt to the recipe. MAKES 24 LARGE OR 48 SMALL BARS

24 saltine crackers
1 cup (2 sticks) unsalted butter
1 cup firmly packed light or dark brown sugar
1 cup sweetened flaked coconut
1½ cups semisweet chocolate chips
1 cup roughly chopped macadamia nuts

1. Preheat the oven to 375°F. Line a 13 x 9 x 2-inch baking pan with aluminum foil, letting the ends of the foil extend over the sides of the pan.

2. Place the crackers on the bottom of the foil-lined pan, 4 crackers wide by 6 crackers long.

3. In a medium-size saucepan over medium heat, melt the butter. Add the brown sugar and, stirring gently, bring to a boil. Let boil for 2 minutes, then pour evenly over the crackers. Sprinkle the coconut, chocolate chips, and nuts in even layers on top. Place in the oven for 5 minutes.

4. Remove from the oven and gently press the mixture down with the back of a spoon. Let cool for 15 to 20 minutes, then refrigerate for 10 to 15 minutes, until the chocolate is set.

5. Remove from the refrigerator and lift the foil holding the bars onto a cutting board. Cut into 24 large or 48 small bars. To freeze, place 2 bars back to back and cover with plastic wrap. Put the wrapped bars in a freezer bag and freeze for up to 3 months.

Chocolate–Peanut Butter Bars: Omit the coconut and substitute 3/4 cup peanut butter chips for an equal amount of the chocolate chips. **MAKES 24 LARGE OR 48 SMALL BARS**

Pecan Pie Bars

These bars are very sweet, like pecan pie. The little bit of salt helps balance the sugar. If you want a shot of chocolate, substitute chocolate graham crackers or sprinkle a cup of semisweet chocolate chips over the graham crackers before you pour the hot caramel sauce over them. MAKES 24 LARGE OR 48 SMALL BARS

9 whole graham crackers

1 cup (2 sticks) unsalted butter

1 cup firmly packed light or dark brown sugar

1/8 teaspoon kosher or sea salt

2 1/2 cups pecan halves

1. Preheat the oven to 375°F. Line a 13 x 9 x 2-inch baking pan with heavy-duty aluminum foil, letting the ends of the foil extend over the sides of the pan.

2. Place the graham crackers in a single layer on the bottom of the foil-lined pan. Break 2 of the crackers into sections to fit; you should have 1 section left over (you have our permission to eat it).

3. In a medium-size saucepan over medium heat, melt the butter. Add the brown sugar and, stirring gently, bring to a boil. Let boil for 2 minutes, add the salt, and pour evenly over the crackers. Add the pecans in an even layer. Place in the oven for 5 minutes.

4. Remove from the oven and gently press the pecans down. Let cool for about 15 minutes, then refrigerate for another 15 minutes, until the mixture is set.

5. Remove from the refrigerator and lift the foil holding the bars onto a cutting board. Cut into 24 large or 48 small bars. To freeze, place 2 bars back to back and cover with plastic wrap. Put the wrapped bars in a freezer bag and freeze for up to 3 months.

Almond Cookie Brittle

Mix all the ingredients together in a bowl, pat the mixture into a baking sheet, bake, and then break into pieces—perfect for making with children or grandchildren. This one is from our book *Easy Grilling & Simple Smoking with the BBQ Queens* (Pig Out Publications, 1997). MAKES ABOUT 24 PIECES

1 cup (2 sticks) unsalted butter, very soft but not melted
1 cup sugar
1 teaspoon kosher or sea salt
2 teaspoons almond extract
2 cups all-purpose flour
1 cup sliced almonds

1. Preheat the oven to 350°F.

2. In a large bowl, beat the butter, sugar, salt, and almond extract together until creamy. Stir in the flour gradually, beating until just blended. Press the dough into a

16 x 10 x 1-inch baking sheet (or one with similar dimensions). Press the sliced almonds evenly on top of the dough. Bake for 20 minutes for chewier brittle or 25 minutes for crunchier brittle.

3. Let cool in the pan. For more uniform pieces, score with a knife while still warm, then break into pieces when completely cooled. For more random pieces, let cool completely, invert onto a counter or cutting board, and break apart. Store in an airtight container.

Substitutions and Additions: For the almonds, you can substitute 1 cup white chocolate chips and 1 cup sweetened dried cranberries to make White Chocolate–Cranberry Brittle. Or top with $^1/_2$ cup sweetened flaked coconut, $^1/_2$ cup sliced almonds, and $^1/_2$ cup semisweet chocolate chips to make Almond Joy Brittle. **MAKES 24 PIECES**

Rice Krispies Treats

This retro snack from Kellogg is a winner with both adults and children. Watch their happy faces when they munch on these treats. **MAKES TWENTY-FOUR 2-INCH SQUARES**

3 tablespoons unsalted butter
4 cups miniature marshmallows
6 cups Kellogg's Rice Krispies cereal

1. Melt the butter in a large saucepan over low heat. Add the marshmallows and stir until completely melted. Remove from the heat. Stir in the cereal and coat well.

2. Coat a 13 x 9 x 2-inch baking pan with nonstick cooking spray. Evenly press the mixture into the pan using the back of a buttered spatula. The mixture will be sticky. Let cool on the counter or in the refrigerator.

3. When completely cooled, cut into 2-inch squares. Serve immediately, or wrap individual squares in plastic, then place in a sealable plastic bag and keep in the refrigerator or freezer for 1 to 2 days. Remove when ready to serve.

Grill Gals

She Sizzles Seashells by the Seashore Menu

Oyster, Prosciutto, and Bay Leaf Skewers
Grilled Clams with Lemon Butter Drizzle
Tequila-Lime Scallop Skewers
Zucchini-Stuffed Tomatoes with Basil

Bonnie Tandy Leblang, registered dietitian, cookbook author, and syndicated food columnist, doesn't live too far from Long Island Sound in Connecticut. "No one can resist the aromas of sizzling kabobs or vegetables cooking on an outdoor grill," she says. "Patio cooking is the way to entertain friends on long summer evenings." Her menu reflects that, as she offers a sampling of three different kinds of shellfish, all of which cook very quickly on her charcoal grill, in recipes we have adapted.

The shellfish can be ready and waiting at the grill on ice as your guests arrive. If you use a charcoal grill, keep a charcoal chimney full of coals handy in case you linger too long with your guests, forget about cooking, and the coals die out. (Or use a gas grill. Or persuade one of your gentleman callers to "man" the grill for a while.) Serve the grilled shellfish with a side dish full of the best summer flavors and maybe some fruit that you grill as the coals are dying down. You could enjoy this menu tapas style—little bites of a progression of courses: grill the oysters first and enjoy them hot, then put the clams on the grill, followed by the scallop skewers.

Oyster, Prosciutto, and Bay Leaf Skewers

Fresh bay leaves are often available with other packaged herbs in the grocery store. Bay plants are available from nurseries—just pluck the leaves off the plant. If you can't find fresh bay, simmer 3 dried bay leaves in the basting mixture over low heat for about 5 minutes, remove from the heat, and infuse for 30 minutes. Remove the bay leaves and baste as directed. SERVES 6 AS AN APPETIZER

18 fresh shucked oysters

6 thin slices prosciutto, each cut lengthwise into thirds

6 wooden skewers, soaked in water for at least 30 minutes before grilling

18 fresh bay leaves (see headnote)

MUSTARD BASTING SAUCE

1/2 cup Dijon mustard

1/4 cup rice vinegar or dry white wine

1/4 cup honey

1 tablespoon toasted sesame oil

1. Rinse the oysters under cold running water and pat dry. Wrap each oyster with a piece of prosciutto and arrange the oysters on a skewer, with a fresh bay leaf touching each one. Don't crowd the oysters on the skewer, or they will take longer to cook through. Remind your guests to remove the bay leaves before eating the oysters.

2. To make the basting sauce, mix all the ingredients together in a small bowl.

3. Prepare a hot fire in a grill.

4. Place the skewers on the grill grate and use a spoon to drizzle them with one-third of the basting mixture. Cover and grill for 4 to 5 minutes. When the oysters are opaque on the bottom, turn the skewers and baste with a brush. Cover and cook for 3 to 4 minutes, until the oysters are opaque all the way through. Brush again with the basting mixture and serve hot. (If you're grilling all three shellfish dishes, close the lid so the grill stays hot.)

Grilled Clams with Lemon Butter Drizzle

Hard-shell clams will pop open on a very hot grill, just like when you steam them. Use a perforated grill rack or two so you don't lose any in the coals. Discard any that have opened and won't close before cooking or that have not opened after cooking. You can scrub and rinse the clams about 1 hour before your guests arrive. Keep them in the refrigerator until 15 minutes before grilling. **SERVES 6 AS AN APPETIZER**

3 pounds hard-shell clams

1 recipe Lemon Butter Drizzle (page 87)

2 tablespoons chopped fresh herbs, such as Italian parsley, chives, tarragon, and/or basil, for garnish

1. Scrub and rinse the clams under cold running water.

2. Prepare a hot fire in a grill.

3. Keep the drizzle warm in a metal container by the grill.

4. Place the clams on perforated grill racks. Cover and grill for 4 to 5 minutes, until they open.

5. Transfer the clams to a large platter and drizzle with the lemon butter. Garnish with the chopped herbs and serve. (If you're grilling all three shellfish dishes, place the cover back on the grill so it stays hot.)

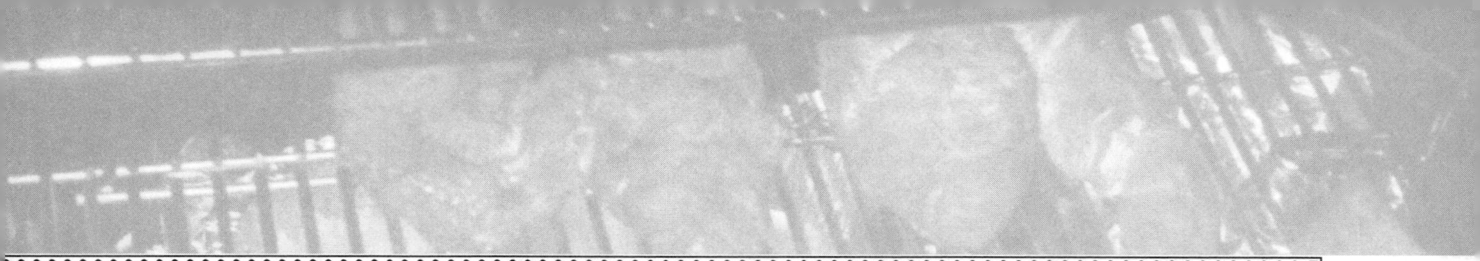

Tequila-Lime Scallop Skewers

If you love margaritas, as we do, this is a great way to get that flavor on the grill.

SERVES 6 AS AN APPETIZER

18 large sea scallops

TEQUILA-LIME MARINADE

1/4 cup tequila

1/4 cup fresh lime juice (4 to 5 limes)

1/4 cup olive oil

2 cloves garlic, minced

1 tablespoon minced shallot

6 wooden skewers, soaked in water for at least 30 minutes before grilling

1. Rinse the scallops under cold running water and pat dry.

2. To make the marinade, combine all the ingredients in a small bowl. Place the scallops in a large sealable plastic bag and pour the marinade over. Seal the bag and refrigerate for 30 minutes.

3. Prepare a hot fire in a grill.

4. Remove the scallops, reserving the marinade. Thread 3 scallops lengthwise onto each skewer, leaving space between them. Place the remaining marinade in a small saucepan, bring to a boil, and continue to boil for 2 minutes. Transfer to a heatproof bowl and place by the grill.

5. Place the skewers on the grill grate and use a spoon to drizzle them with one-third of the marinade mixture. Cover and grill for 4 to 5 minutes. When the scallops are opaque on the bottom, turn the skewers and baste with a brush. Cover and cook for 3 to 4 minutes, until the scallops are opaque all the way through. Brush again with the marinade and serve hot. (If you're grilling the vegetable dish next, place the cover back on the grill so it stays hot.)

Zucchini-Stuffed Tomatoes with Basil

This is an easy, delicious way to serve the best of summer. **SERVES 6 AS AN APPETIZER**

6 large ripe beefsteak (or other large) tomatoes, cored and hollowed out, leaving about a 1/2-inch wall of tomato pulp inside

2 or 3 small zucchini, finely diced

1 shallot, minced

1/4 cup fresh basil leaves, shredded

6 tablespoons freshly grated Parmesan cheese

6 tablespoons extra virgin olive oil

1. Coat 2 disposable aluminum pans with nonstick cooking spray. Set the hollowed-out tomatoes in the pans. If necessary, cut off part of the bottom of the tomatoes so they sit evenly. In a medium-size bowl, combine the zucchini, shallot, basil, and Parmesan. Fill the tomatoes evenly with the mixture. Drizzle each tomato with 1 tablespoon olive oil.

2. Prepare a hot fire in a grill.

3. Place the tomatoes on the grill, cover, and cook until they are bronzed and softened, 8 to 10 minutes. Serve hot, at room temperature, or cold. (If you're going to grill fruit for dessert, place the cover back on the grill so it stays hot.)

Grilled Fish Steaks

Although fish steaks are uniform in thickness and thicker than fish fillets, you grill them the same way, over a hot fire for about 10 minutes per inch of thickness. A halibut steak, for example, is usually about 3/4 inch thick. That means you would grill the steak for about 7 minutes total, turning once halfway through.

We suggest that you start with halibut or salmon steaks, because they're mild-flavored yet fairly firm in texture, so they stay together well on the grill. When you get the hang of those, try tuna steaks, which you grill to medium or medium-rare, or swordfish steaks, using an oiled perforated grill rack and two big fish spatulas to turn the steaks only once.

In general, fish should not be marinated for more than 30 minutes. Otherwise, the delicate flesh could be "cooked," which is not desirable. SERVES 4

4 fish steaks
Olive oil
Fine kosher or sea salt and freshly ground black pepper to taste

1. Prepare a hot fire in a grill. Oil the grill grate or a perforated grill rack.
2. Brush or spray the steaks on both sides with olive oil. Place the fish on the grill rack and grill for 10 minutes per inch of thickness, turning once halfway through. A fish steak is done when it begins to flake when tested with a fork in the center.
3. Remove from the grill, season with salt and pepper, and serve hot.

Crowning Glories

Serve these steaks with:

Vietnamese Drizzle *(page 87)*
Roasted Red Pepper Sauce *(page 94)*
Hearts of Palm Salad *(page 283)*

Down Under Grilled Fish Steaks with Lime-Ginger Marinade: The tropical climate in the northern part of Australia promotes the growth of citrus and ginger, both distinctive elements in this marinade. We like to use 1-inch-thick swordfish, halibut, or salmon steaks here. In a small bowl, whisk together 1/4 cup fresh lime juice (4 to 5 limes), 2 tablespoons vegetable oil, 1 teaspoon Dijon mustard, 1 teaspoon grated fresh ginger (if using a microplane, you don't need to peel), and 1/4 teaspoon each cayenne pepper and freshly ground black pepper. Arrange 4 fish steaks in a deep baking dish and pour the marinade over. Marinate for up to 30 minutes, turning 2 or 3 times. Remove from the marinade and grill as directed above. Serve hot. **SERVES 4**

Lime-Grilled Swordfish with Charred Tomato-Chipotle Salsa: Our mouths water whenever we think about this big-flavor dish, adapted from one by our barbecue buddy Paul Kirk. We could eat the salsa by the spoonful, but usually we save it to serve with luscious lime-grilled swordfish. In a small bowl, combine 3 tablespoons fresh lime juice, 3 tablespoons olive oil, and 2 minced garlic cloves. Rub the mixture over four 8-ounce swordfish steaks cut 1 inch thick. Place in a baking dish and refrigerate for 30 minutes, then grill as directed above. Serve with Charred Tomato-Chipotle Salsa (page 162). **SERVES 4**

Seared Rare Tuna Steaks with Toasted Sesame Oil: In a small bowl, combine 2/3 cup soy sauce, 1/4 cup rice vinegar, 2 tablespoons toasted sesame oil, and 1 tablespoon grated fresh ginger (if using a microplane, you don't need to peel). In a shallow bowl, place four 6-ounce tuna steaks cut at least 1 inch thick. Add 3/4 cup of the marinade and let sit for 15 minutes, turning the steaks a couple of times. Reserve the rest of the marinade for drizzling over the cooked steaks. Grill as directed above, searing the tuna on both sides, for 5 to 6 minutes total. The tuna should still be rare in the center but browned and charred on the edges. Serve with a drizzle of the reserved marinade. **SERVES 4**

Smoked Fish Fillets

Imagine being able to reach into your freezer and take out a moist, delicious smoked fish fillet whenever you want. In the BBQ Queens' humble opinion, that's a real frozen asset. You are then just minutes away from a fabulous appetizer such as Smoked Fish Pâté with Dill and Lemon (page 276), a brunch dish such as Smoked Trout Benedict with Confetti Hash (right), or that French bistro favorite, smoked haddock with mashed potatoes.

You can smoke any fish fillet, but our favorites are Pacific cod or whitefish, catfish, salmon, trout, and walleye (pike) because of their general availability, great flavor, and pleasing texture. When you're going to the trouble to smoke anything, we always recommend that you smoke intentionally for leftovers that you can wrap and freeze. Don't let an opportunity to give yourself the gift of time—for making future dishes—go up in smoke!

In its simplest and purest form, a fish fillet in the smoker needs little more than oil, salt, and pepper. The oil adds moisture to the fish so it won't dry out. Smoking at 225 to 250°F will take 45 to 60 minutes for fish steaks or fillets. The more fish placed on a smoker, the longer it will take to smoke. Smoked fish will keep, tightly covered, in the refrigerator for up to 2 weeks and in the freezer for up to 3 months. **SERVES 4**

SUGGESTED WOOD: **Alder, maple, pecan, or a combination**

Two 8-ounce fish fillets
2 tablespoons olive oil
Fine kosher or sea salt and freshly ground black pepper to taste

1. Brush or spray the fillets with the olive oil and season with salt and pepper.
2. Prepare an indirect fire in a smoker.
3. Place the fish in the smoker, close the lid, and smoke at 225 to 250°F until the fish is opaque and the flesh is just beginning to flake when you test it with a fork, 45 to 60 minutes. Serve hot or at room temperature.

Crowning Glories

Smoked fish fillets are delicious served with:

Hearts of Palm Salad *(page 283)*
Charred Tomato-Chipotle Salsa *(page 162)*
Hot Shallot Vinaigrette *(page 85)*

Smoked Fish with Sauce Verte: Easy-to-make *sauce verte*, pale green with fresh herbs, is great with either smoked or grilled fish fillets or steaks. In a blender or food processor, combine 1 cup mayonnaise (lowfat is okay), 1/2 cup roughly chopped fresh Italian parsley, 1/4 cup chopped fresh dill, 1/4 cup chopped fresh tarragon, 1 tablespoon chopped fresh chives, 1 tablespoon tarragon vinegar, and 2 tablespoons drained capers. Process until smooth. Cover and refrigerate for at least 1 hour or up to 3 days to let the flavors blend. Smoke 4 fish fillets as described above. Serve with a dollop of sauce. **SERVES 4**

Smoked Trout Benedict with Confetti Hash: This is one of our favorite ways to enjoy smoked trout—especially if we've smoked it ahead of time and have it on hand in the freezer. For a great presentation, cook the hash in a large skillet, then divide it into 4 mini cast-iron skillets and top with the remaining ingredients. Nestle each small skillet on a

Great Vegetable Side Dishes

For a simply grilled chicken breast or fish fillet, you want a side dish that is also quick to cook. These delicious vegetable dishes fill the bill.

Haricots Verts with Lemon, Garlic, and Parsley

This dish is adapted from a recipe by Nancy Verde Barr in *Make It Italian* (Alfred A. Knopf, 2002). Normally, we don't go for frozen green beans, but frozen *haricots verts*, those tiny French green beans, have good flavor and a uniform size, and are already trimmed. So why not? This recipe can be doubled or tripled. It just might replace the green bean casserole on your holiday table. The gremolata is also good on grilled chicken breasts, grilled fish fillets or steaks, or any grilled vegetable. SERVES 4

One 12-ounce package frozen *haricots verts*

GREMOLATA

3 large cloves garlic, minced
3 tablespoons olive oil
2 tablespoons minced fresh Italian parsley
2 teaspoons grated lemon zest

Fine kosher or sea salt and freshly ground black pepper to taste

1. Bring a pot of salted water to a boil. Add the beans and cook until tender-crisp, 5 to 6 minutes.

2. While the beans are cooking, make the gremolata by combining the garlic, olive oil, parsley, and lemon zest in a small bowl.

3. When the beans are done, drain immediately, plunge into a bowl of ice water, and let cool for 2 minutes. Drain and transfer to a serving bowl. Pour the gremolata over the beans and toss to blend. Season with salt and pepper and serve immediately.

Baby Carrots Braised in Late-Harvest Riesling

Put this dish on to braise before you go out to the grill, and it will be done when your chicken or fish is. After a dinner party, Judith found that she had some wine left over (as is usually the case with dessert wines), so she dreamed up this dish. SERVES 4

2 tablespoons unsalted butter
2 cups baby carrots
1/2 teaspoon ground white pepper
1/4 teaspoon freshly grated nutmeg
1/4 cup late-harvest Riesling or other dessert wine, sherry, or Marsala
1/4 cup chicken broth
Sea salt to taste

In a medium-size saucepan over medium-high heat, melt the butter and stir in the carrots. Sprinkle on the white pepper and nutmeg and stir to coat the carrots. Cook for 2 minutes, stirring. Pour in the wine and broth and bring to a boil. Reduce the heat to low, cover, and simmer until done, about 10 minutes. Season with salt and serve immediately.

Sautéed Baby Spinach with Olive Oil and Garlic

So simple, yet so good! SERVES 4

2 tablespoons olive oil
1/4 teaspoon red pepper flakes
2 cloves garlic, cut into slivers
1 pound baby spinach leaves
Kosher or sea salt and freshly ground black pepper to taste

Heat the olive oil in a large skillet over medium-high heat. When the oil is hot, add the red pepper flakes and garlic. Stir, then add the spinach and toss until the leaves have wilted and are glistening, 2 to 3 minutes. Season with salt and pepper and serve immediately.

folded napkin placed on a dinner plate. Have ready 4 small smoked trout fillets (see above). In a skillet, melt 3 tablespoons unsalted butter over medium-high heat. Add 1/2 cup chopped green onions and 1 minced garlic clove and cook, stirring, for 2 minutes. Stir in one 19-ounce package defrosted frozen southern-style hash-brown potatoes (about 3 1/2 cups) and cook, stirring occasionally, until the potatoes have browned. Stir in 1/2 cup chopped roasted red and/or yellow peppers (from a jar) and season with kosher or sea salt and freshly ground black pepper to taste. Set in a preheated 250°F oven to keep warm. To poach the eggs (one at a time), coat a medium-size skillet with nonstick cooking spray and fill halfway with hot water. Bring to a simmer over medium-high heat, then reduce the heat to medium-low. Break 1 large egg into a 1-cup measure. Place the cup, sideways, as close to the simmering water as possible and slide the egg into the water. Repeat with 3 more eggs. Simmer until the whites have set, 3 to 5 minutes. Remove with a slotted spoon and drain on paper towels. To assemble the dish, place one-quarter of the hash on a plate, top with a smoked trout fillet and a poached egg, and spoon a little Food Processor or Blender Hollandaise (page 97) over all. Garnish with fresh herb sprigs. **SERVES 4**

Smoked Fish Pâté with Dill and Lemon: In our book *Fish & Shellfish, Grilled & Smoked* (The Harvard Common Press, 2002), we make this pâté with smoked trout. It's so good that we've branched out to use smoked salmon, catfish, and cod—just as yummy. Remove any remaining skin or bones from 1 cup flaked smoked fish fillet (about 4 ounces) and place in a food processor. Add 1/2 cup (1 stick) softened unsalted butter, 1 tablespoon chopped fresh dill, and 1 teaspoon grated lemon zest and process until smooth. Serve the pâté in a crock, garnished with more chopped fresh dill and surrounded with sesame crackers or slices of French or pumpernickel bread. **MAKES ABOUT 2/3 CUP**

Planked Fish or Shellfish

Planked fish or shellfish is one of the easiest, most foolproof ways you can grill seafood. It won't fall through the grill grate, you don't have to turn it, and if you undercook it, you can always zap it in the microwave for a few seconds.

The BBQ Queens plank using a dual-heat fire, meaning that one side of the grill is hot and the other side medium. You put a presoaked plank with the food arranged on it over medium heat, close the grill lid, and cook. (For more information on planking, see Planking 101 on page 42.) Just make sure you have a spray bottle of water handy in case you have a flare-up.

Purchase skinless fish for planking. You want the flesh to touch the wood plank for maximum wood flavor. When you're planking, as in grilling, the thickness of the fish (measured at the thickest part) usually determines the timing. Meaty fish such as tuna and shark, as well as shellfish, will take less time than other fish. For example, a 1/2-inch-thick fish fillet or steak will take 10 to 12 minutes to cook all the way through on a plank. A 3/4-inch-thick fillet or steak will take 12 to 15 minutes. Large shrimp, however, will take only 6 to 8 minutes to cook. We like our halibut and salmon steaks planked until cooked through, but if you like yours served more underdone, adjust the timing. To test whether your fish is done, carefully use the tines of a fork to see whether the fish is beginning to flake in the center but still looks moist. Shellfish should be opaque all the way through. SERVES 4

One 15 x 6 1/2 x 3/8-inch plank, soaked in water for at least 1 hour before grilling

1 salmon fillet, about 3/4 inch thick, skin removed

Mustard-Mayo-Dill Slather (page 66)

1. Prepare a dual-heat fire, with a hot fire on one side and a medium fire on the other.

2. Compare the length of the plank with the length of the salmon fillet and trim the salmon to fit the plank, if necessary. Place the salmon on a baking sheet and spread the flesh side with the mustard slather. Bring outside.

3. Place the plank on the grill grate over the hot fire until it begins to char and pop. Turn the plank over and move to the medium-heat side. Carefully place the salmon slather side up on the charred side of the plank. Cover the grill and cook until the fish begins to flake when tested with a fork in the thickest part, 12 to 15 minutes.

Crowning Glories

Adorn and serve this with:

Chopped fresh herbs

Finely chopped green onions, bell peppers, and tomatoes

Grilled Asparagus *(page 117)*

Oak-Planked Peppercorn Tuna Steaks with Orange Mayonnaise: Served on a bed of couscous, this dish is lusciously flavorful, retaining the wonderful texture and taste of fresh tuna. We like our tuna served medium, so if you like yours more rare or more well done, adjust the time on the grill. The mayonnaise is also delicious on other types of planked or grilled fish as well as in chicken salad. Combine 1/2 cup lowfat mayonnaise, 1/4 cup fresh orange juice (1 to 2 oranges), and 1 teaspoon grated orange zest in a bowl. Cover and refrigerate until ready to serve. Place four 4- to 6-ounce tuna steaks cut about 3/4 inch thick on a baking sheet. Lightly spray or brush with olive oil and season with coarse kosher or sea salt to taste. Firmly press 2 tablespoons crushed multicolored peppercorn blend (pink, green, black, and white peppercorns) into the steaks and bring outside. Prepare an oak plank as directed above. Place the steaks on the prepared plank, cover the grill, and cook for about 10 minutes for medium. To serve, place a dollop of the orange mayonnaise on each steak. **SERVES 4**

Cedar-Planked Shrimp Chimichurri: This is a delicious way to serve shrimp (or scallops) on a plank. Make 1 recipe Chimichurri Sauce (page 346). Place 1 pound peeled and deveined large shrimp in a sealable plastic bag and drizzle with half the sauce. Seal the bag and marinate in the refrigerator for 30 minutes. Bring the shrimp outside. Prepare a cedar plank as directed above. Place the shrimp in a single layer on the prepared plank. Cover the grill and cook until the shrimp are opaque all the way through, 6 to 8 minutes. To serve, drizzle with some of the reserved sauce and pass the rest at the table. **SERVES 4**

Sensational Salads

Salads provide another counterpoint of flavor for a meal from the grill or smoker. Sometimes gently flavored and almost insubstantial, sometimes savory and filling, salads round out a meal with their crunchy fresh texture and great color. For the best flavor, use ingredients in season.

Mediterranean Salad with Lemon-Sumac Vinaigrette

This light, refreshing salad is perfect for the hottest days of summer. Sumac is a dark red powder made from dried sumac berries. In the Midwest, cones of staghorn sumac ripen in late summer and fall and were used by fur traders to make a sour, citrusy drink. Middle Eastern sumac is used as a spice and in blends such as za'atar (combined with sesame, salt, and dried thyme). Sumac is available online from better spice emporiums, such as Penzeys Spices (see Resource Guide, page 446). We love this salad with rotisserie, grilled, or smoked chicken, or with burgers or grilled flatbread. **SERVES 4**

SALAD

2 cups torn romaine lettuce leaves
1/2 cucumber, peeled, seeded, and chopped
1 large ripe beefsteak tomato, chopped
4 green onions
Leaves from 1 bunch fresh mint, coarsely chopped
Leaves from 1 bunch fresh Italian parsley, coarsely chopped

LEMON-SUMAC VINAIGRETTE

1 clove garlic, minced
1/2 teaspoon fine sea salt
Juice of 1/2 lemon
1/4 cup olive oil
1/2 teaspoon ground sumac

1. To make the salad, place all the ingredients in a large salad bowl.

2. To make the vinaigrette, whisk together the garlic, salt, and lemon juice in a small bowl. Drizzle in the olive oil, whisking to blend, then sprinkle in the sumac and whisk again. Pour over the salad, toss, and serve immediately.

Moroccan Orange, Fennel, and Olive Salad

Sweet fennel, tangy oranges, and pungent black olives combine for an impressive salad that will wow guests in any season. We love this paired with grilled, rotisserie, or smoked lamb, chicken, or shellfish. SERVES 4

SALAD

2 small fennel bulbs, tops trimmed and bulbs thinly sliced crosswise

2 oranges, peeled and sectioned

24 oil- or brine-cured Niçoise or Kalamata olives, pitted

1/2 cup thin, bitter salad greens, such as mizuna or frisée

1 tablespoon snipped fresh chives

ORANGE-FENNEL VINAIGRETTE

1/4 cup extra virgin olive oil

Juice of 1 orange

1 tablespoon minced shallot

1/2 teaspoon fennel seeds, toasted in a dry skillet over medium heat until fragrant, then ground

1. To make the salad, combine all the ingredients in a large salad bowl.

2. To make the vinaigrette, whisk together all the ingredients in a small bowl. Pour over the salad, toss to blend, and serve immediately.

Kath's Cucumbers

Karen's mother-in-law, Katherine Abernathy, taught her to make these favorite cucumbers for Karen's husband, Dick. Karen likes to jazz them up a bit with minced garlic and dill, but Dick prefers them plain. He doesn't mind if a red onion is used once in a while, though. Karen likes the red onion because it turns the mixture a pretty pale pink. Substitute a can of drained sliced beets for the cucumber, and you have pickled beets. A big plus to these pickled salads is that they keep refrigerated for several days. SERVES 12

1 medium-size cucumber, peeled or unpeeled
1 medium-size onion
1/2 cup distilled white vinegar
1 1/2 cups water
6 tablespoons sugar
2 tablespoons salt
1 or 2 cloves garlic (optional), minced
1 teaspoon chopped fresh dill (optional)

Slice the cucumber 1/8 inch thick. Peel and slice the onion 1/8 inch thick. In a large glass jar with a tight-fitting lid, alternate slices of cucumber and onion until they reach the top of the jar. Pour in the vinegar, close the lid, and shake to coat. Add the remaining ingredients, close, and gently shake to dissolve the salt and sugar. Taste and adjust the seasoning so that the brine is sweet and sour. This is best made a day ahead and refrigerated to let the flavors develop. It will keep in the refrigerator for up to 2 weeks.

Elaborate Yet Easy Cucumbers in Poppy Seed Dressing

Take the easy way out and buy bottled poppy seed dressing, if you like. We especially enjoy brands made with Vidalia onion. SERVES 4

1 cucumber, thinly sliced

1/4 cup dried apricots, chopped

1/4 cup walnut or pistachio halves, toasted in a 350°F oven until lightly browned, about 15 minutes

2 tablespoons snipped fresh chives

1/2 cup bottled Vidalia onion–poppy seed dressing

In a large bowl, combine all the ingredients. Serve immediately, or cover and keep refrigerated for up to 1 week.

Cauliflower, Roasted Red Pepper, and Cured Olive Salad

Make this salad early in the day to let the flavors blend. It is colorful and portable, perfect for a bring-a-dish dinner. SERVES 6 TO 8

1 large head cauliflower, cut into florets

1/3 cup olive oil

2 cloves garlic, minced

2 teaspoons balsamic vinegar

8 anchovy fillets, chopped

1 1/2 cups pitted oil- or brine-cured olives, drained

1 1/2 cups roasted red peppers (from a jar), drained

1/4 cup pine nuts, toasted in a dry skillet over medium heat until golden

2 to 3 teaspoons chopped fresh herbs, such as oregano, thyme, and/or chives

Sea salt and freshly ground black pepper to taste

1. Prepare a large pot of boiling water. Add the cauliflower and blanch for 3 minutes. Drain in a colander.

2. In a large bowl, whisk together the olive oil, garlic, vinegar, and anchovies. Add the remaining ingredients, including the cauliflower, and toss to blend. Let sit at room temperature for several hours before serving, or refrigerate for up to 1 week.

Hearts of Palm Salad

This is another excellent warm-weather salad that is quick to assemble and can stand at room temperature without any ill effects. Present it in a lovely crystal serving bowl.

SERVES 6

One 14-ounce can hearts of palm, drained and cut into 1-inch pieces
2 cups cherry or grape tomatoes, some cut in half
1/3 cup extra virgin olive oil
3 tablespoons white wine vinegar
1 clove garlic, minced
1/2 teaspoon fine sea salt
1 teaspoon chopped fresh herbs, such as basil, thyme, chives, and/or tarragon
3 tablespoons freshly grated Romano cheese
Freshly ground black pepper to taste

1. In a medium-size serving bowl, combine the hearts of palm and tomatoes.

2. In a jar with a tight-fitting lid, combine the olive oil, vinegar, garlic, salt, and herbs and shake vigorously to blend. Pour over the hearts of palm and tomatoes and toss. Sprinkle with the cheese and season with pepper. Serve immediately, let sit at room temperature for several hours before serving, or refrigerate overnight.

Italian Bean Salad

Bean salads can be made several days ahead and kept refrigerated until ready to serve. They can withstand the summer heat on a buffet table, too. SERVES 12

1 cup chopped red onion
1 cup seeded and chopped red, green, or yellow bell pepper
One 15-ounce can garbanzo beans, drained and rinsed
Two 15-ounce cans cannellini beans, drained and rinsed
1/4 cup red wine vinegar
1/4 cup extra virgin olive oil
1 teaspoon freshly ground black pepper
1/2 teaspoon kosher salt

In a medium-size serving bowl, combine the onion, bell pepper, and both beans. In a jar with a tight-fitting lid, combine the vinegar, olive oil, pepper, and salt and shake vigorously to blend. Pour over the salad and toss to coat evenly. Serve immediately, or refrigerate for up to 1 week.

BBQ QUEEN
1

Smoked Whole Fish

If you have a fisherman in your family, you've heard all the stories about the one that got away. But every so often, you think that *none* got away. You have a glut of fresh fish and don't know what to do.

Why not try smoking a whole fish? You'll end up with a moist, succulent, tender fish with the haunting aroma of wood smoke. Our favorite whole fish to smoke are freshwater trout and ocean fish such as mackerel. Obviously, you'll want a fish that will fit in your grill or smoker, usually in the 3- to 4-pound range.

If you're buying a whole fish, the of freshness is in the eyes—of the beholder and the fish. If the fish's eyes look cloudy, as if they have cataracts, the fish is old and will not taste great. The eyes should be clear and brilliant. A whole fish bought at the store will already be cleaned and scaled for you.

Smoking a whole fish takes 1 to 1 1/2 hours. And because the fish is subjected to the heat for a longer time than fillets or steaks, a basting sauce is a good idea to help keep it moist. Apple juice, apple cider, or a mixture of dry white wine, lemon juice, and melted butter makes for an easy sauce. Remember, the more fish you place in the smoker, the longer it will take to smoke. Serve portions right from the whole fish. A whole smoked fish will keep, tightly covered, in the refrigerator for up to 2 weeks or in the freezer for up to 3 months. SERVES 4 TO 6

SUGGESTED WOOD: Apple, cherry, hickory, oak, or pecan

One 3- to 4-pound whole fish, cleaned and scaled
6 sprigs fresh herbs, such as tarragon, dill, chives, and/or Italian parsley
6 thin lemon slices
1/2 cup dry white wine
1/4 cup (1/2 stick) unsalted butter, melted
1/4 cup fresh lemon juice (about 2 lemons)
Coarse kosher or sea salt and freshly ground black pepper to taste

1. Prepare an indirect fire in a smoker.
2. In the cavity of the fish, place the herb sprigs and lemon slices. In a disposable aluminum pan, combine the wine, butter, and lemon juice. Place the fish in the pan and spoon some of the basting liquid over it. Sprinkle with salt and pepper. Place the pan in the smoker, close the lid, and smoke at 225 to 250°F until the fish is opaque and the flesh is just beginning to flake when you test it with a fork, 1 1/2 to 2 hours. Serve hot.

Crowning Glories

Serve your fish up with:

Moroccan Orange, Fennel, and Olive Salad *(page 280)*

Smoked Chile Beurre Blanc *(page 99)*

Roasted Red Pepper Aioli *(page 110)*

Happy, Happy, Happy Hour Salmon: Martini lovers will have most of these ingredients on hand. This recipe is adapted from Karen's *Best Little Barbecue Cookbook* (Celestial Arts, 2000). Serve it with a spring herb risotto and Grilled Asparagus (page 117). In a small saucepan, combine 1/4 cup gin or vodka, 1/4 cup dry vermouth, 1/4 cup fresh lemon juice (about 2 lemons), 3 tablespoons melted unsalted butter, 1 tablespoon prepared horseradish, 1/2 teaspoon hot pepper sauce, 1 minced garlic clove, and 2 tablespoons juniper berries. Bring to a boil, then remove from the heat and set aside. Rinse one scaled and cleaned 3- to 4-pound whole salmon and pat dry with paper towels. Place on top of a sheet of heavy-duty aluminum foil large enough to hold the fish. Place 1 sliced lemon and 6 sprigs fresh dill in the cavity of the fish. Crimp 3 sides of the foil to hold in the basting sauce (the fourth side will fold over). Pour the sauce over the salmon, fold the foil over the fish, and crimp the edges together. Place on the grill or smoker rack, close, and smoke as directed above for 1 hour. Open the packet, but make sure the edges stay crimped to hold in the baste. Continue to smoke until the fish is opaque and begins to flake when tested with a fork, about 1 hour more. Serve hot. **SERVES 4 TO 6**

Happy, Happy, Happy Hour Salmon Spread: If you have leftover smoked salmon, turn it into this luscious cocktail spread. In a medium-size bowl, combine 1 cup smoked salmon pieces with one 8-ounce package softened cream cheese, 1 minced garlic clove, 1/2 teaspoon hot pepper sauce, 1 teaspoon dillweed, and 2 tablespoons fresh lemon juice (or to taste). Season with fine kosher or sea salt and freshly ground black pepper to taste. Serve with cocktail crackers, small slices of pumpernickel bread, or toasted rounds of French bread. **MAKES ABOUT 2 CUPS**

Apple Cider–Smoked Trout with Horseradish Cream: We love this recipe from our fish book so much, we've adapted it here. Taking the skin off the trout first allows the smoke to penetrate the fish more easily. Just about any fish can be smoked this way. Have ready 1 quart apple cider. Bring a large pot of water to a boil. Using tongs, dip four 14- to 16-ounce cleaned whole trout, one at a time, into the boiling water for 20 to 30 seconds. Remove from the pot and peel off the skin. Brush each trout with 1/2 cup of the cider, sprinkle with BBQ Queens' All-Purpose Rub (page 49), and place cut side down and splayed open in a disposable aluminum pan. Fill the water pan in your smoker with the remaining apple cider. Place the trout in the smoker, cover, and smoke as directed above until the fish begins to flake when tested with a fork, 1 1/2 to 2 hours. While the trout is smoking, make the horseradish cream by blending together 3/4 cup sour cream, 3 tablespoons prepared horseradish, and 3 tablespoons chopped fresh Italian parsley in a small bowl. Season with fine kosher or sea salt and freshly ground black pepper to taste. Serve the trout hot or cold, with a dollop of the cream. **SERVES 4**

Grilled Oysters, Clams, or Mussels in the Shell

Oysters of all kinds, littleneck clams, and mussels are absolutely delicious cooked on the grill, and they look very impressive. Scrub them first under cold running water, then all you have to do is grill them on a perforated grill rack over a hot fire.

You really don't have to worry about overcooking shellfish in the shell, because the shells pop open when they're done. What you do have to worry about is making sure you don't cook any mollusk with a cracked shell or one that is already partially open. Also, any mollusk that doesn't open on the grill should be discarded. SERVES 4

36 oysters, littleneck clams, or mussels in the shell
Melted unsalted butter
Fine kosher or sea salt and freshly ground pepper to taste

1. Scrub the oysters under cold running water and discard any that do not close to the touch or have broken shells. Place on an oiled perforated grill rack.

2. Prepare a hot fire in a grill.

3. Place the grill rack over direct heat and close the lid. Grill for 6 to 8 minutes, using grill tongs to remove the mollusks as they pop open and taking care not to spill the juices out of the shells. Transfer to a big bowl and keep warm until ready to serve.

4. To eat, pry each oyster off the shell, dip in melted butter, and season with salt and pepper.

Italian-Style Grilled Lobster

Send someone to the fish market and have someone else fire up the grill. When your lobsters (which you will have had the fishmonger cut in half) arrive, you're ready to grill. Brush both halves of each lobster with olive oil and grill, flesh side down, for 3 to 4 minutes, until you see grill marks. Turn with grill tongs to cook on the shell side until the flesh is opaque all the way through. Serve hot, in the shell, with a drizzle of extra virgin olive oil, a squeeze of fresh lemon juice, and a sprinkling of chopped fresh Italian parsley.

Crowning Glories

Serve these babies with:

Cocktail sauce

Amogio *(page 72)*

Vietnamese Drizzle *(page 87)*

Grilled Oysters in Pesto: Now that we're not limited to months with an *r* in them to eat oysters (an old adage), you can grill your favorite oysters and top them with pesto made from fresh summer basil. Enjoy these in their shells as an appetizer or removed from their shells and tossed with hot pasta for a fragrantly delicious main course. This recipe makes more pesto than you really need for the oysters, unless you want to toss them with pasta, but we believe you can never have too much pesto on hand! Cover and refrigerate any leftovers. Grill 36 oysters on the half shell as directed above, spooning about 1 teaspoon prepared pesto over each oyster before they go on the grill. Cook for 3 to 5 minutes, until the pesto is bubbling and the edges of the oysters have begun to curl. Serve hot. **SERVES 4**

Grilled Littleneck Clams with Pernod Butter: Figure 6 to 8 of these small clams per person, says Grill Gal Lisa Mayer (see page 292), then always add an extra dozen or two. There are never any leftovers! To make the Pernod butter, melt 1/2 cup (1 stick) unsalted butter in a small saucepan over medium heat. Remove from the heat and stir in 2 tablespoons Pernod or other anise-flavored liqueur and 3 tablespoons chopped fresh tarragon. Set aside. Grill the clams as directed above and serve on a platter with little cups of the Pernod butter on the side for dipping. **SERVES 4**

Black Fettuccine with Grilled Mussels, Garlic, and Parsley: Black fettuccine is colored with squid ink and makes a dramatic presentation with grilled mussels. Even if you use regular fettuccine, however, the delicate flavors of the grilled mussels and dry white wine make this a singular pasta dish to serve guests. We adapted this recipe from our book *Fish & Shellfish, Grilled & Smoked* (The Harvard Common Press, 2002). Grill 3 pounds mussels as directed above over a hot fire in a grill wok or perforated grill rack using mesquite or hickory wood chips soaked in water for at least 30 minutes before grilling. Set aside to let cool slightly. Meanwhile, cook 1 pound black or regular fettuccine according to the package directions until *al dente*. Drain (reserving 1/4 cup of the cooking water), return to the pot, toss with 2 tablespoons olive oil, and cover to keep warm. Heat 3 tablespoons olive oil in a medium-size saucepan. Add 1 minced garlic clove and cook, stirring, until golden, 2 to 3 minutes. Pour in 1/4 cup dry white wine and the reserved pasta cooking water and bring to a boil. Reduce the heat to a simmer and stir in 2 tablespoons chopped fresh Italian parsley. When the mussels are cool enough to handle, remove them from their shells using a paring knife. Add the mussels to the olive oil and wine sauce and stir to combine. Season with fine kosher or sea salt and freshly ground black pepper to taste. Transfer the warm pasta to a large serving bowl. Pour the mussels and sauce over the hot pasta, toss to coat, and serve immediately. **SERVES 4**

Grilled Shrimp, Scallops, or Squid

We hate to admit it, but Karen and Judith remember watching *Queen for a Day* on daytime television during the 1950s. The woman with the best hard-luck story became Queen for a Day, complete with crown, cape, scepter, and lots of prizes.

You don't have to have a hard-luck story to be Queen for a Day at your house. You just have to serve one of these delicious grilled shellfish dishes for ample praise. Choose from shrimp of all sizes (from medium-size to those huge Alaskan spot prawns), large sea scallops, and squid (also called calamari). The trick is not to overcook them, or the texture will be rubbery. (If necessary, pop not-quite-done shellfish in the microwave for 30 seconds on high to finish cooking.) Use a hot fire and a perforated grill rack to cook the fish.

Size does matter when it comes to timing. Smaller shrimp and thin-bodied squid will cook in 2 to 3 minutes total, turning once. Large, meaty sea scallops (the smaller bay scallops are too small for the grill, unless you want to toss them in a grill wok) and Alaskan spot prawns will take about 6 minutes. We prefer to grill shellfish more on one side than the other. For example, grill large sea scallops for 4 minutes on one side, then grill on the other side for 1 to 2 minutes. This technique results in a top "crust" and a softer bottom. SERVES 4

1 pound any size shrimp, peeled and deveined, large sea scallops, or cleaned squid (about 12 bodies and 12 tentacles)

Olive oil

Fine kosher or sea salt and freshly ground black pepper to taste

1. Brush or spray the shellfish with olive oil and season with salt and pepper.

2. Prepare a hot fire in a grill.

3. Place the shellfish on a perforated grill rack and grill, turning once, until opaque but still translucent in the center. Smaller shrimp and squid will take about 2 minutes, sea scallops and large prawns about 6 minutes. Serve hot.

Crowning Glories

These are super served with:

Chive Pesto *(page 64)*

Raspberry Beurre Blanc *(page 101)*

Kimizu *(page 103)*

Grilled Shrimp or Scallops in Thai Green Curry Sauce: Pink shrimp or ivory scallops nestled in a pale green and aromatic sauce is a dish worthy of the finest cubic zirconia tiara. Before grilling, whisk together 3 tablespoons green curry paste and one 11-ounce can unsweetened coconut milk (open the can first and stir the milk with a fork to blend) in a medium-size saucepan. Bring to a boil and cook for 1 minute. Stir in 1/2 cup finely chopped green onions, 3 kaffir lime leaves (very fragrant green leaves available at Asian markets and better grocery stores; you can freeze them and use frozen) or 1/2 teaspoon grated lime zest, 1 tablespoon Asian fish sauce, and 1 tablespoon packed light brown sugar. Bring to a boil again and cook for 2 minutes. Keep warm while you grill the shellfish (see above). To serve, ladle the sauce onto individual plates, place the grilled shellfish on top, and garnish with chopped fresh basil and cilantro. **SERVES 4**

Grilled Shrimp with Nuevo Latino Cocktail Sauce: Turn on the CD player and let the Latin music carry you south of the border. Go for hot and spicy! Include some sipping treats, such as Mojitos, Sangria! (page 250), margaritas, or Mexican beer; serve the shrimp in margarita glasses; and everything will be party perfect. In a large bowl, combine 1/2 cup prepared chili sauce, 1/2 cup chunky salsa, 1/4 cup fresh lime juice (4 to 5 limes), 1/4 cup chopped fresh cilantro, 1/2 teaspoon hot pepper sauce, and 1 minced garlic clove and mix well. Add about 1 pound grilled shrimp (see above) roughly chopped into bite-size pieces.

(Reserve 6 whole shrimp before chopping.) Place 1/4 cup shredded lettuce in the bottom of each of 6 margarita glasses. Divide the shrimp mixture evenly among the glasses. Garnish each glass with a lime wedge, cilantro sprig, and 1 whole shrimp. Serve warm or chilled. **SERVES 6**

Grilled Scallops with Fennel, Red Pepper, and Lemon-Tarragon Vinaigrette: With this dish's eye-popping presentation and flavor, you won't believe how easy it is to make. We got the original idea from California chef John Ash and took it from there. Trim, quarter, and core 1 large fennel bulb, then slice 1/4 inch thick. Prepare a large red bell pepper for grilling, slicing it into strips (see Grilled Peppers, page 142). Brush or spray 12 large sea scallops with olive oil. Grill the fennel and red pepper on a perforated grill rack over a hot fire, turning once, until marked on both sides and tender, about 10 minutes. Transfer to a platter. Grill the scallops as directed above. To serve, divide the fennel slices and pepper strips among 4 plates, place 3 scallops on each plate, and drizzle with Lemon-Tarragon Vinaigrette (page 75). Garnish with fresh tarragon sprigs and serve immediately. **SERVES 4**

Grilled Stuffed Calamari with Thousand-Herb Sauce: If you've had calamari only deep-fried as an appetizer, you're long overdue for a switch. Make sure your fire is really, really hot before you throw these babies on the grill. Place 1 pound cleaned calamari (about 12 bodies and 12 tentacles) in a medium-size bowl. Add 1/4 cup olive oil, 1/4 teaspoon red pepper flakes, 1 minced garlic clove, and fine kosher or sea salt and freshly ground black pepper to taste and toss to coat. Cover and marinate in the refrigerator for 30 minutes. In a small bowl, combine 1/2 cup fresh bread crumbs, 2 tablespoons extra virgin olive oil, the grated zest of 1 lemon, 1 tablespoon coarsely chopped fresh Italian parsley, and 1/4 teaspoon red pepper flakes until well blended. Remove the calamari from the marinade. Stuff each calamari with 2 teaspoons of the bread crumb mixture. Season the bodies and tentacles with salt and pepper and grill on a perforated grill rack over a really hot fire for 1 to 2 minutes per side. Serve with Thousand-Herb Sauce (page 192). **SERVES 6**

Grill Gals

She Spends Summers Off at the Jersey Shore Menu

Grilled Prosciutto and Basil–Wrapped Shrimp with Garlic Dipping Sauce
Grilled Bruschetta with Jersey Tomatoes
Grilled Lobster
Blueberry-Peach Tart with Macaroon Crust

Karen's barbecue buddy Lisa Readie Mayer grew up on the New Jersey shore and loves nothing more than spending summer evenings at the beach barbecuing with her family. Lisa is a freelance writer who writes about grills and other outdoor living products. Sometimes her vocation also becomes her avocation, as in this seashore feast.

This end-of-summer dinner party is an annual event at the Mayer house, with husband David and daughters Emily and Hannah pitching in to help. The exact menu varies from year to year, but it always includes foods the area is known for—seafood, Jersey tomatoes, sweet corn, peaches, and blueberries—and much of it is prepared on the grill. Lisa tries to buy whatever she can at her local farmers' market and the seafood market right near the fishing-boat docks.

"We start out with drinks and hors d'oeuvres on our deck overlooking the water," Lisa says. "Dinner is served informally, picnic table style, and we set out colorful sand pails to hold the lobster shells. Dessert is served during a break in the dancing that usually kicks up after dinner."

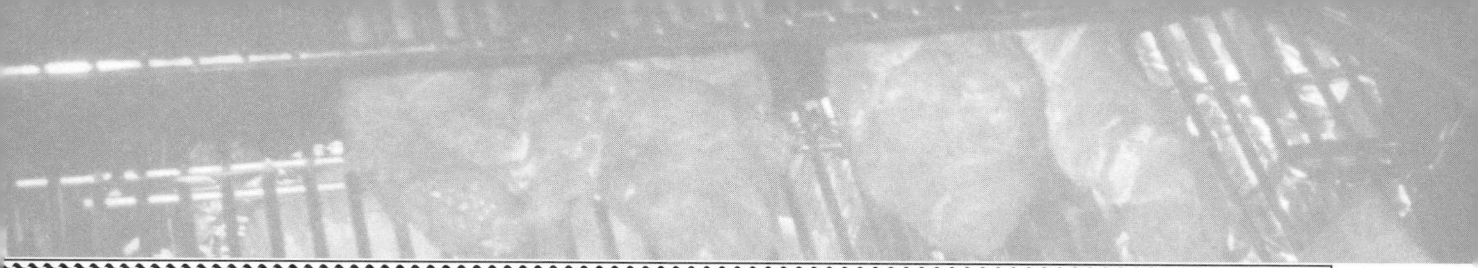

Grilled Prosciutto and Basil–Wrapped Shrimp with Garlic Dipping Sauce

These skewers are yummy and easy to make, even though they look very sophisticated. SERVES 8

24 fresh basil leaves

12 thin slices prosciutto, each cut in half lengthwise

24 extra-large shrimp, peeled and deveined, or large sea scallops

24 bamboo skewers, soaked in water for at least 30 minutes before grilling

GARLIC DIPPING SAUCE

1/3 cup red wine vinegar

2 tablespoons Dijon mustard

1 large clove garlic, chopped

1 cup olive oil

1. Place one basil leaf at the short end of a slice of prosciutto and a shrimp on top of the basil. Roll the shrimp in the prosciutto, then thread lengthwise onto a skewer. Repeat with the remaining basil, prosciutto, and shrimp. Place the skewers on a baking sheet and refrigerate until ready to cook.

2. To make the sauce, combine the vinegar, mustard, and garlic in a food processor or blender. With the machine running, add the olive oil in a slow, steady stream. Process until combined. Ten to 15 minutes before you are ready to grill, spoon about one-third of the sauce over the shrimp skewers to marinate. Transfer the rest of the dipping sauce to a small bowl.

3. Prepare a medium-hot fire in a grill. Grill the shrimp, turning often, until opaque, about 6 minutes.

4. Arrange the cooked skewers on a platter and serve with the dipping sauce on the side.

Grilled Bruschetta with Jersey Tomatoes

To make grilled bruschetta toasts, slice a baguette or other peasant-style bread into 1/2-inch-thick slices. Toast the bread on the grill until lightly browned on each side. Remove from the grill and lightly rub one side of each toast with a peeled garlic clove.
SERVES 8

8 ripe Roma tomatoes, cut in half, seeded, and cut into small dice
1/2 cup extra virgin olive oil
1/2 teaspoon coarse salt, or to taste
1/2 teaspoon freshly ground black pepper, or to taste
12 fresh basil leaves (more or less to taste), torn or snipped into small pieces
1 clove garlic, pressed
Bruschetta toasts (see headnote)

1. Combine all the ingredients except the toasts in a medium-size bowl. Let stand at room temperature for about 30 minutes to meld the flavors. Adjust the seasonings, if necessary.

2. To serve, place a spoonful of the tomato mixture on each toast, or serve the topping and toasts separately and let guests help themselves.

Grilled Lobster

If you've never had lobster on the grill, now is your chance. SERVES 8

Eight 1 1/4- to 1 1/2-pound lobsters
Melted unsalted butter and cocktail sauce for serving

1. Have the fishmonger cut the lobsters in half lengthwise and remove the vein and sack from the head.

2. Build a hot fire in a grill.

3. Oil a perforated grill rack. Place the lobsters cut side down on the grill rack and cook for 6 to 8 minutes. Turn the lobsters over and cook until the flesh is firm and white, another 6 to 8 minutes. Serve with melted butter and cocktail sauce.

Blueberry-Peach Tart with Macaroon Crust

From the crust to the topping, every layer of this dessert is lip-smackin' good. The bonus is that it's also an easy one to put together. If you make it a day ahead, you'll have time to touch up your lipstick and give that 'do another spray before dinner.

MAKES ONE 11-INCH TART; SERVES 10

CRUST

11 soft coconut macaroon cookies (Lisa uses Archway)

1 cup ground pecans

3 tablespoons unsalted butter, melted

FILLING

1/2 cup heavy cream

One 8-ounce package cream cheese, softened

1/3 cup sugar

2 teaspoons orange juice

1 teaspoon vanilla extract

1/2 teaspoon almond extract

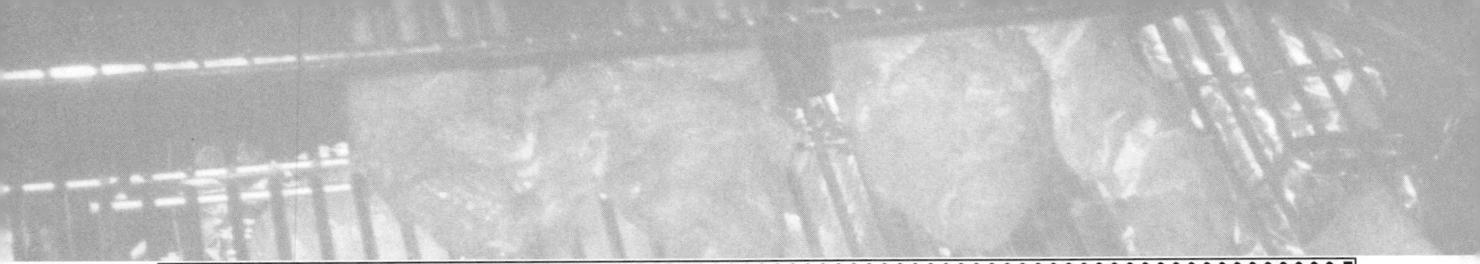

TOPPING

2 medium-size ripe peaches, peeled, pitted, and thinly sliced

2 tablespoons fresh lemon juice

1 pint fresh blueberries, picked over for stems

½ cup apricot preserves

1. Preheat the oven to 350°F.

2. To make the crust, crumble the macaroons (you should have at least 2 cups). Combine the macaroons, pecans, and melted butter in a large bowl. Press the mixture into an 11-inch tart pan with a removable bottom, pressing it into the bottom and up the sides of the pan. Bake until golden, 15 to 18 minutes. Set on a wire rack to cool.

3. To make the filling, in a chilled medium-size bowl with an electric mixer, beat the heavy cream on medium speed until soft peaks form. Set aside. In a large bowl, beat the cream cheese and sugar together on medium speed until fluffy. Add the orange juice and extracts and beat until smooth. Gently fold in the whipped cream. Spread the mixture evenly into the cooled crust, cover with plastic wrap, and refrigerate for 2 to 4 hours.

4. To make the topping, toss the peach slices with the lemon juice to prevent discoloration. Arrange the peaches and blueberries over the filling. In a small saucepan, heat the apricot preserves until just melted. Brush or spoon the glaze over the fruit. Carefully remove the sides of the pan and transfer the tart to a serving platter. Cut into slices and serve.

Stir-Grilled Shellfish

Shellfish is one of the easiest choices to stir-grill because it cooks fast and doesn't fall apart. If you want to marinate shellfish ahead of time, allow 30 minutes at most. Shrimp is probably the easiest and most widely available shellfish to begin with. We prefer to use a 15-inch grill wok for 2 pounds of shrimp so the shrimp are not crowded and will cook evenly and quickly. If you have a 12-inch grill wok, you may want to grill the shrimp in two batches. This recipe works well for scallops and squid, too, but the time may need to be adjusted slightly. SERVES 4

2 pounds large shrimp, peeled and deveined
2 to 3 tablespoons olive oil
2 to 3 tablespoons lemon pepper seasoning
1/2 teaspoon kosher salt

1. Place the shrimp in a large bowl. Drizzle with the olive oil, sprinkle with the lemon pepper and salt, and toss to coat.

2. Prepare a hot fire in a grill.

3. Coat a 15-inch grill wok with nonstick cooking spray. Over the sink, add the shrimp and let any excess oil drain off. Place the wok directly over the fire and stir-grill, tossing the shrimp with wooden paddles or grill spatulas until opaque and just firm to the touch, 12 to 15 minutes. Close the lid for 2 to 3 minutes to heat the shrimp all the way through, especially if the outdoor temperature is a bit cool. Serve warm, or let cool, refrigerate, and serve chilled.

Crowning Glories

Stir-grilled shellfish is delicious served over aromatic scented rice or a thin pasta such as linguine. It is complemented by any of the following rubs, marinades, or sauces:

Zesty Sugar and Spice Rub *(page 52)*
Fennel and Orange Marinade *(page 72)*
Smoked Garlic and Cilantro Cream Sauce *(page 93)*

"Wonton"-Wrapped Stir-Grilled Shellfish: Use grilled shrimp or scallops and serve as an appetizer or light supper. You'll need 1 pound stir-grilled peeled and deveined large shrimp or bay scallops, twelve 8 1/4-inch rice paper wrappers, 1 cup rinsed fresh bean sprouts, and 12 fresh basil leaves. Prepare each wrap by placing each rice paper wrapper in a bowl of hot water for 8 to 10 seconds, until completely wet. Lay the wrapper on a damp towel. Place 3 shrimp down the center of the wrapper. Top with sprouts and a basil leaf. Roll the wrapper tightly around the shrimp, folding the ends in. Repeat with the remaining wrappers and shrimp. Serve with Lemon-Tarragon Vinaigrette (page 75). **SERVES 4**

Grilled Squid Linguine with Amogio: Cook 1 pound linguine according to the package directions until *al dente*. Divide the pasta among 4 or 6 plates. Top each with a grilled squid (see headnote) and drizzle with 3 to 4 tablespoons Amogio (page 72). **SERVES 4 TO 6**

Stir-Grilled Scallop Po'boy Sandwiches: In a large bowl, combine 1 pound sea scallops, 2 cups cored and shredded Napa cabbage, and 3/4 cup Tandoori Marinade (page 74). Let sit at room temperature for 30 minutes. Using a slotted spoon, remove the scallops and cabbage from the marinade and stir-grill as directed above. Divide the scallops and cabbage among 4 hoagie-style or ciabatta rolls. Serve extra marinade on the side. **SERVES 4**

BBQ QUEEN

Here's the Beef

Where's the beef? Right here in this chapter. Americans love beef on the grill, from the popular and economical hamburger to the most expensive steak. People who economize on everything else still like to dine at fancy steakhouses and pay exorbitant prices (compared to other meats) for a prime cut. Beef is primal for Americans. It's all about how our country won the West. So before you decide to throw a steak on the grill or a brisket in the smoker, you need to know how to shop for beef. Let's begin with understanding how beef is graded. The FDA puts beef into three categories—prime, choice, and select (which you rarely see).

The average grocery store usually carries a selection of choice-grade steaks and filets that are 3/4 to 1 inch thick. Butcher shops, upscale grocers, and some specialty gourmet shops offer top choice and even prime (which used to be almost impossible to find) cuts. A butcher will also cut thicker steaks for you.

Steaks for grilling will be prime or choice grade. Let your eyes be your guide and select steaks with a nice, even marbling of fat throughout. The marbling should be thin white veins of fat, which make for tender, juicy, and flavorful eating.

For smoking tougher cuts of meat such as brisket and roasts, choice is often just fine because of the slow cooking time and low temperature, which are the double-barreled secrets to making these cuts of meat desirable and delicious.

It can be confusing shopping for steak, so here's a short rundown of the most popular steaks for the grill. (The same steak may have a different name in different parts of the country. We may use several names for the same steak, so bear with us.) The best and more expensive steaks include Delmonico, boneless rib-eye, Spencer, beauty, filet mignon, tenderloin, *filet de boeuf*, tournedo, Châteaubriand, T-bone, porterhouse, strip, rib, top loin, and shell. Less expensive steaks tend to be thinner and tougher cuts from the shoulder, flank, and round or butt of the cow. These steaks often have a very distinctive grain running through them. They are very flavorful grilled hot and fast to medium-rare, then thinly cut against the grain for best eating. They include shoulder, chuck, London broil, flat iron, blade, sirloin tip, steak tip, cube, minute, skirt, fajita, Philadelphia, flank, charcoal, jiffy, and hangar.

In this chapter, we also tell you how to rotisserie cook and plank beef, and there are certain cuts that take to these treatments better than others. Beef tenderloin works well for grilling, smoking, planking, skewering, and rotisserie cooking—just about anything! For the rotisserie, you want a large boneless roast, whether it's a boneless prime rib, tri-tip, whole beef tenderloin, or sirloin roast.

And, of course, we advise you how to smoke beef. The true American slow-smoked barbecue choice is brisket, but other roasts and tender cuts smoke well, too. Consider sirloin, tri-tip, blade, chuck, rump, rib, boneless rib-eye, tenderloin, standing rib, and beef ribs.

Grilled Burgers 303
- Dolled-Up Caesar Burgers 304
- Greek-Style Lamb Burgers with Cilantro-Mint Chutney 304
- Fourth of July Pilgrim Burgers with Dried Cranberry Relish 305
- Asian Tuna Burgers with Wasabi Mayo 305

Grilled Flank, Skirt, Hangar, or Other Thin Steak 307
- Bistro-Style Steak with Red Wine–Shallot Sauce 308
- Citrus-Grilled Beef Fajitas 308
- Grilled Steak Marinated in Beer, Herbs, and Morels 309
- Grilled Steak Salad with Caper Vinaigrette 309

NEW WAVE STEAK
- *Branding Iron Beef with Ancho Mayonnaise* 311
- *Batayaki Beef with Spicy Lemon-Soy Sauce* 312
- *Beef Filet Salad with Orange-Cumin Vinaigrette* 313

GRILL GALS: SHE GRILLS EVERYTHING MENU
- *Balsamic-Marinated Vegetables on the Grill* 314
- *Charcoal-Grilled Rib-Eye Steak* 315

Grilled Boneless Steak 316
- Steakhouse-Style Filet Mignon 317
- Grilled Peppercorn Filet Mignon with Cognac Sauce 317
- Philadelphia Garlic Rib-Eye Steak 318
- Grilled Strip Steak with Chile–Ginger–Green Onion Sauce 318
- Seduction Strip Steak with Roquefort-Bacon Butter 318

FAVORITE STEAKHOUSE SIDE DISHES
- *Classic Creamed Spinach* 319
- *Fried Onion Slivers* 320
- *Olive Oil Smashed Potatoes* 320
- *Decadent Garlic Mashed Potatoes* 321
- *Stewed and Scalloped Tomatoes* 322

Grilled Bone-In Steak 323
- Korean-Style Bone-In Steak 323
- Grilled T-Bone Steak with Smoked Tomato and Grilled Red Onion Relish 324
- Sicilian Bistecca 324

Grilled Thick-Cut Steak 325
- Black and Bleu Beef 326
- Prairie-Style Hay-Smoked Steak 326

BISTRO SIDE DISHES
- *Haricots Verts Salad with Mustard-Shallot Vinaigrette* 327
- *Homemade Frites* 328
- *Celery Root Rémoulade* 328
- *Bistro Grated Carrot Salad* 329

Grilled Beef Skewers 330
- Grilled Beef Skewers with Spicy Tomato-Chile Sauce 331
- Tamarind and Yogurt Beef Kabobs with Warm Pita Breads 331
- Beef Skewers with Quick Peanut Sauce 331

GRILL GALS: SHE GRILLS FOR A TASTE OF HOME MENU
- *Kabuli Kabobs* 333
- *Salata (Afghani Fresh Chopped Vegetable Salad)* 335

Grilled Beef Tenderloin 336
- Grilled Tenderloin with Sour Cream, Bacon, and Mushroom Sauce 337
- Chez Panisse–Style Grilled Beef Tenderloin 337

Smoked Beef Tenderloin 338
- Peppery Smoked Beef Tenderloin 339
- Smoked Porcini Beef Tenderloin 339
- Smoked Beef BLT 339

GRILL GALS: THIS 'QUE QUEEN IS A KANSAS CITY GRILL QUEEN MENU
- *Grilled Herbed and Spiced Beef Tenderloin Salad* 341
- *Grilled Herbed and Spiced Beef Tenderloin* 342
- *Grilled Turkey Roulade with Lemon-Basil Sauce* 343
- *Kathy's Chicken Wings* 344
- *Smoky Meatballs* 345

Planked Beef Tenderloin 346
- Argentinean Hickory-Planked Beef Tenderloin with Chimichurri Sauce 346
- Gorgonzola Filet Mignon on a Plank 347
- Slathered Beef Filet on a Plank 347

Rotisserie Beef Roast 347
- Uptown Rotisserie Beef Roast with Peppercorn Beurre Blanc 348

Downtown Rotisserie Beef Roast with BBQ Queens' Barbecued Beans 348

Lemon Pepper Beef Roast with Butter Baste 348

Rotisserie Boneless Prime Rib Roast with Blackened Seasoning 349

Smoked Beef Rib Roast 349

Smoked Rib Roast with Yorkshire Pudding 350

Rosemary Pesto Smoked Rib Roast 350

Smoked Rib Roast Sandwiches 350

BBQ BABES: SHE'S A TIARA-TOTIN' TEXAS QUEEN OF THE 'QUE MENU

Slow-Smoked Texas-Style Brisket 353

Mozzarella and Tomato Salad with Two Dressings 354

Smoked Brisket 356

Kansas City–Style Barbecued Brisket 357

Two-Step Shortcut Barbecued Brisket 358

Barbecued Brisket Dip 358

Burnt Ends 358

Burnt Ends Sandwich 358

AND NOW FOR SOMETHING COMPLETELY DIFFERENT

Barbecued Corned Beef with Mustard-Beer Slather and Smoked Potato Salad 359

Rustic Reuben 360

Grilled Burgers

To grill an outstanding burger, you *could* follow the meticulous directions in *Cook's Illustrated* magazine, down to patting the burgers so there is an infinitesimal depression in the middle and a corresponding thickness of a few millimeters around the perimeter. As BBQ Queens, we try to limit the use of calipers in cooking. Our mantra is "Keep it simple first, then jazz it up later."

Whether your burger is made from ground beef, turkey, chicken, pork, lamb, fish, or vegetables, make sure it is moist. With beef, you don't want to use lean ground round, or you will get a shoe-leather burger. We like ground chuck with about an 80-to-20 ratio of lean to fat; even 75 to 25 is fine. For turkey, chicken, or tuna, you will be adding ingredients to the ground meat, as you would for a meat loaf. Those extra ingredients will help keep the meat moist.

Don't work the ground meat too much. Gently pat the mixture into a burger, then leave it alone. If you work a burger for more than a minute, that's too long. Just gather the meat together and press it firmly into a burger shape. Ideally, that's about 5 inches in diameter and 1 1/2 to 2 inches high. You need a burger diameter that will fit on your bread or bun, and you want a burger thick enough to stay juicy. As some people have been known to say, this isn't rocket science.

As usual, we prefer a hot fire. Let the burgers cook without turning for 3 to 4 minutes, then turn and cook on the other side. This gives a nice char to the exterior. If you want a more well-done burger, after it has grilled on both sides, move it to a cooler part of the grill (on a raised shelf or on the perimeter) to cook longer. We like to cook extra (rare) burgers for leftovers, then reheat them for lunch the next day.

If you like, brush the cut surfaces of accompanying hamburger buns with melted butter or olive oil and place them cut sides down on the grill grate for about 1 minute, until you have grill marks. Then serve them with the burgers. SERVES 4

1 pound ground chuck or other ground meat
Fine kosher or sea salt and freshly ground black pepper to taste
Hamburger buns and condiments of your choice

1. Prepare a hot fire in a grill, with mesquite for a kiss of smoke (see page 13), if you like.

2. Form the ground meat into four 5-inch-diameter burgers, 1 1/2 to 2 inches thick. Grill the burgers for 3 to 4 minutes per side, turning once, for medium-rare. Serve with grilled or plain buns and condiments.

Crowning Glories

Instead of ketchup and the usual fixin's, try topping your burger with:

Aioli ***(pages 104–105 and 110)***

Simply Delicious Bordelaise Sauce ***(page 91)***

Mustard-Mayo Slather ***(page 66)***

Dolled-Up Caesar Burgers: These are very similar to what they serve up at the Split T in Oklahoma City. In this part of the country, people prefer their hamburgers "dolled up." We can relate. The Caesar-style dressing has raw egg yolk, so use egg substitute if that is a concern. In a bowl, combine 1 minced garlic clove, 2 to 3 shredded romaine lettuce leaves, $1/2$ cup mayonnaise, $1/4$ cup freshly grated Parmesan cheese, 1 large egg yolk, 2 tablespoons olive oil, $1/2$ teaspoon freshly ground black pepper, and 1 mashed anchovy fillet. Spread on top of each grilled hamburger and serve. **SERVES 4**

Greek-Style Lamb Burgers with Cilantro-Mint Chutney: You can make burgers from just about any ground meat or fish, but these lamb burgers are really something special. We adapted this recipe from one by Grill Guy Robert Chirico of Greenfield, Massachusetts. The burgers taste very fresh, and the mixture of sirloin and lamb makes for a more economical and milder-tasting blend. Serve them on grilled pita breads, with lettuce leaves and slices of fresh tomato and red onion. The chutney is also delicious with grilled fish or chicken, lamb chops, or kabobs. A little blob of Tzatziki (page 112) on each burger would not go amiss. To make the chutney, combine $1/2$ cup plain yogurt, 2 tablespoons finely chopped green onions, $1/4$ cup seeded and chopped jalapeños, $1\,1/2$ tablespoons grated fresh ginger (if using a microplane, you don't need to peel), $3/4$ cup chopped fresh cilantro, $1/3$ cup fresh mint leaves, 2 minced large garlic cloves, $1/2$ teaspoon fine kosher or sea salt, and $1/4$ teaspoon sugar in a blender or food processor and blend thoroughly. Cover and refrigerate for at least several hours or up to 24 hours. To make the burgers, combine 1 pound ground sirloin; 1 pound lean ground lamb; $1/2$ cup crumbled feta cheese (about 2 ounces); $1/3$ cup pitted, drained, and minced oil-cured Kalamata or Niçoise olives; and 1 teaspoon fine kosher or sea salt in a large bowl and mix lightly but thoroughly. Form into 6 patties (each large enough to fit inside a pita bread), handling the meat mixture as little as possible. Brush the patties with $1/4$ cup olive oil, then sprinkle with a mixture of 1 teaspoon each ground cumin and ground coriander. Grill as directed above over a medium-hot fire, about 4 minutes per side for medium-rare. During the last few minutes of cooking, place 6 pita breads on the outer edge of the grill and turn to toast lightly on both sides. Place a patty inside a pita bread pocket, spoon some chutney on top, and serve. **SERVES 6**

Fourth of July Pilgrim Burgers with Dried Cranberry Relish: You've heard of fusion food, a tasty combination of two different culinary traditions. Well, this is fusion holiday food. Take turkey, cranberries, and Pilgrims from Thanksgiving and dude them up for Fourth of July. Why not? Grill these turkey burgers over medium-high heat so they stay moist. In a large bowl, combine 1½ pounds ground turkey, ½ cup seasoned dry bread crumbs, ½ cup finely diced onion, 2 minced garlic cloves, 1 teaspoon fine kosher or sea salt, and ½ teaspoon ground white pepper. Gently form into four 1-inch-thick burgers. Prepare a medium-hot fire and cook the burgers for 7 to 8 minutes on each side. Serve with mayonnaise, Dried Cranberry Relish (page 175), and lettuce leaves on toasted buns. **SERVES 4**

Asian Tuna Burgers with Wasabi Mayo: Fellow Harvard Common Press coauthors Jane Murphy and Liz Yeh Singh are the Burger Queens. In *The Great Big Burger Book* (2003), they offer a huge range of burgers, from ground meats to steak sandwiches, with some delicious vegetarian options as well. We love this recipe, which can be made using salmon, shrimp, catfish, tilapia, poultry, beef, pork—you get the picture. We also like to use a fish or meat fillet marinated in mayonnaise. To make the wasabi mayo, combine ¼ cup plus 2 tablespoons mayonnaise, 3 tablespoons minced green onions, 2 teaspoons grated fresh ginger (if using a microplane, you don't need to peel), 2 teaspoons soy sauce, and 1 teaspoon wasabi paste or powder (available at Asian markets) in a food processor until smooth. Taste and adjust the seasonings. (This will keep, tightly covered, in the refrigerator for up to 1 week.) Cut one ¾-pound tuna steak into ¼-inch dice and mince another ¾-pound tuna steak. Combine the tuna, 2 minced garlic cloves, 2 teaspoons grated fresh ginger, 1 tablespoon toasted sesame oil, 3 tablespoons soy sauce, ¼ cup chopped green onions, ½ teaspoon salt, and ¼ teaspoon freshly ground black pepper in a large bowl. Form into six 1-inch-thick patties. Grill the burgers over a medium-hot fire until browned on both sides and to the desired degree of doneness (the middle can still be reddish pink), 5 to 7 minutes total. Serve on toasted sesame seed buns and top with the mayo. **SERVES 6**

The BBQ Queens' Burger Condiment Bar

Along with assorted breads and rolls, provide a royal feast of favorites for your next grilled burger bash.

Assorted cheese slices, crumbles, or smoked cheese (see pages 36 and 169–175)

Assorted greens

Crisp-cooked bacon

Sliced tomatoes

Caramelized onions

Bell pepper rings

Grilled onions, mushrooms, peppers, and/or tomatoes (see the vegetables chapter)

Assorted mustards, mayonnaise, and ketchup

Mustard-Mayo Slather (page 66)

Rustic Aioli (page 104)

Ancho Mayonnaise (page 311)

Roquefort-Bacon Butter (page 318)

Thai Chile-Peanut Dressing (page 80)

The Doctor Is In Apricot-Bourbon Barbecue Sauce and variations (page 90)

Grilled Tomatillo Salsa (page 163) or prepared salsa

Chili sauce

Guacamole

Horseradish

Fresh herbs

Grilled Flank, Skirt, Hangar, or Other Thin Steak

The whole steak scene had gotten a bit ho-hum. Very predictable. You knew what cuts were available: rib-eye, strip, sirloin, flank. You knew what to do with them. And then, all of a sudden, things changed. There were new cuts and names, such as beef bavette and skirt, hangar, flat iron, patio, and charcoal steak. Wassup? (as a hip-hop queen might ask).

The change is partly a result of consumer interest in ethnic foods, hence the loose-grained skirt steak (the diaphragm muscle on a steer and the first choice for making great fajitas) and the beef bavette (cut from the flank for the French bistro steak and *frites* combo). Both can be hard to find at the grocery store but are readily available at butcher shops and from online vendors such as Niman Ranch.

In addition, the National Cattlemen's Beef Association, based in Colorado, has championed new "moderately priced" options such as the flat iron steak, cut from the beef chuck, and the western griller, cut from the bottom round. Cube steak, a.k.a. minute steak, has been around for a while. It is cut from the round and cubed twice to tenderize this tasty but tough piece of meat and make it great for grilling (a minute per side, not surprisingly). The hangar steak comes from the flank and is actually a thick muscle. It is much tougher than flank steak but is a bistro favorite and is also referred to as onglet.

All of these steaks have a chewy texture but great beef flavor. You need to tenderize them either by marinating them for at least an hour (preferably 8 hours) or pounding them with a meat tenderizer or mallet. Then you grill them over a hot fire to medium-rare. The final crucial step is slicing them properly to serve. Before you marinate a steak, locate the direction of the grain in the meat, which is easy to do. The grain consists of the lines of muscle fiber, which usually go in one direction. File that information away, grill your steak, and cut the meat against the grain, on the diagonal, holding your knife at a 45-degree angle (so it's slanted, not straight up and down). Perfecto!

For the marinade, we suggest Garlic-Citrus Marinade (page 70), Provençal Red Wine Marinade (page 70), or Homemade Teriyaki Marinade (page 69). SERVES 4

Marinade of your choice (see headnote)

1 1/2 pounds beef bavette or flank, skirt, hangar, flat iron, or western griller steak

1. Place the marinade and steak in a sealable plastic bag and refrigerate for at least 1 hour or up to 8 hours.

2. Prepare a hot fire in a grill.

3. Remove the meat from the marinade and pat dry. Grill for 2 to 3 minutes per side for medium-rare. Let the meat rest for 5 minutes, then cut against the grain, on the diagonal and at a 45-degree angle, into slices about 1/4 inch thick. Serve warm.

BBQ Tip: Judith's dad, whose family ran a butcher shop in Ohio for several generations, would run a flat steak like flank through the cuber once to tenderize it a little more. Ask the butcher to do that, then go home and marinate the steak before grilling for scrumptious results.

Crowning Glories

Put this over the top with:

Simply Delicious Bordelaise Sauce *(page 91)*

Potato Gratin with White Cheddar Cheese *(page 412)*

Haricots Verts with Lemon, Garlic, and Parsley *(page 274)*

Bistro-Style Steak with Red Wine–Shallot Sauce: In a mortar with a pestle, or with a meat mallet or the edge of a skillet, crush 2 tablespoons black peppercorns. Press the peppercorns and 2 tablespoons coarse kosher or sea salt into the surface of 1 1/2 pounds of the flat steak of your choice. Let rest for 30 minutes. To make the sauce, melt 3 tablespoons unsalted butter in a medium-size skillet over medium heat. Add 1 cup minced shallot (about 8 medium-size shallots) and cook, stirring, until transparent, about 5 minutes. Stir in 3/4 cup dry red wine and 3/4 cup beef broth and simmer until very thick, about 30 minutes. Season with kosher or sea salt and freshly ground black pepper to taste. Keep warm. When ready to grill, spray the coated steaks lightly with olive oil and grill over a hot fire, 2 to 3 minutes per side for rare. Let rest for 5 minutes, then slice against the grain and serve with the warm sauce, Homemade Frites (page 328), Dijon mustard, and fresh watercress. **SERVES 4**

Citrus-Grilled Beef Fajitas: These are the definitive fajitas. Substitute the same weight in boneless, skinless chicken breasts, if you like. Make 1 recipe of Garlic-Citrus Marinade (page 70). Place 1 1/2 pounds of the flat steak of your choice in a sealable plastic bag and pour the marinade over. Seal the bag and marinate in the refrigerator for at least 2 hours or overnight. Prepare 1 recipe Stir-Grilled Vegetables (page 166) and keep warm. Grill the steak for 2 to 3 minutes on each side for medium-rare, or until the beef is to your desired doneness. Let rest for several minutes before slicing against the grain. To serve, place garnishes such as guacamole, chopped tomato, shredded lettuce, salsa, and shredded cheese in attractive bowls on the table. Arrange the meat, stir-grilled vegetables, and warm flour tortillas on a large platter and let your family or guests have at it. **SERVES 6**

Grilled Steak Marinated in Beer, Herbs, and Morels: This is a hearty yet lean dish of prairie favorites—wheat beer, steak, and morels—adapted from a recipe by midwesterner-at-heart Larry Forgione, who made his mark at An American Place in New York City. In a large bowl, combine 1 cup amber or wheat beer, 1 1/2 cups chicken broth, 1 cup tomato juice, 1/4 cup dried morels or 1/2 cup fresh morels, 2 tablespoons chopped fresh oregano, 2 tablespoons chopped fresh thyme, 1 tablespoon Worcestershire sauce, 1/2 teaspoon hot pepper sauce, and 2 bay leaves. Pour half of the marinade into a baking dish and reserve the other half. Place 1 1/2 pounds flat or thin steak of your choice in the dish, turning to coat. Marinate for 1 hour at room temperature, turning the steak every 15 minutes. Meanwhile, melt 2 tablespoons unsalted butter in a medium-size skillet over medium-high heat. Add 2 tablespoons chopped green onions and cook, stirring, until tender, about 4 minutes. Add the reserved marinade and heat through. Season with fine kosher or sea salt and freshly ground black pepper to taste. Keep warm. Remove the steak from the marinade and pat dry. Sprinkle with salt and pepper and grill as directed above. Let rest for 5 minutes, then slice against the grain, nap with the sauce, and serve. **SERVES 4**

Grilled Steak Salad with Caper Vinaigrette: This is cooking for the sexes. Women want a light dish, men want meat. They get both in this refreshing yet man-pleasing salad any time of the year. For easy entertaining, layer the salad ingredients (minus the flank steak and vinaigrette) in a bowl, cover, and refrigerate for several hours or overnight. In a small bowl, combine 2 tablespoons drained capers, 3 tablespoons fresh lemon juice, 1/2 cup red wine vinegar, 1 cup extra virgin olive oil, and fine kosher or sea salt and freshly ground black pepper to taste. Place 1 1/2 pounds flank steak in a sealable plastic bag and pour half of the vinaigrette over the meat. Seal the bag and marinate in the refrigerator for at least 1 hour or overnight. In a large salad bowl, assemble 1/2 sliced large red onion, 8 ounces sliced fresh mushrooms, 1 cup grape tomatoes, 12 ounces trimmed fresh green beans cooked in boiling water until just crisp (about 3 minutes), 1 cup drained marinated artichoke hearts cut into bite-size pieces, and 1 bunch coarsely chopped watercress or fresh Italian parsley. Grill the steak as directed above, then let the meat rest for 5 minutes. Slice against the grain, then place on top of the salad. Pour the reserved vinaigrette over the salad and toss to blend. Serve immediately. **SERVES 6**

New Wave Steak

America's fascination and fixation with steak dates back only a hundred years or so. It became popular when the West opened up in the 1870s and cowboys drove herds of wild Texas longhorns, descended from cattle abandoned by the Spanish, up to the railroad cars in Abilene, Kansas.

In these years right after the Civil War, the "carpetbagger steak" came into being—a thick steak with a pocket cut in the side that was stuffed with fresh oysters, then cooked on a griddle for city folk. Cowboys herding the rowdy, rangy longhorns north from the southernmost tip of Texas enjoyed steak and beans most nights for supper. However, they enjoyed their tough and lean longhorn steak charred and well done, cooked to death in a cast-iron skillet over an open fire. (Perhaps "enjoyed" is not quite the right term.)

America's cattle industry—and a more tender steak's popularity—began to grow as European cattle breeds such as the Hereford and Aberdeen Angus were introduced to this country and cross-bred with the longhorn. By the late 1800s, a good steak sizzled on a hot griddle was what workingmen wanted when they ate out in cow towns such as Kansas City and Omaha.

In the 1950s, steak entered another evolutionary cycle. Charcoal briquettes, developed as an offshoot business to make use of wooden crates left over from automobile manufacturing at the Ford plant in Detroit, tempted a whole new generation of men to get outside and grill that steak. Charcoal grilling added a spectacular flavor dimension that we still crave.

Flash forward to the 1960s and 1970s, when college-age baby boomers discovered world travel. Cheap airfares, a "do your own thing" ideal, and a good dose of wanderlust sent a whole generation abroad. It's no accident that Julia Child was so successful in introducing French cooking to an American audience at this time. We were open to new ideas and eager to learn. Châteaubriand, *steak au poivre*, and steak Diane became familiar haute cuisine dishes.

Steak is still what we crave today, whether we're queens or kings. According to steak expert William Rice, retired *Chicago Tribune* columnist and author of *Steak Lover's*

***Cookbook* (Workman, 1997), "The steak dinner is the feast of choice for special occasions and a symbol of American well-being and prosperity."**

In the recipes that follow, a new wave of creativity takes steak into the new millennium.

Branding Iron Beef with Ancho Mayonnaise

This recipe is adapted from one created by chef Dan Palmer and featured in Judith's *Prairie Home Cooking* (The Harvard Common Press, 1999). Toasting the ancho chile brings out the flavor, which is milder in heat than a jalapeño or serrano. SERVES 4 AS AN APPETIZER

1 pound sirloin tip
Extra virgin olive oil
Fine kosher or sea salt and freshly ground black pepper to taste
1 small dried ancho chile, cut in half, stemmed, and seeded
1 cup good-quality mayonnaise
2 tablespoons capers, drained, for garnish

1. If your outdoor grill has enough BTUs to blacken redfish, build a very hot fire in the grill. If not, heat a cast-iron skillet on the hottest burner on your stove. (Open the windows and turn on the exhaust fan if cooking indoors, because this will create lots of smoke.) Paint all sides of the sirloin tip with olive oil and season with salt and pepper. When the grill or skillet is extremely hot, blacken the beef for about 1 minute on each side, then remove from the heat.

2. While the beef is cooling, heat a small skillet over high heat. Add the ancho chile and toast until fragrant, 1 to 2 seconds on each side. Transfer to a small bowl and add just enough hot water to cover. Let steep for about 10 minutes. Remove the chile and pat dry. Place in a food processor with the mayonnaise and process until smooth and slightly pink. Cover and refrigerate.

3. When the beef is completely cool, wrap in plastic and put in the freezer to firm (but not freeze), 20 to 30 minutes. If you have one, use a mandoline to cut the beef paper-thin and arrange the slices around the perimeter of 4 chilled serving plates. If you wish, pour the ancho mayonnaise into a squeeze bottle and squirt a design over the beef; you can also drizzle the mayonnaise over. Garnish each plate with capers and serve immediately.

Batayaki Beef with Spicy Lemon-Soy Sauce

Batayaki is a Japanese cooking style in which thin slices of meat and small cut vegetables are cooked right at the table and served with a dipping sauce and steamed rice. Do this inside using a grill pan or electric grill or outside using a grill wok or perforated grill rack. SERVES 4

SPICY LEMON-SOY SAUCE

Juice of 1 lemon

1/4 cup soy sauce

1 teaspoon Korean chile bean sauce (*kochujang*) or other hot pepper paste

1 teaspoon toasted sesame oil

1/2 teaspoon dashi (instant Oriental soup stock; available at Japanese markets)

1 cup thinly shredded daikon (Oriental radish)

1 bunch green onions, cut into 2-inch pieces

1 1/2 pounds sirloin tip, very thinly sliced

12 fresh shiitake mushrooms, stems removed and caps sliced

1 large yellow onion, sliced and separated into rings

8 ounces fresh bean sprouts, rinsed

5 tablespoons vegetable oil

1. To make the sauce, combine all the ingredients in a small bowl. Ladle into 4 individual bowls and top each with 1/4 cup daikon and 1 tablespoon green onions.

2. Brush the beef slices, mushrooms, onion, and bean sprouts with the vegetable oil. Using a hot electric skillet at the table or a grill pan on the stovetop over high heat, or using a grill wok or perforated grill rack on a hot grill outside, cook the beef, mushrooms,

and onion on both sides until done to your satisfaction. Sizzle the bean sprouts a little bit. Arrange the cooked foods on a platter and serve, having guests dip them into the sauce as desired.

Beef Filet Salad with Orange-Cumin Vinaigrette

This dish, adapted from a recipe in William Rice's *Steak Lover's Cookbook* (Workman, 1997), is one that Monique King, chef at Chicago's Soul Kitchen, serves at room temperature. SERVES 4

Two 8-ounce filet mignon steaks, about 1 inch thick, at room temperature

1 tablespoon olive oil

8 cups mesclun or mixed baby greens

ORANGE-CUMIN VINAIGRETTE

3 tablespoons extra virgin olive oil

1 tablespoon fresh orange juice

1 tablespoon sherry vinegar

$1\frac{1}{2}$ teaspoons minced green onions

1 teaspoon grated orange zest

$\frac{1}{4}$ teaspoon ground cumin

Kosher or sea salt and ground white pepper to taste

1. Prepare a hot fire in a grill.

2. Pat the steaks dry and lightly coat with the olive oil. Grill for 2 to 3 minutes per side for medium-rare. Set aside and let cool.

3. Put the greens in a large bowl.

4. To make the vinaigrette, combine all the ingredients in a small bowl. Pour all but 1 tablespoon over the greens, tossing to coat evenly. Divide the greens among 4 plates. Cut the steaks into $\frac{1}{4}$-inch-thick slices and arrange the slices on top of the greens. Drizzle the remaining dressing on top and serve.

Grill Gals

She Grills Everything Menu

Balsamic-Marinated Vegetables on the Grill
Charcoal-Grilled Rib-Eye Steak

Celina Tio is the executive chef at the renowned American Restaurant in Kansas City. Her previous position was with Disney in Orlando, Florida. She has more energy than two chefs put together and enjoys rock climbing in her spare(!) time. When she has friends over for dinner or caters a meal during the summer, she favors a dish she calls "Everything Grilled"—basically, a charcoal-grilled rib-eye steak accompanied by grilled vegetables that have been marinated in balsamic vinegar. It all cooks at the same time, and cleanup is easy. We find that cooking the vegetables—especially the onion slices, which can fall apart—on a perforated grill rack is the way to go.

Balsamic-Marinated Vegetables on the Grill

Who doesn't like balsamic vinegar? Nobody we know. This marinade darkens and deepens the flavors of the grilled vegetables. If you like, use a perforated grill rack so you don't lose any vegetables to the flames. SERVES 6

1/2 cup olive oil
1/4 cup balsamic vinegar
1 eggplant, ends trimmed and sliced 1/4 inch thick
2 zucchini, ends trimmed and sliced on the diagonal 1/4 inch thick

1 yellow summer squash, ends trimmed and sliced on the diagonal 1/4 inch thick

3 Yukon Gold potatoes, sliced 1/4 inch thick

2 red onions, sliced 1/4 inch thick

4 portobello mushrooms, stems and gills removed

1. Combine the olive oil and vinegar in a large sealable plastic bag. Add the vegetables, seal, and marinate for at least 1 hour.

2. When ready to cook, prepare a hot fire in a grill.

3. Remove the vegetables from the marinade and place in a large bowl. Grill the onions, potatoes, and mushrooms directly on the grill grate until soft, about 7 minutes per side. Transfer to a large platter and keep warm.

4. Place an oiled grill wok or perforated grill rack over the grill grate. Grill the eggplant, zucchini, and yellow squash until soft, about 4 minutes per side. Depending on the size of your grill rack, you may need to grill these in 2 batches.

5. Just before the last batch of vegetables goes on the grill, you may begin grilling the steaks. Arrange the cooked vegetables on the platter and serve with the steaks.

Charcoal-Grilled Rib-Eye Steak

SERVES 6

Six 8-ounce rib-eye steaks, 3/4 inch thick

Kosher or sea salt and freshly ground black pepper to taste

1. Prepare a hot fire in a grill.

2. Season the steaks with salt and pepper. Grill for 7 minutes per side for medium. Place on a platter and serve hot.

Grilled Boneless Steak

Boneless steaks come in all shapes, sizes, and degrees of tenderness, from the chewy charcoal steak cut from the beef chuck to the more tender and flavorful sirloin or strip steak to the fabulously tender filet mignon.

The BBQ Queens' favorites are the filet mignon and rib-eye, great steaks for the grill because of their tenderness and good marbling of fat throughout. Cut from the long piece of rib section meat known as standing rib roast or prime rib, boneless rib-eye steaks are usually about 3/4 inch thick. Filet mignon can be cut into steaks up to 3 inches thick, but Grill Gals like us prefer 1-inch cuts.

We love really tender boneless steaks grilled over mesquite charcoal or on a gas grill. The key is a hot-as-you-can-get-it fire. We both like our tender steaks steakhouse style—with a spice rub or flavoring paste applied to the meat, which is then cooked over a hot fire to get a charred crust, while the center remains rare to medium.

Strip steak, also known as Kansas City or New York strip, is a he-man kind of steak—thick, meaty, full of beef flavor, and somewhat chewy. Karen's husband, Dick, loves this cut, so they grill it a lot at their house. Cut from the hindquarter or the middle section of the steer's back, the strip steak starts out as a T-bone steak, part tenderloin and part top loin. The butcher cuts out the tenderloin from one side of the T-bone, then removes the T-bone area entirely and—voilà!—a boneless, elongated strip steak, usually cut about 1 inch thick.

Because strip, sirloin, or chuck steaks are a little chewier than rib-eye or filet mignon, we use a slightly lower fire—medium-hot rather than hot. Full-flavored strip steaks and their like need a sauce or accompaniment with big flavor as well. You can marinate a strip steak, but we prefer an accompanying sauce, condiment, or relish for a better flavor contrast. We love this best served with Smoked Tomato and Grilled Red Onion Relish (page 324), Chile–Ginger–Green Onion Sauce (page 318), or Roquefort-Bacon Butter (page 318). You can grill this steak indoors using a grill pan, if you wish. We're gonna give you a lot of recipes for this type of steak, because there are so many ways to enjoy it.

SERVES 4

Four 8-ounce filet mignon, rib-eye, boneless sirloin, or strip steaks, 1 inch thick

Olive oil

Coarse kosher or sea salt and freshly ground black pepper or lemon pepper seasoning to taste

1. Brush the steaks lightly with olive oil and season with salt and pepper. Set aside.
2. Prepare a hot fire in a grill.

3. Close the lid and grill for 3 minutes per side for medium-rare.

Crowning Glories

Keep it simple and serve with a baked potato and a green salad, or have a rhinestone-tiara kind of night and top your steaks with:

Simply Delicious Bordelaise Sauce *(page 91)*

Smoked Tomato and Grilled Red Onion Relish *(page 324)*

Rustic Béarnaise Sauce *(page 98)*

Roasted Cherry Tomatoes with Frizzled Herbs *(page 208)*

Steakhouse-Style Filet Mignon: The secret to great steakhouse steak flavor is to sear the meat over high heat in a seasoned cast-iron skillet or a heavy anodized grill pan—indoors or out—similar to blackening fish. If your outdoor grill doesn't have the upper-level BTUs to do this, use your stovetop indoors. (Open the windows and turn your kitchen fan on high—this is smoky business.) Searing will produce that blackened, charred exterior and rarish, pink, juicy interior you're looking for—what's termed "black and blue" by New York steakhouses. For a really divine version, spread Porcini Paste (page 65) on the filets and omit dipping them in butter or oil. Prepare a hot fire in a grill or turn your stovetop burner to high, and heat a cast-iron skillet or grill pan over the coals or burner until the bottom begins to turn gray, about 20 minutes. Have ready four 6-ounce filet mignon steaks cut about 2 inches thick. Pour 2 tablespoons clarified butter or olive oil on a plate and dip each steak in it. Sear the steaks for 2 to 3 minutes per side for medium-rare, a little longer for medium. Season with salt and pepper. Accompany with Classic Creamed Spinach (page 319) and Fried Onion Slivers (page 320). **SERVES 6**

Grilled Peppercorn Filet Mignon with Cognac Sauce: This dish deserves a *real* rhinestone tiara! You'll need a seasoned cast-iron skillet you can use on the grill. Prepare a hot fire and place the skillet over direct heat for 20 to 30 minutes before grilling. Meanwhile, press 1/4 cup cracked black peppercorns and kosher salt to taste into the surface of four 6- to 8-ounce filet mignon steaks cut 1 1/2 to 2 inches thick. Spray the filets with olive oil and place in the hot skillet. Close the grill and cook until a thick crust forms on the bottom, 7 to 8 minutes. Turn and dot each with 1 1/2 teaspoons unsalted butter. Close the grill and cook for another 7 to 8 minutes for medium-rare. Transfer the steaks to a plate near the grill to keep warm. Add 1/4 cup heavy cream, 1/4 cup cognac, and 1/2 cup demi-glace (made from concentrate that you can get at gourmet shops and better grocery stores) or good-quality chicken broth to the skillet. Whisk together, then cook until slightly thickened, 3 to 4 minutes. Nap each filet with sauce and serve. **SERVES 4**

Philadelphia Garlic Rib-Eye Steak: In a shallow pie pan, make a paste of 1/4 cup minced garlic (about 8 cloves), 1/4 cup olive oil, 1/4 cup sweet Hungarian paprika, 1 teaspoon seasoned salt, and 1 teaspoon freshly ground black pepper. Dredge four 8-ounce, 1-inch-thick rib-eye (or other boneless) steaks in this mixture and let marinate at room temperature for 30 minutes. Grill the steaks over a hot fire for 3 minutes per side for medium-rare. Serve with Grilled Asparagus (page 117) and a potato casserole (see pages 412–413). **SERVES 4**

Grilled Strip Steak with Chile–Ginger–Green Onion Sauce: In a small skillet, heat 1 tablespoon vegetable oil over medium-high heat. Add 1 teaspoon minced garlic, 1 teaspoon grated fresh ginger (if using a microplane, you don't need to peel), and 1/4 teaspoon red pepper flakes. Cook, stirring, until the garlic and ginger have softened, about 4 minutes. Stir in 1/2 cup mirin (a sweet Japanese wine) or sweet sake, 1/4 cup soy sauce, and 1 tablespoon sugar and bring to a boil. In a small jar with a tight-fitting lid, place 2 tablespoons cornstarch and 1 tablespoon cold water. Cover and shake to blend. Whisk the mixture into the sauce until thickened, about 5 minutes. Keep warm while you grill four 8-ounce, 1-inch-thick strip steaks as directly above. Just before serving, stir 1/4 cup sliced green onions into the sauce. Slice the steak and serve with the sauce spooned over. This sauce is also good with grilled fish, chicken, pork, or vegetables. **SERVES 4**

Seduction Strip Steak with Roquefort-Bacon Butter: Food writer M. F. K. Fisher had menus to both seduce—and un-seduce—would-be lovers. Use this dish for taste-bud seduction, at the very least (unless your intended doesn't like blue cheese, of course). To make the butter, place 2 sticks unsalted butter minus 1 tablespoon in a medium-size bowl. Melt the remaining 1 tablespoon butter in a small skillet over medium heat. Add 6 diced shallots and cook, stirring, until browned, about 6 minutes. Transfer to the bowl along with 3 slices crumbled crisp-cooked bacon, 1/2 cup crumbled Roquefort or other blue cheese, 1 tablespoon snipped fresh chives, and 1 tablespoon Worcestershire sauce. Using a fork or potato masher, mash the butter and place in the middle of a sheet of waxed paper or plastic wrap. Partially cover and roll into a long cylinder. Cover and refrigerate until firm, about 2 hours. (This may be stored in a sealed plastic bag in the freezer for up to 6 months.) Grill four 8-ounce, 1-inch-thick strip steaks as directed above. Serve topped with large pats of the butter, which will pleasingly melt over the hot steaks. Also try the butter on grilled or smoked chicken or pork or on a baked potato. **SERVES 4**

Favorite Steakhouse Side Dishes

Since the time the first American steakhouses graced the big cities, side dishes like these have offered counterpoint flavors to the great taste of steak.

Classic Creamed Spinach

Creamed spinach has been a classic American steakhouse favorite for generations, and for good reason. Fresh baby spinach makes the most tender side dish, almost melting in your mouth. Mellow with cream and gently spiced with freshly grated nutmeg, this is good enough to enjoy on its own, but it's also delicious with steak, roast chicken, or fish or shellfish. SERVES 4

1½ pounds fresh spinach, washed well and trimmed of heavy stems
1 tablespoon unsalted butter
1 tablespoon all-purpose flour
¾ cup half-and-half
Kosher or sea salt, ground white pepper, and freshly grated nutmeg to taste

1. Place the spinach, with the rinse water still clinging to it, in a large pot. Turn the heat to high and cover. When steam begins to escape from under the lid, about 3 minutes, remove the pot from the heat, leave the cover on, and let the spinach steam while you make the sauce.

2. In a small saucepan, melt the butter over medium heat. Stir in the flour and cook until the flour smell disappears, about 2 minutes. Whisk in the half-and-half and stir to remove any lumps. Let the sauce come to a boil to thicken. Stir into the spinach and season with salt, white pepper, and nutmeg. Serve immediately.

Fried Onion Slivers

Judith loves to serve these with filet mignon or rib-eye steak, along with creamed spinach. The Bravo restaurant chain serves these slivers atop a grilled chicken and feta cheese salad with citrus dressing. (Yum!) You'll think of even more ways to enjoy them. We use a mandoline to cut the onion paper-thin and a candy thermometer to check the temperature of the oil. (You also may use an electric skillet or deep-fat fryer.) These "slivers" are actually the thinnest of thin onion rings. SERVES 4

1 large yellow onion, sliced paper-thin
1/2 cup all-purpose flour
3 cups peanut oil
Fine sea salt to taste

1. Toss the onion slices with the flour in a medium-size bowl until well coated.
2. Heat the peanut oil in a deep saucepan or electric skillet to 350°F. Fry the onions in batches, without crowding them, until golden brown, 7 to 8 minutes. Remove from the oil using a slotted spoon and drain on paper towels. Immediately season with salt. Keep warm in a low oven until all the slices have been fried. Serve immediately.

Olive Oil Smashed Potatoes

So easy, and so good! Use the best olive oil you can find, because this flavors the potatoes. SERVES 4

4 large baking potatoes, peeled and roughly chopped
1/4 cup extra virgin olive oil, or to you taste
1 teaspoon fine sea salt
1 teaspoon freshly ground black pepper or ground white pepper

1. Place the potatoes in a medium-size saucepan with enough water to cover. Bring to a boil and continue to boil until the potatoes are tender, 12 to 15 minutes.
2. Drain off the water and use a potato masher or fork to smash the potatoes with the olive oil in the pan. Season with salt and pepper and serve hot.

Decadent Garlic Mashed Potatoes

Julia Child was always ahead of her time. This recipe first appeared on her *French Chef* television program in the 1970s. Today, it's a perfect accompaniment to grilled steak.

SERVES 6 TO 8

GARLIC SAUCE

2 heads garlic (about 30 cloves)

1/4 cup (1/2 stick) unsalted butter

2 tablespoons all-purpose flour

1 cup milk, heated

MASHED POTATOES

2 1/2 pounds baking potatoes, peeled and roughly chopped

1/4 cup (1/2 stick) unsalted butter

3 to 4 tablespoons heavy cream to taste

Fine kosher or sea salt and freshly ground black pepper to taste

1. To make the sauce, separate the garlic cloves from the heads and drop them into boiling water. Boil for 2 minutes, drain, and peel. (This blanches and mellows the garlic so it's not overpowering.) In a small, heavy saucepan, melt the butter over medium-low heat. Add the peeled garlic cloves and flour and cook for 2 minutes. Whisk in the hot milk and continue to whisk until thick and creamy, about 5 minutes. Keep warm.

2. Meanwhile, make the mashed potatoes. Place the potatoes in a large saucepan with salted water to cover. Bring to a boil and continue to boil until tender, 15 to 20 minutes. Drain off the water and use a potato masher or fork to mash the potatoes in the pan, adding the butter, cream and salt and pepper. Mash in the garlic sauce and serve hot.

Stewed and Scalloped Tomatoes

There are stewed tomatoes and there are stewed tomatoes. Some come straight from the can and are just heated up. Others, like this recipe, are graced with a few simple but delicious additions—such as crème fraîche—that make all the difference. SERVES 6 TO 8

1/2 cup sour cream (lowfat is okay)
1/2 cup heavy cream
Two 15-ounce cans stewed tomatoes, with their juice
2 cups fresh bakery or artisanal bread cut into 1-inch cubes
1/4 cup (1/2 stick) unsalted butter, melted

1. Preheat the oven to 350°F. Butter a 13 x 9-inch baking dish.

2. In a large bowl, whisk together the sour cream and heavy cream to make crème fraîche. Fold in the tomatoes and spoon half the mixture into the prepared pan. Dot the top with half the bread cubes and drizzle with half the butter. Spoon the remaining tomato mixture on top of the bread cubes, then dot the surface with the remaining bread cubes and drizzle with the remaining butter. Bake until bubbling and browned, 25 to 30 minutes. Serve hot.

Grilled Bone-In Steak

Sometimes you just gotta have a primeval hunk of grilled meat with a bone to gnaw. Happily, you have lots of choices for this type of steak. A premium rib steak is a rib-eye with the bone left in, tender and juicy from the marbling of fat throughout. The T-bone, cut from the short loin, has a tender filet mignon side and a chewier New York or strip steak side, with a T-shaped bone separating them. The bigger porterhouse is a T-bone steak on steroids, with a more generous portion on the filet side. A chewier, beefier strip steak can also have the bone left in. In that case, it could be called a Kansas City, New York strip, Delmonico, shell, or club steak—depending on where you live and shop. Most bone-in steaks are cut about 1 inch thick.

We like a hot fire and a simple preparation for this kind of steak. Just a little brush of olive oil and maybe a spicy rub (or simply salt and pepper), and you're good to go. SERVES 4

4 bone-in steaks of your choice, about 1 inch thick

Olive oil

Cajun Steak Rub (page 58) or fine kosher or sea salt and freshly ground black pepper to taste

1. Brush or spray the steaks with olive oil.

2. Prepare a hot fire in a grill.

3. Grill the steaks on each side for 3 to 4 minutes for medium-rare. An instant-read meat thermometer inserted in the center near the bone should register 140°F.

Crowning Glories

Enjoy your steak in glorious nakedness (its, not yours, though that's an idea) or gild it with your choice of:

Simply Delicious Bordelaise Sauce *(page 91)*

Mustard-Cornichon Beurre Blanc *(page 100)*

Rustic Béarnaise Sauce *(page 98)*

Korean-Style Bone-In Steak: A Korean-style marinade flavors this steak before it sizzles on the grill. In a large sealable plastic bag, combine $1/3$ cup soy sauce; 2 tablespoons rice wine, rice vinegar, or dry sherry; 1 teaspoon toasted sesame oil; 3 tablespoons vegetable oil;

1 finely chopped small red chile (with or without seeds); 4 minced garlic cloves; 1/4 cup sugar; and 4 thinly sliced green onions. Add 4 bone-in steaks cut about 1 inch thick, seal, and marinate in the refrigerator for at least 2 hours or up to 8 hours, turning the meat at least once. When ready to grill, remove from the marinade, pat dry, and grill as directed above. **SERVES 4**

Grilled T-Bone Steak with Smoked Tomato and Grilled Red Onion Relish: In a small skillet, heat 2 tablespoons olive oil over medium heat. Add 2 minced garlic cloves and cook, stirring, until golden, about 4 minutes. Combine with 2 tablespoons drained capers in a medium-size bowl. Set aside. Slice 2 medium-size red onions, arrange the slices on a microwavable tray, and precook in the microwave on high for 1 1/2 to 2 minutes. Brush the onion slices with 1 tablespoon olive oil, place in a grill basket, and grill for 10 to 12 minutes, turning once. Peel 2 smoked tomatoes (see page 37) and chop the tomato pulp coarsely. Chop the grilled onions. Toss the tomatoes and onions with the garlic oil and capers. Season with kosher or sea salt and freshly ground black pepper to taste. Grill 4 T-bone steaks cut about 1 inch thick as directed above. Spoon the relish over the steaks and serve. This relish also is good with grilled fish, chicken, or pork. **SERVES 4**

Sicilian Bistecca: Culinary wizard Gino Corte's family came to Kansas City from a Sicilian farming community—Poggioreale, about 40 minutes inland from the port city of Palermo. They brought with them the tradition of their own amogio marinade plus seasoned bread crumbs to add flavor notes to everything from artichokes to chicken. In America, where beef was plentiful and relatively cheap, they added that treatment to steak, and it's delicious. First, make the Corte family's version of amogio by whisking together 1/3 cup olive oil, 1/4 cup fresh lemon juice (about 2 lemons), 4 minced garlic cloves, several fresh oregano sprigs or 1 teaspoon dried oregano, 10 cracked black peppercorns, and 3 large bay leaves in a medium-size bowl. Place 2 large bone-in steaks cut 1 inch thick in a glass dish or sealable plastic bag. Pour in the marinade, cover or seal, and refrigerate for at least 2 hours, turning the meat several times. Meanwhile, cut several slices from a good loaf of bread and toast on a baking sheet in a preheated 350°F oven for about 15 minutes. Let cool, then process into crumbs in a food processor or blender. In a medium-size bowl, mix together 3/4 cup of the bread crumbs, 1/2 teaspoon dried oregano, and fine kosher or sea salt and freshly ground black pepper to taste. Remove the steaks from the marinade, without patting them dry. Transfer the bread crumbs to a large plate and dredge the steaks in the crumbs to coat evenly. The steaks should have a thick crust of crumbs. Grill as directed above, first coating the grill grate well with oil. Serve with lemon wedges. **SERVES 4 TO 6**

Grilled Thick-Cut Steak

Keep it simple, stupid, could be the slogan for this type of steak. Grill one huge slab of beef, then slice it and serve. It's easier to cook a thick-cut steak just right, because there's a greater margin of error than with a thinner steak. Grill a thick steak for a minute or two longer, and it's no big deal.

Steaks that are cut thickly usually come from the sirloin or hip section. These include the triangular-shaped tri-tip from the bottom sirloin and the really thick porterhouse from the rib section. Sometimes you'll see them packaged as "double sirloin," but mostly you have to ask the butcher to cut this type of steak for you.

A huge slab of meat like this can go with any kind of flavoring, from Asian or Italian to French bistro or American prairie.

Because this type of steak is more tender than a skirt or flank steak, just cut it across the grain into slices of whatever thickness you want. SERVES 8 TO 12

1 large or 4 smaller steaks of your choice, 2 to 3 inches thick
Olive oil
Fine kosher or sea salt and freshly ground black pepper to taste

1. Brush or spray the steaks with olive oil.
2. Prepare a hot fire in a grill.
3. Grill the steaks for 12 to 15 minutes per side for medium-rare. An instant-read meat thermometer inserted in the center should register 140°F.
4. Season with salt and pepper and let rest for 10 to 15 minutes before slicing against the grain and serving.

Crowning Glories

Serve this with:

Rustic Grill-Roasted Potato Salad *(page 148)*
Grilled Goat Cheese Tomatoes *(page 160)*
Matchstick-cut cucumber, daikon radish, and green onions with Vietnamese Drizzle *(page 87)*
Grilled Mushrooms *(page 132)* **with Wheat Beer Vinaigrette** *(page 77; see headnote for sauce variation)*

Black and Bleu Beef: The term "black and blue (or bleu)" refers to a steak that's charred on the outside and rare on the inside—our personal favorite way of grilling a thick steak. You'll need a hotter than hot fire or a really hot, seasoned large cast-iron griddle or skillet. Brush melted unsalted butter or olive oil on the surface of four 2-inch-thick filet mignon steaks and season with coarse kosher or sea salt and freshly ground black pepper to taste. Wait until you can hold your hand over the fire (or griddle or skillet) for only 3 to 4 seconds, then put the steaks on. Let sizzle for 6 to 7 minutes, turn over, and let sizzle for 6 to 7 minutes more, until an instant-read meat thermometer inserted in the center registers 130°F. Serve with Rustic Béarnaise Sauce (page 98) for an out-of-body experience. **SERVES 4**

Prairie-Style Hay-Smoked Steak: "The following recipe will yield, I promise you, one of the best steaks you have ever eaten," says Kansas City barbecuer Ardie Davis, a.k.a. Remus Powers, Ph.B. (see page 44). Ardie's recipe appeared in Judith's *Prairie Home Cooking* (The Harvard Common Press, 1999), and we repeat it here—we know a good thing when we taste it. From Kansas City, we drive north or south beyond suburbia to farm country, where we buy cider and doughnuts, and a small bale of hay. (You can also buy hay at feed stores.) You actually grill this steak, but the hay smokes as it smolders, giving the steak a little kiss of smoke. You have to use a charcoal grill for this recipe, as the hay has to burn away, and that could clog the jets of a gas grill. You need 1 huge tri-tip or porterhouse steak or 4 Kansas City strip steaks cut 2 to 3 inches thick. Place a large handful (about 3 cups for all of you type A's) of hay (or wheat straw) on a platter and set the steaks on the hay. Sprinkle lightly with 1 tablespoon coarse kosher or sea salt and let sit at room temperature for about 2 hours. You want the moisture from the steaks to permeate the hay. Prepare a hot fire in a charcoal grill and use oak chips for a kiss of smoke (see page 13). Remove the steaks from the hay (pick off any stray pieces from the meat), reserving the moistened hay, and grill for about 3 minutes on each side. Using grill mitts, carefully remove the grate with the steaks still on it and set aside. Drop the hay over the hot coals and return the grate to the grill. Cover and grill-smoke the steaks for 15 to 20 minutes, turning them so both sides absorb the smoky flavor. When medium-rare to medium, about 140°F on an instant-read meat thermometer, transfer to a platter, drizzle with 1 tablespoon extra virgin olive oil, and season with kosher or sea salt and freshly ground black pepper to taste. Pass lemon wedges at the table. **SERVES 4**

Bistro Side Dishes

"Bistro style" has become a buzzword for somewhat sophisticated yet casual food. Envision zinc-topped bars, black-and-white tile flooring, colorful dishes served on plain white china, and a Gallic flair to it all. We love bistro side dishes with all kinds of plainly grilled or smoked foods. Our hands-down favorite is Haricot Verts Salad with Mustard-Shallot Vinaigrette, which we enjoyed at a bistro in the eighth arrondissement of Paris. A few days later, we shopped the local markets and made it from taste memory when we stayed at Anne Willan's Château du Fey in Burgundy with our culinary book club. Don't fret, though; all of these dishes are *magnifique*!

Haricots Verts Salad with Mustard-Shallot Vinaigrette

Haricots verts **are those tiny, thin French green beans that start to come on the market in late spring. Judith grows them in her garden. These beans should be cooked until just slightly crunchy, then dressed warm with the vinaigrette. Use a lighter olive oil, not extra virgin, as you don't want the olive oil flavor to dominate here. If you want the beans to stay a vivid green, plunge them into ice water after cooking, let cool, and then drain before proceeding with the recipe.** SERVES 4

1 pound *haricots verts* or young, thin green beans, tops trimmed

MUSTARD-SHALLOT VINAIGRETTE

1 large shallot, diced

1 tablespoon Dijon mustard

1/4 cup white wine vinegar

1/2 cup olive oil

Fine kosher or sea salt and freshly ground black pepper to taste

1. Put the beans in a large pot with enough water to cover. Bring to a boil and cook until crisp-tender, 1 to 2 minutes. Drain in a colander and rinse under cold running water for 30 seconds to refresh the color but still keep them slightly warm. Let drain for 1 minute, then transfer to a serving bowl.

2. To make the vinaigrette, whisk the shallot, mustard, and vinegar together in a small bowl. Slowly drizzle in the olive oil, whisking to blend. Season with salt and pepper. Pour over the beans, toss to coat, and serve immediately.

Homemade Frites

Basically, these are homemade French fries, but they sound better as *frites*, don't they? The secrets to great *frites* include cutting them thin and keeping the oil at or around 350°F. A deep fryer is great, but you can also use an electric skillet or a deep skillet and a candy thermometer. SERVES 4 TO 6

4 large Idaho potatoes, peeled
Vegetable oil for frying
Coarse kosher or sea salt to taste

1. Cut the potatoes lengthwise into 1/4-inch-thick slices, then cut each slice into 1/4-inch-wide strips. Place the strips in a bowl of ice water for 15 minutes.
2. Drain the water from the potatoes and pat very dry with paper towels.
3. Add 2 inches of vegetable oil to a deep fryer or skillet. If using a skillet, place over medium-high heat. When the oil reaches 350°F, place half the potatoes in the hot oil and cook, turning if necessary, until the potatoes turn golden brown, 5 to 7 minutes. Transfer to paper towels and season with salt. Keep warm in a low oven while you prepare the second batch. Serve immediately.

Celery Root Rémoulade

Bulbous, knobby celery root—which tastes like a cross between celery and potato—is a traditional European vegetable usually available in American markets during the cooler months. You can quarter and peel it, then grate it in a food processor for serving raw in a salad like this one. Or peel it, cut it into cubes, and sauté it in olive oil for a wonderful change from fried potatoes. Either way, work fast, as celery root tends to

darken (like raw potato). True Parisian rémoulade is mustard-based, not like our New Orleans rémoulade, which is more like tartar sauce. This recipe is adapted from one by the well-known cookbook author and Francophile Patricia Wells, the BBQ Queens' American friend in Paris. SERVES 4 TO 6

1/2 cup sour cream
1/2 cup heavy cream
2 tablespoons fresh lemon juice
2 tablespoons Dijon mustard (we prefer the Maille brand for this)
One 1-pound celery root
Coarse kosher or sea salt and freshly ground black pepper to taste

1. In a large bowl, whisk together the sour cream and heavy cream until smooth. Whisk in the lemon juice and mustard. Set aside.

2. Peel and quarter the celery root, then grate in a food processor or by hand on the large holes of a box grater. As you grate each quarter, transfer it to the dressing in the bowl and stir to coat. This keeps the celery root from darkening. Season with salt and pepper. Serve at room temperature or chilled.

Bistro Grated Carrot Salad

This is simplicity itself. SERVES 4 TO 6

4 cups finely shredded carrot (about 6 medium-size carrots)
1 tablespoon fresh lemon juice
1 tablespoon olive oil
2 tablespoons tarragon or raspberry vinegar
Finely chopped fresh Italian parsley for garnish

Place the grated carrot in a large bowl. In a small bowl, stir together the lemon juice, olive oil, and vinegar. Drizzle the dressing over the carrot and toss to blend. Serve at once, garnished with parsley.

Grilled Beef Skewers

The BBQ Queens decree that skewered beef is only as good as the beef you buy. With that said, our choices for skewering include beef from good-quality cuts such as rib-eye steak, sirloin, and tenderloin. You can also vary the type of skewer you use (see pages 29–32 for your options and how to grill skewers), from the standard bamboo skewer, which needs to be soaked in water for at least 30 minutes before grilling, to fresh rosemary branches. If you can, buy flat bamboo skewers, or purchase two-prong metal skewers so the meat won't spin on the stick. You can also thread the meat onto two skewers, which accomplishes the same thing as the double-prong metal skewers. (See how clever we are!)

While the beef skewers are grilling, grill Cheesy Grilled Pepper Boats (page 143) or Char-Grilled Baby Summer Squash (page 155) as an accompaniment. Drizzle a dipping sauce over the finished skewers, if you like. We are particularly fond of amogio, which we also use to marinate the beef before grilling. SERVES 6

1 1/2 pounds boneless sirloin, cut into 24 cubes
1 recipe Amogio (page 72) or 1 3/4 cups bottled Italian-style vinaigrette
6 wooden skewers, soaked in water for at least 30 minutes before grilling

1. Place the beef in a baking dish or sealable plastic bag and pour half the amogio over. Cover or seal and refrigerate for at least 30 minutes or up to 2 hours.

2. Prepare a hot fire in a grill.

3. Thread the beef cubes onto the skewers, 4 to a skewer. Grill, turning once with grill tongs, for 3 to 4 minutes per side for medium. Drizzle a little of the remaining amogio on each skewer and serve.

Crowning Glories

Try making beef skewers sprinkled with a spicy rub (before grilling) or served with a side sauce, such as:

Tricolored Peppercorn Rub *(page 62)*
Asian Barbecue Sauce *(page 90)*
Peanut Butter Dipping Sauce *(page 118)*

Grilled Beef Skewers with Spicy Tomato-Chile Sauce: This delicious Thai-style sauce is a great dipping sauce for beef, pork, fish, or poultry. In a medium-size skillet over medium heat, heat 1 tablespoon red pepper flakes for about 1 minute. Add 1 cup chopped white onion, 4 chopped garlic cloves, and 4 chopped Roma tomatoes and cook, stirring, for 5 to 7 minutes. In a large bowl, combine 1/4 cup Asian fish sauce, the juice and grated zest of 2 limes, and 1/4 cup firmly packed dark brown sugar. Add the tomato mixture and combine using a hand-held blender (or process in an electric blender). Don't overblend; you want the sauce to be a little chunky. Grill the beef skewers as described above and serve with the sauce. **SERVES 6**

Tamarind and Yogurt Beef Kabobs with Warm Pita Breads: Begin with a small bowl filled with 1/2 cup hot water. Add 1 to 2 ounces tamarind pulp (available at Asian markets), soaking it for about 30 minutes. In a large bowl, combine 1 1/2 cups plain yogurt, 3 tablespoons unsweetened coconut milk, 2 tablespoons ground coriander, 1 tablespoon ground cumin, and 1 teaspoon chili powder. Drain the tamarind pulp and add the liquid to the yogurt mixture. Transfer half of the sauce to a small serving bowl and reserve. Cut 1 1/2 pounds boneless sirloin into 24 cubes and marinate in the remaining sauce for about 1 hour. Drain, then thread the beef onto skewers and grill as directed above. While grilling, warm 6 pita breads on the grill. Serve the beef with the pitas and reserved yogurt sauce for dipping. **SERVES 6**

Beef Skewers with Quick Peanut Sauce: In a small bowl, combine 1/4 cup crunchy peanut butter, 1/4 cup unsweetened coconut milk, 1 tablespoon ground cumin, 1 teaspoon red pepper flakes, 1/2 teaspoon ground cinnamon, and kosher salt to taste. (If you like a thicker sauce, use either more peanut butter or less coconut milk.) Grill the skewers as directed above and serve with the sauce. **SERVES 6**

Grill Gals

She Grills for a Taste of Home Menu

Kabuli Kabobs

Salata (Afghani Fresh Chopped Vegetable Salad)

Entrepreneur and go-getter Latifa Raoufi grew up in Kabul, Afghanistan, during the 1950s and 1960s. Her father was a diplomat working for King Shah Zahir and the Afghani royal family. Latifa's family, who spoke Farsi, lived in the old section of upper-class Kabul when her father wasn't on diplomatic assignment in New York, Cairo, or Bombay. Photos taken during the 1960s show a thriving city, with the clear blue Kabul River, landscaped parks, beautiful old flat-roofed buildings of sun-bleached mud brick, a crowded central bazaar with many vendors, the rounded domes of mosques, and the Hindu Kush mountains in the background. Just beyond Kabul were lush irrigated fields where all kinds of vegetables and fruits were grown.

"In the 1950s, Kabul looked like the city of Lyon in France," remembers Latifa, who was a little girl then. "It was beautiful. We had so much luxury. We bought all of our food fresh."

In the kitchen compound, the Raoufi family had four raised brick hearths, each made from two mud-brick squat pillars with an iron grill rack placed atop them. Wood and charcoal fires burned under the grill racks. Pots and pans were coated on the outside with mud for easier cleanup after cooking over the open fire. "When the pots were cleaned, the maids would take them outside again and coat them with fresh mud," Latifa recalls. "Then they would turn the pots upside down to dry in the sun."

When the Soviets invaded Afghanistan in 1979, Latifa fled the country in a daring escape, hidden in the back of a truck with only a little money and her passport. She came to the United States and has made a success of her life here. But when she gets homesick from time to time, she goes to the kitchen to re-create taste memories from another time, another place.

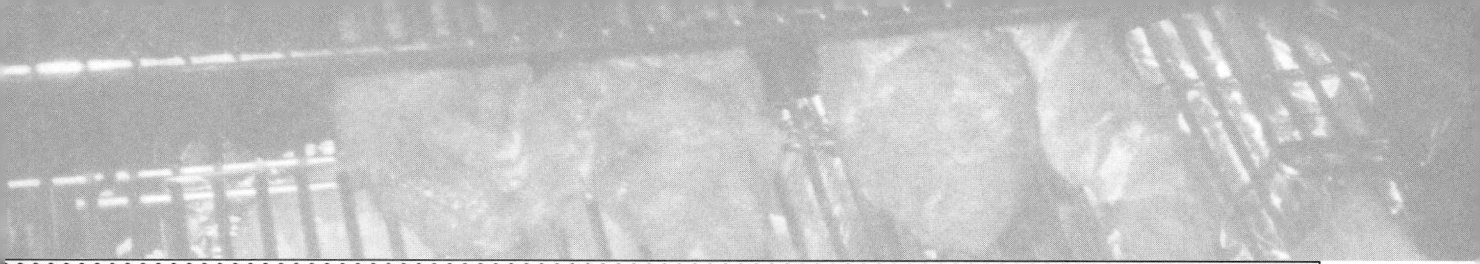

Kabuli Kabobs

A traditional evening meal in pre-1979 Kabul might have five different courses. The first course might include grilled flatbreads with different fillings (such as Bolani, page 182) and kabobs served on platters and eaten out of hand. As a sweet ending to a meal, the Raoufi family often ate dried fruits and nuts, accompanied by green tea flavored with ground cardamom. Make the kabobs the day before you plan to serve them, because they need to be refrigerated overnight. The onion also may be prepared the day before. **SERVES 10**

BEEF TENDERLOIN KABOBS

3 pounds beef tenderloin, cut into 2 x 1-inch pieces
Juice of 2 lemons
1 head garlic, cloves minced
1/4 teaspoon cayenne pepper, or more to taste
1/2 teaspoon kosher or sea salt

MINCED BEEF KABOBS

1 pound ground sirloin
2 tablespoons ground coriander
1 bunch fresh cilantro, minced
4 cloves garlic, minced
Juice of 1 lemon
1 large egg

1 large onion, peeled
Juice of 1 lemon
1/4 teaspoon kosher or sea salt
20 wooden skewers, soaked in water for at least 30 minutes before grilling
10 flatbreads or pita breads
2 large ripe tomatoes
Edible flowers and fresh cilantro or mint sprigs for garnish

1. To make the beef tenderloin kabobs, rinse the meat, pat dry, and place in a large dish or sealable plastic bag. In a small bowl, combine the lemon juice, garlic, cayenne, and salt. Pour over the meat, cover or seal, and marinate in the refrigerator overnight, turning several times.

2. To make the minced beef kabobs, combine all the ingredients in a medium-size bowl, using your hands or a rubber spatula to blend. Cover and refrigerate overnight.

3. Cut the onion into quarters, then cut each quarter into paper-thin half-moons. Place the onion slices in a colander and rinse well with water. Transfer to a medium-size bowl and sprinkle with the lemon juice and salt. Set aside to marinate for at least 1 hour or overnight.

4. Prepare a medium-hot fire in a grill.

5. Thread the marinated beef tenderloin kabobs onto 10 of the skewers and set aside. Form the cold minced beef mixture into ten 6-inch logs. Thread each log lengthwise onto a skewer (handle the logs gently so they don't fall apart). Grill all the kabobs until still a bit pink in the middle, turning once, 5 to 10 minutes total.

6. To serve, arrange the flatbreads on a platter. Cut the tomatoes into quarters. Place the kabobs on top of the breads. Garnish with the marinated onion slices, tomato quarters, flowers, and herb sprigs. Serve hot or at room temperature.

To eat the kabobs in the traditional way, place a flatbread on your plate and slide the kabobs off 2 skewers (one of each type) into the center of the bread. Add some tomatoes and onions (or Salata; right) and wrap the flatbread around the filling.

Salata (Afghani Fresh Chopped Vegetable Salad)

Kabuli cooks have special ways to tame the fire and tears provoked by fresh onions, as you will see in this recipe. Use *salata* as you would *pico de gallo,* a relish made with hot and sweet peppers, other vegetables, and seasonings. SERVES 6

2 large onions, peeled
1/4 teaspoon fine kosher or sea salt
Juice of 2 lemons
2 large ripe tomatoes
1 medium-size cucumber, peeled
Juice of 1 lime

1. Cut the onions into quarters, then cut each quarter into paper-thin half-moons. Place the onion slices in a colander and rinse well with water. Transfer to a medium-size bowl and sprinkle with the salt and lemon juice. Set aside for at least 1 hour to marinate.

2. Cut the tomatoes into quarters, then cut each quarter into paper-thin half-moons and place in a large bowl. Cut the cucumber in half lengthwise, then cut into paper-thin slices. Add to the bowl. Stir in the marinated onion, then the lime juice. Toss to blend and taste for seasoning. Add more salt or lime juice, if necessary. Serve at room temperature.

Grilled Beef Tenderloin

This dish has become special occasion or holiday fare in Judith's family. Although pricey, beef tenderloin repays your outlay with a great entrée—and great leftovers—requiring minimal effort. The BBQ Queens like to grill beef tenderloin with a little char on the exterior, leaving the interior rosy and juicy.

We prefer a plain grilled tenderloin accompanied by a jazzy sauce or two, but you can soak, sprinkle, slather, or sauce this cut to your heart's content. It will always be delicious. Have your butcher prepare the tenderloin first by removing the silverskin and tying it up into a nice, evenly shaped roast.

Grilling a great beef tenderloin starts with a really hot fire—preferably one made with mesquite charcoal—but you can still have a mighty fine tenderloin on a gas grill. You'll want the heat very hot to get that char.

It's also important to turn the tenderloin every 4 to 5 minutes so it cooks evenly all over. During the last 10 minutes of cooking, insert an instant-read meat thermometer in the middle of the meat and watch it as you would a new hairdresser—like a hawk. You can always zap an underdone tenderloin in the microwave, but a well-done tenderloin can't be fixed. (You don't want to see the BBQ Queens cry, now, do you?)

For a royal feast, serve your tenderloin with Grilled Asparagus (page 117) and/or Grilled Mushrooms (page 132). SERVES 10 TO 12

One 6- to 8-pound beef tenderloin, trimmed of any fat and silverskin
Melted unsalted butter
Fine kosher or sea salt and freshly ground black pepper to taste

1. Brush the tenderloin with melted butter, then season with salt and pepper.

2. Prepare a hot fire in a grill, using mesquite chips for a kiss of smoke (see page 13), if you like.

3. Place the tenderloin on the grill, close the lid, and grill, turning a quarter turn every 5 minutes for the first 10 minutes. Turn, brush again with melted butter, and insert a heatproof meat thermometer in the middle of the tenderloin. Continue to grill with the lid closed until the thermometer registers 130°F (for rare) or the meat is firm yet a little springy to the touch, 10 to 12 minutes.

4. Remove from the grill and let rest for 5 minutes. Remove the twine, slice, and serve to frenzied accolades.

BBQ Tip: Judith learned a few beef tenderloin tips from her father. One is to watch for when whole beef tenderloin goes on sale. Then buy it, bring it home, and sharpen that knife. You can get extra savings on beef tenderloin if you trim it yourself, which is easy to do. The whole tenderloin will have a thick end and taper down to a thin end. Trim off any fat and silverskin. Cut the size tenderloin you want to grill whole, then cut the rest of the tenderloin into 1-inch-thick steaks. Cut the tapered end into chunks for kabobs. Wrap well and freeze until you're ready to grill, up to 3 months.

Crowning Glories

Why hold back? Gild that beef lily with one of the following:

Poblano Cream Sauce *(page 93)*

Smoked Chile Beurre Blanc *(page 99)*

Peppercorn Beurre Blanc *(page 102)*

Grilled Tenderloin with Sour Cream, Bacon, and Mushroom Sauce: When Judith's family grills a tenderloin, this is the sauce they serve with it, adapted from a recipe in the Junior League of Pasadena's *California Heritage Cookbook* (Doubleday, 1976). In a large skillet, cook 12 ounces sliced bacon until crisp, then transfer to paper towels to drain. Pour off all but 2 tablespoons of the fat and cook 4 ounces sliced fresh mushrooms until softened, 3 to 5 minutes. Transfer to a medium-size bowl and let cool. When cooled, add 1 1/2 cups sour cream, 2 teaspoons prepared horseradish, 1 tablespoon grated onion (we use a microplane grater), and 2 tablespoons finely chopped fresh Italian parsley and mix. Crumble the bacon into the sauce and mix again. Grill the tenderloin as described above and serve with the sauce on the side. **SERVES 8**

Chez Panisse–Style Grilled Beef Tenderloin: It was a perfect spring night in Berkeley, California—a light breeze, the air a little cool and clear. The BBQ Queens were dining at Chez Panisse—or should we say paying long overdue homage to culinary queen and Grill Gal Alice Waters, who confesses that her "picky eater" childhood birthday menu was always green beans and rare charcoal-grilled steak. We had a fabulous meal, a fabulous experience. When you enjoy beef tenderloin prepared this way, adapted from Waters's *Chez Panisse Menu Cookbook* (Random House, 1982), you'll share in the fabulous-ness. Place one 6- to 8-pound trimmed beef tenderloin in a deep casserole dish. Scatter 2 sliced medium-size onions, 2 crumbled bay leaves, and 10 to 12 black peppercorns around the beef. Pour one 750 ml bottle dry red wine over the beef, then add 10 to 12 sprigs fresh Italian parsley and 1/2 cup olive oil. Cover and refrigerate, turning several times, for up to 12 hours. When ready to grill, remove the meat from the marinade and pat dry. Brush with olive oil and season with kosher or sea salt and freshly ground black pepper to taste. Grill as directed above, then slice and serve. **SERVES 8**

Smoked Beef Tenderloin

When you really want to wow your guests, serve them a beef tenderloin that's slightly charred on the outside, smoky and tender inside.

The only trick to this is our two-step process of putting grill marks on the meat first, then smoking it, because this speeds up the process a bit and makes for a better presentation. But you don't want to build a fire in a grill *and* a smoker. That's just not queenly; it's fussy.

Here's how we do it. If we're using a charcoal or gas grill as a smoker, we simply sear the tenderloin over direct heat, then move it over to the indirect side to smoke. If we're using a three-part bullet-shaped water smoker, we place the smoker's grill rack over the bottom third (which contains the heating element or coals) and sear the meat on the grill rack. Then we remove the grill rack, place the middle section of the smoker back over the heating element or coals, place the grill rack back on top of the middle section, cover, and smoke the tenderloin as usual. If we're using a traditional smoker, we use a grill pan indoors to get the grill marks, then put the meat in the smoker.

Because the beef tenderloin is so thick and meaty, we prefer a smoke that will match its heft—mesquite or hickory. SERVES 8

SUGGESTED WOOD: Mesquite or hickory

1/4 cup olive oil

2 cloves garlic, minced

1 tablespoon finely chopped fresh rosemary

1/2 teaspoon fine kosher or sea salt

Freshly ground black pepper to taste

One 4-pound beef tenderloin, at room temperature, trimmed of any fat and silverskin

1. In a small bowl, combine the olive oil, garlic, rosemary, salt, and pepper. Slather the beef with the mixture and set aside.

2. Prepare an indirect fire in a smoker.

3. On the direct side of the smoker or in a grill pan over high heat indoors, sear the meat on all sides until you can see grill marks. Remove from the heat.

4. Place the beef in a disposable aluminum pan in the smoker. Insert a heatproof meat thermometer in the center of the meat. Cover and smoke at 225 to 250°F until the internal temperature is 135 to 140°F for rare, about 3 hours. Remove from the smoker, remove the thermometer from the meat, and wrap tightly in plastic. Allow to rest for 15 to 20 minutes, then unwrap, slice, and serve.

Crowning Glories

This is heavenly served with:

Simply Delicious Bordelaise Sauce *(page 91)*

White Truffle Aioli *(page 105)*

Smoked Chile Beurre Blanc *(page 99)*

Peppery Smoked Beef Tenderloin: Make 1 recipe Tricolored Peppercorn Rub (page 62), add 1/4 cup olive oil, and slather over a 4-pound trimmed beef tenderloin. Smoke as directed above. Slice and serve with Peppercorn Beurre Blanc (page 102) for a beaucoup fabulous finish. **SERVES 8**

Smoked Porcini Beef Tenderloin: Use Porcini Paste (page 65) to slather a 4-pound trimmed beef tenderloin. Smoke as directed above. During the last hour of smoking, add portobello mushrooms to smoke as directed on page 134. To serve, slice the tenderloin and drizzle the meat and portobellos with Simply Delicious Bordelaise Sauce (page 91). **SERVES 8**

Smoked Beef BLT: Begin with an artisanal loaf of bread, such as Asiago-herb or rosemary-garlic. Slather 1 slice of bread with mustard and another with aioli (see pages 104–105 and 110). Layer thin slices of the smoked beef (as much as you like) on the bread. Top with 3 slices crisp-cooked bacon, a crisp fresh lettuce leaf, and a couple thin slices of home-grown tomatoes. **SERVES 1**

Grill Gals

This 'Que Queen Is a Kansas City Grill Queen Menu

Grilled Herbed and Spiced Beef Tenderloin Salad
Grilled Herbed and Spiced Beef Tenderloin
Grilled Turkey Roulade with Lemon-Basil Sauce
Kathy's Chicken Wings
Smoky Meatballs

'Que Queen team member Kathy Smith is also a member of our Kansas City Cookbook Club. We all cook, eat, and share recipes at least once a month. When the cookbook club meets at Kathy's house, she almost always prepares something from the grill. She and her husband, Don, have traveled to South America and are particularly fond of Brazilian cuisine. This comes through in the recipes Kathy favors, which often have the earthy taste of ground cumin and coriander, plus fresh cilantro.

Kathy, along with 'Que Queen Dee Barwick, cooks up huge quantities of from-scratch soups and casseroles for the homeless. Volunteers deliver the food weekly to homeless people around the city.

An avid cookbook and food magazine devotee, Kathy scours the pages of books and magazines to add new recipes to her repertoire. Her salad is great alone or with other freshly grilled or leftover grilled meats, such as poultry, shellfish, or pork. The turkey roulade recipe can be made ahead and refrigerated, then sliced and served cold. It would also be divine in place of the beef on the salad.

Grilled Herbed and Spiced Beef Tenderloin Salad

Kathy found this recipe in an old *Food & Wine* magazine. While testing it, we decided that it would also be delicious with pork tenderloin, poultry, or even shrimp. Kathy heartily agreed. Here is our revised version. SERVES 6

DRESSING

1/2 cup mayonnaise
1/2 cup freshly grated Romano cheese
3 tablespoons Dijon mustard
3 tablespoons fresh lime juice
2 anchovy fillets, mashed
2 cloves garlic, minced
1 tablespoon Worcestershire sauce
Tabasco sauce to taste
Kosher salt and freshly ground black pepper to taste

SALAD

2 large heads romaine lettuce
4 large ripe beefsteak tomatoes, cut into wedges
2 large ripe avocados, peeled, pitted, and diced
6 slices bacon, cooked crisp and crumbled
1 small red onion, chopped
1/2 cup salted sunflower seeds, CornNuts, or other salty nuts
2 pounds Grilled Herbed and Spiced Beef Tenderloin (recipe follows), thinly sliced

1. To make the dressing, combine all the ingredients in a medium-size bowl. Stir to blend and check the seasoning. Cover and refrigerate until ready to use. (The dressing may be made a day ahead.)

2. To make the salad, rinse and dry the lettuce and tear into bite-size pieces. Toss with half the dressing. Mound on a large platter and surround with the tomato wedges and diced avocado. Sprinkle the bacon, onion, and sunflower seeds over the salad. Arrange the sliced meat on top and serve, passing the remaining dressing at the table.

Grilled Herbed and Spiced Beef Tenderloin

Take advantage of this delicious marinade and use it for fish, shellfish, pork, and poultry, too. Add a satay or Peanut Butter Dipping Sauce (page 118), and you'll be in flavor heaven. SERVES 6

1/4 cup chopped fresh Italian parsley
1/4 cup chopped fresh cilantro
2 tablespoons extra virgin olive oil
1 tablespoon ground coriander
1 tablespoon ground cumin
2 cloves garlic, minced
1 tablespoon coarse kosher salt
2 tablespoons freshly ground black pepper
2 pounds beef tenderloin, trimmed of any fat and silverskin
Handful of wood chips, soaked in water for at least 30 minutes before grilling

1. In a large, shallow glass dish, combine all the ingredients except the beef and wood chips. Stir to blend, then add the meat and turn to coat thoroughly. Cover and refrigerate for 1 to 2 hours.

2. Prepare a hot indirect fire in a grill.

3. Remove the meat from the marinade and pat dry. Grill over the hot fire, searing it by turning it a quarter turn at a time until well browned all over, about 12 minutes total.

4. Place the meat on the indirect side of the grill and tent with heavy-duty aluminum foil or cover with a disposable aluminum pan. Add the wood chips to the fire. Close the lid and roast-smoke until an instant-read meat thermometer inserted in the thickest part of the beef registers 125 to 130°F for medium-rare, 25 to 30 minutes. Transfer to a platter and let rest for 10 to 15 minutes before slicing.

Grilled Turkey Roulade with Lemon-Basil Sauce

This is another adaptable recipe, which Kathy first discovered in an issue of *Gourmet* magazine. Try substituting chicken paillards or beef tenderloin for the turkey and, of course, adjusting the cooking time for the meat you choose. SERVES 6

One 2-pound turkey tenderloin
Kosher salt and freshly ground black pepper to taste
One 12-ounce jar fire-roasted red peppers, drained and cut into strips
4 ounces Brie, cut into strips
1 cup sour cream
Juice and grated zest of 1 lemon
1/2 cup chopped fresh basil

1. Place the turkey on a cutting board and cut in half crosswise. Pound each half as you would to create a paillard (see page 191). Season with salt and pepper, then divide the red pepper slices evenly between them, leaving a 1/4-inch border around the edges. Place the Brie on top of the peppers. Gently roll up each turkey fillet so the filling stays in place and does not squeeze out. Tie the roulades with kitchen twin in 3 or 4 places. Season again with salt and pepper. Cover and refrigerate for 1 to 4 hours.

2. In a small bowl, combine the sour cream, lemon juice and zest, and basil. Cover and refrigerate until ready to serve.

3. Prepare a medium-hot indirect fire in a grill.

4. Grill the roulades directly over the fire, searing them on all sides, about 15 minutes total. Move to the indirect side of the grill and close the lid. Cook for about 10 minutes, then open the grill, turn the roulades, close the lid, and cook for another 5 to 10 minutes, until an instant-read meat thermometer inserted in the center of each registers 170°F.

5. Transfer to a cutting board and let stand for 10 to 15 minutes. Remove the twine carefully and cut into 1/2-inch-thick slices. Serve warm with the sauce.

Kathy's Chicken Wings

Kathy is an adventurous cook. She likes to follow a recipe exactly first, then experiment the second time around. You won't need to do that with this classic chicken wing recipe. It's a winner just as it is. Try serving it with our Creamy Blue Cheese Dressing (page 111). SERVES 10 TO 12

3 pounds chicken wings
1 teaspoon kosher or sea salt
1 teaspoon sweet Hungarian paprika
1 teaspoon onion powder
1 teaspoon lemon pepper seasoning
1/2 teaspoon red pepper flakes
1/2 teaspoon garlic powder

1. Rinse the wings and pat dry. In a large sealable plastic bag, combine the remaining ingredients. Add the chicken, seal the bag, and shake to coat evenly. Place the wings on a baking sheet and let stand at room temperature for 30 to 60 minutes.

2. Prepare a hot fire in a grill.

3. Grill the wings in a single layer, turning and rotating, for 20 to 30 minutes. They are done when the joints move easily and can be torn apart. Serve hot.

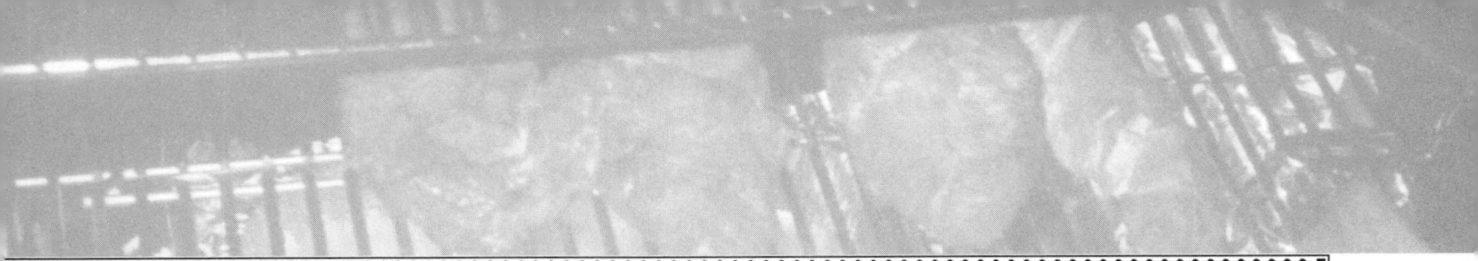

Smoky Meatballs

Ever try meatballs on the grill or in the smoker? If not, here's your chance. We start with Kathy's very good recipe, which makes big meatballs that won't fall through the grill grate. These can also be baked at 350°F for 30 to 40 minutes or sautéed over high heat for 20 to 25 minutes. Serve them with marinara sauce, horseradish cocktail sauce, or Spicy Tomato-Chile Sauce (page 331). MAKES 12 MEATBALLS

1 pound ground beef
3 large eggs
1/2 cup fresh Italian bread crumbs
1/2 cup freshly grated Romano cheese, or more to taste
3 cloves garlic, minced
2 tablespoons chopped fresh Italian parsley
2 tablespoons chopped fresh basil
3/4 teaspoon kosher salt
1/2 teaspoon freshly ground black pepper

1. In a large bowl, combine all the ingredients. Shape into 12 large meatballs. Place in a covered container and refrigerate for at least 8 hours to allow the flavors to meld and the meatballs to firm up.

2. To grill the meatballs, prepare a hot fire. Grill for about 15 minutes, turning several times so they are charred all over. To smoke the meatballs, prepare an indirect fire at 250°F. Place the meatballs directly on the grill grate or in a disposable aluminum pan on the indirect side of the smoker. Smoke for 1 hour. Serve hot.

Planked Beef Tenderloin

We love to plank, and anything that is tender planks well. Our sublime beef tenderloin is perfection. Favored woods for planking beef are oak, maple, pecan, and hickory. Fruitwood planks are nice, too, but you may have to cut your own. For detailed instructions on planking, see page 42.

Serve planked tenderloin with A Platter of Fresh Tomatoes (page 206), Fiesta Bread (page 178), and an earthy Cabernet or a fruity Merlot. It doesn't get much easier—or better—than this. SERVES 4

Four 4-ounce beef tenderloin steaks, 3/4 inch thick

Fine kosher or sea salt and freshly ground black pepper to taste

One 15 x 6 1/2 x 3/8-inch oak or maple plank, soaked in water for at least 1 hour before grilling

1. Prepare a dual-heat fire, with a hot fire on one side and a medium fire on the other.

2. Place the tenderloin steaks on a baking sheet, season with salt and pepper, and bring outside. Place the plank over direct heat for 4 to 5 minutes, until it begins to smoke and pop. Turn the plank over and move to the medium-heat side. Carefully place the steaks on the charred side of the plank. Cover and cook until an instant-read meat thermometer inserted in the center registers 125 to 130°F for medium-rare, about 12 minutes. Serve hot.

Crowning Glories

You can dress these steaks up with a fancy rub, drizzle with a vinaigrette, or serve with a scrumptious side sauce:

BBQ Queens' Photo Op Barbecue Rub *(page 58)*

Hot Shallot Vinaigrette *(page 85)*

Smoked Chile Beurre Blanc *(page 99)*

Bourbon-Mustard Cream Sauce *(page 377)*

Argentinean Hickory-Planked Beef Tenderloin with Chimichurri Sauce: Argentinean restaurants often serve *churrasco* beef that is planked upright around a blazing fire. This recipe gives you much the same flavor, but in an easier preparation. The sauce—made with four different fresh herbs, along with garlic and sherry vinegar—is a robust accompaniment to the gentle smokiness of the beef. To make the sauce, in a food processor combine 1/2 cup fresh Italian parsley leaves, 1/4 cup fresh cilantro leaves, 1/4 cup fresh mint leaves, 2 tablespoons fresh oregano leaves, 1/4 cup chopped yellow onion, 3 peeled garlic cloves, 1/2 teaspoon cayenne pepper, 1/2 teaspoon fine kosher or sea salt, 1/2 teaspoon freshly ground black pepper, 1/3 cup olive oil, 1/3 cup sherry vinegar, and 1/4 cup water. Process until smooth. (The sauce is best served the same day but will keep, covered, in the refrigerator for up to 5 days.) Prepare the planked beef as directed above using a hickory plank. Serve with the sauce. **SERVES 4**

Gorgonzola Filet Mignon on a Plank: Plank the tenderloin steaks as directed above, first placing 1 tablespoon crumbled Gorgonzola on top of each filet. Serve with additional crumbled Gorgonzola on the side and big fat grilled asparagus spears (see page 117). **SERVES 4**

Slathered Beef Filet on a Plank: Plank the steaks as directed above, first slathering each one with 1 to 2 tablespoons Porcini Paste (page 65). **SERVES 4**

Rotisserie Beef Roast

Once you've rotisserie cooked your first rib-eye or sirloin tip roast, there's no going back to plain old roasting. The flavor of smoke and char is a sensational component to the tender meatiness of the beef. To us, roasted-in-the-oven prime rib is now a little lackluster. We prefer rib-eye roasts for tenderness, but sirloin tip or tri-tip roasts are also mighty tasty, if just a little chewier.

Because rotisserie cooking is a bit of a production, why not make it part of the theatrics of entertaining a crowd? Judith recently made this dish for her son Nick's college graduation party, and nary a speck was left over. SERVES 12

One 6-pound boneless rib-eye or sirloin tip roast, rolled and tied
2 cloves garlic, cut into slivers
2 tablespoons olive oil
1 tablespoon fresh lemon juice
Kosher or sea salt and freshly ground black pepper to taste

1. Make 1-inch-deep slits in the roast in several places, then press the garlic slivers into the slits. Combine the olive oil and lemon juice in a cup and rub the roast all over with it. Season with salt and pepper.

2. Set up a grill for rotisserie cooking (see page 33). Prepare a medium fire (around 350°F). Push the rotisserie rod through the center of the roast so it is balanced, then place on the spit. Cover and roast until an instant-read meat thermometer inserted in the center registers 120°F for rare or 140°F for medium-rare, about 2 hours.

3. Place the roast on a serving platter and tent with aluminum foil to keep warm. Let rest for 20 minutes before slicing and serving.

Crowning Glories

Rotisserie beef roast is delicious served with a fancy-schmancy beurre blanc or plain old barbecue sauce; heirloom vegetables, baked beans, or potato salad; or:

Grilled Onions with Thyme and Garlic Cream ***(page 138)***

Potato Gratin with White Cheddar Cheese ***(page 412)***

Grilled Asparagus ***(page 117)***

Uptown Rotisserie Beef Roast with Peppercorn Beurre Blanc: We don't mind the hot flashes we get from *this* combination! It's wonderful. Simply substitute Tricolored Peppercorn Rub (page 62) for the salt and pepper when you're preparing the roast for the spit. Rotisserie cook the roast as directed above. Serve with a double (or triple) recipe of Peppercorn Beurre Blanc (page 102). (Make the beurre blanc one batch at a time, but keep all the batches warm together in one pan.) **SERVES 12**

Downtown Rotisserie Beef Roast with BBQ Queens' Barbecued Beans: This is closer to the down-home barbecuer's idea of barbecue. Substitute BBQ Queens' All-Purpose Rub (page 49) for the salt and pepper when you're preparing the roast for the spit. Rotisserie cook the roast as directed above, but instead of an 11 x 9-inch disposable pan with liquid under the roast, top it with a second pan of BBQ Queens' Barbecued Beans (page 107). Cook the beans with the roast, stirring them every 30 minutes. (The beans will catch all the delicious drippings.) Serve the beef and beans with Smoky Barbecue Sauce (page 90). **SERVES 12**

Lemon Pepper Beef Roast with Butter Baste: This treatment makes sirloin tip taste as luscious as rib-eye roast. Substitute lemon pepper seasoning for the black pepper when you're preparing the roast for the spit. Rotisserie cook the roast as directed above, basting with a brushful of softened unsalted butter (about 1 stick total) every 15 minutes. **SERVES 12**

Rotisserie Boneless Prime Rib Roast with Blackened Seasoning: This is perfect for a New Year's Day feast or a Super Bowl gathering. Substitute your favorite blackened seasoning or Cajun Steak Rub (page 58) for the pepper when you're preparing the roast for the spit. Rotisserie cook the roast as directed above. Let rest for 15 minutes before slicing. SERVES 12

Smoked Beef Rib Roast

A standing rib roast often is the main culinary attraction for a special occasion or holiday dinner. Generally, it is cooked in the oven, but the BBQ Queens are here to tell you that there's a more savory and memorable way to serve this expensive holiday classic. Smoke that sucker!

A smoked rib roast has all that good char on the exterior, and the somewhat bland meat of your mother's standard roasted rib roast is revved up with a smoky flavor. Even traditionalists who don't like anyone messing with their holiday favorites love beef roast this way. By using the smoker, you also free up the oven for other dishes. You can have someone keep an eye on it outside (and get him out from underfoot in the kitchen). Hie thee hence to the smoker for this dish. The BBQ Queens have spoken.

Because the beef roast is so thick and meaty, we prefer to match it with a thick and meaty smoke—mesquite or hickory. Just don't use too much. With smoke, as with makeup, more is not necessarily better.

Go uptown with the roast and serve a wine-enriched sauce or Yorkshire Pudding (page 350), or go downtown with traditional barbecue fixin's—your pick. SERVES 8

SUGGESTED WOOD: **Mesquite or hickory**

One 4- to 6-pound standing rib roast, at room temperature
1/4 cup olive oil
1 tablespoon granulated garlic
1/2 cup cracked black peppercorns

1. Prepare a fire in a smoker.

2. Trim some of the white fat from the roast. Discard it or save it for Yorkshire Pudding (below). Rub the roast with the olive oil and press the granulated garlic and cracked pepper into the meat. Insert a heatproof meat thermometer in the center of the roast. Place fat side up on a rack in the smoker. Cover and smoke at 225 to 250°F, until the meat thermometer registers 140°F for rare, 3 to 3½ hours.

3. Remove the roast from the smoker, remove the thermometer, and wrap the roast tightly in plastic wrap. Allow to rest for 15 to 20 minutes, then unwrap, slice, and serve.

Crowning Glories

Smoked beef rib roast is wonderful with:

Mediterranean-Style Stir-Grilled Mushrooms and Olives *(page 168)*

BBQ Queens' Smoked Potato Casserole *(page 153)*

Cheesy Italian Pesto Bread *(page 177)*

Smoked Rib Roast with Yorkshire Pudding: If you're going to the trouble of making a smoked rib roast, why not go all out and make decadent Yorkshire pudding? If you've never had really good Yorkshire pudding—a cross between a soufflé and a risen savory pancake—now's your chance. When you're trimming the white fat from the rib roast, reserve 1 cup. Smoke the roast as described above. About 45 minutes before you're ready to eat, preheat the oven to 450°F. In a heavy, square glass baking dish, combine the fat, ¼ teaspoon freshly ground black pepper, and ½ teaspoon granulated garlic. Cover loosely with aluminum foil and place in the oven for 7 to 10 minutes, until the fat has melted and slightly browned. Meanwhile, in a small bowl, whisk 2 large eggs. Add 1 cup all-purpose flour, 1 cup whole milk, ¼ teaspoon fine kosher or sea salt, and 2 tablespoons vegetable oil and whisk to a smooth batter. Remove the baking dish from the oven and carefully pour the batter over the hot fat. Return the baking dish to the oven and bake for 10 minutes, then reduce the oven temperature to 350°F and bake until puffed and golden, another 10 to 15 minutes. Cut immediately into squares and serve hot with slices of rib roast. **SERVES 8**

Rosemary Pesto Smoked Rib Roast: A big, beefy roast can stand up to the assertive flavor of Rosemary Pesto (page 62), so slather it on the meat, then smoke as described above. **SERVES 8**

Smoked Rib Roast Sandwiches: If you have any leftover smoked rib roast (which is doubtful), make these memorable sandwiches. Start with crusty ciabatta or other artisanal bread, cut into 12 to 16 slices. In a small bowl, combine 1/2 cup mayonnaise, 1 teaspoon prepared horseradish, and 1 teaspoon Cajun or blackened seasoning of your choice. Slather half the bread slices with the mayonnaise mixture. Layer on slices of smoked rib roast and arugula or other assertive greens and top with the remaining bread slices. Then dig in! **SERVES 6 TO 8**

Fourth of July All-American Barbecue

The BBQ Queens have an extra-special reason for celebrating the Fourth of July. On that day, America made a bold step in declaring its independence from England, King George III, and his queen! That paved the way for democracy—and opened the door to real rhinestone royalty like us. Two centuries later, you can become whatever kind of queen you want to be—BBQ, Sweet Potato, or even Silver Queen Corn Queen. Like the athletic shoe ads say, just do it!

The same goes for putting on a big barbecue bash (and we mean barbecue as in slow smoking, not grilling). Nothing else will do but red, white, and blue for Uncle Sam's birthday. Decorate with miniature flags stuffed in bouquets of red and blue carnations and lots of baby's breath. Fire up that smoker and put in the brisket, beans, and potatoes. Post your favorite male courtier outside (with a supply of beer) and have him keep an eye on things. Meanwhile, because you know everyone's coming, you can bake a cake (see pages 394–397). Howd'yado, howd'yado, howd'yado!

Fourth of July All-American Barbecue Menu

Smoked Brisket *(page 356)*

BBQ Queens' Barbecued Beans *(page 107)*

BBQ Queens' Smoked Potato Casserole *(page 153)*

Smoky Barbecue Sauce *(page 90)*

S'mores *(page 262)*

Toasted Coconut Ice Cream with Hot Fudge Ganache and Toasted Pecans *(page 440)*

BBQ Babes

She's a Tiara-Totin' Texas Queen of the 'Que Menu

Slow-Smoked Texas-Style Brisket
Mozzarella and Tomato Salad with Two Dressings

Dotty Griffith (above, left) was born and raised on Texas barbecue—beef brisket barbecue to be exact. Texas is cattle country, and beef is king of this state. So when we asked Dotty if she would be one of our BBQ Babes and share her delicious brisket recipe with us, her reply was that she'd be honored. We say to Dotty, "Back at ya!"

Dotty is the dining editor and restaurant critic for the *Dallas Morning News*. Formerly, Dotty was the paper's food editor, and that's when Karen first met her and became her publisher for a collection of restaurant recipes titled *Dallas Cuisine* (Two Lane Press, 1993). This now out-of-print cookbook includes a wonderful mozzarella and tomato salad recipe from Paula Lambert (above, right), owner of the renowned Mozzarella Company in Dallas (and a good friend of Dotty's). We include it here and suggest serving it with BBQ Babe Paris Permenter's Texas-Style Pinto Beans (page 106).

Slow-Smoked Texas-Style Brisket

Dotty says, "Brisket is a big, flat, stringy piece of meat, but when slow-smoked, it becomes fork tender and delicious." Her method for cooking brisket is to allow about one hour of cooking per pound of meat, plus a little more in case the fire gets too low or the meat's just tough and stubborn. "And remember," Dotty says, "brisket, like any other meat on the barbecue, takes longer to cook when the weather is cold."

Another Texas buddy of Dotty's is Dean Fearing, lauded chef of the Mansion on Turtle Creek in Dallas. His tip for perfect brisket is an internal temperature of 185 to 200°F. If the meat registers 210°F, it will be too dry. SERVES 10 TO 12

SUGGESTED WOOD: **Oak or mesquite**

One 8- to 10-pound beef brisket, left untrimmed (it should have a thick layer of fat on one side)

$^{1}/_{2}$ cup Texas Two-Steppin' Mesquite Rub (page 59), or kosher or sea salt and freshly ground black pepper to taste

8 to 10 wood chunks, soaked in water for at least 1 hour before grilling, or 2 to 3 cups wood chips, soaked in water for at least 30 minutes before grilling

Warm barbecue sauce of your choice for serving (optional)

Dill pickle slices, sliced onion, and/or pickled jalapeños for serving

1. Generously coat all sides of the brisket, particularly the fat layer, with the rub. Cover and let the meat come to room temperature, about 1 hour.

2. If using a charcoal smoker, prepare an indirect fire. Add the wood chunks when the temperature inside the smoker is about 300°F. When the fire has burned down to glowing embers or the coals are covered with gray ash (225 to 250°F), place a pan of water over the fire. Place the brisket on the grate beside the water pan but not directly over the heat.

If using a gas grill, turn on one burner and close the lid. Heat the grill to 225 to 250°F. Put the wood chips in a smoker box or in an aluminum foil packet poked with

holes and place directly over the flames. Place a pan of water over the flames, too. Place the brisket on the grate beside the water pan but not directly over the heat.

3. Close the lid and smoke the brisket, turning every hour or so. Tend the charcoal fire by adding wood (or wood embers from a separate fire) or coals to keep it from going out and to keep the temperature inside the smoker at 225 to 250°F. Keep a steady 225 to 250°F internal temperature inside the gas grill by adjusting the temperature knob. The brisket is done when it is charred and tender and an instant-read meat thermometer inserted in the center registers 180 to 190°F, 8 to 10 hours.

4. Remove the brisket from the smoker or grill and allow to rest for about 20 minutes. Trim off the fat layer and cut the brisket into thin slices across the grain. Serve with warm barbecue sauce, if desired. (Or stack several slices in a sandwich bun spread lightly with barbecue sauce.) Serve with pickles, onions, and jalapeños on the side.

Mozzarella and Tomato Salad with Two Dressings

Paula Lambert is a cheesemaker who founded the Mozzarella Company in Dallas in 1982. We especially love her handcrafted fresh mozzarella. This recipe is adapted from Dotty's book *Dallas Cuisine*. SERVES 4

1 pound fresh mozzarella
2 large ripe beefsteak tomatoes
8 lettuce leaves
Dressing of your choice (recipes follow)
Fresh basil or cilantro leaves for garnish

Slice the mozzarella and tomatoes uniformly about 1/4 inch thick. Alternate the slices over the lettuce on a platter or on individual salad plates. Drizzle with dressing, garnish with basil leaves, and serve.

Basil Vinaigrette

You can also use this as a drizzle over grilled or smoked meats, fish, or vegetables.
MAKES ABOUT 1/2 CUP

1/4 cup olive oil
2 tablespoons balsamic vinegar
6 to 8 fresh basil leaves
Kosher salt and freshly ground black pepper to taste

Combine all the ingredients in a food processor and whirl until well blended. Taste for salt and pepper.

Southwestern Dressing

This yummy dressing also goes well with poultry and fish and can be used as a marinade or basting sauce, too. MAKES ABOUT 1/2 CUP

1/4 cup olive oil
2 tablespoons red wine vinegar
1 clove garlic, chopped
1 tablespoon chopped fresh cilantro leaves
2 tablespoons chopped canned green chiles
Fine kosher salt and freshly ground black pepper to taste

Combine all the ingredients in a small bowl and whisk to blend.

Smoked Brisket

Beef brisket comes from the front end of the steer, basically the breast area. It's a tough, stringy piece of meat, which makes it perfect for long, slow cooking. Many people have slow roasted a brisket in the oven with the traditional onion gravy to follow, but slow smoking a brisket gives it even more flavor.

The BBQ Queens recommend two methods for smoking your brisket: the long way—about 15 hours—in the smoker, or the shortcut method, which we explain below. We love both, but the reality is, you don't always have 15 hours to tend a fire outdoors.

If you *are* going to devote that much time to a recipe, we think you should get some bang for your buck and smoke two briskets at once. Wrap and freeze one, if you like, to serve for another occasion. Plus, two briskets will yield enough burnt ends for a couple of tasty sandwiches (see page 358). If you choose to smoke only one brisket, cut the recipe in half and smoke for 8 hours total.

We slather the brisket first with a mustard mixture, then sprinkle on a zesty, spicy rub. Then it's into the smoker, where we baste it occasionally with apple juice. When it's done, we slice it on the diagonal, across the grain of the meat (as you do for flank steak), for maximum tenderness. Lots of barbecuers cut a notch in the corner of the meat before it goes on the smoker so they know which way the grain runs; after the brisket has smoked and shrunk, it can be hard to tell.

Make sure you save any trimmings from your smoked brisket. If necessary, freeze them to use later in heavenly BBQ Queens' Barbecued Beans (page 107) or Barbecued Brisket Dip (page 358). SERVES 24

SUGGESTED WOOD: **Apple, hickory, pecan, or a combination; a little mesquite mixed in is quite good, but mesquite alone can be too bitter for long smoking**

Two 10- to 12-pound beef briskets

2 recipes Mustard-Mayo Slather (page 66)

2 recipes BBQ Queens' All-Purpose Rub (page 49)

1 quart apple juice

1. Brush the briskets all over with the slather, then sprinkle evenly with the rub. Set aside for 15 minutes, until the surface of the meat is tacky to the touch.

2. Prepare an indirect fire in a smoker.

3. Cover and smoke the briskets at 225 to 250°F. After 2 hours, start basting with apple juice every 30 minutes. The briskets are done when you can insert a grill fork into the meat and twist easily. An instant-read meat thermometer inserted in the thickest part should register 165°F. This will take about 15 hours total.

4. Let the meat rest for 15 minutes, then slice on the diagonal and across the grain, arrange on a platter, and serve.

BBQ Tip: The meat will stay juicier if you slice it 1/4 inch thick. If it is not fall-apart tender, however, it is better to slice it paper-thin. Or, if you prefer chopped or pulled brisket, slice it 1 inch thick, then pull the meat apart. If the meat doesn't pull easily, chop it up. Toss it with a small amount of BBQ Queens' Love Potion for the Swine (page 89) for a sublime touch.

Crowning Glories

Smoked brisket is traditionally served piled high on a nondescript white bread and topped with barbecue sauce, such as Smoky Barbecue Sauce (page 90); also serve it with:

BBQ Queens' Barbecued Beans *(page 107)*

BBQ Queens' Smoked Potato Casserole *(page 153)*

Layered Vinegar Slaw *(page 80)*

Kansas City–Style Barbecued Brisket: There are two main styles of barbecued brisket—Texas style, which is mildly smoked and very tender, and Kansas City style, which is more heavily smoked and slightly chewy. For KC style, you need to coat the briskets with olive oil, then sprinkle on a rub composed of 1/2 cup sweet Hungarian paprika, 1/4 cup cayenne pepper, 1/4 cup granulated garlic, and 1/4 cup freshly ground black pepper. Use hickory wood for the smoke flavor. Smoke the briskets at 225 to 250°F for 12 hours and begin basting every 30 minutes with apple juice after 4 hours of cooking. After 12 hours, remove the briskets from the smoker, wrap well in a double thickness of plastic wrap and a sheet of heavy-duty aluminum foil, and return to the smoker. (At 225 to 250°F, the plastic wrap will not melt.) Smoke the briskets for another 2 to 3 hours, until tender. Unwrap, slice, and serve. **SERVES 24**

Two-Step Shortcut Barbecued Brisket: Sometimes you end up with a moister brisket by taking a shortcut. You still get the smoky flavor this way, but you also get a juicier end result. Slather and rub the briskets as described above and smoke for 3 hours, basting twice with apple juice. Then bring them inside, wrap in 2 sheets of aluminum foil, and finish in a preheated 300°F oven for 3 to 3½ hours. The briskets are done when you can pierce the meat with a fork and twist easily. Unwrap, slice, and serve. **SERVES 24**

Barbecued Brisket Dip: Smoke for leftovers, we always say. With all the time you've spent smoking a brisket, it only makes sense to freeze some for dishes like this that you can make later. We adapted our recipe from one by our barbecue buddy Ardie Davis, also known as Remus Powers, Ph.B. To make the dip, in a large bowl combine 1 pound (about 2 cups) chopped barbecued brisket; ½ cup chopped onion; 1 minced garlic clove; 1¼ cups barbecue sauce of your choice; one 4-ounce can drained and chopped jalapeños; one 8-ounce package softened cream cheese; and ⅓ cup freshly grated Pecorino Romano, Asiago, or Parmesan cheese. Spoon into a greased 13 x 11-inch baking dish and bake at 350°F until browned and bubbling, 20 to 30 minutes. Serve hot with French bread or crackers. **SERVES 8**

Burnt Ends: When you're doing several briskets at a time, you can make a tasty dish of burnt ends. Burnt ends come from the thinnest part of the brisket, which is too thin to slice. After the brisket has come out of the smoker, trim off the burnt ends. Chop them into small, bite-size pieces, then brush them with the mustard slather and sprinkle with the rub (see above). Put them in a disposable aluminum pan, tightly wrap with foil, and return to the smoker (or a 300°F oven) for 1 to 2 hours, until you can shred them easily. **MAKES 2 TO 4 CUPS**

Burnt Ends Sandwich: One of our favorite decadent sandwiches—the Poor Russ—is made from burnt ends of both beef brisket and pork butt, courtesy of Jack Fiorella's Jack Stack in Kansas City. To make a burnt ends sandwich, use burnt ends that have been slow cooked twice as described above, then shredded and piled on a slice of bread. Add lots of barbecue sauce and top with another bread slice. That's durn good eatin'. **SERVES 1**

And Now for Something Completely Different

Barbecued Corned Beef with Mustard-Beer Slather and Smoked Potato Salad

Sometimes it's good to leave Venus for Mars and get a guy's take on barbecue. Plus, a girl's got to have some guy friends, right? Former Chicago superstation WGN anchor Dave Eckert has two not-so-secret passions—slow-smoked barbecue and great wine. Now taping another season of *Culinary Travels with Dave Eckert,* shown on public television stations nationwide, Eckert loves to experiment with barbecue and pair different smoked meats with wines.

For a recent gathering at his Liberty, Missouri, home, Eckert dreamed up this new take on corned beef and offered it to the BBQ Queens to try. Our decree: divine! Dave's advice: "Try to find a corned beef brisket that has a decent layer of fat on one side. This will help keep the meat tender during the cooking process." And make sure you cook for leftovers, because this barbecued corned beef makes a killer Rustic Reuben (page 360). SERVES 8

SUGGESTED WOOD: Oak

CORNED BEEF WITH MUSTARD SLATHER

One 5-pound corned beef brisket
One 12-ounce bottle Carolina-style mustard-based barbecue sauce
One 12-ounce can or bottle beer

SMOKED POTATO SALAD

2 pounds small new potatoes, pricked all over with a paring knife
2 bunches green onions, sliced
1 cup mayonnaise
Kosher or sea salt and ground white pepper to taste

Hearty, peasant-style rye bread for serving

1. To prepare the brisket, rinse and pat dry. Prepare a mop by combining about half the bottle of barbecue sauce with half the beer. (Drink the rest!) Stir well. The mop should be runny but still have the full flavor of the sauce. (A thicker mixture with more sauce will have a tendency to burn.)

2. Prepare an indirect fire in a grill or smoker.

3. Place the brisket fat side up on the indirect side of the grill and smoke at 250°F. Using a brush or dish mop, slather the meat thoroughly with the mop and close the lid. Mop the meat every 30 to 45 minutes. The brisket should brown slowly but not burn. If the meat is turning black too quickly, turn down the heat or close the vents on the grill to lower the temperature. If the meat is not browning, move the brisket closer to the heat.

4. After about 2 hours, flip the brisket over and continue mopping.

5. To make the potato salad, arrange the potatoes on the rack of the grill or smoker. Remove the potatoes from the smoker after 2 hours. They should fall apart when pierced with a fork. (The brisket, depending on its size and the heat of your grill, should be done at about the same time.) Combine the potatoes, green onions, mayonnaise, and salt and pepper in a large bowl. Gently pierce the potatoes so they make a chunky salad.

6. To serve, cut the brisket on the diagonal, against the grain of the meat, into thin slices. Serve with the warm smoked potato salad and the bread. Pass the rest of the barbecue sauce at the table.

Rustic Reuben: Pile thin slices of barbecued corned beef on a slice of artisanal rye bread. Top with drained deli sauerkraut, a slice of Swiss cheese, a dollop of mustard-based barbecue sauce, and another slice of bread. Coat a skillet with nonstick cooking spray and grill over medium-high heat on both sides until the bread is toasted and the cheese has melted. Serve hot. **SERVES 1**

Bringing Home the Bacon: Pork

Pork is probably the meat that gains the most from both the hot fire of the grill and the low heat of the smoker. From grilled thin-cut pork chops, which take minutes, to smoked pork butt, which takes hours, and all the goodies in between, you've got mighty good eatin'. When the BBQ Queens go out to strut our saucy stuff, we're constantly amazed at the number of people who still haven't grilled a pork tenderloin. If you're one of them, this chapter is especially for you. You have definitely been missing out. For hot and fast grilling, we recommend already-tender cuts such as chops, pork tenderloin, and sausages. Try those very thin breakfast-style pork chops grilled the Roman *scottadito* (to scorch the fingers) way as we do in our master recipe for Grilled Lamb Chops (page 420). Yum! Grill Gal Julie Fox's pork tenderloin, marinated in a heady blend of Worcestershire sauce and mustard, tastes fabulous (page 391).

You'll want a big cut of pork for the rotisserie, such as a pork loin (which also tastes great slow smoked). For low and slow smoking, we recommend a tougher cut, such as a pork butt or ribs. And when you anoint either one with BBQ Queens' Love Potion for the Swine (page 89), you'll understand why we gave that name to that barbecue sauce.

Now, get oinking out there.

BBQ-2

Grilled Hot Diggity Dogs 365

Grilled Chicken and Apple Sausage with Honey-Almond Grilling Glaze 365

Grilled Seafood Sausage with Cucumber and Tzatziki 366

Wisconsin Dilly Beer Brat Sandwiches 366

Rebecca's 'Que Queen Extraordinaire Spicy Pork Sausage 367

Smoked Sausage 368

Smoked Italian Sausage and Artichoke Soup 369

BBQ Queens' Choucroute Garnie with Smoked Bratwurst 369

Red Beans and Rice with Smoked Sausage 369

BBQ BABES: SHE'S A POWDERPUFF AT HEART MENU

Bill's Better Than the Average Barbecue Sauce 370

Cheesy Wild Rice 371

Pistachio Sausage 372

Spiral Herbed Smoked Pork Loin with Apricot-Dijon Glaze 373

Fresh Fruit Tart 374

Grilled Thick-Cut Pork Chops 376

Grilled Pork Chops with Red Wine, Vinegar, and Herb Marinade 377

Grilled Pork Chops with Honey-Apple Marinade and Baste 377

Grilled Pork Chops with Bourbon-Mustard Cream Sauce 377

DEVILISHLY GOOD EGGS

Classic Deviled Eggs 379

Caper-Stuffed Eggs 380

Deviled Eggs with Grilled Shrimp 380

Mediterranean Stuffed Eggs 381

Grilled Thin-Cut Pork Chops, Pork Steaks, or Ham Steaks 382

Vinegar-Mopped Country Cured Ham Steaks 382

Sweet Chops or Ham Steaks with Brown Sugar Basting Sauce 383

Ham, Cheddar, and Apricot Chutney Pizza 384

Smoked Pork Ribs 384

Asian-Style Ribs 385

Raspberry Barbecued Ribs 385

Country-Style Ribs 386

Indoor-Outdoor Kiss of Fire and Smoke Ribs 387

Grilled Pork Tenderloin or Center-Cut Pork Loin Fillet 388

Sesame and Soy–Marinated Pork Tenderloin 389

Grilled Pork Tenderloin with Cilantro-Peanut Dipping Sauce 389

Grilled Pork Tenderloin with Chipotle Dipping Sauce 389

Grilled Pork Tenderloin with Mustard-Herb Dipping Sauce 389

GRILL GALS: SHE WANTS Y'ALL TO COME OVER FOR DINNER MENU

Grilled Pork Tenderloin in Worcestershire Marinade 391

Slow-Simmered Baby Lima Beans 392

Asiago-Garlic Grits 392

Lemon-Scented Peach Crisp 393

YOU TAKE THE CAKE

Cranberry-Almond Torte with Cranberry Drizzle 394

Orange Marmalade Bundt Cake 396

Grilled Pound Cake with Hot Fudge Ganache and Sweetened Berries 397

Rotisserie Pork Loin 398

Herb-Marinated Rotisserie Pork Loin 398

Ancho and Chipotle–Rubbed Rotisserie Pork Loin 399

Bourbon Pecan-Stuffed Rotisserie Pork Loin 399

Rotisserie Pork Loin Sandwiches 399

BBQ BABES: SHE'S THE FLOWER OF THE FLAMES MENU

Raspberry and Mustard–Glazed Pork Roast 400

Kiss of Smoke Beef Tenderloin Black Forest 402

Cola-Marinated Smoked Flank Steak 403

Smoked Pork Loin 404

Slathered and Rubbed Smoked Pork Loin 405

Tuscan-Style Porchetta 405

BBQ Queens' Choucroute Garnie 405

NOT ON THE DISCOVERY CHANNEL: SMOKE-ROASTING

Smoke-Roasted Pork Loin with Herbed Pear Stuffing 407

Smoke-Roasted Potatoes with Garlic and Rosemary 408

Smoked Pork Butt 409

Spicy Orange Barbecued Pork Butt 410

Butts in a Bag 410

Piggy Sandwich 411

Double-Smoked Ham 411

POTATO CASSEROLES WITH A ROYAL TOUCH

Potato Gratin with White Cheddar Cheese 412

Oven-Roasted Saffron Potatoes 413

Double-Smoked Ham with Pineapple-Ginger Salsa 414

Karen's Double-Smoked Ham Salad Sandwiches 414

RISE AND SHINE: BREAKFAST IN THE GREAT OUTDOORS

Campfire Skillet Scones 415

Breakfast S'mores 416

Grilled Hot Diggity Dogs

In the Midwest, where we both live, we're in sausage heaven. Ethnic groups of all kinds settled in our region, bringing their best sausage varieties with them. In Kansas City alone, we can find all kinds of Slavic, German, Polish, Italian, Cajun, Chinese, Swedish, and French sausages—even English bangers.

We're also blessed to have great markets (such as Whole Foods Market) that offer boutique sausages made from salmon, chicken, turkey, buffalo, and the more common pork and beef. So if you haven't done so already, it's time to graduate from the hot dog to something MORE (as the queen of inspirational day-to-day living, Sarah Ban Breathnach, would say).

Grilling great unsmoked link sausage means a medium to medium-hot fire and turning them frequently with grill tongs. Sausage already has fat in the mixture, which will sizzle out during cooking, so you don't need olive oil. It's already seasoned, too, so you don't need salt and pepper. If you like, you can glaze the sausage as you grill it with barbecue sauce. To see whether sausage is done, slice it in the thickest part; if the juices run clear and the interior looks cooked through, it is. To be extra safe, you could use an instant-read meat thermometer inserted in the center; when it registers 170°F, your sausage is fully cooked.

Smoked sausage is not usually grilled, but you can brush it with olive oil and get some grill marks on it, if you like. You can also grill breakfast sausage patties, using a perforated grill rack and keeping a spray bottle with water handy for flare-ups. SERVES 8

2 pounds link sausage, such as Italian, Polish, andouille, chicken, or bratwurst

1. Prepare a medium fire in a grill.
2. Grill the sausage, turning every 4 to 5 minutes, until cooked through, 10 to 15 minutes total, depending on the diameter of the sausage. Serve hot.

Crowning Glories

Have a griller's feast and serve your sausage with mountains of:

Grilled Potatoes *(page 147)*

Grilled Peppers *(page 143)*

Grilled Onions *(page 137)*

Grilled Chicken and Apple Sausage with Honey-Almond Grilling Glaze: The glaze adds a touch of savory sweetness to the sausage. Grill 2 pounds chicken and apple link sausage as directed above, brushing with Honey Almond Grilling Glaze (page 88) and turning frequently. **SERVES 8**

Grilled Seafood Sausage with Cucumber and Tzatziki: Slice an English cucumber paper-thin; sprinkle with 1 teaspoon chopped fresh dill, 1/2 teaspoon ground white pepper, and 1/2 teaspoon garlic salt; arrange on a platter. Grill 2 pounds seafood link sausage as directed above, then place over the cucumber. Pass a bowl of Tzatziki (page 112) at the table, along with Wood-Grilled Flatbreads (page 176), if desired. **SERVES 8**

Wisconsin Dilly Beer Brat Sandwiches: In Wisconsin, grilling a brat is an art form, much like smoking a slab of ribs is in Kansas City. When the weather permits at the "frozen tundra of Lambeau Field," and sometimes when it doesn't, Green Bay Packers fans fire up their grills in the parking lot and wolf down a few of these delicious sandwiches to keep warm. Putting the brats in cold water before grilling ensures juicy sausage, and the beer pot serves two purposes: to add a last touch of flavor to the grilled brats and to keep them warm before serving. Thinly slice 1 large white onion, then separate into rings. In a large bowl, combine 1/2 cup sugar, 2 teaspoons kosher or sea salt, 1 teaspoon dillweed, 1/4 cup water, and 1/2 cup distilled white vinegar. Add the onion rings, submerging them in the marinade. Cover and refrigerate, stirring occasionally, for at least 1 hour. An hour before grilling, put 12 bratwurst sausage in a pan of cold water. Make a beer pot by pouring three 12-ounce bottles microbrew beer into a clean 3-pound coffee can or other similar container that can sit on the side of the grill. Grill the sausage and, as they're cooked, place them in the beer pot. Cut 1 dozen hard rolls or kaiser rolls almost in half horizontally and toast them cut sides down on the grill. To serve, split each brat lengthwise and place in a toasted roll. Place some dilly onion rings on top of the brat and add your favorite condiments. **SERVES A HUNGRY DOZEN**

Rebecca's 'Que Queen Extraordinaire Spicy Pork Sausage

Beckie Baker has been on two barbecue teams that compete in contests around the country. One is the glittery 'Que Queens, to which Karen and Judith belong. The other was Powderpuff Barbecue, a team that included her husband, John, and friends Bill and Janeyce Michel-Cupito. Beckie says, with her characteristic quirky humor, that "even though my main responsibility was mascot, I was also responsible for the sausage category. It was not a mandatory category, so there was not a lot I could screw up. This is the final recipe, after several trials and changes." SERVES 10 TO 12

One 5-pound boneless Boston butt or pork shoulder, trimmed of some fat

2 tablespoons fine kosher or sea salt

2 tablespoons freshly ground black pepper

3 tablespoons crumbled dried sage

1 teaspoon ground coriander

$\frac{1}{2}$ to $1\frac{1}{2}$ teaspoons cayenne pepper, to your taste

1 tablespoon crumbled dried thyme

$1\frac{1}{4}$ teaspoons sugar

$\frac{1}{4}$ cup chopped garlic

1 cup apple juice

1. Cut the pork into chunks. Attach a $\frac{1}{8}$-inch plate to a meat grinder and finely grind the pork in batches, twice.

2. In a large bowl, combine all the remaining ingredients. Add the ground pork and mix thoroughly. Form the mixture into patties or logs before grilling. Or use the meat grinder's stuffing attachment to stuff the mixture into lengths of 31- to 34-millimeter rinsed pork casings, available at wholesale meat companies. Tie off the sausage at 6- to 8-inch intervals with kitchen twine. The sausage will keep in the refrigerator for up to 1 week and in the freezer for 4 to 6 months.

BBQ Tip: **When grilling link sausage, sprinkle 1 envelope unflavored gelatin over 4 cups warm water in a medium-size bowl. Let the gelatin soften, then dissolve, until the liquid is a light, clear beige. Add 1 tablespoon light corn syrup. Soak the sausage links in the mixture for 10 minutes before grilling, then baste with the mixture while grilling. The mixture will caramelize, giving the sausage a nice color and slight sweetness.**

Smoked Sausage

Because sausage is often a category at barbecue competitions, many teams have developed their own sausage recipes (see Beckie Baker's and Janeyce Michel-Cupito's recipes on pages 367 and 372). The teams lovingly tend their homemade sausage as the links bronze to a fine turn on the smoker, along with the ribs, pork butt, brisket, and other goodies they are also smoking for the contest.

The BBQ Queens love a good, smoked hot sausage, but we probably wouldn't fire up the smoker in the backyard for sausage alone. Like smoked vegetables, we are more likely to smoke sausage alongside something else: a whole chicken, ribs, a brisket, or whatever else we're cooking.

Also, you don't have to make your own to enjoy sausage. In Kansas City, we're lucky to have three wonderful Italian sausage companies that make sweet and mild or hot and spicy varieties that are wonderful smoked. Smoke whatever sausage you like best. Even already-smoked sausage is delicious with another kiss of smoke, much like Double-Smoked Ham (page 411).

Smoked sausage can be kept in the refrigerator for up to 2 weeks or in the freezer for up to 3 months. It's one of our favorite convenience foods, ready to thaw and eat as is or as part of a soup, stew, or casserole.

Smoked over fruitwood, this dish has big flavor with very few calories. SERVES 4

SUGGESTED WOOD: Apple, hickory, or pecan

1 to 2 pounds link sausage, such as Italian, Polish, or bratwurst, 1½ to 2 inches in diameter

1. Prepare a fire in a smoker.

2. Place the sausage in a disposable aluminum pan, cover, and smoke at 225 to 250°F until cooked through and bronzed, 2 to 2½ hours. Serve hot.

Crowning Glories

Smoked sausage is stellar topped with:

Stir-Grilled Vegetables *(page 166)*

Raspberry-Jalapeño Barbecue Sauce *(page 90)*

Grated or sliced cheese, such as provolone, cheddar, or mozzarella

Smoked Italian Sausage and Artichoke Soup: The smokiness of the sausage ratchets up the flavor of this soup, adapted from a recipe in Judith's *Prairie Home Cooking* (The Harvard Common Press, 1999). If you use canned fire-roasted tomatoes (such as the Muir Glen brand), so much the better. In a large soup pot, sauté 1 diced red onion and 2 minced garlic cloves in 2 tablespoons olive oil over medium-high heat until softened, about 5 minutes. Cut 1 pound smoked Italian link sausage (see above), one 14-ounce can drained or one 9-ounce package defrosted frozen artichoke hearts, and one 28-ounce can undrained whole Roma tomatoes into bite-size pieces and add to the pot. Pour in 3 cups chicken broth, then add 1 teaspoon each dried oregano, dried basil, and fennel seeds. Bring to a boil, reduce the heat to medium-low, and simmer, uncovered, for 30 minutes. If desired, add 1/4 pound penne and cook until *al dente*, about 15 minutes more. Taste for seasoning and serve. **SERVES 6**

BBQ Queens' Choucroute Garnie with Smoked Bratwurst: Substitute 1 pound smoked bratwurst (see above) for the Polish sausage in BBQ Queens' Choucroute Garnie (page 405) for a rib-sticking entrée when you entertain in cold weather. **SERVES 10 TO 12**

Red Beans and Rice with Smoked Sausage: This dish is pure comfort food, whether you're Cajun or not. Traditionally, already-smoked andouille is used, but the recipe tastes great with any smoked hot and spicy pork sausage. In a large slow cooker or large pot, combine 2 pounds dried red kidney beans, 2 pounds smoked link sausage (see above), 1/2 pound diced smoked pork jowl (available at the butcher counter), 1/2 cup chopped yellow onion, 1/2 cup seeded and chopped green bell pepper, 1 tablespoon vegetable oil, 2 tablespoons sugar, and kosher or sea salt to taste. Mix together and add enough water to cover by 1 inch. Cook on low for 10 hours, stirring occasionally all the way to the bottom of the pan, until the beans are tender and the mixture has thickened. Serve over rice. **SERVES 10 TO 12**

BBQ Babes

She's a Powderpuff at Heart Menu

Bill's Better Than the Average Barbecue Sauce
Cheesy Wild Rice
Pistachio Sausage
Spiral Herbed Smoked Pork Loin with Apricot-Dijon Glaze
Fresh Fruit Tart

Janeyce Michel-Cupito (above, left) never does anything halfway. For years, she put her all into a very successful retail career. During that time, she and her husband, Bill, along with their friends John and Beckie Baker (see Beckie's sausage recipe on page 368), formed the Powderpuff Barbeque team, which competed on the barbecue contest circuit—very successfully, of course. Along the way, they garnered lots of ribbons and several state championships.

The team created many of their own recipes to wow the judges. Because they're not competing anymore and have gone on to new pursuits, Janeyce can share some of their best barbecue secrets here.

Bill's Better Than the Average Barbecue Sauce

This recipe originated when Janeyce's barbecue team needed a new sauce and the team members decided to have a contest among themselves. Janeyce's husband, Bill, wanted to do a really basic, nothing-to-object-to sweet red sauce, so he found some basic recipes, plugged them into the computer, averaged the ingredients, and made this sauce. He won, and they've been enjoying his sauce ever since. MAKES ABOUT 6 CUPS

Three 6-ounce cans tomato paste
3 cups cider vinegar
1/2 cup Worcestershire sauce

1 1/2 cups firmly packed light or dark brown sugar
1/3 cup light corn syrup
1/2 cup honey
1/3 cup molasses
1 medium-size onion, finely minced
2 tablespoons sweet Hungarian paprika
1 tablespoon freshly ground black pepper
2 tablespoons celery salt
2 tablespoons granulated garlic
1 tablespoon liquid smoke flavoring

Combine all the ingredients in a 3-quart saucepan. Bring to a boil, reduce the heat to low, and simmer for about 2 hours, until the flavors blend. Use immediately, or pour into a covered container and keep refrigerated for several months.

Cheesy Wild Rice

This is a wonderful accompaniment to slow-smoked ribs, turkey, pork loin, beef brisket, or chicken. SERVES 6 TO 8

One 6-ounce package long-grain and wild rice mix
4 ounces fresh mushrooms, sliced or chopped
2 1/2 cups water
One 10-ounce package frozen chopped spinach, defrosted
3/4 cup chopped onion
1 tablespoon unsalted butter
2 teaspoons Dijon mustard
1/4 teaspoon freshly grated nutmeg
One 8-ounce package cream cheese, cubed

1. Preheat the oven to 375°F. In a 13 x 9-inch baking dish, combine the rice mix and mushrooms.

2. In a medium-size saucepan, combine the water, spinach, onion, butter, and mustard. Bring to a boil, remove from the heat, and stir in the nutmeg and cream cheese until melted and smooth. Pour over the rice mixture.

3. Bake, covered with aluminum foil, until browned and bubbling, about 40 minutes. Remove from the oven and let stand for 10 minutes before serving.

Pistachio Sausage

This is one of Janeyce's to-die-for sausage recipes. It tastes great either grilled or slow smoked. SERVES 10 TO 12

3 pounds coarsely ground pork butt
1/2 cup unsalted shelled pistachios
1 tablespoon minced fresh Italian parsley
1 tablespoon fine kosher or sea salt
1 teaspoon freshly ground black pepper, plus more for coating
1/2 teaspoon red pepper flakes
1 clove garlic, minced

1. In a large bowl, combine all the ingredients. Divide the mixture into 4 parts. Roll each portion into a long roll about 1 1/2 inches in diameter. Wrap in plastic and refrigerate overnight to blend the flavors.

2. Prepare a medium-hot fire in a grill. Unwrap each roll and coat with pepper.

3. Grill until all sides are nicely browned and an instant-read meat thermometer inserted in the center of a roll registers 160°F, about 12 minutes. To serve, slice each roll into portions.

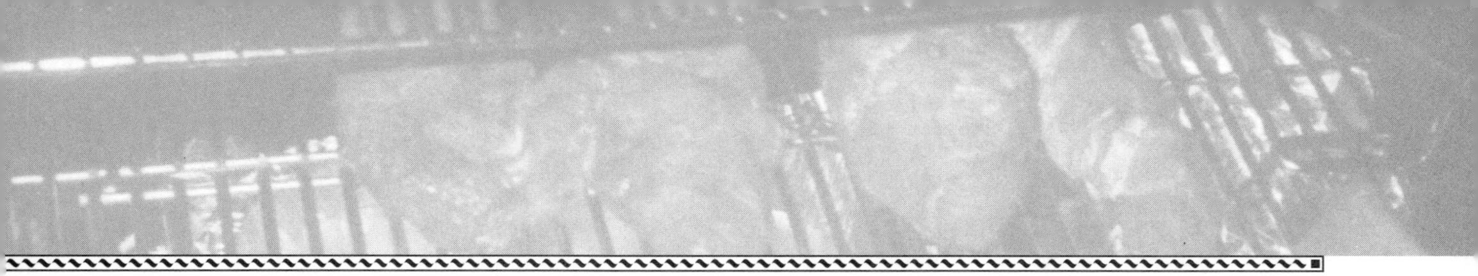

Spiral Herbed Smoked Pork Loin with Apricot-Dijon Glaze

This dish looks as great as it tastes. It's a wonderful entrée to serve a crowd. The herb filling creates a spiral design when you slice the pork loin. SERVES 10 TO 12

SUGGESTED WOOD: A combination of apple, oak, and hickory

1/4 cup (1/2 stick) unsalted butter

1/2 cup finely minced onion

2 tablespoons finely minced fresh Italian parsley

2 tablespoons finely minced fresh sage

2 tablespoons finely minced fresh rosemary

Fine kosher or sea salt and freshly ground black pepper to taste

One 4-pound boneless pork loin roast, cut and pounded with a tenderizer to form a 1/2-inch-thick rectangle

1 recipe Apricot-Dijon Glaze (recipe follows)

1. Melt the butter in a small skillet over medium heat. Add the onion and cook, stirring, until soft, about 5 minutes. Add the herbs and season with salt and pepper. Stir, remove from heat, and let cool for 10 minutes. Spread over the pork loin rectangle. Roll up the pork loin, starting from a long end and tying with kitchen twine at 3-inch intervals. Place in a disposable aluminum pan.

2. Prepare a fire in a smoker.

3. Cover and smoke over indirect heat at 225 to 250°F until an instant-read meat thermometer inserted in the thickest part of the roast registers 160°F and the meat is quite tender, 4 to 5 hours. During the last hour of cooking, brush the meat every 15 minutes with the glaze. Let rest for 15 minutes before slicing and serving.

Apricot-Dijon Glaze

The sweetness of the apricot preserves and the savory Dijon mustard and balsamic vinegar create a sweet yet savory glaze for all kinds of smoked pork, turkey, or chicken dishes. MAKES ABOUT 1 CUP

1/4 cup apricot preserves
1/4 cup Dijon mustard
1/4 cup cider vinegar
1 tablespoon balsamic vinegar
1 large clove garlic, minced
1/4 teaspoon cayenne pepper

Combine all the ingredients in a small bowl. This glaze will keep, covered, in the refrigerator for up to 2 weeks.

Fresh Fruit Tart

This is a lovely light dessert for after the heavy barbecue meal. MAKES ONE 10-INCH TART; SERVES 8

CRUST

1/2 cup sliced almonds
1/2 cup shelled hazelnuts
1/4 cup Splenda granular sweetener
1/4 cup whey protein powder (available in the health food section of better grocery stores)
1/2 teaspoon ground cinnamon
6 tablespoons (3/4 stick) unsalted butter, cut into 6 pieces

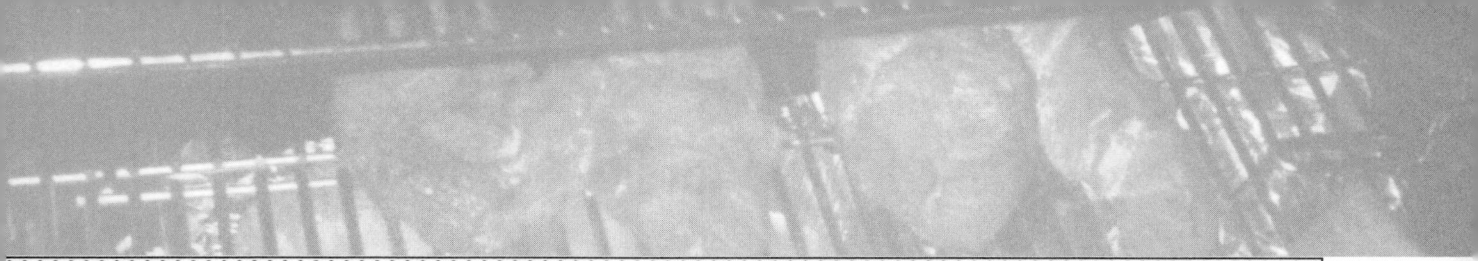

FILLING

One 8-ounce package cream cheese, softened

1/4 cup Splenda granular sweetener

1/2 teaspoon almond extract

TOPPING

Fruit of your choice, such as fresh strawberries, kiwis, raspberries, and/or oranges, or canned apricots

2 tablespoons fresh lemon juice

1/2 teaspoon almond extract

1/3 cup sugar-free apricot preserves

1. Preheat the oven to 400°F.

2. To make the crust, coat a 10-inch tart pan with nonstick cooking spray. In a food processor, process the almonds and hazelnuts until finely ground. Add the Splenda, whey protein powder, cinnamon, and butter and process until the mixture starts to come together into a mass. With your fingers, press the mixture evenly into the prepared pan. Bake for 5 minutes, then remove from the oven and let cool. Place in the refrigerator until cold to the touch.

3. To make the filling, combine the cream cheese, Splenda, and almond extract in the food processor. Process until smooth, then spread in the cold crust.

4. To make the topping, prepare the fruit: slice the strawberries, peel and thinly slice the kiwis, use the raspberries whole, peel and section the oranges, or slice the apricots. Arrange over the filling in slightly overlapping circles. In a small bowl, mix the lemon juice, almond extract, and apricot preserves together until smooth, then brush over the fruit. This tart is best served the same day it is made. Serve at room temperature or chilled.

Grilled Thick-Cut Pork Chops

Thick-cut pork chops—usually center cut from the loin and at least 1 inch thick, bone-in or boneless—can be delicious. In our part of the country, the Midwest, these chops are called Iowa chops. Traditionally, thick pork chops were served "carpetbagger style"—stuffed with a bread crumb and celery dressing—quickly browned on both sides and then braised in chicken broth until tender. We love these chops on the grill, too, but there is a trick to getting them just right: temperature. You need medium heat to produce flavorful and just done, yet still juicy, chops. A bath in a marinade beforehand helps, too.

Over medium heat, cooking will take about 10 minutes per side for a 1-inch-thick chop, longer for thicker chops. For a little razzle-dazzle, try seasoning them with Porcini Paste (page 65) or Spicy Orange Rub (page 51) or marinating them in Garlic-Citrus Marinade (page 70) or Rosemary-Mustard Marinade (page 71) before grilling.

All of these recipes also work well with veal chops. Once the province of upscale Italian restaurants, veal chops are now becoming more popular on the grill. SERVES 4

Four center-cut pork chops, 1 inch thick (about 11 ounces each)
Olive oil
Fine kosher or sea salt and freshly ground black pepper to taste

1. Prepare a medium fire in a grill.
2. Brush or spray the chops on both sides with olive oil. Grill directly over the fire for about 10 minutes per side, or until an instant-read meat thermometer inserted in the thickest part of the chop registers 155°F. Season with salt and pepper and serve hot.

Crowning Glories

A simply grilled thick-cut pork chop is delicious served with:

Smoked Chile Beurre Blanc *(page 99)*
Winter Blood Orange, Fennel, and Black Olive Relish *(page 424)*
Potato Gratin with White Cheddar Cheese *(page 412)*

Grilled Pork Chops with Red Wine, Vinegar, and Herb Marinade: This marinade, in the European hunter's tradition of preparing wild boar, tastes great with pork chops. In a baking dish or sealable plastic bag, combine 1 cup dry red wine, 1 1/2 tablespoons red wine vinegar, 1 teaspoon juniper berries, 2 bay leaves, 2 tablespoons chopped fresh rosemary, and 3 chopped garlic cloves. Add four 1-inch-thick center-cut pork chops, turning to coat. Cover or seal and marinate in the refrigerator for at least 4 hours or up to 8 hours, turning several times. When ready to cook, remove the chops from the marinade and transfer the marinade to a saucepan. Bring to a boil and cook for 2 minutes, swirling in 2 tablespoons unsalted butter. Grill the chops as directed above and serve the sauce over them. **SERVES 4**

Grilled Pork Chops with Honey-Apple Marinade and Baste: The sweetness of the honey and apple cider accentuates the sweetness of the pork. In a baking dish or sealable plastic bag, combine 1 1/2 cups apple cider, 1/4 cup fresh lemon juice (about 2 lemons), 1/4 cup soy sauce, 2 tablespoons clover or other medium-colored honey, 1 minced garlic clove, and kosher or sea salt and freshly ground black pepper to taste. Add four 1-inch-thick center-cut pork chops, turning to coat. Cover or seal and marinate in the refrigerator for at least 4 hours or up to 24 hours, turning several times. When ready to cook, remove the chops from the marinade and transfer the marinade to a saucepan. Bring to a boil and cook for 2 minutes, then swirl in 2 tablespoons unsalted butter. Grill the chops as directed above, basting with the cooked marinade every 3 minutes. Serve hot. **SERVES 10**

Grilled Pork Chops with Bourbon-Mustard Cream Sauce: This sauce is a true "crowning glory" to a luscious, moist chop hot off the grill. In a small saucepan, bring 1/2 cup bourbon to a boil and continue to boil until reduced by half, about 5 minutes. Set aside. In a medium-size skillet, melt 2 tablespoons unsalted butter over medium-high heat. Add 2 tablespoons finely chopped onion and 1 cup thinly sliced fresh mushrooms. Cook, stirring, until the onion is transparent and the mushrooms are lightly browned, about 5 minutes. Stir in 1/8 teaspoon dried thyme, 1 tablespoon Dijon mustard, 1/2 cup heavy cream, and the reduced bourbon and cook for 1 minute to blend the flavors. Keep warm. Grill the pork chops as directed above. Top the chops with the sauce, sprinkle with chopped fresh Italian parsley, and serve. **SERVES 4**

Devilishly Good Eggs

Karen's family holds bragging rights to making unusually good deviled eggs. The trick, says Karen, is to hard-boil the eggs and peel them while they are still warm. Then combine the yolk mixture ingredients while still warm, too. It goes without saying, they are best when served the day they are made.

A true deviled egg always has a little something hot in it, such as hot sauce, red pepper flakes, or a spicy pepper blend, as well as something a little sour, such as vinegar, to take away the "eggy" taste. If you skip the hot stuff, you have just a stuffed egg. But oh what stuffings you can create! Try adding any leftover grilled or smoked fare to the stuffing mixture, such as chopped grilled shrimp, chicken, or pork. Even chopped grilled bell peppers and onions are "eggsellent" choices.

Quick-as-a-wink flavored deviled eggs are only a tube of sun-dried tomato paste, anchovy paste, or tapenade (black olive paste) away. Just add 1 to 2 tablespoons of your favorite paste to the Classic Deviled Eggs recipe below.

As BBQ Queens, we recommend that you invest in containers or plates with indentations made specifically for deviled eggs.

How to Hard-Boil an Egg: Place the eggs in a single layer in a saucepan. Fill with cold water to cover. Place over medium heat until the water just begins to boil. Lower the heat slightly and cook for 5 minutes. Remove the pan from the heat and let sit for 8 minutes. Drain the hot water from the pan and replace with cold tap water. Let sit for a couple of minutes more. Then peel the eggs, while still warm. They will be perfect.

Classic Deviled Eggs

Delicious served as an appetizer or side dish with your barbecue. MAKES 12

6 hard-boiled large eggs, still warm

3 tablespoons mayonnaise

1 tablespoon Dijon mustard

1 tablespoon fresh lemon juice

1 teaspoon Worcestershire sauce, preferably white

1/8 teaspoon hot pepper sauce

Fine kosher or sea salt and freshly ground black pepper to taste

Finely chopped fresh chives for garnish (optional)

1. Peel the eggs, then cut in half lengthwise. Remove the yolks from the whites and place the yolks in a small bowl. Place the whites cut side up on a plate and set aside.

2. Mash the yolks with a fork. Add the mayonnaise, mustard, lemon juice, Worcestershire, and hot sauce and mash until the mixture just begins to be smooth. Season with salt and pepper.

3. Stuff the whites with the yolk mixture, mounding the tops. If desired, sprinkle with chives. Cover loosely and refrigerate for at least 1 hour or up to 8 hours. The eggs will keep, covered, in the refrigerator for 2 to 3 days but are best eaten the day they are made.

Caper-Stuffed Eggs

These are a little tangier and more piquant than regular deviled eggs. MAKES 24

12 hard-boiled large eggs, still warm
1/2 cup extra virgin olive oil
2 tablespoons fresh lemon juice
1/4 cup chopped fresh Italian parsley
3 tablespoons plus 1 teaspoon capers, drained
Fine kosher or sea salt and freshly ground black pepper to taste

1. Peel the eggs, then cut in half lengthwise. Remove the yolks from the whites and place the yolks in a small bowl. Place the whites cut side up on a plate and set aside.

2. Mash the yolks with a fork. Add 1/4 cup of the olive oil, the lemon juice, the parsley, 3 tablespoons of the capers, and the salt and pepper. Mash until the mixture just begins to be smooth. Gradually blend in the remaining 1/4 cup olive oil until smooth and fluffy. Taste for salt and pepper.

3. Stuff the whites with the yolk mixture, mounding the tops. Sprinkle the eggs with the remaining 1 teaspoon capers. Cover loosely and refrigerate for at least 1 hour or up to 8 hours. The eggs will keep, covered, in the refrigerator for 2 to 3 days but are best eaten the day they are made.

Deviled Eggs with Grilled Shrimp

This is a great way to use leftover grilled shrimp. You may substitute salad shrimp, crabmeat, or smoked trout. MAKES 12

6 hard-boiled large eggs, still warm
3 tablespoons mayonnaise
1 tablespoon Dijon mustard
1 tablespoon fresh lemon juice
1/8 teaspoon hot pepper sauce
1/4 cup plus 1 tablespoon chopped grilled shrimp (see page 289)
Fine kosher or sea salt and freshly ground black pepper to taste

1. Peel the eggs, then cut in half lengthwise. Remove the yolks from the whites and place the yolks in a small bowl. Place the whites cut side up on a plate and set aside.

2. Mash the yolks with a fork. Add the mayonnaise, mustard, lemon juice, and hot sauce and mash until the mixture just begins to be smooth. Add 1/4 cup of the shrimp. Season with salt and pepper.

3. Stuff the whites with the yolk mixture, mounding the tops. Top each egg with a bit of the remaining 1 tablespoon chopped shrimp. Cover loosely and refrigerate for at least 1 hour or up to 8 hours. The eggs will keep, covered, in the refrigerator for 2 to 3 days but are best eaten the day they are made.

Mediterranean Stuffed Eggs

Cured olives and roasted red peppers are to die for in these incredible party-perfect eggs. MAKES 24

12 hard-boiled large eggs, still warm
1/2 cup extra virgin olive oil
2 tablespoons fresh lemon juice
1/4 cup plus 1 tablespoon pitted, drained, and chopped oil- or brine-cured olives
1/4 cup chopped roasted red peppers (homemade, see page 145, or from a jar)
Fine kosher or sea salt and freshly ground black pepper to taste

1. Peel the eggs, then cut in half lengthwise. Remove the yolks from the whites and place the yolks in a small bowl. Place the whites cut side up on a plate and set aside.

2. Mash the yolks with a fork. Add 1/4 cup of the olive oil, the lemon juice, 1/4 cup of the olives, the red peppers, and salt and pepper. Mash until the mixture just begins to be smooth. Gradually blend in the remaining 1/4 cup olive oil until smooth and fluffy. Taste for salt and pepper.

3. Stuff the whites with the yolk mixture, mounding the tops. Sprinkle the eggs with the remaining 1 tablespoon olives. Cover loosely and refrigerate for at least 1 hour or up to 8 hours. The eggs will keep, covered, in the refrigerator for 2 to 3 days but are best eaten the day they are made.

Grilled Thin-Cut Pork Chops, Pork Steaks, or Ham Steaks

We wish we were as lean and mean as these quick-to-prepare thin-cut pork chops, pork steaks, and ham steaks. They are perfect for weeknight suppers or feeding a crowd because they cook up so fast and easy.

Tender pork chops cut from the loin can be bone-in or butterflied (with the bone out and opened like a book for even faster cooking). Pork steaks are a tougher cut of meat, usually cut from the pork shoulder, and do well with a bit of a marinade. Ham steaks can be sliced about 1/2 inch thick from a boneless precooked ham. Ham will cook the quickest because it has already been precooked and needs only to heat through and develop those pretty grill marks.

Grill fresh fruit at the same time. Fresh pineapple slices and peach and plum halves are wonderful accompaniments to pork and cook quickly. SERVES 4

Four bone-in pork chops or steaks, boneless butterflied pork chops, or ham steaks, 1/2 inch thick

2 tablespoons mustard of your choice

1. Prepare a hot fire in a grill.

2. Slather the meat on both sides with the mustard. (It can be applied several hours in advance and allowed to marinate in the refrigerator.) Place the meat directly over the fire. Grill until the meat is juicy and slightly pink in the center, 3 to 4 minutes per side.

Crowning Glories

Serve your chops or steaks with:

Fennel and Orange Drizzling Sauce *(page 73)*

Red Cabbage and Apple Slaw *(page 83)*

Vinegar-Mopped Country Cured Ham Steaks: You have probably heard of Smithfield ham, a country cured ham that is saltier and drier than most hams. Have a Smithfield ham or a similar brand sliced about 1/2 inch thick for this recipe. Grill it with a mustard slather as directed above for 4 to 5 minutes per side, but in addition, mop it with a baste of 1/4 cup strong black coffee and 1/4 cup cider vinegar. This lip-smackin' treat is dynamite for breakfast, served with eggs and stone-ground grits seasoned with butter, fine kosher or sea salt, and ground white pepper to taste. **SERVES 4**

Sweet Chops or Ham Steaks with Brown Sugar Basting Sauce: Throw some fresh pineapple slices or peach halves on the grill along with the chops or steaks and use this sweet basting sauce on both. To make the sauce, melt 1/4 cup (1/2 stick) unsalted butter in a small saucepan. Remove from the heat and whisk in 1/2 cup firmly packed light or dark brown sugar; 2 tablespoons each fresh lemon juice, grated orange zest, and dry mustard, and 1/2 teaspoon red pepper flakes. Grill the chops or steaks over a medium-hot fire, basting with the sauce. **SERVES 4**

The 'Que Queens Versus the Male Chauvinist Pigs in the Battle of the Sexes Barbecue Contest

Mid-morning: "Luckily, the charity teams only competed in three categories: pork, brisket, and ribs. The pork shoulder and beef brisket had been on the fire since midnight. At mid-morning, they were ready to go in the warming box after several dips in the sauce. The Queens didn't marinate with sauce until the end, but they did put a marinade on the pork shoulder and a dry rub on the ribs and brisket before they started the cooking process."

Noon: "It was time to get on the tiaras and the royal sashes. The queens had separated their ribs, pulled their pork and sliced their brisket. . . They had put out their wares, one meat category at a time. . . Participants paid their two bucks and picked up a ballot and a sample from each tray. . . And . . . Once again, the women beat the men in the barbeque Battle of the Sexes."

Check out this and other adventures of Heaven Lee in _Revenge of the Barbeque Queens_ (St. Martin's Press, 1997), one of a series of culinary mystery novels written by our fellow 'Que Queen Lou Jane Temple.

Ham, Cheddar, and Apricot Chutney Pizza: This pizza is a snazzy way to use leftover ham or turkey. You can buy a jar of chutney, but this homemade version is really a snap. Combine $1\frac{1}{2}$ cups apricot preserves, $\frac{1}{2}$ teaspoon grated fresh ginger (if using a microplane, you don't need to peel), $\frac{1}{2}$ cup golden raisins, 1 minced garlic clove, 2 tablespoons fresh lemon juice, 1 teaspoon ground cinnamon, and $\frac{1}{2}$ teaspoon ground white pepper in a medium-size bowl. (This will keep, covered, in the refrigerator for several weeks.) To make the pizza, begin with a flatbread such as a pita bread or Boboli as your base. Spread 2 to 3 tablespoons Dijon mustard over the bread. Thinly slice 4 to 5 ounces grilled ham and scatter over the pizza. Sprinkle 1 cup finely shredded cheddar cheese over the meat. Finish by spooning small dollops of the chutney over everything. Bake for about 10 minutes in a preheated 350°F oven. SERVES 6 TO 8

Smoked Pork Ribs

When competition barbecuers start talking about ribs, they divide into four camps: those who favor St. Louis–cut ribs, Kansas City–cut ribs, spareribs, and baby back ribs. St. Louis–cut and Kansas City–cut ribs and spareribs are all bigger and tougher than baby backs, coming from the side of the hog. Because we're kinder, gentler, and daintier than those beefy barbecue guys, we prefer the smaller and more tender baby backs, which come from the area on either side of the backbone. If presented with a platter of heavenly smoked spareribs, however, takers we will be.

Our all-female barbecue team, the 'Que Queens, has won the Battle of the Sexes Barbecue Contest in Kansas City several times with the following recipe. Don't cringe at the thought of squeeze-bottle margarine and honey. This glazing technique really does make the ribs melt-in-your-mouth good!

As a side note, when we were preparing these ribs for a St. Louis television program, we met a young television anchorwoman. She remarked on our tiaras and said she had one of her own. Like a complete dork, Judith asked what kind of queen she was. This former Miss America, Debbye Turner, graciously answered. Then she taught us the four queen waves, which we pass on to you on page 224.

One bit of essential technique is to pull off the membrane from the underside of the ribs in one motion. We usually use needle-nose pliers (or heavy-duty tweezers) for this, grabbing a corner of the membrane, then pulling and tugging until we get it all off. The ribs have to be cold when you do this, or you can't grab the membrane easily. Do it the night before, then sprinkle with the rub, cover, and refrigerate for the best flavor. SERVES 8

SUGGESTED WOOD: A combination of hickory and cherry

3 whole slabs (1 to 1½ pounds each) baby back ribs

Memphis Blue-Ribbon Rib Rub (page 49) or Prizewinning Rib Rub (page 50)

1 cup clover or other medium-colored honey

One 12-ounce squeeze bottle Parkay margarine

One 14-ounce ounce bottle smoky, spicy barbecue sauce of your choice

1. The day before cooking, remove the membrane from the back of the ribs. Sprinkle with the rub on both sides. Cover and refrigerate overnight.

2. Prepare an indirect fire in a smoker.

3. Cover and smoke the ribs at 225 to 250°F. After 2 hours, the rib meat should have pulled back from the tips of the bones. Turn the ribs over and drizzle with half of the honey and half of the margarine. Brush to distribute the honey and margarine evenly over the surface of the meat. Cover and cook for 30 minutes.

4. Turn the ribs again, drizzle with the remaining honey and margarine, and brush the meat again. Cover and cook for 30 minutes.

5. As a glaze, brush the ribs on both sides with some of the barbecue sauce, then smoke for a final 15 minutes. To serve, leave as whole slabs or cut into individual ribs. Serve the remaining sauce on the side.

Crowning Glories

Barbecued ribs are traditionally served with:

BBQ Queens' Barbecued Beans ***(page 107)***

BBQ Queens' Smoked Potato Casserole ***(page 153)***

BBQ Queens' Love Potion for the Swine ***(page 89)***

Asian-Style Ribs: Instead of a typical barbecue rub, make a triple batch of Zesty Sugar and Spice Rub (page 52) or Five-Spice Asian Paste (page 64) and sprinkle or slather on the ribs. Smoke and baste with the honey and margarine as directed above, then finish with Asian Barbecue Sauce (page 90) during the last 30 minutes of smoking. Brush the ribs with some of the sauce to glaze them, then serve the rest at the table. **SERVES 8**

Raspberry Barbecued Ribs: Flower of the Flames barbecue guru Karen Putman (see page 400) inspired this recipe. After you've removed the membrane from the ribs, brush them with one 12-ounce bottle raspberry vinaigrette. Cover and refrigerate overnight. The next day, remove the ribs from the marinade, pat dry, and sprinkle with Memphis

Blue-Ribbon Rib Rub (page 49) or Prizewinning Rib Rub (page 50). Smoke and baste with the honey and margarine as directed above, then finish with Raspberry-Jalapeño Barbecue Sauce (page 90) during the last 30 minutes of smoking. Brush the ribs with some of the sauce to glaze, then serve the rest at the table. **SERVES 8**

Country-Style Ribs: Country-style ribs aren't ribs at all, but fingers of boneless meat cut from the pork shoulder—the same cut of meat known as pork butt. Country-style ribs also benefit from slow smoking, and they're usually tender in about 2 hours. To make these, slather 4 pounds country-style ribs with Mustard-Mayo Slather (page 66) and sprinkle with either Memphis Blue-Ribbon Rib Rub (page 49) or Prizewinning Rib Rub (page 50). Cover and smoke at 225 to 250°F for about 2 hours, turning halfway through (these don't get the honey-Parkay treatment). The ribs are done when they feel tender when pierced with a knife. Serve with your favorite barbecue sauce on the side. **SERVES 8**

Z
Zapatos
Shoes
Z

Indoor-Outdoor Kiss of Fire and Smoke Ribs

Our editor, Pam Hoenig, coaxed us into trying oven-roasted ribs finished on the outdoor grill for a kiss of fire. She acknowledged that for passionate barbecuers this method may seem sacrilegious. Although they don't have the depth of flavor that slow-smoked ribs do, they're still mighty tasty.

The trick to this recipe is preparing two or more slabs at a time, so they can be layered on top of each other and rotated during the oven-roasting process, which keeps the meat moist. Then take them out to the grill to finish. If you don't want to venture outdoors at all (not a queenly thing to do, mind you), the ribs can be sauced and finished in the oven as well. Brush them with barbecue sauce, lay them out flat (not layered), and roast for a final 15 minutes. We like a spicy sauce to finish, but any kind of glaze would do.

Leftover slabs can be double-wrapped in aluminum foil, then plastic wrap, and frozen for up to 3 months. Defrost, unwrap, place on a baking sheet, and warm in a 350°F oven until heated through. SERVES 8

4 whole slabs (1 to 1 1/2 pounds each) baby back ribs
1/2 cup Ole Hickory Rub (page 60)
1 cup hickory chips, soaked in water for at least 30 minutes before grilling
2 cups BBQ Queens' Love Potion for the Swine (page 89)

1. Preheat the oven to 350°F. Line a baking sheet with aluminum foil.

2. Remove the membrane from the back of the ribs with a paring knife, heavy-duty tweezers, or needle-nose pliers. Sprinkle 2 tablespoons of the rub on the top of each slab of ribs. Stack the ribs in two piles on the prepared baking sheet. Bake for about 2 1/2 hours, rotating the ribs every 30 to 45 minutes.

3. Remove the ribs from the oven. (At this point, the ribs could be cooled, wrapped in foil, and refrigerated for up to 2 days before finishing on the grill.)

4. Prepare a hot fire in a grill, adding the hickory chips.

5. Brush both sides of the ribs with sauce and place on the grill. Turn and baste the ribs with additional sauce. Grill for about 15 minutes, until the sauce has caramelized.

Grilled Pork Tenderloin or Center-Cut Pork Loin Fillet

It amazes us how many people have never grilled pork tenderloin or the new, more economical center-cut pork loin fillet. If you're one of those people, this recipe is for you. We give it our royal seal of approval. In a single word and with a wave of our tongs, pork tenderloin is superb!

Pork tenderloin or center-cut pork loin fillet is a great party food. Several tenderloins can go on the grill at once. The meat holds well and can be served hot, at room temperature, or chilled. We once char-grilled 30 tenderloins for a barbecue party of 100 dietitians. It was our first foray into catering, so it was quite by accident that they turned out beautifully. Here's how we did it: We charred about 10 tenderloins at a time over a very hot fire of mesquite hardwood lump charcoal. This took only 7 to 8 minutes per batch, and the pork was crispy on the outside and very rare on the inside. We transferred the charred pork to a cooler and transported it to the dinner destination. Then we cut it into 2-inch-thick slices, placed the slices in a hotel chafing dish, and set the dish out on the buffet. An hour later, the buffet opened. Our pork was a perfect medium and the hit of the party.

Be sure to purchase pork tenderloin or center-cut pork loin fillet, not pork loin roast. Pork tenderloin often comes two tenderloins to a package; a single center-cut pork loin fillet is usually available in about a 1½-pound package. Tenderloins vary in weight from 8 to 16 ounces. Plan on a serving size of 8 ounces—the same for the larger and slightly chewier pork loin fillet. If not all of the meat is eaten, you'll have leftovers for eating cold with peanut dipping sauce, and there's nothing wrong with that.

SERVES 8

4 pork tenderloins or 2 center-cut pork loin fillets (3½ to 4 pounds total)
2 tablespoons olive oil
Fine kosher or sea salt and freshly ground black pepper to taste

1. Prepare a hot fire in a grill.

2. Lightly coat the tenderloins with the olive oil and season with salt and pepper. Place directly over the fire. Grill the tenderloins for 2 to 3 minutes per side (the center-cut pork loin fillets for 5 to 7 minutes per side), turning a quarter turn at a time, until an instant-read meat thermometer inserted in the thickest part registers 145°F and the meat is juicy and slightly pink in the center.

3. Let rest for about 5 minutes, then cut on the diagonal into 1- to 2-inch-thick slices. Transfer to a platter and serve.

Crowning Glories

This meat is delicious served with:

Hearts of Palm Salad ***(page 283)***

Grilled Asparagus ***(page 117)***

Grilled romaine ***(page 127)***

Sesame and Soy–Marinated Pork Tenderloin: Try this pungent Asian-style marinade with just about any meat, fish, or vegetable. In a large bowl, combine 1/2 cup soy sauce, 2 tablespoons toasted sesame oil, 2 minced garlic cloves, and 5 thin slices peeled fresh ginger. Place the tenderloins (or loin fillets) in the bowl, cover, and marinate in the refrigerator for 1 to 2 hours. Grill as directed above and serve. **SERVES 8**

Grilled Pork Tenderloin with Cilantro-Peanut Dipping Sauce: In a small bowl, combine 3/4 cup crunchy peanut butter, 1/4 cup soy sauce, 1/4 cup rice vinegar, 1/4 cup fresh lime juice (4 to 5 limes), 2 tablespoons jalapeño honey, 1 tablespoon toasted sesame oil, and 1 to 2 tablespoons chopped fresh cilantro. To make a thinner sauce, add a little more lime juice. Grill the tenderloins (or loin fillets) as directed above. Serve hot or chilled with this sauce on the side. **SERVES 8 AS A MAIN COURSE OR 16 TO 20 AS AN APPETIZER**

Grilled Pork Tenderloin with Chipotle Dipping Sauce: This simple sauce can be mildly spicy or red-hot depending on the amount of chipotle chiles used. Try it with beef and shellfish, too. In a food processor, combine 2 cups prepared chili sauce, 1 canned chipotle chile in adobo sauce plus 1 teaspoon sauce, 1 tablespoon honey, 1 tablespoon fresh lemon juice, and 1/2 teaspoon kosher salt. Pulse 2 or 3 times to chop the chipotle and blend. Grill the tenderloins (or loin fillets) as described above and serve with the sauce. **SERVES 8**

Grilled Pork Tenderloin with Mustard-Herb Dipping Sauce: The BBQ Queens come from sturdy European stock. Judith has quite a bit of German blood; Karen is half Slavic and is married to Dick, whose family is of German descent. Why are we telling you this? Because we love mustard and mustard sauces. Another member of barbecue royalty, "the Baron of Barbecue," otherwise known as Paul Kirk, is a master at making sauces and rubs. Here we have adapted one of the recipes from his most recent book, *Paul Kirk's Championship Barbecue* (The Harvard Common Press, 2004). In a medium-size bowl, combine 2 cups sour cream, 1/4 cup German-style whole-grain mustard, 1/4 cup Dijon mustard, 1 tablespoon snipped fresh chives, 1 tablespoon chopped fresh tarragon, 1 tablespoon brandy, 1/2 teaspoon kosher salt, and 1/4 teaspoon freshly ground black pepper. Grill the tenderloins (or loin fillets) as directed above. Serve with the sauce on the side. **SERVES 8**

Grill Gals

She Wants Y'all to Come Over for Dinner Menu

Grilled Pork Tenderloin in Worcestershire Marinade
Slow-Simmered Baby Lima Beans
Asiago-Garlic Grits
Lemon-Scented Peach Crisp

Judith's sister, Julie Fox, never used to say "y'all," but she does now that she lives in Atlanta. Although she's still not into sweetened ice tea, Julie loves to frequent the farmers' market near her home to buy great regional produce. In July, she brings home boxes of juice-running-down-your-arm Georgia peaches and tender fresh baby lima beans for a grill menu that Scarlett O'Hara would have loved. Unlike some who might think that women "don't know nuthin' 'bout grillin'," Julie is the grillmaster in her household.

She marinates the pork tenderloins the night before, slowly simmers the lima beans after she comes home from the market on Saturday morning, and then bakes the peach crisp and stirs up the grits right before she sizzles the pork on her gas grill. The bonus with this menu is that *everything* tastes as good or even better the next day.

Grilled Pork Tenderloin in Worcestershire Marinade

The hearty, savory marinade is also yummy with chicken and steaks. SERVES 8

WORCESTERSHIRE MARINADE

1/2 cup olive oil

1/4 cup soy sauce

1/2 cup Worcestershire sauce

2 tablespoons Dijon mustard

3/4 teaspoon kosher or sea salt

1 tablespoon freshly ground black pepper

1/2 cup red or white wine vinegar

2 tablespoons chopped fresh Italian parsley

2 cloves garlic, minced

1/2 cup fresh lemon juice (3 to 4 lemons)

Four 8-ounce pork tenderloins, trimmed of any fat and silverskin

Olive oil

1. To make the marinade, combine all the ingredients in a large baking dish. Reserve 1 cup of the marinade and refrigerate. Place the pork tenderloins in the remaining marinade, turn to coat, cover with plastic wrap, and refrigerate for 4 hours or overnight.

2. Prepare a hot fire in a grill.

3. Remove the pork from the marinade, discarding the marinade. Pat dry with paper towels and spray with olive oil. Grill until an instant-read meat thermometer inserted in the thickest part registers 145°F for medium, about 5 minutes per side.

4. Let rest for 10 minutes before slicing. Meanwhile, bring the reserved marinade to a boil over high heat, drizzle over the tenderloin slices on a platter, and serve.

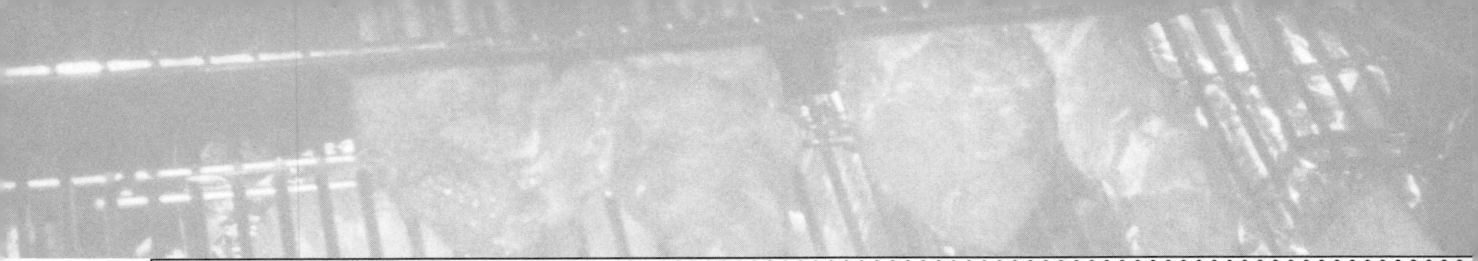

Slow-Simmered Baby Lima Beans

If you have bad memories of big old lima beans, stop right there. These young whipper-snappers are tender, toothsome, and flavorful. SERVES 8

4 cups fresh or three 10-ounce packages defrosted frozen baby lima beans

4 cups water

$1\frac{1}{2}$ tablespoons chicken flavor base (available in the soup section of most grocery stores)

4 slices bacon, cooked crisp and crumbled

Place all the ingredients in a large saucepan and bring to a boil. Reduce the heat to low, cover, and simmer until the beans are tender, 3 to 4 hours. Check periodically, adding more water, if necessary. Serve hot.

Asiago-Garlic Grits

There are cheese grits and then there are *these* cheese grits! If you can't find stone-ground grits, use the old-fashioned kind, not instant. It's okay to use quick-cooking grits, but they will take less time to cook and be less textured than stone-ground grits. SERVES 8

2 cups water

1 cup chicken broth

1 tablespoon chopped garlic

1 cup white or yellow stone-ground grits

1 cup heavy cream

1 cup freshly grated Asiago cheese

Fine kosher or sea salt and ground white pepper to taste

Combine the water, broth, and garlic in a large saucepan. Bring to a boil and slowly whisk in the grits. Cook over low heat, stirring frequently, until the grits thicken to a porridge consistency, about 15 minutes. Remove from the heat and stir in the cream and cheese. Season with salt and white pepper and serve.

Lemon-Scented Peach Crisp

We love the tart taste of lemon with everything—especially peaches. SERVES 8

6 cups peeled, pitted, and sliced fresh peaches
2 cups sugar
1 tablespoon quick-cooking tapioca
Juice and grated zest of 1 lemon
1 cup all-purpose flour
½ cup (1 stick) unsalted butter, softened

1. Preheat the oven to 375°F. Butter a 13 x 9-inch baking dish.

2. In a large bowl, combine the peaches, 1 cup of the sugar, the tapioca, and lemon juice. Spoon into the prepared baking dish. In a medium-size bowl, combine the remaining 1 cup sugar, the flour, and lemon zest. Using your fingers, rub the butter into the flour mixture to form large crumbs. Sprinkle these evenly over the fruit. Bake until lightly browned and bubbly, about 35 minutes. Serve warm.

You Take the Cake

Unfussy, big-flavor, homemade cakes are perfect to serve a crowd at your backyard feast—or for totin' over to someone else's. We've rounded up three of our favorite cakes that pay big dividends for minimal time and effort. We think it's a good idea to give your guests some time to digest all that savory food from the grill or smoker before offering them a sweet treat, perhaps with a coffee bar.

Cranberry-Almond Torte with Cranberry Drizzle

Our friend (and fellow culinary instructor and cookbook author) Ann Lund brought this torte to a meeting, where it was promptly devoured. Everyone asked for the recipe—the highest praise. Ann says she keeps bags of cranberries in the freezer year-round just to use for this easy-to-assemble cake. And the drizzle is divine. **MAKES ONE 9-INCH TORTE; SERVES 8**

CRANBERRY-ALMOND TORTE

1 cup sugar
One 8-ounce can almond paste
1/4 cup (1/2 stick) unsalted butter, softened
3 large eggs
1 tablespoon vanilla extract
1/4 cup all-purpose flour
2 cups frozen cranberries (don't defrost them)

CRANBERRY DRIZZLE

One 11-ounce can frozen cranberry juice concentrate, defrosted
1/4 cup sugar
1 tablespoon cornstarch
1 tablespoon cold water
3 tablespoons amaretto or other almond-flavored liqueur

1. Preheat the oven to 350°F. Grease and flour a 9-inch springform pan.

2. To make the torte, in a food processor, process the sugar, almond paste, butter, eggs, and vanilla together until smooth. Transfer the batter to a bowl. Stir in the flour, then the still-frozen cranberries. Spoon into the prepared pan and bake until a cake tester inserted in the center comes out clean, 35 to 40 minutes.

3. Let cool on a wire rack for 15 minutes, then run a knife around the pan to loosen the torte. Remove the pan and let the torte cool completely.

4. To make the drizzle, combine the cranberry juice concentrate and sugar in a medium-size saucepan and bring to a boil. Stir together the cornstarch and cold water, then stir the mixture into the juice and let boil for 1 minute. Remove from the heat and stir in the amaretto.

5. To serve, slice the torte and pour a little drizzle over each slice. Store any leftover torte, covered, at room temperature for 4 to 5 days. Store the drizzle in the refrigerator for up to 1 week.

BBQ QUEEN
1

Orange Marmalade Bundt Cake

This Bundt cake is a simpler version of the famous cake from author Jan Karon's Mitford series of novels about the fictional North Carolina town. The secret? (Don't faint!) A doctored-up cake mix. This is delish. **SERVES 8 TO 12**

CAKE

One yellow cake mix with pudding

4 large eggs

1/2 cup vegetable oil, such as canola, corn, or light olive oil

1 cup orange juice

1 tablespoon grated orange zest

ORANGE SYRUP AND MARMALADE TOPPING

1/2 cup orange juice

1/4 cup sugar

One 12-ounce jar orange marmalade, melted and cooled

1/3 cup lowfat sour cream

3 cups whipped cream (about 1 1/2 cups heavy cream, whipped to firm peaks) or lowfat whipped topping

Threads of orange zest from 1 orange for garnish

1. Preheat the oven to 325°F. Generously grease a 12-cup tube or Bundt pan.

2. To make the cake, in a large bowl mix together the cake mix, eggs, oil, orange juice, and zest with an electric mixer until smooth. Pour into the prepared pan and bake until a cake tester inserted near the center comes out clean, 55 to 60 minutes. Set on a wire rack.

3. To make the topping, combine the orange juice and sugar in a small bowl, stirring until dissolved. Poke lots of holes in the top of the hot cake with a toothpick. Slowly pour the juice over the cake, making sure that it is absorbed. Let the cake cool completely, then loosen the sides with a knife and remove from the pan. Set on the rack again.

4. Spread the melted orange marmalade over the cake. Combine the sour cream and whipped cream and spread over the marmalade. Sprinkle the top with the orange zest. Refrigerate for at least 2 hours before serving. Store in the refrigerator, covered, for up to 3 days.

Grilled Pound Cake with Hot Fudge Ganache and Sweetened Berries

Pound cake is a delicious basic that can be served with fresh seasonal fruit or frozen fruit. Pair the cake and fruit with a favorite dessert sauce, such as lemon, vanilla, or chocolate, or a liqueur, and garnish with fresh lemon balm or spearmint leaves or citrus zest. Or make the whole thing into a sundae with ice cream or sorbet.

You can find prepared pound cake in the freezer or bakery section of most grocery stores or make your own from a mix or from scratch. SERVES 8

4 cups fresh seasonal berries, such as strawberries, blueberries, or raspberries
1/2 cup sugar, or to taste
1 pound cake
Hot Fudge Ganache (page 440)

1. About 30 minutes before serving, place the berries in a bowl and sprinkle with the sugar. This will bring out the juice in the berries.

2. Cut the pound cake into slices and toast on a clean grill over medium-high heat until grill marks appear, about 2 minutes per side. (Or toast in a toaster.) Serve the toasted pound cake with a spoonful of sweetened berries and a drizzle of ganache.

Rotisserie Pork Loin

Rotisserie pork loin is a great crowd-pleaser. It stays moist and juicy, it slices beautifully, and it tastes fabulous. And unlike the queens of yore, you don't need any minions (scullery maids, knife boys, wenches in general) to help you. The rotisserie does all the work, and you take all the credit. In about 3 hours, you have a spectacular entrée that is wonderful served with a complementary sauce, or with a green salad and a potato casserole (see pages 412–413).

Check the maximum weight that your rotisserie motor can handle, then buy your pork loin. Cook two at a time and plan for delicious leftovers. SERVES 6 TO 8

One 5- to 6- pound boneless pork loin roast
1 recipe Mustard-Mayo-Orange Slather (page 66)
1 recipe Spicy Orange Rub (page 51)

1. Brush the pork loin all over with the slather and sprinkle evenly with the rub. Let sit at room temperature for 15 minutes, until the slather feels tacky to the touch.

2. Set up your grill for rotisserie cooking (see page 33). Prepare a medium fire (around 350°F). Push the rotisserie rod through the center of the roast so that the meat is balanced, then place on the spit. Cover and cook until an instant-read meat thermometer inserted in the center registers 145°F for medium, 3 to 4 hours total. (If you like your pork more well done, aim for 155 to 165°F.) Let rest for 10 minutes before slicing and serving.

Crowning Glories

Rotisserie pork loin is dynamite served with a sauce, such as:

Fennel and Orange Drizzling Sauce *(page 73)*

The Doctor Is In Apricot-Bourbon Barbecue Sauce *(page 90; you can glaze the pork with this or serve it on the side)*

Raspberry-Jalapeño Barbecue Sauce *(page 90; you can glaze the pork with this or serve it on the side)*

Herb-Marinated Rotisserie Pork Loin: This is another way to go with pork loin, marinating it instead of using a slather and rub. We love this dish served with a complementary but different herb sauce, such as Thousand-Herb Sauce (page 192) or Chimichurri Sauce (page

346). To make the marinade, combine 2 fresh bay leaves or 1 teaspoon powdered bay leaf, 1 teaspoon dried thyme, 6 minced garlic cloves, the juice of 2 lemons, and 1/4 cup olive oil in a small bowl. Brush the mixture all over the loin. Cover with plastic wrap and refrigerate for at least 1 hour or overnight. Season with kosher or sea salt and freshly ground black pepper to taste, then cook on the rotisserie as directed above. **SERVES 6 TO 8**

Ancho and Chipotle-Rubbed Rotisserie Pork Loin: You can find ground chipotle and ancho chile in the grocery store under the McCormick label or buy them from your favorite spice emporium. In a small bowl, mix together 1 tablespoon ground chipotle chile, 1 tablespoon ground ancho chile, 1/4 cup grated onion, 1 tablespoon minced garlic, 2 tablespoons olive oil, 1 tablespoon ground cumin, 2 teaspoons coarse kosher or sea salt, and 1 teaspoon freshly ground black pepper. Wearing rubber gloves or using a rubber spatula, rub the paste all over the pork loin. Cover with plastic wrap and marinate in the refrigerator for at least 6 hours or overnight. Unwrap and cook on the rotisserie as directed above. **SERVES 6 TO 8**

Bourbon Pecan-Stuffed Rotisserie Pork Loin: The bourbon in the stuffing and marinade brings out the natural sweetness in the pork. We love this! (Because we're so sweet ourselves.) Have the butcher butterfly a 5- to 6-pound pork loin for you. To make the stuffing, finely snip (using kitchen shears) 1/2 cup dried apricots, 1/2 cup sweetened dried cranberries, and 1/2 cup sweetened dried pineapple into a medium-size bowl. Pour over 1 cup bourbon and let soak and soften for 1 hour, then stir in 1/2 cup finely chopped pecans. Drain the liquid from the stuffing, reserving it. Spread the stuffing over the surface of the pork loin, leaving a 1-inch border. Roll up and tie at 4-inch intervals with kitchen twine. Place the rolled pork loin in a large sealable plastic bag, pour in the reserved stuffing liquid, and turn to coat. Seal the bag and marinate in the refrigerator for at least 1 hour or overnight, turning occasionally. Season with kosher or sea salt and freshly ground black pepper to taste, then cook on the rotisserie as directed above. This is great served with The Doctor Is In Apricot-Bourbon Barbecue Sauce (page 90). **SERVES 6 TO 8**

Rotisserie Pork Loin Sandwiches: Depending on which rotisserie pork loin you make, you can enjoy the leftovers in one of the following sandwiches: sliced Rotisserie Pork Loin with sliced ripe tomatoes, pitted, drained, and sliced oil- or brine-cured Kalamata olives, arugula, and aioli (see pages 104–105 and 110) on country bread; shredded Ancho and Chipotle–Rubbed Rotisserie Pork Loin with assorted greens or *pico de gallo* and Chipotle Vinaigrette (page 86), rolled up in a flour tortilla; sliced Bourbon Pecan-Stuffed Rotisserie Pork Loin with shredded iceberg lettuce and The Doctor Is In Apricot-Bourbon Barbecue Sauce (page 90) on ciabatta. **SERVES AS MANY AS YOU HAVE LEFTOVERS FOR**

BBQ Babes

She's the Flower of the Flames Menu

Raspberry and Mustard–Glazed Pork Roast
Kiss of Smoke Beef Tenderloin Black Forest
Cola-Marinated Smoked Flank Steak

When she began barbecuing on the competition circuit in the mid-1980s, Karen Putman was one of the few women in the game. And she was a big winner. Her fellow competitors dubbed her "the Flower of the Flames." Her barbecue was and still is a force to be reckoned with, and we're proud to say she's one of the original 'Que Queens. She has won hundreds of barbecue and chef competition awards, national and international. Here are some of her greatest hits.

Raspberry and Mustard–Glazed Pork Roast

One of Karen's signature flavors is raspberry, combined here with orange juice and zest, spicy barbecue sauce, and whole-grain mustard to make a superb glaze that you can almost drink as an elixir—the true sign of a queenly sauce. SERVES 8

RASPBERRY AND MUSTARD GLAZE

1 1/2 cups spicy barbecue sauce of your choice
One 12-ounce bag individually frozen raspberries, defrosted
2 tablespoons grated orange zest
1/4 cup fresh orange juice (1 to 2 oranges)
1/4 cup whole-grain mustard

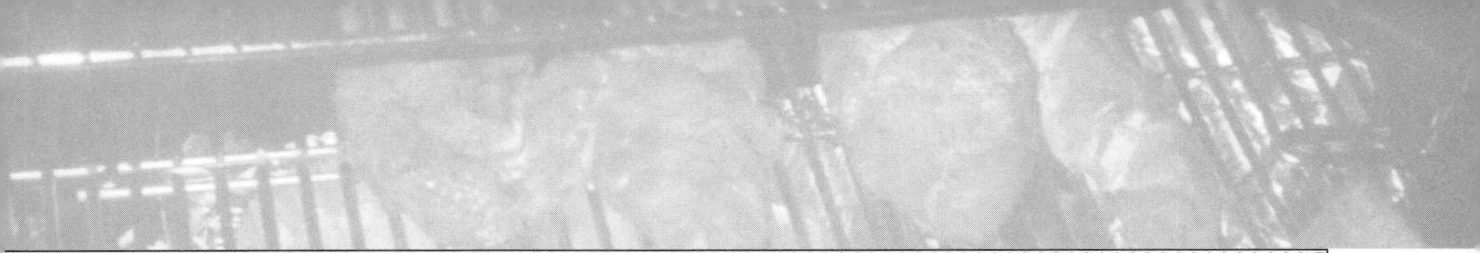

1 teaspoon finely grated fresh ginger (if using a microplane, you don't need to peel)

½ teaspoon fine kosher or sea salt

¼ teaspoon cayenne pepper

One 3½- to 4-pound boneless pork loin roast, tied

4 or 5 apple wood chunks (optional), soaked in water for at least 1 hour before grilling

1. To make the glaze, combine all the ingredients in a medium-size bowl. Divide in half, using one half for basting and reserving the other half for serving.

2. Prepare an indirect fire with a temperature of 250°F.

3. Place a wire rack 4 to 6 inches over a drip pan, then place the roast on the rack. Cover the grill, opening the vents slightly. Cook the roast for 45 minutes and turn. To maintain a constant temperature, add more charcoal and the apple wood chunks, if desired. Cover and continue to cook, basting the roast with the glaze every 10 minutes for the next 45 minutes of cooking. The roast is done when there is still a slight tinge of pink in the center and an instant-read meat thermometer inserted in the center registers 160 to 165°F.

4. Remove from the grill, wrap in plastic, and let stand for 15 minutes before slicing. Serve with the reserved glaze.

Kiss of Smoke Beef Tenderloin Black Forest

Chef Putman creates recipes all the time, and she often enters them in culinary contests, which she usually wins. In this one, she first sears the tenderloins over a hot fire, then transfers them to the indirect side of a grill to finish cooking and get that kiss of smoke. Her concoction for beef tenderloin is an elegant way to serve a crowd. Be sure to serve Decadent Garlic Mashed Potatoes (page 321) with this. Nothing else will do. SERVES 16

SUGGESTED WOOD: Cherry

One 16-ounce can pitted dark sweet cherries, drained
4 large cloves garlic, minced
1/2 cup dry red wine, such as a Burgundy or Cabernet Sauvignon
1/3 cup extra virgin olive oil
Two 5-pound beef tenderloins, trimmed of any fat and silverskin
Fine kosher or sea salt and freshly ground black pepper to taste

1. In a medium-size bowl, combine the cherries, garlic, wine, and olive oil. Cover and refrigerate overnight so the flavors will meld.

2. Prepare a hot indirect fire in a grill.

3. Split the tenderloins lengthwise, but not all the way through. Fill each with the cherry mixture and tie closed at 2-inch intervals with kitchen twine.

4. Grill the meat directly over the hot fire for 10 minutes per side, turning a quarter turn at a time. Move the tenderloins to the indirect side of the grill, cover, and grill until an instant-read meat thermometer inserted in the thickest part registers 120°F for medium-rare and 135°F for medium, 10 to 15 minutes. Slice and serve.

Cola-Marinated Smoked Flank Steak

Coca-Cola makes for a very southern marinade that is sometimes used to glaze smoked ham and other cuts of pork. Chef Putman shows her creativity by applying this to a beef flank steak, a cut that is usually grilled. SERVES 6 TO 8

SUGGESTED WOOD: Fruitwood, hickory, mesquite, oak, or maple

One 4- to 5-pound flank steak

COLA MARINADE

2 cups cola (Karen uses Coca-Cola)
1 cup vegetable oil
1 cup distilled white vinegar
3 cloves garlic, minced
Fine kosher or sea salt and freshly ground black pepper to taste

1. Place the meat in a shallow dish or sealable plastic bag.

2. To make the marinade, combine all the ingredients in a large bowl. Pour two-thirds of it over the meat. Reserve the rest for basting. (Keep refrigerated until ready to use.) Cover or seal and marinate in the refrigerator for at least 8 hours or overnight.

3. Prepare a 200°F fire in a smoker or grill.

4. Remove the meat from the marinade, discarding the marinade. Place in the smoker, cover, and smoke for 6 to 7 hours, basting with the reserved marinade every 30 minutes after the first hour of cooking. The meat is done when it is tender and an instant-read meat thermometer inserted in the thickest part registers about 180°F. Slice on the diagonal and serve.

Smoked Pork Loin

Instead of a safe for our crown jewels, we regard the freezer as the true repository of our culinary gems. We like to buy pork loin on sale, then stow it in the freezer to become a frozen asset. There are so many delicious ways to cook a pork loin on the grill or in the smoker. You can brush on a mustard slather, then sprinkle with a rub, or go for a more basic treatment, as we suggest here.

When a family in Judith's neighborhood was undergoing a medical crisis, Judith smoked a large pork loin and made it the centerpiece of a dinner she brought over to them. The report back was that nary a speck was left over the next day. People in distress have to eat, and what better time to have the food be really, really good? SERVES 8 TO 10

SUGGESTED WOOD: **Apple, cherry, hickory, oak, or a combination**

One 5- to 6-pound boneless pork loin roast
1/4 cup olive oil
3 tablespoons freshly ground black pepper
1 tablespoon garlic salt
2 cups apple juice

1. Brush the pork with the olive oil, then sprinkle with the pepper and garlic salt. Set aside for 15 minutes.

2. Prepare an indirect fire in a smoker.

3. Cover and smoke the pork loin at 225 to 250°F for about 30 minutes per pound. After half an hour, start basting with the apple juice every 30 minutes. The pork loin is done when an instant-read meat thermometer inserted in the center registers 145°F, 3 to 3 1/2 hours. Let rest for 15 minutes, then slice and serve.

Crowning Glories

Smoked pork loin is delicious served with:

Honeyed Barbecue Sauce *(page 90; glaze the pork with this or serve it on the side)*

Smoked (or Grilled) Onion Marmalade *(page 141)*

Pineapple-Ginger Salsa *(page 414)*

Slathered and Rubbed Smoked Pork Loin: You can smoke pork loin using the same preparation as for Rotisserie Pork Loin (page 398). Try slathering a 5- to 6-pound boneless pork roast with Mustard-Mayo-Orange Slather (page 66), then sprinkling on Spicy Orange Rub (page 51). Let sit for at least 15 minutes, until the surface feels tacky to the touch. Place the roast in a disposable aluminum pan and smoke as directed above. A great finishing touch would be Fennel and Orange Drizzling Sauce (page 73). **SERVES 8 TO 10**

Tuscan-Style Porchetta: When Judith and her family went to Tuscany, this rolled and tied roast with a savory filling was part of the Fourth of July feast they enjoyed outdoors. In Tuscany, you can buy roasted porchetta—with its thick collar of fat—at market stalls or butcher shops. We lightened it up a little and smoked instead of roasted it, so you won't miss that collar of fat, we promise! Have your butcher butterfly a 5- to 6-pound boneless pork roast. Combine 2 cups peeled garlic cloves and 1/2 cup olive oil in a baking dish and bake at 350°F until softened, 30 to 40 minutes. Let cool. In a food processor, puree 1 bunch fresh Italian parsley with the roasted garlic, any olive oil remaining in the pan, and the juice of 1 lemon. Spread three-quarters of the paste over the surface of the pork loin, then sprinkle with 1 1/2 teaspoons freshly ground black pepper, 1 teaspoon fine kosher or sea salt, and 1 1/2 teaspoons fennel seeds. Roll up from a long side and tie with kitchen twine at intervals. Slather the remaining paste over the rolled loin, place in a disposable aluminum pan, and smoke as directed above. **SERVES 8 TO 10**

BBQ Queens' Choucroute Garnie: Some of Karen's family is from Yugoslavia and Judith's from Germany, so this dish is soul food to us. Use smoked pork loin as the centerpiece of a hearty sauerkraut supper with all the trimmings. It's a great recipe to serve a crowd on a cold night. Preheat the oven to 350°F. In a large roasting pan, place a 5- to 6-pound pork loin smoked as described above, 2 pounds drained deli or freshly made sauerkraut (not canned), 2 tablespoons juniper berries, 2 tablespoons caraway seeds, 1 cup dry white wine, 1 cup chicken broth, 4 large or 8 small bratwurst sausage, and 1 pound smoked or Polish link sausage. Cover and braise for 1 hour. Check periodically, adding more wine and broth, if necessary. Serve hot, with whole-grain mustard and freshly grated horseradish to pass at the table. **SERVES 10 TO 12**

Not on the Discovery Channel: Smoke-Roasting

Sometimes necessity really is the mother of invention.

When the BBQ Queens traveled far to do a cooking class at a school that shall remain nameless, we realized that only one inept person—who took 15 minutes to chop an onion—was going to help us prepare the four-course dinner. The school also had no smoker (which they assured us they had). Luckily, we had brought a small one with us. But that meant we couldn't slow smoke a pork roast and a potato dish *and* get everything else ready.

First, shock set in, then momentary panic. Finally, we talked ourselves down from the ledge and knew we had to pull this off some way. That's when we invented our version of smoke-roasting—although we found out later that lots of barbecuers, such as Paul Kirk, had come to the technique under similar circumstances.

Smoke-roasting is a combination of low and slow smoking (at 225 to 250°F) and hot and fast roasting (at 450°F). You use both your smoker and your oven. You can either smoke first and roast later, or the opposite. Your food will be a little crispier if you smoke first and roast later (which we prefer), a little softer if you roast and then smoke. What you get is roasted food with a touch of caramelization and a smoky aroma and flavor. Heavenly!

Smoke-roasting works with any dish that you would just roast, namely pork or beef roasts, whole chickens or turkeys, or vegetable dishes.

Smoke-Roasted Pork Loin with Herbed Pear Stuffing

We adapted one of our own recipes from *Easy Grilling & Simple Smoking* (Pig Out Publications, 1997) for this dish. Have your butcher butterfly the roast. Smoking it takes about 2 hours; smoke-roasting saves you a sometimes crucial half-hour. But the big benefit is the flavor and texture. SERVES 6 TO 8

SUGGESTED WOOD: Apple or cherry

HERBED PEAR STUFFING

2 tablespoons unsalted butter
4 ripe but firm pears, peeled, cored, and chopped
1 medium-size yellow onion, diced
4 stalks celery, diced
3 sprigs fresh tarragon, chopped
1 tablespoon chopped fresh oregano
1 tablespoon chopped fresh rosemary
1/2 teaspoon freshly grated nutmeg
1/2 teaspoon ground allspice
4 slices homemade or good-quality store-bought bread, crumbled

One 3- to 4-pound boneless pork loin roast, butterflied
1/2 teaspoon fine kosher or sea salt, or more to taste
Ground white pepper to taste
2 tablespoons freshly ground black pepper
2 teaspoons garlic salt
3 cups apple juice
1 or 2 yellow onions, cut in half

1. Prepare an indirect fire in a smoker.
2. To make the stuffing, melt the butter in a large skillet over medium heat. Add the pears, onion, celery, herbs, and spices and cook, stirring often, until the onion is

translucent, 6 to 8 minutes. Stir in enough of the bread crumbs to bind the mixture together, then remove from the heat.

3. Lay the butterflied pork loin on a work surface and season with the salt and white pepper. Spread the stuffing over the meat. Roll up the loin, starting with a long side. Tie the roll together at intervals with kitchen twine. Sprinkle with the black pepper and garlic salt. Place the tied and rolled pork loin in a disposable aluminum pan with 2 cups of the apple juice and the onion halves.

4. Smoke at 225 to 250°F, with the lid closed, for 1 hour. Meanwhile, preheat the oven to 400°F.

5. Transfer the roast to the oven and baste with the remaining 1 cup apple juice. Cook until an instant-read meat thermometer inserted in the center registers 155°F, about 30 minutes. Remove from the oven. Let sit for 10 minutes before slicing and serving.

Smoke-Roasted Potatoes with Garlic and Rosemary

This is a splendid way to update regular roasted potatoes with a kiss of smoke. SERVES 6

3 large baking potatoes, peeled and quartered
3 large sweet potatoes, peeled and quartered
10 large cloves garlic, peeled
1/2 cup olive oil
2 tablespoons fresh rosemary leaves
Fine kosher or sea salt and freshly ground black pepper to taste

1. Prepare an indirect fire in a smoker.

2. In a large disposable aluminum pan, combine the potatoes and garlic. Drizzle with the olive oil and toss to blend. Sprinkle with the rosemary, season with salt and pepper, and toss again. Smoke at 225 to 250°F, with the lid closed, for 1 hour. Meanwhile, preheat the oven to 400°F.

3. Toss the potatoes again, then transfer to the oven and finish cooking until the potatoes are fork tender, about 30 minutes. Serve hot.

Smoked Pork Butt

Pork butt is a large, usually boneless (the shoulder blade is removed), somewhat cylindrical piece of meat from the upper shoulder of a hog. Pork butt is also sold as Boston butt. A pork butt weighs anywhere from 3½ to 9 pounds, and it's muscular, riddled with fat, and chewy, chewy, chewy. That is, until you slow smoke it. Then it's fabulous—smoky, moist, meltingly tender, and full of flavor. The same goes for the pork shoulder blade roast (bone-in). It takes longer to smoke but is very tasty and often cheap to buy.

You can either slice or pull apart a slow-smoked pork butt to serve as is, with a sauce, or piled on bread, Carolina-style, with a vinegary coleslaw on top—the Piggy Sandwich (page 411). It's where the bun meets the butt, and it's delicious.

The BBQ Queens recommend smoking two smaller pork butts, because that will save you some time. Two 3½-pound pork butts will still take about 8 hours to slow smoke, but a 7-pound pork butt could take 10 to 12 hours. We love to use apple, hickory, oak, pecan, or a combination of these woods and slow smoke at a constant temperature of 225 to 250°F.

We slather our pork butts with a mustard mixture, sprinkle on a zesty rub, and then smoke for a good 8 hours, maybe longer, depending on the weather. We baste occasionally with apple juice. When it's done, people just salivate as we pull it apart. The charred exterior, tender pink interior, and delicious aroma are irresistible. Pork butt is a great smoked meat to serve a crowd.

Hoisin sauce is wonderful slathered all over pork butt. In the spring and summer, when fresh herbs are plentiful, be sure to chop some and add to whatever slather you plan to use.

Make sure you save any trimmings from your smoked pork butt. If necessary, freeze them to use later in heavenly BBQ Queens' Barbecued Beans (page 107). SERVES 12

SUGGESTED WOOD: Apple, pecan, oak, or hickory, or a combination

Two 3½-pound boneless pork butts
Mustard-Mayo Slather (page 66)
BBQ Queens' All-Purpose Rub (page 49)
2 cups apple juice

1. Brush the pork butts with the slather, then sprinkle with the rub. Set aside for 15 minutes, until the surface of the meat is tacky to the touch.

2. Prepare an indirect fire in a smoker.

3. Cover and smoke the pork butts at 225 to 250°F. After 4 hours, start basting with apple juice every 30 minutes. The butts are done when you can insert a grill fork into the meat and twist, about 4 hours more. An instant-read meat thermometer inserted in the center should register 165°F. Pull the meat apart while it is still hot, arrange on a platter, and serve.

Crowning Glories

Barbecued pork butt is traditionally served piled on a bun and topped with a vinegary coleslaw, or serve with:

BBQ Queens' Barbecued Beans *(page 107)*

BBQ Queens' Smoked Potato Casserole *(page 153)*

Smoky Barbecue Sauce *(page 90)*

Spicy Orange Barbecued Pork Butt: Traditional barbecued pork butt, a staple category at barbecue competitions, is nothing short of wonderful. But if you prepare it a lot, sometimes you get a hankerin' for pork butt a different way. This is it. Use Mustard-Mayo-Orange Slather (page 66) and sprinkle the pork butts with Spicy Orange Rub (page 51). Slow smoke as directed above, then accompany with Fennel and Orange Drizzling Sauce (page 73). **SERVES 12**

Butts in a Bag: We couldn't resist this. The name alone made us chuckle. We got this unusual but folksy recipe from Ardie Davis, known on the barbecue circuit as Remus Powers, Ph.B. Like beer can chicken, this recipe has developed a following, and for good reason—it works! The only extras you need, in addition to our basic slow-smoked pork butts, are 4 medium-size brown paper grocery bags, about the size for a small order of groceries. Slather and rub the 2 pork butts as directed above with the slather and rub of your choice, then smoke them for 4 hours. Slide each pork butt into a grocery bag, then double-bag it by sliding the open end of the bag into a second grocery bag. The idea is to totally enclose the pork butt. Place the bagged butts in the smoker and continue to smoke, without basting, for another 4 hours, until the meat is tender. (Don't worry, the bags won't burn at 250°F. Don't try this, though, if you use a kamado-style smoker, which smokes foods at a higher heat.) Remove the bags, pull apart the meat, and serve this moister, even more delicious pork butt. **SERVES 12**

Piggy Sandwich: In the Carolinas, barbecued pork sandwiches are an art form and one of the best ways to enjoy slow-smoked pork butt. Finely chop some of the hot pork butt, mix it with a little barbecue sauce, if you like, and pile some of the meat on the bottom of a toasted bun. Top with a vinegar-based coleslaw, such as Layered Vinegar Slaw (page 80), crown with the top of the bun, and you're in hog heaven! **SERVES 1**

Double-Smoked Ham

Yes, we know that precooked ham is smoked once already. And we know you shouldn't experiment with new dishes on dinner guests—or cooking school students. But we found out how wonderful a double-smoked ham tastes while experimenting, er, we mean teaching a class, in Indiana.

You can double-smoke two different kinds of ham. The easiest one to use is a good-quality, presliced bone-in ham. Because it is presliced, the smoke penetrates farther into the meat in a shorter amount of time—about an hour is just fine—even tented with aluminum foil in a stovetop smoker (see page 34). You don't want to smoke a sliced ham for very long, or it will dry out.

But if you want a mahogany-colored ham with lots of smoke and have some time on your hands, don't buy the spiral cut. Instead, purchase either a country cured whole ham, such as a Smithfield, or a precooked whole ham, such as a Hormel Cure 81. You need the covering on the outside of the ham so that the inner meat doesn't dry out. You'll be able to smoke this whole ham for anywhere from 2 to 10 hours, depending on your desire for smokiness.

You don't even need a glaze on a double-smoked ham, but this one is fairly simple. SERVES 8 TO 10

SUGGESTED WOOD: Apple, hickory, pecan, or oak, or a combination

MUSTARD-APRICOT GLAZE

2 cups apricot preserves
2 1/2 teaspoons dry mustard
1 1/2 tablespoons cider vinegar

One 5- to 7-pound bone-in precooked or smoked ham (shank or butt)
20 whole cloves

1. To make the glaze, combine all the ingredients in a small bowl.

Potato Casseroles with a Royal Touch

Having a number of rich and hearty potato casseroles in your culinary arsenal is as important as knowing the four queen waves (see page 224). Whether you're grilling or smoking (or broiling, frying, poaching, or baking) the main part of your dinner, a potato casserole always comes in handy. You can feed vegetarians, children, the elderly, terminally hungry adolescent boys, picky eaters, those who need fattening up, and those who don't. Here are two of the BBQ Queens' favorites.

Potato Gratin with White Cheddar Cheese

This comes from our culinary instructor and friend Ann Lund, author of her self-published *Dining in Style*. We first tried this at a Somerset Vineyard dinner in Kansas (yes, you read that right). The Burgundy-style wines were wonderful, and one of the stars of the gourmet potluck gathering was this gratin. In company, we were both circumspect and only ate a small square each. At home, we would have cut ourselves a generous slab! We use a mandoline to cut the potatoes. This gratin takes about 2 hours to bake, but it's well worth the time and energy. Don't plan on any leftovers.

SERVES 12 TO 16

- 3 cups heavy cream
- 3/4 cup finely chopped shallot
- 2 teaspoons chopped fresh rosemary
- 2 teaspoons kosher or sea salt
- 3/4 teaspoon freshly ground black pepper
- 4 pounds russet potatoes, peeled and sliced 1/4 inch thick
- 2 cups finely shredded sharp white cheddar cheese

1. Preheat the oven to 375°F. Butter a 13 x 9-inch baking dish.

2. Pour the cream into a microwave-safe bowl and heat on high for 2 minutes. Or pour into a medium-size saucepan and warm over medium heat. Remove from the heat and stir in the shallot, rosemary, salt, and pepper. Cover and let infuse for 30 minutes.

3. Layer half the potato slices in the prepared baking dish, overlapping them to fit. Sprinkle with three-quarters of the cheese. Arrange the remaining potatoes on top of the cheese and pour the cream mixture over. Sprinkle with the remaining cheese.

4. Cover with aluminum foil and bake for 1 hour. Remove the foil and bake until the top is golden and bubbling, about 45 minutes. Let cool for 10 minutes before cutting into squares.

Oven-Roasted Saffron Potatoes

We prefer new or red potatoes for the color of their skins paired with the wonderful tinge of yellow from the saffron. Serve these amazingly aromatic potatoes with grilled pork, lamb, or fish. SERVES 8

1 large pinch of saffron threads (about 1/2 teaspoon)
2 cups chicken broth
16 small new or red potatoes, cut in half
1 tablespoon unsalted butter, melted
Fine kosher or sea salt and cracked black peppercorns to taste

1. Preheat the oven to 400°F. Oil a large baking dish.

2. Carefully toast the saffron in a small saucepan over high heat for 1 minute. Immediately add the broth, stir to blend, and bring to a simmer.

3. In a large bowl, toss the potatoes with the melted butter and season with salt and cracked pepper. Arrange in the prepared dish and pour the saffron broth over all. Roast, turning the potatoes once, until they are tender and the broth has reduced to a rich glaze, 20 to 30 minutes. Serve immediately.

2. Coat the ham with the glaze, reserving any leftover glaze. Stud the ham with the cloves and let stand for 1 hour to marinate.

3. Meanwhile, prepare an indirect fire in a smoker.

4. Put the ham in a disposable aluminum pan and place in the smoker. Cover and smoke at 225 to 250°F. Baste with additional glaze and pan juices after the first hour of smoking. Continue to smoke until the ham is bronzed and reaches the desired smokiness. A spiral-cut ham will take at least 1 hour or up to 2 hours without drying out. A whole ham will take 2 to 8 hours. Remove from the smoker and serve.

Crowning Glories

Double-smoked ham is out of this world served with:

Layered Vinegar Slaw *(page 80)*

Potato Gratin with White Cheddar Cheese *(page 412)*

Texas-Style Pinto Beans *(page 106)*

Double-Smoked Ham with Pineapple-Ginger Salsa: The smoky ham is so good you'll dice it for soup, put it in pasta, and make decadent hoagie sandwiches with it. Or you can serve it sliced with a delicious condiment on the side, such as this salsa. Combine the following ingredients in a food processor: 2 cups peeled, cored, and chopped fresh pineapple; 3 tablespoons peeled and chopped fresh ginger; 1/4 cup firmly packed light brown sugar; and 1/4 cup fresh lime juice (4 to 5 limes). (This salsa will keep in the refrigerator for up to 1 week.) Smoke the ham as directed above and serve with the salsa. **SERVES 8 TO 10**

Karen's Double-Smoked Ham Salad Sandwiches: Karen has been making ham salad sandwiches for years, and her coworkers Mary Ann Duckers and Dee Barwick proclaim them the best. When Judith heard this, she quizzed Karen on what she did to make them so special. Because Karen doesn't use a recipe, it took several questions to figure out the secret: she added the hard-boiled eggs while still warm. To make the ham salad, hard-boil 4 or 5 large eggs (see page 378). While the eggs are cooling a bit, process several chunks of double-smoked ham in a food processor. You need about 2 cups ground ham. Add 1/4 cup mayonnaise, 2 tablespoons Dijon mustard, and 2 tablespoons fresh lemon juice and pulse. Peel the eggs while still warm and put them in the food processor whole. Pulse to combine. Spread the slightly warm ham salad on 4 slices of fresh sourdough bread, top with 4 more bread slices, and enjoy. **SERVES 4**

Rise and Shine: Breakfast in the Great Outdoors

You should have a breakfast picnic at least once in your life, preferably on a cool and sunny May morning before the bugs have come to life again. A breakfast outdoors is perfect for a family gathering. The kids can run around, and the adults can get breakfast on the grill and the table.

Bring everything (freshly brewed coffee in a large thermos, for example) to a park, or relax in your own backyard, with the coffeemaker perking in the kitchen. Scramble the eggs or sauté the hash in a large greased skillet over a medium-hot fire in the grill, Girl Scout style.

Double-Smoked Ham *(page 411)*
Scrambled eggs
Smoked Trout Benedict with Confetti Hash *(page 273)*
Campfire Skillet Scones (recipe follows) with butter, jams, and jellies
Breakfast S'mores (recipe follows)

Campfire Skillet Scones

Portable and pleasing, these scones are adapted from a recipe in Judith's *Prairie Home Breads* (The Harvard Common Press, 2001). Her first experience with campfire cooking was during Girl Scout weekends at Camp Butterworth in Loveland, Ohio. If you're camping, simply place the dry ingredients in a sealable plastic bag, then mix up the batter right before you bake the scones. The key is a large, seasoned cast-iron skillet.

MAKES 8 SCONES

2 cups all-purpose flour

2 tablespoons sugar

2 $^1/_2$ teaspoons baking powder

1 teaspoon fine kosher or sea salt

2 teaspoons cream of tartar

3 tablespoons instant nonfat dry milk

6 tablespoons ($^3/_4$ stick) unsalted butter, cut into small pieces

$^1/_4$ cup water

1 large egg, lightly beaten

1. Prepare a medium-hot campfire or grill fire. Grease a well-seasoned 12-inch cast-iron skillet. In a medium-size bowl, combine the dry ingredients. With your fingertips, work in the butter until the mixture resembles coarse crumbs. Stir in the water and egg until a dough forms.

2. Turn the dough out onto a floured work surface. Flour your hands and pat or press the dough into an 8-inch round about $^1/_2$ inch thick. Cut the round into 8 wedges and arrange the wedges about $^1/_2$ inch apart in the skillet.

3. Place the pan over the campfire or grill fire and cook until the scones have risen and are browned on top, 10 to 15 minutes. Serve warm.

Breakfast S'mores

Send the kids to look for suitable twigs. Then thread a piece of fruit or two (try fresh banana or pineapple chunks, whole firm strawberries, or large peach or nectarine slices), along with a marshmallow, onto each twig and roast over the grill or campfire until the marshmallow gets squishy. Eat right away.

A Little Lamb

Some people still need their arms twisted to try lamb. If you're one of those (and even if you're not), read on. Gone are the days when older mutton was dressed as younger lamb, with a stronger flavor than we really liked. Sometimes the only lamb available was imported, frozen, from New Zealand. Today you can often get delicious, tender lamb that is raised locally. It's lighter in color, finer in flavor, and not at all strong. When paired with garlic, herbs, dry wines, and other seasonings, lamb is one of the BBQ Queens' favorite meats to grill or smoke. We love grilled butterflied leg of lamb and those thin little lamb chops cooked over a hot, hot, hot fire.

There are two tricks to achieving great-tasting lamb. One is to trim off as much of the hard white fat as you can, because this can contribute a stronger flavor than you might like. The second is to grill or rotisserie cook lamb to a medium doneness at most. Well-done lamb on the grill or rotisserie can be dry and strong-flavored. (By contrast, slow-smoked lamb is delicious well done. The smoke counteracts the stronger well-done flavor, and the longer, slower cooking time results in a very tender and juicy meat.)

One reason to eat more lamb—from chops to burgers to skewers to racks to leg cuts—is that there is so much you can do with it on the grill, smoker, or rotisserie. For the grill, we recommend smaller, more tender cuts, such as chops, lamb loin, rack of lamb, or steaks (or cubes of meat destined for skewers) cut from the leg. For the outdoor smoker, we recommend larger cuts of meat that benefit from long, slow cooking, such as boneless butterflied or bone-in leg of lamb, rack of lamb, or lamb shoulder. And for the rotisserie, a boneless butterflied leg of lamb is just perfect.

We hope that we've piqued your interest in baaaaarbecued lamb, and we encourage you to experiment with several of our recipes in this chapter.

Grilled Lamb Chops 420

Lamb Chops with Chiles and Mint 421

Lamb Chops with Rosemary, Garlic, and Lemon Baste 421

Spring Grill Platter with Aioli 421

Grilled Rack of Lamb 422

Rosemary Pesto Rack of Lamb 423

Grilled Marinated Rack of Lamb with Apricot and Cognac-Cabernet Sauce 423

Baaaaarbecued Rack of Lamb 423

FOUR SEASONS OF RELISH

Winter Blood Orange, Fennel, and Black Olive Relish 424

Springtime Strawberry, Toasted Almond, and Spinach Relish 425

Summer Tomato, Pine Nut, and Caper Relish 425

Autumn Roasted Red Pepper and Cannellini Bean Relish 426

Grilled Lamb Skewers 427

Mediterranean-Rubbed Lamb Kabobs with Lemon Butter Drizzle 428

Sambar-Spiced South Indian Lamb Kabobs with Tomato, Garlic, and Chile Chutney 428

Tapas-Style Lamb Brochettes 428

Grilled Leg of Lamb 429

Simple Stuffed Leg of Lamb 430

Rustic Spinach Pesto–Stuffed Leg of Lamb 430

Grilled Lamb, Pear, and Pistou Salad 430

Rotisserie Leg of Lamb 431

Rotisserie Leg of Lamb with Smoked Ratatouille 432

Pasta Salad with Rotisserie Lamb and Eggplant 432

Rotisserie Lamb Sandwiches with Matchstick Vegetables and Tzatziki 433

BBQ BABES: SHE CONDUCTS A ROTISSERIE SMEAR CAMPAIGN MENU

Garlic-Marinated Rolled Leg of Lamb 434

Smear of Your Choice: Sweet Moroccan Spice Paste, Santa Fe Herb Paste, or Mediterranean Herb Paste 435

Sweet-Hot Mustard-Glazed Salmon 437

Smoked Leg of Lamb 438

Smoked Butterflied Leg of Lamb Pinot Noir 438

Tandoori-Marinated Smoked Butterflied Leg of Lamb 439

BBQ Queens' Smoked Stuffed Leg of Lamb 439

EASY AS 1-2-3 ICE CREAMS AND SORBETS

Toasted Coconut Ice Cream with Hot Fudge Ganache and Toasted Pecans 440

Fresh Peach Crumble Ice Cream 441

Pineapple Sorbet in Grilled Pineapple Rings 442

Grilled Lamb Chops

Succulently thin baby lamb chops, grilled in the Roman *scottadito* (to scorch the fingers) way, are best when they're treated in the simplest manner. Bone-in chops cut from either the shoulder or the loin work well in this dish. Flatten the meat first (as you would for boneless, skinless chicken breasts; see page 191) with the side of a saucer or the flat side of a chef's knife. Don't try to flatten the bones; just leave them be. Then give the chops a touch of olive oil, a sprinkling of fresh rosemary, and the high heat of the grill. You want the chops seared and somewhat charred on the outside yet moist and tender inside. In this case, flare-ups from the olive oil are your friend!

These chops get done so quickly that you'll want to have everything else prepared and ready to go. Serve them, rustic style, on a platter garnished with lemon wedges. SERVES 4

12 thin lamb chops, cut from the shoulder or loin, pounded to a 1/2-inch thickness

1/4 cup olive oil

2 teaspoons fresh rosemary leaves

Coarse kosher or sea salt and coarsely ground black pepper to taste

Lemon wedges for garnish

1. Place the lamb chops in a single layer in a baking dish or on a baking sheet. Drizzle with the olive oil and turn to coat each chop. Sprinkle the rosemary over the chops, then marinate for 15 to 30 minutes at room temperature.

2. Prepare a hot fire in a grill.

3. When the coals are at their hottest, season the chops with salt and pepper. Remove from the marinade and place on the grill rack. As the olive oil drips onto the coals, you will have flare-ups, but that's good. The flames will rise up for several seconds, then die down, giving your chops a bit of char. (Keep a spray bottle of water nearby just in case things get out of hand.) Cook the chops for 1 to 2 minutes per side, until definite grill marks appear, for medium-rare. Serve on a platter with lemon wedges.

Crowning Glories

Bring these babies forth topped with your choice of:

Smoked Chile Beurre Blanc *(page 99)*

Raspberry Beurre Blanc *(page 101)*

Chimichurri Sauce *(page 346)*

Lamb Chops with Chiles and Mint: A fresh-tasting chile and mint paste flavors the lamb before grilling. In a bowl, using a fork, make a paste of 2 minced garlic cloves, the juice of 1/2 lemon, 2 seeded and minced small hot chiles, 1/2 cup chopped fresh mint, 1/2 cup olive oil, and kosher or sea salt and freshly ground black pepper to taste. Spread the paste over 12 thin lamb chops pounded to a 1/2-inch thickness. Marinate at room temperature for 15 to 30 minutes, then grill as directed above. **SERVES 4**

Lamb Chops with Rosemary, Garlic, and Lemon Baste: Spread Rosemary, Garlic, and Lemon Baste (page 68) over 12 thin lamb chops pounded to a 1/2-inch thickness. Marinate at room temperature for 15 to 30 minutes, then grill as directed above. **SERVES 4**

Spring Grill Platter with Aioli: We like aioli, that wonderful garlicky mayonnaise, on just about everything. And we like to experiment with riffs on the traditional wintertime Provençal aioli platter of cooked salt cod and roasted vegetables. The virtues of an updated aioli platter are that it looks appealingly rustic, tastes great, and is perfect for casual entertaining. Make 1 recipe Rustic Aioli (page 104) ahead of time and keep covered in the refrigerator. Drizzle fingerling or new potatoes with olive oil and sprinkle with kosher or sea salt and freshly ground black pepper to taste. Roast in a 400°F oven until tender, 35 to 40 minutes, then keep warm. Grill 12 thin lamb chops pounded to a 1/2-inch thickness as directed above. Prepare 1 recipe Grilled Asparagus (page 117) at the same time. Heap the lamb chops in the middle of a platter, then surround them with the asparagus, roasted potatoes, and pitted and drained oil- or brine-cured Niçoise or Kalamata olives. Serve the aioli on the side. **SERVES 4**

Grilled Rack of Lamb

If you love rack of lamb roasted, you'll really love it grilled. The key is a medium-hot fire, turning the lamb every 15 minutes, and cooking it medium-rare. Serve it with Mustard-Cornichon Beurre Blanc (page 100), and you'll be in heaven.

For the mildest flavor, buy the best and youngest lamb you can find. Today's lamb is grain-fed, which gives it great flavor and texture. Naturally tender, lamb should have a deep pinkish red to a dull brick red color, and the fat should be hard, white, and waxy.

Have the butcher remove the chine bone and attached feather bones from the racks and trim the fat and tissue from the rib bones, a process known as "frenching the bones." To french the bones yourself, take a sharp boning or paring knife and trim the meat back from the bones about 1 inch down the rib.

When you are served rack of lamb in a restaurant, the bones usually have frilly paper "hats" on the ends. You can buy these "chop frills" in gourmet shops, but the lamb is just as good without them.

SERVES 4 TO 6

4 racks of lamb (about 1½ pounds each), trimmed of fat and frenched
Olive oil
Coarse kosher or sea salt and ground white pepper to taste

1. Prepare a medium-hot fire in a grill.
2. Rub the lamb with olive oil, then season with salt and white pepper.
3. Grill the lamb, with the lid down and turning every 15 minutes, until an instant-read meat thermometer inserted in the thickest part registers 135 to 140°F for medium-rare, about 45 minutes. Transfer to a cutting board and let rest for 10 minutes before cutting into chops and serving.

Crowning Glories

Serve your racks with:

Basil Oil Mashed Potatoes *(page 258)*
Peppercorn Beurre Blanc *(page 102)*
Pistachio-Pomegranate Sauce *(page 96)*

Rosemary Pesto Rack of Lamb: When it's going to be roasted, rack of lamb usually gets some kind of mustard or herb paste slathered on it. That's not practical when you grill it, as the paste falls off when you turn the lamb. But Rosemary Pesto (page 62) works well. Slather it all over each rack of lamb and marinate, covered, in the refrigerator for at least 4 hours or up to 12 hours. Then grill as directed above and serve with Roasted Red Pepper Sauce (page 94). **SERVES 4 TO 6**

Grilled Marinated Rack of Lamb with Apricot and Cognac-Cabernet Sauce: Luscious! Use the demi-glace concentrate you can buy at gourmet shops or better grocery stores and reconstitute it, or substitute good-quality chicken broth. In a medium-size bowl, whisk together 2 cups olive oil, 1/2 cup chopped garlic (that's not a typo!), 10 sprigs fresh thyme, 6 sprigs fresh rosemary, and 1 tablespoon cracked black peppercorns. Place the lamb in a baking pan large enough to hold it and drizzle the marinade over. Cover and refrigerate, turning several times, for at least 4 hours or up to 12 hours. When ready to grill, remove the lamb from the marinade and pat dry. While the lamb is grilling as directed above, make the sauce by combining 1 cup Cabernet Sauvignon, 6 sprigs fresh thyme, 3 sprigs fresh rosemary, 3 finely chopped shallots, and 5 minced garlic cloves in a medium-size saucepan over high heat. Bring to a boil and let continue to boil until reduced to 1/3 cup, about 10 minutes. (Go out and turn the lamb, then come back in.) Remove the herb sprigs and whisk in 1 1/2 cups reconstituted demi-glace and 1/3 cup apricot preserves until smooth. Keep at a simmer. Right before serving, whisk in 1 tablespoon cognac and 2 tablespoons unsalted butter until the butter melts. Serve the racks of lamb napped with the sauce. Pass the rest of the sauce at the table. **SERVES 4 TO 6**

Baaaaarbecued Rack of Lamb: Rack of lamb is most often roasted or grilled, but you can also slow smoke it. Set up an indirect fire in your grill (see pages 10–12), using the wood of your choice (we like apple, pecan, or hickory with lamb). Paint the lamb with a mustard slather (see page 66) and sprinkle with garlic salt and lemon pepper seasoning. Place the lamb on your grill or smoker. Cook, with the lid down, at 250 to 300°F until an instant-read meat thermometer inserted in the thickest part registers 135 to 140°F for medium-rare, 2 to 3 hours. Let rest for 15 minutes before serving. **SERVES 4 TO 6**

Four Seasons of Relish

Relish is a wonderful accompaniment to simply grilled fish, chicken, pork, beef, or lamb and can be tailored to what's available seasonally. A relish is composed of fruit and/or vegetables, oil, and seasonings, and is uncooked. Here are four recipes to whet your appetite and grace your plate.

Winter Blood Orange, Fennel, and Black Olive Relish

Blood oranges, which are smaller, more reddish orange, and slightly more puckery than other varieties, come on the market in January and February. Grab some up to make this relish. Before sectioning the oranges, grate the rind into a freezer bag to save for other dishes. SERVES 4

4 blood oranges, peeled and sectioned

1 fennel bulb, trimmed, quartered, cored, and thinly sliced

1 medium-size red onion, thinly sliced and separated into rings

1/2 cup pitted oil- or brine-cured black olives, such as Gaeta or Kalamata, drained

1/2 cup extra virgin olive oil

Fine kosher or sea salt and freshly ground black pepper to taste

In a medium-size bowl, combine the orange sections, fennel, onion, and olives. Drizzle with olive oil, season with salt and pepper, and stir to blend. This is best served the same day at room temperature.

Springtime Strawberry, Toasted Almond, and Spinach Relish

Use tender baby spinach and juicy sweet strawberries. SERVES 4

- **1 cup fresh strawberries, hulled and cut in half**
- **1/4 cup sliced almonds, toasted in a dry skillet over medium heat until medium brown**
- **1 cup baby spinach leaves**
- **1/4 cup balsamic vinegar**
- **1/4 cup extra virgin olive oil**
- **Kosher salt and freshly ground black pepper to taste**

In a medium-size bowl, combine the strawberries, almonds, and spinach. Drizzle with the vinegar and olive oil, season with salt and pepper, and stir to blend. This is best served the same day at room temperature.

Summer Tomato, Pine Nut, and Caper Relish

Use the juiciest, freshest cherry tomatoes for this aromatic and delicious relish. SERVES 4

- **16 small cherry tomatoes, cut in half**
- **1/4 cup pine nuts, toasted in a dry skillet over medium heat until medium brown**
- **1/4 cup golden raisins**
- **2 tablespoons capers, drained**
- **1/2 cup pitted oil- or brine-cured black olives, such as Gaeta or Kalamata, drained**
- **1/2 cup extra virgin olive oil**
- **Kosher salt and freshly ground black pepper to taste**

In a medium-size bowl, combine the tomatoes, pine nuts, raisins, capers, and olives. Drizzle with the olive oil, season with salt and pepper, and stir to blend. This is best served the same day at room temperature.

Autumn Roasted Red Pepper and Cannellini Bean Relish

You can throw this one together in minutes. SERVES 4

One 15-ounce can cannellini beans, drained and rinsed
1/2 cup chopped roasted red peppers (homemade, see page 145, or from a jar)
1/2 cup finely chopped fresh basil
1 clove garlic, minced
1/4 cup extra virgin olive oil
Kosher salt and freshly ground black pepper to taste

In a medium-size bowl, combine the beans, red peppers, basil, and garlic. Drizzle with the olive oil, season with salt and pepper, and stir to blend. This is best served the same day at room temperature.

Grilled Lamb Skewers

Grilling lamb on a skewer seems like a simple thing to do. Flavor some chunks of lamb with something, thread them onto a stick, and then grill and eat. People do this all over the world. And therein lies the difficulty—choosing a few from the many, many recipes for this dish.

Karen acquired a taste for tapas from her travels in Spain and Portugal. Judith loves south Indian food from her London days. And we both love Mediterranean food. So deciding on which flavors we wanted to showcase here was relatively easy. Just know that you can take these skewers in any direction you like, from Greek (marinated in a vinaigrette with oregano and mint) to French (slathered with Rosemary Pesto, page 62) to Persian (soaked in Tandoori Marinade, page 74, then served with plain yogurt and a sprinkling of sour-tasting sumac on pita bread) to California cool (marinated in Rosemary-Mustard Marinade, page 71, then served with fresh avocado slices and cherry tomatoes).

You can also vary the type of skewer you use (see page 29 for your options and how to grill skewers), from the standard bamboo skewer, which needs to be soaked in water for at least 30 minutes before grilling, to fresh rosemary branches or spikes of sugarcane. In the case of metal skewers, the BBQ Queens like to use two-prong skewers so the meat doesn't spin on the stick.

We prefer to use boneless leg of lamb for skewers, but lamb loin (expensive but tender) and lamb shoulder (cheap but chewy) work as well. Trim off any fat and gristle and try to keep the cubes as uniform as possible, because they will cook more evenly if they're the same size.

While the lamb skewers are grilling, you could also grill onions (page 137), squash (page 154), and/or tomatoes (page 159) at the same time. SERVES 6

2 pounds lean, boneless leg of lamb, trimmed of fat and cut into 1 1/2-inch cubes
1 cup vinaigrette of your choice, homemade or bottled
1/4 cup extra virgin olive oil

1. Place the lamb in a sealable plastic bag and pour the vinaigrette over. Seal and refrigerate for 1 to 2 hours (preferable) or up to 12 hours.

2. Prepare a hot fire in a grill.

3. Remove the lamb from the marinade and thread onto 6 skewers, leaving a little room between the pieces. Pour the olive oil into a small bowl. Carry the oil with a basting brush and the skewers out to the grill. Grill the skewers, turning and basting with oil, for about 8 minutes, until the meat is browned but still pink in the center. Serve hot.

Crowning Glories

Serve these with your choice of:

Bolani *(page 182)*

Fennel and Orange Drizzling Sauce *(page 73)*

Kimizu *(page 103)*

Mediterranean-Rubbed Lamb Kabobs with Lemon Butter Drizzle: Tender pieces of lamb cut from the leg work well for this recipe. The kabobs can be served with rice or couscous and grilled onion slices (see page 138). Place the lamb cubes in a bowl and sprinkle with about 1 teaspoon Lavender Salt (page 55) and freshly ground black pepper to taste. Cover and refrigerate for 1 to 2 hours. Meanwhile, make the Lemon Butter Drizzle (page 87). Grill the kabobs as directed above, basting with the drizzle. **SERVES 6**

Sambar-Spiced South Indian Lamb Kabobs with Tomato, Garlic, and Chile Chutney: Serve this dish with a pitcher of fresh lemonade to which you've added 1 teaspoon or more bottled rose water for a refreshing hot-weather meal. To make the marinade, in a small bowl combine 4 teaspoons ground coriander, 1 teaspoon ground cumin, 1/4 teaspoon cayenne pepper, 1/4 teaspoon freshly ground black pepper, and 1/4 teaspoon turmeric. Add 1/3 cup vegetable oil, 2 minced garlic cloves, 2 teaspoons finely grated fresh ginger (if using a microplane, you don't need to peel), 1/4 teaspoon ground fennel seeds (use a mortar and pestle), 1 teaspoon kosher or sea salt, and 1/4 cup finely chopped fresh tomato. Place 2 pounds lamb cubes (see above) in a sealable plastic bag. Pour the spice mixture over the lamb, seal the bag, and marinate in the refrigerator for 1 to 2 hours (preferable) or up to 12 hours. Meanwhile, make the chutney. Combine 2 cups chopped fresh tomatoes, 2 minced garlic cloves, 2 teaspoons seeded and minced green chile (such as serrano, Thai, or jalapeño), and 1/4 cup finely chopped fresh cilantro. Add fresh lemon juice and kosher or sea salt to taste. (This can be made up to 1 day in advance and refrigerated.) Skewer, grill, and baste the lamb with olive oil as directed above. Serve with the chutney. **SERVES 6**

Tapas-Style Lamb Brochettes: Enjoy these skewers with a pitcher of Sangria! (page 250) or small glasses of chilled fino sherry. Place 2 pounds lamb cubes in a sealable plastic bag and add half 1 recipe Chimichurri Sauce (page 346) mixed with 1 teaspoon sweet Hungarian paprika. Seal the bag and marinate in the refrigerator for 1 to 2 hours (preferable) or up to 12 hours. Skewer, grill, and baste with olive oil as directed above. Serve the brochettes drizzled with the remaining sauce. **SERVES 6**

Grilled Leg of Lamb

Pamper yourself royally by having your butcher butterfly a leg of lamb. Otherwise, it will take you at least 15 minutes to do the trimming, and unless you are really adept at this, the lamb will look as if you massacred the poor thing. So call in the order, then waltz into the butcher shop and go home with a pretty cut of meat.

For this simple recipe, we are grilling the lamb flat. We're not pounding it out to an even thickness, but you can, if you wish, especially if you plan to stuff and roll it. This is something you can also ask the butcher to do.

Another delicious and timesaving tip is to buy a prepared pesto or tapenade (black olive paste) to spread on the lamb, then roll and tie it. Now we're talking tasty, easy, and pretty when sliced.

Lamb is best cooked medium-rare, 125 to 130°F at the thickest part of the meat. Well done is not a pleasant option, because the meat will be tough and dry. If there are thinner portions of the leg, they will automatically cook more, so you can please all of your guests with medium-rare and medium lamb from the same prepared leg. SERVES 8

One 6- to 7-pound leg of lamb, boned, trimmed of fat, and butterflied
1/2 cup Dijon mustard
Kosher salt and freshly ground black pepper to taste

1. Place the butterflied lamb in a shallow dish, slather the mustard on both sides, and season with salt and pepper. Cover and refrigerate for at least 4 hours or up to 12 hours.
2. Prepare a medium-hot fire in a grill.
3. Grill the lamb over medium-high heat until nicely browned and an instant-read meat thermometer inserted in the thickest part registers 125 to 130°F for medium-rare to medium, about 15 minutes per side. Let rest for 10 to 15 minutes, then slice, arrange on a platter, and serve.

Crowning Glories

Anoint your leg before grilling with your choice of:

Rosemary Salt *(page 56)*
Southwest Heat *(page 215)*
Texas Two-Steppin' Mesquite Rub *(page 59)*

Simple Stuffed Leg of Lamb: Preparing this recipe may be as easy as opening your pantry or refrigerator door. Do you see any store-bought condiments that can be spread on your leg of lamb? Maybe a jar of marmalade with a sprinkling of garlic, or some mint jelly mixed with chopped fresh mint from your garden? Do you have any garlic, sun-dried tomato, or anchovy paste that comes in a tube? What about a jar of chutney or a porcini mushroom sauce? Of course, you can also thumb through the rubs and marinades chapter for appealing recipes. To begin, lay out a butterflied and flattened 6- to 7-pound leg of lamb and slather it on one side with about 1 cup prepared pesto, tapenade (black olive paste), or other condiment of your choice. Roll up lengthwise, jellyroll style, and tie with kitchen twine at 1-inch intervals. Grill over a medium-hot fire for about 10 minutes per side, turning it a quarter turn each time, until an instant-read meat thermometer inserted in the center registers 125 to 130°F for medium-rare to medium. Let rest for 10 to 15 minutes before slicing and serving. **SERVES 8**

Rustic Spinach Pesto–Stuffed Leg of Lamb: This takes just a bit more effort. To make the spinach mixture, heat 3 tablespoons olive oil in a medium-size skillet over high heat. Add 1 pound roughly chopped fresh spinach leaves and 2 minced large garlic cloves and cook, stirring, for about 2 minutes. Transfer the cooked spinach to a medium-size bowl. Add 1/2 cup fresh bread crumbs, 1/4 cup golden raisins, 1/4 cup pine nuts, 1/4 cup chopped fresh Italian parsley, one 3-ounce package softened cream cheese, 1/2 teaspoon fine kosher or sea salt, and 1/2 teaspoon freshly ground black pepper and mix well. Lay out a butterflied and flattened 6- to 7-pound leg of lamb and spread with the spinach mixture. Roll up lengthwise, jellyroll style, and tie with kitchen twine at 1-inch intervals. Grill over a medium-hot fire for about 10 minutes per side, turning it a quarter turn each time, until an instant-read meat thermometer inserted in the center registers 125 to 130°F for medium-rare to medium. Let rest for 10 to 15 minutes before slicing and serving. **SERVES 8**

Grilled Lamb, Pear, and Pistou Salad: This is a great way to use grilled lamb leftovers. Chop sliced grilled lamb into bite-size pieces so that you have about 1 cup. Arrange salad greens on 4 plates and top with the grilled lamb. Peel and core 1 ripe but firm pear, cut into thin slices, and place over the lamb. In a small bowl, whisk together 2 tablespoons freshly grated Parmesan cheese, 16 coarsely chopped fresh basil leaves, 1/4 cup olive oil, and 2 1/2 tablespoons balsamic vinegar. Season with kosher or sea salt and freshly ground black pepper to taste. Drizzle the dressing over the salads and serve. For a great garnish, draw a vegetable peeler over a large, flat piece of Parmesan cheese, letting the thin shavings fall directly onto the salads. **SERVES 4**

Rotisserie Leg of Lamb

Even people who say they don't like lamb, like lamb cooked this way. The first key is to buy fresh lamb, not frozen, for a better flavor. Locally raised is better yet. The second key it to trim the lamb of most of the fat, which can carry a stronger flavor. The third key is to get the exterior of the lamb caramelized and charred on the outside and cooked to medium doneness—at the most!—on the inside. A steady 350°F on the grill and a meat thermometer are your trusty culinary friends.

There's so much you can do, serving-wise, with a leg of lamb. Serve it high style, sliced and napped with a wonderful sauce, such as piquant Mustard-Cornichon Beurre Blanc (page 100). Serve it more casually, Mediterranean style, with warm pita bread, hummus, and a fresh salad. Add any leftovers to a big-flavor pasta salad. SERVES 6 TO 12

One 4- to 9-pound leg of lamb, boned (have your butcher do this for you) and trimmed of fat

1 recipe Provençal Red Wine Marinade (page 70)

1. Place the lamb in a baking dish and pour the marinade over. Cover with plastic wrap and marinate in the refrigerator for at least 4 hours or overnight, turning it several times.

2. Remove the lamb from the marinade, shaking off any excess. Transfer the remaining marinade to a medium-size saucepan, bring to a boil, and continue to boil for 5 minutes, then set aside.

3. Set up your grill for rotisserie cooking (see page 33). Prepare a medium fire (around 350°F). Place a rotisserie clamp on the end of the lamb. Push the rotisserie rod through the center of the lamb so the meat is balanced, secure the other clamp, and place on the spit. Insert a heatproof meat thermometer in the thickest part of the meat, away from the bone. Make sure it is positioned so that you can read it and it will turn freely as the meat turns. Place the spit on the rotisserie. Cover and cook the lamb, basting every 30 minutes with the reserved marinade, until the thermometer registers 135 to 140°F for medium-rare, 2 to 2½ hours. Let rest for 15 minutes before slicing and serving.

Crowning Glories

Rotisserie leg of lamb is delicious served with a fresh tomato salad and warm flatbread or with:

Smoked Garlic and Cilantro Cream Sauce ***(page 93)***

Tomato-Fennel Sauce ***(page 95)***

Tzatziki ***(page 112)***

Rotisserie Leg of Lamb with Smoked Ratatouille: Why not do two things at once when you're cooking the lamb? Smoked ratatouille is a new twist on the Provençal classic: the marinade and juices that drip from the lamb will flavor the vegetables. Peel 1 medium-size eggplant and cut into large chunks. Place in a double thickness of disposable aluminum pans (one placed inside the other) along with 1 pint cherry or grape tomatoes, 2 medium-size zucchini cut into large chunks, 1 yellow onion cut into large chunks, 1 teaspoon dried herbes de Provence, 1/2 cup olive oil and 6 peeled garlic cloves. Toss well to blend. Place the pans under the lamb on the spit and add 1 cup water. Cover and cook as directed above. Slice the lamb and serve with the ratatouille. **SERVES 6 TO 12**

Pasta Salad with Rotisserie Lamb and Eggplant: If you know that your leg of lamb isn't likely to be consumed in one meal, plan ahead to make this yummy salad with the leftovers. The salad can be served warm, at room temperature, or chilled, but we like it best at room temperature. Before you rotisserie the lamb, place 2 cups diced but not peeled eggplant in a double thickness of disposable aluminum pans (one placed inside the other) and drizzle with 2 tablespoons olive oil. Place the pans under the lamb and cook until the eggplant is tender, about 1 hour. Let cool, cover, and refrigerate. The next day, arrange one 12-ounce bag baby spinach leaves on 4 to 6 plates. Cook 1/2 pound small dried pasta (penne, farfalle, wheels, or rings) according to the package directions until *al dente*. Drain well and toss with 1 tablespoon olive oil. Transfer the pasta to a large bowl. With a wooden spoon, mix in the reserved eggplant, 2 cups finely chopped rotisserie lamb; 2 teaspoons drained capers; and 8 pitted, drained, and sliced oil- or brine-cured Kalamata olives. To a triple recipe of Lemon-Garlic Mayonnaise (page 103), add 1 teaspoon fresh thyme leaves and 1 teaspoon grated lemon zest. Stir to combine. Spoon the mayonnaise over the pasta mixture and toss well to blend. Serve over the baby spinach leaves. **SERVES 4 TO 6**

Rotisserie Lamb Sandwiches with Matchstick Vegetables and Tzatziki: Instead of the Provençal Red Wine Marinade, use a double recipe of Tandoori Marinade (page 74) to marinate the lamb. Prepare 1 recipe Tzatziki (page 112). Rotisserie cook the lamb as directed above. Meanwhile, use the julienne blade on a mandoline or food processor (or a chef's knife) to cut 2 small zucchini, 1 peeled and seeded cucumber, 1 peeled carrot, and 1 small red onion into matchsticks. Place in a medium-size bowl, add 1 cup of the tzatziki, and toss. Slice the lamb, slip slices into warm pita breads, and add a spoonful of the vegetables to each. Pass the rest of the tzatziki at the table. **SERVES 6 TO 8**

BBQ Babes

She Conducts a Rotisserie Smear Campaign Menu

Garlic-Marinated Rolled Leg of Lamb

Smear of Your Choice: Sweet Moroccan Spice Paste, Santa Fe Herb Paste, or Mediterranean Herb Paste

Sweet-Hot Mustard-Glazed Salmon

We may be queens in our working lives, but we're basically nice girls at heart. If we were going to start a smear campaign, we'd prefer the kind that our culinary instructor and cookbook author friend Diane Phillips conducts. She concocts all kinds of delicious savory pastes and glazes to smear on food as it cooks on the rotisserie in her southern California backyard. She likes cooking that way so much, she created an entire cookbook of recipes—*The Ultimate Rotisserie Cookbook* (The Harvard Common Press, 2002)—from which we adapted these dishes.

Maybe you wouldn't do all of these dishes on the same day, or maybe you would. The lamb takes longer and by the time it's resting, ready to be carved, you've got the salmon twirling around in the rotisserie basket. Or you could do the salmon first and serve it warm or chilled as an appetizer, then serve the lamb as the main course.

Garlic-Marinated Rolled Leg of Lamb

The garlic marinade works well with any of the three pastes, so decide on your flavor and enjoy the results. SERVES 6

GARLIC MARINADE

1/2 cup olive oil

1/4 cup red wine vinegar

4 cloves garlic, minced

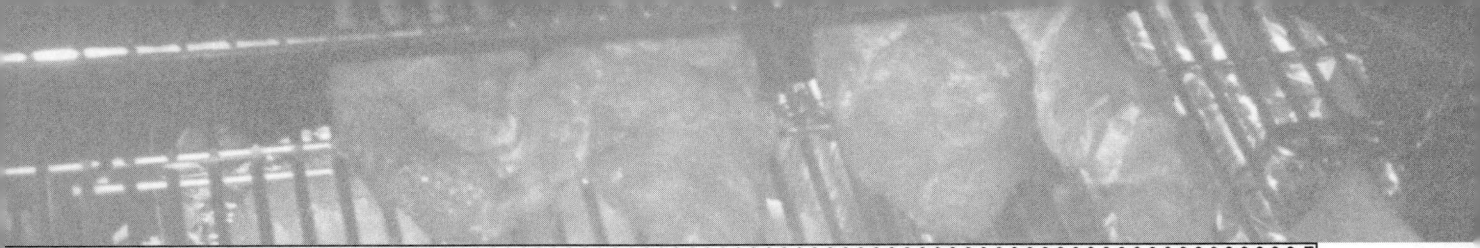

1 1/2 teaspoons fine kosher or sea salt
1/2 teaspoon freshly ground black pepper

One 3- to 4-pound boneless rolled leg of lamb, tied
Flavoring paste of your choice (recipes follow)

1. To make the marinade, combine all the ingredients in a 1-gallon sealable plastic bag.

2. Add the lamb to the bag, seal, and marinate in the refrigerator for at least 6 hours or overnight.

3. Remove the lamb from the marinade and pat dry. Smear your choice of paste over the lamb and cook on the rotisserie as directed on page 431 until an instant-read meat thermometer inserted in the thickest part registers 155°F for medium, 2 to 2 1/2 hours.

4. Remove the lamb from the spit, cover loosely with aluminum foil, and let rest for 10 to 15 minutes. Remove the twine and carve the lamb. Serve hot.

Sweet Moroccan Spice Paste

We love coriander and cumin together, the yin and yang of flavors, as in this heady paste, which is delicious on chicken, pork, or lamb. MAKES ABOUT 1/2 CUP

3 cloves garlic, minced
2 tablespoons olive oil
2 tablespoons firmly packed light brown sugar
1/2 teaspoon sweet Hungarian paprika
1/4 teaspoon ground coriander
1/4 teaspoon ground cumin

Combine all the ingredients in a small bowl. This paste will keep, covered, in the refrigerator for up to 2 days.

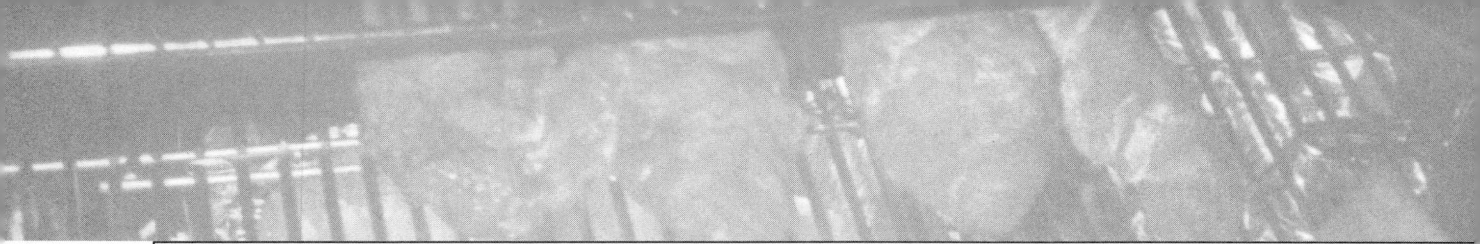

Santa Fe Herb Paste

Various levels of heat and a sweet spiciness make this herb and spice paste a winner on beef, lamb, or pork. MAKES ABOUT 1 CUP

1/2 cup finely chopped fresh cilantro
1/4 cup olive oil
2 tablespoons firmly packed light brown sugar
2 tablespoons fresh lime juice
2 teaspoons ground cumin
5 cloves garlic, minced
1 dried ancho chile, crushed

Combine all the ingredients in a small bowl. This paste will keep, covered, in the refrigerator for up to 3 days.

Mediterranean Herb Paste

Assertively flavored, this paste is great on anything destined for the grill. MAKES ABOUT 1/2 CUP

Grated zest of 2 lemons
6 cloves garlic, minced
2 tablespoons chopped fresh rosemary
1 tablespoon Dijon mustard
1 1/2 teaspoons fine kosher or sea salt
1 teaspoon freshly ground black pepper
Pinch of red pepper flakes

Combine all the ingredients in a small bowl. This paste will keep, covered, in the refrigerator for up to 4 days.

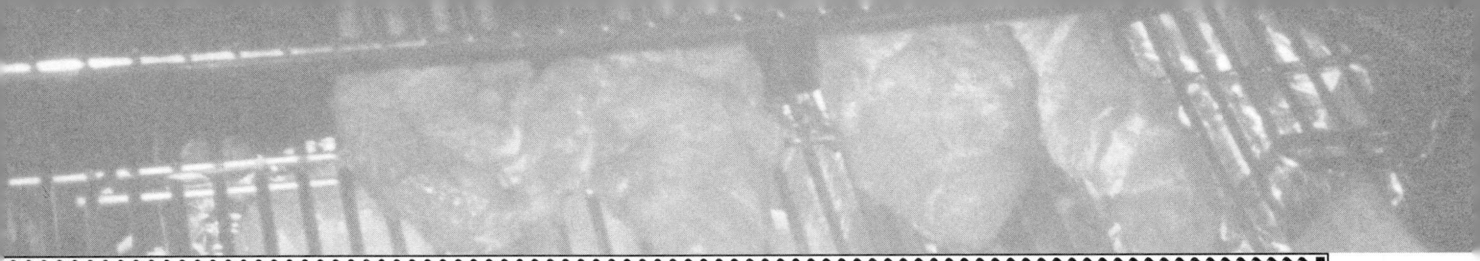

Sweet-Hot Mustard-Glazed Salmon

There are so many delicious ways to do salmon on the grill. This recipe is yet another. Serve over mixed field greens as a main dish salad, or with Tzatziki (page 112) or Charred Tomato-Chipotle Salsa (page 162) as an appetizer. **SERVES 6**

1 cup Dijon mustard

1/2 cup clover or other medium-colored honey

1 tablespoon fresh lemon juice

2 pounds salmon fillets

1. Coat a rotisserie basket with nonstick cooking spray.

2. In a small saucepan over medium heat, combine the mustard, honey, and lemon juice. Bring to a simmer.

3. Reserve half of the glaze for serving. Liberally brush the other half over the salmon, then cook on the rotisserie as directed in the box on page 40 until just cooked through, 15 to 20 minutes. The center will still be a bit undercooked, but it will continue to cook once removed from the heat.

4. Remove the salmon from the basket and brush with the reserved glaze. Serve immediately, or refrigerate and serve cold.

Smoked Leg of Lamb

When the bone is removed and the meat butterflied, a leg of lamb is even easier to smoke. Pamper yourself royally by having your butcher butterfly a leg of lamb, or do it yourself, if you like. You can flavor lamb in so many ways and accompany it with so many different side dishes that we wonder why more people don't smoke it. We've decided that we're now on a mission—a butterflied leg of lamb mission. This is a great dish to serve at a gathering, and with the recent upsurge of interest in Middle Eastern food, you can enjoy smoked leg of lamb as part of a traditional American barbecue or a Mediterranean feast. SERVES 6 TO 8

SUGGESTED WOOD: Apple, cherry, hickory, oak, or pecan

One 6- to 8-pound leg of lamb, boned, trimmed of fat, and butterflied
1/4 cup olive oil
2 tablespoons minced garlic
3 tablespoons lemon pepper seasoning

1. Prepare an indirect fire in a smoker.

2. Rub the butterflied leg of lamb all over with the olive oil, garlic, and lemon pepper. Place the lamb in the smoker, cover, and smoke at 225 to 250°F until an instant-read meat thermometer inserted in the thickest part registers 140 to 145°F for medium-rare, 3 to 4 hours. Let rest for 15 minutes before slicing and serving.

Crowning Glories

Smoked leg of lamb is delicious served with:

Oven-Roasted Saffron Potatoes *(page 413)*

Chimichurri Sauce *(page 346)*

Classic Creamed Spinach *(page 319)*

Smoked Butterflied Leg of Lamb Pinot Noir: Now you don't have to wonder which wine to serve with lamb. It says it all in the title. We love this accompanied by a vinaigrette-dressed spinach, pasta, or rice salad tossed with crumbled goat cheese, toasted pine nuts, and dried currants. For the Pinot Noir marinade, whisk together 2 cups olive oil, 1 cup Pinot Noir or other dry red wine, 1 sliced red onion, 1 tablespoon chopped garlic, 3 bay leaves, 1 tablespoon dried herbes de Provence, and 1 teaspoon lemon pepper seasoning. Place the lamb in a shallow pan or sealable plastic bag and add the marinade. Cover or seal and let marinate in the refrigerator for at least 1 hour or up to 12 hours. Drain and pat dry, then smoke as directed above. **SERVES 6 TO 8**

Tandoori-Marinated Smoked Butterflied Leg of Lamb: For a Mediterranean spin on this recipe, place the lamb in a shallow pan or sealable plastic bag and add 1 recipe Tandoori Marinade (page 74). Cover or seal and marinate in the refrigerator overnight. Drain and pat dry, then smoke as directed above. Serve with grilled pita bread and Tzatziki (page 112). **SERVES 6 TO 8**

BBQ Queens' Smoked Stuffed Leg of Lamb: We've adapted this recipe from one in *Easy Grilling & Simple Smoking with the BBQ Queens* (Pig Out Publications, 1999). We like to use a combination of hickory and apple wood for this dish. The hickory provides a heavier smoke, while the apple supplies sweetness. Make the stuffing by trimming 1 pound fresh spinach of any heavy stems. Take 10 to 12 large leaves and stack them on top of one another. Roll into a cigar shape and cut crosswise into 1/8-inch shreds. Repeat with the remaining spinach. In a medium-size skillet, heat 3 tablespoons olive oil over high heat. Stir in the spinach and 2 minced large garlic cloves. Cook, tossing and stirring often, for about 2 minutes, until the moisture has evaporated from the spinach. Transfer to a medium-size bowl and add 1/2 cup fresh bread crumbs, 1/4 cup golden raisins, 1/4 cup pine nuts, 1/4 cup chopped fresh basil, one 3-ounce package softened cream cheese, 1/2 teaspoon fine kosher or sea salt, and 1/4 teaspoon freshly ground black pepper. Mix well. Lay out the butterflied and trimmed leg of lamb and spread with the spinach mixture. Roll up lengthwise, jelly-roll style, and tie at 1-inch intervals with kitchen twine. Smoke as directed above until an instant-read meat thermometer inserted in the thickest part registers at least 160°F for medium, 5 to 6 hours. Let rest for 15 minutes before slicing and serving. **SERVES 6 TO 8**

Easy as 1-2-3 Ice Creams and Sorbets

Nothing cools the palate after a spicy barbecue meal like ice cream or sorbet. As "the BBQ Queen of Easy," Karen has found some delicious shortcuts to homemade ice cream. We know you'll like the fact that you don't have to make the custard the day before, then chill it overnight. These recipes are for when you have a spur-of-the-moment yen for good ice cream.

If you want to add crunch to any of these ice creams, get creative with store-bought granola cereal, your favorite cookies (store-bought or homemade, crumbled), or toasted nuts (pecans, almonds, walnuts, or others).

Made from canned fruit in heavy syrup, the sorbets included here don't get any easier.

Toasted Coconut Ice Cream with Hot Fudge Ganache and Toasted Pecans

Judith and her father introduced Karen to Aglamesi's coconut ice cream in Cincinnati. Their favorite way to devour this delicious treat is topped with hot fudge ganache and toasted pecans. Divine! MAKES ABOUT 1 QUART

1 cup pecan halves

TOASTED COCONUT ICE CREAM

1 cup sweetened flaked coconut

3 cups heavy cream

1 tablespoon coconut extract

HOT FUDGE GANACHE

1 cup heavy cream

$1\frac{1}{2}$ cups semisweet chocolate chips

1. Preheat the oven to 350°F. Spread the pecans on a baking sheet and bake until the nuts begin to brown and smell toasted, about 10 minutes. Set aside to cool. (The nuts will keep in the freezer for several months.)

2. To make the ice cream, spread the flaked coconut on a baking sheet and bake until it begins to brown, 8 to 10 minutes. Remove from the oven and set aside to cool.

3. Pour the heavy cream and coconut extract into an ice cream maker and begin to freeze according to the manufacturer's directions. After 5 minutes, add the cooled coconut and finish freezing the ice cream.

4. To make the ganache, place the heavy cream in a large glass bowl and microwave on high until it just begins to boil, 2 to 3 minutes. Or bring the cream to a boil in a small, heavy saucepan on the stovetop. Remove from the microwave or heat, add the chocolate chips, and let sit for 5 minutes (do not stir). Gently stir the mixture to create a shiny, dark chocolate sauce. (This will keep in the refrigerator for up to 1 month.)

5. Serve the ice cream topped with ganache and a handful of toasted pecans.

Fresh Peach Crumble Ice Cream

When the dog days of summer hit, your hair goes limp, and not even a tiara can perk up your "do," buy some juicy ripe peaches at the farmers' market and get out your bowl and spoon for a real summer treat. MAKES ABOUT 1 QUART

2 large ripe peaches
3 cups heavy cream
1 teaspoon almond extract
1 cup crumbled shortbread cookies

1. Peel the peaches over a bowl to catch any of the juices. Slice the peaches or cut into chunks, discarding the pits. Set aside.

2. Pour the heavy cream and almond extract into an ice cream maker and begin to freeze according to the manufacturer's directions. After 5 minutes, add the peaches and crumbled cookies. Finish freezing the ice cream, then serve.

Pineapple Sorbet in Grilled Pineapple Rings

Grill Gal Melanie Barnard first shared this sorbet recipe with us while she was representing the Canned Food Alliance. We thought the pineapple sorbet was so delicious and easy to make that we've made variations using canned plums, mandarin oranges, grapefruit sections, and cherries. Freeze the unopened can of crushed pineapple for at least 2 days before making this recipe. We love to use it to doll up grilled fresh pineapple rings. SERVES 6

PINEAPPLE SORBET

One 20-ounce can crushed pineapple in heavy syrup, frozen in the unopened can

3 tablespoons dark rum or 2 teaspoons rum flavoring

3 tablespoons well-stirred canned cream of coconut

GRILLED PINEAPPLE RINGS

1 large fresh pineapple, peeled and cored

1. To make the sorbet, submerge the unopened can of frozen pineapple in hot water for 1 minute. Open the can and pour the pineapple and syrup into a food processor. Process until smooth. Add the rum and cream of coconut and process to mix. Serve immediately, or freeze for up to 8 hours before serving.

2. To make the pineapple rings, right before serving, cut the pineapple into 1-inch-thick-rings and place on a medium-hot grill. Grill until the pineapple has browned and softened, about 2 minutes per side. To serve, place a scoop of pineapple sorbet in each grilled pineapple ring.

Mandarin Orange Sorbet: Freeze 2 unopened 10-ounce cans mandarin oranges overnight or for at least 8 hours to make sure they're frozen solid. Proceed as directed above, substituting 3 tablespoons orange-flavored liqueur or orange extract for the rum and cream of coconut. For extra zing, add 1 tablespoon grated orange zest. **MAKES ABOUT 2½ CUPS**

Resource Guide

BARBECUE AND GRILL MANUFACTURERS

Many manufacturers produce outdoor barbecues and grills. Only a few are listed here. We suggest that you visit a local dealer that offers a variety of grills, as well as service. Happy grilling and smoking!

Alfresco Gourmet Grills
7039 East Slauson Boulevard
Commerce, GA 90040
(888) 383-8800
www.alfrescogrills.com

Manufacturer of gas grills and smokers. Outdoor kitchen concepts with bartending centers and refrigeration units.

Barbeques Galore
U.S. Headquarters
10 Orchard Road, Suite 200
Lake Forest, CA 92630
(800) 752-3085
www.bbqgalore.com

Australian gas grill manufacturer with a U.S. retail division of more than 60 stores nationwide. Also carries barbecue utensils, accessories, books, woods, charcoal, and more.

BBQ Pits by Klose
2216 West 34th Street
Houston, TX 77018
(800) 487-7487
www.bbqpits.com

David Klose carries ready-made smokers in just about every size—from 24-inch models to huge commercial rigs. Also custom-makes smokers.

Big Green Egg
3414 Clairmont Road
Atlanta, GA 30319
(404) 321-4658
www.biggreenegg.com

Large producer of an egg-shaped, ceramic kamado combination smoker/grill that cooks at a higher temperature than traditional cookers.

Brinkmann Corporation
4215 McEwen Road
Dallas, TX 75244
(800) 527-0717
www.thebrinkmanncorp.com

Manufacturer of bullet-shaped charcoal and electric water smokers and grills.

Cajun Grill/Percy Guidry Manufacturing
204 Wilson Street
Lafayette, LA 70501
(800) 822-4766
www.cajungrill.com

Manufacturers of the Cajun Grill and the Cajun Smoker, plus a variety of barbecue accessories, rubs, and sauces.

Char-Broil/W.C. Bradley
P.O. Box 1240
Columbus, GA 31902
(800) 352-4111
www.charbroil.com

Manufacturer of gas and electric grills and barbecue accessories. Also the maker of the New Braunfels heavy-gauge steel smokers and grills.

CM International
P.O. Box 60220
Colorado Springs, CO 80960
(888) 563-0227
www.cameronssmoker.com
Manufacturer of the Camerons Stovetop Smokers. Also a supplier of wood grilling and baking planks and fine wood chips, including corncob pellets and pecan shells.

Cookshack
2304 North Ash Street
Ponca City, OK 74601
(800) 423-0698
www.cookshackamerica.com
Manufacturer of residential and commercial barbecues, grills, cookstoves, ranges, and ovens.

DCS (Dynamic Cooking Systems)
5800 Skylab Road
Huntington Beach, CA 92647
(800) 433-8466
www.dcsappliances.com
Manufacturer of upscale stainless steel gas grills.

Empire Comfort Systems
918 Freeburg Avenue
Belleville, IL 62220
(800) 443-8648
www.broilmaster.com
Manufacturer of the Broilmaster gas grills, smokers, and portable cookers.

Fiesta Gas Grills
One Fiesta Drive
Dickson, TN 37055
(800) 396-3838
www.fiestagasgrills.com
Manufacturer of mid-priced gas grills and barbecues.

Grills to Go
5659 West San Madele Way
Fresno, CA 93722
(877) 869-2253
www.grillstogo.com
Manufacturer of towable commercial charcoal, wood, and gas barbecue grills.

Hasty-Bake
7656 East 46th Street
Tulsa, OK 74145
(800) 426-6836
www.hastybake.com
Manufacturer of the Hasty-Bake oven, a charcoal grill/smoker that has a pulley system to raise and lower the grill grates over the fire. Side door for refueling is nifty, too.

Kingfisher Kookers
1107 South Main
Kingfisher, OK 73750
(866) 542-5665
www.kingfisherkookers.com
Manufacturer of Kingfisher Kookers, grills and smokers in all shapes and sizes.

KitchenAid
P.O. Box 218
St. Joseph, MI 49084
(800) 422-1230
www.kitchenaid.com
Major appliance manufacturer of, among other products, outdoor cooking systems, refrigeration products, and refreshment systems.

Magma Products
3940 Pixie Avenue
Lakewood, CA 90712
(800) 866-2462
www.magmaproducts.com
Manufacturers of Del Mar and Magma brands. These gas and charcoal cookers are compact units professionally designed for boats and small patios.

Napoleon Gourmet Grills
214 Bayview Drive
Barrie, Ontario
Canada L4N 4Y8
(888) 726-2220
www.napoleongrills.com
Manufacturer of stainless steel gas and charcoal grills.

Robert H. Peterson Company
14742 East Proctor Avenue
City of Industry, CA 91746
(800) 332-0240
www.rhpeterson.com
Manufacturer of the widely distributed and popular Fire Magic grills. Models include smokers and charcoal, gas, electric, and infrared grills.

Traeger Industries
P.O. Box 829
1385 East College Street
Mount Angel, OR 97362
(800) 872-3437
www.traegerindustries.com
Manufacturer of the original electric-powered wood pellet grill/smoker. Compressed wood pellets are funneled into the firebox and provide both fuel and flavor.

Viking Range Corporation
111 Front Street
Greenwood, MS 38930
(888) 845-4641
www.vikingrange.com
Manufacturer of stainless steel gas grill outdoor kitchens and professional-quality appliances for the home.

Weber-Stephen Products Co.
200 East Daniels Road
Palatine, IL 60067-6266
(800) 446-1071
www.weber.com
Manufacturer of the original Weber grill since 1951. Grills, smokers, and all their accessories, as well as the Weber Smokey Mountain Cooker, a charcoal chimney starter, and more.

Wolf Appliance Company
P.O. Box 44848
Madison, WI 53744
(800) 332-9513
www.wolfappliance.com
Manufacturer of stainless steel outdoor gas grills, as well as professional indoor kitchens for the home.

BARBECUE BOOKS, SPICES, CATALOGS, NEWSLETTERS, AND CLASSES

Passionate barbecuers are always in search of information about outdoor cooking. Give some of these companies a try.

BBQ Queens
www.bbqqueens.com
Official online site of the BBQ Queens, Karen Adler and Judith Fertig. Features tips and recipes for outdoor cooking, where the BBQ Queens are teaching culinary classes, and information about their books.

Grill Lover's Catalog
P.O. Box 1300
Columbus, GA 31902
(800) 241-8981
www.grilllovers.com
Catalog offering charcoal and gas grills, cookbooks, sauces and seasonings, and accessories for the grill.

Kansas City *Bullsheet*
Kansas City Barbeque Society
11514 Hickman Mills Drive
Kansas City, MO 64134
(800) 963-5227
www.rbjb.com/rbjb/kcbs.htm
Monthly newspaper published by the Kansas City Barbeque Society featuring everything barbecue.

Lawry's Foods
222 East Huntington Drive
Monrovia, CA 91016
(626) 930-8870
www.lawrys.com
Manufacturer of good-quality marinades and spice blends available at grocery stores nationwide.

McCormick & Company
226 Schilling Circle
Hunt Valley, MD 21031
(800) 632-5847
www.mccormick.com
Manufacturer of good-quality spices and flavorings available at grocery stores nationwide.

National Barbecue News

P.O. Box 981
Douglas, GA 31534-0981
(800) 385-0002
www.barbecuenews.com

Monthly newspaper featuring barbecue events and columns. Also the official newspaper of the National Barbecue Association.

Old World Spices & Seasonings Company

4601 Emanuel Cleaver II Boulevard
Kansas City, MO 64130
(800) 241-0070
www.oldworldspices.com

Manufacturer of spices, sauces, and seasonings, including custom products.

Paul Kirk Pitmaster Classes

(800) 963-5227
(816) 765-5891
E-mail: bbqbaron@hotmail.com

Paul Kirk, the Baron of Barbecue, presents one-day classes in which students spend 12 grueling hours cooking and presenting the four competition barbecue meats—brisket, pork butt, pork ribs, and chicken. Classes are usually organized by state or local barbecue association. Barbecue videos and sauces are also available.

Penzeys Spices

19300 West Janacek Court
Brookfield, WI 53045
(800) 741-7787
www.penzeys.com

Online source and catalog sales for spices, herbs, and seasonings. Fresh products are available in larger quantities, too.

Pig Out Publications

207 East Gregory
Kansas City, MO 64114
(800) 877-3119
www.pigoutpublications.com

BBQ Queen Karen Adler owns this company, which offers more than 200 barbecue cookbooks.

The Spice House

1031 North Old World Third Street
Milwaukee, WI 53203
(414) 272-0977
www.thespicehouse.com

Large selection of spices and seasonings.

Vanns Spices

6105 Oakleaf Avenue
Baltimore, MD 21215
(800) 583-1693
www.vannsspices.com

High-quality spices and seasonings with no chemicals or additives. Private labeling and custom blending offered.

Zach's Spice Company

1001 Georgia Avenue
Deer Park, TX 77536
(800) 460-0521
www.zachsspice.com

Specializes in ingredients for barbecuing and grilling in general, as well as those for making sausage, dry rubs, and barbecue sauces.

WOOD PRODUCTS

Look for wood products at stores nearby because they are moderately expensive to ship. However, some specialty woods and wood products are available only in certain regions of the country. If you can't find something locally, try these sources.

Acadian Woods

117 Twenty-fifth Avenue
Madawaska, ME 04756
(321) 698-5826
www.acadian-woods.com

Manufacturer of white cedar grilling and baking planks from the northern Maine woods.

American Wood Products
9540 Riggs Street
Overland Park, KS 66212
(800) 223-9046
Bags of mesquite lump charcoal, as well as a variety of woods—mesquite, pecan, hickory, grape, oak, apple, cherry, sassafras, peach, and alder—in logs, slabs, chunks, and chips.

Barbecuewood.com
P.O. Box 8163
Yakima, WA 98098
(509) 961-3420
www.barbecuewood.com
A variety of wood grilling and baking planks in alder, cherry, cedar, maple, white oak, and hickory. Also wood chunks and chips in hard-to-find varieties such as apricot, as well as all the usual woods used for smoking.

BBQr's Delight
P.O. Box 8727
6109 Celia Road
Pine Bluff, AR 71611
(877) 275-9591
www.bbqrsdelight.com
Compressed wood pellets for fuel and smoke in hickory, mesquite, pecan, apple, cherry, oak, black walnut, mulberry, orange, Jack Daniel's, sugar maple, and more.

Blue Moon Woods
P.O. Box 207
2350 Sopchoppy Highway
Sopchoppy, FL 32358-0207
(888) 959-9291
www.bluemoonwoods.com
A unique line of presoaked wood products that come in convenient pull-ring cans placed directly on the grill. You grill, the wood smokes, and there is no mess. Presoaked woods come in hickory, pecan, mesquite, oak, wild cherry, and more.

Chigger Creek Products
4200 Highway D
Syracuse, MO 65354
(660) 298-3188
www.bbqads.com/chigger/chigger.htm
Hardwood lump charcoal, as well as a variety of woods—hickory, apple, cherry, pecan, grape, sugar maple, alder, oak, mesquite, peach, sassafras, persimmon, pear, apple-hickory, and cherry-oak blends—in chips, chunks, and logs.

CM International
See page 444.
Wood grilling and baking planks.

Fairlane Bar-BQ Wood
12520 Third Street
Grandview, MO 64030
(816) 761-1350
Specializes in mesquite, pecan, hickory, oak, apple, cherry, and sassafras chunks.

Peoples Woods
75 Mill Street
Cumberland, RI 02864
(800) 729-5800
www.peopleswoods.com
Natural lump charcoal and smoking woods.

Sautee Cedar Company
328 Commerce Boulevard, Unit 8
Bogart, GA 30622
(866) 728-8332
www.sauteecedar.com
Aromatic western red cedar grilling planks. Custom packaging available.

WW Wood
P.O. Box 398
Pleasanton, TX 78064
(830) 569-2501
www.woodinc.com
Smoking and grilling woods.

Measurement Equivalents

Please note that all conversions are approximate.

Liquid Conversions

U.S.	Metric
1 tsp	5 ml
1 tbs	15 ml
2 tbs	30 ml
3 tbs	45 ml
1/4 cup	60 ml
1/3 cup	75 ml
1/3 cup + 1 tbs	90 ml
1/3 cup + 2 tbs	100 ml
1/2 cup	120 ml
2/3 cup	150 ml
3/4 cup	180 ml
3/4 cup + 2 tbs	200 ml
1 cup	240 ml
1 cup + 2 tbs	275 ml
1 1/4 cups	300 ml
1 1/3 cups	325 ml
1 1/2 cups	350 ml
1 2/3 cups	375 ml
1 3/4 cups	400 ml
1 3/4 cups + 2 tbs	450 ml
2 cups (1 pint)	475 ml
2 1/2 cups	600 ml
3 cups	720 ml
4 cups (1 quart)	945 ml (1,000 ml is 1 liter)

Weight Conversions

U.S./U.K.	Metric
1/2 oz	14 g
1 oz	28 g
1 1/2 oz	43 g
2 oz	57 g
2 1/2 oz	71 g
3 oz	85 g
3 1/2 oz	100 g
4 oz	113 g
5 oz	142 g
6 oz	170 g
7 oz	200 g
8 oz	227 g
9 oz	255 g
10 oz	284 g
11 oz	312 g
12 oz	340 g
13 oz	368 g
14 oz	400 g
15 oz	425 g
1 lb	454 g

Oven Temperature Conversions

°F	Gas Mark	°C
250	1/2	120
275	1	140
300	2	150
325	3	165
350	4	180
375	5	190
400	6	200
425	7	220
450	8	230
475	9	240
500	10	260
550	Broil	290

Index

A

Aioli
  Easy, The Doctor Is In, 110
  platter, ideas for, 135
  Rustic, 104
  and Smoked Potato Gratin, 152–53
  variations on, 110
  White Truffle, 105
Almond
  Cookie Brittle, 264–65
  -Cranberry Torte with Cranberry Drizzle, 394–95
  -Honey Grilling Glaze, 88
  Joy Brittle, 265
  Toasted, Strawberry, and Spinach Relish, Springtime, 425
Apple and Red Cabbage Slaw, 83
Apple-Rosemary Salsa, 234
Apples, Grilled Stuffed, 244
Apricot and Cognac-Cabernet Sauce, 423
Apricot and Cognac-Glazed Duck, 241
Apricot-Bourbon Barbecue Sauce, The Doctor Is In, 90
Apricot Chutney, 384
Apricot-Dijon Glaze, 374
Apricot-Mustard Glaze, 411
Artichoke(s)
  –Pecorino Romano Glaze, Planked Chicken Breasts with, 194
  Pizza, Grilled, on Parmesan-Herb Crust, 185–86
  and Smoked Italian Sausage Soup, 369
Asparagus
  and Beef Saddlebags, Smoky, 171–72
  Grilled, 117
  Asian-Style, with Peanut Butter Dipping Sauce, 118
  Frittata, 118
  with Shaved Parmigiano-Reggiano, 118
  Spring Grill Platter with Aioli, 421
  Vegetable Platter with Fresh Basil Vinaigrette, 129–30
  Stir-Grilled, with Chicken and Shaved Parmigiano-Reggiano, 199

B

Bacon
  -Roquefort Butter, 318
  Smoked Beef BLT, 339
  Sour Cream, and Mushroom Sauce, 337
Baker, Beckie, 367
Barbecue Sauce
  Apricot-Bourbon, The Doctor Is In, 90
  BBQ Queens' Love Potion for the Swine, 89
  Bill's Better Than the Average, 370–71
  glazing foods with, 15, 26
  variations, 90
Barwick, Dee, 340
Basil
  Fresh, Vinaigrette, 85
  Lemon Sauce, 343
  Mayonnaise, 213
  Oil Mashed Potatoes, 258
  Vinaigrette, 355
Bastes
  applying to grilled foods, 14–15
  applying to smoked foods, 26
  Brown Sugar Basting Sauce, 383
  Honey-Apple, 377
  Lemon Butter Drizzle, 87
  liquid mixtures for, 15, 26
  Orange-Ginger, 261
  Orange-Honey, 246
  Rosemary, Garlic, and Lemon, 68
Battle of the Sexes Barbecue Contest, 197
Bean(s)
  Baked, Easy Southern-Style, 109
  Baked, Jazzy Java, 108
  Barbecued, BBQ Queens', 107
  Cannellini, and Roasted Red Pepper Relish, Autumn, 426
  Haricots Verts Salad with Mustard-Shallot Vinaigrette, 327–28
  Haricots Verts with Lemon, Garlic, and Parsley, 274
  Lima, Baby, Slow-Simmered, 392
  Pinto, Texas-Style, 106–7
  Red, and Rice with Smoked Sausage, 369
  Salad, Italian, 284
Béarnaise Sauce, Rustic, 98
Beef
  buying, 299–300
  Grilled
    and Asparagus Saddlebags, Smoky, 171–72
    Batayaki, with Spicy Lemon-Soy Sauce, 312–13
    best cuts for, 300
    Black and Bleu, 326
    Branding Iron, with Ancho Mayonnaise, 311–12
    Burgers, 303
    Burgers, Dolled-Up Caesar, 304
    Fajitas, Citrus-Grilled, 308–9
    Filet Mignon, Peppercorn, with Cognac Sauce, 317–18

Beef, Grilled (*cont.*)
Filet Mignon, Steakhouse-Style, 317
Filet Salad with Orange-Cumin Vinaigrette, 313
grilling times, 16
Kabobs, Kabuli, 333–34
Kabobs, Tamarind and Yogurt, with Warm Pita Breads, 331
Sicilian Bistecca, 324
Skewers, 330
Skewers with Quick Peanut Sauce, 331
Skewers with Spicy Tomato-Chile Sauce, 331
Smoky Meatballs, 345
Steak, Bistro-Style, with Red Wine–Shallot Sauce, 308
Steak, Bone-In, 323
Steak, Bone-In, Korean-Style, 323–24
Steak, Boneless, 316–17
Steak, Flank, Skirt, Hangar, or Other Thin, 307–8
Steak, Prairie-Style Hay-Smoked, 326
Steak, Rib-Eye, Charcoal-Grilled, 315
Steak, Rib-Eye, Philadelphia Garlic, 318
Steak, Strip, Seduction, with Roquefort-Bacon Butter, 318
Steak, Strip, with Chile–Ginger–Green Onion Sauce, 318
Steak, T-Bone, with Smoked Tomato and Grilled Red Onion Relish, 324
Steak, Thick-Cut, 325
Steak Marinated in Beer, Herbs, and Morels, 309
Steak Salad with Caper Vinaigrette, 309
Tenderloin, 336–37
Tenderloin, Chez Panisse–Style, 337–38
Tenderloin, Herbed and Spiced, 342–43
Tenderloin, Herbed and Spiced, Salad, 341–42
Tenderloin with Sour Cream, Bacon, and Mushroom Sauce, 337
testing for doneness, 16, 17
marinating times, 67
Planked
Gorgonzola Filet Mignon, 347
Hickory-, Tenderloin, Argentinean, with Chimichurri Sauce, 346–47
Slathered, 347
Tenderloin, 346
Rotisserie Roast, 347–48
Boneless Prime Rib, with Blackened Seasoning, 349
Downtown, with BBQ Queens' Barbecued Beans, 348
Lemon Pepper, with Butter Baste, 348
Uptown, with Peppercorn Beurre Blanc, 348
Smoked
best cuts for, 300
BLT, 339
Brisket, 356–57
Brisket, Barbecued, Dip, 358
Brisket, Kansas City–Style Barbecued, 357
Brisket, Texas-Style Slow-Smoked, 353–54
Brisket, Two-Step Shortcut Barbecued, 358
Burnt Ends, 358
Burnt Ends Sandwich, 358
Corned, Barbecued, with Mustard-Beer Slather, 359–60
Flank Steak, Cola-Marinated, 403
Rib Roast, 349–50
Rib Roast, Rosemary Pesto, 350
Rib Roast Sandwiches, 350–51
Rib Roast with Yorkshire Pudding, 350
Rustic Reuben, 360
Smoky Meatballs, 345
Tenderloin, 338–39
Tenderloin, Kiss of Smoke, Black Forest, 402
Tenderloin, Peppery, 339
Tenderloin, Porcini, 339
testing for doneness, 28
timetable for, 27
Smoked Greek Stuffed Tomatoes, 164
steaks, popularity of, 310–11
steaks, types of, 300
Stovetop Smoked Tenderloin, 39
Super Sicilian Sandwich, 184
Beurre Blanc
Mustard-Cornichon, 100
Peppercorn, 102
Raspberry, 101
Smoked Chile, 99
Blueberry-Peach Tart with Macaroon Crust, 295–96
Bordelaise Sauce, Simply Delicious, 91
Boss Hawg barbecue team, 197
Bourbon-Mustard Cream Sauce, 377
Bourbon Pecan-Stuffed Rotisserie Pork Loin, 399
Bread(s). *See also* Pizza
Bolani (Afghani Flatbreads with Fresh Herb Filling), 182
Bruschetta with Jersey Tomatoes, 294
Campfire Skillet Scones, 415–16
Cheesy Italian Pesto, 177
Fiesta, 178
grilled, testing for doneness, 16
Rustic, with Smoked Tomato and Basil Butter, 177–78
Sticks, Grilled Leaf-Wrapped, 181–82
Wood-Grilled Flatbreads, 176
Broccoli Slaw, Crunchy, with Thai Chile-Peanut Dressing, 80
Burgers
Caesar, Dolled-Up, 304
condiments for, 306
Fourth of July Pilgrim, with Dried Cranberry Relish, 305
Grilled, 303
grilled, testing for doneness, 17
grilling times, 16
Lamb, Greek-Style, with Cilantro-Mint Chutney, 304–5
preparing, tips for, 303
Tuna, Asian, with Wasabi Mayo, 305
"Burgers," Grilled Portobello Mushroom, 133
"Burgers," Grilled Tomato, with Herbed Cream Cheese, 160

Butter. *See also* Beurre Blanc
Lemon Drizzle, 87
Pernod, 288
Roquefort-Bacon, 318
Smoked Tomato and Basil, 177–78

C

Cabbage. *See also* Sauerkraut
Blue Cheese Coleslaw, 79
Frozen Asset Slaw, 82
Grilled Greens, 126–27
Layered Vinegar Slaw, 80–81
Red, and Apple Slaw, 83
Red, and Radicchio, Grilled, with Herbed Caesar Dressing, 127
Caesar Burgers, Dolled-Up, 304
Caesar Dressing, Herbed, 127
Caesar Salad, Curlicue Chicken, 196–97
Caesar Salad, Grilled Romaine, 127
Caesar Vinaigrette, Citrus, 84
Cake
Cranberry-Almond Torte with Cranberry Drizzle, 394–95
Grilled Pound, with Hot Fudge Ganache and Sweetened Berries, 397
Orange Marmalade Bundt, 396–97
Calamari. *See* Squid
Caper, Tomato, and Pine Nut Relish, Summer, 425
Caper-Stuffed Eggs, 380
Caper Vinaigrette, 309
Carrot(s)
Baby, Braised in Late-Harvest Riesling, 275
Grated, Salad, Bistro, 329
Vegetable Ribbon Skewers, 156
Cauliflower, Roasted Red Pepper, and Cured Olive Salad, 282–83
Celery Root Rémoulade, 328–29
charcoal, hardwood, 8
charcoal briquettes, 8
charcoal chimney, 8–9
charcoal grills
adding smoke flavors, 11, 21, 24
adjusting temperature in, 25
lighting fire in, 8–9
preparing direct fire in, 10–11
preparing indirect fire in, 11, 19
rotisserie unit on, 33
selection criteria, 4
signs of hot fire in, 13
smoking foods in, 11, 19, 25
Cheese
Asiago-Garlic Grits, 392–93
Blue, Coleslaw, 79
Blue, Dressing, Creamy, 111
Brie and Basil–Stuffed Turkey Breast, 227
Cheesy Grilled Pepper Boats, 143
Cheesy Italian Pesto Bread, 177
Cream, Herbed, Grilled Tomato "Burgers" with, 160
Fennel and Feta Salad, 128
Fiesta Bread, 178
Goat, and Grilled Vegetable Terrine, 130–31
Goat, and Tapenade, Smoked Vegetable Confit on Country Bread with, 158
Goat, Cream Sauce, Smoked Turkey, and Sun-Dried Tomatoes, Penne with, 227
Goat, Grilled Eggplant, and Peppers with Balsamic-Thyme Vinaigrette, 124
Goat, Grilled Portobellos with Garlic, Pine Nuts, Basil, and, 133
Goat, Grilled Tomatoes, 160
Goat, Herbed, or Boursin, Grilled Drumsticks or Thighs Stuffed with, 211–12
Gorgonzola Filet Mignon on a Plank, 347
Grilled, in a Sarong, 128
Grilled Artichoke Pizza on Parmesan-Herb Crust, 185–86
Grilled Asparagus with Shaved Parmigiano-Reggiano, 118
Grilled Eggplant Roll-Ups with Feta-Olive-Lemon Filling, 126
Grilled Pizza with Caramelized Onions and Brie, 180–81
Ham, Cheddar, and Apricot Chutney Pizza, 384
Mozzarella and Tomato Salad with Two Dressings, 354–55
Pecorino Romano–Artichoke Glaze, 194
Planked
Hickory-, with Dried Cranberry Relish, 175
Maple-, with Tricolored Peppers, 175
Semisoft, 174
Roquefort-Bacon Butter, 318
Smoked
Cheesy Smashed Potatoes, 170
Dip, Crunchy, 170
Dip, Homemade Vegetable Crisps with, 170–71
Goat, Salad, 170
Gouda and Tomato Pasta Salad, 173
Mozzarella, Tomato, and Fresh Basil Salad, 173
Sandwich, Grilled, Smoky, 173
Semisoft, 172–73
Smoky Beef and Asparagus Saddlebags, 171–72
Soft, 169–70
Stovetop, Soft, 36
-Stuffed Bone-In Chicken Breasts, Grilled, 200–201
White Cheddar, Potato Gratin with, 412–13
Cherry(ies)
Dried Sweet, –Port Sauce, 237
Kiss of Smoke Beef Tenderloin Black Forest, 402
Chicken
Grilled
and Apple Sausage with Honey-Almond Grilling Glaze, 365–66
Burgers, 303
Butterflied, Rosemary-Scented, 205
Drumsticks or Thighs Stuffed with Herbed Goat Cheese or Boursin, 211–12
grilling times, 16
half a chicken, method for, 201
Hot Diggity Dogs, 365
testing for doneness, 16, 17, 201
Wings, Kathy's, 344
Wings Amogio, 211
Wings and Things, 210–11
Wings and Things, Sizzling, with Sage Butter and Romano Cheese, 211
Grilled Bone-In, Skin-On Breasts, 199–200
Cheese-Stuffed, 200–201

Chicken, Grilled Bone-In, Skin-On Breasts (*cont.*)
and Fresh Greens Salad, 201
Pesto, Sandwich with Cranberry Preserves, 201
Grilled Boneless, Skinless Breasts, 191
Cubano, with Picadillo Olive Salsa, 192
Indoors, 192
Lemonata, 192
Sicilian, One-Dish-Meal, 192–93
with Thousand-Herb Sauce, 192
Grilled, Skewers, 195
Caesar Salad, Curlicue, 196–97
Chopstix, with Gingered Teriyaki Glaze, 196
Satay, 196
marinating times, 67
Planked Boneless, Skinless Breasts, 193–94
Balsamic-Thyme, with Peppers and Onions, 194
with Pecorino Romano–Artichoke Glaze, 194
Rotisserie, 217–18
French Tarragon, 218
Puerto Rican–Style, 218
Sandwich, Karen's Famous, 218–19
Smoked
Barbecued, on Fire, 213
Breasts, and Green Chile Soup, 216
Breasts, with Southwest Heat, 215
Italian Barbecued, 220
Pulled, Salad with Basil Mayonnaise, 213
Rosemary-Garlic, 220
Salad, Chopped, 213
Sesame-Soy Marinated, 221
testing for doneness, 28
timetable for, 27
and Vegetable Lasagna, 221
Whole, 219–20
whole, method for, 201
Wings and Things, 212
Stir-Grilled
Asian Lettuce Wraps, 168–69
with Asparagus and Shaved Parmigiano-Reggiano, 199
and Summer Vegetable Pasta with Fresh Basil Vinaigrette, 199
Tequila-Lime, 199
and Vegetables, 198
Chile(s)
Ancho Mayonnaise, 311–12
Charred Tomato–Chipotle Salsa, 162–63
Chipotle Barbecue Sauce, 90
Chipotle Dipping Sauce, 389
Chipotle Vinaigrette, 86
–Ginger–Green Onion Sauce, 318
Green, and Smoked Chicken Soup, 216
Grilled, Rellenos with Baby Shrimp, 143–44
Grilled, Sauce, Pick a Peck of, 145–46
Poblano Cream Sauce, 93
Raspberry-Jalapeño Barbecue Sauce, 90
Smoked, Beurre Blanc, 99
smoked, preparing, 140
Smoked Chicken Breasts with Southwest Heat, 215
Smoky Chipotle Corn Pudding, 122–23
Southwestern Dressing, 355
Southwest Heat, 215
Tomato, and Garlic Chutney, 428
Chimichurri Sauce, 346–47
Chive Pesto, 64
Chocolate
Almond Joy Brittle, 265
-Coconut-Macadamia Bars, 262–63
Hot Fudge Ganache, 440–41
–Peanut Butter Bars, 263
S'mores, 262
White, –Cranberry Brittle, 265
Chutney
Apricot, 384
Cilantro-Mint, 304
Tomato, Garlic, and Chile, 428
Cilantro
-Mint Chutney, 304
-Peanut Dipping Sauce, 389
Santa Fe Herb Paste, 436
and Smoked Garlic Cream Sauce, 93–94
Clams, Grilled
with Lemon Butter Drizzle, 268
Littleneck, with Pernod Butter, 288
in the Shell, 287
Coconut
Almond Joy Brittle, 265
Chocolate-Macadamia Bars, 262–63
Toasted, Ice Cream, 440–41
Cognac and Apricot Glaze, 241
coleslaw. *See* Slaws
Colwin, Laurie, 63
Corn
cobs and husks, grilling with, 23
Grilled, 119
Green Chile and Smoked Chicken Soup, 216
Layered Salad, 120
Relish, Southwestern-Style, 120
and Smoked Vegetable Pudding, 120
Smoked
Chipotle Pudding, Smoky, 122–23
Green Chile and Smoked Chicken Soup, 216
Ham, and Hominy Casserole, 123
in the Husks, 121–22
Sliced Tomato, and Slivered Red Onion Salad, 122
and Tomato Salad, Fresh, 203
Cornish Game Hens
Grilled, à la Chez Panisse, 246
Grilled Game Birds, 245
with Orange-Honey Baste, 246
Cranberry(ies)
-Almond Torte with Cranberry Drizzle, 394–95
Bourbon Pecan-Stuffed Rotisserie Pork Loin, 399
Dried, Relish, Hickory-Planked Cheese with, 175
-Orange Salsa, 227
–White Chocolate Brittle, 265
Cucumber(s)
Elaborate Yet Easy, in Poppy Seed Dressing, 282
Grilled Gazpacho, 155
Kath's, 281
Tzatziki, 112

D

Davis, Ardie, 44
Desserts
Almond Cookie Brittle, 264–65

Almond Joy Brittle, 265
Blueberry-Peach Tart with Macaroon Crust, 295–96
Chocolate-Coconut-Macadamia Bars, 262–63
Chocolate–Peanut Butter Bars, 263
Cranberry-Almond Torte with Cranberry Drizzle, 394–95
Fresh Fruit Tart, 374–75
Fresh Peach Crumble Ice Cream, 441–42
Grilled Pound Cake with Hot Fudge Ganache and Sweetened Berries, 397
Lemon-Scented Peach Crisp, 393
Mandarin Orange Sorbet, 442
Orange Marmalade Bundt Cake, 396–97
Pecan Pie Bars, 263–64
Pineapple Sorbet in Grilled Pineapple Rings, 442
Rice Krispie Treats, 265
S'mores, 262
Toasted Coconut Ice Cream with Hot Fudge Ganache and Toasted Pecans, 440–41
White Chocolate–Cranberry Brittle, 265
Dips
Barbecued Brisket, 358
Crunchy Smoked Cheese, 170
Smoky Cheese, Homemade Vegetable Crisps with, 170–71
dressings. *See* Salad dressings; Vinaigrettes
drinks. *See* Sangria!
Duck
domestic, about, 236
Grilled
Breast, Salad, 237
Paillards, 235
Paillards with Dried Sweet Cherry–Port Sauce, 237
whole, method for, 236
Smoked
Apricot and Cognac-Glazed, 241
on a Beer Can, 239
Breasts, 239
with Five-Spice Asian Paste, 239
Whole, 238
whole, method for, 236
and Wild Rice Soup, 239
wild, about, 236
Dukka, 61

E

Eggplant
Grilled, 123–24
Balsamic-Marinated Vegetables on the Grill, 314–15
–Garlic Sauce, Fettuccine with, 126
Peppers, and Goat Cheese with Balsamic-Thyme Vinaigrette, 124
Roll-Ups with Feta-Olive-Lemon Filling, 126
Salad, Warm Asian, 125
Spread, Sonoma Farmers' Market, 124–25
Vegetable and Goat Cheese Terrine, 130–31
Vegetable Platter with Fresh Basil Vinaigrette, 129–30
Smoked
Pasta Salad with Rotisserie Lamb and, 432
Rotisserie Leg of Lamb with Smoked Ratatouille, 432
Vegetable Confit, 158
Vegetable Confit on Country Bread with Tapenade and Goat Cheese, 158
Eggs
Beelzebub's Bloody Marys, 204
Caper-Stuffed, 380
Deviled, Classic, 379
Deviled, with Grilled Shrimp, 380–81
Grilled Asparagus Frittata, 118
hard-boiling, 378
Mediterranean Stuffed, 381
Smoked Trout Benedict with Confetti Hash, 273–76
electric grills, 5, 9–10, 24, 25
electric smoker ovens, 10, 12–13, 21, 24
Elk, Drunk, 242–43

F

Fajitas, Citrus-Grilled Beef, 308–9
Fennel
Blood Orange, and Black Olive Relish, Winter, 424
and Feta Salad, 128
Grilled, and Red Potato Salad, 148
Grilled, Red Pepper, and Lemon-Tarragon Vinaigrette, Grilled Scallops with, 291
Orange, and Olive Salad, Moroccan, 280
and Orange Drizzling Sauce, 73
and Orange Marinade, 72–73
Salt, 56
-Tomato Sauce, 95
Fish
Grilled
Asian Tuna Burgers with Wasabi Mayo, 305
cooking times for, 256
general rules for, 256
grilling times, 16
preparing for grill, 256
Skewers, 259–60
testing for doneness, 16, 17
Grilled Fillets, 257
with Basil Oil Mashed Potatoes and Warm Citrus Garnish, 258
Caribbean Grouper on Sugar Cane Skewers, 260–61
Herb-, 258
Japanese-Style, 258–59
Skewers, 259–60
Sweet-Hot Mustard-Glazed Salmon, 437
Veracruzano, 258
Grilled Steaks, 271
Lime-, Swordfish with Charred Tomato-Chipotle Salsa, 272
with Lime-Ginger Marinade, Down Under, 271–72
Seared Rare Tuna Steaks with Toasted Sesame Oil, 272
Skewers, 259–60
Thai-Style Halibut on Lemongrass Skewers, 260
marinating times, 67, 256
Oak-Planked Peppercorn Tuna Steaks with Orange Mayonnaise, 278
Planked, 277
rotisserie cooking, 40
Smoked
Apple Cider–, Trout with Horseradish Cream, 286–87

Fish, Smoked (*cont.*)
cooking times for, 256
general rules for, 256
Happy, Happy, Happy Hour Salmon, 286
Happy, Happy, Happy Hour Salmon Spread, 286
preparing for smoker, 256
Whole, 285
Smoked Fillets, 272–73
Pâté with Dill and Lemon, 276
with Sauce Verte, 273
Smoked Trout Benedict with Confetti Hash, 273–76
Smoked Tomato with Tuna, Lemon, and Herbs, 165
substitution chart, 254–55
Fox, Julie, 390
Frittata, Grilled Asparagus, 118
Fruit. *See also specific fruits*
Breakfast S'Mores, 416
Fresh, Tart, 374–75
Grilled Duck Breast Salad, 237

G

Game Birds. *See also* Duck
Grilled, 245
Cornish Game Hens à la Chez Panisse, 246
Cornish Game Hens with Orange-Honey Baste, 246
Quail Salad with Spiced Pears and Mushrooms, Warm, 246–47
Smoked
and Pasta, 249
Pheasant and Quail, Bacon-Wrapped, 248
pheasant breasts, 249
preparing for cooking, 236
Salad, 248
Small, 247–48
Garlic
-Citrus Marinade, 70
-Herb Pizza Dough, 180
Marinade, 434–35
Mashed Potatoes, Decadent, 321
Rib-Eye Steak, Philadelphia, 318
and Rosemary, Smoke-Roasted Potatoes with, 408
-Rosemary Smoked Chicken, 220
Sauce, 321
Sauce, Dipping, 293
Smoked
and Cilantro Cream Sauce, 93–94
preparing, 140
and Tomatoes, Fettuccine with, 165
Tuscan-Style Porchetta, 405
gas grills
adding "kiss of smoke," 13–14
adding smoke flavors, 12, 13–14, 20, 21, 24
adjusting temperature in, 25
lighting, 9
natural gas for, 3
preparing direct fire in, 11
preparing indirect fire in, 12, 20
propane fuel for, 3
rotisserie cooking on, 33
selection criteria, 3–4
smoking foods in, 12, 20
Gazpacho, Grilled, 155
Gingered Teriyaki Glaze, 196
Ginger-Pineapple Salsa, 414
Glaze
applying to grilled foods, 15
applying to smoked foods, 26
Apricot and Cognac, 241
Apricot-Dijon, 374
barbecue sauces used as, 15, 26
Gingered Teriyaki, 196
Honey-Almond Grilling, 88
Mustard-Apricot, 411
Orange and Tarragon, 261
Pecorino Romano–Artichoke, 194
Raspberry and Mustard, 400–401
sugar-based, types of, 15, 26
Gravy, Traditional Rotisserie Turkey, 229
Greasehouse University, 44
Greens. *See also* Cabbage; Fennel; Lettuce; Spinach
Beef Filet Salad with Orange-Cumin Vinaigrette, 313
Fennel and Feta Salad, 128
Fresh, and Grilled Chicken Salad, 201
Grilled, 126–27
Grilled Cheese in a Sarong, 128
Grilled Lamb, Pear, and Pistou Salad, 430
Grilled Radicchio and Red Cabbage with Herbed Caesar Dressing, 127
Smoked Game Bird Salad, 248
Smoked Goat Cheese Salad, 170
Warm Grilled Quail Salad with Spiced Pears and Mushrooms, 246–47
Gremolata, 274
Griffith, Dotty, 352
grilling foods, 8–17
adding smoke flavors, 11, 12, 13–14, 20
bastes for, 14–15
compared with smoking foods, 2
doneness, testing for, 16–17
doneness chart for, 16
glazes for, 15
grilling times, 15–17
grilling timetable, 16
heat temperatures for, 13
lid position for, 11, 14
methods and tips for, 14–15
rotisserie cooking, 33, 40
stir-grilling, 32
utensils for, 6–7, 41
grills. *See also specific grill types*
baskets for, 6, 40
cleaning, 14
lid position for, 11, 14
preparing food for, 14
racks for, 6
types of, 2–3
Grits, Asiago-Garlic, 392–93
Grits, Smoked Tomato, 164
Grouper, Caribbean, on Sugar Cane Skewers, 260–61

H

Halibut, Thai-Style, on Lemongrass Skewers, 260
Ham
Double-Smoked, 411–14
with Pineapple-Ginger Salsa, 414
Salad Sandwiches, Karen's, 414
Stovetop, 38
Grilled
Cheddar, and Apricot Chutney Pizza, 384
Steaks, 382
Steaks, Country Cured, Vinegar-Mopped, 382–83

Steaks, Sweet, with Brown Sugar Basting Sauce, 383
Smoked Corn, and Hominy Casserole, 123
Hearts of Palm Salad, 283
Herb(s). *See also specific herbs*
adding smoky flavor with, 23
Chimichurri Sauce, 346–47
flavoring grilled foods with, 30–31
Fresh, Aioli, 110
Frizzled, Roasted Cherry Tomatoes with, 208
-Grilled Fish, 258
Herbed Caesar Dressing, 127
-Lemon Marinade, Aromatic, 68–69
-Marinated Rotisserie Pork Loin, 398–99
Mediterranean Salad with Lemon-Sumac Vinaigrette, 279–80
Sauce Verte, 273
stalks, as brushes, 15
stalks, as skewers, 29, 30–31
Thousand-, Sauce, 192
Hollandaise, Food Processor or Blender, 97
Hominy, Smoked Corn, and Ham Casserole, 123
Honey-Almond Grilling Glaze, 88
Honey-Apple Marinade and Baste, 377
Honey-Basted Smoked Onions, 141
Honeyed Barbecue Sauce, 90
Honey-Orange Baste, 246
Horseradish Aioli, 110
Horseradish Cream, 286–87
Horseradish Sauce, Spicy, 223
Hughes, Betty, 171

I

Ice Cream, Fresh Peach Crumble, 441–42
Ice Cream, Toasted Coconut, 440–41

J

Jamison, Cheryl, 214

K

Kallas, Rose, 171
Kamado grills, 5, 10, 12, 21
Kansas City Barbeque Society, 44, 232
Kimizu, 103
Kirk, Paul, 44, 46

L

Lamb
cooking, tips for, 418
Grilled
best cuts for, 418
Brochettes, Tapas-Style, 428
Burgers, 303
Burgers, Greek-Style, with Cilantro-Mint Chutney, 304–5
Chops, 420
Chops with Chiles and Mint, 421
Chops with Rosemary, Garlic, and Lemon Baste, 421
grilling times, 16
Kabobs, Mediterranean-Rubbed, with Lemon Butter Drizzle, 428
Kabobs, Sambar-Spiced South Indian, with Tomato, Garlic, and Chile Chutney, 428
Leg of, 429
Leg of, Rustic Spinach Pesto–Stuffed, 430
Leg of, Simple Stuffed, 430
Pear, and Pistou Salad, 430
Rack of, 422
Rack of, Marinated, with Apricot and Cognac-Cabernet Sauce, 423
Rack of, Rosemary Pesto, 423
Skewers, 427
Spring Grill Platter with Aioli, 421
testing for doneness, 16, 17
marinating times, 67
Rotisserie
and Eggplant, Pasta Salad with, 432
Leg of, 431
Leg of, Garlic-Marinated Rolled, 434–35
Leg of, with Smoked Ratatouille, 432
Sandwiches with Matchstick Vegetables and Tzatziki, 433
Smoked
best cuts for, 418
Leg of, 438
Leg of, Butterflied, Pinot Noir, 438–39
Leg of, Butterflied, Tandoori-Marinated, 439
Leg of, Stuffed, BBQ Queens', 439
Rack of, Baaaaarbecued, 423
testing for doneness, 28
timetable for, 27
Smoked Greek Stuffed Tomatoes, 164
Lasagna, Smoked Chicken and Vegetable, 221
Lavender Salt, 55
Leblang, Bonnie Tandy, 266
Lemongrass Marinade, 74
Lemon(s)
Amogio, 72
Basil Sauce, 343
Butter Drizzle, 87
-Garlic Mayonnaise, 103
Grilled Chicken Lemonata, 192
-Herb Marinade, Aromatic, 68–69
-Soy Sauce, Spicy, 312
-Sumac Vinaigrette, 279–80
-Tarragon Vinaigrette, 75–76
Lettuce
Curlicue Chicken Caesar Salad, 196–97
Grilled Greens, 126–27
Grilled Romaine and Green Onions with Lemon and Olives, 127–28
Grilled Romaine Caesar Salad, 127
Mediterranean Salad with Lemon-Sumac Vinaigrette, 279–80
Wraps, Stir-Grilled Asian, 168–69
Lime(s)
Garlic-Citrus Marinade, 70
-Tequila Marinade, 73
Lobster, Grilled, 294–95
Lobster, Grilled, Italian-Style, 288

M

Macadamia-Chocolate-Coconut Bars, 262–63
Mango-Lemon Sauce, 92
Marinades
Amogio, 72
Cola, 403
compared with vinaigrettes, 67
Fennel and Orange, 72–73

Marinades (*cont.*)
Garlic, 434–35
Garlic-Citrus, 70
Honey-Apple, 377
Lemon Butter Drizzle, 87
Lemongrass, 74
Lemon-Herb, Aromatic, 68–69
Lime-Ginger, 271–72
Red Wine, Provençal, 70
Red Wine, Vinegar, and Herb, 377
Rosemary-Mustard, 71
Sesame and Soy, 389
Sesame-Soy, 221
Tandoori, 74–75
Tequila-Lime, 73
Teriyaki, Homemade, 69
for vegetables, reusing, 119
Worcestershire, 391
working with, 67
Marmalade, Smoked (or Grilled) Onion, 141
Mayer, Lisa Readie, 292
Mayonnaise. *See also* Aioli
Ancho, 311–12
Basil, 213
Lemon-Garlic, 103
Mustard-Mayo-Dill Slather, 66
Mustard-Mayo-Orange Slather, 66
Mustard-Mayo Slather, 66
Mustard-Mayo-Tarragon Slather, 66
Orange, 278
Wasabi, 305
Meatballs, Smoky, 345
Michel-Cupito, Janeyce, 370
Moose, Debbie, 202
Mushroom(s)
Bourbon-Mustard Cream Sauce, 377
Grilled, 132
Balsamic-Marinated Vegetables on the Grill, 314–15
Batayaki Beef with Spicy Lemon-Soy Sauce, 312–13
Portobello, "Burgers," 133
Portobellos with Garlic, Pine Nuts, Basil, and Goat Cheese, 133
Smoked Chicken and Vegetable Lasagna, 221
Grilled Artichoke Pizza on Parmesan-Herb Crust, 185–86
Grilled Steak Salad with Caper Vinaigrette, 309
Porcini Paste, 65
Smoked, 134
Bisque, 136
PLT, 136
Porcini Beef Tenderloin, 339
Smoked Chicken and Vegetable Lasagna, 221
Stuffed, 136
Sour Cream, and Bacon Sauce, 337
Stir-Grilled
and Olives, Mediterranean-Style, 168
Vegetables, Thai-Style, in Lemongrass Marinade, 167
Warm Grilled Quail Salad with Spiced Pears and, 246–47
Mussels, Grilled
with Garlic and Parsley, Black Fettuccine with, 288–89
in the Shell, 287
Mustard
Apricot-Dijon Glaze, 374
-Apricot Glaze, 411
-Bourbon Cream Sauce, 377
-Cornichon Beurre Blanc, 100
-Glazed Salmon, Sweet-Hot, 437
-Herb Dipping Sauce, 389
-Mayo-Dill Slather, 66
-Mayo-Orange Slather, 66
-Mayo Slather, 66
-Mayo-Tarragon Slather, 66
and Raspberry Glaze, 400–401
-Shallot Vinaigrette, 327–28

N

Nut(s). *See also* Almond
Bourbon Pecan-Stuffed Rotisserie Pork Loin, 399
Chocolate-Coconut-Macadamia Bars, 262–63
Dukka, 61
Peanut-Thai Chile Dressing, 80
Pecan Pie Bars, 263–64
Pistachio-Pomegranate Sauce, 96
Pistachio Sausage, 372
Toasted Pecans, 440–41

O

Olive(s)
Black, Blood Orange, and Fennel Relish, Winter, 424
Cured, Cauliflower, and Roasted Red Pepper Salad, 282–83
and Fire-Roasted Tomato Topping, Grilled Pizza with, 180
Orange, and Fennel Salad, Moroccan, 280
Queen-Size Spiced, 145
Salsa, Picadillo, 192
Stir-Grilled, and Mushrooms, Mediterranean-Style, 168
Onion(s)
Caramelized, and Brie, Grilled Pizza with, 180–81
Fried, Slivers, 320
Grilled, 137
Green, 138
Green, and Romaine, with Lemon and Olives, 127–28
Marmalade, 141
Red, and Smoked Tomato Relish, 324
Red, and Sweet Potato Skewers, 151
Red, Slices, 138
Soufflé, 138
with Thyme and Garlic Cream, 138–39
Planked, and Peppers, Balsamic-Thyme Chicken with, 194
Smoked, 139–41
Honey-Basted, 141
Marmalade, 141
Pickled Brewpub, 142
Tart, 141
Orange(s)
Blood, and Raspberry Sauce, 92
Blood, Fennel, and Black Olive Relish, Winter, 424
-Cumin Vinaigrette, 313
Fennel, and Olive Salad, Moroccan, 280
and Fennel Drizzling Sauce, 73
and Fennel Marinade, 72–73
-Fennel Vinaigrette, 280
Garlic-Citrus Marinade, 70
-Ginger Baste, 261
-Ginger Baste, Aussie Shrimp on the Barbie with, 261

-Honey Baste, 246
Mandarin, Sorbet, 442
Marmalade Bundt Cake, 396–97
Mayonnaise, 278
Rub, Spicy, 51
and Tarragon Glaze, 261
Order of the Magic Mop, 44
Oyster(s), Grilled
in Pesto, 288
Prosciutto, and Bay Leaf Skewers, 267
in the Shell, 287

P

Pasta
Black Fettuccine with Grilled Mussels, Garlic, and Parsley, 288–89
Fettuccine with Grilled Eggplant–Garlic Sauce, 126
Fettuccine with Smoked Garlic and Tomatoes, 165
Grilled Squid Linguine with Amogio, 298
Linguine with Smoked Butternut Squash, Fresh Sage, and Morel Cream Sauce, 158
One-Dish-Meal Grilled Chicken Sicilian, 192–93
Penne with Smoked Turkey, Goat Cheese Cream Sauce, and Sun-Dried Tomatoes, 227
Salad, Smoked Gouda and Tomato, 173
Salad with Rotisserie Lamb and Eggplant, 432
Smoked Chicken and Vegetable Lasagna, 221
Smoked Game Birds and, 249
Stir-Grilled Chicken and Summer Vegetable, with Fresh Basil Vinaigrette, 199
Pastes
about, 46
Chive Pesto, 64
Five-Spice Asian, 64–65
Mediterranean Herb, 436
Porcini, 65
Rosemary Pesto, 62–63
Santa Fe Herb, 436
Sweet Moroccan Spice, 435
Peach-Blueberry Tart with Macaroon Crust, 295–96
Peach Crisp, Lemon-Scented, 393
Peach Crumble Ice Cream, Fresh, 441–42
Peanut Butter
–Chocolate Bars, 263
Cilantro-Peanut Dipping Sauce, 389
Dipping Sauce, Asian-Style Asparagus with, 118
Quick Peanut Sauce, 331
Peanut-Thai Chile Dressing, 80
Pear, Grilled Lamb, and Pistou Salad, 430
Pears, Spiced, and Mushrooms, Warm Grilled Quail Salad with, 246–47
Pecan Pie Bars, 263–64
Pecans, Toasted, 440–41
Pecan-Stuffed Bourbon Rotisserie Pork Loin, 399
Peppercorn Beurre Blanc, 102
Peppercorn Rub, Tricolored, 62
Pepper(s). *See also* Chile(s)
Grilled, 142–43
Boats, Cheesy, 143
Eggplant, and Goat Cheese with Balsamic-Thyme Vinaigrette, 124
Gazpacho, 155
Red, Fennel, and Lemon-Tarragon Vinaigrette, Grilled Scallops with, 291
Sauce, Pick a Peck of, 145–46
Tricolored, Maple-Planked Cheese with, 175
Vegetable and Goat Cheese Terrine, 130–31
Vegetable Platter with Fresh Basil Vinaigrette, 129–30
Grill-Roasted, 145
Mediterranean Stuffed Eggs, 381
Roasted Red, Aioli, 110
Roasted Red, and Cannellini Bean Relish, Autumn, 426
Roasted Red, Cauliflower, and Cured Olive Salad, 282–83
Roasted Red, Sauce, 94
smoked, preparing, 140
Smoked Chile Beurre Blanc, 99
Stir-Grilled
Balsamic-Thyme Vegetables, 167
Red Bell, with Garlic and Thyme, 168
Vegetables, 166
Pesto
Aioli, 110
Bread, Cheesy Italian, 177
Chive, 64
Grilled Oysters in, 288
Rosemary, 62–63
Pheasant and Quail, Bacon-Wrapped Smoked, 248
Pheasant breasts, smoked, 249
Phillips, Diane, 434
Pineapple
Bourbon Pecan-Stuffed Rotisserie Pork Loin, 399
-Ginger Salsa, 414
Sorbet in Grilled Pineapple Rings, 442
Pistachio-Pomegranate Sauce, 96
Pistachio Sausage, 372
Pizza
Dough, Food Processor, 179
Dough, Garlic-Herb, 180
Grilled, 179–80
Artichoke, on Parmesan-Herb Crust, 185–86
with Caramelized Onions and Brie, 180–81
with Fire-Roasted Tomato and Olive Topping, 180
Ham, Cheddar, and Apricot Chutney, 384
party, ideas for, 181
plank cooking, 42–43
Pomegranate-Pistachio Sauce, 96
Porcini Beef Tenderloin, Smoked, 339
Porcini Paste, 65
Pork. *See also* Bacon; Ham
Grilled
Burgers, 303
Chops, Sweet, with Brown Sugar Basting Sauce, 383
Chops, Thick-Cut, 376
Chops, Thin-Cut, 382
Chops with Bourbon- Mustard Cream Sauce, 377
Chops with Honey-Apple Marinade and Baste, 377

Pork, Grilled (*cont.*)
Chops with Red Wine, Vinegar, and Herb Marinade, 377
grilling times, 16
Hot Diggity Dogs, 365
Loin Fillet, Center-Cut, 388
Ribs, Indoor-Outdoor Kiss of Fire and Smoke, 387
Sausage, Pistachio, 372
sausage links, tips for, 367
Steaks, 382
Tenderloin, 388
Tenderloin, Sesame and Soy-Marinated, 389
Tenderloin in Worcestershire Marinade, 391
Tenderloin with Chipotle Dipping Sauce, 389
Tenderloin with Cilantro-Peanut Dipping Sauce, 389
Tenderloin with Mustard-Herb Dipping Sauce, 389
testing for doneness, 16, 17
Wisconsin Dilly Beer Brat Sandwiches, 366
marinating times, 67
Rotisserie Loin, 398
Ancho and Chipotle-Rubbed, 399
Bourbon Pecan-Stuffed, 399
Herb-Marinated, 398–99
Sandwiches, 399
Sausage, Spicy, Rebecca's 'Que Queen Extraordinaire, 367
Smoked
BBQ Queens' Choucroute Garnie, 405
Bratwurst, BBQ Queens' Choucroute Garnie with, 369
Butt, 409–10
Butt, Spicy Orange Barbecued, 410
Butts in a Bag, 410
Loin, 404
Loin, Slathered and Rubbed, 405
Loin, Spiral Herbed, with Apricot-Dijon Glaze, 373
Piggy Sandwich, 411
Ribs, 384–85
Ribs, Asian-Style, 385
Ribs, Country-Style, 386
Ribs, Rasberry Barbecued, 385–86
Roast, Raspberry and Mustard–Glazed, 400–401
Sausage, 368
Sausage, Italian, and Artichoke Soup, 369
Sausage, Red Beans and Rice with, 369
Stovetop,Tenderloin, 38–39
testing for doneness, 28
timetable for, 27
Tuscan-Style Porchetta, 405
Smoke-Roasted Loin, with Herbed Pear Stuffing, 407–8
Potato(es). *See also* Sweet Potato(es)
Gratin with White Cheddar Cheese, 412–13
Grilled, 147
Antipasto Skewers, 151
Balsamic-Marinated Vegetables on the Grill, 314–15
Red, and Fennel Salad, 148
Skewered, 149–50
Whole, 148
Grill-Roasted, Salad, Rustic, 148
Homemade Frites, 328
Homemade Vegetable Crisps with Smoky Cheese Dip, 170–71
Mashed, Basil Oil, and Warm Citrus Garnish, Grilled Fish with, 258
Mashed, Decadent Garlic, 321
Oven-Roasted Saffron, 413
Salad, Creamy Dijon, for a Crowd, 151
Smashed, Olive Oil, 320
Smashed, Smoked Cheesy, 170
Smoked, 152
and Aioli Gratin, 152–53
Casserole, BBQ Queens', 153
New or Fingerling, Platter, 153
Salad, 359–60
Soup, 153
Smoked Trout Benedict with Confetti Hash, 273–76
Smoked Turkey Hash, 231
Smoke-Roasted, with Garlic and Rosemary, 408
Powderpuff Barbeque team, 367, 370
Prather, Rozane Miceli, 183
Pudding
Chipotle Corn, Smoky, 122–23
Grilled Corn and Smoked Vegetable, 120
Yorkshire, Smoked Rib Roast with, 350
Putman, Karen, 400

Q

Quail
Grilled, Salad with Spiced Pears and Mushrooms, Warm, 246–47
Grilled Game Birds, 245
Smoked, and Pheasant, Bacon-Wrapped, 248
Smoked Small Game Birds, 247–48
Queen waves, 224–25

R

Radicchio
Grilled Greens, 126–27
and Red Cabbage, Grilled, with Herbed Caesar Dressing, 127
Raoufi, Latifa, 332
Raspberry
Barbecued Ribs, 385–86
Beurre Blanc, 101
and Blood Orange Sauce, 92
-Jalapeño Barbecue Sauce, 90
and Mustard Glaze, 400–401
Relish
Blood Orange, Fennel, and Black Olive, Winter, 424
Dried Cranberry, 175
Grilled Corn, Southwestern-Style, 120
Roasted Red Pepper and Cannellini Bean, Autumn, 426
Smoked Tomato and Grilled Red Onion, 324
Strawberry, Toasted Almond, and Spinach, Springtime, 425
Tomato, Pine Nut, and Caper, Summer, 425
Rice
Durn Good, 243
Wild, and Smoked Duck Soup, 239
Wild, Cheesy, 371–72
Rosemary
-Apple Salsa, 234
Garlic, and Lemon Baste, 68

-Garlic Smoked Chicken, 220
Mediterranean Herb Paste, 436
-Mustard Marinade, 71
Pesto, 62–63
Pesto Rack of Lamb, 423
Pesto Smoked Rib Roast, 350
Salt, 56
-Scented Grilled Butterflied Chicken, 205
rotisserie cooking, 33, 40
Rubs
about, 46
All-Purpose, BBQ Queens', 49
Barbecue, BBQ Queens' Photo Op, 58–59
Dukka, 61
Fair for Fowl, 51
Fennel Salt, 56
Fireworks, 60
Lavender Salt, 55
Lemon Pepper, Spicy Red-Hot, 53
McCormick seasonings, 59
Mesquite, Texas Two-Steppin', 59
Ole Hickory, 60–61
Orange, Spicy, 51
pantry ingredients for, 50
Peppercorn, Tricolored, 62
Rib, Memphis Blue-Ribbon, 49
Rib, Prizewinning, 50
Rosemary Salt, 56
Smoked Hickory Salt, 57
Southwest Heat, 215
Spicy, Savory Seasoned Salt, 56–57
Steak, Cajun, 58
Sugar and Spice, Zesty, 52

S

Saffron Potatoes, Oven-Roasted, 413
Saffron Vinaigrette, 76
Salad. *See also* Slaws
Bean, Italian, 284
Beef Filet, with Orange-Cumin Vinaigrette, 313
Cauliflower, Roasted Red Pepper, and Cured Olive, 282–83
Celery Root Rémoulade, 328–29
Chicken Caesar, Curlicue, 196–97
Dijon Potato, Creamy, for a Crowd, 151
Eggplant, Warm Asian, 125
Elaborate Yet Easy Cucumbers in Poppy Seed Dressing, 282
Fennel and Feta, 128
Fresh Corn and Tomato, 203
Fresh Greens and Grilled Chicken, 201
Grated Carrot, Bistro, 329
Grilled Corn Layered, 120
Grilled Duck Breast, 237
Grilled Herbed and Spiced Beef Tenderloin, 341–42
Grilled Lamb, Pear, and Pistou, 430
Grilled Quail, with Spiced Pears and Mushrooms, Warm, 246–47
Grilled Radicchio and Red Cabbage with Herbed Caesar Dressing, 127
Grilled Red Potato and Fennel, 148
Grilled Romaine and Green Onions with Lemon and Olives, 127–28
Grilled Romaine Caesar, 127
Grilled Steak, with Caper Vinaigrette, 309
Grill-Roasted Potato, Rustic, 148
Haricots Verts, with Mustard-Shallot Vinaigrette, 327–28
Hearts of Palm, 283
Kath's Cucumbers, 281
Mediterranean, with Lemon-Sumac Vinaigrette, 279–80
Mozzarella and Tomato, with Two Dressings, 354–55
Orange, Fennel, and Olive, Moroccan, 280
Pasta, with Rotisserie Lamb and Eggplant, 432
A Platter of Fresh Tomatoes, 206–7
Pulled Smoked Chicken, with Basil Mayonnaise, 213
Roma Tomato, Italian, 207
Salata (Afghani Fresh Chopped Vegetable), 335
Smoked Chicken, Chopped, 213
Smoked Corn, Sliced Tomato, and Slivered Red Onion, 122
Smoked Game Bird, 248
Smoked Goat Cheese, 170
Smoked Gouda and Tomato Pasta, 173
Smoked Mozzarella, Tomato, and Fresh Basil, 173
Smoked Potato, 359–60
Smoked Tomato with Tuna, Lemon, and Herbs, 165
Salad dressings. *See also* Vinaigrettes
Creamy Blue Cheese, 111
Herbed Caesar, 127
Southwestern, 355
Thai Chile-Peanut, 80
Salmon
Planked, 277
Smoked, Happy, Happy, Happy Hour, 286
Smoked, Happy, Happy, Happy Hour, Spread, 286
Sweet-Hot Mustard-Glazed, 437
Salsa
Charred Tomato–Chipotle, 162–63
Cranberry-Orange, 227
Grilled Tomatillo, 163
Picadillo Olive, 192
Pineapple-Ginger, 414
Rosemary-Apple, 234
Salt
Fennel, 56
Lavender, 55
Rosemary, 56
Smoked Hickory, 57
Spicy, Savory Seasoned, 56–57
types of, 54–55
Sandwiches
Burnt Ends, 358
Double-Smoked Ham Salad, Karen's, 414
Grilled Cheese, Smoky, 173
Pesto Chicken, with Cranberry Preserves, 201
Piggy, 411
Rotisserie Chicken, Karen's Famous, 218–19
Rotisserie Lamb, with Matchstick Vegetables and Tzatziki, 433
Rotisserie Pork Loin, 399
Rotisserie Turkey, Day-After, 229
Rustic Reuben, 360
Smoked Beef BLT, 339
Smoked PLT, 136
Smoked Rib Roast, 350–51
Smoked Turkey and Monterey Jack Club, 231
Smoked Vegetable Confit on Country Bread with Tapenade and Goat Cheese, 158

Sandwiches (*cont.*)
Stir-Grilled Scallop Po'boy, 298
Super Sicilian, 184
Wisconsin Dilly Beer Brat, 366
Sangria!, 250
Sauce. *See also* Aioli; Barbecue Sauce; Salsa
Ancho Mayonnaise, 311–12
Apricot and Cognac-Cabernet, 423
BBQ Queens' Love Potion for the Swine, 89
Béarnaise, Rustic, 98
Bordelaise, Simply Delicious, 91
Bourbon- Mustard Cream, 377
Brown Sugar Basting, 383
Chile–Ginger–Green Onion, 318
Chimichurri, 346–47
Chipotle Dipping, 389
Cilantro-Peanut Dipping, 389
Cocktail, Nuevo Latino, 290–91
Creamy Blue Cheese Dressing, 111
Dried Sweet Cherry–Port, 237
emulsion, about, 97
Fennel and Orange Drizzling, 73
Garlic, 321
Garlic Dipping, 293
Grilled Eggplant–Garlic, 126
Grilled Peppers, Pick a Peck of, 145–46
Hollandaise, Food Processor or Blender, 97
Horseradish, Spicy, 223
Hot Fudge Ganache, 440–41
Kimizu, 103
Lemon Basil, 343
Lemon Butter Drizzle, 87
Lemon-Garlic Mayonnaise, 103
Lemon-Soy, Spicy, 312
Mango-Lemon, 92
Mustard-Cornichon Beurre Blanc, 100
Mustard-Herb Dipping, 389
Orange Mayonnaise, 278
Peanut, Quick, 331
Peanut Butter Dipping, 118
Peppercorn Beurre Blanc, 102
Pistachio-Pomegranate, 96
Poblano Cream, 93
Raspberry and Blood Orange, 92
Raspberry Beurre Blanc, 101
Red Wine–Shallot, 308
Roasted Red Pepper, 94
Smoked Butternut Squash, Fresh Sage, and Morel Cream, 158
Smoked Chile Beurre Blanc, 99
Smoked Garlic and Cilantro Cream, 93–94
Sour Cream, Bacon, and Mushroom, 337
Thai Green Curry, 290
Thousand-Herb, 192
Tomato-Chile, Spicy, 331
Tomato-Fennel, 95
Traditional Rotisserie Turkey Gravy, 229
Tzatziki, 112
Verte, 273
Vietnamese Drizzle, 87
Wasabi Mayo, 305
Sauerkraut
BBQ Queens' Choucroute Garnie, 405
BBQ Queens' Choucroute Garnie with Smoked Bratwurst, 369
Rustic Reuben, 360
Sausage(s)
Grilled
Chicken and Apple, with Honey-Almond Grilling Glaze, 365–66
Hot Diggity Dogs, 365
Pistachio, 372
Seafood, with Cucumber and Tzatziki, 366
Wisconsin Dilly Beer Brat Sandwiches, 366
links, cooking tip for, 367
Pork, Spicy, Rebecca's 'Que Queen Extraordinaire, 367
Smoked, 368
BBQ Queens' Choucroute Garnie, 405
BBQ Queens' Choucroute Garnie with Smoked Bratwurst, 369
Italian, and Artichoke Soup, 369
Red Beans and Rice with, 369
Scallop(s)
Grilled, 289–90
with Fennel, Red Pepper, and Lemon-Tarragon Vinaigrette, 291
Skewers, Orange and Tarragon–Glazed, 261
Skewers, Tequila-Lime, 269
in Thai Green Curry Sauce, 290
Stir-Grilled, Po'boy Sandwiches, 298
Stir-Grilled Shellfish, "Wonton"-Wrapped, 298
Scones, Campfire Skillet, 415–16
Seafood. *See also* Fish; Shellfish
Sausage, Grilled, with Cucumber and Tzatziki, 366
Sesame and Soy Marinade, 389
Sesame-Soy Marinated Chicken, Smoked, 221
Shallot(s)
–Red Wine Sauce, 308
smoked, preparing, 140
Vinaigrette, Hot, 85
Shellfish. *See also* Scallop(s); Shrimp
Grilled
Calamari, Stuffed, with Thousand-Herb Sauce, 291
Clams with Lemon Butter Drizzle, 268
Littleneck Clams with Pernod Butter, 288
Lobster, 294–95
Lobster, Italian-Style, 288
Mussels, Garlic, and Parsley, Black Fettuccine with, 288–89
Oyster, Prosciutto, and Bay Leaf Skewers, 267
Oysters, Clams, or Mussels in the Shell, 287
Oysters in Pesto, 288
Skewers, 259–60
Squid, 289–90
testing for doneness, 16, 17
marinating times, 67
Planked, 277
Stir-Grilled, 297
Squid Linguine with Amogio, 298
"Wonton"-Wrapped, 298
Shrimp
Baby, Grilled Chiles Rellenos with, 143–44
Cedar-Planked, Chimichurri, 278
Grilled, 289–90
Aussie, on the Barbie with Orange-Ginger Baste, 261
Deviled Eggs with, 380–81

with Nuevo Latino Cocktail Sauce, 290–91
Prosciutto and Basil–Wrapped, with Garlic Dipping Sauce, 293
in Thai Green Curry Sauce, 290
Stir-Grilled, 297
Stir-Grilled Shellfish, "Wonton"-Wrapped, 298
Stovetop Smoked, 37
Silver Queen Corn Queen, 202
skewers, 7, 29–32
Slather, Mustard-Mayo, 66
slathers, about, 46
Slaws
Blue Cheese Coleslaw, 79
Broccoli, Crunchy, with Thai Chile-Peanut Dressing, 80
Frozen Asset, 82
Layered Vinegar, 80–81
Red Cabbage and Apple, 83
Summer Squash, Mediterranean, 81
types of, 78
Smith, Kathy, 340
smoke flavor
adding to charcoal grill, 11
adding to gas grill, 12, 13–14, 20
"kiss of," gas grilling with, 13–14
non-wood, types of, 23
for plank cooking, 42, 43
wood, types of, 21–24
smokers. *See also* electric smoker ovens; water smokers
adding smoke flavors, 21, 24
adjusting temperature in, 25
competition-style, 20
judging temperature of, 25
placing food in, 25
selection criteria, 18
stovetop, 21, 34–36
types of, 18
smoking foods, 18–28
bastes for, 26
compared with grilling, 2
doneness chart for, 28
glazes for, 26
heat temperatures for, 19–21
lid position for, 25
methods and tips for, 25–26
plank cooking, 42–43
preparations for, 19, 24–25
preparing food for, 25
smoke-roasting, about, 406
smoking time, estimating, 26
smoking timetable, 27
stovetop smoking, 34–36
utensils for, 6–7, 41
S'mores, 262
S'mores, Breakfast, 416
Sorbet, Mandarin Orange, 442
Sorbet, Pineapple, in Grilled Pineapple Rings, 442
Soup
Green Chile and Smoked Chicken, 216
Grilled Gazpacho, 155
Smoked Duck and Wild Rice, 239
Smoked Italian Sausage and Artichoke, 369
Smoked Mushroom Bisque, 136
Smoked Potato, 153
Sour Cream, Bacon, and Mushroom Sauce, 337
Spinach
Baby, Sautéed, with Olive Oil and Garlic, 275
BBQ Queens' Smoked Stuffed Leg of Lamb, 439
Cheesy Wild Rice, 371–72
Creamed, Classic, 319
Grilled Cheese in a Sarong, 128
Grilled Corn Layered Salad, 120
Pasta Salad with Rotisserie Lamb and Eggplant, 432
Pesto–Stuffed Leg of Lamb, Rustic, 430
Strawberry, and Toasted Almond Relish, Springtime, 425
Spreads
Eggplant, Sonoma Farmers' Market, 124–25
Salmon, Happy, Happy, Happy Hour, 286
Smoked Fish Pâté with Dill and Lemon, 276
Squash. *See also* Summer Squash; Zucchini
Smoked, 157
Smoked Acorn, Spicy, 159
Smoked Butternut, Fresh Sage, and Morel Cream Sauce, Linguine with, 158
Squid
Grilled, 289–90
Grilled, Linguine with Amogio, 298
Grilled Stuffed Calamari with Thousand-Herb Sauce, 291
stir-grilling, technique for, 32
stovetop smokers
adding wood chips to, 21
checking food in, 35
cleaning, 36
description of, 34
recipes for, 36–39
smoking foods in, 34–35
Strawberry, Toasted Almond, and Spinach Relish, Springtime, 425
Summer Squash. *See also* Zucchini
Grilled, 154
Balsamic-Marinated Vegetables on the Grill, 314–15
Char-Grilled Baby, 155
Vegetable Platter with Fresh Basil Vinaigrette, 129–30
Vegetable Ribbon Skewers, 156
Slaw, Mediterranean, 81
Smoked, 157
Vegetable Confit, 158
Vegetable Confit on Country Bread with Tapenade and Goat Cheese, 158
Stir-Grilled
Balsamic-Thyme Vegetables, 167
Chicken and Summer Vegetable Pasta with Fresh Basil Vinaigrette, 199
with Fresh Herbs, 167–68
Tequila-Lime Chicken, 199
Sweet Potato(es)
Grilled, 147
Grilled, and Red Onion Skewers, 151
Homemade Vegetable Crisps with Smoky Cheese Dip, 170–71
Smoked, 152
Smoke-Roasted, with Garlic and Rosemary, 408
Swordfish, Lime-Grilled, with Charred Tomato-Chipotle Salsa, 272

T

Tamarind and Yogurt Beef Kabobs with Warm Pita Breads, 331
Tandoori Marinade, 74–75
Tarragon and Orange Glaze, 261
Tarragon Grilled Turkey Breast, 223
Tarragon Rotisserie Chicken, French, 218
Tarts
Blueberry-Peach, with Macaroon Crust, 295–96
Fresh Fruit, 374–75
Grilled Vegetable, 149
Smoked Onion, 141
Tomato, Late-Harvest, 209
temperature, in grills, 13
temperature, in smokers, 25
Tequila-Lime Chicken, Stir-Grilled, 199
Tequila-Lime Marinade, 73
Tequila-Lime Scallop Skewers, 269
Teriyaki Glaze, Gingered, 196
Teriyaki Marinade, Homemade, 69
thermometers, 7, 41
Tio, Celina, 314
Tofu
Stir-Grilled Asian Lettuce Wraps, 168–69
Thai-Style Stir-Grilled Vegetables in Lemongrass Marinade, 167
Tomatillo, Grilled, Salsa, 163
Tomato(es)
Charred, –Chipotle Salsa, 162–63
-Chile Sauce, Spicy, 331
and Corn Salad, Fresh, 203
-Fennel Sauce, 95
Fire-Roasted, and Olive Topping, Grilled Pizza with, 180
Fresh, A Platter of, 206–7
Garlic, and Chile Chutney, 428
Grilled, 159
BBQ Queens' Grilled Antipasto Platter, 144
"Burgers" with Herbed Cream Cheese, 160
Goat Cheese, 160
Provençal, 160–61
Provençal, Indoor, 161
Roma, with Anchovy, Garlic, and Parsley, 160
Vegetable Platter with Fresh Basil Vinaigrette, 129–30
Zucchini-Stuffed, with Basil, 270
Grilled Gazpacho, 155
Jersey, Grilled Bruschetta with, 294
and Mozzarella Salad with Two Dressings, 354–55
Picadillo Olive Salsa, 192
Pine Nut, and Caper Relish, Summer, 425
Roasted Cherry, with Frizzled Herbs, 208
Roma, Salad, Italian, 207
Sliced, Smoked Corn, and Slivered Red Onion Salad, 122
Smoked, 161
Aioli, 110
and Basil Butter, Rustic Bread with, 177–78
and Garlic, Fettuccine with, 165
and Gouda Pasta Salad, 173
Greek Stuffed, 164
and Grilled Red Onion Relish, 324
Grits, 164
Rotisserie Leg of Lamb with Smoked Ratatouille, 432
Stovetop, 37–38
with Tuna, Lemon, and Herbs, 165
Vegetable Confit, 158
Vegetable Confit on Country Bread with Tapenade and Goat Cheese, 158
Smoked Beef BLT, 339
Smoked Mozzarella, and Fresh Basil Salad, 173
Stewed and Scalloped, 322
Stir-Grilled
Balsamic-Thyme Vegetables, 167
Chicken and Summer Vegetable Pasta with Fresh Basil Vinaigrette, 199
Chicken and Vegetables, 198
Tequila-Lime Chicken, 199
Vegetables, Thai-Style, in Lemongrass Marinade, 167
Tart, Late-Harvest, 209
Torte, Cranberry-Almond, with Cranberry Drizzle, 394–95
Trout, Apple Cider–Smoked, with Horseradish Cream, 286–87
Trout, Smoked, Benedict with Confetti Hash, 273–76
Tuna
Burgers, Asian, with Wasabi Mayo, 305
Lemon, and Herbs, Smoked Tomato with, 165
Steaks, Peppercorn, Oak-Planked, with Orange Mayonnaise, 278
Steaks, Seared Rare, with Toasted Sesame Oil, 272
Turkey
Grilled
Burgers, 303
Burgers, Fourth of July Pilgrim, with Dried Cranberry Relish, 305
Roulade with Lemon-Basil Sauce, 343–44
testing for doneness, 16, 17
Grilled Breast
Fillets, Bacon-Wrapped, 223
Steaks with Spicy Horseradish Sauce, 223
Tarragon, 223
Tenderloin Steaks, 222–23
Rotisserie, 228–29
Gravy, Traditional, 229
Sandwich, Day-After, 229
Smoked
Apple-, 233
Hash, 231
and Monterey Jack Club Sandwiches, 231
testing for doneness, 28
timetable for, 27
Whole, 230
Smoked Breast
Apple-, 233
Boneless, 226
Brie and Basil–Stuffed, 227
with Cranberry-Orange Salsa, 227
Goat Cheese Cream Sauce, and Sun-Dried Tomatoes, Penne with, 227
Stir-Grilled Asian Lettuce Wraps, 168–69
Tzatziki, 112

U

utensils, for grilling, 6–7, 41

V

Veal, grilled, testing for doneness, 16, 17
Vegetable(s). *See also specific vegetables*
Grilled
Balsamic-Marinated, 314–15
BBQ Queens' Grilled Antipasto Platter, 144
and Goat Cheese Terrine, 130–31
Platter with Fresh Basil Vinaigrette, 129–30
Ribbon Skewers, 156
Skewered, 149–50
Tart, 149
testing for doneness, 16, 17
marinating times, 67
rotisserie cooking, 40
Smoked
Confit, 158
Confit on Country Bread with Tapenade and Goat Cheese, 158
and Grilled Corn Pudding, 120
Stir-Grilled, 166
Balsamic-Thyme, 167
and Chicken, 198
Thai-Style, in Lemongrass Marinade, 167
Venison, Drunk, 242–43
Vinaigrettes
Balsamic-Thyme, 84
Basil, 355
Basil, Fresh, 85
Caper, 309
Chipotle, 86
Citrus Caesar, 84
Lemon-Sumac, 279–80
Lemon-Tarragon, 75–76
Mustard-Shallot, 327–28
Orange-Cumin, 313
Orange-Fennel, 280
Saffron, 76
Shallot, Hot, 85
using as marinade, 67
Wheat Beer, 77

W

Wasabi Mayo, 305
water smokers
adding smoke flavors to, 24
charcoal, lighting, 19
description of, 5, 8
electric, lighting, 10, 20
electric, smoking times on, 26
gas, lighting, 10, 20
grilling foods in, 8, 12, 19
smoking foods in, 8, 12, 19–20, 26
Weaver, Candy, 240
Weber kettle grills, 4
Wells, Carolyn, 232
Wine
Red, Marinade, Provençal, 70
Red, –Shallot Sauce, 308
Red, Vinegar, and Herb Marinade, 377
Sangria!, 250
woks, 32
"Wonton"-Wrapped Stir-Grilled Shellfish, 298
wood chips, 21, 24
wood chunks, 24
wood flavors. *See* smoke flavor
wood pellet grills
adding smoke flavors, 24
adjusting temperature in, 13
description of, 5
electric-fired, lighting, 9–10
indirect grilling in, 12
smoking foods in, 12, 21
wood pellets, 5, 24, 41
wood "sticks" or logs, 24
Worcestershire Marinade, 391

Y

Yogurt
Tandoori Marinade, 74–75
Tzatziki, 112

Z

Zucchini
Grilled
Balsamic-Marinated Vegetables on the Grill, 314–15
Char-Grilled Baby Summer Squash, 155
Gazpacho, 155
Summer Squash, 154
Vegetable and Goat Cheese Terrine, 130–31
Vegetable Ribbon Skewers, 156
Mediterranean Summer Squash Slaw, 81
Smoked, 157
Rotisserie Leg of Lamb with Smoked Ratatouille, 432
Vegetable Confit, 158
Vegetable Confit on Country Bread with Tapenade and Goat Cheese, 158
Stir-Grilled
Balsamic-Thyme Vegetables, 167
Chicken and Summer Vegetable Pasta with Fresh Basil Vinaigrette, 199
Chicken and Vegetables, 198
Summer Squash with Fresh Herbs, 167–68
Tequila-Lime Chicken, 199
-Stuffed Tomatoes with Basil, 270

World Index Maps / Welt Indexkarten / Indice de Mapas del Mundo
Index des Cartes du Monde / Índice de Mapas do Mundo

RUSSIA
24
76
80
86
88
89
BELARUS
UKRAINE
78
MOLD.
KAZAKHSTAN
MONGOLIA
Black Sea
84
85
Caspian Sea
TURKEY
130
UZBEKISTAN
TURKMENISTAN
KYRG.
TAJIKISTAN
CHINA
104
105
98
KOREA
92
94
Beijing (Peking)
271
Seoul
271
Shanghai
106
93b
174m
102
107
100
T'aipei
TAIWAN
Hong Kong
175d
SYRIA
IRAQ
Tehrān
267
IRAN
128
AFGHANISTAN
PAKISTAN
123
120
Delhi
272
NEPAL
124
BHUTAN
INDIA
Calcutta
272
126
MYANMAR
142
132
EGYPT
Red Sea
SAUDI
ARABIA
OMAN
Bombay
272
122
SRI LANKA
LAOS
THAILAND
Krung Thep (Bangkok)
269
CAMBODIA
VIETNAM
Thanh-pho Ho Chi Minh (Saigon)
269
110
Manila
269
116
PHILIPPINES
Pacific Ocean
175c
175b
140
SUDAN
ERITREA
YEMEN
DJIBOUTI
144
ETHIOPIA
SOMALIA
KENYA
UGANDA
ZAIRE
TANZANIA
154
MALAWI
ZAMBIA
ZIMBABWE
MOZAMBIQUE
56
Johannesburg
273
SWAZILAND
LESOTHO
158
COMOROS
157a
MADAGASCAR
157b
157c
MAURITIUS
REUNION
MALAYSIA
114
Singapore
BRUNEI
BORNEO
112
SUMATRA
INDONESIA
CELEBES
115a
Jakarta
JAVA
LESSER SUNDA ISLANDS
115b
Indian Ocean
NEW GUINEA
PAPUA NEW GUINEA
164
SOLOMON ISLANDS
175e
VANUATU
175f
NEW CALEDONIA
175g
FIJI
AUSTRALIA
162
166
171a
168a
168b
170
Sydney
274
171b
169
Melbourne
274
TASMANIA
NEW ZEALAND
172
176
178
230
242
244
22
72
74
90
134
136
118
108
138
160

Alison —

Happy Birthday 1994

& lots of love

Dad & Liz

& Amanda & Andrew

RAND McNALLY

THE NEW INTERNATIONAL ATLAS
DER NEUE INTERNATIONALE ATLAS
EL NUEVO ATLAS INTERNACIONAL
LE NOUVEL ATLAS INTERNATIONAL
O NÔVO ATLAS INTERNACIONAL

TWENTY-FIFTH ANNIVERSARY EDITION

Rand McNally International Atlas Staff

Publisher
Andrew McNally III
Andrew McNally IV

Corporate Advisory Group
John S. Bakalar
Henry J. Feinberg
Jayne L. Fenton
Michael W. Dobson, Ph. D.

Editorial and Cartographic Direction
Russell L. Voisin
Jon M. Leverenz
V. Patrick Healy

Art and Design Direction
Chris Arvetis
Gordon Hartshorne

Coordination
David C. Zapenski
Stephen Steiner

Geographic Research and Index
Susan Hudson
Keith Jennerjohn
Felix A. Lopez
Raymond T. Tobiaski
Richard L. Forstall (Consultant)

Cartographic Editorial
Robert K. Argersinger
Winifred V. Farbman

Cartographic Compilation
Jill M. Stift
Nina Lusterman
Lynn N. Jasmer
Larry K. Tyler

Cartographic Production
Jim Purvis
Charlene Smith
Patty Porter
Barbara Smith
Wanda McDonald

Composition and Typesetting
Rajani Veeramachaneni

Terrain Illustrators
Ivan Barcaba
Evelyn Mitchell
Mary Jo Schrader

Advisory Board

Dr. Manlio Castiglioni
Italy

Dr. Arch C. Gerlach
United States

Dr. Ir. Cornelis Koeman
Netherlands

Dr. André Libault
Brazil

Brig. D. E. O. Thackwell
United Kingdom

Robert J. Voskuil
United States

Dr. Akira Watanabe
Japan

International Map Advisors

Europe
Prof. Dr. Emil Meynen
Germany
Dr. Sandor Rado
Hungary

Asia
Dr. Hisashi Sato
Japan

Australia
R. O. Buchanan
United Kingdom

Anglo-America
Dr. Arch C. Gerlach
United States

Latin America
Dr. André Libault
Brazil
Dra. Consuelo Soto Mora
Mexico
Dr. Jorge A. Vivó Escoto
Mexico

Metropolitan Area Maps
Prof. Harold M. Mayer
United States

The Real World

Developed by Rand McNally with Dr. Marvin W. Mikesell, University of Chicago. Artimus Keiffer, Kent State University, contributed the section on communication.

Editors
Jon M. Leverenz, Brett R. Gover.

Design Direction
John C. Nelson, Donna M. McGrath; designer: Vito M. DePinto.

Maps by the Cartographic Department of Rand McNally.

Satellite image on pages xvi-A•1: Mendoza, Argentina. Processed by Earth Information Systems Corporation, Austin, TX.; Laser film by Cirrus Technology, Inc., Nashua, NH. Data for communication section from TeleGeography, Inc., Washington, D.C.

The New International Atlas
25th Anniversary Edition

Printed in the United States of America.

Library of Congress Cataloging-in-Publication Data
Rand McNally and Company.
The new international atlas. -- 25th anniversary ed.
p. cm..
Includes index.
ISBN 0-528-83693-5
1. Atlases. I. Title.
G1021.R23 1994 <G&M>
912--dc20
94-15784
CIP
MAP

Foreword

Twenty-five years ago Rand McNally first published *The New International Atlas*. It was created through the cooperative efforts of an international cadre of cartographers, geographers, designers, and editors, under the leadership and direction of Rand McNally. The goal was to bring to a worldwide audience the most comprehensive, authoritative, and handsome atlas possible.

In the quarter of a century since the first printing, the *Atlas* has continued to portray with unsurpassed accuracy the Earth's surface and patterns of human settlement, and to chronicle the geographic changes affecting our lives. During this period it has been redesigned several times, and new maps have been added to the original selection. Today *The New International Atlas* is used throughout the world and is considered the standard of excellence for world reference atlases.

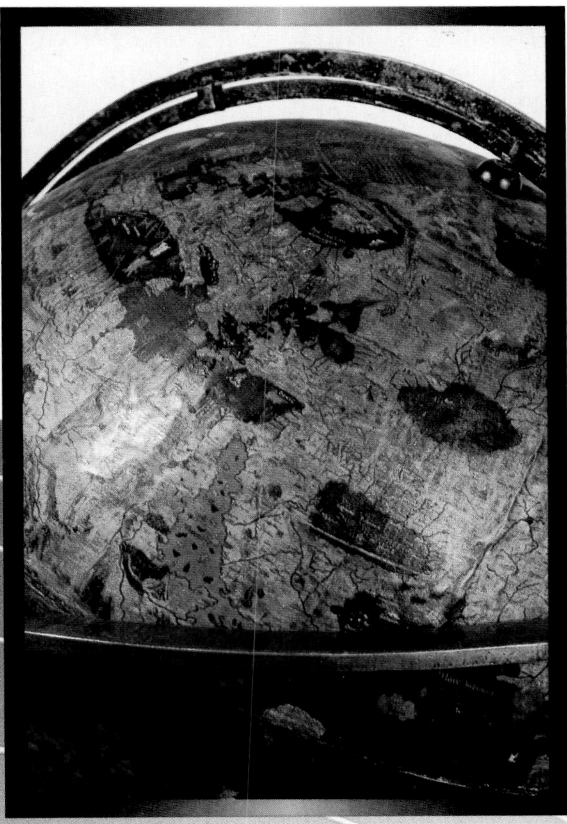

The editorial policies for the *Atlas* have been established with international use in mind. This approach has been carried into the maps through the utilization of the metric system of measurement, and through strong emphasis on the use of local geographic names. Essentially all names are in the local language; however, English is used for names of geographic features which cross international borders, and as an alternate form for major cities. The names of countries appear on most of the maps both in English and in the locally official forms.

Generic terms for physical features (mountain, island, cape, etc.) also appear in their local forms, not in English. Short glossaries translating the most common of these terms appear in the margins of most maps. A complete glossary of all the generic terms can be found toward the back of the *Atlas*. In the index to the *Atlas*, the translation of generic terms is aided by the use of symbols.

The coverage of the world's regions has also been planned with international use in mind. There is an approximate balance between North America, Europe, and Asia, each with more than one-fifth of the total map pages. Africa, Australia/Oceania, and South America together account for the remaining one-third.

Another significant feature of the *Atlas* is the classification of the maps into five separate series, while using a limited number of map scales. This allows ready comparison of the nature and size of the Earth's regions. Each series has its own distinctive style and content. In the first of these series, the continents are portrayed at 1:24,000,000 in natural colors, as they might appear from about 4,000 miles in space. The series also includes maps of the oceans at 1:48,000,000 and the world at 1:75,000,000.

In the next series, the major world regions are uniformly portrayed at 1:12,000,000. These maps are primarily political in style and content. The third series covers virtually the entire inhabited area of the Earth at either 1:6,000,000 for the less dense regions, or 1:3,000,000 for Europe, most of North America, and the densest portions of South and East Asia. Physical and cultural detail are given approximately equal emphasis in this series.

In the fourth series, the scale of 1:1,000,000 has been used to portray key regions in each continent, selected for their exceptional importance, high population density, or complexity of development. The emphasis is on cultural detail, though relief is also shown. In the fifth and final series, the world's major metropolitan areas are mapped at 1:300,000. This series emphasizes the complex patterns characteristic of large urban areas.

The sequence of maps in the *Atlas* begins with the series of world, continent, and ocean maps. Next are the three series of regional maps, arranged within major regions from smallest scale (1:12,000,000) to largest scale (1:1,000,000). The metropolitan maps (1:300,000) have been kept together in one section following the regional maps.

The map symbols used for specific features, shown on the Legend to Maps, are generally alike on all of the map scales, though reduced in size for smaller scales. The art form called shaded relief is used to symbolize the Earth's terrain on the maps in the *Atlas*. It uses variations from light through dark tones to give the maps their three-dimensional appearance. The expert craftsmanship used to depict the surface features in this manner adds beauty, drama, and important information to the maps, as well as a unique quality to the *Atlas*. On the 1:6,000,000 and 1:3,000,000 maps, the shaded relief appears in combination with altitude tints which represent variations in elevation.

In the concluding part of the *Atlas* are various tables and summaries for general reference, beginning with the comprehensive glossary of geographic terms. Following this is the World Information Table which lists the area, population, and political status for each major political unit. The world's largest metropolitan areas are then listed, followed by a list of the world's major cities and their populations. Finally, the Index provides map location references—map page, latitude and longitude—for more than 160,000 places.

Vorwort

Vor fünfundzwanzig Jahren veröffentlichte Rand McNally zum ersten Mal *Den Neuen Internationalen Atlas*. Dieses Werk wurde durch die Zusammenarbeit einer internationalen Gruppe von Kartographen, Geographen, Designern und Herausgebern unter der Leitung und Aufsicht von Rand McNally geschaffen. Das Ziel war, einem weltweiten Publikum den umfassendsten, autoritativsten und attraktivsten Atlas bereitzustellen.

Im Vierteljahrhundert seit der ersten Ausgabe zeigt der Atlas weiterhin die Erdoberfläche und die menschliche Besiedlung mit großer Genauigkeit und stellt die geographischen Veränderungen dar, die unser Leben beeinflussen. In diesem Zeitraum wurde der Atlas mehrmals revidiert und die ursprüngliche Auswahl durch neue Landkarten erweitert. Heute wird *Der Neue Internationale Atlas* überall in der Welt benutzt und als Norm für ausgezeichnete Weltatlanten betrachtet.

Die redaktionellen Richtlinien für den *Atlas* wurden im Hinblick auf internationale Benutzung aufgestellt. Daher werden metrische Maßeinheiten und sowie örtliche geographische Namen benutzt. Im Prinzip erscheinen alle Namen in der jeweiligen Landessprache, jedoch wird Englisch für die Bezeichnung geographischer Merkmale, die Staatsgrenzen überschreiten, sowie als Alternativform für Großstädte eingesetzt. Die Ländernamen erscheinen auf den meisten Landkarten sowohl auf Englisch als auch in den örtlich geltenden Formen.

Gatungsbegriffe für geographische Eigenschaften (Gebirge, Inseln, Buchten usw.) werden ebenfalls in der jeweiligen Landessprache und nicht auf Englisch angegeben. Kurze Glossare mit Übersetzungen der üblichsten Begriffe erscheinen am Rande der meisten Landkarten. Ein vollständiges Glossar aller Gattungsnamen ist nahe dem Ende des *Atlasses* zu finden. Im Index für den gesamten *Atlas* wird die Übersetzung generischer Ausdrücke durch Symbole vereinfacht.

Auch die Behandlung der Weltregionen wurde nach internationalen Gesichtspunkten gestaltet. Die Behandlung von Nordamerika, Europa und Asien nimmt jeweils den gleichen Raum ein, und jeder dieser Kontinente umfaßt mehr als ein Fünftel der gesamten Landkartenseiten. Afrika, Australien/Ozeanien und Südamerika nehmen das restliche Drittel ein.

Ein weiteres wesentliches Merkmal des *Atlasses* ist die Klassifizierung der Landkarten in fünf getrennte Serien, wobei eine begrenzte Anzahl von Maßstäben eingesetzt wird. Dies ermöglicht mühelose Vergleiche der Bodenbeschaffenheit und der Größe der jeweiligen Erdregionen. Jede dieser Serien hat ihren eigenen distinktiven Stil und Inhalt. Die erste Serie zeigt die Kontinente im Maßstab 1:24 000 000 in Naturfarben, wie sie in einer Entfernung von 6600 Kilometern über der Erde sichtbar sind. Diese Serie enthält auch die Karten der Meere im Maßstab 1:48 000 000 und der Welt im Maßstab 1: 75 000 000.

In der folgenden Serie werden die größten Weltregionen gleichartig im Maßstab 1:12 000 000 dargestellt. Diese Landkarten sind in Stil und Inhalt hauptsächlich politisch gegliedert. Die dritte Serie deckt

die gesamten Besiedlungsgebiete der Erde entweder im Maßstab 1:6 000 000 bei den weniger dicht besiedelten Bereichen oder 1:3 000 000 bei Europa, einem Großteil von Nordamerika und sowie bei den am dichtesten besiedelten Gebiete in Süd- und Ostasien. Physische und kulturelle Details werden ungefähr gleichartig in dieser Serie betont.

Bei der vierten Serie wird der Maßstab 1:1 000 000 eingesetzt, um Schlüsselgebiete jedes Kontinents nach Wichtigkeit, Bevölkerungsdichte oder Komplexität der Entwicklung darzustellen. Die Betonung liegt auf kulturellem Detail, aber auch Relief wird gezeigt. Die fünfte und letzte Serie stellt die Bevölkerungszentren im Maßstab von 1:300 000 dar. Diese Serie hebt die komplexen Muster, die für große Stadtgebiete charakteristsich sind, hervor.

Die Abfolge der Karten im *Atlas* beginnt mit einer Anzahl von Welt-, Kontinent- und Meereskarten. Danach folgen drei Serien von regionalen Landkarten, die innerhalb größerer Gebiete von kleinerem Maßstab (1:12 000 000) bis größerem Maßstab (1:1 000 000) angeordnet sind. Die Großstadtkarten (1:300 000) sind in einem Teil nach den regionalen Landkarten zusammengefaßt.

Die Landkartensymbole für bestimmte Merkmale, die in der Legende der Landkarten auftreten, sind bei allen Maßstäben allgemein gleichartig, obwohl sie bei kleineren Maßstäben ebenfalls verkleinert sind. Schattierte Reliefkarten symbolisieren die Erdoberfläche auf den Landkarten im *Atlas*. Variationen von hellen und dunklen Farbtönen geben den Landkarten ein dreidimensionales Aussehen. Diese kartographische Kunstform, die zur Darstellung der Oberflächeneigenschaften eingesetzt wird, gibt den Landkarten Schönheit, Eindrucksstärke, bietet wichtige Informationen und verleiht dem *Atlas* eine einzigartige Qualität. Auf den Landkarten im Maßstab 1:6 000 000 und 1:3 000 000 wird schattierte Reliefdarstellung zusammen mit Höhenfarbtönen eingesetzt und zeigt Höhenunterschiede.

Am Ende des *Atlasses* sind zahlreiche Tabellen und Zusammenfassungen als allgemeine Referenz zu finden, die mit einem umfassenden Glossar geographischer Begriffe beginnen. Danach folgt eine Weltinformationstabelle mit Bereichen, Bevölkerung und politischem Status der wesentlichsten Staaten. Dann werden die größten Bevölkerungsgebiete sowie eine Liste der Großstädte und deren Bevölkerungszahlen aufgeführt. Schließlich gibt der Index Hinweise auf die Landkarten mit Seitenzahlen sowie Breiten- und Längengraden für mehr als 160 000 Orte.

Prefacio

Vinte-cinco anos atrás a Rand McNally publicou *O Novo Atlas Internacional* pela primeira vez. Ele foi criado através dos esforços cooperativos de um quadro internacional de cartógrafos, geógrafos, desenhistas e editores, sob a liderança e direção da Rand McNally. A meta era trazer à uma audiência mundial o atlas mais compreensivo, autoritário e simpático possível.

Neste quarto de século desde a primeira impressão, o *Atlas* continuou a retratar a superfície da Terra e os padrões de colonização humana com grande exatidão, e o registro das mudanças geográficas que afetam as nossas vidas. Durante este período, ele foi redesenhado diversas vezes, e novos mapas foram somados à seleção original. Hoje, *O Novo Atlas Internacional* é utilizado ao redor do mundo e é considerado como sendo o padrão de excelência para os atlases mundiais de referência.

As políticas editoriais para o *Atlas* foram estabelecidas tendo em mente o uso internacional. Esta aproximação foi levada aos mapas através da utilização do sistema métrico de medições, e pela forte ênfase ao uso dos nomes geográficos locais. Essencialmente todos os nomes estão na lingua local; porém, o Inglês é utilizado para os nomes das características geográficas que cruzam fronteiras internacionais, e como uma forma alternativa para cidades principais. Os nomes dos países aparecem na maioria dos mapas tanto em Inglês como na forma oficial local.

Têrmos genéricos para características físicas (montanha, ilha, cabo, etc.) também aparecem em sua forma local, não em Inglês. Glossários curtos traduzindo os mais comuns destes têrmos aparecem nas margens da maioria dos mapas. Um glossário completo de todos os têrmos genéricos pode ser encontrado ao final do *Atlas*. No índice do *Atlas*, uma tradução dos têrmos genéricos é auxiliada pelo uso de símbolos.

A cobertura das regiões mundiais também foram planejadas com o uso internacional em mente. Existe um balanço aproximado entre a América do Norte, Europa e Asia, cada um com mais de um quinto do total de páginas de mapas. África, Austrália/Oceania, e América do Sul juntos compõem o um-terço restante.

Outra característica significante do *Atlas* é a classificação dos mapas em cinco séries separadas, enquanto usando um número limitado de escalas de mapas. Isto permite uma rápida comparação da natureza e do tamanho da regiões da Terra. Cada série possui seu próprio estilo e conteúdo distintos. Na primeira destas séries, os continentes estão retratados na escala de 1:24.000.000 em cores naturais, como eles poderiam parecer de aproximadamente 4.000 milhas no espaço. A série também inclui mapas dos oceanos em 1:48.000.000 e o mundo em 1:75.000.000.

Na próxima série, as principais regiões mundiais são retratadas uniformemente em 1:12.000.000. Estes mapas são primáriamente políticos quanto ao estilo e conteúdo. A terceira série cobre virtualmente todas as áreas habitadas da Terra em 1:6.000.000 para as regiões menos densas, ou 1:3.000.000 para a Europa, a maior parte da América do Norte, e as porções mais densas do Sul e do Leste da Asia. Uma ênfase aproximadamente igual aos detalhes físicos e culturais é dada nesta série.

Na quarta série, a escala de 1:1.000.000 foi utilizada para retratar as regiões chave de cada continente, selecionados pela sua excepcional importância, alta densidade populacional, ou complexidade do desenvolvimento. A ênfase é sobre o detalhe cultural, embora relevo também seja mostrado. Na quinta e última série, as principais áreas metropolitanas mundiais são mapeadas em 1:300.000. Esta série enfatiza os padrões complexos característicos de grandes áreas urbanas.

A sequência de mapas no *Atlas* inicia com a série de mapas do mundo, continente e oceano. A seguir vem três séries de mapas regionais, arranjados dentro de regiões principais desde a menor escala (1:12.000.000) até a maior escala (1:1.000.000). Os mapas metropolitanos (1:300.000) foram mantidos juntos numa seção seguinte aos mapas regionais.

Os símbolos de mapa utilizados para características específicas, mostrados na Inscrição dos Mapas, são geralmente os mesmos em todas as escalas dos mapas, embora reduzidos em tamanho para as escalas menores. A forma de arte chamada relevo sombreado é utilizado para simbolizar o terreno da Terra nos mapas do *Atlas*. A forma utiliza variações dos tons claros aos escuros para dar aos mapas sua aparência tri-dimensional. O artesanato especializado utilizado para retratar as característicass da superfície desta forma soma beleza, drama e informações importantes aos mapas, como também uma qualidade sem igual ao *Atlas*. Nos mapas de 1:6.000.000 e 1:3.000.000, o relevo sombreado aparece em combinação com matizes de altitude que representam variações na elevação.

Na parte que conclui o *Atlas* existem várias tabelas e sumários para referência geral, começando com o glossário compreensivo de têrmos geográficos. Em seguida a isso, está a Tabela de Informação do Mundo, que lista a área, população e status político para cada unidade política. As maiores áreas metropolitanas estão então listadas, seguidas por uma lista das maiores cidades do mundo e suas populações. Finalmente, o Índice proporciona referências de localização de mapas - página do mapa, latitude e longitude - para mais de 160.000 lugares.

Préface

Le *Nouvel Atlas International* fut publié pour la première fois par Rand McNally il y a vingt-cinq ans. Cet atlas fut le produit de la collaboration d'une équipe internationale de cartographes, de géographes, de concepteurs et de rédacteurs travaillant sous la direction de Rand McNally. Le but était de mettre un atlas faisant autorité, aussi complet et bien présenté que possible, à la disposition de lecteurs dans le monde entier.

Tout au long du quart de siècle qui s'est écoulé depuis sa première impression, l'*Atlas* a continué à illustrer avec une grande précision la surface de la Terre et son peuplement humain, et à faire la chronique des changements géographiques qui affectent notre vie. Pendant cette période, de nouvelles cartes ont été ajoutées à la sélection initiale, et sa conception même a été refondue à plusieurs reprises. Aujourd'hui, *Le Nouvel Atlas International* est utilisé dans le monde entier et est considéré comme la norme d'excellence pour les atlas mondiaux de référence.

Sur le plan rédactionnel, l'*Atlas* a véritablement été conçu pour un public international. Cette approche a été appliquée aux cartes en utilisant le système métrique et en employant autant que possible les noms géographiques locaux. En règle générale, tous les noms sont imprimés dans la langue du pays concerné ; cependant, la langue anglaise est utilisée pour les noms de structures géographiques qui dépassent les frontières internationales, et les grandes villes sont indiquées à la fois en anglais et dans la langue locale. Sur la plupart des cartes, les noms des pays sont indiqués en anglais et selon la forme officielle locale.

Les termes génériques pour les traits physiques (montagne, île, cap, etc.) apparaissent également dans leur forme locale plutôt que systématiquement en anglais. De brefs glossaires traduisant les termes génériques les plus usuels figurent en marge de la plupart des cartes. Un glossaire complet de tous les termes génériques est inclus vers la fin de l'*Atlas*. Dans l'index de l'*Atlas*, la compréhension des termes génériques est facilitée par l'emploi de symboles.

Le nombre de pages consacrées aux différents continents a également été décidé en pensant au public international. Il existe un équilibre approximatif entre l'Amérique du Nord, l'Europe et l'Asie - chacun de ces continents occupant plus de 20 pour cent du nombre total des pages de cartes. L'Afrique, l'Australie/Océanie et l'Amérique du Sud occupent ensemble le tiers restant des pages de cartes.

Une autre particularité intéressante de l'*Atlas* est la classification des cartes en cinq séries distinctes avec un nombre limité d'échelles. Ceci permet de comparer facilement la nature et la superficie des régions de la Terre. Chaque série a un style et un contenu distinctifs. Dans la première de ces séries, les continents sont représentés à l'échelle de 1:24 000 000 en couleurs naturelles, exactement comme ils apparaîtraient si vous les regardiez depuis plus de 6 000 km dans l'espace. Cette série comprend également des cartes des océans à 1:48 000 000 et du monde à 1:75 000 000.

Dans la série suivante, les principales régions du monde sont représentées de façon uniforme à l'échelle de 1:12 000 000. Ces cartes sont principalement politiques par leur style et par leurs détails. La troisième série couvre virtuellement toute la surface habitée de la Terre à l'échelle de 1:6 000 000 pour les régions faiblement peuplées ou de 1:3 000 000 pour l'Europe, la plus grande partie de l'Amérique du Nord et les régions à forte densité de population de l'Asie du Sud et de l'Est. Les cartes de cette série donnent une attention identique aux détails physiques et aux détails culturels.

Dans la quatrième série, l'échelle de 1:1 000 000 a été utilisée pour présenter les régions clés de chaque continent en raison de leur importance exceptionnelle, de leur forte densité de population ou de la complexité de leur développement. Les détails culturels sont mis en valeur, mais le relief y apparaît également. Dans la cinquième et dernière série, les principales agglomérations métropolitaines du monde sont présentées à l'échelle de 1:300 000. Cette série de cartes montre les caractéristiques complexes des grandes zones urbanisées.

La séquence de cartes de l'*Atlas* commence par les cartes du monde, des continents et des océans. Puis on trouve les trois séries de cartes régionales arrangées pour chaque grande région depuis la plus petite échelle (1:12 000 000) jusqu'à la plus grande (1:1 000 000). Toutes les cartes des zones métropolitaines (1:300 000) ont été regroupées dans la même section, à la suite des cartes régionales.

Les symboles des cartes utilisés pour des caractéristiques spécifiques, qui apparaissent sur la Légende des cartes, sont généralement les mêmes pour toutes les échelles de cartes, mais en dimensions réduites pour les échelles les plus petites. La méthode graphique dite du relief ombré est utilisée pour symboliser les traits physiques de la Terre sur les cartes de l'*Atlas*. Elle utilise des variations allant du plus clair au plus sombre pour donner aux cartes leur aspect tridimensionnel. Cette technique complexe qui est utilisée pour représenter les particularités de la surface terrestre de cette manière ajoute de la beauté, un aspect spectaculaire et des renseignements importants aux cartes, ainsi qu'une qualité unique à l'*Atlas*. Sur les cartes à une échelle de 1:6 000 000 et de 1:3 000 000, le relief ombré apparaît combiné avec des nuances de hauteurs qui représentent des variations diverses de l'altitude.

Enfin, dans la dernière partie de l'*Atlas*, on trouvera divers tableaux et résumés pour référence générale, en commençant par un glossaire complet des termes géographiques. Ce glossaire est suivi du Tableau des informations mondiales, qui indique la superficie, la population et le statut politique de chacune des principales unités politiques. La section suivante énumère les grandes zones métropolitaines du monde, puis les plus grandes villes du monde, ainsi que leur population. Enfin, l'*Index* donne les références nécessaires pour permettre de localiser plus de 160 000 points dans l'Atlas - page de la carte, latitude et longitude.

Prefácio

Hace veinticinco años Rand McNally publicó por primera vez *El Nuevo Atlas Internacional*. El mismo fue creado gracias a los esfuerzos de colaboración de un plantel internacional de cartógrafos, geógrafos, diseñadores y revisores, bajo el liderazgo y dirección de Rand McNally. El objetivo consistía en poner a la disposición de un público mundial el atlas más completo, más fidedigno y más hermoso posible.

Durante el cuarto de siglo desde su primera impresión, el *Atlas* ha seguido ilustrando con gran exactitud la superficie de la Tierra y las tendencias de las poblaciones, además de registrar los cambios geográficos que afectan nuestras vidas. Durante este período el diseño ha sido modificado varias veces, habiéndose añadido nuevos mapas a la selección original. Hoy día *El Nuevo Atlas Internacional* se utiliza en el mundo entero y es considerado como la norma por excelencia entre los atlas de referencia mundial.

Los principios editoriales que han guiado la elaboración del *Atlas* han sido establecidos teniendo presente el uso a nivel internacional. Este enfoque ha sido incorporado en los mapas mediante la utilización del sistema métrico de medidas y mediante un énfasis acentuado en el uso de los nombres geográficos locales. Esencialmente, todos los nombres aparecen en el idioma local; sin embargo, se ha utilizado el inglés para los nombres de rasgos geográficos que cruzan los confines internacionales y como forma alternativa para ciudades importantes. Los nombres de países aparecen tanto en inglés como en el idioma oficial de la localidad.

También los términos genéricos de accidentes físicos (como montañas, islas, cabos, etc.) figuran en los idiomas locales y no en inglés. En el margen de la mayoría de los mapas aparecen breves glosarios con la traducción de los términos más comunes. Un glosario completo de todos los términos genéricos se encuentra hacia el final del *Atlas*. En el índice alfabético del *Atlas*, la traducción de los términos genéricos es facilitada mediante el uso de símbolos.

También la cobertura de las regiones del mundo ha sido planificada teniendo presente el uso internacional. Existe un equilibrio aproximado entre Norteamérica, Europa y Asia, dedicando a cada continente más de un quinto del total de páginas con mapas. Africa, Australia/Oceanía y América del Sur comprenden, juntas, el tercio restante.

Otra característica significativa del *Atlas* está representada por la clasificación de los mapas en cinco series independientes, aun utilizando un número limitado de escalas. Esto permite una comparacón rápida de la naturaleza y dimensiones de las regiones terrestres. Cada serie está dotada de un estilo y contenido bien distinto. En la primera de estas series, los continentes están representados con una escala de 1:24.000.000 a colores naturales, tal como podrían aparecer desde una distancia de 4.000 millas en el espacio. La serie comprende también mapas de los océanos a una escala de 1:48.000.000 y del mundo a 1:75.000.000.

En la serie subsiguiente, se ilustran las principales regiones del mundo a una escala uniforme de 1:12.000.000. El estilo y el contenido de estos mapas es principalmente político. La tercera serie abarca prácticamente la totalidad de la superficie poblada de la Tierra a una escala de 1:6.000.000 para las regiones menos densamente pobladas o a 1:3.000.000 para Europa, la mayor parte de Norteamérica y las partes de mayor densidad de Asia del Sur y Asia Oriental. En esta serie se ha dedicado aproximadamente el mismo grado de énfasis a los detalles físicos y culturales.

En la cuarta serie, se ha utilizado una escala de 1:1.000.000 para ilustrar las regiones clave de cada continente, seleccionadas en base a su importancia excepcional, alta densidad de población o complejidad de desarrollo. Se ha prestado énfasis al detalle cultural, aun cuando se muestren también los relieves. En la quinta y última serie se han cartografiado las áreas metropolitanas de gran envergadura a una escala de 1:300.000. Esta serie pone énfasis en los patrones característicos de las grandes áreas urbanas.

La secuencia de mapas en el *Atlas* comienza con la serie de mapas del mundo, de los continentes y de los océanos. Seguidamente, aparecen las tres series de mapas regionales, dispuestas dentro de las regiones principales con escalas a partir desde la más pequeña (1:12.000.000) a la más grande (1:1.000.000). Los mapas metropolitanos (1:300.000) se han reunido juntos en una sola sección, a continuación de los mapas regionales.

Los símbolos utilizados en los mapas con respecto a accidentes específicos, indicados en la Leyenda de Mapas, son por lo general similares en todas las escalas, pero de dimensiones reducidas en el caso de escalas más pequeñas. La forma gráfica conocida como relieve sombreado se utiliza para simbolizar el terreno de la Tierra en los mapas del *Atlas*. Se hace uso de variaciones de tonos claros y oscuros para dar el aspecto tridimensional a los mapas. La pericia artística empleada para ilustrar de esta manera las características de superficie añade belleza, drama e información importante a los mapas, así como una calidad exclusiva al *Atlas*. En los mapas con escalas de 1:6.000.000 y 1:3.000.000, el relieve sombreado aparece en combinación con los matices de altitudes que representan las diferencias de altura.

En la parte final del *Atlas* figuran varias tablas y resúmenes como referencia general, comenzando con el glosario completo de los términos geográficos. A continuación de ello, aparece la Tabla de Información del Mundo que indica datos de superficie, población y estado político de cada unidad política importante. Luego se enumeran las áreas metropolitanas más grandes del mundo, seguidas por una lista de las principales ciudades del mundo y su población. Por último, el Indice alfabético proporciona referencias para la ubicación de los mapas como, por ejemplo, la página del mapa, latitud y longitud, correspondientes a más de 160.000 localidades.

Summary of Contents

Advisors, Contributors, Editors, and Staff ii
Foreword iii
Summary of Contents vi
List of Maps vii
Legend to Maps x-xii
Regional and World Index Maps xiii-xv
The Real World (Thematic maps of the world) xvi-A•24
Maps (see List of Maps, vii) 1-288
- World, Ocean, and Continent Maps 1-19
- Regional Maps 20-258
- Metropolitan Area Maps 259-288

Glossary and Abbreviations of Geographical Terms 289
World Information Table 296
Metropolitan Areas Table 300
Populations of Cities and Towns 301
Index 317

Sumario del Contenido

Asesores, Colaboradores, Redactores, y Ayudantes ii
Prefacio iv
Sumario del Contenido vi
Lista de Mapas viii
Leyendas para Mapas x-xii
Indice de los Mapas Regionales y del Mundo xiii-xv
El Mundo Real (Mapas temáticos del Mundo) xvi-A•24
Mapas (véase Lista de Mapas, viii) 1-288
- Mapas del Mundo, Océanos, y Continentes) 1-19
- Mapas Regionales 20-258
- Mapas de las Áreas Metropolitanas 259-288

Glosario y Abreviaciones de Términos Geográficos 289
Tabla de Información Mundial 296
Tabla de las Áreas Metropolitanas 300
Habitantes en las Ciudades y Poblaciones 301
Indice 317

Inhaltsverzeichnis

Berater, Mitarbeiter, Herausgeber, und Redaktion ii
Vorwort iii-iv
Inhaltsverzeichnis vi
Kartenverzeichnis vii
Zeichenerklärung x-xii
Regionale- und Weld Indexkarten xiii-xv
Die Echte Welt (Thematische Landkarten der Welt) xvi-A•24
Karten (siehe Kartenverzeichnis, vii) 1-288
- Weldlarten, Karten der Ozeane und Erdteile 1-19
- Regionalkarten 20-258
- Karten von Stadregionen 259-288

Verzeichnis und Abkürzungen Geographischer Begriffe 289
Welt Informationstabelle 296
Tabelle der Stadtregionen 300
Einwohnerzahlen von Gross-Städten 301
Register 317

Table des Matières

Conseillers, Collaborateurs, Rédacteurs et Personnel ii
Préface v
Table des Matières vi
Liste des Cartes viii
Légende des Cartes x-xii
Index des Cartes Régionales et des Cartes du Monde xiii-xv
Le Monde en Realité (Cartes thématique du monde) xvi-A•24
Cartes (voir Liste des Cartes, viii) 1-288
- Cartes du Monde, des Océans, et des Continents 1-19
- Carte Régionales 20-258
- Cartes des Zones Métropolitaines 259-288

Glossaire et Abréviations de Termes Géographique 289
Table d'Informations Mondiales 296
Table des Zones Métropolitaines 300
Population des Grands Centres et des Villes 301
Index 317

Sumário

Assessores, Colaboradores, y Editores ii
Prefácio v
Sumário vi
Lista de Mapas ix
Legendas dos Mapas x-xii
Mapas de Índice Regionais e do Mundo xiii-xv
O Mundo Real (Mapas temáticos do Mundo) xvi-A•24
Mapas (ver a Lista de Mapas, ix) 1-288
- Mapas do Mundo, dos Oceanos, y Continentes) 1-19
- Mapas Regionais 20-258
- Mapas das Áreas Metropolitanas 259-288

Glossário e Abreviações de Termos Geográficos 289
Tabela de Informações Mundiais 296
Tabela das Áreas Metropolitanas 300
Populaçaõ dos Centros Urbanos 301
Indice 317

Lists of Maps

World, Ocean and Continent Maps

* Introduction 1
1:75 World: Political 2–3
1:75 World: Physical 4–5
1:48 Pacific and Indian Oceans 6–7
1:48 Atlantic Ocean 8
1:24 Antarctica 9
1:24 Europe and Africa 10–11
1:24 Asia 12–13
1:24 Australia and Oceania 14–15
1:24 North America 16–17
1:24 South America 18–19

Regional Maps

Introduction 20–21

Eurasia

1:12 Europe 22–23
1:6 Northern Europe 24–25
1:3 Southern Scandinavia 26–27
1:3 British Isles 28–29
1:3 Central Europe 30–31
1:3 France and the Alps 32–33
1:3 Spain and Portugal 34–35
1:3 Italy 36–37
1:3 Southeastern Europe 38–39
1:1 Stockholm - Karlstad 40
1:1 København - Malmö - Kiel 41
1:1 London - Birmingham - Cardiff 42–43
1:1 Dublin - Manchester - Newcastle upon Tyne 44–45
1:1 Glasgow - Edinburgh - Aberdeen 46–47
1:1 Dublin - Belfast - Cork 48–49
1:1 Paris - London - Bruxelles 50–51
1:1 Amsterdam - Düsseldorf - Hamburg 52–53
1:1 Berlin - Hamburg - Praha 54–55
1:1 Bruxelles - Frankfurt - Stuttgart 56–57
1:1 Zürich - Genève - Strasbourg 58–59
1:1 Nürnberg - München 60
1:1 Wien - Brno - Linz 61
1:1 Lyon - Marseille - Milano 62–63
1:1 München - Venezia - Firenze 64–65
1:1 Roma - Firenze - Napoli 66–67
1:1 Napoli - Messina - Bari 68–69
1:1 Palermo - Catania - Messina 70
1:1 Cagliari - Sassari 71
1:12 Northwest Asia 72–73
1:12 Northeast Asia 74–75
1:3 Baltic and Moscow Regions 76–77
1:3 Ukraine 78–79
1:3 Volga Region 80–81
1:1 Moskva - Tula - Tver' 82
1:1 Donets'k - Luhans'k - Rostov 83
1:3 Caucasus and Transcaucasia 84
1:3 Tashkent Region 85
1:6 Central Russia and Kazakhstan 86–87
1:6 Lake Baikal Region 88
1:6 Far Eastern Russia 89
1:12 China, Japan and Korea 90–91
1:3 Japan 92–93
1:1 Tōkyō - Nagoya - Kyōto 94–95
1:1 Ōsaka - Hiroshima - Fukuoka 96–97
1:3 Northeast China and Korea 98–99
1:3 East and Southeast China 100–101
1:6 Interior China 102–103
1:1 Shenyang -Fushun (Mukden - Fushun) 104
1:1 Beijing - Tianjin (Peking - Tientsin) 105
1:1 Shanghai - Nanjing (Shanghai - Nanking) 106
1:1 Chongqing - Chengdu (Chungking - Chengtu) 107
1:12 Southeast Asia 108–109
1:6 Myanmar, Thailand and Indochina 110–111
1:6 Malaysia and Western Indonesia 112–113
1:3 Malaya, Singapore and Northern Sumatra 114
1:3 Java • Lesser Sunda Islands 115
1:3 Philippines 116–117
1:12 India, Pakistan and Southwest Asia 118–119
1:6 Northern India and Pakistan 120–121
1:6 Southern India and Sri Lanka 122
1:3 Punjab and Kashmir 123
1:3 Ganges Lowland and Nepal 124–125
1:1 Calcutta - Dhaka - Jamshedpur 126–127
1:6 The Middle East 128–129
1:3 Turkey and Cyprus 130–131
1:1 Yerushalayim - Dimashq (Jerusalem - Damascus) 132–133

Africa

1:12 Western North Africa 134–135
1:12 Eastern North Africa 136–137
1:12 Southern Africa 138–139
1:6 Egypt and Sudan 140–141
1:1 Al-Qāhirah - As-Suways (Cairo - Suez) 142–143
1:6 Ethiopia, Somalia and Yemen 144–145
1:6 Libya and Chad 146–147
1:6 Northwestern Africa 148–149
1:6 West Africa 150–151
1:6 Western Congo Basin 152–153
1:6 East Africa and Eastern Congo Basin 154–155
1:6 Southern Africa and Madagascar 156–157
1:3 South Africa 158–159

Australia/Oceania

1:12 Australia 160–161
1:6 Western and Central Australia 162–163
1:6 Northern Australia and New Guinea 164–165
1:6 Eastern Australia 166–167
1:1 Perth • Adelaide 168
1:1 Melbourne - Geelong - Ballarat 169
1:1 Sydney - Newcastle 170
1:1 Brisbane • Canberra 171
1:3 New Zealand 172–173
Various Scales
Islands of the Pacific 174–175

Anglo America

1:12 Canada 176–177
1:12 United States 178–179
1:6 Alaska and Yukon 180–181
1:3 Southwestern Canada 182–183
1:3 South-Central Canada 184–185
1:3 Southeastern Canada 186–187
1:3 Northeastern United States 188–189
1:3 Great Lakes Region 190–191
1:3 Southeastern United States 192–193
1:3 Mississippi Valley 194–195
1:3 Southern Great Plains 196–197
1:3 Northern Great Plains 198–199
1:3 Southern Rocky Mountains 200–201
1:3 Northwestern United States 202–203
1:3 California and Nevada 204–205
1:1 Montréal - Québec 206
1:1 Boston - New York - Albany 207
1:1 New York - Philadelphia - Washington - Norfolk 208–209
1:1 New York - Buffalo 210–211
1:1 Toronto - Ottawa 212–213
1:1 Pittsburgh - Cleveland - Detroit 214–215
1:1 Chicago - Detroit - Milwaukee 216–217
1:1 Indianapolis - Cincinnati - Louisville 218
1:1 St. Louis - Springfield 219
1:1 Miami - Tampa - Orlando 220–221
1:1 Houston - Dallas - Austin 222–223
1:1 Vancouver - Seattle - Portland 224–225
1:1 San Francisco - Reno - Bakersfield 226–227
1:1 Los Angeles - San Diego 228
Various Scales
Hawaii 229

Latin America

1:12 Middle America 230–231
1:6 Mexico 232–233
1:3 Central Mexico 234–235
1:3 Central America 236–237
1:6 Caribbean Region 238–239
Various Scales
Islands of the West Indies 240–241
1:12 Northern South America 242–243
1:12 Southern South America 244–245
1:6 Colombia, Ecuador, Venezuela and Guyana 246–247
1:6 Peru, Bolivia and Western Brazil 248–249
1:6 Northeastern Brazil 250–251
1:6 Central Argentina and Chile 252–253
1:6 Southern Argentina and Chile 254
1:6 Southeastern Brazil 255
1:1 Rio de Janeiro - São Paulo 256–257
1:1 Buenos Aires - Montevideo 258

Metropolitan Area Maps (1:300,000)

Introduction 259
London 260
Paris 261
Manchester - Liverpool 262
Ruhr Area 263
Berlin • Wien • Budapest 264
Sankt Peterburg • Moskva 265
Madrid • Milano • Lisboa • Barcelona 266
Roma • Athinai • İstanbul • Tehrān 267
Tōkyō - Yokohama 268
Krung Thep (Bangkok) • Thanh Pho Ho Chi Minh (Saigon) • Jakarta • Shanghai • T'aipei • Manila 269
Ōsaka - Kōbe - Kyōto 270
Beijing (Peking) • Sŏul • Singapore • Hong Kong 271
Delhi • Bombay • Calcutta 272
Lagos • Kinshasa - Brazzaville • Al-Qāhirah (Cairo) • Johannesburg 273
Sydney • Melbourne 274
Montréal • Toronto 275
New York 276–277
Chicago 278
Cleveland • Pittsburgh 279
Los Angeles 280
Detroit - Windsor 281
San Francisco - Oakland - San Jose 282
Boston 283
Buffalo - Niagara Falls • Baltimore • Washington 284
Philadelphia 285
Ciudad de México • La Habana • Caracas • Lima • Santiago 286
Rio de Janeiro • São Paulo 287
Buenos Aires 288

* Scale in millions

Kartenverzeichnis

Weltkarten, Karten der Ozeane und Erdteile

* Einleitung 1
1:75 Erde: Politisch 2–3
1:75 Erde: Physisch 4–5
1:48 Pazifischer und Indischer Ozean 6–7
1:48 Atlantischer Ozean 8
1:24 Antarktis 9
1:24 Europa und Afrika 10–11
1:24 Asien 12–13
1:24 Australien und Ozeanien 14–15
1:24 Nordamerika 16–17
1:24 Südamerika 18–19

Regionalkarten

Einleitung 20–21

Eurasien

1:12 Europa 22–23
1:6 Nordeuropa 24–25
1:3 Südskandinavien 26–27
1:3 Britische Inseln 28–29
1:3 Mitteleuropa 30–31
1:3 Frankreich und die Alpen 32–33
1:3 Spanien und Portugal 34–35
1:3 Italien 36–37
1:3 Südosteuropa 38–39
1:1 Stockholm - Karlstad 40
1:1 København - Malmö - Kiel 41
1:1 London - Birmingham - Cardiff 42–43
1:1 Dublin - Manchester - Newcastle upon Tyne 44–45
1:1 Glasgow - Edinburgh - Aberdeen 46–47
1:1 Dublin - Belfast - Cork 48–49
1:1 Paris - London - Bruxelles 50–51
1:1 Amsterdam - Düsseldorf - Hamburg 52–53
1:1 Berlin - Hamburg - Praha 54–55
1:1 Bruxelles - Frankfurt - Stuttgart 56–57
1:1 Zürich - Genève - Strasbourg 58–59
1:1 Nürnberg - München 60
1:1 Wien - Brno - Linz 61
1:1 Lyon - Marseille - Milano 62–63
1:1 München - Venezia - Firenze 64–65
1:1 Roma - Firenze - Napoli 66–67
1:1 Napoli - Messina - Bari 68–69
1:1 Palermo - Catania - Messina 70
1:1 Cagliari - Sassari 71
1:12 Nordwestasien 72–73
1:12 Nordostasien 74–75
1:3 Baltenland und Mittelrussland 76–77
1:3 Ukraine 78–79
1:3 Wolgagebiet 80–81
1:1 Moskva - Tula - Tver' 82
1:1 Donets'k - Luhans'k - Rostov 83
1:3 Kaukasus und Transkaukasien 84
1:3 Taschkentgebiet 85
1:6 Mittelrussland und Kasachstan 86–87
1:6 Baikalseegebiet 88
1:6 Russlands Ferne Osten 89
1:12 China, Japan und Korea 90–91
1:3 Japan 92–93
1:1 Tōkyō - Nagoya - Kyōto 94–95
1:1 Ōsaka - Hiroshima - Fukuoka 96–97
1:3 Nordostchina und Korea 98–99
1:3 Ost- und Südostchina 100–101
1:6 Innerchina 102–103
1:1 Shenyang -Fushun (Mukden - Fushun) 104
1:1 Beijing - Tianjin (Peking - Tientsin) 105
1:1 Shanghai - Nanjing (Shanghai - Nanking) 106
1:1 Chongqing - Chengdu (Chungking - Chengtu) 107
1:12 Südostasien 108–109
1:6 Myanmar, Thailand und Indochina 110–111
1:6 Malaysia und westliches Indonesien 112–113
1:3 Malaya, Singapur und Nordsumatra 114
1:3 Java • Kleine Sundainseln 115
1:3 Philippinen 116–117
1:12 Indien, Pakistan und Südwestasien 118–119
1:6 Nordindien und Pakistan 120–121
1:6 Südindien und Sri Lanka 122
1:3 Pandschab und Kaschmir 123
1:3 Gangestiefland und Nepal 124–125
1:1 Calcutta - Dhaka - Jamshedpur 126–127
1:6 Vorderasien 128–129
1:3 Türkei und Zypern 130–131
1:1 Yerushalayim - Dimashq (Jerusalem - Damascus) 132–133

Afrika

1:12 West Nordafrika 134–135
1:12 Ost Nordafrika 136–137
1:12 Südafrika 138–139
1:6 Ägypten und Sudan 140–141
1:1 Al-Qāhirah - As-Suways (Cairo - Suez) 142–143
1:6 Äthiopien, Somalia und Jemen 144–145
1:6 Libyen und Tschad 146–147
1:6 Nordwestafrika 148–149
1:6 Westafrika 150–151
1:6 Westliches Kongobecken 152–153
1:6 Ostafrika und Östliches Kongobecken 154–155
1:6 Südafrika und Madagaskar 156–157
1:3 Republik Südafrika 158–159

Australien/Ozeanien

1:12 Australien 160–161
1:6 West-und Mittelaustralien 162–163
1:6 Nordaustralien und Neuguinea 164–165
1:6 Ostaustralien 166–167
1:1 Perth • Adelaide 168
1:1 Melbourne - Geelong - Ballarat 169
1:1 Sydney - Newcastle 170
1:1 Brisbane • Canberra 171
1:3 Neuseeland 172-173
verschiedene Massstäbe
Pazifische Inseln 174–175

Anglo-Amerika

1:12 Kanada 176–177
1:12 Vereinigte Staaten 178–179
1:6 Alaska und Yukon 180–181
1:3 Südwestkanada 182–183
1:3 Südliches Mittelkanada 184–185
1:3 Südostkanada 186–187
1:3 Nordöstliche Vereinigte Staaten 188–189
1:3 Grosse Seen-Region 190–191
1:3 Südöstliche Vereinigte Staaten 192–193
1:3 Mississippi-Tiefland 194–195
1:3 Südliche Grosse Ebenen 196–197
1:3 Nördliche Grosse Ebenen 198–199
1:3 Südliches Felsengebirge 200–201
1:3 Nordwestliche Vereinigte Staaten 202–203
1:3 Kalifornien und Nevada 204–205
1:1 Montréal - Québec 206
1:1 Boston - New York - Albany 207
1:1 New York - Philadelphia - Washington - Norfolk 208–209
1:1 New York - Buffalo 210–211
1:1 Toronto - Ottawa 212–213
1:1 Pittsburgh - Cleveland - Detroit 214–215
1:1 Chicago - Detroit - Milwaukee 216–217
1:1 Indianapolis - Cincinnati - Louisville 218
1:1 St. Louis - Springfield 219
1:1 Miami - Tampa - Orlando 220–221
1:1 Houston - Dallas - Austin 222–223
1:1 Vancouver - Seattle - Portland 224–225
1:1 San Francisco - Reno - Bakersfield 226–227
1:1 Los Angeles - San Diego 228
verschiedene Massstäbe
Hawaii 229

Latein-Amerika

1:12 Mittelamerika 230–231
1:6 Mexiko 232–233
1:3 Mittelmexiko 234–235
1:3 Zentralamerika 236–237
1:6 Mittelamerikanische Inselwelt 238–239
verschiedene Massstäbe
Westindische Inseln 240–241
1:12 Südamerika, nördlicher Teil 242–243
1:12 Südamerika, südlicher Teil 244–245
1:6 Kolumbien, Ecuador, Venezuela und Guayana 246–247
1:6 Peru, Bolivien und westliches Brasilien 248–249
1:6 Nordostbrasilien 250–251
1:6 Mittelargentinien und Mittelchile 252–253
1:6 Südliches Argentinien und südliches Chile 254
1:6 Südostbrasilien 255
1:1 Rio de Janeiro - São Paulo 256–257
1:1 Buenos Aires - Montevideo 258

Karten Von Stadtregionen (1:300 000)

Einleitung 259
London 260
Paris 261
Manchester - Liverpool 262
Ruhr Area 263
Berlin • Wien • Budapest 264
Sankt Peterburg • Moskva 265
Madrid • Milano • Lisboa • Barcelona 266
Roma • Athinai • İstanbul • Tehrān 267
Tōkyō - Yokohama 268
Krung Thep (Bangkok) • Thanh Pho Ho Chi Minh (Saigon) • Jakarta • Shanghai • T'aipei • Manila 269
Ōsaka - Kōbe - Kyōto 270
Beijing (Peking) • Sŏul • Singapore • Hong Kong 271
Delhi • Bombay • Calcutta 272
Lagos • Kinshasa - Brazzaville • Al-Qāhirah (Cairo) • Johannesburg 273
Sydney • Melbourne 274
Montréal • Toronto 275
New York 276–277
Chicago 278
Cleveland • Pittsburgh 279
Los Angeles 280
Detroit - Windsor 281
San Francisco - Oakland - San Jose 282
Boston 283
Buffalo - Niagara Falls • Baltimore • Washington 284
Philadelphia 285
Ciudad de México • La Habana • Caracas • Lima • Santiago 286
Rio de Janeiro • São Paulo 287
Buenos Aires 288

* Maßstab in Millionen

Lista de Mapas

Mapas del Mundo, Océanos y Continentes

* Introducción 1
1:75 Mundo: Político 2–3
1:75 Mundo: Físico 4–5
1:48 Océanos Pacífico e Indico 6–7
1:48 Océano Atlántico 8
1:24 Antártida 9
1:24 Europa y África 10–11
1:24 Asia 12–13
1:24 Australia y Oceanía 14–15
1:24 América del Norte 16–17
1:24 América del Sur 18–19

Mapas Regionales

Introducción 20–21

Eurasia

1:12 Europa 22–23
1:6 Europe Septentrional 24–25
1:3 Escandinavia Meridional 26–27
1:3 Islas Británicas 28–29
1:3 Europa Central 30–31
1:3 Francia y los Alpes 32–33
1:3 España y Portugal 34–35
1:3 Italia 36–37
1:3 Europa Sud-oriental 38–39
1:1 Stockholm - Karlstad 40
1:1 København - Malmö - Kiel 41
1:1 London - Birmingham - Cardiff 42–43
1:1 Dublin - Manchester - Newcastle upon Tyne 44–45
1:1 Glasgow - Edinburgh - Aberdeen 46–47
1:1 Dublin - Belfast - Cork 48–49
1:1 Paris - London - Bruxelles 50–51
1:1 Amsterdam - Düsseldorf - Hamburg 52–53
1:1 Berlin - Hamburg - Praha 54–55
1:1 Bruxelles - Frankfurt - Stuttgart 56–57
1:1 Zürich - Genève - Strasbourg 58–59
1:1 Nürnberg - München 60
1:1 Wien - Brno - Linz 61
1:1 Lyon - Marseille - Milano 62–63
1:1 München - Venezia - Firenze 64–65
1:1 Roma - Firenze - Napoli 66–67
1:1 Napoli - Messina - Bari 68–69
1:1 Palermo - Catania - Messina 70
1:1 Cagliari - Sassari 71
1:12 Asia Nor-occidental 72–73
1:12 Asia Nor-oriental 74–75
1:3 Regiones de Báltico y de Moscú 76–77
1:3 Ucrania 78–79
1:3 Región del Volga 80–81
1:1 Moskva - Tula - Tver' 82
1:1 Donets'k - Luhans'k - Rostov 83
1:3 Cáucaso y Transcaucasia 84
1:3 Región de Tachkent 85
1:6 Rusia Central e Kazajstan 86–87
1:6 Región del Lago Baikal 88
1:6 Extremo Oriente Ruso 89
1:12 China, Japón y Corea 90–91
1:3 Japón 92–93
1:1 Tōkyō - Nagoya - Kyōto 94–95
1:1 Ōsaka - Hiroshima - Fukuoka 96–97
1:3 China Nor-oriental y Corea 98–99
1:3 Este y Sudeste de la China 100–101
1:6 China Interior 102–103
1:1 Shenyang -Fushun (Mukden - Fushun) 104
1:1 Beijing - Tianjin (Peking - Tientsin) 105
1:1 Shanghai - Nanjing (Shanghai - Nanking) 106
1:1 Chongqing - Chengdu (Chungking - Chengtu) 107
1:6 Asia Sud-oriental 108–109
1:6 Myanmar, Siam e Indochina 110–111
1:6 Malasia e Indonesia Occidental 112–113
1:3 Malaya, Singapur y Sumatra Septentrional 114
1:3 Java • Islas Menores de la Sonda 115
1:3 Filipinas 116–117
1:12 India, Pakistán y Asia Sud-occidental 118–119
1:6 India Septentrional y Pakistán 120–121
1:6 India Meridional y Sri Lanka 122
1:3 Punjab y Cachemira 123
1:3 Llanuras del Ganges y Nepal 124–125
1:1 Calcutta - Dhaka - Jamshedpur 126–127
1:6 El Medio Oriente 128–129
1:3 Turquía y Chipre 130–131
1:1 Yerushalayim - Dimashq (Jerusalem - Damascus) 132–133

África

1:12 Región Occidental de Africa Septentrional 134–135
1:12 Región Oriental de Africa Septentrional 136–137
1:12 África Meridional 138–139
1:6 Egipto y Sudán 140–141
1:1 Al-Qāhirah - As-Suways (Cairo - Suez) 142–143
1:6 Etiopía, Somalia y Yemen 144–145
1:6 Libia y el Chad 146–147
1:6 África Nor-occidental 148–149
1:6 África Occidental 150–151
1:6 Cuenca Occidental del Congo 152–153
1:6 África Oriental y Cuenca Oriental del Congo 154–155
1:6 África Meridional y Madagascar 156–157
1:3 Sudáfrica 158–159

Australia/Oceanía

1:12 Australia 160–161
1:6 Australia Centro-occidental 162–163
1:6 Australia Septentrional y Nueva Guinea 164–165
1:6 Australia Oriental 166–167
1:1 Perth • Adelaide 168
1:1 Melbourne - Geelong - Ballarat 169
1:1 Sydney - Newcastle 170
1:1 Brisbane • Canberra 171
1:3 Nueva Zelanda 172-173
Varias Escalas
Islas del Pacífico 174–175

América Anglosajona

1:12 Canadá 176–177
1:12 Estados Unidos 178–179
1:6 Alaska y Yukón 180–181
1:6 Canadá Sud-occidental 182–183
1:6 Centro Meridional del Canadá 184–185
1:6 Canadá Sud-oriental 186–187
1:3 Nor-este de los Estados Unidos 188–189
1:6 Región de los Grandes Lagos 190–191
1:6 Sud-este de los Estados Unidos 192–193
1:6 Valle del Misisipí 194–195
1:6 Grandes Llanos: zona meridional 196–197
1:6 Grandes Llanos: zona septentrional 198–199
1:6 Montañas Rocosas: zona meridional 200–201
1:6 Nor-oeste de los Estados Unidos 202–203
1:6 California y Nevada 204–205
1:1 Montréal - Québec 206
1:1 Boston - New York - Albany 207
1:1 New York - Philadelphia - Washington - Norfolk 208–209
1:1 New York - Buffalo 210–211
1:1 Toronto - Ottawa 212–213
1:1 Pittsburgh - Cleveland - Detroit 214–215
1:1 Chicago - Detroit - Milwaukee 216–217
1:1 Indianapolis - Cincinnati - Louisville 218
1:1 St. Louis - Springfield 219
1:1 Miami - Tampa - Orlando 220–221
1:1 Houston - Dallas - Austin 222–223
1:1 Vancouver - Seattle - Portland 224–225
1:1 San Francisco - Reno - Bakersfield 226–227
1:1 Los Angeles - San Diego 228
Varias Escalas
Hawaii 229

América Latina

1:12 México, Centroamérica y Las Antillas 230–231
1:6 México 232–233
1:3 México Central 234–235
1:3 América Central 236–237
1:6 Región del Caribe 238–239
Varias Escalas
Islas de las Antillas 240–241
1:12 América del Sur: zona septentrional 242–243
1:12 América del Sur: zona meridional 244–245
1:6 Colombia, Ecuador, Venezuela y Guyana 246–247
1:6 Perú, Bolivia y Brasil Occidental 248–249
1:6 Brasil Nor-oriental 250–251
1:6 Argentina y Chile: zonas centrales 252–253
1:6 Argentina y Chile: zonas meridionales 254
1:6 Brazil Sud-oriental 255
1:1 Rio de Janeiro - São Paulo 256–257
1:1 Buenos Aires - Montevideo 258

Mapas de las Áreas Metropolitanas (1:300 000)

Introducción 259
London 260
Paris 261
Manchester - Liverpool 262
Ruhr Area 263
Berlin • Wien • Budapest 264
Sankt Peterburg • Moskva 265
Madrid • Milano • Lisboa • Barcelona 266
Roma • Athínai • İstanbul • Tehrān 267
Tōkyō - Yokohama 268
Krung Thep (Bangkok) • Thanh Pho Ho Chi Minh (Saigon) • Jakarta • Shanghai • T'aipei • Manila 269
Ōsaka - Kōbe - Kyōto 270
Beijing (Peking) • Sŏul • Singapore • Hong Kong 271
Delhi • Bombay • Calcutta 272
Lagos • Kinshasa - Brazzaville • Al-Qāhirah (Cairo) • Johannesburg 273
Sydney • Melbourne 274
Montréal • Toronto 275
New York 276–277
Chicago 278
Cleveland • Pittsburgh 279
Los Angeles 280
Detroit - Windsor 281
San Francisco - Oakland - San Jose 282
Boston 283
Buffalo - Niagara Falls • Baltimore • Washington 284
Philadelphia 285
Ciudad de México • La Habana • Caracas • Lima • Santiago 286
Rio de Janeiro • São Paulo 287
Buenos Aires 288

* Escala en millones

Liste des Cartes

Cartes du Monde, Des Océans et des Continents

* Introduction 1
1:75 Monde: Politique 2–3
1:75 Monde: Physique 4–5
1:48 Océans Pacifique et Indien 6–7
1:48 Océan Atlantique 8
1:24 Antarctique 9
1:24 Europe et Afrique 10–11
1:24 Asie 12–13
1:24 Australie et Océanie 14–15
1:24 Amérique du Nord 16–17
1:24 Amérique du Sud 18–19

Cartes Régionales

Introduction 20–21

Eurasie

1:12 Europe 22–23
1:6 Europe Septentrionale 24–25
1:3 Scandinavie Méridionale 26–27
1:3 Îles Britanniques 28–29
1:3 Europe Centrale 30–31
1:3 France et Alpes 32–33
1:3 Espagne et Portugal 34–35
1:3 Italie 36–37
1:3 Europe du Sud-Est 38–39
1:1 Stockholm Karlstad 40
1:1 København - Malmö - Kiel 41
1:1 London - Birmingham - Cardiff 42–43
1:1 Dublin - Manchester - Newcastle upon Tyne 44–45
1:1 Glasgow - Edinburgh - Aberdeen 46–47
1:1 Dublin - Belfast - Cork 48–49
1:1 Paris - London - Bruxelles 50–51
1:1 Amsterdam - Düsseldorf - Hamburg 52–53
1:1 Berlin - Hamburg - Praha 54–55
1:1 Bruxelles - Frankfurt - Stuttgart 56–57
1:1 Zürich - Genève - Strasbourg 58–59
1:1 Nürnberg - München 60
1:1 Wien - Brno - Linz 61
1:1 Lyon - Marseille - Milano 62–63
1:1 München - Venezia - Firenze 64–65
1:1 Roma - Firenze - Napoli 66–67
1:1 Napoli - Messina - Bari 68–69
1:1 Palermo - Catania - Messina 70
1:1 Cagliari - Sassari 71
1:12 Asie du Nord-Ouest 72–73
1:12 Asie du Nord-Est 74–75
1:3 Républiques Baltes et la Région de Moscou 76–77
1:3 Ukraine 78–79
1:3 Région de la Volga 80–81
1:1 Moskva - Tula - Tver' 82
1:1 Donets'k - Luhans'k - Rostov 83
1:3 Caucasie et Transcaucasie 84
1:3 Région de Tachkent 85
1:6 Russie Centrale et Kazakhstan 86–87
1:6 Région du Lac Baïkal 88
1:6 Extrême-Orient Russe 89
1:12 Chine, Japon et Corée 90–91
1:3 Japon 92–93
1:1 Tōkyō - Nagoya - Kyōto 94–95
1:1 Ōsaka - Hiroshima - Fukuoka 96–97
1:3 Nord-Est de la Chine et Corée 98–99
1:3 Chine de l'Est et du Sud-Est 100–101
1:6 Chine Intérieure 102–103
1:1 Shenyang -Fushun (Mukden - Fushun) 104
1:1 Beijing - Tianjin (Peking - Tientsin) 105
1:1 Shanghai - Nanjing (Shanghai - Nanking) 106
1:1 Chongqing - Chengdu (Chungking - Chengtu) 107
1:12 Asie du Sud-Est 108–109
1:6 Myanmar, Thaïlande et Indochine 110–111
1:6 Malaisie et Indonésie Occidentale 112–113
1:3 Malaya, Singapour et Sumatra Septentrional 114
1:3 Java • Petites Îles de la Sonde 115
1:3 Philippines 116–117
1:12 Inde, Pakistan et Asie du Sud-Ouest 118–119
1:6 Inde Septentrionale et Pakistan 120–121
1:6 Inde Méridionale et Sri Lanka 122
1:3 Punjab et Cachemire 123
1:3 Plaine du Gange et Népal 124–125
1:1 Calcutta - Dhaka - Jamshedpur 126–127
1:6 Le Moyen-Orient 128–129
1:3 Turquie et Chypre 130–131
1:1 Yerushalayim Dimashq (Jerusalem - Damascus) 132–133

Afrique

1:12 Afrique du Nord Occidentale 134–135
1:12 Afrique du Nord Orientale 136–137
1:12 Afrique Méridionale 138–139
1:6 Égypte et Soudan 140–141
1:1 Al-Qāhirah - As-Suways (Cairo - Suez) 142–143
1:6 Ethiopie, Somalie et Yemen 144–145
1:6 Libye et Tchad 146–147
1:6 Afrique du Nord-Ouest 148–149
1:6 Afrique Occidentale 150–151
1:6 Bassin du Congo, partie Occidentale 152–153
1:6 Afrique Orientale et Bassin du Congo, partie Orientale 154–155
1:6 Afrique Méridionale et Madagascar 156–157
1:3 Afrique du Sud 158–159

Australie/Océanie

1:12 Australie 160–161
1:6 Australie Occidentale et Centrale 162–163
1:6 Australie Septentrionale et Nouvelle Guinée 164–165
1:6 Australie Orientale 166–167
1:1 Perth • Adelaide 168
1:1 Melbourne - Geelong - Ballarat 169
1:1 Sydney - Newcastle 170
1:1 Brisbane • Canberra 171
1:3 Nouvelle Zélande 172–173
Echelles Variées
Îles du Pacifique 174–175

Amérique Anglo-Saxonne

1:12 Canada 176–177
1:12 États-Unis 178–179
1:6 Alaska et Yukon 180–181
1:3 Sud-Ouest du Canada 182–183
1:3 Canada Central, partie Méridionale 184–185
1:3 Sud-Est du Canada 186–187
1:3 Nord-Est des États-Unis 188–189
1:3 Région des Grands Lacs 190–191
1:3 Sud-Est des États-Unis 192–193
1:3 Vallée du Mississippi 194–195
1:3 Grandes Plaines, partie Méridionale 196–197
1:3 Grandes Plaines, partie Septentrionale 198–199
1:3 Montagnes Rocheuses, partie Méridionale 200–201
1:3 Nord-Ouest des États-Unis 202–203
1:3 Californie et Nevada 204–205
1:1 Montréal - Québec 206
1:1 Boston - New York - Albany 207
1:1 New York - Philadelph Washington - Norfolk 208–209
1:1 New York - Buffalo 210–211
1:1 Toronto - Ottawa 212-
1:1 Pittsburgh - Cleveland Detroit 214–215
1:1 Chicago - Detroit - Milwaukee 216–217
1:1 Indianapolis - Cincinna Louisville 218
1:1 St. Louis - Springfield
1:1 Miami - Tampa - Orlando 220–221
1:1 Houston - Dallas - Austin 222–223
1:1 Vancouver - Seattle - Portland 224–225
1:1 San Francisco - Reno - Bakersfield 226–227
1:1 Los Angeles - San Diego 228
Echelles Variées
Hawaï 229

Amérique Latine

1:12 Mexique, Amérique Centrale et Région de Caraïbes 230 -231
1:6 Mexique 232–233
1:3 Mexique Central 234–2
1:3 Amérique Centrale 236–237
1:6 Région des Caraïbes 238–239
Echelles Variées
Îles des Antilles 240–2
1:12 Amérique du Sud Septentrionale 242–
1:12 Amérique du Sud Méridionale 244–245
1:6 Colombie, Équateur, Venezuela et Guyane 246–247
1:6 Pérou, Bolivie et Brésil Occidental 248–249
1:6 Nord-Est du Brésil 250–251
1:6 Argentine et Chili, partie Centrales 252–253
1:6 Argentine et Chili, partie Méridionales 254
1:6 Sud-Est du Brésil 255
1:1 Rio de Janeiro - São Paulo 256–257
1:1 Buenos Aires - Montevideo 258

Cartes des Zones Métropolitaines (1:300 000)

Introduction 259
London 260
Paris 261
Manchester - Liverpool 262
Ruhr Area 263
Berlin • Wien • Budapest 264
Sankt Peterburg • Moskva 265
Madrid • Milano • Lisboa • Barcelona 266
Roma • Athínai • İstanbul • Tehrān 267
Tōkyō - Yokohama 268
Krung Thep (Bangkok) • Thanh Pho Ho Chi Minh (Saigon) • Jakarta • Shanghai • T'aipei • Manila 269
Ōsaka - Kōbe - Kyōto 270
Beijing (Peking) • Sŏul • Singapore • Hong Kong 271
Delhi • Bombay • Calcutta 272
Lagos • Kinshasa - Brazzaville Al-Qāhirah (Cairo) • Johannesburg 273
Sydney • Melbourne 274
Montréal • Toronto 275
New York 276–277
Chicago 278
Cleveland • Pittsburgh 279
Los Angeles 280
Detroit - Windsor 281
San Francisco - Oakland - San Jose 282
Boston 283
Buffalo - Niagara Falls • Baltimore • Washington 284
Philadelphia 285
Ciudad de México • La Habana Caracas • Lima • Santiago 2
Rio de Janeiro • São Paulo 28
Buenos Aires 288

* Echelle en millions

Lista de Mapas

Mapas do Mundo, dos Oceanos e dos Continentes

* Introdução 1
1:75 Mundo: Político 2–3
1:75 Mundo: Físico 4–5
1:48 Oceanos Pacífico e Índico 6–7
1:48 Oceano Atlântico 8
1:24 Antártida 9
1:24 Europa e África 10–11
1:24 Ásia 12–13
1:24 Austrália e Oceania 14–15
1:24 América do Norte 16–17
1:24 América do Sul 18–19

Mapas Regionais

Introdução 20–21

Eurásia

1:12 Europa 22–23
1:6 Europa Setentrional 24–25
1:3 Escandinávia Meridional 26–27
1:3 Ilhas Britânicas 28–29
1:3 Europa Central 30–31
1:3 França e os Alpes 32–33
1:3 Espanha e Portugal 34–35
1:3 Itália 36–37
1:3 Europa Sul-oriental 38–39
1:1 Stockholm - Karlstad 40
1:1 København - Malmö - Kiel 41
1:1 London - Birmingham - Cardiff 42–43
1:1 Dublin - Manchester - Newcastle upon Tyne 44–45
1:1 Glasgow - Edinburgh - Aberdeen 46–47
1:1 Dublin - Belfast - Cork 48–49
1:1 Paris - London - Bruxelles 50–51
1:1 Amsterdam - Düsseldorf - Hamburg 52–53
1:1 Berlin - Hamburg - Praha 54–55
1:1 Bruxelles - Frankfurt - Stuttgart 56–57
1:1 Zürich - Genève - Strasbourg 58–59
1:1 Nürnberg - München 60
1:1 Wien - Brno - Linz 61
1:1 Lyon - Marseille - Milano 62–63
1:1 München - Venezia - Firenze 64–65
1:1 Roma - Firenze - Napoli 66–67
1:1 Napoli - Messina - Bari 68–69
1:1 Palermo - Catania - Messina 70
1:1 Cagliari - Sassari 71
1:12 Ásia do Norte Ocidental 72–73
1:12 Ásia do Norte Oriental 74–75
1:3 Regiões do Báltico e de Moscou 76–77
1:3 Ucrânia 78–79
1:3 Região do Volga 80–81
1:1 Moskva - Tula - Tver' 82
1:1 Donets'k - Luhans'k - Rostov 83
1:3 Cáucaso e Transcaucásia 84
1:3 Região do Taschkent 85
1:6 Rússia Central e Casaquistão 86–87
1:6 Região do Lago Baikal 88
1:6 Extremo Oriente Russo 89
1:12 China, Japão e Coréia 90–91
1:3 Japão 92–93
1:1 Tōkyō - Nagoya - Kyōto 94–95
1:1 Ōsaka - Hiroshima - Fukuoka 96–97
1:3 Nordeste da China e Coréia 98–99
1:3 Leste e Sudeste da China 100–101
1:6 China Interior 102–103
1:1 Shenyang -Fushun (Mukden - Fushun) 104
1:1 Beijing - Tianjin (Peking - Tientsin) 105
1:1 Shanghai - Nanjing (Shanghai - Nanking) 106
1:1 Chongqing - Chengdu (Chungking - Chengtu) 107
1:12 Sudeste Asiático 108–109
1:6 Myanmar, Tailândia e Indochina 110–111
1:6 Malásia e Indonésia Ocidental 112–113
1:3 Malaia, Cingapura e Sumatra Setentrional 114
1:3 Java • Ilhas Menores da Sonda 115
1:3 Filipinas 116–117
1:12 Índia, Paquistão e Ásia do Sudoeste 118–119
1:6 Índia Setentrional e Paquistão 120–121
1:6 Índia Meridional e Sri Lanka 122
1:3 Punjab e Cachemira 123
1:3 Planície do Ganges e Nepal 124–125
1:1 Calcutta - Dhaka - Jamshedpur 126–127
1:6 Oriente Médio 128–129
1:3 Turquia e Chipre 130–131
1:1 Yerushalayim - Dimashq (Jerusalem - Damascus) 132–133

África

1:12 África do Norte Ocidental 134–135
1:12 África do Norte Oriental 136–137
1:12 África Meridional 138–139
1:6 Egito e Sudão 140–141
1:1 Al-Qāhirah - As-Suways (Cairo - Suez) 142–143
1:6 Etiópia, Somália e Iêmen 144–145
1:6 Líbia e Tchad 146–147
1:6 África Norte-ocidental 148–149
1:6 África Ocidental 150–151
1:6 Bacia Ocidental do Congo 152–153
1:6 África Oriental e Bacia Oriental do Congo 154–155
1:6 África Meridional e Madagascar 156–157
1:3 África do Sul 158–159

Austrália/Oceania

1:12 Austrália 160–161
1:6 Austrália Ocidental e Central 162–163
1:6 Austrália Setentrional e Nova Guiné 164–165
1:6 Austrália Oriental 166–167
1:1 Perth • Adelaide 168
1:1 Melbourne - Geelong - Ballarat 169
1:1 Sydney - Newcastle 170
1:1 Brisbane • Canberra 171
1:3 Nova Zelândia 172–173
Várias Escalas
Ilhas do Pacífico 174–175

América Anglosaxônica

1:12 Canadá 176–177
1:12 Estados Unidos 178–179
1:6 Alasca e Yukon 180–181
1:3 Canadá: Sudoeste 182–183
1:3 Canadá Central, parte meridional 184–185
1:3 Canadá: Sudeste 186–187
1:3 Estados Unidos: Nordeste 188–189
1:3 Região dos Grandes Lagos 190–191
1:3 Estados Unidos: Sudeste 192–193
1:3 Vale do Mississippi 194–195
1:3 Grandes Planícies: zona meridional 196–197
1:3 Grandes Planícies: zona setentrional 198–199
1:3 Montanhas Rochosas: zona meridional 200–201
1:3 Noroeste dos Estados Unidos 202–203
1:3 Califórnia e Nevada 204–205
1:1 Montréal Québec 206
1:1 Boston - New York - Albany 207
1:1 New York - Philadelphia - Washington - Norfolk 208–209
1:1 New York - Buffalo 210–211
1:1 Toronto - Ottawa 212–213
1:1 Pittsburgh - Cleveland - Detroit 214–215
1:1 Chicago - Detroit - Milwaukee 216–217
1:1 Indianapolis - Cincinnati - Louisville 218
1:1 St. Louis - Springfield 219
1:1 Miami - Tampa - Orlando 220–221
1:1 Houston - Dallas - Austin 222–223
1:1 Vancouver - Seattle - Portland 224–225
1:1 San Francisco - Reno - Bakersfield 226–227
1:1 Los Angeles - San Diego 228
Várias Escalas
Havaí 229

América Latina

1:12 México, América Central e Antilhas 230–231
1:6 México 232–233
1:3 México Central 234–235
1:3 América Central 236–237
1:6 Região do Caribe 238–239
Várias Escalas
Ilhas do Caribe (Índias Ocidentais) 240–241
1:12 América do Sul: zona setentrional 242–243
1:12 América do Sul: zona meridional 244–245
1:6 Colômbia, Equador, Venezuela e Guiana 246–247
1:6 Peru, Bolívia e Brasil Ocidental 248–249
1:6 Brasil: Nordeste 250–251
1:6 Argentina e Chile: zonas centrais 252–253
1:6 Argentina e Chile: zonas meridionais 254
1:6 Brasil: Sudeste 255
1:1 Rio de Janeiro - São Paulo 256–257
1:1 Buenos Aires - Montevideo 258

Mapas das Áreas Metropolitanas (1:300 000)

Introdução 259
London 260
Paris 261
Manchester - Liverpool 262
Ruhr Area 263
Berlin • Wien • Budapest 264
Sankt Peterburg • Moskva 265
Madrid • Milano • Lisboa • Barcelona 266
Roma • Athínai • İstanbul • Tehrān 267
Tōkyō - Yokohama 268
Krung Thep (Bangkok) • Thanh Pho Ho Chi Minh (Saigon) • Jakarta • Shanghai • T'aipei • Manila 69
Ōsaka - Kōbe - Kyōto 270
Beijing (Peking) • Sŏul • Singapore • Hong Kong 271
Delhi • Bombay • Calcutta 272
Lagos • Kinshasa - Brazzaville • Al-Qāhirah (Cairo) • Johannesburg 273
Sydney • Melbourne 274
Montréal • Toronto 275
New York 276–277
Chicago 278
Cleveland • Pittsburgh 279
Los Angeles 280
Detroit - Windsor 281
San Francisco - Oakland - San Jose 282
Boston 283
Buffalo - Niagara Falls • Baltimore • Washington 284
Philadelphia 285
Rio de Janeiro • São Paulo 287
Buenos Aires 288

* Escalas em milhões

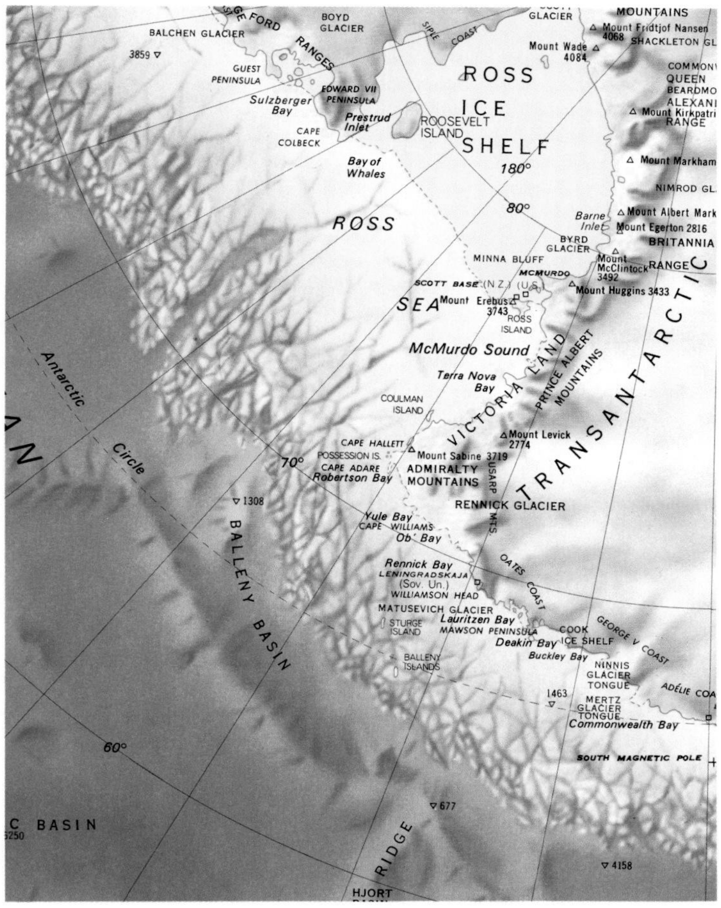

ROSS ICE SHELF
ROSS SEA
McMurdo Sound
VICTORIA LAND
TRANSANTARCTIC
Antarctic Circle
BALLENY BASIN
ROOSEVELT ISLAND
Bay of Whales
RENNICK GLACIER
ADMIRALTY MOUNTAINS
Commonwealth Bay
SOUTH MAGNETIC POLE

The design and color of the map symbols are consistent throughout the Regional and Metropolitan Area maps, although the size of the symbol varies with scale. An asterisk marks those symbols which appear only on the 1:300,000 scale maps.

The symbol 80-81 in the margin of a map directs the reader to a map of the adjoining area.

A separate legend on page 1 identifies the land and submarine features which appear on the World, Ocean, and Continent maps.

Der Entwurf und die Farbe der Kartensymbole sind einheitlich für alle Regionalkarten und Karten von Stadtregionen, während die Grösse des Symbols sich mit dem Massstab ändert. Ein Stern kennzeichnet diejenigen Symbole, welche nur auf den Karten im Masstab 1:300 000 erscheinen.

Kennzeichen 80-81 am rande einer Karte ist ein Hinweis für den Leser, die Karte eines angrenzenden Gebietes nachzuschlagen.

Eine andere Legende auf Seite 1 identifiziert die Land- und untermeerischen Phänomene, die auf den Weltkarten, Karten der Ozeane und Erdteile erscheinen.

El diseño y el color de los símbolos cartográficos son uniformes para todas los mapas regionales y de las áreas metropolitanas, aunque el tamaño del símbolo varía según la escala. Un asterisco distingue los símbolos que aparecen sólo en los mapas a 1:300 000.

El símbolo 80-81 al margen de un mapa dirige al lector a un mapa del área adyacente.

Otra leyenda, en la página 1, identifica la topografía terrestre y submarina que se encuentra en los mapas del Mundo, Océanos y Continentes.

La couleur et la forme des symboles cartographiques des cartes régionales et des cartes des zones métropolitaines sont identiques, bien que la grandeur des signes carie selon l'échelle. Un astérisque accompagne les symboles qui n'apparaissent que sur les cartes au 1:300 000.

Le symbole 80-81 en marge d'une carte renvoie le lecteur à une carte de la région voisine.

Pour les cartes du monde, des océans et des continents une légende séparée, à la page 1, donne le sens des symboles représentant les paysages continentaux et les formes de relief sous-marin.

A cor e a forma dos símbolos cartográficos dos mapas regionais e das áreas metropolitanas são idênticos, ainda que a dimensão do símbolo varie segundo a escala. Um asterisco distingue os símbolos que só aparecem nos mapas da escala de 1:300 000.

O símbolo 80-81 à margem de um mapa, remete o leitos a um mapa da região vizinha.

Nos mapas do mundo, dos oceanos e dos continentes uma legenda separada, na pág. 1, indica o sentido dos símbolos representativos das paisagens continentais e das formas do relevo submarino.

Symbol	***Hydrographic Features***	***Hydrographische Objekte***	***Elementos Hidrográficos***	***Données Hydrographiques***	***Acidentes Hidrográficos***
	Shoreline	Uferlinie	Línea costanera	Trait de côte	Linha costeira
	Undefined or Fluctuating Shoreline	Unbestimmte oder Veränderliche Uferlinie	Línea costanera indefinida o fluctuante	Trait de côte indéfini ou fluctuant	Linha costeira indefinida ou flutuante
Amur	River, Stream	Fluss, Strom	Río, Corriente	Rivière, Cours d'eau	Rio, curso d'água
	Intermittent Stream	Periodischer Fluss	Corriente intermitente	Cours d'eau périodique	Rio, curso d'água intermitente
SALTO ÁNGEL	Rapids, Falls	Stromschnellen, Wasserfälle	Rápidos, Cascadas	Rapides, Chutes d'eau	Corredeiras, quedas d'água
764 ▽	Depth of Water	Wassertiefe	Profundidad del aqua	Profondeur bathymétrique	Profundidade da água
8428 ▼	Greatest Depth (Atlantic, Indian, Pacific oceans)	Grösste Tiefe (Atlantischer, Indischer, Pazifischer Ozean)	Profundidad más grande (Océanos Atlántico, Índico, Pacífico)	Profondeur maximum (océans Atlantique, Indien, Pacifique)	Profundidade máxima (oceanos Atlântico, Índico, Pacífico)
Canal du Midi	Navigable Canal	Schiffbarer Kanal	Canal navegable	Canal navigable	Canal navegável
	Irrigation or Drainage Canal	Be- oder Entwässerungskanal	Canal de irrigación o desagüe	Canal d'irrigation ou de drainage	Canal de irrigação ou drenagem
Los Angeles Aqueduct	Aqueduct	Aquädukt	Acueducto	Aqueduc	Aqueduto
	Pier, Breakwater	Landungsbrücke, Wellenbrecher	Embarcadero, Rompeolas	Jetée, Brise-lames	Cais, Quebra-mar
GREAT BARRIER REEF	Reef	Riff	Arrecife	Récif	Recife
Kumdah ○	Uninhabited Oasis	Unbewohnte Oase	Oasis deshabitado	Oasis inhabitée	Oásis desabitado
L.Victoria	Lake, Reservoir	See, Stausee	Lago, Embalse	Lac, Réservoir	Lago, reservatório (represa)
	Intermittent Lake, Reservoir	Periodischer See, Stausee	Lago o Embalse intermitente	Lac ou Réservoir périodique	Lago, reservatório (represa) intermitente
Tuz Golu	Salt Lake	Salzsee	Lago salado	Lac salé	Lago salgado
	Dry Lake Bed	Trockener Seeboden	Lecho de lago seco	Fond de lac asséché	Leito de lago seco
The Everglades	Swamp	Sumpf	Pantano	Marais	Pântano
RIMO GLACIER	Glacier	Gletscher	Glaciar	Glacier	Geleira
(395)	Lake Surface Elevation	Seehöhe	Elevación del lago	Cote du niveau du lac	Altitude do nível do lago

Symbol	***Topographic Features***	***Topographische Objekte***	***Elementos Topográficos***	***Données Topographiques***	***Acidentes Topográficos***
Matterhorn 4478 △	Elevation Above Sea Level	Höhe über dem Meeresspiegel	Elevación sobre del nivel del mar	Cote au-dessus du niveau de la mer	Altitude acima do nível do mar
76 ▽	Elevation Below Sea Level	Höhe unter dem Meeresspiegel	Elevación bajo del nivel del mar	Cote au-dessous du niveau de la mer	Altitude abaixo do nível do mar
Mount Cook 3764 ▲	Highest Elevation in Country	Höchster Punkt des Landes	Elevación más alta en el país	Cote la plus élevée d'un pays	Altitude mais elevada de um país
133 ▼	Lowest Elevation in Country	Tiefster Punkt des Landes	Elevación más baja en el país	Cote la plus basse d'un pays	Altitude mais baixa de um país
(106)	Elevation of City	Höhenangabe einer Stadt	Elevación de ciudad	Altitude d'une ville	Altitude de uma cidade
Khyber Pass 1067	Mountain Pass	Pass	Paso	Col de montagne	Passo (de montanha)
*	Rock	Fels	Roca	Rocher	Rocha
	Lava	Lava	Lava	Lave	Lava
	Sand Area	Sandgebiet	Area de arena	Région sableuse, Erg	Região arenosa, Erg
	Salt Flat	Salzebene	Salar	Dépression salée	Depressão salgada
A N D E S KUNLUN SHAN	Mountain Range, Plateau, Valley, etc.	Gebirge, Hochebene, Tal, usw.	Sierra, Meseta, Valle, etc.	Chaîne de montagnes, Plateau, Vallée, etc.	Cadeia de montanhas, Planalto, Vale, etc.
BAFFIN ISLAND NUNIVAK ISLAND	Island	Insel	Isla	Île	Ilha
POLUOSTROV KAMČATKA CABO DE HORNOS	Peninsula, Cape, Point, etc.	Halbinsel, Kap, Landspitze, usw.	Península, Cabo, Punta, etc.	Péninsule, Cap, Pointe, etc.	Península, Cabo, Ponta, etc.
	Elevations and depths are given in meters	Höhen und Tiefen sind in Metern angegeben	Elevaciones y profundidades se dan en metros	Cotes et profondeurs sont indiquées en mètres	Altitudes e profundidades são apresentadas em metros
	Highest Elevation and Lowest Elevation of a continent are underlined	Höchster und tiefster Punkt innerhalb eines Erdteils sind unterstrichen	Elevación más alta y más baja de un continente se subrayan	La cote la plus haute et la cote la plus basse d'un continent sont soulignées	As altitudes mais e menos elevadas de um continente são sublinhadas

	English	Deutsch	Español	Français	Português
	Inhabited Localities	***Bewohnte Orte***	***Lugares Poblados***	***Lieux Habités***	***Lugares Habitados***
	The symbol represents the number of inhabitants within the locality	Die Signatur entspricht der Einwohnerzahl des Ortes	El símbolo representa el número de habitantes dentro del lugar	Le symbole représente le nombre d'habitants de la localité	O símbolo representa o número de habitantes do lugar
	1:300,000 1:3,000,000 · 1:1,000,000 1:6,000,000	· 0–10,000 ○ 10,000–25,000 ⊙ 25,000–100,000 ▣ 100,000–250,000 ▣ 250,000–1,000,000 ■ >1,000,000	1:12,000,000	· 0–50,000 ⊙ 50,000–100,000 ▣ 100,000–250,000 ▣ 250,000–1,000,000 ■ >1,000,000	1:24,000,000 1:48,000,000 · 0–100,000 ⊙ 100,000–1,500,000x ■ >1,500,000
Écommoy Lisieux **Rouen** Trouville **Orléans** **PARIS**	The size of type indicates the relative economic and political importance of the locality	Die Schriftgrösse entspricht der relativen wirtschaftlichen und politischen Bedeutung des Ortes	El tamaño del tipo de imprenta indica la relativa importancia económica y política del lugar	La dimension des caractères indique l'importance économique et politique relative d'une localité	A dimensão dos caracteres tipográficos indica a importância econômica e política relativa do lugar
Hollywood □ *Westminster*	Section of a City, Neighborhood	Stadtteil, Nachbarschaft	Sección de una ciudad, Barrio	Arrondissement, Quartier	Seção de uma cidade, Bairro
Northland Center ■	*Major Shopping Center	Haupteinkaufszentrum	Mercado principal	Centre commercial important	Centro comercial importante
BYRD □ *Bir Safājah* ○ *Kumdah* ○	Scientific Station Inhabited Oasis Uninhabited Oasis	Wissenschaftliche Station Bewohnte Oase Unbewohnte Oase	Estación científica Oasis habitado Oasis deshabitado	Station scientifique Oasis habitée Oasis inhabitée	Estação científica Oásis habitado Oásis desabitado
	Urban Area (area of continuous industrial, commercial, and residential development)	Stadtgebiet (ausgedehntes industrie-, Geschäfts- und Wohngebiet)	Zona urbanizada (área de desarrollo industrial, comercial y residencial)	Zone urbanisée (zone d'occupation continue par des industries, des commerces, des habitations)	Zona urbanizada (área de ocupação contínua por indústrias, estabelecimentos comerciais e habitações)
	*Major Industrial Area	Hauptindustriegebiet	Zona principal industrial	Région industrielle importante	Zona industrial importante
	*Wooded Area	Wald	Área de bosque	Région boisée	Área verde
	*Local Park or Recreational Area	Park oder Erholungsgebiet	Parque municipal o área de recreo	Parc municipal ou zone de loisirs	Parque municipal ou área de lazer

	English	Deutsch	Español	Français	Português
	Political Boundaries	***Politische Grenzen***	***Límites Políticos***	***Frontières Politiques***	***Fronteiras e Limites***
	International (First-order political unit)	**Staatsgrenze** (Politische Einheit erster Ordnung)	**Internacionales** (Unidad política de primer orden)	**Internationales** (Entités politiques de premier ordre)	**Internacionais** (Unidade política de primeiro nível)
1:1** HUNGARY 1:.3, 1:3, 1:6 HUNGARY 1:24, 1:48 HUNGARY 1:12	Demarcated, Undemarcated, and Administrative	Markiert, unmarkiert, verwaltungstechnisch	Demarcado, No demarcado, y Administrativo	Délimitées, Non-délimitées, Administratives	Delimitados, Não delimitados, Administrativos
1:1 1:.3, 1:3, 1:6 1:24, 1:48 1:12	Disputed de facto	Umstritten de facto	Disputado de hecho	Contestées de facto	Contestados de fato
1:1 1:.3, 1:3, 1:6 1:24, 1:48 1:12	Disputed de jure	Umstritten de jure	Disputado de derecho	Contestées de jure	Contestados de direito
1:1 1:.3, 1:3, 1:6 1:24, 1:48 1:12	Indefinite or Undefined	Unklar oder Unbestimmt	Indefinido o No determinado	Imprécises ou Non définies	Imprecisos ou Não definidos
1:.3, 1:3, 1:6 1:24, 1:48 1:12	Demarcation Line	Demarkationslinie	Línea de demarcación	Ligne de démarcation	Linha de demarcação
	Internal	**Verwaltungsgrenze**	**Internos**	**Intérieures**	**Limites Internos**
1:1 PERNAMBUCO 1:3, 1:6 PERNAMBUCO 1:12	State, Province, etc. (Second-order political unit)	Land, Provinz, usw. (Politische Einheit zweiter Ordnung)	Estado, Provincia, etc. (Unidad política de segundo orden)	État, Province, etc. (Subdivision administrative de deuxième ordre)	Estado, Província, etc. (Unidade política de segundo nível)
1:1 SIENA 1:.3, 1:1 WESTCHESTER	County, Oblast, etc. (Third-order political unit)	Grafschaft, Oblast, usw. (Politische Einheit dritter Ordnung)	Condado, Oblast, etc. (Unidad política de tercer orden)	Comté, Oblast, etc. (Subdivision administrative de troisième ordre)	Condado, Oblast, etc. (Unidade política de terceiro nível)
1:.3, 1:1 *ISERLOHN*	Okrug, Kreis, etc. (Fourth-order political unit)	Okrug, Kreis, usw. (Politische Einheit vierter Ordnung)	Okrug, Kreis, etc. (Unidad política de cuarto orden)	Okrug, Kreis, etc. (Subdivision administrative de quatrième ordre)	Okrug, Kreis, etc. (Unidade política de quarto nível)
1:.3, 1:1	City or Municipality (may appear in combination with another boundary symbol)	Stadt oder Gemeinde (kann zusammen mit einem anderen Begrenzungssymbol erscheinen)	Ciudad o Municipio (puede aparecer en combinación con otro símbolo de límite)	Ville ou Municipalité (peut paraître en combinaison avec un autre symbole de limites politiques)	Cidade ou Munic ipalidade (Pode aparecer em combinação com outro símbolo de limite político)
NORMANDIE	Historical Region (No boundaries indicated)	Historische Landschaft (Grenzen werden nicht gezeigt)	Región Histórica (Sin indicación de límites)	Région Historique (Sans indication de frontières)	Região Histórica (Sem indicação de fronteiras)
	Capitals of Political Units	**Hauptstädte politischer Einheiten**	**Capitales de Unidades Políticas**	**Capitales d'Entités Politiques**	**Capitais de Unidades Políticas**
BUDAPEST	Independent Nation	Unabhängiger Staat	Nación independiente	État indépendant	Estado independente
Cayenne	Dependency (Colony, protectorate, etc.)	Abhängiges Gebiet (Kolonie, Protektorat, usw.)	Dependencia (Colonia, protectorado, etc.)	Territoire dépendant (Colonie, protectorat, etc.)	Dependência (Colônia, protetorado, etc.)
GALAPAGOS (Ecuador)	Administering Country	Verwaltender Staat	País administrador	Pays administrateur	País administrador
Recife	State, Province, etc.	Land, Provinz, usw.	Estado, Provincia, etc.	État, Province, etc.	Estado, Província, etc.
Ambāla **Johnstown**	County, Oblast, etc.	Grafschaft, Oblast, usw.	Condado, Oblast, etc.	Comté, Oblast, etc.	Condado, Oblast, etc.
Iserlohn	Okrug, Kreis, etc.	Okrug, Kreis, usw.	Okrug, Kreis, etc.	Okrug, Kreis, etc.	Okrug, Kreis, etc.

**Scale in millions

Scale	Symbol	English	Deutsch	Español	Français	Português
		Transportation	***Verkehr***	***Transporte***	***Transports***	***Transporte***
		Road	**Strasse**	**Camino**	**Route**	**Rodovia**
1:.3* 1:1 1:3, 1:6 1:12	PASSAIC EXPWY. (I-80) PENNSYLVANIA TURNPIKE	Primary	Erster Ordnung	Principal	de premier ordre	Principal
1:.3 1:1 1:3, 1:6	BERLINER RING	Secondary	Zweiter Ordnung	Secundario	de second ordre	Secundária
1:.3 1:1		Tertiary	Dritter Ordnung	Terciario	de troisième ordre	Terciária
1:3 1:1 1:3, 1:6		Minor Road, Trail	Weg, Pfad	Rodera, Vereda	Route secondaire, Piste	Caminho, trilha
		Railway	**Eisenbahn**	**Ferrocarril**	**Voie ferrée**	**Ferrovia**
1:.3 1:1 1:3, 1:6 1:12		Primary	Hauptbahn	Principal	Principale	Principal
1:.3 1:1		Secondary	Sonstige Bahn	Secundario	Secondaire	Secundária
1:.3		*Rapid Transit	Schnellverkehr	Tránsito rápido	Métro	Trânsito rápido (metrô)
1:.3 1:1 1:3, 1:6	LONDON (HEATHROW) AIRPORT DULLES INTERNATIONAL AIRPORT	Airport	Flughafen	Aeropuerto	Aéroport	Aeroporto
	SÜD-BAHNHOF	Rail or Air Terminal	Bahnhof oder Flughafengebäude	Terminal ferroviaria o aéro	Gare ou aérogare	Terminal ferroviário ou aéreo (estação)
	REICHS-BRÜCKE	Bridge	Brücke	Puente	Pont	Ponte
	GREAT ST. BERNARD TUNNEL	Tunnel	Tunnel	Túnel	Tunnel	Túnel
	Houston Ship Channel	Shipping Channel	Schiffahrtsrinne	Canal maritimo	Chenal maritime	Canal marítimo
	Canal du Midi	Navigable Canal	Schiffbarer Kanal	Canal navegable	Canal navigable	Canal navegável
		Intracoastal Waterway	Küstenschiffahrtsweg	Via fluvial Intracostera	Canal côtier	Via costeira interna
	TO MALMÖ	Ferry	Fähre	Balsadera	Bac	Balsa
		Miscellaneous Cultural Features	***Sonstige Objekte***	***Elementos Culturales Misceláneos***	***Éléments Culturels Divers***	***Acidentes Culturais Diversos***
	PARQUE NACIONAL LANÍN	National or State Park or Monument	National- oder Naturpark oder Denkmal	Parque o Monumento nacional o provincial	Parc ou Monument national ou régional	Parque ou Monumento nacional ou regional
	EDISON NAT. HIST. SITE	National or State Historic(al) Site, Memorial	Historische Stätte, Gedenkstätte	Sitio histórico nacional o provincial, Monumento	Site historique national ou régional, Mémorial	Sitio histórico nacional ou regional, Monumento histórico
	SEMINOLE IND. RES.	Indian Reservation	Indianerreservation	Reserva de indios	Réserve indienne	Reserva indígena
	FORT DIX	Military Installation	Militäranlage	Instalación militar	Installation militaire	Instalação militar
	GREENWOOD CEMETERY	*Cemetery	Friedhof	Cementerio	Cimetière	Cemitério
	SORBONNE	Point of Interest (Battlefield, museum, temple, university, etc.)	Sehenswürdigkeit (Schlachtfeld, Museum, Tempel, Universität, usw.)	Punto de interés (Campo de batalla, museo, templo, universidad, etc.)	Curiosité (Champ de bataille, musée, temple, université, etc.)	Pontos de interesse (Campo de batalha, museu, templo, universidade, etc.)
	STEPHANSDOM	Church, Monastery	Kirche, Kloster	Iglesia, Monasterio	Église, Monastère	Igreja, Mosteiro
	UXMAL	Ruins	Ruinen	Ruinas	Ruines	Ruínas
	WINDSOR CASTLE	Castle	Burg, Schloss	Castillo	Château	Castelo
		*Lighthouse	Leuchtturm	Faro	Phare	Farol
	ASWĀN DAM	Dam	Damm	Presa	Barrage	Represa (barragem)
		*Lock	Schleuse	Esclusa	Écluse	Eclusa
	Crib	*Water Intake Crib	Wasseraufnahmestation	Toma de agua	Prise d'eau	Captação de água
		Quarry or Surface Mine	Steinbruch oder Tagebau	Cantera o Mina de hoyo abierto	Carrière ou Mine à ciel ouvert	Pedreira ou mina a céu aberto
		Subsurface Mine	Bergwerk	Mina subterránea	Mine souterraine	Mina subterrânea
		*Oil Well	Ölbohrturm	Pozo de petróleo	Puits de pétrole	Poço de petróleo
		Alternate Names	***Alternative Namensformen***	***Nombres Alternativos***	***Variantes Toponymiques***	***Variantes Toponímicas***
	MOSKVA **MOSCOW**	English or second official language names are shown in reduced size lettering	Englische Namen oder Namen in einer zweiten offiziellen Sprache erscheinen in kleineren Schriftgrössen	Los topónimos en inglés o un segundo idioma oficial se muestran en tipo de imprenta mas pequeño	Les toponymes en anglais ou dans la seconde langue officielle sont indiqués en caractères plus petits	Os topônimos em inglês ou num segundo idioma oficial aparecem em tipologia menor
	Ventura **(San Buenaventura)**	Historical or other alternates in the local language are shown in parentheses	Historische oder alternative Namensformen einheimischen Sprache erscheinen in Klammern	Los nombres históricos y alternativos locales se muestran en paréntesis	Les noms historiques de lieux ou les variantes toponymiques locales sont mis entre parenthèses	Os topônimos históricos ou as variantes toponímicos locais aparecem entre parênteses
		Metric-English Equivalents	***Umrechnung metrischer Masse in englische Masse***	***Métrico-Equivalentes Ingleses***	***Equivalences métriques des mesures anglaises***	***Equivalentes métricos das medidas inglesas***
		Areas represented by one square centimeter at various map scales	Flächen die einem cm² in den verschiedenen Kartenmassstäben entsprechen	Áreas representados por un centímetro cuadrado a varias escalas de mapas	Surface représentée par un cm² aux échelles indiquées	Áreas representadas por cm² nas escalas indicadas nos mapas

1:300,000	1:1,000,000	1:3,000,000	1:6,000,000	1:12,000,000	1:24,000,000	1:48,000,000
9 km²	100 km²	900 km²	3,600 km²	14,400 km²	57,600 km²	230,400 km²
3.48 square miles	39 square miles	348 square miles	1,390 square miles	5,558 square miles	22,234 square miles	88,934 square miles

Meter = 3.28 feet Kilometer = 0.62 mile Meter² (m²) = 10.76 square feet Kilometer² (km²) = 0.39 square mile

Meters	Feet
6000	19685
4000	13124
3000	9843
2000	6562
1000	3281
500	1640
200	656
0	0
0	0
200	656
1000	3281
3000	9843
6000	19685
9000	29520

English	Deutsch	Español	Français	Português
Elevation tints shown only on 1:3,000,000 and 1:6,000,000 scale maps	Höhenschichten erscheinen nur auf Karten im Massstab 1:3 000 000 und 1:6 000 000	Se indica las tintas de elevación sólo en los mapas de escala 1:3 000 000 y 1:6 000 000	Teintes hypsométriques exprimées seulement sur cartes à 1:3 000 000 et 1:6 000 000	Indicaram-se as graduações de cor hipsomé-tricas somente nos mapas de escalas 1:3 000 000 e 1:6 000 000

*Scale in millions

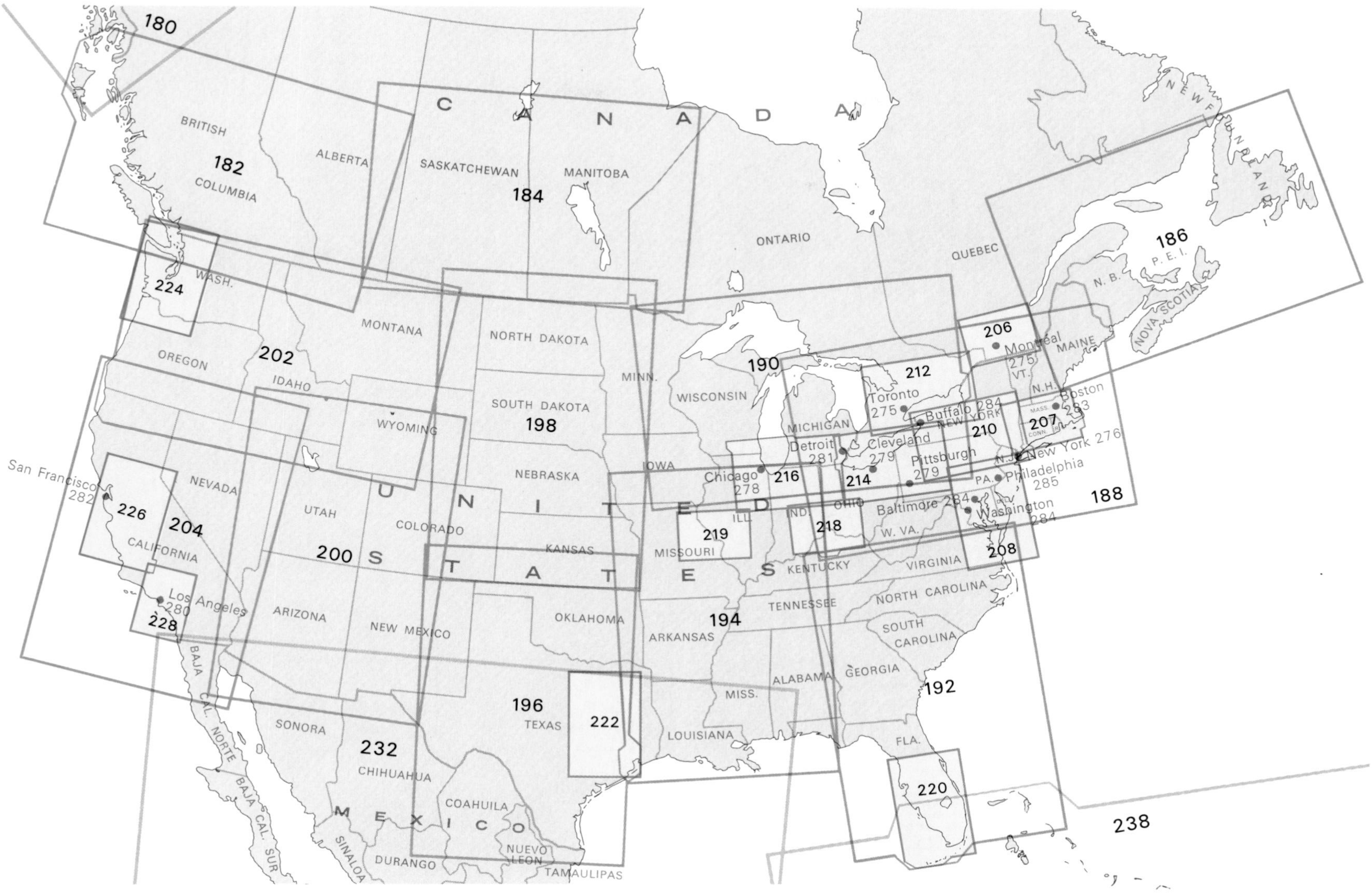
180
182
BRITISH COLUMBIA
ALBERTA
C A N A D A
SASKATCHEWAN
MANITOBA
184
ONTARIO
QUEBEC
186
NEWFOUNDLAND
P.E.I.
N.B.
NOVA SCOTIA
MAINE
224
WASH.
MONTANA
NORTH DAKOTA
OREGON
202
IDAHO
WYOMING
SOUTH DAKOTA
198
MINN.
WISCONSIN
190
MICHIGAN
212
Toronto 275
206
Montréal 275
VT.
N.H.
Buffalo 284
NEW YORK
210
207
Boston 283
MASS.
CONN.
New York 276
Philadelphia 285
188
San Francisco 282
226
NEVADA
204
CALIFORNIA
UTAH
200
COLORADO
NEBRASKA
IOWA
Chicago 278
216
Detroit 281
Cleveland 279
214
Pittsburgh 279
PA.
KANSAS
MISSOURI
219
ILL.
IND.
OHIO
218
Baltimore 284
Washington 284
W. VA.
208
U N I T E D S T A T E S
KENTUCKY
VIRGINIA
Los Angeles 280
228
ARIZONA
NEW MEXICO
OKLAHOMA
ARKANSAS
194
TENNESSEE
NORTH CAROLINA
SOUTH CAROLINA
GEORGIA
ALABAMA
MISS.
192
BAJA CAL. NORTE
SONORA
232
CHIHUAHUA
196
TEXAS
222
LOUISIANA
FLA.
220
BAJA CAL. SUR
M E X I C O
COAHUILA
NUEVO LEÓN
SINALOA
DURANGO
TAMAULIPAS
238

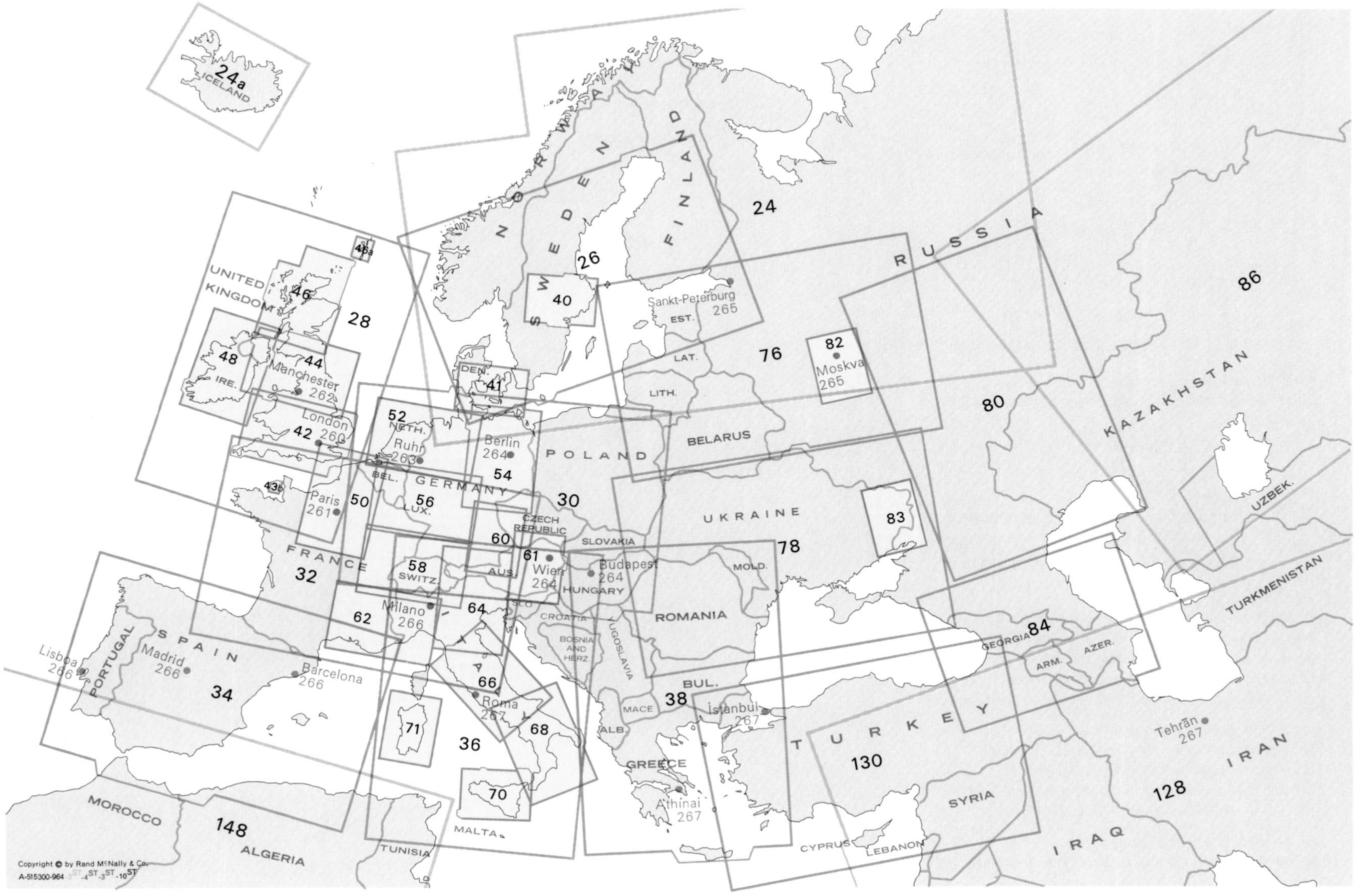
24a
ICELAND
46a
UNITED KINGDOM
46
28
48
IRE.
44
Manchester 262
London 260
42
43b
Paris 261
50
52
NETH.
Ruhr 263
BEL.
LUX.
56
GERMANY
DEN.
41
Berlin 264
54
POLAND
30
N O R W A Y
S W E D E N
40
26
F I N L A N D
24
Sankt-Peterburg 265
EST.
LAT.
LITH.
R U S S I A
76
82
Moskva 265
BELARUS
80
86
K A Z A K H S T A N
UZBEK.
TURKMENISTAN
CZECH REPUBLIC
60
SLOVAKIA
61
Wien 264
AUS.
Budapest 264
HUNGARY
U K R A I N E
83
78
MOLD.
F R A N C E
32
58
SWITZ.
62
Milano 266
64
SLO.
CROATIA
BOSNIA AND HERZ.
YUGOSLAVIA
ROMANIA
84
GEORGIA
ARM.
AZER.
P O R T U G A L
Lisboa 266
S P A I N
Madrid 266
34
Barcelona 266
I T A L Y
66
Roma 267
68
71
36
70
BUL.
38
MACE.
ALB.
İstanbul 267
GREECE
Athínai 267
T U R K E Y
130
SYRIA
CYPRUS
LEBANON
Tehrān 267
I R A N
128
I R A Q
MOROCCO
148
ALGERIA
TUNISIA
MALTA
Copyright © by Rand McNally & Co.
A-515300-964

ALEUTIAN ISLANDS
181a
GREENLAND
ALASKA
180
ICELAND
24a
Atlantic Ocean
UNITED KINGDOM
28
IRE.
GERMANY
30
FRANCE
32
SWITZ.
C A N A D A
182
184
186
202
190
188
198
U N I T E D S T A T E S
204
200
194
196
192
BERMUDA
240a
AZORES
148a
SPAIN
PORTUGAL
34
36
MOROCCO
148
ALGERIA
WESTERN SAHARA
229b 229c
229a
229d
HAWAII
M E X I C O
232
234
Ciudad de México
286
BAHAMAS
PROVIDENCE
240b
240p
JAMAICA
HAITI
DOMINICAN REPUBLIC
PUERTO RICO
240m
241n
241q
238
ANTIGUA 240c
GUADELOUPE 241o
DOMINICA 240d
MARTINIQUE
240e
SAINT LUCIA 241f
BARBADOS 241g
SAINT VINCENT
241h
GRENADA
241k
TRINIDAD AND TOBAGO
241r
NETH. ANTILLES 241s
Caribbean Sea
BELIZE
GUAT.
HONDURAS
NICARAGUA
EL SALVADOR
236
COSTA RICA
Caracas
286
VENEZUELA
GUYANA
SURINAME
FRENCH GUIANA
CAPE VERDE
150a
MAURITANIA
MALI
NIGER
SENEGAL
GAMBIA
GUINEA-BISSAU
GUINEA
SIERRA LEONE
LIBERIA
COTE D'IVOIRE
GHANA
BURKINA FASO
TOGO
BENIN
150
NIGERIA
Lagos
273
CAMEROON
GABON
Pacific Ocean
246
COLOMBIA
ECUADOR
GALAPAGOS ISLANDS
246a
250
B R A Z I L
P E R U
Lima
286
248
BOLIVIA
255
SAMOA ISLANDS
175a
174y
MANUA ISLANDS
São Paulo
287
256
Rio de Janeiro
PARAGUAY
C H I L E
A R G E N T I N A
252
Santiago
286
Buenos Aires
288
URUGUAY
258
254
Atlantic Ocean

MAP COVERAGE / KARTENAUSSCHNITTE
CONTENIDO DEL ATLAS / TABLEAU D'ASSEMBLAGE / ABRANGÊNCIA DO MAPA

148 Page Reference / Seitenangabe
Página de Referencia / Page de Référence / Página de Referência

Map Scale

Manila 269 • 1:300,000

1:1,000,000 | 1:6,000,000

1:3,000,000 | 1:12,000,000

Enlarged maps of Anglo-America and Europe on page XIII.
Vergrösserte Karten von Anglo-Amerika und Europa auf Seite XIII.
Mapas aumentados de América Anglosajona y Europa, página XIII.
Cartes à grande échelle de l'Amérique anglo-saxonne et de l'Europe à la page XIII.
Mapas ampliados da América Anglo-saxônica e da Europa, página XIII.

World, Ocean, and Continent maps on page 2-19.
Weltkarten, Karten der Ozeane und Erdteile auf Seiten 2-19.
Mapas del Mundo, Océanos y Continentes, páginas 2-19.
Cartes du Monde, des Océans et des Continents aux pages 2-19.
Mapas do Mundo, dos Oceanos e dos Continentes, páginas 2-19.

Additional Pacific Ocean Island maps on pages 174-175.
Zusätzliche Karten der Inseln des Pazifischen Ozeans auf Seite 174 175.
Mapas adicionales de las Islas del Océano Pacifico, páginas 174-175.
Cartes supplémentaires des Îles de l'Océan Pacifique aux pages 174-175.
Mapas suplementares das ilhas do Oceano Pacífico, páginas 174-175.

RUSSIA
Pacific Ocean
Indian Ocean
KAZAKHSTAN
MONGOLIA
CHINA
INDIA
IRAN
TURKEY
EGYPT
SAUDI ARABIA
SUDAN
ETHIOPIA
KENYA
TANZANIA
MOZAMBIQUE
MADAGASCAR
AUSTRALIA
NEW GUINEA
NEW ZEALAND
INDONESIA
MALAYSIA
BORNEO
JAVA
THAILAND
MYANMAR
PHILIPPINES
KOREA
TAIWAN
NEPAL
PAKISTAN
AFGHANISTAN
TURKMENISTAN
OMAN
YEMEN
SOMALIA
SRI LANKA
SOLOMON ISLANDS
Black Sea
Caspian Sea
Red Sea
Tehrān 267
Delhi 272
Calcutta 272
Bombay 272
Shanghai 269
Hong Kong 271
Manila 269
Singapore 271
Jakarta 269
Sydney 274
Melbourne 274
24
76
78
80
84
85
86
88
89
92
94
96
98
100
102
104
105
106
107
110
112
114
115a
115b
116
120
122
123
124
126
128
130
132
140
142
144
154
157a
157b
157c
162
164
166
168a
168b
169
170
171a
171b
172
174m
175b
175c
175d
175e
175f
175g

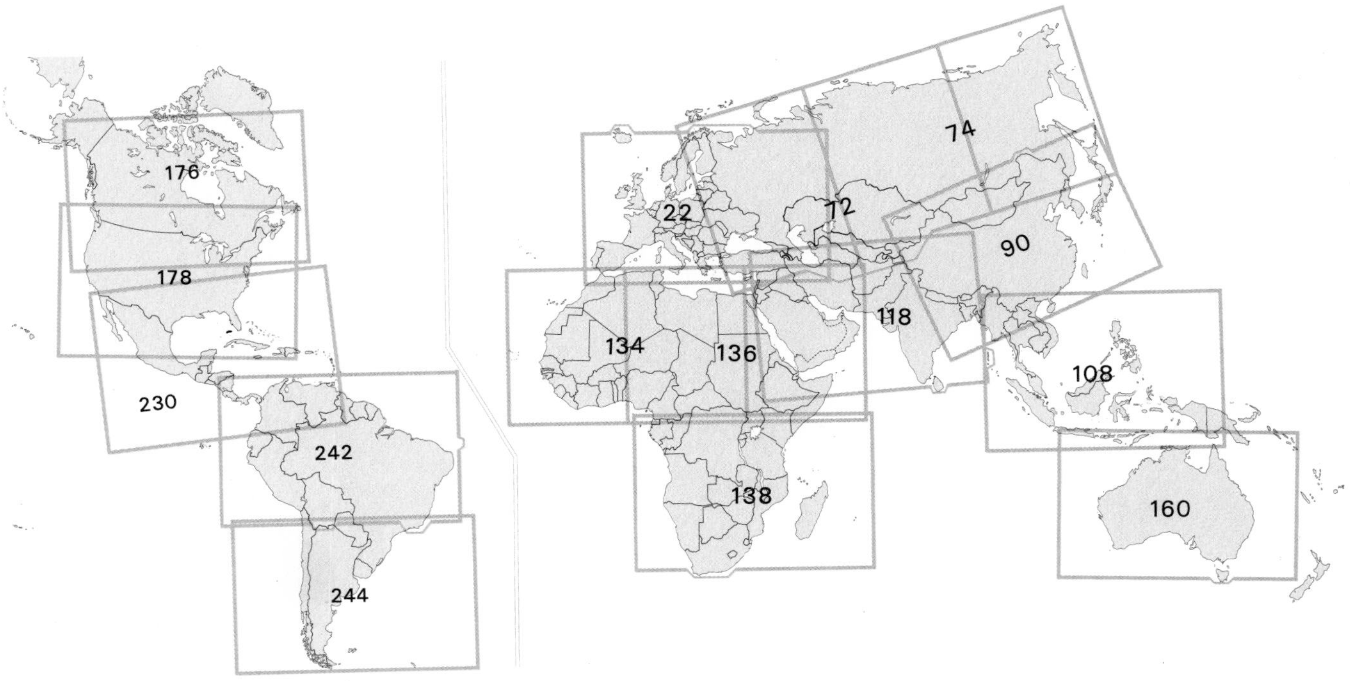
176
178
230
242
244
22
72
74
90
118
134
136
138
108
160

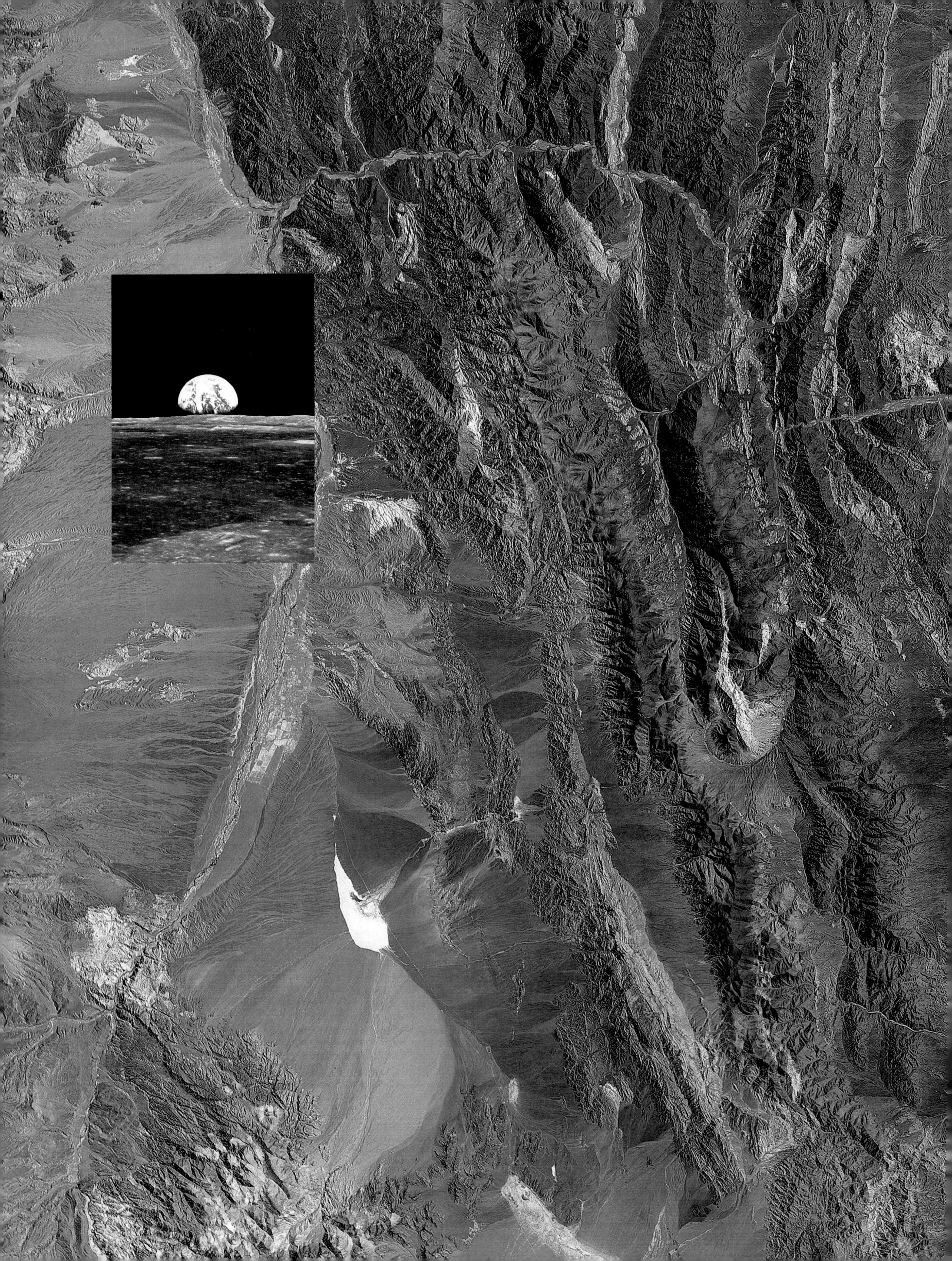

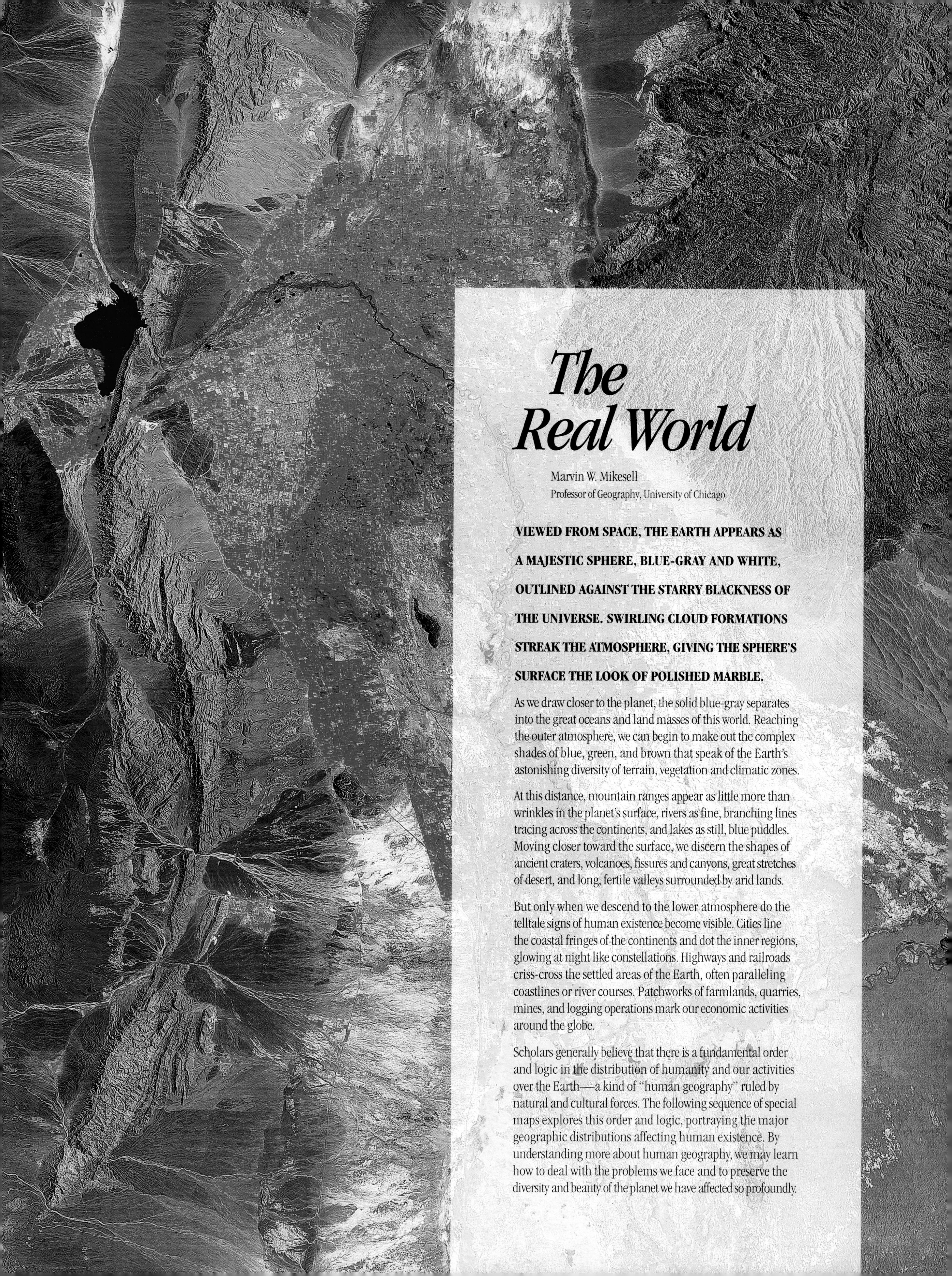

The Real World

Marvin W. Mikesell
Professor of Geography, University of Chicago

VIEWED FROM SPACE, THE EARTH APPEARS AS A MAJESTIC SPHERE, BLUE-GRAY AND WHITE, OUTLINED AGAINST THE STARRY BLACKNESS OF THE UNIVERSE. SWIRLING CLOUD FORMATIONS STREAK THE ATMOSPHERE, GIVING THE SPHERE'S SURFACE THE LOOK OF POLISHED MARBLE.

As we draw closer to the planet, the solid blue-gray separates into the great oceans and land masses of this world. Reaching the outer atmosphere, we can begin to make out the complex shades of blue, green, and brown that speak of the Earth's astonishing diversity of terrain, vegetation and climatic zones.

At this distance, mountain ranges appear as little more than wrinkles in the planet's surface, rivers as fine, branching lines tracing across the continents, and lakes as still, blue puddles. Moving closer toward the surface, we discern the shapes of ancient craters, volcanoes, fissures and canyons, great stretches of desert, and long, fertile valleys surrounded by arid lands.

But only when we descend to the lower atmosphere do the telltale signs of human existence become visible. Cities line the coastal fringes of the continents and dot the inner regions, glowing at night like constellations. Highways and railroads criss-cross the settled areas of the Earth, often paralleling coastlines or river courses. Patchworks of farmlands, quarries, mines, and logging operations mark our economic activities around the globe.

Scholars generally believe that there is a fundamental order and logic in the distribution of humanity and our activities over the Earth—a kind of "human geography" ruled by natural and cultural forces. The following sequence of special maps explores this order and logic, portraying the major geographic distributions affecting human existence. By understanding more about human geography, we may learn how to deal with the problems we face and to preserve the diversity and beauty of the planet we have affected so profoundly.

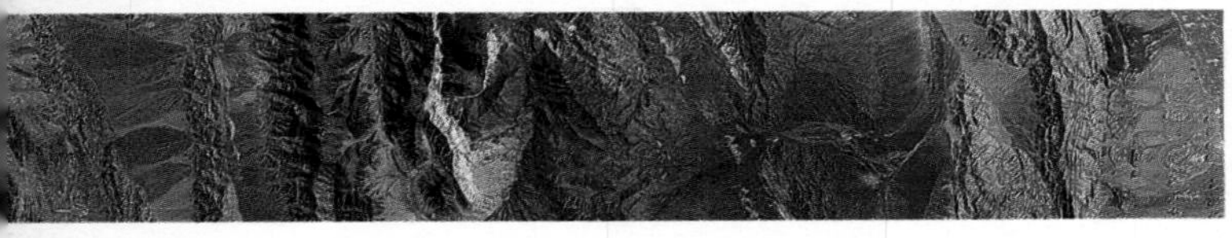

THE SURFACE OF OUR PLANET EXISTS IN A CONSTANT STATE OF CHANGE: CONTINENTS DRIFT TO NEW POSITIONS; OCEANS SHRINK AND DISAPPEAR WHILE NEW ONES ARE BEING born; mountain ranges rise and gradually vanish. But on a human time scale, geologic processes are so gradual as to be almost unnoticeable. Only in the sudden, violent moments of an earthquake, a volcanic eruption, or a major storm do we glimpse the powerful forces that shape the face of our planet.

The greatest shaping force is the movement of the brittle crustal pieces that make up the Earth's surface. These pieces, called "tectonic plates," float on a dense fluid portion of the upper mantle. Convection currents rising from the lower mantle keep them in constant motion—colliding, moving apart, sliding over or under one another. The result is the tremendously varied terrain depicted on the relief map on these pages.

Asia's massive Himalayan mountains were born when the Indo-Australian Plate collided with the Eurasian Plate, crumpling the crustal material at the plate edges and slowly thrusting it upward to heights of five and a half miles above sea level. The Red Sea and Africa's great Rift Valley were created through a different kind of tectonic process: the African plate is literally splitting apart. Eventually, the land east of the rift will be torn from the continent to form an enormous offshore island.

In the vast Pacific Ocean, volcanic activity is creating a long chain of islands as the Pacific Plate slides over a "hot spot" in the mantle. The Hawaiian Islands are the newest additions to this chain, which stretches northwest all the way to Russia's Kamchatka Peninsula.

Besides plate movement, wind and water are the most powerful forces shaping the Earth's surface. Wind and rain carry away soil and sediment, while rivers sculpt valleys and gorges, such as the Grand Canyon, and create fertile flood plains and deltas. The advance and retreat of glaciers during the great ice ages vastly altered terrain in the northern latitudes. Norway's fjords and North America's Great Lakes are among the glaciers' legacies.

Over the last few centuries, humans have had an increasingly significant impact on the face of the Earth. We have turned arid regions into farmlands, and have made forests and grasslands into deserts. We have reclaimed land from the sea and dammed rivers to create new lakes. Our mining and quarrying operations have left huge scars on the landscape.

Today, as population soars and technology leaps forward, our potential for changing the face of the earth, and our responsibility to change it for the better, is greater than ever.

180° 150° 120° 90° 60°
Arctic Ocean
QUEEN ELIZABETH ISLANDS
BAFFIN ISLAND
NORTH AMERICA
GREAT BASIN
GREAT PLAINS
APPALACHIAN MOUNTAINS
Mississippi
Pacific Ocean
HAWAIIAN ISLANDS
WEST INDIES
Atlant
Ocea
Equator
ARCHIPIÉLAGO DE COLÓN (GALÁPAGOS ISLANDS)
Amazon
SOUTH AMERICA
PAMPA
Pacific Ocean
60° 30° 0° 30° 60°
0 1000 2000 3000 Km.
0 1000 2000 3000 Mi.
Equatorial Scale
© Rand McNally
X-510000-792-1E-1E-1E-3B
180° 150° 120° 90° 60°

CONTINENTAL DRIFT

Geologic evidence indicates that the Earth's landmasses have migrated to their present positions over millions of years. These maps illustrate the positions of the continents in the past and where they are at present.

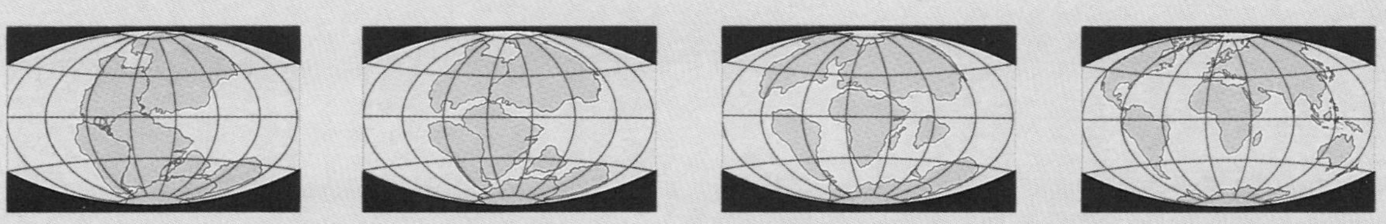

225 million years ago.
All of the world's land masses were joined together, forming a single supercontinent which we call Pangaea. Panthalassa is the name given to the single ancestral ocean. The Tethys Sea, predecessor of the Mediterranean Sea, separated Eurasia and Africa.

180 million years ago.
Pangaea split up. The northern block of continents, Laurasia, drifted northward, and the southern block, Gondwanaland, broke up into South America/ Africa, India, and Australia/ Antarctica.

65 million years ago.
Madagascar moved away from Africa, and the Tethys Sea all but disappeared as the Mediterranean Sea began to form. The ocean basins took shape as South America moved from Africa and India headed toward a collision with Asia. Australia was still joined with Antarctica.

The present day.
India has completed its northward migration and collided with Asia to form the Himalayas. Australia and Antarctica have separated, and North America has split from Eurasia, leaving Greenland as an island between them. During the past 65 million years, nearly one-half of the world's ocean floor has been created.

THE EARTH
This map utilizes shaded relief and varied colors to depict our planet's surface as it looks cloaked in summer vegetation. Country boundaries and all cities have been left off the map in order to highlight the Earth's natural features—continents, islands, oceans, lakes, rivers, mountain ranges, deserts, and plains. However, the textures and colors of the map can only hint at the variety and beauty found in the real world.

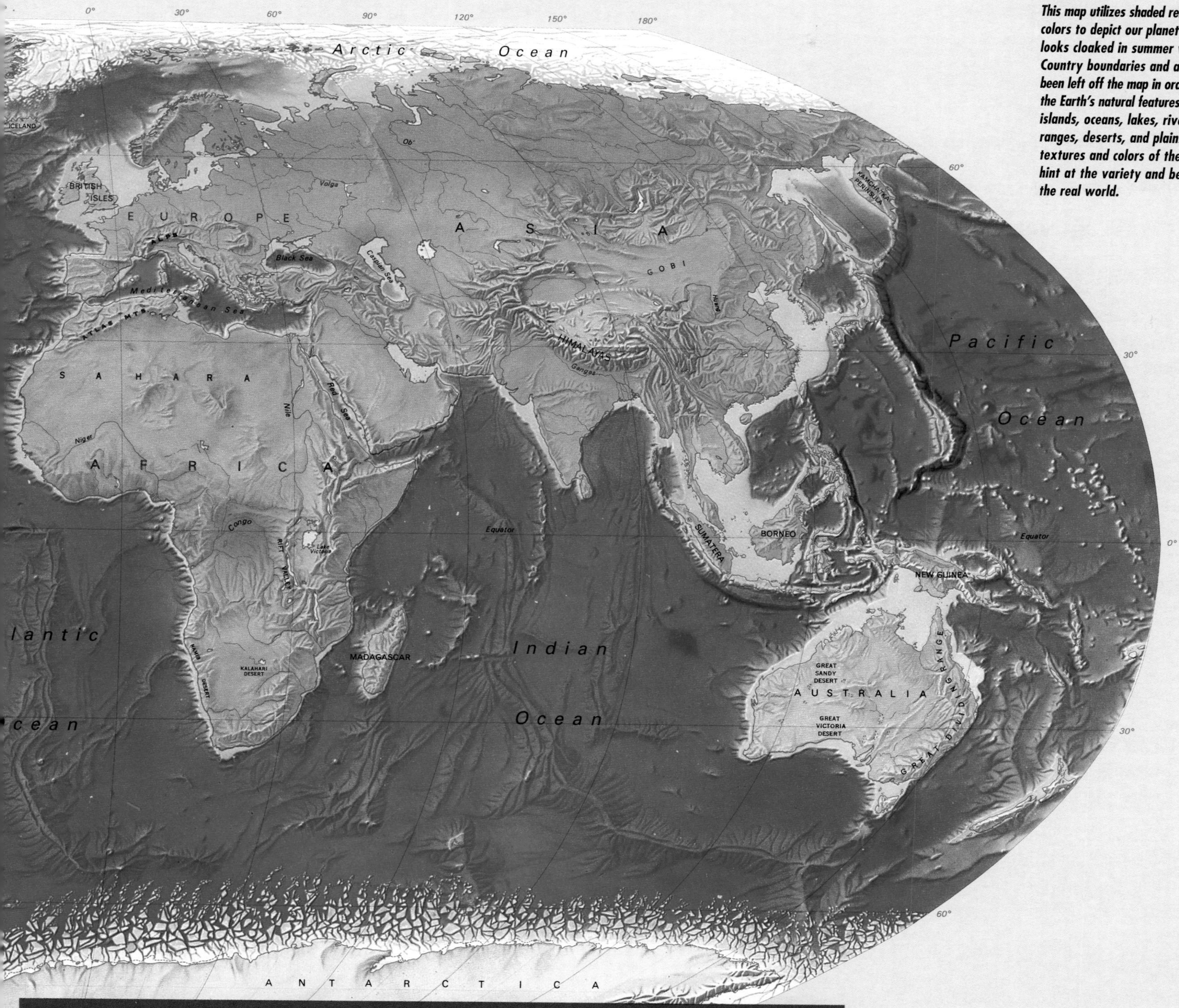

0°
30°
60°
90°
120°
150°
180°
Arctic Ocean
ICELAND
BRITISH ISLES
EUROPE
Volga
Ob'
ASIA
Black Sea
Caspian Sea
GOBI
Mediterranean Sea
ATLAS MTS.
HIMALAYAS
Ganges
Pacific Ocean
SAHARA
Nile
Red Sea
Niger
AFRICA
Congo
Lake Victoria
RIFT VALLEY
Equator
SUMATERA
BORNEO
NEW GUINEA
lantic
cean
MADAGASCAR
KALAHARI DESERT
NAMIB DESERT
Indian Ocean
GREAT SANDY DESERT
AUSTRALIA
GREAT VICTORIA DESERT
GREAT DIVIDING RANGE
ANTARCTICA

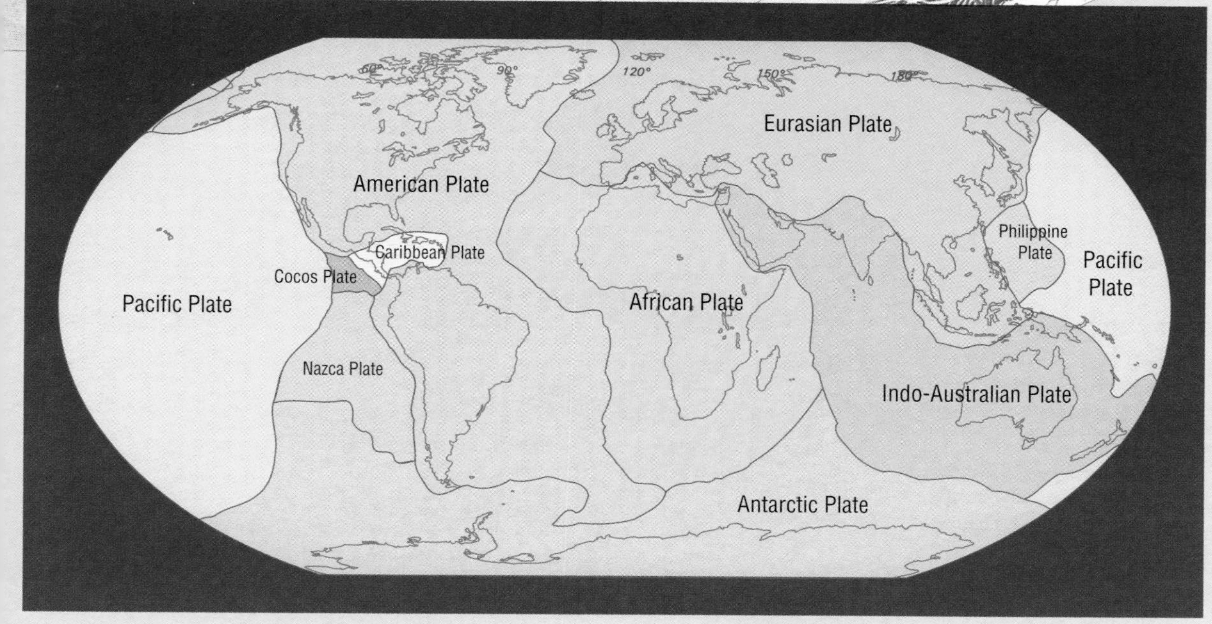

90°
120°
150°
180°
Eurasian Plate
American Plate
Philippine Plate
Pacific Plate
Caribbean Plate
Cocos Plate
Pacific Plate
African Plate
Nazca Plate
Indo-Australian Plate
Antarctic Plate

Subduction Zone
Ocean Ridge Zone

PLATES AND CONTINENTS
The outside crust and uppermost mantle of the Earth, the lithosphere, is divided into six major rigid plates and several smaller platelets. These plates move, driven by convection currents deep in the mantle, and carry the continents along with them. Through this tectonic process, the Earth's crust constantly shifts, is modified and rebuilt. Earthquakes and volcanic activity are associated with plate boundaries. The position of the continents in relation to the plates is shown on the map above.

CLIMATE

WHILE CALM, CLEAR SKIES PREVAIL OVER NORTH AMERICA'S GREAT PLAINS, A VIOLENT HURRICANE BATTERS A CHAIN OF CARIBBEAN ISLANDS. IN EASTERN AFRICA, RAINSTORMS break a two-year drought, but northern European farmers watch their crops dry up in a heat wave. Mild spring winds arrive over Argentina, and in southeast Asia monsoon winds bring lightning and torrential rains.

The infinite variety of our planet's weather is created by the complex relationship of air, water, and land. Air masses ebb and flow around the globe, as moist tropical air moves toward the poles and drier polar air descends toward the equator. The spinning of the Earth helps to direct the air masses. Ocean currents circulate "rivers" of warmer and cooler waters around the globe. Great mountain ranges trap air masses and disrupt the world-wide flow. The 23½° inclination of our planet as it revolves around the sun creates the yearly cycle of seasons.

Over time, this constant interaction of natural forces establishes consistent weather patterns which, in turn, define the major climatic regions of the world, which are depicted on the adjacent map. Within each region, characteristic soils and related plant and animal life evolve.

Generally predictable patterns of weather within these regions have permitted humanity to develop an array of economic and cultural systems, each closely related to the area's normal climatic conditions.

It is the abnormal climatic occurrence—sometimes called a "climatic anomaly"—that causes the most human turmoil, as well as shock to the natural order. For example, a combination of cold Pacific currents and dry air masses makes the northern coast of Chile one of the driest places on Earth. The lifestyle of the region is based upon this prevailing climate. When the phenomenon known as *El Niño* occurs, the usual northerly flow of cold air and water reverses itself, and warm equatorial air and water flow south onto the coast of Chile. These unexpected conditions dramatically increase rainfall, leading to disastrous flooding, and completely disrupting the cultural and natural order.

Today there is growing awareness and concern about humanity's increasing impact on climate. In many large urban areas, the heat-absorbing artificial terrain, combined with air pollution from automobiles and industry, has created "micro-climates" characterized by higher temperatures and excessive smog. A far greater potential problem is global warming resulting from the so-called "greenhouse effect." The burning of fossil fuels adds carbon dioxide to the atmosphere, which causes the atmosphere to trap heat that would normally radiate out into space. If global temperatures rise even a few degrees, the consequences could be disastrous.

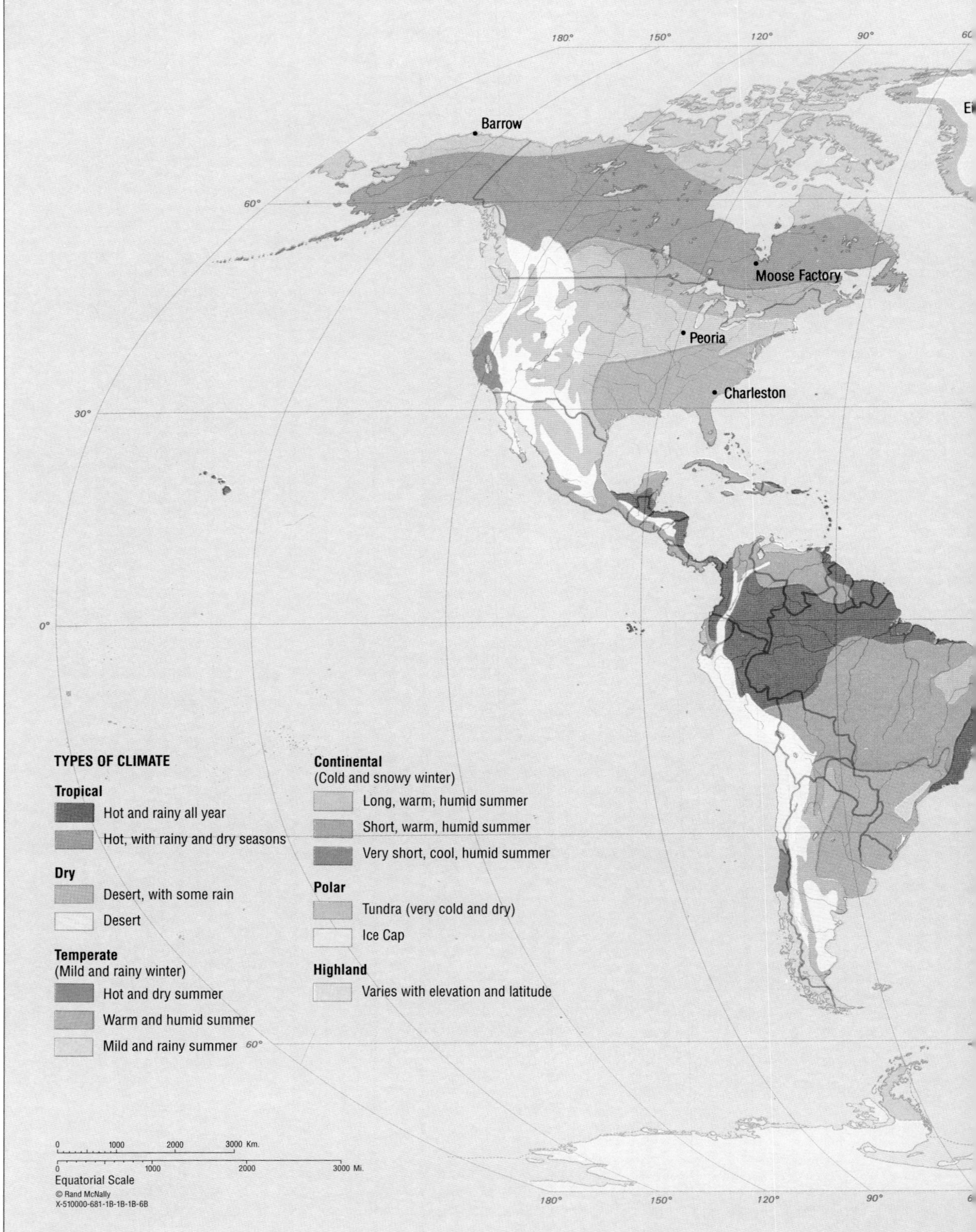
180°
150°
120°
90°
60°
30°
0°
Barrow
Moose Factory
Peoria
Charleston
TYPES OF CLIMATE
Tropical
Hot and rainy all year
Hot, with rainy and dry seasons
Dry
Desert, with some rain
Desert
Temperate
(Mild and rainy winter)
Hot and dry summer
Warm and humid summer
Mild and rainy summer
Continental
(Cold and snowy winter)
Long, warm, humid summer
Short, warm, humid summer
Very short, cool, humid summer
Polar
Tundra (very cold and dry)
Ice Cap
Highland
Varies with elevation and latitude
0 1000 2000 3000 Km.
0 1000 2000 3000 Mi.
Equatorial Scale
© Rand McNally
X-510000-681-1B-1B-1B-6B

EXAMPLES OF TYPES OF CLIMATE

The curved lines on the graphs below show fahrenheit temperatures. The vertical bars show rainfall in inches.

CLIMATE GRAPHS
These graphs show the average monthly temperature and precipitation for typical cities within each of the major climatic regions.

Other elements that influence climate include amount of sunshine and cloud-cover, daily ranges in temperature, wind conditions, and height above sea level.

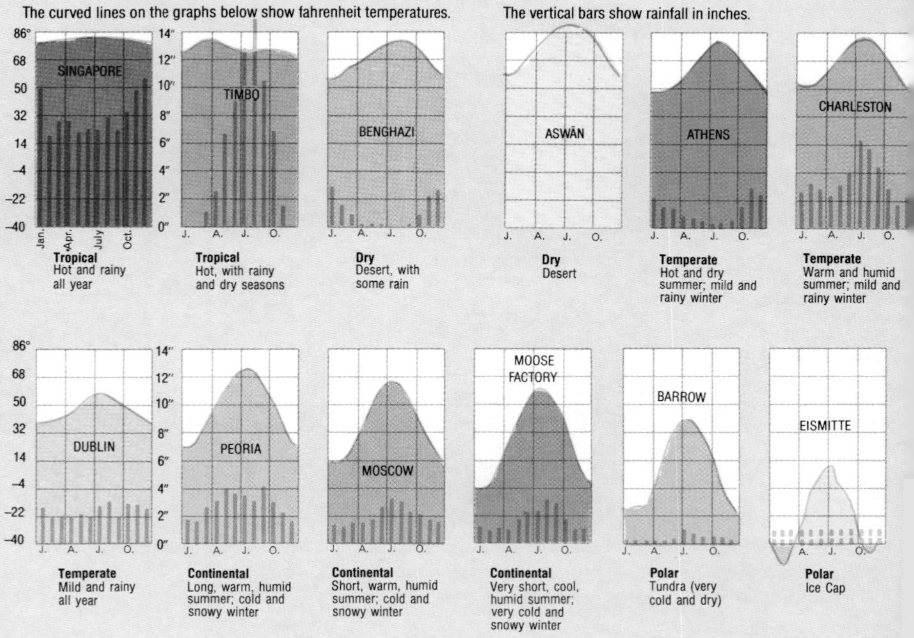
86°
68
50
32
14
–4
–22
–40
14"
12"
10"
8"
6"
4"
2"
0"
SINGAPORE
Jan. Apr. July Oct.
Tropical
Hot and rainy all year
TIMBO
J. A. J. O.
Tropical
Hot, with rainy and dry seasons
BENGHAZI
Dry
Desert, with some rain
ASWĀN
Dry
Desert
ATHENS
Temperate
Hot and dry summer; mild and rainy winter
CHARLESTON
Temperate
Warm and humid summer; mild and rainy winter
DUBLIN
Temperate
Mild and rainy all year
PEORIA
Continental
Long, warm, humid summer; cold and snowy winter
MOSCOW
Continental
Short, warm, humid summer; cold and snowy winter
MOOSE FACTORY
Continental
Very short, cool, humid summer; very cold and snowy winter
BARROW
Polar
Tundra (very cold and dry)
EISMITTE
Polar
Ice Cap

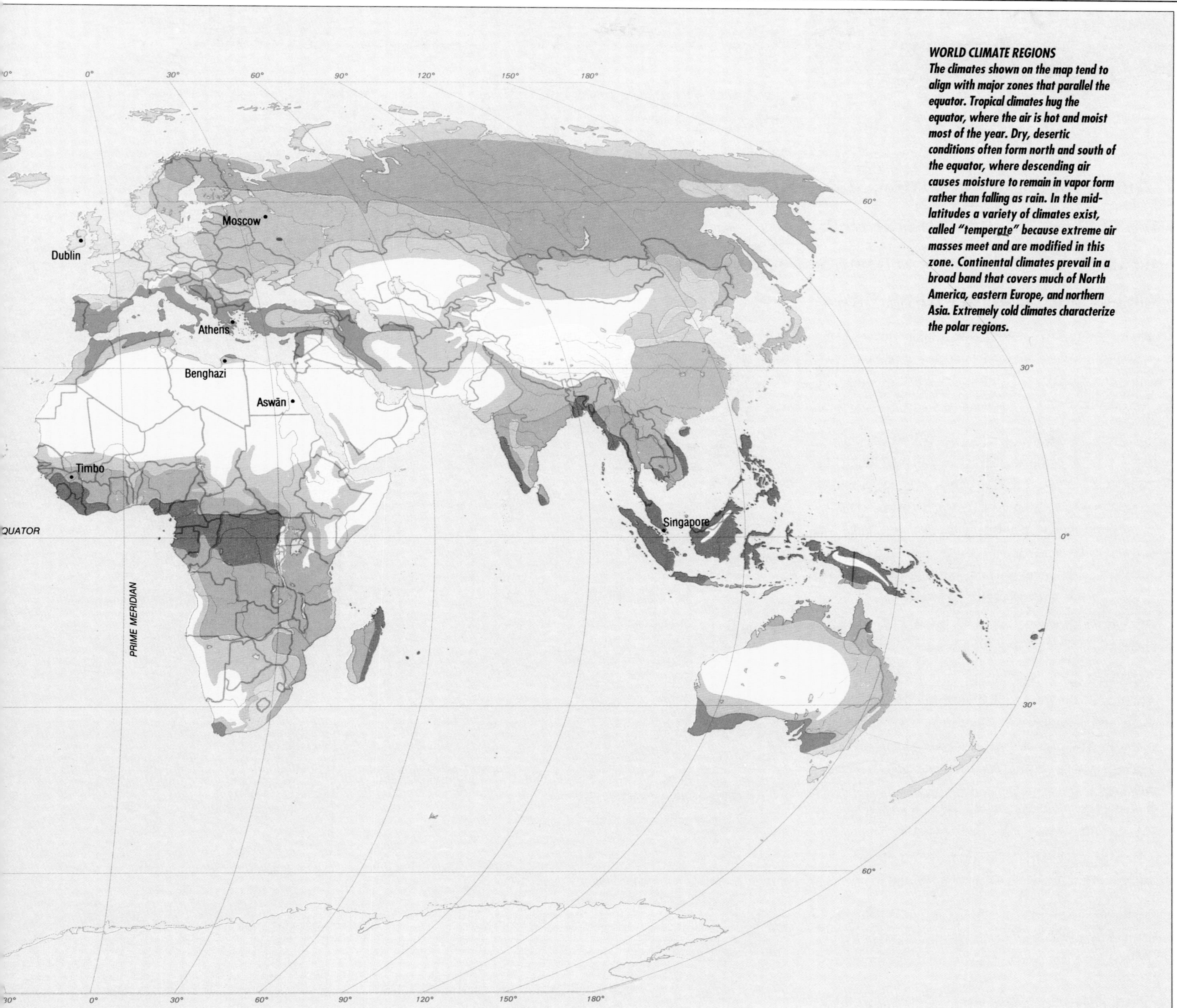

Moscow
Dublin
Athens
Benghazi
Aswān
Timbo
Singapore
QUATOR
PRIME MERIDIAN
0°
30°
60°
90°
120°
150°
180°

WORLD CLIMATE REGIONS

The climates shown on the map tend to align with major zones that parallel the equator. Tropical climates hug the equator, where the air is hot and moist most of the year. Dry, desertic conditions often form north and south of the equator, where descending air causes moisture to remain in vapor form rather than falling as rain. In the mid-latitudes a variety of climates exist, called "temperate" because extreme air masses meet and are modified in this zone. Continental climates prevail in a broad band that covers much of North America, eastern Europe, and northern Asia. Extremely cold climates characterize the polar regions.

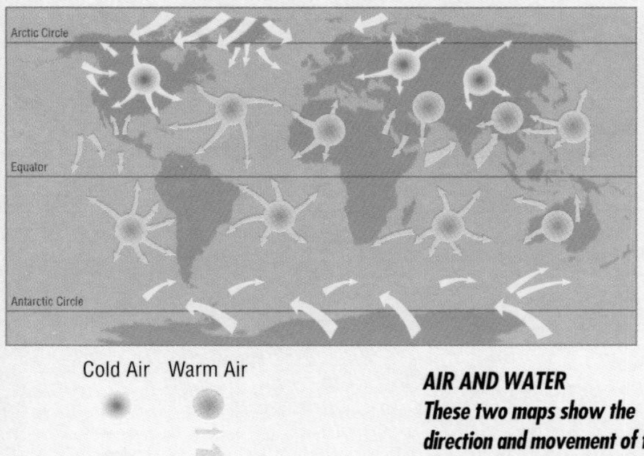

Arctic Circle
Equator
Antarctic Circle
Cold Air
Warm Air

AIR AND WATER

These two maps show the direction and movement of the Earth's major air masses and ocean currents. The world's weather and its climatic regions result from the movement of these huge masses of air and water. The boundaries and direction of these masses are altered by factors such as vertical motion, surface friction, continental and seabed topography, and the Earth's rotation.

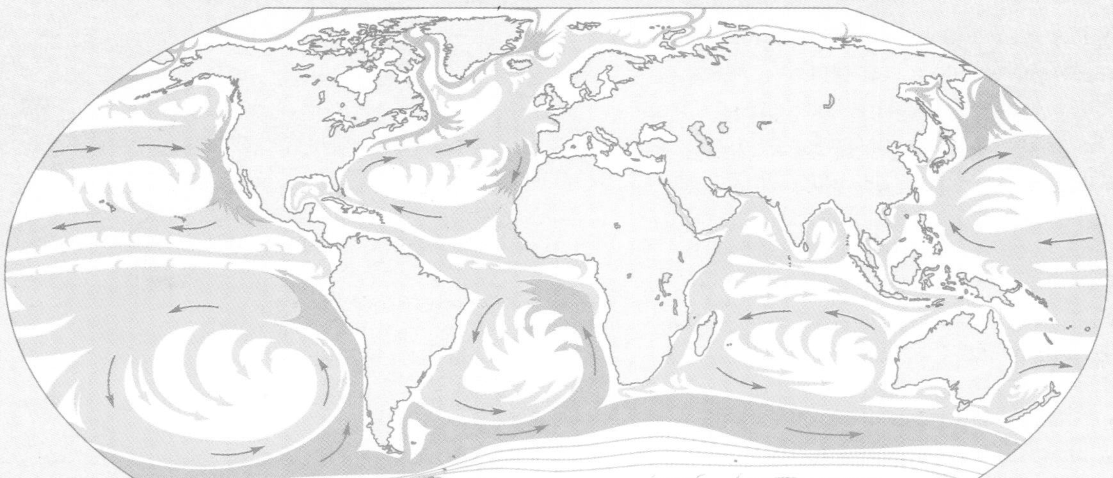

Cold Current
Warm Current

THE HISTORY OF HUMAN SETTLEMENT IS THE STORY OF A SEARCH FOR FERTILE LAND, ABUNDANT SOURCES OF WATER, SUITABLE TERRAIN, AND CLIMATES WITH ADEQUATE growing seasons. Wherever nature supplies all of these elements, human settlements flourish. When they are scarce or disappear, communities are few and may eventually be abandoned.

Since humans began practicing agriculture about 10,000 years ago, the greatest limitation on settlement has been the length of the growing season. Areas with fewer than 90 days free of frost per year are not suitable for most forms of agriculture. Without an abundant food supply, settlements cannot grow beyond a limited size. Outside the regions where agriculture is viable, people must depend on imported food or live by hunting, fishing, and trapping—activities that can support only small communities.

Human settlement is also restricted by the amount of precipitation an area receives. Farming is not practical where annual rainfall is less than 10 inches (24.5 cm) in temperate areas and less than 20 inches (51 cm) in hotter regions. At various times, people have developed large-scale irrigation systems to pipe water into once-arid lands. In this way, human patterns of settlement have appeared in desert areas of the American Southwest, the Middle East, and parts of Africa. However, the process is costly and usually draws heavily on underground reservoirs.

Finally, terrain and soil also limit human settlement. Much of the world is simply too mountainous or the soil too poor for people to settle. At high elevations, the growing season is often too short for cultivation. Taiga forests and equatorial rainforests generally create a thin, acidic soil that is often too infertile to sustain permanent agricultural communities.

Human settlement patterns have shifted dramatically from rural to urban in the last two centuries. Advances in agricultural technology and methods have produced growing food supplies able to support larger and larger urban populations. The industrial and technological revolution has created job opportunities that are nearly always in urban areas. In 1925, approximately 20% of the world's population was urban. Today the figure is approaching 50%. It is estimated that by 2025, five out of eight people will live in cities.

Until the early part of this century, this trend was largely confined to the developed countries, but it has since spread to much of the rest of the world. Today the strongest urbanization trends are in the developing countries of South America and Africa, where the problems indigenous to urban living—overcrowding, pollution, inadequate sanitation, disease—are often magnified by inadequate economic resources.

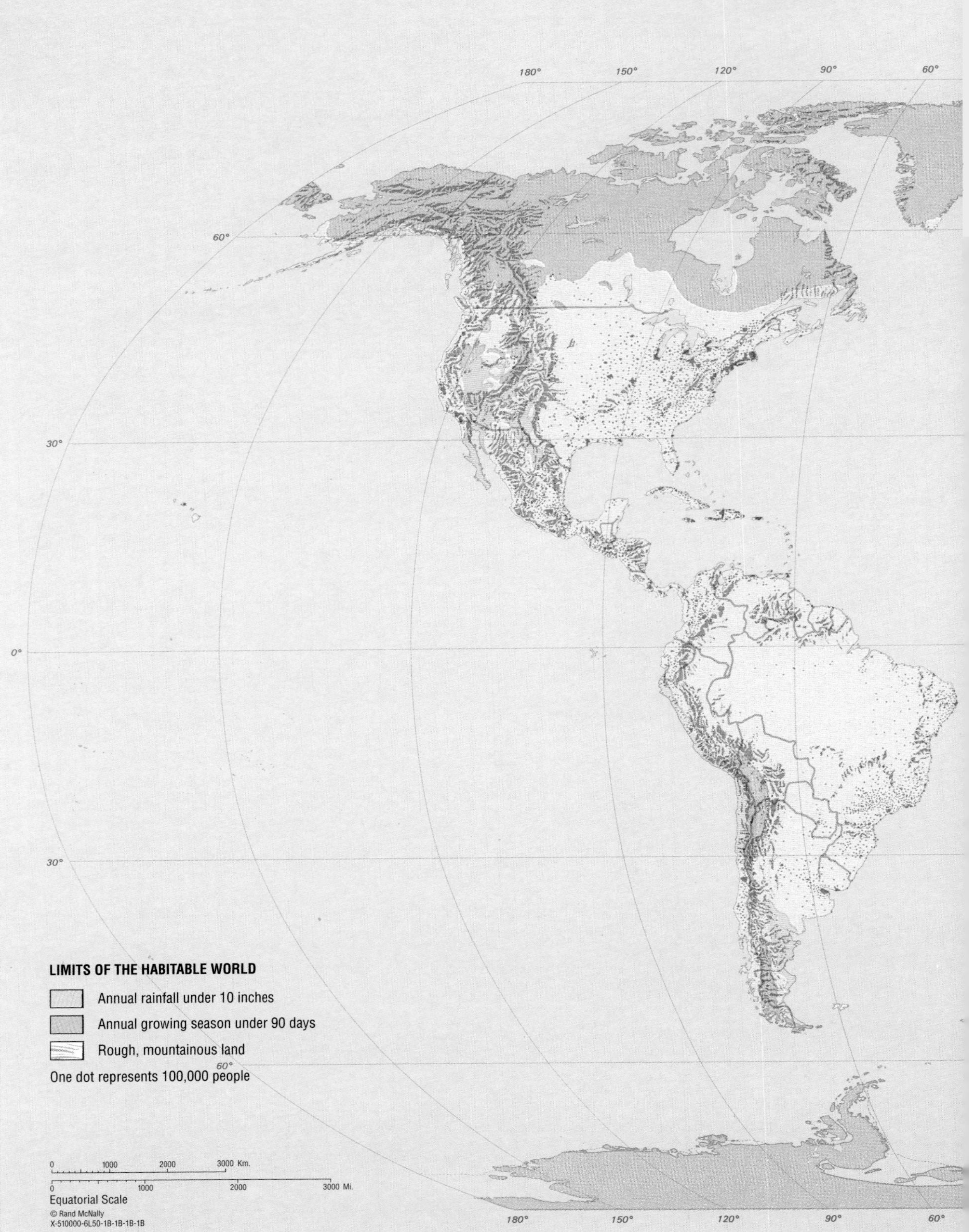
180°
150°
120°
90°
60°
60°
30°
0°
30°
60°
LIMITS OF THE HABITABLE WORLD
Annual rainfall under 10 inches
Annual growing season under 90 days
Rough, mountainous land
One dot represents 100,000 people
0 1000 2000 3000 Km.
0 1000 2000 3000 Mi.
Equatorial Scale
© Rand McNally
X-510000-6L50-1B-1B-1B-1B

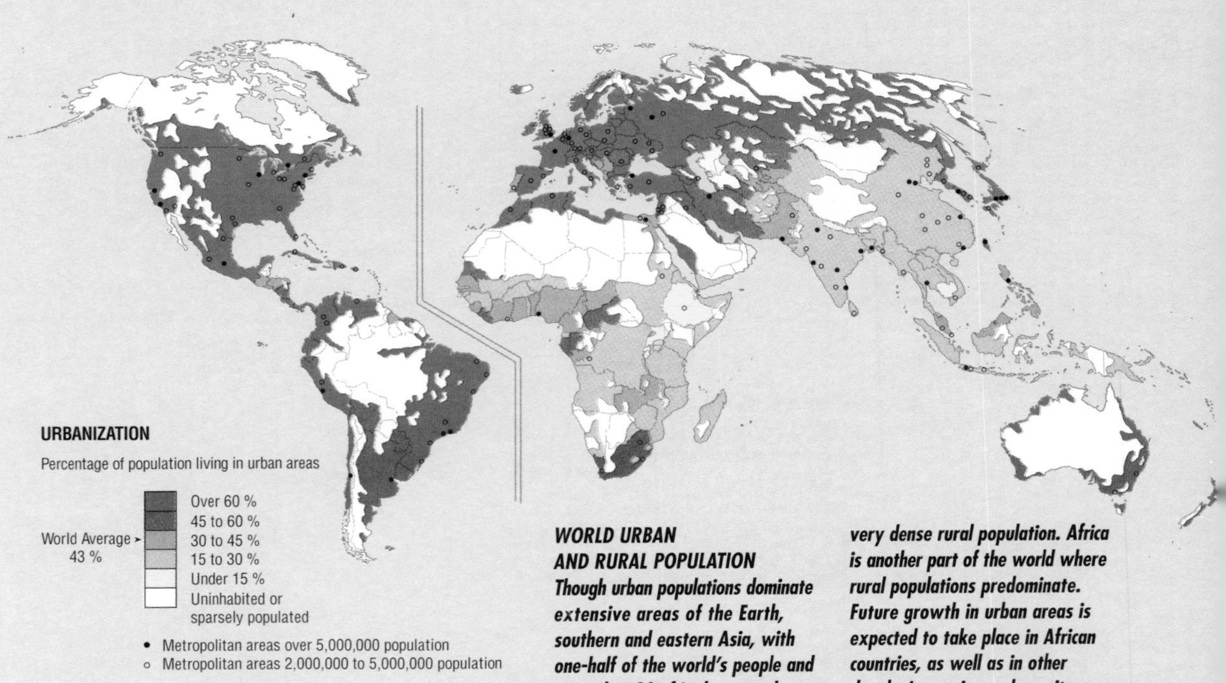
URBANIZATION
Percentage of population living in urban areas
World Average 43 %
Over 60 %
45 to 60 %
30 to 45 %
15 to 30 %
Under 15 %
Uninhabited or sparsely populated
• Metropolitan areas over 5,000,000 population
○ Metropolitan areas 2,000,000 to 5,000,000 population

WORLD URBAN AND RURAL POPULATION
Though urban populations dominate extensive areas of the Earth, southern and eastern Asia, with one-half of the world's people and more than 30 of its largest urban centers, are still characterized by a very dense rural population. Africa is another part of the world where rural populations predominate. Future growth in urban areas is expected to take place in African countries, as well as in other developing regions where city populations are already large.

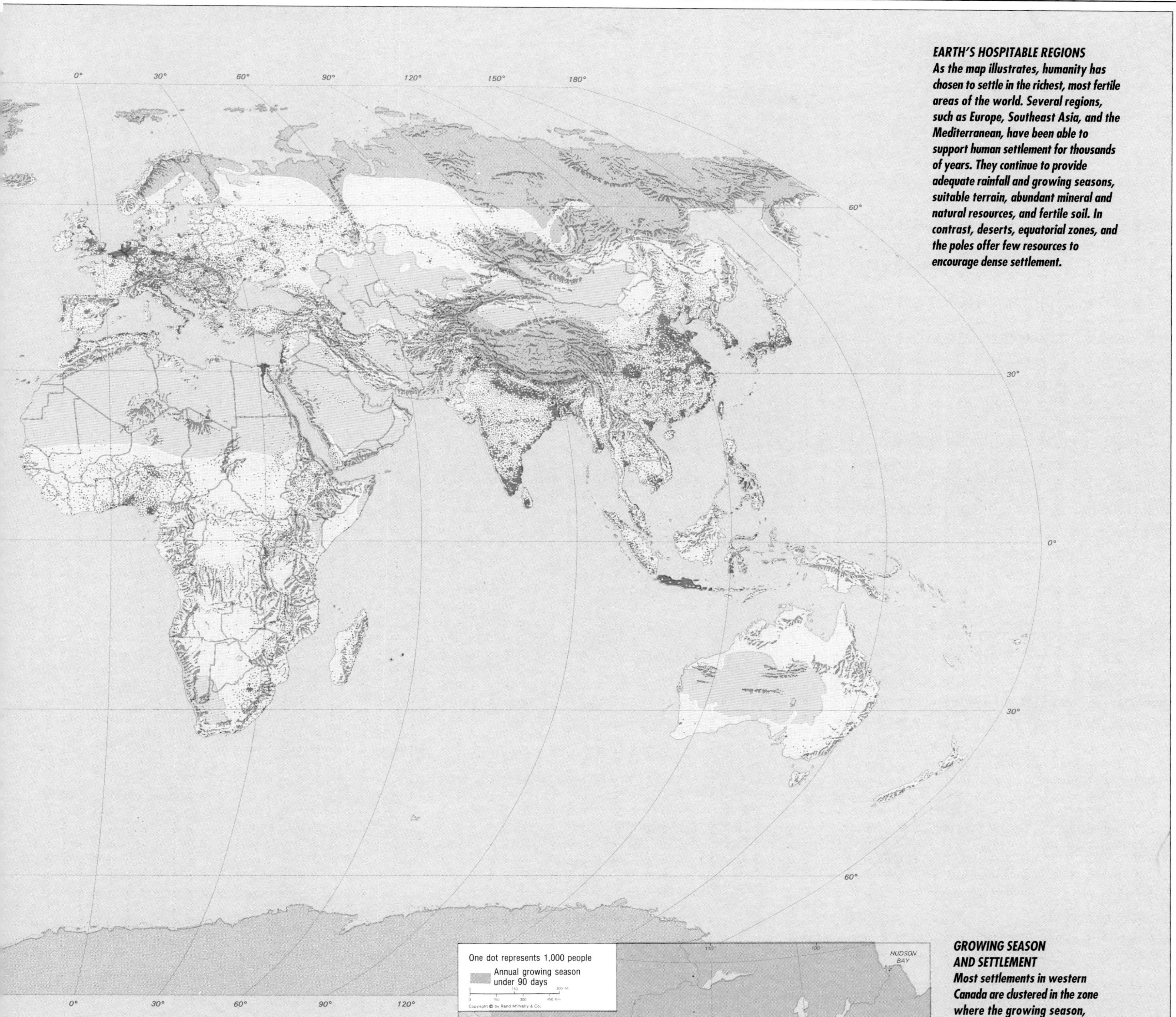
0°
30°
60°
90°
120°
150°
180°
60°
30°
0°
30°
60°
0°
30°
60°
90°
120°

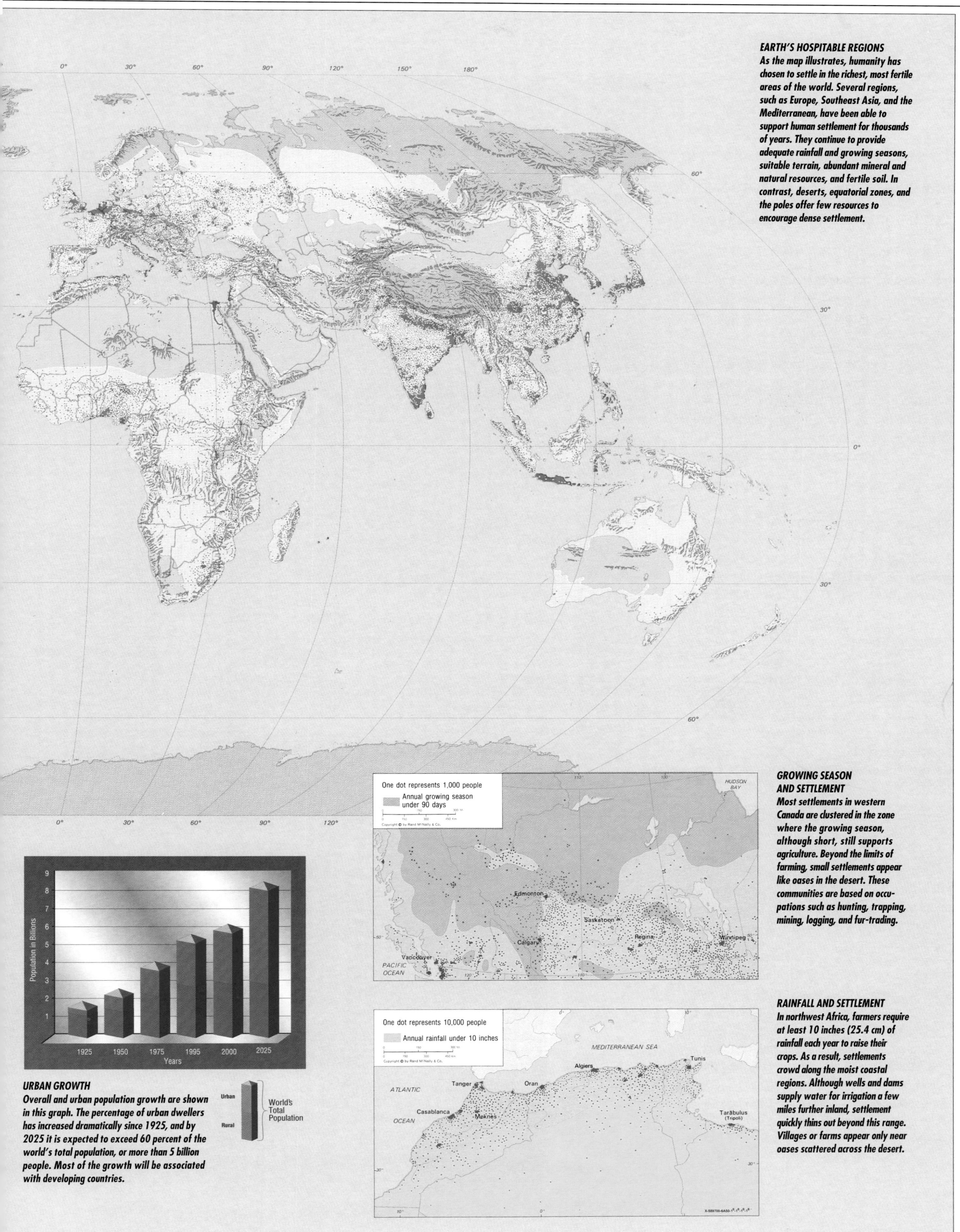

EARTH'S HOSPITABLE REGIONS

As the map illustrates, humanity has chosen to settle in the richest, most fertile areas of the world. Several regions, such as Europe, Southeast Asia, and the Mediterranean, have been able to support human settlement for thousands of years. They continue to provide adequate rainfall and growing seasons, suitable terrain, abundant mineral and natural resources, and fertile soil. In contrast, deserts, equatorial zones, and the poles offer few resources to encourage dense settlement.

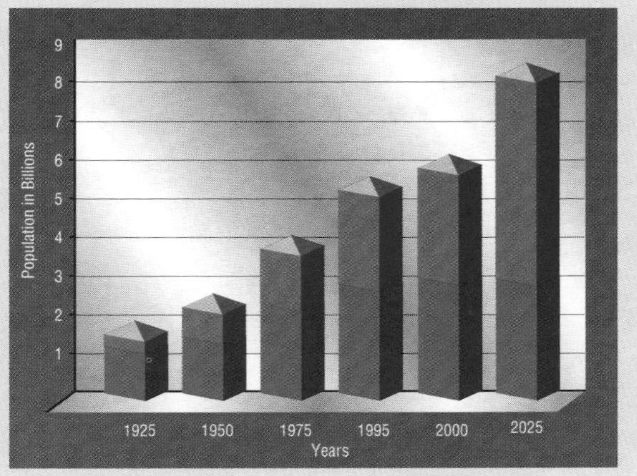
Population in Billions
9
8
7
6
5
4
3
2
1
1925
1950
1975
1995
2000
2025
Years

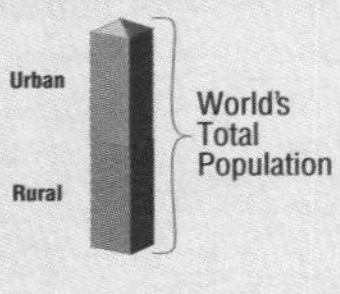
Urban
Rural
World's Total Population

URBAN GROWTH

Overall and urban population growth are shown in this graph. The percentage of urban dwellers has increased dramatically since 1925, and by 2025 it is expected to exceed 60 percent of the world's total population, or more than 5 billion people. Most of the growth will be associated with developing countries.

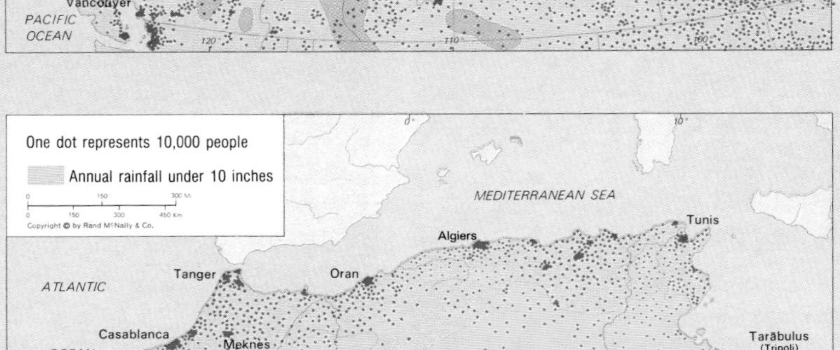
One dot represents 1,000 people
Annual growing season under 90 days
Copyright © by Rand McNally & Co.
HUDSON BAY
Edmonton
Saskatoon
Calgary
Regina
Winnipeg
Vancouver
PACIFIC OCEAN

GROWING SEASON AND SETTLEMENT

Most settlements in western Canada are clustered in the zone where the growing season, although short, still supports agriculture. Beyond the limits of farming, small settlements appear like oases in the desert. These communities are based on occupations such as hunting, trapping, mining, logging, and fur-trading.

One dot represents 10,000 people
Annual rainfall under 10 inches
Copyright © by Rand McNally & Co.
MEDITERRANEAN SEA
Tunis
Algiers
Oran
Tanger
ATLANTIC OCEAN
Casablanca
Meknès
Tarābulus
(Tripoli)

RAINFALL AND SETTLEMENT

In northwest Africa, farmers require at least 10 inches (25.4 cm) of rainfall each year to raise their crops. As a result, settlements crowd along the moist coastal regions. Although wells and dams supply water for irrigation a few miles further inland, settlement quickly thins out beyond this range. Villages or farms appear only near oases scattered across the desert.

POPULATION

NEARLY 1.6 MILLION YEARS AGO, OUR HUMAN ANCESTORS STRUGGLED TO SURVIVE IN THE FORESTS AND FERTILE PLAINS OF EASTERN AFRICA. TODAY, HUMANITY inhabits every continent on earth. World population is approaching 6 billion, with 80 million new lives added every year. More people are alive now than have existed since the dawn of human history.

This explosive growth is fueled not only by a rising birth rate but by longer average life spans and by a sharp reduction in the number of children who die young. With births far outstripping deaths, predictions are that world population will not stablize until the year 2010, when over 10 billion people will share the planet.

The most densely settled parts of the Earth appear in the industrial areas of Europe, North America, and Japan, and the predominantly rural areas of India, China, and Southeast Asia. In developed areas, modern technology has encouraged the growth of large urban districts. The heavily populated rural areas of Asian countries reflect nearly 4,000 years of agricultural civilization.

Even with the surge in population, however, substantial areas of the Earth remain underpopulated or virtually empty. Some regions offer striking contrasts between crowded and open spaces. In Russia, a narrow band of population stretches along the Trans-Siberian Railway. The eastern shore of the Mediterranean Sea, with its crowded coastal fringe of Israel, Lebanon, and Syria, stands out sharply against the barren, uninhabited land beyond.

Several natural and cultural factors help explain the uneven distribution of humanity. Nature imposes limits on agricultural development: many areas are too dry or mountainous or have growing seasons too short to support a large population. The harsher climate and terrain of the polar regions and great deserts of the world show only widely scattered human settlements.

Cultural factors also influence where populations are likely to concentrate. Nearly 2.5 billion people now live in urban centers, half of them in cities that number 500,000 or more. By the year 2000, the urban population in less-developed countries will double, as the rural poor seek greater opportunities in the already-crowded cities. Religion and cultural values also influence a nation's ability to control its birth rate. Until curbing population becomes a worldwide goal, our growing numbers will continue to exert increasing pressure on the Earth's resources.

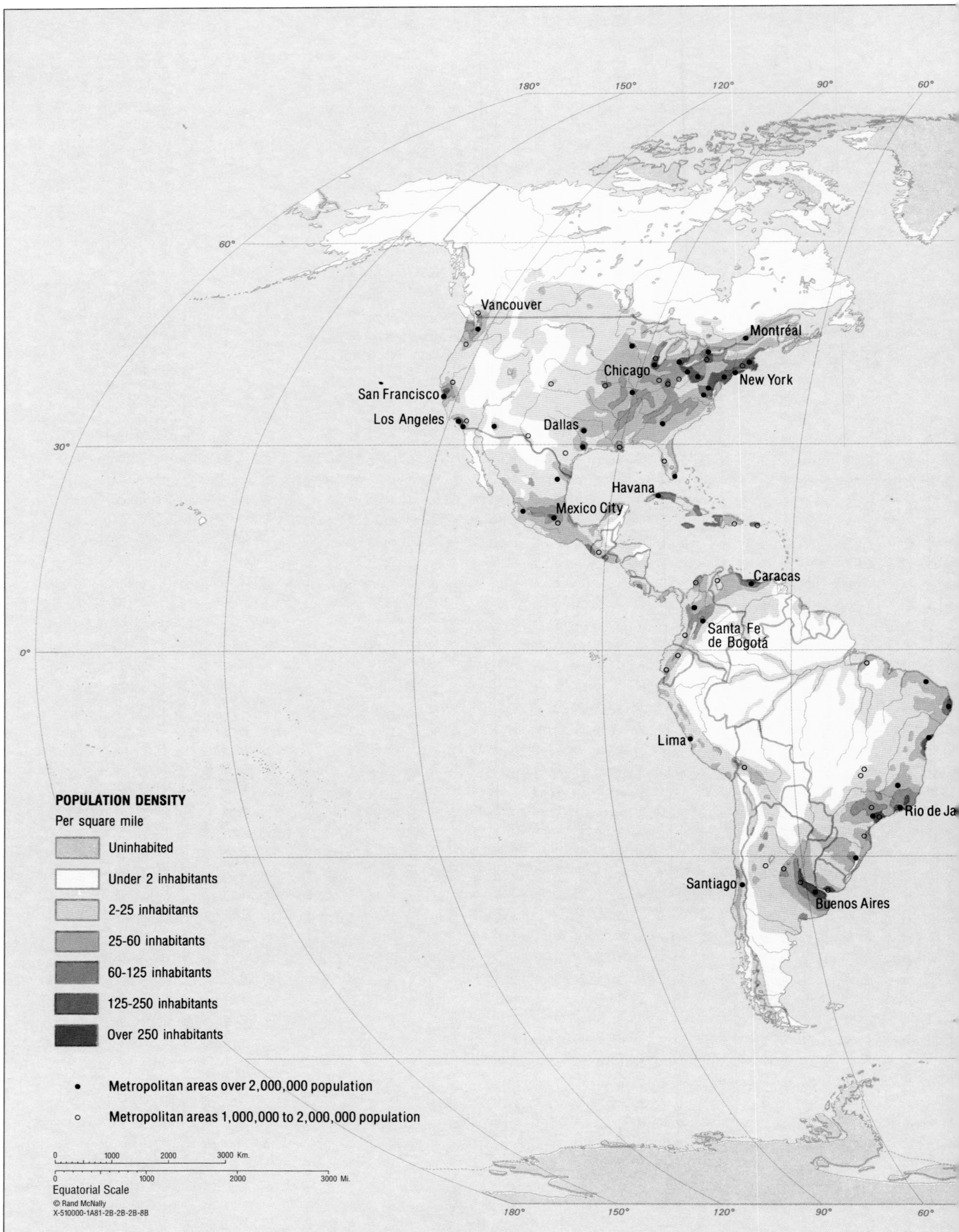

180°
150°
120°
90°
60°
60°
30°
0°
Vancouver
Montréal
Chicago
New York
San Francisco
Los Angeles
Dallas
Havana
Mexico City
Caracas
Santa Fe
de Bogotá
Lima
Rio de Ja
Santiago
Buenos Aires
POPULATION DENSITY
Per square mile
Uninhabited
Under 2 inhabitants
2-25 inhabitants
25-60 inhabitants
60-125 inhabitants
125-250 inhabitants
Over 250 inhabitants
Metropolitan areas over 2,000,000 population
Metropolitan areas 1,000,000 to 2,000,000 population
0 1000 2000 3000 Km.
0 1000 2000 3000 Mi.
Equatorial Scale
© Rand McNally
X-510000-1A81-2B-2B-2B-8B

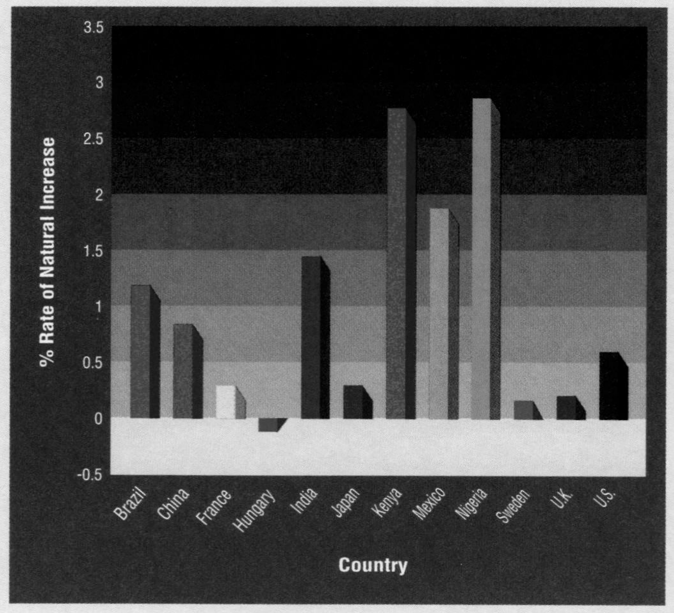

% Rate of Natural Increase
3.5
3
2.5
2
1.5
1
0.5
0
-0.5
Brazil
China
France
Hungary
India
Japan
Kenya
Mexico
Nigeria
Sweden
U.K.
U.S.
Country

POPULATION GROWTH
In densely populated countries, extremely high growth rates can cripple efforts to develop viable economies. Through state-encouraged family planning, China has managed to decrease its growth rate and thus improve the economic well-being of its people. Low rates of growth in industrialized countries have resulted in economies which are able to support relatively high standards of living.

(Rate of natural growth per year = birth rate minus death rate. Immigration and emigration are not included in this formulation.)

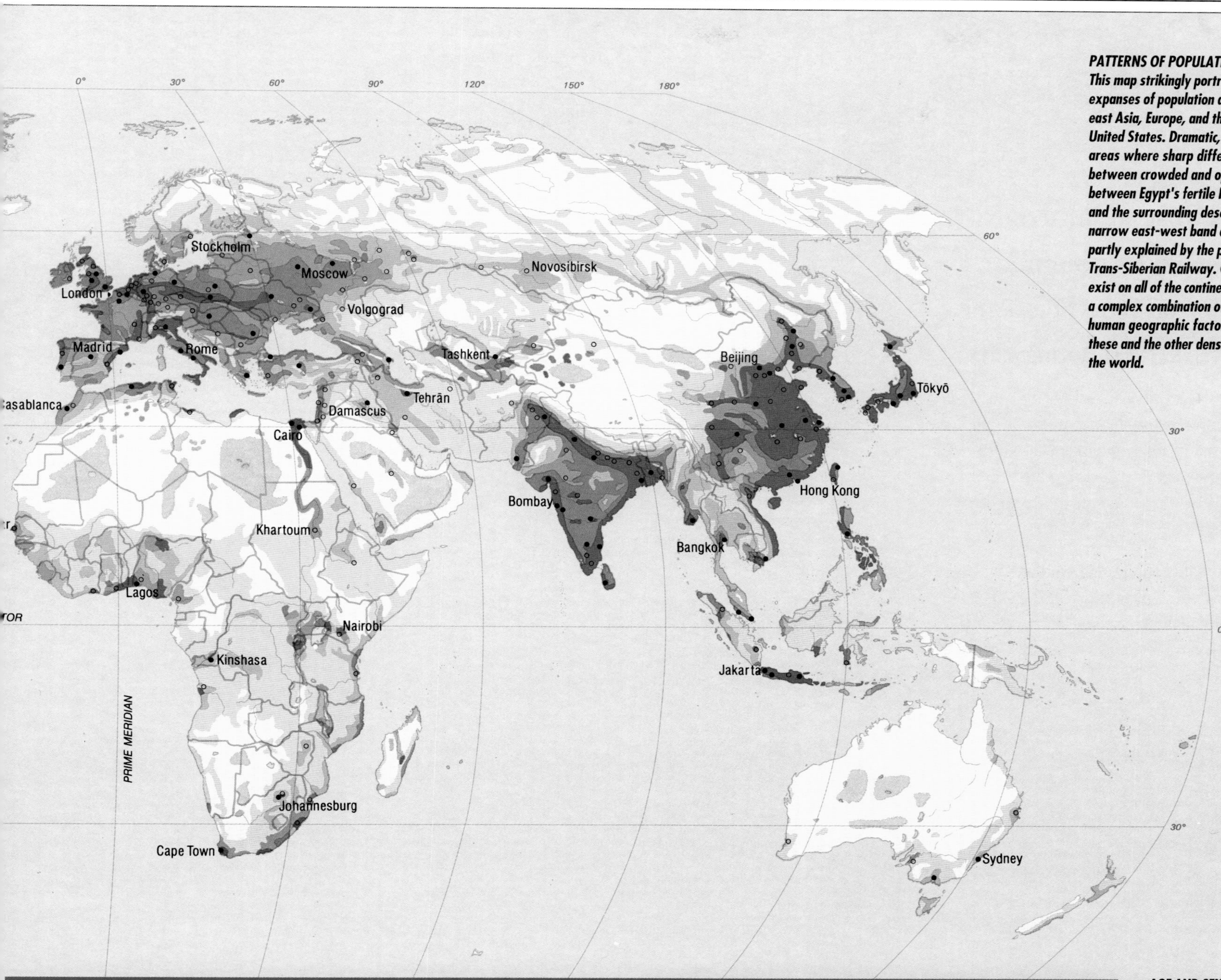
0°
30°
60°
90°
120°
150°
180°
60°
30°
0°
30°
PRIME MERIDIAN
Stockholm
Moscow
London
Volgograd
Novosibirsk
Madrid
Rome
Tashkent
Beijing
Tōkyō
Casablanca
Tehrān
Damascus
Cairo
Bombay
Hong Kong
Khartoum
Bangkok
Lagos
Nairobi
Kinshasa
Jakarta
Johannesburg
Cape Town
Sydney

PATTERNS OF POPULATION DENSITY
This map strikingly portrays the great expanses of population density in southeast Asia, Europe, and the northeastern United States. Dramatic, too, are smaller areas where sharp differences occur between crowded and open places, as between Egypt's fertile Nile River delta and the surrounding desert. Russia's narrow east-west band of population is partly explained by the presence of the Trans-Siberian Railway. Coastal densities exist on all of the continents. It is always a complex combination of physical and human geographic factors that explains these and the other density patterns of the world.

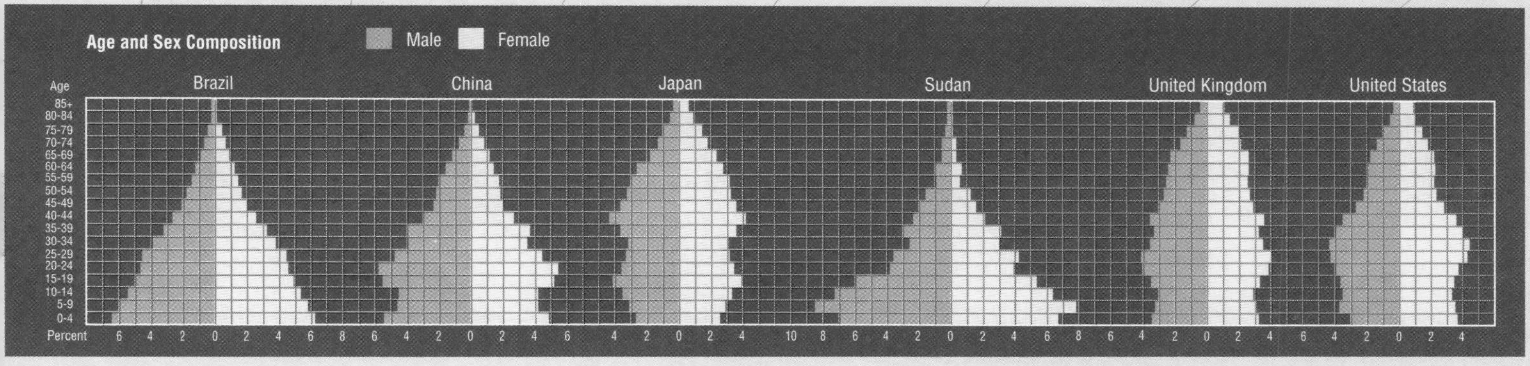
Age and Sex Composition
Male
Female
Brazil
China
Japan
Sudan
United Kingdom
United States
Age
85+
80-84
75-79
70-74
65-69
60-64
55-59
50-54
45-49
40-44
35-39
30-34
25-29
20-24
15-19
10-14
5-9
0-4
Percent
6 4 2 0 2 4 6
8 6 4 2 0 2 4 6
4 2 0 2 4
10 8 6 4 2 0 2 4 6 8
6 4 2 0 2 4
6 4 2 0 2 4

AGE AND SEX COMPOSITION
The varying shapes of these graphs illustrate the vast differences between youth and age throughout the world. Brazil, with a high birth rate and declining death rate, exemplifies many developing countries. Sudan's jagged structure results largely from recurring periods of famine. Typical of many developed countries, Japan's graph shows a declining birth rate. Warfare and family planning are other factors affecting the age composition of countries.

FOOD AND POPULATION
In this cartogram, the size of each country is proportional to the size of its population. Per capita calorie supply is indicated through five gradations of coloration, as shown in the legend. The worst malnutrition problems are found in underdeveloped areas of the world such as India, Bangladesh, and much of Africa. The developed countries of Europe and North America all enjoy calorie supplies well above requirements.

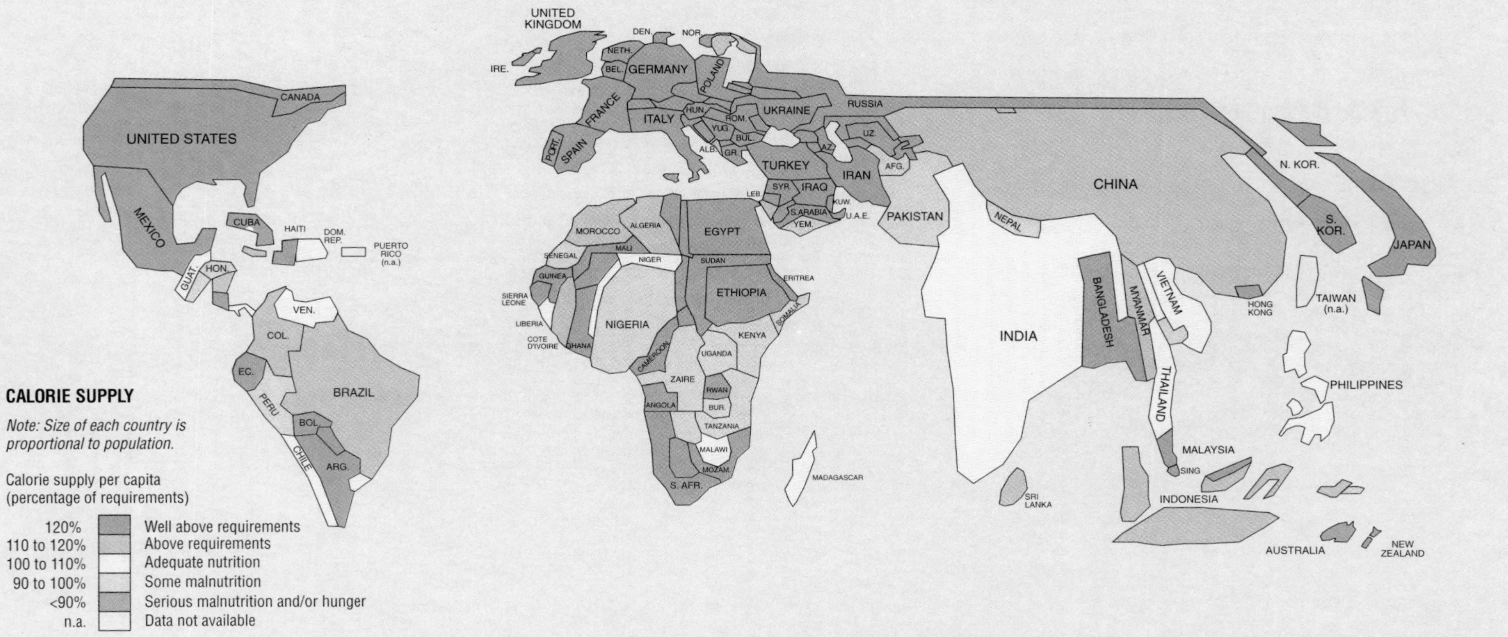
CALORIE SUPPLY
Note: Size of each country is proportional to population.
Calorie supply per capita (percentage of requirements)
120% Well above requirements
110 to 120% Above requirements
100 to 110% Adequate nutrition
90 to 100% Some malnutrition
<90% Serious malnutrition and/or hunger
n.a. Data not available
CANADA
UNITED STATES
MEXICO
CUBA
HAITI
DOM. REP.
PUERTO RICO (n.a.)
GUAT.
HON.
VEN.
COL.
EC.
PERU
BRAZIL
BOL.
CHILE
ARG.
UNITED KINGDOM
IRE.
DEN.
NOR.
NETH.
BEL.
GERMANY
POLAND
FRANCE
PORT.
SPAIN
ITALY
UKRAINE
RUSSIA
TURKEY
IRAN
IRAQ
SYR.
S. ARABIA
YEM.
U.A.E.
AFG.
UZ.
PAKISTAN
NEPAL
CHINA
N. KOR.
S. KOR.
JAPAN
MOROCCO
ALGERIA
EGYPT
SENEGAL
MALI
NIGER
SUDAN
ETHIOPIA
ERITREA
SOMALIA
GUINEA
SIERRA LEONE
LIBERIA
COTE D'IVOIRE
GHANA
NIGERIA
CAMEROON
KENYA
UGANDA
ZAIRE
RWAN.
BUR.
TANZANIA
ANGOLA
MALAWI
MOZAM.
S. AFR.
MADAGASCAR
INDIA
BANGLADESH
MYANMAR
VIETNAM
THAILAND
HONG KONG
TAIWAN (n.a.)
PHILIPPINES
MALAYSIA
SING.
SRI LANKA
INDONESIA
AUSTRALIA
NEW ZEALAND

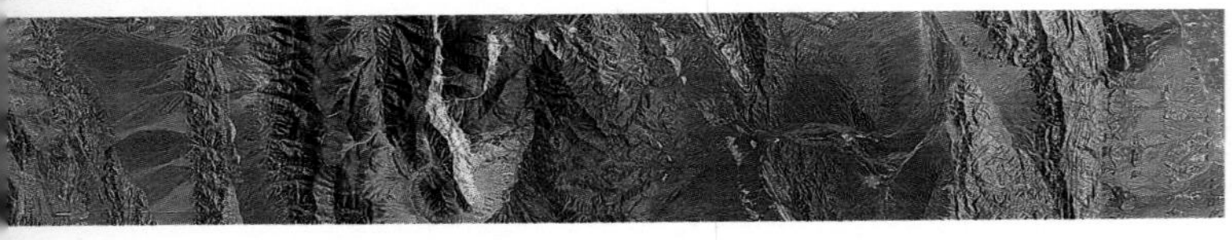

RESOURCES ALONE DO NOT ACCOUNT FOR THE DISTRIBUTION OF INDUSTRIAL DEVELOPMENT AROUND THE WORLD. THE LARGEST OIL AND NATURAL GAS DEPOSITS are in the Sahara and the Persian Gulf region, yet most Middle Eastern countries have little industry beyond refineries. The location and development of industries depend upon several factors—energy, skilled labor, capital and technology, transportation, markets, government planning, and trade alliances.

In North America, industrial sites, large urban markets, and concentrations of resources coincide. These regions are also blessed with abundant skilled labor and large capital markets to fund development. In South America, industrial districts are confined primarily to the main urban centers. Some countries, such as Venezuela and Chile, have adequate natural resources but lack the skilled labor or national markets to sustain industrial development.

Europe, the former Soviet Union, and Japan have developed in widely different ways. In the industrial districts of England, Belgium, northern France, and Germany, large deposits of coal and iron ore have fueled the growth of heavy industries. But in countries where raw materials are scarce, such as Italy, development is due mainly to individual initiative. The pattern of development in the former Soviet Union is tied directly to this region's enormous stores of coal, oil, iron ore, and other natural resources. In contrast, nearly all of Japan's raw materials are imported. Ample capital and skilled labor have made this country a leader in such areas as electronics and automobiles.

Industrial development in other regions of the world reflects a mixture of natural resources and cultural influences. India has only one major industrial district, the product of government initiatives and local supplies of coal and oil. China is taking advantage of rich deposits of coal and iron ore and an abundant labor supply to move rapidly toward modernization. Africa, from an industrial point of view, remains the least developed continent. It has significant hydroelectric potential and mineral resources, but lacks skilled labor and capital.

The trend in industrial development is toward light industries such as electronics and food processing. Concentrations of this type of industry can be found near large urban centers in many countries, including Taiwan, the Philippines, Mexico, and Korea.

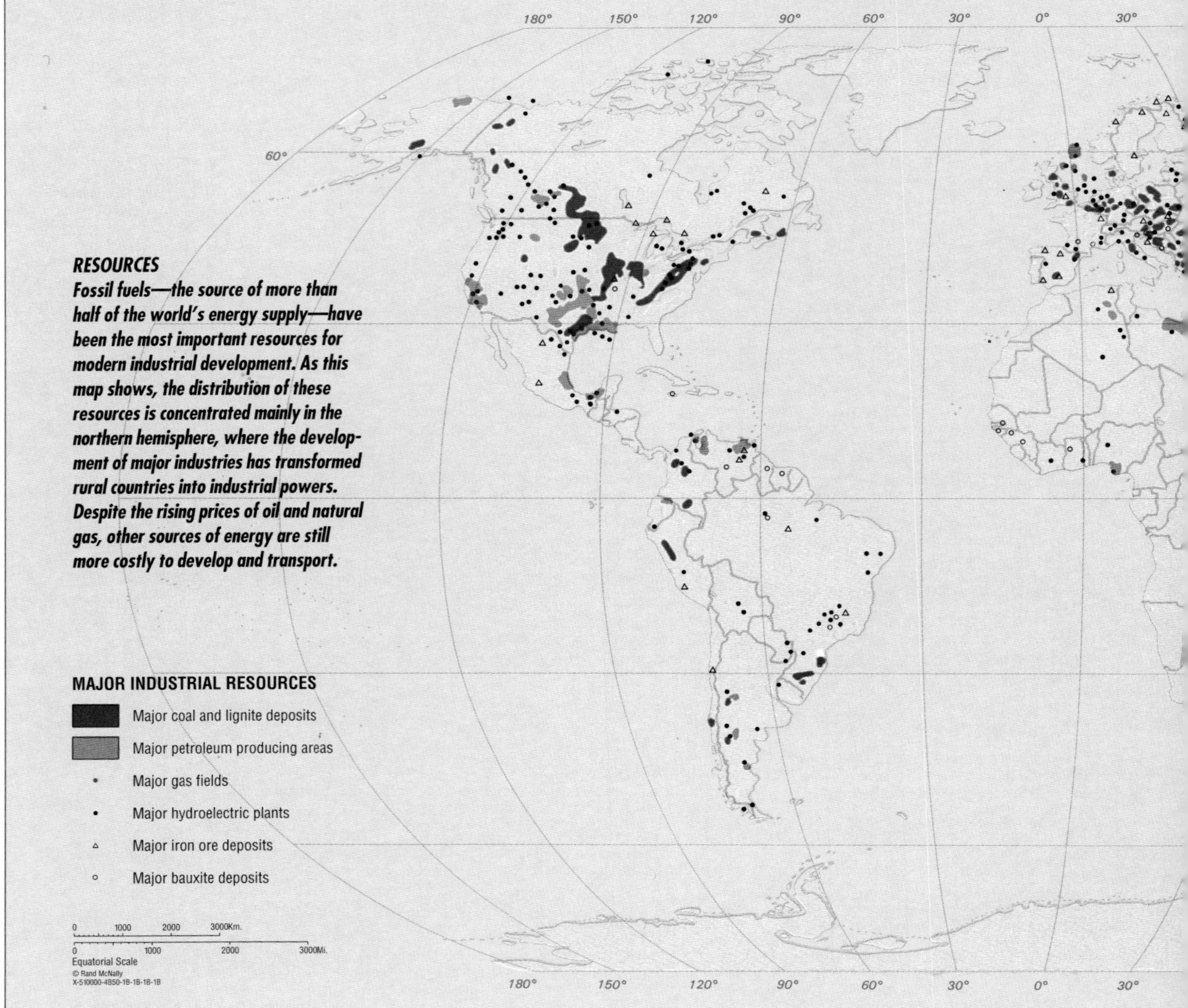
180°
150°
120°
90°
60°
30°
0°
30°
60°
MAJOR INDUSTRIAL RESOURCES
Major coal and lignite deposits
Major petroleum producing areas
Major gas fields
Major hydroelectric plants
Major iron ore deposits
Major bauxite deposits
0 1000 2000 3000Km.
0 1000 2000 3000Mi.
Equatorial Scale
© Rand McNally

RESOURCES
Fossil fuels—the source of more than half of the world's energy supply—have been the most important resources for modern industrial development. As this map shows, the distribution of these resources is concentrated mainly in the northern hemisphere, where the development of major industries has transformed rural countries into industrial powers. Despite the rising prices of oil and natural gas, other sources of energy are still more costly to develop and transport.

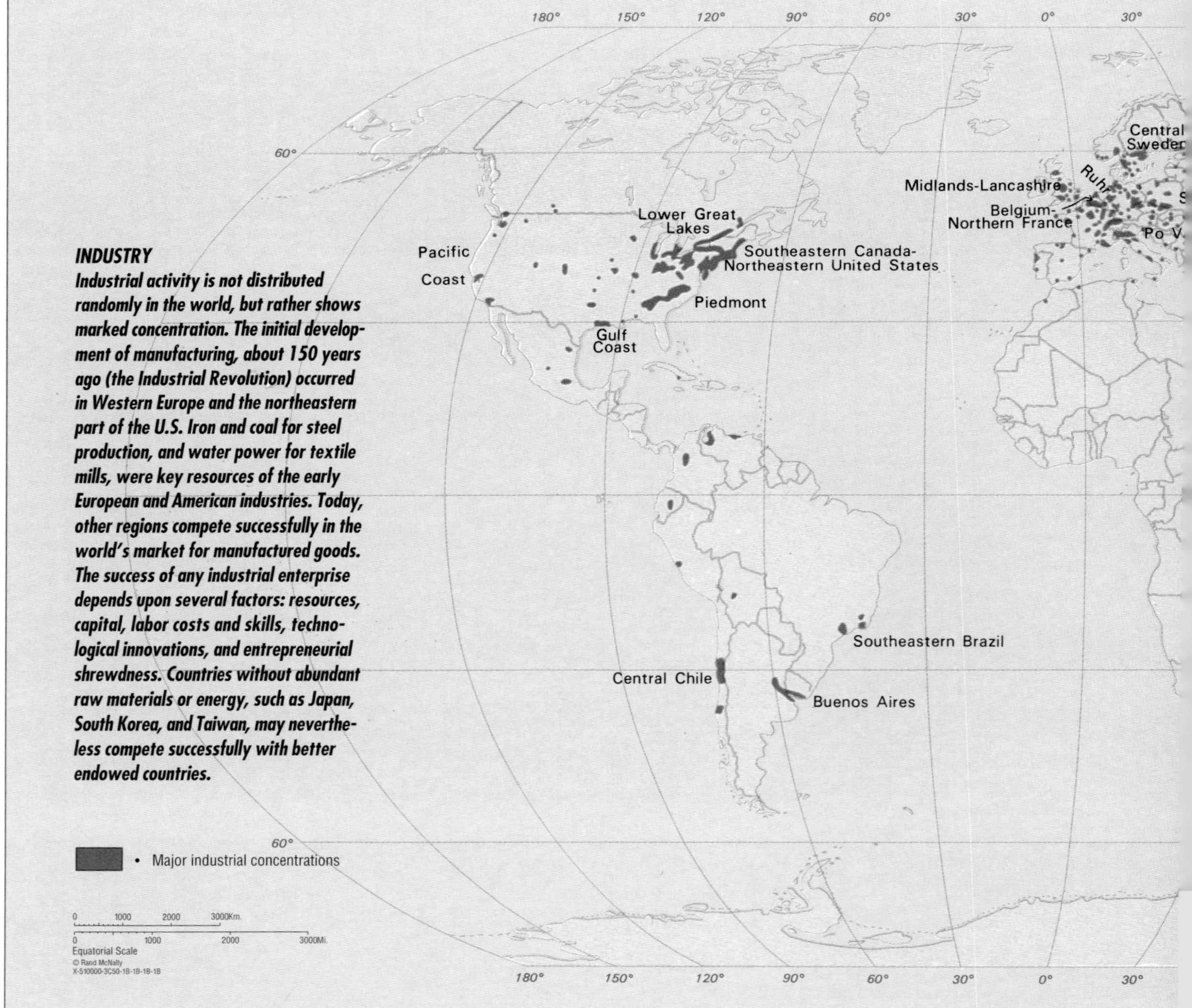
180°
150°
120°
90°
60°
30°
0°
30°
60°
Pacific Coast
Lower Great Lakes
Southeastern Canada-Northeastern United States
Piedmont
Gulf Coast
Midlands-Lancashire
Belgium-Northern France
Ruhr
Central Sweden
Southeastern Brazil
Central Chile
Buenos Aires
Major industrial concentrations
0 1000 2000 3000Km.
0 1000 2000 3000Mi.
Equatorial Scale
© Rand McNally

INDUSTRY
Industrial activity is not distributed randomly in the world, but rather shows marked concentration. The initial development of manufacturing, about 150 years ago (the Industrial Revolution) occurred in Western Europe and the northeastern part of the U.S. Iron and coal for steel production, and water power for textile mills, were key resources of the early European and American industries. Today, other regions compete successfully in the world's market for manufactured goods. The success of any industrial enterprise depends upon several factors: resources, capital, labor costs and skills, technological innovations, and entrepreneurial shrewdness. Countries without abundant raw materials or energy, such as Japan, South Korea, and Taiwan, may nevertheless compete successfully with better endowed countries.

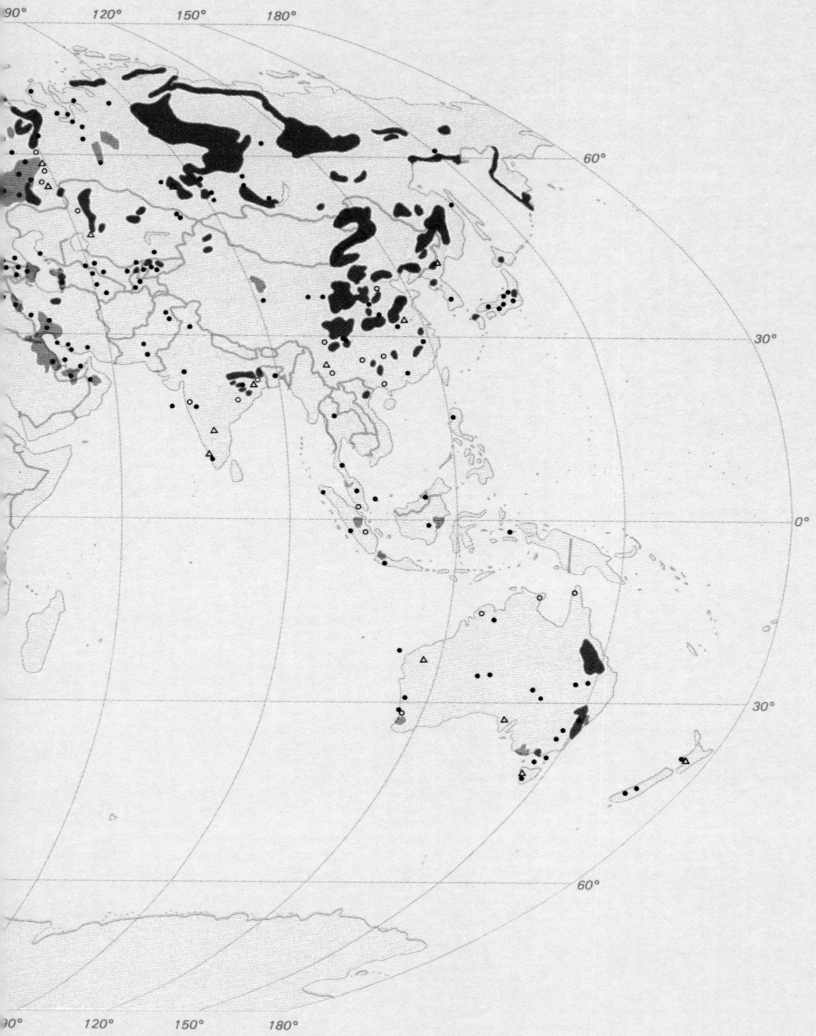
120°
150°
180°
60°
30°
0°
30°
60°
120°
150°
180°

ENERGY PRODUCTION AND CONSUMPTION

A large percentage of the world's energy is used for manufacturing. This fact helps explain the enormous variance—by country and by continent—in the production and consumption of energy. The United States, with only 5% of the world's population, consumes 25% of the world's energy, and nearly five times as much as Africa and South America combined.

However, the United States produces 80% of the energy it consumes, and is therefore less dependent on foreign sources than several other industrialized countries. Germany, for example, produces only 54% of the energy it consumes, and Japan only 7%.

Major energy exporting countries include oil-rich Saudi Arabia, Iran, and Venezuela.

Total World Production: 11,411,215,000 metric tons of coal equivalent
Total World Consumption: 11,037,655,000 metric tons of coal equivalent

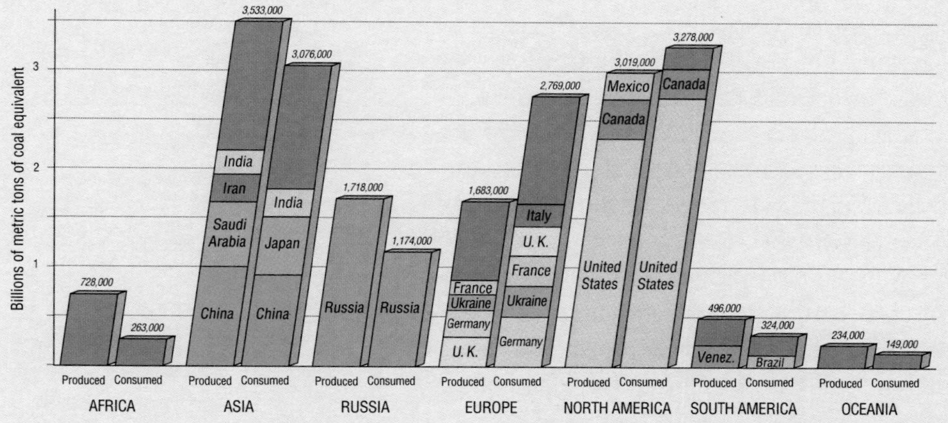
Billions of metric tons of coal equivalent
1
2
3
728,000
263,000
3,533,000
3,076,000
India
Iran
Saudi Arabia
China
India
Japan
China
1,718,000
1,174,000
Russia
Russia
1,683,000
2,769,000
France
Ukraine
Germany
U. K.
Italy
U. K.
France
Ukraine
Germany
3,019,000
3,278,000
Mexico
Canada
United States
Canada
United States
496,000
324,000
Venez.
Brazil
234,000
149,000
Produced Consumed
AFRICA
ASIA
RUSSIA
EUROPE
NORTH AMERICA
SOUTH AMERICA
OCEANIA

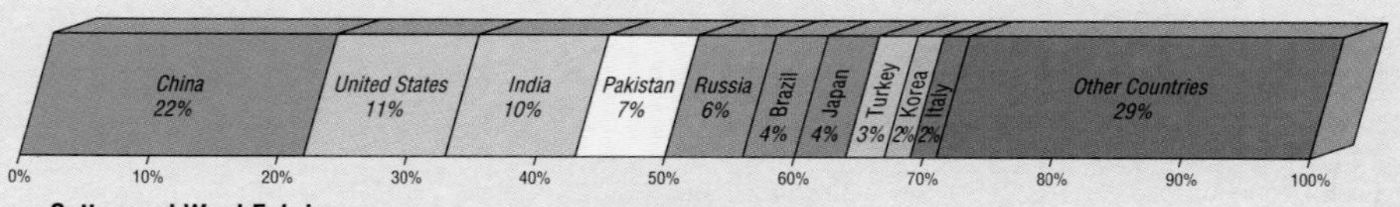
China 22%
United States 11%
India 10%
Pakistan 7%
Russia 6%
Brazil 4%
Japan 4%
Turkey 3%
Korea 2%
Italy 2%
Other Countries 29%
0% 10% 20% 30% 40% 50% 60% 70% 80% 90% 100%

Cotton and Wool Fabrics World Total: 20,189,000 metric tons

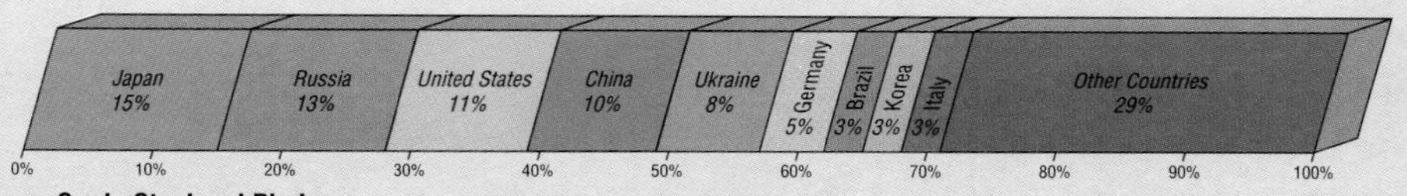
Japan 15%
Russia 13%
United States 11%
China 10%
Ukraine 8%
Germany 5%
Brazil 3%
Korea 3%
Italy 3%
Other Countries 29%
0% 10% 20% 30% 40% 50% 60% 70% 80% 90% 100%

Crude Steel and Pig Iron World Total: 1,305,450,000 metric tons

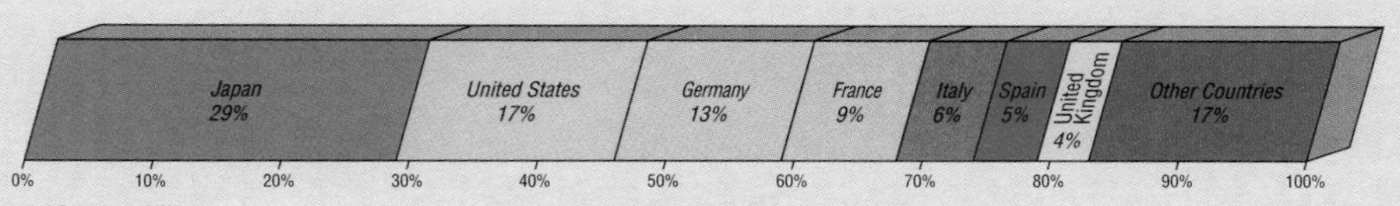
Japan 29%
United States 17%
Germany 13%
France 9%
Italy 6%
Spain 5%
United Kingdom 4%
Other Countries 17%
0% 10% 20% 30% 40% 50% 60% 70% 80% 90% 100%

Automobiles World Total: 34,919,000 automobiles

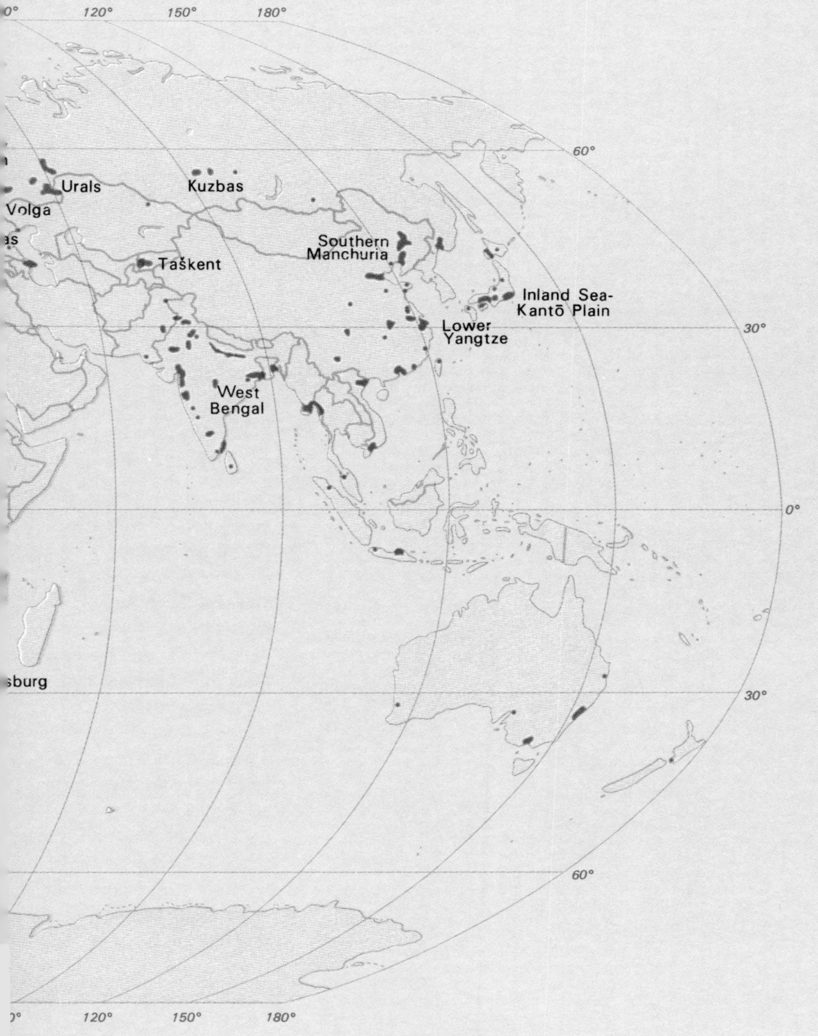
120°
150°
180°
60°
Urals
Volga
Kuzbas
Southern Manchuria
Taškent
Inland Sea-Kantō Plain
Lower Yangtze
30°
West Bengal
0°
30°
60°
120°
150°
180°

MANUFACTURING

These graphs deal with three very different types of manufacturing activities.

Textile manufacturing is a relatively basic industry—it does not require a great deal of technology, capital, or energy. Textiles are basic goods that are needed in every country, regardless of economic status. (It is not surprising that China, with 1.1 billion people, should lead this category.)

Crude steel and pig iron manufacturing provide a raw material that is used in many products, including automobiles, machinery, and building materials.

Automobile production is a rather sophisticated manufacturing activity, requiring significant amounts of energy and capital, and involving sophisticated technology and the complex logistics of assembling many different parts and materials.

More than anything else, the graphs show the industrial dominance of Japan, the U.S., China, and Europe (including Russia), which together produce 48% of the world's cotton and wool fabrics, 65% of the crude steel and pig iron, and 83% of the automobiles.

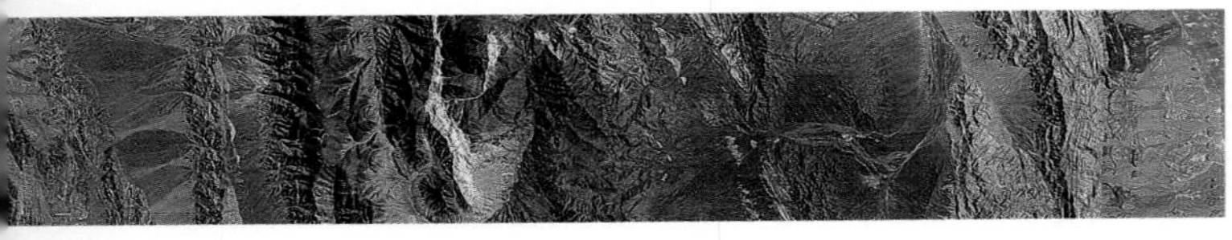

SINCE HUMANS FIRST BEGAN USING TOOLS, CULTIVATING THE SOIL, AND FASHIONING ARTICLES TO TRADE, THEY HAVE MADE USE OF THE EARTH'S RESOURCES TO EARN A living. Economic activities generally fall into two basic categories: herding and farming, and industrial production and commerce.

Nomadic herding and farming are perhaps the oldest economic activities practiced by humans. Today, only a smattering of people in Asia and Africa still follow the nomadic way of life. Farming, however, thrives in nearly every country, ranging from small family or tribal plots to the commercial farms of industrialized countries. Particularly in the United States, small, family-owned farms have given way to huge commercial agribusiness firms. With advanced methods of fertilization and mechanized harvesting, these agricultural businesses can raise enough food to feed the population of the country and still export surpluses around the world.

In contrast, subsistence farming, which produces little or no surplus for sale, is the mainstay of rural populations in Asia, Africa, and parts of South America. The large areas devoted to this type of farming represent essentially closed economic systems. It is in these areas that the challenge of economic development is greatest, for this type of farming is often the struggle on an impoverished people to wrest a living from tiny plots of land. Per capita income may be only a few hundred dollars per year. Release from such grinding poverty and toil is possible only where industries provide an alternative to rural life, and where systems of transportation and storage permit farming on a large scale.

Although subsistence agriculture still occupies large tracts of land in the world, developing countries are seeking to change this state of affairs in the near future. They wish to improve their agricultural output, increase industrialization, and raise their countries' standards of living.

Only a small portion of the Earth's surface is devoted to manufacturing and commerce—the foundations of national wealth and power. These areas generally coincide with the major urban centers of the world. In the United States alone, slightly over one percent of the land provides employment and residence for nearly 70 percent of the population. Urban centers in Europe are somewhat smaller but also account for a disproportionate amount of economic activity. As a result, per capita income in industrialized countries is high.

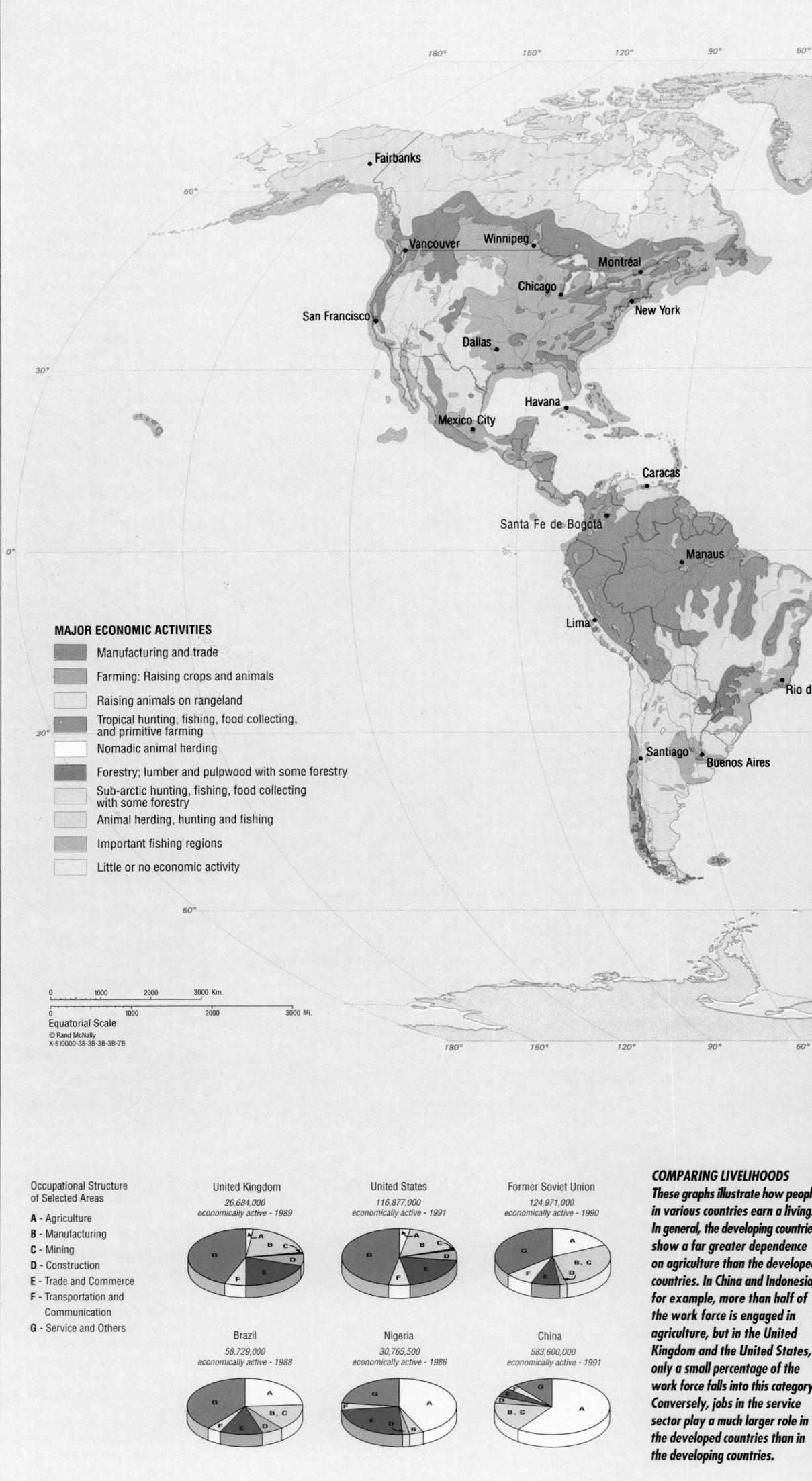

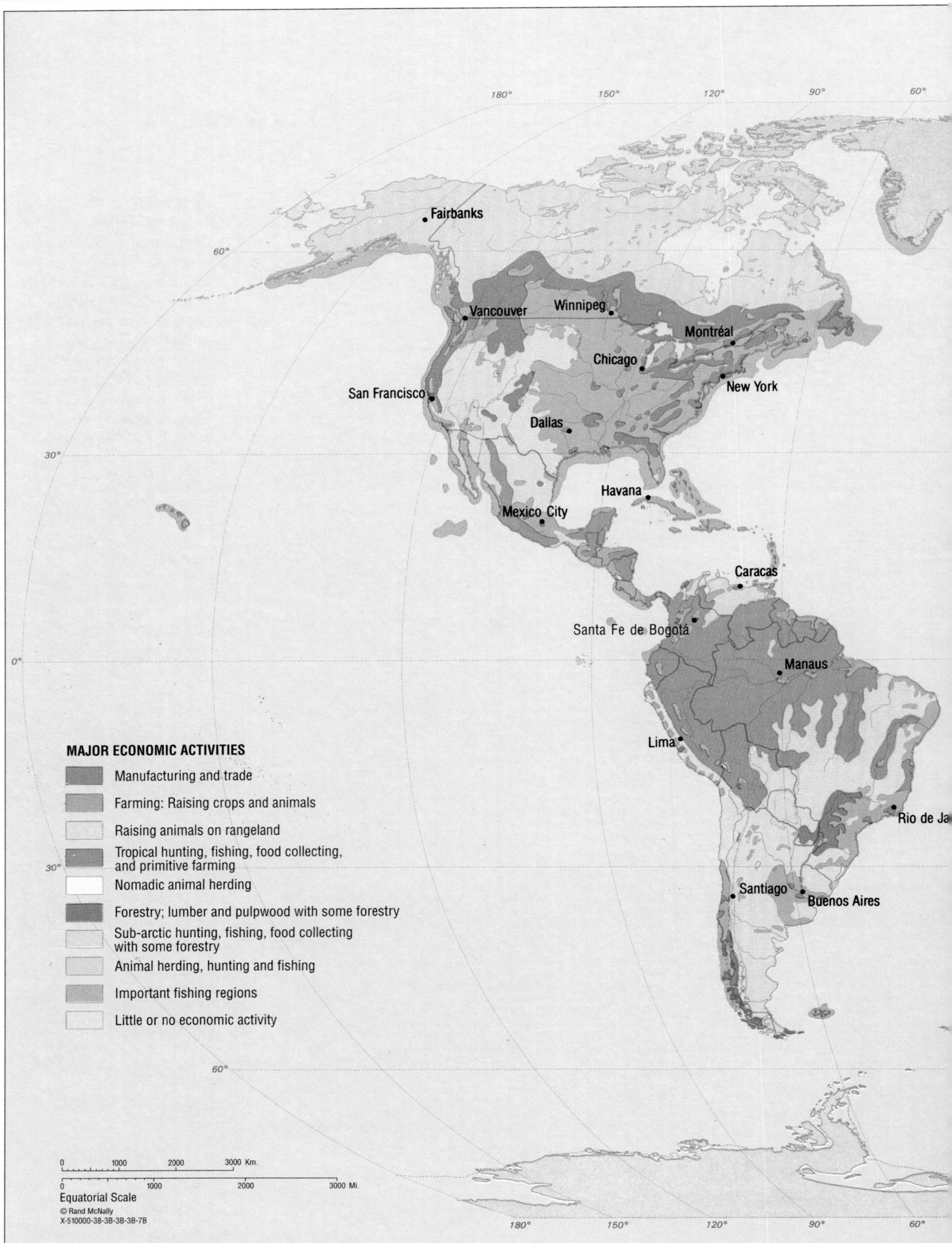
180°
150°
120°
90°
60°
60°
30°
0°
30°
60°
Fairbanks
Vancouver
Winnipeg
Montréal
Chicago
New York
San Francisco
Dallas
Havana
Mexico City
Caracas
Santa Fe de Bogotá
Manaus
Lima
Rio de Ja
Santiago
Buenos Aires
MAJOR ECONOMIC ACTIVITIES
Manufacturing and trade
Farming: Raising crops and animals
Raising animals on rangeland
Tropical hunting, fishing, food collecting, and primitive farming
Nomadic animal herding
Forestry; lumber and pulpwood with some forestry
Sub-arctic hunting, fishing, food collecting with some forestry
Animal herding, hunting and fishing
Important fishing regions
Little or no economic activity
0 1000 2000 3000 Km.
0 1000 2000 3000 Mi.
Equatorial Scale
© Rand McNally
X-510000-38-38-38-38-78

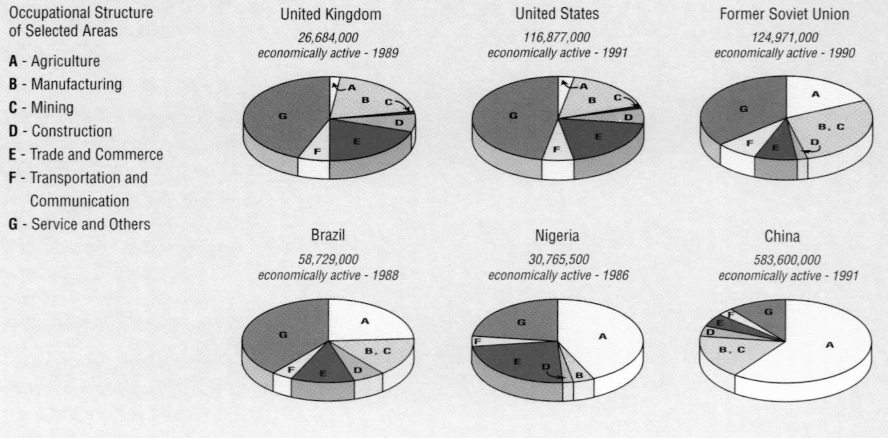
Occupational Structure of Selected Areas
A - Agriculture
B - Manufacturing
C - Mining
D - Construction
E - Trade and Commerce
F - Transportation and Communication
G - Service and Others
United Kingdom
26,684,000 economically active - 1989
United States
116,877,000 economically active - 1991
Former Soviet Union
124,971,000 economically active - 1990
Brazil
58,729,000 economically active - 1988
Nigeria
30,765,500 economically active - 1986
China
583,600,000 economically active - 1991

COMPARING LIVELIHOODS

These graphs illustrate how people in various countries earn a living. In general, the developing countries show a far greater dependence on agriculture than the developed countries. In China and Indonesia, for example, more than half of the work force is engaged in agriculture, but in the United Kingdom and the United States, only a small percentage of the work force falls into this category. Conversely, jobs in the service sector play a much larger role in the developed countries than in the developing countries.

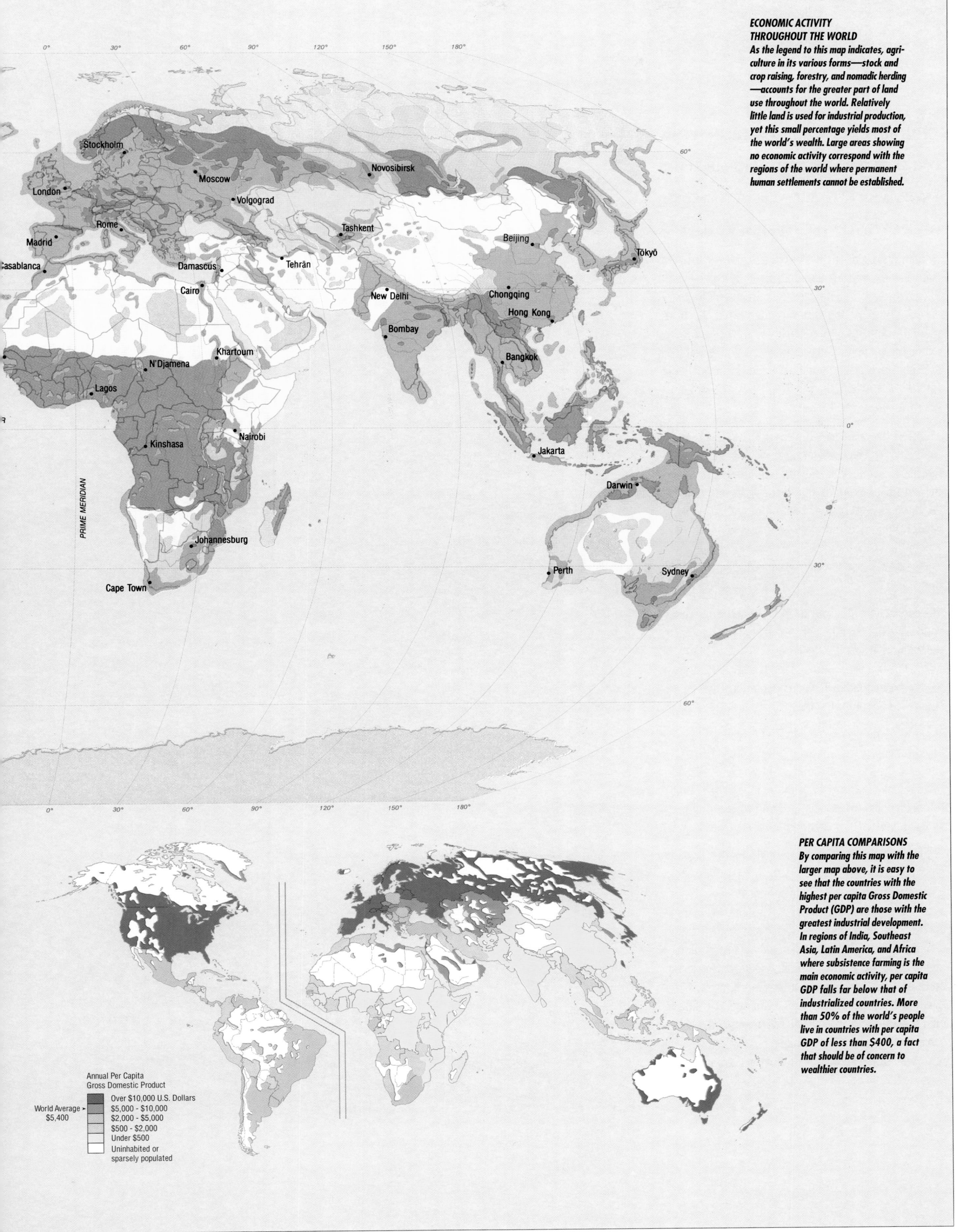

ECONOMIC ACTIVITY THROUGHOUT THE WORLD

As the legend to this map indicates, agriculture in its various forms—stock and crop raising, forestry, and nomadic herding—accounts for the greater part of land use throughout the world. Relatively little land is used for industrial production, yet this small percentage yields most of the world's wealth. Large areas showing no economic activity correspond with the regions of the world where permanent human settlements cannot be established.

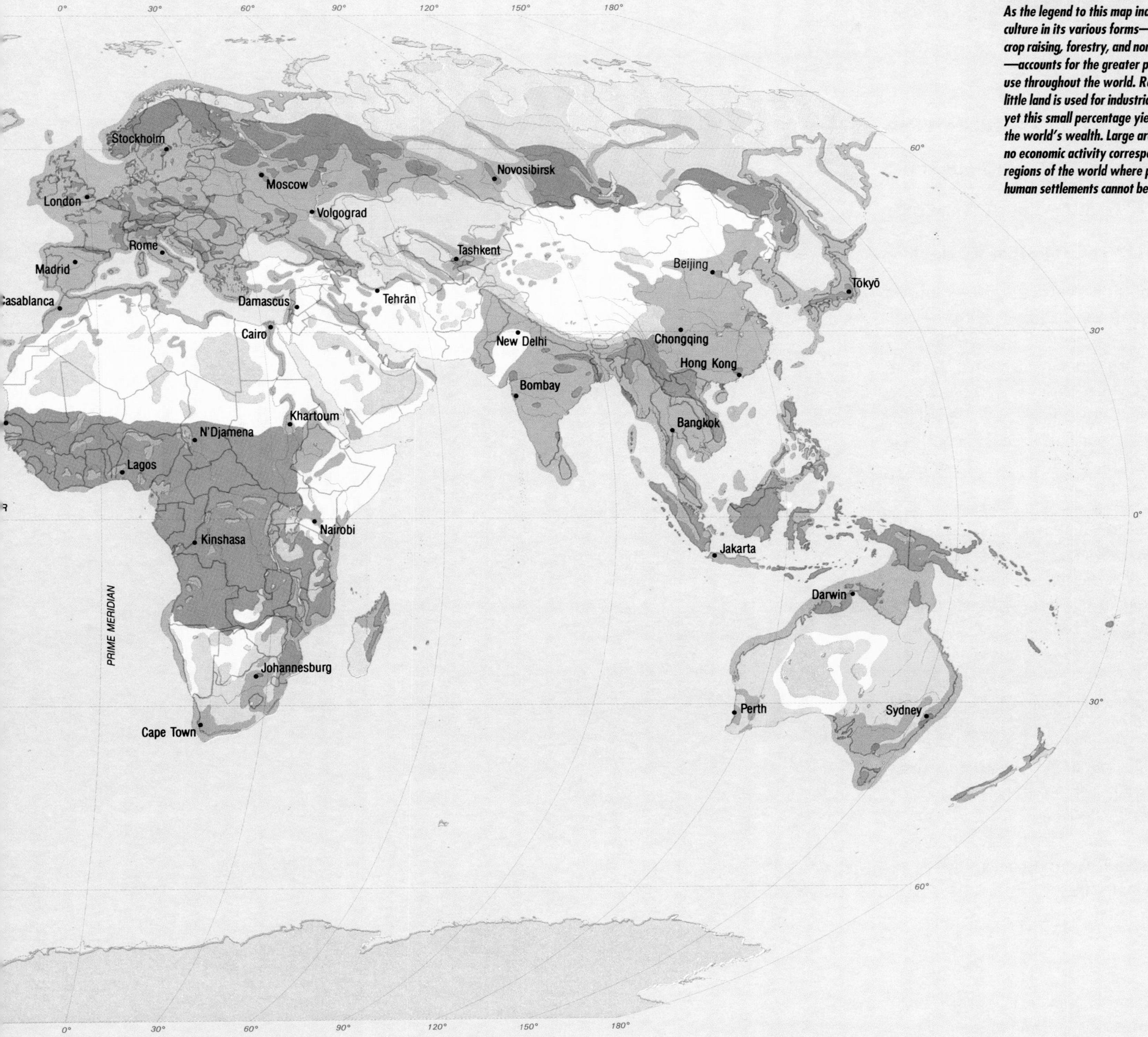
0°
30°
60°
90°
120°
150°
180°
Stockholm
Moscow
London
Volgograd
Novosibirsk
Rome
Madrid
Tashkent
Beijing
Tōkyō
Damascus
Tehrān
Cairo
New Delhi
Chongqing
Hong Kong
Bombay
Khartoum
N'Djamena
Bangkok
Lagos
Nairobi
Kinshasa
Jakarta
Darwin
PRIME MERIDIAN
Johannesburg
Perth
Sydney
Cape Town
60°
30°
0°
30°
60°

PER CAPITA COMPARISONS

By comparing this map with the larger map above, it is easy to see that the countries with the highest per capita Gross Domestic Product (GDP) are those with the greatest industrial development. In regions of India, Southeast Asia, Latin America, and Africa where subsistence farming is the main economic activity, per capita GDP falls far below that of industrialized countries. More than 50% of the world's people live in countries with per capita GDP of less than $400, a fact that should be of concern to wealthier countries.

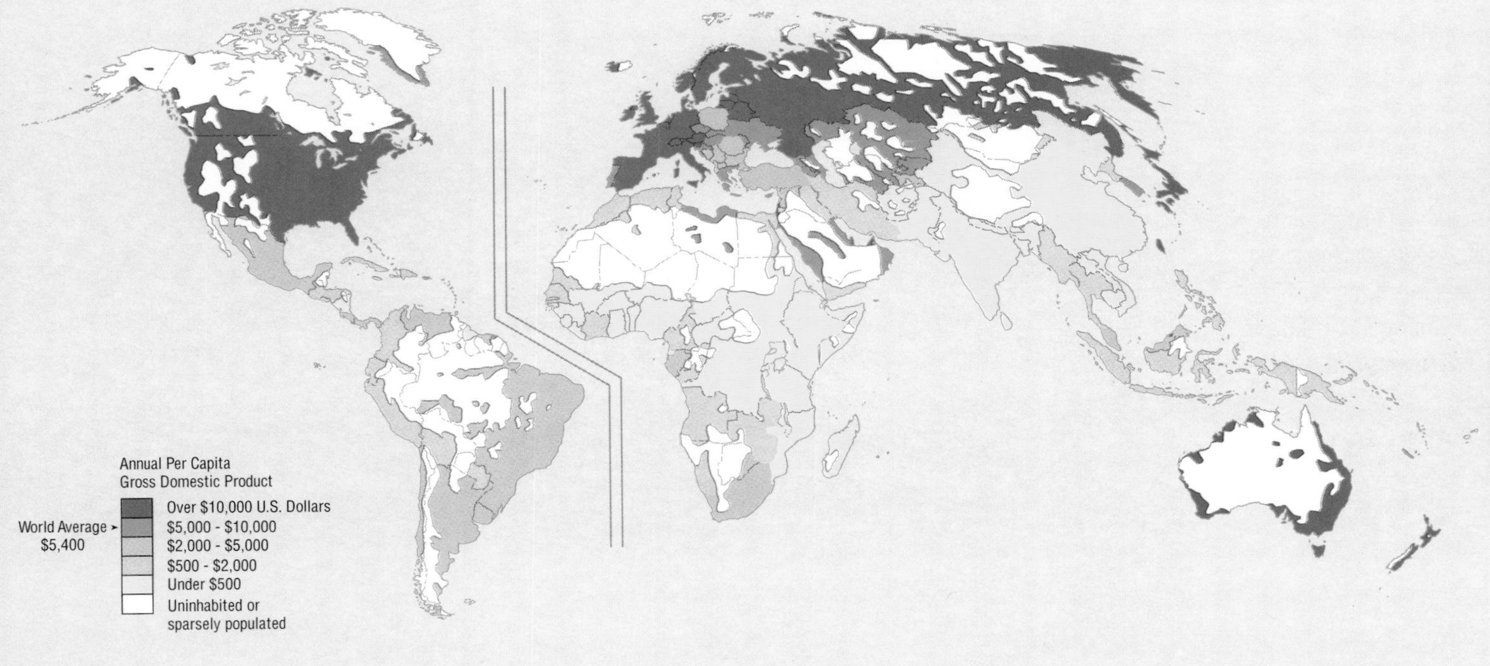
Annual Per Capita
Gross Domestic Product
Over $10,000 U.S. Dollars
$5,000 - $10,000
$2,000 - $5,000
$500 - $2,000
Under $500
Uninhabited or
sparsely populated
World Average
$5,400

ENVIRONMENT

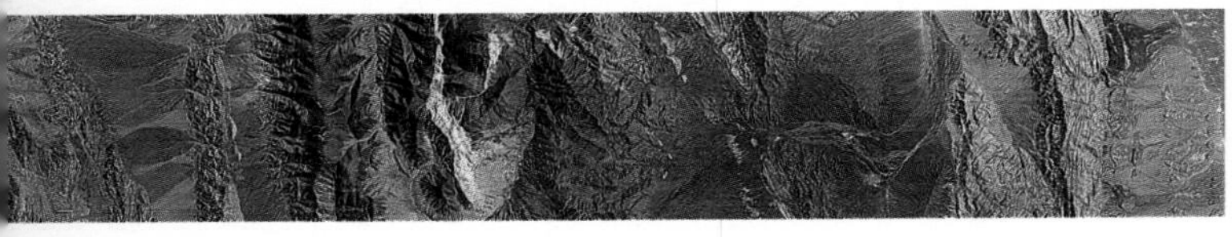

WE HUMANS, UNLIKE ANY OTHER SPECIES ON EARTH, HAVE RADICALLY RESHAPED THE ENVIRONMENT TO SUIT OUR OWN NEEDS. OVER COUNTLESS CENTURIES, WE HAVE cleared vast tracts of forest, dotted the landscape with cities—some covering hundreds of square miles—and altered the natural landscape to such a degree that we can almost speak of a "human-engineered" environment. But this reshaping carries a high price: mass extinctions of plant and animal life, damage to the atmosphere, and pollution on a worldwide scale. In the future, we must learn how to live in the world without destroying it.

The most obvious sign of our efforts to modify the environment has been the clearing of much of the world's forestland. At one time, the mid-latitude zones of both the Old and New Worlds were virtually covered with deciduous and evergreen trees. Over several hundred years, human settlers cleared the forests so vigorously that by the 17th century, wood was in short supply. These latitudes are now the most heavily populated on Earth, with new "forests" of glass, steel, and concrete.

The destruction of the world's forests and the overcultivation and overgrazing of exposed land has damaged the soil and accelerated the erosion process in many areas. The loss of productive land is especially serious today when a rapid increase in population raises the spectre of widespread famine.

Modern technology has enabled us to create artificial environments to live more comfortably in different climates. Central heating and cooling systems keep our buildings at a uniform temperature year-round. Some future planners envision entire dome-covered cities, with climate and temperature controlled by computer.

Pollution of air, water, and soil is perhaps the most pressing problem brought on by human activity. The Earth's atmosphere and hydrosphere are closed circulating systems. Industrial and household wastes are being dumped into these systems at a rate that far exceeds nature's ability to absorb them. Conservation and recycling programs seek to restore the environment and prevent further degradation. But much remains to be done, particularly in developing countries. The future quality of our environment will rest on our ability to cooperate as a world community.

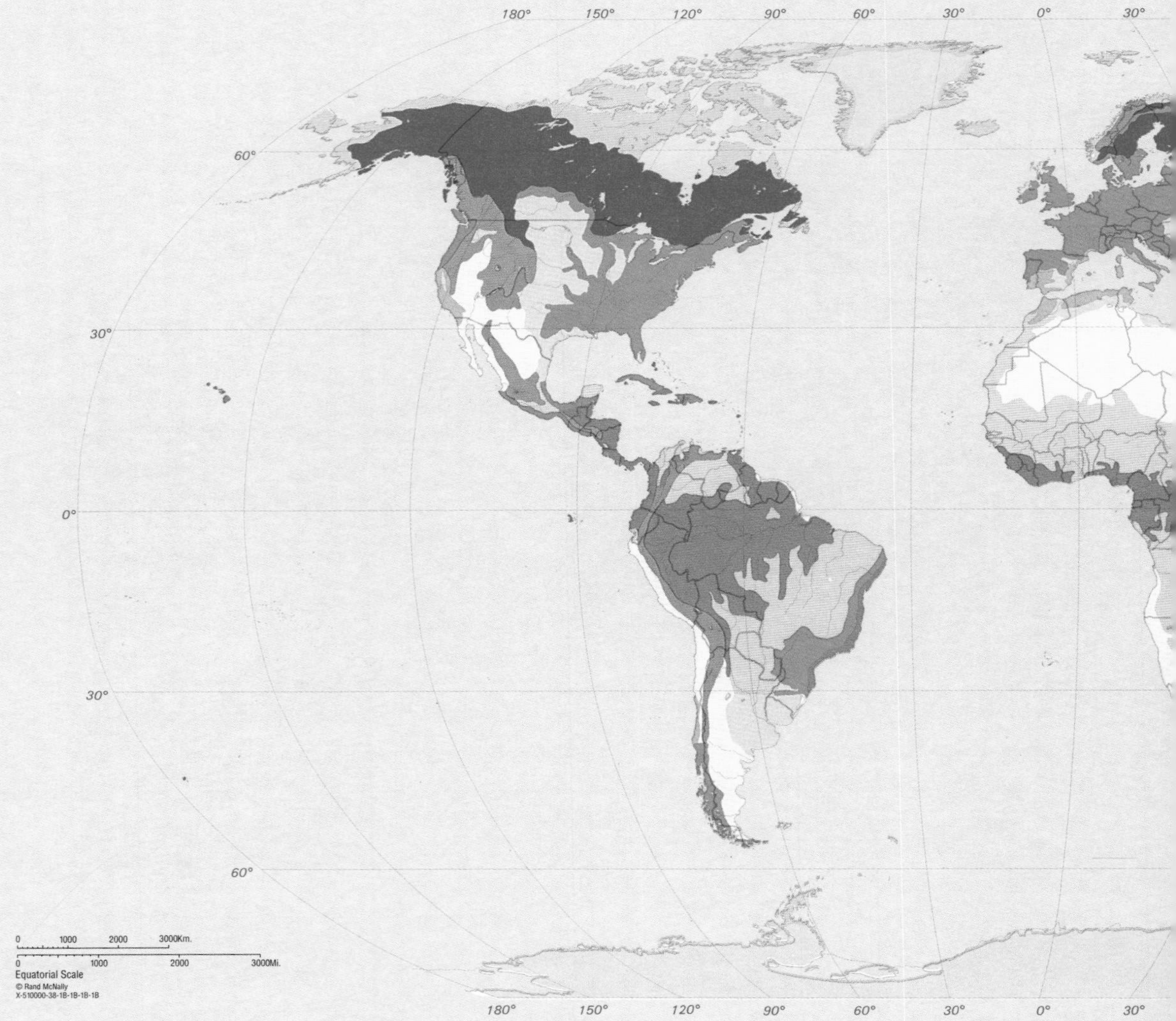
180° 150° 120° 90° 60° 30° 0° 30°
60°
30°
0°
30°
60°
0 1000 2000 3000Km.
0 1000 2000 3000Mi.
Equatorial Scale
© Rand McNally

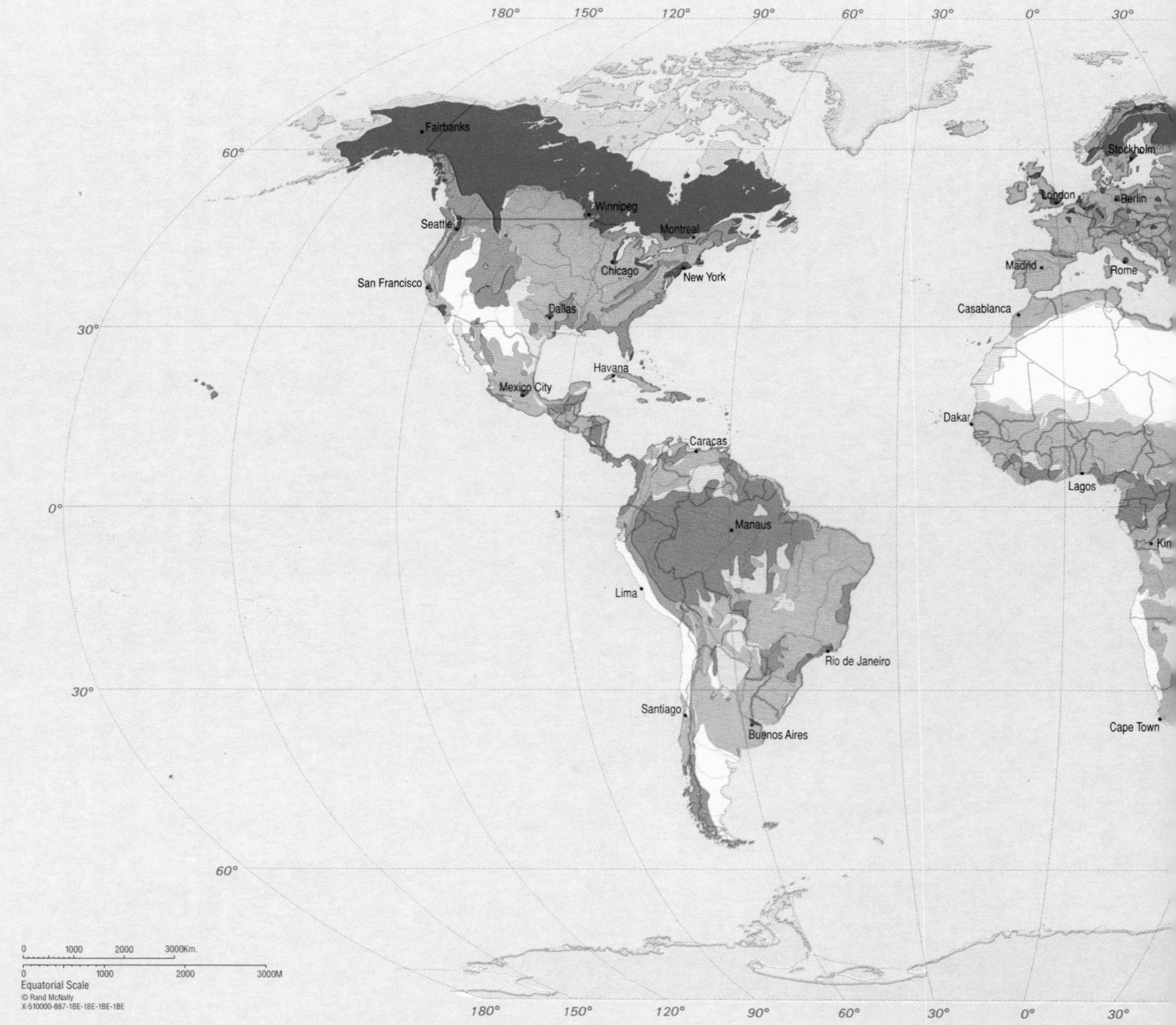
180° 150° 120° 90° 60° 30° 0° 30°
60°
30°
0°
30°
60°
Fairbanks
Stockholm
London
Berlin
Winnipeg
Montreal
Seattle
Chicago
New York
San Francisco
Madrid
Rome
Dallas
Casablanca
Havana
Mexico City
Dakar
Caracas
Lagos
Manaus
Lima
Rio de Janeiro
Santiago
Buenos Aires
Cape Town
0 1000 2000 3000Km.
0 1000 2000 3000M
Equatorial Scale
© Rand McNally

120°
150°
180°
60°
30°
0°
30°
60°
120°
150°
180°

THE NATURAL WORLD

This map shows the world's "natural" vegetation—that is, the vegetation patterns that are thought to have existed before humans began to have a significant impact on the world environment. Tropical and subtropical forests, which harbor a majority of the world's plant species, are clustered near the equator. Savanna and desert regions are found to the north and south of these forests, where hot and dry climates prevail. Mediterranean vegetation, temperate grasslands, and temperate forests appear mainly in the temperate zones of the northern hemisphere, where rainfall is abundant and growing seasons are long. North of these zones are great stretches of the northern coniferous forests called "taiga." The extreme northern and southern latitudes are characterized by tundra and polar ice cap. The world's mountainous regions, though shown here in a uniform color, actually support an incredible diversity of vegetation.

VEGETATION

This legend applies to both maps

Tropical and subtropical forests
Savanna
Desert
Mediterranean
Temperate grassland
Temperate forest
Taiga (northern forests)
Tundra (lichen and moss)
Mountain
Polar and high mountain

120°
150°
180°
60°
Novosibirsk
Tashkent
Beijing
Tehrān
Tōkyō
Shanghai
30°
New Delhi
Chongqing
Calcutta
Hong Kong
Bombay
Bangkok
0°
Jakarta
Darwin
30°
Perth
Sydney
60°
120°
150°
180°

TODAY'S WORLD

The extent to which humans have impacted and reshaped the natural world is evident on this map. The Mediterranean area and most of Europe, once heavily forested, are now cropland, grassland, or near-desert environments. The same is true of south and east Asia. In North America, only pockets remain of the temperate forests and grasslands that once covered much of the central part of the continent. Vast urban areas have sprung up throughout the world, replacing the original environments.

Today, the eyes of the world are on South America, where the vast rain forest of the Amazon basin is being destroyed at a rapid pace to create new cropland and grazing land. This rain forest is thought to play an important role in the Earth's weather systems as well as in the purification of air through the absorption of carbon dioxide and the production of oxygen. Its destruction could be disastrous to the entire world ecosystem.

HUMAN ENVIRONMENTS

This legend applies to the bottom map only

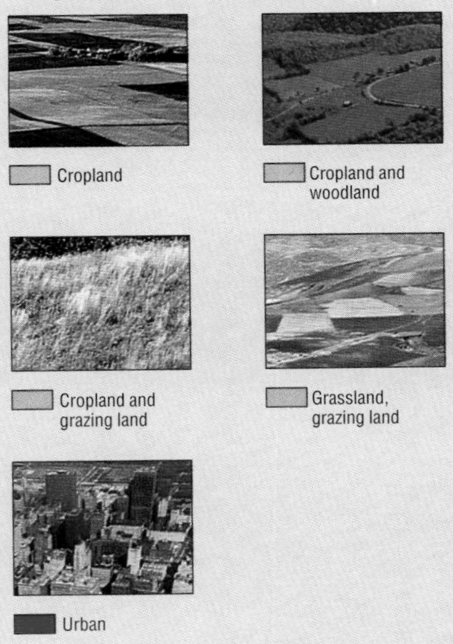

Cropland
Cropland and woodland
Cropland and grazing land
Grassland, grazing land
Urban

TRANSPORTATION

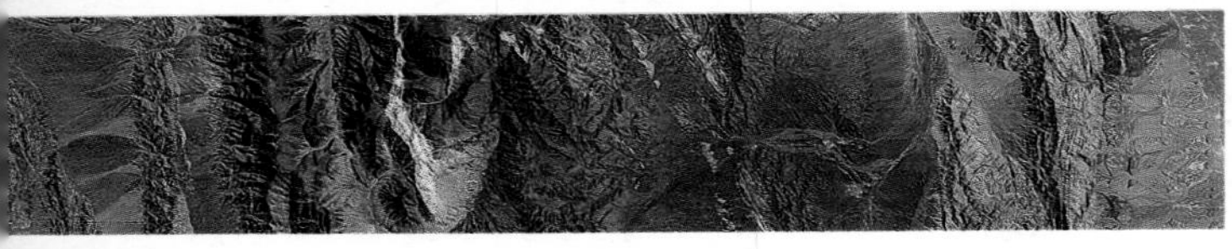

EVERY GREAT CIVILIZATION IN HUMAN HISTORY HAS CREATED A COMPLEX, OFTEN FAR-FLUNG TRANSPORTATION NETWORK LINKING IT TO THE OUTSIDE WORLD. CITIES and industry in any era depend on supply lines and trade routes to survive. As the adjacent map shows, these land and sea routes underscore the world's uneven distribution of human settlement.

The greatest systems of surface transportation are found in North America and Europe, where nearly every inhabited locale can be reached by car, train, bus, or airline. This dense network thins out only in the western United States and in western and northern Canada. The more open network of the former Soviet Union traces the well-populated area west of the Ural Mountains and a narrow corridor between central Asia and Siberia. South America's transportation network is a study in contrasts between densely settled metropolitan areas and the more inaccessible interior regions. Until recently, much of the vast Amazon basin was accessible only via waterways, but development of the rain forest has spurred the construction of new highways and roads. The Pan American Highway, stretching from Mexico to Chile, is a major link among South American countries.

Africa, the Middle East, and Asia are more complex. In Africa, only South Africa, northern Morocco, Algeria, and Tunisia have well-developed transportation systems. The Middle East boasts some of humanity's oldest routes along the sea coast, but further inland the desert has few roads. Only in the oil-producing regions are transportation lines in abundant supply. Vast areas of the Asian continent are sparsely populated, and transportation facilities here are poor or nonexistent. India and Pakistan have roads and rail systems built on a European model, but only Japan's transportation network rivals those of the United States and Europe. In Australia, the transportation lines clearly mark where human settlements end and the "outback" regions begin. A single rail line cuts through the desert, connecting rural settlements with the major cities along the coast.

Transportation patterns also reveal something about the culture and economic development of a country or region. The complex network in Europe, for example, means that every factory, farm, and home is connected into a national and continental system of communication. In contrast, people in more remote areas may not be exposed to new ideas and methods as easily. Whether a country is connected into a vital network of communication or is relatively isolated has a significant impact on its rate of development and progress.

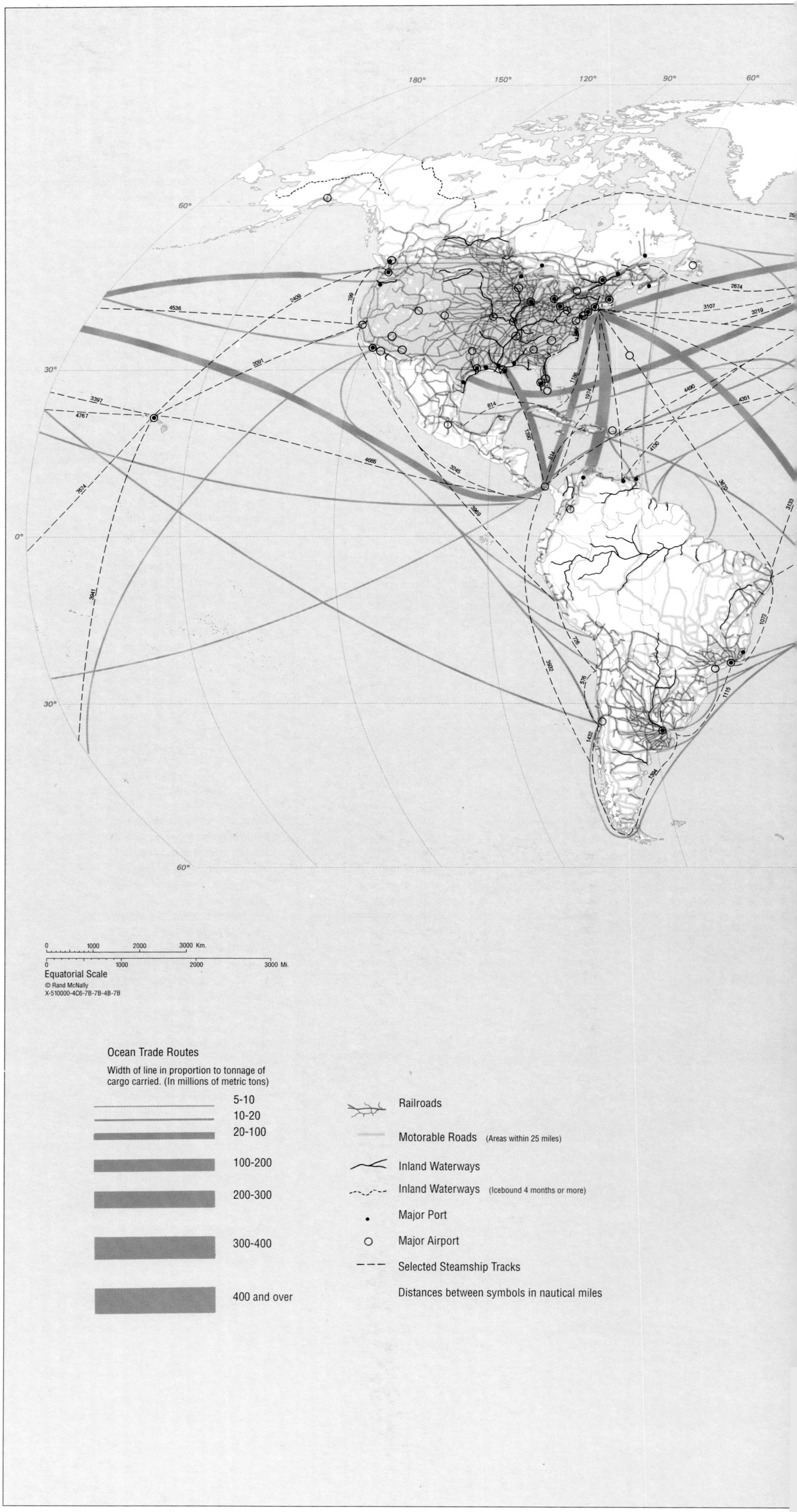

180°
150°
120°
90°
60°
60°
30°
0°
30°
60°
0 1000 2000 3000 Km.
0 1000 2000 3000 Mi.
Equatorial Scale
© Rand McNally
X-510000-4C6-7B-7B-4B-7B
Ocean Trade Routes
Width of line in proportion to tonnage of cargo carried. (In millions of metric tons)
5-10
10-20
20-100
100-200
200-300
300-400
400 and over
Railroads
Motorable Roads (Areas within 25 miles)
Inland Waterways
Inland Waterways (Icebound 4 months or more)
Major Port
Major Airport
Selected Steamship Tracks
Distances between symbols in nautical miles

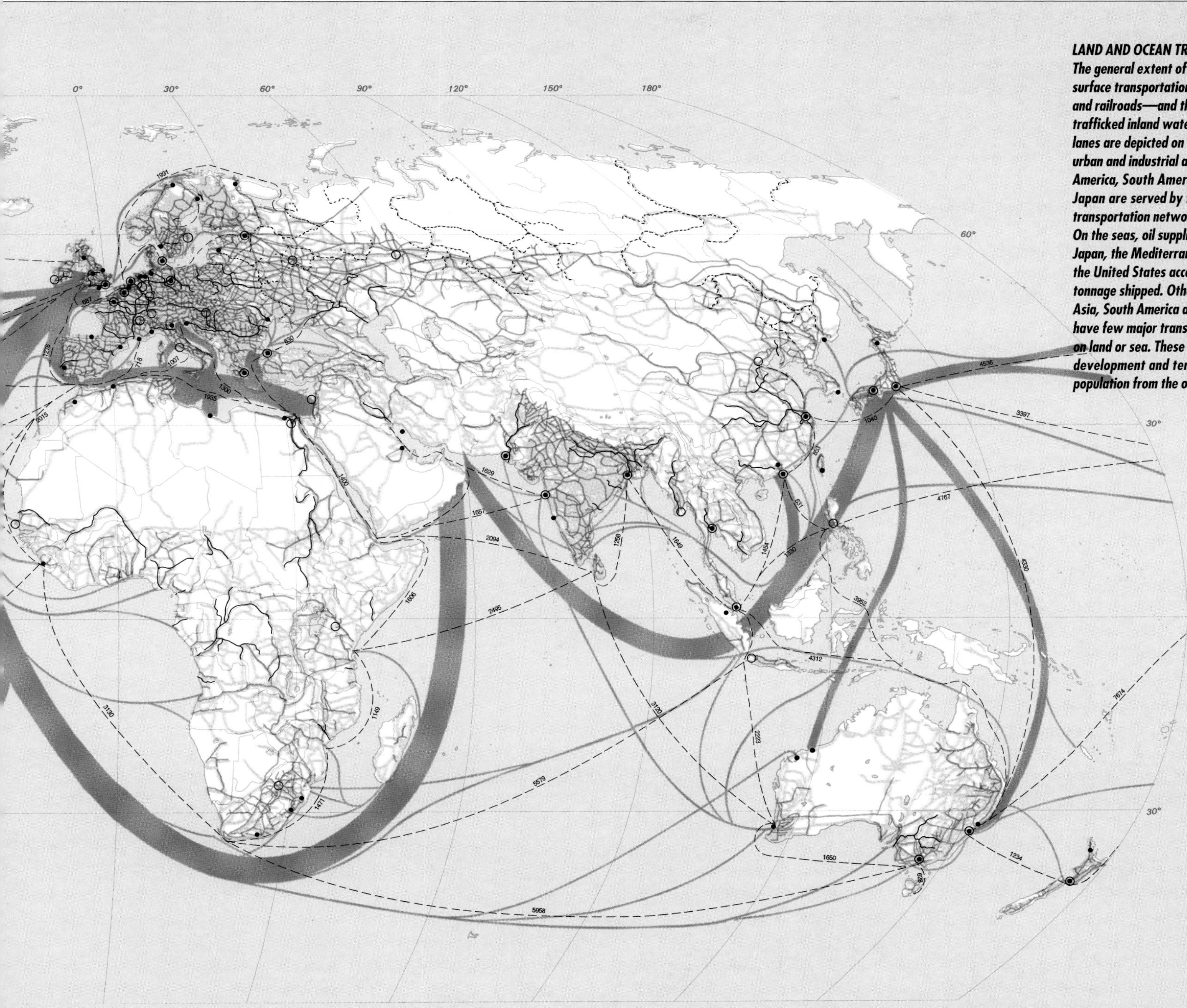
0°
30°
60°
90°
120°
150°
180°
60°
30°
0°
30°

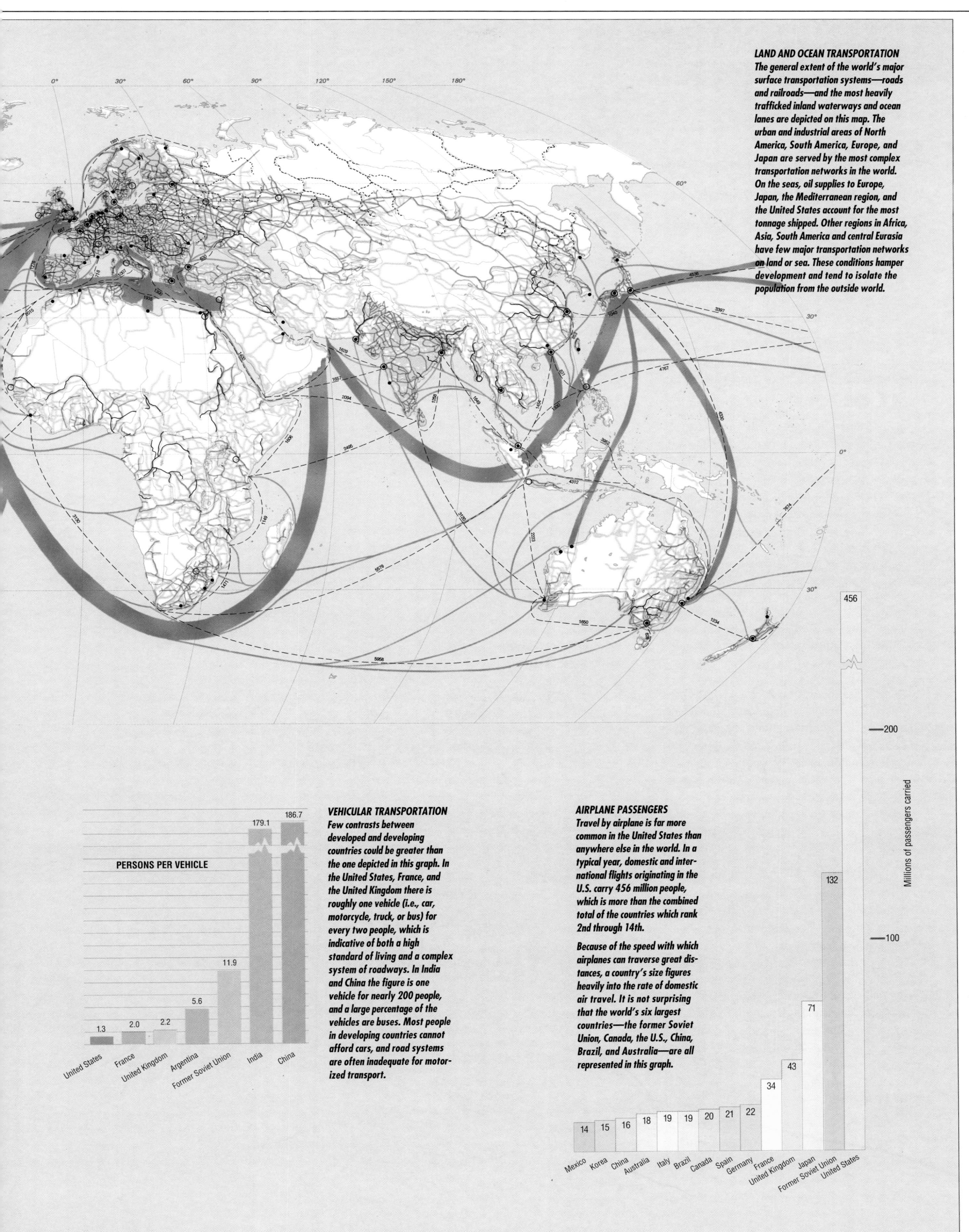

LAND AND OCEAN TRANSPORTATION

The general extent of the world's major surface transportation systems—roads and railroads—and the most heavily trafficked inland waterways and ocean lanes are depicted on this map. The urban and industrial areas of North America, South America, Europe, and Japan are served by the most complex transportation networks in the world. On the seas, oil supplies to Europe, Japan, the Mediterranean region, and the United States account for the most tonnage shipped. Other regions in Africa, Asia, South America and central Eurasia have few major transportation networks on land or sea. These conditions hamper development and tend to isolate the population from the outside world.

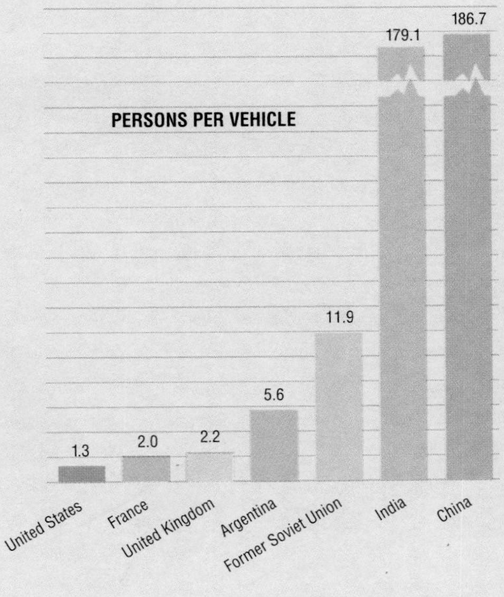
PERSONS PER VEHICLE
1.3
2.0
2.2
5.6
11.9
179.1
186.7
United States
France
United Kingdom
Argentina
Former Soviet Union
India
China

VEHICULAR TRANSPORTATION

Few contrasts between developed and developing countries could be greater than the one depicted in this graph. In the United States, France, and the United Kingdom there is roughly one vehicle (i.e., car, motorcycle, truck, or bus) for every two people, which is indicative of both a high standard of living and a complex system of roadways. In India and China the figure is one vehicle for nearly 200 people, and a large percentage of the vehicles are buses. Most people in developing countries cannot afford cars, and road systems are often inadequate for motorized transport.

AIRPLANE PASSENGERS

Travel by airplane is far more common in the United States than anywhere else in the world. In a typical year, domestic and international flights originating in the U.S. carry 456 million people, which is more than the combined total of the countries which rank 2nd through 14th.

Because of the speed with which airplanes can traverse great distances, a country's size figures heavily into the rate of domestic air travel. It is not surprising that the world's six largest countries—the former Soviet Union, Canada, the U.S., China, Brazil, and Australia—are all represented in this graph.

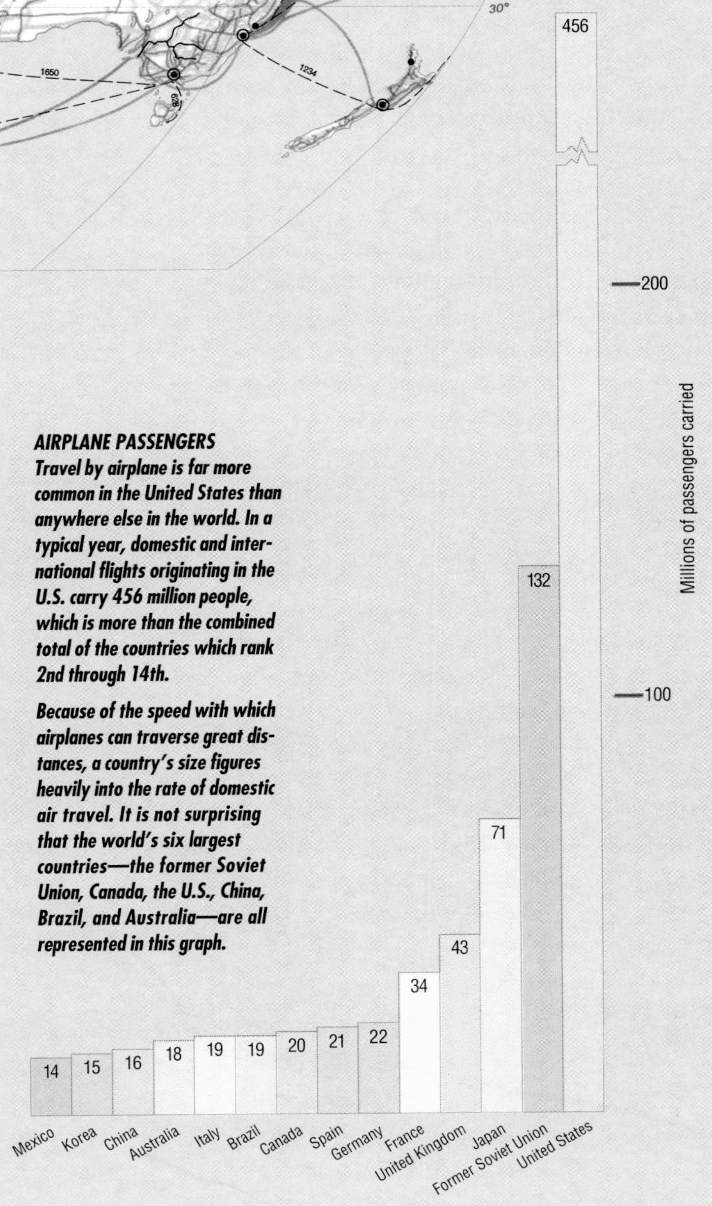
Millions of passengers carried
200
100
14
15
16
18
19
19
20
21
22
34
43
71
132
456
Mexico
Korea
China
Australia
Italy
Brazil
Canada
Spain
Germany
France
United Kingdom
Japan
Former Soviet Union
United States

FEW ACTIVITIES HAVE HAD AS PROFOUND AN IMPACT ON HUMAN DEVELOPMENT AS COMMUNICATION. YET UNLIKE AGRICULTURE OR TRANSPORTATION, COMMUNICATION networks leave little imprint on the landscape. In modern times, this dynamic, invisible network has linked countries around the world, effectively conquering the barriers of time and distance. Today's telecommunications equipment can transmit and receive messages in milliseconds over distances that once took days, even months, to cross.

Throughout history, however, whether a country or region was included in a communications network or relatively isolated greatly affected its rate of cultural evolution. The invention of moveable type and printing in Europe in the 1400s, for example, had a tremendous cultural impact on the Western world. Information could now be disseminated to a wide audience, aiding in the exchange of ideas and new discoveries among the countries of Europe, North Africa, and the Far East. From that time on, the cultural development of these countries began to accelerate. Regions outside this network, such as sub-Saharan Africa and parts of Asia, slowly began to fall behind in technology and economic growth.

In the 1800s, advances in the understanding of electricity led to the invention of the telegraph, telephone, and radio. By 1866, the first transatlantic telegraph cable linked North America and Europe, laying the foundation for the modern era of electronic information exchange. Since the turn of the twentieth century, the explosive growth in communication devices and networks has ushered in the so-called "Information Age," the hallmark of which is the virtual elimination of geographic barriers to communication. Satellites, television and video, computer and data networks, modems, fax machines, electronic and voice mail, and cellular telephones have created a type of global information highway, along which information and communications flow with astonishing speed.

Although its full potential has not yet been realized, this new and vital highway is already beginning to transform the way we live, work, and view the world. For example, computer networking and fax machines allow many people in the service sector to work out of their homes instead of commuting to an office. Global positioning systems make it possible to track ocean-going vessels, trucks and individual parcels. Satellite geographic information systems aid in resource management by revealing global rates of deforestation, flood damage, and suburban sprawl.

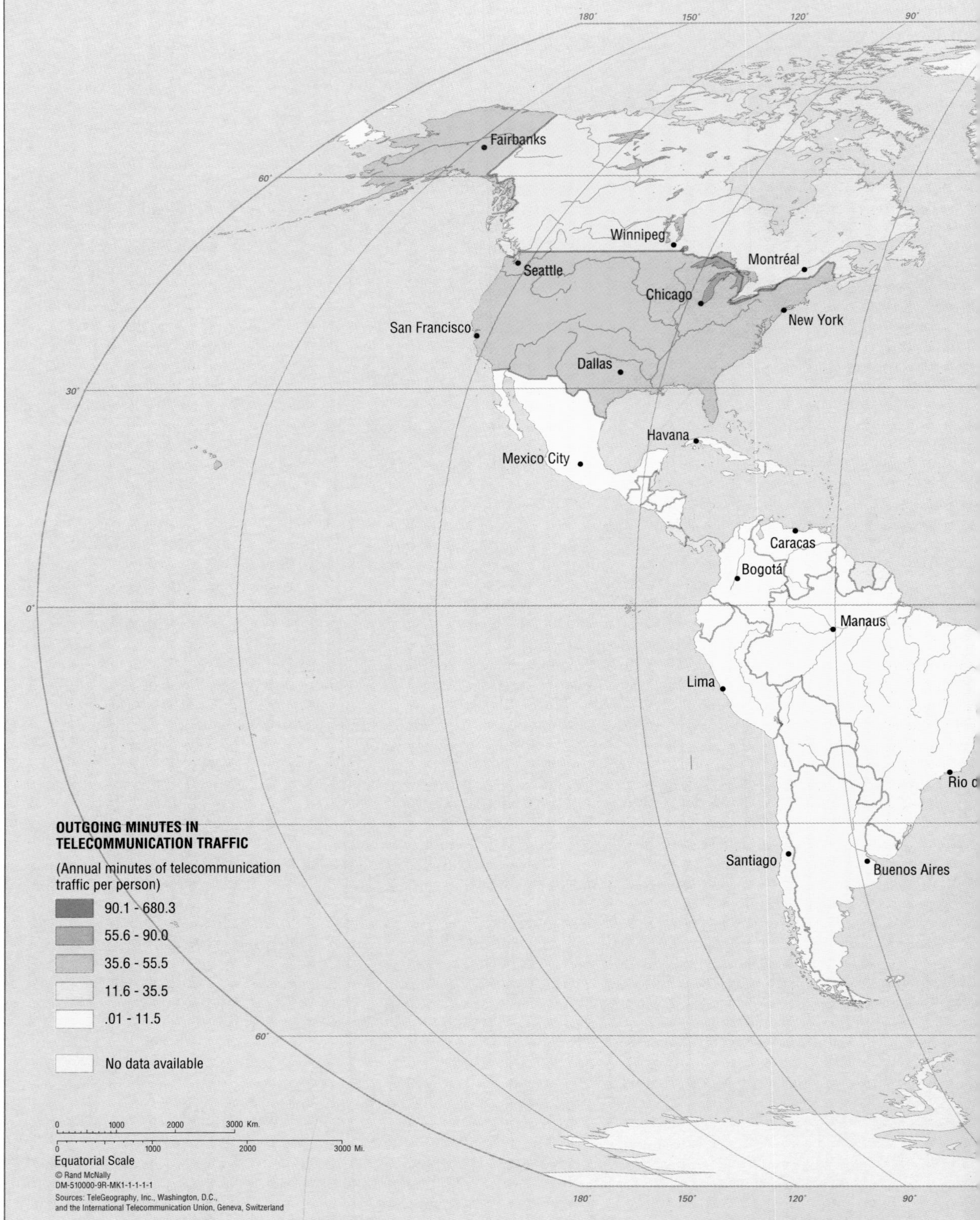

Fairbanks
Winnipeg
Seattle
Montréal
Chicago
San Francisco
New York
Dallas
Havana
Mexico City
Caracas
Bogotá
Manaus
Lima
Santiago
Buenos Aires
OUTGOING MINUTES IN TELECOMMUNICATION TRAFFIC
(Annual minutes of telecommunication traffic per person)
90.1 - 680.3
55.6 - 90.0
35.6 - 55.5
11.6 - 35.5
.01 - 11.5
No data available
Equatorial Scale
© Rand McNally
DM-510000-9R-MK1-1-1-1
Sources: TeleGeography, Inc., Washington, D.C., and the International Telecommunication Union, Geneva, Switzerland

CELLULAR PHONES AND FAX MACHINES

In the short time that they have been available, cellular phones and fax machines have achieved widespread usage in industrialized countries such as Japan, Germany, and the United Kingdom. If the United States were included in this graph, it would dwarf all other countries, with 11,033,000 cellular phones and 6,000,000 fax machines in use as of 1992.

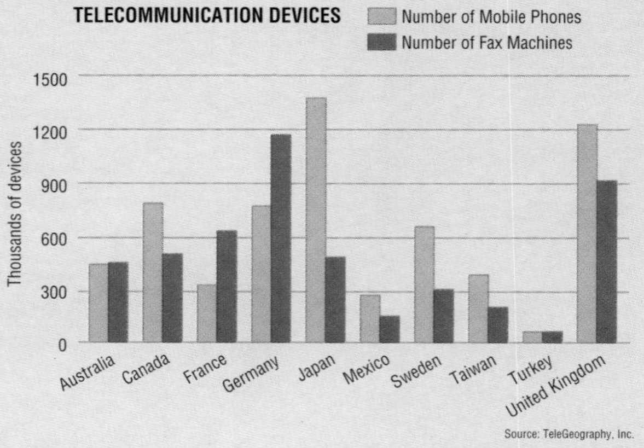

TELECOMMUNICATION DEVICES
Number of Mobile Phones
Number of Fax Machines
Thousands of devices
1500
1200
900
600
300
0
Australia
Canada
France
Germany
Japan
Mexico
Sweden
Taiwan
Turkey
United Kingdom
Source: TeleGeography, Inc.

WORLDWIDE TELECOMMUNICATION

A combination of telephone cables, fiber-optic trunks, sophisticated computer and software systems, orbiting satellites, and transmission towers has created a global corridor for the rapid exchange of information through various mediums, including voice and video communications, fax transmissions, and electronic mail. Traditional geographic barriers such as distance and topography have little impact on this high-tech "information highway."

The map at left depicts worldwide telecommunication traffic on public networks, measured in "Minutes of Telecommunication Traffic" (MiTTs) on a per capita basis.

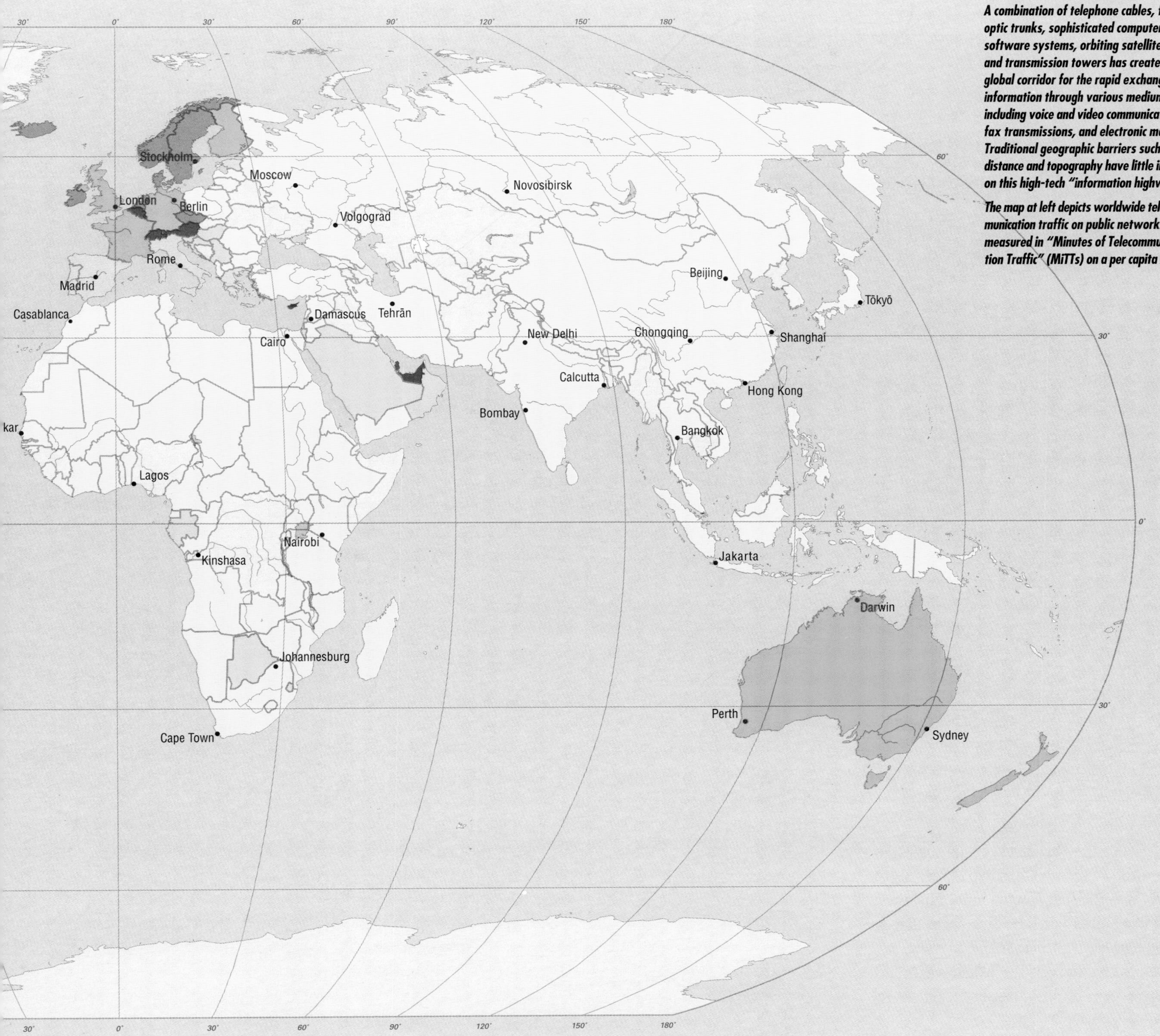

30°
0°
30°
60°
90°
120°
150°
180°
Stockholm
Moscow
Novosibirsk
London
Berlin
Volgograd
Rome
Madrid
Beijing
Tōkyō
Casablanca
Damascus
Tehrān
Cairo
New Delhi
Chongqing
Shanghai
Calcutta
Hong Kong
Bombay
kar
Bangkok
Lagos
Nairobi
Kinshasa
Jakarta
Darwin
Johannesburg
Perth
Sydney
Cape Town
60°
30°
0°

INTERCONTINENTAL COMMUNICATIONS FLOW

As this map strikingly illustrates, the heaviest telecommunications traffic flows east and west in the northern hemisphere. Much of the economic activity of modern industrialized countries is dependent on the rapid communication of data on research and development, pricing, commodities, capital and product markets, and political changes.

© TeleGeography, Inc. 1994

Annual Minutes of Telecommunication Traffic

2.5 bilion — *1 billion* — *500 million* — *100 million*

The width of each band is proportional to the total annual traffic in both directions between each pair of countries.

(This map shows all intercontinental routes with an annual volume of more than 75 million minutes of telecommunication traffic.)

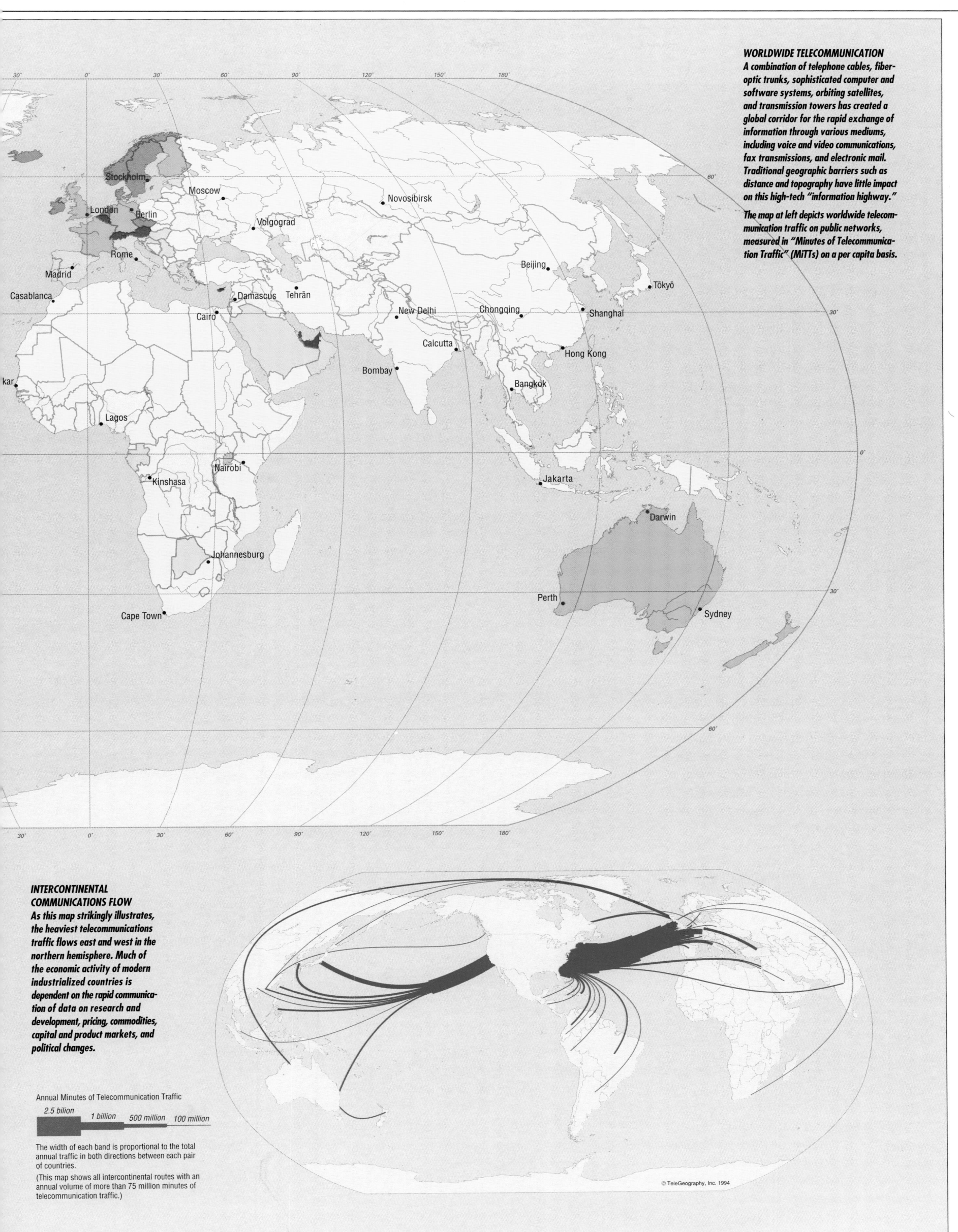

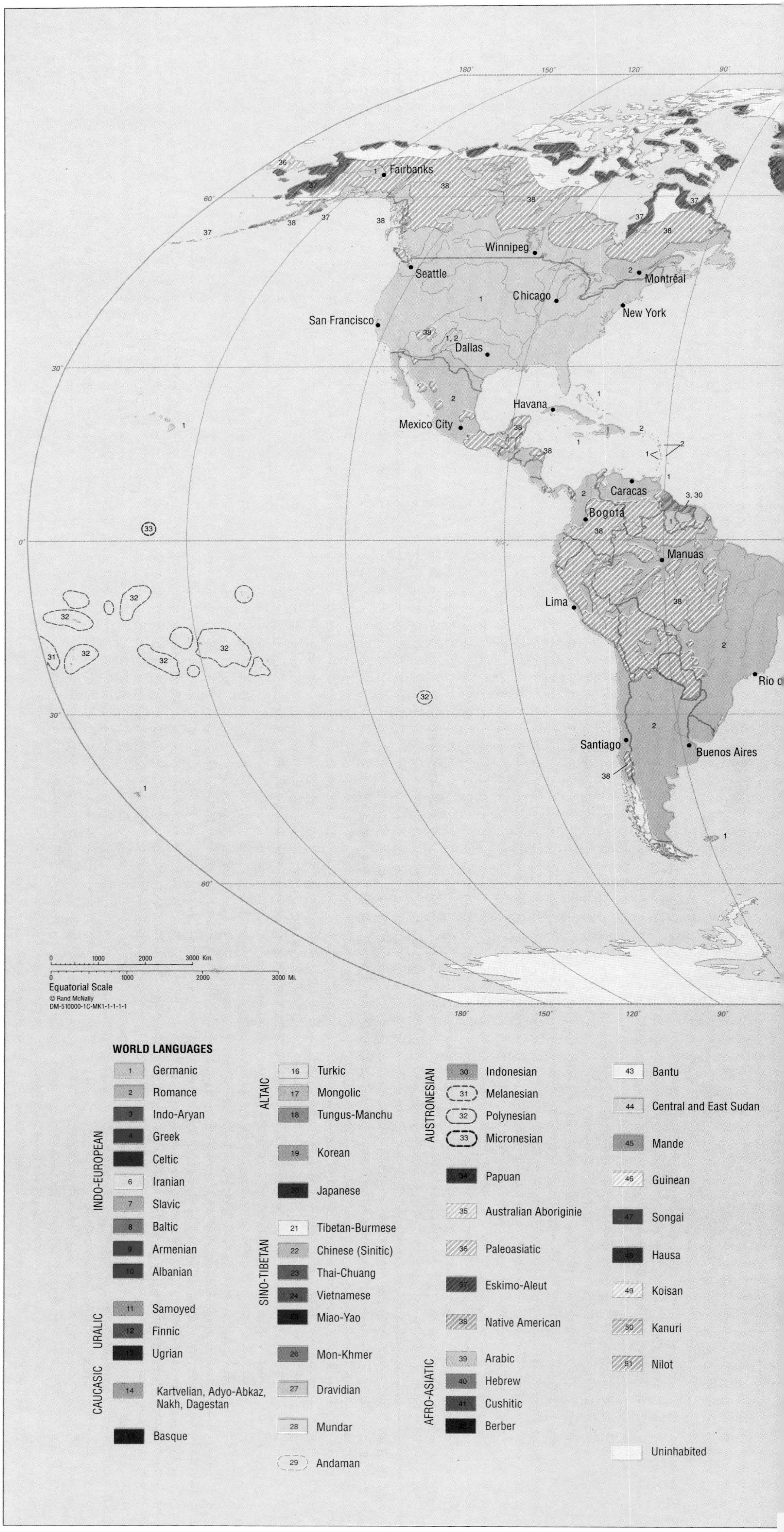
Fairbanks
Winnipeg
Seattle
Montréal
Chicago
New York
San Francisco
Dallas
Havana
Mexico City
Caracas
Bogotá
Manuas
Lima
Rio d
Santiago
Buenos Aires
Equatorial Scale
© Rand McNally
DM-510000-1C-MK1-1-1-1-1
WORLD LANGUAGES
INDO-EUROPEAN
1 Germanic
2 Romance
3 Indo-Aryan
4 Greek
5 Celtic
6 Iranian
7 Slavic
8 Baltic
9 Armenian
10 Albanian
URALIC
11 Samoyed
12 Finnic
13 Ugrian
CAUCASIC
14 Kartvelian, Adyo-Abkaz, Nakh, Dagestan
15 Basque
ALTAIC
16 Turkic
17 Mongolic
18 Tungus-Manchu
19 Korean
20 Japanese
SINO-TIBETAN
21 Tibetan-Burmese
22 Chinese (Sinitic)
23 Thai-Chuang
24 Vietnamese
25 Miao-Yao
26 Mon-Khmer
27 Dravidian
28 Mundar
29 Andaman
AUSTRONESIAN
30 Indonesian
31 Melanesian
32 Polynesian
33 Micronesian
34 Papuan
35 Australian Aboriginie
36 Paleoasiatic
37 Eskimo-Aleut
38 Native American
AFRO-ASIATIC
39 Arabic
40 Hebrew
41 Cushitic
42 Berber
43 Bantu
44 Central and East Sudan
45 Mande
46 Guinean
47 Songai
48 Hausa
49 Koisan
50 Kanuri
51 Nilot
Uninhabited

LANGUAGE, RELIGION, AND ETHNIC IDENTITY—THESE HELP TO DEFINE HUMAN COMMUNITIES IN A WAY THAT TRANSCENDS POLITICAL BOUNDARIES. LANGUAGE, OF

course, is the most effective means of communication among members of a group. It serves as a cohesive force for the members and helps to distinguish one community from another.

The map to the right shows only the major language groups, such as the Germanic branch of the Indo-European family. A map that displayed all known languages would require thousands of colors and labels. The Chinese branch of the Sino-Tibetan family ranks first in the number of speakers. English ranks second, but is the world's most important medium for scientific and commercial communication.

English enjoys absolute predominance in only four countries: the United Kingdom, the U.S., Australia, and New Zealand. However, it is spoken by a majority of people in Ireland and Canada and is the preferred second language in many other countries. French, Spanish, and Russian are also widely used as second languages. The importance of two other languages is suggested by the number of countries in which they have official status: Arabic (18 countries) and Spanish (20 countries).

Religion, like language, is a means of communication and a mechanism that promotes social cohesion. The map here shows the most important universalizing religions (Christianity, Islam, and Buddhism) that are held to be appropriate for all of humankind and so are propagated by missionary activities. Religions associated with particular peoples, such as Judaism and Hinduism, seldom entail missionary activity.

Countries cannot always be neatly divided into religious groups, however. In China, for example, Buddhism, Confucianism, and Taoism are so entwined that one has to speak of a Chinese religious system rather than a Chinese religion. Elsewhere in the world, and especially in Africa, a wide array of tribal religions can be identified, and many of these have incorporated some of the practices and beliefs of one of the universalizing religions. Over time, most religions tend to split into factions or denominations. The division of Christianity into Catholic, Orthodox, and Protestant branches is striking evidence of this tendency, as is the split of the Islamic religion into Sunni and Shi'ite factions after the death of Muhammad in A.D. 632.

The country boundaries that appear as lines under the patterns of religions and languages remind us of an important fact about our world: very few of the 184 member states of the United Nations are nations in the strict or singular sense of the word. Most are a collection

Continued on page A•22

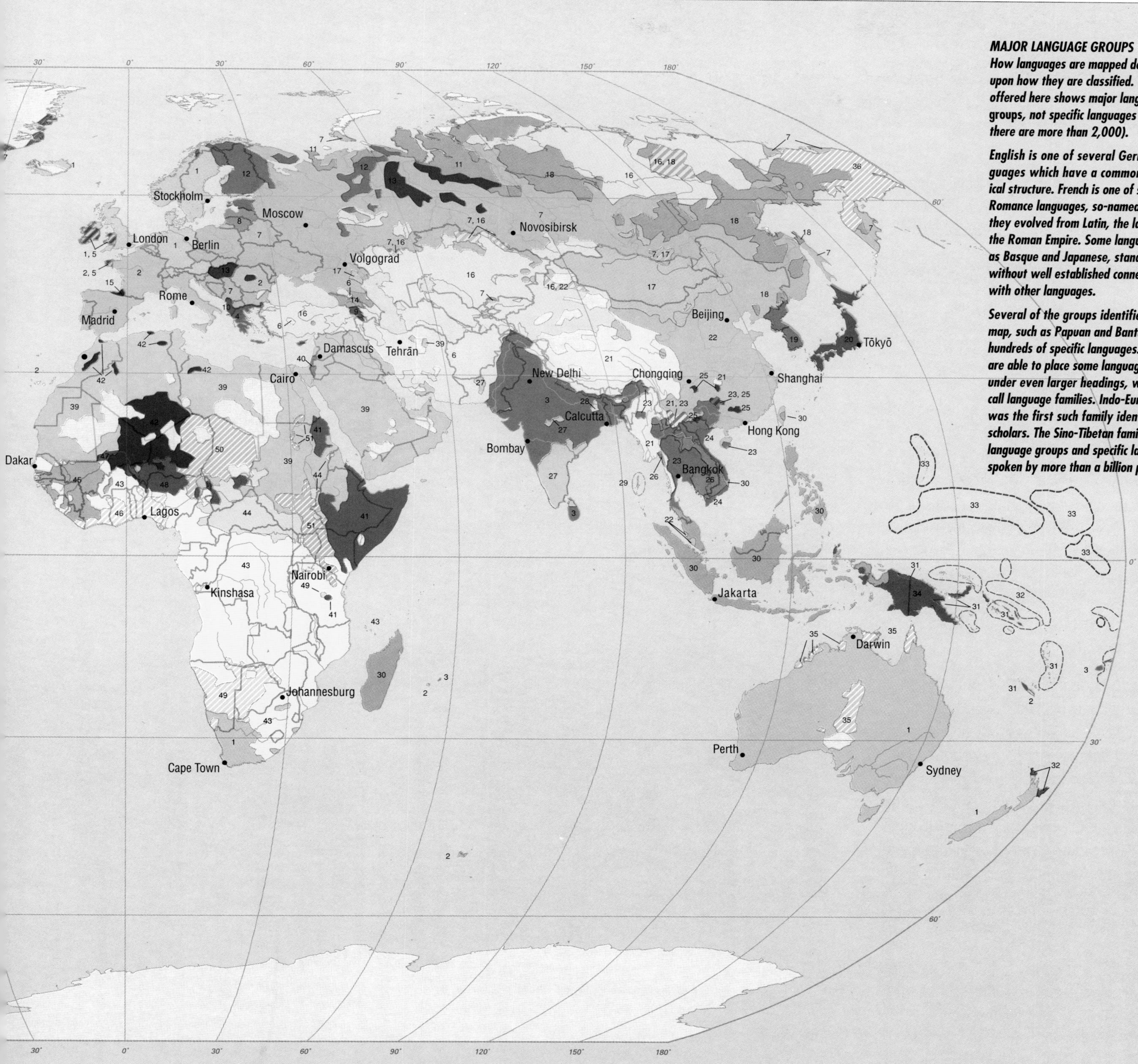
Stockholm
Moscow
London
Berlin
Volgograd
Novosibirsk
Rome
Madrid
Damascus
Tehrān
Cairo
Beijing
Tōkyō
Shanghai
New Delhi
Chongqing
Calcutta
Hong Kong
Bombay
Bangkok
Dakar
Lagos
Nairobi
Kinshasa
Jakarta
Darwin
Johannesburg
Perth
Sydney
Cape Town

MAJOR LANGUAGE GROUPS

How languages are mapped depends upon how they are classified. The map offered here shows major language groups, not specific languages (of which there are more than 2,000).

English is one of several Germanic languages which have a common grammatical structure. French is one of several Romance languages, so-named because they evolved from Latin, the language of the Roman Empire. Some languages, such as Basque and Japanese, stand alone without well established connections with other languages.

Several of the groups identified on this map, such as Papuan and Bantu, include hundreds of specific languages. Linguists are able to place some language groups under even larger headings, which they call language families. Indo-European was the first such family identified by scholars. The Sino-Tibetan family includes language groups and specific languages spoken by more than a billion people.

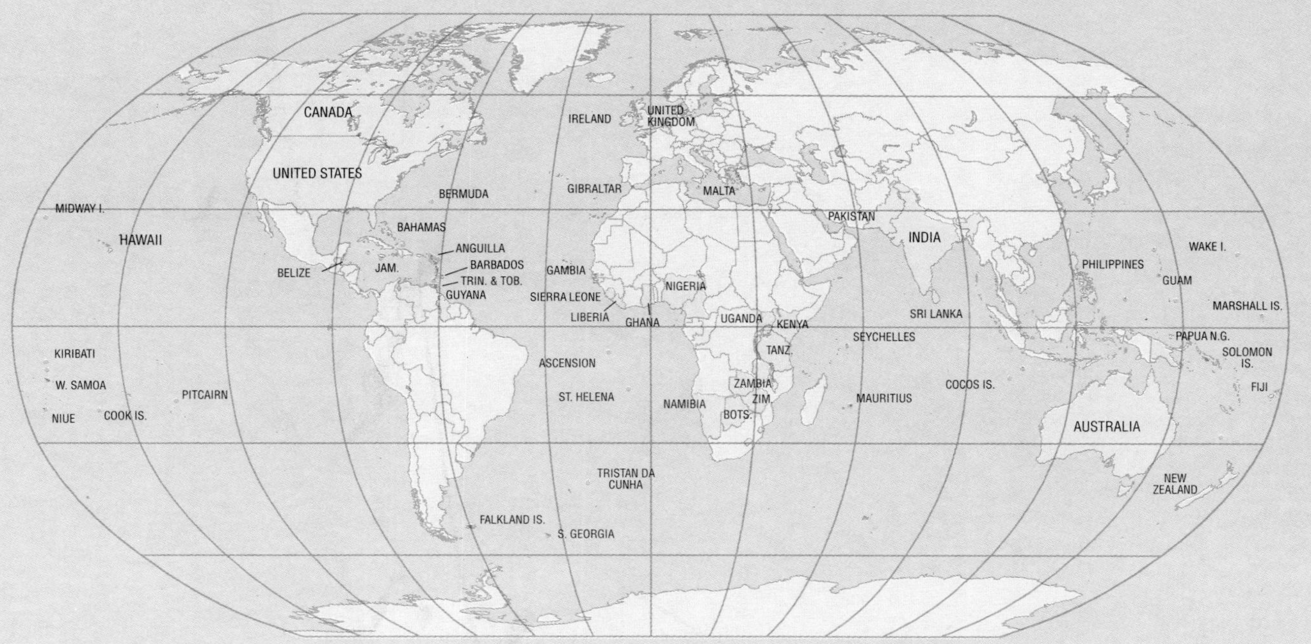
CANADA
IRELAND
UNITED KINGDOM
UNITED STATES
BERMUDA
GIBRALTAR
MALTA
MIDWAY I.
HAWAII
BAHAMAS
PAKISTAN
INDIA
WAKE I.
ANGUILLA
BARBADOS
TRIN. & TOB.
GUYANA
BELIZE
JAM.
GAMBIA
SIERRA LEONE
LIBERIA
GHANA
NIGERIA
UGANDA
KENYA
PHILIPPINES
GUAM
MARSHALL IS.
SRI LANKA
SEYCHELLES
TANZ.
PAPUA N.G.
SOLOMON IS.
KIRIBATI
ASCENSION
W. SAMOA
PITCAIRN
ST. HELENA
ZAMBIA
ZIM.
NAMIBIA
BOTS.
MAURITIUS
COCOS IS.
FIJI
NIUE
COOK IS.
AUSTRALIA
TRISTAN DA CUNHA
NEW ZEALAND
FALKLAND IS.
S. GEORGIA

THE REALM OF ENGLISH

English has become the world's most useful language. This map shows where it has official status. A map showing where English is used without such status would extend its realm to most of the world.

Continued from page A·20

of different groups speaking a variety of languages and maintaining diverse religious and cultural beliefs. In Western Europe, only Denmark and Portugal are homogeneous countries where everyone speaks the same language and belongs to the same church. In Africa, only Tunisia shares this distinction.

It is hard to find a comparable example in the Middle East, even among countries predominantly Islamic in faith and Arabic in speech. Saudi Arabia, if its large foreign labor population is ignored, is the only example of a true nation state in this region. Elsewhere in Asia, Japan and the two Korean states are rare exceptions to the more common pattern of cultural complexity. In Latin America, Spanish or Portuguese speech and Roman Catholicism are cultural common denominators, but Native American languages are still spoken in most countries. In contrast, Argentina and Brazil are cultural melting pots like the United States. Costa Rica and Uruguay may be the only New World states without significant minorities.

The fact that cultural uniformity is so rare, and only one perfect example can be cited (Iceland), means that the familiar political map not only differs from the less familiar maps of language and religion, but may actually conflict with them. Some countries have laws and institutions that permit citizens of different faiths and languages to live in peace and prosperity. For example, the Swiss live in harmony in spite of speaking four languages (German, French, Italian, and Romansch) and having Catholic and Protestant affiliations. Unfortunately, such happy examples of cultural accommodation are offset by numerous instances of tension and conflict. The ethnic warfare within recent decades in Sri Lanka, Bosnia, Sudan, Lebanon, and Rwanda are conspicuous examples of the potential for violence that often exists in states that are not true nation states or have borders that do not coincide with ethnic realities. The collapse of the Soviet Union exposed many problems of this nature.

Since the world is never likely to have only one language or one religion, comparison of maps showing cultural patterns with those indicating political jurisdiction reveals an important truth about our troubled world. In order to understand why ethnic conflict occurs so frequently we need an appropriate vocabulary. We need to be able to distinguish among the following cultural-political categories: *nation states* (homogeneous countries, such as Iceland and Denmark); *multinational states* (countries made up of diverse ethnic and linguistic groups, such as India); *multi-state nations* (multiple countries that share language and religion, such as the Arabic-Islamic realm); *non-nation states* (Vatican City is the only example); and, finally, *non-state nations* (regions where people share language and religion but have no political state, such as Kurdistan and Palestine).

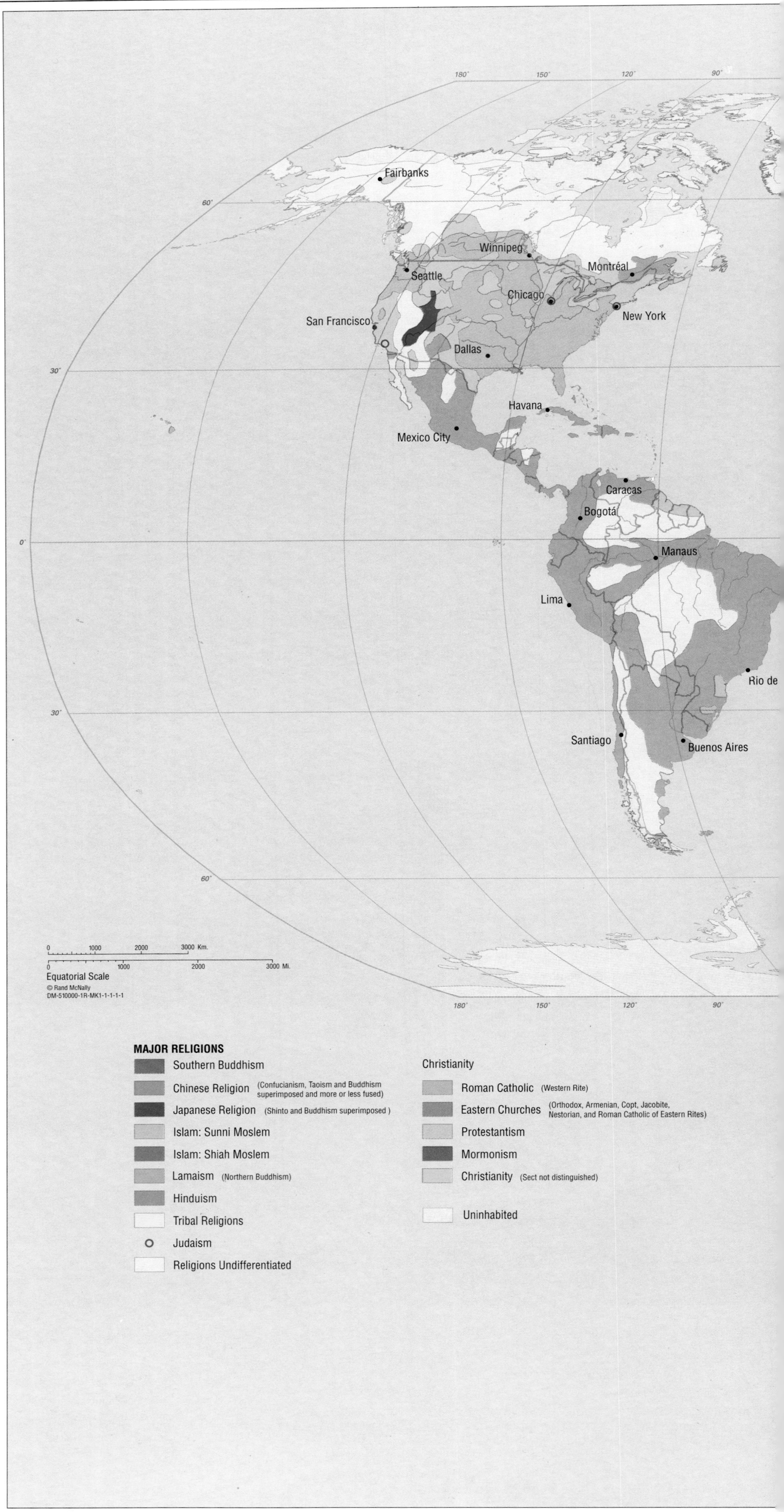
Fairbanks
Winnipeg
Seattle
Montréal
Chicago
New York
San Francisco
Dallas
Havana
Mexico City
Caracas
Bogotá
Manaus
Lima
Rio de
Santiago
Buenos Aires
Equatorial Scale
© Rand McNally
DM-510000-1R-MK1-1-1-1-1
MAJOR RELIGIONS
Southern Buddhism
Chinese Religion (Confucianism, Taoism and Buddhism superimposed and more or less fused)
Japanese Religion (Shinto and Buddhism superimposed)
Islam: Sunni Moslem
Islam: Shiah Moslem
Lamaism (Northern Buddhism)
Hinduism
Tribal Religions
Judaism
Religions Undifferentiated
Christianity
Roman Catholic (Western Rite)
Eastern Churches (Orthodox, Armenian, Copt, Jacobite, Nestorian, and Roman Catholic of Eastern Rites)
Protestantism
Mormonism
Christianity (Sect not distinguished)
Uninhabited

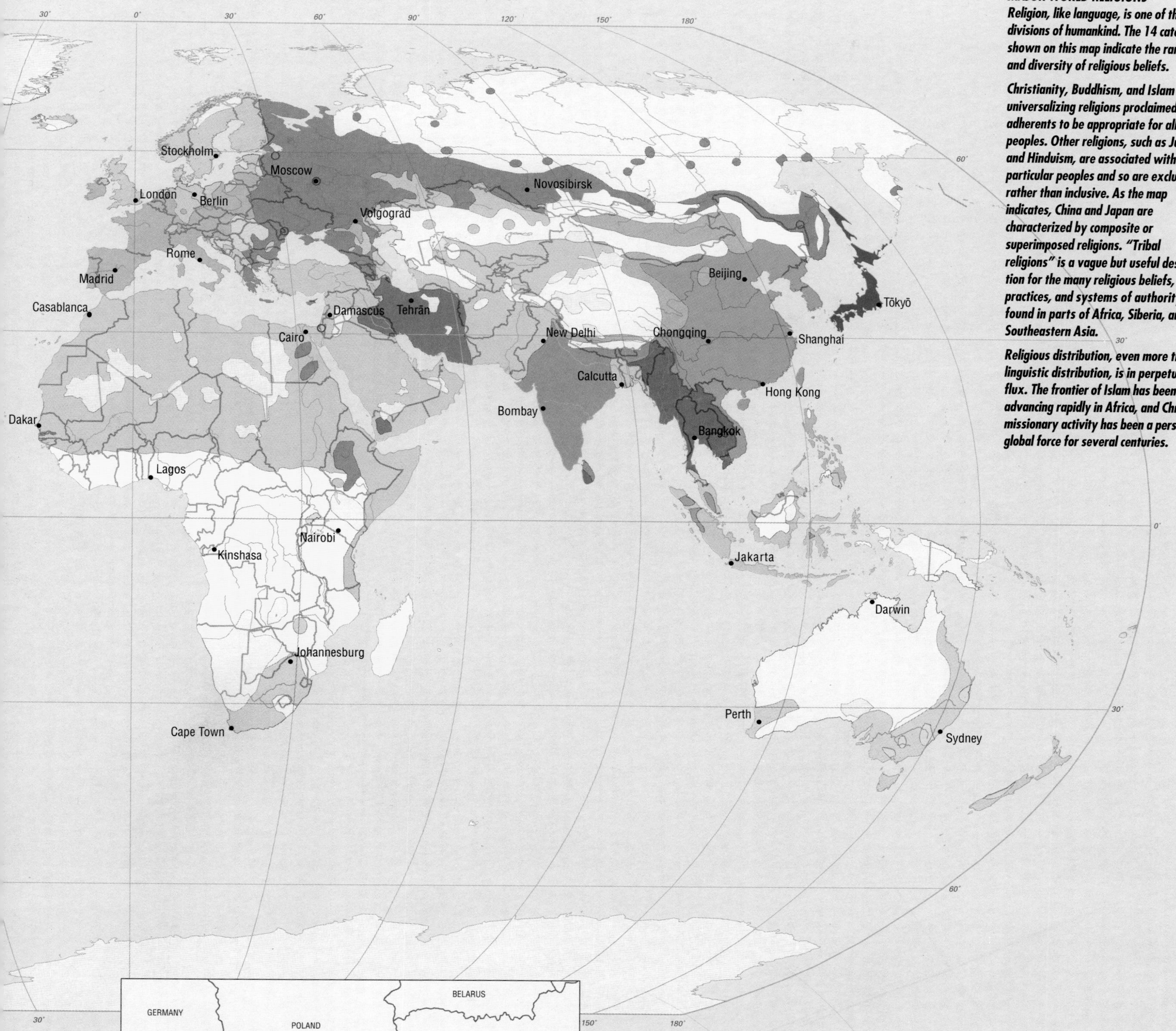

30°
0°
30°
60°
90°
120°
150°
180°
60°
30°
0°
30°
60°
150°
180°
Stockholm
Moscow
London
Berlin
Novosibirsk
Volgograd
Rome
Madrid
Beijing
Casablanca
Damascus
Tehrān
Tōkyō
Cairo
New Delhi
Chongqing
Shanghai
Calcutta
Hong Kong
Bombay
Dakar
Bangkok
Lagos
Nairobi
Kinshasa
Jakarta
Darwin
Johannesburg
Perth
Cape Town
Sydney

MAJOR WORLD RELIGIONS

Religion, like language, is one of the basic divisions of humankind. The 14 categories shown on this map indicate the range and diversity of religious beliefs.

Christianity, Buddhism, and Islam are universalizing religions proclaimed by adherents to be appropriate for all peoples. Other religions, such as Judaism and Hinduism, are associated with particular peoples and so are exclusive rather than inclusive. As the map indicates, China and Japan are characterized by composite or superimposed religions. "Tribal religions" is a vague but useful designation for the many religious beliefs, practices, and systems of authority found in parts of Africa, Siberia, and Southeastern Asia.

Religious distribution, even more than linguistic distribution, is in perpetual flux. The frontier of Islam has been advancing rapidly in Africa, and Christian missionary activity has been a persistent global force for several centuries.

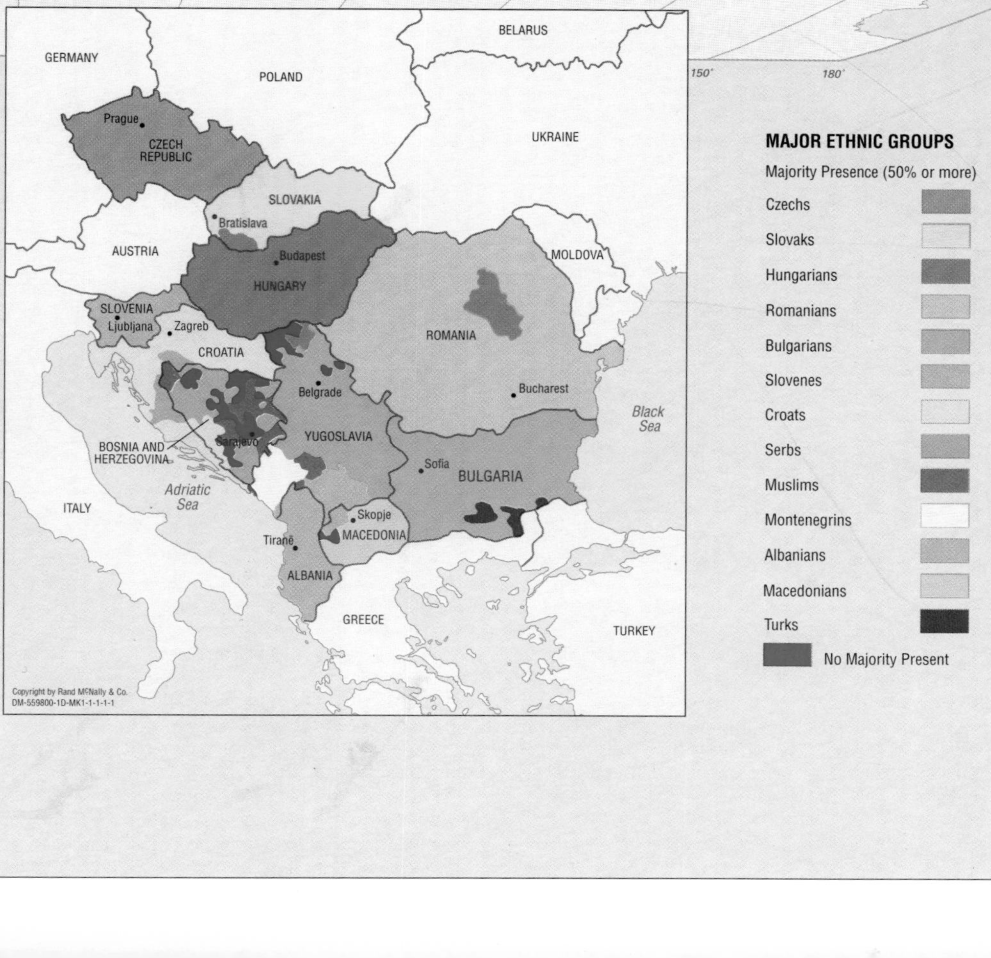

GERMANY
POLAND
BELARUS
UKRAINE
Prague
CZECH REPUBLIC
SLOVAKIA
Bratislava
AUSTRIA
Budapest
HUNGARY
MOLDOVA
SLOVENIA
Ljubljana
Zagreb
CROATIA
ROMANIA
Belgrade
Bucharest
BOSNIA AND HERZEGOVINA
Sarajevo
YUGOSLAVIA
Black Sea
Sofia
BULGARIA
Adriatic Sea
ITALY
Skopje
MACEDONIA
Tiranë
ALBANIA
GREECE
TURKEY
Copyright by Rand McNally & Co.
DM-559800-1D-MK1-1-1-1-1
MAJOR ETHNIC GROUPS
Majority Presence (50% or more)
Czechs
Slovaks
Hungarians
Romanians
Bulgarians
Slovenes
Croats
Serbs
Muslims
Montenegrins
Albanians
Macedonians
Turks
No Majority Present

CULTURAL COMPLEXITY IN EASTERN EUROPE

The boundaries of the states of Eastern Europe have seldom coincided with cultural realities. At present, Hungarians are found not only in Hungary but also in Slovakia, Romania, and Serbia. The former state of Yugoslavia had within its borders Roman Catholic and Eastern Orthodox Christians, Muslims, and speakers of Serbo-Croatian, Slovenian, and Macedonian languages. In Bosnia, ancient disputes among religious and linguistic groups still encourage tension and conflict.

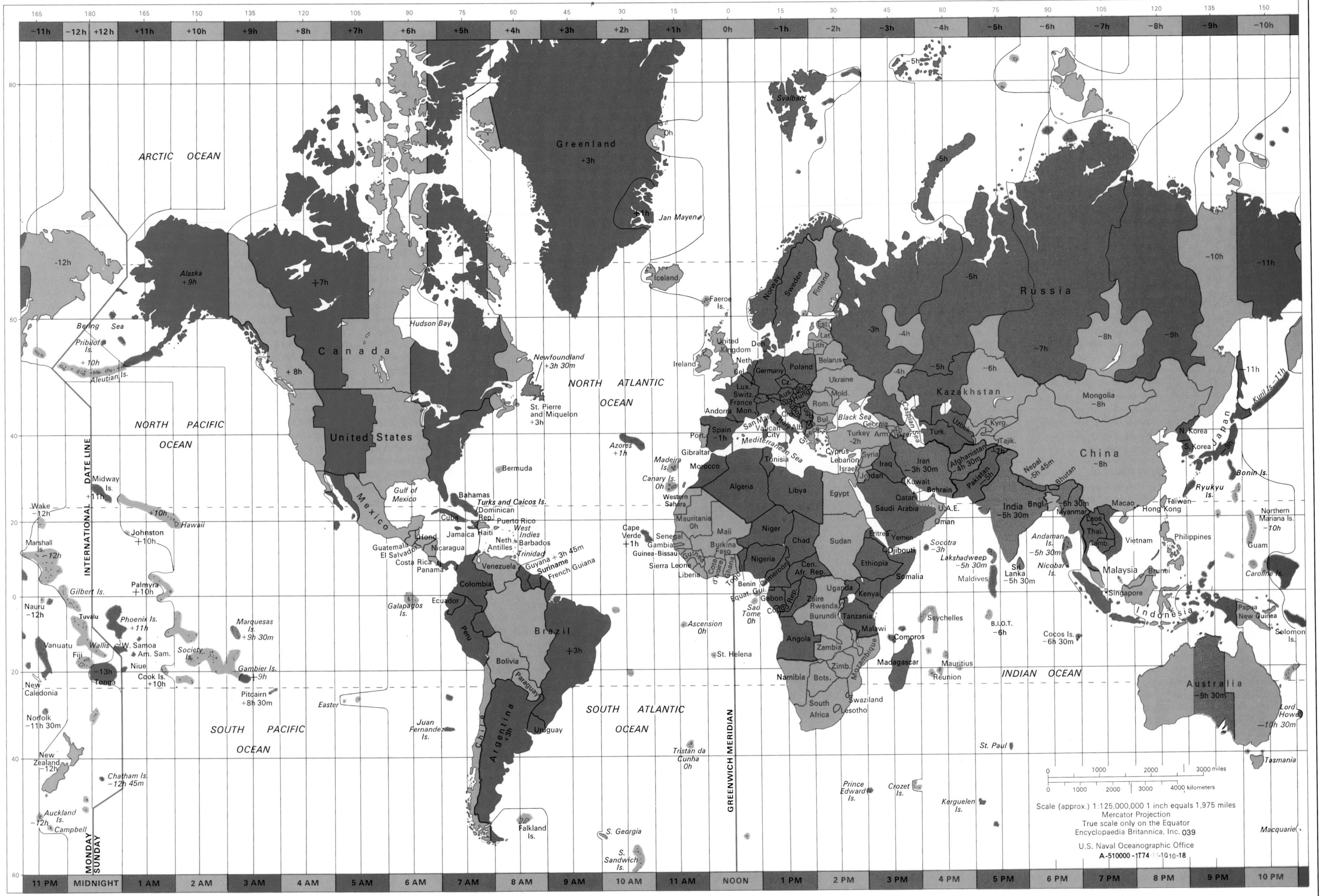

-11h -12h +12h +11h +10h +9h +8h +7h +6h +5h +4h +3h +2h +1h 0h -1h -2h -3h -4h -5h -6h -7h -8h -9h -10h
11 PM MIDNIGHT 1 AM 2 AM 3 AM 4 AM 5 AM 6 AM 7 AM 8 AM 9 AM 10 AM 11 AM NOON 1 PM 2 PM 3 PM 4 PM 5 PM 6 PM 7 PM 8 PM 9 PM 10 PM
ARCTIC OCEAN
NORTH PACIFIC OCEAN
SOUTH PACIFIC OCEAN
NORTH ATLANTIC OCEAN
SOUTH ATLANTIC OCEAN
INDIAN OCEAN
INTERNATIONAL DATE LINE
GREENWICH MERIDIAN
MONDAY
SUNDAY
Greenland +3h
Alaska +9h
Canada
United States
Mexico
Brazil +3h
Argentina +3h
Russia
Kazakhstan
China -8h
Mongolia -8h
India -5h 30m
Australia -9h 30m
Indonesia
Newfoundland +3h 30m
St. Pierre and Miquelon +3h
Hawaii
Chatham Is. -12h 45m
Nepal -5h 45m
Scale (approx.) 1:125,000,000 1 inch equals 1,975 miles
Mercator Projection
True scale only on the Equator
Encyclopaedia Britannica, Inc. 039
U.S. Naval Oceanographic Office
A-510000-1T74 1010-18

Time Zones

- Standard time zone of even-numbered hours from Greenwich time
- Standard time zone of odd-numbered hours from Greenwich time
- Time varies from the standard time zone by half an hour
- Time varies from the standard time zone by other than half an hour

h m hours, minutes

The standard time zone system, fixed by international agreement and by law in each country, is based on a theoretical division of the globe into 24 zones of 15° longitude each. The mid-meridian of each zone fixes the hour for the entire zone. The zero time zone extends 7½° east and 7½° west of the Greenwich meridian, 0° longitude. Since the earth rotates toward the east, time zones to the west of Greenwich are earlier, to the east, later.

Plus and minus hours at the top of the map are added to or subtracted from local time to find Greenwich time. Local standard time can be determined for any area in the world by adding one hour for each time zone counted in an easterly direction from one's own, or by subtracting one hour for each zone counted in a westerly direction. To separate one day from the next, the 180th meridian has been designated as the international date line. On both sides of the line the time of day is the same, but west of the line it is one day later than it is to the east.

Countries that adhere to the international zone system adopt the zone applicable to their location. Some countries, however, establish time zones based on political boundaries, or adopt the time zone of a neighboring unit. For all or part of the year some countries also advance their time by one hour, thereby utilizing more daylight hours each day.

THIS SECTION OPENS with World Political and World Physical maps at the scale of 1:75,000,000. There follow maps of the Pacific, Indian, and Atlantic oceans at the scale 1:48,000,000, the largest scale at which the total expanse of these bodies of water could be portrayed. Finally, a series of continent relief maps at the scale of 1:24,000,000 show a global view of the earth as it would appear from about 4,000 miles in space. The Azimuthal Equal-Area projection is used for the 1:24,000,000 maps, the scale being approximately that of a globe 20 inches in diameter.

The colors of the continent maps portray the land areas as if viewed from space during the growing season, without regard to the fact that the growing seasons are not concurrent in all areas. Underwater features and varying water depths are represented by shaded relief and different color tones. The result is a strong physical portrait of the earth's major land and submarine forms. The legend below shows how these different kinds of terrain and vegetation have been represented. The names of physical features—plateaus, basins, mountain ranges, seas, rivers, lakes, gulfs, trenches, bays, islands—predominate on these maps.

DIESER KARTENTEIL BEGINNT mit politischen und physischen Weltkarten im Massstab 1:75 Millionen. Dann folgen Karten des Pazifischen, Indischen und Atlantischen Ozeans in 1:48 Millionen, dem grössten Massstab, in dem diese Wasserflächen in ihrer ganzen Ausdehnung abgebildet werden konnten. Schliesslich folgt eine Reihe von Reliefkarten der Erdteile in 1:24 Millionen. Sie geben eine Übersicht der Erde, wie sie aus einer Entfernung von ungefähr 6 400 Kilometer aus dem Weltraum gewonnen würde. Den Karten im Massstab 1:24 Millionen liegt ein flächentreuer azimutaler Entwurf zugrunde, dieser Massstab entspricht ungefähr dem eines Globus von 50 cm Durchmesser.

Die Farben der Erdteilkarten bilden jedes Landgebiet so ab, wie es in der Vegetationsperiode aus der Vogelperspektive erschiene, ohne zu berücksichtigen, dass die Vegetationsperioden nicht in allen Gebieten gleichzeitig eintreten. Die Gliederung des Meeresbodens und die unterschiedlichen Meerestiefen werden durch Schummerung und verschiedene Farbstufen dargestellt. Das Ergebnis ist eine anschauliche physische Darstellung der wichtigsten terrestrischen und untermeerischen Formen der Erde. Die untenstehende Zeichenerklärung zeigt, wie diese verschiedenen Geländeformen und Vegetationsgebiete veranschaulicht werden. Namen physischer Objekte—Hochebenen, Becken, Gebirgszüge, Meere, Flüsse, Seen, Buchten, Gräben, Inseln—herrschen in diesen Karten vor.

ESTA SECCIÓN DA PRINCIPIO con los Mapas Políticos y Físicos del Mundo, a una escala de 1:75 000 000. A continuación están los mapas de los océanos Pacífico, Indico y Atlántico a una escala de 1:48 000 000, que es la mayor escala utilizable para la representación de esas masas de agua en toda su extensión. Por último, una serie de mapas del relieve de los continentes, a una escala de 1:24 000 000, proporcionan una vista global de la tierra tal como se apreciaría desde el espacio a una distancia aproximada de 6 400 kilómetros. La proyección azimutal equiárea se usa, para los mapas de 1:24 000 000, a una escala según la cual la tierra se reduciría a un globo de unos 50 cm de diámetro.

Los colores utilizados en los mapas de los continentes representan las diversas regiones de la tierra tal como se verían desde el espacio durante la estación en que la vegetación se desarrolla, sin tomar en cuenta que este fenómeno no se produce simultáneamente en todas las áreas. Las estructuras características del fondo marino y las variaciones de profundidad de los océanos se representan mediante relieve sombreado y distintos matices de color. El resultado es una imagen elocuente de las formas terrestres y submarinas más notables del planeta. La leyenda abajo explica cómo se representan estos diferentes tipos de terreno y vegetación. En estos mapas predomina la nomenclatura de elementos físicos: mesetas, cuencas, sierras, mares, ríos, lagos, golfos, bahías, trincheras, islas.

CETTE PARTIE comprend d'abord des cartes du monde politique et du monde physique à l'échelle de 1:75 000 000. Viennent ensuite les cartes des océans Pacifique, Indien et Atlantique à l'échelle de 1:48 000 000, la plus grande échelle qui a permis la reproduction complète de ces étendues d'eau. Pour terminer, une série de cartes en relief des continents à l'échelle de 1:24 000 000 donne une vue globale de la terre, telle qu'elle apparaîtrait vue de l'espace à une distance d'environ 6 400 kilomètres. La projection azimutale équivalente a été utilisée pour les cartes au 1:24 000 000e, dont l'échelle équivaut à celle d'un globe de 50 cm de diamètre environ.

Les couleurs des cartes font apparaître les continents tels qu'on les verrait de l'espace, pendant la saison de croissance végétale, mais sans tenir compte du fait que cette saison n'apparaît pas partout simultanément. Le relief sous-marin est représenté par un estompage et la profondeur des océans par une variation de la couleur. Il en résulte une reproduction vigoureuse des principaux paysages continentaux et des principales formes sous-marines. La légende ci-dessous indique de quelle façon ils sont cartographiés. Les noms d'éléments topographiques tels que plateaux, bassins, chaînes de montagnes, mers, cours d'eau, lacs, golfes, baies, crêtes, îles et fosses océaniques, prédominent dans ces cartes.

ESTA SEÇÃO PRINCIPIA com os mapas políticos e físicos do Mundo, em escala de 1:75 000 000. Seguem-se os mapas dos oceanos Pacífico, Índico e Atlântico na escala de 1:48 000 000, a maior escala que se pode utilizar para a representação dessas massas de água em toda a sua extensão. Finalmente, uma série de mapas de relevo dos continentes, na escala de 1:24 000 000, proporciona uma visão global da Terra tal como apareceria do espaço a uma distância aproximada de cerca de 6 400 km. A projeção azimutal equiárea foi usada para os mapas da escala de 1:24 000 000, segundo a qual a Terra se apresentaria como um globo de cerca de 50 cm de diâmetro.

As cores utilizadas nos mapas dos continentes representam as massas terrestres tal como apareceriam vistas do espaço durante a estação do crescimento vegetal, sem levar em conta que este fenômeno não se produz simultaneamente em todas as regiões. As características do fundo do mar e as variações de profundidade das águas são representadas por um relevo sombreado e por diferentes matizes de cor. O resultado proporciona uma imagem física eloqüente das principais formas terrestres e submarinas da Terra. As legendas abaixo explicam como foram representados os diversos tipos de terreno e de vegetação. Nestes mapas predomina a nomenclatura dos elementos físicos: planaltos, bacias, cadeias de montanhas, mares, rios, lagos, golfos, baías, fossas, ilhas.

Land Features / Land Phänomene / Elementos de la Tierra
Paysages Continentaux / Acidentes Continentais

Ice and Snow
Eis und Schnee
Hielo y nieve
Glace et neige
Gelo e neve

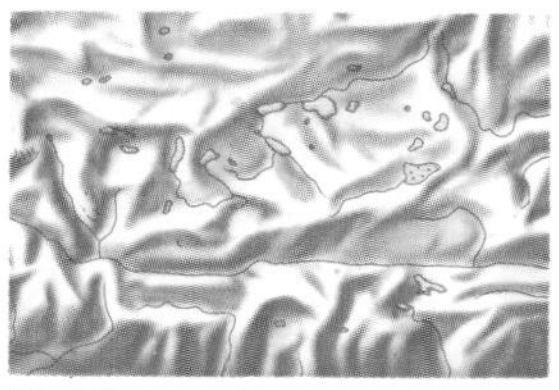

High Barren Area
Hochgebirgswüste
Alta zona árida
Région haute et aride
Alta zona árida

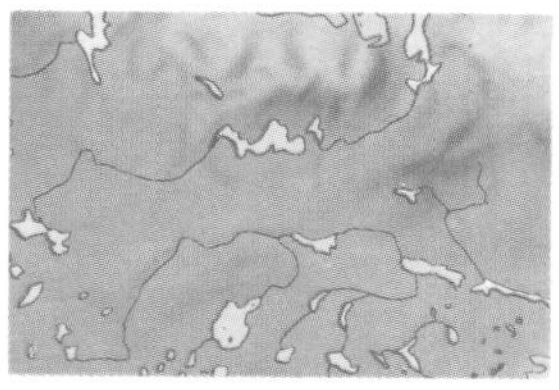

Tundra and Alpine
Tundra und Alpine Vegetation
Tundra y alpina
Toundra et végétation alpine
Tundra e vegetação alpina

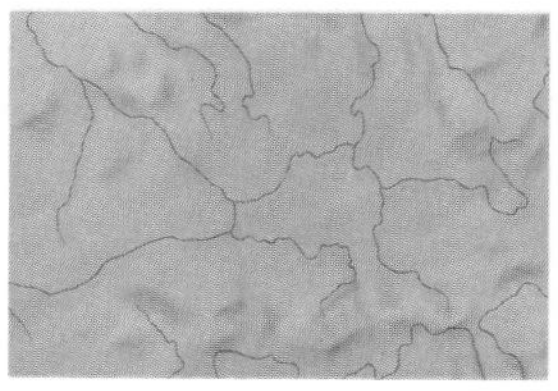

Needleleaf Trees
Nadelwälder
Coníferas
Forêt de conifères
Coníferas

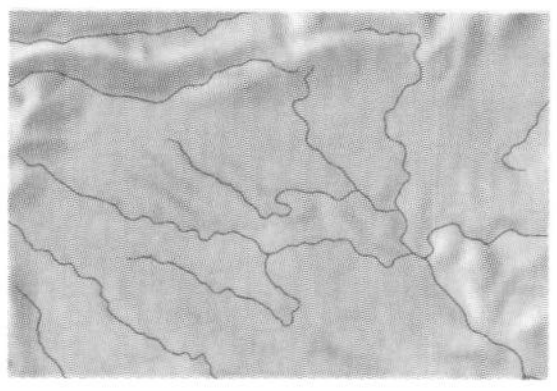

Broadleaf Trees
Laubwälder
Árboles de hojas anchas
Forêt à feuilles caduques
Árvores de folhas caducas

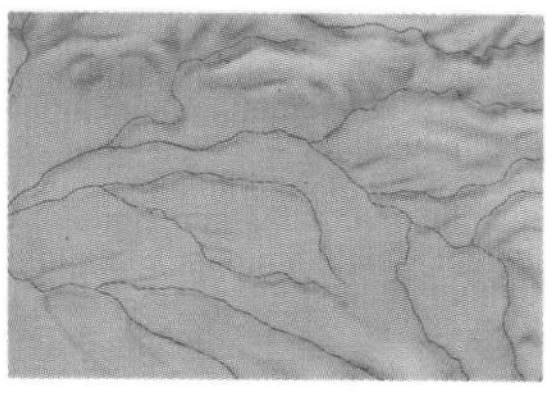

Tropical Rainforest
Tropischer Regenwald
Bosque tropical lluvioso
Forêt tropicale humide
Floresta tropical úmida

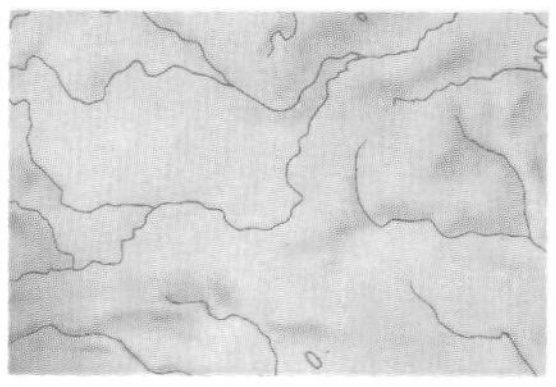

Grassland
Grasland
Pradera
Formations herbacées
Pradaria

Dry Scrub
Trockenes Buschland
Matorral
Brousse sèche
Caatinga

Desert
Wüste
Desierto
Désert
Deserto

Submarine Features / Untermeerische Phänomene
Elementos Submarinos / Formes de Relief Sous-marin / Acidentes do Revelo Submarino

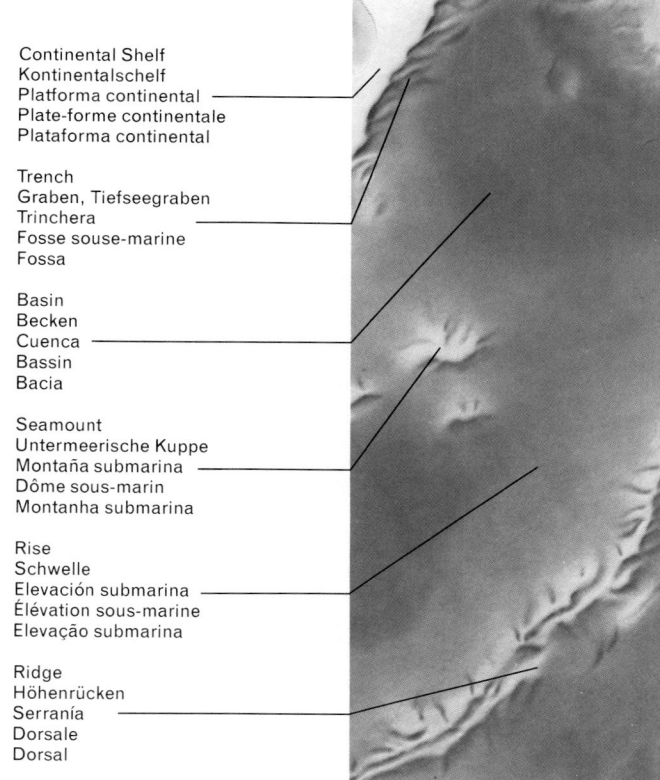

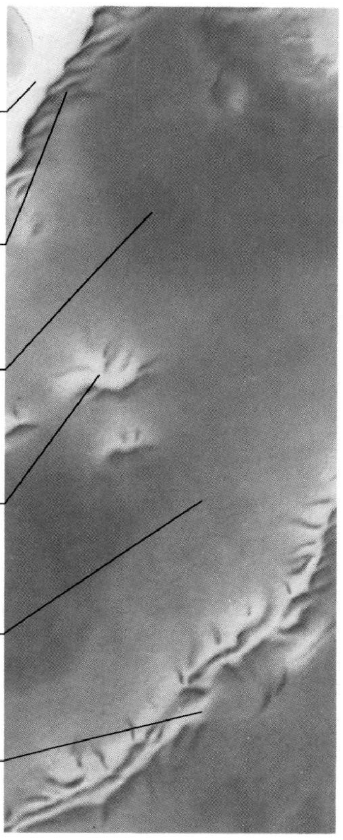
Continental Shelf
Kontinentalschelf
Platforma continental
Plate-forme continentale
Plataforma continental
Trench
Graben, Tiefseegraben
Trinchera
Fosse souse-marine
Fossa
Basin
Becken
Cuenca
Bassin
Bacia
Seamount
Untermeerische Kuppe
Montaña submarina
Dôme sous-marin
Montanha submarina
Rise
Schwelle
Elevación submarina
Élevation sous-marine
Elevação submarina
Ridge
Höhenrücken
Serranía
Dorsale
Dorsal

ARCTIC OCEAN
Beaufort Sea
GREENLAND
(Den.)
Greenland Sea
Thule
Baffin Bay
BAFFIN ISLAND
VICTORIA ISLAND
Godhavn
Godthåb
Angmagssalik
Reykjavík
ICELAND
RUSSIA
UNITED STATES
Arctic Circle
Nome
Fairbanks
Mount McKinley
6194
Anchorage
Inuvik
Yellowknife
Hudson Bay
Churchill
Bering Sea
Gulf of Alaska
Juneau
ROCKY MOUNTAINS
C A N A D A
Edmonton
ALEUTIAN ISLANDS
Calgary
Vancouver
Seattle
Winnipeg
NEWFOUNDLAND
St. John's
Lake Superior
Lake Huron
Quebec
Montréal
Ottawa
Portland
Minneapolis
Toronto
Halifax
NORTH AMERICA
DETROIT
CHICAGO
Boston
NEW YORK
PHILADELPHIA
WASHINGTON
Salt Lake City
Denver
St. Louis
APPALACHIAN MOUNTAINS
SAN FRANCISCO
UNITED STATES
ATLANTIC OCEAN
IRELAND
Glasgow
DUBLIN
Porto
PORTUGAL
LISBOA
GIBRALTAR (U.K.)
RABAT
Casablanca
MOROCCO
P A C I F I C
O C E A N
LOS ANGELES
San Diego
Phoenix
El Paso
Dallas
Atlanta
Houston
New Orleans
AÇORES AZORES (Port.)
ARQUIPÉLAGO DA MADEIRA (Port.)
BERMUDA (U.K.)
ISLAS CANARIAS CANARY ISLANDS (Sp.)
MIDWAY ISLANDS (U.S.)
Tropic of Cancer
Gulf of Mexico
Monterrey
Miami
BAHAMAS
WESTERN SAHARA
MAURITANIA
HAWAIIAN ISLANDS (U.S.)
Honolulu
CABO SAN LUCAS
MEXICO
CIUDAD DE MÉXICO
MEXICO CITY
Guadalajara
LA HABANA
CUBA
DOMINICAN REPUBLIC
HAITI
Port-au-Prince
SANTO DOMINGO
PUERTO RICO (U.S.)
SAN JUAN
JAMAICA
Kingston
Nouakchott
JOHNSTON ATOLL (U.S.)
GUATEMALA
BELIZE
GUATEMALA
HONDURAS
Tegucigalpa
San Salvador
EL SALVADOR
NICARAGUA
Managua
Caribbean Sea
GUADELOUPE (Fr.)
MARTINIQUE (Fr.)
BARBADOS
TRINIDAD AND TOBAGO
Port of Spain
CAPE VERDE
SENEGAL
DAKAR
GAMBIA
Banjul
GUINEA-BISSAU
GUINEA
Conakry
SIERRA LEONE
Freetown
Monrovia
LIBERIA
Bamako
ÎLE CLIPPERTON (Fr)
COSTA RICA
SAN JOSÉ
Panamá
PANAMA
CARACAS
VENEZUELA
GUYANA
Georgetown
Paramaribo
SURINAME
FRENCH GUIANA
Medellín
SANTA FE DE BOGOTÁ
Cali
COLOMBIA
P O L Y N E S I A
Equator
QUITO
ECUADOR
Guayaquil
ARCHIPIÉLAGO DE COLÓN GALAPAGOS ISLANDS (Ec.)
Manaus
Amazon
Belém
Fortaleza
CABO DE SÃO ROQUE
Natal
Recife
KIRIBATI
PHOENIX ISLANDS
Iquitos
TOKELAU (N.Z.)
ÎLES MARQUISES
Trujillo
PERU
B R A Z I L
LIMA
ANDES
SOUTH AMERICA
Salvador
ATLANTIC OCEAN
WALLIS AND FUTUNA (Fr.)
W. SAMOA
AM. SAMOA
Apia
FIJI
ÎLES TUAMOTU
Arequipa
LA PAZ
BOLIVIA
Goiânia
BRASÍLIA
NIUE (N.Z.)
COOK ISLANDS (N.Z.)
FRENCH POLYNESIA
TONGA
Sucre
Belo Horizonte
PARAGUAY
SÃO PAULO
RIO DE JANEIRO
Santos
Tropic of Capricorn
PITCAIRN (U.K.)
Antofagasta
Asunción
Curitiba
ISLA DE PASCUA EASTER ISLAND (Chile)
ISLA SAN AMBROSIO (Chile)
CHILE
International Date Line
Co. Aconcagua
6959
Córdoba
Porto Alegre
Valparaíso
SANTIAGO
Rosario
BUENOS AIRES
URUGUAY
MONTEVIDEO
ARCHIPIÉLAGO JUAN FERNANDEZ (Chile)
P A C I F I C
ARGENTINA
Concepción
Mar del Plata
Bahía Blanca
O C E A N
CHATHAM ISLANDS (N.Z.)
FALKLAND ISLANDS (U.K.)
Punta Arenas
SOUTH GEORGIA (U.K.)
CABO DE HORNOS CAPE HORN
Drake Passage
SOUTH ORKNEY ISLANDS (U.K.)
Antarctic Circle
ANTARCTIC PENINSULA
Bellingshausen Sea
Weddell Sea
Ross Sea
MARIE BYRD LAND
Vinson Massif
4897
ROSS ICE SHELF
A N T A R

ARCTIC OCEAN
Barents Sea
Karskoje more
more Laptevych
NOVOSIBIRSKIJE OSTROVA
ZEML'A FRANCA-IOSIFA
NOVAJA ZEML'A
RUSSIA
E U R O P E
A S I A
KAZAKHSTAN
MONGOLIA
GOBI
C H I N A
ALTAI
TIEN SHAN
HIMALAYAS
Mount Everest 8848
Arctic Circle
Sea of Okhotsk
Bering Sea
Sea of Japan
JAPAN
Black Sea
Caspian Sea
Aral Sea
TURKEY
IRAN
IRAQ
SAUDI ARABIA
PAKISTAN
AFGHANISTAN
INDIA
Arabian Sea
Bay of Bengal
Tropic of Cancer
LIBYA
EGYPT
SUDAN
CHAD
NIGER
ETHIOPIA
ZAIRE
ANGOLA
ZAMBIA
SOUTH AFRICA
MADAGASCAR
A F R I C A
I N D I A N
O C E A N
Equator
Tropic of Capricorn
P A C I F I C
O C E A N
M I C R O N E S I A
M E L A N E S I A
PHILIPPINES
South China Sea
Philippine Sea
I N D O N E S I A
PAPUA NEW GUINEA
A U S T R A L I A
Coral Sea
Tasman Sea
NEW ZEALAND
TASMANIA
S O U T H E R N
O C E A N
Antarctic Circle
ENDERBY LAND
WILKES LAND
A N T A R C T I C A
International Date Line
Copyright © by Rand McNally & Co.
Map prepared by Rand McNally & Co.
A-510000-264
Kilometers
0 1000 2000 3000 Km.
Statute Miles
0 1000 2000 3000 Mi.

One centimeter represents 750 kilometers.
One inch represents approximately 1200 miles.
Robinson Projection
Scale 1:75,000,000

ARCTIC OCEAN
Beaufort Sea
Chukchi Sea
Bering Sea
Gulf of Alaska
Hudson Bay
Baffin Bay
Labrador Sea
GRØNLAND
Greenland Sea
ICELAND
NORTH AMERICA
CANADA
UNITED STATES
MEXICO
ROCKY MOUNTAINS
APPALACHIAN MOUNTAINS
Gulf of Mexico
Caribbean Sea
WEST INDIES
Sargasso Sea
ATLANTIC OCEAN
NORTH AMERICAN BASIN
CAPE VERDE BASIN
GUIANA BASIN
MID-ATLANTIC RIDGE
PACIFIC OCEAN
MENDOCINO FRACTURE ZONE
MURRAY FRACTURE ZONE
CLARION FRACTURE ZONE
CLIPPERTON FRACTURE ZONE
Tropic of Cancer
Equator
Tropic of Capricorn
CENTRAL PACIFIC BASIN
POLYNESIA
HAWAIIAN ISLANDS
SOUTHWEST PACIFIC BASIN
SOUTHEAST PACIFIC BASIN
EAST PACIFIC RISE
CHILE RISE
International Date Line
SOUTH AMERICA
BRAZIL
VENEZUELA
COLOMBIA
BOLIVIA
PARAGUAY
URUGUAY
ARGENTINA
PATAGONIA
ANDES
Amazon
SELVAS
BRAZIL BASIN
ARGENTINE BASIN
FALKLAND PLATEAU
Scotia Sea
Drake Passage
Weddell Sea
Bellingshausen Sea
Amundsen Sea
Ross Sea
ROSS ICE SHELF
MARIE BYRD LAND
Antarctic Circle
ANT

ARCTIC OCEAN
SEVERNAJA ZEML'A
ZEML'A FRANCA-IOSIFA
Barents Sea
Karskoje more
more Laptevych
NOVOSIBIRSKIJE OSTROVA
Vostočno-Sibirskoje more
East Siberian Sea
OSTROV VRANGEL'A
SEVERO-SIBIRSKAJA NIZMENNOST'
SREDNESIBIRSKOJE
PLOSKOGORJE
ZAPADNO-SIBIRSKAJA RAVNINA
SIBIR' SIBERIA
RUSSIA
Arctic Circle
Sea of Okhotsk
Bering Sea
ALEUTIAN BASIN
ALEUTIAN TRENCH
EMPEROR SEAMOUNTS
International Date Line
NORTHWEST PACIFIC BASIN
KAZAKHSTAN
ASIA
MONGOLIA
GOBI
CHINA
Yellow Sea
Sea of Japan
JAPAN
TŌKYŌ
PACIFIC OCEAN
EUROPE
MOSKVA
SANKT-PETERBURG
BERLIN
POLAND
UKRAINE
BELARUS
GERMANY
SWEDEN
FINLAND
NORWAY
ITALY
ROMA
Black Sea
Caspian Sea
TURKEY
İstanbul
Mediterranean Sea
SYRIA
IRAQ
IRAN
TEHRĀN
SAUDI ARABIA
ARABIAN PENINSULA
Red Sea
Persian Gulf
Gulf of Oman
PAKISTAN
INDIA
HIMALAYAS
Mount Everest 8848
K2 8611
CALCUTTA
BOMBAY
Arabian Sea
Bay of Bengal
SRI LANKA
MYANMAR
THAILAND
VIETNAM
South China Sea
PHILIPPINES
Philippine BASIN
MALAYSIA
INDONESIA
BORNEO
JAKARTA
NEW GUINEA
MICRONESIA
MELANESIA
Equator
Tropic of Cancer
Tropic of Capricorn
AFRICA
LIBYA
EGYPT
CHAD
SUDAN
ETHIOPIA
ADIS ABEBA
SOMALIA
NIGERIA
ZAIRE
KINSHASA
TANZANIA
Kilimanjaro
ANGOLA
ZAMBIA
ZIMBABWE
MOZAMBIQUE
NAMIBIA
BOTSWANA
SOUTH AFRICA
CAPE TOWN
Johannesburg
MADAGASCAR
Mozambique Channel
Gulf of Aden
SOMALI BASIN
ARABIAN BASIN
CARLSBERG RIDGE
CHAGOS-LACCADIVE PLATEAU
MID-INDIAN BASIN
MID-INDIAN RIDGE
NINETYEAST RIDGE
WHARTON BASIN
INDIAN OCEAN
MASCARENE ISLANDS
SOUTHWEST INDIAN RIDGE
CROZET BASIN
AGULHAS BASIN
AUSTRALIA
GREAT SANDY DESERT
GIBSON DESERT
GREAT VICTORIA DESERT
GREAT DIVIDING RANGE
Perth
Sydney
Great Australian Bight
SOUTH AUSTRALIAN BASIN
TASMANIA
Tasman Sea
TASMAN BASIN
Coral Sea
Arafura Sea
Timor Sea
NEW ZEALAND
NORTH ISLAND
SOUTH ISLAND
SOUTHEAST INDIAN RIDGE
SOUTHERN OCEAN
SOUTH INDIAN BASIN
ATLANTIC-INDIAN RIDGE
ATLANTIC-INDIAN BASIN
KERGUELEN PLATEAU
Antarctic Circle
ENDERBY LAND
MAC. ROBERTSON LAND
AMERICAN HIGHLAND
WILKES LAND
VICTORIA LAND
Ross Sea
ROSS ICE SHELF
Mount Kirkpatrick 4528
Mount Markham 4282
Mount McClintock 3492
MAUD LAND
ANTARCTICA
Copyright © by Rand McNally & Co.
Map prepared by Rand McNally & Co.
A-510000-764

Kilometers 0 1000 2000 3000 Km.

Statute Miles 0 1000 2000 3000 Mi.

One centimeter represents 750 kilometers.
One inch represents approximately 1200 miles.
Robinson Projection
Scale 1:75,000,000

GREENLAND
ICELAND
Arctic Circle
Norwegian Sea
Barents Sea
NOVAJA ZEML'A
SWEDEN
FINLAND
NORWAY
UNITED KINGDOM
IRELAND
FRANCE
GERMANY
POLAND
UKRAINE
KAZAKHSTAN
RUSSIA
URAL'SKIJE GORY
URAL MOUNTAINS
ZAPADNO-SIBIRSKAJA RAVNINA
SREDNESIBIRSKOJE PLOSKOGORJE
SIBERIA
Sea of Okhotsk
MONGOLIA
GOBI
CHINA
ASIA
TIEN SHAN
ALTAI
KUNLUN SHAN
QING ZANG GAOYUAN
HIMALAYAS
Mount Everest
INDIA
PAKISTAN
AFGHANISTAN
IRAN
IRAQ
TURKEY
SAUDI ARABIA
ARABIAN PENINSULA
Black Sea
Caspian Sea
Aral Sea
MEDITERRANEAN SEA
Red Sea
Gulf of Aden
ARABIAN SEA
Bay of Bengal
SAHARA
Tropic of Cancer
EGYPT
LIBYA
SUDAN
ETHIOPIA
SOMALIA
KENYA
TANZANIA
AFRICA
Equator
ZAMBIA
BOTSWANA
NAMIBIA
SOUTH AFRICA
MADAGASCAR
Mozambique Channel
Tropic of Capricorn
JAPAN
Sea of Japan
Yellow Sea
East China Sea
South China Sea
PHILIPPINES
Philippine Sea
INDOCHINA
THAILAND
MALAYSIA
INDONESIA
GREATER SUNDA ISLANDS
Java Sea
Timor Sea
Arafura Sea
Gulf of Carpentaria
PAPUA NEW GUINEA
GREAT SANDY DESERT
GIBSON DESERT
GREAT VICTORIA DESERT
AUSTRALIA
GREAT DIVIDING RANGE
Great Australian Bight
INDIAN OCEAN
MID-INDIAN RIDGE
MID-INDIAN BASIN
NINETY EAST RIDGE
CHAGOS-LACCADIVE PLATEAU
CARLSBERG RIDGE
SOMALI BASIN
ARABIAN BASIN
MASCARENE BASIN
MASCARENE PLATEAU
WHARTON BASIN
NORTH AUSTRALIAN BASIN
PERTH BASIN
BROKEN RIDGE
SOUTHWEST INDIAN RIDGE
MADAGASCAR BASIN
MADAGASCAR PLATEAU
MOZAMBIQUE PLATEAU
CROZET BASIN
AGULHAS BASIN
ATLANTIC-INDIAN RIDGE
ATLANTIC-INDIAN BASIN
KERGUELEN PLATEAU
SOUTHEAST INDIAN RIDGE
SOUTH INDIAN BASIN
SOUTH AUSTRALIAN BASIN
SOUTHERN OCEAN
Antarctic Circle
ENDERBY LAND
AMERY ICE SHELF
AMERICAN HIGHLAND
WILKES LAND
ANTARCTICA

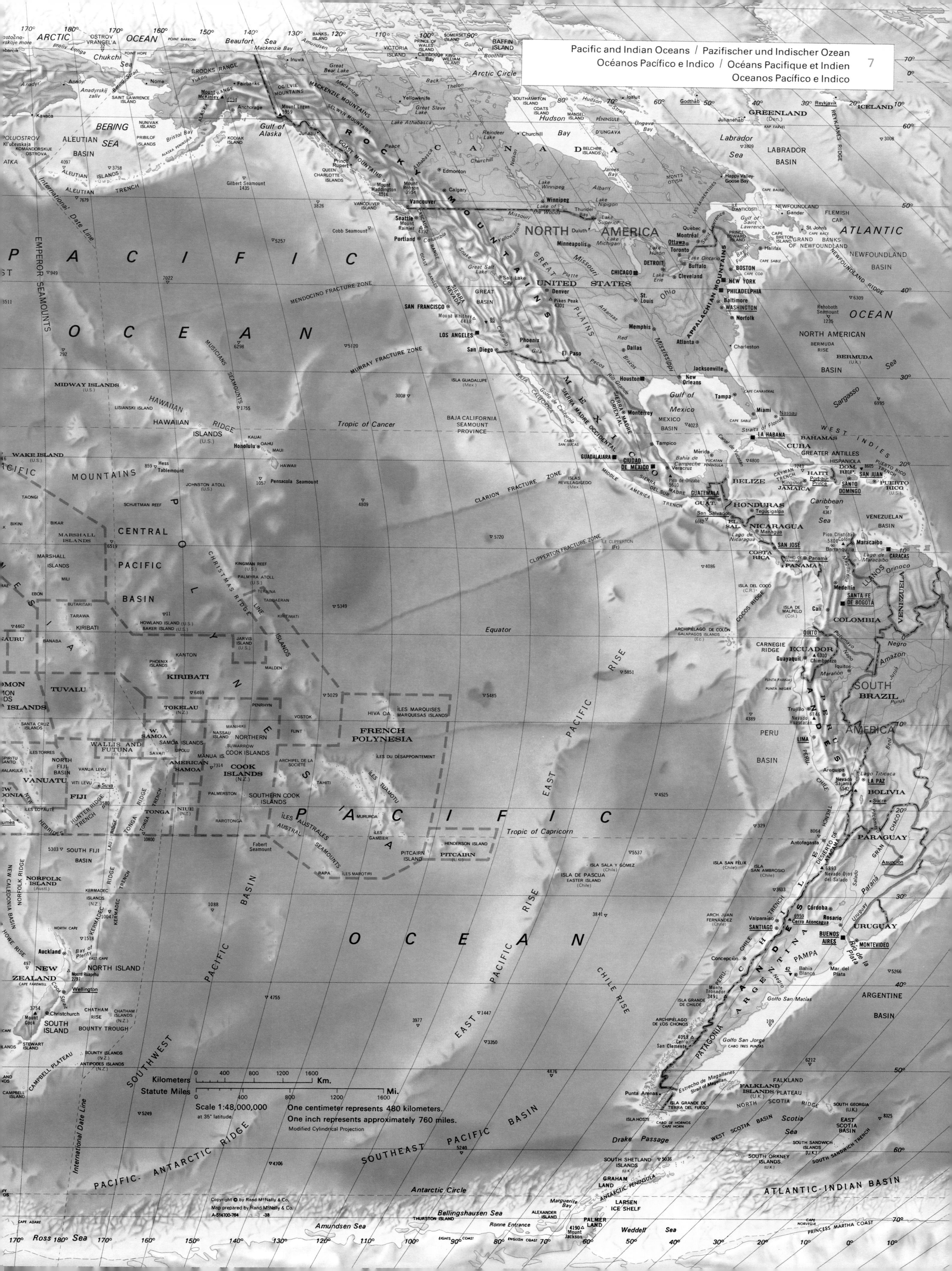
ARCTIC OCEAN
Beaufort Sea
Chukchi Sea
BERING SEA
ALEUTIAN BASIN
Gulf of Alaska
ROCKY MOUNTAINS
CANADA
Hudson Bay
Labrador Sea
GREENLAND (Den.)
ICELAND
NORTH AMERICA
UNITED STATES
Great Basin
Gulf of Mexico
MEXICO
PACIFIC OCEAN
EMPEROR SEAMOUNTS
HAWAIIAN ISLANDS (U.S.)
Honolulu
MIDWAY ISLANDS (U.S.)
WAKE ISLAND (U.S.)
MENDOCINO FRACTURE ZONE
MURRAY FRACTURE ZONE
CLARION FRACTURE ZONE
CLIPPERTON FRACTURE ZONE
Tropic of Cancer
Equator
Tropic of Capricorn
CENTRAL PACIFIC BASIN
KIRIBATI
TUVALU
TOKELAU (N.Z.)
W. SAMOA
AMERICAN SAMOA
WALLIS AND FUTUNA
FIJI
VANUATU
TONGA
NIUE (N.Z.)
COOK ISLANDS (N.Z.)
FRENCH POLYNESIA
PITCAIRN
POLYNESIA
NEW ZEALAND
NORTH ISLAND
SOUTH ISLAND
Wellington
Auckland
EAST PACIFIC RISE
CHILE RISE
SOUTHWEST PACIFIC BASIN
SOUTHEAST PACIFIC BASIN
PACIFIC ANTARCTIC RIDGE
International Date Line
ATLANTIC OCEAN
NORTH AMERICAN BASIN
BERMUDA (U.K.)
Sargasso Sea
CUBA
LA HABANA
BAHAMAS
WEST INDIES
JAMAICA
HAITI
DOM. REP.
PUERTO RICO
Caribbean Sea
BELIZE
GUATEMALA
HONDURAS
EL SAL.
NICARAGUA
COSTA RICA
PANAMA
VENEZUELA
COLOMBIA
ECUADOR
PERU
BOLIVIA
PARAGUAY
CHILE
ARGENTINA
URUGUAY
BRAZIL
SOUTH AMERICA
ANDES
PERU BASIN
ARGENTINE BASIN
PATAGONIA
Drake Passage
Scotia Sea
FALKLAND ISLANDS (U.K.)
SOUTH GEORGIA (U.K.)
SOUTH SHETLAND ISLANDS (U.K.)
SOUTH ORKNEY ISLANDS (U.K.)
SOUTH SANDWICH ISLANDS (U.K.)
ATLANTIC-INDIAN BASIN
Antarctic Circle
Amundsen Sea
Bellingshausen Sea
Weddell Sea
Ross Sea
Kilometers 0 400 800 1200 1600 Km.
Statute Miles 0 400 800 1200 1600 Mi.
Scale 1:48,000,000
at 35° latitude
One centimeter represents 480 kilometers.
One inch represents approximately 760 miles.
Modified Cylindrical Projection
Copyright © by Rand McNally & Co.
Map prepared by Rand McNally & Co.
A-614700-764 -38

8 Atlantic Ocean / Atlantischer Ozean
Océano Atlántico / Océan Atlantique
Oceano Atlântico

GREENLAND
(Den.)
Baffin Bay
Davis Strait
Arctic Circle
Greenland Sea
Norwegian Sea
Barents Sea
ICELAND
FAEROE IS.
NORWEGIAN BASIN
NORTH CANADA
AMERICA
Hudson Bay
Labrador Sea
LABRADOR BASIN
SWEDEN
FINLAND
NORWAY
North Sea
DENMARK
UNITED KINGDOM
IRELAND
NETH.
GERMANY
POLAND
BELARUS
UKRAINE
RUSSIA
EUROPE
FRANCE
SPAIN
PORTUGAL
ITALY
ROMANIA
GREECE
TURKEY
Black Sea
Caspian Sea
Mediterranean Sea
URAL MOUNTAINS
CAUCASUS
ASIA MINOR
SYRIA
IRAQ
LEBANON
ISRAEL
JORDAN
SAUDI ARABIA
EGYPT
LIBYA
ALGERIA
MOROCCO
TUNISIA
ATLAS MOUNTAINS
WESTERN SAHARA
MAURITANIA
SAHARA
MALI
NIGER
CHAD
SUDAN
ETHIOPIA
SENEGAL
GAMBIA
GUINEA-BISSAU
GUINEA
SIERRA LEONE
LIBERIA
COTE D'IV.
GHANA
BURKINA FASO
NIGERIA
CAMEROON
CENTRAL AFRICAN REPUBLIC
AFRICA
GABON
CONGO
ZAIRE
UGANDA
KENYA
RWANDA
BURUNDI
TANZANIA
ANGOLA
ZAMBIA
MALAWI
ZIMBABWE
MOZAMBIQUE
NAMIBIA
BOTSWANA
SOUTH AFRICA
LESOTHO
SWAZILAND
Gulf of Guinea
UNITED STATES
APPALACHIAN MOUNTAINS
Gulf of Mexico
MEXICO
CUBA
BAHAMAS
HAITI
DOM. REP.
JAMAICA
PUERTO RICO
Caribbean Sea
GUATEMALA
BELIZE
HONDURAS
NICARAGUA
COSTA RICA
PANAMA
VENEZUELA
COLOMBIA
GUYANA
SURINAME
FRENCH GUIANA
TRINIDAD AND TOBAGO
ECUADOR
PERU
BRAZIL
BOLIVIA
PARAGUAY
CHILE
ARGENTINA
URUGUAY
SOUTH AMERICA
ANDES
PATAGONIA
FALKLAND ISLANDS
(U.K.)
ATLANTIC OCEAN
NORTH AMERICAN BASIN
WEST EUROPEAN BASIN
Sargasso Sea
AZORES
MID-ATLANTIC RIDGE
CAPE VERDE
CAPE VERDE BASIN
GUIANA BASIN
SIERRA LEONE BASIN
Equator
GUINEA BASIN
BRAZIL BASIN
ANGOLA BASIN
ASCENSION
SAINT HELENA
Tropic of Cancer
Tropic of Capricorn
ARGENTINE BASIN
CAPE BASIN
AGULHAS BASIN
TRISTAN DA CUNHA GROUP
GOUGH ISLAND
BROMLEY PLATEAU
PACIFIC OCEAN
INDIAN OCEAN
SOUTHEAST PACIFIC BASIN
CHILE RISE
Drake Passage
Scotia Sea
SOUTH GEORGIA
SOUTH SANDWICH ISLANDS
SOUTH SHETLAND ISLANDS
SOUTH ORKNEY ISLANDS
Weddell Sea
Bellingshausen Sea
Amundsen Sea
ANTARCTICA
Antarctic Circle
ATLANTIC INDIAN RIDGE
Kilometers 0 400 800 1200 1600 Km.
Statute Miles 0 400 800 1200 1600 Mi.
Scale 1:48,000,000
at 35° latitude.
One centimeter represents 480 kilometers.
One inch represents approximately 760 miles.
Modified Cylindrical Projection
Copyright © by Rand McNally & Co.
Map prepared by Rand McNally & Co.
A-513700-764

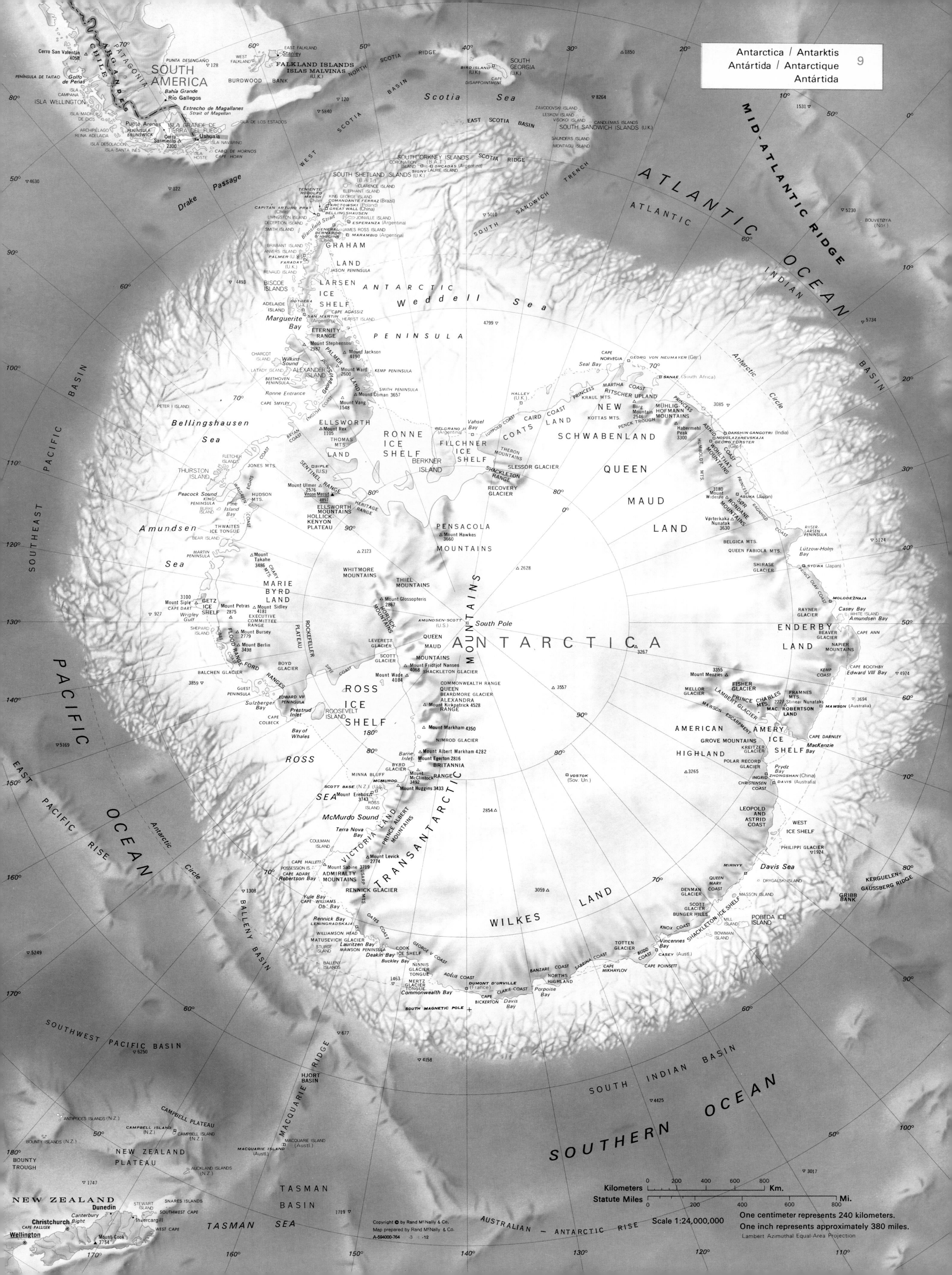
SOUTH AMERICA
PATAGONIA
CHILE
ARGENTINA
ANDES
Cerro San Valentín 4058
PENÍNSULA DE TAITAO
Golfo de Penas
ISLA WELLINGTON
Bahía Grande
Río Gallegos
Estrecho de Magallanes
Strait of Magellan
Punta Arenas
ISLA GRANDE DE TIERRA DEL FUEGO
Ushuaia
Cerro Sarmiento 2300
ISLA DE LOS ESTADOS
ISLA NAVARINO
CABO DE HORNOS
CAPE HORN
PUNTA DESENGAÑO
FALKLAND ISLANDS
ISLAS MALVINAS
(U.K.)
Stanley
BURDWOOD BANK
NORTH SCOTIA RIDGE
SOUTH GEORGIA (U.K.)
Scotia Sea
SCOTIA BASIN
EAST SCOTIA BASIN
WEST SCOTIA BASIN
SOUTH SANDWICH ISLANDS (U.K.)
SOUTH SANDWICH TRENCH
SOUTH ORKNEY ISLANDS
SOUTH SHETLAND ISLANDS (U.K.)
SOUTH SCOTIA RIDGE
Drake Passage
ATLANTIC OCEAN
MID-ATLANTIC RIDGE
ATLANTIC-INDIAN BASIN
BOUVETØYA (Nor.)
Antarctic Circle
GRAHAM LAND
LARSEN ICE SHELF
ANTARCTIC PENINSULA
Weddell Sea
Marguerite Bay
ALEXANDER ISLAND
PALMER LAND
ELLSWORTH LAND
Bellingshausen Sea
PETER I ISLAND
RONNE ICE SHELF
FILCHNER ICE SHELF
BERKNER ISLAND
COATS LAND
NEW SCHWABENLAND
QUEEN MAUD LAND
THURSTON ISLAND
Amundsen Sea
MARIE BYRD LAND
Vinson Massif 4897
ELLSWORTH MOUNTAINS
PENSACOLA MOUNTAINS
Mount Hawkes 3660
THIEL MOUNTAINS
WHITMORE MOUNTAINS
HORLICK MOUNTAINS
South Pole
AMUNDSEN-SCOTT (U.S.)
ANTARCTICA
QUEEN MAUD MOUNTAINS
TRANSANTARCTIC MOUNTAINS
ROCKEFELLER PLATEAU
ROSS ICE SHELF
ROOSEVELT ISLAND
Bay of Whales
ROSS SEA
McMurdo Sound
Mount Erebus 3743
VICTORIA LAND
PRINCE ALBERT MOUNTAINS
ADMIRALTY MOUNTAINS
Mount Markham 4350
Mount Kirkpatrick 4528
ENDERBY LAND
AMERY ICE SHELF
AMERICAN HIGHLAND
PRINCE CHARLES MTS.
LAMBERT GLACIER
MAC. ROBERTSON LAND
VOSTOK (Sov. Un.)
LEOPOLD AND ASTRID COAST
WEST ICE SHELF
Davis Sea
QUEEN MARY COAST
SHACKLETON ICE SHELF
WILKES LAND
KNOX COAST
BUDD COAST
SABRINA COAST
BANZARE COAST
CLARIE COAST
ADÉLIE COAST
GEORGE V COAST
OATES COAST
SOUTH MAGNETIC POLE
DUMONT D'URVILLE (France)
Commonwealth Bay
Porpoise Bay
Vincennes Bay
KERGUELEN-GAUSSBERG RIDGE
GRIBB BANK
PACIFIC OCEAN
SOUTHEAST PACIFIC BASIN
EAST PACIFIC RISE
BALLENY BASIN
BALLENY ISLANDS
SOUTHWEST PACIFIC BASIN
MACQUARIE RIDGE
HJORT BASIN
MACQUARIE ISLAND (Austl.)
CAMPBELL PLATEAU
CAMPBELL ISLAND (N.Z.)
ANTIPODES ISLANDS (N.Z.)
BOUNTY ISLANDS (N.Z.)
BOUNTY TROUGH
NEW ZEALAND PLATEAU
NEW ZEALAND
Dunedin
Christchurch
Wellington
Invercargill
Mount Cook 3754
TASMAN BASIN
TASMAN SEA
AUSTRALIAN - ANTARCTIC RISE
SOUTH INDIAN BASIN
SOUTHERN OCEAN
Kilometers 0 200 400 600 800 Km.
Statute Miles 0 200 400 600 800 Mi.
Scale 1:24,000,000
One centimeter represents 240 kilometers.
One inch represents approximately 380 miles.
Lambert Azimuthal Equal-Area Projection
Copyright © by Rand McNally & Co.
Map prepared by Rand McNally & Co.
A-594000-764 -3 -3 -12

ATLANTIC
OCEAN
MID-ATLANTIC RIDGE
WEST EUROPEAN BASIN
NORWEGIAN BASIN
LOFOTEN BASIN
GREENLAND BASIN
Greenland Sea
Norwegian Sea
Barents Sea
North Sea
Baltic Sea
Black Sea
Caspian Sea
Mediterranean Sea
Adriatic Sea
Tyrrhenian Sea
Ionian Sea
Aegean Sea
Bay of Biscay
Labrador Sea
LABRADOR BASIN
IRMINGER BASIN
ICELAND BASIN
ROCKALL RISE
REYKJANES RIDGE
CANARY BASIN
AZORES-GIBRALTAR RIDGE
CANADA
GREENLAND
ICELAND
NORWAY
SWEDEN
FINLAND
RUSSIA
UKRAINE
BELARUS
POLAND
GERMANY
FRANCE
SPAIN
PORTUGAL
ITALY
UNITED KINGDOM
IRELAND
DENMARK
ROMANIA
HUNGARY
BULGARIA
GREECE
TURKEY
SYRIA
IRAQ
IRAN
SAUDI ARABIA
EGYPT
LIBYA
ALGERIA
TUNISIA
MOROCCO
MAURITANIA
WESTERN SAHARA
KAZAKHSTAN
UZBEKISTAN
TURKMENISTAN
ASIA
EUROPE
URAL'SKIJE GORY
URAL MOUNTAINS
ZAPADNO-SIBIRSKAJA RAVNINA
CAUCASUS
ASIA MINOR
MESOPOTAMIA
ARABIAN PENINSULA
SAHARA
ATLAS MOUNTAINS
ALPS
CARPATHIAN MOUNTAINS
PYRENEES
APPENNINO
MOSKVA
SANKT-PETERBURG
KYYIV
MINSK
WARSZAWA
BERLIN
PRAHA
WIEN
BUDAPEST
BUCURESTI
SOFIJA
BEOGRAD
ATHINAI
ROMA
PARIS
LONDON
DUBLIN
AMSTERDAM
BRUXELLES
KØBENHAVN
OSLO
STOCKHOLM
HELSINKI
TALLINN
RIGA
MADRID
LISBOA
BARCELONA
ISTANBUL
ANKARA
TEHRĀN
BAGHDĀD
DIMASHQ
BAYRŪT
'AMMĀN
AL-QĀHIRAH
AR-RIYĀD
TARĀBULUS
TUNIS
EL DJAZAÏR
RABAT
CASABLANCA
Arctic Circle
Tropic of Cancer

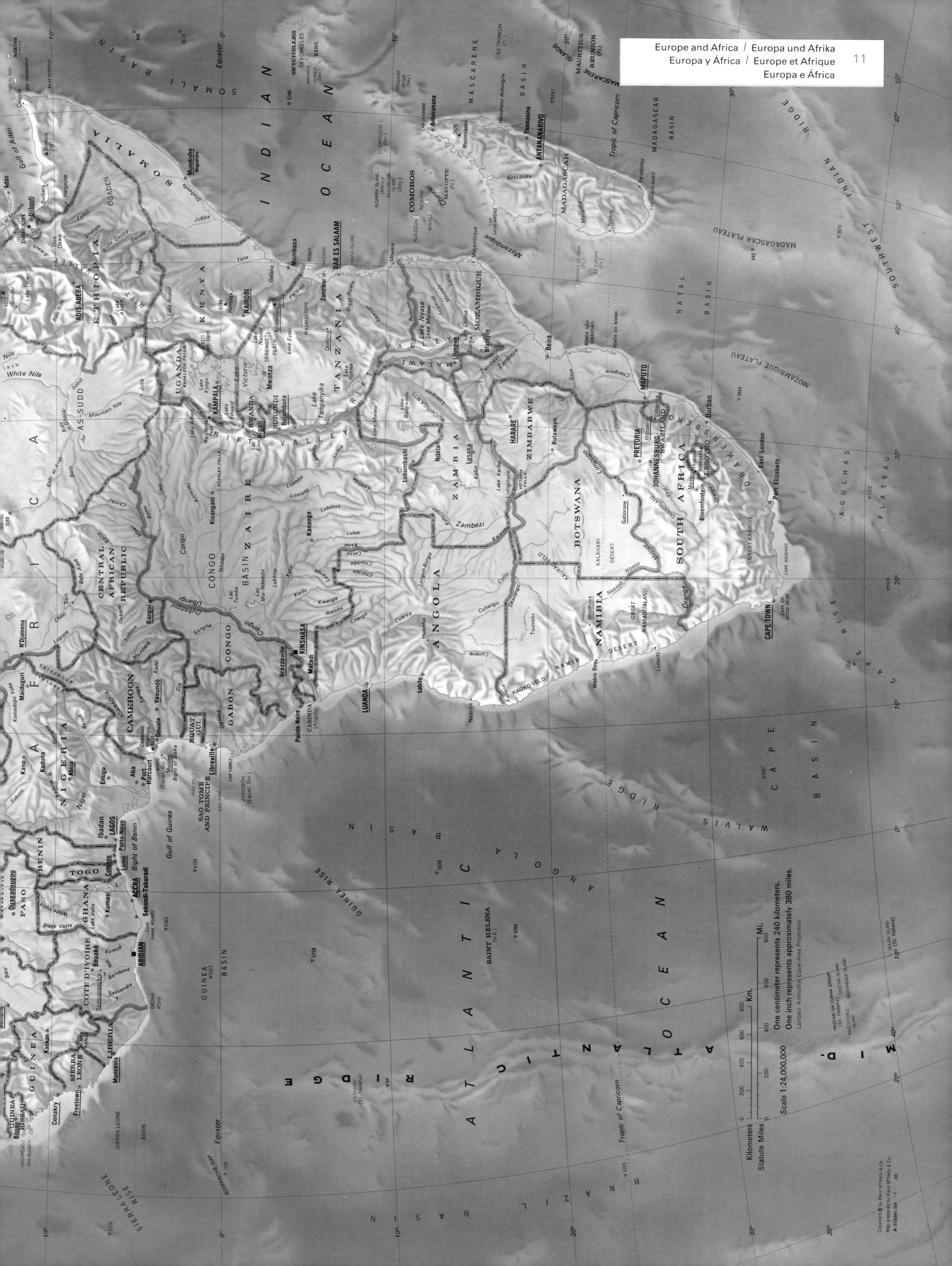
INDIAN OCEAN
ATLANTIC OCEAN
SOMALIA
ETHIOPIA
KENYA
TANZANIA
UGANDA
RWANDA
BURUNDI
ZAIRE
CONGO
GABON
CAMEROON
CENTRAL AFRICAN REPUBLIC
NIGERIA
BENIN
TOGO
GHANA
COTE D'IVOIRE
LIBERIA
SIERRA LEONE
GUINEA
ANGOLA
ZAMBIA
MALAWI
MOZAMBIQUE
ZIMBABWE
BOTSWANA
NAMIBIA
SOUTH AFRICA
LESOTHO
SWAZILAND
MADAGASCAR
COMOROS
SAO TOME AND PRINCIPE
SAINT HELENA (U.K.)
Equator
Tropic of Capricorn
Gulf of Guinea
Bight of Benin
Bight of Biafra
Gulf of Aden
Scale 1:24,000,000
One centimeter represents 240 kilometers.
One inch represents approximately 380 miles.
Lambert Azimuthal Equal-Area Projection
Kilometers
Statute Miles

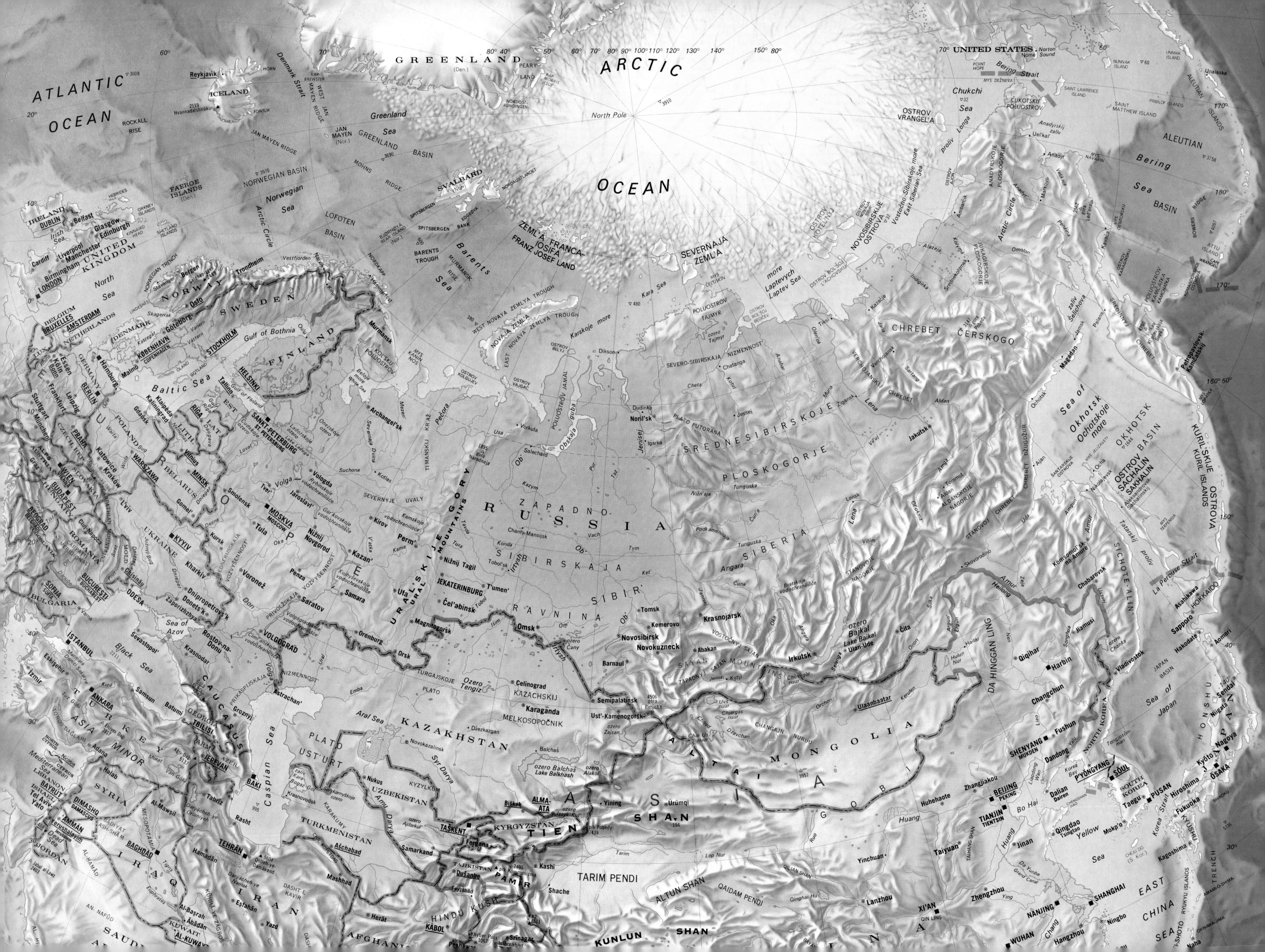

ARCTIC
OCEAN
North Pole
ATLANTIC
OCEAN
GREENLAND
Greenland
Sea
Norwegian
Sea
Barents
Sea
Kara Sea
Laptev Sea
East Siberian Sea
Bering
Sea
Sea of
Okhotsk
UNITED STATES
ICELAND
UNITED
KINGDOM
NORWAY
SWEDEN
FINLAND
RUSSIA
ZAPADNO-
SIBIRSKAJA
RAVNINA
SIBERIA
SREDNESIBIRSKOJE
PLOSKOGORJE
CHREBET ČERSKOGO
URAL'SKIJE GORY
URAL MOUNTAINS
KAZAKHSTAN
MONGOLIA
GOBI
ASIA
TIEN SHAN
KUNLUN SHAN
TARIM PENDI
Caspian
Sea
Black
Sea
Aral Sea
TURKEY
IRAN
IRAQ
SYRIA
CAUCASUS
UKRAINE
BELARUS
POLAND
GERMANY
UZBEKISTAN
TURKMENISTAN
KYRGYZSTAN
TAJIKISTAN
PAMIR
HINDU KUSH
NORTH KOREA
SOUTH KOREA
JAPAN
Sea of
Japan
Yellow
Sea
EAST
CHINA
SEA
KURIL'SKIJE OSTROVA
KURIL ISLANDS
ALEUTIAN
BASIN
Arctic Circle
MOSKVA
SANKT-PETERBURG
LONDON
HELSINKI
STOCKHOLM
Oslo
BERLIN
WARSZAWA
KYYIV
MINSK
Irkutsk
Novosibirsk
Omsk
Jakutsk
Magadan
Vladivostok
Ulaanbaatar
BEIJING
SHANGHAI
PYONGYANG
SOUL
TEHRAN
BAGHDAD
ISTANBUL
ANKARA

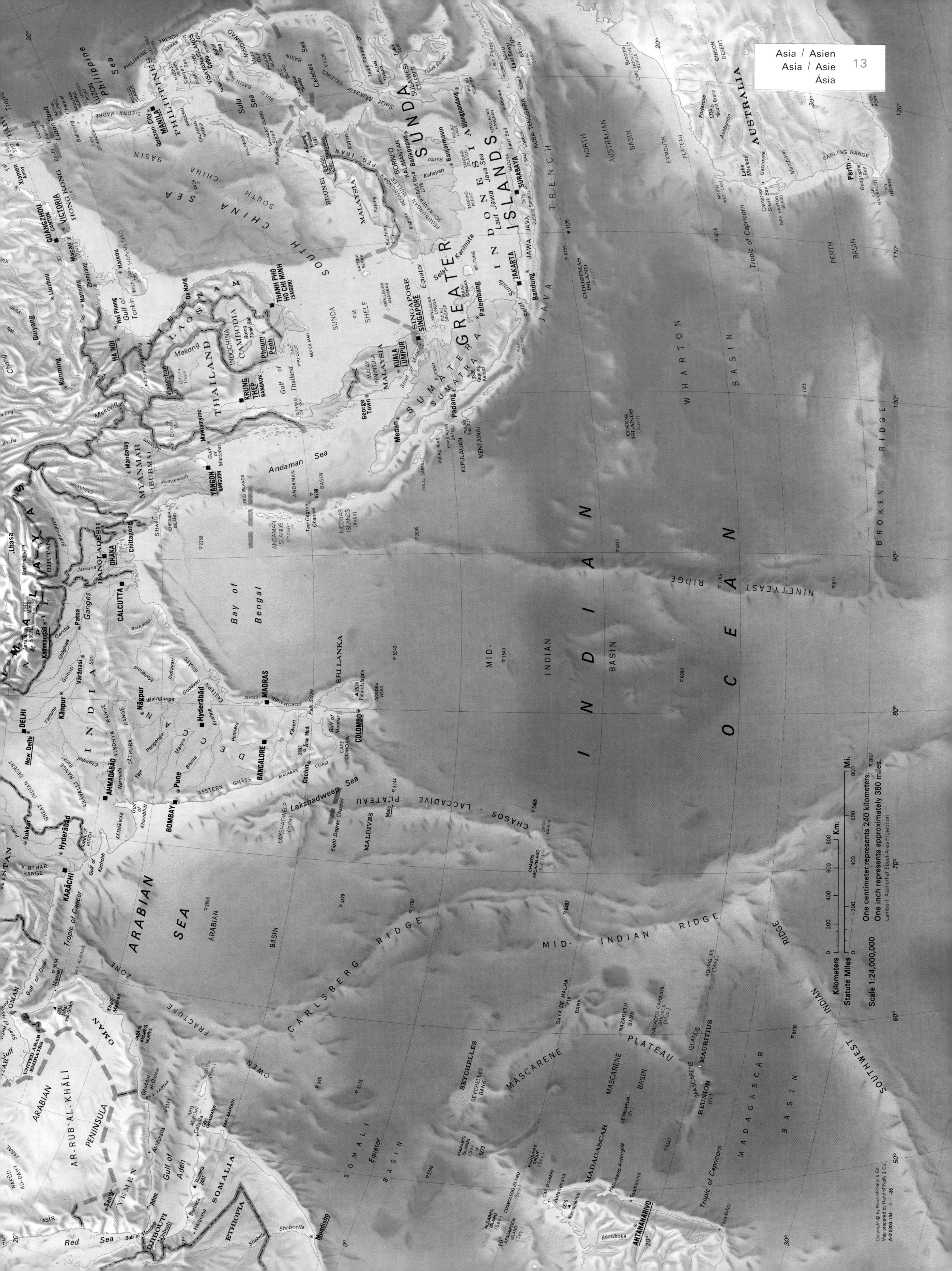
INDIAN OCEAN
ARABIAN SEA
Bay of Bengal
Andaman Sea
SOUTH CHINA SEA
Philippine Sea
Sulu Sea
Celebes Sea
Java Sea
Gulf of Aden
Gulf of Oman
Gulf of Thailand
Lakshadweep Sea
Red Sea
INDIA
SRI LANKA
BANGLADESH
BHUTAN
NEPAL
MYANMAR (BURMA)
THAILAND
LAOS
VIETNAM
CAMBODIA
MALAYSIA
PHILIPPINES
BRUNEI
SINGAPORE
INDONESIA
AUSTRALIA
OMAN
YEMEN
SOMALIA
ETHIOPIA
DJIBOUTI
MADAGASCAR
SEYCHELLES
MALDIVES
MAURITIUS
GREATER SUNDA ISLANDS
BORNEO
SUMATRA
JAVA
ARABIAN PENINSULA
NEW DELHI
DELHI
CALCUTTA
MADRAS
BOMBAY
COLOMBO
DHAKA
YANGON
KRUNG THEP
KUALA LUMPUR
JAKARTA
MANILA
HONG KONG
ANTANANARIVO
MID-INDIAN BASIN
MID-INDIAN RIDGE
CARLSBERG RIDGE
NINETYEAST RIDGE
BROKEN RIDGE
WHARTON BASIN
MASCARENE PLATEAU
MASCARENE BASIN
MADAGASCAR BASIN
SOMALI BASIN
ARABIAN BASIN
JAVA TRENCH
SOUTHWEST INDIAN RIDGE
LACCADIVE CHAGOS PLATEAU
OWEN FRACTURE ZONE
NORTH AUSTRALIAN BASIN
PERTH BASIN
Tropic of Capricorn
Tropic of Cancer
Equator
Kilometers 0 200 400 600 800 Km.
Statute Miles 0 200 400 600 800 Mi.
Scale 1:24,000,000
One centimeter represents 240 kilometers.
One inch represents approximately 380 miles.
Lambert Azimuthal Equal-Area Projection
Copyright © by Rand McNally & Co.

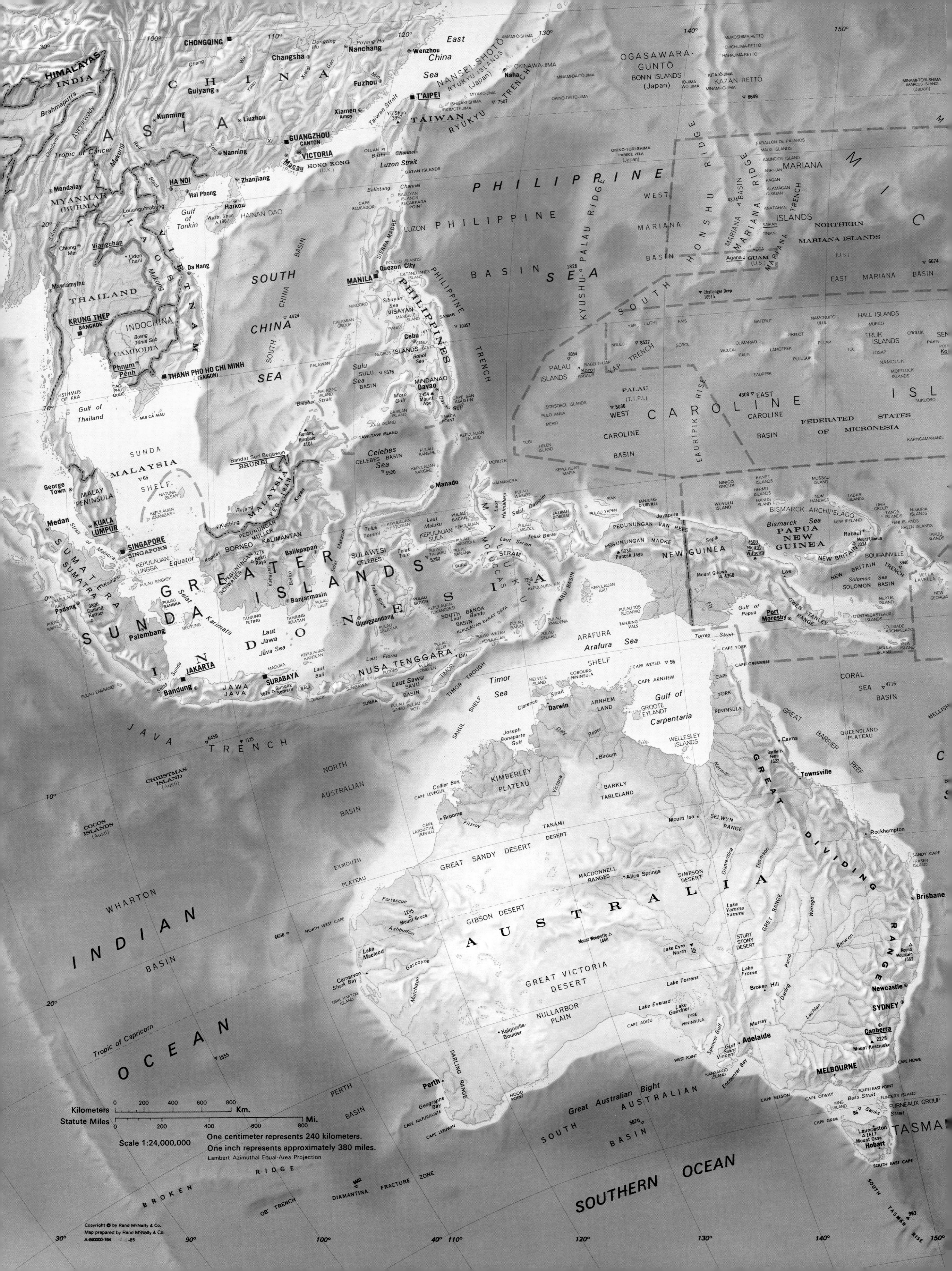
ASIA
CHINA
HIMALAYAS
INDIA
CHONGQING
Changsha
Nanchang
Wenzhou
East China Sea
Guiyang
Fuzhou
Kunming
Liuzhou
Xiamen
T'AIPEI
TAIWAN
GUANGZHOU
CANTON
VICTORIA
HONG KONG (U.K.)
Macau (Port.)
Nanning
Tropic of Cancer
HA NOI
Hai Phong
Zhanjiang
Haikou
HAINAN DAO
Gulf of Tonkin
Mandalay
MYANMAR (BURMA)
LAOS
VIETNAM
Viangchan
Da Nang
THAILAND
KRUNG THEP
BANGKOK
INDOCHINA
CAMBODIA
Phnum Pénh
THANH PHO HO CHI MINH (SAIGON)
Gulf of Thailand
NANSEI-SHOTO
RYUKYU ISLANDS (Japan)
Naha
RYUKYU TRENCH
Luzon Strait
Balintang Channel
LUZON
PHILIPPINE SEA
PHILIPPINE BASIN
MANILA
Quezon City
PHILIPPINES
PHILIPPINE TRENCH
SOUTH CHINA SEA
SOUTH CHINA BASIN
Sulu Sea
SULU BASIN
Cebu
MINDANAO
Davao
OGASAWARA-GUNTO
BONIN ISLANDS (Japan)
KAZAN-RETTO
WEST MARIANA BASIN
KYUSHU-PALAU RIDGE
HONSHU RIDGE
MARIANA RIDGE
MARIANA TRENCH
MARIANA ISLANDS
NORTHERN MARIANA ISLANDS (U.S.)
GUAM (U.S.)
Agana
EAST MARIANA BASIN
Challenger Deep 10915
YAP TRENCH
PALAU ISLANDS
PALAU (T.T.P.I.)
WEST CAROLINE BASIN
CAROLINE ISLANDS
EAST CAROLINE BASIN
EAURIPIK RISE
FEDERATED STATES OF MICRONESIA
HALL ISLANDS
TRUK ISLANDS
SUNDA SHELF
MALAYSIA
BRUNEI
Bandar Seri Begawan
Celebes Sea
CELEBES BASIN
George Town
MALAY PENINSULA
Medan
KUALA LUMPUR
SINGAPORE
Kuching
BORNEO
KALIMANTAN
Balikpapan
SULAWESI
CELEBES
Manado
Equator
GREATER SUNDA ISLANDS
SUMATERA
SUMATRA
Padang
Palembang
Banjarmasin
Ujungpandang
INDONESIA
Laut Jawa
Java Sea
JAKARTA
Bandung
JAWA
JAVA
SURABAYA
Laut Banda
Banda Sea
BANDA BASIN
MOLUCCAS
MALUKU
SERAM
Laut Flores
NUSA TENGGARA
Dili
TIMOR
Laut Sawu
SAVU BASIN
TIMOR TROUGH
Timor Sea
SAHUL SHELF
ARU BASIN
Arafura Sea
ARAFURA SHELF
Torres Strait
NEW GUINEA
Jayapura
PEGUNUNGAN MAOKE
Puncak Jaya
PAPUA NEW GUINEA
Mount Wilhelm
Gulf of Papua
Port Moresby
OWEN STANLEY RANGE
BISMARCK ARCHIPELAGO
Bismarck Sea
Rabaul
NEW BRITAIN
NEW BRITAIN TRENCH
BOUGAINVILLE
Solomon Sea
SOLOMON BASIN
CORAL SEA BASIN
QUEENSLAND PLATEAU
GREAT BARRIER REEF
JAVA TRENCH
CHRISTMAS ISLAND (Austl.)
COCOS ISLANDS (Austl.)
NORTH AUSTRALIAN BASIN
EXMOUTH PLATEAU
WHARTON BASIN
INDIAN OCEAN
Tropic of Capricorn
PERTH BASIN
Darwin
ARNHEM LAND
Gulf of Carpentaria
GROOTE EYLANDT
WELLESLEY ISLANDS
CAPE YORK PENINSULA
Cairns
Townsville
KIMBERLEY PLATEAU
Broome
BARKLY TABLELAND
TANAMI DESERT
GREAT SANDY DESERT
Mount Isa
SELWYN RANGE
MACDONNELL RANGES
Alice Springs
SIMPSON DESERT
AUSTRALIA
GIBSON DESERT
GREAT DIVIDING RANGE
Rockhampton
Brisbane
Lake Eyre North
STURT STONY DESERT
GREAT VICTORIA DESERT
Lake Torrens
Broken Hill
Newcastle
SYDNEY
Canberra
NULLARBOR PLAIN
Kalgoorlie-Boulder
Lake Gairdner
Adelaide
Spencer Gulf
Gulf Saint Vincent
Mount Kosciusko
MELBOURNE
Bass Strait
Perth
DARLING RANGE
Great Australian Bight
SOUTH AUSTRALIAN BASIN
Launceston
Hobart
SOUTHERN OCEAN
DIAMANTINA FRACTURE ZONE
BROKEN RIDGE
SOUTH TASMAN RISE
TASMAN
Kilometers 0 200 400 600 800 Km.
Statute Miles 0 200 400 600 800 Mi.
Scale 1:24,000,000
One centimeter represents 240 kilometers.
One inch represents approximately 380 miles.
Lambert Azimuthal Equal-Area Projection
Copyright © by Rand McNally & Co.
Map prepared by Rand McNally & Co.
A-590000-764

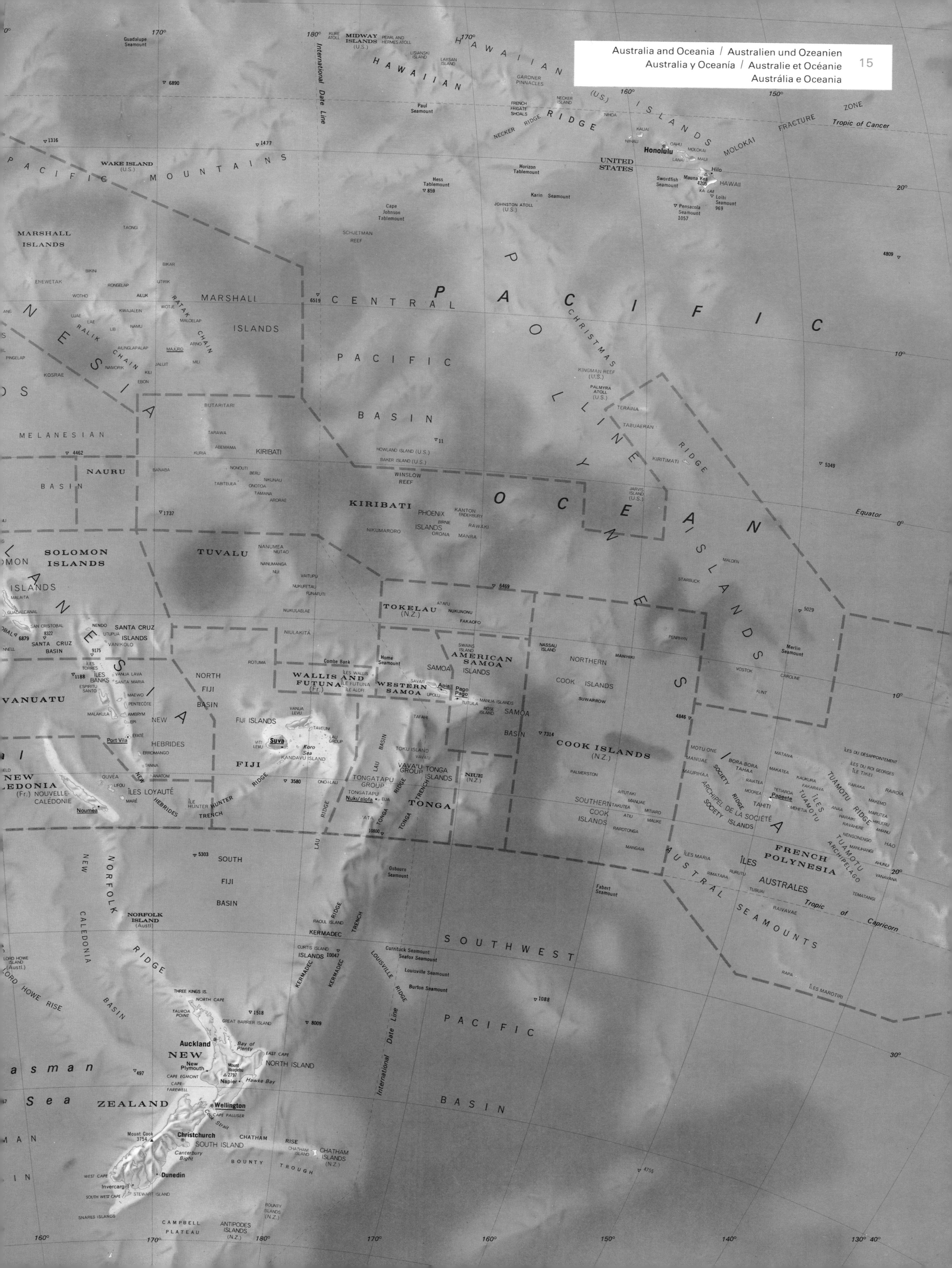
MIDWAY ISLANDS (U.S.)
HAWAIIAN ISLANDS
HAWAIIAN RIDGE
International Date Line
Honolulu
UNITED STATES
Hilo
HAWAII
MOLOKAI FRACTURE ZONE
Tropic of Cancer
WAKE ISLAND (U.S.)
PACIFIC MOUNTAINS
JOHNSTON ATOLL (U.S.)
MARSHALL ISLANDS
MARSHALL ISLANDS
RATAK CHAIN
RALIK CHAIN
MAJURO
CENTRAL PACIFIC BASIN
PACIFIC OCEAN
CHRISTMAS RIDGE
KINGMAN REEF (U.S.)
PALMYRA ATOLL (U.S.)
LINE ISLANDS
POLYNESIA
MICRONESIA
MELANESIA
MELANESIAN BASIN
NAURU
KIRIBATI
HOWLAND ISLAND (U.S.)
BAKER ISLAND (U.S.)
PHOENIX ISLANDS
Equator
SOLOMON ISLANDS
TUVALU
TOKELAU (N.Z.)
SANTA CRUZ ISLANDS
SANTA CRUZ BASIN
AMERICAN SAMOA
WALLIS AND FUTUNA (Fr.)
WESTERN SAMOA
Apia
Pago Pago
SAMOA ISLANDS
NORTH FIJI BASIN
VANUATU
NEW HEBRIDES
Port Vila
FIJI ISLANDS
Suva
FIJI
Koro Sea
TONGA
Nuku'alofa
NIUE (N.Z.)
SAMOA BASIN
NORTHERN COOK ISLANDS
COOK ISLANDS (N.Z.)
SOUTHERN COOK ISLANDS
SOCIETY ISLANDS
ARCHIPEL DE LA SOCIÉTÉ
Papeete
TAHITI
TUAMOTU ARCHIPELAGO
ÎLES TUAMOTU
FRENCH POLYNESIA
ÎLES AUSTRALES
AUSTRAL SEAMOUNTS
Tropic of Capricorn
NEW CALEDONIA (Fr.) NOUVELLE-CALÉDONIE
Nouméa
ÎLES LOYAUTÉ
HUNTER TRENCH
TONGA TRENCH
KERMADEC TRENCH
KERMADEC RIDGE
LOUISVILLE RIDGE
SOUTH FIJI BASIN
NORFOLK ISLAND (Austl.)
NORFOLK RIDGE
NEW CALEDONIA BASIN
LORD HOWE RISE
SOUTHWEST PACIFIC BASIN
Auckland
NEW ZEALAND
NORTH ISLAND
Wellington
Cook Strait
Christchurch
SOUTH ISLAND
Dunedin
Invercargill
CHATHAM RISE
CHATHAM ISLANDS (N.Z.)
BOUNTY TROUGH
Tasman Sea
CAMPBELL PLATEAU
ANTIPODES ISLANDS (N.Z.)
160°
170°
180°
150°
140°
130°
20°
10°
0°
30°
40°

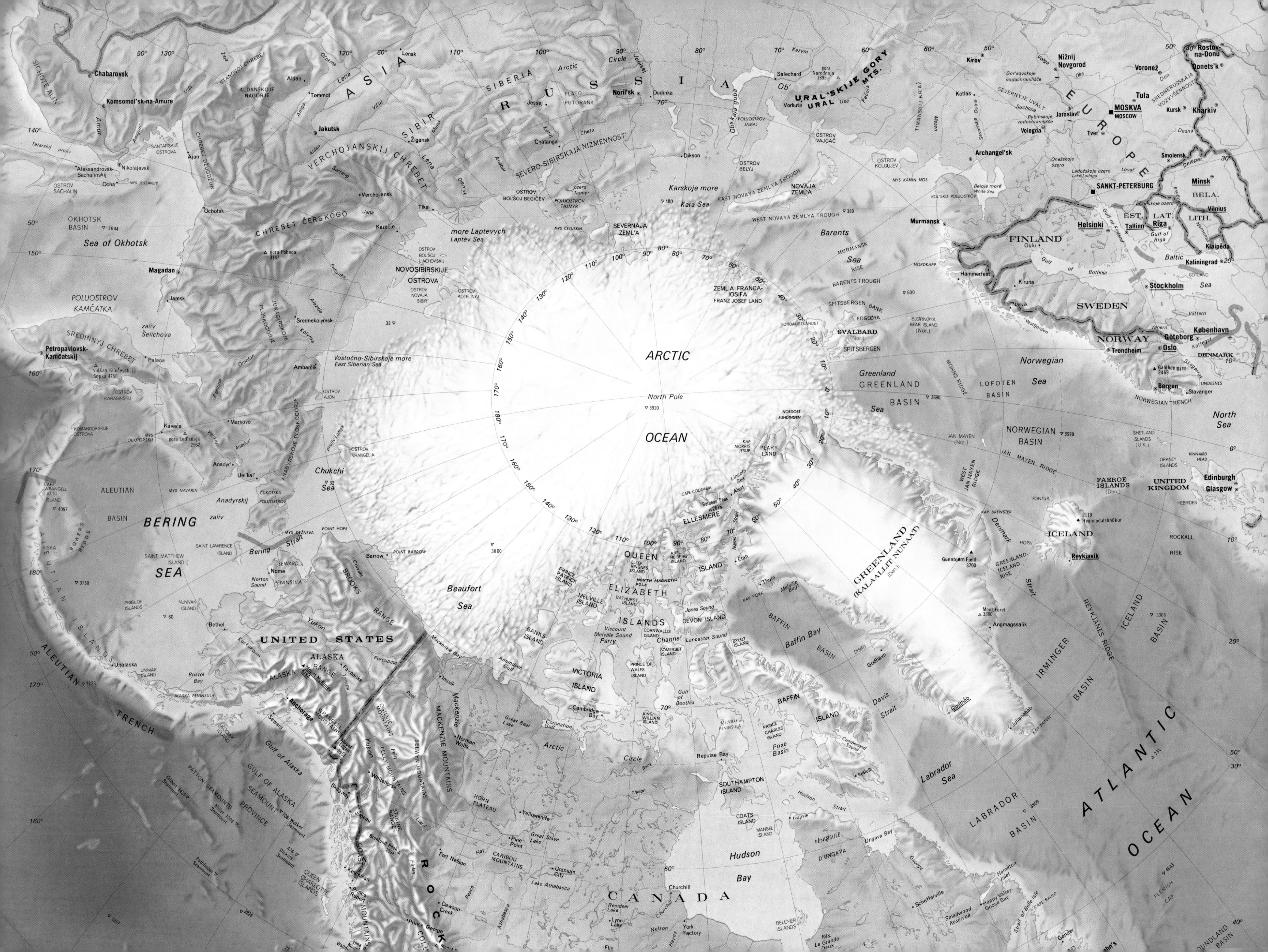

ARCTIC OCEAN
North Pole
ATLANTIC OCEAN
EUROPE
ASIA
RUSSIA
SIBERIA
CANADA
UNITED STATES
ALASKA
GREENLAND (KALAALLIT NUNAAT)
ICELAND
FINLAND
SWEDEN
NORWAY
UNITED KINGDOM
DENMARK
BERING SEA
Sea of Okhotsk
Beaufort Sea
Hudson Bay
Baffin Bay
Labrador Sea
Greenland Sea
Norwegian Sea
North Sea
Barents Sea
Kara Sea
Chukchi Sea
Gulf of Alaska
ALEUTIAN ISLANDS
ALEUTIAN TRENCH
QUEEN ELIZABETH ISLANDS
MACKENZIE MOUNTAINS
BROOKS RANGE
ROCK

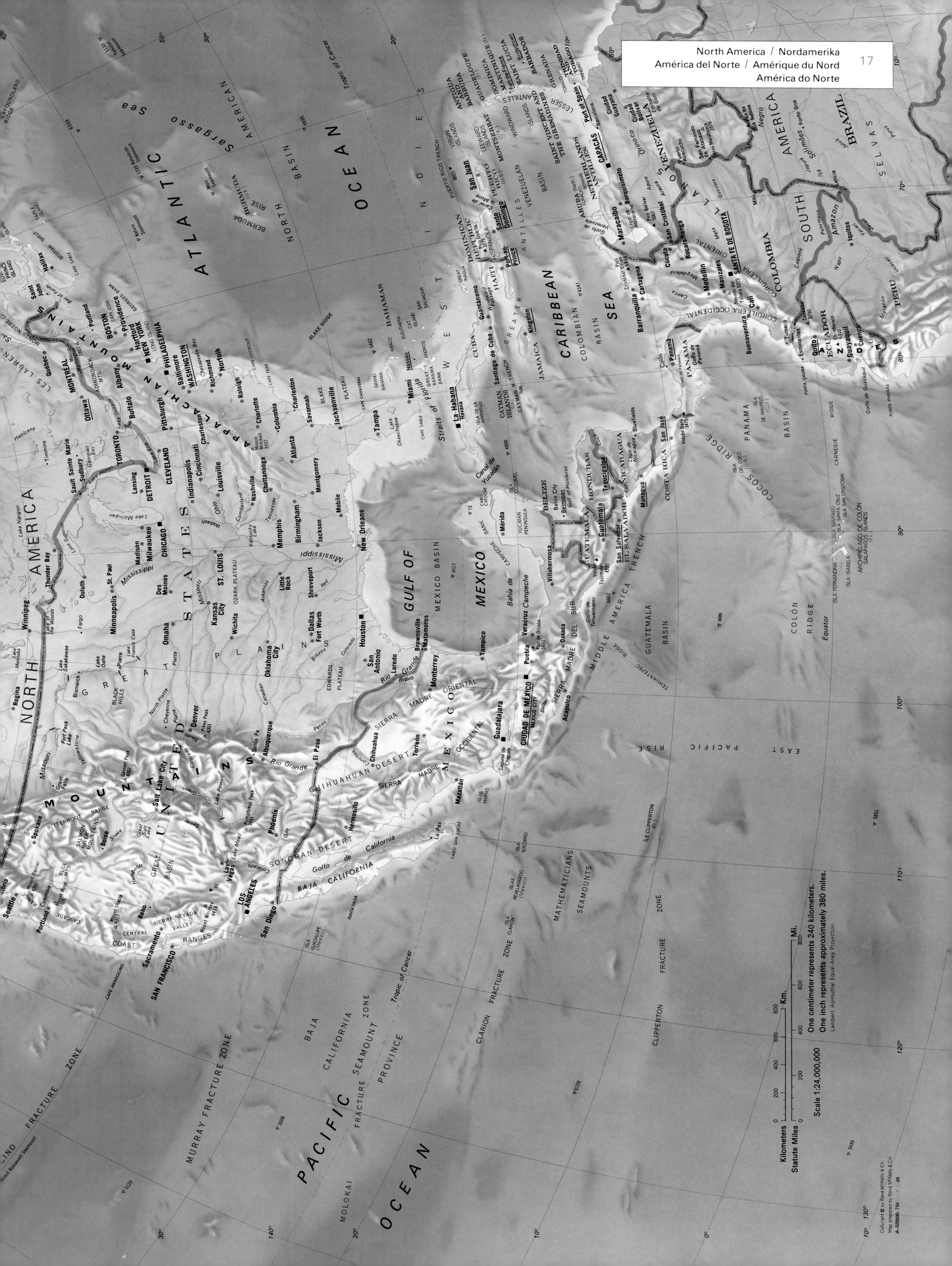
NORTH AMERICA
UNITED STATES
ATLANTIC OCEAN
PACIFIC OCEAN
GULF OF MEXICO
CARIBBEAN SEA
Sargasso Sea
SOUTH AMERICA
MEXICO
WEST INDIES
APPALACHIAN MOUNTAINS
ROCKY MOUNTAINS
GREAT PLAINS
Kilometers
Statute Miles
Scale 1:24,000,000
One centimeter represents 240 kilometers.
One inch represents approximately 380 miles.
Lambert Azimuthal Equal-Area Projection

NORTH AMERICA
UNITED STATES
MEXICO
GULF OF MEXICO
CARIBBEAN SEA
ATLANTIC OCEAN
NORTH AMERICAN BASIN
Sargasso Sea
MID-ATLANTIC RIDGE
Tropic of Cancer
CAPE VERDE BASIN
GUIANA BASIN
AZORES PLATEAU
WEST INDIES
GREATER ANTILLES
LESSER ANTILLES
SOUTH AMERICA
BRAZIL
SELVAS
COLOMBIA
VENEZUELA
ECUADOR
PERU
GUYANA
SURINAME
FRENCH GUIANA
CUBA
HAITI
DOMINICAN REPUBLIC
PUERTO RICO
JAMAICA
BAHAMAS
BELIZE
GUATEMALA
HONDURAS
EL SALVADOR
NICARAGUA
COSTA RICA
PANAMA
TRINIDAD AND TOBAGO
GRENADA
BARBADOS
SAINT LUCIA
SAINT VINCENT AND THE GRENADINES
DOMINICA
ANTIGUA AND BARBUDA
MONTSERRAT
NETHERLANDS ANTILLES
ARUBA
APPALACHIAN MOUNTAINS
ROCKY MTS.
GREAT PLAINS
SIERRA MADRE ORIENTAL
SIERRA MADRE DEL SUR
MIDDLE AMERICA TRENCH
PERU - CHILE TRENCH
COCOS RIDGE
CARNEGIE RIDGE
COLÓN RIDGE
GUATEMALA BASIN
PANAMA BASIN
COLOMBIAN BASIN
VENEZUELAN BASIN
MEXICO BASIN
CAYMAN TRENCH
PUERTO RICO TRENCH
Equator
NEW YORK
PHILADELPHIA
WASHINGTON
CHICAGO
CLEVELAND
ST. LOUIS
CIUDAD DE MÉXICO
La Habana
CARACAS
SANTA FE DE BOGOTÁ
Quito
LIMA
Georgetown
Paramaribo
Cayenne
Kingston
Port-au-Prince
Santo Domingo
San Juan
Port of Spain
Bridgetown
Manaus
Belém
São Luís
Fortaleza
Natal
Recife
Salvador
Iquitos
Guayaquil
Amazon
Orinoco

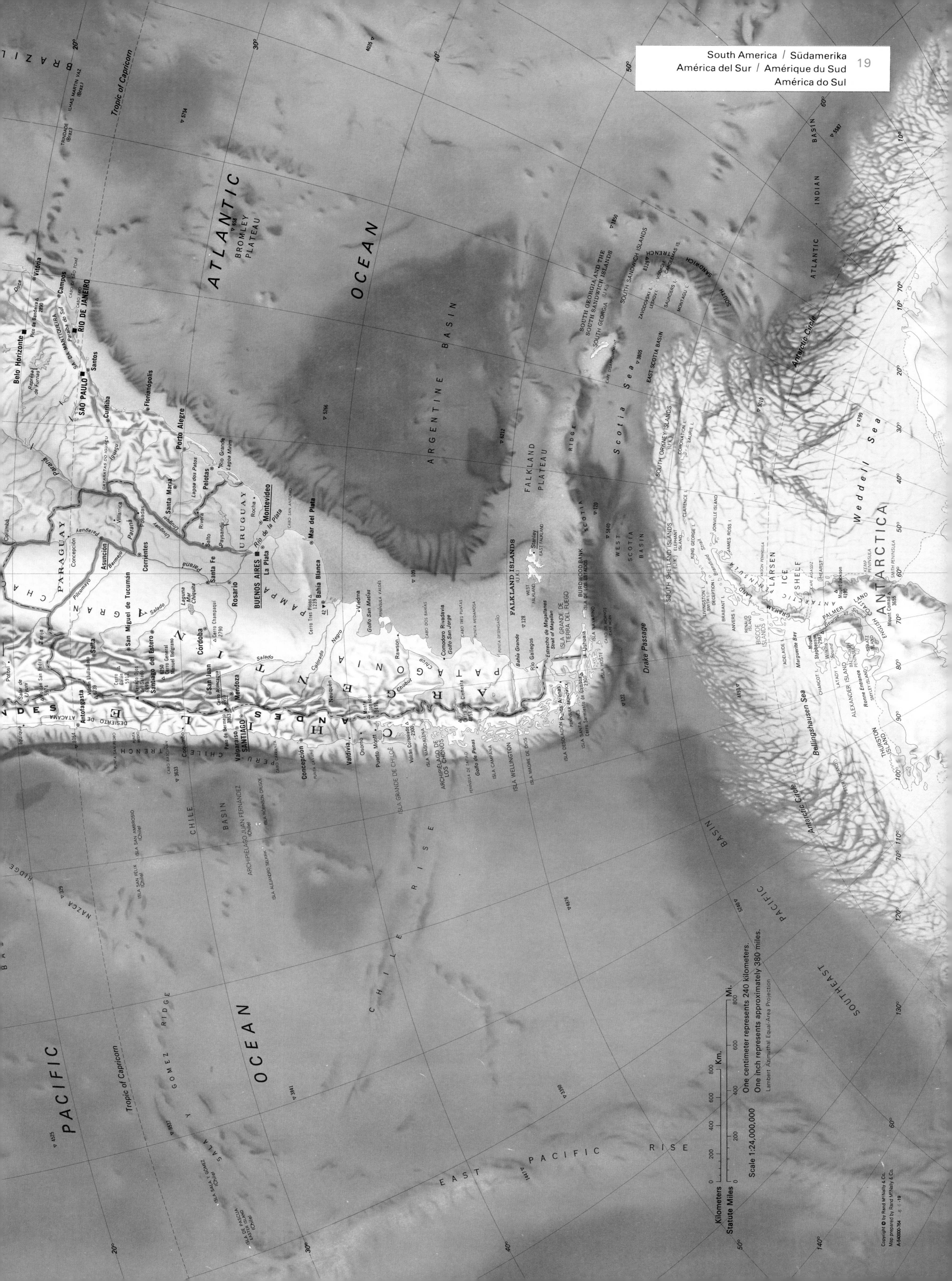
ATLANTIC OCEAN
PACIFIC OCEAN
BROMLEY PLATEAU
ARGENTINE BASIN
FALKLAND PLATEAU
Scotia Sea
Weddell Sea
Bellingshausen Sea
Drake Passage
ANTARCTICA
SOUTH GEORGIA AND THE SOUTH SANDWICH ISLANDS
SOUTH SANDWICH ISLANDS
SOUTH SANDWICH TRENCH
EAST SCOTIA BASIN
WEST SCOTIA BASIN
SOUTH ORKNEY ISLANDS (U.K.)
SOUTH SHETLAND ISLANDS
FALKLAND ISLANDS (U.K.)
Stanley
BURDWOOD BANK
ISLA GRANDE DE TIERRA DEL FUEGO
Estrecho de Magallanes
Ushuaia
Río Gallegos
Punta Arenas
PATAGONIA
PAMPA
URUGUAY
PARAGUAY
BUENOS AIRES
Montevideo
La Plata
Mar del Plata
Bahía Blanca
Rosario
Santa Fe
Córdoba
Mendoza
SANTIAGO
Valparaíso
Concepción
Valdivia
Puerto Montt
Antofagasta
Salta
San Miguel de Tucumán
Santiago del Estero
San Juan
Asunción
Corrientes
Porto Alegre
Florianópolis
Curitiba
SÃO PAULO
Santos
RIO DE JANEIRO
Belo Horizonte
Vitória
Campos
BRAZIL
Tropic of Capricorn
Antarctic Circle
CHILE BASIN
CHILE RISE
EAST PACIFIC RISE
SOUTHEAST PACIFIC BASIN
GOMEZ RIDGE
SALA Y GOMEZ RIDGE
NAZCA RIDGE
ATLANTIC-INDIAN BASIN
Kilometers 0 200 400 600 800 Km.
Statute Miles 0 200 400 600 800 Mi.
Scale 1:24,000,000
One centimeter represents 240 kilometers.
One inch represents approximately 380 miles.
Lambert Azimuthal Equal-Area Projection

THE REGIONAL MAPS consist of three basic series, each distinctive in style, but using common symbols to ensure ease of understanding (see Legend to Maps, pages x-xii). Every major land region, continent or subcontinent, is introduced by one or more maps at the scale of 1:12,000,000. There follow maps at 1:6,000,000 and 1:3,000,000 which cover the region in sections, in greater detail. Except for scale, the 1:6,000,000 and 1:3,000,000 maps are alike. Finally, selected areas of special importance in the region are shown at 1:1,000,000. Each scale is identified by a color bar, and a locater map with the same color may be found in the margin of the map page. A sample area at each of the scales, including centimeter-kilometer and inch-mile equivalents, appears on page 21.

The three basic series differ in content and emphasis. The 1:12,000,000 maps, which are primarily political, present an overview of each region. They show national boundaries and, in some cases, subordinate administrative subdivisions as well. These introductory maps make it possible to compare location, areal extent, and shape among the nations of the world. The distribution of cities, towns and metropolitan areas is shown in the context of broad physical configurations. A selection of the most important railways and highways also appears.

The 1:6,000,000 and 1:3,000,000 maps together constitute about half of the map pages and provide the basic reference coverage of the Atlas. They show sections of regions in great detail—in some cases individual countries (Japan and New Zealand), in others, parts of countries (central Mexico), in still others, larger regions (the Middle East). The more densely settled areas appear at the larger 1:3,000,000 scale, the remaining areas at 1:6,000,000. Maps at these two scales present political and cultural information against the background of a detailed physical portrait of the terrain, which is depicted by both shaded relief and a spectrum of altitude tints. Bathymetric tints are used to show offshore water depths. The transportation pattern shown includes major railways, two classes of roads, and airports that offer either international or jet service. The names and boundaries of political subdivisions are given for selected countries.

In the 1:1,000,000 series, strategic areas that are of special interest because of economic importance, dense settlement, or both, appear in even greater detail. This series is designed to show the pattern of cities, towns, roads, railways, bridges, airports, dams, reservoirs, and other interrelated features reflecting man's dense occupancy in these areas. The most important parks, places of historical interest, and recreational facilities are indicated. Three classes of highways and two classes of railways are shown, and major roads are named. All features are portrayed against a topographic background of shaded relief.

Inhabited places on the regional maps are classified in two distinct ways. Cities and towns of different *population size* are distinguished by the *size and shape of the symbol* that locates the place. The symbol reflects the population within the municipal or corporate limits, exclusive of any suburbs. In countries where the limits of a municipality include rural areas, the symbol represents only the urban or agglomerated population. The *relative political and economic importance* of a place which may be independent of the number of its inhabitants, is indicated by the *size of type* in which its name appears.

DIE REGIONALKARTEN bestehen aus drei Serien, die im Stil verschieden sind, der besseren Lesbarkeit halber aber gemeinsame Kartensignaturen verwenden (siehe "Zeichenerklärung" S. x-xii). Jede Grossregion, jeder Kontinent oder Subkontinent werden durch eine oder mehrere Karten im Massstab 1:12 Millionen eingeleitet. Es folgen sodann Karten in den Massstäben 1:6 und 1:3 Millionen, welche die Region in Teilen und grösseren Einzelheiten darstellen. Die Karten in 1:6 Millionen und 1:3 Millionen unterscheiden sich nur im Massstab. Schliesslich werden ausgewählte Gebiete von besonderer Bedeutung innerhalb der Region in 1:1 Million dargestellt. Jede Massstabsangabe ist durch ein Farbfeld gekennzeichnet, und ein Lagekärtchen in derselben Farbe erscheint am Rand der Kartenseite. Kartenausschnitte als Beispiele für jeden dieser Massstäbe mit Angabe des Verhältnisses Zentimeter zu Kilometer und Zoll zu Meilen sind auf Seite 21 aufgeführt.

Die drei Kartenreihen unterscheiden sich in Inhalt und Betonung. Die Karten im Massstab 1:12 Millionen, die vor allem politische Karten sind, geben einen Überblick über jede Region. Sie zeigen die Staatsgrenzen und in manchen Fällen auch die Grenzen von nachgeordneten Verwaltungseinheiten. Diese einführenden Karten ermöglichen einen Vergleich der Lage, Ausdehnung und Gestalt der Staaten der Erde. Die Verteilung der städtischen Ballungsgebiete, Grossstädte und Städte wird in ihrem Zusammenhang mit dem grossräumigen Formenschatz des Reliefs dargestellt. Gezeigt wird auch eine Auswahl der wichtigsten Eisenbahnlinien und Fernverkehrsstrassen.

Die Karten 1:6 Millionen und 1:3 Millionen machen zusammen mehr als die Hälfte der Kartenseiten aus und bilden den grundlegenden Teil des Atlas. Sie zeigen sehr inhaltsreiche Ausschnitte von Regionen—in einigen Fällen einzeln Länder (Japan und Neuseeland), in anderen Landesteile (Zentralmexiko) und wieder anderen Grossräume (Mittlerer Osten).

Die dichter besiedelten Gebiete sind im Massstab 1:3 Millionen dargestellt, die übrigen Gebiete im Massstab 1:6 Millionen. Die Karten in diesen beiden Massstäben liefern politische und kulturgeographische Informationen vor dem Hintergrund einer detaillierten Geländedarstellung, gekennzeichnet durch Reliefschummerung und eine Skala von Höhenschichten. Tiefenstufen werden verwendet, um die Meerestiefen jenseits der Küsten zu gliedern. Das abgebildete Verkehrsnetz umfasst wichtige Eisenbahnlinien, zwei Klassen von Strassen und Flughäfen, die entweder im internationalen Verkehr oder von Düsenflugzeugen angeflogen werden. Die Verwaltungsgliederung wird für eine grosse Zahl von Staaten gezeigt.

In der Kartenserie 1:1 Million sind mit noch zahlreicheren Einzelheiten zentrale Räume dargestellt, denen infolge ihrer wirtschaftlichen Bedeutung, dichten Besiedlung oder durch beide Faktoren bedingt besonderes Interesse zukommt. Diese Kartenserie wurde entwikelt, um die Verteilung der Grossstädte, Städte, Strassen, Eisenbahnen, Brücken, Flughäfen, Dämme, Stauseen und anderer Objekte zu zeigen, die Ausdruck sind für die dichte Besiedlung. Verzeichnet sind auch die wichtigsten Parks, Örtlichkeiten von historischem Interesse und Erholungsstätten. Drei Strassenklassen und zwei Klassen von Eisenbahnlinien werden unterschieden. Die Darstellung ist mit einer Reliefschummerung unterlegt.

Die Siedlungen auf den Regionalkarten sind auf zwei bestimmte Arten klassifiziert. Grossstädte und Städte unterschiedlicher *Einwohnerzahl* sind durch *Grösse und Form der Signatur* unterschieden, die den Ort lokalisiert. Die Signatur entspricht der Zahl der Einwohner innerhalb der Stadtgrenzen, schliesst also nicht eingemeindete Vororte aus. In Staaten, in denen ländliche Gebiete in die Stadtgemeinden einbezogen sind, entsprechen die Signaturen nur der in den zentralen Siedlungen ansässigen Bevölkerung. Die *relative politische und wirtschaftliche Bedeutung* eines Ortes, die von der Zahl seiner Einwohner unabhängig sein kann, ist ausgedrückt durch die *Schriftgrösse,* in welcher der Ortsname erscheint.

LOS MAPAS REGIONALES integran tres series básicas, cada una con su estilo propio; pero los símbolos usados son en todas los mismos para facilitar su comprensión (véanse las Leyendas para Mapas, páginas x-xii). Cada una de las grandes regiones, continentes o subcontinentes, se presenta a través de uno o varios mapas a la escala de 1:12 000 000. A continuación hay mapas a escalas de 1:6 000 000 y 1:3 000 000 que presentan la región correspondiente en secciones, con mayores detalles. Con excepción de su escala, los mapas de 1:6 000 000 y 1:3 000 000 tienen las mismas características. Por ultimo, aparecen a la escala de 1:1 000 000 áreas de cada región seleccionadas por su importancia. Cada escala se identifica por una barra de color, y un mapa-guía con el mismo color se presenta en el margen de la página de cada mapa. La página 21 ofrece como ejemplo un área-muestra a cada una de las escalas, incluyendo equivalentes en centímetros-kilómetros y pulgadas-millas.

Las tres series básicas son diferentes en contenido y en énfasis. Los mapas a escala de 1:12 000 000, fundamentalmente políticos, ofrecen una vista general de cada región. Indican las fronteras nacionales y, en algunos casos, las subdivisiones administrativas secundarias. Son mapas introductivos que permiten comparar la ubicación, extensión territorial y forma de las distintas naciones. La distribución de ciudades, poblados y áreas metropolitanas se aprecia en un contexto físico esbozado a grandes rasgos. Los detalles incluyen una selección de las vías férras y las carreteras más importantes.

Las series de mapas a 1:6 000 000 y a 1:3 000 000 ocupan entre ambas cerca de la mitad de los mapas del atlas y en ellas se concentra el material de consulta básico de la obra. Los mapas muestran secciones de regiones en gran detalle: en algunos casos países enteros, como Japón y Nueva Zelandia; en otros, partes de países, como el centro de México; y en otros, regiones mas extensas, como el Medio Oriente. Las áreas con mayor densidad de establecimientos humanos se presentan a una escala mayor, la de 1:3 000 000, y las demás a la escala de 1:6 000 000. En estas dos escalas los mapas contienen información política y cultural, sobre un fondo que ilustra en detalle la configuración física del terreno, utilizando sombreado para el relieve y toda una gama de tintes para indicar las altitudes. Un colorido batimétrico señala las variaciones de profundidad en el suelo marino. El esquema de las vías de comunicación incluye las principales vías férreas, dos clases de caminos, y los aeropuertos que ofrecen servicio nacional o internacional de jets. Las subdivisiones políticas secundarias se dan para una selección de varios países.

En la serie de mapas de 1:1 000 000, las áreas estratégicas de especial interés por su importancia económica, su densidad de población, o ambos factores combinados, aparecen aún con mayor detalle. Esta serie se diseñó para mostrar la distribución de ciudades, poblados, caminos, vías férreas, puentes, aeropuertos, presas, embalses y otros elementos similares, que reflejan la densidad de la ocupación humana. También se consignan los parques más importantes, los sitios de interés histórico, los campos de recreo, tres clases de carreteras, y dos de ferrocarriles, se da los nombres de los caminos más importantes. Todos estos elementos aparecen sobre un fondo topográfico de relieve sombreado.

En los mapas regionales se hacen dos clasificaciones distintas de los lugares habitados. Las ciudades y las poblaciones *de diferente densidad de habitantes* se distinguen por la *forma y tamaño del símbolo* que las localiza en el mapa. Este símbolo refleja el tamaño de la poblacióin dentro de sus límites municipales, sin tomar en cuenta los suburbios. En los países donde los límites de una municipalidad incluyen áreas rurales, el símbolo se limita a representar el conglomerado urbano de habitantes. La *importancia económica y política de un lugar,* la cual puede ser independiente del número de sus habitantes, se indica mediante el *tamaño del tipo de imprenta* en que aparece su nombre.

LES CARTES RÉGIONALES sont de trois types principaux, chacun d'un style différent mais avec des symboles communs pour faciliter la compréhension (voir la légende des cartes pages x-xii). Chaque grande région, continent ou subcontinent, est représentée par une ou plusieurs cartes à l'échelle de 1:12 000 000e. Viennent ensuite des cartes au 1:6 000 000e et au 1:3 000 000e qui couvrent la région par sections plus détaillées; hormis la différence d'échelle, ces cartes sont semblables. Enfin, des secteurs particulièrement importants sont représentés au 1:1 000 000e. À chaque échelle correspond une bande colorée et une carte repère de même couleur, dans la marge de chaque page. Un échantillon de cartes aux diverses échelles est représenté à droite. Chaque carte est accompagnée d'une double échelle graphique donnant les rapports centimètre/kilomètre et inch/mille correspondants.

Les trois catégories de cartes diffèrent par le contenu et par ce qu'elles mettent en relief. Les cartes au 1:12 000 000e, qui sont essentiellement politiques, donnent un apercu général de chaque région. Elles indiquent les frontières nationales et, dans certains cas, les subdivisions administratives intérieures. Ces cartes d'introduction permettent de comparer la localisation, la superficie et la forme des pays du monde. La répartition des villes et des zones métropolitaines y apparaît dans le cadre des grandes régions naturelles. Les routes et les voies ferrées les plus importantes y figurent également.

Les cartes au 1:6 000 000e et au 1:3 000 000e forment la moitié de l'Atlas et en constituent la série cartographique essentielle. Elles représentent de façon plus détaillée une partie de pays (centre du Mexique), ou encore des régions plus vestes (Moyen-Orient) ou, parfois, des pays entiers (Japon, Nouvelle-Zélande). Les régiones les plus peuplées sont représentées à plus grande échelle (1;3 000 000e) que les autres (1:6 000 000e). Ces cartes offrent des informations d'ordre politique et culturel sur un fond topographique précis où le relief est indiqué à la fois par un estompage et par des variations de couleur. Différentes teintes de bleu sont utilisées pour symboliser les profondeurs marines. Les réseaux de transport représentés comprennent les principales voies ferrées, deux catégories de routes et les aéroports internationaux ou desservis par des avions à réaction. Les subdivisions politiques d'un certain nombre de pays sont aussi tracées.

Dans la série de cartes au 1:1 000 000e, des régions très importantes, soit du fait de leur densité de population, soit du fait de leur rôle économique, sont représentées d'une manière encore plus détaillée. L'objectif de cette série de cartes est de montrer la répartition des villes, routes, voies ferrées, ponts, aéroports, barrages, lacs de barrages et autres données associées qui traduisent la densité de l'occupation humaine dans ces régions. Les parcs les plus importants, les sites historiques essentiels et les centres de loisirs sont indiqués. Toutes les informations se détachent sur un fond topographique où le relief apparaît en estompage.

Les centres urbains des cartes régionales sont classés de deux manières différentes. *L'importance de la population* des villes est indiquée par *la dimension et la forme du symbole* qui les situe sur la carte. Seule la population comprise dans les limites municipales est prise en considération; dans les pays où des espaces ruraux sont inclus dans les limites d'une municipalité, seule la population urbaine entre en ligne de compte. *L'importance politique et économique relative* d'une ville, qui n'est pas nécessairement liée au nombre d'habitants, est indiquée par la dimension des caractères qui composent son nom.

OS MAPAS REGIONAIS compreendem três séries básicas, cada uma em estilo diferente, mas que empregam os mesmos símbolos para facilitar sua compreensão (Ver as *Legendas dos mapas*, pág. x-xii). Os mapas de cada uma das principais regiões terrestres, continentes ou subcontinentes, são introduzidos por um ou mais mapas na escala 1:12 000 000. Em seguida, vêm mapas, nas escalas de 1:6 000 000 e 1:3 000 000, que apresentam, com maiores detalhes, seções da região considerada. Exceto quanto à escala, os mapas de 1:6 000 000 e 1:3 000 000 têm as mesmas características. Finalmente, aparecem, na escala de 1:1 000 000, os mapas das áreas mais importantes da região considerada. A cada escala corresponde uma barra colorida e um indicador da mesma cor, que se encontra à margem da página de cada mapa. À página 21, acha-se um exemplo de cada escala, bem como a equivalência das relações centímetro/quilômetro e polegada/milha.

As três séries básicas de mapas são diferentes quanto ao conteúdo e à apresentação. Os mapas em escala de 1:12 000 000, que são essencialmente políticos, oferecem uma visão geral de cada região. Indicam as fronteiras nacionais e, em alguns casos, as subdivisões administrativas internas. Esses mapas servem de introdução e permitem avaliar e comparar a posição, superfície e forma dos países do Mundo. Neles está claramente indicada a distribuição das cidades e outros centros urbanos, bem como as principais características da configuração do solo. Encontra-se neles também uma seleção das ferrovias e rodovias mais importantes.

A série de mapas das escalas de 1:6 000 000 e de 1:3 000 000 constituem o principal material de referência do Atlas e representa cerca de metade do conjunto de mapas. Entre eles há mapas detalhados de parte de um país (centro do México), de um país inteiro (Japão e a Nova Zelândia) ou de uma região mais extensa (Oriente Médio). As áreas de maior densidade demográfica são apresentadas em escala maior, a de 1:3 000 000, e as demais, na de 1:6 000 000. Nessas duas escalas, os mapas fornecem informações de ordem política e cultural sobre um fundo que indica a configuração detalhada das particularidades físicas do solo, cujo relevo se destaca por contrastes de sombras e cores. Diversos matizes do azul traduzem o mapa batimétrico da profundidade ao largo das costas. Indicam também os aeroportos internacionais, as principais ferrovias, duas categorias de rodovias. As subdivisões políticas internas de numerosos países estão igualmente assinalados.

Na série de mapas da escala de 1:1 000 000, certas áreas, de interesse estratégico conjugado à importância econômica, densidade demográfica, ou ambos os elementos combinados, aparecem em forma ainda mais detalhada. O objetivo dessa série é representar a distribuição dos grandes centros urbanos, cidades, rodovias, ferrovias, pontes, aeroportos, represas, reservatórios e outras características associadas às grandes densidades demográficas. Indicam-se, também, os parques mais importantes, os lugares de interesse histórico, as áreas de lazer, três categorias de rodovias, e duas de ferrovias; e a nomenclatura dos grandes itinerários rodoviários. Todos esses elementos destacam-se sobre um fundo topográfico do relevo, executado em matizes das diversas cores.

Nos mapas regionais, assinalam-se os centros urbanos de dois modos. A *grandeza da população* das grandes cidades e dos centros urbanos secundários é representada pela *dimensão e forma do símbolo* que as localiza no mapa. O símbolo só reflete a população situada dentro de limites administrativos, sem levar em conta os subúrbios. Nos países onde os limites de uma municipalidade incluem zonas rurais, o símbolo representa apenas a população. A *importância política e econômica* de uma cidade, que não se relaciona necessariamente com o número de seus habitantes, é indicada pela *dimensão* dos caracteres tipográficos com que se compõe o seu nome.

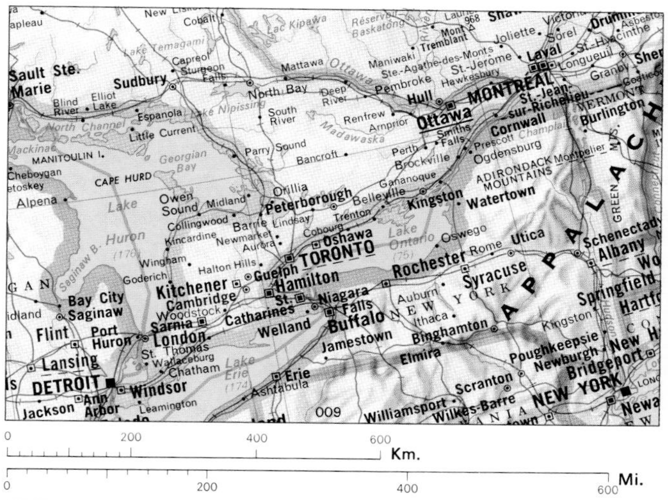

Scale 1:12,000,000 One centimeter represents 120 kilometers. One inch represents approximately 190 miles.

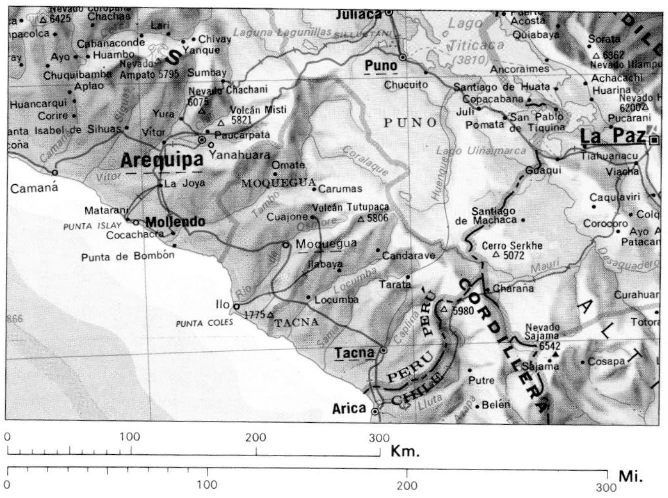

Scale 1:6,000,000 One centimeter represents 60 kilometers. One inch represents approximately 95 miles.

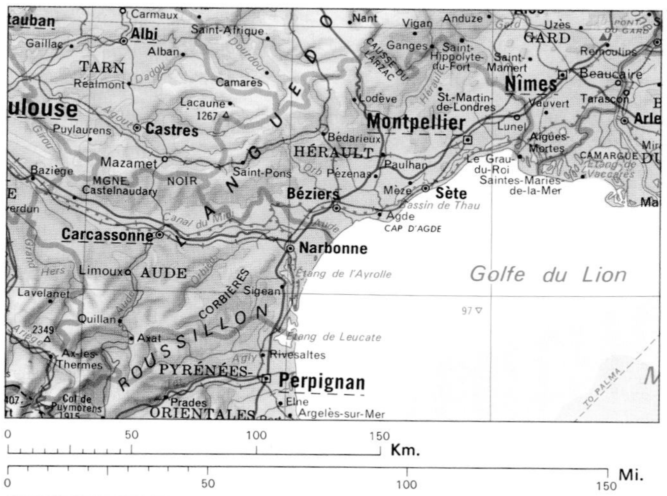

Scale 1:3,000,000 One centimeter represents 30 kilometers. One inch represents approximately 47 miles.

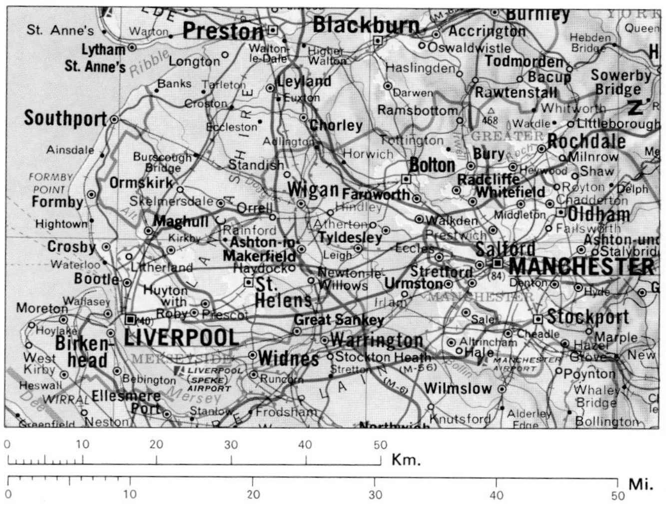

Scale 1:1,000,000 One centimeter represents 10 kilometers. One inch represents approximately 16 miles.

ICELAND
Reykjavík
Arctic Circle
NORWEGIAN SEA
FAEROE ISLANDS (Den.)
SHETLAND ISLANDS
ORKNEY ISLANDS
NORWAY
SWEDEN
Bergen
Oslo
Stavanger
Göteborg
Trondheim
ATLANTIC OCEAN
IRELAND
Dublin
Cork
UNITED KINGDOM
SCOTLAND
Glasgow
Edinburgh
Aberdeen
Belfast
Newcastle
Manchester
Liverpool
Leeds
Birmingham
LONDON
English Channel
CELTIC SEA
NORTH SEA
DENMARK
KØBENHAVN
NETHERLANDS
AMSTERDAM
BRUXELLES
BELGIUM
LUXEMBOURG
GERMANY
Hamburg
BERLIN
München
Frankfurt
Köln
FRANCE
PARIS
Lyon
Marseille
Bordeaux
Toulouse
Nantes
Bay of Biscay
SWITZERLAND
Bern
Zürich
AUSTRIA
WIEN
PRAHA
CZECH REP.
POLAND
HUNGARY
SLOVENIA
CROATIA
BOSNIA AND HERZEGOVINA
ITALY
ROMA
Milano
Torino
Napoli
Genova
Venezia
Firenze
Bologna
CORSE
SARDEGNA
SICILIA
Palermo
Tyrrhenian Sea
Adriatic Sea
Ionian Sea
SPAIN
MADRID
Barcelona
València
Sevilla
Málaga
ISLES BALEARS
PORTUGAL
LISBOA
Porto
MEDITERRANEAN SEA
EL DJAZAÏR
ALGIERS
ALGERIA
MOROCCO
RABAT
Casablanca
ATLAS MOUNTAINS
TUNISIA
TUNIS
MALTA
Valletta
Copyright © by Rand McNally & Co.
Map prepared by Esselte Map Service AB, Stockholm

MAP FORM	-älven	gora	île	islands	-øya	ozero	sea	vodochranilišče
ENGLISH	river	mountain	island	islands	island	lake	sea	reservoir
DEUTSCH	Fluss	Berg	Insel	Inseln	Insel	See	Meer	Stausee
ESPAÑOL	río	montaña	isla	islas	isla	lago	mar	embalse
FRANÇAIS	rivière	montagne	île	îles	île	lac	mer	réservoir
PORTUGUÊS	rio	montanha	ilha	ilhas	ilha	lago	mar	reservatório

Map continues pages 134-135

BARENTS SEA
RUSSIA
FINLAND
ESTONIA
LATVIA
LITHUANIA
BELARUS
UKRAINE
MOLDOVA
ROMANIA
BULGARIA
TURKEY
GEORGIA
ARMENIA
AZERBAIJAN
KAZAKHSTAN
UZBEK.
TURKMENISTAN
SYRIA
IRAQ
IRAN
NORTH CYPRUS
CYPRUS
BLACK SEA
CASPIAN SEA
Sea of Azov
Aral Sea
URAL'SKIJE GORY
URAL MOUNTAINS
ZAPADNO SIBIRSKAJA RAVNINA
CAUCASUS
MOSKVA
MOSCOW
SANKT-PETERBURG
HELSINKI
Tallinn
RIGA
Vilnius
MINSK
KYYIV
Chişinău
BUCUREŞTI
SOFIJA
ANKARA
TBILISI
JEREVAN
BAKI
TEHRĀN
BAGHDĀD
Nicosia

Map continues pages 72-73

Map continues pages 118-119

Kilometers 0 200 400 600 Km.
Statute Miles 0 200 400 600 Mi.

Scale 1:12,000,000

One centimeter represents 120 kilometers.
One inch represents approximately 190 miles.
Miller Oblated Stereographic Projection

Northern Europe / Nordeuropa / Europe Septentrional
Europe Septentrionale / Europa Setentrional

a

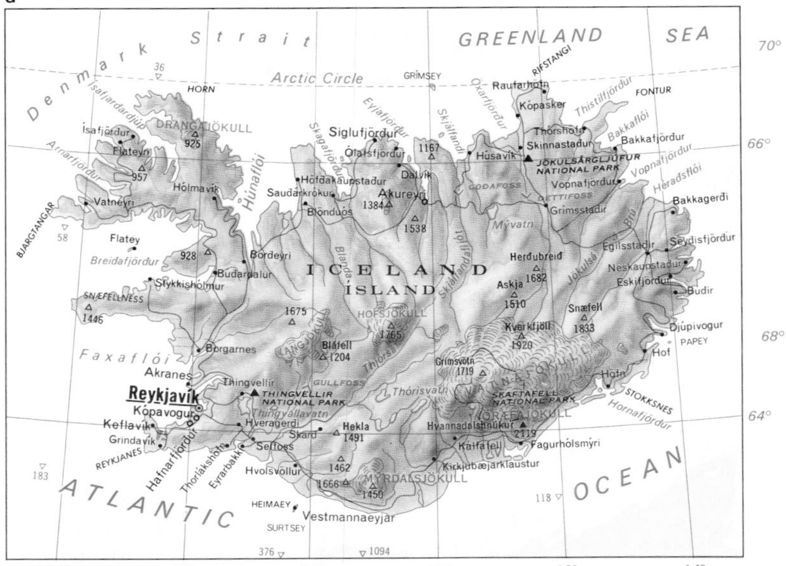
Denmark Strait
GREENLAND SEA
Arctic Circle
ICELAND
ÍSLAND
Reykjavík
Akureyri
Húsavík
Vestmannaeyjar
Faxaflói
ATLANTIC OCEAN
VATNAJÖKULL
MÝRDALSJÖKULL
DRANGAJÖKULL
Hekla 1491

NORWEGIAN SEA
ATLANTIC OCEAN
NORTH SEA
Skagerrak
Kattegat
BALTIC SEA
Gulf of Bothnia
Bottenviken
Bottenhavet
Gulf of Finland
Gulf of Riga
Arctic Circle
Oslo
STOCKHOLM
HELSINKI
HELSINGFORS
KØBENHAVN
COPENHAGEN
Tallinn
RIGA
Vilnius
Göteborg
Bergen
Trondheim
Tampere
Turku
HAMBURG
Gdańsk
Kaliningrad (Königsberg)
RUSSIA
POLAND
FINLAND
SWEDEN
NORWAY
DENMARK
ESTONIA
LATVIA
LIETUVA
LITHUANIA

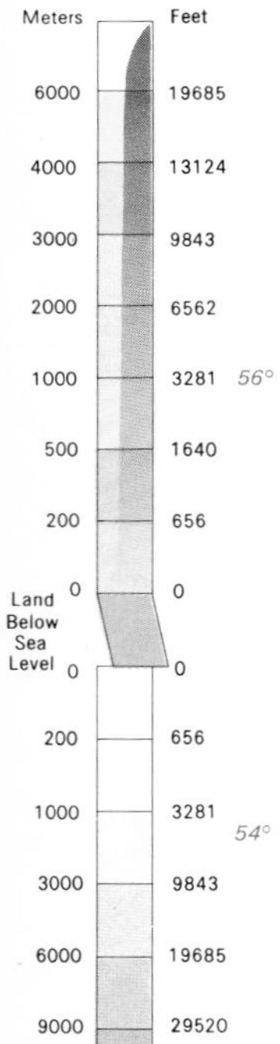
Meters
Feet
6000
19685
4000
13124
3000
9843
2000
6562
1000
3281
500
1640
200
656
0
0
Land Below Sea Level
0
0
200
656
1000
3281
3000
9843
6000
19685
9000
29520

MAP FORM	-älven	-fjorden	guba	-joki	-jökull	lääni	-øya	ozero
ENGLISH	river	fjord, lake	bay	river	glacier	province	island	lake
DEUTSCH	Fluss	Fjord, See	Bucht	Fluss	Gletscher	Provinz	Insel	See
ESPAÑOL	río	fiordo, lago	bahía	río	glaciar	provincia	isla	lago
FRANÇAIS	rivière	fjord, lac	baie	rivière	glacier	province	île	lac
PORTUGUÊS	rio	fiorde, lago	baía	rio	geleira	provincia	ilha	lago

BARENTS SEA
BARENCEVO MORE
PEČORSKOJE MORE
White Sea
Beloje more
OSTROV KOLGUJEV
Češskaja guba
Dvinskaja guba
Onežskaja guba
URAL MOUNTAINS
URAL'SKIJE GORY
Arctic Circle
Murmansk
Archangel'sk
Severodvinsk
Vorkuta
Syktyvkar
Kotlas
Petrozavodsk
ST.-PETERBURG
ST. PETERSBURG
Vologda
Jaroslavl'
Kostroma
Kirov
Iževsk
Kazan'
NIŽNIJ NOVGOROD
GORKY
Čeboksary
MOSKVA
MOSCOW
Tver'
Smolensk
Kaluga
Tula
Rjazan'
Vladimir
Ivanovo
Uljanovsk
SAMARA
Saransk
Sterlitamak
Syzran'
Copyright © by Rand McNally & Co.
Map compiled by Rand McNally & GmbH, Stuttgart
Map produced by Rand McNally & Co.
A-573000-764

Map continues pages 86-87

Map continues pages 76-77

Kilometers 0 100 200 300 Km.
Statute Miles 0 100 200 300 Mi.

Scale 1:6,000,000
One centimeter represents 60 kilometers.
One inch represents approximately 95 miles.
Lambert Conformal Conic Projection

Southern Scandinavia / Südskandinavien / Escandinavia Meridional
Scandinavie Méridionale / Escandinávia Meridional

NORWEGIAN SEA
NORTH SEA
Skagerrak
Kattegat
NORWAY NORGE
SWEDEN SVERIGE
DENMARK DANMARK
GERMANY DTSCHL.
Oslo
STOCKHOLM
KØBENHAVN COPENHAGEN
Göteborg Gothenburg
Bergen
Stavanger
Trondheim
Kristiansand
Malmö
Helsingborg
Uppsala
Meters
Feet
6000 19685
4000 13124
3000 9843
2000 6562
1000 3281
500 1640
200 656
0 0
Land Below Sea Level
200 656
1000 3281
3000 9843
6000 19685
9000 29520

Map continues pages 30-31

MAP FORM	-älven	bugt	-fjället	-fjell	-fjorden	-järvi	-joki	-ö, -ön	-sjön	-vesi
ENGLISH	river	bay	mountain	mountain	fjord, lake	lake	river	island	lake	lake
DEUTSCH	Fluss	Bucht	Berg	Berg	Fjord, See	See	Fluss	Insel	See	See
ESPAÑOL	río	bahía	montaña	montaña	fiordo, lago	lago	río	isla	lago	lago
FRANÇAIS	rivière	baie	montagne	montagne	fjord, lac	lac	rivière	île	lac	lac
PORTUGUÊS	rio	baía	montanha	montanha	fiorde, lago	lago	rio	ilha	lago	lago

Map continues pages 24-25

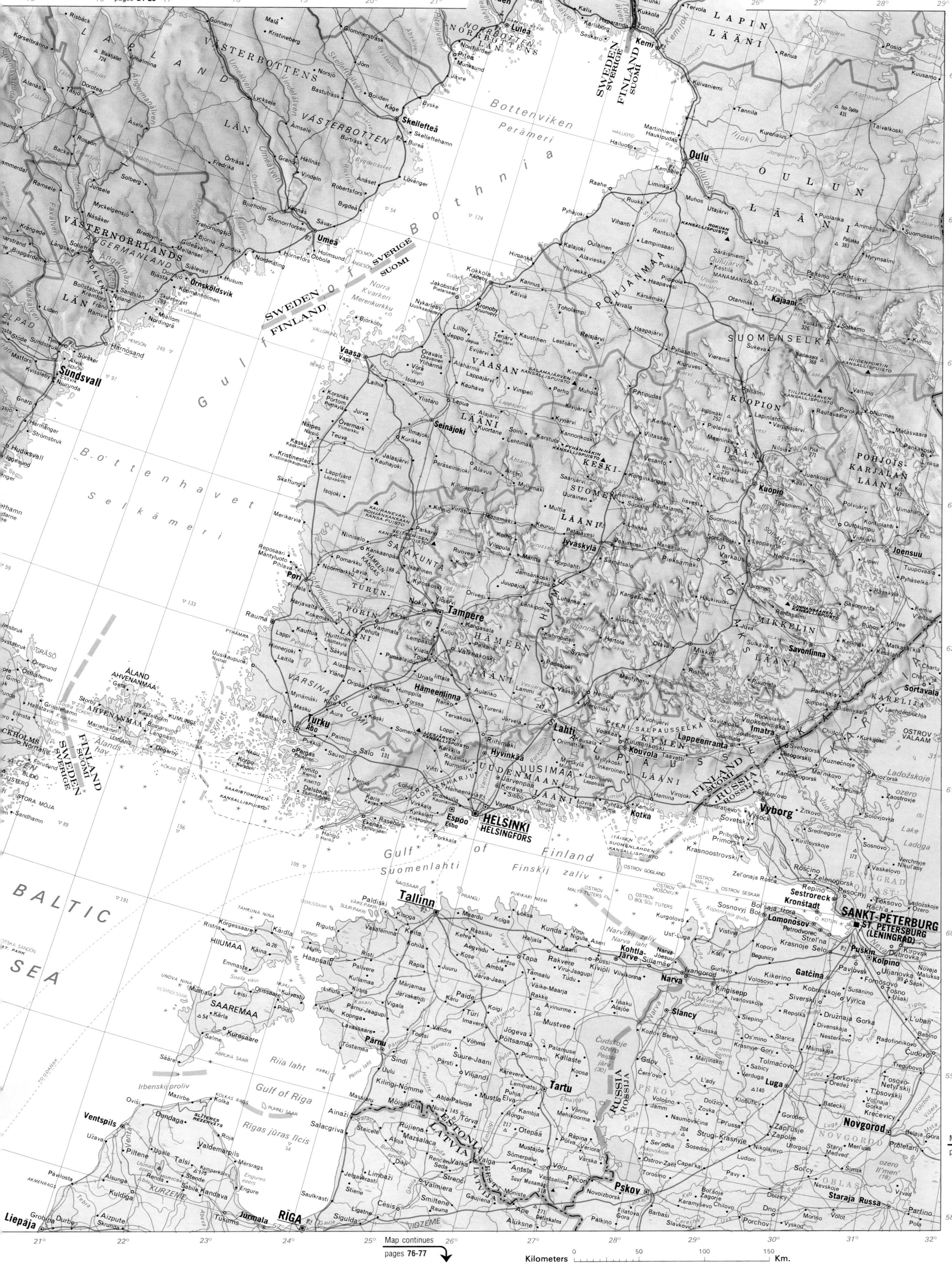
Gulf of Bothnia
Bottenviken
Perämeri
Bottenhavet
Selkämeri
Gulf of Finland
Suomenlahti
Finskij zaliv
BALTIC SEA
Gulf of Riga
Rigas jūras līcis
Riia laht
SWEDEN
SVERIGE
FINLAND
SUOMI
RUSSIA
ROSSIJA
ESTONIA
LATVIA
LAPIN LÄÄNI
OULUN LÄÄNI
VAASAN LÄÄNI
KESKI-SUOMEN LÄÄNI
KUOPION LÄÄNI
POHJOIS-KARJALAN LÄÄNI
MIKKELIN LÄÄNI
HÄMEEN LÄÄNI
TURUN-PORIN LÄÄNI
UUDENMAAN LÄÄNI
KYMEN LÄÄNI
ÅLAND
AHVENANMAA
VÄSTERBOTTENS LÄN
VÄSTERNORRLANDS LÄN
HIIUMAA
SAAREMAA
Luleå
Kemi
Oulu
Skellefteå
Umeå
Vaasa
Sundsvall
Kajaani
Kuopio
Joensuu
Jyväskylä
Seinäjoki
Pori
Tampere
Lahti
Savonlinna
Turku
Åbo
Hämeenlinna
Hyvinkää
Kouvola
Lappeenranta
Imatra
Kotka
Espoo
Esbo
HELSINKI
HELSINGFORS
Vyborg
Tallinn
Narva
Sankt-Peterburg
St. Petersburg
(Leningrad)
Tartu
Pärnu
Pskov
Novgorod
Ventspils
Liepāja
Rīga
Jūrmala
Sortavala
Gatčina
Luga
Kronštadt

Map continues pages 76-77

Map continues pages 76-77

Kilometers 0 50 100 150 Km.

Statute Miles 0 50 100 150 Mi.

Scale 1:3,000,000

One centimeter represents 30 kilometers.

One inch represents approximately 47 miles.

Conic Projection, Two Standard Parallels

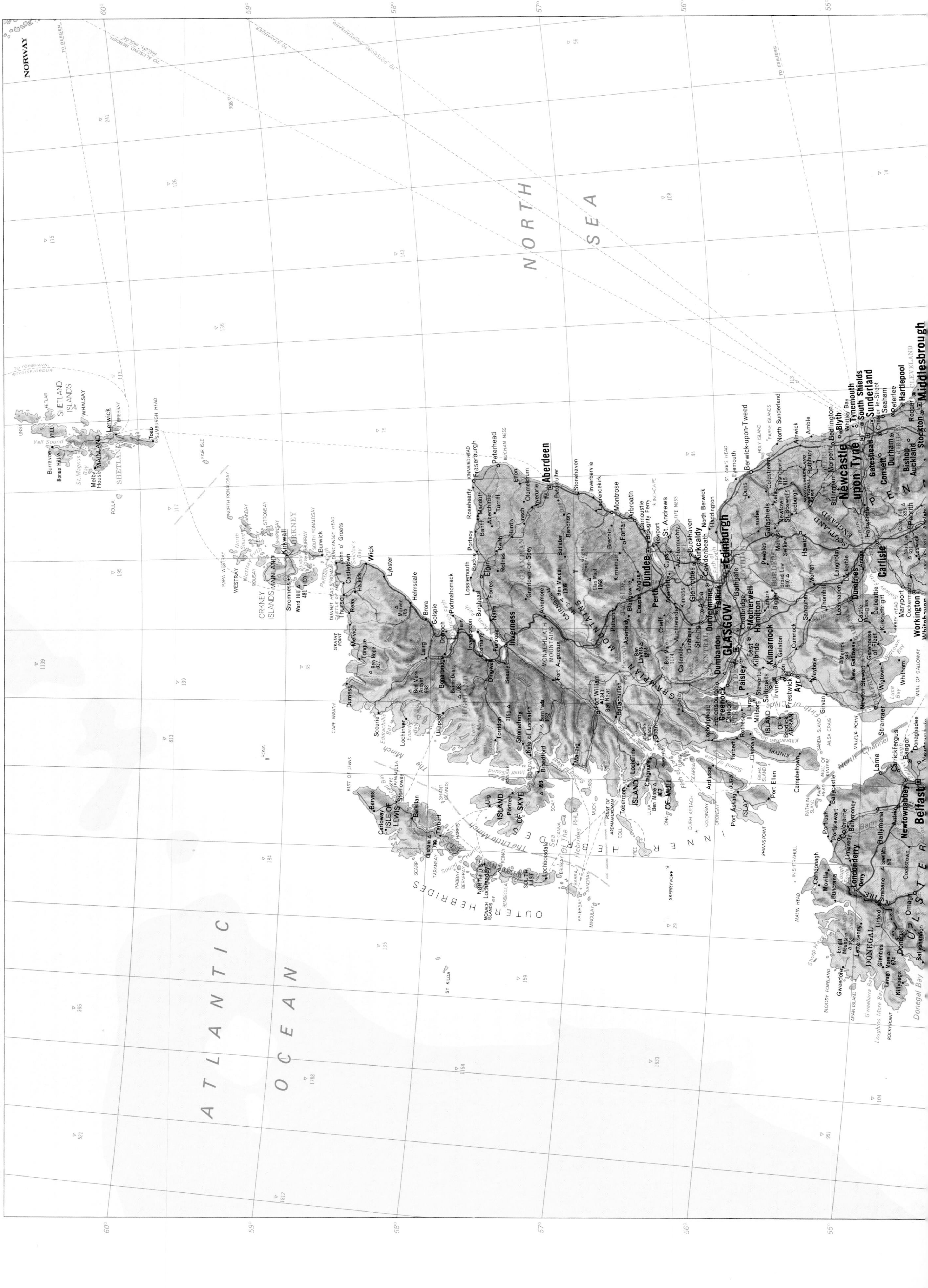
NORTH SEA
ATLANTIC OCEAN
NORWAY
SHETLAND ISLANDS
ORKNEY ISLANDS
OUTER HEBRIDES
Aberdeen
Inverness
Dundee
Perth
Edinburgh
GLASGOW
Newcastle upon Tyne
Sunderland
Middlesbrough
Carlisle
Belfast

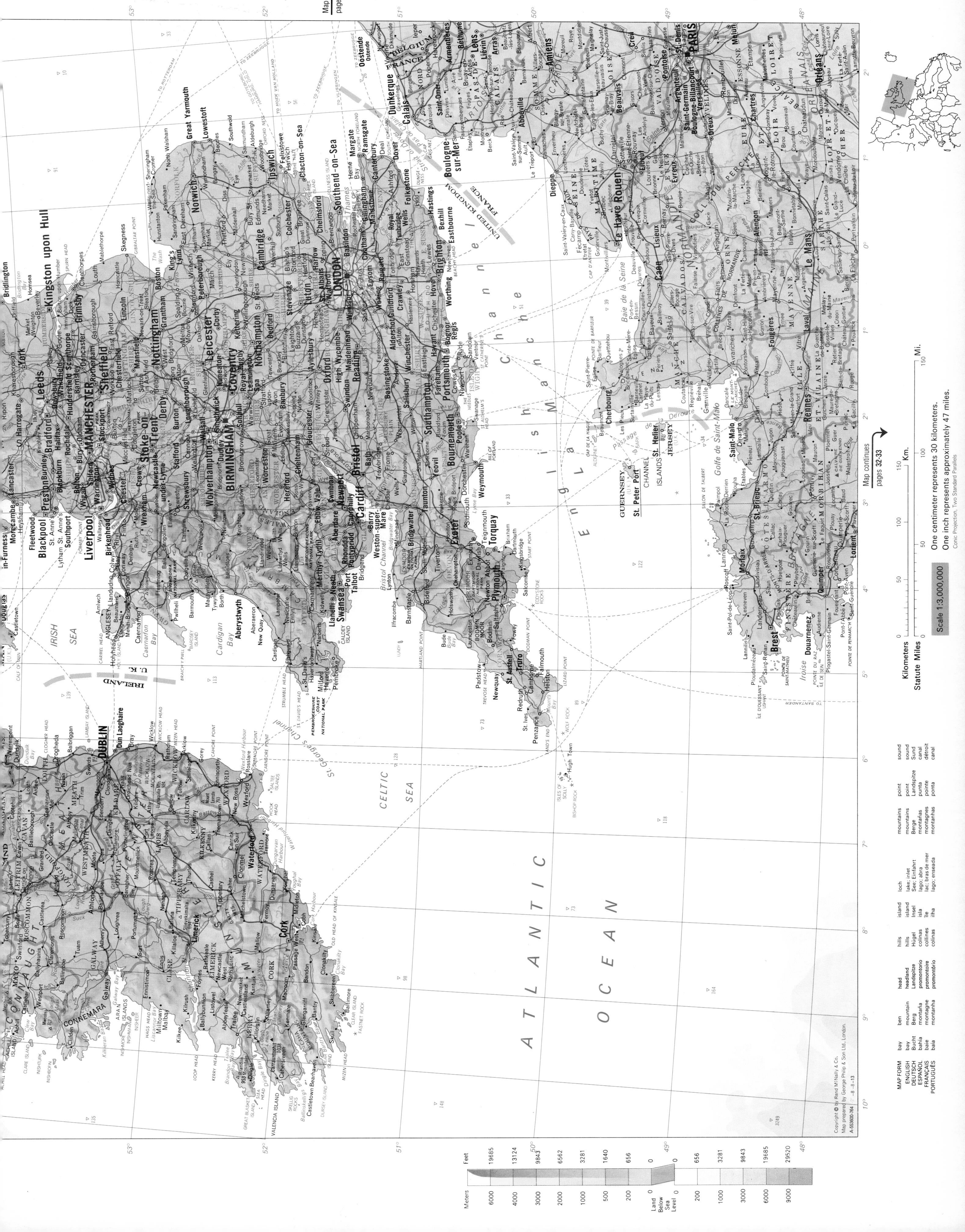
Map continues pages 30-31
Map continues pages 32-33
ATLANTIC OCEAN
CELTIC SEA
IRISH SEA
English Channel
LONDON
DUBLIN
PARIS
Scale 1:3,000,000
One centimeter represents 30 kilometers.
One inch represents approximately 47 miles.
Conic Projection, Two Standard Parallels
Kilometers
Statute Miles
MAP FORM bay ben head hills island loch mountains point sound
ENGLISH bay mountain headland hills island lake; inlet mountains point sound
DEUTSCH Bucht Berg Landspitze Hügel Insel See; Einfahrt Berge Landspitze Sund
ESPAÑOL bahía montaña promontorio colinas isla lago; abra montañas punta canal
FRANÇAIS baie montagne promontoire collines île lac; bras de mer montagnes pointe détroit
PORTUGUÊS baía montanha promontório colinas ilha lago; enseada montanhas ponta canal
Feet
Meters
Land Below Sea Level

Central Europe / Mitteleuropa / Europa Central
Europe Centrale / Europa Central

Map continues pages 26-27

NORTH SEA
WEST FRISIAN ISLANDS
NORTH FRISIAN ISLANDS
Deutsche Bucht
DENMARK
GERMANY
NETHERLANDS
BELGIUM
LUXEMBOURG
FRANCE
SWITZERLAND
AUSTRIA
ÖSTERREICH
AMSTERDAM
BRUXELLES
BRUSSEL
HAMBURG
MÜNCHEN
MUNICH
Bremen
Hannover
Köln
Düsseldorf
Frankfurt a. M.
Stuttgart
Nürnberg
Rotterdam
Antwerpen
Lille
Luxembourg
Strasbourg
Zürich
Bern
Basel
Genève
Lausanne
Innsbruck
Dijon
Reims
Nancy
Metz
Kiel
Lübeck
Rostock
Magdeburg
Kassel
Mannheim
Karlsruhe
Freiburg
Augsburg
Regensburg
ALPS
JURA
Map prepared by Rand McNally & Co.

Map continues pages 28-29

Meters	Feet
6000	19685
4000	13124
3000	9843
2000	6562
1000	3281
500	1640
200	656
Land Below Sea Level 0	0
0	0
200	656
1000	3281
3000	9843
6000	19685
9000	29520

MAP FORM	Bucht	Gebirge	jezioro	Kanal	park narodowy	See	Wald
ENGLISH	bay	range	lake, lagoon	canal	national park	lake	forest, mountains
DEUTSCH	Bucht	Gebirge	See, Haff	Kanal	Nationalpark	See	Wald
ESPAÑOL	bahía	sierra	lago, laguna	canal	parque nacional	lago	bosque, montañas
FRANÇAIS	baie	chaîne	lac, lagune	canal	parc national	lac	forêt, montagnes
PORTUGUÊS	baía	serra	lago, laguna	canal	parque nacional	lago	floresta, montanhas

Kilometers 0 50 100 150 Km.
Statute Miles 0 50 100 Mi.

Scale 1:3,000,000

One centimeter represents 30 kilometers.
One inch represents approximately 47 miles.
Conic Projection, Two Standard Parallels.

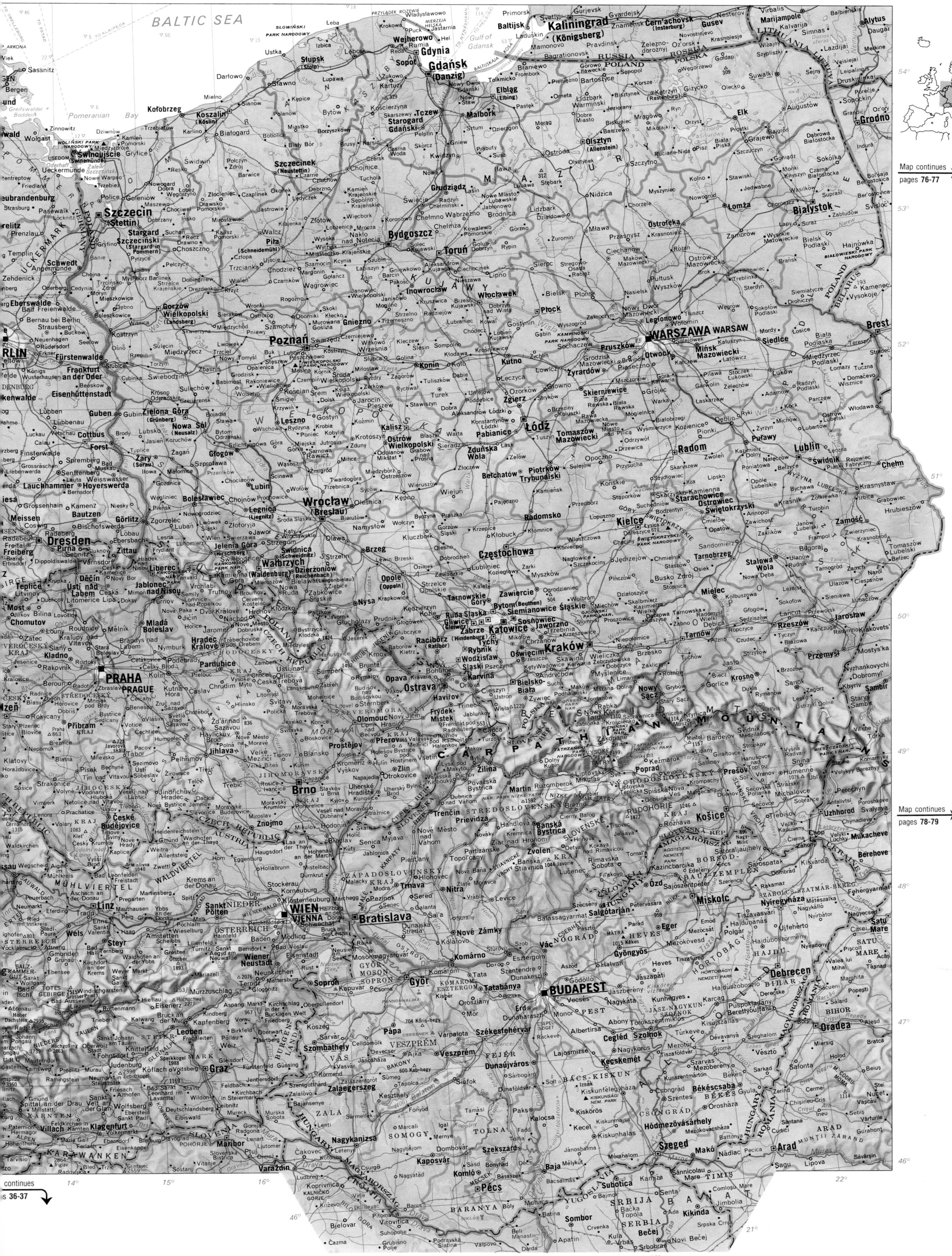

BALTIC SEA
Gulf of Gdansk
Pomeranian Bay
Kaliningrad (Königsberg)
Gdańsk (Danzig)
Gdynia
Szczecin (Stettin)
Bydgoszcz
Toruń
Olsztyn (Allenstein)
Białystok
Poznań
WARSZAWA WARSAW
Łódź
Lublin
Wrocław (Breslau)
Częstochowa
Kielce
Radom
Katowice
Kraków
Rzeszów
Dresden
PRAHA PRAGUE
Ostrava
Brno
Bratislava
WIEN VIENNA
Linz
Graz
Košice
Miskolc
BUDAPEST
Debrecen
Szeged
Pécs
Győr
Oradea
Arad
Grodno
Brest
CARPATHIAN MOUNTAINS
POLAND
CZECH REPUBLIC
SLOVAKIA
AUSTRIA
HUNGARY
ROMANIA
UKRAINE
BELARUS
LITHUANIA
CROATIA
SERBIA
RUSSIA

Map continues
pages 76-77

Map continues
pages 78-79

continues
s 36-37

Map continues pages 28-29

English Channel
La Manche
ATLANTIC OCEAN
Bay of Biscay
UNITED KINGDOM
FRANCE
Strait of Dover
Pas de Calais
CHANNEL ISLANDS
GUERNSEY (UK)
St. Peter Port
JERSEY (UK)
St. Helier
PARIS
Rouen
Le Havre
Caen
Cherbourg
Rennes
Nantes
Brest
Angers
Le Mans
Tours
Orléans
Limoges
Poitiers
Bordeaux
Toulouse
Montpellier
Clermont-Ferrand
Perpignan
Lille
Amiens
Dunkerque
Calais
Boulogne-sur-Mer
Pau
Bayonne
Biarritz
Donostia San Sebastián
Bilbao
Santander
Vitoria Gasteiz
Pamplona
Burgos
ANDORRA
Andorra
PYRÉNÉES
MASSIF CENTRAL
BRETAGNE
NORMANDIE
Plymouth
Exeter
Southampton
Portsmouth
Brighton
Torquay
Bournemouth

Meters / Feet
6000 19685
4000 13124
3000 9843
2000 6562
1000 3281
500 1640
200 656
0 0
Land Below Sea Level
0 0
200 656
1000 3281
3000 9843
6000 19685
9000 29520

Map continues pages 34-35

MAP FORM	canal	cap	île	lago	mont (e)	monts	pointe	See
ENGLISH	canal	cape	island	lake	mount	mountains	point	lake
DEUTSCH	Kanal	Kap	Insel	See	Berg	Berge	Landspitze	See
ESPAÑOL	canal	cabo	isla	lago	monte	montes	punta	lago
FRANÇAIS	canal	cap	île	lac	mont	monts	pointe	lac
PORTUGUÊS	canal	cabo	ilha	lago	monte	montes	ponta	lago

Map continues pages 30-31

MEDITERRANEAN SEA
LIGURIAN SEA
ADRIATIC SEA
Gulf of Venice
MARSEILLE
Marseille
Toulon
Nice
Cannes
Genova
Torino
MILANO
Venezia
Bologna
Firenze
Livorno
Lyon
Grenoble
Genève
Lausanne
Bern
Basel
Zürich
Innsbruck
Salzburg
MÜNCHEN
Augsburg
Stuttgart
Strasbourg
Nancy
Metz
Luxembourg
Frankfurt a. M.
Mannheim
Nürnberg
Regensburg
Köln
Bonn
Aachen
Liège
Koblenz
PRAHA
Trieste
Verona
Padova
Bergamo
Brescia
CORSE
CORSICA
Bastia
ALPS
APPENNINO
Copyright © by Rand McNally & Co.
Map prepared by Rand McNally GmbH, Stuttgart.
A-559495-764 -9 -6 -16

Map continues pages 36-37

Kilometers 0 50 100 150 Km.
Statute Miles 0 50 100 150 Mi.

Scale 1:3,000,000

One centimeter represents 30 kilometers.
One inch represents approximately 47 miles.
Lambert Conformal Conic Projection

Spain and Portugal / Spanien und Portugal / España y Portugal
Espagne et Portugal / Espanha e Portugal

Bay of Biscay
ATLANTIC
OCEAN
ATLANTIC
OCEAN
ALBORÁN SEA
La Coruña
El Ferrol del Caudillo
Gijón
Oviedo
Avilés
Santander
Bilbao
Donostia San Sebastián
Vitoria Gasteiz
Logroño
Burgos
León
Lugo
Santiago de Compostela
Pontevedra
Vigo
Orense
Ponferrada
Palencia
Valladolid
Zamora
Salamanca
Segovia
Ávila
Soria
Guadalajara
MADRID
Alcalá de Henares
Getafe
Toledo
Aranjuez
Talavera de la Reina
Plasencia
Cáceres
Badajoz
Mérida
Ciudad Real
Puertollano
Valdepeñas
Córdoba
Jaén
Linares
Úbeda
Granada
Almería
Málaga
Sevilla Seville
Huelva
Cádiz
Jerez de la Frontera
Algeciras
Gibraltar (U.K.)
Tánger Tangier
Ceuta (Sp.)
Tétouan
Melilla (Sp.)
Nador
Al-Hoceima
Larache
Ksar-el-Kebir
Ouezzane
MOROCCO AL-MAGREB
Porto
Vila Nova de Gaia
Braga
Viseu
Coimbra
Leiria
Santarém
LISBOA LISBON
Setúbal
Évora
Faro
Lagos
Portimão
Golfo de Cádiz
Strait of Gibraltar
CORDILLERA CANTÁBRICA
SISTEMA CENTRAL
SIERRA MORENA
SISTEMAS BÉTICOS
SISTEMA IBÉRICO
CASTILLA LA MANCHA
CASTILLA LEÓN
EXTREMADURA
ANDALUCÍA
GALICIA
ASTURIAS
CANTABRIA
ALGARVE
ALENTEJO
TRAS-OS-MONTES
MINHO
BEIRA
SPAIN ESPAÑA
PORTUGAL
Copyright © by Rand McNally & Co.
Map prepared by Rand McNally GmbH, Stuttgart.
A-559900-764

Meters	Feet
6000	19685
4000	13124
3000	9843
2000	6562
1000	3281
500	1640
200	656
0	0
Land Below Sea Level 0	0
200	656
1000	3281
3000	9843
6000	19685
9000	29520

ESPAÑOL	bahía	cabo	isla	embalse	puerto	punta	ría	sierra
ENGLISH	bay	cape	island	reservoir	port	point	estuary	mountains
DEUTSCH	Bucht	Kap	Insel	Stausee	Hafen	Landspitze	Trichtermündung	Berge
FRANÇAIS	baie	cap	île	réservoir	port	pointe	estuaire	montagnes
PORTUGUÊS	baía	cabo	ilha	reservatório	porto	ponta	estuário	serra

Map continues pages 32-33

Golfe du Lion
MEDITERRANEAN SEA
ILLES BALEARS
BALEARIC ISLANDS
BALEARS
MALLORCA
MAJORCA
MENORCA
MINORCA
EIVISSA
IBIZA
FORMENTERA
Palma
Maó
Ciutadella
Eivissa
BARCELONA
L'Hospitalet de Llobregat
Badalona
Sabadell
Terrassa
Mataró
Tarragona
Reus
Lleida
Girona
Manresa
Vic
Figueres
Zaragoza
Huesca
Teruel
Castelló de la Plana
València
Sagunt
Gandia
Alzira
Alcoi
Elda
Elx
Alacant
Oriola
Murcia
Cartagena
Torrevella
Golf de València
DELTA DE L'EBRE
CATALUNYA
ARAGÓN
VALÈNCIA
ANDORRA
Andorra
PYRÉNÉES
PYRENEES
ROUSSILLON
FRANCE
SPAIN
ESPAÑA
Toulouse
Montauban
Albi
Castres
Carcassonne
Narbonne
Béziers
Sète
Montpellier
Nîmes
Avignon
Arles
Marseille
Toulon
La Seyne
Hyères
Cannes
Nice
Antibes
Aix-en-Provence
Perpignan
Tarbes
Pau
Auch
Mont-de-Marsan
Dax
MONACO
PROVENCE
LANGUEDOC
GASCOGNE
ARMAGNAC
EL DJAZAÏR
ALGIERS
ALGERIA
ALGÉRIE
Wahran
Oran
Mestghanem
Ech Cheliff
(Orleansville)
El Boulaida
Boufarik
Lemdiyya
Tizi-Ouzou
Bejaïa
(Bougie)
Sétif
El Eulma
Bordj Bou Arreridj
Batna
Bou Saâda
Sidi bel Abbès
Sig
Ghilizane
Qasr el-Boukhari
Jijel
ATLAS TELLIEN
MOUNTAINS
KABYLIE
DAHRA
L'OUARSENIS
TITTERI
MONTS DU HODNA
PLAINE DU HODNA

Map continues pages 148-149

Kilometers 0 50 100 150 Km.
Statute Miles 0 50 100 150 Mi.

Scale 1:3,000,000

One centimeter represents 30 kilometers.
One inch represents approximately 47 miles.
Conic Projection, Two Standard Parallels

Map continues pages 38-39

Map continues pages 30-31

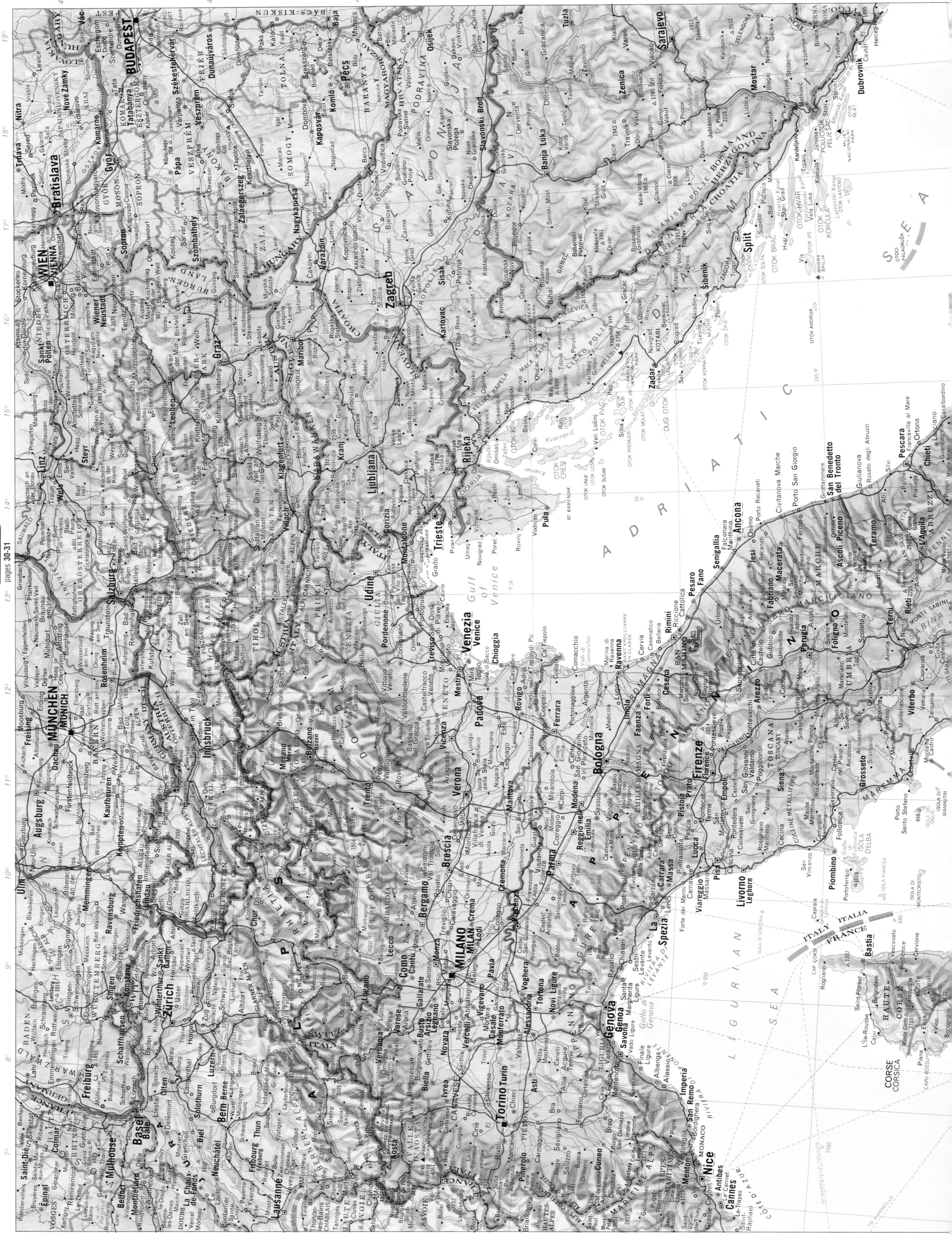
ADRIATIC SEA
LIGURIAN SEA
BUDAPEST
WIEN
MÜNCHEN
MILANO
Venezia
Bologna
Firenze
Zagreb
Ljubljana
Sarajevo
Torino
Genova

Map continues pages 32-33

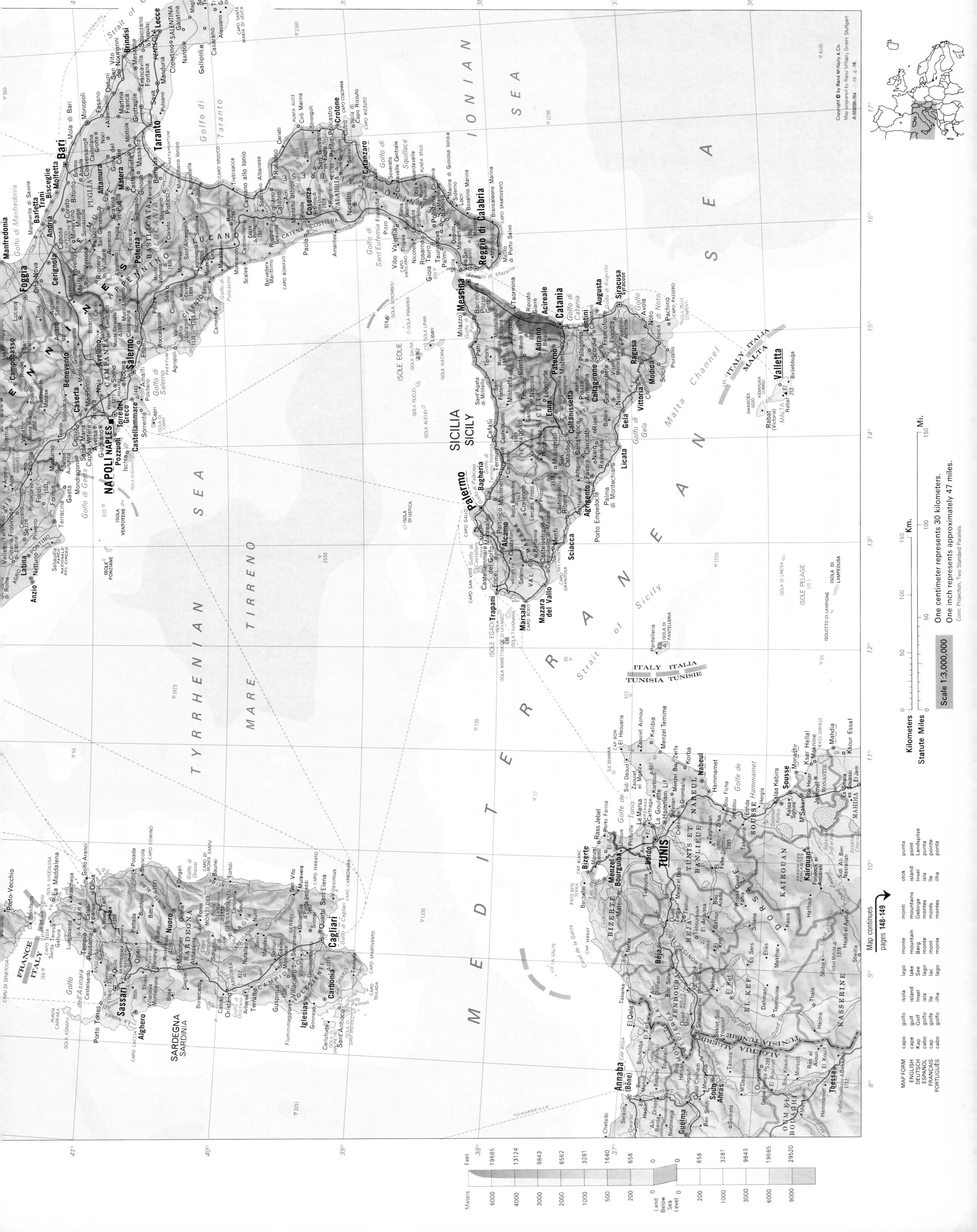
TYRRHENIAN SEA
MARE TIRRENO
IONIAN SEA
MEDITERRANEAN SEA
SICILIA
SICILY
SARDEGNA
SARDINIA
Strait of Sicily
Malta Channel
Strait of Otranto
Golfo di Taranto
NAPOLI NAPLES
Palermo
Messina
Catania
Cagliari
TUNIS
Valletta
Scale 1:3,000,000
One centimeter represents 30 kilometers.
One inch represents approximately 47 miles.
Conic Projection, Two Standard Parallels
Kilometers
Statute Miles
Map continues pages 148-149
Copyright © by Rand McNally & Co.
Map prepared by Rand McNally GmbH, Stuttgart.
MAP FORM: capo, golfo, isola, lago, monte, monti, otok, punta
ENGLISH: cape, gulf, island, lake, mountain, mountains, island, point
DEUTSCH: Kap, Golf, Insel, See, Berg, Gebirge, Insel, Landspitze
ESPAÑOL: cabo, golfo, isla, lago, monte, montes, isla, punta
FRANÇAIS: cap, golfe, île, lac, mont, monts, île, pointe
PORTUGUÊS: cabo, golfo, ilha, lago, monte, montes, ilha, ponta
Meters
Feet
Land Below Sea Level

BLACK SEA
CARPATHIAN MOUNTAINS
BUCUREŞTI
BUDAPEST
BEOGRAD
SOFIJA
Chişinău
Mouths of the Danube

MAP FORM	akra	kólpos	lacul	limni	manastir	muntii	prohod	sea
ENGLISH	cape	bay	lake	lake	monastery	mountains	pass	sea
DEUTSCH	Kap	Bucht	See	See	Kloster	Berge	Pass	Meer
ESPAÑOL	cabo	bahía	lago	lago	monasterio	montañas	paso	mar
FRANÇAIS	cap	baie	lac	lac	monastère	montagnes	col	mer
PORTUGUÊS	cabo	baía	lago	lago	mosteiro	montanhas	passo	mar

Kilometers 0 50 100 150 Km.
Statute Miles 0 50 100 150 Mi.

Scale 1:3,000,000

One centimeter represents 30 kilometers.
One inch represents approximately 47 miles.
Conic Projection, Two Standard Parallels

Map continues pages 30-31
Map continues pages 78-79
Map continues pages 36-37

Map continues pages 130-131

AEGEAN SEA
IONIAN SEA
MEDITERRANEAN SEA
ADRIATIC SEA
Strait of Otranto
Sea of Crete
ATHÍNAI (ATHENS)
ISTANBUL
Thessaloníki (Salonika)
İzmir (Smyrna)
KIKLÁDHES CYCLADES
DHODHEKÁNISOS DODECANESE
KRÍTI CRETE
IONIAN ISLANDS
ITALY
Copyright © by Rand McNally & Co.
Map prepared by Rand McNally GmbH, Stuttgart.

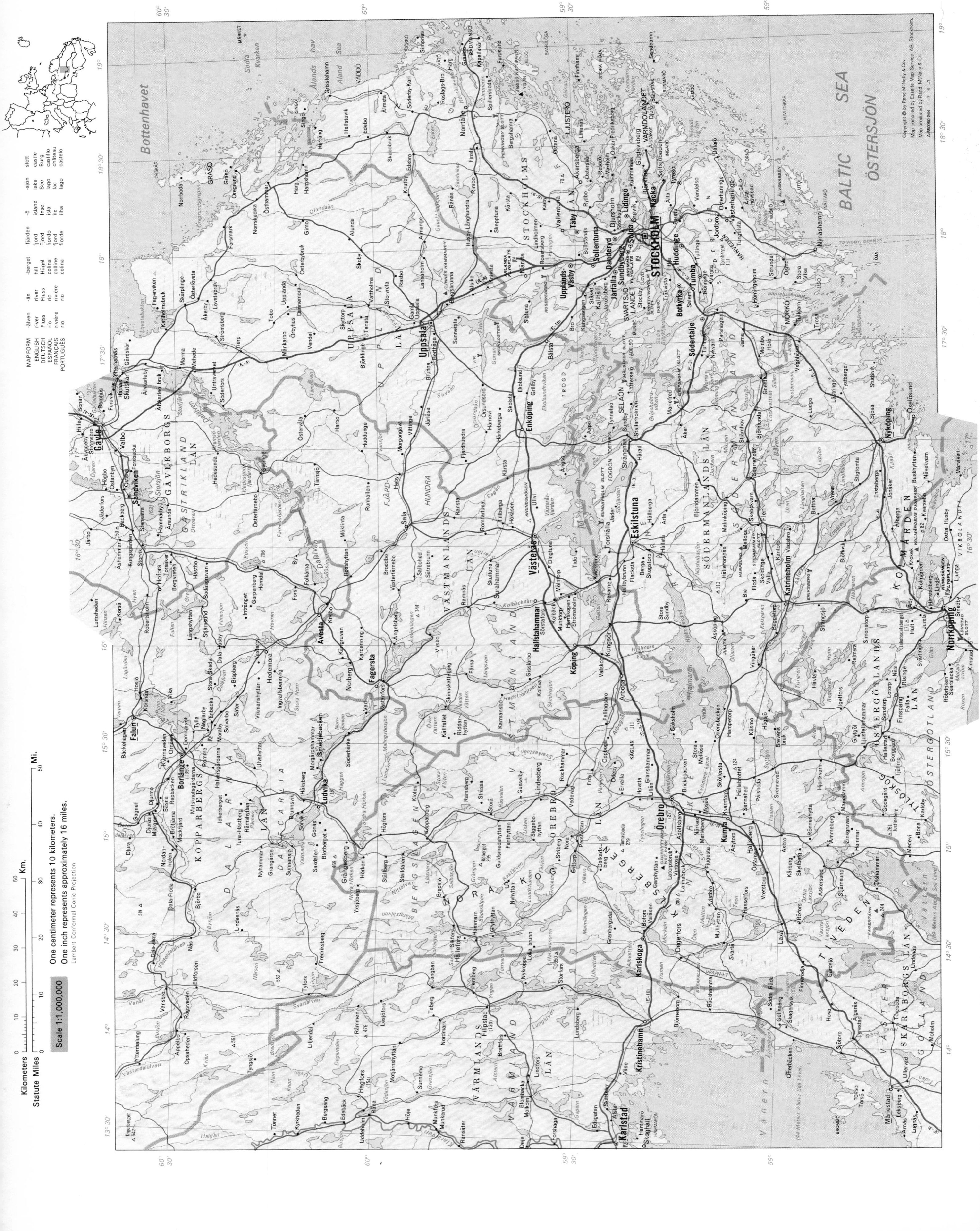
MAP FORM
ENGLISH
DEUTSCH
ESPAÑOL
FRANÇAIS
PORTUGUÊS
-älven river Fluss río rivière rio
-ån river Fluss río rivière rio
-berget hill Hügel colina colline colina
-fjärden fjord Fjord fiordo fjord fiorde
-ö island Insel isla île ilha
-sjön lake See lago lac lago
slott castle Burg castillo château castelo
Kilometers
Statute Miles
Km.
Mi.
Scale 1:1,000,000
One centimeter represents 10 kilometers.
One inch represents approximately 16 miles.
Lambert Conformal Conic Projection
Copyright © by Rand McNally & Co.
Map compiled by Esselte Map Service AB, Stockholm.
Map produced by Rand McNally & Co.
Bottenhavet
BALTIC SEA
ÖSTERSJÖN
STOCKHOLM
STOCKHOLMS LÄN
UPPSALA LÄN
Uppsala
Västerås
VÄSTMANLANDS LÄN
SÖDERMANLANDS LÄN
Eskilstuna
Örebro
ÖREBRO LÄN
KOPPARBERGS LÄN
GÄVLEBORGS LÄN
Gävle
VÄRMLANDS LÄN
Karlstad
Norrköping
Nyköping
Vänern
Vättern
Hjälmaren
Mälaren

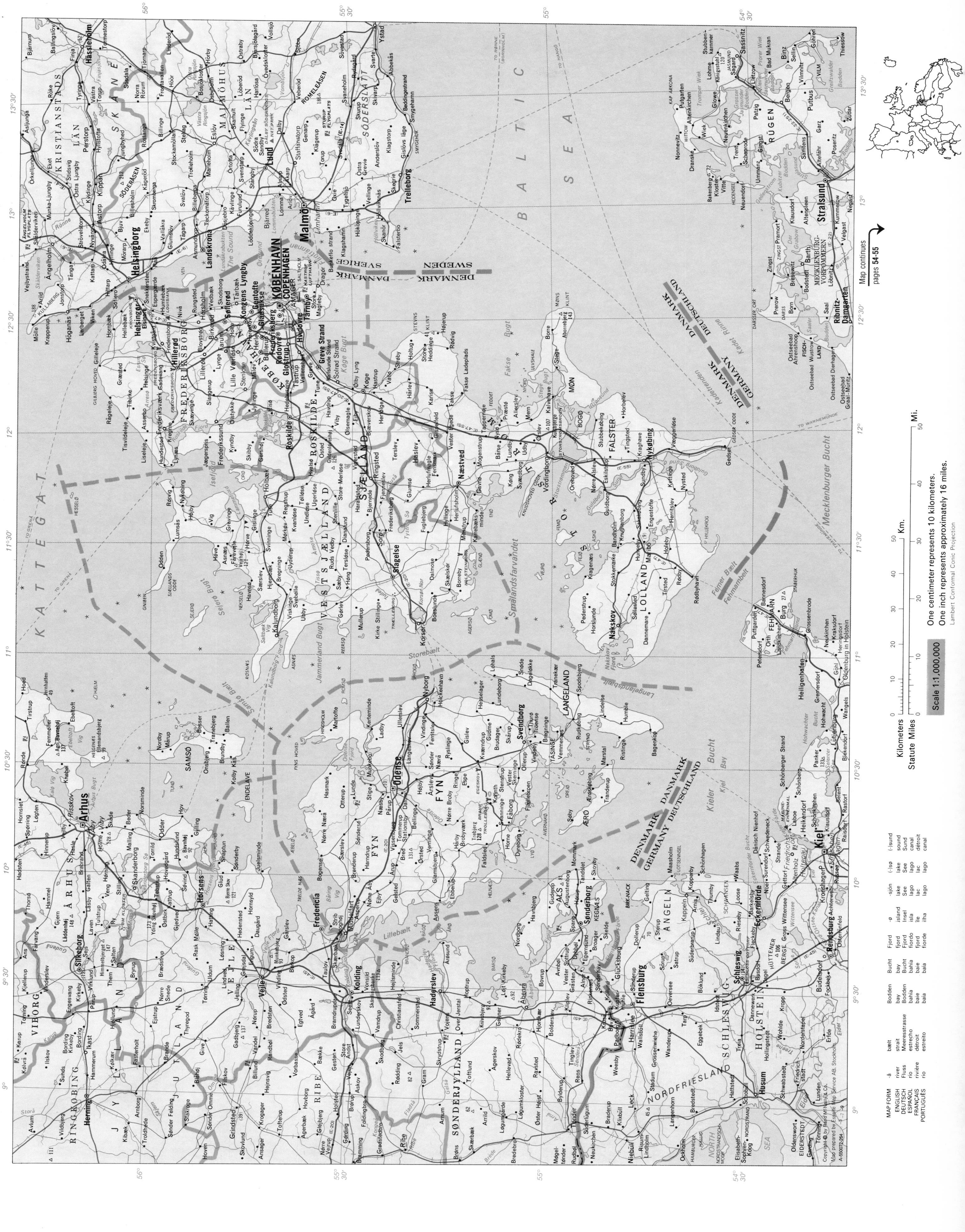
KATTEGAT
BALTIC SEA
KØBENHAVN
COPENHAGEN
Malmö
Kiel
Helsingborg
Helsingør
Roskilde
Odense
Århus
Flensburg
Stralsund
RÜGEN
FYN
SJÆLLAND
LOLLAND
FALSTER
MØN
DANMARK
SVERIGE
DENMARK
SWEDEN
DEUTSCHLAND
GERMANY
Map continues pages 54-55
Kilometers
Statute Miles
Scale 1:1,000,000
One centimeter represents 10 kilometers.
One inch represents approximately 16 miles.
Lambert Conformal Conic Projection
MAPFORM / ENGLISH / DEUTSCH / ESPAÑOL / FRANÇAIS / PORTUGUÊS
Copyright by Rand McNally & Co.
Map prepared by Esselte Map Service AB, Stockholm

St. George's Channel
Cardigan Bay
Bristol Channel
Carmarthen Bay
CAMBRIAN MOUNTAINS
BLACK MOUNTAINS
BRECON BEACONS
SNOWDONIA NATIONAL PARK
PEMBROKESHIRE COAST NATIONAL PARK
EXMOOR
DARTMOOR
BODMIN MOOR
GWYNEDD
CLWYD
POWYS
DYFED
WEST GLAMORGAN
MID GLAMORGAN
SOUTH GLAMORGAN
GWENT
CHESHIRE
SHROPSHIRE
HEREFORD AND WORCESTER
DEVON
CORNWALL
SOMERSET
DORSET
Wrexham
Stoke-on-Trent
Shrewsbury
Wolverhampton
Aberystwyth
Worcester
Hereford
Gloucester
Swansea
Llanelli
Port Talbot
Neath
Rhondda
Merthyr Tydfil
Pontypridd
Caerphilly
Newport
Cardiff
Bristol
Bath
Weston-super-Mare
Taunton
Barnstaple
Exeter
Exmouth
Torquay
Newton Abbot
Plymouth
Newquay
Truro
Falmouth
Penzance
St. Ives
Yeovil
Dorchester
Weymouth
Haverfordwest
Milford Haven
Pembroke
Carmarthen
Cardigan
Bridgwater
TORBAY
Lyme Bay
ENG
a
ISLES OF SCILLY
ATLANTIC OCEAN

Map continues pages 48-49

ENGLISH	bay	drain	forest	head	hill	isle	marsh	point	vale
DEUTSCH	Bucht	Abzugsgraben	Wald	Landspitze	Hügel	Insel	Marsch	Landspitze	Tal
ESPAÑOL	bahia	acquia	bosque	promontorio	colina	isla	pantano	punta	valle
FRANÇAIS	baie	drainage	forêt	promontoire	colline	île	marais	pointe	dépression
PORTUGUÊS	baia	drenagem	floresta	promontório	colina	ilha	pântano	ponta	vale

Map continues
pages 44-45

NORTH SEA
The Wash
Brancaster Roads
NORWICH
Norwich
Great Yarmouth
Lowestoft
King's Lynn
Peterborough
Cambridge
CAMBRIDGESHIRE
Ipswich
Colchester
Harwich
Felixstowe
Clacton-on-Sea
Chelmsford
Southend-on-Sea
LONDON
Luton
Bedford
Northampton
Leicester
Nottingham
Derby
Coventry
Rugby
Oxford
Aylesbury
Reading
Swindon
Newbury
Salisbury
Winchester
Southampton
Portsmouth
Bournemouth
ISLE OF WIGHT
Chichester
Worthing
Brighton
Eastbourne
Hastings
Maidstone
Canterbury
Margate
Ramsgate
Dover
Folkestone
Ashford
Guildford
Reigate
Crawley
Strait of Dover
C H A N N E L
GUERNSEY (U.K.)
St. Peter Port
CHANNEL ISLANDS
JERSEY (U.K.)
St. Helier
ALDERNEY
Passage de la Déroute

Map continues
pages 50-51

Kilometers 0 10 20 30 40 50 Km.

Statute Miles 0 10 20 30 40 50 Mi.

Scale 1:1,000,000

One centimeter represents 10 kilometers.

One inch represents approximately 16 miles.

Lambert Conformal Conic Projection

Map continues pages 46-47

Map continues pages 48-49

North Channel
IRISH SEA
SCOTLAND
NORTHERN IRELAND
IRELAND ÉIRE
UNITED KINGDOM
ISLE OF MAN (U.K.)
ANGLESEY
ISLAND OF ARRAN
DONEGAL
MONAGHAN
CAVAN
LOUTH
MEATH
KILDARE
WICKLOW
CARLOW
WEXFORD
WICKLOW MOUNTAINS
MOURNE MTS.
STRATHCLYDE
GWYNEDD
Lough Neagh
Lough Foyle
Strangford Lough
Luce Bay
Solway Firth
Caernarfon Bay
Tremadog Bay
Londonderry
Derry
Coleraine
Ballymena
Larne
Antrim
Belfast
Bangor
Newtownards
Lisburn
Portadown
Armagh
Newry
Dundalk
Dún Dealgan
Drogheda
Droichead Átha
DUBLIN
BAILE ÁTHA CLIATH
Dún Laoghaire
Bray
Wicklow
Arklow
Douglas
Kilmarnock
Ayr
Irvine
Dumfries
Stranraer
Workington
Whitehaven
Barrow-in-Fu
Holyhead
Bangor
Caernarfon
Llandudno
Colwyn Bay
Rhyl

MAP FORM	bay	dale	firth	forest	head	loch	moor	water
ENGLISH	bay	dale	estuary	forest	head	lake; inlet	moor	water (lake, river)
DEUTSCH	Bucht	Weites Tal	Trichtermündung	Wald	Landspitze	See; Einfahrt	Moor	See, Fluss
ESPAÑOL	bahía	valle	estuario	bosque	promontorio	lago; abra	páramo	lago, río
FRANÇAIS	baie	vallée	estuaire	forêt	promontoire	lac; bras de mer	lande	lac, rivière
PORTUGUÊS	baía	vale	estuário	floresta	promontório	lago; enseada	pântano	lago, rio

NORTH SEA
NEWCASTLE UPON TYNE
Gateshead
South Shields
Sunderland
Middlesbrough
Hartlepool
Darlington
Stockton-on-Tees
Scarborough
Bridlington
Harrogate
York
LEEDS
Bradford
Halifax
Huddersfield
Wakefield
Kingston upon Hull
Grimsby
Scunthorpe
Doncaster
Barnsley
Sheffield
Chesterfield
Lincoln
Nottingham
Derby
Stoke-on-Trent
MANCHESTER
Stockport
Oldham
Bolton
Rochdale
Blackburn
Burnley
Preston
Lancaster
Carlisle
LIVERPOOL
Chester
Wrexham
Crewe
Stafford
Burton upon Trent
Boston
Berwick-upon-Tweed
Hawick
NORTH YORK MOORS
NORTHUMBERLAND NATIONAL PARK
YORKSHIRE DALES NATIONAL PARK
NORTH YORK MOORS NATIONAL PARK
VALE OF PICKERING
VALE OF YORK
The Wash
Map continues pages 42-43

Kilometers 0 10 20 30 40 50 Km.
Statute Miles 0 10 20 30 40 50 Mi.

Scale 1:1,000,000

One centimeter represents 10 kilometers.
One inch represents approximately 16 miles.

Lambert Conformal Conic Projection

ATLANTIC OCEAN
NORTH SEA
ORKNEY ISLANDS
SHETLAND ISLANDS
SHETLAND
FAIR ISLE
WESTRAY
SANDAY
STRONSAY
SHAPINSAY
ROUSAY
EDAY
HOY
SOUTH RONALDSAY
STROMA
Kirkwall
Stromness
Pentland Firth
Thurso
Wick
John o' Groats
Helmsdale
Brora
Golspie
Dornoch
Tain
Invergordon
Dingwall
BLACK ISLE
Nairn
Forres
Elgin
Lossiemouth
Buckie
Banff
Fraserburgh
Moray Firth
HIGHLAND
Ullapool
Kinlochbervie
Durness
CAPE WRATH
Tongue
Lairg
Bonar Bridge
Lochinver
Gairloch
The Minch
Little Minch
Stornoway
LEWIS
HARRIS
Tarbert
NORTH UIST
Lochmaddy
HEBRIDES
BUTT OF LEWIS
FLANNAN ISLANDS
SULE SKERRY
STACK SKERRY
RONA
UNST
YELL
FETLAR
WHALSAY
BRESSAY
Lerwick
Scalloway
MAINLAND
FOULA
PAPA STOUR
SUMBURGH HEAD
FITFUL HEAD
St. Magnus Bay
Yell Sound
Copyright © by Rand McNally & Co.

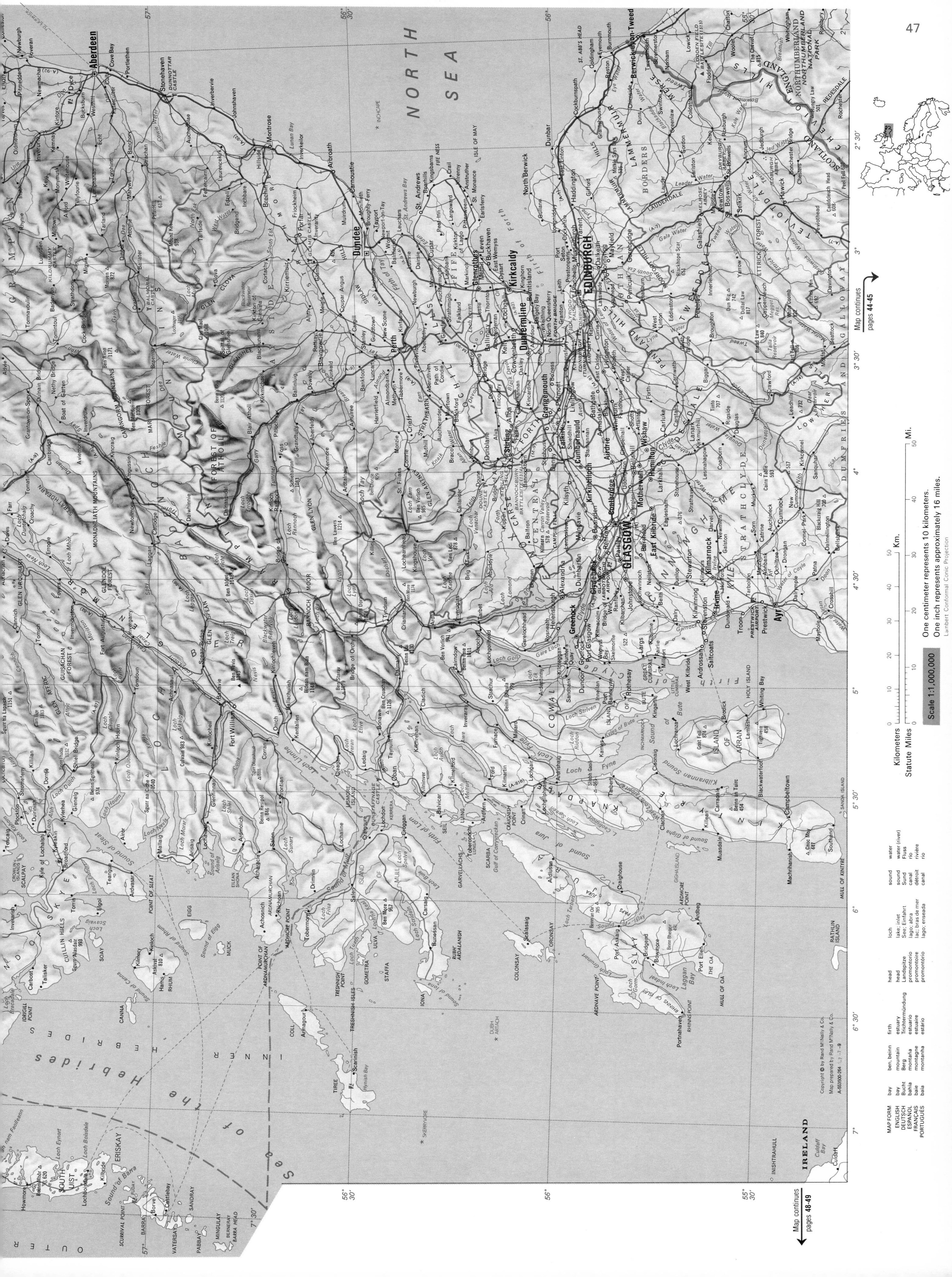
NORTH SEA
Sea of the Hebrides
INNER HEBRIDES
OUTER HEBRIDES
IRELAND
Map continues pages 44-45
Map continues pages 48-49
Scale 1:1,000,000
Kilometers
Statute Miles
Km.
Mi.
One centimeter represents 10 kilometers.
One inch represents approximately 16 miles.
Lambert Conformal Conic Projection
MAP FORM | bay | ben, beinn | firth | head | loch | sound | water
ENGLISH | bay | mountain | estuary | head | lake; inlet | sound | water (river)
DEUTSCH | Bucht | Berg | Trichtermündung | Landspitze | See; Einfahrt | Sund | Fluss
ESPAÑOL | bahía | montaña | estuario | promontorio | lago; abra | canal | río
FRANÇAIS | baie | montagne | estuaire | promontoire | lac; bras de mer | détroit | rivière
PORTUGUÊS | baía | montanha | estuário | promontório | lago; enseada | canal | rio
Copyright © by Rand McNally & Co.
Map prepared by Rand McNally & Co.

Map continues pages 44-45

Map continues pages 46-47

ATLANTIC
OCEAN
IRISH
SEA
North Channel
SCOTLAND
NORTHERN IRELAND
ULSTER
CONNAUGHT
U.K.
IRELAND
EIRE
Belfast
Londonderry
Derry
Coleraine
Ballymena
Larne
Lisburn
Newtownabbey
Bangor
Newtownards
Lurgan
Portadown
Armagh
Newry
Dundalk
Dún Dealgan
Drogheda
Droichead Átha
Omagh
Enniskillen
Strabane
Letterkenny
Donegal
Sligo
Sligeach
Ballina
Castlebar
Westport
Cavan
Monaghan
Dungannon
Cookstown
Lough Neagh
Lough Foyle
Lough Swilly
Donegal Bay
Sligo Bay
Clew Bay
INISHOWEN
SPERRIN MTS.
MOURNE MTS.
BLUE STACK MTS.
DERRYVEAGH MTS.
NEPHIN BEG RANGE
SLIEVE GAMPH
ACHILL ISLAND
CLARE ISLAND
MONAGHAN
CAVAN
LOUTH
MEATH
LEITRIM
SLIGO
ROSCOMMON
MAYO
DONEGAL

Map continues pages 42-43

Scale 1:1,000,000
One centimeter represents 10 kilometers.
One inch represents approximately 16 miles.
Lambert Conformal Conic Projection
Kilometers
Statute Miles
MAP FORM bay harbour head loch mountains, mts. point slieve
ENGLISH bay harbor, harbour head lake; inlet mountains point mountain, mountains
DEUTSCH Bucht Hafen Landspitze See; Einfahrt Berge Landspitze Berg, Berge
ESPAÑOL bahía puerto promontorio lago; abra montañas punta montaña, montañas
FRANÇAIS baie port promontoire lac; bras de mer montagnes pointe montagne, montagnes
PORTUGUÊS baía porto promontório lago; enseada montanhas ponta montanha, montanhas
Copyright © by Rand McNally & Co.
Map prepared by Rand McNally & Co.
CELTIC SEA
St. George's Channel

Map continues pages 56-57

Map continues pages 52-53

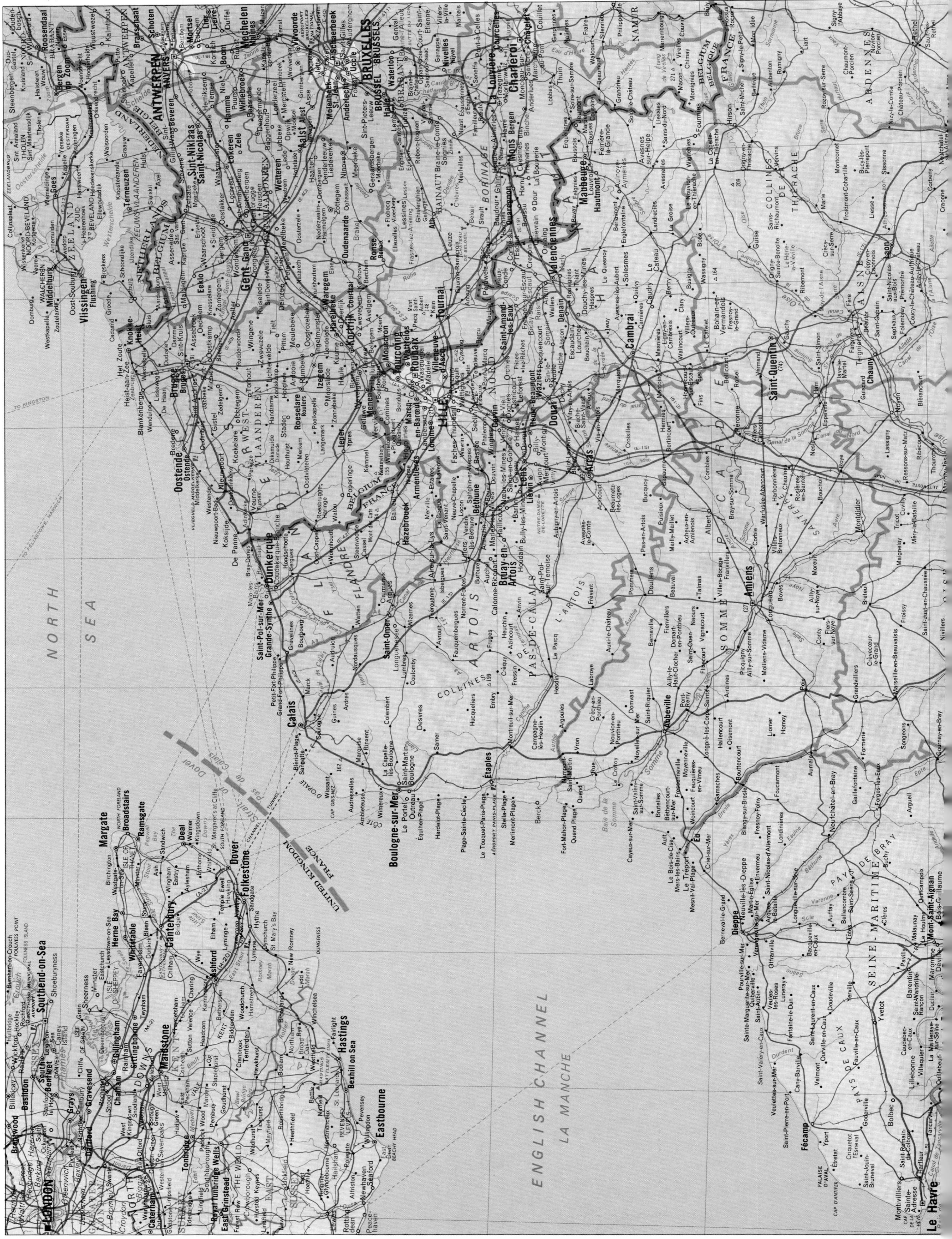
NORTH SEA
ENGLISH CHANNEL
LA MANCHE
Strait of Dover
Pas de Calais
UNITED KINGDOM
FRANCE
BELGIUM
LONDON
Dover
Folkestone
Canterbury
Calais
Boulogne-sur-Mer
Dunkerque
Oostende
Brugge
Gent
Antwerpen
Bruxelles
Brussel
Lille
Amiens
Abbeville
Dieppe
Le Havre
Saint-Quentin
Charleroi
Mons
Tournai
Arras
Cambrai
Valenciennes
Hastings
Eastbourne
Maidstone
Margate
Ramsgate
Fécamp
Laon

Map continues pages 42-43

Map continues pages 58-59

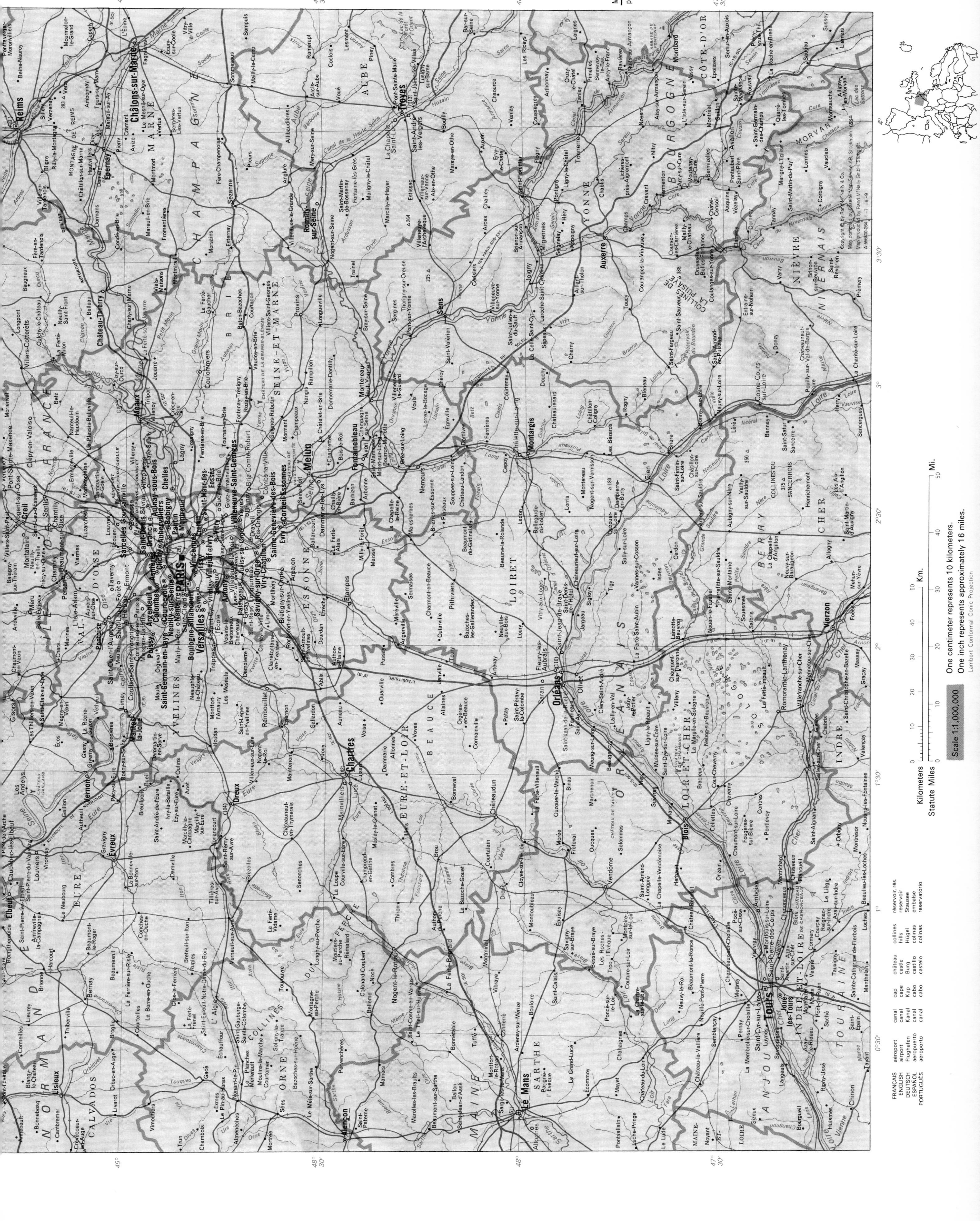
Kilometers
Statute Miles
Scale 1:1,000,000
One centimeter represents 10 kilometers.
One inch represents approximately 16 miles.
Lambert Conformal Conic Projection
FRANÇAIS aéroport canal cap château collines réservoir, rés.
ENGLISH airport canal cape castle hills reservoir
DEUTSCH Flughafen Kanal Kap Burg Hügel Stausee
ESPAÑOL aeropuerto canal cabo castillo colinas embalse
PORTUGUÊS aeroporto canal cabo castelo colinas reservatório

NORTH SEA
FRISIAN
WADDENEILANDEN
Waddenzee
TEXEL
VLIELAND
TERSCHELLING
AMELAND
SCHIERMONNIKOOG
GERMANY DEUTSCHLAND
NETHERLANDS NEDERLAND
FRIESLAND
GRONINGEN
DRENTHE
OVERIJSSEL
GELDERLAND
NOORD-HOLLAND
ZUID-HOLLAND
ZEELAND
NOORD-BRABANT
LIMBURG
BELGIË BELGIQUE
BELGIUM
FLANDERS
IJsselmeer (Zuiderzee)
Markermeer
Den Helder
Alkmaar
Hoorn
Leeuwarden
Groningen
Zwolle
Lelystad
AMSTERDAM
Haarlem
IJmuiden
Utrecht
Amersfoort
Apeldoorn
Arnhem
Nijmegen
's-Gravenhage
The Hague
ROTTERDAM
Dordrecht
Breda
Tilburg
Eindhoven
Venlo
Krefeld
Duisburg
Mönchengladbach
Vlissingen
Flushing
Middelburg
ANTWERPEN
ANVERS
Gent
Gand
Mechelen
Malines

Map continues
pages 50-51

Map continues
pages 56-57

DEUTSCH	Gebirge	Kanal	Moor	Naturpark	Stausee	Talsperre	Wald
ENGLISH	range	canal	moor	reserve	reservoir	dam	forest, mountains
ESPAÑOL	sierra	canal	páramo	reserva	embalse	presa	bosque, montañas
FRANÇAIS	chaîne	canal	lande	réserve	réservoir	barrage	forêt, montagnes
PORTUGUÊS	serra	canal	pântano	reserva natural	reservatório	represa	floresta, montanhas

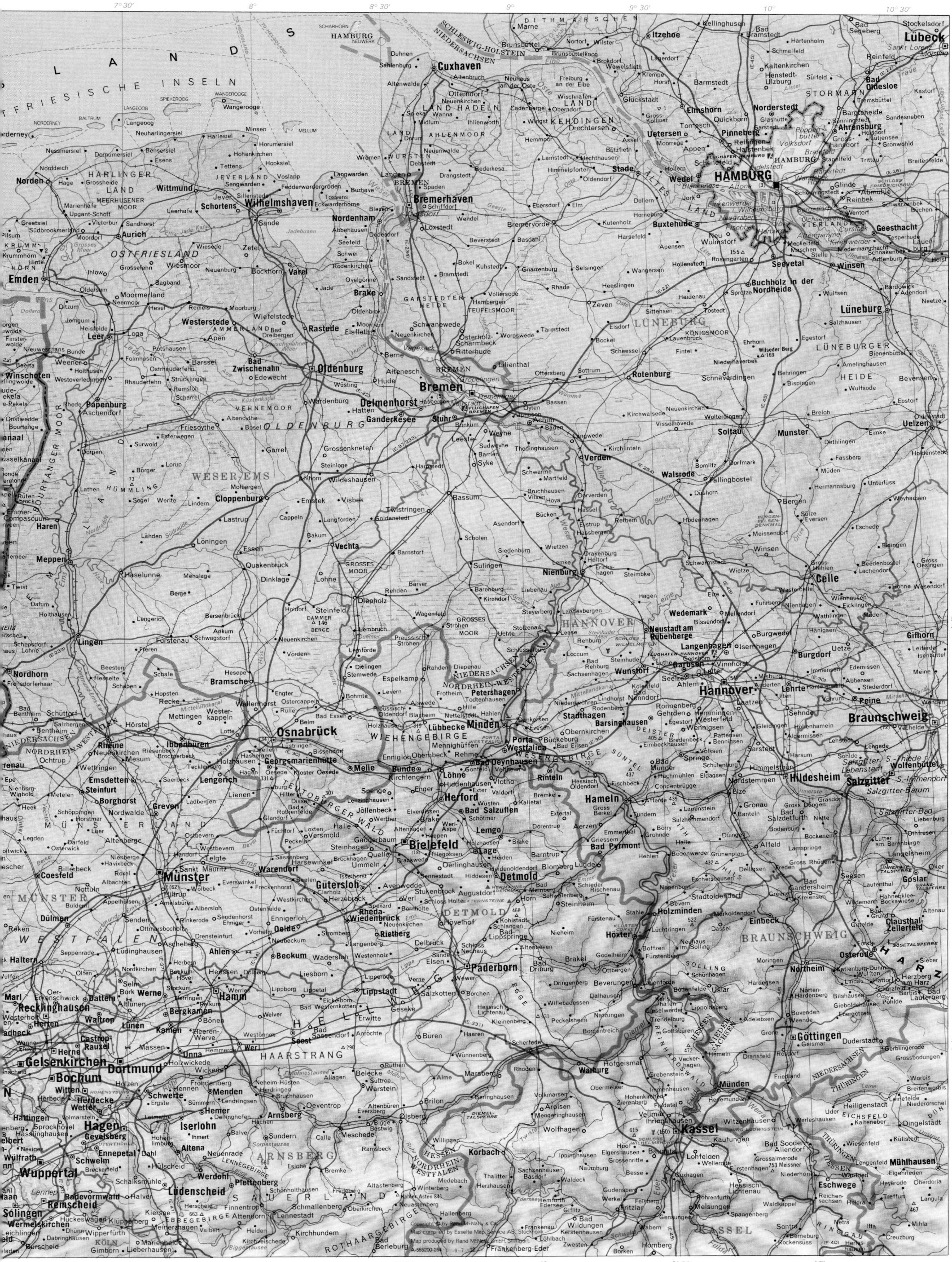

Lübeck
Cuxhaven
Itzehoe
HAMBURG
Bremerhaven
Wilhelmshaven
Emden
Aurich
Leer
Oldenburg
Bremen
Delmenhorst
Cloppenburg
Vechta
Nienburg
Verden
Soltau
Lüneburg
Uelzen
Celle
Hannover
Braunschweig
Wolfenbüttel
Salzgitter
Hildesheim
Hameln
Minden
Osnabrück
Münster
Bielefeld
Detmold
Paderborn
Gütersloh
Hamm
Lippstadt
Soest
Dortmund
Bochum
Gelsenkirchen
Recklinghausen
Hagen
Iserlohn
Lüdenscheid
Wuppertal
Remscheid
Solingen
Kassel
Göttingen
Goslar
Mühlhausen
Höxter
Holzminden
Warburg
Korbach
OSTFRIESISCHE INSELN
OSTFRIESLAND
LÜNEBURGER HEIDE
TEUTOBURGER WALD
WIEHENGEBIRGE
HAARSTRANG
SAUERLAND
ROTHAARGEBIRGE
SOLLING
REINHARDSWALD
HARZ
WESER-EMS
HANNOVER
BRAUNSCHWEIG
DETMOLD
ARNSBERG
KASSEL
MÜNSTER
NIEDERSACHSEN
NORDRHEIN-WESTFALEN
SCHLESWIG-HOLSTEIN
HESSEN
THÜRINGEN
Copyright © by Rand McNally & Co.
Map compiled by Esselte Map Service AB, Stockholm
Map produced by Rand McNally GmbH, Stuttgart

Map continues pages 54-55

Kilometers 0 10 20 30 40 50 Km.

Statute Miles 0 10 20 30 40 50 Mi.

Scale 1:1,000,000

One centimeter represents 10 kilometers.
One inch represents approximately 16 miles.
Lambert Conformal Conic Projection

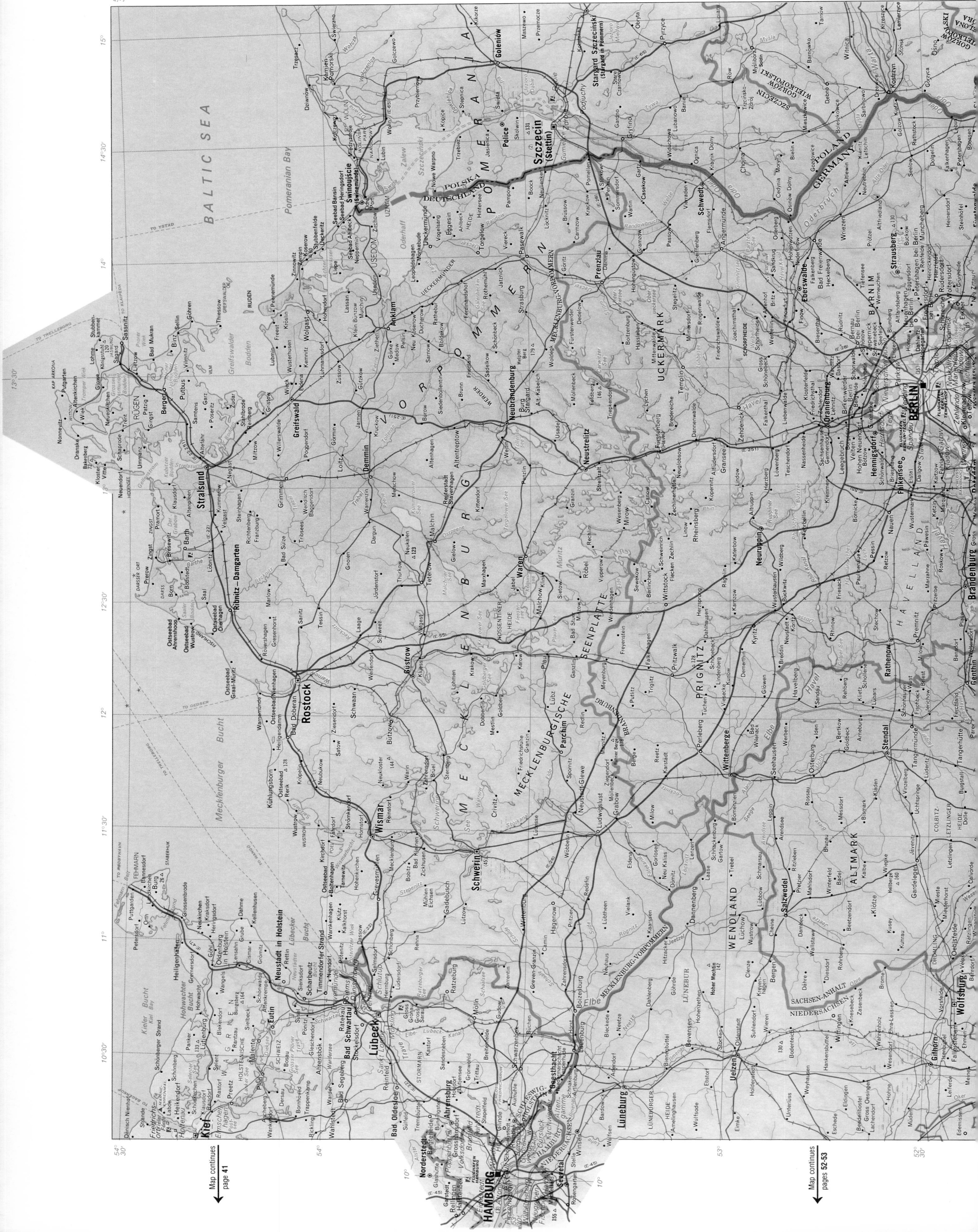
BALTIC SEA
Pomeranian Bay
Mecklenburger Bucht
Szczecin (Stettin)
Stralsund
Rostock
Wismar
Lübeck
Kiel
HAMBURG
BERLIN
Schwerin
Neubrandenburg
Brandenburg
Stendal
Lüneburg
Uelzen
Wolfsburg
Salzwedel
Wittenberge
Neuruppin
Neustrelitz
Greifswald
Güstrow
Parchim
Prenzlau
Eberswalde
Oranienburg
POLSKA
DEUTSCHLAND
POLAND
GERMANY
VORPOMMERN
MECKLENBURG
UCKERMARK
PRIGNITZ
ALTMARK
WENDLAND
HAVELLAND
BARNIM
MECKLENBURGISCHE SEENPLATTE
NIEDERSACHSEN
SACHSEN-ANHALT

Map continues page 41

Map continues pages 52-53

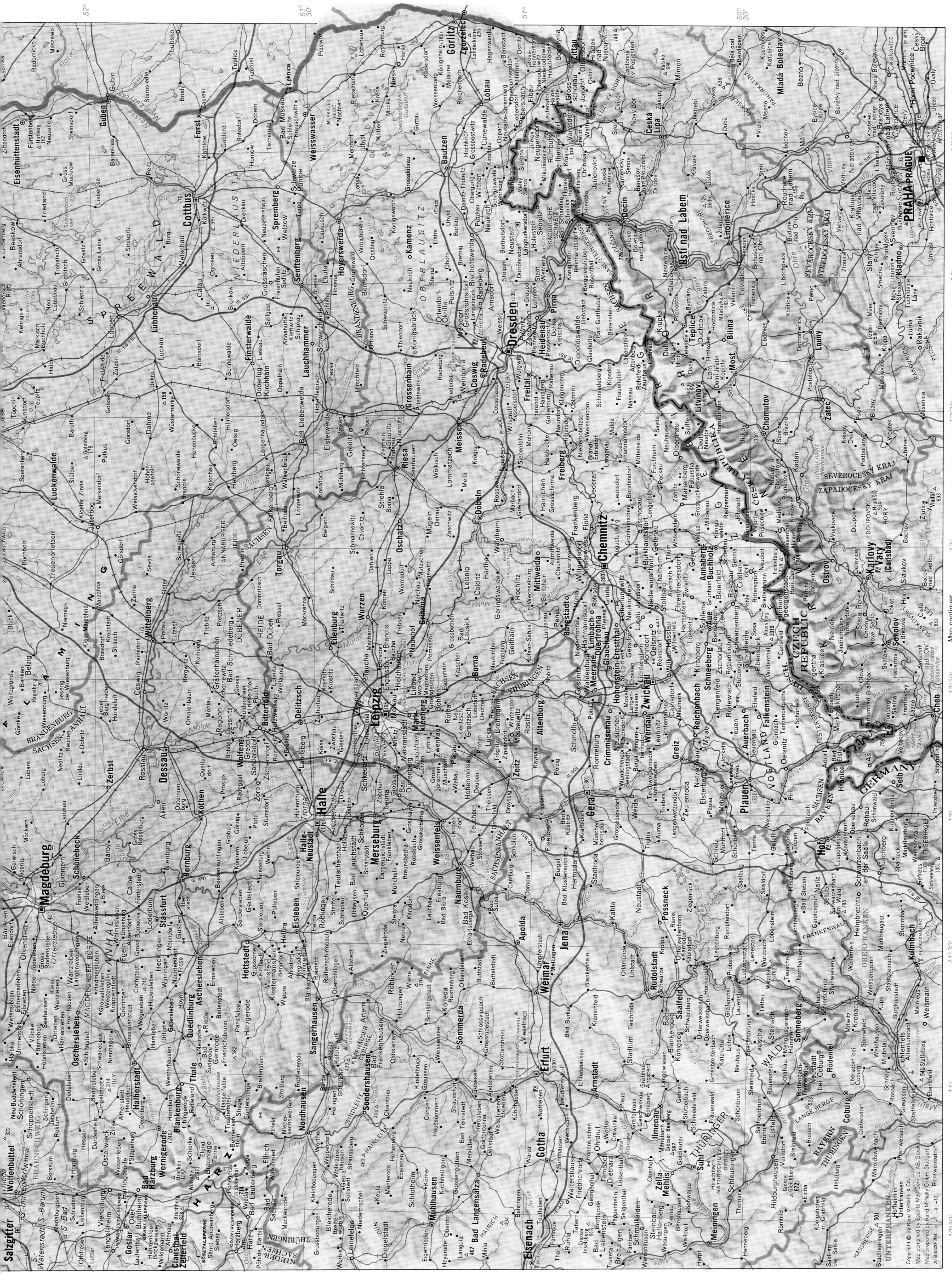

DEUTSCH	Berg, Bg.	Bodden	Bucht	Gebirge	Heide	Kanal	See	Talsperre
ENGLISH	mountain	bay	bay	range	heath	canal	lake	dam
ESPAÑOL	montaña	bahía	bahía	sierra	matorral	canal	lago	presa
FRANÇAIS	montagne	baie	baie	chaîne	lande	canal	lac	barrage
PORTUGUÊS	montanha	baía	baía	serra	charneca	canal	lago	represa

Scale 1:1,000,000

Kilometers 0 10 20 30 40 50 Km.

Statute Miles 0 10 20 30 40 50 Mi.

One centimeter represents 10 kilometers.
One inch represents approximately 16 miles.
Lambert Conformal Conic Projection

Map continues page 60

Map continues pages 56-57

Map continues pages 52-53

Map continues pages 50-51

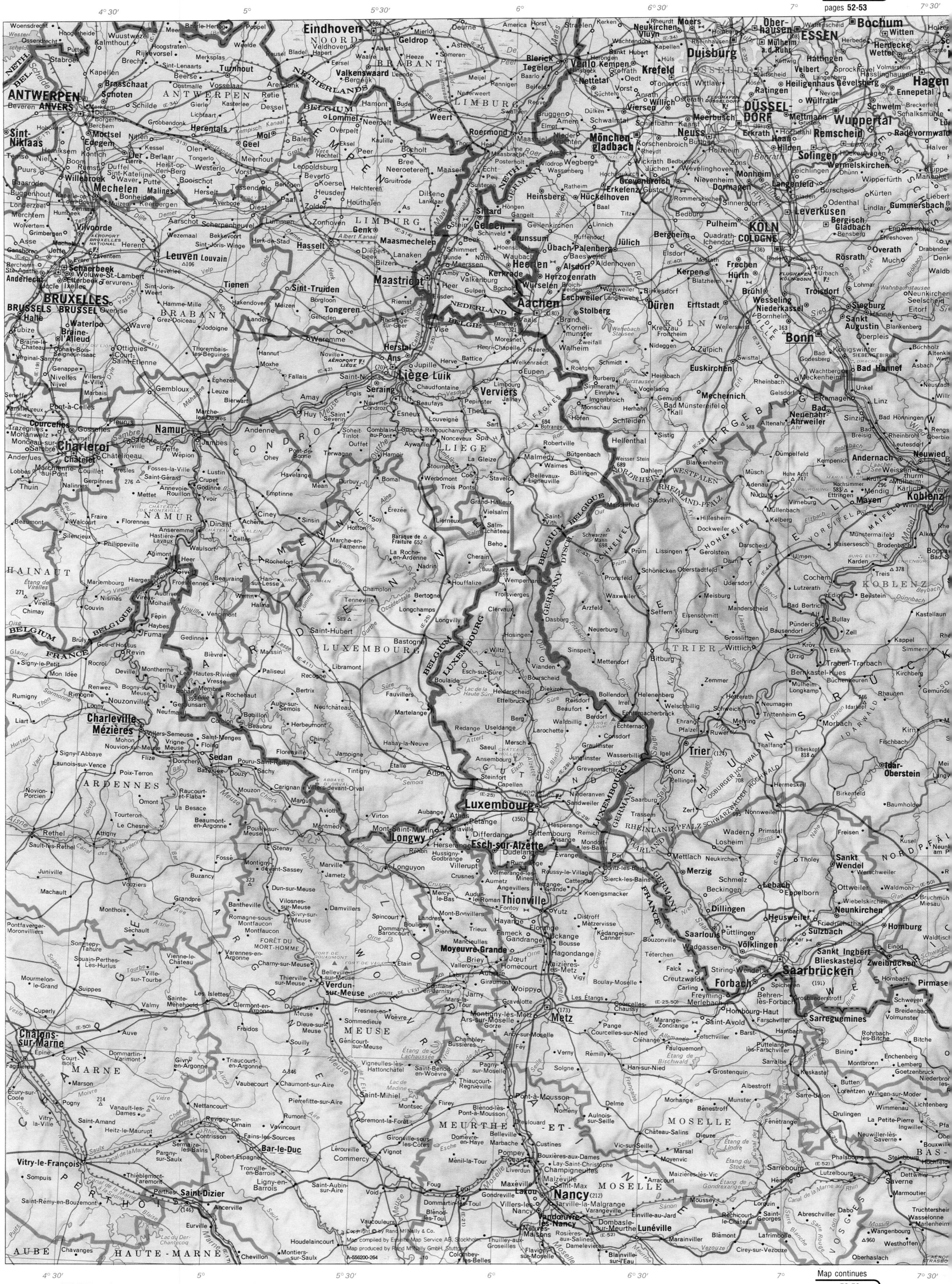
ANTWERPEN
BRUXELLES
Eindhoven
Duisburg
ESSEN
Bochum
DÜSSEL-DORF
Wuppertal
KÖLN
Bonn
Aachen
Maastricht
Liège Luik
Namur
Charleroi
Leuven
Mechelen
Hasselt
Verviers
Trier
Luxembourg
Esch-sur-Alzette
Longwy
Thionville
Metz
Nancy
Saarbrücken
Sedan
Charleville Mézières
Verdun-sur-Meuse
Bar-le-Duc
Saint-Dizier
Vitry-le-François
Châlons-sur-Marne
Koblenz
Lunéville
NETHERLANDS
BELGIUM
BELGIQUE
FRANCE
GERMANY
LUXEMBOURG
ARDENNES
EIFEL
HUNSRÜCK
MOSELLE
MEUSE
MARNE
AUBE
HAUTE-MARNE
4° 30′
5°
5° 30′
6°
6° 30′
7°
7° 30′
51°
50° 30′
50°
49° 30′
49°
48° 30′

Map continues pages 58-59

MAP FORM	aéroport	Berg	canal	chateau	étang	Gebirge	Naturpark	Stausee
ENGLISH	airport	mountain	canal	castle	pond	range	reserve	reservoir
DEUTSCH	Flughafen	Berg	Kanal	Burg	Teich	Gebirge	Naturpark	Stausee
ESPAÑOL	aeropuerto	montaña	canal	castillo	charca	cordillera	reserva	embalse
FRANÇAIS	aéroport	montagne	canal	château	étang	chaîne	réserve	réservoir
PORTUGUÊS	aeroporto	montanha	canal	castelo	lagoa	cordilheira	reserva	reservatório

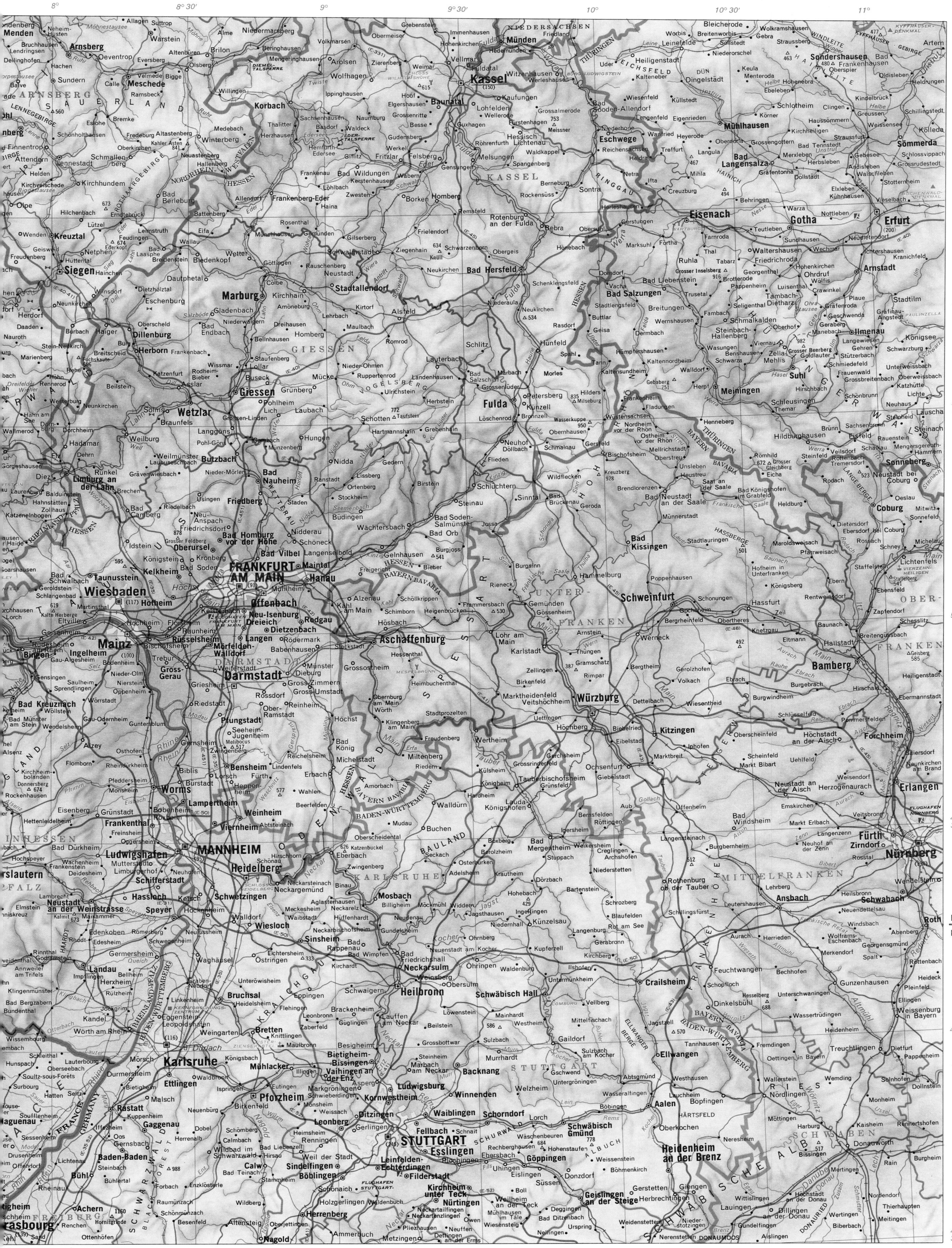

Kassel
Marburg
Giessen
Wetzlar
Siegen
Fulda
Bad Hersfeld
Eisenach
Gotha
Erfurt
Mühlhausen
Göttingen
Münden
Arnsberg
Meschede
Korbach
Frankfurt am Main
Wiesbaden
Mainz
Offenbach
Hanau
Darmstadt
Aschaffenburg
Würzburg
Schweinfurt
Bad Kissingen
Coburg
Bamberg
Erlangen
Fürth
Nürnberg
Mannheim
Ludwigshafen
Heidelberg
Worms
Heilbronn
Karlsruhe
Pforzheim
Stuttgart
Esslingen
Ludwigsburg
Aalen
Heidenheim an der Brenz
Ansbach
Schwäbisch Hall
Crailsheim
Baden-Baden
Landau
Speyer
Bad Kreuznach
Limburg an der Lahn
Bad Homburg vor der Höhe
Suhl
Meiningen
Ilmenau
Arnstadt
Sondershausen
Nördlingen
Göppingen
Reutlingen
Nürtingen
Herrenberg
Nagold
Calw
Böblingen
Sindelfingen

Map continues pages 54-55

Map continues page 60

Kilometers 0 10 20 30 40 50 Km.

Statute Miles 0 10 20 30 40 50 Mi.

Scale 1:1,000,000

One centimeter represents 10 kilometers.
One inch represents approximately 16 miles.

Lambert Conformal Conic Projection

Nancy
Lunéville
Saint-Dizier
Chaumont
Langres
Dijon
Besançon
Dole
Beaune
Chalon-sur-Saône
Le Creusot
Montceau-les-Mines
Mâcon
Bourg-en-Bresse
Lons-le-Saunier
Villefranche
LYON
Villeurbanne
Épinal
Belfort
Montbéliard
Mulhouse
Colmar
Basel
Delémont
Biel
Grenchen
Neuchâtel
Bern
Fribourg
Yverdon
Lausanne
Vevey
Genève
Geneva
Annecy
Oyonnax
Pontarlier
La Chaux-de-Fonds
Vesoul
MARNE
AUBE
HAUTE-MARNE
MEUSE
MEURTHE-ET-MOSELLE
VOSGES
HAUTE-SAÔNE
CÔTE-D'OR
DOUBS
JURA
SAÔNE-ET-LOIRE
AIN
RHÔNE
HAUTE-SAVOIE
SAVOIE
FRANCE
SWITZERLAND
VAUD
NEUCHÂTEL
FRIBOURG
Lac Léman
Lake Geneva
4°30′
5°
5°30′
6°
6°30′
7°
48°30′
48°
47°30′
47°
46°30′
46°

Map continues pages 50-51

MAP FORM	col	Horn	lago	mont	passo	piz, -zo	See	Spitze	val
ENGLISH	pass	peak	lake	mount	pass	peak	lake	peak	valley
DEUTSCH	Pass	Horn	See	Berg	Pass	Gipfel	See	Spitze	Tal
ESPAÑOL	paso	pico	lago	monte	paso	pico	lago	pico	valle
FRANÇAIS	col	cime	lac	mont	col	cime	lac	pico	val
PORTUGUÊS	passo	pico	lago	monte	passo	pico	lago	pico	vale

Map continues pages 56-57

Strasbourg
Freiburg im Breisgau
Tübingen
Reutlingen
Ulm
Augsburg
Kempten
Konstanz
Schaffhausen
Winterthur
Zürich
Luzern
Sankt Gallen
Feldkirch
Vaduz
LIECHTENSTEIN
Chur
Bellinzona
Locarno
Lugano
Como
Lecco
Varese
Verbania
Domodossola
Sondrio
GERMANY
SWITZERLAND
AUSTRIA
ITALY
Bodensee
Lake Constance

Map continues page 60

Map continues pages 64-65

ontinues 62-63

Kilometers 0 10 20 30 40 50 Km.
Statute Miles 0 10 20 30 40 50 Mi.

Scale 1:1,000,000

One centimeter represents 10 kilometers.
One inch represents approximately 16 miles.
Lambert Conformal Conic Projection

Map continues pages 54-55

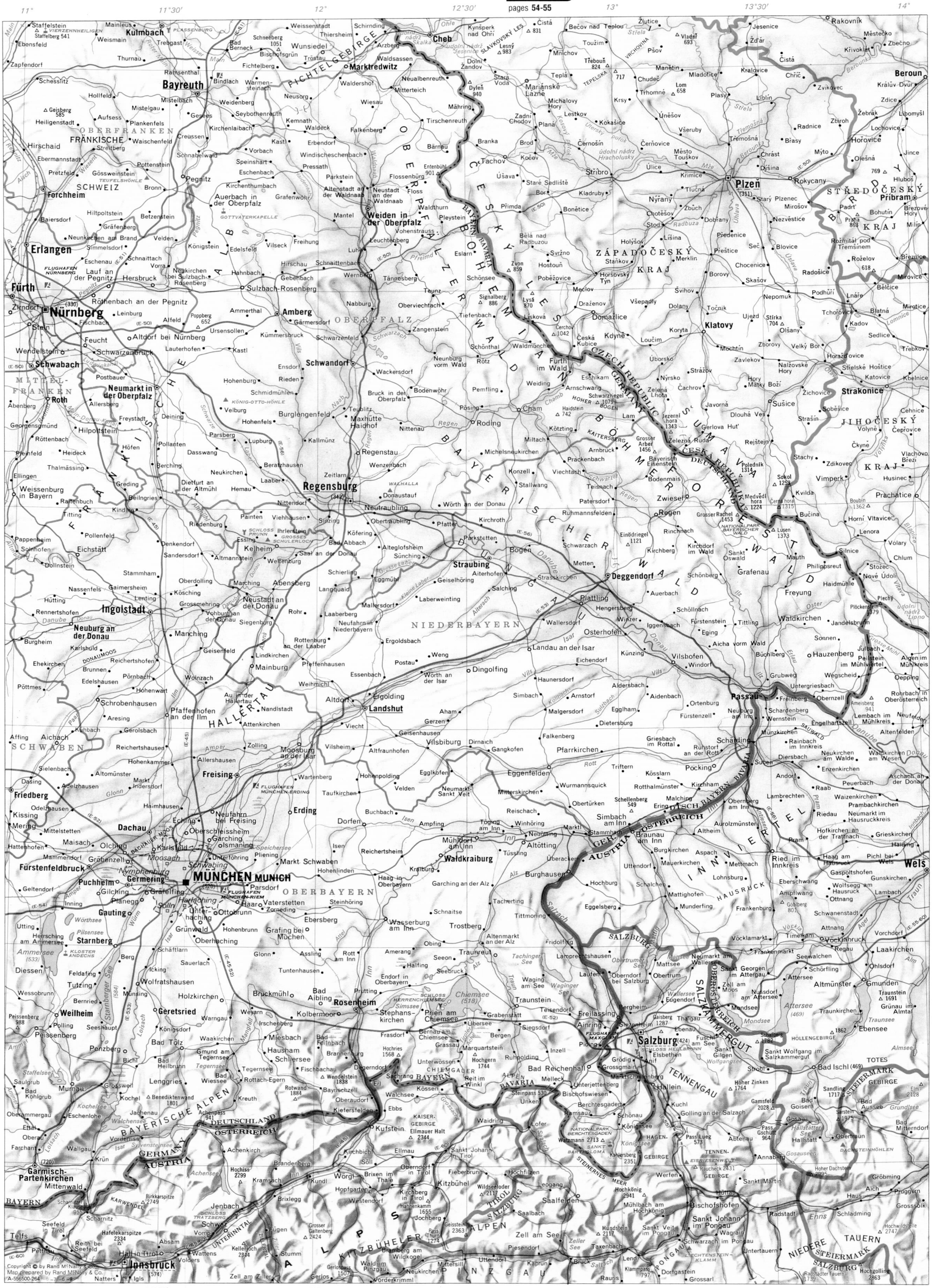
Nürnberg
München
Munich
Regensburg
Ingolstadt
Augsburg
Salzburg
Innsbruck
Passau
Landshut
Erlangen
Fürth
Bayreuth
Plzeň
Cheb
Amberg
Straubing
Deggendorf
Rosenheim
Freising
Dachau
Weiden in der Oberpfalz
Wels
Beroun
Klatovy
Strakonice
Garmisch-Partenkirchen
OBERBAYERN
NIEDERBAYERN
OBERPFALZ
HALLERTAU
INNVIERTEL
SALZKAMMERGUT
BAYERISCHE ALPEN
KITZBÜHELER ALPEN
BAYERISCHER WALD
OBERPFÄLZER WALD
ČESKÝ LES
ŠUMAVA
BÖHMERWALD
FRÄNKISCHE ALB
SCHWABEN
DEUTSCHLAND
ÖSTERREICH
GERMANY
AUSTRIA
CZECH REPUBLIC
ČESKÁ REPUBLIKA
ZÁPADOČESKÝ KRAJ
JIHOČESKÝ KRAJ
STŘEDOČESKÝ KRAJ
Danube
Donau
Isar
Inn
Chiemsee
Ammersee
Starnberger See
Copyright © by Rand McNally & Co.
Map prepared by Rand McNally & Co.
A-556500-264

Map continues pages 56-57

Map continues pages 58-59

Map con page 61

Map continues pages 64-65

DEUTSCH	Berg	Gebirge	Pass	Schloss	See
ENGLISH	mountain	range	pass	castle	lake
ESPAÑOL	montaña	sierra	paso	castillo	lago
FRANÇAIS	montagne	chaîne	col	château	lac
PORTUGUÊS	montanha	serra	passo	castelo	lago

Kilometers 0 10 20 30 40 50 Km.

Statute Miles 0 10 20 30 40 50 Mi.

Scale 1:1,000,000

One centimeter represents 10 kilometers.
One inch represents approximately 16 miles.

Modified Polyconic Projection

continues 60

continues 64-65

Brno
Bratislava
WIEN
VIENNA
Linz
Graz
Maribor
Klagenfurt
České Budějovice
Sopron
Szombathely
Zalaegerszeg
Mosonmagyaróvár
Znojmo
Sankt Pölten
Wiener Neustadt
Krems an der Donau
Leoben
Bruck an der Mur
Kapfenberg
Wolfsberg
JIHOČESKÝ KRAJ
JIHOMORAVSKÝ KRAJ
ZÁPADOSLOVENSKÝ KRAJ
NIEDERÖSTERREICH
OBERÖSTERREICH
STEIERMARK
KÄRNTEN
BURGENLAND
GYŐR-MOSON-SOPRON
VAS
ZALA
WALDVIERTEL
WEINVIERTEL
MÜHLVIERTEL
WIENERWALD
WACHAU
NIEDERE TAUERN
ALPS
KARAWANKEN
KARAVANKE
SLOVENSKE GORICE
PREKOMURJE
MEDUMURJE
BOHEMIAN FOREST
BÖHMER WALD
ČESKÁ REPUBLIKA
ÖSTERREICH
CZECH REPUBLIC
AUSTRIA
SLOVAKIA
MAGYARORSZÁG
AUSTRIA HUNGARY
SLOVENIJA
SLOVENIA
CROATIA
HRVATSKA
Danube
Donau
Drava
Mura
Copyright © 1980, 1987 by Rand McNally & Co.
Map prepared by Rand McNally & Co.

DEUTSCH	Alpe, -n	Berg	Gebirge	Sattel	Schloss	Wald
ENGLISH	mountains	mountain	range	saddle	castle	forest; mountains
ESPAÑOL	montañas	montaña	sierra	paso	castillo	bosque; montañas
FRANÇAIS	montagnes	montagne	chaîne	col	château	forêt; montagnes
PORTUGUÊS	montanhas	montanha	serra	passo	castelo	Floresta; montanhas

Kilometers 0 10 20 30 40 50 Km.

Statute Miles 0 10 20 30 40 50 Mi.

Scale 1:1,000,000

One centimeter represents 10 kilometers.
One inch represents approximately 16 miles.

Lambert Conformal Conic Projection

4°
4°30′
5°
5°30′
6°
6°30′
45°30′
45°
44°30′
44°
43°30′
43°
LYON
Villeurbanne
Vénissieux
Saint-Étienne
Vienne
Valence
Grenoble
Chambéry
Voiron
Le Puy
Privas
Montélimar
Orange
Avignon
Nîmes
Alès
Arles
Montpellier
Sète
Salon-de-Provence
Aix-en-Provence
MARSEILLE
Aubagne
La Ciotat
Toulon
Hyères
Draguignan
Digne
Gap
LYONNAIS
LOIRE
HAUTE-LOIRE
ARDÈCHE
DRÔME
GARD
VAUCLUSE
BOUCHES-DU-RHÔNE
VAR
HÉRAULT
LOZÈRE
HAUTES-ALPES
ALPES-DE-HAUTE-PROVENCE
PROVENCE
SAVOIE
HAUTE-SAVOIE
AIN
PLATEAU DE ISÈRE
CHAMBARAN
VERCORS
DÉVOLUY
CAMARGUE
Golfe du Lion
Golfe d'Aigues-Mortes
Golfe des Saintes-Maries
ÎLES D'HYÈRES
Copyright © by Rand McNally & Co.
Map compiled by Esselte Map Service AB, Stockholm.
Map produced by Rand McNally GmbH, Stuttgart.
A-555800-264

MAP FORM	abbaye	capo	col	île, î.	lac, l.	monte	passo	pic	val (-le)
ENGLISH	abbey	cape	pass	island	lake	mountain	pass	peak	valley
DEUTSCH	Abtei	Kap	Pass	Insel	See	Berg	Pass	Gipfel	Tal
ESPAÑOL	abadía	cabo	paso	isla	lago	montaña	paso	pico	valle
FRANÇAIS	abbaye	cap	col	île	lac	montagne	col	cime	val
PORTUGUÊS	abadia	cabo	passo	ilha	lago	montanha	passo	pico	vale

Map continues pages 58-59

MILANO
MILAN
TORINO TURIN
GENOVA
GENOA
Bergamo
Varese
Como
Lecco
Novara
Vercelli
Biella
Ivrea
Aosta
Asti
Alessandria
Pavia
Piacenza
Vigevano
Voghera
Tortona
Cuneo
Pinerolo
Savona
Imperia
San Remo
Monaco
Menton
Nice
Cannes
Antibes
La Spezia
Rapallo
Chiavari
Sestri Levante
Casale Monferrato
Chivasso
Lodi
Crema
Golfo di Genova
Ligurian Sea
Mar Ligure
MEDITERRANEAN SEA
APPENNINO
APENNINES
ALPES MARITIMES
ALPI MARITTIME
ALPS
RIVIERA DI PONENTE
RIVIERA DI LEVANTE
CÔTE D'AZUR
CORSE
CORSICA
HAUTE-CORSE (Fr.)
7°
7°30'
8°
8°30'
9°
9°30'
45°30'
45°
44°30'
44°
43°30'
43°

Map continues pages 64-65

Kilometers 0 10 20 30 40 50 Km.

Statute Miles 0 10 20 30 40 50 Mi.

Scale 1:1,000,000

One centimeter represents 10 kilometers.

One inch represents approximately 16 miles.

Lambert Conformal Conic Projection

Map continues page 61

Map continues page 60

MÜNCHEN
MUNICH
Innsbruck
Salzburg
Bolzano
Bozen
Merano
Meran
Udine
Trento
Belluno
Villach
Kempten
Garmisch-Partenkirchen
Rosenheim
Kufstein
Lienz
Cortina d'Ampezzo
Bregenz
Dornbirn
Lindau
Sondrio
AUSTRIA
ITALY
GERMANY
SWITZERLAND
SLOVENIA
48°
47° 30'
47°
46° 30'
10°
10° 30'
11°
11° 30'
12°
12° 30'
13°
13° 30'

Map continues pages 58-59

Map continues pages 66-67
Scale 1:1,000,000
One centimeter represents 10 kilometers.
One inch represents approximately 16 miles.
Lambert Conformal Conic Projection
Kilometers
Statute Miles
Copyright © by Rand McNally & Co.
ADRIATIC SEA
MARE ADRIATICO
Gulf of Venice
LIGURIAN SEA
MAR LIGURE

Map continues pages 62-63

Map continues pages 64-65

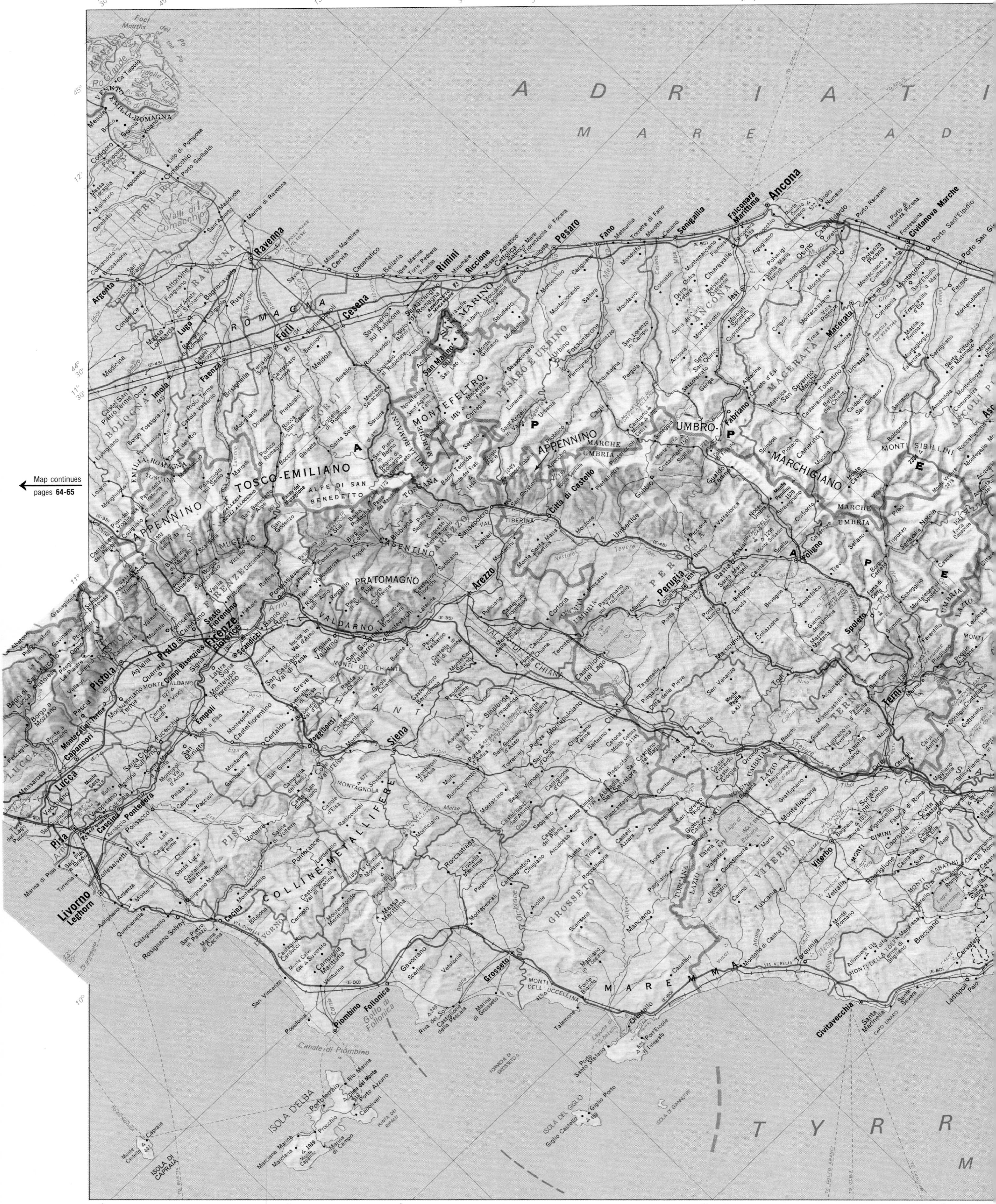
A D R I A T I
M A R E A D
T Y R R
M
Foci del Po
Mouths of the Po
EMILIA-ROMAGNA
Valli di Comacchio
Ravenna
Rimini
Riccione
Pesaro
Fano
Senigallia
Falconara Marittima
Ancona
Civitanova Marche
Cesena
Forlì
Faenza
Imola
Lugo
Argenta
SAN MARINO
San Marino
ROMAGNA
MONTEFELTRO
PESARO E URBINO
Urbino
Jesi
Macerata
Fabriano
Tolentino
APPENNINO TOSCO-EMILIANO
ALPE DI SAN BENEDETTO
APPENNINO UMBRO-MARCHIGIANO
MONTI SIBILLINI
MUGELLO
PRATOMAGNO
CASENTINO
VALDARNO
Firenze
Florence
Prato
Pistoia
Empoli
Lucca
Pisa
Livorno
Leghorn
Arezzo
Siena
Poggibonsi
CHIANTI
MONTAGNOLA
COLLINE METALLIFERE
VAL DI CHIANA
Perugia
Città di Castello
Foligno
Spoleto
Terni
Orvieto
Lago di Bolsena
Viterbo
Tarquinia
Civitavecchia
Grosseto
Orbetello
MAREMMA
MONTI DELL'UCCELLINA
Piombino
Follonica
Golfo di Follonica
Canale di Piombino
ISOLA D'ELBA
Portoferraio
ISOLA DEL GIGLIO
ISOLA DI CAPRAIA
Cecina
TOSCANA
UMBRIA
MARCHE
LAZIO

MAP FORM	golfo	isola	lago	monte	monti	passo	punta
ENGLISH	gulf	island	lake	mountain	mountains	pass	point
DEUTSCH	Golf	Insel	See	Berg	Berge	Pass	Landspitze
ESPAÑOL	golfo	isla	lago	montaña	montañas	paso	punta
FRANÇAIS	golfe	île	lac	montagne	montagnes	col	pointe
PORTUGUÊS	golfo	ilha	lago	montanha	montanhas	passo	ponta

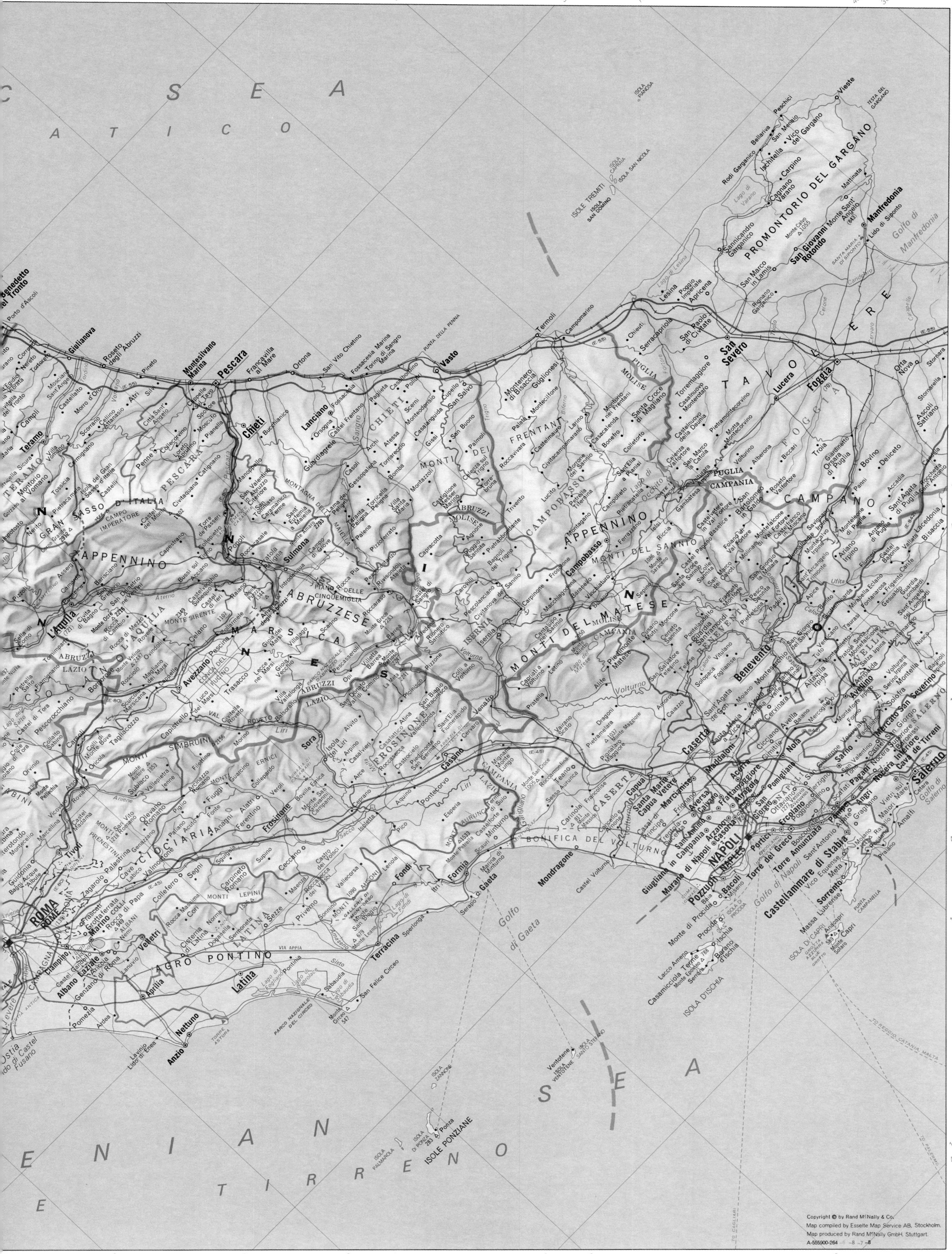

ADRIATIC SEA
PROMONTORIO DEL GARGANO
Golfo di Manfredonia
Manfredonia
Vieste
Foggia
Lucera
San Severo
TAVOLIERE
ISOLE TREMITI
Pescara
Chieti
Vasto
Lanciano
Termoli
Teramo
L'Aquila
Sulmona
Avezzano
Campobasso
Isernia
Benevento
Avellino
Caserta
Capua
NAPOLI
Pozzuoli
Salerno
Castellammare di Stabia
Sorrento
Golfo di Napoli
ISOLA D'ISCHIA
ISOLA DI CAPRI
ROMA
Tivoli
Velletri
Latina
Aprilia
Anzio
Nettuno
Frosinone
Cassino
Sora
Formia
Gaeta
Golfo di Gaeta
Terracina
Fondi
AGRO PONTINO
CIOCIARIA
APPENNINO ABRUZZESE
MONTI DEL MATESE
GRAN SASSO D'ITALIA
MARSICA
ISOLE PONZIANE
TYRRHENIAN SEA
MARE TIRRENO

Map continues pages 68-69

Kilometers 0 10 20 30 40 50 Km.

Statute Miles 0 10 20 30 40 50 Mi.

Scale 1:1,000,000

One centimeter represents 10 kilometers.

One inch represents approximately 16 miles.

Lambert Conformal Conic Projection

ADRIATIC SEA
MARE ADRIATICO
CROATIA
ITALY
TYRRHEN
PROMONTORIO DEL GARGANO
Golfo di Manfredonia
Golfo di Salerno
Golfo di Gaeta
Golfo di Policastro
APPENNINO LUCANO
APPENNINO CAMPANO
VALLO DI DIANO
PIANA DEL SELE
BONIFICA DEL VOLTURNO
PUGLIA
BASILICATA
CAMPANIA
MOLISE
LAZIO
FOGGIA
BARI
MATERA
POTENZA
SALERNO
BRINDISI
TARANTO
CASERTA
Bari
Taranto
Foggia
Manfredonia
San Severo
Lucera
Cerignola
Barletta
Trani
Bisceglie
Molfetta
Andria
Corato
Bitonto
Altamura
Gravina in Puglia
Matera
Monopoli
Mola di Bari
Ostuni
Martina Franca
Grottaglie
Francavilla Fontana
Massafra
Gioia del Colle
Potenza
Melfi
Eboli
Battipaglia
Salerno
Avellino
Benevento
Caserta
Campobasso
NAPOLI
NAPLES
Pozzuoli
Torre del Greco
Castellammare di Stabia
Sorrento
Cava de' Tirreni
Nocera Inferiore
Nola
Aversa
Marcianise
Maddaloni
Cassino
Formia
Gaeta
Fondi
Mondragone
ISOLA D'ISCHIA
ISOLA DI CAPRI
Vieste
Lesina
Agropoli
Amalfi

Map continues pages 66-67

MAP FORM	capo	golfo	isola	lago	monte	monti	punta
ENGLISH	cape	gulf	island	lake	mountain	mountains	point
DEUTSCH	Kap	Golf	Insel	See	Berg	Berge	Landspitze
ESPAÑOL	cabo	golfo	isla	lago	montaña	montañas	punta
FRANÇAIS	cap	golfe	île	lac	montagne	montagnes	pointe
PORTUGUÊS	cabo	golfo	ilha	lago	montanha	montanhas	ponta

Strait of Otranto
Lecce
Otranto
Galatina
Copertino
Nardò
Gallipoli
PENISOLA SALENTINA
CAPO SANTA MARIA DI LEUCA
Golfo di Taranto
IONIAN SEA
MARE IONIO
MARE TIRRENO
Crotone
Isola di Capo Rizzuto
Cirò Marina
Rossano
Corigliano Calabro
SILA GRANDE
SILA PICCOLA
Cosenza
Catanzaro
Catanzaro Lido
Golfo di Squillace
Soverato
Nicastro
Sant'Eufemia Lamezia
Golfo di Sant'Eufemia
Pizzo
Vibo Valentia
Tropea
Golfo di Gioia
Gioia Tauro
Palmi
Bagnara Calabra
Scilla
Villa San Giovanni
Reggio di Calabria
ASPROMONTE
Locri
Siderno
CALABRIA
SICILIA
Messina
Copyright © by Rand McNally & Co.
Map prepared by Rand McNally GmbH, Stuttgart.

Map continues page 70

Kilometers 0 10 20 30 40 50 Km.

Statute Miles 0 10 20 30 40 50 Mi.

Scale 1:1,000,000

One centimeter represents 10 kilometers.

One inch represents approximately 16 miles.

Lambert Conformal Conic Projection

Map continues pages 68-69

Kilometers 0 10 20 30 40 50 Km.

Statute Miles 0 10 20 30 40 50 Mi.

Scale 1:1,000,000

One centimeter represents 10 kilometers.
One inch represents approximately 16 miles.

Lambert Conformal Conic Projection

MAP FORM	capo	golfo	isola	lago	monte	pizzo
ENGLISH	cape	gulf	island	lake	mountain	peak
DEUTSCH	Kap	Golf	Insel	See	Berg	Gipfel
ESPAÑOL	cabo	golfo	isla	lago	montaña	pico
FRANÇAIS	cap	golfe	île	lac	montagne	pic
PORTUGUÊS	cabo	golfo	ilha	lago	montanha	pico

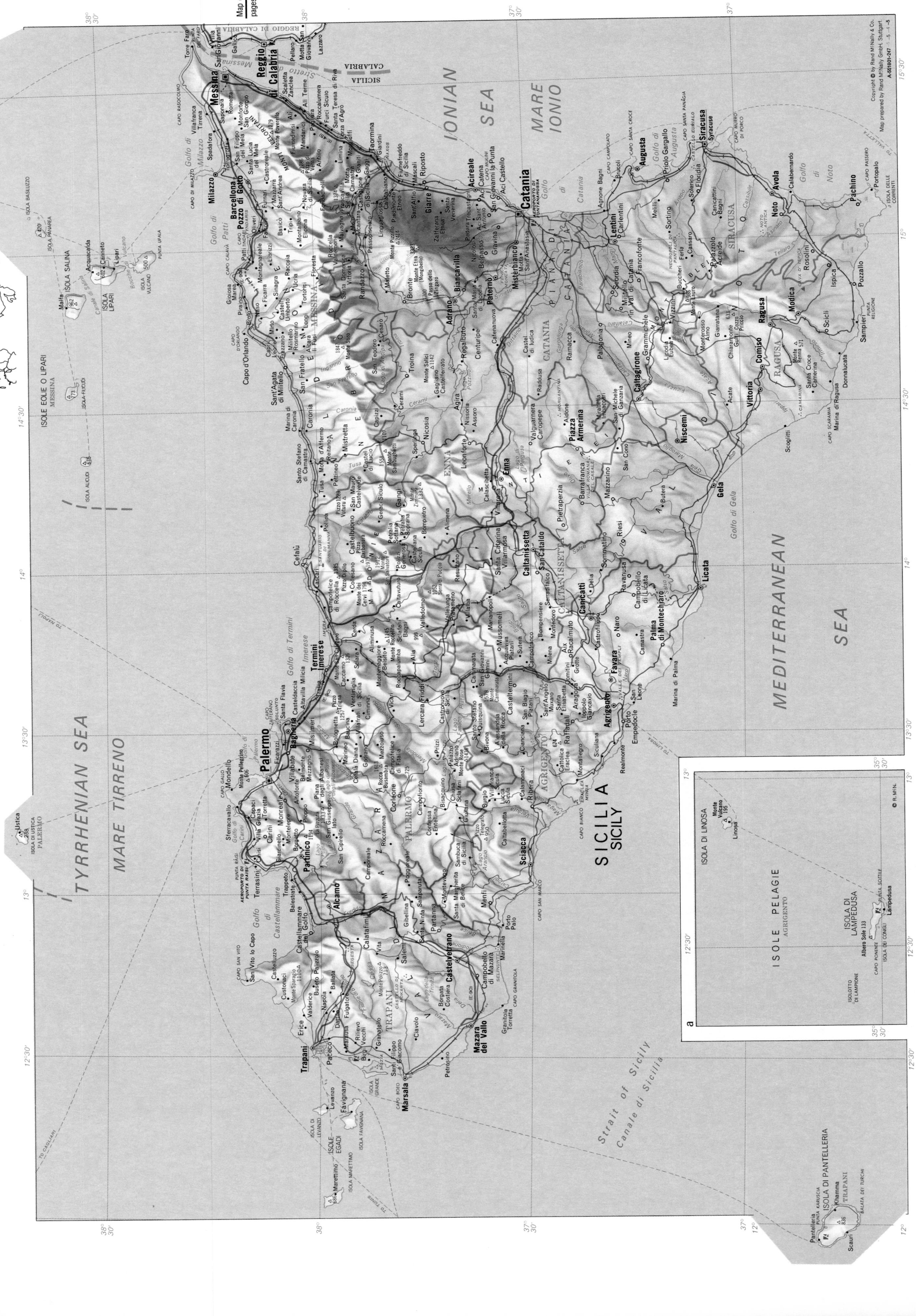

TYRRHENIAN SEA
MARE TIRRENO
IONIAN SEA
MARE IONIO
MEDITERRANEAN SEA
SICILIA
SICILY
Strait of Sicily
Canale di Sicilia
Palermo
Catania
Messina
Reggio di Calabria
Siracusa
Trapani
Marsala
Agrigento
Caltanissetta
Enna
Ragusa
ISOLE EOLIE O LIPARI
ISOLE EGADI
ISOLE PELAGIE
ISOLA DI PANTELLERIA
ISOLA DI LAMPEDUSA
ISOLA DI LINOSA
Copyright © by Rand McNally & Co.
Map prepared by Rand McNally GmbH, Stuttgart

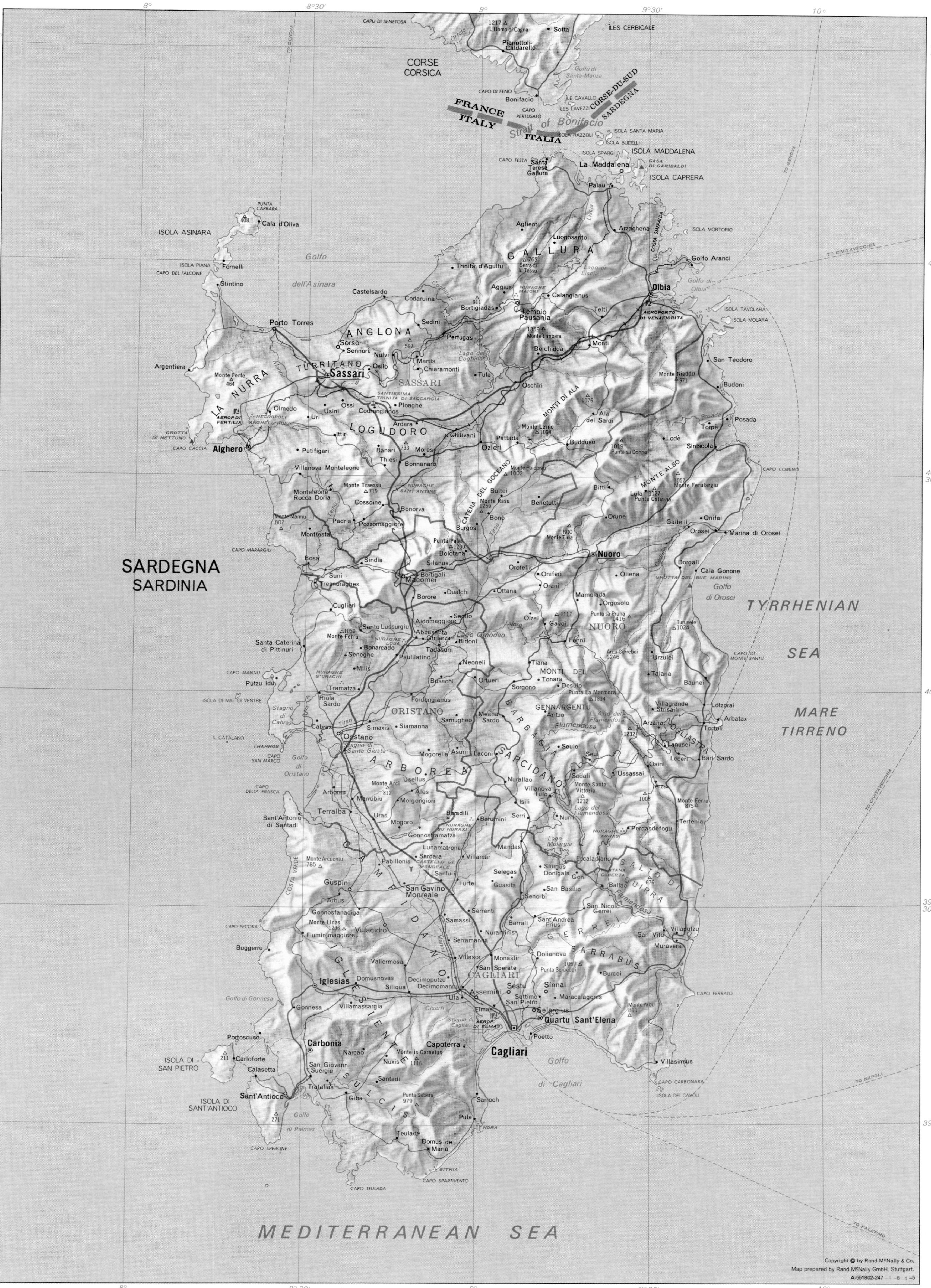
CORSE
CORSICA
Bonifacio
Strait of Bonifacio
FRANCE
ITALY
ITALIA
CORSE-DU-SUD
SARDEGNA
ISOLA MADDALENA
La Maddalena
ISOLA CAPRERA
Santa Teresa Gallura
Palau
ISOLA ASINARA
Golfo dell'Asinara
Stintino
Porto Torres
Castelsardo
ANGLONA
Sassari
TURRITANO
SASSARI
NURRA
Alghero
Argentiera
LOGUDORO
Ozieri
GALLURA
Tempio Pausania
Olbia
Golfo Aranci
Arzachena
Siniscola
Posada
Orosei
Nuoro
NUORO
Oliena
Dorgali
Cala Gonone
Golfo di Orosei
TYRRHENIAN SEA
MARE TIRRENO
SARDEGNA
SARDINIA
Bosa
Macomer
Cuglieri
Oristano
ORISTANO
Golfo di Oristano
ARBOREA
GENNARGENTU
BARBAGIA
OGLIASTRA
Lanusei
Tortolì
Arbatax
Laconi
CAMPIDANO
Sanluri
Guspini
Iglesias
IGLESIENTE
Carbonia
SULCIS
ISOLA DI SAN PIETRO
Carloforte
ISOLA DI SANT'ANTIOCO
Sant'Antioco
Golfo di Palmas
Teulada
Pula
Sarroch
Cagliari
CAGLIARI
Golfo di Cagliari
Quartu Sant'Elena
Villasimius
SARRABUS
GERREI
Muravera
MEDITERRANEAN SEA
TO GENOVA
TO CIVITAVECCHIA
TO NAPOLI
TO PALERMO
Copyright © by Rand McNally & Co.
Map prepared by Rand McNally GmbH, Stuttgart.
A-551802-247

MAP FORM	capo	golfo	isola	lago, l.	monte
ENGLISH	cape	gulf	island	lake	mountain
DEUTSCH	Kap	Golf	Insel	See	Berg
ESPAÑOL	cabo	golfo	isla	lago	montaña
FRANÇAIS	cap	golfe	île	lac	montagne
PORTUGUÊS	cabo	golfo	ilha	lago	montanha

Kilometers 0 10 20 30 40 50 Km.

Statute Miles 0 10 20 30 40 50 Mi.

Scale 1:1,000,000

One centimeter represents 10 kilometers.

One inch represents approximately 16 miles.

Lambert Conformal Conic Projection

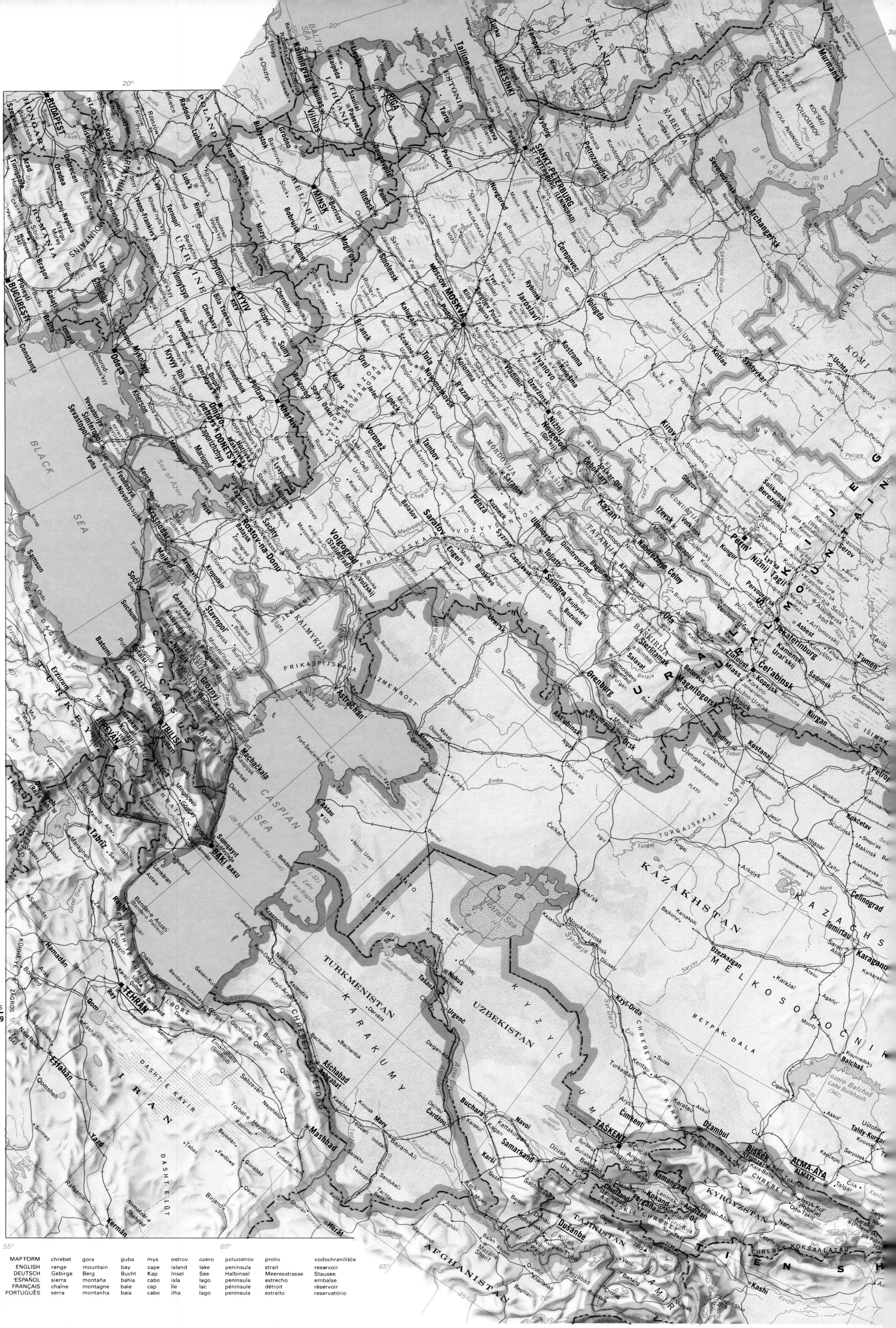

BLACK SEA
Sea of Azov
CASPIAN SEA
Aral Sea
White Sea
UKRAINE
BELARUS
POLAND
LITHUANIA
LATVIA
ESTONIA
FINLAND
HUNGARY
ROMANIA
TURKEY
GEORGIA
KAZAKHSTAN
UZBEKISTAN
TURKMENISTAN
KYRGYZSTAN
TAJIKISTAN
AFGHANISTAN
IRAN
CAUCASUS
KARAKUMY
MOSCOW MOSKVA
SANKT-PETERBURG (LENINGRAD)
KYYIV
MINSK
VILNIUS
RIGA
TALLINN
HELSINKI
BUCUREŞTI
BUDAPEST
TBILISI
JEREVAN
BAKI BAKU
TEHRĀN
TAŠKENT
ALMA-ATA ALMATY
BIŠKEK
DUŠANBE
AŠCHABAD

Map continues pages 22-23

Map continues pages 118-119

MAP FORM	chrebet	gora	guba	mys	ostrov	ozero	poluostrov	proliv	vodochranilišče
ENGLISH	range	mountain	bay	cape	island	lake	peninsula	strait	reservoir
DEUTSCH	Gebirge	Berg	Bucht	Kap	Insel	See	Halbinsel	Meeresstrasse	Stausee
ESPAÑOL	sierra	montaña	bahía	cabo	isla	lago	península	estrecho	embalse
FRANÇAIS	chaîne	montagne	baie	cap	île	lac	péninsule	détroit	réservoir
PORTUGUÊS	serra	montanha	baía	cabo	ilha	lago	península	estreito	reservatório

KARSKOJE MORE
KARA SEA
MORE LAPTEVYCH
LAPTEV SEA
NOVAJA ZEML'A
SEVERNAJA ZEML'A
POLUOSTROV TAJMYR
GORY BYRRANGA
SEVERO - SIBIRSKAJA NIZMENNOST'
PLATO PUTORANA
SREDNE-SIBIRSKOJE PLOSKOGORJE
ZAPADNO-SIBIRSKAJA RAVNINA
RUSSIA
JAKUTIJA
BURJATIJA
STANOVOJE NAGORJE
STANOVOY MOUNTAINS
VOSTOČNYJ SAJAN
ZAPADNYJ SAJAN
SAYAN MOUNTAINS
TUVA
ALTAJ
MONGOLIA
CHINA
XINJIANG UYGUR ZIZHIQU
Novosibirsk
Omsk
Tomsk
Krasnojarsk
Irkutsk
Ulan-Ude
Čita
Barnaul
Kemerovo
Novokuznetsk
Bratsk
Noril'sk
Surgut
Vorkuta
Ulaanbaatar
Semipalatinsk
Ust'-Kamenogorsk
Pavlodar
Arctic Circle
Copyright © by Rand McNally & Co.
Map prepared by Esselte Map Service AB, Stockholm.

Map continues pages 74-75

Map continues pages 90-91

Kilometers 0 200 400 600 Km.
Statute Miles 0 200 400 600 Mi.

Scale 1:12,000,000

One centimeter represents 120 kilometers.
One inch represents approximately 190 miles.
Lambert Conformal Conic Projection

BARENTS SEA
NOVAJA ZEML'A
KARSKOJE MORE
KARA SEA
MORE LAPTEVYCH
LAPTEV SEA
SEVERNAJA ZEML'A
OSTROV KOMSOMOLEC
OSTROV OKT'ABR'SKOJ REVOL'UCII
OSTROV BOL'ŠEVIK
POLUOSTROV TAJMYR
GORY BYRRANGA
SEVERO - SIBIRSKAJA NIZMENNOST'
URAL'SKIJE GORY
Arctic Circle
POLUOSTROV JAMAL
GYDANSKIJ POLUOSTROV
JAMALO-NENECKIJ
NENECKIJ
KOMI
PLATO PUTORANA
SREDNE-SIBIRSKOJE PLOSKOGORJE
ZAPADNO-SIBIRSKAJA RAVNINA
SIBERIA
RUSSIA
KAZAKHSTAN
CHINA
MONGOLIA
ZAPADNYJ SAJAN
VOSTOČNYJ SAJAN
SAJAN MOUNTAINS
ALTAJ
TUVA
CHAKASIJA
BURJATIJA
STANOVOJE NAGORJE
STANOVOY MOUNTAINS
JABLONOVYJ CHREBET
MONGOL ALTAJN NURUU
CHANGAJN NURUU
XINJIANG UYGUR ZIZHIQU
SINKIANG
JUNGGAR PENDI
ozero Bajkal
Lake Baikal
Noril'sk
Vorkuta
Dudinka
Surgut
Omsk
Novosibirsk
Tomsk
Kemerovo
Barnaul
Krasnojarsk
Bratsk
Irkutsk
Angarsk
Ulan-Ude
Čita
Ulaanbaatar
Semipalatinsk
Pavlodar
Ust'-Kamenogorsk
Novokuzneck
Abakan
Copyright © by Rand McNally & Co.
Map prepared by Esselte Map Service AB, Stockholm.

Map continues pages 72-73

Map continues pages 90-91

MAP FORM	chrebet	gora	guba	mys	ostrov	ozero	poluostrov	proliv	vodochranilišče
ENGLISH	range	mountain	bay	cape	island	lake	peninsula	strait	reservoir
DEUTSCH	Gebirge	Berg	Bucht	Kap	Insel	See	Halbinsel	Meeresstrasse	Stausee
ESPAÑOL	sierra	montaña	bahía	cabo	isla	lago	península	estrecho	embalse
FRANÇAIS	chaîne	montagne	baie	cap	île	lac	péninsule	détroit	réservoir
PORTUGUÊS	serra	montanha	baía	cabo	ilha	lago	península	estreito	reservatório

Kilometers 0 200 400 600 Km.
Statute Miles 0 200 400 600 Mi.

Scale 1:12,000,000

One centimeter represents 120 kilometers.
One inch represents approximately 190 miles.
Lambert Conformal Conic Projection

ALASKA
UNITED STATES
Chukchi Sea
Bering Strait
OSTROV VRANGEL'A
proliv Longa
SAINT LAWRENCE ISLAND
NUNIVAK ISLAND
SAINT MATTHEW ISLAND
Gambell
Provideniya
ČUKOTSKIJ POLUOSTROV
Uelen
Lavrentija
Egvekinot
Arctic Circle
zaliv Kresta
Anadyrskij zaliv
Anadyr'
Beringovskij
Bering Sea
ČUKOTSKOJE NAGORJE
ANADYRSKOJE PLOSKOGORJE
EKIATAPSKIJ CHREBET
Mys Šmidta
Vankarem
Pevek
Bilibino
AN'UJSKIJ CHREBET
VOSTOČNO-SIBIRSKOJE MORE
EAST SIBERIAN SEA
NOVOSIBIRSKIJE OSTROVA
OSTROVA DE-LONGA
OSTROVA ANŽU
OSTROV KOTEL'NYJ
OSTROV NOVAJA SIBIR'
OSTROV BOL'ŠOJ L'ACHOVSKIJ
proliv Sannikova
proliv Dmitrija Lapteva
MEDVEŽ'I OSTROVA
Čerskij
Ambarčik
Kolymskaja
KOLYMSKAJA NIZMENNOST'
JUKAGIRSKOJE PLOSKOGORJE
Kolyma
Omolon
Jana
Indigirka
Chroma
Čokurdach
Srednekolymsk
Zyr'anka
Krest-Major
Družina
MOMSKIJ CHREBET
CHREBET ČERSKOGO
gora Pobeda 3147
Ust'-Nera
Oimjakon
Verchojansk
Batagaj
JAKUTIJA
SIBERIA
CHREBET SUNTAR-CHAJATA
CHREBET SETTE-DABAN
Jakutsk
Pokrovsk
Aldan
Amga
Lena
ALDANSKOJE NAGORJE
STANOVOJ CHREBET
Tommot
Nagornyj
Tynda
Skovorodino
Magadan
Tauiskaja guba
Ola
Ochotsk
Ajan
CHREBET DŽUGDŽUR
Nel'kan
Gižiga
Evensk
Zaliv Šelichova
Penžinskaja guba
Gižiginskaja guba
KOR'AKSKOJE NAGORJE
PENŽINSKIJ CHREBET
Kamenskoje
Manily
Korf
Olutorskij zaliv
Karaginskij zaliv
OSTROV KARAGINSKIJ
KOMANDORSKIJE OSTROVA
OSTROV BERINGA
OSTROV MEDNYJ
POLUOSTROV KAMČATKA
SREDINNYJ CHREBET
Petropavlovsk-Kamčatskij
Kl'učevskaja Sopka
Ust'-Kamčatsk
Ust'-Bol'šereck
Kronockij zaliv
Palana
Tigil'
SEA OF OKHOTSK
OCHOTSKOJE MORE
OSTROV IONY
ŠANTARSKIJE OSTROVA
Sachalinskij zaliv
Nikolajevsk-na-Amure
Okha
OSTROV SACHALIN
SAKHALIN
Aleksandrovsk-Sachalinskij
Poronajsk
zaliv Terpenija
MYS TERPENIJA
Južno-Sachalinsk
Korsakov
Cholmsk
zaliv Aniva
Tatarskij proliv
La Perouse Strait
KURIL'SKIJE OSTROVA
KURIL ISLANDS
OSTROV PARAMUŠIR
Severo-Kuril'sk
proliv Kruzenšterna
OSTROV URUP
OSTROV ITURUP
proliv Friza
Kuril'sk
Habomai, Shikotan, Kunashiri, and Etorofu, occupied since 1945, are claimed by Japan pending a final peace treaty
PACIFIC OCEAN
SEA OF JAPAN
Wakkanai
Asahikawa
Sapporo
Otaru
Muroran
Obihiro
Kushiro
Nemuro
HOKKAIDŌ
JAPAN
HONSHŪ
Hakodate
Aomori
Hachinohe
Akita
Morioka
Miyako
Komsomol'sk-na-Amure
Chabarovsk
SICHOTE-ALIN'
BUREINSKIJ CHREBET
Zejskoje vodochranilišče
Zeja
Svobodnyj
Blagoveščensk
Belogorsk
Amur
Birobidžan
JEVREJSKAJA
Sovetskaja Gavan'
Vladivostok
Nachodka
Ussurijsk
Art'om
Dal'nerečensk
Spassk-Dal'nij
Lesozavodsk
zaliv Petra Velikogo
Harbin
Qiqihar Tsitsihar
Mudanjiang
Jixi
Hegang
Jiamusi
Shuangyashan
Yichun
Bei'an
HEILONGJIANG
NEI MONGGOL ZIZHIQU
DA HINGGAN LING
XIAO HINGGAN LING
MANCHURIA
CHINA

Map continues pages 26-27

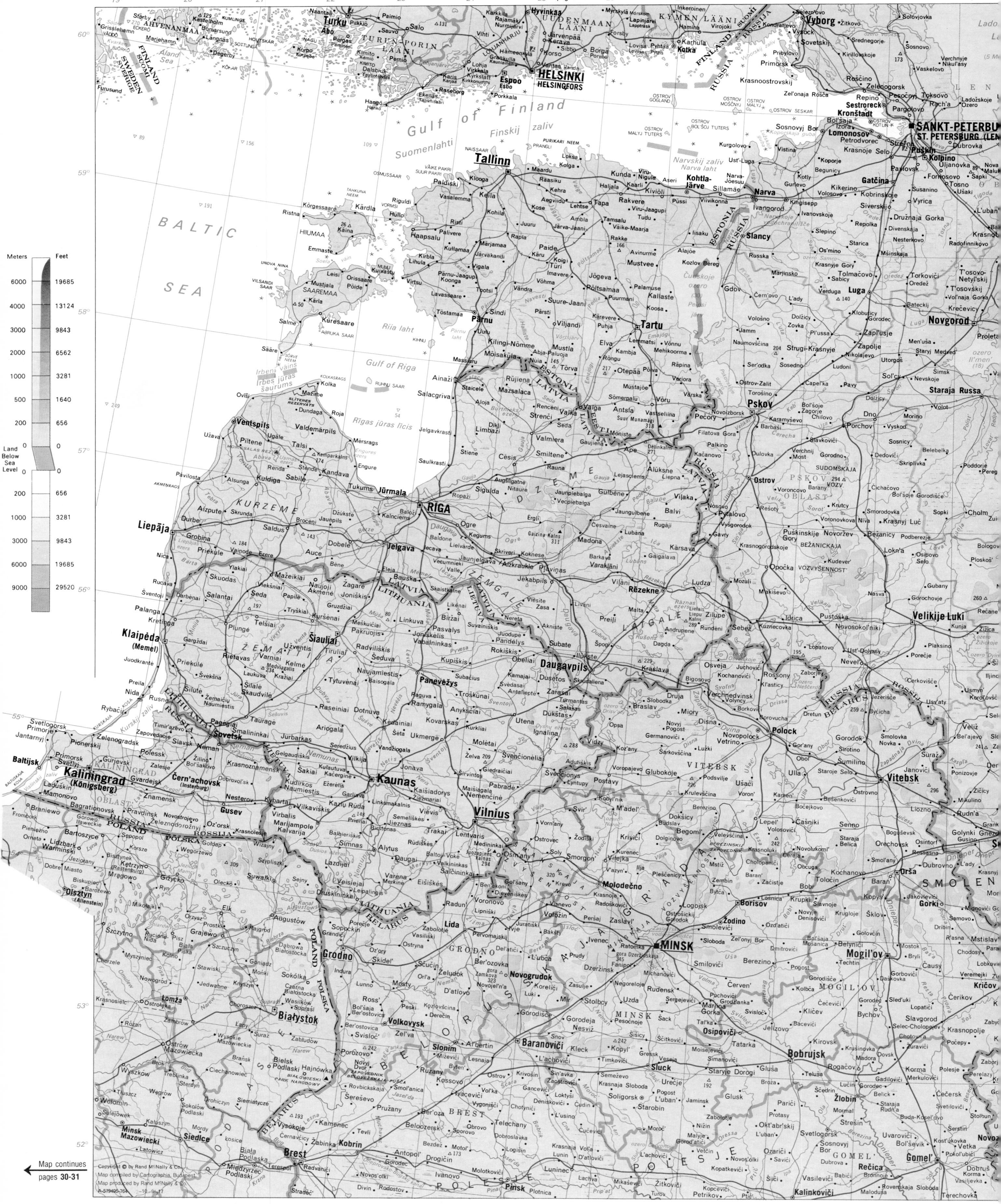
Meters
Feet
6000
19685
4000
13124
3000
9843
2000
6562
1000
3281
500
1640
200
656
0
Land Below Sea Level
Gulf of Finland
Finskij zaliv
Suomenlahti
BALTIC SEA
Gulf of Riga
Rigas jūras līcis
HELSINKI
HELSINGFORS
Tallinn
RIGA
Vilnius
MINSK
SANKT-PETERBURG
ST. PETERSBURG
Kaliningrad
(Königsberg)
Kaunas
Klaipėda
(Memel)
Liepāja
Ventspils
Tartu
Pskov
Novgorod
Vitebsk
Grodno
Brest
Gomel'
Mogil'ov
Daugavpils
Šiauliai
Białystok
Narva
Turku
Åbo
Vyborg
Map continues pages 30-31
Copyright © by Rand McNally & Co.
Map compiled by Cartographia, Budapest
Map produced by Rand McNally & Co.

MAP FORM	gr'ada	ostrov, o.	ozero, o.	vodochranilišče, vdchr.	vozvyšennost', vozv.	zaliv	zapovednik, zapov.
ENGLISH	ridge	island	lake	reservoir	upland	gulf; bay	reserve
DEUTSCH	Höhenrücken	Insel	See	Stausee	Bergland	Golf; Bucht	Reservat
ESPAÑOL	lomerío	isla	lago	embalse	tierras altas	golfo; bahía	reserva
FRANÇAIS	crête	île	lac	réservoir	hautes terres	golfo; baie	réserve
PORTUGUÊS	cordilheira	ilha	lago	reservatório	terras altas	golfo; baía	reserva

Map continues
pages 24-25

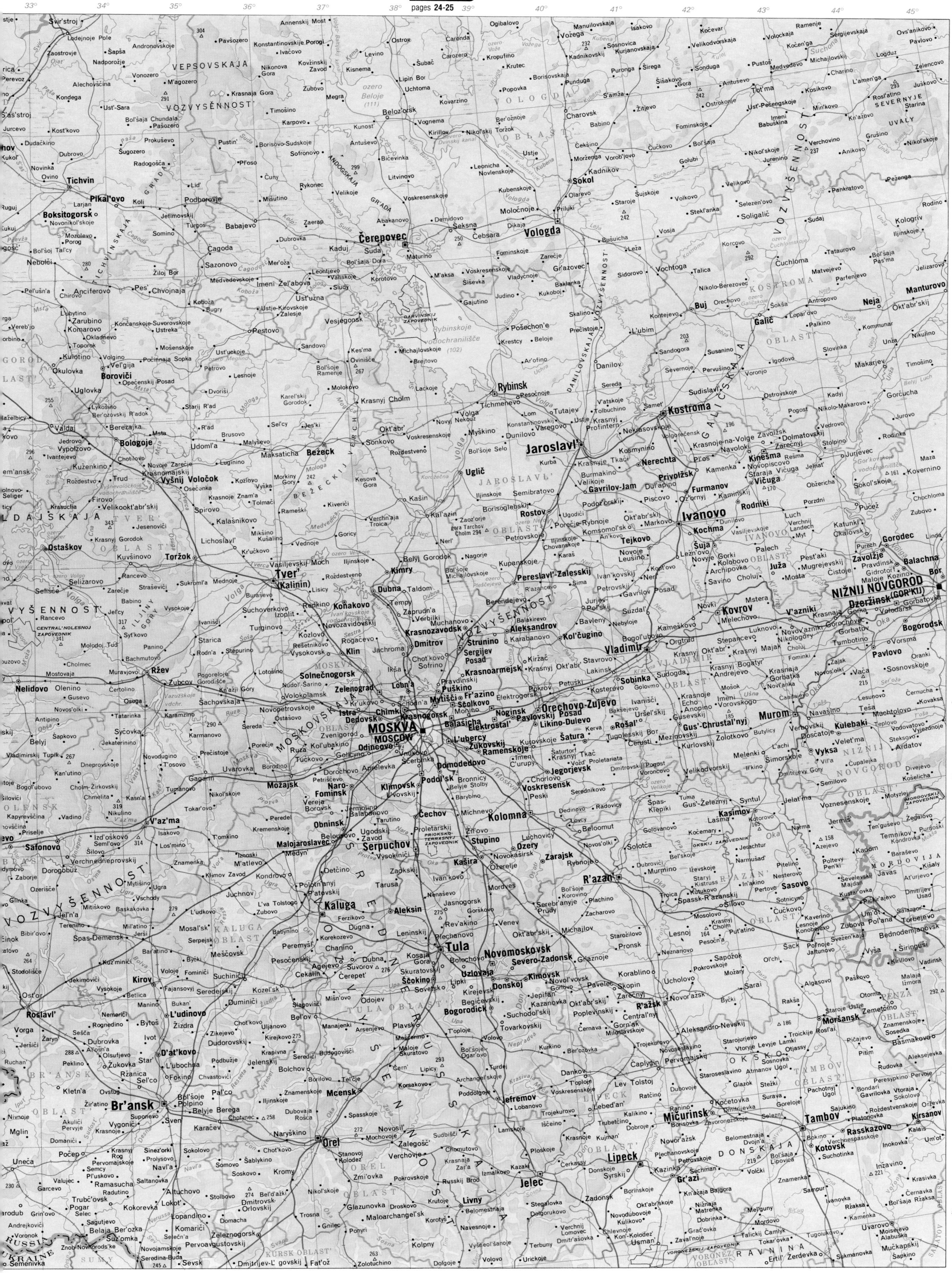
MOSKVA
MOSCOW
Tver' (Kalinin)
Jaroslavl'
Vologda
Čerepovec
Rybinsk
Kostroma
Ivanovo
Vladimir
NIŽNIJ NOVGOROD (GOR'KIJ)
Dzeržinsk
Tula
Kaluga
R'azan'
Br'ansk
Orel
Lipeck
Tambov
Mičurinsk
Jelec
Novomoskovsk
Serpuchov
Kolomna
Murom
Kovrov
Tichvin
Boroviči
Toržok
Ržev
Roslavl'
V'az'ma
Smolensk
VOZVYŠENNOST'
MOSKVA
OBLAST'

Map continues
pages 80-81

Map continues
pages 78-79

Kilometers 0 50 100 150 Km.
Statute Miles 0 50 100 150 Mi.

Scale 1:3,000,000

One centimeter represents 30 kilometers.
One inch represents approximately 47 miles.
Lambert Conformal Conic Projection

Map continues pages 30-31

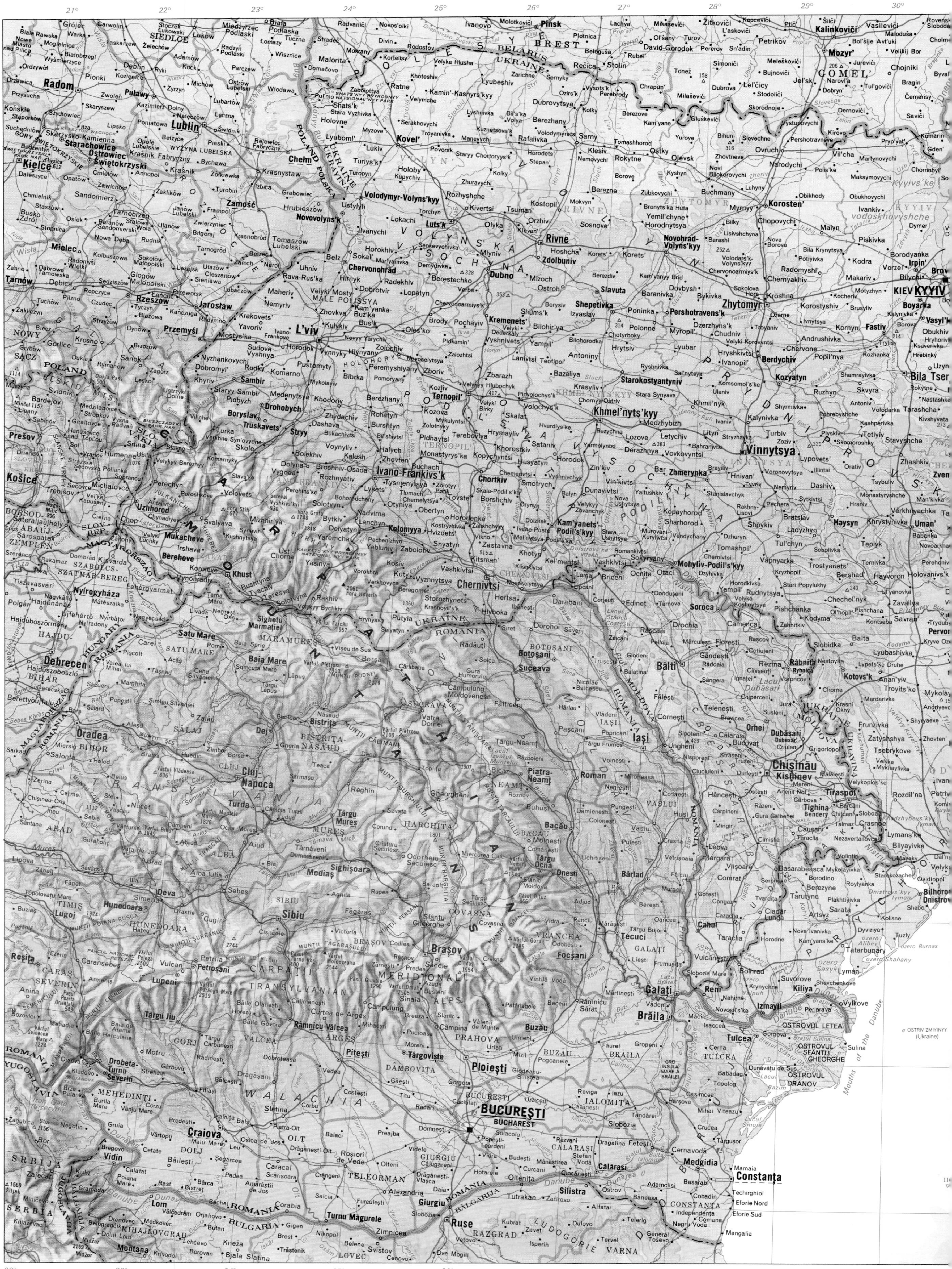
Kyyiv
Kiev
L'viv
Rivne
Zhytomyr
Vinnytsya
Khmel'nyts'kyy
Ternopil'
Ivano-Frankivs'k
Chernivtsi
Lutsk
Kovel'
Chişinău
Kishinev
Iaşi
Galaţi
Brăila
Constanţa
Bucureşti
Bucharest
Ploieşti
Braşov
Sibiu
Cluj-Napoca
Oradea
Craiova
Piteşti
Debrecen
Lublin
Radom
Rzeszów
Przemyśl
Košice
Prešov
Ruse
Vidin
Pinsk
Brest
Mozyr'
Uman'
Tulcea
Izmayil
Reni
Suceava
Botoşani
Bacău
Focşani
Mukacheve
Uzhhorod
Khust
Satu Mare
Baia Mare
BELARUS
UKRAINE
POLAND
ROMANIA
HUNGARY
MOLDOVA
BULGARIA
SRBIJA
SERBIA
YUGOSLAVIA
SLOVAKIA
CARPATHIAN MOUNTAINS
TRANSYLVANIAN ALPS
WALACHIA
Danube

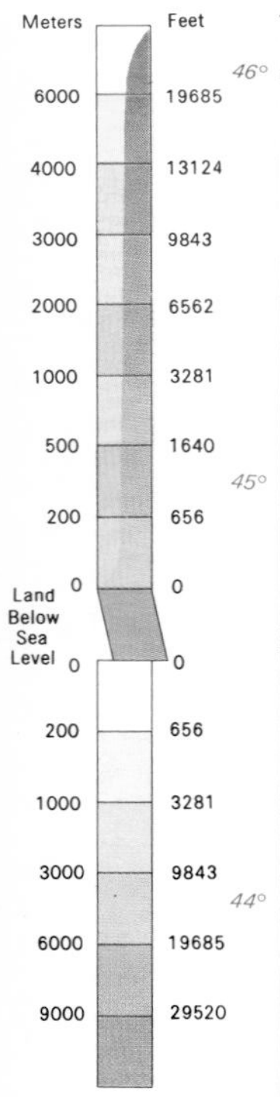
Meters
Feet
6000
19685
4000
13124
3000
9843
2000
6562
1000
3281
500
1640
200
656
0
0
Land Below Sea Level
0
0
200
656
1000
3281
3000
9843
6000
19685
9000
29520

Map continues pages 38-39

MAP FORM	hora	liman	lyman	mys	nyzovyna	ozero	vysochyna	zaliv	zatoka
ENGLISH	mountain	bay	bay	cape	plain	lake	upland	bay	bay
DEUTSCH	Berg	Bucht	Bucht	Kap	Ebene	See	Bergland	Bucht	Bucht
ESPAÑOL	montaña	bahía	bahía	cabo	llanno	lago	tierras altas	bahía	bahía
FRANÇAIS	montagne	baie	baie	cap	plaine	lac	hautes terres	baie	baie
PORTUGUÊS	montanha	baía	baía	cabo	planície	lago	terras altas	baía	baía

Map continues pages 76-77

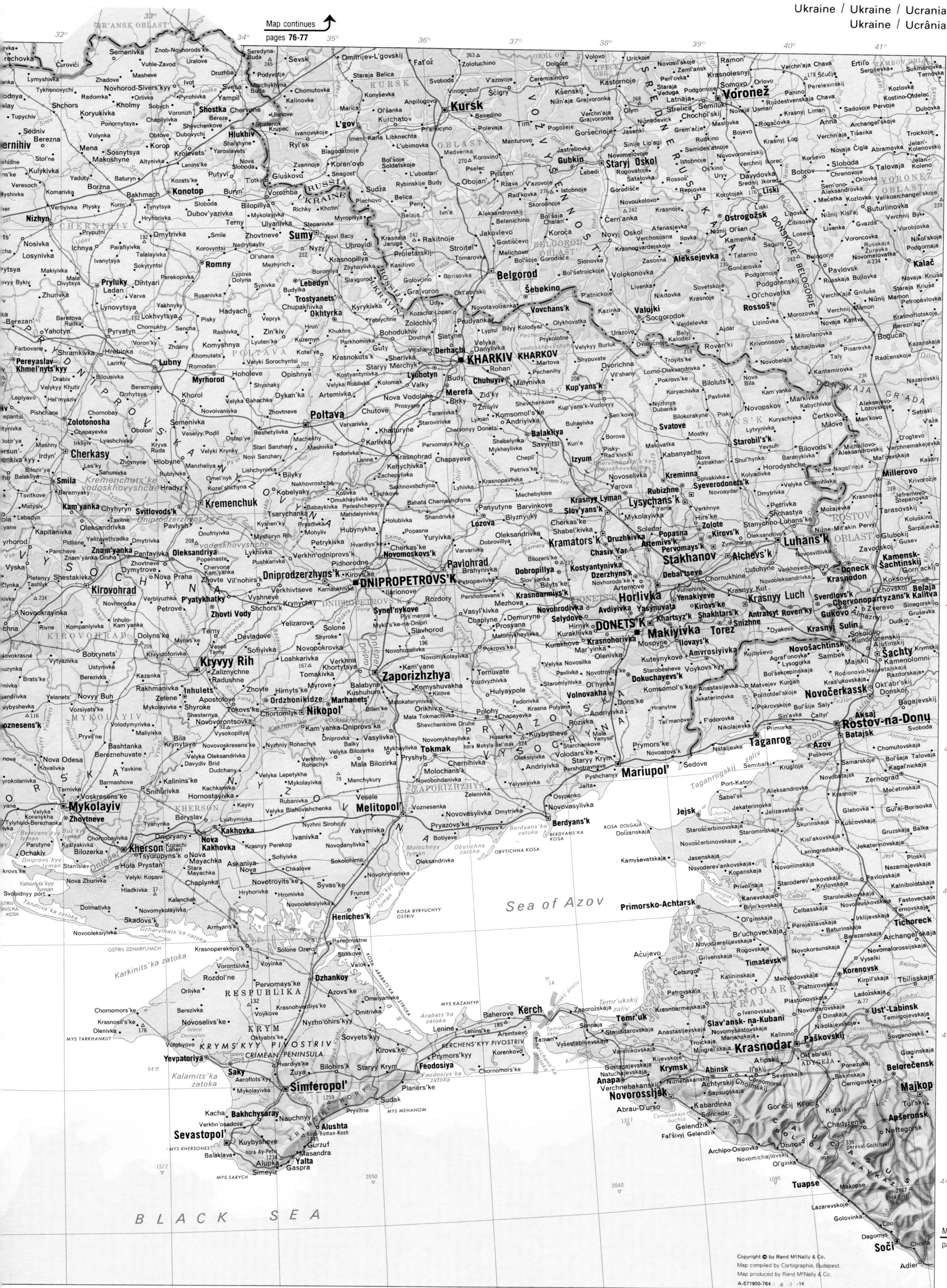
Kursk
Voronež
Staryj Oskol
Belgorod
Sumy
KHARKIV KHARKOV
Poltava
Cherkasy
Kremenchuk
Kirovohrad
Kryvyy Rih
DNIPROPETROVS'K
Dniprodzerzhyns'k
Zaporizhzhya
Nikopol'
Melitopol'
Mykolayiv
Kherson
Horlivka
DONETS'K
Makiyivka
Luhans'k
Mariupol'
Taganrog
Rostov-na-Donu
Novočerkassk
Šachty
Jejsk
Primorsko-Achtarsk
Krasnodar
Novorossijsk
Anapa
Kerch
Feodosiya
Simferopol'
Sevastopol'
Yevpatoriya
Yalta
Alushta
Tuapse
Soči
Majkop
Armavir
Tichoreck
Sea of Azov
BLACK SEA
KRYMS'KYY PIVOSTRIV
CRIMEAN PENINSULA
RESPUBLIKA KRYM
RUSSIA
UKRAINE
Copyright © by Rand McNally & Co.
Map compiled by Cartographia, Budapest.
Map produced by Rand McNally & Co.
A-571900-764

Map continues pages 80-81

Map continues page 84

Kilometers 0 50 100 150 Km.
Statute Miles 0 50 100 150 Mi.

Scale 1:3,000,000
One centimeter represents 30 kilometers.
One inch represents approximately 47 miles.
Lambert Conformal Conic Projection

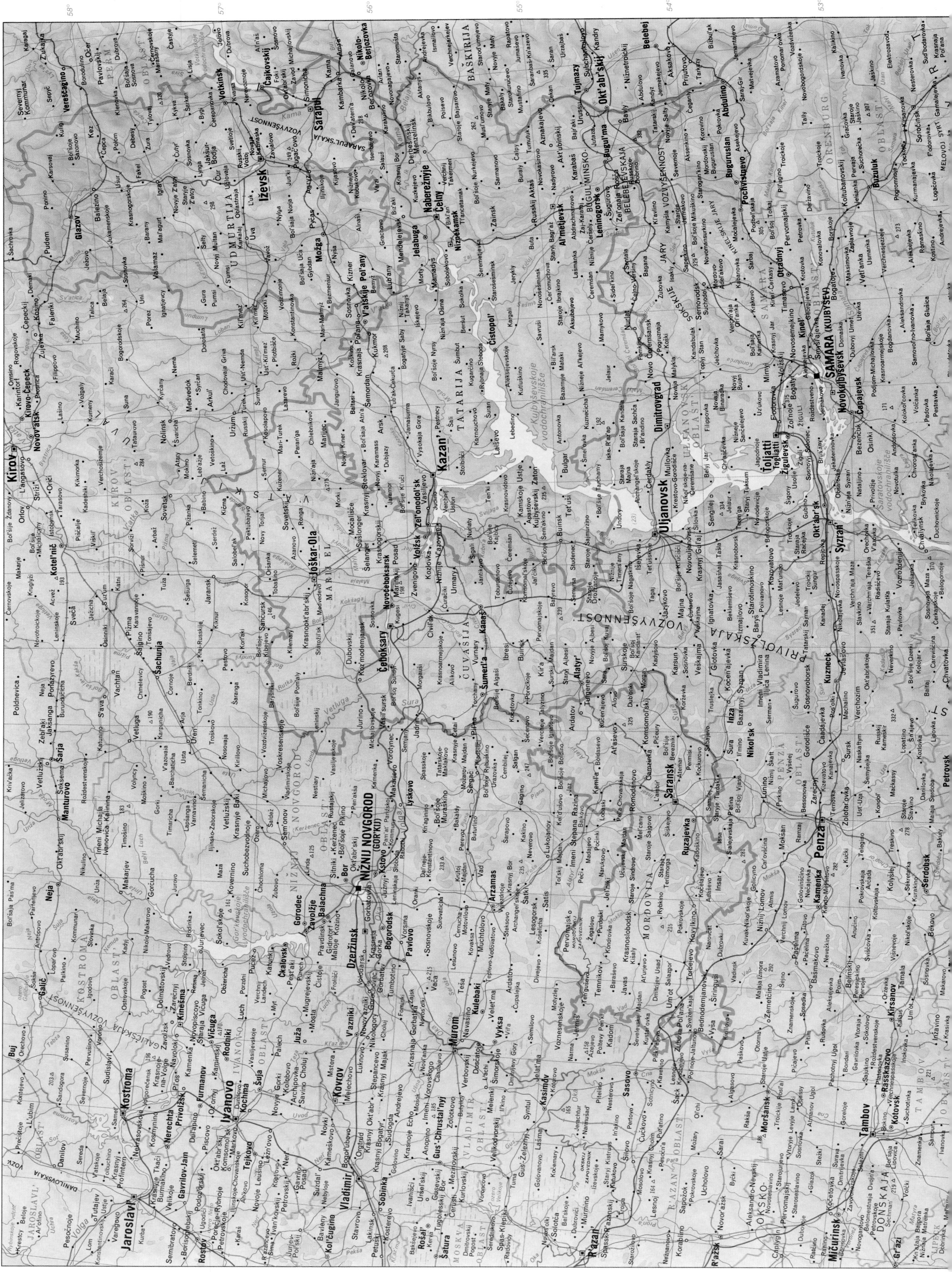
Kirov
Kazan'
Uljanovsk
SAMARA (KUJBYŠEV)
Penza
Saransk
Tambov
Rjazan'
Vladimir
Jaroslavl'
Kostroma
Ivanovo
NIŽNIJ NOVGOROD (GOR'KIJ)
Čeboksary
Iževsk
Toljatti
Syzran'
Dzeržinsk
Murom

Map continues pages 24-25

Map continues pages 76-77

Map continues pages 86-87

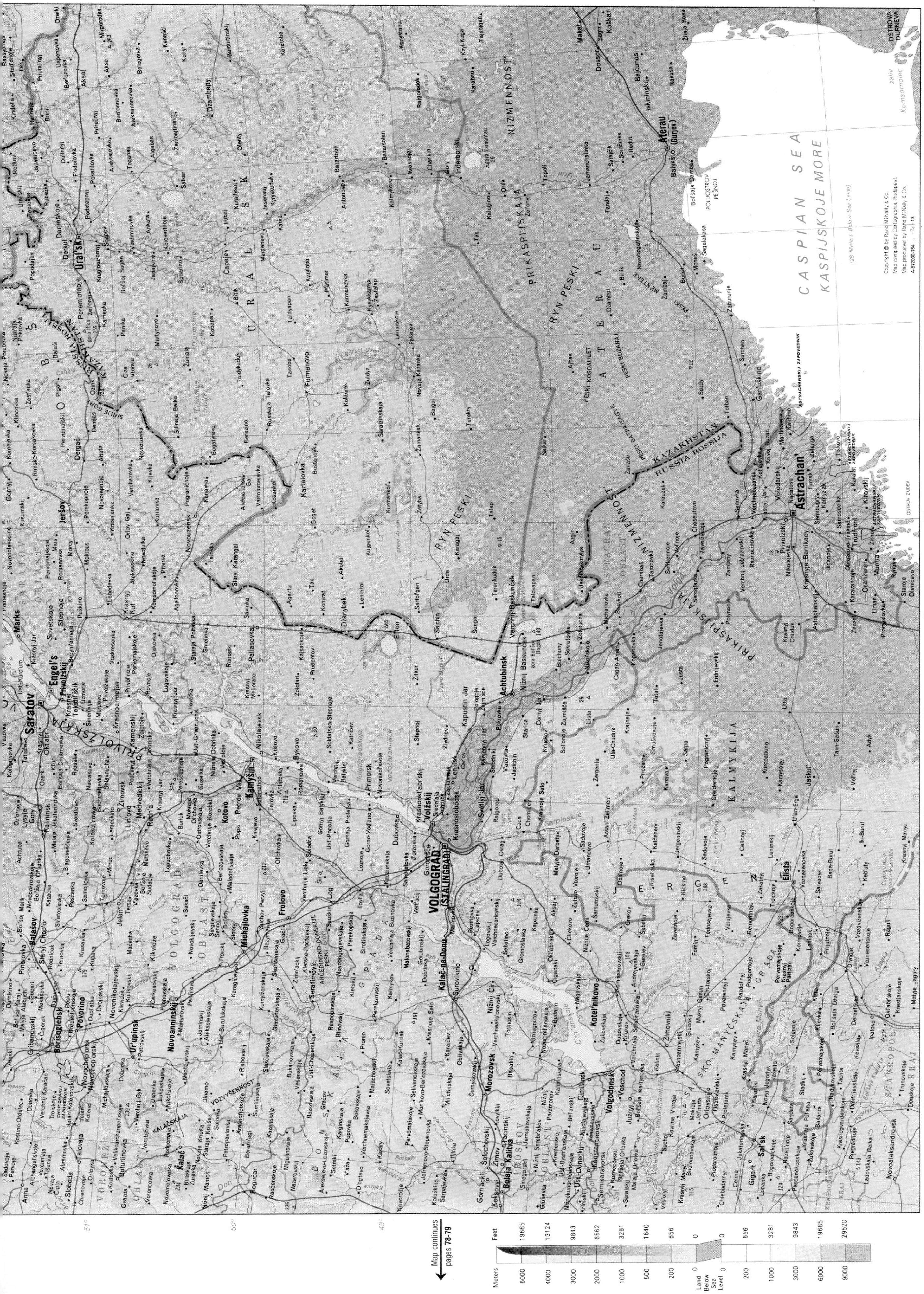
CASPIAN SEA
KASPIJSKOJE MORE
PRIKASPIJSKAJA NIZMENNOST'
RYN-PESKI
KALMYKIJA
ERGENI
PRIVOLŽSKAJA
SAL'SKO-MANYČSKAJA GRADA
KAZAKHSTAN
RUSSIA ROSSIJA
VOLGOGRAD (STALINGRAD)
Saratov
Astrachan'
Atyrau (Gurjev)
Ural'sk
Engel's
Kamyšin
Volžskij
Kalač-na-Donu
Elista
Achtubinsk
Volgodonsk
Morozovsk
Borisoglebsk
Kotel'nikovo
Frolovo
Michajlovka
Uryupinsk
Novoanninskij
Balašov
Pallasovka
Džanybek
Furmanovo
Sal'sk
Gigant
Volga
Ural
Don
Copyright © by Rand McNally & Co.
Map compiled by Cartographia, Budapest
Map produced by Rand McNally & Co.
A-572000-764 -1-1-13

Map continues page 84

Map continues pages 78-79

Scale 1:3,000,000

One centimeter represents 30 kilometers.
One inch represents approximately 47 miles.
Lambert Conformal Conic Projection

Kilometers 0 50 100 150 Km.
Statute Miles 0 50 100 150 Mi.

MAP FORM	gory	ozero	peski	vodochranilišče	vozvyšennost'	zapovednik
ENGLISH	mountains	lake	desert	reservoir	upland	reserve
DEUTSCH	Berge	See	Wüste	Stausee	Bergland	Reservat
ESPAÑOL	montañas	lago	desierto	embalse	tierras altas	reserva
FRANÇAIS	montagnes	lac	désert	réservoir	hautes terres	réserve
PORTUGUÊS	montanhas	lago	deserto	reservatório	terras altas	reserva

Meters	Feet
6000	19685
4000	13124
3000	9843
2000	6562
1000	3281
500	1640
200	656
0	0
Land Below Sea Level 0	0
200	656
1000	3281
3000	9843
6000	19685
9000	29520

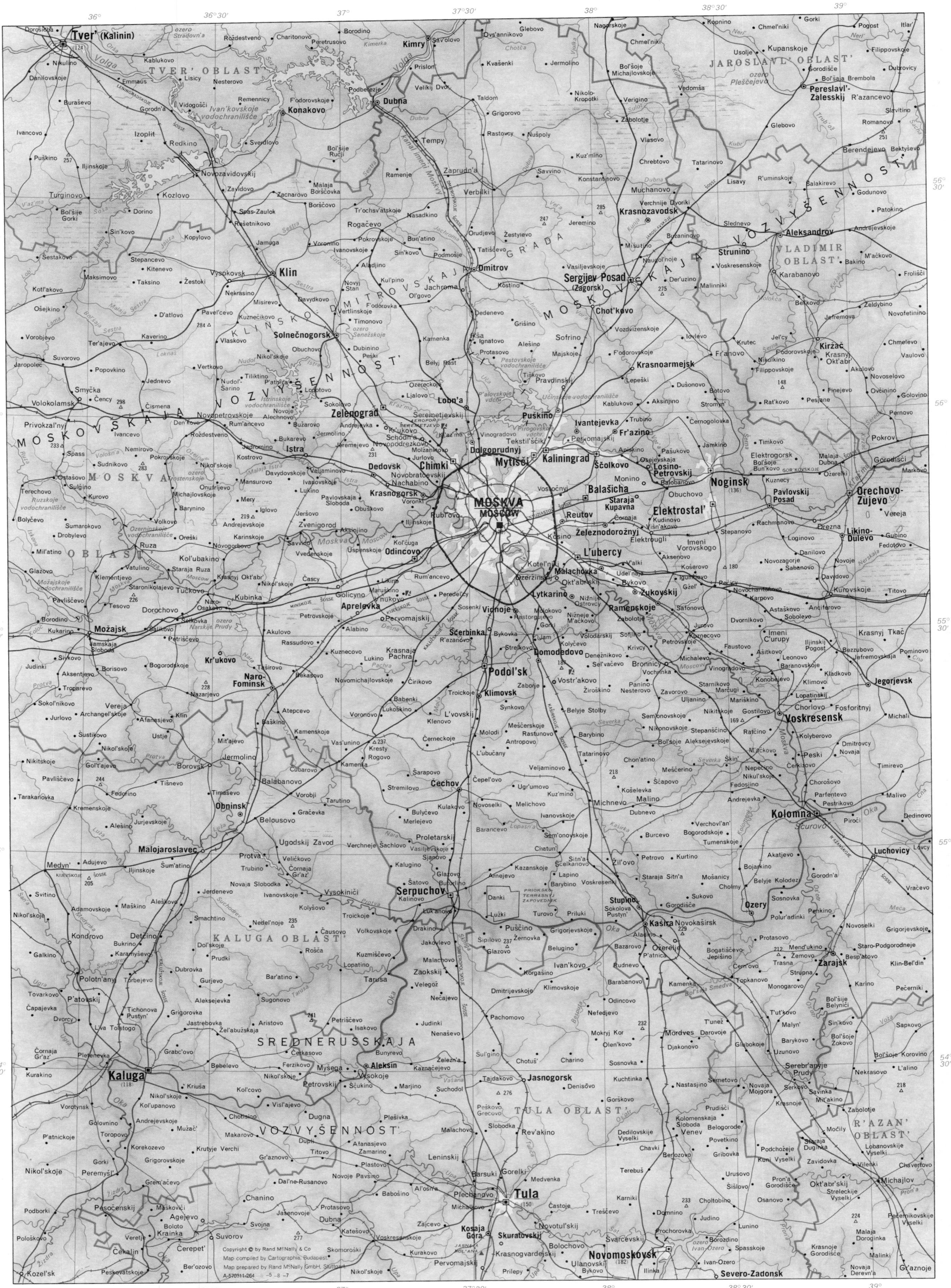
MOSKVA
MOSCOW
Tver' (Kalinin)
Tula
Kaluga
Serpuchov
Kolomna
Podol'sk
Klin
Dubna
Dmitrov
Sergijev Posad (Zagorsk)
Noginsk
Orechovo-Zujevo
Voskresensk
Novomoskovsk
Aleksin
Obninsk
Zelenograd
Mytišči
Kaliningrad
Balašicha
Elektrostal'
Solnečnogorsk
Volokolamsk
Možajsk
Naro-Fominsk
Malojaroslavec
TVER' OBLAST'
JAROSLAVL' OBLAST'
VLADIMIR OBLAST'
MOSKOVSKAJA OBLAST'
KALUGA OBLAST'
TULA OBLAST'
R'AZAN' OBLAST'
MOSKOVSKAJA VOZVYŠENNOST'
KLINSKO-DMITROVSKAJA GRADA
SREDNERUSSKAJA VOZVYŠENNOST'
Ivan'kovskoje vodochranilišče
Volga
Oka
Moskva
36°
36°30'
37°
37°30'
38°
38°30'
39°
56°
55°30'
55°
54°30'
Copyright © by Rand McNally & Co.
Map compiled by Cartographia, Budapest
Map prepared by Rand McNally GmbH, Stuttgart
A-570511-264 -5 -8 -7

MAP FORM	gr'ada	ozero	vodochranilišče, vdchr.	vozvyšennost'	zapovednik
ENGLISH	ridge	lake	reservoir	upland	reserve
DEUTSCH	Höhenrücken	See	Stausee	Bergland	Reservat
ESPAÑOL	lomerío	lago	embalse	tierras altas	reserva
FRANÇAIS	crête	lac	réservoir	hautes terres	réserve
PORTUGUÊS	cordilheira	lago	reservatório	terras altas	reserva

Kilometers 0 10 20 30 40 50 Km.

Statute Miles 0 10 20 30 40 50 Mi.

Scale 1:1,000,000

One centimeter represents 10 kilometers.
One inch represents approximately 16 miles.

Lambert Conformal Conic Projection

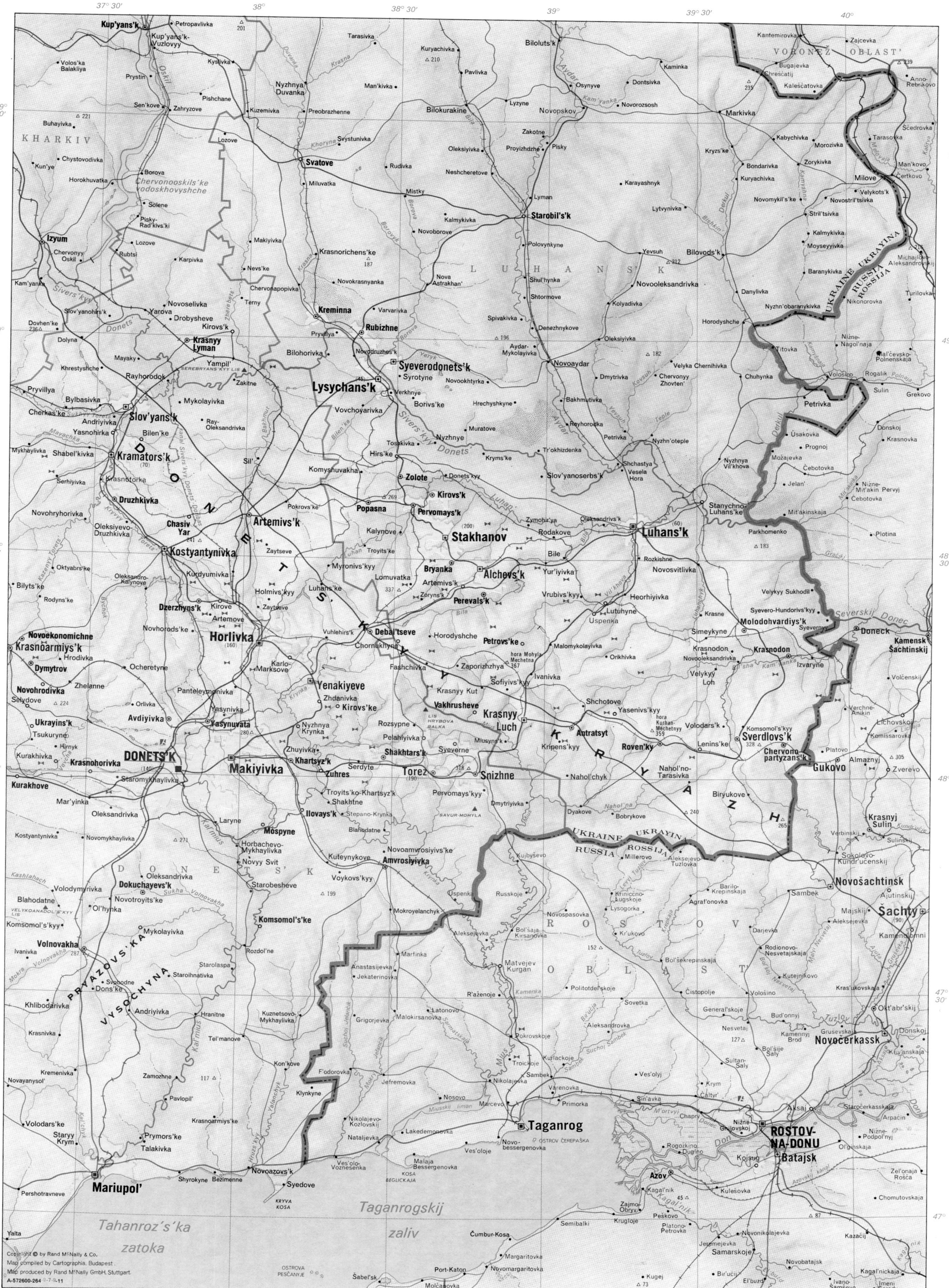

Kup'yans'k
Izyum
Slov'yans'k
Kramators'k
Kostyantynivka
Artemivs'k
Horlivka
DONETS'K
Makiyivka
Krasnoarmiys'k
Volnovakha
Mariupol'
Lysychans'k
Syeverodonets'k
Starobil's'k
Svatove
Kreminna
Rubizhne
Alchevs'k
Stakhanov
Luhans'k
Krasnyy Luch
Sverdlovs'k
Krasnodon
Taganrog
ROSTOV-NA-DONU
Batajsk
Azov
Novočerkassk
Šachty
Novošachtinsk
Gukovo
Doneck
Kamensk Šachtinskij
Millerovo
KHARKIV
D O N E T S' K
L U H A N S' K
V O R O N E Ž O B L A S T'
R O S T O V O B L A S T'
UKRAINE UKRAYINA
RUSSIA ROSSIJA
PRYAZOVS'KA VYSOCHYNA
Tahanroz'ka zatoka
Taganrogskij zaliv
Donets'
Siverskyy Donets'
Severskij Donec
Don
Copyright © by Rand McNally & Co.
Map compiled by Cartographia, Budapest
Map produced by Rand McNally GmbH, Stuttgart
A-572600-264 -7-9-11

MAP FORM	kosa	ostrov, o.	vodoskhovyshche, vdskhv.	vysochyna, vys.	zaliv	zatoka
ENGLISH	spit	island	reservoir	upland	bay	bay
DEUTSCH	Landzunge	Insel	Stausee	Bergland	Bucht	Bucht
ESPAÑOL	lengua de tierra	isla	embalse	tierras altas	bahía	bahía
FRANÇAIS	flèche	île	réservoir	hautes terres	baie	baie
PORTUGUÊS	ponta de terra	ilha	reservatório	terras altas	baía	baía

Kilometers 0 10 20 30 40 50 Km.

Statute Miles 0 10 20 30 40 50 Mi.

Scale 1:1,000,000

One centimeter represents 10 kilometers.

One inch represents approximately 16 miles.

Lambert Conformal Conic Projection

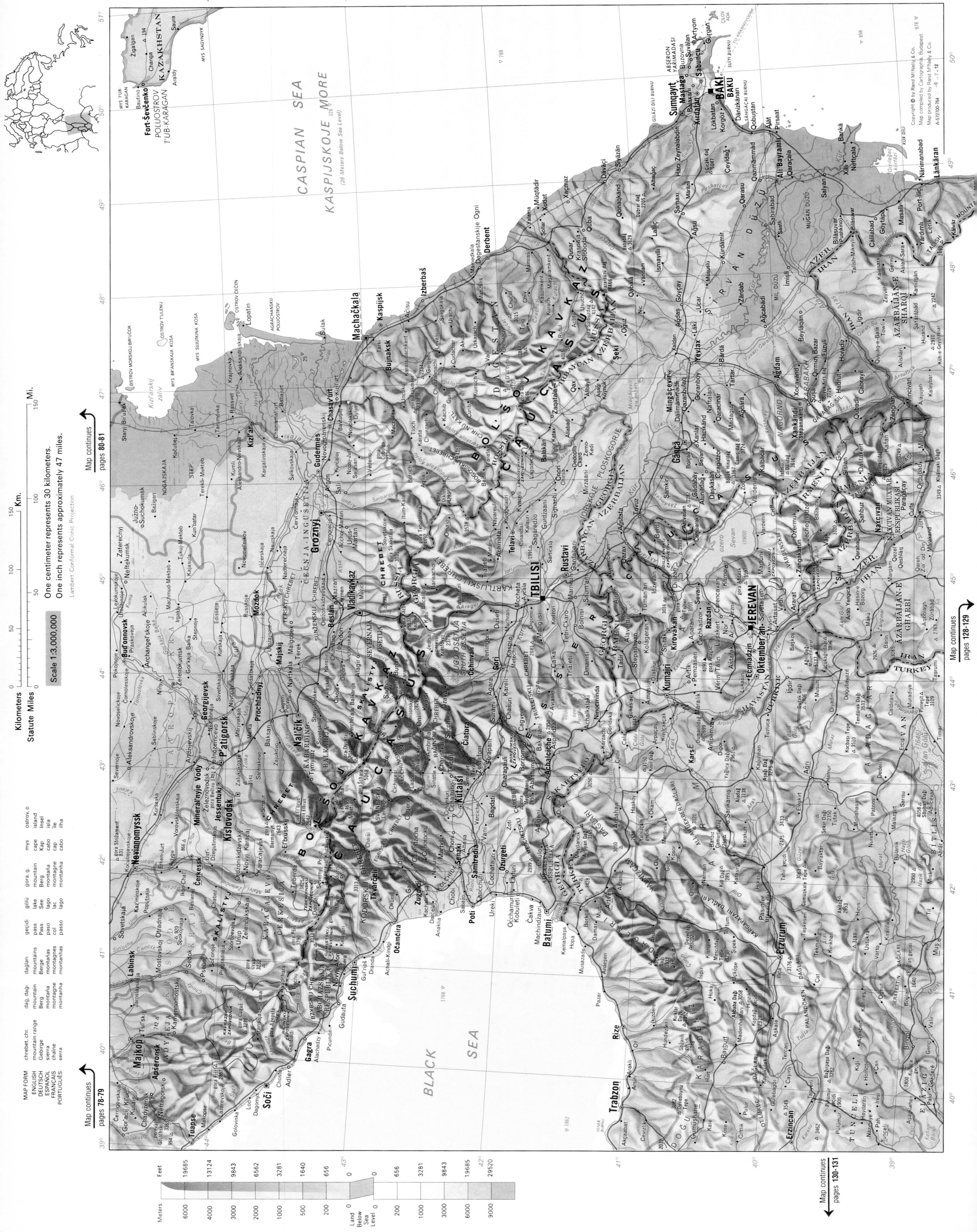
Scale 1:3,000,000
One centimeter represents 30 kilometers.
One inch represents approximately 47 miles.
Lambert Conformal Conic Projection
Kilometers 0 50 100 150 Km.
Statute Miles 0 50 100 150 Mi.
MAP FORM: chrebet, chr. / dag, dagi / daglari / geçidi / gölü / gora, g. / mys / ostrov, o
ENGLISH: mountain range / mountain / mountains / pass / lake / mountain / cape / island
DEUTSCH: Gebirge / Berg / Berge / Pass / See / Berg / Kap / Insel
ESPAÑOL: sierra / montaña / montañas / paso / lago / montaña / cabo / isla
FRANÇAIS: chaîne / montagne / montagnes / col / lac / montagne / cap / île
PORTUGUÊS: serra / montanha / montanhas / passo / lago / montanha / cabo / ilha
Map continues pages 78-79
Map continues pages 80-81
Map continues pages 128-129
Map continues pages 130-131
CASPIAN SEA
KASPIJSKOJE MORE
(28 Meters Below Sea Level)
BLACK SEA
Meters 6000 4000 3000 2000 1000 500 200 0 Land Below Sea Level 0 200 1000 3000 6000 9000
Feet 19685 13124 9843 6562 3281 1640 656 0 0 656 3281 9843 19685 29520
Copyright © by Rand McNally & Co.
Map compiled by Cartographia, Budapest.
Map produced by Rand McNally & Co.

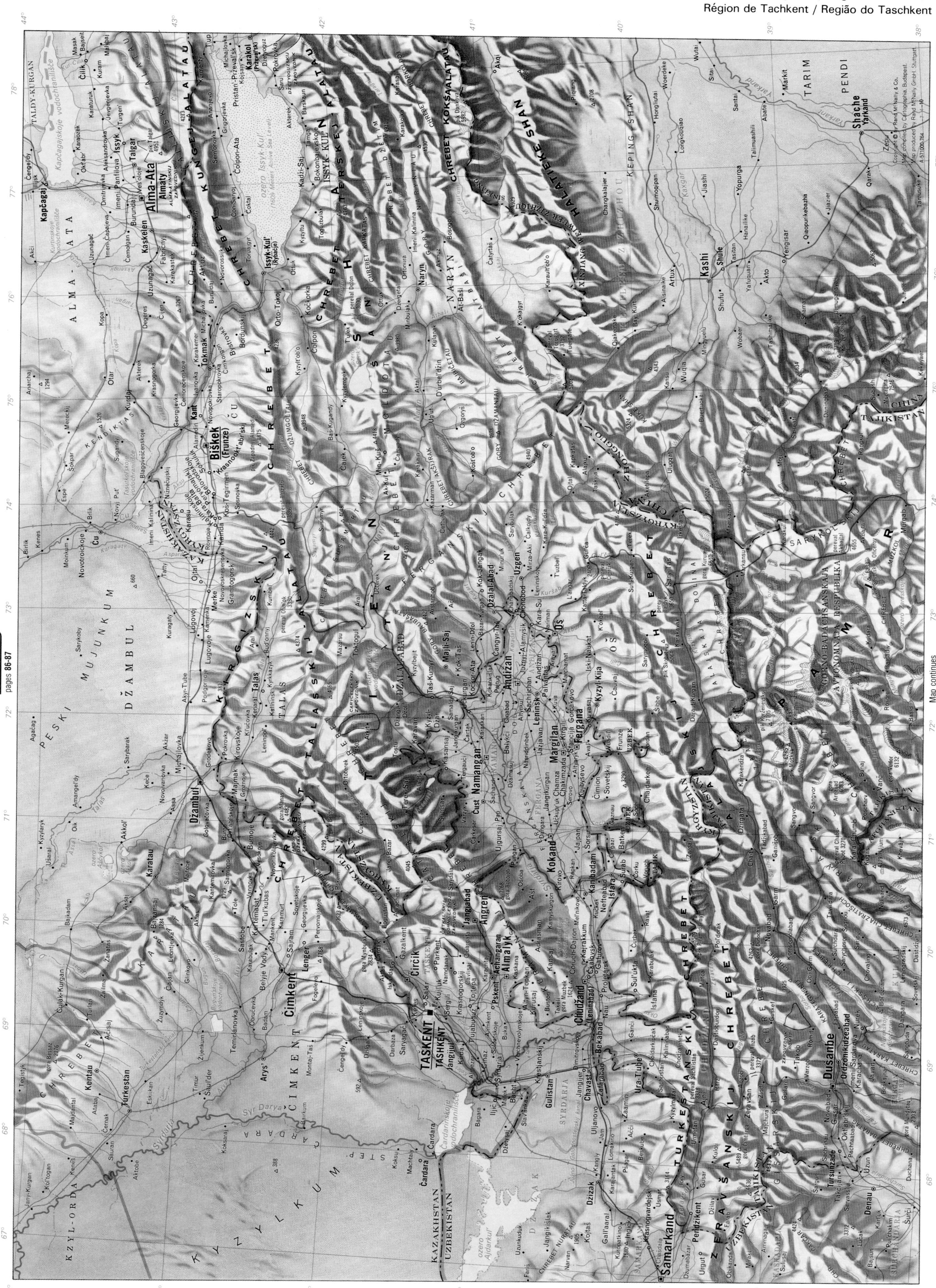
TASHKENT
TASHKENT
Biškek (Frunze)
Alma-Ata
Almaty
Dušanbe
Samarkand
Kashi
Shache
Yarkand
Andižan
Namangan
Kokand
Fergana
Oš
Džambul
Čimkent
Turkestan
Kentau
Talas
Naryn
Tokmak
Kant
Issyk-Kul'
Karakol
KAZAKHSTAN
UZBEKISTAN
TAJIKISTAN
CHINA
MUJUNKUM
K Y Z Y L K U M
TARIM PENDI
Syr Darya

Map continues pages 86-87

Map continues page 123

Kilometers 0 50 100 150 Km.
Statute Miles 0 50 100 150 Mi.

Scale 1:3,000,000
One centimeter represents 30 kilometers.
One inch represents approximately 47 miles.
Lambert Conformal Conic Projection

MAP FORM	chrebet	gora	gory	ozero	pereval	pik
ENGLISH	mountain range	mountain	mountains	lake	pass	peak
DEUTSCH	Gebirge	Berg	Berge	See	Pass	Gipfel
ESPAÑOL	cordillera	montaña	montañas	lago	paso	pico
FRANÇAIS	chaîne	montagne	montagnes	lac	défilé	cime
PORTUGUÊS	cordilheira	montanha	montanhas	lago	passo	pico

Meters	6000	4000	3000	2000	1000	500	200	0	Land Below Sea Level	0	200	1000	3000	6000	9000
Feet	19685	13124	9843	6562	3281	1640	656	0		0	656	3281	9843	19685	29520

Map continues pages 72-73

Map continues pages 24-25

Map continues pages 80-81

Perm'
Kazan'
Iževsk
Ufa
Orenburg
SAMARA
JEKATERINBURG (SVERDLOVSK)
ČEL'ABINSK
Kurgan
T'umen'
Magnitogorsk
Kustanaj
Ural'sk
Akt'ubinsk
Orsk
Petropavlovsk
Kokčetav
Kzyl-Orda
Aral'sk
Džezkazgan
Arkalyk
URAL'SKIJE GORY
KAZAKHSTAN
UZBEKISTAN
RUSSIA
Aral'skoje more
Aral Sea
Caspian Sea
KYZYL-ORDA
AKT'UBINSK
TURGAJ
DŽEZKAZGAN
KARAKALPAK RESPUBLIKA
MANGISTAU
KYZYLKUM
Copyright © by Rand McNally & Co.
Map compiled by Cartographia, Budapest.
Map produced by Rand McNally & Co.

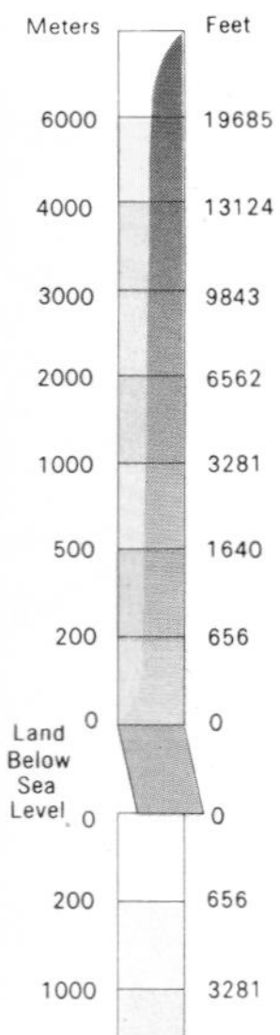
Meters
Feet
6000
19685
4000
13124
3000
9843
2000
6562
1000
3281
500
1640
200
656
0
0
Land Below Sea Level
0
0
200
656
1000
3281
3000
9843
6000
19685
9000
29520

Map continues page 85

MAP FORM	chrebet	gora	hu	ozero	plato	porog
ENGLISH	mountain range	mountain	lake	lake	plateau	waterfall
DEUTSCH	Gebirge	Berg	See	See	Hochebene	Wasserfall
ESPAÑOL	cordillera	montaña	lago	lago	meseta	cascada
FRANÇAIS	chaîne	montagne	lac	lac	plateau	chute d'eau
PORTUGUÊS	cordilheira	montanha	lago	lago	planalto	queda d'agua

TOMSK OBLAST'
NOVOSIBIRSKAJA OBLAST'
OMSKAJA OBLAST'
KEMEROVSKAJA OBLAST'
ALTAJSKIJ KRAJ
KRASNOJARSKIJ KRAJ
CHAKASIJA
TUVA
PAVLODAR
SEMIPALATINSK
KARAGANDA
TALDY-KURGAN
ALMA-ATA
XINJIANG UYGUR ZIZHIQU
JUNGGAR PENDI
DZUNGARIAN BASIN
TIAN SHAN
ALTAJ
MONGOLIA
CHINA
KAZAKHSTAN
RUSSIA
Tomsk
NOVOSIBIRSK
OMSK
Kemerovo
Novokuzneck
Barnaul
Bijsk
Krasnojarsk
Abakan
Pavlodar
Semipalatinsk
Ust'-Kamenogorsk
Rubcovsk
Karaganda
Balchaš
Alma-Ata
Ürümqi
Karamay
Yining
Kapčagaj
Taldy-Kurgan
Ačinsk
Kansk
Minusinsk
Gorno-Altajsk
Slavgorod
Kolpaševo
Asino
Bolotnoje
Leninsk-Kuzneckij
Prokopjevsk
Kisel'ovsk
Mariinsk
Kupino
Karasuk
Tatarsk
Barabinsk
Kujbyšev
Ekibastuz
Ajaguz
Leninogorsk
Zyr'anovsk
Tekeli
Talgar
Turpan
TURPAN PENDI
TURPAN DEPRESSION
BOGDA SHAN
BOROHORO SHAN
Lake Balkhash
WEST SIBERIAN PLAIN
Map continues page 88

Kilometers 0 100 200 300 Km.
Statute Miles 0 100 200 300 Mi.

Scale 1:6,000,000

One centimeter represents 60 kilometers.
One inch represents approximately 95 miles.
Lambert Conformal Conic Projection

Lake Baikal Region / Baikalseegebiet / Región del Lago Baikal / Région du Lac Baïkal / Região do Lago Baikal

Map continues page 89

Map continues pages 74-75

Map continues pages 102-103

Map continues pages 86-87

RUSSIA
MONGOLIA
CHINA
Baikal
Irkutsk
Ulan-Ude
Čita
Ulaanbaatar
Krasnojarsk
Bratsk
Kyzyl
Angarsk
Kansk
Abakan
Ust'-Ilimsk
Ust'-Kut
SAJAN MOUNTAINS
STANOVOJE NAGORJE
JABLONOVYJ CHREBET
VITIMSKOJE PLOSKOGORJE
BURJATIJA
TUVA
IRKUTSK OBLAST'
KRASNOJARSK KRAJ
ČITA OBLAST'

MAP FORM	chrebet	gora	nuruu	nuur	ozero, o.	porog	uul
ENGLISH	mountain range	mountain	mountain range	lake	lake	waterfall	mountains
DEUTSCH	Gebirge	Berg	Gebirge	See	See	Wasserfall	Berge
ESPAÑOL	cordillera	montaña	cordillera	lago	lago	cascada	montañas
FRANÇAIS	chaîne	montagne	chaîne	lac	lac	chute d'eau	montagnes
PORTUGUÊS	cordilheira	montanha	cordilheira	lago	lago	queda d'água	montanhas

Scale 1:6,000,000

One centimeter represents 60 kilometers.
One inch represents approximately 95 miles.
Lambert Conformal Conic Projection

Kilometers 0 100 200 300 Km.
Statute Miles 0 100 200 300 Mi.

Feet	Meters
19685	6000
13124	4000
9843	3000
6562	2000
3281	1000
1640	500
656	200
0	0
Land Below Sea Level	
0	0
656	200
3281	1000
9843	3000
19685	6000
29520	9000

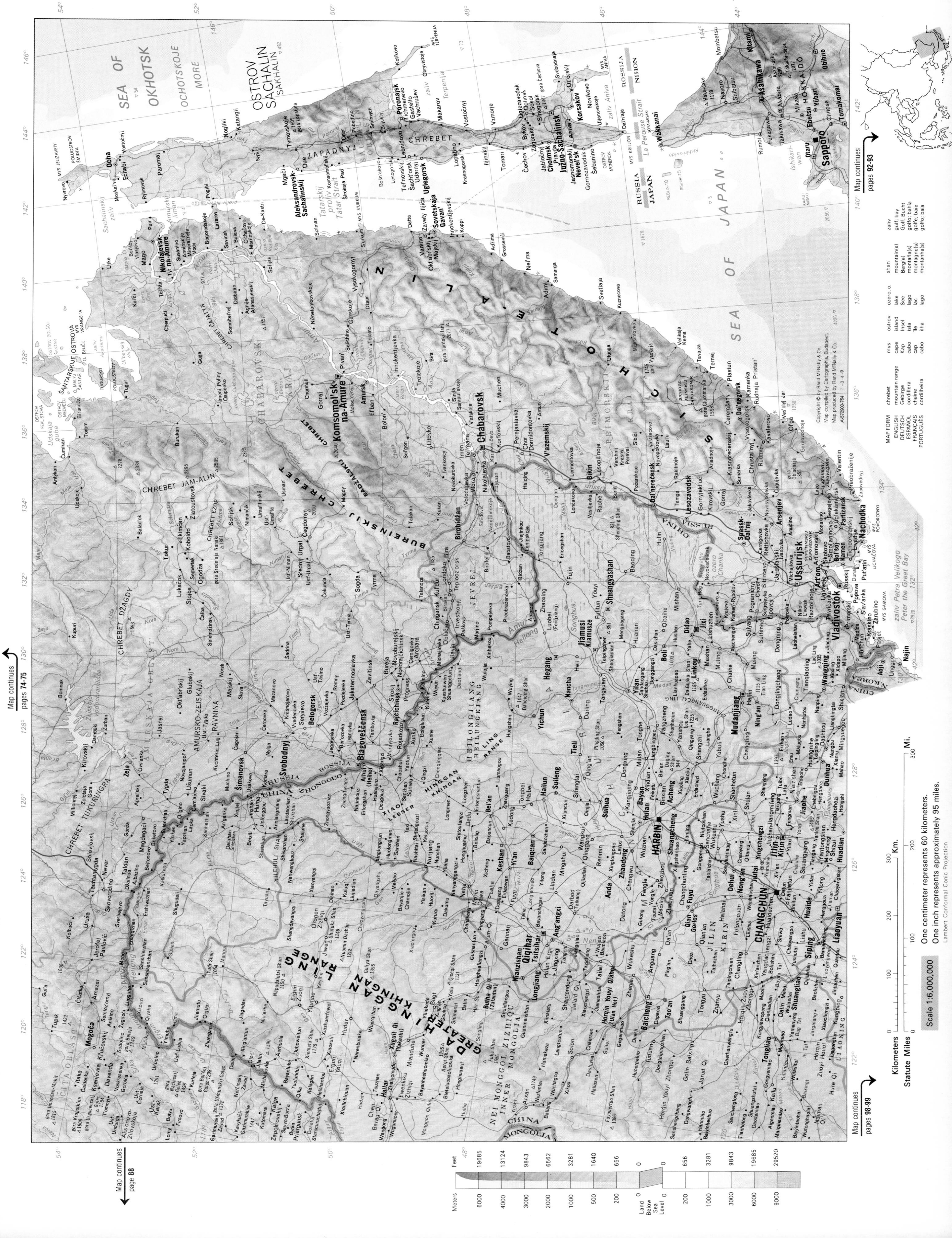
SEA OF OKHOTSK
OCHOTSKOJE MORE
OSTROV SACHALIN
SAKHALIN
SEA OF JAPAN
CHABAROVSK
Chabarovsk
Vladivostok
HARBIN
CHANGCHUN
Qiqihar
Blagoveščensk
Komsomol'sk-na-Amure
Sapporo
HOKKAIDŌ
RUSSIA
JAPAN
CHINA
MONGOLIA
GREATER KHINGAN RANGE
DA HINGGAN LING
BUREINSKIJ CHREBET
SICHOTE-ALIN'
Map continues pages 92-93
Map continues pages 74-75
Map continues pages 98-99
Map continues page 88
Scale 1:6,000,000
One centimeter represents 60 kilometers.
One inch represents approximately 95 miles.
Lambert Conformal Conic Projection
Kilometers
Statute Miles
Copyright © by Rand McNally & Co.
Map compiled by Rand McNally & Co.
Map produced by Cartographia, Budapest.

Map continues pages 74-75

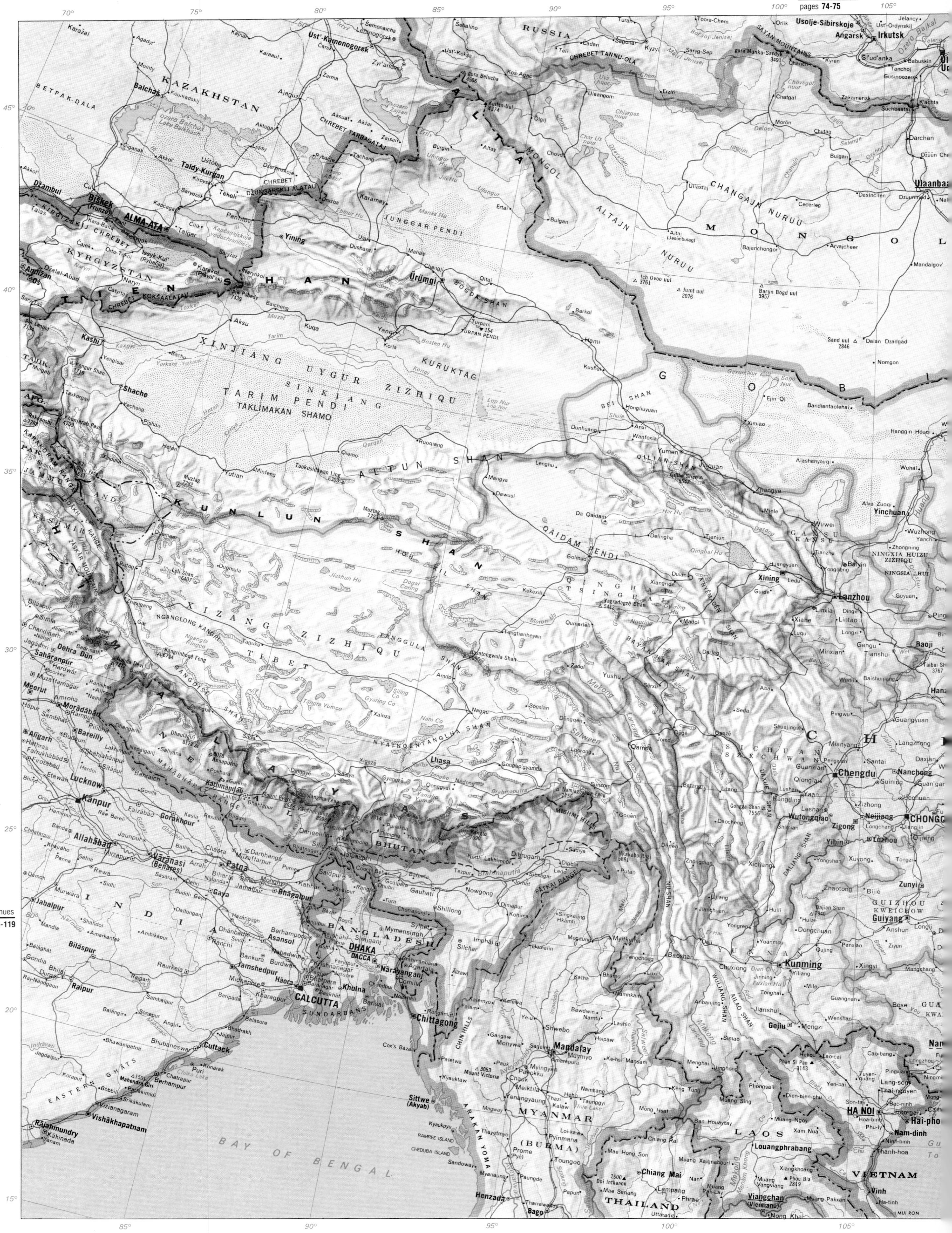
RUSSIA
KAZAKHSTAN
KYRGYZSTAN
TIEN SHAN
XINJIANG UYGUR ZIZHIQU
SINKIANG
TARIM PENDI
TAKLIMAKAN SHAMO
ALTUN SHAN
KUNLUN SHAN
QAIDAM PENDI
QINGHAI
XIZANG ZIZHIQU
TIBET
HIMALAYAS
NEPAL
BHUTAN
INDIA
BANGLADESH
MYANMAR (BURMA)
THAILAND
LAOS
VIETNAM
MONGOL
GOBI
ALTAJ
CHANGAJN NURUU
SICHUAN
YUNNAN
GUIZHOU
BAY OF BENGAL
Ürümqi
Lhasa
Lanzhou
Xining
Chengdu
Kunming
Guiyang
Alma-Ata
Biškek (Frunze)
Ulaanbaatar
Irkutsk
Kathmandu
Calcutta
Dhaka
Chittagong
Mandalay
Chiang Mai
Ha Noi
Patna
Lucknow
Kanpur
Allahābād
Vārānasi (Benares)

Map continues pages 118-119

MAP FORM	bandao	dao	hu	-jima	pendi	shan	-shima
ENGLISH	peninsula	island	lake	island	basin	mountain(s)	island
DEUTSCH	Halbinsel	Insel	See	Insel	Becken	Berg(e)	Insel
ESPAÑOL	península	isla	lago	isla	cuenca	montaña(s)	isla
FRANÇAIS	péninsule	île	lac	île	bassin	montagne(s)	île
PORTUGUÊS	península	ilha	lago	ilha	bacia	montanha(s)	ilha

SEA OF JAPAN
YELLOW SEA
EAST CHINA SEA
SOUTH CHINA SEA
PACIFIC OCEAN
PHILIPPINE SEA
SEA OF OKHOTSK
RUSSIA
MANCHURIA
NORTH KOREA
SOUTH KOREA
JAPAN
TAIWAN
PHILIPPINES
HONSHŪ
HOKKAIDŌ
SHIKOKU
KYŪSHŪ
NEI MONGGOL ZIZHIQU
INNER MONGOLIA
HEILONGJIANG
JILIN
LIAONING
HEBEI
SHANXI
SHANDONG
HENAN
JIANGSU
ANHUI
HUBEI
HUNAN
JIANGXI
ZHEJIANG
FUJIAN
GUANGDONG
BEIJING
PEKING
TIANJIN
TIENTSIN
SHENYANG
MUKDEN
SHANGHAI
WUHAN
GUANGZHOU
CANTON
VICTORIA
HONG KONG
T'AIPEI
P'YŎNGYANG
SŎUL
SEOUL
TŌKYŌ
ŌSAKA
Harbin
Changchun
Dalian
Qingdao
Nanjing
Hangzhou
Fuzhou
Xiamen
Busan
Pusan
Nagoya
Kyōto
Yokohama
Sapporo
Hiroshima
Fukuoka
Nagasaki
Kagoshima
Vladivostok
Chabarovsk
Tropic of Cancer
Copyright © by Rand McNally & Co.
Map prepared by Esselte Map Service AB, Stockholm.
A-569700-264

Map continues
pages 108-109

Kilometers 0 200 400 600 Km.
Statute Miles 0 200 400 600 Mi.

Scale 1:12,000,000
One centimeter represents 120 kilometers.
One inch represents approximately 190 miles.
Lambert Conformal Conic Projection

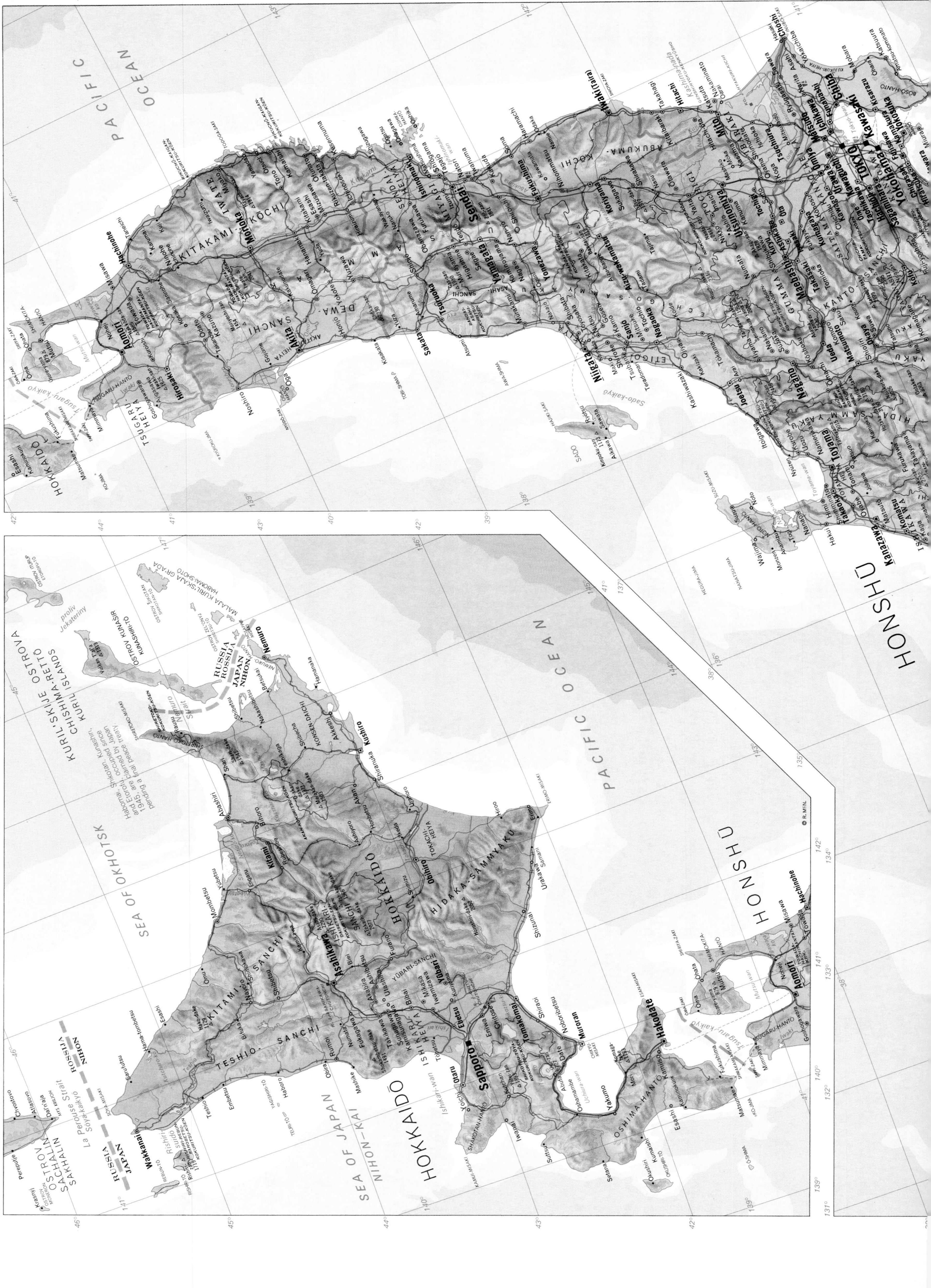
PACIFIC OCEAN
SEA OF JAPAN
NIHON-KAI
SEA OF OKHOTSK
HOKKAIDŌ
HONSHŪ
KURIL'SKIJE OSTROVA
CHISHIMA-RETTŌ
KURIL ISLANDS
La Perouse Strait
Sōya-kaikyō
RUSSIA
JAPAN
NIHON
Tsugaru-kaikyō
Sado-kaikyō
TŌKYŌ
Sapporo
Sendai
Yokohama
Aomori
Hakodate
Asahikawa
a

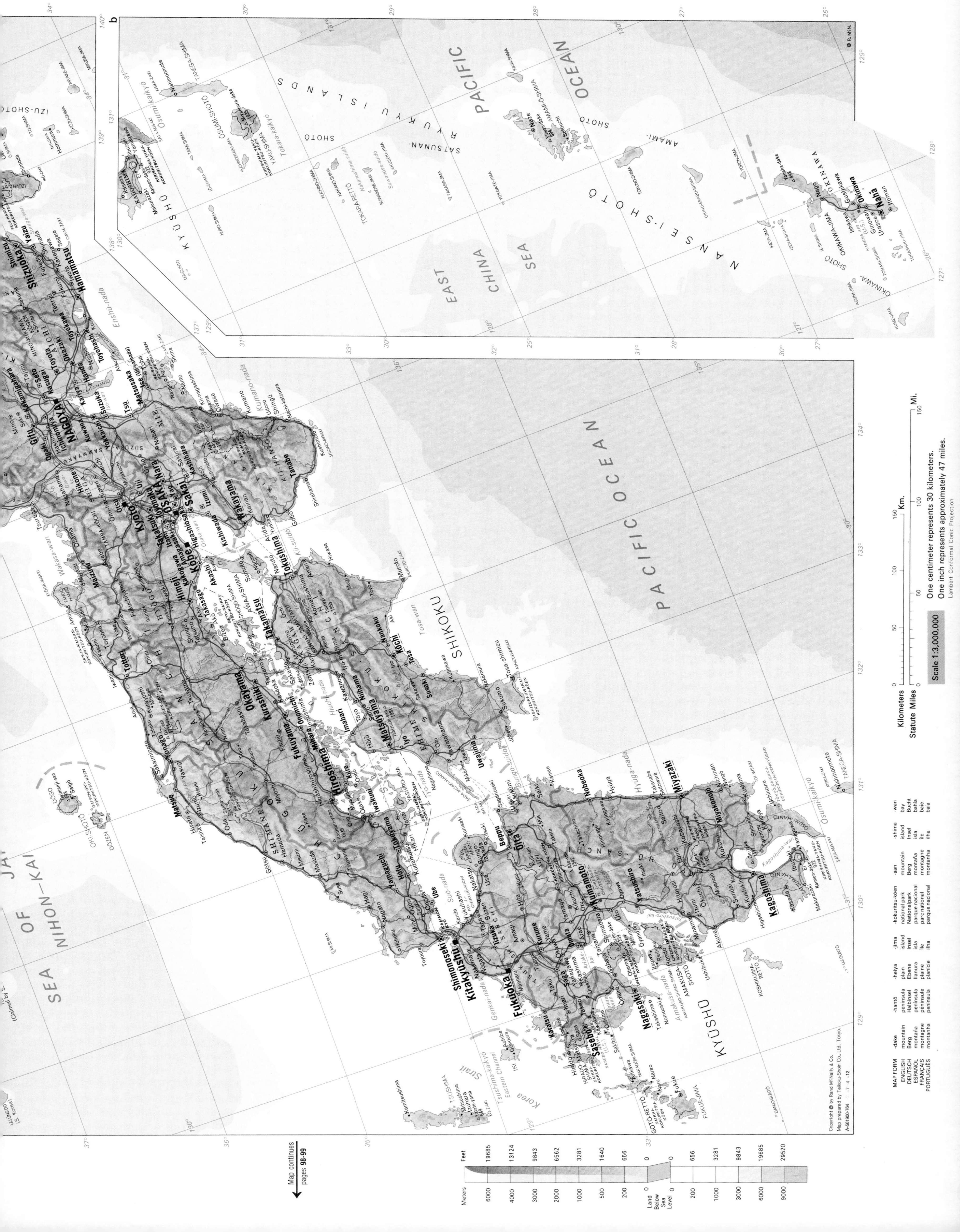
SEA OF JAPAN
NIHON-KAI
PACIFIC OCEAN
EAST CHINA SEA
SHIKOKU
KYŪSHŪ
RYUKYU ISLANDS
NANSEI-SHOTŌ
SATSUNAN-SHOTŌ
AMAMI-SHOTŌ
OKINAWA-SHOTŌ
OKINAWA
OKI-SHOTŌ
Korea Strait
Tsushima-kaikyō
Eastern Channel
TSUSHIMA
GOTŌ-RETTŌ
AMAKUSA-SHOTŌ
TANEGA-SHIMA
YAKU-SHIMA
Ōsumi-kaikyō
Tokara-kaikyō
Kagoshima-wan
Hyūga-nada
Bungo-suidō
Tosa-wan
Kii-suidō
Kumano-nada
Enshū-nada
Wakasa-wan
Osaka-wan
Ise-wan
Suō-nada
Genkai-nada
Shimonoseki
Kitakyūshū
Fukuoka
Sasebo
Nagasaki
Kumamoto
Kagoshima
Miyazaki
Nobeoka
Ōita
Beppu
Hiroshima
Okayama
Kurashiki
Fukuyama
Matsuyama
Takamatsu
Tokushima
Kōchi
Kōbe
Ōsaka
Kyōto
Sakai
Nara
Wakayama
Himeji
Akashi
Nagoya
Gifu
Yokkaichi
Tsu
Shizuoka
Hamamatsu
Toyohashi
Matsue
Tottori
Yamaguchi
Ube
Naha
Naze
IZU-SHOTŌ
Kilometers
Statute Miles
Scale 1:3,000,000
One centimeter represents 30 kilometers.
One inch represents approximately 47 miles.
Lambert Conformal Conic Projection
Map continues pages 98-99
Meters
Feet
Land Below Sea Level
MAP FORM | -dake | -hantō | -heiya | -jima | -kokuritsu-kōen | -san | -shima | -wan
ENGLISH | mountain | peninsula | plain | island | national park | mountain | island | bay
DEUTSCH | Berg | Halbinsel | Ebene | Insel | Nationalpark | Berg | Insel | Bucht
ESPAÑOL | montaña | península | llanura | isla | parque nacional | montaña | isla | bahía
FRANÇAIS | montagne | péninsule | plaine | île | parc national | montagne | île | baie
PORTUGUÊS | montanha | península | planície | ilha | parque nacional | montanha | ilha | baía
Copyright © by Rand McNally & Co.
Map prepared by Teikoku-Shoin Co., Ltd. Tokyo.
A-561900-784

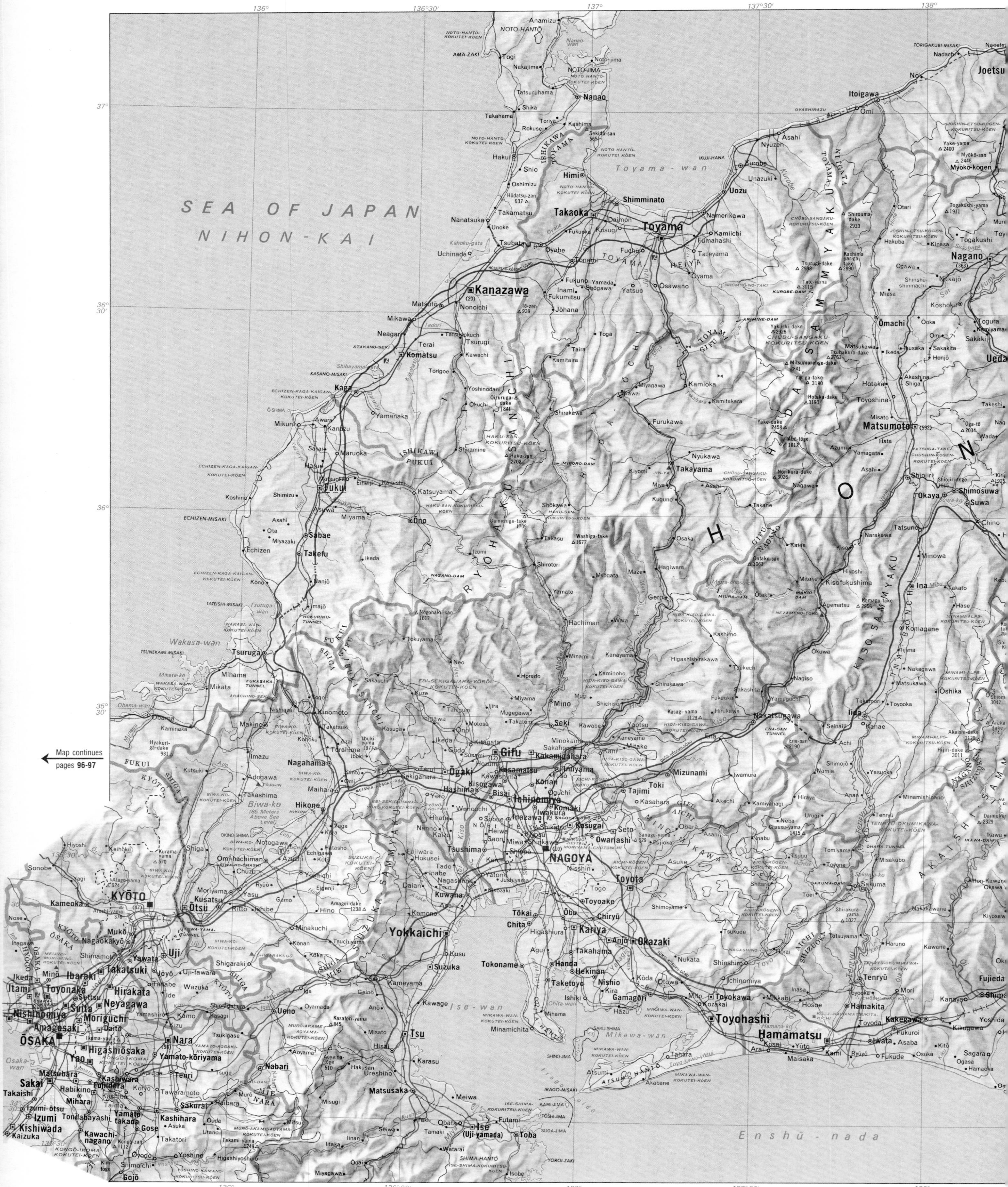
SEA OF JAPAN
NIHON-KAI
Toyama-wan
Wakasa-wan
Ise-wan
Mikawa-wan
Enshū-nada
Biwa-ko
(85 Meters Above Sea Level)
HONSHU
HIDA-SAMMYAKU
KISO-SAMMYAKU
RYŌHAKU-SANCHI
SUZUKA-SAMMYAKU
NOTO-HANTŌ
Anamizu
Togi
Nanao
Shika
Takahama
Hakui
Himi
Shimminato
Takaoka
Toyama
Uozu
Kurobe
Itoigawa
Joetsu
Nagano
Kanazawa
Komatsu
Kaga
Fukui
Sabae
Takefu
Ōno
Tsuruga
Obama
Takayama
Matsumoto
Suwa
Okaya
Ina
Iida
Nakatsugawa
Gifu
Ōgaki
Nagahama
Hikone
Ichinomiya
Inuyama
NAGOYA
Kasugai
Seto
Tajimi
Toyota
Okazaki
Anjō
Kariya
Chita
Tōkai
Handa
Hekinan
Nishio
Gamagōri
Toyokawa
Toyohashi
Hamamatsu
Iwata
Kakegawa
Tenryū
Yokkaichi
Suzuka
Kameyama
Tsu
Matsusaka
Ise (Uji-yamada)
Toba
Nabari
Ueno
KYŌTO
Ōtsu
Kusatsu
Uji
Takatsuki
Ibaraki
Hirakata
Neyagawa
Moriguchi
Toyonaka
Suita
Itami
Nishinomiya
Amagasaki
ŌSAKA
Higashiōsaka
Yao
Nara
Yamato-kōriyama
Tenri
Sakurai
Kashihara
Yamato-takada
Matsubara
Sakai
Izumi
Kishiwada
Kaizuka
Gojō
Kameoka

Map continues
pages 96-97

MAP FORM	-dake	-hantō	-kokutei-kōen	-misaki	-san	-tōge	-wan	-yama	-zaki
ENGLISH	mountain	peninsula	national park	cape	mountain	pass	bay	mountain	point
DEUTSCH	Berg	Halbinsel	Nationalpark	Kap	Berg	Pass	Bucht	Berg	Landspitze
ESPAÑOL	montaña	península	parque nacional	cabo	montaña	paso	bahía	montaña	punta
FRANÇAIS	montagne	péninsule	parc national	cap	montagne	col	baie	montagne	pointe
PORTUGUÊS	montanha	península	parque nacional	cabo	montanha	passo	baía	montanha	ponta

TŌKYŌ
YOKOHAMA
KAWASAKI
Chiba
Utsunomiya
Maebashi
Takasaki
Kōfu
Numazu
Shizuoka
Hachiōji
Yokosuka
Odawara
Mito
Hitachi
Iwaki (Taira)
Chōshi
Kashima-nada
Sagami-wan
Sagami-nada
Suruga-wan
Tōkyō-wan
Tokyo Bay
KANTŌ HEIYA
BŌSŌ-HANTŌ
IZU-HANTŌ
IZU-SHOTŌ
PACIFIC OCEAN
Ō-SHIMA
NII-JIMA
Copyright © by Rand McNally & Co.
Map prepared by Teikoku-Shoin Co., Ltd., Tokyo.

Kilometers 0 10 20 30 40 50 Km.

Statute Miles 0 10 20 30 40 50 Mi.

Scale 1:1,000,000

One centimeter represents 10 kilometers.

One inch represents approximately 16 miles.

Lambert Conformal Conic Projection

130° 30′
131°
131°30′
132°
132° 30′
35° 30′
35°
34° 30′
34°
33° 30′
33°
SEA OF JAPAN
NIHON-KAI
MI-SHIMA
TAKA-SHIMA
KÖYAMA-MISAKI
KAWASHIRI-MISAKI
ŌMI-SHIMA
TSUNO-SHIMA
FUTAOI-JIMA
Hibiki-nada
KITA-NAGATO-KAIGAN-KOKUTEI-KŌEN
Izumo
Taisha
Hirata
Hikawa
Oda
Gōtsu
Hamada
Masuda
Hagi
Nagato
Mine
Yamaguchi
Hōfu
Tokuyama
Kudamatsu
Shinnanyō
Hikari
Yanai
Iwakuni
Ōtake
HIROSHIMA
Itsukaichi
Hatsukaichi
Kure
Higashihiroshima
Miyoshi
Shimonoseki
KITAKYŪSHŪ
Onoda
Ube
Suō-nada
Iyo-nada
Aki-nada
Uwa-kai
Matsuyama
Yawatahama
Uwajima
FUKUOKA
Kasuga
Ōnojō
Chikushino
Munakata
Nakama
Nōgata
Iizuka
Tagawa
Yukuhashi
Buzen
Nakatsu
Usa
Bungo-takada
Kunisaki
Beppu
Ōita
Usuki
Tsukumi
Saiki
Hita
Kurume
Tosu
Amagi
Yame
Chikugo
Yanagawa
Ōmuta
Yamaga
Kikuchi
KYŪSHŪ
SHIMANE
HIROSHIMA
YAMAGUCHI
FUKUOKA
ŌITA
KUMAMOTO
EHIME
KŌCHI

MAP FORM	-jima	-misaki	-san	-sen	-shima	-tōge	-yama	-zen
ENGLISH	island	cape	mountain	mountain	island	pass	mountain	mountain
DEUTSCH	Insel	Kap	Berg	Berg	Insel	Pass	Berg	Berg
ESPAÑOL	isla	cabo	montaña	montaña	isla	paso	montaña	montaña
FRANÇAIS	île	cap	montagne	montagne	île	col	montagne	montagne
PORTUGUÊS	ilha	cabo	montanha	montanha	ilha	passo	montanha	montanha

133° 30′
134°
134° 30′
135°
135° 30′
35°
34°
33° 30′
33°
H O N S H U
SHIKOKU
PACIFIC OCEAN
SAN'IN-KAIGAN-KOKURITSU-KŌEN
DAISEN-OKI-KOKURITSU-KŌEN
SETO-NAIKAI-KOKURITSU-KŌEN
Harima-nada
Ōsaka-wan
Tosa-wan
Kii-suidō
Hiuchi-nada
Mizushima-nada
Miho-wan
Wakasa-wan
AWAJI-SHIMA
IESHIMA-SHOTŌ
SHIWAKU-SHOTŌ
BISAN-SHOTŌ
KII-HANTŌ
TANGO-HANTŌ
MUROTO-ANAN-KAIGAN-KOKUTEI-KŌEN
Tottori
Yonago
Kurayoshi
Sakaiminato
Yasugi
Toyooka
Maizuru
Fukuchiyama
Ayabe
Okayama
Kurashiki
Fukuyama
Onomichi
Himeji
Akashi
KOBE
OSAKA
KYŌTO
Nara
Ōtsu
Sakai
Wakayama
Tokushima
Takamatsu
Kōchi
Niihama
Muroto
Susaki
Ako
Aioi
Kakogawa
Nishinomiya
Amagasaki
Higashiōsaka
Kishiwada
Sumoto
Naruto
Anan
Tanabe
Gobo
Kainan
Marugame
Sakaide
Kanonji
Kawanoe
Iyo-mishima
Saijō
Tsuyama
Takahashi
Nishiwaki
Kasai
Ono
Miki
Sanda
Ikeda
Itami
Toyonaka
Suita
Takatsuki
Ibaraki
Hirakata
Neyagawa
Moriguchi
Uji
Kameoka
Muko
Izumi
Izumi-ōtsu
Kaizuka
Izumi-sano
Kawachi-nagano
Tondabayashi
Yao
Kashiwara
Matsubara
Habikino
Fujiidera
Sakurai
Kashihara
Gose
Tenri
Yamato-kōriyama
Shimotsu
Arida
Hashimoto
Copyright © by Rand McNally & Co.
Map prepared by Teikoku-Shoin Co., Ltd., Tokyo.

Map continues pages 94-95

Kilometers 0 10 20 30 40 50 Km.

Statute Miles 0 10 20 30 40 50 Mi.

Scale 1:1,000,000

One centimeter represents 10 kilometers.

One inch represents approximately 16 miles.

Lambert Conformal Conic Projection

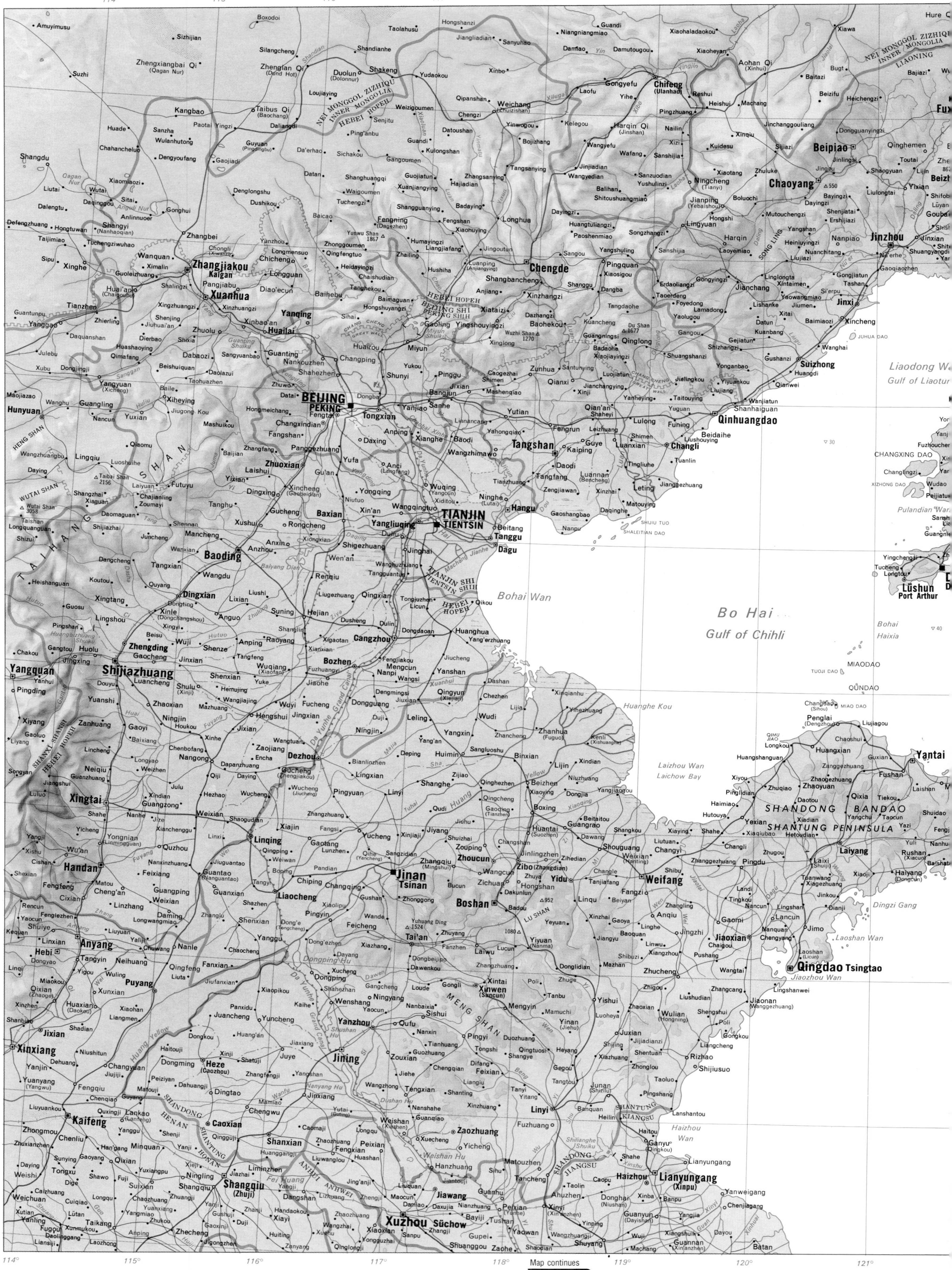
114°
115°
116°
117°
118°
119°
120°
121°
42°
41°
40°
39°
38°
37°
36°
35°
34°
NEI MONGGOL ZIZHIQU
INNER MONGOLIA
HEBEI HOPEH
LIAONING
Chifeng (Ulanhad)
Chengde
Zhangjiakou
Kalgan
Xuanhua
Beipiao
Chaoyang
Jinzhou
Jinxi
Suizhong
Qinhuangdao
Shanhaiguan
Beidaihe
BEIJING
PEKING
Tongxian
Tangshan
TIANJIN
TIENTSIN
Tanggu
Dagu
Hangu
Baoding
Dingxian
Cangzhou
Shijiazhuang
Yangquan
Xingtai
Handan
Anyang
Dezhou
Jinan
Tsinan
Zibo (Zhangdian)
Weifang
Yantai
Qingdao Tsingtao
Jiaoxian
Laiyang
Linyi
Jining
Yanzhou
Xinxiang
Kaifeng
Caoxian
Heze (Caozhou)
Shangqiu (Zhuji)
Xuzhou Süchow
Lianyungang (Xinpu)
Haizhou
Lüshun
Port Arthur
Liaodong Wan
Gulf of Liaotung
Bo Hai
Gulf of Chihli
Bohai Wan
Laizhou Wan
Laichow Bay
Huanghe Kou
SHANDONG BANDAO
SHANTUNG PENINSULA
TAIHANG SHAN
MENG SHAN
HEBEI HOPEH
SHANDONG SHANTUNG
HENAN HONAN
JIANGSU KIANGSU
ANHUI ANHWEI

Map continues
pages 102-103

Meters	Feet
6000	19685
4000	13124
3000	9843
2000	6562
1000	3281
500	1640
200	656
0	0
Land Below Sea Level 0	0
200	656
1000	3281
3000	9843
6000	19685
9000	29520

MAP FORM	dao	-do	-gang	hu	kukrip kongwŏn	-san	shan	wan
ENGLISH	island	island	river	lake	national park	mountain	mountain(s)	bay
DEUTSCH	Insel	Insel	Fluss	See	Nationalpark	Berg	Berg(e)	Bucht
ESPAÑOL	isla	isla	río	lago	parque nacional	montaña	montaña(s)	bahía
FRANÇAIS	île	île	rivière	lac	parc national	montagne	montagne(s)	baie
PORTUGUÊS	ilha	ilha	rio	lago	parque nacional	montanha	montanha(s)	baía

Map continues
pages 100-101

Map continues page 89

MANCHURIA
SHENYANG
MUKDEN
FUSHUN
Anshan
Liaoyang
Benxi
Dandong
Yingkou
Haicheng
Tonghua
Dongfeng
Hailong
Hunjiang
Linjiang
Yanji
Tumen
Faku
Kaiyuan
Tieling
Xinmin
Zhuanghe
Fengcheng
Xiuyan
Gaixian
LIAODONG BANDAO
LIAOTUNG PENINSULA
CHANGBAI SHAN
CHINA
NORTH KOREA
RUSSIA
Paektu-san 2744
Hyesan
Kanggye
Sinŭiju
Ŭiju
Ch'ŏngjin
Kimch'aek
Hamhŭng
Hŭngnam
Wŏnsan
P'YŎNGYANG
Namp'o
Sariwŏn
Haeju
Kaesŏng
HAMGYŎNG SANMAEK
HAMGYŎNG PUKDO
HAMGYŎNG NAMDO
YANGGANG DO
CHAGANG DO
P'YŎNGAN PUKDO
P'YŎNGAN NAMDO
HWANGHAE PUKDO
HWANGHAE NAMDO
KANGWŎN DO
NANGNIM SANMAEK
KANGNAM SANMAEK
MYOHYANG SANMAEK
T'AEBAEK SANMAEK
SOBAEK SANMAEK
SOUTH KOREA
SŎUL
SEOUL
Inch'ŏn
Suwŏn
Ŭijŏngbu
Sŏngnam-si
Ch'unch'ŏn
Kangnŭng
Samch'ŏk
Wŏnju
Ch'ŏngju
Ch'ŏnan
Taejŏn
Kunsan
Chŏnju
Kwangju
Mokp'o
Yŏsu
Chinju
Masan
Pusan
Ulsan
Taegu
P'ohang
Andong
KYŎNGGI DO
CH'UNGCH'ŎNG PUKDO
CH'UNGCH'ŎNG NAMDO
KYŎNGSANG PUKDO
KYŎNGSANG NAMDO
CHŎLLA PUKDO
CHŎLLA NAMDO
SEA OF JAPAN
Korea Bay
YELLOW SEA
Korea Strait
Western Channel
TSUSHIMA
Tongjosŏn-man
Sŏjosŏn-man
Kyŏnggi-man
Copyright © by Rand McNally & Co.
Map compiled by Cartographia, Budapest.
Map produced by Rand McNally & Co.
A-564400-764

Map continues pages 92-93

Kilometers 0 50 100 150 Km.

Statute Miles 0 50 100 150 Mi.

Scale 1:3,000,000

One centimeter represents 30 kilometers.

One inch represents approximately 47 miles.

Lambert Conformal Conic Projection

YELLOW SEA
HUANG HAI
SHANGHAI
NANJING
NANKING
Hangzhou
Hangchow
Suzhou
Soochow
Ningbo
Hefei
Bengbu
Huainan
Xuzhou
WUHAN
Nanchang
Anqing
Jingdezhen
Zhenjiang
Yangzhou
Nantong
Wuxi
Changzhou
Shaoxing
DABIE SHAN
TONGBAI SHAN
FUNIU SHAN
MUFU SHAN
JIULING SHAN
Tai Hu
Chao Hu
Poyang Hu
Hangzhou Wan
JIANGSU
ANHUI
HENAN
HUBEI
ZHEJIANG
JIANGXI
HUNAN

Map continues pages 98-99
Map continues pages 102-103

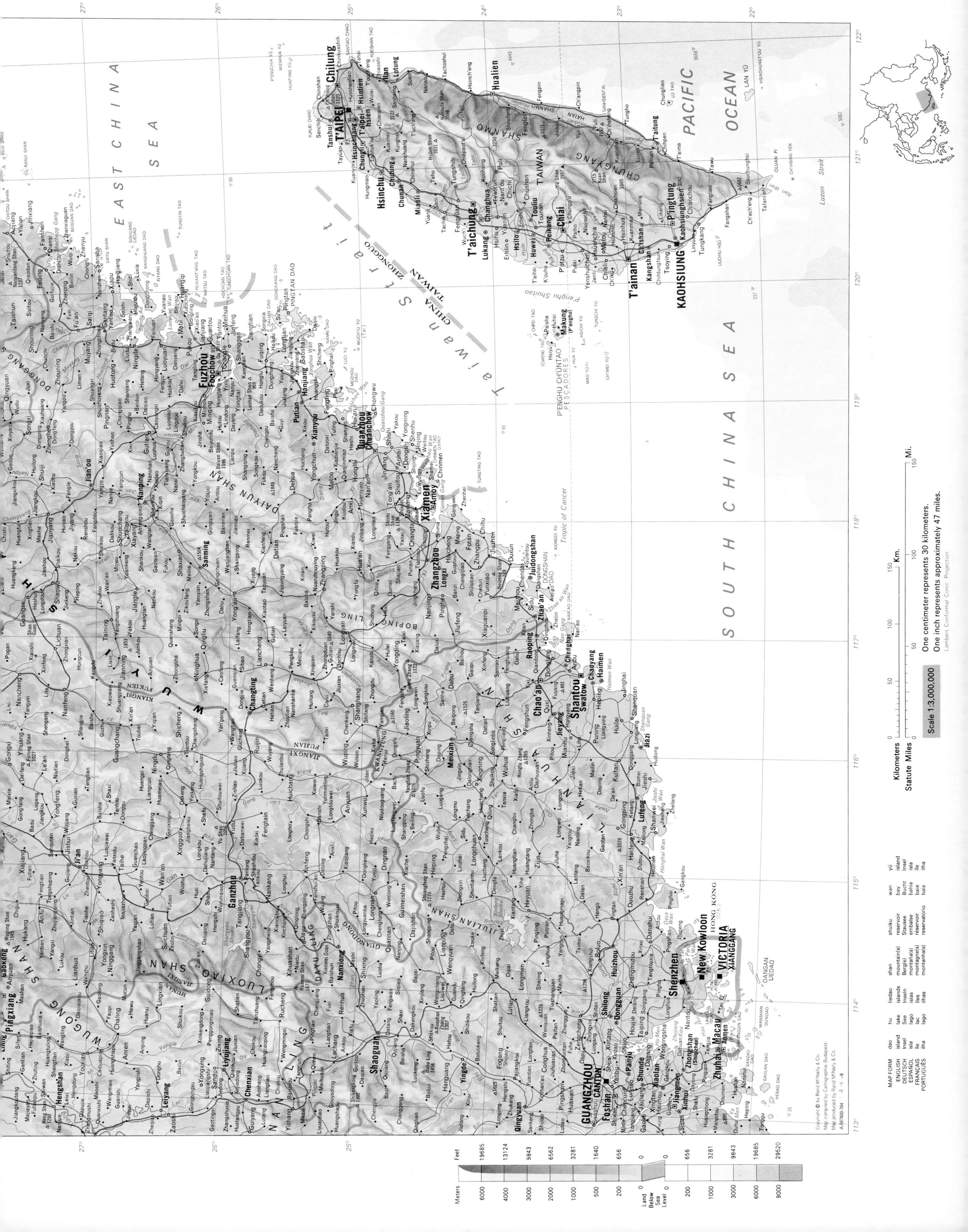
EAST CHINA SEA
SOUTH CHINA SEA
PACIFIC OCEAN
Taiwan Strait
TAIWAN
T'AIPEI
KAOHSIUNG
T'ainan
T'aichung
Chilung
Hualien
Hsinchu
P'ENGHU CH'ÜNTAO
PESCADORES
Tropic of Cancer
Luzon Strait
FUJIAN
JIANGXI
GUANGDONG
HUNAN
Fuzhou
Foochow
Xiamen
Amoy
Quanzhou
Zhangzhou
Shantou
Swatow
Chao'an
Meixian
Ganzhou
Ji'an
Nanping
Sanming
Shaoguan
GUANGZHOU
CANTON
Foshan
Shenzhen
New Kowloon
VICTORIA
XIANGGANG
HONG KONG
Macau
Aomen
Zhuhai
Hengshan
Chenxian
Pingxiang
WUYI SHAN
DAIYUN SHAN
NAN LING
LUOXIAO SHAN
WUGONG SHAN
JIULIAN SHAN
Scale 1:3,000,000
One centimeter represents 30 kilometers.
One inch represents approximately 47 miles.
Kilometers
Statute Miles
Km.
Mi.
Lambert Conformal Conic Projection
MAP FORM
ENGLISH
DEUTSCH
ESPAÑOL
FRANÇAIS
PORTUGUES
dao: island, Insel, isla, île, ilha
hu: lake, See, lago, lac, lago
liedao: islands, Inseln, islas, îles, ilhas
shan: mountain(s), Berg(e), montaña(s), montagne(s), montanha(s)
shuiku: reservoir, Stausee, embalse, réservoir, reservatório
wan: bay, Bucht, bahía, baie, baía
yü: island, Insel, isla, île, ilha
Feet
Meters
Land Below Sea Level
Copyright © by Rand McNally & Co.
Map compiled by Cartographia, Budapest.
Map produced by Rand McNally & Co.
A-567600-764 -2 -5 -9

Map continues pages 98-99

Map continues page 88

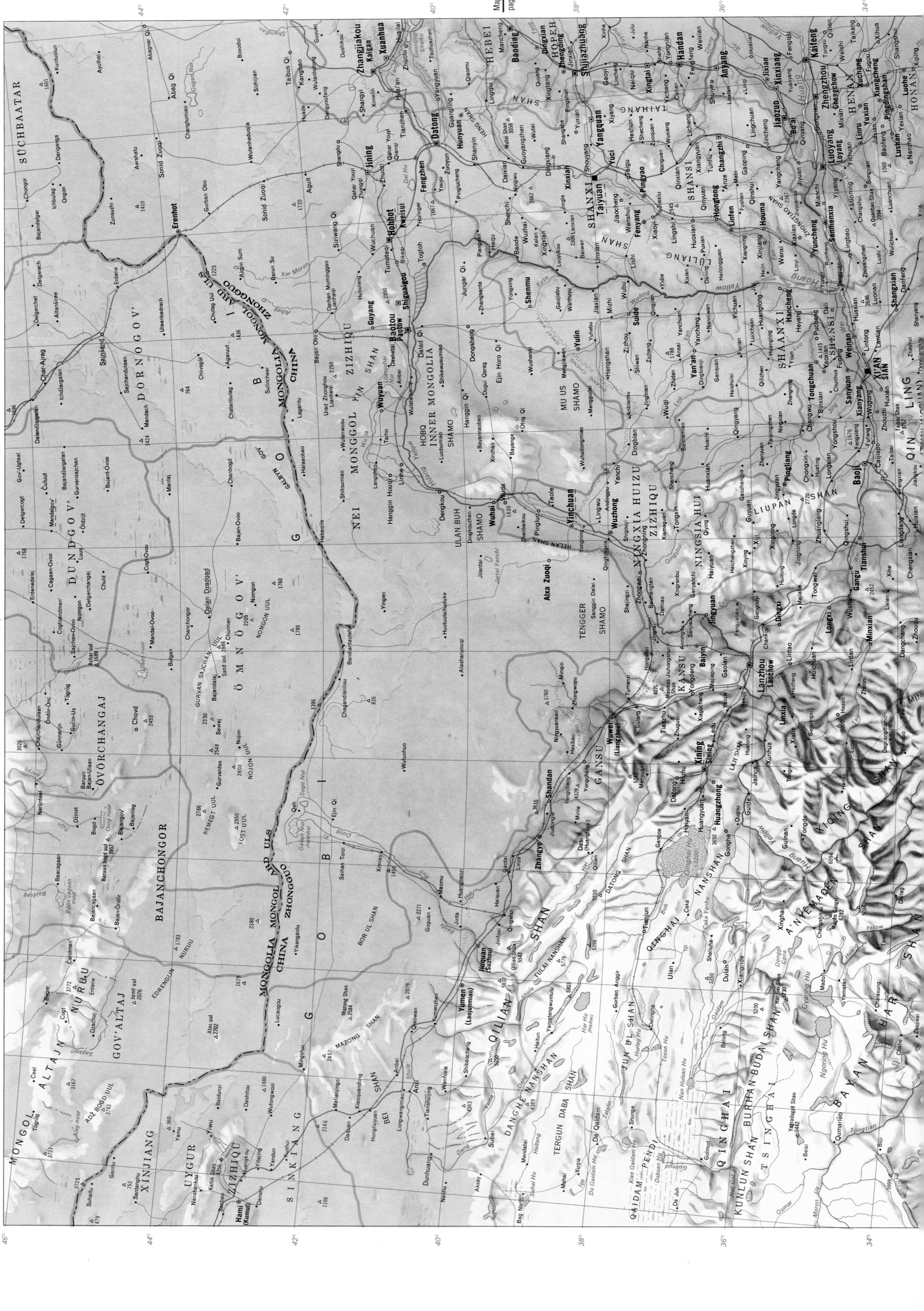
MONGOLIA
CHINA
ZHONGGUO
DORNOGOV'
DUNDGOV'
ÖMNÖGOV'
ÖVÖRCHANGAJ
BAJANCHONGOR
GOV'ALTAJ
SÜCHBAATAR
NEI MONGGOL ZIZHIQU
INNER MONGOLIA
NINGXIA HUIZU ZIZHIQU
GANSU
KANSU
QINGHAI
TSINGHAI
SHANXI
SHANSI
SHAANXI
SHENSI
HEBEI
HOPEH
HENAN
HONAN
XINJIANG UYGUR ZIZHIQU
SINKIANG
GOBI
TENGGER SHAMO
MU US SHAMO
HOBQ SHAMO
ULAN BUH SHAMO
QILIAN SHAN
QIN LING
LIUPAN SHAN
HELAN SHAN
YIN SHAN
TAIHANG SHAN
LÜLIANG SHAN
BAYAN HAR SHAN
QAIDAM PENDI
KUNLUN SHAN
Hohhot
Baotou
Yinchuan
Lanzhou
Xining
Xi'an
Taiyuan
Shijiazhuang
Datong
Zhangjiakou
Erenhot
Zhengzhou
Luoyang
Yumen
Jiuquan
Zhangye
Wuwei
Hami
Dunhuang

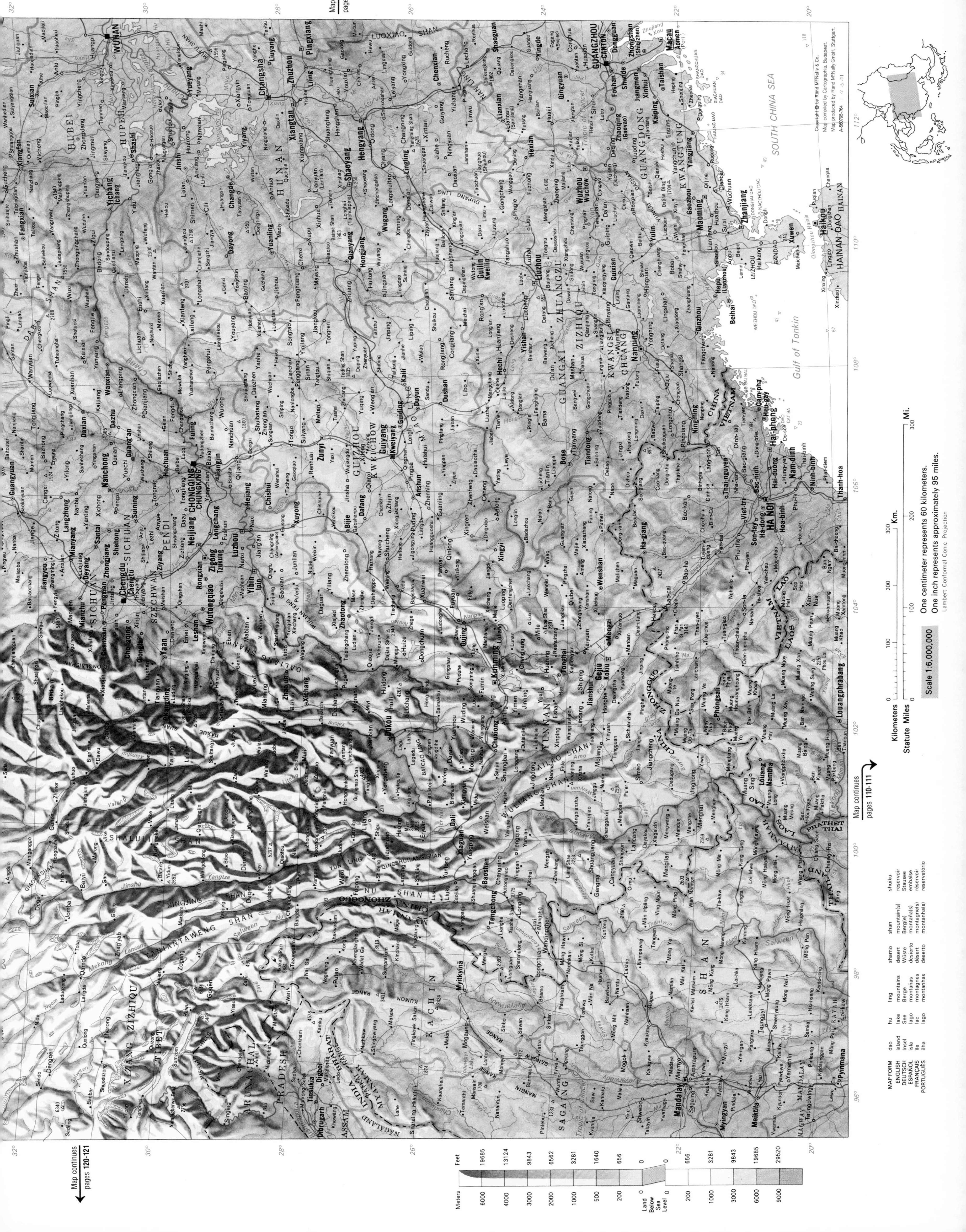
Map continues pages 100-101
Map continues pages 110-111
Map continues pages 120-121
SOUTH CHINA SEA
Gulf of Tonkin
HUBEI
HUNAN
GUANGDONG
GUANGXI ZHUANGZU ZIZHIQU
GUIZHOU
SICHUAN
YUNNAN
XIZANG ZIZHIQU
HAINAN DAO
Kilometers
Statute Miles
Scale 1:6,000,000
One centimeter represents 60 kilometers.
One inch represents approximately 95 miles.
Lambert Conformal Conic Projection
MAP FORM dao hu ling shamo shan shuiku
ENGLISH island lake mountains desert mountain(s) reservoir
DEUTSCH Insel See Berge Wüste Berg(e) Stausee
ESPAÑOL isla lago montañas desierto montaña(s) embalse
FRANÇAIS île lac montagnes désert montagne(s) réservoir
PORTUGUÊS ilha lago montanhas deserto montanha(s) reservatório
Meters Feet
Land Below Sea Level
Copyright © by Rand McNally & Co.
Map compiled by Cartographia, Budapest.
Map produced by Rand McNally GmbH, Stuttgart.

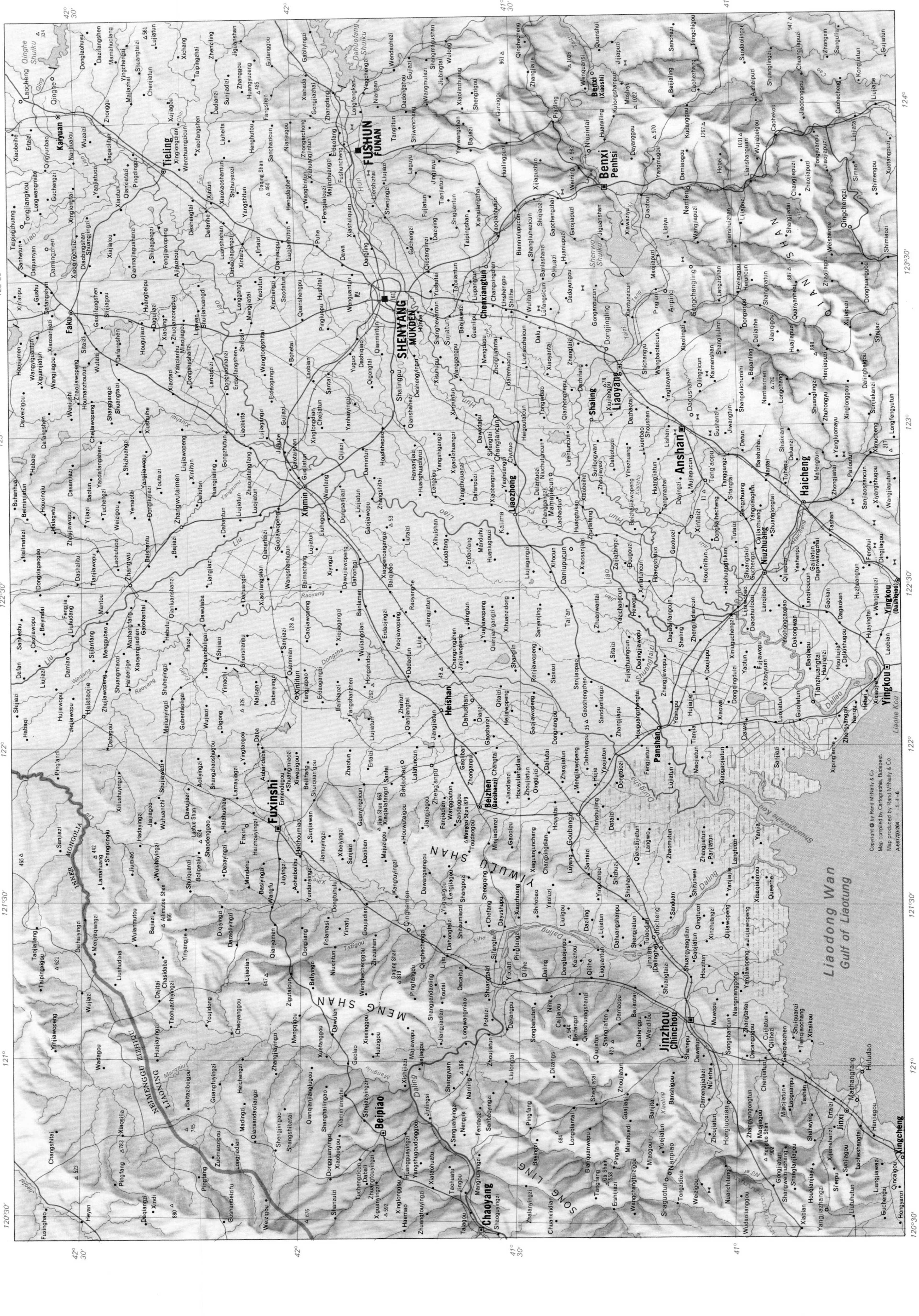
SHENYANG
MUKDEN
FUSHUN
FUNAN
Fuxinshi
Anshan
Liaoyang
Benxi
Penhsi
Jinzhou
Chinchou
Yingkou
Chaoyang
Beipiao
Tieling
Kaiyuan
Faku
Xinmin
Panshan
Haicheng
Heishan
Beizhen
Jinxi
Xingcheng
Liaodong Wan
Gulf of Liaotung
NEIMENGGU ZIZHIQU
INNER MONGOLIA
LIAONING
YIWULU SHAN
SONG LING
MENG SHAN

MAP FORM	kou	shan	shuiku	wan
ENGLISH	estuary	mountain(s)	reservoir	bay
DEUTSCH	Trichtermündung	Berg(e)	Stausee	Bucht
ESPAÑOL	estuario	montaña(s)	embalse	bahía
FRANÇAIS	estuaire	montagne(s)	réservoir	baie
PORTUGUÊS	estuário	montanha(s)	reservatorio	baía

Kilometers 0 10 20 30 40 50 Km.

Statute Miles 0 10 20 30 40 50 Mi.

Scale 1:1,000,000

One centimeter represents 10 kilometers.
One inch represents approximately 16 miles.
Modified Polyconic Projection

BEIJING
PEKING
TIANJIN
TIENTSIN
Bohai Wan
Copyright © by Rand McNally & Co.
Map compiled by Cartographia, Budapest.
Map produced by Rand McNally & Co.
Scale 1:1,000,000
One centimeter represents 10 kilometers.
One inch represents approximately 16 miles.
Modified Polyconic Projection
Kilometers
Statute Miles
Km.
Mi.
MAP FORM hai shan shuiku wa
ENGLISH lake mountain(s) reservoir marsh
DEUTSCH See Berg(e) Stausee Marsch
ESPAÑOL lago montaña(s) embalse pantano
FRANÇAIS lac montagne(s) réservoir marais
PORTUGUÊS lago montanha(s) reservatório pântano

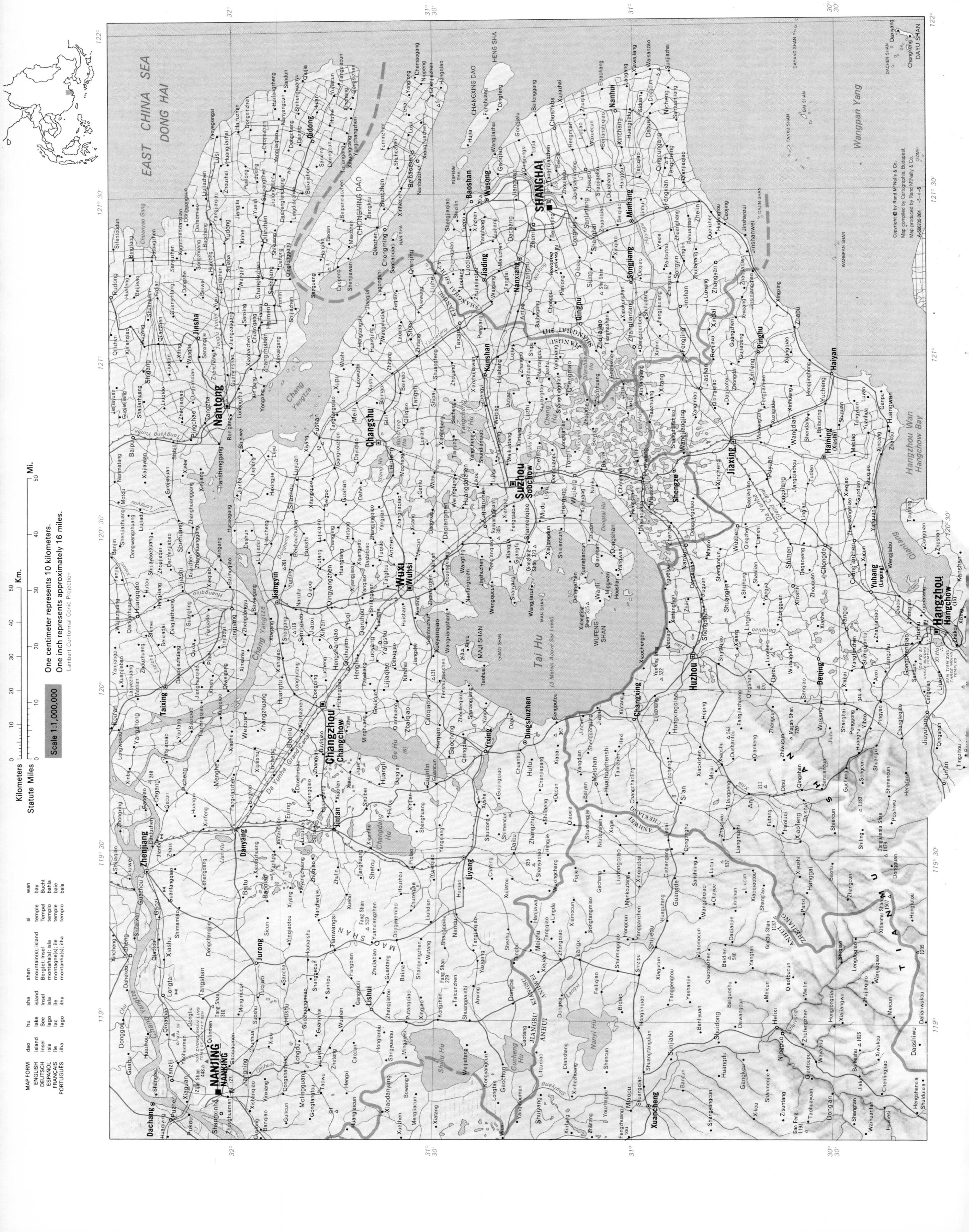
Kilometers 0 10 20 30 40 50 Km.
Statute Miles 0 10 20 30 40 50 Mi.
Scale 1:1,000,000
One centimeter represents 10 kilometers.
One inch represents approximately 16 miles.
Lambert Conformal Conic Projection
MAP FORM dao hu sha shan si wan
ENGLISH island lake island mountain(s); island temple bay
DEUTSCH Insel See Insel Berg(e); Insel Tempel Bucht
ESPAÑOL isla lago isla montaña(s); isla templo bahia
FRANÇAIS île lac île montagne(s); île temple baie
PORTUGUÊS ilha lago ilha montanha(s); ilha templo baia
Copyright © by Rand McNally & Co.
Map compiled by Cartographia, Budapest.
Map produced by Rand McNally & Co.
EAST CHINA SEA
DONG HAI
Wangpan Yang
Hangzhou Wan
Hangchow Bay
Tai Hu
SHANGHAI
NANJING
NANKING
Suzhou
Soochow
Hangzhou
Hangchow
Changzhou
Changchow
Wuxi
Wusih
Nantong
Changshu
Jiaxing
Huzhou
Zhenjiang
Chang Yangtze
CHONGMING DAO

CHONGQING
CHUNGKING
CHENGDU
CHENGTU
ZIGONG
TZUKUNG
Nanchong
Guang'an
Hechuan
Suining
Tongnan
Dazu
Bishan
Jiangjin
Yongchuan
Rongchang
Neijiang
Longchang
Luzhou
Hejiang
Naxi
Anyue
Ziyang
Jianyang
Lezhi
Renshou
Weiyuan
Fushun
Rongxian
Yibin
Ipin
Jiang'an
Nanxi
Leshan
Wutongqiao
Qianwei
Meishan
Pengshan
Xinjin
Shuangliu
Wenjiang
Chongqing
Dayi
Qionglai
Danleng
Jiajiang
Emei
Pujiang
Jingyan
Qijiang
Tongliang
Yuechi
Yangtze
Chang
Jialing
Tuo
Min
Fu
Dadu
Qingyi
Jinsha
LONGQUAN SHAN
DALIANG SHAN
SICHUAN
SZECHWAN
GUIZHOU
KWEICHOW
Scale 1:1,000,000
One centimeter represents 10 kilometers.
One inch represents approximately 16 miles.
Modified Polyconic Projection
Kilometers
Statute Miles
Km.
Mi.
MAP FORM shan shuiku
ENGLISH mountain(s) reservoir
DEUTSCH Berg(e) Stausee
ESPAÑOL montaña(s) embalse
FRANÇAIS montagne(s) réservoir
PORTUGUÊS montanha(s) reservatório
Copyright © by Rand McNally & Co.
Map compiled by Cartographia, Budapest.
Map produced by Rand McNally & Co.

Map continues pages 90-91

Map continues pages 118-119

CHINA
YUNNAN
GUANGXI ZHUANGZU
GUANGDONG
Nanning
Wuzhou
GUANGZHOU (CANTON)
Shantou
Swatow
Chao'an
Foshan
Shenzhen
Dongguan
Aomen Macau
New Kowloon Xinjiulong
VICTORIA XIANGGANG
HONG KONG (U.K.)
Zhanjiang
Beihai
Haikou
HAINAN
HAINAN DAO
Gulf of Tonkin
INDIA
BANGLADESH
Chittagong
MYANMAR (BURMA)
Mandalay
Monywa
Taunggyi
Sittwe (Akyab)
Prome (Pyè)
Henzada
Pathein
Bago
YANGON RANGOON
Mawlamyine
Dawei
BAY OF BENGAL
Preparis North Channel
Preparis South Channel
Coco Channel
ANDAMAN ISLANDS (India)
NORTH ANDAMAN
MIDDLE ANDAMAN
SOUTH ANDAMAN
Port Blair
LITTLE ANDAMAN
ANDAMAN SEA
Ten Degree Channel
CAR NICOBAR
NICOBAR ISLANDS (India)
LITTLE NICOBAR
GREAT NICOBAR
Great Channel
MERGUI ARCHIPELAGO
LAOS
Louangphrabang
Viangchan (Vientiane)
Savannakhét
HA NOI
Hai Phong
Nam Dinh
Vinh
Hue
Da Nang
Qui Nhon
Nha Trang
VIETNAM
INDOCHINA
Chiang Mai
THAILAND
Khon Kaen
Nakhon Ratchasima
KRUNG THEP BANGKOK
Gulf of Thailand
Songkhla
Hat Yai
CAMBODIA
Batdâmbâng
Phnum Pénh
Kâmpóng Saôm
THANH PHO HO CHI MINH (SAIGON)
Can Tho
SOUTH CHINA SEA
XISHA QUNDAO PARACEL ISLANDS (claimed by China, Taiwan and Vietnam)
SPRATLY ISLANDS
MALAYSIA
George Town (Pinang)
Alor Setar
Kota Baharu
Kuala Terengganu
Ipoh
Kuantan
KUALA LUMPUR
Seremban
Melaka
Johor Baharu
SINGAPORE
Medan
Banda Aceh
SUMATERA SUMATRA
Padang
Pekanbaru
Jambi
Palembang
Bengkulu
Pangkalpinang
Tanjungkarang-Telukbetung
KEPULAUAN MENTAWAI
KEPULAUAN NATUNA BESAR
BRUNEI
Bandar Seri Begawan
SABAH
Kota Kinabalu (Jesselton)
SARAWAK
Kuching
Pontianak
BORNEO KALIMANTAN
Balikpapan
Banjarmasin
INDONESIA
GREATER SUNDA ISLANDS
LAUT JAWA JAVA SEA
JAKARTA
BANDUNG
Cirebon
Semarang
Yogyakarta
Surakarta
SURABAYA
Malang
JAWA JAVA
Denpasar
Mataram
INDIAN OCEAN
CHRISTMAS ISLAND (Austl.)

MAP FORM	gulf	gunung	island	kepulauan	pulau	sea	selat	strait
ENGLISH	gulf	mountain	island	islands	island	sea	strait	strait
DEUTSCH	Golf	Berg	Insel	Inseln	Insel	Meer	Meeresstrasse	Meeresstrasse
ESPAÑOL	golfo	montaña	isla	islas	isla	mar	estrecho	estrecho
FRANÇAIS	golfe	montagne	île	îles	île	mer	détroit	détroit
PORTUGUÊS	golfo	montanha	ilha	ilhas	ilha	mar	estreito	estreito

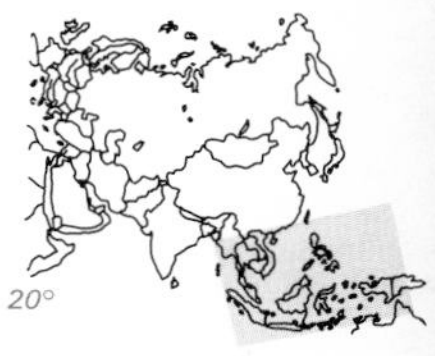

TAIWAN
T'AIWAN
Hualien
Chiai
P'ingtung
T'aitung
Tropic of Cancer
Bashi Channel
Luzon Strait
BATAN ISLANDS
BABUYAN ISLANDS
LUZON
Laoag
Tuguegarao
Baguio
Dagupan
Cabanatuan
San Fernando
PHILIPPINES
MANILA
Quezon City
Cavite
San Pablo
Batangas
Lucena
Naga
Mayon Volcano
Legaspi
Sorsogon
Calapan
MINDORO
Sibuyan Sea
Masbate
SAMAR
Catbalogan
Tacloban
LEYTE
PANAY
Roxas
Iloilo
Bacolod
Cebu
NEGROS
Dumaguete
BOHOL
Surigao
Butuan
Bohol Sea
Cagayan de Oro
MINDANAO
Dipolog
Ozamiz
Iligan
Zamboanga
ZAMBOANGA PENINSULA
Cotabato
Davao
Davao Gulf
General Santos
Moro Gulf
Jolo
SULU ARCHIPELAGO
SEA
CELEBES SEA
KEPULAUAN TALAUD
KEPULAUAN SANGIHE
Manado
MINAHASA
Gorontalo
HALMAHERA
Ternate
Tidore
LAUT MALUKU
MOLUCCA SEA
Halmahera Sea
Teluk Tomini
KEPULAUAN BANGGAI
KEPULAUAN SULA
KEPULAUAN OBI
LAUT SERAM
CERAM SEA
SERAM
CERAM
BURU
Ambon
Kendari
Watampone
PULAU BUTON
Baubau
LAUT BANDA
BANDA SEA
MOLUCCAS
KEPULAUAN KAI
KEPULAUAN ARU
KEPULAUAN TANIMBAR
PULAU YAMDENA
Saumlaki
KEPULAUAN BARAT DAYA
KEPULAUAN BABAR
KEPULAUAN LETI
Flores Sea
FLORES
Ende
SUMBA
Waingapu
Laut Sawu
Savu Sea
TIMOR
Dili
Kupang
TIMOR SEA
ARAFURA SEA
AUSTRALIA
CAPE YORK PENINSULA
Torres Strait
Gulf of Papua
PAPUA NEW GUINEA
NEW GUINEA
Jayapura (Sukarnapura)
Teluk Cenderawasih
JAZIRAH DOBERAI
Manokwari
Sorong
Biak
PEGUNUNGAN VAN REES
PEGUNUNGAN MAOKE
Puncak Jaya
Puncak Trikora
Puncak Mandala
Wewak
Madang
Mount Wilhelm
Mount Hagen
Mount Giluwe
Mount Bosavi
Daru
PULAU YOS SUDARSO
Merauke
PHILIPPINE SEA
PACIFIC OCEAN
Equator
PALAU ISLANDS
BABELTHUAP
Koror
PALAU BELAU
(T.T.P.I.)
CAROLINE ISLANDS
FEDERATED STATES OF MICRONESIA
YAP
ULITHI
NORTHERN MARIANA ISLANDS
(U.S.)
MARIANA ISLANDS
SAIPAN
ROTA
GUAM
(U.S.)
Agana
OKINO-TORI-SHIMA
PAREСE VELA
(Japan)
125°
130°
135°
140°
145°
20°
15°
10°
5°
0°

Map continues pages 160-161

Kilometers 0 200 400 600 Km.
Statute Miles 0 200 400 600 Mi.

Scale 1:12,000,000

One centimeter represents 120 kilometers.
One inch represents approximately 190 miles.
Lambert Conformal Conic Projection

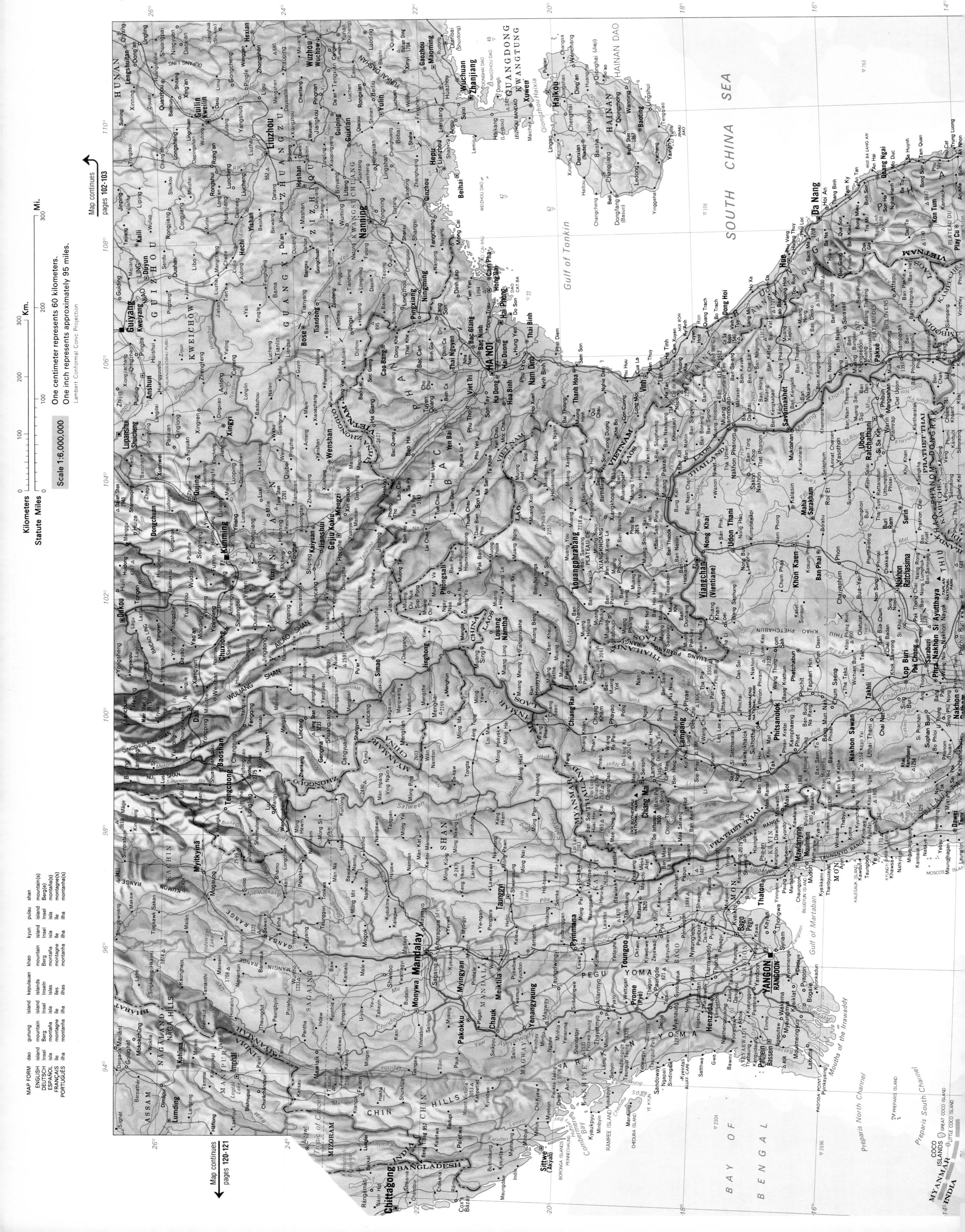
Scale 1:6,000,000
Kilometers 0 100 200 300 Km.
Statute Miles 0 100 200 300 Mi.
One centimeter represents 60 kilometers.
One inch represents approximately 95 miles.
Lambert Conformal Conic Projection
Map continues pages 102-103
Map continues pages 120-121
MAP FORM dao gunung khao kepulauan kyun pulau shan
ENGLISH island mountain mountain islands island island mountain(s)
DEUTSCH Insel Berg Berg Inseln Insel Insel Berg(e)
ESPAÑOL isla montaña montaña islas isla isla montaña(s)
FRANÇAIS île montagne montagne îles île île montagne(s)
PORTUGUÊS ilha montanha montanha ilhas ilha ilha montanha(s)
SOUTH CHINA SEA
Gulf of Tonkin
BAY OF BENGAL
Gulf of Martaban
Mouths of the Irrawaddy

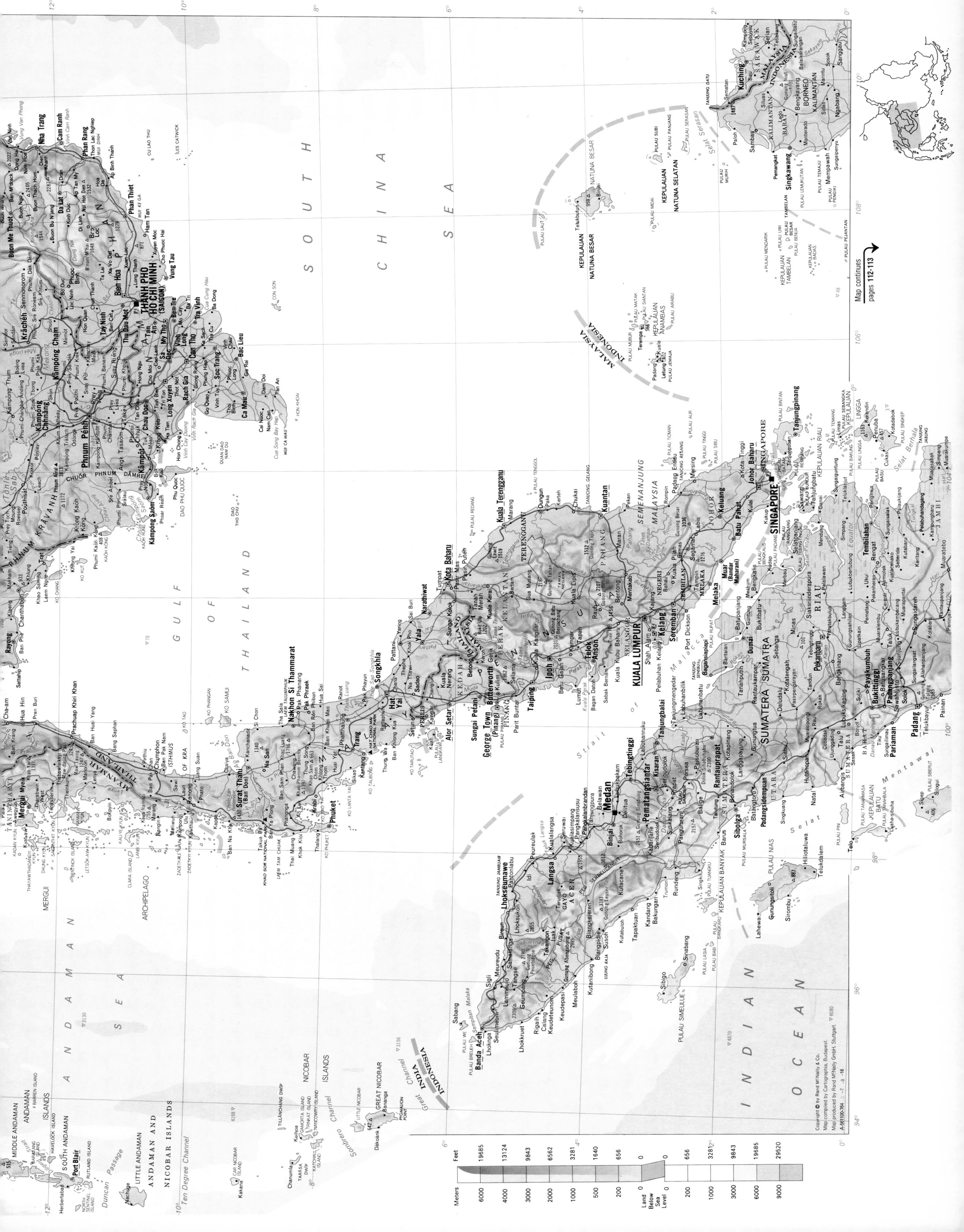
SOUTH CHINA SEA
GULF OF THAILAND
ANDAMAN SEA
INDIAN OCEAN
Strait of Malacca
THANH PHO HO CHI MINH (SAIGON)
Phnum Penh
KUALA LUMPUR
SINGAPORE
Medan
Padang
George Town (Pinang)
Kuala Terengganu
Kuantan
Ipoh
Songkhla
Hat Yai
Phuket
Nakhon Si Thammarat
Surat Thani (Ban Don)
Mergui (Myeik)
SUMATERA SUMATRA
MALAYSIA
INDONESIA
NATUNA BESAR
KEPULAUAN ANAMBAS
NICOBAR ISLANDS
ANDAMAN ISLANDS
Kuching
Map continues pages 112-113
Meters
Feet
Land Below Sea Level
Copyright © by Rand McNally & Co.

Map continues pages 110-111

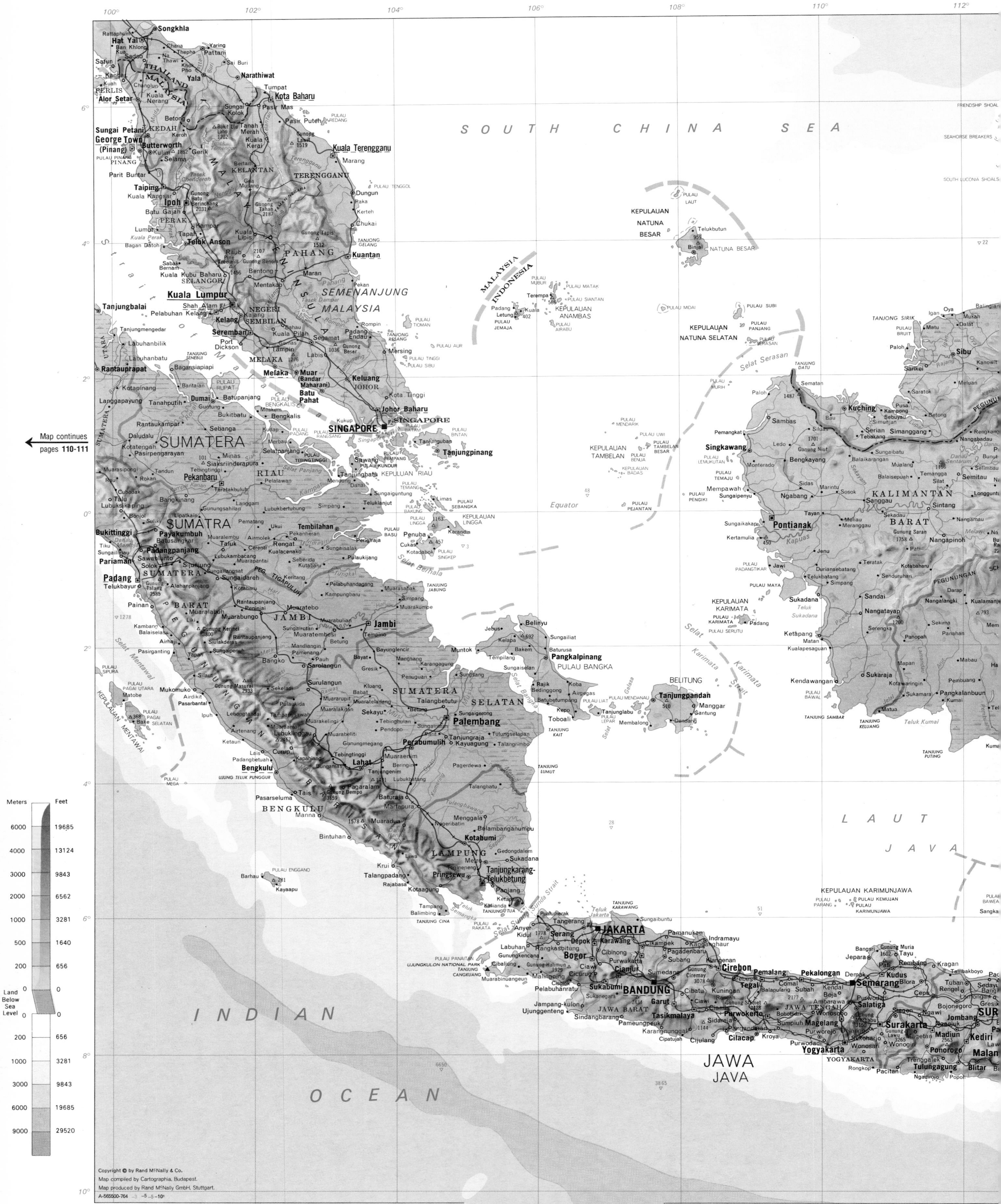
SOUTH CHINA SEA
INDIAN OCEAN
LAUT JAVA
Selat Malaka
SEMENANJUNG MALAYSIA
SUMATERA
SUMATRA
KALIMANTAN BARAT
JAWA
JAVA
KEPULAUAN NATUNA BESAR
KEPULAUAN NATUNA SELATAN
KEPULAUAN ANAMBAS
KEPULAUAN TAMBELAN
KEPULAUAN RIAU
KEPULAUAN LINGGA
PULAU BANGKA
BELITUNG
KEPULAUAN KARIMATA
KEPULAUAN KARIMUNJAWA
KEPULAUAN MENTAWAI
Selat Karimata
Selat Sunda
Sunda Strait
Selat Gelasa
Selat Bangka
Selat Serasan
Selat Mentawai
Equator
MALAYSIA
INDONESIA
SINGAPORE
Kuala Lumpur
Jakarta
Bandung
Semarang
Yogyakarta
Surakarta
Palembang
Padang
Pekanbaru
Jambi
Bengkulu
Tanjungkarang-Telukbetung
Pangkalpinang
Tanjungpandan
Pontianak
Kuching
Sibu
Singkawang
Johor Baharu
Melaka
Seremban
Kuantan
Kuala Terengganu
Kota Baharu
Alor Setar
George Town (Pinang)
Butterworth
Ipoh
Taiping
Teluk Anson
Songkhla
Hat Yai
Bukittinggi
Tanjungpinang
Cirebon
Bogor
Tegal
Pekalongan
Kediri
Blitar
Madiun
Malang
Meters
Feet
6000
19685
4000
13124
3000
9843
2000
6562
1000
3281
500
1640
200
656
0
Land Below Sea Level
200
656
1000
3281
3000
9843
6000
19685
9000
29520
Copyright © by Rand McNally & Co.
Map compiled by Cartographia, Budapest.
Map produced by Rand McNally GmbH, Stuttgart.
A-565500-764

CHRISTMAS ISLAND
(Austl.)
Flying Fish Cove
361
106°

MAP FORM	danau	gunung	kepulauan	pegunungan	pulau	selat	tanjung	teluk
ENGLISH	lake	mountain	islands	mountains	island	strait	cape	bay
DEUTSCH	See	Berg	Inseln	Berge	Insel	Meeresstrasse	Kap	Bucht
ESPAÑOL	lago	montaña	islas	montañas	isla	estrecho	cabo	bahía
FRANÇAIS	lac	montagne	îles	montagnes	île	détroit	cap	baie
PORTUGUÊS	lago	montanha	ilhas	montanhas	ilha	estreito	cabo	baía

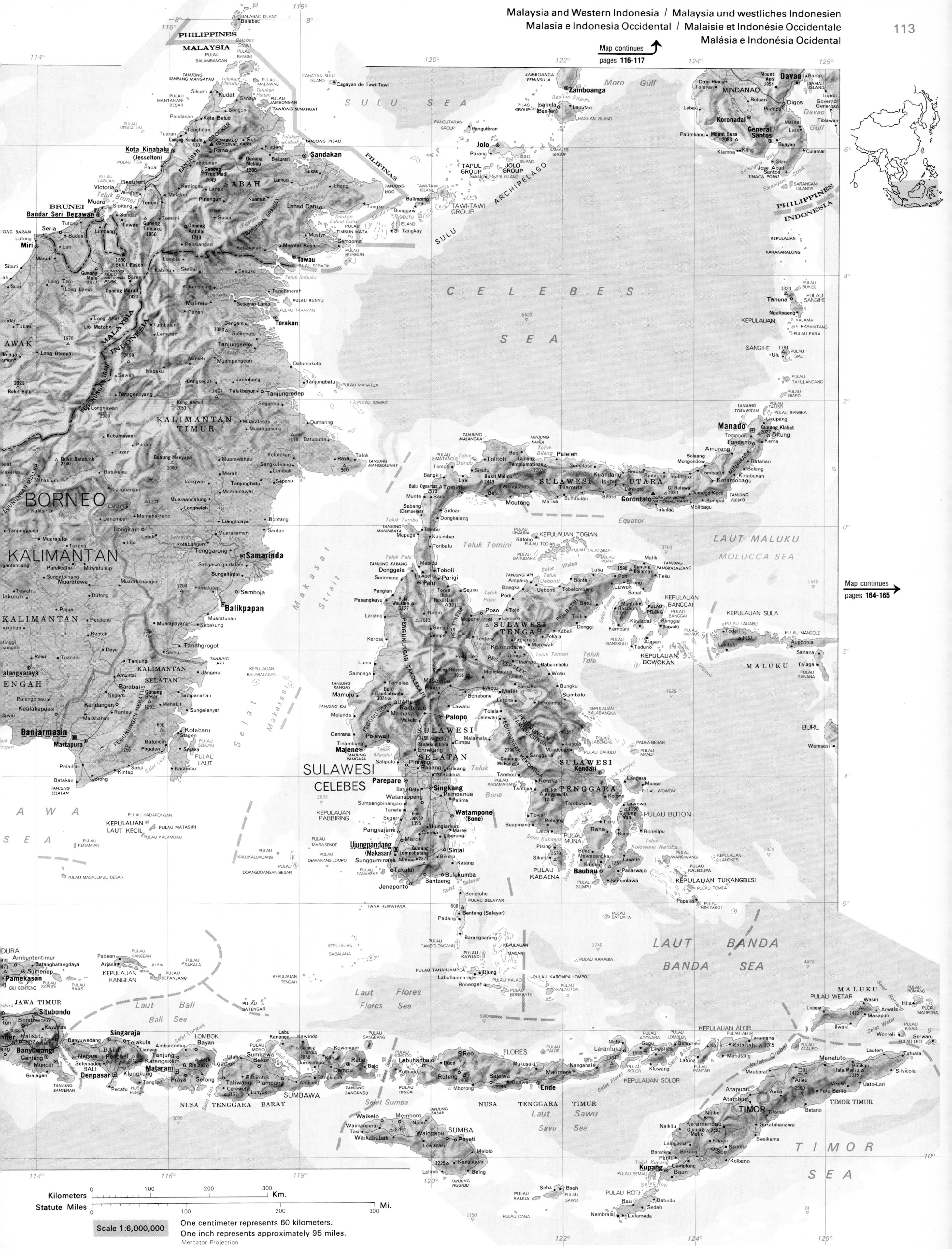
Map continues pages 116-117
Map continues pages 164-165
PHILIPPINES
MALAYSIA
SULU SEA
Moro Gulf
Zamboanga
MINDANAO
Davao
Davao Gulf
General Santos
Koronadal
Kota Kinabalu (Jesselton)
Sandakan
SABAH
BRUNEI
Bandar Seri Begawan
Miri
Tawau
Jolo
TAWI-TAWI GROUP
SULU ARCHIPELAGO
PHILIPPINES INDONESIA
CELEBES SEA
Tarakan
Tanjungredep
KALIMANTAN TIMUR
BORNEO
KALIMANTAN
Samarinda
Balikpapan
Makasar Strait
KALIMANTAN SELATAN
Banjarmasin
Martapura
Manado
SULAWESI UTARA
Gorontalo
Teluk Tomini
KEPULAUAN TOGIAN
Palu
Poso
SULAWESI TENGAH
KEPULAUAN BANGGAI
KEPULAUAN SULA
LAUT MALUKU
MOLUCCA SEA
Equator
MALUKU
Palopo
SULAWESI SELATAN
SULAWESI CELEBES
Parepare
Watampone (Bone)
Ujungpandang (Makasar)
Kendari
SULAWESI TENGGARA
PULAU BUTON
Baubau
KEPULAUAN TUKANGBESI
Teluk Bone
BURU
JAWA SEA
KEPULAUAN LAUT KECIL
Selat Makassar
Benteng (Salayar)
LAUT BANDA
BANDA SEA
Laut Flores
Flores Sea
Laut Bali
Bali Sea
JAWA TIMUR
Pamekasan
Situbondo
Banyuwangi
Singaraja
BALI
Denpasar
LOMBOK
Mataram
SUMBAWA
NUSA TENGGARA BARAT
Selat Sumba
SUMBA
Waingapu
FLORES
Ende
NUSA TENGGARA TIMUR
Laut Sawu
Savu Sea
KEPULAUAN ALOR
PULAU WETAR
Dili
TIMOR TIMUR
TIMOR
Kupang
TIMOR SEA
PULAU ROTI
Kilometers
Statute Miles
Km.
Mi.

Scale 1:6,000,000
One centimeter represents 60 kilometers.
One inch represents approximately 95 miles.
Mercator Projection

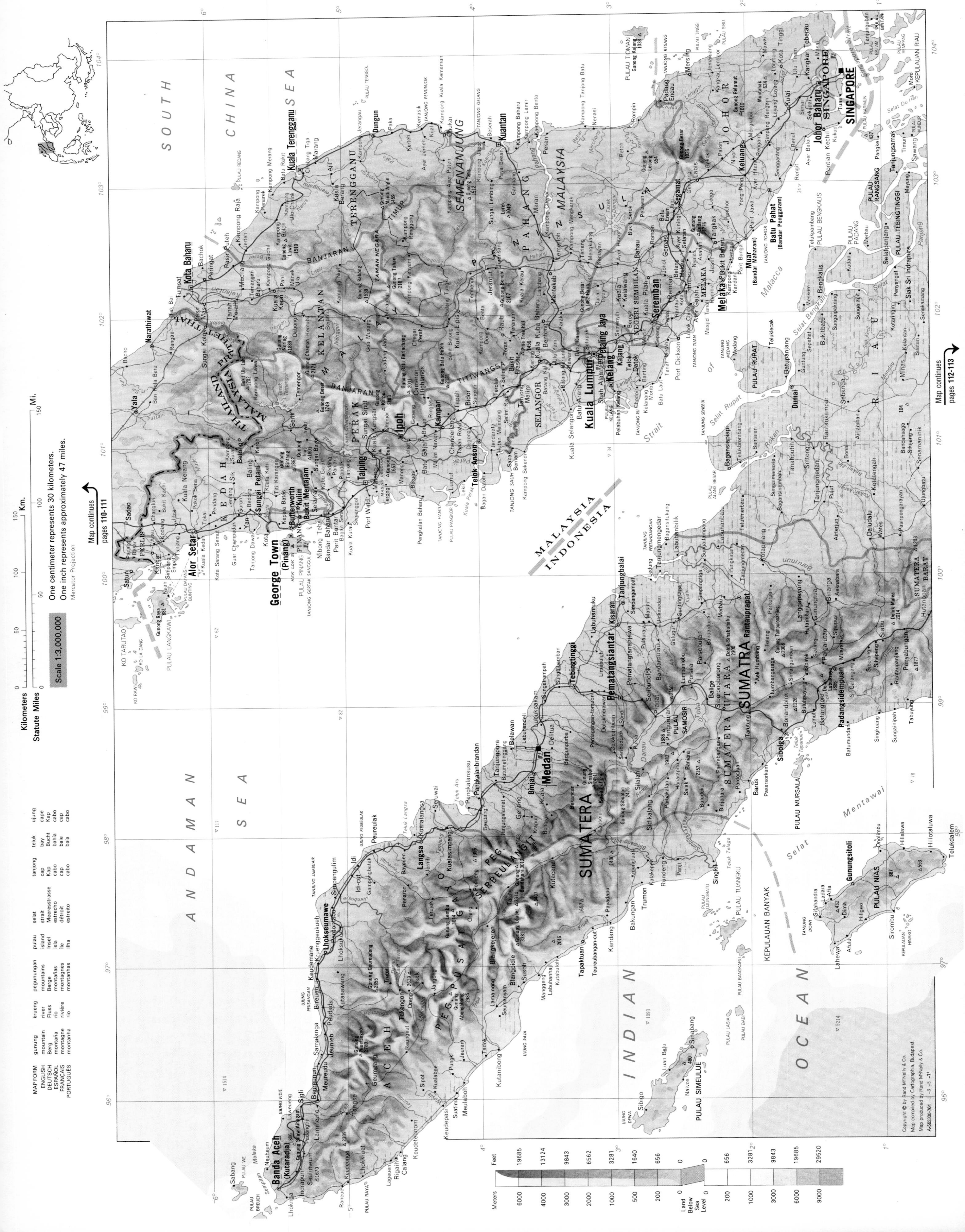
Scale 1:3,000,000
One centimeter represents 30 kilometers.
One inch represents approximately 47 miles.
Mercator Projection
Map continues pages 110-111
Map continues pages 112-113
SOUTH CHINA SEA
ANDAMAN SEA
INDIAN OCEAN
SUMATERA
MALAYSIA
INDONESIA
SINGAPORE
Kuala Lumpur
George Town (Pinang)
Medan

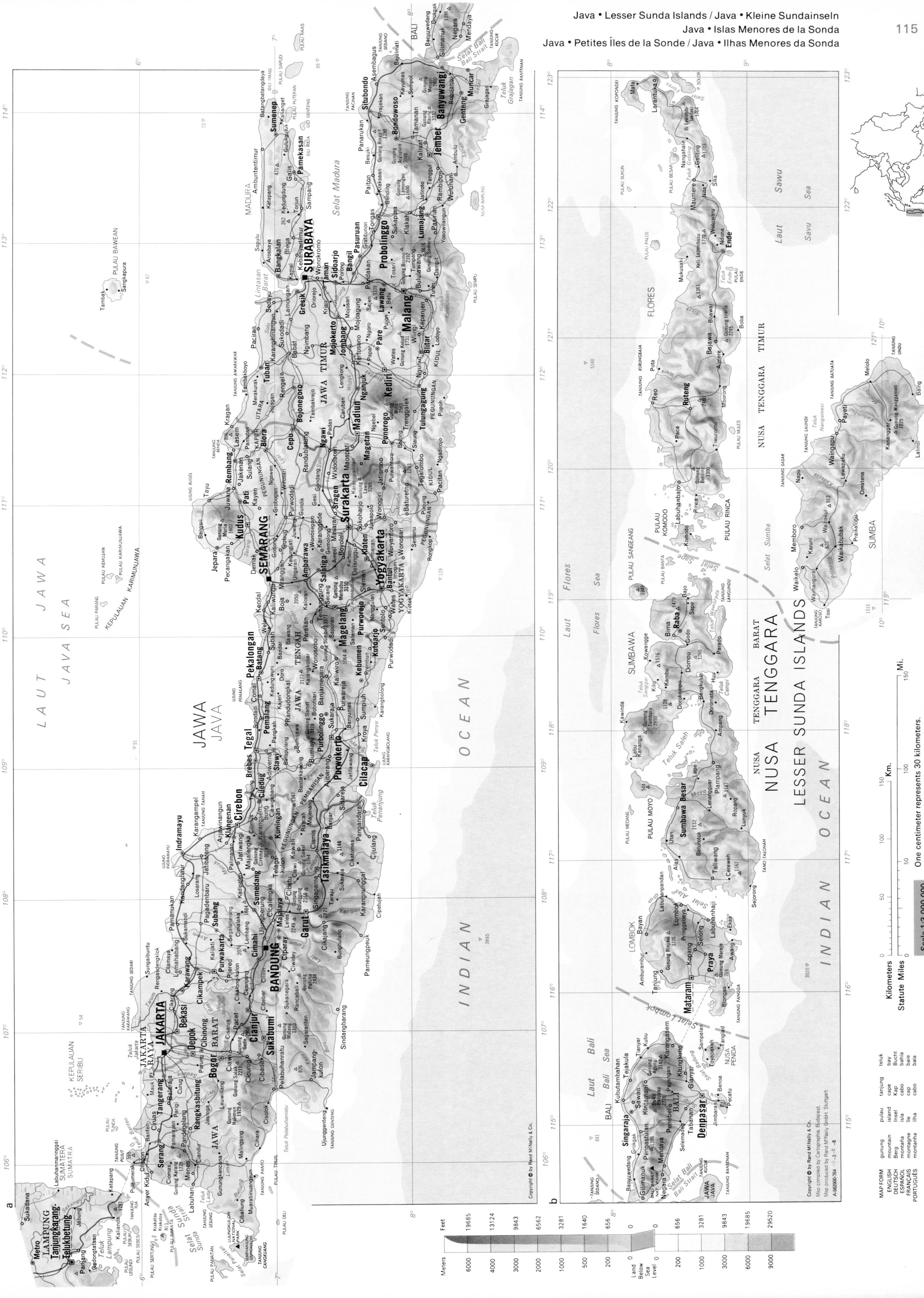
LAUT JAWA
JAVA SEA
JAWA
JAVA
INDIAN OCEAN
JAKARTA
BANDUNG
SEMARANG
SURABAYA
LESSER SUNDA ISLANDS
NUSA TENGGARA
NUSA TENGGARA BARAT
NUSA TENGGARA TIMUR
FLORES
SUMBA
SUMBAWA
LOMBOK
BALI
Laut Flores
Flores Sea
Laut Bali
Bali Sea
Laut Sawu
Savu Sea
Scale 1:3,000,000
One centimeter represents 30 kilometers.
One inch represents approximately 47 miles
Mercator Projection
Kilometers
Statute Miles
MAP FORM gunung pulau tanjung teluk
ENGLISH mountain island cape bay
DEUTSCH Berg Insel Kap Bucht
ESPAÑOL montaña isla cabo bahía
FRANÇAIS montagne île cap baie
PORTUGUÊS montanha ilha cabo baía
Meters
Feet
Land Below Sea Level
Copyright © by Rand McNally & Co.
Map produced by Cartographia, Budapest.
Map produced by Rand McNally GmbH, Stuttgart.

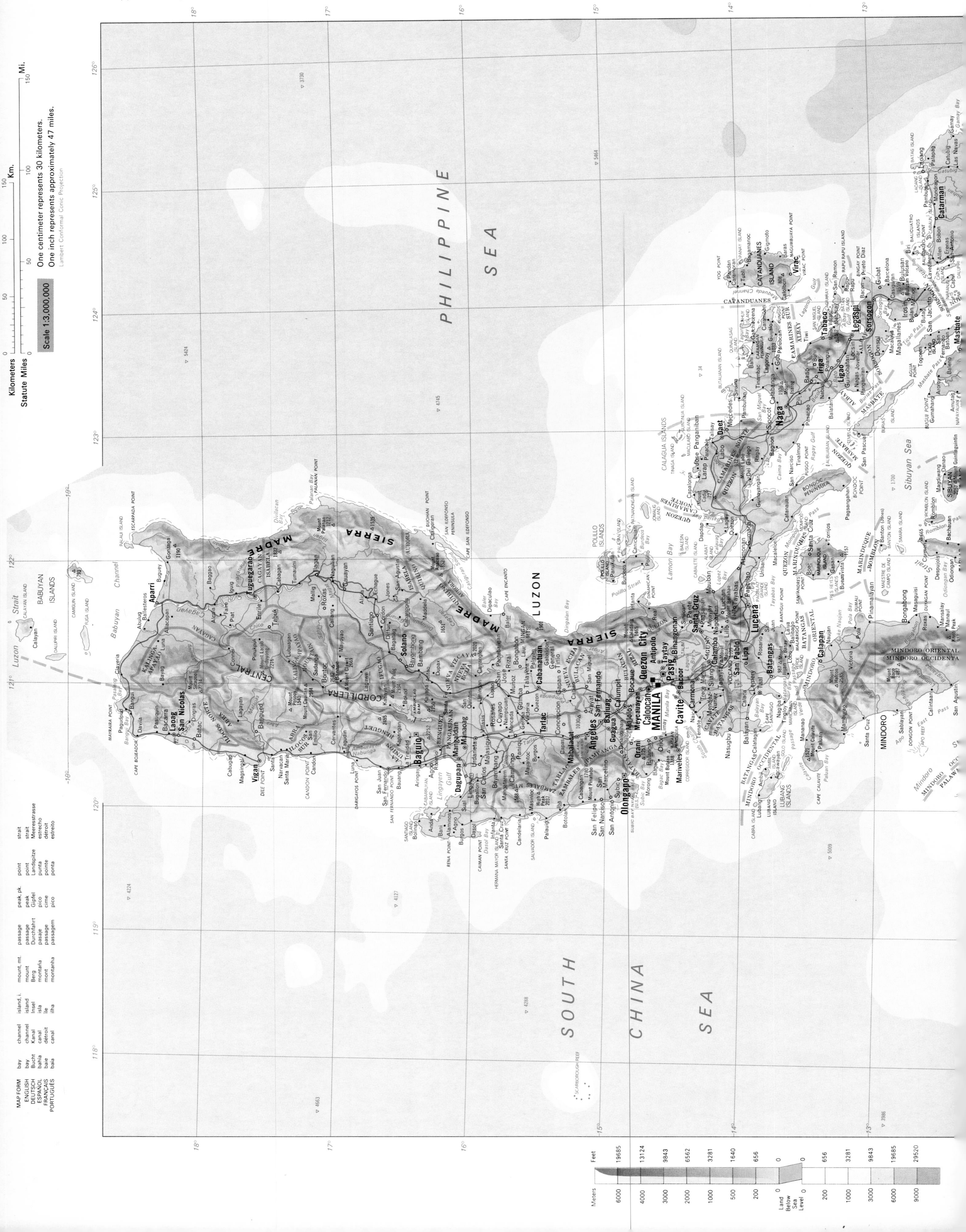
Kilometers
Statute Miles
Scale 1:3,000,000
One centimeter represents 30 kilometers.
One inch represents approximately 47 miles.
Lambert Conformal Conic Projection
PHILIPPINE SEA
SOUTH CHINA SEA
LUZON
MANILA
Quezon City
Luzon Strait
BABUYAN ISLANDS
Sibuyan Sea
MINDORO
MAP FORM bay channel island, i. mount, mt. passage peak, pk. point strait
ENGLISH bay channel island mount passage peak point strait
DEUTSCH Bucht Kanal Insel Berg Durchfahrt Gipfel Landspitze Meeresstrasse
ESPAÑOL bahía canal isla montaña pasaje pico punta estrecho
FRANÇAIS baie canal île mont passage cime pointe détroit
PORTUGUÊS baía canal ilha montanha passagem pico ponta estreito
Feet 19685 13124 9843 6562 3281 1640 656 0 0 656 3281 9843 19685 29520
Meters 6000 4000 3000 2000 1000 500 200 0 Land Below Sea Level 0 200 1000 3000 6000 9000

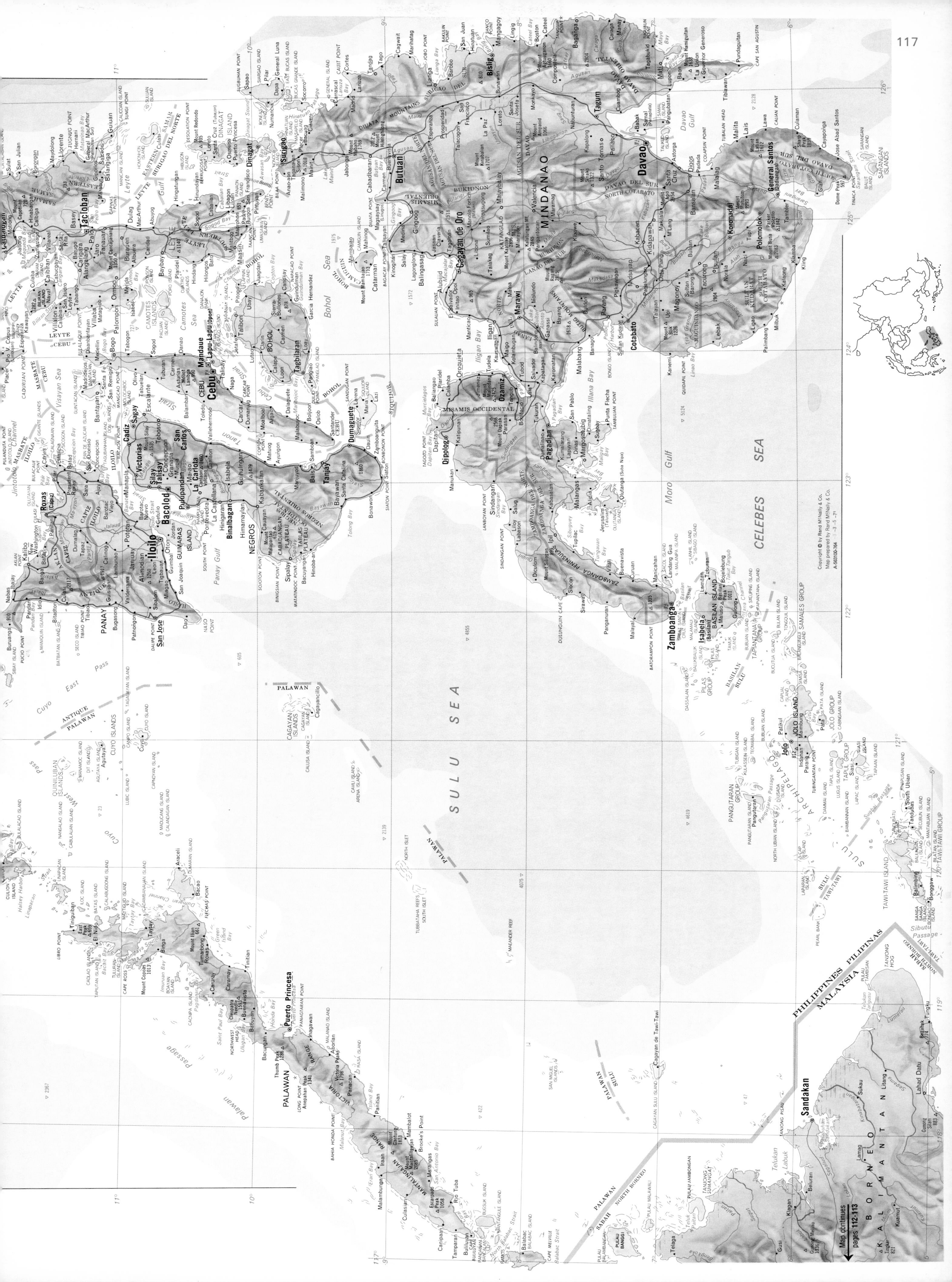
MINDANAO
SULU SEA
CELEBES SEA
Moro Gulf
Bohol Sea
Visayan Sea
Camotes Sea
Panay Gulf
Iligan Bay
Davao Gulf
SULU ARCHIPELAGO
PALAWAN
Puerto Princesa
PANAY
Iloilo
Roxas
NEGROS
Bacolod
Dumaguete
CEBU
Cebu
BOHOL
Tagbilaran
LEYTE
Tacloban
Surigao
Butuan
Cagayan de Oro
Davao
General Santos
Cotabato
Pagadian
Dipolog
Ozamiz
Zamboanga
Isabela
BASILAN ISLAND
Jolo
JOLO ISLAND
TAWI-TAWI GROUP
PHILIPPINES
PILIPINAS
MALAYSIA
SABAH
NORTH BORNEO
Sandakan
BORNEO
KALIMANTAN
Map continues pages 112-113
Copyright by Rand McNally & Co.
Map prepared by Rand McNally & Co.

Map continues pages 22-23

Map continues pages 134-135

TURKEY
ASIA MINOR
SYRIA
LEBANON
ISRAEL
JORDAN
EGYPT
IRAQ
KUWAIT
SAUDI ARABIA
QATAR
BAHRAIN
UNITED ARAB EMIRATES
OMAN
YEMEN
ERITREA
DJIBOUTI
ETHIOPIA
SOMALIA
SUDAN
IRAN
TURKMENISTAN
CASPIAN SEA
MEDITERRANEAN SEA
RED SEA
Persian Gulf
Gulf of Oman
Gulf of Aden
INDIAN
ARAB
Tropic of Cancer
AN-NAFŪD
NAJD
AD-DAHNĀ
AR-RUB' AL-KHĀLI
AL-HIJĀZ
DASHT-E KAVĪR
DASHT-E LŪT
KŪHHĀ-YE ZĀGROS
MESOPOTAMIA
BĀDIYAT ASH-SHĀM
HADRAMAWT
MAKRAN COAST
OGADEN
KARAKUMY
TBILISI
JEREVAN
BAKU
TEHRĀN
BAGHDĀD
DIMASHQ DAMASCUS
BAYRŪT BEIRUT
'AMMĀN
Yerushalayim Jerusalem
AL-KUWAYT
AR-RIYĀD RIYADH
Ad-Dawhah Doha
Al-Manāmah
Abū Zaby Abu Dhabi
Masqat Muscat
San'ā'
Asmera
Djibouti
Makkah Mecca
Al-Madīnah Medina
Jiddah Jeddah
Mashhad
Aşchabad Ashgabat
35°
40°
45°
50°
55°
60°
30°
25°
20°
15°
10°

MAP FORM	gulf	jabal	jazirat	range	ra's	shan
ENGLISH	gulf	mountain	island	range	cape	mountain(s)
DEUTSCH	Golf	Berg	Insel	Gebirge	Kap	Berg(e)
ESPAÑOL	golfo	montaña	isla	sierra	cabo	montaña(s)
FRANÇAIS	golfe	montagne	île	chaîne	cap	montagne(s)
PORTUGUÊS	golfo	montanha	ilha	serra	cabo	montanha(s)

Kilometers 0 200 400 600 Km.
Statute Miles 0 200 400 600 Mi.

Scale 1:12,000,000

One centimeter represents 120 kilometers.
One inch represents approximately 190 miles.
Lambert Conformal Conic Projection

Map continues pages 72-73

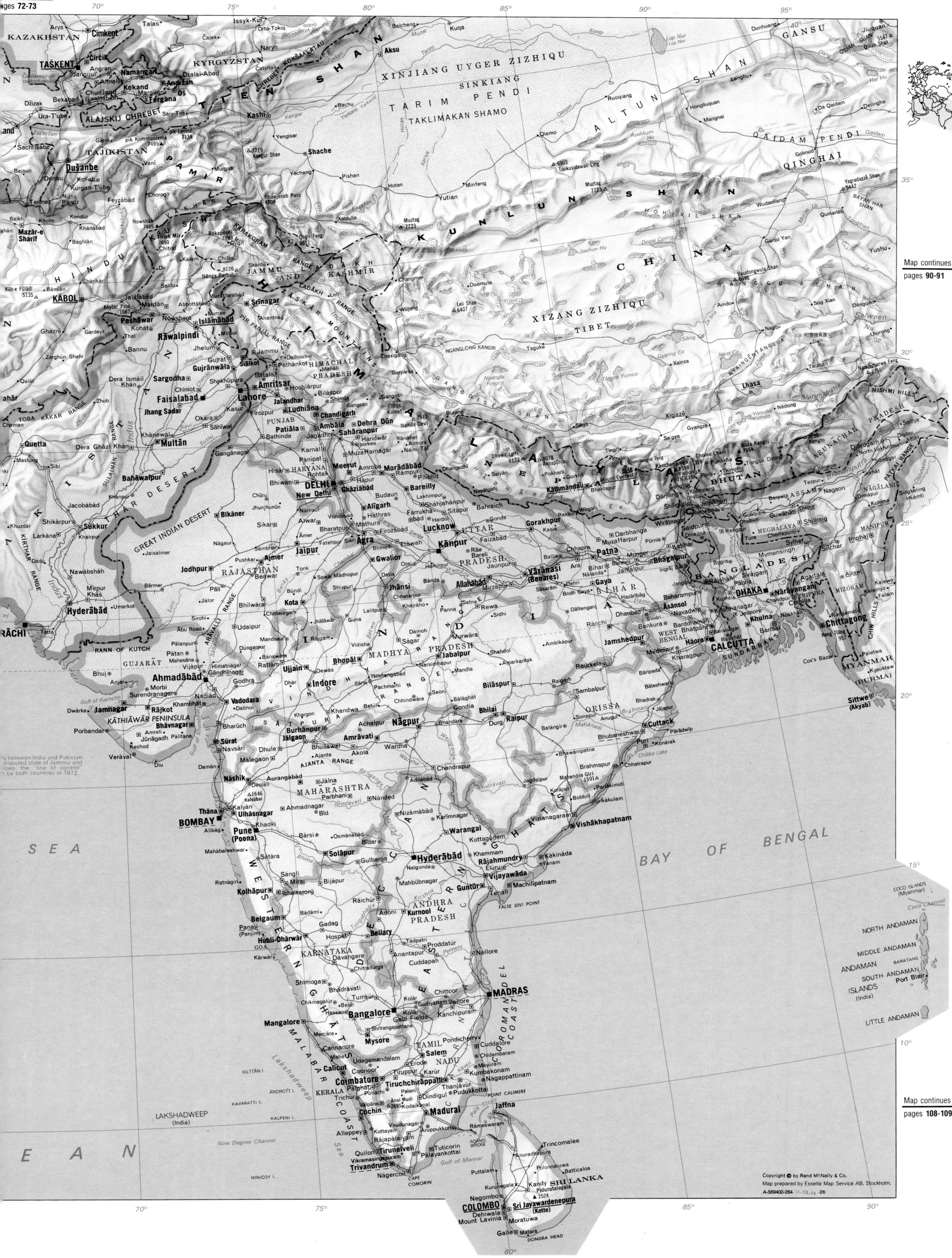
KAZAKHSTAN
KYRGYZSTAN
TAJIKISTAN
XINJIANG UYGER ZIZHIQU
SINKIANG
TARIM PENDI
TAKLIMAKAN SHAMO
ALTUN SHAN
QAIDAM PENDI
QINGHAI
GANSU
KUNLUN SHAN
TIEN SHAN
PAMIR
HINDU KUSH
KARAKORAM
JAMMU AND KASHMIR
XIZANG ZIZHIQU
TIBET
CHINA
HIMALAYAS
NEPAL
BHUTAN
BANGLADESH
MYANMAR (BURMA)
PAKISTAN
INDIA
GREAT INDIAN DESERT
THAR DESERT
PUNJAB
HARYANA
RĀJASTHAN
UTTAR PRADESH
MADHYA PRADESH
BIHAR
WEST BENGAL
ORISSA
GUJARĀT
MAHĀRĀSHTRA
ANDHRA PRADESH
KARNĀTAKA
TAMIL NADU
KERALA
SRI LANKA
ARABIAN SEA
BAY OF BENGAL
INDIAN OCEAN
LAKSHADWEEP (India)
ANDAMAN ISLANDS (India)
KĀBOL
Peshāwar
Islāmābād
Rawalpindi
Lahore
Faisalabad
Multān
Quetta
Hyderābād
KARACHI
Srīnagar
Amritsar
Chandigarh
DELHI
New Delhi
Jaipur
Agra
Lucknow
Kānpur
Vārānasi (Benares)
Patna
Kathmandu
Lhasa
DHAKA
CALCUTTA
Chittagong
Ahmadābād
Bhopāl
Indore
Nāgpur
Sūrat
BOMBAY
Pune (Poona)
Hyderābād
Vishākhapatnam
Bangalore
MADRAS
Mysore
Madurai
Cochin
Trivandrum
Jaffna
COLOMBO
Sri Jayawardenepura (Kotte)
Kandy
Copyright © by Rand McNally & Co.
Map prepared by Esselte Map Service AB, Stockholm.

Map continues pages 90-91

Map continues pages 108-109

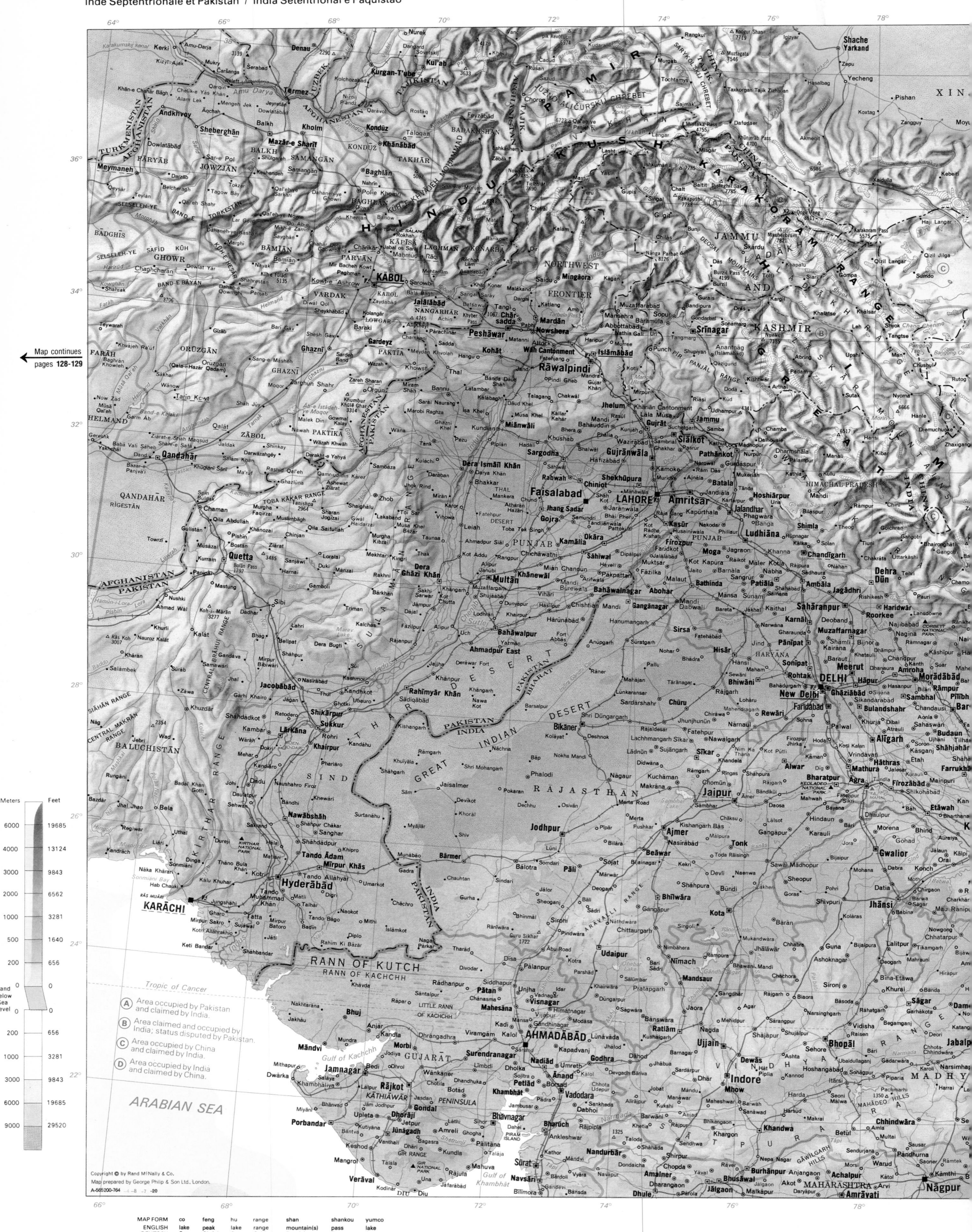

Map continues pages 128-129

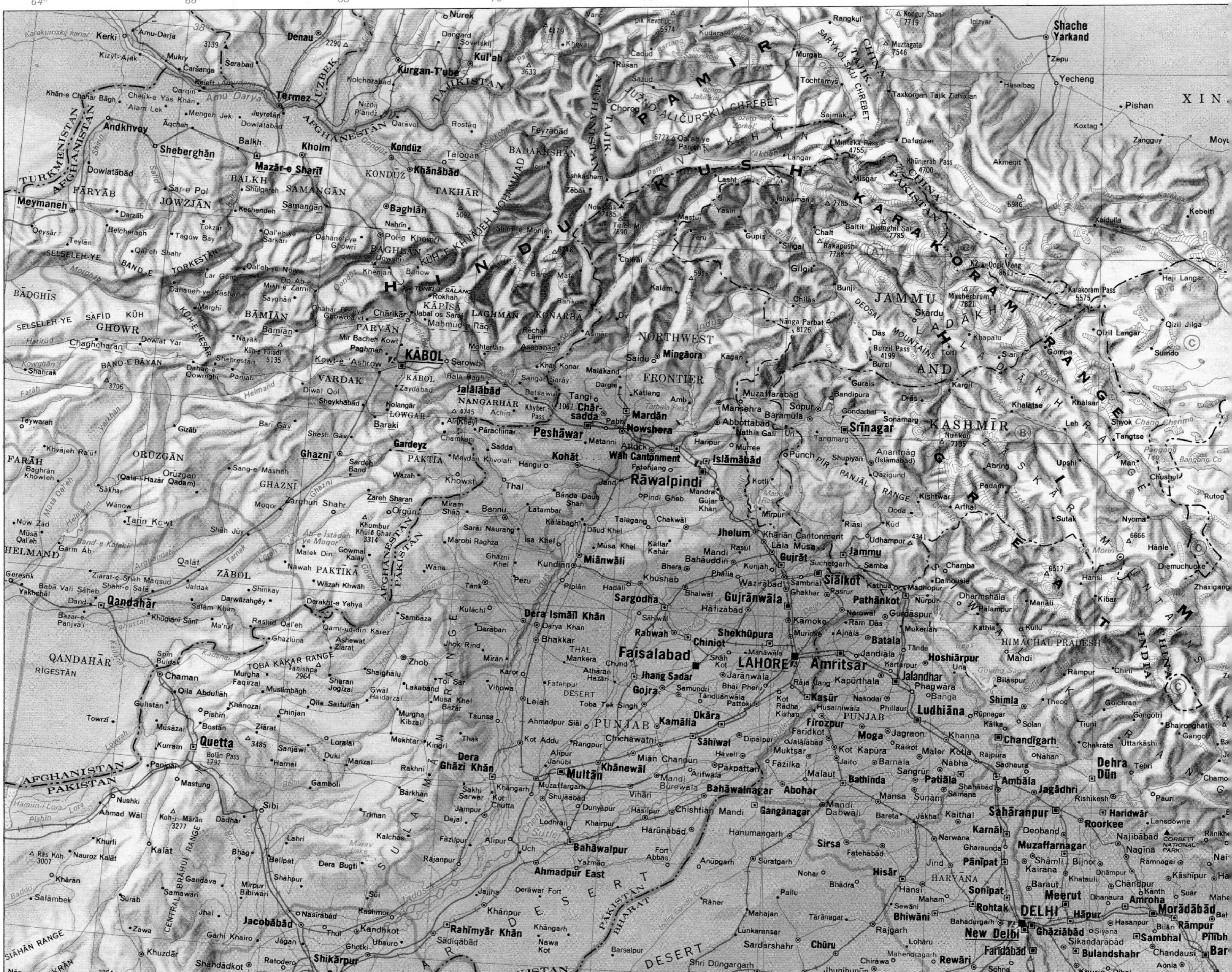
64° 66° 68° 70° 72° 74° 76° 78°
36° 34° 32° 30° 28° 26° 24° 22°
PAMIR
HINDU KUSH
KARAKORAM RANGE
JAMMU AND KASHMIR
NORTHWEST FRONTIER
KĀBOL
Islāmābād
Rāwalpindi
Peshāwar
Lahore
Amritsar
Faisalabad
Multān
Quetta
Qandahār
PUNJAB
SULAIMAN RANGE
KIRTHAR RANGE
BALUCHISTĀN
SIND
THAR DESERT
GREAT INDIAN DESERT
RĀJASTHĀN
DELHI
New Delhi
Jaipur
Jodhpur
Hyderābād
KARĀCHI
RANN OF KUTCH
RANN OF KACHCHH
Tropic of Cancer
AHMADĀBĀD
GUJARĀT
KĀTHIĀWĀR PENINSULA
ARABIAN SEA
Gulf of Kachchh
Gulf of Khambhāt
Indore
Bhopāl
Nāgpur
MAHĀRĀSHTRA
MADHYA
Ⓐ Area occupied by Pakistan and claimed by India.
Ⓑ Area claimed and occupied by India; status disputed by Pakistan.
Ⓒ Area occupied by China and claimed by India.
Ⓓ Area occupied by India and claimed by China.
Copyright © by Rand McNally & Co.
Map prepared by George Philip & Son Ltd., London.
A-565200-764

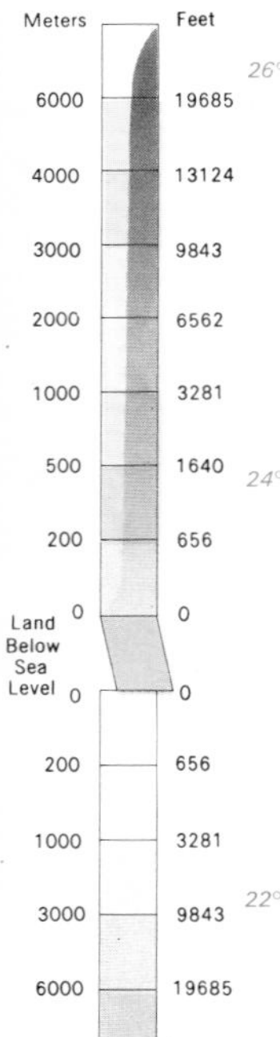
Meters Feet
6000 19685
4000 13124
3000 9843
2000 6562
1000 3281
500 1640
200 656
0 0
Land Below Sea Level
0 0
200 656
1000 3281
3000 9843
6000 19685
9000 29520

MAP FORM	co	feng	hu	range	shan	shankou	yumco
ENGLISH	lake	peak	lake	range	mountain(s)	pass	lake
DEUTSCH	See	Gipfel	See	Gebirge	Berg(e)	Pass	See
ESPAÑOL	lago	pico	lago	sierra	montaña(s)	paso	lago
FRANÇAIS	lac	cime	lac	chaîne	montagne(s)	col	lac
PORTUGUÊS	lago	pico	lago	serra	montanha(s)	passo	lago

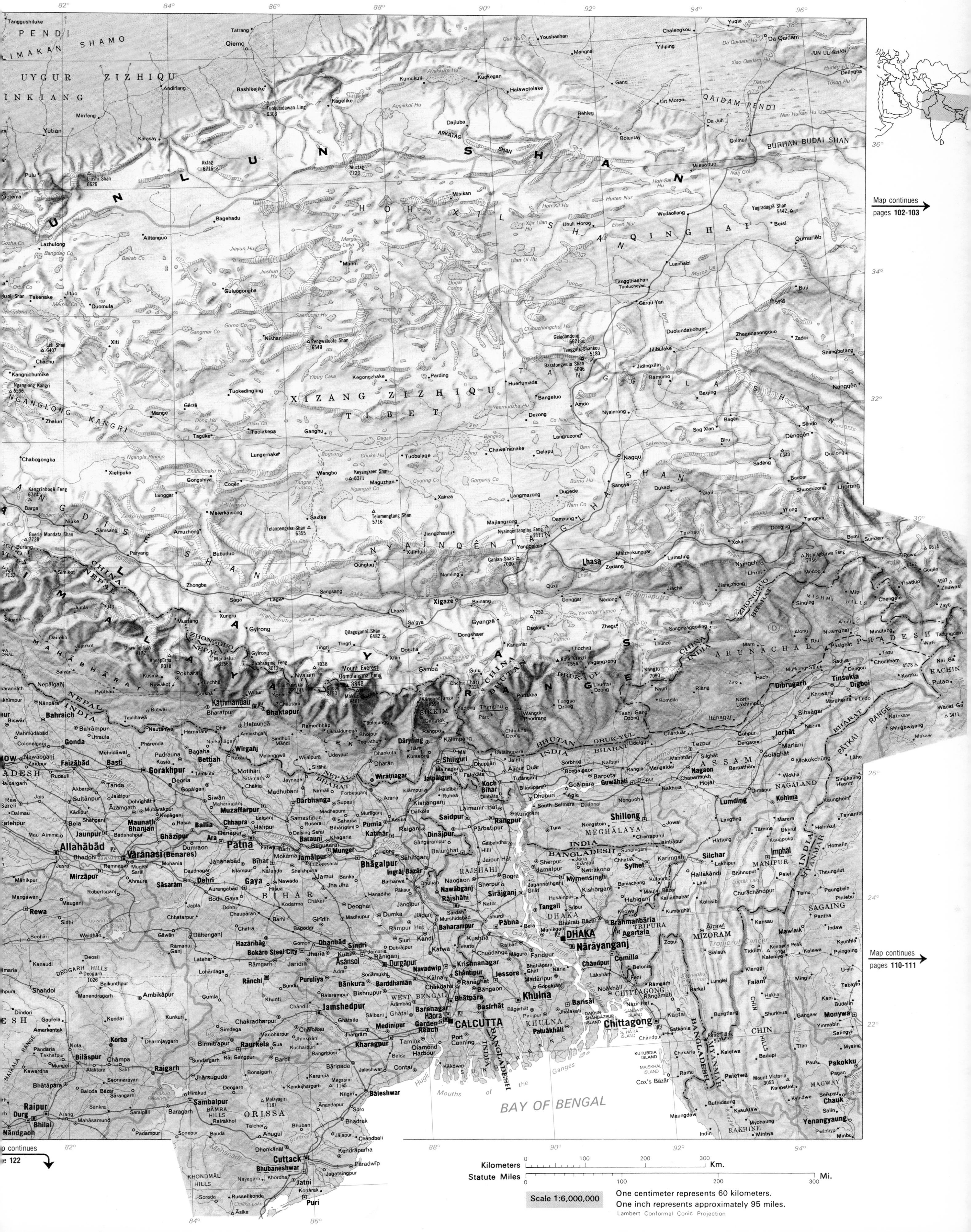
UYGUR ZIZHIQU
KUNLUN SHAN
HOH XIL SHAN
QINGHAI
QAIDAM PENDI
BURHAN BUDAI SHAN
XIZANG ZIZHIQU
TIBET
NYAINQÊNTANGLHA SHAN
GANGDISÊ SHAN
HIMALAYA
GREAT HIMALAYA RANGE
Lhasa
Xigazê
Mount Everest
Qomolangma Feng
8848
Kāthmāndau
NEPAL
SIKKIM
Thimphu
BHUTAN
DRUK-YUL
ARUNACHAL PRADESH
ASSAM
MEGHALAYA
NAGALAND
MANIPUR
MIZORAM
TRIPURA
BIHAR
WEST BENGAL
ORISSA
BANGLADESH
DHAKA
Chittagong
CALCUTTA
Patna
Allahābād
Vārānasi (Benares)
Mouths of the Ganges
BAY OF BENGAL
Tropic of Cancer
MYANMAR
CHIN HILLS
PĀTKAI RANGE
KACHIN
SAGAING
MAGWAY
RAKHINE
Kilometers 0 100 200 300 Km.
Statute Miles 0 100 200 300 Mi.

Map continues pages 102-103

Map continues pages 110-111

Map continues page 122

Scale 1:6,000,000
One centimeter represents 60 kilometers.
One inch represents approximately 95 miles.
Lambert Conformal Conic Projection

Southern India and Sri Lanka / Südindien und Sri Lanka / India Meridional y Sri Lanka / Inde Méridionale et Sri Lanka / Índia Meridional e Sri Lanka

Map continues pages 120-121

ARABIAN SEA
BAY OF BENGAL
INDIAN OCEAN
Laccadive Sea
Lakshadweep Sea
LAKSHADWEEP
Nine Degree Channel
Eight Degree Channel
Gulf of Mannar
Gulf of Khambhāt
SRI LANKA
INDIA BHARAT
MALDIVES
MALDIVE ISLANDS
BOMBAY
HYDERĀBĀD
MADRAS
BANGALORE
COLOMBO
Nāgpur
Pune (Poona)
Madurai
Coimbatore
Mysore
Trivandrum
Vishākhapatnam
Copyright © by Rand McNally & Co.
Map prepared by George Philip & Son Ltd. London
A-565300-764 -2 -3 -5-11

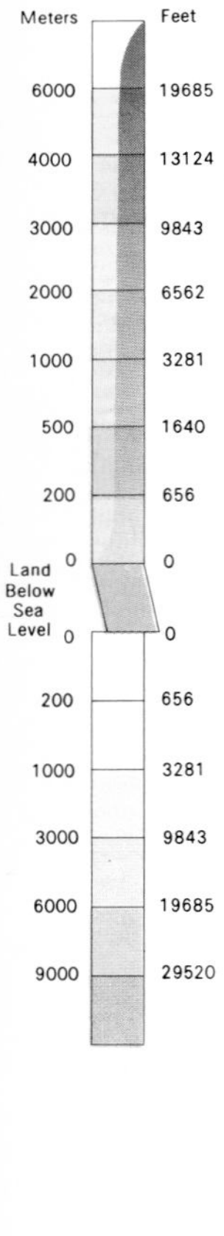
Meters
Feet
6000 19685
4000 13124
3000 9843
2000 6562
1000 3281
500 1640
200 656
0 0
Land Below Sea Level
0 0
200 656
1000 3281
3000 9843
6000 19685
9000 29520

ENGLISH	atoll	hills	island	lagoon	lake	range	reservoir
DEUTSCH	Atoll	Hügel	Insel	Haff	See	Gebirge	Stausee
ESPAÑOL	atolón	colinas	isla	laguna	lago	sierra	embalse
FRANÇAIS	atoll	collines	île	lagune	lac	chaîne	réservoir
PORTUGUÊS	atol	colinas	ilha	laguna	lago	serra	reservatório

Kilometers 0 100 200 300 Km.
Statute Miles 0 100 200 300 Mi.

Scale 1:6,000,000

One centimeter represents 60 kilometers.
One inch represents approximately 95 miles.
Lambert Conformal Conic Projection

Map continues page 85

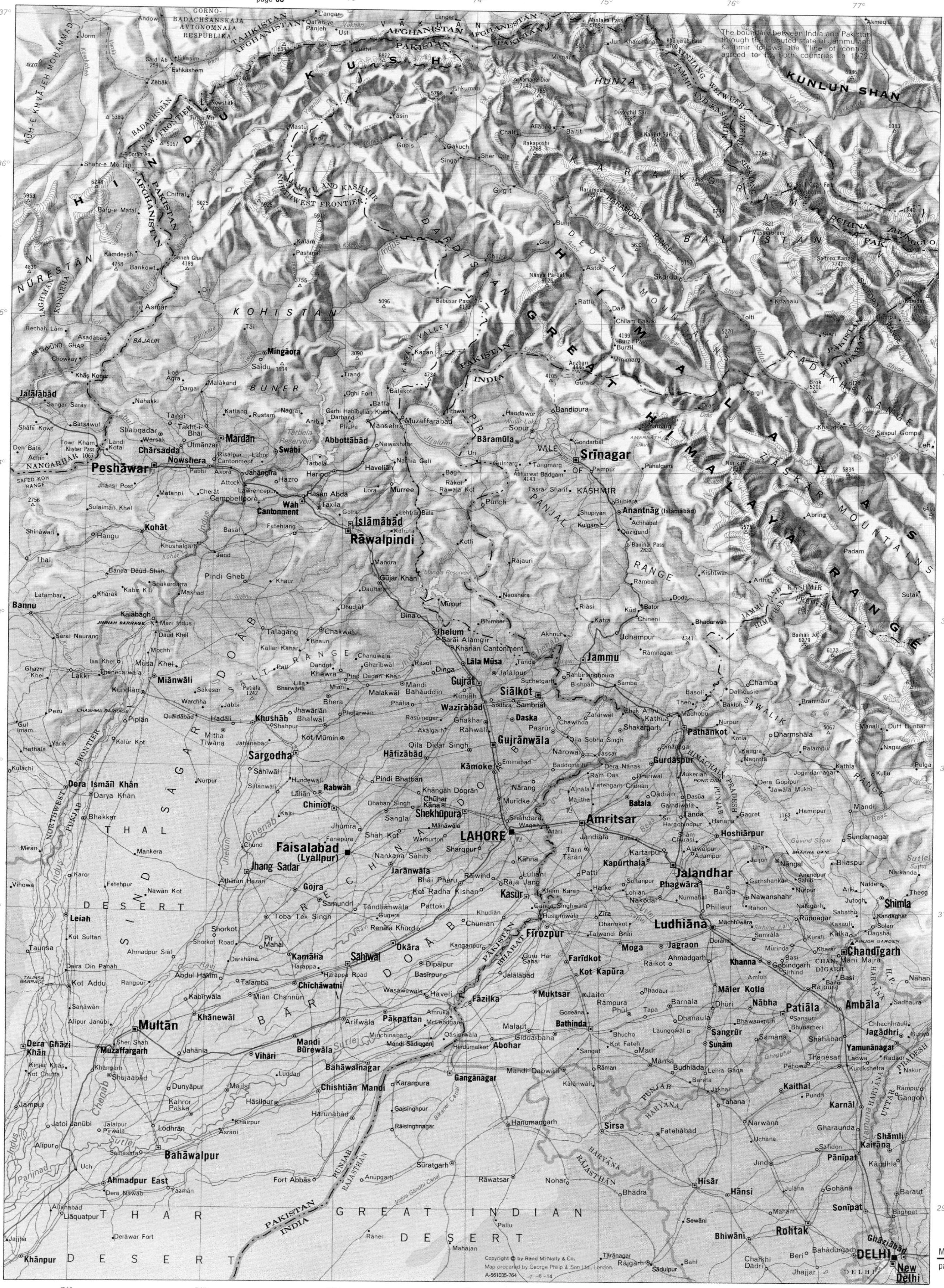
The boundary between India and Pakistan through the disputed state of Jammu and Kashmir follows the "line of control" agreed to by both countries in 1972.
HINDU KUSH
KUNLUN SHAN
KARAKORAM
BALTISTAN
HUNZA
DARDISTAN
KOHISTAN
GREAT HIMALAYA RANGE
ZASKAR MOUNTAINS
LADAKH RANGE
PIR PANJAL RANGE
SALT RANGE
SIWALIK RANGE
SIND SAGAR DOAB
RECHNA DOAB
BARI DOAB
THAL DESERT
THAR DESERT
GREAT INDIAN DESERT
Peshāwar
Islāmābād
Rāwalpindi
Srīnagar
Jammu
Lahore
Amritsar
Faisalabad (Lyallpur)
Multān
Jalandhar
Ludhiāna
Chandīgarh
Shimla
Patiāla
Ambāla
Delhi
New Delhi
Bahāwalpur
Gujrānwāla
Siālkot
Sargodha
Copyright © by Rand McNally & Co.
Map prepared by George Philip & Son Ltd. London.
A-561035-764 7-6-14

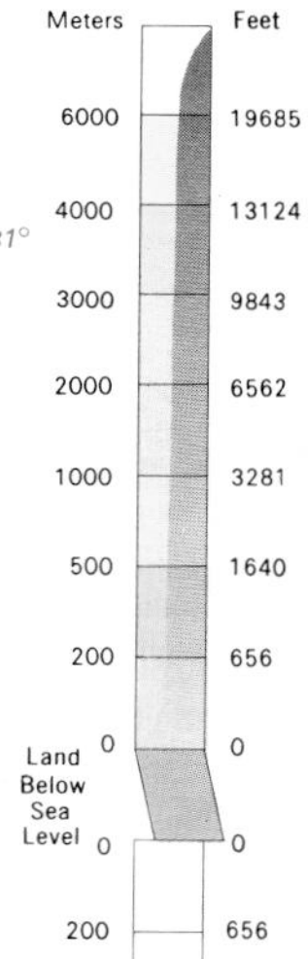
Meters
Feet
6000 19685
4000 13124
3000 9843
2000 6562
1000 3281
500 1640
200 656
0 0
Land Below Sea Level
0 0
200 656
1000 3281
3000 9843
6000 19685
9000 29520

Map continues pages 124-125

MAP FORM	airport	doāb	glacier	pass	range	sar
ENGLISH	airport	upland	glacier	pass	range	mountain
DEUTSCH	Flughafen	Bergland	Gletscher	Pass	Gebirge	Berg
ESPAÑOL	aeropuerto	tierras altas	glaciar	paso	sierra	montaña
FRANÇAIS	aéroport	hautes terres	glacier	col	chaîne	montagne
PORTUGUÊS	aeroporto	terras altas	geleira	passo	serra	montanha

Kilometers 0 50 100 150 Km.
Statute Miles 0 50 100 150 Mi.

Scale 1:3,000,000

One centimeter represents 30 kilometers.
One inch represents approximately 47 miles.
Lambert Conformal Conic Projection

Map continues page 123

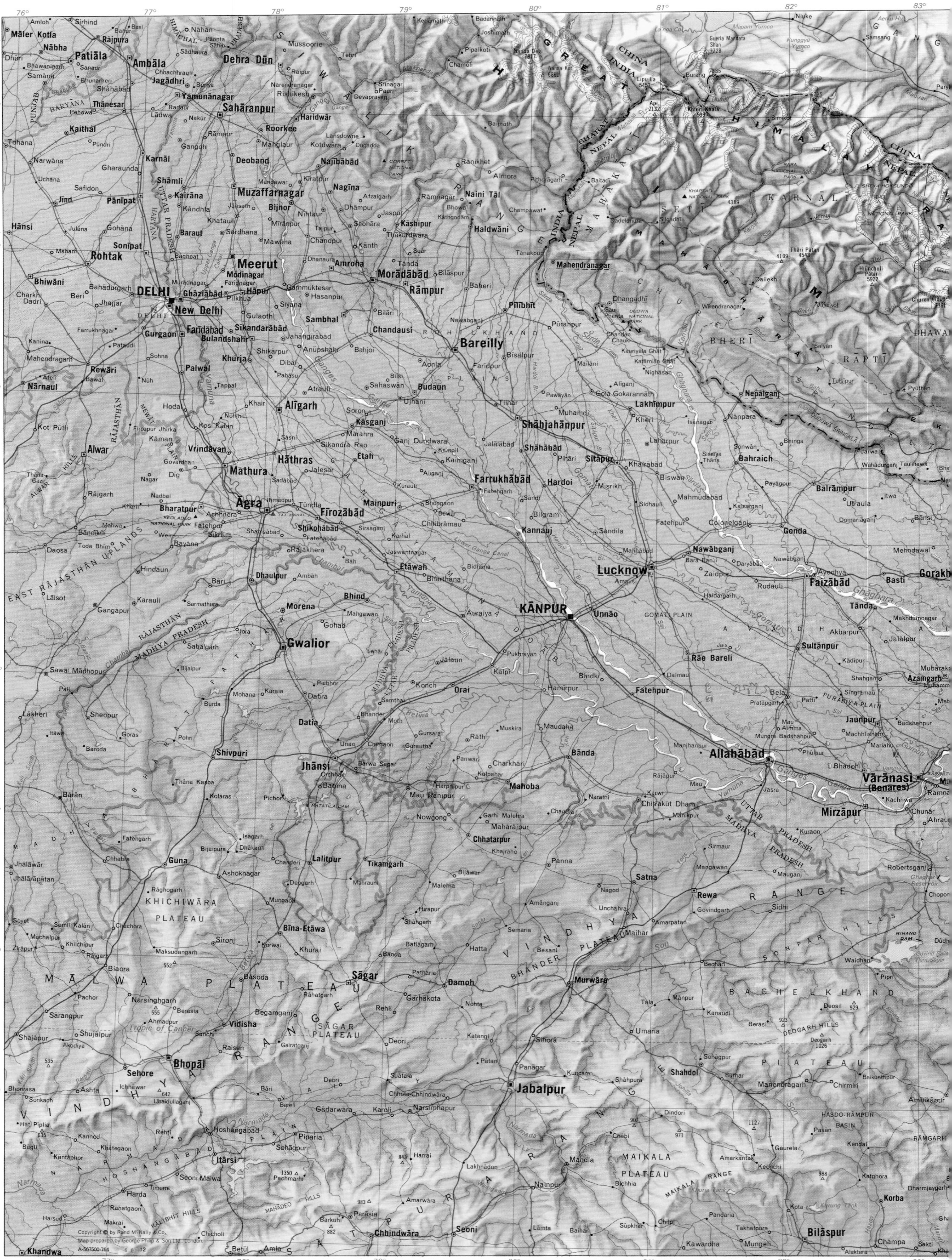
DELHI
New Delhi
Meerut
Morādābād
Bareilly
Shāhjahānpur
Lucknow
KĀNPUR
Allahābād
Vārānasi (Benares)
Āgra
Mathura
Alīgarh
Gwalior
Jhānsi
Sāgar
Bhopāl
Jabalpur
Dehra Dūn
Sahāranpur
Ambāla
Patiāla
Rohtak
Alwar
Faizābād
Gonda
Bahraich
Rewa
Satna
Mirzāpur
Bilāspur
Chhindwāra
Khandwa
Hoshangābād
Vidisha
Guna
Shivpuri
Lalitpur
Tikamgarh
Chhatarpur
Bānda
Fatehpur
Rāe Bareli
Sultānpur
Jaunpur
Azamgarh
Farrukhābād
Hardoi
Sītāpur
Kannauj
Etāwah
Mainpuri
Fīrozābād
Etah
Hāthras
Budaun
Rāmpur
Muzaffarnagar
Roorkee
Haridwār
Naini Tāl
Haldwāni
Mahendranagar
Nepālganj
Murwāra
Damoh
Mandla
Seoni
Itārsi
Sehore
Dhaulpur
Morena
Bhind
Datia
Orai
Mahoba
G R E A T   H I M A L A Y A
M A L W A   P L A T E A U
V I N D H Y A   R A N G E
S Ā T P U R A   R A N G E
MAIKALA PLATEAU
B A G H E L K H A N D
KHICHIWĀRA PLATEAU
EAST RĀJASTHĀN UPLANDS
SIWALIK RANGE
CHINA
INDIA
NEPAL
Tropic of Cancer
Ganges
Yamuna
Ghāghara
Narmada
Chambal
Betwa
Son
Copyright © by Rand McNally & Co.
Map prepared by George Philip & Son Ltd., London

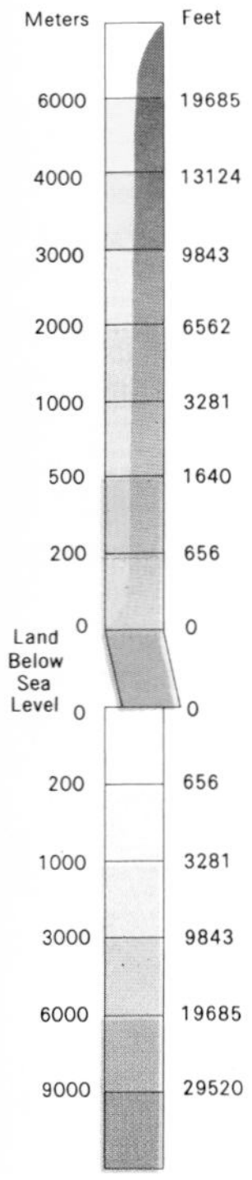
Meters
Feet
6000
19685
4000
13124
3000
9843
2000
6562
1000
3281
500
1640
200
656
0
0
Land Below Sea Level
0
0
200
656
1000
3281
3000
9843
6000
19685
9000
29520

MAP FORM	hills	plains	plateau	range	shan	yumco
ENGLISH	hills	plains	plateau	range	mountains	lake
DEUTSCH	Hügel	Ebenen	Hochebene	Gebirge	Berge	See
ESPAÑOL	colinas	llanos	meseta	sierra	montañas	lago
FRANÇAIS	collines	plaines	plateau	chaîne	montagnes	lac
PORTUGUÊS	colinas	planícies	planalto	serra	montanhas	lago

Kilometers 0 50 100 150 Km.
Statute Miles 0 50 100 150 Mi.

Scale 1:3,000,000

One centimeter represents 30 kilometers.
One inch represents approximately 47 miles.
Lambert Conformal Conic Projection

XIZANG ZIZHIQU
TIBET
NYAINQENTANGLHA SHAN
GREAT HIMALAYA RANGE
Mount Everest 8848
Lhasa
Kathmandau
Bhaktapur
Pokhara
Thimphu
Darjiling
Gangtok
Kalimpang
SIKKIM
BHUTAN
DRUK-YUL
NEPAL
INDIA
BHARAT
CHINA
ZHONGGUO
BANGLADESH
ASSAM
MEGHALAYA
BIHAR
WEST BENGAL
ORISSA
UTTAR PRADESH
Patna
Muzaffarpur
Darbhanga
Gaya
Bhagalpur
Munger
Ranchi
Jamshedpur
Asansol
Durgapur
Barddhaman
CALCUTTA
Haora
Kharagpur
Raurkela
Dhaka (Dacca)
Narayanganj
Comilla
Rajshahi
Khulna
Jessore
Barisal
Rangpur
Dinajpur
Mymensingh
Bokaro Steel City
Hazaribag
CHOTA NAGPUR PLATEAU
RANCHI PLATEAU
HAZARIBAG PLATEAU
Ganges
Brahmaputra
Meghna
GANGES DELTA
Mouths of the Ganges
BAY OF BENGAL
Tropic of Cancer
84°
85°
86°
87°
88°
89°
90°
91°
22°
24°
25°
26°
27°
28°
29°
30°

86° 30'
87°
87° 30'
88°
24°
23° 30'
23°
22° 30'
22°
21° 30'
Madhupur
Giridih
Dumka
Rāmpur Hāt
Jiāganj
Murshidābād
Baharampur
Jāmtāra
Chittaranjan
Kumardhubi
Dhanbād
Katrās
Jharia
Sindri
Kulti
Āsansol
Rānīganj
Burnpur
Sūri
Bolpur
Kandi
Kātwa
Chās
Purūliya
Durgāpur
Bānkura
Barddhamān
Navadwip
Kālna
Bishnupur
Jamshedpur
Ārāmbāg
Ghātāl
Hugli-Chinsurah
Chandannagar
Bhadreswar
Champdāni
Baidyabāti
Serāmpore
Rishra
Konnagar
Pānihāti
Uttarpara-Kotrung
Bally
Baranagar
Hāora
CAL
Garden Reach
Behāla
Budge Budge
Ulubāria
Medinīpur
Kharagpur
Jhārgrām
Ghātsila
Tamlūk
Contai
Bāripada
Baleshwar
Jaleshwar
Haldī
Diamond Harbour
Rājpur
Tropic of Cancer
Pānchet Reservoir
Maithon Reservoir
Morākhi Reservoir
Dāmodar
Ajay
Kāsai
Rūpnārāyan
Hugli
Subarnarekha
BIHĀR
WEST BENGAL
ORISSA
RĀJMAHAL HILLS
RĀRH
GARHJĀT HILLS
MIDNAPORE PLAIN
KĀNTHI COASTAL PLAIN
SĀGAR ISLAND
Ganga Sāgar
BHĀGIRATHI PLAIN

MAP FORM	bay	canal	char	delta	island	plain
ENGLISH	bay	canal	island	delta	island	plain
DEUTSCH	Bucht	Kanal	Insel	Delta	Insel	Ebene
ESPAÑOL	bahía	canal	isla	delta	isla	llanura
FRANÇAIS	baie	canal	île	delta	île	plaine
PORTUGUÊS	baía	canal	ilha	delta	ilha	planície

89°
89° 30′
90°
90° 30′
24°
23° 30′
Tropic of Cancer
23°
22° 30′
22°
21° 30′
Ishurdi
Pābna
Ganges
Padma
Kushtia
Kumārkhāli
Rājbāri
Tangail
Jamuna
Dhaleswari
Mānikganj
Tongi
Narsinghdi
Mīrpur
Gulshan
ZIA INTERNATIONAL AIRPORT
DHAKA DACCA
Nārāyanganj
Munshiganj
Meghna
Faridpur
Chuādanga
Jhenida
Māgura
Kotchāndpur
Jessore
Bangaon
Gobardānga
Khulna
Sātkhira
Bāduria
Basīrhāt
Bāgerhāt
Rāmpāl
Pirojpur
Mādārīpur
Gopālganj
Barisāl
Jhālakāti
Patuākhāli
Bārguna
Chāndpur
Lakshmīpur
Bhola
Shāhbāzpur
Tetulia
DAKHIN SHĀHBĀZPUR ISLAND
RABNABAD ISLANDS
DONMANICK ISLANDS
DALHOUSIE ISLAND
BANGADUNI ISLAND
PUTNEY ISLAND
S U N D A R B A N S
BAY OF BENGAL
BANGLADESH
INDIA
WEST BENGAL
BHARAT
RAJSHAHI
KHULNA
DHAKA
CHITTAGONG
Copyright © by Rand McNally & Co.
Map prepared by George Philip & Son Ltd., London.
A-567900-264

Kilometers 0 10 20 30 40 50 Km.

Statute Miles 0 10 20 30 40 50 Mi.

Scale 1:1,000,000

One centimeter represents 10 kilometers.

One inch represents approximately 16 miles.

Lambert Conformal Conic Projection

Map continues page 84

Map continues pages 130-131

ANKARA
Kırıkkale
Yozgat
Tokat
Sivas
Gümüşhane
Erzincan
Erzurum
Kars
JEREVAN
Gjandža
NAGORNO-KARABAKH
Stepanakert
AZERBAJDŽAN
Kayseri
Konya
Niğde
Malatya
Elazığ
Bingöl
Muş
Van
Bitlis
Diyarbakır
Batman
Siirt
Hakkâri
Nachičevan'
Khvoy
Tabrīz
Orūmīyeh (Reza'iyeh)
Marand
Marāgheh
Mīāneh
Kahramanmaraş
Adıyaman
Şanlıurfa
Mardin
Gaziantep
Adana
Tarsus
İçel
Osmaniye
Ceyhan
İskenderun
Kilis
TOROS DAĞLARI
TURKEY
TÜRKİYE
SYRIA
SŪRIYAH
Antakya
Antioch
Halab Aleppo
Ar-Raqqah
Al-Qāmishlī
Al-Ḥasakah
Dayr az-Zawr
Tall 'Afar
Al-Mawṣil
Mosul
Irbīl
Kirkūk
As-Sulaymānīyah
Mahābād
Saqqez
Sanandaj
Hamadān
Bakhtarān (Kermānshāh)
NORTH CYPRUS
KUZEY KIBRIS
Nicosia
Lefkoşa
Lemesós
Limassol
Gazimağusa
Famagusta
CYPRUS
KIPROS
The Turkish Republic of Northern Cyprus unilaterally declared its independence on November 15, 1983.
MEDITERRANEAN SEA
Al-Lādhiqīyah
Latakia
Ḥamāh
Ḥimṣ Homs
Ṭarābulus
Tripoli
LEBANON
LUBNĀN
BEIRUT BAYRŪT
Ṣaydā Sidon
Ṣūr Tyre
DIMASHQ DAMASCUS
Tudmur (Palmyra)
Abū Kamāl
Euphrates
BĀDIYAT ASH-SHĀM
SYRIAN DESERT
AL-ANBĀR
NĪNAWĀ
Sāmarrā'
Tikrīt
ṢALĀḤ AD-DĪN
MESOPOTAMIA
BAGHDĀD
Ba'qūbah
Al-Fallūjah
Ar-Ramādī
Karbalā'
Al-Ḥillah
An-Najaf
Ad-Dīwānīyah
Al-Kūt
Al-'Amārah
An-Nāṣirīyah
Al-Baṣrah
Basra
Area occupied by Israel since June 1967
ISRAEL
YISRA'EL
'Akko Acre
Hefa Haifa
Netanya
TEL AVIV-YAFO
PALESTINE
Nāblus
Yerushalayim Jerusalem
'AMMĀN
Az-Zarqā'
Irbid
As-Suwaydā'
Ghazzah Gaza
Be'er Sheva'
Dumyāṭ
Būr Sa'īd Port Said
Al-Ismā'īlīyah
Az-Zaqāzīq
As-Suways Suez
Al-'Arīsh
JORDAN
AL-URDUN
IRAQ
AL-'IRAQ
SAUDI ARABIA
AL-'ARABIYAH AS-SU'ŪDIYAH
KUWAIT
AL-KUWAYT
Al-Jahrah
Eilat
Al-'Aqabah
Ma'ān
Tabūk
Sakākah
Al-Jawf
AN-NAFŪD
Ḥā'il
Buraydah
'Unayzah
AR-RIYĀḌ RIYADH
AD-DIBDIBAH
AD-DAHNĀ'
AS-SUMMĀN
AL-ḤIJĀZ
HEJAZ
Al-Madīnah Medina
Yanbu' al-Baḥr
Rābigh
RED SEA
AL-BAḤR AL-AḤMAR
Gulf of Suez
Gulf of Aqaba
SHIBH JAZĪRAT SĪNĀ'
SINAI PENINSULA
Al-Ghurdaqah
Al-Quṣayr
EGYPT
MIṢR
SUDAN
AS-SŪDĀN
Area administered by Sudan
Administrative Boundary
Tropic of Cancer
Meters
Feet
6000 19685
4000 13124
3000 9843
2000 6562
1000 3281
500 1640
200 656
0 0
Land Below Sea Level
0 0
200 656
1000 3281
3000 9843
6000 19685
9000 29520

Map continues pages 140-141

Map continues pages 144-145

MAP FORM	harrat	jabal	jazīreh	kūh	ra's	sabkhat	wādī
ENGLISH	lava flow	mountain	island	mountain	cape	salt marsh	wadi
DEUTSCH	Lavastrom	Berg	Insel	Berg	Kap	Salzmarsch	Wadi
ESPAÑOL	corriente de lava	montaña	isla	montaña	cabo	pantano salado	uadi
FRANÇAIS	coulée de lave	montagne	île	montagne	cap	marais salé	wadi
PORTUGUÊS	corrente de lava	montanha	ilha	montanha	cabo	pântano salgado	uádi

CASPIAN SEA
(28 Meters Below Sea Level)
BAKU
Krasnovodsk
BALKAN
TAŠAUZ
KARAKUM
CENTRAL'NYJE KARAKUMY
ČARDŽOU
Buchara
Kagan
UZBEKISTAN
TURKMENISTAN
Ašchabad
Ashgabat
KOPETDAG
MARY
Mary
Bajram-Ali
Tedžen
Serachs
Sarakhs
Mashhad
MĀZANDARĀN
Gorgān
Gonbad-e Qābūs
Bojnūrd
Qūchān
Neyshābūr
Sabzevār
RESHTEH-YE KŪHHĀ-YE ALBORZ
ELBURZ MOUNTAINS
Qolleh-ye Damāvand
Mount Demavend
5604
TEHRĀN
Tehran
Qazvīn
Karaj
Qom
Semnān
SEMNĀN
DASHT-E KAVĪR
KHORĀSĀN
Torbat-e Heydarīyeh
Bīrjand
Kāshān
ESFAHĀN
Esfahān
Isfahan
Najafābād
Yazd
YAZD
DASHT-E LŪT
Kermān
KERMĀN
Rafsanjān
Sīrjān
Zāhedān
Zābol
Shīrāz
Marv Dasht
Kāzerūn
Būshehr
BŪSHEHR
Bandar-e Būshehr
FARS
Fasā
Jahrom
Fīrūzābād
Bam
HORMOZGĀN
Bandar-e 'Abbās
Qeshm
Strait of Hormuz
Persian Gulf
Arabian Gulf
SĪSTĀN VA BALŪCHESTĀN
BALUCHISTAN
SIAHAN RANGE
CENTRAL MAKRAN RANGE
CHĀGAI HILLS
SANDY DESERT
MAKRAN COAST
Gulf of Oman
Herāt
HERĀT
FARĀH
Farāh
Shīndand
HELMAND
NĪMRŪZ
DASHT-E MĀRGOW
RĪGESTĀN
QANDAHĀR
Qandahār
SAFĪD KŪH
Mazār-e Sharīf
Sheberghān
Andkhvoy
Meymaneh
FĀRYĀB
JOWZJĀN
BALKH
BĀMĪĀN
ORŪZGĀN
ZĀBOL
AFGHANISTAN
AFGHĀNESTĀN
PAKISTAN
IRAN
Kushka
Termez
Karši
Kerki
BAHRAIN
AL-BAHRAYN
Al-Manāmah
Ad-Dammām
Az-Zahrān
Al-Qaṭīf
Al-Khubar
Al-Jubayl
Al-Hufūf
Al-Mubarraz
QATAR
Ad-Dawḥah
Doha
Ar-Rayyān
UNITED ARAB EMIRATES
AL-IMĀRĀT AL-'ARABĪYAH AL-MUTTAḤIDAH
Abū Ẓaby
Abu Dhabi
Dubayy
Ash-Shāriqah
Ra's al-Khaymah
Al-'Ayn
OMAN
'UMĀN
Masqaṭ
Muscat
Maṭraḥ
Ṣuḥār
AL-BĀṬINAH
AL-JABAL AL-AKHḌAR
AL-HAJAR ASH-SHARQI
AR-RUB' AL-KHĀLĪ
SAUDI ARABIA
AL-'ARABĪYAH AS-SU'ŪDĪYAH
Tropic of Cancer
Gwādar
Pasni
Map continues pages 120-121
Copyright © by Rand McNally & Co.
Map prepared by George Philip & Son Ltd., London.

Kilometers 0 100 200 300 Km.

Statute Miles 0 100 200 300 Mi.

Scale 1:6,000,000

One centimeter represents 60 kilometers.

One inch represents approximately 95 miles.

Lambert Conformal Conic Projection

Map continues pages 38-39

BLACK
MEDITERRANEAN SEA
İSTANBUL
ANKARA
İZMİR
Bursa
Eskişehir
Konya
Antalya
Marmara Denizi
Sea of Marmara
Antalya Körfezi
Gulf of Antalya
TAURUS MOUNTAINS
DODECANESE
NORTH CYPRUS
KUZEY KIBRIS
CYPRUS
KIPROS
Nicosia
The Turkish Republic of Northern Cyprus unilaterally declared its independence on November 15, 1983.
Meters
Feet
Land Below Sea Level
Copyright © by Rand McNally & Co.
Map prepared by George Philip & Son Ltd., London.

MAP FORM	burnu	dağ, dağı	dağları	gölü	jabal	körfezi	sabkhat
ENGLISH	cape	mountain	mountains	lake	mountains	bay, gulf	salt marsh
DEUTSCH	Kap	Berg	Berge	See	Berge	Bucht, Golf	Salzmarsch
ESPAÑOL	cabo	montaña	montañas	lago	montañas	bahía, golfo	pantano salado
FRANÇAIS	cap	montagne	montagnes	lac	montagnes	baie, golfe	marais salé
PORTUGUÊS	cabo	montanha	montanhas	lago	montanhas	baía, golfo	pântano salgado

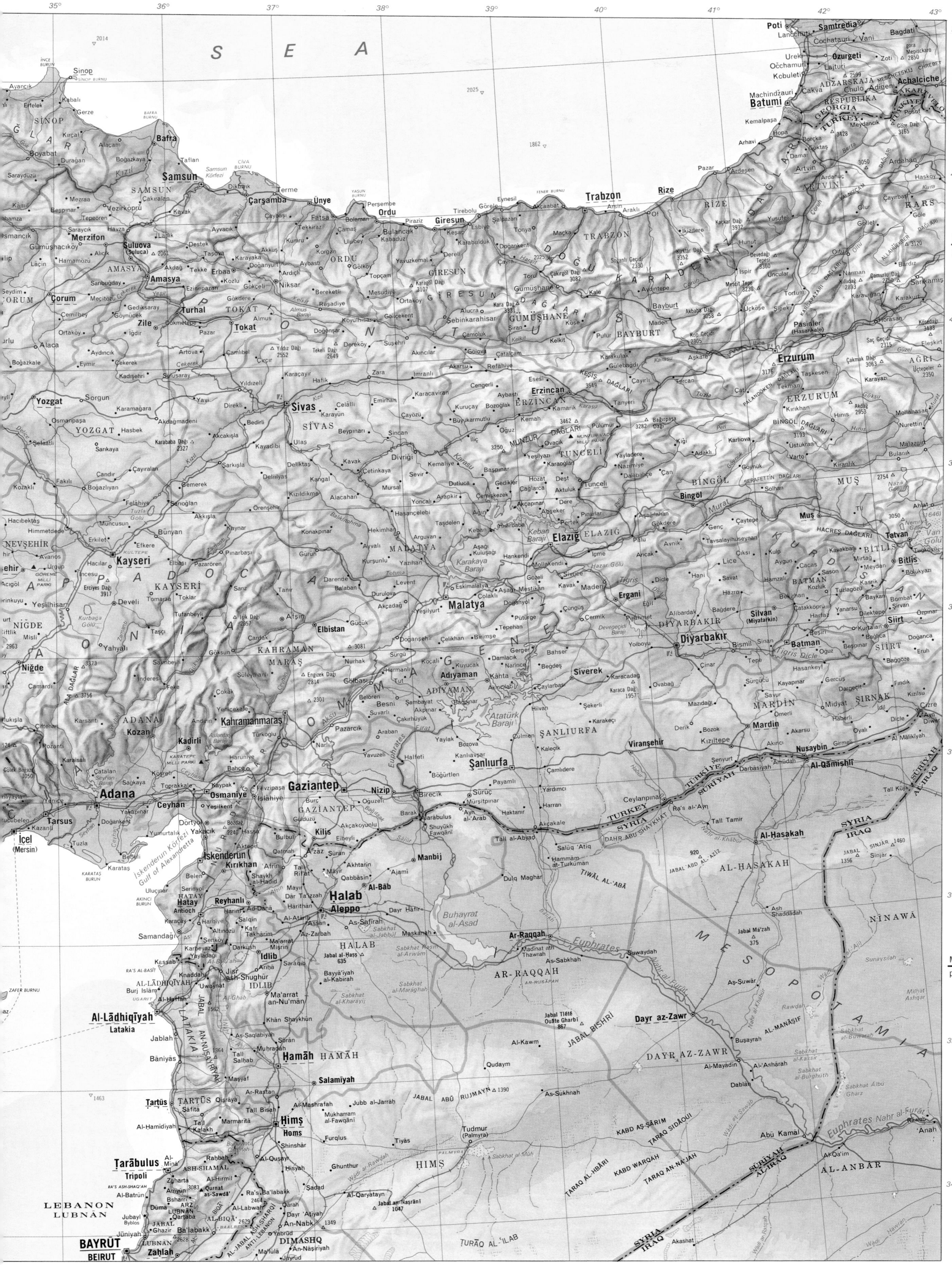
SEA
Sinop
Samsun
Bafra
Ordu
Giresun
Trabzon
Rize
Batumi
Poti
Ozurgeti
Achalciche
Artvin
Ardahan
KARS
Erzurum
Erzincan
Bayburt
Gümüşhane
Tokat
Amasya
Çorum
Merzifon
Turhal
Zile
Yozgat
Sivas
Kayseri
Malatya
Elazığ
Tunceli
Bingöl
Muş
Tatvan
Bitlis
Siirt
Batman
Diyarbakır
Ergani
Siverek
Adıyaman
Kahramanmaraş
Gaziantep
Şanlıurfa
Mardin
Nusaybin
Viranşehir
Kilis
Adana
Osmaniye
Ceyhan
Kozan
Kadirli
Tarsus
İçel
(Mersin)
Niğde
İskenderun
Hatay
Antioch
Reyhanlı
Halab
Aleppo
Idlib
Al-Lādhiqīyah
Latakia
Ḥamāh
Salamīyah
Ḥimṣ
Homs
Ṭarṭūs
Ṭarābulus
Tripoli
BAYRŪT
BEIRUT
Zaḥlah
DIMASHQ
Tudmur
(Palmyra)
Ar-Raqqah
Dayr az-Zawr
Al-Ḥasakah
Al-Qāmishlī
Abū Kamāl
LEBANON
LUBNĀN
SYRIA
TURKEY
IRAQ
MESOPOTAMIA
Euphrates
Tigris
Atatürk Barajı
Buhayrat al-Asad

Map continues page 84

Map continues pages 128-129

Kilometers 0 50 100 150 Km.
Statute Miles 0 50 100 150 Mi.

Scale 1:3,000,000

One centimeter represents 30 kilometers.
One inch represents approximately 47 miles.
Conic Projection, Two Standard Parallels

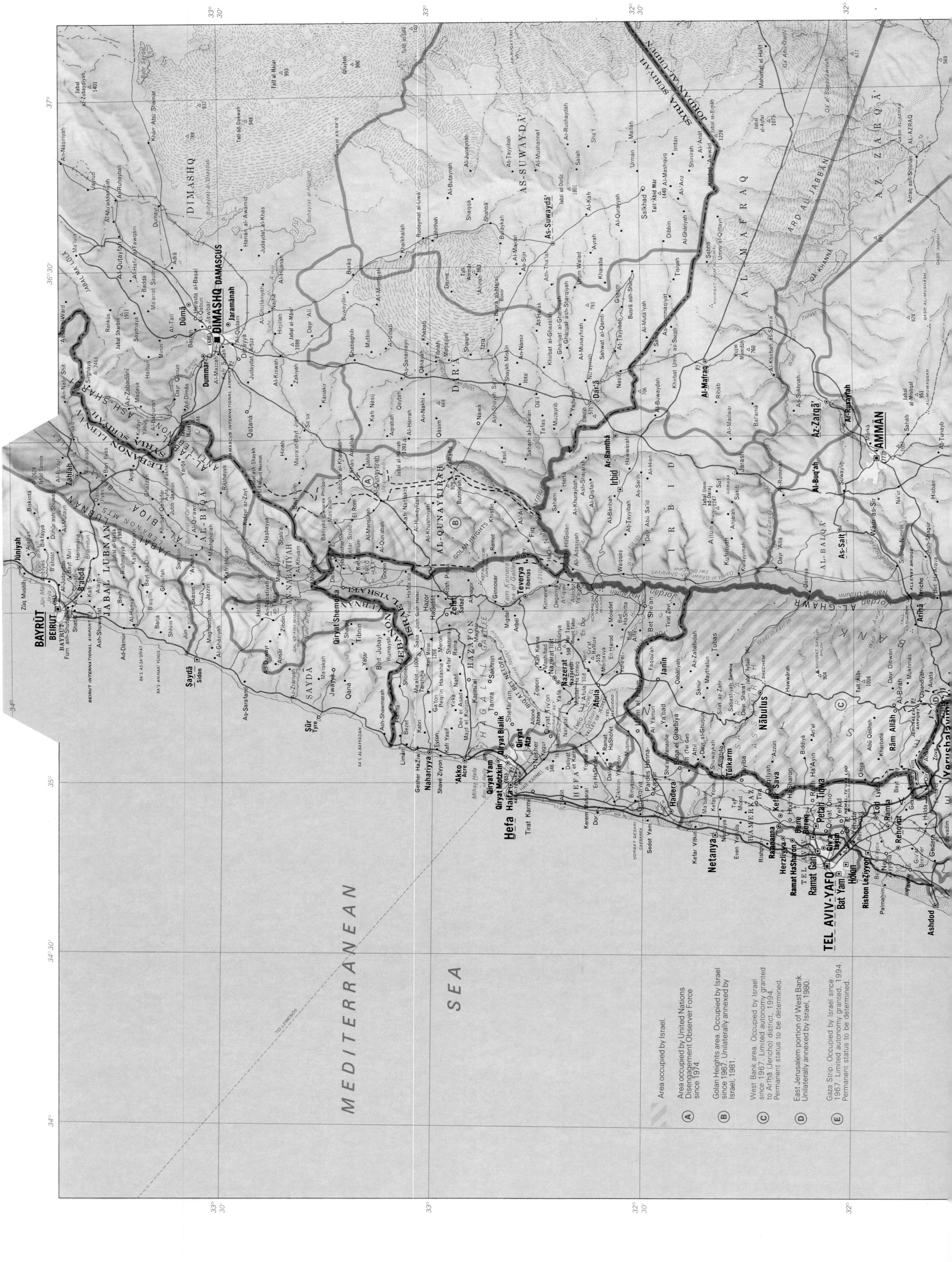
MEDITERRANEAN SEA
DIMASHQ DAMASCUS
BAYRŪT BEIRUT
TEL AVIV-YAFO
'AMMĀN
Area occupied by Israel.
(A) Area occupied by United Nations Disengagement Observer Force since 1974.
(B) Golan Heights area. Occupied by Israel since 1967. Unilaterally annexed by Israel, 1981.
(C) West Bank area. Occupied by Israel since 1967. Limited autonomy granted to Arīḥā (Jericho) district, 1994. Permanent status to be determined.
(D) East Jerusalem portion of West Bank. Unilaterally annexed by Israel, 1980.
(E) Gaza Strip. Occupied by Israel since 1967. Limited autonomy granted, 1994. Permanent status to be determined.

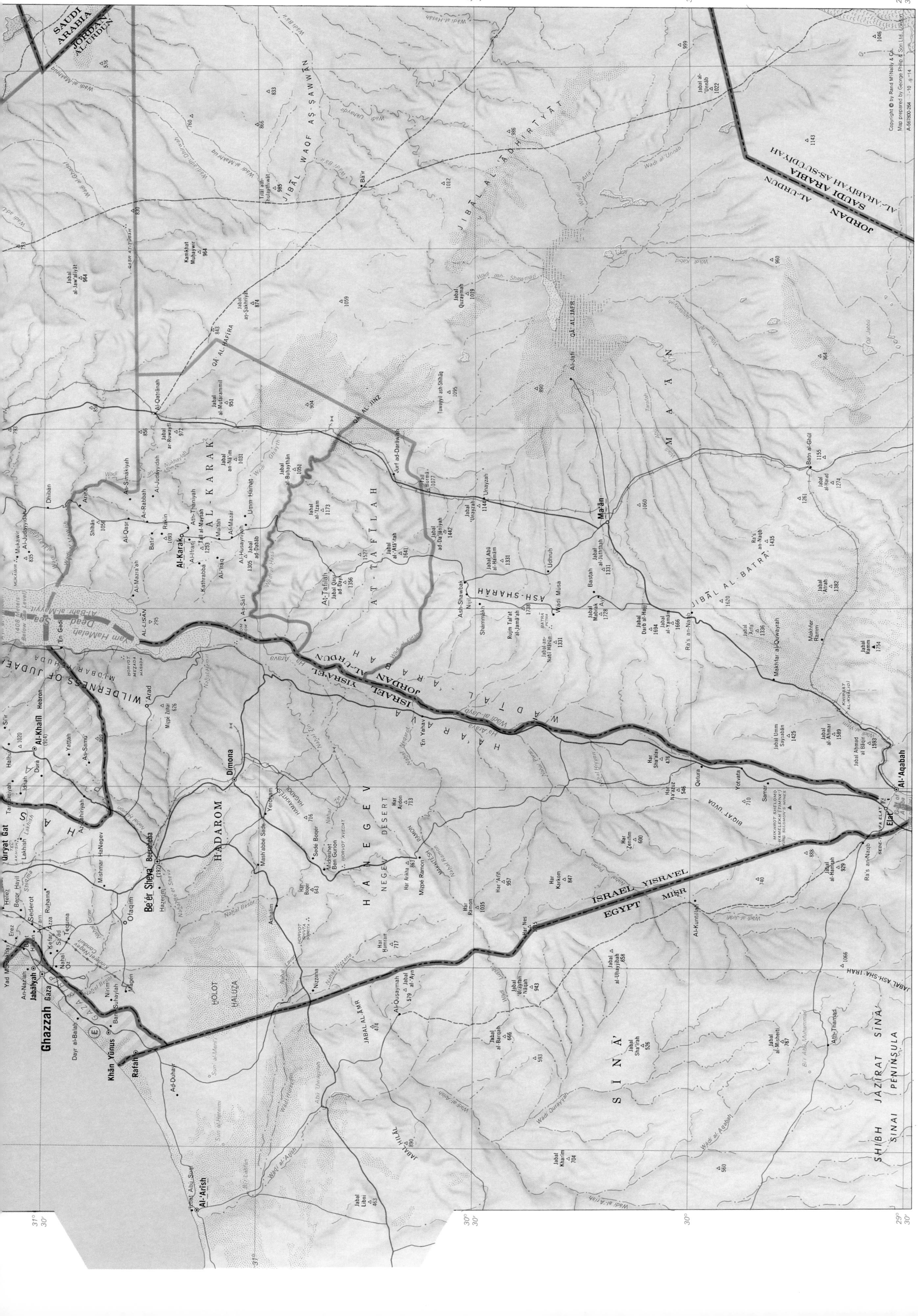
Copyright © by Rand McNally & Co.
Map prepared by George Philip & Son Ltd., London.

MAP FORM	har	jabal	nahr	ra's	sede-te'ufa	tall	wadi
ENGLISH	mountain	mountain(s)	river	cape	airport	mountain	wadi
DEUTSCH	Berg	Berg(e)	Fluss	Kap	Flughafen	Berg	Wadi
ESPAÑOL	montaña	montaña(s)	río	cabo	aeropuerto	montaña	uadi
FRANÇAIS	montagne	montagne(s)	rivière	cap	aéroport	montagne	wadi
PORTUGUÊS	montanha	montanha(s)	rio	cabo	aeroporto	montanha	uadi

Kilometers 0 10 20 30 40 50 Km.

Statute Miles 0 10 20 30 40 50 Mi.

Scale 1:1,000,000

One centimeter represents 10 kilometers.
One inch represents approximately 16 miles.

Lambert Conformal Conic Projection

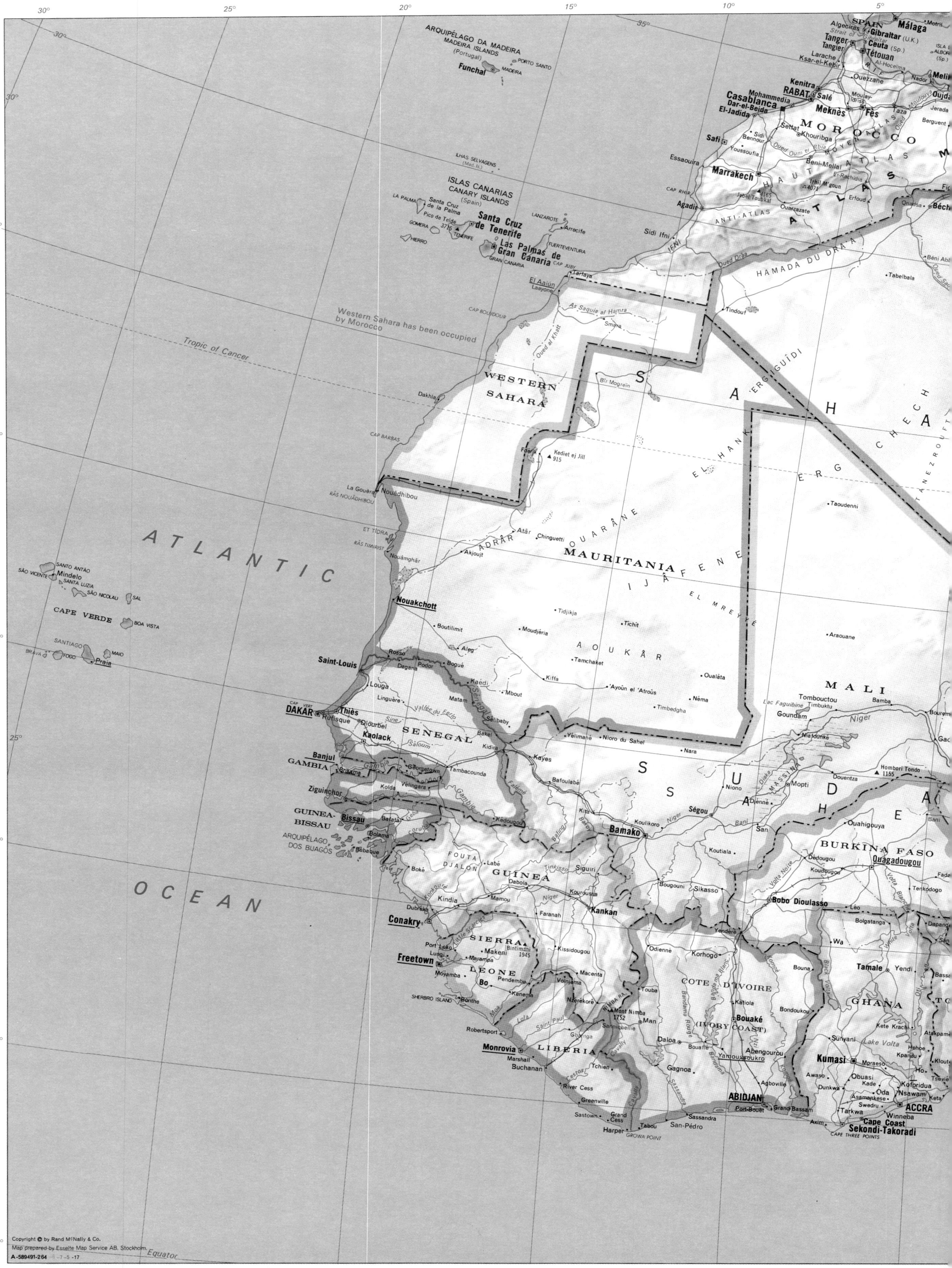
ATLANTIC
OCEAN
ARQUIPÉLAGO DA MADEIRA
MADEIRA ISLANDS
(Portugal)
Funchal
PORTO SANTO
ISLAS CANARIAS
CANARY ISLANDS
(Spain)
Santa Cruz de Tenerife
Las Palmas de Gran Canaria
LANZAROTE
Arrecife
FUERTEVENTURA
GRAN CANARIA
TENERIFE
LA PALMA
GOMERA
HIERRO
ILHAS SELVAGENS
MOROCCO
SPAIN
Málaga
Gibraltar (U.K.)
Tanger
Ceuta (Sp.)
Tétouan
Larache
Ksar-el-Kebir
Kenitra
RABAT
Salé
Casablanca
Dar-el-Beida
Mohammedia
El-Jadida
Meknès
Fès
Safi
Essaouira
Marrakech
Agadir
Sidi Ifni
Oujda
HAUT ATLAS
ANTI-ATLAS
HAMADA DU DRA'A
Tarfaya
El Aaiún
Laayoune
Tindouf
Western Sahara has been occupied by Morocco
Tropic of Cancer
WESTERN SAHARA
Dakhla
Smara
Bir Mogreïn
CAP BOJADOR
CAP BARBAS
La Gouéra
Nouadhibou
RÂS NOUÂDHIBOU
MAURITANIA
ADRÂR
Atâr
Chinguetti
Akjoujt
Nouâmghâr
Nouakchott
Boutilimit
Tidjikja
Tîchît
Moudjéria
Aleg
Kiffa
Tamchakett
Oualâta
Néma
Timbedgha
'Ayoûn el 'Atroûs
AOUKÂR
IJÂFENE
OUARÂNE
EL MREYYÉ
ERG IGUÎDI
ERG CHECH
EL HANK
Taoudenni
Kediet ej Jill 915
SAHARA
CAPE VERDE
SANTO ANTÃO
SÃO VICENTE
Mindelo
SANTA LUZIA
SÃO NICOLAU
SAL
BOA VISTA
SANTIAGO
MAIO
FOGO
BRAVA
Praia
Saint-Louis
Rosso
Podor
Dagana
Bogué
Louga
Linguère
Matam
Kaédi
Mbout
SENEGAL
DAKAR
Thiès
Rufisque
Diourbel
Kaolack
Banjul
GAMBIA
Georgetown
Tambacounda
Kolda
Vélingara
Ziguinchor
Sélibaby
Bakel
Kayes
Kidira
Nioro du Sahel
Yélimané
Nara
MALI
Tombouctou
Timbuktu
Goundam
Bamba
Niger
Araouane
Hombori Tondo 1155
Douentza
Mopti
Djenné
Ségou
San
Bamako
Koulikoro
Koutiala
Sikasso
Bougouni
Kita
Bafoulabé
Kéniéba
Kédougou
SUDAN
GUINEA-BISSAU
Bissau
Bafatá
Bolama
ARQUIPÉLAGO DOS BIJAGÓS
Bubaque
GUINEA
FOUTA DJALON
Labé
Boké
Dabola
Mamou
Kindia
Kouroussa
Kankan
Siguiri
Faranah
Dubréka
Conakry
Kissidougou
Macenta
Nzérékoré
SIERRA LEONE
Freetown
Port Loko
Lunsar
Makeni
Magburaka
Moyamba
Bo
Pendembu
Kenema
SHERBRO ISLAND
Bonthe
Bintimani 1945
Mont Nimba 1752
LIBERIA
Robertsport
Monrovia
Marshall
Buchanan
River Cess
Greenville
Sastown
Grand Cess
Harper
Tchien
Sanniquellie
Ganta
Voinjama
CÔTE D'IVOIRE
(IVORY COAST)
Odienné
Korhogo
Touba
Man
Bouaké
Daloa
Bouaflé
Yamoussoukro
Gagnoa
Abengourou
Agboville
Bondoukou
Bouna
ABIDJAN
Port-Bouët
Grand-Bassam
Sassandra
San-Pédro
Tabou
GROWA POINT
BURKINA FASO
Ouagadougou
Ouahigouya
Koudougou
Dédougou
Bobo Dioulasso
Léo
Tenkodogo
GHANA
Wa
Bolgatanga
Tamale
Yendi
Kintampo
Sunyani
Lake Volta
Kumasi
Obuasi
Koforidua
Dunkwa
Tarkwa
Swedru
Winneba
ACCRA
Cape Coast
Sekondi-Takoradi
Axim
CAPE THREE POINTS
Equator
Copyright © by Rand McNally & Co.
Map prepared by Esselte Map Service AB, Stockholm.
A-589491-264

MAP FORM	bahr, baḥr	chott	jabal	lake	mountains	oued	wahāt
ENGLISH	river, sea	salt marsh	mountain(s)	lake	mountains	wadi	oasis
DEUTSCH	Fluss, Meer	Salzmarsch	Berg(e)	See	Berge	Wadi	Oase
ESPAÑOL	río, mar	pantano salado	montaña(s)	lago	montañas	uadi	oasis
FRANÇAIS	rivière, mer	marais salé	montagne(s)	lac	montagnes	wadi	oasis
PORTUGUÊS	rio, mar	pântano salgado	montanha(s)	lago	montanhas	uādi	oásis

Map continues
pages 22-23

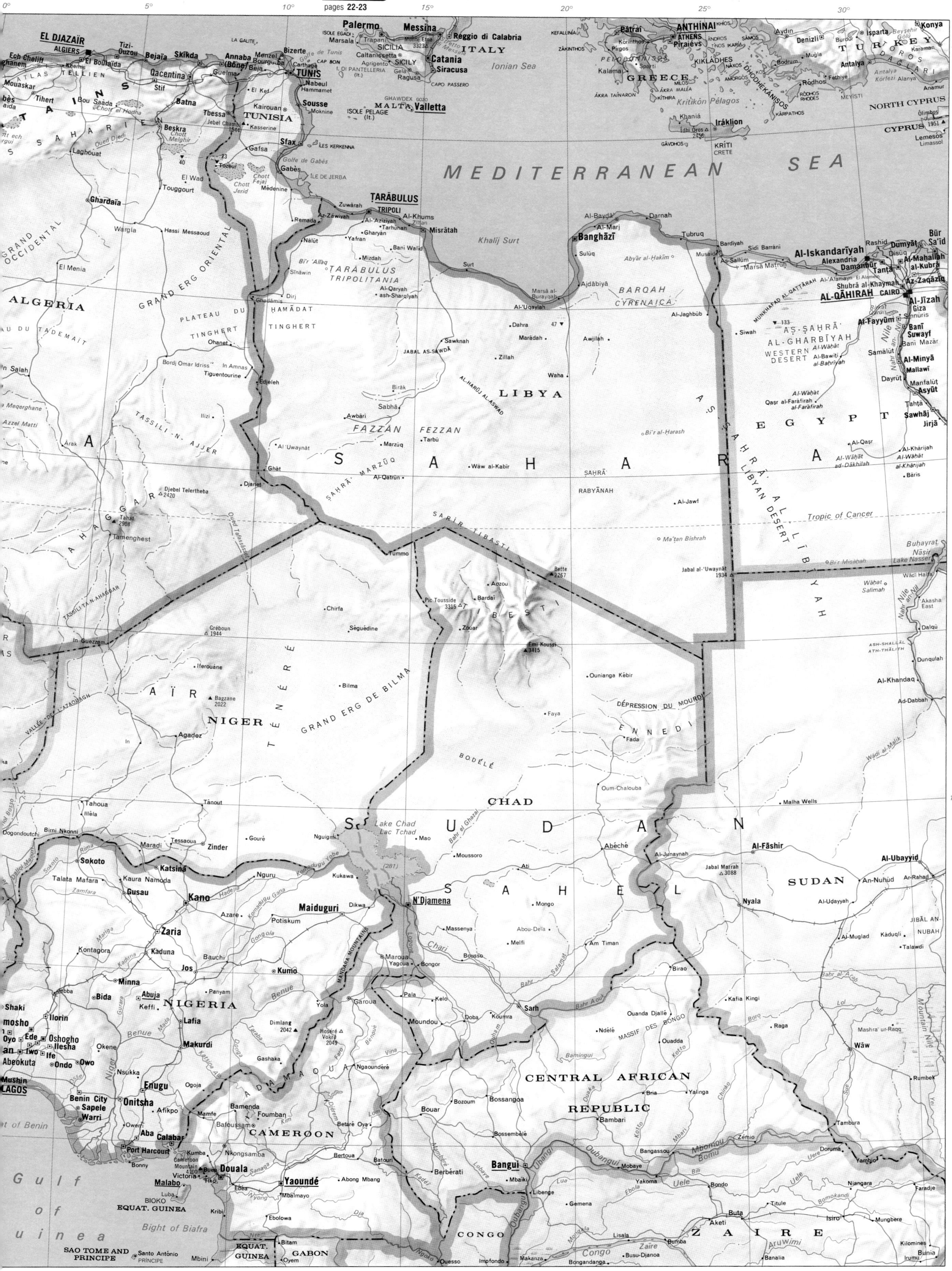
MEDITERRANEAN SEA
ALGERIA
EL DJAZAÏR
ALGIERS
TUNISIA
TUNIS
LIBYA
ṬARĀBULUS
TRIPOLI
Banghāzī
EGYPT
AL-QĀHIRAH
CAIRO
Al-Iskandarīyah
Alexandria
NIGER
CHAD
N'Djamena
SUDAN
NIGERIA
LAGOS
CAMEROON
Yaoundé
Douala
CENTRAL AFRICAN REPUBLIC
Bangui
CONGO
ZAIRE
GABON
EQUAT. GUINEA
Malabo
SAO TOME AND PRINCIPE
ITALY
SICILIA
SICILY
Palermo
Messina
Catania
Siracusa
Ionian Sea
MALTA
Valletta
GREECE
ATHINAI
ATHENS
KRITI
CRETE
TURKEY
CYPRUS
NORTH CYPRUS
Lake Chad
Lac Tchad
SAHARA
SAHEL
SUDAN
AÏR
TÉNÉRÉ
TIBESTI
ENNEDI
AHAGGAR
TASSILI-N-AJJER
GRAND ERG ORIENTAL
GRAND ERG OCCIDENTAL
GRAND ERG DE BILMA
FEZZAN
BARQAH
CYRENAICA
AL-GHARBĪYAH
WESTERN DESERT
LIBYAN DESERT
Tropic of Cancer
Gulf of Guinea
Bight of Biafra
Lake Nasser
Nile
Benue
Niger
Congo
Oubangui
Uele
Khalīj Surt
Golfe de Gabès
Kano
Maiduguri
Zaria
Sokoto
Ibadan
Benin City
Port Harcourt
Enugu
Agadez
Zinder
Tahat 2908
Emi Koussi 3415
Pic Toussidé 3315
Sabhā
Ghadāmis
Misrātah
Ghardaïa
Touggourt
Biskra
Constantine
Annaba
Sfax
Gabès
Jos
Abuja
Makurdi
Garoua
Ngaoundéré
Sarh
Abéché
Al-Fāshir
Al-Ubayyid
Nyala
Berbérati
Bambari
Bossangoa
Faya
Bilma
Tummo
Jabal Marrah 3088
Siwah
Asyūṭ
Al-Minyā
Al-Fayyūm

Map continues
pages 136-137

Map continues
pages 138-139

Kilometers 0 200 400 600 Km.
Statute Miles 0 200 400 600 Mi.

Scale 1:12,000,000

One centimeter represents 120 kilometers.
One inch represents approximately 190 miles.
Miller Oblated Stereographic Projection

Map continues pages 22-23

MEDITERRANEAN SEA
ALGERIA
LIBYA
EGYPT
TUNISIA
NIGER
CHAD
SUDAN
NIGERIA
CAMEROON
CENTRAL AFRICAN REPUBLIC
ZAIRE
CONGO
GABON
EQUAT. GUINEA
SAO TOME AND PRINCIPE
MALI
BENIN
ITALY
GREECE
TURKEY
MALTA
CYPRUS
SAHARA
SAHEL
ATLAS MOUNTAINS
GRAND ERG OCCIDENTAL
GRAND ERG ORIENTAL
PLATEAU DU TADEMAÏT
PLATEAU DU TINGHERT
HAMĀDAT TINGHERT
TASSILI-N-AJJER
AHAGGAR
AÏR
TÉNÉRÉ
GRAND ERG DE BILMA
TIBESTI
BODÉLÉ
ENNEDI
DÉPRESSION DU MOURDI
MASSIF DES BONGO
ADAMAOUA
FAZZAN FEZZAN
ṢAḤRĀ' MARZŪQ
TARĀBULUS TRIPOLITANIA
BARQAH CYRENAICA
AṢ-ṢAḤRĀ' AL-LĪBĪYAH LIBYAN DESERT
AṢ-ṢAḤRĀ' AL-GHARBĪYAH WESTERN DESERT
Tropic of Cancer
Gulf of Guinea
Bight of Benin
Bight of Biafra
Ionian Sea
Khalīj Surt
Lake Chad Lac Tchad
EL DJAZAÏR ALGIERS
TUNIS
ṬARĀBULUS TRIPOLI
AL-QĀHIRAH CAIRO
ATHINAI ATHENS
Valletta
LAGOS
N'Djamena
Bangui
Yaoundé
Malabo
Abuja
Palermo
Messina
Catania
Al-Iskandarīyah Alexandria
Banghāzī
Miṣrātah
Sabhā
Ghardaïa
Constantine
Kano
Maiduguri
Ibadan
Douala
Zinder
Agadez
Tamenghest
Abéché
Al-Fāshir
Nyala
Sarh
Moundou
Bambari
Bette 2267
Emi Koussi 3415
Pic Toussidé 3315
Tahat 2908
Jabal Marrah 3088
Jabal al-'Uwaynāt 1934
Cameroon Mountain 4100

Map continues pages 134-135

Map continues pages 138-139

MAP FORM	bahr, baḩr	chott	jabal	lake	mountains	oued	ra's; ras	wāḩāt
ENGLISH	river, sea	salt marsh	mountain(s)	lake	mountains	wadi	cape	oasis
DEUTSCH	Fluss, Meer	Salzmarsch	Berg(e)	See	Berge	Wadi	Kap	Oase
ESPAÑOL	rio, mar	pantano salado	montaña(s)	lago	montañas	uadi	cabo	oasis
FRANÇAIS	rivière, mer	marais salé	montagne(s)	lac	montagnes	oued	cap	oasis
PORTUGUÊS	rio, mar	pântano salgado	montanha(s)	lago	montanhas	uádi	cabo	oásis

SAUDI ARABIA
AR-RIYĀD
RIYADH
AR · RUB' · AL · KHĀLĪ
AN-NAFŪD
NAJD
AD · DAHNĀ'
IRAN
IRAQ
BAGHDĀD
KUWAIT
AL-KUWAYT
SYRIA
JORDAN
AMMAN
DIMASHQ
DAMASCUS
QATAR
BAHRAIN
UNITED ARAB EMIRATES
OMAN
YEMEN
Ṣan'ā'
'Adan
Aden
ERITREA
Asmera
DJIBOUTI
Djibouti
ETHIOPIA
ADIS ABEBA
ADDIS ABABA
SOMALIA
Muqdisho
Mogadishu
KENYA
UGANDA
Umm Durmān
Omdurman
AL-KHARṬŪM
KHARTOUM
Makkah Mecca
Jiddah
Jeddah
Al-Madīnah
Medina
Persian Gulf
Gulf of Oman
Gulf of Aden
RED SEA
ARABIAN SEA
INDIAN OCEAN
OGADEN
Tropic of Cancer
Equator
Dubayy
Dubai
Abū Ẓaby
Abu Dhabi
Ad-Dawḥah
Doha
Al-Manāmah
Muscat
Esfahān
Shīrāz
Yazd
Kermān
Hargeysa
Bur Sūdān
Port Sudan
Mitsiwa
Al-Mukallā
Suquṭrā Socotra
Lake Rudolf
Lake Tana
Copyright © by Rand McNally & Co.
Map prepared by Esselte Map Service AB, Stockholm.
A-589391 -264 -11-10-24

Map continues
pages 118-119

Kilometers 0 200 400 600 Km.
Statute Miles 0 200 400 600 Mi.

Scale 1:12,000,000
One centimeter represents 120 kilometers.
One inch represents approximately 190 miles.
Miller Oblated Stereographic Projection

Map continues pages 136-137

SAO TOME AND PRINCIPE
EQUATORIAL GUINEA
CAMEROON
GABON
CONGO
ZAIRE
ANGOLA
NAMIBIA
BOTSWANA
ZAMBIA
ZIMBABWE
SOUTH AFRICA
LESOTHO
RWANDA
BURUNDI
ATLANTIC OCEAN
Tropic of Capricorn
KALAHARI DESERT
NAMIB DESERT
CAPRIVI ZIPFEL
OKAVANGO DELTA
KATANGA
OVAMBOLAND
DAMARALAND
GREAT NAMAQUALAND
BUSHMAN LAND
GREAT KARROO
LITTLE KARROO
Libreville
Port Gentil
Brazzaville
KINSHASA (LÉOPOLDVILLE)
Pointe-Noire
LUANDA
Lobito
Benguela
Huambo (Nova Lisboa)
Windhoek
Walvis Bay
Swakopmund
Lüderitz
Kisangani (Stanleyville)
Mbandaka (Coquilhatville)
Kananga (Luluabourg)
Mbuji-Mayi (Bakwanga)
Lubumbashi (Elisabethville)
Likasi (Jadotville)
Kolwezi
Lusaka
Livingstone
Kabwe (Broken Hill)
Ndola
Kitwe
Bulawayo
Gweru
Kigali
Bujumbura
Gaborone
PRETORIA
JOHANNESBURG
Kimberley
Bloemfontein
Durban
Pietermaritzburg
East London
Port Elizabeth
Uitenhage
CAPE TOWN KAAPSTAD
Stellenbosch
Paarl
CAPE OF GOOD HOPE
CAPE AGULHAS
Congo
Zaire
Zambezi
Cuanza
Kasai
Kunene
Okavango
Orange
Vaal
Limpopo
Lake Tanganyika
Lake Kariba
Lake Ngami
5°
10°
15°
20°
25°
30°

MAP FORM	cape	île	island	lake	mountains	plateau
ENGLISH	cape	island	island	lake	mountains	plateau
DEUTSCH	Kap	Insel	Insel	See	Berge	Hochebene
ESPAÑOL	cabo	isla	isla	lago	montañas	meseta
FRANÇAIS	cap	île	île	lac	montagnes	plateau
PORTUGUÊS	cabo	ilha	ilha	lago	montanhas	planalto

INDIAN OCEAN
INDIAN OCEAN
Equator
Tropic of Capricorn
SOMALIA
KENYA
NAIROBI
Nakuru
Kisumu
Machakos
Mombasa
Tanga
Zanzibar
DAR ES SALAAM
Dodoma
Morogoro
Arusha
Moshi
SERENGETI PLAIN
MASAI STEPPE
MAFIA ISLAND
Kilwa Kivinje
Lindi
Mtwara
CABO DELGADO
Lake Nyasa
Lake Malawi
Lilongwe
Zomba
Blantyre
MOZAMBIQUE
Nampula
Nacala
Moçambique
Pemba
Quelimane
Beira
Chinde
Inhambane
Inharrime
Mozambique Channel
COMOROS
Moroni
ARCHIPEL DES COMORES
Dzaoudzi
MAYOTTE (Fr.)
MADAGASCAR
ANTANANARIVO
Antsiranana
Mahajanga
Toamasina
Antsirabe
Fianarantsoa
Toliara
Morondava
Manakara
Farafangana
Taolanaro
Ambovombe
Faradofay
CAP SAINTE-MARIE
CAP D'AMBRE
Hell-Ville
NOSY BE
Antalaha
Sambava
Maroantsetra
SEYCHELLES
Victoria
MAHÉ ISLAND
PRASLIN ISLAND
LA DIGUE
SILHOUETTE
AMIRANTE ISLANDS (Sey.)
ÎLE DESROCHES (Sey.)
PLATTE ISLAND (Sey.)
ALPHONSE ISLAND (Sey.)
COETIVY ISLAND (Sey.)
PROVIDENCE ISLAND (Sey.)
ALDABRA ISLAND (Sey.)
COSMOLEDO I. (Sey.)
ASSUMPTION ISLAND (Sey.)
ASTOVE ISLAND (Sey.)
SAINT PIERRE ISLAND (Sey.)
CERF ISLAND (Sey.)
FARQUHAR GROUP (Sey.)
AGALEGA ISLANDS (Mauritius)
ÎLES GLORIEUSES (Fr.)
ÎLE TROMELIN (Fr.)
BASSAS DA INDIA (Fr.)
ÎLE EUROPA (Fr.)
ÎLE JUAN DE NOVA (Fr.)
MAURITIUS
Port Louis
Curepipe
Mahébourg
REUNION (Fr.)
Saint-Denis
MASCARENE ISLANDS
Copyright © by Rand McNally & Co.
Map prepared by Esselte Map Service AB, Stockholm.
A-589200-264

Kilometers 0 200 400 600 Km.

Statute Miles 0 200 400 600 Mi.

Scale 1:12,000,000

One centimeter represents 120 kilometers.

One inch represents approximately 190 miles.

Miller Oblated Stereographic Projection

Map continues
pages 128-129

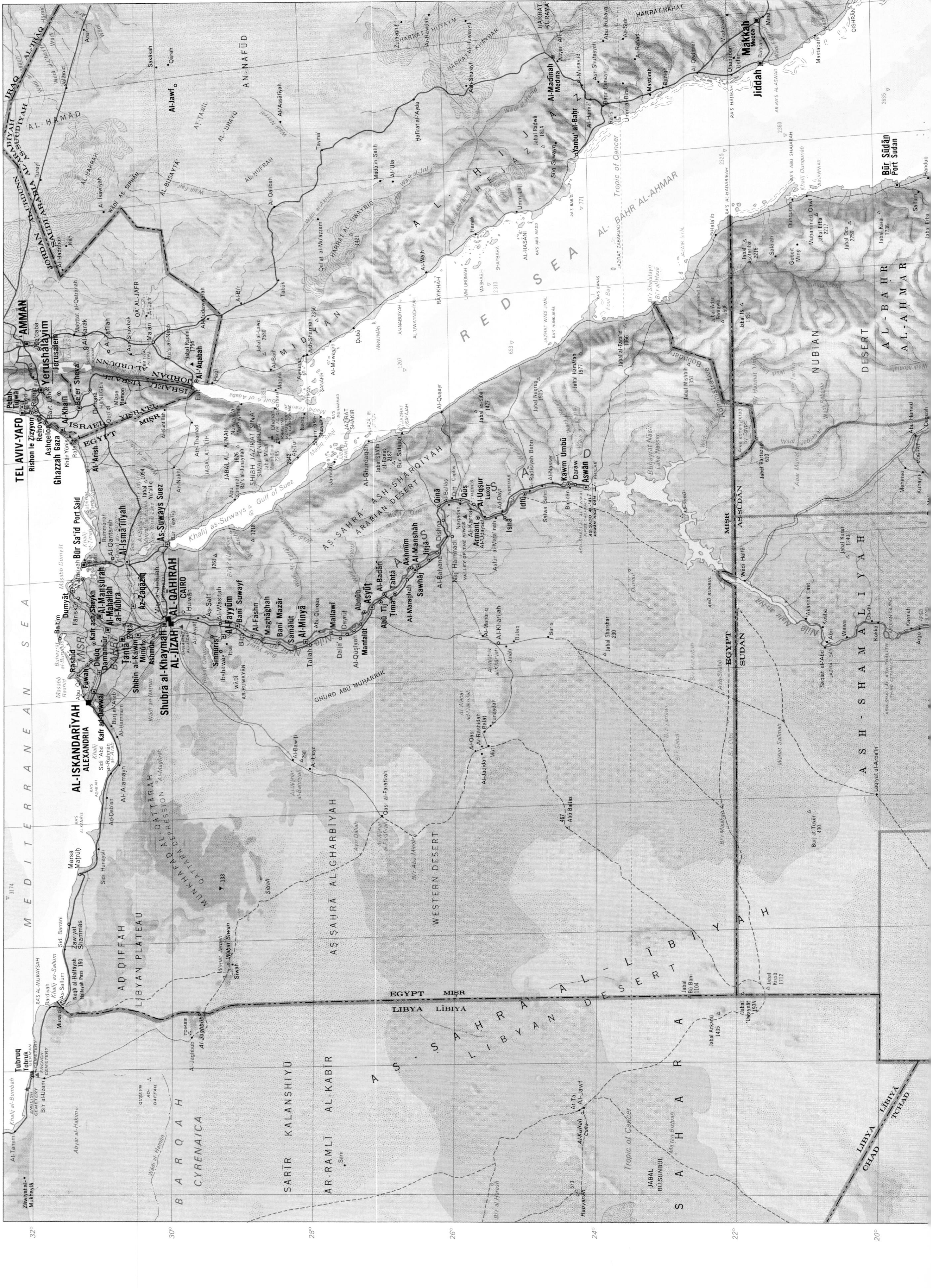
MEDITERRANEAN SEA
RED SEA
AL-BAHR AL-AHMAR
AL-ISKANDARĪYAH
ALEXANDRIA
AL-QĀHIRAH
CAIRO
AL-JĪZAH
TEL AVIV-YAFO
'AMMĀN
Yerushalayim
Makkah
Jiddah
Al-Madīnah
Medina
Aswān
Asyūṭ
Al-Minyā
Būr Sa'īd Port Said
As-Suways Suez
Al-Ismā'īlīyah
Būr Sūdān
Port Sudan
WESTERN DESERT
LIBYAN DESERT
ARABIAN DESERT
NUBIAN DESERT
LIBYAN PLATEAU
AṢ-ṢAḤRĀ' AL-LĪBĪYAH
AṢ-ṢAḤRĀ' ASH-SHARQĪYAH
CYRENAICA
BARQAH
SHIBH JAZĪRAT SĪNĀ'
SINAI PENINSULA
EGYPT
MIṢR
LIBYA
LĪBIYĀ
SUDAN
AS-SŪDĀN
ISRAEL
YISRA'EL
JORDAN
AL-URDUNN
SAUDI ARABIA
AL-'ARABĪYAH AS-SU'ŪDĪYAH
IRAQ
AL-'IRĀQ
CHAD
TCHAD
Tropic of Cancer
Gulf of Suez
Nile
Lake Nasser

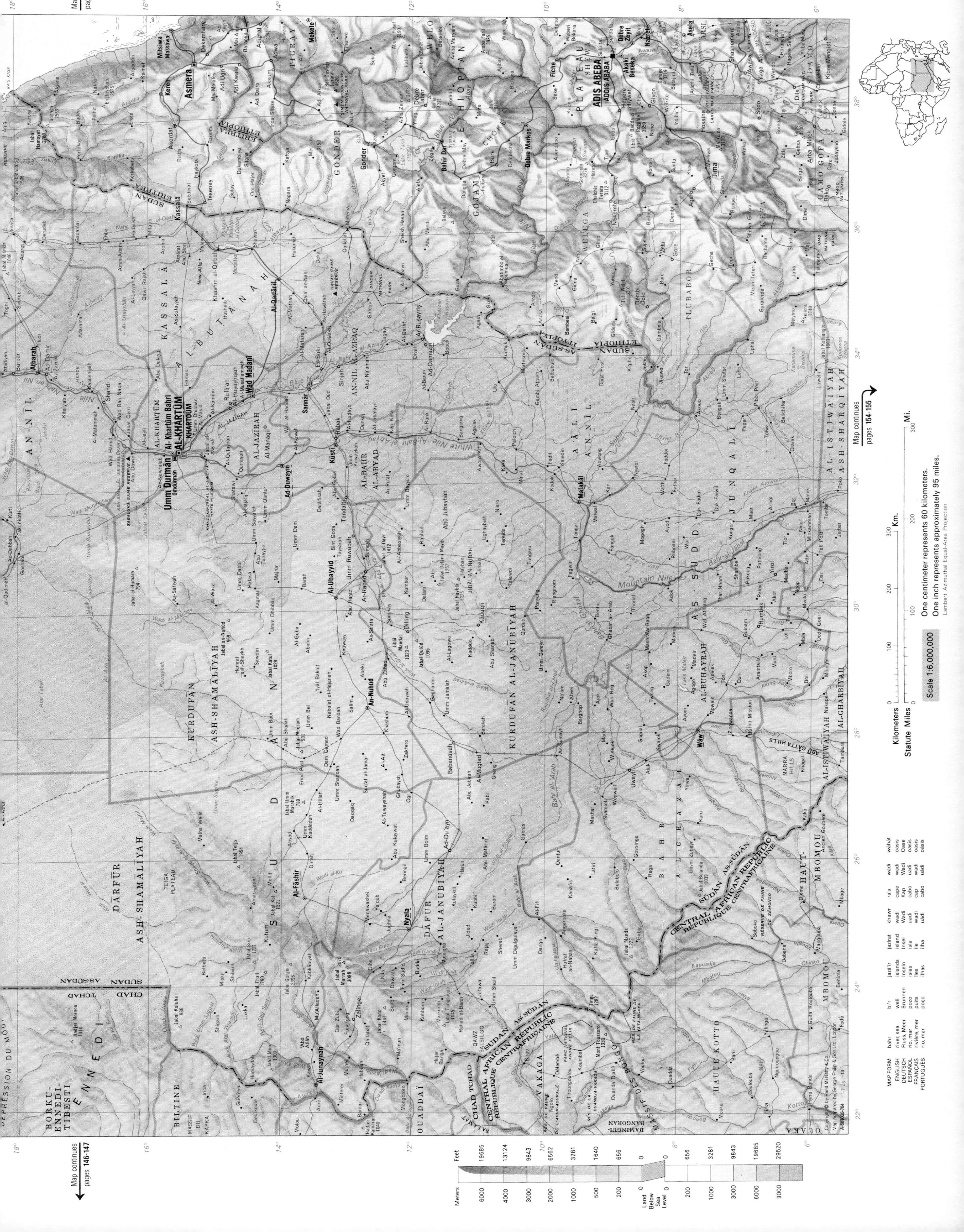
Map continues pages 144-145
Map continues pages 146-147
Map continues pages 154-155
Scale 1:6,000,000
One centimeter represents 60 kilometers.
One inch represents approximately 95 miles.
Lambert Azimuthal Equal-Area Projection
Kilometers
Statute Miles

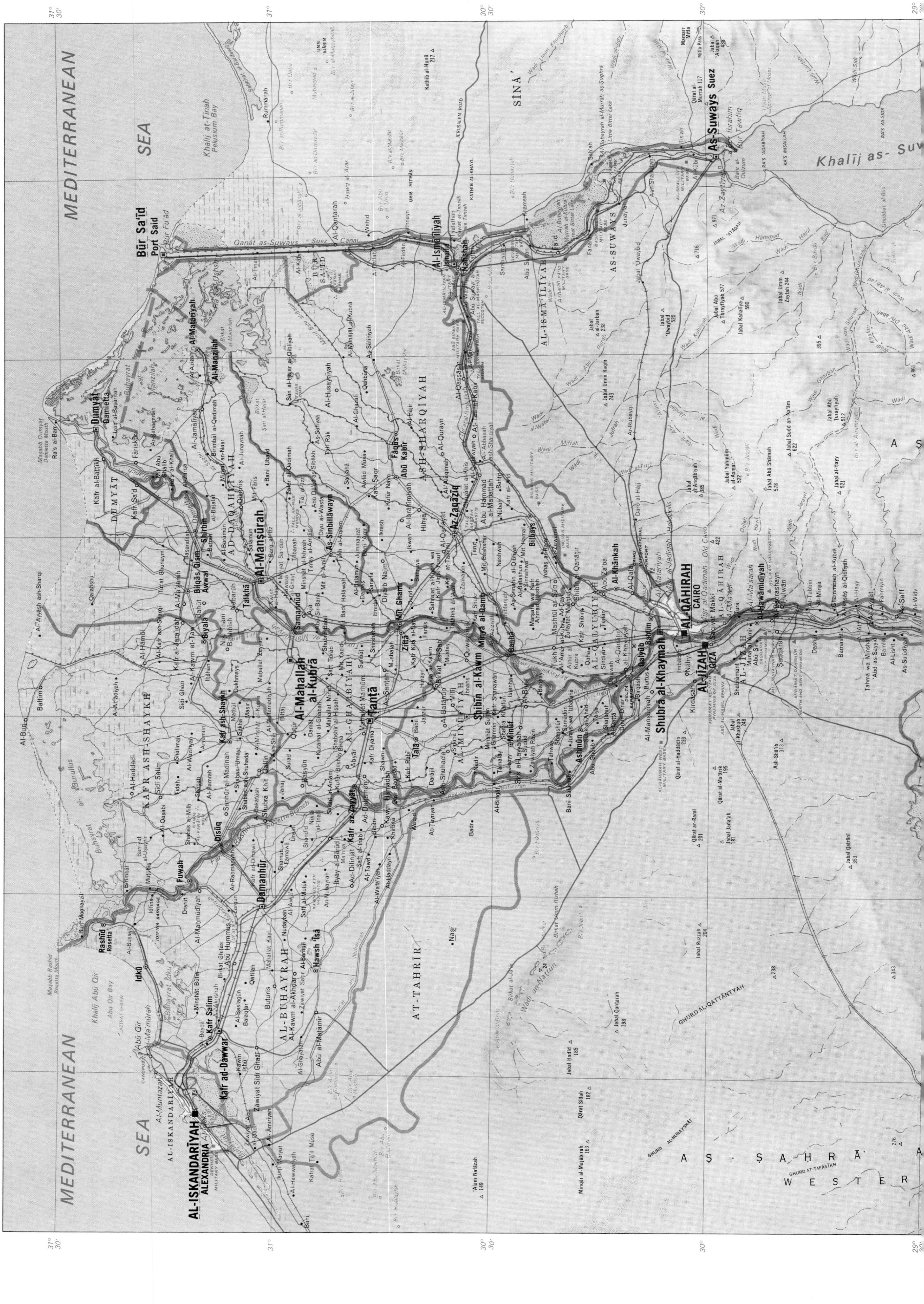
MEDITERRANEAN SEA
MEDITERRANEAN SEA
Būr Sa'īd
Port Said
Qanāt as-Suways
Suez Canal
Dumyāṭ
Damietta
Al-Manṣūrah
Al-Maḥallah al-Kubrā
Ṭanṭā
Az-Zaqāzīq
Al-Ismā'īlīyah
As-Suways
Suez
Khalīj as-Suways
SĪNĀ'
AL-QĀHIRAH
CAIRO
AL-JĪZAH
GIZA
Shubrā al-Khaymah
AL-ISKANDARĪYAH
ALEXANDRIA
Damanhūr
Rashīd
Rosetta
Kafr ad-Dawwār
Kafr ash-Shaykh
Shibīn al-Kawm
Banhā
Bilbays
Idkū
Fuwah
Disūq
AŞ-ŞAḤRĀ'
WESTER

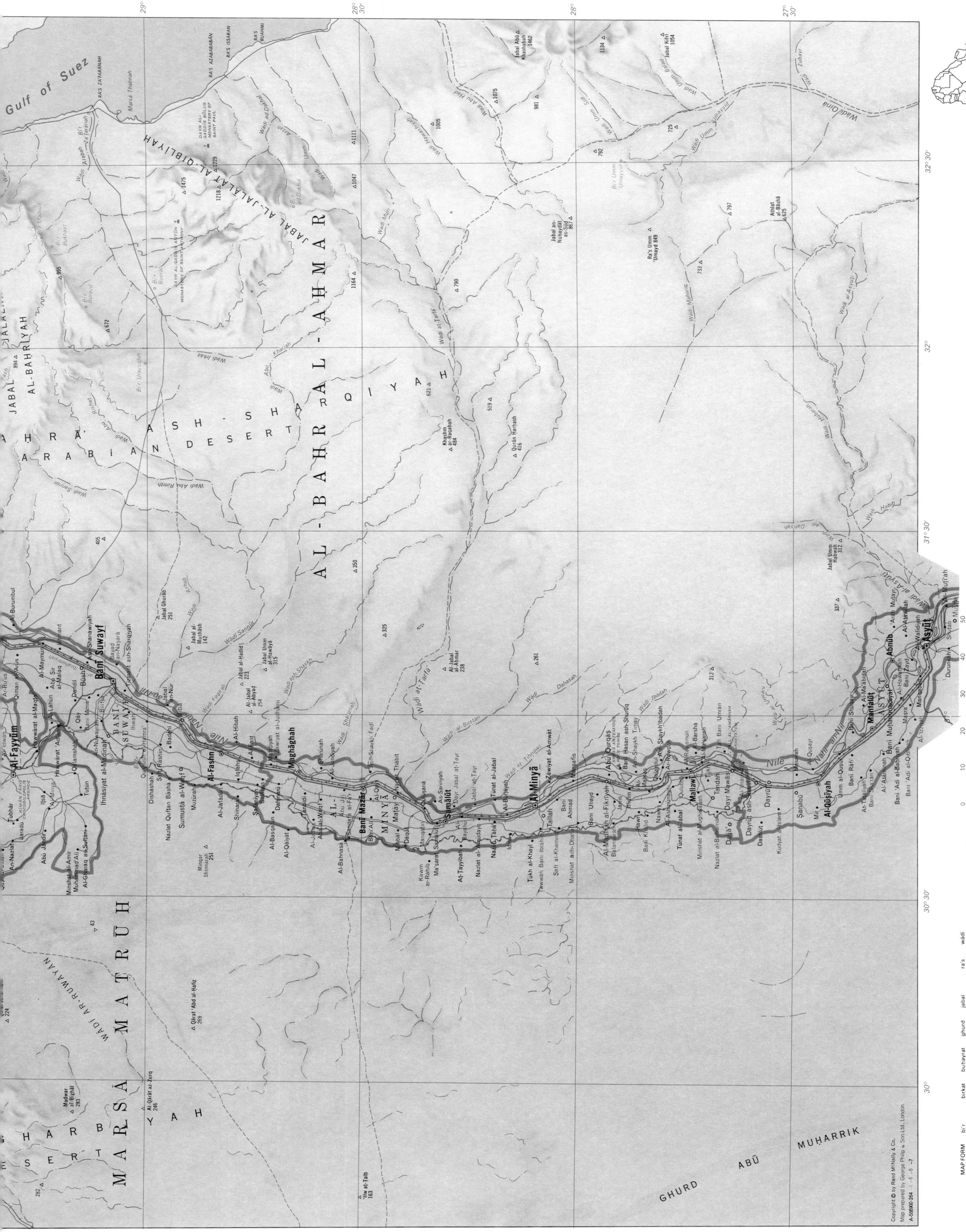
Gulf of Suez
AL-BAHR AL-AHMAR
ARABIAN DESERT
ASH-SHARQIYAH
JABAL AL-JALALAT AL-QIBLIYAH
MARSĀ MATRŪH
GHURD ABŪ MUHARRIK
Nile
Al-Fayyūm
Banī Suwayf
Al-Fashn
Maghāghah
Banī Mazār
Samālūt
Al-Minyā
Abū Qurqāş
Mallawī
Dayrūţ
Al-Qūşīyah
Manfalūţ
Abnūb
Asyūţ
Kilometers
Statute Miles
Scale 1:1,000,000
One centimeter represents 10 kilometers.
One inch represents approximately 16 miles.
Lambert Conformal Conic Projection
MAP FORM bi'r birkat buhayrat ghurd jabal ra's wādī
ENGLISH well lake lake dunes mountain cape wadi
DEUTSCH Brunnen See See Dünen Berg Kap Wadi
ESPAÑOL pozo lago lago dunas montaña cabo uadi
FRANÇAIS puits lac lac dunes montagne cap wadi
PORTUGUÊS poço lago lago dunas montanha cabo uadi
Copyright © by Rand McNally & Co.
Map prepared by George Philip & Son Ltd. London.

RED SEA
AL-BAHR AL-AHMAR
Gulf of Aden
AR-RUB' AL-KHALI
Makkah
Mecca
Jiddah
Jeddah
Şan'ā'
'Adan
Aden
Asmera
Djibouti
Bûr Sûdân
Port Sudan
Al-Ḥudaydah
Al-Mukallā
Ta'izz
Berbera
Gonder
Mekele
Dese
Kassalā
Wad Madani
Atbarah

Map continues pages 128-129

Map continues pages 140-141

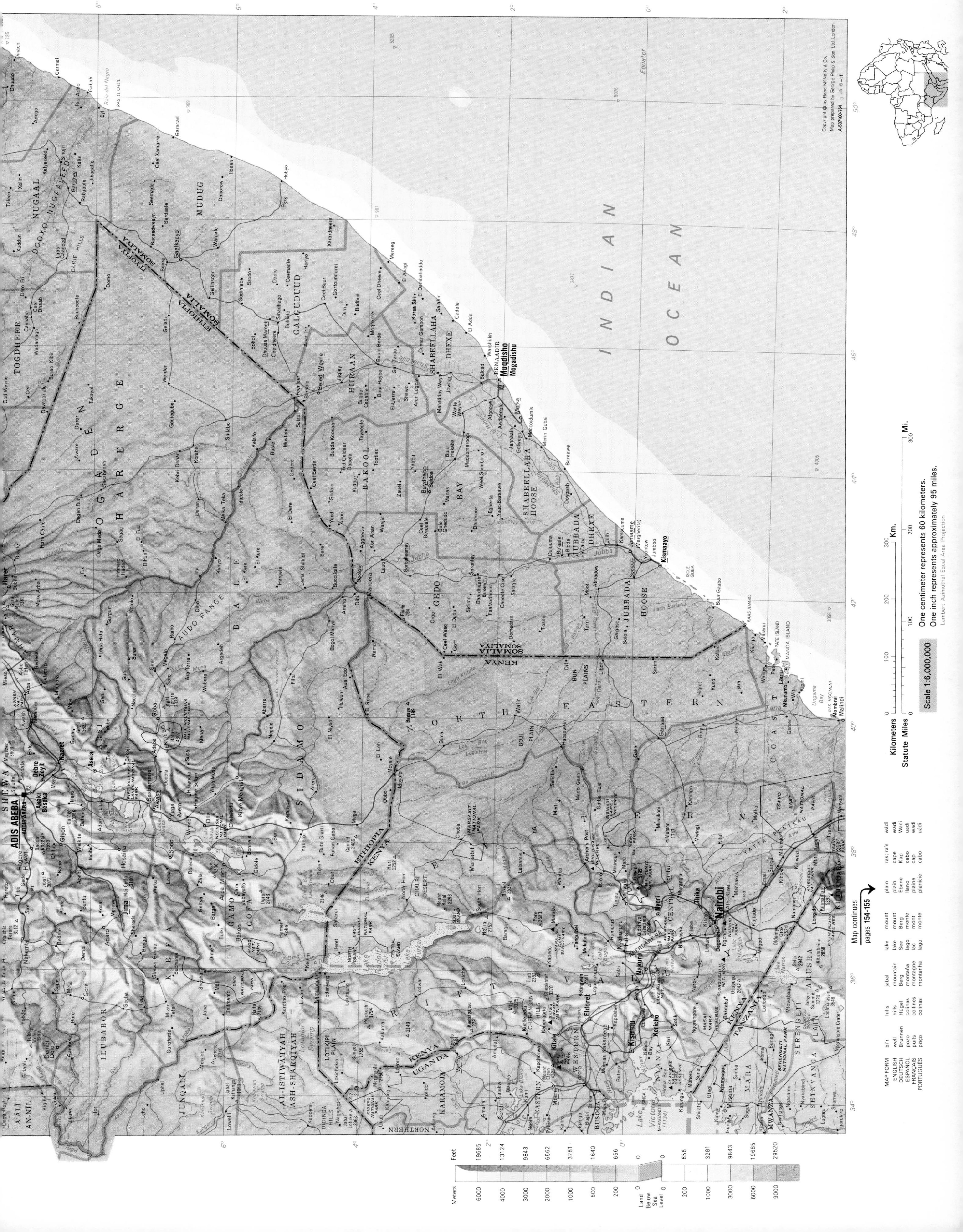
INDIAN OCEAN
ETHIOPIA
SOMALIA
KENYA
TANZANIA
UGANDA
Mogadishu
Muqdisho
Kismaayo
Nairobi
ADIS ABEBA
OGADEN
HARERGE
BALE
SIDAMO
GAMO GOFA
KEFA
ILUBABOR
SHEWA
ARSI
MUDUG
GALGUDUUD
HIIRAAN
BAKOOL
BAY
GEDO
NORTHEASTERN
COAST
RIFT VALLEY
Lake Rudolf (Lake Turkana)
Equator
Copyright © by Rand McNally & Co.
Map prepared by George Philip & Son Ltd, London.
Scale 1:6,000,000
One centimeter represents 60 kilometers.
One inch represents approximately 95 miles.
Lambert Azimuthal Equal-Area Projection
Kilometers
Statute Miles
Map continues pages 154-155
MAP FORM
ENGLISH
DEUTSCH
ESPAÑOL
FRANÇAIS
PORTUGUÊS
Feet
Meters
Land Below Sea Level

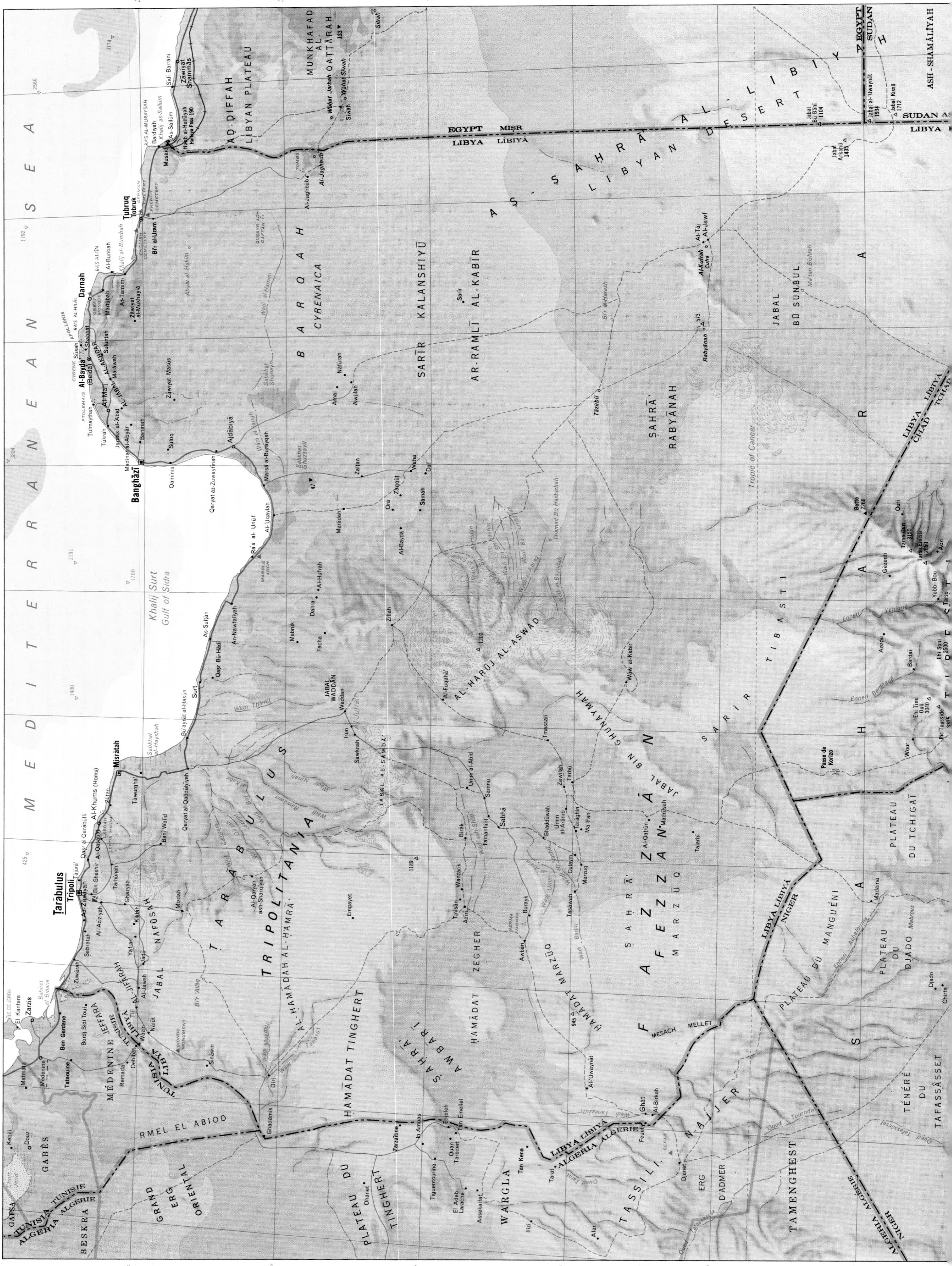
MEDITERRANEAN SEA
Khalij Surt
Gulf of Sidra
Ṭarābulus
Tripoli
Misratah
Banghāzī
Darnah
Ṭubruq
Tobruk
Surt
Ajdābiyā
Al-Bayḍā'
As-Sallūm
Sīdī Barrānī
Bardīyah
Al-Jaghbūb
Sabhā
Marzūq
Ghāt
Ghadāmis
Waddān
Hūn
Awjilah
Zalṭan
Al-Kufrah
Zarzis
Medenine
Tataouine
Ben Gardane
Matmata
Kebili
Douz
Djanet
Illizi
Tamenghest
Bardaï
Aozou
Djado
Madama
Chirfa
BARQAH
CYRENAICA
ṬARĀBULUS
TRIPOLITANIA
FEZZAN
AL-HARŪJ AL-ASWAD
JABAL NAFŪSAH
AL-ḤAMĀDAH AL-ḤAMRĀ'
ḤAMĀDAT TINGHERT
ḤAMĀDAT ZEGHER
ḤAMĀDAT MARZŪQ
ṢAḤRĀ' AWBĀRĪ
ṢAḤRĀ' MARZŪQ
SARĪR KALANSHIYŪ
SARĪR TIBASTI
AR-RAMLĪ AL-KABĪR
AS-ṢAḤRĀ' AL-LĪBĪYAH
LIBYAN DESERT
LIBYAN PLATEAU
AD-DIFFAH
MUNKHAFAḌ AL-QAṬṬĀRAH
ṢAḤRĀ' RABYĀNAH
JABAL BŪ SUNBUL
JABAL BIN GHUNAYMAH
TASSILI N-AJJER
GRAND ERG ORIENTAL
RMEL EL ABIOD
PLATEAU DU TINGHERT
PLATEAU DU DJADO
PLATEAU DU MANGUÉNI
PLATEAU DU TCHIGAÏ
TÉNÉRÉ DU TAFASSÂSSET
MESACH MELLET
ERG D'ADMER
JEFFARA
GABÈS
BESKRA
WARGLA
SAHARA
Tropic of Cancer
EGYPT MIṢR
LIBYA LĪBIYĀ
SUDAN
CHAD TCHAD
NIGER
ALGERIA ALGÉRIE
TUNISIA TUNISIE

Map continues pages 148-149

Map continues pages 140-141

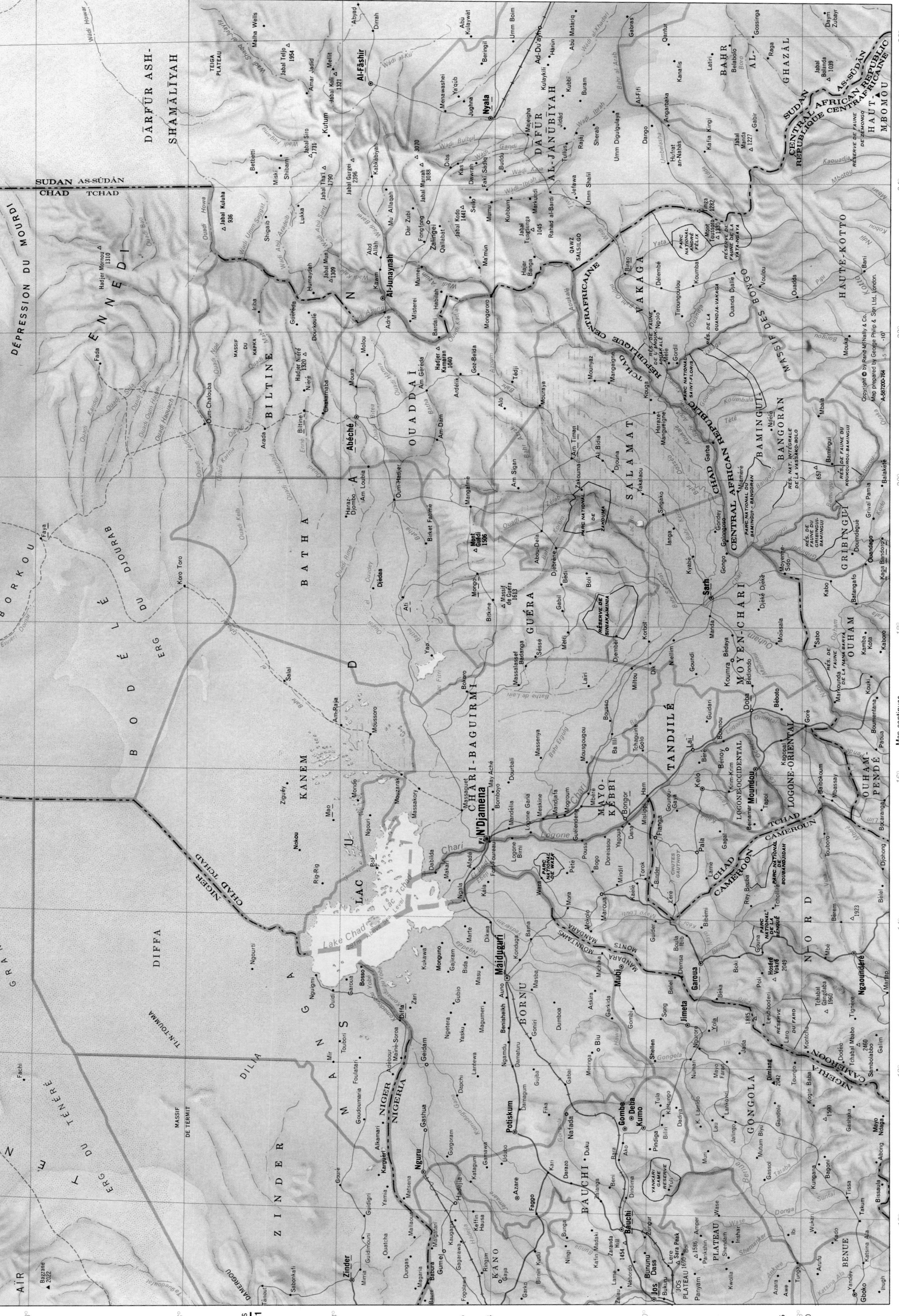
SUDAN AS-SŪDĀN
CHAD TCHAD
DĀRFŪR ASH-SHAMĀLĪYAH
DĀRFŪR AL-JANŪBĪYAH
BORKOU-ENNEDI-TIBESTI
DÉPRESSION DU MOURDI
ENNEDI
BILTINE
OUADDAÏ
BATHA
BODÉLÉ
ERG DU DJOURAB
KANEM
LAC
CHARI-BAGUIRMI
GUÉRA
SALAMAT
MOYEN-CHARI
TANDJILÉ
MAYO-KÉBBI
LOGONE OCCIDENTAL
LOGONE ORIENTAL
CENTRAL AFRICAN REPUBLIC
RÉPUBLIQUE CENTRAFRICAINE
VAKAGA
BAMINGUI-BANGORAN
HAUTE-KOTTO
OUHAM
OUHAM-PENDÉ
GRIBINGUI
MASSIF DES BONGO
BAHR AL-GHAZĀL
HAUT-MBOMOU
NIGER
NIGERIA
CAMEROON
CAMEROUN
DIFFA
ZINDER
MANGA
KAOUAR
GRAND ERG DE BILMA
ERG DU TÉNÉRÉ
AÏR
BORNU
BAUCHI
GONGOLA
BENUE
PLATEAU
NORD
KANO
Lake Chad
N'Djamena
Abéché
Al-Fāshir
Nyala
Sarh
Moundou
Maiduguri
Zinder
Faya

Kilometers 0 100 200 300 Km.
Statute Miles 0 100 200 300 Mi.

Scale 1:6,000,000
One centimeter represents 60 kilometers.
One inch represents approximately 95 miles.
Lambert Azimuthal Equal-Area Projection

Map continues pages 152-153

MAP FORM	bahr	hadjer	jabal	massif	ouadi	ra's	sarir	wādi
ENGLISH	river	mountain	mountain	massif	wadi	cape	desert	wadi
DEUTSCH	Fluss	Berg	Berg	Gebirgsmassiv	Wadi	Kap	Wüste	Wadi
ESPAÑOL	río	montaña	montaña	macizo	uadi	cabo	desierto	uadi
FRANÇAIS	rivière	montagne	montagne	massif	wadi	cap	désert	wadi
PORTUGUÊS	rio	montanha	montanha	maciço	uádi	cabo	deserto	uádi

Feet	Meters
19685	6000
13124	4000
9843	3000
6562	2000
3281	1000
1640	500
656	200
0	0
0	Land Below Sea Level 0
656	200
3281	1000
9843	3000
19685	6000
29520	9000

Map continues pages 150-151

Northwestern Africa / Nordwestafrika / África Nor-occidental
Afrique du Nord-Ouest / África Norte-occidental

Map continues pages 34-35

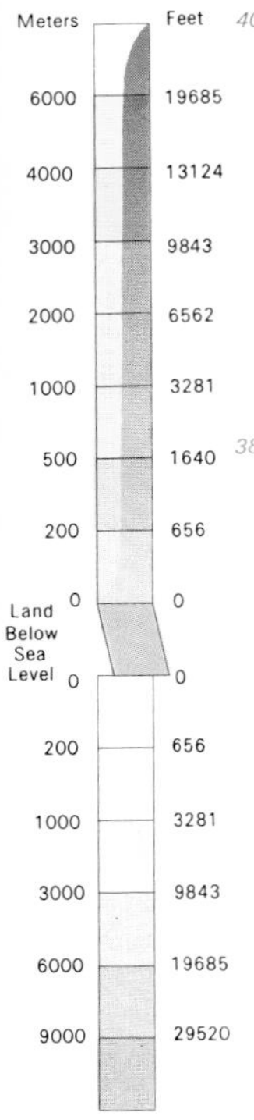
Meters
Feet
6000 19685
4000 13124
3000 9843
2000 6562
1000 3281
500 1640
200 656
0 0
Land Below Sea Level
0 0
200 656
1000 3281
3000 9843
6000 19685
9000 29520

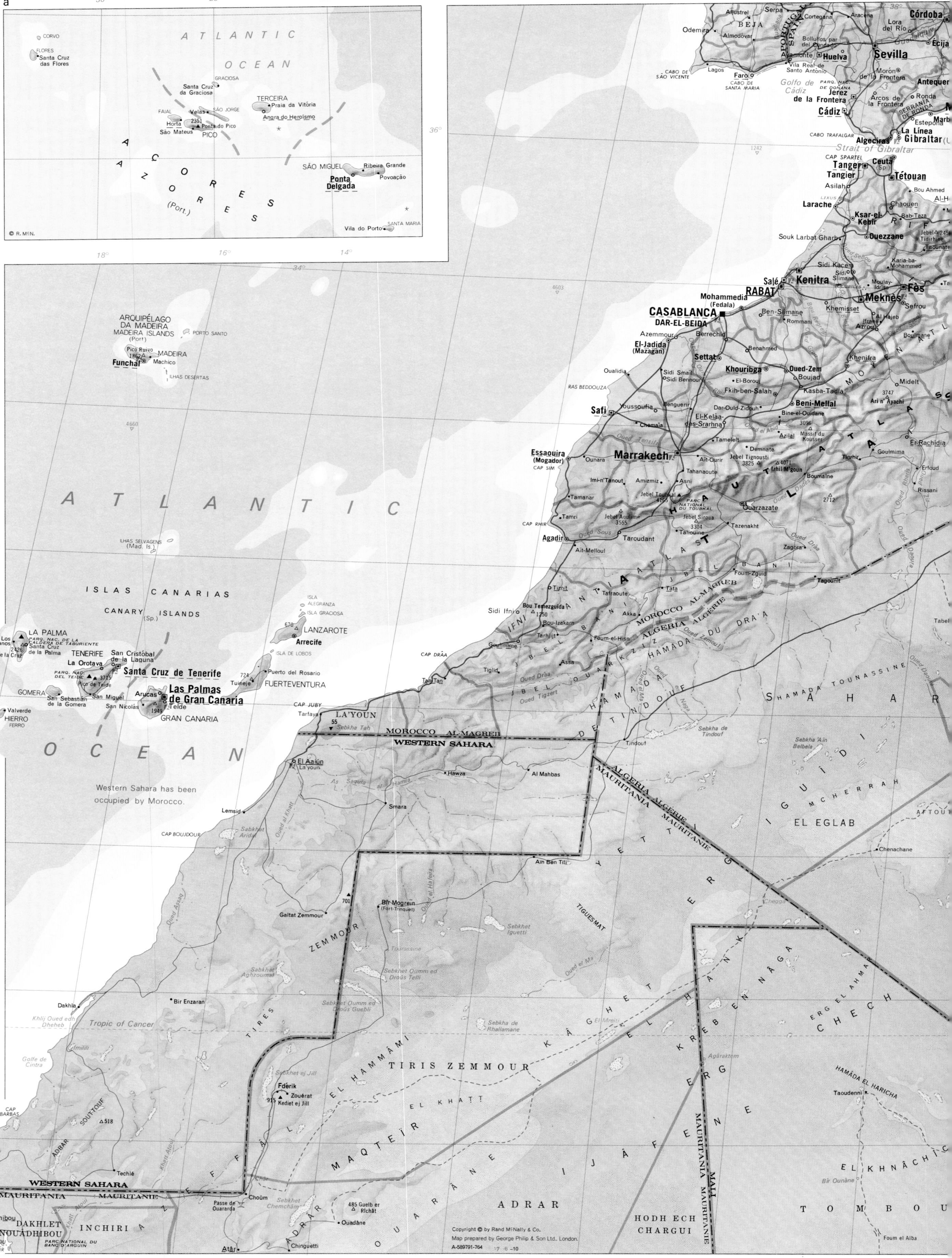
a
ATLANTIC OCEAN
AÇORES (Port.)
CORVO
FLORES
Santa Cruz das Flores
GRACIOSA
Santa Cruz da Graciosa
TERCEIRA
Praia da Vitória
Angra do Heroísmo
FAIAL
Horta
Velas
SÃO JORGE
São Mateus
Ponta do Pico
PICO
2351
SÃO MIGUEL
Ribeira Grande
Ponta Delgada
Povoação
SANTA MARIA
Vila do Porto
© R. MCN.
ARQUIPÉLAGO DA MADEIRA
MADEIRA ISLANDS (Port.)
PORTO SANTO
Pico Ruivo 1862
MADEIRA
Funchal
Machico
ILHAS DESERTAS
ILHAS SELVAGENS (Mad. Is.)
ATLANTIC OCEAN
ISLAS CANARIAS
CANARY ISLANDS (Sp.)
LA PALMA
Los Llanos
Santa Cruz de la Palma
Pico de la Cruz 2426
TENERIFE
San Cristóbal de la Laguna
La Orotava
Pico de Teide 3715
Santa Cruz de Tenerife
GOMERA
San Sebastián de la Gomera
Valverde
HIERRO
Las Palmas de Gran Canaria
Arucas
San Nicolás
Telde
1949
GRAN CANARIA
LANZAROTE
Arrecife
ISLA ALEGRANZA
ISLA GRACIOSA
ISLA DE LOBOS
Puerto del Rosario
Tuineje
FUERTEVENTURA
CAP JUBY
Tarfaya
LA'YOUN
MOROCCO AL-MAGREB
WESTERN SAHARA
El Aaiún
Smara
Hawza
Al Mahbas
Lemsid
CAP BOUJDOUR
Western Sahara has been occupied by Morocco.
Bir Mogrein (Fort-Trinquet)
Galtat Zemmour
ZEMMOUR
Dakhla
Bir Enzaran
Tropic of Cancer
TIRIS ZEMMOUR
Fdérik
Zouérat
Kediet ej Jill
CAP BARBAS
Techlé
WESTERN SAHARA
MAURITANIA MAURITANIE
Nouâdhibou
La Gouèra
DAKHLET NOUÂDHIBOU
INCHIRI
PARC NATIONAL DU BANC D'ARGUIN
Choûm
Atâr
Chinguetti
Ouadâne
ADRAR
HODH ECH CHARGUI
MAQTEÏR
EL KHATT
ALGERIA ALGÉRIE
MAURITANIA MAURITANIE
MALI
EL EGLAB
IGUIDI
Tindouf
HAMADA DE TINDOUF
Chenachane
Taoudenni
HAMÂDA EL HARICHA
EL KHNÂCHICH
TOMBOUCTOU
Foum el Alba
Odemira
Serpa
BEJA
Lagos
Faro
CABO DE SÃO VICENTE
CABO DE SANTA MARIA
Huelva
Sevilla
Córdoba
Écija
Antequera
Jerez de la Frontera
Cádiz
Algeciras
La Línea
Gibraltar
Strait of Gibraltar
CABO TRAFALGAR
CAP SPARTEL
Tanger
Ceuta
Tétouan
Larache
Ksar-el-Kebir
Ouezzane
Souk Larbat Gharb
Kenitra
Salé
RABAT
Mohammedia (Fedala)
CASABLANCA DAR-EL-BEIDA
Meknès
Fès
Khemisset
Azemmour
El-Jadida (Mazagan)
Berrechid
Settat
Khouribga
Oued-Zem
Boujad
Kasba-Tadla
Beni-Mellal
Midelt
Safi
Youssoufia
Benguerir
El-Kelaa-des-Srarhna
Essaouira (Mogador)
CAP SIM
Marrakech
Jebel Toubkal 4165
Jebel Tignousti 3825
Irhil M'goun 4071
Ouarzazate
Er-Rachidia
Agadir
CAP RHIR
Taroudant
Tiznit
Tafraoute
Sidi Ifni
Bou Temezguida
Goulimine
Tan-Tan
CAP DRÂA
Tagounit
Zagora
HAUT ATLAS
MOYEN ATLAS
ANTI ATLAS
JBEL BANI
HAMADA DU DRA'A
SAHARA
Copyright © by Rand McNally & Co.
Map prepared by George Philip & Son Ltd., London.
A-589791-764

Map continues pages 150-151

MAP FORM	cap	chott	djebel	erg	hamada	jbel	oued	sebkha
ENGLISH	cape	intermittent lake	mountain	sand desert	desert	mountain	wadi	salt flat
DEUTSCH	Kap	periodischer See	Berg	Sandwüste	Wüste	Berg	Wadi	Salzebene
ESPAÑOL	cabo	lago intermitente	montaña	desierto arenoso	desierto	montaña	uadi	salar
FRANÇAIS	cap	lac périodique	montagne	désert de sable	désert	montagne	wadi	saline
PORTUGUÊS	cabo	lago intermitente	montanha	deserto arenoso	deserto	montanha	uádi	salina

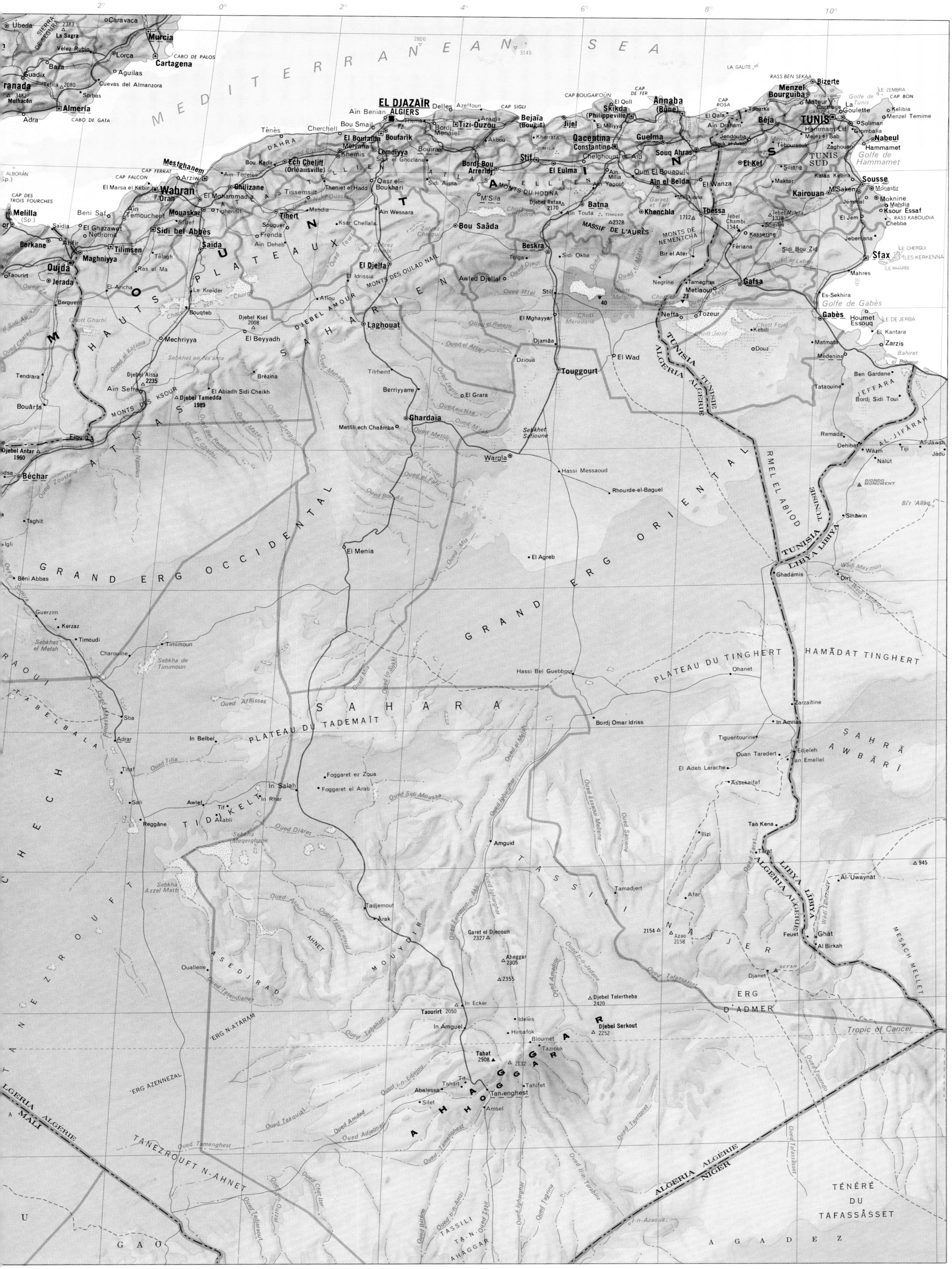
MEDITERRANEAN SEA
EL DJAZAÏR ALGIERS
Wahran Oran
Qacentina Constantine
Annaba (Bône)
TUNIS
Sfax
Gabès
Bizerte
Sousse
Kairouan
Melilla
Oujda
Béchar
Laghouat
Ghardaïa
Touggourt
Wargla
Beskra
El Djelfa
Batna
Stif
Bejaïa (Bougie)
Tizi-Ouzou
Murcia
Cartagena
Almería
Granada
HAUTS PLATEAUX
ATLAS SAHARIEN
MONTS DU HODNA
MASSIF DE L'AURÈS
GRAND ERG OCCIDENTAL
GRAND ERG ORIENTAL
PLATEAU DU TADEMAÏT
PLATEAU DU TINGHERT
HAMĀDAT TINGHERT
SAHARA
TIDIKELT
TASSILI
AHAGGAR
TANEZROUFT
ERG CHECH
In Salah
Adrar
Tamanrasset
Ghadāmis
Ghāt
Djanet
Hassi Messaoud
El Golea
Tropic of Cancer
TUNISIA TUNISIE
ALGERIA ALGÉRIE
LIBYA LIBYA
MALI
NIGER
TÉNÉRÉ DU TAFASSÂSSET
AGADEZ
GAO

Map continues pages 146-147

Kilometers 0 100 200 300 Km.
Statute Miles 0 100 200 300 Mi.

Scale 1:6,000,000
One centimeter represents 60 kilometers.
One inch represents approximately 95 miles.
Lambert Azimuthal Equal-Area Projection

DAKHLET NOUADHIBOU
INCHIRI
AKCHÂR
ADRAR
OUARÂNE
IJÂFENE
PARC NATIONAL DU BANC D'ARGUIN
Nouâmghâr
Atâr
Chinguetti
Akjoujt
ADÂFER EL ABIOD
EL MREYYÉ
TAGANT
DAHR TÎCHÎT
HODH ECH CHARGUI
Sebkhet te-n-Dgâmcha
Nouakchott
TRÂRZA
AOUKÂR
MALI
MAURITANIA
MAURITANIE
'AKLÉ AOUÂNA
TOM
Tidjikja
Boutilimit
BRAKNA
TRARZA
Mederdra
Aleg
Boûmdeïd
Tamchakt
Oualâta
DAHR OUALÂTA
IRIGUI
Kiffa
'Ayoûn el 'Atroûs
HÔD
Néma
DAHR NÉMA
Timbedgha
Rosso
Richard-Toll
Podor
Bogué
Sénégal
EL 'AÇÂBA
AFOLLÉ
HODH EL GHARBI
Saint-Louis
Kaédi
GORGOL
SAINT-LOUIS
Louga
LOUGA
SENEGAL
GUIDIMAKA
Sélibaby
Nioro du Sahel
Nara
Bassikounou
Nampala
Thiès
THIÈS
DIOURBEL
Diourbel
FERLO
Rufisque
DAKAR
CAP VERT
Mbour
KAOLACK
Kaolack
FATICK
Fatick
Kayes
KAYES
Kidira
Bakel
Tambacounda
TAMBACOUNDA
PARC NATIONAL DU NIOKOLO KOBA
KOULIKORO
PARC NATIONAL DE LA BOUCLE DU BAOULÉ
SÉGOU
Ségou
Mopti
CAPE SAINT MARY
Banjul (Bathurst)
GAMBIA
KOLDA
Kolda
ZIGUINCHOR
Ziguinchor
GUINEA-BISSAU
GUINÉ-BISSAU
Bamako
Koulikoro
Kati
Bissau
Bafatá
Gabú
ARQUIPÉLAGO DOS BIJAGÓS
FOUTA DJALON
Labé
GUINEA
GUINÉE
Siguiri
Kankan
SIKASSO
Sikasso
Bobo
Banfora
Kindia
Conakry
Boké
Fria
CAP VERGA
SIERRA LEONE
NORTHERN
Freetown
WESTERN AREA
EASTERN
SOUTHERN
Bo
Kenema
Koidu
LOMA MTS.
Bintimani 1945
Odienné
Korhogo
CÔTE D'IVOIRE
Man
Bouaké
Yamoussoukro
Daloa
Gagnoa
MONTS DU TOURA
NIMBA RANGE
Mont Nimba
PARC NAT. DE LA MARAHOUÉ
PARC NAT. DU MONT PEKO
LIBERIA
Monrovia
Robertsport
Buchanan
BONG RA.
KPOURA
Gbarnga
PUTU RANGE
Greenville
Harper
GROWA POINT
Tabou
San Pédro
Sassandra
ABIDJAN
Grand-Lahou
ATLANTIC OCEAN
GRAIN COAST
IVORY COAST
TURNERS PENINSULA
Sherbro
BANANA ISLANDS
ÎLES DE LOS
Meters
Feet
Land Below Sea Level
a
SANTO ANTÃO
Ribeira Grande
Mindelo
SÃO VICENTE
SANTA LUZIA
SÃO NICOLAU
SAL
BOA VISTA
MAIO
SANTIAGO
Praia
FOGO
BRAVA
CAPE VERDE
CABO VERDE
ATLANTIC
OCEAN
© R. McN.
Copyright © by Rand McNally & Co.
Map prepared by George Philip & Son Ltd., London.
A-589792-764

MAP FORM	coast	dhar	game reserve	ilha	lac	monts	mountains	vallée
ENGLISH	coast	escarpment	game reserve	island	lake	mountains	mountains	valley
DEUTSCH	Küste	Landstufe	Wildpark	Insel	See	Berge	Berge	Tal
ESPAÑOL	costa	escarpa	vedado de caza	isla	lago	montes	montañas	valle
FRANÇAIS	côte	escarpement	réserve à gibier	île	lac	monts	montagnes	vallée
PORTUGUÊS	costa	escarpa	reserva de caça	ilha	lago	montes	montanhas	vale

Map continues pages 148-149

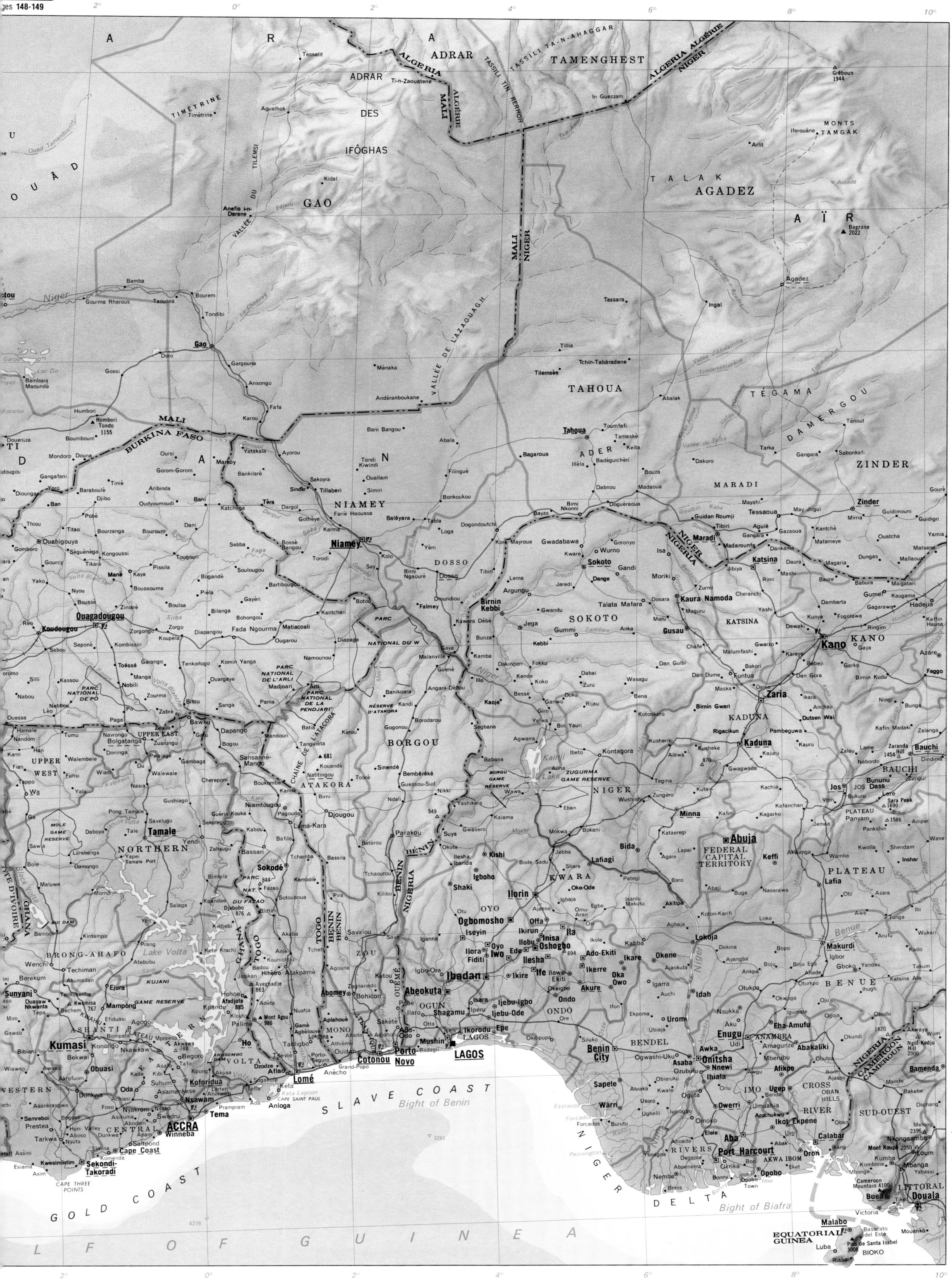
ALGERIA
ADRAR
TAMENGHEST
TASSILI TA-N-AHAGGAR
ADRAR DES IFÔGHAS
TIMÉTRINE
MALI
NIGER
GAO
AGADEZ
AÏR
TAHOUA
TÉGAMA
DAMERGOU
ZINDER
MARADI
NIAMEY
DOSSO
BURKINA FASO
SOKOTO
KATSINA
KANO
KADUNA
BAUCHI
NIGER
PLATEAU
FEDERAL CAPITAL TERRITORY
KWARA
OYO
OGUN
ONDO
BENDEL
ANAMBRA
IMO
RIVERS
CROSS RIVER
BENUE
BORGOU
ATAKORA
ZOU
MONO
ATLANTIQUE
OUÉMÉ
BENIN
TOGO
GHANA
NORTHERN
UPPER EAST
UPPER WEST
BRONG-AHAFO
ASHANTI
EASTERN
VOLTA
WESTERN
CENTRAL
CÔTE D'IVOIRE
NIGERIA
CAMEROON
SUD-OUEST
LITTORAL
EQUATORIAL GUINEA
BIOKO
Niamey
Kano
Kaduna
Abuja
Ibadan
Lagos
Porto-Novo
Cotonou
Lomé
Accra
Kumasi
Ouagadougou
Tamale
Zaria
Jos
Ilorin
Ogbomosho
Enugu
Port Harcourt
Calabar
Douala
Malabo
Agadez
Zinder
Maradi
Sokoto
Gao
Sekondi-Takoradi
Cape Coast
SLAVE COAST
Bight of Benin
GOLD COAST
NIGER DELTA
Bight of Biafra
GULF OF GUINEA
Lake Volta
Kainji Lake
Niger
Benue
Kilometers
Statute Miles

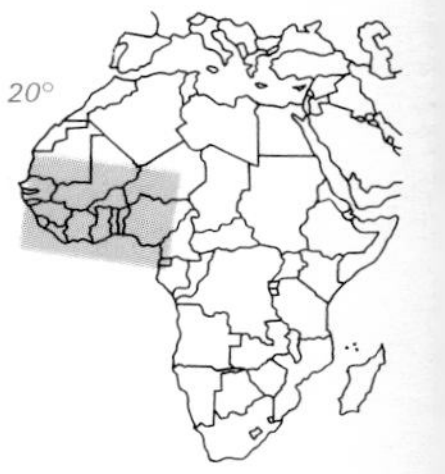

Map continues pages 146-147

Map continues pages 152-153

Kilometers 0 100 200 300 Km.

Statute Miles 0 100 200 300 Mi.

Scale 1:6,000,000

One centimeter represents 60 kilometers.
One inch represents approximately 95 miles.
Lambert Azimuthal Equal-Area Projection

Map continues pages 146-147

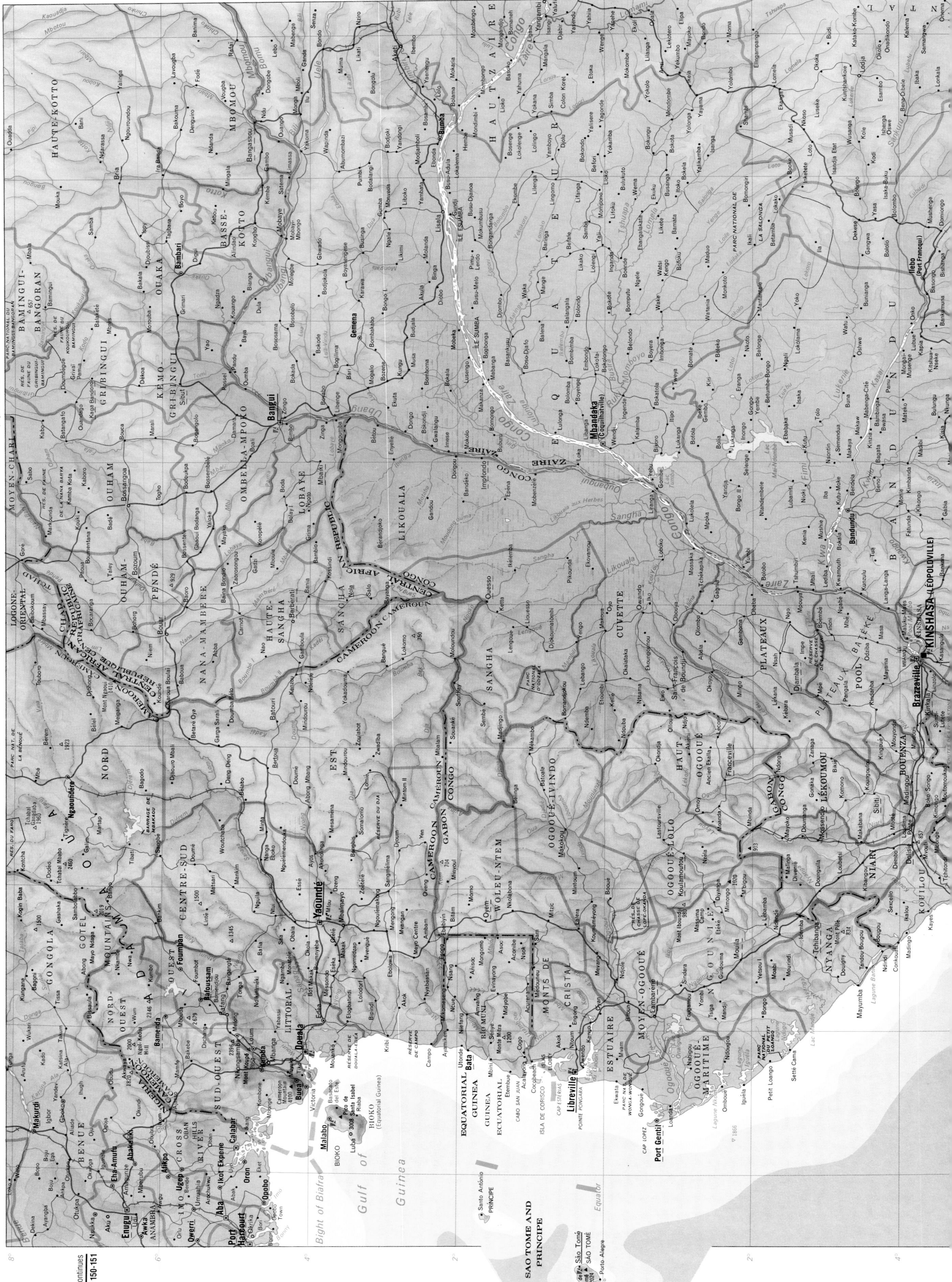
Gulf of Guinea
Bight of Biafra
Equator
CAMEROON
EQUATORIAL GUINEA
GABON
CONGO
ZAIRE
CENTRAL AFRICAN REPUBLIC
SAO TOME AND PRINCIPE
NIGERIA
Bangui
Yaoundé
Douala
Libreville
Port Gentil
Brazzaville
KINSHASA (LÉOPOLDVILLE)
Mbandaka (Coquilhatville)
Malabo
BIOKO (Equatorial Guinea)
São Tomé
Ilebo (Port Francqui)
Bandundu
Ngaoundéré
Bambari
Berbérati
Franceville
Makokou
Lambaréné
Calabar
Enugu
Port Harcourt

Map continues pages 150-151

Map continues pages 154-155

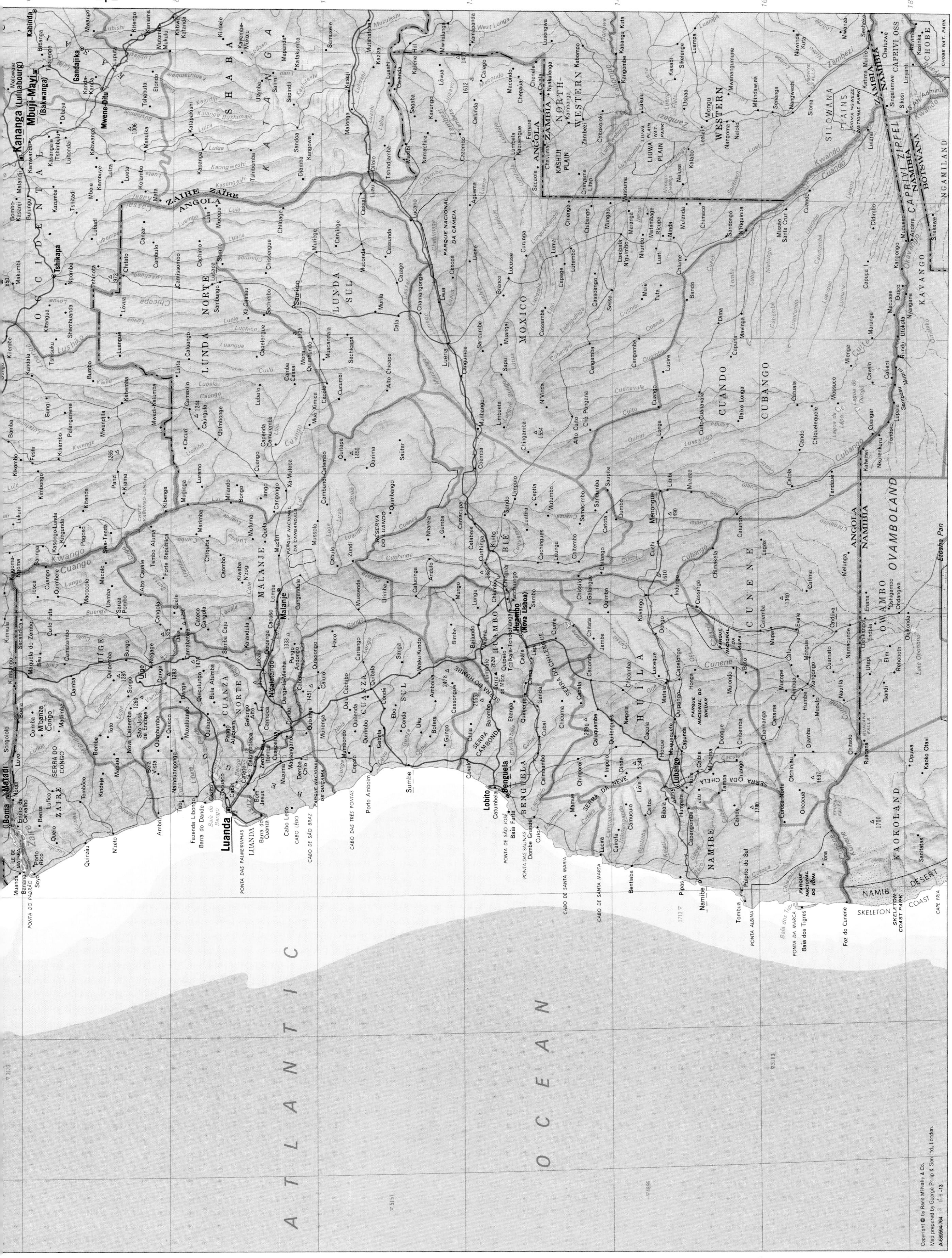
ATLANTIC
OCEAN
ANGOLA
ZAIRE
ZAMBIA
NAMIBIA
BOTSWANA
Luanda
Lobito
Benguela
Huambo (Nova Lisboa)
Malanje
Lubango
Namibe
Menongue
Kananga (Luluabourg)
Mbuji-Mayi (Bakwanga)
Tshikapa
Matadi
Boma
Scale 1:6,000,000
One centimeter represents 60 kilometers.
One inch represents approximately 95 miles.
Lambert Azimuthal Equal-Area Projection
Kilometers
Statute Miles
MAP FORM cabo falls île lac lagune monts ponta serra
ENGLISH cape waterfall island lake lagoon mountains point mountains
DEUTSCH Kap Wasserfall Insel See Haff Berge Landspitze Berge
ESPAÑOL cabo cascada isla lago laguna montes punta sierra
FRANÇAIS cap chute d'eau île lac lagune monts pointe montagnes
PORTUGUÊS cabo queda d'água ilha lago laguna montes ponta serra
Copyright © by Rand McNally & Co.
Map prepared by George Philip & Son Ltd., London.

Map continues pages 156-157

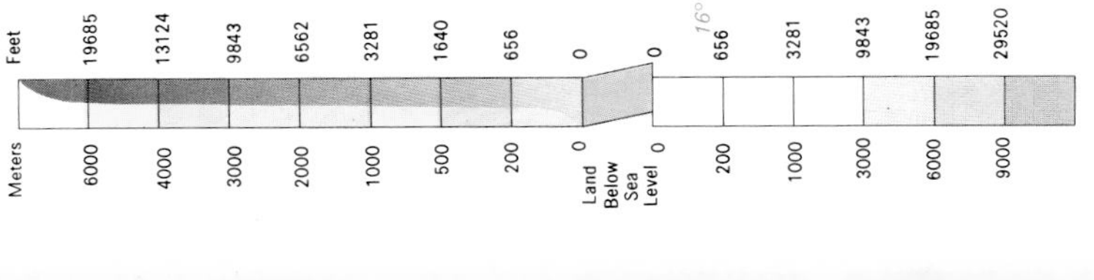
Feet
19685
13124
9843
6562
3281
1640
656
0
Meters
6000
4000
3000
2000
1000
500
200
0
Land Below Sea Level
0
200
1000
3000
6000
9000
656
3281
9843
19685
29520

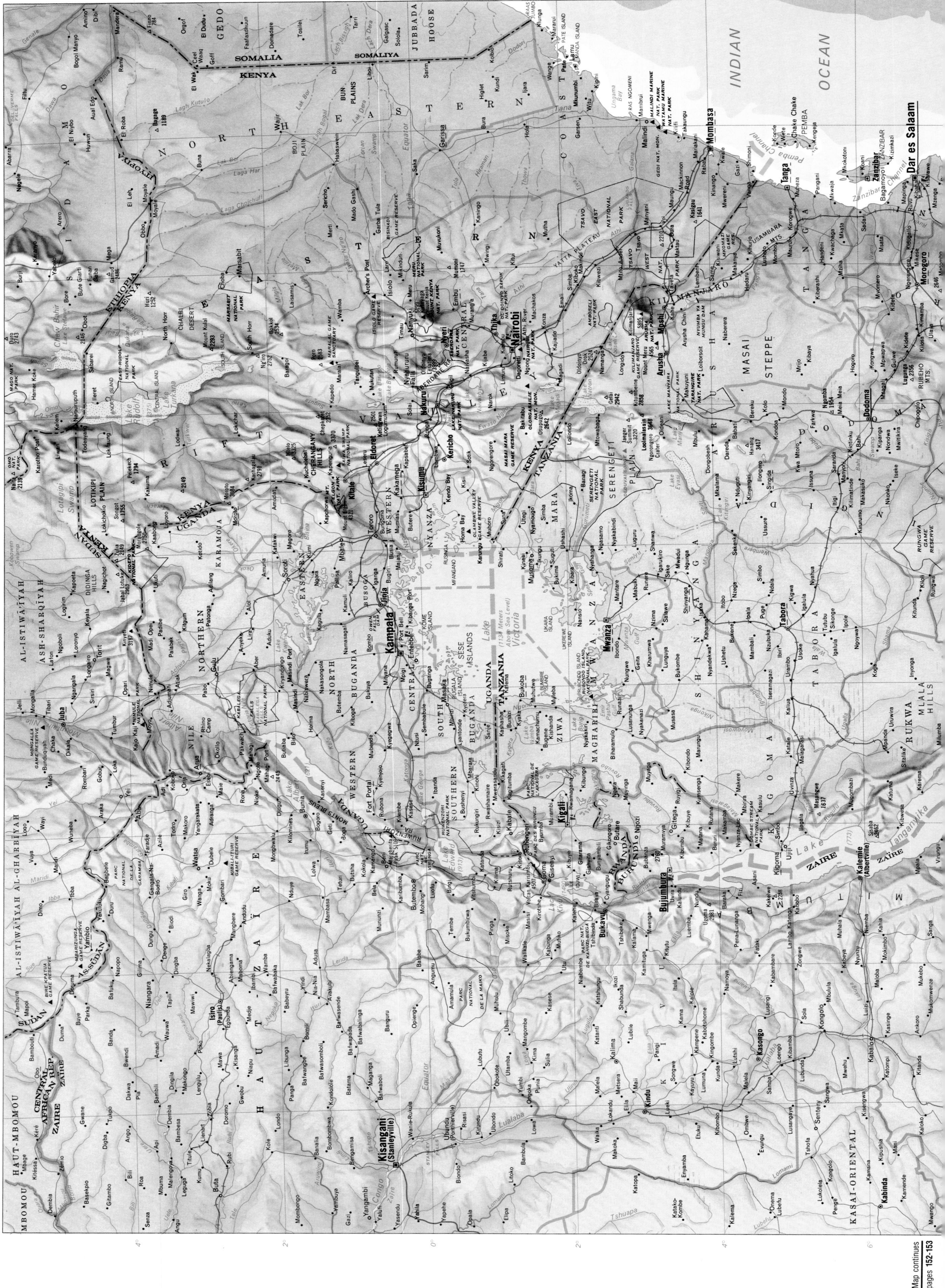
INDIAN OCEAN
Dar es Salaam
Zanzibar
Mombasa
Tanga
Nairobi
Kampala
Kisumu
Mwanza
Kigali
Bujumbura
Kisangani (Stanleyville)
Lake Victoria
Lake Rudolf
Lake Tanganyika
KENYA
UGANDA
TANZANIA
SOMALIA
ETHIOPIA
SUDAN
ZAIRE
RWANDA
BURUNDI
CENTRAL AFRICAN REP.
Equator

Map continues pages 144-145
Map continues pages 140-141
Map continues pages 152-153

Kilometers 0 100 200 300 Km.
Statute Miles 0 100 200 Mi.

Scale 1:6,000,000

One centimeter represents 60 kilometers.
One inch represents approximately 95 miles.
Lambert Azimuthal Equal-Area Projection

ENGLISH	falls	game reserve	island	lake	mountains	national park	plain	swamp
DEUTSCH	Wasserfall	Wildreservat	Insel	See	Berge	Nationalpark	Ebene	Sumpf
ESPAÑOL	cascada	vedado de caza	isla	lago	montañas	parque nacional	llano	pantano
FRANÇAIS	chute d'eau	réserve à gibier	île	lac	montagnes	parc national	plaine	marais
PORTUGUÊS	queda d'água	reserva de caça	ilha	lago	montanhas	parque nacional	planície	pântano

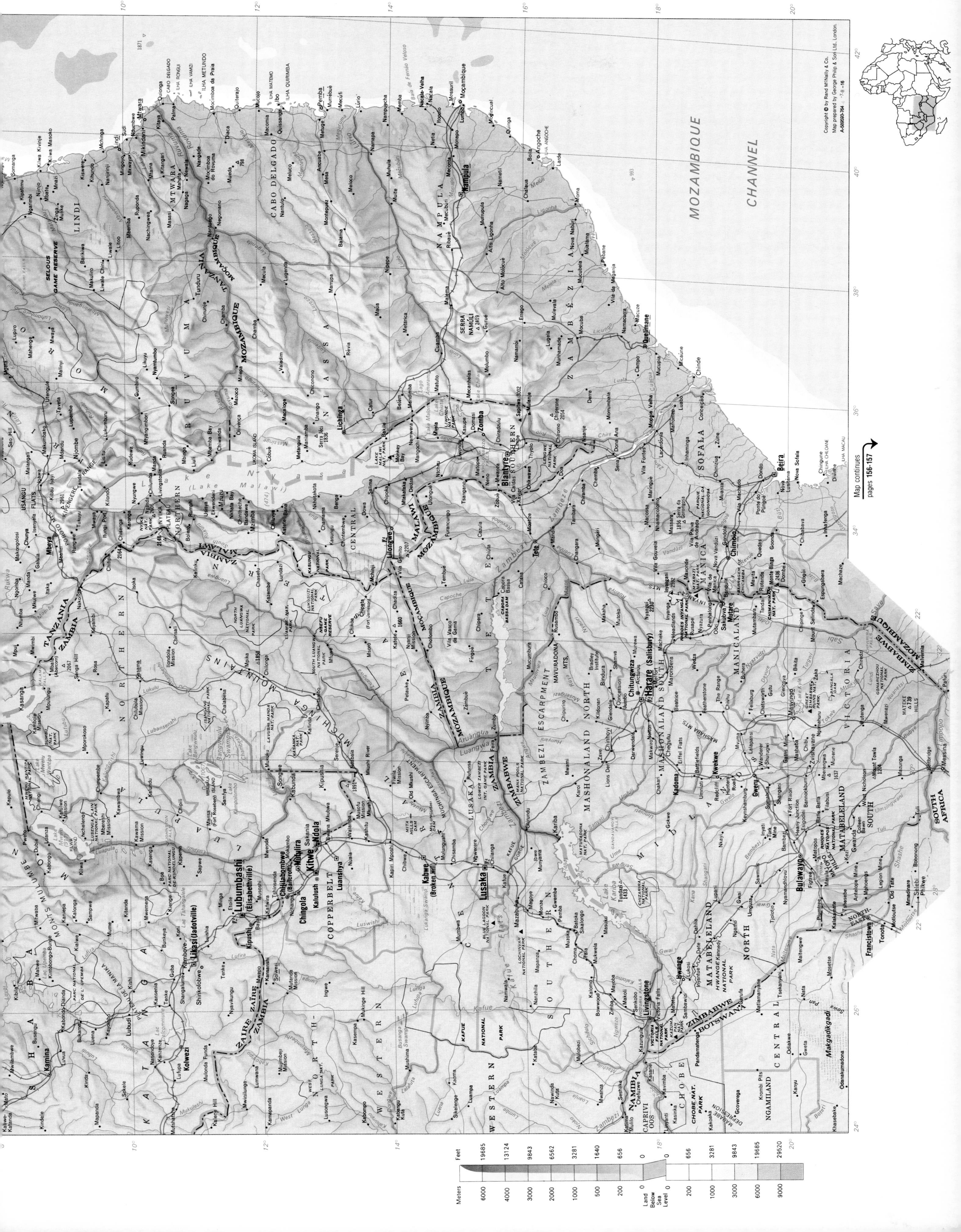
MOZAMBIQUE CHANNEL
Map continues pages 156-157
Copyright © by Rand McNally & Co.
Map prepared by George Philip & Son Ltd., London.
Lake Nyasa (Lake Malawi)
Lilongwe
Blantyre
Zomba
Lusaka
Harare (Salisbury)
Bulawayo
Lubumbashi (Élisabethville)
Likasi (Jadotville)
Kolwezi
Ndola
Kitwe
Livingstone
Beira
Nampula
Quelimane
Tete
Francistown
ZAMBIA
MALAWI
MOZAMBIQUE
ZIMBABWE
TANZANIA
BOTSWANA
NAMIBIA
SOUTH AFRICA
ZAÏRE
Meters
Feet
Land Below Sea Level

Southern Africa and Madagascar / Südafrika und Madagaskar / África Meridional y Madagascar
Afrique Méridionale et Madagascar / África Meridional e Madagascar

Map continues pages 152-153

ATLANTIC OCEAN
NAMIBIA
BOTSWANA
SOUTH AFRICA
SUID-AFRIKA
ANGOLA
ZIMBABWE
KAOKOLAND
OVAMBOLAND
DAMARALAND
GREAT NAMAQUALAND
LITTLE NAMAQUALAND
NAMIB DESERT
KALAHARI DESERT
KAVANGO
NGAMILAND
GHANZI
CENTRAL
KWENENG
BOPHUTHATSWANA
NORTHERN CAPE
WESTERN CAPE
EASTERN CAPE
NORTH WEST
ORANGE FREE STATE
GREAT KAROO
BUSHMAN LAND
ETOSHA NATIONAL PARK
OKAVANGO DELTA
CENTRAL KALAHARI GAME RESERVE
KALAHARI GEMSBOK NATIONAL PARK
Windhoek
Walvis Bay
Swakopmund
Lüderitz
Keetmanshoop
Gaborone
Maun
Upington
Kimberley
Bloemfontein
CAPE TOWN
KAAPSTAD
Port Elizabeth
Oudtshoorn
Worcester
Livingstone
Tropic of Capricorn
CAPE OF GOOD HOPE
CAPE AGULHAS
Copyright © by Rand McNally & Co.
Map prepared by George Philip & Son Ltd., London.
A-589292-764

Meters	Feet
6000	19685
4000	13124
3000	9843
2000	6562
1000	3281
500	1640
200	656
0	0
Land Below Sea Level	
0	0
200	656
1000	3281
3000	9843
6000	19685
9000	29520

MAP FORM	bay	berg, berge	cape	game reserve	ilha	lake	national park
ENGLISH	bay	mountain, mountains	cape	game reserve	island	lake	national park
DEUTSCH	Bucht	Berg, Berge	Kap	Wildpark	Insel	See	Nationalpark
ESPAÑOL	bahía	montaña, montañas	cabo	vedado de caza	isla	lago	parque nacional
FRANÇAIS	baie	montagne, montagnes	cap	réserve à gibier	île	lac	parc national
PORTUGUÊS	baía	montanha, montanhas	cabo	reserva de caça	ilha	lago	parque nacional

Kilometers 0 100 200 300 Km.
Statute Miles 0 100 200 300 Mi.

Scale 1:6,000,000

One centimeter represents 60 kilometers.
One inch represents approximately 95 miles.

Lambert Azimuthal Equal-Area Projection

Map continues
pages 154-155

a
INDIAN OCEAN
NJAZIDJA (GRANDE COMORE)
Moroni
COMOROS
COMORES
ARCHIPEL DES COMORES
MAYOTTE (Fr.)
Dzaoudzi
MOZAMBIQUE CHANNEL
b
MADAGASCAR
MADAGASIKARA
Antsiranana
Mahajanga
ANTANANARIVO
Toamasina
Antsirabe
Fianarantsoa
Toliara
MASSIF DU TSARATANANA
PLATEAU DU BEMARAHA
Tropic of Capricorn
INDIAN OCEAN
MOZAMBIQUE CHANNEL
c
INDIAN
MAURITIUS
Port Louis
RÉUNION
Saint-Denis
MASCARENE ISLANDS
OCEAN
HARARE (SALISBURY)
Chitungwiza
Kwekwe
Gweru
Bulawayo
Masvingo
Mutare
MIDLANDS
MANICALAND
MATABELELAND SOUTH
VICTORIA
ZIMBABWE
MOZAMBIQUE
MANICA
SOFALA
Chimoio
Beira
Quelimane
ZAMBEZIA
Chinde
INHAMBANE
GAZA
Inhambane
Xai-Xai
MAPUTO
NORTHERN TRANSVAAL
Pietersburg
PRETORIA
Nelspruit
EASTERN TRANSVAAL
SWAZILAND
Mbabane
SOUTH AFRICA
ZULULAND
NATAL
Ladysmith
Pietermaritzburg
DURBAN
TRANSKEI
Umtata
INDIAN OCEAN
MOZAMBIQUE CHANNEL
© R. McN.

Map continues pages 156-157

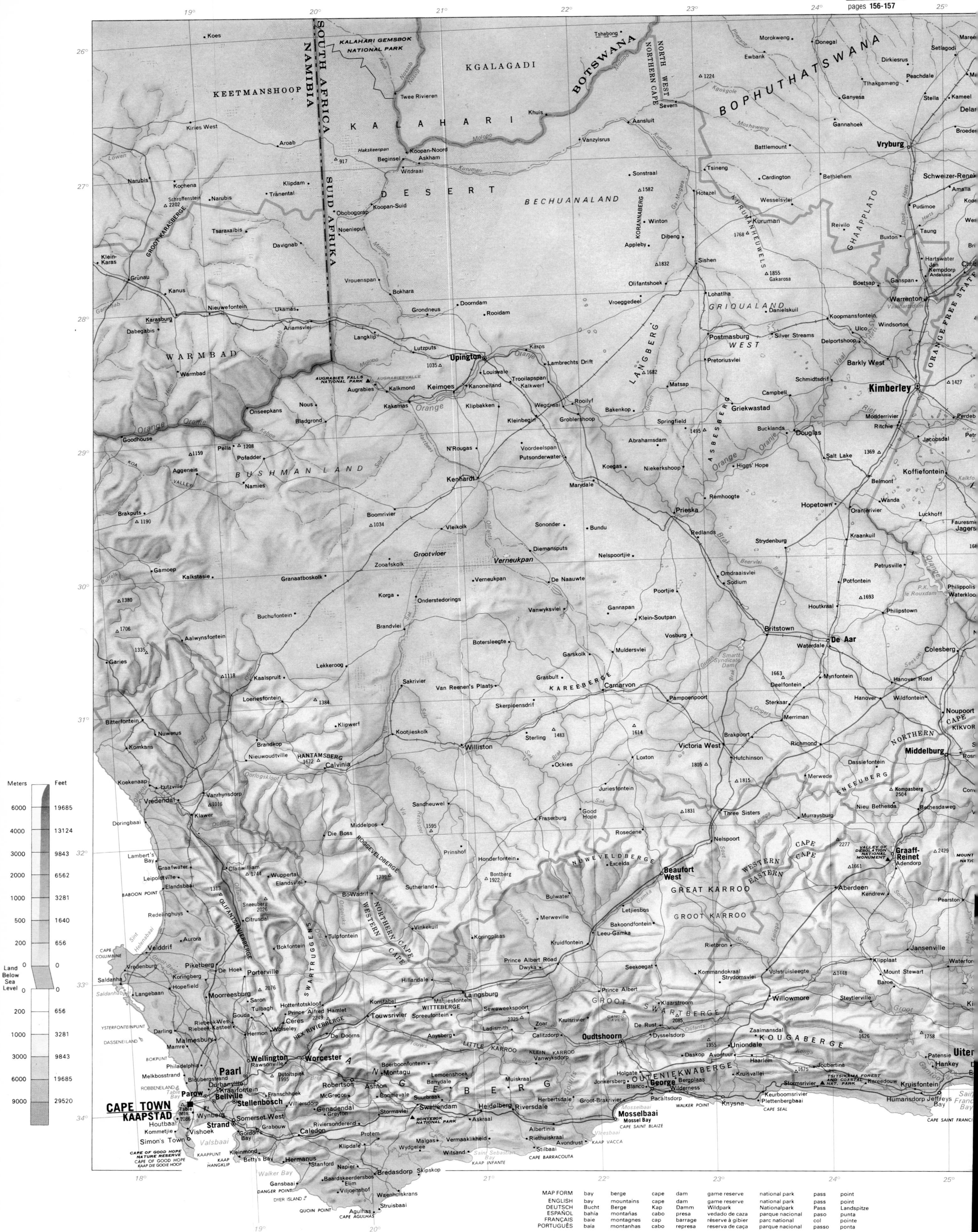
SOUTH AFRICA
NAMIBIA
SUID AFRIKA
BOTSWANA
KGALAGADI
KALAHARI GEMSBOK NATIONAL PARK
KEETMANSHOOP
K A L A H A R I
D E S E R T
BECHUANALAND
BOPHUTHATSWANA
NORTH WEST
NORTHERN CAPE
GRIQUALAND WEST
ORANGE FREE STATE
WARMBAD
B U S H M A N L A N D
AUGRABIES FALLS NATIONAL PARK
Upington
Kimberley
Vryburg
Kenhardt
Prieska
Calvinia
Williston
Carnarvon
Victoria West
Beaufort West
De Aar
Britstown
Middelburg
Graaff-Reinet
GREAT KARROO
GROOT KAROO
NUWEVELDBERGE
KAREEBERGE
SNEEUBERG
ROGGEVELDBERGE
HANTAMSBERG
SWARTRUGGENS
OLIFANTSRIVIERBERGE
GROOT SWARTBERGE
KOUGABERGE
OUTENIEKWABERGE
LANGEBERG
WITTEBERGE
HEX RIVIERBERGE
LITTLE KARROO
KLEIN KAROO
VALLEY OF DESOLATION NATIONAL MONUMENT
BONTEBOK NATIONAL PARK
TSITSIKAMMA FOREST AND COASTAL NAT. PARK
CAPE OF GOOD HOPE NATURE RESERVE
CAPE TOWN
KAAPSTAD
Bellville
Paarl
Stellenbosch
Wellington
Worcester
Oudtshoorn
George
Mosselbaai
Mossel Bay
Knysna
Swellendam
Hermanus
CAPE AGULHAS
Orange
Meters
Feet
6000 19685
4000 13124
3000 9843
2000 6562
1000 3281
500 1640
200 656
0 0
Land Below Sea Level
200 656
1000 3281
3000 9843
6000 19685
9000 29520

MAP FORM	bay	berge	cape	dam	game reserve	national park	pass	point
ENGLISH	bay	mountains	cape	dam	game reserve	national park	pass	point
DEUTSCH	Bucht	Berge	Kap	Damm	Wildpark	Nationalpark	Pass	Landspitze
ESPAÑOL	bahía	montañas	cabo	presa	vedado de caza	parque nacional	paso	punta
FRANÇAIS	baie	montagnes	cap	barrage	réserve à gibier	parc national	col	pointe
PORTUGUÊS	baía	montanhas	cabo	represa	reserva de caça	parque nacional	passo	ponta

Pretoria
JOHANNESBURG
Soweto
Krugersdorp
Benoni
Germiston
Springs
Vereeniging
Potchefstroom
Klerksdorp
Kroonstad
Welkom
Virginia
Bethlehem
Harrismith
Ladysmith
Newcastle
Dundee
Maseru
LESOTHO
DRAKENSBERG
Pietermaritzburg
DURBAN
SWAZILAND
Mbabane
Manzini
Maputo (Lourenço Marques)
MOZAMBIQUE
MOÇAMBIQUE
ZULULAND
Piet Retief
Vryheid
Richard's Bay
Stanger
Port Shepstone
Kokstad
Umtata
TRANSKEI
KAFFRARIA
Queenstown
East London
Oos-Londen
King William's Town
CISKEI
Grahamstown
Port Alfred
Elizabeth
INDIAN
OCEAN
WILD COAST
NATAL
EASTERN CAPE
EASTERN TRANSVAAL
GRIQUALAND EAST
PONDOLAND
Copyright © by Rand McNally & Co.
Map prepared by George Philip & Son Ltd., London.
A-584600-764

Kilometers 0 50 100 150 Km.

Statute Miles 0 50 100 150 Mi.

Scale 1:3,000,000

One centimeter represents 30 kilometers.

One inch represents approximately 47 miles.

Lambert Conformal Conic Projection

Australia / Australien / Australia
Australie / Austrália

Map continues pages 108-109

110°
115°
120°
125°
130°
10°
15°
20°
25°
30°
35°
40°
105°
INDONESIA
JAWA JAVA
Magelang
Madiun
Kediri
Malang
Jember
Tasikmalaya
Cilacap
Yogyakarta
Surakarta
Blitar
Banyuwangi
BALI
Singaraja
Mataram
Denpasar
LOMBOK
Praya
Sumbawa Besar
SUMBAWA
NUSA TENGGARA
LESSER SUNDA ISLANDS
FLORES
Waingapu
Waikabubak
SUMBA
Baing
Laut Sawu
Savu Sea
PULAU SEMAU
Kupang
TIMOR
Soe
PULAU ROTI
PULAU SAWU
Timor Sea
Arafura
HIBERNIA REEF
ASHMORE ISLANDS
CARTIER ISLANDS (Austl.)
MELVILLE ISLAND
BATHURST ISLAND
CAPE CROKER
COBOURG PENINSULA
Van Diemen Gulf
Clarence Strait
Beagle Gulf
Darwin
Humpty Doo
POINT BLAZE
Rum Jungle
ARNHEM
Joseph Bonaparte Gulf
Pine Creek
Katherine
CAPE LONDONDERRY
Admiralty Gulf
BROWSE ISLAND
SCOTT REEF
BONAPARTE ARCHIPELAGO
York Sound
Wyndham
Kununurra
Lake Argyle
Victoria River Downs
Victoria
Daly Waters
ADÈLE ISLAND
BEAGLE REEF
BUCCANEER ARCHIPELAGO
Collier Bay
CAPE LEVEQUE
King Sound
KIMBERLEY PLATEAU
KING LEOPOLD RANGES
DURACK RANGES
Derby
Mount Ord 937
Fitzroy Crossing
Halls Creek
Wave Hill
INDIAN OCEAN
ROWLEY SHOALS
Broome
CAPE LATOUCHE TREVILLE
La Grange
EIGHTY MILE BEACH
NORTHERN TERRITORY
TANAMI DESERT
Lake Gregory
Port Hedland
Goldsworthy
Shay Gap
De Grey
GREAT SANDY DESERT
MONTE BELLO ISLANDS
DAMPIER ARCHIPELAGO
Dampier
Karratha
Roebourne
Marble Bar
Nullagine
Lake White
Lake Wills
Lake Mackay
BARROW ISLAND
MUIRON ISLANDS
NORTH WEST CAPE
Exmouth
Exmouth Gulf
Onslow
Pannawonica
HAMERSLEY RANGE
Fortescue
Wittenoom
Mount Brockman 1132
Mount Bruce 1235
Tom Price
Mount Meharry 1251
Paraburdoo
Newman
Lake Dora
Lake Auld
Lake Disappointment
Lake Macdonald
Mount Leisler 897
Mount Liebig 1524
Mount 1511
MACDONNELL RANGES
POINT CLOATES
Ashburton
Savory
WESTERN AUSTRALIA
GIBSON DESERT
Lake Neale
Lake Amadeus
Mount Olga 1069
Ayers Rock 867
Mount Cockburn 1138
CAPE CUVIER
Lake Macleod
Lyons
Mount Augustus 1105
906 Mount Essendon
Tropic of Capricorn
Geographe Channel
Carnarvon
BERNIER ISLAND
DORRE ISLAND
Shark Bay
Naturaliste Channel
Gascoyne
ROBINSON RANGE
Peak Hill
Lake Carnegie
Lake Gillen
Mount Aloysius 1085
Mount Woodroffe 1440
Wooramel
DIRK HARTOG ISLAND
STEEP POINT
Denham
Murchison
Meekatharra
Nannine
Wiluna
Lake Wells
Cue
Lake Austin
Sandstone
Agnew
Mount Redcliffe 562
Yeo Lake
GREAT VICTORIA DESERT
Kalbarri
Mount Magnet
Yalgoo
Laverton
Malcolm
Lake Carey
Leonora
Lake Ballard
Lake Raeside
Lake Maurice
Northampton
Mullewa
Pindar
HOUTMAN ABROLHOS
Geraldton
Mongers Lake
Lake Barlee
Menzies
Lake Minigwal
Maralinga
Ooldea
Dongara
Three Springs
Lake Moore
Forrest
Deakin
GREEN HEAD
Dalwallinu
Bonnie Rock
Kalgoorlie-Boulder
Coolgardie
Zanthus
Rawlinna
Haig
NULLARBOR PLAIN
Moora
Bencubbin
Bullfinch
Southern Cross
Lake Lefroy
Eucla
CAPE ADIEU
SAINT PETER I.
DARLING RANGE
Northam
Merredin
Kellerberrin
Lake Cowan
Wanneroo
Perth
Fremantle
York
Beverley
Brookton
Hyden
Lake Johnston
Norseman
Eyre
Lake Dundas
POINT CULVER
Pinjarra
Narrogin
Newdegate
Wagin
Ravensthorpe
Esperance
CAPE ARID
Great Australian Bight
Bunbury
Geographe Bay
Collie
CAPE NATURALISTE
Busselton
Nyabing
Katanning
Gnowangerup
Hopetoun
ARCHIPELAGO OF THE RECHERCHE
Esperance Bay
Bridgetown
Manjimup
Bluff Knoll 1096
HOOD POINT
Augusta
Mount Barker
CAPE LEEUWIN
Pemberton
Albany
CAPE VANCOUVER
POINT D'ENTRECASTEAUX
Denmark
WEST CAPE HOWE
King George Sound
SOUTHERN OCEAN
Copyright © by Rand McNally & Co.
Map prepared by Esselte Map Service AB, Stockholm.
A-590200-264 -8-9-17

ENGLISH	bay	cape	island	lake	mount	point	range	reef
DEUTSCH	Bucht	Kap	Insel	See	Berg	Landspitze	Gebirge	Riff
ESPAÑOL	bahía	cabo	isla	lago	montaña	punta	cordillera	arrecife
FRANÇAIS	baie	cap	île	lac	mont	pointe	chaîne	récif
PORTUGUÊS	baía	cabo	ilha	lago	monte	ponta	cordilheira	recife

Coral Sea
PACIFIC OCEAN
Tasman Sea
Solomon Sea
Gulf of Carpentaria
Gulf of Papua
Torres Strait
Bass Strait
PAPUA NEW GUINEA
NEW GUINEA
Port Moresby
SOLOMON ISLANDS
Honiara
GUADALCANAL
CAPE YORK PENINSULA
GREAT BARRIER REEF
GREAT DIVIDING RANGE
QUEENSLAND
GREAT ARTESIAN BASIN
SIMPSON DESERT
STURT STONY DESERT
NEW SOUTH WALES
VICTORIA
AUSTRALIA
TASMANIA
A.C.T.
Canberra
SYDNEY
Brisbane
MELBOURNE
Adelaide
Hobart
Newcastle
Wollongong
Townsville
Cairns
Rockhampton
Launceston
Broken Hill
Mount Isa
Lake Eyre North
Lake Eyre South
Lake Torrens
Lake Frome
FRASER ISLAND
KING ISLAND
FLINDERS ISLAND
KANGAROO ISLAND
LORD HOWE ISLAND (N.S.W.)
Tropic of Capricorn
140°
145°
150°
155°
160°
165°
15°
20°
25°
30°
35°
40°

Kilometers 0 200 400 600 Km.
Statute Miles 0 200 400 600 Mi.

Scale 1:12,000,000

One centimeter represents 120 kilometers.
One inch represents approximately 190 miles.
Lambert Conformal Conic Projection

Western and Central Australia / West-und Mittelaustralien / Australia Centro-occidental
Australie Occidentale et Centrale / Austrália Ocidental e Central

INDIAN OCEAN
GREAT SANDY DESERT
WESTERN AUSTRALIA
GIBSON DESERT
LITTLE SANDY DESERT
HAMERSLEY RANGE
Tropic of Capricorn
Perth
Fremantle
Stirling
Geraldton
Kalgoorlie-Boulder
Broome
Port Hedland
Carnarvon
Esperance
Albany
Bunbury
Shark Bay
ARCHIPELAGO OF THE RECHERCHE
Meters
Feet
Land Below Sea Level
Copyright © by Rand McNally & Co.
Map prepared by George Philip & Son Ltd., London.

ENGLISH	bay	cape	creek, cr.	island, i.	lake, l.	mount	point	range
DEUTSCH	Bucht	Kap	Bach	Insel	See	Berg	Landspitze	Gebirge
ESPAÑOL	bahía	cabo	riachuelo	isla	lago	montaña	punta	cordillera
FRANÇAIS	baie	cap	crique	île	lac	mont	pointe	chaîne
PORTUGUÊS	baía	cabo	riacho	ilha	lago	monte	ponta	cordilheira

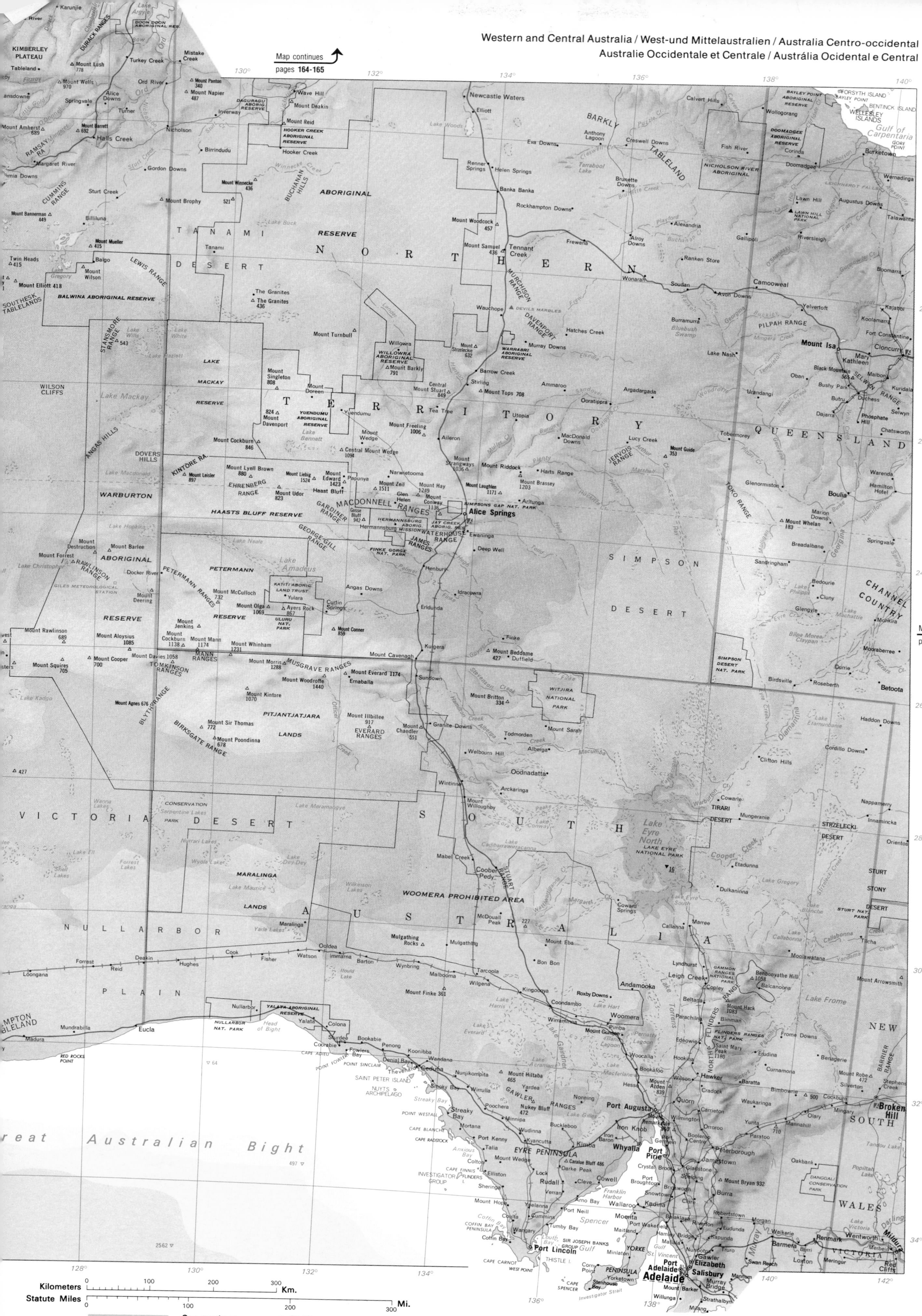
Map continues
pages 164-165
Map continues
pages 166-167
KIMBERLEY PLATEAU
DURACK RANGES
Halls Creek
Turkey Creek
Wave Hill
Mount Deakin
Hooker Creek
HOOKER CREEK ABORIGINAL RESERVE
Birrindudu
Gordon Downs
Sturt Creek
CUMMINS RANGE
Billiluna
Balgo
LEWIS RANGE
BALWINA ABORIGINAL RESERVE
SOUTHESK TABLELANDS
TANAMI DESERT
Tanami
ABORIGINAL RESERVE
NORTHERN TERRITORY
The Granites
Lake Mackay
LAKE MACKAY RESERVE
WILSON CLIFFS
ANGAS HILLS
DOVERS HILLS
KINTORE RA.
WARBURTON
HAASTS BLUFF RESERVE
Haast Bluff
Papunya
Yuendumu
YUENDUMU ABORIGINAL RESERVE
Newcastle Waters
Elliott
Lake Woods
Eva Downs
Renner Springs
Helen Springs
Banka Banka
Rockhampton Downs
Tennant Creek
MURCHISON RANGE
DEVILS MARBLES
Wauchope
DAVENPORT RANGE
Hatches Creek
Murray Downs
WARRABRI ABORIGINAL RESERVE
Barrow Creek
Stirling
Ammaroo
Argadargada
Ti Tree
Utopia
Aileron
MACDONNELL RANGES
Alice Springs
SIMPSONS GAP NAT. PARK
Hermannsburg
HERMANNSBURG ABORIG. MISSION
WATERHOUSE RANGE
JAMES RANGES
FINKE GORGE NAT. PARK
GEORGE GILL RANGE
Ewaninga
Deep Well
Arltunga
Harts Range
Jervois Range
SIMPSON DESERT
Lake Amadeus
PETERMANN RANGES
PETERMANN ABORIGINAL RESERVE
KATITI ABORIG. LAND TRUST
Yulara
Ayers Rock 867
Mount Olga 1069
ULURU NAT. PARK
Curtin Springs
Angas Downs
Henbury
Idracowra
Erldunda
Kulgera
Finke
Mount Cavenagh
MANN RANGES
TOMKINSON RANGES
MUSGRAVE RANGES
Mount Woodroffe 1440
Ernabella
BLYTH RANGE
PITJANTJATJARA LANDS
BIRKSGATE RANGE
EVERARD RANGES
Sundown
WITJIRA NATIONAL PARK
Granite Downs
Todmorden
Welbourn Hill
Oodnadatta
Wintinna
Arckaringa
Mount Willoughby
VICTORIA DESERT
CONSERVATION PARK
MARALINGA LANDS
Maralinga
WOOMERA PROHIBITED AREA
Coober Pedy
STUART RANGE
Mabel Creek
NULLARBOR PLAIN
Cook
Ooldea
Forrest
Deakin
Hughes
Fisher
Watson
Reid
Loongana
Mulgathing Rocks
Tarcoola
Wilgena
Kingoonya
Eucla
Madura
Mundrabilla
Nullarbor
NULLARBOR NAT. PARK
YALATA ABORIGINAL RESERVE
Yalata
Colona
Head of Bight
Great Australian Bight
Fowlers Bay
Penong
Ceduna
Thevenard
Smoky Bay
Streaky Bay
NUYTS ARCHIPELAGO
GAWLER RANGES
EYRE PENINSULA
Port Kenny
Elliston
Lock
Rudall
Cleve
Cowell
Tumby Bay
Port Lincoln
Spencer Gulf
Whyalla
Iron Knob
Port Augusta
Woomera
Roxby Downs
Andamooka
Lake Torrens
Lake Gairdner
Lake Eyre North
LAKE EYRE NATIONAL PARK
Lake Eyre South
Marree
Lyndhurst
Leigh Creek
Beltana
FLINDERS RANGES
FLINDERS RANGES NAT. PARK
Hawker
Quorn
Port Pirie
Peterborough
Jamestown
Burra
Kadina
Wallaroo
YORKE PENINSULA
Gulf St. Vincent
Gawler
Elizabeth
Salisbury
Adelaide
Port Adelaide
Murray Bridge
Mount Barker
Strathalbyn
Renmark
Berri
Barmera
Loxton
Waikerie
Morgan
Broken Hill
Wentworth
Mildura
Merbein
VICTORIA
NEW SOUTH WALES
Lake Frome
Tibooburra
STRZELECKI DESERT
STURT DESERT
STONY DESERT
TIRARI DESERT
Cooper Creek
Innamincka
Nappamerry
Birdsville
SIMPSON DESERT NAT. PARK
Betoota
Haddon Downs
Cordillo Downs
CHANNEL COUNTRY
Bedourie
QUEENSLAND
Boulia
Hamilton Hotel
Springvale
TOKO RANGE
Glenormiston
Tobermorey
Urandangi
Mount Isa
Cloncurry
Mary Kathleen
SELWYN RANGE
Duchess
Camooweal
Avon Downs
PILPAH RANGE
Lake Nash
BARKLY TABLELAND
Anthony Lagoon
Brunette Downs
Alexandria
Alroy Downs
Wonarah
Soudan
Ranken Store
Gallipoli
Lawn Hill
LAWN HILL NATIONAL PARK
Doomadgee
DOOMADGEE ABORIGINAL RESERVE
NICHOLSON RIVER ABORIGINAL
Burketown
Gulf of Carpentaria
WELLESLEY ISLANDS
BENTINCK ISLAND
FORSYTH ISLAND
Wollogorang
Calvert Hills
128°
130°
132°
134°
136°
138°
140°
142°
20°
22°
24°
26°
28°
30°
32°
34°
Kilometers 0 100 200 300 Km.
Statute Miles 0 100 200 300 Mi.

Scale 1:6,000,000

One centimeter represents 60 kilometers.
One inch represents approximately 95 miles.
Lambert Conformal Conic Projection

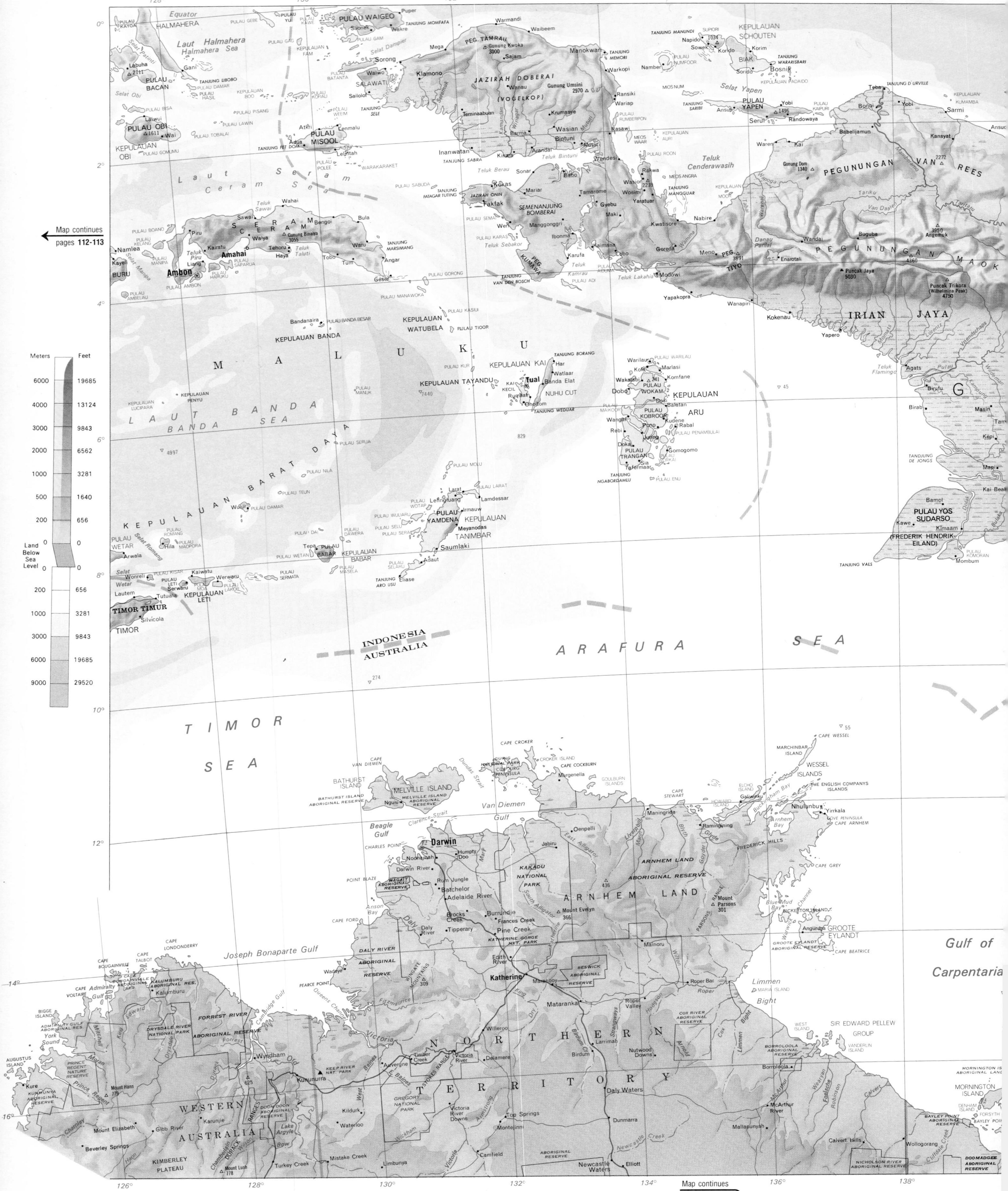
Meters Feet
6000 19685
4000 13124
3000 9843
2000 6562
1000 3281
500 1640
200 656
0 0
Land Below Sea Level
0 0
200 656
1000 3281
3000 9843
6000 19685
9000 29520
Equator
HALMAHERA
PULAU WAIGEO
Laut Halmahera
Halmahera Sea
PULAU BACAN
PULAU OBI
KEPULAUAN OBI
PULAU MISOOL
SALAWATI
Sorong
JAZIRAH DOBERAI
(VOGELKOP)
Manokwari
KEPULAUAN SCHOUTEN
BIAK
PULAU YAPEN
Selat Yapen
Teluk Cenderawasih
PEGUNUNGAN VAN REES
PEGUNUNGAN MAOK
Puncak Jaya 5030
Puncak Trikora (Wilhelmina Peak) 4750
IRIAN JAYA
Laut Seram
Ceram Sea
SERAM
Ambon
Amahai
BURU
Fakfak
Teluk Bintuni
KEPULAUAN BANDA
KEPULAUAN WATUBELA
KEPULAUAN KAI
Tual
KEPULAUAN TAYANDU
KEPULAUAN ARU
MALUKU
LAUT BANDA
BANDA SEA
KEPULAUAN BARAT DAYA
PULAU YAMDENA
KEPULAUAN TANIMBAR
Saumlaki
PULAU WETAR
KEPULAUAN LETI
TIMOR TIMUR
PULAU YOS SUDARSO
(FREDERIK HENDRIK EILAND)
Map continues
pages 112-113
INDONESIA
AUSTRALIA
ARAFURA SEA
TIMOR SEA
BATHURST ISLAND
MELVILLE ISLAND
Van Diemen Gulf
Beagle Gulf
Darwin
WESSEL ISLANDS
Nhulunbuy
GROOTE EYLANDT
Gulf of Carpentaria
ARNHEM LAND
ARNHEM LAND ABORIGINAL RESERVE
KAKADU NATIONAL PARK
Katherine
Joseph Bonaparte Gulf
Wyndham
Kununurra
NORTHERN TERRITORY
WESTERN AUSTRALIA
KIMBERLEY PLATEAU
Daly Waters
Newcastle Waters
SIR EDWARD PELLEW GROUP
MORNINGTON ISLAND
Borroloola
Limmen Bight
126° 128° 130° 132° 134° 136° 138°
0° 2° 4° 6° 8° 10° 12° 14° 16°

Map continues
pages 162-163

MAP FORM	bay	cape	island	kepulauan	mount	pulau	range	tanjung
ENGLISH	bay	cape	island	islands	mount	island	range	cape
DEUTSCH	Bucht	Kap	Insel	Inseln	Berg	Insel	Gebirge	Kap
ESPAÑOL	bahía	cabo	isla	islas	montaña	isla	cordillera	cabo
FRANÇAIS	baie	cap	île	îles	mont	île	chaîne	cap
PORTUGUÊS	baía	cabo	ilha	ilhas	monte	ilha	cordilheira	cabo

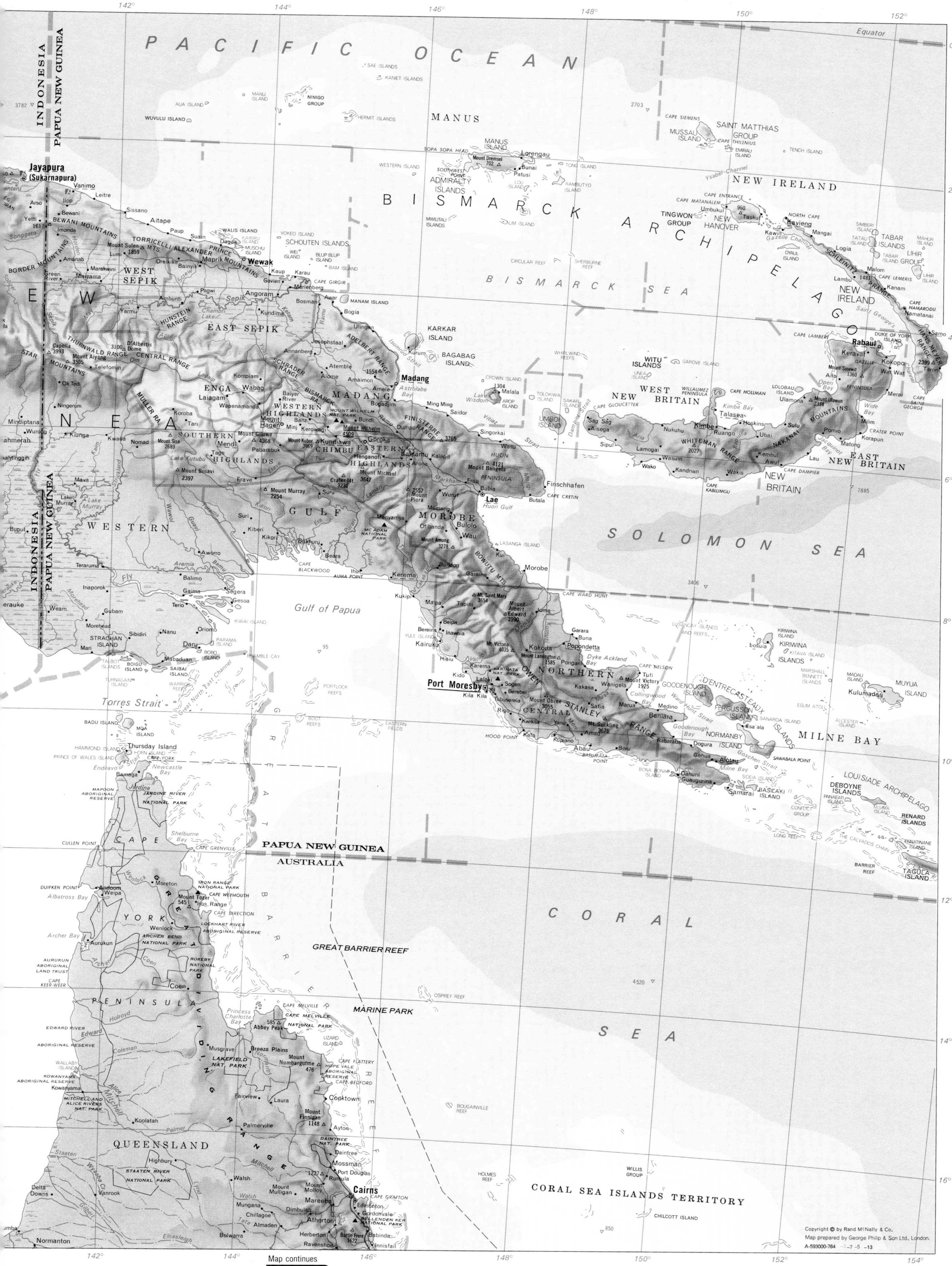
PACIFIC OCEAN
INDONESIA
PAPUA NEW GUINEA
Jayapura (Sukarnapura)
Vanimo
Aitape
Wewak
SCHOUTEN ISLANDS
MANUS
Lorengau
ADMIRALTY ISLANDS
BISMARCK ARCHIPELAGO
BISMARCK SEA
NEW IRELAND
Kavieng
NEW HANOVER
SAINT MATTHIAS GROUP
TABAR ISLANDS
LIHIR GROUP
WEST SEPIK
EAST SEPIK
Angoram
KARKAR ISLAND
BAGABAG ISLAND
Madang
MADANG
ENGA
Wabag
WESTERN HIGHLANDS
Mount Hagen
Mount Wilhelm 4509
SOUTHERN HIGHLANDS
Mendi
CHIMBU
EASTERN HIGHLANDS
Goroka
Kundiawa
NEW BRITAIN
WEST NEW BRITAIN
EAST NEW BRITAIN
Rabaul
Kokopo
Talasea
WITU ISLANDS
Lae
Huon Gulf
Finschhafen
HUON PENINSULA
MOROBE
Bulolo
Wau
GULF
Kerema
WESTERN
Balimo
Daru
Gulf of Papua
SOLOMON SEA
Port Moresby
NORTHERN
Popondetta
Kokoda
CENTRAL
OWEN STANLEY RANGE
Mount Victoria 4035
Mount Albert Edward 3990
TROBRIAND ISLANDS
KIRIWINA ISLANDS
WOODLARK
Kulumadau
MUYUA ISLAND
D'ENTRECASTEAUX ISLANDS
GOODENOUGH ISLAND
FERGUSSON ISLAND
NORMANBY ISLAND
MILNE BAY
Alotau
Samarai
LOUISIADE ARCHIPELAGO
DEBOYNE ISLANDS
RENARD ISLANDS
TAGULA ISLAND
Torres Strait
Thursday Island
PAPUA NEW GUINEA
AUSTRALIA
CAPE YORK PENINSULA
GREAT DIVIDING RANGE
GREAT BARRIER REEF
GREAT BARRIER REEF MARINE PARK
Weipa
Aurukun
Coen
Cooktown
QUEENSLAND
Cairns
Atherton
Innisfail
Normanton
CORAL SEA
CORAL SEA ISLANDS TERRITORY
WILLIS GROUP
CHILCOTT ISLAND
Equator
Copyright © by Rand McNally & Co.
Map prepared by George Philip & Son Ltd., London.
A-593000-764

Map continues pages 166-167

Kilometers 0 100 200 300 Km.
Statute Miles 0 100 200 300 Mi.

Scale 1:6,000,000

One centimeter represents 60 kilometers.
One inch represents approximately 95 miles.
Lambert Conformal Conic Projection

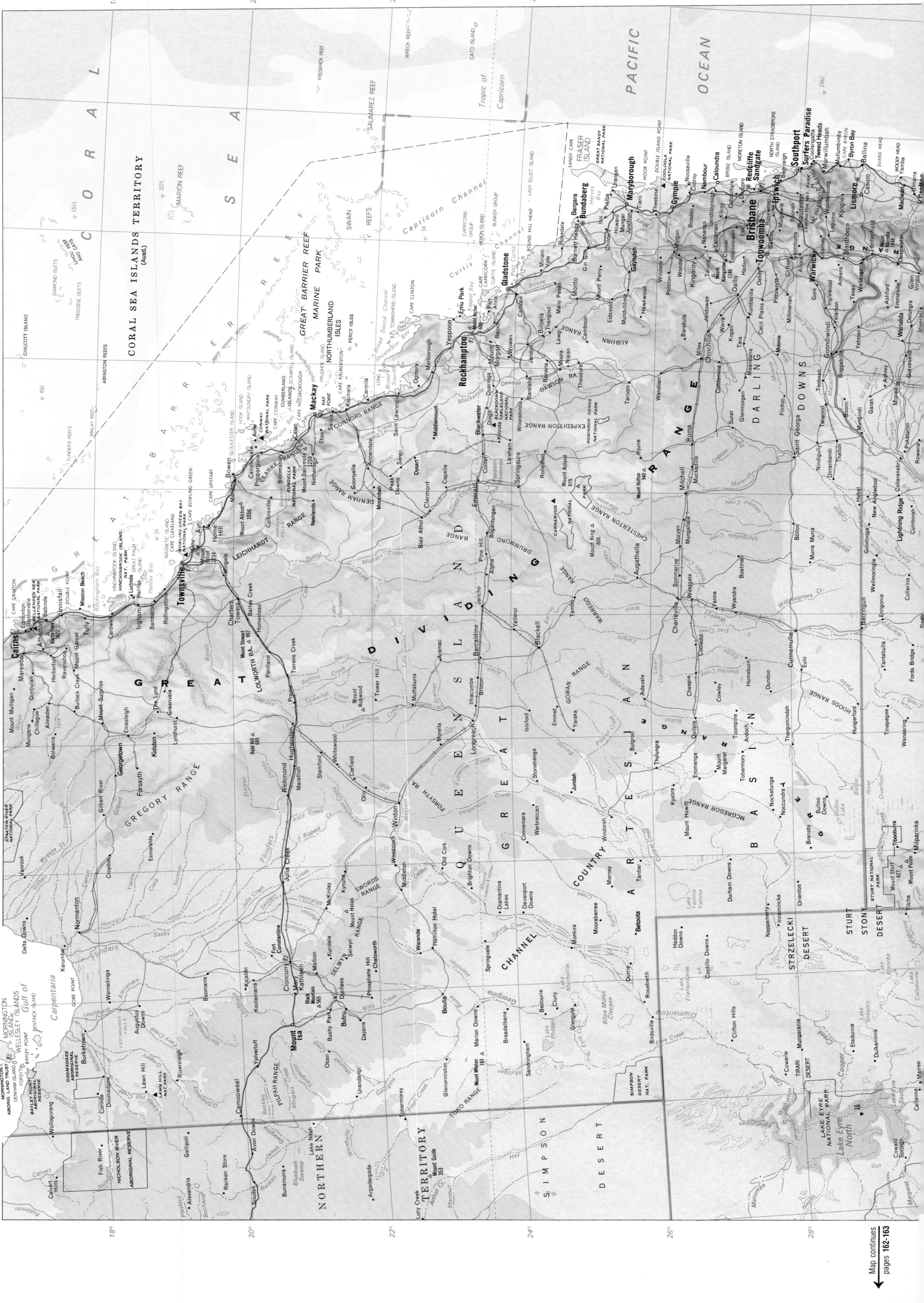
CORAL SEA
PACIFIC OCEAN
CORAL SEA ISLANDS TERRITORY (Austl.)
GREAT BARRIER REEF
GREAT BARRIER REEF MARINE PARK
Tropic of Capricorn
Capricorn Channel
Gulf of Carpentaria
QUEENSLAND
NORTHERN TERRITORY
GREAT DIVIDING RANGE
GREAT ARTESIAN BASIN
CHANNEL COUNTRY
SIMPSON DESERT
STURT STONY DESERT
STRZELECKI DESERT
DARLING DOWNS
GREGORY RANGE
Brisbane
Townsville
Cairns
Rockhampton
Mackay
Mount Isa
Gladstone
Bundaberg
Maryborough
Toowoomba
Ipswich
Southport
Longreach
Charleville
Roma
Lake Eyre North

Map continues pages 164-165

Map continues pages 162-163

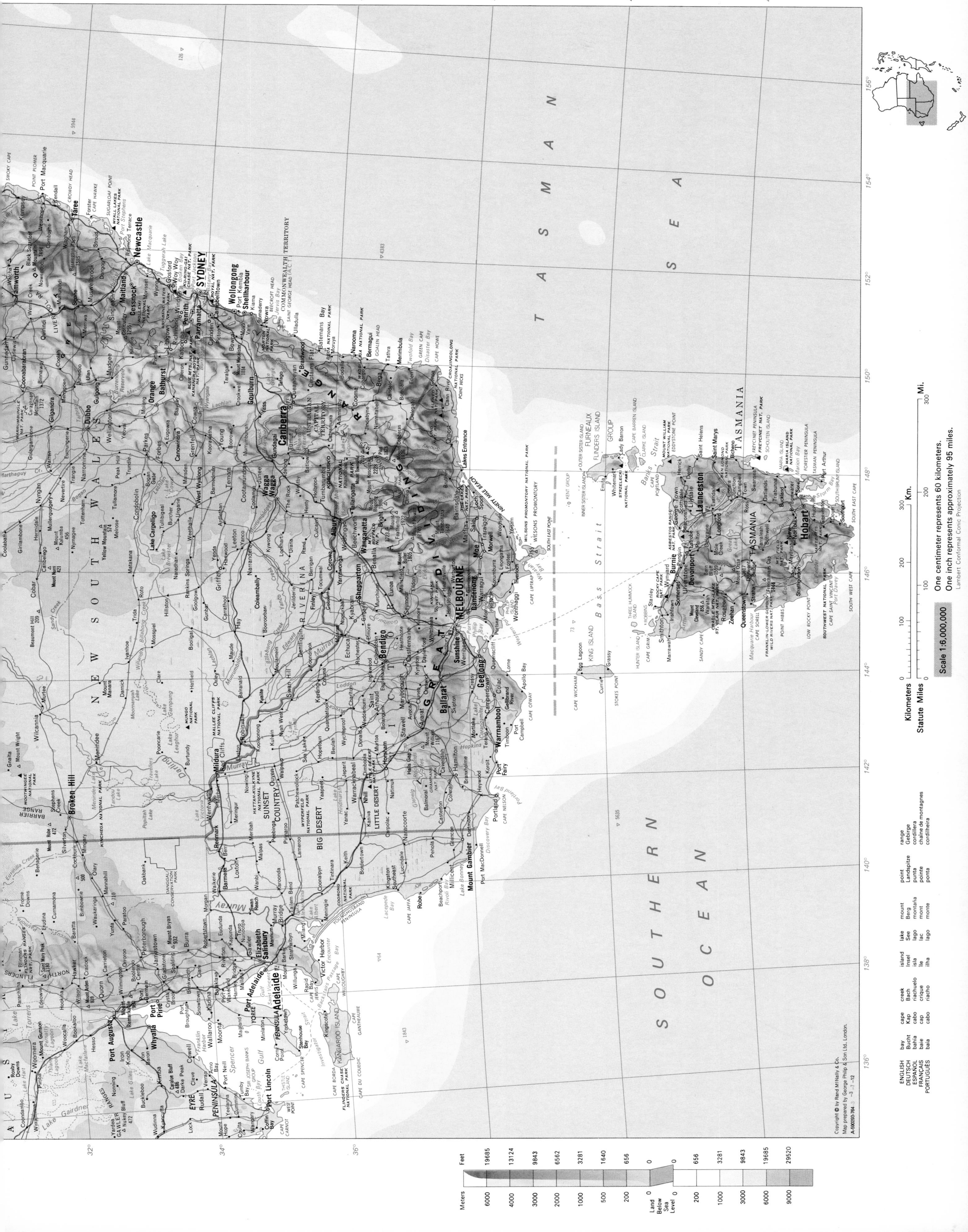
TASMAN SEA
SOUTHERN OCEAN
NEW SOUTH WALES
TASMANIA
SYDNEY
MELBOURNE
Canberra
Adelaide
Hobart
Newcastle
Wollongong
Geelong
Ballarat
Bendigo
Launceston
Bass Strait
KING ISLAND
FLINDERS ISLAND
KANGAROO ISLAND
COMMONWEALTH TERRITORY
GREAT DIVIDING RANGE
Scale 1:6,000,000
One centimeter represents 60 kilometers.
One inch represents approximately 95 miles.
Lambert Conformal Conic Projection
Kilometers
Statute Miles
ENGLISH bay cape creek island lake mount point range
DEUTSCH Bucht Kap Bach Insel See Berg Landspitze Gebirge
ESPAÑOL bahía cabo riachuelo isla lago montaña punta cordillera
FRANÇAIS baie cap crique île lac mont pointe chaîne de montagnes
PORTUGUÊS baía cabo riacho ilha lago monte ponta cordilheira
Copyright © by Rand McNally & Co.
Map prepared by George Philip & Son Ltd, London.
Meters 6000 4000 3000 2000 1000 500 200 0 Land Below Sea Level 0 200 1000 3000 6000 9000
Feet 19685 13124 9843 6562 3281 1640 656 0 0 656 3281 9843 19685 29520

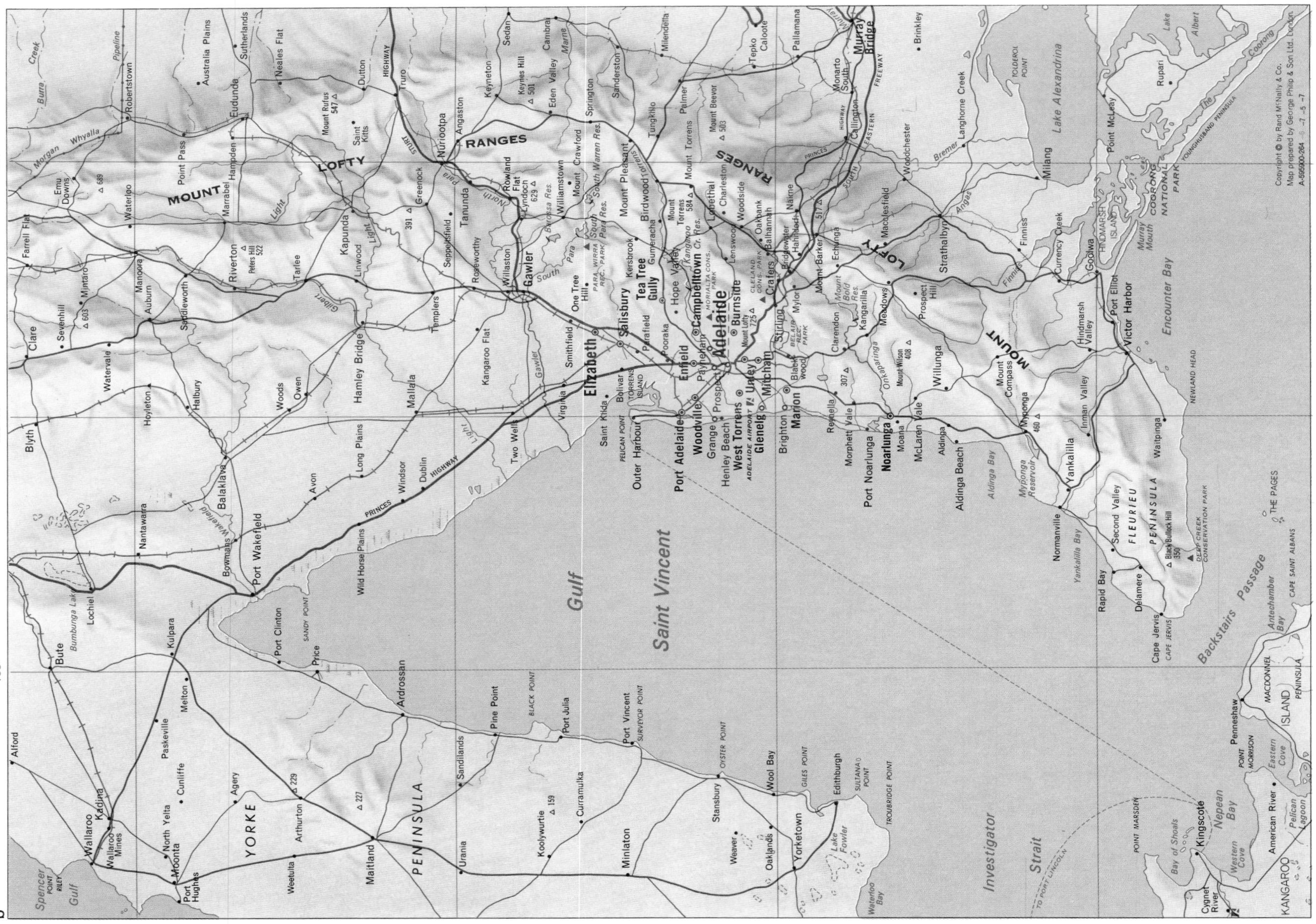
b
Gulf
Saint Vincent
YORKE
PENINSULA
Investigator
Strait
MOUNT
LOFTY
RANGES
Adelaide

ENGLISH	DEUTSCH	ESPAÑOL	FRANÇAIS	PORTUGUES
bay, b.	Bucht	bahía	baie	baía
cape	Kap	cabo	cap	cabo
dam	Damm	dique	barrage	barragem
gulf	Golf	golfo	golfe	golfo
island	Insel	isla	île	ilha
lake, l.	See	lago	lac	lago
peninsula	Halbinsel	península	péninsule	península
point	Landspitze	punta	pointe	ponta

Kilometers 0 10 20 30 40 50 Km.
Statute Miles 0 10 20 30 40 50 Mi.

Scale 1:1,000,000

One centimeter represents 10 kilometers.
One inch represents approximately 16 miles.
Lambert Conformal Conic Projection

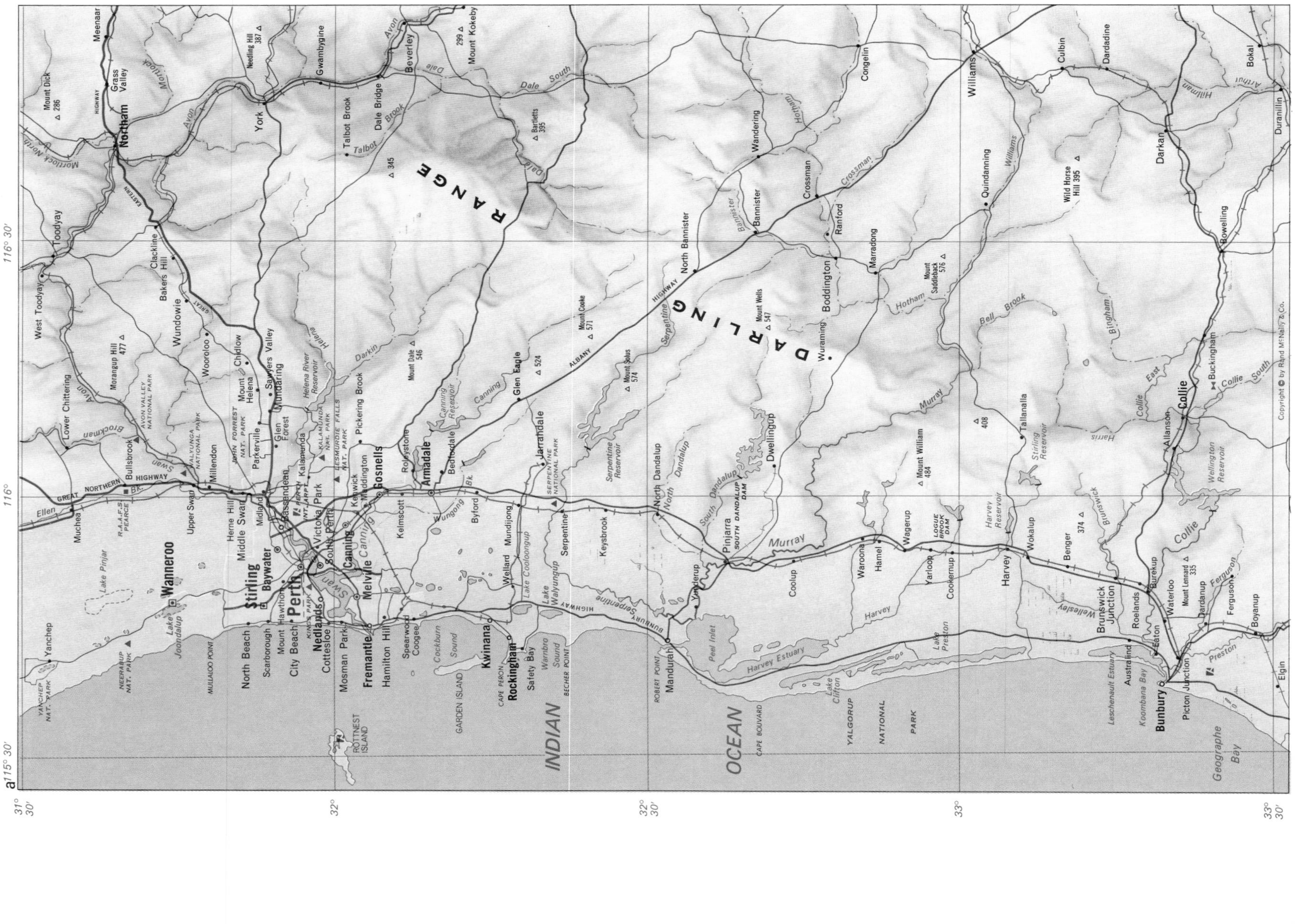
a
INDIAN
OCEAN
DARLING
RANGE
Perth

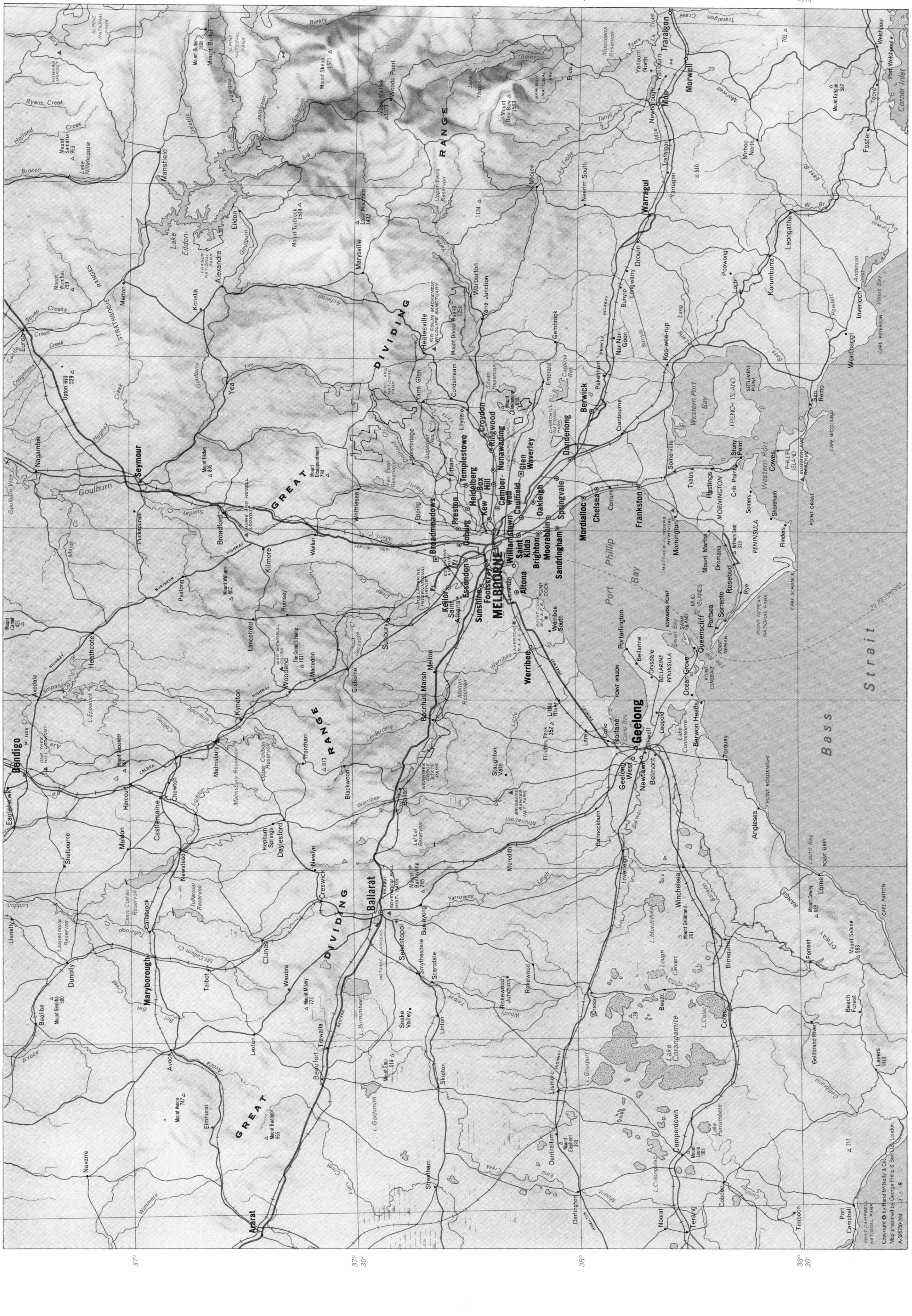
MELBOURNE
Geelong
Ballarat
Bendigo
Seymour
Warragul
Morwell
Traralgon
Frankston
Dandenong
Werribee
Melton
Kyneton
Castlemaine
Maryborough
Ararat
Colac
Camperdown
Torquay
Port Phillip Bay
Western Port Bay
FRENCH ISLAND
PHILLIP ISLAND
Bass Strait
GREAT DIVIDING RANGE
MORNINGTON PENINSULA
BELLARINE PENINSULA
OTWAY RANGES
Lake Eildon
Lake Corangamite
Copyright © by Rand McNally & Co.
Map prepared by George Philip & Son Ltd. London.

ENGLISH	bay, b.	cape	creek, cr.	lake, l.	mount, mt.	point	range, ra.	reservoir, res.
DEUTSCH	Bucht	Kap	Bach	See	Berg	Landspitze	Gebirge	Stausee
ESPAÑOL	bahía	cabo	riachuelo	lago	montaña	punta	cordillera	embalse
FRANÇAIS	baie	cap	crique	lac	mont	pointe	chaîne	réservoir
PORTUGUES	baía	cabo	riacho	lago	monte	ponta	cordilheira	reservatório

Kilometers 0 10 20 30 40 50 Km.

Statute Miles 0 10 20 30 40 50 Mi.

Scale 1:1,000,000

One centimeter represents 10 kilometers.
One inch represents approximately 16 miles.

Lambert Conformal Conic Projection

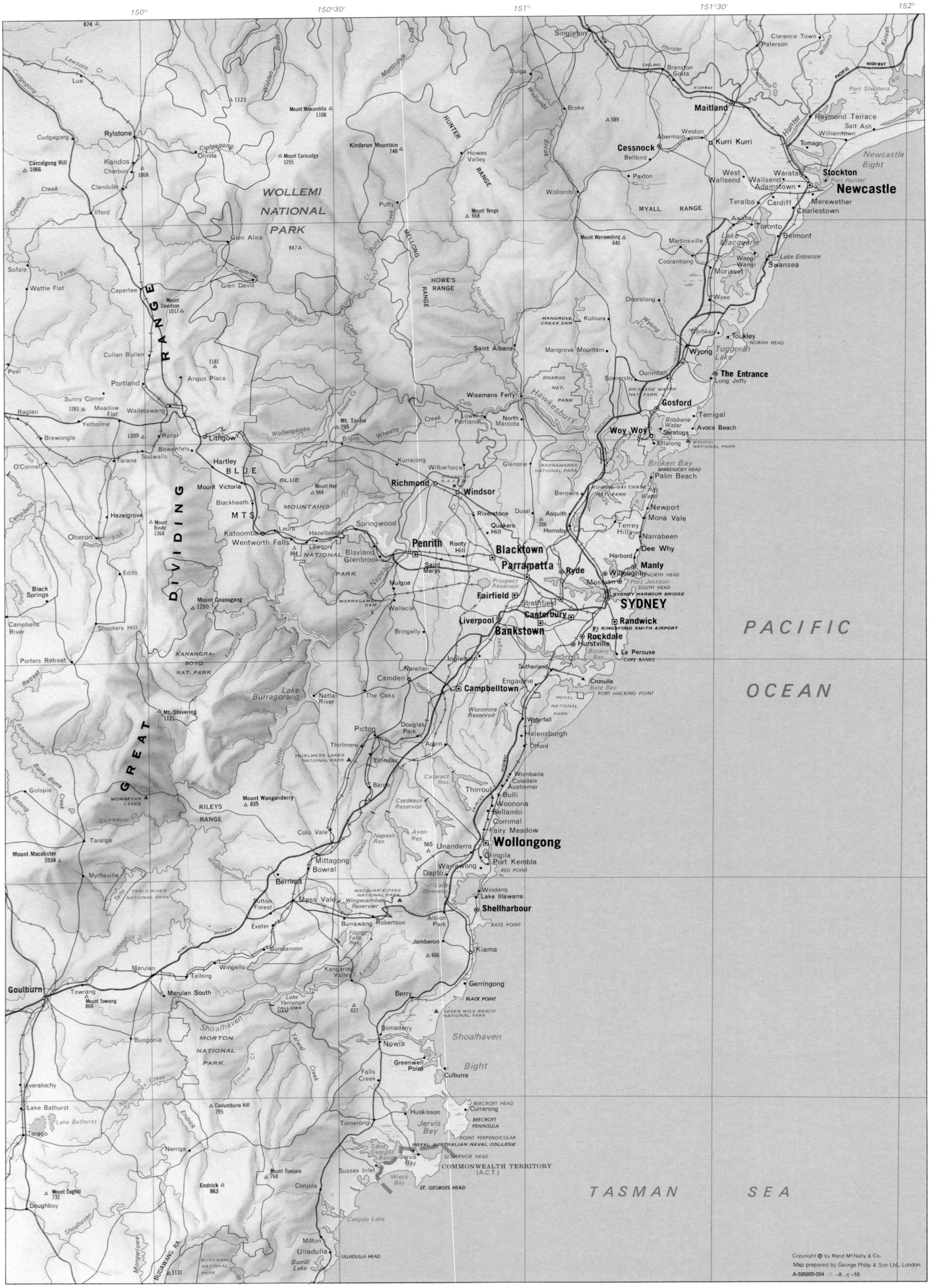

150°
150°30′
151°
151°30′
152°
33°
33° 30′
34°
34° 30′
35°
WOLLEMI NATIONAL PARK
GREAT DIVIDING RANGE
BLUE MTS.
BLUE MOUNTAINS
KANANGRA-BOYD NAT. PARK
MORTON NATIONAL PARK
HUNTER RANGE
MELLONG RANGE
HOWE'S RANGE
MYALL RANGE
RILEYS RANGE
PACIFIC OCEAN
TASMAN SEA
SYDNEY
Newcastle
Wollongong
Parramatta
Blacktown
Penrith
Liverpool
Bankstown
Fairfield
Canterbury
Rockdale
Ryde
Manly
Randwick
Gosford
Maitland
Cessnock
Kurri Kurri
Stockton
Campbelltown
Shellharbour
Lithgow
Goulburn
Singleton
Windsor
Richmond
Katoomba
Wentworth Falls
Picton
Camden
Mittagong
Bowral
Moss Vale
Kiama
Nowra
Jervis Bay
Shoalhaven Bight
Lake Burragorang
Lake Macquarie
Hawkesbury
Port Stephens
Newcastle Bight
KINGSFORD SMITH AIRPORT
SYDNEY HARBOUR BRIDGE
ROYAL NATIONAL PARK
COMMONWEALTH TERRITORY (A.C.T.)
ROYAL AUSTRALIAN NAVAL COLLEGE
Copyright © by Rand McNally & Co.
Map prepared by George Philip & Son Ltd., London.
A-595800-264

ENGLISH	bight	creek, cr.	head	mount	range	reservoir, res.
DEUTSCH	Bucht	Bach	Vorgebirge	Berg	Gebirge	Stausee
ESPAÑOL	ensenada pequeña	riachuelo	promontorio	montaña	cordillera	estanque
FRANÇAIS	anse	crique	promontoire	mont	chaîne	réservoir
PORTUGUÊS	enseada	riacho	promontório	monte	cordilheira	reservatório

Kilometers 0 10 20 30 40 50 Km.

Statute Miles 0 10 20 30 40 50 Mi.

Scale 1:1,000,000

One centimeter represents 10 kilometers.
One inch represents approximately 16 miles.
Lambert Conformal Conic Projection

a

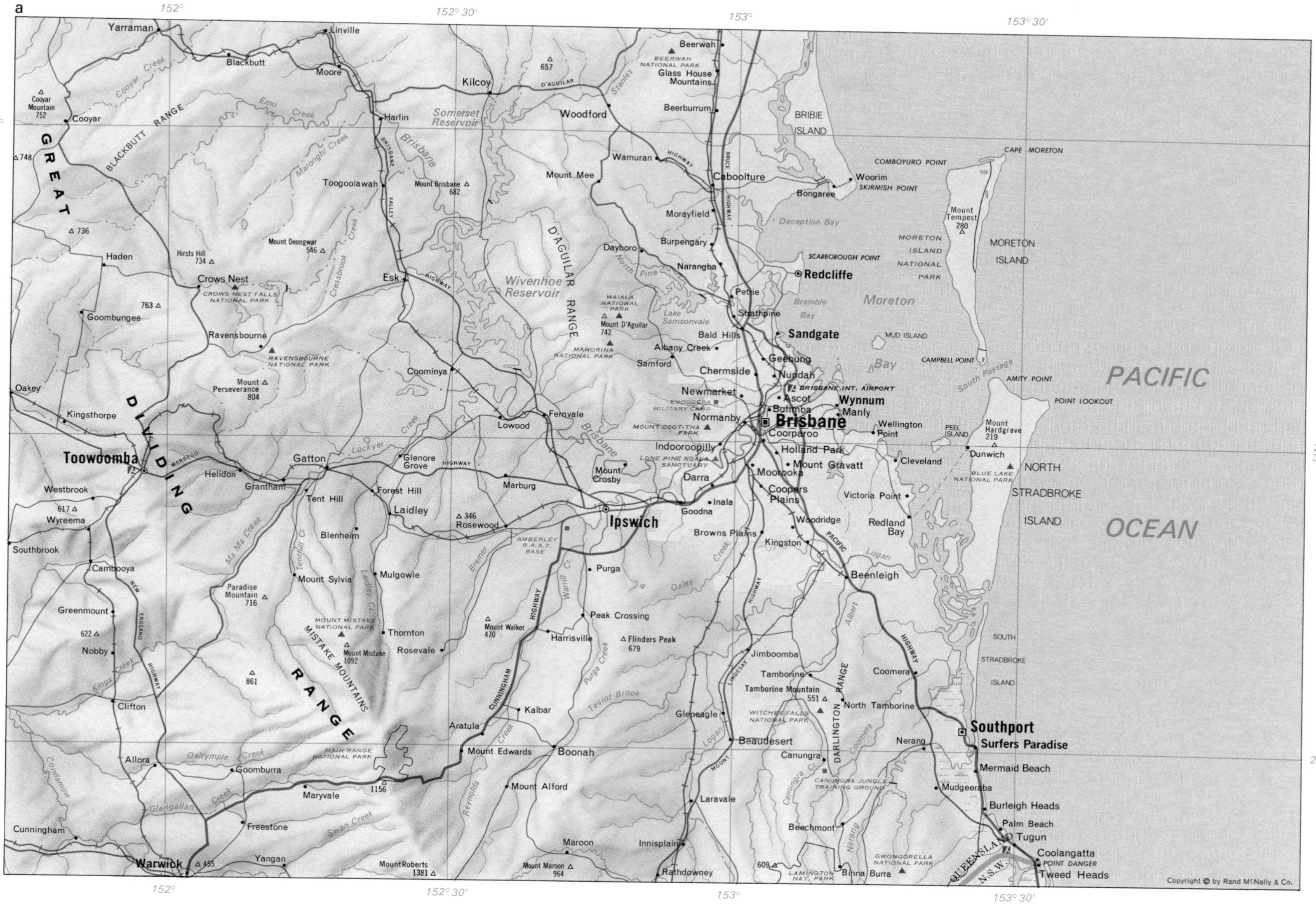
Yarraman
Linville
Blackbutt
Moore
Beerwah
Glass House Mountains
Kilcoy
Woodford
Cooyar
GREAT DIVIDING RANGE
BLACKBUTT RANGE
Harlin
Somerset Reservoir
Beerburrum
BRIBIE ISLAND
Toogoolawah
Wamuran
Caboolture
Mount Mee
Bongaree
Woorim
CAPE MORETON
MORETON ISLAND
Morayfield
Burpengary
Dayboro
Narangba
Deception Bay
Redcliffe
Haden
Crows Nest
Esk
Wivenhoe Reservoir
D'AGUILAR RANGE
Petrie
Strathpine
Sandgate
Moreton Bay
Goombungee
Ravensbourne
Bald Hills
Albany Creek
Samford
Geebung
Chermside
Nundah
Ascot
Oakey
Coominya
Newmarket
Wynnum
Manly
Kingsthorpe
Lowood
Fernvale
Normanby
Brisbane
Coorparoo
Wellington Point
PACIFIC OCEAN
Toowoomba
Helidon
Gatton
Glenore Grove
Indooroopilly
Holland Park
Mount Gravatt
Cleveland
Dunwich
NORTH STRADBROKE ISLAND
Westbrook
Wyreema
Grantham
Tent Hill
Forest Hill
Marburg
Mount Crosby
Darra
Mootooka
Coopers Plains
Inala
Goodna
Victoria Point
Laidley
Rosewood
Ipswich
Redland Bay
Southbrook
Blenheim
Browns Plains
Woodridge
Kingston
Cambooya
Mount Sylvia
Mulgowie
Purga
Beenleigh
Greenmount
Paradise Mountain
Peak Crossing
Nobby
Thornton
Rosevale
Harrisville
Flinders Peak
MISTAKE MOUNTAINS
RANGE
Jimboomba
Tamborine
Tamborine Mountain
North Tamborine
Coomera
SOUTH STRADBROKE ISLAND
Clifton
Kalbar
Aratula
Gleneagle
Beaudesert
Southport
Surfers Paradise
Allora
Mount Edwards
Boonah
Canungra
Nerang
Goomburra
Mermaid Beach
Mount Alford
Mudgeeraba
Maryvale
Laravale
Burleigh Heads
Cunningham
Freestone
Beechmont
Palm Beach
Tugun
Maroon
Innisplain
Coolangatta
Warwick
Yangan
Mount Roberts 1381
Mount Maroon 964
Rathdowney
Binna Burra
Tweed Heads
QUEENSLAND
N.S.W.
Copyright © by Rand McNally & Co.

b

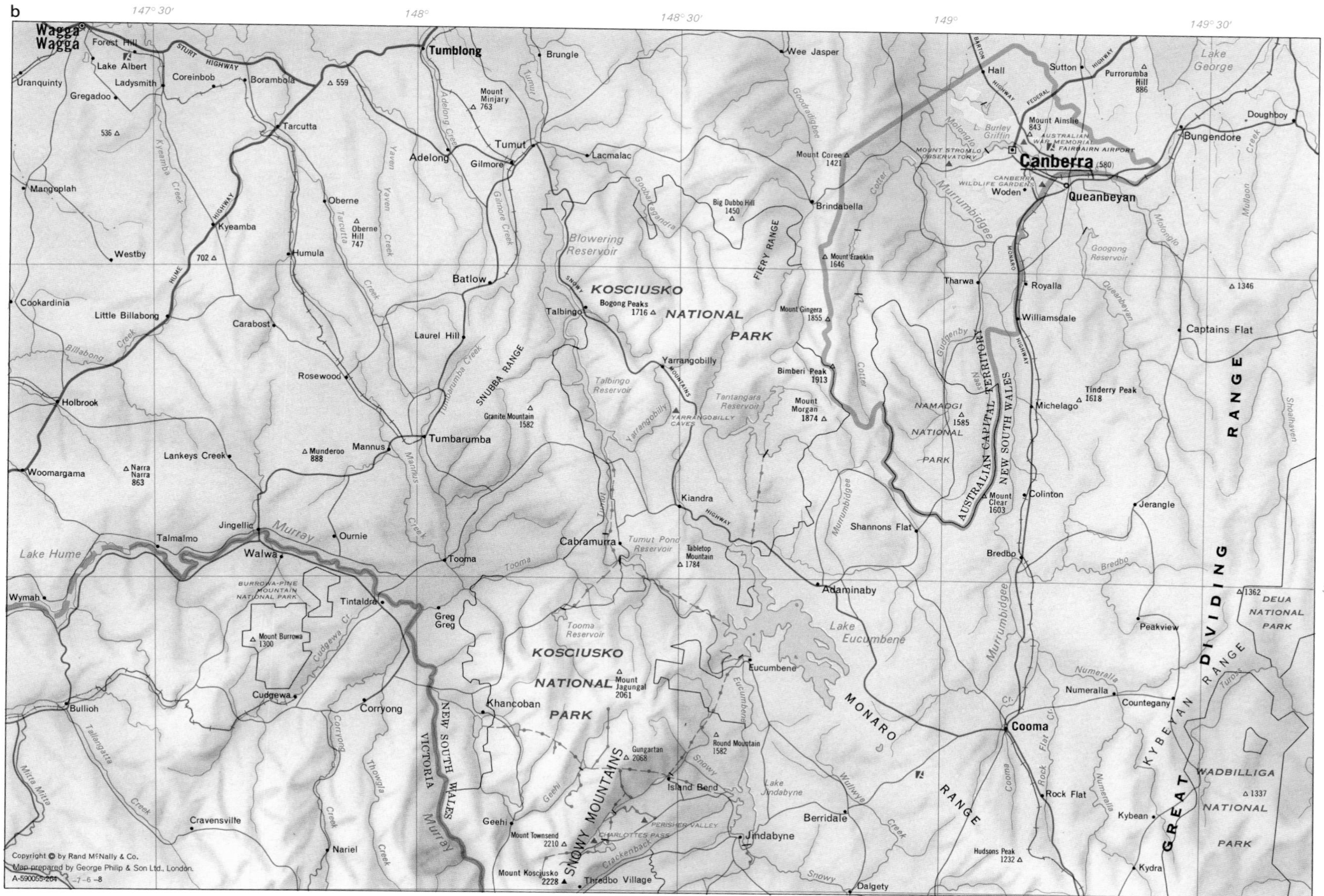
Wagga Wagga
Forest Hill
Lake Albert
Uranquinty
Ladysmith
Coreinbob
Borambola
Tumblong
Brungle
Wee Jasper
Hall
Sutton
Lake George
Gregadoo
Mount Minjary 763
Tarcutta
Adelong
Tumut
Gilmore
Lacmalac
Mount Coree 1421
Mount Ainslie 843
Canberra
Bungendore
Mangoplah
Oberne
Kyeamba
Brindabella
Woden
Queanbeyan
Westby
Humula
Blowering Reservoir
FIERY RANGE
Mount Franklin 1646
Tharwa
Royalla
Cookardinia
Little Billabong
Batlow
KOSCIUSKO NATIONAL PARK
Talbingo
Bogong Peaks 1716
Mount Gingera 1855
Williamsdale
Captains Flat
Carabost
Laurel Hill
Yarrangobilly
Rosewood
Bimberi Peak 1913
Holbrook
Tinderry Peak 1618
Michelago
Granite Mountain 1582
Mount Morgan 1874
NAMADGI NATIONAL PARK
AUSTRALIAN CAPITAL TERRITORY
NEW SOUTH WALES
RANGE
Lankeys Creek
Mannus
Tumbarumba
Munderoo 888
Woomargama
Narra Narra 863
Kiandra
Mount Clear 1603
Colinton
Jerangle
Jingellic
Talmalmo
Ournie
Cabramurra
Tumut Pond Reservoir
Tabletop Mountain 1784
Shannons Flat
Lake Hume
Walwa
Murray
Tooma
Bredbo
Wymah
Tintaldra
Adaminaby
DEUA NATIONAL PARK
Greg Greg
Lake Eucumbene
Peakview
Mount Burrowa 1300
KOSCIUSKO NATIONAL PARK
Mount Jagungal 2061
Eucumbene
MONARO RANGE
Numeralla
Countegany
GREAT DIVIDING RANGE
KYBEYAN RANGE
Cudgewa
Corryong
Khancoban
Bullioh
Cooma
VICTORIA
NEW SOUTH WALES
Round Mountain 1582
Gungartan 2068
Island Bend
SNOWY MOUNTAINS
Lake Jindabyne
Rock Flat
WADBILLIGA NATIONAL PARK
Kybean
Cravensville
Geehi
Mount Townsend 2210
Jindabyne
Berridale
Nariel
Hudsons Peak 1232
Kydra
Mount Kosciusko 2228
Thredbo Village
Dalgety
Copyright © by Rand McNally & Co.
Map prepared by George Philip & Son Ltd., London.

ENGLISH	creek	island	mount	peak	point	range	reservoir
DEUTSCH	Bach	Insel	Berg	Gipfel	Landspitze	Gebirge	Stausee
ESPAÑOL	riachuelo	isla	montaña	pico	punta	cordillera	embalse
FRANÇAIS	crique	île	mont	cime	pointe	chaîne	réservoir
PORTUGUÊS	riacho	ilha	monte	pico	ponta	cordilheira	reservatório

Kilometers 0 10 20 30 40 50 Km.

Statute Miles 0 10 20 30 40 50 Mi.

Scale 1:1,000,000

One centimeter represents 10 kilometers.
One inch represents approximately 16 miles.
Lambert Conformal Conic Projection

New Zealand / Neuseeland / Nueva Zelanda
Nouvelle Zélande / Nova Zelândia

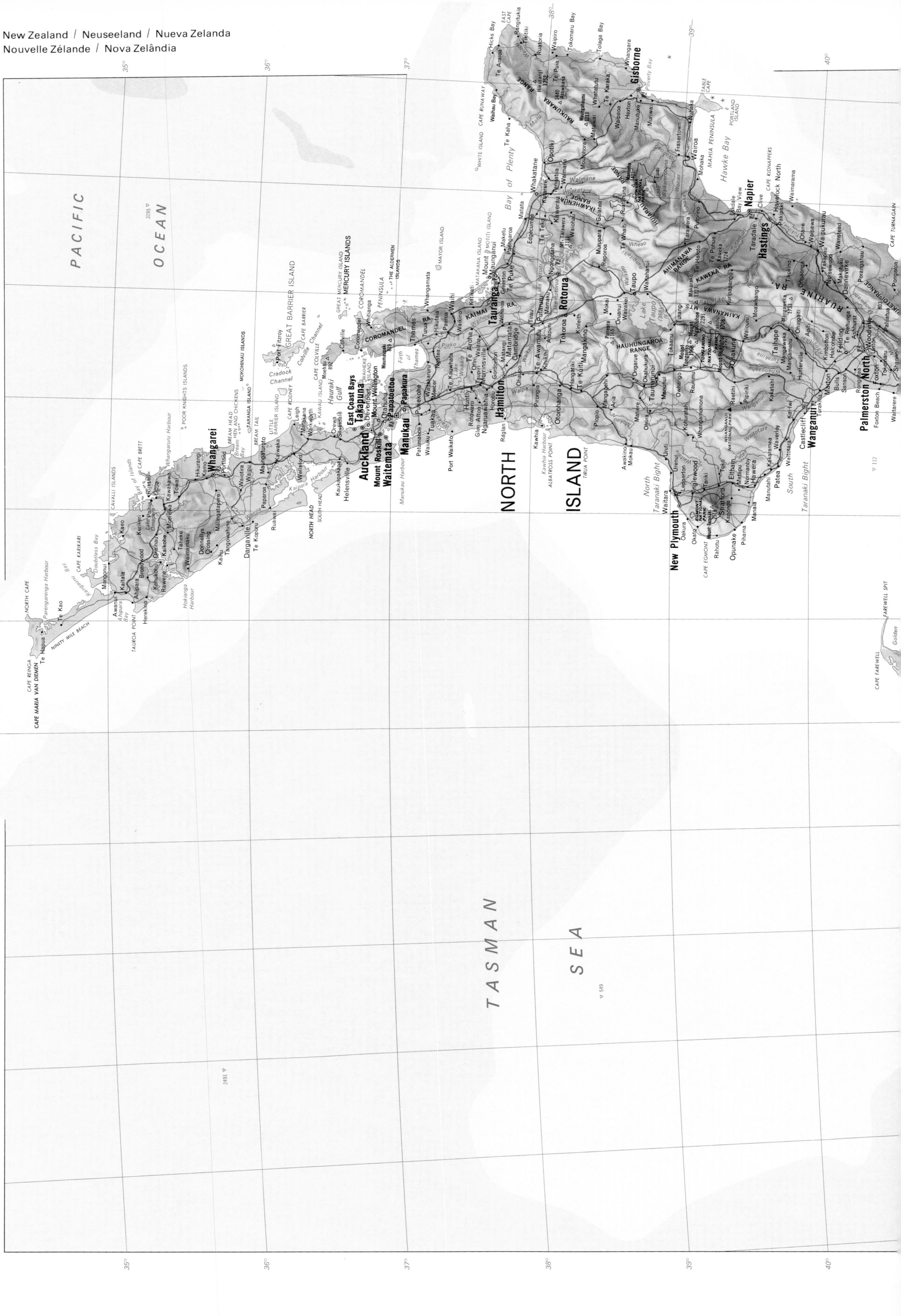
PACIFIC
OCEAN
TASMAN
SEA
NORTH
ISLAND
Auckland
Hamilton
Tauranga
Rotorua
Gisborne
Napier
Hastings
Whangarei
New Plymouth
Wanganui
Palmerston North
Bay of Plenty
Hawke Bay
North Taranaki Bight
South Taranaki Bight
Hauraki Gulf
GREAT BARRIER ISLAND
MERCURY ISLANDS
Taupo
Lake Taupo
NINETY MILE BEACH
CAPE REINGA
CAPE MARIA VAN DIEMEN
NORTH CAPE
EAST CAPE
CAPE EGMONT
CAPE KIDNAPPERS
CAPE TURNAGAIN
CAPE FAREWELL
FAREWELL SPIT
THREE KINGS ISLANDS

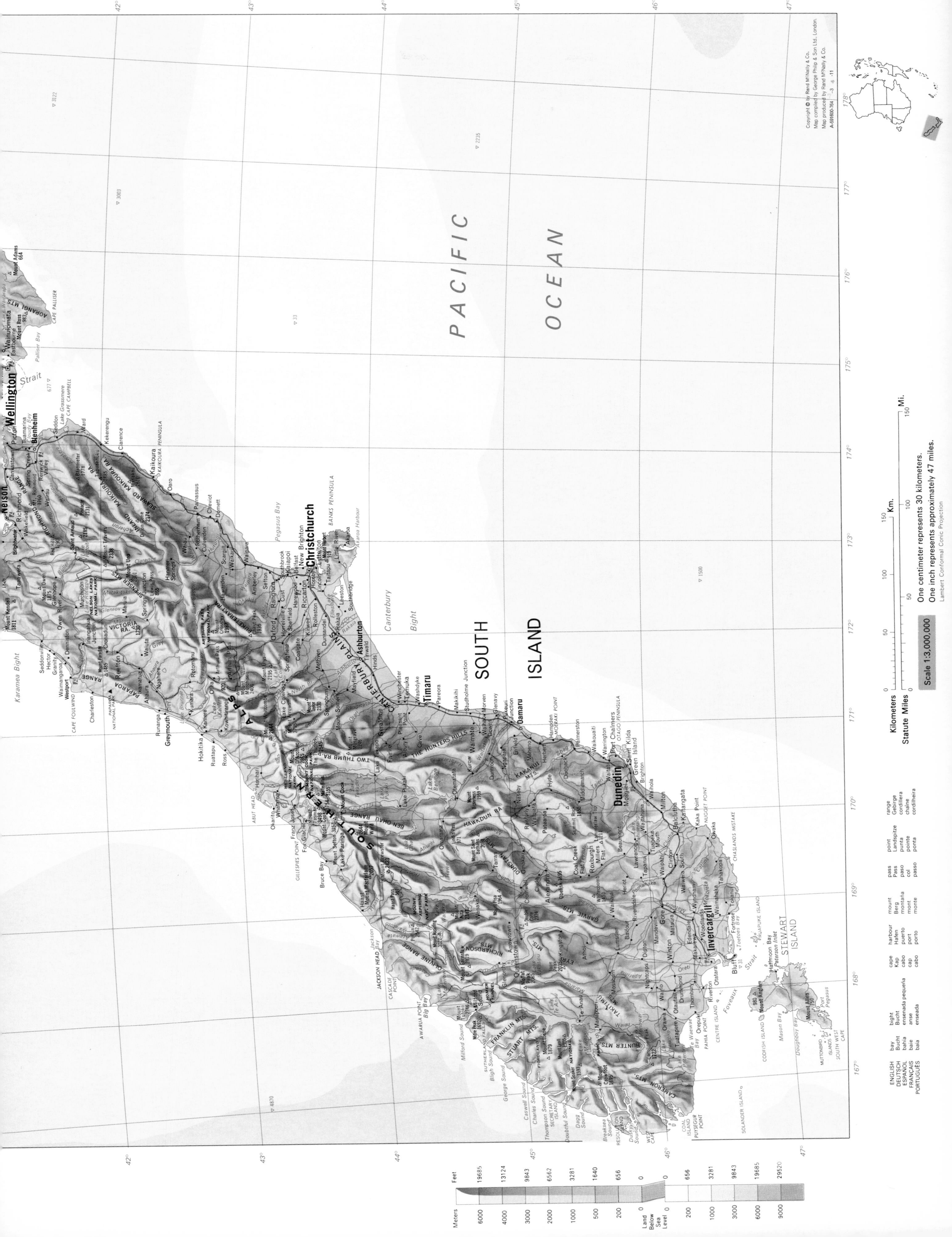
PACIFIC OCEAN
SOUTH ISLAND
STEWART ISLAND
Wellington
Nelson
Blenheim
Kaikoura
Christchurch
Ashburton
Timaru
Oamaru
Dunedin
Invercargill
Greymouth
Hokitika
Westport
Canterbury Bight
Pegasus Bay
Karamea Bight
Foveaux Strait
SOUTHERN ALPS
CANTERBURY PLAINS
BANKS PENINSULA
Kilometers
Statute Miles
Scale 1:3,000,000
One centimeter represents 30 kilometers.
One inch represents approximately 47 miles.
Lambert Conformal Conic Projection
Copyright © by Rand McNally & Co.
Map compiled by George Philip & Son Ltd. London.
Map produced by Rand McNally & Co.
ENGLISH bay bight cape harbour mount pass point range
DEUTSCH Bucht Bucht Kap Hafen Berg Pass Landspitze Gebirge
ESPAÑOL bahía ensenada pequeña cabo puerto montaña paso punta cordillera
FRANÇAIS baie anse cap port mont col pointe chaîne
PORTUGUÊS baía enseada cabo porto monte passo ponta cordilheira
Meters
Feet
Land Below Sea Level

a

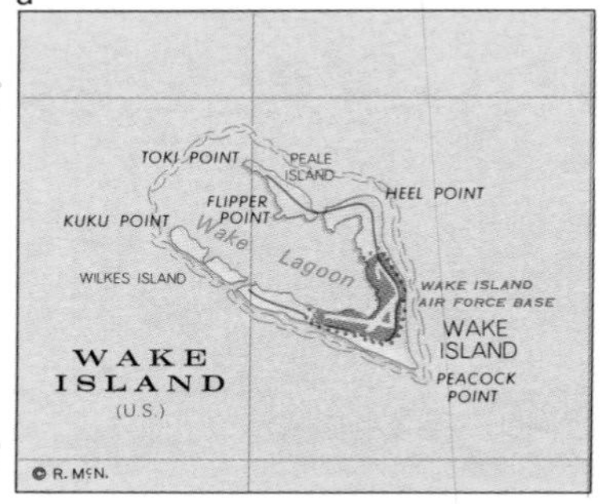
WAKE ISLAND
(U.S.)
TOKI POINT
PEALE ISLAND
FLIPPER POINT
KUKU POINT
HEEL POINT
WILKES ISLAND
WAKE ISLAND
PEACOCK POINT

b

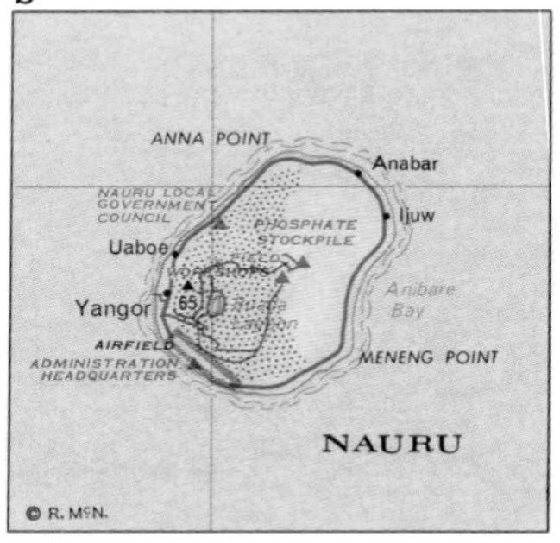
ANNA POINT
Anabar
Ijuw
Uaboe
Yangor
MENENG POINT
NAURU

c

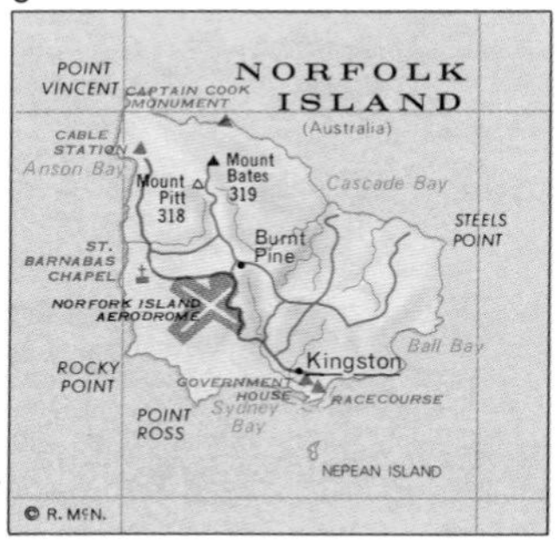
NORFOLK ISLAND
(Australia)
POINT VINCENT
Mount Pitt 318
Mount Bates 319
Burnt Pine
STEELS POINT
Kingston
ROCKY POINT
POINT ROSS
NEPEAN ISLAND

d

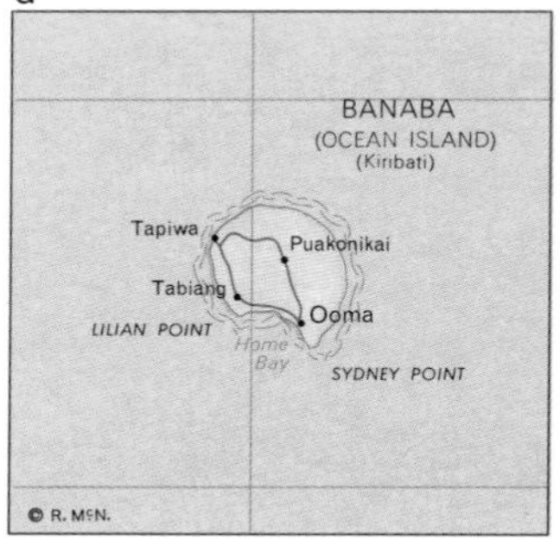
BANABA
(OCEAN ISLAND)
(Kiribati)
Tapiwa
Tabiang
Buakonikai
Ooma
LILIAN POINT
SYDNEY POINT

e

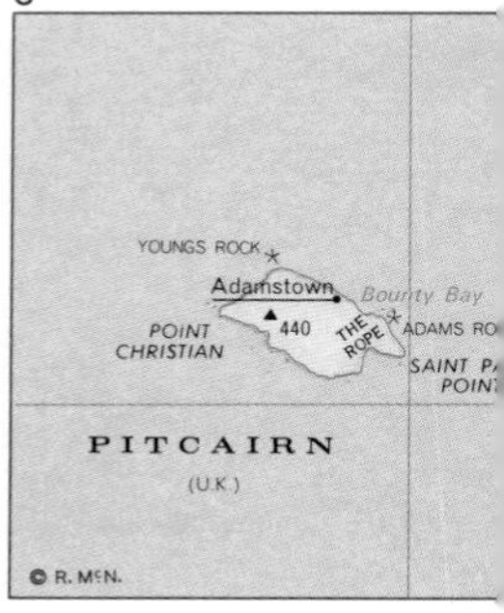
YOUNGS ROCK
Adamstown
440
POINT CHRISTIAN
PITCAIRN
(U.K.)

f

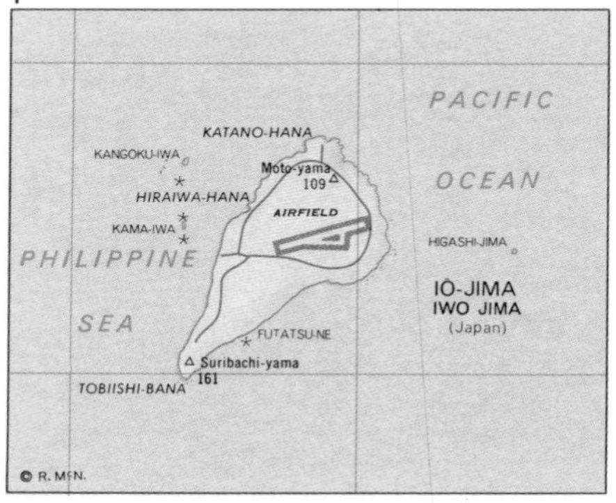
PACIFIC OCEAN
PHILIPPINE SEA
KATANO-HANA
KANGOKU-IWA
Motoyama 109
HIRAIWA-HANA
KAMA-IWA
HIGASHI-JIMA
IŌ-JIMA
IWO JIMA
(Japan)
FUTATSU-NE
Suribachi-yama 161
TOBIISHI-BANA

g

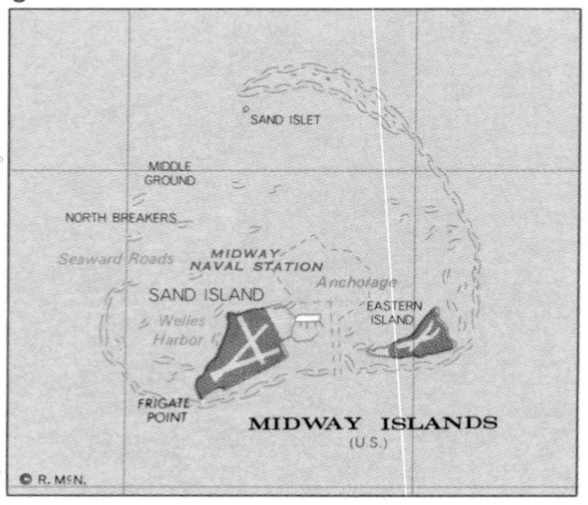
SAND ISLET
MIDDLE GROUND
NORTH BREAKERS
Seaward Roads
MIDWAY NAVAL STATION
SAND ISLAND
Welles Harbor
Anchorage
EASTERN ISLAND
FRIGATE POINT
MIDWAY ISLANDS
(U.S.)

h

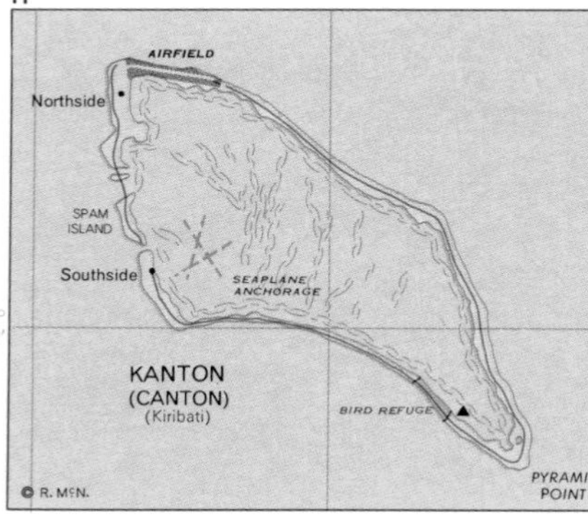
AIRFIELD
Northside
SPAM ISLAND
Southside
SEAPLANE ANCHORAGE
KANTON
(CANTON)
(Kiribati)
BIRD REFUGE
PYRAMID POINT

k

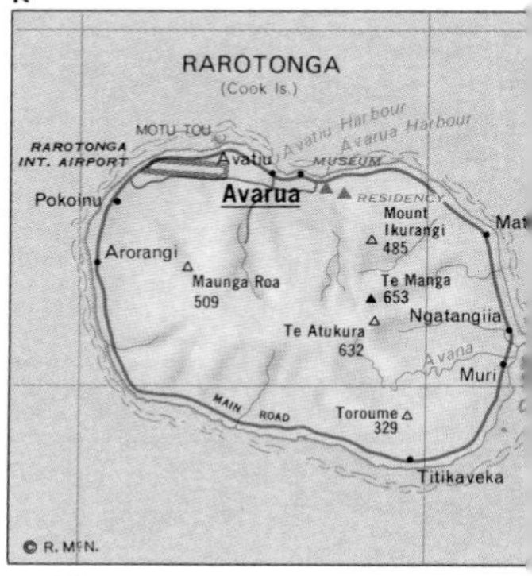
RAROTONGA
(Cook Is.)
Avarua
Pokoinu
Arorangi
Mount Ikurangi 485
Maunga Roa 509
Te Manga 653
Ngatangiia
Te Atukura 632
Muri
Toroume 329
Titikaveka

Kilometers 0 5 10 15 Km.
Statute Miles 0 5 10 15 Mi.

Scale 1:300,000
One centimeter represents 3 kilometers.
One inch represents approximately 4.7 miles.

m

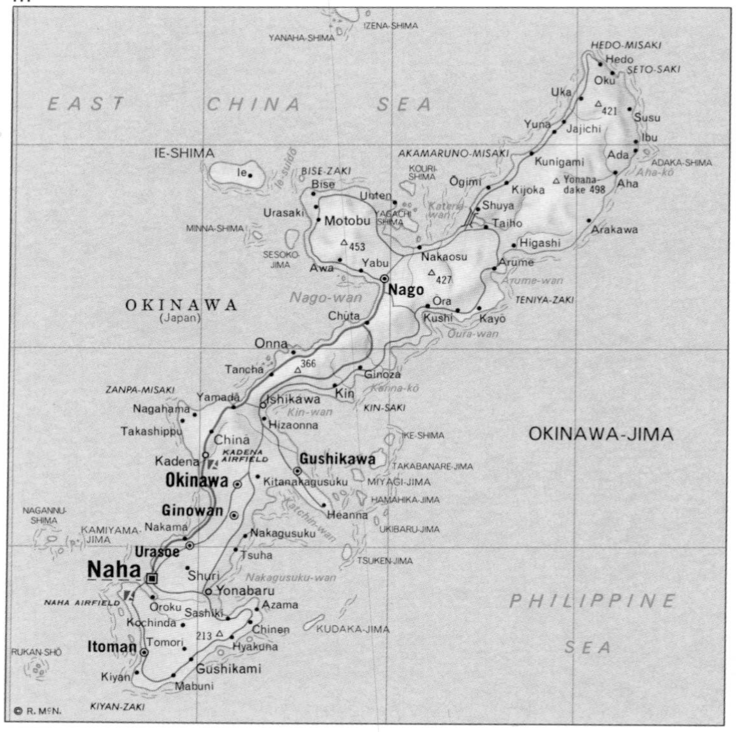
EAST CHINA SEA
HEDO-MISAKI
Hedo
IE-SHIMA
Ie
Motobu
Nago
OKINAWA
(Japan)
Onna
Ishikawa
Gushikawa
Okinawa
Ginowan
Urasoe
Naha
Shuri
Yonabaru
Itoman
Gushikami
OKINAWA-JIMA
PHILIPPINE SEA

n

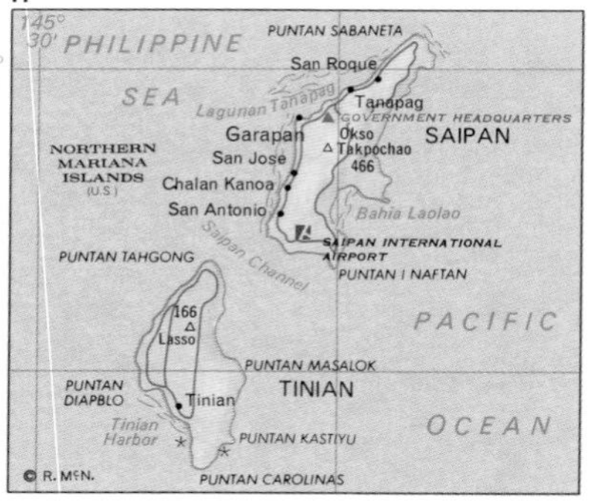
PHILIPPINE SEA
San Roque
Tanapag
Garapan
SAIPAN
San Jose
Chalan Kanoa
San Antonio
NORTHERN MARIANA ISLANDS (U.S.)
TINIAN
Tinian
PACIFIC OCEAN

o

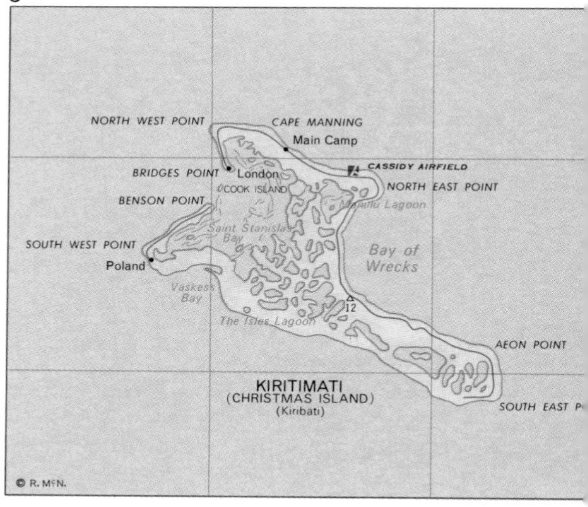
NORTH WEST POINT
CAPE MANNING
Main Camp
London
NORTH EAST POINT
BENSON POINT
SOUTH WEST POINT
Poland
Bay of Wrecks
KIRITIMATI
(CHRISTMAS ISLAND)
(Kiribati)
SOUTH EAST POINT

p

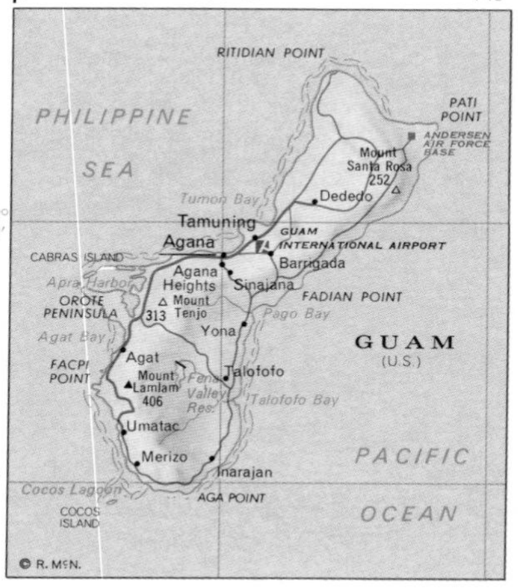
RITIDIAN POINT
PATI POINT
PHILIPPINE SEA
Dededo
Tamuning
Agana
Agana Heights
Barrigada
Sinajana
Yona
Agat
Talofofo
Umatac
Merizo
Inarajan
AGA POINT
GUAM
(U.S.)
PACIFIC OCEAN

q

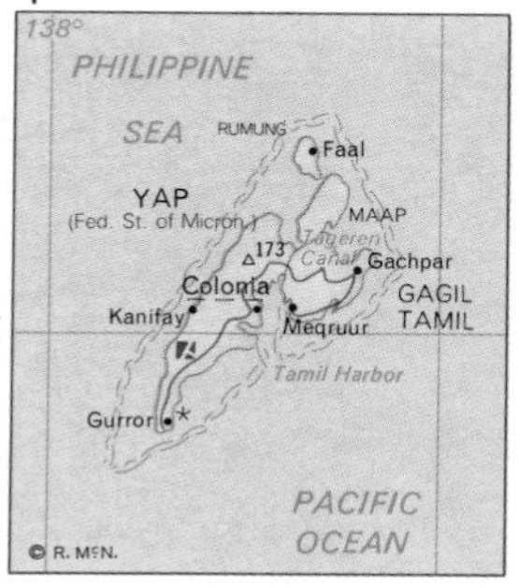
PHILIPPINE SEA
YAP
(Fed. St. of Micron.)
Colonia
Kanifay
Gagil Tamil
Gurror
PACIFIC OCEAN

r

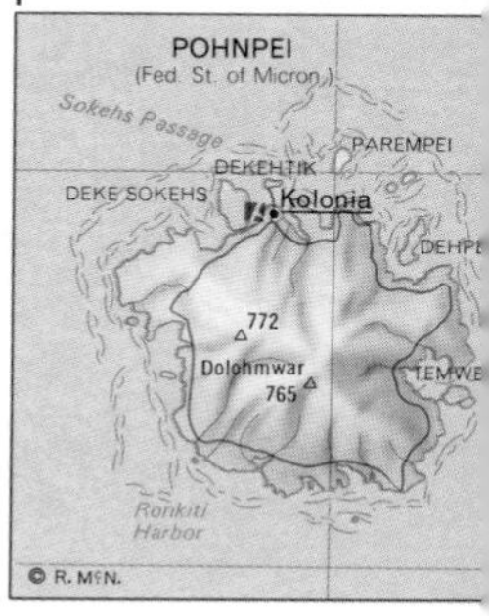
POHNPEI
(Fed. St. of Micron.)
Kolonia
772
Dolohmwar 765

s

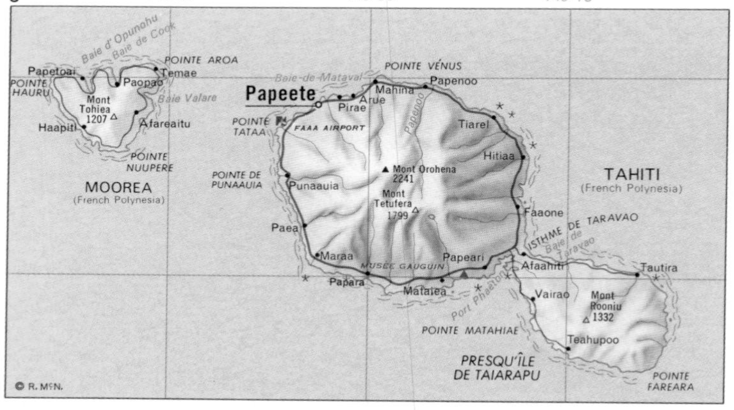
Papetoai
POINTE AROA
Temae
Mont Tohiea 1207
Afareaitu
Haapiti
MOOREA
(French Polynesia)
POINTE VÉNUS
Papeete
Papenoo
Pirae
Tiarei
Hitiaa
Mont Orohena 2241
Punaauia
Paea
Papara
Mataiea
Taravao
Tautira
TAHITI
(French Polynesia)
Mont Rooniu 1332
Teahupoo
PRESQU'ÎLE DE TAIARAPU
POINTE FAREARA

t

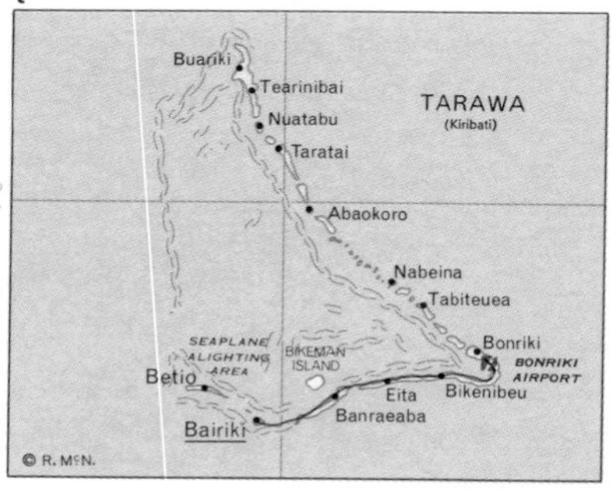
Buariki
Tearinibai
Nuatabu
Taratai
TARAWA
(Kiribati)
Abaokoro
Nabeina
Tabiteuea
Bonriki
Betio
Eita
Bikenibeu
Bairiki
Banraeaba

u

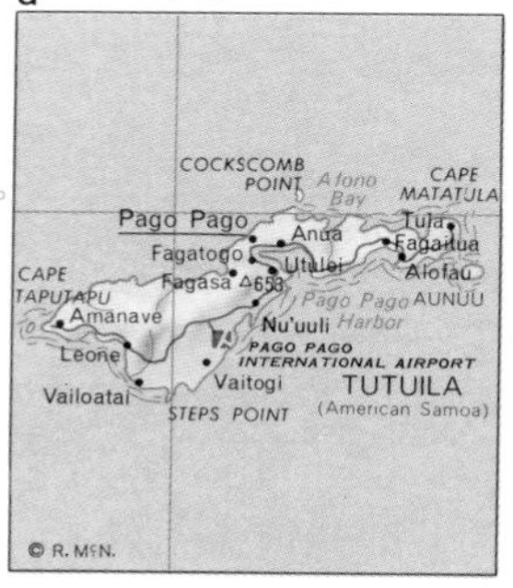
Pago Pago
Fagatogo
Aua
Tula
Leone
Vailoatai
Vaitogi
TUTUILA
(American Samoa)

v

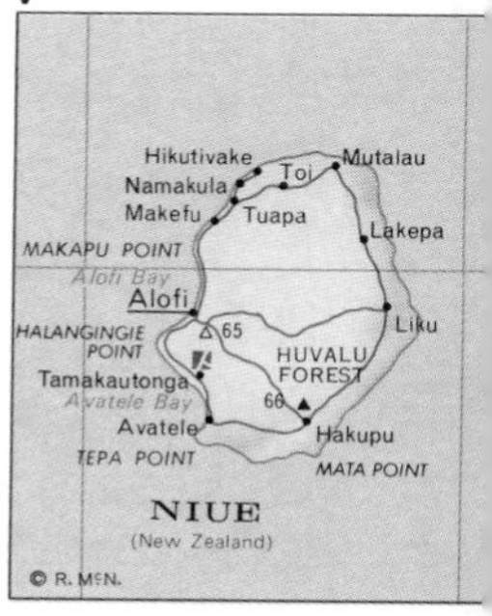
Hikutavake
Mutalau
Namakula
Tuapa
Makefu
Lakepa
Alofi
Liku
Avatele
Hakupu
NIUE
(New Zealand)

w

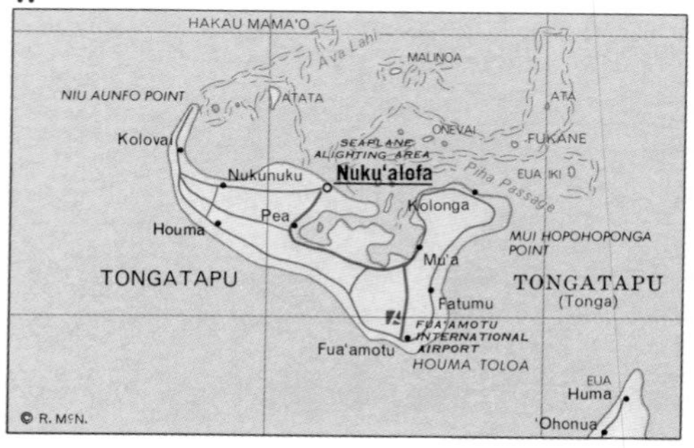
HAKAU MAMA'O
NIU AUNFO POINT
Kolovai
Nukunuku
Nuku'alofa
Houma
Pea
Kolonga
Mu'a
TONGATAPU
(Tonga)
Fatumu
Fua'amotu
HOUMA TOLOA
'Ohonua

x

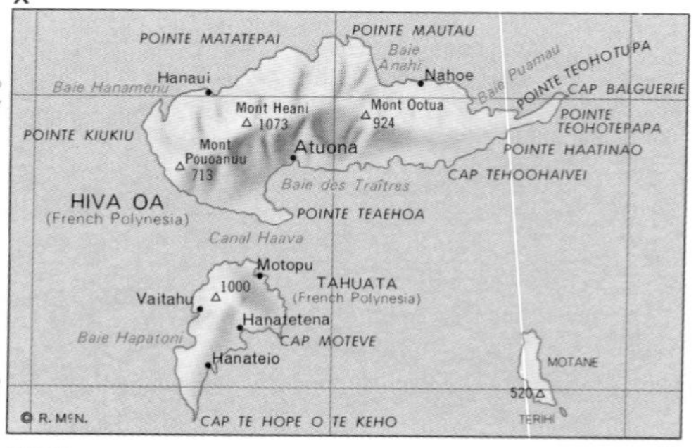
POINTE MATATEPAI
POINTE MAUTAU
Hanaui
Nahoe
Mont Heani 1073
Mont Ootua 924
Atuona
HIVA OA
(French Polynesia)
Vaitahu
Motopu
TAHUATA
(French Polynesia)
Hanatetena
Hanateio
MOTANE

y

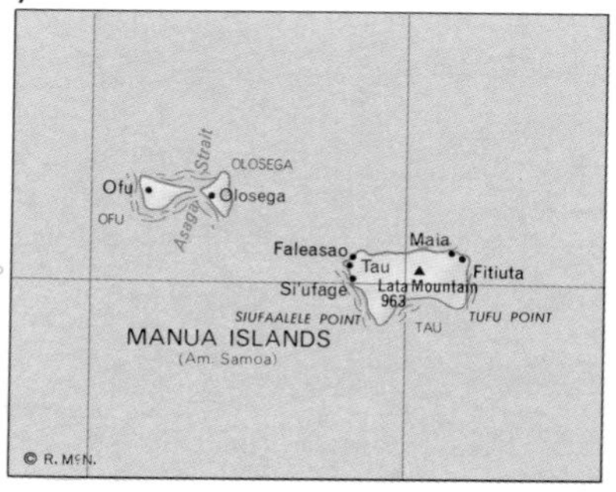
OLOSEGA
Ofu
Olosega
Faleasao
Tau
Maia
Fitiuta
Lata Mountain 963
MANUA ISLANDS
(Am. Samoa)

z

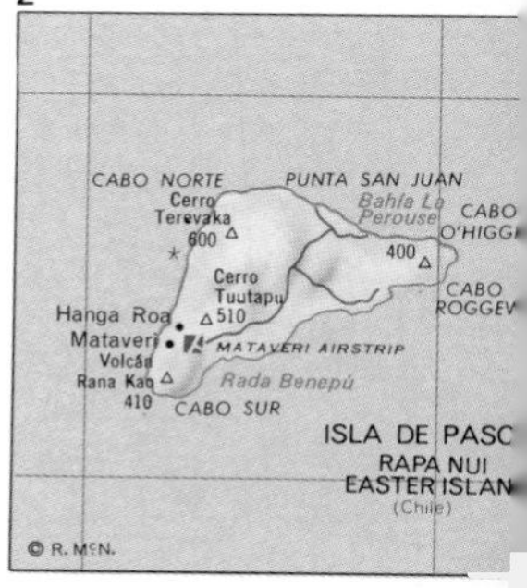
CABO NORTE
PUNTA SAN JUAN
Hanga Roa
Mataveri
ISLA DE PASCUA
RAPA NUI
EASTER ISLAND
(Chile)

MAP FORM	baie	harbor	island	jima	passe	pointe	shima
ENGLISH	bay	harbor	island	island	passage	point	island
DEUTSCH	Bucht	Naturhafen	Insel	Insel	Durchfahrt	Landspitze	Insel
ESPAÑOL	bahía	puerto	isla	isla	pasaje	punta	isla
FRANÇAIS	baie	port	île	île	passage	pointe	île
PORTUGUÊS	baía	porto	ilha	ilha	passagem	ponta	ilha

Kilometers 0 10 20 30 40 50 Km.
Statute Miles 0 10 20 30 40 50 Mi.

Scale 1:1,000,000
One centimeter represents 10 kilometers.
One inch represents approximately 16 miles.
Transverse Mercator Projection

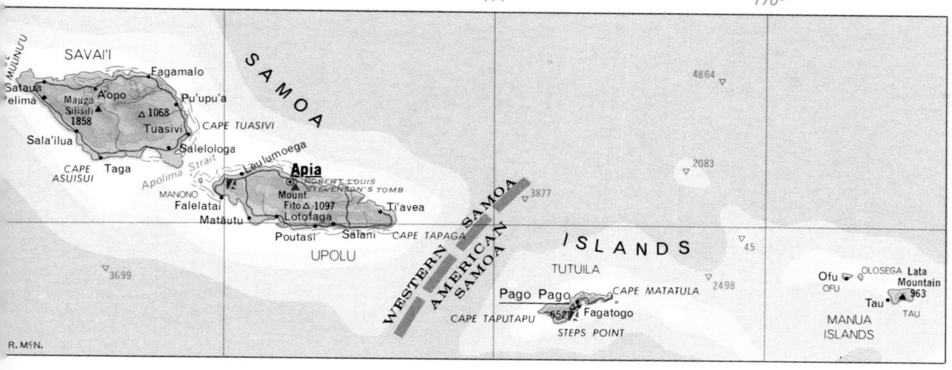
SAVAI'I
SAMOA
Apia
UPOLU
WESTERN SAMOA
AMERICAN SAMOA
ISLANDS
TUTUILA
Pago Pago
Fagatogo
MANUA ISLANDS
Ofu
Tau
CAPE TUASIVI
Falealatai
Lotofaga
Salani
Ti'avea
Sala'ilua
Taga
CAPE ASUISUI
172°
171°
170°
R. McN.

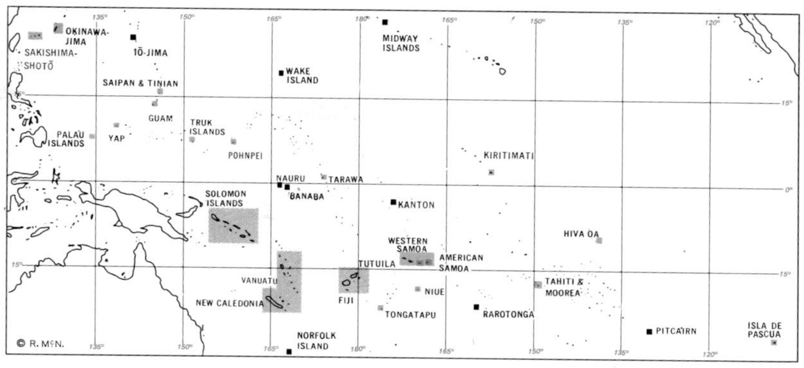
OKINAWA-JIMA
SAKISHIMA-SHOTŌ
IŌ-JIMA
SAIPAN & TINIAN
GUAM
PALAU ISLANDS
YAP
TRUK ISLANDS
POHNPEI
WAKE ISLAND
MIDWAY ISLANDS
KIRITIMATI
NAURU
TARAWA
BANABA
KANTON
SOLOMON ISLANDS
WESTERN SAMOA
TUTUILA
AMERICAN SAMOA
VANUATU
FIJI
NIUE
NEW CALEDONIA
TONGATAPU
RAROTONGA
HIVA OA
TAHITI & MOOREA
NORFOLK ISLAND
PITCAIRN
ISLA DE PASCUA
© R. McN.

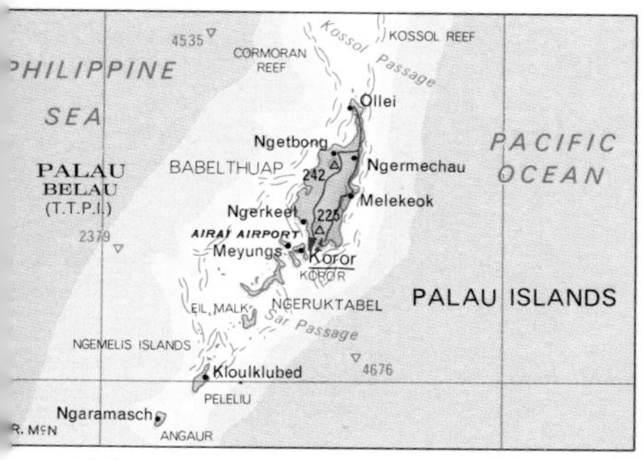
PHILIPPINE SEA
PALAU BELAU (T.T.P.I.)
BABELTHUAP
PACIFIC OCEAN
Ngetbong
Ngermechau
Melekeok
Ngerkeel
AIRAI AIRPORT
Meyungs
Koror
PALAU ISLANDS
KOSSOL REEF
Kossol Passage
Klouklubed
PELELIU
Ngaramasch
ANGAUR
134°
135°
R. McN.

c

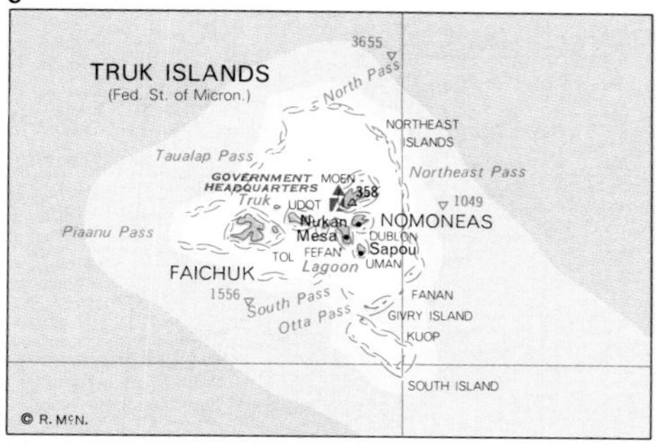
TRUK ISLANDS
(Fed. St. of Micron.)
North Pass
NORTHEAST ISLANDS
Northeast Pass
Piaanu Pass
GOVERNMENT HEADQUARTERS
Nukan
Mesa
NOMONEAS
Sapou
FAICHUK
Truk Lagoon
South Pass
Otta Pass
FANAN
GIVRY ISLAND
KUOP
SOUTH ISLAND
152°
© R. McN.

d

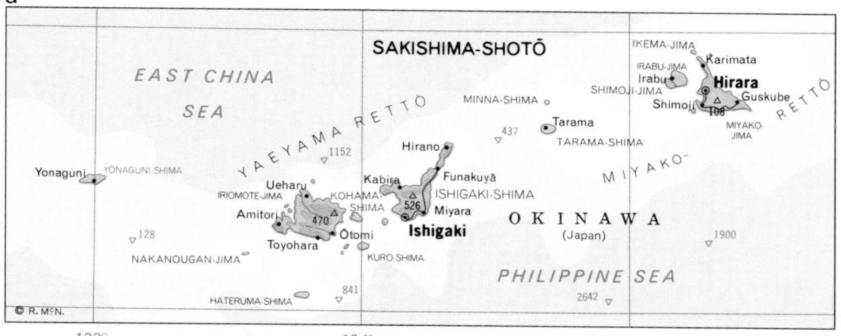
SAKISHIMA-SHOTŌ
EAST CHINA SEA
YAEYAMA RETTŌ
MIYAKO-RETTŌ
IKEMA-JIMA
Karimata
Irabu
Hirara
Guskube
SHIMOJI-JIMA
MINNA-SHIMA
Tarama
TARAMA-SHIMA
Hirano
Yonaguni
YONAGUNI-SHIMA
Uehara
IRIOMOTE-JIMA
Amitori
Kabira
ISHIGAKI-SHIMA
Funakuyā
Miyara
Ishigaki
OKINAWA
(Japan)
Toyohara
Ōtomi
KURO-SHIMA
NAKANOUGAN-JIMA
HATERUMA-SHIMA
PHILIPPINE SEA
25°
24°
123°
124°
125°
R. McN.

Kilometers 0 50 100 150 Km.
Statute Miles 0 50 100 150 Mi.

Scale 1:3,000,000

One centimeter represents 30 kilometers.
One inch represents approximately 47 miles.
Lambert Conformal Conic Projection

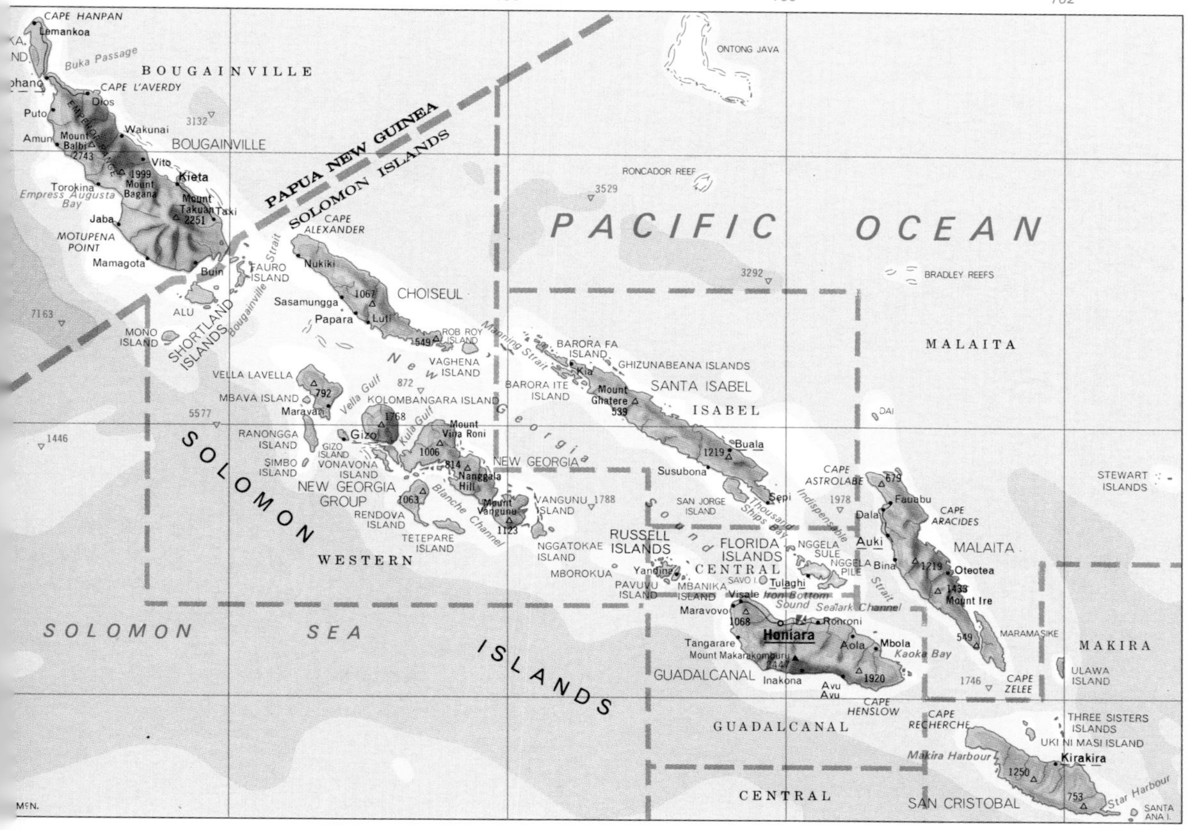
CAPE HANPAN
Buka Passage
BOUGAINVILLE
CAPE L'AVERDY
Wakunai
BOUGAINVILLE
Kieta
Empress Augusta Bay
Torokina
Jaba
MOTUPENA POINT
Mamagota
Buin
PAPUA NEW GUINEA
SOLOMON ISLANDS
CAPE ALEXANDER
ONTONG JAVA
RONCADOR REEF
PACIFIC OCEAN
BRADLEY REEFS
CHOISEUL
Sasamungga
SHORTLAND ISLANDS
MONO ISLAND
ALU
VELLA LAVELLA
KOLOMBANGARA ISLAND
Gizo
NEW GEORGIA GROUP
RENDOVA ISLAND
TETEPARE ISLAND
New Georgia Sound
SANTA ISABEL
ISABEL
Buala
MALAITA
Auki
RUSSELL ISLANDS
FLORIDA ISLANDS
CENTRAL
Tulagi
Honiara
GUADALCANAL
Maravovo
Tangarare
Aola
Mbola
Avu Avu
CAPE HENSLOW
STEWART ISLANDS
MALAITA
MAKIRA
ULAWA ISLAND
THREE SISTERS ISLANDS
UKI NI MASI ISLAND
Kirakira
SAN CRISTOBAL
SANTA ANA I.
SOLOMON SEA
SOLOMON
WESTERN
ISLANDS
156°
158°
160°
162°

f

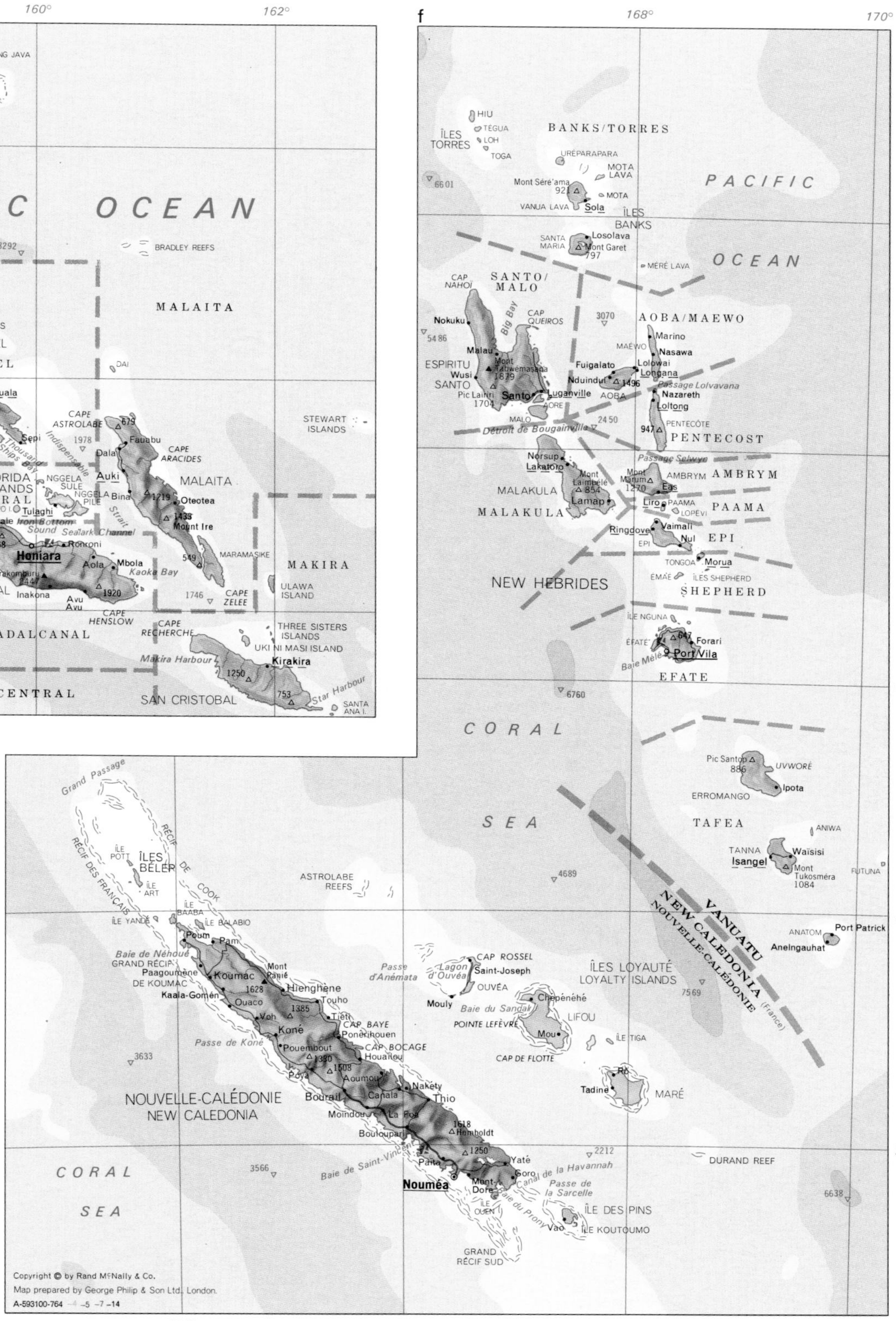
ÎLES TORRES
BANKS/TORRES
MOTA LAVA
VANUA LAVA
Sola
ÎLES BANKS
PACIFIC OCEAN
SANTO/MALO
ESPIRITU SANTO
Santo
Luganville
AOBA/MAEWO
PENTECOST
Lolowai
MALAKULA
Lakatoro
Lamap
AMBRYM
PAAMA
EPI
SHEPHERD
NEW HEBRIDES
EFATE
Port Vila
CORAL SEA
TAFEA
ERROMANGO
TANNA
Isangel
ANEITYUM
VANUATU
NEW CALEDONIA
NOUVELLE-CALÉDONIE (France)
ÎLES BELEP
ÎLES LOYAUTÉ
LOYALTY ISLANDS
OUVÉA
LIFOU
MARÉ
Koumac
Hienghène
Touho
Koné
Poindimié
Houaïlou
Bourail
Canala
Thio
Nouméa
Yaté
ÎLE DES PINS
NOUVELLE-CALÉDONIE
NEW CALEDONIA
CORAL SEA
DURAND REEF
Copyright © by Rand McNally & Co.
Map prepared by George Philip & Son Ltd. London.
A-593100-764 -5 -7 -14
164°
166°
168°
170°
14°
16°
18°
20°
22°

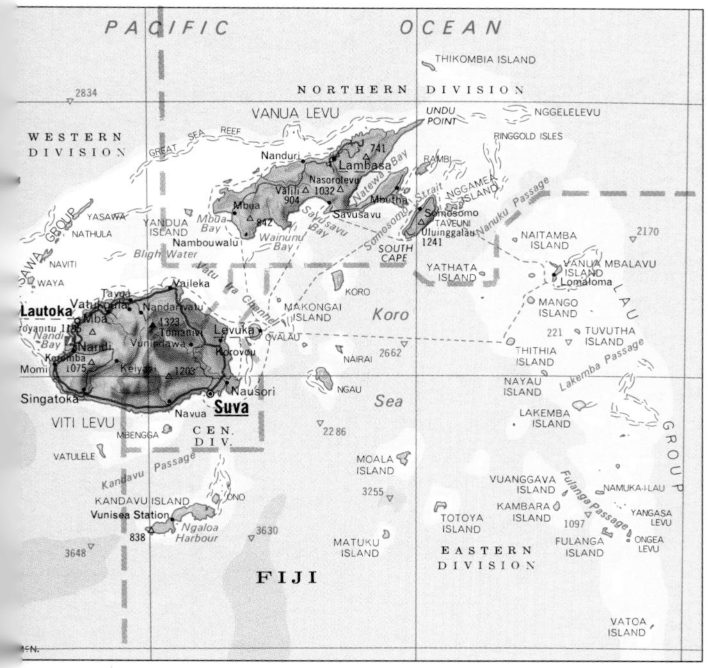
PACIFIC OCEAN
THIKOMBIA ISLAND
NORTHERN DIVISION
VANUA LEVU
WESTERN DIVISION
Nanduri
Lambasa
Savusavu
Labasa
YASAWA
NATHULA
Bligh Water
NAVITI
WAYA
Lautoka
Nandi
Ba
Tavua
Vaileka
Koro Sea
KORO
VITI LEVU
Singatoka
Navua
Suva
Nausori
CEN. DIV.
MBENGGA
VATULELE
KANDAVU ISLAND
Vunisea Station
MOALA ISLAND
TOTOYA ISLAND
MATUKU ISLAND
EASTERN DIVISION
LAKEMBA ISLAND
LAU GROUP
FIJI
VATOA ISLAND
178°
180°
178°
16°

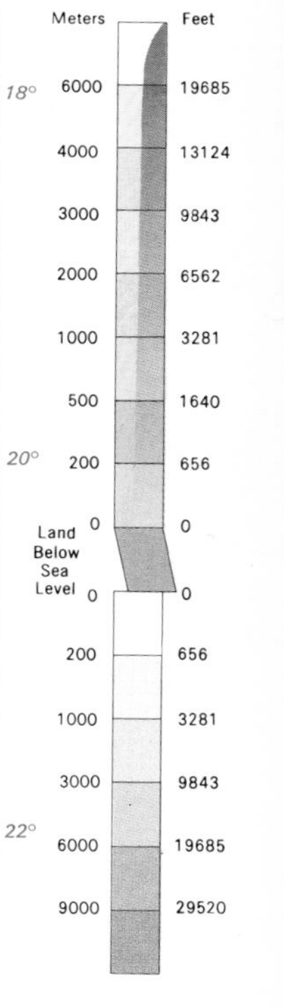
Meters
Feet
6000 19685
4000 13124
3000 9843
2000 6562
1000 3281
500 1640
200 656
0 0
Land Below Sea Level
0 0
200 656
1000 3281
3000 9843
6000 19685
9000 29520

MAP FORM	bay	cape	île	lagoon	mount	point	passage	strait
ENGLISH	bay	cape	island	lagoon	mount	point	passage	strait
DEUTSCH	Bucht	Kap	Insel	Haff	Berg	Landspitze	Durchfahrt	Meeresstrasse
ESPAÑOL	bahía	cabo	isla	laguna	montaña	punta	pasaje	estrecho
FRANÇAIS	baie	cap	île	lagune	mont	pointe	passage	détroit
PORTUGUÊS	baía	cabo	ilha	laguna	monte	ponta	passagem	estreito

Kilometers 0 100 200 300 Km.
Statute Miles 0 100 200 300 Mi.

Scale 1:6,000,000

One centimeter represents 60 kilometers.
One inch represents approximately 95 miles.
Lambert Conformal Conic Projection

Beaufort Sea
PACIFIC OCEAN
Gulf of Alaska
UNITED STATES
CANADA
ALASKA
ALASKA RANGE
NORTHWEST
ALBERTA
SASKATCHEWAN
MANITOBA
BRITISH COLUMBIA
WASHINGTON
OREGON
IDAHO
MONTANA
WYOMING
NORTH DAKOTA
SOUTH DAKOTA
NEBRASKA
MINNESOTA
NEVADA
UTAH
COLORADO
CALIFORNIA
IOWA
ROCKY MOUNTAINS
COAST MOUNTAINS
MACKENZIE MTS
SELWYN MTS.
PELLY MOUNTAINS
CASCADE RANGE
SIERRA NEVADA
GREAT BASIN
VICTORIA ISLAND
BANKS ISLAND
PRINCE OF WALES ISLAND
QUEEN CHARLOTTE ISLANDS
VANCOUVER ISLAND
Fairbanks
Anchorage
Whitehorse
Prince Rupert
Prince George
Edmonton
Calgary
Saskatoon
Regina
Winnipeg
Vancouver
Victoria
Seattle
Tacoma
Spokane
Portland
Salem
Eugene
Boise
Missoula
Great Falls
Helena
Butte
Billings
Bismarck
Fargo
Grand Forks
Minneapolis
Salt Lake City
Ogden
Provo
Reno
Sacramento
SAN FRANCISCO
Oakland
San Jose
Stockton
Modesto
Fresno
Yellowknife
Lethbridge
Medicine Hat
Moose Jaw
Rapid City
Sioux Falls
155°
150°
145°
140°
135°
130°
125°
120°
115°
110°
105°
100°
95°
60°
55°
50°
45°
40°

Map continues
pages **178-179**

ENGLISH	bay	cape	island	lake, l.	mountains, mts.	point	range	strait
DEUTSCH	Bucht	Kap	Insel	See	Berge	Landspitze	Gebirge	Meeresstrasse
ESPAÑOL	bahía	cabo	isla	lago	montañas	punta	sierra	estrecho
FRANÇAIS	baie	cap	île	lac	montagnes	pointe	chaîne	détroit
PORTUGUÊS	baía	cabo	ilha	lago	montanhas	ponta	serra	estreito

GREENLAND
KALAALLIT NUNAAT
(Denmark)
Baffin Bay
Davis Strait
Labrador Sea
ATLANTIC OCEAN
Hudson Bay
Foxe Basin
Ungava Bay
James Bay
Hudson Strait
BAFFIN ISLAND
DEVON ISLAND
ELLESMERE ISLAND
COBURG ISLAND
CAPE PARKER
PHILPOTS ISLAND
CAPE SHERARD
Lancaster Sound
Jones Sound
LEOPOLD ISLAND
CAPE CRAUFORD
CAPE LIVERPOOL
BYLOT ISLAND
CAPE GRAHAM MOORE
BORDEN PENINSULA
BRODEUR PENINSULA
Arctic Bay
Pond Inlet
CAPE ADAIR
CAPE CHRISTIAN
Clyde River
CAPE HENRY KATER
Upernavik
Qeqertaq
SVARTENHUK
NÛGSSUAQ
DISKO
Godhavn
Qeqertarsuaq
Egedesminde
Aasiaat
Holsteinsborg
Sisimiut
Sukkertoppen
Maniitsoq
Godthåb
Nuuk
Frederikshåb
Paamiut
Julianehåb
Qaqortoq
KAP FARVEL
KAP CORT ADELAER
KAP MØSTING
Angmagssalik
GAVE HOLM
Mont Forel
Arctic Circle
CAPE DYER
BROUGHTON ISLAND
CUMBERLAND PENINSULA
Pangnirtung
Cumberland Sound
CAPE MERCY
Iqaluit
HALL PENINSULA
RESOLUTION ISLAND
MELVILLE PENINSULA
SOUTHAMPTON ISLAND
Coral Harbour
CAPE COMFORT
FOXE PENINSULA
Cape Dorset
NOTTINGHAM ISLAND
SALISBURY ISLAND
CAP DE NOUVELLE-FRANCE
MANSEL ISLAND
COATS ISLAND
BUTTON ISLANDS
KILLINIQ ISLAND
CAP HOPES ADVANCE
AKPATOK ISLAND
PÉNINSULE D'UNGAVA
Kangiqsujuaq
Salluit
Povungnituk
Inukjuak
Kuujjuaq
Kangirsuk
TORNGAT MOUNTAINS
NORTH AULATSIVIK ISLAND
SOUTH AULATSIVIK ISLAND
Nain
Hopedale
CAPE HARRISON
Cartwright
LABRADOR
Happy Valley-Goose Bay
North West River
Churchill Falls
Smallwood Reservoir
Battle Harbour
BELLE ISLE
St. Anthony
NEWFOUNDLAND
Corner Brook
Gander
Grand Falls
St. John's
CAPE RACE
CAPE SPEAR
Channel-Port-aux-Basques
ST. PIERRE AND MIQUELON
CAPE BRETON ISLAND
Sydney
Glace Bay
PRINCE EDWARD ISLAND
Charlottetown
Summerside
ÎLES DE LA MADELEINE
ÎLE D'ANTICOSTI
Gulf of St. Lawrence
NOVA SCOTIA
Halifax
Dartmouth
Yarmouth
CAPE SABLE
SABLE ISLAND
NEW BRUNSWICK
Moncton
Saint John
Fredericton
Bay of Fundy
Gulf of Maine
MAINE
Bangor
Augusta
Portland
QUÉBEC
Schefferville
Labrador City
Fermont
Gagnon
Sept-Îles
Havre-St.-Pierre
Baie-Comeau
Chicoutimi
Jonquière
Québec
Trois-Rivières
Shawinigan
Sherbrooke
Drummondville
Montréal
Hull
Ottawa
Chibougamau
Matagami
Rouyn
Val-d'Or
Amos
Chisasibi
La Grande Rivière
Fort Severn
Winisk
Attawapiskat
Moosonee
Fort Albany
Eastmain
Waskaganish
AKIMISKI ISLAND
ONTARIO
Timmins
Kapuskasing
Cochrane
Hearst
Thunder Bay
Lake Nipigon
Sault Ste. Marie
Sudbury
North Bay
Lake Superior
Lake Huron
Georgian Bay
Lake Ontario
Lake Erie
Lake Michigan
Kingston
Peterborough
Oshawa
Toronto
Hamilton
Kitchener
Cambridge
Guelph
London
Sarnia
Windsor
DETROIT
Toledo
Cleveland
Buffalo
Niagara Falls
Rochester
Syracuse
Utica
Albany
Schenectady
Watertown
Burlington
Manchester
Concord
BOSTON
Worcester
Providence
Fall River
New Bedford
CAPE COD
NANTUCKET ISLAND
Springfield
Hartford
New Haven
Bridgeport
NEW YORK
Newark
PHILADELPHIA
Trenton
Allentown
Scranton
Wilkes-Barre
Harrisburg
Williamsport
Binghamton
Elmira
Youngstown
Erie
CHICAGO
Milwaukee
Racine
Kenosha
Madison
Green Bay
Appleton
Oshkosh
Marquette
Escanaba
Flint
Saginaw
Bay City
Lansing
Grand Rapids
Kalamazoo
Battle Creek
Jackson
Ann Arbor
South Bend
Muskegon
MICHIGAN
ADIRONDACK MOUNTAINS
APPALACHIAN MTS.
MONTS NOTRE-DAME
LAURENTIDES
NEWFOUNDLAND
All islands within Hudson Bay, James Bay, and Ungava Bay lie within Northwest Territories
Copyright © by Rand McNally & Co.
Map prepared by Rand McNally & Co.
A-520200-264

Kilometers 0 200 400 600 Km.

Statute Miles 0 200 400 600 Mi.

Scale 1:12,000,000

One centimeter represents 120 kilometers.
One inch represents approximately 190 miles.

Lambert Conformal Conic Projection

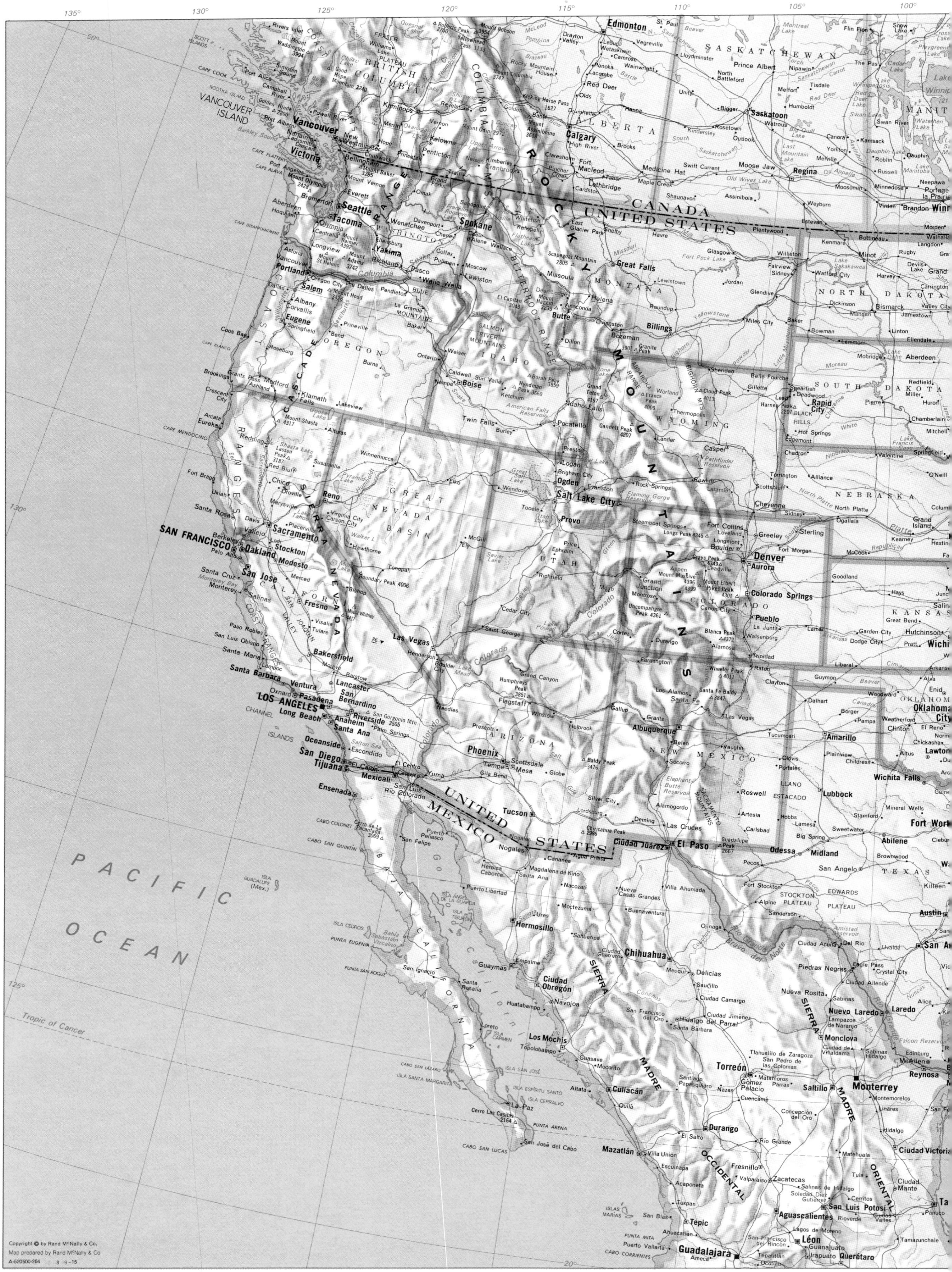
135°
130°
125°
120°
115°
110°
105°
100°
45°
40°
35°
30°
25°
20°
Tropic of Cancer
PACIFIC
OCEAN
VANCOUVER ISLAND
BRITISH COLUMBIA
ALBERTA
SASKATCHEWAN
CANADA
UNITED STATES
MEXICO
WASHINGTON
OREGON
IDAHO
MONTANA
WYOMING
NORTH DAKOTA
SOUTH DAKOTA
NEBRASKA
NEVADA
UTAH
COLORADO
KANSAS
CALIFORNIA
ARIZONA
NEW MEXICO
OKLAHOMA
TEXAS
ROCKY MOUNTAINS
COAST RANGES
CASCADE RANGE
SIERRA NEVADA
GREAT BASIN
SIERRA MADRE OCCIDENTAL
SIERRA MADRE ORIENTAL
BAJA CALIFORNIA
Edmonton
Calgary
Regina
Saskatoon
Vancouver
Victoria
Seattle
Tacoma
Spokane
Portland
Salem
Boise
Helena
Great Falls
Billings
Butte
Salt Lake City
Ogden
Provo
Reno
Sacramento
SAN FRANCISCO
Oakland
San Jose
Fresno
Bakersfield
LOS ANGELES
Long Beach
San Diego
Tijuana
Las Vegas
Phoenix
Tucson
Albuquerque
Santa Fe
El Paso
Ciudad Juárez
Denver
Colorado Springs
Pueblo
Cheyenne
Casper
Rapid City
Bismarck
Amarillo
Lubbock
Odessa
Midland
Wichita Falls
Oklahoma City
Chihuahua
Hermosillo
Ciudad Obregón
Los Mochis
Culiacán
Mazatlán
Durango
Torreón
Monterrey
Saltillo
Nuevo Laredo
Laredo
Zacatecas
Aguascalientes
San Luis Potosí
Tepic
Guadalajara
León
Querétaro
Copyright © by Rand McNally & Co.
Map prepared by Rand McNally & Co
A-520500-264

ENGLISH	bay	cape	desert	island	lake	mountains	peak	range
DEUTSCH	Bucht	Kap	Wüste	Insel	See	Berge	Gipfel	Gebirge
ESPAÑOL	bahía	cabo	desierto	isla	lago	montañas	pico	sierra
FRANÇAIS	baie	cap	désert	île	lac	montagnes	cime	chaîne
PORTUGUÊS	baía	cabo	deserto	ilha	lago	montanhas	pico	serra

Map continues pages 230-231

Map continues
pages 176-177

ONTARIO
QUÉBEC
James Bay
Gulf of Saint Lawrence
MONTS NOTRE-DAME
NEW BRUNSWICK
NOVA SCOTIA
PRINCE EDWARD ISLAND
CAPE BRETON ISLAND
NEWFOUNDLAND
Gulf of Maine
TORONTO
MONTREAL
Ottawa
Québec
Halifax
BOSTON
NEW YORK
PHILADELPHIA
Baltimore
WASHINGTON
DETROIT
CHICAGO
Milwaukee
Cleveland
Pittsburgh
Cincinnati
Indianapolis
Louisville
Nashville
Memphis
Atlanta
Charlotte
Richmond
Norfolk
Birmingham
Jacksonville
New Orleans
Tampa
Orlando
Miami
APPALACHIAN MOUNTAINS
ADIRONDACK MTS.
MICHIGAN
WISCONSIN
IOWA
ILLINOIS
INDIANA
OHIO
PENNSYLVANIA
NEW YORK
WEST VIRGINIA
VIRGINIA
KENTUCKY
TENNESSEE
NORTH CAROLINA
SOUTH CAROLINA
GEORGIA
ALABAMA
MISSISSIPPI
LOUISIANA
ARKANSAS
MISSOURI
FLORIDA
ATLANTIC OCEAN
BERMUDA (U.K.)
GULF OF MEXICO
BAHAMAS
Nassau
Tropic of Cancer
Straits of Florida
WEST INDIES
LA HABANA
CUBA
Santiago de Cuba
HAITI
Port-au-Prince
DOMINICAN REPUBLIC
SANTO DOMINGO
HISPANIOLA
TURKS AND CAICOS ISLANDS (U.K.)
CAYMAN IS. (U.K.)
CARIBBEAN SEA
Canal de Yucatán
YUCATAN PENINSULA
Mérida
Cancún
90°
85°
80°
75°
70°
65°
60°
45°
40°
35°
30°
25°
20°

Kilometers 0 200 400 600 Km.

Statute Miles 0 200 400 600 Mi.

Scale 1:12,000,000

One centimeter represents 120 kilometers.
One inch represents approximately 190 miles.
Albers Conical Equal-Area Projection

ARCTIC
Chukchi Sea
BERING SEA
Anadyrskij zaliv
International Date Line
Arctic Circle
RUSSIA
UNITED STATES
ROSSIJA
Bering Strait
Norton Sound
Kotzebue Sound
Bristol Bay
Kuskokwim Bay
PACIF
ANADYRSKOJE PLOSKOGORJE
EKVYVATAPSKIJ CHREBET
ČUKOTSKIJ AVTONOMNYJ OKRUG
ČUKOTSKIJ POLUOSTROV
Anadyr'
Providenija
Barrow
Wainwright
Point Hope
Kivalina
Kotzebue
Shishmaref
Wales
Teller
Nome
Golovin
Unalakleet
Stebbins
Saint Michael
Bethel
Dillingham
King Salmon
Naknek
Port Heiden
Cold Bay
Sand Point
LISBURNE PENINSULA
DE LONG MOUNTAINS
BROOK
BAIRD MOUNTAINS
SCHWATKA MOUNTAINS
KOBUK VALLEY NATIONAL PARK
SEWARD PENINSULA
KUSKOKWIM
KILBUCK MOUNTAINS
TAYLOR MOUNTAINS
AHKLUN MOUNTAINS
ALASKA PENINSULA
NUSHAGAK PENINSULA
SAINT LAWRENCE ISLAND
Gambell
Savoonga
Northeast Cape
SAINT MATTHEW ISLAND
HALL ISLAND
NUNIVAK ISLAND
NELSON ISLAND
PRIBILOF ISLANDS
Saint Paul Island
Saint George Island
UNIMAK ISLAND
KRENITZIN ISLANDS
SHUMAGIN ISLANDS
UMNAK ISLAND
UNALASKA ISLAND
FOX ISLANDS
ISLANDS OF FOUR MOUNTAINS
ALEUTIAN ISLANDS
ANDREANOF ISLANDS
ATKA ISLAND
ADAK ISLAND
Meters
Feet
6000 19685
4000 13124
3000 9843
2000 6562
1000 3281
500 1640
200 656
0 0
Land Below Sea Level
200 656
1000 3281
3000 9843
6000 19685
9000 29520
ENGLISH bay cape island, i. lake, l. mount, mt. peak, pk. point
DEUTSCH Bucht Kap Insel See Berg Gipfel Landspitze
ESPAÑOL bahía cabo isla lago monte pico punta
FRANÇAIS baie cap île lac mont pic pointe
PORTUGUÊS baía cabo ilha lago monte pico ponta

OCEAN
Beaufort Sea
Gulf of Alaska
BERING SEA
ALEUTIAN ISLANDS
PACIFIC OCEAN
a
Mackenzie Bay
MACKENZIE DELTA
BRITISH MOUNTAINS
RICHARDSON MOUNTAINS
OGILVIE MOUNTAINS
MACKENZIE MOUNTAINS
SELWYN MOUNTAINS
LOGAN MOUNTAINS
CASSIAR MOUNTAINS
COAST MOUNTAINS
ST. ELIAS MOUNTAINS
WRANGELL MOUNTAINS
CHUGACH MOUNTAINS
ALASKA RANGE
YUKON FLATS
KLONDIKE
NORTHWEST TERRITORIES
YUKON
ALASKA
BRITISH COLUMBIA
CANADA
UNITED STATES
ALEXANDER ARCHIPELAGO
QUEEN CHARLOTTE ISLANDS
Dixon Entrance
Hecate Strait
Great Bear Lake
Fairbanks
Anchorage
Juneau
Whitehorse
Dawson
Inuvik
Aklavik
Old Crow
Fort McPherson
Norman Wells
Fort Good Hope
Fort Franklin
Fort Norman
Tuktoyaktuk
Deadhorse
Kaktovik
Arctic Village
Fort Yukon
Circle
Eagle
Tok
Valdez
Cordova
Seward
Kenai
Homer
Haines
Skagway
Yakutat
Sitka
Petersburg
Wrangell
Ketchikan
Prince Rupert
Stewart
Watson Lake
Teslin
Atlin
Carcross
Ross River
Faro
Mayo
Keno Hill
Carmacks
Kodiak
Attu
Shemya Station
Adak
Copyright © by Rand McNally & Co.
Map prepared by Rand McNally & Co.

Map continues pages 176-177

Map continues pages 182-183

Kilometers 0 100 200 300 Km.
Statute Miles 0 100 200 300 Mi.

Scale 1:6,000,000

One centimeter represents 60 kilometers.
One inch represents approximately 95 miles.
Lambert Conformal Conic Projection

Map continues pages 180-181

U.S.
CANADA
Dixon Entrance
Prince Rupert
Kitimat
Terrace
Hazelton
Smithers
Houston
Burns Lake
Vanderhoof
Prince George
Quesnel
Williams Lake
COAST MOUNTAINS
PACIFIC RANGES
KITIMAT RANGES
NECHAKO PLATEAU
FRASER PLATEAU
TWEEDSMUIR PROVINCIAL PARK
STRATHCONA PROVINCIAL PARK
GRAHAM ISLAND
MORESBY ISLAND
QUEEN CHARLOTTE ISLANDS
Hecate Strait
Queen Charlotte Sound
Queen Charlotte Strait
VANCOUVER ISLAND
PACIFIC OCEAN
Strait of Georgia
Strait of Juan de Fuca
VANCOUVER
Victoria
Nanaimo
Port Alberni
Powell River
Courtenay
Campbell River
Port Hardy
Bella Coola
Ocean Falls
Port Angeles
Bellingham
CANADA
UNITED STATES
Meters
Feet
6000 19685
4000 13124
3000 9843
2000 6562
1000 3281
500 1640
200 656
0 0
Land Below Sea Level
200 656
1000 3281
3000 9843
6000 19685
9000 29520

ENGLISH	creek	Indian reserve	inlet	island	lake, l.	mountain	peak	provincial park	sound
DEUTSCH	Bach	Indianerreservation	Einfahrt	Insel	See	Berg	Gipfel	Provinz-Park	Sund
ESPAÑOL	riachuelo	reserva de Indios	abra	isla	lago	montaña	pico	parque de provincia	sonda
FRANÇAIS	crique	réserve indienne	bras de mer	île	lac	montagne	cime	parc provincial	détroit
PORTUGUÊS	riacho	reserva indígena	enseada	ilha	lago	montanha	pico	parque provincial	estreito

Peace River
Fort St. John
Dawson Creek
Grande-Prairie
Edmonton
Red Deer
Calgary
Lethbridge
Kamloops
Vernon
Kelowna
Penticton
Cranbrook
Kalispell
Revelstoke
Golden
Banff
Jasper
Hinton
Edson
Whitecourt
Athabasca
Medicine Hat
Nelson
Trail
Castlegar
Fernie
Creston
Drumheller
Camrose
Wetaskiwin
Lacombe
Olds
Lesser Slave Lake
JASPER NATIONAL PARK
BANFF NATIONAL PARK
GLACIER NATIONAL PARK
ROCKY MOUNTAINS
COLUMBIA MOUNTAINS
MONASHEE MOUNTAINS
SELKIRK MOUNTAINS
PURCELL MOUNTAINS
CASCADE RANGE
BRITISH COLUMBIA
ALBERTA
MONTANA
IDAHO
WASHINGTON
CANADA
UNITED STATES

Map continues pages 184-185

Map continues pages 202-203

Kilometers 0 50 100 150 Km.
Statute Miles 0 50 100 150 Mi.

Scale 1:3,000,000

One centimeter represents 30 kilometers.
One inch represents approximately 47 miles.
Lambert Conformal Conic Projection

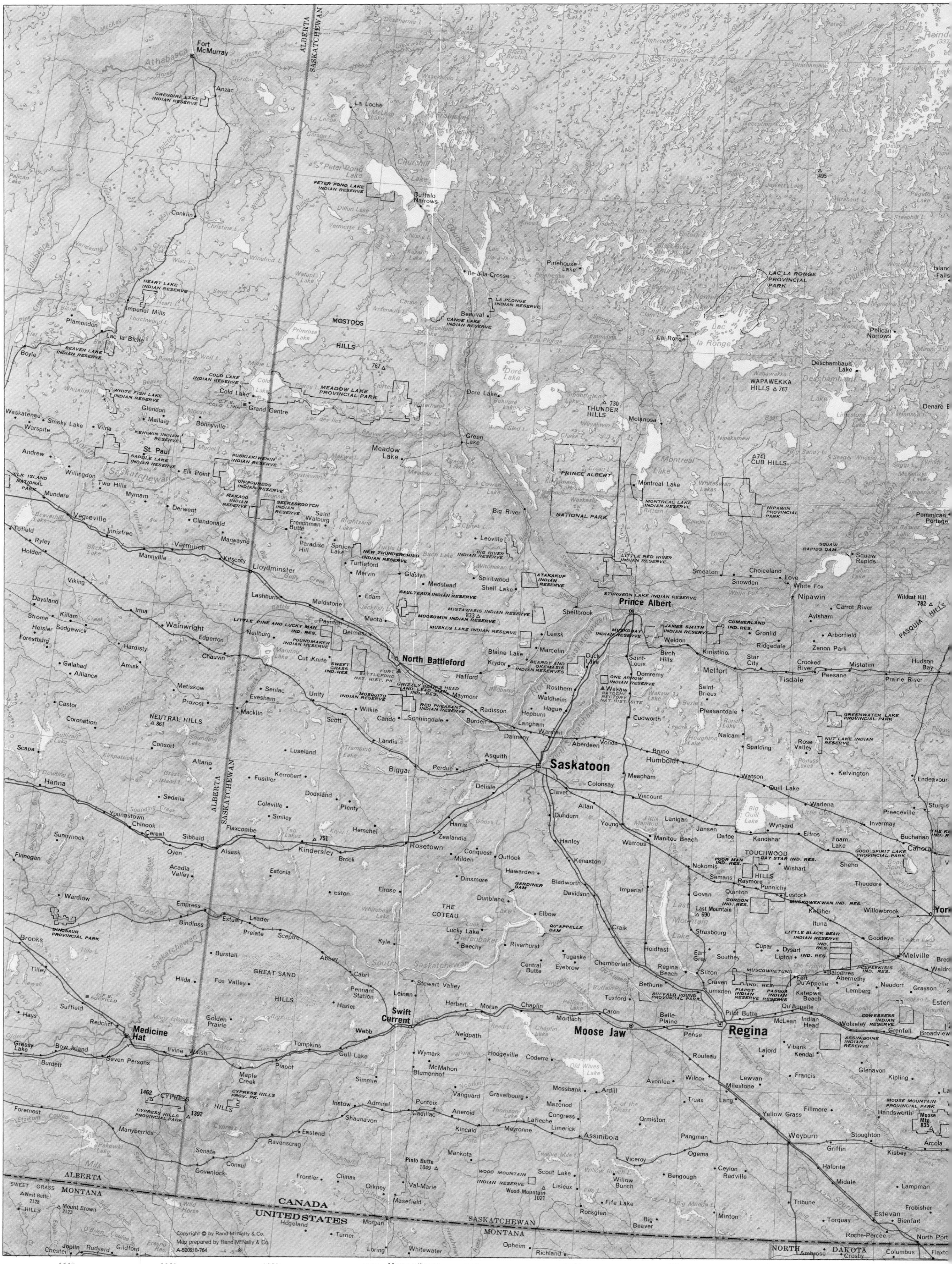
113° 112° 111° 110° 109° 108° 107° 106° 105° 104° 103°
56° 55° 54° 53° 52° 51° 50° 49°
ALBERTA
SASKATCHEWAN
MONTANA
NORTH DAKOTA
CANADA
UNITED STATES
Fort McMurray
Athabasca
Anzac
GREGOIRE LAKE INDIAN RESERVE
La Loche
Peter Pond Lake
PETER POND LAKE INDIAN RESERVE
Churchill Lake
Buffalo Narrows
Conklin
Christina L.
Dillon Lake
Pelican Lake
Île-à-la-Crosse
Pinehouse Lake
LAC LA RONGE PROVINCIAL PARK
La Ronge
Lac la Ronge
Pelican Narrows
Island Falls
HEART LAKE INDIAN RESERVE
Imperial Mills
Plamondon
Lac la Biche
Boyle
BEAVER LAKE INDIAN RESERVE
MOSTOOS HILLS
Primrose Lake
Beauval
LA PLONGE INDIAN RESERVE
CANOE LAKE INDIAN RESERVE
Lac la Plonge
Deschambault Lake
WAPAWEKKA HILLS △ 767
COLD LAKE INDIAN RESERVE
Cold Lake
MEADOW LAKE PROVINCIAL PARK
Grand Centre
Doré Lake
THUNDER HILLS △ 730
Molanosa
Waskatenau
Smoky Lake
Warspite
Vilna
Glendon
Mallaig
Bonnyville
WHITE FISH LAKE INDIAN RESERVE
KEHIWIN INDIAN RESERVE
St. Paul
SADDLE LAKE INDIAN RESERVE
Elk Point
PUSKIAKIWENIN INDIAN RESERVE
Meadow Lake
Green Lake
PRINCE ALBERT NATIONAL PARK
Montreal Lake
CUB HILLS △ 741
Andrew
Willingdon
Two Hills
Mundare
ELK ISLAND NATIONAL PARK
Mynam
Derwent
UNIPOUHEOS INDIAN RESERVE
MAKAOO INDIAN RESERVE
SEEKASKOOTCH INDIAN RESERVE
Saint Walburg
Frenchman Butte
Paradise Hill
Spruce Lake
Turtleford
Big River
MONTREAL LAKE INDIAN RESERVE
NIPAWIN PROVINCIAL PARK
Map continues pages 182-183
Vegreville
Tofield
Innisfree
Ryley
Holden
Clandonald
Marwayne
Vermilion
Mannville
Kitscoty
Lloydminster
Leoville
Spiritwood
Shell Lake
Mervin
Glaslyn
Medstead
LITTLE RED RIVER INDIAN RESERVE
Smeaton
Choiceland
Snowden
White Fox
Love
Nipawin
Squaw Rapids
Viking
Daysland
Killam
Strome
Heisler
Sedgewick
Forestburg
Irma
Wainwright
Edgerton
Lashburn
Maidstone
Paynton
Delmas
Neilburg
Edam
Meota
SAULTEAUX INDIAN RESERVE
MOOSOMIN INDIAN RESERVE
MISTAWASIS INDIAN RESERVE
MUSKEG LAKE INDIAN RESERVE
STURGEON LAKE INDIAN RESERVE
Prince Albert
Shellbrook
Leask
JAMES SMITH INDIAN RESERVE
CUMBERLAND IND. RES.
Gronlid
Aylsham
Carrot River
Wildcat Hill 782 △
PASQUIA HILLS
Arborfield
Zenon Park
Ridgedale
Weldon
Kinistino
Hardisty
Amisk
Chauvin
Galahad
Alliance
Cut Knife
North Battleford
Battleford
Hafford
Blaine Lake
Marcelin
Krydor
Duck Lake
Saint-Louis
Birch Hills
Domremy
Melfort
Star City
Crooked River
Tisdale
Peesane
Mistatim
Hudson Bay
Prairie River
Metiskow
Provost
Castor
Coronation
Senlac
Unity
Evesham
Macklin
Wilkie
Cando
Sonningdale
Maymont
Radisson
Borden
Rosthern
Waldheim
Hepburn
Hague
Langham
Wakaw
Saint-Brieux
Pleasantdale
Cudworth
Naicam
GREENWATER LAKE PROVINCIAL PARK
NEUTRAL HILLS △ 861
Scott
Landis
Dalmeny
Warman
Aberdeen
Vonda
Bruno
Humboldt
Spalding
Rose Valley
NUT LAKE INDIAN RESERVE
Scapa
Consort
Luseland
Perdue
Asquith
Saskatoon
Biggar
Watson
Kelvington
Altario
Kerrobert
Fusilier
Dodsland
Delisle
Colonsay
Meacham
Quill Lake
Endeavour
Hanna
Sedalia
Coleville
Smiley
Plenty
Clavet
Allan
Viscount
Wadena
Preeceville
Sturgis
Youngstown
Chinook
Cereal
Sibbald
Flaxcombe
Herschel
Harris
Dundurn
Young
Lanigan
Jansen
Wynyard
Invermay
Sunnynook
Oyen
Alsask
Kindersley
Brock
Rosetown
Zealandia
Milden
Conquest
Outlook
Hanley
Watrous
Manitou Beach
Dafoe
Kandahar
Elfros
Foam Lake
Buchanan
Finnegan
Acadia Valley
Eatonia
Dinsmore
Hawarden
Kenaston
TOUCHWOOD HILLS
Nokomis
Semans
Raymore
Wishart
Sheho
Theodore
Wardlow
Eston
Elrose
Dunblane
Bladworth
Davidson
Imperial
Govan
Quinton
Punnichy
Lestock
Kelliher
Willowbrook
Yorkton
Empress
Bindloss
Leader
Prelate
Sceptre
THE COTEAU
Lucky Lake
Elbow
Last Mountain Lake
Strasbourg
Ituna
DINOSAUR PROVINCIAL PARK
Brooks
Tilley
Burstall
GREAT SAND HILLS
Kyle
Beechy
Riverhurst
Craik
Holdfast
Earl Grey
Southey
Cupar
Dysart
Lipton
Goodeve
Melville
Hilda
Fox Valley
Abbey
Cabri
Pennant Station
Stewart Valley
Central Butte
Tugaske
Eyebrow
Chamberlain
Regina Beach
Silton
Craven
Lumsden
Bethune
Balcarres
Abernethy
Neudorf
Grayson
Suffield
Hays
Redcliff
Medicine Hat
Golden Prairie
Hazlet
Leinan
Swift Current
Herbert
Morse
Chaplin
Tuxford
Caron
Mortlach
Moose Jaw
Belle Plaine
Pilot Butte
Regina
Fort Qu'Appelle
Qu'Appelle
Indian Head
Wolseley
Grenfell
Broadview
Grassy Lake
Bow Island
Burdett
Seven Persons
Irvine
Walsh
Webb
Tompkins
Gull Lake
Neidpath
Wymark
Hodgeville
Coderre
Pense
Rouleau
Lajord
Vibank
Kendal
Maple Creek
Piapot
Simmie
McMahon
Blumenhof
Glenavon
Kipling
Francis
CYPRESS HILLS PROVINCIAL PARK
CYPRESS HILLS PROV. PK.
Admiral
Shaunavon
Ponteix
Cadillac
Vanguard
Aneroid
Gravelbourg
Mossbank
Ardill
Wilcox
Lewvan
Milestone
Truax
Lang
Yellow Grass
Fillmore
MOOSE MOUNTAIN PROVINCIAL PARK
Handsworth
Foremost
Manyberries
Eastend
Ravenscrag
Kincaid
Meyronne
Lafleche
Mazenod
Congress
Limerick
Assiniboia
Ormiston
Pangman
Weyburn
Stoughton
Arcola
Kisbey
Griffin
Senate
Consul
Govenlock
Pinto Butte 1049 △
Mankota
Viceroy
Ogema
Bengough
Ceylon
Radville
Halbrite
Midale
Lampman
Frontier
Climax
Orkney
Val-Marie
Masefield
WOOD MOUNTAIN INDIAN RESERVE
Wood Mountain 1021
Scout Lake
Lisieux
Willow Bunch
Fife Lake
Rockglen
Big Beaver
Minton
Tribune
Torquay
Estevan
Bienfait
Frobisher
North Portal
SWEET GRASS HILLS
West Butte 2128
Mount Brown 2121
Hogeland
Turner
Morgan
Loring
Whitewater
Opheim
Richland
Joplin
Rudyard
Gildford
Chester
Ambrose
Crosby
Columbus
Roche-Percée
Copyright © by Rand McNally & Co.
Map prepared by Rand McNally & Co.
A-520218-764
Map continues pages 202-203
Map continues pages 198-199

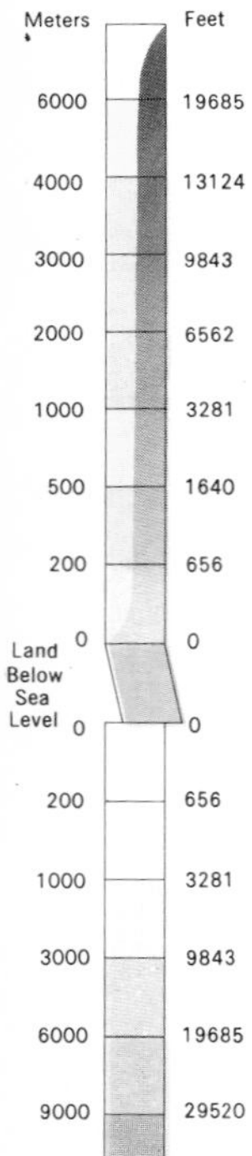
Meters
Feet
6000 19685
4000 13124
3000 9843
2000 6562
1000 3281
500 1640
200 656
0 0
Land Below Sea Level
0 0
200 656
1000 3281
3000 9843
6000 19685
9000 29520

ENGLISH	creek, cr.	hills	Indian reserve	island, i.	lake, l.	provincial park
DEUTSCH	Bach	Hügel	Indianerreservation	Insel	See	Provinz-Park
ESPAÑOL	riachuelo	colinas	reserva de Indios	isla	lago	parque de provincia
FRANÇAIS	crique	collines	réserve indienne	île	lac	parc provincial
PORTUGUÊS	riacho	colinas	reserva indígena	ilha	lago	parque provincial

101°
100°
99°
98°
97°
96°
95°
94°
93°
92°
91°
90°
56°
55°
54°
53°
52°
51°
50°
49°
Port Nelson
York Factory
Thibaudeau
Weir River
Amery
KETTLE RAPIDS DAM
Gillam
Ilford
Shamattawa
Lynn Lake
South Indian Lake
Southern Indian L.
Churchill
Nelson
Hayes
Gods
Nelson House
Thompson
Pikwitonei
Sipiwesk
Thicket Portage
Kississing
Sherridon
Snow Lake
Wabowden
Herb Lake
Oxford House
OXFORD HOUSE INDIAN RESERVE
Gods Lake
Optic Lake
Cranberry Portage
Cross Lake
JENPEG DAM
ROSS ISLAND
Playgreen Lake
Norway House
Island Lake
Red Sucker Lake
WETIKO HILLS
MANITOBA
ONTARIO
Cormorant
The Pas
CLEARWATER LAKE PROVINCIAL PARK
Moose Lake
LIMESTONE POINT
BIG MOSSY POINT
Cedar Lake
Grand Rapids
Opasquia
Sandy Lake
Severn
LONG POINT
Lake Winnipeg
(217)
Lake Winnipegosis
(253)
Pelican Rapids
Mafeking
Hart Mountain 797
Birch River
Bowsman
Swan River
Minitonas
Duck Bay
PINE CREEK INDIAN RESERVE
REINDEER ISLAND
BERENS ISLAND
Berens River
Poplar Hill
Pikangikum
Sturgeon Bay
Camperville
Skownan
Anama Bay
Jackhead Harbour
Matheson Island
Gypsumville
Pine River
DUCK MOUNTAIN
Winnipegosis
Little Bullhead
Ethelbert
Baldy Mountain 832
CRANE RIVER IND. RES.
Steep Rock
FISHER RIVER INDIAN RESERVE
HECLA PROVINCIAL PARK
Uchi Lake
Rorketon
Magnet
PEGUIS INDIAN RESERVE
Sifton
McKenzie Island
Balmertown
Red Lake
Grandview
Gilbert Plains
Dauphin
Ashern
Hodgson
Hecla
Manigotagan
Bissett
Madsen
Ochre River
Ste-Rose-du-Lac
Fisher Branch
Riverton
Arborg
Lake Winnipeg
Bruce Lake
Ear Falls
RIDING MOUNTAIN NATIONAL PARK
Ste-Amélie
EBB AND FLOW INDIAN RESERVE
Laurier
Eriksdale
Victoria Beach
FORT ALEXANDER INDIAN RESERVE
Russell
Angusville
Binscarth
Rossburn
LIZARD POINT INDIAN RESERVE
Oakburn
McCreary
Amaranth
Lundar
Gimli
Pine Falls
Lac Seul
Perrault Falls
Lake Manitoba
(248)
Oak Point
SANDY BAY INDIAN RESERVE
Inwood
Winnipeg Beach
Grand Beach
Great Falls
St-Lazare
Elphinstone
Strathclair
Erickson
ROLLING RIVER INDIAN RESERVE
Langruth
St-Laurent
Teulon
LAC SEUL INDIAN RESERVE
Sioux Lookout
Birtle
Shoal Lake
Plumas
Arden
Minnedosa
Gladstone
LOWER FORT GARRY NATIONAL HISTORIC PARK
Stonewall
Selkirk
Red Lake Road
Richan
McAuley
Miniota
Hamiota
Rapid City
Neepawa
Delta Beach
Poplar Point
Lockport
Beausejour
Vermilion Bay
Dryden
Elkhorn
Rivers
Westbourne
Portage-la-Prairie
Winnipeg
Whitemouth
Kenora
Hawk Lake
Dinorwic
Dyment
Austin
MacGregor
Oakville
Rennie
WHITESHELL PROVINCIAL PARK
Keewatin
Virden
Douglas
Brandon
Carberry
Alexander
Oak Lake
Griswold
SPRUCE WOODS PROV. PARK
Souris
Treherne
Rathwell
Haywood
Starbuck
Elm Creek
Lorette
Ste-Anne-des-Chênes
Niverville
Richer
East Braintree
Waugh
Gold Rock
Sioux Narrows
Wawanesa
Holland
St. Claude
Ste-Agathe
Steinbach
La Broquerie
AULNEAU PENINSULA
Reston
Hartney
Glenboro
Cypress River
Notre-Dame-de-Lourdes
Otterburne
St. Pierre-Jolys
Grunthal
Carman
Woodridge
Angle Inlet
(323)
Crow Lake
Minto
Ninette
Belmont
Swan Lake
Morris
Dunrea
Baldur
Somerset
Miami
Roland
St-Jean-Baptiste
Napinka
Melita
Boissevain
Ninga
Manitou
Pilot Mound
Darlington
Winkler
Vita
Morson
Gainsborough
Deloraine
Killarney
Crystal City
Morden
Altona
Dominion City
Gardenton
Sprague
Middlebro
Waskada
Goodlands
TURTLE MTN. P. P.
Cartwright
Mather
Clearwater
MANITOBA
MINNESOTA
Woods
Lake of the Woods
ONTARIO
MINNESOTA
Turtle Mtn. 767
CANADA
UNITED STATES
Gretna
Emerson
Ridgeville
Warroad
Roseau
Roosevelt
Rainy River
Black Hawk
Mine Centre
Flanders
Westhope
INTERNATIONAL PEACE GARDEN
Hannah
Neche
Walhalla
Pembina
St. Vincent
Badger
Williams
Baudette
Emo
Fort Frances
International Falls
Rainy Lake

Map continues pages 190-191

Kilometers 0 50 100 150 Km.

Statute Miles 0 50 100 150 Mi.

Scale 1:3,000,000

One centimeter represents 30 kilometers.
One inch represents approximately 47 miles.
Lambert Conformal Conic Projection

Southeastern Canada / Südostkanada / Canadá Sud-oriental
Sud-Est du Canada / Canadá: Sudeste

72°
71°
70°
69°
68°
67°
66°
65°
64°
63°
51°
50°
49°
48°
47°
46°
45°
44°
NEWF.
QUÉ.
Mont de Babel
Réservoir Manicouagan
Sept-Îles
Moisie
Port-Cartier
Clarke City
Rivière-au-Tonnerre
Magpie
Mingan
Havre-St-Pierre
Baie-Johan-Beetz
Aguanish
ÎLES DE MINGAN
MINGAN ARCHIPELAGO NAT. PARK
Détroit de Jacques-Cartier
Baie-Ste-Claire
Port-Menier
ÎLE D'ANTICOSTI
Détroit d'Honguedo
Rivière-Pentecôte
Islets-Caribou
Baie-Trinité
POINTE DES MONTS
Godbout
Baie-Comeau
Hauterive
Betsiamites
Forestville
Portneuf-sur-Mer
Sault-au-Mouton
Tadoussac
Alma
Kenogami
Arvida
Jonquière
Chicoutimi
La Baie
Saint Laurent
Saint Lawrence
Ste-Anne-des-Monts
Cap-Chat
Matane
Ste-Félicité
Mont-Joli
Rimouski
Bic
Trois-Pistoles
Rivière-du-Loup
Madeleine-Centre
Rivière-à-Claude
Pointe-à-la-Frégate
St-Yvon
Fontenelle
Gaspé
PARC NATIONAL DE FORILLON
PÉNINSULE DE LA GASPÉSIE
MONTS CHIC CHOCS
Percé
Chandler
Grande-Rivière
Newport
Amqui
Causapscal
New-Richmond
Caplan
Bonaventure
New-Carlisle
Matapédia
Campbellton
Dalhousie
Chaleur Bay
Bathurst
Caraquet
Shippegan
Lamèque
Clermont
La Malbaie
Baie-St-Paul
PARC PROVINCIAL DES LAURENTIDES
Québec
Lauzon
Lévis
Ste-Foy
Beauport
Montmagny
La Pocatière
St-Jean-Port-Joli
Edmundston
Madawaska
Fort Kent
Van Buren
Grand Falls
APPALACHIAN MOUNTAINS
QUÉBEC
NEW BRUNSWICK
MAINE
CANADA
UNITED STATES
Presque Isle
Caribou
Houlton
Woodstock
Newcastle
Chatham
Miramichi Bay
Fredericton
Oromocto
Moncton
Dieppe
Sackville
Amherst
Saint John
St. Stephen
Calais
Eastport
Bangor
Orono
Brewer
Millinocket
Mount Katahdin
Moosehead L.
Waterville
Augusta
Lewiston
Auburn
Bath
Brunswick
Portland
South Portland
Cape Elizabeth
Old Orchard Beach
Saco
Biddeford
Kennebunk
Ogunquit
Cape Porpoise
Bar Harbor
ACADIA NATIONAL PARK
Gulf of Maine
Bay of Fundy
GRAND MANAN ISLAND
PRINCE EDWARD ISLAND
Charlottetown
Summerside
Northumberland Strait
NOVA SCOTIA
Truro
New Glasgow
Pictou
Halifax
Dartmouth
Yarmouth
Digby
Annapolis Royal
Kentville
Wolfville
Windsor
Bridgewater
Lunenburg
Liverpool
Shelburne
Lockeport
Barrington
CAPE SABLE

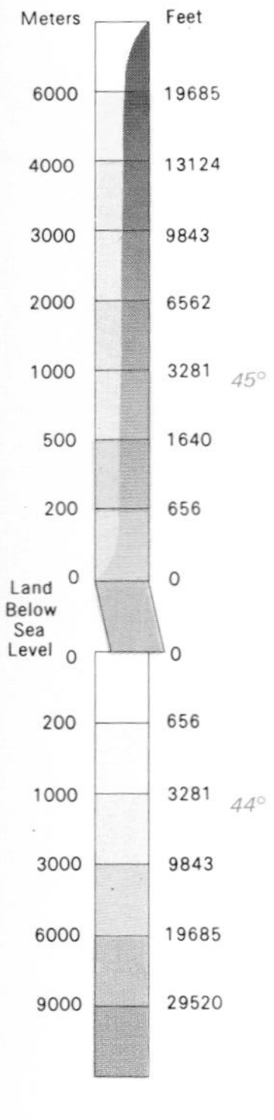
Meters
Feet
6000
19685
4000
13124
3000
9843
2000
6562
1000
3281
500
1640
200
656
0
Land Below Sea Level
0
200
656
1000
3281
3000
9843
6000
19685
9000
29520

Map continues pages **188-189**

ENGLISH	bay	cape	dam	island	lake, l.	mountain	point	strait
DEUTSCH	Bucht	Kap	Damm	Insel	See	Berg	Landspitze	Meeresstrasse
ESPAÑOL	bahía	cabo	presa	isla	lago	montaña	punta	estrecho
FRANÇAIS	baie	cap	barrage	île	lac	montagne	pointe	détroit
PORTUGUÊS	baía	cabo	represa	ilha	lago	montanha	ponta	estreito

LABRADOR
SEA
ATLANTIC
OCEAN
NEWFOUNDLAND
LONG RANGE MOUNTAINS
Corner Brook
St. John's
Gander
Grand Falls
Stephenville
Channel-Port-aux-Basques
Deer Lake
Bonavista
Bonavista Bay
Trinity Bay
Conception Bay
Placentia Bay
Fortune Bay
St. Mary's Bay
Notre Dame Bay
White Bay
Saint George's Bay
AVALON PENINSULA
BURIN PENINSULA
Cabot Strait
SAINT PIERRE AND MIQUELON
(France)
SAINT-PIERRE-ET-MIQUELON
Saint-Pierre
Miquelon
Sydney
North Sydney
Sydney Mines
Glace Bay
CAPE BRETON ISLAND
Louisbourg
SABLE ISLAND
(N.S.)
LA MADELEINE
(Qué.)
Grand-Entrée
ST. PAUL ISLAND
(N.S.)
GROS MORNE NATIONAL PARK
TERRA NOVA NATIONAL PARK
CAPE BRETON HIGHLANDS NATIONAL PARK
Strait of Belle Isle
St. Anthony
Blanc Sablon
Port Saunders
Twillingate
Lewisporte
Botwood
Clarenville
Carbonear
Harbour Grace
Placentia
Marystown
Grand Bank
Burgeo
Ramea
Port aux Basques
Copyright © by Rand McNally & Co.
Map prepared by Rand McNally & Co.
A-520219-764

Kilometers 0 50 100 150 Km.

Statute Miles 0 50 100 150 Mi.

Scale 1:3,000,000

One centimeter represents 30 kilometers.

One inch represents approximately 47 miles.

Lambert Conformal Conic Projection

LAKE MICHIGAN
LAKE HURON
Georgian Bay
LAKE ONTARIO
LAKE ERIE
CANADA
UNITED STATES
MICHIGAN
ONTARIO
OHIO
INDIANA
PENNSYLVANIA
NEW YORK
WEST VIRGINIA
VIRGINIA
KENTUCKY
MARYLAND
DETROIT
TORONTO
CLEVELAND
PITTSBURGH
BUFFALO
CINCINNATI
WASHINGTON
Columbus
Toledo
Lansing
Flint
Saginaw
Grand Rapids
Akron
Dayton
Charleston
Lexington
Hamilton
London
Rochester
Erie
ALLEGHENY MOUNTAINS
MANITOULIN ISLAND
BRUCE PENINSULA

Map continues pages 190-191

Map continues pages 194-195

Map continues pages 192-193

Meters	Feet
6000	19685
4000	13124
3000	9843
2000	6562
1000	3281
500	1640
200	656
0	0
Land Below Sea Level	0
0	
200	656
1000	3281
3000	9843
6000	19685
9000	29520

ENGLISH	bay	creek, cr.	island, i.	lake, l.	mountain, mtn.	point, pt.	reservoir, res.	state park, s.p.
DEUTSCH	Bucht	Bach	Insel	See	Berg	Landspitze	Stausee	Staatspark
ESPAÑOL	bahía	riachuelo	isla	lago	montaña	punta	embalse	parque del estado
FRANÇAIS	baie	crique	île	lac	montagne	pointe	réservoir	parc régional
PORTUGUÊS	baía	riacho	ilha	lago	montanha	ponta	reservatório	parque estadual

Map continues pages 186-187

Trois-Rivières
MONTRÉAL
Ottawa
Sherbrooke
Bangor
Portland
Gulf of Maine
Burlington
Montpelier
Syracuse
Albany
Schenectady
Manchester
BOSTON
Massachusetts Bay
Worcester
Springfield
Hartford
Providence
Cape Cod Bay
Nantucket Sound
New Haven
Bridgeport
Long Island Sound
NEW YORK
Newark
Trenton
PHILADELPHIA
Atlantic City
ATLANTIC
OCEAN
Scranton
Binghamton
Allentown
Wilmington
Dover
Delaware Bay
DELMARVA PENINSULA
Salisbury
ADIRONDACK MOUNTAINS
CATSKILL MOUNTAINS
WHITE MOUNTAINS
GREEN MOUNTAINS
Copyright © by Rand McNally & Co.
Map prepared by Rand McNally & Co.

Kilometers 0 50 100 150 Km.
Statute Miles 0 50 100 150 Mi.

Scale 1:3,000,000

One centimeter represents 30 kilometers.
One inch represents approximately 47 miles.
Albers Conical Equal-Area Projection

Great Lakes Region / Grosse Seen-Region / Región de los Grandes Lagos
Région des Grands Lacs / Região dos Grandes Lagos

Map continues pages 184-185

Map continues pages 198-199

LAKE SUPERIOR
(183 Meters Above Sea Level)
LAKE MICHIGAN
(176 Meters Above Sea Level)
CANADA
UNITED STATES
ONTARIO
MINNESOTA
WISCONSIN
MICHIGAN
IOWA
ILL.
IND.
MISSOURI
Thunder Bay
Duluth
Superior
International Falls
Bemidji
Hibbing
Virginia
Brainerd
St. Cloud
MINNEAPOLIS
St. Paul
Rochester
Mankato
Owatonna
Albert Lea
Austin
Mason City
Fort Dodge
Waterloo
Cedar Falls
Marshalltown
Cedar Rapids
Iowa City
Des Moines
Ottumwa
Oskaloosa
Burlington
Fort Madison
Keokuk
Davenport
Rock Island
Moline
Dubuque
La Crosse
Eau Claire
Wausau
Marshfield
Stevens Point
Wisconsin Rapids
Oshkosh
Appleton
Green Bay
Manitowoc
Sheboygan
Fond du Lac
Madison
Janesville
Beloit
MILWAUKEE
Racine
Kenosha
Waukegan
Rockford
Freeport
Elgin
CHICAGO
Joliet
Aurora
Gary
Hammond
South Bend
Kankakee
Peoria
Pekin
Galesburg
Macomb
Bloomington
Kalamazoo
Grand Rapids
Muskegon
Holland
Marquette
Escanaba
Iron Mountain
Ironwood
Menominee
Marinette
Ashland
ISLE ROYALE
Copyright © by Rand McNally & Co.
Map prepared by Rand McNally & Co.

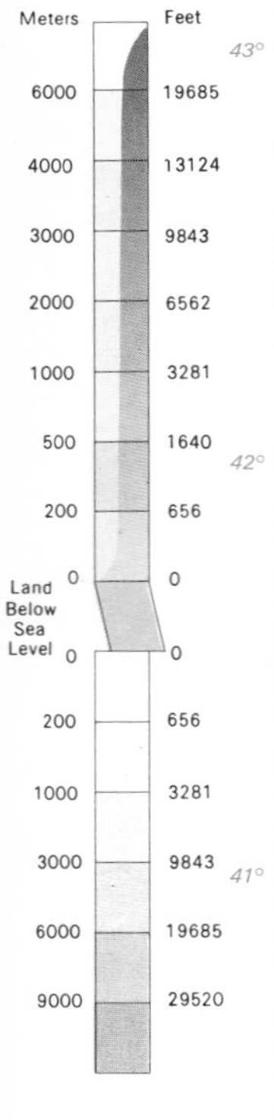

Meters
Feet
6000 19685
4000 13124
3000 9843
2000 6562
1000 3281
500 1640
200 656
0 0
Land Below Sea Level
0 0
200 656
1000 3281
3000 9843
6000 19685
9000 29520

Map continues pages 194-195

ENGLISH	bay	creek, cr.	Indian reservation	island, i.	lake, l.	point	reservoir, res.	state park, s.p.
DEUTSCH	Bucht	Bach	Indianerreservation	Insel	See	Landspitze	Stausee	Staatspark
ESPAÑOL	bahía	riachuelo	reserva de Indios	isla	lago	punta	embalse	parque del estado
FRANÇAIS	baie	crique	réserve indienne	île	lac	pointe	réservoir	parc régional
PORTUGUÊS	baía	riacho	reserva indígena	ilha	lago	ponta	reservatório	parque estadual

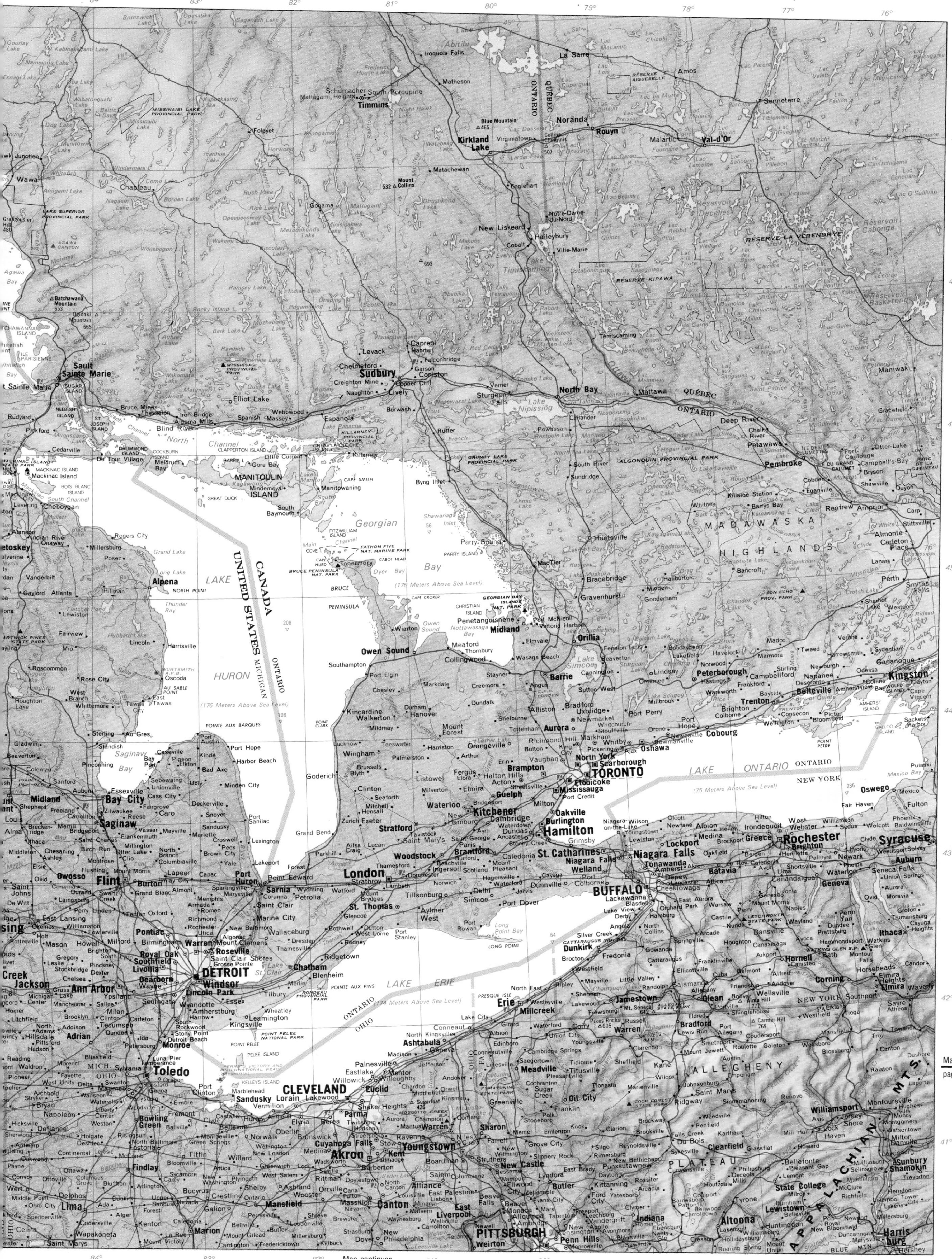
Lake Huron
(176 Meters Above Sea Level)
Georgian Bay
Lake Ontario
(75 Meters Above Sea Level)
Lake Erie
(174 Meters Above Sea Level)
Saginaw Bay
Lake Nipissing
Lake Simcoe
CANADA
UNITED STATES
ONTARIO
QUÉBEC
MICHIGAN
NEW YORK
OHIO
MANITOULIN ISLAND
BRUCE PENINSULA
MADAWASKA HIGHLANDS
ALLEGHENY PLATEAU
APPALACHIAN MTS.
ALGONQUIN PROVINCIAL PARK
TORONTO
DETROIT
Windsor
CLEVELAND
BUFFALO
PITTSBURGH
Hamilton
London
Kingston
Rochester
Syracuse
Toledo
Flint
Saginaw
Sudbury
Timmins
North Bay
Sault Sainte Marie
Erie
Akron
Youngstown
Canton
Lima
Ann Arbor
Lansing
Rouyn
Val-d'Or
Kirkland Lake
Niagara Falls
St. Catharines
Kitchener
Oshawa
Barrie
Owen Sound
Sarnia
Port Huron
Jamestown
Altoona
Harrisburg
Williamsport
Elmira
Ithaca

Map continues pages 188-189

Map continues pages 188-189

Kilometers 0 50 100 150 Km.

Statute Miles 0 50 100 150 Mi.

Scale 1:3,000,000

One centimeter represents 30 kilometers.

One inch represents approximately 47 miles.

Albers Conical Equal-Area Projection

ENGLISH	DEUTSCH	ESPAÑOL	FRANÇAIS	PORTUGUÊS
bay	Bucht	bahía	baie	baía
cape	Kap	cabo	cap	cabo
creek, cr.	Bach	riachuelo	crique	riacho
dam	Damm	presa	barrage	represa
island, I.	Insel	isla	île	ilha
lake, l.	See	lago	lac	lago
mountain, mtn.	Berg	montaña	montagne	montanha
state park, s.p.	Staatspark	parque del estado	parc régional	parque estadual

Kilometers 0 50 100 150 Km.
Statute Miles 0 50 100 150 Mi.

Scale 1:3,000,000
One centimeter represents 30 kilometers.
One inch represents approximately 47 miles.
Albers Conical Equal-Area Projection

Map continues pages 188-189

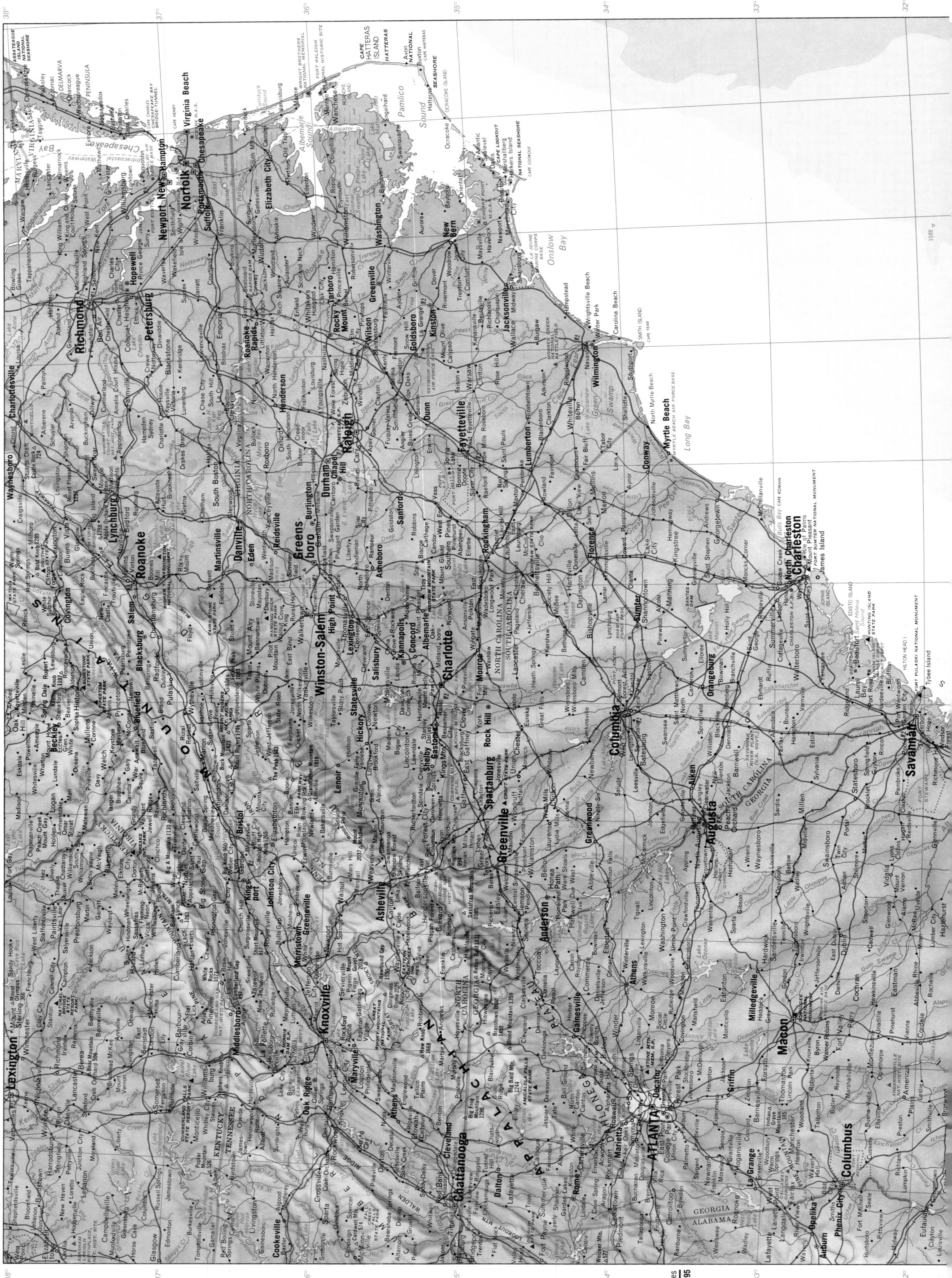

Map continues pages 194-195

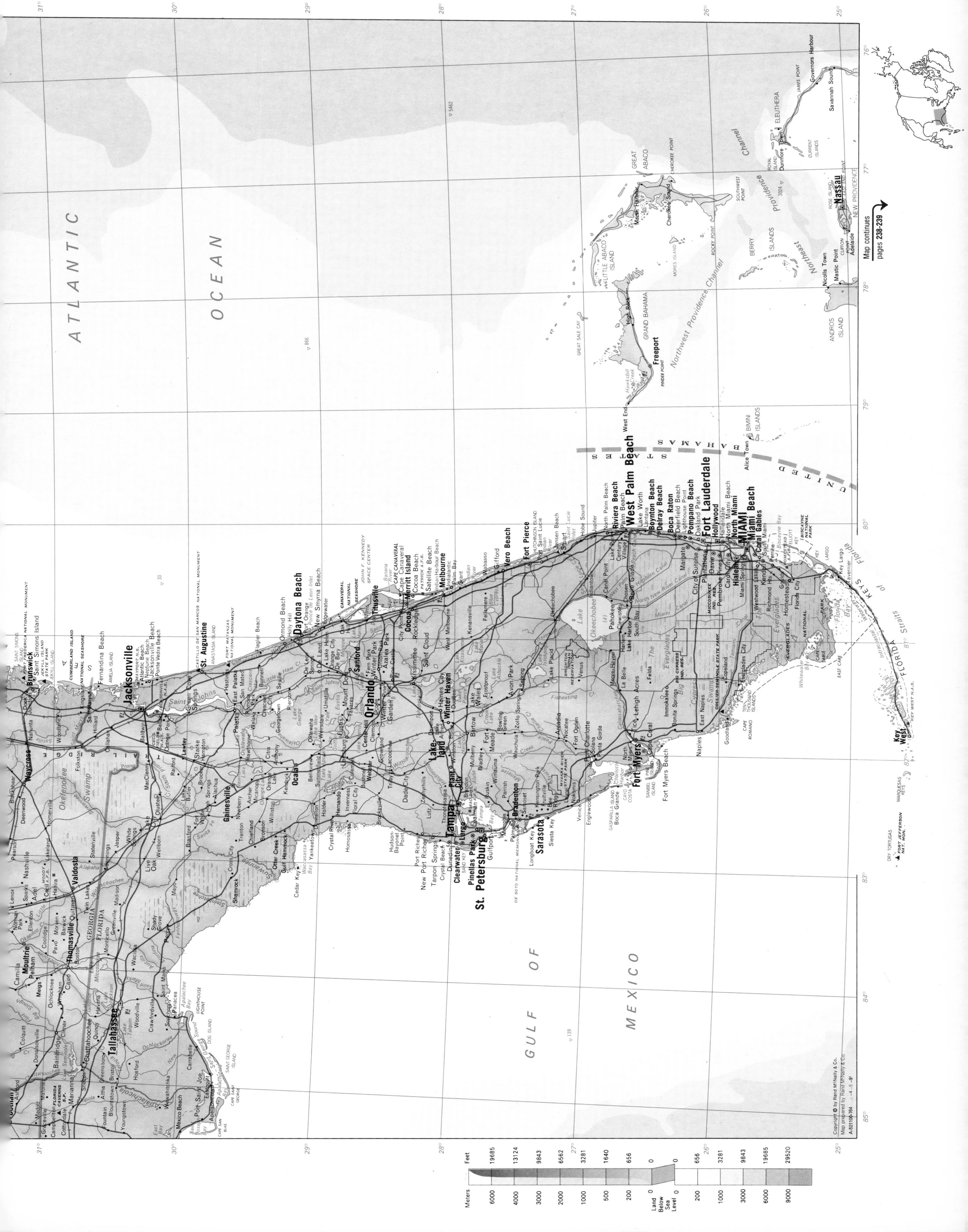
ATLANTIC
OCEAN
GULF OF MEXICO
Jacksonville
St. Augustine
Daytona Beach
Orlando
Tampa
St. Petersburg
Clearwater
Sarasota
Fort Myers
West Palm Beach
Fort Lauderdale
Hollywood
MIAMI
Miami Beach
Key West
Tallahassee
Gainesville
Ocala
Valdosta
Thomasville
Brunswick
Waycross
Freeport
Nassau
GRAND BAHAMA
GREAT ABACO
ANDROS ISLAND
ELEUTHERA
BAHAMAS
UNITED STATES
Map continues pages 238-239
Copyright © by Rand McNally & Co.
Feet
Meters
Land Below Sea Level

Map continues pages 188-189

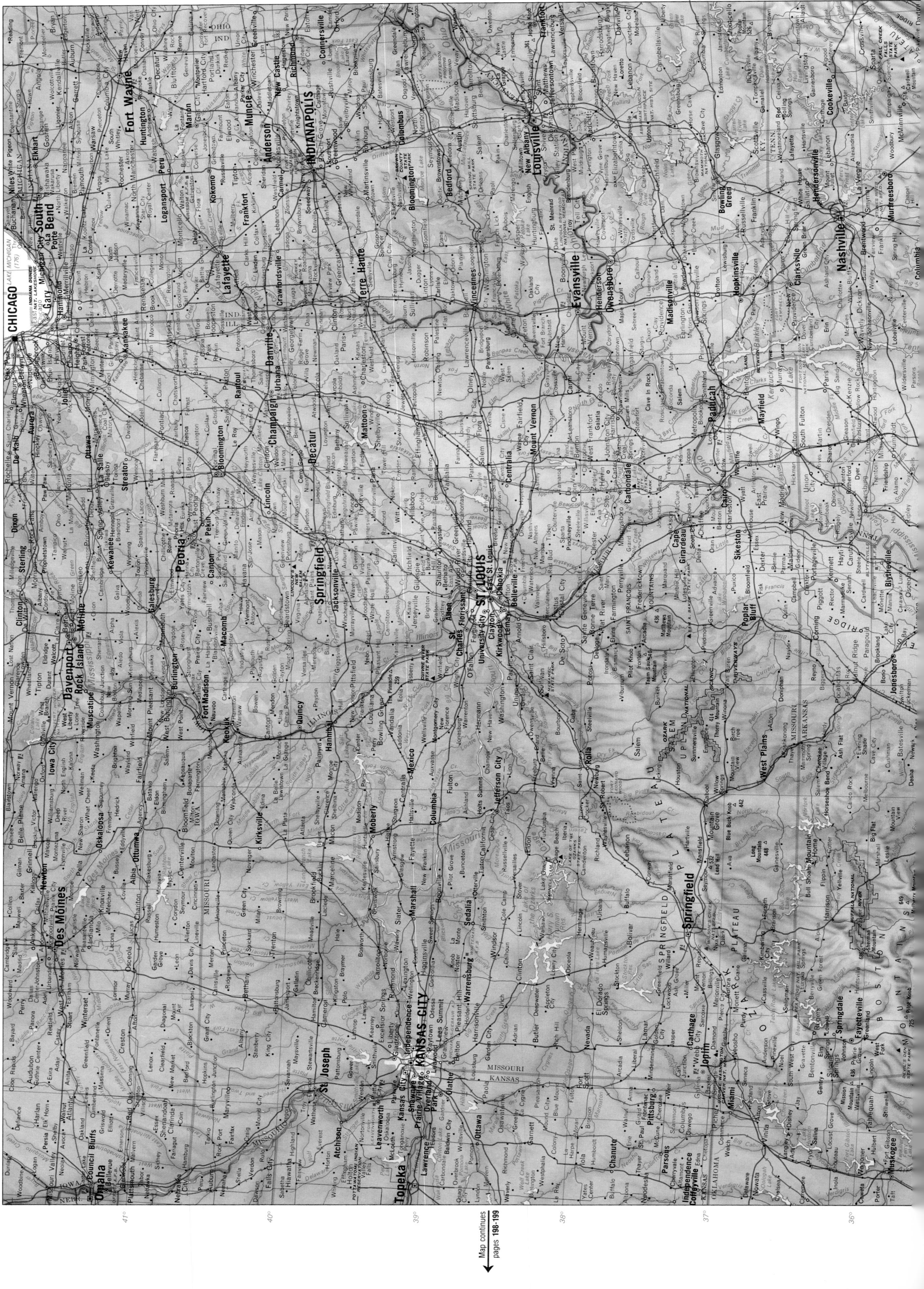
CHICAGO
INDIANAPOLIS
ST. LOUIS
KANSAS CITY
Louisville
Nashville
Springfield
Peoria
Des Moines
Davenport
Evansville
Fort Wayne
Topeka
Omaha

Map continues pages 190-191

Map continues pages 198-199

Map continues pages 192-193

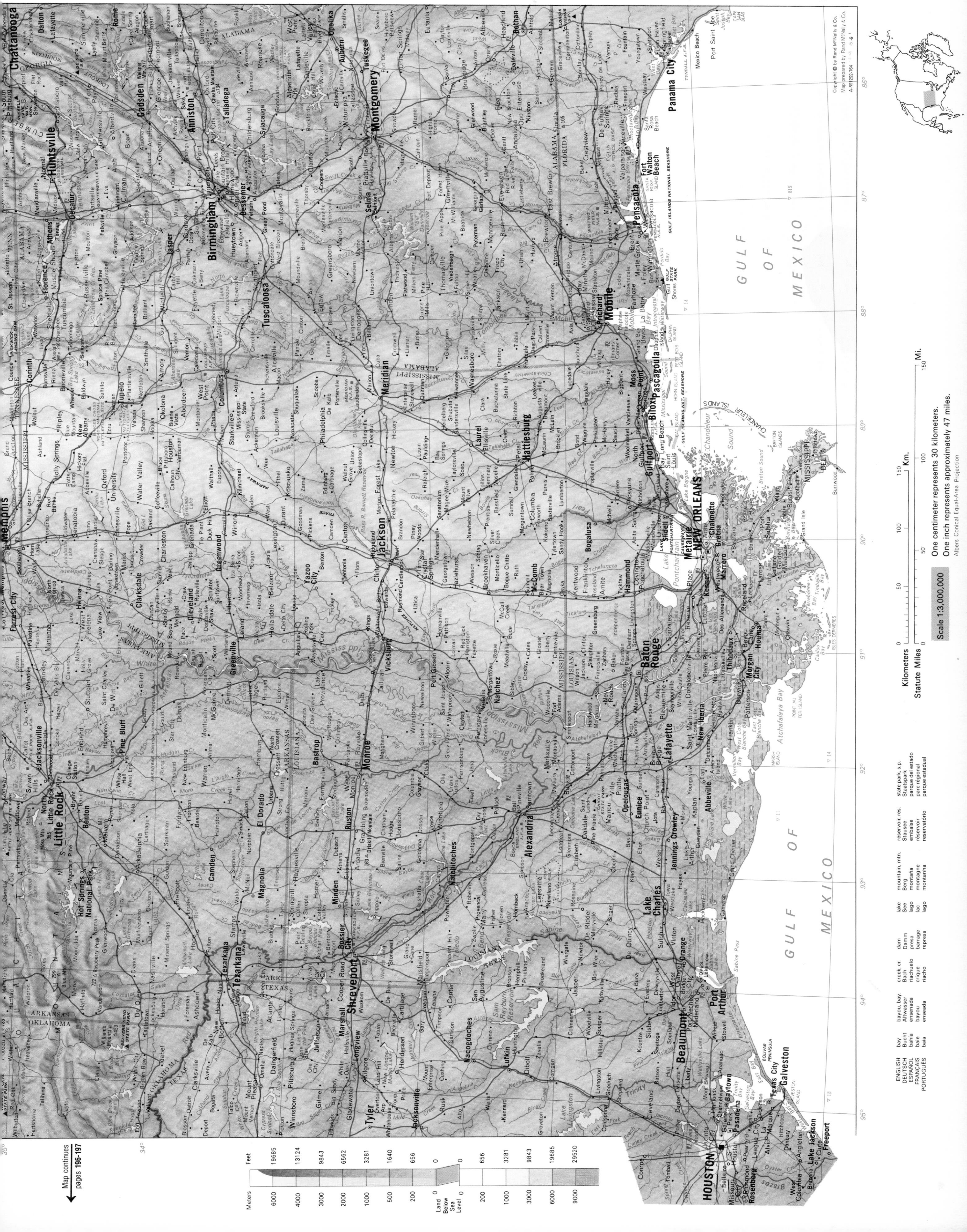
GULF OF MEXICO
Scale 1:3,000,000
One centimeter represents 30 kilometers.
One inch represents approximately 47 miles.
Albers Conical Equal-Area Projection
Kilometers
Statute Miles
Copyright © by Rand McNally & Co.
Map prepared by Rand McNally & Co.
Meters
Feet
Land Below Sea Level
ENGLISH bay bayou, bay creek, cr. dam lake mountain, mtn. reservoir, res. state park, s.p.
DEUTSCH Bucht Altwasser Bach Damm See Berg Stausee Staatspark
ESPAÑOL bahía ensenada riachuelo presa lago montaña embalse parque del estado
FRANÇAIS baie bayou crique barrage lac montagne réservoir parc régional
PORTUGUÊS baía enseada riacho represa lago montanha reservatório parque estadual
HOUSTON
NEW ORLEANS
Memphis
Birmingham
Montgomery
Jackson
Shreveport
Little Rock
Baton Rouge
Mobile

Map continues pages 196-197

Map continues pages 194-195

Map continues pages 198-199

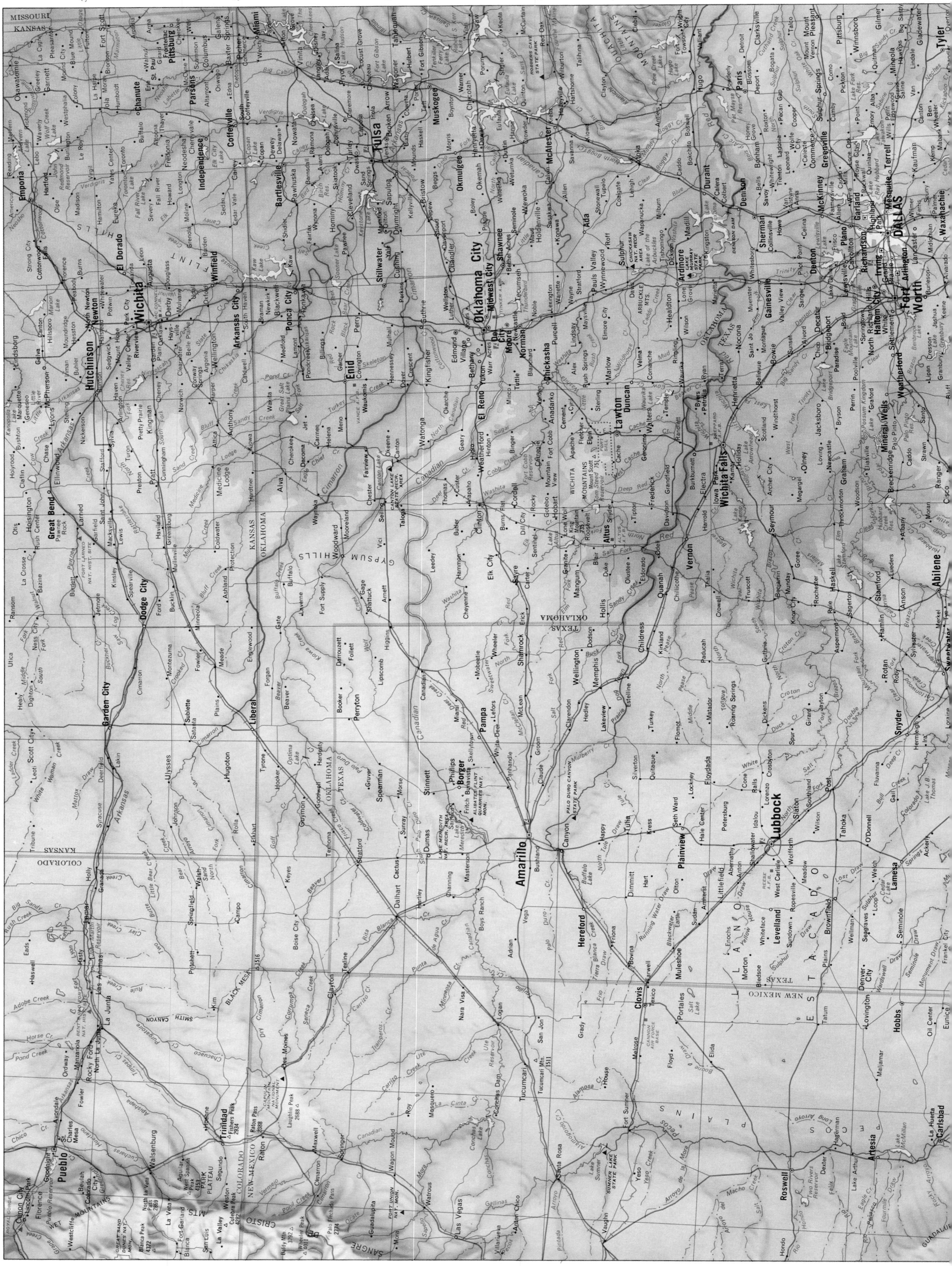
38°
37°
36°
35°
34°
33°
95°
96°
97°
98°
99°
100°
101°
102°
103°
104°
105°
MISSOURI
KANSAS
OKLAHOMA
TEXAS
COLORADO
NEW MEXICO
Wichita
Tulsa
Oklahoma City
Amarillo
Lubbock
DALLAS
Fort Worth
Wichita Falls
Abilene
Dodge City
Garden City
Liberal
Pueblo
Trinidad
Raton
Clovis
Roswell
Hutchinson
Enid
Lawton
GYPSUM HILLS
FLINT HILLS
WICHITA MOUNTAINS
LLANO ESTACADO
PLAINS
SANGRE DE CRISTO MTS

Map continues pages 200-201

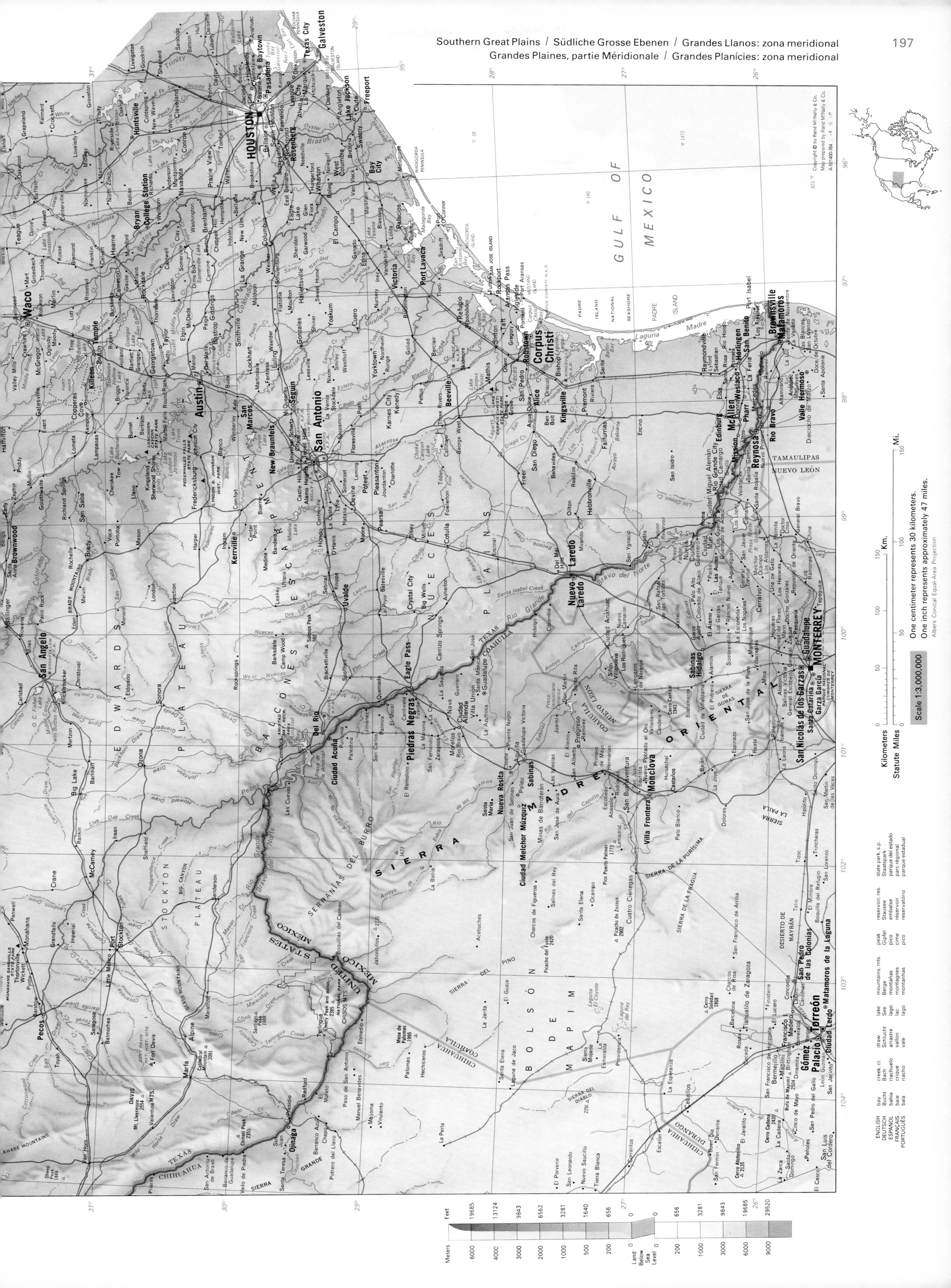
GULF OF MEXICO
Scale 1:3,000,000
One centimeter represents 30 kilometers.
One inch represents approximately 47 miles.
Albers Conical Equal-Area Projection
Kilometers
Statute Miles
Copyright © by Rand McNally & Co.
Map prepared by Rand McNally & Co.
ENGLISH bay creek, cr. draw lake mountains, mts. peak reservoir, res. state park, s.p.
DEUTSCH Bucht Bach Schlucht See Berge Gipfel Stausee Staatspark
ESPAÑOL bahía riachuelo arrastre lago montañas pico embalse parque del estado
FRANÇAIS baie crique vallon lac montagnes cime reservoir parc régional
PORTUGUÊS baía riacho vale lago montanhas pico reservatório parque estadual
Meters
Feet
Land Below Sea Level
HOUSTON
San Antonio
Austin
Corpus Christi
MONTERREY
Torreón

Map continues pages 190-191

Map continues pages 184-185

MANITOBA
ONTARIO
MINNESOTA
NORTH DAKOTA
SOUTH DAKOTA
MONTANA
WYOMING
SASKATCHEWAN
CANADA
UNITED STATES
Winnipeg
Brandon
Grand Forks
Fargo
Moorhead
Bismarck
Minot
Jamestown
Aberdeen
Pierre
Rapid City
Williston
Dickinson
Miles City
St. Cloud
Brainerd
Bemidji
COTEAU DU MISSOURI
BADLANDS
BLACK HILLS
COTEAU DES PRAIRIES

Map continues pages 202-203

Map continues pages 194-195

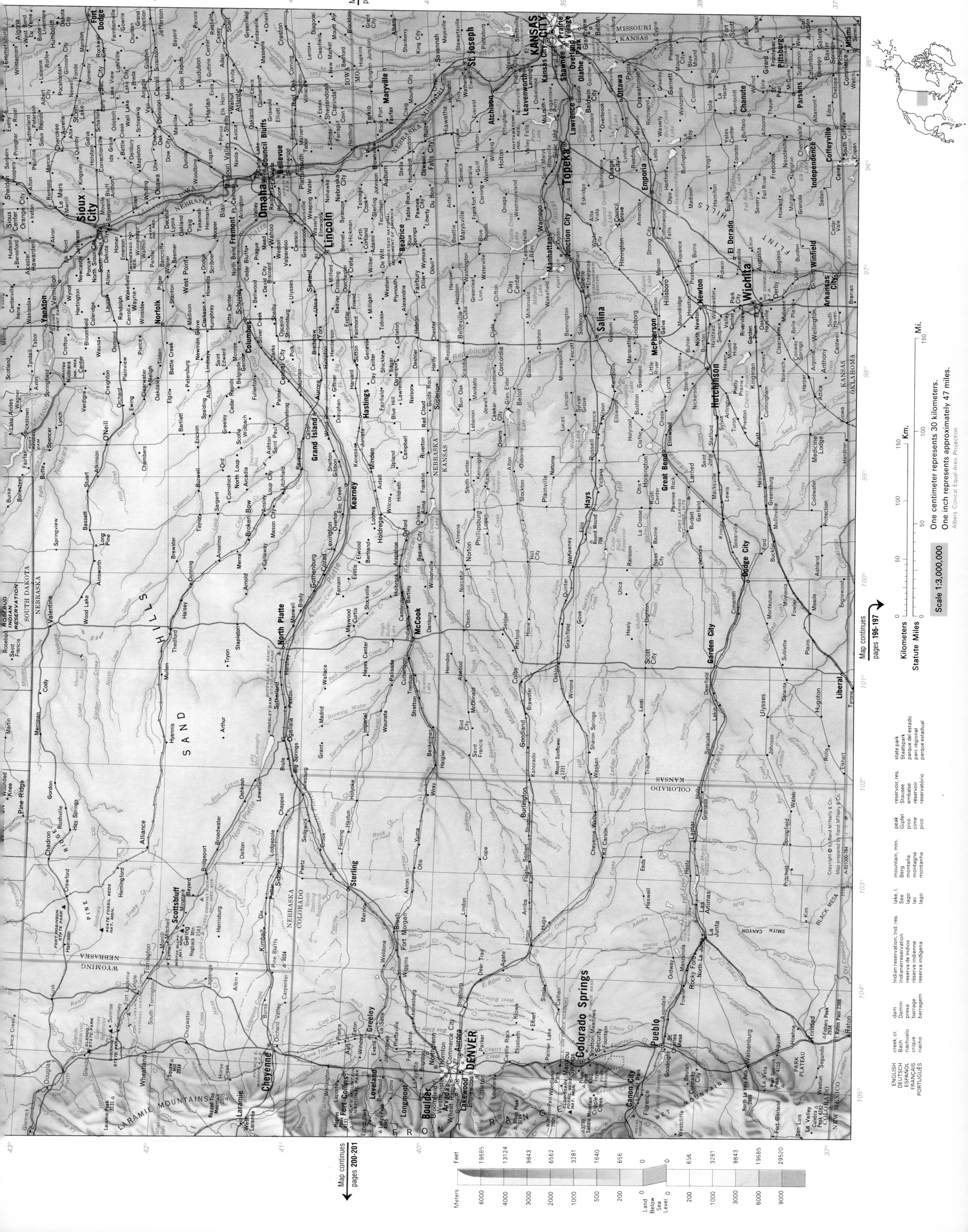
Scale 1:3,000,000
One centimeter represents 30 kilometers.
One inch represents approximately 47 miles.
Albers Conical Equal-Area Projection
Kilometers
Statute Miles
ENGLISH DEUTSCH ESPAÑOL FRANÇAIS PORTUGUÊS
creek, cr. Bach riachuelo crique riacho
dam Damm presa barrage barragem
Indian reservation, Ind. res. Indianerreservation reserva de indios réserve indienne reserva indígena
lake, l. See lago lac lago
mountain, mtn. Berg montaña montagne montanha
peak Gipfel pico cime pico
reservoir, res. Stausee embalse réservoir reservatório
state park Staatspark parque del estado parc régional parque estadual
Copyright © by Rand McNally & Co.
Map prepared by Rand McNally & Co.
Feet
Meters
Land Below Sea Level

Map continues pages 196-197

Map continues pages 200-201

Map continues pages 198-199

Map continues pages 202-203

DENVER
Colorado Springs
Pueblo
Cheyenne
Laramie
Casper
Salt Lake City
Ogden
Provo
Pocatello
Idaho Falls
Twin Falls
Grand Junction
Rock Springs
Boulder
Greeley
Fort Collins
Longmont
Logan
Moab
GREAT SALT LAKE DESERT
GREAT DIVIDE BASIN
WYOMING
IDAHO
UTAH
NEVADA
COLORADO

Map continues pages 204-205

Map continues pages 196-197

Albuquerque
Santa Fe
Las Vegas
Los Alamos
Farmington
Gallup
Flagstaff
Prescott
Phoenix
Scottsdale
Tempe
Mesa
Chandler
Tucson
Nogales
Douglas
Las Cruces
El Paso
Ciudad Juárez
Yuma
Lake Havasu City
North Las Vegas
Las Vegas
Saint George
NEW MEXICO
ARIZONA
UNITED STATES
MEXICO
CHIHUAHUA
SONORA
Golfo de California
DESIERTO DE ALTAR

ENGLISH	DEUTSCH	ESPAÑOL	FRANÇAIS	PORTUGUÊS
creek, cr.	Bach	riachuelo	crique	riacho
Indian reservation	Indianerreservation	reserva de Indios	réserve indienne	reserva indígena
lake	See	lago	lac	lago
mountains	Berge	montañas	montagnes	montanhas
national monument, nat. mon.	Nationaldenkmal	monumento nacional	monument national	monumento nacional
peak	Gipfel	pico	cime	pico
reservoir, res.	Stausee	embalse	réservoir	reservatório
wash	Trockenfluss	uadi	wadi	uádi

Scale 1:3,000,000

One centimeter represents 30 kilometers.
One inch represents approximately 47 miles.

Kilometers 0 50 100 150 Km.
Statute Miles 0 50 100 150 Mi.

Feet	19685	13124	9843	6562	3281	1640	656	0	0	656	3281	9843	19685	29520
Meters	6000	4000	3000	2000	1000	500	200	0 Land Below Sea Level	0	200	1000	3000	6000	9000

Map continues pages 182-183

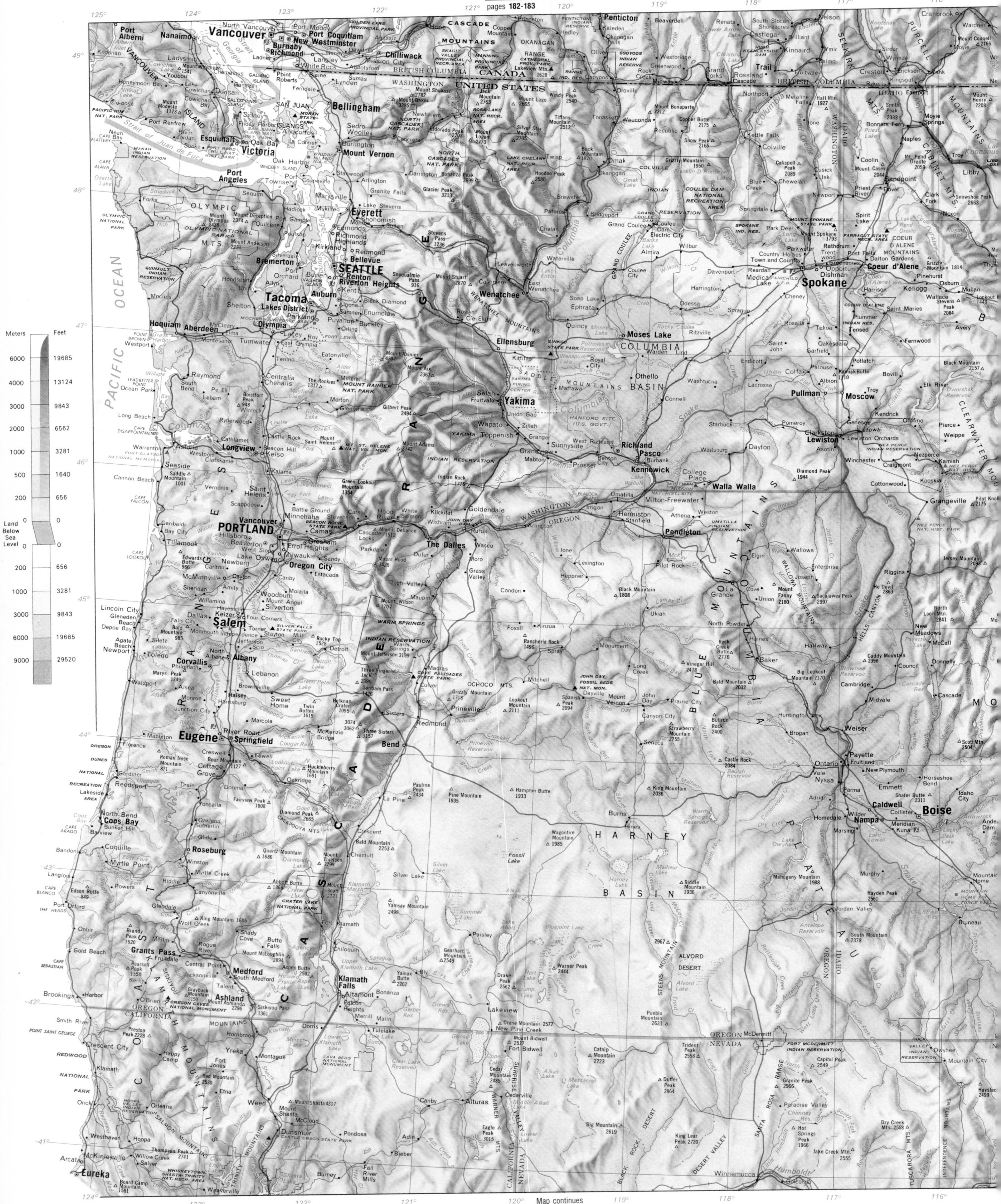
Meters
Feet
6000 19685
4000 13124
3000 9843
2000 6562
1000 3281
500 1640
200 656
0 0
Land Below Sea Level
200 656
1000 3281
3000 9843
6000 19685
9000 29520
BRITISH COLUMBIA
CANADA
UNITED STATES
WASHINGTON
IDAHO
OREGON
CALIFORNIA
NEVADA
PACIFIC OCEAN
Vancouver
Victoria
Bellingham
SEATTLE
Tacoma
Olympia
Everett
Spokane
Yakima
Wenatchee
Ellensburg
Moses Lake
Richland
Pasco
Kennewick
Walla Walla
Lewiston
Pullman
Moscow
Coeur d'Alene
PORTLAND
Salem
Eugene
Corvallis
Albany
Bend
The Dalles
Pendleton
Baker
Burns
Medford
Grants Pass
Klamath Falls
Roseburg
Coos Bay
Boise
Nampa
Caldwell
Eureka
Yreka
Lakeview
Winnemucca
CASCADE RANGE
BLUE MOUNTAINS
COLUMBIA BASIN
HARNEY BASIN
OLYMPIC MTS.
COAST RANGES
KLAMATH MOUNTAINS
OREGON PLATEAU

Map continues pages 204-205

ENGLISH	creek, cr.	Indian reservation	lake, l.	mountain, mtn.	pass	peak	range	reservoir, res.
DEUTSCH	Bach	Indianerreservation	See	Berg	Pass	Gipfel	Gebirge	Stausee
ESPAÑOL	riachuelo	reserva de Indios	lago	montaña	paso	pico	sierra	embalse
FRANÇAIS	crique	réserve indienne	lac	montagne	col	pic	chaîne	réservoir
PORTUGUÊS	riacho	reserva indígena	lago	montanha	passo	pico	serra	reservatório

Map continues pages 184-185

CANADA
UNITED STATES
ALBERTA
SASKATCHEWAN
MONTANA
IDAHO
WYOMING
UTAH
COLORADO
Great Falls
Helena
Missoula
Butte
Anaconda
Bozeman
Billings
Havre
Kalispell
Lewistown
Miles City
Glasgow
Sheridan
Casper
Idaho Falls
Pocatello
Twin Falls
Logan
Ogden
Rock Springs
YELLOWSTONE NATIONAL PARK
GLACIER NATIONAL PARK
BIGHORN BASIN
GREAT DIVIDE BASIN
GREAT SALT LAKE DESERT
SNAKE RIVER PLAIN
BITTERROOT RANGE
ABSAROKA RANGE
WIND RIVER RANGE
BIGHORN MOUNTAINS
LEWIS AND CLARK RANGE
Missouri
Yellowstone
Snake
Fort Peck Lake
Flathead Lake
Copyright © by Rand McNally & Co.
Map prepared by Rand McNally & Co.
A-520597-764

Map continues pages 198-199

Map continues pages 200-201

Kilometers 0 50 100 150 Km.
Statute Miles 0 50 100 150 Mi.

Scale 1:3,000,000
One centimeter represents 30 kilometers.
One inch represents approximately 47 miles.
Albers Conical Equal-Area Projection

Map continues pages 200-201

Map continues pages 202-203

GREAT SALT LAKE DESERT
SNAKE RIVER PLAIN
COLUMBIA PLATEAU
HARNEY BASIN
GREAT BASIN
CASCADE RANGE
COAST RANGES
KLAMATH MOUNTAINS
SIERRA NEVADA
SACRAMENTO VALLEY
BLACK ROCK DESERT
RUBY MOUNTAINS
IDAHO
OREGON
NEVADA
CALIFORNIA
UTAH
SAN FRANCISCO
Oakland
San Jose
Sacramento
Stockton
Reno
Sparks
Carson City
Eureka
Redding
Chico
Medford
Klamath Falls
Twin Falls
Winnemucca
Elko
Fallon
Tonopah
Santa Rosa
Modesto
Roseburg
Grants Pass
Coos Bay

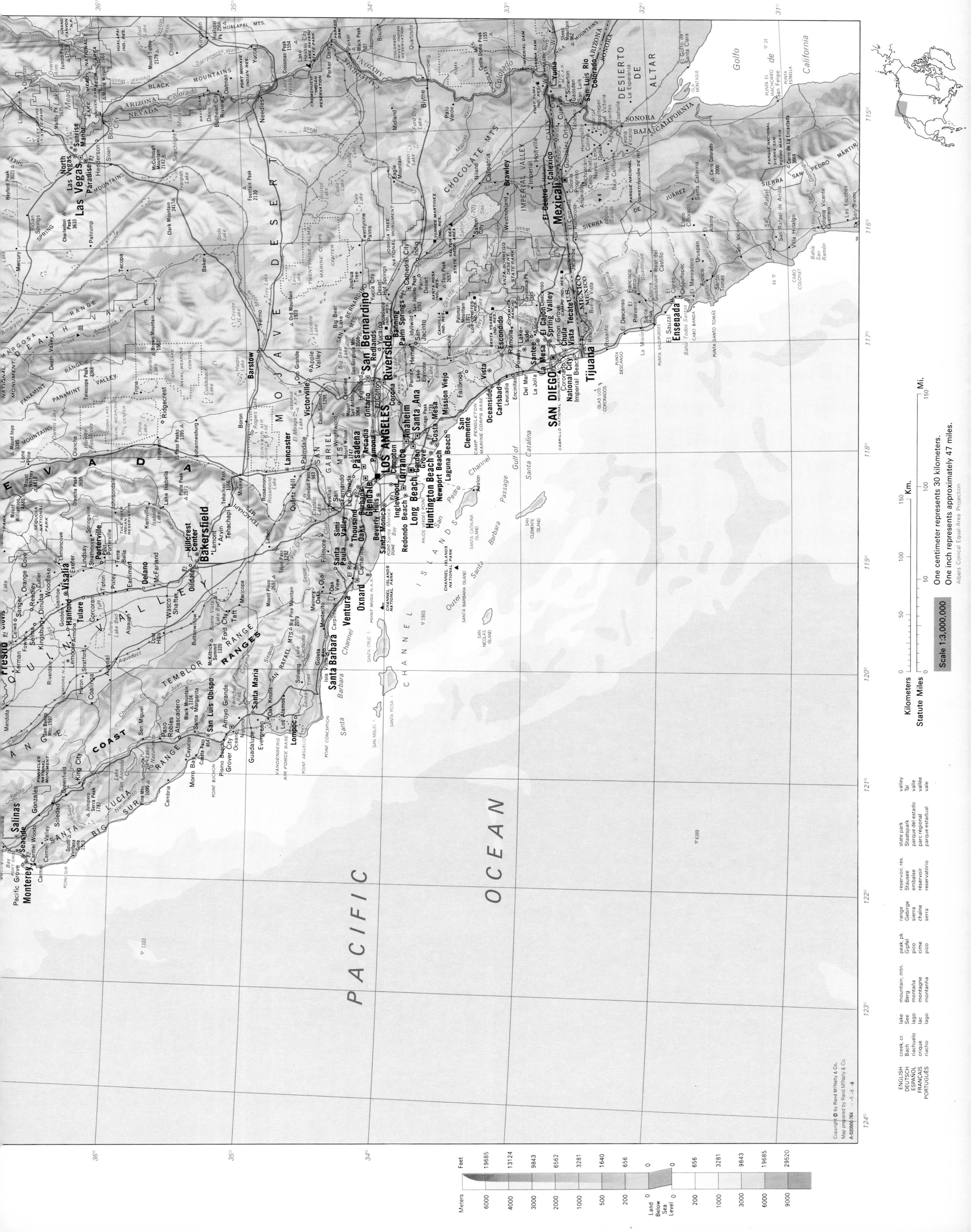
PACIFIC OCEAN
MOJAVE DESERT
LOS ANGELES
SAN DIEGO
Las Vegas
Bakersfield
San Bernardino
Riverside
Santa Barbara
Mexicali
Tijuana
Scale 1:3,000,000
One centimeter represents 30 kilometers.
One inch represents approximately 47 miles.
Albers Conical Equal-Area Projection
Kilometers 0 50 100 150 Km.
Statute Miles 0 50 100 150 Mi.
ENGLISH creek, cr. lake mountain, mtn. peak, pk. range reservoir, res. state park valley
DEUTSCH Bach See Berg Gipfel Gebirge Stausee Staatspark Tal
ESPAÑOL riachuelo lago montaña pico sierra embalse parque del estado valle
FRANÇAIS ruisseau lac montagne cime chaîne réservoir parc régional vallée
PORTUGUÊS riacho lago montanha pico serra reservatório parque estadual vale
Meters 6000 4000 3000 2000 1000 500 200 0 Land Below Sea Level 0 200 1000 3000 6000 9000
Feet 19685 13124 9843 6562 3281 1640 656 0 0 656 3281 9843 19685 29520
Copyright © by Rand McNally & Co.
Map prepared by Rand McNally & Co.

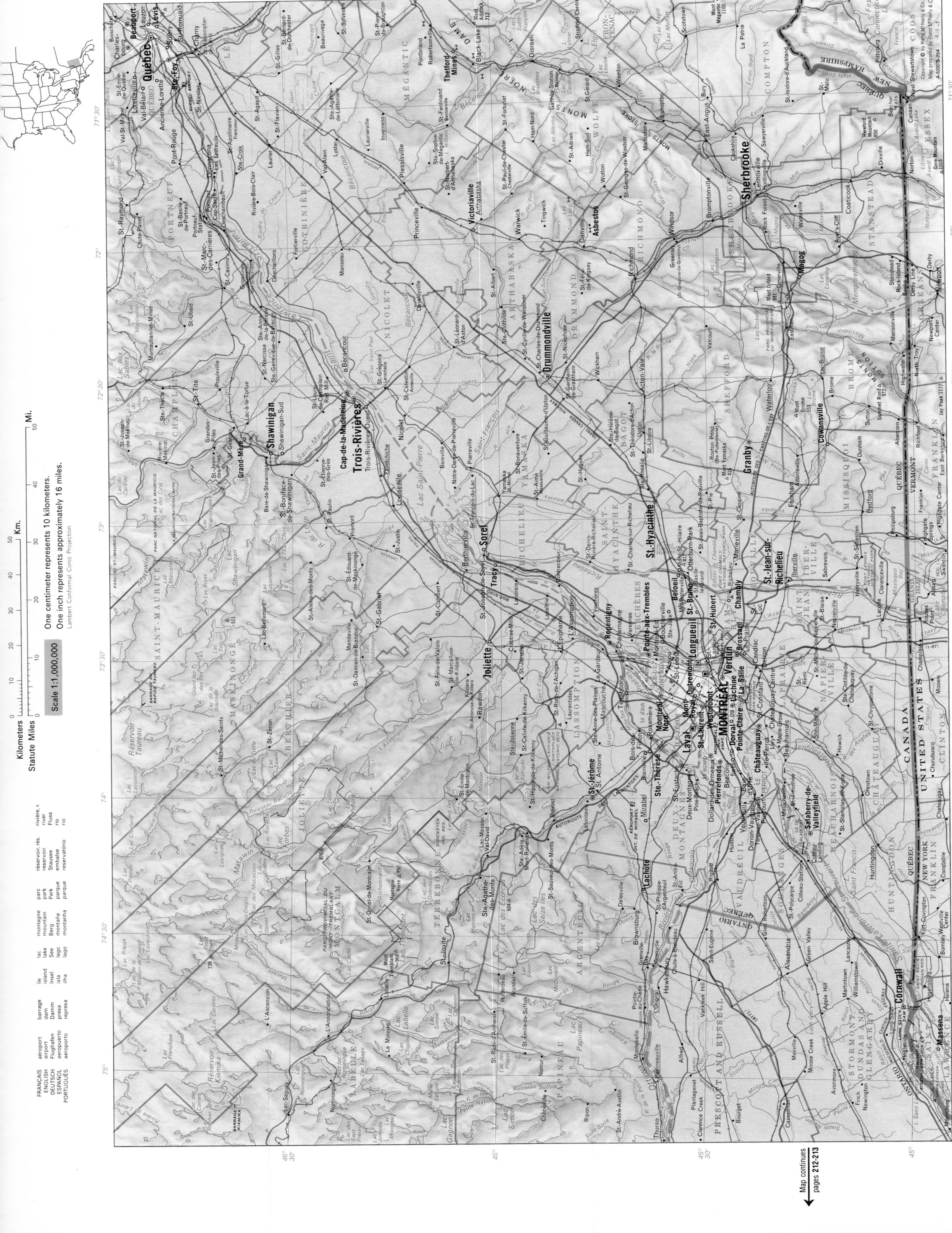
Kilometers 0 10 20 30 40 50 Km.
Statute Miles 0 10 20 30 40 50 Mi.
Scale 1:1,000,000
One centimeter represents 10 kilometers.
One inch represents approximately 16 miles.
Lambert Conformal Conic Projection
FRANÇAIS aéroport barrage île lac montagne parc réservoir, rés. rivière, r.
ENGLISH airport dam island lake mountain park reservoir river
DEUTSCH Flughafen Damm Insel See Berg Park Stausee Fluss
ESPAÑOL aeropuerto presa isla lago montaña parque embalse río
PORTUGUÊS aeroporto represa ilha lago montanha parque reservatório rio
Québec
Lévis
Trois-Rivières
Shawinigan
Drummondville
Sherbrooke
Granby
St.-Hyacinthe
Sorel
Joliette
St.-Jérôme
Laval
MONTRÉAL
Longueuil
Cornwall
Massena
CANADA
UNITED STATES
QUÉBEC
ONTARIO
VERMONT
NEW YORK
NEW HAMPSHIRE
Map continues pages 212-213

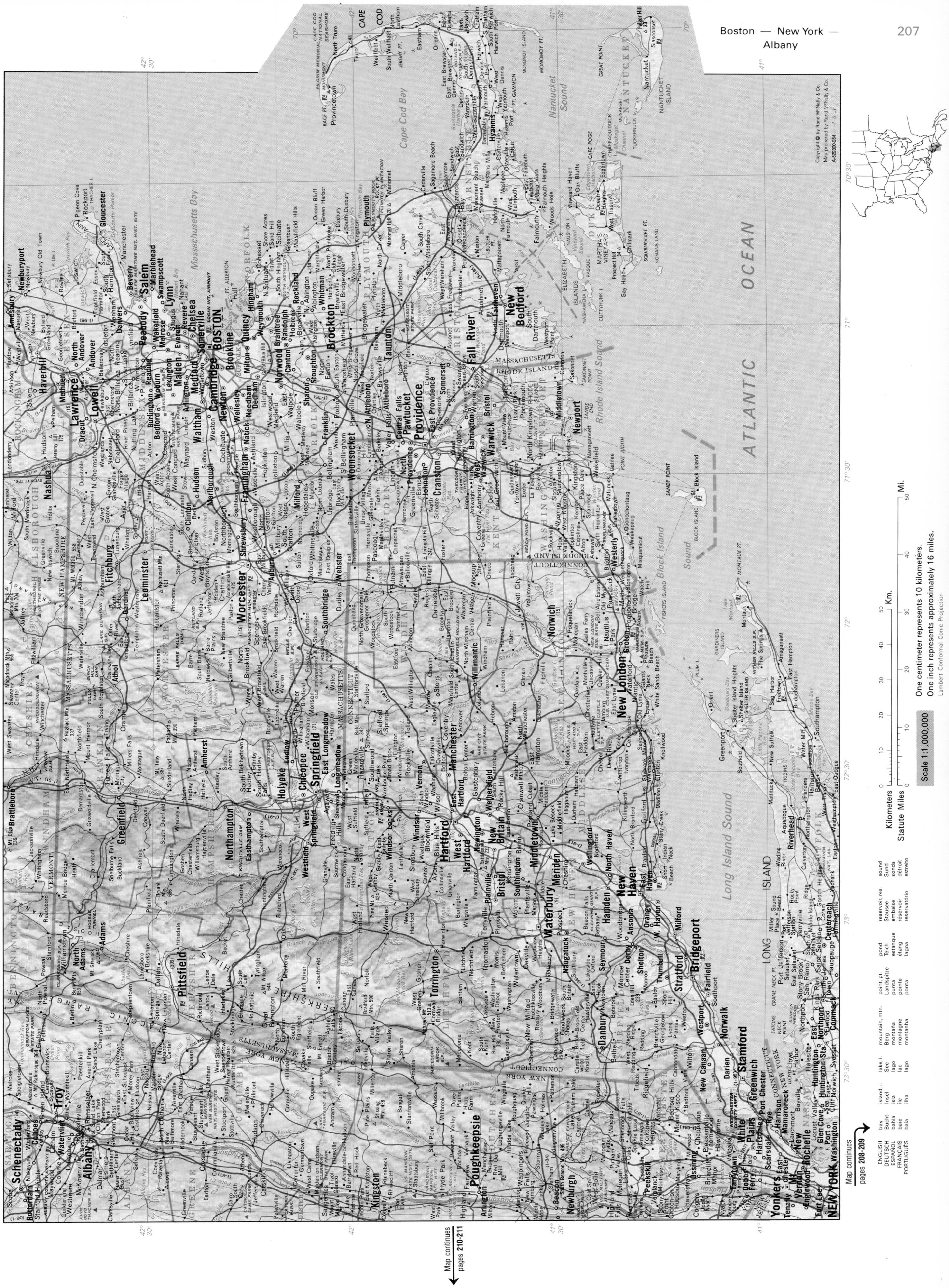
ATLANTIC OCEAN
Scale 1:1,000,000
One centimeter represents 10 kilometers.
One inch represents approximately 16 miles.
Lambert Conformal Conic Projection
Kilometers
Statute Miles
Map continues pages 210-211
Map continues pages 208-209
Long Island Sound
Massachusetts Bay
Cape Cod Bay
Rhode Island Sound
Block Island Sound
Nantucket Sound

Map continues pages 210-211

NEW YORK
NEWARK
PHILADELPHIA
Camden
Trenton
Wilmington
Atlantic City
BALTIMORE
WASHINGTON
Alexandria
Arlington
Annapolis
Harrisburg
Lancaster
Reading
Allentown
Bethlehem
Frederick
Vineland
Dover
Delaware Bay
DELMARVA
APPALACHIAN MOUNTAINS
NEW JERSEY
PENNSYLVANIA
MARYLAND
DELAWARE
VIRGINIA

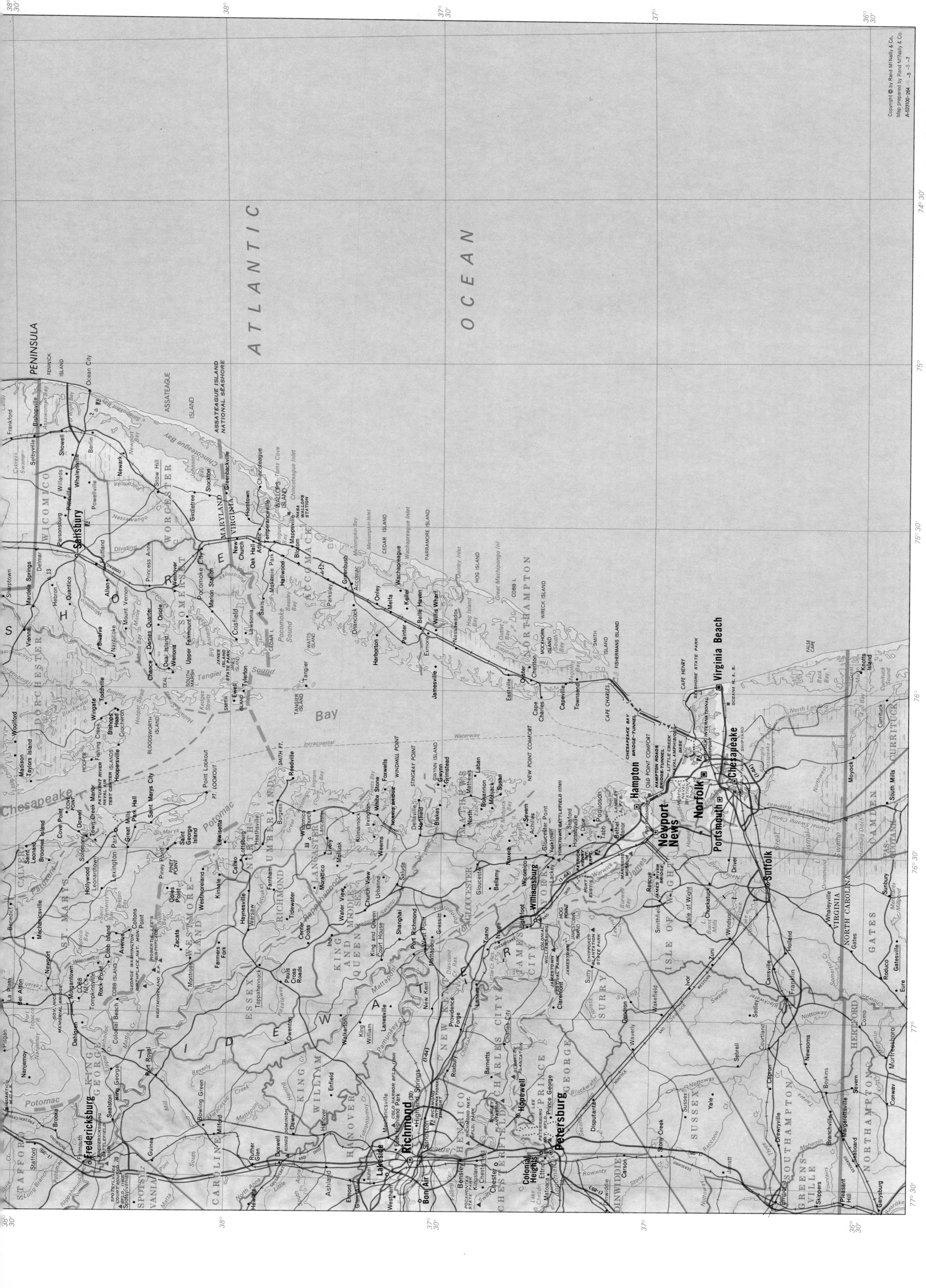
ATLANTIC
OCEAN
Chesapeake
Bay
Potomac
PENINSULA
Norfolk
Virginia Beach
Chesapeake
Portsmouth
Newport News
Hampton
Suffolk
Richmond
Petersburg
Williamsburg
Fredericksburg
Salisbury
Copyright © by Rand McNally & Co.
Map prepared by Rand McNally & Co.

ENGLISH	airport, arpt.	bay	creek, cr.	inlet	island, i.	mountain	point, pt.	reservoir, res.	state park
DEUTSCH	Flughafen	Bucht	Bach	Einfahrt	Insel	Berg	Landspitze	Stausee	Naturpark
ESPAÑOL	aeropuerto	bahía	riachuelo	abra	isla	montaña	punta	embalse	parque provincial
FRANÇAIS	aéroport	baie	crique	bras de mer	île	montagne	pointe	réservoir	parc régional
PORTUGUÊS	aeroporto	baía	riacho	enseada	ilha	montanha	ponta	reservatório	parque estadual

Kilometers 0 10 20 30 40 50 Km.
Statute Miles 0 10 20 30 40 50 Mi.

Scale 1:1,000,000

One centimeter represents 10 kilometers.
One inch represents approximately 16 miles.
Lambert Conformal Conic Projection

Map continues pages 212-213

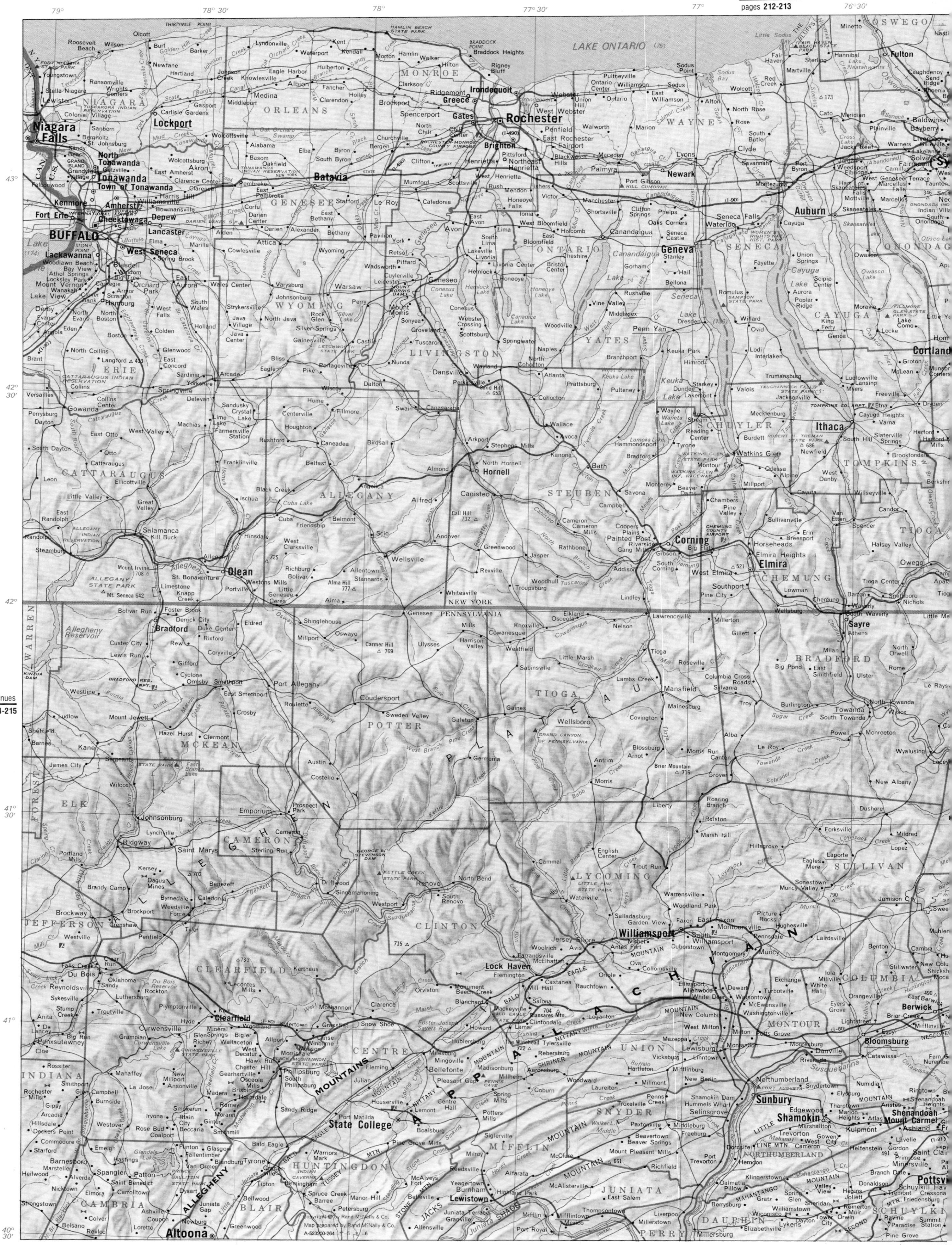
LAKE ONTARIO
NIAGARA
ORLEANS
MONROE
WAYNE
GENESEE
WYOMING
LIVINGSTON
ONTARIO
YATES
SENECA
CAYUGA
ERIE
CATTARAUGUS
ALLEGANY
STEUBEN
SCHUYLER
CHEMUNG
TOMPKINS
TIOGA
NEW YORK
PENNSYLVANIA
WARREN
McKEAN
POTTER
TIOGA
BRADFORD
SULLIVAN
ELK
CAMERON
CLINTON
LYCOMING
JEFFERSON
CLEARFIELD
CENTRE
UNION
MONTOUR
COLUMBIA
INDIANA
CAMBRIA
BLAIR
HUNTINGDON
MIFFLIN
SNYDER
JUNIATA
NORTHUMBERLAND
SCHUYLKILL
DAUPHIN
PERRY
ALLEGHENY PLATEAU
APPALACHIAN MOUNTAINS
Niagara Falls
Lockport
Rochester
Buffalo
Batavia
Tonawanda
Lackawanna
Geneva
Auburn
Ithaca
Corning
Elmira
Olean
Bradford
Hornell
Williamsport
Lock Haven
State College
Altoona
Sunbury
Shamokin
Bloomsburg
Lewistown
Clearfield
Cortland
Sayre
Fulton
Copyright © by Rand McNally & Co.
Map prepared by Rand McNally & Co.
A-523200-264

Map continues pages 214-215

ENGLISH	airport, arpt.	bay	creek, cr.	hill	Island	lake	mountain	reservoir	state park, s.p.
DEUTSCH	Flughafen	Bucht	Bach	Hügel	Insel	See	Berg	Stausee	Naturpark
ESPAÑOL	aeropuerto	bahía	riachuelo	colina	isla	lago	montaña	embalse	parque provincial
FRANÇAIS	aéroport	baie	crique	colline	île	lac	montagne	réservoir	parc régional
PORTUGUÊS	aeroporto	baía	riacho	colina	ilha	lago	montanha	reservatório	parque estadual

NEW YORK

75°30'
75°
74°30'
74°
73°30'
ADIRONDACK MOUNTAINS
HAMILTON
Rome
Utica
Oneida
Ilion
Herkimer
Gloversville
Johnstown
Amsterdam
Glens Falls
Saratoga Springs
Schenectady
Troy
Albany
Cohoes
Watervliet
Rensselaer
Oneonta
Binghamton
Pittsfield
Hudson
Kingston
CATSKILL MOUNTAINS
Poughkeepsie
Newburgh
Beacon
Middletown
Scranton
Wilkes-Barre
Danbury
Bridgeport
Norwalk
Stamford
White Plains
Yonkers
New Rochelle
Mount Vernon
Paterson
Passaic
Clifton
Hackensack
NEWARK
NEW YORK
Jersey City
Bayonne
Elizabeth
Plainfield
Allentown
Bethlehem
Easton
Long Island Sound
ATLANTIC OCEAN

Map continues page 207

Map continues pages 208-209

Kilometers 0 10 20 30 40 50 Km.
Statute Miles 0 10 20 30 40 50 Mi.

Scale 1:1,000,000
One centimeter represents 10 kilometers.
One inch represents approximately 16 miles.
Lambert Conformal Conic Projection

81°
80° 30′
80°
79° 30′
79°
78° 30′
45° 30′
45°
44° 30′
44°
43° 30′
43°
Georgian Bay
(176 Meters Above Sea Level)
Nottawasaga Bay
Lake Simcoe
(219)
LAKE ERIE
(174 Meters Above Sea Level)
Long Point Bay
CANADA
UNITED STATES
ONTARIO
NEW YORK
NIPISSING
PARRY SOUND
MUSKOKA
HALIBURTON
VICTORIA
GREY
SIMCOE
BRUCE
DUFFERIN
DURHAM
YORK
PEEL
WELLINGTON
HURON
WATERLOO
HALTON
PERTH
OXFORD
BRANT
WENTWORTH
HAMILTON
NIAGARA
MIDDLESEX
ELGIN
HALDIMAND-NORFOLK
Parry Sound
Huntsville
Bracebridge
Gravenhurst
Midland
Penetanguishene
Orillia
Barrie
Collingwood
Owen Sound
Meaford
Lindsay
Newmarket
Aurora
Richmond Hill
Markham
Vaughan
North York
Scarborough
East York
York
TORONTO
Etobicoke
Mississauga
Brampton
Oshawa
Whitby
Pickering
Ajax
Newcastle
Oakville
Burlington
Hamilton
Stoney Creek
Saint Catharines
Niagara Falls
Welland
Port Colborne
Guelph
Kitchener
Waterloo
Cambridge
(Galt)
Brantford
Woodstock
London
Stratford
Simcoe
Saint Thomas
Milton
Orangeville
Caledon
Halton Hills
Lockport
Tonawanda
North Tonawanda
BUFFALO
Lackawanna
West Seneca
Cheektowaga
Lancaster
Depew
Amherst
Kenmore
Copyright © by Rand McNally & Co.
Map prepared by Rand McNally & Co.

Map continues pages 214-215

ENGLISH	airport	bay	canal	channel	creek, cr.	Indian reservation	island	lake, l.	point
DEUTSCH	Flughafen	Bucht	Kanal	Kanal	Bach	Indianerreservation	Insel	See	Landspitze
ESPAÑOL	aeropuerto	bahia	canal	canal	riachuelo	reserva de Indios	isla	lago	punta
FRANÇAIS	aéroport	baie	canal	canal	crique	réserve indienne	île	lac	pointe
PORTUGUÊS	aeroporto	baia	canal	canal	riacho	reserva indigena	ilha	lago	ponta

Map continues page 206

ONTARIO
(75 Meters Above Sea Level)
ONTARIO
NEW YORK
QUE.
ONT.
PONTIAC
GATINEAU
PRESCOTT AND RUSSELL
OTTAWA-CARLETON
STORMONT, DUNDAS AND GLENGARRY
LANARK
LEEDS AND GRENVILLE
FRONTENAC
LENNOX AND ADDINGTON
HASTINGS
MADAWASKA
RENFREW
HIGHLANDS
PETERBOROUGH
NORTHUMBERLAND
PRINCE EDWARD
SAINT LAWRENCE
JEFFERSON
LEWIS
OSWEGO
ONEIDA
ONONDAGA
MADISON
CORTLAND
CAYUGA
SENECA
WAYNE
MONROE
ONTARIO
YATES
LIVINGSTON
CHENANGO
Ottawa
Hull
Gatineau
Vanier
Aylmer
Nepean
Gloucester
Kanata
Renfrew
Arnprior
Almonte
Carleton Place
Perth
Smiths Falls
Kemptville
Prescott
Brockville
Ogdensburg
Kingston
Belleville
Trenton
Picton
Napanee
Gananoque
Cape Vincent
Watertown
Carthage
Lowville
Oswego
Fulton
Rome
Utica
Oneida
Syracuse
Auburn
Geneva
Canandaigua
Newark
Rochester
Brighton
Greece
Irondequoit
Gates
Lyons
Sodus
Cazenovia
Hamilton
Bancroft
Marmora
Campbellford
Tweed
Sharbot Lake
Westport
Madoc
Stirling
Sackets Harbor
Lake Ontario
Wellington Bay
Mexico Bay
Oneida L.
Owasco L.
Skaneateles L.
Cayuga L.
Seneca L.
78°
77° 30′
77°
76° 30′
76°
75° 30′
45° 30′
45°
44° 30′
44°
43° 30′
43°

Map continues pages 210-211

Kilometers 0 10 20 30 40 50 Km.

Statute Miles 0 10 20 30 40 50 Mi.

Scale 1:1,000,000

One centimeter represents 10 kilometers.
One inch represents approximately 16 miles.
Lambert Conformal Conic Projection

Map continues
pages 216-217

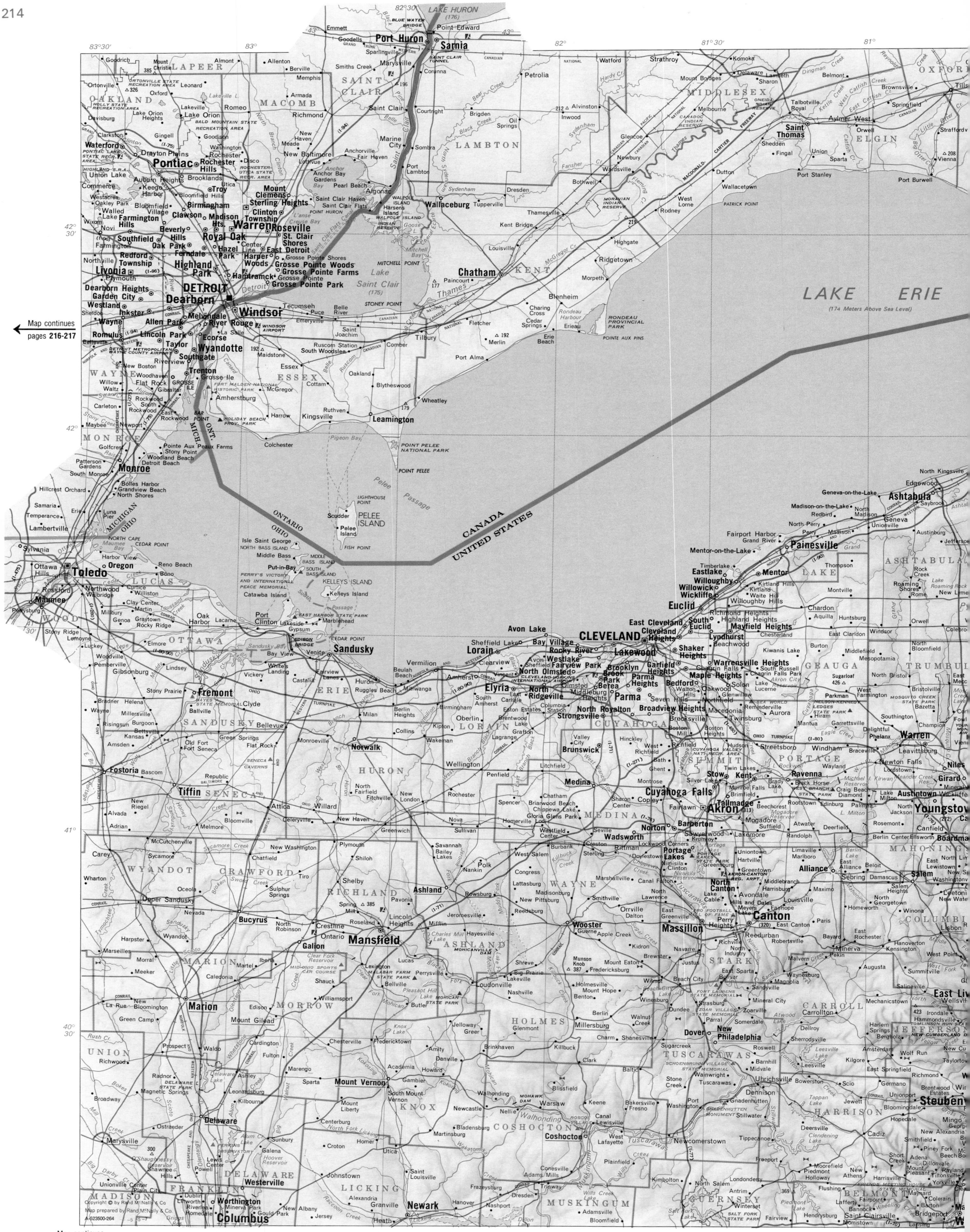
LAKE HURON (176)
BLUE WATER BRIDGE
Point Edward
Port Huron
Sarnia
ST. CLAIR TUNNEL
LAPEER
OAKLAND
MACOMB
SAINT CLAIR
LAMBTON
MIDDLESEX
OXFORD
ELGIN
KENT
ESSEX
WAYNE
MONROE
Petrolia
Strathroy
Saint Thomas
Port Stanley
Aylmer West
Pontiac
Waterford
Rochester Hills
Troy
Birmingham
Warren
Roseville
Royal Oak
Livonia
Dearborn
DETROIT
Windsor
Hamtramck
Grosse Pointe
Lake Saint Clair (175)
Wallaceburg
Chatham
Leamington
Amherstburg
Wyandotte
Trenton
Monroe
Tecumseh
Kingsville
Tilbury
Blenheim
Ridgetown
RONDEAU PROVINCIAL PARK
POINTE AUX PINS
Port Alma
LAKE ERIE
(174 Meters Above Sea Level)
POINT PELEE NATIONAL PARK
POINT PELEE
Pelee Passage
PELEE ISLAND
CANADA
UNITED STATES
ONTARIO
OHIO
MICHIGAN
MICH.
ONT.
Toledo
Oregon
Maumee
Sylvania
LUCAS
WOOD
OTTAWA
Port Clinton
KELLEYS ISLAND
PERRY'S VICTORY AND INTERNATIONAL PEACE MEMORIAL
Put-in-Bay
Sandusky
Fremont
SANDUSKY
ERIE
Huron
Vermilion
Lorain
Elyria
Avon Lake
CLEVELAND
Lakewood
Parma
Euclid
Painesville
Mentor
Ashtabula
ASHTABULA
LAKE
GEAUGA
TRUMBULL
CUYAHOGA
LORAIN
HURON
Norwalk
Fostoria
Tiffin
SENECA
Medina
MEDINA
Akron
Cuyahoga Falls
Kent
PORTAGE
SUMMIT
Warren
Youngstown
MAHONING
Alliance
Canton
Massillon
STARK
Wooster
WAYNE
Ashland
ASHLAND
Mansfield
RICHLAND
CRAWFORD
Bucyrus
Galion
WYANDOT
Upper Sandusky
Marion
MARION
MORROW
Mount Gilead
HOLMES
Millersburg
TUSCARAWAS
Dover
New Philadelphia
CARROLL
COLUMBIANA
East Liverpool
JEFFERSON
Steubenville
HARRISON
Cadiz
KNOX
Mount Vernon
COSHOCTON
Coshocton
UNION
DELAWARE
Delaware
Marysville
Westerville
LICKING
Newark
MUSKINGUM
GUERNSEY
BELMONT
Saint Clairsville
FRANKLIN
MADISON
Worthington
Columbus
Copyright © by Rand McNally & Co.
Map prepared by Rand McNally & Co.
A-523500-264
83°30′
83°
82°30′
82°
81°30′
81°
42° 30′
42°
41° 30′
41°
40° 30′

Map continues
page 218

ENGLISH	airport	creek, cr.	hill	lake, l.	mountain, mtn.	point, pt.	reservoir, res.	state park
DEUTSCH	Flughafen	Bach	Hügel	See	Berg	Landspitze	Stausee	Naturpark
ESPAÑOL	aeropuerto	riachuelo	colina	lago	montaña	punta	embalse	parque provincial
FRANÇAIS	aéroport	crique	colline	lac	montagne	pointe	réservoir	parc régional
PORTUGUÊS	aeroporto	riacho	colina	lago	montanha	ponta	reservatório	parque estadual

Map continues pages 212-213

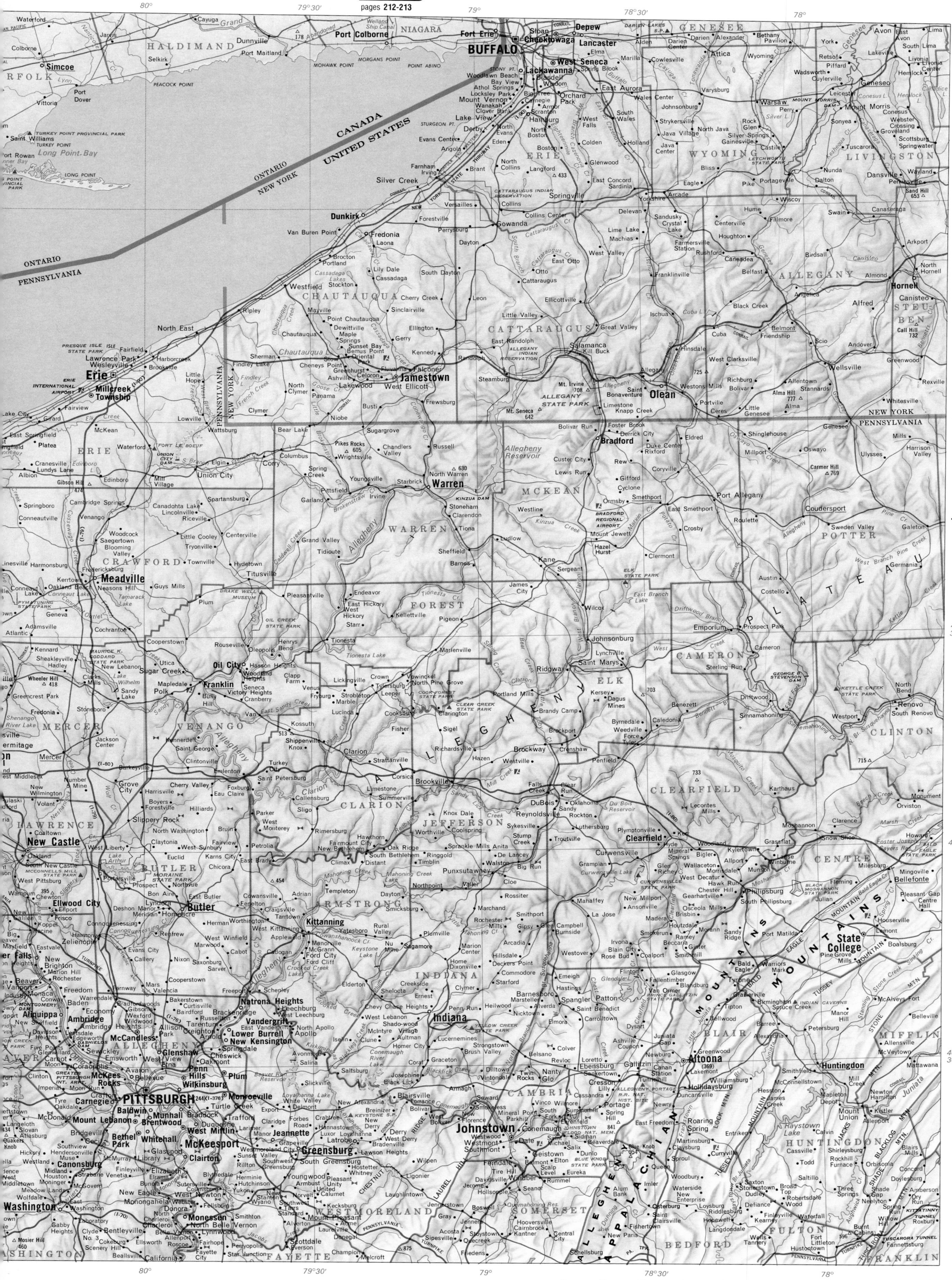

ONTARIO
NEW YORK
PENNSYLVANIA
CANADA
UNITED STATES
BUFFALO
Erie
Jamestown
Warren
Olean
Bradford
Meadville
Franklin
Oil City
New Castle
Butler
Kittanning
Indiana
Johnstown
Altoona
State College
PITTSBURGH
McKeesport
Greensburg
Washington
ALLEGHENY PLATEAU
APPALACHIAN MOUNTAINS
ALLEGHENY MOUNTAINS
CHAUTAUQUA
CATTARAUGUS
ALLEGANY
ERIE
CRAWFORD
WARREN
MCKEAN
POTTER
FOREST
ELK
CAMERON
CLINTON
VENANGO
MERCER
CLARION
JEFFERSON
CLEARFIELD
CENTRE
LAWRENCE
BUTLER
ARMSTRONG
INDIANA
CAMBRIA
BLAIR
HUNTINGDON
WESTMORELAND
SOMERSET
BEDFORD
FULTON
FAYETTE
ALLEGHENY
WYOMING
LIVINGSTON
STEUBEN
HALDIMAND
NIAGARA
GENESEE

Map continues pages 210-211

Kilometers 0 10 20 30 40 50 Km.

Statute Miles 0 10 20 30 40 50 Mi.

Scale 1:1,000,000

One centimeter represents 10 kilometers.

One inch represents approximately 16 miles.

Lambert Conformal Conic Projection

LAKE
MICHIGAN
(176 Meters Above Sea Level)
Madison
Milwaukee
Waukesha
Racine
Kenosha
Janesville
Beloit
Rockford
Waukegan
Evanston
Skokie
CHICAGO
Oak Park
Cicero
Elgin
Aurora
Joliet
Naperville
Hammond
East Chicago
Gary
Michigan City
La Porte
Valparaiso
Kankakee
Ottawa
La Salle
Streator
Pontiac
Normal
Bloomington
Lafayette
West Lafayette
Rantoul
Champaign
De Kalb
WISCONSIN
ILLINOIS
INDIANA
DANE
JEFFERSON
WAUKESHA
MILWAUKEE
RACINE
KENOSHA
WALWORTH
ROCK
GREEN
WINNEBAGO
BOONE
MCHENRY
LAKE
COOK
DU PAGE
KANE
DE KALB
OGLE
LEE
LA SALLE
KENDALL
GRUNDY
WILL
KANKAKEE
LIVINGSTON
IROQUOIS
FORD
MC LEAN
WOODFORD
MARSHALL
DE WITT
PIATT
CHAMPAIGN
VERMILION
PORTER
LA PORTE
STARKE
JASPER
NEWTON
BENTON
WHITE
PULASKI
CARROLL
TIPPECANOE
WARREN
FOUNTAIN
CLINTON
89° 30'
89°
88° 30'
88°
87° 30'
87°
86° 30'
43°
42° 30'
42°
41° 30'
41°
40° 30'
Copyright © by Rand McNally & Co.
Map prepared by Rand McNally & Co.
A-523000-264 -5 -5 -7

Map continues page 219

ENGLISH	airport	creek, cr.	ditch	lake, l.	reservoir	state park, s.p.
DEUTSCH	Flughafen	Bach	Graben	See	Stausee	Naturpark
ESPAÑOL	aeropuerto	riachuelo	acequia	lago	embalse	parque provincial
FRANÇAIS	aéroport	crique	fossé	lac	réservoir	parc régional
PORTUGUÊS	aeroporto	riacho	fosso	lago	reservatório	parque estadual

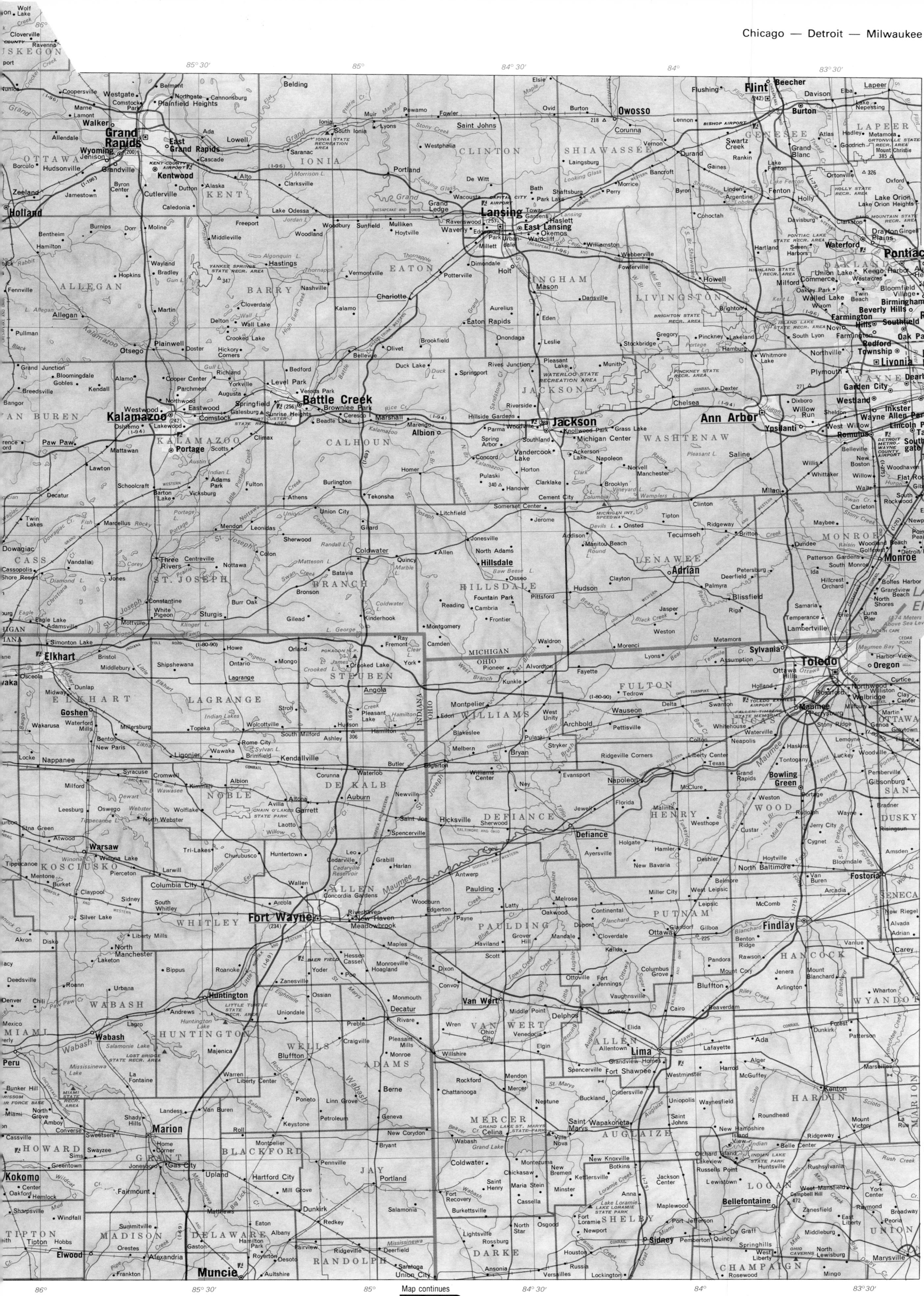

Grand Rapids
Wyoming
Kentwood
Holland
Kalamazoo
Portage
Battle Creek
Lansing
East Lansing
Jackson
Ann Arbor
Flint
Owosso
Pontiac
Warren
DETROIT
Windsor
Dearborn
Livonia
Monroe
Toledo
Adrian
Hillsdale
Coldwater
Elkhart
Goshen
Warsaw
Fort Wayne
Huntington
Wabash
Marion
Kokomo
Muncie
Defiance
Findlay
Lima
Van Wert
Sidney
Bellefontaine
LAKE ERIE
CANADA
U.S.
OTTAWA
KENT
IONIA
CLINTON
SHIAWASSEE
GENESEE
LAPEER
OAKLAND
ALLEGAN
BARRY
EATON
INGHAM
LIVINGSTON
WAYNE
VAN BUREN
KALAMAZOO
CALHOUN
JACKSON
WASHTENAW
CASS
ST. JOSEPH
BRANCH
HILLSDALE
LENAWEE
MONROE
ESSEX
ELKHART
LAGRANGE
STEUBEN
WILLIAMS
FULTON
LUCAS
WOOD
OTTAWA
SANDUSKY
NOBLE
DE KALB
DEFIANCE
HENRY
KOSCIUSKO
WHITLEY
ALLEN
PAULDING
PUTNAM
HANCOCK
SENECA
WABASH
HUNTINGTON
WELLS
ADAMS
VAN WERT
ALLEN
HARDIN
WYANDOT
MIAMI
GRANT
BLACKFORD
JAY
MERCER
AUGLAIZE
LOGAN
MARION
HOWARD
TIPTON
MADISON
DELAWARE
RANDOLPH
DARKE
SHELBY
CHAMPAIGN
UNION
MICHIGAN
INDIANA
OHIO
85° 30′
85°
84° 30′
84°
83° 30′
43°
42° 30′
42°
41° 30′
41°
40° 30′
86°

Map continues pages 214-215

Map continues page 218

Kilometers 0 10 20 30 40 50 Km.

Statute Miles 0 10 20 30 40 50 Mi.

Scale 1:1,000,000

One centimeter represents 10 kilometers.
One inch represents approximately 16 miles.

Lambert Conformal Conic Projection

Map continues pages 214-215

ENGLISH	DEUTSCH	ESPAÑOL	FRANÇAIS	PORTUGUÊS
airport	Flughafen	aeropuerto	aéroport	aeroporto
creek, cr.	Bach	riachuelo	crique	riacho
dam	Damm	presa	barrage	represa
lake	See	lago	lac	lago
reservoir, res.	Stausee	embalse	réservoir	reservatório
ridge	Höhenrücken	serranía	crête	cordilheira
state park	Naturpark	parque provincial	parc régional	parque estadual

Map continues pages 216-217

Scale 1:1,000,000

Kilometers 0 10 20 30 40 50 Km.
Statute Miles 0 10 20 30 40 50 Mi.

One centimeter represents 10 kilometers.
One inch represents approximately 16 miles.

Lambert Conformal Conic Projection

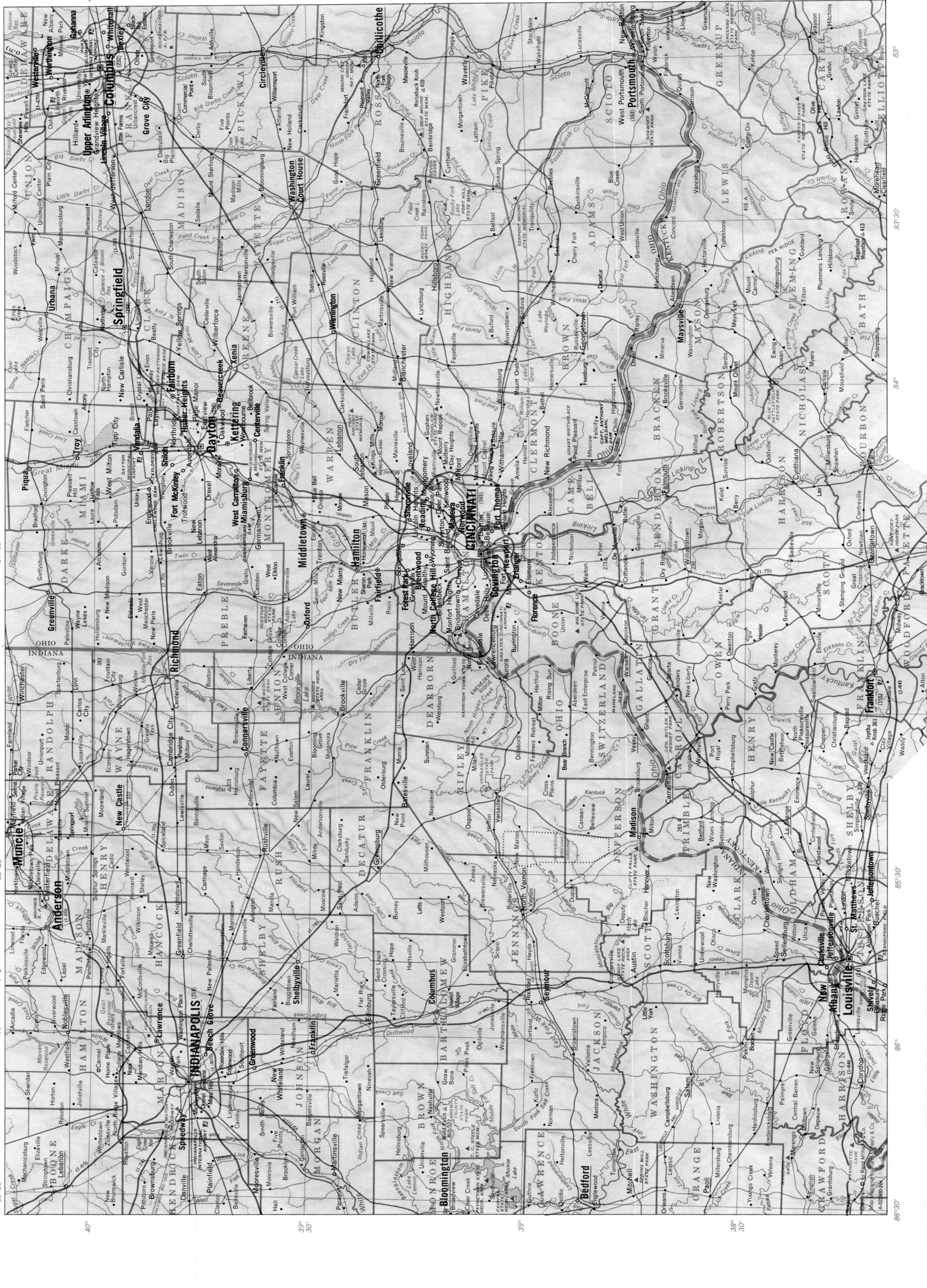

INDIANAPOLIS
CINCINNATI
Louisville
Dayton
Columbus
Richmond
Hamilton
Springfield
Bloomington
Muncie
Anderson
Frankfort
OHIO
INDIANA
KENTUCKY

Map continues pages 216-217

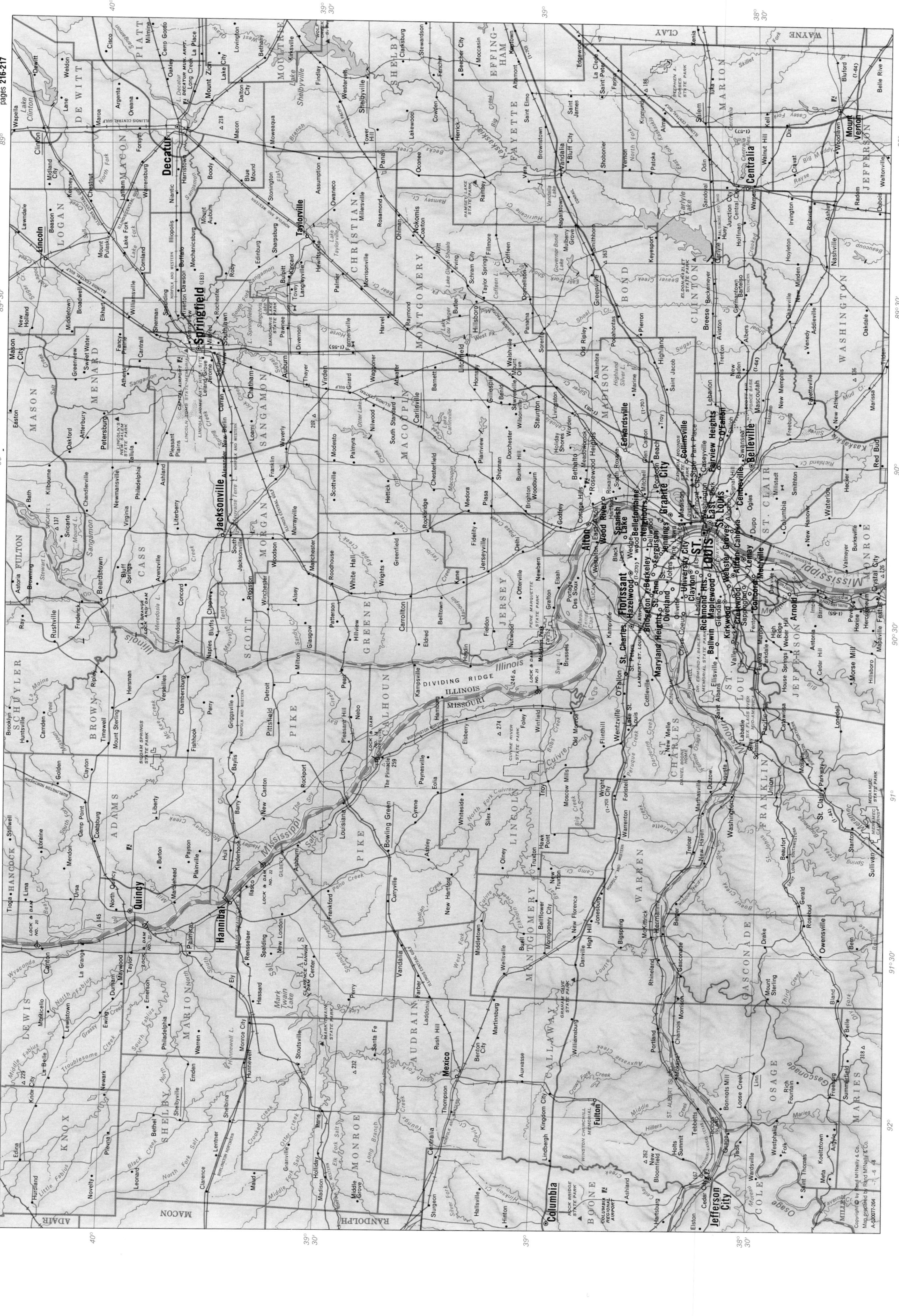
Springfield
St. Louis
East St. Louis
Decatur
Jacksonville
Quincy
Hannibal
Columbia
Jefferson City
Belleville
Alton
Lincoln
Taylorville
Centralia
Mount Vernon
Fulton
Mexico
St. Charles
Florissant
Mississippi
Illinois
Missouri
Kaskaskia
Sangamon
MASON
MENARD
LOGAN
DE WITT
PIATT
MACON
SANGAMON
CHRISTIAN
MOULTRIE
SHELBY
EFFINGHAM
FAYETTE
MONTGOMERY
MACOUPIN
MORGAN
CASS
SCOTT
GREENE
JERSEY
MADISON
BOND
CLINTON
MARION
WASHINGTON
JEFFERSON
ST. CLAIR
MONROE
CALHOUN
PIKE
BROWN
ADAMS
SCHUYLER
FULTON
LINCOLN
ST. CHARLES
WARREN
CALLAWAY
AUDRAIN
RALLS
MARION
LEWIS
KNOX
SHELBY
MONROE
BOONE
OSAGE
GASCONADE
FRANKLIN
COLE
MARIES
ST. LOUIS
DIVIDING RIDGE
ILLINOIS
MISSOURI
Copyright © by Rand McNally & Co.
Map produced by Rand McNally & Co.

ENGLISH	DEUTSCH	ESPAÑOL	FRANÇAIS	PORTUGUÊS
creek, cr.	Bach	riachuelo	crique	riacho
dam	Damm	presa	barrage	represa
island, i.	Insel	isla	île	ilha
lake, l.	See	lago	lac	lago
lock	Schleuse	esclusa	écluse	eclusa
reservoir	Stausee	embalse	réservoir	reservatório
state park	Naturpark	parque provincial	parc régional	parque estadual

Scale 1:1,000,000

Kilometers 0 10 20 30 40 50 Km.

Statute Miles 0 10 20 30 40 50 Mi.

One centimeter represents 10 kilometers.
One inch represents approximately 16 miles.
Lambert Conformal Conic Projection

Kilometers 0 10 20 30 40 50 Km.

Statute Miles 0 10 20 30 40 50 Mi.

Scale 1:1,000,000

One centimeter represents 10 kilometers.
One inch represents approximately 16 miles.
Lambert Conformal Conic Projection

ENGLISH	bay	canal	cape	creek, cr.	inlet	island	key	lake, l.	swamp
DEUTSCH	Bucht	Kanal	Kap	Bach	Einfahrt	Insel	Klippe	See	Sumpf
ESPAÑOL	bahía	canal	cabo	riachuelo	abra	isla	cayo	lago	pantano
FRANÇAIS	baie	canal	cap	crique	bras de mer	île	caye	lac	marais
PORTUGUÊS	baía	canal	cabo	riacho	enseada	ilha	recife	lago	pântano

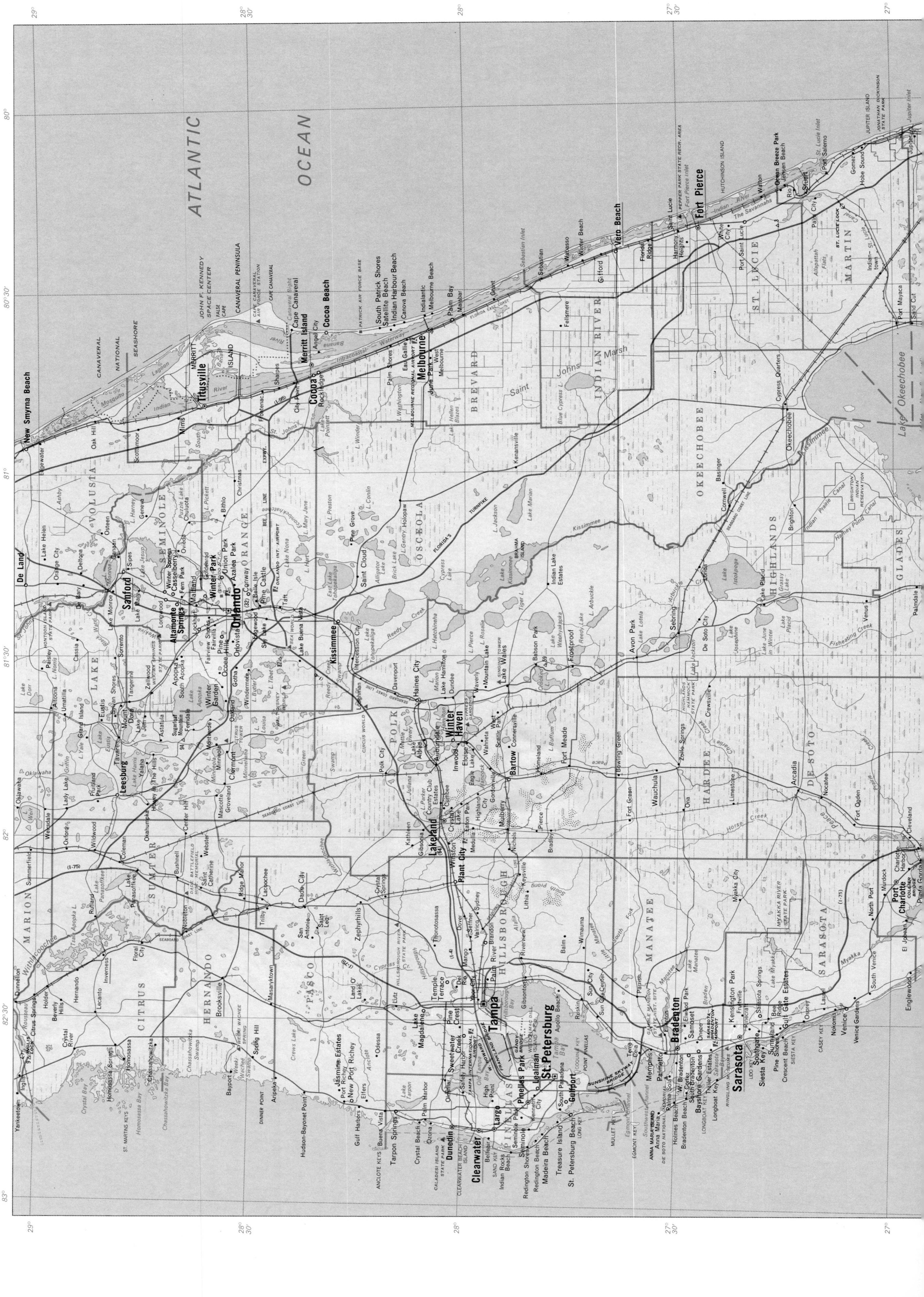
ATLANTIC
OCEAN
Orlando
Tampa
St. Petersburg
Clearwater
Lakeland
Sarasota
Bradenton
Melbourne
Cocoa
Titusville
Fort Pierce
Vero Beach
Kissimmee
Sanford
De Land
New Smyrna Beach
Winter Haven
Winter Park
Leesburg
Dunedin
Largo
Plant City
Bartow
Lake Okeechobee
CITRUS
HERNANDO
PASCO
PINELLAS
HILLSBOROUGH
MANATEE
SARASOTA
POLK
LAKE
SUMTER
MARION
ORANGE
SEMINOLE
VOLUSIA
OSCEOLA
BREVARD
INDIAN RIVER
ST. LUCIE
MARTIN
OKEECHOBEE
HIGHLANDS
HARDEE
DE SOTO
GLADES
CAPE CANAVERAL
JOHN F. KENNEDY SPACE CENTER

Palm Beach
West Palm Beach
Lake Worth
Lantana
Boynton Beach
Delray Beach
Highland Beach
Boca Raton
Deerfield Beach
Pompano Beach
Fort Lauderdale
Hollywood
Miami Beach
North Miami Beach
North Miami
MIAMI
Coral Gables
Key Biscayne
South Miami
Hialeah
Miami Springs
Kendall
Perrine
Homestead
Florida City
Key Largo
Tavernier
Islamorada
Marathon
Big Pine Key
Key West
Naples
Fort Myers
Cape Coral
Sanibel
Captiva
Bonita Springs
Immokalee
Belle Glade
Clewiston
Everglades City
Chokoloskee
Flamingo
PALM BEACH
BROWARD
DADE
HENDRY
COLLIER
LEE
MONROE
EVERGLADES NATIONAL PARK
BISCAYNE NATIONAL PARK
BIG CYPRESS NATIONAL PRESERVE
The Everglades
Florida Bay
Biscayne Bay
FLORIDA KEYS
GULF OF MEXICO
DRY TORTUGAS
Copyright © by Rand McNally & Co.
Map prepared by Rand McNally & Co.

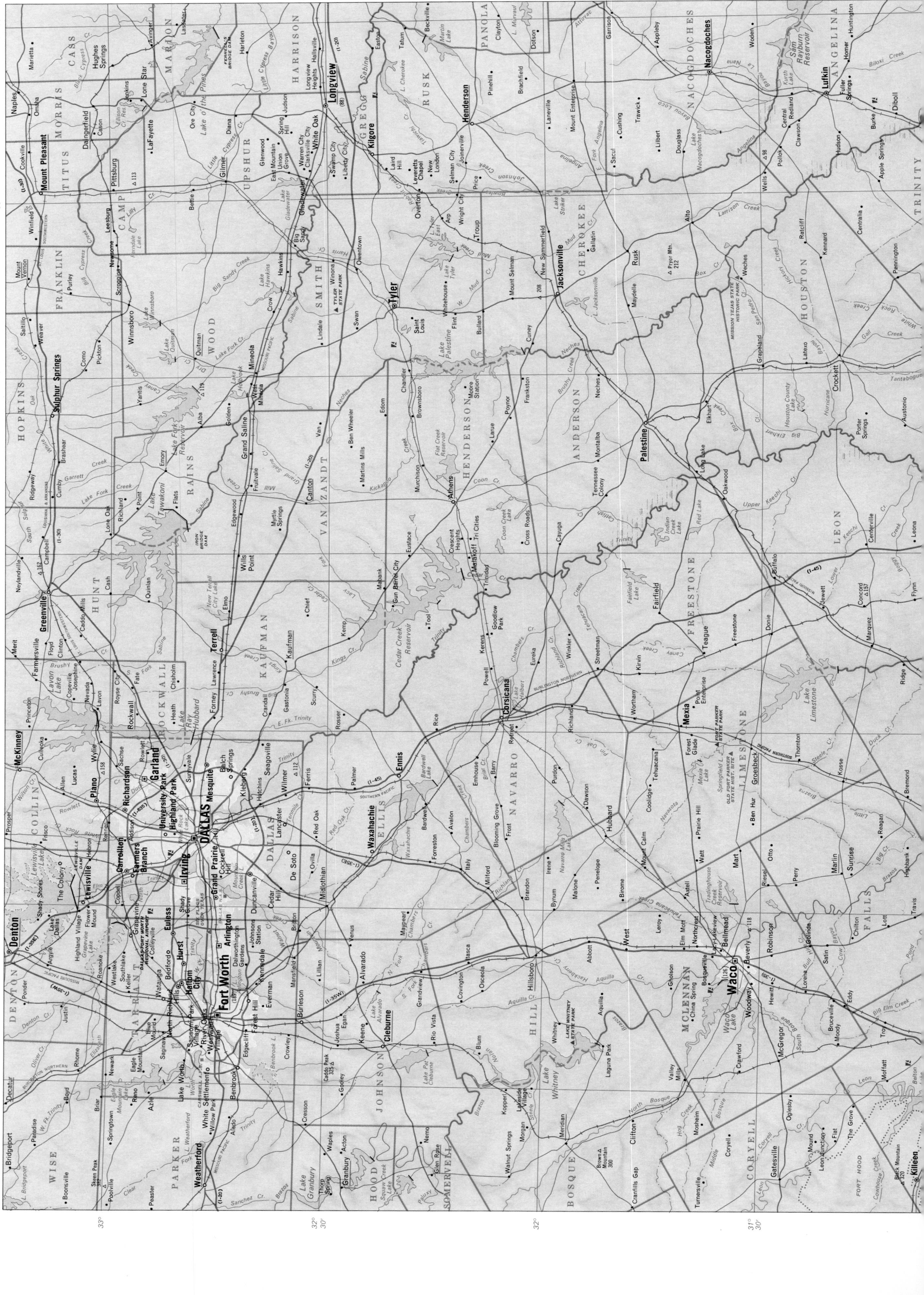
CASS
MORRIS
TITUS
CAMP
MARION
HARRISON
FRANKLIN
HOPKINS
WOOD
UPSHUR
GREGG
PANOLA
RUSK
SMITH
RAINS
HUNT
ROCKWALL
COLLIN
DENTON
WISE
PARKER
TARRANT
DALLAS
KAUFMAN
VAN ZANDT
HENDERSON
CHEROKEE
NACOGDOCHES
ANGELINA
TRINITY
HOUSTON
ANDERSON
LEON
FREESTONE
NAVARRO
ELLIS
JOHNSON
HOOD
SOMERVELL
HILL
BOSQUE
McLENNAN
LIMESTONE
FALLS
CORYELL
DALLAS
Fort Worth
Arlington
Irving
Garland
Mesquite
Grand Prairie
Denton
McKinney
Greenville
Sulphur Springs
Mount Pleasant
Longview
Kilgore
Tyler
Henderson
Nacogdoches
Lufkin
Jacksonville
Palestine
Athens
Corsicana
Ennis
Waxahachie
Cleburne
Weatherford
Hillsboro
Waco
Mexia
Crockett
Terrell
Killeen
Lake Whitney
Cedar Creek Reservoir
Lake Tawakoni
Lake Palestine
Sam Rayburn Reservoir

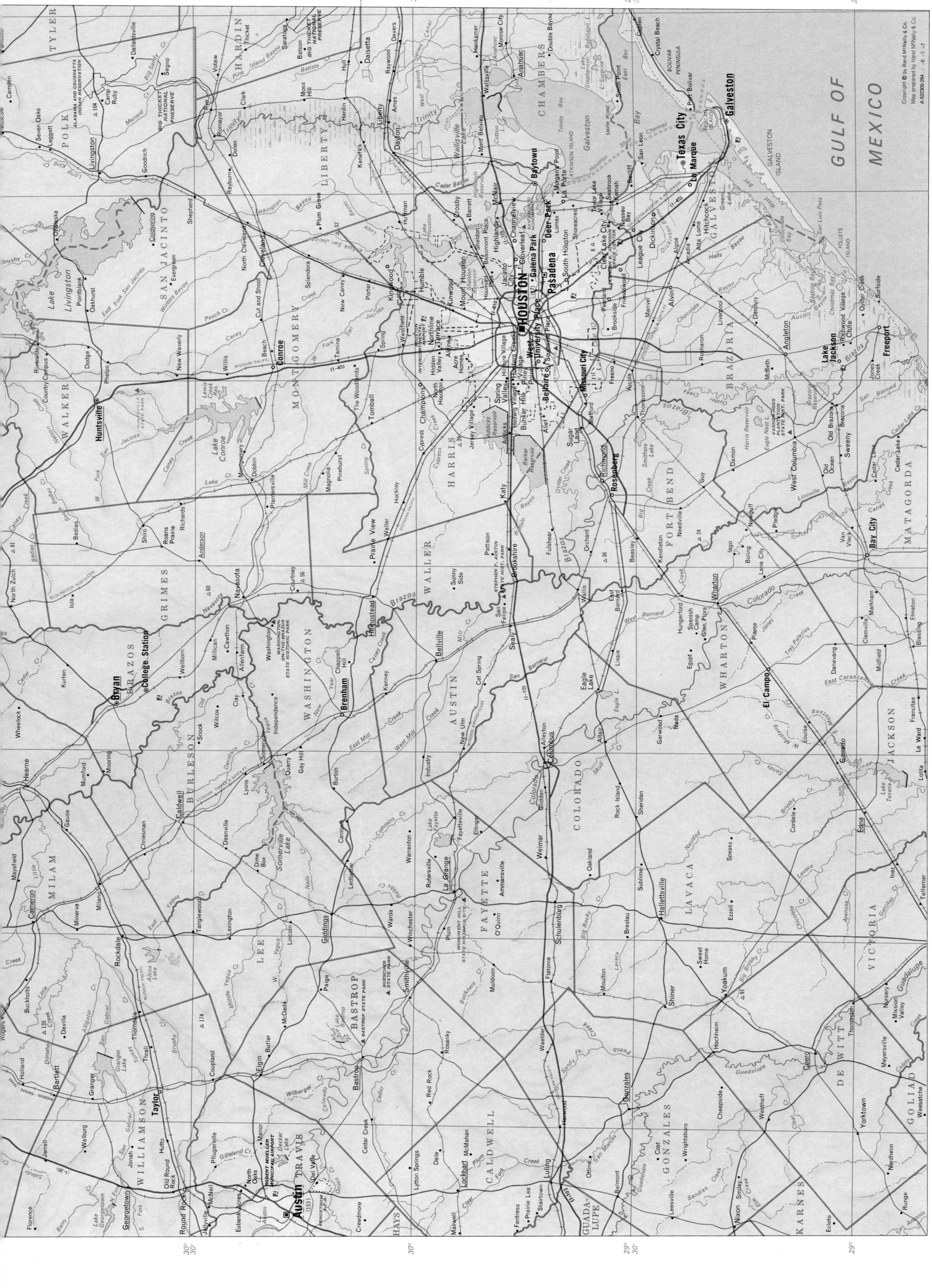
GULF OF MEXICO
HOUSTON
Galveston
Austin
Bryan
College Station
Huntsville
Conroe
Pasadena
Baytown
Texas City
Freeport
Lake Jackson
Bay City
Wharton
Rosenberg
Brenham
La Grange
Columbus
Bastrop
Georgetown
Taylor
Lockhart
Gonzales
Cuero
Victoria
HARRIS
MONTGOMERY
WALKER
GRIMES
WASHINGTON
AUSTIN
WALLER
FORT BEND
BRAZORIA
GALVESTON
CHAMBERS
LIBERTY
SAN JACINTO
POLK
TYLER
HARDIN
BRAZOS
BURLESON
MILAM
LEE
FAYETTE
COLORADO
WHARTON
MATAGORDA
JACKSON
LAVACA
DE WITT
GONZALES
CALDWELL
BASTROP
TRAVIS
WILLIAMSON
HAYS
GUADALUPE
KARNES
GOLIAD
VICTORIA
Copyright © by Rand McNally & Co.
Map prepared by Rand McNally & Co.

Scale 1:1,000,000

Kilometers 0 10 20 30 40 50 Km.

Statute Miles 0 10 20 30 40 50 Mi.

One centimeter represents 10 kilometers.
One inch represents approximately 16 miles.

Lambert Conformal Conic Projection

ENGLISH	DEUTSCH	ESPAÑOL	FRANÇAIS	PORTUGUÊS
airport	Flughafen	aeropuerto	aéroport	aeroporto
bay	Bucht	bahía	baie	baía
bayou	Altwasser	ensenada pantanosa	bayou	enseada pantanosa
creek, cr.	Bach	riachuelo	crique	riacho
island	Insel	isla	île	ilha
lake, l.	See	lago	lac	lago
reservoir	Stausee	embalse	réservoir	reservatório
state park	Naturpark	parque provincial	parc régional	parque estadual

VANCOUVER
North Vancouver
Burnaby
New Westminster
Richmond
Chilliwack
Abbotsford
Nanaimo
Port Alberni
Victoria
Esquimalt
Bellingham
Mount Vernon
Anacortes
Everett
SEATTLE
Bremerton
Tacoma
Port Angeles
Port Townsend
Renton
Auburn
Kent
Bellevue
Strait of Georgia
Strait of Juan de Fuca
Haro Strait
Puget Sound
SAN JUAN ISLANDS
VANCOUVER ISLAND
BRITISH COLUMBIA
WASHINGTON
CANADA
UNITED STATES
CASCADE MOUNTAINS
OLYMPIC MOUNTAINS
OLYMPIC NATIONAL PARK
NORTH CASCADES NATIONAL PARK
WENATCHEE MOUNTAINS
ENTIAT MOUNTAINS
SEYMOUR RANGE
WHATCOM
SKAGIT
SNOHOMISH
CHELAN
KING
KITSAP
MASON
JEFFERSON
CLALLAM
OKANOGAN

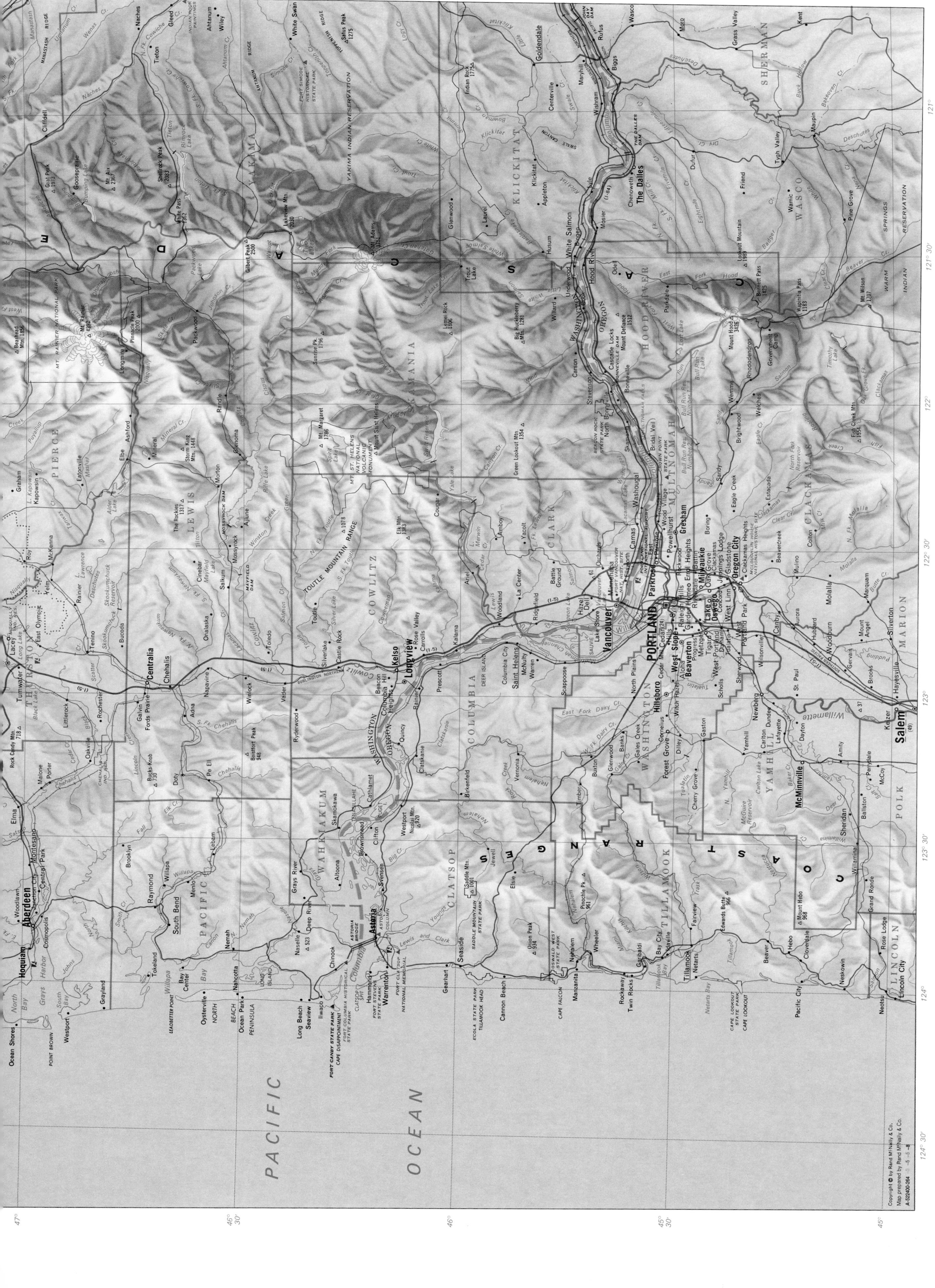
PACIFIC
OCEAN
PORTLAND
Vancouver
Salem
Longview
Kelso
Astoria
Aberdeen
Hoquiam
Centralia
Chehalis
The Dalles
Hillsboro
Beaverton
Gresham
Oregon City
Milwaukie
Lake Oswego
McMinnville
Tillamook
Seaside
Warrenton
Goldendale
Hood River
White Salmon
Camas
Washougal
Mt. Rainier
Mt. Adams
Mount Saint Helens
Mount Hood
WASHINGTON
OREGON
PACIFIC
LEWIS
COWLITZ
WAHKIAKUM
SKAMANIA
KLICKITAT
CLARK
CLATSOP
COLUMBIA
TILLAMOOK
WASHINGTON
YAMHILL
MULTNOMAH
CLACKAMAS
HOOD RIVER
WASCO
SHERMAN
MARION
POLK
LINCOLN
PIERCE
THURSTON
YAKIMA
YAKIMA INDIAN RESERVATION
WARM SPRINGS INDIAN RESERVATION
TOUTLE MOUNTAIN RANGE
CASCADE RANGE
COAST RANGES

Scale 1:1,000,000

Kilometers 0 10 20 30 40 50 Km.

Statute Miles 0 10 20 30 40 50 Mi.

One centimeter represents 10 kilometers.
One inch represents approximately 16 miles.
Lambert Conformal Conic Projection

ENGLISH	bay	cape	channel	creek, cr.	island, I.	lake, l.	mount	peak	strait
DEUTSCH	Bucht	Kap	Kanal	Bach	Insel	See	Berg	Gipfel	Meeresstrasse
ESPAÑOL	bahía	cabo	canal	riachuelo	isla	lago	monte	pico	estrecho
FRANÇAIS	baie	cap	canal	crique	île	lac	mont	cime	détroit
PORTUGUÊS	baía	cabo	canal	riacho	ilha	lago	monte	pico	estreito

Reno
Sparks
Carson City
South Lake Tahoe
Lake Tahoe
SIERRA NEVADA
CARSON RANGE
PINE NUT MOUNTAINS
SWEETWATER MTS.
CATHEDRAL RANGE
YOSEMITE NATIONAL PARK
Sacramento
West Sacramento
North Highlands
Carmichael
Citrus Heights
Roseville
Rancho Cordova
Davis
Woodland
Marysville
Yuba City
Oroville
Stockton
Lodi
Modesto
Manteca
Tracy
Turlock
Fairfield
Vacaville
Vallejo
Napa
Santa Rosa
Petaluma
Concord
Walnut Creek
Antioch
Pittsburg
Berkeley
Oakland
Alameda
San Leandro
Hayward
Fremont
San Mateo
Redwood City
Daly City
SAN FRANCISCO
San Rafael
Novato
Livermore
Pleasanton
SACRAMENTO VALLEY
SAN JOAQUIN
SONOMA MOUNTAINS
EL DORADO
PLACER
AMADOR
CALAVERAS
TUOLUMNE
MARIPOSA
STANISLAUS
CONTRA COSTA
ALAMEDA
SOLANO
YOLO
SUTTER
COLUSA
GLENN
LAKE
NAPA
SONOMA
MARIN
MONO
ALPINE
DOUGLAS
LYON
STOREY
WASHOE
CARSON
NEVADA
CALIFORNIA
39° 30'
39°
38° 30'
38°
37° 30'
119° 30'
120°
120° 30'
121°
121° 30'
122°
122° 30'

Map continues page 228
Scale 1:1,000,000
One centimeter represents 10 kilometers.
One inch represents approximately 16 miles.
Lambert Conformal Conic Projection
Kilometers 0 10 20 30 40 50 Km.
Statute Miles 0 10 20 30 40 50 Mi.
ENGLISH bay canal creek, cr. lake, l. mountain, mtn. pass range reservoir slough
DEUTSCH Bucht Kanal Bach See Berg Pass Gebirge Stausee verlandene Wasserfläche
ESPAÑOL bahía canal riachuelo lago montaña paso sierra embalse pantano
FRANÇAIS baie canal crique lac montagne col chaîne réservoir fondrière
PORTUGUÊS baía canal riacho lago montanha passo serra reservatório pântano
Copyright © by Rand McNally & Co.
Map prepared by Rand McNally & Co.
PACIFIC OCEAN
Monterey Bay
SAN JOAQUIN VALLEY
COAST RANGES
DIABLO RANGE
GABILAN RANGE
SANTA LUCIA RANGE
TEMBLOR RANGE
SALINAS VALLEY
SANTA CRUZ MOUNTAINS
Fresno
Bakersfield
Salinas
Monterey
Santa Cruz
San Luis Obispo
Visalia
Tulare
Hanford
Madera
Los Banos
Paso Robles
Watsonville
Hollister
Gilroy
Coalinga

Map continues pages 226-227

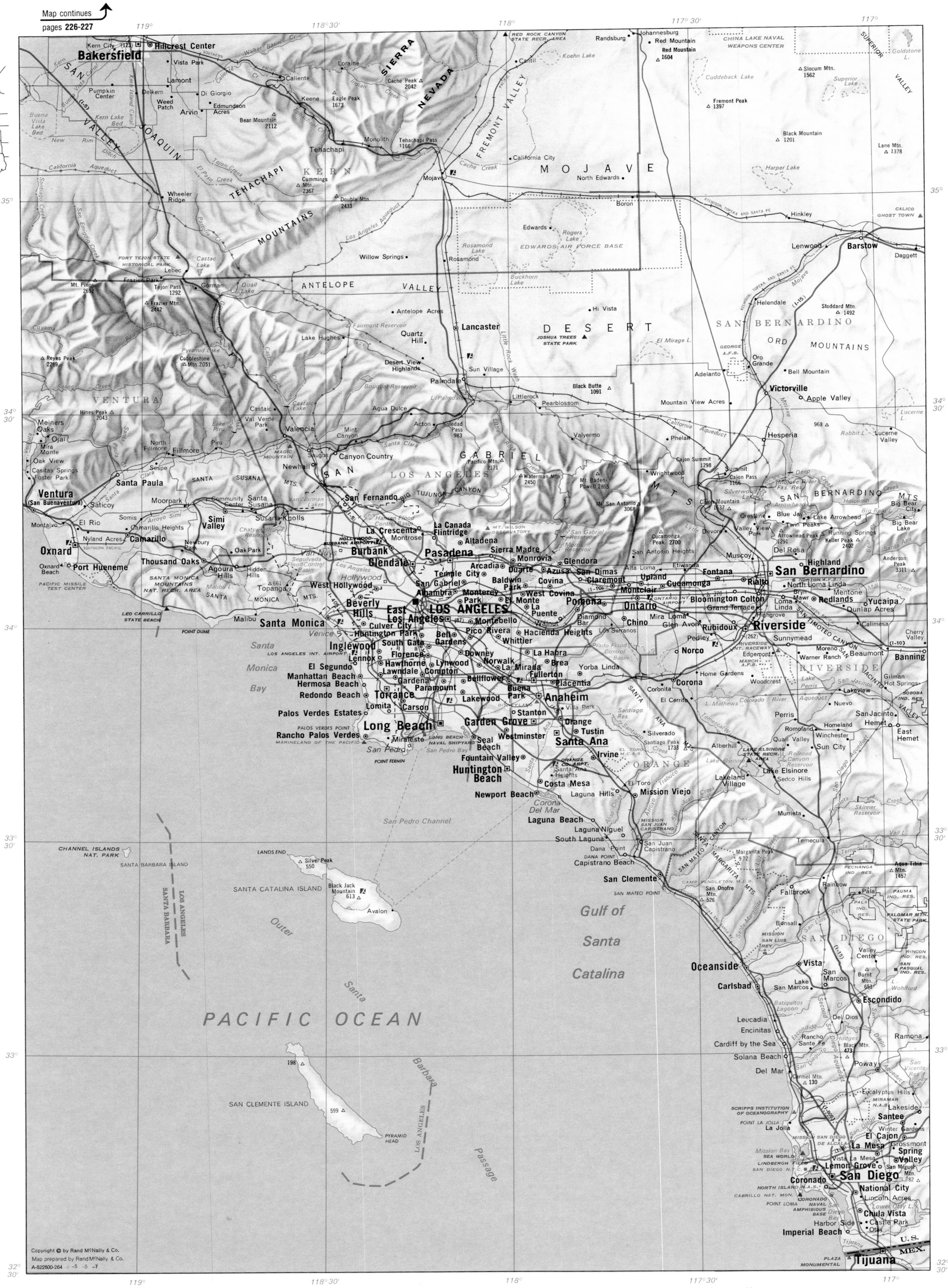
119°
118°30'
118°
117°30'
117°
35°
34° 30'
34°
33° 30'
33°
32° 30'
Bakersfield
Hillcrest Center
Kern City
Vista Park
Lamont
Pumpkin Center
Weed Patch
Arvin
Di Giorgio
Edmundson Acres
Caliente
Loraine
Keene
Eagle Peak 1673
Cache Peak 2042
Bear Mountain 2112
SIERRA NEVADA
SAN JOAQUIN VALLEY
TEHACHAPI MOUNTAINS
Tehachapi
Monolith
Tehachapi Pass 1166
KERN
Cummings Mtn. 2367
Double Mtn. 2433
Wheeler Ridge
California Aqueduct
Los Angeles Aqueduct
FREMONT VALLEY
California City
Mojave
MOJAVE
North Edwards
Boron
Cantil
Koehn Lake
RED ROCK CANYON STATE RECR. AREA
Randsburg
Johannesburg
Red Mountain
Red Mountain 1604
CHINA LAKE NAVAL WEAPONS CENTER
Cuddeback Lake
Fremont Peak 1397
Slocum Mtn. 1562
Superior Lake
SUPERIOR VALLEY
Goldstone L.
Black Mountain 1201
Lane Mtn. 1378
Harper Lake
CALICO GHOST TOWN
Hinkley
Barstow
Daggett
Lenwood
Edwards
Rogers Lake
EDWARDS AIR FORCE BASE
Rosamond Lake
Rosamond
Willow Springs
Buckhorn Lake
FORT TEJON STATE HISTORICAL PARK
Lebec
Castac Lake
Frazier Park
Mt. Pinos 2692
Tejon Pass 1292
Gorman
Frazier Mtn. 2442
Quail Lake
ANTELOPE VALLEY
Antelope Acres
Lancaster
Hi Vista
DESERT
JOSHUA TREES STATE PARK
El Mirage L.
SAN BERNARDINO MOUNTAINS
Helendale
Stoddard Mtn. 1492
Oro Grande
Bell Mountain
Victorville
Apple Valley
Adelanto
Fairmont Reservoir
Lake Hughes
Quartz Hill
Reyes Peak 2289
Cobblestone Mtn. 2051
Pyramid Lake
Desert View Highlands
Palmdale
Sun Village
Black Butte 1091
Littlerock
Pearblossom
Mountain View Acres
Hesperia
Lucerne Valley
VENTURA
Castaic
Castaic Lake
Agua Dulce
Acton
Soledad Pass 983
Hines Peak 2043
Meiners Oaks
Ojai
Mira Monte
Oak View
Casitas Springs
Foster Park
Val Verde Park
Valencia
Mint Canyon
Saugus
Canyon Country
Newhall
North Fillmore
Fillmore
Piru
Santa Paula
Sespe
SAN GABRIEL MTS.
LOS ANGELES
Pacifico Mtn. 2171
Waterman Mtn. 2450
Mt. Baden-Powell 2865
Valyermo
Phelan
Cajon Summit 1298
Summit
Cajon Pass 1166
Wrightwood
Mt. San Antonio 3068
SAN BERNARDINO MTS.
Big Bear City
Big Bear Lake
Lake Arrowhead
Crestline
Blue Jay
Twin Peaks
Running Springs
Arrowhead Peak 1291
Keller Peak 2402
Ventura (San Buenaventura)
Saticoy
Moorpark
Santa Susana
Community Center
San Fernando
Montalvo
El Rio
Somis
Camarillo Heights
Camarillo
Simi Valley
Susana Knolls
Oxnard
Nyland Acres
Port Hueneme
Oxnard Beach
PACIFIC MISSILE TEST CENTER
Thousand Oaks
Newbury Park
Agoura Hills
Hidden Hills
Oak Park
SANTA MONICA MOUNTAINS NAT. RECR. AREA
Topanga
Malibu
LEO CARRILLO STATE BEACH
POINT DUME
La Crescenta
Montrose
La Canada Flintridge
Altadena
Burbank
Glendale
Pasadena
Sierra Madre
Monrovia
Duarte
Azusa
Glendora
San Dimas
Claremont
Upland
Cucamonga
Fontana
Rialto
San Bernardino
Highland
Del Rosa
Muscoy
Devore
Etiwanda
Alta Loma
Arcadia
Temple City
San Gabriel
Alhambra
Monterey Park
Baldwin Park
Covina
West Covina
El Monte
La Puente
Pomona
Montclair
Ontario
Chino
Bloomington
Colton
Grand Terrace
Loma Linda
Redlands
Mentone
Yucaipa
Dunlap Acres
Calimesa
Cherry Valley
Banning
Beaumont
West Hollywood
Beverly Hills
Hollywood
Santa Monica
East Los Angeles
LOS ANGELES
Montebello
Culver City
Huntington Park
Venice
Inglewood
South Gate
Bell Gardens
Pico Rivera
Whittier
Hacienda Heights
Diamond Bar
Walnut
Rubidoux
Riverside
Pedley
Norco
Corona
Sunnymead
Moreno
Edgemont
El Segundo
Lennox
Hawthorne
Lawndale
Florence
Lynwood
Compton
Downey
Norwalk
La Mirada
La Habra
Brea
Fullerton
Placentia
Yorba Linda
Manhattan Beach
Hermosa Beach
Redondo Beach
Torrance
Gardena
Paramount
Bellflower
Lakewood
Buena Park
Anaheim
Lomita
Carson
Long Beach
Stanton
Palos Verdes Estates
Rancho Palos Verdes
San Pedro
Garden Grove
Westminster
Orange
Tustin
Santa Ana
Seal Beach
Fountain Valley
Huntington Beach
Irvine
Costa Mesa
Newport Beach
Corona Del Mar
Laguna Beach
Laguna Hills
El Toro
Mission Viejo
Laguna Niguel
South Laguna
San Juan Capistrano
Dana Point
Capistrano Beach
San Clemente
ORANGE
Lakeland Village
Lake Elsinore
Alberhill
Sedco Hills
Perris
Romoland
Homeland
Winchester
Hemet
East Hemet
San Jacinto
Sun City
Quail Valley
Murrieta
Temecula
Nuevo
Lakeview
Aqua Tibia Mtn. 1457
Fallbrook
Rainbow
Pala
Bonsall
Oceanside
Carlsbad
Vista
San Marcos
Escondido
Valley Center
Leucadia
Encinitas
Cardiff by the Sea
Solana Beach
Del Mar
Rancho Santa Fe
Del Dios
Ramona
Poway
Eucalyptus Hills
Lakeside
Santee
El Cajon
La Mesa
Spring Valley
Lemon Grove
La Jolla
San Diego
Coronado
National City
Lincoln Acres
Chula Vista
Castle Park
Harbor Side
Imperial Beach
Tijuana
U.S.
MEX.
PACIFIC OCEAN
Santa Monica Bay
San Pedro Channel
Gulf of Santa Catalina
Outer Santa Barbara Passage
SANTA CATALINA ISLAND
Avalon
Black Jack Mountain 613
Silver Peak 550
SANTA BARBARA ISLAND
CHANNEL ISLANDS NAT. PARK
SAN CLEMENTE ISLAND
PYRAMID HEAD
LOS ANGELES
SANTA BARBARA
Copyright © by Rand McNally & Co.
Map prepared by Rand McNally & Co.
A-522600-264

ENGLISH	canyon	creek, cr.	lake, l.	mountain, mtn.	pass	peak	point	reservoir, res
DEUTSCH	Cañon	Bach	See	Berg	Pass	Gipfel	Landspitze	Stausee
ESPAÑOL	cañón	riachuelo	lago	montaña	paso	pico	punta	embalse
FRANÇAIS	canyon	crique	lac	montagne	col	cime	pointe	reservoir
PORTUGUÊS	canhão	riacho	lago	montanha	passo	pico	ponta	reservatório

Kilometers 0 10 20 30 40 50 Km.

Statute Miles 0 10 20 30 40 50 Mi.

Scale 1:1,000,000

One centimeter represents 10 kilometers.
One inch represents approximately 16 miles.

Lambert Conformal Conic Projection

a

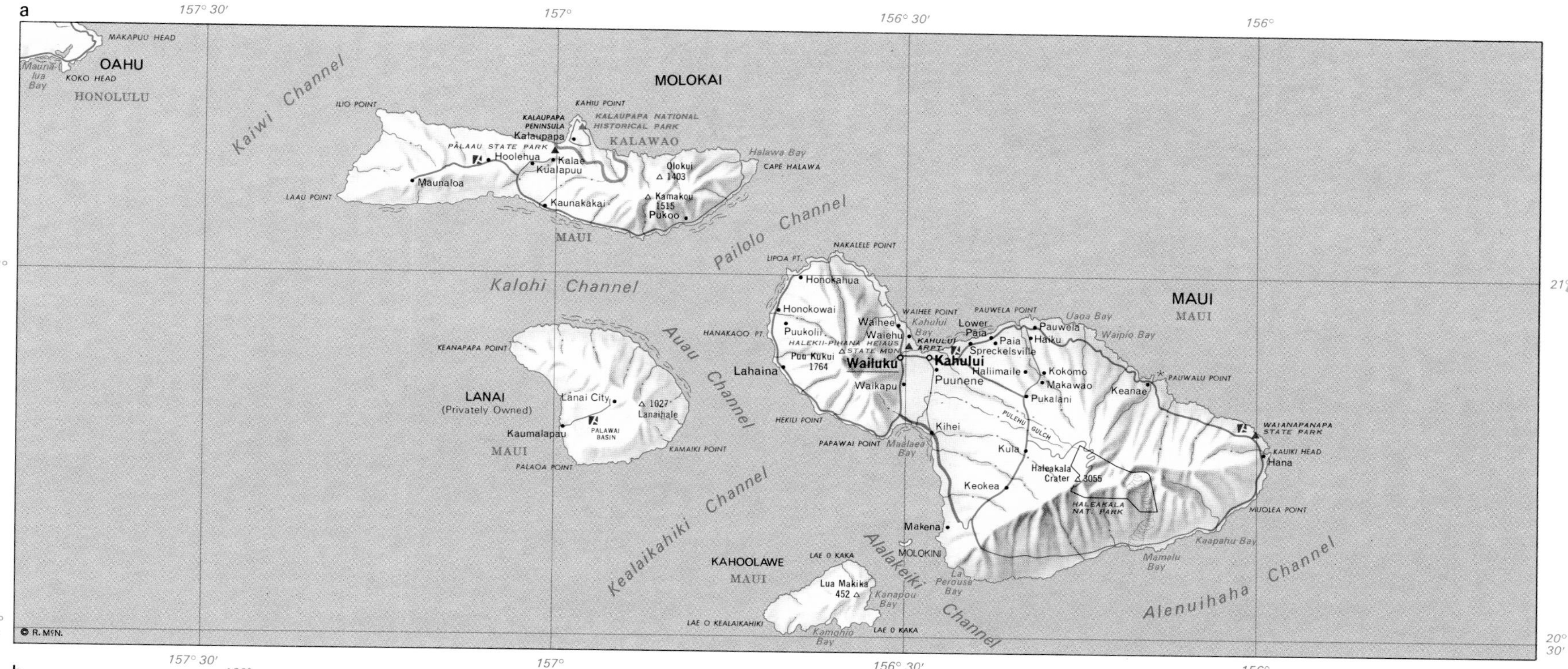
157° 30'
157°
156° 30'
156°
21°
20° 30'
MAKAPUU HEAD
Maunalua Bay
OAHU
KOKO HEAD
HONOLULU
Kaiwi Channel
MOLOKAI
ILIO POINT
KAHIU POINT
KALAUPAPA PENINSULA
KALAUPAPA NATIONAL HISTORICAL PARK
Kalaupapa
KALAWAO
PALAAU STATE PARK
Hoolehua
Kualapuu
Kala
Halawa Bay
CAPE HALAWA
Olokui 1403
LAAU POINT
Maunaloa
Kaunakakai
Kamakou 1515
Pukoo
MAUI
Pailolo Channel
Kalohi Channel
LIPOA PT.
NAKALELE POINT
Honokahua
Honokowai
Puukolii
Puu Kukui 1764
Lahaina
HANAKAOO PT.
Waihee
Waiehu
Wailuku
Waikapu
Kahului
Kahului Bay
Lower Paia
Paia
Spreckelsville
Haiku
Pauwela
PAUWELA POINT
Uaoa Bay
Waipio Bay
Haliimaile
Kokomo
Makawao
Pukalani
Keanae
PAUWALU POINT
Puunene
MAUI
MAUI
KEANAPAPA POINT
LANAI
(Privately Owned)
Lanai City
1027 Lanaihale
PALAWAI BASIN
Kaumalapau
PALAOA POINT
KAMAIKI POINT
MAUI
Auau Channel
HEKILI POINT
PAPAWAI POINT
Maalaea Bay
Kihei
Kula
Haleakala Crater 3055
HALEAKALA NAT. PARK
Keokea
WAIANAPANAPA STATE PARK
KAUIKI HEAD
Hana
MUOLEA POINT
Kealaikahiki Channel
Makena
MOLOKINI
Alalakeiki Channel
Perouse Bay
Kaupahu Bay
Mamalu Bay
KAHOOLAWE
MAUI
LAE O KAKA
Lua Makika 452
Kanapou Bay
Kamohio Bay
LAE O KEALAIKAHIKI
LAE O KAKA
Alenuihaha Channel
© R. McN.

b

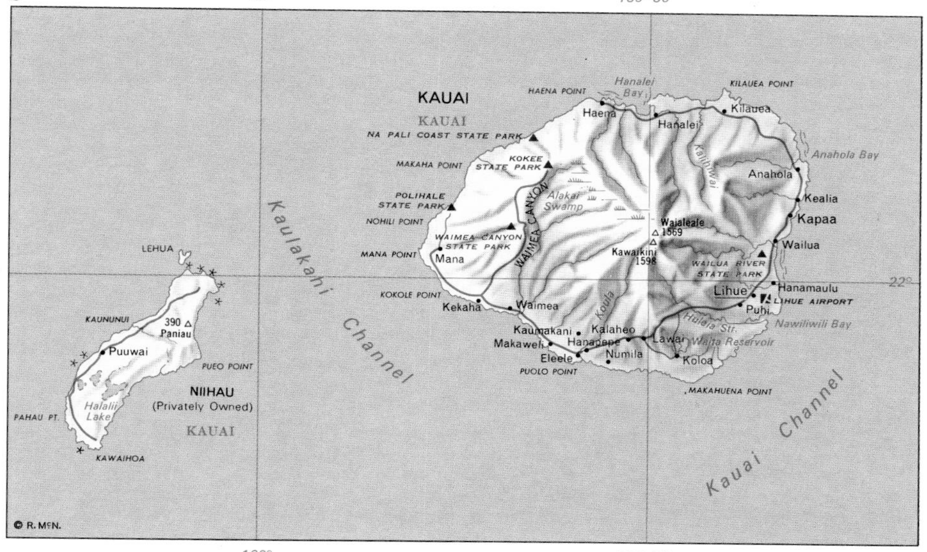
160°
159° 30'
22°
KAUAI
KAUAI
HAENA POINT
Hanalei Bay
KILAUEA POINT
Haena
Hanalei
Kilauea
NA PALI COAST STATE PARK
KOKEE STATE PARK
MAKAHA POINT
POLIHALE STATE PARK
NOHILI POINT
MANA POINT
Mana
WAIMEA CANYON STATE PARK
Alakai Swamp
Waialeale 1569
Kawaikini 1598
Anahola Bay
Anahola
Kealia
Kapaa
Wailua
WAILUA RIVER STATE PARK
Hanamaulu
Lihue
LIHUE AIRPORT
Puhi
Nawiliwili Bay
KOKOLE POINT
Kekaha
Waimea
Kaumakani
Makaweli
Eleele
Hanapepe
Kalaheo
Lawai
Numila
Koloa
PUOLO POINT
MAKAHUENA POINT
Kaulakahi Channel
Kauai Channel
LEHUA
KAUNUNUI
390 Paniau
Puuwai
PUEO POINT
NIIHAU
(Privately Owned)
KAUAI
PAHAU PT.
Halalii Lake
KAWAIHOA
© R. McN.

c

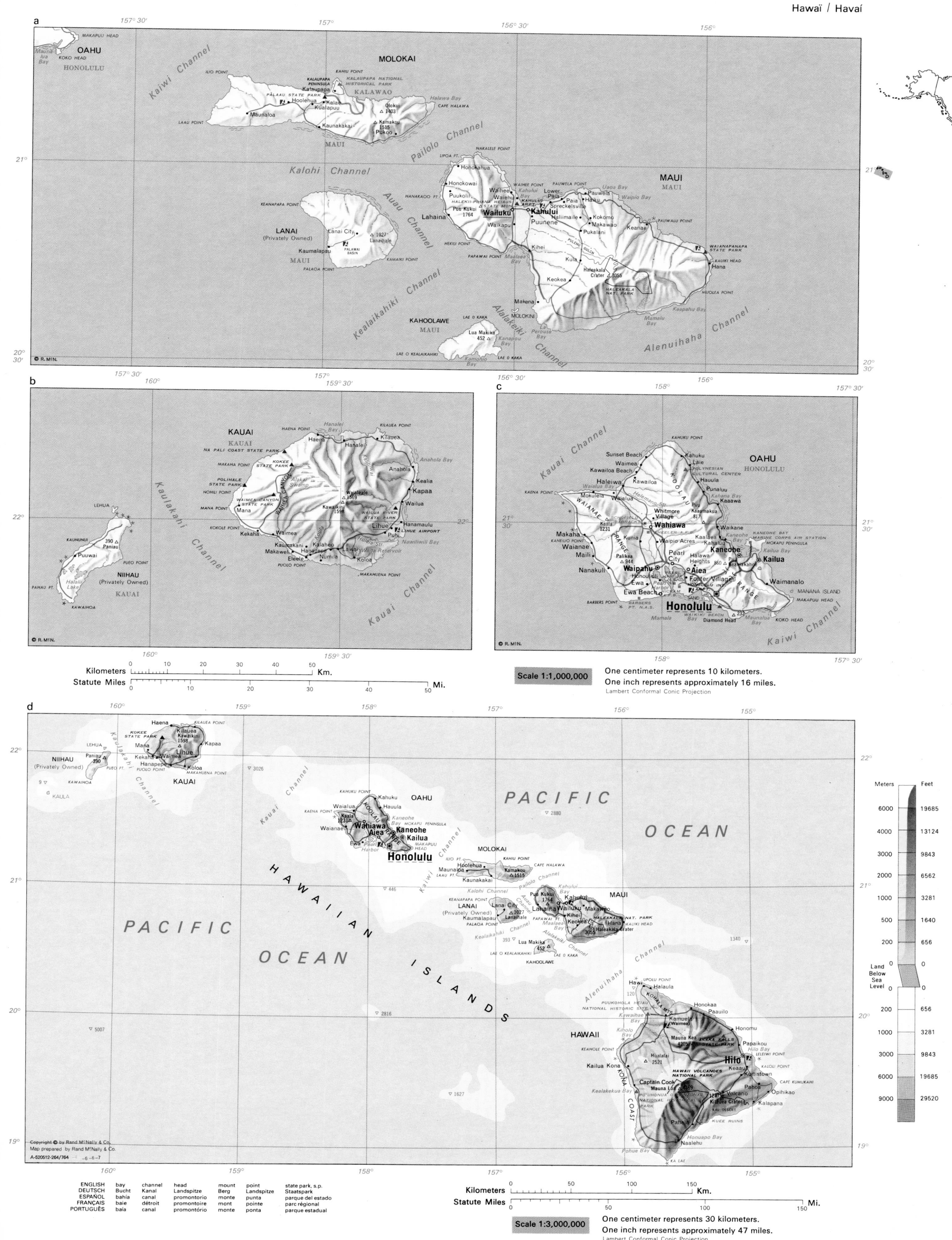

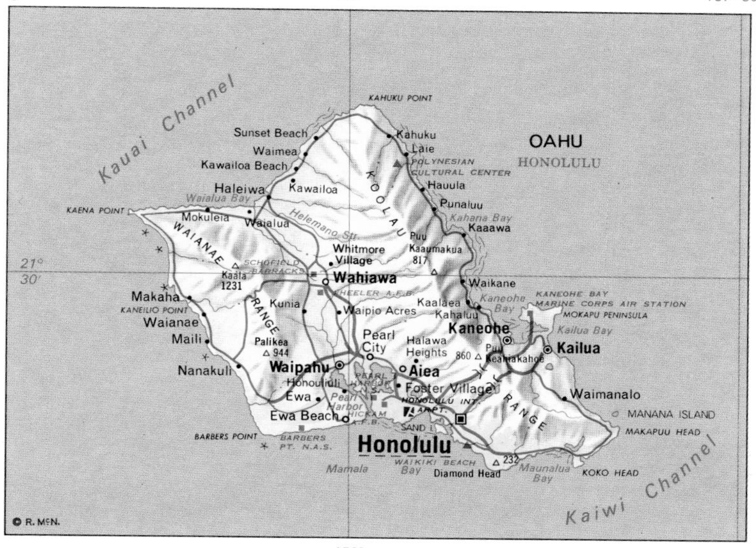
158°
157° 30'
21° 30'
KAHUKU POINT
OAHU
HONOLULU
Kauai Channel
Sunset Beach
Waimea
Kawailoa Beach
Kahuku
Laie
POLYNESIAN CULTURAL CENTER
Hauula
Punaluu
Kahana Bay
Kaaawa
Haleiwa
Waialua Bay
Kawailoa
KAENA POINT
Mokuleia
Waialua
KOOLAU RANGE
WAIANAE RANGE
Whitmore Village
Wahiawa
Puu Kaaumakua 817
Kaala 1231
Makaha
KANEILIO POINT
Waianae
Maili
Nanakuli
Kunia
Waipio Acres
Palikea 944
Pearl City
Waipahu
Honouliuli
Ewa
Ewa Beach
Aiea
Halawa Heights
Kaneohe
Kailua
Kahaluu
Kaalaea
Waikane
KANEOHE BAY MARINE CORPS AIR STATION
MOKAPU PENINSULA
Kailua Bay
Waimanalo
MANANA ISLAND
MAKAPUU HEAD
Foster Village
Pearl Harbor
BARBERS POINT
BARBERS PT. N.A.S.
Honolulu
Mamala Bay
WAIKIKI BEACH
Diamond Head
Maunalua Bay
KOKO HEAD
Kaiwi Channel
© R. McN.

Kilometers 0 10 20 30 40 50 Km.
Statute Miles 0 10 20 30 40 50 Mi.

Scale 1:1,000,000

One centimeter represents 10 kilometers.
One inch represents approximately 16 miles.
Lambert Conformal Conic Projection

d

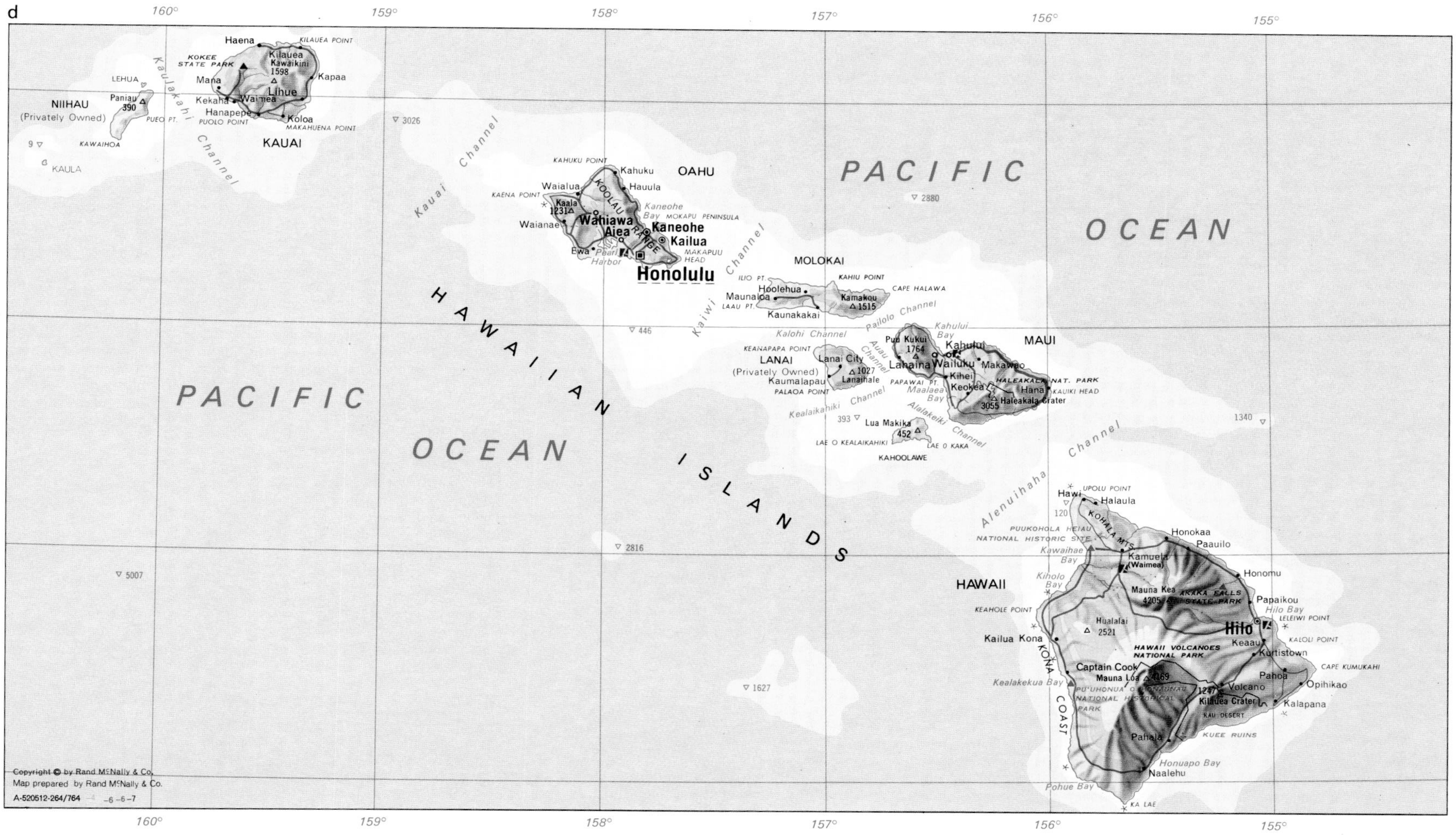
160°
159°
158°
157°
156°
155°
22°
21°
20°
19°
Haena
KILAUEA POINT
KOKEE STATE PARK
Kilauea
Kawaikini 1598
Kapaa
Mana
Lihue
Kekaha
Waimea
Hanapepe
Koloa
PUOLO POINT
MAKAHUENA POINT
KAUAI
LEHUA
NIIHAU
(Privately Owned)
Paniau 390
PUEO PT.
KAWAIHOA
KAULA
Kaulakahi Channel
3026
Kauai Channel
KAHUKU POINT
Kahuku
OAHU
Hauula
KAENA POINT
Waialua
Kaala 1231
Wahiawa
Waianae
Aiea
Kaneohe
Kailua
Ewa
Pearl Harbor
MOKAPU PENINSULA
MAKAPUU HEAD
Honolulu
Kaiwi Channel
PACIFIC
OCEAN
2880
MOLOKAI
ILIO PT.
KAHIU POINT
Hoolehua
Maunaloa
LAAU PT.
Kaunakakai
Kamakou 1515
CAPE HALAWA
Pailolo Channel
446
Kalohi Channel
Kahului Bay
Puu Kukui 1764
Kahului
Wailuku
Lahaina
Makawao
MAUI
KEANAPAPA POINT
LANAI
(Privately Owned)
Lanai City
Kaumalapau
1027 Lanaihale
PALAOA POINT
Auau Channel
PAPAWAI POINT
Maalaea Bay
Kihei
Keokea
HALEAKALA NAT. PARK
Hana
KAUIKI HEAD
3055 Haleakala Crater
Kealaikahiki Channel
Alalakeiki Channel
393
Lua Makika 452
LAE O KEALAIKAHIKI
LAE O KAKA
KAHOOLAWE
1340
Alenuihaha Channel
HAWAIIAN ISLANDS
PACIFIC
OCEAN
2816
5007
Hawi
UPOLU POINT
Halaula
KOHALA MTS.
PUUKOHOLA HEIAU NATIONAL HISTORIC SITE
Kawaihae Bay
Honokaa
Paauilo
Kamuela (Waimea)
Honomu
Mauna Kea 4205
AKAKA FALLS STATE PARK
Papaikou
Hilo Bay
Hilo
LELEIWI POINT
HAWAII
Kiholo Bay
KEAHOLE POINT
Hualalai 2521
Kailua Kona
KONA COAST
KAOLI POINT
Keaau
Kurtistown
HAWAII VOLCANOES NATIONAL PARK
CAPE KUMUKAHI
Kealakekua Bay
Captain Cook
Mauna Loa 4169
Pahoa
Opihikao
Volcano
1247 Kilauea Crater
Kalapana
KAU DESERT
KUEE RUINS
1627
Pahala
Honuapo Bay
Naalehu
Pohue Bay
KA LAE

ENGLISH	bay	channel	head	mount	point	state park, s.p.
DEUTSCH	Bucht	Kanal	Landspitze	Berg	Landspitze	Staatspark
ESPAÑOL	bahía	canal	promontorio	monte	punta	parque del estado
FRANÇAIS	baie	détroit	promontoire	mont	pointe	parc régional
PORTUGUÊS	baía	canal	promontório	monte	ponta	parque estadual

Kilometers 0 50 100 150 Km.
Statute Miles 0 50 100 150 Mi.

Scale 1:3,000,000

One centimeter represents 30 kilometers.
One inch represents approximately 47 miles.
Lambert Conformal Conic Projection

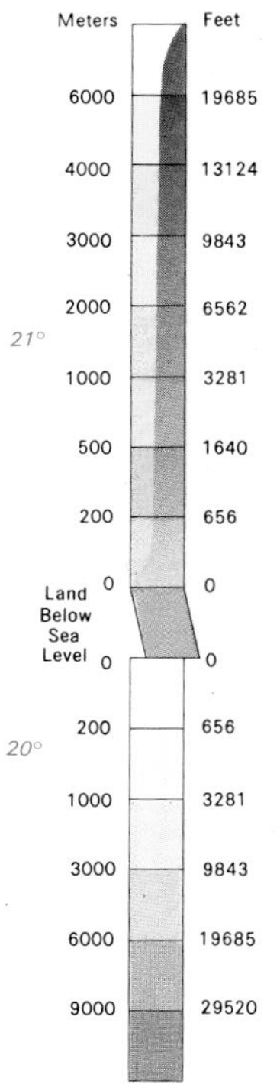
Meters
Feet
6000 19685
4000 13124
3000 9843
2000 6562
1000 3281
500 1640
200 656
0 0
Land Below Sea Level
0 0
200 656
1000 3281
3000 9843
6000 19685
9000 29520

Map continues pages 178-179

UNITED STATES
MEXICO
GULF OF MEXICO
PACIFIC OCEAN
SIERRA MADRE OCCIDENTAL
SIERRA MADRE ORIENTAL
SIERRA MADRE DEL SUR
Golfo de California
BAJA CALIFORNIA
Tropic of Cancer
CIUDAD DE MEXICO
Guadalajara
Monterrey
Chihuahua
Hermosillo
Culiacán
Mazatlán
Acapulco
Veracruz
Puebla
Oaxaca
Mérida
Tampico
Tijuana
Mexicali
San Diego
Phoenix
Tucson
El Paso
Ciudad Juárez
Dallas
Fort Worth
Houston
San Antonio
New Orleans
Oklahoma City
Tulsa
Little Rock
Memphis
Shreveport
Galveston
Corpus Christi
Brownsville
Matamoros
GUATEMALA
BELIZE
EL SALVADOR
YUCATAN PENINSULA
Bahía de Campeche
Golfo de Tehuantepec
ISLAS REVILLAGIGEDO
ÎLE CLIPPERTON (Fr.)
EDWARDS PLATEAU
TEXAS
LOUISIANA
MISSISSIPPI
ARIZONA
NEW MEXICO
CALIFORNIA
OKLAHOMA
ARKANSAS
MISSOURI

ESPAÑOL	cabo	cordillera	golfo	isla, i.	lago, l.	punta	sierra	volcán, vol.
ENGLISH	cape	mountains	gulf	island	lake	point	mountains	volcano
DEUTSCH	Kap	Berge	Golf	Insel	See	Landspitze	Berge	Vulkan
FRANÇAIS	cap	montagnes	golfe	île	lac	pointe	montagnes	volcan
PORTUGUÊS	cabo	cordilheira	golfo	ilha	lago	ponta	serra	vulcão

ATLANTIC OCEAN
Sargasso Sea
BERMUDA (U.K.)
Hamilton
Tropic of Cancer
BAHAMAS
Nassau
ANDROS
Straits of Florida
TURKS AND CAICOS ISLANDS (U.K.)
Grand Turk
WEST INDIES
GREATER ANTILLES
CUBA
LA HABANA
Santiago de Cuba
Guantánamo
CAYMAN IS. (U.K.)
George Town
JAMAICA
Kingston
HAITI
Port-au-Prince
DOMINICAN REPUBLIC
SANTO DOMINGO
HISPANIOLA
PUERTO RICO (U.S.)
San Juan
ANGUILLA (U.K.)
ANTIGUA AND BARBUDA
Saint John's
SAINT KITTS AND NEVIS
Basseterre
MONTSERRAT (U.K.)
GUADELOUPE (Fr.)
Basse-Terre
DOMINICA
Roseau
MARTINIQUE (Fr.)
Fort-de-France
SAINT LUCIA
Castries
BARBADOS
Bridgetown
SAINT VINCENT AND THE GRENADINES
Kingstown
GRENADA
Saint George's
TRINIDAD AND TOBAGO
Port of Spain
LESSER ANTILLES
CARIBBEAN SEA
ARUBA (Neth.)
Oranjestad
NETHERLANDS ANTILLES
Willemstad
VENEZUELA
CARACAS
Maracaibo
COLOMBIA
SANTA FE DE BOGOTÁ
Medellín
Cali
Barranquilla
Cartagena
COSTA RICA
SAN JOSÉ
PANAMÁ
Panamá
BRAZIL
GUYANA
Atlanta
Miami
Tampa
Jacksonville
Charleston
Norfolk
ATLANTIC
Map continues pages 242-243

Kilometers 0 200 400 600 Km.
Statute Miles 0 200 400 600 Mi.

Scale 1:12,000,000
One centimeter represents 120 kilometers.
One inch represents approximately 190 miles.
Oblique Conic Conformal Projection

ARIZONA
NEW MEXICO
UNITED STATES
MEXICO
San Diego
Tijuana
Mexicali
Yuma
San Luis Río Colorado
Tucson
El Paso
Ciudad Juárez
Las Cruces
Carlsbad
Nogales
Ensenada
BAJA CALIFORNIA
BAJA CALIFORNIA SUR
SONORA
CHIHUAHUA
SINALOA
DURANGO
NAYARIT
JALISCO
COLIMA
Hermosillo
Guaymas
Ciudad Obregón
Navojoa
Los Mochis
Culiacán
Mazatlán
Chihuahua
Delicias
Hidalgo del Parral
Durango
Tepic
Puerto Vallarta
Guadalajara
Zapopan
Ciudad Guzmán
Manzanillo
Tecomán
Colima
Torreón
Gómez Palacio
La Paz
San José del Cabo
San Lucas
Golfo de California
SIERRA MADRE OCCIDENTAL
Tropic of Cancer
PACIFIC OCEAN
ISLAS REVILLAGIGEDO (Mex.)
ISLAS MARÍAS
ISLA CEDROS
ISLA TIBURÓN
Bahía Sebastián Vizcaíno
Bahía Magdalena
Bahía de Banderas

Meters	Feet
6000	19685
4000	13124
3000	9843
2000	6562
1000	3281
500	1640
200	656
0	0
Land Below Sea Level 0	0
200	656
1000	3281
3000	9843
6000	19685
9000	29520

ESPAÑOL	bahía	cerro	isla	laguna	presa	punta	río	sierra
ENGLISH	bay	mountain	island	lagoon	reservoir	point	river	mountains
DEUTSCH	Bucht	Berg	Insel	Haff	Stausee	Landspitze	Fluss	Berge
FRANÇAIS	baie	montagne	île	lagune	réservoir	pointe	rivière	montagnes
PORTUGUÊS	baia	montanha	ilha	laguna	reservatório	ponta	rio	serra

Kilometers 0 100 200 300 Km.
Statute Miles 0 100 200 300

Scale 1:6,000,000
One centimeter represents 60 kilometers.
One inch represents approximately 95 miles.
Lambert Conformal Conic Projection

GULF
OF
MEXICO
Bahía de Campeche
Golfo de Tehuantepec
Tropic of Cancer
TEXAS
LOUISIANA
MISSISSIPPI
ALABAMA
EDWARDS
PLATEAU
UNITED STATES
MEXICO
NUEVO LEÓN
TAMAULIPAS
SAN LUIS POTOSÍ
GUANAJUATO
QUERÉTARO
HIDALGO
MÉXICO
MORELOS
PUEBLA
VERACRUZ
OAXACA
GUERRERO
TABASCO
CHIAPAS
CAMPECHE
YUCATÁN
QUINTANA ROO
GUATEMALA
BELIZE
HONDURAS
SIERRA MADRE ORIENTAL
SIERRA MADRE DEL SUR
SIERRA MADRE DE CHIAPAS
ISTMO DE TEHUANTEPEC
YUCATAN PENINSULA
PENÍNSULA DE YUCATÁN
Gulf of Honduras
Dallas
Fort Worth
Houston
San Antonio
Austin
Galveston
Corpus Christi
Brownsville
Shreveport
Jackson
Baton Rouge
New Orleans
Mobile
Monterrey
Saltillo
Tampico
San Luis Potosí
León
Querétaro
Pachuca
CIUDAD DE MÉXICO
MÉXICO CITY
Puebla
Xalapa
Veracruz
Orizaba
Oaxaca
Acapulco
Chilpancingo de los Bravo
Cuernavaca
Toluca
Coatzacoalcos
Villahermosa
Tuxtla Gutiérrez
Ciudad del Carmen
Campeche
Mérida
Progreso
Cancún
Cozumel
Chetumal
Belize City
Belmopan
GUATEMALA
Ciudad Victoria
Matamoros
Reynosa
Nuevo Laredo
Laredo
Ciudad Madero
Tuxpan
Poza Rica
Salina Cruz
Tapachula
San Pedro Sula
Map continues pages 238-239
Map continues pages 236-237

Map continues
pages 232-233

PACIFIC OCEAN
SIERRA MADRE OCCIDENTAL
SIERRA MADRE DEL SUR
GUADALAJARA
Durango
Mazatlán
Zacatecas
Aguascalientes
San Luis Potosí
León
Guanajuato
Querétaro
Tepic
Puerto Vallarta
Colima
Manzanillo
Morelia
Acapulco
Lázaro Cárdenas
ISLAS MARÍAS
Meters
Feet
Land Below Sea Level
Copyright © by Rand McNally & Co.
Map prepared by Rand McNally & Co.

ESPAÑOL	arroyo	boca	cerro	lago	laguna	punta	rio	sierra	volcán
ENGLISH	brook	entrance	butte	lake	lagoon	point	river	ranges	volcano
DEUTSCH	Bach	Einfahrt	Restberg	See	Haff	Landspitze	Fluss	Bergketten	Vulkan
FRANÇAIS	ruisseau	entrée	butte	lac	lagune	pointe	rivière	chaîne	volcan
PORTUGUÊS	riacho	entrada	cerro	lago	laguna	ponta	rio	serra	vulcão

GULF OF MEXICO
Bahia de Campeche
Tropic of Cancer
Golfo de Tehuantepec
ISTMO DE TEHUANTEPEC
SIERRA MADRE DEL SUR
SIERRA MADRE DE CHIAPAS
TAMAULIPAS
SAN LUIS POTOSÍ
VERACRUZ
HIDALGO
PUEBLA
TLAXCALA
MORELOS
GUERRERO
OAXACA
TABASCO
CHIAPAS
Ciudad Victoria
Ciudad Mante
Ciudad Madero
Tampico
Pánuco
Tuxpan
Poza Rica
Papantla
Pachuca
Tulancingo
Teziutlán
Xalapa
Coatepec
Veracruz
Córdoba
Orizaba
Puebla
Atlixco
Tehuacán
Tierra Blanca
Cosamaloapan
San Andrés Tuxtla
Coatzacoalcos
Minatitlán
Acayucan
Villahermosa
Oaxaca
Juchitán de Zaragoza
Salina Cruz
Tuxtla Gutiérrez
San Cristóbal de las Casas
Puerto Escondido
Puerto Ángel
Tonalá
Arriaga
99° 98° 97° 96° 95° 94° 93°
24° 23° 22° 21° 20° 19° 18° 17° 16°

Map continues pages 232-233

Map continues pages 236-237

Kilometers 0 50 100 150 Km.
Statute Miles 0 50 100 150 Mi.

Scale 1:3,000,000
One centimeter represents 30 kilometers.
One inch represents approximately 47 miles.
Lambert Conformal Conic Projection

Map continues pages 232-233

PACIFIC
OCEAN
Gulf of Honduras
Golfo de Fonseca
MEXICO
MÉXICO
GUATEMALA
BELIZE
HONDURAS
EL SALVADOR
GUATEMALA
San Salvador
Tegucigalpa
Managua
Tapachula
Quetzaltenango
Escuintla
Santa Ana
San Miguel
San Pedro Sula
Puerto Cortés
Puerto Barrios
La Ceiba
Choluteca
Chinandega
León
Comayagua
Siguatepeque
PETÉN
ALTA VERAPAZ
BAJA VERAPAZ
CHIAPAS
SIERRA MADRE DE CHIAPAS
SIERRA DE LAS MINAS
ISLAS DE LA BAHÍA
ISLA DE ROATÁN
Meters
Feet
6000
19685
4000
13124
3000
9843
2000
6562
1000
3281
500
1640
200
656
0
0
Land Below Sea Level
0
0
200
656
1000
3281
3000
9843
6000
19685
9000
29520
92°
91°
90°
89°
88°
87°
14°
13°
12°
11°
10°
9°
8°

Map continues pages 234-235

ESPAÑOL	bahía	cerro	cordillera	isla	lago	laguna	punta	sierra	volcán
ENGLISH	bay	mountain	mountains	island	lake	lagoon	point	mountains	volcano
DEUTSCH	Bucht	Berg	Berge	Insel	See	Haff	Landspitze	Berge	Vulkan
FRANÇAIS	baie	montagne	montagnes	île	lac	lagune	pointe	montagnes	volcan
PORTUGUÊS	baía	montanha	cordilheira	ilha	lago	laguna	ponta	serra	vulcão

CARIBBEAN
SEA
LA MOSQUITIA
GRACIAS A DIOS
MONTAÑAS DE COLÓN
COSTA DE MOSQUITOS
ZELAYA
COSTA
CORDILLERA ISABELIA
CORDILLERA DARIENSE
CORDILLERA CHONTALEÑA
SERRANÍAS HUAPÍ
SERRANÍAS DE YOLAINA
HONDURAS
NICARAGUA
COSTA RICA
PANAMÁ
JINOTEGA
MATAGALPA
BOACO
CHONTALES
RÍO SAN JUAN
ALAJUELA
HEREDIA
GUANACASTE
CARTAGO
LIMÓN
SAN JOSÉ
PUNTARENAS
BOCAS DEL TORO
CHIRIQUÍ
VERAGUAS
COCLÉ
COLÓN
HERRERA
LOS SANTOS
CORDILLERA CENTRAL
ISTMO DE PANAMÁ
ARCHIPIÉLAGO DE BOCAS DEL TORO
Golfo de los Mosquitos
Golfo de Panamá
Golfo Dulce
Golfo de Chiriquí
Golfo de Nicoya
Bahía de Coronado
Bahía de Punta Gorda
Lago de Nicaragua
SAN ANDRÉS Y PROVIDENCIA (Colombia)
ISLA DE PROVIDENCIA
San Andrés
CAYOS DE ALBUQUERQUE
CAYOS DEL ESTE SUDESTE
ISLAS DEL MAÍZ (Nic.)
CAYOS MISKITOS
MISKITOS REEF
QUITASUEÑO
CAYO DE SERRANA
CAYOS DE RONCADOR
CAYO DE SERRANILLA (Colombia)
CAYOS CAJONES
CAYOS BECERRO
CAYOS VIVORILLO
CAYOS COCOROCUMA
ARRECIFES DE LA MEDIA LUNA
ARRECIFE EDINBURGH
Edinburgh Channel
CABO GRACIAS A DIOS
Cabo Gracias a Dios
CABO CAMARÓN
CABO FALSO
Santa Rosa de Aguán
Limón
Iriona
Brus Laguna
Puerto Lempira
Paya
Dulce Nombre de Culmí
Wampú
Valencia
San Ramón
Waspam
Bilwaskarma
Bocay
Bonanza
Yablis
Puerto Cabezas
La Rosita
Siuna
La Luz
Wounta
Tungla
Prinzapolka
La Cruz de Río Grande
San Pedro del Norte
La Barra
Matiguás
Camoapa
Comalapa
Santo Domingo
La Libertad
Santo Tomás
Villa Sandino
Juigalpa
Acoyapa
Muelle de los Bueyes
Rama
Bluefields
El Bluff
San Ubaldo
Morrito
Altagracia
San Miguelito
Punta Gorda
Cárdenas
San Carlos
Los Chiles
El Castillo de La Concepción
San Juan del Norte
Colorado
Upala
Caño Negro
Liberia
Bagaces
Tilarán
Cañas
Fortuna
Arenal
Altamira
Venecia
Puerto Viejo
Quesada
Juntas
Filadelfia
Santa Cruz
Nicoya
San Antonio
Mansión
Lepanto
Paquera
Tambor
Cabuya
CABO BLANCO
Puntarenas
SAN JOSÉ
Desamparados
Alajuela
Heredia
Cartago
Turrialba
Guápiles
Siquirres
Puerto Limón
Vesta
Puerto Viejo
Suretka
Parrita
Quepos
San Isidro
Palmares
Dominical
Buenos Aires
Ciudad Cortés
Palmar Sur
Golfito
Puerto Jiménez
Puerto Armuelles
La Concepción
David
Boquerón
Dolega
Bocas del Toro
Almirante
Changuinola
Chiriquí Grande
Bahía Azul
Remedios
Tolé
Las Lajas
Santiago
La Mesa
Atalaya
Montijo
Sona
Las Palmas
Santa Fe
Calobre
Aguadulce
Santa María
Chitré
La Arena
Pesé
Ocú
Penonomé
Antón
Natá
Olá
La Pintada
El Valle
San Carlos
Chame
Río Hato
Bejuco
La Chorrera
Panamá
Balboa
Taboga
Colón
Cristóbal
Portobelo
Nombre de Dios
Nuevo Chagres
Palmas Bellas
Miguel de la Borda
Escobal
Gamboa
Paraíso
Lago Gatún
Volcán Barú 3475
Cerro Chirripó 3819
Volcán Irazú 3432
Volcán Arenal 1633
Cerro Saslaya 1650
PUNTA MANZANILLO
PUNTA BURICA
PUNTA MONA
PUNTA CAHUITA
PUNTA GORDA
PUNTA DE PERLAS
PUNTA MONO
PUNTA LLORONA
PUNTA SALSIPUEDES
PUNTA BANCO
PUNTA CHAME
PUNTA JUDAS
PUNTA QUEPOS
PUNTA LEONA
ISLA DEL VENADO
ISLA SEVILLA
ISLA BOCA BRAVA
ISLA PARIDA
ISLAS SECAS
ISLA DEL CAÑO
ISLA ESCUDO DE VERAGUAS
ISLA COLÓN
ISLA BASTIMENTOS
ISLA DE OMETEPE
ISLA SAN BERNARDO
(31 Meters Above Sea Level)
85°
84°
83°
82°
81°
80°
15°
14°
13°
12°
11°
10°
9°
8°

Map continues pages 246-247

Kilometers 0 50 100 150 Km.

Statute Miles 0 50 100 150 Mi.

Scale 1:3,000,000

One centimeter represents 30 kilometers.
One inch represents approximately 47 miles.
Lambert Conformal Conic Projection

Caribbean Region / Mittelamerikanische Inselwelt / Región del Caribe
Région des Caraïbes / Região do Caribe

Map continues pages 232-233

Map continues pages 236-237

GULF OF MEXICO
UNITED STATES
FLORIDA
Fort Myers
West Palm Beach
Fort Lauderdale
Hollywood
Hialeah
MIAMI
Miami Beach
Coral Gables
Key West
Straits of Florida
GRAND BAHAMA
Freeport
ABACO
Nassau
NEW PROVIDENCE
ANDROS
ELEUTHERA
EXUMA
GREAT BAHAMA BANK
LA HABANA
HAVANA
Matanzas
Cárdenas
Pinar del Río
Santa Clara
Cienfuegos
Sancti Spíritus
Ciego de Ávila
Camagüey
Holguín
Bayamo
Manzanillo
Santiago de Cuba
Guantánamo
CUBA
ISLA DE LA JUVENTUD
(ISLA DE PINOS)
CAYMAN ISLANDS
(U.K.)
George Town
GREATER
Montego Bay
Kingston
Spanish Town
JAMAICA
YUCATAN PENINSULA
PENÍNSULA DE YUCATÁN
Cancún
MEXICO
QUINTANA ROO
Canal de Yucatán
Gulf of Honduras
ISLAS DE LA BAHÍA
La Ceiba
Tegucigalpa
HONDURAS
NICARAGUA
LA MOSQUITIA
Managua
León
Granada
Lago de Nicaragua
Bluefields
COSTA RICA
SAN JOSÉ
Puerto Limón
PANAMÁ
Colón
Panamá
PACIFIC OCEAN
CARIBBEAN
SAN ANDRÉS Y PROVIDENCIA
(Col.)
Barranquilla
Cartagena
Copyright © by Rand McNally & Co.
Map prepared by Rand McNally & Co.
A-530100-764

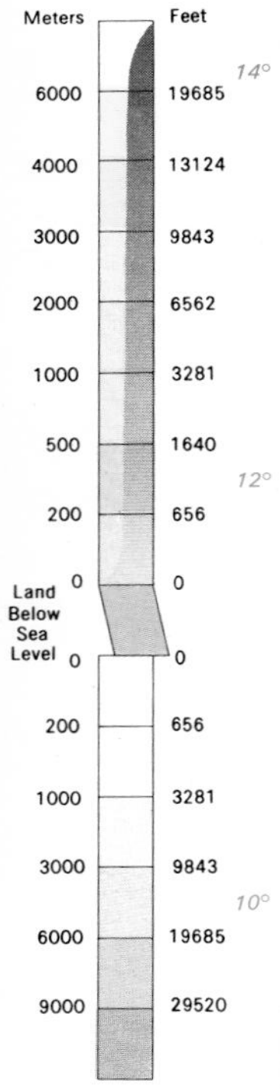
Meters
Feet
6000
19685
4000
13124
3000
9843
2000
6562
1000
3281
500
1640
200
656
0
0
Land Below Sea Level
0
200
656
1000
3281
3000
9843
6000
19685
9000
29520

MAP FORM	bahía	cabo	cerro	channel	golfo	isla	passage	pico	punta
ENGLISH	bay	cape	mountain	channel	gulf	isle	passage	peak	point
DEUTSCH	Bucht	Kap	Berg	Kanal	Golf	Insel	Durchfahrt	Gipfel	Landspitze
ESPAÑOL	bahía	cabo	cerro	canal	golfo	isla	pasaje	pico	punta
FRANÇAIS	baie	cap	montagne	détroit	golfe	île	passage	cime	pointe
PORTUGUÊS	baía	cabo	montanha	canal	golfo	ilha	passagem	pico	ponta

ATLANTIC OCEAN
Sargasso Sea
Tropic of Cancer
TURKS AND CAICOS ISLANDS (U.K.)
CAICOS ISLANDS
GREAT INAGUA
SILVER BANK
INDIES
HAITI
HAÏTI
HISPANIOLA
Port-au-Prince
Cap-Haïtien
Santiago
SANTO DOMINGO
DOMINICAN REPUBLIC
REPÚBLICA DOMINICANA
PUERTO RICO (U.S.)
SAN JUAN
Mayagüez
Ponce
BRITISH VIRGIN ISLANDS
VIRGIN ISLANDS (U.S.)
Charlotte Amalie
Road Town
SAINT CROIX
ANGUILLA
SAINT KITTS AND NEVIS
Basseterre
ANTIGUA AND BARBUDA
Saint John's
MONTSERRAT (U.K.)
Plymouth
GUADELOUPE
Pointe-à-Pitre
Basse-Terre
DOMINICA
Roseau
MARTINIQUE (Fr.)
Fort-de-France
SAINT LUCIA
Castries
SAINT VINCENT AND THE GRENADINES
Kingstown
BARBADOS
Bridgetown
GRENADA
Saint George's
TRINIDAD AND TOBAGO
Port of Spain
LESSER ANTILLES
SEA
ARUBA
Oranjestad
NETHERLANDS ANTILLES
NEDERLANDSE ANTILLEN
Willemstad
CURAÇAO
BONAIRE
Maracaibo
CARACAS
Valencia
Barquisimeto
Maracay
Cumaná
Barcelona
Ciudad Bolívar
COLOMBIA
VENEZUELA
Map continues pages 246-247

Kilometers 0 100 200 300 Km.
Statute Miles 0 100 200 300 Mi.

Scale 1:6,000,000

One centimeter represents 60 kilometers.
One inch represents approximately 95 miles.
Lambert Conformal Conic Projection

Islands of the West Indies / Westindische Inseln / Islas de las Antillas
Îles des Antilles / Ilhas do Caribe (Índias Ocidentais)

a

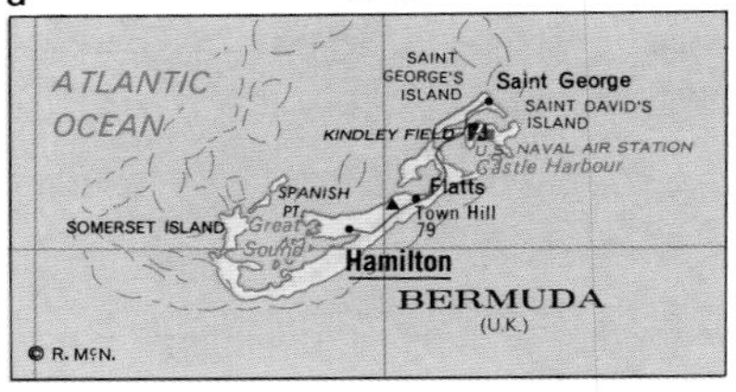
ATLANTIC OCEAN
Saint George
Hamilton
BERMUDA
(U.K.)
© R. McN.

b

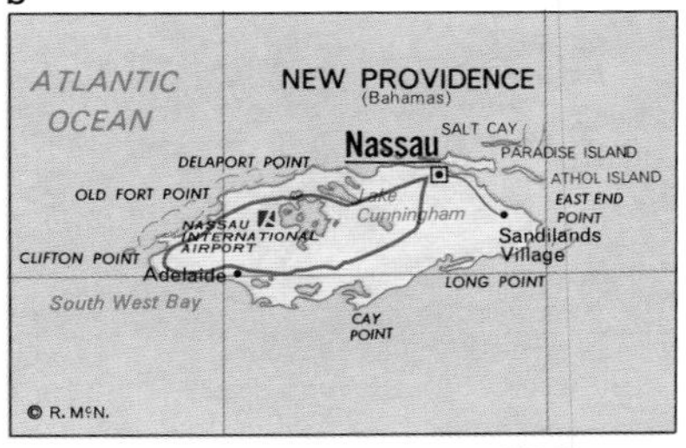
ATLANTIC OCEAN
NEW PROVIDENCE
(Bahamas)
Nassau
South West Bay
© R. McN.

c

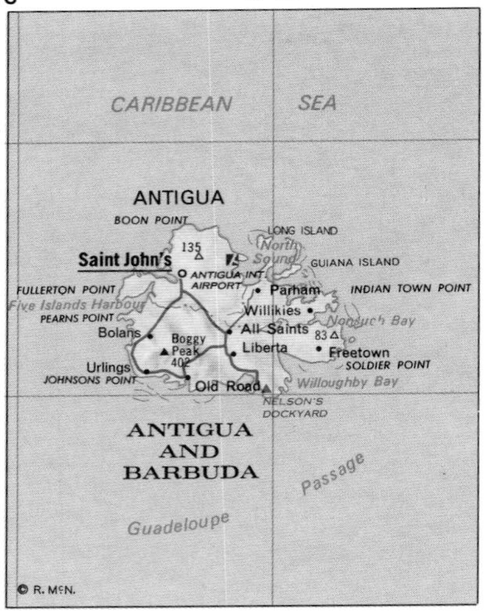
CARIBBEAN SEA
ANTIGUA
Saint John's
ANTIGUA AND BARBUDA
Guadeloupe Passage
© R. McN.

d

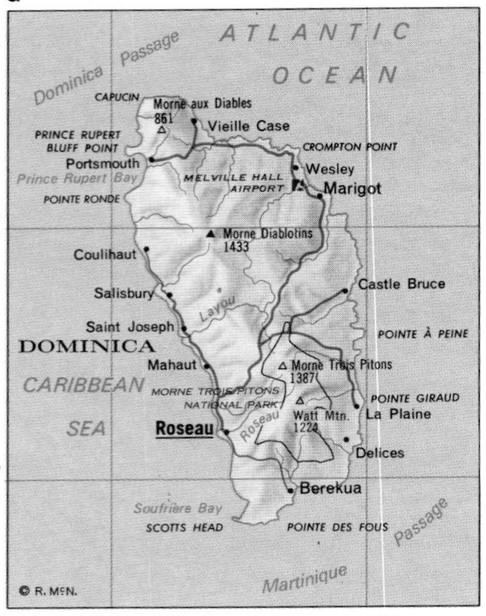
ATLANTIC OCEAN
Dominica Passage
DOMINICA
CARIBBEAN SEA
Roseau
Martinique Passage
© R. McN.

e

ATLANTIC OCEAN
Martinique Passage
Fort-de-France
MARTINIQUE
CARIBBEAN SEA
Saint Lucia Channel
© R. McN.

m

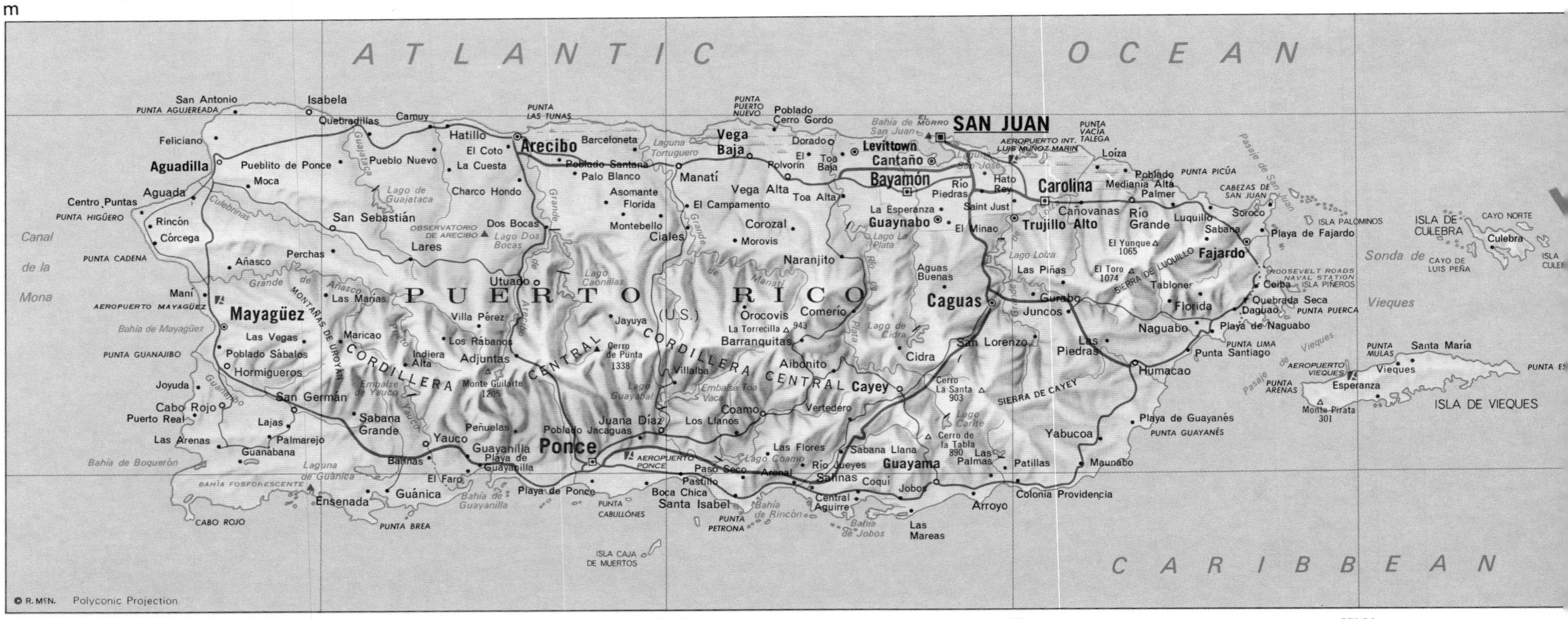
ATLANTIC OCEAN
SAN JUAN
PUERTO RICO (U.S.)
Mayagüez
Ponce
Caguas
Arecibo
Bayamón
ISLA DE CULEBRA
ISLA DE VIEQUES
CARIBBEAN
© R. McN. Polyconic Projection

p

GULF OF MEXICO
LA HABANA
HAVANA
Matanzas
Cárdenas
Pinar del Río
Cienfuegos
Santa Clara
Sancti Spíritus
Nueva Gerona
ISLA DE LA JUVENTUD (ISLA DE PINOS)
CARIBBEAN SEA
CAYMAN ISLANDS (U.K.)
Copyright © by Rand McNally & Co.
Map prepared by Rand McNally & Co.
A-532200-264/764

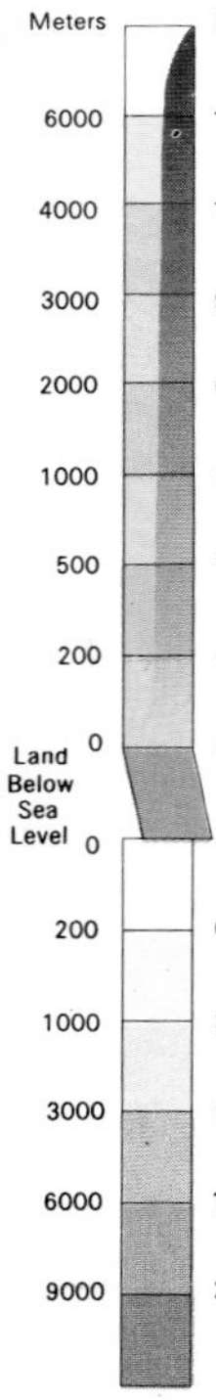
Meters
Feet
6000 19685
4000 13124
3000 9843
2000 6562
1000 3281
500 1640
200 656
0 0
Land Below Sea Level
0 0
200 656
1000 3281
3000 9843
6000 19685
9000 29520

MAP FORM	bahía	cayo	channel	ensenada	golfo	island	mount	passage	point
ENGLISH	bay	cay	channel	bayou	gulf	island	mount	passage	point
DEUTSCH	Bucht	Klippe	Kanal	Altwasser	Golf	Insel	Berg	Durchfahrt	Landspitze
ESPAÑOL	bahía	cayo	canal	ensenada	golfo	isla	montaña	pasaje	punta
FRANÇAIS	baie	caye	détroit	bayou	golfe	île	mont	passage	pointe
PORTUGUÊS	baía	baixio	canal	enseada	golfo	ilha	montanha	passagem	ponta

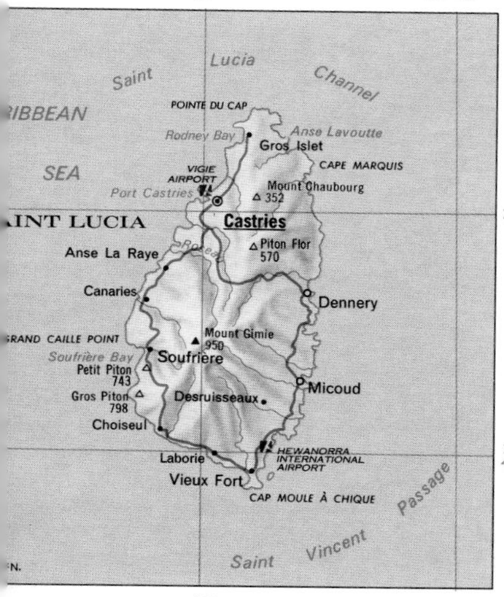
Saint Lucia Channel
CARIBBEAN SEA
SAINT LUCIA
Castries
Gros Islet
Pointe du Cap
Cape Marquis
Mount Chaubourg 352
Piton Flor 570
Anse La Raye
Canaries
Dennery
Mount Gimie 950
Soufrière
Petit Piton 743
Gros Piton 798
Desruisseaux
Micoud
Choiseul
Laborie
Vieux Fort
Hewanorra International Airport
Cap Moule à Chique
Saint Vincent Passage

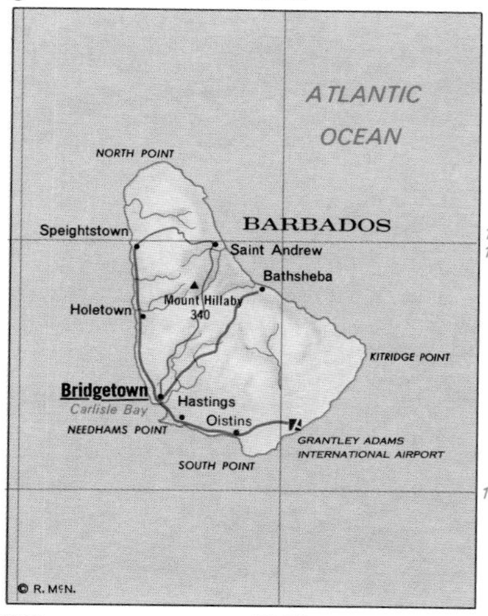
g
ATLANTIC OCEAN
BARBADOS
North Point
Speightstown
Saint Andrew
Bathsheba
Holetown
Mount Hillaby 340
Bridgetown
Carlisle Bay
Needhams Point
Hastings
Oistins
Kitridge Point
South Point
Grantley Adams International Airport
© R. McN.

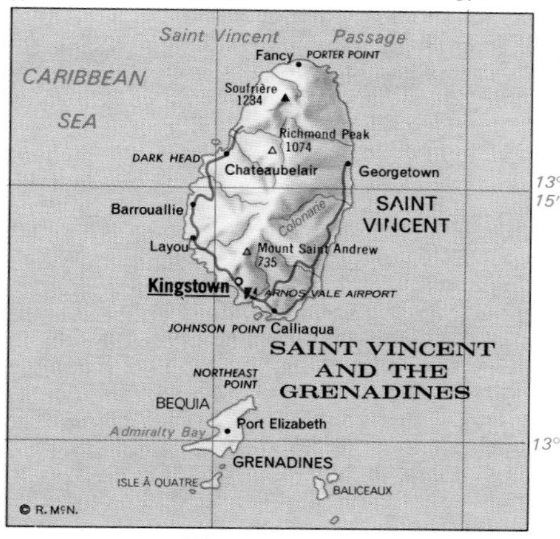
h
Saint Vincent Passage
CARIBBEAN SEA
Fancy
Porter Point
Soufrière 1234
Richmond Peak 1074
Dark Head
Chateaubelair
Georgetown
SAINT VINCENT
Barrouallie
Layou
Mount Saint Andrew 735
Kingstown
Arnos Vale Airport
Johnson Point
Calliaqua
SAINT VINCENT AND THE GRENADINES
Northeast Point
Bequia
Admiralty Bay
Port Elizabeth
GRENADINES
Isle à Quatre
Baliceaux
© R. McN.

k
CARIBBEAN SEA
Ronde Island
Tanga Langua
Green Island
Victoria
Sauteurs
Gouyave
Mount Saint Catherine 840
Tivoli
Grand Roy
Grenville
Telescope Point
Grenville Bay
Molinière Point
Mount Sinai 703
Marquis
Saint George's
Grande Anse Bay
Point Salines
Point Salines International Airport
Prickly Point
Point of Fort Jeudy
GRENADA
© R. McN.

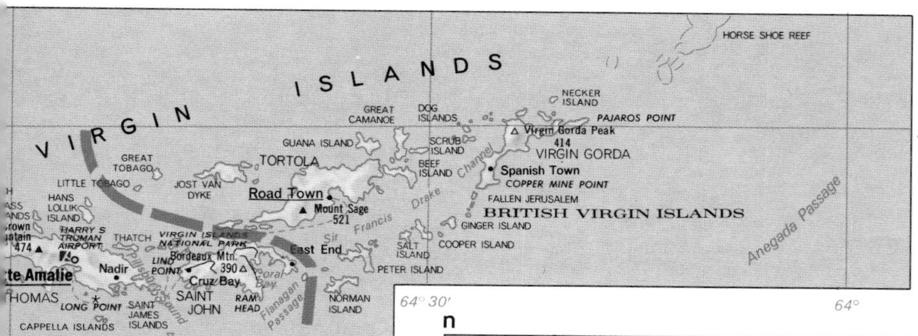
VIRGIN ISLANDS
Horse Shoe Reef
Necker Island
Pajaros Point
Virgin Gorda Peak 414
VIRGIN GORDA
Great Camanoe
Dog Islands
Scrub Island
Guana Island
Tortola
Great Tobago
Jost Van Dyke
Little Tobago
Beef Island
Road Town
Mount Sage 521
Spanish Town
Copper Mine Point
Fallen Jerusalem
BRITISH VIRGIN ISLANDS
Ginger Island
Cooper Island
Salt Island
Peter Island
Anegada Passage
Francis Drake Channel
Cruz Bay
East End
Saint John
Ram Head
Norman Island
Charlotte Amalie
Saint Thomas
Long Point
Nadir
Cappella Islands
Saint James Islands
VIRGIN ISLANDS (U.S.)
Frenchcap Cay
SEA

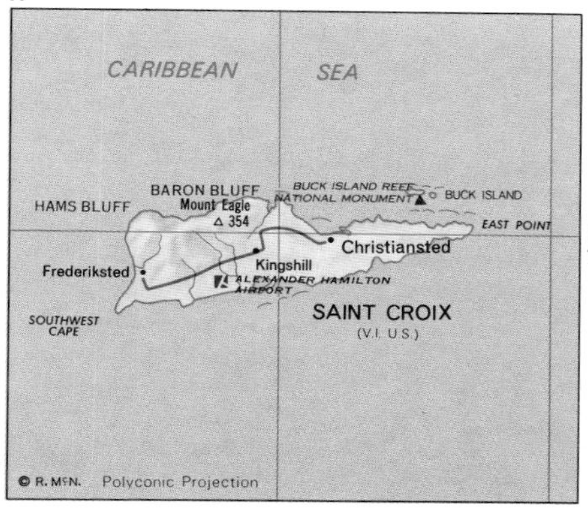
n
CARIBBEAN SEA
Hams Bluff
Baron Bluff
Mount Eagle 354
Buck Island Reef National Monument
Buck Island
East Point
Christiansted
Frederiksted
Kingshill
Alexander Hamilton Airport
Southwest Cape
SAINT CROIX (V.I. U.S.)
© R. McN. Polyconic Projection

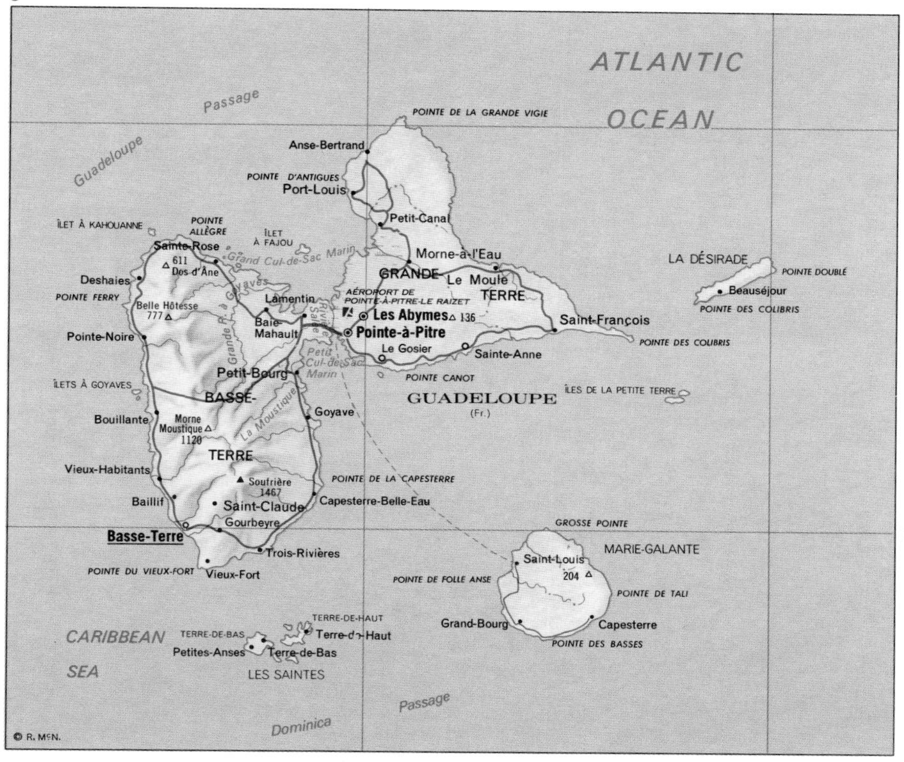
o
ATLANTIC OCEAN
Guadeloupe Passage
Pointe de la Grande Vigie
Anse-Bertrand
Pointe d'Antigues
Port-Louis
Petit-Canal
Îlet à Kahouanne
Pointe Allègre
Îlet à Fajou
Sainte-Rose
Grand Cul-de-Sac Marin
Morne-à-l'Eau
GRANDE-TERRE
Le Moule
LA DÉSIRADE
Pointe Doublé
Beauséjour
Pointe des Colibris
Deshaies
Pointe Ferry
Lamentin
Aéroport de Pointe-à-Pitre-Le Raizet
Les Abymes
Pointe-à-Pitre
Saint-François
Pointe des Colibris
Baie-Mahault
Le Gosier
Sainte-Anne
Pointe-Noire
Petit-Bourg
Pointe Canot
Îlets à Goyaves
BASSE-TERRE
Îles de la Petite Terre
GUADELOUPE (Fr.)
Bouillante
Goyave
Vieux-Habitants
Soufrière 1467
Pointe de la Capesterre
Baillif
Saint-Claude
Capesterre-Belle-Eau
Gourbeyre
Basse-Terre
Trois-Rivières
Pointe du Vieux-Fort
Vieux-Fort
Grosse Pointe
MARIE-GALANTE
Saint-Louis
Pointe de Folle Anse
Pointe de Tali
Grand-Bourg
Capesterre
Pointe des Basses
CARIBBEAN SEA
Terre-de-Bas
Terre-de-Haut
Petites-Anses
LES SAINTES
Dominica Passage
© R. McN.

Kilometers 0 10 20 30 40 50 Km.
Statute Miles 0 10 20 30 40 50 Mi.

Scale 1:1,000,000
One centimeter represents 10 kilometers.
One inch represents approximately 16 miles.
Transverse Mercator Projection (except as noted)

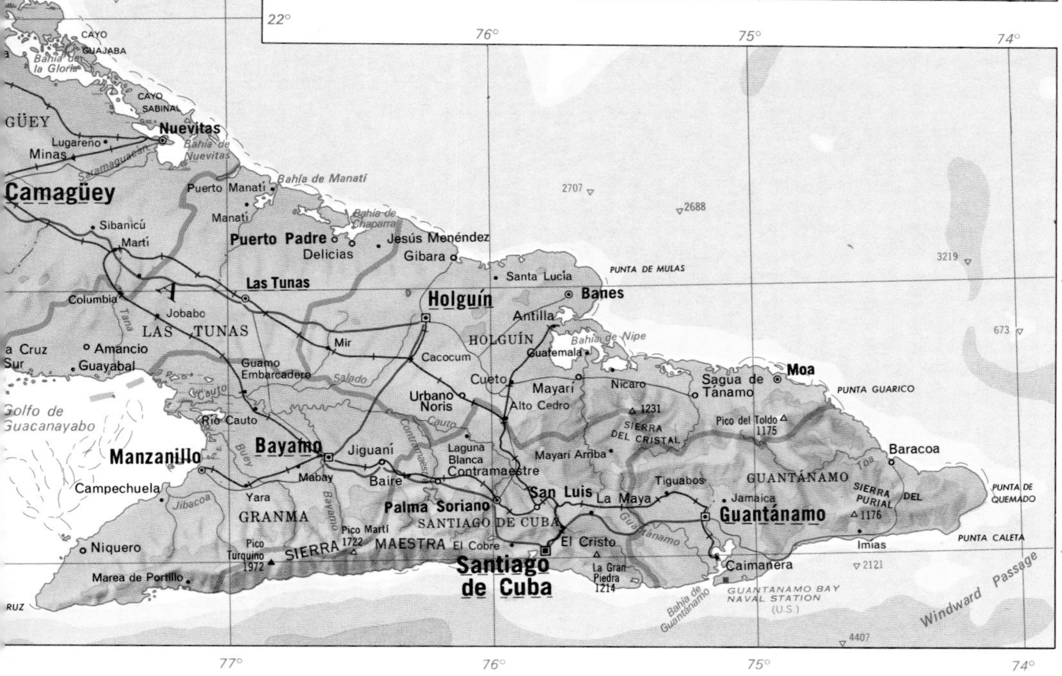
ATLANTIC OCEAN
GREAT BAHAMA BANK
Cay Lobos (Bahamas)
CAMAGÜEY
Nuevitas
Lugareño
Minas
Camagüey
Bahía de Manatí
Puerto Manatí
Manatí
Sibanicú
Martí
Puerto Padre
Delicias
Jesús Menéndez
Gibara
Las Tunas
Santa Lucía
Holguín
Banes
Punta de Mulas
Columbia
Jobabo
LAS TUNAS
Antilla
Amancio
Guayabal
Mir
HOLGUÍN
Guamo Embarcadero
Cacocum
Moa
Punta Guarico
Cueto
Mayarí
Nicaro
Sagua de Tánamo
Golfo de Guacanayabo
Río Cauto
Urbano Noris
Alto Cedro
Manzanillo
Bayamo
Jiguaní
Laguna Blanca
Contramaestre
Baracoa
Campechuela
Yara
Mabay
Baire
San Luis
La Maya
GUANTÁNAMO
GRANMA
Palma Soriano
Guantánamo
SANTIAGO DE CUBA
Niquero
Pico Turquino 1972
SIERRA MAESTRA
El Cobre
El Cristo
Imías
Punta Caleta
Marea de Portillo
Santiago de Cuba
Caimanera
Guantanamo Bay Naval Station (U.S.)
Windward Passage

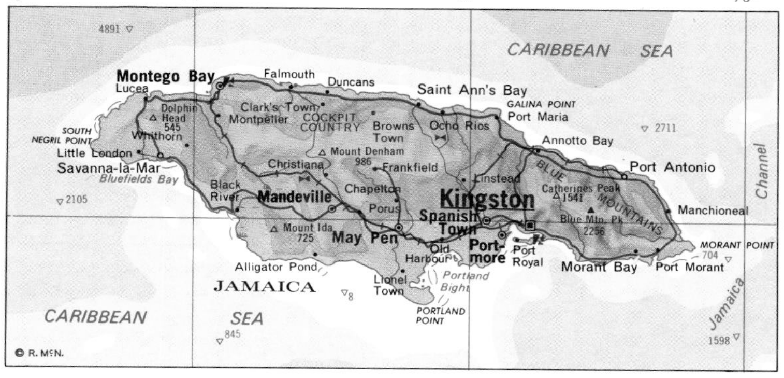
q
CARIBBEAN SEA
Montego Bay
Lucea
Falmouth
Duncans
Saint Ann's Bay
Galina Point
Port Maria
Dolphin Head 545
Whitehorn
Clark's Town
Montpelier
COCKPIT COUNTRY
Browns Town
Ocho Rios
Annotto Bay
South Negril Point
Little London
Savanna-la-Mar
Bluefields Bay
Mount Denham 986
Frankfield
Christiana
Port Antonio
Black River
Mandeville
Chapelton
Porus
Kingston
Spanish Town
Catherines Peak 1541
Blue Mtn. Pk. 2256
BLUE MOUNTAINS
Manchioneal
Mount Ida 725
May Pen
Old Harbour
Portmore
Port Royal
Morant Point
Alligator Pond
JAMAICA
Lionel Town
Portland Bight
Portland Point
Morant Bay
Port Morant
Jamaica Channel
CARIBBEAN SEA
© R. McN.

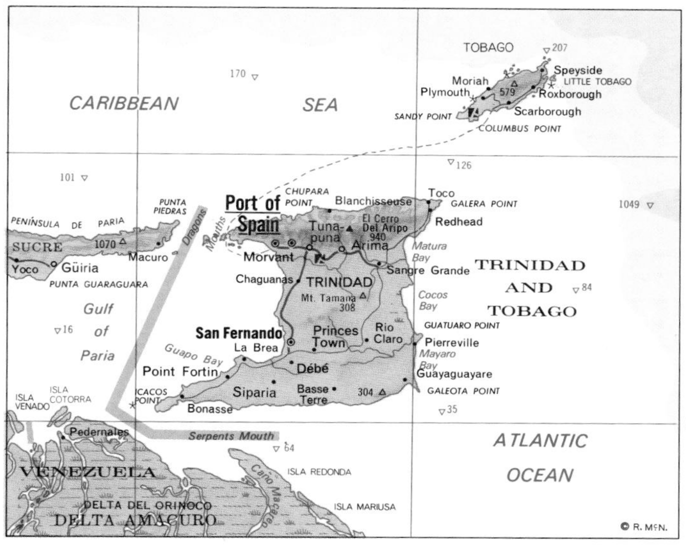
r
CARIBBEAN SEA
TOBAGO
Speyside
Little Tobago
Moriah
Plymouth
Roxborough
Sandy Point
Scarborough
Columbus Point
Península de Paria
Punta Piedras
Chupara Point
Port of Spain
Blanchisseuse
Toco
Galera Point
El Cerro del Aripo 940
Redhead
SUCRE
Güiria
Yoco
Punta Guaraguara
Macuro
Tunapuna
Arima
Morvant
Chaguanas
Matura Bay
Sangre Grande
TRINIDAD AND TOBAGO
TRINIDAD
Mt. Tamana 308
Cocos Bay
Gulf of Paria
San Fernando
La Brea
Princes Town
Rio Claro
Guatuaro Point
Pierreville
Mayaro Bay
Guapo Bay
Point Fortin
Débé
Guayaguayare
Galeota Point
Icacos Point
Siparia
Basse Terre
Isla Cotorra
Bonasse
Pedernales
Serpents Mouth
VENEZUELA
DELTA DEL ORINOCO
DELTA AMACURO
Isla Redonda
Isla Marilusa
ATLANTIC OCEAN
© R. McN.

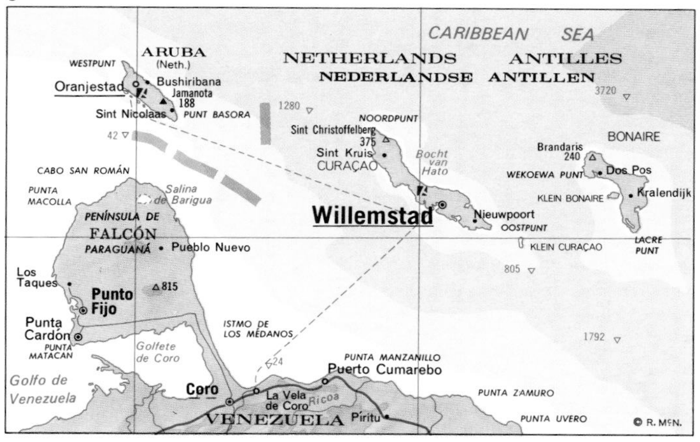
s
CARIBBEAN SEA
ARUBA (Neth.)
Westpunt
Oranjestad
Bushiribana
Jamanota 188
Sint Nicolaas
Punt Basora
NETHERLANDS ANTILLES
NEDERLANDSE ANTILLEN
Noordpunt
Sint Christoffelberg 375
Sint Kruis
CURAÇAO
Bocht van Hato
BONAIRE
Brandaris 240
Dos Pos
Wekoewa Punt
Klein Bonaire
Kralendijk
Cabo San Román
Punta Macolla
Salina de Bariqua
Península de Paraguaná
FALCÓN
Willemstad
Nieuwpoort
Oostpunt
Klein Curaçao
Lacre Punt
Pueblo Nuevo
Los Taques
Punto Fijo
Punta Cardón
Punta Matacán
Golfete de Coro
Istmo de los Médanos
Golfo de Venezuela
Punta Manzanillo
Puerto Cumarebo
Coro
La Vela de Coro
Punta Zamuro
VENEZUELA
Píritu
Punta Uvero
© R. McN.

Kilometers 0 50 100 150 Km.
Statute Miles 0 50 100 150 Mi.

Scale 1:3,000,000
One centimeter represents 30 kilometers.
One inch represents approximately 47 miles.
Lambert Conformal Conic Projection

Map continues pages 230-231

CARIBBEAN SEA
PACIFIC OCEAN
NICARAGUA
COSTA RICA
PANAMÁ
COLOMBIA
VENEZUELA
ECUADOR
PERU
BOLIVIA
CHILE
ARGENTINA
ACRE
AMAZONAS
RONDÔNIA
SELVA
LLANOS
ALTIPLANO
ANDES
CORDILLERA OCCIDENTAL
CORDILLERA CENTRAL
CORDILLERA ORIENTAL
CORDILLERA REAL
LESSER ANTILLES
ARUBA (Neth.)
NETHERLANDS ANTILLES
SAINT VINCENT AND THE GRENADINES
Managua
Masaya
Granada
SAN JOSÉ
Panamá
Colón
Barranquilla
Cartagena
Santa Marta
Maracaibo
CARACAS
Valencia
Barquisimeto
Medellín
Cali
Manizales
SANTA FE DE BOGOTÁ
Bucaramanga
Cúcuta
QUITO
Guayaquil
Cuenca
Iquitos
Trujillo
Chiclayo
Chimbote
Callao
LIMA
Huancayo
Cusco
Arequipa
LA PAZ
Cochabamba
Sucre
Potosí
Oruro
Santa Cruz de la Sierra
Arica
Tacna
Iquique
Porto Velho
Rio Branco
Amazon
Solimões
Equator
Copyright © by Rand McNally & Co.
Map prepared by Esselte Map Service AB, Stockholm.

Kilometers 0 200 400 600 Km.

Statute Miles 0 200 400 600 Mi.

Scale 1:12,000,000

One centimeter represents 120 kilometers.
One inch represents approximately 190 miles.
Oblique Conic Conformal Projection

ATLANTIC OCEAN
Equator
Tropic of Capricorn
55°
50°
45°
40°
35°
10°
5°
0°
15°
20°
Georgetown
Paramaribo
SURINAME
FRENCH GUIANA
Cayenne
CABO ORANGE
TUMUC-HUMAC MTS.
AMAPÁ
Macapá
ILHA DE MARAJÓ
CABO MAGUARI
Belém
Amazonas
Santarém
PARÁ
Represa de Tucuruí
Marabá
SERRA DOS CARAJÁS
Imperatriz
São Luís
MARANHÃO
Teresina
Parnaíba
Fortaleza
CEARÁ
ATOL DAS ROCAS
ILHA FERNANDO DE NORONHA (Brazil)
CABO DE SÃO ROQUE
Natal
RIO GRANDE DO NORTE
PIAUÍ
Mossoró
Campina Grande
João Pessoa
PONTA DO SEIXAS
PARAÍBA
PERNAMBUCO
Recife
Olinda
Caruaru
Juazeiro do Norte
Petrolina
Juazeiro
ALAGOAS
Maceió
SERGIPE
Aracaju
SERRA DO CACHIMBO
TOCANTINS
Palmas
ILHA DO BANANAL
BRAZIL
BAHIA
Feira de Santana
Salvador
ILHA DE TINHARÉ
Vitória da Conquista
Ilhéus
Itabuna
MATO GROSSO
PLANALTO DO MATO GROSSO
Cuiabá
Rondonópolis
GOIÁS
BRASÍLIA
D.F.
PLANALTO CENTRAL
Anápolis
Goiânia
Montes Claros
MINAS GERAIS
Governador Valadares
ESPÍRITO SANTO
Belo Horizonte
Vitória
Vila Velha
MATO GROSSO DO SUL
Corumbá
Campo Grande
Uberlândia
Uberaba
Ribeirão Preto
SÃO PAULO
Presidente Prudente
Campinas
São José dos Campos
Juiz de Fora
Volta Redonda
Petrópolis
Niterói
RIO DE JANEIRO
CABO FRIO
CABO DE SÃO TOMÉ
Campos
SÃO PAULO
Santo André
Santos
São Vicente
ILHA DE SÃO SEBASTIÃO
ILHA GRANDE

MAP FORM	cerro	cordillera	ilha	lago	nevado	península	serra
ENGLISH	mountain	range	island	lake	mountain	peninsula	mountains
DEUTSCH	Berg	Gebirge	Insel	See	Berg	Halbinsel	Berge
ESPAÑOL	montaña	cordillera	isla	lago	montaña	península	montañas
FRANÇAIS	montagne	chaîne	île	lac	montagne	péninsule	montagnes
PORTUGUÊS	montanha	cordilheira	ilha	lago	montanha	península	montanhas

Map continues pages 244-245

Map continues pages 242-243

PACIFIC OCEAN
CHILE
ARGENTINA
BOLIVIA
Tropic of Capricorn
ANDES
PATAGONIA
CHACO
ATACAMA
Antofagasta
Salta
San Miguel de Tucumán
Santiago del Estero
Córdoba
Santa Fe
Rosario
BUENOS AIRES
Asunción
Resistencia
La Serena
Coquimbo
San Juan
Mendoza
Valparaíso
Viña del Mar
SANTIAGO
Rancagua
Talca
Chillán
Concepción
Talcahuano
Temuco
Valdivia
Osorno
Puerto Montt
Bahía Blanca
Neuquén
Comodoro Rivadavia
Río Gallegos
Punta Arenas
Puerto Natales
Ushuaia
ISLA GRANDE DE CHILOÉ
ARCHIPIÉLAGO DE LOS CHONOS
ISLA WELLINGTON
ISLA GRANDE DE TIERRA DEL FUEGO
ISLA DE LOS ESTADOS
ARCHIPIÉLAGO JUAN FERNÁNDEZ (Chile)
ISLA SAN FÉLIX (Chile)
ISLA SAN AMBROSIO (Chile)
FALKL ISLAN (U.K.)
WEST FALKLAND
Golfo San Matías
Golfo San Jorge
Estrecho de Magallanes
Copyright © by Rand McNally & Co.
Map prepared by Esselte Map Service AB, Stockholm.
A-549200-264 -6 -8 -10

MAP FORM	cerro, co.	golfo	ilha	isla	lago	lagoa	monte	salar
ENGLISH	butte	gulf	island	isle	lake	lake	mountain	saltflat
DEUTSCH	Restberg	Golf	Insel	Insel	See	See	Berg	Salzebene
ESPAÑOL	cerro	golfo	isla	isla	lago	lago	montaña	salobral
FRANÇAIS	butte	golfe	île	île	lac	lac	montagne	salina
PORTUGUÊS	colina	golfo	ilha	ilha	lago	lago	montanha	salina

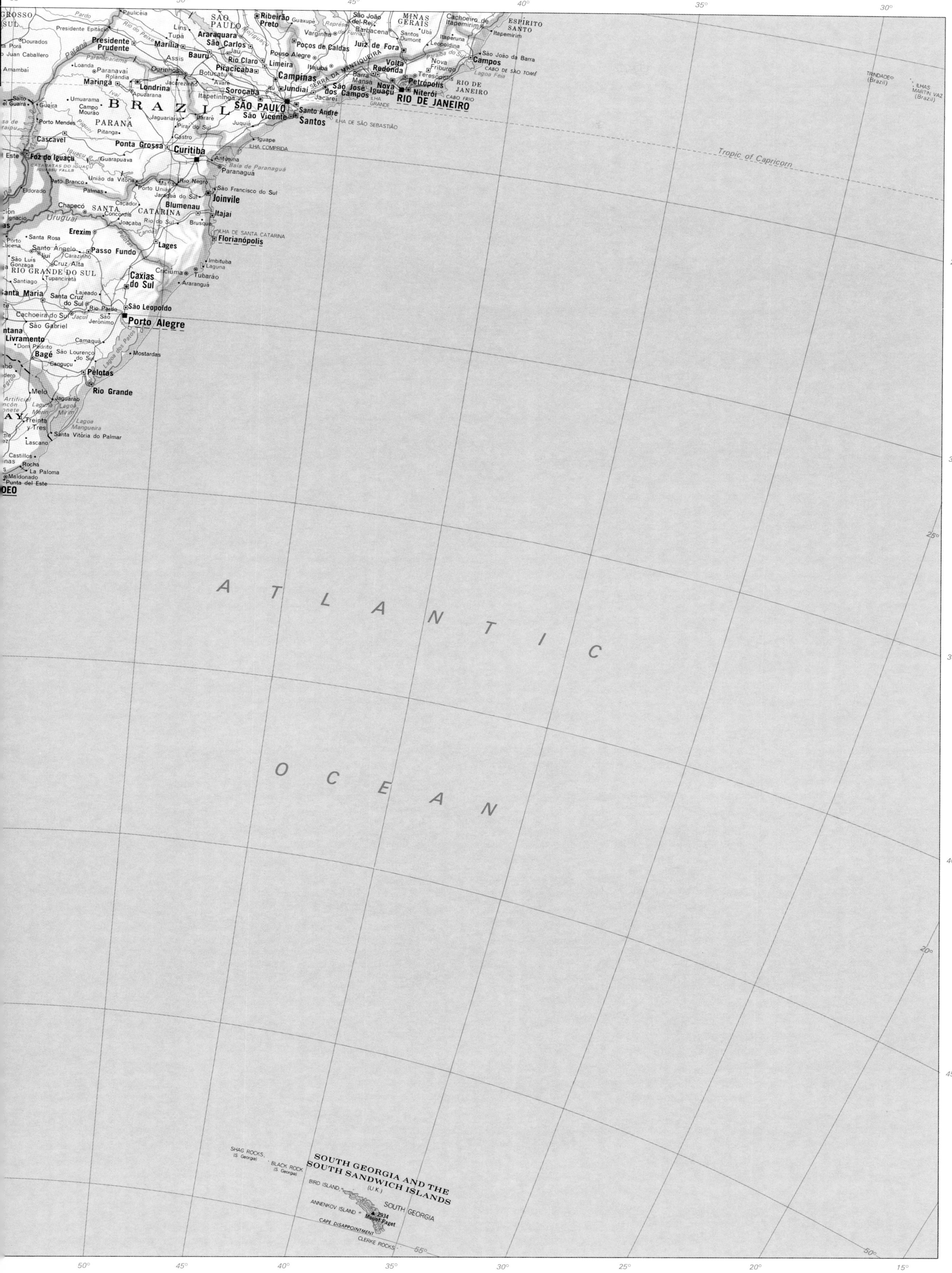
BRAZIL
SÃO PAULO
RIO DE JANEIRO
MINAS GERAIS
ESPIRITO SANTO
PARANA
SANTA CATARINA
RIO GRANDE DO SUL
Ribeirão Preto
Araraquara
São Carlos
Presidente Prudente
Marília
Bauru
Piracicaba
Campinas
Sorocaba
Jundiaí
São José dos Campos
Santo André
São Vicente
Santos
Londrina
Maringá
Juiz de Fora
Volta Redonda
Barra Mansa
Nova Iguaçu
Niterói
Petrópolis
Campos
Ponta Grossa
Curitiba
Paranaguá
Foz do Iguaçu
Cascavel
Joinvile
Blumenau
Itajaí
Florianópolis
Lages
Erexim
Passo Fundo
Caxias do Sul
Santa Maria
São Leopoldo
Porto Alegre
Pelotas
Rio Grande
Bagé
Livramento
Melo
Criciúma
Tubarão
Uruguai
Tropic of Capricorn
TRINDADE (Brazil)
ILHAS MARTIN VAZ (Brazil)
ATLANTIC
OCEAN
SOUTH GEORGIA AND THE SOUTH SANDWICH ISLANDS (U.K.)
SHAG ROCKS (S. Georgia)
BLACK ROCK (S. Georgia)
BIRD ISLAND
ANNENKOV ISLAND
SOUTH GEORGIA
Mount Paget 2934
CAPE DISAPPOINTMENT
CLERKE ROCKS
55°
50°
45°
40°
35°
30°
25°
20°
15°

Kilometers 0 200 400 600 Km.

Statute Miles 0 200 400 600 Mi.

Scale 1:12,000,000

One centimeter represents 120 kilometers.

One inch represents approximately 190 miles.

Oblique Conic Conformal Projection

Map continues pages 238-239

CARIBBEAN SEA
PACIFIC OCEAN
NICARAGUA
SAN ANDRÉS Y PROVIDENCIA (Col.)
Puerto Limón
Colón
Panamá
David
Santiago
ARCH. DE LAS PERLAS
ISLA DE COIBA
Barranquilla
Santa Marta
Cartagena
Riohacha
Maracaibo
Cabimas
Ciudad Ojeda
Valledupar
Montería
Sincelejo
Magangué
Cúcuta
San Cristóbal
Mérida
Bucaramanga
Medellín
Quibdó
Manizales
Pereira
Armenia
Ibagué
SANTA FE DE BOGOTÁ
Villavicencio
Tunja
Buenaventura
Cali
Palmira
Popayán
Neiva
Florencia
Pasto
Tumaco
Esmeraldas
Ibarra
QUITO
Santo Domingo de los Colorados
Manta
Portoviejo
Ambato
Riobamba
Guayaquil
Machala
Cuenca
Loja
Tumbes
Talara
Sullana
Iquitos
a
PACIFIC OCEAN
ARCHIPIÉLAGO DE COLÓN
GALAPAGOS ISLANDS
GALÁPAGOS (Ec.)
ISLA ISABELA
ISLA SANTA CRUZ
ISLA SAN CRISTÓBAL
Copyright © by Rand McNally & Co.
Map prepared by Rand McNally & Co.

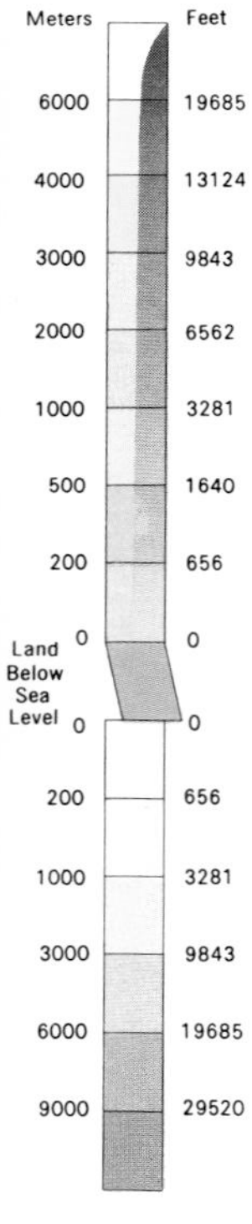
Meters
Feet
6000
19685
4000
13124
3000
9843
2000
6562
1000
3281
500
1640
200
656
0
0
Land Below Sea Level
0
0
200
656
1000
3281
3000
9843
6000
19685
9000
29520

MAP FORM	bahía	cabo	cerro, co.	golfo	igarapé	isla, i.	lago, l.	punta	volcán, vol.
ENGLISH	bay	cape	butte	gulf	river	island	lake	point	volcano
DEUTSCH	Bucht	Kap	Restberg	Golf	Fluss	Insel	See	Landspitze	Vulkan
ESPAÑOL	bahía	cabo	cerro	golfo	río	isla	lago	punta	volcán
FRANÇAIS	baie	cap	butte	golfe	rivière	île	lac	pointe	volcan
PORTUGUÊS	baía	cabo	colina	golfo	rio	ilha	lago	ponta	vulcão

Map continues pages 248-249

Map continues
pages 238-239

NETHERLANDS ANTILLES
NEDERLANDSE ANTILLEN
BONAIRE
Kralendijk
LESSER ANTILLES
ISLAS LAS AVES (Ven.)
ISLAS LOS ROQUES (Ven.)
ISLA LA ORCHILA (Ven.)
ISLA BLANQUILLA (Ven.)
ISLAS LOS HERMANOS (Ven.)
ISLAS LOS TESTIGOS (Ven.)
CARRIACOU
GRENADINES
Victoria
Saint George's
GRENADA
TOBAGO
Speyside
Scarborough
TRINIDAD AND TOBAGO
Port of Spain
Arima
Sangre Grande
San Fernando
Point Fortin
Siparia
Princes Town
Rio Claro
GALERA POINT
GALEOTA POINT
ATLANTIC OCEAN
NUEVA ESPARTA
ISLA DE MARGARITA
La Asunción
Juangriego
Porlamar
Boca de Pozo
Punta de Piedras
Carúpano
ISLA LA TORTUGA (Ven.)
DISTRITO FEDERAL
Maiquetía
Petare
CARACAS
Los Teques
Guarenas
MIRANDA
Puerto Cabello
Maracay
Valencia
CARABOBO
ARAGUA
San Juan de los Morros
Tucacas
Chichiriviche
San Juan de los Cayos
Tocuyo de la Costa
PUNTA TUCACAS
CABO CODERA
Puerto la Cruz
Barcelona
Pozuelos
Cumaná
SUCRE
Cariaco
Casanay
Golfo de Cariaco
Río Caribe
PENÍNSULA DE PARIA
Gulf of Paria
Güiria
Yoco
Irapa
Maturín
MONAGAS
Caripito
Anaco
El Tigre
San Tomé
San José de Guanipa
ANZOÁTEGUI
DELTA AMACURO
Tucupita
ORINOCO
Boca Grande
Ciudad Guayana
Ciudad Bolívar
Soledad
Upata
El Palmar
Guasipati
El Callao
Tumeremo
El Dorado
El Manteco
BOLÍVAR
Canaima
SALTO ANGEL / ANGEL FALLS
Auyán Tepuy 2950
LA GRAN SABANA
PARQUE NACIONAL CANAIMA
Tirá Tepuy 2620
Mount Roraima 2875
Santa Elena de Uairén
PAKARAIMA MOUNTAINS
Luepa
Cerro Guaiquinima 2100
Cerro Campanero 2200
Cerro Bolívar
Ciudad Piar
La Paragua
Arabelo
Cacurí
Cerro Uquila 2500
GUÁRICO
Calabozo
Valle de la Pascua
Espino
PARQUE NACIONAL AGUARO-GUARIQUITO
Camaguán
San Fernando
APURE
Achaguas
Arichuna
San Juan de Payara
Cunaviche
La Urbana
Santa Rosa
Caicara de Orinoco
Maripa
Cerro Mato 1863
COJEDES
Acarigua
Barquisimeto
Puerto Páez
Puerto Carreño
VENEZUELA
COLOMBIA
Puerto Ayacucho
Cerro Guanay 2300
Cerro Yaví 2441
Samariapo
Morganito
Puerto Nariño
Cerro Ovana 1978
San Fernando de Atabapo
Puerto Inírida
Santa Bárbara
AMAZONAS
Cerro Marahuaca 2579
Cerro Duida 2400
La Esmeralda
Yavita
Maroa
Victorino
SIERRA PARIMA
San Felipe
San Carlos de Río Negro
Santa Rosa de Amanadona
Cucuí
Cerro Avispa 2112
Pico Tamacuarí 2340
Pico da Neblina 3014
BRAZIL
ILHA PEDRO II
PARQUE NACIONAL DO PICO DA NEBLINA
Içana
Taraquá
Uaupés
Negro
Tapurucuara
ILHA TAMANQUARÉ
AMAZONAS
Barcelos
Carvoeiro
Moura
Represa Balbina
Japurá
Maraã
ILHA MAPIXARI
PARQUE NACIONAL DO JAÚ
ARQUIPÉLAGO DAS ANAVILHANAS
Airão
Manaus
Manacapuru
Caapiranga
Anamã
Anori
Codajás
Beruri
Coari
Tefé
Alvarães
Fonte Boa
Tamaniquá
Tonantins
Copatana
Santo Antônio do Içá
Amaturá
São Paulo de Olivença
Rita do Weil
Juruá
Carauari
Concórdia
Jutaí
Solimões
Amazon
Purus
Madeira
Lago Badajós
Lago Piorini
Lago Coari
Lago Mamiá
Lago Aiapuá
Anamã
Autazes
Careiro
ILHA DO CAREIRO
Itacoatiara
Murutinga
Nova Olinda do Norte
Axinim
Borba
Canumã
Novo Aripuanã
Itapiranga
Urucará
Urucurituba
Parintins
Barreirinha
Maués
TUPINAMBARANA
ILHA DO RISCO
Nhamundá
Faro
Terra Santa
Lago do Erepecuru
PARQUE NACIONAL DA AMAZÔNIA
PARÁ
Trombetas
CACHOEIRA DAS ILHAS
RORAIMA
Boa Vista
Caracaraí
São José de Anauá
Boiaçu
Uraricoera
ILHA DE MARACÁ
Conceição do Maú
Equator
Branco
GUYANA
BARIMA-WAINI
Morawhanna
Mabaruma
Matthews Ridge
POMEROON-SUPENAAM
ESSEQUIBO ISLANDS-WEST DEMERARA
DEMERARA-MAHAICA
MAHAICA-BERBICE
Georgetown
Anna Regina
Charity
Queenstown
Suddie
Parika
Vreed en Hoop
Mahaicony Village
Fort Wellington
Bush Lot
Rosignol
Rosehall
New Amsterdam
Linden
Bartica
Rockstone
Wismar
CUYUNI-MAZARUNI
UPPER DEMERARA-BERBICE
Ituni
Issano
Potaro Landing
Tumatumari
Mahdia
KAIETEUR NATIONAL PARK
KAIETEUR FALL
POTARO-SIPARUNI
Holmia
Orinduik
Mount Makarapan 934
Lethem
Saint Ignatius
KANUKU MOUNTAINS
UPPER TAKUTU-UPPER ESSEQUIBO
Dadanawa
Isherton
KAMOA MOUNTAINS
ACARAI MOUNTAINS
EAST BERBICE-CORENTYNE
Corriverton
Nieuw Nickerie
Wageningen
NICKERIE
CORONIE
Apoera
Bakhuis
SIPALIWINI
WILHELMINA GEB.
Juliana Top 1230
KAYSER GEBERGTE
SURINAME
Corentyne

Map continues
pages 250-251

Kilometers 0 100 200 300 Km.

Statute Miles 0 100 200 300 Mi.

Scale 1:6,000,000

One centimeter represents 60 kilometers.
One inch represents approximately 95 miles.

Oblique Conic Conformal Projection

Peru, Bolivia and Western Brazil / Peru, Bolivien und westliches Brasilien / Perú, Bolivia y Brasil Occidental
Pérou, Bolivie et Brésil Occidental / Peru, Bolívia e Brasil Ocidental

PACIFIC
OCEAN
CORDILLERA OCCIDENTAL
CORDILLERA CENTRAL
CORDILLERA ORIENTAL
ANDES
LORETO
UCAYALI
ACRE
MADRE DE DIOS
PUNO
AREQUIPA
LIMA
Callao
Trujillo
Chiclayo
Piura
Sullana
Chimbote
Huaraz
Huánuco
Cerro de Pasco
Huancayo
Ayacucho
Cusco
Arequipa
Juliaca
Puno
Tacna
Arica
Iquique
Tocopilla
Ica
Pisco
Nazca
Pucallpa
Yurimaguas
Moyobamba
Tarapoto
Cajamarca
Chincha Alta
Mollendo
Ilo
Cruzeiro do Sul
Meters
Feet
6000 19685
4000 13124
3000 9843
2000 6562
1000 3281
500 1640
200 656
0 0
Land Below Sea Level
0 0
200 656
1000 3281
3000 9843
6000 19685
9000 29520
Copyright © by Rand McNally & Co.
Map prepared by Rand McNally & Co.
A-549792-764

MAP FORM	cerro	cordillera	isla, i.	lago, l.	nevado	punta	rio	serra
ENGLISH	mountain	mountains	island	lake	mountain	point	river	mountains
DEUTSCH	Berg	Berge	Insel	See	Berg	Landspitze	Fluss	Berge
ESPAÑOL	montaña	montañas	isla	lago	nevado	punta	rio	sierra
FRANÇAIS	montagne	montagnes	île	lac	montagne	pointe	rivière	montagnes
PORTUGUÊS	montanha	montanhas	ilha	lago	pico nevado	ponta	rio	serra

Map continues pages 246-247

AMAZONAS
SELVAS
PARÁ
RONDÔNIA
MATO GROSSO
MATO GROSSO DO SUL
PANDO
BENI
COCHABAMBA
SANTA CRUZ
CHUQUISACA
POTOSÍ
TARIJA
ALTO PARAGUAY
CHACO BOREAL
NUEVA ASUNCIÓN
BOQUERÓN
GRAN CHACO
SALTA
JUJUY
ARGENTINA
BRAZIL
BOLIVIA
BRASIL
PARAGUAY
SERRA DO CACHIMBO
SERRA DOS APIACÁS
SERRA DO NORTE
SERRA DO TOMBADOR
CHAPADA DOS PARECIS
PLANALTO DO MATO GROSSO
SERRA FORMOSA
SERRA DE MARACAJU
SERRA DA BODOQUENA
SERRANÍA DE HUANCHACA
SERRANÍA DE SANTIAGO
SERRANÍA DE AGUARAGUE
CORDILLERA REAL
CORDILLERA ORIENTAL
ALTIPLANO
Salar de Uyuni
Lago Poopó
Pantanal de São Lourenço
Porto Velho
Rio Branco
Humaitá
Ariquemes
Ji-Paraná
Vilhena
Guajará-Mirim
Trinidad
Cochabamba
Santa Cruz de la Sierra
Oruro
Sucre
Potosí
Tarija
Cuiabá
Várzea Grande
Cáceres
Rondonópolis
Corumbá
Campo Grande
Dourados
Ponta Porã
Pedro Juan Caballero
Puerto Suarez
Madeira
Purus
Guaporé
Mamoré
Beni
Paraguai
Pilcomayo
Juruena
Aripuanã
Machado
Scale 1:6,000,000

Kilometers 0 100 200 300 Km.

Statute Miles 0 100 200 300 Mi.

Scale 1:6,000,000

One centimeter represents 60 kilometers.
One inch represents approximately 95 miles.
Oblique Conic Conformal Projection

Map continues pages 250-251

Map continues page 255

Map continues pages 252-253

Paramaribo
Lelydorp
New Amsterdam
Nieuw Nickerie
Totness
Corriverton
CORONIE
NICKERIE
SARAMACCA
PARA
WANICA
COMMEWIJNE
MAROWIJNE
BROKOPONDO
SIPALIWINI
EAST BERBICE-CORENTYNE
KAYSER GEBERGTE
WILHELMINA GEB.
ORANJE GEB.
TUMUC-HUMAC MOUNTAINS
SURINAME
GUYANA
FRENCH GUIANA
GUYANE FRANÇAISE
BRAZIL
BRASIL
SAINT-LAURENT-DU-MARONI
CAYENNE
Cayenne
Kourou
Saint-Laurent-du-Maroni
Maripasoula
Saül
Saint-Georges
Oiapoque
PARQUE NACIONAL DO CABO ORANGE
CABO ORANGE
AMAPÁ
Macapá
Serra do Navio
Calçoene
Amapá
ILHA DE MARACÁ
ILHA CAVIANA DE FORA
ILHA MEXIANA
ILHA DE MARAJÓ
ILHA GRANDE DO GURUPÁ
Equator
Amazonas
Amazon
AMAZONAS
Belém
Castanhal
Capanema
Bragança
Abaetetuba
Cametá
Breves
Almeirim
Prainha
Monte Alegre
Alenquer
Óbidos
Oriximiná
Santarém
Parintins
Itacoatiara
Maués
Altamira
TRANSAMAZÔNICA
RODOVIA
Itaituba
PARQUE NACIONAL DA AMAZÔNIA
Tucuruí
Represa de Tucuruí
Jacundá
Marabá
Imperatriz
Açailândia
MARANHÃO
P A R Á
SERRA DOS CARAJÁS
Carajás
Araguaína
Carolina
Balsas
Conceição do Araguaia
Redenção
SERRA DO CACHIMBO
Cachimbo
Alta Floresta
SERRA DOS APIACÁS
MATO GROSSO
SERRA FORMOSA
SERRA DO TOMBADOR
SERRA DO RONCADOR
SERRA DO ESTRONDO
TOCANTINS
Palmas
Porto Nacional
Gurupi
Paraíso do Tocantins
Miracema do Tocantins
Tocantinópolis
ILHA DO BANANAL
PARQUE NACIONAL DO ARAGUAIA
CHAPADA DAS MANGABEIRAS
Sinop
Juara
Porto dos Gaúchos
Tapajós
Xingu
Tocantins
Araguaia
Meters
Feet
6000
19685
4000
13124
3000
9843
2000
6562
1000
3281
500
1640
200
656
0
Land Below Sea Level
9000
29520

Map continues pages 246-247

Map continues pages 248-249

Map continues page 255

MAP FORM	cabo	cachoeira, cach.	ilha, i.	lago, l.	riacho	ribeirão, rão.	rio, r.	serra, sa.
ENGLISH	cape	waterfall	island	lake	creek	creek	river	mountains
DEUTSCH	Kap	Wasserfall	Insel	See	Bach	Bach	Fluss	Berge
ESPAÑOL	cabo	cascada	isla	lago	riachuelo	riachuelo	río	montañas
FRANÇAIS	cap	chute d'eau	île	lac	crique	crique	rivière	montagnes
PORTUGUÊS	cabo	queda d'água	ilha	lago	riacho	riacho	rio	montanhas

ATLANTIC
OCEAN
Equator
ATOL DAS ROCAS
ILHA FERNANDO DE NORONHA (Brazil)
CABO DE SÃO ROQUE
PONTA DO SEIXAS
PONTA DE JERICOACOARA
CEARÁ
RIO GRANDE DO NORTE
PARAÍBA
PERNAMBUCO
ALAGOAS
SERGIPE
PIAUÍ
BAHIA
SERRA GRANDE
CHAPADA DO ARARIPE
Reprêsa de Sobradinho
FORTALEZA
Natal
João Pessoa
RECIFE
Olinda
Maceió
Aracaju
Teresina
Parnaíba
Sobral
Crateús
Mossoró
Campina Grande
Caruaru
Juàzeiro do Norte
Crato
Petrolina
Juàzeiro
Paulo Afonso
Arcoverde
Garanhuns
Arapiraca
Picos
Floriano
Caxias
Codó
Timon
Senhor do Bonfim
Alagoinhas
Estância
Itabaiana
Lagarto
Xique-Xique
Copyright © by Rand McNally & Co.
Map prepared by Rand McNally & Co.

Kilometers 0 100 200 300 Km.
Statute Miles 0 100 200 300 Mi.

Scale 1:6,000,000
One centimeter represents 60 kilometers.
One inch represents approximately 95 miles.
Oblique Conic Conformal Projection

Map continues pages 248-249

PACIFIC
OCEAN
Tropic of Capricorn
BOLIVIA
CHILE
ARGENTINA
POTOSÍ
TARIJA
BOQUERÓN
JUJUY
SALTA
PUNA
ANTOFAGASTA
ATACAMA
DESIERTO DE ATACAMA
CORDILLERA DOMEYKO
A N D E S
TUCUMÁN
CATAMARCA
SANTIAGO DEL ESTERO
CHACO AUSTRAL
GRAN CHACO
LA RIOJA
CÓRDOBA
SANTA FE
SAN JUAN
COQUIMBO
VALPARAISO
MENDOZA
SAN LUIS
LA PAMPA
BUENOS AIRES
NEUQUÉN
RÍO NEGRO
LA ARAUCANÍA
BIOBÍO
MAULE
O'HIGGINS
LIBERTADOR GENERAL BERNARDO O'HIGGINS
REGION METROPOLITANA
PAMPA
Antofagasta
Calama
Chuquicamata
Tocopilla
Copiapó
La Serena
Coquimbo
Viña del Mar
Valparaíso
SANTIAGO
Rancagua
Curicó
Talca
Linares
Chillán
Concepción
Talcahuano
Los Ángeles
Temuco
San Salvador de Jujuy
Salta
San Miguel de Tucumán
Santiago del Estero
San Fernando del Valle de Catamarca
La Rioja
Córdoba
San Juan
Mendoza
San Luis
Río Cuarto
San Rafael
Santa Rosa
Bahía Blanca
Neuquén
Cipolletti
Salinas Grandes
Copyright © by Rand McNally & Co.
Map prepared by Rand McNally & Co.
A-540191-764

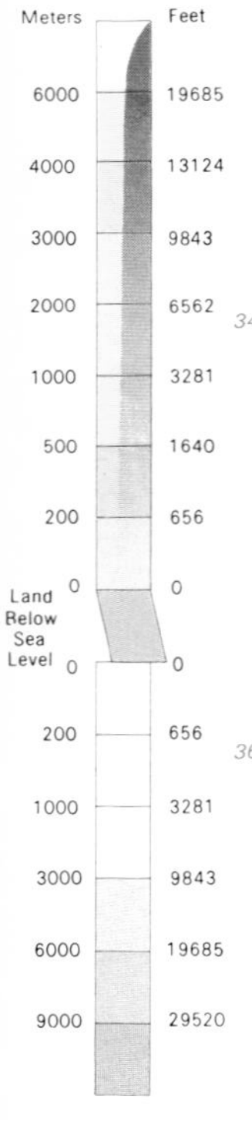
Meters
Feet
6000 19685
4000 13124
3000 9843
2000 6562
1000 3281
500 1640
200 656
0 0
Land Below Sea Level
0 0
200 656
1000 3281
3000 9843
6000 19685
9000 29520

Map continues page 254

MAP FORM	cabo	cerro	cuchilla	ilha	laguna	punta	salar	sierra	volcán
ENGLISH	cape	mountain	hills	island	lagoon; lake	point	saltflat	mountains	volcano
DEUTSCH	Kap	Berg	Hügel	Insel	Haff; See	Landspitze	Salzebene	Berge	Vulkan
ESPAÑOL	cabo	cerro	cuchilla	isla	laguna	punta	salobral	sierra	volcán
FRANÇAIS	cap	montagne	collines	île	lagune; lac	pointe	salina	montagnes	volcan
PORTUGUÊS	cabo	montanha	colina	ilha	laguna	ponta	salina	serra	vulcão

Map continues page 255

ATLANTIC
OCEAN
MATO GROSSO DO SUL
SÃO PAULO
PARANÁ
SANTA CATARINA
RIO GRANDE DO SUL
PRESIDENTE HAYES
CONCEPCIÓN
AMAMBAY
SAN PEDRO
CANINDEYÚ
ALTO PARANÁ
CAAGUAZÚ
CORDILLERA
CENTRAL
PARAGUARÍ
GUAIRÁ
CAAZAPÁ
ITAPÚA
MISIONES
ÑEEMBUCÚ
CORRIENTES
ENTRE RIOS
Asunción
Concepción
Pedro Juan Caballero
Ciudad del Este
Encarnación
Posadas
Corrientes
Formosa
Goya
Uruguaiana
Concordia
Salto
Paysandú
Gualeguaychú
Mercedes
Tacuarembó
Rivera
Santana do Livramento
Melo
Minas
Las Piedras
MONTEVIDEO
BUENOS AIRES
La Plata
Avellaneda
Mar del Plata
Tandil
Necochea
Dolores
Bahía Samborombón
SÃO PAULO
Campinas
Santos
Sorocaba
Bauru
Marília
Presidente Prudente
Londrina
Maringá
Curitiba
Ponta Grossa
Paranaguá
Joinvile
Blumenau
Florianópolis
Lages
Criciúma
Tubarão
Caxias do Sul
Passo Fundo
Santa Maria
PORTO ALEGRE
Pelotas
Rio Grande
Bagé
Alegrete
Lagoa dos Patos
Lagoa Mirim

Kilometers 0 100 200 300 Km.
Statute Miles 0 100 200 300 Mi.

Scale 1:6,000,000
One centimeter represents 60 kilometers.
One inch represents approximately 95 miles.
Oblique Conic Conformal Projection

Southern Argentina and Chile / Südliches Argentinien und südliches Chile / Argentina y Chile: zonas meridionales
Argentine et Chili, parties Méridionales / Argentina e Chile: zonas meridionais

Map continues pages 252-253

PACIFIC OCEAN
ATLANTIC OCEAN
LA ARAUCANÍA
NEUQUÉN
LA PAMPA
BUENOS AIRES
RÍO NEGRO
LOS LAGOS
CHUBUT
SANTA CRUZ
AISÉN DEL GENERAL CARLOS IBÁÑEZ DEL CAMPO
MAGALLANES Y DE LA ANTÁRTICA CHILENA
PATAGONIA
LOS ANDES
ISLA GRANDE DE TIERRA DEL FUEGO
FALKLAND ISLANDS (U.K.)
WEST FALKLAND
EAST FALKLAND
Bahía Blanca
Neuquén
Temuco
Valdivia
Osorno
Puerto Montt
San Carlos de Bariloche
Esquel
Trelew
Rawson
Puerto Madryn
Viedma
Comodoro Rivadavia
Coihaique
Puerto Deseado
Río Gallegos
Puerto Natales
Punta Arenas
Ushuaia
Stanley
CHILE
ARGENTINA
Copyright © by Rand McNally & Co.
Map prepared by Rand McNally & Co.
A-548400-764

Meters / Feet

Meters	Feet
6000	19685
4000	13124
3000	9843
2000	6562
1000	3281
500	1640
200	656
0	0
Land Below Sea Level	
0	0
200	656
1000	3281
3000	9843
6000	19685
9000	29520

MAP FORM	bahia	cabo	cerro	isla	lago	monte	punta
ENGLISH	bay	cape	mountain, hill	isle	lake	mountain	point
DEUTSCH	Bucht	Kap	Berg, Hügel	Insel	See	Berg	Landspitze
ESPAÑOL	bahía	cabo	cerro	isla	lago	monte	punta
FRANÇAIS	baie	cap	montagne, colline	île	lac	montagne	pointe
PORTUGUÊS	baia	cabo	montanha, colina	ilha	lago	monte	ponta

Kilometers 0 100 200 300 Km.

Statute Miles 0 100 200 300 Mi.

Scale 1:6,000,000

One centimeter represents 60 kilometers.
One inch represents approximately 95 miles.

Oblique Conic Conformal Projection

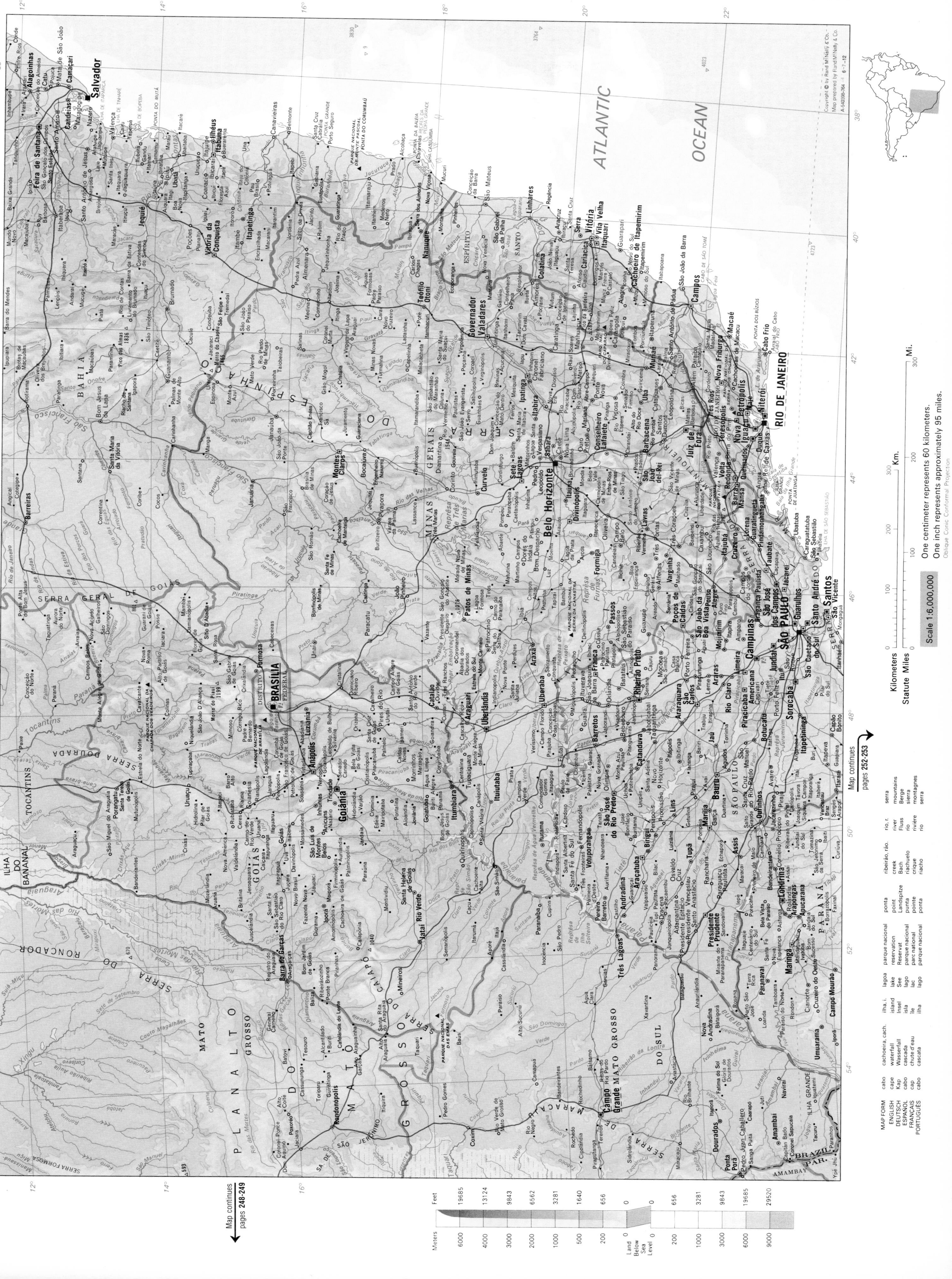
ATLANTIC
OCEAN
Salvador
Brasília
Belo Horizonte
Rio de Janeiro
São Paulo
Vitória
Goiânia
Campo Grande
Scale 1:6,000,000
One centimeter represents 60 kilometers.
One inch represents approximately 95 miles.
Oblique Conic Conformal Projection
Kilometers
Statute Miles

Map continues pages 250-251
Map continues pages 248-249
Map continues pages 252-253

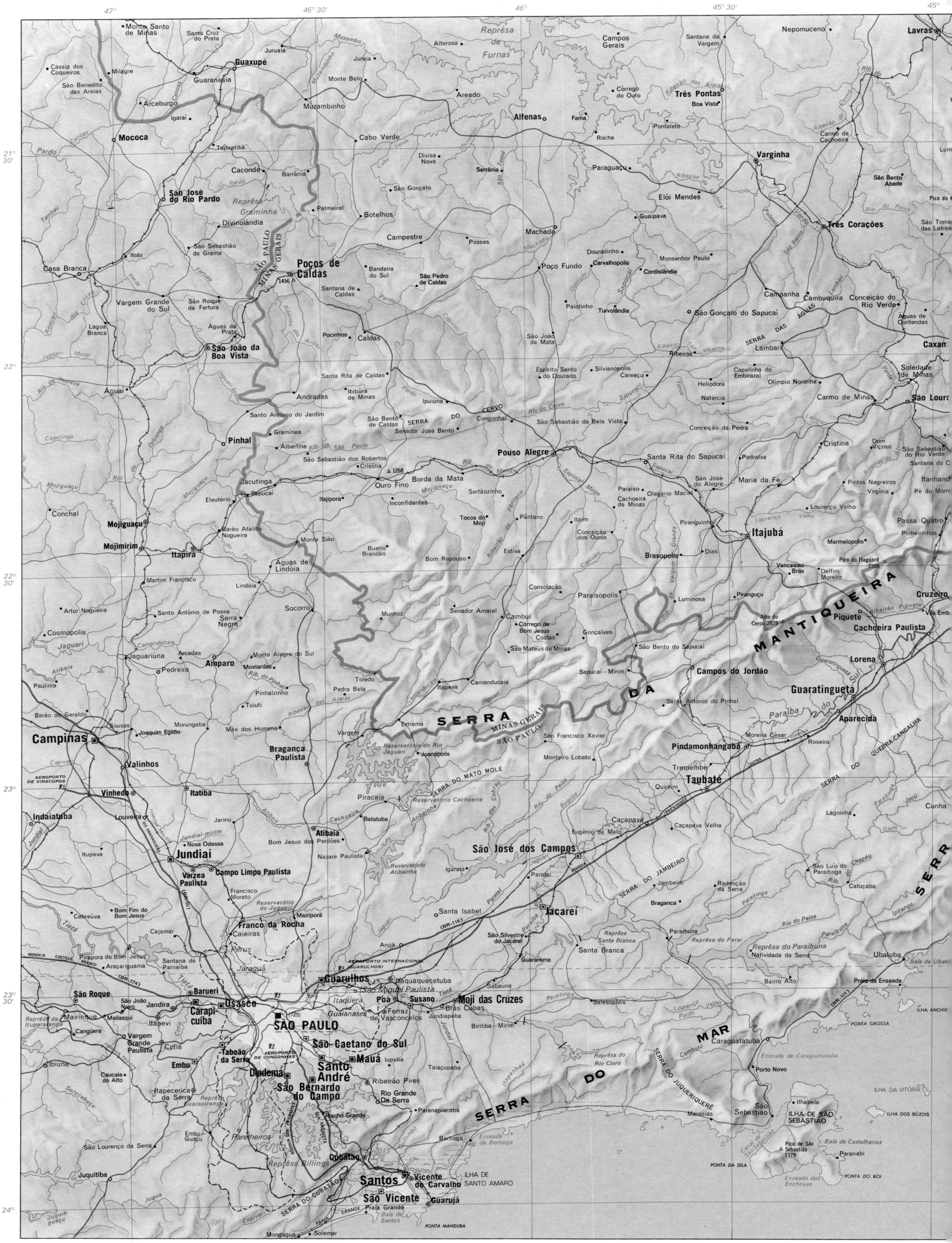

47°
46° 30'
46°
45° 30'
45°
21° 30'
22°
22° 30'
23°
23° 30'
24°
Represa de Furnas
Guaxupé
Mococa
São José do Rio Pardo
Poços de Caldas
Alfenas
Três Pontas
Varginha
Três Corações
Lavras
Pouso Alegre
Itajubá
Campinas
Jundiaí
Bragança Paulista
Atibaia
São José dos Campos
Jacareí
Taubaté
Pindamonhangaba
Guaratinguetá
Aparecida
Lorena
Cruzeiro
Cachoeira Paulista
Campos do Jordão
Guarulhos
Osasco
SÃO PAULO
São Caetano do Sul
Santo André
São Bernardo do Campo
Mauá
Diadema
Moji das Cruzes
Cubatão
Santos
São Vicente
Guarujá
Vicente de Carvalho
ILHA DE SANTO AMARO
Caraguatatuba
São Sebastião
ILHA DE SÃO SEBASTIÃO
Ubatuba
SERRA DA MANTIQUEIRA
SERRA DO MAR
SÃO PAULO
MINAS GERAIS

MAP FORM	baía	enseada	ilha	pico	ponta	represa	ribeirão	rio	serra
ENGLISH	bay	bay	island	peak	point	reservoir	stream	river	mountains
DEUTSCH	Bucht	Bucht	Insel	Gipfel	Landspitze	Stausee	Bach	Fluss	Berge
ESPAÑOL	bahía	bahía	isla	pico	punta	estanque	corriente de agua	río	sierra
FRANÇAIS	baie	baie	île	cime	pointe	réservoir	cours d'eau	rivière	montagnes
PORTUGUÊS	baía	enseada	ilha	pico	ponta	represa	ribeirão	rio	serra

44° 30'
44°
43° 30'
43°
21° 30'
22°
22° 30'
23°
23° 30'
24°
42° 30'
Nazareno
Mecuco de Minas
Itutinga
São Sebastião da Vitória
Barbacena
1176
Padre Brito
Mercês
Rodeiro
Diamante de Ubá
Miraí
Santa Bárbara do Tugúrio
Correia de Almeida
Paiva
Rio Pomba
Piraúba
Santana do Campestre
Santana de Cataguases
Caquende
Arcângelo
Emboabas
Antônio Carlos
Oliveira Fortes
Aracitaba
Tabuleiro
Guarani
Astolfo Dutra
Dona Euzébia
Cataguarino
Sereno
São Manuel de Guaiaçu
1434
Cataguases
Represa de Camargos
Carrancas
Madre de Deus de Minas
Piedade do Rio Grande
Ibertioga
Santos Dumont
Conceição do Formoso
São João da Serra
Descoberto
Itamarati de Minas
Vista Alegre
Ribeiro Junqueira
Piacatuba
Ewbank da Câmara
Dores do Paraibuna
Paraíso Garcia
Santa Rita do Ibitipoca
Monte Criminoso
1108
Piau
Rio Novo
Goianá
São João Nepomuceno
Itupi
Leopoldina
Paula Lima
Bias Fortes
Santana do Garambéu
Campolide
Coronel Pacheco
Carlos Alves
Roça Grande
Taruaçu
Rochedo de Minas
Tebas
Argirita
São Vicente de Minas
Minduri
Andrelândia
Rosário de Minas
Pedro Teixeira
Chácara
Bicas
Guarará
Maripá de Minas
São Domingos
Providência
Água-Viva
Trimonte
Angustura
Volta Grande
MANTIQUEIRA
São José dos Lopes
Juiz de Fora
Pregos
Senador Cortes
Santo Antônio do Aventureiro
São Domingos da Bocaina
Olaria
Lima Duarte
Torreões
Matias Barbosa
Sarandira
Pequeri
Engenho Novo
Porto Velho do Cunha
Serranos
Seritinga
Alto da Cachoeira Grande 1695
Mar de Espanha
Além Paraíba
Arantina
Bom Jardim de Minas
Aiuruoca
Tabuão
Santa Bárbara do Monte Verde
Belmiro Braga
Simão Pereira
Saudade
Santana do Deserto
Benjamim Constant
Paraíba do Sul
Jamapará
Carmo
Barra de São Francisco
Carvalhos
Liberdade
Três Ilhas
Afonso Arinos
Comendador Levy Gasparian
Chiador
Sapucaia
Penha Longa
Nossa Senhora da Aparecida
Sumidouro
Anta
Duas Barras
Franceses dos Carvalhos
DA
Itaboca
São Sebastião do Barreado
Rio Prêto
Porto das Flores
Manuel Duarte
Três Rios
Moura Brasil
Bemposta
São José do Rio Preto
Mitra do Bispo 2195
Alagoa
Santa Rita de Jacutinga
Bocaina de Minas
Pentagna
Rio das Flores
Paraíba do Sul
Salutaris
Abarracamento
Tábuas
Werneck
Areal
Riograndina
Conselheiro Paulino
Campo do Coelho
Passa Vinte
Mirantão
Santa Isabel do Rio Prêto
Ribeirão de São Joaquim
Valença
Andrade Pinto
Inconfidência
Posse
Bom Sucesso
Nova Friburgo
SERRA
MINAS GERAIS
RIO DE JANEIRO
Falcão
Fumaça
Conservatória
Sebastião de Lacerda
Avelar
Pico das Agulhas Negras 2787
Pedra Selada
Nossa Senhora do Amparo
São José do Turvo
Ipiabas
Barão de Juparanã
Pedro do Rio
Itaipava
Nhunguaçu
MAR
ÓRGÃOS
Porto Real
Quatis
Boa Esperança
PARQUE NACIONAL DO ITATIAIA
Agulhas Negras
Floriano
Volta Redonda
Dorândia
Barra do Piraí
Vassouras
Ferreiros
Pati do Alferes
Teresópolis
Pedra do Sino 2218
DO
PARQUE NACIONAL DA SERRA DOS ÓRGÃOS
DOS
Resende
Sacra Família do Tinguá
Miguel Pereira
Cascatinha
Pico Dedo de Deus 1675
Subaio
Cachoeiras de Macacu
Várzea
Engenheiro Passos
Itatiaia
Represa do Funil
Vargem Alegre
Pinheiral
Santanésia
Governador Portela
Petrópolis
Barra Mansa
Babilônia
Mendes
Conrado
Engenheiro Paulo de Frontin
Xerém
Santo Aleixo
Guapimirim
Gaviões
Areias
Pirangaí
Rialto
Paracambi
Tinguá
Inhomirim
Piabetá
Japuíba
Arrozal
Taireta
Jaceruba
Papucaia
São José do Barreiro
Arapeí
Bananal
Getulândia
Piraí
Japeri
Imbariê
Majé
Pouso Sêco
Cava
Campos Elísios
Suruí
Sambaetiba
SERRA DA BOCAINA
Morro Tira Chapéu 2085
Rio Claro
Passa Três
Represa do Ribeirão das Lajes
Monumento
Queimados
Belford Roxo
Guia de Pacobaíba
Porto das Caixas
Rio Bonito
Tanguá
Praça Cruzeiro
São José
MAR
SERRA DA CARIOCA
Seropédica
Nova Iguaçu
Coelho da Rocha
Duque de Caxias
Itambi
Itaboraí
Mesquita
Jardim Paraíso
Nilópolis
Olinda
São João de Meriti
São Mateus
Monjolo
Boa Esperança
PARQUE NACIONAL DE BOCAINA
Lídice
Itaguaí
Bangu
São Gonçalo
Cabuçu
Alto da Serra
Paciência
Inhoaíba
Realengo
Madureira
Jacarepaguá
Neves
Sete Pontes
Ipiíba
Sampaio Correia
Manuel Ribeiro
Coroa Grande
Santa Cruz
Cosmo
Campo Grande
1125
RIO DE JANEIRO
Niterói
Inoã
Maricá
Bracuí
Mambucaba
Betero
Mangaratiba
Muriqui
Itacurussá
ILHA DE ITACURUSSÁ
AEROPORTO BARTOLOMEU DE GUSMÃO
Sepetiba
Baía de Sepetiba
Lagoa de Jacarepaguá
Morro do Corcovado 740
Pão de Açúcar Sugar Loaf 404
AEROPORTO SANTOS DUMONT
Lagoa Piratininga
Itaipu
Lagoa de Maricá
Ponta Negra
PONTA NEGRA
Saquarema
Cunhambebe
Pedra de Guaratiba
Ipanema
Tarituba
Angra dos Reis
Jacuecanga
Conceição de Jacareí
Ilha
ILHAS COMPRIDA
ILHAS MARICÁS
São Roque
ILHA DA JIBÓIA
Baía da
Pico da Marambaia 641
RESTINGA DA MARAMBAIA
ILHA DA MARAMBAIA
ILHA RASA DE GUARATIBA
ILHA REDONDA
ILHA DO ARAÚJO
Praia de Araçatiba
Abraão
ILHA GRANDE
PONTA DE CASTELHANOS
Ilha Grande
ILHA DO ALGODÃO
PONTA DOS MEROS
ILHA JORGE GREGO
Parati
Parati-Mirim
Pico do Cairoçu 1070
PONTA DE JUATINGA
COUVES
Tropic of Capricorn
ATLANTIC OCEAN
Copyright © by Rand McNally & Co.
Map prepared by Rand McNally & Co.
A-542200-264

Kilometers 0 10 20 30 40 50 Km.

Statute Miles 0 10 20 30 40 50 Mi.

Scale 1:1,000,000

One centimeter represents 10 kilometers.

One inch represents approximately 16 miles.

Polyconic Projection

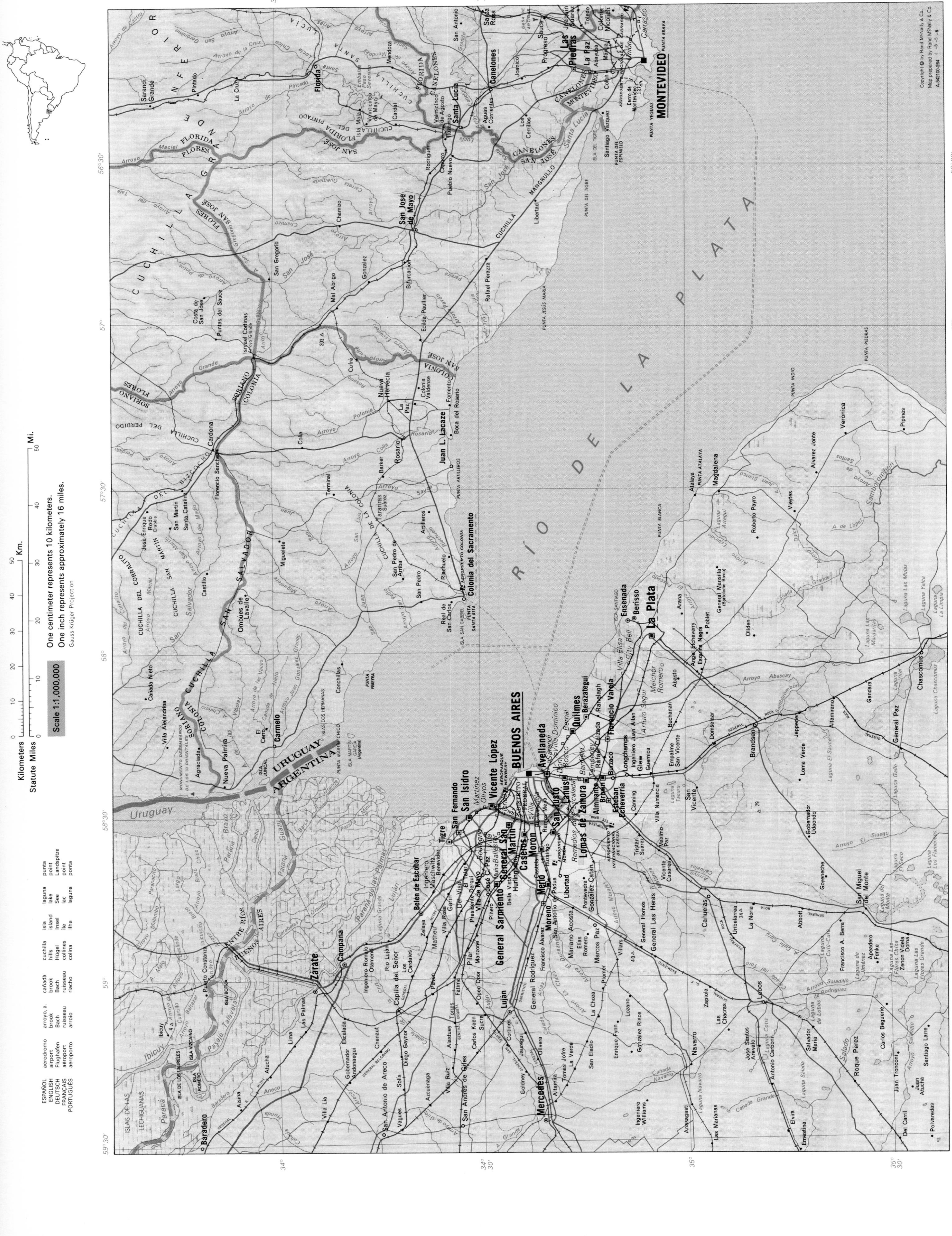
ESPAÑOL aeródromo arroyo, a. cañada cuchilla isla laguna punta
ENGLISH airport brook brook hills island lake point
DEUTSCH Flughafen Bach Bach Hügel Insel See Landspitze
FRANÇAIS aéroport ruisseau ruisseau collines île lac point
PORTUGUÊS aeroporto arroio riacho colina ilha laguna ponta
Scale 1:1,000,000
One centimeter represents 10 kilometers.
One inch represents approximately 16 miles.
Gauss-Krüger Projection
Kilometers
Statute Miles
Copyright © by Rand McNally & Co.
Map prepared by Rand McNally & Co.
RÍO DE LA PLATA
BUENOS AIRES
MONTEVIDEO
La Plata
Colonia del Sacramento
San José de Mayo
Canelones
Florida
URUGUAY
ARGENTINA
Zárate
Campana
Luján
Mercedes
Quilmes
Avellaneda
Tigre
San Isidro
Vicente López
Juan L. Lacaze
Rosario
Carmelo
Nueva Palmira
Chascomús

THIS SECTION CONSISTS of 60 maps of the world's major metropolitan areas, at the scale of 1:300,000. The maps show the generalized land-use patterns in and around each city—the total urban extent, major industrial areas, parks and preserves, and wooded areas. Airports are shown, as are many details of the highway and rail transportation networks. Selected points of interest appear, such as Fisherman's Wharf and Chinatown in San Francisco, the Welcome monument in Jakarta, the Temple of the Jade Buddha in Shanghai, and the Cristo Redentor statue in Rio de Janeiro.

The maps name and locate a great number of towns, villages, and suburbs, and also sections or neighborhoods within limits of the larger cities. Prominent physical features, including elevations, named and unnamed, have been indicated to give a general impression of the local topography. Shaded relief has been omitted, however, to permit display of such details as streams, parks, airport runways, important public buildings and monuments, and the names of major streets. The corporate limits of major cities are also outlined. For the symbols used on these maps see the Legend to Maps.

Maps of major world cities usually vary widely in scale, and heretofore have not been consistent in design and coverage. For this section, a special effort has been made to portray these varied metropolitan areas in as standard and comparable a fashion as possible. However, for a few cities (notably several in Asia) there has not been adequate source material to include certain information, such as major industrial areas and corporate limits.

The order of presentation is generally regional, with some exceptions where for ease of comparison major capitals or industrial centers or cities located in similar physical surroundings have been juxtaposed. Many American cities and some European cities, with their lower densities and more extensive areas, require larger maps than do Asiatic cities of comparable population. The total land area and population within the confines of each map are stated in the margin as a further aid to comparison.

DIESER KARTENTEIL UMFASST 60 Karten der bedeutendsten Stadtregionen der Erde im Massstab 1:300 000. Die Karten zeigen in generalisierter Form die Landnutzung in und um jede Stadt: die gesamte Ausdehnung des verstädterten Gebietes, wichtige Industriegebiete, Parks, Landflächen in Gemeinbesitz und Wald. Flughäfen werden ebenso dargestellt wie viele Einzelheiten des Strassen- und Eisenbahnnetzes. Bekannte Sehenswürdigkeiten sind eingetragen wie die "Fisherman's Wharf" und "Chinatown" in San Francisco, das Willkomm-Denkmal in Jakarta, der Tempel des Jade-Buddhas in Shanghai and die "Cristo Redentor"-Statue in Rio de Janeiro.

Die Karten verzeichnen Name and Lage einer grossen Zahl von Städten, Dörfern, Vororten ebenso wie eingemeindete Ortsteile bei grösseren Städten. Hervortretende physische Formen wie benannte und unbenannte Erhebungen sind aufgenommen, um eine allgemeine Vorstellung des lokalen Reliefs zu geben. Auf die Schummerung wurde jedoch verzichtet, um klar solche Einzelheiten wie Flüsse, Parks, Start- und Landebahnen der Flughäfen, bedeutende öffentliche Gebäude und Denkmäler sowie die Namen der wichtigsten Strassen herausstellen zu können. Eingetragen sind ferner die Gemeindegrenzen der wichtigsten Städte. Zu den auf diesen Karten verwendeten Signaturen siehe "Zeichenerklärung".

Karten der bedeutendsten Weltstädte differieren normalerweise sehr stark in ihren Massstäben und sind daher uneinheitlich in ihrer Gestaltung und Begrenzung. Deshalb wurde in diesem Kartenteil besonderer Wert darauf gelegt, die verschiedenen städtischen Ballungsgebiete in möglichst einheitlicher und vergleichbarer Form darzustellen. Für einige Städte, vor allem mehrere asiatische, war das Quellenmaterial jedoch nicht ausreichend genug, um gewisse Informationen wie Hauptindustriegebiete oder Stadtgrenzen einzutragen.

Im allgemeinen sind diese Karten nach regionalen Gesichtspunkten geordnet. Um Vergleiche zu erleichtern wurden einige Ausnahmen gemacht, indem wichtige Hauptstädte, Industriezentren oder Städte in vergleichbarer landschaftlicher Lage einander gegenübergestellt wurden. Viele americkanische und einige europäische Städte mit ihrer geringen Bevölkerungsdichte, aber ausgedehnteren Fläche erfordern eine grössere Kartenfläche als asiatische Städte von vergleichbarer Bevölkerungszahl. Die gesamte Landfläche und die Bevölkerung innerhalb des dargestellten Gebietes ist am Kartenrand verzeichnet als ein weiteres Hilfsmittel für Vergleiche.

INTEGRAN ESTA SECCION 60 mapas de las áreas metropolitanas más importantes del mundo, a la escala de 1:300 000. Los mapas muestran los patrones de uso del suelo dentro de cada ciudad y en sus alrededores—la extensión total del conglomerado urbano, las principales áreas industriales, parques y reservas, y zonas boscosas. Aparecen los aeropuertos, así como muchos otros detalles de las redes de carreteras y ferrocarriles. Se seleccionaron también puntos de interés, como el Muelle de los Pescadores y el Barrio Chino de San Francisco, el monumento de Bienvenida de Jakarta, el Templo del Buda de Jade de Shanghai y la estatua del Cristo Redentor de Rio de Janeiro.

Los mapas incluyen los nombres y la ubicación de gran número de ciudades, poblaciones menores, suburbios, e inclusive barrios y distritos de algunas de las ciudades más importantes. Las características físicas sobresalientes, e incluso algunas elevaciones con o sin nombre, están indicados para dar una impresión general de la topografía local. Se omitió sin embargo el relieve sombreado, lo cual permite mostrar detalles como ríos y arroyos, parques, pistas de aterrizaje, edificios y monumentos públicos notables y los nombres de las calles principales. También están marcados los límites territoriales de las ciudades más grandes. Para la interpretación de los símbolos usados en estos mapas, véanse Leyendas para Mapas.

Los mapas de las ciudades más importantes del mundo varían generalmente en escala, y hasta ahora no han sido consistentes ni en diseño ni en contenido. En esta sección hemos hecho un esfuerzo de presentar las distintas áreas metropolitanas en la forma más uniforme posible, para facilitar sus comparaciones. Para algunas ciudades (la mayoría de ellas en Asia), no fué posible obtener de las propias fuentes material adecuado para la inclusión de ciertos datos, tales como las mayores áreas industriales y los límites municipales.

Los mapas de áreas metropolitanas se presentan por regiones, a excepción de unos cuantos que aparecen yuxtapuestos para facilitar la comparación entre grandes capitales, o centros comerciales, o ciudades ubicadas en contextos físicos similares. Muchas ciudades de América y algunas ciudades de Europa, por su baja densidad de población y su área extensa, requieren mapas más grandes que los ocupados por ciudades asiáticas con poblaciones comparables. Al margen de cada mapa se anotaron el área total y la población de territorio representado, lo cual facilita también las comparaciones.

CETTE PARTIE COMPREND 60 cartes des principales zones métropolitaines à l'échelle du 1:300 000ᵉ. Les cartes représentent les principaux types d'occupation du sol des villes et de leurs environs, c'est-à-dire de toute la zone urbanisée, les principales zones industrielles, les parcs et réserves naturelles, et les régions boisées. Les aéroports sont aussi représentés ainsi que de nombreux éléments des réseaux routier et ferroviaire. Certains lieux particulièrement intéressants sont indiqués, tels que le quai des pêcheurs et la ville chinoise à San Francisco, le monument de la Bienvenue à Jakarta, le temple du Bouddha de Jade à Shanghai et la statue du Christ Rédempteur à Rio de Janeiro.

Les cartes permettent de localiser un grand nombre de villes, villages et banlieues, ainsi que des quartiers de grandes villes. Les caractéristiques topographiques notables, comme les hauteurs sont indiquées même si elles ne portent pas de nom, pour donner une idée du site de l'aire métropolitaine. L'estompage du relief est omis cependant pour permettre de représenter cours d'eau, parcs, pistes d'envol des aéroports, monuments et bâtiments publics importants, noms des principales rues, ainsi que les limites municipales des grandes villes. (Pour la signification des symboles voir légende.)

En général, les échelles des cartes des grandes villes du monde varient considérablement, et jusqu'ici la présentation et le contenu de ces cartes n'étaient pas comparables. Dans cette partie de l'Atlas, un effort spécial a été fait pour représenter les diverses zones métropolitaines de manière aussi homogène que possible. Cependant, dans certains cas (en Asie notamment), les documents de base n'étaient pas assez complets pour qu'il fût possible d'inclure avec précision des données comme les zones industrielles et les limites municipales.

L'ordre de présentation est régional, avec des exceptions quand, pour faciliter les comparaisons, de grandes capitales de grands centres industriels ou encore des villes possédant un même environnement naturel, sont juxtaposés. Beaucoup de villes américaines et quelques villes européennes ont une faible densité de population et une étendue considérable; elles requièrent, par conséquent, des cartes plus grandes que des villes asiatiques de population similaire. La superficie et la population de chaque carte sont indiquées dans la marge.

INTEGRAM ESTA SEÇÃO 60 mapas das áreas metropolitanas mais importantes do mundo, em escala de 1:300 000. Os mapas mostram os principais tipos de uso do solo em cada cidade e seus arredores, seja, a extensão total da zona urbanizada, as principais áreas industriais, os parques e reservas, e as áreas florestais. Mostram os aeroportos, e muitos detalhes das redès rodo e ferroviária. Indicam também pontos de interesse, selecionados, tais como o Cais dos Pescadores e o Bairro Chinês de San Francisco, o monumento de Boasvindas, em Jakarta, o templo do Buda de Jade, em Shanghai, e a Estátua do Cristo Redentor, no Rio de Janeiro.

Os mapas apresentam o nome e a localização de grande número de cidades, vilas e subúrbios, e incluem bairros das cidades mais importantes. Foram indicadas as características físicas principais, inclusive elevações, com ou sem nome, com o objetivo de proporcionar uma idéia geral da topografia local. No entanto, omitiu-se o sombreado do relevo, para permitir a indicação de detalhes tais como cursos d'água, parques, pistas de aeroportos, edifícios públicos e monumentos notáveis, e os nomes das principais ruas, bem como os limites municipais das grandes cidades. Para a interpretação dos símbolos usados nesses mapas, ver as *Legendas dos mapas*.

Os mapas das cidades mais importantes do mundo variam consideravelmente, de modo geral, quanto à escala, e até o presente não são comparáveis nem na forma de apresentação nem no conteúdo. Nesta seção, fez-se um esforço especial para representar as diversas áreas metropolitanas do modo mais uniforme e comparável possível. No entanto, para algumas cidades, a maioria das quais da Ásia, não foi possível obter fontes fidedignas de informações, tais como áreas industriais principais e limites municipais.

A ordem de apresentação dos mapas das áreas metropolitanas é geralmente regional, exceto em certos casos em que, para facilidade de comparação, capitais ou centros industriais e cidades importantes localizadas em meio físico semelhante foram justapostos. Muitas cidades da América e algumas da Europa, por sua baixa densidade demográfica e áreas mais extensas, exigem mapas maiores que as cidades asiáticas de população comparável. À margem de cada mapa indicam-se a área terrestre e a população total do território representado, também para maior facilidade de comparação.

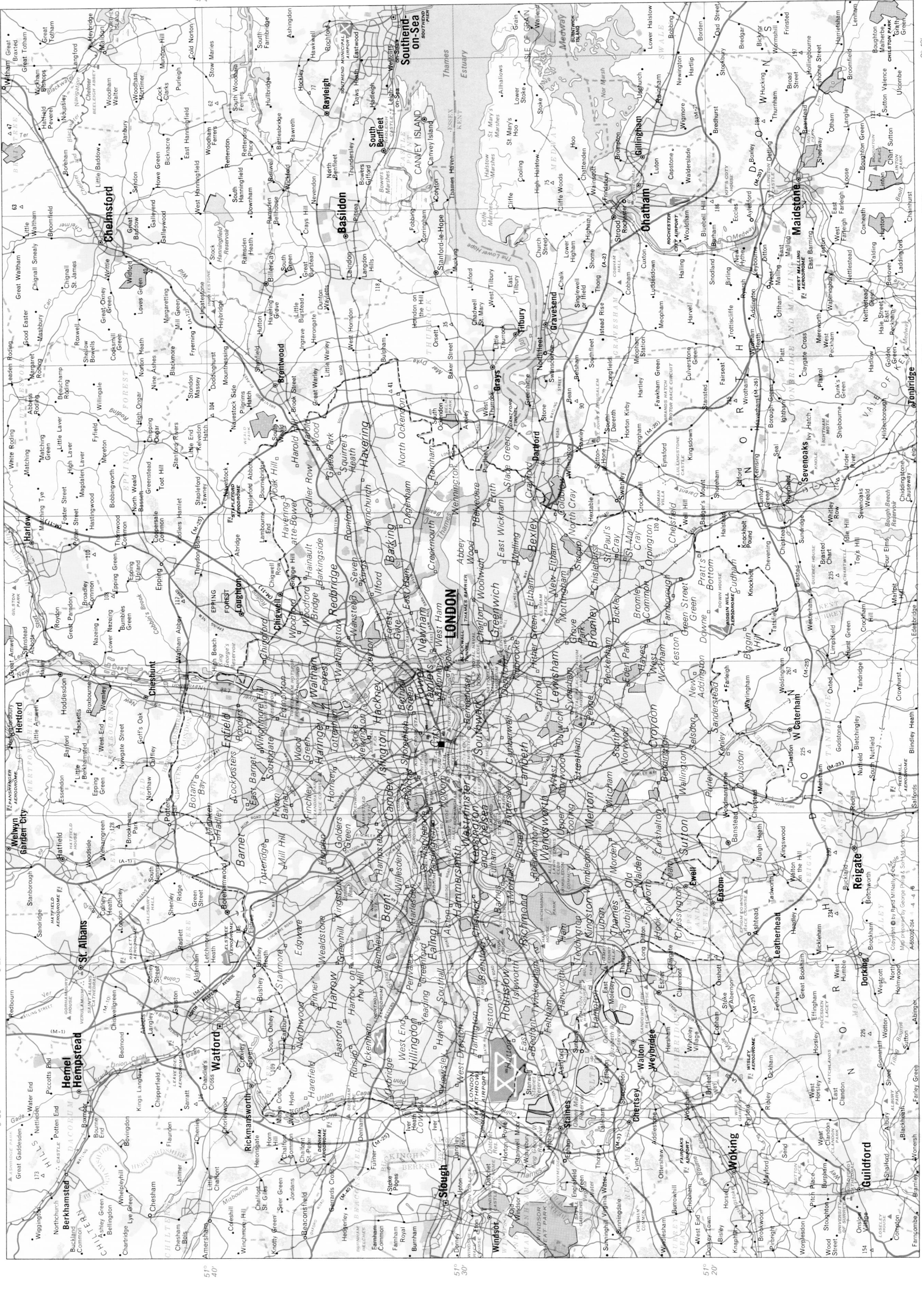

ENGLISH	DEUTSCH	ESPAÑOL	FRANÇAIS	PORTUGUÊS
aerodrome	Flughafen	aeropuerto	aéroport	aeroporto
canal	Kanal	canal	canal	canal
castle	Burg	castillo	château	castelo
palace	Palast	palacio	palais	palácio
park	Park	parque	parc	parque
race course	Rennbahn	hipódromo	champ de course	hipódromo
road	Landstrasse	camino	route	rodovia
station	Bahnhof	estación	gare	estação

AREA 6,400 km²
POPULATION 10,325,000

Kilometers 0 5 10 15 Km.
Statute Miles 0 5 10 15 Mi.

Scale 1:300,000
One centimeter represents 3 kilometers.
One inch represents approximately 4.7 miles.

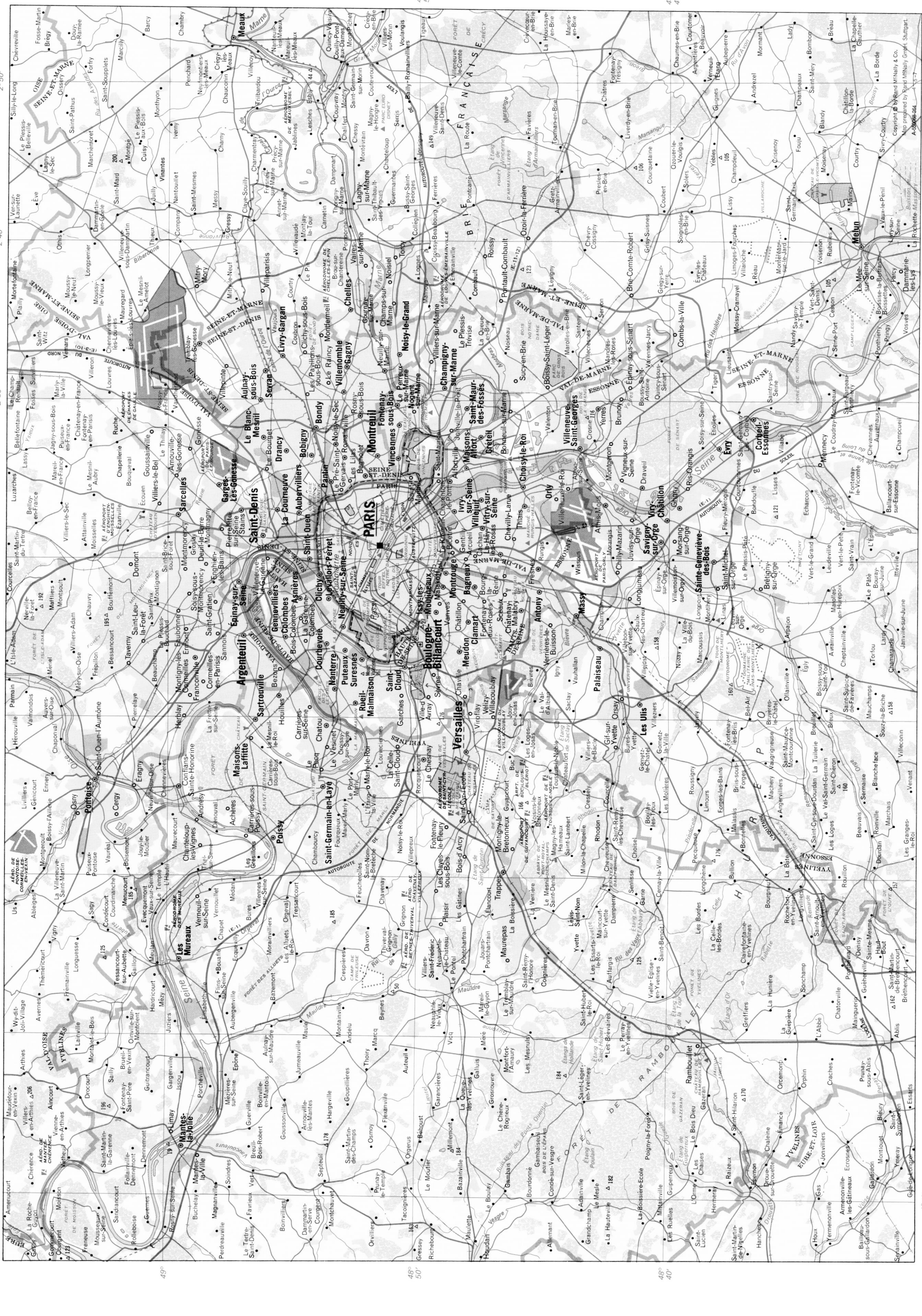
PARIS
Versailles
Saint-Denis
Melun
Meaux
Rambouillet
Copyright © by Rand McNally & Co.
Map prepared by Rand McNally GmbH, Stuttgart.

Kilometers 0 5 10 15 Km.

Statute Miles 0 5 10 15 Mi.

Scale 1:300,000

One centimeter represents 3 kilometers.
One inch represents approximately 4.7 miles.

FRANÇAIS	ENGLISH	DEUTSCH	ESPAÑOL	PORTUGUÊS
aérodrome	airport	Flughafen	aeropuerto	aeroporto
bois	woods	Gehölz	bosques	bosques
château	castle	Burg	castillo	castelo
étang	pond	Teich	charca	lagoa
forêt	forest	Wald	bosque	floresta
ruisseau	brook	Bach	arroyo	arroio

AREA: 6,500 km²
POPULATION: 9,800,000

Kilometers 0 5 10 15 Km.

Statute Miles 0 5 10 15 Mi.

Scale 1:300,000

One centimeter represents 3 kilometers.
One inch represents approximately 4.7 miles.

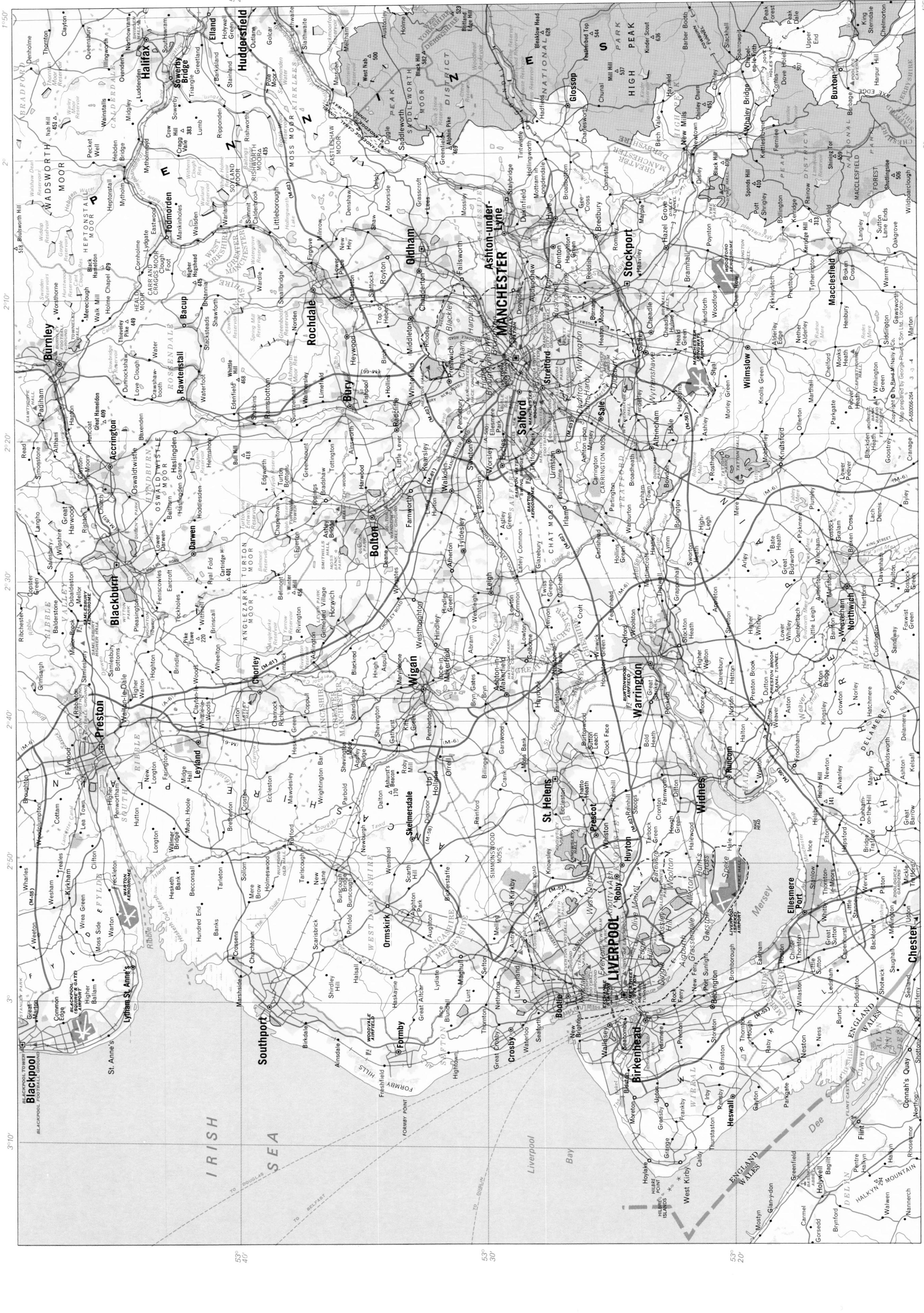

ENGLISH	bank	canal	hill	moor	park	railway station	reservoir	tower
DEUTSCH	Bank	Kanal	Hügel	Ried	Park	Bahnhof	Stausee	Turm
ESPAÑOL	banco	canal	colina	páramo	parque	terminal ferroviaria	estanque	torre
FRANÇAIS	banque	canal	colline	lande	parc	gare	réservoir	tour
PORTUGUÊS	banco	canal	colina	charneca	parque	estação ferroviária	reservatório	torre

AREA 5,650 km²
POPULATION 6,275,000

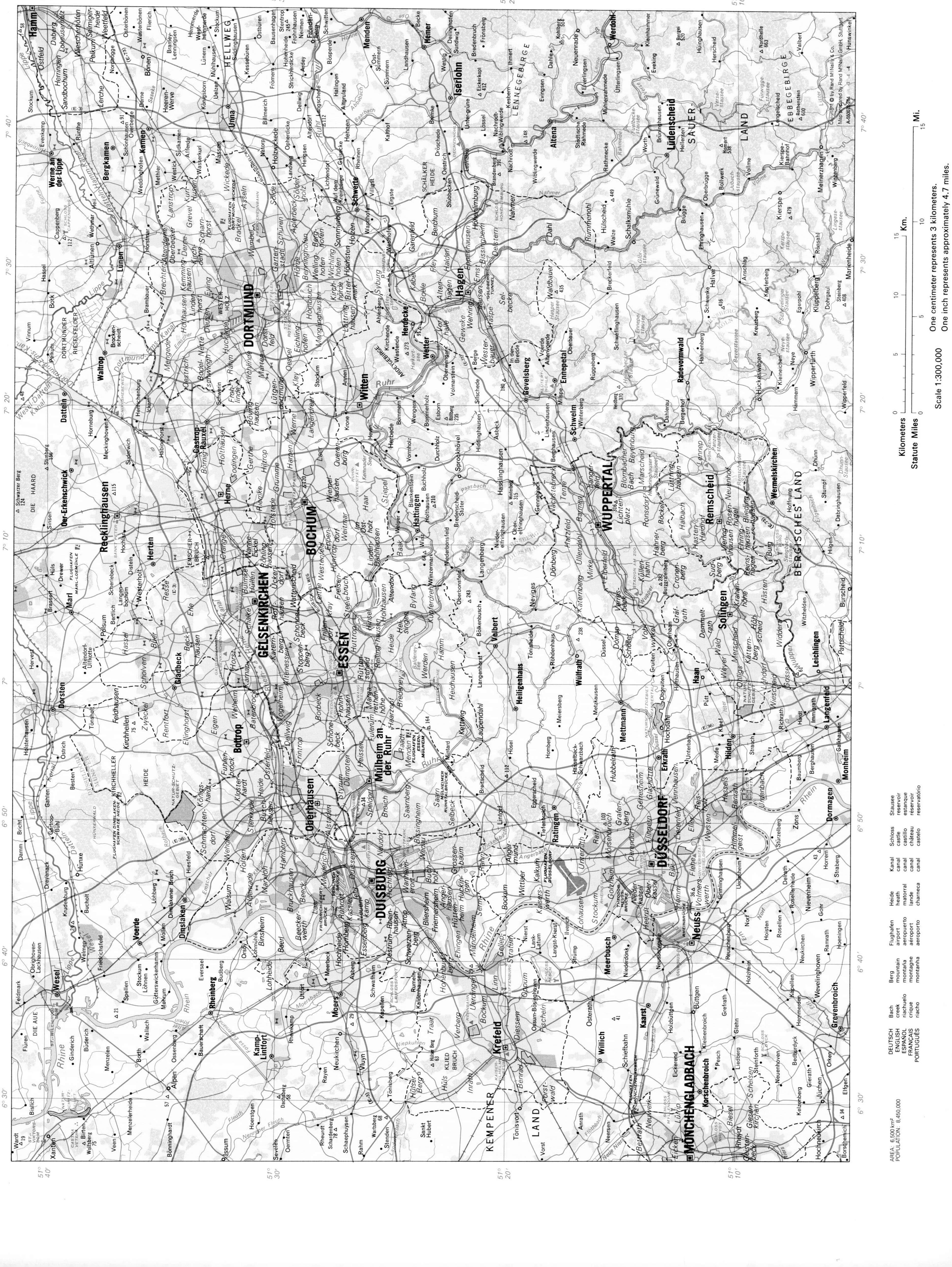
Hamm
Dortmund
Bochum
Essen
Gelsenkirchen
Duisburg
Mülheim an der Ruhr
Oberhausen
Düsseldorf
Wuppertal
Hagen
Remscheid
Solingen
Krefeld
Mönchengladbach
Neuss
Recklinghausen
Herne
Witten
Iserlohn
Lüdenscheid
Bottrop
Gladbeck
Dorsten
Marl
Wesel
Moers
Ratingen
Velbert
Hattingen
Castrop-Rauxel
Lünen
Unna
Kamen
Bergkamen
Schwerte
Herdecke
Wetter
Gevelsberg
Schwelm
Ennepetal
Altena
Menden
Hemer
Dinslaken
Voerde
Kamp-Lintfort
Rheinberg
Viersen
Kempen
Willich
Kaarst
Meerbusch
Mettmann
Hilden
Langenfeld
Leichlingen
Haan
Monheim
Dormagen
Grevenbroich
Heiligenhaus
Wülfrath
Erkrath
Radevormwald
Wermelskirchen
Herten
Datteln
Waltrop
Werne an der Lippe
Bönen
Xanten
Rhein
Ruhr
Lippe
Emscher
Wupper
Rhine
HELLWEG
LENNEGEBIRGE
EBBEGEBIRGE
SAUERLAND
BERGISCHES LAND
KEMPENER LAND
DIE HAARD
Kilometers 0 5 10 15 Km.
Statute Miles 0 5 10 15 Mi.
Scale 1:300,000
One centimeter represents 3 kilometers.
One inch represents approximately 4.7 miles.
AREA: 6,500 km²
POPULATION: 8,450,000
DEUTSCH | ENGLISH | ESPAÑOL | FRANÇAIS | PORTUGUÊS
Bach | creek | riachuelo | crique | riacho
Berg | mountain | montaña | montagne | montanha
Flughafen | airport | aeropuerto | aéroport | aeroporto
Heide | heath | brezal | lande | charneca
Kanal | canal | canal | canal | canal
Schloss | castle | castillo | château | castelo
Stausee | reservoir | embalse | réservoir | reservatório
Copyright © by Rand McNally & Co.
Made by Rand McNally GmbH, Stuttgart

a

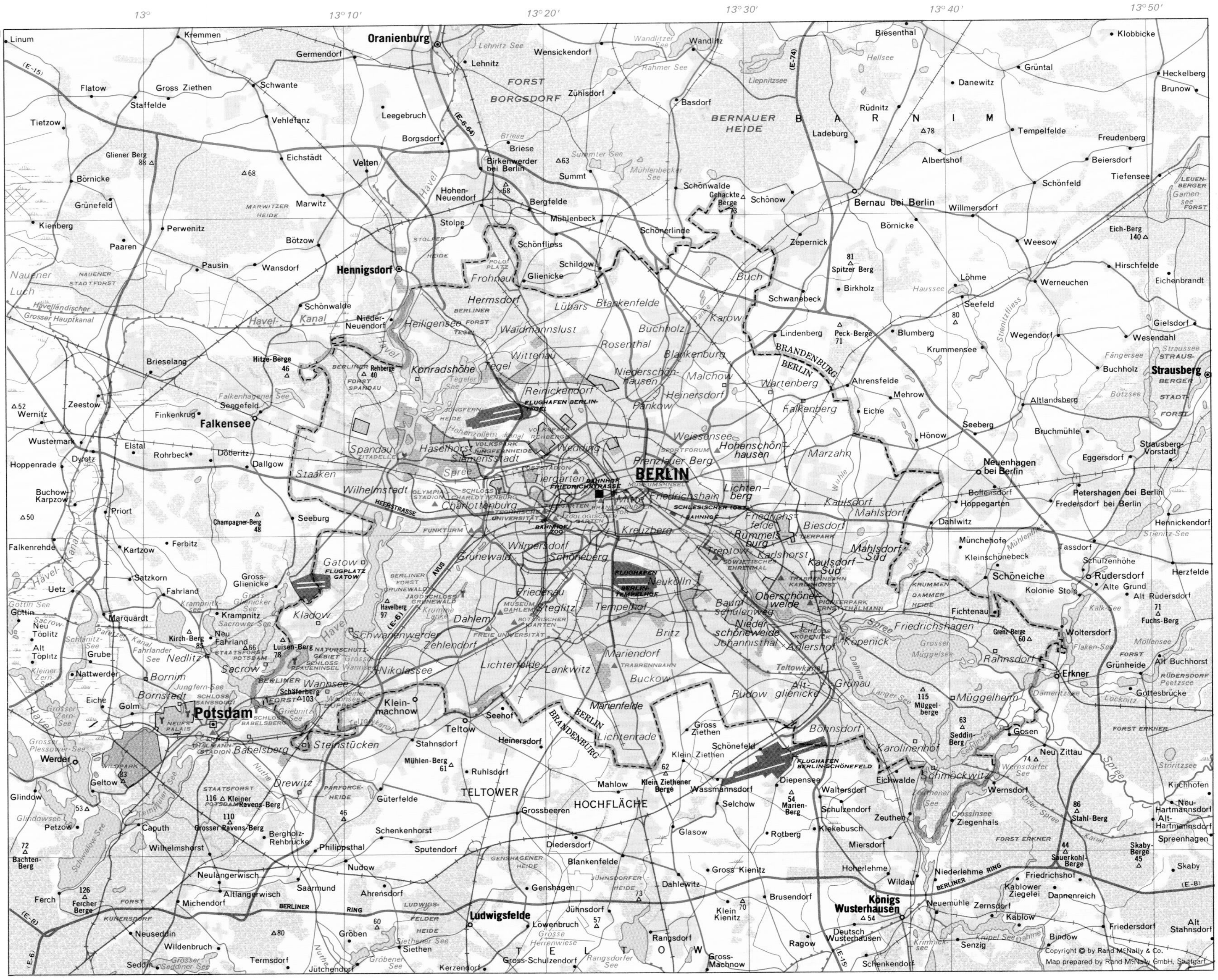
Oranienburg
Hennigsdorf
Falkensee
Potsdam
BERLIN
Spandau
Charlottenburg
Wilmersdorf
Schöneberg
Tempelhof
Neukölln
Köpenick
Pankow
Weissensee
Reinickendorf
Zehlendorf
Steglitz
Kreuzberg
Lichtenberg
Treptow
Ludwigsfelde
Königs Wusterhausen
Strausberg
Bernau bei Berlin
Erkner
Teltow
BARNIM
TELTOWER HOCHFLÄCHE
BERNAUER HEIDE
FLUGHAFEN BERLIN-TEGEL
FLUGHAFEN BERLIN-TEMPELHOF
FLUGHAFEN BERLIN-SCHÖNEFELD
Copyright © by Rand McNally & Co.
Map prepared by Rand McNally GmbH, Stuttgart.

b

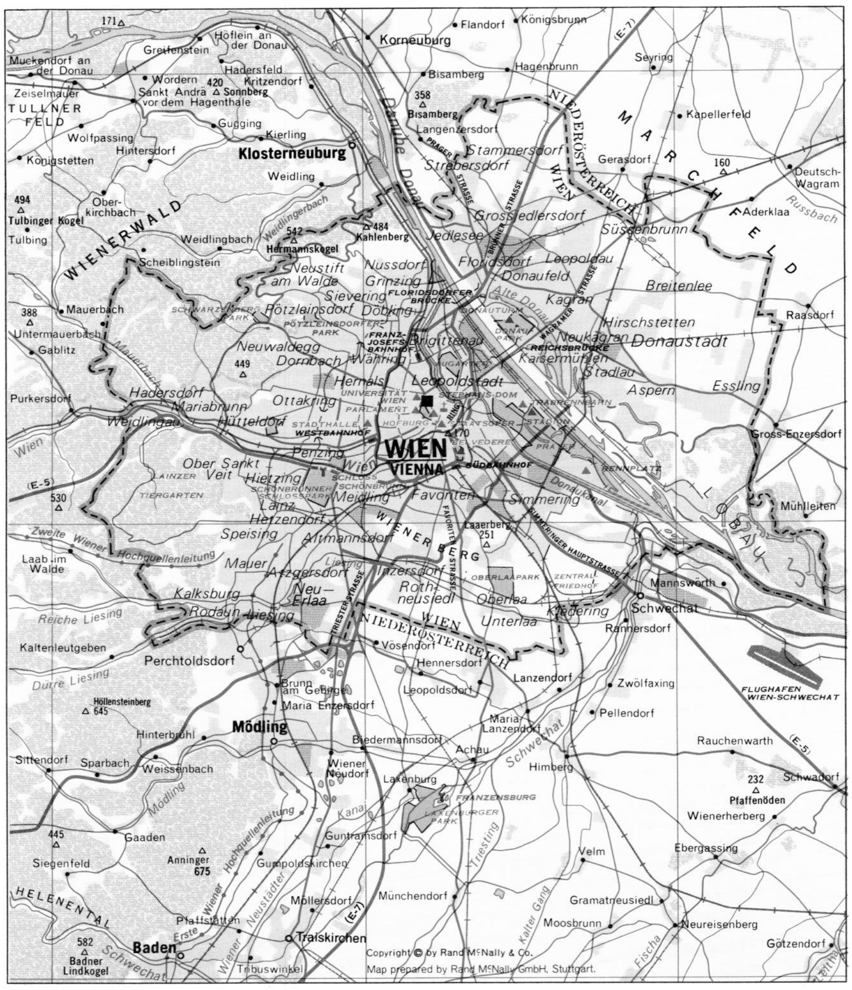
Korneuburg
Klosterneuburg
WIEN
VIENNA
WIENERWALD
MARCHFELD
Donaustadt
Floridsdorf
Leopoldstadt
Favoriten
Simmering
Schwechat
Mödling
Perchtoldsdorf
Baden
Traiskirchen
FLUGHAFEN WIEN-SCHWECHAT
Copyright © by Rand McNally & Co.
Map prepared by Rand McNally GmbH, Stuttgart.

c

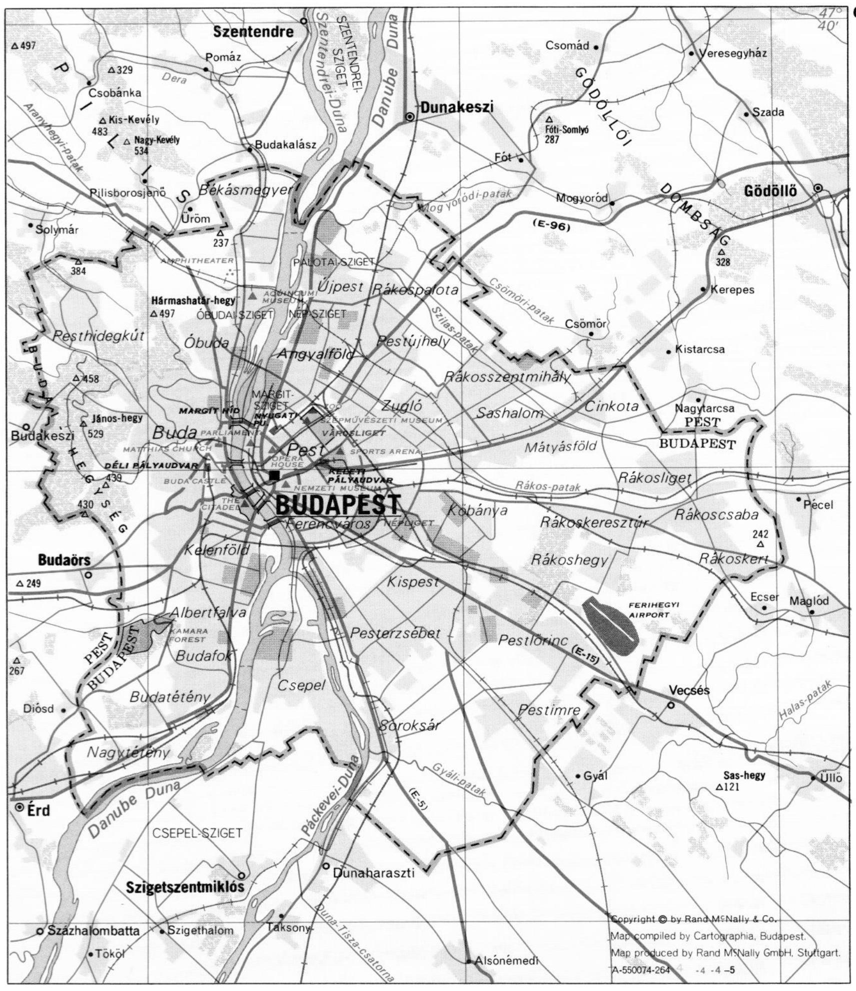
Szentendre
Dunakeszi
Gödöllő
BUDAPEST
Buda
Pest
Óbuda
Újpest
Kispest
Pesterzsébet
Csepel
Budaörs
Érd
Vecsés
Szigetszentmiklós
CSEPEL-SZIGET
FERIHEGYI AIRPORT
Copyright © by Rand McNally & Co.
Map compiled by Cartographia, Budapest.
Map produced by Rand McNally GmbH, Stuttgart.
A-550074-264 -4 -4 -5

	AREA (km²)	POPULATION
BERLIN	3,700	3,550,000
WIEN	1,300	1,825,000
BUDAPEST	1,300	2,450,000

MAP FORM	Berg	Berge	hegy	Heide	Schloss	See	sziget
ENGLISH	hill	hills	mountain	heath	castle	lake	island
DEUTSCH	Berg	Berge	Berg	Heide	Schloss	See	Insel
ESPAÑOL	colina	colinas	montaña	lande	castillo	lago	isla
FRANÇAIS	colline	collines	montagne	lande	château	lac	île
PORTUGUÊS	colina	colinas	montanha	charneca	castelo	lago	ilha

Kilometers 0 5 10 15 Km.

Statute Miles 0 5 10 15 Mi.

Scale 1:300,000

One centimeter represents 3 kilometers.

One inch represents approximately 4.7 miles.

a

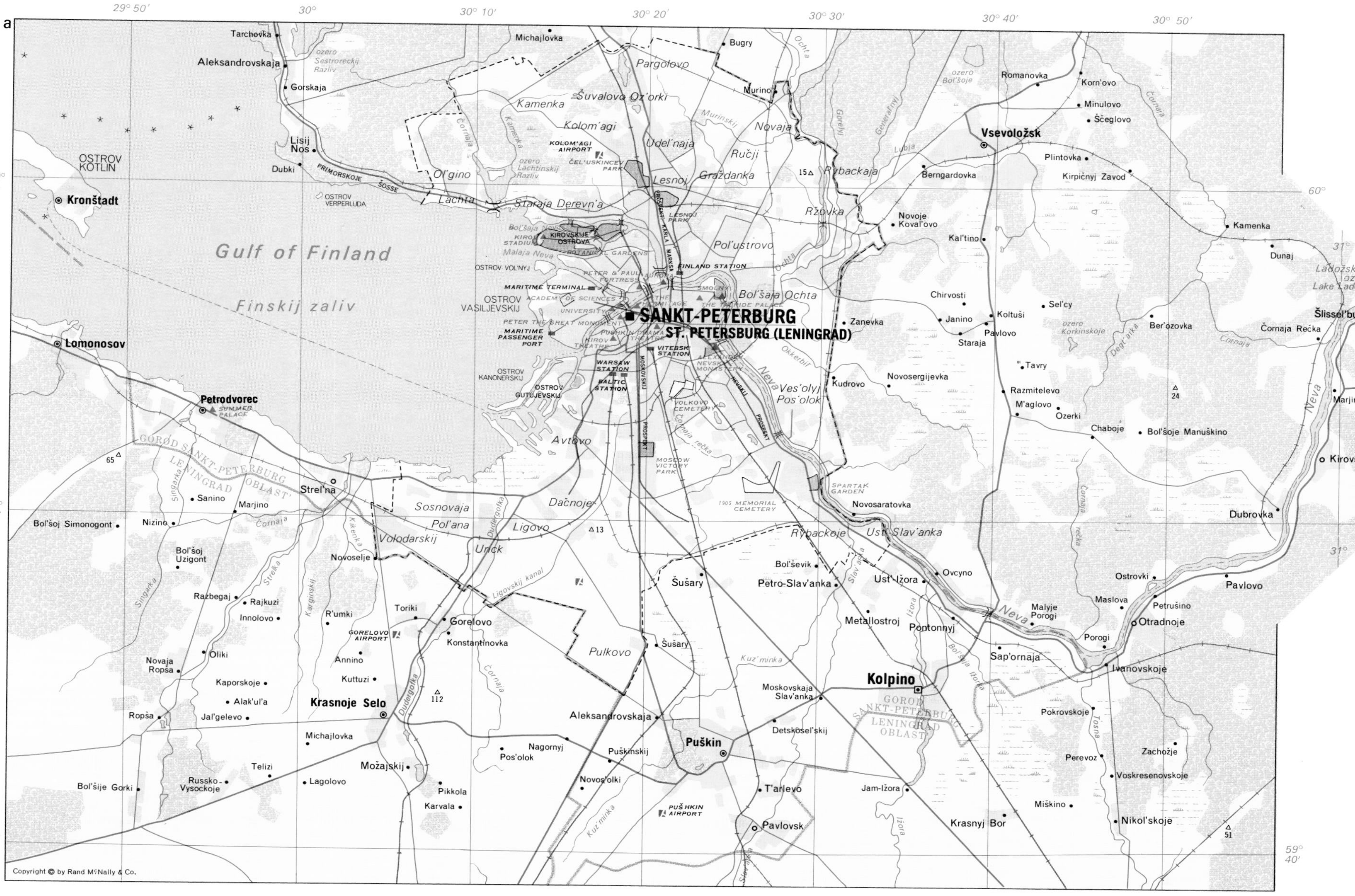

29° 50′
30°
30° 10′
30° 20′
30° 30′
30° 40′
30° 50′
60°
59° 50′
59° 40′
Gulf of Finland
Finskij zaliv
OSTROV KOTLIN
Kronštadt
Lomonosov
Petrodvorec
Strel'na
SANKT-PETERBURG
ST. PETERSBURG (LENINGRAD)
OSTROV VASILJEVSKIJ
Neva
Vsevoložsk
Kolpino
Puškin
Pavlovsk
Krasnoje Selo
Šlissel'burg
Kirovsk
Otradnoje
Ladožskoje ozero
Lake Ladoga
Tarchovka
Aleksandrovskaja
Gorskaja
Lisij Nos
Dubki
Michajlovka
Pargolovo
Bugry
Murino
Kamenka
Šuvalovo
Oz'orki
Kolom'agi
Udel'naja
Novaja
Ručji
Lesnoj
Graždanka
Ol'gino
Lachta
Staraja Derevn'a
Poľustrovo
Boľšaja Ochta
Rževka
Avtovo
Dačnoje
Ligovo
Uryck
Volodarskij
Sosnovaja Poľana
Pulkovo
Šušary
Rybackoje
Ust'-Slav'anka
Ves'olyj Pos'olok
Kudrovo
Zanevka
Janino
Koltuši
Kaľtino
Romanovka
Minulovo
Ščeglovo
Plintovka
Berngardovka
Kamenka
Dunaj
Ber'ozovka
Čornaja Rečka
Marjino
Dubrovka
Pavlovo
Ostrovki
Maslova
Petrušino
Porogi
Ivanovskoje
Sap'ornaja
Pontonnyj
Metallostroj
Ust'-Ižora
Ovcyno
Novosaratovka
Petro-Slav'anka
Boľševik
Gorelovo
Konstantinovka
Toriki
Annino
Kuttuzi
R'umki
Novoselje
Nizino
Sanino
Marjino
Boľšoj Simonogont
Boľšoj Uzigont
Razbegaj
Rajkuzi
Innolovo
Oliki
Novaja Ropsa
Kaporskoje
Alak'ul'a
Jaľgelevo
Ropša
Michajlovka
Telizi
Russko-Vysockoje
Boľšije Gorki
Lagolovo
Možajskij
Pikkola
Karvala
Nagornyj Pos'olok
Aleksandrovskaja
Puškinskij
Novos'olki
T'arlevo
Detskoseľskij
Moskovskaja Slav'anka
Jam-Ižora
Krasnyj Bor
Pokrovskoje
Perevoz
Zachožje
Voskresenovskoje
Miškino
Nikoľskoje
GOROD SANKT-PETERBURG
LENINGRAD OBLAST'
Copyright © by Rand McNally & Co.

b

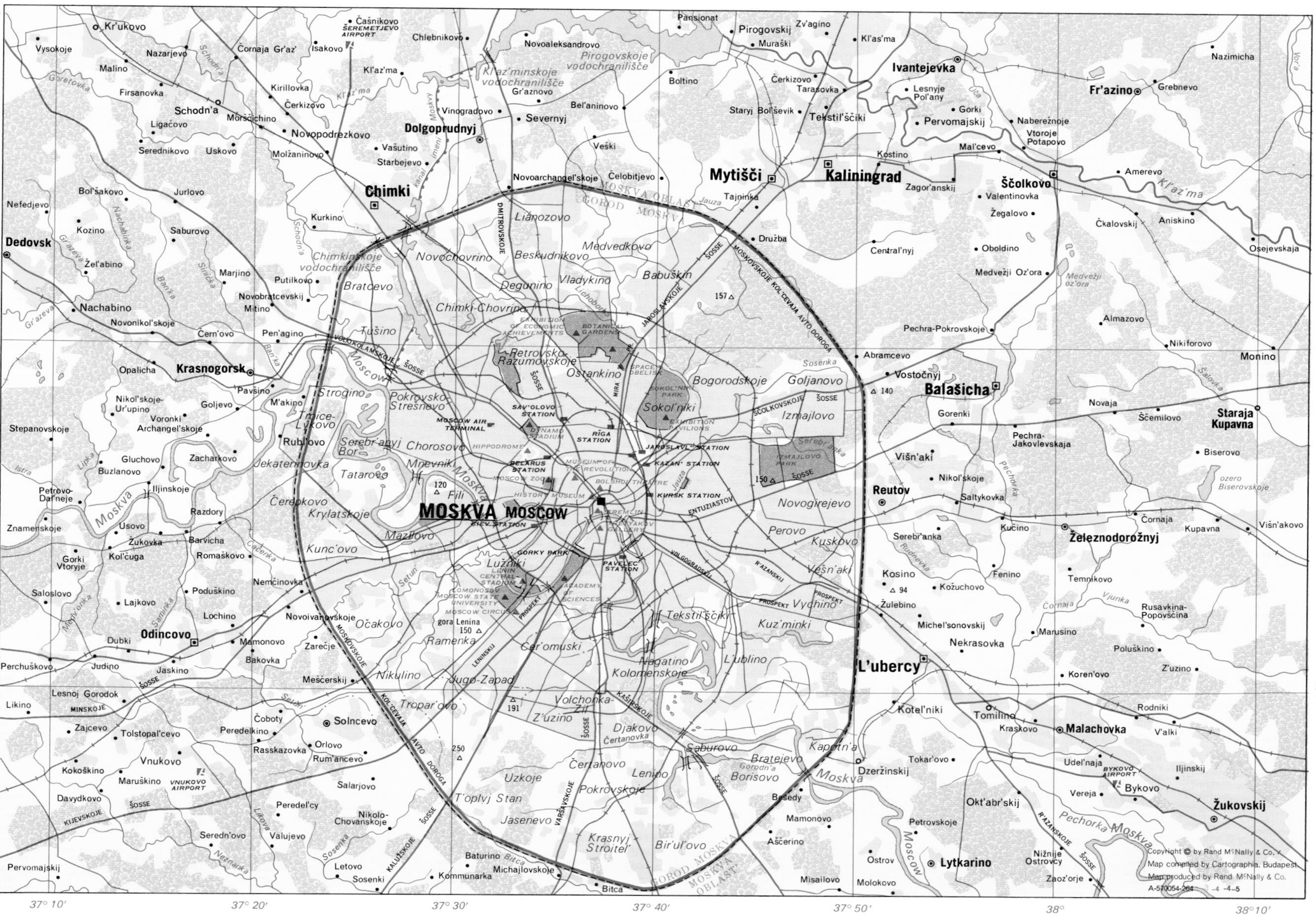

37° 10′
37° 20′
37° 30′
37° 40′
37° 50′
38°
38° 10′
55° 50′
55° 40′
MOSKVA MOSCOW
Moskva
Chimki
Dolgoprudnyj
Mytišči
Kaliningrad
Ivantejevka
Fr'azino
Ščolkovo
Balašicha
Reutov
Železnodorožnyj
L'ubercy
Dzeržinskij
Lytkarino
Odincovo
Krasnogorsk
Dedovsk
Solncevo
Malachovka
Žukovskij
Staraja Kupavna
Monino
Kr'ukovo
Vysokoje
Nazarjevo
Čornaja Gr'az'
Isakovo
Šeremetjevo Airport
Chlebnikovo
Pansionat
Pirogovskij
Zv'agino
Kl'as'ma
Pirogovskoje vodochranilišče
Kl'az'minskoje vodochranilišče
Bol'tino
Tarasovka
Lesnyje Pol'any
Pervomajskij
Nazimicha
Grebnevo
Novopodrezkovo
Vinogradovo
Severnyj
Lianozovo
Medvedkovo
Babuškin
Beskudnikovo
Vladykino
Degunino
Novochovrino
Chimkinskoje vodochranilišče
Bratcevo
Tušino
Strogino
Ostankino
Bogorodskoje
Goljanovo
Izmajlovo
Sokol'niki
Perovo
Novogrejevo
Kuskovo
Vešn'aki
Vychino
Kuz'minki
L'ublino
Nagatino
Kolomenskoje
Tekstil'ščiki
Čer'omuški
Ramenka
Očakovo
Nikulino
Jugo-Zapad
Tropar'ovo
Z'uzino
Volchonka-Zil
Djakovo
Saburovo
Bratejevo
Borisovo
Kapotn'a
Čertanovo
Lenino
Pokrovskoje
Uzkoje
T'oplyj Stan
Jasenevo
Krasnyj Stroitel'
Bir'ul'ovo
Mnevniki
Krylatskoje
Kunc'ovo
Mazilovo
Fili
Tatarovo
Tušino
Vostočnyj
Kosino
Žulebino
Kraskovo
Tomilino
Bykovo
Vnukovo
Vnukovo Airport
Bykovo Airport
Nachabino
Mitino
Pavšino
Znamenskoje
Usovo
Barvicha
Nemčinovka
Zarečje
Mamonovo
Bakovka
Jaskino
Perchuškovo
Judino
Lesnoj Gorodok
Likino
Zajcevo
Tolstopal'cevo
Kokoškino
Maruškino
Davydkovo
Salarjevo
Peredel'cy
Nikolo-Chovanskoje
Valujevo
Seredn'ovo
Pervomajskij
Letovo
Sosenki
Kommunarka
Baturino
Michajlovskoje
Bitca
Misailovo
Molokovo
Ostrov
Mamonovo
Aščerino
Besedy
Petrovskoje
Nižnije Ostrovcy
Zaoz'orje
Vereja
Oktʼabrʼskij
Udel'naja
Il'jinskij
Tokar'ovo
Kotel'niki
Rodniki
Vlasov
Koren'ovo
Z'uzino
Marusino
Poluškino
Rusavkina-Popovščina
Temnikovo
Fenino
Kučino
Kupavna
Višn'akovo
Saltykovka
Nikol'skoje
Pechra-Jakovlevskaja
Gorenki
Novaja
Ščemilovo
Biserovo
Nikiforovo
Almazovo
Pechra-Pokrovskoje
Abramcevo
Medvežji Oz'ora
Oboldino
Žegalovo
Čkalovskij
Anisikno
Osejevskaja
Amerevo
Central'nyj
Zagor'anskij
Družba
Tajninka
Kostino
Mal'cevo
Nabereznoje
Vtoroje Potapovo
GOROD MOSKVA
MOSKVA OBLAST'
Copyright © by Rand McNally & Co.
Map compiled by Cartographia, Budapest.
Map produced by Rand McNally & Co.
A-570054-264 -4 -4-5

	AREA (km²)	POPULATION
SANKT-PETERBURG	2,800	4,850,000
MOSKVA	3,200	9,950,000

MAP FORM	ostrov	ozero	štadion	vodochranilišče	vokzal
ENGLISH	island	lake	stadium	reservoir	rail terminal
DEUTSCH	Insel	See	Stadion	Stausee	Bahnhof
ESPAÑOL	isla	lago	estadio	estanque	terminal ferroviaria
FRANÇAIS	île	lac	stade	reservoir	gare
PORTUGUÊS	ilha	lago	estádio	reservatório	estação ferroviária

Kilometers 0 5 10 15 Km.

Statute Miles 0 5 10 15 Mi.

Scale 1:300,000

One centimeter represents 3 kilometers.

One inch represents approximately 4.7 miles.

	AREA (km²)	POPULATION
MADRID	1,250	3,875,000
MILANO	1,900	3,975,000
LISBOA	1,150	2,150,000
BARCELONA	950	3,825,000

MAP FORM	aeroporto	arroyo	estación	ponta	ribeira	riera
ENGLISH	airport	brook	station	point	creek	creek
DEUTSCH	Flughafen	Bach	Bahnhof	Landspitze	Bach	Bach
ESPAÑOL	aeropuerto	arroyo	estación	punta	riachuelo	riera
FRANÇAIS	aéroport	ruisseau	gare	pointe	crique	crique
PORTUGUÊS	aeroporto	arroio	estação	ponta	riacho	riacho

Kilometers 0 5 10 15 Km.

Statute Miles 0 5 10 15 Mi.

Scale 1:300,000

One centimeter represents 3 kilometers.

One inch represents approximately 4.7 miles

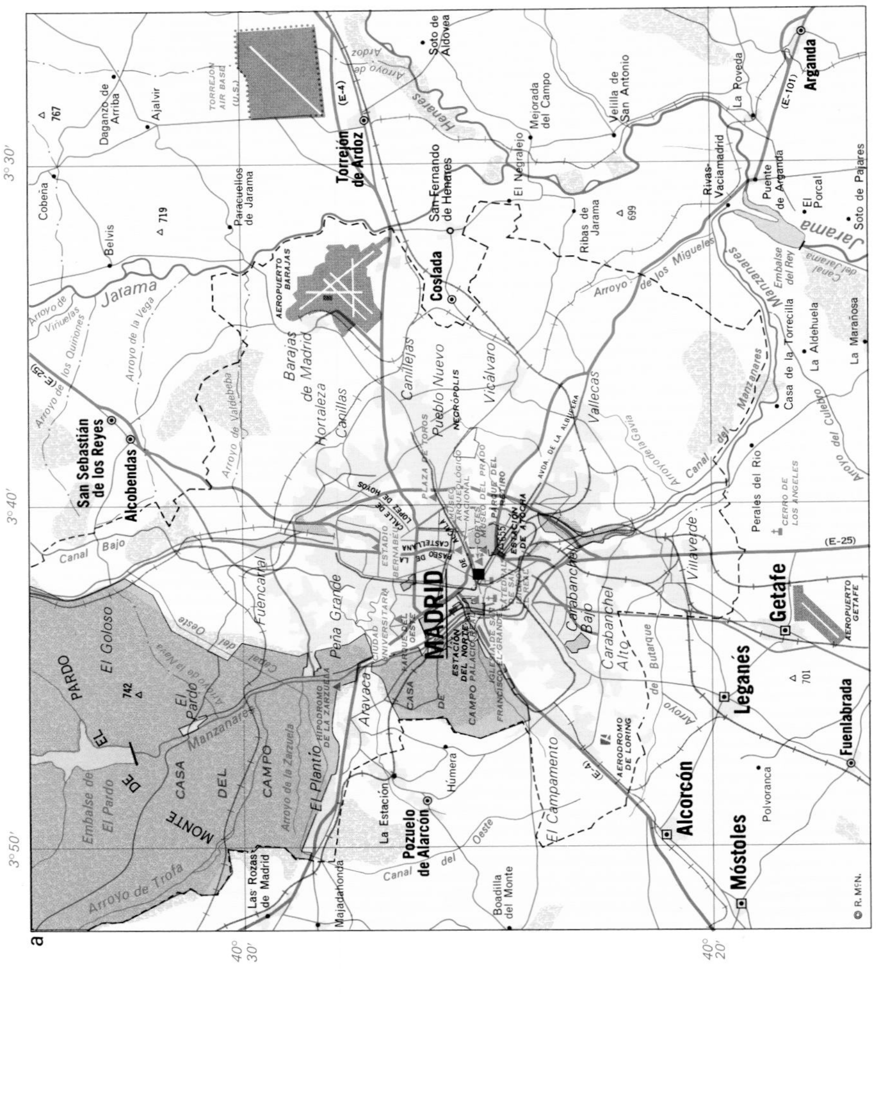
a
MADRID
Alcorcón
Móstoles
Leganés
Getafe
Fuenlabrada
Coslada
Torrejón de Ardoz
San Sebastián de los Reyes
Alcobendas
Pozuelo de Alarcón
Arganda
AEROPUERTO BARAJAS
© R.McN.

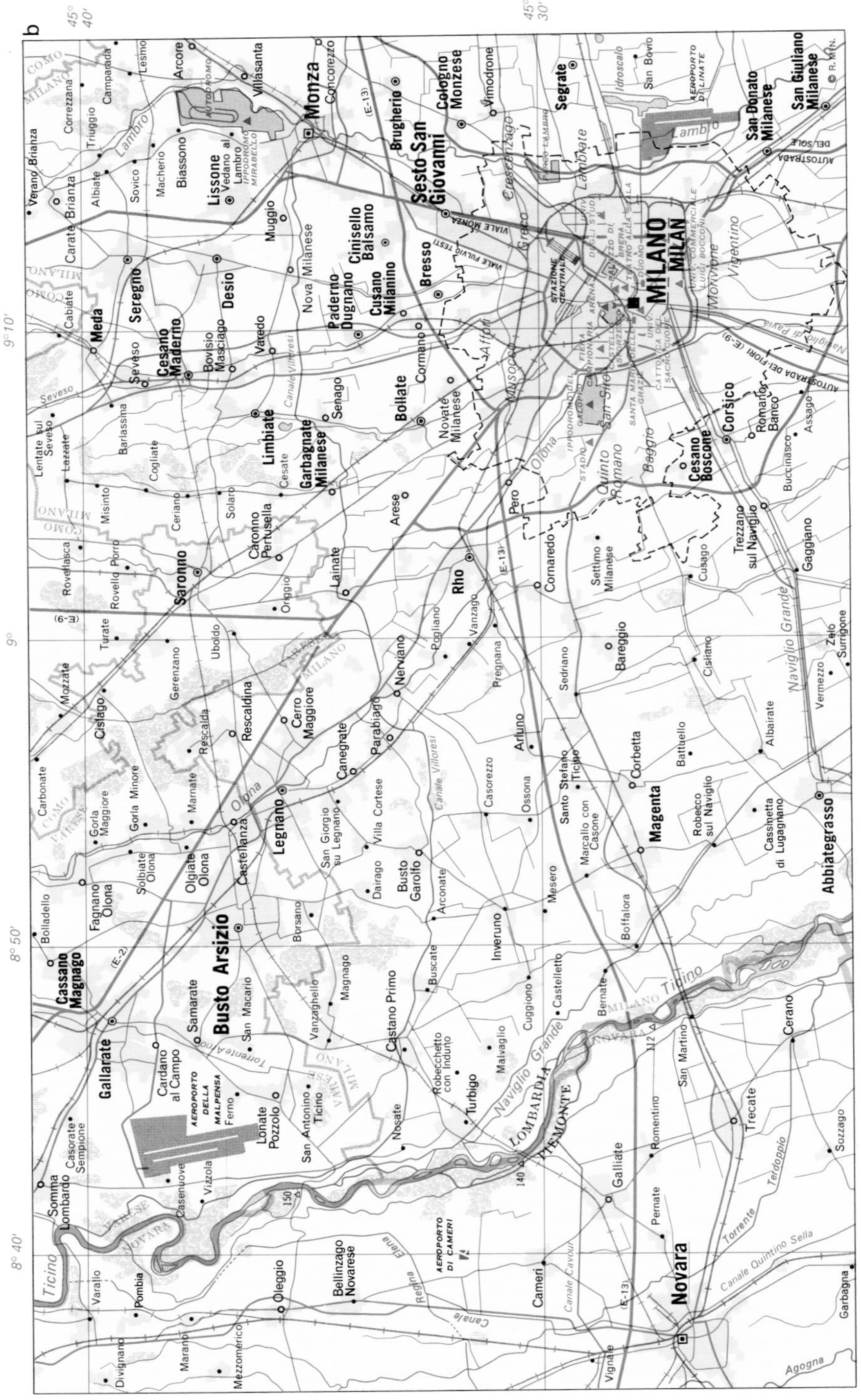
b
MILANO
MILAN
Monza
Sesto San Giovanni
Busto Arsizio
Legnano
Gallarate
Novara
Rho
Saronno
Abbiategrasso
Magenta
AEROPORTO DELLA MALPENSA
© R.McN.

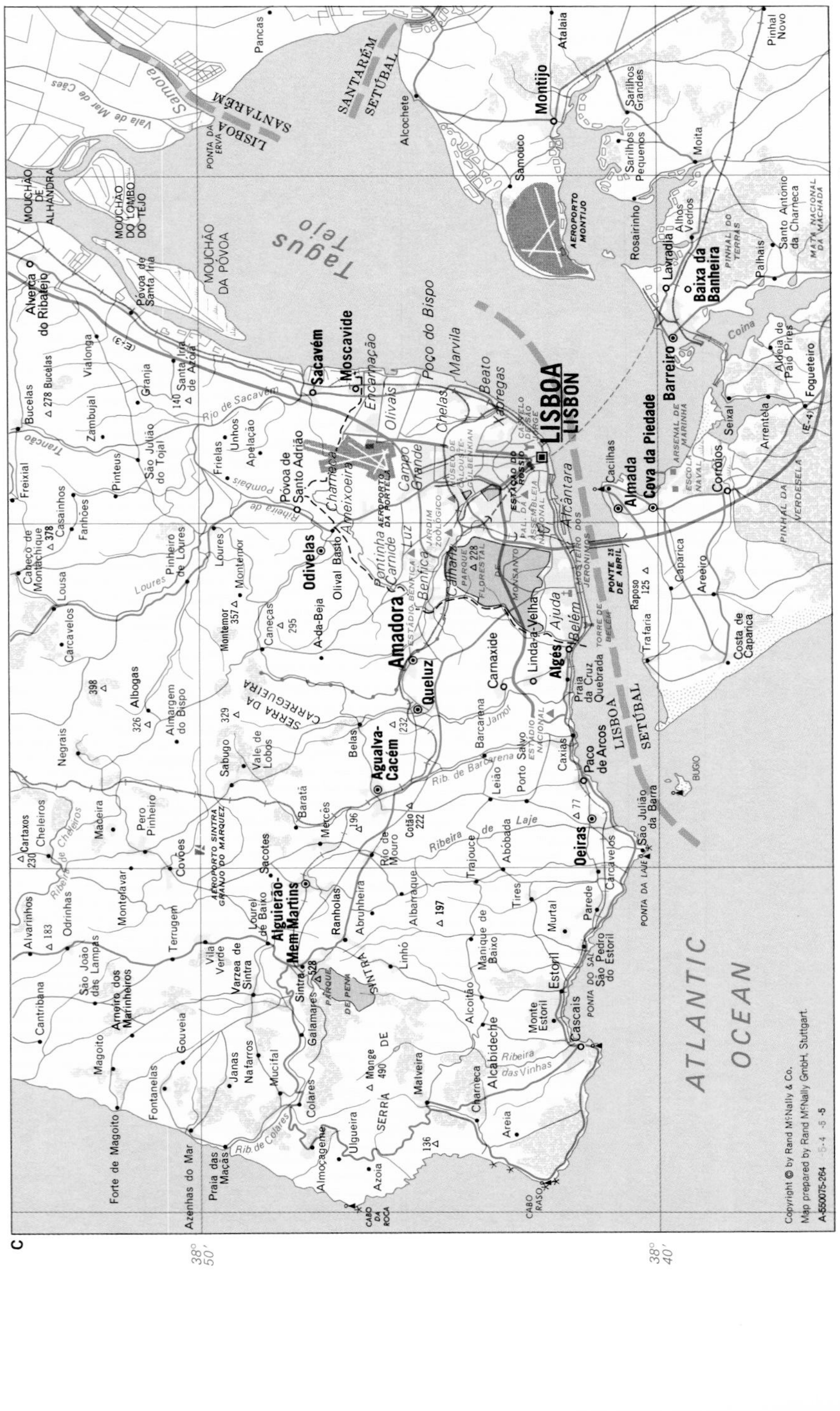
c
LISBOA
LISBON
Amadora
Queluz
Odivelas
Almada
Barreiro
Cascais
Oeiras
Sintra
Montijo
Tagus
Tejo
ATLANTIC OCEAN
Copyright © by Rand McNally & Co.
Map prepared by Rand McNally GmbH, Stuttgart.

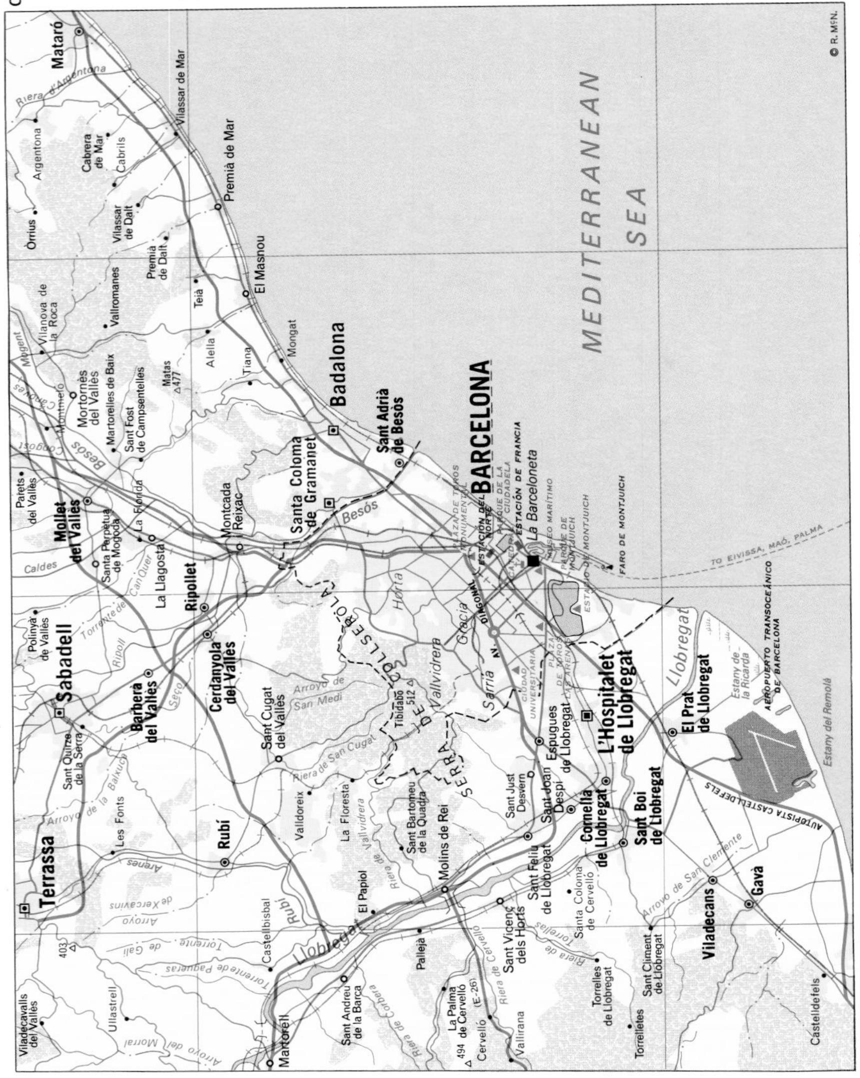
d
BARCELONA
Badalona
Sabadell
Terrassa
Mataró
L'Hospitalet de Llobregat
El Prat de Llobregat
Santa Coloma de Gramanet
Cornellà de Llobregat
MEDITERRANEAN SEA
© R.McN.

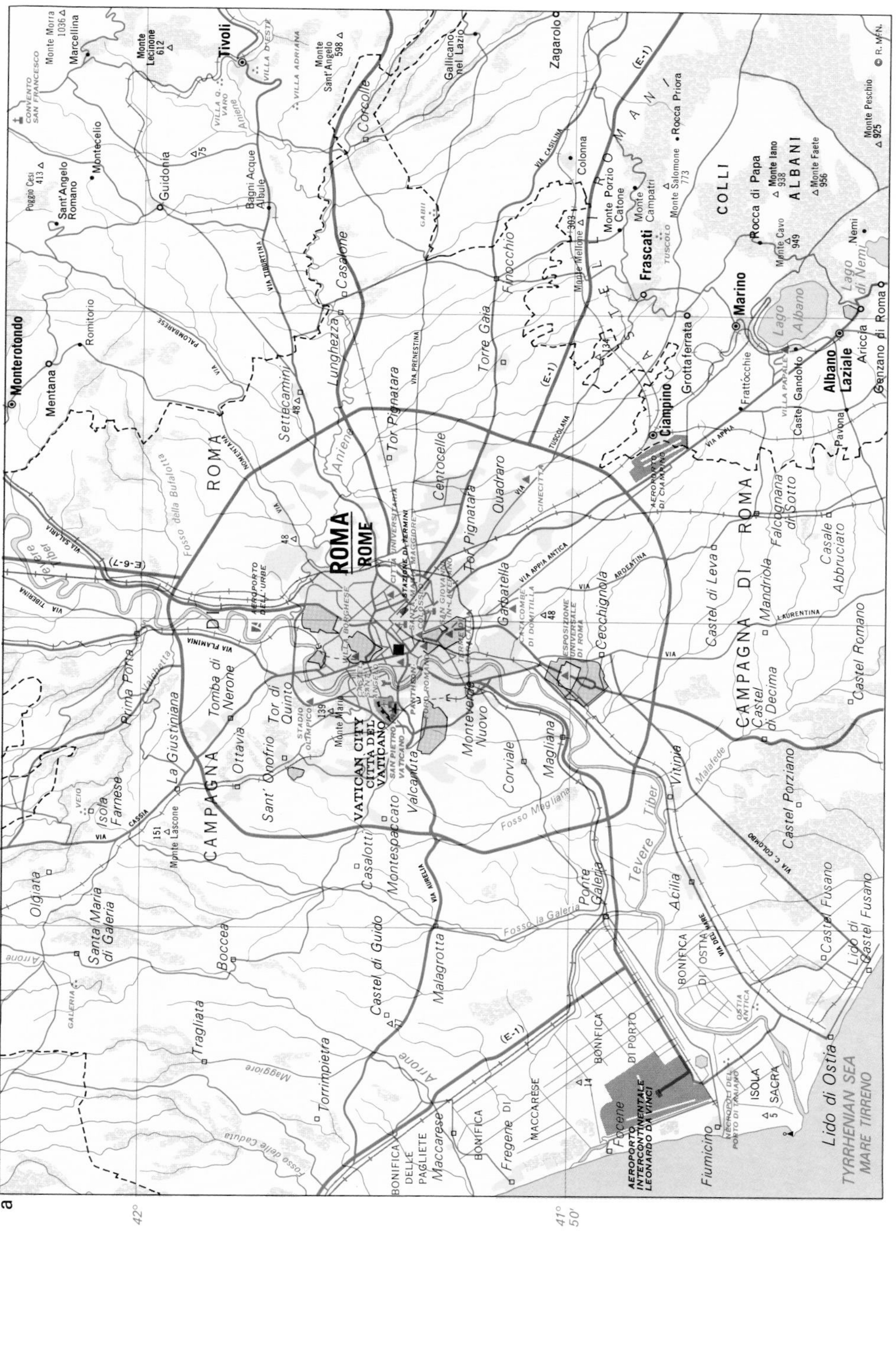
a
ROMA
ROME

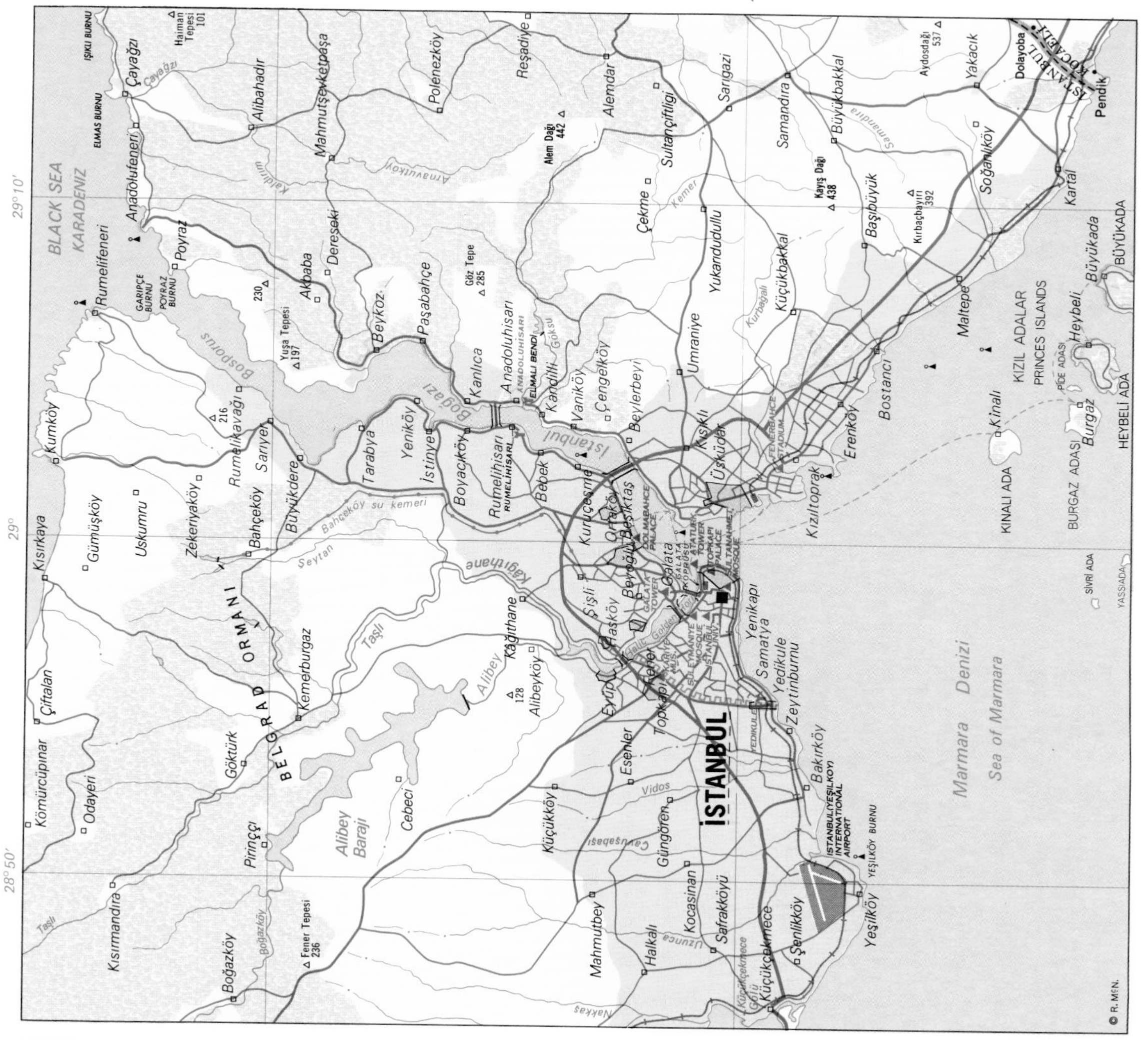
b
İSTANBUL

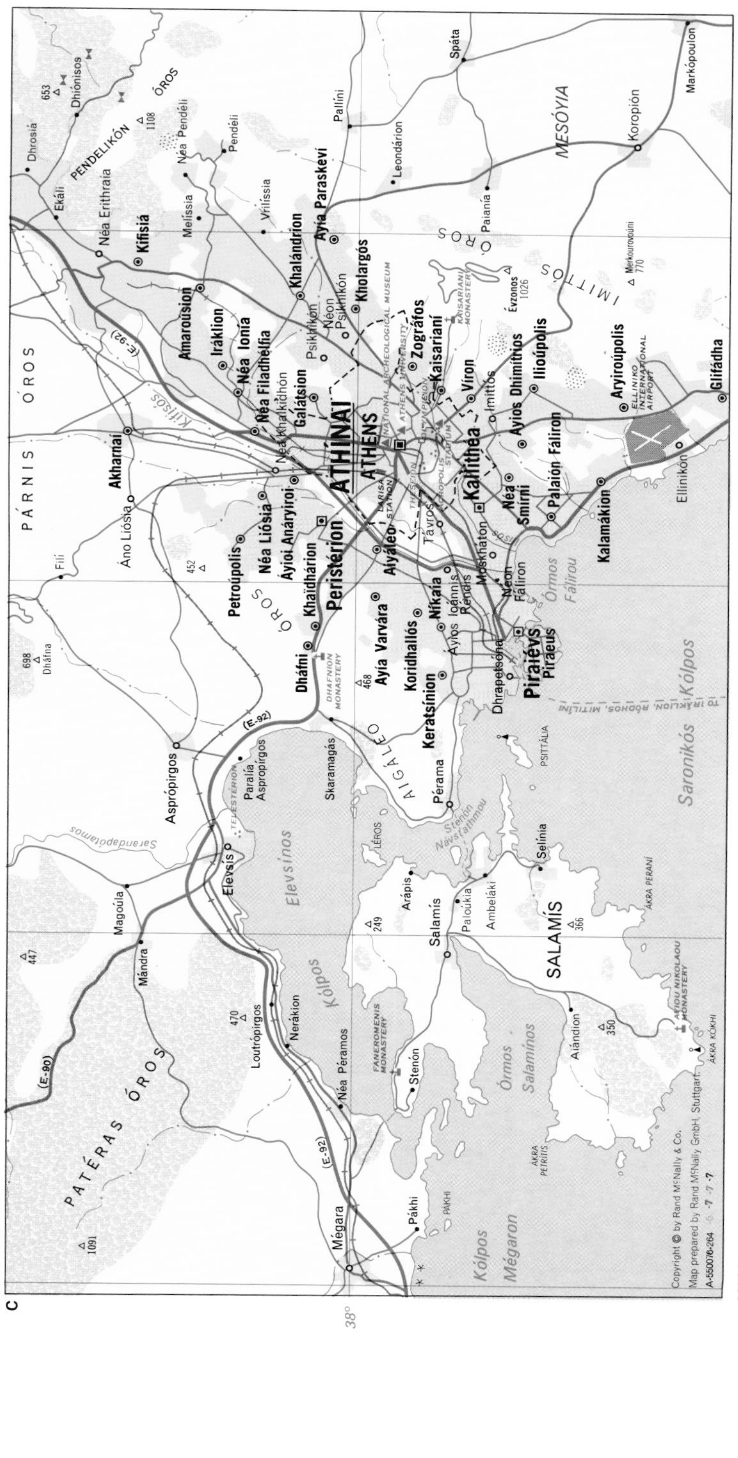
c
ATHÍNAI
ATHENS

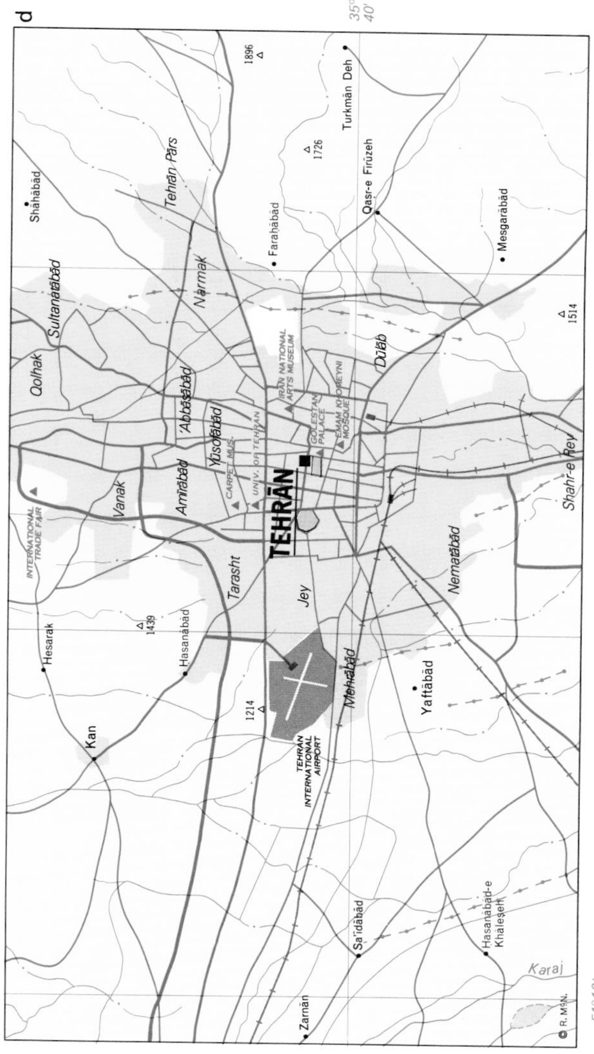
d
TEHRĀN

Kilometers 0 5 10 15 Km.
Statute Miles 0 5 10 15 Mi.

Scale 1:300,000
One centimeter represents 3 kilometers.
One inch represents approximately 4.7 miles.

	AREA (km²)	POPULATION
ROMA	2,000	3,250,000
ATHÍNAI	1,100	3,350,000
İSTANBUL	1,300	4,300,000
TEHRĀN	950	5,200,000

MAP FORM	ada	burnu	camii	deresi	fosso	moni	monte
ENGLISH	island	cape	mosque	river	brook	monastery	mount
DEUTSCH	Insel	Kap	Moschee	Fluss	Bach	Kloster	Berg
ESPAÑOL	isla	cabo	mezquita	río	arroyo	monasterio	monte
FRANÇAIS	île	cap	mosquée	rivière	ruisseau	monastère	mont
PORTUGUÊS	ilha	cabo	mesquita	rio	arroio	mosteiro	monte

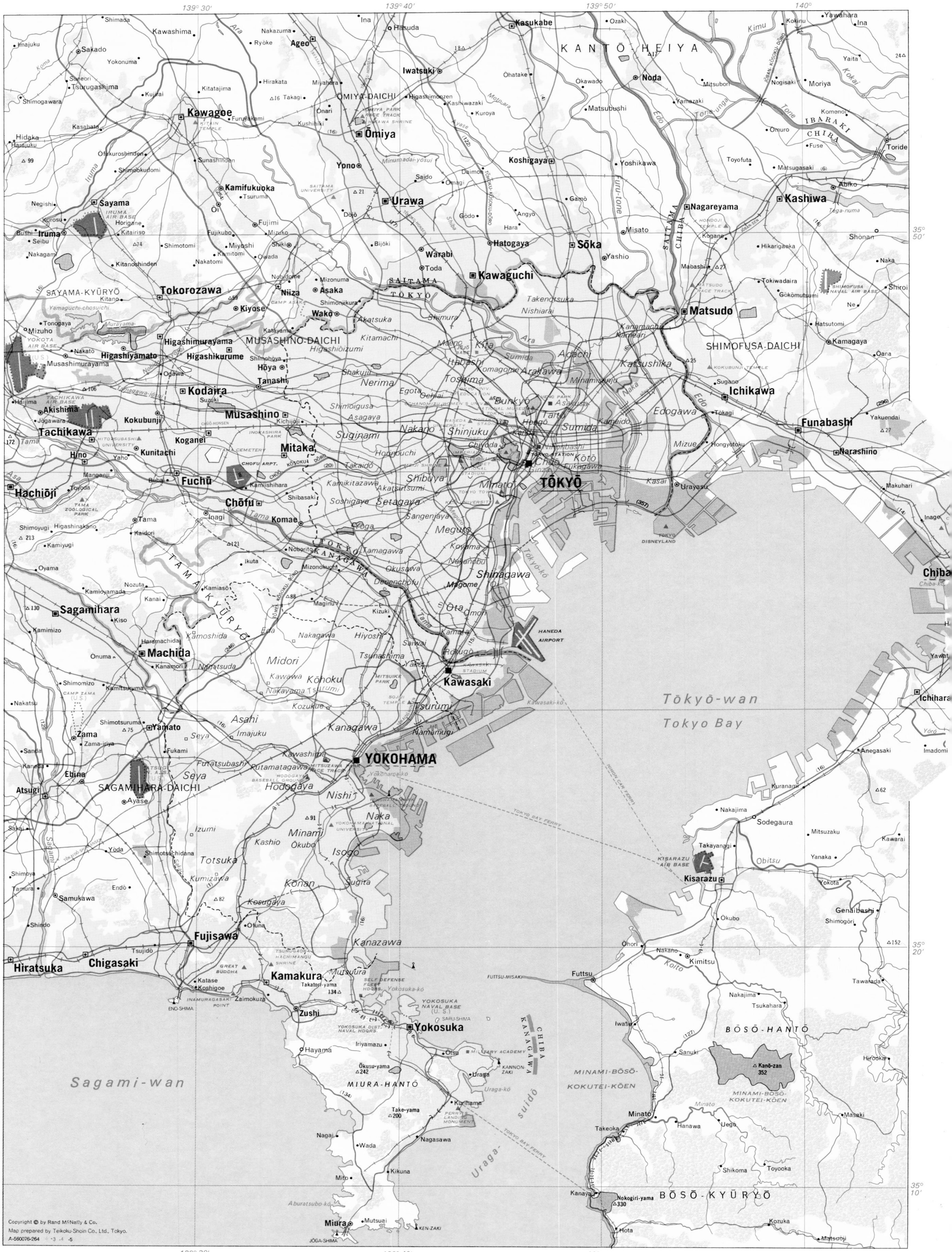
139° 30'
139° 40'
139° 50'
140°
35° 50'
35° 40'
35° 30'
35° 20'
35° 10'
KANTŌ-HEIYA
Kasukabe
Iwatsuki
Noda
Ageo
Kawagoe
Ōmiya
Urawa
Koshigaya
Nagareyama
Kashiwa
Abiko
Toride
Moriya
IBARAKI
CHIBA
SAITAMA
TŌKYŌ
Sayama
Iruma
Tokorozawa
Sōka
Hatogaya
Warabi
Kawaguchi
Matsudo
SAYAMA-KYŪRYŌ
MUSASHINO-DAICHI
SHIMOFUSA-DAICHI
Higashimurayama
Higashiyamato
Higashikurume
Kodaira
Musashino
Tachikawa
Kokubunji
Kunitachi
Koganei
Mitaka
Hino
Hachiōji
Fuchū
Chōfu
Komae
Ichikawa
Funabashi
Narashino
Chiba
Nerima
Itabashi
Kita
Adachi
Katsushika
Edogawa
Arakawa
Toshima
Bunkyō
Taitō
Sumida
Suginami
Nakano
Shinjuku
Chiyoda
Chūō
Kōtō
Minato
Shibuya
Setagaya
Meguro
Shinagawa
Ōta
TŌKYŌ
Urayasu
TOKYO DISNEYLAND
TŌKYŌ
KANAGAWA
TAMA-KYŪRYŌ
Sagamihara
Machida
Kawasaki
HANEDA AIRPORT
Tōkyō-wan
Tokyo Bay
Yamato
Zama
Ebina
Atsugi
SAGAMIHARA-DAICHI
YOKOHAMA
Hodogaya
Kanagawa
Tsurumi
Totsuka
Isogo
Kanazawa
Fujisawa
Chigasaki
Hiratsuka
Kamakura
Zushi
Yokosuka
MIURA-HANTŌ
Sagami-wan
Uraga-suidō
Miura
Kisarazu
BŌSŌ-HANTŌ
BŌSŌ-KYŪRYŌ
MINAMI-BŌSŌ-KOKUTEI-KŌEN
Kanō-zan 352
Nokogiri-yama 330
Futtsu
Kimitsu
Ichihara
Copyright © by Rand McNally & Co.
Map prepared by Teikoku-Shoin Co., Ltd., Tokyo.
A-560076-264

AREA (km²): 5,350
POPULATION: 24,350,000

MAP FORM	air base	camp	-daichi	-kō	-shima	temple	-yama
ENGLISH	air base	camp	plateau	harbor	island	temple	mountain
DEUTSCH	Luftstützpunkt	Lager	Hochebene	Hafen	Insel	Tempel	Berg
ESPAÑOL	base aérea	campo	meseta	puerto	isla	templo	montaña
FRANÇAIS	base aérienne	camp	plateau	port	île	temple	montagne
PORTUGUÊS	base aérea	campo	planalto	porto	ilha	templo	montanha

Kilometers 0 5 10 15 Km.
Statute Miles 0 5 10 15 Mi.

Scale 1:300,000
One centimeter represents 3 kilometers.
One inch represents approximately 4.7 miles.

a

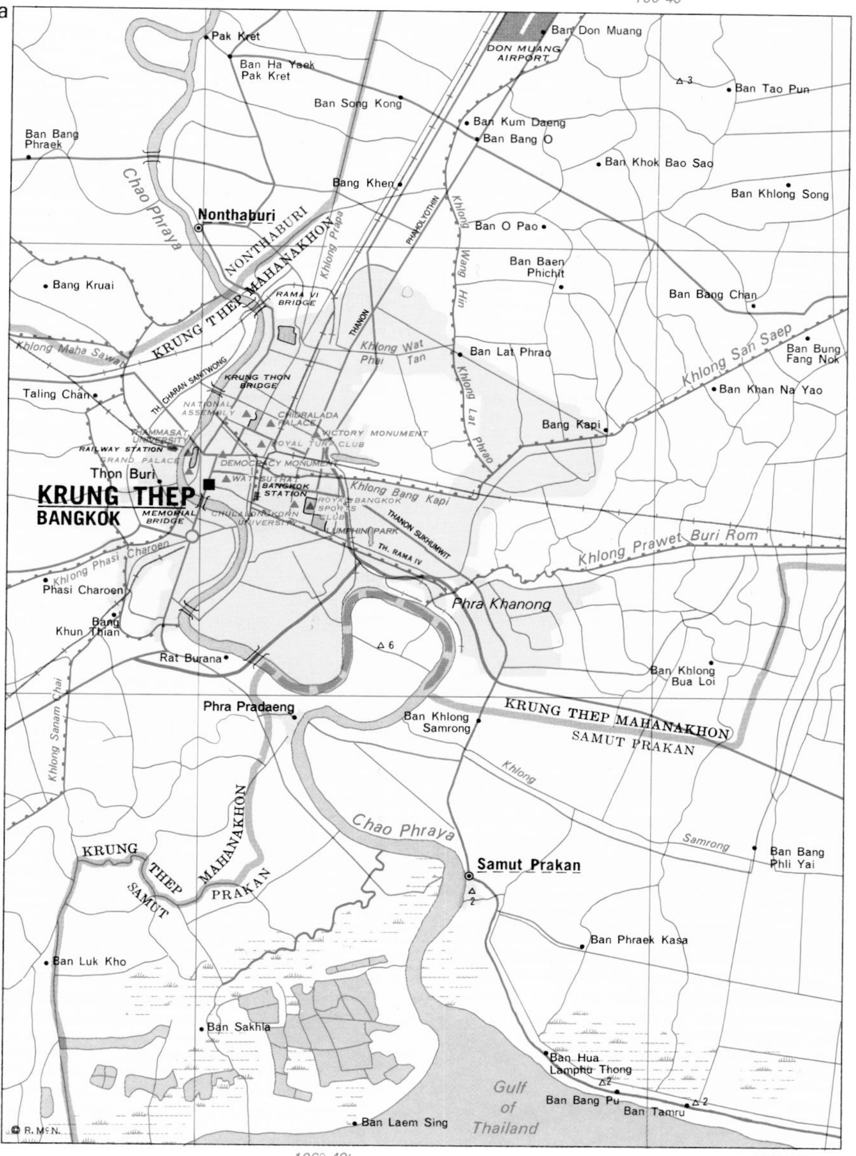
100°30'
100°40'
13° 50'
13° 40'
Pak Kret
Ban Don Muang
DON MUANG AIRPORT
Ban Ha Yaek Pak Kret
Ban Tao Pun
Ban Song Kong
Ban Kum Daeng
Ban Bang O
Ban Bang Phraek
Ban Khok Bao Sao
Bang Khen
Ban Khlong Song
Chao Phraya
Nonthaburi
NONTHABURI
KRUNG THEP MAHANAKHON
Ban O Pao
Ban Baen Phichit
Bang Kruai
Ban Bang Chan
Khlong Maha Sawat
Khlong San Saep
Ban Lat Phrao
Ban Bung Fang Nok
Taling Chan
Ban Khan Na Yao
Bang Kapi
KRUNG THEP
BANGKOK
Thon Buri
Khlong Bang Kapi
Khlong Prawet Buri Rom
Phasi Charoen
Bang Khun Thian
Phra Khanong
Rat Burana
Ban Khlong Bua Loi
Phra Pradaeng
Ban Khlong Samrong
KRUNG THEP MAHANAKHON
SAMUT PRAKAN
Chao Phraya
Samut Prakan
Ban Bang Phli Yai
KRUNG THEP MAHANAKHON
SAMUT PRAKAN
Ban Phraek Kasa
Ban Luk Kho
Ban Sakhla
Ban Hua Lamphu Thong
Ban Bang Pu
Ban Tamru
Ban Laem Sing
Gulf of Thailand
© R. McN.

b

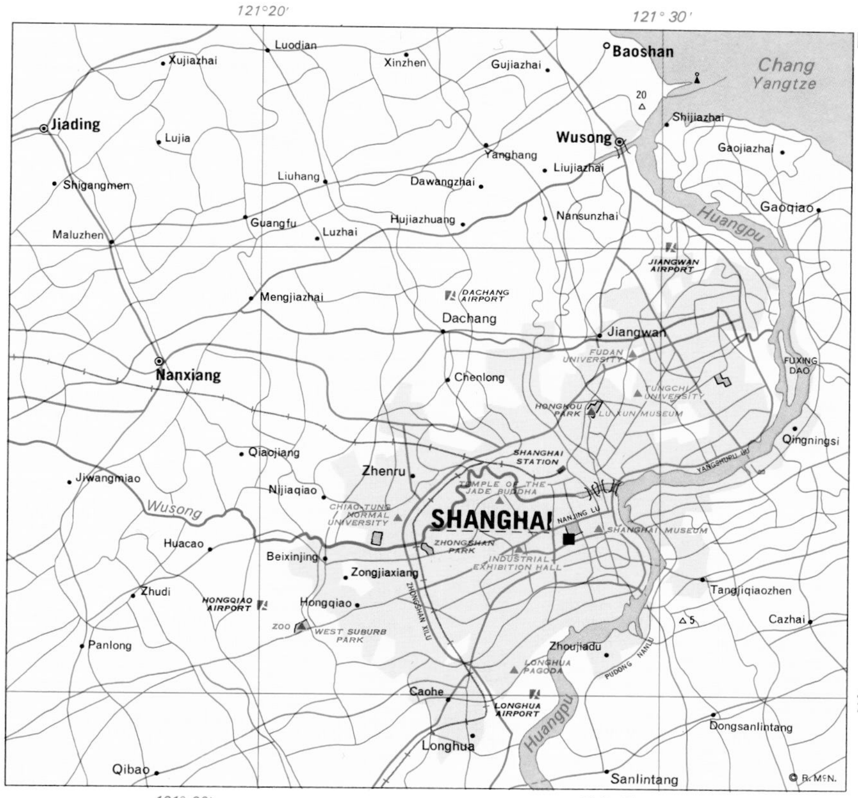
121°20'
121° 30'
31° 20'
31° 10'
Luodian
Baoshan
Xujiazhai
Xinzhen
Gujiazhai
Chang Yangtze
Jiading
Lujia
Wusong
Shijiazhai
Gaojiazhai
Yanghang
Liujiazhai
Shigangmen
Liuhang
Dawangzhai
Gaoqiao
Guangfu
Hujiazhuang
Nansunzhai
Maluzhen
Luzhai
Huangpu
JIANGWAN AIRPORT
DACHANG AIRPORT
Mengjiazhai
Dachang
Jiangwan
FUDAN UNIVERSITY
Nanxiang
Chenlong
Qingningsi
Qiaojiang
Zhenru
Jiwangmiao
Nijiaqiao
SHANGHAI
Wusong
Huacao
Beixinjing
Zongjiaxiang
Zhudi
HONGQIAO AIRPORT
Hongqiao
Tangjiqiaozhen
Cazhai
Panlong
Zhoujiadu
LONGHUA PAGODA
Caohe
LONGHUA AIRPORT
Longhua
Dongsanlintang
Qibao
Sanlintang
© R. McN.

c

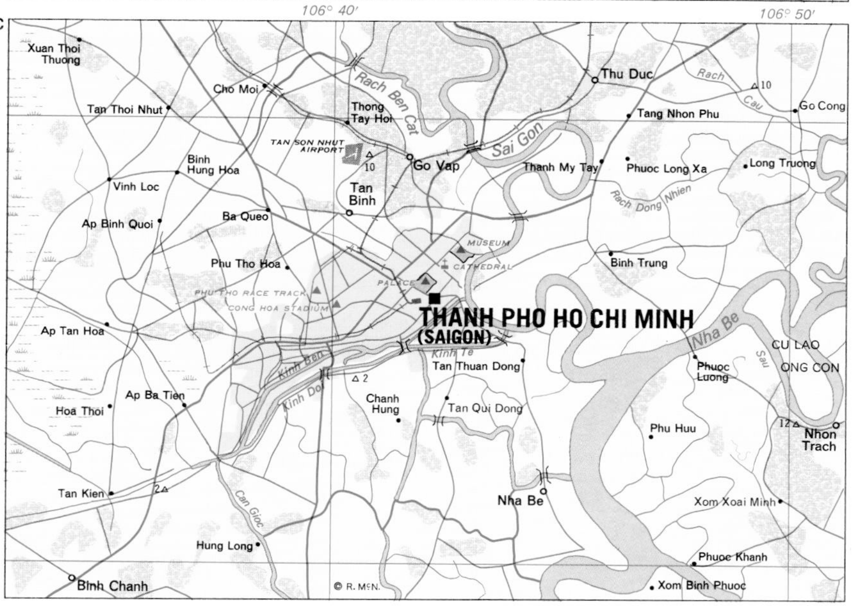
106° 40'
106° 50'
10° 50'
10° 40'
Xuan Thoi Thuong
Thu Duc
Cho Moi
Tan Thoi Nhut
Thong Tay Hoi
Tang Nhon Phu
Go Cong
TAN SON NHUT AIRPORT
Go Vap
Sai Gon
Binh Hung Hoa
Thanh My Tay
Phuoc Long Xa
Long Truong
Vinh Loc
Tan Binh
Ap Binh Quoi
Ba Queo
Binh Trung
Phu Tho Hoa
THANH PHO HO CHI MINH
(SAIGON)
Ap Tan Hoa
Tan Thuan Dong
Nha Be
CU LAO ONG CON
Phuoc Luong
Ap Ba Tien
Chanh Hung
Tan Qui Dong
Hoa Thoi
Phu Huu
Nhon Trach
Tan Kien
Nha Be
Xom Xoai Minh
Hung Long
Phuoc Khanh
Binh Chanh
Xom Binh Phuoc
© R. McN.

d

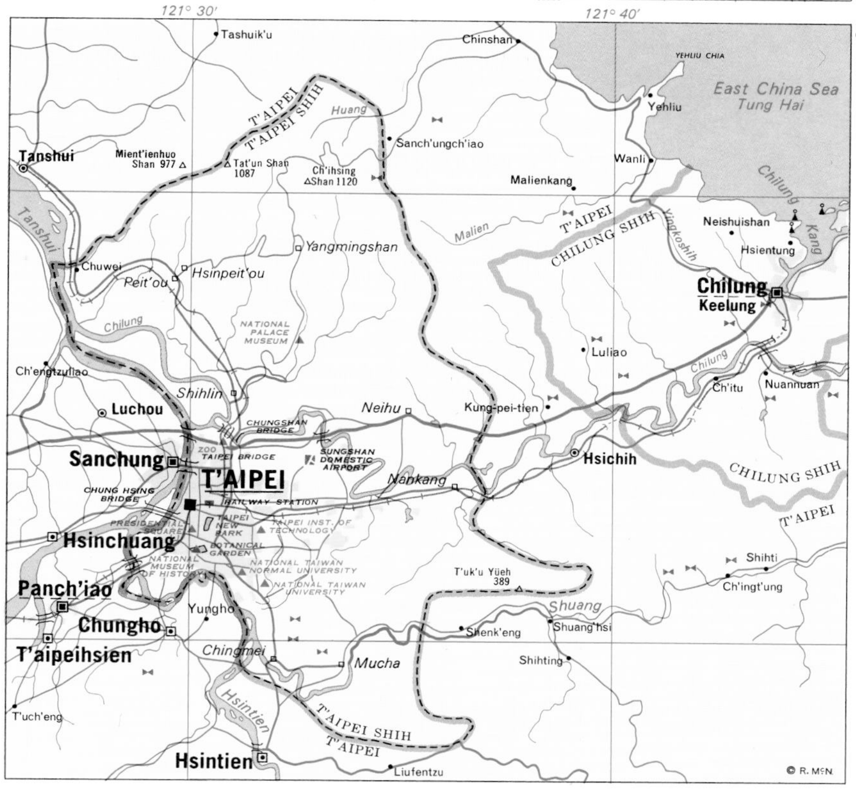
121° 30'
121° 40'
25° 10'
25°
Tashuik'u
Chinshan
East China Sea
Tung Hai
Yehliu
Tanshui
Mien'tienhuo Shan 977
Tat'un Shan 1087
Ch'ihsing Shan 1120
Sanch'ungch'iao
Malienkang
Wanli
T'AIPEI SHIH
Yangmingshan
T'AIPEI
CHILUNG SHIH
Neishuishan
Hsientung
Chuwei
Hsinpeit'ou
Peit'ou
Chilung
Keelung
NATIONAL PALACE MUSEUM
Luliao
Ch'engtzuliao
Shihlin
Luchou
Neihu
Kung-pei-tien
Nuannuan
Ch'itu
Sanchung
T'AIPEI
Hsichih
Nankang
CHILUNG SHIH
T'AIPEI
Hsinchuang
Shihti
Ch'ingt'ung
T'uk'u Yüeh 389
Panch'iao
Chungho
Yungho
Shenk'eng
Shuang'hsi
T'aipeihsien
Mucha
Shihting
T'uch'eng
T'AIPEI SHIH
T'AIPEI
Hsintien
Liufentzu
© R. McN.

e

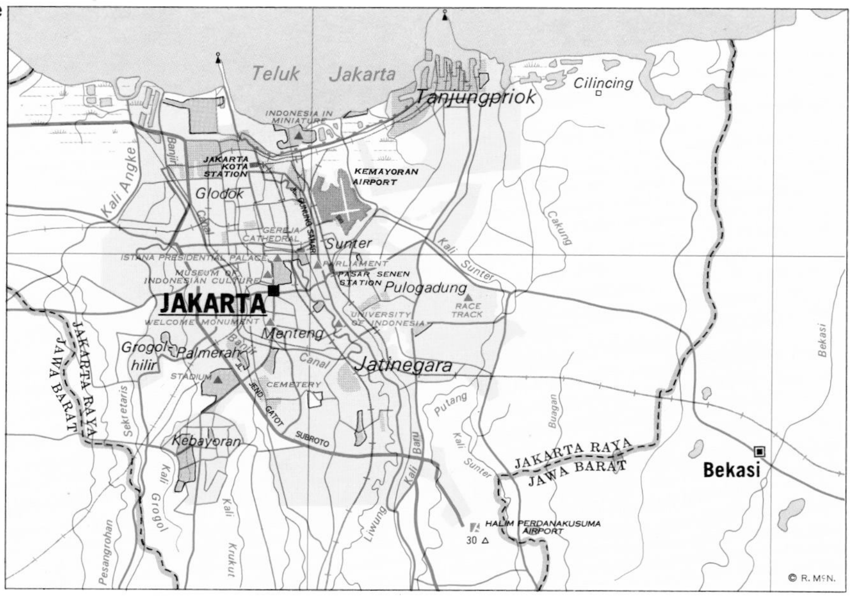
6° 10'
106°50'
107°
Teluk Jakarta
Tanjungpriok
Cilincing
KEMAYORAN AIRPORT
Glodok
Sunter
Pulogadung
JAKARTA
Menteng
Grogol
Palmerah
Jatinegara
JAKARTA RAYA
JAWA BARAT
Kebayoran
JAKARTA RAYA
JAWA BARAT
Bekasi
HALIM PERDANAKUSUMA AIRPORT
© R. McN.

f

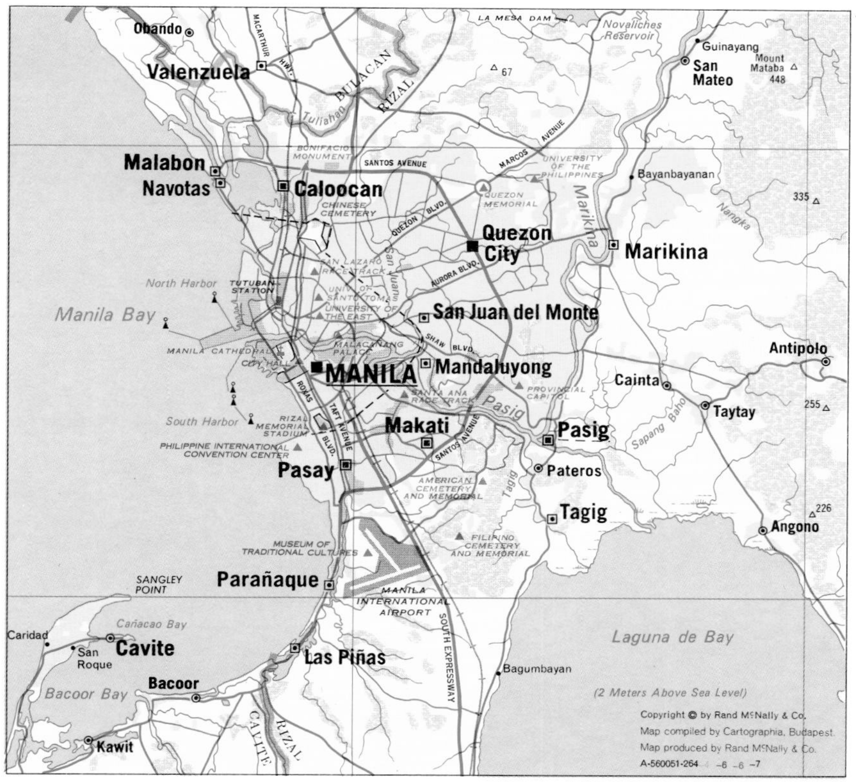
14° 40'
14° 30'
121°
121°10'
Obando
Valenzuela
San Mateo
Malabon
Navotas
Caloocan
Quezon City
Marikina
Manila Bay
San Juan del Monte
MANILA
Mandaluyong
Antipolo
Cainta
Taytay
Makati
Pasig
Pasay
Pateros
Tagig
Angono
Parañaque
Cavite
Las Piñas
Laguna de Bay
(2 Meters Above Sea Level)
Bacoor
Bacoor Bay
Kawit
Copyright © by Rand McNally & Co.
Map compiled by Cartographia, Budapest
Map produced by Rand McNally & Co.
A-560051-264

	AREA (km²)	POPULATION
KRUNG THEP (BANGKOK)	1,450	5,300,000
SAI-GON	750	2,400,000
JAKARTA	700	6,450,000
SHANGHAI	1,000	8,400,000
T'AIPEI	950	4,125,000
MANILA	650	5,900,000

MAP FORM	kali	khlong	monument	shan
ENGLISH	stream	stream	monument	mountain
DEUTSCH	Bach	Bach	Denkmal	Berg
ESPAÑOL	corriente de agua	corriente de agua	monumento	montaña
FRANÇAIS	cours d'eau	cours d'eau	monument	montagne
PORTUGUÊS	corrente de água	corrente de água	monumento	montanha

Kilometers 0 5 10 15 Km.

Statute Miles 0 5 10 15 Mi.

Scale 1:300,000

One centimeter represents 3 kilometers.

One inch represents approximately 4.7 miles.

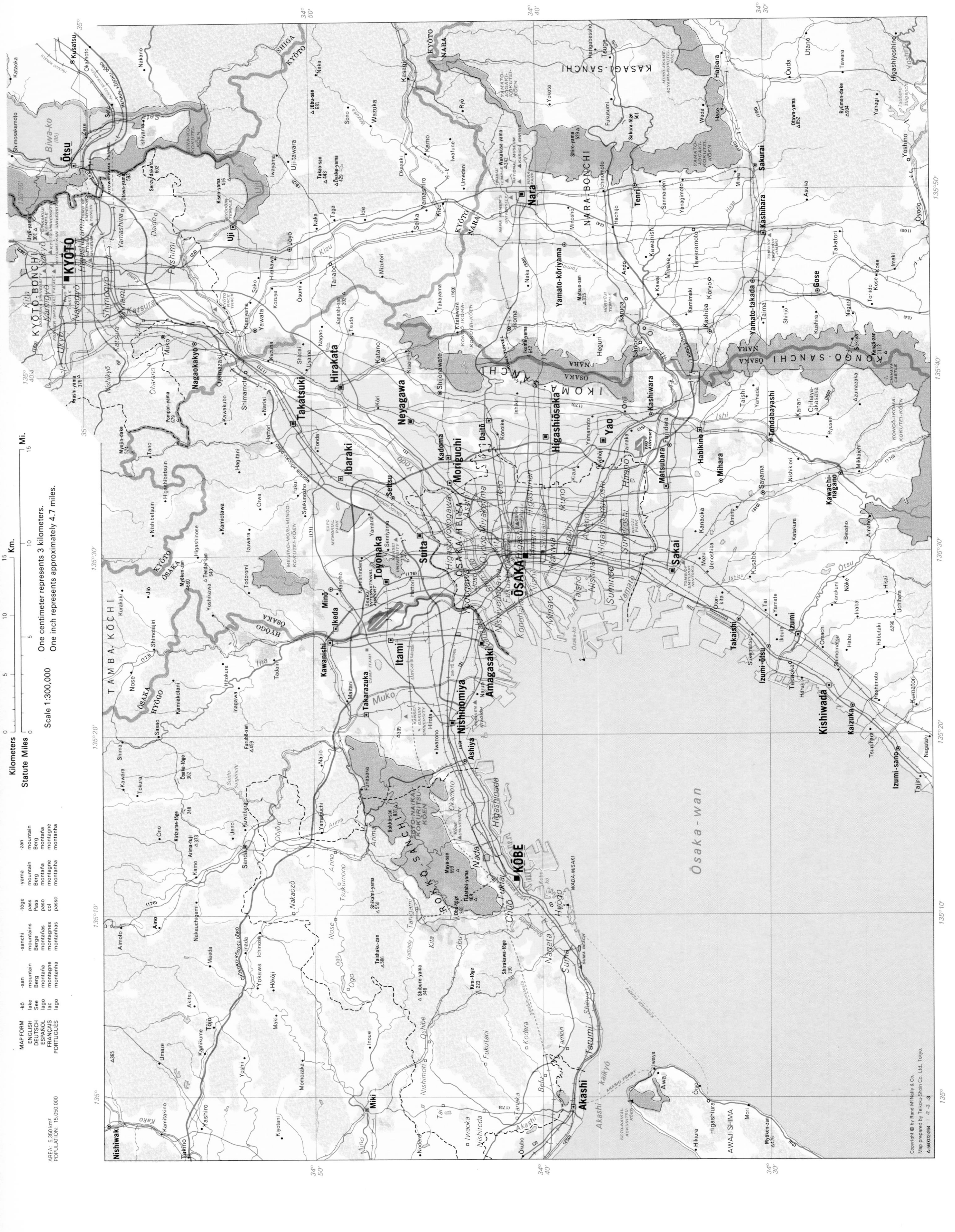
Kilometers
Statute Miles
Scale 1:300,000
One centimeter represents 3 kilometers.
One inch represents approximately 4.7 miles.
MAP FORM -kō -san -sanchi -tōge -yama -zan
ENGLISH lake mountain mountains pass mountain mountain
DEUTSCH See Berg Berge Pass Berg Berg
ESPAÑOL lago montaña montañas paso montaña montaña
FRANÇAIS lac montagne montagnes col montagne montagne
PORTUGUÊS lago montanha montanhas passo montanha montanha
AREA 5,350 km²
POPULATION 15,050,000
KYŌTO
Ōtsu
Biwa-ko
KYŌTO-BONCHI
Uji
Nara
NARA-BONCHI
Tenri
Sakurai
Kashihara
Yamato-kōriyama
Takatsuki
Hirakata
Neyagawa
Ibaraki
Suita
Toyonaka
Moriguchi
Kadoma
Higashiōsaka
Yao
ŌSAKA
Sakai
Amagasaki
Nishinomiya
Itami
Ikeda
Takarazuka
Kawanishi
Ashiya
KŌBE
Akashi
Kishiwada
Kaizuka
Izumi-sano
Izumi-ōtsu
Takaishi
Izumi
Kawachi-nagano
Tondabayashi
Ōsaka-wan
Akashi-kaikyō
AWAJI-SHIMA
ROKKŌ-SANCHI
IKOMA-SANCHI
KONGŌ-SANCHI
KASAGI-SANCHI
TAMBA-KŌCHI
SETO-NAIKAI-KOKURITSU-KŌEN
Miki
Nishiwaki
Sanda
Copyright © by Rand McNally & Co.
Map prepared by Teikoku-Shoin Co., Ltd., Tokyo.

a

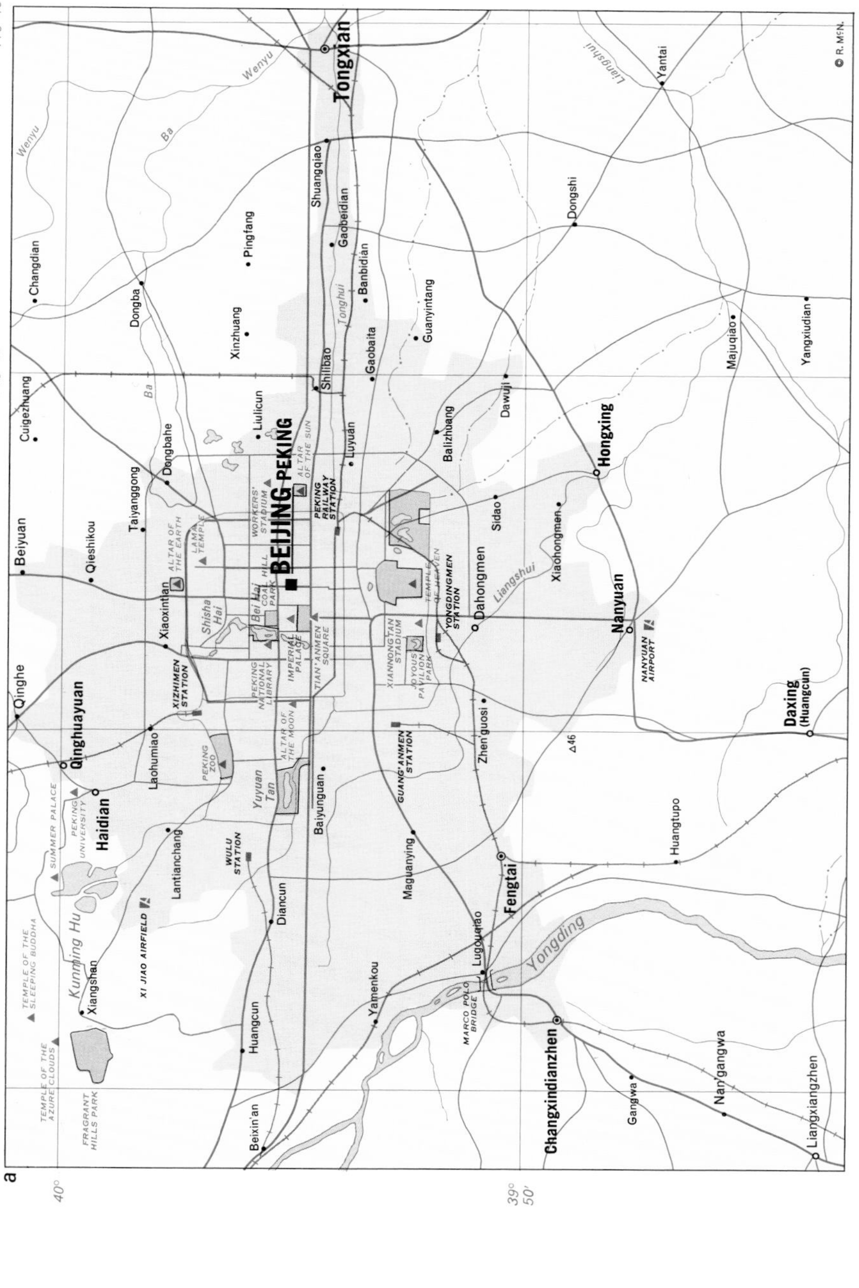

b

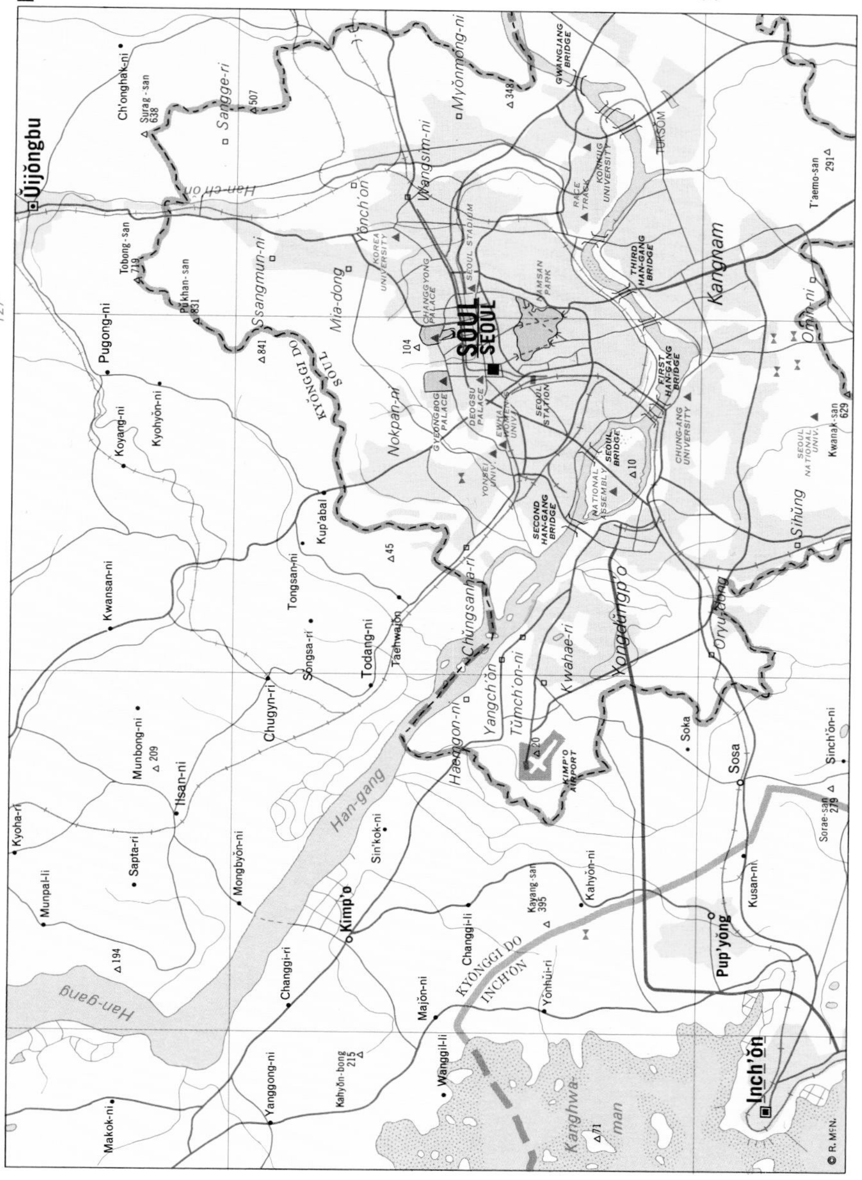

c

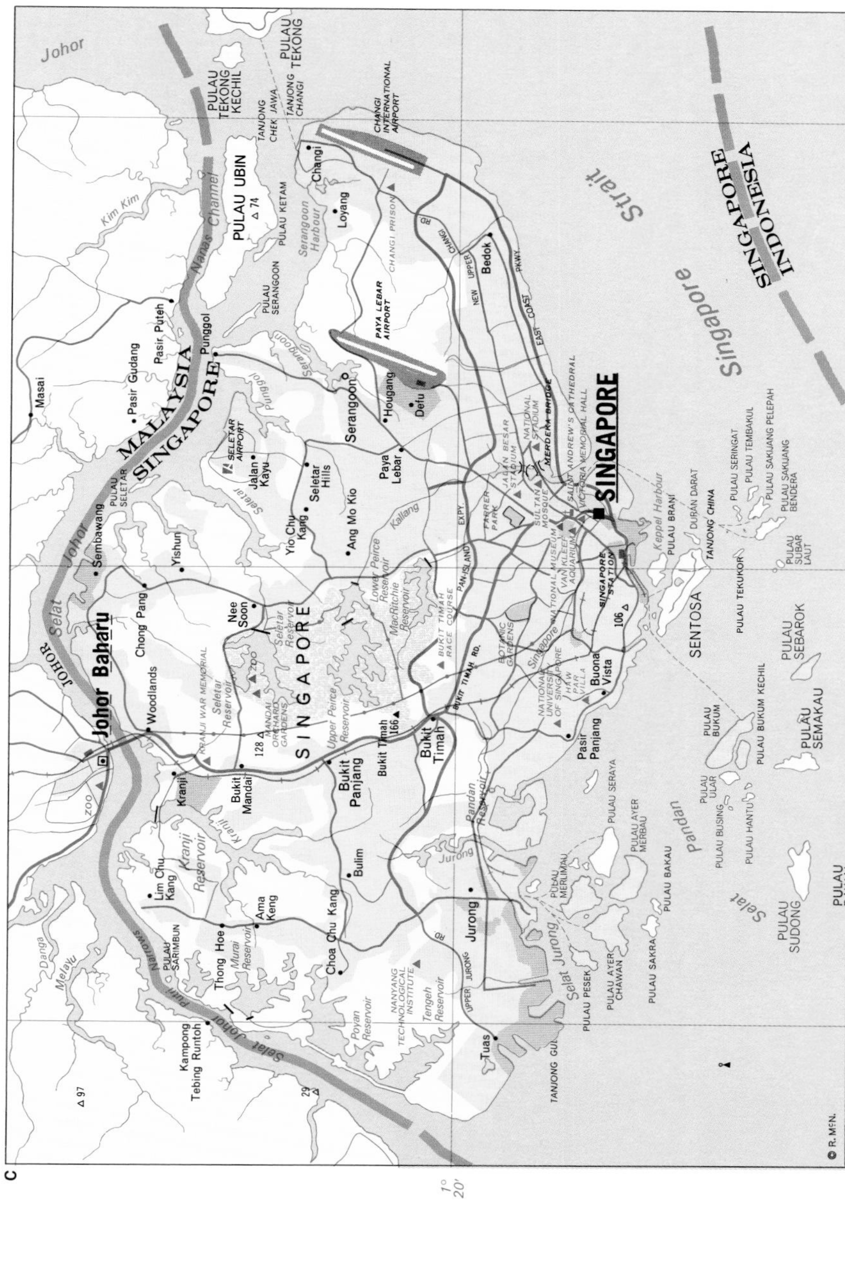

d

	AREA (km²)	POPULATION
BEIJING (PEKING)	1,550	5,300,000
SŎUL	1,450	9,300,000
SINGAPORE	900	2,600,000
HONG KONG	650	4,450,000

MAP FORM	ENGLISH	DEUTSCH	ESPAÑOL	FRANÇAIS	PORTUGUES
airport	airport	Flughafen	aeropuerto	aéroport	aeroporto
chau	island	Insel	isla	île	ilha
island	island	Insel	isla	île	ilha
park	park	Park	parque	parc	parque
peak	peak	Gipfel	pico	cime	pico
reservoir	reservoir	Stausee	estanque	réservoir	reservatório
wan	bay	Bucht	bahía	baie	baía

Scale 1:300,000

One centimeter represents 3 kilometers.
One inch represents approximately 4.7 miles.

	AREA (km²)	POPULATION
DELHI	1,400	5,500,000
BOMBAY	1,050	8,250,000
CALCUTTA	3,100	11,200,000

ENGLISH	airport	dock	island	lake	point	railroad station	road	temple
DEUTSCH	Flughafen	Dock	Insel	See	Punkt	Bahnhof	Landstrasse	Tempel
ESPAÑOL	aeropuerto	muelle	isla	lago	punta	terminal ferroviaria	camino	templo
FRANÇAIS	aéroport	quai	île	lac	pointe	gare	route	temple
PORTUGUÊS	aeroporto	cais	ilha	lago	ponta	estação ferroviária	rodovia	templo

Kilometers 0 5 10 15 Km.

Statute Miles 0 5 10 15 Mi.

Scale 1:300,000

One centimeter represents 3 kilometers.
One inch represents approximately 4.7 miles.

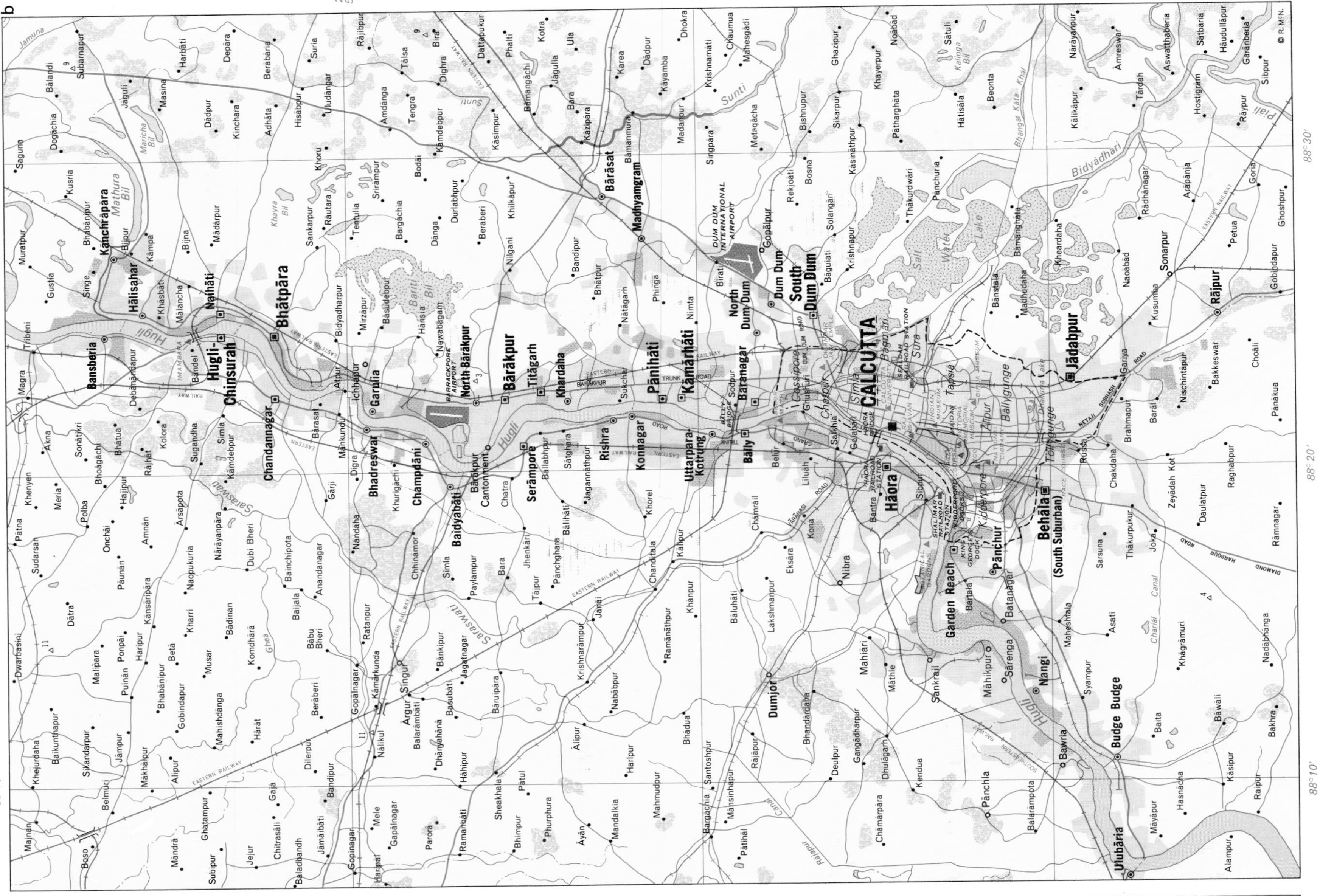
b
CALCUTTA
Hāora
Behāla (South Suburban)
Garden Reach
Dum Dum
South Dum Dum
North Dum Dum
Bārākpur
Hugli-Chinsurah
Bhātpāra
Hālisahar
Kānchrapāra
Naihāti
Bānsbēria
Serampore
Rishra
Konnagar
Uttarpara-Kotrung
Bally
Baranagar
Kāmārhāti
Pānihāti
Khardaha
Titāgarh
Chandannagar
Bhadreswar
Champdāni
Baidyabāti
Budge Budge
Uluberia
Jādabpur
Rājpur
Bārāsat
Madhyamgram
Nangi
Dumjor
Hugli
DUM DUM INTERNATIONAL AIRPORT
88°10'
88°20'
88°30'
22°30'
22°40'
22°50'
© R. McN.

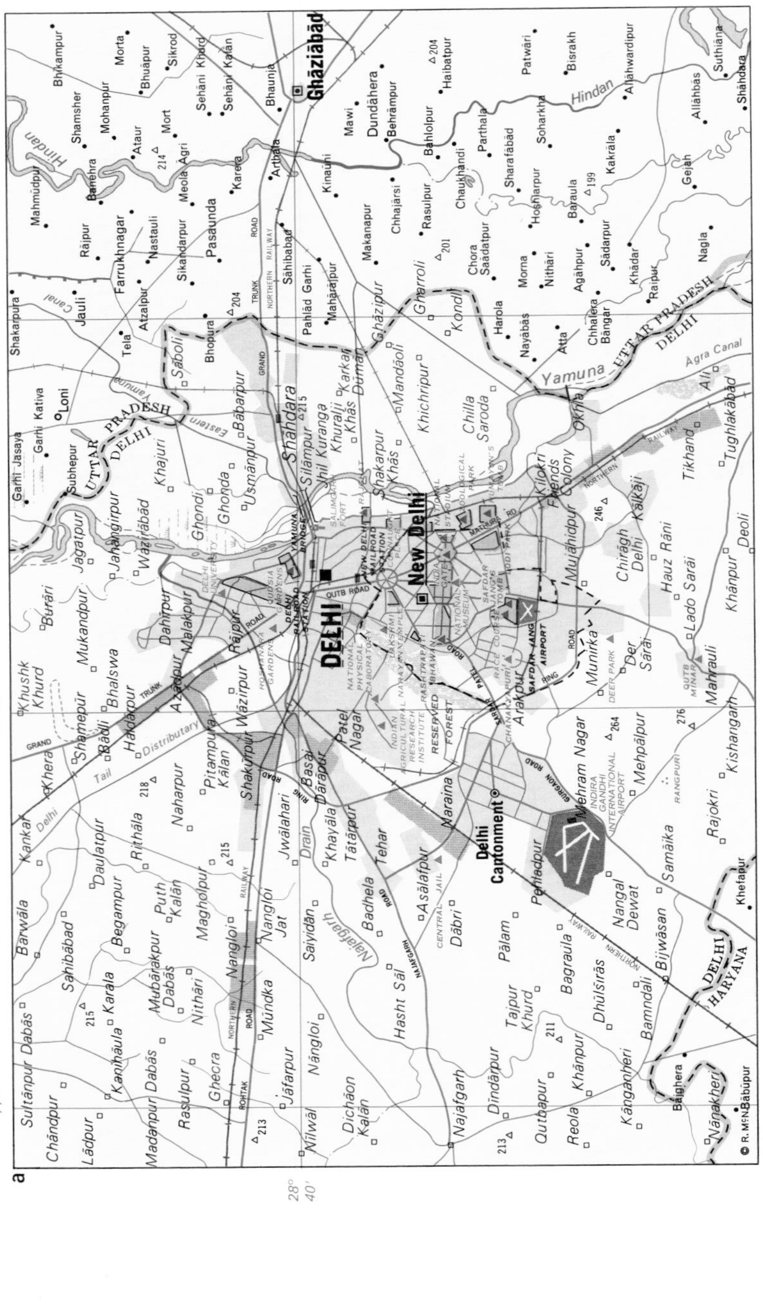
a
DELHI
New Delhi
Delhi Cantonment
Ghāziābād
Shāhdara
Yamuna
Hindan
UTTAR PRADESH
DELHI
HARYANA
77°
77°10'
77°20'
28°40'
© R. McN.

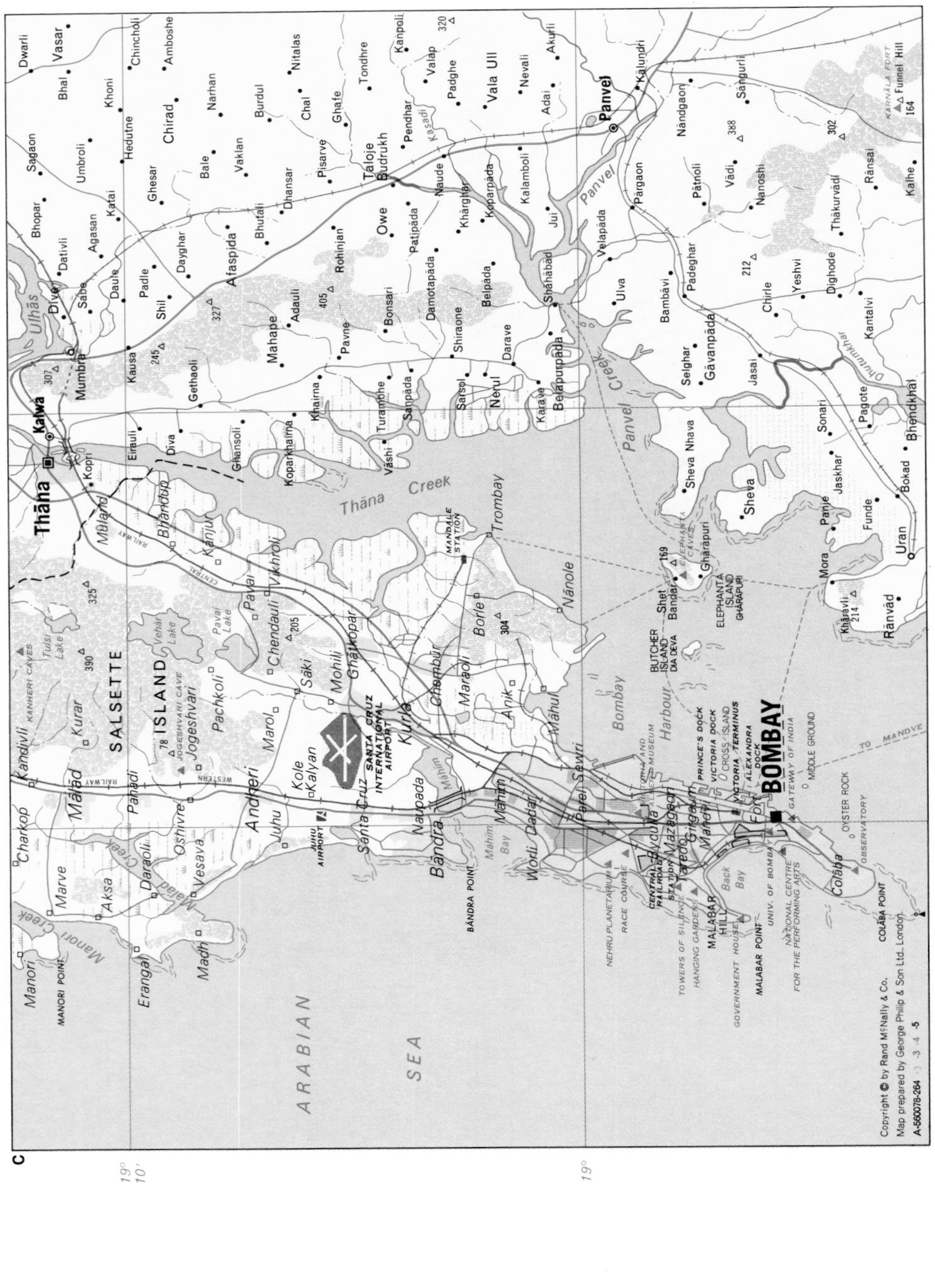
c
BOMBAY
Thāna
Thāna Creek
Panvel
SALSETTE ISLAND
ARABIAN SEA
Trombay
Bāndra
Kurla
Andheri
Chembur
SANTA CRUZ INTERNATIONAL AIRPORT
ELEPHANTA ISLAND
BUTCHER ISLAND
Bombay Harbour
Colāba
Mahim Bay
Back Bay
72°50'
73°
19°
19°10'
Copyright © by Rand McNally & Co.
Map prepared by George Philip & Son Ltd., London.

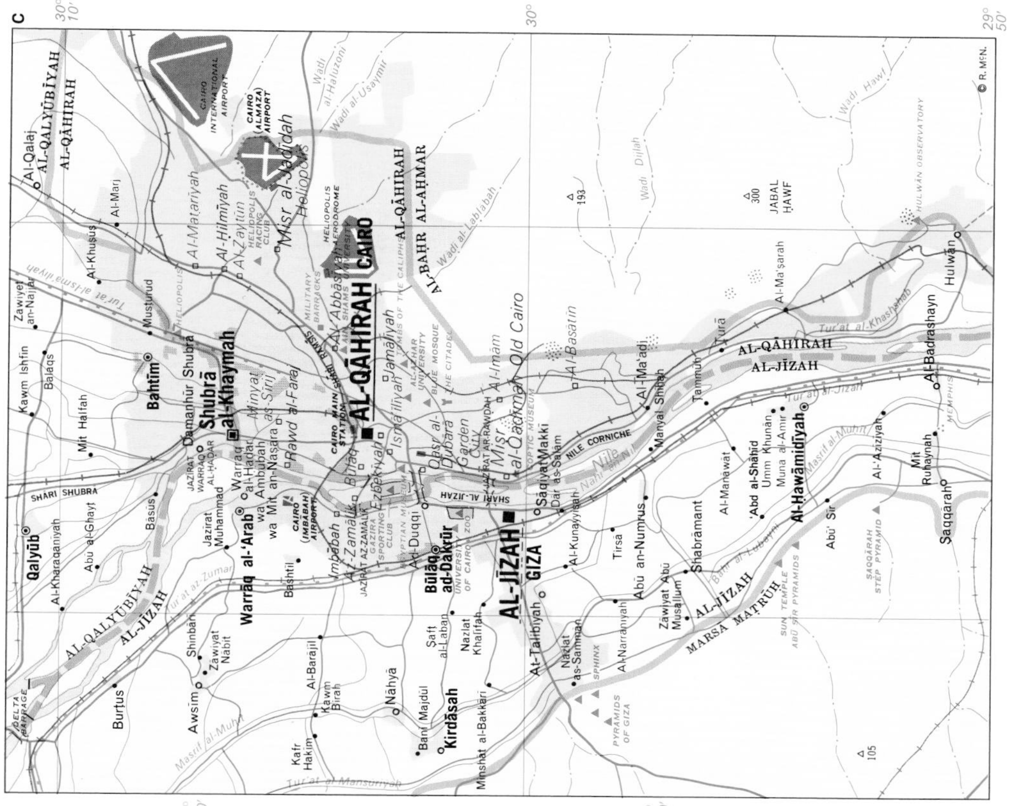
c
AL-QĀHIRAH
CAIRO
GIZA
AL-JĪZAH
Shubrā al-Khaymah
Nile

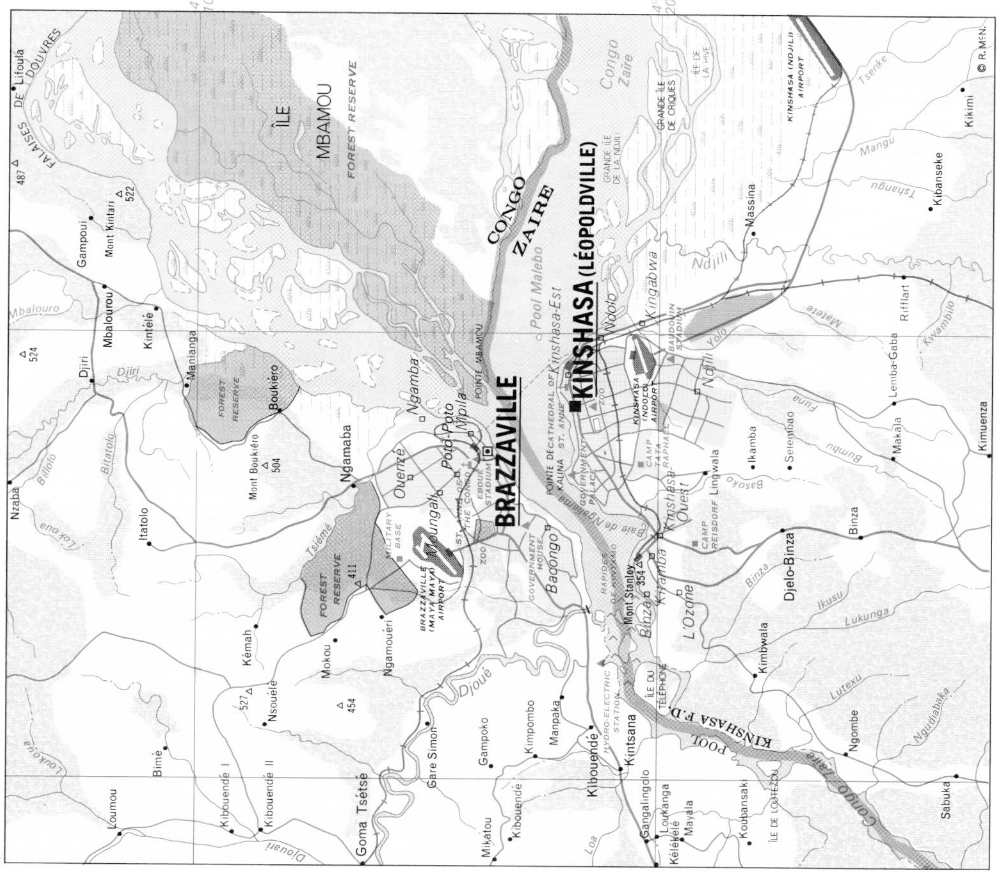
b
KINSHASA (LÉOPOLDVILLE)
BRAZZAVILLE
CONGO
ZAIRE
Pool Malebo
ÎLE MBAMOU

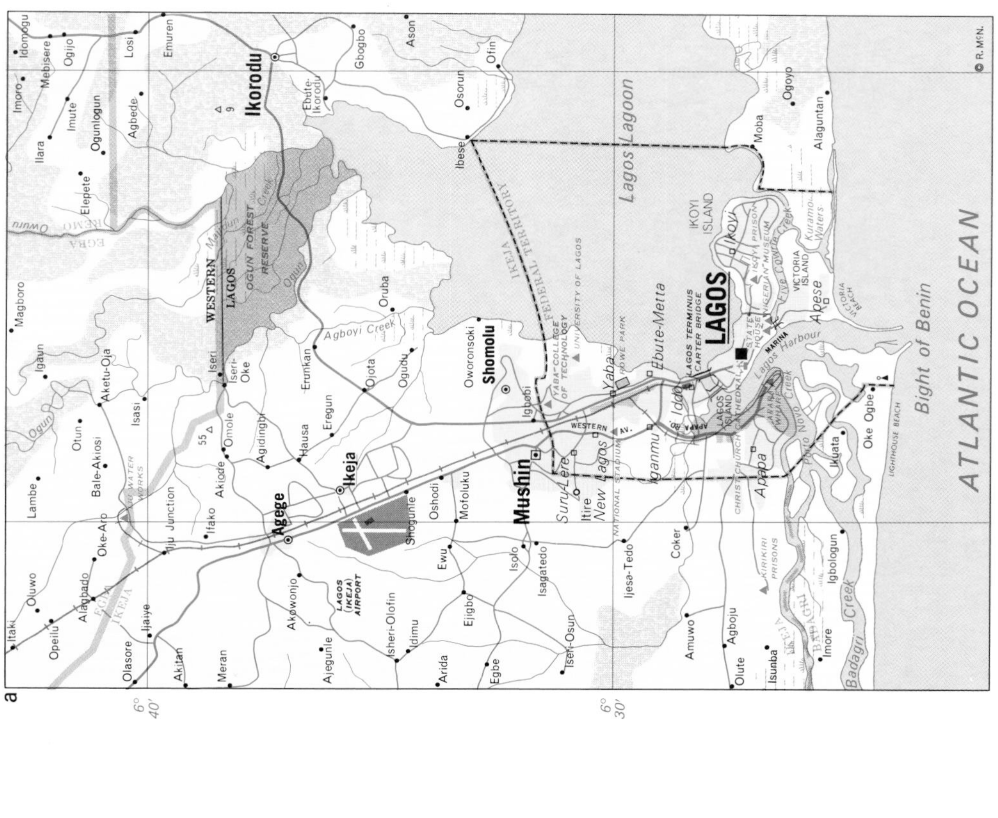
a
LAGOS
Ikeja
Agege
Mushin
Shomolu
Ikorodu
Lagos Lagoon
Bight of Benin
ATLANTIC OCEAN

d
JOHANNESBURG
Soweto
Roodepoort
Krugersdorp
Randfontein
Westonaria
Germiston
Alberton
Boksburg
Benoni
Brakpan
Springs
Kempton Park
Randburg
Alexandra
Edenvale

	AREA (km²)	POPULATION
LAGOS	750	2,400,000
KINSHASA-BRAZZAVILLE	1,150	2,750,000
AL-QĀHIRAH (CAIRO)	1,200	8,900,000
JOHANNESBURG	2,650	3,300,000

MAP FORM	airport	creek	dam	île	park	race course	tur'at	wadi
ENGLISH	airport	creek	dam	island	park	race course	canal	wadi
DEUTSCH	Flughafen	Bach	Damm	Insel	Park	Rennbahn	Kanal	Wadi
ESPAÑOL	aeropuerto	riachuelo	presa	isla	parque	hipódromo	canal	uadi
FRANÇAIS	aéroport	crique	barrage	île	parc	champ de course	canal	wadi
PORTUGUÊS	aeroporto	riacho	represa	ilha	parque	hipódromo	canal	uadi

Scale 1:300,000
One centimeter represents 3 kilometers.
One inch represents approximately 4.7 miles.

a

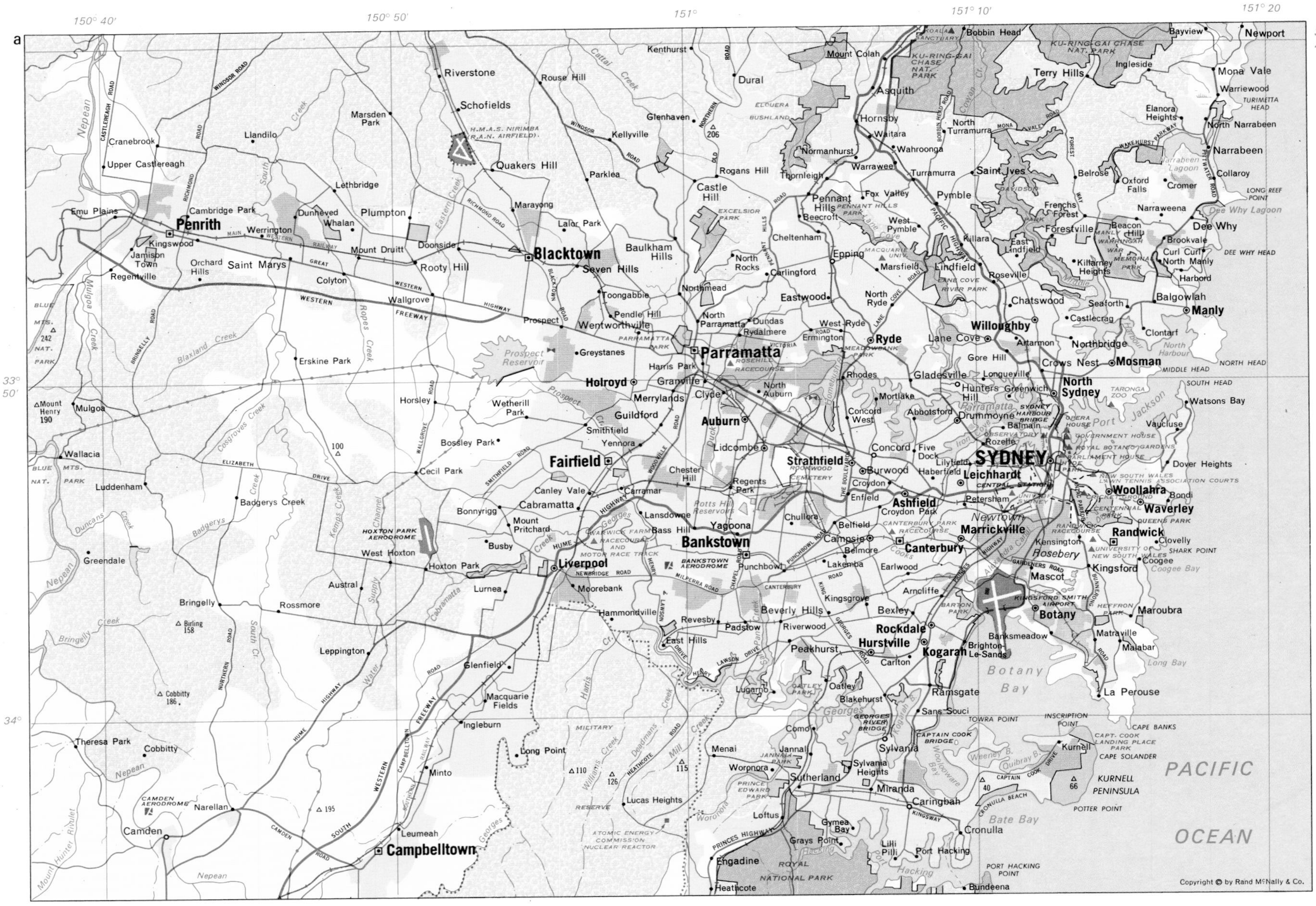

150° 40'
150° 50'
151°
151° 10'
151° 20'
33° 40'
33° 50'
34°
Riverstone
Schofields
Rouse Hill
Kenthurst
Dural
Mount Colah
Bobbin Head
Bayview
Newport
Mona Vale
Terry Hills
Ingleside
Asquith
Hornsby
Waitara
Wahroonga
North Turramurra
Turramurra
Saint Ives
Pymble
Warrawee
Narrabeen
North Narrabeen
Collaroy
Marsden Park
Llandilo
Cranebrook
Upper Castlereagh
Quakers Hill
Kellyville
Glenhaven
Castle Hill
Rogans Hill
Parklea
Marayong
Lethbridge
Plumpton
Dunheved
Whalan
Emu Plains
Cambridge Park
Penrith
Werrington
Kingswood
Jamison Town
Regentville
Orchard Hills
Saint Marys
Mount Druitt
Doonside
Rooty Hill
Blacktown
Seven Hills
Baulkham Hills
Lalor Park
Colyton
Wallgrove
Prospect
Toongabbie
Wentworthville
Pendle Hill
Northmead
North Rocks
Carlingford
Cheltenham
Epping
Marsfield
Beecroft
Pennant Hills
Killara
Lindfield
Roseville
Chatswood
Willoughby
Seaforth
Manly
Balgowlah
Harbord
Curl Curl
North Manly
Dee Why
Forestville
Frenchs Forest
Oxford Falls
Cromer
Belrose
Narraweena
Castlecrag
Clontarf
Northbridge
Artarmon
Crows Nest
Mosman
Lane Cove
Gore Hill
North Sydney
Greenwich
Hunters Hill
Gladesville
Ryde
North Ryde
West Ryde
Eastwood
Ermington
Rydalmere
Dundas
Parramatta
Harris Park
Granville
Holroyd
Greystanes
Erskine Park
Mount Henry 190
Mulgoa
Wallacia
Luddenham
Horsley
Wetherill Park
Smithfield
Guildford
Merrylands
Clyde
Auburn
Lidcombe
Rhodes
Concord West
Concord
Mortlake
Abbotsford
Drummoyne
Five Dock
Haberfield
Strathfield
Burwood
Croydon
Enfield
Ashfield
Leichhardt
Balmain
SYDNEY
Watsons Bay
Vaucluse
Dover Heights
Bondi
Woollahra
Waverley
Randwick
Clovelly
Coogee
Kingsford
Maroubra
Malabar
Matraville
La Perouse
Botany
Mascot
Kensington
Rosebery
Newtown
Petersham
Marrickville
Canterbury
Campsie
Belmore
Lakemba
Earlwood
Arncliffe
Bexley
Rockdale
Kogarah
Hurstville
Carlton
Brighton-Le-Sands
Banksmeadow
Botany Bay
Ramsgate
Sans Souci
Kingsgrove
Beverly Hills
Riverwood
Peakhurst
Oatley
Blakehurst
Lugarno
Padstow
Revesby
Panania
East Hills
Bankstown
Yagoona
Punchbowl
Chullora
Belfield
Lansdowne
Bass Hill
Chester Hill
Regents Park
Yennora
Fairfield
Cecil Park
Bossley Park
Canley Vale
Cabramatta
Bonnyrigg
Mount Pritchard
Busby
Liverpool
Moorebank
Hammondville
West Hoxton
Hoxton Park
Lurnea
Austral
Badgerys Creek
Greendale
Bringelly
Rossmore
Leppington
Glenfield
Macquarie Fields
Ingleburn
Long Point
Minto
Campbelltown
Leumeah
Narellan
Camden
Cobbitty
Theresa Park
Menai
Woronora
Jannali
Como
Sutherland
Sylvania
Sylvania Heights
Miranda
Caringbah
Kurnell
Cronulla
Gymea Bay
Grays Point
Lilli Pilli
Port Hacking
Loftus
Engadine
Heathcote
Bundeena
Lucas Heights
Kurnell Peninsula
Captain Cook Bridge
Cape Banks
Cape Solander
Inscription Point
Potter Point
Port Hacking Point
Bate Bay
PACIFIC OCEAN
Royal National Park
Kingsford Smith Airport
Prospect Reservoir
Hoxton Park Aerodrome
Bankstown Aerodrome
Camden Aerodrome
Nepean
Georges
North Head
South Head
Middle Head
Long Reef Point
Copyright © by Rand McNally & Co.

b

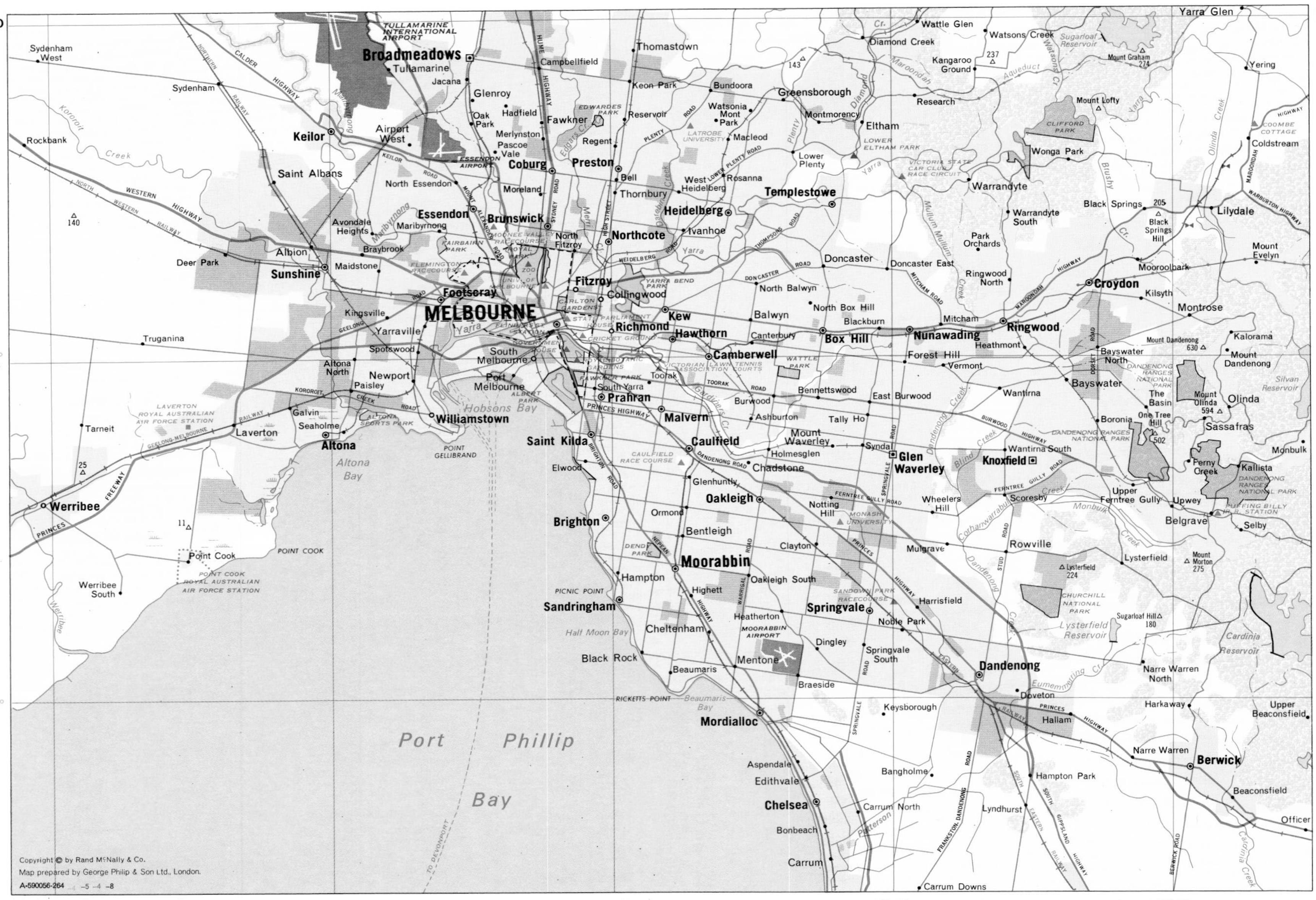

144° 40'
144° 50'
145°
145° 10'
145° 20'
37° 40'
37° 50'
38°
Tullamarine International Airport
Broadmeadows
Tullamarine
Jacana
Glenroy
Hadfield
Oak Park
Campbellfield
Thomastown
Keon Park
Bundoora
Greensborough
Montmorency
Eltham
Research
Kangaroo Ground
Watsons Creek
Diamond Creek
Wattle Glen
Yarra Glen
Yering
Coldstream
Mount Lofty
Wonga Park
Warrandyte
Warrandyte South
Park Orchards
Black Springs
Lilydale
Mount Evelyn
Mooroolbark
Croydon
Kilsyth
Montrose
Ringwood
Ringwood North
Mitcham
Nunawading
Box Hill
Blackburn
Forest Hill
Vermont
Heathmont
Bayswater
Bayswater North
Boronia
The Basin
Olinda
Sassafras
Kallista
Ferny Creek
Upwey
Upper Ferntree Gully
Belgrave
Selby
Monbulk
Kalorama
Mount Dandenong
Sydenham West
Sydenham
Keilor
Airport West
Essendon Airport
Fawkner
Reservoir
Regent
Preston
Coburg
Pascoe Vale
Merlynston
Watsonia
Macleod
Rosanna
Lower Plenty
Templestowe
Heidelberg
Ivanhoe
West Heidelberg
Bell
Thornbury
Northcote
Brunswick
Moreland
Essendon
North Essendon
Rockbank
Saint Albans
Avondale Heights
Maribyrnong
Braybrook
Albion
Sunshine
Deer Park
Maidstone
Footscray
Kingsville
Yarraville
Spotswood
MELBOURNE
Fitzroy
North Fitzroy
Collingwood
Richmond
Kew
Hawthorn
Camberwell
Balwyn
North Balwyn
Doncaster
Doncaster East
Canterbury
Burwood
East Burwood
Wantirna
Wantirna South
Bennettswood
Ashburton
Malvern
Prahran
Toorak
South Yarra
South Melbourne
Port Melbourne
Saint Kilda
Elwood
Caulfield
Glenhuntly
Chadstone
Holmesglen
Mount Waverley
Syndal
Glen Waverley
Knoxfield
Scoresby
Wheelers Hill
Notting Hill
Oakleigh
Ormond
Bentleigh
Brighton
Clayton
Mulgrave
Rowville
Lysterfield
Moorabbin
Highett
Oakleigh South
Hampton
Sandringham
Cheltenham
Heatherton
Springvale
Noble Park
Harrisfield
Dandenong
Dingley
Springvale South
Mentone
Braeside
Black Rock
Beaumaris
Mordialloc
Keysborough
Doveton
Hallam
Narre Warren North
Narre Warren
Harkaway
Upper Beaconsfield
Berwick
Beaconsfield
Officer
Hampton Park
Lyndhurst
Bangholme
Aspendale
Edithvale
Chelsea
Bonbeach
Carrum
Carrum North
Carrum Downs
Truganina
Altona North
Altona
Newport
Paisley
Galvin
Seaholme
Williamstown
Laverton
Tarneit
Werribee
Werribee South
Point Cook
Point Gellibrand
Hobsons Bay
Altona Bay
Port Phillip Bay
Half Moon Bay
Picnic Point
Ricketts Point
Beaumaris Bay
Moorabbin Airport
Cardinia Reservoir
Churchill National Park
Dandenong Ranges National Park
Copyright © by Rand McNally & Co.
Map prepared by George Philip & Son Ltd., London.
A-590056-264

	AREA (km²)	POPULATION
MELBOURNE	2,600	2,425,000
SYDNEY	2,800	2,850,000

ENGLISH	bay, b.	bridge	creek, cr.	highway	point	road
DEUTSCH	Bucht	Brücke	Bach	Landstrasse	Landspitze	Landstrasse
ESPAÑOL	bahía	puente	riachuelo	camino	punta	camino
FRANÇAIS	baie	pont	crique	route	pointe	route
PORTUGUÊS	baía	ponte	riacho	rodovia	ponta	rodovia

Kilometers 0 5 10 15 Km.
Statute Miles 0 5 10 15 Mi.

Scale 1:300,000

One centimeter represents 3 kilometers.
One inch represents approximately 4.7 miles.

a

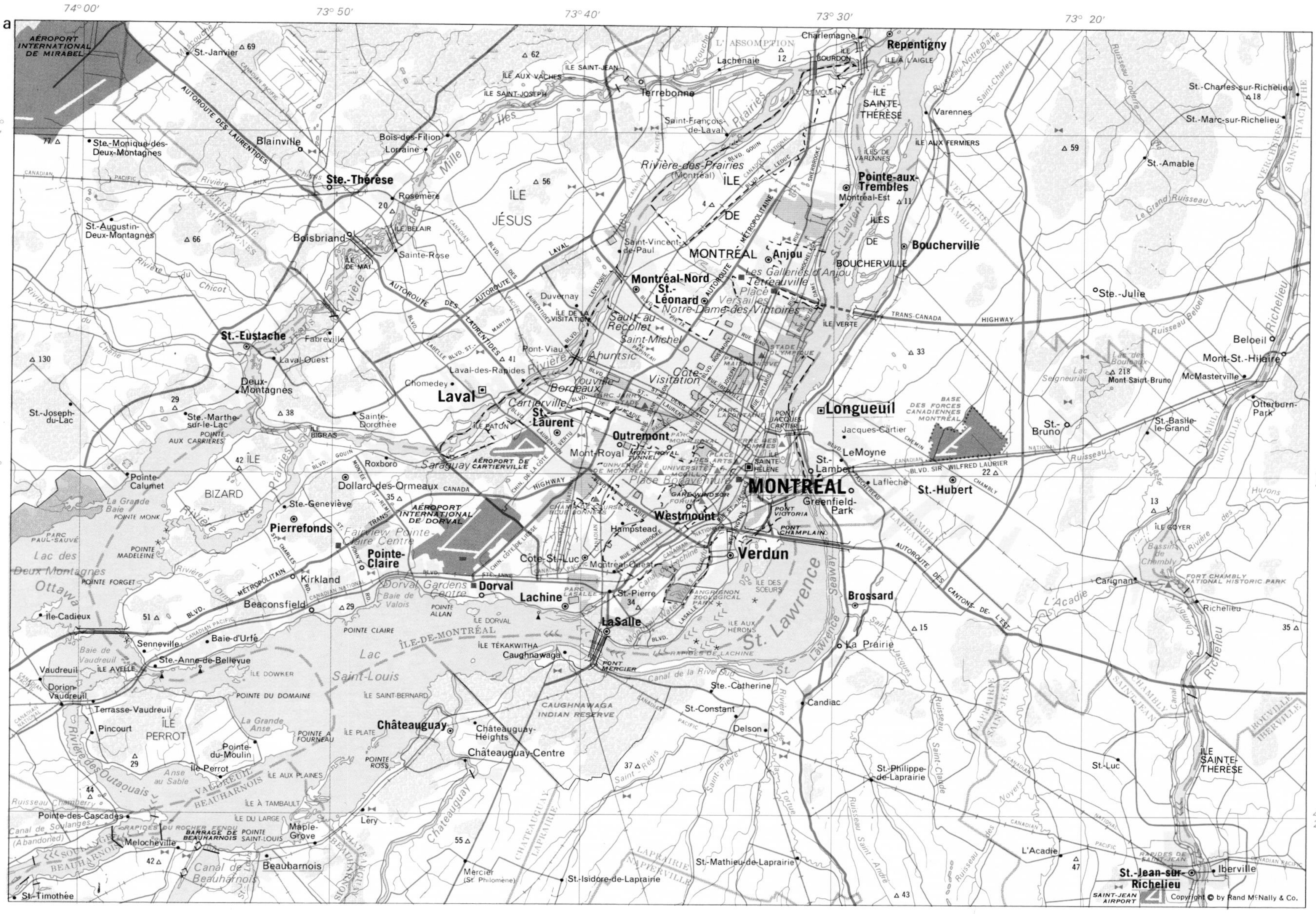

AÉROPORT INTERNATIONAL DE MIRABEL
St.-Janvier
Repentigny
Charlemagne
Lachenaie
Terrebonne
ÎLE SAINT-JEAN
ÎLE AUX VACHES
ÎLE SAINT-JOSEPH
ÎLE BOURDON
ÎLE À L'AIGLE
ÎLE SAINTE-THÉRÈSE
Varennes
St.-Charles-sur-Richelieu
St.-Marc-sur-Richelieu
Saint-François-de-Laval
Bois-des-Filion
Lorraine
Blainville
Ste.-Monique-des-Deux-Montagnes
AUTOROUTE DES LAURENTIDES
Mille Îles
Rivière-des-Prairies (Montréal)
ÎLE AUX FERMIERS
St.-Amable
Ste.-Thérèse
Rosemère
ÎLE JÉSUS
ÎLE DE MONTRÉAL
Pointe-aux-Trembles
Montréal-Est
ÎLES DE BOUCHERVILLE
Boucherville
St.-Augustin-Deux-Montagnes
Boisbriand
Sainte-Rose
Saint-Vincent-de-Paul
Anjou
Les Galeries d'Anjou
Montréal-Nord
St.-Léonard
Duvernay
Sault-au-Récollet
Ste.-Julie
St.-Eustache
Fabreville
Laval-Ouest
Pont-Viau
Ahuntsic
Laval-des-Rapides
Chomedey
Deux-Montagnes
Laval
Cartierville
Bordeaux
Beloeil
Mont-St.-Hilaire
McMasterville
Longueuil
BASE DES FORCES CANADIENNES MONTRÉAL
St.-Bruno
Otterburn-Park
St.-Joseph-du-Lac
Ste.-Marthe-sur-le-Lac
Sainte-Dorothée
St.-Laurent
Outremont
Jacques-Cartier
LeMoyne
St.-Basile-le-Grand
ÎLE BIZARD
Roxboro
AÉROPORT DE CARTIERVILLE
Mont-Royal
St.-Lambert
Pointe-Calumet
Dollard-des-Ormeaux
MONTRÉAL
Greenfield-Park
St.-Hubert
Ste.-Geneviève
AÉROPORT INTERNATIONAL DE DORVAL
Westmount
Pierrefonds
Hampstead
Verdun
Pointe-Claire
Côte-St.-Luc
Montréal-Ouest
Lac des Deux Montagnes
Kirkland
Dorval
Lachine
Carignan
FORT CHAMBLY NATIONAL HISTORIC PARK
Beaconsfield
St.-Pierre
Brossard
Île-Cadieux
LaSalle
Richelieu
Baie-d'Urfé
Senneville
St. Lawrence
La Prairie
Ste.-Anne-de-Bellevue
Vaudreuil
Dorion-Vaudreuil
Lac Saint-Louis
ÎLE-DE-MONTRÉAL
Caughnawaga
PONT MERCIER
Ste.-Catherine
CAUGHNAWAGA INDIAN RESERVE
Terrasse-Vaudreuil
St.-Constant
Candiac
Pincourt
ÎLE PERROT
Châteauguay
Châteauguay-Heights
Delson
Pointe-du-Moulin
Châteauguay-Centre
Île-Perrot
St.-Philippe-de-Laprairie
St.-Luc
ÎLE SAINTE-THÉRÈSE
Pointe-des-Cascades
Léry
Maple-Grove
Melocheville
Beauharnois
Canal de Beauharnois
L'Acadie
St.-Mathieu-de-Laprairie
Mercier (St. Philomène)
St.-Isidore-de-Laprairie
St.-Jean-sur-Richelieu
Iberville
St.-Timothée
SAINT-JEAN AIRPORT
Copyright © by Rand McNally & Co.

b

Caledon East
Bolton
Richmond Hill
Markham
Mono Road Station
Teston
Buttonville
BUTTONVILLE AIRFIELD
Unionville
Box Grove
Cedar Grove
Pickering
Ajax
Kleinburg
MAPLE AIRFIELD
Maple
Richvale
Cherrywood
Nashville
McMICHAEL ART COLLECTION
Veillore
CANADA'S WONDERLAND
Sherwood
Hagerman Corners
Armadale
Sandhill
Langstaff
Milliken
Dunbarton
Wildfield
Thornhill
Frenchman's Bay
Fairport
Concord
Doncaster
Steeles Corners
Fairport Beach
Elder Mills
Pine Grove
Tullamore
Castlemore
Vaughan
Edgeley
Newton Brook
Agincourt
Rosebank Station
Stanley Mills
Willowdale
Fairview Mall
Port Union
Ebenezer
North York
Maryvale
Scarborough Centre
Woburn
West Hill
Claireville
Lansing
Woodbill
Thistletown
Don Mills
Wexford
Scarborough
Snelgrove
Rexdale
Nortonville
Bramalea
Weston
Leaside
Scarborough Bluffs
Malton
LESTER B. PEARSON INTERNATIONAL AIRPORT
Mount Dennis
York
East York
Brampton
Forest Hill
Birch Cliff
Mount Charles
Rosedale
Pleasant
Yorkville
Springbrook
BRAMPTON AIRFIELD
TORONTO
Etobicoke
Islington
Swansea
Derry West
Norval
Huttonsville
Summerville
Toronto Harbour
Churchville
Meadowvale
Britannia
Burnhamthorpe
Mimico
Sherway Centre
Long Branch
New Toronto
GIBRALTAR POINT
Streetsville
Mississauga
LAKE ONTARIO
(75 Meters Above Sea Level)
Hornby
Port Credit
Erindale
Omagh
Boyne
Trafalgar
Glenarchy
Oakville
CANADA
UNITED STATES
Copyright © by Rand McNally & Co.
Map prepared by Rand McNally & Co.
A-520080-264 -3 -4 -5

	AREA (km²)	POPULATION
MONTRÉAL	3,100	2,875,000
TORONTO	2,100	2,850,000

MAP FORM	île	park	rapides	rivière	ruisseau
ENGLISH	island	park	rapids	river	brook
DEUTSCH	Insel	Park	Stromschnellen	Fluss	Bach
ESPAÑOL	isla	parque	rápidos	río	arroyo
FRANÇAIS	île	parc	rapides	rivière	ruisseau
PORTUGUÊS	ilha	parque	rápidos	rio	arroio

Kilometers 0 5 10 15 Km.

Statute Miles 0 5 10 15 Mi.

Scale 1:300,000

One centimeter represents 3 kilometers.

One inch represents approximately 4.7 miles.

74°40'
74°30'
74°20'
74°10'
74°
41° 10'
41°
40° 50'
40° 40'
40° 30'
40° 20'
NEW YORK
Newark
Jersey City
Paterson
Elizabeth
Hackensack
Staten Island
Manhattan
Brooklyn
Hoboken
Morristown
New Brunswick
Princeton
Perth Amboy
Plainfield
Edison
Piscataway
Somerville
Dover
Clifton
Passaic
Bayonne
Union City
West New York
Irvington
Bloomfield
Montclair
Livingston
Westfield
Linden
Rahway
Sayreville
East Brunswick
Middletown
Raritan Bay
Sandy Hook
NEW YORK
NEW JERSEY
WATCHUNG MTS.
RAMAPO MTS.
L. Hopatcong

ENGLISH	bay	brook, br.	creek	harbor	island	lake, l.	point	pond
DEUTSCH	Bucht	Bach	Bach	Hafen	Insel	See	Landspitze	Teich
ESPAÑOL	bahía	arroyo	riachuelo	puerto	isla	lago	punta	charca
FRANÇAIS	baie	ruisseau	crique	port	île	lac	pointe	etang
PORTUGUÊS	baía	arroio	riacho	porto	ilha	lago	ponta	lagoa

For complete glossary see page I • 1.

73°40'
73°30'
73°20'
73°10'
41° 10'
41°
40° 50'
40° 40'
40° 30'
40° 20'
NEW YORK
CONNECTICUT
Bridgeport
Fairfield
Westport
Norwalk
New Canaan
Darien
Stamford
Greenwich
Port Chester
Rye
White Plains
Scarsdale
Harrison
Mamaroneck
New Rochelle
Pelham
Chappaqua
Pleasantville
Armonk
Thornwood
Hawthorne
Valhalla
Hartsdale
Eastchester
Larchmont
NORWALK ISLANDS
Long Island Sound
CAUMSETT STATE PARK
SUNKEN MEADOW STATE PARK
Glen Cove
Oyster Bay
Huntington
Huntington Station
Northport
Commack
Smithtown
Centereach
Coram
Selden
Port Jefferson
Stony Brook
Setauket
Holbrook
Ronkonkoma
Lake Ronkonkoma
Hauppauge
Central Islip
Brentwood
Deer Park
Bay Shore
Islip
West Islip
Babylon
West Babylon
Lindenhurst
Amityville
Copiague
Massapequa
Wantagh
Seaford
Merrick
Bellmore
Freeport
Baldwin
Oceanside
Rockville Centre
Hempstead
Uniondale
East Meadow
Levittown
Hicksville
Plainview
Bethpage
Farmingdale
Syosset
Jericho
Melville
Dix Hills
Mineola
Garden City
Franklin Square
Elmont
Valley Stream
Lynbrook
Long Beach
Great Neck
Manhasset
Roslyn
Port Washington
Floral Park
Jamaica
Flushing
Bayside
JOHN F. KENNEDY INTERNATIONAL AIRPORT
JONES BEACH STATE PARK
ROBERT MOSES STATE PARK
FIRE ISLAND
FIRE ISLAND NATIONAL SEASHORE
Great South Bay
LONG ISLAND
Patchogue
Sayville
Bayport
Blue Point
Medford
Farmingville
MAC ARTHUR AIRPORT
ATLANTIC OCEAN
Copyright © by Rand McNally & Co.
Map prepared by Rand McNally & Co.
A-520060-264

Kilometers 0 5 10 15 Km.

Statute Miles 0 5 10 15 Mi.

Scale 1:300,000

One centimeter represents 3 kilometers.

One inch represents approximately 4.7 miles.

88°
87° 50′
87° 40′
87° 30′
87° 20′
42° 20′
42° 10′
42°
41° 50′
41° 40′
41° 30′
LAKE MICHIGAN
(176 Meters Above Sea Level)
ILLINOIS
INDIANA
Waukegan
North Chicago
GREAT LAKES NAVAL TRAINING CENTER
Lake Forest
Highland Park
Glencoe
Winnetka
Wilmette
Evanston
Skokie
Northbrook
Deerfield
Glenview
Des Plaines
Park Ridge
Niles
Arlington Heights
Palatine
Buffalo Grove
Wheeling
Mount Prospect
Hoffman Estates
Schaumburg
Elk Grove Village
CHICAGO-O'HARE INTERNATIONAL AIRPORT
Addison
Glendale Heights
Carol Stream
Lombard
Elmhurst
Glen Ellyn
Wheaton
Downers Grove
Woodridge
Bolingbrook
Lisle
Romeoville
Lockport
Joliet
Crest Hill
Maywood
Oak Park
Berwyn
Cicero
CHICAGO
SEARS TOWER
NAVY PIER
CHICAGO MIDWAY AIRPORT
Burbank
Oak Lawn
Evergreen Park
Blue Island
Orland Park
Oak Forest
Harvey
Tinley Park
Chicago Heights
Dolton
Calumet City
Hammond
East Chicago
Whiting
Gary
Lansing
Highland
Merrillville
Dyer
Schererville
Griffith
Munster
Matteson
Libertyville
Mundelein
Vernon Hills
Lake Zurich
Barrington
Copyright © by Rand McNally & Co.
Map prepared by Rand McNally & Co.

ENGLISH	airport	creek, cr.	harbor	lake, l.	park	woods
DEUTSCH	Flughafen	Bach	Hafen	See	Park	Gehölz
ESPAÑOL	aeropuerto	riachuelo	puerto	lago	parque	bosques
FRANÇAIS	aéroport	crique	port	lac	parc	bois
PORTUGUÊS	aeroporto	riacho	porto	lago	parque	bosques

Kilometers 0 5 10 15 Km.

Statute Miles 0 5 10 15 Mi.

Scale 1:300,000

One centimeter represents 3 kilometers.
One inch represents approximately 4.7 miles.

a

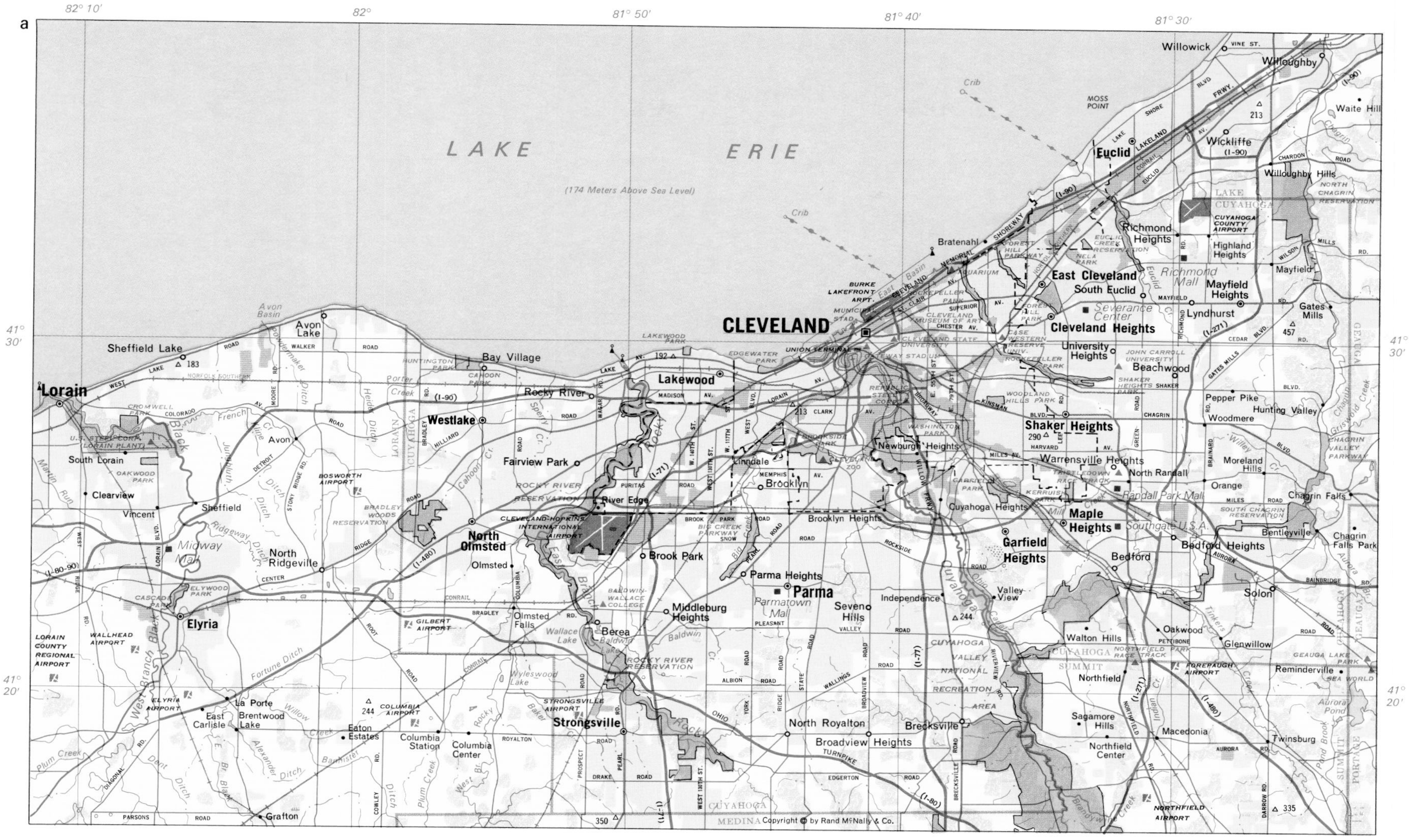
LAKE ERIE
(174 Meters Above Sea Level)
CLEVELAND
Lorain
Elyria
Lakewood
Parma
Euclid
East Cleveland
Cleveland Heights
Shaker Heights
Garfield Heights
Maple Heights
Westlake
North Olmsted
Strongsville
Copyright © by Rand McNally & Co.

b

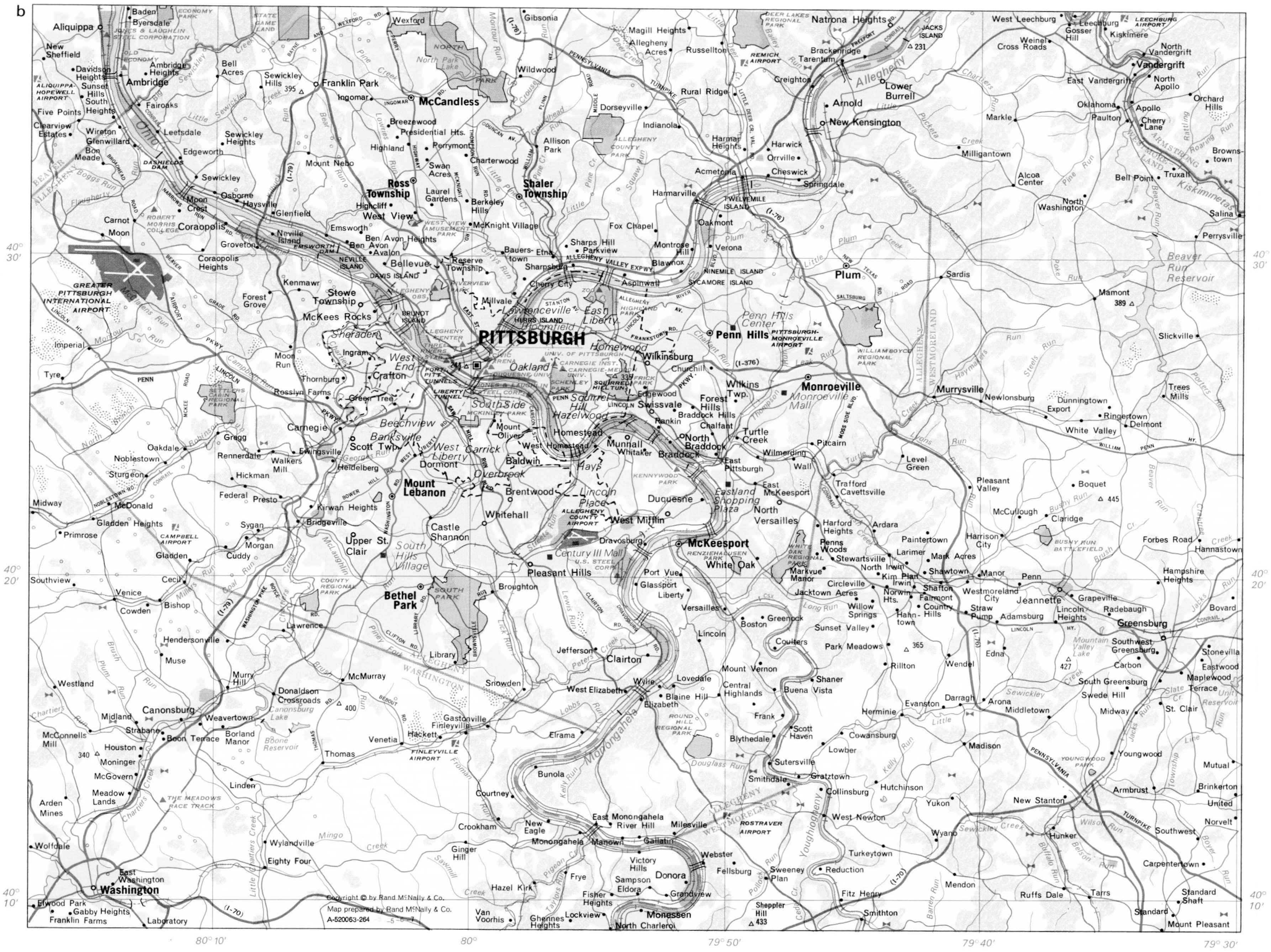
PITTSBURGH
McKeesport
McCandless
Ross Township
Shaler Township
Penn Hills
Monroeville
Plum
Mount Lebanon
Bethel Park
Canonsburg
Washington
Greensburg
Copyright © by Rand McNally & Co.
Map prepared by Rand McNally & Co.
A-520063-264

ENGLISH	creek, cr.	ditch	island	lake, l.	park	reservoir	run	
DEUTSCH	Bach	Graben	Insel	See	Park	Stausee	Bach	
ESPAÑOL	riachuelo	acequia	isla	lago	parque	embalse	arroyo	
FRANÇAIS	crique	fossé	île	lac	parc	réservoir	ruisseau	
PORTUGUÊS	riacho	fosso	ilha	lago	parque	reservatório	córrego	

Kilometers 0 5 10 15 Km.

Statute Miles 0 5 10 15 Mi.

Scale 1:300,000

One centimeter represents 3 kilometers.
One inch represents approximately 4.7 miles.

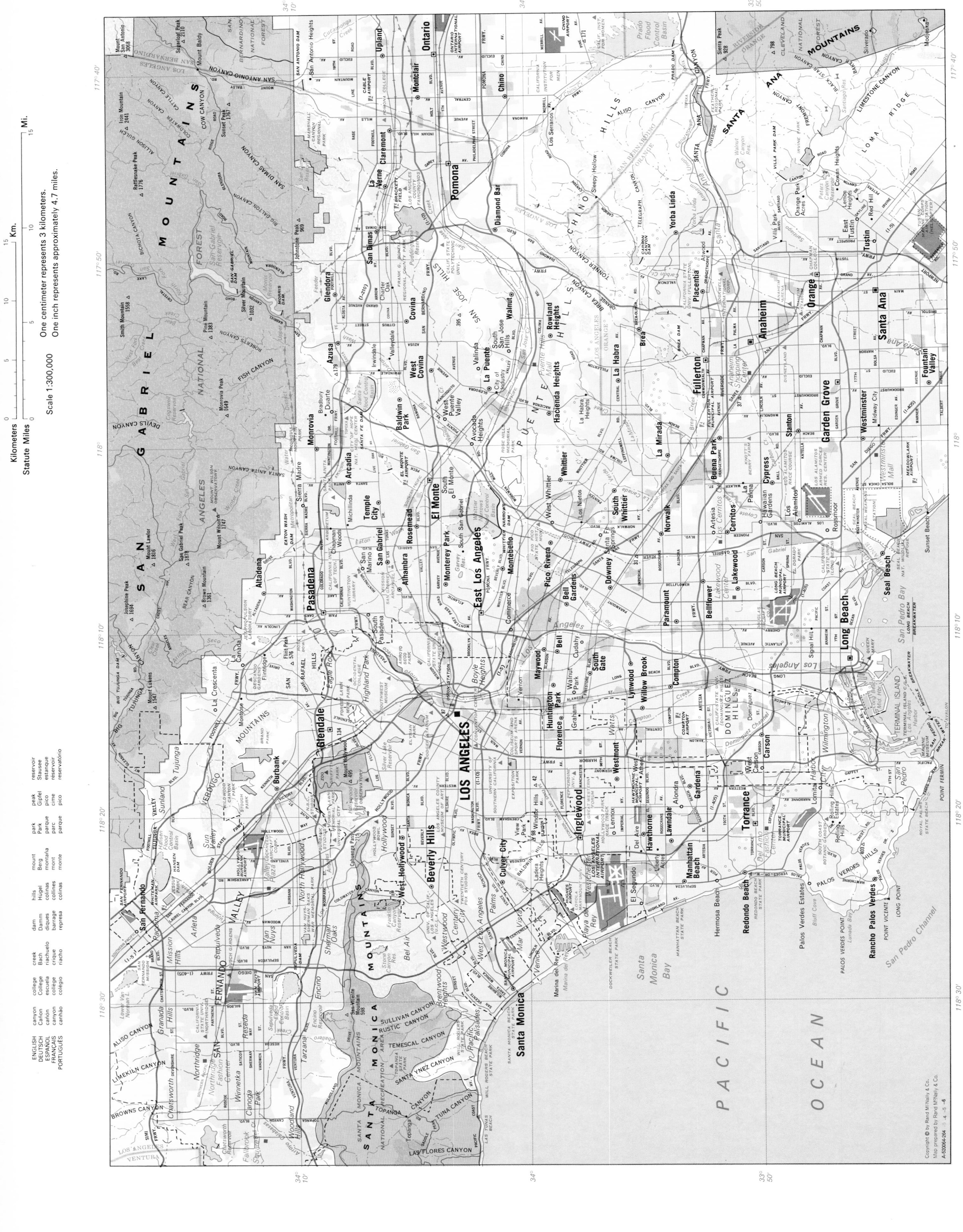
Kilometers 0 5 10 15 Km.
Statute Miles 0 5 10 15 Mi.
Scale 1:300,000
One centimeter represents 3 kilometers.
One inch represents approximately 4.7 miles.
ENGLISH canyon college creek dam hills mount park peak reservoir
DEUTSCH Canon College Bach Damm Hügel Berg Park Gipfel Stausee
ESPAÑOL cañón escuela riachuelo diques colinas montaña parque pico estanque
FRANÇAIS canyon college crique barrage collines mont parc cime reservoir
PORTUGUÊS canhão colégio riacho represa colinas monte parque pico reservatório
SAN GABRIEL MOUNTAINS
SAN GABRIEL NATIONAL FOREST
ANGELES NATIONAL FOREST
SANTA MONICA MOUNTAINS
SAN FERNANDO VALLEY
SANTA ANA MOUNTAINS
PUENTE HILLS
CHINO HILLS
SAN JOSE HILLS
LOS ANGELES
Pasadena
Glendale
Burbank
Santa Monica
Beverly Hills
Long Beach
Anaheim
Santa Ana
Orange
Fullerton
Pomona
Ontario
Torrance
Inglewood
Whittier
El Monte
Santa Monica Bay
San Pedro Bay
PACIFIC OCEAN
Copyright © by Rand McNally & Co.
Map prepared by Rand McNally & Co.

DETROIT
Windsor
UNITED STATES
CANADA
MICHIGAN
ONTARIO
Lake Saint Clair
(175 Meters Above Sea Level)
Anchor Bay
Pontiac
Ann Arbor
Ypsilanti
Dearborn
Warren
Livonia
Southfield
Troy
Royal Oak
Sterling Heights
Rochester Hills
Waterford
Farmington Hills
Novi
Westland
Taylor
Wyandotte
Southgate
Lincoln Park
Allen Park
Inkster
Garden City
Dearborn Heights
Redford Township
Highland Park
Hamtramck
Grosse Pointe
Grosse Pointe Park
Grosse Pointe Farms
Grosse Pointe Woods
Grosse Pointe Shores
Harper Woods
St. Clair Shores
Eastpointe
Roseville
Mount Clemens
Clinton Township
Madison Heights
Hazel Park
Ferndale
Oak Park
Berkley
Birmingham
Bloomfield Hills
Auburn Hills
Utica
Tecumseh
St. Clair Beach
Belle River
Amherstburg
La Salle
Essex
Romulus
Belleville
Plymouth
Northville
Wayne
Trenton
Grosse Ile
Flat Rock
Kilometers
Statute Miles
Km.
Mi.
Scale 1:300,000
One centimeter represents 3 kilometers.
One inch represents approximately 4.7 miles.
Copyright © by Rand McNally & Co.
Map prepared by Rand McNally & Co.
ENGLISH bay channel creek, cr. island lake, l. point
DEUTSCH Bucht Kanal Bach Insel See Landspitze
ESPAÑOL bahía canal riachuelo isla lago punta
FRANÇAIS baie détroit crique île lac pointe
PORTUGUÊS baía canal riacho ilha lago ponta

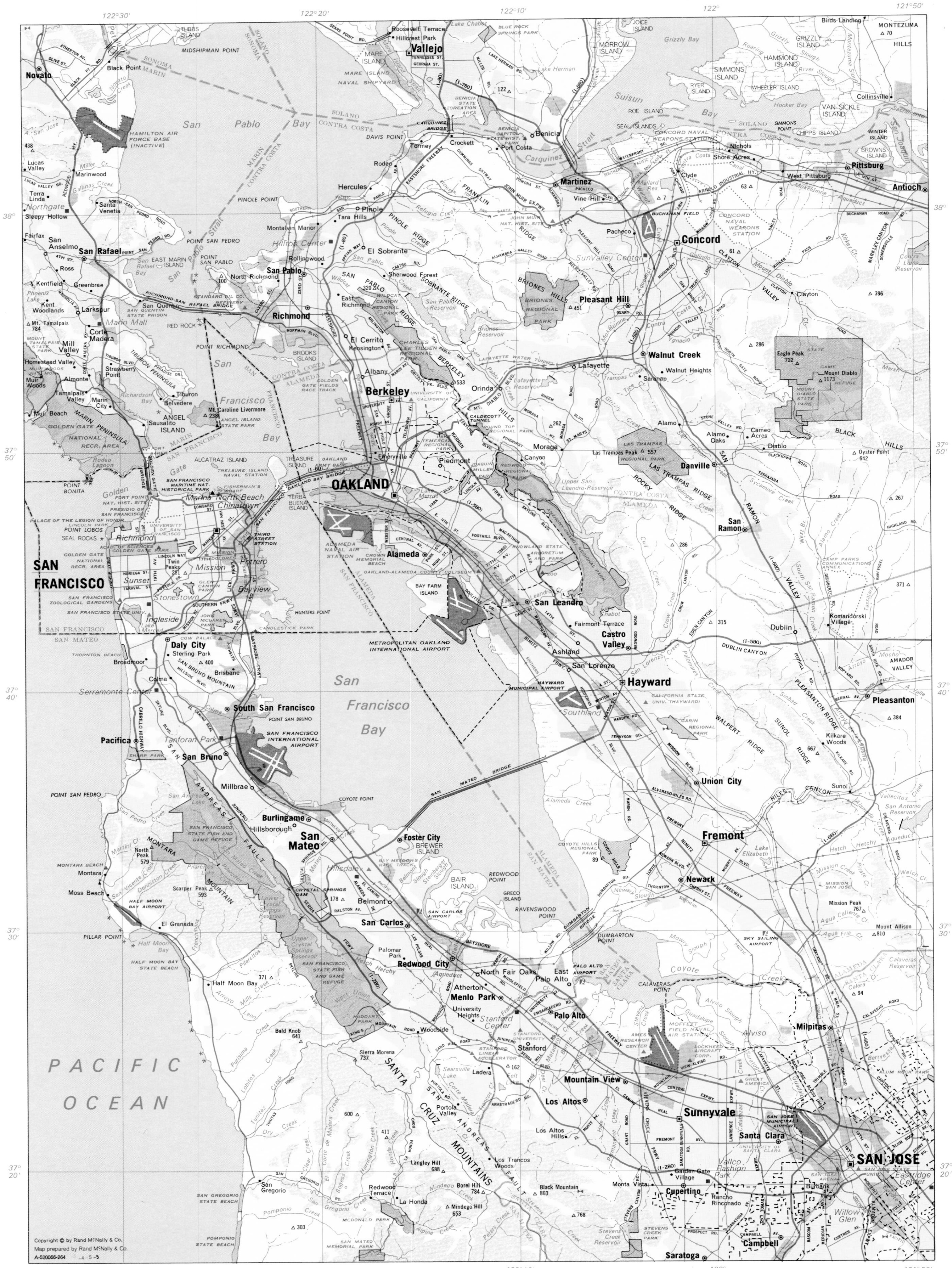
122°30'
122°20'
122°10'
122°
121°50'
38°
37° 50'
37° 40'
37° 30'
37° 20'
Novato
Vallejo
Benicia
Martinez
Concord
Pittsburg
Antioch
Pleasant Hill
Walnut Creek
San Rafael
San Pablo
Richmond
Berkeley
OAKLAND
Alameda
San Leandro
Castro Valley
Hayward
Danville
San Ramon
Dublin
Pleasanton
Union City
Fremont
Newark
Milpitas
SAN FRANCISCO
Daly City
South San Francisco
Pacifica
San Bruno
Millbrae
Burlingame
San Mateo
Foster City
San Carlos
Redwood City
Menlo Park
Palo Alto
Mountain View
Los Altos
Sunnyvale
Santa Clara
SAN JOSE
Cupertino
Saratoga
Campbell
Half Moon Bay
San Gregorio
La Honda
San Pablo Bay
Suisun Bay
San Francisco Bay
PACIFIC OCEAN
SANTA CRUZ MOUNTAINS
SAN ANDREAS FAULT
Mount Diablo 1173
SAN FRANCISCO INTERNATIONAL AIRPORT
METROPOLITAN OAKLAND INTERNATIONAL AIRPORT
SAN MATEO BRIDGE
DUMBARTON BRIDGE
Copyright © by Rand McNally & Co.
Map prepared by Rand McNally & Co.

ENGLISH	bay	beach	creek, cr.	island	lake	point	reservoir
DEUTSCH	Bucht	Strand	Bach	Insel	See	Punkt	Stausee
ESPAÑOL	bahía	playa	riachuelo	isla	lago	punta	estangue
FRANÇAIS	baie	plage	crique	île	lac	pointe	réservoir
PORTUGUÊS	baía	praia	riacho	ilha	lago	ponta	reservatório

Kilometers 0 5 10 15 Km.

Statute Miles 0 5 10 15 Mi.

Scale 1:300,000

One centimeter represents 3 kilometers.
One inch represents approximately 4.7 miles.

71° 20'
71° 10'
71°
70° 50'
70° 40'
42° 40'
42° 30'
42° 20'
42° 10'
42°
ATLANTIC OCEAN
Massachusetts Bay
Ipswich Bay
Cape Ann
BOSTON
Boston Harbor
LOGAN INTERNATIONAL AIRPORT
Cambridge
Somerville
Chelsea
Brookline
Newton
Waltham
Watertown
Arlington
Medford
Malden
Everett
Revere
Winthrop
Lynn
Nahant
Swampscott
Marblehead
Salem
Peabody
Beverly
Danvers
Gloucester
Rockport
Manchester
Ipswich
Newburyport
PLUM ISLAND
PARKER RIVER NATIONAL WILDLIFE REFUGE
Haverhill
Methuen
Lawrence
North Andover
Andover
Lowell
Dracut
Chelmsford
Tewksbury
Billerica
Wilmington
Reading
Wakefield
Woburn
Burlington
Lexington
Bedford
Concord
Lincoln
Maynard
Sudbury
Wayland
Weston
Wellesley
Needham
Natick
Framingham
Dedham
Milton
Quincy
Braintree
Weymouth
Hingham
Hull
Cohasset
Scituate
Norwood
Canton
Randolph
Holbrook
Stoughton
Brockton
Sharon
Walpole
Foxboro
Franklin
Mansfield
Norton
Abington
Rockland
Hanover
Marshfield
Duxbury
Kingston
Plymouth
Bridgewater
Halifax
Whitman
Nashua
Hudson
Pelham
Windham
Salem
NEW HAMPSHIRE
MASSACHUSETTS
RHODE ISLAND
North Attleboro
Plymouth Bay
Kingston Bay
Copyright © by Rand McNally & Co.
Map prepared by Rand McNally & Co.
A-520067-264

ENGLISH	bay	brook	island, i.	lake, l.	point	pond	reservation
DEUTSCH	Bucht	Bach	Insel	See	Landspitze	Teich	Reservat
ESPAÑOL	bahía	arroyo	isla	lago	punta	charca	parque nacional
FRANÇAIS	baie	ruisseau	île	lac	pointe	étang	réservation
PORTUGUÊS	baía	arroio	ilha	lago	ponta	lagoa	parque nacional

Kilometers 0 5 10 15 Km.

Statute Miles 0 5 10 15 Mi.

Scale 1:300,000

One centimeter represents 3 kilometers.
One inch represents approximately 4.7 miles.

Kilometers 0 5 10 15 Km.
Statute Miles 0 5 10 15 Mi.

Scale 1:300,000

One centimeter represents 3 kilometers.
One inch represents approximately 4.7 miles.

ENGLISH	airport	bridge	creek, cr.	island, i.	park	point	run	university
DEUTSCH	Flughafen	Brücke	Bach	Insel	Park	Landspitze	Bach	Universität
ESPAÑOL	aeropuerto	puente	riachuelo	isla	parque	punta	arroyo	universidad
FRANÇAIS	aéroport	pont	crique	île	parc	pointe	ruisseau	université
PORTUGUÊS	aeroporto	ponte	riacho	ilha	parque	ponta	córrego	universidade

b

BALTIMORE
Towson
Parkville
Essex
Dundalk
Catonsville
Columbia
Chesapeake Bay

c

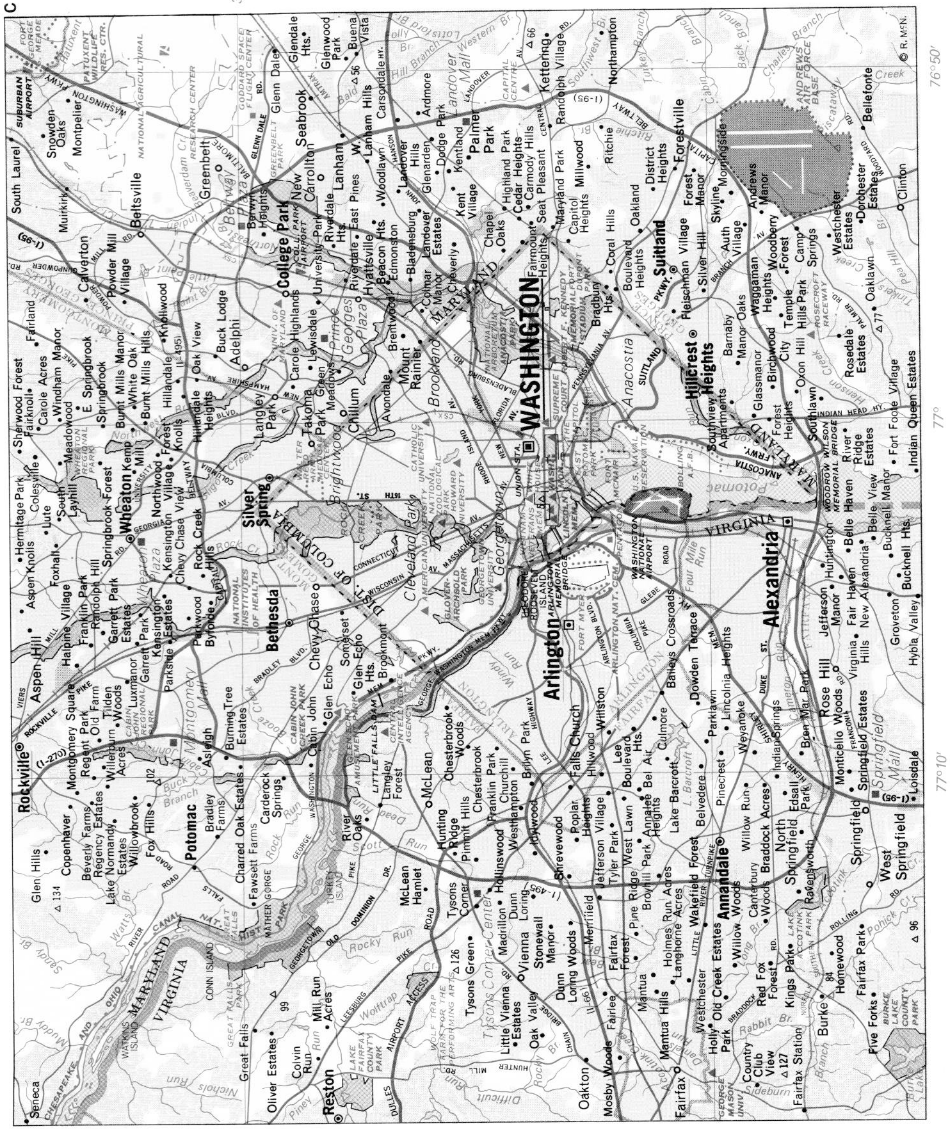
WASHINGTON
Arlington
Alexandria
Bethesda
Silver Spring
Rockville
College Park

a

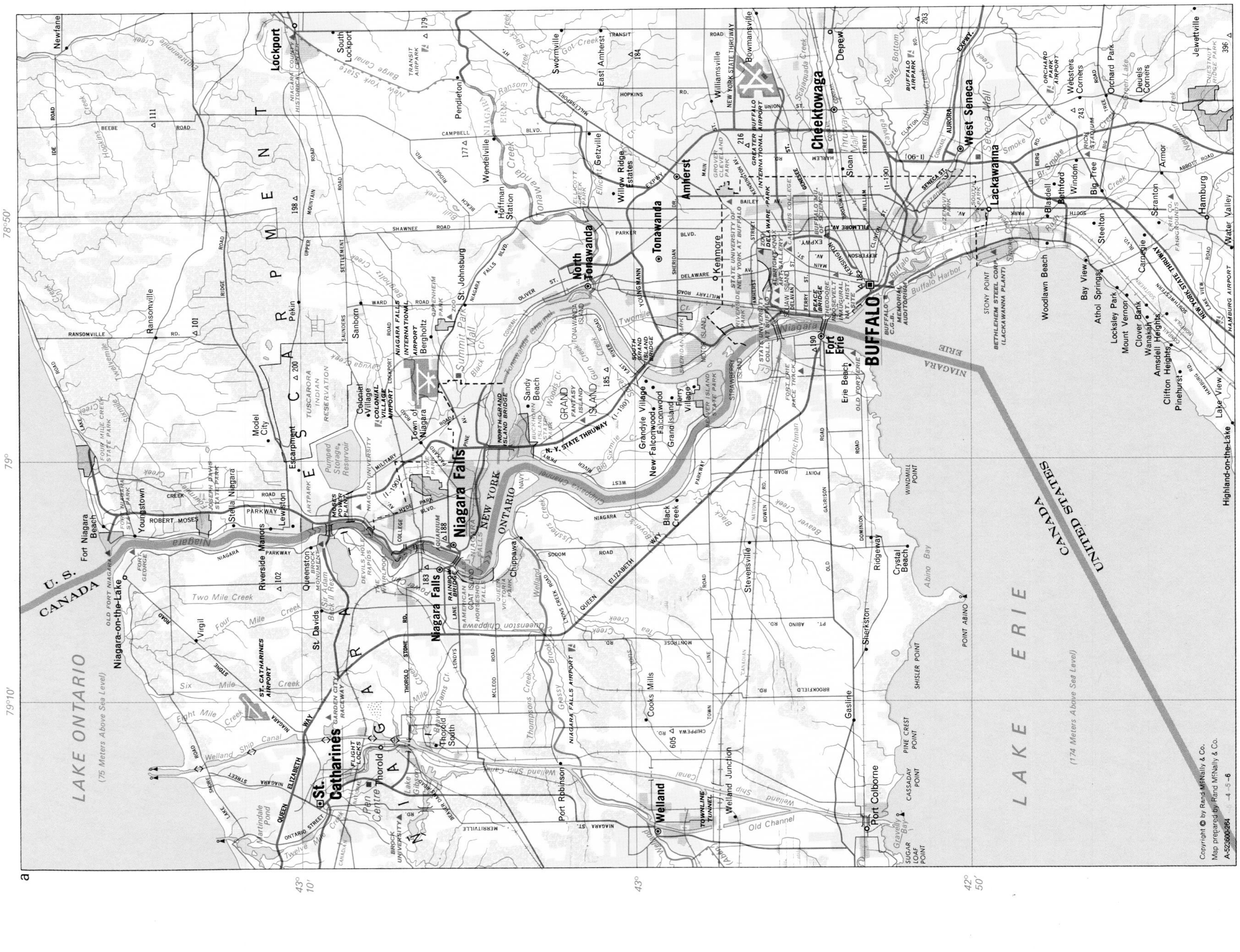
LAKE ONTARIO
LAKE ERIE
BUFFALO
Niagara Falls
St. Catharines
Lockport
Tonawanda
Cheektowaga
Welland
CANADA
UNITED STATES

PHILADELPHIA
Camden
Trenton
Wilmington
Chester
Norristown
Pottstown
Levittown
Willingboro
Cherry Hill
Pennsauken
Cheltenham
Upper Darby
Drexel Hill
Havertown
Warminster
Downingtown
West Chester
New Castle
Pennsville
Newark
Glassboro
Woodbury
Mount Holly
Burlington
Bristol
Morrisville
Ewing Township
WHARTON STATE FOREST
PINE BARRENS
DELAWARE
NEW JERSEY
PENNSYLVANIA
ENGLISH airport bridge college creek,cr. island,i. lake,l. run state park
DEUTSCH Flughafen Brücke College Bach Insel See Bach Staatspark
ESPAÑOL aeropuerto puente escuela riachuelo isla lago arroyo parque del estado
FRANÇAIS aeroport pont college crique île lac ruisseau parc régional
PORTUGUÊS aeroporto ponte escola riacho ilha lago córrego parque estadual
Kilometers 0 5 10 15 Km.
Statute Miles 0 5 10 15 Mi.
Scale 1:300,000
One centimeter represents 3 kilometers.
One inch represents approximately 4.7 miles.
Copyright by Rand McNally & Co.
Map prepared by Rand McNally & Co.

a

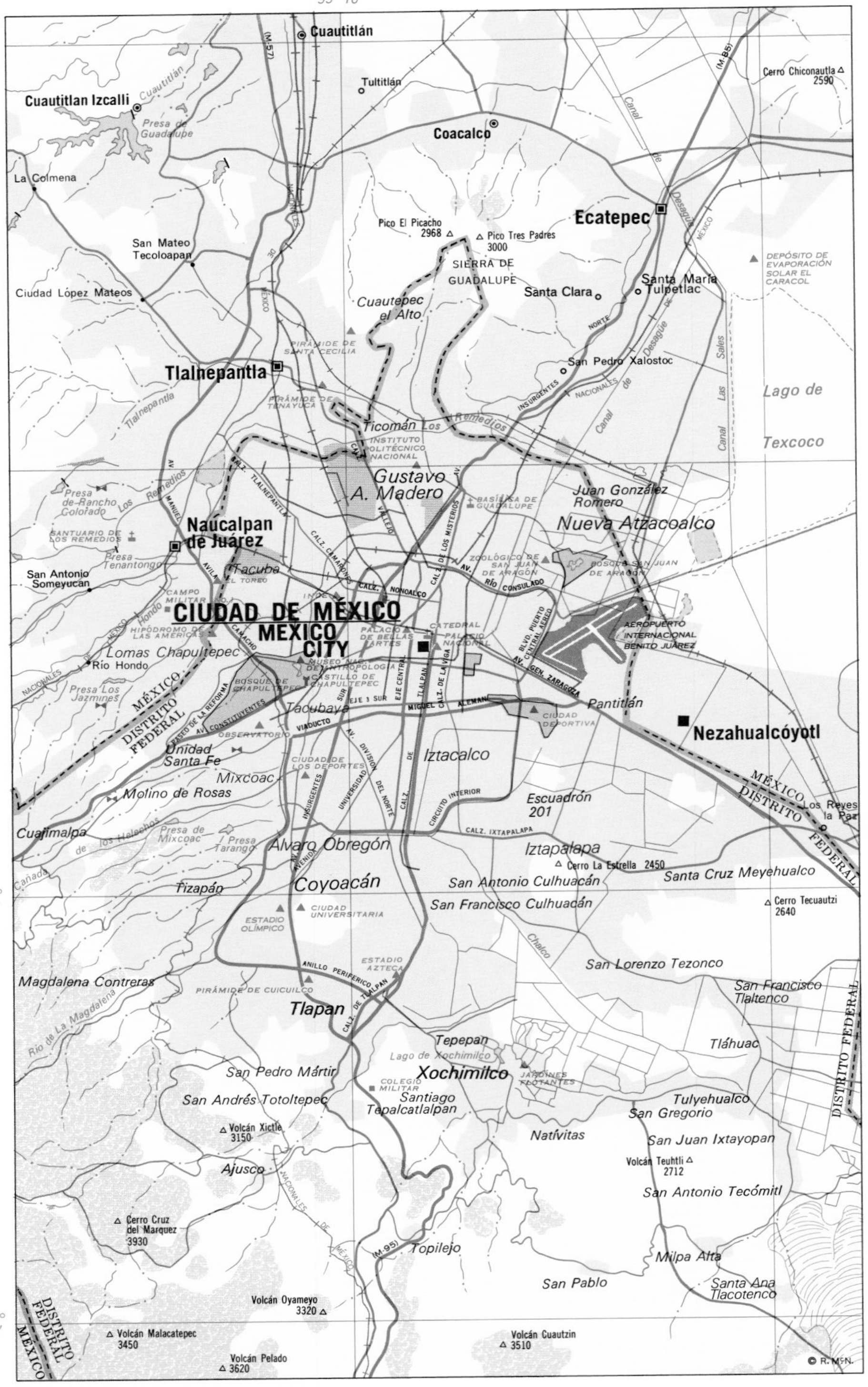
CIUDAD DE MÉXICO
MEXICO CITY
Cuautitlán
Cuautitlan Izcalli
Tultitlán
Coacalco
Ecatepec
La Colmena
San Mateo Tecoloapan
Ciudad López Mateos
Cuautepec el Alto
Santa Clara
Santa María Tulpetlac
San Pedro Xalostoc
Tlalnepantla
Lago de Texcoco
Gustavo A. Madero
Naucalpan de Juárez
Juan González Romero
Nueva Atzacoalco
San Antonio Someyucan
Tacuba
Lomas Chapultepec
Río Hondo
Tacubaya
Unidad Santa Fe
Mixcoac
Molino de Rosas
Cuajimalpa
Pantitlán
Nezahualcóyotl
Iztacalco
Escuadrón 201
Álvaro Obregón
Coyoacán
Iztapalapa
Tizapán
San Antonio Culhuacán
San Francisco Culhuacán
Santa Cruz Meyehualco
Magdalena Contreras
Tlalpan
San Lorenzo Tezonco
San Francisco Tlaltenco
Tláhuac
San Pedro Mártir
San Andrés Totoltepec
Xochimilco
Tepepan
Santiago Tepalcatlalpan
Tulyehualco
San Gregorio
Nativitas
San Juan Ixtayopan
San Antonio Tecómitl
Ajusco
Topilejo
Milpa Alta
San Pablo
Santa Ana Tlacotenco
Volcán Xictle 3150
Cerro Cruz del Marquez 3930
Volcán Oyameyo 3320
Volcán Malacatepec 3450
Volcán Pelado 3620
Volcán Cuautzin 3510
Volcán Teuhtli 2712
Cerro Tecuautzi 2640
Cerro La Estrella 2450
Cerro Chiconautla 2590
Pico El Picacho 2968
Pico Tres Padres 3000
SIERRA DE GUADALUPE
Los Reyes la Paz
MÉXICO
DISTRITO FEDERAL
© R. McN.

b

GULF OF MEXICO
LA HABANA
HAVANA
Cojímar
Casablanca
Vedado
Miramar
Regla
Guanabacoa
Playa
Lawton
Mariano
San Luis
Mantilla
El Calvario
Los Pinos
Santa Fé
Arroyo Naranjo
Cotorro
Playa Baracoa
Calabazar
Punta Brava
Bauta
Santiago de las Vegas
CIUDAD DE LA HABANA
LA HABANA
Bejucal
Laguna de Ariguanabo
Cuatro Caminos
© R. McN.

c

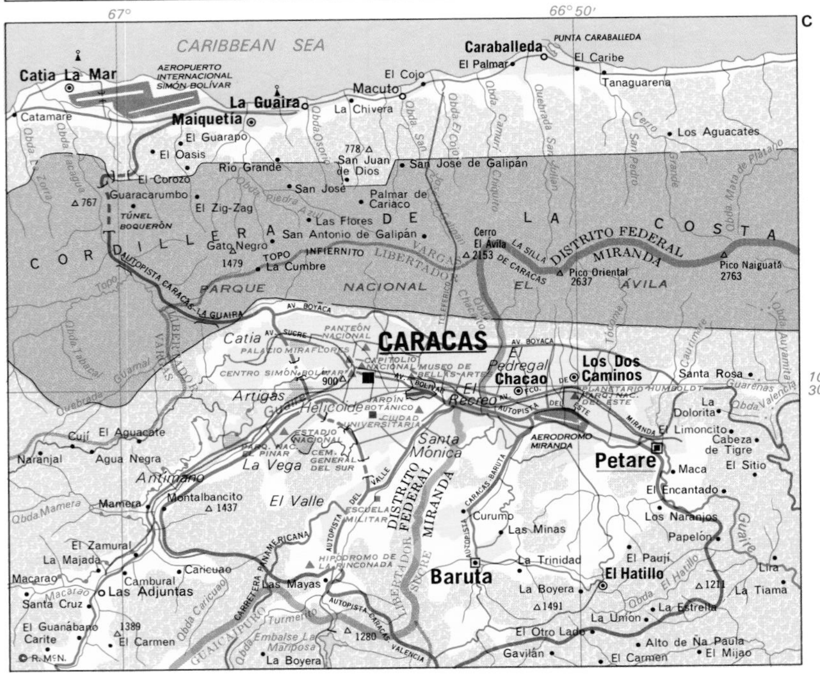
CARIBBEAN SEA
Caraballeda
Catia La Mar
Macuto
La Guaira
Maiquetía
El Caribe
Tanaguarena
Los Aguacates
San José de Galipán
CORDILLERA DE LA COSTA
DISTRITO FEDERAL
MIRANDA
Pico Oriental 2637
Pico Naiguatá 2763
PARQUE NACIONAL EL ÁVILA
CARACAS
Catia
Chacao
Los Dos Caminos
Petare
Santa Rosa
El Hatillo
Baruta
El Valle
La Vega
Antímano
Santa Mónica
Las Minas
La Trinidad
Las Adjuntas
El Carmen
El Jarillo
Gavilán
© R. McN.

d

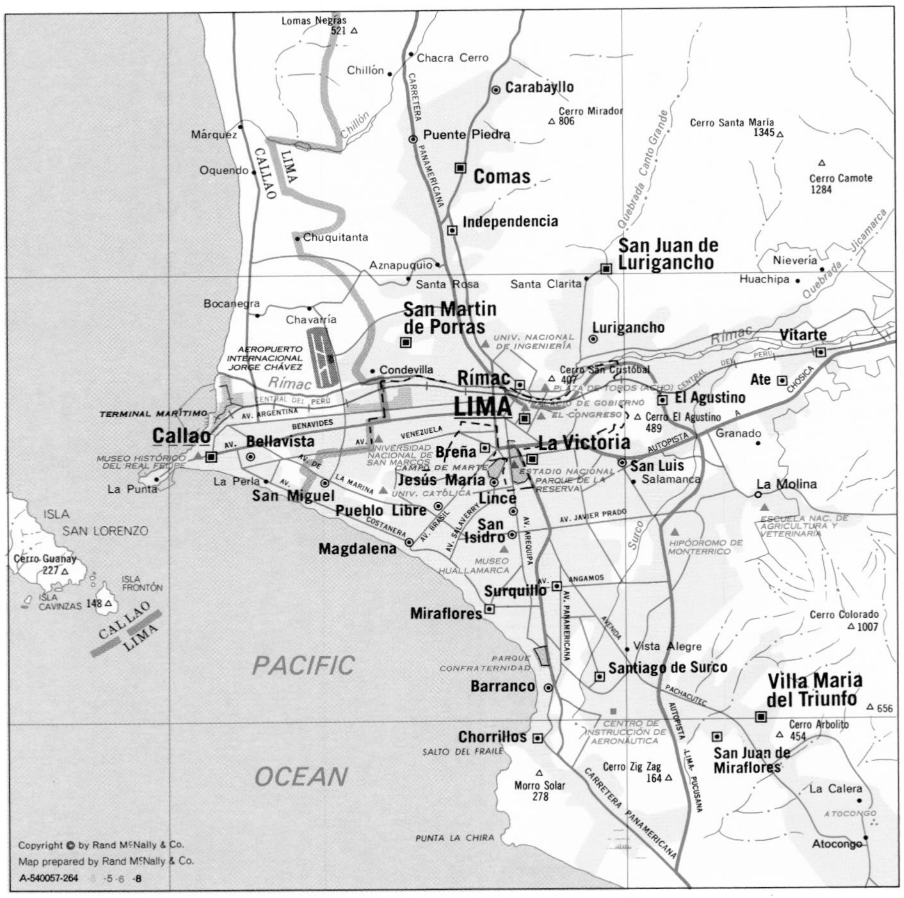
Lomas Negras 521
Chillón
Chacra Cerro
Carabayllo
Puente Piedra
Comas
Márquez
Oquendo
CALLAO
LIMA
Independencia
San Juan de Lurigancho
Chuquitanta
Aznapuquio
Santa Rosa
Santa Clarita
Bocanegra
San Martín de Porras
Lurigancho
Vitarte
Rímac
LIMA
El Agustino
Ate
Callao
Bellavista
La Victoria
Breña
Jesús María
San Luis
La Molina
San Miguel
Pueblo Libre
Lince
San Isidro
La Punta
Magdalena
ISLA SAN LORENZO
Miraflores
Surquillo
PACIFIC OCEAN
Barranco
Santiago de Surco
Villa María del Triunfo
Chorrillos
San Juan de Miraflores
Atocongo
La Calera
Copyright © by Rand McNally & Co.
Map prepared by Rand McNally & Co.
A-540057-264

e

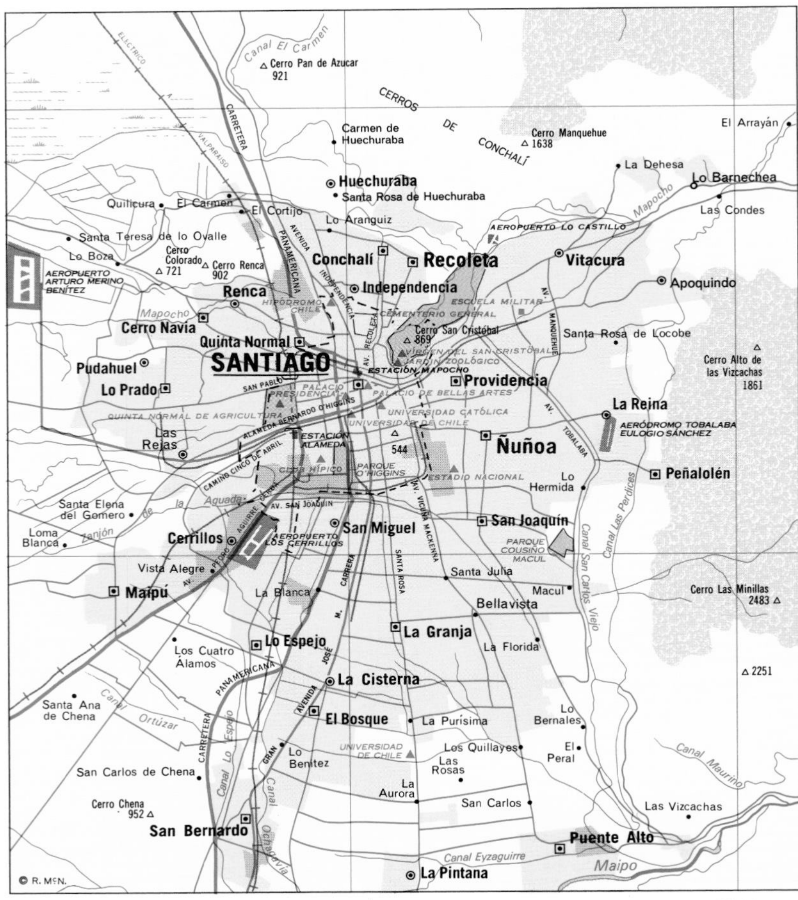
Cerro Pan de Azucar 921
CERROS DE CONCHALÍ
Huechuraba
Quilicura
El Arrayán
Lo Barnechea
Las Condes
Recoleta
Conchalí
Vitacura
Apoquindo
Independencia
Renca
Cerro Navia
Quinta Normal
SANTIAGO
Providencia
Pudahuel
Lo Prado
La Reina
Ñuñoa
Peñalolén
San Joaquín
Cerrillos
San Miguel
Maipú
Lo Espejo
La Granja
La Cisterna
El Bosque
San Bernardo
Puente Alto
La Pintana
Las Vizcachas
© R. McN.

ESPAÑOL	arroyo	castillo	isla	laguna	presa	quebrada
ENGLISH	brook	castle	island	lagoon	reservoir	creek
DEUTSCH	Bach	Burg	Insel	Haff	Stausee	Bach
FRANÇAIS	ruisseau	château	île	lagune	réservoir	crique
PORTUGUÊS	arroio	castelo	ilha	laguna	reservatório	riacho

Kilometers 0 5 10 15 Km.

Statute Miles 0 5 10 15 Mi.

Scale 1:300,000

One centimeter represents 3 kilometers.
One inch represents approximately 4.7 miles.

a

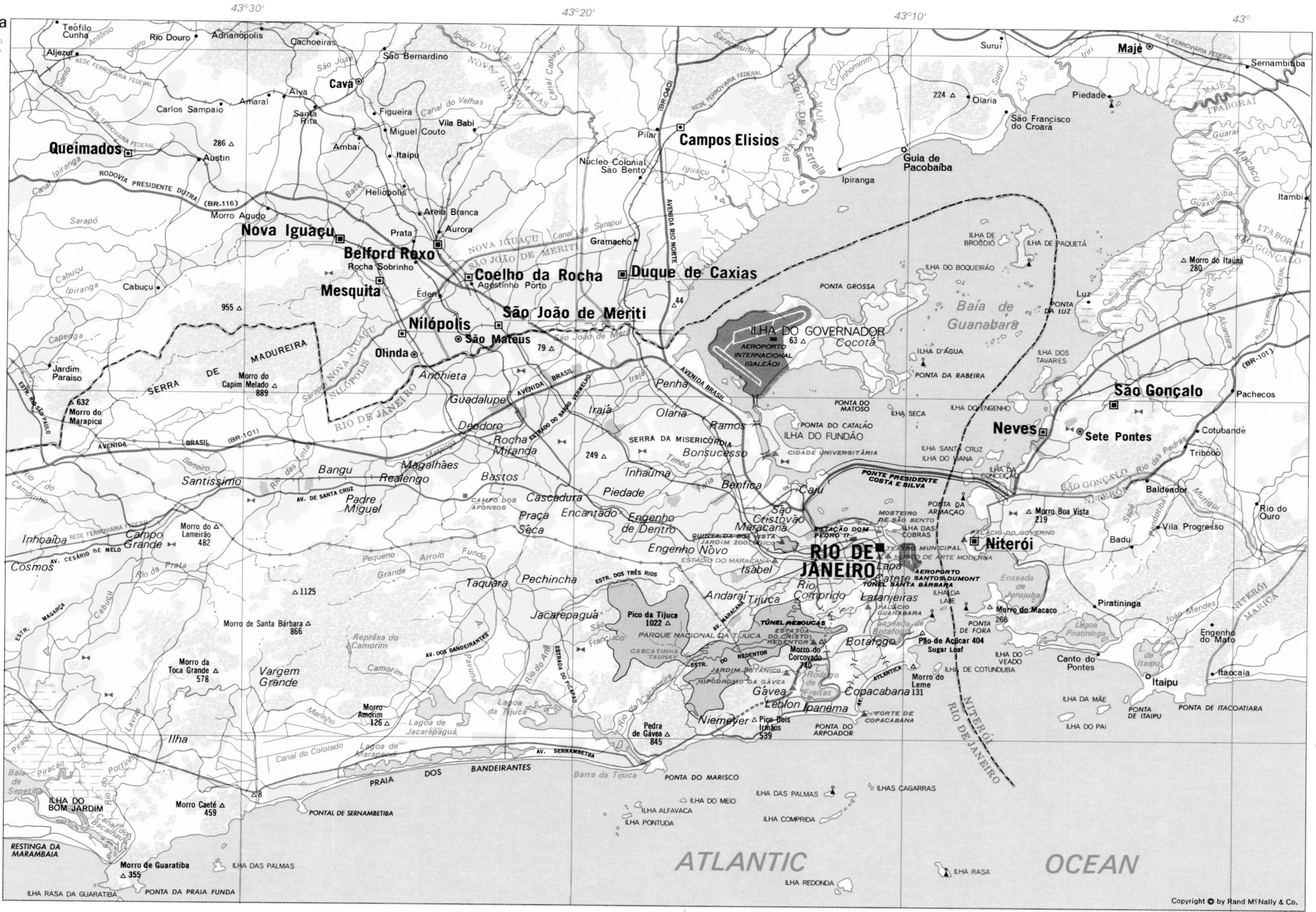

43°30'
43°20'
43°10'
43°
22° 40'
22° 50'
23°
Teófilo Cunha
Aljezur
Rio Douro
Adrianópolis
Cachoeiras
São Bernardino
Cava
Carlos Sampaio
Amaral
Figueira
Vila Babi
Miguel Couto
Queimados
Austin
Ambaí
Itaipu
Pilar
Campos Elísios
Surui
Majé
Sernambitiba
Olaria
Piedade
São Francisco do Croará
Guia de Pacobaíba
Ipiranga
Itambi
Morro Agudo
Nova Iguaçu
Heliópolis
Areia Branca
Aurora
Prata
Belford Roxo
Rocha Sobrinho
Coelho da Rocha
Agostinho Porto
Duque de Caxias
Gramacho
Mesquita
Cabuçu
São João de Meriti
Nilópolis
São Mateus
Olinda
Anchieta
RIO DE JANEIRO
Guadalupe
Deodoro
Irajá
Penha
ILHA DO GOVERNADOR
AEROPORTO INTERNACIONAL (GALEÃO)
Cocotá
Baía de Guanabara
PONTA GROSSA
ILHA DE PAQUETÁ
Luz
São Gonçalo
Pachecos
Neves
Sete Pontes
Cotubandé
Tribobó
SERRA DE MADUREIRA
Jardim Paraíso
Morro do Marapicu
Morro do Capim Melado 889
Bangu
Realengo
Magalhães
Bastos
Rocha Miranda
Madureira
Santíssimo
Padre Miguel
Cascadura
Piedade
Inhaúma
Bonsucesso
Ramos
SERRA DA MISERICÓRDIA
ILHA DO FUNDÃO
CIDADE UNIVERSITÁRIA
PONTE PRESIDENTE COSTA E SILVA
Baldeador
Rio do Ouro
Inhoaíba
Campo Grande
Cosmos
Morro do Lameirão 482
Praça Sêca
Encantado
Engenho de Dentro
Engenho Nôvo
Benfica
Caju
São Cristóvão
Maracanã
RIO DE JANEIRO
Niterói
Badu
Vila Progresso
Taquara
Pechincha
Jacarepaguá
Pico da Tijuca 1022
PARQUE NACIONAL DA TIJUCA
Andaraí
Tijuca
Isabel
Rio Comprido
Laranjeiras
Catete
Lapa
AEROPORTO SANTOS DUMONT
Botafogo
Pão de Açúcar 404 Sugar Loaf
Morro do Corcovado 710
Morro de Santa Bárbara 866
Morro da Toca Grande 578
Vargem Grande
Piratininga
Engenho do Mato
Itacoaiaba
Itaipu
Gávea
Leblon
Ipanema
Copacabana
Morro do Leme 131
Niemeyer
Pico Dois Irmãos 539
Pedra de Gávea 845
Morro Amorim 126
Lagoa de Jacarepaguá
Lagoa de Marapendi
Ilha
PRAIA DOS BANDEIRANTES
Barra da Tijuca
PONTA DO MARISCO
ILHAS CAGARRAS
ILHA DAS PALMAS
ILHA COMPRIDA
ILHA ALFAVACA
ILHA PONTUDA
ILHA DO MEIO
PONTAL DE SERNAMBETIBA
ILHA DO BOM JARDIM
Morro Caeté 459
RESTINGA DA MARAMBAIA
Morro de Guaratiba 355
ILHA RASA DA GUARATIBA
PONTA DA PRAIA FUNDA
ATLANTIC OCEAN
ILHA REDONDA
ILHA RASA
ILHA DA MÃE
ILHA DO PAI
PONTA DE ITACOATIARA
Copyright © by Rand McNally & Co.

b

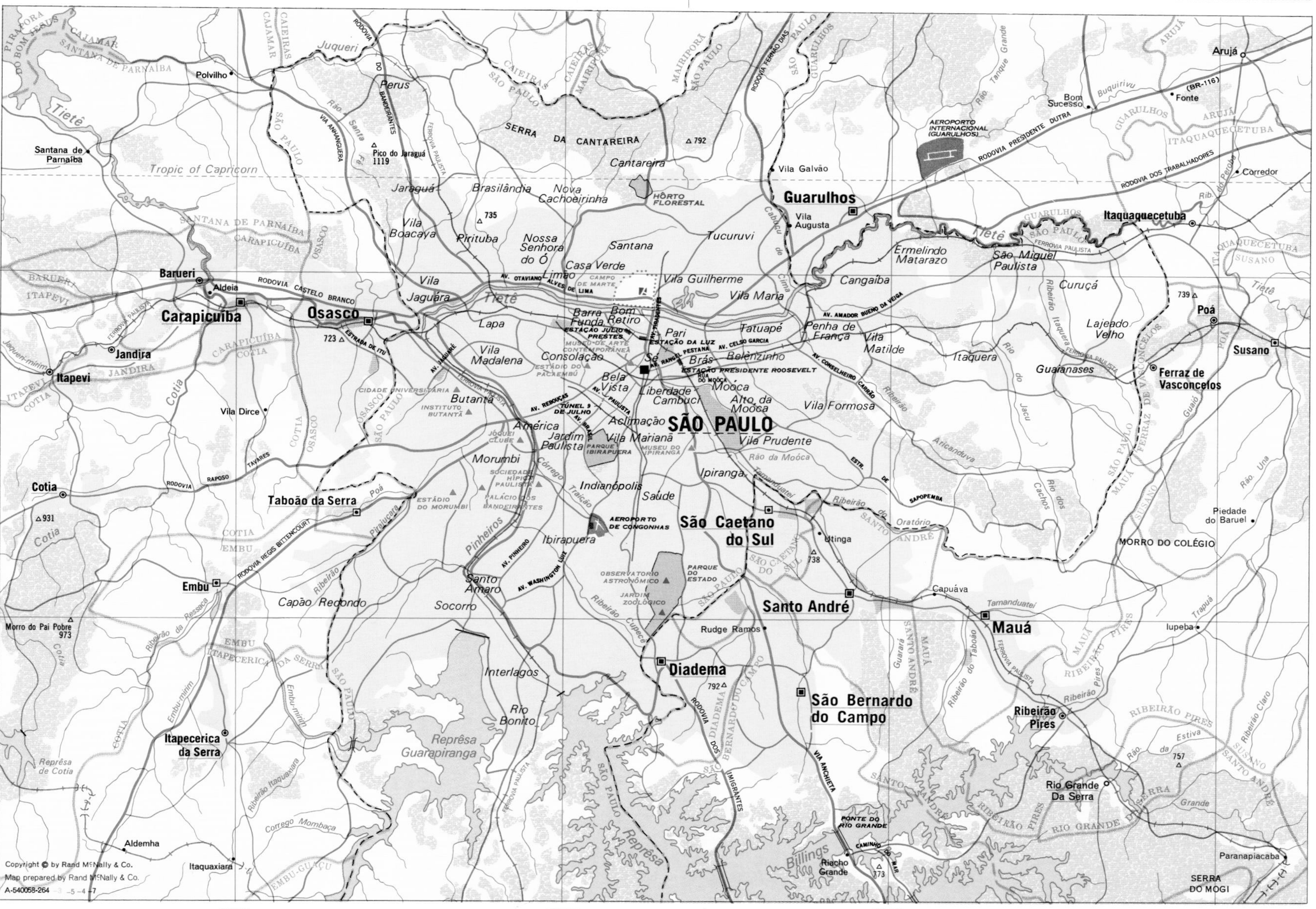

46°50'
46°40'
46°30'
46°20'
23° 30'
23° 40'
Polvilho
Juqueri
Perus
Arujá
Bom Sucesso
Fonte
Santana de Parnaíba
Tropic of Capricorn
Pico do Jaraguá 1119
SERRA DA CANTAREIRA
Cantareira
Vila Galvão
AEROPORTO INTERNACIONAL (GUARULHOS)
Corredor
Jaraguá
Brasilândia
Nova Cachoeirinha
HÔRTO FLORESTAL
Guarulhos
Vila Augusta
Itaquaquecetuba
Vila Boaçava
Pirituba
Nossa Senhora do Ó
Santana
Tucuruvi
Ermelindo Matarazo
São Miguel Paulista
Barueri
Aldeia
Carapicuíba
Osasco
Vila Jaguara
Casa Verde
Limão
Vila Guilherme
Vila Maria
Cangaíba
Curuçá
Poá
Susano
Jandira
Itapevi
Lapa
Barra Funda
Bom Retiro
Pari
Tatuapé
Penha de França
Vila Matilde
Lajeado Velho
Vila Madalena
Consolação
Brás
Belenzinho
Itaquera
Guaianases
Ferraz de Vasconcelos
Vila Dirce
Butantã
Bela Vista
Liberdade
Cambuci
Mooca
Alto da Mooca
Vila Formosa
SÃO PAULO
América
Jardim Paulista
Aclimação
Vila Mariana
Vila Prudente
Morumbi
Cotia
Taboão da Serra
Indianópolis
Saúde
Ipiranga
AEROPORTO DE CONGONHAS
São Caetano do Sul
Piedade do Baruel
MORRO DO COLÉGIO
Ibirapuera
Utinga
Embu
Santo Amaro
Capão Redondo
Socorro
PARQUE DO ESTADO
Santo André
Capuava
Mauá
Morro do Pai Pobre 973
Rudge Ramos
Iupeba
Interlagos
Diadema
São Bernardo do Campo
Ribeirão Pires
Rio Bonito
Itapecerica da Serra
Represa Guarapiranga
Represa de Cotia
Rio Grande Da Serra
Aldemha
Itaquaxiara
Riacho Grande
Billings
Paranapiacaba
SERRA DO MOGI
Copyright © by Rand McNally & Co.
Map prepared by Rand McNally & Co.
A-540058-264

PORTUGUÊS	ilha	lagoa, l.	morro	ponta	reservatório	ribeirão, raó.
ENGLISH	island	lagoon	hill	point	reservoir	creek
DEUTSCH	Insel	Haff	Hügel	Landspitze	Stausee	Bach
ESPAÑOL	isla	laguna	colina	punta	embalse	riachuelo
FRANÇAIS	île	lagune	colline	pointe	réservoir	crique

Kilometers 0 5 10 15 Km.

Statute Miles 0 5 10 15 Mi.

Scale 1:300,000

One centimeter represents 3 kilometers.
One inch represents approximately 4.7 miles.

Kilometers 0 5 10 15 Km.

Statute Miles 0 5 10 15 Mi.

Scale 1:300,000

One centimeter represents 3 kilometers.

One inch represents approximately 4.7 miles.

ESPAÑOL	aeropuerto	arroyo	estación	isla	parque	punta
ENGLISH	airport	brook	station	island	park	point
DEUTSCH	Flughafen	Bach	Bahnhof	Insel	Park	Landspitze
FRANÇAIS	aéroport	ruisseau	gare	île	parc	pointe
PORTUGUÊS	aeroporto	arroio	estação	ilha	parque	ponta

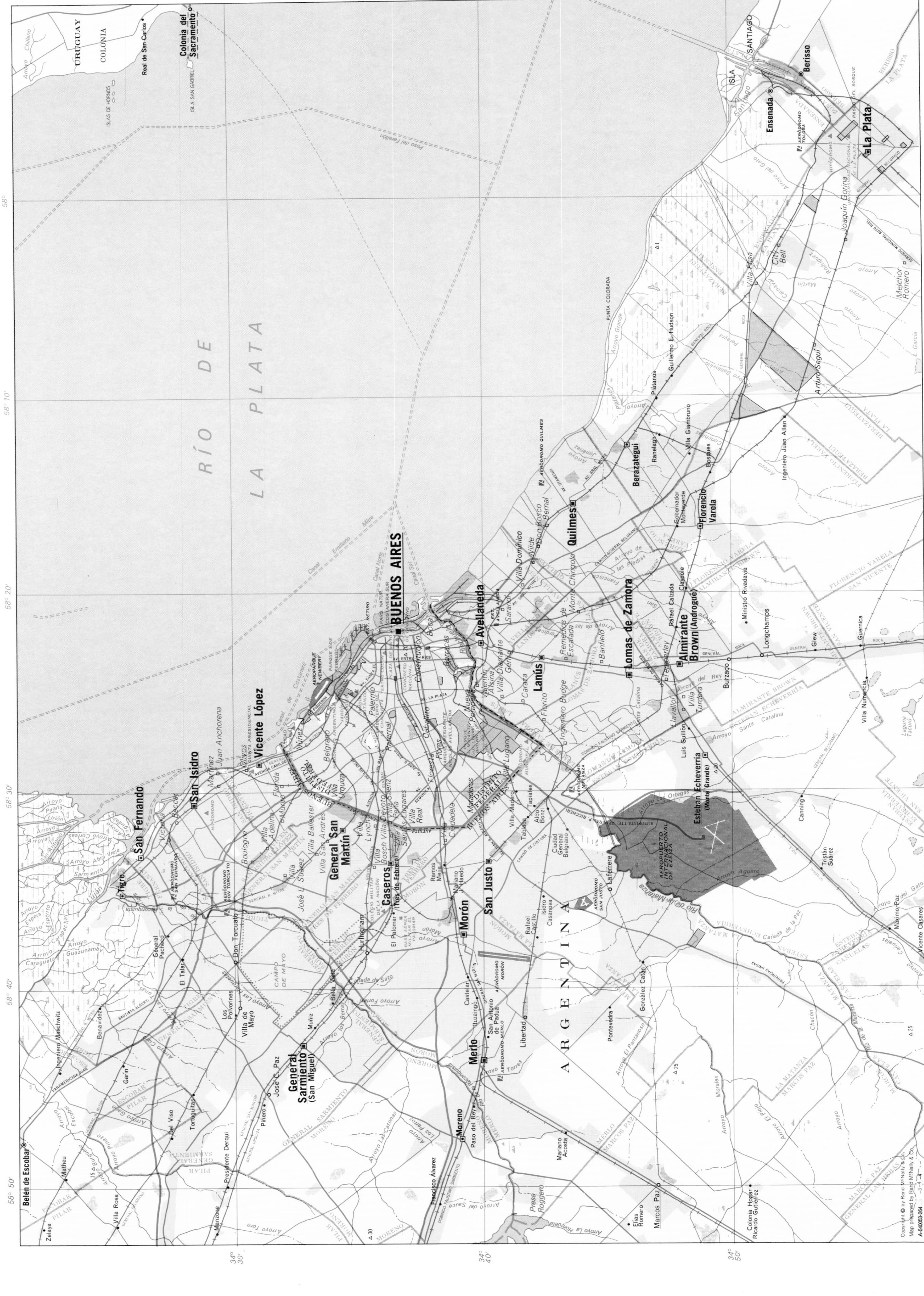
RÍO DE LA PLATA
URUGUAY
COLONIA
Colonia del Sacramento
Real de San Carlos
ARGENTINA
BUENOS AIRES
DISTRITO FEDERAL
Avellaneda
Lanús
Quilmes
Berazategui
Lomas de Zamora
Almirante Brown (Adrogué)
Florencio Varela
Esteban Echeverría (Monte Grande)
AEROPUERTO INTERNACIONAL DE EZEIZA
La Plata
Ensenada
Berisso
Vicente López
San Isidro
San Fernando
Tigre
General San Martín
Caseros (Tres de Febrero)
Morón
San Justo
Merlo
Moreno
General Sarmiento (San Miguel)
Belén de Escobar
AEROPARQUE NEWBERY
PUNTA COLORADA
Copyright © by Rand McNally & Co.

THE MAP FORM column of the glossary lists in alphabetical order the geographical terms, including any abbreviations, that appear on the maps. Terms preceded by a hyphen are those which commonly appear as endings in map names (for example, -san in Fuji-san, -älven in Dalälven). The languages of the terms are identified by abbreviations in *italics* (see Abbreviations of Language Names below). The glossary provides the English, German, Spanish, French, and Portuguese equivalent for each term.

As a rule, the translations were made from the map form to English, then from English into the other four languages. Since the glossary terms and translations refer to specific map features, some may vary from the customary dictionary definitions of the terms.

IN DER SPALTE "Geographische Begriffe" werden alle Begriffe und Abkürzungen in alphabetischer Ordnung aufgeführt, die in den Karten erscheinen. Begriffe mit vorgesetztem Bindestrich erscheinen normalerweise als Wortendungen in Kartennamen (z.B. -san in Fuji-san, -älven in Dalälven). In *Kursivschrift* sind die jeweiligen Abkürzungen angegeben für die Sprachen, in denen der Begriff wiedergegeben ist (siehe unten: Abkürzungen der Sprachen). Das Verzeichnis gibt für jeden Begriff den entsprechenden Ausdruck in englisch, deutsch, spanisch, französisch, und portugiesisch.

In der Regel wurde der Begriff in der Karte ins Englische übersetzt und dann vom Englischen in die vier anderen Sprachen. Da die Begriffe und Übersetzungen sich auf bestimmte Objekte in der Karte beziehen, können einige von ihnen von den in den üblichen Wörterbüchern aufgeführten Begriffsbestimmungen abweichen.

LOS TÉRMINOS GEOGRÁFICOS que aparecen en los mapas, incluyendo abreviaciones, son presentados en la columna de Términos Geográficas del Glosario, en orden alfabético. Los términos que están precedidos por un guión aparecen frecuentemente como terminaciones de los nombres en los mapas (por ejemplo, -san en Fuji-san, -älvan en Dalälven). Los idiomas que representan los términos están identificados por medio de abreviaciones en *cursiva* (véase abajo, Abreviaciones de los Idiomas Extranjeros). El Glosario provee el equivalente para cada término en inglés, alemán, español, francés y portugués.

Generalmente las traducciones están hechas de las formas originales de la terminología de los mapas que aparecen primero en inglés, y luego se traducen a las otras cuatro lenguas. Algunos términos y traducciones pueden aparecer distintas a las usadas en los diccionarios generales porque se refieren a los rasgos particulares de los mapas.

LE GLOSSAIRE cite par ordre alphabétique les termes géographiques et les abréviations utilisées. Les mots précédés d'un tiret sont des suffixes (par exemple, -san dans Fuji-san, -älven dans Dalälven). La langue d'origine du nom cité est indiquée par une abréviation en *italique* (voir Abréviations des noms de langues, ci-dessous). Le Glossaire donne chaque nom en anglais, allemand, espagnol, français, et portugais.

En général, les termes géographiques des cartes ont d'abord été traduits en anglais, puis de l'anglais dans les quatre autres langues. Les définitions de certains termes sont adaptées aux particularités de l'Atlas. Il peut arriver qu'elles diffèrent des définitions habituelles données par les dictionnaires.

A COLUNA 'TERMINOLOGIA', do *Glossário*, contém todos os termos geográficos que figuram nos mapas, em ordem alfabética e com as respectivas abreviações. Os termos precedidos por um hífen são os que freqüentemente aparecem nos mapas como sufixos de nomes tais como *-san* (em Fuji-san), *-älven* (em Dalälven). As línguas em que os termos são expressos estão identificadas por abreviações em *grifo* (ver abaixo, 'Abreviações das línguas estrangeiras'). O Glossário fornece o equivalente de cada termo em inglês, alemão, espanhol, português e francês.

De modo geral, as traduções foram feitas das formas originais da terminologia usada nos mapas para o inglês, e, em seguida, do inglês para as outras quatro línguas. Uma vez que os termos geográficos e traduções do *Glossário* referem-se a acidentes específicos de cada mapa, é possível que algumas definições sejam diferentes das consignadas nos dicionários gerais das línguas.

Abbreviations of Language Names / Abkürzungen der Nationalsprachen / Abreviaciones de los Idiomas Extranjeros Abréviations des Noms de Langues / Abreviações dos Idiomas Estrangeiros

	ENGLISH	DEUTSCH	ESPAÑOL	FRANCAIS	PORTUGUÊS
Afk.	Afrikaans	Afrikaans	Africano	Afrikaans	Afrikaans
Alb.	Albanian	Albanisch	Albanesa	Albanais	Albanês
Ara.	Arabic	Arabisch	Árabe	Arabe	Árabe
Ber.	Berber	Berberisch	Bereber	Berbère	Berbere
Ben.	Bengali	Bengali	Bengali	Bengali	Bengali
Blg.	Bulgarian	Bulgarisch	Búlgaro	Bulgare	Búlgaro
Bur.	Burmese	Burmanisch	Birmano	Birman	Birmanês
Cat.	Catalan	Katalanisch	Catalán	Catalan	Catalão
Cbd.	Cambodian	Kambodschanisch	Camboyano	Cambodgien	Cambojano
Ch.	Chinese	Chinesisch	Chino	Chinois	Chinês
Czech	Czech	Tschechisch	Checo	Tchèque	Tcheco
Dan.	Danish	Dänisch	Danés	Danois	Dinamarquês
Du.	Dutch	Niederländisch	Holandés	Néerlandais	Holandês
Eng.	English	Englisch	Inglés	Anglais	Inglês
Est.	Estonian	Estnisch	Estonio	Esthonien	Estoniano
Finn.	Finnish	Finnisch	Finés	Finnois	Finlandês
Flm.	Flemish	Flämisch	Flamenco	Flamand	Flamengo
Fr.	French	Französisch	Francés	Français	Francês
Gae.	Gaelic	Gälisch	Gaélico	Gaélique	Gaélico
Ger.	German	Deutsch	Alemán	Allemand	Alemão
Gr.	Greek	Griechisch	Griego	Grec	Grego
Hau.	Hausa	Haussa	Hausa	Haoussa	Haussa
Heb.	Hebrew	Hebräisch	Hebreo	Hébreu	Hebraico
Hung.	Hungarian	Ungarisch	Húngaro	Hongrois	Húngaro
Ice.	Icelandic	Isländisch	Islandés	Islandais	Islandês
Indon.	Indonesian	Indonesisch	Indonesio	Indonésien	Indonésio
It.	Italian	Italienisch	Italiano	Italien	Italiano

	ENGLISH	DEUTSCH	ESPAÑOL	FRANCAIS	PORTUGUÊS
Jap.	Japanese	Japanisch	Japonés	Japonais	Japonês
Kor.	Korean	Koreanisch	Coreano	Coréen	Coreano
Lao.	Laotian	Laotisch	Laosiano	Laotien	Laosiano
Lapp.	Lappish	Lappisch	Lapón	Lapon	Lapão
Latv.	Latvian	Lettisch	Letón	Letton	Letão
Lith.	Lithuanian	Litauisch	Lituano	Lithuanien	Lituano
Mal.	Malay	Malaiisch	Malayo	Malais	Malaio
Mong.	Mongolian	Mongolisch	Mogol	Mongol	Mongol
Nor.	Norwegian	Norwegisch	Norvego	Norvégien	Norueguês
Pas.	Pashto	Paschtu	Pushtu	Pachtou	Pachtu
Per.	Persian	Persisch	Persa	Persan	Persa
Pol.	Polish	Polnisch	Polaco	Polonais	Polonês
Poly.	Polynesian	Polynesisch	Polinesio	Polynésien	Polinésio
Port.	Portuguese	Portugiesisch	Portugués	Portugais	Português
Rom.	Romanian	Rumänisch	Rumano	Roumain	Romeno
Rus.	Russian	Russisch	Ruso	Russe	Russo
S./C.	Serbo-Croatian	Serbokroatisch	Servio-croata	Serbo-croate	Servo-croata
Sin.	Sinhalese	Singhalesisch	Cingalés	Cinghalais	Cingalês
Slo.	Slovak	Slowakisch	Eslovaco	Slovaque	Eslovaco
Sp.	Spanish	Spanisch	Español	Espagnol	Espanhol
Swe.	Swedish	Schwedisch	Sueco	Suédois	Sueco
Thai	Thai	Thai	Tai	Thaï	Tailandês
Tib.	Tibetan	Tibetisch	Tibetano	Tibétain	Tibetano
Tur.	Turkish	Türkisch	Turco	Turc	Turco
Ukr.	Ukrainian	Ukrainisch	Ucranio	Ukrainien	Ucraniano
Viet.	Vietnamese	Vietnamesisch	Vietnamita	Vietnamien	Vietnamita
Welsh	Welsh	Walisisch	Galés	Gallois	Galês

A

ENGLISH	DEUTSCH	Map Form Geographische Begriffe Términos Geográficos Termes Géographiques Termos Geográficos	ESPAÑOL	FRANCAIS	PORTUGUÊS
river	Fluss	**-å** *Dan., Nor., Swe.*	río	rivière	rio
brook	Bach	**a., arroyo** *Sp.*	arroyo	ruisseau	córrego
river	Fluss	**āb** *Per.*	río	rivière	rio
army base	Heeres-stützpunkt	**a.b., army base** *Eng.*	base del ejército	base d'armée	base militar
well	Brunnen	**ābār** *Ara.*	pozo	puits	poço
abbey	Abtei	**abb., abbazia** *It.*	abadía	abbaye	abadia
abbey	Abtei	**abbaye** *Fr.*	abadía	abbaye	abadia
abbey	Abtei	**abbazia** *It.*	abadía	abbaye	abadia
abbey	Abtei	**abbey** *Eng.*	abadía	abbaye	abadia
aboriginal reserve	Eingeborenen-schutzgebiet	**aboriginal reserve** *Eng.*	zona de aborígenes	réserve d'indigènes	reserva indígena
abbey	Abtei	**Abtei** *Ger.*	abadía	abbaye	abadia
ditch	Graben	**acequia** *Sp.*	acequia	fossé	fosso
reservoir	Stausee	**ačude** *Port.*	embalse	réservoir	açude
island(s)	Insel(n)	**ada(lar)** *Tur.*	isla(s)	île(s)	ilha(s)
island	Insel	**adası** *Tur.*	isla	île	ilha
mountains	Berge	**adrar** *Ber.*	montañas	montagnes	montanhas
Atomic Energy Commission	Atomenergie-kommission	**A.E.C., Atomic Energy Commission** *Eng.*	Comisión de Energía Atomica	Commission de l'Énergie Atomique	Comissão de Energia Atômica
airport	Flughafen	**aérd., aérodrome** *Fr.*	aeródromo	aérodrome	aeródromo
airport	Flughafen	**aeródromo** *Port., Sp.*	aeródromo	aérodrome	aeródromo
airport	Flughafen	**aeroparque** *Sp.*	aeroparque	aéroport	aeroporto
airport	Flughafen	**aéroport** *Fr.*	aeropuerto	aéroport	aeroporto
airport	Flughafen	**aeroporto** *It., Port.*	aeropuerto	aéroport	aeroporto
airport	Flughafen	**aeropuerto** *Sp.*	aeropuerto	aéroport	aeroporto
air force base	Luftwaffen-stützpunkt	**a.f.b., air force base** *Eng.*	base aeronáutica	base aérienne	base aérea
wadi	Wadi	**ahzar** *Ara.*	uadi	wadi	uádi
peak	Gipfel	**aiguille** *Fr.*	pico	aiguille	pico
air base	Luftstützpunkt	**air base** *Eng.*	base aérea	base aérienne	base aérea
airfield	Flugplatz	**airfield** *Eng.*	camp de aviación	aérodrome	campo de pouso
air force base	Luftwaffen-stützpunkt	**air force base** *Eng.*	base aeronáutica	base aérienne	base aérea
airport	Flughafen	**airport** *Eng.*	aeropuerto	aéroport	aeroporto
cape	Kap	**ákra, akrotírion** *Gr.*	cabo	cap	cabo
hill	Hügel	**'alam, 'alāmat** *Ara.*	colina	colline	colina

ENGLISH	DEUTSCH	Map Form Geographische Begriffe Términos Geográficos Termes Géographiques Termos Geográficos	ESPAÑOL	FRANCAIS	PORTUGUÊS
avenue	Allee	**alameda** *Sp.*	alameda	avenue	avenida
alps	Alpen	**alpes** *Fr.*	alpes	alpes	alpes
alps	Alpen	**alpi** *It.*	alpes	alpes	alpes
mountains, hills	Berge, Hügel	**altos** *Sp.*	altos	montagnes, collines	montanhas, colinas
river	Fluss	**-älv,-älven** *Swe.*	río	rivière	rio
amusement park	Vergnügungs-park	**amusement park** *Eng.*	parque de diversiones	parc récréatif	parque de diversões
river	Fluss	**-ån** *Swe.*	río	rivière	rio
anchorage	Ankerplatz	**anchorage** *Eng.*	ancladero	ancrage	ancoradouro
bay	Bucht	**angra** *Sp.*	angra	baie	baía
cove	kleine Bucht	**anse** *Fr.*	ensenada	anse	enseada
bay	Bucht	**ao** *Ch.*	bahía	baie	baía
bay	Bucht	**ao** *Thai*	bahía	baie	baía
aqueduct	Aquädukt	**aqueduc** *Fr.*	acueducto	aqueduc	aqueduto
aqueduct	Aquädukt	**aqueduct** *Eng.*	acueducto	aqueduc	aqueduto
archipelago	Archipel	**archipel** *Fr.*	archipiélago	archipel	arquipélago
archipelago	Archipel	**archipelag** *Rus.*	archipiélago	archipel	arquipélago
archipelago	Archipel	**archipelago** *Eng.*	archipiélago	archipel	arquipélago
archipelago	Archipel	**archipiélago** *Sp.*	archipiélago	archipel	arquipélago
arm	Arm	**arm** *Eng.*	brazo	bras	braço de rio
army base	Heeres-stützpunkt	**army base** *Eng.*	base del ejército	base d'armée	base militar
airport	Flughafen	**arpt., aéroport** *Fr.* **aeroporto** **aeropuerto** **airport**	aeropuerto	aéroport	aeroporto
archipelago	Archipel	**arquipélago** *Port.*	archipiélago	archipel	arquipélago
reef	Riff	**arrecife** *Sp.*	arrecife	récif	recife
brook	Bach	**arroyo** *Sp.*	arroyo	ruisseau	córrego, arroio
hills	Hügel	**-ås,-åsen** *Swe.*	colinas	collines	colinas
ridge	Höhenrücken	**'assâbet** *Ara.*	sierra	crête	serra
atoll	Atoll	**atol** *Port.*	atolón	atoll	atol
atoll	Atoll	**atoll** *Eng., Fr.*	atolón	atoll	atol
auditorium	Auditorium	**aud., auditorium** *Eng.*	auditorio	auditorium	auditório
race course	Rennbahn	**autodrome** *Fr.*	autódromo	autodrome	autódromo
race course	Rennbahn	**autodromo** *It.*	autódromo	autodrome	autódromo
expressway	Autobahn	**autopista** *Sp.*	autopista	autoroute	via expressa

Glossary and Abbreviations of Geographical Terms / Verzeichnis und Abkürzungen Geographischer Begriffe
Glosario y Abreviaciones de Términos Geográficos / Glossaire et Abréviations de Termes Géographiques
Glossário e Abreviações de Termos Geográficos

ENGLISH	DEUTSCH	Map Form / Geographische Begriffe / Términos Geográficos / Termes Géographiques / Termos Geográficos	ESPAÑOL	FRANCAIS	PORTUGUÊS
avenue	Allee	**av., avenida** *Port., Sp.* **avenue**	avenida	avenue	avenida
channel	Kanal	**ava** *Poly.*	canal, estrecho	canal, détroit	canal, estreito
avenue	Allee	**avenida** *Port., Sp.*	avenida	avenue	avenida
spring	Quelle	**'ayn** *Ara.*	manantial	source	manancial, fonte

B

ENGLISH	DEUTSCH	Map Form	ESPAÑOL	FRANCAIS	PORTUGUÊS
bay	Bucht	**baai** *Du.*	bahía	baie	baía
strait	Meeresstrasse	**bab** *Ara.*	estrecho	détroit	estreito
brook, creek	Bach	**Bach** *Ger.*	arroyo, riachuelo	ruisseau, crique	córrego, arroio
hill	Hügel	**-backen** *Swe.*	colina	colline	colina
bay	Bucht	**badia** *Cat.*	bahía	baie	baía
desert	Wüste	**bādiyat** *Ara.*	desierto	désert	deserto
strait	Meeresstrasse	**bælt** *Dan.*	estrecho	détroit	estreito
bay	Bucht	**bahía** *Sp.*	bahía	baie	baía
inlet	Einfahrt	**bahiret** *Ara.*	abra	bras de mer	enseada, estuário
railroad station	Bahnhof	**Bahnhof** *Ger.*	estación de ferrocarril	gare	estação ferroviária
river, sea	Fluss, Meer	**bahr, bahr** *Ara.*	río, mar	rivière, mer	rio, mar
reservoir	Stausee	**bahrat** *Ara.*	embalse	réservoir	reservatório
bay	Bucht	**baía** *Port.*	bahía	baie	baía
bay	Bucht	**baie** *Fr.*	bahía	baie	baía
reef, sand bar	Riff, Sandbarre	**bajo** *Sp.*	bajo	récif, banc de sable	recife, banco de areia
gorge	Schlucht	**balka** *Rus.*	garganta	gorge	garganta
dome	Kuppe	**ballon** *Fr.*	domo	ballon	domo
marsh	Marsch	**balta** *Rom.*	pantano	marais	pântano
cape	Kap	**-bana** *Jpn.*	cabo	cap	cabo
marsh	Marsch	**bañados** *Sp.*	bañados	marais	pântano
island	Insel	**-banare** *Jpn.*	isla	île	ilha
bank	Bank	**banco** *Sp.*	banco	banc	banco
peninsula	Halbinsel	**bandao** *Ch.*	península	péninsule	península
bank	Bank	**bank** *Eng.*	banco	banc	banco
shoal	Untiefe	**-banken** *Swe.*	bajo	haut-fond	escolho
sand bar	Sandbarre	**barra** *Sp.*	barra	banc de sable	banco de areia
dam	Damm	**barrage** *Fr.*	presa	barrage	represa
ravine	Tobel	**barranca** *Sp.*	barranca	ravin	ravina
air base	Luftstützpunkt	**base aérea** *Sp.*	base aérea	base aérienne	base aérea
basilica	Basilika	**basílica** *Sp.*	basílica	basilique	basílica
basilica	Basilika	**basilique** *Fr.*	basílica	basilique	basílica
basin	Becken	**basin** *Eng.*	cuenca	bassin	bacia
basin	Becken	**bassin** *Fr.*	cuenca	bassin	bacia
marsh	Marsch	**batakliği** *Tur.*	pantano	marais	pântano
river	Fluss	**batang** *Indon.*	río	rivière	rio
river	Fluss	**batha** *Ara.*	río	rivière	rio
marsh	Marsch	**bātlāq** *Per.*	pantano	marais	pântano
battlefield	Schlachtfeld	**battlefield** *Eng.*	campo de batalla	champ de bataille	campo de batalha
mountain	Berg	**batu** *Mal.*	montaña	montagne	montanha
bay	Bucht	**bay** *Eng.*	bahía	baie	baía
bayou	Altwasser	**bayou** *Fr., Eng.*	ensenada pantanosa	bayou	enseada pantanosa
beach	Strand	**beach** *Eng.*	playa	plage	praia
mountain	Berg	**bein, beinn** *Gae.*	montaña	montagne	montanha
snowcapped mountains	Schneegipfel	**belogorje** *Rus.*	nevados	montagnes neigeuses	picos nevados
mountain	Berg	**ben** *Gae.*	montaña	montagne	montanha
mountain, hill	Berg	**Berg** *Ger.*	montaña, colina	montagne, colline	montanha, colina
mountains	Gebirge	**-berg** *Afk.*	montañas	montagnes	montanhas
hill(s), mountain(s)	Hügel, Berg(e)	**-berg** *Swe.*	colina(s), montaña(s)	colline(s), montagne(s)	colina(s), montanha(s)
mountains	Berge	**Berge** *Ger.*	montañas	montagnes	montanhas
mountains	Berge	**-berge** *Afk.*	montañas	montagnes	montanhas
hills, mountains	Hügel, Berge	**-bergen** *Swe.*	colinas, montañas	collines, montagnes	colinas, montanhas
hill, mountain	Hügel, Berg	**-berget** *Swe.*	colina, montaña	colline, montagne	colina, montanha
upland	Bergland	**Bergland** *Ger.*	tierras altas	hautes terres	terras altas
battlefield	Schlachtfeld	**bfld., battlefield** *Eng.*	campo de batalla	champ de bataille	campo de batalha
mountain, hill	Berg	**Bg., Berg** *Ger.*	montaña, colina	montagne, colline	montanha, colina
bridge	Brücke	**bge., bridge** *Eng.*	puente	pont	ponte
bight (bay)	Bucht	**bight** *Eng.*	bahía	baie	baía, enseada
bill (point)	Landspitze	**bill** *Eng.*	punta	pointe	ponta
valley	Tal	**biq'at** *Heb.*	valle	vallée	vale
well	Brunnen	**bi'r** *Ara.*	pozo	puits	poço
lake	See	**birkat** *Ara.*	lago	lac	lago
mountains	Berge	**bjeshkët** *Alb.*	montañas	montagnes	montanhas
brook	Bach	**bk., brook** *Eng.*	arroyo	ruisseau	córrego, arroio
upland	Bergland	**blaenau** *Welsh*	tierras altas	hautes terres	terras altas
bluff(s)	Steilufer	**bluff(s)** *Eng.*	acantilado(s)	falaise(s)	falésia(s)
boulevard	Boulevard	**blvd., boulevard** *Fr., Eng.*	boulevar	boulevard	bulevar
mountain	Berg	**b'nom** *Viet.*	montaña	montagne	montanha
river mouth	Flussmündung	**boca** *Sp.*	boca	embouchure	foz
river mouth, pass	Flussmündung, Pass	**bocca** *It.*	boca, paso	embouchure, col	foz, passo
bay	Bucht	**bocht** *Du.*	bahía	baie	baía
bay	Bodden	**Bodden** *Ger.*	bahía	baie	baía
lake	See	**bæng** *Cbd.*	lago	lac	lago
bog	Moor	**bog** *Eng.*	pantano	fondrière	pântano
strait	Meeresstrasse	**boğazı** *Tur.*	estrecho	détroit	estreito
range	Gebirge	**bogd** *Mong.*	sierra	chaîne	cordilheira
woods	Gehölz	**bois** *Fr.*	bosque	bois	bosque
enclosed basin	Becken	**bolsón** *Sp.*	bolsón	bassin fermée	bacia fechada
forest	Wald	**bory** *Pol.*	bosque	forêt	floresta
forest	Wald	**bosque** *Sp.*	bosque	forêt	floresta
boulevard	Boulevard	**boulevard** *Fr., Eng.*	boulevar	boulevard	bulevar
branch	Arm	**br., branch** *Eng.*	brazo	bras	braço
stream distributary	Flussarm	**braţul** *Rom.*	brazo de río	bras	braço de rio
breakwater	Wellenbrecher	**breakwater** *Eng.*	rompeolas	brise-lames	quebra-mar
glacier	Gletscher	**-breen** *Nor.*	glaciar	glacier	geleira
bridge	Brücke	**bridge** *Eng.*	puente	pont	ponte
marsh	Bruch	**Bruch** *Ger.*	pantano	marais	pântano
bridge	Brücke	**Brücke** *Ger.*	puente	pont	ponte
bridge	Brücke	**brug** *Du.*	puente	pont	ponte
bay	Bucht	**Bucht** *Ger.*	bahía	baie	baía
bay	Bucht	**buchta** *Rus.*	bahía	baie	baía
mountain	Berg	**bufa** *Sp.*	bufa	montagne	montanha
bay	Bucht	**bugt** *Dan.*	bahía	baie	baía
lake	See	**buḩayrah** *Ara.*	lago	lac	lago
lake, lagoon	See, Lagune, Haff	**buḩayrat** *Ara.*	lago, laguna	lac, lagune	lago, laguna
mountain, hill	Berg, Hügel	**bukit** *Indon., Mal.*	montaña, colina	montagne, colline	montanha, colina
bay	Bucht	**-bukten** *Swe.*	bahía	baie	baía
mountain	Berg	**bulu** *Indon.*	montaña	montagne	montanha
castle	Burg	**Burg** *Ger.*	castillo	château	castelo
hill	Hügel	**burj** *Ara.*	colina	colline	colina
brook	Bach	**burn** *Gae.*	riachuelo	crique	riacho
cape	Kap	**burnu, burun** *Tur.*	cabo	cap	cabo
bay	Busen	**Busen** *Ger.*	bahía	baie	baía
butte(s)	Restberg(e)	**butte(s)** *Eng., Fr.*	butte(s)	butte(s)	colina, outeiro

C

ENGLISH	DEUTSCH	Map Form	ESPAÑOL	FRANCAIS	PORTUGUÊS
cape	Kap	**c., cabo** *Sp.* **cap** **cape**	cabo	cap	cabo
street	Strasse	**c., calle** *Sp.*	calle	rue	rua
peaks	Gipfel	**cabezas** *Sp.*	cabezas	cimes	picos
cape	Kap	**cabo** *Port., Sp.*	cabo	cap	cabo
waterfall	Wasserfall	**cachoeira** *Port.*	cascada	chute d'eau	cachoeira
street	Strasse	**calle** *Sp.*	calle	rue	rua
parkway	Ferienstrasse	**calzada** *Sp.*	calzada	allée de parc	alameda de parque
mosque	Moschee	**camii** *Tur.*	mezquita	mosqée	mesquita
road	Landstrasse	**camino** *Sp.*	camino	route	rodovia
camp	Lager	**camp** *Eng., Fr.*	campo	camp	campo
plain	Ebene	**campo** *It.*	llanura	plaine	planície
brook, ravine	Bach, Tobel	**cañada** *Sp.*	cañada	ruisseau, ravin	ravina
canal	Kanal	**canal** *Eng.*	canal	canal	canal
canal, channel	Kanal	**canal** *Fr., Port., Sp.*	canal	canal	canal
canal, channel	Kanal	**canale** *It.*	canal	canal	canal
stream distributary	Flussarm	**caño** *Sp.*	caño	bras	braço de rio, igarapé
canyon	Cañon	**cañón** *Sp.*	cañón	canyon	canhão
canyon	Cañon	**canyon** *Eng.*	cañón	canyon	canhão
plateau	Hochebene	**cao nguyen** *Viet.*	meseta	plateau	planalto
cape	Kap	**cap** *Fr., Cat.*	cabo	cap	cabo
cape	Kap	**cape** *Eng.*	cabo	cap	cabo
capitol	Kapitol	**capitolio** *Sp.*	capitolio	capitole	capitólio
cape	Kap	**capo** *It.*	cabo	cap	cabo
captain	Kapitän	**capt., captain** *Eng.*	capitán	capitaine	capitão
highway	Strasse	**carretera** *Sp.*	carretera	route	rodovia
valley	Tal	**carse** *Gae.*	valle	vallée	vale
waterfall	Wasserfall	**cascada** *Sp.*	cascada	chute d'eau	queda d'água
waterfall	Wasserfall	**cascata** *It.*	cascada	chute d'eau	queda d'água
castle	Burg, Schloss	**castel, castello** *It.*	castillo	château	castelo
castle	Burg, Schloss	**castelo** *Port.*	castillo	château	castelo
castle	Burg, Schloss	**castillo** *Sp.*	castillo	château	castelo
castle	Burg, Schloss	**castle** *Eng.*	castillo	château	castelo
cataracts	Katarakten	**cataratas** *Port., Sp.*	cataratas	cataractes	cataratas
cathedral	Kathedrale	**catedral** *Sp.*	catedral	cathédrale	catedral
range	Gebirge	**catena** *Sp.*	catena	chaîne	cordilheira
cathedral	Kathedrale	**cathedral** *Eng.*	catedral	cathédrale	catedral
causeway	Dammweg	**causeway** *Eng.*	calzada	chaussée	calçada
upland	Bergland	**causse** *Fr.*	tierras altas	causse	terras altas
cave(s)	Höhle(n)	**cave(s)** *Eng.*	cueva(s)	caverne(s)	caverna(s)
cay (islet)	Klippe	**cay** *Eng.*	cayo	caye	baixio
cay(s), islet(s)	Klippe(n)	**cayo(s)** *Sp.*	cayo(s)	caye(s)	baixio(s)
cemetery	Friedhof	**cementerio** *Sp.*	cementerio	cimetière	cemitério
cemetery	Friedhof	**cemetery** *Eng.*	cementerio	cimetière	cemitério
mountain(s), hill(s)	Berg(e), Hügel	**cerro(s)** *Sp.*	cerro(s)	montagne(s), colline(s)	montanha(s), colina(s)
range	Gebirge	**chaîne** *Fr.*	sierra	chaîne	cordilheira
channel	Kanal	**channel** *Eng.*	canal, estrecho	canal, détroit	canal, estreito
hills	Hügel	**chapada** *Port.*	colinas	collines	chapada
island	Insel	**char** *Ben.*	isla	île	ilha
castle	Burg, Schloss	**château** *Fr.*	castillo	château	castelo
road	Landstrasse	**chemin** *Fr.*	camino	chemin	rodovia
bay	Bucht	**chhâk** *Cbd.*	bahía	baie	baía
lake	See	**chi** *Ch.*	lago	lac	lago
harbor, harbour	Hafen	**chiang** *Ch.*	puerto	port	porto
cape	Kap	**chiao** *Ch.*	cabo	cap	cabo
road	Landstrasse	**chin., chemin** *Fr.*	camino	chemin	rodovia
river	Fluss	**-ch'ŏn** *Kor.*	río	rivière	rio
reservoir	Stausee	**-chŏsuji** *Kor.*	embalse	réservoir	reservatório
intermittent lake, salt marsh	periodischer See, Salzmarsch	**chott** *Ara.*	lago intermitente, pantano salado	lac périodique, marais salé	lago intermitente, pântano salgado
range	Gebirge	**chr., chrebet** *Rus.*	sierra	chaîne	cordilheira
mountains	Berge	**chuŏr phnum** *Cbd.*	montañas	montagnes	montanhas
church	Kirche	**church** *Eng.*	iglesia	église	igreja
waterfalls	Wasserfälle	**chutes** *Fr.*	cascadas	chutes d'eau	quedas d'água
marsh	Marsch	**ciénaga** *Sp.*	ciénaga	marais	pântano
peak	Gipfel	**cima** *It., Sp.*	cima	cime	pico
peak	Gipfel	**cime** *Fr.*	cima	cime	pico
cemetery	Friedhof	**cimetière** *Fr.*	cementerio	cimetière	cemitério
city	Stadt	**città** *It.*	ciudad	ville	cidade
city	Stadt	**city** *Eng.*	ciudad	ville	cidade
city	Stadt	**ciudad** *Sp.*	ciudad	ville	cidade
claypan	Tonpfanne	**claypan** *Eng.*	capa de arcilla	couche argilleuse	camada de argila
cliff(s)	Kliff(e)	**cliff(s)** *Eng.*	risco(s)	falaise(s)	falésia(s)
lake	See	**co** *Tib.*	lago	lac	lago
mountain	Berg	**co** *Viet.*	montaña	montagne	montanha
mountain, hill	Berg, Hügel	**co., cerro** *Sp.*	cerro	montagne, colline	montanha, colina
coast	Küste	**coast** *Eng.*	costa	côte	costa
coast guard station	Küstenwacht-station	**coast guard station** *Eng.*	estación de los guardacostas	station des gardescôte	estação de guarda costeira
pass	Pass	**col** *Fr.*	paso	col	passo
college	Hochschule	**colegio** *Sp.*	colegio	collège	colégio
hill(s)	Hügel	**colina(s)** *Sp.*	colina(s)	colline(s)	colina(s)
college	Hochschule	**coll., college** *Eng.*	colegio	collège	colégio
hills	Hügel	**colli** *It.*	colinas	collines	colinas
hills	Hügel	**colline** *It.*	colinas	collines	colinas
hills	Hügel	**collines** *Fr.*	colinas	collines	colinas
common	Gemeindeland	**common** *Eng.*	campo común	commune	terra comum
islands	Inseln	**con** *Viet.*	islas	îles	ilhas
plain	Ebene	**conca** *It.*	llanura	plaine	planície
convent	Nonnenkloster	**convent** *Eng.*	convento	couvent	convento
convent	Nonnenkloster	**convento** *It., Port., Sp.*	convento	couvent	convento
range	Gebirge	**cord., cordillera** *Sp.*	cordillera	chaîne	cordilheira
mountain	Berg	**corno** *It.*	montaña	montagne	montanha
brook	Bach	**córrego** *Port.*	arroyo	ruisseau	córrego
coast	Küste	**costa** *Sp.*	costa	côte	costa
coast, hills	Küste, Hügel	**côte** *Fr.*	costa, colinas	côte	costa, colinas
hills	Hügel	**coteau** *Fr.*	colinas	coteau	colinas
coulee	breite Schlucht	**coulee** *Eng.*	rambla	coulée	barranco
coulee	breite Schlucht	**coulée** *Fr.*	rambla	coulée	barranco
county park	Park	**county park** *Eng.*	parque del condado	parc de comté	parque de condado
convent	Nonnenkloster	**couvent** *Fr.*	convento	couvent	convento
cove	kleine Bucht	**cove** *Eng.*	ensenada	anse	enseada
brook	Bach	**cr., creek** *Eng.*	riachuelo	crique	riacho
crag	Felsspitze	**crag** *Eng.*	despeñadero	pointe de rocher	despenhadeiro
crater	Krater	**crater** *Eng.*	cráter	cratère	cratera
crater	Krater	**cratère** *Fr.*	cráter	cratère	cratera
creek	Bach	**creek** *Eng.*	riachuelo	crique	riacho
peak	Gipfel	**croda** *It.*	pico	cime	pico
canal	Kanal	**csatorna** *Hung.*	canal	canal	canal
bay	Bucht	**cua** *Viet.*	bahía	baie	baía
hills, ridge	Hügel, Höhenrücken	**cuchilla** *Sp.*	cuchilla	collines, crête	coxilha
caves	Höhen	**cuevas** *Sp.*	cuevas	cavernes	cavernas
cove	kleine Bucht	**cul-de-sac** *Fr.*	ensenada	cul-de-sac	enseada
mountains	Berge	**culmea** *Rom.*	montañas	montagnes	montanhas
summit	Gipfel	**cumbre** *Sp.*	cumbre	sommet	cume

D

ENGLISH	DEUTSCH	Map Form	ESPAÑOL	FRANCAIS	PORTUGUÊS
mountain	Berg	**dağ, dağı** *Tur.*	montaña	montagne	montanha
mountains	Berge	**dāgh** *Per.*	montañas	montagnes	montanhas
mountains	Berge	**dağlar, dağları** *Tur.*	montañas	montagnes	montanhas
hill	Hügel	**dahr** *Ara.*	colina	colline	colina
plateau	Hochebene	**-dai, -daichi** *Jpn.*	meseta	plateau	planalto
mountain	Berg	**-dake** *Jpn.*	montaña	montagne	montanha
valley	Tal	**-dal, -dalen** *Nor., Swe.*	valle	vallée	vale
dale	weites Tal	**dale** *Eng.*	valle ancho	vallée large	vale aberto
dam	Damm	**dam** *Eng.*	presa	barrage	represa
lake	See	**danau** *Indon.*	lago	lac	lago
island	Insel	**dao** *Ch., Viet.*	isla	île	ilha
marsh	Marsch	**daqq** *Per.*	pantano	marais	pântano
lake	See	**daryācheh** *Per.*	lago	lac	lago
desert	Wüste	**dasht** *Per.*	desierto	désert	deserto
monastery	Kloster	**dayr** *Ara.*	monasterio	monastère	mosteiro
deep	Tiefe	**deep** *Eng.*	fosa marina	fossé marin	fossa submarina
delta	Delta	**delta** *Eng., Fr., Sp.*	delta	delta	delta

ENGLISH	DEUTSCH	Map Form Geographische Begriffe Términos Geográficos Termes Géographiques Termos Geográficos	ESPAÑOL	FRANCAIS	PORTUGUÊS
sea	Meer	**deniz, denizi** *Tur.*	mar	mer	mar
monument	Denkmal	**Denkmal** *Ger.*	monumento	monument	monumento
pass	Pass	**deo** *Viet.*	paso	col	passo
depression	Senke	**depression** *Eng.*	depresión	dépression	depressão
river	Fluss	**deresi** *Tur.*	río	rivière	rio
desert	Wüste	**desert** *Eng.*	desierto	désert	deserto
desert	Wüste	**desierto** *Sp.*	desierto	désert	deserto
strait	Meeresstrasse	**détroit** *Fr.*	estrecho	détroit	estreito
escarpment	Landstufe	**dhar** *Ara.*	escarpa	escarpement	escarpa
canal	Kanal	**dhiórix** *Gr.*	canal	canal	canal
lake, marsh	See, Marsch	**dian** *Ch.*	lago, pantano	lac, marais	lago, pântano
channel	Kanal	**diep** *Du.*	canal, estrecho	canal, détroit	canal, estreito
dike	Deich	**dijk** *Du.*	dique	digue	dique
district	Distrikt	**district** *Eng.*	distrito	district	distrito
district	Distrikt	**distrito** *Sp.*	distrito	district	distrito
ditch	Graben	**ditch** *Eng.*	acequia	fossé	fosso
mountain(s)	Berg(e)	**djebel** *Ara.*	montaña(s)	montagne(s)	montanha(s)
fjord	Fjord	**-djúp** *Ice.*	fiordo	fjord	fiorde
channel, sound	Kanal, Sund	**-djupet** *Swe.*	canal, sonda	canal, détroit	canal, estreito
zoo	Zoo	**djurpark** *Swe.*	parque zoológico	zoo	jardim zoológico
island	Insel	**-do** *Kor.*	isla	île	ilha
interfluve	Erhebung	**doāb** *Per.*	interfluvio	interfluve	interflúvio
dock	Dock	**dock** *Eng.*	muelle	quai	doca
mountain	Berg	**doi** *Thai*	montaña	montagne	montanha
valley	Tal	**dolina** *Rus.*	valle	vallée	vale
mountain	Berg	**dolok** *Indon.*	montaña	montagne	montanha
hills	Hügel	**dombrovidék** *Hung.*	colinas	collines	colinas
hills	Hügel	**dombvidék** *Hung.*	colinas	collines	colinas
peak	Gipfel	**dos** *Fr.*	pico	dos	pico
downs (hills)	Hügelland	**downs** *Eng.*	colinas	collines	terras baixas (colinas)
drive	Fahrweg	**dr., drive** *Eng.*	calzada	avenue	avenida
drain (water-course)	Abzugsgraben	**drain** *Eng.*	desaguadero	drainage	escoadouro
draw (ravine)	kleines Tal	**draw** *Eng.*	valle pequeño	ravine	bacia, vale
drive	Fahrweg	**drive** *Eng.*	calzada	avenue	avenida
dry lake	Trockensee	**dry lake** *Eng.*	lago seco	lac asséché	lago seco
dunes	Dünen	**dunes** *Eng., Fr.*	dunas	dunes	dunas

E

east	Ost	**e., east** *Eng.*	este	est	leste
school	Schule	**école** *Fr.*	escuela	école	escola
mountain	Berg	**-egga** *Nor.*	montaña	montagne	montanha
memorial	Ehrenmal	**Ehrenmal** *Ger.*	monumento	memorial	monumento
river	Fluss	**-elv,-elva** *Nor.*	río	rivière	rio
reservoir	Stausee	**embalse** *Sp.*	embalse	réservoir	reservatório
pier	Landungsbrücke	**embarcadero** *Sp.*	embarcadero	jetée	cais
valley	Tal	**‘emeq** *Heb.*	valle	vallée	vale
monument	Denkmal	**emlékmü** *Hung.*	monumento	monument	monumento
spring	Quelle	**‘en** *Heb.*	manantial	source	fonte, manancial
cove	kleine Bucht	**enseada** *Port.*	ensenada	anse	enseada
cove	kleine Bucht	**ensenada** *Sp.*	ensenada	anse	enseada
entrance	Einfahrt	**entrance** *Eng.*	entrada	entrée	entrada
forest	Wald	**erdö** *Hung.*	bosque	forêt	floresta
sand desert	Sandwüste	**erg** *Ara.*	desierto arenoso	désert de sable	deserto arenoso
escarpment	Landstufe	**escarpment** *Eng.*	escarpa	escarpement	escarpa
school	Schule	**escuela** *Sp.*	escuela	école	escola
highland	Hochland	**espigão** *Port.*	región montañosa	pays montagneux	espigão
station	Bahnhof, Stützpunkt	**est., estação** *Port.*	estación	station	estação
		estación			
stadium	Stadion	**estadio** *Sp.*	estadio	stade	estádio
reservoir	Stausee	**estanque** *Sp.*	estanque	réservoir	reservatório
estuary	Trichtermündung	**estero** *Sp.*	estero	estuaire	estuário
road	Landstrasse	**estr., estrada** *Port.*	camino	route	estrada
strait	Meeresstrasse	**estrecho** *Sp.*	estrecho	détroit	estreito
estuary	Trichtermündung	**estuary** *Eng.*	estuario	estuaire	estuário
pond	Teich	**étang** *Fr.*	charca	étang	lagoa, açude
expressway	Autobahn	**expy., expressway** *Eng.*	autopista	autoroute	via expressa
island	Insel	**-ey** *Ice.*	isla	île	ilha
lake	See	**ežeras** *Lith.*	lago	lac	lago
lake	See	**ezers** *Latv.*	lago	lac	lago

F

faculty (school)	Fakultät	**faculté** *Fr.*	facultad	faculté	faculdade
fairground	Ausstellungsgelände	**fairground** *Eng.*	campo para ferias	champ de foire	terreno para feiras
cliff	Kliff	**falaise** *Fr.*	risco	falaise	falésia
fall(s) (waterfall)	Wasserfall	**falls(s)** *Eng.*	cascada	chute d'eau	queda d'água
waterfall	Fall	**Fall** *Ger.*	cascada	chute d'eau	queda d'água
waterfall	Wasserfall	**-fallet** *Swe.*	cascada	chute d'eau	queda d'água
river	Fluss	**far'** *Ara.*	río	rivière	rio
lighthouse	Leuchtturm	**faro** *Sp.*	faro	phare	farol
upland	Bergland	**farsh** *Ara.*	tierras altas	hautes terres	terras altas
fell (mountain, hill)	ödes Hügelland	**fell** *Eng.*	colina rocosa	colline rocheuse	colina rochosa
mountain	Berg	**-fell** *Ice.*	montaña	montagne	montanha
mountain	Berg	**feng** *Ch.*	montaña	montagne	montanha
upland	Bergland	**fennsík** *Hung.*	tierras altas	hautes terres	terras altas
ferry	Fähre	**ferry** *Eng.*	balsadera	bac	balsa
lake	See	**fertö** *Hung.*	lago	lac	lago
fortress	Feste	**Feste** *Ger.*	fortaleza	fort	fortaleza
estuary, strait	Trichtermündung, Meeresstrasse	**firth** *Eng.*	estuario, estrecho	estuaire, détroit	estuário, estreito
mountain(s)	Berg(e)	**fjäll(en)** *Swe.*	montaña(s)	montagne(s)	montanha(s)
mountain	Berg	**fjället** *Swe.*	montaña	montagne	montanha
fjord	Fjord	**fjärden** *Swe.*	fiordo	fjord	fiorde
mountain	Berg	**-fjell, -fjellet** *Nor.*	montaña	montagne	montanha
mountain	Berg	**-fjöll** *Ice.*	montaña	montagne	montanha
fjord	Fjord	**-fjord** *Nor.*	fiordo	fjord	fiorde
fjord, lake	Fjord, See	**-fjorden** *Nor., Swe.*	fiordo, lago	fjord, lac	fiorde, lago
fjord, bay	Fjord, Bucht	**-fjörur** *Ice.*	fiordo, bahía	fjord, baie	fiorde, baía
fork	Arm	**fk., fork** *Eng.*	brazo	bras	braço de rio
flat	Flachland	**flat** *Eng.*	llano	plat	planície
river	Fluss	**-fljót** *Ice.*	río	rivière	rio
bay	Bucht	**-flói** *Ice.*	bahía	baie	baía
flood control basin	Hochwasserrückhaltebecken	**flood control basin** *Eng.*	cuenca para controlar la inundación	bassin de contrôle d'inondation	bacia de controle de inundações
airport	Flugplatz	**Flughafen** *Ger.*	aeropuerto	aéroport	aeroporto
airport	Flugplatz	**Flugplatz** *Ger.*	aeropuerto	aérodrome	aeroporto
airport	Flughafen	**flygplats** *Swe.*	aeródromo	aérodrome	aeroporto
river mouth, pass	Flussmündung, Pass	**foce** *It.*	desembocadura, paso	embouchure, col	desembocadura, foz, passo
canal	Kanal	**föcsatorna** *Hung.*	canal	canal	canal
glacier	Gletscher	**-fonn** *Nor.*	glaciar	glacier	geleira
spring	Quelle	**fontaine** *Fr.*	manantial	fontaine	fonte, manancial
pass	Pass	**forca** *It.*	paso	col	passo
inlet	Förde	**Förde** *Ger.*	abra	bras de mer	enseada, estuário
foreland	Vorland	**foreland** *Eng.*	promontorio	promontoire	promontório
forest	Wald	**forest** *Eng.*	bosque	forêt	floresta
forest reserve	Waldreservat	**forest reserve** *Eng.*	reserva de bosque	réserve forestière	reserva florestal

ENGLISH	DEUTSCH	Map Form Geographische Begriffe Términos Geográficos Termes Géographiques Termos Geográficos	ESPAÑOL	FRANCAIS	PORTUGUÊS
forest	Wald	**forêt** *Fr.*	bosque	forêt	floresta
waterfall	Wasserfall	**-forsen** *Swe.*	cascada	chute d'eau	queda d'água
forest	Forst	**Forst** *Ger.*	bosque	forêt	floresta
fort	Fort	**fort** *Eng., Fr.*	fuerte	fort	forte
waterfall	Wasserfall	**-foss** *Ice.*	cascada	chute d'eau	queda d'água
waterfall	Wasserfall	**-fossen** *Nor.*	cascada	chute d'eau	queda d'água
brook	Bach	**fosso** *It.*	arroyo	ruisseau	córrego
pass	Pass	**foum** *Ara.*	paso	col	passo
fracture zone	Bruchzone	**fracture zone** *Eng.*	zona de fractura	zone de faille	zona de fratura
freeway	Autobahn	**frwy., freeway** *Eng.*	autopista	autoroute	via expressa
fort	Fort	**ft., fort** *Eng., Fr.*	fuerte	fort	forte
stream distributary	Flussarm	**furo** *Port.*	brazo de río	bras	furo

G

mountain, hill	Berg, Hügel	**g., gora** *Rus.*	montaña, colina	montagne, colline	montanha, colina
mountain	Berg	**g., gunong** *Mal.*	montaña	montagne	montanha
		gunung			
mountain	Berg	**-gai'sa** *Lapp.*	montaña	montagne	montanha
tunnel	Tunnel	**galleria** *It.*	túnel	tunnel	túnel
gallery	Galerie	**gallery** *Eng.*	galería	galerie	galeria
game farm	Wildfarm	**game farm** *Eng.*	criadero de caza	ferme de gibier	fazenda de caça
game park	Wildpark	**game park** *Eng.*	vedado de caza	parc à gibier	parque de caça
game refuge	Wildgehege	**game refuge** *Eng.*	refugio de caza	refuge de gibier	refúgio de caça
game reserve	Wildreservat	**game reserve** *Eng.*	vedado de caza	réserve à gibier	reserva de caça
game sanctuary	Wildschutzgebiet	**game sanctuary** *Eng.*	vedado de caza	réserve à gibier	santuário de caça
bay	Bucht	**gang** *Ch.*	bahía	baie	baía
river	Fluss	**-gang** *Kor.*	río	rivière	rio
gap	Pass	**gap** *Eng.*	paso	col	passo
intermittent lake	periodischer See	**garaet** *Ara.*	lago intermitente	lac périodique	lago intermitente
garden	Garten	**gard., garden** *Eng.*	jardín	jardin	jardim
gardens	Gärten	**gardens** *Eng.*	jardines	jardins	jardins
mountain	Berg	**garet** *Ara.*	montaña	montagne	montanha
lake	See	**-gata** *Jpn.*	lago	lac	lago
gate	Tor	**gate** *Eng.*	puerta	porte	portão
mountain torrent	Wildbach	**gave** *Fr.*	torrente	gave	torrente
range	Gebirge	**gebergte** *Du.*	sierra	chaîne	cordilheira
range	Gebirge	**Gebirge** *Ger.*	sierra	chaîne	cordilheira
pass	Pass	**gečidi** *Tur.*	paso	col	passo
oasis, well	Oase, Brunnen	**ghadīr** *Ara.*	oasis, pozo	oasis, puits	oásis, poço
mountains	Gebirge	**ghar** *Pas.*	montañas	montagnes	montanhas
spring	Quelle	**ghayl** *Ara.*	manantial	source	manancial
bay	Bucht	**ghubbat** *Ara.*	bahía	baie	baía
dunes	Dünen	**ghurd** *Ara.*	dunas	dunes	dunas
island	Insel	**gili** *Indon.*	isla	île	ilha
peak	Gipfel	**Gipfel** *Ger.*	pico	cime	pico
hill	Hügel	**giva't** *Heb.*	colina	colline	colina
bay	Bucht	**gji** *Alb.*	bahía	baie	baía
glacier	Gletscher	**glacier** *Eng., Fr.*	glaciar	glacier	geleira
lake	See	**göl** *Tur.*	lago	lac	lago
bald mountains	kahle Berge	**gol'cy** *Rus.*	montañas calvas	monts chauves	montanhas calvas
gulf	Golf	**golf** *Cat.*	golfo	golfe	golfo
golf course	Golfplatz	**golf course** *Eng.*	campo de golf	champ de golf	campo de golfe
gulf	Golf	**golfe** *Fr.*	golfo	golfe	golfo
bay	Bucht	**golfete** *Sp.*	golfete	baie	baía
gulf	Golf	**golfo** *It., Sp.*	golfo	golfe	golfo
lake	See	**gölü** *Tur.*	lago	lac	lago
mountain, hill	Berg, Hügel	**gora** *Rus.*	montaña, colina	montagne, colline	montanha, colina
mountains	Berge	**gora** *S./C.*	montañas	montagnes	montanhas
mountain	Berg	**góra** *Pol.*	montaña	montagne	montanha
gorge	Schlucht	**gorge** *Eng., Fr.*	garganta	gorge	garganta
mountains, hills	Berge, Hügel	**gorje** *S./C.*	montañas, colinas	montagnes, collines	montanhas, colinas
ruins	Ruinen	**gorodišče** *Rus.*	ruinas	ruines	ruínas
mountains, hills	Berge, Hügel	**gory** *Rus.*	montañas, colinas	montagnes, collines	montanhas, colinas
mountains	Berge	**góry** *Pol.*	montañas	montagnes	montanhas
sinkhole	Schluckloch	**gouffre** *Fr.*	sumidero	gouffre	sumidouro
wadi	Wadi	**goulbin** *Hau.*	uadi	wadi	uádi
ditch	Graben	**Graben** *Ger.*	acequia	fossé	fosso
ridge	Höhenrücken	**gr'ada** *Rus.*	sierra	crête	cordilheira
mountain	Berg	**gradište** *Blg.*	montaña	montagne	montanha
ridges	Höhenrücken	**gr'ady** *Rus.*	sierras	crêtes	cordilheira
general	General	**gral., general** *Eng., Sp.*	general	général	geral
ridge	Grat	**Grat** *Ger.*	sierra	crête	cordilheira
grotto	Grotte	**grotta** *It.*	gruta	grotte	gruta
grotto	Grotte	**grotte** *Fr.*	gruta	grotte	gruta
group	Gruppe	**group** *Eng.*	grupo	groupe	grupo
island	Insel	**-grund** *Swe.*	isla	île	ilha
group	Gruppe	**grupo** *Sp.*	grupo	groupe	grupo
group	Gruppe	**groppo** *It.*	grupo	groupe	grupo
pass	Pass	**guan** *Ch.*	paso	col	passo
bay	Bucht	**guba** *Rus.*	bahía	baie	baía
mountain	Berg	**guelb** *Ara.*	montaña	montagne	montanha
gulch	Wildbachschlucht	**gulch** *Eng.*	quebrada	ravin	quebrada
gulf	Golf	**gulf** *Eng.*	golfo	golfe	golfo
mountain	Berg	**gunong** *Mal.*	montaña	montagne	montanha
mountain	Berg	**gunung** *Indon.*	montaña	montagne	montanha
islands	Inseln	**-guntō** *Jpn.*	islas	îles	ilhas

H

upland	Bergland	**hadabat** *Ara.*	tierras altas	hautes terres	terras altas
mountain	Berg	**hadjer** *Ara.*	montaña	montagne	montanha
lagoon	Haff	**Haff** *Ger.*	laguna	lagune	laguna
sea, lake	Meer, See	**hai** *Ch.*	mar, lago	mer, lac	mar, lago
strait	Meeresstrasse	**haixia** *Ch.*	estrecho	détroit	estreito
reef	Riff	**hakau** *Poly.*	arrecife	récif	recife
peninsula	Halbinsel	**Halbinsel** *Ger.*	península	péninsule	península
hall	Halle	**hall** *Eng., Fr.*	salón	hall	hall
peninsula	Halbinsel	**-halvøya** *Nor.*	península	péninsule	península
beach	Strand	**-hama** *Jpn.*	playa	plage	praia
desert	Wüste	**hamada** *Ara.*	desierto	désert	deserto
plateau	Hochebene	**hammādat** *Ara.*	meseta	plateau	planalto
lake, marsh	See, Marsch	**hāmūn** *Per.*	lago, pantano	lac, marais	lago, pântano
point	Landspitze	**-hana** *Jpn.*	punta	pointe	ponta
peninsula	Halbinsel	**-hantō** *Jpn.*	península	péninsule	península
mountain, hill	Berg, Hügel	**har** *Heb.*	montaña, colina	montagne, colline	montanha, colina
harbor, harbour	Hafen	**harbor, harbour** *Eng.*	puerto	port	porto
mountains, hills	Berge, Hügel	**hare** *Heb.*	montañas, colinas	montagnes, collines	montanhas, colinas
ridge	Höhenrücken	**-harju** *Finn.*	sierra	crête	cordilheira
lava flow	Lavastrom	**harrat** *Ara.*	corriente de lava	coulée de lave	corrente de lava
hills	Hügel	**hauteurs** *Fr.*	colinas	hauteurs	colinas
sea, bay	Meer, Bucht	**-hav** *Swe.*	mar, bahía	mer, baie	mar, baía
harbor, harbour	Hafen	**havre** *Fr.*	puerto	havre	porto
oasis	Oase	**hawd** *Ara.*	oasis	oasis	oásis
lake	See	**hawr** *Ara.*	lago	lac	lago
harbor, harbour	Hafen	**hbr., harbor, harbour** *Eng.*	puerto	port	porto
headquarters	Hauptquartier	**hdqrs., headquarters** *Eng.*	cuartel general	guartier général	quartel-general
river	Fluss	**he** *Ch.*	río	rivière	rio
head (headland)	Landspitze	**head** *Eng.*	promontorio	promontoire	promontório

ENGLISH	DEUTSCH	Map Form / Geographische Begriffe / Términos Geográficos / Termes Géographiques / Termos Geográficos	ESPAÑOL	FRANCAIS	PORTUGUÊS
heath	Heide	**heath** *Eng.*	matorral	lande	charneca
mountain(s)	Berg(e)	**hegy(ség)** *Hung.*	montaña(s)	montagne(s)	montanha(s)
heath	Heide	**Heide** *Ger.*	matorral	lande	charneca
plain	Ebene	**-heiya** *Jpn.*	llanura	plaine	planície
hills	Hügel	**-heuwells** *Afk.*	colinas	collines	colinas
highland	Hochland	**highland** *Eng.*	región montañosa	pays montagneux	terras altas
highway	Strasse	**highway** *Eng.*	carretera	route	rodovia
hill(s)	Hügel	**hill(s)** *Eng.*	colina(s)	colline(s)	colina(s)
race course	Rennbahn	**hipódromo** *Sp.*	hipódromo	hippodrome	hipódromo
race course	Rennbahn	**hippodrome** *Fr.*	hipódromo	hippodrome	hipódromo
historical	historisch	**hist., historical** *Eng.*	histórico	historique	histórico
historical park	historischer Park	**historical park** *Eng.*	parque histórico	parc historique	parque histórico
historic(al) site	historische Stätte	**historic(al) site** *Eng.*	sitio histórico	site historique	sítio histórico
Her Majesty's Air Station (U.K.)	Luftwaffen-stützpunkt (V.K.)	**H.M.A.S., Her Majesty's Air Station** *Eng.*	Real Estación Aeronáutica (R.U.)	Station Aérienne Royale (R.U.)	Estação Aérea Real (R.U.)
river	Fluss	**ho** *Ch.*	río	rivière	rio
reservoir	Stausee	**-ho** *Kor.*	embalse	réservoir	reservatório
mountain	Berg	**-hø** *Nor.*	montaña	montagne	montanha
plateau	Hochebene	**Hochebene** *Ger.*	meseta	plateau	planalto
forest	Hochwald	**Hochwald** *Ger.*	bosque	forêt	floresta
mountain	Berg	**-högarna** *Swe.*	montaña	montagne	montanha
height	Höhe	**Höhe** *Ger.*	altura	hauteur	elevação
cave(s)	Höhle(n)	**Höhle(n)** *Ger.*	cueva(s)	caverne(s)	caverna(s)
island	Insel	**-holm** *Dan.*	isla	île	ilha
hook	Haken	**hook** *Eng.*	gancho	crochet	cabo, promontório
mountain	Berg	**hora** *Czech, Slo.*	montaña	montagne	montanha
mountain, hill	Berg, Hügel	**hora** *Ukr.*	montaña, colina	montagne, colline	montanha, colina
point, peak	Horn	**Horn** *Ger.*	punta, pico	pointe, cime	ponta, pico
ruin	Ruine	**ḥorva** *Heb.*	ruina	ruine	ruína
mountains	Berge	**hory** *Czech, Slo.*	montañas	montagnes	montanhas
mountains, hills	Berge, Hügel	**hory** *Ukr.*	montañas, colinas	montagnes, collines	montanhas, colinas
hospital	Krankenhaus	**hospital** *Eng., Sp.*	hospital	hôpital	hospital
point	Landspitze	**houma** *Poly.*	punta	pointe	ponta
house	Haus	**house** *Eng.*	casa	maison	casa
island	Insel	**hsü** *Ch.*	isla	île	ilha
lake, reservoir	See, Stausee	**hu** *Ch.*	lago, embalse	lac, réservoir	lago, reservatório
hill	Hügel	**Hügel** *Ger.*	colina	colline	colina
cape	Huk	**Huk** *Ger.*	cabo	cap	cabo
cape	Huk	**-huk** *Swe.*	cabo	cap	cabo
highway	Strasse	**hy., highway** *Eng.*	carretera	route	rodovia
			I		
island	Insel	**i., isla** *Sp.* **island**	isla	île	ilha
icefield	Eisdecke	**icefield** *Eng.*	helero	champ de glace	geleira
ice shelf	Schelfeis	**ice shelf** *Eng.*	corniza glacial	barrière de glace	banco de gelo
ice tongue	Eiszunge	**ice tongue** *Eng.*	lengua de glaciar	langue glaciaire	língua de geleira
dunes	Dünen	**idehan** *Ber.*	dunas	dunes	dunas
river	Fluss	**ig., igarapé** *Port.*	río	rivière	igarapé
church	Kirche	**iglesia** *Sp.*	iglesia	église	igreja
lake	See	**-ike** *Jpn.*	lago	lac	lago
island(s)	Insel(n)	**île(s)** *Fr.*	isla(s)	île(s)	ilha(s)
islet(s)	kleine Insel(n)	**îlet(s)** *Fr.*	isleta(s)	îlet(s)	ilhota(s)
island(s)	Insel(n)	**ilha(s)** *Port.*	isla(s)	île(s)	ilha(s)
islet(s)	kleine Insel(n)	**ilhéu(s)** *Port.*	isleta(s)	îlot(s)	ilhéu(s)
island	Insel	**illa** *Cat.*	isla	île	ilha
islands	Inseln	**illes** *Cat.*	islas	îles	ilhas
hill, upland	Hügel, Bergland	**'ilw** *Ara.*	colina, tierras altas	colline, hautes terres	colina, terras altas
hill	Hügel	**'ilwat** *Ara.*	colina	colline	colina
Indian reservation	Indianer-reservation	**Ind. res., Indian reservation** *Eng.*	reserva de Indios	réserve indienne	reserva indígena
inlet	Einfahrt	**inlet** *Eng.*	abra	bras de mer	enseada
island(s)	Insel(n)	**Insel(n)** *Ger.*	isla(s)	île(s)	ilha(s)
institute	Institut	**inst., institute** *Eng.*	instituto	institut	instituto
international	international	**int., international** *Eng.*	internacional	international	internacional
race course	Rennbahn	**ippodromo** *It.*	hipódromo	hippodrome	hipódromo
wadi	Wadi	**irhazer** *Ber.*	uadi	wadi	uádi
dunes	Dünen	**'irq** *Ara.*	dunas	dunes	dunas
islands	Inseln	**is., islands** *Eng.* **islas**	islas	îles	ilhas
island	Insel	**isla** *Sp.*	isla	île	ilha
island(s)	Insel(n)	**island(s)** *Eng.*	isla(s)	île(s)	ilha(s)
islands	Inseln	**islas** *Sp.*	islas	îles	ilhas
isle(s)	Insel(n)	**isle(s)** *Eng.*	isla(s)	île(s)	ilha(s)
islet(s)	kleine Insel(n)	**islet(s)** *Eng.*	isleta(s)	îlot(s)	ilhota(s)
islet	kleine Insel	**islote** *Sp.*	islote	îlot	ilhota
island	Insel	**isola** *It.*	isla	île	ilha
islands	Inseln	**isole** *It.*	islas	îles	ilhas
islet	kleine Insel	**isolotto** *It.*	isleta	îlot	ilhota
isthmus	Landenge	**isthme** *Fr.*	istmo	isthme	istmo
isthmus	Landenge	**isthmus** *Eng.*	istmo	isthme	istmo
isthmus	Landenge	**istmo** *Sp.*	istmo	isthme	istmo
island	Insel	**-iwa** *Jpn.*	isla	île	ilha
			J		
mountain(s)	Berg(e)	**jabal** *Ara.*	montaña(s)	montagne(s)	montanha(s)
cave	Höhle	**jama** *S./C.*	cueva	caverne	caverna
caves	Höhlen	**jame** *S./C.*	cuevas	cavernes	cavernas
garden	Garten	**jardin** *Fr.*	jardín	jardin	jardim
garden	Garten	**jardín** *Sp.*	jardín	jardin	jardim
gardens	Gärten	**jardines** *Sp.*	jardines	jardins	jardins
lake	See	**järv** *Est.*	lago	lac	lago
lake	See	**-järvi** *Finn.*	lago	lac	lago
mountains	Berge	**jary** *Rus.*	montañas	montagnes	montanhas
lake	See	**-jaur** *Lapp.*	lago	lac	lago
islands	Inseln	**jazā'ir** *Ara.*	islas	îles	ilhas
peninsula	Halbinsel	**jazirah** *Indon.*	península	péninsule	península
island	Insel	**jazīrat** *Ara.*	isla	île	ilha
island	Insel	**jazīreh** *Per.*	isla	île	ilha
reservoir	Stausee	**jazovir** *Blg.*	embalse	réservoir	reservatório
mountain(s)	Berg(e)	**jbel** *Ara.*	montaña(s)	montagne(s)	montanha(s)
lake	See	**jezero** *S./C.*	lago	lac	lago
lake, lagoon	See, Lagune, Haff	**jezioro** *Pol.*	lago, laguna	lac, lagune	lago, laguna
river	Fluss	**jiang** *Ch.*	río	rivière	rio
cape	Kap	**jiao** *Ch.*	cabo	cap	cabo
mountains	Berge	**jibāl** *Ara.*	montañas	montagnes	montanhas
island	Insel	**-jima** *Jpn.*	isla	île	ilha
saddle (pass)	Joch	**Joch** *Ger.*	paso	col	passo
river	Fluss	**-joki** *Finn.*	río	rivière	rio
glacier	Gletscher	**-jøkulen** *Nor.*	glaciar	glacier	geleria
glacier	Gletscher	**-jökull** *Ice.*	glaciar	glacier	geleria
gulf	Golf	**jūras līcis** *Latv.*	golfo	golfe	golfo
islands	Inseln	**juzur** *Ara.*	islas	îles	ilhas
			K		
mountains	Berge	**kabīr** *Per.*	montañas	montagnes	montanhas
dunes	Dünen	**kahal** *Ara.*	dunas	dunes	dunas
sea	Meer	**-kai** *Jpn.*	mar	mer	mar
strait	Meeresstrasse	**-kaikyō** *Jpn.*	estrecho	détroit	estreito
mountain	Berg	**-kaise** *Lapp.*	montaña	montagne	montanha
navy installation	Anlage de Marine	**ka.j., kaijō-jieitai** *Jpn.*	estación de la marina	installation navale	instalação naval
brook	Bach	**kali** *Indon.*	riachuelo	crique	riacho
mountain	Berg	**kalns** *Latv.*	montaña	montagne	montanha
ridge	Kamm	**Kamm** *Ger.*	sierra	crête	serra

ENGLISH	DEUTSCH	Map Form / Geographische Begriffe / Términos Geográficos / Termes Géographiques / Termos Geográficos	ESPAÑOL	FRANCAIS	PORTUGUÊS
canal	Kanal	**kanaal** *Du.*	canal	canal	canal
canal, channel	Kanal	**Kanal** *Ger.*	canal	canal	canal
canal, channel	Kanal	**kanal** *Rus., S./C., Swe., Ukr.*	canal	canal	canal
canal, channel	Kanal	**kana** *Pol.*	canal	canal	canal
canal, channel	Kanal	**kanalen** *Swe.*	canal	canal	canal
canal, channel	Kanal	**kanava** *Finn.*	canal	canal	canal
pass	Pass	**kandao** *Pas.*	paso	col	passo
river	Fluss	**-kang** *Kor.*	río	rivière	rio
moor	Moor	**-kangas** *Finn.*	páramo	lande	charneca
national park	Nationalpark	**kansallis-puisto** *Finn.*	parque nacional	parc national	parque nacional
island	Insel	**kaŏh** *Cbd.*	isla	île	ilha
cape	Kap	**Kap** *Ger.*	cabo	cap	cabo
gorge	Schlucht	**kapija** *S./C.*	garganta	gorge	garganta
cape	Kap	**-kapp** *Nor.*	cabo	cap	cabo
dunes	Dünen	**kathīb** *Ara.*	dunas	dunes	dunas
desert	Wüste	**kavīr** *Per.*	desierto	désert	deserto
mountain	Berg	**kawlat** *Ara.*	montaña	montagne	montanha
hill	Hügel	**kawm** *Ara.*	colina	colline	colina
mountain	Berg	**kedīet** *Ara.*	montaña	montagne	montanha
lake	See	**kenohan** *Indon.*	lago	lac	lago
cape	Kap	**kep** *Alb.*	cabo	cap	cabo
islands	Inseln	**kepulauan** *Indon.*	islas	îles	ilhas
key(s), cay(s)	Klippe(n)	**key(s)** *Eng.*	cayo(s)	caye(s)	baixio(s)
intermittent lake	periodischer See	**khabrat** *Ara.*	lago intermitente	lac périodique	lago intermitente
gulf	Golf	**khalīj** *Ara.*	golfo	golfe	golfo
mountain	Berg	**khao** *Bur., Thai*	montaña	montagne	montanha
mountain	Berg	**khashm** *Ara.*	montaña	montagne	montanha
wadi	Wadi	**khatt** *Ara.*	uadi	wadi	uádi
wadi, river	Wadi, Fluss	**khawr** *Ara.*	uadi, río	wadi, rivière	uádi, rio
dam	Damm	**khazzān** *Ara.*	presa	barrage	represa
river, canal	Fluss, Kanal	**khlong** *Thai*	río, canal	rivière, canal	rio, canal
range	Gebirge	**khrebet** *Ukr.*	sierra	chaîne	cordilheira
dunes	Dünen	**khubb** *Ara.*	dunas	dunes	dunas
kill (river, channel)	Fluss, Kanal	**kill** *Eng.*	río, canal	rivière, canal	rio, canal
cemetery	Friedhof	**kladb., kladbišče** *Rus.*	cementerio	cimetière	cemitério
cloister	Kloster	**klasztory** *Pol.*	claustro	cloître	claustro, convento
cloister, monastery	Kloster	**Kloster** *Ger.*	claustro, monasterio	cloître, monastère	claustro, mosteiro
knob	Kuppe	**knob** *Eng.*	protuberancia	bosse	cerro, colina
island	Insel	**ko** *Thai*	isla	île	ilha
lake, lagoon	See, Lagune, Haff	**-ko** *Jpn.*	lago, laguna	lac, lagune	lago, laguna
harbor, harbour	Hafen	**-kō** *Jpn.*	puerto	port	porto
highland	Hochland	**-kōchi** *Jpn.*	región montañosa	pays montagneux	terras altas
mountain	Kogel	**Kogel** *Ger.*	montaña	montagne	montanha
plateau	Hochebene	**-kogen** *Jpn.*	meseta	plateau	planalto
mountains	Berge	**koh** *Per.*	montañas	montagnes	montanhas
air force installation	Anlage der Luftwaffe	**ko.j., kōkū-jieitai** *Jpn.*	estación aeronáutica	installation aérienne	instalação da força aérea
national park	Nationalpark	**-kokuritsu-kōen** *Jpn.*	parque nacional	parc national	parque nacional
national park	Nationalpark	**-kokutei-kōen** *Jpn.*	parque nacional	parc national	parque nacional
bay	Bucht	**kólpos** *Gr.*	bahía	baie	baía
mountain	Berg	**kong** *Indon.*	montaña	montagne	montanha
peak	Kopf	**Kopf** *Ger.*	pico	cime	pico
bridge	Brücke	**köprüsü** *Tur.*	puente	pont	ponte
gulf, bay	Golf, Bucht	**körfezi** *Tur.*	golfo, bahía	golfe, baie	golfo, baía
spit	Landzunge	**kosa** *Rus., Ukr.*	lengua de tierra	flèche	ponta de terra
rapids	Stromschnellen	**-koski** *Finn.*	rápidos	rapides	rápidos
pass	Pass	**kotal** *Per.*	paso	col	passo
basin	Becken	**kotlina** *Pol.*	cuenca	bassin	bacia
bay, pass	Bucht, Pass	**kou** *Ch.*	bahía, paso	baie, col	baía, passo
ridge	Höhenrücken	**kr'až** *Rus.*	sierra	crête	serra
escarpment	Landstufe	**kreb** *Ara.*	escarpa	escarpement	escarpa
fort	Fort	**krepost'** *Rus.*	fuerte	fort	forte
national park	Nationalpark	**krk., kokuritsu-kōen** *Jpn.*	parque nacional	parc national	parque nacional
ridge	Höhenrücken	**kryazh** *Ukr.*	sierra	crête	serra
national park	Nationalpark	**ktk., kokutei-kōen** *Jpn.*	parque nacional	parc national	parque nacional
bay	Bucht	**kuala** *Mal.*	bahía	baie	baía
mountain(s)	Berg(e)	**kūh(ha)** *Per.*	montaña(s)	montagne(s)	montanha(s)
hill	Hügel	**-kulle** *Swe.*	colina	colline	colina
dome	Kuppe	**Kuppe** *Ger.*	domo	dôme	domo
strait	Meeresstrasse	**-kurkku** *Finn.*	estrecho	détroit	estreito
channel	Kanal	**kyle** *Gae.*	canal, estrecho	canal, détroit	canal, estreito
island	Insel	**kyun** *Bur.*	isla	île	ilha
hills	Hügel	**-kyūryū** *Jpn.*	colinas	collines	colinas
			L		
lake	See	**l., lac** *Fr.* **lago lagoa lake**	lago	lac	lago, lagoa
pass	Pass	**la** *Tib.*	paso	col	passo
province	Provinz	**lääni** *Finn.*	provincia	province	província
lake(s)	See(n)	**lac(s)** *Fr.*	lago(s)	lac(s)	lago(s)
lake	See	**lacul** *Rom.*	lago	lac	lago
cape	Kap	**laem** *Thai*	cabo	cap	cabo
lagoon, lake	Lagune, Haff, See	**lag., laguna** *Sp.*	laguna	lagune, lac	laguna
lake	See	**lago** *It., Port., Sp.*	lago	lac	lago
lake, lagoon	See, Lagune, Haff	**lagoa** *Port.*	lago, laguna	lac, lagune	lagoa
lagoon	Lagune, Haff	**lagoon** *Eng.*	laguna	lagune	laguna
lakes	Seen	**lagos** *Port., Sp.*	lagos	lacs	lagos
lagoon, lake	Lagune, Haff, See	**laguna** *Sp.*	laguna	lagune, lac	laguna, lago
lagoon	Lagune, Haff	**lagune** *Fr.*	laguna	lagune	laguna
bay	Bucht	**laht** *Est.*	bahía	baie	baía
gulf	Golf	**-lahti** *Finn.*	golfo	golfe	golfo
lake(s)	See(n)	**lake(s)** *Eng.*	lago(s)	lac(s)	lago(s)
county	Grafschaft	**län** *Swe.*	condado	comté	condado
lake	Lanke (See)	**Lanke** *Ger.*	lago	lac	lago
sea	Meer	**laut** *Indon.*	mar	mer	mar
lava flow	Lavastrom	**lava flow** *Eng.*	corriente de lava	coulée de lave	corrente de lava
hill, mountain	Hügel, Berg	**law** *Eng.*	colina, montaña	colline, montagne	colina, montanha
mountains, forest	Berge, Wald	**les** *Czech*	montañas, bosque	montagnes, forêt	montanhas, floresta
forest	Wald	**les** *Rus.*	bosque	forêt	floresta
level (plain)	Niveau (Ebene)	**level** *Eng.*	nivel (llano)	niveau (plaine)	planície
islands	Inseln	**liedao** *Ch.*	islas	îles	ilhas
lighthouse	Leuchtturm	**lighthouse** *Eng.*	faro	phare	farol
estuary	Trichter-mündung	**liman** *Rus.*	estuario	estuaire	estuário
bay	Bucht	**limanı** *Tur.*	bahía	baie	baía
lake	See	**límni** *Gr.*	lago	lac	lago
mountain(s), peak	Berg(e), Gipfel	**ling** *Ch.*	montaña(s), pico	montagne(s), pic	montanha(s), pico
forest	Wald	**lis** *Ukr.*	bosque	forêt	floresta
plain(s)	Ebene(n)	**llano(s)** *Sp.*	llano(s)	plaine(s)	planície(s)
lake, reservoir	See, Stausee	**llyn** *Welsh*	lago, embalse	lac, réservoir	lago, reservatório
lake, inlet	See, Einfahrt	**loch** *Gae.*	lago, abra	lac, bras de mer	lago, angra
lock	Schleuse	**lock** *Eng.*	esclusa	écluse	eclusa
lock and dam	Damm mit Schleuse	**lock and dam** *Eng.*	presa y esclusa	écluse et barrage	represa e esclusa

ENGLISH	DEUTSCH	Map Form / Geographische Begriffe / Términos Geográficos / Termes Géographiques / Termos Geográficos	ESPAÑOL	FRANCAIS	PORTUGUÊS
gorge	Schlucht	**log** *Rus.*	garganta	gorge	garganta
mountain	Berg	**loi** *Bur.*	montaña	montagne	montanha
hills	Hügel	**lomas** *Sp.*	lomas	collines	colinas
lake	See	**lough** *Gae.*	lago	lac	lago
lowland	Tiefland	**lowland** *Eng.*	tierra baja	terrain bas	terras baixas
marsh	Luch (Bruch)	**Luch** *Ger.*	pantano	marais	pântano
island	Insel	**-luoto** *Finn.*	isla	île	ilha
estuary	Trichter-mündung	**lyman** *Ukr.*	estuario	estuaire	estuário

M

ENGLISH	DEUTSCH	Map Form	ESPAÑOL	FRANCAIS	PORTUGUÊS
mountains	Berge	**m., munţii** *Rom.*	montañas	montagnes	montanhas
island	Insel	**-maa** *Est.*	isla	île	ilha
strait	Meeresstrasse	**madīq** *Ara.*	estrecho	détroit	estreito
river	Fluss	**mae** *Thai*	río	rivière	rio
depression	Senke	**makhtesh** *Heb.*	depresión	dépression	depressão
bay	Bucht	**-man** *Kor.*	bahía	baie	baía
monastery	Kloster	**manastir** *S./C.*	monasterio	monastère	mosteiro
sea	Meer	**mar** *Sp., It.*	mar	mer	mar
marsh	Marsch	**marais** *Fr.*	pantano	marais	pântano
sea	Meer	**mare** *It.*	mar	mer	mar
marine corps air station	Flugstützpunkt des Marine-Corps	**marine corps air station** *Eng.*	estación aeronáutica de la infantería de marina	station aérienne de fusiliers marins	estação aérea de fuzileiros navais
marine corps base	Marine-Corps-Stützpunkt	**marine corps base** *Eng.*	base de la infantería de marina	base de fusiliers marins	base de fuzileiros navais
bay	Bucht	**marsā** *Ara.*	bahía	baie	baía
marsh	Marsch	**Marsch** *Ger.*	pantano	marais	pântano
marsh(es)	Marsch(en)	**marsh(es)** *Eng.*	pantano(s)	marais	pântano(s)
river mouth	Flussmündung	**maşabb** *Ara.*	desembocadura	embouchure	desembocadura
canal	Kanal	**maşrif** *Ara.*	canal	canal	canal
massif	Gebirgsmassiv	**massif** *Eng., Fr.*	macizo	massif	maciço
marine corps air station	Flugstützpunkt des Marine-Corps	**m.c.a.s., marine corps air station** *Eng.*	estación aeronáutica de la infantería de marina	station aérienne de fusiliers marins	estação aérea de fuzileiros navais
marine corps base	Marine-Corps-Stützpunkt	**m.c.b., marine corps base** *Eng.*	base de la infantería de marina	base de fusiliers marins	base de fuzileiros navais
meadow	Wiese	**meadow** *Eng.*	prado	prairie	pradaria
dunes	Dünen	**médanos** *Sp.*	médanos	dunes	dunas
sea, lake	Meer	**Meer** *Ger.*	mar, lago	mer, lac	mar, lago
sea, lake	Meer	**-meer** *Afk., Du.*	mar, lago	mer, lac	mar, lago
hills	Hügel	**melkosopočnik** *Rus.*	colinas	collines	colinas
memorial	Gedenkstätte	**mem., memorial** *Eng.*	monumento	mémorial	monumento
peninsula	Halbinsel	**menanjung** *Indon.*	península	péninsule	península
sea	Meer	**mer** *Fr.*	mar	mer	mar
mesa	Tafelberg	**mesa** *Sp.*	mesa	mesa	mesa
plateau	Hochebene	**meseta** *Sp.*	meseta	plateau	planalto
middle	Mittel-	**mid., middle** *Eng.*	medio	moyen	médio, central
spit	Landzunge	**mierzeja** *Pol.*	lengua de tierra	flèche	ponta de terra
bay	Bucht	**mifraz** *Heb.*	bahía	baie	baía
mines	Bergwerke	**mikhrot** *Heb.*	minas	mines	minas
military	militärisch	**mil., military** *Eng.*	militar	militaire	militar
harbor, harbour	Hafen	**-minato** *Jpn.*	puerto	port	porto
mine	Bergwerk	**mine** *Eng., Fr.*	mina	mine	mina
mountain	Berg	**-mine** *Jpn.*	montaña	montagne	montanha
cliff	Kliff	**minqār** *Ara.*	risco	falaise	falésia
cape	Kap	**-misaki** *Jpn.*	cabo	cap	cabo
mission	Mission	**mission** *Eng., Fr.*	misión	mission	missão
monument	Denkmal	**mon., monument** *Eng., Fr.*	monumento	monument	monumento
monastery	Kloster	**monasterio** *Sp.*	monasterio	monastère	mosteiro
monastery	Kloster	**monastero** *It.*	monasterio	monastère	mosteiro
monastery	Kloster	**monastery** *Eng.*	monasterio	monastère	mosteiro
monastery	Kloster	**moní** *Gr.*	monasterio	monastère	mosteiro
mount	Berg	**mont** *Fr.*	monte	mont	monte
mountain	Berg	**montagna** *It.*	montaña	montagne	montanha
mountain(s)	Berg(e)	**montagne(s)** *Fr.*	montaña(s)	montagne(s)	montanha(s)
mountain(s)	Berg(e)	**montaña(s)** *Sp.*	montaña(s)	montagne(s)	montanha(s)
mount	Berg	**monte** *It., Port., Sp.*	monte	mont	monte
mountains	Berge	**montes** *Port., Sp.*	montes	monts	montes
mountains	Berge	**monti** *It.*	montes	monts	montes
mountains	Berge	**monts** *Fr.*	montes	monts	montes
monument	Denkmal	**monument** *Eng., Fr.*	monumento	monument	monumento
moor	Moor	**moor** *Eng.*	páramo	lande	pântano
moor	Moor	**Moor** *Ger.*	páramo	lande	pântano
sea	Meer	**more** *Rus., Ukr.*	mar	mer	mar
mountain	Berg	**-mori** *Jpn.*	montaña	montagne	montanha
mountain	Berg	**morne** *Fr.*	montaña	morne	montanha
hill, mountain	Hügel, Berg	**morro** *Port., Sp.*	morro	colline, montagne	morro
mosque	Moschee	**mosque** *Eng.*	mezquita	mosquée	mesquita
island, rock	Insel, Fels	**motu** *Poly.*	isla, roca	île, rocher	ilha, rochedo
island	Insel	**mouchão** *Port.*	isla	île	mouchão
mound	Erdhügel	**mound** *Eng.*	montículo	tertre	montículo
mount	Berg	**mount** *Eng.*	monte	mont	monte
mountain(s)	Berg(e)	**mountain(s)** *Eng.*	montaña(s)	montagne(s)	montanha(s)
mouth (river mouth)	Mündung	**mouth** *Eng.*	desembocadura	embouchure	desembocadura
mount	Berg	**mt., mount** *Eng.*	monte	mont	monte
mountain	Berg	**mtn., mountain** *Eng.*	montaña	montagne	montanha
mountains	Berge	**mts., mountains** *Eng.*	montañas	montagnes	montanhas
point	Landspitze	**mui** *Viet.*	punta	pointe	ponta
headland	Landspitze	**mull** *Gae.*	promontorio	promontoire	promontório
depression	Senke	**munkhafad** *Ara.*	depresión	dépression	depressão
mountain	Berg	**muntele** *Rom.*	montaña	montagne	montanha
mountains	Berge	**munţii** *Rom.*	montañas	montagnes	montanhas
museum	Museum	**museo** *It., Sp.*	museo	musée	museu
museum	Museum	**Museum** *Ger.*	museo	musée	museu
museum	Museum	**museum** *Eng.*	museo	musée	museu
museum	Museum	**múzeum** *Hung.*	museo	musée	museu
museum	Museum	**muzej** *Rus.*	museo	musée	museu
cape	Kap	**mys** *Rus., Ukr.*	cabo	cap	cabo

N

ENGLISH	DEUTSCH	Map Form	ESPAÑOL	FRANCAIS	PORTUGUÊS
north	Nord	**n., north** *Eng.*	norte	nord	norte
sea, gulf	Meer, Golf	**-nada** *Jpn.*	mar, golfo	mer, golfe	mar, golfo
desert	Wüste	**nafūd** *Ara.*	desierto	désert	deserto
plateau, mountains	Hochebene, Berge	**nagorje** *Rus.*	meseta, montañas	plateau, montagnes	planalto, montanhas
river	Fluss	**nahr** *Ara.*	río	rivière	rio
sea	Meer	**-naikai** *Jpn.*	mar	mer	mar
salt flat	Salzebene	**namakzār** *Per.*	salar	saline	salina
narrows	Meeresenge	**narrows** *Eng.*	angostura	goulet	estreito
peninsula	Halbinsel	**-näs** *Swe.*	península	péninsule	península
naval air station	Flugstützpunkt der Marine	**n.a.s., naval air station** *Eng.*	estación aeronáutica de la marina	station de forces aériennes navales	estação aérea da marinha
National Aeronautics and Space Administration	Nationale Aeronautik-und Weltraum-Behörde	**N.A.S.A., National Aeronautics and Space Administration** *Eng.*	Administración Nacional Aeronáutica y Espacial	Administration Nationale de l'Espace et Aéronautique	Administração Nacional do Espaço e Aeronáutica
national park	Nationalpark	**nasjonal park** *Nor.*	parque nacional	parc national	parque nacional
national	national	**nat., national** *Eng., Fr.*	nacional	national	nacional
national battlefield site	Schlachtfeld	**national battlefield site** *Eng.*	campo de batalla nacional	champ de bataille national	campo de batalha nacional
national cemetery	Nationalfriedhof	**national cemetery** *Eng.*	cementerio nacional	cimetière national	cemitério nacional
national forest	Wald in Gemeinbesitz	**national forest** *Eng.*	bosque nacional	forêt nationale	floresta nacional
national historical park	Park an historischer Stätte	**national historical park** *Eng.*	parque histórico nacional	parc historique national	parque histórico nacional
national historical site	historische Stätte	**national historical site** *Eng.*	lugar histórico nacional	site historique national	sítio histórico nacional
national laboratory	staatliche Forschungs-anstalt	**national laboratory** *Eng.*	laboratorio nacional	laboratoire national	laboratório nacional
national memorial	nationale Gedenkstätte	**national memorial** *Eng.*	monumento nacional	memorial national	monumento nacional
national military park	Park bei einem Schlachtfeld	**national military park** *Eng.*	parque militar nacional	parc militaire national	parque militar nacional
national monument	National-denkmal	**national monument** *Eng.*	monumento nacional	monument national	monumento nacional
national park	Nationalpark	**national park** *Eng.*	parque nacional	parc nationale	parque nacional
national recreation area	Ausflugsgebiet	**national recreation area** *Eng.*	campo nacional de recreo	région de récréation national	área de lazer nacional
national seashore	öffentlicher Badestrand	**national seashore** *Eng.*	playa nacional	plage nationale	praia nacional
national park	Nationalpark	**natsional'nyy park** *Ukr.*	parque nacional	parc nationale	parque nacional
reserve	Naturpark	**Naturpark** *Ger.*	reserva natural	réserve naturelle	reserva natural
nature reserve	Natur-schutzgebiet	**Naturschutzgebiet** *Ger.*	reserva natural	réserve naturelle	reserva natural
naval air station	Flugstützpunkt der Marine	**naval air station** *Eng.*	estación aeronáutica de la marina	station de forces aériennes navales	estação aérea da marinha
naval base	Flotten-stützpunkt	**naval base** *Eng.*	base naval	base navale	base naval
naval station	Marinestation	**naval station** *Eng.*	estación naval	station navale	estação naval
naval base	Flotten-stützpunkt	**n.b., naval base** *Eng.*	base naval	base navale	base naval
rock	Fels	**-ne** *Jpn.*	roca	rocher	rochedo
neck	Landenge	**neck** *Eng.*	istmo	isthme	istmo
necropolis (cemetery)	Friedhof	**necrópolis** *Sp.*	necrópolis	nécropole	necrópole
cape	Kap	**neem** *Est.*	cabo	cap	cabo
peninsula, point	Halbinsel, Landspitze	**-nes** *Ice., Nor.*	península, punta	péninsule, pointe	península, ponta
promontory	Vorgebirge	**ness** *Gae.*	promontorio	promontoire	promontório
snowcapped mountain(s)	Schneegipfel	**nev.(s)., nevado(s)** *Sp.*	nevado(s)	montagne(s) neigeuse(s)	pico(s) nevado(s)
mountain	Berg	**ngoc** *Viet.*	montaña	montagne	montanha
cape	Kap	**nina** *Est.*	cabo	cap	cabo
islands	Inseln	**nísoi** *Gr.*	islas	îles	ilhas
island	Insel	**nísos** *Gr.*	isla	île	ilha
lowland	Tiefland	**nizina** *Rus.*	tierra baja	terrain bas	terras baixas
lowland	Tiefland	**nižina** *Slo.*	tierra baja	terrain bas	terras baixas
lowland	Tiefland	**nizmennost'** *Rus.*	tierra baja	terrain bas	terras baixas
cape	Kap	**nos** *Blg.*	cabo	cap	cabo
naval station	Marinestation	**n.s., naval station** *Eng.*	estación naval	station navale	estação naval
nature reserve	Natur-schutzgebiet	**Nsg., Natur-schutzgebiet** *Ger.*	reserva natural	réserve naturelle	reserva natural
mountain	Berg	**nui** *Viet.*	montaña	montagne	montanha
lake	See	**-numa** *Jpn.*	lago	lac	lago
mountains	Berge	**nuruu** *Mong.*	montañas	montagnes	montanhas
island	Insel	**nusa** *Indon.*	isla	île	ilha
lake	See	**nuur** *Mong.*	lago	lac	lago
lowland	Tiefland	**nyzovyna** *Ukr.*	tierra baja	terrain bas	terras baixas

O

ENGLISH	DEUTSCH	Map Form	ESPAÑOL	FRANCAIS	PORTUGUÊS
island	Insel	**-ø** *Dan., Nor.*	isla	île	ilha
island	Insel	**-ö** *Swe.*	isla	île	ilha
island	Insel	**o., ostrov** *Rus.*	isla	île	ilha
islands	Inseln	**-öarna** *Swe.*	islas	îles	ilhas
oasis	Oase	**oasis** *Eng., Fr., Sp.*	oasis	oasis	oásis
observatory	Observatorium	**observatorio** *Sp.*	observatorio	observatoire	observatório
observatory	Observatorium	**observatory** *Eng.*	observatorio	observatoire	observatório
ocean	Ozean	**ocean** *Eng.*	océano	océan	oceano
island	Insel	**-ön** *Swe.*	isla	île	ilha
mountains	Berge	**óri** *Gr.*	montañas	montagnes	montanhas
bay	Bucht	**órmos** *Gr.*	bahía	baie	baía
mountain(s)	Berg(e)	**óros** *Gr.*	montaña(s)	montagne(s)	montanha(s)
island	Insel	**ostriv** *Ukr.*	isla	île	ilha
island(s)	Insel(n)	**ostrov(a)** *Rus.*	isla(s)	île(s)	ilha(s)
island	Insel	**ostrovul** *Rom.*	isla	île	ilha
islands	Inseln	**otoci** *S./C.*	islas	îles	ilhas
island	Insel	**otok** *S./C.*	isla	île	ilha
wadi	Wadi	**ouadi** *Ara.*	uadi	wadi	uádi
wadi	Wadi	**oued** *Ara.*	uadi	wadi	uádi
outlet	Abfluss	**outlet** *Eng.*	desagüe	débouché	escoadouro
island	Insel	**-øy, -øya** *Nor.*	isla	île	ilha
lake	See	**oz., ozero** *Rus., Ukr.*	lago	lac	lago
lakes	Seen	**ozera** *Rus.*	lagos	lacs	lagos

P

ENGLISH	DEUTSCH	Map Form	ESPAÑOL	FRANCAIS	PORTUGUÊS
hills	Hügel	**pahorkatina** *Czech*	colinas	collines	colinas
palace	Palast	**pal., palace** *Eng.*	palacio	palais	palácio
palace	Palast	**palacio** *Sp.*	palacio	palais	palácio
palace	Palast	**palais** *Fr.*	palacio	palais	palácio
palace	Palast	**palazzo** *It.*	palacio	palais	palácio
palace	Palast	**paleis** *Du.*	palacio	palais	palácio
railroad station	Bahnhof	**pályaudvar** *Hung.*	estacion ferrocarril	gare	estação ferroviária
monument	Denkmal	**pam'atnik** *Rus.*	monumento	monument	monumento
plain	Ebene	**pampa** *Sp.*	pampa	plaine	pampa
basin	Becken	**pánev** *Czech*	cuenca	bassin	bacia
swamp	Sumpf	**pantanal** *Port., Sp.*	pantanal	marais	pantanal
marsh, swamp, reservoir	Marsch, Sumpf, Stausee	**pantano** *Sp.*	pantano	marais, réservoir	Pântano
moor	Moor	**páramo** *Sp.*	páramo	lande	pântano
park	Park	**parc** *Fr.*	parque	parc	parque
national park	Nationalpark	**parc national** *Fr.*	parque nacional	parc national	parque nacional
park	Park	**parco** *It.*	parque	parc	parque
national park	Nationalpark	**parco nazionale** *It.*	parque nacional	parc national	parque nacional
provincial park	Naturpark	**parc provincial** *Fr.*	parque de la provincia	parc provincial	parque provincial
park	Park	**Park** *Ger.*	parque	parc	parque
park	Park	**park** *Eng.*	parque	parc	parque
national park	Nationalpark	**park narodowy** *Pol.*	parque nacional	parc national	parque nacional
parkway	Ferienstrasse	**parkway** *Eng.*	calzada	allée de parc	alameda de parque
park	Park	**parque** *Port., Sp.*	parque	parc	parque
national park	Nationalpark	**parq. nac., parque nacional** *Port., Sp.*	parque nacional	parc national	parque nacional
beach	Strand	**part** *Hung.*	playa	plage	praia
strait	Meeresstrasse	**pas** *Fr.*	estrecho	détroit	estreito
passage	Durchfahrt	**pasaje** *Sp.*	pasaje	passage	passagem
pass	Pass	**paso** *Sp.*	paso	col	passo
pass	Pass	**Pass** *Ger.*	paso	col	passo
pass	Pass	**pass** *Eng.*	paso	col	passo
passage	Durchfahrt	**passage** *Eng., Fr.*	pasaje	passage	passagem
passage	Durchfahrt	**passe** *Fr.*	pasaje	passe	passagem
pass	Pass	**passo** *It.*	paso	col	passo
pass	Pass	**pasul** *Rom.*	paso	col	passo
brook	Bach	**patak** *Hung.*	riachuelo	crique	riacho
peak(s)	Gipfel	**peak(s)** *Eng.*	pico(s)	pic(s)	pico(s)
cave	Höhle	**pečina** *S./C.*	cueva	caverne	caverna
mountain	Berg	**pedra** *Port.*	montaña	montagne	montanha
mountains	Berge	**peg., pegunungan** *Indon.*	montañas	montagnes	montanhas
sea	Meer	**pélagos** *Gr.*	mar	mer	mar

ENGLISH	DEUTSCH	Map Form / Geographische Begriffe / Términos Geográficos / Termes Géographiques / Termos Geográficos	ESPAÑOL	FRANCAIS	PORTUGUÊS
peninsula	Halbinsel	**pen., peninsula** *Eng.*	península	péninsule	península
peak, rock	Gipfel, Fels	**peña** *Sp.*	peña	pic, rocher	penha
peak, large rock	Gipfel, grosser Fels	**peñasco** *Sp.*	peñasco	pic, rocher	penhasco
basin	Becken	**pendi** *Ch.*	cuenca	bassin	bacia
peninsula	Halbinsel	**peninsula** *Eng.*	península	péninsule	península
peninsula	Halbinsel	**península** *Sp.*	península	péninsule	península
peninsula	Halbinsel	**péninsule** *Fr.*	península	péninsule	península
rock	Fels	**peñón** *Sp.*	peñón	rocher	rochedo
pass	Pass	**pereval** *Rus., Ukr.*	paso	col	passo
strait	Meeresstrasse	**pertuis** *Fr.*	estrecho	pertuis	estreito
sand desert	Sandwüste	**peski** *Rus.*	desierto arenoso	désert de sable	deserto arenoso
mountain	Berg	**phnum** *Cbd.*	montaña	montagne	montanha
mountain	Berg	**phou** *Lao.*	montaña	montagne	montanha
mountain	Berg	**phu** *Thai*	montaña	montagne	montanha
cape	Kap	**pi** *Ch.*	cabo	cap	cabo
plain	Ebene	**piano** *It.*	llanura	plaine	planície
peak	Gipfel	**pic** *Fr.*	pico	pic	pico
peak	Gipfel	**picacho** *Sp.*	picacho	pic	pico
peak	Gipfel	**picco** *It.*	pico	pic	pico
peak(s)	Gipfel	**pico(s)** *Port., Sp.*	pico(s)	pic(s)	pico(s)
pier	Landungsbrücke	**pier** *Eng.*	embarcadero	jetée	cais
mountain	Berg	**-piggen** *Nor.*	montaña	montagne	montanha
peak	Gipfel	**pik** *Rus.*	pico	pic	pico
forest	Wald	**pinhal** *Port.*	bosque	forêt	pinhal
peak	Gipfel	**pique** *Fr.*	pico	pique	pico
pyramid	Pyramide	**pirâmide** *Sp.*	pirámide	pyramide	pirâmide
peak(s)	Gipfel	**piton(s)** *Fr.*	pico(s)	piton(s)	pico(s)
peninsula	Halbinsel	**pivostriv** *Ukr.*	península	péninsule	península
peak	Gipfel	**piz, pizzo** *It.*	pico	pic	pico
peak	Gipfel	**pk., peak** *Eng.*	pico	pic	pico
parkway	Ferienstrasse	**pkwy., parkway** *Eng.*	calzada	allée de parc	avenida
plain	Ebene	**plain** *Eng.*	llanura	plaine	planície
plain	Ebene	**plaine** *Fr.*	llanura	plaine	planície
plains	Ebenen	**plains** *Eng.*	llanura	plaines	planícies
plateau	Hochebene	**planalto** *Port.*	meseta	plateau	planalto
planetarium	Planetarium	**planetario** *Sp.*	planetario	planétarium	planetário
planetarium	Planetarium	**planetarium** *Eng.*	planetario	planétarium	planetário
mountain, range	Berg, Gebirge	**planina** *S./C.*	montaña, sierra	montagne, chaîne	montanha, cordilheira
plateau	Hochebene	**plateau** *Eng., Fr.*	meseta	plateau	planalto
plateau	Hochebene	**plato** *Afk., Blg., Rus.*	meseta	plateau	planalto
beach	Strand	**playa** *Sp.*	playa	plage	praia
square	Platz	**plaza** *Sp.*	plaza	place	praça
plateau	Hochebene	**plošina** *Czech*	meseta	plateau	planalto
plateau	Hochebene	**ploskogorje** *Rus.*	meseta	plateau	planalto
pass	Pass	**poarta** *Rom.*	paso	col	passo
hill	Hügel	**poggio** *It.*	colina	colline	colina
point	Landspitze	**point** *Eng.*	punta	pointe	ponta
point	Landspitze	**pointe** *Fr.*	punta	pointe	ponta
island	Insel	**pol** *Du.*	isla	île	ilha
plain, basin	Ebene, Becken	**polje** *S./C.*	llanura, cuenca	plaine, bassin	planície, bacia
peninsula	Halbinsel	**poluostrov** *Rus.*	península	péninsule	península
peninsula	Halbinsel	**poluotok** *S./C.*	península	péninsule	península
pond	Teich	**pond** *Eng.*	charca	étang	lago
peak	Gipfel	**-pong** *Kor.*	pico	cime	pico
bridge	Brücke	**pont** *Fr.*	puente	pont	ponte
point	Landspitze	**ponta, pontal** *Port.*	punta	pointe	ponta, pontal
bridge	Brücke	**ponte** *Port.*	puente	pont	ponte
pool	Tümpel	**pool** *Eng.*	charco	étang	charco
rapids	Stromschnellen	**porog** *Rus.*	rápidos	rapides	rápidos
port	Hafen	**port** *Eng., Fr.*	puerto	port	porto
port	Hafen	**porto** *It.*	puerto	port	porto
strait	Meeresstrasse	**porthmós** *Gr.*	estrecho	détroit	estreito
provincial park	Naturpark	**p.p., provincial park** *Eng.*	parque de la provincia	parc provincial	parque provincial
beach	Strand	**praia** *Port.*	playa	plage	praia
reservoir	Stausee	**přehr., přehradová nádrž** *Czech*	embalse	réservoir	reservatório
reservoir, dam	Stausee, Damm	**presa** *Sp.*	presa	réservoir, barrage	represa
peninsula	Halbinsel	**presqu'île** *Fr.*	península	presqu'île	península
reservoir	Stausee	**priehradová nádrž** *Slo.*	embalse	réservoir	reservatório
pass	Pass	**priesmyk** *Slo.*	paso	col	passo
prison	Gefängnis	**prison** *Eng.*	prisión	prison	prisão
pass	Pass	**prohod** *Blg.*	paso	col	passo
strait	Meeresstrasse	**proliv** *Rus.*	estrecho	détroit	estreito
promontory	Vorgebirge	**promontorio** *It., Sp.*	promontorio	promontoire	promontório
promontory	Vorgebirge	**promontory** *Eng.*	promontorio	promontoire	promontório
strait	Meeresstrasse	**protoka** *Ukr.*	estrecho	détroit	estreito
provincial park	Naturpark	**prov. park, provincial park** *Eng.*	parque de la provincia	parc provincial	parque provincial
reservoir	Stausee	**prudy** *Rus.*	embalse	réservoir	reservatório
pass	Pass	**průsmyk** *Czech*	paso	col	passo
pass	Pass	**przeęcz** *Pol.*	paso	col	passo
cape	Kap	**przylądek** *Pol.*	cabo	cap	cabo
point	Landspitze	**pt., point** *Eng.*	punta	pointe	ponta
railroad station	Bahnhof	**pu., pályaudvar** *Hung.*	estación de ferrocarril	gare	estação ferroviária
port	Hafen	**puerto** *Sp.*	puerto	port	porto
peak	Gipfel	**puig** *Cat.*	pico	cime	pico
island	Insel	**pulau** *Indon., Mal.*	isla	île	ilha
upland	Bergland	**puna** *Sp.*	puna	hautes terres	terras altas
peak	Gipfel	**puncak** *Indon.*	pico	cime	pico
point	Landspitze	**punt** *Du.*	punta	pointe	ponta
point, peak	Landspitze, Gipfel	**punta** *It., Sp.*	punta	pointe, cime	ponta
point	Landspitze	**puntilla** *Sp.*	puntilla	pointe	ponta pequena
forest	Wald	**puszcza** *Pol.*	bosque	forêt	floresta
pyramid	Pyramide	**pyramid** *Eng.*	pirámide	pyramide	pirâmide

Q

ENGLISH	DEUTSCH	Map Form	ESPAÑOL	FRANCAIS	PORTUGUÊS
salt flat	Salzebene	**qā'** *Ara.*	salar	saline	salina
canal	Kanal	**qanāt** *Ara.*	canal	canal	canal
hill	Hügel	**qārat** *Ara.*	colina	colline	colina
hills	Hügel	**qārāt** *Ara.*	colinas	collines	colinas
dunes	Dünen	**qawz** *Ara.*	dunas	dunes	dunas
brook	Bach	**qbda., quebrada** *Sp.*	quebrada	crique	arroio
mountain	Berg	**qolleh** *Per.*	montaña	montagne	montanha
canal	Kanal	**-qu** *Ch.*	canal	canal	canal
quarry	Steinbruch	**quarry** *Eng.*	cantera	carrière	pedreira
brook	Bach	**quebrada** *Sp.*	quebrada	crique	arroio
rapids	Stromschnellen	**quedas** *Port.*	rápidos	rapides	quedas
islands	Inseln	**qundao** *Ch.*	islas	îles	ilhas
hill	Hügel	**qūr** *Ara.*	colina	colline	colina
mountain	Berg	**qurnat** *Ara.*	montaña	montagne	montanha

R

ENGLISH	DEUTSCH	Map Form	ESPAÑOL	FRANCAIS	PORTUGUÊS
river	Fluss	**r., rio** *Port.* **río** **river** **rivière**	río	rivière	rio
range	Gebirge	**ra., range** *Eng.*	sierra	chaîne	cordilheira
Royal Australian Air Force Station	Luftwaffenstützpunkt (Austl.)	**R.A.A.F.S., Royal Australian Air Force Station** *Eng.*	Real Estación Aeronáutica (Austl.)	Station Aérienne Royale (Austl.)	Real Estação da Força Aérea Australiana
race course	Rennbahn	**race course** *Eng.*	hipódromo	champ de course	hipódromo
race track	Rennbahn	**race track** *Eng.*	hipódromo	champ de course	hipódromo
raceway	Rennbahn	**raceway** *Eng.*	hipódromo	champ de course	hipódromo
river	Fluss	**rach** *Viet.*	río	rivière	rio
anchorage	Ankerplatz	**rada** *Sp.*	rada	ancrage	ancoradouro
cape	Kap	**rags** *Latv.*	cabo	cap	cabo
railroad	Eisenbahn	**railroad** *Eng.*	ferrocarril	chemin de fer	ferrovia
railway	Eisenbahn	**railway** *Eng.*	ferrocarril	chemin de fer	ferrovia
railway station	Bahnhof	**railway station** *Eng.*	estacion de ferrocarril	gare	estação ferroviária
dunes	Dünen	**ramlat** *Ara.*	dunas	dunes	dunas
range(s)	Gebirge	**range(s)** *Eng.*	sierra(s)	chaîne(s)	cordilheira(s)
river	Fluss	**rão., ribeirão** *Port.*	río	rivière	rio, ribeirão
rapids	Stromschnellen	**rapides** *Fr.*	rápidos	rapides	rápidos
rapids	Stromschnellen	**rapids** *Eng.*	rápidos	rapides	rápidos
wadi	Wadi	**raqabat** *Ara.*	uadi	wadi	uádi
cape	Kap	**ras, ra's** *Ara.*	cabo	cap	cabo
cape	Kap	**rās** *Per.*	cabo	cap	cabo
ravine	Tobel	**ravine** *Eng.*	barranca	ravin	ravina
plain	Ebene	**ravnina** *Rus.*	llanura	plaine	planície
canal	Kanal	**rayyāh** *Ara.*	canal	canal	canal
flood plain	Überschwemmungsebene	**razlivy** *Rus.*	llanura de inundación	lit d'inondation	planície de inundação
road	Landstrasse	**rd., road** *Eng.*	camino	route	rodovia
reef	Riff	**récif** *Fr.*	arrecife	récif	recife
reefs	Riffe	**recifes** *Port.*	arrecifes	récifs	recifes
reefs	Riffe	**récifs** *Fr.*	arrecifes	récifs	recifes
reef(s)	Riff(e)	**reef(s)** *Eng.*	arrecife(s)	récif(s)	recife(s)
regional park	Regionalpark	**regional park** *Eng.*	parque regional	parc régional	parque regional
mountain	Berg	**-rei** *Jpn.*	montaña	montagne	montanha
race course	Rennbahn	**Rennbahn** *Ger.*	hipódromo	champ de course	hipódromo
dam, reservoir	Damm, Stausee	**represa** *Port.*	presa, embalse	barrage, réservoir	represa
airport	Flughafen	**repülőtér** *Hung.*	aeropuerto	aéroport	aeroporto
reservoir	Stausee	**res., reservoir** *Eng.*	embalse	réservoir	reservatório
reservation	Reservat	**reservation** *Eng.*	reservación	réservation	reserva
reservoir	Stausee	**reservatório** *Port.*	embalse	réservoir	reservatório
reserve	Reservat	**reserve** *Eng.*	reserva	réserve	reserva
reserve	Reservat	**réserve** *Fr.*	reserva	réserve	reserva
game reserve	Wildreservat	**réserve de chasse** *Fr.*	vedado de caza	réserve de chasse	reserva de caça
reservoir	Stausee	**reservoir** *Eng.*	embalse	réservoir	reservatório
reservoir	Stausee	**réservoir** *Fr.*	embalse	réservoir	reservatório
beach	Strand	**restinga** *Port.*	playa	plage	praia
islands	Inseln	**-retto** *Jpn.*	islas	îles	ilhas
ria (inlet)	Ria	**ria** *Sp.*	ría	ria	ria
brook	Bach	**riacho** *Port., Sp.*	riacho	crique	riacho
brook	Bach	**riachuelo** *Sp.*	riachuelo	crique	riacho
brook	Bach	**rib., ribeira** *Port.*	riachuelo	crique	ribeira
river	Fluss	**ribeirão** *Port.*	río	rivière	ribeirão
ridge	Höhenrücken	**ridge** *Eng.*	sierra	crête	serra
moor	Ried	**Ried** *Ger.*	páramo	lande	pântano
brook	Bach	**riera** *Sp., Cat.*	riera	crique	riacho
national museum	Reichsmuseum	**rijksmuseum** *Du.*	museo nacional	musée national	museu nacional
army installation	Anlage des Heeres	**rikujō-jieitai** *Jpn.*	estación del ejército	installation militaire	instalação militar
river	Fluss	**rio** *Port.*	río	rivière	rio
river	Fluss	**río** *Sp.*	río	rivière	rio
river	Fluss	**riozinho** *Port.*	río	rivière	riozinho
rise (submarine)	Schwelle (untermeerische)	**rise** *Eng.*	elevación (submarina)	élévation (sous-marine)	elevação (submarina)
river	Fluss	**river** *Eng.*	río	rivière	rio
brook	Bach	**rivera** *Sp.*	rivera	ruisseau	córrego
coast	Küste	**riviera** *It.*	costa	côte	costa
river	Fluss	**rivière** *Fr.*	río	rivière	rio
army installation	Anlage des Heeres	**r.j., rikujō-jieitai** *Jpn.*	estación del ejército	installation militaire	instalação do exército
road	Landstrasse	**road** *Eng.*	camino	route	rodovia
roads (anchorage)	Ankerplatz	**roads** *Eng.*	ancladero	ancrage	ancoradouro
rock	Fels	**roca** *Sp.*	roca	rocher	rochedo
rock, mountain	Fels, Berg	**rocca** *It.*	roca, montaga	rocher, montagne	rochedo, montanha
rock(s)	Fels(en)	**rock(s)** *Eng.*	roca(s)	rocher(s)	rochedo(s)
cape	Kap	**rt** *S./C.*	cabo	cap	cabo
brook	Bach	**rû** *Fr.*	arroyo	rû	córrego
mountains	Berge	**rudohorie** *Slo.*	montañas	montagnes	montanhas
brook	Bach	**ruisseau** *Fr.*	arroyo	ruisseau	córrego
mountain	Berg	**rujm** *Ara.*	montaña	montagne	montanha
run (stream)	Bach	**run** *Eng.*	arroyo	ruisseau	córrego

S

ENGLISH	DEUTSCH	Map Form	ESPAÑOL	FRANCAIS	PORTUGUÊS
south	Süd	**s., south** *Eng.*	sur	sud	sul
range	Gebirge	**sa., serra** *Port.*	sierra	chaîne	cordilheira
island	Insel	**saar** *Est.*	isla	île	ilha
savanna	Savanne	**sabana** *Sp.*	sabana	savane	savana
salt marsh, lagoon	Salzmarsch, Lagune, Haff	**sabkhat** *Ara.*	pantano salado, laguna	marais salé, lagune	pântano salgado, laguna
dam	Damm	**sadd** *Ara.*	presa	barrage	represa
wadi	Wadi	**saguia** *Ara.*	uadi	wadi	uádi
desert	Wüste	**sahrā'** *Ara.*	desierto	désert	deserto
cape	Kap	**-saki** *Jpn.*	cabo	cap	cabo
salt flat	Salzebene	**salar** *Sp.*	salar	saline	salina
salt marsh, salt flat	Salzmarsch, Salzebene	**salina(s)** *Sp.*	salina(s)	marais salé, saline	salina(s)
salt marsh, salt flat	Salzmarsch, Salzebene	**salines** *Fr.*	pantano salado, salinas, salar	salines	pântano salgado, salinas
salt flat	Salzebene	**salt flat** *Eng.*	salar	saline	salina
salt lake	Salzsee	**salt lake** *Eng.*	lago salado	lac salé	lago salgado
salt marsh	Salzmarsch	**salt marsh** *Eng.*	pantano salado	marais salé	pântano salgado
waterfall	Wasserfall	**salto(s)** *Port., Sp.*	salto(s)	chute d'eau	salto(s)
reservoir	Stausee	**samudra** *Sin.*	embalse	réservoir	reservatório
range	Gebirge	**-sammyaku** *Jpn.*	sierra	chaîne	cordilheira
mountain	Berg	**-san** *Jpn., Kor.*	montaña	montagne	montanha
mountains	Berge	**-sanchi** *Jpn.*	montañas	montagnes	montanhas
mountains	Berge	**-sanmaek** *Kor.*	montañas	montagnes	montanhas
shrine	Schrein	**santuario** *It., Sp.*	santuario	châsse	santuário
mountain	Berg	**sar** *Pas.*	montaña	montagne	montanha
island	Insel	**sari** *Est.*	isla	île	ilha
desert	Wüste	**sarīr** *Ara.*	desierto	désert	deserto
saddle (pass)	Sattel	**Sattel** *Ger.*	paso	col	passo
strait	Meeresstrasse	**šaurums** *Latv.*	estrecho	détroit	estreito
waterfall	Wasserfall	**saut** *Fr.*	cascada	saut	queda d'água
castle	Schloss	**Schloss** *Ger.*	castillo	château	castelo
gorge	Schlucht	**Schlucht** *Ger.*	garganta	gorge	garganta
school	Schule	**school** *Eng.*	escuela	école	escola
sea	Meer	**sea** *Eng.*	mar	mer	mar
seamount	untermeerische Kuppe	**seamount** *Eng.*	montaña submarina	montagne sous-marine	montanha submarina
sea scarp	Abbruch	**sea scarp** *Eng.*	cantil	escarpement sous-marine	escarpa submarina
dry lake	Trockensee	**sebjet** *Ara.*	lago seco	lac asséché	lago seco
salt flat	Salzebene	**sebkha** *Ara.*	salar	saline	salina
intermittent lake	periodischer See	**sebkra** *Ara.*	lago intermitente	lac périodique	lago intermitente
salt marsh	Salzmarsch	**sebkret** *Ara.*	pantano salado	marais salé	pântano salgado
airport	Flughafen	**sede-te'ufa** *Heb.*	aeropuerto	aéroport	aeroporto
saddle (pass)	Sattel	**sedlo** *Czech*	paso	col	passo
lake(s)	See(n)	**See(n)** *Ger.*	lago(s)	lac(s)	lago(s)
strait	Meeresstrasse	**selat** *Indon.*	estrecho	détroit	estreito
peninsula	Halbinsel	**semenanjung** *Indon.*	península	péninsule	península
seminary	Seminar	**seminary** *Eng.*	seminario	séminaire	seminário
mountain	Berg	**-sen** *Jpn.*	montaña	montagne	montanha
sound	Sund	**seno** *Sp.*	seno	détroit	estreito
mountains	Gebirge	**serra** *Cat.*	montañas	montagnes	montanhas
range, mountain	Gebirge, Berg	**serra** *Port.*	sierra	chaîne, montagne	serra

ENGLISH	DEUTSCH	Map Form / Geographische Begriffe / Términos Geográficos / Termes Géographiques / Termos Geográficos	ESPAÑOL	FRANCAIS	PORTUGUÊS
ridge(s)	Höhenrücken	**serranía(s)** *Sp.*	serranía(s)	crête(s)	serrania(s)
island	Insel	**sha** *Ch.*	isla	île	ilha
rapids	Stromschnellen	**shallāl** *Ara.*	rápidos	rapides	rápidos
desert	Wüste	**shamo** *Ch.*	desierto	désert	deserto
mountain(s), island	Berg(e), Insel	**shan** *Ch.*	montaña(s), isla	montagne(s), île	montanha(s), ilha
pass	Pass	**shankou** *Ch.*	paso	col	passo
mountains	Berge	**shanmo** *Ch.*	montañas	montagnes	montanhas
bay	Bucht	**sharm** *Ara.*	bahía	baie	baía
peninsula	Halbinsel	**shibh jazīrat** *Ara.*	península	péninsule	península
island	Insel	**-shima** *Jpn.*	isla	île	ilha
reef	Riff	**-shō** *Jpn.*	arrecife	récif	recife
shoal(s)	Untiefe(n)	**shoal(s)** *Eng.*	bajo(s)	haut-fond(s)	baixio(s)
islands	Inseln	**-shotō** *Jpn.*	islas	îles	ilhas
shrine	Schrein	**shrine** *Eng.*	santuario	châsse	santuário
river	Fluss	**shui** *Ch.*	río	rivière	rio
reservoir	Stausee	**shuiku** *Ch.*	embalse	réservoir	reservatório
strait	Meeresstrasse	**shuitao** *Ch.*	estrecho	détroit	estreito
temple	Tempel	**si** *Ch.*	templo	temple	templo
range, ridge	Gebirge, Höhenrücken	**sierra** *Sp.*	sierra	chaîne, crête	serra
rapids	Stromschnellen	**šivera** *Rus.*	rápidos	rapides	rápidos
lake	See	**-sjø** *Nor.*	lago	lac	lago
lakes	Seen	**-sjöarna** *Swe.*	lagos	lacs	lagos
lake	See	**-sjøen** *Nor.*	lago	lac	lago
lake, bay	See, Bucht	**-sjön** *Swe.*	lago, bahía	lac, baie	lago, baía
island	Insel	**skär** *Swe.*	isla	île	ilha
forest	Wald	**-skog, -skogen** *Swe.*	bosque	forêt	floresta
mountain	Berg	**slieve** *Gae.*	montaña	montagne	montanha
castle	Schloss	**slot** *Du.*	castillo	château	castelo
castle	Schloss	**slott** *Swe.*	castillo	château	castelo
slough (swamp)	verlandende Wasserfläche	**slough** *Eng.*	pantano	fondrière	pântano, brejo
ridge	Höhenrücken	**snía., serranía** *Sp.*	serranía	crête	serrania
snowfield	Schneefeld	**snowfield** *Eng.*	ventisquero	champ de neige	campo de neve
lake	See	**-sø** *Dan.*	lago	lac	lago
sound	Sund	**sonda** *Sp.*	sonda	détroit	estreito
sound	Sund	**sound** *Eng.*	sonda	détroit	estreito
cave, tunnel	Höhle, Tunnel	**souterrain** *Fr.*	cueva, túnel	souterrain	caverna, túnel
state park	Naturpark	**s.p., state park** *Eng.*	parque provincial	parc régional	parque estadual
cave	Höhle	**špilja** *S./C.*	cueva	caverne	caverna
spit	Landzunge	**spit** *Eng.*	lengua de tierra	flèche	ponta de terra
peak	Spitze	**Spitze** *Ger.*	pico	cime	pico
spring	Quelle	**spr., spring** *Eng.*	manantial	source	fonte, manancial
square	Platz	**sq., square** *Eng.*	plaza	place	praça
range, ridge	Gebirge, Höhenrücken	**srra., sierra** *Sp.*	sierra	chaîne, crête	serra
saint	Sankt	**st., saint** *Eng., Fr.*	san, santa, santo	saint	são, santa, santo
street	Strasse	**st., street** *Eng.*	calle	rue	rua
saint	Sankt	**sta., santa** *Port., Sp.*	santa	sainte	santa
station	Bahnhof, Stützpunkt	**sta., station** *Eng., Fr.*	estación	station	estação
stadium	Stadion	**stad., stadium** *Eng.*	estadio	stade	estádio
stadium	Stadion	**stadio** *It.*	estadio	stade	estádio
stadium	Stadion	**Stadion** *Ger.*	estadio	stade	estádio
stadium	Stadion	**stadion** *Rus.*	estadio	stade	estádio
stadium	Stadion	**stadium** *Eng.*	estadio	stade	estádio
state beach	öffentlicher Badestrand	**state beach** *Eng.*	playa provincial	plage régionale	praia estadual
state forest	Wald in Gemeinbesitz	**state forest** *Eng.*	bosque provincial	forêt régionale	floresta estadual
state historical park	Park an historischer Stätte	**state historical park** *Eng.*	parque histórico provincial	parc historique régional	parque histórico estadual
state park	Naturpark	**state park** *Eng.*	parque provincial	parc régional	parque estadual
state recreation area	Ausflugsgebiet	**state recreation area** *Eng.*	zona de recreo provincial	zone récréative regionale	área de lazer estadual
station	Bahnhof, Stützpunkt	**station** *Eng., Fr.*	estación	station	estação
reservoir	Stausee	**Stausee** *Ger.*	embalse	réservoir	reservatório
station	Bahnhof, Stützpunkt	**stazione** *It.*	estación	station	estação
saint	Sankt	**ste., sainte** *Fr.*	santa	sainte	santa
mountains	Berge	**stěny** *Czech*	montañas	montagnes	montanhas
steppe	Steppe	**step'** *Rus.*	estepa	steppe	estepe
peak	Gipfel	**štít** *Slo.*	pico	cime	pico
saint	Sankt	**sto., santo** *Port., Sp.*	santo	saint	santo
strait(s)	Meeresstrasse	**strait(s)** *Eng.*	estrecho	détroit	estreito
stream	Strom	**stream** *Eng.*	corriente de agua	cours d'eau	curso d'água
street	Strasse	**street** *Eng.*	calle	rue	rua
strait	Meeresstrasse	**stretto** *It.*	estrecho	détroit	estreito
spit	Landzunge	**strilka** *Ukr.*	lengua de tierra	flèche	ponta de terra
stream	Strom	**Strom** *Ger.*	corriente de agua	cours d'eau	curso d'água
stream	Strom	**-ström, -strömmen** *Swe.*	corriente de agua	cours d'eau	curso d'água
river	Fluss	**-su** *Kor.*	río	rivière	rio
channel	Kanal	**-suidō** *Jpn.*	canal, estrecho	canal, détroit	canal, estreito
sound	Sund	**Sund** *Ger.*	sonda	détroit	estreito
sound	Sund	**-sund** *Swe.*	sonda	détroit	estreito
swamp	Sumpf	**swamp** *Eng.*	pantano	marais	pântano
ridge	Höhenrücken	**syrt** *Tur.*	sierra	crête	serra
island	Insel	**sziget** *Hung.*	isla	île	ilha

T

ENGLISH	DEUTSCH	Map Form	ESPAÑOL	FRANCAIS	PORTUGUÊS
tableland	Tafelland	**tableland** *Eng.*	mesa, altiplano	plateau	planalto
woods	Gehölz	**taillis** *Fr.*	bosque	taillis	bosque
reef	Riff	**taka** *Indon.*	arrecife	récif	recife
mountain	Berg	**-take** *Jpn.*	montaña	montagne	montanha
waterfall	Wasserfall	**-taki** *Jpn.*	cascada	chute d'eau	queda d'água
valley	Tal	**Tal** *Ger.*	valle	vallée	vale
mountain	Berg	**tall** *Ara.*	montaña	montagne	montanha
mountain, hill	Berg, Hügel	**tallat** *Ara.*	montaña, colina	montagne, colline	montanha, colina
hills	Hügel	**tallāt** *Ara.*	colinas	collines	colinas
dam	Talsperre	**Talsperre** *Ger.*	presa	barrage	represa
point	Landspitze	**-tangar, -tangi** *Ice.*	punta	pointe	ponta
cape	Kap	**tanjong** *Mal.*	cabo	cap	cabo
cape	Kap	**tanjung** *Indon.*	cabo	cap	cabo
island	Insel	**tao** *Ch.*	isla	île	ilha
hills	Hügel	**taraq** *Ara.*	colinas	collines	colinas
lake	See	**tasek** *Mal.*	lago	lac	lago
lake	See	**tasik** *Indon.*	lago	lac	lago
plateau	Hochebene	**tassili** *Ber.*	meseta	plateau	planalto
mountain	Berg	**taung** *Bur.*	montaña	montagne	montanha
range	Gebirge	**taungdan** *Bur.*	sierra	chaîne	cordilheira
theatre	Theater	**teatro** *It., Sp.*	teatro	théâtre	teatro
bay	Bucht	**teluk** *Indon.*	bahía	baie	baía
temple	Tempel	**temple** *Eng., Fr.*	templo	temple	templo
church	Kirche	**templom** *Hung.*	iglesia	église	igreja
desert	Wüste	**ténéré** *Ber.*	desierto	désert	deserto
peak, hill	Gipfel, Hügel	**tepe, tepesi** *Tur.*	pico, colina	cime, colline	pico, colina
territory	Territorium	**territory** *Eng.*	territorio	territoire	território
lagoon	Lagune, Haff	**thale** *Thai*	laguna	lagune	laguna
mountains	Berge	**thiu khao** *Thai*	montañas	montagnes	montanhas
mountain	Berg	**-tind,-tinderne** *Nor.*	montaña	montagne	montanha
ridge	Höhenrücken	**tiwāl** *Ara.*	sierra	crête	serra
mountain	Berg	**-tjåkko, tjåure** *Lapp.*	montaña	montagne	montanha
island	Insel	**-to** *Kor.*	isla	île	ilha
island	Insel	**-tō** *Jpn.*	isla	île	ilha
lake	See	**tó** *Hung.*	lago	lac	lago
pass	Pass	**-tōge** *Jpn.*	paso	col	passo
island	Insel	**tokong** *Mal.*	isla	île	ilha
lake	See	**tônlé** *Cbd.*	lago	lac	lago
mountain torrent	Wildbach	**torrente** *It., Sp.*	torrente	torrent	torrente
tower	Turm	**tower** *Eng.*	torre	tour	torre
turnpike	gebührenpflichtige Autobahn	**tpk., turnpike** *Eng.*	camino con peaje	grande route à péage	rodovia com pedágio
lake	See	**-träsk** *Swe.*	lago	lac	lago
trench	Tiefseegraben	**trench** *Eng.*	trinchera	tranchée	fossa submarina
trough	Tiefseegraben	**trough** *Eng.*	trinchera	tranchée	fossa submarina
volcano	Vulkan	**tulūl** *Ara.*	volcán	volcan	vulcão
tunnel	Tunnel	**túnel** *Sp.*	túnel	tunnel	túnel
tunnel	Tunnel	**tunnel** *Eng., Fr.*	túnel	tunnel	túnel
hill, mountain	Hügel, Berg	**-tunturi** *Finn.*	colina, montaña	colline, montagne	colina, montanha
island	Insel	**tuo** *Ch.*	isla	île	ilha
canal	Kanal	**tur'at** *Ara.*	canal	canal	canal
turnpike	gebührenpflichtige Autobahn	**turnpike** *Eng.*	camino con peaje	grande route à péage	rodovia com pedágio

U-V

ENGLISH	DEUTSCH	Map Form	ESPAÑOL	FRANCAIS	PORTUGUÊS
cape	Kap	**ujung** *Indon.*	cabo	cap	cabo
lagoon	Lagune, Haff	**-umi** *Jpn.*	laguna	lagune	laguna
United Nations	Vereinte Nationen	**U.N., United Nations** *Eng.*	Naciones Unidas	Nations Unies	Nações Unidas
canal	Kanal	**-unga** *Jpn.*	canal	canal	canal
university	Universität	**univ., universidad** *Sp.* **universidade università university**	universidad	université	universidade
university	Universität	**Universität** *Ger.*	universidad	université	universidade
university	Universität	**université** *Fr.*	universidad	université	universidade
university	Universität	**universitet** *Rus.*	universidad	université	universidade
upland	Bergland	**upland** *Eng.*	tierras altas	hautes terres	terras altas
lake	See	**-ura** *Jpn.*	lago	lac	lago
mountain(s)	Berg(e)	**uul** *Mong.*	montaña(s)	montagne(s)	montanha(s)
elevation(s)	Höhe(n)	**uval(y)** *Rus.*	altura(s)	élévation(s)	elevação(ões)
spring	Quelle	**'uyūn** *Ara.*	manantial	source	fonte, manancial
hill	Hügel	**-vaara** *Finn.*	colina	colline	colina
strait	Meeresstrasse	**väin** *Est.*	estrecho	détroit	estreito
valley	Tal	**val** *Fr., It.*	valle	val	vale
valley	Tal	**valle** *It., Sp.*	valle	vallée	vale
valley	Tal	**vallée** *Fr.*	valle	vallée	vale
waterfall	Wasserfall	**vallen** *Du.*	cascada	chute d'eau	queda d'água
valley	Tal	**valley** *Eng.*	valle	vallée	vale
valley	Tal	**vallon** *Fr.*	valle	vallon	vale
mountain	Berg	**vârful** *Rom.*	montaña	montagne	montanha
lake	See	**-vatn** *Ice., Nor.*	lago	lac	lago
lake	See	**-vatnet** *Nor.*	lago	lac	lago
lake	See	**-vattnet** *Swe.*	lago	lac	lago
reservoir	Stausee	**vdchr., vodochranilišče** *Rus.*	embalse	réservoir	reservatório
hills	Hügel	**-veden** *Swe.*	colinas	collines	colinas
upland	Bergland	**verch** *Rus.*	tierras altas	hautes terres	terras altas
lake	See	**-vesi** *Finn.*	lago	lac	lago
viaduct	Viadukt	**viaducto** *Sp.*	viaducto	viaduc	viaduto
plateau	Hochebene	**-vidda** *Nor.*	meseta	plateau	planalto
gulf	Golf	**-viken** *Swe.*	golfo	golfe	golfo
bay	Bucht	**vinh** *Viet.*	bahía	baie	baía
airport	Flughafen	**vliegveld** *Du.*	aeropuerto	aéroport	aeroporto
channel	Kanal	**vliet** *Du.*	canal, estrecho	canal, détroit	canal, estreito
canal	Kanal	**vodnyj put'** *Rus.*	canal	canal	canal
reservoir	Stausee	**vodochranilišče** *Rus.*	embalse	réservoir	reservatório
reservoir	Stausee	**vodoskhovyshche** *Ukr.*	embalse	réservoir	reservatório
railroad station	Bahnhof	**vokzal** *Rus.*	estación de ferrocarril	gare	estação ferroviária
volcano	Vulkan	**vol., volcán** *Sp.* **volcano**	volcán	volcan	vulcão
pass	Pass	**vorota** *Rus.*	paso	col	passo
upland	Bergland	**vozvyšennost'** *Rus.*	tierras altas	hautes terres	terras altas
mountain	Berg	**vrâh** *Blg.*	montaña	montagne	montanha
mountains	Berge	**vrchovina** *Czech, Slo.*	montañas	montagnes	montanhas
mountains	Berge	**vrchy** *Slo.*	montañas	montagnes	montanhas
peak	Gipfel	**vrh** *S./C.*	pico	cime	pico
volcano	Vulkan	**vulkan** *Rus.*	volcán	volcan	vulcão
bay	Bucht	**vung** *Viet.*	bahía	baie	baía
mountain, hill	Berg, Hügel	**-vuori** *Finn.*	montaña, colina	montagne, colline	montanha, colina
upland	Bergland	**vysochyna** *Ukr.*	tierras altas	hautes terres	terras altas

W-Z

ENGLISH	DEUTSCH	Map Form	ESPAÑOL	FRANCAIS	PORTUGUÊS
west	West	**w., west** *Eng.*	oeste	ouest	oeste
marsh	Marsch	**wa** *Ch.*	pantano	marais	pântano
wadi	Wadi	**wādī** *Ara.*	uadi	wadi	uádi
oasis	Oase	**wāhat, wāhāt** *Ara.*	oasis	oasis	oásis
forest, mountains	Wald	**Wald** *Ger.*	bosque, montañas	forêt, montagnes	floresta, montanhas
bay	Bucht	**wan** *Ch., Jap.*	bahía	baie	baía
wash	Wadi	**wash** *Eng.*	uadi	wadi	uádi
waterfalls	Wasserfälle	**Wasserfälle** *Ger.*	cascadas	chutes d'eau	quedas d'água
water (lake, river)	Wasser (See, Fluss)	**water** *Eng.*	agua (lago, río)	eau (lac, rivière)	água (lago, rio)
waterway	Wasserstrasse	**waterway** *Eng.*	canal	canal	canal
pond	Weiher	**Weiher** *Ger.*	charca	étang	charco
well	Brunnen	**well** *Eng.*	pozo	puits	poço
bay	Wiek	**Wiek** *Ger.*	bahía	baie	baía
woods	Gehölz	**woods** *Eng.*	bosque	bois	bosque
water (lake, river)	Wasser (See, Fluss)	**wr., water** *Eng.*	agua (lago, río)	eau (lac, rivière)	água (lago, rio)
strait	Meeresstrasse	**xia** *Ch.*	estrecho	détroit	estreito
lake, sea	See, Meer	**yam** *Heb.*	lago, mar	lac, mer	lago, mar
mountain	Berg	**-yama** *Jpn.*	montaña	montagne	montanha
bay	Bucht	**yang** *Ch.*	bahía	baie	baía
peninsula	Halbinsel	**yarımadası** *Tur.*	península	péninsule	península
mountain	Berg	**yebel** *Ara.*	montaña	montagne	montanha
rock, island	Fels, Insel	**yen** *Ch.*	roca, isla	rocher, île	rochedo, ilha
mountains	Berge	**yoma** *Bur.*	montañas	montagnes	montanhas
island	Insel	**yu** *Ch.*	isla	île	ilha
lake	See	**yumco** *Tib.*	lago	lac	lago
canal	Kanal	**yunhe** *Ch.*	canal	canal	canal
intermittent lake	periodischer See	**zahrez** *Ara.*	lago intermitente	lac périodique	lago intermitente
point	Landspitze	**-zaki** *Jpn.*	punta	pointe	ponta
lagoon	Lagune, Haff	**zalew** *Pol.*	laguna	lagune	laguna
gulf, bay	Golf, Bucht	**zaliv** *Rus.*	golfo, bahía	golfe, baie	golfo, baía
reserve	Reservat	**zapov., zapovednik** *Rus.*	reserva	réserve	reserva
gulf, bay	Golf, Bucht	**zatoka** *Ukr.*	golfo, bahía	golfe, baie	golfo, baía
sea, lake	Meer, See	**zee** *Du.*	mar, lago	mer, lac	mar, lago
autonomous province	autonome Provinz	**zizhiqu** *Ch.*	provincia autónoma	province autonome	província autônoma
zoo	Zoo	**zoo** *Eng.*	parque zoológico	zoo	jardim zoológico

THIS TABLE gives the area, population, population density, capital, and political status for every country in the world. The political units listed are categorized by political status in the last column of the table, as follows: A—independent countries; B—internally independent political entities which are under the protection of another country in matters of defense and foreign affairs; C—colonies and other dependent political units; and D—the major administrative subdivisions of Australia, Canada, China, the United Kingdom, and the United States. For comparison, the table also includes the continents and the world. For units categorized B, the names of protecting countries are specified in the political-status column. For units categorized C, the names of administering countries are given in parentheses in the first column.

The populations are estimates for January 1, 1994, made by Rand McNally on the basis of official data, United Nations estimates, and other available information.

IN DIESER ÜBERSICHT sind Fläche, Bevölkerung, Bevölkerungsdichte, Hauptstadt und politischer Status für jedes Land der Erde aufgeführt. Die politischen Einheiten sind in der letzten Spalte der Tabelle nach ihrem politischen Status wie folgt gegliedert: A—souveräne Staaten; B—innenpolitisch unabhängige Länder unter der Protektion eines anderen Landes in Angelegenheiten der Aussenpolitik und Verteidigung; C—Kolonien oder anderweitig abhängige Gebiete; D—die wichtigsten Verwaltungseinheiten von Australien, Kanada, China, dem Vereinigten Königreich und den Vereinigten Staaten. Für Vergleiche enthält die Übersicht auch Angaben über die Kontinente und die Welt. Für die unter B eingestuften Einheiten ist der Name des Schutzstaates in der Spalte Politischer Status aufgeführt. Für die unter C eingestuften Gebiete steht der Name des die Verwaltung ausübenden Landes in Klammern in der ersten Spalte.

Die Bevölkerungsangaben sind Schätzungen zum 1. Januar 1994, die Rand McNally auf der Grundlage amtlicher Zahlen, Schätzungen der Vereinten Nationen und anderer zugänglicher Informationen berechnet hat.

EL CUADRO ABAJO incluye la extensión, población y densidad de población, la capital y el estado político de todos los países del mundo. Las entidades políticas nombradas están clasificadas de acuerdo a su estado político en la última columna de la tabla, de esta manera: A—países independientes; B—entidades políticas internamente independientes las cuales se encuentran bajo la protección de otro país en cuanto a asuntos de defensa nacional y relaciones con el extranjero; C—colonias y otras entidades políticas dependientes; y D—las mayores subdivisiones administrativas de Australia, Canadá, China, el Reino Unido, y los Estados Unidos. Para servir de medida comparativa, el cuadro también incluye los continentes y el mundo. Para las entidades de la clasificación B, los nombres de los países protectores están especificados en la columna de estado político. Para las unidades bajo la categoría C, los nombres de los países administradores se encuentran entre paréntesis en la primera columna.

Las poblaciones son los estimados de Rand McNally, tomados el 1o. de Enero de 1994, en base a datos oficiales, estimados de las Naciones Unidas y varias otras informaciones disponibles.

CETTE TABLE donne, pour chaque pays du monde, les renseignements suivants: superficie, population, densité de population, capitale, statut politique. Les entités politiques sont classées, selon leur statut, dans la dernière colonne du tableau: A—pays indépendants; B—entités politiques indépendants intérieurement, mais qui se trouvent sous la protection d'un autre pays pour leur défense et leurs relations extérieures; C—colonies et autres entités politiques dépendantes; D—principales subdivisions administratives de l'Australie, du Canada, de la Chine, du Royaume-Uni, des États-Unis. Pour permettre les comparaisons, la table comprend aussi les continents et le monde. Pour les entités politiques de la catégorie B, les noms des pays protecteurs sont spécifiés dans la colonne "statut politique". Pour celles de la catégorie C, les noms des pays administrateurs sont mis entre parenthèses dans la première colonne.

Les chiffres concernant la population sont des estimations au 1er janvier 1994, établies par Rand McNally, d'après les sources officielles, les estimations des Nations Unies et autres informations disponibles.

A TABELA que se segue apresenta a área, a população, a densidade demográfica, a capital e o estatuto político de todos os países do mundo. As unidades políticas relacionadas na tabela estão classificadas de acordo com o respectivo estatuto político na última coluna, do seguinte modo: A—países independentes; B—unidades políticas internamente independentes mas que se encontram sob a proteção de outro país no tocante a assuntos de defesa nacional e negócios extrenos; C—colônias e outras unidades políticas dependentes; e D—subdivisões administrativas principais da Austrália, Canadá, China, Reino Unido e Estados Unidos. Para fins de comparabilidade, a tabela também inclui os continentes e o mundo. No tocante ás unidades classificadas em B, os nomes dos países protetores estão especificados na coluna relativa ao estatuto político. Para as unidades da categoria C, os nomes dos países administradores figuram entre parênteses na primeira coluna.

Os dados relativos à população são estimativas de Rand McNally para 1 de janeiro de 1994, com base em dados oficiais, estimativas das Nações Unidas e outras informações disponíveis.

NAME / NAME / NOMBRE / NOM / NOME — English / Englisch / Inglés / Anglais / Inglês	Local / Einheimisch / Local / Local / Local	AREA / FLÄCHE / AREA / SUPERFICIE / ÁREA — sq. km.	sq. mi.	POPULATION / BEVÖLKERUNG / POBLACIÓN / POPULATION / POPULAÇÃO	DENSITY PER / BEVÖLKERUNGSDICHTE PRO / DENSIDAD POR / DENSITÉ / DENSIDADE POR — sq. km.	sq. mi.	CAPITAL / HAUPSTADT / CAPITAL / CAPITALE / CAPITAL	POLITICAL STATUS / POLITISCHER STATUS / ESTADO POLITICO / STATUS POLITIQUE / ESTATUTO POLITICO
†Afghanistan	Afghānestān	652,225	251,826	16,595,000	25	66	Kābol (Kabul)	A
Africa	. . .	30,300,000	11,700,000	683,700,000	23	58	. . .	. . .
Alabama, U.S.	Alabama	135,775	52,423	4,202,000	31	80	Montgomery	D
Alaska, U.S.	Alaska	1,700,139	656,424	597,000	0.4	0.9	Juneau	D
†Albania	Shqipëri	28,748	11,100	3,424,000	119	308	Tiranë	A
Alberta, Can.	Alberta	661,190	255,287	2,599,000	3.9	10	Edmonton	D
†Algeria	Algérie (French) / Djazaïr (Arabic)	2,381,741	919,595	26,780,000	11	29	El Djazaïr (Algiers)	A
American Samoa (U.S.)	American Samoa (English) / Amerika Samoa (Samoan)	199	77	53,000	266	688	Pago Pago	C
†Andorra	Andorra	453	175	58,000	128	331	Andorra	B(Sp., Fr.)
†Angola	Angola	1,246,700	481,354	11,040,000	8.9	23	Luanda	A
Anguilla	Anguilla	91	35	7,000	77	200	The Valley	B(U.K.)
Anhwei, China	Anhui	139,000	53,668	58,850,000	423	1,097	Hefei	D
Antarctica	. . .	14,000,000	5,400,000	(1)	. . .	. . .	. . .	. . .
†Antigua and Barbuda	Antigua and Barbuda	442	171	64,000	145	374	St. John's	A
†Argentina	Argentina	2,780,400	1,073,519	33,635,000	12	31	Buenos Aires and Viedma (3)	A
Arizona, U.S.	Arizona	295,276	114,006	3,943,000	13	35	Phoenix	D
Arkansas, U.S.	Arkansas	137,742	53,182	2,438,000	18	46	Little Rock	D
†Armenia	Hayastan	29,800	11,506	3,743,000	126	325	Jerevan	A
Aruba	Aruba	193	75	68,000	352	907	Oranjestad	B(Neth.)
Asia	. . .	44,900,000	17,300,000	3,385,900,000	75	196	. . .	. . .
†Australia	Australia	7,682,300	2,966,155	17,950,000	2.3	6.1	Canberra	A
Australian Capital Territory, Austl.	Australian Capital Territory	2,400	927	303,000	126	327	Canberra	D
†Austria	Österreich	83,856	32,377	7,913,000	94	244	Wien (Vienna)	A
†Azerbaijan	Azärbaycan	86,600	33,436	7,481,000	86	224	Bakı (Baku)	A
†Bahamas	Bahamas	13,939	5,382	270,000	19	50	Nassau	A
†Bahrain	Al-Bahrayn	691	267	572,000	828	2,142	Al-Manāmah	A
†Bangladesh	Bangladesh	143,998	55,598	115,240,000	800	2,073	Dhaka (Dacca)	A
†Barbados	Barbados	430	166	260,000	605	1,566	Bridgetown	A
†Belarus	Byelarus'	207,600	80,155	10,380,000	50	129	Minsk	A
†Belgium	Belgique (French) / België (Flemish)	30,518	11,783	10,050,000	329	853	Bruxelles (Brussels)	A
†Belize	Belize	22,963	8,866	205,000	8.9	23	Belmopan	A
†Benin	Bénin	112,600	43,475	5,292,000	47	122	Porto-Novo and Cotonou	A
Bermuda (U.K.)	Bermuda	54	21	76,000	1,407	3,619	Hamilton	C
†Bhutan	Druk-Yul	46,500	17,954	1,707,000	37	95	Thimphu	B(India)
†Bolivia	Bolivia	1,098,581	424,165	7,582,000	6.9	18	La Paz and Sucre	A
†Bosnia and Herzegovina	Bosna i Hercegovina	51,129	19,741	4,442,000	87	225	Sarajevo	A
†Botswana	Botswana	582,000	224,711	1,424,000	2.4	6.3	Gaborone	A
†Brazil	Brasil	8,511,996	3,286,500	151,310,000	18	46	Brasília	A
British Columbia, Can.	British Columbia (English) / Colombie-Britannique (French)	947,800	365,948	3,354,000	3.5	9.2	Victoria	D
British Indian Ocean Territory (U.K.)	British Indian Ocean Territory	60	23	(1)	. . .	. . .	. . .	C
British Virgin Islands (U.K.)	British Virgin Islands	153	59	13,000	85	220	Road Town	C
†Brunei	Brunei	5,765	2,226	279,000	48	125	Bandar Seri Begawan	A
†Bulgaria	Bălgarija	110,994	42,855	8,813,000	79	206	Sofija (Sofia)	A
†Burkina Faso	Burkina Faso	274,200	105,869	9,922,000	36	94	Ouagadougou	A
†Burundi	Burundi	27,830	10,745	6,015,000	216	560	Bujumbura	A
California, U.S.	California	424,002	163,707	31,905,000	75	195	Sacramento	D
†Cambodia	Kâmpŭchéa	181,035	69,898	10,010,000	55	143	Phnum Pénh (Phnom Penh)	A
†Cameroon	Cameroun (French) / Cameroon (English)	475,440	183,568	12,845,000	27	70	Yaoundé	A
†Canada	Canada	9,970,610	3,849,674	27,950,000	2.8	7.3	Ottawa	A
†Cape Verde	Cabo Verde	4,033	1,557	414,000	103	266	Praia	A
Cayman Islands (U.K.)	Cayman Islands	259	100	32,000	124	320	George Town	C
†Central African Republic	République centrafricaine	622,984	240,535	3,089,000	5.0	13	Bangui	A
†Chad	Tchad	1,284,000	495,755	6,149,000	4.8	12	N'Djamena	A
Chekiang, China	Zhejiang	101,800	39,305	43,455,000	427	1,106	Hangzhou	D
†Chile	Chile	756,626	292,135	13,795,000	18	47	Santiago	A
†China (excl. Taiwan)	Zhongguo	9,556,100	3,689,631	1,184,060,000	124	321	Beijing (Peking)	A
Christmas Island (Austl.)	Christmas Island	135	52	1,300	9.6	25	The Settlement	C
Cocos (Keeling) Islands (Austl.)	Cocos (Keeling) Islands	14	5.4	600	43	111	. . .	C
†Colombia	Colombia	1,141,748	440,831	35,085,000	31	80	Santa Fe de Bogotá	A
Colorado, U.S.	Colorado	269,620	104,100	3,528,000	13	34	Denver	D
†Comoros (excl. Mayotte)	Comores (French) / Al-Qumur (Arabic)	2,235	863	508,000	227	589	Moroni	A
†Congo	Congo	342,000	132,047	2,403,000	7.0	18	Brazzaville	A
Connecticut, U.S.	Connecticut	14,358	5,544	3,272,000	228	590	Hartford	D
Cook Islands	Cook Islands	236	91	19,000	81	209	Avarua	B(N.Z.)
†Costa Rica	Costa Rica	51,100	19,730	3,285,000	64	166	San José	A
†Cote d'Ivoire	Côte d'Ivoire	322,500	124,518	13,930,000	43	112	Abidjan and Yamoussoukro	A
†Croatia	Hrvatska	56,538	21,829	4,796,000	85	220	Zagreb	A
†Cuba	Cuba	110,861	42,804	11,015,000	99	257	La Habana (Havana)	A
†Cyprus (excl. North Cyprus)	Kípros (Greek) / Kıbrıs (Turkish)	5,896	2,276	574,000	97	252	Nicosia (Levkosía)	A
Cyprus, North	Kuzey Kıbrıs	3,355	1,295	193,000	58	149	Nicosia (Lefkoşa)	A
†Czech Republic	Česká Republika	78,864	30,450	10,400,000	132	342	Praha (Prague)	A
Delaware, U.S.	Delaware	6,447	2,489	700,000	109	281	Dover	D
†Denmark	Danmark	43,094	16,639	5,181,000	120	311	København (Copenhagen)	A

NAME / NAME / NOMBRE / NOM / NOME English / Englisch Inglés / Anglais / Inglês	Local / Einheimisch Local / Local / Local	AREA / FLÄCHE AREA / SUPERFICIE / ÁREA sq. km.	sq. mi.	POPULATION BEVÖLKERUNG POBLACIÓN POPULATION POPULAÇÃO	DENSITY PER BEVÖLKERUNGSDICHTE PRO / DENSIDAD POR DENSITÉ / DENSIDADE POR sq. km.	sq. mi.	CAPITAL HAUPTSTADT CAPITAL CAPITALE CAPITAL	POLITICAL STATUS POLITISCHER STATUS ESTADO POLÍTICO STATUS POLITIQUE ESTATUTO POLÍTICO
District of Columbia, U.S.	District of Columbia	177	68	576,000	3,254	8,471	Washington	D
†Djibouti	Djibouti	23,200	8,958	579,000	25	65	Djibouti	A
†Dominica	Dominica	790	305	87,000	110	285	Roseau	A
†Dominican Republic	República Dominicana	48,442	18,704	7,715,000	159	412	Santo Domingo	A
†Ecuador	Ecuador	272,045	105,037	10,515,000	39	100	Quito	A
†Egypt	Miṣr	1,001,449	386,662	56,820,000	57	147	Al-Qāhirah (Cairo)	A
†El Salvador	El Salvador	21,041	8,124	5,179,000	246	637	San Salvador	A
England, U.K.	England	130,410	50,352	48,320,000	371	960	London	D
†Equatorial Guinea	Guinea Ecuatorial	28,051	10,831	379,000	14	35	Malabo	A
†Eritrea	Ērtra	93,679	36,170	3,540,000	38	98	Asmera	A
†Estonia	Eesti	45,100	17,413	1,608,000	36	92	Tallinn	A
†Ethiopia	Ītyop'iya	1,157,603	446,953	54,170,000	47	121	Adis Abeba	A
Europe	. . .	9,900,000	3,800,000	709,300,000	72	187	. . .	. . .
Faeroe Islands	Føroyar	1,399	540	48,000	34	89	Tórshavn	B(Den.)
Falkland Islands (U.K.) (2)	Falkland Islands	12,173	4,700	2,200	0.2	0.5	Stanley	C
†Fiji	Fiji (French / Viti (Fijian)	18,274	7,056	759,000	42	108	Suva	A
†Finland	Suomi (Finnish) / Finland (Swedish)	338,145	130,559	5,056,000	15	39	Helsinki (Helsingfors)	A
Florida, U.S.	Florida	170,313	65,758	13,855,000	81	211	Tallahassee	D
†France (excl. Overseas Departments)	France	547,026	211,208	57,680,000	105	273	Paris	A
French Guiana (Fr.)	Guyane française	91,000	35,135	134,000	1.5	3.8	Cayenne	C
French Polynesia (Fr.)	Polynésie française	3,521	1,359	211,000	60	155	Papeete	C
Fukien, China	Fujian	120,000	46,332	31,375,000	261	677	Fuzhou	D
†Gabon	Gabon	267,667	103,347	1,127,000	4.2	11	Libreville	A
†Gambia	Gambia	10,689	4,127	919,000	86	223	Banjul	A
Gaza Strip	. . .	378	146	745,000	1,971	5,103	. . .	. . .
Georgia, U.S.	Georgia	153,953	59,441	6,875,000	45	116	Atlanta	D
†Georgia	Sakartvelo	69,700	26,911	5,646,000	81	210	Tbilisi	A
†Germany	Deutschland	356,955	137,822	80,930,000	227	587	Berlin and Bonn	A
†Ghana	Ghana	238,533	92,098	16,595,000	70	180	Accra	A
Gibraltar (U.K.)	Gibraltar	6.0	2.3	32,000	5,333	13,913	Gibraltar	C
Golan Heights	. . .	1,176	454	29,000	25	64	. . .	. . .
†Greece	Ellás	131,957	50,949	10,500,000	80	206	Athínai (Athens)	A
Greenland	Kalaallit Nunaat (Inuit) / Grønland (Danish)	2,175,600	840,004	57,000		0.1	Godthåb (Nuuk)	B(Den.)
†Grenada	Grenada	344	133	91,000	265	684	St. George's	A
Guadeloupe (incl. Dependencies) (Fr.)	Guadeloupe	1,780	687	424,000	238	617	Basse-Terre	C
Guam (U.S.)	Guam	541	209	147,000	272	703	Agana	C
†Guatemala	Guatemala	108,889	42,042	10,510,000	97	250	Guatemala	A
Guernsey (incl. Dependencies)	Guernsey	78	30	63,000	808	2,100	St. Peter Port	B(U.K.)
†Guinea	Guinée	245,857	94,926	6,274,000	26	66	Conakry	A
†Guinea-Bissau	Guiné-Bissau	36,125	13,948	1,078,000	30	77	Bissau	A
†Guyana	Guyana	214,969	83,000	732,000	3.4	8.8	Georgetown	A
Hainan, China	Hainan	34,000	13,127	6,867,000	202	523	Haikou	D
†Haiti	Haïti	27,750	10,714	6,411,000	231	598	Port-au-Prince	A
Hawaii, U.S.	Hawaii	28,313	10,932	1,167,000	41	107	Honolulu	D
Heilungkiang, China	Heilongjiang	469,000	181,082	36,945,000	79	204	Harbin	D
Honan, China	Henan	167,000	64,479	89,520,000	536	1,388	Zhengzhou	D
†Honduras	Honduras	112,088	43,277	5,206,000	46	120	Tegucigalpa	A
Hong Kong (U.K.)	Hong Kong (English) / Xianggang (Chinese)	1,072	414	5,890,000	5,494	14,227	Hong Kong (Victoria)	C
Hopeh, China	Hebei	190,000	73,359	63,940,000	337	872	Shijiazhuang	D
Hunan, China	Hunan	210,000	81,081	63,580,000	303	784	Changsha	D
†Hungary	Magyarország	93,030	35,919	10,295,000	111	287	Budapest	A
Hupeh, China	Hubei	187,400	72,356	56,480,000	301	781	Wuhan	D
†Iceland	Ísland	103,000	39,769	262,000	2.5	6.6	Reykjavík	A
Idaho, U.S.	Idaho	216,456	83,574	1,089,000	5.0	13	Boise	D
Illinois, U.S.	Illinois	150,007	57,918	11,750,000	78	203	Springfield	D
†India (incl. part of Jammu and Kashmir)	India (English) / Bharat (Hindi)	3,203,975	1,237,062	906,770,000	283	733	New Delhi	A
Indiana, U.S.	Indiana	94,328	36,420	5,733,000	61	157	Indianapolis	D
†Indonesia	Indonesia	1,948,732	752,410	198,810,000	102	264	Jakarta	A
Inner Mongolia, China	Nei Monggol	1,183,000	456,759	22,495,000	19	49	Hohhot	D
Iowa, U.S.	Iowa	145,754	56,276	2,827,000	19	50	Des Moines	D
†Iran	Īrān	1,638,057	632,457	63,940,000	39	101	Tehrān	A
†Iraq	Al-'Irāq	438,317	169,235	19,335,000	44	114	Baghdād	A
†Ireland	Ireland (English) / Éire (Gaelic)	70,285	27,137	3,563,000	51	131	Dublin (Baile Átha Cliath)	A
Isle of Man	Isle of Man	572	221	72,000	126	326	Douglas	B(U.K.)
†Israel	Yisra'el (Hebrew) / Isrā'īl (Arabic)	20,770	8,019	4,950,000	238	617	Yerushalayim (Jerusalem)	A
†Italy	Italia	301,277	116,324	56,670,000	188	487	Roma (Rome)	A
†Jamaica	Jamaica	10,991	4,244	2,538,000	231	598	Kingston	A
†Japan	Nihon	377,801	145,870	124,840,000	330	856	Tōkyō	A
Jersey	Jersey	116	45	86,000	741	1,911	St. Helier	B(U.K.)
†Jordan	Al-Urdun	91,000	35,135	3,858,000	42	110	'Ammān	A
Kansas, U.S.	Kansas	213,110	82,282	2,568,000	12	31	Topeka	D
Kansu, China	Gansu	450,000	173,746	23,445,000	52	135	Lanzhou	D
†Kazakhstan	Kazakhstan	2,717,300	1,049,156	17,190,000	6.3	16	Alma-Ata (Almaty)	A
Kentucky, U.S.	Kentucky	104,665	40,411	3,813,000	36	94	Frankfort	D
†Kenya	Kenya	582,646	224,961	28,280,000	49	126	Nairobi	A
Kiangsi, China	Jiangxi	166,600	64,325	39,550,000	237	615	Nanchang	D
Kiangsu, China	Jiangsu	102,600	39,614	70,210,000	684	1,772	Nanjing (Nanking)	D
Kiribati	Kiribati	811	313	77,000	95	246	Bairiki	A
Kirin, China	Jilin	187,000	72,201	25,815,000	138	358	Changchun	D
†Korea, North	Chosŏn-minjujuŭi-inmīn-konghwaguk	120,538	46,540	22,735,000	189	489	P'yŏngyang	A
†Korea, South	Taehan-min'guk	99,016	38,230	44,250,000	447	1,157	Sŏul (Seoul)	A
†Kuwait	Al-Kuwayt	17,818	6,880	1,734,000	97	252	Al-Kuwayt (Kuwait)	A
Kwangsi Chuang, China	Guangxi Zhuangzu	236,300	91,236	44,285,000	187	485	Nanning	D
Kwangtung, China	Guangdong	178,000	68,726	65,830,000	370	958	Guangzhou (Canton)	D
Kweichow, China	Guizhou	170,000	65,637	33,985,000	200	518	Guiyang	D
†Kyrgyzstan	Kyrgyzstan	198,500	76,641	4,645,000	23	61	Biškek (Frunze)	A
†Laos	Lao	236,800	91,429	4,601,000	19	50	Viangchan (Vientiane)	A
†Latvia	Latvija	63,700	24,595	2,556,000	40	104	Rīga	A
†Lebanon	Lubnān	10,400	4,015	3,566,000	343	888	Bayrūt (Beirut)	A
†Lesotho	Lesotho	30,355	11,720	1,907,000	63	163	Maseru	A
Liaoning, China	Liaoning	145,700	56,255	41,325,000	284	735	Shenyang (Mukden)	D
†Liberia	Liberia	99,067	38,250	2,901,000	29	76	Monrovia	A
†Libya	Lībiyā	1,759,540	679,362	4,917,000	2.8	7.2	Tarābulus (Tripoli)	A
†Liechtenstein	Liechtenstein	160	62	30,000	188	484	Vaduz	A
†Lithuania	Lietuva	65,300	25,212	3,777,000	58	150	Vilnius	A
Louisiana, U.S.	Louisiana	134,275	51,843	4,332,000	32	84	Baton Rouge	D
†Luxembourg	Luxembourg (French) / Lezebuurg (Luxembourgish)	2,586	998	401,000	155	402	Luxembourg	A
Macau (Port.)	Macau	17	6.6	380,000	22,353	57,576	Macau	C
†Macedonia	Makedonija	25,713	9,928	2,198,000	85	221	Skopje	A
†Madagascar	Madagasikara (Malagasy) / Madagascar (French)	587,041	226,658	13,110,000	22	58	Antananarivo	A
Maine, U.S.	Maine	91,653	35,387	1,245,000	14	35	Augusta	D
†Malawi	Malaŵi	118,484	45,747	8,942,000	75	195	Lilongwe	A
†Malaysia	Malaysia	329,758	127,320	19,060,000	58	150	Kuala Lumpur	A
†Maldives	Maldives	298	115	246,000	826	2,139	Male'	A
†Mali	Mali	1,248,574	482,077	8,922,000	7.1	19	Bamako	A
†Malta	Malta	316	122	365,000	1,155	2,992	Valletta	A
Manitoba, Can.	Manitoba	649,950	250,947	1,118,000	1.7	4.5	Winnipeg	D
†Marshall Islands	Marshall Islands	181	70	52,000	287	743	Majuro (island)	A
Martinique (Fr.)	Martinique	1,100	425	377,000	343	887	Fort-de-France	C
Maryland, U.S.	Maryland	32,135	12,407	5,006,000	156	403	Annapolis	D
Massachusetts, U.S.	Massachusetts	27,337	10,555	6,106,000	223	578	Boston	D
†Mauritania	Mauritanie (French) / Mūrītāniyā (Arabic)	1,025,520	395,956	2,142,000	2.1	5.4	Nouakchott	A

NAME / NAME / NOMBRE / NOM / NOME English / Englisch Inglés / Anglais / Inglês	Local / Einheimisch Local / Local / Local	AREA / FLÄCHE AREA / SUPERFICIE / ÁREA sq. km.	sq. mi.	POPULATION BEVÖLKERUNG POBLACIÓN POPULATION POPULAÇÃO	DENSITY PER BEVÖLKERUNGSDICHTE PRO / DENSIDAD POR DENSITÉ / DENSIDADE POR sq. km.	sq. mi.	CAPITAL HAUPSTADT CAPITAL CAPITALE CAPITAL	POLITICAL STATUS POLITISCHER STATUS ESTADO POLITICO STATUS POLITIQUE ESTATUTO POLITICO
†Mauritius (incl. Dependencies)	Mauritius	2,040	788	1,110,000	544	1,409	Port Louis	A
Mayotte (Fr.) (4)	Mayotte	374	144	91,000	243	632	Dzaoudzi and Mamoudzou (3)	C
†Mexico	México	1,967,183	759,534	90,870,000	46	120	Ciudad de México (Mexico City)	A
Michigan, U.S.	Michigan	250,738	96,810	9,550,000	38	99	Lansing	D
†Micronesia, Federated States of	Federated States of Micronesia	702	271	119,000	170	439	Kolonia and Paliker (3)	A
Midway Islands (U.S.)	Midway Islands	5.2	2.0	500	96	250	. . .	C
Minnesota, U.S.	Minnesota	225,182	86,943	4,539,000	20	52	St. Paul	D
Mississippi, U.S.	Mississippi	125,443	48,434	2,646,000	21	55	Jackson	D
Missouri, U.S.	Missouri	180,546	69,709	5,266,000	29	76	Jefferson City	D
†Moldova	Moldova	33,700	13,012	4,425,000	131	340	Chişinău (Kishinev)	A
†Monaco	Monaco	1.9	0.7	31,000	16,316	44,286	Monaco	A
†Mongolia	Mongol Ard Uls	1,566,500	604,829	2,314,000	1.5	3.8	Ulaanbaatar (Ulan Bator)	A
Montana, U.S.	Montana	380,850	147,046	830,000	2.2	5.6	Helena	D
Montserrat (U.K.)	Montserrat	102	39	13,000	127	333	Plymouth	C
†Morocco (excl. Western Sahara)	Al-Magrib	446,550	172,414	28,095,000	63	163	Rabat	A
†Mozambique	Moçambique	799,380	308,642	16,585,000	21	54	Maputo	A
†Myanmar	Myanmar	676,577	261,228	43,630,000	64	167	Yangon (Rangoon)	A
†Namibia	Namibia	824,272	318,253	1,555,000	1.9	4.9	Windhoek	A
Nauru	Nauru (English) / Naoero (Nauruan)	21	8.1	10,000	476	1,235	Yaren District	A
Nebraska, U.S.	Nebraska	200,358	77,358	1,635,000	8.2	21	Lincoln	D
†Nepal	Nepāl	147,181	56,827	20,660,000	140	364	Kāṭhmāṇḍāũ	A
†Netherlands	Nederland	41,864	16,164	15,320,000	366	948	Amsterdam and 's-Gravenhage (The Hague)	A
Netherlands Antilles	Nederlandse Antillen	800	309	192,000	240	621	Willemstad	B(Neth.)
Nevada, U.S.	Nevada	286,368	110,567	1,375,000	4.8	12	Carson City	D
New Brunswick, Can.	New Brunswick (English) / Nouveau-Brunswick (French)	73,440	28,355	755,000	10	27	Fredericton	D
New Caledonia (Fr.)	Nouvelle-Calédonie	19,058	7,358	179,000	9.4	24	Nouméa	C
Newfoundland, Can.	Newfoundland (English) / Terre-Neuve (French)	405,720	156,649	587,000	1.4	3.7	St. John's	D
New Hampshire, U.S.	New Hampshire	24,219	9,351	1,167,000	48	125	Concord	D
New Jersey, U.S.	New Jersey	22,590	8,722	7,915,000	350	907	Trenton	D
New Mexico, U.S.	New Mexico	314,939	121,598	1,608,000	5.1	13	Santa Fe	D
New South Wales, Austl.	New South Wales	801,600	309,500	6,117,000	7.6	20	Sydney	D
New York, U.S.	New York	141,089	54,475	18,375,000	130	337	Albany	D
†New Zealand	New Zealand	270,534	104,454	3,486,000	13	33	Wellington	A
†Nicaragua	Nicaragua	129,640	50,054	4,267,000	33	85	Managua	A
†Niger	Niger	1,267,000	489,191	8,754,000	6.9	18	Niamey	A
†Nigeria	Nigeria	923,768	356,669	94,550,000	102	265	Lagos and Abuja	A
Ningsia Hui, China	Ningxia Huizu	66,400	25,637	4,855,000	73	189	Yinchuan	D
Niue	Niue	259	100	1,900	7.3	19	Alofi	B(N.Z.)
Norfolk Island (Austl.)	Norfolk Island	36	14	2,700	75	193	Kingston	C
North America	. . .	24,700,000	9,500,000	444,600,000	18	47	. . .	. . .
North Carolina, U.S.	North Carolina	139,397	53,821	6,955,000	50	129	Raleigh	D
North Dakota, U.S.	North Dakota	183,123	70,704	632,000	3.5	8.9	Bismarck	D
Northern Ireland, U.K.	Northern Ireland	14,144	5,461	1,605,000	113	294	Belfast	D
Northern Mariana Islands	Northern Mariana Islands	477	184	49,000	103	266	Saipan (island)	B(U.S.)
Northern Territory, Austl.	Northern Territory	1,346,200	519,771	172,000	0.1	0.3	Darwin	D
Northwest Territories, Can.	Northwest Territories (English) / Territoires du Nord-Ouest (French)	3,426,320	1,322,910	56,000	. . .	. . .	Yellowknife	D
†Norway (incl. Svalbard and Jan Mayen)	Norge	386,975	149,412	4,301,000	11	29	Oslo	A
Nova Scotia, Can.	Nova Scotia (English) / Nouvelle-Écosse (French)	55,490	21,425	922,000	17	43	Halifax	D
Oceania (incl. Australia)	. . .	8,500,000	3,300,000	28,000,000	3.3	8.5	. . .	. . .
Ohio, U.S.	Ohio	116,103	44,828	11,155,000	96	249	Columbus	D
Oklahoma, U.S.	Oklahoma	181,049	69,903	3,242,000	18	46	Oklahoma City	D
†Oman	'Umān	212,457	82,030	1,659,000	7.8	20	Masqaṭ (Muscat)	A
Ontario, Can.	Ontario	1,068,580	412,581	10,315,000	9.7	25	Toronto	D
Oregon, U.S.	Oregon	254,819	98,386	3,009,000	12	31	Salem	D
†Pakistan (incl. part of Jammu and Kashmir)	Pākistān	879,902	339,732	126,090,000	143	371	Islāmābād	A
Palau	Palau (English) / Belau (Palauan)	508	196	16,000	31	82	Koror and Melekeok (3)	B(U.S.)
†Panama	Panamá	75,517	29,157	2,592,000	34	89	Panamá	A
†Papua New Guinea	Papua New Guinea	462,840	178,704	3,989,000	8.6	22	Port Moresby	A
†Paraguay	Paraguay	406,752	157,048	4,297,000	11	27	Asunción	A
Peking, China	Beijing	16,800	6,487	11,365,000	676	1,752	Beijing (Peking)	D
Pennsylvania, U.S.	Pennsylvania	119,291	46,058	12,145,000	102	264	Harrisburg	D
†Peru	Perú	1,285,216	496,225	23,305,000	18	47	Lima	A
†Philippines	Philippines (English) / Pilipinas (Tagalog)	300,000	115,831	66,190,000	221	571	Manila	A
Pitcairn (incl. Dependencies) (U.K.)	Pitcairn	49	19	100	2.0	5.3	Adamstown	C
†Poland	Polska	313,895	121,196	38,540,000	123	318	Warszawa (Warsaw)	A
†Portugal	Portugal	91,985	35,516	9,961,000	108	280	Lisboa (Lisbon)	A
Prince Edward Island, Can.	Prince Edward Island (English) / Île-du Prince-Édouard (French)	5,660	2,185	140,000	25	64	Charlottetown	D
Puerto Rico	Puerto Rico	9,104	3,515	3,801,000	418	1,081	San Juan	B(U.S.)
†Qatar	Qaṭar	11,427	4,412	502,000	44	114	Ad-Dawḥah (Doha)	A
Quebec, Can.	Québec	1,540,680	594,860	7,070,000	4.6	12	Québec	D
Queensland, Austl.	Queensland	1,727,200	666,876	3,111,000	1.8	4.7	Brisbane	D
Reunion (Fr.)	Réunion	2,510	969	643,000	256	664	Saint-Denis	C
Rhode Island, U.S.	Rhode Island	4,002	1,545	1,012,000	253	655	Providence	D
†Romania	România	237,500	91,699	22,770,000	96	248	Bucureşti (Bucharest)	A
†Russia	Rossija	17,075,400	6,592,849	150,500,000	8.8	23	Moskva (Moscow)	A
†Rwanda	Rwanda	26,338	10,169	8,196,000	311	806	Kigali	A
St. Helena (incl. Dependencies) (U.K.)	St. Helena	314	121	7,000	22	58	Jamestown	C
†St. Kitts and Nevis	St. Kitts and Nevis	269	104	45,000	167	433	Basseterre	A
†St. Lucia	St. Lucia	616	238	151,000	245	634	Castries	A
St. Pierre and Miquelon (Fr.)	Saint-Pierre-et-Miquelon	242	93	7,000	29	75	Saint-Pierre	C
†St. Vincent and the Grenadines	St. Vincent and the Grenadines	388	150	115,000	296	767	Kingstown	A
†San Marino	San Marino	61	24	24,000	393	1,000	San Marino	A
†Sao Tome and Principe	São Tomé e Príncipe	964	372	125,000	130	336	São Tomé	A
Saskatchewan, Can.	Saskatchewan	652,330	251,866	1,006,000	1.5	4.0	Regina	D
†Saudi Arabia	Al-'Arabīyah as-Su'ūdīyah	2,149,690	830,000	16,585,000	7.7	20	Ar-Riyāḍ (Riyadh)	A
Scotland, U.K.	Scotland	78,789	30,421	5,130,000	65	169	Edinburgh	D
†Senegal	Sénégal	196,712	75,951	8,522,000	43	112	Dakar	A
†Seychelles	Seychelles	453	175	72,000	159	411	Victoria	A
Shanghai, China	Shanghai	6,200	2,394	13,970,000	2,253	5,835	Shanghai	D
Shansi, China	Shanxi	156,000	60,232	30,075,000	193	499	Taiyuan	D
Shantung, China	Shandong	153,000	59,074	88,450,000	578	1,497	Jinan	D
Shensi, China	Shaanxi	205,000	79,151	34,455,000	168	435	Xi'an (Sian)	D
†Sierra Leone	Sierra Leone	72,325	27,925	4,538,000	63	163	Freetown	A
†Singapore	Singapore	636	246	2,834,000	4,456	11,520	Singapore	A
Sinkiang Uighur, China	Xinjiang Uygur	1,600,000	617,764	15,865,000	9.9	26	Ürümqi	D
†Slovakia	Slovenská Republika	49,035	18,933	5,342,000	109	282	Bratislava	A
†Slovenia	Slovenija	20,253	7,820	1,986,000	98	254	Ljubljana	A
†Solomon Islands	Solomon Islands	28,370	10,954	376,000	13	34	Honiara	A
†Somalia	Somaliya	637,657	246,201	6,541,000	10	27	Muqdisho (Mogadishu)	A
†South Africa	South Africa (English) / Suid-Afrika (Afrikaans)	1,219,909	471,010	42,320,000	35	90	Pretoria, Cape Town, and Bloemfontein	A
South America	. . .	17,800,000	6,900,000	304,500,000	17	44	. . .	. . .
South Australia, Austl.	South Australia	984,000	379,925	1,495,000	1.5	3.9	Adelaide	D

NAME / NAME / NOMBRE / NOM / NOME English / Englisch Inglés / Anglais / Inglês	Local / Einheimisch Local / Local / Local	AREA / FLÄCHE AREA / SUPERFICIE / ÁREA sq. km.	sq. mi.	POPULATION BEVÖLKERUNG POBLACIÓN POPULATION POPULAÇÃO	DENSITY PER BEVÖLKERUNGSDICHTE PRO / DENSIDAD POR DENSITÉ / DENSIDADE POR sq. km.	sq. mi.	CAPITAL HAUPSTADT CAPITAL CAPITALE CAPITAL	POLITICAL STATUS POLITISCHER STATUS ESTADO POLITICO STATUS POLITIQUE ESTATUTO POLITICO
South Carolina, U.S.	South Carolina	82,898	32,007	3,657,000	44	114	Columbia	D
South Dakota, U.S.	South Dakota	199,745	77,121	726,000	3.6	9.4	Pierre	D
South Georgia and the South Sandwich Islands (U.K.)	South Georgia and the South Sandwich Islands	3,755	1,450	(1)	. . .	. . .	. . .	C
†Spain	España	504,750	194,885	38,640,000	77	198	Madrid	A
Spanish North Africa (Sp.) (5)	Plazas de Soberanía en el Norte de África	32	12	142,000	4,438	11,833	. . .	C
†Sri Lanka	Sri Lanka	64,652	24,962	17,970,000	278	720	Colombo and Sri Jayawardenapura	A
†Sudan	As-Sūdān	2,505,813	967,500	28,900,000	12	30	Al-Kharṭūm (Khartoum)	A
†Suriname	Suriname	163,820	63,251	418,000	2.6	6.6	Paramaribo	A
†Swaziland	Swaziland	17,364	6,704	854,000	49	127	Mbabane and Lobamba	A
†Sweden	Sverige	449,964	173,732	8,747,000	19	50	Stockholm	A
Switzerland	Schweiz (German) / Suisse (French) / Svizzera (Italian)	41,293	15,943	7,001,000	170	439	Bern (Berne)	A
†Syria	Sūrīyah	185,180	71,498	13,695,000	74	192	Dimashq (Damascus)	A
Szechwan, China	Sichuan	570,000	220,078	112,250,000	197	510	Chengdu	D
Taiwan	T'aiwan	36,002	13,900	20,945,000	582	1,507	T'aipei	A
†Tajikistan	Tajikistan	143,100	55,251	5,720,000	40	104	Dušanbe	A
†Tanzania	Tanzania	945,087	364,900	27,450,000	29	75	Dar es Salaam and Dodoma	A
Tasmania, Austl.	Tasmania	67,800	26,178	483,000	7.1	18	Hobart	D
Tennessee, U.S.	Tennessee	109,158	42,146	5,058,000	46	120	Nashville	D
Texas, U.S.	Texas	695,676	268,601	17,925,000	26	67	Austin	D
†Thailand	Prathet Thai	513,115	198,115	58,960,000	115	298	Krung Thep (Bangkok)	A
Tibet, China	Xizang	1,220,000	471,045	2,250,000	1.8	4.8	Lhasa	D
Tientsin, China	Tianjin	11,300	4,363	9,235,000	817	2,117	Tianjin (Tientsin)	D
†Togo	Togo	56,785	21,925	4,142,000	73	189	Lomé	A
Tokelau (N.Z.)	Tokelau	12	4.6	1,500	125	326	. . .	C
Tonga	Tonga	747	288	104,000	139	361	Nuku'alofa	A
†Trinidad and Tobago	Trinidad and Tobago	5,128	1,980	1,288,000	251	651	Port of Spain	A
Tsinghai, China	Qinghai	720,000	277,994	4,618,000	6.4	17	Xining	D
†Tunisia	Tunisie (French) / Tunis (Arabic)	163,610	63,170	8,605,000	53	136	Tunis	A
†Turkey	Türkiye	779,452	300,948	61,540,000	79	204	Ankara	A
†Turkmenistan	Turkmenistan	488,100	188,456	3,935,000	8.1	21	Aščhabad (Ashgabat)	A
Turks and Caicos Islands (U.K.)	Turks and Caicos Islands	500	193	13,000	26	67	Grand Turk	C
Tuvalu	Tuvalu	26	10	10,000	385	1,000	Funafuti	A
†Uganda	Uganda	241,139	93,104	18,425,000	76	198	Kampala	A
†Ukraine	Ukrayina	603,700	233,090	52,240,000	87	224	Kyyiv (Kiev)	A
†United Arab Emirates	Al-Imārāt al-'Arabīyah al-Muttaḥidah	83,600	32,278	2,692,000	32	83	Abū Ẓaby (Abu Dhabi)	A
†United Kingdom	United Kingdom	244,101	94,249	57,960,000	237	615	London	A
†United States	United States	9,809,431	3,787,425	259,390,000	26	68	Washington	A
†Uruguay	Uruguay	177,414	68,500	3,181,000	18	46	Montevideo	A
Utah, U.S.	Utah	219,902	84,904	1,842,000	8.4	22	Salt Lake City	D
†Uzbekistan	Üzbekiston	447,400	172,742	22,240,000	50	129	Taškent (Toshkent)	A
†Vanuatu	Vanuatu	12,190	4,707	160,000	13	34	Port Vila	A
Vatican City	Città del Vaticano	0.4	0.2	900	2,250	4,500	Città del Vaticano (Vatican City)	A
†Venezuela	Venezuela	912,050	352,145	20,460,000	22	58	Caracas	A
Vermont, U.S.	Vermont	24,903	9,615	585,000	23	61	Montpelier	D
Victoria, Austl.	Victoria	227,600	87,877	4,566,000	20	52	Melbourne	D
†Vietnam	Viet Nam	330,036	127,428	72,080,000	218	566	Ha Noi	A
Virginia, U.S.	Virginia	110,771	42,769	6,485,000	59	152	Richmond	D
Virgin Islands (U.S.)	Virgin Islands	344	133	97,000	282	729	Charlotte Amalie	C
Wake Island (U.S.)	Wake Island	7.8	3.0	300	38	100	. . .	C
Wales, U.K.	Wales	20,758	8,015	2,905,000	140	362	Cardiff	D
Wallis and Futuna (Fr.)	Wallis et Futuna	255	98	14,000	55	143	Mata-Utu	C
Washington, U.S.	Washington	184,674	71,303	5,188,000	28	73	Olympia	D
West Bank (Incl. Jericho)	. . .	6,078	2,347	1,190,000	240	622	. . .	. . .
Western Australia, Austl.	Western Australia	2,525,500	975,101	1,703,000	0.7	1.7	Perth	D
Western Sahara	. . .	266,000	102,703	208,000	0.8	2.0	El Aaiún (Laayone)	. . .
†Western Samoa	Western Samoa (English) / Samoa i Sisifo (Samoan)	2,831	1,093	168,000	59	154	Apia	A
West Virginia, U.S.	West Virginia	62,759	24,231	1,816,000	29	75	Charleston	D
Wisconsin, U.S.	Wisconsin	169,653	65,503	5,058,000	30	77	Madison	D
Wyoming, U.S.	Wyoming	253,349	97,818	467,000	1.8	4.8	Cheyenne	D
†Yemen	Al-Yaman	527,968	203,850	10,840,000	21	53	San'ā'	A
Yugoslavia	Jugoslavija	102,173	39,449	10,730,000	105	272	Beograd (Belgrade)	A
Yukon Territory, Can.	Yukon Territory	483,450	186,661	28,000	0.1	0.2	Whitehorse	D
Yunnan, China	Yunnan	394,000	152,124	38,720,000	98	255	Kunming	D
†Zaire	Zaïre	2,345,095	905,446	41,675,000	18	46	Kinshasa	A
†Zambia	Zambia	752,614	290,586	8,625,000	11	30	Lusaka	A
†Zimbabwe	Zimbabwe	390,759	150,873	10,605,000	27	70	Harare (Salisbury)	A
WORLD	. . .	150,100,000	57,900,000	5,556,000,000	37	96	. . .	. . .

† Member of the United Nations (1993).
. . . None, or not applicable.
(1) No permanent population.
(2) Claimed by Argentina.
(3) Future capital.
(4) Claimed by Comoros.
(5) Comprises Ceuta, Melilla, and several small islands.

† Mitglied der Vereinten Nationen (1993).
. . . Kein(e), oder nicht anwendbar.
(1) Bevölkerungszahl schwankend.
(2) Von Argentinien beansprucht.
(3) Zukünftige Hauptstadt.
(4) Von Komoren beansprucht.
(5) Umfasst Ceuta, Melilla und mehrere kleine Inseln.

† Miembro de las Naciones Unidas (1993).
. . . Ninguno, o no se aplica.
(1) Sin población permanente.
(2) Reclamado por la Argentina.
(3) Capital futura.
(4) Reclamado por las Comores.
(5) Comprende Ceuta, Melilla y various islas pequeñas.

† Membre des Nations Unies (1993).
. . . Pas d'information, ou pas applicable.
(1) Pas de population permanente.
(2) Revendiqué par l'Argentine.
(3) Capitale future.
(4) Revendiqué par les Comores.
(5) Inclus Ceuta, Melilla et plusieurs petites îles.

† Membro das Nações Unidas (1993).
. . . Inexistente ou não aplicável.
(1) Sem população permanente.
(2) Reivindicado pela Argentina.
(3) Capital futuro.
(4) Reivindicado pelas Comores.
(5) Compreende Ceuta, Melilla e várias ilhas pequenas.

THIS TABLE lists the major metropolitan areas of the world according to their estimated population on January 1, 1994. For convenience in reference, the areas are grouped by major region with the total for each region given. The number of areas by population classification is given in parentheses with each size group.

For ease of comparison, each metropolitan area has been defined by Rand McNally according to consistent rules. A metropolitan area includes a central city, neighboring communities linked to it by continuous built-up areas, and more distant communities if the bulk of their population is supported by commuters to the central city. Some metropolitan areas have more than one central city; in such cases each central city is listed.

IN DIESER TABELLE sind die Hauptmetropolen der Welt verzeichnet, gemessen nach ihrer Bevölkerung, die nach dem Stand vom 1. Januar 1994 geschätzt wurde. Zur besseren Übersicht sind die Zonen nach grösseren Regionen gruppiert, wobei die Gesamtzahl für jede Region angegeben ist. Die Anzahl der Zonen ist nach Bevölkerung klassifiziert und in Klammern hinter denen nach Grössen sortierten Gruppen angegeben.

Zum einfacheren Vergleich ist jede Metropole von Rand McNally nach übereinstimmenden Massstäben definiert worden. Eine Metropole schliesst eine zentrale Stadt mit benachbarten Gemeinden, die mit ihr durch ununterbrochen bebaute Gebiete verbunden sind ein, sowie weiter entfernte Gemeinden, wenn der grösste Teil ihrer Bevölkerung von den Pendlern unterhalten wird. Einige Metropolen haben mehr als eine zentrale Stadt; in solchen Fällen ist jede dieser zentralen Städte angeführt.

ESTA TABLA indica las principales áreas metropolitanas del mundo, de acuerdo con su población calculada al 1 de enero de 1994. Para facilitar las referencias, las áreas se han agrupado por regiones principales, indicándose el total para cada región. El número de áreas, clasificadas por población, se indica entre paréntesis en los grupos de cada tamaño.

Para facilitar las comparaciones, Rand McNally ha definido cada área metropolitana de acuerdo con reglas consistentes. Un área metropolitana incluye una ciudad central, localidades vecinas vinculadas con ella mediante sectores construídos y contínuos, y localidades más distantes, si el grueso de su población lo constituye un núcleo que diariamente viaja a la ciudad central. Algunas áreas metropolitanas incluyen más de una ciudad central; en tales casos se indica cada una dichas ciudades.

CETTE TABLE contient la liste des aires métropolitaines les plus considérables dans le monde pour ce qui est du peuplement a la date du 1 er janvier 1994. Afin de faciliter la consultation, on a groupé les aires par grandes régions en indiquant la population totale pour chaque région, et, entre parenthéses, le nombre d'aires comprises dans celle-ci.

Afin de rendre plus faciles les comparaisons, Rand McNally a défini chaque aire métropolitaine selorègles cohérentes: une aire métropolitaine englobe une citè centrale ou métropole et l'environnement urbain continu qui s'y rattache; elle inclut également des agglomérations éloignées de la métropole lorsque la population de ces dernières est pour sa májorité constituée d'habitants se rendant quotidiennement dans la cité ou est situé le lieu de travail de ceux-ci. On trouvera quelques aires métropolitaines pourvues de plus d'une métropole. Dans ce cas, chaque métropole est mentionnée.

A TABELA que se segúe relaciona as principais áreas metropolitanas do mundo, de acordo com as respectivas populações, estimadas para 1 de janeiro de 1994. Para facilidade de referência, as áreas metropolitanas foram agrupadas dentro das regiões maiores, indicando-se, entre parênteses, os totais de cada região maior e o número de áreas metropolitanas, classificadas segundo a população, compreendidas em cada uma.

Para fins de comparabilidade, Rand McNally definiu cada área metropolitana de acordo com regras uniformes. Uma área metropolitana inclui uma cidade central, as localidades vizinhas ligadas a ela por áreas construídas contínuas, e as localidades mais distantes, desde que a maior parte de suas respectivas populações dependa economicamente da cidade central e que para ela viaje diariamente. Algumas áreas metropolitanas incluem mais de uma cidade central; em tais casos, indicam-se ambas as cidades.

CLASSIFICATION KLASSIFIZIERT CLASIFICADAS CLASSIFICATION CLASSIFICAÇÃO	ANGLO-AMERICA ANGLO-AMERIKA AMÉRICA ANGLOSAJONA AMÉRIQUE ANGLO-SAXONNE AMÉRICA ANGLO-SAXÔNICA	LATIN AMERICA LATEIN-AMERIKA AMÉRICA LATINA AMÉRIQUE LATINE AMÉRICA LATINA	EUROPE-RUSSIA EUROPA-RUSSLAND EUROPA-RUSIA EUROPE RUSSIE EUROPA RÚSSIA	ASIA ASIEN ASIA ASIE ÁSIA	AFRICA-OCEANIA AFRIKA-OZEANIEN AFRICA-OCEANÍA AFRIQUE-OCÉANIE ÁFRICA-OCEANIA
Over 25,000,000 (1)				**Tōkyō-Yokohama**	
15,000,000-25,000,000 (5)	**New York**	**Ciudad de México (Mexico City) São Paulo**		**Ōsaka-Kōbe-Kyōto Sŏul (Seoul)**	
10,000,000-15,000,000 (13)	**Los Angeles**	**Buenos Aires Rio de Janeiro**	**London Moskva (Moscow) Paris**	**Bombay Calcutta Delhi-New Delhi Jakarta Manila Shanghai**	**Al-Qāhirah (Cairo)**
5,000,000-10,000,000 (22)	**Chicago Philadelphia-Trenton-Wilmington San Francisco-Oakland-San Jose Toronto**	**Lima Santa Fe de Bogotá Santiago**	**Essen-Dortmund-Duisburg (Ruhr Area) Sankt-Peterburg (St. Petersburg)**	**Beijing (Peking) Dhaka (Dacca) Hyderābād İstanbul Karāchi Krung Thep (Bangkok) Madras Nagoya T'aipei Tehrān Tianjin (Tientsin) Victoria (Hong Kong)**	**Lagos**
3,000,000-5,000,000 (40)	**Boston Dallas-Fort Worth Detroit-Windsor Houston Miami-Fort Lauderdale Montréal San Diego-Tijuana Washington**	**Belo Horizonte Caracas Guadalajara Porto Alegre**	**Athínai (Athens) Barcelona Berlin Kyyiv (Kiev) Madrid Milano (Milan) Roma (Rome)**	**Ahmadābād Baghdād Bangalore Guangzhou (Canton) Harbin Kuala Lumpur Lahore Pusan Shenyang (Mukden) Singapore Surabaya Thanh Pho Ho Chi Minh (Saigon) Wuhan Yangon (Rangoon)**	**Al-Iskandarīyah (Alexandria) Casablanca El Djazaïr (Algiers) Johannesburg Kinshasa Melbourne Sydney**
2,000,000-3,000,000 (64)	**Atlanta Baltimore Cleveland Minneapolis-St. Paul Phoenix Pittsburgh St. Louis Seattle-Tacoma**	**Curitiba Fortaleza La Habana (Havana) Medellín Monterrey Recife Salvador San Juan Santo Domingo**	**Amsterdam Birmingham Bruxelles (Brussels) București (Bucharest) Budapest Donets'k-Makiyivka Frankfurt am Main Hamburg Katowice-Bytom-Gliwice Kharkiv Leeds-Bradford Lisboa (Lisbon) Liverpool Manchester München (Munich) Napoli (Naples) Nižnij Novgorod (Gorky) Stuttgart Warszawa (Warsaw) Wien (Vienna)**	**ʻAmman Ankara Bakı (Baku) Bandung Changchun Chengdu (Chengtu) Chittagong Chongqing (Chungking) Colombo Dalian (Dairen) Dimashq (Damascus) Fukuoka İzmir Kānpur Nanjing (Nanking) Pune (Poona) P'yongyang Sapporo-Otaru Taegu Taškent Tel Aviv-Yafo Xi'an (Sian)**	**Abidjan Adis Abeba Al-Kharṭūm-Umm Durmān (Khartoum-Omdurman) Cape Town Durban**
Total/Gesamtzahl Total/Total/Total (145)	**22**	**20**	**32**	**57**	**14**

ALL URBAN CENTERS of 50,000 or more population and many other important or well-known cities and towns are listed in the following table. The populations are from recent censuses (designated C) or official estimates (designated E) for the dates specified. For a few cities, only unofficial estimates are available (designated U). For comparison, the total population of each country is also given. For each country, the date stated for the total population also applies to the cities, except those for which another date is specified.

Population estimates for 1994 for countries may be found in the World Information Table.

A population figure in parentheses and preceded by a star (★) is the population of a city's entire metropolitan area. To permit meaningful comparisons of metropolitan areas, these have been defined by Rand McNally according to consistent rules (see introduction to Metropolitan Areas Table), and in some cases may differ somewhat from the officially recognized metropolitan areas. Where a town is located within the metropolitan area of another city, that city's name is given in parentheses preceded by a star (★). The capital of a country is denoted by CAPITAL letters.

ALLE STÄDTISCHEN ZENTREN mit 50 000 oder mehr Einwohnern und zahlreiche andere bedeutende oder bekannte Städte sind in der folgenden Tabelle zusammengestellt. Die Bevölkerungszahlen stammen von neuesten Zählungen (mit C gekennzeichnet) oder amtlichen Schätzungen (E) zu den angegebenen Zeitpunkten. Für einige wenige Städte waren lediglich inoffizielle Schätzungen erhältlich (U). Zu Vergleichszwecken ist ferner die Gesamtbevölkerung jedes Landes angegeben. Das Bezugsjahr für die Einwohnerzahl eines Landes betrifft auch die Städte mit Ausnahme jener, bei denen ein anderes Datum angegeben ist.

Schätzungen der Bevölkerungszahlen der Länder für 1994 finden sich in der Welt-Informationstabelle.

Bevölkerungszahlen in Klammern mit vorangestelltem Stern (★) beziehen sich auf die gesamte Stadtregion einer Stadt. Um sinnvolle Vergleiche von Stadtregionen zu ermöglichen, wurden diese von Rand McNally nach einheitlichen Regeln festgelegt (siehe Einleitung: Tabelle der Stadtregionen), weshalb sie in einigen Fällen etwas von der offiziellen Abgrenzung von Stadtregionen abweichen können. Ist eine Stadt in die Stadtregion einer anderen Grossstadt einbezogen, so wird der Name der Stadtregion mit vorangestelltem Stern (★) in Klammern aufgeführt. Die Hauptstadt eines Landes wird durch GROSSBUCHSTABEN hervorgehoben.

TODAS LOS CENTROS URBANOS de 50 000 habitantes o más y muchos otros de importancia así como bien conocidas ciudades y pueblos están incluídos en la tabla que se presenta a continuación. El número de habitantes indicados está tomado del censo más reciente (cifras identificadas con la letra C) o estimados oficiales (E) para las fechas especificadas. Para algunas ciudades, sólo existen informes no oficiales (U). Para medida de comparación, la población total de cada país se encuentra incluída también.

Para permitir una comparación, se da la población total de cada país, referente al mismo año que se usa para las ciudades principles, excepto para aquellas en las que se especifica otra fecha. El número de habitantes para 1994 para los países, se encuentra en la Tabla de Información Mundial.

La segunda cifra para la población que aparece en paréntesis y está precedida por una estrella (★) constituye la población de un área metropolitana entera. Para permitir comparaciones validas de áreas metropolitanas, éstas fueron definidas por Rand McNally siguiendo las reglas establecidas para estos propósitos (véase la Introducción a la Tabla de las Areas Metropolitanas), y en algunas ocasiones pueden ser un poco distintas de las áreas metropolitanas oficialmente reconocidas. Cuando una población se encuentra dentro de los límites de un área metropolitana de otra ciudad, el nombre de ésta se da entre paréntesis precedido por una (★). La capital de un país se indica con letras MAYÚSCULAS.

TOUTES LES VILLES de plus de 50 000 habitants et des villes moins peuplées, mais célèbres ou importantes, sont mentionnées dans la table ci-dessous. Les chiffres donnant la population proviennent de recensements récents (référence C), ou d'estimations officielles (référence E), aux dates indiquées. Pour quelques villes, on dispose seulement d'estimations non officielles (référence U). La population totale de chaque pays est également donnée, ce qui permet des comparaisons. Dans chaque pays, la date des renseignements est identique pour les villes et le pays, sauf indication contraire.

On trouvera dans la table d'informations mondiales les estimations de la population en 1994 pour chaque pays.

Les chiffres entre parenthèses, précédés d'une étoile (★), indiquent la population de l'ensemble de la zone métropolitaine. Pour permettre d'établir des comparaisons significatives entre les zones métropolitaines, ces dernières ont été définies selon des critères uniformes par Rand McNally & Company (voir l'introduction à la table des zones métropolitaines). Parfois, les limites des zones métropolitaines ainsi définies diffèrent des limites officielles. Quand une ville fait partie de la zone métropolitaine d'une autre ville, le nom de celle-ci, précédé d'une étoile (★), est mis entre parenthèses. Le nom des capitales de pays est écrit en lettres MAJUSCULES.

TODOS OS CENTROS URBANOS de 50 000 habitantes e mais, bem como muitas outras cidades e vilas importantes ou muito conhecidas figuram na tabela que se apresenta em sequida. Os dados relativos à população referem-se a censos recentes (identificadas com a letra C), ou a estimativas oficiais (E) nas datas indicadas. Para algumas cidades só existem estimativas não oficiais (U). Para fins de comparabilidade, apresenta-se também a população total de cada país.

Para cada país, a data de referência da população total aplica-se também às cidades exceto quando especificado em contrário. As estimativas da população dos países para 1994 encontra-se na *Tabela de informaçoes mundiais.*

Um dado de população apresentado entre parênteses e precedido por uma estrela (★), refere-se à população de toda a área metropolitana. Para fins de comparabilidade, as áreas metropolitanas foram definidas por Rand McNally segundo regras coerentes (ver a 'Introdução' à *Tabela das áreas metropolitanas),* e em certos casos podem ser um pouco diferentes das áreas metropolitanas oficialmente reconhecidas. Quando um centro urbano esta localizado dentro dos limites da área metropolitana de outro, seu nome figura entre parênteses precedido por uma estrela (★). A capital de um país é indicada por letras MAIÚSCULAS.

AFGHANISTAN / Afghānestān

1988 E	17,672,000
Herāt	177,300
Jalālābād (1982E)	58,000
• KĀBOL	1,424,400
Kondūz (1982E)	57,000
Mazār-e Sharīf	130,600
Qandahār	225,500

ALBANIA / Shqipëri

1989 C	3,182,400
Durrës	82,700
Elbasan	80,700
Korçë	63,600
Shkodër	79,900
• TIRANË	238,100
Vlorë	71,700

ALGERIA / Algérie / Djazaïr

1987 C	23,038,942
Aïn el Beïda	61,997
Aïn Oussera	44,270
Aïn Témouchent	47,479
Annaba (Bône)	305,526
Bab Ezzouar (★El Djazaïr)	55,211
Barika	56,488
Batna	181,601
Béchar	107,311
Bejaïa (Bougie)	114,534
Beskra	128,281
Bordj Bou Arreridj	84,264
Bordj el Kiffan (★El Djazaïr)	61,035
Boufarik	41,305
Bou Saâda	66,688
Ech Cheliff (Orléansville)	129,976
El Boulaïda	170,935
• EL DJAZAÏR (ALGIERS) (★2,547,983)	1,507,241
El Djelfa	84,207
El Eulma	67,933
El Wad	70,073
Ghardaïa	89,415
Ghilizane	80,091
Guelma	77,821
Jijel	62,793
Khemis	55,335
Khenchla	69,743
Laghouat	67,214
Lemdiyya	85,195
Maghniyya	52,275
Messaad	47,460
Mestghanem	114,037
Mouaskar	64,691
M'Sila	65,805
Qacentina	440,842
Saïda	80,825
Sidi bel Abbès	152,778
Skikda	128,747
Souq Ahras	83,015
Stif	170,182
Tbessa	107,559
Tihert	95,821
Tilimsen	126,882
Tizi-Ouzou	61,163
Touggourt	70,645
Wahran	628,558
Wargla	81,721

AMERICAN SAMOA / Amerika Samoa

1980 C	32,279
• PAGO PAGO	3,075

ANDORRA

1991 E	54,507
• ANDORRA	20,437

ANGOLA

1989 E	9,739,100
Benguela (1983E)	155,000
Huambo (Nova Lisboa) (1983E)	203,000
Lobito (1983E)	150,000
• LUANDA	1,459,900
Lubango (1984E)	95,915
Namibe (1981E)	100,000

ANGUILLA

1984 C	6,680
South Hill	961
• THE VALLEY	1,042

ANTIGUA AND BARBUDA

1977 E	72,000
• SAINT JOHN'S	24,359

ARGENTINA

1991 C	32,608,560
Almirante Brown (★Buenos Aires)	448,762
Avellaneda (★Buenos Aires)	346,620
Bahía Blanca	255,145
Berazategui (★Buenos Aires)	244,881
Berisso (★Buenos Aires)	72,703
• BUENOS AIRES (★11,000,000)	2,960,976
Campana (★Buenos Aires)	67,267
Caseros (Tres de Febrero) (★Buenos Aires)	349,221
Comodoro Rivadavia	124,151
Concordia	116,491
Córdoba (★1,260,000)	1,148,305
Corrientes	257,766
Ensenada (★Buenos Aires)	47,192
Esteban Echeverría (★Buenos Aires)	274,303
Florencio Varela (★Buenos Aires)	249,006
Formosa	153,855
General San Martín (★Buenos Aires)	407,506
General Sarmiento (San Miguel) (★Buenos Aires)	646,891
Godoy Cruz (★Mendoza)	179,468
Gualeguaychú	64,620
Junín	70,138
Lanús (★Buenos Aires)	466,755
La Plata (★Buenos Aires)	520,449
La Rioja	104,494
Las Heras (★Mendoza)	145,823
Lomas de Zamora (★Buenos Aires)	572,769
Mar del Plata	519,707
Mendoza (★770,000)	121,739
Mercedes	77,137
Merlo (★Buenos Aires)	386,304
Moreno (★Buenos Aires)	285,964
Morón (★Buenos Aires)	641,541
Necochea	59,775
Neuquén	167,078
Olavarría	72,821
Paraná	206,848
Pergamino	78,200
Pilar (★Buenos Aires)	113,428
Presidencia Roque Sáenz Peña	64,476
Posadas	201,943
Punta Alta	56,165
Quilmes (★Buenos Aires)	509,445
Rafaela	67,086
Resistencia (★291,083)	228,199
Río Cuarto	134,677
Rosario (★1,190,000)	894,645
Salta	367,099
San Carlos de Bariloche	77,750
San Fernando (★Buenos Aires)	141,496
San Fernando del Valle de Catamarca (★133,050)	110,269
San Francisco (★58,536)	55,828
San Isidro (★Buenos Aires)	299,022
San Juan (★353,476)	119,492
San Justo (★Buenos Aires)	1,111,811
San Lorenzo (★Rosario)	38,509
San Luis	110,353
San Miguel de Tucumán (★622,348)	470,604
San Nicolás de los Arroyos	114,752
San Rafael	94,776
San Salvador de Jujuy	181,318
Santa Fe (★394,888)	342,796
Santiago del Estero (★255,000)	189,490
Tandil	90,427
Tigre (★Buenos Aires)	253,748
Trelew	78,089
Venado Tuerto	58,678
Vicente López (★Buenos Aires)	289,142
Villa Krause (★San Juan)	83,266
Villa María	64,763
Villa Nueva (★Mendoza)	200,595
Zárate	77,877

ARMENIA / Hayastan

1989 C	3,283,000
Abovjan (1987E)	53,000
Ečmiadzin (★Jerevan) (1987E)	53,000
• JEREVAN (★1,315,000)	1,199,000
Kirovakan (1987E)	169,000
Kumajri	120,000
Razdan (1987E)	56,000

ARUBA

1987 E	64,763
• ORANJESTAD	19,800

AUSTRALIA

1991 C	16,850,330
Adelaide (★1,023,597)	14,843
Albury (★72,871)	40,154
Auburn (★Sydney)	48,566
Ballarat (★78,342)	34,501
Bankstown (★Sydney)	153,904
Bayswater (★Perth)	44,010
Bendigo (★67,315)	30,134
Berwick (★Melbourne)	69,144
Blacktown (★Sydney)	211,710
Blue Mountains (★Sydney)	69,420
Box Hill (★Melbourne)	45,139
Brisbane (★1,334,017)	751,115
Broadmeadows (★Melbourne)	102,996
Brunswick (★Melbourne)	39,886
Camberwell (★Melbourne)	83,799
Campbelltown (★Sydney)	137,879
CANBERRA (★303,846)	276,162
Canning (★Perth)	65,967
Canterbury (★Sydney)	129,232
Caulfield (★Melbourne)	67,776
Coburg (★Melbourne)	50,625
Cockburn (★Perth)	50,380
Coffs Harbour	51,520
Dandenong (★Melbourne)	57,275
Darwin (★78,400)	70,072
Doncaster (★Melbourne)	102,898
Enfield (★Adelaide)	61,502
Essendon (★Melbourne)	52,721
Fairfield (★Sydney)	175,099
Footscray (★Melbourne)	46,844
Frankston (★Melbourne)	84,986
Geelong (★145,325)	13,036
Gosford	128,956
Gosnells (★Perth)	69,560
Heidelberg (★Melbourne)	60,468
Hobart (★181,832)	47,106
Holroyd (★Sydney)	79,132
Hurstville (★Sydney)	63,757
Ipswich (★Brisbane)	73,299
Keilor (★Melbourne)	106,076
Knox (★Melbourne)	121,982
Kogarah (★Sydney)	46,518
Lake Macquarie (★Newcastle)	162,026

▲ Population of an entire municipality, commune, or district, including rural area.
• Largest city in country.
★ Population or designation of the metropolitan area, including suburbs.
C Census. **E** Official estimate. **U** Unofficial estimate.

▲ Bevölkerung eines ganzen städtischen Verwaltungsgebietes, eines Kommunalbezirkes oder eines Distrikts, einschliesslich ländlicher Gebiete.
• Grösste Stadt des Landes.
★ Bevölkerung oder Bezeichnung der Stadtregion einschliesslich Vororte.
C Volkszählung. **E** Offizielle Schätzung. **U** Inoffizielle Schätzung.

▲ Población de un municipio, comuna o distrito entero, incluyendo sus áreas rurales.
• Ciudad más grande de un país.
★ Población o designación de un área metropolitana, incluyendo los suburbios.
C Censo. **E** Estimado oficial. **U** Estimado no oficial.

▲ Population d'une municipalité, d'une commune ou d'un district, zone rurale incluse.
• Ville la plus peuplée du pays.
★ Population de l'agglomération (ou nom de la zone métropolitaine englobante).
C Recensement. **E** Estimation officielle. **U** Estimation non officielle.

▲ População de um municipio, comuna ou distrito, inclusive as respectivas áreas rurais.
• Maior cidade de um país.
★ População ou indicação de uma área metropolitana.
C Censo. **E** Estimativa oficial. **U** Estimativa não oficial.

Launceston (★93,581)	59,646
Leichhardt (★Sydney)	58,484
Liverpool (★Sydney)	98,203
Logan (★Brisbane)	142,595
Mackay (★53,934)	23,052
Malvern (★Melbourne)	41,340
Marion (★Adelaide)	73,942
Marrickville (★Sydney)	78,023
Melbourne (★3,022,439)	60,476
Melville (★Perth)	84,838
Mitcham (★Adelaide)	60,939
Moorabbin (★Melbourne)	94,161
Newcastle (★427,824)	131,305
Noarlunga (★Adelaide)	80,882
Northcote (★Melbourne)	46,547
North Sydney (★Sydney)	50,446
Nunawading (★Melbourne)	91,468
Oakleigh (★Melbourne)	55,151
Parramatta (★Sydney)	132,798
Penrith (★Sydney)	149,630
Perth (★1,143,249)	80,517
Prahran (★Melbourne)	42,193
Preston (★Melbourne)	76,996
Randwick (★Sydney)	115,349
Redcliffe (★Brisbane)	47,799
Rockdale (★Sydney)	84,074
Rockhampton (★62,797)	59,394
Ryde (★Sydney)	90,197
Saint Kilda (★Melbourne)	45,481
Salisbury (★Adelaide)	106,007
Shoalhaven	68,287
Southport (★324,429)	157,857
South Sydney (★Sydney)	77,818
Springvale (★Melbourne)	89,478
Stirling (★Perth)	172,731
Sunshine (★Melbourne)	94,020
• Sydney (★3,538,749)	13,501
Tea Tree Gully (★Adelaide)	83,969
Toowoomba	81,043
Townsville (★101,398)	87,288
Wagga Wagga	53,447
Wanneroo (★Perth)	167,873
Waverley (★Melbourne)	118,265
Waverley (★Sydney)	59,095
West Torrens (★Adelaide)	42,863
Willoughby (★Sydney)	51,503
Wollongong (★235,966)	173,764
Woodville (★Adelaide)	78,824
Woollahra (★Sydney)	49,904

AUSTRIA / **Österreich**

1991 C	7,795,786
Bruck an der Mur (★50,000)	14,046
Graz (★265,000)	237,810
Innsbruck (★200,000)	118,112
Klagenfurt (★118,000)	89,415
Leoben (★47,600)	28,897
Linz (★352,000)	203,044
Neunkirchen (★45,000)	10,216
Salzburg (★185,000)	143,978
Sankt Pölten (★69,500)	50,026
Steyr (★58,000)	39,337
Villach (★66,500)	54,640
Wels (★68,000)	52,594
• WIEN (VIENNA) (★1,900,000)	1,539,848

AZERBAIJAN / **Azərbaycan**

1991 E	7,136,600
Äli Bayramlı	61,500
• BAKI (★2,020,000)	1,080,500
Gäncä	282,200
Mingäçevir	90,900
Naxçıvan	61,700
Şeki	57,800
Sumqayıt (★Bakı)	236,200
Xankändi (Stepanakert)	55,200

BAHAMAS

1990 C	254,685
Freeport (▲171,542)	28,200
• NASSAU	141,000

BAHRAIN / **Al-Baḥrayn**

1988 E	473,000
• AL-MANĀMAH (★273,000) (1986E)	82,700
Al-Muḥarraq (★Al-Manāmah)	78,000
Jidd Ḥafṣ (★Al-Manāmah)	48,000

BANGLADESH

1991 C	104,766,143
Barisāl	180,014
Begamganj (1981C)	69,623
Bhairab Bāzār	75,747
Bogra	93,114
Brāhmanbāria	114,297
Chāndpur	84,067
Chittagong (★2,342,662)	1,566,070
Chuādanga	65,222
Comilla (1981C)	164,509
• DHAKA (DACCA) (★6,537,308)	3,637,892
Dinājpur	136,657
Farīdpur	72,927
Gopālpur	45,174
Gulshan (★Dhaka) (1981C)	215,444
Jamālpur	108,416
Jessore	176,398
Jhenida	69,501
Khulna (★966,096)	601,051
Kishorganj	64,676
Kurīgrām	62,075
Kushtia	71,706
Mādārīpur	46,842
Mīrpur (★Dhaka) (1981C)	349,031
Mymensingh	138,662
Naogaon	109,156
Nārāyanganj (★Dhaka)	288,008
Narsinghdi	100,120
Nawābganj	131,260
Noākhāli	73,766
Pābna	113,146
Patuākhāli	50,344
Rājshāhi (★560,013)	324,532
Rangpur	220,849
Saidpur	110,494
Sātkhira	81,199
Sherpur	63,030
Sirājganj	100,003
Sītākunda (★Chittagong) (1981C)	237,520
Sylhet	114,284
Tangail	111,783
Tongi (★Dhaka)	165,099

BARBADOS

1980 C	244,228
• BRIDGETOWN (★115,000)	7,466

BELARUS / **Byelarus'**

1991 E	10,260,400
Baranoviči	166,700
Bobrujsk	223,000
Borisov	150,200
Brest	277,000
Gomel'	503,300
Grodno	284,800
Kobrin	48,300
Lida	95,000
• MINSK (★1,694,000)	1,633,600
Mogil'ov	363,000
Molodečno	93,500
Mozyr'	103,000
Novopolock	96,600
Orša	125,300
Pinsk	123,800
Polock	78,700
Rečica	69,400
Sluck	60,100
Soligorsk	96,000
Vitebsk	361,500
Žlobin	60,800
Žodino	56,000

BELGIUM / **België** / **Belgique**

1987 E	9,864,751
Aalst (Alost) (★Bruxelles)	77,113
Anderlecht (★Bruxelles)	88,849
Antwerpen (★1,100,000)	479,748
Bastogne (▲11,699)	6,900
Brugge (Bruges) (★223,000)	117,755
• BRUXELLES (★2,385,000)	136,920
Charleroi (★480,000)	209,395
Etterbeek (★Bruxelles)	44,240
Forest (★Bruxelles)	48,266
Genk (★Hasselt)	61,391
Gent (Gand) (★465,000)	233,856
Hasselt (★290,000)	65,563
Ixelles (★Bruxelles)	76,241
Kortrijk (Courtrai) (★202,000)	76,216
La Louvière (★147,000)	76,340
Leuven (Louvain) (★173,000)	84,583
Liège (Luik) (★750,000)	200,891
Mechelen (Malines) (★121,000)	75,808
Molenbeek-St.-Jean (★Bruxelles)	69,764
Mons (Bergen) (★242,000)	89,697
Mouscron (★Lille, France)	53,713
Namur (★147,000)	102,670
Oostende (Ostende) (★122,000)	68,318
Roeselare (Roulers)	51,963
Saint-Gilles (★Bruxelles)	42,482
Schaerbeek (★Bruxelles)	104,919
Seraing (★Liège)	61,731
Sint-Niklaas (Saint-Nicolas)	68,082
Spa	9,645
Tournai (Doornik) (▲66,998)	44,900
Uccle (★Bruxelles)	75,876
Verviers (★101,000)	53,498
Waterloo (★Bruxelles)	25,232
Woluwe-Saint-Lambert (Sint-Lambrechts-Woluwe) (★Bruxelles)	47,887

BELIZE

1990 C	184,340
• Belize City	43,621
BELMOPAN	5,256

BENIN / **Bénin**

1984 E	3,825,000
Abomey	53,000
• COTONOU (1992C)	533,212
Parakou	92,000
PORTO-NOVO	164,000

BERMUDA

1985 E	56,000
• HAMILTON (★15,000)	1,676

BHUTAN / **Druk-Yul**

1982 E	1,333,000
• THIMPHU	12,000

BOLIVIA

1990 E	7,314,000
Cochabamba	413,300
• LA PAZ	1,125,600
Montero (1988E)	84,100
Oruro	207,700
Potosí	120,100
Santa Cruz de la Sierra	696,100
SUCRE	101,400
Tarija	74,600
Trinidad	51,900

BOSNIA AND HERZEGOVINA / **Bosna i Hercegovina**

1987 E	4,400,464
Banja Luka (▲193,890)	130,900
• SARAJEVO (▲479,688)	341,200
Tuzla (▲129,967)	67,300
Zenica (▲144,869)	67,500

BOTSWANA

1991 C	1,326,796
Francistown	65,244
• GABORONE	133,468
Selebi Phikwe	39,772

BRAZIL / **Brasil**

1991 C	146,917,459
Abaetetuba (▲100,016)	55,442
Abreu e Lima (▲76,568)	70,099
Alagoinhas (▲116,740)	97,819
Alegrete (▲78,879)	67,505
Almirante Tamandaré (▲66,090)	51,240
Altamira (▲120,441)	48,452
Alvorada (▲142,020) (★Porto Alegre)	132,582
Americana	153,592
Ananindeua (▲88,035)	73,941
Anápolis (▲239,047)	222,400
Anil (▲695,199)	81,879
Antônio Bezerra (▲1,765,794) (★Fortaleza)	193,682
Aparecida de Goiânia (▲178,326)	48,804
Apucarana (▲94,914)	80,048
Aracaju	401,676
Araçatuba (▲159,499)	146,977
Araguaína (▲103,396)	81,729
Araguari (▲91,202)	80,568
Arapiraca (▲165,379)	131,449
Arapongas (▲64,531)	59,996
Araraquara (▲166,732)	101,302
Araras (▲87,355)	79,002
Araucária (▲61,767)	53,522
Araxá	67,919
Arcoverde (▲55,790)	49,479
Assis (▲85,265)	72,004
Atibaia (▲86,193)	74,658
Avaré (▲61,063)	56,232
Bacabal (▲98,875)	64,844
Bagé (▲118,736)	89,372
Barbacena (▲99,895)	80,682
Barra Alegre (▲179,710)	58,445
Barra do Piraí (▲78,426)	59,202
Barra Mansa (▲171,671) (★Volta Redonda)	145,112
Barreiras (▲92,439)	70,701
Barreiros (▲139,318) (★Florianópolis)	58,694
Barretos (▲95,538)	88,935
Barueri (▲130,383)	66,722
Bauru	254,690
Bayeux (★João Pessoa)	77,047
Bebedouro (▲67,752)	60,792
Belém (★1,355,000)	765,476
Belford Roxo (▲1,293,611) (★Rio de Janeiro)	337,698
Belo Horizonte (★3,340,000)	1,529,566
Betim (★Belo Horizonte)	162,462
Birigui	70,547
Blumenau (▲211,862)	185,200
Boa Vista (▲142,902)	118,928
Botucatu (▲90,620)	81,528
Bragança Paulista (▲108,602)	88,336
Brás Cubas (▲273,255)	65,538
BRASÍLIA	1,513,470
Brusque	53,438
Cabo (▲126,756)	68,594
Cabo Frio (▲84,635)	70,251
Caçapava (▲65,889)	58,145
Cáceres (▲77,475)	51,891
Cachoeira do Sul (▲89,148)	69,780
Cachoeirinha (★Porto Alegre)	87,976
Cachoeiro de Itapemirim (▲143,763)	112,099
Camaçari (▲113,615)	88,302
Camarajibe	99,431
Cambé (▲73,803)	66,767
Campina Grande	298,331
Campinas (★1,290,000)	759,032
Campo Comprido (▲1,313,094) (★Curitiba)	105,631
Campo Grande	516,403
Campo Mourão (▲82,280)	69,966
Campos (▲388,747)	277,482
Campos Elísios (▲665,343) (★Rio de Janeiro)	197,833
Candeias (▲67,936)	61,432
Canoas (★Porto Alegre)	269,234
Capuáva (▲615,112)	92,950
Carapicuíba (▲283,653) (★São Paulo)	207,264
Carapina (▲221,510) (★Vit2oria)	141,234
Carazinho (▲58,770)	49,010
Cariacica (▲274,455) (★Vitória)	91,888
Caruaru (▲213,573)	180,654
Cascatinha (▲255,261)	56,890
Cascavel (▲192,884)	175,332
Castanhal (▲101,963)	90,364
Catanduva	88,024
Caucaia (▲165,015) (★Fortaleza)	66,379
Cava (▲1,293,611)	59,506
Cavaleiro (▲486,774) (★Recife)	120,065
Caxias (▲146,730)	85,332
Caxias do Sul (▲290,969)	262,983
Chapecó (▲122,889)	93,697
Codó (▲111,679)	58,163
Coelho da Rocha (▲424,689) (★Rio de Janeiro)	152,045
Colatina (▲106,712)	71,094
Colombo (▲117,658) (★Curitiba)	110,161
Conselheiro Lafaiete (▲88,843)	82,619
Contagem (▲448,991) (★Belo Horizonte)	195,705
Corumbá (▲88,290)	75,235
Cotia (▲106,822)	90,469
Coxipó da Ponte (▲401,303)	140,130
Crato (▲91,413)	56,374
Criciúma (▲146,162)	99,375
Cruz Alta (▲68,784)	61,860
Cruzeiro	65,935
Cubatão (★Santos)	90,572
Cuiabá (▲401,303)	252,784
Curitiba (★1,815,000)	841,882
Diadema (★São Paulo)	305,068
Divinópolis (▲151,382)	141,984
Dourados (▲135,786)	116,817
Dracena (▲39,576)	33,856
Duque de Caxias (▲665,343) (★Rio de Janeiro)	325,903
Embu (★São Paulo)	155,851
Erechim (▲72,292)	61,509
Esteio (★Porto Alegre)	70,449
Eunápolis (▲70,561)	63,553
Feira de Santana (▲405,848)	340,034
Fernandópolis (▲56,125)	51,216
Ferraz de Vasconcelos (▲95,973) (★São Paulo)	65,319
Florianópolis (★420,000)	191,664
Formosa (▲62,974)	49,135
Fortaleza (★2,040,000)	743,335
Foz do Iguaçu	186,362
Franca	227,613
Francisco Morato	83,361
Franco da Rocha	79,534
Garanhuns (▲103,365)	86,593
Goiabeiras (▲258,243) (★Vitória)	74,086
Goiânia (★1,130,000)	912,136
Governador Valadares (▲230,403)	210,396
Gravataí (▲181,019) (★Porto Alegre)	166,954
Guaíba (▲83,119)	72,739
Guarapari (▲61,594)	54,994
Guaratinguetá (▲102,005)	84,660
Guarujá (▲209,814) (★Santos)	98,918
Guarulhos (▲786,355) (★São Paulo)	546,417
Gurupi (▲56,741)	51,005
Hortolândia (▲226,225)	78,011
Ibes (▲265,251) (★Vitória)	91,071
Icoraci (▲1,244,688) (★Belém)	67,458
Igapó (▲606,681)	117,251
Igarassu (▲79,713) (★Recife)	48,598
Ijuí (▲75,169)	58,627
Ilhéus (▲223,482)	135,117
Imbariê (▲665,343)	100,687
Imperatriz (▲276,440)	209,970
Indaiatuba (▲100,816)	91,752
Inhomirim (▲191,249)	76,031
Ipatinga (▲179,710)	120,025
Ipiíba (▲778,831) (★Rio de Janeiro)	121,785
Itabira (▲85,284)	71,287
Itaboraí (▲161,398)	72,410
Itabuna (▲185,165)	170,434
Itaguaí (▲113,019)	48,274
Itaipu (▲435,658)	35,072
Itaituba (▲116,541)	62,278
Itajaí	114,558
Itajubá (▲74,618)	68,469
Itambi (▲161,398)	48,891
Itapecerica da Serra (▲92,854) (★São Paulo)	84,479
Itaperuna (▲78,017)	55,484
Itapetininga (▲105,071)	84,703
Itapeva (▲81,858)	55,658
Itapevi (★São Paulo)	107,983
Itaquaquecetuba (★São Paulo)	164,665
Itaquari (▲274,455) (★Vitória)	169,145
Itatiba (▲61,587)	54,044
Itaúna	61,891
Itú (▲107,176)	88,838
Ituiutaba (▲84,581)	78,211
Itumbiara (▲79,457)	68,673
Jaboatão (▲486,774) (★Recife)	81,178
Jaboticabal (▲59,130)	53,027
Jacareí (▲163,843)	144,141
Jandira	62,573
Japeri (▲1,293,611)	65,576
Jaraguá do Sul (▲76,994)	62,578
Jardim Presidente Dutra (▲786,355) (★São Paulo)	229,987
Jataí (▲65,921)	53,431
Jaú (▲94,138)	80,331
Jequié (▲144,572)	114,542
Ji-Paraná (▲97,719)	75,384
João Monlevade	57,413
João Pessoa (★670,000)	497,308
Joinvile	326,208
Juàzeiro128,691) (★Petrolina)	95,676
Juazeiro do Norte	163,527
Juiz de Fora	377,538
Jundiaí (▲288,644)	265,599
Jurema (▲165,015) (★Fortaleza)	75,463
Justinópolis (▲143,696) (★Belo Horizonte)	85,452
Lages (▲151,100)	137,169
Lavras (▲65,857)	60,690
Leme	64,525
Limeira (▲207,416)	177,591
Linhares (▲119,501)	73,082
Lins (▲59,218)	54,868
Londrina (▲389,959)	355,062
Lorena (▲73,167)	67,766
Luziânia (▲207,425)	194,128
Macaé (▲100,642)	57,581
Macapá (▲179,252)	146,523
Maceió (▲628,241)	554,727
Manaus	1,005,634
Marabá (▲122,231)	102,364
Marília (▲160,872)	144,906
Maringá	225,516
Matão	59,694
Mauá (★São Paulo)	294,631
Mesquita (▲1,293,611) (★Rio de Janeiro)	141,326
Messejana (▲1,765,794) (★Fortaleza)	229,507
Moji das Cruzes (▲273,255) (★São Paulo)	138,995
Mojiguaçu (▲107,440)	92,440
Mojimirim (▲64,750)	57,395
Mondubim (▲1,765,794) (★Fortaleza)	331,591
Monjolo (▲778,831) (★Rio de Janeiro)	137,974
Montes Claros (▲249,565)	223,046
Mossoró (▲191,959)	177,020
Muriaé (▲84,507)	65,406
Muribeca dos Guararapes (▲486,774) (★Recife)	217,905
Natal (▲606,681)	459,827
Neves (▲778,831) (★Rio de Janeiro)	151,067
Nilópolis (▲157,936) (★Rio de Janeiro)	104,671
Niterói (▲435,658) (★Rio de Janeiro)	400,586
Nossa Senhora do Socorro	67,443
Nova Brasília (▲178,326) (★Goiânia)	126,701
Nova Friburgo (▲166,975)	111,020
Nova Iguaçu (▲1,293,611) (★Rio de Janeiro)	562,062
Nova Veneza (▲226,225)	82,203
Novo Hamburgo (★Porto Alegre)	201,334
Novo Mundo (▲1,313,094) (★Curitiba)	71,508
Olinda (★Recife)	341,059
Olinda (▲157,936)	53,265
Osasco (★São Paulo)	566,949
Ourinhos (▲76,912)	70,690
Palhoça (▲68,298) (★Florianópolis)	58,097
Paracatu (▲62,709)	49,656
Pará de Minas (▲61,066)	51,679
Paranaguá (▲107,601)	88,110
Paranavaí (▲71,173)	61,043
Parangaba (▲1,765,794) (★Fortaleza)	267,679
Parauapebas (▲53,312)	27,452
Parnaíba (▲127,992)	105,131
Parnamirim (▲63,253)	48,534
Parque Industrial (▲448,991) (★Belo Horizonte)	223,660
Passo do Sabão (▲169,079) (★Porto Alegre)	63,140
Passo Fundo (▲147,239)	135,158
Passos (▲84,618)	74,218
Patos (▲81,292)	76,378
Patos de Minas (▲102,766)	83,670
Paulista (▲211,017) (★Recife)	53,566
Paulo Afonso (▲86,594)	74,326
Pelotas (▲290,660)	260,510
Petrolina (★300,000)	123,857
Petrópolis (▲255,261) (★Rio de Janeiro)	164,849
Pindamonhangaba (▲101,939)	71,449
Pinhais (▲106,764) (★Curitiba)	71,973
Pinheirinho (▲1,313,094) (★Curitiba)	117,516
Piracicaba (▲283,634)	223,170
Poá (★São Paulo)	72,151
Poços de Caldas	105,223
Ponta Grossa	219,955
Porto Alegre (★2,850,000)	1,247,352
Porto Velho (▲286,471)	226,196
Porto Velho (▲161,611)	56,973

▲ Population of an entire municipality, commune, or district, including rural area.
• Largest city in country.
★ Population or designation of the metropolitan area, including suburbs.
C Census. **E** Official estimate. **U** Unofficial estimate.

▲ Bevölkerung eines ganzen städtischen Verwaltungsgebietes, eines Kommunalbezirkes oder eines Distrikts, einschliesslich ländlicher Gebiete.
• Grösste Stadt des Landes.
★ Bevölkerung oder Bezeichnung der Stadtregion einschliesslich Vororte.
C Volkszählung. **E** Offizielle Schätzung. **U** Inoffizielle Schätzung.

Pouso Alegre (▲81,776)	73,875
Praia da Conceição (▲211,017) (★Recife)	97,635
Praia Grande (▲123,494)	97,173
Presidente Prudente	157,618
Queimados (▲1,293,611) (★Rio de Janeiro)	124,121
Recife (★2,880,000)	1,296,995
Resende (▲91,605)	52,261
Ribeirão Pires	62,240
Ribeirão Preto	416,186
Rio Branco (▲196,871)	136,457
Rio Claro	130,364
Rio de Janeiro (★11,050,000)	5,473,909
Rio Grande (▲172,408)	157,608
Rio Verde (▲95,894)	76,818
Rondonópolis (▲126,082)	87,307
Salto	72,076
Salvador (★2,340,000)	2,070,296
Santa Bárbara d'Oeste	141,230
Santa Cruz do Sul (▲117,779)	74,295
Santa Felicidade (▲1,313,094) (★Curitiba)	53,560
Santa Inês (▲64,655)	54,006
Santa Maria (▲217,604)	193,294
Santana do Livramento (▲80,145)	72,950
Santarém (▲264,779)	168,153
Santa Rita (▲94,412) (★João Pessoa)	74,396
Santa Rosa (▲58,262)	48,211
Santo André (▲615,112) (★São Paulo)	518,272
Santo Ângelo (▲76,461)	59,688
Santo Antônio de Jesus (▲64,198)	52,770
Santos (★1,165,000)	415,554
São Benedito (▲137,686) (★Belo Horizonte)	91,733
São Bernardo do Campo (★São Paulo)	550,030
São Borja (▲63,766)	52,493
São Caetano do Sul (★São Paulo)	149,203
São Carlos (▲158,186)	100,502
São Cristóvão	46,172
São Gabriel (▲59,024)	47,668
São Gonçalo (▲778,831) (★Rio de Janeiro)	296,021
São João da Boa Vista (▲69,090)	60,845
São João del-Rei (▲72,741)	63,680
São João de Meriti (▲424,689) (★Rio de Janeiro)	220,742
São José do Rio Preto	263,454
São José dos Campos (▲442,009)	385,879
São José dos Pinhais (▲128,170) (★Curitiba)	99,154
São Leopoldo (★Porto Alegre)	160,228
São Lourenco da Mata (▲85,889) (★Recife)	68,479
São Luís (★710,000)	164,334
São Mateus (▲424,689)	51,902
• São Paulo (★16,925,000)	9,393,753
São Vicente (★Santos)	268,467
Sapiranga (▲58,522)	51,387
Sapucaia do Sul (★Porto Alegre)	104,626
Serra (▲221,510)	62,398
Sertãozinho (▲78,753)	68,874
Sete Lagoas	139,910
Sete Pontes (▲778,831) (★Rio de Janeiro)	71,984
Sobral (▲127,459)	92,805
Sorocaba	348,952
Sumaré (▲226,225)	64,673
Susano (▲159,142) (★São Paulo)	110,414
Taboão da Serra (★São Paulo)	159,894
Tatuí (▲76,662)	68,808
Taubaté (▲206,416)	185,790
Teixeira de Freitas (▲85,227)	73,107
Telêmaco Borba (▲64,854)	50,774
Teófilo Otoni (▲140,676)	96,382
Teresina (★665,000)	556,073
Teresópolis (▲120,712)	96,516
Timon (▲107,394) (★Teresina)	90,577
Timóteo (▲58,393)	48,340
Toledo (▲94,857)	67,343
Três Corações (▲57,053)	49,138
Três Lagoas (▲68,067)	60,716
Três Rios (▲81,163)	60,201
Tubarão (▲95,058)	83,262
Tucuruí (▲81,635)	46,011
Tupã (▲61,290)	53,282
Ubá (▲66,422)	52,673
Uberaba (▲211,356)	198,565
Uberlândia	355,191
Umbará (▲1,313,094) (★Curitiba)	64,523
Umuarama (▲100,185)	66,995
Uruguaiana (▲117,437)	103,160
Valinhos (▲67,867)	59,896
Varginha (▲88,045)	82,263
Várzea Grande (▲161,611)	96,379
Várzea Paulista	67,911
Venda Nova (▲2,017,127) (★Belo Horizonte)	481,470
Viamão (▲169,079)	75,782
Vicente de Carvalho (▲209,814) (★Santos)	110,881
Vila Dirce (▲283,653)	59,144
Vila Velha (▲265,251) (★Vitória)	113,664
Vila Xavier (▲166,732)	50,922
Vitória (★810,000)	184,157
Vitória da Conquista (▲224,896)	179,868
Vitória de Santo Antão (▲106,661)	84,116
Volta Redonda (★430,000)	219,988
Votorantim	79,150
Votuporanga (▲66,037)	59,604

BRITISH VIRGIN ISLANDS

1980 C	12,034
• ROAD TOWN	2,479

BRUNEI

1981 C	192,832
• BANDAR SERI BEGAWAN (★64,000)	22,777
Seria	23,415

BULGARIA / Bâlgarija

1989 E	8,986,636
Asenovgrad	58,568
Blagoevgrad	74,236
Burgas	200,464
Dimitrovgrad	57,102
Dobrič	112,582
Gabrovo	80,930
Haskovo	93,609
Jambol	97,414
Kărdžali	58,995
Kazanlăk	63,776
Kjustendil	55,620
Loveč	50,872
Montana	55,203
Pazardžik	83,451
Pernik	97,930
Pleven	136,287
Plovdiv	364,162
Razgrad	56,494
Ruse	190,720
Silistra	56,907
Sliven	109,432
• SOFIJA (★1,205,000)	1,136,875
Stara Zagora	158,151
Šumen	107,973
Varna	306,300
Veliko Tărnovo	71,709
Vidin	65,892
Vraca	81,992

BURKINA FASO

1985 C	7,964,705
Bobo Dioulasso	228,668
Koudougou	51,926
• OUAGADOUGOU	441,514
Ouahigouya	38,902

BURUNDI

1990 C	5,356,266
• BUJUMBURA	226,628

CAMBODIA / Kâmpŭchéa

1990 E	8,567,582
Bătdâmbâng	94,412
Kâmpóng Saôm	67,452
• PHNUM PÉNH	620,000
Prey Vêng	41,456
Siĕmréab	76,434
Ta Khmau	34,947

CAMEROON / Cameroun

1987 C	9,312,429
Bafoussam	92,331
Bamenda	95,455
• Douala	712,251
Foumban	46,920
Garoua	122,584
Kumba	63,911
Maroua	111,630
Ngaoundéré	62,468
Nkongsamba	76,887
YAOUNDE	560,785

CANADA

1991 C	27,296,859

CANADA: ALBERTA

1991 C	2,545,553
Calgary (★754,033)	710,677
Edmonton (★839,924)	616,741
Lethbridge	60,974
Medicine Hat (★52,681)	43,625
Red Deer	58,134

CANADA: BRITISH COLUMBIA

1991 C	3,282,061
Burnaby (★Vancouver)	158,858
Chilliwack (★60,251)	49,531
Delta (★Vancouver)	95,577
Kamloops (★67,856)	67,057
Kelowna (★111,846)	75,950
Matsqui (★113,562)	68,064
Nanaimo (★73,547)	60,129
Prince George	69,653
Richmond (★Vancouver)	126,624
Saanich (★Victoria)	245,173
Surrey (★Vancouver)	84,021
Vancouver (★1,602,502)	471,844
Victoria (★287,897)	71,228

CANADA: MANITOBA

1991 C	1,091,942
Winnipeg (★652,354)	616,790

CANADA: NEW BRUNSWICK

1991 C	723,900
Fredericton (★71,869)	46,466
Moncton (★106,503)	57,010
Saint John (★124,981)	74,969

CANADA: NEWFOUNDLAND

1991 C	568,474
Saint John's (★171,859)	95,770

CANADA: NORTHWEST TERRITORIES

1991 C	57,649
Yellowknife	15,179

CANADA: NOVA SCOTIA

1991 C	899,942
Dartmouth (★Halifax)	67,798
Halifax (★320,501)	114,455
Sydney (★116,100)	26,063

CANADA: ONTARIO

1991 C	10,084,885
Ajax (★Toronto)	57,350
Barrie (★92,165)	62,728
Brampton (★Toronto)	234,445
Brantford (★97,106)	81,997
Burlington (★Hamilton)	129,575
Cambridge (Galt) (★Kitchener)	92,772
Cornwall (★53,545)	47,137
East York (★Toronto)	102,696
Etobicoke (★Toronto)	309,993
Gloucester (★Ottawa)	101,677
Guelph (★97,213)	87,976
Hamilton (★599,760)	318,499
Kingston (★136,401)	56,597
Kitchener (★356,421)	168,282
Leamington (★35,792)	14,182
London (★381,522)	303,165
Markham (★Toronto)	153,811
Mississauga (★Toronto)	463,388
Nepean (★Ottawa)	107,627
Newcastle	49,479
Niagara Falls (★Saint Catharines)	75,399
North Bay (★63,285)	55,405
North York (★Toronto)	562,564
Oakville (★Toronto)	114,670
Oshawa (★240,104)	129,344
OTTAWA (★920,857)	313,987
Peterborough (★98,060)	68,371
Pickering (★Toronto)	68,631
Richmond Hill (★Toronto)	80,142
Saint Catharines (★364,552)	129,300
Sarnia (★87,870)	74,376
Sault Sainte Marie (★101,800)	81,476
Scarborough (★Toronto)	524,598
Stoney Creek (★Hamilton)	49,968
Sudbury (★157,613)	92,884
Thunder Bay (★124,427)	113,946
• Toronto (★3,893,046)	635,395
Vaughan (★Toronto)	111,359
Waterloo (★Kitchener)	71,181
Whitby (★Oshawa)	61,281
Windsor (★262,075)	191,435
York (★Toronto)	140,525

CANADA: PRINCE EDWARD ISLAND

1991 C	129,765
Charlottetown (★57,472)	15,396

CANADA: QUÉBEC

1991 C	6,895,963
Beauport (★Québec)	69,158
Brossard (★Montréal)	64,793
Charlesbourg (★Québec)	70,788
Chicoutimi (★160,928)	62,670
Drummondville (★60,092)	35,462
Gatineau (★Ottawa)	92,284
Hull (★Ottawa)	60,707
Jonquière (★Chicoutimi)	57,933
La Salle (★Montréal)	73,804
Laval (★Montréal)	314,398
Lévis (★Québec)	39,452
Longueuil (★Montréal)	129,874
Montréal (★3,127,242)	1,017,666
Montréal-Nord (★Montréal)	85,516
Pierrefonds (★Montréal)	48,735
Québec (★645,550)	167,517
Repentigny (★Montréal)	49,630
Sainte-Foy (★Québec)	71,133
Saint-Hubert (★Montréal)	74,027
Saint-Jean-sur-Richelieu (★68,378)	37,607
Saint-Laurent (★Montréal)	72,402
Saint-Léonard (★Montréal)	73,120
Shawinigan (★61,672)	19,931
Sherbrooke (★139,194)	76,429
Trois-Rivières (★136,303)	49,426
Verdun (★Montréal)	61,307

CANADA: SASKATCHEWAN

1991 C	988,928
Regina (★191,692)	179,178
Saskatoon (★210,023)	186,058

CANADA: YUKON

1991 C	27,797
Whitehorse	17,925

CAPE VERDE / Cabo Verde

1990 C	341,491
Mindelo	47,109
• PRAIA	61,644

CAYMAN ISLANDS

1988 E	25,900
• GEORGE TOWN	13,700

CENTRAL AFRICAN REPUBLIC / République centrafricaine

1984 E	2,517,000
• BANGUI	473,817
Bouar (1982E)	48,000

CHAD / Tchad

1988 E	5,428,000
Abéché	40,000
Moundou	100,000
• N'DJAMENA	500,000
Sarh	76,835

CHILE

1982 C	11,329,736
Antofagasta (1990E)	218,800
Apoquindo (★Santiago)	175,735
Arica (1990E)	177,300
Calama	81,684
Cerrillos (★Santiago)	67,013
Cerro Navia (★Santiago)	137,777
Chillán (1990E)	146,000
Concepción (★710,000) (1990E)	306,500
Conchalí (★Santiago)	157,884
Copiapó	69,045
Coquimbo	62,186
Coronel (★Concepción)	65,918
Curicó	60,550
El Bosque (★Santiago)	143,717
Huechuraba (★Santiago)	56,313
Independencia (★Santiago)	86,724
Iquique (1990E)	148,500
La Cisterna (★Santiago)	95,863
La Florida (★Santiago)	191,883
La Granja (★Santiago)	109,168
La Pintana (★Santiago)	73,932
La Reina (★Santiago)	80,452
La Serena (1990E)	105,600
Las Rejas (★Santiago)	147,918
Linares	46,433
Lo Espejo (★Santiago)	124,462
Lo Prado (★Santiago)	103,575
Los Angeles	70,529
Lota (★Concepción)	47,133
Macul (★Santiago)	113,100
Maipú (★Santiago)	114,117
Ñuñoa (★Santiago)	168,919
Osorno (1990E)	117,400
Ovalle	43,023
Pedro Aguirre Cerda (★Santiago)	145,207
Peñalolén (★Santiago)	137,298
Providencia (★Santiago)	115,449
Pudahuel (★Santiago)	97,578
Puente Alto (★Santiago) (1990E)	187,400
Puerto Montt (1990E)	106,500
Punta Arenas (1990E)	120,000
Quilpué (★Valparaíso) (1990E)	107,400
Quinta Normal (★Santiago)	128,989
Rancagua (1990E)	190,400
Recoleta (★Santiago)	164,292
Renca (★Santiago)	93,928
San Antonio	61,486
San Bernardo (★Santiago) (1990E)	188,200
San Joaquín (★Santiago)	123,904
San Miguel (★Santiago)	88,764
San Ramón (★Santiago)	99,410
• SANTIAGO (★4,100,000)	232,667
Talca (1990E)	164,500
Talcahuano (★Concepción) (1990E)	246,900
Temuco (1990E)	211,700
Valdivia (1990E)	113,500
Vallenar	38,375
Valparaíso (★690,000) (1990E)	276,800
Villa Alemana (★Valparaíso)	55,766
Viña del Mar (★Valparaíso) (1990E)	281,100
Vitacura (★Santiago)	72,038

CHINA / Zhongguo

1988 E	999,999,999
Abagnar Qi (▲100,700) (1986E)	71,700
Acheng (1985E)	100,304
Aihui (▲135,000) (1986E)	76,700
Aksu (▲345,900) (1986E)	143,100
Altay (▲141,700) (1986E)	62,800
Anci (Langfang) (▲522,800) (1986E)	122,100
Anda (▲425,500) (1986E)	130,200
Ankang (1985E)	89,188
Anqing (▲433,900) (1986E)	213,200
Anshan	1,330,000
Anshun (▲214,700) (1986E)	128,800
Anyang (▲541,900) (1986E)	361,200
Baicheng (▲282,000) (1986E)	198,600
Baiquan (1985E)	50,996
Baiyin (▲301,900) (1986E)	157,100
Baoding (▲535,100) (1986E)	423,200
Baoji (▲359,500) (1986E)	286,200
Baoshan (▲688,400) (1986E)	52,300
Baotou (Paotow)	1,130,000
Baoying (1985E)	50,479
Bei'an (▲440,500) (1986E)	199,500
Beihai (▲175,900) (1986E)	119,000
BEIJING (PEKING) (★7,320,000)	6,710,000
Beipiao (▲603,700) (1986E)	180,900
Bengbu (▲612,600) (1986E)	403,900
Benxi (Penhsi)	860,000
Bijie (1985E)	54,871
Binxian (▲177,900) (1986E)	86,700
Binxian (1982C)	127,326
Boli (1985E)	61,990
Bose (▲271,400) (1986E)	82,000
Boshan (1975U)	100,000
Boxian (1985E)	63,222
Boxing (1982C)	57,554
Boyang (1985E)	60,688
Butha Qi (Zalantun) (▲389,500) (1986E)	111,300
Cangshan (Bianzhuang) (1982C)	79,334
Cangzhou (▲293,600) (1986E)	196,700
Changchun (▲2,000,000)	1,822,000
Changde (▲220,800) (1986E)	178,200
Changge (1982C)	67,002
Changji (▲233,400) (1986E)	110,500
Changqing (1982C)	65,094
Changsha	1,230,000
Changshou (1985E)	51,923
Changshu (▲998,000) (1986E)	281,300
Changtu (1985E)	49,937
Changyi (1982C)	64,513
Changzhi (▲463,400) (1986E)	273,000
Changzhou (Changchow) (1986E)	522,700
Chao'an (▲1,214,500) (1986E)	265,400
Chaoxian (▲739,500) (1986E)	116,800
Chaoyang, Guangdong prov. (1985E)	85,968
Chaoyang, Liaoning prov. (▲318,900) (1986E)	180,300
Chengde (▲330,400) (1986E)	226,600
Chengdu (Chengtu) (▲2,960,000)	1,884,000
Chenghai (1985E)	50,631
Chenxian (▲191,900) (1986E)	143,500
Chifeng (Ulanhad) (▲882,900) (1986E)	299,000
Chongqing (Chungking) (▲2,890,000)	2,502,000
Chuxian (▲365,000) (1986E)	113,300
Chuxiong (▲379,400) (1986E)	67,700
Da'an (1985E)	70,552
Dachangzhen (1975U)	50,000
Dalian (Dairen)	2,280,000
Dandong (1986E)	579,800
Daqing (▲880,000)	640,000
Dashiqiao (1985E)	68,898
Datong (1985E)	55,529
Datong (▲1,040,000)	810,000
Dawa (1985E)	142,581
Daxian (▲209,400) (1986E)	142,000
Dehui (1985E)	60,247
Dengfeng (1982C)	49,746
Deqing (1982C)	48,726
Deyang (▲753,400) (1986E)	184,800
Dezhou (▲276,200) (1986E)	161,300
Didao (1975U)	50,000
Dinghai (1985E)	50,161
Dongchuan (Xincun) (▲275,100) (1986E)	67,400
Dongguan (▲1,208,500) (1986E)	254,900
Dongsheng (▲121,300) (1986E)	57,500
Dongtai (1985E)	65,788
Dongying (▲514,400) (1986E)	178,100
Dukou (▲551,200) (1986E)	380,200
Dunhua (▲448,000) (1986E)	217,100
Duyun (▲386,600) (1986E)	123,800
Echeng (▲938,000) (1986E)	217,400
Enshi (▲679,000) (1986E)	84,300
Erenhot (1986E)	7,200
Ergun Zuoqi (1985E)	55,970
Feixian (1982C)	73,246
Fengcheng (1985E)	66,745
Foshan (▲312,700) (1986E)	243,500
Fujin (1985E)	60,948
Fuling (▲973,500) (1986E)	166,300
Fushun (Funan)	1,290,000
Fuxian (Wafangdian) (▲960,700) (1986E)	246,200
Fuxin	700,000
Fuyang (▲195,200) (1986E)	143,400
Fuyu, Heilongjiang prov. (1985E)	48,670
Fuyu, Jilin prov. (1985E)	98,373
Fuzhou, Fujian prov. (▲1,240,000)	910,000

▲ Población de un municipio, comuna o distrito entero, incluyendo sus áreas rurales.
• Ciudad más grande de un país.
★ Población o designación de un área metropolitana, incluyendo los suburbios.
C Censo. E Estimado oficial. U Estimado no oficial.

▲ Population d'une municipalité, d'une commune ou d'un district, zone rurale incluse.
• Ville la plus peuplée du pays.
★ Population de l'agglomération (ou nom de la zone métropolitaine englobante).
C Recensement. E Estimation officielle. U Estimation non officielle.

▲ População de um município, comuna ou distrito, inclusive as respectivas áreas rurais.
• Maior cidade de um país.
★ População ou indicação de uma área metropolitana.
C Censo. E Estimativa oficial. U Estimativa não oficial.

Fuzhou, Jiangxi prov. (▲171,800) (1986E)	106,700
Gaixian (1985E)	67,587
Ganhe (1985E)	48,128
Ganzhou (▲346,000) (1986E)	191,600
Gaoqing (Tianzhen) (1982C)	70,411
Gaoyou (1985E)	57,844
Gejiu (Kokiu) (▲341,700) (1986E)	193,600
Golmud (1986E)	60,300
Gongchangling (1982C)	49,281
Guanghua (▲420,000) (1986E)	104,400
Guangyuan (▲805,500) (1986E)	162,200
Guangzhou (Canton) (▲3,420,000)	3,100,000
Guanxian, Shandong prov. (1982C)	49,782
Guanxian, Sichuan prov. (1985E)	65,039
Guilin (Kweilin) (▲457,500) (1986E)	324,200
Guixian (1985E)	61,970
Guiyang (Kweiyang) (▲1,430,000)	1,030,000
Haicheng (▲984,800) (1986E)	210,700
Haifeng (1985E)	50,401
Haikou (▲289,600) (1986E)	209,200
Hailar (▲163,549) (1986E)	180,000
Hailin (1985E)	58,909
Hailong (Meihekou) (▲534,200) (1986E)	117,500
Hailun (1985E)	83,448
Haiyang (Dongcun) (1982C)	77,098
Hami (Kumul) (▲270,300) (1986E)	146,400
Hancheng (▲304,200) (1986E)	66,600
Handan (▲1,030,000)	870,000
Hangu (1975U)	100,000
Hangzhou (Hangchow)	1,290,000
Hanzhong (▲415,000) (1986E)	151,700
Harbin	2,710,000
Hebi (▲321,600) (1986E)	158,500
Hechi (▲266,800) (1986E)	74,400
Hechuan (1985E)	65,237
Hefei (▲930,000)	740,000
Hegang (1986E)	588,300
Helong (1985E)	62,665
Hengshui (▲286,500) (1986E)	83,100
Hengyang (▲601,300) (1986E)	419,200
Heshan (▲109,600) (1986E)	42,000
Heze (Caozhou) (▲1,001,500) (1986E)	115,400
Hohhot (▲830,000)	670,000
Hongjiang (▲67,000) (1986E)	54,300
Horqin Youyi Qianqi (Ulan Hot) (▲192,100) (1986E)	129,100
Hotan (▲122,800) (1986E)	71,700
Houma (▲158,500) (1986E)	67,000
Huadian (1985E)	75,183
Huai'an (1985E)	65,673
Huaibei (▲447,200) (1986E)	252,100
Huaide (▲899,400) (1986E)	187,600
Huaihua (▲427,100) (1986E)	102,000
Huainan (▲1,110,000)	700,000
Huaiyin (Wangying) (▲382,500) (1986E)	201,700
Huanan (1985E)	66,596
Huanggang (1982C)	65,961
Huangshi (1986E)	451,900
Huayun (Huarong) (▲313,500) (1986E)	81,000
Huinan (Chaoyang) (1985E)	52,429
Huizhou (▲182,100) (1986E)	117,000
Hulan (1985E)	74,989
Hunjiang (Badaojiang) (▲687,700) (1986E)	442,600
Huzhou (▲964,400) (1986E)	208,500
Jiading (1985E)	60,718
Jiamusi (Kiamusze) (▲557,700) (1986E)	429,800
Ji'an (▲184,300) (1986E)	132,200
Jiangling (1985E)	77,887
Jiangmen (▲231,700) (1986E)	168,800
Jiangyin (1985E)	66,476
Jiangyou (1985E)	72,663
Jian'ou (1985E)	55,180
Jiaohe (1985E)	51,504
Jiaojiang (▲385,200) (1986E)	82,300
Jiaoxian (1985E)	51,869
Jiaozuo (▲509,900) (1986E)	335,400
Jiawang (1975U)	50,000
Jiaxing (▲686,500) (1986E)	210,200
Jiayuguan (▲102,100) (1986E)	73,800
Jiexiu (1985E)	51,300
Jieyang (1985E)	98,531
Jilin (Kirin)	1,200,000
Jinan (Tsinan) (▲2,140,000)	1,546,000
Jinchang (Baijiazui) (▲136,000) (1986E)	90,500
Jincheng (▲612,700) (1986E)	99,900
Jingdezhen (Kingtechen) (▲569,700) (1986E)	304,000
Jingmen (▲946,500) (1986E)	227,000
Jinhua (▲799,900) (1986E)	147,800
Jining, Nei Monggol prov. (1986E)	163,300
Jining, Shandong prov. (▲765,700) (1986E)	222,600
Jinshi (▲219,700) (1986E)	73,700
Jinxi (▲634,300) (1986E)	223,100
Jinxian (1985E)	95,761
Jinzhou (Chinchou) (▲810,000)	710,000
Jishou (▲194,500) (1986E)	59,500
Jishu (1985E)	75,587
Jiujiang (▲382,300) (1986E)	248,500
Jiuquan (Suzhou) (▲269,900) (1986E)	56,300
Jiutai (1985E)	63,021
Jixi (▲820,000)	700,000
Jixian (1985E)	59,725
Juancheng (1982C)	54,110
Junan (Shizilu) (1982C)	90,222
Junxian (▲423,400) (1986E)	97,000
Juxian (1982C)	51,666
Kaifeng (▲629,100) (1986E)	458,800
Kaili (▲342,100) (1986E)	96,600
Kaiping (1985E)	54,145
Kaiyuan (▲342,100) (1986E)	96,600
Kaiyuan (1985E)	85,762
Karamay (▲168,868) (1986E)	185,300
Kashi (▲194,500) (1986E)	146,300
Keshan (1985E)	65,088
Korla (▲219,000) (1986E)	129,400
Kunming (▲1,550,000)	1,310,000
Kunshan (1985E)	44,645
Kuqa (1985E)	63,847
Kuytun (1986E)	60,200
Laiwu (▲1,041,800) (1986E)	143,500
Langxiang (1985E)	64,658
Lanxi (1985E)	53,236
Lanxi (▲606,800) (1986E)	70,500

Lanzhou (Lanchow) (▲1,420,000)	1,297,000
Lechang (1986E)	56,913
Lengshuijiang (▲277,600) (1986E)	101,700
Lengshuitan (▲362,000) (1986E)	60,900
Leshan (▲972,300) (1986E)	307,300
Lhasa (▲107,700) (1986E)	84,400
Lianyungang (Xinpu) (▲459,400) (1986E)	288,000
Liaocheng (▲724,300) (1986E)	119,000
Liaoyang (▲576,900) (1986E)	442,600
Liaoyuan (1986E)	370,400
Liling (▲856,300) (1986E)	107,100
Linfen (▲530,100) (1986E)	157,600
Lingling (▲515,300) (1986E)	72,700
Lingyuan (1985E)	66,825
Linhai (1985E)	52,653
Linhe (▲365,900) (1986E)	99,800
Linkou (1985E)	52,936
Linqing (▲603,000) (1986E)	87,000
Linqu (1982C)	84,196
Linxia (▲150,200) (1986E)	72,900
Linyi (▲1,365,000) (1986E)	190,000
Liuzhou	680,000
Longjiang (1985E)	51,156
Longyan (▲378,500) (1986E)	114,500
Loudi (▲254,300) (1986E)	84,200
Lu'an (▲163,400) (1986E)	122,600
Lufeng (1985E)	53,015
Luohe (▲159,100) (1986E)	102,300
Luoyang (Loyang) (▲1,090,000)	760,000
Luzhou (▲360,300) (1986E)	237,800
Ma'anshan (▲367,000) (1986E)	258,900
Manzhouli (1986E)	116,600
Maoming (▲434,900) (1986E)	118,600
Meixian (▲740,600) (1986E)	169,000
Mengyin (1982C)	70,602
Mianyang, Sichuan prov. (▲848,500) (1986E)	233,900
Minhang (1975U)	60,000
Mishan (1985E)	54,919
Mixian (1982C)	64,776
Mudanjiang	650,000
Nahe (1985E)	49,725
N'aizishen (1985E)	51,982
Nancha (1975U)	50,000
Nanchang (▲1,260,000)	1,090,000
Nanchong (▲238,100) (1986E)	158,000
Nanjing (Nanking)	2,390,000
Nanning (▲1,000,000)	720,000
Nanpiao (1982C)	67,274
Nanping (▲420,800) (1986E)	157,100
Nantong (▲411,000) (1986E)	308,800
Nanyang (▲294,800) (1986E)	199,400
Neihuang (1982C)	56,039
Neijiang (▲298,500) (1986E)	191,100
Ning'an (1985E)	49,334
Ningbo (▲1,050,000)	570,000
Ningyang (1982C)	55,424
Nong'an (1985E)	55,966
Nunjiang (1985E)	59,276
Orogen Zizhiqi (1985E)	48,042
Panshan (▲343,100) (1986E)	248,100
Panshi (1985E)	59,270
Pingdingshan (▲819,900) (1986E)	363,200
Pingliang (▲362,500) (1986E)	85,400
Pingxiang, Jiangxi prov. (▲1,286,700) (1986E)	368,700
Pingyi (1982C)	89,373
Pingyin (1982C)	62,827
Potou (▲456,100) (1986E)	59,000
Puqi (1985E)	65,239
Putian (▲265,400) (1986E)	64,600
Putuo (1985E)	50,962
Puyang (▲1,086,100) (1986E)	131,000
Qian Gorlos (1985E)	79,494
Qingdao (Tsingtao)	1,300,000
Qinggang (1985E)	43,075
Qingjiang, Jiangsu prov. (▲246,617) (1982C)	150,000
Qingjiang, Jiangxi prov. (1985E)	42,698
Qingyuan (1985E)	51,756
Qinhuangdao (Chinwangtao) (▲436,000) (1986E)	307,500
Qinzhou (▲923,400) (1986E)	97,100
Qiqihar (Tsitsihar) (▲1,330,000)	1,180,000
Qitaihe (▲309,900) (1986E)	166,400
Qixia (1982C)	54,158
Qixian (1982C)	53,041
Quanzhou (Chuanchou) (▲436,000) (1986E)	157,000
Qujing (▲758,000) (1986E)	135,000
Quxian (▲704,800) (1986E)	124,000
Raoping (1985E)	54,831
Rizhao (▲970,300) (1986E)	93,300
Rongcheng (1982C)	52,878
Rugao (1985E)	50,643
Rui'an (1985E)	57,993
Sanmenxia (Shanxian) (▲150,000) (1986E)	79,000
Sanming (▲214,300) (1986E)	144,900
• Shanghai (★9,300,000)	7,220,000
Shangqiu (Zhuji) (▲199,400) (1986E)	135,400
Shangrao (▲142,500) (1986E)	113,000
Shangshui (1982C)	50,191
Shantou (Swatow) (▲790,000)	560,000
Shanwei (1985E)	61,234
Shaoguan (1986E)	363,100
Shaowu (▲266,700) (1986E)	81,400
Shaoxing (▲250,900) (1986E)	167,100
Shaoyang (▲465,900) (1986E)	218,600
Shashi (1986E)	253,700
Shenxian (1982C)	50,208
Shenyang (Mukden) (▲4,370,000)	3,910,000
Shenzhen (▲231,900) (1986E)	189,600
Shiguaigou (1975U)	50,000
Shihezi (▲549,300) (1987E)	304,700
Shijiazhuang	1,220,000
Shiyan (▲332,600) (1986E)	227,300
Shizuishan (▲317,400) (1986E)	225,500
Shouguang (1982C)	83,400
Shuangcheng (1985E)	91,163
Shuangliao (1985E)	67,326
Shuangyashan (1986E)	427,300
Shuicheng (▲2,216,500) (1986E)	363,500
Shulan (1986E)	50,582
Shunde (1985E)	50,262
Siping (▲357,800) (1986E)	280,100
Sishui (1982C)	82,990
Songjiang (1985E)	71,864
Songjianghe (1985E)	53,023
Suifenhe (▲21,700) (1986E)	13,900
Suihua (▲732,100) (1986E)	200,400
Suileng (1985E)	68,399
Suining (▲1,174,900) (1986E)	118,500
Suixian (▲1,281,600) (1986E)	187,700

Suqian (1985E)	50,742
Suxian (▲218,600) (1986E)	123,300
Suzhou (Soochow)	740,000
Tai'an (▲1,325,400) (1986E)	215,900
Taiyuan (▲1,980,000)	1,700,000
Taizhou (▲210,800) (1987E)	143,200
Tancheng (1982C)	61,857
Tangshan (▲1,440,000)	1,080,000
Tao'an (1985E)	76,269
Tengxian (1985E)	53,254
Tianjin (Tientsin) (▲5,540,000)	4,950,000
Tianshui (▲953,200) (1986E)	209,500
Tiefa (▲146,367) (1982C)	60,000
Tieli (1985E)	102,527
Tieling (▲454,100) (1986E)	326,100
Tongchuan (▲393,200) (1986E)	268,900
Tonghua (▲367,400) (1986E)	290,200
Tongliao (▲253,100) (1986E)	190,100
Tongling (▲216,400) (1986E)	182,900
Tongren (1985E)	50,307
Tongxian (1985E)	97,168
Tumen (▲99,700) (1986E)	77,600
Tunxi (▲104,500) (1986E)	61,800
Turpan (▲196,800) (1986E)	52,300
Ürümqi	1,060,000
Wangkui (1985E)	52,021
Wangqing (1985E)	61,237
Wanxian (▲280,800) (1986E)	138,700
Weifang (▲1,042,200) (1986E)	312,500
Weihai (▲220,800) (1986E)	83,000
Weinan (▲699,400) (1986E)	111,300
Weishan (Xiazhen) (1982C)	57,932
Weixian (Hanting) (1982C)	50,180
Wenzhou (▲530,600) (1986E)	372,200
Wuchang (1985E)	64,403
Wuhai (1986E)	266,000
Wuhan	3,570,000
Wuhu (▲502,200) (1986E)	396,000
Wulian (Hongning) (1982C)	51,718
Wusong (1982C)	64,017
Wuwei (Liangzhou) (▲804,000) (1986E)	115,500
Wuxi (Wuhsi)	880,000
Wuzhong (▲402,400) (1986E)	48,600
Wuzhou (Wuchow) (▲261,500) (1986E)	194,800
Xiaguan (▲395,800) (1986E)	112,100
Xiamen (Amoy) (▲546,400) (1986E)	343,700
Xi'an (Sian) (▲2,580,000)	2,210,000
Xiangfan (▲421,200) (1986E)	314,900
Xiangtan (▲511,100) (1986E)	389,500
Xianning (▲402,200) (1986E)	122,200
Xianyang (▲641,800) (1986E)	285,900
Xiaogan (▲1,204,400) (1986E)	125,500
Xiaoshan (1985E)	63,074
Xichang (▲161,000) (1986E)	105,000
Xinghua (1985E)	75,573
Xinglongzhen (1982C)	52,961
Xingtai (▲350,800) (1986E)	265,600
Xinhui (1985E)	77,381
Xining (Sining)	620,000
Xinmin (1985E)	47,900
Xintai (▲1,157,300) (1986E)	171,400
Xinwen (Suncun) (1975U)	50,000
Xinxian (▲398,600) (1986E)	74,200
Xinxiang (▲540,500) (1986E)	411,000
Xinyang (▲234,200) (1986E)	169,100
Xinyu (▲610,600) (1986E)	140,200
Xuancheng (1985E)	52,387
Xuanhua (1975U)	140,000
Xuanwei (1982C)	70,081
Xuchang (▲247,200) (1986E)	167,800
Xuguit Qi (Yakeshi) (1986E)	390,000
Xuzhou (Süchow)	860,000
Yaan (▲277,600) (1986E)	89,200
Yan'an (▲259,800) (1986E)	86,700
Yancheng (▲1,251,400) (1986E)	258,400
Yangcheng (1982C)	57,255
Yangjiang (1986E)	91,433
Yangquan (▲478,900) (1986E)	295,100
Yangzhou (▲417,300) (1986E)	321,500
Yanji (▲216,900) (1986E)	175,000
Yanji (Longjing) (1985E)	55,035
Yanling (1982C)	52,679
Yantai (Chefoo) (▲717,300) (1986E)	327,000
Yanzhou (1985E)	48,972
Yaxian (Sanya) (▲321,700) (1986E)	70,500
Yi'an (1986E)	54,253
Yibin (Ipin) (▲636,500) (1986E)	218,800
Yichang (Ichang) (1986E)	410,500
Yichuan (1982C)	58,914
Yichun, Heilongjiang prov.	840,000
Yichun, Jiangxi prov. (▲770,200) (1986E)	132,600
Yidu (1985E)	54,838
Yilan (1985E)	50,436
Yima (▲84,800) (1986E)	53,700
Yinan (Jiehu) (1982C)	67,803
Yinchuan (▲396,900) (1986E)	268,200
Yingchengzi (1985E)	59,072
Yingkou (▲480,000) (1986E)	366,900
Yingtan (▲116,200) (1986E)	64,500
Yining (Kuldja) (▲232,000) (1986E)	153,200
Yiyang (▲365,000) (1986E)	155,300
Yiyuan (Nanma) (1982C)	53,800
Yong'an (▲269,000) (1986E)	105,100
Yongchuan (1985E)	70,444
Yuci (▲420,700) (1986E)	171,000
Yueyang (▲411,300) (1986E)	239,500
Yulin, Guangxi Zhuangzu prov. (▲1,228,800) (1986E)	115,600
Yulin, Shaanxi prov. (1985E)	51,610
Yumen (Laojunmiao) (▲160,100) (1986E)	84,300
Yuncheng, Shandong prov. (1982C)	54,262
Yuncheng, Shansi prov. (▲434,900) (1986E)	87,000
Yunyang (1982C)	54,903
Yushu (1985E)	57,222
Yuyao (▲772,700) (1986E)	169,700
Zaozhuang (▲1,592,000) (1986E)	292,200
Zhangjiakou (Kalgan) (▲640,000)	500,000
Zhangye (▲394,200) (1986E)	73,000
Zhangzhou (Longxi) (▲310,400) (1986E)	159,400
Zhanjiang (▲920,900) (1986E)	335,500
Zhaodong (1985E)	99,836
Zhaoqing (Gaoyao) (▲187,600) (1986E)	145,700
Zhaotong (▲546,600) (1986E)	77,500
Zhaoyuan (1985E)	42,426
Zhaoyuan (1982C)	56,389
Zhengzhou (Chengchow) (▲1,580,000)	1,150,000

Zhenjiang (1986E)	412,400
Zhongshan (Shiqizhen) (▲1,059,700) (1986E)	238,700
Zhoucun (1975U)	50,000
Zhoukouzhen (▲220,400) (1986E)	110,500
Zhuhai (▲155,000) (1986E)	88,800
Zhumadian (▲149,500) (1986E)	99,400
Zhuoxian (1985E)	54,523
Zhuzhou (Chuchow) (▲499,600) (1986E)	344,800
Zibo (Zhangdian) (▲2,370,000)	840,000
Zigong (Tzukung) (▲909,300) (1986E)	361,700
Zixing (▲334,300) (1986E)	97,100
Ziyang (1985E)	57,349
Zouping (1982C)	49,274
Zouxian (1985E)	61,578
Zunyi (▲347,600) (1986E)	236,600

COLOMBIA

1985 C	27,867,326
Armenia	187,130
Barrancabermeja	137,406
Barranquilla (★1,140,000)	899,781
Bello (★Medellín)	212,861
Bucaramanga (★550,000)	352,326
Buenaventura	160,342
Buga	82,992
Cali (★1,400,000)	1,350,565
Cartagena	531,426
Cartago	97,791
Ciénaga	56,860
Cúcuta (★445,000)	379,478
Dos Quebradas (★Pereira)	101,480
Duitama	56,390
Envigado (★Medellín)	91,391
Florencia	66,430
Floridablanca (★Bucaramanga)	143,824
Girardot	70,078
Ibagué	292,965
Itagüí (★Medellín)	137,623
Magangué	49,160
Maicao	46,033
Malambo (★Barranquilla)	52,584
Manizales (★330,000)	299,352
Medellín (★2,095,000)	1,468,089
Montería	157,466
Neiva	194,556
Ocaña	51,443
Palmira	175,186
Pasto	197,407
Pereira (★390,000)	233,271
Popayán	141,964
• SANTA FE DE BOGOTÁ (★4,260,000)	3,982,941
Santa Marta	177,922
Sincelejo	120,537
Soacha (★Santa Fe de Bogotá)	109,051
Sogamoso	64,437
Soledad (★Barranquilla)	165,791
Tuluá	99,721
Tunja	93,792
Valledupar	142,771
Villa Rosario (★Cúcuta)	63,615
Villavicencio	178,685
Zipaquirá	45,676

COMOROS / Al-Qumur / Comores

1990 E	452,742
• MORONI	23,432

CONGO

1989 C	2,188,367
• BRAZZAVILLE	693,712
Dolisie	57,991
Pointe-Noire	350,139

COOK ISLANDS

1986 C	18,155
• AVARUA	9,678

COSTA RICA

1988 E	2,851,000
Alajuela (▲147,400)	33,800
Desamparados (★San José) (1984C)	43,352
Puerto Limón (▲62,600)	40,400
Puntarenas (▲86,400)	34,100
• SAN JOSÉ (★1,355,000)	278,600

CÔTE D'IVOIRE (IVORY COAST)

1988 C	10,815,694
Abengourou	59,114
• ABIDJAN	1,929,079
Agboville	46,045
Bouaké	329,850
Daloa	121,842
Divo	72,350
Gagnoa	85,563
Korhogo	109,445
Man	89,575
San Pédro	70,611
YAMOUSSOUKRO	106,786

CROATIA / Hrvatska

1987 E	4,673,517
Osijek (▲162,490)	106,800
Rijeka (▲199,282)	166,400
Split	191,074
• ZAGREB	697,925

CUBA

1991 E	10,694,465
Bayamo	139,061
Camagüey	286,404
Cárdenas (▲84,590)	69,800
Ciego de Ávila	101,620
Cienfuegos	136,233
Florida	51,442
Guantánamo	215,864
Holguín	236,967
• LA HABANA (HAVANA) (★2,210,000)	2,119,059
Las Tunas	126,678
Manzanillo	108,668
Matanzas	119,510
Morón	49,793
Palma Soriano (▲124,543)	66,600
Pinar del Río	136,303
Sancti Spíritus	97,522
Santa Clara	203,753
Santiago de Cuba	434,541

▲ Population of an entire municipality, commune, or district, including rural area.
• Largest city in country.
★ Population or designation of the metropolitan area, including suburbs.
C Census. **E** Official estimate. **U** Unofficial estimate.

▲ Bevölkerung eines ganzen städtischen Verwaltungsgebietes, eines Kommunalbezirkes oder eines Distrikts, einschliesslich ländlicher Gebiete.
• Grösste Stadt des Landes.
★ Bevölkerung oder Bezeichnung der Stadtregion einschliesslich Vororte.
C Volkszählung. **E** Offizielle Schätzung. **U** Inoffizielle Schätzung.

CYPRUS / Kıbrıs / Kípros

1982 C	512,097
Lárnax (Larnaca) (★48,330)	35,823
Lemesós (Limassol) (★107,161)	74,782
• NICOSIA (LEVKOSÍA) (★185,000)	48,221

CYPRUS, NORTH / Kuzey Kıbrıs

1985 E	160,287
Gazimağusa (Famagusta)	19,428
• NICOSIA (LEFKOŞA)	37,400

CZECH REPUBLIC / Česká Republika

1991 C	10,298,731
Brno (★450,000)	387,986
Česká Lípa	39,667
České Budějovice (★114,000)	97,283
Český Těšín (★Třinec)	28,737
Cheb	31,847
Chomutov (★80,000)	53,191
Děčín (★72,000)	55,112
Frýdek-Místek (★Ostrava)	65,067
Havířov (★Ostrava)	86,267
Hodonín	30,736
Hradec Králové (★113,000)	99,889
Jablonec nad Nisou (★Liberec)	45,918
Jihlava	52,271
Karlovy Vary (Carlsbad)	56,291
Karviná (★Ostrava)	68,368
Kladno (★88,500)	71,735
Kolín	31,582
Kroměříž (★38,500)	28,962
Liberec (★175,000)	101,934
Litvínov (★Most)	29,085
Mladá Boleslav	44,471
Most (★135,000)	70,675
Nový Jičín	29,028
Olomouc (★126,000)	105,690
Opava (★78,000)	63,601
Orlová (★Ostrava)	36,307
Ostrava (★760,000)	327,553
Pardubice	94,857
Písek	29,542
Plzeň (★210,000)	173,129
• PRAHA (★1,328,000)	1,212,010
Přerov	51,341
Příbram	36,869
Prostějov	50,102
Šumperk	30,446
Tábor (★55,500)	36,329
Teplice (★94,000)	53,039
Třebíč	39,348
Třinec (★87,500)	45,189
Trutnov	31,957
Ústí nad Labem (★115,000)	99,739
Valašské Meziříčí	28,153
Vsetín	31,584
Zlín (★124,000)	84,634
Znojmo	39,910

DENMARK / Danmark

1992 E	5,162,126
Ålborg (▲156,614)	115,200
Århus (▲267,873)	207,300
Ballerup (★København)	45,476
Esbjerg (▲81,843)	72,200
Fredericia (▲46,617)	28,700
Frederiksberg (★København)	86,372
Gentofte (★København)	66,077
Gladsakse (★København)	60,604
Helsingør (Elsinore) (★København)	56,794
Horsens (▲55,123)	47,200
Hvidovre (★København)	48,754
• KØBENHAVN (★1,670,000)	464,566
Kolding (▲57,982)	42,700
Kongens Lyngby (★København)	49,612
Odense (▲179,487)	142,800
Randers	61,440
Rønne	15,236
Roskilde (▲50,158) (★København)	40,700
Vejle (▲51,845)	45,700

DJIBOUTI

1991 E	508,541
• DJIBOUTI	329,337

DOMINICA

1984 E	77,000
• ROSEAU	9,348

DOMINICAN REPUBLIC / República Dominicana

1990 E	7,169,800
Barahona	80,400
La Romana	147,800
La Vega	192,300
Mao	58,400
Puerto Plata	94,900
San Cristóbal	137,500
San Francisco de Macorís	165,300
San Juan de la Maguana	129,700
San Pedro de Macorís	144,300
Santiago de los Caballeros	489,500
• SANTO DOMINGO	2,411,900

ECUADOR

1990 C	9,648,189
Ambato	124,166
Babahoyo	50,285
Cuenca	194,981
Eloy Alfaro (★Guayaquil)	82,359
Esmeraldas	98,558
• Guayaquil	1,508,444
Ibarra	80,991
La Libertad	50,108
Loja	94,305
Machala	144,197
Manta	125,505
Milagro	93,637
Portoviejo	132,937
Quevedo	86,910
QUITO (★1,300,000)	1,100,847
Riobamba	94,505
Santo Domingo de los Colorados	114,422

EGYPT / Mişr

1986 C	48,205,049
Abnūb	48,302
Abū Kabīr	68,394
Abū Tīj	48,518
Akhmīm	70,494
Al-'Arīsh	67,337
Al-Fayyūm	213,070
Al-Hawāmidīyah (★Al-Qāhirah)	73,298
Al-Iskandarīyah (Alexandria) (★3,350,000)	2,926,859
Al-Ismā'īlīyah (★235,000)	158,045
Al-Jīzah (Giza) (★Al-Qāhirah)	1,883,189
Al-Maḥallah al-Kubrā	306,509
Al-Manṣūrah (★375,000)	317,508
Al-Manzilah	54,918
Al-Maṭarīyah	73,315
Al-Minyā	179,060
• AL-QĀHIRAH (CAIRO) (★9,300,000)	6,068,695
Al-Qanāṭir al-Khayrīyah	49,361
Al-Uqṣur (Luxor)	126,160
Armant	54,618
Ashmūn	54,450
As-Sinbillāwayn	60,159
As-Suways (Suez)	327,717
Aswān	190,579
Asyūṭ	272,986
Az-Zaqāzīq	244,354
Bahtīm (★Al-Qāhirah)	275,807
Banhā	115,701
Banī Mazār	47,982
Banī Suwayf	152,476
Bilbays	96,511
Bilqās Qism Awwal	73,040
Biyalā	47,702
Būlāq ad-Dakrūr (★Al-Qāhirah)	148,787
Būr Sa'īd (Port Said)	401,172
Būsh	54,655
Damanhūr	188,939
Dikirnis	48,616
Disūq	78,316
Dumyāṭ (Damietta)	89,069
Fāqūs	48,365
Hawsh 'Īsā	53,619
Idkū	70,724
Jirjā	71,564
Kafr ad-Dawwār (★Al-Iskandarīyah)	198,244
Kafr ash-Shaykh	103,301
Kafr az-Zayyāt	58,276
Kawm Umbū	52,506
Maghāghah	50,916
Mallawī	98,632
Manfalūṭ	52,281
Marsā Maṭrūḥ	43,157
Minūf	69,673
Mīt Ghamr (★100,000)	91,927
Qalyūb	84,413
Qinā	119,917
Rashīd (Rosetta)	51,789
Samālūṭ	62,404
Sāqiyat Makkī	51,062
Sawhāj	132,649
Shibīn al-Kawm	132,209
Shubrā al-Khaymah (★Al-Qāhirah)	714,594
Sinnūris	55,187
Ṭahṭā	58,457
Ṭalkhā (★Al-Manṣūrah)	54,923
Ṭanṭā	336,517
Ṭimā	46,824
Warrāq al-'Arab (★Al-Qāhirah)	127,108
Ziftā (★Mīt Ghamr)	69,253

EL SALVADOR

1985 E	5,337,896
Delgado (★San Salvador)	67,684
Mejicanos (★San Salvador)	91,465
Nueva San Salvador (★San Salvador)	53,688
San Miguel	88,520
• SAN SALVADOR (★920,000)	462,652
Santa Ana	137,879
Soyapango (★San Salvador)	60,000

EQUATORIAL GUINEA / Guinea Ecuatorial

1983 C	300,000
• MALABO	31,630

ERITREA

1991 E	2,951,000
• ASMERA (1990E)	358,100
Mitsiwa (1986E)	16,576

ESTONIA / Eesti

1991 E	1,581,800
Kohtla-Järve	74,700
Narva	83,000
Pärnu	54,200
• TALLINN	481,500
Tartu	115,300

ETHIOPIA / Ityopiya

1986 E	44,927,000
• ADIS ABEBA (★1,990,000) (1990E)	1,912,500
Akaki Beseka (★Adis Abeba)	58,977
Awasa	39,693
Bahir Dar	59,951
Debre Zeyit	55,706
Dese	77,459
Dire Dawa (1990E)	127,400
Gonder	88,344
Harer	67,977
Jima	67,470
Mekele	66,640
Nazret	83,091

FAEROE ISLANDS / Føroyar

1990 E	47,946
• TÓRSHAVN	14,767

FALKLAND ISLANDS

1991 C	2,050
• STANLEY	1,557

FIJI

1986 C	715,375
Lautoka (★39,057)	28,728
• SUVA (★141,273)	69,665

FINLAND / Suomi

1992 E	5,029,002
Espoo (Esbo) (★Helsinki)	175,670
• HELSINKI (HELSINGFORS) (★1,040,000)	497,542
Joensuu	48,182
Jyväskylä (★93,000) (1990E)	67,026
Kotka	56,515
Kouvola (★53,821)	32,066
Kuopio	81,593
Lahti (★108,000)	93,414
Lappeenranta	55,358
Oulu (★121,000) (1990E)	102,280
Pori	76,432
Tampere (★241,000)	173,797
Turku (Åbo) (★228,000)	159,403
Vaasa (Vasa)	53,764
Vantaa (Vanda) (★Helsinki)	157,274

FRANCE

1990 C	56,614,493
Aix-en-Provence (★Marseille)	123,842
Ajaccio	58,315
Albi (★54,359)	46,579
Alès (★76,856)	41,037
Amiens (★156,120)	131,872
Angers (★208,282)	141,404
Angoulême (★102,908)	42,876
Annecy (★126,729)	49,644
Antibes (★Cannes)	63,248
Antony (★Paris)	57,771
Argenteuil (★Paris)	93,096
Arles (★54,309)	39,000
Armentières (★57,738)	25,219
Arras (★79,607)	38,983
Asnières [-sur-Seine] (★Paris)	71,850
Aubervilliers (★Paris)	67,557
Aulnay-sous-Bois (★Paris)	82,314
Avignon (★181,136)	86,939
Bastia (★52,446)	37,845
Bayonne (★164,378)	40,051
Beauvais (★57,704)	54,190
Belfort (★77,844)	50,125
Besançon (★122,623)	113,828
Béthune (★261,535)	24,556
Béziers (★76,304)	70,996
Blois (★65,132)	49,318
Bondy (★Paris)	46,676
Bordeaux (★760,000)	210,336
Boulogne-Billancourt (★Paris)	101,743
Boulogne-sur-Mer (★91,249)	43,678
Bourg-en-Bresse (★55,784)	40,972
Bourges (★94,731)	75,609
Brest (★201,480)	147,956
Brive-la-Gaillarde (★64,379)	49,765
Bruay-en-Artois (★Béthune)	24,927
Caen (★191,490)	112,846
Calais (★101,768)	75,309
Cambrai (★48,133)	33,092
Cannes (★335,647)	68,676
Carcassonne	43,470
Castres (★46,482)	44,812
Châlons-sur-Marne (★61,452)	48,423
Chalon-sur-Saône (★77,764)	54,575
Chambéry (★103,283)	54,120
Champigny-sur-Marne (★Paris)	79,486
Charleville-Mézières (★67,213)	57,008
Chartres (★85,933)	39,595
Châteauroux (★67,090)	50,969
Châtellerault (★36,298)	34,678
Cherbourg (★92,045)	27,121
Cholet	55,132
Clamart (★Paris)	47,227
Clermont-Ferrand (★254,416)	136,181
Clichy (★Paris)	48,030
Cognac (★27,468)	19,528
Colmar (★83,816)	63,498
Colombes (★Paris)	78,513
Compiègne (★67,057)	41,896
Courbevoie (★Paris)	65,389
Creil (★97,119)	31,956
Créteil (★Paris)	82,088
Denain (★Valenciennes)	19,544
Dieppe (★43,348)	35,894
Dijon (★230,451)	146,703
Douai (★199,562)	42,175
Drancy (★Paris)	60,707
Dunkerque (★190,879)	70,331
Elbeuf (★53,886)	16,604
Épinal (★62,140)	36,732
Épinay-sur-Seine (★Paris)	48,762
Évreux (★57,968)	49,103
Évry (★Paris)	45,531
Fontainebleau (★35,706)	15,714
Fontenay-sous-Bois (★Paris)	51,868
Forbach (★98,758)	27,076
Fréjus (★73,967)	41,486
Gennevilliers (★Paris)	44,818
Grenoble (★404,733)	150,758
Hagondange (★112,061)	8,222
Hayange (★Thionville)	15,638
Issy-les-Moulineaux (★Paris)	46,127
Ivry-sur-Seine (★Paris)	53,619
La Rochelle (★100,264)	71,094
La Seyne-sur-Mer (★Toulon)	59,968
Laval (★56,855)	50,473
Le Blanc-Mesnil (★Paris)	46,956
Le Havre (★253,627)	195,854
Le Mans (★189,107)	145,502
Lens (★323,174)	35,017
Le Puy (★43,499)	21,743
Levallois-Perret (★Paris)	47,548
Lille (★1,050,000)	172,142
Limoges (★170,065)	133,464
Longwy (★41,300)	15,439
Lorient (★115,488)	59,271
Lourdes	16,300
Lyon (★1,335,000)	415,487
Mâcon (★46,714)	37,275
Maisons-Alfort (★Paris)	53,375
Mantes-la-Jolie (★Paris)	45,087
Marseille (★1,225,000)	800,550
Martigues (★Marseille)	31,300
Maubeuge (★102,772)	34,989
Meaux (★63,006)	48,305
Melun (★107,705)	35,319
Menton (★Monaco, Monaco)	29,141
Mérignac (★Bordeaux)	57,273
Metz (★193,117)	119,594
Meudon (★Paris)	45,339
Montargis (★52,804)	15,020
Montbéliard (★117,510)	29,005
Montceau-les-Mines (★47,283)	22,999
Montluçon (★63,018)	44,248
Montpellier (★248,303)	207,996
Montreuil-sous-Bois (★Paris)	94,754
Moulins (★41,715)	22,799
Moyeuvre-Grande (★Hagondange)	9,203
Mulhouse (Mülhausen) (★223,856)	108,357
Nancy (★329,447)	99,351
Nanterre (★Paris)	84,565
Nantes (★496,078)	244,995
Neuilly-sur-Seine (★Paris)	61,768
Nevers (★58,915)	41,968
Nice (★516,740)	342,439
Nîmes (★138,527)	128,471
Niort (★65,792)	57,012
Noisy-le-Grand (★Paris)	54,032
Noisy-le-Sec (★Paris)	36,309
Orléans (★243,153)	105,111
Orly (★Paris)	21,646
Pantin (★Paris)	47,303
• PARIS (★10,275,000)	2,152,423
Pau (★144,674)	82,157
Périgueux (★63,322)	30,280
Perpignan (★157,873)	105,983
Pessac (★Bordeaux)	51,055
Poissy (★Paris)	36,745
Poitiers (★107,625)	78,894
Quimper (★65,954)	59,437
Reims (★206,437)	180,620
Rennes (★245,065)	197,536
Roanne (★77,160)	41,756
Rodez (★39,017)	24,701
Romans-sur-Isère (★49,212)	32,734
Roubaix (★Lille)	97,746
Rouen (★380,161)	102,723
Rueil-Malmaison (★Paris)	66,401
Saint-Brieuc (★83,861)	44,752
Saint-Chamond (★81,795)	38,878
Saint-Denis (★Paris)	89,988
Saint-Dizier (★40,097)	33,552
Saint-Étienne (★313,338)	199,396
Saint-Lô (★2,760)	21,546
Saint-Malo	48,057
Saint-Maur-des-Fossés (★Paris)	77,206
Saint-Nazaire (★131,511)	64,812
Saint-Ouen (★Paris)	42,343
Saint-Quentin (★71,113)	60,644
Sarcelles (★Paris)	56,833
Sartrouville (★Paris)	50,329
Sevran	48,478
Soissons (★46,168)	29,829
Strasbourg (★415,000)	252,338
Suresnes (★Paris)	35,998
Tarbes (★77,787)	47,566
Thionville (★132,413)	39,712
Toulon (★437,553)	167,619
Toulouse (★650,000)	358,688
Tourcoing (★Lille)	93,765
Tours (★282,152)	129,509
Troyes (★122,763)	59,255
Valence (★107,965)	63,437
Valenciennes (★338,392)	38,441
Vénissieux (★Lyon)	60,444
Verdun-sur-Meuse (★26,711)	20,753
Versailles (★Paris)	87,789
Vichy (★61,566)	27,714
Villefranche (★55,249)	29,542
Villejuif (★Paris)	48,405
Villeneuve-d'Ascq (★Lille)	65,320
Villeurbanne (★Lyon)	116,872
Vitry-sur-Seine (★Paris)	82,400
Wattrelos (★Lille)	43,675

FRENCH GUIANA / Guyane française

1982 C	73,022
• CAYENNE	38,091

FRENCH POLYNESIA / Polynésie française

1988 C	188,814
• PAPEETE (★80,000)	23,555

GABON

1985 E	1,312,000
Franceville	58,800
Lambaréné	49,500
• LIBREVILLE	235,700
Port Gentil	124,400

GAMBIA

1983 C	687,817
• BANJUL (★160,000)	44,188
Brikama	19,624

GAZA STRIP

1992 E	667,000
Ghazzah (1986E)	235,000
Khān Yūnis (1986E)	98,370
Rafah (1967C)	49,812

GEORGIA / Sakartvelo

1991 E	5,464,200
Batumi	137,500
Gori	70,100
Kutaisi	238,200
Poti	51,100
Rustavi (★Tbilisi)	161,900
Suchumi	120,000
• TBILISI (★1,460,000)	1,279,000
Zugdidi	50,600

GERMANY / Deutschland

1991 E	79,753,227
Aachen (★540,000)	241,861
Aalen (★78,000)	64,781
Ahlen	54,169
Albstadt	49,021
Alsdorf (★Aachen)	46,935
Altenburg	48,926
Amberg	43,111
Arnsberg	75,864
Aschaffenburg (★150,000)	64,098
Augsburg (★420,000)	256,877
Baden-Baden	51,849
Bad Homburg (★Frankfurt am Main)	51,820
Bad Oeynhausen	46,475
Bad Salzuflen (★Herford)	53,771
Bamberg (★122,000)	70,521
Bautzen	48,588
Bayreuth (★87,000)	72,345
Bergheim (★Köln)	58,146
Bergisch Gladbach (★Köln)	104,037
Bergkamen (★Essen)	49,761
BERLIN (★4,150,000)	3,433,695
Bielefeld (★535,000)	319,037
Bitterfeld (★105,000)	17,988
Bocholt	68,936
Bochum (★Essen)	396,486
BONN (★575,000)	292,234
Bottrop (★Essen)	118,936
Brandenburg	89,889
Braunschweig (★320,000)	258,833
Bremen (★790,000)	551,219
Bremerhaven (★180,000)	130,446
Castrop-Rauxel (★Essen)	79,037
Celle	72,260

▲ Población de un municipio, comuna o distrito entero, incluyendo sus áreas rurales.
• Ciudad más grande de un país.
★ Población o designación de un área metropolitana, incluyendo los suburbios.
C Censo. **E** Estimado oficial. **U** Estimado no oficial.

▲ Population d'une municipalité, d'une commune ou d'un district, zone rurale incluse.
• Ville la plus peuplée du pays.
★ Population de l'agglomération (ou nom de la zone métropolitaine englobante).
C Recensement. **E** Estimation officielle. **U** Estimation non officielle.

▲ População de um municipio, comuna ou distrito, inclusive as respectivas áreas rurais.
• Maior cidade de um país.
★ População ou indicação de uma área metropolitana.
C Censo. **E** Estimativa oficial. **U** Estimativa não oficial.

Chemnitz (★500,000)	294,244
Coburg	44,246
Cottbus	125,891
Cuxhaven	56,090
Dachau (★München)	35,387
Darmstadt (★315,000)	138,920
Delmenhorst (★Bremen)	75,154
Dessau (★138,000)	96,754
Detmold	70,074
Dinslaken (★Essen)	65,313
Dormagen (★Köln)	58,260
Dorsten (★Essen)	78,035
Dortmund (★Essen)	599,055
Dresden (★870,000)	490,571
Duisburg (★Essen)	535,447
Düren (★108,000)	86,508
Düsseldorf (★1,225,000)	575,794
Eberswalde	52,586
Eisenach	45,220
Eisenhüttenstadt	50,216
Emden	50,735
Erfurt	208,989
Erlangen (★Nürnberg)	102,440
Eschweiler (★Aachen)	54,675
• Essen (★5,050,000)	626,973
Esslingen (★Stuttgart)	91,685
Euskirchen	49,654
Flensburg (★98,000)	86,977
Frankenthal (★Mannheim)	46,966
Frankfurt am Main (★1,935,000)	644,865
Frankfurt an der Oder	86,131
Freiberg	48,609
Freiburg (★235,000)	191,029
Friedrichshafen	54,129
Fulda (★74,000)	56,289
Fürth (★Nürnberg)	103,362
Garbsen (★Hannover)	60,776
Garmisch-Partenkirchen	26,837
Gelsenkirchen (★Essen)	293,714
Gera	129,037
Giessen (★155,000)	74,497
Gladbeck (★Essen)	80,267
Göppingen (★155,000)	54,957
Görlitz	72,237
Goslar (★72,000)	46,251
Gotha	54,525
Göttingen	121,831
Greifswald	66,251
Grevenbroich (★Düsseldorf)	60,835
Gummersbach	50,965
Gütersloh (★Bielefeld)	86,807
Hagen (★Essen)	214,449
Halberstadt	45,364
Halle (★455,000)	310,234
Hamburg (★2,385,000)	1,652,363
Hameln (★65,000)	58,539
Hamm	179,639
Hanau (★Frankfurt am Main)	86,913
Hannover (★1,000,000)	513,010
Hattingen (★Essen)	58,241
Heidelberg (★Mannheim)	136,796
Heidenheim (★80,000)	50,532
Heilbronn (★245,000)	115,843
Herford (★120,000)	63,893
Herne (★Essen)	178,132
Herten (★Essen)	69,245
Hilden (★Düsseldorf)	54,782
Hildesheim (★126,000)	105,291
Hof	52,913
Hoyerswerda	64,888
Hürth (★Köln)	50,808
Ingolstadt (★145,000)	105,489
Iserlohn	96,314
Jena	102,518
Kaiserslautern (★130,000)	99,351
Kamen (★Essen)	46,160
Karlsruhe (★505,000)	275,061
Kassel (★375,000)	194,268
Kempten (Allgäu)	61,906
Kerpen (★Köln)	57,337
Kiel (★325,000)	245,567
Kleve	45,963
Koblenz (★170,000)	108,733
Köln (★1,810,000)	953,551
Konstanz	75,089
Krefeld (★Essen)	244,020
Landshut	59,066
Langenfeld (★Düsseldorf)	53,455
Langenhagen (★Hannover)	47,432
Leipzig (★720,000)	511,079
Leverkusen (★Köln)	160,919
Lingen	49,137
Lippstadt	62,345
Lübeck (★250,000)	214,758
Lüdenscheid	79,401
Ludwigsburg (★Stuttgart)	82,343
Ludwigshafen (★Mannheim)	162,173
Lüneburg	61,870
Lünen (★Essen)	87,845
Magdeburg (★400,000)	278,807
Mainz (★Wiesbaden)	179,486
Mannheim (★1,525,000)	310,411
Marburg	74,146
Marl (★Essen)	91,467
Meerbusch (★Düsseldorf)	52,104
Menden	56,527
Merseburg (★Halle)	42,905
Minden (★121,000)	78,145
Moers (★Essen)	104,595
Mönchengladbach (★410,000)	259,436
Mülheim an der Ruhr (★Essen)	177,681
München (Munich) (★1,900,000)	1,229,026
Münster	259,438
Neubrandenburg	89,284
Neumünster	80,743
Neunkirchen/Saar (★125,000)	51,536
Neuss (★Düsseldorf)	147,019
Neustadt an der Weinstrasse	51,988
Neu-Ulm (★Ulm)	46,264
Neuwied (★157,000)	62,075
Norderstedt (★Hamburg)	68,450
Nordhausen	46,422
Nordhorn	49,359
Nürnberg (★1,065,000)	493,692
Oberhausen (★Essen)	223,840
Offenbach (★Frankfurt am Main)	114,992
Offenburg	52,964
Oldenburg	143,131
Osnabrück (★270,000)	163,168
Paderborn	120,680
Passau	50,328
Peine	46,654
Pforzheim (★230,000)	112,944
Pirmasens	47,680
Pirna (★Dresden)	41,798
Plauen	71,774
Potsdam (★Berlin)	139,794
Ratingen (★Düsseldorf)	91,007
Ravensburg (★75,000)	45,650
Recklinghausen (★Essen)	125,060
Regensburg (★180,000)	121,691
Remscheid (★Wuppertal)	123,155
Reutlingen (★170,000)	103,687
Rheine	70,452
Riesa	45,440
Rosenheim	56,340
Rostock	248,088
Rüsselsheim (★Wiesbaden)	59,430
Saarbrücken (★365,000)	191,694
Saarlouis (★115,000)	38,160
Salzgitter	114,355
Sankt Augustin (★Bonn)	51,886
Schwäbisch Gmünd	60,081
Schwedt	50,633
Schweinfurt (★105,000)	54,483
Schwerin	127,447
Schwerte (★Essen)	50,696
Siegburg (★175,000)	35,441
Siegen (★192,000)	109,174
Sindelfingen (★Stuttgart)	58,805
Solingen (★Wuppertal)	165,401
Speyer	46,553
Stendal	48,532
Stolberg (★Aachen)	57,231
Stralsund	72,780
Stuttgart (★2,005,000)	579,988
Suhl	54,731
Trier (★122,000)	97,835
Troisdorf (★Siegburg)	64,430
Tübingen	80,372
Ulm (★215,000)	110,529
Unna (★Essen)	61,552
Velbert (★Essen)	89,253
Viersen (★Mönchengladbach)	77,453
Villingen-Schwenningen	78,218
Weimar	60,326
Wesel	59,631
Wetzlar (★96,000)	51,737
Wiesbaden (★790,000)	260,301
Wilhelmshaven (★122,000)	90,561
Wismar	55,509
Witten (★Essen)	105,403
Wittenberg	49,682
Wolfenbüttel (★Braunschweig)	52,032
Wolfsburg	128,510
Worms (★Mannheim)	76,503
Wuppertal (★845,000)	383,660
Würzburg (★195,000)	127,777
Zweibrücken (★100,000)	33,918
Zwickau (★180,000)	114,632

GHANA

1987 E	13,577,538
• ACCRA (★1,390,000)	949,113
Ashiaman (★Accra) (1984C)	49,427
Cape Coast (1984C)	57,653
Koforidua (1984C)	54,400
Kumasi (★540,000)	385,192
Obuasi (1984C)	60,146
Sekondi (★175,352) (1984C)	32,355
Tafo (★Kumasi) (1984C)	50,432
Takoradi (★Sekondi) (1984C)	61,527
Tamale (★171,661)	151,069
Tema (★179,076) (★Accra)	109,975
Teshie (★Accra) (1984C)	62,954

GIBRALTAR

1988 E	30,077
• GIBRALTAR	30,077

GREECE / Ellás

1991 C	10,264,156
Aiyáleo (★Athínai)	79,560
Akharnaí	60,062
Amaroúsion (★Athínai)	63,619
Ampelókipoi (★Thessaloníki) (1981C)	40,033
• ATHÍNAI (ATHENS) (★3,096,775)	748,110
Áyios Dhimítrios (★Athínai)	57,387
Ermoúpolis (★16,008)	12,987
Galátsion (★Athínai)	56,972
Glifádha (★Athínai)	62,310
Ilioúpolis (★Athínai)	72,623
Ioánnina	56,496
Iráklion (★127,600)	117,167
Kalámai (★45,090)	43,838
Kalamariá (★Thessaloníki) (1981C)	51,676
Kallithéa (★Athínai)	110,738
Kardhítsa	30,451
Kateríni (★48,021)	46,304
Kavála	58,576
Keratsínion (★Athínai)	71,845
Khalándrion (★Athínai)	72,286
Khalkís	51,482
Khaniá (★65,519)	50,077
Khíos (★27,405)	21,261
Koridhallós (★Athínai)	63,033
Kórinthos (Corinth)	28,903
Lárisa (★125,623)	113,426
Návplion	11,453
Néa Ionía (★Athínai)	60,364
Néa Liósia (★Athínai)	78,029
Neápolis (★Thessaloníki) (1981C)	31,464
Néa Smírni (★Athínai)	69,319
Níkaia (★Athínai)	87,924
Palaión Fáliron (★Athínai)	60,974
Pátrai (★172,763)	155,180
Peristérion (★Athínai)	145,854
Piraiévs (Piraeus) (★Athínai)	169,622
Ródhos (Rhodes)	43,619
Sérrai	50,875
Spárti (Sparta) (★15,496)	14,043
Thessaloníki (Salonika) (★739,998)	377,951
Tríkala	48,810
Trípolis	21,772
Véroia	38,871
Víron (★Athínai)	57,149
Vólos (★106,142)	77,907
Zográfos (★Athínai)	78,570

GREENLAND / Grønland / Kalaallit Nunaat

1990 E	55,558
Egedesminde (Aasiaat)	3,308
• GODTHÅB (NUUK)	12,217
Holsteinsborg (Sisimiut)	4,871

GRENADA

1991 C	90,691
• SAINT GEORGE'S (★25,000)	4,439

GUADELOUPE

1982 C	328,400
BASSE-TERRE (★26,600)	13,656
Les Abymes (★Pointe-à-Pitre)	56,165
• Pointe-à-Pitre (★83,000)	25,310

GUAM

1990 C	133,152
• AGANA (★50,000)	1,139

GUATEMALA

1989 E	8,935,395
Escuintla	60,673
• GUATEMALA (★1,400,000)	1,057,210
Quetzaltenango	88,769

GUERNSEY

1991 C	58,867
• SAINT PETER PORT (★36,000)	16,648

GUINEA / Guinée

1986 E	6,225,000
• CONAKRY	800,000
Kankan	100,000
Kindia	80,000
Labé	110,000
Nzérékoré (1983C)	55,356

GUINEA-BISSAU / Guiné-Bissau

1988 E	945,000
• BISSAU	125,000

GUYANA

1983 E	918,000
• GEORGETOWN (★188,000)	78,500

HAITI / Haïti

1987 E	5,531,802
Cap-Haïtien	72,161
Gonaïves	37,034
• PORT-AU-PRINCE (★880,000)	797,000

HONDURAS

1988 C	4,443,721
Choluteca	54,481
El Progreso	60,058
La Ceiba	68,764
San Pedro Sula (★375,000)	287,350
• TEGUCIGALPA	576,661

HONG KONG

1986 C	5,395,997
Kowloon (Jiulong) (★Victoria)	774,781
Kwai Chung (★Victoria)	131,362
New Kowloon (Xinjiulong) (★Victoria)	1,526,910
Sha Tin (★Victoria)	355,810
Sheung Shui	87,206
Tai Po	119,679
Tsuen Wan (Quanwan) (★Victoria)	514,241
Tuen Mun (★Victoria)	262,458
• VICTORIA (★4,770,000) (1991C)	1,250,993
Yuen Long	75,740

HUNGARY / Magyarország

1990 C	10,374,823
Békéscsaba	67,609
• BUDAPEST (★2,515,000)	2,016,774
Debrecen	212,235
Dunaújváros	59,028
Eger	61,892
Győr	129,338
Hódmezővásárhely	51,180
Kaposvár	71,788
Kecskemét	102,516
Miskolc	196,442
Nagykanizsa	54,052
Nyíregyháza	114,152
Ózd	43,592
Pécs	170,039
Salgótarján	47,822
Sopron	55,083
Szeged	175,301
Székesfehérvár	108,958
Szolnok	78,328
Szombathely	85,617
Tatabánya	74,277
Vác	34,015
Veszprém	63,867
Zalaegerszeg	62,212

ICELAND / Ísland

1991 E	259,577
Akureyri	14,436
• REYKJAVÍK (★149,482)	99,623

INDIA / Bharat

1991 C	846,302,688
Abohar	107,163
Achalpur	96,229
Ādilābād	84,255
Ādityapur (★Jamshedpur)	77,803
Ādoni	136,182
Agartala	157,358
Āgra (★948,063)	891,790
Āgra Cantonment (★Āgra)	49,755
Ahmadābād (★3,312,216)	2,876,710
Ahmadnagar (★222,088)	181,339
Āīzawl	155,240
Ajmer	402,700
Akola	328,034
Akot	65,681
Alandur (★Madras)	125,244
Alīgarh	480,520
Alīpur Duār (★102,815)	65,241
Allahābād (★844,546)	792,858
Alleppey (★264,969)	174,666
Alwal (★Hyderābād)	66,471
Alwar (★210,146)	205,086
Amalner	76,442
Ambājogāi	57,159
Ambāla (★259,227)	119,338
Ambāla Cantonment (★Ambāla Sadar)	49,017
Ambāla Sadar	90,872
Ambāsamudram (★59,661)	33,893
Ambattur (★Madras)	215,424
Ambikāpur (★53,227)	50,277
Āmbūr	75,911
Amrāvati	421,576
Amreli (★69,366)	67,827
Amritsar	708,835
Amroha	137,061
Anakāpalle	84,336
Ānand (★174,480)	110,266
Anantapur	174,924
Anjār	51,209
Ankleshwar (★78,100)	51,739
Ara	157,082
Arakkonam	71,928
Arcot (★114,760)	45,205
Arni	54,898
Aruppukkottai	78,976
Asansol (★763,939)	262,188
Ashoknagar-Kalyangarh (★Hābra)	96,747
Āttūr	55,667
Auraiya	50,772
Aurangābād (★592,709)	573,272
Avadi (★Madras)	183,215
Āzamgarh	78,567
Badagara (★102,430)	72,434
Bagaha	34,327
Bāgalkot	76,903
Bahādurgarh	56,524
Baharampur (★126,400)	115,144
Bahraich	135,400
Baidyabāti (★Calcutta)	90,081
Bālāghāt (★67,151)	62,178
Bālāngīr	69,920
Bāleshwar (★101,829)	85,442
Ballarpur (★92,436)	83,511
Ballia	84,063
Bālly (★Calcutta)	184,474
Bālly (★Calcutta)	73,322
Balrāmpur	59,619
Bālurghāt (★126,225)	119,796
Bānda	96,795
Bangalore (★4,130,288)	2,660,088
Bangaon	79,571
Bānkura	114,876
Bansberia (★Calcutta)	93,520
Bānswāra (★67,908)	66,632
Bāpatla	62,536
Bārākpur (★Calcutta)	133,265
Bārān	57,719
Baranagar (★Calcutta)	224,821
Bārāsat (★Calcutta)	102,660
Baraut	67,705
Barddhamān	245,079
Bareilly (★617,350)	587,211
Bargarh	51,205
Bāripada (★69,240)	49,619
Bārmer	68,625
Barnāla	75,430
Bārsi	88,810
Basīrhāt	101,409
Basti	87,371
Batala (★103,367)	86,006
Bathinda	159,114
Beāwar (★106,721)	105,363
Begusarai (★84,018)	71,424
Bela	65,945
Belampalli	66,780
Belgaum (★402,412)	326,399
Bellary	245,391
Bettiah	92,653
Betūl	63,534
Bhadohi	64,010
Bhadrak	76,435
Bhadrāvati (★149,257)	55,475
Bhadrāvati New Town (★Bhadrāvati)	74,928
Bhadreswar (★Calcutta)	72,474
Bhāgalpur (★260,119)	253,225
Bhandāra	71,813
Bharatpur (★156,880)	148,519
Bharūch (★139,029)	133,102
Bhātpāra (★Calcutta)	304,952
Bhavāni (★97,160)	35,198
Bhāvnagar (★405,225)	402,338
Bhawānipatna	51,062
Bhilai (★685,474)	386,159
Bhīlwāra	183,965
Bhīmavaram	121,314
Bhind	109,755
Bhiwandi (★392,214)	379,070
Bhiwāni	121,629
Bhopāl	1,062,771
Bhubaneshwar	411,542
Bhuj (★121,009)	102,176
Bhusāwal (★159,799)	145,143
Bīd	112,434
Bīdar (★132,408)	108,016
Bihār	201,323
Bijāpur (★193,131)	186,939
Bijnor (★73,900)	66,486
Bīkāner	416,289
Bilāspur (★229,615)	179,833
Bilīmora (★51,039)	42,052
Birlapur (★65,482)	20,320
Birnagar (★92,208)	20,015
Bishnupur	56,128
Bodhan	64,406
Bodināyakkanūr	66,500
Bokāro Steel City (★398,890)	333,683
Bolpur	52,760
• Bombay (★12,596,243)	9,925,891
Botād	64,603
Brahmapur	210,418
Brajrajnagar	69,667
Budaun	116,695
Budge Budge (★Calcutta)	72,951
Bulandshahr	127,201
Buldāna	52,767
Bulsār (★111,775)	57,909
Būndi	65,047
Burhānpur	172,710
Calcutta (★11,021,918)	4,399,819
Calicut (★801,190)	419,831
Cannanore (★Tellicherry)	65,238
Chaībāsa	56,729
Chākdaha	74,769
Chakradharpur (★47,666)	32,737
Chālisgaon	77,420
Champdāni (★Calcutta)	101,067
Chandannagar (★Calcutta)	120,378
Chandausi	82,748
Chandīgarh (★575,829)	504,094
Chāndpur	55,825
Chandrapur	226,105
Changanācheri	52,445
Channapatna	55,209
Chāpra	136,877
Chās	65,207
Chhatarpur (★75,594)	72,824
Chhindwāra (★96,858)	93,650
Chidambaram (★67,949)	58,740
Chikmagalūr	60,816
Chilakalūrupet	79,142
Chingleput	54,127
Chintāmani	50,394
Chīrāla (★142,778)	80,861
Chitradurga (★103,435)	87,069

▲ Population of an entire municipality, commune, or district, including rural area.
• Largest city in country.
★ Population or designation of the metropolitan area, including suburbs.
C Census. **E** Official estimate. **U** Unofficial estimate.

▲ Bevölkerung eines ganzen städtischen Verwaltungsgebietes, eines Kommunalbezirkes oder eines Distrikts, einschliesslich ländlicher Gebiete.
• Grösste Stadt des Landes.
★ Bevölkerung oder Bezeichnung der Stadtregion einschliesslich Vororte.
C Volkszählung. **E** Offizielle Schätzung. **U** Inoffizielle Schätzung.

Chittaranjan (★65,689)	47,186
Chittaurgarh	71,569
Chittoor	133,462
Chopda	49,234
Chūru	82,464
Cochin (★1,140,605)	564,589
Coimbatore (★1,100,746)	816,321
Contai	53,484
Coonoor (★100,687)	48,003
Cuddalore	144,561
Cuddapah (★215,866)	121,463
Cuttack (★440,295)	403,418
Dabgram	147,217
Dabhoi	50,641
Dāhod (★96,632)	66,500
Dāltenganj	56,323
Damoh (★105,043)	95,661
Dānāpur (★Patna)	84,616
Dandeli	52,701
Darbhanga	218,391
Darjiling	73,062
Datia	64,477
Dāvangere (★287,233)	266,082
Dehra Dūn (★368,053)	270,159
Dehri	93,694
Delhi (★8,419,084)	7,206,704
Delhi Cantonment (★Delhi)	94,393
Deoband	66,208
Deoghar (★85,902)	76,380
Deolāli (★Nāsik)	44,331
Deoria	82,168
Dewās	164,364
Dhamtari	69,357
Dhanbad (★815,005)	151,789
Dhār	59,246
Dhārāpuram	48,393
Dharmapuri	59,318
Dharmavaram	78,961
Dhaulpur	68,533
Dholka (★54,352)	49,860
Dhorāji (★79,479)	77,748
Dhrāngadhra	57,961
Dhuburi	66,216
Dhule	278,317
Dibrugarh (★125,667)	120,127
Dimāpur	57,182
Dindigul	182,477
Dīsa	62,435
Dod Ballāpur	54,609
Dum Dum (★Calcutta)	40,961
Durg (★Bhilai)	150,645
Durgāpur	425,836
Elūru	212,866
Erode (★361,755)	159,323
Etah	78,458
Etāwah	124,072
Faizābād (★176,922)	124,437
Farīdābad (★Delhi)	617,717
Farīdkot	58,244
Farrukhābād (★208,727)	194,657
Fatehpur	117,675
Fathpur	66,387
Fāzilka	58,028
Fīrozābād (★270,536)	215,128
Fīrozpur	78,738
Fīrozpur Cantonment	53,094
Gadag	134,051
Gandhidham	104,585
Gāndhinagar	123,359
Ganga Ghat	50,260
Gangānagar	161,482
Gangāpur (★68,886)	53,689
Gangāwati (★85,515)	64,843
Gangtok	25,024
Gārulia (★Calcutta)	80,918
Gaya (★294,427)	219,675
Ghāziābād (★511,759)	454,156
Ghāzīpur	76,547
Girīdīh	78,097
Godhra (★100,662)	96,813
Gokāk	52,080
Gonda	95,553
Gondal (★81,611)	80,584
Gondia	109,470
Gopichettipālaiyam	48,364
Gorakhpur	505,566
Gudivāda	101,656
Gudiyāttam (★90,557)	83,232
Gūdūr	55,984
Gulbarga (★310,920)	304,099
Guna	100,490
Guntakal	107,592
Guntūr	471,051
Gurdāspur	54,733
Gurgaon (★135,884)	121,486
Guruvayur (★118,632)	20,216
Guwāhāti	584,342
Gwalior (★717,780)	690,765
Hābra (★196,970)	100,223
Hājīpur	87,687
Haldwāni	104,195
Hālisahar (★Calcutta)	114,028
Hānsi	59,653
Hanumāngarh (★82,733)	78,525
Hāora (★Calcutta)	950,435
Hāpur	146,262
Hardoi	88,651
Haridwār (★187,392)	147,305
Harihar	66,647
Hassan (★108,706)	90,803
Hāthras	113,285
Hazārībāg	97,824
Himatnagar	51,461
Hindaun	60,780
Hindupur	104,651
Hinganghāt	78,715
Hingoli	54,457
Hisār (★181,255)	172,677
Hoshangābād	70,914
Hoshiārpur	122,705
Hospet (★134,799)	96,322
Hubli-Dhārwār	648,298
Hugli-Chinsurah (★Calcutta)	151,806
Hyderābād (★4,344,437)	30,443,896
Ichaikaronji (★235,979)	214,950
Imphāl (★202,839)	198,535
Indore (★1,109,056)	1,091,674
Ingrāj Bāzār (★177,164)	139,204
Itānagar	16,545
Itārsi (★84,626)	77,334
Jabalpur (★888,916)	741,927
Jabalpur Cantonment (★Jabalpur)	56,124
Jagādhri (★Yamunānagar)	67,386
Jagdalpur (★84,578)	66,154
Jagtiāl	67,591
Jahānābād	52,332
Jaipur (★1,518,235)	1,458,483
Jalandhar	509,510

Jālgaon	242,193
Jālna	174,985
Jalpāiguri	68,732
Jamālpur	86,112
Jamkhandi	48,143
Jammu (★223,361) (1981C)	206,135
Jāmnagar (★381,646)	341,637
Jamshedpur (★829,171)	460,577
Jaora (★56,023)	54,997
Jaunpur	136,062
Jaypur	65,246
Jetpur (★95,397)	73,560
Jhānsi (★368,154)	300,850
Jharia (★Dhanbād)	69,641
Jhārsuguda	65,054
Jhunjhunūn	72,187
Jīnd	85,315
Jodhpur	666,279
Jorhāt (★112,030)	58,358
Jūnāgadh (★167,110)	130,484
Kadaiyanallūr	68,819
Kadiri	63,378
Kagaznagar	57,535
Kairāna	56,079
Kaithal	71,142
Kākināda (★327,541)	279,980
Kalamassery (★Cochin)	54,342
Kālol (★92,550)	82,137
Kalyān (★Bombay)	1,014,557
Kāmāreddi	48,666
Kāmārhāti (★Calcutta)	266,889
Kambam	52,435
Kāmthi (★127,151)	78,612
Kānchipuram (★171,129)	144,955
Kānchrāpāra (★Calcutta)	100,194
Kānnangād (★118,214)	57,165
Kannauj	58,932
Kānpur (★2,029,889)	1,874,409
Kānpur Cantonment (★Kānpur)	95,021
Kapra (★Hyderābād)	87,747
Kapūrthala	64,567
Karād	56,819
Kāraikāl	61,804
Kāraikkudi (★110,926)	71,965
Kāranja	48,866
Karauli	49,008
Karīmnagar	148,583
Karnāl (★176,131)	173,751
Karūr (★113,669)	73,418
Kārwār	51,022
Kāsaragod	50,126
Kāsganj	75,634
Kāshīpur	69,870
Katihār (★154,367)	135,436
Kātwa	55,541
Kāvali	65,910
Kāyankulam	67,151
Keshod	50,172
Khadki Cantonment (★Pune)	78,323
Khambhāt (★89,834)	76,746
Khāmgaon	73,692
Khammam (★149,077)	127,992
Khandwa	145,133
Khanna	71,990
Kharagpur (★264,842)	177,989
Kharagpur Railway Settlement (★Kharagpur)	84,252
Khardaha	88,358
Khargone	66,786
Khurja	80,305
Kishanganj	64,568
Kishangarh Bās	81,948
Koch Bihār (★92,820)	71,215
Kodarma	53,577
Kohīma	51,418
Kolār	83,287
Kolār Gold Fields (★156,746)	72,485
Kolhāpur (★418,538)	406,370
Konnagar (★Calcutta)	62,200
Korba	124,501
Kota	537,371
Kot Kapūra	62,430
Kottagūdem (★102,137)	80,440
Kottayam (★166,552)	63,155
Kovilpatti	78,834
Krishnagiri	60,315
Krishnanagar	121,110
Kukatpalle (★Hyderābād)	186,963
Kulti (★Asansol)	108,518
Kumārapālaiyam (★Bhavāni)	57,672
Kumbakonam (★150,540)	139,483
Kundla (★65,785)	64,815
Kurasia (★71,708)	15,898
Kurichi (★Coimbatore)	64,796
Kurnool (★275,360)	236,800
Lādnūn	48,205
Lakhīmpur	79,951
Lalbahadur Nagar (★Hyderābād)	155,514
Lalitpur	79,870
Lalitpur	79,870
Lātūr	197,408
Luckeesarai	53,360
Lucknow (★1,669,204)	1,619,115
Lucknow Cantonment (★Lucknow)	50,089
Ludhiāna	1,042,740
Machilīpatnam (Bandar)	159,110
Madanapalle	73,820
Madgaon (Margao) (★72,400)	58,951
Mādhavaram (★Madras)	49,256
Madhubani	53,747
Madras (★5,421,985)	3,841,396
Madurai (★1,085,914)	940,989
Mahbūbnagar	116,833
Mahesāna (★109,950)	88,201
Mahoba	56,247
Mahuva (★64,144)	59,912
Mainpuri	76,735
Makrāna (★66,720)	59,714
Malappuram (★142,204)	49,692
Malaut	56,868
Mālegaon	342,595
Māler Kotla	88,600
Malkajgiri (★Hyderābād)	127,178
Malkāpur	51,311
Mancheriyal	52,657
Mandsaur	95,907
Mandya	120,265
Mangalagiri	59,152
Mangalore (★426,341)	273,304
Mango (★Jamshedpur)	108,100
Manjeri	69,334
Manmād	61,312
Mannārgudi	56,552
Mānsa	55,089
Mathura (★235,922)	226,691
Maunath Bhanjan	136,697
Mawāna	51,701
Māyūram	76,837

Medinīpur	125,498
Meerut (★849,799)	753,778
Meerut Cantonment (★Meerut)	96,021
Melappālaiyam (★Tirunelveli)	68,347
Mettuppālaiyam	63,479
Mhow (★83,796)	74,987
Mira Bhayandar (★Bombay)	175,605
Miraj (★Sāngli)	121,593
Miryalaguda	65,879
Mirzāpur	169,336
Modinagar (★123,279)	101,660
Moga (★110,958)	108,304
Mokāma	59,528
Morādābād (★443,701)	429,214
Morbi (★120,117)	90,357
Morena	147,124
Mormugao (★90,429)	83,367
Motihāri (★83,255)	77,432
Mubārakpur (★62,733)	45,376
Muktsar	66,383
Munger	150,112
Murwāra	163,431
Muzaffarnagar (★247,624)	240,609
Muzaffarpur	241,107
Mysore (★653,345)	480,692
Nābha	54,421
Nadiād (★170,217)	167,051
Nagaon	93,350
Nāgappattinam (★99,745)	86,489
Nāgaur	68,194
Nagda	79,622
Nāgercoil	190,084
Nagīna	58,513
Nāgpur (★1,664,006)	1,624,752
Naihāti (★Calcutta)	132,701
Najībābād	66,860
Nalasopara (★Bombay)	67,732
Nalgonda	84,910
Nānded (★309,316)	275,083
Nandurbār	78,378
Nandyāl	119,813
Nangi (★Calcutta)	52,956
Narasapur	56,362
Narasaraopet	88,726
Nārnaul	51,976
Nāshik (★725,341)	656,925
Navadwip (★155,905)	125,037
Navsāri (★190,946)	126,089
Nawābganj (★77,234)	64,582
Nawāda	53,174
Nawalgarh	51,190
Nedumangād	49,875
Neemuch (★90,474)	86,439
Nellore	316,606
New Bārākpur (★Calcutta)	63,795
New Bombay (★Bombay)	307,724
NEW DELHI (★Delhi)	301,297
Neyveli (★126,889)	118,080
Nipāni	51,624
Nirmal	57,761
Nizāmābād	241,034
North Bārākpur (★Calcutta)	100,606
North Dum Dum (★Calcutta)	149,965
Ongole (★128,648)	100,836
Orai	98,716
Osmānābād	68,019
Pālakodu	56,969
Palani (★76,209)	68,907
Pālanpur (★90,269)	80,657
Pālayankottai (★Tirunelveli)	98,399
Pālghāt (★180,033)	123,289
Pāli	136,842
Pallavaram (★Madras)	111,866
Palwal	59,168
Palwancha	53,102
Panaji (Panjim) (★85,515)	43,349
Pandharpur	79,902
Pānihāti (★Calcutta)	275,990
Pānīpat	191,212
Panruti	51,394
Panvel	58,986
Paramakkudi	72,321
Parbhani	190,255
Parli	72,670
Pātan (★97,025)	96,112
Pathānkot (★128,198)	123,930
Patiāla (★253,706)	238,368
Patna (★1,099,647)	917,243
Pattukkottai	58,062
Payyannūr	64,032
Periyakulam	46,744
Petlād	48,552
Phagwāra (★88,316)	83,163
Pīlibhīt	106,605
Pilkhua	51,162
Pimpri-Chinchwad (★Pune)	517,083
Pollāchi (★127,132)	86,897
Pondicherry (★401,437)	203,065
Ponmalai (★Tiruchchirāppalli)	69,639
Ponnāni	51,770
Ponnūru Nidubrolu	54,363
Porbandar (★160,167)	116,671
Port Blair	74,955
Proddatūr	133,914
Pudukkottai	99,058
Puliyangudi	53,287
Pune (Poona) (★2,493,987)	1,566,651
Pune Cantonment (★Pune)	82,139
Puri	125,199
Pūrnia (★136,918)	114,912
Puruliya	92,386
Pusad	55,931
Quilon (★362,572)	139,852
Qutubullapur (★Hyderābād)	106,591
Rabkavi Banhatti	60,609
Rāe Bareli	129,904
Rāichūr (★170,577)	157,551
Raiganj (★159,266)	151,045
Raigarh (★90,265)	86,767
Raipur (★462,694)	438,639
Rājahmundry (★401,397)	324,851
Rājapālaiyam	114,202
Rajendranagar (★Hyderābād)	84,520
Rajhara-Jharandalli	55,996
Rājkot (★654,490)	559,407
Rāj Nāndgaon	125,371
Rājpur (★86,451)	60,175
Rājpura	70,983
Rāmanagaram	50,437
Rāmanāthapuram	52,879
Rāmgarh (★82,328)	51,264
Rāmpur	243,742
Rānāghāt (★127,035)	62,532
Rānchi (★614,795)	599,306
Rānībennur	67,442
Rānīganj (★155,823)	61,997
Ratangarh	55,079
Ratlām (★195,776)	183,375
Ratnāgiri	56,529

Raurkela (★398,864)	215,509
Raurkela Civil Township (★152,690) (★Raurkela)	142,408
Rāyagāda	48,247
Rewa	128,981
Rewāri	75,342
Rishīkesh (★71,704)	44,487
Rishra (★Calcutta)	102,815
Robertson Pet (★Kolār Gold Fields)	68,230
Rohtak	216,096
Roorkee (★91,139)	80,262
Rudrapur	61,280
Sāgar (★257,119)	195,346
Sahāranpur	374,945
Saharsa	80,149
Sahaswān	51,080
Sāhibganj	49,257
Salem (★578,291)	366,712
Sāmalkot	48,760
Sambalpur (★193,297)	131,138
Sambhal	150,869
Sangamner	49,061
Sangareddi	50,123
Sāngli (★363,751)	193,197
Sangrūr	56,419
Sankarankovil	48,846
Sardārshahr	67,954
Sarni	84,379
Sāsarām	98,122
Sātāra	95,180
Satna (★160,500)	156,630
Sawāi Mādhopur (★77,690)	72,165
Secunderābād Cantonment (★Hyderābād)	171,148
Sehore	71,456
Seoni	64,532
Serampore (★Calcutta)	137,028
Serilungampalle (★Hyderābād)	72,320
Shahdol (★60,529)	55,508
Shāhjahānpur (★260,403)	237,713
Shāmli	70,853
Shāntipur	109,956
Shikohābād	62,829
Shiliguri	216,950
Shillong (★223,366)	131,719
Shimoga (★193,028)	179,258
Shivpuri	108,277
Shrirampur (★79,052)	71,368
Siddhapur (★51,794)	50,770
Siddipet	54,091
Sikandarābād	60,992
Sīkar	148,272
Silchar	115,483
Silvassa	11,725
Simla (★110,360)	82,054
Sindri (★Dhānbād)	72,333
Sircilla	50,048
Sirsa	112,841
Sītāmarhi (★67,336)	44,935
Sītāpur	121,842
Siuri	54,298
Sivakāsi (★102,175)	65,593
Siwān	83,125
Solāpur (★620,846)	604,215
Sonīpat	143,922
South Dum Dum (★Calcutta)	232,811
Srīkākulam	88,883
Srikalahasti	88,883
Srīnagar (★606,002) (1981C)	594,775
Srīrangam (★Tiruchchirāppalli)	70,109
Srīvilliputtūr	68,644
Sujāngarh	70,843
Sultānpur	76,533
Sūrat (★1,518,950)	1,498,817
Surendranagar (★166,466)	106,110
Suriāpet	60,630
Tādepallegūdem	88,878
Tādpatri	71,068
Talipparamba	60,226
Tāmbaram (★Madras)	107,187
Tānda	70,605
Tanuku	62,913
Tellicherry (★463,962)	103,579
Tenāli	143,726
Tenkāsi	55,189
Tezpur	55,084
Thāna (★Bombay)	803,389
Thānesar	81,255
Thanjāvūr	202,013
Theni-Allinagaram	60,050
Thiruvārūr	49,195
Thrippunithura (★Cochin)	51,078
Tīkamgarh	54,173
Tindivanam	61,579
Tinsukia	73,918
Tiruchchirāppalli (★711,862)	387,223
Tiruchengodu	63,027
Tirunelveli (★366,869)	135,825
Tirupati (★188,904)	174,369
Tiruppattūr	55,282
Tiruppur (★306,237)	235,661
Tirūr	49,453
Tiruvalla	54,780
Tiruvannāmalai	109,196
Tirūvottiyūr (★Madras)	168,642
Titāgarh (★Calcutta)	114,085
Tonk	100,079
Trichūr (★275,053)	74,604
Trivandrum (★826,225)	524,006
Ttruchchendūr (★75,301)	27,420
Tumkūr (★179,877)	138,903
Tuticorin (★280,091)	199,854
Udagamandalam	81,763
Udaipur	308,571
Udamalpet	58,678
Udgīr	70,453
Ujjain	362,266
Ulhāsnagar (★Bombay)	369,077
Ulubāria	155,172
Unjha	51,003
Unnāo	107,425
Upleta	51,801
Uppal Kalan (★Hyderābād)	75,644
Uttarpara-Kotrung (★Calcutta)	101,268
Vadodara (★1,126,824)	1,031,346
Vālpārai	106,523
Vāniyambādi (★92,307)	72,428
Vārānasi (Benares) (★1,030,863)	929,270
Vasai (Bassein) (★83,734)	39,781
Veerappanchattiram (★Erode)	61,649
Vejalpur (★Ahmadābād)	92,116
Vellore (★310,776)	175,061
Verāval (★120,178)	93,976
Vidisha	92,922
Vijayawāda (★845,756)	701,827
Vikramasingapuram	49,834
Viluppuram	88,788
Viramgām	50,698

▲ Población de un municipio, comuna o distrito entero, incluyendo sus áreas rurales.
● Ciudad más grande de un país.
★ Población o designación de un área metropolitana, incluyendo los suburbios.
C Censo. **E** Estimado oficial. **U** Estimado no oficial.

▲ Population d'une municipalité, d'une commune ou d'un district, zone rurale incluse.
● Ville la plus peuplée du pays.
★ Population de l'agglomération (ou nom de la zone métropolitaine englobante).
C Recensement. **E** Estimation officielle. **U** Estimation non officielle.

▲ População de um município, comuna ou distrito, inclusive as respectivas áreas rurais.
● Maior cidade de um país.
★ População ou indicação de uma área metropolitana.
C Censo. **E** Estimativa oficial. **U** Estimativa não oficial.

Virār (★Bombay)	57,600
Virudunagar	70,971
Vishākhapatnam (★1,057,118)	752,037
Visnagar (★59,647)	57,869
Vizianagaram (★177,022)	160,359
Vriddhāchalam	52,819
Wadhwan (★Surendranager)	49,791
Warangal (★137,757)	447,657
Wardha	102,985
Wāshīm	49,140
Yamunānagar (★219,754)	144,346
Yavatmāl (★121,816)	108,578
Yemmiganur	65,089

INDONESIA

1990 C	179,378,946
Ambon (▲275,888)	205,193
Balikpapan	344,147
Banda Aceh (Kuturaja) (▲184,650)	143,360
Bandung (★2,220,000)	2,058,122
Banjarmasin	480,737
Bantul (▲696,944)	13,700
Banyuwangi (▲1,455,010)	92,800
Batang (▲591,647)	55,200
Bekasi (▲951,509) (★Jakarta)	146,400
Bengkulu	170,183
Binjai (▲181,866)	127,184
Blitar (★150,000)	118,933
Bogor (★620,000)	271,341
Bojonegoro (▲1,104,031)	63,700
Brebes (▲1,521,835)	49,500
Bukittinggi	83,753
Cianjur (▲1,420,228)	108,700
Cibinong (▲1,812,734)	264,100
Cikampek (▲1,152,405)	91,200
Cilacap (▲1,487,308)	141,900
Ciledug (▲1,244,151)	293,000
Cimahi (▲1,909,459) (★Bandung)	196,900
Ciparay (▲1,909,456)	135,300
Cirebon (★315,000)	254,477
Denpasar (▲663,390)	209,500
Depok (▲1,812,734) (★Jakarta)	382,000
Dili (▲123,475)	12,900
Dumai (▲904,375)	71,500
Garut (▲1,478,757)	145,900
Genteng (▲1,455,010)	60,900
Gorontalo (▲119,745)	94,058
Gresik (▲856,853)	102,000
Indramayu (▲1,226,609)	32,700
• JAKARTA (★10,200,000)	8,227,746
Jambi	339,786
Jayapura (Sukarnapura) (▲246,389)	101,200
Jember (▲2,062,554)	190,000
Jepara (▲827,657)	36,200
Jombang (▲1,048,805)	65,700
Karawang (▲1,152,405)	143,300
Kebumen (▲1,120,982)	48,300
Kediri	249,538
Kendari (▲488,471)	70,700
Kisaran (▲884,594)	66,600
Klangenang (▲1,035,575)	291,200
Klaten (▲1,056,135)	120,400
Kudus (▲631,322)	182,600
Kuningan (▲739,360)	33,100
Kupang (▲522,944)	111,300
Lumajang (▲924,894)	62,100
Madiun (★200,000)	170,050
Magelang (★180,000)	123,156
Majalaya (▲1,909,459)	176,600
Malang	695,089
Manado	320,600
Mataram (▲859,273)	276,300
Medan	1,730,052
Mojokerto	99,707
Muncar (▲1,455,010)	48,100
Padang (▲631,263)	477,064
Padangsidempuan (▲954,184)	72,100
Palangkaraya	112,511
Palembang	1,144,047
Palu (▲784,647)	56,500
Pangkalpinang	113,129
Pare (▲1,343,125)	51,400
Parepare (▲101,421)	84,093
Pasuruan (★190,000)	152,075
Pati (▲1,064,115)	54,900
Payakumbuh (▲90,838)	50,475
Pekalongan (★430,000)	242,714
Pekanbaru	398,621
Pemalang (▲1,114,228)	86,200
Pematangsiantar (★250,000)	219,316
Perabumulih (▲582,396)	59,500
Ponorogo (▲837,055)	59,500
Pontianak	396,658
Pringsewu (▲1,825,040)	58,300
Probolinggo (▲176,906)	131,077
Purwakarta (▲437,327)	62,300
Purwokerto (▲1,348,825)	158,300
Purworejo (▲700,788)	38,600
Salatiga	98,012
Samarinda (▲407,174)	334,851
Semarang	1,249,230
Serang (▲1,201,742)	84,900
Sibolga	71,559
Sidoarjo (▲1,167,467)	76,800
Singaraja (▲540,150)	59,200
Singkawang (▲574,156)	64,000
Situbondo (▲574,156)	63,800
Sorong (▲199,085)	77,900
Subang (▲1,037,394)	52,700
Sukabumi (★250,000)	119,938
Sumedang (▲718,488)	42,900
Sumenep (▲933,746)	53,300
Surabaya	2,473,272
Surakarta (★590,000)	503,827
Taman (▲1,167,467)	88,100
Tangerang (▲1,244,151)	99,100
Tanjungbalai	107,751
Tanjungkarang-Telukbetung (▲636,418)	457,927
Tanjungpinang	105,820
Tarakan (▲232,494)	61,300
Tasikmalaya (▲1,444,242)	194,000
Tebingtinggi	116,749
Tegal (★510,000)	229,553
Tembilahan (▲4,878,066)	62,700
Tuban (▲977,716)	54,700
Tulungagung (▲890,032)	97,000
Ujungpandang (Makasar)	944,372
Yogyakarta (★540,000)	412,059

IRAN / Īrān

1986 C	49,445,010
Ābādān	21,879
Abhar	41,628
Āghā Jārī	64,102
Ahar	62,145
Ahvāz	579,826
Alīgūdarz	53,843
Āmol	118,242
Andīmeshk	56,288
Arāk	265,349
Ardabīl	281,973
Bābol	115,320
Bābol Sar	28,589
Bākhtarān (Kermānshāh)	560,514
Bam	50,709
Bandar-e 'Abbās	201,642
Bandar-e Anzalī (Bandar-e Pahlavī)	87,063
Bandar-e Būshehr	120,787
Bandar-e Māh Shahr	71,808
Behbahān	78,694
Behshahr	52,461
Bīrjand	81,798
Bojnūrd	93,392
Borāzjān	67,061
Borūjerd	183,879
Dezfūl	151,420
Do Gonbadān	51,107
Do Rūd	62,517
Emāmshahr (Shāhrūd)	78,950
Eşfahān (★1,175,000)	986,753
Eslāmābād	73,362
Eslāmshahr (★Tehrān)	215,129
Fasā	64,771
Ganāveh	41,883
Gonbad-e Qābūs	87,100
Gorgān	139,430
Hamadān	272,499
Īlām	89,035
Jahrom	77,174
Karaj (★Tehrān)	275,100
Kāshān	138,599
Kāshmar	49,259
Kāzerūn	73,444
Kermān	257,284
Khomeynīshahr (★Eşfahān)	104,647
Khorramābād	208,592
Khorramshahr (1976C)	146,706
Khvoy	115,343
Mahābād	75,238
Malāyer	103,640
Marāgheh	100,679
Marand	71,394
Marv Dasht	79,132
Mashhad	1,463,508
Masjed-e Soleymān	104,787
Mīāndoāb	59,551
Mīāneh	65,959
Nahāvand	52,265
Najafābād	129,058
Naqadeh	52,275
Neyshābūr	109,258
Orūmīyeh (Reẕā'īyeh)	300,746
Qā'emshahr	109,288
Qazvīn	248,591
Qom	543,139
Qomsheh	73,367
Qūchān	66,531
Rafsanjān	66,498
Rasht	290,897
Sabzevār	129,103
Salmās	50,573
Sanandaj	204,537
Saqqez	81,351
Sārī	141,020
Sāveh	64,081
Semnān	64,891
Shahr-e Kord	75,080
Shīrāz	848,289
Shīrvān	48,688
Shūshtar	65,840
Sīrjān	90,072
Tabrīz	971,482
• TEHRĀN (★7,500,000)	6,042,584
Torbat-e Ḩeydarīyeh	72,068
Varāmīn	58,311
Yazd	230,483
Zābol	75,105
Zāhedān	281,923
Zanjān	215,261

IRAQ / Al 'Irāq

1985 E	15,584,987
Ad-Dīwānīyah (1970E)	62,300
Al-'Amārah	131,785
Al-Başrah	616,700
Al-Ḩillah	215,249
Al-Kūt	73,022
Al-Mawşil	570,926
An-Najaf	242,603
An-Nāşirīyah	138,842
Ar-Ramādī	137,388
As-Samāwah	75,293
As-Sulaymānīyah	279,424
• BAGHDĀD (1987C)	3,841,268
Ba'qūbah	114,516
Irbīl	333,903
Karbalā'	184,574
Kirkūk (1970E)	207,900

IRELAND / Éire

1986 C	3,540,643
Cork (★173,694)	133,271
• DUBLIN (BAILE ÁTHA CLIATH) (★1,140,000)	502,749
Dún Laoghaire (★Dublin)	54,715
Galway	47,104
Limerick (★76,557)	56,279
Waterford (★41,054)	39,529

ISLE OF MAN

1991 C	69,788
• DOUGLAS (★30,000)	22,214

ISRAEL / Isrā'īl / Yisra'el

1991 E	4,713,800
Ashdod	83,900
Ashqelon	59,700
Bat Yam (★Tel Aviv-Yafo)	141,300
Be'ér Sheva (Beersheba)	122,000
Bene Beraq (★Tel Aviv-Yafo)	116,700
Elat	26,300
Giv'atayim (★Tel Aviv-Yafo)	46,600
Ḩefa (★450,000)	245,900
Herzliyya (★Tel Aviv-Yafo)	77,200
Ḩolon (★Tel Aviv-Yafo)	156,700
Kefar Sava (★Tel Aviv-Yafo)	61,100
Lod (Lydda) (★Tel Aviv-Yafo)	43,300
Nazerat (Nazareth) (★77,000)	53,600
Netanya (★Tel Aviv-Yafo)	132,200
Petaḩ Tiqwa (★Tel Aviv-Yafo)	144,000
Ra'ananna (★Tel Aviv-Yafo)	53,600
Ramat Gan (★Tel Aviv-Yafo)	119,500
Reḩovot (★Tel Aviv-Yafo)	80,300
Rishon LeẔiyyon (★Tel Aviv-Yafo)	139,500
• Tel Aviv-Yafo (★1,735,000)	339,400
YERUSHALAYIM (AL-QUDS) (JERUSALEM) (★560,000)	524,500

ITALY / Italia

1991 C	56,411,290
Afragola (★Napoli)	59,940
Alessandria (▲93,351)	74,000
Altamura	57,462
Ancona	103,268
Andria	82,556
Arezzo (▲91,623)	74,200
Asti (▲74,497)	62,800
Avellino	54,343
Aversa (★Napoli)	50,361
Bari (★475,000)	341,273
Barletta	86,215
Benevento (▲62,683)	51,900
Bergamo (★345,000)	115,655
Biella	50,993
Bitonto	49,792
Bologna (★525,000)	411,803
Bolzano	100,380
Brescia	196,766
Brindisi	91,778
Busto Arsizio (★Milano)	77,001
Cagliari (★305,000)	211,719
Caltanissetta	62,853
Campobasso (▲51,307)	44,400
Carpi (▲60,794)	49,600
Carrara (★Massa)	68,480
Caserta	68,811
Casoria (▲79,315) (★Napoli)	57,800
Castellammare di Stabia (★Napoli)	68,720
Catania (★550,000)	330,037
Catanzaro	103,802
Cava de'Tirreni (★Salerno)	52,610
Cerignola	54,971
Cesena (▲89,497)	72,200
Chieti	57,535
Cinisello Balsamo (★Milano)	75,606
Civitavecchia	50,856
Collegno (★Torino)	47,192
Cologno Monzese (★Milano)	50,853
Como (★165,000)	85,955
Cosenza (★150,000)	104,483
Cremona	75,160
Crotone (▲61,813)	54,300
Cuneo (▲55,838)	47,900
Empoli (▲42,790)	32,300
Ercolano (★Napoli)	60,869
Ferrara (▲140,600)	110,700
Firenze (★640,000)	402,316
Foggia	155,042
Foligno (▲53,518)	42,500
Forlì (▲109,755)	90,600
Gela	79,718
Genova (Genoa) (★805,000)	675,639
Giugliano in Campania (★Napoli)	59,091
Grosseto (▲71,373)	57,000
Imola (▲62,352)	48,800
Imperia	41,278
L'Aquila (▲67,818)	43,100
La Spezia (★185,000)	101,701
Latina (▲105,543)	72,700
Lecce	102,344
Lecco	45,859
Legnano (★Milano)	50,068
Livorno	171,265
Lucca	86,437
Manfredonia	58,157
Mantova (▲54,228)	46,800
Marsala	77,218
Massa (★145,000)	67,779
Matera	54,872
Messina	274,846
Mestre (▲317,837) (★Venezia)	181,900
• Milano (Milan) (★3,750,000)	1,371,008
Modena	177,501
Molfetta	66,658
Moncalieri (★Torino)	58,433
Monopoli (▲43,019)	33,100
Monza (★Milano)	121,151
Napoli (Naples) (★2,875,000)	1,024,601
Nicastro (▲69,660)	53,700
Nocera Inferiore	49,021
Novara	103,349
Padova (★270,000)	218,186
Palermo	697,162
Parma	173,991
Pavia	80,073
Perugia (▲150,576)	109,500
Pesaro (▲90,341)	78,700
Pescara	128,553
Piacenza	102,252
Pisa	101,500
Pistoia (▲87,275)	73,900
Pordenone	50,222
Portici (★Napoli)	67,824
Potenza (▲68,499)	58,800
Pozzuoli (▲75,706) (★Napoli)	67,100
Prato (★215,000)	165,364
Quartu Sant'Elena	60,852
Ragusa	69,423
Ravenna (▲136,724)	87,000
Reggio di Calabria	178,496
Reggio nell'Emilia (▲131,880)	108,800
Rho (★Milano)	51,646
Rimini (▲130,896)	114,800
Rivoli (★Torino)	51,884
ROMA (★3,175,000)	2,693,383
Salerno (★250,000)	153,436
San Benedetto del Tronto	45,220
San Giorgio a Cremano (★Napoli)	62,168
San Remo	59,247
San Severo	55,376
Sassari	120,011
Savona (★112,000)	68,997
Scandicci (★Firenze)	53,264
Sesto Fiorentino (★Firenze)	46,899
Sesto San Giovanni (★Milano)	85,175
Siena	57,745
Siracusa	125,444
Taranto	232,200
Teramo (▲52,490)	36,100
Terni (▲109,809)	93,400
Torino (★1,550,000)	961,916
Torre Annunziata (★Napoli)	50,346
Torre del Greco (★Napoli)	101,456
Trani	49,337
Trapani (▲69,273)	59,700
Trento (▲102,124)	83,100
Treviso	83,886
Trieste (Triest) (Trst)	231,047
Udine (★126,000)	98,322
Varese	85,461
Venezia (Venice) (★420,000)	85,100
Vercelli	50,207
Verona	258,946
Viareggio (▲60,559)	51,500
Vicenza	109,333
Vigevano	61,380
Viterbo (▲60,213)	48,700
Vittoria	56,970

JAMAICA

1990 E	2,392,000
• KINGSTON (★820,000)	661,600
Montego Bay (★155,700)	80,500
Portmore (★Kingston) (1982C)	73,426
Spanish Town (▲358,600) (★Kingston)	96,100

JAPAN / Nihon

1990 C	123,611,167
Abiko (★Tōkyō)	120,628
Ageo (★Tōkyō)	194,947
Aizu-wakamatsu	119,080
Akashi (★Ōsaka)	270,722
Akigawa (★Tōkyō)	50,387
Akishima (★Tōkyō)	105,372
Akita	302,362
Akō	51,131
Amagasaki (★Ōsaka)	498,999
Anan (▲59,044)	47,000
Anjō	142,251
Aomori	287,808
Arao (★Ōmuta)	59,507
Asahikawa	359,071
Asaka (★Tōkyō)	103,617
Ashikaga	167,686
Ashiya (★Ōsaka)	87,524
Atami	47,291
Atsugi (★Tōkyō)	197,282
Ayase (★Tōkyō)	77,926
Beppu	130,334
Bisai (★Nagoya)	55,880
Chiba (★Tōkyō)	829,455
Chichibu	60,915
Chigasaki (★Tōkyō)	201,675
Chikushino (★Fukuoka)	70,303
Chiryū (★Nagoya)	54,059
Chita (★Nagoya)	75,433
Chitose	78,946
Chōfu (★Tōkyō)	197,677
Chōshi	85,138
Daitō (★Ōsaka)	126,460
Dazaifu (★Fukuoka)	62,402
Ebetsu (★Sapporo)	97,201
Ebina (★Tōkyō)	105,822
Eniwa	55,615
Fuchū (★Tōkyō)	209,396
Fuchū	45,739
Fuchū	50,060
Fuji (★370,000)	222,490
Fujieda (★Shizuoka)	119,815
Fujiidera (★Ōsaka)	65,922
Fujimi (★Tōkyō)	94,864
Fujinomiya (★Fuji)	117,092
Fujioka (▲60,981)	50,100
Fujisawa (★Tōkyō)	350,330
Fuji-yoshida	54,804
Fukaya (▲94,017)	75,600
Fukuchiyama (▲66,506)	56,700
Fukui	252,743
Fukuoka (★1,750,000)	1,237,062
Fukushima	277,528
Fukuyama	365,612
Funabashi (★Tōkyō)	533,270
Furukawa (▲64,230)	51,200
Fussa (★Tōkyō)	58,062
Gamagōri	84,819
Gifu	410,324
Ginowan	75,905
Gotemba	79,557
Gushikawa	54,018
Gyōda	83,181
Habikino (★Ōsaka)	115,049
Hachinohe	241,057
Hachiōji (★Tōkyō)	466,347
Hadano (★Tōkyō)	155,620
Hagi	50,618
Hakodate	307,249
Hamada	49,135
Hamakita	81,157
Hamamatsu	534,620
Hanamaki (▲70,514)	55,000
Handa (★Nagoya)	99,550
Hannō (★Tōkyō)	73,214
Hashima	61,460
Hasuda (★Tōkyō)	59,706
Hatogaya (★Tōkyō)	56,440
Hatsukaichi (★Hiroshima)	63,441
Hekinan	65,899
Higashihiroshima (★Hiroshima)	94,209
Higashikurume (★Tōkyō)	113,818
Higashimatsuyama	84,394
Higashimurayama (★Tōkyō)	134,002
Higashiōsaka (★Ōsaka)	518,319
Higashiyamato (★Tōkyō)	75,132
Hikari (★Tokuyama)	47,611
Hikone	99,519
Himeji (★660,000)	454,360
Himi (▲60,766)	51,400
Hino (★Tōkyō)	165,928
Hirakata (★Ōsaka)	390,788
Hiratsuka (★Tōkyō)	245,950
Hirosaki (▲174,704)	133,800
Hiroshima (★1,575,000)	1,085,705
Hita (▲64,695)	57,100
Hitachi	202,141
Hōfu	117,634
Honjō	59,098
Hōya (★Tōkyō)	95,146
Hyūga	58,442
Ibaraki (★Ōsaka)	254,078
Ichihara (★Tōkyō)	257,716
Ichikawa (★Tōkyō)	436,596
Ichinomiya (★Nagoya)	262,434
Ichinoseki (▲61,967)	50,100
Iida (▲91,859)	64,700
Iizuka (★110,000)	83,131
Ikeda (★Ōsaka)	104,218
Ikoma (★Ōsaka)	99,604
Imabari	123,114
Imari (▲60,882)	50,000
Ina (▲60,062)	49,500
Inagi (★Tōkyō)	58,635
Inazawa (★Nagoya)	96,274
Inuyama (★Nagoya)	69,801
Iruma (★Tōkyō)	137,585
Isahaya	90,683
Ise (Uji-yamada)	104,164
Isehara (★Tōkyō)	89,567
Isesaki	115,938

▲ Population of an entire municipality, commune, or district, including rural area.
• Largest city in country.
★ Population or designation of the metropolitan area, including suburbs.
C Census. **E** Official estimate. **U** Unofficial estimate.

▲ Bevölkerung eines ganzen städtischen Verwaltungsgebietes, eines Kommunalbezirkes oder eines Distrikts, einschliesslich ländlicher Gebiete.
• Grösste Stadt des Landes.
★ Bevölkerung oder Bezeichnung der Stadtregion einschliesslich Vororte.
C Volkszählung. **E** Offizielle Schätzung. **U** Inoffizielle Schätzung.

Ishinomaki	121,976
Itami (★Ōsaka)	186,134
Itō	71,223
Iwaki (Taira)	355,812
Iwakuni	109,530
Iwamizawa	80,417
Iwata	83,521
Iwatsuki (★Tōkyō)	106,462
Izumi (★Ōsaka)	146,127
Izumi (★Sendai)	124,216
Izumi-ōtsu (★Ōsaka)	67,035
Izumi-sano (★Ōsaka)	88,866
Izumo (▲82,679)	69,600
Joetsu	130,116
Jōyō (★Ōsaka)	84,770
Kadoma (★Ōsaka)	142,297
Kaga	69,196
Kagoshima	536,752
Kainan (★Wakayama)	48,596
Kaizuka (★Ōsaka)	79,234
Kakamigahara	129,680
Kakegawa (▲72,795)	59,000
Kakogawa (★Ōsaka)	239,803
Kamagaya (★Tōkyō)	95,052
Kamaishi	52,484
Kamakura (★Tōkyō)	174,307
Kameoka	85,283
Kamifukuoka (★Tōkyō)	58,761
Kanazawa	442,868
Kani (★Nagoya)	80,012
Kanoya (▲77,655)	61,500
Kanuma (▲90,043)	74,900
Karatsu (▲79,207)	70,500
Kariya (★Nagoya)	120,126
Kasai	51,784
Kasaoka (▲59,619)	52,700
Kashihara (★Ōsaka)	115,554
Kashiwa (★Tōkyō)	305,058
Kashiwara (★Ōsaka)	76,819
Kashiwazaki (▲88,309)	75,300
Kasuga (★Fukuoka)	88,699
Kasugai (★Nagoya)	266,599
Kasukabe (★Tōkyō)	188,823
Katano (★Ōsaka)	65,308
Katsuta	109,825
Kawachi-nagano (★Ōsaka)	108,767
Kawagoe (★Tōkyō)	304,854
Kawaguchi (★Tōkyō)	438,680
Kawanishi (★Ōsaka)	141,253
Kawasaki (★Tōkyō)	1,173,603
Kesennuma	65,578
Kimitsu (▲89,242)	76,100
Kiryū	126,446
Kisarazu	123,433
Kishiwada (★Ōsaka)	188,563
Kitaibaraki	51,093
Kitakyūshū (★1,525,000)	1,026,455
Kitami	107,247
Kitamoto (★Tōkyō)	63,929
Kiyose (★Tōkyō)	67,539
Kōbe (★Ōsaka)	1,477,410
Kōchi	317,069
Kodaira (★Tōkyō)	164,013
Kōfu	200,626
Koga (★Tōkyō)	58,231
Koganei (★Tōkyō)	105,899
Kokubunji (★Tōkyō)	100,982
Komae (★Tōkyō)	74,189
Komaki (★Nagoya)	124,441
Komatsu	106,075
Kōnan (★Nagoya)	93,837
Kōnosu (★Tōkyō)	72,435
Kōriyama	314,642
Koshigaya (★Tōkyō)	285,259
Kudamatsu (★Tokuyama)	53,030
Kuki (★Tōkyō)	66,852
Kumagaya	152,124
Kumamoto	579,306
Kunitachi (★Tōkyō)	65,833
Kurashiki	414,693
Kure (★Hiroshima)	216,723
Kuroiso (▲52,344)	41,900
Kurume	228,347
Kusatsu (★Ōsaka)	94,767
Kushiro	205,639
Kuwana (★Nagoya)	97,909
Kyōto (★Ōsaka)	1,461,103
Machida (★Tōkyō)	349,050
Maebashi	286,261
Maizuru	96,333
Marugame	75,606
Matsubara (★Ōsaka)	135,919
Matsudo (★Tōkyō)	456,210
Matsue	142,956
Matsumoto	200,715
Matsusaka	118,725
Matsuyama	443,322
Mihara	85,518
Miki (★Ōsaka)	76,501
Minō (★Ōsaka)	122,120
Misato (★Tōkyō)	128,376
Mishima (★Numazu)	105,418
Mitaka (★Tōkyō)	165,564
Mito	234,968
Miura (★Tōkyō)	52,440
Miyako	58,503
Miyakonojō (▲130,153)	106,200
Miyazaki	287,352
Mobara	83,437
Moriguchi (★Ōsaka)	157,372
Morioka	235,434
Moriyama	58,561
Mukō (★Ōsaka)	52,928
Munakata	68,265
Muroran (★195,000)	117,855
Musashimurayama (★Tōkyō)	65,562
Musashino (★Tōkyō)	139,077
Mutsu	48,470
Nabari	68,933
Nagahama	55,485
Nagano	347,026
Nagaoka	185,938
Nagaokakyō (★Ōsaka)	77,191
Nagareyama (★Tōkyō)	140,059
Nagasaki	444,599
Nagoya (★4,800,000)	2,154,793
Naha	304,836
Nakama (★Kitakyūshū)	49,216
Nakatsu	66,388
Nakatsugawa	53,722
Nanao	50,103
Nara (★Ōsaka)	349,349
Narashino (★Tōkyō)	151,471
Narita	86,708
Naruto	64,575
Naze	46,306
Neyagawa (★Ōsaka)	256,524
Niigata	486,097
Niihama	129,149
Niitsu (▲63,999)	55,700
Niiza (★Tōkyō)	138,919
Nishinomiya (★Ōsaka)	426,909
Nishio	95,197
Nobeoka	130,624
Noboribetsu (★Muroran)	55,571
Noda (★Tōkyō)	114,475
Nōgata	62,530
Noshiro (▲55,915)	47,800
Numazu (★495,000)	211,732
Obihiro	167,384
Ōbu (★Nagoya)	69,720
Ōdate (▲68,195)	58,500
Odawara	193,417
Ōgaki	148,281
Ōita	408,501
Ōkawa	45,704
Okaya	59,849
Okayama	593,730
Okazaki	306,822
Okegawa (★Tōkyō)	69,029
Okinawa	105,845
Okinawa	105,852
Ōme (★Tōkyō)	125,960
Ōmi-hachiman (★Ōsaka)	66,066
Ōmiya (★Tōkyō)	403,776
Ōmura	73,435
Ōmuta (★225,000)	150,453
Ōnojō (★Fukuoka)	75,214
Onomichi	97,103
Ōsaka (★16,900,000)	2,623,801
Ōta	139,801
Otaru (★Sapporo)	163,211
Ōtsu (★Ōsaka)	260,018
Owariashi (★Nagoya)	65,675
Oyama (▲142,262)	120,000
Sabae	62,283
Saga	169,963
Sagamihara (★Tōkyō)	531,542
Saijō	56,821
Saiki	52,323
Sakado (★Tōkyō)	95,740
Sakai (★Ōsaka)	807,765
Sakaide	63,876
Sakata	100,811
Saku (▲62,003)	50,000
Sakura (★Tōkyō)	144,688
Sakurai	60,262
Sanda (▲64,560) (★Ōsaka)	54,500
Sanjō	85,823
Sano	83,484
Sapporo (★1,900,000)	1,671,742
Sasebo	244,677
Satte	54,342
Sayama (★Tōkyō)	157,309
Sayama (★Ōsaka)	54,319
Seki	68,386
Sendai, Kagoshima pref. (▲71,735)	58,000
Sendai, Miyagi pref. (★1,175,000)	918,398
Sennan (★Ōsaka)	60,065
Seto	126,340
Settsu (★Ōsaka)	87,453
Shibata (▲78,170)	63,600
Shijōnawate (★Ōsaka)	50,035
Shiki (★Tōkyō)	63,491
Shimada (▲73,810)	64,500
Shimizu (★Shizuoka)	241,523
Shimodate (▲66,028)	54,100
Shimonoseki (★Kitakyūshū)	262,635
Shiogama (★Sendai)	62,025
Shizuoka (★975,000)	472,196
Sōka (★Tōkyō)	206,132
Suita (★Ōsaka)	345,206
Suwa	52,464
Suzuka	174,105
Tachikawa (★Tōkyō)	152,824
Tagajō (★Sendai)	58,456
Tagawa	57,700
Tajimi (★Nagoya)	94,036
Takaishi (★Ōsaka)	65,086
Takamatsu	329,684
Takaoka (★220,000)	175,466
Takarazuka (★Ōsaka)	201,862
Takasago (★Ōsaka)	93,273
Takasaki	236,461
Takatsuki (★Ōsaka)	359,867
Takayama	65,243
Takefu	70,187
Takikawa	49,591
Tama (★Tōkyō)	144,489
Tamano	73,238
Tanabe (▲69,859)	59,100
Tanashi (★Tōkyō)	75,144
Tatebayashi	76,221
Tenri	68,815
Tochigi	86,216
Toda (★Tōkyō)	87,599
Tōkai (★Nagoya)	97,358
Toki	64,946
Tokoname (★Nagoya)	51,784
Tokorozawa (★Tōkyō)	303,040
Tokushima	263,356
Tokuyama (★250,000)	110,900
● TŌKYŌ (★30,300,000)	8,163,573
Tomakomai	160,118
Tondabayashi (★Ōsaka)	110,447
Toride (★Tōkyō)	81,665
Tosu	55,877
Tottori	142,467
Toyama	321,254
Toyoake (★Nagoya)	62,160
Toyohashi	337,982
Toyokawa	111,730
Toyonaka (★Ōsaka)	409,837
Toyota	332,336
Tsu	157,177
Tsuchiura	127,471
Tsuruga	68,041
Tsuruoka	99,889
Tsushima (★Nagoya)	59,343
Tsuyama	89,400
Ube (★230,000)	175,053
Ueda	119,435
Ueno (▲60,242)	51,400
Uji (★Ōsaka)	177,010
Uozu	49,514
Urasoe	89,994
Urawa (★Tōkyō)	418,271
Urayasu (★Tōkyō)	115,675
Usa (▲50,829)	38,600
Ushiku	60,693
Utsunomiya	426,795
Uwajima	68,034
Wakayama (★495,000)	396,553
Wakkanai	48,232
Wakō (★Tōkyō)	56,890
Warabi (★Tōkyō)	73,620
Yachiyo (★Tōkyō)	148,615
Yaizu (★Shizuoka)	112,186
Yamagata	249,487
Yamaguchi	129,461
Yamato (★Tōkyō)	194,866
Yamato-kōriyama (★Ōsaka)	92,949
Yamato-takada (★Ōsaka)	68,237
Yao (★Ōsaka)	277,568
Yashio (★Tōkyō)	72,473
Yatsushiro (▲108,135)	88,300
Yawata (★Ōsaka)	75,758
Yokkaichi	274,180
Yokohama (★Tōkyō)	3,220,331
Yokosuka (★Tōkyō)	433,358
Yonago	131,453
Yonezawa	94,760
Yono (★Tōkyō)	79,060
Yotsukaidō (★Tōkyō)	72,157
Yukuhashi	65,711
Zama (★Tōkyō)	112,102
Zushi (★Tōkyō)	56,704

JERSEY

1991 C	84,082
● SAINT HELIER (★46,500)	28,123

JORDAN / Al-Urdun

1989 E	3,111,000
Al-Baq'ah (★'Ammān)	63,985
● 'AMMĀN (★1,625,000)	936,300
Ar-Ruṣayfah (★'Ammān)	72,580
As-Salt	47,585
Az-Zarqā' (★'Ammān)	318,055
Irbid	167,785

KAZAKHSTAN

1991 E	16,793,100
Aktau	169,000
Akt'ubinsk	265,300
● ALMA-ATA (ALMATY) (★1,190,000)	1,156,200
Arkalyk	64,900
Aterau	152,500
Balchaš	87,600
Čelinograd	286,000
Čimkent	407,900
Džambul	312,300
Džetygara	48,900
Džezkazgan	111,100
Ekibastuz	138,900
Karaganda	608,600
Kentau	65,100
Kokčetav	143,300
Kustanaj	233,900
Kzyl-Orda	158,200
Leninogorsk	69,500
Leninsk	73,000
Pavlodar	342,500
Petropavlovsk	247,400
Rudnyj	128,800
Šachtinsk	65,300
Saptajev	61,400
Šaran'	62,600
Ščučinsk	56,000
Semipalatinsk	344,700
Taldy-Kurgan	124,500
Temirtau	213,100
Turkestan	81,200
Ural'sk	214,000
Ust'-Kamenogorsk	332,900
Žanatas	53,000
Zyr'anovsk	53,800

KENYA

1990 E	24,870,000
Eldoret (1979C)	50,503
Kisumu (1984E)	167,100
Machakos (1983E)	92,300
Meru (1979C)	72,049
Mombasa	537,000
● NAIROBI	1,505,000
Nakuru (1984E)	101,700

KIRIBATI

1990 C	72,298
BAIRIKI	2,226
● Bikenibeu	5,055

KOREA, NORTH / Chosŏn-minjujuŭi-inmīn-konghwaguk

1981 E	18,317,000
Ch'ŏngjin	490,000
Haeju (1983E)	213,000
Hamhŭng (1970E)	150,000
Hŭngnam (1976E)	260,000
Kaesŏng	259,000
Kanggye (1967E)	130,000
Kimch'aek (Sŏngjin) (1967E)	265,000
Namp'o	241,000
● P'YŎNGYANG	2,355,000
Sinŭiju	305,000
Songnim (1944C)	53,035
Wŏnsan	398,000

KOREA, SOUTH / Taehan-min'guk

1990 C	43,520,199
Andong	116,932
Ansan (★Sŏul)	252,157
Anyang (★Sŏul)	480,668
Bucheon (★Sŏul)	667,777
Changsŭngp'o	48,614
Changwŏn (★Masan)	323,138
Chech'on	102,037
Cheju	232,687
Chinhae	120,207
Chinju	258,365
Chŏmch'on	47,802
Ch'ŏnan	211,382
Ch'ŏngju	497,429
Chŏnju	86,850
Chŏnju, Chŏlla Pukdo prov.	517,104
Ch'unch'ŏn	174,153
Ch'ungju	129,994
Ch'ungmu	92,159
Hanam (★Sŏul)	101,278
Inch'ŏn (★Sŏul)	1,818,293
Iri	203,401
Kangnŭng	152,605
Kimch'ŏn	81,349
Kimhae	106,166
Kimje	55,136
Kongju	65,195
Kumi	206,101
Kŭmsŏng (1985C)	58,897
Kunp'o (★Sŏul)	99,956
Kunsan	218,216
Kwachŏn (★Sŏul)	72,328
Kwangju	1,144,695
Kwangmyŏng (★Sŏul)	328,803
Kyŏngju	141,895
Kyŏngsan	60,524
Masan (★625,000)	496,639
Mikŭm (★Sŏul)	74,688
Miryang	52,995
Mokp'o	253,423
Naju	55,306
Namwŏn	63,121
Ŏnyang	66,379
Osan	59,492
P'ohang	318,595
Pusan (★3,800,000)	3,797,566
P'yŏngt'aek	79,238
Samch'ŏnp'o	62,824
Sangju	51,875
Shihŭng (★Sŏul)	107,190
Sŏgwipo	88,292
Sŏkch'o	73,796
Sŏngnam (★Sŏul)	540,764
Songtan	77,460
Sŏsan	55,930
● SŎUL (★15,850,000)	10,627,790
Sunch'ŏn	167,209
Suwŏn (★Sŏul)	644,968
T'aebaek	89,770
Taech'ŏn	56,922
Taegu	2,228,834
Taejŏn	1,062,084
Tongduchŏn	71,448
Tonghae	89,162
Tongkwang	70,118
Ŭijŏngbu (★Sŏul)	212,368
Ŭiwang	96,892
Ulsan	682,978
Wŏnju	173,013
Yŏch'ŏn	63,802
Yŏngch'ŏn	48,890
Yŏngju	84,335
Yŏsu	173,164

KUWAIT / Al-Kuwayt

1985 C	1,697,301
Abraq Khīṭān (★Al-Kuwayt)	45,120
Al-Aḥmadī (★285,000)	26,899
Al-Farwānīyah (★Al-Kuwayt)	68,701
Al-Fuḥayḥīl (★Al-Aḥmadī)	50,081
Al-Jahrah (★Al-Kuwayt)	111,222
● AL-KUWAYT (★1,375,000)	44,335
As-Sālimīyah (★Al-Kuwayt)	153,359
Aṣ-Ṣulaybīyah (★Al-Kuwayt)	51,314
Ḥawallī (★Al-Kuwayt)	145,126
Qalīb ash-Shuyūkh (★Al-Kuwayt)	114,771
South Khīṭān (★Al-Kuwayt)	69,256
Subahiya (★Al-Aḥmadī)	60,787

KYRGYZSTAN

1991 E	4,422,200
● BIŠKEK	631,300
Džalal-Abad	74,200
Kara-Balta	55,000
Karakol (Prževal'sk)	64,300
Oš	218,700
Tokmak	71,200

LAOS / Lao

1985 C	3,584,803
Savannakhét (1975E)	53,000
● VIANGCHAN (VIENTIANE)	377,409

LATVIA / Latvija

1991 E	2,680,500
Daugavpils	129,000
Jelgava	74,500
Jūrmala (★Rīga)	66,500
Liepāja	114,900
● RĪGA (★1,005,000)	910,200
Ventspils	50,400

LEBANON / Lubnān

1982 E	2,637,000
● BAYRŪT (★1,675,000)	509,000
Ṣaydā	105,000
Ṣūr (Tyre) (1970E)	12,500
Ṭarābulus (Tripoli) (★950,000)	198,000

LESOTHO

1986 C	1,577,536
● MASERU	98,017

LIBERIA

1986 E	2,221,000
● MONROVIA	465,000

LIBYA / Lībiyā

1988 E	3,772,500
Al-Bayḍā (Beida) (1984C)	67,120
Banghāzī	446,250
Darnah (1984C)	62,179
Miṣrātah	121,669
● ṬARĀBULUS (TRIPOLI)	591,062
Ṭubruq (Tobruk) (1984C)	75,282

LIECHTENSTEIN

1992 E	29,386
● VADUZ	4,887

LITHUANIA / Lietuva

1992 C	3,746,400
Alytus	77,500
Kaunas	433,600
Klaipėda (Memel)	208,300
Marijampolė	52,300
Panevėžys	132,300
Šiauliai	149,000
● VILNIUS	596,900

LUXEMBOURG

1991 C	384,062
Esch-sur-Alzette (★83,000)	24,012
● LUXEMBOURG (★136,000)	75,377

MACAU

1989 E	452,300
● MACAU	452,300

▲ Población de un municipio, comuna o distrito entero, incluyendo sus áreas rurales.
● Ciudad más grande de un país.
★ Población o designación de un área metropolitana, incluyendo los suburbios.
C Censo. E Estimado oficial. U Estimado no oficial.

▲ Population d'une municipalité, d'une commune ou d'un district, zone rurale incluse.
● Ville la plus peuplée du pays.
★ Population de l'agglomération (ou nom de la zone métropolitaine englobante).
C Recensement. E Estimation officielle. U Estimation non officielle.

▲ População de um município, comuna ou distrito, inclusive as respectivas áreas rurais.
● Maior cidade de um país.
★ População ou indicação de uma área metropolitana.
C Censo. E Estimativa oficial. U Estimativa não oficial.

MACEDONIA / Makedonija

1987 E	2,064,581
Bitola (▲143,090)	76,200
• SKOPJE (▲547,214)	444,900

MADAGASCAR / Madagasikara

1988 E	11,238,000
• ANTANANARIVO	1,250,000
Antsirabe (▲100,000)	52,700
Antsiranana	220,000
Fianarantsoa	300,000
Mahajanga	200,000
Toamasina	230,000
Toliara	150,000

MALAWI / Malaŵi

1987 C	7,988,507
• Blantyre	333,120
LILONGWE	223,318
Mzuzu	51,904

MALAYSIA

1980 C	13,136,109
Alor Setar	69,435
Batu Pahat	64,727
Butterworth (★George Town)	77,982
George Town (Pinang) (★495,000)	248,241
Ipoh	293,849
Johor Baharu (★Singapore, Singapore)	246,395
Kelang	192,080
Keluang	50,315
Kota Baharu	167,872
Kota Kinabalu (Jesselton)	55,997
• KUALA LUMPUR (★1,475,000)	919,610
Kuala Terengganu	180,296
Kuantan	131,547
Kuching	72,555
Melaka	87,494
Miri	52,125
Muar (Bandar Maharani)	65,151
Petaling Jaya (★Kuala Lumpur)	207,805
Sandakan	70,420
Seremban	132,911
Sibu	85,231
Taiping	146,000
Telok Anson	49,148

MALDIVES

1990 C	213,215
• MALE'	55,130

MALI

1987 C	7,696,348
• BAMAKO	658,275
Gao	55,266
Kayes	50,993
Koutiala	48,698
Mopti	74,771
Ségou	88,135
Sikasso	73,859
Tombouctou (Timbuktu)	31,962

MALTA

1991 E	355,910
• VALLETTA (★215,000)	9,199

MARSHALL ISLANDS

1980 C	30,873
• Jarej-Uliga-Delap	8,583

MARTINIQUE

1982 C	328,566
• FORT-DE-FRANCE (★116,017)	99,844

MAURITANIA / Mauritanie / Mūrītāniyā

1987 E	2,007,000
• NOUAKCHOTT	285,000

MAURITIUS

1989 E	1,081,669
Beau Bassin-Rose Hill (★Port Louis)	94,236
Curepipe (★Port Louis)	66,704
• PORT LOUIS (★420,000)	141,870
Quatre Bornes (★Port Louis)	65,759
Vacoas-Phoenix (★Port Louis)	56,335

MAYOTTE

1985 E	67,205
• DZAOUDZI (★6,979)	5,865

MEXICO / México

1990 C	81,249,645
Acámbaro	52,248
Acapulco de Juárez	515,374
Aguascalientes	440,425
Apatzingán de la Constitución	76,643
Apodaca	103,364
Atlixco	74,233
Buenavista	114,653
Campeche	150,518
Cancún	167,730
Cárdenas	61,017
Celaya	214,856
Chalco (★Ciudad de México)	224,190
Chetumal	94,158
Chicoloapan de Juárz	57,306
Chihuahua	516,153
Chilpancingo de los Bravo	97,165
Chimalhuacán	235,587
Cholula de Rivadabia (★Puebla)	53,673
Ciudad Acuña	52,983
Ciudad del Carmen	83,806
• CIUDAD DE MÉXICO (★14,100,000)	8,235,744
Ciudad Guzmán	72,619
Ciudad Hidalgo	48,476
Ciudad Juárez (★El Paso, Tex., U.S.A.)	789,522
Ciudad Lerdo (★Torreón)	46,593
Ciudad López Mateos	315,059
Ciudad Madero (★Tampico)	160,331
Ciudad Mante	76,799
Ciudad Obregón	219,980
Ciudad Valles	91,402
Ciudad Victoria	194,996
Coacalco	151,255
Coatzacoalcos	198,817
Colima	106,967
Comitan de Dominguez	48,299
Córdoba	130,695
Cortazar	45,579
Cuauhtémoc	6,938
Cuautitlán Izcalli (★Ciudad de México)	313,238
Cuernavaca	279,187
Culiacán	415,046
Delicias	87,412
Durango	348,036
Ecatepec (★Ciudad de México)	1,218,135
Ensenada	169,426
Fresnillo	75,118
Garza García (★Monterrey)	113,017
General Escobedo	96,962
Gómez Palacio (★Torreón)	164,092
Guadalajara (★2,430,000)	1,650,042
Guadalupe (★Monterrey)	535,332
Guadalupe	46,433
Guamúchil	49,635
Guanajuato	73,108
Guasave	49,338
Guaymas	87,484
Hermosillo	406,417
Heroica Zitácuaro	66,983
Hidalgo del Parral	88,197
Iguala	83,412
Irapuato	265,042
Ixtapaluca	115,711
Jiutepec	82,845
Juchitán de Zaragoza	53,666
Lagos de Moreno	63,646
La Paz	137,641
La Piedad de Cabadas	62,625
Las Choapas	43,868
León	758,279
Los Mochis	162,659
Los Reyes la Paz	134,544
Manzanillo	67,697
Matamoros (★Brownsville, Tex., U.S.A.)	266,055
Matehuala	54,713
Mazatlán	262,705
Mérida	523,422
Metepec	116,203
Mexicali (★460,000)	438,377
Minatitlán	142,060
Monclova	177,792
Monterrey (★2,015,000)	1,068,996
Morelia	428,486
Naucalpan de Juárez (★Ciudad de México)	845,960
Navojoa	82,618
Nezahualcóyotl (★Ciudad de México)	1,255,456
Nogales	105,873
Nuevo Laredo (★Laredo, Tex., U.S.A.)	218,413
Oaxaca de Juárez	212,818
Ocotlán	62,595
Orizaba (★215,000)	114,216
Pachuca	174,013
Papantla de Olarte	46,075
Piedras Negras	96,178
Poza Rica	151,739
Puebla (★1,200,000)	1,007,170
Puerto Vallarta	93,503
Querétaro	385,503
Reynosa	265,663
Río Bravo	67,092
Sahuayo de José María Morelos	50,463
Salamanca	123,190
Salina Cruz	61,656
Saltillo	420,947
San Andrés Tuxtla	49,658
San Cristóbal de las Casas	73,388
San Francisco del Rincón	52,291
San Juan del Río	61,652
San Luis Potosí (★600,000)	489,238
San Luis Río Colorado	95,461
San Martín Texmelucan	57,519
San Miguel de Allende	48,935
San Nicolás de los Garza (★Monterrey)	436,603
San Pablo de las Salinas	84,217
Santa Catarina (★Monterrey)	162,707
Silao	50,828
Soledad de Graciano Sanchez	123,943
Tampico (★440,000)	272,690
Tapachula	138,858
Tecomán	60,938
Tehuacán	139,450
Temixco	65,058
Tepatitlán de Morelos	54,036
Tepic	206,967
Texcoco de Mora (★Ciudad de México)	74,194
Tijuana (★San Diego, Calif., U.S.A.)	698,752
Tlalnepantla (★Ciudad de México)	702,270
Tlaquepaque (★Guadalajara)	328,031
Tlaxcala de Xicoténcatl	50,486
Toluca de Lerdo	327,865
Tonalá	151,190
Torreón (★690,000)	439,436
Tulancingo	75,477
Tuxpan	69,224
Tuxtepec	62,788
Tuxtla Gutiérrez	289,626
Uruapan del Progreso	187,623
Valle de Santiago	56,009
Veracruz (★540,000)	438,821
Villa Frontera	58,216
Villahermosa	261,231
Villa Nicolás Romero	148,342
Xalapa	279,451
Zacatecas	100,051
Zamora de Hidalgo	109,751
Zapopan (★Guadalajara)	668,323

MICRONESIA, FEDERATED STATES OF

1985 E	94,534
• KOLONIA	6,306

MOLDOVA

1991 E	4,366,300
Bălţi	161,800
• CHIŞINĂU (KISHINEV)	676,700
Râbniţa (Rybnica)	62,900
Tighina	133,000
Tiraspol	186,000

MONACO

1990 C	29,972
• MONACO (★87,000)	29,972

MONGOLIA / Mongol Ard Uls

1989 E	2,040,000
Darchan (1985E)	69,800
• ULAANBAATAR	548,400

MONTSERRAT

1980 C	11,606
• PLYMOUTH	1,568

MOROCCO / Al-Magreb

1982 C	20,419,555
Agadir	110,479
Beni-Mellal	95,003
Berkane	60,490
• Casablanca (Dar-el-Beida) (★2,475,000)	2,139,204
El-Jadida (Mazagan)	81,455
Fès (★535,000)	448,823
Kenitra	188,194
Khemisset	58,925
Khouribga	127,181
Ksar-el-Kebir	73,541
Larache	63,893
Marrakech (★535,000)	439,728
Meknès (★375,000)	319,783
Mohammedia (Fedala) (★Casablanca)	105,120
Nador	62,040
Oued-Zem	58,744
Oujda	260,082
RABAT (★980,000)	518,616
Safi	197,309
Salé (★Rabat)	289,391
Settat	65,203
Sidi Kacem	55,833
Sidi Slimane	50,457
Tanger (Tangier) (★370,000)	266,346
Tan-Tan	41,451
Taza	77,216
Temera (★Rabat)	48,644
Tétouan	199,615

MOZAMBIQUE / Moçambique

1989 E	15,326,476
Beira	291,604
Chimoio (1986E)	86,928
Inhambane (1986E)	64,274
• MAPUTO	1,069,727
Nacala	101,615
Nampula	197,379
Pemba (1986E)	50,215
Quelimane	78,520
Tete (1986E)	56,178
Xai-Xai (1986E)	51,620

MYANMAR (BURMA)

1983 C	34,124,908
Bago (Pegu)	150,528
Chauk	51,437
Dawei (Tavoy)	69,882
Henzada	82,005
Kale	52,628
Lashio	88,590
Magway	54,881
Mandalay	532,949
Mawlamyine (Moulmein)	219,961
Maymyo	63,782
Meiktila	96,496
Mergui (Myeik)	88,600
Mogok	49,392
Monywa	106,843
Myingyan	77,060
Myitkyinā	56,427
Nyaunglebin	55,194
Pakokku	71,860
Pathein (Bassein)	144,096
Prome (Pyè)	83,332
Pyinmana	52,962
Sagaing	46,212
Shwebo	52,185
Sittwe (Akyab)	107,621
Taunggyi	108,231
Thaton	61,790
Toungoo	65,861
• YANGON (RANGOON) (★2,800,000)	2,705,039
Yenangyaung	62,582

NAMIBIA

1988 E	1,760,000
Walvis Bay (★22,999) (1991C)	12,383
• WINDHOEK	114,500

NEPAL / Nepāl

1981 C	15,022,839
Bhaktapur	48,472
• KĀTHMĀNDAU (★320,000)	235,160
Wirātnagar	93,544

NETHERLANDS / Nederland

1992 E	15,129,150
Alkmaar (★124,000)	91,817
Almelo	63,383
Alphen aan den Rijn	63,573
Amersfoort	104,390
Amstelveen (★Amsterdam)	71,939
• AMSTERDAM (★1,875,000)	713,407
Apeldoorn	148,745
Arnhem (★305,000)	132,928
Assen	50,880
Bergen op Zoom	47,259
Breda (★165,000)	126,709
Delft (★'s-Gravenhage)	90,066
Den Helder	61,225
Deventer	68,004
Dordrecht (★209,000)	111,791
Ede (▲96,044)	50,700
Eindhoven (★384,000)	193,966
Emmen (▲93,107)	37,000
Enschede (★252,000)	147,199
Geleen (★179,000)	33,922
Gouda	67,416
Groningen (★208,000)	169,387
Haarlem (★Amsterdam)	149,788
Haarlemmermeer (▲100,659) (★Amsterdam)	14,000
Heerlen (★267,500)	53,600
Helmond	70,574
Hengelo (★Enschede)	76,726
Hilversum (★Amsterdam)	84,674
Hoorn	59,028
IJmuiden (★Amsterdam)	61,506
Kerkrade (★Heerlen)	53,364
Leeuwarden	86,405
Leiden (★190,000)	112,976
Maastricht (★163,000)	118,152
Nieuwegein (★Utrecht)	58,882
Nijmegen (★242,000)	146,344
Oss	52,132
Purmerend (★Amsterdam)	62,504
Ridderkerk (★Rotterdam)	45,834
Rijswijk (★'s-Gravenhage)	47,456
Roosendaal	61,354
Rotterdam (★1,120,000)	589,707
Schiedam (★Rotterdam)	71,117
'S-GRAVENHAGE (THE HAGUE) (★773,000)	445,287
's-Hertogenbosch (★200,000)	93,171
Soest (★Amersfoort)	41,693
Spijkenisse (★Rotterdam)	69,655
Tilburg (★235,000)	160,618
Utrecht (★528,000)	232,705
Veenendaal	50,791
Venlo (★88,000)	64,890
Vlaardingen (★Rotterdam)	73,893
Vlissingen (Flushing) (▲43,913)	25,000
Zaanstad (★Amsterdam)	131,273
Zeist (★Utrecht)	59,211
Zoetermeer (★'s-Gravenhage)	100,623
Zwolle	97,131

NETHERLANDS ANTILLES / Nederlandse Antillen

1990 E	189,687
• WILLEMSTAD (★130,000) (1981C)	31,883

NEW CALEDONIA / Nouvelle-Calédonie

1989 C	164,173
• NOUMÉA (★97,581)	65,110

NEW ZEALAND

1991 C	3,434,950
• Auckland (★855,571)	315,668
Christchurch (★307,179)	292,858
Dunedin	116,577
Hamilton (★148,625)	101,448
Invercargill	56,148
Lower Hutt (★Wellington)	94,540
Manukau (★Auckland)	226,147
Napier (★110,216)	51,645
Palmerston North (★70,951)	70,318
Rotorua (★53,702)	45,144
Takapuna (★Auckland)	74,360
Tauranga (★70,803)	46,308
Waitemata (★Auckland)	136,716
WELLINGTON (★375,000)	150,301
Whangarei (★44,183)	40,101

NICARAGUA

1985 E	3,272,100
Chinandega	75,000
Granada (1981E)	64,642
León	101,000
• MANAGUA	682,000
Masaya	75,000
Matagalpa	68,000

NIGER

1988 C	7,220,089
Agadez	49,361
Maradi	104,386
• NIAMEY	392,165
Tahoua	49,948
Zinder	119,838

NIGERIA

1987 E	101,907,000
Aba	239,800
Abakaliki	56,800
Abeokuta	341,300
ABUJA (1993U)	250,000
Ado-Ekiti	287,000
Afikpo	65,790
Agege	83,810
Akure	129,600
Amaigbo	53,690
Apomu	49,570
Aramoko	48,280
Asaba	47,410
Awka	88,800
Azare	50,020
Bauchi	68,840
Benin City	183,200
Bida	100,200
Calabar	139,800
Deba	110,600
Duku	52,880
Ede	245,200
Effon-Alaiye	122,300
Ejigbo	84,570
Emure-Ekiti	58,750
Enugu	252,500
Epe	80,560
Erin-Oshogbo	59,940
Eruwa	49,140
Fiditi	49,440
Gboko	49,390
Gbongan	53,990
Gombe	86,120
Gusau	126,200
Ibadan	1,144,000
Idah	50,550
Idanre	56,080
Ife	237,000
Ifon-Oshogbo	65,980
Igbasa-Odo	48,040
Igboho	85,230
Igbo-Ora	68,060
Igede-Ekiti	56,570
Ihiala	73,240
Ijebu-Igbo	78,680
Ijebu-Ode	124,900
Ijero-Ekiti	76,420
Ikare	112,500
Ikerre	195,400
Ikire	94,450
Ikirun	144,900
Ikole	71,860
Ikorodu	147,700
Ikot Ekpene	69,440
Ila	210,800
Ilawe-Ekiti	147,300
Ilesha	302,100
Ilobu	159,000
Ilorin	380,000
Inisa	95,630
Ipoti-Ekiti	53,220
Ise-Ekiti	82,580
Iseyin	173,500
Iwo	289,100

▲ Population of an entire municipality, commune, or district, including rural area.
• Largest city in country.
★ Population or designation of the metropolitan area, including suburbs.
C Census. **E** Official estimate. **U** Unofficial estimate.

▲ Bevölkerung eines ganzen städtischen Verwaltungsgebietes, eines Kommunalbezirkes oder eines Distrikts, einschliesslich ländlicher Gebiete.
• Grösste Stadt des Landes.
★ Bevölkerung oder Bezeichnung der Stadtregion einschliesslich Vororte.
C Volkszählung. **E** Offizielle Schätzung. **U** Inoffizielle Schätzung.

Jega (1985E)	47,000
Jimeta	66,130
Jos	164,700
Kaduna	273,200
Kano	538,300
Katsina	165,000
Kaura Namoda	52,910
Keffi	57,790
Kishi	77,210
Kumo	118,200
Lafia	97,810
Lafiagi	57,580
• LAGOS (★3,800,000)	1,213,000
Lalupon	56,130
Lere	49,670
Maiduguri	255,100
Makurdi	98,350
Minna	109,300
Mubi	51,190
Mushin (★Lagos)	266,100
Nguru	78,770
Nsukka	47,760
Ode-Ekiti	48,910
Offa	157,500
Ogbomosho	582,900
Oka	114,400
Oke-Mesi	55,040
Okwe	52,550
Olupona	65,720
Ondo	135,300
Onitsha	298,200
Opobo	64,620
Oron	62,260
Oshogbo	380,800
Owerri (1985E)	37,000
Owo	146,600
Oyan	50,930
Oyo	204,700
Pindiga	64,130
Port Harcourt	327,300
Potiskum	56,490
Sapele	111,200
Shagamu	93,610
Shaki	139,000
Shomolu (★Lagos)	120,700
Sokoto	163,700
Ugep	81,910
Umuahia	52,550
Uyo	60,500
Warri	100,700
Zaria	302,800

NIUE

1989 C	2,267
• ALOFI	706

NORTHERN MARIANA ISLANDS

1980 C	16,780
• Chalan Kanoa	2,678
Garapan	2,063

NORWAY / Norge

1987 E	4,190,000
Bærum (★Oslo) (1985E)	83,000
Bergen (★239,000)	209,320
Drammen (★73,000) (1985E)	50,700
Fredrikstad (★52,000) (1983E)	27,618
Hammerfest (1983E)	7,208
Kristiansand (1985E)	62,200
Narvik (1983E)	19,080
• OSLO (★720,000)	452,415
Skien (★77,981) (1985E)	46,700
Stavanger (★132,000) (1985E)	94,200
Tromsø (1985E)	47,800
Trondheim	135,010

OMAN / 'Umān

1983 E	1,131,000
• MASQAT (MUSCAT)	30,000
Maṭraḥ (1971E)	14,000
Ṣūr	30,000

PAKISTAN / Pākistān

1981 C	84,253,644
Abbottābād (★65,996)	32,188
Ahmadpur East	56,979
Attock (★39,986)	26,233
Bahāwalnagar	74,533
Bahāwalpur (★180,263)	152,009
Bannu (★43,210)	35,170
Bhakkar	41,934
Chārsadda	62,530
Chīchāwatni	50,241
Chiniot	105,559
Chishtiān Mandi	61,959
Daska	55,555
Dera Ghāzi Khān	102,007
Dera Ismāīl Khān (★68,145)	64,358
Drigh Road Cantonment (★Karāchi)	56,742
Faisalabad (Lyallpur)	1,104,209
Gojra	68,000
Gujrānwāla (★658,753)	600,993
Gujrānwāla Cantonment (★Gujrānwāla)	57,760
Gujrāt	155,058
Hāfizābād	83,464
Hyderābād (★800,000)	702,539
Hyderābād Cantonment (★Hyderābād)	48,990
ISLAMABAD (★Rāwalpindi)	204,364
Jacobābād	79,365
Jarānwāla	69,459
Jhang Sadar	195,558
Jhelum (★106,462)	92,646
Kamālia	61,107
Kāmoke	71,097
• Karāchi (★5,300,000)	4,901,627
Karāchi Cantonment (★Karāchi)	181,981
Kasūr	155,523
Khairpur	61,447
Khānewāl	89,090
Khānpur	70,589
Khāriān Cantonment (★51,506)	16,042
Khushāb	56,274
Kohāt (★77,604)	55,832
Lahore (★3,025,000)	2,707,215
Lahore Cantonment (★Lahore)	245,474
Lārkāna	123,890
Leiah	51,482
Malir Cantonment (★Karāchi)	47,588
Mandi Būrewāla	86,311
Mardān (★147,977)	141,842
Miānwāli	59,159
Mingāora	88,078
Mīrpur Khās	124,371
Multān (★732,070)	696,316
Muzaffargarh	53,000
Nawābshāh	102,139
Nowshera (★74,913)	38,875
Okāra (★153,483)	127,455
Pākpattan	69,820
Peshāwar (★566,248)	506,896
Peshāwar Cantonment (★Peshāwar)	59,352
Quetta (★285,719)	244,842
Rahīmyār Khān (★132,635)	119,036
Rāwalpindi (★1,040,000)	457,091
Rāwalpindi Cantonment (★Rāwalpindi)	337,752
Sādiqābād	63,935
Sāhīwal	150,954
Sargodha (★291,362)	231,895
Sargodha Cantonment (★Sargodha)	59,467
Shekhūpura	141,168
Shikārpur	88,138
Shorkot (★50,568)	18,533
Siālkot (★302,009)	258,147
Sukkur	190,551
Tando Ādam	62,744
Turbat	52,337
Vihāri	53,799
Wāh Cantonment	122,335
Wazīrābād	62,725

PALAU / Belau

1986 C	13,873
• KOROR	8,629

PANAMA / Panamá

1990 C	2,315,047
Balboa (▲11,327) (★Panamá)	3,500
Colón (★96,000)	54,469
David	65,635
• PANAMÁ (★770,000)	411,549
San Miguelito (★Panamá)	242,529

PAPUA NEW GUINEA

1990 C	3,534,038
Lae	78,265
• PORT MORESBY	193,242
Rabaul	16,883

PARAGUAY

1992 C	4,123,550
• ASUNCIÓN (★700,000)	502,426
Caaguazú	38,200
Capiatá	83,189
Ciudad del Este	133,896
Encarnación	55,359
Fernando de la Mora (★Asunción)	95,287
Lambaré (★Asunción)	99,681
Pedro Juan Caballero	53,601
San Lorenzo (★Asunción)	133,311

PERU / Perú

1981 C	17,031,221
Arequipa (★446,942)	108,023
Ayacucho (★69,533)	57,432
Barranco (★Lima)	46,478
Breña (★Lima)	112,398
Cajamarca	62,259
Callao (★Lima)	264,133
Cerro de Pasco (★66,373)	55,597
Chiclayo (★279,527)	213,095
Chimbote	223,341
Chorrillos (★Lima)	141,881
Chosica	65,139
Cusco (★184,550)	89,563
Huacho	43,398
Huancayo (★164,954)	84,845
Huánuco	61,812
Ica	114,786
Iquitos	178,738
Jesús María (★Lima)	83,179
Juliaca	87,651
La Victoria (★Lima)	270,778
• LIMA (★4,608,010)	371,122
Lince (★Lima)	80,456
Magdalena (★Lima)	55,535
Miraflores (★Lima)	103,453
Pisco	55,604
Piura (★207,934)	144,609
Pucallpa	112,263
Pueblo Libre (★Lima)	83,985
Puno	67,397
Rímac (★Lima)	184,484
San Isidro (★Lima)	71,203
San Martin de Porras (★Lima)	404,856
Santiago de Surco (★Lima)	146,636
Sullana	89,037
Surquillo (★Lima)	134,158
Tacna	97,173
Talara	57,351
Trujillo (★354,301)	202,469
Tumbes	47,936
Vitarte (★Lima)	145,504

PHILIPPINES / Pilipinas

1990 C	60,477,000
Angeles	236,685
Antipolo (▲207,842)	83,641
Bacolod	364,000
Bacoor (★Manila)	159,685
Baguio	183,102
Baliuag	89,719
Biñan (★Manila)	134,553
Binangonan	127,561
Bislig (▲81,615) (1980C)	49,498
Bocaue	67,243
Butuan (▲228,000)	99,000
Cabanatuan (▲173,065)	74,966
Cagayan de Oro (▲340,000)	255,000
Cainta (★Manila)	126,839
Calamba (▲173,453)	97,623
Caloocan (★Manila)	761,011
Carmona (★Manila)	28,247
Cavite (★195,000)	91,641
Cebu (★825,000)	610,000
Cotabato	127,000
Dagupan	122,247
Davao (▲850,000)	569,300
Dumaguete	80,000
General Santos (Dadiangas) (▲250,000)	157,600
Guagua	88,290
Iloilo	311,000
Isabela (Basilan) (▲49,891) (1980C)	11,491
Jolo (1980C)	52,429
Lapu-Lapu (Opon)	146,000
Las Piñas (★Manila)	296,851
Legaspi (▲121,000)	63,000
Lucena	150,624
Mabalacat (▲121,115)	64,261
Makati (★Manila)	452,734
Malabon (★Manila)	278,380
Malolos	125,178
Mandaluyong (★Manila)	244,538
Mandaue (★Cebu)	180,000
Mangaldan	65,947
• MANILA (★9,650,000)	1,598,918
Marawi	92,000
Marikina (★Manila)	310,010
Meycauayan (★Manila)	123,982
Muntinglupa (★Manila)	276,972
Naga	115,000
Navotas (★Manila)	186,799
Olongapo	193,327
Pagadian (▲107,000)	52,400
Parañaque (★Manila)	307,717
Pasay (★Manila)	366,623
Pasig (★Manila)	397,309
Puerto Princesa (▲92,147)	47,461
Quezon City (★Manila)	1,666,766
San Fernando	157,851
San Juan del Monte (★Manila)	126,708
San Pablo (▲161,630)	80,671
San Pedro	156,486
Santa Cruz	76,603
Santa Rosa (★Manila)	94,719
Tacloban	138,000
Tagbilaran	56,000
Tagig (★Manila)	266,080
Taytay (★Manila)	112,403
Valenzuela (★Manila)	340,050
Zamboanga (▲444,000)	107,000

PITCAIRN

1988 C	59
• ADAMSTOWN	59

POLAND / Polska

1991 E	38,183,200
Będzin (★Katowice)	76,200
Bełchatów	57,400
Biała Podlaska	53,100
Białystok	270,600
Bielsko-Biała	181,300
Bydgoszcz	381,500
Bytom (Beuthen) (★Katowice)	231,200
Chełm	66,400
Chorzów (★Katowice)	131,900
Częstochowa	258,000
Dąbrowa Górnicza (★Katowice)	136,900
Dzierżoniów (Reichenbach) (★89,000)	38,000
Elbląg (Elbing)	126,100
Ełk	52,400
Gdańsk (Danzig) (★909,000)	465,100
Gdynia (★Gdańsk)	251,500
Gliwice (Gleiwitz) (★Katowice)	214,200
Głogów	73,300
Gniezno	70,400
Gorzów Wielkopolski (Landsberg an der Warthe)	124,300
Grudziądz	102,300
Inowrocław	77,700
Jastrzębie-Zdrój	103,700
Jaworzno (★Katowice)	99,500
Jelenia Góra (Hirschberg)	93,400
Kalisz	106,200
• Katowice (★2,778,000)	366,800
Kędzierzyn Kozle	71,700
Kielce	214,200
Konin	80,300
Koszalin (Köslin)	108,700
Kraków (★828,000)	750,500
Krosno	49,700
Kutno	50,400
Legionowo (★Warszawa)	50,800
Legnica (Liegnitz)	105,200
Leszno	58,300
Łódź (★1,061,000)	848,200
Łomża	59,300
Lubin	82,300
Lublin (★389,000)	351,400
Mielec	61,800
Mysłowice (★Katowice)	93,800
Nowy Sącz	78,200
Olsztyn (Allenstein)	162,900
Opole (Oppeln)	128,400
Ostrołęka	50,700
Ostrowiec Świętokrzyski	78,600
Ostrów Wielkopolski	73,300
Pabianice (★Łódź)	75,200
Piekary Śląskie (★Katowice)	68,500
Piła (Schneidemühl)	72,300
Piotrków Trybunalski	81,000
Płock	123,400
Poznań (★672,000)	590,100
Pruszków (★Warszawa)	53,700
Przemyśl	68,500
Puławy	85,700
Racibórz (Ratibor)	64,400
Radom	228,500
Radomsko	50,400
Ruda Śląska (★Katowice)	171,000
Rybnik	144,000
Rzeszów	153,000
Siedlce	72,000
Siemianowice Śląskie (★Katowice)	81,100
Skarżysko-Kamienna	50,900
Słupsk (Stolp)	101,200
Sopot (★Gdańsk)	46,700
Sosnowiec (★Katowice)	259,400
Stalowa Wola	70,000
Starachowice	56,600
Stargard Szczeciński (Stargard in Pommern)	71,000
Starogard Gdański	49,500
Suwałki	61,300
Świdnica (Schweidnitz)	63,300
Świętochłowice (★Katowice)	60,500
Świnoujście (Swinemünde)	43,300
Szczecin (Stettin) (★449,000)	413,400
Tarnów	121,200
Tarnowskie Góry (★Katowice)	74,100
Tczew	59,500
Tomaszów Mazowiecki	69,900
Toruń	202,300
Tychy (★Katowice)	191,700
Wałbrzych (Waldenburg) (★207,000)	141,000
WARSZAWA (★2,323,000)	1,655,700
Włocławek	122,200
Wodzisław Śląski	111,800
Wrocław (Breslau)	643,200
Zabrze (Hindenburg) (★Katowice)	205,000
Zamość	61,800
Zawiercie	56,600
Zgierz (★Łódź)	59,000
Zielona Góra (Grünberg)	114,100
Żory	67,000

PORTUGAL

1981 C	9,833,014
Amadora (★Lisboa)	95,518
Barreiro (★Lisboa)	50,863
Braga	63,033
Coimbra	74,616
• LISBOA (★2,250,000)	807,167
Ponta Delgada	21,187
Porto (★1,225,000)	327,368
Setúbal	77,885
Vila Nova de Gaia (★Porto)	62,469

PUERTO RICO

1990 C	3,522,037
Arecibo (★160,500)	49,545
Bayamón (▲220,262) (★San Juan)	202,103
Caguas (▲133,447) (★San Juan)	92,429
Carolina (▲177,806) (★San Juan)	162,404
Guaynabo (▲92,886) (★San Juan)	73,385
Mayagüez (★200,600)	83,010
Ponce (★232,700)	159,151
• SAN JUAN (★1,877,000)	426,832

QATAR / Qaṭar

1986 C	369,079
• AD-DAWḤAH (DOHA) (★310,000)	217,294
Ar-Rayyān (★Ad-Dawḥah)	91,996

REUNION / Réunion

1982 C	515,814
• SAINT-DENIS (▲109,072)	84,400

ROMANIA / România

1992 C	22,760,449
Alba Iulia	71,254
Alexandria	58,582
Arad	190,088
Bacău	204,495
Baia Mare	148,815
Bistrița	87,793
Botoșani	126,204
Brăila	234,706
• BUCUREȘTI (BUCHAREST) (★2,300,000)	2,064,474
Buzău	148,247
Călărași	76,886
Cluj-Napoca	328,008
Constanța	350,476
Craiova	303,520
Deva	78,366
Drobeta-Turnu Severin	115,526
Focșani	101,296
Galați	325,788
Giurgiu	74,236
Hunedoara	81,198
Iași	342,994
Lugoj	50,983
Medgidia	46,586
Mediaș	64,488
Miercurea-Ciuc	46,029
Onești	59,008
Oradea	220,848
Petroșani (★76,000)	52,532
Piatra Neamț	123,175
Pitești	179,479
Ploiești (★310,000)	252,073
Râmnicu Vâlcea	113,356
Reșița	96,798
Roman	80,192
Satu Mare	131,859
Sfântu Gheorghe	68,070
Sibiu	169,696
Slatina	85,336
Slobozia	55,614
Suceava	114,355
Târgoviște	97,876
Târgu Jiu	98,267
Târgu Mureș	163,625
Tecuci	46,735
Timișoara	334,278
Tulcea	97,500
Turda	61,135
Vaslui	80,151
Zalău	68,322

RUSSIA

1991 E	148,542,700
Abakan	157,300
Achtubinsk	50,800
Ačinsk	122,000
Alapajevsk	50,300
Alatyr'	47,700
Aleksandrov	68,600
Aleksin	74,200
Al'metjevsk	132,700
Amursk	59,600
Anapa	55,900
Angarsk	268,500
Anžero-Sudžensk	107,000
Apatity	88,600
Archangel'sk	420,400
Armavir	162,200
Arsenjev	71,200
Art'om	70,100
Arzamas	111,800
Asbest	84,900
Astrachan'	511,900
Azov	80,700
Balakovo	201,300
Balašicha (★Moskva)	137,600
Balašov	97,300
Barnaul (★673,000)	606,800
Batajsk (★Rostov-na-Donu)	93,300
Belebej	54,500
Belgorod	311,400
Belogorsk	74,300
Belorečensk	51,900
Beloreck	73,100
Belovo	92,900
Berdsk (★Novosibirsk)	80,400
Berezniki	199,700
Ber'ozovskij	51,900

▲ Población de un municipio, comuna o distrito entero, incluyendo sus áreas rurales.
• Ciudad más grande de un país.
★ Población o designación de un área metropolitana, incluyendo los suburbios.
C Censo. **E** Estimado oficial. **U** Estimado no oficial.

▲ Population d'une municipalité, d'une commune ou d'un district, zone rurale incluse.
• Ville la plus peuplée du pays.
★ Population de l'agglomération (ou nom de la zone métropolitaine englobante).
C Recensement. **E** Estimation officielle. **U** Estimation non officielle.

▲ População de um municipio, comuna ou distrito, inclusive as respectivas áreas rurais.
• Maior cidade de um país.
★ População ou indicação de uma área metropolitana.
C Censo. **E** Estimativa oficial. **U** Estimativa não oficial.

Bijsk	234,600
Birobidžan	86,300
Blagoveščensk	211,000
Bor (★Niñij Novgorod)	64,500
Borisoglebsk	72,100
Boroviči	62,800
Br'ansk	458,900
Bratsk	259,400
Bud'onnovsk	57,500
Bugul'ma	91,100
Buguruslan	54,100
Buj	32,900
Bujnaksk	57,900
Buzuluk	85,100
Čajkovskij	88,300
Čapajevsk	96,000
Čebarkul'	50,700
Čeboksary	436,000
Čechov	60,200
Čel'abinsk (★1,325,000)	1,148,300
Čeremchovo	73,600
Čerepovec	315,900
Čerkessk	117,000
Černogorsk	79,700
Chabarovsk	613,300
Chasavjurt	72,800
Chimki (★Moskva)	135,500
Cholmsk	51,800
Čistopol'	66,600
Čita	376,300
Čusovoj	58,000
Derbent	81,500
Dimitrovgrad	127,000
Dmitrov	65,600
Dolgoprudnyj (★Moskva)	71,100
Domodedovo (★Moskva)	56,300
Doneck	48,900
Dubna	67,200
Dzeržinsk (★Nižnij Novgorod)	286,700
Elektrostal'	153,000
Elista	92,700
Engel's (★Saratov)	183,600
Fr'azino (★Moskva)	54,000
Furmanov	45,900
Gatčina (★Sankt-Peterburg)	80,600
Gelendžik	48,600
Georgijevsk	63,700
Georgiu-Dež	54,600
Glazov	106,000
Gorno-Altajsk	47,500
Gr'azi	47,700
Groznyj	401,400
Gubkin	76,400
Gukovo	67,700
Gus'-Chrustal'nyj	77,000
Inta	60,900
Irbit	51,300
Irkutsk	640,500
Išim	65,900
Išimbaj	71,000
Iskitim	68,700
Ivanovo	482,200
Ivantejevka (★Moskva)	53,200
Iževsk	646,800
Jakutsk	193,300
Jarcevo	54,000
Jaroslavl'	638,100
Jefremov	56,600
Jegorjevsk	74,200
Jejsk	79,400
Jelec	121,300
Jelizovo	48,700
Jermolajevo	65,600
Jessentuki	86,300
Joškar-Ola	247,800
Jurga	94,000
Južno-Sachalinsk	164,000
Kaliningrad (★Moskva)	161,500
Kaliningrad (Königsberg)	408,100
Kaluga	315,500
Kamensk-Šachtinskij	73,100
Kamensk-Ural'skij	208,700
Kamyšin	124,400
Kanaš	56,100
Kandalakša	54,300
Kansk	109,900
Kaspijsk	61,900
Kazan' (★1,165,000)	1,107,300
Kemerovo	520,700
Kimry	62,000
Kinel'	33,800
Kinešma	104,900
Kingisepp	50,600
Kiriši	53,100
Kirov	491,200
Kirovo-Čepeck	95,600
Kisel'ovsk (★Prokopjevsk)	126,900
Kislovodsk	116,800
Kizel	36,600
Klimovsk (★Moskva)	57,600
Klin	95,100
Klincy	71,200
Kogalym	48,200
Kol'čugino	45,600
Kolomna	163,500
Kolpino (★Sankt-Peterburg)	144,500
Komsomol'sk-na-Amure	318,800
Kopejsk (★Čel'abinsk)	78,300
Korkino	44,800
Korsakov	45,300
Kostroma	281,800
Kotlas	68,900
Kovrov	161,900
Krasnodar	631,200
Krasnogorsk (★Moskva)	91,700
Krasnojarsk	924,400
Krasnokamensk	67,000
Krasnokamsk	57,800
Krasnoturjinsk	67,200
Krasnoufimsk	46,100
Krasnoural'sk	34,800
Krasnyj Sulin	43,200
Kropotkin	76,600
Krymsk	51,100
Kstovo (★Nižnij Novgord)	65,300
Kujbyšev	51,600
Kungur	81,800
Kurgan	363,800
Kursk	433,300
Kušva	43,300
Kuzneck	100,000
Kyzyl	88,000
Labinsk	58,600
Leninogorsk	63,300
Leninsk-Kuzneckij	133,400
Lesosibirsk	69,300
Lipeck	460,100
Livny	52,600
Lobn'a (★Moskva)	61,000
L'ubercy (★Moskva)	164,900
Lys'va	77,800
Lytkarino (★Moskva)	51,700
Machačkala	333,500
Magadan	154,900
Magnitogorsk	443,900
Majkop	152,500
Mcensk	49,200
Meleuz	55,200
Meždurečensk	107,500
Miass	169,700
Michajlovka	58,700
Mičurinsk	109,400
Mineral'nyje Vody	72,500
Minusinsk	74,200
Mončegorsk	68,100
Moršansk	50,500
• MOSKVA (MOSCOW) (★13,150,000)	8,801,500
Murmansk	472,900
Murom	126,000
Mytišči (★Moskva)	153,900
Naberežnyje Čelny	510,100
Nachodka	164,500
Nadym	52,200
Nal'čik	240,600
Naro-Fominsk	58,800
Nazarovo	65,200
Neftejugansk	65,500
Ner'ungri	77,200
Nevinnomyssk	123,300
Nikolo-Berjozovka	110,500
Nižnekamsk	196,200
Nižnevartovsk	247,400
Nižnij Novgorod (Gorky) (★2,025,000)	1,445,000
Nižnij Tagil	439,200
Njagan	59,800
Noginsk	122,700
Nojabr'sk	88,900
Noril'sk	169,000
Novgorod	233,800
Novoaltajsk (★Barnaul)	55,200
Novočeboksarsk	119,300
Novočerkassk	188,500
Novodvinsk	50,300
Novokujbyševsk (★Samara)	113,200
Novokuzneck	601,900
Novomoskovsk, Tula oblast' (★365,000)	145,800
Novorossijsk	188,600
Novošachtinsk	107,300
Novosibirsk (★1,600,000)	1,446,300
Novotroick	107,600
Novyj Urengoj	93,600
Obninsk	103,700
Odincovo (★Moskva)	128,400
Okt'abr'skij	106,700
Omsk (★1,190,000)	1,166,800
Orechovo-Zujevo (★205,000)	136,800
Orel	345,200
Orenburg	556,500
Orsk	272,200
Osinniki	63,200
Otradnyj	49,600
Partizansk	50,000
P'atigorsk	131,100
Pavlovo	72,200
Pavlovskij Posad	70,800
Pečora	65,500
Penza	551,100
Perm' (★1,180,000)	1,110,400
Pervoural'sk	143,700
Petrodvorec (★Sankt-Peterburg)	83,800
Petropavlovsk-Kamčatskij	272,900
Petrozavodsk	277,400
Podol'sk (★Moskva)	208,500
Polevskoj	71,900
Prochladnyj	58,500
Prokopjevsk (★410,000)	272,600
Pskov	207,500
Puškin (★Sankt-Peterburg)	95,300
Puškino (★Moskva)	75,800
Ramenskoje	88,800
Rasskazovo	49,800
R'azan'	527,200
Reutov (★Moskva)	68,900
Revda	66,000
Roslavl'	60,700
Rossoš'	58,900
Rostov-na-Donu (★1,165,000)	1,027,600
Rubcovsk	172,500
Ruzajevka	52,100
Rybinsk	252,600
Ržev	70,900
Šachty	227,700
Šadrinsk	87,500
Safonovo	56,300
Sajanogorsk	53,000
Salavat	151,400
Sal'sk	61,700
Samara (★1,505,000)	1,257,300
Sankt-Peterburg (Saint Petersburg) (★5,525,000)	4,466,800
Saransk	319,600
Sarapul	110,600
Saratov (★1,155,000)	911,100
Šatka	51,100
Ščelkovo (★Moskva)	109,600
Ščokino	68,800
Šelechov	48,600
Sergijev Posad (Zagorsk)	115,600
Serov	103,800
Serpuchov	141,200
Severodvinsk	251,500
Severomorsk	66,200
Slav'ansk-Na-Kubani	58,500
Smolensk	349,800
Soči	341,500
Sokol	46,700
Solikamsk	110,200
Solnečnogorsk (★Moskva)	56,700
Sosnovyj Bor	56,700
Spassk-Dal'nij	61,100
Staryj Oskol	181,900
Stavropol'	328,300
Sterlitamak	252,200
Stupino	74,600
Šuja	69,000
Surgut	261,100
Sverdlovsk (★1,620,000)	1,375,400
Svetlogorsk	71,600
Svobodnyj	80,900
Syktyvkar	224,000
Syzran'	174,900
Taganrog	293,600
Talnach	65,600
Tambov	309,600
Tichoreck	67,600
Tichvin	71,800
Tobol'sk	96,800
Toljatti	654,700
Tomsk	505,600
Toržok	50,500
Troick	89,800
Tuapse	63,800
Tujmazy	59,800
Tula (★640,000)	543,600
Tulun	53,700
T'umen'	494,200
Tver'	455,300
Tyndinskij	64,700
Uchta	112,100
Ufa (★1,118,000)	1,097,000
Uglič	40,000
Ulan-Ude	362,400
Uljanovsk	648,300
Usinsk	52,300
Usolje-Sibirskoje	106,800
Ussurijsk	160,200
Ust'-Ilimsk	112,200
Ust'-Kut	61,800
Uzlovaja (★Novomoskovsk)	64,000
V'az'ma	59,900
Velikije Luki	115,400
Verchn'aja Pyšma (★Sverdlovsk)	53,500
Verchn'aja Salda	55,100
Vičuga	49,700
Vidnoje (★Moskva)	56,900
Vladikavkaz	306,000
Vladimir	355,600
Vladivostok	648,000
Volchov	50,100
Volgodonsk	180,700
Volgograd (Stalingrad) (★1,360,000)	1,007,300
Vologda	289,200
Vol'sk	65,500
Volžsk	62,000
Volžskij (★Volgograd)	278,400
Vorkuta	117,400
Voronež	900,000
Voskresensk	81,400
Votkinsk	104,500
Vyborg	81,100
Vyksa	62,200
Vyšnij Voločok	64,600
Zarinsk	51,800
Zelenograd (★Moskva)	162,700
Železnodorožnyj (★Moskva)	99,300
Železnogorsk	89,200
Zel'onodol'sk	97,000
Žigulevsk	45,000
Zlatoust	208,200
Žukovskij	101,300

RWANDA

1991 C	6,762,145
• KIGALI	232,733

SAINT HELENA

1987 C	5,644
• JAMESTOWN	1,413

SAINT KITTS AND NEVIS

1980 C	44,404
• BASSETERRE	14,725
Charlestown	1,771

SAINT LUCIA

1987 E	142,342
• CASTRIES	53,933

SAINT PIERRE AND MIQUELON / Saint-Pierre-et-Miquelon

1982 C	6,041
• SAINT-PIERRE	5,371

SAINT VINCENT AND THE GRENADINES

1987 E	112,589
• KINGSTOWN (★28,936)	19,028

SAN MARINO

1989 E	23,000
• SAN MARINO	2,794

SAO TOME AND PRINCIPE / São Tomé e Príncipe

1991 C	117,504
• SÃO TOMÉ	5,245

SAUDI ARABIA / Al-'Arabīyah as-Su'ūdīyah

1980 E	9,229,000
Abhā (1974C)	30,150
Ad-Dammām	200,000
Al-Hufūf (1974C)	101,271
Al-Khubar (1974C)	48,817
Al-Madīnah (Medina)	290,000
Al-Mubarraz (1974C)	54,325
AR-RIYĀD (RIYADH)	1,250,000
At-Tā'if	300,000
Buraydah (1974C)	69,940
Hā'il (1974C)	40,502
• Jiddah (Jeddah)	1,300,000
Khamīs Mushayt (1974C)	49,581
Makkah (Mecca)	550,000
Najran (1974C)	47,501
Tabūk (1974C)	74,825

SENEGAL / Sénégal

1988 C	6,892,720
• DAKAR	1,490,450
Diourbel	77,548
Kaolack	152,007
Louga	52,763
Saint-Louis	160,689
Thiès	184,902
Ziguinchor	124,283

SEYCHELLES

1984 E	64,718
• VICTORIA	23,000

SIERRA LEONE

1985 C	3,515,812
Bo	59,768
• FREETOWN (★525,000)	469,776
Kenema	52,473
Koidu	82,474
Makeni	49,038

SINGAPORE

1990 C	2,690,100
• SINGAPORE (★3,025,000)	2,690,100

SLOVAKIA / Slovenská Republika

1991 C	5,268,935
Banská Bystrica	85,007
• BRATISLAVA	441,453
Komárno	37,370
Košice	234,840
Martin	58,338
Michalovce	38,866
Nitra	89,888
Nové Zámky	42,851
Poprad	52,878
Považská Bystrica	39,801
Prešov	87,788
Prievidza	53,393
Spišská Nová Ves	39,187
Trenčín	56,733
Trnava	71,641
Žilina	83,853
Zvolen	41,935

SLOVENIA / Slovenija

1987 E	1,936,606
• LJUBLJANA (▲316,607)	233,200
Maribor (▲187,651)	107,400

SOLOMON ISLANDS

1986 C	285,176
• HONIARA	30,413

SOMALIA / Somaliya

1984 E	5,423,000
Berbera	65,000
Hargeysa	70,000
Kismaayo	70,000
Marka	60,000
• MUQDISHO	600,000

SOUTH AFRICA / Suid-Afrika

1991 C	30,986,920
Alberton (★Johannesburg)	76,642
Alexandra (★Johannesburg)	124,586
Atteridgeville (★Pretoria)	92,008
Bellville (★Cape Town)	78,822
Benoni (★Johannesburg)	113,501
Bloemfontein (★280,000)	126,867
Boksburg (★Johannesburg)	119,890
Botshabelo (★Bloemfontein)	117,926
Brakpan (★Johannesburg)	53,522
CAPE TOWN (KAAPSTAD) (★1,900,000)	854,616
Carletonville (★175,000)	118,699
Daveyton (★Johannesburg)	151,659
Diepmeadow (★Johannesburg)	241,099
Durban (★1,740,000)	715,669
East London (Oos-Londen) (★365,000)	102,325
Edendale (★Pietermaritzburg)	72,063
Elsies River (★Cape Town)	82,045
Evaton (★Vereeniging)	201,026
Galeshewe (★Kimberley)	72,118
Ga-Rankuwa (1980C)	48,300
Germiston (★Johannesburg)	134,005
Grassy Park (★Cape Town)	52,675
Guguletu (★Cape Town)	54,635
• Johannesburg (★4,000,000)	712,507
Kagiso (★Johannesburg)	61,680
Katlehong (★Johannesburg)	201,785
Kempton Park (★Johannesburg)	106,606
Kimberley (★160,000)	80,082
Klerksdorp (★275,000)	58,923
Krugersdorp (★Johannesburg)	81,584
Kwa Mashu (★Durban)	156,679
KwaNdengezi (★Durban)	50,835
KwaNobuhle (★Port Elizabeth)	92,381
Kwa-Thema (★Johannesburg)	81,345
Ladysmith (★37,885)	29,589
Lekoa (Shapeville) (★Vereeniging)	217,582
Madadeni (★Newcastle)	95,931
Mafikeng (★16,000) (1980C)	6,500
Mamelodi (★Pretoria)	154,845
Mangaung (★Bloemfontein)	125,545
Mdantsane (★East London) (1986E)	242,823
Ntuzuma (★Durban)	102,310
Nyanga (★Cape Town)	92,896
Osizweni (★Durban)	78,079
Paarl (★Cape Town)	73,415
Parow (★Cape Town)	68,081
Pietermaritzburg (★265,000)	156,473
Pinetown (★Durban)	70,001
Port Elizabeth (★810,000)	303,353
PRETORIA (★1,100,000)	525,583
Randburg (★Johannesburg)	90,557
Randfontein (★Johannesburg)	51,940
Roodepoort-Maraisburg (★Johannesburg)	162,632
Sandton (★Johannesburg)	101,197
Soshanguve (★Pretoria)	146,334
Soweto (★Johannesburg)	596,632
Springs (★Johannesburg)	72,647
Tembisa (★Johannesburg)	209,238
Thabong (★Welkom)	88,547
Uitenhage (★Port Elizabeth)	67,581
Umlazi (★Durban)	299,275
Umtata (1978E)	30,000
Vanderbijlpark (★Vereeniging)	67,291
Vereeniging (★675,000)	70,255
Verwoerdburg (★Pretoria)	80,552
Vosloosrus (★Johannesburg)	76,015
Welkom (★156,658)	68,111
Westonaria (★Johannesburg)	57,177

SPAIN / España

1988 E	39,217,804
Alacant (Alicante)	261,051
Albacete	125,997
Alcalá de Guadaira	50,935
Alcalá de Henares (★Madrid)	150,021
Alcobendas (★Madrid)	73,455
Alcoi (Alcoy)	66,074
Alcorcón (★Madrid)	139,796
Algeciras	99,528
Almería	157,644
Avilés (★131,000)	87,811
Badajoz (▲122,407)	106,400
Badalona (★Barcelona)	225,229
Baracaldo (★Bilbao)	113,502
Barcelona (★4,040,000)	1,714,355
Bilbao (★985,000)	384,733
Burgos	160,561
Cáceres	71,598
Cádiz (★240,000)	156,591
Cartagena (▲172,710)	70,000

▲ Population of an entire municipality, commune, or district, including rural area.
• Largest city in country.
★ Population or designation of the metropolitan area, including suburbs.
C Census. **E** Official estimate. **U** Unofficial estimate.

▲ Bevölkerung eines ganzen städtischen Verwaltungsgebietes, eines Kommunalbezirkes oder eines Distrikts, einschliesslich ländlicher Gebiete.
• Grösste Stadt des Landes.
★ Bevölkerung oder Bezeichnung der Stadtregion einschliesslich Vororte.
C Volkszählung. **E** Offizielle Schätzung. **U** Inoffizielle Schätzung.

Castelló de la Plana	131,809
Ciudad Real	56,300
Córdoba	302,301
Cornellà de Llobregat (★Barcelona)	86,866
Coslada (★Madrid)	68,765
Donostia (San Sebastián) (★285,000)	177,622
Dos Hermanas (▲68,456)	60,600
Elda	56,756
El Ferrol del Caudillo (★129,000)	86,503
El Prat de Llobregat (★Barcelona)	64,193
El Puerto de Santa María (▲62,285)	49,900
Elx (Elche) (▲180,256)	158,300
Fuenlabrada (★Madrid)	128,872
Gernika-Lumo (Guernica y Luno) (▲17,836) (1981C)	12,214
Getafe (★Madrid)	135,367
Gijón	262,156
Granada	263,334
Granollers (★Barcelona)	49,045
Guadalajara	61,309
Huelva	137,826
Irún	54,886
Jaén	106,435
Jerez de la Frontera (▲183,007)	156,200
La Coruña	248,862
La Línea	60,956
Las Palmas de Gran Canaria (▲366,347)	319,000
Leganés (★Madrid)	168,403
León (★159,000)	136,558
L'Hospitalet de Llobregat (★Barcelona)	278,449
Linares	58,622
Lleida (Lérida) (▲109,795)	91,500
Logroño	119,038
Lugo (▲78,795)	68,700
• MADRID (★4,650,000)	3,102,846
Málaga	574,456
Manresa	65,607
Mataró	100,817
Mérida	52,368
Móstoles (★Madrid)	181,648
Murcia (▲314,124)	149,800
Orense	106,042
Oviedo (▲190,073)	168,900
Palencia	76,692
Palma (▲314,608)	249,000
Pamplona	180,598
Parla (★Madrid)	66,253
Portugalete (★Bilbao)	57,813
Puertollano	52,284
Reus	83,800
Rubí (★Barcelona)	48,807
Sabadell (★Barcelona)	189,489
Salamanca	159,342
San Baudilio de Llobrega (★Barcelona)	77,502
San Cristóbal de la Laguna (▲111,533)	25,900
San Fernando (★Cádiz)	81,975
San Sebastián de los Reyes (★Madrid)	51,653
Santa Coloma de Gramanet (★Barcelona)	136,042
Santa Cruz de Tenerife	215,228
Santander (▲190,795)	166,800
Santiago de Compostela (▲88,110)	68,800
Santurce-Antiguo (★Bilbao)	52,334
Segovia	54,402
Sevilla (★945,000)	663,132
Talavera de la Reina	68,158
Tarragona (▲109,586)	63,500
Tarrasa (★Barcelona)	161,410
Toledo	59,551
Torrejón de Ardoz (★Madrid)	83,267
Torrent (★València)	55,751
València (★1,270,000)	743,933
Valladolid	331,461
Vigo (▲271,128)	179,500
Vitoria (Gasteiz)	204,264
Zamora	62,047
Zaragoza	582,239

SPANISH NORTH AFRICA / Plazas de Soberanía en el Norte de África

1988 E	122,905
• Ceuta	67,188
Melilla	55,717

SRI LANKA

1989 E	16,806,000
Battaramulla (★Colombo) (1981C)	56,535
Batticaloa	50,000
• COLOMBO (★2,050,000)	612,000
Dehiwala-Mount Lavinia (★Colombo)	193,000
Galle	83,000
Jaffna	128,000
Kandy	103,000
Moratuwa (★Colombo)	166,000
Negombo	64,000
SRI JAYAWARDENEPURA (KOTTE) (★Colombo)	108,000
Trincomalee	49,000

SUDAN / As-Sūdān

1983 C	20,594,197
Al-Fāshir	84,298
• AL-KHARTŪM (★1,450,000)	473,597
Al-Kharṭūm Baḥrī (★Al-Kharṭūm)	340,857
Al-Qaḍārif	116,876
Al-Ubayyiḍ	137,582
'Aṭbarah	72,836
Būr Sūdān (Port Sudan)	206,038
Jūbā	84,377
Kassalā	141,429
Kūstī	89,135
Nyala	111,693
Umm Durmān (Omdurman) (★Al-Kharṭūm)	526,192
Wad Madanī	145,015
Wāw	90,960

SURINAME

1988 E	392,000
• PARAMARIBO (★296,000)	241,000
Wanica (★Paramaribo)	55,000

SWAZILAND

1986 C	712,131
LOBAMBA	
Manzini (★30,000)	18,084
• MBABANE	38,290

SWEDEN / Sverige

1991 E	8,590,630
Borås (▲101,766)	59,400
Eskilstuna (▲89,765)	59,800
Gävle (▲88,568)	67,300
Göteborg (★710,894)	433,042
Halmstad (▲80,061)	48,900
Helsingborg (▲109,267)	82,000
Huddinge (★Stockholm)	73,829
Järfälla (★Stockholm)	56,359
Jönköping (▲111,486)	76,300
Karlstad (▲76,467)	53,100
Linköping (▲122,268)	82,700
Luleå (▲68,412)	42,700
Lund (▲87,681) (★Malmö)	63,700
Malmö (★475,224)	233,887
Mölndal (★Göteborg)	52,028
Nacka (★Stockholm)	64,056
Norrköping (▲120,522)	82,600
Örebro (▲120,944)	86,000
Södertälje (▲81,786) (★Stockholm)	58,100
Sollentuna (★Stockholm)	51,377
Solna (★Stockholm)	51,841
• STOCKHOLM (★1,491,726)	674,452
Sundsvall (▲93,808)	50,300
Täby (★Stockholm)	56,714
Trollhättan (▲51,047)	41,000
Tumba (★Stockholm)	68,542
Umeå (▲91,258)	61,300
Uppsala (▲167,508)	110,000
Västerås (▲119,761)	98,300
Växjö (▲69,547)	48,000

SWITZERLAND / Schweiz / Suisse / Svizzera

1990 C	6,873,687
Aarau (★59,500)	16,481
Arbon (★41,400)	11,043
Baden (★73,200)	15,718
Basel (Bâle) (★587,000)	178,428
BERN (BERNE) (★300,400)	136,338
Biel (Bienne) (★83,100)	51,893
Fribourg (Freiburg) (★62,500)	36,355
Genève (Geneva) (★470,000)	171,042
Lausanne (★265,000)	128,112
Locarno (★42,200)	13,796
Lugano (★94,700)	25,344
Luzern (★165,000)	61,034
Neuchâtel (★67,500)	33,579
Sankt Gallen (★127,000)	75,237
Schaffhausen (★53,800)	34,225
Thun (★79,500)	38,211
Vevey (★65,900)	15,968
Winterthur (★110,500)	86,959
Zug (★69,000)	21,705
• Zürich (★870,000)	365,043

SYRIA / Sūrīyah

1988 E	11,338,000
Al-Hasakah (1981C)	73,426
Al-Lādhiqīyah (Latakia)	249,000
Al-Qāmishlī	126,236
Ar-Raqqah	113,000
As-Suwaydā'	46,844
Dar'ā (1981C)	49,534
Dārayyā (★Dimashq)	53,204
Dayr az-Zawr	112,000
• DIMASHQ (DAMASCUS) (★2,000,000)	1,326,000
Dūmā (★Dimashq)	66,130
Halab (Aleppo) (★1,335,000)	1,261,000
Hamāh	222,000
Ḥimṣ	447,000
Idlib (1981C)	51,682
Jaramānah (★Dimashq)	96,681
Kābir aṣ Saghīr	47,728
Madīnat ath Thawrah	58,151
Ṭarṭūs (1981C)	52,589

TAIWAN / T'aiwan

1991 E	20,352,966
Changhua (▲215,224)	165,000
Chiai (1992E)	258,713
Chilung (1992E)	357,000
Chungho (★T'aipei)	374,339
Chungli	269,804
Chutung (1988E)	104,797
Fangshan (★Kaohsiung)	290,777
Fengyüan (▲151,642)	121,100
Hsichih (★T'aipei) (1980C)	70,031
Hsinchu (1992E)	330,576
Hsinchuang (★T'aipei)	299,174
Hsintien (★T'aipei)	225,517
Hualien	107,552
Ilan (▲81,751) (1980C)	70,900
Kangshan (1980C)	78,049
Kaohsiung (★1,900,000) (1992E)	1,401,239
Lotung (1980C)	57,925
Lukang (1980C)	72,019
Miaoli (1980C)	81,500
Nant'ou (1980C)	84,038
P'ingchen (★T'aipei)	147,030
P'ingtung (▲210,801)	172,400
Sanchung (★T'aipei)	375,996
Shulin (★T'aipei)	111,993
Tach'i (1980C)	67,209
T'aichung (1992E)	785,182
T'ainan (1992E)	692,116
• T'AIPEI (★6,200,000) (1992E)	2,706,453
T'aipeihsien (★T'aipei)	538,954
T'aitung (▲108,196)	79,100
Taoyüan	241,263
T'oufen (1980C)	66,536
T'uch'eng (▲136,928) (★T'aipei)	80,300
Yangmei (1980C)	84,353
Yüanlin (▲121,251)	53,200
Yungho (★T'aipei)	249,736
Yungkang (▲136,705)	70,900

TAJIKISTAN

1991 E	5,358,300
Chudžand (Leninabad)	164,500
• DUŠANBE	582,400
Kul'ab	79,300
Kurgan-T'ube	58,400

TANZANIA

1985 E	21,733,000
Arusha (1984E)	69,000
• DAR ES SALAAM	1,096,000
DODOMA	85,000
Iringa (1984E)	67,000
Kigoma (1978C)	50,044
Mbeya	194,000
Morogoro (1984E)	72,000
Moshi (1984E)	62,000
Mtwara (1978C)	48,510
Mwanza	252,000
Tabora	214,000
Tanga	172,000
Ujiji (1967C)	21,369
Zanzibar	133,000

THAILAND / Prathet Thai

1991 E	56,961,030
Chiang Mai	161,541
Chon Buri	45,763
Hat Yai	142,351
Khon Kaen	131,478
• KRUNG THEP (BANGKOK) (★7,060,000)	5,620,591
Nakhon Ratchasima	202,503
Nakhon Sawan	108,569
Nakhon Si Thammarat	74,219
Nonthaburi (★Krung Thep)	264,201
Pattaya	64,731
Phitsanulok	77,672
Phra Nakhon Si Ayutthaya	60,561
Phuket	42,913
Sakon Nakhon	47,869
Samut Prakan (★Krung Thep)	71,538
Samut Sakhon	55,509
Saraburi	64,915
Songkhla	82,167
Trang	48,589
Ubon Ratchathani	98,950
Udon Thani	78,489
Yala	68,834

TOGO

1987 E	3,148,000
• LOMÉ	500,000
Sokodé	55,000

TONGA

1986 C	94,535
• NUKU'ALOFA	21,265

TRINIDAD AND TOBAGO

1990 C	1,234,388
• PORT OF SPAIN (★370,000)	50,878
San Fernando (★75,000)	30,092

TUNISIA / Tunis / Tunisie

1984 C	6,975,450
Ariana (★Tunis)	98,655
Bardo (★Tunis)	65,669
Ben Arous (★Tunis)	52,105
Bizerte	94,509
Gabès	92,258
Gafsa	60,970
Hammam Lif (★Tunis)	47,009
Houmt Essouk	92,269
Kairouan	72,254
Kasserine	47,606
La Goulette (★Tunis)	61,609
Menzel Bourguiba	51,399
Sfax (★310,000)	231,911
Sousse (★160,000)	83,509
• TUNIS (★1,225,000)	596,654
Zarzis	49,063

TURKEY / Türkiye

1990 C	56,473,035
Adana	916,150
Adıyaman	100,045
Afyon	95,643
Ağrı	58,038
Akhisar	73,944
Aksaray	90,698
Akşehir	51,746
Alanya	52,460
Amasya	57,288
ANKARA (★2,650,000)	2,559,471
Antalya	378,208
Aydın	107,011
Bafra	65,600
Balıkesir	170,589
Bandırma	77,444
Batman	147,347
Bilecik	23,273
Bolu	60,789
Burdur	56,432
Bursa	834,576
Çanakkale	53,995
Ceyhan	85,308
Cizre	50,023
Çorlu	74,681
Çorum	116,810
Darıca	53,560
Denizli	204,118
Diyarbakır	381,144
Düzce	61,878
Edirne	102,345
Elazığ	204,603
Elbistan	54,741
Ereğli, Konya prov.	74,283
Ereğli, Zonguldak prov.	63,987
Erzincan	91,772
Erzurum	242,391
Esenyurt (★İstanbul)	70,280
Eskişehir	413,082
Gaziantep	603,434
Gebze (★İstanbul)	159,116
Gelibolu	18,670
Gemlik	50,237
Giresun	67,604
Gölcük	64,911
Gümüşhane	26,014
Hakkâri	30,407
Hatay (Antioch)	123,871
İçel (Mersin)	422,357
İnegöl	71,120
İskenderun	154,807
Isparta	112,117
• İstanbul (★7,550,000)	6,620,241
İzmir (★1,900,000)	1,757,414
İzmit	256,882
Kadirli	55,061
Kahramanmaraş	228,129
Karabük	105,373
Karaman	76,525
Kars	78,455
Kastamonu	51,560
Kayseri	421,362
Kilis	82,882
Kırıkkale	185,431
Kırşehir	73,538
Kızıltepe	60,134
Konya	513,346
Körfez	65,786
Kozan	54,451
Kütahya	130,994
Lüleburgaz	52,384
Malatya	281,776
Manisa	158,928
Mardin	53,005
Muş	44,019
Nazilli	80,277
Nevşehir	52,719
Niğde	55,035
Nizip	58,604
Nusaybin	49,671
Ödemiş	51,620
Ordu	102,107
Osmaniye	123,307
Polatlı	60,158
Rize	52,031
Sakarya	171,225
Salihli	70,861
Samsun	303,979
Şanlıurfa	276,528
Siirt	68,320
Silvan (Miyafarkin)	59,865
Sinop	25,537
Sivas	221,512
Siverek	63,049
Söke	50,866
Soma	49,977
Sultanbeyli (★İstanbul)	82,298
Tarsus	187,508
Tatvan	54,071
Tekirdağ	80,442
Tokat	83,058
Trabzon	143,941
Tunceli	24,513
Turgutlu	73,634
Turhal	68,384
Uşak	105,270
Van	153,111
Viranşehir	57,461
Yalova (★İstanbul)	65,823
Yozgat	50,335
Zonguldak (★220,000)	116,725

TURKMENISTAN

1991 E	3,714,100
• AŠCHABAD (ASHGABAT)	412,200
Čardžou	166,400
Krasnovodsk	59,500
Mary	94,900
Nebit-Dag	89,100
Tašauz	117,000

TURKS AND CAICOS ISLANDS

1990 C	11,465
• GRAND TURK	3,691

TUVALU

1979 C	7,349
• FUNAFUTI	2,191

UGANDA

1991 C	16,582,700
Jinja	60,979
• KAMPALA	773,463
Masaka	49,070
Mbale	53,634

UKRAINE / Ukrayina

1991 E	51,944,400
Alchevs'k	126,000
Antratsyt (★Krasnyy Luch)	72,800
Artemivs'k	90,800
Berdyans'k	135,200
Berdychivv	93,400
Bila Tserkva	204,400
Bilhorod-Dnistrovs'kyy	56,800
Boryspil' (★Kyyiv)	52,700
Brovary (★Kyyiv)	84,800
Bryanka (★Stakhanov)	64,500
Cherkasy	302,200
Chernihiv	305,700
Chernivtsi	258,800
Chervonohrad	74,000
Dniprodzerzhyns'k (★Dnipropetrovs'k)	284,400
Dnipropetrovs'k (★1,600,000)	1,189,300
Donets'k (★2,125,000)	1,121,300
Drohobych	79,200
Druzhkivka (★Kramators'k)	74,400
Dymytrov (★Krasnoarmiys'k)	63,800
Dzerzhyns'k (★Horlivka)	50,500
Dzhankoy	54,500
Enerhodar	51,500
Fastiv	54,400
Feodosiya	85,600
Horlivka (★700,000)	336,600
Illichivs'k (★Odesa)	56,000
Ivano-Frankivs'k	225,800
Izmayil	95,100
Izyum	64,800
Kalush	69,400
Kam'yanets'-Podil's'kyy	104,900
Kerch	178,300
Kharkiv (Kharkov) (★2,050,000)	1,622,800
Khartsyz'k (★Donets'k)	69,300
Kherson	365,400
Khmel'nyts'kyy	244,500
Kirovohrad	277,900
Kolomyya	66,200
Komsomol's'k	53,000
Konotop	97,700
Korosten'	67,500
Kostyantynivka	107,800
Kovel'	69,700
Kramators'k (★515,000)	201,300
Krasnoarmiys'k (★180,000)	73,300
Krasnodon (★165,000)	54,800
Krasnyy Luch (★320,000)	113,400
Kremenchuk	240,600
Kryvyy Rih	724,000
• KYYIV (KIEV) (★3,250,000)	2,635,000
Lozova	74,100
Lubny	60,300
Luhans'k (★650,000)	503,900
Luts'k	209,500
L'viv	802,200
Lysychans'k (★415,000)	126,400
Makiyivka (★Donets'k)	423,900
Marhanets'	54,700
Mariupol' (Ždanov)	521,800

▲ Población de un municipio, comuna o distrito entero, incluyendo sus áreas rurales.
• Ciudad más grande de un país.
★ Población o designación de un área metropolitana, incluyendo los suburbios.
C Censo. **E** Estimado oficial. **U** Estimado no oficial.

▲ Population d'une municipalité, d'une commune ou d'un district, zone rurale incluse.
• Ville la plus peuplée du pays.
★ Population de l'agglomération (ou nom de la zone métropolitaine englobante).
C Recensement. **E** Estimation officielle. **U** Estimation non officielle.

▲ População de um município, comuna ou distrito, inclusive as respectivas áreas rurais.
• Maior cidade de um país.
★ População ou indicação de uma área metropolitana.
C Censo. **E** Estimativa oficial. **U** Estimativa não oficial.

Melitopol'	176,900
Mukacheve	88,000
Mykolayiv	511,600
Nikopol'	159,000
Nizhyn	82,000
Nova Kakhovka	59,000
Novohrad-Volyns'kyy	56,100
Novomoskovs'k	76,600
Novovolyns'k	56,400
Odesa (★1,185,000)	1,100,700
Okhtyrka	52,000
Oleksandriya	104,900
Pavlohrad	134,300
Pervomays'k (★Stakhanov)	52,000
Pervomays'k	83,800
Poltava	320,100
Pryluky	72,900
Rivne	239,300
Romny	57,300
Roven'ky	58,500
Rubizhne (★Lysychans'k)	75,100
Sevastopol'	366,200
Shakhtars'k (★Torez)	73,100
Shepetivka	51,900
Shostka	95,200
Simferopol'	352,600
Slov'yans'k (★Kramators'k)	137,100
Smila	81,100
Snizhne (★Torez)	68,900
Stakhanov (★700,000)	112,700
Stryy	68,200
Sumy	300,900
Sverdlovs'k (★145,000)	83,700
Svitlovods'k	57,900
Syeverodonets'k (★Lysychans'k)	133,300
Ternopil'	218,400
Torez (★320,000)	88,100
Uman'	92,700
Uzhhorod	122,600
Vinnytsya	380,900
Yalta	89,300
Yenakiyeve (★Horlivka)	120,100
Yevpatoriya	110,500
Zaporizhzhya	896,600
Zhovti Vody	63,900
Zhytomyr	297,500

UNITED ARAB EMIRATES / Al-Imārāt al-'Arabīyah al-Muttaḥidah

1980 C	980,000
ABŪ ZABY (ABU DHABI)	242,975
Al-'Ayn	101,663
Ash-Shāriqah	125,149
• Dubayy	265,702
Ra's al-Khaymah	42,000

UNITED KINGDOM

1981 C	55,678,079

UNITED KINGDOM: ENGLAND

1981 C	46,220,955
Aldershot (★London)	53,665
Ashton-under-Lyne (★Manchester)	43,605
Aylesbury	51,999
Barnsley	76,783
Barrow-in-Furness	50,174
Basildon (★London)	94,800
Basingstoke	73,027
Bath	84,283
Bebington (★Liverpool)	62,618
Bedford	75,632
Beeston and Stapleford (★Nottingham)	64,785
Benfleet (★London)	50,783
Birkenhead (★Liverpool)	99,075
Birmingham (★2,675,000)	1,013,995
Blackburn (★221,900)	109,564
Blackpool (★280,000)	146,297
Bognor Regis	50,323
Bolton (★Manchester)	143,960
Bootle	70,860
Bournemouth (★315,000)	142,829
Bracknell (★London)	52,257
Bradford (★Leeds)	293,336
Brentwood (★London)	51,212
Brighton (★420,000)	134,581
Bristol (★630,000)	413,861
Burnley (★160,000)	76,365
Burton upon Trent	59,040
Bury (★Manchester)	61,785
Bury Saint Edmunds	30,563
Cambridge	87,111
Cannock (★Birmingham)	54,503
Canterbury	34,546
Carlisle	72,206
Carlton (★Nottingham)	46,053
Chatham (★London)	65,835
Cheadle and Gatley (★Manchester)	59,478
Chelmsford (★London)	91,109
Cheltenham	87,188
Cheshunt (★London)	49,616
Chester	80,154
Chesterfield (★127,000)	73,352
Clacton-on-Sea	39,618
Colchester	87,476
Corby	48,704
Coventry (★645,000)	318,718
Crawley (★London)	80,113
Crewe	59,097
Crosby (★Liverpool)	54,103
Darlington	85,519
Dartford (★London)	62,032
Derby (★275,000)	218,026
Dewsbury (★Leeds)	49,612
Doncaster	74,727
Dover	33,461
Dudley (★Birmingham)	186,513
Dunstable (★Luton)	48,436
Durham	38,105
Eastbourne	86,715
Eastleigh (★Southampton)	58,585
Ellesmere Port (★Liverpool)	65,829
Epsom and Ewell (★London)	65,830
Esher / Molesey (★London)	46,688
Exeter	88,235
Fareham / Portchester (★Portsmouth)	55,563
Farnborough (★London)	48,063
Folkestone	42,949
Frimley and Camberley (★London)	45,108
Gateshead (★Newcastle)	91,429
Gillingham (★London)	92,531
Gloucester (★115,000)	106,526
Gosport (★Portsmouth)	69,664
Gravesend (★London)	53,450
Grays (★London)	45,881
Greasby / Moreton (★Liverpool)	56,410
Great Yarmouth	54,777
Grimsby (★145,000)	91,532
Guildford (★London)	61,509
Halesowen (★Birmingham)	57,533
Halifax	76,675
Harlow (★London)	79,150
Harrogate	63,637
Hartlepool (★Middlesbrough)	91,749
Hastings	74,979
Havant (★Portsmouth)	50,098
Hemel Hempstead (★London)	80,110
Hereford	48,277
Hertford (★London)	21,350
High Wycombe (▲156,800)	69,575
Hove (★Brighton)	65,587
Huddersfield (▲377,400)	147,825
Huyton-with-Roby (★Liverpool)	62,011
Ipswich	129,661
Keighley (★Leeds)	49,188
Kidderminster	50,385
Kingston upon Hull (★350,000)	322,144
Kingswood (★Bristol)	54,736
Kirkby (★Liverpool)	52,825
Lancaster	43,902
Leeds (★1,540,000)	445,242
Leicester (★495,000)	324,394
Lincoln	79,980
Littlehampton	46,028
Liverpool (★1,525,000)	538,809
• LONDON (★11,100,000)	6,574,009
Loughborough	44,895
Lowestoft	59,430
Luton (★220,000)	163,209
Macclesfield	47,525
Maidenhead (★London)	59,809
Maidstone	86,067
Manchester (★2,775,000)	437,612
Mansfield (★198,000)	71,325
Margate	53,137
Middlesbrough (★580,000)	158,516
Middleton (★Manchester)	51,373
Milton Keynes	36,886
Newcastle-under-Lyme (★Stoke-on-Trent)	73,208
Newcastle upon Tyne (★1,300,000)	199,064
Northampton	154,172
Norwich (★230,000)	169,814
Nottingham (★655,000)	273,300
Nuneaton (★Coventry)	60,337
Oldbury / Smethwick (★Birmingham)	153,268
Oldham (★Manchester)	107,095
Oxford (★230,000)	113,847
Penzance	18,501
Peterborough	113,404
Plymouth (★290,000)	238,583
Poole (★Bournemouth)	122,815
Portsmouth (★485,000)	174,218
Preston (★250,000)	166,675
Ramsgate	36,678
Reading (★200,000)	194,727
Redditch (★Birmingham)	61,639
Reigate / Redhill (★London)	48,241
Rochdale (★Manchester)	97,292
Rotherham (★Sheffield)	122,374
Royal Leamington Spa (★Coventry)	56,552
Royal Tunbridge Wells	57,699
Rugby	59,039
Runcorn (★Liverpool)	63,995
Saint Albans (★London)	76,709
Saint Helens	114,397
Sale (★Manchester)	57,872
Salford (★Manchester)	96,525
Salisbury	36,890
Scarborough	36,665
Scunthorpe	79,043
Sheffield (★710,000)	470,685
Shrewsbury	57,731
Slough (★London)	106,341
Solihull (★Birmingham)	93,940
Southampton (★415,000)	211,321
Southend-on-Sea (★London)	155,720
Southport (★Liverpool)	88,596
South Shields (★Newcastle)	86,488
Stafford	60,915
Staines (★London)	51,949
Stevenage	74,757
Stockport (★Manchester)	135,489
Stockton-on-Tees (★Middlesbrough)	86,699
Stoke-on-Trent (★440,000)	272,446
Stourbridge (★Birmingham)	55,136
Stratford-upon-Avon	20,941
Stretford (★Manchester)	47,522
Sunderland (★Newcastle)	195,064
Sutton Coldfield (★Birmingham)	102,572
Swindon	127,348
Tamworth	63,260
Taunton	47,793
Torquay (★112,400)	54,430
Wakefield (★Leeds)	74,764
Wallasey (★Liverpool)	62,465
Walsall (★Birmingham)	177,923
Walton and Weybridge (★London)	50,031
Warrington	81,366
Washington (★Newcastle)	48,856
Waterlooville (★Portsmouth)	57,296
Watford (★London)	109,503
West Bromwich (★Birmingham)	153,725
Weston-super-Mare	60,821
Widnes	55,973
Wigan (★Manchester)	88,725
Woking (★London)	92,667
Wolverhampton (★Birmingham)	263,501
Worcester	75,466
Worthing (★Brighton)	90,687
York (★145,000)	123,126

UNITED KINGDOM: NORTHERN IRELAND

1990 E	1,589,400
Bangor (★Belfast)	72,600
Belfast (★685,000)	295,100
Castlereagh (★Belfast)	58,100
Londonderry (Derry)	100,500
Lurgan (★63,000) (1981C)	20,991
Newtownabbey (★Belfast)	72,900

UNITED KINGDOM: SCOTLAND

1990 E	5,102,400
Aberdeen	211,080
Ayr (★100,000) (1981C)	48,493
Clydebank (★Glasgow) (1981C)	51,832
Coatbridge (1981C)	50,831
Cumbernauld (★Glasgow)	50,700
Dundee	172,860
Dunfermline (★125,817) (1981C)	52,105
East Kilbride (★Glasgow)	70,500
Edinburgh (★630,000)	434,520
Falkirk (★148,171) (1981C)	36,372
Glasgow (★1,800,000)	689,210
Greenock (★101,000) (1981C)	58,436
Hamilton (★Glasgow) (1981C)	51,666
Irvine (★94,000)	56,000
Kilmarnock (★84,000) (1981C)	51,799
Kirkcaldy (★148,171) (1981C)	46,356
Motherwell (★Glasgow) (1981C)	30,616
Paisley (★Glasgow) (1981C)	84,330
Perth (1981C)	41,916
Stirling (★61,000) (1981C)	36,640

UNITED KINGDOM: WALES

1981 C	2,790,462
Cardiff (★625,000)	262,313
Cwmbran (★Newport)	44,592
Llanelli	45,336
Merthyr Tydfil	38,893
Neath (★Swansea)	48,687
Newport (★310,000)	115,896
Pontypool (★Newport)	36,064
Port Talbot (★130,000)	40,078
Rhondda (★Cardiff)	70,980
Swansea (★275,000)	172,433
Wrexham	39,929

UNITED STATES

1990 C	248,709,873

UNITED STATES: ALABAMA

1990 C	4,040,587
Anniston (★116,034)	26,623
Auburn (★61,100)	33,830
Birmingham (★907,810)	265,968
Decatur (★131,556)	48,761
Dothan (★130,964)	53,589
Florence (★131,327)	36,426
Gadsden (★99,840)	42,523
Huntsville (★238,912)	159,789
Mobile (★476,923)	196,278
Montgomery (★292,517)	187,106
Tuscaloosa (★150,522)	77,759

UNITED STATES: ALASKA

1990 C	550,043
Anchorage (★248,400)	226,338
Fairbanks (★59,500)	30,843
Juneau	26,751

UNITED STATES: ARIZONA

1990 C	3,665,228
Chandler (★Phoenix)	90,533
Glendale (★Phoenix)	148,134
Mesa (★Phoenix)	288,091
Nogales (★Nogales, Mexico)	19,489
Phoenix (★2,122,101)	900,013
Scottsdale (★Phoenix)	130,069
Tempe (★Phoenix)	141,865
Tucson (★666,880)	405,390
Yuma (★106,895)	54,923

UNITED STATES: ARKANSAS

1990 C	2,350,725
Fayetteville (★113,409)	42,099
Fort Smith (★175,911)	72,798
Hot Springs National Park (★56,500)	32,462
Jonesboro (★49,300)	46,535
Little Rock (★513,117)	175,795
North Little Rock (★Little Rock)	61,741
Pine Bluff (★85,487)	57,140

UNITED STATES: CALIFORNIA

1990 C	29,760,021
Alameda (★Oakland)	76,459
Alhambra (★Los Angeles)	82,106
Anaheim (★2,410,556) (★Los Angeles)	266,406
Antioch (★Oakland)	62,195
Arden (★Sacramento)	62,900
Bakersfield (★543,477)	174,820
Baldwin Park (★Los Angeles)	69,330
Bellflower (★Los Angeles)	61,815
Berkeley (★Oakland)	102,724
Buena Park (★Anaheim)	68,784
Burbank (★Los Angeles)	93,643
Calexico (★Mexicali, Mexico)	18,633
Camarillo (★Oxnard)	52,303
Carlsbad (★San Diego)	63,126
Carmichael (★Sacramento)	48,702
Carson (★Los Angeles)	83,995
Cerritos (★Los Angeles)	53,240
Chico (★182,120)	40,079
Chino (★Riverside)	59,682
Chula Vista (★San Diego)	135,163
Citrus Heights (★Sacramento)	112,800
Clovis (★Fresno)	50,323
Compton (★Los Angeles)	90,454
Concord (★Oakland)	111,348
Corona (★Riverside)	76,095
Costa Mesa (★Anaheim)	96,357
Cucamonga (★Riverside)	101,409
Daly City (★San Francisco)	92,311
Diamond Bar (★Los Angeles)	53,672
Downey (★Los Angeles)	91,444
East Los Angeles (★Los Angeles)	126,379
El Cajon (★San Diego)	88,693
El Monte (★Los Angeles)	106,209
El Toro (★Anaheim)	62,685
Escondido (★San Diego)	108,635
Eureka (★89,800)	27,025
Fairfield (★Vallejo)	77,211
Fontana (★Riverside)	87,535
Fountain Valley (★Anaheim)	53,691
Fremont (★Oakland)	173,339
Fresno (★667,490)	354,202
Fullerton (★Anaheim)	114,144
Gardena (★Los Angeles)	49,847
Garden Grove (★Anaheim)	143,050
Glendale (★Los Angeles)	180,038
Hacienda Heights (★Los Angeles)	58,200
Hawthorne (★Los Angeles)	71,349
Hayward (★Oakland)	111,498
Hemet (★Riverside)	36,094
Huntington Beach (★Anaheim)	181,519
Huntington Park (★Los Angeles)	56,065
Inglewood (★Los Angeles)	109,602
Irvine (★Anaheim)	110,330
La Habra (★Anaheim)	51,266
Lakewood (★Los Angeles)	73,557
La Mesa (★San Diego)	52,931
Lancaster (★189,300) (★Los Angeles)	97,291
Livermore (★Oakland)	56,741
Lodi (★Stockton)	51,874
Lompoc (★Santa Barbara)	37,649
Long Beach (★Los Angeles)	429,433
Los Angeles (★14,531,529)	3,485,398
Lynwood (★Los Angeles)	61,945
Merced (★178,403)	56,216
Milpitas (★San Jose)	50,686
Mission Viejo (★Anaheim)	72,820
Modesto (★370,522)	164,730
Montebello (★Los Angeles)	59,564
Monterey (★Salinas)	31,954
Monterey Park (★Los Angeles)	60,738
Mountain View (★San Jose)	67,460
Napa (★Vallejo)	61,842
National City (★San Diego)	54,249
Newport Beach (★Anaheim)	66,643
Norwalk (★Los Angeles)	94,279
Oakland (★2,082,914) (★San Francisco)	372,242
Oceanside (★San Diego)	128,398
Ontario (★Riverside)	133,179
Orange (★Anaheim)	110,658
Oxnard (★669,016) (★Los Angeles)	142,216
Palm Springs (★Riverside)	40,181
Palo Alto (★San Jose)	55,900
Pasadena (★Los Angeles)	131,591
Pico Rivera (★Los Angeles)	59,177
Pleasanton (★Oakland)	50,553
Pomona (★Los Angeles)	131,723
Porterville (★Visalia)	29,563
Rancho Cordova (★Sacramento)	48,731
Redding (★147,036)	66,462
Redlands (★Riverside)	60,394
Redondo Beach (★Los Angeles)	60,167
Redwood City (★San Francisco)	66,072
Rialto (★Riverside)	72,388
Richmond (★Oakland)	87,425
Riverside (★2,588,793) (★Los Angeles)	226,505
Rosemead (★Los Angeles)	51,638
Sacramento (★1,481,102)	369,365
Salinas (★355,660)	108,777
San Bernardino (★Riverside)	164,164
San Diego (★2,949,000)	1,110,549
San Francisco (★6,253,311)	723,959
San Jose (★1,497,577) (★San Francisco)	782,248
San Leandro (★Oakland)	68,223
San Mateo (★San Francisco)	85,486
Santa Ana (★Anaheim)	293,742
Santa Barbara (★369,608)	85,571
Santa Clara (★San Jose)	93,613
Santa Cruz (★229,734) (★San Francisco)	49,040
Santa Maria (★Santa Barbara)	61,284
Santa Monica (★Los Angeles)	86,905
Santa Rosa (★388,222) (★San Francisco)	113,313
Santee (★San Diego)	52,902
Simi Valley (★Oxnard)	100,217
South Gate (★Los Angeles)	86,284
South San Francisco (★San Francisco)	54,312
South Whittier (★Los Angeles)	51,100
Spring Valley (★San Diego)	54,600
Stockton (★480,628)	210,943
Sunnyvale (★San Jose)	117,229
Thousand Oaks (★Oxnard)	104,352
Torrance (★Los Angeles)	133,107
Tustin (★Anaheim)	50,689
Union City (★Oakland)	53,762
Upland (★Riverside)	63,374
Vacaville (★Vallejo)	71,479
Vallejo (★451,186) (★San Francisco)	109,199
Ventura (San Buenaventura) (★Oxnard)	92,575
Visalia (★311,921)	75,636
Vista (★San Diego)	71,872
Walnut Creek (★Oakland)	60,569
Watsonville (★Santa Cruz)	31,099
West Covina (★Los Angeles)	96,086
Westminster (★Anaheim)	78,118
Whittier (★Los Angeles)	77,671
Yorba Linda (★Anaheim)	52,422
Yuba City (★122,643)	27,437

UNITED STATES: COLORADO

1990 C	3,294,394
Arvada (★Denver)	89,235
Aurora (★Denver)	222,103
Boulder (★225,339) (★Denver)	83,312
Colorado Springs (★397,014)	281,140
Denver (★1,848,319)	467,610
Fort Collins (★186,136)	87,758
Grand Junction (★85,200)	29,034
Greeley (★131,821)	60,536
Lakewood (★Denver)	126,481
Longmont (★Boulder)	51,555
Loveland (★Fort Collins)	37,352
Pueblo (★123,051)	98,640
Thornton (★Denver)	55,031
Westminster (★Denver)	74,625

UNITED STATES: CONNECTICUT

1990 C	3,287,116
Bridgeport (★443,722) (★New York, N.Y.)	141,686
Bristol (★79,488) (★Hartford)	60,640
Danbury (★187,867) (★New York, N.Y.)	65,585
East Hartford (★Hartford)	50,452
Fairfield (★Bridgeport)	53,418
Greenwich (★Stamford)	58,441
Hamden (★New Haven)	53,100
Hartford (★1,085,837)	139,739
Manchester (★Hartford)	51,000
Meriden (★New Haven)	59,479
Milford (★Bridgeport)	48,168
New Britain (★148,188) (★Hartford)	75,491
New Haven (★530,180)	130,474
New London (★266,819)	28,540
Norwalk (★127,378) (★New York, N.Y.)	78,331
Stamford (★202,557) (★New York, N.Y.)	108,056
Stratford (★Bridgeport)	49,389
Torrington (★58,800)	33,687
Waterbury (★221,629)	108,961
West Hartford (★Hartford)	59,100
West Haven (★New Haven)	54,021

▲ Population of an entire municipality, commune, or district, including rural area.
• Largest city in country.
★ Population or designation of the metropolitan area, including suburbs.
C Census. **E** Official estimate. **U** Unofficial estimate.

▲ Bevölkerung eines ganzen städtischen Verwaltungsgebietes, eines Kommunalbezirkes oder eines Distrikts, einschliesslich ländlicher Gebiete.
• Grösste Stadt des Landes.
★ Bevölkerung oder Bezeichnung der Stadtregion einschliesslich Vororte.
C Volkszählung. **E** Offizielle Schätzung. **U** Inoffizielle Schätzung.

UNITED STATES: DELAWARE

1990 C	666,168
Dover (★78,900)	27,630
Wilmington (★Philadelphia, Pa.)	71,529

UNITED STATES: DISTRICT OF COLUMBIA

1990 C	606,900
WASHINGTON (★3,923,574)	606,900

UNITED STATES: FLORIDA

1990 C	12,937,926
Boca Raton (★West Palm Beach)	61,492
Brandon (★Tampa)	57,985
Cape Coral (★Fort Myers)	74,991
Carol City (★Miami)	52,800
City of Sunrise (★Fort Lauderdale)	64,407
Clearwater (★Tampa)	98,784
Daytona Beach (★370,712)	61,921
De Land (★Daytona Beach)	16,491
Fort Lauderdale (★1,255,488) (★Miami)	149,377
Fort Myers (★335,113)	45,206
Fort Pierce (★251,071)	36,830
Fort Walton Beach (★143,776)	21,471
Gainesville (★204,111)	84,770
Hialeah (★Miami)	188,004
Hollywood (★Fort Lauderdale)	121,697
Jacksonville (★906,727)	635,230
Kendall (★Miami)	53,100
Lakeland (★405,382)	70,576
Largo (★Tampa)	65,674
Melbourne (★398,978)	59,646
Miami (★3,192,582)	358,548
Miami Beach (★Miami)	92,639
Naples (★152,099)	19,505
Ocala (★194,833)	42,045
Orlando (★1,072,748)	164,693
Panama City (★126,994)	34,378
Pembroke Pines (★Fort Lauderdale)	65,452
Pensacola (★344,406)	58,165
Plantation (★Fort Lauderdale)	66,692
Pompano Beach (★Fort Lauderdale)	72,411
Saint Petersburg (★Tampa)	238,629
Sarasota (★277,776)	50,961
Tallahassee (★233,598)	124,773
Tampa (★2,067,959)	280,015
Venice (★Sarasota)	16,922
West Palm Beach (★863,518)	67,643
Winter Haven (★Lakeland)	24,725

UNITED STATES: GEORGIA

1990 C	6,478,216
Albany (★112,561)	78,122
Athens (★156,267)	45,734
Atlanta (★2,833,511)	394,017
Augusta (★396,809)	44,639
Columbus (★243,072)	178,681
Macon (★281,103)	106,612
Rome (★74,900)	30,326
Savannah (★242,622)	137,560
Valdosta (★64,000)	39,806
Warner Robins (★Macon)	43,726

UNITED STATES: HAWAII

1990 C	1,108,229
Hilo (★47,600)	37,808
Honolulu (★836,231)	365,272

UNITED STATES: IDAHO

1990 C	1,006,749
Boise (★205,775)	125,738
Idaho Falls (★72,700)	43,929
Lewiston (★44,300)	28,082
Nampa (★70,500)	28,365
Pocatello (★56,700)	46,080

UNITED STATES: ILLINOIS

1990 C	11,430,602
Arlington Heights (★Chicago)	75,460
Aurora (★356,884) (★Chicago)	99,581
Bloomington (★129,180)	51,972
Champaign (★173,025)	63,502
Chicago (★8,065,633)	2,783,726
Cicero (★Chicago)	67,436
Danville (★68,000)	33,828
Decatur (★117,206)	83,885
De Kalb (★52,200)	34,925
Des Plaines (★Chicago)	53,223
East Saint Louis (★Saint Louis, Mo.)	40,944
Elgin (★Aurora)	77,010
Evanston (★Chicago)	73,233
Galesburg (★40,600)	33,530
Joliet (★389,650) (★Chicago)	76,836
Kankakee (★96,255)	27,575
Mount Prospect (★Chicago)	53,170
Naperville (★Chicago)	85,351
Oak Lawn (★Chicago)	56,182
Oak Park (★Chicago)	53,648
Peoria (★339,172)	113,504
Quincy (★50,600)	39,681
Rockford (★283,719)	139,426
Schaumburg (★Chicago)	68,586
Skokie (★Chicago)	59,432
Springfield (★189,550)	105,227
Waukegan (★Chicago)	69,392
Wheaton (★Chicago)	51,464

UNITED STATES: INDIANA

1990 C	5,544,159
Anderson (★130,669)	59,459
Bloomington (★108,978)	60,633
Columbus (★59,000)	31,802
Elkhart (★156,198)	43,627
Evansville (★278,990)	126,272
Fort Wayne (★363,811)	173,072
Gary (★604,526) (★Chicago, Il.)	116,646
Hammond (★Gary)	84,236
Indianapolis (★1,249,822)	731,327
Kokomo (★96,946)	44,962
Lafayette (★130,598)	43,764
Marion (★76,900)	32,618
Michigan City (★55,600)	33,822
Muncie (★119,659)	71,035
Richmond (★64,100)	38,705
South Bend (★247,052)	105,511
Terre Haute (★130,812)	57,483

UNITED STATES: IOWA

1990 C	2,776,755
Ames (★65,400)	47,198
Cedar Rapids (★168,767)	108,751
Clinton (★39,600)	29,201
Council Bluffs (★Omaha, Ne.)	54,315
Davenport (★350,861)	95,333
Des Moines (★392,928)	193,187
Dubuque (★86,403)	57,546
Iowa City (★96,119)	59,738
Mason City	29,040
Sioux City (★115,018)	80,505
Waterloo (★146,611)	66,467

UNITED STATES: KANSAS

1990 C	2,477,574
Hutchinson (★46,800)	39,308
Kansas City (★Kansas City, Mo.)	149,767
Lawrence (★81,798)	65,608
Manhattan (★47,400)	37,712
Olathe (★Kansas City, Mo.)	63,352
Overland Park (★Kansas City, Mo.)	111,790
Salina (★42,700)	42,303
Topeka (★160,976)	119,883
Wichita (★485,270)	304,011

UNITED STATES: KENTUCKY

1990 C	3,685,296
Bowling Green (★59,100)	40,641
Covington (★Cincinnati, Oh.)	43,264
Frankfort	25,968
Lexington (★348,428)	225,366
Louisville (★952,662)	269,063
Owensboro (★87,189)	53,549
Paducah (★63,000)	27,256

UNITED STATES: LOUISIANA

1990 C	4,219,973
Alexandria (★131,556)	49,188
Baton Rouge (★528,264)	219,531
Bossier City (★Shreveport)	52,721
Houma (★182,842)	96,982
Kenner (★New Orleans)	72,033
Lafayette (★208,740)	94,440
Lake Charles (★168,134)	70,580
Metairie (★New Orleans)	149,428
Monroe (★142,191)	54,909
New Iberia (★49,000)	31,828
New Orleans (★1,238,816)	496,938
Shreveport (★334,341)	198,525

UNITED STATES: MAINE

1990 C	1,227,928
Augusta (★56,700)	21,325
Bangor (★88,745)	33,181
Lewiston (★88,141)	39,757
Portland (★215,281)	64,358

UNITED STATES: MARYLAND

1990 C	4,781,468
Annapolis (★Baltimore)	33,187
Baltimore (★2,382,172)	736,014
Bethesda (★Washington, D.C.)	62,936
Columbia (★Baltimore)	75,883
Cumberland (★101,643)	23,706
Dundalk (★Baltimore)	65,800
Hagerstown (★121,393)	35,445
Salisbury (★72,400)	20,592
Silver Spring (★Washington, D.C.)	76,046
Towson (★Baltimore)	49,445
Wheaton (★Washington, D.C.) (1989)	58,300

UNITED STATES: MASSACHUSETTS

1990 C	6,016,425
Amherst (★44,700)	17,824
Boston (★4,171,643)	574,283
Brockton (★189,478) (★Boston)	92,788
Brookline (★Boston)	54,718
Cambridge (★Boston)	95,802
Chicopee (★Springfield)	56,632
Fall River (★157,272) (★Providence, R.I.)	92,703
Fitchburg (★102,797)	41,194
Framingham (★Boston)	64,989
Haverhill (★Lawrence)	51,418
Lawrence (★393,516) (★Boston)	70,207
Lowell (★273,067) (★Boston)	103,439
Lynn (★Salem)	81,245
Malden (★Boston)	53,884
Medford (★Boston)	57,407
New Bedford (★175,641)	99,922
Newton (★Boston)	82,585
Northampton (★Springfield)	29,289
Pittsfield (★79,250)	48,622
Quincy (★Boston)	84,985
Somerville (★Boston)	76,210
Springfield (★529,519)	156,983
Taunton (★59,700)	49,832
Waltham (★Boston)	57,878
Weymouth (★Boston)	54,063
Worcester (★436,905)	169,759

UNITED STATES: MICHIGAN

1990 C	9,295,297
Ann Arbor (★282,937) (★Detroit)	109,592
Battle Creek (★135,982)	53,540
Benton Harbor (★161,378)	12,818
Clinton Township (★Detroit)	77,900
Dearborn (★Detroit)	89,286
Dearborn Heights (★Detroit)	60,838
Detroit (★4,665,236)	1,027,974
East Lansing (★Lansing)	50,677
Farmington Hills (★Detroit)	74,652
Flint (★430,459)	140,761
Grand Rapids (★688,399)	189,126
Holland (★Grand Rapids)	30,745
Jackson (★149,756)	37,446
Kalamazoo (★223,411)	80,277
Lansing (★432,674)	127,321
Livonia (★Detroit)	100,850
Monroe (★62,600) (★Detroit)	22,902
Muskegon (★158,983)	40,283
Pontiac (★Detroit)	71,166
Port Huron (★Sarnia, Canada)	33,694
Redford Township (★Detroit)	54,387
Roseville (★Detroit)	51,412
Royal Oak (★Detroit)	65,410
Saginaw (★399,320)	69,512
Saint Clair Shores (★Detroit)	68,107
Sault Sainte Marie	14,689
Southfield (★Detroit)	75,728
Sterling Heights (★Detroit)	117,810
Taylor (★Detroit)	70,811
Troy (★Detroit)	72,884
Warren (★Detroit)	144,864
Westland (★Detroit)	84,724
Wyoming (★Grand Rapids)	63,891

UNITED STATES: MINNESOTA

1990 C	4,375,099
Bloomington (★Minneapolis)	86,335
Brooklyn Park (★Minneapolis)	56,381
Burnsville (★Minneapolis)	51,288
Coon Rapids (★Minneapolis)	52,978
Duluth (★239,971)	85,493
Mankato (★48,400)	31,477
Minneapolis (★2,464,124)	368,383
Plymouth (★Minneapolis)	50,889
Rochester (★106,470)	70,745
Saint Cloud (★190,921)	48,812
Saint Paul (★Minneapolis)	272,235

UNITED STATES: MISSISSIPPI

1990 C	2,573,216
Biloxi (★197,125)	46,319
Columbus (★52,100)	23,799
Greenville (★48,500)	45,226
Gulfport (★Biloxi)	40,775
Hattiesburg (★71,600)	41,882
Jackson (★395,396)	196,637
Laurel (★47,300)	18,827
Meridian (★60,600)	41,036
Natchez (★45,700)	19,460
Pascagoula (★115,243)	25,899
Vicksburg (★43,500)	20,908

UNITED STATES: MISSOURI

1990 C	5,117,073
Cape Girardeau (★59,100)	34,438
Columbia (★112,379)	69,101
Florissant (★Saint Louis)	51,206
Independence (★Kansas City)	112,301
Jefferson City (★60,100)	35,481
Joplin (★134,910)	40,961
Kansas City (★1,566,280)	435,146
Saint Charles (★Saint Louis)	54,555
Saint Joseph (★83,083)	71,852
Saint Louis (★2,444,099)	396,685
Springfield (★240,593)	140,494

UNITED STATES: MONTANA

1990 C	799,065
Billings (★113,419)	81,151
Butte (★33,900)	33,336
Great Falls (★77,691)	55,097
Helena	24,569
Missoula (★65,700)	42,918

UNITED STATES: NEBRASKA

1990 C	1,578,385
Grand Island (★42,200)	39,386
Lincoln (★213,641)	191,972
Omaha (★618,262)	335,795

UNITED STATES: NEVADA

1990 C	1,201,833
Carson City	40,443
Henderson (★Las Vegas)	64,942
Las Vegas (★741,459)	258,295
Paradise (★Las Vegas)	124,682
Reno (★254,667)	133,850
Sparks (★Reno)	53,367
Sunrise Manor (★Las Vegas)	95,362

UNITED STATES: NEW HAMPSHIRE

1990 C	1,109,252
Concord (★73,300)	36,006
Manchester (★147,809)	99,567
Nashua (★180,557) (★Boston, Ma.)	79,662
Portsmouth (★223,578)	25,925

UNITED STATES: NEW JERSEY

1990 C	7,730,188
Atlantic City (★319,416)	37,986
Bayonne (★Jersey City)	61,444
Bloomfield (★Newark)	45,061
Brick Township (★New York, N.Y.)	66,473
Camden (★Philadelphia, Pa.)	87,492
Cherry Hill (★Philadelphia, Pa.)	69,319
Clifton (★New York, N.Y.)	71,742
East Orange (★Newark)	73,552
Edison (★New York, N.Y.)	88,680
Elizabeth (★Newark)	110,002
Irvington (★Newark)	59,774
Jersey City (★553,099) (★New York, N.Y.)	228,537
Middletown (★New York, N.Y.)	62,298
Newark (★1,824,321) (★New York, N.Y.)	275,221
Passaic (★New York, N.Y.)	58,041
Paterson (★New York, N.Y.)	140,891
Trenton (★325,824) (★Philadelphia, Pa.)	88,675
Union (★Newark)	50,024
Union City (★Jersey City)	58,012
Vineland (★138,053) (★Philadelphia, Pa.)	54,780

UNITED STATES: NEW MEXICO

1990 C	1,515,069
Albuquerque (★480,577)	384,736
Farmington (★50,300)	33,997
Las Cruces (★135,510)	62,126
Roswell (★50,600)	44,654
Santa Fe (★117,043)	55,859

UNITED STATES: NEW YORK

1990 C	17,990,455
Albany (★874,304)	101,082
Auburn (★52,900)	31,258
Binghamton (★264,497)	53,008
Buffalo (★1,189,288)	328,123
Cheektowaga (★Buffalo)	84,387
Elmira (★95,195)	33,724
Glens Falls (★118,539)	15,023
Hempstead (★New York)	49,453
Irondequoit (★Rochester)	52,322
Ithaca (★82,700)	29,541
Jamestown (★141,895)	34,681
Kingston (★88,200)	23,095
Levittown (★New York)	53,286
Lockport (★57,500) (★Buffalo)	24,426
Mount Vernon (★New York)	67,153
Newburgh (★102,300) (★New York)	26,454
New Rochelle (★New York)	67,265
• New York (★18,087,251)	7,322,564
Niagara Falls (★220,756) (★Buffalo)	61,840
Poughkeepsie (★259,462)	28,844
Rochester (★1,002,410)	231,636
Schenectady (★Albany)	65,566
Syracuse (★659,864)	163,860
Troy (★Albany)	54,269
Utica (★316,633)	68,637
West Seneca (★Buffalo)	47,866
Yonkers (★New York)	188,082

UNITED STATES: NORTH CAROLINA

1990 C	6,628,637
Asheville (★174,821)	61,607
Burlington (★108,213)	39,498
Charlotte (★1,162,093)	395,934
Durham (★Raleigh)	136,611
Fayetteville (★274,566)	75,695
Gastonia (★Charlotte)	54,732
Goldsboro (★94,200)	40,709
Greensboro (★942,091)	183,521
Hickory (★221,700)	28,301
High Point (★Greensboro)	69,496
Jacksonville (★149,838)	30,013
Kannapolis (★Charlotte)	29,696
Raleigh (★735,480)	207,951
Rocky Mount (★83,400)	48,997
Salisbury (★Charlotte)	23,087
Wilmington (★120,284)	55,530
Winston-Salem (★Greenboro)	143,485

UNITED STATES: NORTH DAKOTA

1990 C	638,800
Bismarck (★83,831)	49,256
Fargo (★153,296)	74,111
Grand Forks (★70,683)	49,425
Minot (★39,800)	34,544

UNITED STATES: OHIO

1990 C	10,347,115
Akron (★657,575) (★Cleveland)	223,019
Alliance (★Canton)	23,376
Ashtabula (★40,900)	21,633
Brunswick (★Cleveland)	28,230
Canton (★394,106)	84,161
Cincinnati (★1,744,124)	364,040
Cleveland (★2,759,823)	505,616
Cleveland Heights (★Cleveland)	54,052
Columbus (★1,377,419)	632,910
Dayton (★951,270)	182,044
East Liverpool (★44,400)	13,654
Elyria (★Lorain)	56,746
Euclid (★Cleveland)	54,875
Hamilton (★291,479) (★Cincinnati)	61,368
Kettering (★Dayton)	60,569
Lakewood (★Cleveland)	59,718
Lancaster (★Columbus)	34,507
Lima (★154,340)	45,549
Lorain (★271,126) (★Cleveland)	71,245
Mansfield (★126,137)	50,627
Marion (★53,900)	34,075
Middletown (★107,200) (★Cincinnati)	46,022
Newark (★Columbus)	44,389
Parma (★Cleveland)	87,876
Portsmouth (★64,300)	22,676
Sandusky (★79,800)	29,764
Springfield (★Dayton)	70,487
Steubenville (★142,523)	22,125
Toledo (★614,128)	332,943
Warren (★Youngstown)	50,793
Youngstown (★492,619)	95,732
Zanesville (★67,800)	26,778

UNITED STATES: OKLAHOMA

1990 C	3,145,585
Broken Arrow (★Tulsa)	58,043
Edmond (★Oklahoma City)	52,315
Enid (★56,735)	45,309
Lawton (★111,486)	80,561
Midwest City (★Oklahoma City)	52,267
Muskogee (★49,500)	37,708
Norman (★Oklahoma City)	80,071
Oklahoma City (★958,839)	444,719
Tulsa (★708,954)	367,302

UNITED STATES: OREGON

1990 C	2,842,321
Beaverton (★Portland)	53,310
Corvallis (★98,700)	44,757
Eugene (★282,912)	112,669
Gresham (★Portland)	68,235
Medford (★146,389)	46,951
Portland (★1,477,895)	437,319
Salem (★278,024)	107,786

UNITED STATES: PENNSYLVANIA

1990 C	11,881,643
Abington (★Philadelphia)	59,300
Allentown (★686,688)	105,090
Altoona (★130,542)	51,881
Bensalem (★Philadelphia)	56,788
Bethlehem (★Allentown)	71,428
Bristol (★Philadelphia)	57,129
Butler (★86,500)	15,714
Coatesville (★93,400) (★Philadelphia)	11,038
Erie (★275,572)	108,718
Hanover (★York)	14,399
Harrisburg (★587,986)	52,376
Haverford (★Philadelphia)	49,848
Hazleton (★Scranton)	24,730
Johnstown (★241,247)	28,134
Lancaster (★422,822)	55,551
Lebanon (★Harrisburg)	24,800
Lower Merion Township (★Philadelphia)	58,003
New Castle (★68,400)	28,334
Oil City (★42,000)	11,949
Penn Hills (★Pittsburgh)	51,430
Philadelphia (★5,899,345)	1,585,577
Pittsburgh (★2,242,798)	369,879
Pottstown (★88,300) (★Philadelphia)	21,831
Pottsville (★54,200)	16,603
Reading (★336,523)	78,380
Scranton (★734,175)	81,805
Sharon (★121,003)	17,493

▲ Población de un municipio, comuna o distrito entero, incluyendo sus áreas rurales.
• Ciudad más grande de un país.
★ Población o designación de un área metropolitana, incluyendo los suburbios.
C Censo. **E** Estimado oficial. **U** Estimado no oficial.

▲ Population d'une municipalité, d'une commune ou d'un district, zone rurale incluse.
• Ville la plus peuplée du pays.
★ Population de l'agglomération (ou nom de la zone métropolitaine englobante).
C Recensement. **E** Estimation officielle. **U** Estimation non officielle.

▲ População de um municipio, comuna ou distrito, inclusive as respectivas áreas rurais.
• Maior cidade de um país.
★ População ou indicação de uma área metropolitana.
C Censo. **E** Estimativa oficial. **U** Estimativa não oficial.

State College (★123,786)	38,923
Uniontown (★53,200) (★Pittsburgh)	12,034
Upper Darby (★Philadelphia)	84,054
Washington (★66,000) (★Pittsburgh)	15,864
Wilkes-Barre (★Scranton)	47,523
Williamsport (★118,710)	31,933
York (★417,848)	42,192

UNITED STATES: RHODE ISLAND

1990 C	1,003,464
Cranston (★Providence)	76,060
East Providence (★Providence)	50,380
Newport (★64,500)	28,227
Pawtucket (★329,384) (★Providence)	72,644
Providence (★1,141,510)	160,728
Warwick (★Providence)	85,427

UNITED STATES: SOUTH CAROLINA

1990 C	3,486,703
Anderson (★145,196)	26,184
Charleston (★506,875)	80,414
Columbia (★453,331)	98,052
Florence (★114,344)	29,813
Greenville (★640,861)	58,282
North Charleston (★Charleston)	70,218
Rock Hill (★Charlotte, N.C.)	41,643
Spartanburg (★Greenville)	43,467
Sumter (★90,300)	41,943

UNITED STATES: SOUTH DAKOTA

1990 C	696,004
Pierre	12,906
Rapid City (★81,343)	54,523
Sioux Falls (★123,809)	100,814

UNITED STATES: TENNESSEE

1990 C	4,877,185
Bristol (★Johnson City)	23,421
Chattanooga (★433,210)	152,466
Clarksville (★169,439)	75,494
Jackson (★77,982)	48,949
Johnson City (★436,047)	49,381
Kingsport (★Johnson City)	36,365
Knoxville (★604,816)	165,121
Memphis (★981,747)	610,337
Murfreesboro (★Nashville)	44,922
Nashville (★985,026)	487,969

UNITED STATES: TEXAS

1990 C	16,986,510
Abilene (★119,655)	106,654
Amarillo (★187,547)	157,615
Arlington (★Fort Worth)	261,721
Austin (★781,572)	465,622
Baytown (★Houston)	63,850
Beaumont (★361,226)	114,323
Brownsville (★460,000)	98,962
Bryan (★121,862)	55,002
Carrollton (★Dallas)	82,169
College Station (★Bryan)	52,456
Corpus Christi (★349,894)	257,453
Dallas (★3,885,415)	1,006,877
Denton (★Dallas)	66,270
El Paso (★650,000)	515,342
Fort Worth (★1,332,053) (★Dallas)	447,619
Freeport (★88,600) (★Houston)	11,389
Galveston (★217,399) (★Houston)	59,070
Garland (★Dallas)	180,650
Grand Prairie (★Dallas)	99,616
Harlingen (★Brownsville)	48,735
Houston (★3,711,043)	1,630,553
Irving (★Dallas)	155,037
Killeen (★255,301)	63,535
Laredo (★354,000)	122,899
Longview (★162,431)	70,311
Lubbock (★222,636)	186,206
Lufkin (★56,000)	30,206
McAllen (★383,545)	84,021
Mesquite (★Dallas)	101,484
Midland (★106,611)	89,443
Odessa (★118,934)	89,699
Pasadena (★Houston)	119,363
Plano (★Dallas)	128,713
Port Arthur (★Beaumont)	58,724
Richardson (★Dallas)	74,840
San Angelo (★98,458)	84,474
San Antonio (★1,302,099)	935,933
Sherman (★95,021)	31,601
Temple (★Killeen)	46,109
Texarkana (★120,132)	31,656
Tyler (★151,309)	75,450
Victoria (★74,361)	55,076
Waco (★189,123)	103,590
Wichita Falls (★122,378)	96,259

UNITED STATES: UTAH

1990 C	1,722,850
Logan (★60,300)	32,762
Ogden (★Salt Lake City)	63,909
Orem (★Provo)	67,561
Provo (★263,590)	86,835
Salt Lake City (★1,072,227)	159,936
Sandy (★Salt Lake City)	75,058
West Valley City (★Salt Lake City)	86,976

UNITED STATES: VERMONT

1990 C	562,758
Burlington (★131,439)	39,127
Montpelier (★52,800)	8,247
Rutland (★53,000)	18,230

UNITED STATES: VIRGINIA

1990 C	6,187,358
Alexandria (★Washington, D.C.)	111,183
Annandale (★Washington, D.C.)	50,975
Arlington (★Washington, D.C.)	170,936
Charlottesville (★131,107)	40,341
Chesapeake (★Norfolk)	151,976
Danville (★108,711)	53,056
Hampton (★Norfolk)	133,793
Lynchburg (★142,199)	66,049
Martinsville (★67,100)	16,162
Newport News (★Norfolk)	170,045
Norfolk (★1,396,107)	261,229
Portsmouth (★Norfolk)	103,907
Richmond (★865,640)	203,056
Roanoke (★224,477)	96,397
Suffolk (★Norfolk)	52,141
Virginia Beach (★Norfolk)	393,069

UNITED STATES: WASHINGTON

1990 C	4,866,692
Bellevue (★Seattle)	86,874
Bellingham (★127,780)	52,179
Bremerton (★189,731)	38,142
Everett (★Seattle)	69,961
Lakes District (★Tacoma)	58,412
Longview (★67,100)	31,499
Olympia (★161,238)	33,840
Pasco (★Richland)	20,337
Seattle (★2,559,164)	516,259
Spokane (★361,364)	177,196
Tacoma (★586,203) (★Seattle)	176,664
Yakima (★188,823)	54,827

UNITED STATES: WEST VIRGINIA

1990 C	1,793,477
Beckley (★64,300)	18,296
Charleston (★250,454)	57,287
Clarksburg (★53,800)	18,059
Fairmont (★53,700)	20,210
Huntington (★312,529)	54,844
Morgantown (★71,500)	25,879
Parkersburg (★149,169)	33,862
Wheeling (★159,301)	34,882

UNITED STATES: WISCONSIN

1990 C	4,891,769
Appleton (★315,121)	65,695
Beloit (★Janesville)	35,573
Eau Claire (★137,543)	56,856
Fond du Lac (★52,400)	37,757
Green Bay (★194,594)	96,466
Janesville (★139,510)	52,133
Kenosha (★128,181) (★Chicago, Il.)	80,352
La Crosse (★97,904)	51,003
Madison (★367,085)	191,262
Manitowoc (★57,300)	32,520
Milwaukee (★1,607,183)	628,088
Oshkosh (★Appleton)	55,006
Racine (★175,034) (★Milwaukee)	84,298
Sheboygan (★103,877)	49,676
Waukesha (★Milwaukee)	56,958
Wausau (★115,400)	37,060
Wauwatosa (★Milwaukee)	49,366
West Allis (★Milwaukee)	63,221

UNITED STATES: WYOMING

1990 C	453,588
Casper (★61,226)	46,742
Cheyenne (★73,142)	50,008

URUGUAY

1985 C	2,955,241
Las Piedras (★Montevideo)	58,288
Melo	42,615
Mercedes	36,702
Minas	34,661
• MONTEVIDEO (★1,550,000)	1,251,647
Paysandú	76,191
Rivera	57,316
Salto	80,823

UZBEKISTAN

1991 E	20,708,200
Almalyk	116,400
Andižan	298,300
Angren	132,600
Bekabad	82,800
Buchara	249,600
Çhodžejli	61,200
Čirčik (★Taškent)	158,400
Denau	49,300
Džizak	109,700
Fergana	193,700
Gulistan	54,500
Jangijul'	56,900
Kagan	49,800
Karši	168,000
Kattakurgan	59,600
Kokand	175,000
Margilan	124,900
Namangan	319,200
Navoi	111,600
Nukus	179,600
Şachrichan	47,600
Šachrisabz	53,200
Samarkand	370,500
• TAŠKENT (TASHKENT) (★2,325,000)	2,113,300
Termez	90,400
Urgenč	130,400

VANUATU

1989 C	142,944
• PORT VILA (★23,000)	19,311

VATICAN CITY / Città del Vaticano

1988 E	766

VENEZUELA

1990 C	18,105,265
Acarigua	116,551
Anaco	61,386
Araure	55,299
Barcelona	221,792
Barinas	153,630
Barquisimeto	625,450
Baruta (★Caracas)	182,941
Cabimas	165,755
Cagua	73,465
Calabozo	79,578
• CARACAS (★4,000,000)	1,822,465
Carora	70,715
Carúpano	92,333
Catia La Mar (★Caracas)	100,104
Chacao (★Caracas)	66,897
Ciudad Bolívar	225,340
Ciudad Guayana	453,047
Ciudad Ojeda (Lagunillas)	73,473
Coro	124,506
Cumaná	212,432
El Limón	90,030
El Tigre	93,229
Guacara	100,766
Guanare	84,904
Guarenas (★Caracas)	134,158
La Asunción	16,552
La Victoria	77,326
Los Dos Caminos (★Caracas)	59,141
Los Teques (★Caracas)	140,617
Maiquetía (★Caracas)	62,834
Maracaibo	1,249,670
Maracay	354,196
Mariara	69,404
Maturín	206,654
Mérida	170,902
Palo Negro	50,718
Petare (★Caracas)	338,417
Porlamar	62,732
Pozuelos (1981C)	80,342
Puerto Ayacucho	36,107
Puerto Cabello	128,825
Puerto la Cruz	115,731
Punto Fijo	88,681
San Carlos	50,708
San Cristóbal	220,675
San Felipe	65,509
San Fernando	72,716
San Juan de los Morros	67,791
Trujillo	33,241
Tucupita	41,117
Turmero	174,280
Valencia	903,621
Valera	97,012
Valle de la Pascua	67,100
Villa de Cura	51,096

VIETNAM / Viet Nam

1989 C	64,411,668
Bac Giang	50,879
Bac Lieu	83,483
Bien Hoa	273,879
Buon Me Thuot	97,044
Ca Mau	81,901
Cam Pha	105,336
Can Tho	208,078
Chau Doc	50,935
Da Lat	102,583
Da Nang	369,734
Hai Duong	53,370
Hai Phong (▲1,447,523)	351,919
HA NOI (★1,275,000)	905,939
Hoa Binh	69,323
Hon Gai	123,102
Hue	211,718
Long Xuyen	128,814
Minh Hai (1979C)	72,517
My Tho	104,724
Nam Dinh	165,629
Nha Trang	213,460
Phan Rang	71,111
Phan Thiet	114,236
Play Cu	76,991
Qui Nhon	159,852
Rach Gia	137,784
Sa Dec	50,733
Soc Trang	87,899
Soc Trang	87,899
Tan An	50,288
Thai Binh	57,640
Thai Nguyen	124,871
Thanh Hoa	84,951
• Thanh Pho Ho Chi Minh (Saigon) (★3,300,000)	2,796,229
Tra Vinh	47,785
Tuy Hoa	54,081
Uong Bi	49,595
Viet Tri	73,347
Vinh	110,793
Vinh Long	81,620
Vung Tau	123,528
Yen Bai	58,645

VIRGIN ISLANDS OF THE UNITED STATES

1990 C	101,809
• CHARLOTTE AMALIE (★32,000)	12,331

WALLIS AND FUTUNA / Wallis et Futuna

1983 E	12,408
• MATÂ'UTU	815
Ono (1976C)	624

WEST BANK

1992 E	1,653,000
Al - Quds (Jerusalem) (★Yerushalayim, Israel)	285,000
Arīḥā (Jericho) (Independent City) (1967C)	6,829
Bayt Laḥm (Bethlehem) (1971E)	25,000
Nābulus (1971E)	64,000

WESTERN SAHARA

1982 E	142,000
• EL AAIÚN	93,875

WESTERN SAMOA / Samoa i Sisifo

1981 C	156,349
• APIA	33,170

YEMEN / Al-Yaman

1990 E	15,267,000
‘Adan (★318,000) (1984E)	176,100
Al-Ḥudaydah (1986C)	155,110
Al-Mukallā (1984E)	58,000
• ṢAN‘Ā' (1986C)	427,150
Ta‘izz (1986C)	178,043

YUGOSLAVIA / Jugoslavija

1991 C	10,337,920
• BEOGRAD (★1,554,826)	1,136,786
Čačak	72,392
Kragujevac	146,607
Kraljevo	56,616
Kruševac	58,114
Leskovac	61,963
Niš	175,555
Novi Pazar	51,906
Novi Sad	178,896
Pančevo (★Beograd)	72,717
Podgorica	118,059
Priština (▲244,830) (1987E)	125,400
Šabac	54,829
Smederevo	64,257
Sombor	48,789
Subotica1)	100,219
Užice	53,666
Valjevo	58,324
Vranje	51,695
Zrenjanin	81,382

ZAIRE / Zaïre

1984 C	30,729,443
Bandundu	63,642
Beni	44,141
Boma	197,617
Bukavu	167,950
Bumba	51,197
Bunia	59,598
Butembo	73,312
Gandajika	64,878
Gbadolite	27,063
Gemena	63,052
Goma	77,908
Ilebo (Port-Francqui)	53,887
Isiro	78,268
Kalemie (Albertville)	73,528
Kamina	62,789
Kananga (Luluabourg)	298,693
Kikwit	149,296
Kindu	66,812
• KINSHASA (LÉOPOLDVILLE) (1986E)	3,000,000
Kipushi	53,207
Kisangani (Stanleyville)	317,581
Kolwezi	416,122
Likasi (Jadotville)	213,862
Lubumbashi (Élisabethville)	564,830
Matadi	138,798
Mbandaka (Coquilhatville)	137,291
Mbuji-Mayi (Bakwanga)	486,235
Mwene-Ditu	94,560
Tshikapa	116,016
Uvira	74,432

ZAMBIA

1990 C	7,818,447
Chililabombwe (Bancroft) (★76,848)	35,200
Chingola	167,954
Kabwe (Broken Hill)	166,519
Kalulushi	75,197
Kitwe (★338,207)	247,100
Livingstone	82,218
Luanshya (★146,275)	79,500
• LUSAKA	982,362
Mufulira (★152,944)	85,000
Ndola	376,311

ZIMBABWE

1983 E	7,740,000
Bulawayo	429,000
Chitungwiza (★Harare)	202,000
Gweru (1982C)	78,940
• HARARE (★890,000)	681,000
Mutare (1982C)	75,358

▲ Population of an entire municipality, commune, or district, including rural area.

• Largest city in country.
★ Population or designation of the metropolitan area, including suburbs.
C Census. **E** Official estimate.
U Unofficial estimate.

▲ Bevölkerung eines ganzen städtischen Verwaltungsgebietes, eines Kommunalbezirkes oder eines Distrikts, einschliesslich ländlicher Gebiete.

• Grösste Stadt des Landes.
★ Bevölkerung oder Bezeichnung der Stadtregion einschliess lich Vororte.
C Volkszählung. **E** Offizielle Schätzung.
U Inoffizielle Schätzung.

▲ Población de un municipio, comuna o distrito entero, incluyendo sus áreas rurales.

• Ciudad más grande de un país.
★ Población o designación de un área metropolitana, incluyendo los suburbios.
C Censo. **E** Estimado oficial.
U Estimado no oficial.

▲ Population d'une municipalité, d'une commune ou d'un district, zone rurale incluse.

• Ville la plus peuplée du pays.
★ Population de l'agglomération (ou nom de la zone métropolitaine englobante).
C Recensement. **E** Estimation officielle.
U Estimation non officielle.

▲ População de um municipio, comuna ou distrito, inclusive as respectivas áreas rurais.

• Maior cidade de um país.
★ População ou indicação de uma área metropolitana.
C Censo. **E** Estimativa oficial.
U Estimativa não oficial.

The index includes in a single alphabetical list some 170,000 names appearing on the maps. Each name is followed by a page reference to one or more maps and by the location of the feature on the map, in coordinates of latitude and longitude. If a page contains several maps, a lowercase letter identifies the particular map. The page reference for two-page maps is always to the left-hand page.

Most map features are indexed to the largest-scale map on which they appear. However, a feature usually is not indexed to a Metropolitan Area map if it is also shown on another map where it can be seen in a broader setting. Countries, mountain ranges, and other extensive features are generally indexed to the largest-scale map that shows them in their entirety.

The order in which index information is presented is shown in the English, German, Spanish, French, and Portuguese headings at the center of each two-page spread.

For example:

ENGLISH			
Name	Page	Lat.°′	Long.°′

The features indexed are of three types: *point, areal,* and *linear.* For *point* features (for example, cities, mountain peaks, dams), latitude and longitude coordinates give the location of the point on the map. For *areal* features (countries, mountain ranges, etc.), the coordinates generally indicate the approximate center of the feature. For *linear* features (rivers, canals, aqueducts), the coordinates locate a terminating point—for example, the mouth of a river, or the point at which a feature reaches the map margin.

Name Forms Names in the index, as on the maps, are generally in the local language and insofar as possible are spelled according to official practice. Diacritical marks are included, except that those used to indicate tone, as in Vietnamese, are usually not shown. Most features that extend beyond the boundaries of one country have no single official name, and these are usually named in English. Many English, German, Spanish, French, and Portuguese names, which may not be shown on the maps, appear in the index as cross references. All cross references are indicated by the symbol →. A name that appears in a shortened version on the map due to space limitations is given in full in the index, with the portion that is omitted on the map enclosed in brackets, for example, Acapulco [de Juárez].

Transliteration For names in languages not written in the Roman alphabet, the locally official transliteration system has been used where one exists. Thus, names in Russia and Bulgaria have been transliterated according to the systems adopted by the academies of science of these countries. Similarly, the transliteration for mainland Chinese names follows the Pinyin system, which has been officially adopted in mainland China. For languages with no one locally accepted transliteration system, notably Arabic, transliteration in general follows closely a system adopted by the United States Board on Geographic Names.

Alphabetization Names are alphabetized in the order of the letters of the English alphabet. Spanish *ll* and *ch,* for example, are not treated as distinct letters. Furthermore, diacritical marks are disregarded in alphabetization—German or Scandinavian *ä* or *ö* are treated as *a* or *o.*

The names of physical features may appear inverted, since they are always alphabetized under the proper, not the generic, part of the name, thus: "Gibraltar, Strait of)(." Otherwise every entry, whether consisting of one word or more, is alphabetized as a single continuous entity. "Lakeland," for example, appears after "La Crosse" and before "La Salle." Names beginning with articles (Le Havre, Den Helder, Al-Qāhirah, As-Suways) are not inverted. Names beginning with "St." and "Sainte" are alphabetized as though spelled "Saint."

In the case of identical names, towns are listed first, then political divisions, then physical features. Entries that are completely identical (including symbols, discussed below) are distinguished by abbreviations of their official country names and are sequenced alphabetically by country name. The many duplicate names in Canada, the United Kingdom, and the United States are further distinguished by abbreviations of the names of their primary subdivisions. (See list of abbreviations on pages 319-320).

Abbreviation and Capitalization Abbreviation and styling have been standardized for all languages. A period is used after every abbreviation even when this may not be the local practice. The abbreviation "St." is used only for "Saint." "Sankt" and other forms of the term are spelled out.

All names are written with an initial capital letter except for a few Dutch names, such as 's-Gravenhage. Capitalization of noninitial words in a name generally follows local practice.

Symbols The symbols that appear in the index represent graphically the broad categories of the features named, for example, ʌ for mountain (Everest, Mount ʌ). An abbreviated key to the symbols, in the five atlas languages, appears at the foot of each pair of index pages. Superior numbers following some symbols in the index indicate finer distinctions, for example, ʌ^{1} for volcano (Fuji-san ʌ^{1}). A complete list of the symbols and superior numbers is given on page I•1.

Das Register umfasst in alphabetischer Anordnung etwa 170 000 in den Karten erscheinende Namen. Nach jedem Namen folgt die Seitenangabe zu einer oder mehreren Karten und die Lageangabe des Objektes in der Karte mit geographischer Länge und Breite. Enthält eine Seite mehrere Karten, so wird die betreffende Karte durch einen Kleinbuchstaben gekennzeichnet. Die Seitenangabe für Doppelseiten bezieht sich immer auf die linke Seite.

Die Verweise für die meisten Objekte in den Karten beziehen sich auf die Karte mit dem grössten Massstab. Normalerweise werden jedoch Verweise auf Objekte in den Karten der Stadtregionen nicht gegeben, wenn sie auf einer anderen Karte in grösserem Zusammenhang dargestellt sind. Die Lageangaben für Länder, Gebirgszüge und andere ausgedehnte Objekte beziehen sich allgemein auf die Karte grössten Massstabes, die sie in ihrer ganzen Ausdehnung zeigt.

Die Anordnung, in welcher die Lageangabe erfolgt, geht aus den englischen, deutschen, spanischen, französischen und portugiesischen Überschriften in der Mitte jeder Doppelseite hervor.

Zum Beispiel:

DEUTSCH			
Name	Seite	Breite°′	Länge°′ E = Ost

Die aufgeführten Objekte gliedern sich in drei Gruppen: *punkt-, flächen-* und *linienförmige* Objekte. Bei *punktförmigen* Objekten (z.B. Städte, Berge, Dämme) beziehen sich die Angaben nach Länge und Breite auf die Signatur in der Karte. Bei *flächenhaften* Objekten (Länder, Gebirgszüge usw.) verweisen die Koordinaten im allgemeinen auf das ungefähre Zentrum des Objektes. Bei *linienhaften* Objekten (Flüsse, Kanäle, Wasserleitungen) beziehen sich die Koordinaten auf einen bestimmten Punkt, z.B. die Mündung eines Flusses oder den Punkt, an dem das Objekt den Kartenrand schneidet.

Namengebung Wie in den Karten so sind auch im Register die Namen im allgemeinen in der örtlichen Namensform wiedergegeben und soweit als möglich in der amtlichen Schreibweise. Diakritische Zeichen wurden gesetzt; sie wurden nur dort weggelassen, wo sie, wie im Vietnamesischen, Tonhöhen kennzeichnen. Meist haben Objekte, die sich über die Grenzen eines Landes hinaus erstrecken, keinen einzelnen offiziellen Namen; normalerweise sind sie daher englisch beschriftet. Viele englische, deutsche, spanische, französische und portugiesische Namensformen, die nicht in den Karten enthalten sind, erscheinen im Register als Kreuzverweis. Alle Kreuzverweise werden durch das Symbol → gekennzeichnet. Namen, die aus Platzgründen in abgekürzter Form in der Karte erscheinen, werden im Register voll ausgeschrieben, wobei der auf der Karte weggelassene Teil in Klammern gesetzt ist, z.B. Acapulco [de Juárez].

Transkription Für die Transkription von Namen aus Sprachen, die nicht im lateinischen Alphabet geschrieben werden, wurde das offizielle Transkriptionssystem benutzt, sofern ein solches vorhanden ist. So wurden die Namen in Russland und in Bulgarien nach dem von den wissenschaftlichen Akademien dieser Länder angewandten System transkribiert. Entsprechend wurden die Namen auf dem chinesischen Festland nach dem Pinyin-System übertragen, das offiziell in der Volksrepublik China eingeführt wurde. Bei Sprachen, für die ein allgemein anerkanntes Transkriptionssystem nicht vorliegt, vor allem für Arabisch, erfolgte die Transkription in enger Anlehnung an das vom United States Board on Geographic Names angewandte System.

Alphabetische Ordnung Die alphabetische Ordnung der Namen entspricht der Reihenfolge der Buchstaben im englischen Alphabet. So werden z.B. das spanische *ll* und *ch* nicht als besondere Buchstaben behandelt. Ferner wurden diakritische Zeichen beim Alphabetisieren nicht berücksichtigt, das deutsche oder skandinavische *ä* oder *ö* als *a* oder *o* behandelt.

Physische Objekte können umgestellt erscheinen, da sie immer nach dem Eigennamen und nicht nach dem Gattungsbegriff eingeordnet wurden, z.B. "Gibraltar, Strait of)(." Ansonsten wurde jeder Eintrag, ob er aus einem Wort oder aus mehreren besteht, als eine einzige Einheit behandelt. So ist z.B. "Lakeland" nach "La Crosse," aber vor "La Salle" aufgeführt. Namen, die mit einem Artikel beginnen, wurden nicht umgestellt (Le Havre, Den Helder, Al-Qāhirah, As-Suways). Namen, die mit "St." und "Sainte" beginnen, sind der Schreibweise "Saint" nach eingeordnet.

Wo Namensgleichheit besteht, werden zunächst die Städte aufgeführt, dann politische Einheiten und schliesslich physische Objekte. Eintragungen, die vollkommen identisch sind (einschliesslich der weiter unten erläuterten Symbole), werden durch Hinzufügung der Abkürzung des offiziellen Ländernamens unterschieden und sind den Ländernamen nach alphabetisch geordnet. Die zahlreichen identischen Namen in Kanada, dem Vereinigten Königreich und den Vereinigten Staaten sind darüber hinaus noch durch Abkürzungen der obersten Verwaltungseinheit unterschieden. (Siehe Verzeichnis der Abkürzungen, Seite 319-320).

Abkürzungen und Grossschreibung Abkürzung und Schreibweise wurden für alle Sprachen vereinheitlicht. Nach jeder Abkürzung steht ein Punkt, auch wenn dies nicht der jeweiligen Gepflogenheit entspricht. Die Abkürzung "St." wird ausschliesslich für "Saint" gebraucht. "Sankt" und andere Formen dieses Begriffes werden ausgeschrieben.

Der erste Buchstabe eines Namens wird gross geschrieben, ausgenommen einige holländische Namen wie 's-Gravenhage. Die Grossschreibung der weiteren Worte eines zusammengesetzten Namens folgt im allgemeinen der landesüblichen Schreibweise.

Symbole Die im Register verwendeten Symbole veranschaulichen graphisch die zahlreichen Kategorien der benannten Objekte, z.B. ʌ = Berg (Everest, Mount ʌ). Eine kurzgefasste Erläuterung der Symbole erscheint in jeder der fünf Sprachen des Atlas am Fusse jeder Doppelseite des Registers. Hochgestellte Ziffern hinter Symbolen im Register bezeichnen feinere Unterscheidungen, z.B. ʌ^{1} = Vulkan (Fuji-san ʌ^{1}). Eine vollständige Übersicht der Symbole und hochgestellten Ziffern findet sich auf Seite I•1.

El índice contiene en una sola lista alfabética, alrededor de 170 000 nombres que aparecen en los mapas. Después de cada nombre está indicada la página o las páginas de referencia, en los cuales se encuentran los mismos, y las coordinadas de la latitud y la longitud del lugar del rasgo. Si una página contiene various mapas, letras minúsculas identifican el mapa correspondiente. Para mapas que ocupan dos páginas, la página de referencia siempre es la de la izquierda.

La mayoría de los nombres que figuran en el índice, se efiere a los mapas en la escala más grande. Sin embargo, un nombre no se refiere en un mapa metropolitano si ya aparece en otro mapa, donde se muestra en un marco de mayor proporción. Los países, sierras y otros rasgos extensivos se refieren generalmente en el índice en los mapas de escalas mayores en que se muestran completos.

En orden en que la información del índice se presenta, aparece en un encabezamiento al centro de cada par de páginas, en inglés, alemán, español, francés y portugués.

Por ejemplo:

ESPAÑOL			
Nombre	Página	Lat.°′	Long.°′ W = Oeste

Los rasgos anotados en el índice son de tres tipos: *el punto, el área y la extensión linear.* Para rasgos que indican *el punto* (como por ejemplo, las ciudades, picos de montañas, presas), las coordinadas de latitud y longitud indican la posición exacta del punto sobre el mapa. Respecto a *las áreas* (como países, sierras, etc.), las coordinadas indican usualmente el centro aproximado del rasgo particular. En cuanto a *los rasgos lineares* (ríos, canales, acueductos) las coordinadas indican los puntos terminales, por ejemplo, la boca de un río, o el punto en que un rasgo físico alcanza el margen del mapa.

Las Formas de los Nombres Los nombres que aparecen en el índice, así como también en los mapas, se dan en general en el idioma local, y en tanto que es posible siguen la ortografía oficialmente aceptada. Incluímos también marcas diacríticas, excepto las que se usan para indicar tono, como en la lengua vietnamita. A causa de que la mayoría de los rasgos que se extienden más allá de las fronteras de un país no tienen un solo nombre oficial, éstos se denominan usualmente en inglés. Muchos nombres, en inglés, alemán, español, francés y portugués, que pueden no figurar en el mapa, se dan como referencia de una página a otra en el índice. Todas las referencias que pasan a otras páginas se indican con el símbolo →. Un nombre que aparece en el mapa en forma abreviada, debido a la limitación de espacio, en el índice figura en su forma completa, poniendo entre paréntesis angulares la parte omitida en el mapa, por ejemplo Acapulco [de Juárez].

"Trasliteración" Para los nombres escritos en los idiomas que no usan el alfabeto latino, el sistema oficial de trasliteración ha sido utilizado donde localmente existe. Así, los nombres de Rusia y de Bulgaria se trasliteran conforme a los sistemas aceptados por las academias de las ciencias de sus respectivos países. De la misma manera, la trasliteración de los nombres en chino continental siguen el sistema Pinyin que ha sido oficialmente adoptado en este país. Para idiomas sin ningún sistema localmente aceptado de trasliteración, particularmente para el árabe, éstos se trasliteran usando por lo general un sistema adoptado por el United States Board on Geographic Names.

Alfabetización Los nombres se han ordenado de acuerdo con el alfabeto inglés. Las letras del alfabeto en español *ll* y *ch* por ejemplo, no se han considerado letras separadas. Además, los signos diacríticos no se toman en cuenta en la alfabetización — en alemán o escadinavo letras *ä* u *ö* se tratan como *a* u *o*.

Los nombres de los rasgos físicos algunas veces se invierten, ya que se ordenan alfabéticamente según la parte propia y no genérica del nombre. Así por ejemplo, en el caso del Estrecho de Gibraltar aparece: Gibraltar, Strait of ᴗ. Por lo demás, cada renglón, sea una palabra o una frase, se alfabetiza como una unidad. Por ejemplo, "Lakeland" aparece después de "La Crosse" y antes de "La Salle." Los nombres que comienzan con artículos (Le Havre, Den Helder, Al-Qāhirah, As-Suways) no están invertidos. Nombres que empiezan con "St." y "Sainte" se alfabetizan como "Saint".

En los casos de nombres idénticos, las poblaciones aparecen primero, las divisiones políticas después y finalmente los rasgos físicos. En caso de ser completamente idénticos (incluyendo los símbolos, discutidos más abajo) se distinguen por medio de abreviaciones de los nombres oficiales de los países a que pertenecen y son puestos en orden alfabético, de acuerdo al nombre de cada país. Hay muchos nombres duplicados en Canadá, el Reino Unido y los Estados Unidos de América, y éstos se distinguen además, por sus subdivisiones primarias. (Vease abajo, la lista de abreviaciones en las páginas 319-320).

Abreviaciones y Mayúsculas Las abreviaciones y el uso de las mayúsculas se han hecho uniformes para todos los idiomas. Se usa un punto al final de la abreviación, aun cuando en algunos casos no sea ésta la práctica local. La abreviación "St." se usa sólo para "Saint." Las otras formas del mismo término, como "Sankt," se escriben completas.

La mayúscula se usa al comienzo de todos los nombres a excepción de algunos holandeses, como 's-Gravenhage. Las palabras que no son iniciales, se dan con mayúscula o minúscula, según la práctica local.

Símbolos Los símbolos que aparecen en el índice representan gráficamente las grandes categorías de los rasgos que se han ido nombrando, por ejemplo, $\wedge$ para montaña (Everest, Mount $\wedge$). Una clave abreviada para los símbolos aparece en los cinco idiomas del atlas al pie de cada par de páginas del índice. Los números que siguen más arriba del símbolo indican alguna diferencia más precisa, pro ejemplo, $\wedge^1$ para un volcán (Fuji- san $\wedge^1$). Una lista completa de símbolos y números superiores aparece en la página I•1.

L'index rassemble en une seule liste alphabétique, quelque 170 000 noms qui figurent sur les cartes. Chaque nom est suivi d'un renvoi à une ou plusieurs pages de cartes et de coordonnées géographiques qui permettent de localiser ce qu'il désigne. Si une page contient plusieurs cartes, une lettre minuscule permet d'identifier chaque carte. Pour les cartes en double page, la référence indiquée est toujours celle de la page de gauche.

En général, l'index renvoie aux cartes où l'information recherchée est reproduite à la plus grande échelle; cependant, les cartes de zones métropolitaines ne sont pas utilisées si le terme géographique figure sur une autre carte dans un contexte plus large. Pour les éléments de grande dimension comme les pays et les chaînes de montagnes, l'index renvoie généralement à la carte à grande échelle qui les représente en entier.

L'ordre des informations de l'index est rappelé en tête de chaque double page dans les cinq langues: anglais, allemand, espagnol, français et portugais.

Par exemple:

FRANÇAIS

Nom	Page	Lat.°'	Long.°' W = Ouest

Les termes de l'index désignent des réalités géographiques de type *ponctuel, spatial* ou *linéaire*. Leur position est déterminée par les coordonnées géographiques du lieu quand les données sont de type *ponctuel* (villes, sommets, barrages, etc.), quand elles sont de type *spatial* (pays, chaînes de montagnes, etc.) par les coordonnées du centre approximatif de la zone considérée, et, quand elles sont du type *linéaire* (aqueducs, canaux, etc.) par les coordonnées soit d'un point terminal comme l'embouchure d'un cours d'eau, soit du point où les limites de la carte les interrompent.

Forme des Toponymes Les noms de l'index comme ceux des cartes sont généralement reproduits dans la langue locale et, dans la mesure du possible, selon leur orthographe officielle. Les signes diacritiques sont conservés, à l'exclusion de ceux qui servent à indiquer le ton, comme en vietnamien. La plupart des données géographiques qui s'étendent au-delà des frontières d'un pays sont nommées souvent en anglais, car elles n'ont pas de nom officiel unique. Beaucoup de noms anglais, allemands, espagnols, français et portugais, qui ne se trouvent pas sur les cartes, sont cités dans l'index sous forme de renvois. Tous les renvois sont signalés par le symbole (→). Un nom écrit sur la carte sous forme abrégée, par manque de place, figure en entier dans l'index; la partie omise est entre crochets, par exemple: Acapulco [de Juárez].

Transcription des Noms Pour les noms qui viennent de langues n'utilisant pas l'alphabet romain, le système local et officiel de transcription a été utilisé là où il existait. Ainsi, les noms russes et bulgares ont été transcrits selon les systèmes adoptés par les académies des sciences de ces pays. De même, pour la transcription des noms de la Chine continentale, on a employé le système Pinyin, officiellement adopté en Chine continentale. Pour les langues qui n'ont pas de système officiel de transcription en alphabet romain, notamment l'arabe, la transcription suit généralement de près le système adopté par le United States Board on Geographic Names (Comité américain pour les noms géographiques).

Ordre Alphabétique Les noms sont classés dans l'ordre de l'alphabet anglais. Les *ll* et *ch* espagnols, par exemple, ne sont pas traités comme des lettres séparées. De plus, on ne tient pas compte des signes diacritiques: le *ä* et le *ö* allemand ou scandinave correspondent au *a* et *o* sans tréma.

Les noms des données physiques peuvent se trouver inversés car ils sont toujours classés suivant le nom propre. Exemple: "Gibraltar, Strait of ᴗ." Par ailleurs, les noms composés d'un ou plusieurs mots sont considérés comme une seule entité. Exemple: "Lakeland" est inscrit après "La Crosse" et avant "La Salle." Les noms qui commencent par un article (Le Havre, Den Helder, Al-Qāhirah, As-Suways) ne sont pas inversés. Les noms qui commencent par "St." ou "Sainte" sont classés comme s'ils s'écrivaient "Saint."

Dans le cas de noms identiques, les villes sont inscrites d'abord, puis les divisions politiques, et ensuite les données physiques. Les noms qui sont tout à fait identiques (y compris les symboles qui s'y rapportent) se distinguent par leur pays d'origine, noté en abrégé dans l'ordre alphabétique. Les noms que l'on rencontre plusieurs fois, au Canada, au Royaume-Uni et aux Etats-Unis se distinguent grâce à l'abréviation de la première subdivision administrative de ce pays (voir la liste des abréviations de la page 319-320).

Abréviations et Majuscules L'usage des abréviations a été standardisé pour toutes les langues. Un point suit chaque abréviation, même quand ce n'est pas l'usage dans certaines langues. L'abréviation "St." sert uniquement pour le mot "Saint." "Sankt" et les autres formes du mot "Saint" sont écrites en entier.

Tous les noms commencent par une majuscule, sauf quelques noms des Pays-Bas comme 's-Gravenhage. Certains noms prennent une majuscule, même s'ils ne se trouvent pas au début du terme; on a adopté, en général, l'orthographe locale.

Symboles Les symboles utilisés dans l'index donnent une représentation graphique des réalités géographiques mentionnées. Par exemple, $\wedge$ pour une montagne (Everest, Mount $\wedge$). Une explication abrégée des symboles dans les cinq langues de l'Atlas se trouve au bas de chaque double page de l'index. Les indices qui accompagnent certains symboles permettent une distinction plus précise. Par exemple, $\wedge^1$ pour volcan (Fujisan $\wedge^1$). Une liste complète des symboles et indices est donnée à la page I•1.

O Índice contém, numa só lista alfabética, cerca de 170,000 nomes que figuram nos mapas. Segue-se a cada nome a referência a um ou mais mapas e a localização do acidente geográfico no mapa pelas respectivas coordenadas de latitude e longitude. A referência a mapas que ocupam duas páginas fica sempre na página da esquerda. A maior parte dos acidentes geográficos estão indexados no mapa em que aparecem em escala maior. No entanto, um acidente geográfico não é geralmente indexado num mapa de Área Metropolitana se também figura em outro mapa em que aparece em contexto mais amplo. Os países, cordilheiras e outros acidentes geográficos de maior extensão estão geralmente indexados no mapa em escala maior que os apresente em seu todo.

A ordem em que as informações são apresentadas no Índice figura no cabeçalho, a cada duas páginas, em inglês, alemão, espanhol, francês e PORTUGUÊS.

Por exemplo:

PORTUGUÊS

Nome	Página	Lat.°'	Long.°' W = Oeste

Os acidentes indexados são de três tipos: *Ponto, espacial* (área) e *linear* (extensão). Para acidentes que indicam *pontos* (como, por exemplo, cidades, picos de montanhas, represas), as coordenadas de latitude e longitude indicam a posição exata do ponto no mapa. No que se refere aos *acidentes espaciais* (como países, cordilheiras etc.), as coordenadas geralmente indicam o centro aproximado do acidente específico. Quanto aos *acidentes lineares* (rios, canais, aquedutos), as coordenadas localizam os pontos terminais, como, por exemplo, a foz de um rio, ou o ponto em que um acidente físico atinge a margem do mapa.

Formas dos nomes Os nomes que aparecem no Índice, assim como também nos mapas, são geralmente apresentados na língua local, e tanto quanto possível, seguem a ortografia oficial. Usam-se, também, os sinais diacríticos, exceto os que indicam tom, como na língua vietnamita. A maioria dos acidentes geográficos que se estendem além das fronteiras de um só país não possuem um nome oficial único; nesses casos, estão geralmente indicados em inglês. Muitos nomes em inglês, alemão, espanhol, português e francês podem não figurar nos mapas, mas aparecem no Índice como referências remissivas. Todas essas referências são indicadas pelo símbolo (→). Um nome que aparece no mapa em forma abreviada devido a limitações de espaço, figura no Índice em sua forma completa, com a parte omitida no mapa entre chaves (por exemplo, Acapulco [de Juárez]).

Transliteração Para os nomes escritos em línguas que não usam o alfabeto latino, foi utilizado o sistema oficial de transliteração, sempre que este existia. Assim, os nomes da Rússia e da Bulgária foram transliterados de acordo com os sistemas adotados pelas academias de ciências desses países. Do mesmo modo, a transliteração dos nomes da China continental seguem o sistema Pinyin, que foi oficialmente adotado nesse país. Para as línguas que não possuem um sistema de transliteração adotado oficialmente, em especial o árabe, a transliteração geralmente segue de perto o sistema adotado pelo Conselho de Nomes Geográficos dos Estados Unidos (United States Board on Geographic Names).

Alfabetação Os nomes foram ordenados de acordo com o alfabeto inglês. Por exemplo, o espanhol *ll* e *ch* não foram considerados como letras separadas. Ademais, os sinais diacríticos não foram considerados na alfabetação. Por exemplo, em alemão ou escandinavo as letras *ä* ou *ö* foram tratradas como *a* ou *o*.

Os nomes dos acidentes físicos podem aparecer, às vezes, invertidos, já que foram sempre alfabetados pela parte específica e não genérica do nome, como, por exemplo, *Gibraltar, estreito de* ᴗ. Por outro lado, cada entrada do Índice, quer constituída por uma só palavra ou mais de uma, foi alfabetada como uma unidade contínua. Por exemplo, "Lakeland" aparece depois de "La Grosse" e antes de "La Salle". Os nomes que começam por artigo (Le Havre, Den Helder, Al-Qāhirah, As-Suways) não são invertidos. Os nomes que começam por "St." e "Sainte" são alfabetados como se fossem soletrados "Saint".

Nos casos de nomes idênticos, as cidades estão relacionadas em primeiro lugar; depois as divisões políticas e em seguida os acidentes físicos. As entradas completamente idênticas (inclusive símbolos, mencionados mais abaixo), distinguem-se pelas abreviaturas dos nomes oficiais dos países a que pertencem e são arrolados na ordem alfabética do nome do país. Os muitos nomes repetidos no Canadá, no Reino Unido e nos Estados Unidos, são ainda diferenciados pelas abreviaturas dos nomes das respectivas subdivisões primárias (Ver a lista de abreviaturas, das páginas 319-320).

Abreviações e uso de maiúsculas As abreviaturas e o estilo foram normalizados em todas as línguas. Usa-se um ponto depois de cada abreviatura, mesmo que não seja essa a prática local. A abreviatura "St." só é usada para "Saint". As outras formas do termo, tal como "Sankt", são escritas por extenso.

Todos os nomes são escritos com a inicial maiúscula exceto em alguns nomes holandeses, como 's-Gravenhage. O uso de maiúsculas em palavras não iniciais de um nome segue geralmente a prática local.

Símbolos Os símbolos que aparecem no Índice representam graficamente as grandes categorias dos acidentes indicados, por exemplo, $\wedge$ para montanha (Everest, Mount $\wedge$). Uma chave abreviada dos símbolos nas cinco línguas do Atlas figura no pé de cada par de páginas do Índice. Os números altos que acompanham certos símbolos do Índice indicam diferenças mais precisas, como, por examplo, $\wedge^1$ para vulcão (Fuji-san $\wedge^1$). Uma lista completa de símbolos e números altos aparece à pág. I•1.

	LOCAL NAME	ENGLISH	DEUTSCH	ESPAÑOL	FRANÇAIS	PORTUGUÊS
Ab., Can.	Alberta	Alberta	Alberta	Alberta	Alberta	Alberta
Afg.	Afghānestān	Afghanistan	Afghanistan	Afganistán	Afghanistan	Afeganistão
Afr.	. . .	Africa	Afrika	Africa	Afrique	África
Ak., U.S.	Alaska	Alaska	Alaska	Alaska	Alaska	Alasca
Al., U.S.	Alabama	Alabama	Alabama	Alabama	Alabama	Alabama
Alg.	Algérie / Djazaïr	Algeria	Algerien	Argelia	Algérie	Argélia
Am. Sam.	American Samoa / Amerika Samoa	American Samoa	Amerikanisch-Samoa	Samoa Americana	Samoa américaines	Samoa Americana
And.	Andorra	Andorra	Andorra	Andorra	Andorre	Andorra
Ang.	Angola	Angola	Angola	Angola	Angola	Angola
Anguilla	Anguilla	Anguilla	Anguilla	Anguilla	Anguilla	Anguilla
Ant.	. . .	Antarctica	Antarktis	Antártida	Antarctique	Antártida
Antig.	Antigua and Barbuda	Antigua and Barbuda	Antigua und Barbuda	Antigua y Barbuda	Antigua-et-Barbuda	Antígua e Barbuda
Ar., U.S.	Arkansas	Arkansas	Arkansas	Arkansas	Arkansas	Arkansas
Arg.	Argentina	Argentina	Argentinien	Argentina	Argentine	Argentina
Ar. Su.	Al-ʿArabīyah as-Suʿūdīyah	Saudi Arabia	Saudi-Arabien	Arabia Saudita	Arabie saoudite	Arábia Saudita
Aruba	Aruba	Aruba	Aruba	Aruba	Aruba	Aruba
Asia	. . .	Asia	Asien	Asia	Asie	Ásia
Austl.	Australia	Australia	Australien	Australia	Australie	Austrália
Az., U.S.	Arizona	Arizona	Arizona	Arizona	Arizona	Arizona
Azer.	Azerbaijan	Azerbaijan	Aserbaidschan	Azerbaidján	Azerbaïdjan	Azerbaijão
Ba.	Bahamas	Bahamas	Bahamas	Bahamas	Bahamas	Bahamas
Bahr.	Al-Baḥrayn	Bahrain	Bahrain	Bahrein	Bahreïn	Bahrein
Barb.	Barbados	Barbados	Barbados	Barbados	Barbade	Barbados
B.C., Can.	British Columbia / Colombie-Britannique	British Columbia	Britisch Kolumbien	Columbia Británica	Colombie britannique	Colúmbia Britânica
Bdi.	Burundi	Burundi	Burundi	Burundi	Burundi	Burundi
Bel.	Belgique / België	Belgium	Belgien	Bélgica	Belgique	Bélgica
Belize	Belize	Belize	Belize	Belice	Bélize	Belize
Bela.	Belarus	Belarus	Belorussland	Bielorrusia	Biélorussie	Bielorrússia
Bénin	Bénin	Benin	Benin	Benin	Bénin	Benin
Ber.	Bermuda	Bermuda	Bermuda	Bermudas	Bermudes	Bermudas
B.I.O.T.	British Indian Ocean Territory	British Indian Ocean Territory	Britisch-Indien Ozean-Territorium	Territorio Británico del Océano Indico	Territoire britannique de l'océan Indien	Território Britânico do Oceano Indico
Blg.	Bâlgarija	Bulgaria	Bulgarien	Bulgaria	Bulgarie	Bulgária
Bngl.	Bangladesh	Bangladesh	Bangladesch	Bangladesh	Bangladesh	Bangladesh
Bol.	Bolivia	Bolivia	Bolivien	Bolivia	Bolivie	Bolívia
Bos.	Bosna i Hercegovina	Bosnia and Hercegovina	Bosnien und Herzegowina	Bosnia y Herzegovina	Bosnie et Herzégovine	Bósnia e Herzegovina
Bots.	Botswana	Botswana	Botswana	Botswana	Botswana	Botsuana
Bra.	Brasil	Brazil	Brasilien	Brasil	Brésil	Brasil
Bru.	Brunei	Brunei	Brunei	Brunei	Brunéi	Brunei
Br. Vir. Is.	British Virgin Islands	British Virgin Islands	Britische Jungferninseln	Islas Vírgenes Británicas	Îles Vierges britanniques	Virgens Britânicas, Ilhas
Burkina	Burkina Faso	Burkina Faso	Burkina Faso	Burkina Faso	Burkina Faso	Burkina Faso
Ca., U.S.	California	California	Kalifornien	California	Californie	Califórnia
Cam.	Cameroun / Cameroon	Cameroon	Kamerun	Camerún	Cameroun	Camarão
Can.	Canada	Canada	Kanada	Canadá	Canada	Canadá
Cay. Is.	Cayman Islands	Cayman Islands	Caiman-Inseln	Islas Caimán	Îles Caïmanes	Cayman, Ilhas
Centraf.	République centrafricaine	Central African Republic	Zentralafrikanische Republik	República Centroafricana	République centrafricaine	Centro-Africana, República
Česká Rep.	Česká Republika	Czech Republic	Tschechische Republik	República Checa	République Tcheque	República Tcheca
Chile	Chile	Chile	Chile	Chile	Chili	Chile
Christ. I.	Christmas Island	Christmas Island	Weihnachtsinsel	Isla Christmas	Île Christmas	Christmas, Ilha
C. Iv.	Côte d'Ivoire	Cote d'Ivoire	Côte d'Ivoire	Côte d'Ivoire	Côte d'Ivoire	Côte d'Ivoire
C.M.I.K.	Chosŏn-minjujuŭi-inmīn-konghwaguk	Korea, North	Nordkorea	Corea del Norte	Corée du Nord	Coréia do Norte
Co., U.S.	Colorado	Colorado	Colorado	Colorado	Colorado	Colorado
Cocos Is.	Cocos (Keeling) Islands	Cocos (Keeling) Islands	Cokos-Inseln	Islas Cocos (Keeling)	Îles Cocos (Keeling)	Cocos (Keeling), Ilhas
Col.	Colombia	Colombia	Kolumbien	Colombia	Colombie	Colômbia
Comores	Comores / Al-Qumur	Comoros	Komoren	Comoras	Comores	Comores
Congo	Congo	Congo	Kongo	Congo	Congo	Congo
Cook Is.	Cook Islands	Cook Islands	Cook-Inseln	Islas Cook	Îles Cook	Cook, Ilhas
C.R.	Costa Rica	Costa Rica	Costa Rica	Costa Rica	Costa Rica	Costa Rica
Ct., U.S.	Connecticut	Connecticut	Connecticut	Connecticut	Connecticut	Connecticut
Cuba	Cuba	Cuba	Kuba	Cuba	Cuba	Cuba
C.V.	Cabo Verde	Cape Verde	Kap Verde	Cabo Verde	Cap-Vert	Cabo Verde
Dan.	Danmark	Denmark	Dänemark	Dinamarca	Danemark	Dinamarca
D.C., U.S.	District of Columbia	District of Columbia	District of Columbia	District of Columbia	District of Columbia	Distrito de Columbia
De., U.S.	Delaware	Delaware	Delaware	Delaware	Delaware	Delaware
Dji.	Djibouti	Djibouti	Djibouti	Djibouti	Djibouti	Djibouti
Dom.	Dominica	Dominica	Dominica	Dominica	Dominique	Dominica
Dtsch.	Deutschland	Germany	Deutschland	Alemania	Allemagne	Alemanha
D.Y.	Druk-Yul	Bhutan	Bhutan	Bhután	Bhoutan	Butã
Ec.	Ecuador	Ecuador	Ecuador	Ecuador	Équateur	Equador
Eesti	Eesti	Estonia	Estland	Estonia	Estonie	Estónia
Ellás	Ellás	Greece	Griechenland	Grecia	Grèce	Grécia
El Sal.	El Salvador	El Salvador	El Salvador	El Salvador	El Salvador	El Salvador
Eng., U.K.	England	England	England	Inglaterra	Angleterre	Inglaterra
Erit.	Eritrea	Eritrea	Eritrea	Eritrea	Erythrée	Eritréia
Esp.	España	Spain	Spanien	España	Espagne	Espanha
Europe	. . .	Europe	Europa	Europa	Europe	Europa
Falk. Is.	Falkland Islands	Falkland Islands	Falkland-Inseln	Islas Malvinas	Îles Falkland	Falkland, Ilhas
Fiji	Fiji	Fiji	Fidschi	Fiji	Fidji	Fiji (Fidji)
Fl., U.S.	Florida	Florida	Florida	Florida	Floride	Flórida
Før.	Føroyar	Faeroe Islands	Färöer	Islas Feroe	Îles Féroé	Faeroe, Ilhas
Fr.	France	France	Frankreich	Francia	France	França
Ga., U.S.	Georgia	Georgia	Georgia	Georgia	Georgie	Geórgia
Gabon	Gabon	Gabon	Gabun	Gabón	Gabon	Gabão
Gam.	Gambia	Gambia	Gambia	Gambia	Gambie	Gâmbia
Gaza	. . .	Gaza Strip	Gazastreifen	Franja de Gaza	Bande de Gaza	Faixa de Gaza
Ghana	Ghana	Ghana	Ghana	Ghana	Ghana	Gana
Gib.	Gibraltar	Gibraltar	Gibraltar	Gibraltar	Gibraltar	Gibraltar
Golan	. . .	Golan Heights	Golan-Höhen	Alturas de Golán	Hauteurs de Golan	Colinas de Golan
Gren.	Grenada	Grenada	Grenada	Granada	Grenade	Grenada
Guad.	Guadeloupe	Guadeloupe	Guadeloupe	Guadalupe	Guadeloupe	Guadalupe
Guam	Guam	Guam	Guam	Guam	Guam	Guam
Guat.	Guatemala	Guatemala	Guatemala	Guatemala	Guatemala	Guatemala
Guernsey	Guernsey	Guernsey	Guernsey	Guernsey	Guernesey	Guernsey
Gui.-B.	Guiné-Bissau	Guinea-Bissau	Guinea-Bissau	Guinea-Bissau	Guinée-Bissau	Guiné-Bissau
Gui. Ecu.	Guinea Ecuatorial	Equatorial Guinea	Äquatorial-guinea	Guinea Ecuatorial	Guinée équatoriale	Guiné Equatorial
Guinée	Guinée	Guinea	Guinea	Guinea	Guinée	Guiné
Guy.	Guyana	Guyana	Guyana	Guyana	Guyane	Guiana
Guy. fr.	Guyane française	French Guiana	Französisch-Guayana	Guayana Francesa	Guyane française	Guiana Francesa
Haï.	Haïti	Haiti	Haiti	Haití	Haïti	Haiti
Haya.	Hayastan	Armenia	Armenien	Armenia	Arménie	Arménia
Hi., U.S.	Hawaii	Hawaii	Hawaii	Hawaii	Hawaii	Havaí
H.K.	Hong Kong	Hong Kong	Hongkong	Hong Kong	Hong-Kong	Hong Kong
Hond.	Honduras	Honduras	Honduras	Honduras	Honduras	Honduras
Hrv.	Hrvatska	Croatia	Kroatien	Croacia	Croatie	Croácia
Ia., U.S.	Iowa	Iowa	Iowa	Iowa	Iowa	Iowa
I.A.M.	Al-Imārāt al-ʿArabīyah al-Muttaḥidah	United Arab Emirates	Vereinigte Arabische Emirate	Emiratos Arabes Unidos	Émirats arabes unis	Emirados Árabes Unidos
Id., U.S.	Idaho	Idaho	Idaho	Idaho	Idaho	Idaho
Il., U.S.	Illinois	Illinois	Illinois	Illinois	Illinois	Illinois
In., U.S.	Indiana	Indiana	Indiana	Indiana	Indiana	Indiana
India	India / Bharat	India	Indien	India	Inde	Índia
Indon.	Indonesia	Indonesia	Indonesien	Indonesia	Indonésie	Indonésia
I. of Man	Isle of Man	Isle of Man	Insel Man	Isla de Man	Île de Man	Man, Ilha de
Īrān	Īrān	Iran	Iran	Irán	Iran	Irã
ʿĪrāq	Al-ʿĪrāq	Iraq	Irak	Iraq	Iraq	Iraque
Ire.	Ireland / Éire	Ireland	Irland	Irlanda	Irlande	Irlanda
Ísland	Ísland	Iceland	Island	Islandia	Islande	Islândia
It.	Italia	Italy	Italien	Italia	Italie	Itália
Ityo.	Ityopiya	Ethiopia	Äthiopien	Etiopía	Éthiopie	Etiópia
Jam.	Jamaica	Jamaica	Jamaika	Jamaica	Jamaïque	Jamaica
Jersey	Jersey	Jersey	Jersey	Jersey	Jersey	Jersey
Jugo.	Jugoslavija	Yugoslavia	Jugoslawien	Yugoslavia	Yougoslavie	Iugoslávia
Kal. Nun.	Kalaallit Nunaat / Grønland	Greenland	Grönland	Groenlandia	Groenland	Groenlândia
Kâm.	Kâmpŭchéa	Cambodia	Kambodscha	Camboya	Cambodge	Camboja
Kaz.	Kazachstan	Kazakhstan	Kasachstan	Kazajstán	Kazakhstan	Cazaquistão
Kenya	Kenya	Kenya	Kenia	Kenya	Kenya	Quênia
Kıbrıs	Kuzey Kıbrıs	Cyprus, North	Türkische Republik Nordzypern	República Turca de Chipre del Norte	République turque du Nord de Chypre	República Turca do Norte de Chipre
Kípros	Kípros / Kıbrıs	Cyprus	Zypern	Chipre	Chypre	Chipre
Kiribati	Kiribati	Kiribati	Kiribati	Kiribati	Kiribati	Kiribati
Ks., U.S.	Kansas	Kansas	Kansas	Kansas	Kansas	Kansas
Kuwayt	Al-Kuwayt	Kuwait	Kuwait	Kuwait	Koweït	Kuwait
Ky., U.S.	Kentucky	Kentucky	Kentucky	Kentucky	Kentucky	Kentucky
Kyrg.	Kyrgyzstan	Kyrgyzstan	Kirgisistan	Kirguizia	Kirghizistan	Quirguistão
La., U.S.	Louisiana	Louisiana	Louisiana	Luisiana	Louisiane	Louisiana
Lao	Lao	Laos	Laos	Laos	Laos	Lao
Lat.	Latvija	Latvia	Lettland	Letonia	Lettonie	Letónia
Leso.	Lesotho	Lesotho	Lesotho	Lesotho	Lesotho	Lesoto
Liber.	Liberia	Liberia	Liberia	Liberia	Libéria	Libéria
Lībiyā	Lībiyā	Libya	Libyen	Libia	Libye	Líbia
Liech.	Liechtenstein	Liechtenstein	Liechtenstein	Liechtenstein	Liechtenstein	Liechtenstein
Liet.	Lietuva	Lithuania	Litauen	Lituania	Lithuanie	Lituânia
Lubnān	Lubnān	Lebanon	Libanon	Líbano	Liban	Líbano
Lux.	Luxembourg	Luxembourg	Luxemburg	Luxemburgo	Luxembourg	Luxemburgo
Ma., U.S.	Massachusetts	Massachusetts	Massachusetts	Massachusetts	Massachusetts	Massachusetts
Macau	Macau	Macao	Macao	Macao	Macao	Macau
Madag.	Madagasikara / Madagascar	Madagascar	Madagaskar	Madagascar	Madagascar	Madagascar
Magreb	Al-Magreb	Morocco	Marokko	Marruecos	Maroc	Marrocos
Magy.	Magyarország	Hungary	Ungarn	Hungría	Hongrie	Hungria
Mak.	Makedonija	Macedonia	Makedonien	Macedonia	Macédoine	Macedonia
Malaŵi	Malaŵi	Malawi	Malawi	Malawi	Malawi	Malaui
Malay.	Malaysia	Malaysia	Malaysia	Malasia	Malaisie	Malásia
Mald.	Maldives	Maldives	Malediven	Maldivas	Maldives	Maldivas
Mali	Mali	Mali	Mali	Malí	Mali	Mali
Malta	Malta	Malta	Malta	Malta	Malte	Malta
Marsh. Is.	Marshall Islands	Marshall Islands	Marshall Islands	Islas Marshall	Îles Marshall	Marshall Islands
Mart.	Martinique	Martinique	Martinique	Martinica	Martinique	Martinica
Maur.	Mauritanie / Mūrītāniyā	Mauritania	Mauretanien	Mauritania	Mauritanie	Mauritânia
Maus.	Mauritius	Mauritius	Mauritius	Mauricio	Maurice	Maurício
Mayotte	Mayotte	Mayotte	Mayotte	Mayotte	Mayotte	Mayotte
Mb., Can.	Manitoba	Manitoba	Manitoba	Manitoba	Manitoba	Manitoba
Md., U.S.	Maryland	Maryland	Maryland	Maryland	Maryland	Maryland
Me., U.S.	Maine	Maine	Maine	Maine	Maine	Maine
Méx.	México	Mexico	Mexiko	México	Mexique	México
Mi., U.S.	Michigan	Michigan	Michigan	Michigan	Michigan	Michigan
Micron.	Federated States of Micronesia	Micronesia, Federated States of	Federated States of Micronesia	Estado Federal de Micronesia	États fédérés de Micronésie	Federated States of Micronesia
Mid. Is.	Midway Islands	Midway Islands	Midway-Inseln	Islas Midway	Îles Midway	Midway, Ilhas
Miṣr	Miṣr	Egypt	Ägypten	Egipto	Égypte	Egito
Mn., U.S.	Minnesota	Minnesota	Minnesota	Minnesota	Minnesota	Minnesota
Mo., U.S.	Missouri	Missouri	Missouri	Misuri	Missouri	Missouri
Moç.	Moçambique	Mozambique	Mosambik	Mozambique	Mozambique	Moçambique
Mol.	Moldova	Moldova	Moldawien	Moldavia	Moldavie	Moldávia
Monaco	Monaco	Monaco	Monaco	Mónaco	Monaco	Mônaco
Mong.	Mongol Ard Uls	Mongolia	Mongolei	Mongolia	Mongolie	Mongólia
Monts.	Montserrat	Montserrat	Montserrat	Montserrat	Montserrat	Montserrat
Ms., U.S.	Mississippi	Mississippi	Mississippi	Misisipi	Mississippi	Mississippi
Mt., U.S.	Montana	Montana	Montana	Montana	Montana	Montana
Mya.	Myanmar	Myanmar	Myanmar	Myanmar	Myanmar	Myanmar
N.A.	. . .	North America	Nordamerika	América del Norte	Amérique du Nord	América do Norte
Namibia	Namibia	Namibia	Namibia	Namibia	Namibie	Namíbia
Nauru	Nauru / Naoero	Nauru	Nauru	Nauru	Nauru	Nauru
N.B., Can.	New Brunswick / Nouveau-Brunswick	New Brunswick	Neubraunschweig	Nueva Brunswick	Nouveau-Brunswick	Nova Brunswick
N.C., U.S.	North Carolina	North Carolina	Nord Karolina	Carolina del Norte	Caroline du Nord	Carolina do Norte
N. Cal.	Nouvelle-Calédonie	New Caledonia	Neukaledonien	Nueva Caledonia	Nouvelle Calédonie	Nova Caledônia
N.D., U.S.	North Dakota	North Dakota	Nord Dakota	Dakota del Norte	Dakota du Nord	Dakota do Norte
Ne., U.S.	Nebraska	Nebraska	Nebraska	Nebraska	Nebraska	Nebraska
Ned.	Nederland	Netherlands	Niederlande	Países Bajos	Pays-Bas	Países Baixos
Ned. Ant.	Nederlandse Antillen	Netherlands Antilles	Niederländische Antillen	Antillas Neerlandesas	Antilles néerlandaises	Antilhas Holandesas
Nepāl	Nepāl	Nepal	Nepal	Nepal	Népal	Nepal
Nf., Can.	Newfoundland / Terre-Neuve	Newfoundland	Neufundland	Terranova	Terre-Neuve	Terra Nova
N.H., U.S.	New Hampshire	New Hampshire	New Hampshire	Nuevo Hampshire	New Hampshire	Nova Hampshire
Nic.	Nicaragua	Nicaragua	Nicaragua	Nicaragua	Nicaragua	Nicarágua
Nig.	Nigeria	Nigeria	Nigeria	Nigeria	Nigéria	Nigéria
Niger	Niger	Niger	Niger	Níger	Niger	Níger
Nihon	Nihon	Japan	Japan	Japón	Japon	Japão
N. Ire., U.K.	Northern Ireland	Northern Ireland	Nordirland	Irlanda del Norte	Irlande du Nord	Irlanda do Norte
Niue	Niue	Niue	Niue	Niue	Nioué	Niue

	LOCAL NAME	ENGLISH	DEUTSCH	ESPAÑOL	FRANÇAIS	PORTUGUÊS
N.J., U.S.	New Jersey	New Jersey	New Jersey	Nueva Jersey	New Jersey	Nova Jersey
N.M., U.S.	New Mexico	New Mexico	New Mexico	Nuevo México	Nouveau-Mexique	Nova México
N. Mar. Is.	Northern Mariana Islands	Northern Mariana Islands	Northern Mariana Islands	Islas Marianas	Îles Mariannes du Nord	Northern Mariana Islands
Nor.	Norge	Norway	Norwegen	Noruega	Norvège	Noruega
Norf. I.	Norfolk Island	Norfolk Island	Norfolk-Insel	Isla Norfolk	Île Norfolk	Norfolk, Ilha
N.S., Can.	Nova Scotia / Nouvelle-Écosse	Nova Scotia	Neu Schottland	Nueva Escocia	Nouvelle-Écosse	Nova Scotia
N.T., Can.	Northwest Territories / Territoires du Nord-Ouest	Northwest Territories	Nord-West Territorien	Territorios del Noroeste	Territoires du Nord-Ouest	Territórios do Noroeste
Nv., U.S.	Nevada	Nevada	Nevada	Nevada	Nevada	Nevada
N.Y., U.S.	New York	New York	New York	Nueva York	New York	Nova York
N.Z.	New Zealand	New Zealand	Neuseeland	Nueva Zelanda	Nouvelle-Zélande	Nova Zelândia
Oc.	. . .	Oceania	Ozeanien	Oceanía	Océanie	Oceania
Oh., U.S.	Ohio	Ohio	Ohio	Ohio	Ohio	Ohio
Ok., U.S.	Oklahoma	Oklahoma	Oklahoma	Oklahoma	Oklahoma	Oklahoma
On., Can.	Ontario	Ontario	Ontario	Ontario	Ontario	Ontário
Or., U.S.	Oregon	Oregon	Oregon	Oregón	Oregon	Oregon
Öst.	Österreich	Austria	Österreich	Austria	Autriche	Austria
Pa., U.S.	Pennsylvania	Pennsylvania	Pennsylvanien	Pensilvania	Pennsylvanie	Pennsylvania
Pāk.	Pākistān	Pakistan	Pakistan	Pakistán	Pakistan	Paquistão
Palau	Palau / Belau	Palau	Palau	Palau	Palau (Belau)	Palau
Pan.	Panamá	Panama	Panama	Panamá	Panama	Panamá
Pap. N. Gui.	Papua New Guinea	Papua New Guinea	Papua-Neuguinea	Papua Nueva Guinea	Papouasie-Nouvelle Guinée	Papua-Nova Guiné
Para.	Paraguay	Paraguay	Paraguay	Paraguay	Paraguay	Paraguai
P.E., Can.	Prince Edward Island / Île-du-Prince-Édouard	Prince Edward Island	Prinz Edward-Insel	Isla Príncipe Eduardo	Île-du-Prince Édouard	Príncipe Eduardo, Ilha do
Perú	Perú	Peru	Peru	Perú	Pérou	Peru
Pil.	Pilipinas / Philippines	Philippines	Philippinen	Filipinas	Philippines	Filipinas
Pit.	Pitcairn	Pitcairn	Pitcairn	Pitcairn	Pitcairn	Pitcairn
Pol.	Polska	Poland	Polen	Polonia	Pologne	Polônia
Poly. fr.	Polynésie française	French Polynesia	Französisch-Polynesien	Polinesia Francesa	Polynésie française	Polinésia Francesa
Port.	Portugal	Portugal	Portugal	Portugal	Portugal	Portugal
P.Q., Can.	Québec	Quebec	Quebec	Quebec	Québec	Québec
P.R.	Puerto Rico	Puerto Rico	Puerto Rico	Puerto Rico	Porto Rico	Porto Rico
P.S.N.Á.	Plazas de Soberanía en el Norte de África	Spanish North Africa	Spanisch-Nordafrika	Plazas de Soberanía en el Norte de África	Afrique du Nord espagnole	África do Norte Espanhola
Qatar	Qaṭar	Qatar	Katar	Qatar	Qatar	Qatar
Rep. Dom.	República Dominicana	Dominican Republic	Dominikanische Republik	República Dominicana	République dominicaine	Dominicana, República
Réu.	Réunion	Reunion	Réunion	Reunión	Réunion	Reunião
R.I., U.S.	Rhode Island	Rhode Island	Rhode Island	Rhode Island	Rhode Island	Rhode Island
Rom.	România	Romania	Rumänien	Rumania	Roumanie	Romênia
Ross.	Rossija	Russia	Russland	Rusia	Russie	Rússia
Rw.	Rwanda	Rwanda	Ruanda	Rwanda	Rwanda	Ruanda
S.A.	. . .	South America	Südamerika	América del Sur	Amérique du Sud	América do Sul
S. Afr.	South Africa / Suid-Afrika	South Africa	Südafrika	Sudáfrica	Afrique du Sud	África do Sul
Sak.	Sakartvelo	Georgia	Georgien	Georgia	Géorgie	Geórgia
S.C., U.S.	South Carolina	South Carolina	Süd Karolina	Carolina del Sur	Caroline du Sud	Carolina do Sul
Schw.	Schweiz / Suisse / Svizzera	Switzerland	Schweiz	Suiza	Suisse	Suíça
Scot., U.K.	Scotland	Scotland	Schottland	Escocia	Écosse	Escócia
S.D., U.S.	South Dakota	South Dakota	Süd Dakota	Dakota del Sur	Dakota du Sud	Dakota do Sul
Sén.	Sénégal	Senegal	Senegal	Senegal	Sénégal	Senegal
Sey.	Seychelles	Seychelles	Seschellen	Seychelles	Seychelles	Seychelles
Shq.	Shqipëri	Albania	Albanien	Albania	Albanie	Albânia
Sing.	Singapore	Singapore	Singapur	Singapur	Singapour	Cingapura
Sk., Can.	Saskatchewan	Saskatchewan	Saskatchewan	Saskatchewan	Saskatchewan	Saskatchewan
S.L.	Sierra Leone	Sierra Leone	Sierra Leone	Sierra Leona	Sierra Leone	Serra Leoa
S. Lan.	Sri Lanka	Sri Lanka	Sri Lanka	Sri Lanka	Sri Lanka	Sri Lanka
Slvk.	Slovensko	Slovakia	Slowakei	Eslovaquia	Slovaquie	Eslováquia
Slvn.	Slovenija	Slovenia	Slowenien	Eslovenia	Slovénie	Eslovênia
S. Mar.	San Marino	San Marino	San Marino	San Marino	Saint-Marin	San Marino
Sol. Is.	Solomon Islands	Solomon Islands	Salomonen	Islas Salomón	Îles Salomon	Salomão, Ilhas
Som.	Somaliya	Somalia	Somalia	Somalia	Somalie	Somália
St. Hel.	St. Helena	St. Helena	Sankt Helena	Santa Elena	Sainte-Hélène	Santa Helena
St. K./N.	St. Kitts and Nevis	St. Kitts and Nevis	Sankt Kitts und Nevis	San Kitts y Nevis	Saint-Kitts-et-Nevis	São Kitts e Nevis

	LOCAL NAME	ENGLISH	DEUTSCH	ESPAÑOL	FRANÇAIS	PORTUGUÊS
St. Luc.	St. Lucia	St. Lucia	Sankt Lucia	Santa Lucía	Sainte-Lucie	Santa Lúcia
S. Tom./P.	São Tomé e Príncipe	Sao Tome and Principe	São Tomé und Principe	Santo Tomé y Príncipe	Sao Tomé-et-Principe	São Tomé e Príncipe
St. P./M.	Saint-Pierre-et-Miquelon	St. Pierre and Miquelon	Saint-Pierre und Miquelon	San Pedro y Miquelón	Saint-Pierre-et-Miquelon	São Pedro e Miquelon
St. Vin.	St. Vincent and the Grenadines	St. Vincent and the Grenadines	Sankt Vincent und die Grenadinen	San Vicente y las Granadinas	Saint-Vincent-et-Grenadines	São Vicente e Granadinas
Süd.	As-Sūdān	Sudan	Sudan	Sudán	Soudan	Sudão
Suomi	Suomi / Finland	Finland	Finnland	Finlandia	Finlande	Finlândia
Sur.	Suriname	Suriname	Suriname	Suriname	Suriname	Suriname
Sūrīy.	Sūrīyah	Syria	Syrien	Siria	Syrie	Síria
Sve.	Sverige	Sweden	Schweden	Suecia	Suède	Suécia
Swaz.	Swaziland	Swaziland	Swasiland	Swazilandia	Swaziland	Suazilândia
T.a.a.f.	Terres australes et antarctiques françaises	French Southern and Antarctic Territories	Französische Süd- und Antarktis-Gebiete	Tierras Australes y Antárticas Francesas	Terres australes et antarctiques françaises	Terras Austrais e Antárticas Francesas
Taehan	Taehan-min'guk	Korea, South	Südkorea	Corea del Sur	Corée du Sud	Coréia do Sul
T'aiwan	T'aiwan	Taiwan	Taiwan	Taiwán	Taïwan	Taiwan (Formosa)
Taj.	Tajikistan	Tajikistan	Tadschikistan	Tadjikistán	Tadjikistan	Tajiquistão
Tan.	Tanzania	Tanzania	Tansania	Tanzanía	Tanzanie	Tanzânia
Tchad	Tchad	Chad	Tschad	Chad	Tchad	Tchad
T./C. Is.	Turks and Caicos Islands	Turks and Caicos Islands	Turks- und Caicos-Inseln	Islas Turcas y Caicos	Îles Turques et Caïques	Turcas e Caicos, Ilhas
Thai	Prathet Thai	Thailand	Thailand	Tailandia	Thaïlande	Tailândia
Tn., U.S.	Tennessee	Tennessee	Tennessee	Tennessee	Tennessee	Tennessee
Togo	Togo	Togo	Togo	Togo	Togo	Togo
Tok.	Tokelau	Tokelau	Tokelau	Tokelau	Tokélaou	Tokelau
Tonga	Tonga	Tonga	Tonga	Tonga	Tonga	Tonga
Trin.	Trinidad and Tobago	Trinidad and Tobago	Trinidad und Tobago	Trinidad y Tabago	Trinité-et-Tobago	Trinidad e Tobago
Tun.	Tunisie / Tunis	Tunisia	Tunesien	Túnez	Tunisie	Tunísia
Tür.	Türkiye	Turkey	Türkei	Turquía	Turquie	Turquia
Turk.	Turkmenistan	Turkmenistan	Turkmenistan	Turkmenia	Turkmenistan	Turquemenistão
Tuvalu	Tuvalu	Tuvalu	Tuvalu	Tuvalu	Tuvalu	Tuvalu
Tx., U.S.	Texas	Texas	Texas	Texas	Texas	Texas
Ug.	Uganda	Uganda	Uganda	Uganda	Ouganda	Uganda
U.K.	United Kingdom	United Kingdom	Vereinigtes Königreich	Reino Unido	Royaume-Uni	Reino Unido
Ukr.	Ukraina	Ukraine	Ukraine	Ucrania	Ukraine	Ucrânia
'Umān	'Umān	Oman	Oman	Omán	Oman	Omã
Ur.	Uruguay	Uruguay	Uruguay	Uruguay	Uruguay	Uruguai
Urd.	Al-Urdun	Jordan	Jordanien	Jordania	Jordanie	Jordânia
U.S.	United States	United States	Vereinigte Staaten	Estados Unidos	États-Unis	Estados Unidos
Ut., U.S.	Utah	Utah	Utah	Utah	Utah	Utah
Uzb.	Uzbekistan	Uzbekistan	Usbekistan	Uzbekistán	Ouzbekistan	Usbequistão
Va., U.S.	Virginia	Virginia	Virginia	Virginia	Virginie	Virgínia
Vanuatu	Vanuatu	Vanuatu	Vanuatu	Vanuatu	Vanuatu	Vanuatu
Vat.	Città del Vaticano	Vatican City	Vatikanstadt	Ciudad del Vaticano	Cité du Vatican	Vaticano
Ven.	Venezuela	Venezuela	Venezuela	Venezuela	Venezuela	Venezuela
Viet	Viet Nam	Vietnam	Vietnam	Viet Nam	Viet Nam	Vietnam
Vir. Is., U.S.	Virgin Islands (U.S.)	Virgin Islands (U.S.)	Amerikanische Jungferninseln	Islas Vírgenes (americanas)	Îles Vierges (américaines)	Virgens Americanas, Ilhas
Vt.	Vermont	Vermont	Vermont	Vermont	Vermont	Vermont
Wa., U.S.	Washington	Washington	Washington	Washington	Washington	Washington
Wake I.	Wake Island	Wake Island	Wake	Isla Wake	Île Wake	Wake
Wales, U.K.	Wales	Wales	Wales	Gales	Galles	Gales
Wal./F.	Wallis et Futuna	Wallis and Futuna	Wallis und Futuna	Wallis y Futuna	Wallis et Futuna	Wallis e Futuna
W.B.	. . .	West Bank	Westufer	Ribera Oeste	Cisjordanie	Margem Oeste
Wi., U.S.	Wisconsin	Wisconsin	Wisconsin	Wisconsin	Wisconsin	Wisconsin
W. Sah.	. . .	Western Sahara	Westliche Sahara	Sahara Occidental	Sahara occidental	Saara Ocidental
W. Sam.	Western Samoa / Samoa i Sisifo	Western Samoa	Westsamoa	Samoa Occidental	Samoa-Occidental	Samoa Ocidental
W.V., U.S.	West Virginia	West Virginia	West Virginia	Virginia Occidental	Virginie Occidentale	Virgínia Ocidental
Wy., U.S.	Wyoming	Wyoming	Wyoming	Wyoming	Wyoming	Wyoming
Yaman	Al-Yaman	Yemen	Jemen	Yemen	Yémen	Iêmen
Yis.	Yisra'el / Isrā'īl	Israel	Israel	Israel	Israël	Israel
Yk., Can.	Yukon Territory	Yukon Territory	Yukon	Yukón	Yukon	Yukon
Zaïre	Zaïre	Zaire	Zaire	Zaire	Zaïre	Zaire
Zam.	Zambia	Zambia	Sambia	Zambia	Zambie	Zâmbia
Zhg.	Zhongguo	China	China	China	Chine	China
Zimb.	Zimbabwe	Zimbabwe	Simbabwe	Zimbabwe	Zimbabwe	Zimbabwe

Key to Index Symbols

The symbols below represent the categories into which the physical and cultural features are classified in the Index. Broad categories appear in **boldface** type. Symbols with superior numbers identify subcategories.

Schlüssel zu den Symbolen des Registers

Die folgenden Symbole veranschaulichen die Kategorien, nach denen physische und kulturgeographische Objekte im Register geordnet sind. Die Oberbegriffe sind in **Fettdruck** hervorgehoben. Symbole mit hochgestellten Nummern kennzeichnen Unterbegriffe.

Clave de los Símbolos del Índice

Los símbolos abajo representan las categorías dentro de las cuales están clasificados los rasgos físicos y culturales que están incluídos en el Índice. Las grandes categorías aparecen en **negrilla**. Los símbolos que tienen números en su parte superior identifican las subcategorías.

Signification des Symboles de l'Index

Les symboles ci-dessous représentent les catégories sous lesquelles les données physiques et culturelles sont classées dans l'index. Les symboles en caractèter **gras** correspondent aux catégories principales. Ceux suivis d'un indice désignent les subdivisions d'une même catégorie.

Chave dos Símbolos do Índice

Os símbolos abaixo representam as categorias em que estão classificados os acidentes físicos e culturais no Índice. As grandes categorias aparecem em **negrito**. Os símbolos acompanhados de números altos identificam as subcategorias.

ENGLISH	DEUTSCH	ESPAÑOL	FRANÇAIS	PORTUGUÊS
∧ **Mountain**	**Berg**	**Montaña**	**Montagne**	**Montanha**
∧[1] Volcano	Vulkan	Volcán	Volcan	Vulcão
∧[2] Hill	Hügel	Colina	Colline	Colina
⋏ **Mountains**	**Gebirge**	**Montañas**	**Montagnes**	**Montanhas**
⋏[1] Plateau	Hochebene	Meseta	Plateau	Planalto
⋏[2] Hills	Hügel	Colinas	Collines	Colinas
)(**Pass**	**Paß**	**Paso**	**Col**	**Passo**
V **Valley, Canyon**	**Tal, Cañon**	**Valle, Cañón**	**Vallée, Canyon**	**Vale, Canhão**
≚ **Plain**	**Ebene**	**Llano**	**Plaine**	**Planície**
≚[1] Basin	Becken	Cuenca	Bassin	Bacia
≚[2] Delta	Delta	Delta	Delta	Delta
≻ **Cape**	**Kap**	**Cabo**	**Cap**	**Cabo**
≻[1] Peninsula	Halbinsel	Península	Péninsule	Península
≻[2] Spit, Sand Bar	Landzunge, Sandbarre	Lengua de Tierra, Bajo	Flèche, Banc de sable	Ponta de Terra, Banco de Areia
I **Island**	**Insel**	**Isla**	**Île**	**Ilha**
I[1] Atoll	Atoll	Atolón	Atoll	Atol
I[2] Rock	Fels	Roca	Rocher	Rochedo
II **Islands**	**Inseln**	**Islas**	**Îles**	**Ilhas**
II[1] Rocks	Felsen	Rocas	Rochers	Rochedos
± **Other Topographic Features**	**Andere Topographische Objekte**	**Otros Elementos Topográficos**	**Autres données topographiques**	**Outros Acidentes Topográficos**
±[1] Continent	Erdteil	Continente	Continent	Continente
±[2] Coast, Beach	Küste, Strand	Costa, Playa	Côte, Plage	Costa, Praia
±[3] Isthmus	Landenge	Istmo	Isthme	Istmo
±[4] Cliff	Kliff	Risco	Falaise	Falésia
±[5] Cave, Caves	Höhle, Höhlen	Cueva, Cuevas	Caverne, Cavernes	Caverna, Cavernas
±[6] Crater	Krater	Cráter	Cratère	Cratera
±[7] Depression	Senke	Depresión	Dépression	Depressão
±[8] Dunes	Dünen	Dunas	Dunes	Dunas
±[9] Lava Flow	Lavastrom	Corriente de Lava	Coulée de lave	Corrente de Lava
≏ **River**	**Fluß**	**Río**	**Rivière, Fleuve**	**Rio**
≏[1] River Channel	Flussarm	Brazo de Río	Bras de rivière	Canal de Rio
≊ **Canal**	**Kanal**	**Canal**	**Canal**	**Canal**
≊[1] Aqueduct	Aquädukt	Acueducto	Aqueduc	Aqueduto
∟ **Waterfall, Rapids**	**Wasserfall, Stromschnellen**	**Cascada, Rápidos**	**Chute d'eau, Rapides**	**Quedas d'água, Rápidos**
ʯ **Strait**	**Meeresstraße**	**Estrecho**	**Détroit**	**Estreito**
⊂ **Bay, Gulf**	**Bucht, Golf**	**Bahía, Golfo**	**Baie, Golfe**	**Baía, Golfo**
⊂[1] Estuary	Trichtermündung	Estuario	Estuaire	Estuário
⊂[2] Fjord	Fjord	Fiordo	Fjord	Fiorde
⊂[3] Bight	Bucht	Bahía	Baie	Enseada
⊜ **Lake, Lakes**	**See, Seen**	**Lago, Lagos**	**Lac, Lacs**	**Lago, Lagos**
⊜[1] Reservoir	Stausee	Embalse	Réservoir, Retenue	Reservatório
⩩ **Swamp**	**Sumpf**	**Pantano**	**Marais**	**Pântano**
⊓ **Ice Features, Glacier**	**Eis- und Gletscherformen**	**Accidentes Glaciales, Glaciar**	**Formes glaciaires, Glacier**	**Acidentes Glaciares, Geleira**
╤ **Other Hydrographic Features**	**Andere Hydrographische Objekte**	**Otros Elementos Hidrográficos**	**Autres données hydrographiques**	**Outros Acidentes Hidrográficos**
╤[1] Ocean	Ozean	Océano	Océan	Oceano
╤[2] Sea	Meer	Mar	Mer	Mar
╤[3] Anchorage	Ankerplatz	Ancladero	Ancrage	Ancoradouro
╤[4] Oasis, Well, Spring	Oase, Brunnen, Quelle	Oasis, Pozo, Manantial	Oasis, Puits, Source	Oásis, Poço, Fonte, Manancial

ENGLISH	DEUTSCH	ESPAÑOL	FRANÇAIS	PORTUGUÊS
✢ **Submarine Features**	**Untermeerische Objekte**	**Accidentes Submarinos**	**Formes de relief sous-marin**	**Acidentes Submarinos**
✢[1] Depression	Senke	Depresión	Dépression	Depressão
✢[2] Reef, Shoal	Riff, Untiefe	Arrecife, Bajo	Récif, Haut-fond	Recife, Baixio
✢[3] Mountain, Mountains	Berg, Gebirge	Montaña, Montañas	Montagne, Montagnes	Montanha, Montanhas
✢[4] Slope, Shelf	Abhang, Schelf	Talud, Plataforma	Talus, Plateau continental	Talude, Plataforma
□ **Political Unit**	**Politische Einheit**	**Unidad Política**	**Entité politique**	**Unidade Política**
□[1] Independent Nation	Unabhängiger Staat	Nación Independiente	État indépendant	País Independente
□[2] Dependency	Abhängiges Gebiet	Dependencia	Dépendance	Dependência
□[3] State, Canton, Republic	Land, Kanton, Republik	Estado, Cantón, República	État, Canton, République	Estado, Cantão, República
□[4] Province, Region, Oblast	Provinz, Landschaft, Oblast	Provincia, Región, Oblast	Province, Région, Oblast	Província, Região, Oblast
□[5] Department, District, Prefecture	Département, Distrikt, Präfektur	Departamento, Distrito, Prefectura	Département, District, Préfecture	Departamento, Distrito, Prefeitura
□[6] County	Grafschaft	Condado	Comté	Condado
□[7] City, Municipality	Stadt, Stadtkreis	Ciudad, Municipalidad	Ville, Municipalité	Cidade, Municipalidade
□[8] Miscellaneous	Verschiedenes	Misceláneo	Divers	Diversos
□[9] Historical	Historisch	Histórico	Historique	Sítio Histórico
ʊ **Cultural Institution**	**Kulturelle Institution**	**Institución Cultural**	**Institution culturelle**	**Instituição Cultural**
ʊ[1] Religious Institution	Religiöse Institution	Institución Religiosa	Institution religieuse	Instituição Religiosa
ʊ[2] Educational Institution	Erziehungsinstitution	Institución Educacional	Établissement d'éducation	Estabelecimento de Ensino
ʊ[3] Scientific, Industrial Facility	Wissenschaftliche, Industrielle Anlage	Institución Científica o Industrial	Établissement scientifique ou industriel	Estabelecimento Científico ou Industrial
⊥ **Historical Site**	**Historische Stätte**	**Sitio Histórico**	**Site historique**	**Sítio Histórico**
♠ **Recreational Site**	**Erholungs- und Ferienort**	**Sitio de Recreo**	**Centre de loisirs**	**Área de Lazer**
⊠ **Airport**	**Flughafen**	**Aeropuerto**	**Aéroport**	**Aeroporto**
■ **Military Installation**	**Militäranlage**	**Instalación Militar**	**Installation militaire**	**Instalação Militar**
◆ **Miscellaneous**	**Verschiedenes**	**Misceláneo**	**Divers**	**Diversos**
◆[1] Region	Region	Región	Région	Região
◆[2] Desert	Wüste	Desierto	Désert	Deserto
◆[3] Forest, Moor	Wald, Moor	Bosque, Páramo	Forêt, Lande	Floresta, Pântano
◆[4] Reserve, Reservation	Reservat	Reserva, Reservación	Réserve	Reserva
◆[5] Transportation	Verkehr	Transporte	Transport	Transporte
◆[6] Dam	Damm	Presa	Barrage	Represa
◆[7] Mine, Quarry	Bergwerk, Steinbruch	Mina, Cantera	Mine, Carrière	Mina, Pedreira
◆[8] Neighborhood	Nachbarschaft	Barrio	Quartier	Arredores, Vizinhança
◆[9] Shopping Center	Einkaufszentrum	Mercado	Centre commercial	Shopping Center

A

Aa ≏	**50**	51.01 N	2.06 E
Aach	**58**	47.50 N	8.51 E
Aachen	**56**	50.47 N	6.05 E
Aach im Allgäu	**58**	47.31 N	9.58 E
Aach-Linz	**58**	47.54 N	9.11 E
Aadorf	**58**	47.30 N	8.54 E
Aaiun → El Aaiún	**148**	27.09 N	13.12 W
Aalen	**56**	48.50 N	10.05 E
A'ālī an-Nīl □[4]	**140**	9.30 N	31.00 E
Aalsmeer	**52**	52.16 N	4.45 E
Aalst (Alost), Bel.	**50**	50.56 N	4.02 E
Aalst, Ned.	**52**	51.23 N	5.29 E
Aalten	**52**	51.56 N	6.35 E
Aalter	**50**	51.05 N	3.27 E
Aalwynsfontein	**158**	30.27 S	18.38 E
Äänekoski	**26**	62.36 N	25.44 E
Aansluit	**158**	26.44 S	22.28 E
Aar ≏	**56**	50.23 N	8.00 E
Aarau	**58**	47.23 N	8.03 E
Aarberg	**58**	47.03 N	7.16 E
Aarburg	**58**	47.19 N	7.54 E
Aardenburg	**52**	51.16 N	3.27 E
Aare ≏	**58**	47.37 N	8.13 E
Aareschlucht ♠	**58**	46.44 N	8.12 E
Aargau □[3]	**58**	47.30 N	8.10 E
Aarle-Rixtel	**52**	51.31 N	5.38 E
Aaronsburg	**210**	40.54 N	77.27 W
Aarschot	**56**	50.59 N	4.50 E
Aarwangen	**58**	47.15 N	7.46 E
Aazanèn	**34**	35.13 N	3.10 W
Aba, Nig.	**150**	5.06 N	7.21 E
Aba, Zaïre	**154**	3.52 N	30.14 E
Aba, Zhg.	**102**	33.06 N	101.59 E
Abā al-Bawl, Qurayn ∧[2]	**128**	24.56 N	51.13 E
Abā al-Waqf	**142**	28.35 N	30.46 E
Abā as-Su'ūd	**144**	17.29 N	44.08 E
Abacaxis ≏	**242**	3.54 S	58.47 W
Abaco I	**238**	26.28 N	77.05 W
Abacou, Pointe ≻	**238**	18.03 N	73.47 W
Abadab, Jabal ∧	**140**	18.53 N	35.59 E
Ābādān	**128**	30.20 N	48.16 E
Ābādeh	**128**	31.10 N	52.37 E
Abadia dos Dourados	**255**	18.28 S	47.24 W
Abadiânia	**255**	16.06 S	48.48 W
Abadla	**148**	31.01 N	2.44 W
Abaeté	**255**	19.09 S	45.27 W
Abaeté ≏	**255**	18.02 S	45.12 W
Abaetetuba	**250**	1.42 S	48.54 W
Abagajtuj	**88**	49.35 N	117.49 E
Abagnar Qi	**102**	43.58 N	116.04 E
Abag Qi	**102**	43.53 N	114.33 E
Abaí	**252**	26.01 S	55.57 W
Abaj, Kaz.	**86**	49.38 N	72.52 E
Abaj, Ross.	**86**	50.27 N	85.05 E
Abaji	**150**	8.28 N	6.57 E
Abajo Mountains ⋏	**200**	37.50 N	109.25 W
Abajo Peak ∧	**200**	37.51 N	109.28 W
Abak	**150**	4.57 N	7.47 E
Abakaliki	**150**	6.21 N	8.06 E
Abakan	**86**	53.43 N	91.26 E
Abakan ≏	**86**	53.43 N	91.30 E
Abakanovo	**76**	59.18 N	37.39 E
Abakanskij chrebet ⋏	**86**	52.20 N	88.50 E
Abala, Congo	**152**	1.21 S	15.30 E
Abala, Niger	**150**	14.56 N	3.26 E
Abalak, Niger	**150**	15.27 N	6.17 E
Abalak, Ross.	**86**	58.08 N	68.36 E
Abalemma, Vallée d' V	**150**	15.34 N	6.23 E
Abalessa	**148**	22.54 N	4.50 E
Aban	**88**	56.41 N	96.04 E
Abancay	**248**	13.35 S	72.55 W
Abanga ≏	**152**	0.20 S	10.30 E
Abano Terme	**64**	45.21 N	11.47 E
Abaokoro	**174t**	1.29 N	173.02 E
Abar Irir	**144**	4.53 N	46.10 E
Abar Kūh	**128**	31.08 N	53.17 E
Abarra	**144**	5.23 N	39.58 E
Abarracamento	**256**	22.12 S	43.30 W
Abaša	**84**	42.12 N	42.13 E
Abascay, Arroyo ≏	**258**	35.17 S	58.07 W
Abashiri	**92a**	44.01 N	144.17 E
Abasolo, Méx.	**196**	27.12 N	101.24 W
Abasolo, Méx.	**196**	25.57 N	100.24 W
Abasolo, Méx.	**204**	32.39 N	115.21 W
Abasolo, Méx.	**232**	25.18 N	104.40 W
Abasolo, Méx.	**232**	24.04 N	98.22 W
Abasolo, Méx.	**234**	20.27 N	101.32 W
Abasolo del Valle	**234**	17.44 N	95.29 W
Abasto	**258**	34.58 S	58.06 W
Abastumani	**84**	41.46 N	42.50 E
Abate	**85**	39.03 N	77.36 E
Abate Alonia, Lago di ⊜	**68**	41.01 N	15.45 E
Abatimbo el Gumas	**144**	10.36 N	35.13 E
Abatskij	**86**	56.18 N	70.28 E
Abau	**164**	10.11 S	148.42 E
Abava ≏	**76**	57.06 N	21.54 E
Abay → Blue Nile ≏	**140**	15.38 N	32.31 E
Abaya, Lake ⊜	**144**	6.20 N	37.55 E
Abayuba	**258**	34.51 S	56.14 W
Abaza	**86**	52.39 N	90.06 E
Abba	**152**	5.20 N	15.11 E
Abbabach ≏	**263**	51.28 N	7.41 E
Abbadia San Salvatore	**66**	42.53 N	11.41 E
'Abbāsābād ◆[8]	**267d**	35.44 N	51.25 E
Abbasanta	**71**	40.08 N	8.49 E
Abbaye, Étang de l' ⊜	**261**	48.41 N	1.56 E
Abbé, Lac (Lake Abe) ⊜	**144**	11.06 N	41.50 E
Abbehausen	**52**	53.29 N	8.26 E
Abbekås	**41**	55.24 N	13.36 E
Abbensen	**52**	52.23 N	10.11 E
Abbert ≏	**48**	53.25 N	8.53 W
Abbess Roding	**260**	51.47 N	0.17 E
Abbeville, Fr.	**50**	50.06 N	1.50 E
Abbeville, Ga., U.S.	**192**	31.59 N	83.18 W
Abbeville, La., U.S.	**194**	29.58 N	92.08 W
Abbeville, Ms., U.S.	**194**	34.30 N	89.30 W
Abbeville, S.C., U.S.	**192**	34.10 N	82.22 W
Abbey	**184**	50.43 N	108.45 W
Abbeydorney	**48**	52.19 N	9.41 W
Abbeyfeale	**48**	52.24 N	9.18 W
Abbey Head ≻	**44**	54.46 N	3.58 W
Abbeyleix	**48**	52.55 N	7.20 W
Abbey Peak ∧	**164**	14.18 S	144.29 E
Abbey Wood ◆[8]	**260**	51.29 N	0.08 E
Abbiategrasso	**62**	45.24 N	8.54 E
Abbot, Mount ∧	**166**	20.03 S	147.45 E
Abbots Bromley	**42**	52.48 N	1.52 W
Abbotsbury	**42**	50.40 N	2.36 W
Abbotsford, Austl.	**274a**	33.51 S	151.08 E
Abbotsford, B.C., Can.	**224**	49.03 N	122.17 W
Abbotsford, Wi., U.S.	**190**	44.56 N	90.18 W
Abbots Langley	**42**	51.43 N	0.25 W
Abbott, Arg.	**258**	35.17 S	58.48 W
Abbott, Tx., U.S.	**222**	31.53 N	97.04 W
Abbottābād	**123**	34.09 N	73.13 E
Abbott Butte ∧	**202**	42.57 N	122.33 W
Abbottstown	**208**	39.53 N	76.59 W
Abchazskaja Respublika □[3]	**84**	43.10 N	41.00 E
Abcoude	**52**	52.16 N	4.58 E
'Abd al-'Azīz, Jabal ⋏	**130**	36.25 N	40.20 E
'Abd al-Ḥafiẓ, Qārat ∧[2]	**142**	28.53 N	30.08 E
'Abd al-Kūrī I	**118**	12.12 N	52.13 E
'Abd Allāh	**140**	13.30 N	23.02 E
'Abd Allāh, Khawr ʯ	**128**	29.50 N	48.20 E
'Abd al-Shāhīd	**273c**	29.55 N	31.13 E
Ābdānān	**128**	32.58 N	47.26 E
Ábdēra ⊥	**38**	40.59 N	24.58 E
Abdrachmanovo	**80**	54.46 N	52.30 E
Abdul Hakīm	**123**	30.33 N	72.07 E
Abdulino	**80**	53.42 N	53.40 E
Abdulovo	**80**	54.16 N	53.27 E
Abe ≏	**94**	34.56 N	138.24 E
Abe, Lake (Lac Abbé) ⊜	**144**	11.06 N	41.50 E
Abéché	**146**	13.49 N	20.49 E
Abéjar	**34**	41.48 N	2.47 W
Abejonal, Cerro ∧	**236**	11.39 N	86.10 W
Abejorral	**246**	5.47 N	75.26 W
Abekr	**140**	12.43 N	28.55 E
Abelek	**140**	7.23 N	28.46 E
Abel Tasman National Park ♠	**172**	40.55 S	173.00 E
Abelti	**144**	8.10 N	37.34 E
Abemama I[1]	**14**	0.21 N	173.51 E
Abenberg	**56**	49.14 N	10.57 E
Abengourou	**150**	6.44 N	3.29 W
Abeno ◆[8]	**270**	34.38 N	135.32 E
Abenójar	**34**	38.53 N	4.21 W
Åbenrå	**41**	55.02 N	9.26 E
Åbenrå Fjord ⊂	**41**	55.03 N	9.34 E
Abens ≏	**60**	48.51 N	11.46 E
Abensberg	**60**	48.49 N	11.51 E
Abeokuta	**150**	7.10 N	3.26 E
Aber	**154**	2.12 N	32.21 E
Aberaeron	**42**	52.15 N	4.15 W
Aberaman	**42**	51.42 N	3.25 W
Aberavon → Port Talbot	**42**	51.36 N	3.47 W
Abercarn	**42**	51.39 N	3.08 W
Aberchirder	**46**	57.33 N	2.38 W
Abercorn, P.Q., Can.	**206**	45.02 N	72.40 W
Abercorn → Mbala, Zam.	**154**	8.50 S	31.22 E
Abercrombie ≏	**170**	34.09 S	149.40 E
Aberdare	**42**	51.43 N	3.27 W
Aberdare National Park ♠	**154**	0.30 S	36.45 E
Aberdare Range ⋏	**154**	0.25 S	36.38 E
Aberdaron	**42**	52.49 N	4.43 W
Aberdeen, Sk., Can.	**184**	52.19 N	106.17 W
Aberdeen (Xianggangzi), H.K.	**271d**	22.15 N	114.09 E
Aberdeen, S. Afr.	**158**	32.29 S	24.05 E
Aberdeen, Scot., U.K.	**46**	57.10 N	2.04 W
Aberdeen, Id., U.S.	**202**	42.56 N	112.50 W
Aberdeen, Md., U.S.	**208**	39.30 N	76.09 W
Aberdeen, Ms., U.S.	**194**	33.49 N	88.32 W
Aberdeen, N.C., U.S.	**192**	35.07 N	79.25 W
Aberdeen, Oh., U.S.	**218**	38.39 N	83.45 W
Aberdeen, S.D., U.S.	**198**	45.27 N	98.29 W
Aberdeen, Wa., U.S.	**224**	46.58 N	123.48 W
Aberdeen Lake ⊜	**176**	64.27 N	99.00 W
Aberdeen Lake ⊜[1]	**194**	33.55 N	88.30 W
Aberdeen Proving Ground ■	**208**	39.25 N	76.10 W
Aberdour	**46**	56.03 N	3.19 W
Aberdulais	**42**	51.41 N	3.48 W
Aberdyfi	**42**	52.33 N	4.02 W
Aberfeldy	**46**	56.37 N	3.54 W
Aberfoyle	**46**	56.11 N	4.23 W
Abergavenny	**42**	51.50 N	3.00 W
Abergele	**44**	53.17 N	3.34 W
Abergwynfi	**42**	51.40 N	3.35 W
Abergynolwyn	**42**	52.40 N	3.58 W
Aberjona ≏	**283**	42.27 N	71.08 W
Abermain	**170**	32.49 S	151.25 E
Abernathy	**196**	33.50 N	101.51 W
Abernethy, Sk., Can.	**184**	50.45 N	103.25 W
Abernethy, Scot., U.K.	**46**	56.20 N	3.19 W
Aberporth	**42**	52.09 N	4.33 W
Abersoch	**42**	52.50 N	4.29 W
Abersychan	**42**	51.44 N	3.04 W
Abert, Lake ⊜	**202**	42.38 N	120.13 W
Abertillery	**42**	51.45 N	3.09 W
Aberuthven	**46**	56.19 N	3.39 W
Aberystwyth	**42**	52.25 N	4.05 W
Abessinien, Hochland von → Ethiopian Plateau ⋏[1]	**144**	9.00 N	38.00 E
Abetone	**66**	44.08 N	10.40 E
Abez'	**24**	66.32 N	61.42 E
Abhā	**144**	18.13 N	42.30 E
Abhar	**128**	36.09 N	49.13 E
Abharwat ∧	**123**	34.02 N	74.25 E
Abhayāpuri	**124**	26.20 N	90.40 E
Abhaynagar	**126**	23.01 N	89.28 E
Abiaca Creek ≏	**194**	33.20 N	90.15 W
Abid, Oued el ≏	**148**	32.18 N	7.03 W
Ābidīn	**140**	13.33 N	29.38 E
'Abīdīyah	**140**	18.14 N	33.57 E
Abidjan	**150**	5.19 N	4.02 W
'Ābid Mār, Tall ∧	**132**	32.26 N	36.42 E
Abiengama	**154**	2.35 N	27.46 E
Abiko	**94**	35.52 N	140.03 E
Abilene, Ks., U.S.	**198**	38.55 N	97.12 W
Abilene, Tx., U.S.	**196**	32.26 N	99.43 W
Abingdon, Eng., U.K.	**42**	51.41 N	1.17 W
Abingdon, Il., U.S.	**190**	40.48 N	90.24 W
Abingdon, Il., U.S.	**194**	40.48 N	90.24 W

≏ River	Fluß	Río	Rivière	Rio
≊ Canal	Kanal	Canal	Canal	Canal
∟ Waterfall, Rapids	Wasserfall, Stromschnellen	Cascada, Rápidos	Chute d'eau, Rapides	Cascata, Rápidos
ʯ Strait	Meeresstraße	Estrecho	Détroit	Estreito
⊂ Bay, Gulf	Bucht, Golf	Bahía, Golfo	Baie, Golfe	Baía, Golfo
⊜ Lake, Lakes	See, Seen	Lago, Lagos	Lac, Lacs	Lago, Lagos
⩩ Swamp	Sumpf	Pantano	Marais	Pântano
⊓ Ice Features, Glacier	Eis- und Gletscherformen	Accidentes Glaciales	Formes glaciaires	Acidentes glaciares
╤ Other Hydrographic Features	Andere Hydrographische Objekte	Otros Elementos Hidrográficos	Autres données hydrographiques	Outros acidentes hidrográficos

✢ Submarine Features	Untermeerische Objekte	Accidentes Submarinos	Formes de relief sous-marin	Acidentes submarinos
□ Political Unit	Politische Einheit	Unidad Politica	Entité politique	Unidade política
ʊ Cultural Institution	Kulturelle Institution	Institución Cultural	Institution culturelle	Instituição cultural
⊥ Historical Site	Historische Stätte	Sitio Histórico	Site historique	Sitio histórico
♠ Recreational Site	Erholungs- und Ferienort	Sitio de Recreo	Centre de loisirs	Area de Lazer
⊠ Airport	Flughafen	Aeropuerto	Aéroport	Aeroporto
■ Military Installation	Militäranlage	Instalación Militar	Installation militaire	Instalação militar
◆ Miscellaneous	Verschiedenes	Misceláneo	Divers	Diversos

Abingdon, Va., U.S. 192 36.42 N 81.58 W
Abinger 260 51.12 N 0.24 W
Abington, Ct., U.S. 207 41.51 N 72.00 W
Abington, Ma., U.S. 207 42.06 N 70.56 W
Abington, Pa., U.S. 208 40.07 N 75.07 W
Abington Reefs ◆[2] 166 18.00 S 149.36 E
Abino, Point > 212 42.50 N 79.05 W
Abino Bay c 284a 42.51 N 79.05 W
Abinsk 78 44.52 N 38.09 E
Abiod, Rmel el ⊥[8] 148 31.30 N 9.30 E
Abiquiu 200 36.12 N 106.19 W
Abiquiu Reservoir ⊜[1] 200 36.18 N 106.32 W
Abiseo ≐ 248 7.18 S 76.50 W
Abiseo, Parque Nacional ♦ 248 7.35 S 77.10 W
Abisko 24 68.20 N 18.51 E
Abisko Nationalpark ♦ 24 68.20 N 18.30 E
Abita Springs 194 30.28 N 90.02 W
Abitau ≐ 176 59.53 N 109.03 W
Abitibi ≐ 176 51.03 N 80.55 W
Abitibi, Lake ⊜ 190 48.42 N 79.45 W
Abiy Adi 144 13.26 N 39.03 E
Abiyata, Lake ⊜ 144 7.37 N 38.36 E
Abja-Paluoja 76 58.08 N 25.21 E
Abkhazia → Abchazskaja Respublika □[3] 84 43.10 N 41.00 E
Ableiges 261 49.05 N 1.59 E
Ablis 50 48.31 N 1.50 E
Ablon-sur-Seine 261 48.43 N 2.25 E
Abnūb 142 27.16 N 31.09 E
Åbo → Turku 26 60.27 N 22.17 E
Abóbada 266c 38.43 N 9.20 W
Abodom 150 5.32 N 0.49 W
Abohar 123 30.09 N 74.11 E
Aboisso 150 5.28 N 3.12 W
Abomey 150 7.11 N 1.59 E
Abondance 58 46.17 N 6.44 E
Abong 146 6.59 N 10.44 E
Abongabong, Gunung ∧ 114 4.15 N 96.48 E
Abong Mbang 152 3.59 N 13.10 E
Abonnema 150 4.43 N 6.47 E
Abony 30 47.11 N 20.01 E
Aborigen, pik ∧ 74 61.59 N 149.19 E
Aborlan 116 9.26 N 118.33 E
Aborrebjerg ∧[2] 41 54.59 N 12.32 E
Aboso 150 5.22 N 1.56 W
Abō-tōge)(94 36.11 N 137.35 E
Abou 144 4.21 N 43.03 E
Abou-Deïa 146 11.27 N 19.17 E
Abounamy ≐ 250 4.24 N 54.26 W
Aboyne 46 57.05 N 2.50 W
Abra □[4] 116 17.35 N 120.50 E
Abra ≐ 116 17.31 N 120.23 E
Abraão 256 23.08 S 44.10 W
Abraham Lake ⊜[1] 182 52.15 N 116.23 W
Abraham Lincoln Birthplace National Historic Site ⊥ 194 37.32 N 85.44 W
Abrahamsdam 158 29.08 S 22.39 E
Abraka 150 5.50 N 6.05 E
Abram 262 53.31 N 2.35 W
Abramcevo 265b 55.50 N 37.50 E
Abramovka 78 51.12 N 41.01 E
Abramovskaja 24 65.11 N 51.43 E
Abram S. Hewitt State Forest ♦ 276 41.11 N 74.22 W
Abrantes 34 39.28 N 8.12 W
Abra Pampa 252 22.43 S 65.42 W
Abraq, Wādī al- V 146 26.27 N 18.48 E
Abrau-D'urso 78 44.43 N 37.37 E
Abra Vieja, Arroyo ≐ 288 34.26 S 58.34 W
Abre-Campo 255 20.18 S 42.29 W
Abrego 246 8.05 N 73.13 W
Abreojos, Punta > 232 26.42 N 113.35 W
Abreschviller 58 48.38 N 7.06 E
Abreu e Lima 250 7.54 S 34.53 W
'Abrī, Sūd. 140 11.40 N 30.28 E
'Abrī, Sūd. 140 20.48 N 30.20 E
Abriachan 46 57.22 N 4.24 W
Abridge 260 51.39 N 0.07 E
Abriès 62 44.47 N 6.56 E
Abring 123 33.42 N 76.35 E
Abriola 68 40.30 N 15.49 E
Abrud 38 46.17 N 23.04 E
Abruka saar I 76 58.10 N 22.30 E
Abrunheira 266c 38.46 N 9.21 W
Abruzzi □[4] 66 42.20 N 13.45 E
Abruzzo, Parco Nazionale d' ♦ 66 41.45 N 13.45 E
Absam 64 47.18 N 11.30 E
Absaroka Range ⋏ 202 44.45 N 109.50 W
Absarokee 202 45.31 N 109.26 W
Abscon 50 50.20 N 3.18 E
Absdorf 61 48.24 N 15.59 E
Absecon 208 39.25 N 74.29 W
Absecon Bay c 208 39.24 N 74.28 W
Abşeker 130 38.55 N 39.11 E
Abşeron yarımadası >[1] 84 40.30 N 50.00 E
Abtenau 64 47.33 N 13.21 E
Abtsgmünd 56 48.54 N 10.00 E
Abtsteinach 56 49.33 N 8.47 E
Abu 96 34.30 N 131.28 E
Abu ≐ 96 34.25 N 131.24 E
Abū Ahl ⊤[4] 142 30.06 N 43.45 E
Abū 'Alāwī, Wādī V 142 30.07 N 31.51 E
Abū al-Ghayt 273c 30.09 N 31.11 E
Abū al-Hamām, Jabal ∧ 132 30.27 N 35.38 E
Abū al-Hawl (Sphinx) ⊥ 142 29.59 N 31.08 E
Abū 'Alī I 128 27.20 N 49.33 E
Abū al-Khaṣīb 128 30.27 N 47.59 E
Abū al-Maṭāmīr 142 30.55 N 30.11 E
Abū al-'Urūq, Bi'r ⊤[4] 142 30.45 N 32.23 E
Abū an-Numrus 273c 29.57 N 31.12 E
Abū 'Aradeib, Wādī V 140 14.12 N 23.06 E
Abū 'Arīsh 144 16.57 N 42.50 E
Abū Ballās ∧[2] 140 24.26 N 27.39 E
Abū Daraj, Ra's > 142 29.23 N 32.34 E
Abū Dā'ūd, Ra's > 128 23.19 N 58.55 E
Abū Dā'ūd as-Sibākh 142 30.55 N 31.34 E
Abū Dawm 140 16.10 N 32.36 E
Abū Dawm, Wādī V 140 18.28 N 31.49 E
Abu Dhabi → Abū Zaby 128 24.28 N 54.22 E
Abū Dhi'ābah, Wādī V 142 29.37 N 32.06 E
Abū Dīs 140 19.08 N 33.34 E
Abū Dulayq 140 15.54 N 33.49 E
Abufari 248 5.25 S 62.59 W
Abū Gatta Hills ⋏[2] 140 6.06 N 27.44 E
Abū Gelba 140 13.11 N 31.52 E
Abū Ghālib 142 30.16 N 30.56 E
Abū Habl, Khawr V 140 12.49 N 31.15 E
Abū Hād, Wādī V 142 28.20 N 32.49 E
Abū Hadīmah, Bi'r ⊤ 142 30.44 N 29.51 E
Abū Hamad 140 19.32 N 33.19 E
Abū Hamād al-Mahattah 142 30.32 N 31.40 E
Abū Harāz, Sūd. 140 12.58 N 29.52 E
Abū Harāz, Sūd. 140 19.04 N 32.07 E
Abū Hasan, Jabal ∧ 144 17.42 N 42.54 E
Abū Hummuṣ 142 31.06 N 30.19 E
Abū Hushsh, Bi'r ⊤[4] 142 30.49 N 29.57 E
Abuja 150 9.12 N 7.11 E
Abū Jābirah 140 11.04 N 26.51 E
Abū Jandīr 142 29.14 N 30.41 E
Abū Jīrj 142 28.32 N 30.47 E
Abū Jubayhah 140 11.27 N 31.14 E
Abū Kabīr 142 30.44 N 31.40 E
Abū Kamāl 130 34.27 N 40.55 E
Abū Kharjah, Wādī V 142 28.38 N 31.44 E
Abū Khashabah, Jabal ∧ 142 28.08 N 32.52 E
Abūksāh 142 29.23 N 30.42 E
Abū Kulaywāt 140 12.20 N 26.00 E
Abukuma ≐ 92 38.02 N 140.56 E
Abukuma-kōchi ⋏ 92 37.30 N 140.45 E
Abū Latt I 144 19.58 N 40.08 E
Abulug 116 18.27 N 121.27 E
Abulug ≐ 116 18.29 N 121.25 E
Abū Madd, Ra's > 128 24.50 N 37.07 E
Abū Makhlūf, Bi'r ⊤[4] 142 30.28 N 29.42 E
Abū Maṭāriq 140 10.58 N 26.17 E
Abu Mendi 144 11.47 N 35.43 E
Abū Minqār, Bi'r ⊤[4] 140 26.30 N 27.35 E
Abumombazi 152 3.42 N 22.10 E
Abū Muhammad, Bi'r ⊤[4] 132 29.43 N 34.13 E
Abū Muḥarrik, Ghurd ⊥[8] 140 27.50 N 29.40 E
Abū Mūsā I 128 25.52 N 55.03 E
Abuna 248 9.42 S 65.23 W
Abunã (Abunā) ≐ 248 9.41 S 65.23 W
Abū Na'āmah 140 12.44 N 34.08 E
Abune Yosef ∧ 144 12.10 N 39.12 E
Abū Qarḍ, Qā' ≐ 132 32.08 N 37.11 E
Abū Qashsh 132 31.57 N 35.11 E
Abū Qīr ◆[8] 142 31.19 N 30.04 E
Abū Qīr, Khalīj (Abu Qir Bay) c 142 31.23 N 30.13 E
Abū Qurqāṣ 142 27.56 N 30.50 E
Aburatsubo-kō c 268 35.09 N 139.38 E
Abū Rimth, Wādī V, Miṣr 142 28.45 N 31.27 E
Abū Rimth, Wādī V, Miṣr 142 30.21 N 31.53 E
Abū Rīshat, Wādī V 142 28.54 N 31.37 E
Abu Road 120 24.29 N 72.47 E
Abū Rubayq 128 23.44 N 39.42 E
Abū Rujmayn, Jabal ⋏[2] 130 34.52 N 38.20 E
Abū Sant, Wādī V 140 14.11 N 23.06 E
Abū Shajarah, Ra's > 140 21.04 N 37.14 E
Abū Shāmah, Jabal ∧ 142 29.52 N 31.38 E
Abū Shanab, Sūd. 140 10.47 N 29.32 E
Abū Shanab, Sūd. 140 13.57 N 27.47 E
Abū Shaykhāt, Dahr ∧[2] 132 36.36 N 39.40 E
Abu Simbel → Abū Sunbul ⊥ 140 22.22 N 31.38 E
Abū Sīr 273c 29.53 N 31.13 E
Abū Sīr al-Malaq 142 29.15 N 31.05 E
Abū Sīr-Banā 142 30.55 N 31.15 E
Abū Sīr Pyramids ⊥ 273c 29.54 N 31.12 E
Abū Sulṭān 142 30.25 N 32.19 E
Abū Sunbul ⊥ 140 22.22 N 31.38 E
Abū Suwayr al-Mahattah 142 30.34 N 32.07 E
Abū Suwayr Military Base ■ 142 30.34 N 32.06 E
Abuta 92a 42.33 N 140.46 E
Abū Ṭabaq, Bi'r ⊤[4] 140 17.35 N 28.31 E
Abū Ṭarafah, Wādī V 132 30.12 N 36.13 E
Abut Head > 172 43.07 S 170.15 E
Abū Tīj 140 27.02 N 31.19 E
Abū Tunaytin 140 14.24 N 31.01 E
Abū Turayfīyah, Jabal ∧, Miṣr 142 29.58 N 32.06 E
Abū Turayfīyah, Jabal ∧, Miṣr 142 29.42 N 31.49 E
Abū 'Uwayjilah ⊤[4] 132 30.50 N 34.07 E
Abuye Meda ∧ 144 10.28 N 39.44 E
Abuyog 116 10.45 N 125.01 E
Abū Zabad 140 12.21 N 29.15 E
Abū Za'bal 142 30.15 N 31.21 E
Abū Zaby (Abu Dhabi) 128 24.28 N 54.22 E
Abū Zanīmah 140 29.03 N 33.06 E
Abwong 140 9.07 N 32.12 E
Åby 40 58.40 N 16.11 E
Aby ◆[8] 41 56.09 N 10.10 E
Aby, Lagune c 150 5.15 N 3.14 W
Abyad 140 13.46 N 26.28 E
Abyad, Al-Bahr al- → White Nile ≐ 140 15.38 N 32.31 E
Abyad, Wādī al- V 142 29.38 N 32.13 E
Abyälven ≐ 26 65.01 N 21.24 E
Abyār 142 30.50 N 30.52 E
Abyār 'Alī 128 24.25 N 39.32 E
Åbybro 26 57.09 N 9.45 E
Abydos 162 21.25 S 118.54 E
Abyei 140 9.36 N 28.26 E
Åbyggeby 40 60.44 N 17.07 E
Åbytorp 40 59.07 N 15.04 E
Abzanovo 86 53.50 N 58.36 E
Acacías 246 3.59 N 73.46 W
Academia 214 40.25 N 82.28 W
Academy Corners 208 41.57 N 77.23 W
Academy of Sciences ◆[3] 282 37.46 N 122.28 W
Acadia National Park ♦ 188 44.18 N 68.15 W
Acadia Valley 184 51.08 N 110.13 W
Acahay 252 25.55 S 57.09 W
Açailandia 250 4.57 S 47.29 W
Acajete 234 19.06 N 97.57 W
Acajutiba 250 11.40 S 38.01 W
Acajutla 236 13.36 N 89.50 W
Acala 234 16.34 N 92.48 W
Acalayong 152 1.05 N 9.40 E
Acámbaro 234 20.02 N 100.44 W
Acampo 226 38.10 N 121.13 W
Acandí 246 8.32 N 77.14 W
Acaponeta 234 22.30 N 105.22 W
Acaponeta ≐ 234 22.20 N 105.37 W
Acapulco [de Juárez] 234 16.51 N 99.55 W
Acará 250 1.57 S 48.11 W
Acará ≐ 250 1.40 S 48.25 W
Acará, Lago ⊜ 246 3.39 S 62.40 W
Acarai ≐ 250 2.02 S 52.15 W
Acarai Mountains ⋏ 246 1.30 N 58.15 W
Acará-Mirim ≐ 250 1.58 S 48.12 W
Acaraú 250 2.53 S 40.07 W
Acaraú ≐ 250 2.51 S 40.08 W
Acaray ≐ 252 25.29 S 54.42 W
Acari, Bra. 250 6.31 S 36.38 W
Acarí, Perú 248 15.26 S 74.37 W
Acari ≐, Bra. 248 5.18 S 59.42 W
Acari ≐, Bra. 255 16.00 S 45.03 W
Acarí ≐, Perú 248 15.39 S 74.39 W
Acarigua 246 9.33 N 69.12 W
Acâş 38 47.33 N 22.47 E
Acate 70 37.02 N 14.28 E
Acate ≐ 70 37.00 N 14.20 E
Acatic 234 20.47 N 102.53 W
Acatlán ≐ 234 18.04 N 98.19 W
Acatlán de Juárez 234 20.26 N 103.38 W
Acatlán de Osorio 234 18.12 N 98.03 W
Acatlán de Pérez Figueroa 234 18.32 N 96.37 W
Acatzingo [de Hidalgo] 234 18.59 N 97.47 W
Acay, Nevado de ∧ 252 24.21 S 66.12 W
Acayucan 234 17.57 N 94.55 W
Accadia 68 41.10 N 15.20 E
Acceglio 62 44.28 N 7.00 E
Aččen, mys > 180 64.45 N 175.30 W
Accettura 68 40.29 N 16.09 E
Ačchoj-Martan 84 43.11 N 45.18 E
Ačči 85 39.57 N 68.14 E
Acciano 66 42.10 N 13.43 E
Accokeek 208 38.40 N 77.02 W
Accomac 208 37.43 N 75.39 W
Accomack □[6] 208 37.45 N 75.40 W
Accord, Ma., U.S. 283 42.10 N 70.53 W
Accord, N.Y., U.S. 210 41.47 N 74.13 W
Accord Brook ≐ 283 42.10 N 70.53 W
Accord Pond ⊜ 283 42.10 N 70.53 W
Accotink Creek ≐ 284c 38.46 N 77.15 W
Accotink Creek, Bear Branch ≐ 284c 38.52 N 77.15 W
Accotink Creek, Long Branch ≐ 284c 38.48 N 77.13 W
Accoville 192 37.46 N 81.50 W
Accra 150 5.33 N 0.13 W
Accra ≐ 150 5.40 N 0.10 W
Accrington 44 53.46 N 2.21 W
Accumoli 66 42.42 N 13.15 E
Acebuches 232 28.15 N 102.43 W
Aceguá 252 31.52 S 54.09 W
Aceh □[4] 114 4.00 N 97.00 E
Aceh ≐ 114 5.36 N 95.20 E
Acerentia ⊥ 68 39.16 N 16.49 E
Acerenza 68 40.48 N 15.57 E
Acerno 68 40.44 N 15.03 E
Acerra 68 40.57 N 14.22 E
Acevedo 252 33.45 S 60.27 W
Achacachi 248 16.03 S 68.43 W
Achaguas 246 7.46 N 68.14 W
Achalciche 84 41.38 N 42.59 E
Achali-Kindgi 84 42.48 N 41.16 E
Achalkalaki 84 41.25 N 43.29 E
Achalpur 120 21.16 N 77.31 E
Achangaran 85 40.54 N 69.37 E
Achao 254 42.28 S 73.30 W
Achar 252 32.25 S 56.10 W
Acharacle 46 56.44 N 5.47 W
Achar uul ∧ 102 45.10 N 103.45 E
Achau 264b 48.05 N 16.23 E
Achavanich 46 58.22 N 3.24 W
Achelouma, Enneri V 146 21.55 N 13.35 E
Achêne 56 50.16 N 5.03 E
Acheng 89 45.32 N 126.59 E
Achenkirch 64 47.31 N 11.42 E
Achénouma 146 19.08 N 12.55 E
Achen Pass)(64 47.35 N 11.38 E
Achensee ⊜ 64 47.28 N 11.42 E
Achères 261 48.58 N 2.04 E
Achern 56 48.37 N 8.04 E
Acheron ≐, Austl. 169 37.14 S 145.42 E
Acheron ≐, N.Z. 172 42.24 S 172.58 E
Acheux-en-Amiénois 50 50.04 N 2.32 E
Achhābal 123 33.41 N 75.14 E
Achhnera 124 27.11 N 77.46 E
Achí, Col. 246 8.34 N 74.33 W
Achi, Nihon 94 35.27 N 137.45 E
Achiasi 150 5.52 N 1.00 W
Achicourt 50 50.16 N 2.46 E
Achigan, Lac de l' ⊜ 206 45.56 N 73.58 W
Achiguate ≐ 236 13.55 N 90.55 W
Achill 28 53.56 N 9.54 W
Achilles 208 37.17 N 76.27 W
Achill Head > 48 53.59 N 10.13 W
Achill Island I 48 54.00 N 10.00 W
Achill Sound 48 53.55 N 9.58 W
Achim 52 53.00 N 9.02 E
Achin 120 34.08 N 70.42 E
Achiras 252 33.10 S 65.00 W
Achir-Ula, gora ∧ 88 50.21 N 94.31 E
Achmeta 84 42.02 N 45.13 E
Achnasaul 46 56.58 N 4.59 W
Achnasheen 46 57.35 N 5.06 W
Achol 140 6.34 N 31.31 E
Achosnich 46 56.45 N 6.06 W
Achterwasser c 54 54.00 N 13.57 E
Achterwehr 54 54.19 N 9.57 E
Achthuizen 52 51.42 N 4.16 E
Achtuba 80 51.37 N 44.22 E
Achtuba ≐ 80 46.42 N 48.00 E
Achtubinsk 80 48.17 N 46.10 E
Achty 84 41.28 N 47.43 E
Achtyrskij 78 44.52 N 38.20 E
Achuapa 236 13.03 N 86.35 W
Achur'an (Arpaçay) ≐ 84 40.06 N 43.39 E
Achwa ≐ 154 3.43 N 31.55 E
Aci 85 41.17 N 73.02 E
Aci Castello 70 37.33 N 15.08 E
Aci Catena 70 37.36 N 15.08 E
Acıgöl ⊜ 130 38.35 N 34.31 E
Acı Göl ⊜ 130 37.50 N 29.54 E
Acikak 88 54.11 N 103.18 E
Ačikulak 84 44.34 N 44.50 E
Acilia ◆[8] 267a 41.47 N 12.22 E
Ačimovy Vtoryje 86 60.04 N 75.12 E
Ačinsk 86 56.17 N 90.30 E
Acıpayam 130 37.25 N 29.22 E
Acireale 70 37.37 N 15.10 E
Ačisaj 85 43.35 N 68.53 E
Aci Sant'Antonio 70 37.36 N 15.07 E
Ačisu 84 42.38 N 47.40 E
Ačit 86 56.48 N 57.54 E
Ačit nuur ⊜ 86 49.30 N 90.32 E
Ackerly 196 32.32 N 101.43 W
Ackerman 194 33.18 N 89.10 W
Ackermanville 210 40.49 N 75.17 W
Ackerson Lake ⊜ 216 42.11 N 84.20 W
Ackley 190 42.33 N 93.03 W
Acklins I 238 22.26 N 73.58 W
Acklins, Bight of c[3] 238 22.30 N 74.15 W
Acland, Mount ∧ 166 24.55 S 148.05 E
Acle 42 52.38 N 1.33 E
Aclimação ◆[8] 287b 23.34 S 46.37 W
Acme, Ab., Can. 182 51.30 N 113.30 W
Acme, Pa., U.S. 214 40.08 N 79.26 W
Acme, Wa., U.S. 224 48.43 N 122.12 W
Acmetonia 279b 40.32 N 79.49 W
Acobamba 248 12.48 S 74.34 W
Acolla 248 11.44 S 75.34 W
Acoma Indian Reservation ◆[4] 200 34.52 N 107.40 W
Acomayo, Perú 248 13.55 S 71.41 W
Acomayo, Perú 248 9.46 S 76.05 W
Aconcagua, Cerro ∧ 252 32.39 S 70.01 W
Aconchi 232 29.50 N 110.12 W
Aconibe 152 1.18 N 10.56 E
Acopiara 250 6.06 S 39.27 W
Açores (Azores) II 148a 38.30 N 28.00 W
Acoria 248 12.37 S 74.53 W
Acorizal 248 15.12 S 56.22 W
Acornhoek 156 24.37 S 31.02 E
Acosta 214 40.07 N 79.04 W
Acoyapa 236 11.58 N 85.10 W
Acoyapa ≐ 236 11.48 N 85.16 W
Acquabona, Passo di)(68 39.02 N 16.20 E
Acquacalda 70 38.31 N 14.57 E
Acqualagna 66 43.37 N 12.40 E
Acquanegra sul Chiese 64 45.10 N 10.26 E
Acquapendente 66 42.44 N 11.52 E
Acquappesa 68 39.29 N 15.57 E
Acquarossa 58 46.28 N 8.57 E
Acquasanta Terme 66 42.46 N 13.24 E
Acquasparta 66 42.41 N 12.33 E
Acquaviva 66 43.57 N 12.25 E
Acquaviva delle Fonti 68 40.54 N 16.50 E
Acquaviva Platani 70 37.34 N 13.42 E
Acqui Terme 62 44.41 N 8.28 E
Acra 210 42.19 N 74.03 W
Acraman, Lake ⊜ 162 32.02 S 135.26 E
Acre → 'Akko 132 32.55 N 35.05 E
Acre □[3] 248 9.00 S 70.00 W
Acre ≐ 248 8.45 S 67.22 W
Acre Homes 222 29.53 N 95.27 W
Acri 68 39.29 N 16.23 E
Acropolis ⊥ 267c 37.58 N 23.43 E
Acrotambo, Cerro ∧ 248 8.50 S 76.50 W
Acton, On., Can. 212 43.37 N 80.02 W
Acton, Ca., U.S. 228 34.28 N 118.11 W
Acton, Ma., U.S. 207 42.29 N 71.26 W
Acton, Tx., U.S. 222 32.27 N 97.41 W
Acton ◆[8] 260 51.30 N 0.16 W
Acton Bridge 262 53.16 N 2.36 W
Acton Homes 158 28.36 S 29.26 E
Acton Lake ⊜ 218 39.34 N 84.45 W
Acton Turville 42 51.32 N 2.17 W
Acton-Vale 206 45.39 N 72.34 W
Actopan 234 20.16 N 98.56 W
Actopan ≐ 234 19.25 N 96.20 W
Açu 250 5.34 S 36.54 W
Açuã ≐ 248 7.12 S 64.11 W
Açucena 255 19.04 S 42.32 W
Acuitzio del Canje 234 19.29 N 101.20 W
Ačujevo 78 45.43 N 37.45 E
Acuña 252 29.55 S 57.58 W
Acurauá ≐ 248 7.37 S 70.48 W
Acurenam 152 1.02 N 10.40 E
Acushnet 207 41.41 N 70.55 W
Acuto 66 41.47 N 13.10 E
Acvež 80 58.21 N 47.46 E
Acworth 192 34.03 N 84.40 W
Ada, Ghana 150 5.47 N 0.24 E
Ada, Jugo. 38 45.48 N 20.08 E
Ada, Nihon 174m 26.44 N 128.19 E
Ada, Mi., U.S. 216 42.57 N 85.29 W
Ada, Mn., U.S. 198 47.18 N 96.31 W
Ada, Oh., U.S. 216 40.46 N 83.49 W
Ada, Ok., U.S. 196 34.46 N 96.40 W
Ada, Mount ∧ 180 56.41 N 134.40 W
Adaba 144 7.00 N 39.24 E
A-da-Beja 266c 38.47 N 9.14 W
'Adabīyah, Ra's > 142 29.52 N 32.30 E
Adachi ◆[8] 268 35.45 N 139.48 E
Adachi-yama ∧ 96 33.51 N 130.55 E
Adado, Ras > 144 11.20 N 48.40 E
Adâfer el Abiod ◆[1] 150 19.30 N 10.00 W
Adai 272c 19.01 N 73.08 E
Adailo 144 14.28 N 40.52 E
Adainville 261 48.43 N 1.39 E
Adair, Ia., U.S. 198 41.22 N 94.19 W
Adair, Ok., U.S. 196 36.26 N 95.16 W
Adair □[6] 219 40.08 N 92.22 W
Adair, Bahía de c 200 31.30 N 113.48 W
Adair, Cape > 176 71.24 N 71.13 W
Adairsville 192 34.22 N 84.56 W
Adairville 194 36.40 N 86.51 W
Adaja ≐ 34 41.32 N 4.52 W
Adajevka 86 51.47 N 62.06 E
Adak, Ross. 24 66.30 N 59.38 E
Adak, Ak., U.S. 180 51.54 N 176.35 W
Adaka-shima I 174m 26.45 N 128.20 E
Adak Island I 180 51.45 N 176.40 W
Adakli 130 39.14 N 40.30 E
Ådalen V 26 63.10 N 17.16 E
Ādam 118 22.24 N 57.32 E
Adam, Mount ∧ 254 51.35 S 59.55 W
Adamantina 255 21.42 S 51.04 W
Adamaoua ⋏ 152 7.00 N 12.00 E
Adamawa → Adamaoua ⋏ 152 7.00 N 12.00 E
Adamclisi 38 44.05 N 27.57 E
Adamello ∧ 64 46.10 N 10.35 E
Adaminaby 171b 36.03 S 148.43 E
Adami Tulu 144 7.52 N 38.42 E
Adamovka 86 51.32 N 59.56 E
Adamovskoje 82 54.52 N 35.57 E
Adamów 50 51.45 N 22.17 E
Ādampur 123 31.26 N 75.43 E
Adams, In., U.S. 218 39.22 N 85.33 W
Adams, Ma., U.S. 207 42.37 N 73.07 W
Adams, Mn., U.S. 190 43.33 N 92.43 W
Adams, Ne., U.S. 198 40.27 N 96.30 W
Adams, N.Y., U.S. 212 43.48 N 76.01 W
Adams, N.D., U.S. 198 48.25 N 98.04 W
Adams, Tn., U.S. 194 36.34 N 87.03 W
Adams, Wi., U.S. 190 43.57 N 89.49 W
Adams □[6], Il., U.S. 219 39.56 N 91.23 W
Adams □[6], In., U.S. 216 40.50 N 84.56 W
Adams □[6], Oh., U.S. 218 38.48 N 83.32 W
Adams □[6], Pa., U.S. 208 39.48 N 77.15 W
Adams ≐ 182 50.52 N 119.35 W
Adams, Mount ∧, N.Z. 172 41.19 S 175.46 E
Adams, Mount ∧, Wa., U.S. 224 46.12 N 121.28 W
Adams Bridge ◆[2] 122 9.04 N 79.37 E
Adamsburg 279b 40.19 N 79.40 W
Adams Center 212 43.51 N 76.00 W
Adams Creek ≐ 224 46.18 N 121.40 W
Adams Lake ⊜ 182 51.13 N 119.33 W
Adams Mills 214 40.09 N 81.57 W
Adams National Historic Site ⊥ 283 42.15 N 71.01 W
Adams Park 216 42.08 N 85.29 W
Adams Park ♦ 275b 43.48 N 79.09 W
Adams Peak ∧ 122 6.48 N 80.30 E
Adams Rock I[2] 174e 25.04 S 130.05 W
Adamston 208 40.02 N 74.05 W
Adamstown, Austl. 170 32.56 S 151.44 E
Adamstown, Pit. 174e 25.04 S 130.05 W
Adamstown, Md., U.S. 208 39.18 N 77.28 W
Adamstown, Pa., U.S. 208 40.14 N 76.03 W
Adamsville, P.Q., Can. 206 45.17 N 72.47 W
Adamsville, Mi., U.S. 216 41.47 N 86.00 W
Adamsville, Oh., U.S. 214 40.04 N 81.53 W
Adamsville, Pa., U.S. 214 41.31 N 80.22 W
Adamsville, Tn., U.S. 194 35.14 N 88.23 W
'Adan (Aden) 144 12.45 N 45.12 E
Adana 130 37.01 N 35.18 E
Adana □[4] 130 37.20 N 35.45 E
Adanero 34 40.56 N 4.36 W
Adarama 140 17.05 N 34.54 E
Adare 48 52.34 N 8.48 W
Adare, Cape > 9 71.17 S 170.14 E
Adar Gwagwa, Jabal ∧ 140 22.15 N 35.20 E
Adarot 140 17.50 N 36.07 E
Adaševo 80 53.56 N 44.19 E
Adauli 272c 19.06 N 73.02 E
Adaut 164 8.08 S 131.07 E
Adavale 166 25.55 S 144.36 E
Adda ≐, It. 36 45.08 N 9.53 E
Adda ≐, Sūd. 140 9.51 N 24.50 E
Ad-Dab'ah 140 31.02 N 28.26 E
Ad-Dabbah 140 18.03 N 30.57 E
Ad-Dafīnah 128 23.18 N 41.58 E
Ad-Dafrah ◆[1] 128 23.25 N 53.25 E
Ad-Dahnā' ◆[2] 128 24.30 N 48.10 E
Ad-Daljamūn 142 30.48 N 30.50 E
Ad-Damazin 140 11.49 N 34.23 E
Ad-Dāmir 140 17.35 N 33.58 E
Ad-Dammām 128 26.26 N 50.07 E
Ad-Dāmūr 132 33.44 N 35.27 E
Ad-Dānā 130 36.13 N 36.46 E
Ad-Daqahlīyah □[4] 142 31.10 N 31.30 E
Ad-Darb 144 17.43 N 42.15 E
Ad-Dawādimī 128 24.28 N 44.18 E
Ad-Dawhah (Doha) 128 25.17 N 51.32 E
Ad-Dayr, Miṣr 140 25.20 N 32.35 E
Ad-Dayr, Miṣr 142 30.20 N 31.36 E
Adderbury 42 52.00 N 1.17 W
Ad-Dibdibah ◆[1] 128 28.00 N 46.30 E
Addicks 222 29.47 N 95.39 W
Addicks Reservoir ⊜[1] 222 29.49 N 95.40 W
Addieville 219 38.23 N 89.29 W
Ad-Diffah (Libyan Plateau) ◆[1] 140 30.30 N 25.30 E
Ad-Dilam 128 23.59 N 47.12 E
Ad-Dilinjāt 142 30.50 N 30.30 E
Ad-Dīmās 132 33.35 N 36.05 E
Addingham 44 53.57 N 1.53 W
Addington 260 51.18 N 0.03 W
Addis 194 30.21 N 91.15 W
Addis Ababa → Adis Abeba 144 9.02 N 38.42 E
Addison, Il., U.S. 216 41.55 N 87.59 W
Addison, Mi., U.S. 216 41.59 N 84.21 W
Addison, N.Y., U.S. 210 42.06 N 77.14 W
Addison, Tx., U.S. 222 32.57 N 96.49 W
Addison Creek ≐ 278 41.51 N 87.51 W
Ad-Dīwānīyah 128 31.59 N 44.56 E
Addlestone 260 51.22 N 0.30 W
Addo 158 33.32 S 25.45 E
Addo Elephant National Park ♦ 158 33.29 S 25.46 E
Ad-Du'ayn 140 11.26 N 26.09 E
Ad-Duhayr 132 31.11 N 34.08 E
Ad-Duqqī 273c 30.04 N 31.15 E
Ad-Duwayd 128 30.15 N 42.17 E
Ad-Duwaym 140 14.00 N 32.19 E
Ad-Duwayr 132 33.23 N 35.25 E
Adébour 146 13.20 N 11.54 E
Adego 144 8.58 N 49.35 E
Adel, Ga., U.S. 192 31.08 N 83.25 W
Adel, Ia., U.S. 190 41.36 N 94.01 W
Adelaida → Adelaide 168b 34.55 S 138.35 E
Adelaide, Austl. 168b 34.55 S 138.35 E
Adelaide, Ba. 240b 25.00 N 77.31 W
Adelaide, S. Afr. 158 32.42 S 26.20 E
Adelaide Airport ✈ 168b 34.58 S 138.32 E
Adelaide Island I 9 67.15 S 68.30 W
Adelaide Peninsula >[1] 176 68.09 N 97.45 W
Adelaide River 164 13.15 S 131.06 E
Adelanto 228 34.34 N 117.24 W
Adelbert Range ⋏ 164 4.35 S 145.10 E
Adelboden 58 46.30 N 7.33 E
Adelebsen 52 51.34 N 9.45 E
Adèle Island I 160 15.32 S 123.09 E
Adelfia 68 41.00 N 16.52 E
Adélie Coast ⊥[2] 9 67.00 S 139.00 E
Adelong 171b 35.19 S 148.03 E
Adelong Creek ≐ 171b 35.06 S 148.02 E
Adelphi 284c 39.00 N 76.58 W
Adelphia 208 40.13 N 74.15 W
Adelphi University ⊥[2] 276 40.43 N 73.36 W
Adelsheim 56 49.24 N 9.23 E
Adelsö I 40 59.23 N 17.30 E
Adelzhausen 60 48.21 N 11.08 E
Aden → 'Adan 144 12.45 N 45.12 E
Aden, Gulf of c 136 12.30 N 48.00 E
Adena 214 40.13 N 80.52 W
Adenau 50 50.23 N 6.55 E
Adendorf 52 53.17 N 10.26 E
Adendorp 158 32.20 S 24.33 E
Ader ⋏[1] 150 14.50 N 5.15 E
Aderklaa 264b 48.17 N 16.32 E
Adéta 150 7.08 N 0.44 E
Adhāta 272b 22.52 N 88.32 E
'Adhirīyāt, Jibāl al- ⋏[2] 132 30.25 N 36.48 E
Adi 154 3.24 N 30.48 E
Adi, Pulau I 164 4.18 S 133.26 E
Adiaké 150 5.16 N 3.17 W
Adi Arkay 144 13.27 N 37.57 E
Adi Dairo 144 14.23 N 38.12 E
Adieu, Cape > 162 31.59 S 132.09 E
Adigala 144 10.25 N 42.14 E
Adige (Etsch) ≐ 64 45.10 N 12.20 E
Adigeni 84 41.42 N 42.42 E
Adigrat 144 14.17 N 39.28 E
Adigüzel Barajı ⊜[1] 130 38.10 N 29.15 E
Adi Keyih 144 14.51 N 39.22 E
Adi Kwala 144 14.38 N 38.50 E
Ādilābād 122 19.40 N 78.32 E
Adilang 154 2.44 N 33.29 E
Adilcevaz 84 38.44 N 42.44 E
Adimi 89 47.20 N 138.56 E
Adin 204 41.11 N 120.56 W
Adinkerke 50 51.04 N 2.36 E
Adirondack Mountains ⋏ 188 44.00 N 74.00 W
Adirondack Park ♦ 188 44.00 N 74.20 W
Adis Abeba (Addis Ababa) 144 9.02 N 38.42 E
Adis Zemen 144 12.07 N 37.47 E
Adi Ugri 144 14.53 N 38.49 E
Adiwerna 115a 6.56 S 109.07 E
Adiyaman 130 37.46 N 38.17 E
Adiyaman □[4] 130 37.45 N 38.30 E
Adjan 112 2.11 N 113.12 E
Adjelman, Oued V 148 22.09 N 3.47 E
Adjohon 150 6.42 N 2.28 E
Adjud 38 46.04 N 27.11 E
Adjumani 154 3.22 N 31.47 E
Adjuntas 240m 18.10 N 66.43 W
Adler 78 43.27 N 39.55 E
Adler Planetarium ⊥ 278 41.52 N 87.37 W
Adlershof ◆[8] 264a 52.26 N 13.33 E
Adlington 44 53.37 N 2.36 W
Adlington Hall ⊥ 262 53.19 N 2.09 W
Adliswil 58 47.19 N 8.32 E
Admer, Erg d' ◆[2] 148 24.00 N 9.15 E
Admiral 184 49.43 N 108.01 W
Admiralitäts-Inseln → Admiralty Islands II 164 2.10 S 147.00 E
Admiralty Bay c, St. Vin. 241h 13.00 N 61.16 W
Admiralty Bay c, Ak., U.S. 180 70.53 N 155.45 W
Admiralty Gulf c 160 14.20 S 125.50 E
Admiralty Gulf Aboriginal Reserve ◆[4] 164 14.40 S 125.30 E
Admiralty Inlet c, N.T., Can. 176 73.00 N 86.00 W
Admiralty Inlet c, Wa., U.S. 224 48.05 N 122.39 W
Admiralty Island I, N.T., Can. 176 69.30 N 101.00 W
Admiralty Island I, Ak., U.S. 180 57.50 N 134.30 W
Admiralty Islands II 164 2.10 S 147.00 E
Admiralty Mountains ⋏ 9 71.45 S 168.30 E
Admont 61 47.34 N 14.27 E
Adna 224 46.38 N 123.04 W
Ado ≐ 94 35.19 N 136.05 E
Adobe Creek ≐, Ca., U.S. 282 37.26 N 122.06 W
Adobe Creek ≐, Co., U.S. 198 38.05 N 103.18 W
Ado-Ekiti 150 7.38 N 5.12 E
Adogawa 94 35.20 N 136.02 E
Adok 140 8.11 N 30.19 E
Adolfo López Mateos 232 28.28 N 107.20 W
Adolfo López Mateos, Presa ⊜[1] 232 25.13 N 107.25 W
Adolfsberg 40 59.15 N 15.10 E
Adolphus Reach ⊥ 212 44.05 N 76.55 W
Adonara, Pulau I 112 8.20 S 123.10 E
Ādoni 122 15.38 N 77.17 E
Ado-Odo 150 6.36 N 2.56 E
Adorf 54 50.19 N 12.15 E
Adoua, Korén V 150 14.37 N 6.40 E
Adour ≐ 32 43.32 N 1.32 W
Adowa → Adwa 144 14.10 N 38.55 E
Adra, Esp. 34 36.44 N 3.01 W
Ādra, India 126 23.30 N 86.40 E
'Adrā, Sūrīy. 132 33.37 N 36.30 E
Adranga 154 2.54 N 30.26 E
Adrano 70 37.40 N 14.50 E
Adrar 148 27.54 N 0.17 W
Adrar □[4] 150 20.05 N 11.00 W
Adrar □[5] 148 26.00 N 1.00 W
Adrâr ◆[1] 134 20.30 N 13.30 W
Adraskan 128 33.39 N 62.16 E
Adrasman 85 40.38 N 69.58 E
Adré 146 13.28 N 22.12 E
Adrī 146 27.32 N 13.14 E
Adria 64 45.03 N 12.03 E
Adrian, Ga., U.S. 192 32.31 N 82.35 W
Adrian, Mi., U.S. 216 41.53 N 84.02 W
Adrian, Mn., U.S. 198 43.38 N 95.55 W
Adrian, Mo., U.S. 194 38.23 N 94.21 W
Adrian, Oh., U.S. 214 41.03 N 83.20 W
Adrian, Or., U.S. 202 43.44 N 117.04 W
Adrian, Pa., U.S. 214 40.53 N 79.32 W
Adrian, Tx., U.S. 196 35.16 N 102.40 W
Adrian, W.V., U.S. 188 38.54 N 80.16 W
Adrianople → Edirne 130 41.40 N 26.34 E
Adrianópolis 287a 22.39 S 43.30 W
Adrianovka 88 51.34 N 114.30 E
Adriatico, Mar → Adriatic Sea ⊤[2] 22 42.30 N 16.00 E
Adriatic Sea ⊤[2] 22 42.30 N 16.00 E
Adriatique, Mer → Adriatic Sea ⊤[2] 22 42.30 N 16.00 E
Adriatisches Meer → Adriatic Sea ⊤[2] 22 42.30 N 16.00 E
Adrigole 48 51.40 N 9.42 W
Adro 64 45.37 N 9.57 E
Adrogué → Almirante Brown 258 34.48 S 58.23 W
Adstock, Mont ∧ 206 46.02 N 71.12 W
Adua 164 1.55 S 129.50 E
Aduard 52 53.15 N 6.26 E
Adujevo 82 54.59 N 35.59 E
Aduku 154 2.01 N 32.43 E
A Dun ≐ 110 13.24 N 108.28 E
Adur ≐ 42 50.49 N 0.16 W
Adusa 154 1.23 N 28.01 E
Adutiškis 76 55.09 N 26.36 E
Advance 194 37.06 N 89.54 W
Adventure, Bahía c 254 44.50 S 74.45 W
Advie 46 57.23 N 3.27 W
Advocate Harbour 186 45.20 N 64.47 W
Adwa 144 14.10 N 38.55 E
Adwick le Street 44 53.34 N 1.11 W
Adyča ≐ 74 68.13 N 134.41 E
Adyge 84 44.19 N 41.57 E
Adygea → Adygeja □[3] 72 45.00 N 40.00 E
Adygeja □[3] 72 45.00 N 40.00 E
Adyk 80 45.48 N 45.38 E
Adžarskaja Respublika □[3] 84 41.40 N 42.00 E
Adž Bogd uul ⋏ 102 44.52 N 95.10 E
Adžima 89 48.08 N 139.40 E
Adzopé 150 6.06 N 3.52 W
Adz'va ≐ 24 66.36 N 59.28 E
Adz'vavom 24 66.36 N 59.12 E
Ae, Water of ≐ 44 55.08 N 3.27 W
Æbelø I 41 55.38 N 10.12 E
Aegean Sea ⊤[2] 38 38.30 N 25.00 E
Aegerisee ⊜ 58 47.07 N 8.38 E
Aegina → Aíyina I 38 37.46 N 23.26 E
Aegviidu 76 59.17 N 25.37 E
Aek Humbang 114 1.59 N 99.11 E
Aeknabara 114 1.17 N 99.45 E
Aeon Point > 174o 1.46 N 157.11 W
Aerhuola 89 51.01 N 120.10 E
Aerku Hu ⊜ 120 30.43 N 82.55 E
Ærø I 41 54.53 N 10.20 E
Aeroflots'kyj 78 45.43 N 34.01 E
Aeron ≐ 42 52.14 N 4.16 W
Aeronáutica, Centro de Instrucción de ◆[2] 286d 12.09 S 77.00 W
Ærøskøbing 41 54.53 N 10.25 E
Aerqi Shan ∧ 89 48.35 N 121.07 E
Aershatu 102 44.11 N 113.36 E
Aerzen 52 52.03 N 9.16 E
Aesch 58 47.28 N 7.36 E
Aeschi 58 46.40 N 7.42 E
Aetna 182 49.08 N 113.15 W
Afaahiti 174s 17.43 S 149.19 W
Afadé 146 12.14 N 14.38 E
Afadjoto ∧[2] 150 7.05 N 0.35 E
'Afak 128 32.04 N 45.15 E
Afan ≐ 42 51.35 N 3.48 W
Afanasjeva 78 50.47 N 38.36 E
Afanasjevo, Ross. 24 58.52 N 53.12 E
Afanasjevo, Ross. 82 54.20 N 37.01 E
Afanasjevo, Ross. 82 55.18 N 36.12 E
Afanasjevskoje 86 56.49 N 58.17 E
Afándou 36 36.17 N 28.10 E
Afar 148 25.30 N 8.22 E
Afareaitu 174s 17.33 S 149.47 W
Afars and Issas → Djibouti □[1] 144 11.30 N 43.00 E
Afaspida 272c 19.08 N 73.04 E
Afdem 144 9.28 N 41.00 E
Afferde, Dtsch. 52 52.06 N 9.25 E
Afferde, Dtsch. 263 51.34 N 7.39 E
Affery 150 6.19 N 3.57 W
Affi 64 45.33 N 10.46 E
Affing 58 48.27 N 10.58 E
Afflisses, Oued V 148 28.29 N 1.09 E
Affoltern am Albis 58 47.17 N 8.27 E
Affori ◆[8] 266b 45.31 N 9.10 E
Affric ≐ 46 57.19 N 4.50 W
Affric, Glen V 46 57.17 N 4.56 W
Affton 219 38.33 N 90.19 W
Afghānestān → Afghanistan □[1] 118 33.00 N 65.00 E
Afghanistan (Afghānestān) □[1] 118 33.00 N 65.00 E
Afgooye 144 2.09 N 45.07 E
Afia 114 1.23 N 97.32 E
'Afīf 128 23.55 N 42.56 E
Afikpo 150 5.53 N 7.56 E
Afipskij 78 44.55 N 38.50 E
Afiqim 132 32.40 N 35.35 E
Afjord 26 63.58 N 10.12 E
Aflao 150 6.05 N 1.08 E
Aflenz Kurort 61 47.32 N 15.14 E
Aflou 148 34.07 N 2.06 E
Afmadow 144 0.31 N 42.04 E
Afodo 144 10.14 N 34.39 E
Afogados da Ingazeira 250 7.45 S 37.39 W
Afognak Island I 180 58.15 N 152.30 W
Afollé ⋏[2] 150 16.55 N 10.25 W
Afonicha 24 68.13 N 53.17 E
Afono Bay c 174u 14.15 S 170.39 W
Afonso Arinos 256 22.00 S 43.20 W
Afonso Bezerra 250 5.30 S 36.30 W
Afonso Claudio 255 20.05 S 41.08 W
Afonsos, Campo dos ■ 287a 22.53 S 43.23 W
Afragola 68 40.55 N 14.18 E
Afram ≐ 150 7.00 N 0.52 W
Africa ⊥[1] 4 10.00 N 22.00 E
Africa ⊥[1] 10 10.00 N 22.00 E
Africa del Sur → South Africa □[1] 156 30.00 S 26.00 E
Africo 68 38.04 N 15.59 E
Afrika → Africa ⊥[1] 10 10.00 N 22.00 E
Afrikanda 24 67.25 N 32.43 E
'Afrīn 130 36.31 N 36.52 E
'Afrīn ≐ 130 36.22 N 36.28 E
Afrique → Africa ⊥[1] 10 10.00 N 22.00 E
Afrique du Sud (République d') → South Africa □[1] 156 30.00 S 26.00 E
Afritz 64 46.43 N 13.48 E
Afşin 130 38.15 N 36.55 E
Afsluitdijk ◆[5] 52 53.00 N 5.15 E
Afton, De., U.S. 285 39.49 N 75.29 W
Afton, Ia., U.S. 194 41.01 N 94.11 W
Afton, N.Y., U.S. 210 42.13 N 75.31 W
Afton, Ok., U.S. 196 36.41 N 94.57 W
Afton, Wi., U.S. 216 42.36 N 89.04 W
Afton, Wy., U.S. 200 42.43 N 110.55 W
Aftout ◆[1] 148 26.40 N 3.48 W
Afuá 250 0.10 S 50.23 W
'Afula 132 32.36 N 35.17 E
'Afula 'Illit 132 32.38 N 35.20 E
Afulu 114 1.17 N 97.15 E
Afyon 130 38.45 N 30.33 E
Afyon □[4] 130 38.40 N 30.30 E
Afyonkarahisar → Afyon 130 38.45 N 30.33 E
Afzalgarh 124 29.24 N 78.41 E
Aga, Nor. 26 60.18 N 6.36 E
Aga, Ross. 88 51.12 N 115.10 E
Aga ≐ 88 51.30 N 115.50 E
Agačag 85 44.03 N 71.58 E
Ağaçören 130 38.52 N 33.56 E
Agadez 150 16.58 N 7.59 E
Agadez □[5] 146 19.45 N 12.00 E
Agadez, Ighazer oua-n- V 150 17.28 N 6.26 E
Agadir 148 30.26 N 9.36 W
Agadir □[4] 148 30.40 N 8.55 W
Agâdîr, Râs > 148 20.34 N 16.32 W
Agadyr' 86 48.17 N 72.53 E
Agafonovka 80 50.36 N 47.26 E
Agāhpur 272a 28.34 N 77.22 E
Agaie 150 9.03 N 6.18 E
Ägäisches Meer → Aegean Sea ⊤[2] 38 38.30 N 25.00 E
Agalak 140 11.01 N 32.42 E
Agalega Islands II 138 10.24 S 56.37 E
Agal Terara ∧ 144 6.57 N 40.08 E
Agan ≐ 72 61.23 N 74.35 E

Symbols in the index entries represent the broad categories identified in the key at the right. Symbols with superior numbers (⋏[1]) identify subcategories (see complete key on page *I · 1*).

Symbole im Register stellen die rechts im Schlüssel erklärten Kategorien dar. Symbole mit hochgestellten Ziffern (⋏[1]) bezeichnen Unterabteilungen einer Kategorie (vgl. vollständiger Schlüssel auf Seite *I · 1*).

Los símbolos incluídos en el texto del índice representan las grandes categorías identificadas con la clave a la derecha. Los símbolos con numeros en su parte superior (⋏[1]) identifican las subcategorías (véase la clave completa en la página *I · 1*).

Les symboles de l'index représentent les catégories indiquées dans la légende à droite. Les symboles suivis d'un indice (⋏[1]) représentent des sous-catégories (voir légende complète à la page *I · 1*).

Os símbolos incluídos no texto do índice representam as grandes categorias identificadas com a chave à direita. Os símbolos com números em sua parte superior (⋏[1]) identificam as subcategorias (veja-se a chave completa à página *I · 1*).

∧ Mountain	Berg	Montaña	Montagne	Montanha
⋏ Mountains	Gebirge	Montañas	Montagnes	Montanhas
)(Pass	Paß	Paso	Col	Passo
V Valley, Canyon	Tal, Cañon	Valle, Cañón	Vallée, Canyon	Vale, Canhão
≚ Plain	Ebene	Llano	Plaine	Planície
> Cape	Kap	Cabo	Cap	Cabo
I Island	Insel	Isla	Île	Ilha
II Islands	Inseln	Islas	Îles	Ilhas
⊥ Other Topographic Features	Andere Topographische Objekte	Otros Elementos Topográficos	Autres données topographiques	Outros acidentes topográficos

ESPAÑOL · FRANÇAIS · PORTUGUÊS

Nombre / Nom / Nome	Página / Page / Página	Lat.°'	Long.°' W = Oeste / W = Ouest / W = Oeste
Agana	174p	13.28 N	144.45 E
Agana Heights	174p	13.28 N	144.45 E
Agano ≃	92	37.57 N	139.08 E
Agapa	74	71.27 N	89.15 E
Aga Point >	174p	13.15 N	144.43 E
Agapovka	86	53.18 N	59.28 E
Agar	120	23.42 N	76.01 E
Agara	84	42.03 N	43.49 E
Agâraktem ⊤4	148	23.11 N	6.20 W
Ågård	41	55.35 N	9.26 E
Agaro	144	7.50 N	36.40 E
Agartala	120	23.49 N	91.16 E
Agartu	80	49.49 N	47.06 E
Agaru	140	10.59 N	34.44 E
Agaruut	102	43.10 N	109.26 E
Agasan	272c	19.11 N	73.04 E
Agassiz	224	49.14 N	121.46 W
Agassiz, Cape >	9	68.29 S	62.56 W
Agassiz Pool ⊜	198	48.20 N	95.58 W
Agat	174p	13.24 N	144.39 E
Agat Bay c	174p	13.24 N	144.39 E
Agate	198	39.27 N	103.56 W
Agate Beach	202	44.40 N	124.03 W
Agate Fossil Beds National Monument ♠	198	42.25 N	103.43 W
Agathonísion I	38	37.28 N	27.00 E
Agats	164	5.33 S	138.08 E
Agatsuma	94	36.34 N	138.50 E
Agatsuma ≃	94	36.30 N	139.01 E
Agatti Island I	122	10.50 N	72.12 E
Agattu Island I	181a	52.25 N	173.35 E
Agattu Strait ᥕ	181a	52.35 N	173.25 E
Agawa	96	33.34 N	133.10 E
Agawa ≃	190	47.21 N	84.38 W
Agawa Bay c	190	47.20 N	84.42 W
Agawa Canyon V	190	47.27 N	84.29 W
Agawam, Ma., U.S.	207	42.04 N	72.36 W
Agawam, Mt., U.S.	182	48.00 N	112.10 W
Agay	62	43.26 N	6.51 E
Agazzano	62	44.57 N	9.31 E
Agbaja	150	7.58 N	6.38 E
Agbede	273a	6.40 N	3.29 E
Agbélouvé	150	6.40 N	1.10 E
Agboju	273a	6.28 N	3.17 E
Agboville	150	5.56 N	4.13 W
Agboyi Creek ≃	273a	6.34 N	3.25 E
Ağcabädi	84	40.03 N	47.28 E
Agcawayan	116	13.46 N	120.16 E
Ağdam	84	39.59 N	46.57 E
Ağdärä	84	40.12 N	46.48 E
Ağdaş	84	40.38 N	47.28 E
Agde	32	43.19 N	3.28 E
Agde, Cap d' >	32	43.16 N	3.30 E
Agege	273a	6.37 N	3.20 E
Agejevo	82	54.10 N	36.29 E
Agematsu	94	35.47 N	137.42 E
Agen	32	44.12 N	0.37 E
Agency	190	40.59 N	92.18 W
Agency Lake ⊜	202	42.32 N	121.58 W
Ageo	94	35.58 N	139.36 E
Agepsta, gora ʌ	84	43.32 N	40.30 E
Ager ≃	60	48.05 N	13.51 E
Agerbæk	41	55.36 N	8.48 E
Agerskov	41	55.07 N	9.08 E
Agersø I	41	55.12 N	11.12 E
Agery	168b	34.10 S	137.44 E
Ágfalva	61	47.41 N	16.31 E
Aggeneis	158	29.03 S	18.51 E
Agger ≃	56	50.48 N	7.11 E
Aggherar	144	4.03 N	42.40 E
Aggius	71	40.56 N	9.04 E
Aggstein ⊥	61	48.18 N	15.25 E
Aggteleki Nemzeti Park ♠	30	48.30 N	20.32 E
Āghā Jārī	128	30.42 N	49.50 E
Aghleam	48	54.08 N	10.07 W
Aghzoumal, Sabkhat ⊜	148	24.21 N	12.52 W
Agia	124	26.05 N	90.32 E
Agidingbi	273a	6.38 N	3.21 E
Agimont	56	50.10 N	4.48 E
Ağın	130	38.57 N	38.43 E
Agincourt ◆8	275b	43.48 N	79.17 W
Aginskoje, Ross.	86	55.15 N	94.55 E
Aginskoje, Ross.	88	51.06 N	114.32 E
Agira	70	37.39 N	14.31 E
Aglasterhausen	56	49.21 N	8.59 E
Ağlasun	130	37.40 N	30.32 E
Agliana	66	43.54 N	11.00 E
Agliano	62	44.47 N	8.15 E
Aglientu	71	41.05 N	9.07 E
Agly ≃	32	42.47 N	3.02 E
Agna	64	45.10 N	11.58 E
Agnadello	62	45.26 N	9.33 E
Agnes, Mount ʌ	162	26.51 S	128.59 E
Agnes Lake ⊜	190	48.13 N	91.21 W
Agnew	162	28.01 S	120.30 E
Agnew Lake ⊜1	190	46.22 N	81.45 W
Agnews Hill ʌ2	48	54.51 N	5.56 W
Agnibilékrou	150	7.08 N	3.12 W
Agnije-Afanasjevskij	89	51.57 N	138.45 E
Agnita	38	45.59 N	24.38 E
Agno, Pil.	116	16.07 N	119.48 E
Agno, Schw.	58	46.00 N	8.54 E
Agno ≃, It.	64	45.31 N	11.22 E
Agno ≃, Pil.	116	16.02 N	120.08 E
Agnone	66	41.48 N	14.22 E
Agnone Bagni ◆8	70	37.18 N	15.06 E
Ago	92	34.20 N	136.51 E
Agogna ≃	62	45.04 N	8.54 E
Agogo, Ghana	150	6.47 N	1.04 W
Agogo, Sūd.	140	7.49 N	28.52 E
Agoo	116	16.20 N	120.22 E
Agordat → Akordat	144	15.33 N	37.53 E
Agordo	64	46.17 N	12.02 E
Agostinho Pôrto	287a	22.47 S	43.23 W
Agostitlán	234	19.33 N	100.41 W
Agou, Mont ʌ	150	6.52 N	0.46 E
Agouna	150	7.34 N	1.42 E
Agoura Hills	228	34.08 N	118.44 W
Agout ≃	32	43.47 N	1.41 E
Agoza ⊥	146	18.30 N	23.45 E
Āgra	124	27.11 N	78.01 E
Āgra Canal ≍	272a	28.34 N	77.18 E
Agrachanskij poluostrov >1	84	43.42 N	47.36 E
Agraciada	258	33.48 S	58.15 W
Agrado	246	2.15 N	75.46 W
Agraf'novka	83	47.45 N	39.29 E
Agram → Zagreb	36	45.48 N	15.58 E
Agramonte	240p	22.41 N	81.07 W
Agrate Brianza	62	45.34 N	9.21 E
Ágreda	34	41.51 N	1.56 W
Ağrı	84	39.44 N	43.03 E
Ağrı ▫4	84	39.30 N	43.15 E
Agri ≃	68	40.13 N	16.44 E
Agri Bavnehøj ʌ2	41	56.14 N	10.33 E
Ağrı Dağı (Mount Ararat) ʌ	84	39.42 N	44.18 E
Agrigento	70	37.18 N	13.35 E
Agrigento ▫4	70	37.27 N	13.30 E
Agrihan I	108	18.46 N	145.40 E
Agrínion	38	38.37 N	21.24 E
Agrio ≃	252	38.21 S	69.43 W
Agropoli	68	40.21 N	15.00 E
Agro Pontino ◆1	66	41.25 N	12.55 E
Agryz	80	56.33 N	53.00 E
Ağstafa	84	41.08 N	45.28 E
Ağsu	84	40.34 N	48.24 E
Agtuuganon, Mount ʌ	116	7.48 N	126.12 E
Agua, Ilha d' I	287a	22.49 S	43.10 W
Agua, Volcán de ʌ1	236	14.28 N	90.45 W
Água Branca, Bra.	250	9.17 S	37.55 W
Água Branca, Bra.	250	7.31 S	37.40 W
Água Branca, Bra.	250	5.53 S	42.38 W
Agua Brava, Laguna c	234	22.10 N	105.32 W
Agua Caliente, Méx.	232	27.27 N	108.32 W
Agua Caliente, Méx.	234	23.20 N	105.20 W
Agua Caliente Creek ≃	282	37.29 N	121.56 W
Agua Caliente Grande	232	26.31 N	108.22 W
Aguacate	240p	22.59 N	81.49 W
Aguachica	246	8.19 N	73.38 W
Água Clara	255	20.27 S	52.52 W
Aguada	240m	18.23 N	67.11 W
Aguada, Zanjón de la ≃	286e	33.30 S	70.47 W
Aguada Cecilio	254	40.51 S	65.51 W
Aguada de Guerra	254	41.04 S	68.25 W
Aguada de Pasajeros	240p	22.23 N	80.51 W
Aguadas	246	5.37 N	75.27 W
Aguadilla	240m	18.26 N	67.09 W
Água Doce	252	27.00 S	51.33 W
Agua Dulce, Méx.	234	18.08 N	94.08 W
Aguadulce, Pan.	236	8.15 N	80.33 W
Agua Dulce, Ca., U.S.	228	34.30 N	118.23 W
Agua Dulce, Tx., U.S.	196	27.47 N	97.54 W
Agua Fria ≃	200	33.23 N	112.21 W
Agua Fria Creek ≃	282	37.28 N	121.56 W
Aguaí	256	22.04 S	46.58 W
Agualeguas	232	26.18 N	99.34 W
Água Limpa	255	18.06 S	48.46 W
Agualva-Cacém	266c	38.46 N	9.18 W
Aguán ≃	236	15.57 N	85.44 W
Aguanaval ≃	232	25.28 N	102.53 W
Agua Negra	286c	10.28 N	67.01 W
Aguanish	186	50.13 N	62.05 W
Aguanus ≃	186	50.13 N	62.05 W
Aguapeí ≃, Bra.	248	15.53 S	58.25 W
Aguapeí ≃, Bra.	255	21.03 S	51.47 W
Aguapey ≃	252	29.07 S	56.36 W
Água Preta, Igarapé ≃	246	1.41 S	63.48 W
Agua Prieta	232	31.18 N	109.34 W
Aguaragüe, Serranía de ⋏	248	21.30 S	63.40 W
Aguaray	252	22.16 S	63.44 W
Aguaray-Guazú ≃, Para.	252	24.47 S	57.19 W
Aguaray-Guazú ≃, Para.	252	24.05 S	56.40 W
Aguarico ≃	246	0.59 S	75.11 W
Aguaro-Guariquito, Parque Nacional ♠	246	8.10 N	66.50 W
Aguaruto	232	24.47 N	107.29 W
Aguas ≃	34	37.09 N	1.49 W
Águas, Serra das ʌ	256	21.55 S	45.25 W
Aguasabon ≃	190	48.46 N	87.07 W
Águas Belas	250	9.07 S	37.07 W
Aguas Buenas	240m	18.15 N	66.06 W
Aguascalientes, Méx.	200	32.18 N	115.10 W
Aguascalientes, Méx.	234	21.53 N	102.18 W
Aguascalientes ▫3	234	22.00 N	102.30 W
Aguascalientes, Río de ≃	234	21.23 N	102.28 W
Aguas Corrientes	258	34.31 S	56.24 W
Águas da Prata	256	21.56 S	46.43 W
Águas de Contendas	256	21.54 S	45.01 W
Águas de Lindóia	256	22.29 S	46.39 W
Águas Formosas	255	17.05 S	40.57 W
Aguasvivas ≃	34	41.20 N	0.25 W
Agua Tibia ʌ	228	33.24 N	116.59 W
Água Vermelha, Represa de ⊜1	255	20.00 S	50.00 W
Agua-Viva	256	21.41 S	42.33 W
Aguayo	252	31.40 S	65.54 W
Aguaytía ≃	248	8.08 S	74.37 W
Agua Zarca	200	31.10 N	110.59 W
Agu Bay c	176	70.18 N	86.30 W
Agudos	255	22.28 S	49.00 W
Águeda	34	40.34 N	8.27 W
Águeda ≃	34	41.02 N	6.56 W
Aguelhok	150	19.28 N	0.52 E
Aguema	152	12.03 S	21.49 E
Aguenier, Lac ⊜	186	50.43 N	68.13 W
Agugliano	66	43.32 N	13.23 E
Agui	94	34.55 N	136.55 E
Aguié	150	13.30 N	7.47 E
Aguijan I	108	14.51 N	145.34 E
Aguila	200	33.56 N	113.10 W
Aguilar, Esp.	34	37.31 N	4.39 W
Aguilar, Co., U.S.	198	37.24 N	104.39 W
Aguilares, Arg.	252	27.26 S	65.37 W
Aguilares, El Sal.	236	13.58 N	89.12 W
Águilas	34	37.24 N	1.35 W
Aguililla	234	18.44 N	102.44 W
Aguirre ≃	246	8.28 N	61.02 W
Aguirre, Arroyo ≃	288	34.46 S	58.35 W
Aguirre, Bahía c	254	54.57 S	65.50 W
Aguit	102	41.52 N	112.56 E
Aguita Zarc	234	23.10 N	104.28 W
Aguja, Cerro ʌ	254	42.11 S	71.51 W
Aguja, Punta >	248	5.48 S	81.06 W
Aguja Point >	116	12.42 N	123.23 E
Agujas, Cabo de las → Agulhas, Cape >	158	34.52 S	20.00 E
Agujereada, Punta >	240m	18.31 N	67.08 W
Agujita	196	27.53 N	101.09 W
Agul ≃	88	55.44 N	95.41 E
Agulai	144	13.41 N	39.35 E
Agulhas	158	34.50 S	20.03 E
Agulhas, Cape >	158	34.52 S	20.00 E
Agulhas Basin ✣1	8	47.00 S	27.00 E
Agulhas Negras	256	22.28 S	44.27 W
Agulhas Negras, Pico das ʌ	256	22.23 S	44.38 W
Agulhas Plateau ✣3	10	40.00 S	26.00 E
Agung, Gunung ʌ	115b	8.21 S	115.30 E
Aguni-jima I	93b	26.35 N	127.14 E
Agusan ≃	116	9.00 N	125.31 E
Agusan del Norte ▫4	116	9.00 N	125.30 E
Agusan del Sur ▫4	116	8.30 N	125.40 E
Agustín Codazzi	246	10.02 N	73.14 W
Agutaya	116	11.09 N	120.56 E
Agutaya Island I	116	11.09 N	120.58 E
Ağva	130	41.09 N	29.50 E
Agvali	84	42.33 N	46.06 E
Agwarra	150	10.42 N	4.35 E
Ägypten → Egypt ▫1	140	27.00 N	30.00 E
Aha	174m	26.43 N	128.17 E
Ahaggar (Hoggar) ⋏	148	23.00 N	6.30 E
Ahaggar, Tassili ta-n- ⋏1	148	21.00 N	6.00 E
Aha Hills ⋏2	156	19.45 S	21.10 E
Aha-kō c	174m	26.43 N	128.18 E
Aham	60	48.32 N	12.28 E
Ahar	128	38.28 N	47.04 E
Ahar ≃	128	38.32 N	47.31 E
Ahascragh	48	53.24 N	8.20 W
Ahaura	172	42.21 S	171.32 E
Ahaura ≃	172	42.21 S	171.31 E
Ahaus	52	52.04 N	7.00 E
Aheggar ʌ	148	24.43 N	5.39 E
Ahfir	148	34.57 N	2.17 W
Ahimanawa Range ⋏	172	39.00 S	176.27 E
Ahipara	172	35.10 S	173.10 E
Ahipara Bay c	172	35.10 S	173.07 E
'Āhirah	132	32.53 N	36.28 E
Ahırlı	130	37.14 N	32.08 E
Ahklun Mountains ⋏	180	59.15 N	161.00 W
Ahlat, Tür.	128	38.45 N	42.29 E
Ahlat, Tür.	130	38.45 N	42.29 E
Ahlbeck	54	53.40 N	14.11 E
Ahlem	52	52.23 N	9.40 E
Ahlen	52	51.46 N	7.53 E
Ahlenberg	263	51.25 N	7.28 E
Ahlenmoor ◆3	52	53.40 N	8.45 E
Ahlhorn	52	52.54 N	8.14 E
Ahlsdorf	54	51.32 N	11.28 E
Ahmadābād	120	23.02 N	72.37 E
Aḥmadābād-e Sarjām	128	35.51 N	59.36 E
Aḥmad al-Bāqir, Jabal ʌ	132	29.36 N	35.08 E
Ahmadgarh	123	30.41 N	75.50 E
Ahmadnagar	122	19.05 N	74.44 E
Ahmadpur, India	124	23.31 N	77.13 E
Ahmadpur, India	126	23.50 N	87.42 E
Ahmadpur East	123	29.09 N	71.16 E
Ahmadpur Siāl	123	30.41 N	71.46 E
Ahmad Wāl	120	29.25 N	65.56 E
Aḥmar, Al-Baḥr al- → Red Sea ⊤2	136	20.00 N	38.00 E
Ahmar, 'Erg el ◆2	148	23.30 N	4.54 W
Aḥmar, Jabal al- ʌ	132	29.40 N	35.09 E
Ahmar Mountains ⋏	144	9.15 N	41.00 E
Ahmedabad → Ahmadābād	120	23.02 N	72.37 E
Ahmetli	130	38.31 N	27.57 E
Ahmic Lake ⊜	190	45.37 N	79.42 W
Ahnet ⋏	148	24.58 N	2.57 E
Ahnet, Tanezrouft n- ◆2	148	22.15 N	1.30 E
Ahoada	150	5.05 N	6.38 E
Ahoghill	48	54.51 N	6.22 W
Ahome	232	25.55 N	109.11 W
Ahon, Tarso ʌ	146	20.23 N	18.18 E
Ahornspitz ʌ	64	47.08 N	11.56 E
Ahoskie	192	36.17 N	76.59 W
Ahousat	182	49.17 N	126.04 W
Ahr ≃	56	50.33 N	7.17 E
Ahram	128	28.52 N	51.16 E
Ahrāmāt Dahshūr (North and Bent Pyramids) ⊥	142	29.48 N	31.13 E
Ahrāmāt Maydūm (Maydūm Pyramid) ⊥	142	29.23 N	31.10 E
Ahraura	124	25.01 N	83.01 E
Ahrensbök	54	54.00 N	10.34 E
Ahrensburg	52	53.40 N	10.14 E
Ahrensdorf, Dtsch.	54	52.10 N	14.05 E
Ahrensdorf, Dtsch.	264a	52.19 N	13.12 E
Ahrensfelde	264a	52.35 N	13.35 E
Ahrgebirge ⋏	56	50.30 N	6.50 E
Ahtanum	224	46.34 N	120.37 W
Ahtanum Creek ≃	202	46.32 N	120.31 W
Ahtanum Ridge ʌ	224	46.30 N	120.50 W
Ähtäri	26	62.34 N	24.06 E
Ähtärinjärvi ⊜	26	62.40 N	24.03 E
Ähtävänjoki ≃	26	63.38 N	22.48 E
Ahtopol	38	42.06 N	27.57 E
Ahu	98	34.27 N	118.39 E
Ahuacatlán, Méx.	234	21.03 N	104.29 W
Ahuacatlán, Méx.	234	20.00 N	97.52 W
Ahuachapán	236	13.55 N	89.51 W
Ahuacuotzingo	234	17.42 N	98.56 W
Ahualulco de Mercado	234	20.42 N	103.59 W
Ahuijullo	234	19.05 N	103.05 W
Ahuijullo ≃	234	18.49 N	103.37 W
Ahumada, Méx.	204	32.30 N	115.30 W
Ahumada, Méx.	232	30.37 N	106.31 W
Ahun	32	46.05 N	2.05 E
Ahuntsic ◆8	275a	45.33 N	73.39 W
Ahunui I1	14	19.39 S	140.25 W
Ahuriri ≃	172	44.33 S	170.11 E
Åhus	26	55.55 N	14.17 E
Ahuzhen	98	34.27 N	118.39 E
Ahvāz	128	31.19 N	48.42 E
Ahvenanmaa ▫4	26	60.15 N	20.00 E
Ahwahnee	226	37.21 N	119.43 W
Aḥwar	144	13.31 N	46.42 E
Ahwa-ri	98	35.54 N	129.02 E
Ai ≃	98	40.13 N	124.30 E
Aialik Cape >	180	59.42 N	149.31 W
Aiándion	267c	37.55 N	23.28 E
Aiapuá	246	4.29 S	62.04 W
Aiapuá, Lago ⊜	246	4.27 S	62.08 W
Aibag ≃	102	42.40 N	110.42 E
Aibonito	240m	18.08 N	66.16 W
Aich	64	47.25 N	13.49 E
Aichach	60	48.28 N	11.08 E
Aicha vorm Wald	60	48.41 N	13.18 E
Aichi ▫5	94	35.00 N	137.15 E
Aichi-kōgen-kokutei-kōen ♠	94	35.10 N	137.25 E
Aichi-yōsui ≍	94	34.42 N	136.57 E
Aichstetten	58	47.54 N	10.04 E
Aidenbach	60	48.34 N	13.06 E
Aidomaggiore	71	40.10 N	8.51 E
Aidone	70	37.25 N	14.27 E
Aidong	102	24.46 N	107.21 E
Aiduma, Pulau I	164	3.58 S	134.06 E
Aiea	229c	21.22 N	157.56 W
Aiello Calabro	68	39.07 N	16.10 E
Aigáleo Óros ʌ2	267c	38.00 N	23.37 E
Aigburth ◆8	262	53.22 N	2.55 W
Aigen im Mühlkreis	60	48.39 N	13.58 E
Aigenmiao	89	43.36 N	120.50 E
Aigle	58	46.19 N	6.58 E
Aigle, Île à l' I	275a	45.42 N	73.28 W
Aigle, Lac à l' ⊜	186	51.12 N	65.25 W
Aignay-le-Duc	58	47.40 N	4.44 E
Aigre	32	45.54 N	0.01 E
Aiguá	252	34.12 S	54.45 W
Aiguebelette, Lac d' ⊜	62	45.33 N	5.48 E
Aiguebelette-le-Lac	62	45.32 N	5.49 E
Aiguebelle	62	45.32 N	6.18 E
Aiguebelle, Réserve ♠	190	48.33 N	78.45 W
Aigueperse	32	46.01 N	3.12 E
Aigues ≃	62	44.07 N	4.43 E
Aigues-Mortes	62	43.34 N	4.11 E
Aigues-Mortes, Golfe d' c	62	43.31 N	4.03 E
Aigüestortes, Parc National d' ♠	34	42.30 N	1.01 E
Aigues-Vives	62	43.44 N	4.10 E
Aiguilles	62	44.47 N	6.52 E
Aiguines	62	43.46 N	6.15 E
Aigurande	32	46.26 N	1.50 E
Aihui (Heihe)	89	50.16 N	127.28 E
Aija	248	9.46 S	77.38 W
Aikawa, Nihon	92	38.02 N	138.15 E
Aikawa, Nihon	94	35.32 N	139.17 E
Aiken	192	33.33 N	81.43 W
Aikens Lake ⊜	184	51.12 N	95.20 W
Ailao Shan ⋏	102	24.08 N	101.25 E
Ailefroide	62	44.53 N	6.27 E
Aileron	162	22.39 S	133.20 E
Ailette ≃	50	49.35 N	3.10 E
Aileu	112	8.43 S	125.34 E
Ailimutou Shan ʌ	104	42.19 N	121.25 E
Ailingen	58	47.41 N	9.29 E
Ailinglapalap I1	14	7.23 N	168.46 E
Ailinzhuang	105	39.27 N	117.36 E
Aillant-sur-Tholon	50	47.52 N	3.21 E
Aille ≃	62	43.26 N	6.30 E
Ailly-le-Haut-Clocher	50	50.05 N	2.00 E
Ailly-sur-Noye	50	49.45 N	2.22 E
Ailly-sur-Somme	50	49.55 N	2.12 E
Ailo	164	4.50 S	151.40 E
Ailsa Craig	190	43.08 N	81.33 W
Ailsa Craig I	44	55.16 N	5.07 W
Ailuk I1	14	10.20 N	169.56 E
Aim	74	58.50 N	134.12 E
Aimargues	62	43.41 N	4.12 E
Aime	62	45.33 N	6.39 E
Aimere	115b	8.50 S	120.52 E
Aimi	96	35.22 N	133.22 E
Aimogasta	252	28.33 S	66.49 W
Aimorés	255	19.30 S	41.04 W
Aimoto	270	34.59 N	135.10 E
Ain ▫5	32	46.10 N	5.20 E
Ain ≃	58	45.48 N	5.10 E
Aïn Arnat	34	36.11 N	5.19 E
Aïn Azel	34	35.49 N	5.31 E
Ainaži	76	57.52 N	24.21 E
'Aïn Belbela, Sebkha ≚	148	27.30 N	5.20 W
Aïn Benian	148	36.48 N	2.55 E
Aïn Ben Tili	148	26.00 N	9.32 W
Aïn Berda	36	36.39 N	7.35 E
Aïn Bessem	34	36.18 N	3.40 E
Aincourt	261	49.04 N	1.47 E
Aïn Defla	34	36.16 N	1.58 E
Aïn Deheb	148	34.51 N	1.33 E
Aïn Draham	148	36.47 N	8.42 E
Aine ≃	56	50.23 N	5.31 E
Aïn el Beïda	148	35.50 N	7.27 E
Aïn el Hadjel	34	35.40 N	3.53 E
Aïn el Kebira	34	36.22 N	5.30 E
Aïn Milia	148	36.02 N	6.34 E
Aino	270	34.57 N	135.10 E
Aino-shima I, Nihon	96	33.45 N	130.23 E
Aino-shima I, Nihon	96	33.59 N	130.50 E
Aïn Oulmène	34	35.55 N	5.18 E
Ainring	64	47.48 N	12.56 E
Ainsdale	44	53.36 N	3.02 W
Aïn Sefra	148	32.45 N	0.35 W
Ain Shams University ʊ2	273c	30.03 N	31.17 E
Ainslie, Mount ʌ	171b	35.16 S	149.10 E
Ainslie Lake ⊜	186	46.08 N	61.12 W
Ainsworth, Eng., U.K.	262	53.35 N	2.22 W
Ainsworth, Ne., U.S.	198	42.33 N	99.51 W
Aïn Taghrout	34	36.08 N	5.05 E
Aïn Tedelès	148	36.00 N	0.18 E
Aïn Témouchent	148	35.18 N	1.08 W
Aïn Touta	148	35.23 N	5.54 E
Aintree	262	53.29 N	2.56 W
Aintree Race Course ♠	262	53.28 N	2.56 W
Aïn Wessara	148	35.27 N	2.54 E
Aïn Yagout	148	35.47 N	6.25 E
Aio	96	34.00 N	131.26 E
Aioi	96	34.48 N	134.28 E
Aiome	164	5.10 S	144.45 E
Aiora	34	39.04 N	1.03 W
Aipe	246	3.13 N	75.15 W
Aiquara	255	14.07 S	39.52 W
Aiquile	248	18.10 S	65.10 W
Aïr ⋏	150	18.00 N	8.30 E
Airabu, Pulau I	112	2.46 N	106.14 E
Airai Airport ⊠	175b	7.22 N	134.33 E
Airaines	50	49.58 N	1.57 E
Airão	246	1.56 S	61.22 W
Airasca	62	44.55 N	7.29 E
Airbangis	110	0.12 N	99.23 E
Airdikit	112	2.40 S	101.15 E
Airdrie, Ab., Can.	182	51.18 N	114.02 W
Airdrie, Scot., U.K.	46	55.52 N	3.59 W
Aire ≃, Fr.	56	49.19 N	4.49 E
Aire ≃, Eng., U.K.	44	53.44 N	0.54 W
Aire-sur-l'Adour	32	43.42 N	0.16 W
Aire-sur-la-Lys	50	50.38 N	2.24 E
Air Force Island I	176	67.55 N	74.10 W
Airgegas	112	2.42 S	106.25 E
Airgin Sum	102	42.58 N	111.08 E
Airhaji	112	1.57 S	100.53 E
Airjamban	114	1.13 N	101.14 E
Airlie	166	20.16 S	148.43 E
Airmolek	112	0.22 S	102.17 E
Airmont	276	41.06 N	74.06 W
Airola	68	41.04 N	14.33 E
Airole	62	43.52 N	7.33 E
Airolo	58	46.32 N	8.37 E
Airor	46	57.04 N	5.46 W
Airport West	274b	37.44 S	144.53 E
Airtenang	112	3.08 S	101.43 E
Airterjun	114	1.20 N	100.27 E
Airuno	62	45.45 N	9.25 E
Airvault	32	46.50 N	0.08 W
Aisch ≃	56	49.46 N	11.01 E
Aisega	164	5.44 S	148.21 E
Aisén del General Carlos Ibáñez del Campo ▫4	254	46.30 S	73.30 W
Aisey-sur-Seine	58	47.45 N	4.35 E
Aishihik	180	61.35 N	137.30 W
Aishihik Lake ⊜	180	61.25 N	137.06 W
Ai-shima I	96	34.30 N	131.17 E
Aisinaike	85	39.47 N	75.47 E
Aislingen	56	48.30 N	10.27 E
Aisne ▫5	50	49.30 N	3.30 E
Aisne ≃	32	49.26 N	2.50 E
Aisne à la Marne, Canal de l' ≍	50	49.24 N	3.55 E
Aïssa, Djebel ʌ	148	32.51 N	0.30 W
Aïssey	58	47.16 N	6.20 E
Aist ≃	61	48.14 N	14.35 E
Aisy-sur-Armançon	50	47.39 N	4.13 E
Aitana, Serra d' ʌ	34	38.44 N	0.16 W
Aitape	164	3.08 S	142.21 E
Aiterach ≃	60	48.54 N	12.38 E
Aiterhofen	60	48.51 N	12.37 E
Aith	46a	60.16 N	1.23 W
Aitkin	190	46.31 N	93.42 W
Aït-Melloul	148	30.21 N	9.31 W
Aitolikón	38	38.27 N	21.22 E
Aït-Ourir	148	31.38 N	7.42 W
Aitrach	58	47.56 N	10.05 E
Aitutaki I1	14	18.52 S	159.45 W
Ait Youssef ou Ali	34	35.13 N	3.55 W
Aiuaba	250	6.38 S	40.07 W
Aiud	38	46.19 N	23.44 E
Aiún → El Aaiún	148	27.09 N	13.12 W
Aiuruoca	256	21.58 S	44.36 W
Aiuruoca ≃, Bra.	256	21.42 S	44.22 W
Aiuruoca ≃, Bra.	256	21.32 S	44.26 W
Aiva	287a	22.42 S	43.28 W
Aiviekste ≃	76	56.37 N	25.45 E
Aix, Mount ʌ	224	46.47 N	121.15 W
Aix-en-Othe	50	48.13 N	3.44 E
Aix-en-Provence	62	43.32 N	5.26 E
Aix-la-Chapelle → Aachen	56	50.47 N	6.05 E
Aix-les-Bains	62	45.42 N	5.55 E
Aiyáleo	267c	37.59 N	23.41 E
Aiyang, Mount ʌ	164	5.05 S	141.19 E
Aiyansh	182	55.17 N	129.03 W
Aíyina	38	37.44 N	23.27 E
Aíyina I	38	37.46 N	23.26 E
Aiyínion	38	40.30 N	22.33 E
Aíyion	38	38.15 N	22.05 E
Āīzawl	120	23.44 N	92.43 E
Aizhaipuzi	104	40.57 N	124.01 E
Aizkraukle	76	56.38 N	25.13 E
Aizpute	76	56.43 N	21.38 E
Aizu-bange	92	37.34 N	139.49 E
Aizu-wakamatsu	92	37.30 N	139.56 E
Aj ≃	86	56.08 N	57.40 E
Ajā	142	30.57 N	31.17 E
Ajā', Jabal ⋏	128	27.20 N	41.45 E
'Ajab Shīr	128	37.28 N	45.54 E
Ajaccio	36	41.55 N	8.44 E
Ajaguz	86	47.56 N	80.23 E
Ajaguz ≃	86	46.42 N	79.15 E
Ajajú ≃	246	0.59 N	72.20 W
Ajalpan	234	18.22 N	97.15 W
'Ajaltūn	132	33.58 N	35.41 E
Ajalvir	266a	40.32 N	3.29 W
'Ajamī	130	36.28 N	37.42 E
Ajan, Ross.	74	56.27 N	138.10 E
Ajan, Ross.	88	54.43 N	110.55 E
Ajan ≃	74	70.10 N	95.50 E
Ajana	162	27.57 S	114.38 E
Ajanta	122	20.32 N	75.45 E
Ajanta Range ⋏	122	20.30 N	76.00 E
Ajaokuta	150	7.28 N	6.39 E
Ajarani ≃	246	1.33 N	61.16 W
Ajasse	150	8.17 N	4.48 E
Ajasso	150	5.52 N	8.52 E
Ajat ≃	86	52.54 N	63.02 E
Ajax	212	43.51 N	79.02 W
Ajay ≃	126	23.39 N	88.08 E
Ajbas	80	47.51 N	49.37 E
Ajdābiyā	146	30.48 N	20.14 E
Ajdabul'	86	52.42 N	68.59 E
Ajdar	78	50.03 N	38.56 E
Ajdarkul', ozero ⊜1	72	40.45 N	67.20 E
Ajdarly	86	44.32 N	65.50 E
Ajdovščina	36	45.53 N	13.53 E
Ajdyrlinskij	86	52.03 N	59.50 E
Ajegunle	273a	6.36 N	3.17 E
Ajgurka ≃	80	45.46 N	43.12 E
Ajgyrkol', ozero ⊜	80	48.15 N	52.50 E
Ajhūr al-Kubrā	142	30.18 N	31.09 E
Aji	96	34.23 N	134.08 E
Ajibar	144	10.52 N	38.40 E
Ajibarang	115a	7.25 S	109.04 E
Ajigasawa	94	40.47 N	140.12 E
'Ajjī, Wādī al- V	130	35.19 N	41.09 E
Ajijic	234	20.18 N	103.17 W
Ajil	114	5.05 N	103.05 E
Ājimganj	126	24.14 N	88.15 E
Ajimu	96	33.26 N	131.21 E
Ajipuzicun	104	42.16 N	123.33 E
Ajisu	96	34.00 N	131.22 E
Ajjer, Tassili-n- ⋏1	148	25.10 N	8.00 E
Ajka	30	47.07 N	17.34 E
Ajke, ozero ⊜	86	50.57 N	61.36 E
Ajkino	24	62.15 N	49.56 E
'Ajlūn	132	32.20 N	35.45 E
Ajlune	224	46.31 N	122.26 W
'Ajmah, Jabal al- ⋏	140	29.12 N	34.02 E
Ajmer	120	26.27 N	74.38 E
Ajnāla	123	31.51 N	74.48 E
Ajni	85	39.23 N	68.32 E
Ajo	200	32.22 N	112.51 W
Ajo, Cabo de >	34	43.31 N	3.35 W
Ajok	140	9.15 N	28.27 E
Ajon, ostrov I	74	69.50 N	168.40 E
Ajoya	232	24.04 N	106.22 W
Ajrag nuur ⊜	88	48.54 N	93.28 E
'Ajramīyah, Bi'r al- ⊤4	142	29.39 N	31.50 E
Ajrum	84	41.13 N	44.53 E
Ajryk	86	50.30 N	76.48 E
Ajsary	86	53.18 N	71.52 E
Ajtos	38	42.42 N	27.15 E
Ajuchitlán del Progreso	234	18.09 N	100.29 W
Ajuda ◆8	266c	38.43 N	9.12 W
Ajusco	204	31.35 N	116.25 W
Ajusco ◆8	286a	19.14 N	99.12 W
Ajuta ≃	83	47.34 N	40.07 E
Ajuterique	236	14.20 N	87.43 W
Ajutinskij	83	47.46 N	40.08 E
Ajuy	116	11.10 N	123.01 E
Ajuy Bay c	116	11.10 N	123.02 E
Aka ≃	92	38.54 N	139.50 E
Akaba	150	7.57 N	1.03 E
Akabane	94	34.37 N	137.12 E
Akabira	92a	43.34 N	142.03 E
Akabli	148	26.42 N	1.22 E
Akabori	94	36.22 N	139.14 E
Akademii, zaliv c	89	54.15 N	138.05 E
Akagera (Kagera) ≃	154	0.57 S	31.47 E
Akagera, Parc National de l' ♠	154	1.30 S	30.35 E
Akagi, Nihon	94	36.33 N	139.03 E
Akagi, Nihon	96	35.00 N	132.43 E
Akagi-san ʌ	94	36.33 N	139.11 E
Akaishi-dake ʌ	94	35.27 N	138.09 E
Akaishi-sammyaku ⋏	94	35.18 N	138.07 E
Akaka Falls State Park ♠	229d	19.52 N	155.09 W
Akaki Beseka	144	8.52 N	38.47 E
Akālgarh	123	32.16 N	73.49 E
Akalkot	122	17.32 N	76.13 E
Akamaruno-misaki >	174m	26.44 N	128.09 E
Akámas, Akrotírion >	130	35.06 N	32.17 E
Akan	92a	43.06 N	144.10 E
Akana-tōge)(	96	34.57 N	132.44 E
Akan-kokuritsu-kōen ♠	92a	43.30 N	144.15 E
Akaoka	96	33.32 N	133.43 E
Ak-Aral	86	49.10 N	90.57 E
Akaroa	172	43.48 S	172.58 E
Akaroa Harbour c	172	43.50 S	172.56 E
Åkarp	41	55.39 N	13.07 E
Akarsu, Tür.	130	39.56 N	38.38 E
Akarsu, Tür.	130	37.14 N	41.04 E
Akasaki	96	35.31 N	133.38 E
'Akasha East	140	21.05 N	30.43 E
Akashat	130	33.45 N	39.58 E
Akashi	96	34.38 N	134.59 E
Akashi ≃	270	34.38 N	134.59 E
Akashi-kaikyō ᥕ	96	34.37 N	135.02 E
Akashina	94	36.21 N	137.56 E
Akatani-ko ⊜1	94	36.43 N	138.54 E
Akatjevo	82	54.59 N	38.45 E
Akatova	76	55.09 N	31.48 E
Akatsuka ◆8	268	35.46 N	139.39 E
Akatsutsumi ◆8	268	35.39 N	139.39 E
Akbaba ◆8	267b	41.09 N	29.06 E
Akbaba Dağı ʌ	130	40.12 N	40.51 E
Akbajtal	85	38.32 N	73.49 E
Akbajtal, pereval)(	85	38.32 N	73.40 E
Akbarpur, India	124	24.39 N	83.58 E
Akbarpur, India	124	26.25 N	82.33 E
Akbeit	86	51.38 N	70.02 E
Akbou	148	36.28 N	4.32 E
Akbulak, Kaz.	86	49.26 N	80.28 E
Akbulak, Ross.	86	51.01 N	55.37 E
Akbura ≃	85	40.39 N	72.36 E
Akçaabat	130	41.02 N	39.34 E
Akçadağ	130	38.21 N	37.59 E
Akçakale	130	36.41 N	38.56 E
Akcakışla	130	39.33 N	36.22 E
Akçakoca	130	41.05 N	31.09 E
Akçakoyunlu	130	36.46 N	37.38 E
Akçaova, Tür.	130	37.30 N	28.02 E
Akçaova, Tür.	130	41.03 N	29.57 E
Akçapınar	130	38.57 N	38.57 E
Akčatau	86	47.59 N	74.02 E
Akçay	130	36.36 N	29.45 E
Akçay ≃	130	37.50 N	28.15 E
Akchâr ◆1	150	20.00 N	14.30 W
Akči	85	44.00 N	76.20 E
Akdağ	130	40.43 N	36.00 E
Akdağ ʌ	130	39.29 N	41.54 E
Akdağmadeni	130	39.40 N	35.54 E
Akdala	86	45.02 N	74.35 E
Akdoğan	130	35.06 N	33.41 E
Ak-Dovurak	86	51.16 N	90.31 E
Akechi	94	35.18 N	137.23 E
Akehama	96	33.19 N	132.26 E
Akeley	190	47.00 N	94.43 W
Aken	54	51.51 N	12.02 E
Akeno, Nihon	94	36.15 N	140.02 E
Akeno, Nihon	94	35.46 N	138.26 E
Åker	40	59.15 N	17.05 E
Åkerby	40	60.25 N	17.46 E
Åkersberga	40	59.29 N	18.18 E
Akershus ▫6	26	60.00 N	11.10 E
Akersloot	52	52.34 N	4.44 E
Akespe	86	46.48 N	60.31 E
Aketi	152	2.44 N	23.46 E
Aketilepa	85	39.57 N	74.03 E
Aketu-Oja	273a	6.41 N	3.23 E
Åkforsån ≃	40	58.54 N	16.28 E
Akgöl ⊜	130	38.58 N	31.48 E
Akharnaí	38	38.05 N	23.44 E
Akhḍar, Al-Jabal al- ⋏, Lībiyā	146	32.30 N	21.30 E
Akhḍar, Al-Jabal al- ⋏, 'Umān	128	23.15 N	57.20 E
Akhelóös ≃	38	38.36 N	21.14 E
Akh Gol ⊜	84	39.33 N	44.47 E
Akhiok	180	56.57 N	154.10 W
Akhisar	130	38.55 N	27.51 E
Akhmīm	140	26.34 N	31.44 E
Akhnūr	123	32.54 N	74.44 E
Akhtarīn	130	36.31 N	37.20 E
Aki, Nihon	96	33.30 N	133.54 E
Aki, Nihon	96	33.28 N	131.43 E
Aki ≃, Nihon	94	35.41 N	139.21 E
Aki ≃, Nihon	96	33.30 N	133.55 E
Akiachak	180	60.55 N	161.27 W
Akiak	180	60.55 N	161.12 W
Akiéni	152	1.11 S	13.53 E
Akima	88	53.06 N	115.44 E
Akimiski Island I	176	53.00 N	81.20 W
Aki-nada ⊤2	96	34.05 N	132.48 E
Akıncı	130	37.10 N	40.52 E
Akıncı Burun >	130	36.19 N	35.47 E
Akıncılar, Tür.	130	40.06 N	38.21 E
Akıncılar, Tür.	130	37.45 N	38.50 E
Akiode	273a	6.38 N	3.21 E
Åkirkeby	26	55.04 N	14.56 E
Akishima	94	35.41 N	139.22 E
Akišma ≃	89	52.08 N	132.40 E
Akita	92	39.43 N	140.07 E
Akita-heiya ≚	92	39.45 N	140.10 E
Akitan	273a	6.39 N	3.16 E
Akitipa	150	8.17 N	6.16 E
Akitkan, chrebet ⋏	88	57.05 N	109.05 E
Akitsu, Nihon	96	34.19 N	132.50 E
Akitsu, Nihon	270	34.56 N	135.06 E
Akiyama	94	35.34 N	139.05 E
Akiyoshi-dai ⋏1	96	34.15 N	131.15 E
Akiyoshi-dai-kokutei-kōen ♠	96	34.15 N	131.17 E
Akiyoshi-do ⊥5	96	34.14 N	131.19 E
Akjar	86	51.50 N	58.14 E
Akjoujt	150	19.45 N	14.23 W
Akka	148	29.22 N	8.14 W
Akkala	86	43.43 N	59.31 E
Akkani	180	65.30 N	171.10 W
Akkerman → Bilhorod-Dnistrovs'kyy	78	46.12 N	30.20 E
Akkermanovka	86	51.11 N	58.12 E
Akkerwoude	52	53.17 N	5.58 E
Akkeshi	92a	43.02 N	144.51 E
Akkışla	130	39.00 N	36.11 E
'Akko (Acre)	132	32.55 N	35.05 E
Akkol', Kaz.	85	43.25 N	70.47 E
Akkol', Kaz.	86	45.02 N	75.40 E
Akkol', ozero ⊜	85	43.24 N	70.40 E
Akkol'skij	86	52.12 N	75.05 E
Akköy	130	37.29 N	27.15 E
Akkra → Accra	150	5.33 N	0.13 W
Akkrum	52	53.03 N	5.50 E
Ak-Kul'	85	41.41 N	74.16 E
Akkuş	130	40.49 N	37.01 E
Aklan ▫4	116	11.40 N	122.20 E
Aklan ≃	116	11.44 N	122.20 E
Aklan Point >	116	11.44 N	122.22 E
Aklavik	180	68.12 N	135.00 W
'Aklé 'Aouâna ◆1	150	18.00 N	5.30 W
Akmeņrags >	76	56.51 N	21.03 E
Akmeqit	120	37.01 N	76.59 E
Akmeşe	130	40.51 N	30.12 E
Akmuz	85	41.16 N	76.09 E
Ākna	272b	22.59 N	88.21 E
Aknet, gora ʌ	86	50.51 N	75.40 E
Aknīste	76	56.10 N	25.45 E
Aknoul	148	34.43 N	3.49 W
Ako, Nig.	146	10.17 N	10.58 E
Akō, Nihon	96	34.45 N	134.24 E
Akoba	80	49.28 N	47.25 E
Akobo	140	7.47 N	33.01 E
Akobo (Akūbū) ≃	140	7.47 N	33.03 E
Akodiya	124	23.23 N	76.36 E
Akok, Cam.	152	2.46 N	10.18 E
Akok, Gabon	152	0.31 N	9.45 E
Akola	122	20.44 N	77.00 E
Akonolinga	152	3.47 N	12.15 E
Akop	140	8.21 N	29.05 E
Akor	150	14.53 N	6.58 W
Akora	123	34.00 N	72.08 E
Akordat	144	15.33 N	37.53 E
Akören	130	37.27 N	32.23 E
Akosombo Dam ◆6	150	6.16 N	0.03 E
Akot, India	120	21.11 N	77.04 E
Akot, Sūd.	140	6.33 N	30.03 E
Akoupé	150	6.23 N	3.54 W
Akowonjo	273a	6.37 N	3.19 E
Akpatok Island I	176	60.25 N	68.00 W
Akpınar, Tür.	130	37.34 N	38.13 E
Akpınar, Tür.	130	39.17 N	33.40 E
Akqi	85	40.52 N	77.58 E
Åkrafjorden c2	26	59.46 N	6.06 E
Akranes	24a	64.18 N	22.02 W
Åkrehamn	26	59.16 N	5.11 E
Akrítas, Ákra >	38	36.43 N	21.54 E
Akrofuom	150	6.07 N	1.39 W
Akrokórinthos ⊥	38	37.54 N	22.56 E
Akron, Co., U.S.	198	40.09 N	103.12 W
Akron, In., U.S.	216	41.02 N	86.01 W
Akron, Ia., U.S.	198	42.49 N	96.33 W
Akron, N.Y., U.S.	210	43.01 N	78.29 W
Akron, Oh., U.S.	214	41.04 N	81.31 W
Akron, Pa., U.S.	208	40.09 N	76.12 W
Akron-Canton Regional Airport ⊠	214	40.55 N	81.27 W
Akron City Reservoir ⊜1	214	41.20 N	81.17 W
Akrotíri	130	34.36 N	32.57 E
Akša	88	50.16 N	113.17 E
Aksa ◆8	272c	19.10 N	72.48 E
Aksaj, Kaz.	80	51.09 N	53.00 E
Aksaj, Kaz.	85	43.22 N	70.12 E
Aksaj, Ross.	80	47.58 N	43.59 E
Aksaj, Ross.	83	47.15 N	39.52 E
Aksaj (Toxkan) ≃, Asia	85	40.55 N	78.16 E
Aksaj ≃, Ross.	83	47.15 N	39.53 E
Aksaj ≃, Ross.	84	43.32 N	46.51 E
Aksakovo	80	54.02 N	54.09 E
Aksaray	130	38.23 N	34.03 E
Aksaray ▫4	130	38.30 N	34.00 E
Aksarka	74	66.36 N	67.46 E
Akšatau	86	49.23 N	54.36 E
Aksaut ≃	84	43.55 N	41.42 E
Aksay	102	39.28 N	94.15 E
Aksayqin Hu ⊜	120	35.12 N	79.50 E
Akşehir	130	38.21 N	31.25 E
Akşehir Gölü ⊜	130	38.30 N	31.28 E
Akseki	130	37.02 N	31.48 E
Aksengir ≃	85	43.40 N	76.14 E
Aksenkino	80	53.59 N	53.06 E
Aksenovo	82	55.40 N	38.15 E
Aksentjevo	82	55.25 N	35.54 E
Akšij	86	47.37 N	55.56 E
Akšijrak, chrebet ⋏	85	41.20 N	74.15 E
Aksinjino, Ross.	82	55.44 N	36.59 E
Aksinjino, Ross.	82	56.02 N	38.12 E
Aks'onovo	88	58.51 N	101.43 E
Aks'onovo-Zilovskoje	88	53.04 N	117.32 E
Aksoran, gora ʌ	86	48.27 N	75.32 E
Akstafa ≃	84	41.15 N	45.26 E
Aksu, Kaz.	80	50.56 N	53.06 E
Aksu, Kaz.	86	52.28 N	71.59 E
Aksu, Kaz.	86	45.37 N	79.30 E
Aksu, Tür.	130	36.58 N	30.50 E
Aksu, Zhg.	90	41.10 N	80.20 E
Aksu ≃, Asia	85	43.22 N	73.54 E
Aksu ≃, Kaz.	86	46.20 N	78.15 E
Aksu ≃, Tür.	130	37.25 N	36.54 E
Aksu ≃, Tür.	130	36.51 N	30.54 E
Aksu-Ajuly	86	48.47 N	73.40 E
Aksuart, ozero ⊜	86	51.24 N	64.28 E
Aksuat, Kaz.	86	51.32 N	64.34 E
Aksuat, Kaz.	86	47.45 N	82.40 E
Aksuat, Kaz.	86	48.16 N	83.50 E
Aksubajevo	80	54.52 N	50.50 E
Aksu-Džabaglinskij zapovednik ♠	85	42.20 N	70.35 E
Aksum	144	14.08 N	38.43 E
Aktag ʌ	120	36.45 N	84.40 E
Aktal	85	41.25 N	75.03 E
Aktanyš	80	55.43 N	54.05 E
Aktas, Kaz.	85	42.57 N	70.04 E
Aktas, Kaz.	86	48.02 N	66.21 E
Aktas, Kaz.	86	49.47 N	72.59 E
Aktas, Kaz.	86	50.06 N	76.40 E
Aktaš, Ross.	86	50.18 N	87.44 E
Aktaš, Uzb.	85	41.38 N	69.44 E
Aktaş Gölü ⊜	84	41.15 N	43.12 E
Aktasty	86	50.44 N	61.43 E
Aktau, Kaz.	72	43.35 N	51.05 E
Aktau, Kaz.	86	50.16 N	73.02 E
Aktau, gora ʌ	86	48.00 N	71.45 E
Aktepe	130	36.44 N	36.27 E
Akterek, Kaz.	85	43.22 N	75.18 E
Akterek, Kyrg.	85	42.14 N	77.45 E
Akto	85	39.08 N	75.57 E
Aktobe	85	43.13 N	67.46 E
Aktogaj, Kaz.	86	44.27 N	76.42 E
Aktogaj, Kaz.	86	48.18 N	74.58 E
Aktogaj, Kaz.	86	46.57 N	79.40 E
Aktubek	86	48.37 N	71.06 E
Akt'ubinsk ▫4	86	48.30 N	58.30 E

≃ River	Fluß	Río	Rivière	Rio
≍ Canal	Kanal	Canal	Canal	Canal
⌊ Waterfall, Rapids	Wasserfall, Stromschnellen	Cascada, Rápidos	Chute d'eau, Rapides	Cascata, Rápidos
ᥕ Strait	Meeresstraße	Estrecho	Détroit	Estreito
c Bay, Gulf	Bucht, Golf	Bahía, Golfo	Baie, Golfe	Baía, Golfo
⊜ Lake, Lakes	See, Seen	Lago, Lagos	Lac, Lacs	Lago, Lagos
≚ Swamp	Sumpf	Pantano	Marais	Pântano
⊼ Ice Features, Glacier	Eis- und Gletscherformen	Accidentes Glaciales	Formes glaciaires	Acidentes glaciares
⊤ Other Hydrographic Features	Andere Hydrographische Objekte	Otros Elementos Hidrográficos	Autres données hydrographiques	Outros acidentes hidrográficos
✣ Submarine Features	Untermeerische Objekte	Accidentes Submarinos	Formes de relief sous-marin	Acidentes submarinos
▫ Political Unit	Politische Einheit	Unidad Política	Entité politique	Unidade política
ʊ Cultural Institution	Kulturelle Institution	Institución Cultural	Institution culturelle	Instituição cultural
⊥ Historical Site	Historische Stätte	Sitio Histórico	Site historique	Sítio histórico
♠ Recreational Site	Erholungs- und Ferienort	Sitio de Recreo	Centre de loisirs	Área de Lazer
⊠ Airport	Flughafen	Aeropuerto	Aéroport	Aeroporto
■ Military Installation	Militäranlage	Instalación Militar	Installation militaire	Instalação militar
◆ Miscellaneous	Verschiedenes	Misceláneo	Divers	Diversos

ENGLISH — Name / Page / Lat.°' / Long.°'

DEUTSCH — Name / Seite / Breite°' / Länge°' E = Ost

Name	Page	Lat.°'	Long.°'
Akt'ubinskij	80	54.49 N	52.47 E
Aktuluk	130	39.03 N	39.32 E
Aktumsyk	86	46.40 N	57.19 E
Akt'uz	85	42.54 N	76.07 E
Aku	150	6.42 N	7.20 E
Akūbū (Akobo) ≃	140	7.47 N	33.03 E
Akui ≃	96	34.06 N	134.33 E
Akula	152	2.22 N	20.11 E
Akuliči Pervyje	76	53.11 N	33.13 E
Akulovo, Ross.	82	55.31 N	36.42 E
Akulovo, Ross.	82	56.05 N	38.59 E
Akumadan	150	7.24 N	1.57 W
Akune	92	32.01 N	130.11 E
Akun Island I	180	54.12 N	165.35 W
Akure	150	7.15 N	5.12 E
Akureyri	24a	65.44 N	18.08 W
Akurli	272c	19.01 N	73.08 E
Akuša	84	42.17 N	47.21 E
Akuse	150	6.06 N	0.08 E
Akuseki-jima I	93b	29.27 N	129.37 E
Akutan	180	54.08 N	165.46 W
Akutan Island I	180	54.10 N	165.55 W
Akutan Pass ⊔	180	54.00 N	166.10 W
Akuticha	86	52.27 N	84.29 E
Akwa Ibom ▫3	150	4.50 N	7.50 E
Akwanga	150	8.55 N	8.23 E
Akwatia	150	6.04 N	0.49 W
Akwawa ∧2	150	6.27 N	0.25 W
Akwaya	152	6.30 N	9.40 E
Akyab → Sittwe	110	20.09 N	92.54 E
Akyazı	130	40.41 N	30.37 E
Akyel	144	12.33 N	37.04 E
Akyr-T'ube	85	42.59 N	72.07 E
Akyurt	130	40.08 N	33.06 E
Akžajkyn, ozero ⊜	86	44.55 N	67.46 E
Akžal, Kaz.	86	47.47 N	74.02 E
Akžal, Kaz.	86	49.13 N	81.25 E
Akžar, Kaz.	85	43.08 N	71.38 E
Akžar, Kaz.	86	47.35 N	83.42 E
Akžaryk	86	48.34 N	75.30 E
Ål	26	60.38 N	8.34 E
Ala	64	45.45 N	11.00 E
Ala ≃	86	42.42 N	89.12 E
Alà, Monti di ⋏	71	40.40 N	9.14 E
Al-Ab'ādīyah	142	31.22 N	31.07 E
Alabama	210	43.06 N	78.23 W
Alabama ▫3, U.S.	178	32.50 N	87.00 W
Alabama ▫3, U.S.	194	32.50 N	87.00 W
Alabama ≃	194	31.08 N	87.57 W
Alabama and Coushatta Indian Reservation ◆4	222	30.43 N	94.42 W
Alabaster	194	33.14 N	86.48 W
Alabat Island I	116	14.07 N	122.03 E
Al-'Abbāsah ash-Sharqīyah	142	30.32 N	31.43 E
Al-'Abbāsīyah	140	12.10 N	31.18 E
Al-'Abbāsīyah ◆8	273c	30.04 N	31.17 E
Alabino	82	55.31 N	37.01 E
Āl-'Ābis	144	18.04 N	43.10 E
Alabuga ≃	85	41.26 N	74.41 E
Ala-Buka	85	41.23 N	71.30 E
Alaca	130	40.10 N	34.51 E
Alacahan	130	39.07 N	37.37 E
Alacalı	130	41.11 N	29.27 E
Alaçam	130	41.37 N	35.37 E
Alaçam Dağları ⋏	130	39.20 N	28.32 E
Alacant	34	38.21 N	0.29 W
Alacant ▫4	34	38.30 N	0.45 W
Alaçatı	130	38.16 N	26.23 E
Alachadzy	84	43.14 N	40.18 E
Alachua	192	29.47 N	82.29 W
Alacrán, Arrecife ✢2	232	22.24 N	89.42 W
Alacranes, Presa ⊜1	240p	22.45 N	80.08 W
Aladağ	130	37.02 N	32.41 E
Aladağ ∧, Tür.	84	40.11 N	42.49 E
Aladağ ∧, Tür.	130	37.44 N	35.09 E
Aladağlar ⋏, Tür.	84	39.20 N	43.35 E
Ala Dağlar ⋏, Tür.	130	37.55 N	35.13 E
Al-'Adasīyah	132	32.40 N	35.37 E
Alà dei Sardi	71	40.39 N	9.20 E
Aladino	82	54.49 N	38.12 E
Aladinskij, porog ∟	86	58.24 N	95.29 E
Ala di Stura	62	45.19 N	7.19 E
Aladjino	82	56.21 N	37.04 E
Aladža manastir ◉1	38	43.17 N	28.01 E
Alafia ≃	220	27.52 N	82.23 W
Alafia, South Prong ≃	220	27.51 N	82.08 W
Alagbado	273a	6.41 N	3.18 E
Alagna Valsesia	62	45.51 N	7.56 E
Alag nuur ⊜	102	45.09 N	94.28 E
Alagoa	256	22.10 S	44.38 W
Alagoa Grande	250	7.03 S	35.38 W
Alagoa Nova	250	7.04 S	35.46 W
Alagoas ▫3	250	9.00 S	36.00 W
Alagoinhas	255	12.07 S	38.26 W
Alagón	34	41.46 N	1.07 W
Alagón ≃	34	39.44 N	6.53 W
Alaguntan	273a	6.26 N	3.30 E
Alah ≃	116	6.53 N	124.33 E
Alahanpanjang	112	1.05 S	100.47 E
Alahärmä	26	63.14 N	22.51 E
Alaior	34	39.56 N	4.08 E
Al-Ait	140	12.22 N	27.27 E
Al-'Ajamīyīn	142	29.20 N	30.43 E
Alajärvi	26	63.00 N	23.49 E
Alajku	85	40.18 N	74.25 E
Alajõe	76	59.01 N	27.26 E
Alajskaja dolina V	85	39.30 N	73.00 E
Alajskij chrebet ⋏	85	39.45 N	72.00 E
Alajuela	236	10.01 N	84.13 W
Alajuela ▫4	236	10.30 N	84.30 W
Alajuela, Lago ⊜1	236	9.15 N	79.35 W
Ālājūjeh	84	38.57 N	46.41 E
Alakai Swamp ≡	229b	22.08 N	159.35 W
Alakamisy	157b	21.19 S	47.14 E
Alakanuk	180	62.41 N	164.37 W
Alaknanda ≃	124	30.08 N	78.36 E
Alakol', ozero ⊜	86	46.10 N	81.45 E
Al-'Akrīshah	142	31.08 N	30.09 E
Alaktara	124	22.01 N	82.26 E
Alak'ul'a	265a	59.44 N	29.56 E
Alakurtti	24	66.57 N	30.18 E
Al-'Āl	132	32.48 N	35.44 E
Alalakeiki Channel ⊔	229a	20.35 N	156.30 W
Al-'Alamayn	140	30.49 N	28.57 E
Al-'Alāqimah	142	30.37 N	31.38 E
Alalaú ≃	246	0.30 S	61.09 W
Al-'Amādīyah	128	37.06 N	43.29 E
Alamagan I	108	17.36 N	145.50 E
Al-'Amārah	128	31.50 N	47.09 E
Al-'Amār al-Kubrā	142	30.21 N	31.08 E
Alamata	144	12.25 N	39.33 E
Alamdānga	124	23.46 N	88.57 E
Alameda, Esp.	34	37.12 N	4.39 W
Alameda, Ca., U.S.	226	37.45 N	122.14 W
Alameda, N.M., U.S.	200	35.11 N	106.37 W
Alameda ▫6	226	37.35 N	121.55 W
Alameda, Estación ◆5	286e	33.27 S	70.41 W
Alameda Creek ≃	226	37.35 N	122.09 W
Alameda Naval Air Station ■	226	37.47 N	122.18 W
Alamedin	85	42.54 N	74.37 E
Alamein → Al-'Alamayn	140	30.49 N	28.57 E
Alamillo	200	31.02 N	110.35 W
Alaminos	116	16.10 N	119.59 E
Al-'Āmirīyah	142	31.01 N	29.48 E
'Alam Lek	128	37.02 N	65.57 E
Álamo, Méx.	234	20.55 N	97.41 W
Alamo, Ca., U.S.	226	37.51 N	122.02 W
Alamo, Ga., U.S.	192	32.08 N	82.46 W
Alamo, Mi., U.S.	216	42.22 N	85.43 W
Alamo, Nv., U.S.	204	37.21 N	115.09 W
Alamo, Tn., U.S.	194	35.47 N	89.07 W
Alamo ≃	204	33.14 N	115.39 W
Alamo Creek ≃	282	37.42 N	121.55 W
Alamo Creek, West Branch ≃	282	37.45 N	121.55 W
Alamogordo	200	32.53 N	105.57 W
Alamogordo Creek ≃	196	34.40 N	104.23 W
Alamo Heights	196	29.29 N	98.27 W
Alamo Indian Reservation ◆4	200	34.30 N	107.30 W
Alamo Lake ⊜1	200	34.20 N	113.30 W
Alamo Oaks	282	37.51 N	121.59 W
Alamor	246	4.02 S	80.02 W
Alamos, Méx.	196	26.25 N	100.25 W
Álamos, Méx.	232	27.01 N	108.56 W
Álamos, Río de los ≃	196	27.53 N	101.12 W
Alamosa	200	37.28 N	105.52 W
Alamosa ≃	200	37.22 N	105.46 W
Alamosa Creek ≃, N.M., U.S.	196	34.26 N	103.58 W
Alamosa Creek ≃, N.M., U.S.	200	33.20 N	107.21 W
Alamosa East	200	37.28 N	105.49 W
Álamos de Márquez	232	28.40 N	103.30 W
Ālampur, Bngl.	126	23.49 N	89.06 E
Alampur, India	272b	22.25 N	88.08 E
Alanäs	26	64.10 N	15.42 E
Al-'Ānāt	132	32.21 N	36.48 E
Al-Anbār ▫4	128	33.45 N	41.45 E
Āland	122	17.34 N	76.34 E
Åland (Ahvenanmaa) II	26	60.15 N	20.00 E
Aland ≃	54	53.02 N	11.34 E
Åland-Inseln → Åland II	26	60.15 N	20.00 E
Ålands hav ▾2	26	60.00 N	19.30 E
Alandur	122	13.02 N	80.15 E
Alangalang	116	11.12 N	124.51 E
Alang-besar, Pulau I	114	2.12 N	100.39 E
Alanje	236	8.24 N	82.33 W
Alano di Piave	64	45.55 N	11.52 E
Alanson	190	45.26 N	84.47 W
Alanya	130	36.33 N	32.01 E
Al-'Anz	132	32.23 N	36.38 E
Alaotra, Lac ⊜	157b	17.30 S	48.30 E
Alapaha	192	31.23 N	83.13 W
Alapaha ≃	192	30.26 N	83.06 W
Alapajevsk	86	57.52 N	61.42 E
Alaplı	130	41.11 N	31.24 E
Al-'Aqabah	132	29.31 N	35.00 E
'Alaqah, Jabal ∧	142	29.59 N	32.53 E
Alaquines	234	22.08 N	99.36 W
Al-'Arabīyah as-Su'ūdīyah → Saudi Arabia ▫1	118	25.00 N	45.00 E
Alarcón	34	39.33 N	2.05 W
Alarcón, Embalse de ⊜1	34	39.36 N	2.10 W
Al-'Arīsh	132	31.08 N	33.48 E
Al-'Armah ⋏1	128	25.30 N	46.30 E
Alarobia Vohiposa	157b	20.59 S	47.09 E
Alas	115b	8.32 S	117.00 E
Alas ≃, Indon.	114	3.05 N	97.55 E
Alaš ≃, Ross.	86	51.15 N	90.54 E
Alas, Selat ⊔	115b	8.40 S	116.40 E
Alasan	112	1.45 S	123.19 E
Alasdair, Sgurr ∧	46	57.12 N	6.14 W
Alaşehir	130	38.21 N	28.32 E
Alashanyouqi	102	40.02 N	103.33 E
Al-'Ashārah	130	34.55 N	40.34 E
Al-Ashmūnayn	142	27.47 N	30.49 E
Alaska	216	42.50 N	85.29 W
Alaska ▫3	180	65.00 N	153.00 W
Alaska, Gulf of C	16	58.00 N	146.00 W
Alaska Peninsula ≻1	180	57.00 N	158.00 W
Alaska Range ⋏	180	62.30 N	150.00 W
Al-'Assāfīyah	128	28.21 N	39.08 E
Alassio	62	44.00 N	8.10 E
Alastaro	26	60.56 N	22.55 E
Alastuey	258	34.25 S	59.13 W
Älät, Azer.	84	39.57 N	49.25 E
Alat, Uzb.	128	39.26 N	63.48 E
Al-'Aṭāminah	142	27.20 N	30.50 E
Alatan'aola → Xin Barag Youqi	88	48.41 N	116.53 E
Al-Atārib	130	36.08 N	36.49 E
Al-Aṭāwilah	142	27.14 N	31.13 E
Al-'Aṭf	142	29.39 N	31.16 E
Al-'Athāmīn ⋏	128	30.22 N	43.40 E
Alatna ≃	180	66.34 N	152.34 W
Alatri	66	41.43 N	13.21 E
Al-'Aṭrūn	140	18.11 N	26.36 E
Alatyr'	80	54.51 N	46.36 E
Alatyr' ≃	80	54.52 N	46.36 E
Alausí	246	2.12 S	78.50 W
Alava, Cape ≻	224	48.10 N	124.43 W
Alaverdi	84	41.08 N	44.39 E
Alavieska	26	64.10 N	24.18 E
Alavus	26	62.35 N	23.37 E
Alaw ≃	44	53.18 N	4.32 W
Alaw, Llyn ⊜1	44	53.20 N	4.22 W
Alawa	150	10.20 N	6.39 E
Alāwalpur	123	31.26 N	75.39 E
Al-'Awjā'	142	30.58 N	30.32 E
Al-'Awsajīyah	128	26.49 N	41.41 E
'Ālayh	132	33.48 N	35.36 E
Al-'Ayn	128	24.13 N	55.46 E
Al-'Ayn ▾4	140	16.36 N	29.19 E
Al-'Ayyāsh ash-Sharqī	142	31.33 N	31.13 E
Al-'Ayyāṭ	142	29.37 N	31.15 E
Alazani ≃	84	41.05 N	46.40 E
Alazeja ≃	74	70.51 N	153.34 E
Al-Azhar University ◉2	273c	30.03 N	31.16 E
Al'Azīzah	142	31.11 N	31.57 E
Al-'Azīzīyah, Lībiyā	146	32.32 N	13.01 E
Al-'Azīzīyah, Miṣr	142	30.29 N	31.18 E
Al-'Azīzīyah, Miṣr	273c	29.52 N	31.15 E
Al-Azraq ◆1	132	31.52 N	36.50 E
Alb ≃	58	47.35 N	8.08 E
Alba, It.	62	44.42 N	8.02 E
Alba, Mi., U.S.	190	44.58 N	84.58 W
Alba, Pa., U.S.	210	41.42 N	76.50 W
Alba, Tx., U.S.	222	32.48 N	95.38 W
Alba ▫6	38	46.15 N	23.30 E
Alba, Foum de)(	148	20.27 N	3.36 W
Al-Bāb	130	36.22 N	37.31 E
Albacete	34	38.59 N	1.51 W
Albacete ▫4	34	38.50 N	1.50 W
Albachten	52	51.55 N	7.31 E
Albacina	66	43.21 N	13.01 E
Al-Bad'	128	28.25 N	35.04 E
Al-Badārī	140	26.59 N	31.25 E
Alba de Tormes	34	40.49 N	5.31 W
Al-Badrashayn	142	29.51 N	31.16 E
Ålbæk	26	57.36 N	10.25 E
Al-Bahnasā	142	28.32 N	30.39 E
Al-Baḥr al-Abyaḍ ▫4	140	13.15 N	32.25 E
Al-Baḥr al-Aḥmar ▫4, Miṣr	142	28.45 N	32.00 E
Al-Baḥr al-Aḥmar ▫4, Sūd.	140	20.00 N	35.15 E
Al-Baḥrayn → Bahrain ▫1	128	26.00 N	50.30 E
Albaida	34	38.51 N	0.31 W
Albairate	266b	45.25 N	8.56 E
Alba Iulia	38	46.04 N	23.35 E
Al-Bajalāt	142	31.10 N	31.37 E
Al-Bājūr	142	30.26 N	31.02 E
Al-Bakātūsh	142	31.03 N	30.48 E
Al-Balāmūn	142	30.49 N	31.26 E
Al-Balāshūn	142	30.26 N	31.26 E
Al-Ballāḥ	142	30.46 N	32.19 E
Al-Ballāṣ	140	26.01 N	32.46 E
Al-Balqā' ▫8	132	32.00 N	35.40 E
Al-Bālū'ah ⊜	130	35.55 N	36.28 E
Al-Balyanā	140	26.14 N	32.00 E
Alban	32	43.54 N	2.28 E
Albanel, Lac ⊜	176	50.55 N	73.12 W
Albanella	68	40.30 N	15.08 E
Albani, Colli ⋏2	66	41.45 N	12.45 E
Albania, Col.	246	1.21 N	75.57 W
Albania, Col.	246	11.01 N	72.40 W
Albania (Shqipëri) ▫1, Europe	22	41.00 N	20.00 E
Albania (Shqipëri) ▫1, Europe	38	41.00 N	20.00 E
Albanie → Albania ▫1	38	41.00 N	20.00 E
Albanien → Albania ▫1	38	41.00 N	20.00 E
Albano, Lago ⊜	66	41.45 N	12.40 E
Albano, Monte ⋏	66	43.50 N	10.58 E
Albano di Lucania	68	40.35 N	16.02 E
Albano Laziale	66	41.44 N	12.39 E
Albany, Austl.	162	35.02 S	117.53 E
Albany, Ca., U.S.	226	37.53 N	122.17 W
Albany, Ga., U.S.	192	31.34 N	84.09 W
Albany, Il., U.S.	190	41.47 N	90.13 W
Albany, In., U.S.	216	40.18 N	85.14 W
Albany, Ky., U.S.	194	36.41 N	85.08 W
Albany, Mn., U.S.	190	45.37 N	94.34 W
Albany, Mo., U.S.	194	40.14 N	94.19 W
Albany, N.Y., U.S.	210	42.39 N	73.45 W
Albany, Oh., U.S.	188	39.13 N	82.12 W
Albany, Or., U.S.	202	44.38 N	123.06 W
Albany, Tx., U.S.	196	32.43 N	99.17 W
Albany, Wi., U.S.	190	42.42 N	89.26 W
Albany ▫6	210	42.39 N	73.45 W
Albany ≃	176	52.17 N	81.31 W
Albany County Airport ⊠	210	42.45 N	73.48 W
Albany Creek	171a	27.21 S	152.58 E
Albany Park ◆8	278	41.58 N	87.43 W
Al-Baq'ah	132	32.05 N	35.53 E
Al-Barājīl	273c	30.04 N	31.09 E
Al-Barāmūn	142	31.07 N	31.26 E
Albardón	252	31.26 S	68.32 W
Albaredo d'Adige	64	45.19 N	11.16 E
Al-Bāriḥah	132	32.34 N	35.50 E
Al-Barnūjī	142	30.56 N	30.23 E
Albaron	62	43.37 N	4.28 E
Albaron ∧	62	45.20 N	7.07 E
Albarracín	34	40.25 N	1.26 W
Al-Barrah	128	24.55 N	45.52 E
Albarraque	266c	38.46 N	9.21 W
Al-Barshā	142	27.43 N	30.54 E
Al-Barun	140	11.44 N	33.30 E
Al-Basātīn ◆8	273c	29.59 N	31.16 E
Al-Baslaqūn	142	31.06 N	30.08 E
Al-Basqalūn	142	28.42 N	30.44 E
Al-Baṣrah (Basra)	128	30.30 N	47.47 E
Al-Baṣrah ▫4	128	30.20 N	47.35 E
Al-Batānūn	142	30.37 N	30.59 E
Al-Baṭḥā'	128	31.06 N	45.53 E
Al-Bāṭinah ◆1	128	23.45 N	57.20 E
Albatross Bay C	164	12.45 S	141.43 E
Albatross Point ≻	172	38.06 S	174.41 E
Al-Batrūn	130	34.15 N	35.39 E
Al-Baṭrūnah	132	33.39 N	36.02 E
Al-Bauga	140	18.16 N	33.55 E
Al-Bawīṭī	140	28.21 N	28.52 E
Albay ▫4	116	13.00 N	123.40 E
Al-Bayahū	142	28.16 N	30.44 E
Al-Bayḍā (Beida), Lībiyā	146	28.22 N	18.55 E
Al-Bayḍā' (Beida), Lībiyā	146	32.46 N	21.43 E
Al-Bayḍā', Miṣr	142	31.10 N	30.05 E
Albay Gulf C	116	13.10 N	124.00 E
Albazino	89	53.23 N	124.05 E
Albbruck	58	47.35 N	8.07 E
Albegna ≃	66	42.30 N	11.11 E
Albemarle	192	35.13 N	80.13 W
Albemarle and Chesapeake Canal ≍	208	36.43 N	76.15 W
Albemarle Sound ⊔	192	36.03 N	76.12 W
Albenga	62	44.03 N	8.13 E
Albens	62	45.47 N	5.57 E
Alberche ≃	34	39.58 N	4.46 W
Alberdi	252	26.10 S	58.09 W
Alberene	192	37.53 N	78.37 W
Alberga, Austl.	162	27.12 S	135.28 E
Ålberga, Sve.	40	58.44 N	16.34 E
Alberga Creek ≃	162	27.06 S	135.33 E
Albergaria-a-Velha	34	40.42 N	8.29 W
Alberhill	228	33.44 N	117.23 W
Alberic	34	39.07 N	0.31 W
Alberni Inlet C	182	49.07 N	124.50 W
Alberobello	68	40.47 N	17.15 E
Alberona	68	41.26 N	15.07 E
Albero Sole ∧	70a	35.31 N	12.32 E
Albers	219	38.33 N	89.37 W
Alberschwende	58	47.27 N	9.49 E
Albersloh	52	51.52 N	7.43 E
Albert	50	50.00 N	2.39 E
Albert ≃	171a	27.42 S	153.15 E
Albert, Lake ⊜, Afr.	154	1.40 N	31.00 E
Albert, Lake ⊜, Austl.	166	35.38 S	139.17 E
Alberta	194	32.13 N	87.24 W
Alberta ▫4, Can.	176	54.00 N	113.00 W
Alberta ▫4, Can.	182	54.00 N	113.00 W
Alberta, Mount ∧	182	52.18 N	117.28 W
Albert Canyon	182	51.08 N	117.52 W
Albert City	198	42.46 N	94.56 W
Albert Edward, Mount ∧	164	8.23 S	147.24 E
Albert Edward Bay C	176	69.32 N	103.00 W
Albert Falls	158	29.27 S	30.25 E
Albertfalva ◆8	264c	47.27 N	19.02 E
Alberti	252	35.02 S	60.16 W
Al'bertin	76	53.05 N	25.23 E
Albertina	256	22.12 S	46.37 W
Albertinia	158	34.13 S	21.36 E
Albertirsa	30	47.15 N	19.38 E
Albert Kanaal (Canal Albert) ≍	56	50.39 N	5.37 E
Albert Lea	190	43.38 N	93.22 W
Albert Markham, Mount ∧	9	81.23 S	158.12 E
Albert Nile ≃	154	3.36 N	32.02 E
Alberto, Lago → Albert, Lake ⊜	154	1.40 N	31.00 E
Alberto Eduardo → Albert Edward, Mount ∧	164	8.23 S	147.24 E
Alberton, P.E., Can.	186	46.49 N	64.04 W
Alberton, S. Afr.	273d	26.16 S	28.08 E
Alberton, Mt., U.S.	202	47.00 N	114.29 W
Albert Park ♠	274b	37.51 S	144.57 E
Albert Peak ∧	182	51.02 N	117.51 W
Albertshof	264a	52.42 N	13.40 E
Albertson	276	40.46 N	73.38 W
Albertson Brook ≃	285	39.41 N	74.43 W
Albertson Brook, Blue Anchor Branch ≃	285	39.42 N	74.49 W
Albertson Brook, Pump Branch ≃	285	39.42 N	74.49 W
Albertville, Fr.	62	45.41 N	6.23 E
Albertville, Al., U.S.	194	34.16 N	86.12 W
Albertville → Kalemie, Zaïre	154	5.56 S	29.12 E
Albestroff	56	48.56 N	6.51 E
Albettone	64	45.21 N	11.35 E
Albi	32	43.56 N	2.09 E
Albia, Ia., U.S.	190	41.01 N	92.48 W
Albia, N.Y., U.S.	210	42.43 N	73.39 W
Albiate	266b	45.39 N	9.15 E
Al Bidia	146	10.33 N	20.13 E
Albidona	68	39.55 N	16.28 E
Albignasego	64	45.21 N	11.52 E
Albin	198	41.25 N	104.05 W
Albina	250	5.30 N	54.03 W
Albina, Ponta ≻	152	15.51 S	11.44 E
Albinea	64	44.37 N	10.36 E
Albino	62	45.46 N	9.47 E
Albion, Austl.	274b	37.47 S	144.49 E
Albion, B.C., Can.	224	49.11 N	122.33 W
Albion, Ca., U.S.	204	39.13 N	123.46 W
Albion, Id., U.S.	202	42.24 N	113.34 W
Albion, Il., U.S.	194	38.22 N	88.03 W
Albion, In., U.S.	216	41.23 N	85.25 W
Albion, Ia., U.S.	190	42.06 N	92.59 W
Albion, Mi., U.S.	216	42.14 N	84.45 W
Albion, Ne., U.S.	198	41.41 N	98.00 W
Albion, N.J., U.S.	285	39.47 N	74.56 W
Albion, N.Y., U.S.	210	43.14 N	78.11 W
Albion, Pa., U.S.	214	41.53 N	80.22 W
Albion, R.I., U.S.	207	41.57 N	71.27 W
Albion, Wa., U.S.	202	46.47 N	117.14 W
Albion, Wi., U.S.	216	42.52 N	89.04 W
Albion Airstrip ⊠	285	39.46 N	74.58 W
Albion Park	170	34.34 S	150.47 E
Al-Biqā' ▫4	130	34.00 N	36.00 E
Al-Biqā' V	128	33.50 N	36.00 E
Al-Bi'r	128	28.50 N	36.19 E
Al-Bīrah	132	31.54 N	35.13 E
Al-Birīgāt	142	30.30 N	30.49 E
Al-Birk	144	18.13 N	41.33 E
Al-Birkah	146	24.54 N	10.11 E
Al-Birkah ▾4	144	22.12 N	40.43 E
Albisola Marina	62	44.19 N	8.30 E
Albisola Superiore	62	44.20 N	8.31 E
Albizzate	62	45.43 N	8.44 E
Alblasserdam	52	51.52 N	4.40 E
Albo, Monte ∧	71	40.32 N	9.35 E
Albocàsser	34	40.21 N	0.02 E
Albogas	266c	38.51 N	9.15 W
Alborán, Isla de I	34	35.58 N	3.02 W
Alborán Sea ▾2	34	36.00 N	3.00 W
Ålborg	26	57.03 N	9.56 E
Ålborg Bugt C	26	56.45 N	10.30 E
Alborz, Reshteh-ye Kūhhā-ye (Elburz Mountains) ⋏	128	36.00 N	53.00 E
Albreda	182	52.38 N	119.09 W
Albright-Knox Art Gallery ◉	284a	42.56 N	78.53 W
Albrighton	42	52.38 N	2.16 W
Albstadt	58	48.13 N	9.01 E
Albuch ⋏	56	48.15 N	9.50 E
Albuera	116	10.55 N	124.42 E
Albufeira	34	37.05 N	8.15 W
Ālbū Gharz, Sabkhat ⊜	130	34.45 N	41.15 E
Al-Buḥayrah ▫4, Miṣr	142	30.59 N	30.12 E
Al-Buḥayrah ▫4, Sūd.	140	7.30 N	29.30 E
Albula ≃	58	46.42 N	9.27 E
Al-Bunbah	146	32.24 N	23.08 E
Albuñol	34	36.47 N	3.12 W
Albuquerque, Bra.	248	19.23 S	57.26 W
Albuquerque, N.M., U.S.	200	35.05 N	106.39 W
Albuquerque, Cayos de II	236	12.10 N	81.50 W
Al-Buraymī	128	24.15 N	55.45 E
Alburg	206	44.58 N	73.18 W
Al-Burj	142	31.35 N	30.59 E
Al-Burjāyah	142	28.09 N	30.44 E
Alburno, Monte ∧	68	40.33 N	15.17 E
Alburquerque	34	39.13 N	7.00 W
Alburtis	208	40.31 N	75.36 W
Al-Burumbul	142	29.19 N	31.14 E
Albury, Austl.	166	36.05 S	146.55 E
Albury, N.Z.	172	44.14 S	170.52 E
Albury, Eng., U.K.	260	51.13 N	0.30 W
Albury Park ♠	260	51.13 N	0.29 W
Al-Buṣaylī	142	31.20 N	30.24 E
Al-Busayṭā' ≚	128	29.30 N	38.45 E
Al-Buṭānah ◆1	140	15.00 N	34.40 E
Al-Buṭaynah	132	32.57 N	36.42 E
Al-Buwayḍah	132	32.28 N	36.04 E
Al-Buzūn	144	15.35 N	50.55 E
Albuzzano	62	45.11 N	9.16 E
Alby, Fr.	62	45.49 N	6.01 E
Alby, Sve.	26	62.30 N	15.28 E
Alca	248	15.08 S	72.46 W
Alcabideche	266c	38.44 N	9.24 W
Alcácer do Sal	34	38.22 N	8.30 W
Alcains	34	39.55 N	7.27 W
Alcala	116	17.54 N	121.39 E
Alcalá de Guadaira	34	37.20 N	5.50 W
Alcalá de Henares	34	40.29 N	3.22 W
Alcalá la Real	34	37.28 N	3.56 W
Alcalde	200	36.05 N	106.03 W
Alcamachi ≃	248	16.08 S	66.50 W
Alcamo	70	37.59 N	12.58 E
Alčan ≃	89	46.38 N	134.22 E
Alcanadre ≃	34	41.37 N	0.12 E
Alcanar	34	40.33 N	0.29 E
Alcañices	34	41.42 N	6.21 W
Alcañiz	34	41.03 N	0.08 W
Alcântara, Bra.	250	2.24 S	44.24 W
Alcántara, Esp.	34	39.43 N	6.53 W
Alcantara, Pil.	116	12.16 N	122.03 E
Alcântara ◆8	266c	38.42 N	9.10 W
Alcantara ≃	70	37.49 N	15.16 E
Alcántara, Embalse de ⊜1	34	39.45 N	6.25 W
Alcantarilla	34	37.58 N	1.13 W
Alcantilado	255	16.23 S	53.31 W
Alcara li Fusi	70	38.01 N	14.42 E
Alcaraz	34	38.40 N	2.29 W
Alcarrache ≃	34	38.16 N	7.24 W
Alcatraz Island I	282	37.49 N	122.26 W
Alcaudete	34	37.36 N	4.05 W
Alcázar de San Juan	34	39.24 N	3.12 W
Alcazarquivir → Er-Rachidia	148	31.58 N	4.25 W
Alcester, Eng., U.K.	42	52.13 N	1.52 W
Alcester, S.D., U.S.	198	43.01 N	96.37 W
Alcester Island I	164	9.35 S	152.25 E
Alchevs'k	83	48.30 N	38.47 E
Alcira (Gigena)	252	32.45 S	64.20 W
Alcoa	192	35.47 N	83.58 W
Alcoa Center	279b	40.33 N	79.39 W
Alcoa Lake ⊜1	222	30.34 N	97.03 W
Alcobaça, Bra.	255	17.30 S	39.13 W
Alcobaça, Port.	34	39.33 N	8.59 W
Alcobaça ≃	255	17.32 S	39.12 W
Alcobendas	34	40.32 N	3.38 W
Alcochete	266c	38.45 N	8.58 W
Alcockspruit	158	27.55 S	30.01 E
Alcoi	34	38.42 N	0.28 W
Alcoi ≃	34	38.59 N	0.09 W
Alcoitão	266c	38.44 N	9.24 W
Alcolea del Pinar	34	41.02 N	2.28 W
Alcolu	192	33.45 N	80.12 W
Alcomunga	234	18.25 N	97.02 W
Alconbury Brook ≃	42	52.19 N	0.12 W
Alconchel	34	38.31 N	7.04 W
Alcony	218	40.01 N	84.04 W
Alcorcón	266a	40.21 N	3.50 W
Alcorn	194	31.52 N	91.09 W
Alcorta	252	33.32 S	61.07 W
Alcoutim	34	37.28 N	7.28 W
Alcova Reservoir ⊜1	200	42.32 N	106.45 W
Alcove	210	42.28 N	73.55 W
Alcove Reservoir ⊜1	210	42.29 N	73.57 W
Alcovy ≃	192	33.26 N	83.50 W
Alcubierre	34	41.48 N	0.27 W
Alcúdia	34	39.52 N	3.07 E
Alcúdia, Badia d' C	34	39.48 N	3.13 E
Alcyon Lake ⊜	285	39.44 N	75.08 W
Aldabra Island I	138	9.25 S	46.22 E
Aldama, Méx.	232	28.51 N	105.54 W
Aldama, Méx.	234	22.55 N	98.04 W
Aldama, Arroyo ≃	286b	23.05 N	82.15 W
Aldan, Ross.	74	58.37 N	125.24 E
Aldan, Pa., U.S.	285	39.55 N	75.17 W
Aldan ≃	74	63.28 N	129.35 E
Aldanskoje nagorje ⋏1	74	57.00 N	127.00 E
Aldbourne	42	51.31 N	1.37 W
Aldbrough	44	53.50 N	0.07 W
Aldbury	42	51.48 N	0.36 W
Alde ≃	42	52.03 N	1.28 E
Aldea Apeleg	254	44.41 S	70.51 W
Aldeburgh	42	52.09 N	1.35 E
Aldeia de Paio Pires	266c	38.38 N	9.05 W
Aldeia Nova de Santo Bento	34	37.55 N	7.25 W
Aldeia Velha	256	22.47 S	42.55 W
Aldemha	287b	23.45 S	46.53 W
Alden, Il., U.S.	216	42.27 N	88.31 W
Alden, Ia., U.S.	190	42.31 N	93.22 W
Alden, Mn., U.S.	190	43.40 N	93.34 W
Alden, N.Y., U.S.	210	42.54 N	78.29 W
Alden, Pa., U.S.	210	41.10 N	76.00 W
Alden Center	212	42.55 N	78.32 W
Aldenham	260	51.40 N	0.21 W
Aldenhoven	56	50.53 N	6.16 E
Aldenrade ◆8	263	51.31 N	6.44 E
Alder, Ben ∧	46	56.48 N	4.28 W
Alder Creek ≃	202	45.50 N	119.56 W
Aldergrove	224	49.04 N	122.28 W
Alder Lake ⊜1	224	46.45 N	122.15 W
Alderley Edge	44	53.18 N	2.15 W
Aldermaston	42	51.23 N	1.09 W
Alderney I	43b	49.43 N	2.12 W
Alder Peak ∧	226	35.53 N	121.22 W
Aldersbach	60	48.36 N	13.05 E
Aldershot	42	51.15 N	0.47 W
Alderson	192	37.44 N	80.38 W
Alderton	224	47.10 N	122.14 W
Alderwood Manor	224	47.49 N	122.17 W
Aldine	222	29.54 N	95.24 W
Aldinga	168b	35.17 S	138.29 E
Aldinga Bay C	168b	35.20 S	138.25 E
Aldinga Beach	168b	35.18 S	138.27 E
Aldingen	58	48.05 N	8.41 E
Aldino	64	46.23 N	11.20 E
Aldo Bonzi	288	34.42 S	58.31 W
Aldridge	42	52.36 N	1.55 W
Aldwell, Lake ⊜1	224	48.05 N	123.34 W
Alechovščina	76	60.25 N	33.52 E
Aled ≃	44	53.14 N	3.34 W
Aledo, Il., U.S.	190	41.11 N	90.44 W
Aledo, Tx., U.S.	222	32.42 N	97.36 W
Alefa	144	11.57 N	36.52 E
Aleg	150	17.03 N	13.55 W
Alegranza, Isla I	148	29.23 N	13.30 W
Alegre	255	20.46 S	41.32 W
Alegre ≃	248	15.01 S	59.57 W
Alegres Mountain ∧	200	34.09 N	108.11 W
Alegrete	252	29.46 S	55.46 W
Alej ≃	86	52.52 N	83.36 E
Alejandría → Al-Iskandarīyah	142	31.12 N	29.54 E
Alejandro, Isla → Alexander Island I	9	71.00 S	70.00 W
Alejandro Roca	252	33.21 S	63.43 W
Alejandro Selkirk, Isla (Isla Más Afuera) I	244	33.45 S	80.46 W
Alejo Ledesma	252	33.37 S	62.37 W
Alejsk	86	52.28 N	82.45 E
Aleknagik	180	59.17 N	158.38 W
Aleknagik, Lake ⊜	180	59.20 N	158.45 W
Aleksandrijskaja	84	43.54 N	47.08 E
Aleksandro-Nevskaja	84	43.55 N	46.35 E
Aleksandro-Nevskij	80	53.28 N	40.13 E
Aleksandrov	82	56.24 N	38.43 E
Aleksandrov Gaj	80	50.09 N	48.34 E
Aleksandrovka, Kaz.	80	50.47 N	52.59 E
Aleksandrovka, Kaz.	85	43.27 N	77.20 E
Aleksandrovka, Kaz.	86	53.07 N	69.50 E
Aleksandrovka, Ross.	78	46.47 N	39.01 E
Aleksandrovka, Ross.	80	52.36 N	50.37 E
Aleksandrovka, Ross.	83	47.26 N	39.13 E
Aleksandrovka, Ross.	86	56.32 N	90.47 E
Aleksandrovka, Ross.	86	52.43 N	54.17 E
Aleksandrovskaja, Ross.	265a	60.03 N	29.59 E
Aleksandrovskaja, Ross.	265a	59.44 N	30.21 E
Aleksandrovskij	78	51.03 N	36.44 E
Aleksandrovskij Šl'uz	86	59.26 N	89.20 E
Aleksandrovskij Zavod	88	50.55 N	117.57 E
Aleksandrovskoje, Ross.	84	44.42 N	43.00 E
Aleksandrovskoje, Ross.	86	56.44 N	85.23 E
Aleksandrovskoje, Ross.	86	60.26 N	77.50 E
Aleksandrovsk-Sachalinskij	89	50.54 N	142.10 E
Aleksandrów Kujawski	30	52.52 N	18.42 E
Aleksandrów Łódzki	30	51.49 N	19.19 E
Aleksaskino	80	50.57 N	47.42 E
Aleksejevka, Kaz.	80	50.58 N	52.25 E
Aleksejevka, Kaz.	86	53.31 N	69.30 E
Aleksejevka, Kaz.	86	51.59 N	70.59 E
Aleksejevka, Kaz.	86	47.16 N	81.34 E
Aleksejevka, Kaz.	86	48.25 N	85.40 E
Aleksejevka, Ross.	78	50.37 N	38.42 E
Aleksejevka, Ross.	80	52.35 N	51.17 E
Aleksejevka, Ross.	80	53.15 N	50.30 E
Aleksejevka, Ross.	80	53.02 N	42.46 E
Aleksejevka, Ross.	80	51.49 N	43.56 E
Aleksejevka, Ross.	80	52.18 N	48.01 E
Aleksejevka, Ross.	82	54.41 N	36.34 E
Aleksejevka, Ross.	83	47.38 N	38.49 E
Aleksejevka, Ross.	83	47.41 N	39.54 E
Aleksejevka, Ross.	86	52.30 N	79.33 E
Aleksejevka, Ross.	86	54.31 N	81.08 E
Aleksejevka, Ross.	86	55.22 N	72.03 E
Aleksejevo-Lozovskoje	78	49.24 N	40.39 E
Aleksejevo-Tuzlovka	83	47.50 N	39.24 E
Aleksejevsk	88	57.50 N	108.23 E
Aleksejevskaja	80	50.17 N	42.11 E
Aleksejevskoje	80	55.18 N	50.06 E
Aleksin	82	54.31 N	37.05 E
Aleksinac	38	43.32 N	21.43 E
Alella	266d	41.30 N	2.18 E
Alemanha → Germany ▫1	30	51.00 N	10.00 E
Alemania	252	25.36 S	65.38 W
Alemania → Germany ▫1	30	51.00 N	10.00 E
Alem Dağı ∧	267b	41.04 N	29.12 E
Alemdar ◆8	267b	41.03 N	29.14 E
Além Paraíba	256	21.52 S	42.41 W
Alençon	50	48.26 N	0.05 E
Alenquer	250	1.56 S	54.46 W
Alentejo ▫9	34	38.00 N	8.00 W
Alenuihaha Channel ⊔	229a	20.26 N	156.00 W
Aléoutiennes, Îles → Aleutian Islands II	180	52.00 N	176.00 W
Alep → Ḥalab	130	36.12 N	37.10 E
Aleppo → Ḥalab	130	36.12 N	37.10 E
Aléria	36	42.05 N	9.30 E
Alert	16	82.29 N	62.22 W
Alert Bay	182	50.35 N	126.55 W
Alès, Fr.	62	44.08 N	4.05 E
Ales, It.	71	39.46 N	8.49 E
Aleșd	38	47.04 N	22.24 E
Alešino, Ross.	82	56.09 N	37.45 E
Alešino, Ross.	82	55.04 N	36.05 E
Aleški	80	51.38 N	41.46 E
Aleškovo	82	54.53 N	36.23 E
Alessandria	62	44.54 N	8.37 E
Alessandria ▫4	62	44.49 N	8.42 E
Alessandria del Carretto	68	39.57 N	16.23 E
Alessandria della Rocca	70	37.34 N	13.27 E
Alessano	68	39.53 N	18.20 E
Ålestrup	26	56.42 N	9.30 E
Ålesund	26	62.28 N	6.09 E
Aletschhorn ∧	58	46.28 N	8.00 E
Alëuten → Aleutian Islands II	180	52.00 N	176.00 W
Aleutianas, Islas → Aleutian Islands II	180	52.00 N	176.00 W
Aleutian Basin ✢1	16	57.00 N	177.00 E
Aleutian Islands II	180	52.00 N	176.00 W
Aleutian Range ⋏	180	59.00 N	155.00 W
Aleutian Trench ✢1	6	51.00 N	170.00 W
Aleutka	74	45.57 N	150.10 E
Alevina, mys ≻	74	58.50 N	151.20 E
Ale Water ≃	46	55.31 N	2.35 W
Alex	196	34.54 N	97.46 W
Alexander, Mb., Can.	184	49.50 N	100.17 W
Alexander, Il., U.S.	219	39.43 N	90.02 W
Alexander, N.Y., U.S.	210	42.54 N	78.16 W
Alexander, N.D., U.S.	198	47.50 N	103.38 W
Alexander ≃	132	32.24 N	34.52 E
Alexander, Cape ≻	175e	6.35 S	156.30 E
Alexander, Mount ∧, Austl.	162	22.39 S	115.32 E
Alexander, Mount ∧, Austl.	169	36.59 S	144.18 E
Alexander Archipelago II	180	56.30 N	134.00 W
Alexander Bay	156	28.40 S	16.30 E
Alexander City	194	32.56 N	85.57 W
Alexander Dam ⊜1	273d	26.13 S	28.25 E
Alexander Ditch ≍	279a	41.20 N	82.05 W
Alexander Hamilton Airport ⊠	241n	17.42 N	64.48 W
Alexander Indian Reserve ◆4	182	53.48 N	113.58 W
Alexander Island I	9	71.00 S	70.00 W
Alexander Nevsky Monastery ◉1	265a	59.55 N	30.24 E
Alexandra, Austl.	169	37.12 S	145.43 E
Alexandra, N.Z.	172	45.15 S	169.24 E
Alexandra, S. Afr.	273d	26.06 S	28.05 E
Alexandra ≃	166	18.14 S	139.54 E
Alexandra Canal ≍	274a	33.56 S	151.10 E
Alexandra Falls ∟	176	60.29 N	116.18 W
Alexandra Park ♠	262	53.27 N	2.15 W
Alexandra Park Race Course ♠	260	51.36 N	0.08 W
Alexandretta → İskenderun	130	36.37 N	36.07 E
Alexandretta, Gulf of → İskenderun Körfezi C	130	36.30 N	35.40 E
Alexandria, Austl.	166	19.05 S	136.40 E
Alexandria, Bra.	250	6.25 S	38.01 W
Alexandria, B.C., Can.	182	52.38 N	122.27 W
Alexandria, On., Can.	206	45.19 N	74.38 W
Alexandria → Al-Iskandarīyah, Miṣr	142	31.12 N	29.54 E
Alexandria, Rom.	38	43.58 N	25.20 E
Alexandria, S. Afr.	158	33.40 S	26.24 E
Alexandria, Scot., U.K.	46	55.59 N	4.36 W
Alexandria, In., U.S.	216	40.15 N	85.40 W
Alexandria, Ky., U.S.	218	38.57 N	84.23 W
Alexandria, La., U.S.	194	31.18 N	92.26 W
Alexandria, Mn., U.S.	198	45.53 N	95.22 W
Alexandria, Mo., U.S.	194	40.21 N	91.27 W
Alexandria, Ne., U.S.	198	40.14 N	97.23 W
Alexandria, Oh., U.S.	214	40.05 N	82.37 W
Alexandria, Pa., U.S.	214	40.34 N	78.06 W
Alexandria, S.D., U.S.	198	43.39 N	97.46 W
Alexandria, Tn., U.S.	194	36.04 N	86.02 W
Alexandria, Va., U.S.	208	38.48 N	77.02 W
Alexandria Bay	212	44.20 N	75.55 W
Alexandrie → Al-Iskandarīyah	142	31.12 N	29.54 E
Alexandrina, Lake ⊜	168b	35.26 S	139.10 E
Alexandroúpolis	38	40.50 N	25.52 E
Alexis	190	41.03 N	90.33 W
Alexis Creek	182	52.05 N	123.17 W
Alexis Indian Reserve ◆4	182	53.46 N	114.30 W
Alezio	68	40.04 N	18.03 E
Alf	56	50.03 N	7.07 E
Ālfādānga	126	23.18 N	89.42 E
Al-Fahmīyīn	142	29.36 N	31.17 E
Al-Fallūjah	128	33.20 N	43.46 E
Alfambra	34	40.33 N	1.02 W
Alfambra ≃	34	40.21 N	1.07 W
Al-Fant	142	28.46 N	30.53 E
Alfarata	208	40.39 N	77.27 W
Al-Farḍah	144	14.51 N	48.27 E
Alfaro	34	42.11 N	1.45 W
Alfarràs	34	41.49 N	0.35 E
Al-Fāshir	140	13.38 N	25.21 E
Al-Fashn	142	28.49 N	30.54 E
Alfatar	38	43.57 N	27.17 E
Alfavaca, Ilha I	287a	23.02 S	43.18 W
Al-Fāw	128	29.58 N	48.29 E
Al-Fayyūm	142	29.19 N	30.50 E
Al-Fayyūm ▫4	142	29.19 N	30.48 E
Al-Fāzah	144	14.08 N	43.05 E
Alfbach ≃	56	50.03 N	7.08 E
Alfedena	66	41.44 N	14.02 E
Alfeld, Dtsch.	52	51.59 N	9.50 E
Alfeld, Dtsch.	60	49.26 N	11.33 E
Alfenas	256	21.25 S	45.57 W
Alfianello	64	45.16 N	10.10 E
Al-Fifi	140	10.03 N	25.01 E
Alfiós ≃	38	37.40 N	21.33 E
Al-Firdān	142	30.41 N	32.20 E
Alföld ≚	30	47.00 N	20.00 E
Alfonsine	66	44.30 N	12.03 E
Alford, Austl.	168b	33.49 S	137.49 E
Alford, Eng., U.K.	44	53.16 N	0.10 E
Alford, Scot., U.K.	46	57.13 N	2.42 W
Alfortville	261	48.49 N	2.25 E
Ålfotbreen ⌂	26	61.45 N	5.40 E
Alfred, On., Can.	206	45.34 N	74.53 W
Alfred, Me., U.S.	188	43.28 N	70.43 W
Alfred, N.Y., U.S.	210	42.15 N	77.47 W
Alfred National Park ♠	166	37.35 S	149.20 E
Alfredo M. Terrazas	234	21.28 N	98.51 W
Alfreton	44	53.06 N	1.23 W
Alfriston	42	50.48 N	0.10 E
Alfta	26	61.21 N	16.05 E
Al-Fujayrah	128	25.06 N	56.21 E
Al-Fuqahā'	146	27.50 N	16.22 E
Al-Furzul	132	33.52 N	35.56 E
Alga	86	49.46 N	57.20 E
Algabas, Kaz.	80	50.39 N	52.07 E
Algabas, Kaz.	86	44.41 N	78.06 E
Algabas, Kaz.	86	48.21 N	81.39 E
Algači	88	50.43 N	117.47 E
Ålgarås	40	58.48 N	14.14 E
Ålgård	26	58.46 N	5.51 E
Al-Garef	140	12.03 N	34.19 E
Algarrobal	252	28.08 S	70.39 W
Algarrobo, Arg.	252	38.53 S	63.08 W
Algarrobo, Arg.	252	31.44 S	68.18 W
Algarrobo, Chile	252	33.22 S	71.40 W
Algarrobo del Águila	252	36.26 S	67.09 W
Algarve ▫9	34	37.10 N	8.15 W
Algás ≃	34	41.08 N	0.39 E
Algasovo	76	53.41 N	41.40 E
Al-Gebir	140	13.43 N	29.49 E
Algeciras, Col.	246	2.35 N	75.18 W
Algeciras, Esp.	34	36.08 N	5.30 W
Algemesí	34	39.11 N	0.26 W
Algena	144	17.19 N	38.31 E
Alger → El Djazaïr, Alg.	148	36.47 N	3.03 E
Alger, Oh., U.S.	216	40.42 N	83.50 W
Alger, Baie d' C	34	36.50 N	3.15 E
Algeria (Algérie) ▫1, Afr.	134	28.00 N	3.00 E
Algeria (Algérie) ▫1, Afr.	148	28.00 N	3.00 E
Algérie → Algeria ▫1	148	28.00 N	3.00 E
Algerien → Algeria ▫1	148	28.00 N	3.00 E
Algermissen	52	52.15 N	9.58 E
Algés	266c	38.42 N	9.13 W
Al-Ghāb ⊜	130	35.30 N	36.18 E
Al-Gharaq as-Sulṭānī	142	29.08 N	30.42 E
Al-Gharbīyah ▫4	142	30.45 N	31.00 E
Al-Ghāriyah	132	32.23 N	36.39 E
Al-Ghāṭ	128	26.00 N	45.03 E
Al-Ghawr V	132	31.50 N	35.30 E
Al-Ghayatah	142	30.57 N	30.06 E
Al-Ghayḍah	118	16.12 N	52.15 E
Al-Ghazālah	128	26.48 N	41.19 E
Al-Ghazālī	142	30.49 N	31.49 E
Al-Ghāzīyah	132	33.31 N	35.22 E
Alghero	71	40.34 N	8.19 E
Al-Ghurayfah	128	24.00 N	56.29 E

Symbols in the index entries represent the broad categories identified in the key at the right. Symbols with superior numbers (⋏1) identify subcategories (see complete key on page *I · 1*).

Symbole im Register stellen die rechts im Schlüssel erklärten Kategorien dar. Symbole mit hochgestellten Ziffern (⋏1) bezeichnen Unterabteilungen einer Kategorie (vgl. vollständiger Schlüssel auf Seite *I · 1*).

Los símbolos incluídos en el texto del índice representan las grandes categorías identificadas con la clave a la derecha. Los símbolos con numeros en su parte superior (⋏1) identifican las subcategorías (véase la clave completa en la página *I · 1*).

Les symboles de l'index représentent les catégories indiquées dans la légende à droite. Les symboles suivis d'un indice (⋏1) représentent des sous-catégories (voir légende complète à la page *I · 1*).

Os símbolos incluídos no texto do índice representam as grandes categorias identificadas com a chave à direita. Os símbolos com números em sua parte superior (⋏1) identificam as subcategorias (veja-se a chave completa à página *I · 1*).

∧	Mountain	Berg	Montaña	Montagne	Montanha
⋏	Mountains	Gebirge	Montañas	Montagnes	Montanhas
)(	Pass	Paß	Paso	Col	Passo
V	Valley, Canyon	Tal, Cañon	Valle, Cañón	Vallée, Canyon	Vale, Canhão
≚	Plain	Ebene	Llano	Plaine	Planície
≻	Cape	Kap	Cabo	Cap	Cabo
I	Island	Insel	Isla	Île	Ilha
II	Islands	Inseln	Islas	Îles	Ilhas
≛	Other Topographic Features	Andere Topographische Objekte	Otros Elementos Topográficos	Autres données topographiques	Outros acidentes topográficos

ESPAÑOL Nombre	Página	Lat.°'	Long.°' W = Oeste

Al-Ghurdaqah 140 27.14 N 33.50 E
Algier — El Djazaïr 148 36.47 N 3.03 E
Algiers — El Djazaïr 148 36.47 N 3.03 E
Alginet 34 39.16 N 0.28 W
Algoa 222 29.24 N 95.11 W
Algoabaai c 158 33.50 S 25.50 E
Algodão, Ilha do I 256 23.13 S 44.36 W
Algodón ≃ 246 2.23 S 71.56 W
Algodones 200 35.22 N 106.28 W
Algodor ≃ 34 39.55 N 3.53 W
Algoma 190 44.36 N 87.25 W
Algoma Mills 190 46.10 N 82.50 W
Algona, Ia., U.S. 190 43.04 N 94.13 W
Algona, Wa., U.S. 224 47.16 N 122.15 W
Algonac 214 42.37 N 82.31 W
Algonquin 216 42.09 N 88.17 W
Algonquin Lake ⊜ 216 42.40 N 85.20 W
Algonquin Provincial Park ♠ 190 45.45 N 78.26 W
Algood 194 36.11 N 85.26 W
Algorta, Esp. 34 43.22 N 3.01 W
Algorta, Ur. 252 32.25 S 57.23 W
Alguierão-Mem Martins 266c 38.48 N 9.20 W
Al-Haddādī 142 31.20 N 30.47 E
Al-Haddayn 142 30.44 N 30.38 E
Al-Hadīthah 128 34.07 N 42.23 E
Al-Hadr 128 35.35 N 42.44 E
Al-Haffah 130 35.35 N 36.02 E
Al-Hafīr Al-Fawqānī 132 33.42 N 36.28 E
Al-Hajālīj 140 14.36 N 31.54 E
Al-Hajarah ◆ 1 128 30.00 N 44.00 E
Al-Hajar al-Gharbī ⋏ 128 24.10 N 56.15 E
Al-Hajar ash-Sharqī ⋏ 128 22.45 N 59.00 E
Al Hajeb 148 33.43 N 5.13 W
Al-Hājir 142 30.41 N 31.49 E
Al-Halfāyah 128 31.49 N 47.26 E
Al-Hamād ≚ 128 32.00 N 39.30 E
Alhama de Granada 34 37.00 N 3.59 W
Alhama de Murcia 34 37.51 N 1.25 W
Al-Hamal ◆ 1 128 23.30 N 49.45 E
Alhambra, Ca., U.S. 228 34.05 N 118.07 W
Alhambra, Il., U.S. 219 38.53 N 89.44 W
Al-Hamīdīyah 130 34.43 N 35.56 E
Al-Hammām 140 30.50 N 29.23 E
Al-Hamrā', Ar. Su. 128 23.57 N 38.52 E
'Al-Hamrā', Lubnān 132 33.42 N 35.27 E
Al-Hamrah 142 31.10 N 30.52 E
Al-Hāmūl 142 31.19 N 31.10 E
Alhandra 250 7.26 S 34.54 W
Alhandra, Mouchão de I 266c 38.54 N 9.00 W
Al-Harāk 132 32.44 N 36.18 E
Al-Harīq 128 23.37 N 46.31 E
Al-Hārrah 132 33.03 N 36.00 E
Al-Harrah • 9 128 31.00 N 38.30 E
Al-Harūj al-Aswad ⋏ 2 146 27.00 N 17.10 E
Al-Hasakah 130 36.29 N 40.45 E
Al-Hasakah □ 8 130 36.30 N 41.00 E
Al-Hasānī I 128 24.58 N 37.05 E
Alhaurín el Grande 34 36.38 N 4.41 W
Al-Hawāmidīyah 273c 29.54 N 31.15 E
Al-Hawātah 140 13.25 N 34.38 E
Al-Hawātikah 142 27.16 N 31.01 E
Al-Hawrah 144 13.49 N 47.37 E
Al-Hawtah 144 15.50 N 48.27 E
Al-Hawwārīyah 142 30.58 N 29.41 E
Al-Hayy, 'Irāq 128 32.10 N 46.03 E
Al-Hayy, Misr 142 29.39 N 31.18 E
Al-Hayyānīyah 128 28.38 N 42.45 E
Al-Hayz 140 28.02 N 28.39 E
Al-Hībah 142 28.45 N 30.55 E
Al-Hījānah 132 33.21 N 36.33 E
Al-Hijāz ◆ 1 118 24.30 N 38.30 E
Al-Hillah, 'Irāq 128 32.29 N 44.25 E
Al-Hillah, Sūd. 140 13.27 N 27.08 E
Al-Hilmīyah ◆ 8 273c 30.07 N 31.19 E
Al-Hindīyah 128 32.33 N 44.13 E
Al-Hirmil 130 34.23 N 36.23 E
Al-Hisn 132 32.29 N 35.52 E
Al-Hoceïma 148 35.15 N 3.55 W
Al-Hoceïma □ 4 148 35.00 N 4.30 W
Al Hoceïma, Baie d' c 34 35.20 N 3.50 W
Alhos Vedros 266c 38.39 N 9.02 W
Alhucemas, Peñón de I 34 35.13 N 3.53 W
Al-Hudayb 140 13.00 N 32.50 E
Al-Hudaydah 144 14.48 N 42.57 E
Al-Hufrah 146 29.10 N 18.02 E
Al-Hufrah ◆ 1 128 28.40 N 38.30 E
Al-Hufūf 128 25.22 N 49.34 E
Al-Hulwah 128 23.27 N 46.47 E
Al-Humayshah 144 13.41 N 45.52 E
Al-Humrah ◆ 1 128 23.20 N 54.30 E
Al-Husayhisah 140 14.44 N 33.18 E
Al-Husaynīyah 142 30.52 N 31.55 E
Al-Husaynīyah ⫧ 4 144 17.48 N 44.27 E
Al-Huwaylizah 132 33.02 N 35.51 E
Al-Huwaymī 144 14.05 N 47.44 E
Al-Huwayyit 128 25.36 N 40.23 E
Alì 70 38.02 N 15.25 E
Ali ◆ 8 272a 28.31 N 77.18 E
'Ālī, As-Sadd al- (Aswān High Dam) ◆ 6 140 23.58 N 32.52 E
Alía, Esp. 34 39.27 N 5.13 W
Alia, It. 70 37.47 N 13.43 E
Äliabad, Azer. 84 41.29 N 46.37 E
'Alīābād, Īrān 128 36.57 N 54.59 E
Alīābād, Pāk. 123 36.18 N 74.37 E
Aliade 150 7.16 N 8.28 E
Aliaga, Esp. 34 40.40 N 0.42 W
Aliağa, Tür. 130 38.48 N 26.59 E
Aliákmon ≃ 38 40.30 N 22.36 E
Aliákmonos, Tekhnití Límni ⊜ 1 38 40.15 N 22.00 E
Aliaksin, Cape ≻ 180 55.30 N 160.43 W
'Alī al-Gharbī 128 32.27 N 46.41 E
Aliança 250 7.35 S 35.13 W
Aliano 68 40.19 N 16.14 E
Alībāg 122 18.39 N 72.54 E
Alibahadır ◆ 8 267b 41.11 N 29.12 E
Alibardak 130 38.06 N 40.25 E
Alibates Flint Quarries National Monument ♠ 196 35.35 N 101.39 W
Älibäyli 84 41.23 N 46.49 E
Äli Bayramlı 84 39.56 N 48.56 E
Alibey ≃ 267b 41.03 N 28.56 E
Alibey, ozero ⊜ 78 45.48 N 30.02 E
Alibey Adası I 130 39.20 N 26.38 E
Alibey Barajı ⊜ 1 267b 41.07 N 28.55 E
Alibeyköy ◆ 8 267b 41.04 N 28.56 E
Alibijaban Island I 116 13.20 N 122.43 E
Alibori ≃ 150 11.56 N 3.17 E
Al-Ibrāhīmīyah 142 30.57 N 31.35 E
Alibunar 38 45.05 N 20.58 E
Alicante — Alacant 34 38.21 N 0.29 W
Alice, S. Afr. 158 32.47 S 26.50 E
Alice, Tx., U.S. 196 27.45 N 98.04 W
Alice ≃, Austl. 164 15.22 S 141.58 E
Alice ≃, Austl. 166 24.02 S 144.50 E
Alice, Punta ≻ 68 39.24 N 17.10 E
Alice Arm 182 55.29 N 129.29 W
Alicedale 158 33.19 S 26.05 E
Alice Downs 162 17.45 S 127.56 E
Alice Springs 162 23.42 S 133.53 E
Alice Superiore 62 45.28 N 7.47 E
Alice Town 238 25.44 N 79.17 W
Aliceville 194 33.07 N 88.09 W
Alicia, Pil. 116 16.45 N 121.42 E
Alicia, Pil. 116 7.30 N 122.55 E
Alıcık 130 40.49 N 35.21 E
Alick Creek ≃ 166 20.25 S 142.00 E
Alicudi, Isola I 70 38.32 N 14.21 E
Alicurá, Embalse de ⊜ 1 254 40.40 S 71.00 W
Al-'Idwah 142 29.21 N 30.55 E
Alief 222 29.43 N 95.35 W

FRANÇAIS Nom	Page	Lat.°'	Long.°' W = Ouest

Alife 68 41.20 N 14.20 E
Al-Ifranj 132 31.11 N 35.41 E
Alīganj, India 124 28.07 N 80.36 E
Alīganj, India 124 27.30 N 79.11 E
Alīgarh 124 27.53 N 78.05 E
Alignements de Carnac ⊥ 32 47.35 N 3.05 W
Alīgūdarz 128 33.24 N 49.41 E
Alijos, Islas II 232 24.57 N 115.44 W
'Alī Kheyl 120 33.57 N 69.43 E
Al-Ikhşāş al-Qiblīyah 142 29.42 N 31.17 E
Al-Ikhwān II 118 12.08 N 53.10 E
Alikovo 80 55.45 N 46.45 E
Alima ≃ 152 1.36 S 16.36 E
Al-Imām ◆ 8 273c 30.01 N 31.10 E
Al-Imārāt al-'Arabīyah al-Muttaḥidah — United Arab Emirates □ 1 128 24.00 N 54.00 E
Al-'Imārīyah 142 27.37 N 30.53 E
Alimena 70 37.42 N 14.07 E
Alimini Grande ⊜ 68 40.12 N 18.27 E
Alimini Piccolo ⊜ 68 40.10 N 18.27 E
Aliminusa 70 37.52 N 13.47 E
Alim Island I 164 2.55 S 147.05 E
Alimkent 85 40.58 N 69.11 E
Alimodian 116 10.49 N 122.26 E
Alindao 152 5.02 N 21.13 E
Alingsås 26 57.56 N 12.31 E
Ālipur, India 272b 22.43 N 88.12 E
Alipur, India 272b 22.55 N 88.11 E
Alīpur, Pāk. 123 29.23 N 70.55 E
Ālīpur ◆ 8 126 22.31 N 88.20 E
Ālīpur Duār 124 26.29 N 89.44 E
Alīpur Janūbi 123 30.13 N 71.18 E
Aliquippa 214 40.38 N 80.14 W
Aliquippa-Hopewell Airport ⊠ 279b 40.35 N 80.17 W
Alīrājpur 120 22.19 N 74.21 E
Al-'Irāq 132 31.05 N 35.39 E
Al-'Irāq — Iraq □ 1 128 33.00 N 44.00 E
Al-'Irqah 144 13.30 N 47.22 E
Ali-Sabieh 144 11.09 N 42.42 E
Al-'Īsāwīyah 128 30.38 N 37.53 E
Aliseda 34 39.26 N 6.41 W
Alise-Sainte-Reine 58 47.32 N 4.29 E
Alīshārī 84 39.02 N 47.15 E
Al-Iskandarīyah (Alexandria) 142 31.12 N 29.54 E
Al-Iskandarīyah □ 4 142 31.10 N 29.53 E
Al-Ismā'īlīyah (Ismailia) 142 30.35 N 32.16 E
Al-Ismā'īlīyah □ 4 142 30.30 N 32.15 E
Al-Ismā'īlīyah Military Base ■ 142 30.35 N 32.14 E
Aliso Canyon ∨, Ca., U.S. 280 34.18 N 118.33 W
Aliso Canyon ∨, Ca., U.S. 280 33.53 N 117.40 W
Aliso Creek ≃ 228 33.31 N 117.45 W
Al-Istiwā'īyah al-Gharbīyah □ 4 140 5.55 N 28.15 E
Al-Istiwā'īyah ash-Sharqīyah □ 4 154 4.30 N 33.00 E
Alistráti 38 41.04 N 23.57 E
Alitak, Cape ≻ 180 56.51 N 154.21 W
Alitak Bay c 180 57.00 N 154.05 W
Alitanguo 120 35.10 N 83.30 E
Alì Terme 70 38.01 N 15.26 E
Alivérion 38 38.24 N 24.02 E
Aliwal North 158 30.45 S 26.45 E
Alix 182 52.24 N 113.11 W
Al-'Izzīyah 142 27.13 N 30.59 E
Al-Jabal al-Abyad ʌ 2 142 28.46 N 31.00 E
Al-Jabal al-Ahmar ʌ 2 142 28.19 N 31.07 E
Al-Jabalayn 140 12.36 N 32.48 E
Al-Jadīdah 140 25.34 N 28.51 E
Al-Jafādūn 142 28.50 N 30.48 E
Al-Jafr 132 30.18 N 36.13 E
Al-Jāfūrah ◆ 2 128 24.14 N 50.00 E
Al-Jaghbūb 146 29.45 N 24.31 E
Al-Jaghbūb ⫧ 4 146 29.40 N 24.43 E
Al-Jahrah 128 29.20 N 47.40 E
Al-Jamālīyah 142 31.11 N 31.51 E
Al-Jarnūs 142 28.36 N 30.43 E
Al-Jawf, Ar. Su. 128 29.50 N 39.52 E
Al-Jawf, Lībiyā 146 24.11 N 23.19 E
Al-Jawsh 146 32.00 N 11.40 E
Al-Jaylī 140 16.01 N 32.36 E
Al-Jazā'ir — Algeria □ 1 148 28.00 N 3.00 E
Al-Jazīrah □ 4 140 14.30 N 33.20 E
Al-Jazīrah ◆ 1 140 14.25 N 33.00 E
Aljezur, Bra. 287a 22.40 S 43.36 W
Aljezur, Port. 34 37.19 N 8.48 W
Al-Jibāb 132 33.06 N 36.15 E
Al-Jifārah 128 23.59 N 45.11 E
Al-Jifārah (Jeffara) ≚ 146 32.30 N 11.45 E
Al-Jīzah (Giza), Misr 142 30.01 N 31.13 E
Al-Jīzah, Urd. 132 31.43 N 35.58 E
Al-Jīzah □ 4 142 29.46 N 31.18 E
Al-Jubayl 128 27.01 N 49.40 E
Al-Jubayn 140 12.07 N 35.10 E
Aljucén ≃ 34 38.56 N 6.25 W
Al-Judaydah 132 33.54 N 35.34 E
Al-Judayyidah, Urd. 132 31.32 N 35.39 E
Al-Judayyidah, Urd. 132 31.15 N 35.49 E
Al-Jufrah ⫧ 4 146 29.10 N 16.00 E
Al-Julaydah ⫧ 4 128 29.03 N 45.38 E
Al-Junaynah, Misr 142 31.06 N 31.41 E
Al-Junaynah, Sūd. 140 13.27 N 22.27 E
Al-Junaynah, Sūrīy. 132 32.54 N 36.44 E
Al-Jundīyah 142 28.34 N 30.50 E
Aljustrel 34 37.52 N 8.10 W
Al-Kāb 142 30.57 N 32.18 E
Al-Kabrit Military Base ■ 142 30.15 N 32.29 E
Al-Kafr 132 32.38 N 36.38 E
Al-Kafr ash-Sharqī 142 31.17 N 31.10 E
Al-Kahfah 128 27.04 N 43.02 E
Alkali Creek ≃, Ab., Can. 184 50.52 N 110.30 W
Alkali Creek ≃, Wy., U.S. 202 43.16 N 107.40 W
Alkali Lake 182 51.47 N 122.14 W
Alkali Lake ⊜, Nv., U.S. 204 41.42 N 119.50 W
Alkali Lake ⊜, Or., U.S. 202 42.58 N 120.02 W
Alkamari 146 13.24 N 11.07 E
Al-Kāmilīn 140 15.05 N 33.11 E
Al-Karabah 140 18.33 N 33.42 E
Al-Karak 132 31.11 N 35.42 E
Al-Karak □ 8 132 31.10 N 35.45 E
Al-Karnak 140 25.43 N 32.39 E
Al-Kawah 140 13.44 N 32.30 E
Al-Kawd 144 13.05 N 45.22 E
Al-Kawm 130 35.11 N 38.52 E
Al-Kawm al-Akhdar 142 30.58 N 30.17 E
Al-Kawm At-Tawīl 142 31.12 N 31.05 E
Alken 56 50.15 N 7.26 E
Al-Khabrā' 128 26.04 N 43.33 E
Al-Khābūrah 128 23.59 N 57.08 E
Al-Khafaqān ⊜ 128 23.24 N 40.24 E
Al-Khalīl (Hebron) 132 31.32 N 35.06 E
Al-Khālis 128 33.49 N 44.32 E
Al-Khandaq 140 18.36 N 30.34 E
Al-Khānkah 142 30.13 N 31.21 E
Al-Kharaqānīyah 273c 30.10 N 31.10 E
Al-Khārijah 140 25.26 N 30.33 E
Al-Khartūm (Khartoum) 140 15.36 N 32.32 E
Al-Khartūm □ 4 140 15.45 N 32.30 E
Al-Khartūm Bahrī 140 15.38 N 32.33 E
Al-Khasab 128 26.12 N 56.15 E
Al-Khatam ◆ 1 128 24.00 N 55.10 E
Al-Khirbah as-Samrā' 132 32.11 N 36.10 E
Al-Khiyām 132 33.19 N 35.36 E
Al-Khubar 128 26.17 N 50.12 E
Al-Khums (Homs) 146 32.39 N 14.16 E
Al-Khuraybah, Urd. 132 32.40 N 35.52 E
Al-Khuraybah, Yaman 144 15.06 N 48.19 E

PORTUGUÊS Nome	Página	Lat.°'	Long.°' W = Oeste

Al-Khurmah 144 21.54 N 42.03 E
Al-Khushnīyah 132 33.00 N 35.48 E
Al-Khuşūş 273c 30.09 N 31.19 E
Al-Kifl 128 32.14 N 44.22 E
Al-Kiswah 132 33.21 N 36.14 E
Alkmaar 52 52.37 N 4.44 E
Alkoven 61 48.17 N 14.06 E
Al-Kūbrī 142 30.02 N 32.33 E
Al-Kūfah 128 32.02 N 44.24 E
Al-Kufrah (Cufra) ⫧ 4 146 24.20 N 23.15 E
Al-Kunayyisah 273c 29.59 N 31.11 E
Al-Kuntillah 140 30.00 N 34.41 E
Al-Kūt 128 32.25 N 45.49 E
Al-Kuwayt 128 29.20 N 47.59 E
Al-Kuwayt — Kuwait □ 1 128 29.30 N 47.45 E
Alkvettern ⊜ 40 59.25 N 14.21 E
Allaben 210 42.07 N 74.22 W
Al-Labwah 130 34.12 N 36.21 E
Allacapan 116 18.15 N 121.35 E
Allach-Jun' 74 61.08 N 138.03 E
Allada 150 6.39 N 2.09 E
Al-Lādhiqīyah (Latakia) 130 35.31 N 35.47 E
Al-Lādhiqīyah □ 8 130 35.30 N 36.00 E
Allagash ≃ 186 47.05 N 69.02 W
Allagen 56 51.28 N 8.14 E
Al-Lagowa 140 11.24 N 29.08 E
Allahābād, India 124 25.27 N 81.51 E
Allāhābād, Pāk. 123 28.57 N 70.53 E
Allāhbās 272a 28.31 N 77.25 E
Allahüekber Dağları ⋏ 130 40.35 N 42.32 E
Al-Lāhūn 142 29.13 N 30.59 E
Allāhwardipur 272a 28.33 N 77.26 E
Allaines 50 48.12 N 1.50 E
Allaire State Park ♠ 208 40.08 N 74.08 W
Allakaket 180 66.34 N 152.41 W
Allaman 58 46.28 N 6.24 E
Allamuchy 210 40.55 N 74.48 W
Allan 184 51.53 N 106.04 W
Allan, Pointe ≻ 275a 45.26 N 73.45 W
Allanche 32 45.14 N 2.56 E
Alland 61 48.03 N 16.05 E
Allan Island I 224 48.28 N 122.42 W
Allanmyo 110 19.22 N 95.13 E
Allanridge 158 27.55 S 26.44 E
Allanson 168a 33.20 S 116.06 E
Allanton 46 55.47 N 3.51 W
Allan Water ≃ 46 56.08 N 3.56 W
Allapattah Flats ≚ 220 27.29 N 82.34 W
'Allāq, Bi'r ⫧ 4 146 31.05 N 11.42 E
'Allāqī, Wādī al- ∨ 140 22.42 N 33.12 E
Allard, Lac ⊜ 186 50.32 N 63.31 W
Allardt 194 36.22 N 84.53 W
Allariz 34 42.11 N 7.48 W
Allatoona Lake ⊜ 1 192 34.08 N 84.38 W
Allauch 62 43.20 N 5.29 E
Al-Layyah 140 16.16 N 35.25 E
Alldays 156 22.44 S 29.04 E
Alle, Bel. 56 49.51 N 4.58 E
Alle, Schw. 58 47.26 N 7.08 E
Ålleberg ʌ 2 26 58.08 N 13.36 E
Allegan 216 42.31 N 85.51 W
Allegan □ 6 216 42.35 N 85.53 W
Allegan, Lake ⊜ 216 42.33 N 85.55 W
Allegany 210 42.05 N 78.29 W
Allegany □ 6 210 42.13 N 78.02 W
Allegany Indian Reservation ◆ 4 210 42.10 N 78.47 W
Allegany State Park ♠ 210 42.04 N 78.44 W
Alleghany 226 39.28 N 120.51 W
Alleghe 64 46.24 N 12.01 E
Allegheny □ 6 214 40.26 N 79.59 W
Allegheny ≃ 214 40.27 N 80.00 W
Allegheny Acres 279b 40.37 N 79.53 W
Allegheny Center ʊ 279b 40.27 N 80.01 W
Allegheny County Airport ⊠ 279b 40.21 N 79.56 W
Allegheny County Park ♠ 279b 40.34 N 79.55 W
Allegheny Mountains ⋏ 188 38.30 N 80.00 W
Allegheny Observatory ʊ 3 279b 40.29 N 80.01 W
Allegheny Plateau ⋏ 1 188 41.30 N 78.00 W
Allegheny Portage Railroad National Historic Site ⊥ 214 40.28 N 78.32 W
Allegheny Reservoir ⊜ 1 214 42.00 N 78.56 W
Allègre 62 45.12 N 3.42 E
Allègre, Pointe ≻ 241o 16.22 N 61.45 W
Allemagne — Germany □ 1 30 51.00 N 10.00 E
Allemands, Lac Des ⊜ 194 29.55 N 90.35 W
Allemanskraaldam ⊜ 1 158 28.16 S 27.07 E
Allemant 261 48.45 N 1.37 E
Allemont 62 45.08 N 6.02 E
Allen, Arg. 252 38.58 S 67.50 W
Allen, Pil. 116 12.30 N 124.17 E
Allen, Md., U.S. 208 38.17 N 75.41 W
Allen, Mi., U.S. 216 41.57 N 84.46 W
Allen, Ne., U.S. 198 42.24 N 96.50 W
Allen, Ok., U.S. 196 34.52 N 96.24 W
Allen, Pa., U.S. 208 40.10 N 77.05 W
Allen, S.D., U.S. 198 43.16 N 101.55 W
Allen, Tx., U.S. 222 33.06 N 96.40 W
Allen, Wa., U.S. 224 48.31 N 122.23 W
Allen □ 6, In., U.S. 216 41.04 N 85.09 W
Allen □ 6, Oh., U.S. 216 40.46 N 84.06 W
Allen ≃ 44 54.58 N 2.19 W
Allen, Lough ⊜ 48 54.08 N 8.08 W
Allen, Mount ʌ, N.Z. 172 47.05 S 167.48 E
Allen, Mount ʌ, Ak., U.S. 180 62.14 N 142.13 W
Allenby Bridge ◆ 5 132 31.52 N 35.52 E
Allendale, Il., U.S. 194 38.32 N 87.43 W
Allendale, Mi., U.S. 216 42.58 N 85.57 W
Allendale, N.J., U.S. 276 41.02 N 74.07 W
Allendale, S.C., U.S. 192 33.00 N 81.18 W
Allendale Town 44 54.54 N 2.15 W
Allende, Méx. 232 28.20 N 100.51 W
Allende, Méx. 234 18.09 N 94.16 W
Allendorf 56 51.02 N 8.38 E
Allenfarm 222 30.24 N 96.14 W
All England Lawn Tennis Club ♠ 260 51.26 N 0.13 W
Allen Grove 216 42.35 N 88.41 W
Allen Park 216 42.15 N 83.12 W
Allenport, Pa., U.S. 214 40.20 N 77.53 W
Allenport, Pa., U.S. 214 40.06 N 79.51 W
Allensbach 58 47.43 N 9.03 E
Allenstein — Olsztyn 30 53.48 N 20.29 E
Allensville 214 40.32 N 77.49 W
Allenton, Mi., U.S. 214 42.55 N 82.57 W
Allenton, R.I., U.S. 207 41.32 N 71.28 W
Allentown, N.J., U.S. 208 40.10 N 74.35 W
Allentown, N.Y., U.S. 210 42.05 N 78.03 W
Allentown, Oh., U.S. 216 40.46 N 84.12 W
Allentown, Pa., U.S. 208 40.36 N 75.28 W
Allentsteig 61 48.42 N 15.20 E
Allenwood, N.J., U.S. 208 40.12 N 74.13 W
Allenwood, N.Y., U.S. 276 40.48 N 73.44 W
Allenwood, Pa., U.S. 210 41.07 N 76.54 W
Alleppey 122 9.29 N 76.19 E
Aller ≃ 30 52.57 N 9.11 E
Allerona 66 42.49 N 11.58 E
Allersberg 60 49.15 N 11.15 E
Allershausen 60 48.26 N 11.36 E
Allerslev 41 55.05 N 12.03 E
Allerton, Ia., U.S. 190 40.42 N 93.21 W
Allerton, Ma., U.S. 283 42.18 N 70.53 W
Allerton ◆ 8 262 53.22 N 2.53 W
Allerton, Point ≻ 207 42.18 N 70.53 W
Allestree 42 52.57 N 1.29 W
Allevard 62 45.24 N 6.04 E
Alley Park ♠ 276 40.45 N 73.44 W
Alleyton 222 29.43 N 96.29 W
Allgäu ◆ 1 58 47.35 N 10.10 E
Allgäuer Alpen ⋏ 58 47.20 N 10.25 E
Allhallows 260 51.28 N 0.39 E

Alli ≃ 68 38.51 N 16.40 E
Alliance, Ab., Can. 182 52.26 N 111.47 W
Alliance, Ne., U.S. 198 42.12 N 102.58 W
Alliance, Oh., U.S. 214 40.54 N 81.06 W
Allibaudières 50 48.35 N 4.07 E
Al-Lidām 144 20.29 N 44.50 E
Allier □ 5 32 46.25 N 3.00 E
Allier ≃ 32 46.58 N 3.04 E
Alligator ≃ 192 35.58 N 75.58 W
Alligator Creek ≃, Ga., U.S. 192 31.58 N 82.22 W
Alligator Creek ≃, Tx., U.S. 222 30.42 N 97.07 W
Alligator Lake ⊜ 220 28.13 N 81.13 W
Alligator Pond 241q 17.52 N 77.34 W
Alligny-en-Morvan 50 47.12 N 4.10 E
Allihies 48 51.38 N 10.03 W
Allinagaram 122 10.02 N 77.30 E
Allinge 26 55.16 N 14.49 E
Allington Castle ⊥ 260 51.17 N 0.31 E
Al-Lisān ≻ 1 132 31.17 N 35.28 E
Al-Lisht 142 29.34 N 31.14 E
Allison 190 42.45 N 92.47 W
Allison, Mount ʌ 282 37.30 N 121.52 W
Allison Gulch ∨ 280 34.16 N 117.44 W
Allison Park 214 40.34 N 79.57 W
Alliste 68 39.57 N 18.05 E
Alliston 212 44.09 N 79.52 W
Al-Līth 144 20.09 N 40.16 E
Allmendingen 58 48.20 N 9.43 E
Alloa 46 56.07 N 3.49 W
Allochio, Galleria degli ◆ 5 66 44.03 N 11.30 E
Allogny 50 47.13 N 2.19 E
Allonby 44 54.46 N 3.25 W
Alloné Abba 132 32.44 N 35.10 E
Allonnes, Fr. 50 48.20 N 1.40 E
Allonnes, Fr. 50 47.58 N 0.09 E
Allora 171a 28.02 S 151.59 E
Allos 62 44.14 N 6.38 E
Allos, Col d')(62 44.18 N 6.36 E
Allott, Mount ʌ 2 162 26.06 S 124.46 E
Allouez 190 44.28 N 88.00 W
Alloway 208 39.33 N 75.21 W
Alloway Creek ≃ 208 39.27 N 75.30 W
Allport 214 40.58 N 78.12 W
Allred Peak ʌ 200 40.32 N 108.33 W
All Saints 240c 17.03 N 61.48 W
Allschwil 58 47.33 N 7.33 E
Allstedt 54 51.24 N 11.23 E
Allston ◆ 8 283 42.22 N 71.08 W
Alluets, Forêt des ♠ 261 48.55 N 1.55 E
Al-Luhayyah 144 15.42 N 42.42 E
Allumette Lake ⊜ 190 45.53 N 77.13 W
Allumettes, Île des I 190 45.50 N 77.05 W
Allumiere 66 42.09 N 11.54 E
Allview Estates 208 39.12 N 76.51 W
Allyn 224 47.23 N 122.49 W
Alm ≃ 60 48.05 N 13.55 E
Alma, N.B., Can. 186 45.36 N 64.57 W
Alma, P.Q., Can. 186 48.33 N 71.39 W
Alma, Ar., U.S. 194 35.28 N 94.13 W
Alma, Ga., U.S. 192 31.32 N 82.27 W
Alma, Il., U.S. 219 38.43 N 88.55 W
Alma, Ks., U.S. 198 39.01 N 96.17 W
Alma, Mi., U.S. 190 43.22 N 84.39 W
Alma, Ne., U.S. 198 40.05 N 99.21 W
Alma, N.Y., U.S. 210 42.01 N 78.03 W
Alma, Wi., U.S. 190 44.19 N 91.54 W
Al-Ma'ābidah 142 27.20 N 31.01 E
Al-Ma'ādī ◆ 8 142 29.58 N 31.15 E
Alma-Ata (Almaty) 85 43.15 N 76.57 E
Alma-Ata □ 8 86 44.00 N 77.00 E
Alma-Atinskij zapovednik ♠ 85 43.10 N 77.25 E
Alma Center 190 44.26 N 90.54 W
Almada 34 38.41 N 9.09 W
Almaden, Austl. 166 17.20 S 144.41 E
Almadén, Esp. 34 38.46 N 4.50 W
Almadén de la Plata 34 37.52 N 6.04 W
Al-Madīnah (Medina) 128 24.28 N 39.36 E
Al-Madīnah al-Fikrīyah 142 27.56 N 30.49 E
Al-Madwar 132 32.17 N 36.00 E
Al-Mafāzah 140 13.36 N 34.33 E
Al-Mafraq 132 32.21 N 36.12 E
Al-Mafraq □ 8 132 32.15 N 36.30 E
Almafuerte 252 32.12 S 64.15 W
Al-Maghārīm 144 15.01 N 47.51 E
Al-Maghrah ⫧ 4 140 30.14 N 28.56 E
Almagor 132 32.55 N 35.36 E
Almagre, Laguna c 234 23.48 N 97.48 W
Al-Magreb — Morocco □ 1 148 32.00 N 5.00 W
Almagro 34 38.53 N 3.43 W
Almagro Island I 116 11.56 N 124.18 E
Al-Mahallah al-Kubrā 142 30.58 N 31.10 E
Al-Mahārīq 140 25.37 N 30.39 E
Al Mahbas 148 27.13 N 9.44 W
Alma Hill ʌ 2 210 42.03 N 78.01 W
Al-Mahmūdīyah 142 31.11 N 30.32 E
Al-Mahras 142 27.49 N 30.48 E
Al-Mahsamah 142 30.34 N 32.01 E
Al-Majdal 132 32.47 N 36.30 E
Al-Majma'ah 128 25.54 N 45.20 E
Almājului, Munții ⋏ 38 44.43 N 22.12 E
Al-Maks ◆ 8 142 31.09 N 29.51 E
Al-Mālikīyah 130 37.10 N 42.08 E
Almalyk 85 40.50 N 69.35 E
Al-Ma'mūrah ◆ 8 142 31.18 N 30.03 E
Al-Manāmah 128 26.13 N 50.35 E
Al-Manāqil 140 14.15 N 32.59 E
Al-Manāsif ◆ 1 130 35.17 N 40.50 E
Al-Manāwāt 273c 29.55 N 31.14 E
Almanor, Lake ⊜ 204 40.15 N 121.08 W
Almansa 34 38.52 N 1.05 W
Al-Manshāh 140 26.28 N 31.48 E
Al-Mansūrah, Golan 132 33.08 N 35.48 E
Al-Mansūrah, Misr 142 31.03 N 31.23 E
Al-Mansūrīyah 142 30.08 N 31.05 E
Almanza 34 42.39 N 5.02 W
Al-Manzilah 142 31.09 N 31.56 E
Almanzor ʌ 34 40.15 N 5.18 W
Almanzora ≃ 34 37.14 N 1.46 W
Almar ≃ 34 40.54 N 5.29 W
Al-Marāghah 140 26.42 N 31.36 E
Almargem do Bispo 266c 38.51 N 9.16 W
Al-Marj 146 32.30 N 20.54 E
Al-Marj ◆ 8 273c 30.09 N 31.20 E
Almas 250 11.33 S 47.09 W
Almaș ≃ 38 47.14 N 23.19 E
Almas, Pico das ʌ 255 13.33 S 41.56 W
Al-Ma'sarah, Misr 142 27.42 N 30.52 E
Al-Ma'sarah, Misr 142 31.13 N 31.19 E
Al-Ma'sarah ◆ 8 142 29.54 N 31.17 E
Al-Mashqūq 132 32.24 N 36.43 E
Al-Mashrafah 130 34.50 N 36.52 E
Al-Masīd 140 15.15 N 32.57 E
Almassora 34 39.57 N 0.03 W
Al-Matammah 140 16.43 N 33.22 E
Al-Matarīyah 142 31.11 N 32.02 E
Al-Matarīyah ◆ 8 142 30.07 N 31.19 E
Al-Matnah 140 13.47 N 35.03 E
Al-Mawsil (Mosul) 128 36.20 N 43.08 E
Al-Mayādīn 130 35.01 N 40.27 E
Al-Maymūn 142 29.14 N 31.12 E
Almazán 34 41.29 N 2.32 W
Al-Mazār, Urd. 132 31.04 N 35.42 E
Almazar, Uzb. 85 40.59 N 68.54 E
Almaznyj 83 48.02 N 40.03 E
Almazovo 265b 55.51 N 38.02 E
Al-Mazra'ah 132 31.16 N 35.31 E
Al-Mazzah 132 33.30 N 36.15 E
Alme 56 51.28 N 8.37 E
Almeer 52 52.20 N 5.14 E
Almeida 34 40.43 N 6.54 W
Almeirim, Bra. 250 1.32 S 52.34 W
Almeirim, Port. 34 39.12 N 8.38 W
Almelo 52 52.21 N 6.39 E
Almena 198 39.53 N 99.42 W
Almenara 255 16.11 S 40.42 W
Almenar de Soria 34 41.41 N 2.12 W
Almendares ≃ 286b 23.08 N 82.25 W

Almendra, Embalse de ⊜ 1 34 41.15 N 6.10 W
Almendralejo 34 38.41 N 6.24 W
Almenêches 50 48.42 N 0.07 E
Al'menevo 86 54.57 N 63.34 E
Almenno San Salvatore 62 45.45 N 9.35 E
Almería 34 36.50 N 2.27 W
Almería □ 4 34 37.10 N 2.25 W
Almería, Golfo de c 34 36.46 N 2.30 W
Al'metjevsk 80 54.53 N 52.20 E
Al'mež 24 60.03 N 48.03 E
Älmhult 26 56.33 N 14.08 E
Al-Midhnab 128 25.54 N 44.14 E
Al-Mīnā' 130 34.27 N 35.49 E
Almina, Punta ≻ 34 35.53 N 5.15 W
Almino Afonso 250 6.09 S 37.46 W
Al-Minshāt al-Kubrā 142 31.03 N 30.54 E
Al-Minūfīyah □ 4 142 30.30 N 31.00 E
Al-Minyā, Misr 142 28.06 N 30.45 E
Al-Minyā, Misr 142 29.45 N 31.18 E
Al-Minyā, Misr 142 29.14 N 30.45 E
Al-Minyā □ 4 142 28.26 N 30.42 E
Al-Miqdādīyah 128 33.59 N 44.56 E
Almira 202 47.42 N 118.56 W
Almirantazgo, Islas — Admiralty Islands II 164 2.10 S 147.00 E
Almirantazgo, Montes — Admiralty Mountains ⋏ 9 71.45 S 168.30 E
Almirante 236 9.18 N 82.24 W
Almirante, Bahía de c 236 9.20 N 82.18 W
Almirante Brown 258 34.48 S 58.23 W
Almirante Brown □ 5 288 34.50 S 58.20 W
Almirante Guillermo Brown, Parque ♠ 288 34.40 S 58.28 W
Almirante Latorre 252 29.38 S 70.58 W
Almirante Montt, Golfo ʉ 254 51.55 S 72.45 W
Almirós 38 39.11 N 22.46 E
Almiroú, Kólpos c 38 35.23 N 24.20 E
Al-Mismīyah 132 33.08 N 36.23 E
Almo 202 42.06 N 113.37 W
Almoçageme 266c 38.48 N 9.28 W
Almodôvar 34 37.31 N 8.04 W
Almodóvar del Campo 34 38.43 N 4.10 W
Almolonga 236 14.49 N 91.30 W
Almond, N.Y., U.S. 210 42.19 N 77.44 W
Almond, Wi., U.S. 190 44.15 N 89.24 W
Almond ≃, Scot., U.K. 46 56.25 N 3.27 W
Almond ≃, Scot., U.K. 46 55.58 N 3.18 W
Almondbank 46 56.24 N 3.33 W
Almondsbury 42 51.34 N 2.34 W
Almonesson 208 39.49 N 75.06 W
Almont 214 42.55 N 83.02 W
Almont ≃ 261 48.32 N 2.40 E
Almonte, On., Can. 212 45.14 N 76.12 W
Almonte, Esp. 34 37.15 N 6.31 W
Almonte, Ca., U.S. 282 37.53 N 122.32 W
Almora 124 29.37 N 79.40 E
Almsee ⊜ 64 47.45 N 13.57 E
Älmsta 40 59.58 N 18.48 E
Al-Mu'addamīyah 132 33.45 N 36.39 E
Al-Mubarraz, Ar. Su. 128 25.25 N 49.35 E
Al-Mubarraz, Ar. Su. 144 22.17 N 46.44 E
Al-Mudawwarah 128 29.19 N 35.59 E
Almudébar 34 42.03 N 0.35 W
Al-Muglad 140 11.02 N 27.44 E
Al-Muharraq 128 26.16 N 50.37 E
Al-Mukallā 144 14.32 N 49.08 E
Al-Mukhā (Mocha) 144 13.19 N 43.15 E
Al-Munājāt al-Kubrā 142 30.50 N 32.01 E
Almuñécar 34 36.43 N 3.41 W
Almunge 40 59.53 N 18.03 E
Al-Muntazah ◆ 8 142 31.17 N 30.01 E
Almus 130 40.23 N 36.55 E
Al-Musallamīyah 140 14.34 N 33.21 E
Al-Musayfirah 132 32.37 N 36.20 E
Al-Musayjīd 128 24.05 N 39.06 E
Al-Musayyib 128 32.47 N 44.18 E
Almus Barajı ⊜ 1 130 40.20 N 37.00 E
Al-Mushannaf 132 32.44 N 36.46 E
Al-Musharrak Qiblī 142 29.23 N 30.34 E
Al-Mutā'iyah 132 32.29 N 36.17 E
Al-Mu'tamadīyah 142 31.02 N 31.05 E
Al-Mutayn 132 33.54 N 35.44 E
Al-Muthannā □ 4 128 30.30 N 45.15 E
Al-Mutī'ah 142 27.08 N 31.18 E
Al-Muwaqqar ⊥ 132 31.49 N 36.06 E
Al-Muwassam 144 16.25 N 42.20 E
Al-Muwayh 144 22.45 N 41.36 E
Al-Muwaylih 128 27.41 N 35.27 E
Aln ≃ 44 55.23 N 1.37 W
Alnarp 41 55.39 N 13.05 E
Al-Narrānīyah 273c 29.58 N 31.10 E
Al'n'aš 80 56.44 N 54.43 E
Alnaši 80 56.11 N 52.28 E
Al-Nasser 140 24.32 N 32.55 E
Alne ≃ 42 52.13 N 1.52 W
Alness 46 57.41 N 4.15 W
Alnmouth 44 55.23 N 1.36 W
Alnön I 26 62.25 N 17.26 E
Alnor 41 54.55 N 9.36 E
Alnwick 44 55.25 N 1.42 W
Alnwick Indian Reserve ◆ 4 212 44.10 N 78.06 W
Alo 146 11.47 N 20.53 E
Aloândia 255 17.43 S 49.29 W
Alofau 174u 14.16 S 170.36 W
Alofi 174v 19.01 S 169.55 W
Alofi, Île I 14 14.21 S 178.02 W
Alofi Bay c 174v 19.01 S 169.56 W
Aloha 224 45.29 N 122.51 W
Aloha, Lake ⊜ 226 38.52 N 120.09 W
Aloi 154 2.17 N 33.10 E
Aloja 76 57.46 N 24.53 E
Alondra 280 33.55 N 118.15 W
Along 120 28.18 N 94.39 E
Alónnisos 38 39.08 N 23.50 E
Alónnisos I 38 39.13 N 23.55 E
Alor, Kepulauan II 112 8.15 S 124.30 E
Alor, Pulau I 112 8.15 S 124.45 E
Alor, Selat ʉ 112 8.20 S 123.48 E
Álora 34 36.48 N 4.42 W
Alor Gajah 114 2.23 N 102.13 E
Alor Setar 114 6.07 N 100.22 E
Alor Star — Alor Setar 114 6.07 N 100.22 E
Alorton 219 38.36 N 90.08 W
Al'oškino 88 58.35 N 100.32 E
Al'ošn'a, Ross. 76 53.38 N 33.29 E
Al'ošn'a, Ross. 82 54.14 N 37.16 E
Alosno 34 37.33 N 7.07 W
Alost — Aalst 50 50.56 N 4.02 E
Alotau 164 10.14 S 150.30 E
Alouette ≃ 224 49.16 N 122.42 W
Alouette Lake ⊜ 224 49.19 N 122.28 W
Alovo 80 54.38 N 46.27 E
Aloxe-Corton 58 47.04 N 4.52 E
Aloysius, Mount ʌ 162 26.01 S 128.34 E
Alpachiri 252 37.22 S 63.46 W
Alpaugh 226 35.53 N 119.29 W
Alpen 52 51.35 N 6.30 E
Alpen — Alps ⋏ 32 46.25 N 10.00 E
Alpena, Ar., U.S. 194 36.17 N 93.17 W
Alpena, Mi., U.S. 190 45.03 N 83.25 W
Alpena, S.D., U.S. 198 44.10 N 98.21 W
Alpercatas ≃ 250 6.02 S 44.19 W
Alpes — Alps ⋏ 32 46.25 N 10.00 E
Alpes-de-Haute-Provence □ 5 62 44.10 N 6.00 E
Alpes Dináricos — Dinara ⋏ 36 43.50 N 16.35 E
Alpes-Maritimes □ 5 62 44.00 N 7.10 E
Alpes Marítimos — Maritime Alps ⋏ 62 44.15 N 7.10 E

Alpes Transilvanos — Carpații Meridionali ⋏ 38 45.30 N 24.15 E
Alpha, Austl. 166 23.39 S 146.38 E
Alpha, Il., U.S. 190 41.12 N 90.23 W
Alpha, Mi., U.S. 190 46.02 N 88.22 W
Alpha, N.J., U.S. 210 40.40 N 75.09 W
Alpharetta 192 34.04 N 84.17 W
Alphen aan den Rijn 52 52.07 N 4.40 E
Alphington 42 50.42 N 3.31 W
Alphin Pike ʌ 2 262 53.31 N 2.00 W
Alphonse Island I 138 7.00 S 52.45 E
Alpi — Alps ⋏ 32 46.25 N 10.00 E
Alpi, Monte ʌ 68 40.07 N 15.59 E
Alpiarça 34 39.15 N 8.35 W
Alpi Dinariche — Dinara ⋏ 36 43.50 N 16.35 E
Alpignano 62 45.06 N 7.31 E
Alpilles, Chaîne des ⋏ 2 62 43.45 N 4.50 E
Alpine, Az., U.S. 200 33.50 N 109.08 W
Alpine, Ca., U.S. 204 32.50 N 116.47 W
Alpine, N.J., U.S. 276 40.57 N 73.55 W
Alpine, N.Y., U.S. 210 42.19 N 76.44 W
Alpine, Tx., U.S. 196 30.21 N 103.39 W
Alpine □ 6 226 38.41 N 119.47 W
Alpine Creek ≃ 282 37.19 N 122.17 W
Alpine National Park ♠ 166 37.00 S 147.15 E
Alpinópolis 255 20.52 S 46.23 W
Alpi Retiche — Rhaetian Alps ⋏ 58 46.30 N 10.00 E
Alpirsbach 58 48.21 N 8.23 E
Alplaus Kill ≃ 210 42.51 N 73.54 W
Alpnachstad 58 46.57 N 8.17 E
Alps ⋏ 22 46.25 N 10.00 E
Alpsee ⊜ 58 47.34 N 10.10 E
Alpu 130 39.47 N 30.58 E
Al-Qābil 128 23.57 N 55.48 E
Al-Qābūn 132 33.33 N 36.20 E
Al-Qadam 132 33.28 N 36.17 E
Al-Qadārif 140 14.02 N 35.24 E
Al-Qadīmah 144 22.21 N 39.09 E
Al-Qādisīyah □ 4 128 31.55 N 45.00 E
Al-Qāhirah (Cairo), Misr 142 30.03 N 31.15 E
Al-Qāhirah (Cairo), Misr 273c 30.03 N 31.15 E
Al-Qāhirah □ 4 142 30.02 N 31.17 E
Al-Qāhirah West Military Base ■ 142 30.06 N 30.56 E
Al-Qahmah 144 18.00 N 41.41 E
Al-Qā'im 128 34.21 N 41.07 E
Al-Qā'īyah ⫧ 4 128 26.27 N 45.35 E
Al-Qāiyāt 142 28.40 N 30.41 E
Al-Qalaj 142 30.11 N 31.21 E
Al-Qalībah 128 28.32 N 37.42 E
Al-Qalyūbīyah □ 4 142 30.18 N 31.18 E
Al-Qāmishlī 130 37.02 N 41.14 E
Al-Qanātir al-Khayrīyah 142 30.12 N 31.08 E
Al-Qanāyāt 142 30.37 N 31.28 E
Al-Qantarah 142 30.52 N 32.19 E
Al-Qaryah ash-Sharqīyah 146 30.24 N 13.36 E
Al-Qaryatayn 130 34.14 N 37.14 E
Al-Qasabāt 146 32.35 N 14.03 E
Al-Qasābī 142 31.16 N 30.41 E
Al-Qasr, Misr 140 25.42 N 28.53 E
Al-Qasr, Urd. 132 31.19 N 35.45 E
Al-Qassāsīn 142 30.34 N 31.56 E
Al-Qatīf 128 26.33 N 50.00 E
Al-Qatrānah 132 31.15 N 36.03 E
Al-Qatrūn 146 24.56 N 14.38 E
Al-Qattā 142 30.13 N 30.58 E
Al-Qattāwīyah 142 30.33 N 31.40 E
Al-Qays 142 28.29 N 30.47 E
Al-Qaysūmah 128 28.16 N 46.03 E
Al-Qir'awn 132 33.34 N 35.43 E
Al-Qişfah 132 32.38 N 35.52 E
Al-Quds — Yerushalayim 132 31.46 N 35.14 E
Alquízar 240p 22.48 N 82.35 W
Al-Qun'abah 132 33.08 N 35.40 E
Al-Qunaytirah 132 33.07 N 35.49 E
Al-Qunaytirah □ 8 132 33.00 N 35.50 E
Al-Qunfudhah 144 19.08 N 41.05 E
Al-Qurayn 142 30.37 N 31.44 E
Al-Qurayyah 132 32.32 N 36.36 E
Al-Qurnah 128 31.00 N 47.26 E
Al-Qusaymah 132 30.40 N 34.22 E
Al-Qusayr, Misr 128 26.06 N 34.17 E
Al-Qusayr, Misr 142 27.27 N 30.52 E
Al-Qusayr, Sūrīy. 130 34.31 N 36.35 E
Al-Qūsīyah 142 27.26 N 30.49 E
Al-Qutayfah 132 33.44 N 36.36 E
Al-Qutaynah 140 14.52 N 32.21 E
Al-Quway'īyah 128 24.03 N 45.15 E
Al-Quwaysī 140 13.20 N 34.05 E
Alrø I 41 55.51 N 10.05 E
Alroy Downs 162 19.18 S 136.04 E
Als I 41 54.59 N 9.55 E
Alsace □ 9 58 48.30 N 7.30 E
Alsace, Ballon d' ʌ 58 47.50 N 6.51 E
Alsager 44 53.06 N 2.17 W
Alsask 184 51.23 N 109.59 W
Alsasua 34 42.54 N 2.10 W
Alsdorf 56 50.53 N 6.10 E
Alsea 202 44.22 N 123.35 W
Alsea ≃ 202 44.26 N 124.05 W
Alsek ≃ 180 59.10 N 138.10 W
Alsen 198 48.37 N 98.42 W
Alseno 64 44.54 N 9.59 E
Alsenz 56 49.43 N 7.49 E
Alsenz ≃ 56 49.49 N 7.51 E
Alsey 219 39.34 N 90.25 W
Alsfeld 56 50.45 N 9.16 E
Als Fjord c 2 41 55.02 N 9.38 E
Alsh, Loch c 46 57.15 N 5.39 W
Al-Shallūfa Military Base ■ 142 30.03 N 32.32 E
Alsike 40 59.45 N 17.45 E
Alsina 252 33.54 S 59.23 W
Alsip 216 41.40 N 87.44 W
Alsleben 54 51.42 N 11.41 E
Alsónémedi 264c 47.19 N 19.10 E
Alstaden ◆ 8 263 51.28 N 6.50 E
Ålstäket 40 59.20 N 18.28 E
Alstätte 52 52.08 N 6.55 E
Alstead ≃ 184 55.50 N 107.26 W
Alster 40 59.24 N 13.36 E
Alster ≃ 52 53.36 N 9.59 E
Alsterbro 26 56.57 N 15.55 E
Alstern ⊜ 40 59.40 N 13.55 E
Alston 44 54.49 N 2.26 W
Alsunga 76 56.59 N 21.34 E
Alswede 52 52.20 N 8.33 E
Alt ≃ 44 53.32 N 3.03 W
Alta, Nor. 24 69.55 N 23.12 E
Älta, Sve. 40 59.16 N 18.11 E
Alta, Ca., U.S. 226 39.12 N 120.49 W
Alta, Ia., U.S. 198 42.40 N 95.17 W
Alta, Cachoeira ʟ 250 5.46 S 54.28 W
Alta, Mount ʌ 172 44.30 S 168.58 E
Altadena 228 34.11 N 118.07 W
Alta Floresta 250 9.57 S 56.06 W
Alta Gracia, Arg. 252 31.40 S 64.26 W
Altagracia, Nic. 236 11.34 N 85.35 W
Altagracia, Ven. 246 10.43 N 71.32 W
Altagracia de Orituco 246 9.52 N 66.23 W
Alta Hill 226 39.14 N 121.04 W
Al Tahoe 226 38.57 N 119.59 W
Altai ⋏ 90 48.00 N 90.00 E
Altair 222 29.34 N 96.28 W
Altaj, Mong. 86 48.18 N 89.35 E
Altaj (Jesönbulag), Mong. 90 46.20 N 96.18 E
Altaj, Ross. 86 53.27 N 91.48 E
Altaj □ 3 86 51.00 N 86.00 E
Altajskij 86 51.58 N 85.22 E
Alta Loma, Ca., U.S. 228 34.07 N 117.36 W
Alta Loma, Tx., U.S. 222 29.22 N 95.04 W

≃ River	Fluß	Río	Rivière	Rio
≅ Canal	Kanal	Canal	Canal	Canal
ʟ Waterfall, Rapids	Wasserfall, Stromschnellen	Cascada, Rápidos	Chute d'eau, Rapides	Cascata, Rápidos
ʉ Strait	Meeresstraße	Estrecho	Détroit	Estreito
c Bay, Gulf	Bucht, Golf	Bahía, Golfo	Baie, Golfe	Baía, Golfo
⊜ Lake, Lakes	See, Seen	Lago, Lagos	Lac, Lacs	Lago, Lagos
≡ Swamp	Sumpf	Pantano	Marais	Pântano
⍓ Ice Features, Glacier	Eis- und Gletscherformen	Accidentes Glaciales	Formes glaciaires	Acidentes glaciares
⫧ Other Hydrographic Features	Andere Hydrographische Objekte	Otros Elementos Hidrográficos	Autres données hydrographiques	Outros acidentes hidrográficos

✣ Submarine Features	Untermeerische Objekte	Accidentes Submarinos	Formes de relief sous-marin	Acidentes submarinos
□ Political Unit	Politische Einheit	Unidad Politica	Entité politique	Unidade política
ʊ Cultural Institution	Kulturelle Institution	Institución Cultural	Institution culturelle	Instituição cultural
⊥ Historical Site	Historische Stätte	Sitio Histórico	Site historique	Sitio histórico
♠ Recreational Site	Erholungs- und Ferienort	Sitio de Recreo	Centre de loisirs	Area de Lazer
⊠ Airport	Flughafen	Aeropuerto	Aéroport	Aeroporto
■ Military Installation	Militäranlage	Instalación Militar	Installation militaire	Instalação militar
◆ Miscellaneous	Verschiedenes	Misceláneo	Divers	Diversos

Altamaha ≃ 192 31.19 N 81.17 W
Altamira, Arg. 258 34.40 S 59.22 W
Altamira, Bra. 250 3.12 S 52.12 W
Altamira, Chile 252 25.47 S 69.51 W
Altamira, C.R. 236 10.30 N 84.23 W
Altamira, Méx. 234 22.24 N 97.55 W
Altamira, Las Cuevas de ≐[5] 34 43.18 N 4.08 W
Altamirano, Arg. 258 35.21 S 58.09 W
Altamirano, Méx. 196 25.55 N 97.47 W
Altamont, Il., U.S. 219 39.03 N 88.44 W
Altamont, Ks., U.S. 198 37.11 N 95.17 W
Altamont, N.Y., U.S. 210 42.42 N 74.02 W
Altamont, Or., U.S. 202 42.12 N 121.44 W
Altamont, Tn., U.S. 194 35.25 N 85.43 W
Altamonte Springs 220 28.39 N 81.21 W
Altamura 68 40.50 N 16.33 E
Altamura, Isla I 232 25.00 N 108.10 W
Altan, Ross. 88 49.31 N 111.32 E
Altan, Ross. 88 49.53 N 109.04 E
Altanbulag, Mong. 88 50.19 N 106.30 E
Altanbulag, Mong. 88 47.41 N 106.22 E
Altan-Cögor 86 49.03 N 90.27 E
Altanširee 102 45.35 N 110.27 E
Altar 232 30.43 N 111.44 W
Altar ≃ 232 30.39 N 111.53 W
Altar, Desierto de ◆[2] 232 31.50 N 114.15 W
Altar de Los Sacrificios ⊥ 232 16.28 N 90.32 W
Altare 62 44.20 N 8.20 E
Altario 184 51.55 N 110.09 W
Altarnun 42 50.37 N 4.30 W
Altar of the Earth ⊍[1] 271a 39.57 N 116.24 E
Altar of the Moon ⊍[1] 271a 39.55 N 116.20 E
Altar of the Sun ⊍[1] 271a 39.54 N 116.27 E
Altar Wash V 200 32.05 N 111.19 W
Altaskij Kraj ▫[8] 86 52.30 N 83.00 E
Altastenberg 56 51.11 N 8.28 E
Altata, Méx. 232 24.38 N 107.55 W
Altata, Ross. 80 51.07 N 48.44 E
Alta Verapaz ▫[5] 236 15.40 N 90.00 W
Altavilla Irpina 68 41.00 N 14.47 E
Altavilla Milicia 70 38.02 N 13.32 E
Altavilla Silentina 68 40.32 N 15.08 E
Altaville 226 38.05 N 120.33 W
Alta Vista, Ks., U.S. 198 38.51 N 96.29 W
Altavista, Va., U.S. 192 37.06 N 79.17 W
Altay, Ross. 86 60.20 N 68.58 E
Altay, Zhg. 86 47.52 N 88.07 E
Altay → Altaj ▫[3] 86 51.00 N 86.00 E
Alt Buchhorst 264a 52.26 N 13.51 E
Altdöbern 54 51.39 N 14.02 E
Altdorf, Dtsch. 60 48.34 N 12.07 E
Altdorf, Schw. 58 46.53 N 8.39 E
Altdorf bei Nürnberg 60 49.23 N 11.21 E
Alte Donau ⊜ 264b 48.14 N 16.26 E
Alteelva ≃ 24 69.58 N 23.23 E
Altefähr 54 54.20 N 13.07 E
Alteglofsheim 60 48.55 N 12.12 E
Alte Grund 264a 52.28 N 13.47 E
Altena 56 51.17 N 7.40 E
Altenahr 56 50.31 N 6.59 E
Altenau 52 51.48 N 10.26 E
Altenbeken 52 51.46 N 8.56 E
Altenberg 54 50.46 N 13.45 E
Altenberge 52 52.03 N 7.27 E
Altenbruch 52 53.49 N 8.46 E
Altenbüren 56 51.23 N 8.30 E
Altenburg, Dtsch. 54 50.59 N 12.26 E
Altenburg, Öst. 61 48.38 N 15.35 E
Altenderne Oberbecker ◆[8] 263 51.35 N 7.33 E
Altendorf 263 51.29 N 7.40 E
Altendorf ◆[8] 263 51.25 N 7.06 E
Altendorf-Ulfkotte 263 51.38 N 7.00 E
Altenesch 52 53.08 N 8.37 E
Altenessen ◆[8] 263 51.29 N 7.00 E
Altenfelden 60 48.29 N 13.58 E
Altengamme ◆[8] 52 53.25 N 10.16 E
Altenhagen, Dtsch. 52 52.03 N 8.38 E
Altenhagen, Dtsch. 54 53.45 N 13.06 E
Altenhagen ◆[8] 263 51.22 N 7.28 E
Altenhof 54 52.55 N 13.43 E
Altenholz 41 54.24 N 10.07 E
Altenkirchen, Dtsch. 54 54.38 N 13.20 E
Altenkirchen (Westerwald), Dtsch. 56 50.41 N 7.38 E
Altenkrempe 54 54.08 N 10.49 E
Altenkunstadt 54 50.07 N 11.14 E
Altenmarkt an der Alz 60 48.00 N 12.32 E
Altenoythe 52 53.02 N 7.52 E
Altenpleen 54 54.21 N 12.57 E
Altenstadt an der Waldnaab 60 49.48 N 12.10 E
Altensteig 56 48.35 N 8.37 E
Altentreptow 54 53.42 N 13.14 E
Altenvoerde 263 51.18 N 7.22 E
Altenwalde 52 53.49 N 8.40 E
Altenweddingen 54 52.00 N 11.31 E
Alte Oder ≃ 54 52.52 N 14.09 E
Alter do Chão 34 39.12 N 7.40 W
Alterosa 256 21.15 S 46.08 W
Alter Rhein ≃ 263 51.35 N 6.36 E
Altes Land ◆[1] 52 53.33 N 9.38 E
Altevatnet ⊜ 24 68.32 N 19.30 E
Altfraunhofen 60 48.27 N 12.10 E
Altfriedland 54 52.38 N 14.12 E
Altglashütten 58 47.51 N 8.06 E
Alt-Glienicke ◆[8] 264a 52.25 N 13.32 E
Altgruland 263 51.27 N 7.41 E
Altha 192 30.34 N 85.07 W
Altham 262 53.47 N 2.21 W
Alt-Hartmannsdorf 264a 52.21 N 13.50 E
Althea Lake ⊜ 283 42.40 N 71.23 W
Altheim 60 48.15 N 13.13 E
Altheimer 194 34.19 N 91.50 W
Althofen 61 46.54 N 14.27 E
Altıağaç 84 40.50 N 48.54 E
Altınekin 130 38.19 N 32.53 E
Altinho 250 8.29 S 36.04 W
Altınoluk 130 39.34 N 26.44 E
Altinópolis 255 21.02 S 47.23 W
Altınova 130 39.13 N 26.47 E
Altınözü 130 36.08 N 36.12 E
Altıntaş 130 39.04 N 30.07 E
Altınyaka 130 36.34 N 30.21 E
Altiplano ⋏[1] 248 18.00 S 68.00 W
Alt Käbelich 54 53.29 N 13.29 E
Altkirch 58 47.37 N 7.15 E
Altlandsberg 54 52.33 N 13.43 E
Altlangerwisch 264a 52.19 N 13.04 E
Altlewin 54 52.42 N 14.16 E
Altlüdersdorf 54 53.02 N 13.11 E
Altlünen 52 51.38 N 7.31 E
Altmannsdorf ◆[8] 264b 48.10 N 16.20 E
Altmannstein 60 48.54 N 11.39 E
Altmar 212 43.31 N 76.00 W
Altmark ◆[1] 54 52.40 N 11.20 E
Altmittweida 54 50.58 N 12.57 E
Altmühl ≃ 60 48.54 N 11.54 E
Altmünster 64 47.54 N 13.45 E
Altnaharra 46 58.16 N 4.27 W
Alto, Mi., U.S. 216 42.51 N 85.22 W
Alto, Tx., U.S. 222 31.39 N 95.04 W
Alto, Cerro ∧, Méx. 234 20.50 N 100.22 W
Alto, Cerro ∧, Ca., U.S. 226 35.25 N 120.43 W
Alto Anapu ≃ 250 2.15 S 51.27 W
Alto Araguaia 255 17.19 S 53.12 W
Alto Cauale 152 7.34 S 16.16 E
Alto Cedro 240p 20.31 N 75.58 W
Alto Chicapa 152 10.53 S 19.14 E
Alto Coité 255 15.47 S 54.20 W
Alto Cuito 152 13.27 S 18.49 E
Alto da Moóca ◆[8] 287b 23.34 S 46.35 W
Alto da Serra 256 22.53 S 44.14 W
Alto de las Vizcachas, Cerro ∧ 286e 33.25 S 70.26 W
Alto del Carmen 252 28.46 S 70.30 W
Alto de Ña Paula 286c 10.24 N 66.48 W
Alto do Rio Doce 255 21.02 S 43.25 W
Altofonte 70 38.03 N 13.18 E
Alto Garças 255 16.56 S 53.32 W
Alto Ligonha 154 15.30 S 38.20 E
Alto Longá 250 5.15 S 42.12 W
Alto Lucero 234 19.37 N 96.43 W
Alto Molócuè 154 15.38 S 37.42 E
Altomonte 68 39.42 N 16.08 E
Altomünster 60 48.23 N 11.15 E
Alton, On., Can. 212 43.52 N 80.04 W
Alton, Eng., U.K. 42 51.09 N 0.59 W
Alton, Il., U.S. 219 38.53 N 90.11 W
Alton, Ia., U.S. 198 42.59 N 96.00 W
Alton, Ks., U.S. 198 39.28 N 98.56 W
Alton, Ky., U.S. 218 38.04 N 84.55 W
Alton, Mo., U.S. 194 36.41 N 91.23 W
Alton, N.H., U.S. 188 43.27 N 71.13 W
Alton, N.Y., U.S. 210 43.13 N 76.59 W
Alton, R.I., U.S. 207 41.26 N 71.43 W
Altona, Austl. 162 27.34 S 120.00 E
Altona, Austl. 169 37.52 S 144.50 E
Altona, Mb., Can. 184 49.06 N 97.33 W
Altona, In., U.S. 216 41.21 N 85.09 W
Altona ◆[8] 52 53.32 N 9.56 E
Altona Bay c 274b 37.53 S 144.51 E
Altona North 274b 37.50 S 144.51 E
Altona Sports Park ♦ 274b 37.52 S 144.52 E
Altoona, Al., U.S. 194 34.01 N 86.19 W
Altoona, Fl., U.S. 220 28.57 N 81.38 W
Altoona, Ia., U.S. 190 41.39 N 93.28 W
Altoona, Ks., U.S. 198 37.31 N 95.39 W
Altoona, Pa., U.S. 214 40.31 N 78.23 W
Altoona, Wa., U.S. 224 46.16 N 123.39 W
Altoona, Wi., U.S. 190 44.48 N 91.26 W
Alto Pacajá ≃ 250 3.07 S 50.20 W
Alto Paraguai 248 14.30 S 56.31 W
Alto Paraguay ▫[5] 248 21.00 S 58.45 W
Alto Paraíso de Goiás 255 14.07 S 47.31 W
Alto Paraná ▫[5] 252 25.00 S 54.50 W
Alto Parnaíba 250 9.06 S 45.57 W
Alto Purús ≃ 248 9.34 S 70.36 W
Alto Río Mayo 254 45.35 S 71.06 W
Alto Río Senguer 254 45.02 S 70.50 W
Altos 250 5.03 S 42.28 W
Alto Santo 250 5.31 S 38.15 W
Alto Sucuriú 255 19.19 S 52.47 W
Altotonga 234 19.46 N 97.14 W
Altötting 60 48.13 N 12.40 E
Alto Volta → Burkina Faso ▫[1] 150 13.00 N 1.30 W
Alto Yurua ≃ 248 9.24 S 72.43 W
Altrincham 44 53.24 N 2.21 W
Alt Rüdersdorf 264a 52.28 N 13.49 E
Altruppin 54 52.56 N 12.50 E
Altshausen 58 47.56 N 9.32 E
Alt Stahnsdorf 264a 52.17 N 13.53 E
Altstätten 58 47.23 N 9.33 E
Alt Töplitz 264a 52.26 N 12.55 E
Altuchovo 76 52.40 N 34.20 E
Āltūn Kūprī 128 35.45 N 44.09 E
Altun Shan ⋏ 90 38.00 N 88.00 E
Alturas 204 41.29 N 120.32 W
Altus, Ar., U.S. 194 35.26 N 93.45 W
Altus, Ok., U.S. 196 34.38 N 99.20 W
Altus, Lake ⊜[1] 196 34.56 N 99.18 W
Altus Air Force Base ■ 196 34.40 N 99.16 W
Altusried 58 47.48 N 10.13 E
Altyaryk 85 40.23 N 71.30 E
Altykarasu 86 49.12 N 55.52 E
Altynaj 86 57.04 N 62.00 E
Altynasar ⊥ 86 45.10 N 63.07 E
Altynivka 78 51.27 N 33.10 E
Altynkul' 85 40.48 N 72.10 E
Altyntau 86 44.08 N 68.03 E
Altyn-Topkan 85 40.38 N 69.35 E
Alu I 175e 7.02 S 155.47 E
Al-Ubayyiḍ 140 13.11 N 30.13 E
Alubijid 116 8.35 N 124.29 E
Alucra 130 40.20 N 38.46 E
Al-'Udaysāt 140 25.35 N 32.29 E
Al-Uḍayyah 140 12.03 N 28.17 E
Aluk 140 8.26 N 27.27 E
Alūksne 76 57.25 N 27.03 E
Al-'Ulā 128 26.37 N 37.52 E
Alum Bank 214 40.14 N 78.34 W
Alum Creek ≃ 218 39.53 N 82.54 W
Alum Creek Lake ⊜[1] 214 40.15 N 82.58 W
Aluminé 254 39.13 S 70.57 W
Aluminé ≃ 254 39.50 S 70.53 W
Aluminé, Lago ⊜ 252 38.55 S 71.09 W
Alum Rock 226 37.21 N 121.49 W
Alum Rock Park ♦ 282 37.24 N 121.49 W
Alunda 40 60.04 N 18.05 E
Alunitdağ 84 40.32 N 46.03 E
Alupka 78 44.26 N 34.03 E
Al-'Uqaylah 146 30.16 N 19.12 E
Al-'Uqayr 128 25.39 N 50.12 E
Al-Uqṣur (Luxor) 140 25.41 N 32.39 E
Al-'Urayq ≐[8] 128 29.10 N 39.15 E
Al-'Urayq ◆[1] 128 24.47 N 42.55 E
Al-Urdun → Jordan ▫[1] 128 31.00 N 36.00 E
Al-Urdunn → Jordan ≃ 132 31.46 N 35.33 E
Alushta 78 44.42 N 34.24 E
Al-'Uṭayshān ▼[4] 140 16.25 N 34.30 E
Al-'Uwaynāt 146 25.46 N 10.34 E
Al-'Uwaynidhīyah I 128 26.37 N 36.05 E
Al-'Uyaynah 128 24.54 N 46.23 E
Alva, Scot., U.K. 46 56.09 N 3.48 W
Alva, Fl., U.S. 220 26.42 N 81.36 W
Alva, Ok., U.S. 196 36.48 N 98.39 W
Alva ≃ 34 40.18 N 8.15 W
Alvada 214 41.03 N 83.24 W
Alvaiázere 34 39.49 N 8.23 W
Alvaneu-Bad 58 46.40 N 9.39 E
Älvängen 26 57.58 N 12.07 E
Alvanley 262 53.16 N 2.45 W
Alvarado, Méx. 234 18.46 N 95.46 W
Alvarado, Tx., U.S. 222 32.24 N 97.12 W
Alvarado, Lake ⊜[1] 222 32.23 N 97.15 W
Alvarães 246 3.12 S 64.50 W
Álvarez Jonte 258 35.19 S 57.28 W
Alvarinhos 266c 38.54 N 9.22 W
Álvaro Obregón 234 19.50 N 101.05 W
Álvaro Obregón ◆[8] 286a 19.21 N 99.12 W
Álvaro Obregón, Presa ⊜[1] 232 27.55 N 109.52 W
Alvastra ⊥ 26 58.18 N 14.39 E
Alvdal 26 62.07 N 10.39 E
Älvdalen 26 61.14 N 14.02 E
Alvear 252 29.06 S 56.33 W
Alvechurch 42 52.21 N 1.57 W
Alverca 34 38.54 N 9.02 W
Alverda 214 40.38 N 78.52 W
Alvernia, Mount ∧[2] 238 24.15 N 75.24 W
Alverton 214 40.08 N 79.35 W
Alves 46 57.38 N 3.27 W
Alvesta 26 56.54 N 14.33 E
Alveston 42 51.36 N 2.32 W
Alviano, Lago di ⊜[1] 66 42.36 N 12.15 E
Alvik, Nor. 26 60.26 N 6.26 E
Alvik, Sve. 26 62.25 N 17.24 E
Alvin, Il., U.S. 216 40.19 N 87.37 W
Alvin, Tx., U.S. 222 29.25 N 95.14 W
Alvinópolis 255 20.06 S 43.03 W
Alvinston 214 42.49 N 81.52 W
Alviso ◆[8] 282 37.26 N 121.58 W
Alviso Slough ≃ 282 37.27 N 122.02 W
Alvito, It. 66 41.41 N 13.45 E
Alvito, Port. 34 38.15 N 7.59 W
Älvkarleby 40 60.34 N 17.27 E
Älvkarleö bruk 40 60.32 N 17.24 E
Alvord 196 33.22 N 97.42 W
Alvord Desert ◆[2] 202 42.30 N 118.25 W
Alvord Lake ⊜ 202 42.23 N 118.36 W
Alvordton 216 41.40 N 84.26 W
Alvra, Pass d')(58 46.35 N 9.50 E
Älvros 26 62.03 N 14.39 E
Älvsborgs Län ▫[6] 26 58.00 N 12.30 E
Älvsbyn 24 65.39 N 20.59 E
Älvsnabben ⊥ 40 58.59 N 18.10 E
Al-Wafā'īyah 142 30.46 N 30.36 E
Al-Wajh 128 26.15 N 36.26 E
Al-Wakrah 128 25.10 N 51.36 E
Al-Walīdīyah 142 27.12 N 31.10 E
Alwar 124 27.34 N 76.36 E
Alwar Hills ⋏[2] 124 27.20 N 76.15 E
Al-Wāṣifīyah 142 30.35 N 32.10 E
Al-Wāsiṭah 142 29.20 N 31.12 E
Alwaye 122 10.07 N 76.21 E
Al-Wazīrīyah 142 31.11 N 30.57 E
Al-Wazz 140 15.01 N 30.10 E
Alwen ≃ 44 52.58 N 3.24 W
Al-Widy 142 29.31 N 31.16 E
Alxa Zuoqi 102 38.50 N 105.32 E
Al-Yamāmah → As-Sulaymānīyah 128 24.09 N 47.19 E
Al-Yaman → Yemen ▫[1] 144 15.00 N 47.00 E
Al Yāmūn 132 32.29 N 35.14 E
Alygdžer 88 53.38 N 98.16 E
Alyn and Deeside ▫[8] 262 53.16 N 3.02 W
Alypsatar 86 48.03 N 80.21 E
Alyth 46 56.37 N 3.13 W
Alytus 76 54.24 N 24.03 E
Alz ≃ 60 48.16 N 12.49 E
Alzamaj 88 55.33 N 98.39 E
Alzano Lombardo 62 45.44 N 9.43 E
Al-Zarqa 142 31.13 N 31.38 E
Alzenau 56 50.05 N 9.04 E
Alzette ≃ 56 49.52 N 6.07 E
Alzey 56 49.45 N 8.07 E
Alzira (Alcira) 34 39.09 N 0.26 W
Amab, Khawr V 140 17.08 N 34.51 E
Amacayacu, Parque Nacional ♦ 246 3.45 S 70.10 W
Amacuro ≃ 246 8.32 N 60.28 W
Amacuzac ≃ 234 17.53 N 99.12 W
Amadeus, Lake ⊜ 162 24.50 S 130.45 E
Āmādi, Bngl. 126 22.28 N 89.19 E
Amadi, Zaïre 154 3.35 N 26.47 E
Amadjuak Lake ⊜ 176 65.00 N 71.00 W
Amador ▫[6] 226 38.21 N 120.46 W
Amadora 266c 38.45 N 9.14 W
Amador City 226 38.25 N 120.56 W
Amador Valley V 282 37.41 N 121.51 W
Amagansett 207 40.58 N 72.08 W
Amagasaki 96 34.43 N 135.25 E
Amagase 96 33.15 N 131.02 E
Amager I 41 55.37 N 12.37 E
Amagi 96 33.25 N 130.39 E
Amagi-san ∧ 94 34.51 N 139.00 E
Amagi-yugashima 94 34.53 N 138.56 E
Amagoi-dake ∧ 94 35.01 N 136.23 E
Amagunze 150 6.20 N 7.40 E
Amahai 164 3.20 S 128.55 E
Amaichá del Valle 252 26.36 S 65.55 W
Amaimon 164 5.10 S 145.25 E
Amajac ≃ 234 21.15 N 98.46 W
Amaka ≃ 236 14.14 N 85.07 W
Ama Keng 271c 1.24 N 103.42 E
Amak Island I 180 55.25 N 163.07 W
Amakusa-nada ▼[2] 92 32.35 N 130.05 E
Amakusa-shotō II 92 32.20 N 130.15 E
Amakusa-Shimo-shima I 92 32.20 N 130.05 E
Amal, Lībiyā 146 29.25 N 21.10 E
Åmål, Sve. 26 59.03 N 12.42 E
Amalāpuram 122 16.35 N 82.01 E
Amalat ≃ 88 54.49 N 115.12 E
Amalfi, Col. 246 6.55 N 75.04 W
Amalfi, It. 68 40.38 N 14.36 E
Amalia 158 27.16 S 25.03 E
Amaliás 38 37.49 N 21.23 E
Amalner 120 21.03 N 75.04 E
Amamaki-zan ∧ 94 36.25 N 140.09 E
Amambaí 255 23.05 S 55.13 W
Amambaí ≃ 255 23.22 S 53.56 W
Amambay ▫[5] 252 23.00 S 56.00 W
Amami-Ō-shima I 93b 28.15 N 129.20 E
Amami-shotō II 93b 28.16 N 129.21 E
Amamula 154 0.18 S 27.50 E
Amana 190 41.48 N 91.52 W
Amanã ≃, Bra. 250 4.25 S 57.34 W
Amana ≃, Ven. 238 9.45 N 62.39 W
Amanã, Lago ⊜ 246 2.35 S 64.40 W
Amanab 164 3.35 S 141.13 E
Amanave 174u 14.19 S 170.49 W
Amance 58 47.48 N 6.04 E
Amancey 58 47.02 N 6.05 E
Amancio 240p 20.49 N 77.35 W
Amanda 188 39.38 N 82.44 W
Amanda Park 224 47.28 N 123.54 W
Amandola 66 42.59 N 13.21 E
Amānganj 124 24.26 N 80.02 E
Amangel'dy, Kaz. 85 43.43 N 71.07 E
Amangel'dy, Kaz. 86 50.10 N 65.13 E
Amangel'dy, Kaz. 86 49.52 N 59.00 E
Åmänningen ⊜ 40 59.57 N 15.56 E
Amano 270 34.26 N 135.33 E
Amanotkel' 86 46.07 N 61.34 E
Amantea 68 39.08 N 16.05 E
Amantogaj 86 50.22 N 65.33 E
Amanu I[1] 14 17.48 S 140.46 W
Amanzimtofi 158 30.03 S 30.53 E
Amapá 250 2.03 N 50.48 W
Amapá ▫[3] 250 1.00 N 52.00 W
Amapa ≃ 234 18.18 N 96.19 W
Amapala 236 13.17 N 87.40 W
Amapala, Punta de > 236 13.10 N 87.54 W
Amapari ≃ 250 0.43 N 51.32 W
Amaraji 250 8.24 S 35.27 W
Amaral 287a 22.42 S 43.29 W
Amaramba, Lago ⊜ 154 14.30 S 35.55 E
Amarante 250 6.14 S 42.50 W
Amarante do Maranhão 250 5.36 S 46.45 W
Amaranth 184 50.36 N 98.43 W
Amarapura 110 21.54 N 96.03 E
Amărăştii de Jos 38 43.59 N 24.10 E
'Amārat Abū Sinn 140 15.21 N 35.45 E
Amarāvati ≃ 122 10.51 N 78.11 E
Amarda 126 21.47 N 87.08 E
Amareleja 34 38.12 N 7.14 W
Amares 34 41.38 N 8.21 W
Amargosa 255 13.02 S 39.36 W
Amargosa ≃ 204 36.13 N 116.48 W
Amargosa Range ⋏ 204 36.15 N 116.45 W
Amarillo 196 35.13 N 101.49 W
Amarillo, Mar → Yellow Sea ▼[2] 90 36.00 N 123.00 E
'Amar Jadīd 140 14.28 N 25.14 E
Amarkantak 124 22.40 N 81.45 E
Amarnāth 122 19.11 N 73.10 E
Amarnāth Cave ≐[5] 123 34.13 N 75.31 E
Amaro, Monte ∧ 66 42.05 N 14.05 E
Amaroni 68 38.47 N 16.27 E
Amaroúsion 267c 38.03 N 23.49 E
Amarpātan 124 24.19 N 80.59 E
Amarube-saki > 96 35.40 N 134.32 E
Amarume 92 38.50 N 139.55 E
Amarwāra 124 22.18 N 79.10 E
Amasa 190 46.13 N 88.26 W
Amaseno ≃ 66 41.19 N 13.11 E
Amasija 84 40.58 N 43.46 E
Amasra 130 41.45 N 32.24 E
Amasya 130 40.39 N 35.51 E
Amasya ▫[4] 130 40.45 N 35.30 E
Amataurá 246 3.29 S 68.06 W
Amatignak Island I 181a 51.15 N 179.08 W
Amatikulu 158 29.06 S 31.27 E
Amatique, Bahía de c 236 15.55 N 88.45 W
Amatitán 234 20.50 N 103.43 W
Amatitlán 236 14.29 N 90.37 W
Amatitlán, Lago de ⊜ 236 14.27 N 90.34 W
Amatlán de Cañas 234 20.52 N 104.27 W
Amatlán de los Reyes 234 18.50 N 96.55 W
Amatrice 66 42.38 N 13.17 E
Amatsu-kominato 94 35.07 N 140.10 E
Amau 164 10.02 S 148.34 E
Amausi 124 26.46 N 80.51 E
Amawalk 210 41.17 N 73.46 W
Amay 56 50.33 N 5.19 E
Ama-zaki > 94 37.08 N 136.40 E
Amazar 89 53.54 N 120.53 E
Amazon (Solimões) (Amazonas) ≃ 242 0.10 S 49.00 W
Amazonas ▫[3] 242 5.00 S 63.00 W
Amazonas ▫[5], Col. 246 1.00 S 72.00 W
Amazonas ▫[5], Perú 248 5.30 S 78.00 W
Amazonas ▫[8] 246 3.30 N 66.00 W
Amazonas → Amazon ≃ 242 0.10 S 49.00 W
Amazônia, Parque Nacional da ♦ 250 4.30 S 56.30 W
Amb 123 34.19 N 72.51 E
Ambāh 124 26.43 N 78.14 E
Ambahikily 157b 21.36 S 43.41 E
Ambahita 157b 24.01 S 45.16 E
Ambaí 287a 22.43 S 43.28 W
Ambājogāi 122 18.44 N 76.23 E
Ambakaka 157b 24.10 S 46.17 E
Ambāla 124 30.21 N 76.50 E
Ambāla Airport ⊠ 123 30.22 N 76.50 E
Ambalabe 157b 18.24 S 49.10 E
Ambalafany 157b 22.32 S 47.36 E
Ambalangoda 122 6.14 N 80.03 E
Ambalanjanakomby 157b 16.42 S 47.05 E
Ambalavao 157b 21.50 S 46.56 E
Ambam 152 2.23 N 11.17 E
Amba Maryam 144 11.26 N 39.17 E
Ambanja 157b 13.41 S 48.27 E
Ambar 248 10.44 S 77.16 W
Ambararata 157b 15.03 S 48.33 E
Ambarawa 115a 7.15 S 110.24 E
Ambarčik, Ross. 74 69.39 N 162.20 E
Ambarčik, Ross. 88 55.09 N 95.46 E
Ambargasta, Salinas de ≐ 252 29.15 S 64.30 W
Ambarijeby 157b 14.56 S 47.41 E
Ambarnyj 24 65.56 N 33.43 E
Ambaro, Baie d' c 157b 13.23 S 48.38 E
Ambāsamudram 122 8.42 N 77.28 E
Ambassador Bridge ◆[5] 281 42.20 N 83.05 W
Ambato, Ec. 246 1.15 S 78.37 W
Ambato, Madag. 157b 13.24 S 48.29 E
Ambato Boeny 157b 16.28 S 46.43 E
Ambatofinandrahana 157b 20.33 S 46.48 E
Ambatolampy 157b 19.23 S 47.25 E
Ambatomainty 157b 17.41 S 45.40 E
Ambatomanoina 157b 18.18 S 47.37 E
Ambatondrazaka 157b 17.50 S 48.25 E
Ambatosoratra 157b 17.34 S 48.32 E
Ambeláki 267c 37.57 N 23.32 E
Ambelau, Pulau I 164 3.51 S 127.12 E
Ámbelos, Ákra > 38 39.56 N 23.55 E
Ambenja 157b 15.17 S 46.58 E
Amber ≃ 44 53.04 N 1.29 W
Amberes → Antwerpen 50 51.13 N 4.25 E
Amberg, Dtsch. 60 49.27 N 11.52 E
Amberg, Wi., U.S. 190 45.30 N 87.59 W
Ambergris Cay I 232 18.03 N 87.56 W
Ambérieu-en-Bugey 58 45.57 N 5.21 E
Amberley 172 43.10 S 172.44 E
Amberley Royal Australian Air Force Base ■ 171a 27.37 S 152.41 E
Amberson 214 40.10 N 77.41 W
Ambert 62 45.33 N 3.45 E
Ambevongo 157b 15.27 S 47.27 E
Ambia 216 40.29 N 87.31 W
Ambidédi 150 14.35 N 11.47 W
Ambikānagar 126 22.57 N 86.46 E
Ambikāpur 124 23.07 N 83.12 E
Ambil 116 13.49 N 120.20 E
Ambil Island I 116 13.48 N 120.18 E
Ambilobe 157b 13.12 S 49.04 E
Ambinanindrano 157b 20.20 S 48.19 E
Ambinanitelo 157b 15.21 S 49.35 E
Ambinda 157b 16.25 S 45.52 E
Ambivy 157b 21.31 S 44.02 E
Ambjörby 26 60.30 N 13.10 E
Ambla 76 59.11 N 25.51 E
Amble 44 55.20 N 1.34 W
Ambler, Ak., U.S. 180 67.05 N 157.52 W
Ambler, Pa., U.S. 208 40.09 N 75.13 W
Ambleside 44 54.26 N 2.58 W
Ambleteuse 50 50.49 N 1.36 E
Amblève ≃ 56 50.28 N 5.36 E
Ambo 248 10.07 S 76.10 W
Amboahangy 157b 24.15 S 46.22 E
Amboasary, Madag. 157b 18.26 S 48.16 E
Amboasary, Madag. 157b 25.02 S 46.23 E
Ambodifototra 157b 16.59 S 49.52 E
Ambodilazana 157b 18.06 S 49.10 E
Ambodiriana 157b 17.55 S 49.18 E
Ambohibary 157b 19.20 S 46.17 E
Ambohidratrimo 157b 18.50 S 47.26 E
Ambohidray 157b 18.36 S 48.18 E
Ambohimahamasina 157b 21.56 S 47.11 E
Ambohimahasoa 157b 21.07 S 47.13 E
Ambohimanga du Sud 157b 20.52 S 47.36 E
Ambohimitombo 157b 20.43 S 47.26 E
Amboina → Ambon 164 3.43 S 128.12 E
Amboise 50 47.25 N 0.59 E
Amboíva 152 11.32 S 14.44 E
Ambon 164 3.43 S 128.12 E
Ambon, Pulau I 164 3.40 S 128.10 E
Ambondro 157b 25.13 S 45.44 E
Ambonnay 50 49.04 N 4.10 E
Amboseli, Lake ⊜ 154 2.37 S 37.08 E
Amboseli National Park ♦ 154 2.30 S 37.15 E
Amboshe 272c 19.09 N 73.08 E
Ambositra 157b 20.31 S 47.15 E
Ambovombe 157b 25.11 S 46.05 E
Amboy, Il., U.S. 190 41.42 N 89.19 W
Amboy, In., U.S. 216 40.36 N 85.55 W
Amboy, Mn., U.S. 190 43.53 N 94.09 W
Amboy, Wa., U.S. 224 45.54 N 122.26 W
Ambre, Cap d' > 157b 11.57 S 49.17 E
Ambre, Montagne d' ∧ 157b 12.30 S 49.10 E
Ambridge 214 40.35 N 80.13 W
Ambridge Heights 214 40.36 N 80.13 W
Ambridge Reservoir ⊜[1] 214 40.34 N 80.21 W
Ambrières 32 48.24 N 0.38 W
Ambriz 152 7.50 S 13.06 E
Ambrolauri 84 42.31 N 43.09 E
Ambronay 58 46.00 N 5.21 E
Ambrose 198 48.57 N 103.28 W
Ambrose Brook ≃ 276 40.33 N 74.32 W
Ambrose Channel ⌣ 276 40.32 N 74.02 W
Ambrosia Lake 200 35.25 N 107.49 W
Ambrym ▫[8] 175f 16.15 S 168.12 E
Ambrym I 175f 16.15 S 168.10 E
Ambuklao Dam ◆[6] 116 16.28 N 120.45 E
Ambulong Island I 116 12.12 N 121.01 E
Ambulu 115a 8.21 S 113.36 E
Ambuntentimur 115a 6.54 S 113.45 E
Ambunti 164 4.14 S 142.50 E
Āmbūr 122 12.47 N 78.42 E
Amburambur 115b 8.15 S 116.18 E
Amburayan Nabunga ≃ 116 16.55 N 120.27 E
Amby 56 50.53 N 5.44 E
Amchitka Island I 181a 51.30 N 179.00 E
Amchitka Pass ⌣ 181a 51.30 N 179.30 W
'Amd 144 15.18 N 48.00 E
Am-Dam 146 12.46 N 20.29 E
Āmdānga 272b 22.49 N 88.31 E
Amded, Oued V 148 22.09 N 3.15 E
Amden 58 47.09 N 9.11 E
Amderma 72 69.45 N 61.39 E
Amdo 120 32.18 N 91.04 E
Ameagle 188 37.56 N 81.25 W
Ameca 234 20.33 N 104.02 W
Ameca ≃ 234 20.41 N 105.18 W
Amecameca [de Juárez] 234 19.07 N 98.46 W
Ameghino 252 34.50 S 62.27 W

ENGLISH

Name	Page	Lat.°′	Long.°′
Ameglia	64	44.04 N	9.57 E
Ameisberg ∧	60	48.33 N	13.50 E
Ameixoeira ◆[8]	266c	38.47 N	9.10 W
Ameland I	52	53.25 N	5.45 E
Amele	164	5.16 S	145.42 E
Amelia, It.	66	42.33 N	12.25 E
Amelia, Oh., U.S.	218	39.01 N	84.13 W
Amelia, Passo d')(	66	42.36 N	12.32 E
Amelia Court House	192	37.20 N	77.58 W
Amelia Earhart Peak ∧	226	37.47 N	119.17 W
Amelia Island I	192	30.37 N	81.27 W
Amelinghausen	52	53.08 N	10.13 E
Amelsbüren	52	51.53 N	7.37 E
Amendolara	68	39.57 N	16.35 E
Ameng	102	23.50 N	104.32 E
Amenia	210	41.50 N	73.33 W
Amenucourt	261	49.06 N	1.39 E
Āmer	120	26.59 N	75.52 E
Amerang	60	48.00 N	12.18 E
Amerevo	265b	55.55 N	38.03 E
America	52	51.26 N	5.59 E
América del Norte → North America ≐[1]	16	45.00 N	100.00 W
América del Sur → South America ≐[1]	18	15.00 S	60.00 W
American ≃, Ca., U.S.	226	38.36 N	121.30 W
American ≃, Wa., U.S.	224	46.58 N	121.08 W
American, Middle Fork ≃	226	38.55 N	121.02 W
American, North Fork ≃	226	38.43 N	121.09 W
American, South Fork ≃	226	38.43 N	121.09 W
Americana	255	22.45 S	47.20 W
American Canyon	226	38.10 N	122.15 W
American Cemetery and Memorial ◆	269f	14.33 N	121.03 E
American Falls	202	42.47 N	112.51 W
American Falls ∟	284a	43.05 N	79.04 W
American Falls Reservoir ⊜[1]	202	42.45 N	112.45 W
American Fork	200	40.22 N	111.47 W
American Highland ⋏[1]	9	72.30 S	78.00 E
American Lake ⊜	224	47.07 N	122.34 W
American Museum of Natural History ⊍	276	40.47 N	73.59 W
Americano	250	1.19 S	48.04 W
American River	168b	35.47 S	137.47 E
American Samoa ▫[2], Oc.	14	14.20 S	170.00 W
American Samoa ▫[2], Oc.	175a	14.20 S	170.00 W
American University ⊍[2]	284c	38.56 N	77.05 W
Américas, Hipódromo de las ♦	286a	19.26 N	99.13 W
Americus, Ga., U.S.	192	32.04 N	84.13 W
Americus, Ks., U.S.	198	38.30 N	96.15 W
Amerikanisches Hochland → American Highland ⋏[1]	9	72.30 S	78.00 E
Ameringkogel ∧	61	47.04 N	14.48 E
Amérique du Nord → North America ≐[1]	16	45.00 N	100.00 W
Amern	56	51.14 N	6.15 E
Amerongen	52	52.00 N	5.27 E
Amersfoort, Ned.	52	52.09 N	5.24 E
Amersfoort, S. Afr.	158	27.01 S	29.51 E
Amersham	42	51.40 N	0.38 W
Amery, Austl.	162	31.09 S	117.05 E
Amery, Mb., Can.	184	56.34 N	94.03 W
Amery, Wi., U.S.	190	45.18 N	92.21 W
Amery Ice Shelf ⊓	9	69.30 S	72.00 E
Ames, Ia., U.S.	190	42.02 N	93.37 W
Ames, N.Y., U.S.	210	42.50 N	74.36 W
Ames, Tx., U.S.	222	30.03 N	94.46 W
Amesbury, Eng., U.K.	42	51.10 N	1.45 W
Amesbury, Ma., U.S.	207	42.51 N	70.55 W
Ames Long Pond ⊜	283	42.05 N	71.07 W
Ames Nowell State Park ♦	283	42.07 N	70.59 W
Ames Pond ⊜	283	42.38 N	71.13 W
Ames Research Center ⊍[3]	282	37.25 N	122.04 W
Amet Sound ⌣	186	45.47 N	63.13 W
Amfíklia	38	38.38 N	22.35 E
Amfilokhía	38	38.51 N	21.10 E
Ámfissa	38	38.31 N	22.24 E
Amfreville-la-Campagne	50	49.13 N	0.57 E
Amfreville-les-Champs	50	49.19 N	1.19 E
Amga	74	60.53 N	132.00 E
Amga ≃	74	62.38 N	134.32 E
Am Géréda	146	12.52 N	21.10 E
Amguema	180	66.58 N	179.16 W
Amguema ≃	180	68.10 N	177.40 W
Amguid	148	26.26 N	5.22 E
Amgun' ≃	89	52.56 N	139.40 E
Amherst, N.S., Can.	186	45.49 N	64.14 W
Amherst, Ma., U.S.	207	42.22 N	72.31 W
Amherst, N.H., U.S.	207	42.51 N	71.37 W
Amherst, N.Y., U.S.	210	42.58 N	78.48 W
Amherst, Oh., U.S.	214	41.23 N	82.13 W
Amherst, Tx., U.S.	196	34.01 N	102.25 W
Amherst, Va., U.S.	192	37.35 N	79.03 W
Amherst, Wi., U.S.	190	44.27 N	89.17 W
Amherst, Mount ∧	162	18.11 S	126.59 E
Amherstburg	214	42.06 N	83.06 W
Amherstdale	188	37.47 N	81.48 W
Amherst Island I	212	44.08 N	76.45 W
Amherstview	212	44.13 N	76.38 W
Ami	94	36.02 N	140.14 E
Amianan Island I	108	21.07 N	121.57 E
Amiata, Monte ∧	66	42.53 N	11.37 E
Amicalola Falls State Park ♦	192	34.33 N	84.15 W
Amidon	198	46.28 N	103.19 W
Amiens, Austl.	166	28.35 S	151.49 E
Amiens, Fr.	50	49.54 N	2.18 E
Amili, India	120	28.26 N	95.52 E
Amili, Zhg.	120	28.25 N	95.52 E
Amīn as-Samālūsī, Bi'r ▼[4]	142	29.52 N	30.02 E
Amīndīvi Islands II	122	11.23 N	72.23 E
Aminga	252	28.50 S	66.54 W
Amini Island I	122	11.07 N	72.44 E
Amino, Ityo.	144	4.31 N	41.49 E
Amino, Nihon	96	35.41 N	135.02 E
Aminuis	156	23.43 S	19.21 E
Amīrābād	128	36.04 N	54.10 E
Amīrābād ◆[8]	267d	35.43 N	51.23 E
Amirante Islands II	138	6.00 S	53.10 E
Amirauté, Îles de l' → Admiralty Islands II	164	2.10 S	147.00 E
Amisk	182	52.33 N	111.04 W
Amisk Lake ⊜	184	54.35 N	102.13 W
Amistad, Parque Internacional de la ♦	236	9.25 N	83.10 W
Amistad, Presa de la (Amistad Reservoir) ⊜[1]	196	29.34 N	101.15 W
Amistad National Recreation Area ♦	196	29.32 N	101.12 W
Amistad Reservoir (Presa de la Amistad) ⊜[1]	196	29.34 N	101.15 W
Amite	194	30.43 N	90.30 W
Amite ≃	194	30.12 N	90.35 W
Amite, East Fork ≃	194	30.58 N	90.51 W
Amiterno ⊥	66	42.21 N	13.19 E
Amitori	175d	24.18 N	123.41 E
Amity, Ar., U.S.	194	34.15 N	93.27 W

DEUTSCH

Name	Seite	Breite°′	Länge°′ E = Ost
Amity, Oh., U.S.	214	40.03 N	83.17 W
Amity, Or., U.S.	224	45.06 N	123.12 W
Amity Point >	171a	27.24 S	153.27 E
Amityville	276	40.40 N	73.25 W
Amixtlán	234	20.03 N	97.48 W
Amizmiz	148	31.14 N	8.14 W
Āmjhori ∧	126	21.51 N	86.19 E
Āmjhupi	126	23.45 N	88.42 E
Āmla, Bngl.	126	23.54 N	88.56 E
Amla, India	124	21.56 N	78.07 E
Āmlāgora	126	22.50 N	87.20 E
Amlekhganj	124	27.17 N	84.59 E
Åmli	26	58.47 N	8.30 E
Amlia Island I	180	52.06 N	173.30 W
Amloh	124	30.37 N	76.14 E
Am Loubia	146	13.39 N	20.08 E
Amlwch	44	53.25 N	4.20 W
'Amm-Adām	140	16.22 N	36.06 E
Ammagan	85	38.56 N	67.15 E
'Ammān	132	31.57 N	35.56 E
'Ammān ▫[8]	132	31.45 N	36.15 E
Ammanford	42	51.48 N	3.59 W
Ämmänsaari	26	64.53 N	28.55 E
Ammansville	222	29.47 N	96.51 W
'Ammār, Tall ∧[2]	132	32.53 N	36.29 E
Ammarnäs	24	65.56 N	16.09 E
Ammaroo	162	21.45 S	135.15 E
Åmmeberg	40	58.52 N	15.00 E
Ammeloe	52	52.05 N	6.47 E
Ammendorf ◆[8]	54	51.25 N	11.59 E
Ammer ≃	64	47.57 N	11.08 E
Ammerån ≃	26	63.09 N	16.13 E
Ammerbuch	56	48.33 N	8.58 E
Ammer Gebirge ⋏	64	47.35 N	10.55 E
Ammerland ◆[1]	52	53.15 N	8.00 E
Ammerman Mountain ∧	180	68.21 N	141.03 W
Ammerschwihr	58	48.07 N	7.17 E
Ammersee ⊜	60	48.00 N	11.08 E
Ammerthal	60	49.26 N	11.45 E
Ammon	202	43.28 N	111.57 W
Ammonoosuc ≃	188	44.10 N	72.02 W
Amnān	272b	22.56 N	88.18 E
Amnat Charoen	110	15.51 N	104.38 E
Amnay ≃	116	12.58 N	120.46 E
Amne Machin Shan → A'nyêmaqên Shan ⋏	102	34.30 N	100.00 E
Amnicon ≃	190	46.41 N	91.52 W
Amnok-kang (Yalu) ≃	98	39.55 N	124.22 E
Amo ≃, Asia	124	26.16 N	89.36 E
Amo ≃, Zhg.	102	22.58 N	101.44 E
Āmol	128	36.23 N	52.20 E
Amolar	248	18.01 S	57.30 W
Amöneburg	56	50.48 N	8.55 E
Amorbach	56	49.39 N	9.13 E
Amorgós	38	36.50 N	25.54 E
Amorgós I	38	36.50 N	25.59 E
Amorim, Morro ∧[2]	287a	23.00 S	43.26 W
Amorinópolis	255	16.36 S	51.08 W
Amorosi	68	41.12 N	14.28 E
Amory	194	33.59 N	88.29 W
Amos	190	48.35 N	78.07 W
Åmose ≃	41	55.35 N	11.18 E
Åmot, Nor.	26	59.35 N	8.00 E
Åmot, Nor.	26	59.54 N	9.54 E
Åmotfors	26	59.46 N	12.22 E
Amour → Amur ≃	74	52.56 N	141.10 E
Amour, Djebel ⋏	148	34.00 N	2.15 E
Amoy → Xiamen	100	24.28 N	118.07 E
Amozoc	234	19.02 N	98.03 W
Ampana	112	0.51 S	121.32 E
Ampanavoana	157b	15.41 S	50.22 E
Ampang	115b	8.47 S	118.00 E
Ampanihy	157b	24.42 S	44.45 E
Ampaoid, Mount ∧	116	7.57 N	125.41 E
Amparafaravola	157b	17.35 S	48.13 E
Amparihy, Madag.	157b	16.40 S	44.49 E
Amparihy, Madag.	157b	23.57 S	47.20 E
Amparo	256	22.42 S	46.45 W
Ampasibe	157b	22.56 S	46.58 E
Ampasinambo	157b	20.31 S	48.00 E
Ampasindava, Baie d' c	157b	13.16 S	48.43 E
Ampasindava, Presq'île d' >[1]	157b	13.45 S	48.00 E
Ampato, Nevado ∧	248	15.50 S	71.52 W
Ampel	115a	7.27 S	110.32 E
Amper	150	9.20 N	9.43 E
Amper ≃	60	48.30 N	11.58 E
Ampezzo	64	46.25 N	12.48 E
Ampezzo, Valle d' V	64	46.30 N	12.10 E
Ampfing	60	48.16 N	12.25 E
Ampflwang	64	48.05 N	13.34 E
Amphion-les-Bains	58	46.23 N	6.32 E
Ampisikina	157b	12.57 S	49.49 E
Ampleforth	44	54.12 N	1.06 W
Ampollino, Lago ⊜	68	39.12 N	16.37 E
Ampombiantambo	157b	12.42 S	48.57 E
Amposta	34	40.43 N	0.35 E
Ampotaka	157b	25.03 S	44.41 E
Ampoza	157b	22.20 S	44.44 E
Ampthill	42	52.02 N	0.30 W
Ampuis	62	45.29 N	4.49 E
Ampus	62	43.36 N	6.23 E
Amqui	186	48.28 N	67.26 W
Āmr, Jabal al- ⋏	132	30.45 N	34.20 E
Amraoti → Amrāvati	120	20.56 N	77.45 E
Amrāvati	120	20.56 N	77.45 E
Am-Raya	146	14.00 N	16.35 E
Amreli	120	21.37 N	71.14 E
Āmreswar	272b	22.28 N	88.34 E
Amriswil	58	47.33 N	9.18 E
Amritsar	123	31.35 N	74.53 E
Amroha	124	28.55 N	78.28 E
Amrūka	123	30.19 N	73.53 E
Amrum I	30	54.39 N	8.21 E
Amsdell Heights	284a	42.45 N	78.54 W
Amsden	214	41.13 N	83.20 W
Amsel	148	22.37 N	5.26 E
Åmsele	26	64.32 N	19.20 E
Am Sigan	146	11.41 N	19.51 E
Amsoldingen	58	46.43 N	7.35 E
Amsteg	58	46.46 N	8.41 E
Amstel ≃	52	52.22 N	4.54 E
Amstelmeer ⊜	52	52.52 N	4.45 E
Amstelveen	52	52.18 N	4.51 E
Amsterdam, Ned.	52	52.22 N	4.54 E
Amsterdam, S. Afr.	158	26.35 S	30.45 E
Amsterdam, N.Y., U.S.	210	42.56 N	74.11 W
Amsterdam, Oh., U.S.	214	40.28 N	80.55 W
Amsterdam, Île I	6	37.52 S	77.32 E
Amsterdam-Rijnkanaal ≚	52	51.57 N	5.20 E
Amstetten	61	48.07 N	14.53 E
Amston	207	41.37 N	72.20 W
Āmta	126	22.35 N	88.01 E
Amt'ae-do I	98	34.50 N	126.07 E
Āmtala	126	23.55 N	88.27 E
Amtāli	126	22.08 N	90.14 E
Am Timan	146	11.02 N	20.17 E
Amtrak Station ◆[5]	281	42.19 N	83.04 W
Amubri	236	9.31 N	82.56 W
'Āmūdah	130	37.05 N	40.54 E
Amu-Darja	128	37.53 N	65.15 E
Amu Darya (Amudarja) ≃	72	43.40 N	59.01 E
Amudat	154	1.57 N	34.57 E
Amugulang → Xin Barag Zuoqi	88	48.14 N	118.18 E
Amukta Island I	180	52.29 N	171.15 W
Amukta Pass ⌣	180	52.25 N	172.00 W
Amulree	46	56.30 N	3.47 W
Amun	175e	5.57 S	154.45 E
Amundsen Bay c	9	66.55 S	50.00 E
Amundsen Gulf c	176	71.00 N	124.00 W
Amundsen-Scott ⊍[3]	9	90.00 S	0.00
Amundsen Sea ▼[2]	9	72.30 S	112.00 W

Symbols in the index entries represent the broad categories identified in the key at the right. Symbols with superior numbers (⋏[1]) identify subcategories (see complete key on page I · 1).

Symbole im Register stellen die rechts im Schlüssel erklärten Kategorien dar. Symbole mit hochgestellten Ziffern (⋏[1]) bezeichnen Unterabteilungen einer Kategorie (vgl. vollständiger Schlüssel auf Seite I · 1).

Los símbolos incluídos en el texto del índice representan las grandes categorías identificadas con la clave a la derecha. Los símbolos con numeros en su parte superior (⋏[1]) identifican las subcategorías (véase la clave completa en la página I · 1).

Les symboles de l'index représentent les catégories indiquées dans la légende à droite. Les symboles suivis d'un indice (⋏[1]) représentent des sous-catégories (voir légende complète à la page I · 1).

Os símbolos incluídos no texto do índice representam as grandes categorias identificadas com a chave à direita. Os símbolos com números em sua parte superior (⋏[1]) identificam as subcategorias (veja-se a chave completa à página I · 1).

∧ Mountain	Berg	Montaña	Montagne	Montanha
⋏ Mountains	Gebirge	Montañas	Montagnes	Montanhas
)(Pass	Paß	Paso	Col	Passo
V Valley, Canyon	Tal, Cañon	Valle, Cañón	Vallée, Canyon	Vale, Canhão
= Plain	Ebene	Llano	Plaine	Planície
> Cape	Kap	Cabo	Cap	Cabo
I Island	Insel	Isla	Île	Ilha
II Islands	Inseln	Islas	Îles	Ilhas
≐ Other Topographic Features	Andere Topographische Objekte	Otros Elementos Topográficos	Autres données topographiques	Outros acidentes topográficos

ESPAÑOL

Nombre	Página	Lat.°′	Long.°′ W = Oeste
Amung, Mount ∧	164	7.26 S	146.36 E
Amungen ⊜	26	61.09 N	15.39 E
Amuntai	112	2.26 S	115.15 E
Amur (Heilong) ≃	74	52.56 N	141.10 E
ʻAmūr, Wādī V	140	18.56 N	33.34 E
Amurang	112	1.11 N	124.35 E
Amuria	154	2.01 N	33.38 E
Amursk	89	50.13 N	136.52 E
Amurskaja Oblast' □[8]	89	53.00 N	129.00 E
Amurskij liman c	89	52.45 N	141.40 E
Amursko-Zejskaja ravnina ⩘[1]	89	52.30 N	128.30 E
Amurzet	89	47.42 N	131.05 E
Amutag	116	12.23 N	123.16 E
Amuwo	273a	6.28 N	3.18 E
Amuyimusu	98	42.25 N	113.21 E
Amuzhong	120	30.33 N	84.28 E
Amvamg	152	1.45 N	10.29 E
Amvrakikós Kólpos c	38	39.00 N	21.00 E
Amvrosiyivka	83	47.47 N	38.29 E
Amwom, Khawr V	140	7.50 N	31.13 E
Amyl ≃	86	53.47 N	92.54 E
Amyūn	130	34.18 N	35.49 E
Amz'a	80	56.13 N	54.23 E
Amzi, Oued ti-n- V	148	20.30 N	4.35 E
An	110	19.47 N	94.02 E
Anaa I[1]	14	17.25 S	145.30 W
Anabanua	112	3.57 S	120.04 E
Anabar	174b	0.30 S	166.57 E
Anabar ≃	74	73.08 N	113.36 E
ʻAnabtā	132	32.19 N	35.07 E
Anabuki	96	34.02 N	134.11 E
Anacapri	68	40.33 N	14.13 E
Anaco	246	9.27 N	64.28 W
Anacoco	194	31.15 N	93.20 W
Anacoco, Bayou ≃	194	30.52 N	93.34 W
Anaconda	202	46.07 N	112.56 W
Anaconda Range ⩘	202	45.55 N	113.30 W
Anacortes	224	48.30 N	122.36 W
Anacostia ◆[8]	284c	38.52 N	76.59 W
Anacostia ≃	284c	38.52 N	77.01 W
Anacostia, Little Paint Branch ≃	284c	39.01 N	76.56 W
Anacostia, Northeast Branch ≃	284c	38.57 N	76.57 W
Anacostia, Paint Branch ≃	284c	38.58 N	76.55 W
Anacostia Park ♦	284c	38.54 N	76.58 W
Anacuao, Mount ∧	116	16.16 N	121.53 E
Anadarko	196	35.04 N	98.14 W
Anadia	250	9.42 S	36.18 W
Anadolufeneri ◆[8]	267b	41.12 N	29.09 E
Anadoluhisarı ⊥	267b	41.04 N	29.03 E
Anadyr'	180	64.45 N	177.29 E
Anadyr' ≃	74	64.55 N	176.05 E
Anadyrskaja nizmennost' ≚	180	65.30 N	176.00 E
Anadyrskij liman c	180	64.30 N	177.45 E
Anadyrskij zaliv c	180	64.00 N	179.00 W
Anadyrskoje ploskogorje ⩘[1]	180	67.00 N	174.00 E
Anáfi I	38	36.21 N	25.50 E
Anagni	66	41.44 N	13.09 E
ʻĀnah	128	34.28 N	41.56 E
Anaheim	228	33.50 N	117.54 W
Anaheim Arena ♦	280	33.48 N	117.52 W
Anaheim Shopping Center ◆[9]	280	33.51 N	117.56 W
Anaheim Stadium ♦	280	33.51 N	117.57 W
Anaheim Union Canal ≍	280	33.54 N	117.52 W
Anahi, Baie c	174x	9.45 S	138.56 W
Anahim Lake	182	52.28 N	125.18 W
Anahola	229b	22.08 N	159.18 W
Anahola Bay c	229b	22.09 N	159.18 W
Anáhuac, Méx.	196	25.48 N	97.45 W
Anáhuac, Méx.	232	27.14 N	100.09 W
Anáhuac, Méx.	232	28.25 N	106.40 W
Anahuac, Tx., U.S.	222	29.46 N	94.41 W
Anahuac, Lake ⊜	222	29.48 N	94.41 W
Anaimala	122	10.35 N	76.56 E
Ānai Mudi ∧	122	10.10 N	77.04 E
Anajás	250	0.59 S	49.57 W
Anajás, Ilha I	250	0.20 S	50.30 W
Anajatuba	250	3.16 S	44.37 W
Anakāpalle	122	17.41 N	83.01 E
Anaklia	84	42.24 N	41.34 E
Anaktuvuk ≃	180	69.32 N	151.30 W
Anaktuvuk Pass	180	68.10 N	151.50 W
Analalava	157b	14.38 S	47.45 E
Analapatsy	157b	25.10 S	46.42 E
Analavoka	157b	22.33 S	46.30 E
Analomink	210	41.03 N	75.13 W
Anamã	246	3.35 S	61.22 W
Anamã, Lago ⊜	246	3.32 S	61.35 W
Anama Bay	184	51.56 N	98.05 W
Ana María, Cayos de II	240p	21.29 N	78.46 W
Ana María, Golfo de c	240p	21.25 N	78.40 W
Anambas, Kepulauan II	112	3.00 N	106.00 E
Anambra □[3]	150	6.30 N	7.20 E
Anambra ≃	150	6.11 N	6.46 E
Anamizu	94	37.14 N	136.54 E
Anamoose	198	47.52 N	100.14 W
Anamosa	190	42.06 N	91.17 W
Anamu ≃	250	0.56 N	57.03 W
Anamur	130	36.06 N	32.50 E
Anamur Burnu ›	130	36.03 N	32.48 E
Anan, Nihon	94	35.19 N	137.49 E
Anan, Nihon	96	33.55 N	134.39 E
Ānand	120	22.34 N	72.56 E
Ananda	150	7.17 N	4.16 W
Anandanagar	272b	22.51 N	88.16 E
Ānandapur, India	120	21.14 N	86.07 E
Ānandapur, India	126	22.34 N	87.25 E
Anandpur Sahib	123	31.15 N	76.30 E
Ananea	248	14.42 S	69.33 W
Ananindeua	250	1.22 S	48.23 W
Ananjevo	85	42.45 N	77.40 E
Anantapur	122	14.41 N	77.36 E
Anantnāg (Islāmābād)	123	33.44 N	75.09 E
Anan'yiv	78	47.40 N	29.55 E
Anao-aon	116	9.47 N	125.25 E
Anapa	78	44.53 N	37.19 E
Anapo ≃	70	37.03 N	15.15 E
Anápolis	255	16.20 S	48.58 W
Anapu ≃	250	1.53 S	50.53 W
Anapurus	250	3.40 S	43.06 W
Anār, Īrān	128	30.53 N	55.18 E
Anar, Kaz.	86	50.38 N	72.27 E
Anāra	126	23.28 N	86.33 E
Anārak	128	33.20 N	53.42 E
Anarchaj	85	44.02 N	75.15 E
Anār Darreh	128	32.46 N	61.39 E
Anaš	86	54.52 N	91.00 E
Anasagasti	258	35.01 S	59.24 W
Añasco	240m	18.17 N	67.08 W
Änäset	26	64.16 N	21.03 E
Anastácio	255	21.31 S	54.08 W
Anastasia Island I	192	29.48 N	81.16 W
Anastasijevka	83	47.34 N	38.31 E
Anastasijevskaja	78	45.13 N	37.53 E
ʻAnātā	132	31.49 N	35.16 E
Anatahan I	108	16.22 N	145.40 E
Anatolikí Makedhonía kaí Thráki □[4]	38	41.00 N	25.00 E
Anatolivka	78	46.48 N	31.13 E
Anatom I	175f	20.12 S	169.45 E
Añatuya	252	28.28 S	62.50 W
Anauá ≃	246	0.58 N	61.21 W
Anaurilândia	255	22.03 S	52.45 W
Anavilhanas, Arquipélago das II	246	2.42 S	60.45 W
Anawalt	192	37.20 N	81.26 W
Anbanjing	102	23.57 N	100.55 E
Anbei, Zhg.	102	40.45 N	96.06 E
Anbei, Zhg.	102	40.49 N	108.56 E
Anbianbu	102	37.39 N	108.11 E
Anbo	98	39.51 N	122.19 E
Anbu	100	23.28 N	116.44 E
Anbyŏn	98	39.03 N	127.32 E

FRANÇAIS

Nom	Page	Lat.°′	Long.°′ W = Ouest
Ancarano	66	42.50 N	13.44 E
Ancash □[5]	248	9.30 S	77.45 W
Ancaster, On., Can.	212	43.12 N	80.00 W
Ancaster, Eng., U.K.	44	52.59 N	0.32 W
Ancasti	252	28.49 S	65.30 W
Ancasti, Sierra de ⩘	252	28.50 S	65.39 W
Ance ≃, Fr.	62	45.17 N	4.08 E
Ance ≃, Fr.	62	44.58 N	3.40 E
Ancenis	32	47.22 N	1.11 W
Ancerville	58	48.38 N	5.02 E
Anchang	100	30.09 N	120.30 E
Anchau	150	10.59 N	8.23 E
Anchieta ◆[8]	287a	22.49 S	43.24 W
Anchieta, Ilha I	256	23.33 S	45.04 W
Anch'ing → Anqing	100	30.31 N	117.02 E
Ancho, Canal ʊ	254	49.54 S	74.23 W
Ancholme ≃	44	53.41 N	0.32 W
Anchor	216	40.34 N	88.32 W
Anchorage	180	61.13 N	149.54 W
Anchor Bay c	214	42.38 N	82.45 W
Anchor Bay Gardens	214	42.39 N	82.49 W
Anchorena	252	35.41 S	65.27 W
Anchor Point	180	59.46 N	151.52 W
Anchor Point ›	180	59.47 N	151.52 W
Anchorville	214	42.42 N	82.41 W
Anchuras	34	39.29 N	4.50 W
Anci (Langfang)	105	39.31 N	116.41 E
Ancien Ekalla	152	1.27 S	14.00 E
Ancien Goubéré	140	5.51 N	26.46 E
Ancienne-Lorette	206	46.48 N	71.21 W
Anciferovo, Ross.	76	58.58 N	34.01 E
Anciferovo, Ross.	82	55.33 N	38.49 E
Ancipa, Lago di ⊜	70	37.50 N	14.34 E
Anclitas, Cayo I	240p	20.48 N	78.54 W
Anclote ≃	220	39.59 N	88.49 W
Anclote Keys II	220	28.12 N	82.51 W
Ancón, Méx.	234	22.35 N	101.11 W
Ancón, Perú	248	11.47 S	77.11 W
Ancona, It.	66	43.38 N	13.30 E
Ancona, S. Afr.	158	27.40 S	26.32 E
Ancona □[4]	66	43.33 N	13.10 E
Ancón de Sardinas, Bahía de c	246	1.30 N	79.00 W
Ancoraimes	248	15.54 S	68.58 W
Ancram	210	42.03 N	73.38 W
Ancre ≃	50	49.54 N	2.28 E
Ancrum	46	55.31 N	2.35 W
Ancuabe	154	12.58 S	39.54 E
Ancud	254	41.52 S	73.50 W
Ancud, Golfo de c	254	42.05 S	73.00 W
Ancy-le-Franc	50	47.46 N	4.10 E
Ancy-sur-Moselle	56	49.03 N	6.04 E
Anda, Pil.	116	16.17 N	119.57 E
Anda, Zhg.	89	46.24 N	125.19 E
Andacollo, Arg.	252	37.11 S	70.41 W
Andacollo, Chile	252	30.14 S	71.06 W
Andahuaylas	248	13.39 S	73.23 W
Andaingo	157b	18.12 S	48.17 E
Andāl	124	23.36 N	87.12 E
Andalgalá	252	27.36 S	66.19 W
Andalo	64	46.10 N	11.00 E
Åndalsnes	26	62.34 N	7.42 E
Andalucía □[4]	34	37.30 N	4.30 W
Andalucía □[9]	34	37.36 N	4.30 W
Andalusia, Al., U.S.	194	31.19 N	86.29 W
Andalusia, Pa., U.S.	285	40.04 N	74.58 W
Andaman and Nicobar Islands □[8]	110	11.00 N	93.00 E
Andaman Basin ✢[1]	12	10.00 N	94.00 E
Andamanen → Andaman Islands II	110	12.00 N	92.45 E
Andaman Islands II	110	12.00 N	92.45 E
Andaman Sea ⊤[2]	110	10.00 N	95.00 E
Andamarca, Bol.	248	18.49 S	67.31 W
Andamarca, Perú	248	11.46 S	74.44 W
Andamooka	166	30.27 S	137.12 E
Andance	62	45.14 N	4.47 E
Andapa	157b	14.39 S	49.39 E
Andara	152	18.03 S	21.27 E
Andaraí	255	12.48 S	41.20 W
Andaraí ◆[8]	287a	22.56 S	43.15 W
Andarax ≃	34	36.48 N	2.26 W
Andaray	248	15.49 S	72.50 W
Andau	61	47.46 N	17.02 E
Andechs, Kloster ᵾ[1]	64	47.58 N	11.10 E
Andeer	58	46.36 N	9.26 E
Andelfingen	58	47.36 N	8.41 E
Andelle ≃	50	49.19 N	1.14 E
Andelot	58	48.15 N	5.18 E
Andelot-en-Montagne	58	46.51 N	5.56 E
Andelu	261	48.53 N	1.50 E
Anden → Andes ⩘	18	20.00 S	67.00 W
Andenes	24	69.16 N	16.08 E
Andenne	56	50.29 N	5.06 E
Andéranboukane	150	15.26 N	3.02 E
Ånderdalen Nasjonalpark ♦	24	69.14 N	17.17 E
Anderlecht	50	50.50 N	4.18 E
Anderlues	50	50.24 N	4.16 E
Andermatt	58	46.38 N	8.36 E
Andernach	56	50.26 N	7.24 E
Andersen Air Force Base ■	174p	13.35 N	144.56 E
Anderslöv	41	55.26 N	13.22 E
Anderson, Al., U.S.	194	34.55 N	87.15 W
Anderson, Ak., U.S.	180	64.21 N	149.10 W
Anderson, Ca., U.S.	204	40.26 N	122.17 W
Anderson, In., U.S.	218	40.06 N	85.40 W
Anderson, Mo., U.S.	194	36.39 N	94.26 W
Anderson, S.C., U.S.	192	34.30 N	82.39 W
Anderson, Tx., U.S.	222	30.29 N	95.59 W
Anderson □[6], Ky., U.S.	218	38.05 N	84.55 W
Anderson □[6], Tx., U.S.	222	31.47 N	95.40 W
Anderson ≃	180	69.43 N	128.58 W
Anderson, Mount ∧	224	47.43 N	123.20 W
Anderson Creek ≃	194	33.18 N	94.26 W
Anderson Dam	202	43.30 N	115.30 W
Anderson Inlet c	169	38.39 S	145.48 E
Anderson Island I	224	47.10 N	122.42 W
Anderson Lake ⊜	182	50.41 N	122.07 W
Anderson Lake ⊜[1]	226	37.11 N	121.37 W
Anderson Peak ∧	228	34.08 N	116.53 W
Anderson Ranch Reservoir ⊜[1]	202	43.25 N	115.20 W
Andersonville	218	39.30 N	85.17 W
Andersonville National Historic Site ⊥	192	32.12 N	84.07 W
Anderstorp	26	57.17 N	13.38 E
Anderten	52	52.21 N	9.51 E
Anderton	262	53.17 N	2.32 W
Andes, Col.	246	5.40 N	75.53 W
Andes, N.Y., U.S.	210	42.12 N	74.47 W
Andes ⩘	18	20.00 S	67.00 W
Andes, Lake ⊜	198	43.11 N	98.27 W
Andeville	50	49.15 N	2.10 E
Andevoranto	157b	18.57 S	49.06 E
Andfjorden ʊ	24	69.10 N	16.20 E
Andheri ◆[8]	272c	19.07 N	72.51 E
Andhra Lake ⊜	122	18.54 N	73.32 E
Andhra Pradesh □[3]	122	16.00 N	79.00 E
Andijk	52	52.45 N	5.12 E
Andijskoje Kojsu ≃	84	42.47 N	46.48 E
Andikíthira I	38	35.52 N	23.18 E
Andilamena	157b	17.01 S	48.35 E
Andimákhia	38	36.48 N	27.07 E
Andīmeshk	128	32.27 N	48.21 E
Andingpu	102	37.58 N	107.02 E
Anding Zhan	105	39.38 N	116.29 E
Andíparos I	38	37.00 N	25.03 E
Andirá ≃	250	2.45 S	56.49 W
Andirá, Riozinho do ≃	248	9.21 S	67.31 W
Andırın	130	37.34 N	36.20 E
Andirlang	120	37.36 N	83.50 E
Andisleben	54	51.04 N	10.56 E
Ándissa	38	39.14 N	25.59 E
Andižan	85	40.45 N	72.22 E

PORTUGUÊS

Nome	Página	Lat.°′	Long.°′ W = Oeste
Andižan □[4]	85	40.45 N	72.15 E
Andkhvoy	120	36.56 N	65.08 E
Andlau-au-Val	58	48.23 N	7.25 E
Ando	270	34.37 N	135.46 E
Andoam	164	12.40 S	141.55 E
Andoas	246	2.50 S	76.30 W
Andoga ≃	76	59.10 N	37.27 E
Andogskaja gr'ada ∧	76	59.25 N	37.30 E
Andolsheim	58	48.04 N	7.25 E
Andomskij Pogost	24	61.14 N	36.36 E
Andong, Taehan	98	36.35 N	128.44 E
Andong, Zhg.	100	30.16 N	121.13 E
Andong-chŏsuji ⊜[1]	98	36.41 N	128.49 E
Andong-ni	98	39.28 N	127.27 E
Andora	62	43.59 N	8.08 E
Andorf	60	48.23 N	13.35 E
Andorno Micca	62	45.37 N	8.03 E
Andorra	34	42.30 N	1.31 E
Andorra □[1], Europe	22	42.30 N	1.30 E
Andorra □[1], Europe	34	42.30 N	1.30 E
Andorre → Andorra □[1]	34	42.30 N	1.30 E
Andover, Eng., U.K.	42	51.13 N	1.28 W
Andover, Ct., U.S.	207	41.44 N	72.22 W
Andover, Me., U.S.	188	44.38 N	70.45 W
Andover, Ma., U.S.	207	42.39 N	71.08 W
Andover, N.J., U.S.	210	40.59 N	74.44 W
Andover, N.Y., U.S.	210	42.09 N	77.47 W
Andover, Oh., U.S.	214	41.36 N	80.34 W
Andover, S.D., U.S.	198	45.24 N	97.54 W
Andowj	123	37.02 N	71.27 E
Andøya I	24	69.08 N	15.54 E
Andradas	256	22.04 S	46.34 W
Andrade Pinto	256	22.14 S	43.22 W
Andradina	255	20.54 S	51.23 W
Andramasina	157b	19.11 S	47.35 E
Andranopasy	157b	21.17 S	43.44 E
Andranovory	157b	23.08 S	44.10 E
Andrate	62	45.32 N	7.53 E
Andreafsky ≃	180	62.02 N	163.16 W
Andreafsky, East Fork ≃	180	62.03 N	163.07 W
Andreanof Islands II	180	52.00 N	176.00 W
Andreapol'	76	56.39 N	32.15 E
Andreas, I. of Man	44	54.22 N	4.26 W
Andreas, Pa., U.S.	208	40.45 N	75.48 W
André Félix, Parc National ♦	146	9.25 N	23.20 E
Andrejevka, Kaz.	86	52.59 N	67.23 E
Andrejevka, Kaz.	86	45.50 N	80.35 E
Andrejevka, Ross.	80	55.42 N	54.23 E
Andrejevka, Ross.	80	52.19 N	51.55 E
Andrejevka, Ross.	82	55.07 N	38.37 E
Andrejevka, Ross.	82	55.59 N	37.08 E
Andrejevo	80	55.56 N	41.08 E
Andrejevsk	88	58.06 N	114.08 E
Andrejevskaja	80	47.21 N	43.02 E
Andrejevskoje, Ross.	82	54.23 N	36.12 E
Andrejevskoje, Ross.	82	56.24 N	39.01 E
Andrejevskoje, Ross.	82	55.46 N	36.35 E
Andrejkoviči	76	52.25 N	33.00 E
Andrelândia	256	21.44 S	44.18 W
Andrésy	261	48.59 N	2.04 E
Andretta	68	40.56 N	15.19 E
Andrew	182	53.53 N	112.21 W
Andrew, Mount ∧	162	32.52 S	122.56 E
Andrews, In., U.S.	216	40.51 N	85.36 W
Andrews, Mi., U.S.	216	41.57 N	86.22 W
Andrews, N.C., U.S.	192	35.12 N	83.49 W
Andrews, S.C., U.S.	192	33.18 N	79.17 W
Andrews, Tx., U.S.	196	32.19 N	102.32 W
Andrews Air Force Base ■	208	38.48 N	76.52 W
Andrews Manor	284c	38.49 N	76.54 W
Andrezel	261	48.37 N	2.49 E
Andrézieux Bouthéon	62	45.32 N	4.16 E
Andria	68	41.13 N	16.18 E
Andriamena	157b	17.26 S	47.30 E
Andriandampy	157b	22.45 S	45.41 E
Andriba	157b	17.36 S	46.55 E
Andrija, Otok I	36	43.02 N	15.45 E
Andrijevica	38	42.44 N	19.46 E
Andriyevo-Ivanivka	78	47.28 N	30.28 E
Andriyivka, Ukr.	78	47.06 N	36.35 E
Andriyivka, Ukr.	78	49.32 N	36.38 E
Andriyivka, Ukr.	83	47.28 N	37.39 E
Andriyivka, Ukr.	83	48.49 N	37.33 E
Androka	157b	25.02 S	44.05 E
Andronovskoje	76	60.39 N	34.46 E
Andropov → Rybinsk	76	58.03 N	38.52 E
Ándros	38	37.50 N	24.57 E
Andros I, Ba.	238	24.26 N	77.57 W
Ándros I, Ellás	38	37.45 N	24.42 E
Androscoggin ≃	188	43.55 N	69.55 W
Androsovka	80	52.41 N	49.35 E
Andros Town	238	24.43 N	77.47 W
Āndrott Island I	122	10.50 N	73.41 E
Andrupene	76	56.11 N	27.23 E
Andrushivka	78	50.01 N	29.01 E
Andr'ušino	86	59.12 N	62.59 E
Andrychów	30	49.52 N	19.21 E
Andudu	154	2.29 N	28.41 E
Andújar	34	38.03 N	4.04 W
Andulo	152	11.30 S	16.45 E
Anduze	62	44.03 N	3.59 E
Andžijevskij	84	44.14 N	43.05 E
Âne, Dos d' ∧	241o	16.19 N	61.46 W
Aneby	26	57.50 N	14.48 E
Anécho	150	6.14 N	1.36 E
Anecón Grande, Cerro ∧	254	41.25 S	70.16 W
Anefis i-n-Darane	150	18.03 N	0.36 E
Anegada I	238	18.45 N	64.20 W
Anegada, Bahía c	254	40.15 S	62.15 W
Anegada Passage ʊ	238	18.30 N	63.40 W
Anegam	200	32.22 N	112.01 W
Anegasaki	268	35.28 N	140.02 E
Anelngauhat	175f	20.14 S	169.44 E
Añelo	252	38.21 S	68.47 W
Anémata, Passe d' ʊ	175f	20.31 S	166.12 E
Anenii Noi	38	46.52 N	29.14 E
Anepahan Peak ∧	116	9.40 N	118.25 E
Aneroid	184	49.43 N	107.20 W
Anet	50	48.51 N	1.26 E
Aneta	198	47.40 N	97.59 W
Aneto, Pico de ∧	34	42.38 N	0.40 E
Aney	146	19.24 N	12.56 E
Anfeng, Zhg.	100	33.06 N	120.08 E
Anfeng, Zhg.	100	32.44 N	120.24 E
Anfengqiao	100	26.41 N	118.08 E
Anfo	64	45.46 N	10.29 E
Anfu	100	27.23 N	114.37 E
Anfuzhen, Zhg.	107	28.47 N	104.41 E
Anfuzhen, Zhg.	107	29.21 N	105.28 E
Anga	88	53.58 N	106.12 E
Angamacutiro [de la Unión]	234	20.10 N	101.41 W
Angamos, Punta ›	252	23.01 S	70.32 W
Angangueo	234	19.37 N	100.18 W
Ang'angxi	89	47.09 N	123.48 E
An'ganka	89	52.18 N	126.17 E
Angao	100	33.08 N	112.22 E
Angar	164	3.39 S	130.50 E
Angara ≃	88	58.06 N	93.00 E
Angara-Débou	150	11.19 N	3.03 E
Angarbaka	140	9.44 N	24.44 E
Āngāria	126	22.29 N	90.22 E
Angarsk	88	52.34 N	103.54 E
Angas ≃	168b	35.23 S	138.59 E
Angas Downs	162	24.49 S	132.14 E
Angas Hills ⩘[2]	162	22.55 S	128.00 E
Angastaco	252	25.38 S	66.11 W
Angaston	168b	34.30 S	139.02 E
Angat ≃	116	14.53 N	120.46 E
Angatuba	255	23.29 S	48.25 W
Angaul	88	53.49 N	100.18 E
Angaur I	175b	6.54 N	134.09 E
Angden Pass)(	124	29.43 N	86.17 E
Angduo	102	32.20 N	98.55 E
Ånge	26	62.31 N	15.37 E
Ángel, Salto (Angel Falls) ∟	246	5.57 N	62.30 W

Angel City	220	28.20 N	80.40 W
Ángel de la Guarda, Isla I	232	29.20 N	113.25 W
Angeles	116	15.09 N	120.35 E
Angeles National Forest ♦	280	34.15 N	117.56 W
Angel Etcheverry	258	35.02 S	58.04 W
Angel Falls → Ángel, Salto ∟	246	5.57 N	62.30 W
Ängelholm	41	56.15 N	12.51 E
Ängelholm flygplats ⊠	41	56.20 N	12.51 E
Angelica	210	42.18 N	78.00 W
Angelina □[6]	222	31.17 N	94.42 W
Angelina ≃	194	30.53 N	94.12 W
Angelina, East Fork ≃	222	31.50 N	94.56 W
Angel Island I	282	37.52 N	122.26 W
Angellala Creek ≃	166	26.40 S	146.08 E
Angeln ◆[1]	41	54.39 N	9.44 E
Angelo ≃	162	23.43 S	117.45 E
Angel R. Cabada	234	18.35 N	95.26 W
Ängelsberg	40	59.58 N	16.00 E
Angels Camp	226	38.04 N	120.33 W
Angels Creek ≃	226	38.01 N	120.33 W
Angelus, Lake ⊜	281	42.41 N	83.20 W
Angemuk ∧	164	3.30 S	138.34 E
Anger	61	47.16 N	15.42 E
Angera	62	45.46 N	8.35 E
Angerbach ≃	263	51.23 N	6.44 E
Angereb ≃	144	13.51 N	36.08 E
Angeren	52	51.55 N	5.58 E
Angerhausen ◆[8]	263	51.23 N	6.44 E
Ångermanälven ≃	26	62.48 N	17.56 E
Ångermanland □[9]	26	63.30 N	18.05 E
Angermund ◆[8]	263	51.20 N	6.47 E
Angermünde	54	53.01 N	14.00 E
Angern, Dtsch.	54	52.21 N	11.44 E
Angern, Öst.	61	48.22 N	16.50 E
Angers	32	47.28 N	0.33 W
Angerville	50	48.19 N	2.00 E
Angervilliers	261	48.36 N	2.04 E
Ängesön I	26	63.43 N	20.55 E
Angevillers	56	49.23 N	6.02 E
Anggowala, Bukit ∧	112	4.15 S	121.44 E
Anghelu Ruiu, Necropoli ⊥	71	40.38 N	8.20 E
Anghiari	66	43.32 N	12.03 E
Angical	255	12.00 S	44.42 W
Angical do Piauí	250	6.05 S	42.44 W
Angicos	250	5.40 S	36.36 W
Angier	192	35.30 N	78.44 W
Angijak Island I	176	65.40 N	62.15 W
Angikuni Lake ⊜	176	62.13 N	99.50 W
Angke, Kali ≃	269e	6.06 S	106.46 E
Angkor Wat ⊥	110	13.26 N	103.52 E
Ângk Tasaôm	110	11.01 N	104.41 E
Anglais, Baie des c	186	49.15 N	68.07 W
Anglais, Jardin ♦	261	48.38 N	1.49 E
Anglais, Rivière des (English) ≃	206	45.13 N	73.50 W
Angle	42	51.41 N	5.06 W
Angle Inlet	198	49.21 N	95.04 W
Anglem, Mount ∧	172	46.44 S	167.56 E
Anglesea	169	38.25 S	144.11 E
Anglesey I	44	53.17 N	4.22 W
Anglet	32	43.29 N	1.31 W
Angleterre → England □[8]	28	52.30 N	1.30 W
Angleton	222	29.10 N	95.25 W
Anglezarke Moor ◆[3]	262	53.40 N	2.33 W
Anglezarke Reservoir ⊜[1]	262	53.39 N	2.35 W
Angling ≃	184	56.45 N	93.36 W
Angling Lake ⊜	184	53.55 N	93.52 W
Anglona ◆[1]	71	40.50 N	8.45 E
Anglo-Normandes, Îles → Channel Islands II	28	49.20 N	2.20 W
Anglure	50	48.35 N	3.49 E
Angmagssalik	176	65.36 N	37.41 W
Angmering	42	50.48 N	0.28 W
Ang Mo Kio	271c	1.22 N	103.51 E
Ango	154	4.02 N	25.52 E
Angoche	154	16.15 S	39.54 E
Angoche, Ilha I	154	16.20 S	39.50 E
Angohrān	128	26.35 N	57.54 E
Angol	252	37.48 S	72.43 W
Angola, In., U.S.	216	41.38 N	84.59 W
Angola, N.Y., U.S.	210	42.38 N	79.01 W
Angola □[1], Afr.	138	12.30 S	18.30 E
Angola □[1], Afr.	152	12.30 S	18.30 E
Angola Basin ✢[1]	10	15.00 S	3.00 E
Angola Lake Shore	214	42.37 N	79.05 W
Angono	269f	14.31 N	121.09 E
Angoon	180	57.30 N	134.35 W
Angora → Ankara	130	39.56 N	32.52 E
Angoram	164	4.04 S	144.04 E
Angostura, Méx.	232	25.22 N	108.11 W
Angostura → Ciudad Bolívar, Ven.	246	8.08 N	63.33 W
Angostura, Presa de la ⊜[1]	234	16.10 N	92.40 W
Angostura Reservoir ⊜[1]	198	43.18 N	103.27 W
Angoulême	32	45.39 N	0.09 E
Angoumois □[9]	32	45.30 N	0.05 W
Angra, Meos I	164	2.42 S	134.50 E
Angra do Heroísmo	148a	38.39 N	27.13 W
Angra do Heroísmo □[5]	148a	38.50 N	27.30 W
Angra dos Reis	256	23.00 S	44.18 W
Angren	85	41.01 N	70.12 E
Angren ≃	85	40.48 N	68.53 E
Angri	68	40.44 N	14.34 E
Angrignon Zoological Park ♦	275a	45.26 N	73.36 W
Angrogna	62	44.50 N	7.13 E
Ängsö	40	59.32 N	16.51 E
Ängsö Nationalpark ♦	40	59.39 N	18.44 E
Ang Thong	110	14.35 N	100.27 E
Angu	154	3.33 N	24.28 E
Angu ≃	256	21.48 S	42.30 W
Angualasto	252	30.03 S	69.09 W
Anguang	89	45.31 N	123.45 E
Anguchang	107	29.30 N	103.39 E
Anguciana, Cerro ∧	236	8.50 N	83.07 W
Anguilas, Arroyo ≃	288	34.26 S	58.31 W
Anguilla	194	32.58 N	90.49 W
Anguilla □[2], N.A.	230	18.15 N	63.05 W
Anguilla □[2], N.A.	238	18.15 N	63.05 W
Anguilla Cays II	238	23.31 N	79.33 W
Anguillara Sabazia	66	42.05 N	12.16 E
Anguillara Veneta	64	45.08 N	11.53 E
Anguille, Cape ›	186	47.55 N	59.25 W
Anguli Nur ⊜	98	41.13 N	114.32 E
Angumu	154	0.07 S	27.42 E
Anguo	98	38.25 N	115.19 E
Anguozhuang	105	39.44 N	117.59 E
Anguruga	164	14.00 S	136.29 E
Angus	212	44.19 N	79.53 W
Angus Place	170	33.20 S	150.06 E
Angustura	256	21.45 S	42.41 W
Angusville	184	50.44 N	101.01 W
Angwa ≃	154	15.51 S	30.35 E
Angwin	226	38.34 N	122.26 W
Angyalföld ◆[8]	264c	47.33 N	19.05 E
Angyō	268	35.51 N	139.46 E
An Hai, Viet	110	15.13 N	108.56 E
Anhai, Zhg.	100	24.45 N	118.27 E
Anhalt □[9]	54	52.00 N	11.30 E
Anholt	52	51.52 N	6.27 E
Anholt I	26	56.42 N	11.34 E
Anhovo	64	46.03 N	13.37 E
Anhua	102	28.18 N	111.14 E
Anhuai	100	33.04 N	117.50 E
Anhui (Anhwei) □[4]	100	32.00 N	117.00 E
Anhŭng	98	36.41 N	126.10 E
Anhwei → Anhui □[4]	100	32.00 N	117.00 E
Aniak	180	61.35 N	159.33 W

Aniak ≃	180	61.34 N	159.30 W
Aniakchak National Monument ♦	180	56.50 N	157.50 W
Anibare Bay c	174b	0.32 S	166.57 E
Aniche	50	50.20 N	3.15 E
Anicuns	255	16.28 S	49.58 W
Anié	150	7.45 N	1.12 E
Anié ≃	150	7.40 N	1.18 E
Anie, Pic d' ∧	32	42.57 N	0.43 W
Aniene ≃	66	41.56 N	12.30 E
Anif	64	47.45 N	13.04 E
Anik ◆[8]	272c	19.02 N	72.53 E
Anikino, Ross.	86	56.32 N	73.56 E
Anikino, Ross.	88	53.26 N	120.20 E
Anikovo	76	59.23 N	43.45 E
Anil	250	2.32 S	44.14 W
Anil, Rio do ≃	287a	22.59 S	43.21 W
Animas	200	31.56 N	108.48 W
Animas ≃	200	36.43 N	108.13 W
Animas Peak ∧	200	31.35 N	108.47 W
Animas Valley V	200	31.45 N	108.50 W
Anin	110	15.40 N	97.46 E
Anina	38	45.05 N	21.51 E
Anipemza	84	40.27 N	43.37 E
Aniskino	82	55.54 N	38.06 E
Añisoc	152	1.51 N	10.46 E
Anita, Ia., U.S.	198	41.26 N	94.45 W
Anita, Pa., U.S.	214	41.00 N	78.58 W
Anıtkaya	130	38.57 N	30.18 E
Aniva	89	46.43 N	142.32 E
Aniva, mys ›	89	46.01 N	143.25 E
Aniva, zaliv c	89	46.16 N	142.48 E
Anivorano	157b	18.44 S	48.58 E
Anivorano Nord	157b	12.44 S	49.13 E
Aniwa I	175f	19.17 S	169.35 E
Anizy-le-Château	50	49.30 N	3.27 E
Anjad	120	22.02 N	75.03 E
Anjan	26	63.41 N	12.49 E
Anjangaon	120	21.10 N	77.18 E
Anjār, India	120	23.08 N	70.01 E
ʻAnjar, Lubnān	132	33.42 N	35.54 E
ʻAnjarah	132	32.18 N	35.45 E
Anjavimihavana	157b	12.32 S	49.16 E
Anji	106	30.43 N	119.41 E
Anjiabe	157b	12.07 S	49.20 E
Anjiang	105	40.45 N	117.38 E
Anjigami Lake ⊜	190	47.51 N	84.34 W
Anjō	94	34.57 N	137.05 E
Anjou	206	45.36 N	73.33 W
Anjou □[9]	32	47.20 N	0.30 W
Anjozorobe	157b	18.24 S	47.52 E
Anju, C.M.I.K.	98	39.36 N	125.40 E
Anju, Zhg.	100	31.45 N	113.11 E
Anju, Zhg.	107	30.21 N	105.27 E
Anjudin	24	62.33 N	58.12 E
Anjuzhen	107	29.59 N	106.02 E
Anka	150	12.07 N	5.55 E
Ankang	102	32.42 N	109.05 E
Ankara	130	39.56 N	32.52 E
Ankara □[4]	130	39.50 N	32.50 E
Ankara ≃	130	39.51 N	31.55 E
Ankaramena	157b	21.57 S	46.39 E
Ankaratra ⩘	157b	19.25 S	47.12 E
Ankarimbelo	157b	22.08 S	47.20 E
Ankaroaka ∧	157b	17.48 S	48.32 E
Ankarsrum	26	57.42 N	16.19 E
Ankasakasa	157b	16.21 S	44.52 E
Ankata	80	50.44 N	51.34 E
Ankavandra	157b	18.46 S	45.18 E
Ankazoabo	157b	22.18 S	44.31 E
Ankazobe	157b	18.21 S	47.07 E
Ankazomiriotra	157b	19.38 S	46.32 E
Ankeny	190	41.43 N	93.36 W
An Khe	110	13.57 N	108.39 E
Ankilimalinika	157b	22.58 S	43.45 E
Ankilizato	157b	20.25 S	45.01 E
Anking → Anqing	100	30.31 N	117.02 E
Ankisabe	157b	19.17 S	46.29 E
Anklam	54	53.51 N	13.41 E
Ankleshwar	120	21.36 N	73.00 E
Ankober	144	9.35 N	39.44 E
Ankoro	154	6.45 S	26.57 E
Ankororoka	157b	25.30 S	45.11 E
Ankou	100	25.03 N	113.24 E
An'kovo	80	56.57 N	39.57 E
Ankpa	150	7.23 N	7.37 E
Ankum	52	52.32 N	7.52 E
Ankwe ≃	150	8.03 N	9.26 E
Anlinnuoer	98	41.11 N	114.31 E
Anliu	100	23.42 N	115.42 E
Anloga	150	5.47 N	0.50 E
Anlong	102	25.02 N	105.31 E
Ânlóng Vêng	110	14.14 N	104.05 E
Anlu	100	31.17 N	113.40 E
Anma-do I	98	35.21 N	126.02 E
Anmyŏn-do I	98	36.30 N	126.22 E
Ånn ⊜	26	63.16 N	12.34 E
Ann, Cape ›, Ant.	9	66.10 S	51.22 E
Ann, Cape ›, Ma., U.S.	283	42.39 N	70.38 W
Anna, Ross.	78	51.29 N	40.25 E
Anna, Il., U.S.	194	37.27 N	89.14 W
Anna, Oh., U.S.	216	40.23 N	84.10 W
Anna, Tx., U.S.	196	33.21 N	96.33 W
Anna, Lake ⊜[1]	188	38.04 N	77.45 W
Annaba (Bône)	148	36.54 N	7.46 E
Annaba □[5]	148	36.50 N	8.00 E
An-Nabaṭīyah □[4]	132	33.20 N	35.30 E
An-Nabaṭīyah at-Taḥtā	132	33.23 N	35.29 E
Annaberg, Öst.	61	47.52 N	15.22 E
Annaberg, Öst.	64	47.31 N	13.26 E
Annaberg-Buchholz	54	50.35 N	13.00 E
An-Nabī Shīt	132	33.52 N	36.07 E
An-Nabk	130	34.01 N	36.44 E
An-Nabqīyah I	128	26.44 N	36.01 E
Annaburg	54	51.44 N	13.03 E
Annaburger Heide ◆[3]	54	51.40 N	13.05 E
An-Nafūd ◆[2]	128	28.30 N	41.00 E
Annagassan	48	53.53 N	6.20 W
Annahütte	54	51.34 N	13.53 E
An-Najaf	128	31.59 N	44.20 E
An-Najaf □[4]	128	31.00 N	44.00 E
Annaka	94	36.19 N	138.54 E
An-Nakhl, Miṣr	140	29.55 N	33.45 E
An-Nakhl, Sūrīy.	132	33.00 N	36.07 E
Annalee ≃	48	54.03 N	7.24 W
Annalee Heights	208	38.51 N	77.10 W
Annalong	48	54.06 N	5.53 W
Annam → Trung Phan □[9]	110	15.00 N	108.00 E
Anna Maria	220	27.31 N	82.44 W
Anna Maria Island I	220	27.30 N	82.43 W
An-Nāmir	132	32.47 N	36.13 E
Annamitique, Chaîne ⩘	110	17.00 N	106.00 E
Annan	44	54.59 N	3.16 W
Annan ≃	44	54.59 N	3.16 W
Annanberg	164	4.55 S	144.40 E
Annandale, Austl.	166	21.57 S	148.22 E
Annandale, Mn., U.S.	190	45.15 N	94.07 W
Annandale, N.J., U.S.	210	40.38 N	74.52 W
Annandale, Va., U.S.	208	38.49 N	77.11 W
Annandale V	44	55.10 N	3.25 W
Annandale-on-Hudson	210	42.01 N	73.54 W
Anna Pink, Bahía c	254	45.50 S	74.50 W
Anna Plains	162	19.17 S	121.37 E
Anna Point ›	174b	0.30 S	166.56 E
Annapolis	208	38.58 N	76.29 W
Annapolis Basin c	186	44.39 N	65.42 W
Annapolis Royal	186	44.45 N	65.31 W
Annapūrṇa ∧	124	28.34 N	83.50 E
Annapūrṇapratham ∧	124	28.31 N	84.08 E
An-Naqīrah ⊤[4]	128	27.53 N	48.15 E
Ann Arbor	216	42.16 N	83.43 W
Ann Arbor Municipal Airport ⊠	281	42.14 N	83.45 W
Anna Regina	246	7.16 N	58.30 W
Annaricken Brook ≃	285	40.03 N	74.42 W
An-Nāṣirīyah, ʻIrāq	128	31.02 N	46.16 E

An-Nāṣirīyah, Sūrīy.	130	33.52 N	36.49 E
Annaspan ⊜	158	28.33 S	25.47 E
An-Nawfalāb	140	15.52 N	32.32 E
An-Nawfalīyah	146	30.47 N	17.50 E
An-Nazlah	132	31.32 N	34.29 E
An-Nazlat	142	29.19 N	30.39 E
Annbank	44	55.28 N	4.30 W
Annean, Lake ⊜	162	26.54 S	118.14 E
Anne Arundel □[6]	208	38.59 N	76.30 W
Annebault	50	49.15 N	0.04 E
Annecy	58	45.54 N	6.07 E
Annecy, Lac d' ⊜	58	45.51 N	6.11 E
Annecy-le-Vieux	58	45.55 N	6.09 E
Annemasse	58	46.12 N	6.15 E
Annen	263	51.27 N	7.22 E
Annenkov Island I	244	54.29 S	37.05 W
Annenskij Most	76	60.45 N	37.10 E
Annenskoje	86	53.08 N	60.26 E
Anner ≃	48	52.22 N	7.39 W
Annestown	48	52.08 N	7.17 W
Annet I	42a	49.54 N	6.21 W
Annet-sur-Marne	261	48.56 N	2.43 E
Annette	182	55.03 N	131.34 W
Annette Island I	182	55.10 N	131.28 W
Annevoie-Rouillon	56	50.21 N	4.50 E
Annezin	50	50.32 N	2.37 E
Annfield Plain	44	54.51 N	1.45 W
An Nhon	110	13.53 N	109.06 E
Anniangniang	89	51.33 N	125.49 E
Annicco	62	45.14 N	9.52 E
An-Nīl □[4]	140	19.00 N	33.00 E
An-Nīl al-Azraq □[4]	140	12.00 N	34.00 E
Anning	102	24.59 N	102.18 E
Anningdu	102	36.56 N	104.31 E
Anninger ∧	264b	48.03 N	16.15 E
Annino	265a	59.46 N	30.03 E
Anninskije Mineral'nyje Vody	89	52.44 N	140.12 E
Annisquam	283	42.39 N	70.41 W
Annisquam ≃	283	42.39 N	70.41 W
Anniston	194	33.39 N	85.49 W
Annobón I	138	1.25 S	5.36 E
Annonay	62	45.14 N	4.40 E
Annopol	30	50.54 N	21.52 E
Anno-Rebrikovo	83	49.36 N	40.12 E
Annot	62	43.58 N	6.40 E
Annotto Bay	241q	18.16 N	76.46 W
Annsjön ⊜	40	58.48 N	15.26 E
An-Nubayrah	142	30.54 N	30.35 E
An-Nuhūd	140	12.42 N	28.26 E
An-Nuʻmān I	128	27.08 N	35.46 E
An-Nuʻmānīyah	128	32.32 N	45.25 E
An-Nuwayrah	142	29.06 N	30.59 E
Annville, Ky., U.S.	192	37.19 N	83.58 W
Annville, Pa., U.S.	208	40.19 N	76.30 W
Annweiler am Trifels	56	49.12 N	7.58 E
Anō	94	34.46 N	136.27 E
Anoia	68	38.27 N	16.05 E
Anoia ≃	34	41.28 N	1.56 E
Anoka	190	45.11 N	93.23 W
Áno Liósia	267c	38.05 N	23.42 E
Año Nuevo Bay c	226	37.07 N	122.19 W
Anopino	80	55.42 N	40.40 E
Anori, Bra.	246	3.47 S	61.38 W
Anorí, Col.	246	7.05 N	75.08 W
Anorotsangana	157b	13.56 S	47.55 E
Anosibe	157b	19.26 S	48.13 E
Anosyennes, Chaînes ⩘	157b	24.30 S	46.50 E
Anotaié ≃	250	3.29 N	52.04 W
Anpilogovo	78	51.47 N	36.01 E
Anping, Zhg.	98	38.16 N	115.30 E
Anping, Zhg.	98	34.01 N	115.07 E
Anping, Zhg.	100	26.33 N	113.22 E
Anping, Zhg.	104	41.11 N	123.26 E
Anping, Zhg.	105	39.43 N	116.53 E
Anpu	102	21.27 N	110.00 E
ʻAnqābīyah, Jabal al- ∧[2]	142	30.01 N	31.37 E
Anqing	100	30.31 N	117.02 E
Anqiu	98	36.25 N	119.10 E
Anrath	56	51.17 N	6.28 E
Anren, Zhg.	100	28.04 N	119.20 E
Anren, Zhg.	100	26.42 N	113.16 E
Anrenzhen	107	30.31 N	103.38 E
Anröchte	52	51.33 N	8.19 E
Ans, Bel.	56	50.39 N	5.32 E
Ans, Dan.	41	56.19 N	9.36 E
Ansager	41	55.42 N	8.45 E
Ansai	102	36.54 N	109.10 E
ʻAnṣār	132	33.23 N	35.21 E
Ansbach	56	49.17 N	10.34 E
Anschan → Anshan	104	41.08 N	122.59 E
Anschlag	263	51.10 N	7.29 E
Anse	58	45.56 N	4.43 E
Anseba ≃	144	17.03 N	37.24 E
Anse-Bertrand	241o	16.29 N	61.31 W
Anse-d'Hainault	238	18.30 N	74.27 W
Anse La Raye	241f	13.57 N	61.03 W
Anselmo	198	41.37 N	99.51 W
Anseremme	56	50.15 N	4.54 E
Anserma	246	5.13 N	75.48 W
Ansfelden	61	48.13 N	14.17 E
Anshan	104	41.08 N	122.59 E
Anshun	102	26.15 N	105.56 E
Ansina	252	31.54 S	55.28 W
Ansley	198	41.17 N	99.22 W
Anson	196	32.45 N	99.53 W
Anson Bay c, Austl.	164	13.20 S	130.06 E
Anson Bay c, Norf. I.	174c	29.01 S	167.55 E
Anson Creek ≃	212	44.53 N	79.03 W
Ansŏng	98	37.02 N	127.16 E
Ansongo	150	15.40 N	0.30 E
Ansonia, Ct., U.S.	207	41.20 N	73.04 W
Ansonia, Oh., U.S.	216	40.12 N	84.38 W
Ansonville, N.C., U.S.	192	35.06 N	80.06 W
Ansonville, Pa., U.S.	214	40.51 N	78.34 W
Ansouis	62	43.44 N	5.28 E
Ansted	188	38.08 N	81.05 W
Anstey	42	52.40 N	1.11 W
Anstruther	46	56.13 N	2.42 W
Anstruther Lake ⊜	212	44.45 N	78.12 W
Ansudu	164	2.08 S	139.20 E
Ansus	164	1.44 S	135.49 E
Anta, Bra.	256	22.03 S	42.59 W
Anta, Perú	248	13.29 S	72.09 W
Antabamba	248	14.19 S	72.55 W
Antalaha	157b	14.53 S	50.16 E
Antalieptė	76	55.40 N	25.51 E
Antalivtsi	78	48.38 N	22.31 E
Antalya	130	36.53 N	30.42 E
Antalya □[4]	130	37.00 N	31.00 E
Antalya, Gulf of → Antalya Körfezi c	130	36.30 N	31.00 E
Antalya Körfezi c	130	36.30 N	31.00 E
Antambohobe	157b	22.20 S	46.47 E
An Tan	110	15.26 N	108.39 E
Antanambao Manampotsy	157b	19.29 S	48.34 E
Antanambe	157b	16.26 S	49.52 E
Antananarivo	157b	18.55 S	47.31 E
Antananarivo □[4]	157b	19.00 S	47.00 E
Antanetibe	157b	18.27 S	46.42 E
Antanifotsy	157b	19.39 S	47.19 E
Antanimieva	157b	22.12 S	43.44 E
Antanimora	157b	24.49 S	45.40 E
Antar, Djebel ∧	148	31.57 N	1.56 W
Antarctica ±[1]	9	87.00 S	60.00 E
Antarctic Peninsula ›[1]	9	69.30 S	65.00 W
Antarctique, Péninsule → Antarctic Peninsula ›[1]	9	69.30 S	65.00 W
Antarctiques territoires britanniques → British Antarctic Territory □[2]	9	60.00 S	45.00 W
Antarktis → Antarctica ±[1]	9	87.00 S	60.00 E

	English	Deutsch	Español	Français	Português
≃	River	Fluß	Río	Rivière	Rio
≍	Canal	Kanal	Canal	Canal	Canal
∟	Waterfall, Rapids	Wasserfall, Stromschnellen	Cascada, Rápidos	Chute d'eau, Rapides	Cascata, Rápidos
ʊ	Strait	Meeresstraße	Estrecho	Détroit	Estreito
c	Bay, Gulf	Bucht, Golf	Bahía, Golfo	Baie, Golfe	Baía, Golfo
⊜	Lake, Lakes	See, Seen	Lago, Lagos	Lac, Lacs	Lago, Lagos
≚	Swamp	Sumpf	Pantano	Marais	Pântano
⊼	Ice Features, Glacier	Eis- und Gletscherformen	Accidentes Glaciales	Formes glaciaires	Acidentes glaciares
⊤	Other Hydrographic Features	Andere Hydrographische Objekte	Otros Elementos Hidrográficos	Autres données hydrographiques	Outros acidentes hidrográficos

	English	Deutsch	Español	Français	Português
✢	Submarine Features	Untermeerische Objekte	Accidentes Submarinos	Formes de relief sous-marin	Acidentes submarinos
□	Political Unit	Politische Einheit	Unidad Politica	Entité politique	Unidade política
ᵾ	Cultural Institution	Kulturelle Institution	Institución Cultural	Institution culturelle	Instituição cultural
⊥	Historical Site	Historische Stätte	Sitio Histórico	Site historique	Sitio histórico
♦	Recreational Site	Erholungs- und Ferienort	Sitio de Recreo	Centre de loisirs	Area de Lazer
⊠	Airport	Flughafen	Aeropuerto	Aéroport	Aeroporto
■	Military Installation	Militäranlage	Instalación Militar	Installation militaire	Instalação militar
◆	Miscellaneous	Verschiedenes	Misceláneo	Divers	Diversos

Name	Page	Lat.°′	Long.°′
Antártica, Península → Antarctic Peninsula ≻[1]	9	69.30 S	65.00 W
Antas	250	10.23 S	38.20 W
Antas, Ribeirão das ≃	256	21.47 S	46.36 W
Antas, Rio das ≃	252	29.04 S	51.21 W
An Teallach ∧	46	57.48 N	5.14 W
Antechamber Bay ⊂	168b	35.48 S	138.05 E
Antegnate	62	45.29 N	9.47 E
Antela, Laguna de ⊜	34	42.07 N	7.41 W
Antelope Acres	228	34.44 N	118.19 W
Antelope Creek ≃, Nv., U.S.	204	40.00 N	117.24 W
Antelope Creek ≃, S.D., U.S.	198	45.19 N	102.27 W
Antelope Creek ≃, Wy., U.S.	198	43.29 N	105.23 W
Antelope Island I	202	40.57 N	112.12 W
Antelope Mine	154	21.02 S	28.27 E
Antelope Peak ∧	204	41.19 N	114.58 W
Antelope Reservoir ⊜[1]	202	42.54 N	117.13 W
Antelope Valley V	228	34.45 N	118.20 W
Antelope Wash V	204	39.33 N	116.17 W
Antenor Navarro	250	6.44 S	38.27 W
Antequera, Esp.	34	37.01 N	4.33 W
Antequera, Para.	252	24.08 S	57.07 W
Antero Reservoir ⊜[1]	200	39.00 N	105.55 W
Anterselva, Lago d' ⊜	64	46.53 N	12.10 E
Anterselva di Sopra	64	46.52 N	12.08 E
Antes Fort	210	41.12 N	77.14 W
Antetikireja	157b	14.42 S	47.29 E
Antevamena	157b	21.02 S	44.08 E
Antey-Saint-André	62	45.48 N	7.36 E
Anthéor	62	43.26 N	6.53 E
Anthon	198	42.23 N	95.51 W
Anthony, Fl., U.S.	192	29.17 N	82.06 W
Anthony, Ks., U.S.	198	37.09 N	98.01 W
Anthony, N.M., U.S.	200	32.00 N	106.36 W
Anthony, R.I., U.S.	207	41.41 N	71.32 W
Anthony, Tx., U.S.	200	31.59 N	106.36 W
Anthony Chabot Regional Park ♦	282	37.45 N	122.06 W
Anthony Creek ≃	188	37.54 N	80.20 W
Anthony Lagoon	162	17.59 S	135.32 E
Anthony Peak ∧	204	39.51 N	122.58 W
Anti-Atlas ⋇	148	30.00 N	8.30 W
Antibes	62	43.35 N	7.07 E
Antibes, Cap d' ≻	62	43.32 N	7.07 E
Anticosti, Île d' I	186	49.30 N	63.00 W
Antiesen ≃	60	48.22 N	13.24 E
Antietam Creek, West Branch ≃	208	39.41 N	77.37 W
Antietam National Battlefield ♦	188	39.24 N	77.47 W
Antifer, Cap d' ≻	50	49.41 N	0.10 E
Antignano	66	43.30 N	10.19 E
Antigo	190	45.08 N	89.09 W
Antigonish	186	45.35 N	61.55 W
Antigorio, Valle V	58	46.18 N	8.20 E
Antigua I	240c	17.03 N	61.48 W
Antigua and Barbuda □[1], N.A.	230	17.03 N	61.48 W
Antigua and Barbuda □[1], N.A.	240c	17.03 N	61.48 W
Antigua Guatemala	236	14.34 N	90.44 W
Antigua International Airport ⊠	240c	17.09 N	61.47 W
Antigues, Pointe d' ≻	241o	16.26 N	61.33 W
Antiguo Morelos	234	22.33 N	99.05 W
Anti-Lebanon → Sharqī, Al-Jabal ash- ⋇	132	33.35 N	36.00 E
Antilla, Arg.	252	26.07 S	64.36 W
Antilla, Cuba	240p	20.50 N	75.45 W
Antillas, Archipiélago de las → West Indies II	230	19.00 N	70.00 W
Antillas Holandesas → Netherlands Antilles □[2]	241s	12.15 N	69.00 W
Antilles hollandaise → Netherlands Antilles □[2]	241s	12.15 N	69.00 W
Antilles néerlandaises → Netherlands Antilles □[2]	241s	12.15 N	69.00 W
Antillo	70	37.58 N	15.15 E
Anṭilyās	132	33.55 N	35.35 E
Antímano ⊕[8]	286c	10.28 N	66.59 W
Antimony	200	38.07 N	111.59 W
Anting	106	31.18 N	121.09 E
Antioch → Hatay, Tür.	130	36.14 N	36.07 E
Antioch, Ca., U.S.	226	38.00 N	121.48 W
Antioch, Il., U.S.	216	42.28 N	88.05 W
Antioquia	246	6.33 N	75.50 W
Antioquia □[5]	246	7.00 N	75.30 W
Antipino, Ross.	76	55.55 N	33.16 E
Antipino, Ross.	86	57.49 N	66.34 E
Antipino, Ross.	86	59.01 N	55.10 E
Antipodes Islands II	9	49.40 S	178.47 E
Antipolo	116	14.35 N	121.10 E
Antipovka	80	49.50 N	45.20 E
Antiquarian Museum ʊ	283	42.27 N	71.20 W
Antique □[4]	116	11.00 N	121.45 E
Antizana ∧[1]	246	0.30 S	78.08 W
Antler ≃	184	49.08 N	101.00 W
Antlers	196	34.13 N	95.37 W
Antoetra	157b	20.46 S	47.20 E
Antofagasta	252	23.39 S	70.24 W
Antofagasta □[4]	252	23.30 S	69.00 W
Antofagasta de la Sierra	252	26.04 S	67.25 W
Antofalla, Salar de ≚	252	25.44 S	67.45 W
Antofalla, Volcán ∧[1]	252	25.34 S	67.55 W
Antoing	50	50.34 N	3.27 E
Antolana ∧	157b	17.04 S	48.09 E
Antón, Pan.	236	8.24 N	80.16 W
Anton, Tx., U.S.	196	33.49 N	102.10 W
Anton Chico	200	35.12 N	105.08 W
Antongila, Helodrano ⊂	157b	15.45 S	49.50 E
Antonia	219	38.21 N	90.27 W
Antonibe	157b	15.07 S	47.24 E
Antonina	252	25.27 S	48.43 W
Antonina do Norte	250	6.43 S	39.58 W
Antoniny	78	49.49 N	26.52 E
Antonio Amaro	232	24.16 N	104.01 W
Antonio Carboni	258	35.12 S	59.20 W
Antônio Carlos	256	21.19 S	43.45 W
Antonio de Biedma	254	47.29 S	66.30 W
Antonio Escobedo	234	20.46 N	103.57 W
Antônio Lemos	250	1.22 S	50.50 W
Antônio Prado	252	28.51 S	51.17 W
Antonito	200	37.05 N	106.00 W
Antoniv	78	49.37 N	29.47 E
Antón Lizardo, Punta ≻	234	19.03 N	95.58 W
Antonovka, Kaz.	86	53.19 N	68.26 E
Antonovka, Kaz.	86	45.38 N	80.15 E
Antonovka, Ross.	80	54.55 N	49.30 E
Antonovo	80	49.23 N	51.47 E
Antony	50	48.45 N	2.18 E
Antopol'	76	52.12 N	24.47 E
Antou	100	26.07 N	118.11 E
Antraigues	62	44.43 N	4.21 E
Antrain	32	48.27 N	1.29 W
Antratsit → Antratsyt	83	48.06 N	39.06 E
Antratsyt	83	48.06 N	39.06 E
Antrift ≃	56	50.54 N	9.15 E
Antrim, N. Ire., U.K.	48	54.43 N	6.13 W
Antrim, Oh., U.S.	214	40.06 N	81.23 W
Antrim, Pa., U.S.	210	41.37 N	77.18 W
Antrodoco	66	42.25 N	13.05 E
Antronapiana	58	46.03 N	8.07 E
Antropologia, Museo Nacional de ʊ	286a	19.25 N	99.11 W
Antropovo, Ross.	80	58.26 N	43.00 E
Antropovo, Ross.	82	55.15 N	37.39 E
Antsakabary	157b	15.03 S	48.56 E
Antsalova	157b	18.40 S	44.37 E
Antsenavolo	157b	21.24 S	48.03 E
Antsiafabositra	157b	17.18 S	46.57 E
Antsirabe, Madag.	157b	14.00 S	49.59 E
Antsirabe, Madag.	157b	15.57 S	48.58 E
Antsirabe, Madag.	157b	19.51 S	47.02 E
Antsiranana	157b	12.16 S	49.17 E
Antsiranana □[4]	157b	13.30 S	49.10 E
Antsla	76	57.50 N	26.32 E
Antsohihy	157b	14.52 S	47.59 E
Anttis	24	67.16 N	22.52 E
Antu (Songjiang)	98	42.32 N	128.18 E
Antufash, Jazīrat I	144	15.42 N	42.25 E
Antulai, Gunong ∧	112	4.40 N	116.21 E
Antun'	89	47.36 N	135.46 E
Antung → Dandong	98	40.08 N	124.20 E
Antuševo, Ross.	76	59.54 N	37.40 E
Antuševo, Ross.	76	59.59 N	42.18 E
Antwerp → Antwerpen, Bel.	50	51.13 N	4.25 E
Antwerp, N.Y., U.S.	212	44.11 N	75.36 W
Antwerp, Oh., U.S.	216	41.10 N	84.44 W
Antwerpen (Anvers)	50	51.13 N	4.25 E
Antwerpen □[4]	56	51.10 N	4.50 E
Antykan	89	54.55 N	135.12 E
Anua	174u	14.16 S	170.40 W
Anučino, Ross.	80	52.58 N	43.52 E
Anučino, Ross.	89	43.58 N	133.02 E
Anugul	120	20.51 N	85.06 E
Anŭi	98	35.38 N	127.48 E
An'uj ≃	89	49.18 N	136.27 E
An'ujsk	74	68.18 N	161.38 E
An'ujskij chrebet ⋇, Ross.	74	67.30 N	166.00 E
Anujskij chrebet ⋇, Ross.	86	51.30 N	84.55 E
Anundshögen ⊥	40	59.38 N	16.37 E
Anūpgarh	123	29.11 N	73.13 E
Anūpshahr	124	28.22 N	78.16 E
Ānūr	126	22.55 N	87.39 E
Anuradhapura	122	8.21 N	80.23 E
Anvers → Antwerpen	50	51.13 N	4.25 E
Anversa degli Abruzzi	66	41.59 N	13.48 E
Anvers Island I	9	64.33 S	63.35 W
Anvik	180	62.40 N	160.12 W
Anvik ≃	180	62.39 N	160.14 W
Anvil Peak ∧	181a	52.00 N	179.35 E
Anvil Range ⋇	180	62.30 N	133.50 W
Anvin	50	50.27 N	2.15 E
Anxi, Zhg.	100	25.06 N	118.12 E
Anxi, Zhg.	100	25.15 N	115.06 E
Anxi, Zhg.	102	40.32 N	95.51 E
Anxi, Zhg.	106	30.25 N	120.01 E
Anxian	102	31.40 N	104.32 E
Anxiang	102	29.23 N	112.09 E
Anxin (Xin'anzhen)	105	38.55 N	115.55 E
Anxing	106	31.24 N	119.06 E
Anxious Bay ⊂	162	33.25 S	134.35 E
Anyama	150	5.30 N	4.03 W
Anyang, Taehan	98	37.23 N	126.55 E
Anyang, Zhg.	98	36.06 N	114.21 E
Anyang ≃	98	36.01 N	114.46 E
Anyeke	154	2.24 N	32.31 E
A'nyêmaqên Shan ⋇	102	34.30 N	100.00 E
Anyer Kidul	115a	6.04 S	105.53 E
Anyi	100	28.50 N	115.31 E
Anykščiai	76	55.32 N	25.06 E
Anyox	182	55.25 N	129.49 W
Anysberg	158	33.31 S	20.46 E
Anyuan, Zhg.	100	26.36 N	116.38 E
Anyuan, Zhg.	100	27.37 N	113.54 E
Anyuan, Zhg.	100	25.08 N	115.28 E
Anyuanyi → Tianzhu	102	37.14 N	102.59 E
Anyue	107	30.06 N	105.21 E
Anza-Borrego Desert State Park ♦	204	33.00 N	116.26 W
Anzac	184	56.27 N	111.02 W
Anzaldo	248	17.50 S	65.55 W
Anzano di Puglia	68	41.07 N	15.17 E
Anzbari ∧	123	34.40 N	74.50 E
Anze	102	36.11 N	112.16 E
Anžero-Sudžensk	86	56.07 N	86.00 E
Anzhen	106	31.36 N	120.28 E
Anzhou	105	38.52 N	115.49 E
Anzhuang	106	31.04 N	121.01 E
Anzi, It.	68	40.31 N	15.55 E
Anzi, Zaïre	152	0.52 S	23.24 E
Anzicun	105	39.46 N	115.50 E
Anzin	50	50.22 N	3.30 E
Anzio	66	41.27 N	12.37 E
Anzoátegui □[3]	246	9.00 N	64.30 W
Anzob	85	39.10 N	68.48 E
Anzob, pereval)(	85	39.07 N	68.52 E
Anzola dell'Emilia	64	44.33 N	11.11 E
Anzon ≃	62	45.45 N	3.57 E
Anžu, ostrova II	74	75.30 N	143.00 E
Aoba I	175f	15.25 S	167.50 E
Aoba / Maewo □[8]	175f	15.05 S	168.00 E
Aogaki	96	35.14 N	135.00 E
Aoga-shima I	90	32.28 N	139.46 E
Aohaibolihu	104	42.01 N	121.32 E
Aohandaba	104	42.05 N	121.59 E
Aohan Qi (Xinhui)	98	42.19 N	119.59 E
Aoíz	34	42.47 N	1.22 W
Aoji	98	42.31 N	130.23 E
Aojiang	100	27.37 N	120.33 E
Aojiao	100	23.37 N	117.26 E
Aola	175e	9.32 S	160.29 E
Aoliyingzi	104	42.14 N	121.58 E
Ao Luk	110	8.23 N	98.43 E
Aomar	34	36.30 N	3.47 E
Aomen → Macau	100	22.14 N	113.35 E
Aomori	92	40.49 N	140.45 E
Aonla	124	28.17 N	79.09 E
Aono-yama ∧	96	34.27 N	131.48 E
Aóös (Vijosë) ≃	38	40.37 N	19.20 E
A'opo	175a	13.29 S	172.30 W
Aôral, Phnum ∧	110	12.02 N	104.10 E
Aorangi Mountains ⋇	172	41.26 S	175.20 E
Aore I	175f	15.35 S	167.10 E
Aorere ≃	172	40.41 S	172.40 E
Aoshang	100	25.42 N	113.00 E
Ao-shima I, Nihon	96	33.55 N	134.44 E
Ao-shima I, Nihon	96	33.44 N	132.29 E
Aosta	62	45.44 N	7.20 E
Aosta □[4]	58	45.45 N	7.20 E
Aosta, Valle d' V	62	45.46 N	7.25 E
Aoste	62	45.35 N	5.36 E
Aotou	100	22.44 N	114.33 E
Aoudaghost ⊥	150	17.25 N	10.40 W
Aouderas	150	17.37 N	8.26 E
Aoudour, Oued ≃	34	35.02 N	5.02 W
Aouk, Bahr ≃	146	8.51 N	18.53 E
Aoukalé ≃	146	9.17 N	22.42 E
Aouk-Aoukalé, Réserve de Faune de l' ⊕[4]	146	10.00 N	21.15 E
Aoukâr ⊕[1]	150	18.00 N	9.30 W
Aoulime, Jebel ∧	148	30.48 N	8.50 W
Aoumou	175f	21.24 S	165.50 E
Aourou	150	14.57 N	11.35 W
Aoya	96	35.31 N	133.59 E
Aoyama	94	34.40 N	136.11 E
Aoyama-tōge)(	94	34.40 N	136.16 E
Aozi	146	21.04 N	18.41 E
Aozou	146	21.49 N	17.25 E
Apa ≃	252	22.06 S	58.00 W
Apache	196	34.53 N	98.21 W
Apache Junction	200	33.24 N	111.32 W
Apache Lake ⊜[1]	200	33.36 N	111.16 W
Apache Peak ∧	200	31.49 N	110.25 W
Apalachee ≃	192	33.32 N	83.17 W
Apalachee Bay ⊂	192	30.00 N	84.13 W
Apalaches → Appalachian Mountains ⋇	178	41.00 N	77.00 W
Apalachicola	192	29.43 N	84.59 W
Apalachicola ≃	192	29.44 N	84.59 W
Apalachicola Bay ⊂	192	29.40 N	85.00 W
Apalachin	210	42.04 N	76.09 W
Apam	150	5.17 N	0.44 W
Apan	234	19.43 N	98.25 W
Apanas, Laguna de ⊜[1]	236	13.11 N	85.59 W
Apango	234	17.44 N	99.20 W
Apapa ⊕[8]	273a	6.27 N	3.22 E
Apapa Wharf ⊕[5]	273a	6.23 N	3.23 E
Apaporis ≃	246	1.23 S	69.25 W
Aparados da Serra, Parque Nacional de ♦	252	29.30 S	50.32 W
Aparan	84	40.36 N	44.23 E
Aparecida	256	22.50 S	45.14 W
Aparima ≃	172	46.20 S	168.01 E
Aparri	116	18.22 N	121.39 E
Apartadó	246	7.54 N	76.39 W
Apaseo El Grande	234	20.33 N	100.41 W
Apastovo	80	55.11 N	48.30 E
Apatin	38	45.40 N	18.59 E
Apatity	24	67.34 N	33.18 E
Apatou	250	5.09 N	54.20 W
Apatzingán de la Constitución	234	19.05 N	102.21 W
Apaxtla de Castrejón	234	18.09 N	99.52 W
Apayacu ≃	246	3.19 S	71.51 W
Ap Ba Tien	269c	10.44 N	106.36 E
Ap Binh Quoi	269c	10.48 N	106.36 E
Ap Binh Thanh	110	11.11 N	108.42 E
Apcheron, Péninsule de l' → Abşeron yarımadası ≻[1]	84	40.30 N	50.00 E
Ape	76	57.32 N	26.40 E
Apeadero Funke	258	35.28 S	58.59 W
Apecchio	66	43.33 N	12.25 E
Ape Dale V	42	52.30 N	2.45 W
Apeganau Lake ⊜	184	55.35 N	99.35 W
Apelação	266c	38.49 N	9.08 W
Apeldoorn	52	52.13 N	5.58 E
Apeleg, Arroyo ≃	254	44.58 S	70.07 W
Apen	52	53.13 N	7.48 E
Apenes	224	49.16 N	124.41 W
Apeninos → Appennino ⋇	36	43.00 N	13.00 E
Apenninen → Appennino ⋇	36	43.00 N	13.00 E
Apennines → Appennino ⋇	36	43.00 N	13.00 E
Apennins → Appennino ⋇	36	43.00 N	13.00 E
Apensen	52	53.26 N	9.37 E
Apese ⊕[8]	273a	6.25 N	3.25 E
Apetlon	61	47.45 N	16.50 E
Apex	192	35.43 N	78.51 W
Apex Mountain ∧	180	62.28 N	138.04 W
Api	154	3.40 N	25.26 E
Api ∧	124	30.00 N	80.57 E
Api, Tanjung ≻	112	0.48 S	121.39 E
Apía, Col.	246	5.05 N	75.58 W
Apia, W. Sam.	175a	13.50 S	171.44 W
Apiacá ≃	250	9.16 S	57.03 W
Apiacás, Serra dos ⋇[1]	248	10.15 S	57.15 W
Apiaí	252	24.31 S	48.50 W
Apiaú ≃	246	2.39 N	61.12 W
Apice	68	41.07 N	14.56 E
Apipilulco	234	18.11 N	99.41 W
Apishapa ≃	198	38.08 N	103.57 W
Apiti	172	39.58 S	175.53 E
Apizaco	234	19.25 N	98.09 W
Apizolaya	232	24.50 N	102.15 W
Aplahoué	150	6.56 N	1.41 E
Aplao	248	16.05 S	72.31 W
Ap Lei Chau I	271d	22.15 N	114.09 E
Aplerbeck ⊕[8]	263	51.29 N	7.33 E
Aplinskij, porog ∟	88	58.28 N	100.32 E
Apo	234	19.25 N	102.25 W
Apo, Mount ∧	116	6.59 N	125.16 E
Apodi	250	5.39 S	37.48 W
Apodi ≃	250	4.56 S	37.10 W
Apo East Pass ⋃	116	12.40 N	120.40 E
Apoera	250	5.12 N	57.10 W
Apolakkiá	38	36.06 N	27.50 E
Apolda	54	51.01 N	11.31 E
Apolima Strait ⋃	175a	13.50 S	172.10 W
Apolinario Saravia	252	24.25 S	64.02 W
Apollo	214	40.34 N	79.34 W
Apollo Bay	166	38.45 S	143.40 E
Apollo Beach	220	27.45 N	82.25 W
Apollonia ⊥	146	32.54 N	21.58 E
Apolo	248	14.43 S	68.31 W
Apón ≃	246	10.06 N	72.23 W
Aponguao ≃	246	4.48 N	61.36 W
Apopa	236	13.48 N	89.11 W
Apopka	220	28.40 N	81.30 W
Apopka, Lake ⊜	220	28.37 N	81.38 W
Apoquindo	286e	33.24 S	70.32 W
Aporá	250	11.39 S	38.05 W
Aporé	255	18.58 S	52.01 W
Aporé ≃	255	19.27 S	50.57 W
Apo Reef ⊹[2]	116	12.40 N	120.29 E
Aporema	250	1.14 N	50.49 W
Aporo	234	19.41 N	100.25 W
Apostle Islands II	190	46.50 N	90.30 W
Apostle Islands National Lakeshore ♦	190	46.55 N	91.00 W
Apóstoles	252	27.55 S	55.46 W
Apostolove	78	47.39 N	33.44 E
Appalachen → Appalachian Mountains ⋇	178	41.00 N	77.00 W
Appalaches, Monts → Appalachian Mountains ⋇	178	41.00 N	77.00 W
Appalachia	192	36.54 N	82.46 W
Appalachian Mountains ⋇	178	41.00 N	77.00 W
Äppelbo	40	60.30 N	14.00 E
Appelhülsen	52	51.54 N	7.25 E
Appen	52	53.40 N	9.44 E
Appennino (Apennines) ⋇	36	43.00 N	13.00 E
Appennino, Galleria dell' ⊕[5]	66	44.10 N	11.10 E
Appennino Abruzzese ⋇	66	42.00 N	14.00 E
Appennino Calabrese ⋇	68	39.00 N	16.30 E
Appennino Campano ⋇	66	41.30 N	15.00 E
Appennino Ligure ⋇	62	44.30 N	9.00 E
Appennino Lucano ⋇	68	40.30 N	16.00 E
Appennino Tosco-Emiliano ⋇	36	44.00 N	11.30 E
Appennino Umbro-Marchigiano ⋇	66	43.20 N	12.45 E
Appenweier	58	48.32 N	7.59 E
Appenzell	58	47.20 N	9.25 E
Appenzell-Ausser Rhoden □[3]	58	47.22 N	9.28 E
Appenzell-Inner Rhoden □[3]	58	47.18 N	9.25 E
Appiano (Eppan)	64	46.28 N	11.15 E
Appiano Gentile	62	45.44 N	8.59 E
Appin	170	34.12 S	150.47 E
Appingedam	52	53.18 N	6.52 E
Apple ≃, U.S.	190	42.11 N	90.14 W
Apple ≃, Wi., U.S.	190	45.09 N	92.45 W
Appleby, S. Afr.	158	27.39 S	22.36 E
Appleby, Eng., U.K.	44	54.36 N	2.29 W
Appleby, Tx., U.S.	222	31.43 N	94.36 W
Apple Creek	214	40.45 N	81.50 W
Apple Creek ≃, Il., U.S.	219	39.22 N	90.37 W
Apple Creek ≃, Mo., U.S.	194	37.35 N	89.32 W
Apple Creek ≃, N.D., U.S.	198	46.40 N	100.46 W
Applecross	46	57.25 N	5.49 W
Appledore	42	51.03 N	4.10 W
Applegate	226	39.06 N	120.59 W
Applegate ≃	202	42.26 N	123.27 W
Apple Hill	206	45.13 N	74.46 W
Apple Orchard Mountain ∧	192	37.31 N	79.31 W
Apples	58	46.34 N	6.25 E
Apple Springs	222	31.13 N	94.58 W
Appleton, Eng., U.K.	262	53.21 N	2.33 W
Appleton, Mn., U.S.	198	45.11 N	96.01 W
Appleton, Wa., U.S.	224	45.48 N	121.16 W
Appleton, Wi., U.S.	190	44.15 N	88.24 W
Appleton City	194	38.11 N	94.01 W
Apple Valley	228	34.30 N	117.11 W
Applewold	214	40.47 N	79.36 W
Appley Bridge	262	53.35 N	2.43 W
Appling	192	33.32 N	82.18 W
Appoigny	50	47.53 N	3.32 E
Appomattox	192	37.21 N	78.49 W
Appomattox ≃	192	37.18 N	77.18 W
Appomattox Court House National Historical Park ♦	192	37.23 N	78.48 W
Approuague ≃	250	4.38 N	51.58 W
Apra Harbor ⊂	174p	13.27 N	144.38 E
Aprelevka	82	55.33 N	37.04 E
Aprel'sk	88	58.10 N	114.34 E
Aprel'skij	89	53.30 N	126.16 E
Apremont	58	46.13 N	5.40 E
Apremont-la-Forêt	56	48.51 N	5.38 E
Aprica, Passo d')(	64	46.09 N	10.09 E
Apricena	68	41.47 N	15.27 E
Aprigliano	68	39.14 N	16.20 E
April ≃	164	4.18 S	142.26 E
Aprilia	66	41.36 N	12.39 E
Apscheron → Abşeron yarımadası ≻[1]	84	40.30 N	50.00 E
Apšeronsk	84	44.28 N	39.44 E
Apshawa	276	41.01 N	74.22 W
Apsley	212	44.45 N	78.06 W
Apt	62	43.53 N	5.24 E
Aptakisic	278	42.12 N	87.56 W
Ap Tan Hoa	269c	10.45 N	106.35 E
Ap Tan My	110	11.43 N	108.49 E
Aptos	226	36.58 N	121.53 W
Apuane, Alpi ⋇	64	44.09 N	10.15 E
Apuaú ≃	246	2.32 S	60.48 W
Apucarana	255	23.33 S	51.29 W
Apulia Station	210	42.49 N	76.05 W
Apure □[3]	246	7.10 N	68.50 W
Apure ≃	246	7.37 N	66.25 W
Apurímac □[5]	248	14.00 S	73.00 W
Apurímac ≃	248	11.48 S	74.03 W
Apurito	246	7.56 N	68.27 W
Āq ≃	84	38.59 N	45.27 E
Aqaba, Gulf of ⊂	128	29.00 N	34.40 E
Aqabah, Wādī al- V	132	30.14 N	33.53 E
Āqbolāgh	84	38.54 N	44.32 E
Āqchah	120	36.56 N	66.11 E
ʿAqīq	140	18.14 N	38.12 E
ʿAqīq, Khalīj ⊂	140	18.20 N	38.10 E
ʿAqīq, Wādī al- V	128	24.17 N	40.10 E
Aq Qalʿeh	128	37.01 N	54.30 E
Aqqikkol Hu ⊜	120	37.05 N	88.05 E
ʿAqrabah	132	33.06 N	36.00 E
ʿAqrah	128	36.45 N	43.54 E
Aquarius Plateau ⋇[1]	200	38.05 N	111.40 W
Aquasco	208	38.35 N	76.43 W
Aquashicola	210	40.49 N	75.35 W
Aquashicola Creek ≃	210	40.47 N	75.37 W
Äquatorial-Guinea → Equatorial Guinea □[1]	152	2.00 N	9.00 E
Aquebogue	207	40.56 N	72.37 W
Aqueduct Race Track ♦	276	40.40 N	73.50 W
Aquia Creek ≃	208	38.23 N	77.18 W
Aquiaulne ≃	50	47.37 N	2.30 E
Aquidabã	250	10.17 S	37.02 W
Aquidabã ≃	248	20.58 S	57.50 W
Aquidabán ≃	252	23.11 S	57.32 W
Aquidauana	248	20.28 S	55.48 W
Aquidauana ≃	248	19.44 S	56.50 W
Aquila, Méx.	234	18.36 N	103.30 W
Aquila, Schw.	58	46.31 N	8.57 E
Aquileia	64	45.46 N	13.22 E
Aquiles Serdán, Méx.	232	28.36 N	105.53 W
Aquiles Serdán, Méx.	232	25.38 N	97.50 W
Aquili, Cachoeira ∟	250	11.08 S	55.22 W
Aquilla, Oh., U.S.	214	41.34 N	81.09 W
Aquilla, Tx., U.S.	222	31.51 N	97.13 W
Aquilla Creek ≃	222	31.40 N	97.10 W
Aquilonia	68	41.00 N	15.29 E
Aquin	238	18.17 N	73.24 W
Aquincumi Museum ʊ	264c	47.34 N	19.03 E
Aquino	66	41.30 N	13.42 E
Aquio ≃	246	2.42 N	67.34 W
Ara	124	25.34 N	84.40 E
Ara ≃, Esp.	34	42.25 N	0.09 E
Ara ≃, Ire.	48	52.24 N	7.56 W
Ara ≃, Nihon	92	38.09 N	139.25 E
Ara ≃, Nihon	94	35.39 N	139.51 E
Arab	194	34.19 N	86.29 W
ʿArab, Baḥr al- ≃	140	9.02 N	29.28 E
ʿArab, Khalīj al- ⊂	140	30.55 N	29.05 E
Arab, Oued el V	148	34.41 N	6.31 E
Arab, Shatt al- ≃	128	29.57 N	48.34 E
ʿArab, Wādī al- V	132	32.35 N	35.35 E
ʿArabābād	128	33.02 N	57.41 E
ʿArabah, Wādī V	142	29.07 N	32.39 E
ʿArabah, Wādī al- (Ha'Arava) V	132	30.10 N	35.10 E
Arabako □[4]	34	42.50 N	2.45 W
Araban	130	37.26 N	37.41 E
Arabats'ka zatoka ⊂	78	45.20 N	35.30 E
Arabba	64	46.30 N	11.52 E
Arabelo	246	4.55 N	64.13 W
Arabi	194	29.57 N	90.00 W
Arabian Basin ⊹[1]	12	11.30 N	65.00 E
Arabian Desert → Sharqīyah, Aṣ-Ṣaḥrā' ash- ⊕[2]	140	28.00 N	32.00 E
Arabian Gulf → Persian Gulf ⊂	128	27.00 N	51.00 E
Arabian Peninsula ≻[1]	12	25.00 N	45.00 E
Arabian Sea ⊻[2]	118	15.00 N	65.00 E
Arabia Saudita → Saudi Arabia □[1]	118	25.00 N	45.00 E
Arabie, Mer d' → Arabian Sea ⊻[2]	118	15.00 N	65.00 E
Arabie Saoudite → Saudi Arabia □[1]	118	25.00 N	45.00 E
Arabique, Péninsule → Arabian Peninsula ≻[1]	12	25.00 N	45.00 E
Arabisches Meer → Arabian Sea ⊻[2]	118	15.00 N	65.00 E
ʿArab Muṭayr	142	27.16 N	31.14 E
Ara-Bure, porog ∟	88	53.00 N	100.12 E
Äräb Yengicä	84	39.29 N	44.58 E
Araç	130	41.15 N	33.21 E
Araçá ≃	246	0.25 S	62.55 W
Aracaju	250	10.55 S	37.04 W
Araçariguama	256	23.26 S	47.04 W
Aracataca	246	10.36 N	74.12 W
Aracati	250	4.34 S	37.46 W
Araçatuba	255	21.12 S	50.25 W
Araceli	116	10.33 N	119.59 E
Aracena	34	37.53 N	6.33 W
Arâches-les-Carroz	58	46.02 N	6.39 E
Arachino-seki ⊥	94	35.33 N	136.05 E
Araci	250	11.20 S	38.57 W
Aracides, Cape ≻	175e	8.39 S	161.01 E
Aracitaba	256	21.20 S	43.23 W
Aracoiaba	250	4.23 S	38.49 W
Aracruz	255	19.49 S	40.16 W
Araçuaí	255	16.52 S	42.04 W
Araçuaí ≃	255	16.46 S	42.02 W
Arad, Rom.	38	46.11 N	21.20 E
ʿArad, Yis.	132	31.15 N	35.13 E
Arad □[6]	38	46.20 N	21.40 E
Arada, Hond.	236	14.48 N	88.18 W
Arada, Tchad	146	15.01 N	20.40 E
Aradeo	68	40.08 N	18.08 E
Aradhíppou	130	34.57 N	33.35 E
Arafali	144	15.05 N	39.45 E
Arafune-san ∧	94	36.12 N	138.38 E
Arafura Sea ⊻[2]	164	9.00 S	133.00 E
Arafura Shelf ⊹[4]	14	10.00 S	137.00 E
Aragac, gora ∧	84	40.32 N	44.14 E
Aragarças	255	15.55 S	52.15 W
Arago, Cape ≻	202	43.18 N	124.25 W
Aragon	192	34.02 N	85.03 W
Aragón □[4]	34	41.30 N	0.30 W
Aragón ≃	34	42.13 N	1.44 W
Aragona	70	37.24 N	13.37 E
Aragua □[3]	246	10.00 N	67.10 W
Araguacema	250	8.50 S	49.34 W
Araguaçu	255	12.49 S	49.51 W
Aragua de Barcelona	246	9.28 N	64.49 W
Aragua de Maturín	246	9.58 N	63.29 W
Araguaia ≃	242	5.21 S	48.41 W
Araguaia, Braço Menor ≃	250	9.50 S	50.10 W
Araguaia, Parque Nacional do ♦	250	12.00 S	50.20 W
Araguaína	250	7.12 S	48.12 W
Araguainha	255	16.49 S	53.05 W
Araguao, Caño ≃[1]	246	9.15 N	60.50 W
Araguari	255	18.38 S	48.11 W
Araguari ≃, Bra.	250	1.15 N	49.55 W
Araguari ≃, Bra.	255	18.21 S	48.40 W
Araguatins	250	5.38 S	48.07 W
Aragvi ≃	84	41.50 N	44.43 E
ʿĀrah, Ra's al- ≻	144	12.36 N	43.56 E
Arai, Nihon	94	37.01 N	138.15 E
Arai, Nihon	94	34.41 N	137.34 E
Ārāihāzar	126	23.47 N	90.40 E
Araioses	250	2.53 S	41.55 W
Arak, Alg.	148	25.18 N	3.45 E
Arāk, Īrān	128	34.05 N	49.41 E
Araka	154	4.20 N	30.23 E
Arakamčečen, ostrov I	180	64.45 N	172.30 W
Arakan, porog ∟	88	57.35 N	96.36 E
Arakan Yoma ⋇	110	19.00 N	94.40 E
Arakawa, Nihon	94	35.57 N	139.02 E
Arakawa, Nihon	174m	26.39 N	128.15 E
Arakawa ⊕[8]	268	35.47 N	139.47 E
Arakawa-dake ∧	94	35.30 N	138.10 E
Arákhova	38	38.29 N	22.35 E
Árakhthos ≃	38	39.01 N	21.03 E
Arakkonam	122	13.06 N	79.40 E
Araklı	130	40.57 N	40.03 E
Arakmeer, gora ∧	84	42.38 N	46.49 E
Arakpur ⊕[8]	272a	28.35 N	77.10 E
Aral, Kyrg.	85	42.32 N	72.40 E
Aral, Kyrg.	85	41.50 N	73.03 E
Araldy	84	44.18 N	50.24 E
Aral Sea ⊻[2]	86	45.00 N	60.00 E
Aral'sk	86	46.48 N	61.40 E
Aralsor, ozero ⊜, Kaz.	80	48.42 N	52.24 E
Aralsor, ozero ⊜, Kaz.	80	49.05 N	48.12 E
Aralsul'fat	86	46.50 N	61.58 E
Aramá ≃	250	1.06 S	50.40 W
Aramac	166	22.59 S	145.14 E
Aramac ≃	166	23.02 S	144.31 E
Aramari	255	12.04 S	38.30 W
Ārāmbāg	126	22.53 N	87.47 E
Aramberri	232	24.06 N	99.49 W
Aramia ≃	164	7.55 S	143.22 E
Aramon	62	43.53 N	4.41 E
Arampampa	248	17.55 S	66.04 W
Aramtalla	140	6.47 N	29.13 E
Ārān	128	34.04 N	51.29 E
Arana	258	35.00 S	57.54 W
Arancio, Lago ⊜	70	37.38 N	13.05 E
Aranda de Duero	34	41.41 N	3.41 W
Arandai	164	2.10 S	133.01 E
Arandas	234	20.42 N	102.21 W
Aranđelovac	38	44.18 N	20.35 E
Arandis	156	22.24 S	15.00 E
Aran Fawddwy ∧	42	52.47 N	3.41 W
Arang	120	21.12 N	81.58 E
Aranhegyi-patak ≃	264c	47.34 N	19.04 E
Ārāni, Bngl.	126	24.17 N	88.52 E
Arani, Bol.	248	17.34 S	65.46 W
Ārani, India	122	12.40 N	79.17 E
Aran Island I	48	54.58 N	8.33 W
Aran Islands II	48	53.07 N	9.43 W
Aranjuez	34	40.02 N	3.36 W
Aranos	156	24.09 S	19.09 E
Aransas ≃	196	28.04 N	97.14 W
Aransas Pass	196	27.54 N	97.08 W
Arantāngi	122	10.10 N	78.59 E
Arantina	256	21.56 S	44.15 W
Aranyaprathet	110	13.41 N	102.30 E
Arao	96	32.57 N	130.28 E
Araouane	150	18.54 N	3.33 W
Arapa, Laguna ⊜	248	15.10 S	70.01 W
Arapaho	196	35.34 N	98.57 W
Arapahoe	198	40.18 N	99.54 W
Arapaho National Recreation Area ♦	200	40.07 N	105.48 W
Arāpānja	272b	22.26 N	88.28 E
Arapawa Island I	172	41.11 S	174.19 E
Arapeí	256	22.41 S	44.27 W
Arapey	252	30.58 S	57.32 W
Arapey Chico ≃	252	30.57 S	57.30 W
Arapey Grande ≃	252	30.55 S	57.49 W
Arapiraca	250	9.45 S	36.39 W
Arapiri, Ilha I	250	2.04 S	54.56 W
Arápis	267c	37.59 N	23.32 E
Arapiuns ≃	250	2.18 S	55.00 W
Arapkir	130	39.03 N	38.30 E
Arapongas	255	23.23 S	51.27 W
Arapoti	255	24.08 S	49.50 W
Arapuni	172	38.04 S	175.39 E
Araquil ≃	34	42.48 N	1.45 W
ʿArʿar	128	30.59 N	41.02 E
ʿArʿar, Wādī V	128	31.23 N	42.26 E
Araracuara	246	0.38 S	72.15 W
Araranguá	252	28.56 S	49.29 W
Araraquara	255	21.47 S	48.10 W
Araras	255	22.22 S	47.23 W
Araras, Açude ⊜[1]	250	4.20 S	40.28 W
Araras, Ribeirão das ≃, Bra.	256	22.52 S	46.37 W
Araras, Ribeirão das ≃, Bra.	256	21.18 S	45.45 W
Ararat, Austl.	169	37.17 S	142.56 E
Ararat, Haya.	84	39.50 N	44.42 E
Ararat, Mount → Ağrı Dağı ∧	84	39.42 N	44.18 E
Arari	250	3.28 S	44.47 W
Arari, Lago ⊜	250	0.37 S	49.07 W
Arāria	124	26.08 N	87.24 E
Araripe	250	7.12 S	40.08 W
Araripe, Chapada do ⋇[1]	250	7.20 S	40.00 W
Araripina	250	7.33 S	40.34 W
Ararirá ≃	246	0.30 S	63.33 W
Arar Lugole	144	3.16 N	45.28 E
Araruama, Lagoa de ⊂	255	22.53 S	42.12 W
Araruna	250	6.32 S	35.44 W
Aras (Araz) ≃	84	39.56 N	48.28 E
ʿAras, Ḥawḍ al- ⊻[4]	142	30.51 N	32.32 E
Arashi-yama ∧[2]	270	35.01 N	135.40 E
Åråsviken ⊂	40	59.02 N	14.01 E
Ara Terra	144	6.38 N	40.57 E
Áratos	38	41.05 N	25.33 E
Aratuípe	255	13.05 S	39.00 W
Aratula	171a	27.59 S	152.32 E
Arau	114	6.26 N	100.16 E
Arauá ≃, Bra.	246	4.06 S	63.36 W
Arauã ≃, Bra.	248	7.59 S	65.14 W
Arauá ≃, Bra.	248	5.40 S	60.48 W
Arauca	246	7.05 N	70.45 W
Arauca □[5]	246	6.40 N	71.00 W
Arauca ≃	246	7.24 N	66.35 W
Araucária	252	25.35 S	49.25 W
Arauco	252	37.15 S	73.19 W
Arauco, Golfo de ⊂	252	37.11 S	73.25 W
Araújo, Ilha do I	256	23.09 S	44.42 W
Araújos	255	19.56 S	45.04 W
Arauquita	246	7.02 N	71.25 W
Araure	246	9.34 N	69.13 W
Aravaca ⊕[8]	266a	40.28 N	3.46 W
Aravaipa Creek ≃	200	32.50 N	110.43 W
Arāvalli Range ⋇	120	25.00 N	73.30 E
Aravan	85	40.32 N	72.30 E
Arawata ≃	172	44.00 S	168.41 E
Araxá	255	19.35 S	46.55 W
Araya	246	10.34 N	64.15 W
Araya, Punta de ≻	246	10.38 N	64.18 W
Arayat	116	15.10 N	120.46 E
Araz (Aras) ≃	84	39.56 N	48.28 E
Arba	144	9.01 N	40.23 E
Arba ≃	34	41.52 N	1.18 W
Arbagar	88	51.56 N	116.15 E
Ārbālia	126	22.41 N	88.47 E
Arba Minch	144	6.02 N	37.33 E
Arbatax	71	39.56 N	9.42 E
Arbaž	80	57.41 N	48.18 E
Arbedo	58	46.12 N	9.03 E
Arbél	132	32.49 N	35.29 E
Arbesbach	61	48.29 N	14.57 E
Arbia ≃	66	43.08 N	11.28 E
Arboga	40	59.24 N	15.50 E
Arbogaån ≃	40	59.26 N	16.04 E
Arbois	58	46.54 N	5.46 E
Arboledas	252	36.53 S	61.29 W
Arboletes	246	8.51 N	76.26 W
Arbolito, Cerro ∧[2]	286d	12.10 S	76.57 W
Arbon	58	47.31 N	9.26 E
Arbonne	50	48.25 N	2.34 E
Arborea	71	39.46 N	8.35 E
Arborea ⊕[1]	71	39.50 N	8.50 E
Arborfield	184	53.06 N	103.39 W
Arborg	184	50.55 N	97.15 W
Arbrå	26	61.29 N	16.23 E
Arbroath	46	56.34 N	2.35 W
Arbu, Monte ∧	71	39.15 N	9.27 E
Arbuckle	226	39.01 N	122.03 W
Arbuckle, Lake ⊜	220	27.41 N	81.24 W
Arbuckle Creek ≃	220	27.26 N	81.17 W
Arbuckle Mountains ⋇	196	34.25 N	97.20 W
Arbuckles, Lake of the ⊜[1]	196	34.25 N	97.00 W
Arbury Hills	216	41.33 N	87.51 W
Arbus	71	39.32 N	8.36 E
Arbutus Lake ⊜	276	40.31 N	74.10 W
Arbuzovo	76	56.21 N	32.27 E
Arbuzynka	78	47.53 N	31.19 E
Arc ≃, Fr.	62	43.31 N	5.07 E
Arc ≃, Fr.	62	45.34 N	6.12 E
Arc, Bayou des ≃	194	35.00 N	91.30 W
Arcachon	32	44.37 N	1.12 W
Arcachon, Bassin d' ⊂	32	44.40 N	1.10 W
Arcadas	256	22.42 S	46.52 W
Arcade, It.	64	45.47 N	12.13 E
Arcade, Ca., U.S.	226	34.02 N	118.15 W
Arcade, N.Y., U.S.	210	42.32 N	78.25 W
Arcadia, Ca., U.S.	228	34.08 N	118.02 W
Arcadia, Fl., U.S.	220	27.12 N	81.51 W
Arcadia, In., U.S.	218	40.10 N	86.01 W
Arcadia, Ia., U.S.	198	42.01 N	95.02 W
Arcadia, Ks., U.S.	198	37.38 N	94.37 W
Arcadia, La., U.S.	194	32.32 N	92.55 W
Arcadia, Mi., U.S.	190	44.29 N	86.13 W
Arcadia, Mo., U.S.	194	37.35 N	90.37 W
Arcadia, Ne., U.S.	198	41.25 N	99.07 W
Arcadia, Oh., U.S.	216	41.06 N	83.31 W
Arcadia, Pa., U.S.	214	40.47 N	78.51 W
Arcadia, S.C., U.S.	192	34.57 N	81.59 W
Arcadia, Tx., U.S.	222	29.23 N	95.07 W
Arcadia, Wi., U.S.	190	44.15 N	91.30 W
Arcângelo	256	21.18 S	44.19 W
Arcanum	218	39.59 N	84.33 W
Arcas, Cayos II	232	20.12 N	91.58 W
Arcata	204	40.52 N	124.04 W
Arcatao	236	14.05 N	88.45 W
Arc de Triomphe ⊥	261	48.53 N	2.17 E
Arc Dome ∧	204	38.50 N	117.21 W
Arce	66	41.35 N	13.34 E
Arceburgo	256	21.22 S	46.56 W
Arčeda ≃	80	49.52 N	43.10 E
Arčedinsko-Donskije peski ⊕[2]	80	49.33 N	43.15 E
Arcelia	234	18.17 N	100.16 W
Arcen	52	51.29 N	6.11 E
Arc-en-Barrois	58	47.57 N	5.00 E
Arces	50	48.05 N	3.36 E
Arc-et-Senans	58	47.02 N	5.46 E
Arcevia	66	43.30 N	12.56 E
Archambault, Lac ⊜	206	46.18 N	74.15 W
Archangaj □[8]	88	48.00 N	101.30 E
Archangel → Archangel'sk	24	64.34 N	40.32 E
Archangel'sk	24	64.34 N	40.32 E
Archangel'skaja	78	45.41 N	40.15 E
Archangel'sk Oblast' □[4]	24	63.00 N	42.00 E
Archangel'skoje, Ross.	76	53.16 N	37.42 E
Archangel'skoje, Ross.	78	51.27 N	40.55 E
Archangel'skoje, Ross.	80	55.13 N	44.05 E
Archangel'skoje, Ross.	80	54.26 N	48.40 E
Archangel'skoje, Ross.	82	55.19 N	35.58 E
Archangel'skoje, Ross.	84	44.37 N	44.05 E
Archangel'skoje, Ross.	265b	55.47 N	37.18 E
Archara	89	49.27 N	130.07 E
Archara ≃	89	49.13 N	129.53 E
Archbald	210	41.29 N	75.32 W
Archbold	216	41.31 N	84.18 W
Archdale	192	35.54 N	79.58 W
Archer	192	29.31 N	82.31 W
Archer ≃	164	13.28 S	141.41 E
Archer, Lake ⊜	283	42.04 N	71.20 W
Archer, Mount ∧	166	23.20 S	150.34 E
Archer Bay ⊂	164	13.25 S	141.43 E
Archer Bend National Park ♦	164	13.30 S	142.20 E
Archer City	196	33.35 N	98.37 W
Archer's Post	154	0.39 N	37.41 E
Arches	58	48.07 N	6.32 E
Arches National Park ♦	200	38.42 N	109.45 W
Archi	66	42.05 N	14.23 E
Archiac	32	45.31 N	0.18 W
Archidona	34	37.05 N	4.23 W
Archipo-Osipovka	78	44.22 N	38.33 E
Archipovka	80	56.38 N	41.14 E
Archipovo	24	66.26 N	45.52 E
Archonskaja	84	43.07 N	44.30 E
Archshofen	56	49.27 N	10.04 E
Archville	276	41.07 N	73.52 W
Arci, Monte ∧	71	39.47 N	8.44 E
Arcidosso	66	42.52 N	11.33 E
Arcille	66	42.48 N	11.15 E
Arcinazzo Romano	66	41.48 N	13.12 E
Arcisate	62	45.54 N	8.52 E
Arcis-sur-Aube	50	48.32 N	4.08 E
Arckaringa	162	27.56 S	134.45 E
Arckaringa Creek ≃	162	28.10 S	135.22 E
Arc-les-Gray	58	47.27 N	5.35 E
Arco, It.	64	45.55 N	10.53 E
Arco, Id., U.S.	202	43.38 N	113.17 W
Arco de Baúlhe	34	41.29 N	7.58 W
Arcola, Sk., Can.	184	49.37 N	102.30 W
Arcola, It.	64	44.07 N	9.54 E
Arcola, Il., U.S.	194	39.41 N	88.18 W
Arcola, In., U.S.	216	41.06 N	85.17 W
Arcola, Ms., U.S.	194	33.16 N	90.52 W
Arcola, Pa., U.S.	285	40.09 N	75.27 W
Arcola, Tx., U.S.	222	29.31 N	95.27 W
Arconate	266b	45.32 N	8.51 E
Arcore	266b	45.38 N	9.19 E

Symbols in the index entries represent the broad categories identified in the key at the right. Symbols with superior numbers (⋇[1]) identify subcategories (see complete key on page *I · 1).*

Symbole im Register stellen die rechts im Schlüssel erklärten Kategorien dar. Symbole mit hochgestellten Ziffern (⋇[1]) bezeichnen Unterabteilungen einer Kategorie (vgl. vollständiger Schlüssel auf Seite *I · 1).*

Los símbolos incluídos en el texto del índice representan las grandes categorías identificadas con la clave a la derecha. Los símbolos con numeros en su parte superior (⋇[1]) identifican las subcategorías (véase la clave completa en la página *I · 1).*

Les symboles de l'index représentent les catégories indiquées dans la légende à droite. Les symboles suivis d'un indice (⋇[1]) représentent des sous-catégories (voir légende complète à la page *I · 1).*

Os símbolos incluídos no texto do índice representam as grandes categorias identificadas com a chave à direita. Os símbolos com números em sua parte superior (⋇[1]) identificam as subcategorias (veja-se a chave completa à página *I · 1).*

∧ Mountain	Berg	Montaña	Montagne	Montanha
⋇ Mountains	Gebirge	Montañas	Montagnes	Montanhas
)(Pass	Paß	Paso	Col	Passo
V Valley, Canyon	Tal, Cañon	Valle, Cañón	Vallée, Canyon	Vale, Canhão
≚ Plain	Ebene	Llano	Plaine	Planície
≻ Cape	Kap	Cabo	Cap	Cabo
I Island	Insel	Isla	Île	Ilha
II Islands	Inseln	Islas	Îles	Ilhas
⊥ Other Topographic Features	Andere Topographische Objekte	Otros Elementos Topográficos	Autres données topographiques	Outros acidentes topográficos

ESPAÑOL — Nombre | Página | Lat.°′ | Long.°′ W = Oeste
FRANÇAIS — Nom | Page | Lat.°′ | Long.°′ W = Ouest
PORTUGUÊS — Nome | Página | Lat.°′ | Long.°′ W = Oeste

Nombre	Página	Lat.°′	Long.°′ W = Oeste
Arcos	255	20.17 S	45.32 W
Arcos de la Frontera	34	36.45 N	5.48 W
Arcot	122	12.54 N	79.20 E
Arcoverde	250	8.25 S	37.04 W
Arctic Bay	176	73.02 N	85.11 W
Arctic Ocean ⊤[1]	16	85.00 N	170.00 E
Arctic Red ≃	180	67.27 N	133.46 W
Arctic Red River	180	67.27 N	133.46 W
Arctic Village	180	68.08 N	145.19 W
Arctique, Océan Glacial → Arctic Ocean ⊤[1]	16	85.00 N	170.00 E
Arctowski ʊ[3]	9	62.09 S	58.28 W
Arcturus	154	17.47 S	31.20 E
Arcueil	261	48.48 N	2.20 E
Arcuentu, Monte ∧	71	39.35 N	8.33 E
Arcvašen	84	40.38 N	45.32 E
Arcy-sur-Cure	50	47.36 N	3.45 E
Ard, Loch ⊜	46	56.11 N	4.28 W
Arḍ, Ra's al- ›	128	29.21 N	48.05 E
Arda ≃, Europe	38	41.39 N	26.29 E
Arda ≃, It.	64	45.02 N	10.02 E
Ardabīl	128	38.15 N	48.18 E
Ardagger	61	48.11 N	14.50 E
Ardagh	48	52.28 N	9.04 W
Ardahan	130	41.07 N	42.41 E
Ardakān, Īrān	128	30.16 N	52.01 E
Ardakān, Īrān	128	32.19 N	53.59 E
Ardal	128	31.59 N	50.39 E
Ardalanish, Rubh' ›	46	56.17 N	6.18 W
Årdalsfjorden ⊂[2]	26	61.12 N	7.30 E
Årdalstangen	26	61.14 N	7.43 E
Ardanuç	130	41.08 N	42.04 E
Ardara, Ire.	48	54.46 N	8.25 W
Árdara, It.	71	40.37 N	8.48 E
Ardara, Pa., U.S.	279b	40.22 N	79.44 W
Ardarroch	46	57.25 N	5.38 W
Ardatov, Ross.	80	55.15 N	43.06 E
Ardatov, Ross.	80	54.51 N	46.13 E
Ardbeg	46	55.39 N	6.05 W
Ardcharnich	46	57.51 N	5.05 W
Ardea	66	41.36 N	12.33 E
Ardèche □[5]	62	44.40 N	4.20 E
Ardèche ≃	62	44.16 N	4.39 E
Ardee	48	53.52 N	6.33 W
Ardélik	146	12.26 N	21.25 E
Arden, Mb., Can.	184	50.17 N	99.14 W
Arden, Ca., U.S.	226	38.36 N	121.23 W
Arden, De., U.S.	208	39.48 N	75.29 W
Arden, Forest of ◆[3]	42	52.23 N	1.42 W
Arden, Mount ∧	166	32.09 S	137.59 E
Ardenay-sur-Mérize	50	48.00 N	0.25 E
Arden Mines	279b	40.12 N	80.17 W
Ardennes □[5]	32	49.40 N	4.40 E
Ardennes ◆[1]	56	50.10 N	5.45 E
Ardennes, Canal des ≍	50	49.26 N	4.02 E
Ardenno	58	46.10 N	9.39 E
Ardentinny	46	56.03 N	4.55 W
Ardenza	66	43.31 N	10.19 E
Arderin ∧[2]	48	53.02 N	7.40 W
Ardersier	46	57.34 N	4.02 W
Ardeşen	130	41.12 N	41.00 E
Ardestān	128	33.22 N	52.23 E
Ardey	263	51.28 N	7.43 E
Ardeygebirge ⋏[2]	263	51.25 N	7.23 E
Ardez	58	46.46 N	10.11 E
Ardfern	46	56.10 N	5.32 W
Ardglass	48	54.16 N	5.37 W
Ardgroom	48	51.42 N	9.52 W
Ardıçlı	130	40.40 N	37.00 E
Ardila ≃	34	38.12 N	7.28 W
Ardill	184	49.53 N	105.49 W
Ardino	38	41.35 N	25.08 E
Ardlethan	166	34.21 S	146.54 E
Ardlui	46	56.18 N	4.43 W
Ardlussa	46	56.02 N	5.47 W
Ardmolich	46	56.49 N	5.41 W
Ardmore, Ire.	48	51.57 N	7.43 W
Ardmore, Al., U.S.	194	34.59 N	86.50 W
Ardmore, In., U.S.	216	41.41 N	86.19 W
Ardmore, Md., U.S.	284c	38.56 N	76.51 W
Ardmore, Ok., U.S.	196	34.10 N	97.08 W
Ardmore, Pa., U.S.	208	40.01 N	75.18 W
Ardmore Point ›, Scot., U.K.	46	56.39 N	6.07 W
Ardmore Point ›, Scot., U.K.	46	55.42 N	6.01 W
Ardnamurchan ›[1]	46	56.43 N	6.00 W
Ardnamurchan, Point of ›	46	56.44 N	6.13 W
Ardnaree	48	54.06 N	9.08 W
Ardnave Point ›	46	55.54 N	6.20 W
Ardoch	166	27.26 S	144.08 E
Ardon, Ross.	84	43.12 N	44.18 E
Ardon, Schw.	58	46.13 N	7.15 E
Ardon ≃	84	43.17 N	44.18 E
Ardon, Har ∧	132	30.38 N	34.57 E
Ardooie	50	50.59 N	3.12 E
Ardore	68	38.11 N	16.10 E
Ardoux ≃	50	47.42 N	1.35 E
Ardoz, Arroyo de ≃	266a	40.26 N	3.27 W
Ardres	50	50.51 N	1.59 E
Ardres ≃	50	49.18 N	3.40 E
Ardrishaig	46	56.01 N	5.27 W
Ardrossan, Austl.	168b	34.25 S	137.55 E
Ardrossan, Scot., U.K.	46	55.39 N	4.49 W
Ardsley, Eng., U.K.	44	53.32 N	1.28 W
Ardsley, N.Y., U.S.	276	41.00 N	73.50 W
Ardtalnaig	46	56.31 N	4.06 W
Arduan Island I	140	19.55 N	30.22 E
Ardusson ≃	50	48.30 N	3.32 E
Ardvasar	46	57.04 N	5.54 W
Åre	26	63.24 N	13.04 E
Areado	256	21.21 S	46.09 W
Areal	256	22.14 S	43.07 W
Arèches	62	45.41 N	6.34 E
Arecibo	240m	18.28 N	66.43 W
Arecibo, Observatorio de ʊ[3]	240m	18.20 N	66.46 W
Areco ≃	258	33.56 S	59.16 W
Areeiro	266c	38.39 N	9.12 W
Arefjevo	86	57.01 N	90.40 E
Areguá	252	25.18 S	57.25 W
Areia, Bra.	250	6.58 S	35.42 W
Areia, Port.	266c	38.43 N	9.08 W
Areia, Ribeirão da ≃	255	16.07 S	45.52 W
Areia Branca, Bra.	250	4.56 S	37.07 W
Areia Branca, Bra.	287a	22.44 S	43.25 W
Areias	256	22.35 S	44.42 W
Arena	68	38.34 N	16.13 E
Arena, Point ›	204	38.57 N	123.44 W
Arena, Punta ›	232	23.33 N	109.28 W
Arena de la Ventana, Punta ›	232	24.04 N	109.52 W
Arena Island I	116	9.14 N	120.46 E
Arenal, C.R.	236	10.29 N	84.53 W
Arenal, P.R.	240m	17.59 N	66.19 W
Arenal, Laguna de ⊜	236	10.32 N	84.56 W
Arenal, Volcán ∧[1]	236	10.28 N	84.44 W
Arenápolis	248	14.26 S	56.49 W
Arenas, Cayo I	232	22.08 N	91.24 W
Arenas, Punta ›	240m	18.07 N	65.35 W
Arenas, Punta de ›	254	53.09 S	68.13 W
Arenas de San Pedro	34	40.12 N	5.05 W
Arendal	26	58.27 N	8.48 E
Arendonk	56	51.19 N	5.05 E
Arendsee	54	52.53 N	11.30 E
Arendsee ⊜	54	52.53 N	11.30 E
Arendtsville	208	39.55 N	77.18 W
Arenes ≃	266d	41.29 N	2.02 E
Arenig Fawr ∧	42	52.55 N	3.45 W
Arenillas	246	3.33 S	80.04 W
Arenosa Creek ≃	196	28.52 N	96.44 W
Arenys de Mar	34	41.35 N	2.33 E
Arenzano	62	44.24 N	8.41 E
Arenzville	219	39.53 N	90.22 W
Arequipa	248	16.24 S	71.33 W
Arequipa □[5]	248	16.00 S	72.15 W
Arequito	252	33.09 S	61.28 W
Arero	144	4.45 N	38.49 E
Arês, Bra.	250	6.11 S	35.09 W
Arès, Fr.	32	44.46 N	1.08 W
Arese	266b	45.33 N	9.05 E
Aresing	60	48.32 N	11.18 E
Åreskutan ∧	26	63.26 N	13.06 E
Areuse ≃	58	46.56 N	6.53 E
Arévalo	34	41.04 N	4.43 W
Arezzo	66	43.25 N	11.53 E
Arezzo □[4]	66	43.32 N	11.50 E
Arfa', Jabal ∧	132	29.51 N	35.27 E
'Arfā', Wādī al- ∨	132	30.16 N	36.34 E
Arga ≃	34	42.18 N	1.47 W
Argada	88	54.14 N	110.41 E
Argadargada	166	21.40 S	136.40 E
Argajaš	86	55.29 N	60.52 E
Argamasilla de Alba	34	39.07 N	3.06 W
Arganda	34	40.18 N	3.26 W
Argao	116	9.52 N	123.36 E
Arga-Sala ≃	74	68.30 N	112.12 E
Argedeb	144	6.10 N	41.10 E
Argegno	58	45.56 N	9.08 E
Argel → El Djazaïr	148	36.47 N	3.03 E
Argelès-Gazost	32	43.01 N	0.06 W
Argelès-sur-Mer	32	42.33 N	3.01 E
Argelia → Algeria □[1]	148	28.00 N	3.00 E
Argen ≃	58	47.35 N	9.33 E
Argens ≃	62	43.24 N	6.44 E
Argent	158	26.04 S	28.50 E
Argent, Côte d' ≛[2]	32	43.30 N	1.30 W
Argenta, It.	66	44.37 N	11.50 E
Argenta, Il., U.S.	219	39.58 N	88.49 W
Argentan	32	48.45 N	0.01 W
Argentat	32	45.06 N	1.56 E
Argentera	62	44.24 N	6.57 E
Argentera ∧	62	44.10 N	7.18 E
Argenteuil	50	48.57 N	2.15 E
Argenteuil □[6]	206	45.45 N	74.30 W
Argentia	186	47.18 N	53.59 W
Argentiera	71	40.44 N	8.09 E
Argentière	58	45.59 N	6.56 E
Argentières	261	48.39 N	2.52 E
Argentina □[1]	244	34.00 S	64.00 W
Argentina ≃	62	43.50 N	7.51 E
Argentine	216	42.47 N	83.51 W
Argentine → Argentina □[1]	244	34.00 S	64.00 W
Argentine Basin ⊹[1]	18	45.00 S	45.00 W
Argentinien → Argentina □[1]	244	34.00 S	64.00 W
Argentino, Hipódromo ✦	288	34.34 S	58.26 W
Argentino, Lago ⊜	254	50.13 S	72.25 W
Argentona	266d	41.33 N	2.24 E
Argentona, Riera d' ≃	266d	41.31 N	2.26 E
Argenton-Château	32	46.59 N	0.27 W
Argenton-sur-Creuse	32	46.35 N	1.31 E
Argentré	32	48.05 N	0.39 W
Argent-sur-Sauldre	50	47.33 N	2.27 E
Argeș □[6]	38	45.00 N	24.45 E
Argeș ≃	38	44.04 N	26.37 E
Arghandāb ≃	128	31.27 N	64.23 E
Arghastān ≃	120	31.23 N	65.45 E
Argirita	256	21.37 S	42.50 W
Argıthanı	130	38.17 N	31.43 E
Argo	140	19.31 N	30.25 E
Ārgoal	126	21.58 N	87.38 E
Argo Island I	140	19.25 N	30.27 E
Argolikós Kólpos ⊂	38	37.33 N	22.45 E
Argonia	198	37.15 N	97.45 W
Argonne	190	45.39 N	88.52 W
Argonne ◆[1]	56	49.30 N	5.00 E
Argonne National Laboratory ʊ[3]	216	41.43 N	87.58 W
Argopuro, Gunung ∧	115a	7.57 S	113.33 E
Árgos, Ellás	38	37.39 N	22.44 E
Argos, In., U.S.	216	41.14 N	86.15 W
Árgos Orestikón	38	40.28 N	21.16 E
Argostólion	38	38.10 N	20.30 E
Argoules	50	50.21 N	1.50 E
Argueil	50	49.32 N	1.31 E
Arguello, Point ›	204	34.35 N	120.39 W
Argun	84	43.16 N	45.52 E
Argun ≃	84	43.22 N	45.55 E
Argun' (Ergun) ≃, Asia	74	53.20 N	121.28 E
Argungu	150	12.45 N	4.31 E
Arguni, Teluk ⊂	164	3.06 S	133.42 E
Ārgur	272b	22.48 N	88.13 E
Argut	86	49.51 N	87.03 E
Argut ≃	86	50.16 N	86.43 E
Arguvan	130	38.47 N	38.17 E
Argyle, Austl.	162	33.32 S	115.46 E
Argyle, Mn., U.S.	198	48.19 N	96.49 W
Argyle, Mo., U.S.	219	38.18 N	92.02 W
Argyle, N.Y., U.S.	210	43.14 N	73.30 W
Argyle, Tx., U.S.	222	33.07 N	97.11 W
Argyle, Lake ⊜[1]	164	16.15 S	128.45 E
'Arhāb, Wādī ∨	142	28.55 N	31.09 E
Arhavi	130	41.22 N	41.16 E
Arhéa Epídavros ⊥	38	37.37 N	23.02 E
Århus	41	56.09 N	10.13 E
Århus □[6]	41	56.15 N	10.05 E
Århus Bugt ⊂	41	56.09 N	10.18 E
Aria	172	38.33 S	174.59 E
Aria ≃	164	5.45 S	149.15 E
Ariadnoje	89	45.08 N	134.25 E
Ariah	126	23.33 N	86.20 E
Ariake-kai ⊂	92	33.00 N	130.20 E
Ariāl Khān ≃	126	23.56 N	90.46 E
Ariamácina, Lago di ⊜[1]	68	39.20 N	16.32 E
Ariamsvlei	156	28.07 S	19.49 E
Ariana	36	36.52 N	10.12 E
Ariano, Isola d' I	64	45.00 N	12.10 E
Ariano Irpino	68	41.09 N	15.05 E
Ariano nel Polesine	64	44.56 N	12.07 E
Ariari ≃	246	2.35 N	72.47 W
Arias	252	33.38 S	62.25 W
Arias, Arroyo de ≃	258	34.17 S	56.06 W
Arias, Cañada ≃	258	34.39 S	58.59 W
Ariaú	250	3.11 S	57.14 W
Aribinda	150	14.14 N	0.52 W
Arica, Chile	248	18.29 S	70.20 W
Arica, Col.	246	2.08 S	71.47 W
Arıcak	130	38.33 N	39.48 E
Aricanduva, Ribeirão ≃	287b	23.32 S	46.33 W
Ariccia	66	41.43 N	12.40 E
Arichat	186	45.31 N	61.01 W
Arichuna	246	7.42 N	67.08 W
Arid, Cape ›	162	34.00 S	123.09 E
Arida, Nig.	273a	6.34 N	3.16 E
Arida, Nihon	96	34.05 N	135.07 E
Arida ≃	96	34.05 N	135.06 E
Aridal, Sabkhat ⊜	148	26.12 N	14.05 W
Aridhaía	38	40.59 N	22.03 E
Ariège □[5]	32	43.00 N	1.30 E
Ariège ≃	32	43.31 N	1.25 E
Ariel, Wa., U.S.	224	45.57 N	122.34 W
Ari'el, W.B.	132	32.06 N	35.06 E
Arienzo	68	41.01 N	14.30 E
Arieș ≃	38	46.26 N	23.59 E
'Arif, Har ∧	132	30.26 N	34.44 E
Ārifwāla	123	30.17 N	73.04 E
Ariguanabo, Laguna de ⊜	286b	22.56 N	82.33 W
Ariguaní ≃	246	9.35 N	73.46 W
Arīḥā, Sūrīy.	130	35.48 N	36.36 E
Arīḥā, Urd.	132	31.25 N	35.47 E
Arīḥā (Jericho), W.B.	132	31.52 N	35.27 E
Arikaree ≃	198	40.01 N	101.56 W
Arikaree, North Fork ≃	198	39.39 N	102.57 W
Arikawa	92	32.59 N	129.07 E
Arikha, Har ∧[2]	132	30.39 N	34.47 E
Arild	41	56.16 N	12.34 E
Arima	241r	10.38 N	61.17 W
Arima ◆[8]	270	34.48 N	135.15 E
Arima ≃	270	34.52 N	135.15 E
Arima-fuji ∧[2]	270	34.55 N	135.14 E
Arimine-dam ◆[6]	94	36.29 N	137.27 E
Arinagour	46	56.37 N	6.31 W
Aringay	116	16.26 N	120.21 E
Arino ◆[8]	270	34.50 N	135.14 E
Arinos ≃	248	10.25 S	58.20 W
Arinthod	58	46.23 N	5.34 E
Ario de Rosales	234	19.12 N	101.43 W
Ariogala	76	55.16 N	23.30 E
Aripeka	220	28.25 N	82.39 W
Ariporo ≃	246	6.03 N	69.54 W
Aripuanã	248	9.10 S	60.38 W
Aripuanã ≃	248	5.07 S	60.24 W
Ariquemes	248	9.56 S	63.04 W
Arisa ≃	246	7.32 N	64.00 W
Arisaig	46	56.51 N	5.51 W
Arisaig, Sound of ⊂	46	56.51 N	5.51 W
'Arīsh, Wādī al- ∨	140	31.09 N	33.49 E
Arismendi	246	8.29 N	68.22 W
Aristazabal Island I	182	52.30 N	129.05 W
Aristes	210	40.49 N	76.20 W
Aristizábal, Cabo ›	254	45.13 S	66.31 W
Aristovo	82	54.37 N	36.40 E
Arıt	130	41.41 N	32.39 E
Aritao	116	16.18 N	121.02 E
Ariton	194	31.36 N	85.43 W
Aritzo	71	39.57 N	9.12 E
Arivonimamo	157b	19.01 S	47.15 E
Ariyalūr	122	11.08 N	79.05 E
Arizaro, Salar de ≚	252	24.42 S	67.45 W
Arizgoiti	34	43.13 N	2.54 W
Arizona	252	35.43 S	65.18 W
Arizona □[3], U.S.	178	34.00 N	112.00 W
Arizona □[3], U.S.	200	34.00 N	112.00 W
Arizpe	232	30.20 N	110.10 W
Arja	80	57.30 N	46.00 E
Årjäng	26	59.23 N	12.08 E
Arjasa	112	6.51 S	115.16 E
Arjawinangun	115a	6.39 S	108.24 E
Arjay	192	36.48 N	83.38 W
Arjeplog	24	66.00 N	17.58 E
Arjona, Col.	246	10.15 N	75.21 W
Arjona, Esp.	34	37.56 N	4.03 W
Arka	74	60.03 N	142.12 E
Arkabutla Lake ⊜[1]	194	34.45 N	90.06 W
Arkadak	80	51.58 N	43.28 E
Arkadelphia	194	34.07 N	93.03 W
Arkaig, Loch ⊜	46	56.58 N	5.08 W
Arkalyk	86	50.13 N	66.50 E
Arkansas □[3], U.S.	178	34.50 N	92.30 W
Arkansas □[3], U.S.	194	34.50 N	92.30 W
Arkansas ≃	178	33.48 N	91.04 W
Arkansas, Salt Fork ≃	196	36.36 N	97.03 W
Arkansas City, Ar., U.S.	194	33.36 N	91.12 W
Arkansas City, Ks., U.S.	198	37.03 N	97.02 W
Arkansas Post National Memorial ⊥	194	33.55 N	91.26 W
Arkanū, Jabal ∧	146	22.13 N	24.41 E
Arkatag Shan ⋏	120	36.48 N	89.10 E
Arken-Āhon ∧	146	20.05 N	18.25 E
Arkhangélos	38	36.12 N	28.08 E
Arkhangel'sk → Archangel'sk	24	64.34 N	40.32 E
Arki	123	31.09 N	76.58 E
Árki I	38	37.22 N	26.45 E
Arkit	85	41.47 N	71.58 E
Arklow	48	52.48 N	6.09 W
Arkoma	194	35.21 N	94.26 W
Arkona, Kap ›	54	54.41 N	13.26 E
Arkösund	26	58.30 N	16.56 E
Arkport	210	42.23 N	77.41 W
Arktičeskij, mys ›	74	81.15 N	95.45 E
Arktičeskogo Instituta, ostrova II	74	75.20 N	81.55 E
Arkul'	80	57.17 N	50.03 E
Arkville	210	42.08 N	74.37 W
Arkwright	207	41.43 N	71.33 W
Ärla	40	59.17 N	16.40 E
Arlan	80	55.58 N	54.15 E
Arlan, gora ∧	128	39.40 N	54.33 E
Arlanc	62	45.25 N	3.44 E
Arlanda flygplats ⊠	40	59.37 N	17.55 E
Arlanza ≃	34	42.06 N	4.09 W
Arlanzón ≃	34	42.03 N	4.17 W
Arlbergpass)(	64	47.08 N	10.12 E
Arlberg-Tunnel ◆[5]	64	47.08 N	10.12 E
Arlee	202	47.09 N	114.05 W
Arles	62	43.40 N	4.38 E
Arles à Port de Bouc, Canal d' ≍	62	43.40 N	4.37 E
Arlesey	42	52.01 N	0.14 W
Arlesheim	58	47.30 N	7.37 E
Arleta ◆[8]	280	34.15 N	118.26 W
Arleux	50	50.17 N	3.06 E
Arley	262	53.19 N	2.30 W
Arli	150	11.35 N	1.28 E
Arli, Parc National de l' ✦	150	11.35 N	1.30 E
Arlington, S. Afr.	158	28.06 S	27.54 E
Arlington, Ga., U.S.	192	31.26 N	84.43 W
Arlington, In., U.S.	218	39.38 N	85.34 W
Arlington, Ia., U.S.	190	42.44 N	91.40 W
Arlington, Ks., U.S.	198	37.53 N	98.10 W
Arlington, Ky., U.S.	194	36.47 N	89.00 W
Arlington, Ma., U.S.	207	42.24 N	71.09 W
Arlington, Mn., U.S.	190	44.36 N	94.04 W
Arlington, Ne., U.S.	198	41.27 N	96.21 W
Arlington, N.Y., U.S.	210	41.41 N	73.53 W
Arlington, Oh., U.S.	216	40.53 N	83.39 W
Arlington, Or., U.S.	202	45.43 N	120.11 W
Arlington, S.D., U.S.	198	44.21 N	97.07 W
Arlington, Tn., U.S.	194	35.18 N	89.40 W
Arlington, Tx., U.S.	222	32.44 N	97.06 W
Arlington, Vt., U.S.	210	43.04 N	73.09 W
Arlington, Va., U.S.	208	38.52 N	77.06 W
Arlington, Wa., U.S.	224	48.11 N	122.07 W
Arlington □[6]	284c	38.50 N	77.10 W
Arlington, Lake ⊜[1]	222	32.42 N	97.13 W
Arlington Heights, Il., U.S.	216	42.05 N	87.58 W
Arlington Heights, Ma., U.S.	283	42.25 N	71.11 W
Arlington International Race Course ✦	278	42.05 N	88.00 W
Arlington Memorial Bridge ◆[5]	284c	38.53 N	77.03 W
Arlington Mill Reservoir ⊜[1]	283	42.48 N	71.13 W
Arlington National Cemetery ◆	284c	38.53 N	77.04 W
Arlit	150	19.00 N	7.38 E
Arlod	58	46.06 N	5.49 E
Arlon	56	49.41 N	5.49 E
Arlöv	41	55.39 N	13.05 E
Arltunga	162	23.26 S	134.41 E
Arl'uk	86	55.26 N	84.50 E
Arluno	62	45.30 N	8.56 E
Arly ≃	62	45.40 N	6.23 E
Arlyn Oaks	276	40.40 N	73.27 W
Arm ≃	184	50.46 N	105.00 W
Arma	198	37.32 N	94.42 W
Armação, Ponta da ›	287a	22.53 S	43.08 W
Armada	214	42.50 N	82.53 W
Armadale, Austl.	168a	32.09 S	116.00 E
Armadale, On., Can.	275b	43.50 N	79.15 W
Armadale, S. Afr.	273d	26.17 S	27.57 E
Armadale, Scot., U.K.	46	55.54 N	3.42 W
Arma di Taggia	62	43.50 N	7.51 E
Armageddon → Tel Megiddo ⊥	132	32.35 N	35.11 E
Armagh, N. Ire., U.K.	48	54.21 N	6.39 W
Armagh, Pa., U.S.	214	40.27 N	79.02 W
Armagnac □[9]	32	43.45 N	0.10 E
Armah, Wādī ∨	144	18.12 N	51.02 E
Armainvilliers, Étang d' ⊜	261	48.45 N	2.44 E
Armainvilliers, Forêt d' ✦	261	48.45 N	2.45 E
Armance ≃	50	47.59 N	3.43 E
Armançon ≃, Fr.	50	47.57 N	3.30 E
Armançon ≃, Fr.	58	47.33 N	4.17 E
Armant	140	25.37 N	32.32 E
Armavir	72	45.00 N	41.08 E
Armazém	252	28.16 S	49.01 W
Armbrust	214	40.13 N	79.33 W
Armells Creek ≃	202	47.37 N	108.40 W
Armenia	246	4.31 N	75.41 W
Armenia □[9]	84	40.30 N	43.30 E
Armenia □[1], Asia	72	40.00 N	45.00 E
Armenia (Hayastan) □[1], Asia	84	40.00 N	45.00 E
Armenija → Armenia □[1]	72	40.00 N	45.00 E
Armeniș	38	45.12 N	22.19 E
Armenistís	38	37.36 N	26.08 E
Armeniya → Armenia □[1]	72	40.00 N	45.00 E
Armeno	62	45.49 N	8.26 E
Armenonville-les-Gâtineaux	261	48.33 N	1.39 E
Armentières	50	50.41 N	2.53 E
Armento	68	40.18 N	16.04 E
Armería	234	18.56 N	103.58 W
Armería ≃	234	18.52 N	103.59 W
Armero	246	4.58 N	74.54 W
Armidale	166	30.31 S	151.39 E
Armijo	200	35.03 N	106.40 W
Armitage	42	52.44 N	1.53 W
Armit Lake ⊜	176	64.10 N	91.32 W
Armizonskoje	86	55.57 N	67.42 E
Armona	226	36.19 N	119.42 W
Armonk	276	41.07 N	73.42 W
Armor	210	42.44 N	78.48 W
Armori	122	20.28 N	79.59 E
Armour	198	43.19 N	98.20 W
Armoy, Fr.	58	46.21 N	6.31 E
Armoy, N. Ire., U.K.	48	55.07 N	6.20 W
Armstrong, Arg.	252	32.47 S	61.36 W
Armstrong, B.C., Can.	182	50.27 N	119.12 W
Armstrong, Il., U.S.	216	40.18 N	87.53 W
Armstrong, Ia., U.S.	198	43.23 N	94.28 W
Armstrong, Mo., U.S.	194	39.16 N	92.42 W
Armstrong □[6]	214	40.49 N	79.32 W
Armstrong ≃	164	16.46 S	131.12 E
Armstrong, Mount ∧	180	63.12 N	133.16 W
Armstrong Station	176	50.18 N	89.02 W
Armthorpe	44	53.32 N	1.03 W
Ārmūr	122	18.48 N	78.17 E
Armutlu	130	40.31 N	28.50 E
Armyans'k	78	46.07 N	33.41 E
Arnå ≃	41	54.57 N	8.53 E
Arnaccio	66	43.40 N	10.27 E
Arnaía	38	40.29 N	23.35 E
Arnarfjörður ⊂[2]	24a	65.45 N	23.40 W
Årnäs	40	58.41 N	13.35 E
Arnaud ≃	176	59.59 N	69.46 W
Arnaudville	194	30.24 N	91.56 W
Arnavad, gora ∧	85	38.33 N	71.31 E
Arnavutköy ≃	267b	41.13 N	29.12 E
Arnay-le-Duc	58	47.08 N	4.29 E
Arnaz	62	45.38 N	7.43 E
Arnborg	41	56.01 N	8.59 E
Arnbruck	60	49.08 N	13.00 E
Arncliffe	274a	33.56 S	151.09 E
Arneburg	54	52.40 N	12.00 E
Arnedo	34	42.13 N	2.06 W
Arneiro dos Marinheiros	266c	38.51 N	9.25 W
Arneiroz	250	6.20 S	40.08 W
Arnejevo	82	54.58 N	37.35 E
Arnemuiden	52	51.30 N	3.41 E
Årnes	26	60.09 N	11.28 E
Arnett	196	36.08 N	99.46 W
Arney ≃	48	54.16 N	7.37 W
Arnhem	52	51.59 N	5.55 E
Arnhem, Cape ›	164	12.21 S	136.21 E
Arnhem Bay ⊂	164	12.20 S	136.12 E
Arnhem Land ◆[1]	164	13.10 S	134.30 E
Arnhem Land Aboriginal Reserve ◆[4]	164	13.10 S	134.30 E
Arni	64	44.04 N	10.15 E
Arnis	41	54.38 N	9.56 E
Árnissa	38	40.48 N	21.50 E
Arno I[1]	14	7.05 N	171.41 E
Arno ≃	66	43.41 N	10.17 E
Arno, Torrente ≃	266b	45.42 N	8.48 E
Arno Bay	166	33.54 S	136.34 E
Arnold, B.C., Can.	224	49.08 N	122.03 W
Arnold, Eng., U.K.	44	53.00 N	1.08 W
Arnold, Ca., U.S.	204	38.15 N	120.21 W
Arnold, Md., U.S.	208	39.01 N	76.30 W
Arnold, Mn., U.S.	190	46.52 N	92.05 W
Arnold, Mo., U.S.	219	38.25 N	90.22 W
Arnold, Ne., U.S.	198	41.25 N	100.11 W
Arnold, Pa., U.S.	214	40.34 N	79.46 W
Arnold ≃	164	15.19 S	134.06 E
Arnold Arboretum ✦	283	42.18 N	71.08 W
Arnold Mills	283	41.58 N	71.23 W
Arnold Mills Reservoir ⊜[1]	283	41.59 N	71.25 W
Arnolds Park	198	43.22 N	95.08 W
Arnoldstein	64	46.33 N	13.43 E
Arnon ≃	50	47.13 N	2.01 E
Arnos Vale Airport ⊠	241h	13.09 N	61.13 W
Arnot	210	41.39 N	77.07 W
Arnouville-lès-Gonesse	261	49.00 N	2.25 E
Arnouville-lès-Mantes	261	48.55 N	1.44 E
Arnoya ≃	34	42.15 N	8.09 W
Arnprior	212	45.26 N	76.21 W
Arnsberg	56	51.24 N	8.03 E
Arnsberg □[5]	52	51.20 N	8.00 E
Arnschwang	60	49.16 N	12.49 E
Arnsdorf	54	51.05 N	13.59 E
Arnside	44	54.12 N	2.50 W
Arnstadt	54	50.50 N	10.57 E
Arnstein	56	49.58 N	9.58 E
Arnstorf	60	48.34 N	12.49 E
Arnum	41	55.15 N	8.59 E
Årø I	41	55.15 N	9.45 E
Aro ≃	246	8.01 N	64.11 W
Aroa	246	10.26 N	68.54 W
Aroa ≃	246	10.40 N	68.19 W
Aroa, Pointe ›	174s	17.28 S	149.46 W
Aroab	156	26.47 S	19.40 E
Aroali	126	24.03 N	87.56 E
Arochukwu	150	5.23 N	7.55 E
Aroeiras	250	7.31 S	35.41 W
Ar'ofino	80	58.16 N	39.15 E
Arolla	58	46.02 N	7.29 E
Arolsen	56	51.23 N	9.01 E
Aroma	140	15.49 N	36.08 E
Aroma Park	216	41.04 N	87.48 W
Aromas	226	36.53 N	121.39 W
Aromaševo	86	56.52 N	68.39 E
Arona, It.	62	45.46 N	8.34 E
Arona, Pap. N. Gui.	164	6.20 S	146.00 E
Arona, Pa., U.S.	279b	40.16 N	79.39 W
Aroostook ≃	186	46.48 N	67.45 W
Arop Island I	164	5.20 S	147.05 E
Aropuk Lake ⊜	180	61.12 N	163.50 W
Arorae I	14	2.38 S	176.49 E
Arorangi	174k	21.13 S	159.49 W
Aroroy	116	12.31 N	123.24 E
Aros ≃	232	29.09 N	109.40 W
Arosa	58	46.47 N	9.41 E
Arosa, Ría de ⊂[1]	34	42.28 N	8.57 W
Arosbaya	115a	6.56 S	112.51 E
Årøsund	41	55.16 N	9.45 E
Aro Usu, Tanjung ›	164	8.20 S	130.45 E
Arowhana ∧	172	38.07 S	177.52 E
Arp	222	32.13 N	95.03 W
Arpa ≃	84	39.28 N	44.57 E
Arpaçay	84	40.52 N	43.20 E
Arpaçay (Achur'an) ≃	84	40.06 N	43.39 E
Arpačin	83	47.14 N	40.11 E
Arpaia	68	41.02 N	14.33 E
Arpajon	50	48.35 N	2.15 E
Ārpāra	126	23.23 N	89.23 E
Arpino	66	41.39 N	13.36 E
Arpoador, Ponta do ›	287a	22.59 S	43.12 W
Arquà Petrarca	64	45.16 N	11.43 E
Arquà Polesine	64	45.01 N	11.45 E
Arquata del Tronto	66	42.46 N	13.18 E
Arquata Scrivia	62	44.41 N	8.53 E
Arque	248	17.48 S	66.23 W
Arques	50	50.44 N	2.17 E
Arques-la-Bataille	50	49.53 N	1.08 E
Ar-Rabaḍ	128	23.11 N	39.32 E
Ar-Rabbah	132	31.16 N	35.44 E
Arracourt	58	48.44 N	6.32 E
Ar-Radīsīyah Baḥrī	140	24.57 N	32.53 E
Ar-Rafīd	132	32.57 N	35.53 E
Arraga	252	28.04 S	64.14 W
Arrah	150	6.40 N	3.58 W
Ar-Rahad	140	12.43 N	30.39 E
Ar-Raḥāminah	142	31.18 N	31.45 E
Ar-Raḥmānīyah	142	31.06 N	30.38 E
Arraial do Cabo	255	22.58 S	42.01 W
Arraias	255	12.56 S	46.57 W
Arraias ≃, Bra.	250	11.10 S	53.35 W
Arraias ≃, Bra.	255	12.28 S	47.18 W
'Arrām, Wādī ∨	132	32.55 N	36.10 E
Ar-Ramādī	128	33.25 N	43.17 E
Ar-Ramthā	132	32.34 N	36.00 E
Arran, Island of I	46	55.35 N	5.15 W
Ar-Rank	140	11.45 N	32.48 E
Arran Lake ⊜	212	44.29 N	81.16 W
Ar-Raqqah	130	35.56 N	39.01 E
Ar-Raqqah □[8]	130	36.00 N	39.00 E
Arras	50	50.17 N	2.47 E
Arras, Nuraghe ⊥	71	39.40 N	9.25 E
Ar-Rāshidah	140	25.35 N	28.56 E
Ar-Rass	128	25.52 N	43.28 E
Ar-Rastan	130	34.55 N	36.44 E
Arrats ≃	32	44.06 N	0.52 E
Ar-Rawḍah, Ar. Su.	128	26.05 N	40.37 E
Ar-Rawḍah, Miṣr	142	27.48 N	30.52 E
Ar-Rawḍah, Miṣr	142	29.27 N	31.00 E
Ar-Rawḍah, Yaman	144	14.28 N	47.17 E
Ar-Rāwuk	144	15.45 N	48.54 E
Ar-Rayramūn	142	27.45 N	30.52 E
Ar-Rayyāḥ ar-Minūfīya ≍	142	30.20 N	31.00 E
Ar-Rayyāḥ at-Tawfīqī ≍	142	30.11 N	31.07 E
Ar-Rayyān	128	25.18 N	51.27 E
Arrecife	148	28.57 N	13.32 W
Arrecifes	252	34.03 S	60.07 W
Arrée, Montagnes d' ⋏	32	48.26 N	3.55 W
Arregui, Laguna ⊜	258	35.05 S	57.33 W
Arrentela	266c	38.38 N	9.06 W
Arresø ⊜	41	55.58 N	12.08 E
Arrey	200	32.50 N	107.19 W
Arriaga	234	16.14 N	93.54 W
Arriba	198	39.17 N	103.16 W
Arrild	41	55.09 N	8.58 E
Ar-Riyāḍ (Riyadh)	128	24.38 N	46.43 E
Arrochar	46	56.12 N	4.44 W
Arroio Grande	252	32.14 S	53.05 W
Arrojado ≃	255	13.24 S	44.20 W
Arronches	34	39.07 N	7.17 W
Arrone ≃, It.	66	41.52 N	12.11 E
Arrone ≃, It.	66	42.18 N	11.38 E
Arros ≃	32	43.40 N	0.02 W
Arroscia ≃	62	44.03 N	8.11 E
Arroux ≃	32	46.29 N	3.58 E
Arrow ≃, Eng., U.K.	42	52.12 N	2.43 W
Arrow ≃, Eng., U.K.	42	52.09 N	1.53 W
Arrow, Lough ⊜	48	54.04 N	8.21 W
Arrow Creek ≃	202	47.43 N	109.50 W
Arrowhead, Lake ⊜[1], Ca., U.S.	228	34.15 N	117.11 W
Arrowhead, Lake ⊜[1], Tx., U.S.	196	33.40 N	98.20 W
Arrowhead Peak ∧	228	34.13 N	117.16 W
Arrowhead Provincial Park ✦	212	45.24 N	79.13 W
Arrowhead Village	208	40.04 N	74.07 W
Arrow Lake ⊜	190	48.08 N	90.18 W
Arrowrock Reservoir ⊜[1]	202	43.36 N	115.51 W
Arrowsmith	216	40.27 N	88.38 W
Arrowsmith, Mount ∧, Austl.	166	30.09 S	141.50 E
Arrowsmith, Mount ∧, B.C., Can.	224	49.13 N	124.36 W
Arrowsmith, Mount ∧, N.Z.	172	43.21 S	170.59 E
Arrowtown	172	44.56 S	168.50 E
Arrowwood	182	50.44 N	113.09 W
Arroyan, Arroyo ≃[1]	288	34.24 S	58.32 W
Arroyito	252	31.25 S	63.03 W
Arroyo	240m	17.58 N	66.04 W
Arroyo de la Luz	34	39.29 N	6.35 W
Arroyo Grande, Ca., U.S.	204	35.07 N	120.35 W
Arroyo Grande → Ismael Cortinas, Ur.	258	33.58 S	57.06 W
Arroyo Hondo	200	36.32 N	105.40 W
Arroyo Naranjo ◆[8]	286b	23.02 N	82.23 W
Arroyo Seco	252	33.14 S	60.50 W
Arroyo Seco Park ✦	280	34.06 N	118.12 W
Arroyos y Esteros	252	25.04 S	57.06 W
Arrozal	256	22.37 S	44.03 W
Ar-Ru'at	140	12.21 N	32.17 E
Ar-Rub' al-Khālī ◆[2]	118	20.00 N	51.00 E
Ar-Rubayqī	142	30.10 N	31.46 E
Ar-Ruḥaybah	132	33.45 N	36.42 E
Ar-Rukhaymīyah ⊤[4]	128	29.14 N	45.35 E
Ar-Rumaythah	128	31.32 N	45.12 E
Ar-Rummān	132	32.10 N	35.50 E
Ar-Ruqayyah ⊥	132	32.47 N	37.05 E
Ar-Ruṣāfah ⊥	130	35.37 N	38.45 E
Ar-Ruṣayfah	132	32.01 N	36.03 E
Ar-Ruṣayriṣ	140	11.51 N	34.23 E
Ar-Rushaydah	132	32.40 N	36.50 E
Ar-Ruṭbah	128	33.02 N	40.17 E
Ar-Ru'ūs	142	29.21 N	31.04 E
Ar-Ruways	128	26.08 N	51.13 E
Års	26	56.48 N	9.32 E
Aršan, Ross.	88	51.54 N	102.27 E
Aršan, Ross.	88	53.54 N	99.54 E
Arsanjān	128	29.56 N	53.18 E
Aršan'-Zel'men'	80	47.36 N	44.36 E
Ārsāpota	272b	22.55 N	88.18 E
Arsbeck	56	51.08 N	6.12 E
Arsenal de Marinha ■	266c	38.39 N	9.09 W
Arsenal Football Club ✦	260	51.33 N	0.06 W
Arsenault Lake ⊜	184	55.06 N	108.30 W
Arsenjev	89	44.10 N	133.15 E
Arsenjevka ≃	89	44.54 N	133.35 E
Arsenjevo	76	53.44 N	36.40 E
Ars-en-Ré	32	46.12 N	1.31 W
Arsi □[4]	144	8.00 N	39.40 E
Arsiè	64	45.59 N	11.45 E
Arsiero	64	45.48 N	11.21 E
Arsikere	122	13.20 N	76.15 E
Arsin	130	40.58 N	39.56 E
Arsintsevo	78	45.17 N	36.25 E
Arsk	80	56.06 N	49.54 E
Arslanbob	85	41.21 N	72.56 E
Årslev	41	55.18 N	10.29 E
Arso	164	2.56 S	140.47 E
Arsoli	66	42.02 N	13.01 E
Ársos	130	34.50 N	32.46 E
Ars-sur-Formans	58	45.59 N	4.49 E
Ars-sur-Moselle	56	49.05 N	6.04 E
Årsta havsbad	40	59.05 N	18.10 E
Arsufhsa ≃	84	39.08 N	46.50 E
Årsunda	40	60.32 N	16.44 E
Art, Île I	175f	19.43 S	163.38 E
Árta, Ellás	38	39.09 N	20.59 E
Artà, Esp.	34	39.42 N	3.21 E
Artarmon	274a	33.49 S	151.11 E
Artašat	84	39.59 N	44.33 E
Arta Terme	64	46.28 N	13.01 E
Arteaga	234	18.28 N	102.25 W
Arteche	116	12.17 N	125.22 E
Arte Contemporânea, Museu de ʊ	287b	23.32 S	46.38 W
Artegna	64	46.14 N	13.09 E
Artemare	62	45.52 N	5.42 E
Artemisa	240p	22.49 N	82.46 W
Artemivka	78	49.46 N	35.04 E
Artemivs'k, Ukr.	83	48.27 N	38.42 E
Artemivs'k, Ukr.	83	48.35 N	38.00 E
Artemón	38	36.59 N	24.43 E
Artémou	150	15.31 N	12.16 W
Artemove	83	48.22 N	37.53 E
Artemovsk → Artemivs'k	83	48.35 N	38.00 E
Artèn	64	46.00 N	11.50 E
Artenay	50	48.05 N	1.53 E
Artern	54	51.22 N	11.17 E
Artesia → Mosomane, Bots.	156	24.04 S	26.15 E
Artesia, Ca., U.S.	280	33.51 N	118.04 W
Artesia, Ms., U.S.	194	33.24 N	88.38 W
Artesia, N.M., U.S.	196	32.50 N	104.24 W
Artesia Lake ⊜	226	38.57 N	119.22 W
Artesian	198	44.00 N	97.55 W
Arth	58	47.04 N	8.31 E
Arthabaska	206	46.02 N	71.55 W
Arthabaska □[6]	206	46.05 N	72.00 W
Arthal	123	33.16 N	76.11 E
Arthala	272a	28.40 N	77.24 E
Arthies	261	49.06 N	1.48 E
Arthonnay	50	47.56 N	4.13 E
Arthur, On., Can.	212	43.50 N	80.32 W
Arthur, Il., U.S.	194	39.43 N	88.28 W
Arthur, Ne., U.S.	198	41.34 N	101.41 W
Arthur, N.D., U.S.	198	47.06 N	97.13 W
Arthur, Tn., U.S.	192	36.32 N	83.40 W
Arthur ≃, Austl.	166	41.03 S	144.40 E
Arthur ≃, Austl.	168a	33.31 S	116.50 E
Arthur, Lake ⊜[1]	214	40.57 N	80.05 W
Arthur Creek ≃	162	22.55 S	136.45 E
Arthur Kill ⊔	276	40.30 N	74.15 W
Arthurs Pass	172	42.57 S	171.34 E
Arthurs Pass)(	172	42.54 S	171.34 E
Arthur's Pass National Park ✦	172	42.50 S	171.40 E
Arthurs Seat ∧[2]	169	38.21 S	144.57 E
Arthur's Town	238	24.38 N	75.42 W
Arthurton	168b	34.16 S	137.45 E
Arti	86	56.26 N	58.32 E
Artibonite ≃	238	19.15 N	72.47 W
Artico, Océano → Arctic Ocean ⊤[1]	16	85.00 N	170.00 E
Artigas	252	30.24 S	56.28 W
Artigas ◆[8]	286c	10.30 N	66.56 W
Artigas, Casa de ⊥	258	34.39 S	56.03 W
Artik	84	40.37 N	43.59 E
Artilleros	258	34.22 S	57.34 W
Artilleros, Punta ›	258	34.28 S	57.32 W
Artillery Lake ⊜	176	63.09 N	107.52 W
Artlenburg	52	53.22 N	10.29 E
Artney, Glen ∨	46	56.20 N	4.04 W
Artois □[9]	50	50.30 N	2.30 E
Artois, Collines de l' ⋏[2]	50	50.25 N	2.10 E
Art'om	89	43.22 N	132.13 E
Art'omovsk	86	54.21 N	93.26 E
Art'omovskij, Ross.	86	57.21 N	61.54 E
Art'omovskij, Ross.	88	58.12 N	114.45 E
Art'omovskij, Ross.	89	43.27 N	132.22 E
Artova	130	40.03 N	36.19 E
Artpark ✦	284a	43.10 N	79.03 W
Artrutx, Cap d' ›	34	39.56 N	3.48 E
Artsyz	78	46.00 N	29.26 E
Artuby ≃	62	43.44 N	6.22 E
Artur Nogueira	256	22.35 S	47.09 W
Arturo Merino Benítez, Aeropuerto ⊠	286e	33.23 S	70.49 W
Arturo Segui ◆[8]	258	34.51 S	58.09 W
Artvin	130	41.11 N	41.49 E
Artvin □[4]	130	41.05 N	42.00 E
Artybaš	86	51.48 N	87.16 E
Artyk	74	64.12 N	145.06 E
Artyom	84	40.28 N	50.20 E
Aru, Kepulauan II	164	6.00 S	134.30 E
Aru, Tanjung ›	112	2.10 S	116.34 E
Aru, Teluk ⊂	114	4.09 N	98.12 E
Arua	154	3.01 N	30.55 E
Aruã ≃	250	2.39 S	55.38 W
Aruaddin	144	16.15 N	38.43 E
Aruanã	255	14.54 S	51.05 W
Aruângua (Luangwa) ≃	154	15.36 S	30.25 E
Aruba □[2], N.A.	230	12.30 N	69.58 W
Aruba □[2], N.A.	241s	12.30 N	69.58 W
Aru Basin ⊹[1]	14	5.00 S	134.00 E
Arucas	148	28.07 N	15.31 W
Arue	174s	17.32 S	149.32 W
Arufu	150	7.50 N	9.14 E
Arujá	256	23.24 S	46.20 W
Arujá □[7]	287b	23.24 S	46.20 W
Arumanduba	250	1.29 S	52.29 W
Arume	174m	26.36 N	128.07 E
Arume-wan ⊂	174m	26.35 N	128.08 E
Aruṇ (Pong) ≃, Asia	124	26.49 N	87.09 E
Arun ≃, Eng., U.K.	42	50.48 N	0.33 W
Arunāchal Pradesh □[3]	120	28.30 N	95.00 E
Arundel, P.Q., Can.	206	45.58 N	74.37 W
Arundel, Eng., U.K.	42	50.51 N	0.34 W
Arun Qi	89	48.07 N	123.28 E
Årup	41	55.23 N	10.04 E
Aruppukkottai	122	9.31 N	78.06 E
Arurandeua ≃	250	3.43 S	48.50 W
Arusha	154	3.22 S	36.41 E
Arusha □[4]	154	4.00 S	36.15 E
Arusha Chini	154	3.35 S	37.20 E
Arusha National Park ✦	154	3.17 S	36.56 E
Arut ≃	112	2.42 S	111.34 E
Aruvi ≃	122	8.49 N	79.55 E
Aruwimi ≃	138	1.13 N	23.36 E
Arvada	200	39.48 N	105.05 W
Arvagh	48	53.55 N	7.34 W
Arvajcheer	90	46.15 N	102.48 E
Arve ≃	58	46.12 N	6.08 E
Arverne ◆[8]	276	40.35 N	73.48 W
Arves, Les Aiguilles d' ∧	62	45.08 N	6.21 E
Arvi	120	20.59 N	78.14 E
Arvida	186	48.25 N	71.11 W
Arvidsjaur	24	65.35 N	19.07 E
Arvier	62	45.42 N	7.11 E
Arvieux	62	44.46 N	6.44 E
Arvika	26	59.39 N	12.36 E
Arvillard	62	45.27 N	6.07 E
Arvin	228	35.12 N	118.49 W
Arvo, Lago ⊜	68	39.14 N	16.29 E
Arvon, Mount ∧	190	46.45 N	88.09 W
Arvonia	192	37.40 N	78.20 W
Arvorezinha	252	28.53 S	52.10 W
Arwal	124	25.15 N	84.41 E
Arwala	112	7.41 S	126.49 E
Arxan	89	47.11 N	119.57 E
Aryamūn	142	31.11 N	30.54 E
Aryiroúpolis	267c	37.54 N	23.45 E
Arys'	85	42.26 N	68.48 E
Arys' ≃	85	42.48 N	68.12 E
Arys, ozero ⊜	86	45.50 N	66.20 E
Arzachena	71	41.05 N	9.23 E
Arzamas	80	55.23 N	43.50 E
Arzana	71	39.55 N	9.31 E
Arzano	68	40.55 N	14.16 E
Arzberg	60	50.04 N	12.12 E
Arzew, Golfe d' ⊂	34	35.50 N	0.10 W
Arzew, Salines d' ⊜	34	35.40 N	0.15 W
Arzfeld	56	50.05 N	6.16 E
Arzignano	64	45.31 N	11.20 E
Arziw	148	35.51 N	0.19 W
Arz Lubnān ◆[3]	130	34.14 N	36.03 E
Arzni	84	40.19 N	44.36 E
Arzon ≃	62	45.11 N	3.54 E
Arzúa	34	42.56 N	8.09 W
As, Bel.	56	51.01 N	5.35 E

≃	River	Fluß	Río	Rivière	Rio
≍	Canal	Kanal	Canal	Canal	Canal
∟	Waterfall, Rapids	Wasserfall, Stromschnellen	Cascada, Rápidos	Chute d'eau, Rapides	Cascata, Rápidos
⊔	Strait	Meeresstraße	Estrecho	Détroit	Estreito
⊂	Bay, Gulf	Bucht, Golf	Bahía, Golfo	Baie, Golfe	Baía, Golfo
⊜	Lake, Lakes	See, Seen	Lago, Lagos	Lac, Lacs	Lago, Lagos
≚	Swamp	Sumpf	Pantano	Marais	Pântano
✱	Ice Features, Glacier	Eis- und Gletscherformen	Accidentes Glaciales	Formes glaciaires	Formas glaciares
⊤	Other Hydrographic Features	Andere Hydrographische Objekte	Otros Elementos Hidrográficos	Autres données hydrographiques	Outros acidentes hidrográficos
⊹	Submarine Features	Untermeerische Objekte	Accidentes Submarinos	Formes de relief sous-marin	Acidentes submarinos
□	Political Unit	Politische Einheit	Unidad Politica	Entité politique	Unidade política
ʊ	Cultural Institution	Kulturelle Institution	Institución Cultural	Institution culturelle	Institução cultural
⊥	Historical Site	Historische Stätte	Sitio Histórico	Site historique	Sitio histórico
✦	Recreational Site	Erholungs- und Ferienort	Sitio de Recreo	Centre de loisirs	Area de Lazer
⊠	Airport	Flughafen	Aeropuerto	Aéroport	Aeroporto
■	Military Installation	Militäranlage	Instalación Militar	Installation militaire	Instalação militar
◆	Miscellaneous	Verschiedenes	Misceláneo	Divers	Diversos

Aš, Česká Rep. 54 50.10 N 12.10 E
Ås, Nor. 26 59.40 N 10.48 E
Asa, Nihon 96 34.33 N 132.26 E
Aša, Ross. 86 55.00 N 57.16 E
Asa ≏, Nihon 94 35.39 N 139.26 E
Asa ≏, Nihon 96 34.01 N 131.09 E
Asa ≏, Ven. 246 6.50 N 63.18 W
Asab 156 25.29 S 17.59 E
Asaba, Nig. 150 6.12 N 6.44 E
Asaba, Nihon 94 34.42 N 137.56 E
Asad, Buḥayrat al- ⊜[1] 130 36.00 N 38.10 E
Asadābād, Afg. 120 34.52 N 71.09 E
Asadābād, Īrān 128 34.47 N 48.07 E
Asafo 150 6.11 N 0.28 W
Asaga Strait 174y 14.11 S 169.40 W
Asagaya ✦[8] 268 35.42 N 139.38 E
Aşağıbostancı 130 35.10 N 33.00 E
Aşağıçiğil 130 38.03 N 31.52 E
Aşağı Dağ ∧ 84 40.01 N 43.11 E
Aşağı Köynük 84 41.18 N 47.00 E
Aşağı Kuluşağı 130 38.39 N 38.39 E
Aşağılahan 130 38.25 N 38.39 E
Aşağı Mestikân 130 38.25 N 38.46 E
Asahan 114 2.23 N 102.33 E
Asahan ≏ 114 3.02 N 99.52 E
Asahi, Nihon 94 35.14 N 137.22 E
Asahi, Nihon 94 35.43 N 140.39 E
Asahi, Nihon 94 35.59 N 136.07 E
Asahi, Nihon 94 36.05 N 137.21 E
Asahi, Nihon 94 36.14 N 140.31 E
Asahi, Nihon 94 35.02 N 136.40 E
Asahi, Nihon 94 36.07 N 137.52 E
Asahi, Nihon 94 36.57 N 137.34 E
Asahi, Nihon 96 34.59 N 133.50 E
Asahi, Nihon 96 34.51 N 132.16 E
Asahi, Nihon 96 34.17 N 131.28 E
Asahi ✦[8], Nihon 268 35.29 N 139.33 E
Asahi ✦[8], Nihon 270 34.44 N 135.34 E
Asahi ≏ 96 34.36 N 133.58 E
Asahi-dake ∧, Nihon 92a 43.40 N 142.51 E
Asahi-dake ∧, Nihon 94 37.14 N 139.21 E
Asahigawa
— Asahikawa 92a 43.46 N 142.22 E
Asahi-gawa-daiichi-dam ✦[6] 96 34.53 N 133.22 E
Asahikawa 92a 43.46 N 142.22 E
Asahikawa-chūtonchi, Rikujō-Jieitai- ▪ 92a 43.49 N 142.25 E
Asahi-ko ⊜[1] 96 34.56 N 133.51 E
Asahi-sanchi ⋌ 92 38.25 N 139.50 E
Asaka 94 35.48 N 139.36 E
Asaka, Camp ▪ 268 35.47 N 139.36 E
Asakanskij Golec, gora ∧ 88 50.18 N 109.55 E
Asakawa 94 37.05 N 140.25 E
Asake ≏ 94 35.00 N 136.41 E
Asako 96 35.14 N 134.48 E
Asakura 96 33.23 N 130.44 E
Asakusa ✦[8] 268 35.43 N 139.49 E
Asālafpur ✦[8] 272a 28.38 N 77.05 E
Asale 144 14.22 N 40.32 E
Asale, Lake ⊜ 144 14.19 N 40.18 E
Asamankese 150 5.52 N 0.42 W
Asama-yama ∧ 94 36.24 N 138.31 E
Asanbani, India 126 22.43 N 86.20 E
Asanbāni, India 126 24.07 N 87.27 E
Asani 154 4.25 S 29.05 E
Asankrangwa 150 5.48 N 2.26 W
Asan-man ⊂ 98 36.56 N 126.51 E
Asānsol, India 126 24.14 N 87.17 E
Asānsol, India 126 23.41 N 86.59 E
Asap 86 57.07 N 56.30 E
Asar 88 47.56 N 117.38 E
Åsarna 26 62.39 N 14.21 E
Asarum 26 56.12 N 14.50 E
Asashina 94 36.16 N 138.25 E
Asāsuni 126 22.32 N 89.10 E
Asati 272b 22.29 N 88.14 E
Asa-yama ∧ 96 34.47 N 132.23 E
Asayita 144 11.33 N 41.30 E
Asbach 56 50.40 N 7.25 E
Asbeck 263 51.21 N 7.18 E
Asberg 263 51.26 N 6.40 E
Asbesberg ⋌ 158 28.55 S 23.15 E
Asbest 86 57.00 N 61.30 E
Asbestos 206 45.46 N 71.57 W
Asbestos Range National Park ♦ 166 41.08 S 146.39 E
Asbe Teferi 144 9.02 N 40.58 E
Åsbro 40 59.00 N 15.03 E
Asbury 210 40.41 N 75.00 W
Asbury Park 208 40.13 N 74.01 W
Ascea 68 40.08 N 15.11 E
Ascensión 232 31.06 N 107.59 W
Ascension I 10 7.57 S 14.22 W
Ascent 158 27.12 S 29.03 E
Aščerino 265b 55.36 N 37.46 E
Asch 58 47.57 N 10.49 E
Aschabad (Ashgabat) 128 37.57 N 58.23 E
Aschach an der Donau 61 48.22 N 14.02 E
Aschaffenburg 56 49.59 N 9.09 E
Aschbach Markt 61 48.04 N 14.45 E
Ascheberg, Dtsch. 52 51.47 N 7.37 E
Ascheberg, Dtsch. 54 54.08 N 10.20 E
Aschendorf 52 53.04 N 7.22 E
Aschersleben 54 51.45 N 11.27 E
Asciano 66 43.14 N 11.33 E
Aščikol', ozero ⊜ 86 45.05 N 67.15 E
Aščiozek ≏ 80 49.12 N 48.06 E
Aščitastysor, ozero ⊜ 86 49.19 N 63.59 E
Ascoli Piceno 66 42.51 N 13.34 E
Ascoli Piceno ▫[4] 66 43.01 N 13.34 E
Ascoli Satriano 68 41.12 N 15.34 E
Ascona 58 46.09 N 8.46 E
Ascope 248 7.43 S 79.07 W
Ascot, Austl. 171a 27.26 S 153.04 E
Ascot, Eng., U.K. 42 51.25 N 0.41 W
Ascot ≏ 206 45.21 N 71.51 W
Ascotán 252 21.44 S 68.18 W
Ascros 62 43.55 N 7.01 E
Aščykol', ozero ⊜ 85 43.32 N 70.35 E
Aščysu ≏ 86 49.54 N 78.58 E
Aseb 144 13.00 N 42.45 E
Åseda 26 57.10 N 15.20 E
Asedjrad ⋌[1] 148 24.28 N 1.52 E
Asekejevo 80 53.36 N 52.49 E
Asela 144 7.59 N 39.08 E
Åsele 26 64.10 N 17.20 E
Asemi ≏ 115a 6.14 S 107.42 E
Asembagus 115a 7.45 S 114.14 E
Asembourg 56 49.43 N 6.02 E
Åsen 26 63.36 N 11.03 E
Asendabo 144 9.50 N 37.33 E
Asendorf 52 52.46 N 9.00 E
Asenovgrad 38 42.01 N 24.52 E
Åsensbruk 26 58.48 N 12.25 E
Aseri 76 59.27 N 26.52 E
Asfar, Jabal al- ∧ 132 32.12 N 36.54 E
Asfordby 42 52.46 N 0.57 W
Asfūn al-Maṭāʿinah 140 25.23 N 32.32 E
Åsgårdstrand 26 59.21 N 10.28 E
Ash, Eng., U.K. 42 51.17 N 1.16 E
Ash, Eng., U.K. 42 51.15 N 0.44 W
Ashalim 132 30.58 N 34.40 E
Ashammar 40 60.39 N 16.32 E
Ashanti ▫[4] 150 6.45 N 1.30 W
ʿAsharah, Wādī al- ∨ 142 30.21 N 32.15 E
Asharoken 276 40.56 N 73.22 W
Ashaway 207 41.25 N 71.47 W
Ashbourne, Ire. 48 53.31 N 6.24 W
Ashbourne, Eng., U.K. 44 53.02 N 1.44 W
Ash Brook Swamp Reservation ♦ 276 40.37 N 74.21 W
Ashburn, Ga., U.S. 192 31.42 N 83.39 W
Ashburn, Mo., U.S. 219 39.33 N 91.10 W
Ashburn, Va., U.S. 208 39.02 N 77.29 W
Ashburnham 207 42.38 N 71.54 W
Ashburton, Austl. 274b 37.52 S 145.05 E
Ashburton, N.Z. 172 43.55 S 171.45 E
Ashburton, Eng., U.K. 42 50.31 N 3.45 W
Ashburton ≏, Austl. 162 21.40 S 114.56 E
Ashburton ≏, N.Z. 172 44.04 S 171.48 E
Ashburton, North Branch ≏ 172 43.54 S 171.44 E
Ashburton, South Branch ≏ 172 43.44 S 171.32 E
Ashburton Downs 162 23.24 S 117.04 E
Ashby 207 42.40 N 71.49 W
Ashby, Lake ⊜ 220 28.56 N 81.07 W
Ashby-de-la-Zouch 42 52.46 N 1.28 W
Ashchurch 42 52.00 N 2.07 W
Ash Creek ≏, Ca., U.S. 204 41.05 N 121.08 W
Ash Creek ≏, Ct., U.S. 276 41.08 N 73.14 W
Ashcroft 182 50.43 N 121.17 W
Ashdod, Ma., U.S. 283 42.04 N 70.45 W
Ashdod, Yis. 132 31.49 N 34.40 E
Ashdod, Tel ⊥ 132 31.45 N 34.40 E
Ashdot Ya'aqov 132 32.40 N 35.35 E
Ashdown 194 33.40 N 94.07 W
Asheboro 192 35.42 N 79.48 W
Ashern 184 51.11 N 98.21 W
Asherton 196 28.26 N 99.45 W
Asheville 192 35.36 N 82.33 W
Ashewat Ziārat 120 31.22 N 68.32 E
Asheweig ≏ 176 54.17 N 87.12 W
Ashfield, Austl. 274a 33.53 S 151.08 E
Ashfield, Ma., U.S. 207 42.31 N 72.47 W
Ash Flat 194 36.13 N 91.36 W
Ashford, Austl. 166 29.20 S 151.06 E
Ashford, Eng., U.K. 42 51.08 N 0.53 E
Ashford, Eng., U.K. 260 51.26 N 0.27 W
Ashford, Al., U.S. 194 31.10 N 85.14 W
Ashford, Wa., U.S. 224 46.46 N 122.02 W
Ashford Airport ✈ 42 51.04 N 1.01 E
Ash Fork 200 35.13 N 112.28 W
Ash Grove 194 37.18 N 93.35 W
Ashhurst 172 40.18 S 175.45 E
Ashibe 92 33.48 N 129.46 E
Ashibetsu 92a 43.31 N 142.11 E
Ashida ≏ 96 34.26 N 133.25 E
Ashikaga 94 36.20 N 139.27 E
Ashikagga-gakkō ⊥ 94 36.22 N 139.30 E
Ashingdon 260 51.36 N 0.42 E
Ashington 44 55.12 N 1.35 W
Ashino-ko ⊜ 94 35.13 N 139.00 E
Ashio 94 36.38 N 139.27 E
Ashio-sanchi ⋌ 94 36.35 N 139.30 E
Ashippun 216 43.14 N 88.31 W
Ashippun ≏ 216 43.10 N 88.33 W
Ashitaka-yama ∧ 94 35.12 N 138.49 E
Ashiya, Nihon 96 33.53 N 130.40 E
Ashiya, Nihon 96 34.43 N 135.17 E
Ashiya ≏ 270 34.44 N 135.18 E
Ashiyasu 94 35.38 N 138.23 E
Ashiyoro 92a 43.15 N 143.30 E
Ashizuri-misaki ≻ 92 32.44 N 133.01 E
Ashizuri-Uwakai-kokuritsu-kōen ♦, Nihon 92 32.45 N 132.45 E
Ashizuri-Uwakai-kokuritsu-kōen ♦, Nihon 96 33.07 N 132.27 E
Ashkhabad
— Ašchabad 128 37.57 N 58.23 E
Ashkum 216 40.53 N 87.57 W
Ashland, Al., U.S. 194 33.16 N 85.50 W
Ashland, Ca., U.S. 226 37.41 N 122.06 W
Ashland, Il., U.S. 219 39.53 N 90.00 W
Ashland, Ks., U.S. 198 37.11 N 99.45 W
Ashland, Ky., U.S. 188 38.28 N 82.38 W
Ashland, Me., U.S. 186 46.37 N 68.24 W
Ashland, Ma., U.S. 207 42.15 N 71.27 W
Ashland, Ms., U.S. 194 34.49 N 89.10 W
Ashland, Mo., U.S. 219 38.46 N 92.15 W
Ashland, Mt., U.S. 202 45.35 N 106.16 W
Ashland, Ne., U.S. 198 41.02 N 96.22 W
Ashland, N.H., U.S. 188 43.41 N 71.37 W
Ashland, N.J., U.S. 285 39.51 N 75.00 W
Ashland, N.Y., U.S. 210 42.18 N 74.20 W
Ashland, Oh., U.S. 214 40.52 N 82.19 W
Ashland, Or., U.S. 202 42.11 N 122.42 W
Ashland, Pa., U.S. 208 40.46 N 76.20 W
Ashland, Va., U.S. 208 37.45 N 77.28 W
Ashland, Wi., U.S. 190 46.35 N 90.53 W
Ashland ▫[6] 214 40.52 N 82.19 W
Ashland, Mount ∧ 202 42.05 N 122.43 W
Ashland City 194 36.16 N 87.03 W
Ashley, Austl. 166 29.19 S 149.49 E
Ashley, Eng., U.K. 262 53.21 N 2.20 W
Ashley, Il., U.S. 219 38.20 N 89.11 W
Ashley, In., U.S. 216 41.32 N 85.04 W
Ashley, Mi., U.S. 190 43.11 N 84.28 W
Ashley, Mo., U.S. 219 39.15 N 91.14 W
Ashley, N.D., U.S. 198 46.01 N 99.22 W
Ashley, Oh., U.S. 214 40.24 N 82.57 W
Ashley, Pa., U.S. 210 41.12 N 75.53 W
Ashley ≏ 172 43.16 S 172.42 E
Ashley Creek ≏ 200 40.21 N 109.22 W
Ashley Falls 207 42.03 N 73.20 W
Ashley Green 260 51.44 N 0.35 W
Ashmore 194 39.32 N 88.01 W
Ashmore Islands II 160 12.14 S 123.05 E
Ashmūn 142 30.18 N 30.58 E
Ashokan Reservoir ⊜[1] 210 41.58 N 74.10 W
Ashoknagar 124 24.34 N 77.43 E
Ashqelon 132 31.40 N 34.35 E
Ashridge Park ♦ 260 51.48 N 0.34 W
Ash-Shabakah 128 30.49 N 43.39 E
Ash-Shabb ≂[4] 140 22.19 N 29.46 E
Ash-Shaddādah 130 36.02 N 40.45 E
Ash-Shāghūr 132 31.50 N 35.39 E
Ash-Shāʿib ⋌[2] 142 29.50 N 30.56 E
Ash-Shajarah 132 32.39 N 35.56 E
Ash-Shallūfah 142 30.07 N 32.34 E
Ash-Shamāl ▫[4] 130 34.30 N 36.00 E
Ash-Shamāliyah ▫[4] 140 19.15 N 29.00 E
Ash-Shāmiyah 128 31.57 N 44.36 E
Ash-Shanāwīyah 142 29.08 N 31.08 E
Ash-Sharāh ✦[1] 132 30.20 N 35.30 E
Ash-Shāriqah 128 25.22 N 55.23 E
Ash-Sharmah 128 28.01 N 35.16 E
Ash-Sharqāṭ 128 35.27 N 43.16 E
Ash-Sharqīyah ▫[4] 142 30.48 N 31.38 E
Ash-Sharqīyah ✦[1] 128 27.00 N 49.00 E
Ash-Shatrah 128 31.25 N 46.10 E
Ash-Shawāshinah 142 29.22 N 30.36 E
Ash-Shawbak 132 30.32 N 35.34 E
Ash-Shawmarah 142 33.07 N 35.08 E
Ash-Shaykh Faḍl 142 28.29 N 30.50 E
Ash-Shaykh ʿIbādah 142 27.48 N 30.52 E
Ash-Shaykh Saʿd 132 32.50 N 36.02 E
Ash-Shaykh Timay 142 27.53 N 30.51 E
Ash-Shiḥr 144 14.45 N 49.36 E
Ash-Shīn 132 31.01 N 30.53 E
Ash-Shināfiyah 128 31.35 N 44.39 E
Ash-Shiyāḥ 132 33.51 N 35.30 E
Ash-Shufayyah 128 23.50 N 39.08 E
Ash-Shuhadāʾ 142 30.36 N 30.54 E
Ash-Shumlūl 128 26.31 N 47.19 E
Ash-Shuqayq 144 17.43 N 42.01 E
Ash-Shurayf 128 25.43 N 39.14 E
Ash-Shuwayhāt 128 18.48 N 33.34 E
Ash-Shuwayfāt 132 33.49 N 35.31 E
Ash Slough ≏ 226 37.02 N 120.32 W
Ashta, India 122 16.57 N 74.24 E
Ashta, India 124 23.01 N 76.43 E
Ashtabula 214 41.51 N 80.47 W
Ashtabula ≏ 214 41.54 N 80.47 W
Ashtabula ▫[6] 214 41.44 N 80.46 W
Ashtabula ≏ 214 41.55 N 80.47 W
Ashtabula, East Branch ≏ 214 41.48 N 80.37 W
Ashtabula, Lake ⊜[1] 198 47.11 N 97.58 W
Ashtabula, West Branch ≏ 214 41.48 N 80.38 W
Ashtead 42 51.19 N 0.18 W
Ashton, S. Afr. 158 33.50 S 20.05 E
Ashton, Eng., U.K. 262 53.13 N 2.45 W
Ashton, Id., U.S. 202 44.04 N 111.26 W
Ashton, Il., U.S. 190 41.51 N 89.13 W
Ashton, Ia., U.S. 198 43.18 N 95.47 W
Ashton, Md., U.S. 208 39.08 N 77.00 W
Ashton, Ne., U.S. 198 41.14 N 98.47 W
Ashton, R.I., U.S. 207 41.46 N 71.25 W
Ashton-in-Makerfield 44 53.29 N 2.39 W
Ashton-under-Lyne 44 53.29 N 2.06 W
Ashton upon Mersey 262 53.26 N 2.19 W
Ashuanipi Lake ⊜ 176 52.35 N 66.10 W
Ashuelot ≏ 188 42.46 N 72.29 W
Ashurst's Beacon ∧[2] 262 53.34 N 2.45 W
Ashville, Al., U.S. 194 33.52 N 86.17 W
Ashville, N.Y., U.S. 214 42.06 N 79.23 W
Ashville, Oh., U.S. 218 39.42 N 82.57 W
Ashville, Pa., U.S. 214 40.34 N 78.33 W
Ashwater 42 50.44 N 4.16 W
Ashwaubenon 190 44.30 N 88.06 W
Ashworth Moor Reservoir ⊜[1] 262 53.38 N 2.16 W
Asi (Nahr al-ʿĀṣī) ≏ 130 36.02 N 35.58 E
Asia ▪[1] 4 50.00 N 100.00 E
Asia ▪[1] 12 50.00 N 100.00 E
Asia, Kepulauan II 108 1.03 N 131.18 E
Asiago 64 45.52 N 11.30 E
Asia Menor
— Asia Minor ▫[9] 22 39.00 N 32.00 E
Asia Minor ▫[9] 22 39.00 N 32.00 E
Asid Gulf ⊂ 116 12.07 N 123.30 E
Asie
— Asia ▪[1] 12 50.00 N 100.00 E
Asie Mineure
— Asia Minor ▫[9] 22 39.00 N 32.00 E
Asien
— Asia ▪[1] 12 50.00 N 100.00 E
Āsika 120 19.36 N 84.39 E
Asikuma 150 5.35 N 1.00 W
Asilah 148 35.32 N 6.00 W
Asinara, Golfo dell' ⊂ 71 41.00 N 8.32 E
Asinara, Isola I 71 41.04 N 8.16 E
Asinaro ≏ 70 36.53 N 15.08 E
Asino 86 57.00 N 86.09 E
Asipoquobah Lake ⊜ 184 53.40 N 91.15 W
ʿAsīr ✦[1] 144 19.00 N 42.00 E
Āšītkovo 82 55.26 N 38.36 E
Aşkale 130 39.55 N 40.42 E
Askam in Furness 44 54.11 N 3.13 W
Askaniya-Nova 78 46.27 N 33.52 E
Askarovo 86 53.21 N 58.30 E
Askeaton 48 52.36 N 8.58 W
Asker 26 59.50 N 10.26 E
Askern 44 53.37 N 1.09 W
Askersund 40 58.53 N 14.54 E
Askham 158 26.59 S 20.47 E
Askim 26 59.35 N 11.10 E
Askino 86 56.05 N 56.34 E
Askira 146 10.39 N 12.55 E
Askival ∧ 46 56.59 N 6.17 W
Askiz 86 53.08 N 90.32 E
Askja ∧[1] 24a 65.00 N 16.48 W
Askø I 41 54.54 N 11.30 E
Asköping 40 59.09 N 16.04 E
Askov 41 55.28 N 9.06 E
Askraal 158 34.09 S 20.52 E
Askrigg 44 54.19 N 2.04 W
Askvoll 26 61.21 N 5.04 E
Aslanapa 130 39.13 N 29.52 E
Aslan-Sara 84 39.02 N 48.16 E
Aslantaş Barajı ⊜[1] 130 37.20 N 36.15 E
Åsleigh 284c 39.01 N 77.10 W
Åsljunga 41 56.19 N 13.22 E
Aslyk 86 57.33 N 68.40 E
Aslyk ≏ 86 57.50 N 69.12 E
Asmār 120 35.02 N 71.22 E
Asmara
— Asmera 144 15.20 N 38.53 E
Asmera 144 15.20 N 38.53 E
Åsmundtorp 41 55.53 N 12.56 E
Asnæs 41 55.49 N 11.31 E
Asnæs ≻[1] 41 55.40 N 11.00 E
Åsnen ⊜ 26 56.38 N 14.42 E
Asnebumskit Hill ∧[2] 207 42.18 N 71.54 W
Asnières [-sur-Seine] 50 48.55 N 2.17 E
Asō, Nihon 94 35.59 N 140.29 E
Aso, Nihon 96 32.58 N 131.02 E
Aso ≏ 66 43.06 N 13.51 E
Asoc 152 1.26 N 11.18 E
Aso-kokuritsu-kōen ♦ 92 33.00 N 131.07 E
Asola 64 45.13 N 10.24 E
Asolo 64 45.48 N 11.54 E
Asomante 240m 18.23 N 66.36 W
Ason 273a 6.34 S 3.31 E
Asosa 144 10.03 N 34.32 E
Asotin 202 46.20 N 117.02 W
Aso-san ∧ 92 32.53 N 131.06 E
Asoteriba, Jabal ∧ 140 21.51 N 36.30 E
Asouf, Oued ∨ 148 25.51 N 1.33 E
Asowsches Meer
— Azov, Sea of ≂[2] 78 46.00 N 36.00 E
Asp 38 38.21 N 0.46 W
Aspach 60 48.11 N 13.18 E
Aspach-le-Bas 58 47.46 N 7.09 E
Aspang Markt 61 47.33 N 16.06 E
Aspara ≏ 85 43.17 N 73.28 E
Asparuhovo 38 43.17 N 27.57 E
Aspe, Gave d' ≏ 32 43.12 N 0.36 W
Aspen 200 39.11 N 106.49 W
Aspen Butte ∧ 202 42.19 N 122.05 W
Aspendale 274b 38.02 S 145.07 E
Aspendos ⊥ 130 37.00 N 31.10 E
Aspen Hill 284c 39.04 N 77.04 W
Aspen Knolls 284c 39.05 N 76.55 W
Aspen Lake ⊜ 202 42.18 N 122.00 W
Asperg 56 48.54 N 9.07 E
Aspermont 196 33.08 N 100.13 W
Aspern ✦[8] 264b 48.13 N 16.29 E
Aspers 208 39.59 N 77.13 W
Asperup 41 55.29 N 9.52 E
Aspid, Mount ∧ 184 53.30 N 167.33 W
Aspindza 84 41.36 N 43.15 E
Aspinwall
— Colón, Pan. 236 9.22 N 79.54 W
Aspinwall, Pa., U.S. 279b 40.29 N 79.54 W
Aspiring, Mount ∧ 172 44.23 S 168.44 E
Aspres 62 44.31 N 5.45 E
Aspres-sur-Buëch 62 44.31 N 5.45 E
Aspromonte ⋌ 68 38.10 N 15.55 E
Asprópirgos 267c 38.04 N 23.35 E
Aspull 262 53.34 N 2.35 W
Aspy Bay ⊂ 186 46.55 N 60.25 W
Asquins 50 47.29 N 3.45 E
Asquith, Austl. 274a 33.41 S 151.07 E
Asquith, Sk., Can. 184 52.08 N 107.13 W
Asralt chajrchan ∧ 88 48.29 N 107.24 E
Asrāni 123 29.31 N 72.07 E
Assa, Kaz. 85 43.02 N 71.10 E
Assa, Maroc 148 28.34 N 9.27 W
Assa ≏, Kaz. 85 43.55 N 70.25 E
Assa ≏, Ross. 84 43.14 N 44.39 E
As-Saʿata 140 13.37 N 29.59 E
Assab
— Aseb 144 13.00 N 42.45 E
Assabet ≏ 283 42.28 N 71.21 W
As-Sabkhah 130 35.47 N 39.18 E
As-Sadarah 144 14.30 N 48.04 E
As-Saʿdīyah 128 34.11 N 45.07 E
As-Saff 140 29.34 N 31.17 E
As-Saffānīyah 128 27.58 N 48.47 E
As-Ṣāfī 132 31.02 N 35.28 E
As-Saffīrah 130 36.04 N 37.22 E
As-Ṣāfī 140 15.31 N 30.07 E
Assago 266b 45.24 N 9.08 E
Assai 255 23.22 S 50.49 W
As-Saʿīd ▫[4] 140 26.00 N 32.00 E
Assaikwatamo ≏ 184 56.52 N 95.50 W
Assal, Lac ⊜ 144 11.41 N 42.25 E
ʿAssāl al-Ward 132 33.52 N 36.24 E
As-Sallūmah 140 32.47 N 31.59 E
As-Sallīmah 142 14.02 N 45.46 E
As-Sālimīyah 128 29.20 N 48.05 E
As-Salmān 128 30.30 N 44.32 E
As-Salṭ 132 32.03 N 35.44 E
Assam ▫[3] 120 26.00 N 93.00 E
As-Samāwah 128 31.18 N 45.17 E
As-Samūʿ 132 31.24 N 35.04 E
Assam Valley ∨ 124 26.30 N 90.30 E
ʿAssān 130 36.05 N 37.14 E
As-Sanāfīn Al-Qiblīyah 142 30.27 N 31.18 E
As-Sanamayn 132 33.05 N 36.10 E
As-Santah 142 30.45 N 31.08 E
Assaq, Oued ∨ 148 25.41 N 14.40 W
As-Saqlabiyah 130 35.22 N 36.23 E
As-Sarafand 132 33.27 N 35.18 E
Assaré 250 6.52 S 39.52 W
As-Sarīḥ 132 32.30 N 35.54 E
As-Sarīrīyah 142 28.20 N 30.45 E
Assateague Island I 208 38.05 N 75.10 W
Assateague Island National Seashore ♦ 208 38.00 N 75.15 W
Assawoman Bay ⊂ 208 38.25 N 75.05 W
Assawoman Canal ≡ 208 38.31 N 75.04 W
Assawompset Pond ⊜ 207 41.50 N 70.55 W
Asse 50 50.55 N 4.12 E
Asse ≏ 62 43.53 N 5.53 E
Assean Lake ⊜ 184 56.13 N 96.30 W
Assebroek 50 51.12 N 3.16 E
Assekaifaf 148 28.07 N 8.50 E
Assel 52 53.41 N 9.25 E
Asseln ✦[8] 263 51.32 N 7.35 E
Assembleia Nacional, Palacio da ✪ 266c 38.43 N 9.09 W
Assemini 71 39.17 N 9.00 E
Assen 52 52.59 N 6.34 E
Assendelft 52 52.27 N 4.45 E
Assenede 50 51.14 N 3.45 E
Assens 41 55.16 N 9.55 E
Asserbo 41 56.01 N 12.01 E
Assergi 66 42.25 N 13.30 E
Asseria ⊥ 36 44.02 N 15.39 E
As-Sīb 128 23.41 N 58.11 E
As-Sidr 128 23.27 N 39.45 E
As-Sijn 132 32.47 N 36.28 E
As-Simākīyah 132 31.18 N 35.48 E
As-Sinbillāwayn 142 30.53 N 31.27 E
Assini ⊥ 38 37.36 N 22.48 E
Assiniboia 184 49.38 N 105.59 W
Assiniboine ≏ 184 49.53 N 97.08 W
Assiniboine, Mount ∧ 182 50.52 N 115.39 W
Assiniboine Indian Reserve ✦[4] 184 50.21 N 103.28 W
Assinika ≏ 184 52.37 N 96.10 W
Assinippi 283 42.09 N 70.51 W
Assis 255 22.40 S 50.25 W
Assis Chateaubriand 252 24.29 S 53.32 W
Assiscunk Creek ≏ 285 40.05 N 74.51 W
Assisi 66 43.04 N 12.37 E
Asslar 56 50.35 N 8.28 E
Assling 60 48.00 N 12.00 E
Asso 62 45.52 N 9.16 E
Assodé ≂[4] 150 18.26 N 8.28 E
Assomada 150a 15.06 N 23.41 W
Assonet 207 41.47 N 71.04 W
Assoro 70 37.37 N 14.25 E
As-Subūʿ ⊥ 140 22.45 N 32.34 E
As-Sūdān
— Sudan ▫[1] 140 15.00 N 30.00 E
As-Sudd ✦[1] 140 8.00 N 31.00 E
As-Sufāl 144 14.06 N 48.42 E
As-Sufayyah 140 15.30 N 34.42 E
As-Sūfīyah 140 30.55 N 31.46 E
As-Sukhnah, Sūrīy. 130 34.52 N 38.52 E
As-Sukhnah, Urd. 132 32.08 N 36.04 E
As-Sulaymānīyah, Ar. Su. 128 24.09 N 47.19 E
As-Sulaymānīyah, ʿIrāq 128 35.33 N 45.26 E
As-Sulaymānīyah ▫[4] 128 35.30 N 45.25 E
As-Sulaymī 128 26.17 N 41.21 E
As-Sulayyil 144 20.27 N 45.34 E
As-Sulṭān 146 31.07 N 17.10 E
As-Sumayh 140 9.49 N 27.39 E
As-Summān ✦[1] 128 25.00 N 47.00 E
As-Summāqīyāt 132 32.26 N 36.24 E
Assumption, Il., U.S. 219 39.31 N 89.02 W
Assumption, Oh., U.S. 216 41.40 N 83.54 W
Assumption Island I 138 9.45 S 46.30 E
Assunpink Creek ≏ 285 40.13 N 74.46 W
As-Suʿūdīyah 142 29.33 N 31.14 E
As-Suwār 130 35.30 N 40.39 E
As-Suwaydāʾ 132 32.42 N 36.34 E
As-Suwaydāʾ ▫[8] 132 32.45 N 36.45 E
As-Suways (Suez) 142 29.58 N 32.33 E
As-Suways ▫[4] 142 30.12 N 32.30 E
Assynt, Loch ⊜ 46 58.11 N 5.06 W
Ast 60 48.41 N 11.47 E
Asta, Cima d' ∧ 64 46.10 N 11.36 E
Astaffort 32 44.04 N 0.40 E
Astakós 38 38.32 N 21.05 E
Āstāneh, Īrān 128 37.17 N 49.59 E
Āstāneh, Īrān 128 33.53 N 49.22 E
Astara, Azer. 84 38.28 N 48.52 E
Āstārā, Īrān 128 38.26 N 48.52 E
Astarak 84 40.18 N 44.22 E
Astaškovo 82 55.32 N 38.36 E
Astatula 220 28.43 N 81.44 W
Astemajac de Brizuela 234 20.11 N 103.42 W
Astemar 80 54.11 N 45.24 E
Astemble 164 5.05 S 144.45 E
Atena Lucana 68 40.27 N 15.33 E
Atenango del Río 234 18.05 N 99.06 W
Atenas
— Athínai 38 37.58 N 23.43 E
Atencingo 234 18.30 N 98.36 W
Atengo ≏ 234 21.50 N 104.43 W
Atenguillo 234 20.25 N 104.31 W
Atenguillo ≏ 234 20.55 N 104.38 W
Atenquique 234 19.31 N 103.30 W
Atepecwo 82 55.43 N 38.46 E
Aterau 86 47.07 N 51.56 E
Aterau ▫[4] 86 47.00 N 51.00 E
Aterno ≏ 66 42.11 N 13.51 E
Aterrado, Ribeirão do ≏ 256 22.09 S 45.03 W
Atessa 66 42.04 N 14.27 E
Atfīḥ 142 29.24 N 31.15 E
Atfīḥ, Wādī al- ∨ 142 29.23 N 31.16 E
Ātgharia 126 24.06 N 89.14 E
Atglen 208 39.57 N 75.58 W
Ath 50 50.38 N 3.47 E
Athabasca 182 54.43 N 113.17 W
Athabasca ≏ 176 58.40 N 110.50 W
Athabasca, Lake ⊜ 176 59.07 N 110.00 W
Athalmer 182 50.32 N 116.02 W
Athapapuskow Lake ⊜ 184 54.33 N 101.40 W
Athārabānki ≏[1] 126 22.49 N 89.39 E
Athārbāri Hazāri 124 25.53 N 82.10 E
Athboy 48 53.37 N 6.55 W
Athea 48 52.28 N 9.17 W
Athen
— Athínai 38 37.58 N 23.43 E
Athena 202 45.48 N 118.29 W
Athènes
— Athínai 38 37.58 N 23.43 E
Athenry 48 53.18 N 8.45 W
Athens, Ont., Can. 212 44.38 N 75.57 W
Athens
— Athínai, Ellás 38 37.58 N 23.43 E
Athens, Al., U.S. 194 34.48 N 86.58 W
Athens, Ga., U.S. 192 33.57 N 83.22 W
Athens, Il., U.S. 219 39.57 N 89.43 W
Athens, La., U.S. 194 32.39 N 93.01 W
Athens, Mi., U.S. 216 42.05 N 85.14 W
Athens, N.Y., U.S. 210 42.15 N 73.48 W
Athens, Oh., U.S. 188 39.19 N 82.06 W
Athens, Pa., U.S. 210 41.57 N 76.31 W
Athens, Tn., U.S. 192 35.26 N 84.35 W
Athens, Tx., U.S. 222 32.12 N 95.51 W
Athens, W.V., U.S. 192 37.25 N 81.00 W
Athens, Wi., U.S. 190 45.01 N 90.04 W
Athenstedt 54 51.56 N 10.55 E
Athens University ✪[2] 267c 37.59 N 23.44 E
Asti 62 44.54 N 8.12 E
Asti ▫[4] 62 44.55 N 8.10 E
Astica 252 30.56 S 67.23 W
Astico ≏ 64 45.37 N 11.37 E
Astillero 248 12.36 S 69.13 W
Astipálaia 38 36.33 N 26.21 E
Astipálaia I 38 36.35 N 26.25 E
Astley Bridge 262 53.36 N 2.26 W
Astley Green 262 53.29 N 2.27 W
Astley Hall ⊥ 262 53.39 N 2.38 W
Astola Island I 120 25.07 N 63.51 E
Astolfo Dutra 256 21.19 S 42.52 W
Aston, Eng., U.K. 262 53.18 N 2.40 W
Aston, Pa., U.S. 285 39.52 N 75.26 W
Aston Clinton 42 51.48 N 0.44 W
Aston-on-Trent 42 52.52 N 1.23 W
Astor 123 35.22 N 74.51 E
Astor ≏ 123 35.34 N 74.41 E
Astorga, Bra. 255 23.13 S 51.40 W
Astorga, Esp. 34 42.27 N 6.03 W
Astorga, Pil. 116 6.54 N 125.27 E
Astoria, Il., U.S. 219 40.13 N 90.21 W
Astoria, Or., U.S. 224 46.11 N 123.49 W
Astoria ✦[8] 276 40.46 N 73.55 W
Astoria Bridge ✦[5] 224 46.13 N 123.52 W
Astoria Column ⊥ 224 46.11 N 123.50 W
Astorp 41 56.08 N 12.57 E
Astove Island I 138 10.06 S 47.45 E
Astrachan' 80 46.21 N 48.03 E
Astrachanka 86 51.33 N 69.47 E
Astrachan' Oblast' ▫[4] 80 47.00 N 47.30 E
Astrachanskij 80 46.12 N 47.16 E
Astrachanskij zapovednik ✦[4] 80 46.00 N 48.32 E
Astrakhan
— Astrachan' 80 46.21 N 48.03 E
Astrakhan 222 29.41 N 95.25 W
Astrodome ♦ 175e 8.20 S 160.34 E
Astrolabe, Cape ≻ 164 5.20 S 145.50 E
Astrolabe Bay ⊂ 175i 19.48 S 165.37 E
Astrolabe Reefs ✢[2] 64 45.16 N 8.50 E
Astrudillo 66 41.24 N 12.46 E
Astura, Torre ⊥ 116 10.34 N 123.43 E
Asturias 34 43.20 N 6.00 W
Asturias ▫[4], Esp. 34 43.20 N 6.00 W
Asturias ▫[4], Esp. 34 43.20 N 6.00 W
Asturias ▫[9] 42 52.15 N 1.56 W
Astwood Bank 86 49.31 N 83.03 E
Asubulak 175a 14.17 S 170.42 W
Asuisui, Cape ≻ 94 34.28 N 135.50 E
Asuka 9 71.32 S 24.08 E
Asuka ✪[3] 94 35.08 N 137.19 E
Asuke 252 25.16 S 57.40 W
Asunción 232 27.06 N 114.11 W
Asunción, Bahía ⊂
Asuncion Island I 108 19.40 N 145.24 E
Asunción Ixtaltepec 234 16.30 N 95.03 W
Asunción Mita 236 14.20 N 89.43 W
Asunción Nochixtlán 234 17.28 N 97.14 W
Åsunden ⊜, Sve. 26 57.58 N 15.50 E
Åsunden ⊜, Sve. 26 57.44 N 13.22 E
Asunga, Wādī ∨ 146 13.21 N 22.17 E
Asuni 71 39.52 N 8.56 E
ʿĀṣūr, Tall ∧ 132 31.59 N 35.17 E
Asuwa 94 36.01 N 136.16 E
Asuwa ≏ 94 36.04 N 136.11 E
Aswad, Ar-Raʾs al- ≻ 144 21.22 N 39.08 E
Aswān 140 24.05 N 32.53 E
Aswān High Dam
— ʿĀlī, As-Sadd al- ✦[6] 140 23.58 N 32.52 E
Aswatthaberia 272b 22.26 N 88.32 E
Asy ≏ 85 43.31 N 78.20 E
Asyūṭ 142 27.11 N 31.11 E
Asyūṭ ▫[4] 142 27.20 N 30.50 E
Asyūṭī, Wādī al- ∨ 142 27.11 N 31.16 E
Aszód 30 47.39 N 19.31 E
ʿAta I, Tonga 14 22.20 S 176.12 W
Ata I, Tonga 174w 21.03 S 175.00 W
Atabaj 85 43.30 N 68.20 E
Atabapo ≏ 246 4.03 N 67.42 W
Atabasca
— Athabasca ≏ 176 58.40 N 110.50 W
Atabasca, Lago
— Athabasca, Lake ⊜ 176 59.07 N 110.00 W
Atabey 130 37.57 N 30.39 E
Atacama ▫[4] 252 27.30 S 70.00 W
Atacama, Desierto de ✦[2] 18 24.30 S 69.15 W
Atacama, Puna de ✦[1] 252 24.30 S 67.30 W
Atacama, Salar de ≚ 252 23.30 S 68.15 W
Ataco 246 3.35 N 75.23 W
Atacora, Chaîne de l' ⋌ 150 10.45 N 1.30 E
Atacuari ≏ 246 3.47 S 70.44 W
Atafu I[1] 14 8.33 S 172.30 W
Atagaj 88 55.06 N 99.23 E
Atago-yama ∧, Nihon 94 35.07 N 139.59 E
Atago-yama ∧, Nihon 96 35.03 N 135.37 E
Ātāi ≏[1] 126 22.51 N 89.33 E
ʿAṭʿitah, Jabal al- ∧ 132 30.40 N 35.39 E
Atakakup Indian Reserve ✦[4] 184 53.24 N 106.55 W
Atakano-seki ⊥ 94 36.24 N 136.25 E
Atakora ▫[5] 150 10.00 N 1.35 E
Atakora, Réserve d' ✦[4] 150 11.30 N 2.10 E
Atakpamé 150 7.32 N 1.08 E
Atalaia, Bra. 250 9.31 S 36.02 W
Atalaia, Port. 266c 38.41 N 8.55 W
Atalándi 38 38.39 N 23.00 E
Atalanka 88 54.50 N 103.05 E
Atalaya, Arg. 258 35.02 S 57.32 W
Atalaya, Pan. 236 8.03 N 80.56 W
Atalaya, Perú 248 10.44 S 73.45 W
Atalaya, Cerro ∧, Chile 254 52.45 S 72.42 W
Atalaya, Cerro ∧, Perú 248 12.38 S 71.56 W
Atalaya, Punta ≻ 258 35.01 S 57.31 W
Atamanovka 88 51.56 N 113.37 E
Atamanovo 86 56.24 N 93.36 E
Atambua 112 9.07 S 124.54 E
Atami 94 35.05 N 139.04 E
Atapupu 112 9.00 S 124.51 E
ʿAṭāq 144 14.33 N 46.48 E
ʿAṭāqah, Jabal ∧ 142 29.58 N 32.20 E
Atār 150 20.31 N 13.03 W
Atarm, ʿErg n- ✦[2] 148 23.46 N 1.44 E
Atarés, Castillo de ⊥ 286b 23.08 N 82.21 W
Atāri 123 31.36 N 74.35 E
Atary 80 57.32 N 49.18 E
Atascadero 226 35.29 N 120.40 W
Atascosa ≏ 196 28.26 N 98.12 W
Atʾaševo 80 54.36 N 46.06 E
Atasu 86 48.42 N 71.38 E
Atas uul ∧ 102 43.18 N 96.36 E
Atata I 174w 21.03 S 175.15 W
Atatürk Barajı ⊜[1] 130 37.30 N 38.30 E
Ataturk Tower ⊥ 267b 41.00 N 28.59 E
Atauro, Pulau I 272a 28.43 N 77.24 E
Atbara (ʿAṭbarah) ≏ 112 8.13 S 125.35 E
ʿAṭbarah 140 17.40 N 33.56 E
ʿAṭbarah (Atbara) ≏ 140 17.42 N 33.59 E
Atbasar 86 51.48 N 68.20 E
At-Baši 85 41.10 N 75.48 E
Atbaši ≏ 85 41.24 N 75.38 E
Atbaši, chrebet ∧ 85 40.55 N 75.40 E
Atchafalaya ≏ 194 29.53 N 91.28 W
Atchafalaya Bay ⊂ 194 29.25 N 91.20 W
Atchison 198 39.33 N 95.07 W
Atco 208 39.46 N 74.53 W
Ate 286 12.03 S 76.58 W
Atebubu 150 7.45 N 0.59 W
Ateca 34 41.20 N 1.47 W
Ateichu ≏ 255 12.05 S 53.46 W
Ateleta 66 41.51 N 14.12 E
Ateli 124 28.06 N 76.17 E
Atella 68 40.52 N 15.39 E
Atherley 212 44.36 N 79.22 W
Atherstone 42 52.35 N 1.31 W
Atherton, Austl. 166 17.16 S 145.29 E
Atherton, Eng., U.K. 44 53.31 N 2.31 W
Atherton, Ca., U.S. 226 37.27 N 122.11 W
Athi ≏ 154 2.59 S 38.31 E
Athiainou 130 35.04 N 33.32 E
Athiémé 150 6.35 N 1.40 E
Athies-sous-Laon 50 49.34 N 3.41 E
Athínai (Athens), Ellás 38 37.58 N 23.43 E
Athínai (Athens), Ellás 267c 37.58 N 23.43 E
Āthiopien
— Ethiopia ▫[1] 144 9.00 N 39.00 E
Athi River 154 1.27 S 36.59 E
Athis-Mons 261 48.43 N 2.24 E
Athlat al-Bāshā ∧[2] 142 27.31 N 32.20 E
Athleague 48 53.34 N 8.15 W
Athlone 48 53.25 N 7.56 W
Athni 122 16.44 N 75.04 E
Athok 110 17.12 N 95.05 E
Athol, N.Z. 172 45.31 S 168.35 E
Athol, Ma., U.S. 207 42.35 N 72.13 W
Athol Bay ⊂ 212 43.53 N 77.15 W
Athol Island I 240b 25.05 N 77.16 W
Atholl, Forest of ✦[3] 46 56.50 N 4.00 W
Athol Springs 210 42.46 N 78.52 W
Áthos ∧ 38 40.09 N 24.19 E
Ath-Thaʿlah 132 32.42 N 36.26 E
Ath-Thamad 140 29.41 N 34.18 E
Ath-Tharīyah 132 31.10 N 35.43 E
Athus 56 49.34 N 5.50 E
Athy 48 53.00 N 7.00 W
Ati 146 13.13 N 18.20 E
Atiak 154 3.15 N 32.07 E
Atibaia 256 23.07 S 46.33 W
Atibainha ≏ 256 22.42 S 47.17 W
Atibainha, Reservatório ⊜[1] 256 23.10 S 46.20 W
Atico 248 16.14 S 73.39 W
Aticonipi, Lac ⊜ 186 51.52 N 59.22 W
Atienza 34 41.12 N 2.52 W
Atigun Pass ⋊ 180 68.08 N 149.29 W
Atik Lake ⊜ 184 55.16 N 96.00 W
Atikokan 190 48.45 N 91.37 W
Atikonak Lake ⊜ 176 52.40 N 64.30 W
Atil 200 30.50 N 111.35 W
Atimari ≏ 248 9.04 S 67.23 W
Atimonan 116 14.00 N 121.55 E
Atina 66 41.37 N 13.48 E
Atiparanā ≏[1] 246 1.51 S 65.37 W
Atiquizaya 236 13.58 N 89.46 W
Atirāmpattinam 122 10.21 N 79.24 E
Atitlán, Lago de ⊜ 236 14.42 N 91.12 W
Atitlán, Volcán ∧[1] 236 14.35 N 91.11 W
Atiu I 14 20.02 S 158.07 W
Atka, Ross. 74 60.50 N 151.48 E
Atka, Ak., U.S. 180 52.12 N 174.12 W
Atka Island I 180 52.15 N 174.30 W
Atkaracalar 130 40.50 N 33.04 E
Atkarsk 80 51.52 N 45.00 E
Atkins 194 35.14 N 92.56 W
Atkinson, Il., U.S. 190 41.25 N 90.00 W
Atkinson, Ne., U.S. 198 42.31 N 98.58 W
Atkinson, N.H., U.S. 207 42.50 N 71.08 W
Atkinson, N.C., U.S. 192 34.31 N 78.10 W
Atkinson Island I 222 29.40 N 94.58 W
Atkinson Lake ⊜ 184 55.59 N 94.48 W
Atkri 164 1.44 S 130.04 E
Atlacomulco 234 19.48 N 99.53 W
Atlanta, Ga., U.S. 192 33.44 N 84.23 W
Atlanta, Il., U.S. 194 40.15 N 89.14 W
Atlanta, Mi., U.S. 190 45.00 N 84.08 W
Atlanta, Mo., U.S. 194 39.53 N 92.28 W
Atlanta, N.Y., U.S. 210 42.33 N 77.28 W
Atlanta, Oh., U.S. 218 39.34 N 83.11 W
Atlanta, Tx., U.S. 194 33.06 N 94.09 W
Atlantic, Ia., U.S. 198 41.24 N 95.00 W
Atlantic, N.C., U.S. 192 34.53 N 76.20 W
Atlantic, Pa., U.S. 214 41.30 N 80.21 W
Atlantic, Va., U.S. 208 37.54 N 75.30 W
Atlantic ≏ 208 39.27 N 74.44 W
Atlantic Beach, Fl., U.S. 192 30.20 N 81.23 W
Atlantic Beach, N.Y., U.S. 276 40.35 N 73.44 W
Atlantic City 208 39.21 N 74.25 W
Atlantic Highlands 208 40.24 N 74.02 W
Atlantic-Indian Basin ✢[1] 6 60.00 S 15.00 E
Atlantic-Indian Ridge ✢[3] 4 53.00 S 15.00 E
Atlántico ▫[5] 246 10.45 N 75.00 W
Atlántico, Océano
— Atlantic Ocean ≂[1] 8 5.00 S 25.00 W
Atlantic Ocean ≂[1] 4 5.00 S 25.00 W
Atlantic Ocean ≂[1] 8 5.00 S 25.00 W
Atlantic Peak ∧ 200 42.37 N 109.00 W
Atlántida 252 34.46 S 55.45 W
Atlántida ▫[5] 236 15.40 N 87.00 W
Atlantique 276 40.39 N 73.10 W
Atlantique ▫[5] 150 6.35 N 2.15 E
Atlantique, Océan
— Atlantic Ocean ≂[1] 8 5.00 S 25.00 W
Atlantischer Ozean
— Atlantic Ocean ≂[1] 8 5.00 S 25.00 W
Atlas, Mi., U.S. 216 42.56 N 83.32 W
Atlas, Pa., U.S. 208 40.48 N 76.26 W
Atlasburg 214 40.20 N 80.23 W
Atlas Mountains ∧ 148 33.00 N 2.00 W
Atlasova, ostrov I 74 50.53 N 155.27 E
Atlasovo 92a 46.01 N 142.09 E
Atlas Saharien ∧ 148 33.25 N 1.20 E
Atlas Tellien ⋌ 148 36.00 N 3.00 E
Atlin 180 59.35 N 133.42 W
Atlin Lake ⊜ 180 59.20 N 133.45 W
Atlit 132 32.41 N 34.56 E
Atlixco 234 18.54 N 98.26 W
Ātmakūr 122 15.53 N 78.35 E
Atmanov Ugol 80 53.07 N 41.23 E
Atmis 80 53.28 N 43.57 E
Atmore 194 31.01 N 87.29 W
Atna ≏ — Etna, Monte ∧[1] 70 37.46 N 15.00 E
Atna ≏ 26 61.44 N 10.49 E
Atna Peak ∧ 182 53.57 N 128.03 W
Atnarko ≏ 182 52.22 N 126.04 W
Atnis 88 58.48 N 69.38 E
Atnosen 26 61.44 N 10.49 E
Atō 96 34.24 N 131.43 E
Atocha 248 20.56 S 66.14 W
Atocha, Estación de ✦[5] 266a 40.24 N 3.41 W
Atocongo 286d 12.08 S 76.56 W
Atocongo ⊥ 286d 12.12 S 76.55 W
Atoka 196 34.23 N 96.07 W
Atotonilco 232 24.15 N 102.45 W
Atotonilco, Cerro ∧ 234 20.18 N 104.13 W
Atotonilco, Lago ⊜ 234 20.22 N 103.39 W
Atotonilco de Tula 234 20.00 N 99.13 W
Atotonilco El Alto 234 20.33 N 102.31 W
Atoui, Khaṭṭ ∨ 150 20.04 N 15.59 W
Atoyac 234 20.01 N 103.32 W
Atoyac ≏, Méx. 234 17.05 N 100.29 W
Atoyac ≏, Méx. 234 18.10 N 98.31 W
Atoyac ≏, Méx. 234 16.30 N 97.31 W
Atoyac ≏, Méx. 234 19.02 N 96.08 W
Atoyac de Álvarez 234 17.12 N 100.26 W
Atoyaquillo ≏ 234 18.37 N 97.41 W
Atpur 272b 22.50 N 88.29 E
Atrā 26 59.59 N 8.45 E
ʿAtrah, Jabal ∧ 132 29.50 N 35.34 E
Atrai ≏ 124 24.29 N 89.03 E
Atrak (Atrek) ≏ 128 37.28 N 53.57 E
Atran ≏ 26 56.53 N 12.30 E
Atrato ≏ 246 8.17 N 76.58 W
Atrauli 124 28.02 N 78.17 E
Atrek (Atrak) ≏ 128 37.28 N 53.57 E
Atri 66 42.35 N 13.59 E
Atripalda 68 40.55 N 14.50 E
Atrisco 200 34.59 N 106.41 W

Symbols in the index entries represent the broad categories identified in the key at the right. Symbols with superior numbers (⋌[1]) identify subcategories (see complete key on page I · 1).

Symbole im Register stellen die rechts im Schlüssel erklärten Kategorien dar. Symbole mit hochgestellten Ziffern (⋌[1]) bezeichnen Unterabteilungen einer Kategorie (vgl. vollständiger Schlüssel auf Seite I · 1).

Los símbolos incluidos en el texto del índice representan las grandes categorías identificadas con la clave a la derecha. Los símbolos con números en su parte superior (⋌[1]) identifican las subcategorías (véase la clave completa en la página I · 1).

Les symboles de l'index représentent les catégories indiquées dans la légende à droite. Les symboles suivis d'un indice (⋌[1]) représentent des sous-catégories (voir légende complète à la page I · 1).

Os símbolos incluídos no texto do índice representam as grandes categorias identificadas com a chave à direita. Os símbolos com números em sua parte superior (⋌[1]) identificam as subcategorias (veja-se a chave completa à página I · 1).

ENGLISH	DEUTSCH	ESPAÑOL	FRANÇAIS	PORTUGUÊS
∧ Mountain	Berg	Montaña	Montagne	Montanha
∧ Mountains	Gebirge	Montañas	Montagnes	Montanhas
⋊ Pass	Paß	Paso	Col	Passo
∨ Valley, Canyon	Tal, Cañon	Valle, Cañón	Vallée, Canyon	Vale, Canhão
≚ Plain	Ebene	Llano	Plaine	Planície
≻ Cape	Kap	Cabo	Cap	Cabo
I Island	Insel	Isla	Île	Ilha
II Islands	Inseln	Islas	Îles	Ilhas
✦ Other Topographic Features	Andere Topographische Objekte	Otros Elementos Topográficos	Autres données topographiques	Outros acidentes topográficos

ESPAÑOL

Nombre	Página	Lat.°′	Long.°′ W = Oeste
Atrop ◆ 8	263	51.24 N	6.43 E
Atsion Lake ⊜	285	39.44 N	74.44 W
Atsugi	94	35.27 N	139.22 E
Atsugi-hikōjō ■	94	35.28 N	139.27 E
Atsumi, Nihon	92	38.37 N	139.35 E
Atsumi, Nihon	94	34.37 N	137.07 E
Atsumi-hantō ≻ 1	94	34.39 N	137.15 E
Atta	272a	28.34 N	77.20 E
At-Tabbīn	142	29.47 N	31.18 E
Aṭ-Ṭafīlah	132	30.50 N	35.36 E
Aṭ-Ṭafīlah □ 8	132	30.45 N	35.45 E
At-Taḥrīr □ 4	142	30.40 N	30.15 E
Aṭ-Ṭā'if	144	21.16 N	40.24 E
Attainville	261	49.03 N	2.21 E
At-Tāj	146	24.13 N	23.18 E
Aṭ-Ṭalibīyah	273c	30.00 N	31.11 E
At-Tall	132	33.36 N	36.18 E
Attalla	194	34.01 N	86.05 W
At-Tall al-Kabīr	142	30.34 N	31.47 E
At-Ta'mīm □ 4	128	35.25 N	44.20 E
At-Tamīmī	146	32.20 N	23.04 E
Attapu	110	14.48 N	106.50 E
Attar, Oued el V	148	33.27 N	5.26 E
At-Taṭālīyah	142	27.20 N	30.50 E
Attáviros ∧	38	36.12 N	27.52 E
Attawapiskat	176	52.55 N	82.26 W
Attawapiskat ≃	176	52.57 N	82.18 W
Attawapiskat Lake ⊜	176	52.18 N	87.54 W
Attawaugan	207	41.52 N	71.52 W
Aṭ-Ṭawd	142	30.47 N	30.37 E
Aṭ-Ṭawīl ⋏	128	29.20 N	39.35 E
Aṭ-Ṭayrīyah	142	30.39 N	30.46 E
At-Taysīyah ⩡	128	28.00 N	44.00 E
Aṭ-Ṭayyibah, Miṣr	142	28.16 N	30.39 E
Aṭ-Ṭayyibah, Sūrīy.	132	32.33 N	36.14 E
Aṭ-Ṭayyibah, Sūrīy.	132	32.48 N	36.46 E
Aṭ-Ṭayyibah, Urd.	132	32.33 N	35.43 E
Attel ≃	64	48.01 N	12.11 E
Attendorn	56	51.07 N	7.54 E
Attenhausen	58	47.59 N	10.20 E
Attenkirchen	60	48.30 N	11.46 E
Atterbury	219	40.04 N	89.55 W
Attersee	64	47.55 N	13.33 E
Attersee ⊜	64	47.52 N	13.33 E
Attert ≃	56	49.52 N	6.05 E
Attica, In., U.S.	216	40.17 N	87.14 W
Attica, Ks., U.S.	198	37.14 N	98.13 W
Attica, N.Y., U.S.	210	42.51 N	78.16 W
Attica, Oh., U.S.	214	41.03 N	82.53 W
Attica → Attikí □ 9	38	38.10 N	23.20 E
Attichy	50	49.25 N	3.03 E
Attigliano	66	42.31 N	12.17 E
Attigny	56	49.29 N	4.35 E
Attikí □ 4	38	38.00 N	23.45 E
Attikí □ 9	38	38.10 N	23.20 E
'Attīl	132	32.22 N	35.04 E
Attimis	64	46.11 N	13.16 E
At-Tīnah	142	31.03 N	32.18 E
Attingal	122	8.41 N	76.50 E
Attir	140	6.04 N	30.50 E
Attleboro	207	41.56 N	71.17 W
Attleborough	42	52.31 N	1.01 E
Attnang	60	48.01 N	13.43 E
Attock	123	33.54 N	72.15 E
Attoyac ≃	194	31.29 N	94.18 W
Attu	181a	52.56 N	173.14 E
At-Tubah	144	12.40 N	43.30 E
Attu Island I	181a	52.55 N	173.00 E
Aṭ-Ṭunayb	132	31.48 N	35.57 E
Āttūr, India	122	11.36 N	78.37 E
Aṭ-Ṭūr, Miṣr	140	28.14 N	33.37 E
Aṭ-Ṭuwayshah	140	12.21 N	26.32 E
Aṭ-Ṭuwayyah	128	27.36 N	41.13 E
Attymon	48	53.19 N	8.35 W
Atucatiquini ≃	248	7.44 S	67.57 W
Atucha	258	33.58 S	59.18 W
Atuel ≃	252	36.17 S	66.50 W
Atuel, Bañados del ⁝	252	36.30 S	66.55 W
Atuntaqui	246	0.20 N	78.13 W
Atuona	174x	9.48 S	139.02 W
At'urjevo	80	54.21 N	43.19 E
Atushi	85	39.43 N	76.08 E
Åtvidaberg	26	58.12 N	16.00 E
Atwater, Sk., Can.	184	50.47 N	102.10 W
Atwater, Ca., U.S.	226	37.20 N	120.36 W
Atwater, Il., U.S.	219	39.20 N	89.44 W
Atwater, Mn., U.S.	198	45.08 N	94.46 W
Atwater, Oh., U.S.	214	41.01 N	81.10 W
Atwood, On., Can.	212	43.40 N	81.01 W
Atwood, Ca., U.S.	280	33.52 N	117.50 W
Atwood, Il., U.S.	194	39.48 N	88.28 W
Atwood, In., U.S.	216	41.15 N	85.58 W
Atwood, Ks., U.S.	198	39.48 N	101.02 W
Atwood, Tn., U.S.	194	35.58 N	88.40 W
Atwood Lake ⊜ 1	214	40.33 N	81.13 W
Atzalpur	272a	28.43 N	77.21 E
Atzendorf	54	51.55 N	11.35 E
Atzgersdorf ◆ 8	264b	48.09 N	16.18 E
Au	58	47.19 N	9.59 E
Auagrām	126	23.31 N	87.41 E
Auaiá-Miçu ≃	250	10.51 S	53.08 W
Aua Island I	164	1.27 S	143.04 E
Aual Edo	144	4.14 N	40.37 E
Auari ≃	246	3.33 N	63.48 W
Auau Channel ⊔	229a	20.51 N	156.45 W
Aub	56	49.33 N	10.04 E
Aubá	112	9.02 S	125.22 E
Aubagne	62	43.17 N	5.34 E
Aubange	56	49.35 N	5.48 E
Aube □ 5	32	48.15 N	4.05 E
Aube ≃	32	48.34 N	3.43 E
Aubenas	62	44.37 N	4.23 E
Aubenton	50	49.50 N	4.12 E
Aubepierre	261	48.38 N	2.53 E
Aubergenville	261	48.58 N	1.51 E
Auberive	58	47.47 N	5.03 E
Auberry	226	37.04 N	119.29 W
Aubervilliers	50	48.55 N	2.23 E
Aubetin ≃	50	48.49 N	3.01 E
Aubette ≃	261	49.00 N	1.54 E
Aubigny-en-Artois	50	50.21 N	2.35 E
Aubigny-sur-Nère	50	47.29 N	2.26 E
Aubin	32	44.32 N	2.14 E
Aubinadong ≃	190	46.51 N	83.22 W
Aubonne	58	46.28 N	6.24 E
Auboué	56	49.13 N	5.59 E
Aubrac ⋏	32	44.40 N	3.00 E
Aubrey Cliffs ⩡ 4	200	35.45 N	113.00 W
Aubrey Lake ⊜ 1	190	46.54 N	83.11 W
Aubrives	56	50.06 N	4.46 E
Aubry Lake ⊜	180	67.23 N	126.30 W
Auburn, Austl.	168b	34.01 S	138.41 E
Auburn, Austl.	274a	33.51 S	151.02 E
Auburn, Al., U.S.	194	32.36 N	85.28 W
Auburn, Ca., U.S.	226	38.53 N	121.04 W
Auburn, Il., U.S.	219	39.35 N	89.44 W
Auburn, In., U.S.	216	41.22 N	85.03 W
Auburn, Ky., U.S.	194	37.02 N	86.54 W
Auburn, Me., U.S.	188	44.05 N	70.13 W
Auburn, Ma., U.S.	207	42.11 N	71.50 W
Auburn, Mi., U.S.	190	43.36 N	84.04 W
Auburn, Ne., U.S.	198	40.23 N	95.50 W
Auburn, N.J., U.S.	285	39.42 N	75.22 W
Auburn, N.Y., U.S.	210	42.55 N	76.33 W
Auburn, Pa., U.S.	208	40.35 N	76.05 W
Auburn, Wa., U.S.	224	47.18 N	122.13 W
Auburn ≃	166	25.38 S	151.12 E
Auburndale, Fl., U.S.	220	28.03 N	81.47 W
Auburndale, Ma., U.S.	283	42.21 N	71.22 W
Auburn Heights	216	42.38 N	83.13 W
Auburn Hills, Palace of ♠	281	42.41 N	83.14 W
Auburn Range ⋏	166	25.10 S	150.30 E
Auburn Ravine V	226	38.51 N	121.31 W
Auburn Southeast	210	42.54 N	76.32 W
Aubusson	32	45.57 N	2.11 E
Auby-sur-Semois	56	49.49 N	5.10 E
Auca Mahuida	252	37.53 S	68.31 W
Auca Mahuida, Cerro ∧	252	37.45 S	68.56 W
Aucará	248	14.15 S	74.05 W

FRANÇAIS

Nom	Page	Lat.°′	Long.°′ W = Ouest
Auce	76	56.28 N	22.53 E
Auch	32	43.39 N	0.35 E
Auchel	50	50.30 N	2.28 E
Auchenblae	46	56.54 N	2.26 W
Auchencairn	44	54.51 N	3.53 W
Auchi	150	7.02 N	6.14 E
Auchinleck	44	55.28 N	4.17 W
Auchterarder	46	56.18 N	3.43 W
Auchterderran	46	56.09 N	3.16 W
Auchtermuchty	46	56.17 N	3.15 W
Aucilla ≃	192	30.05 N	83.59 W
Auckland	172	36.52 S	174.46 E
Auckland Islands II	9	50.40 S	166.30 E
Auckland Park ◆ 8	273d	26.11 S	28.00 E
Auckland Park Race Course ♠	273d	26.11 S	28.00 E
Aude □ 5	32	43.05 N	2.30 E
Aude ≃	32	43.13 N	3.14 E
Audenge	32	44.41 N	1.00 W
Audenshaw	262	53.28 N	2.08 W
Audenshaw Reservoirs ⊜ 1	262	53.28 N	2.08 W
Auderghem	50	50.49 N	4.26 E
Audeux	58	47.16 N	5.53 E
Audierne	32	48.01 N	4.32 W
Audincourt	58	47.29 N	6.50 E
Audley	44	53.03 N	2.18 W
Audo Range ⋏	144	6.30 N	41.30 E
Audrain □ 6	219	39.12 N	91.50 W
Audresselles	50	50.49 N	1.36 E
Audruicq	50	50.53 N	2.05 E
Audubon, Ia., U.S.	198	41.43 N	94.55 W
Audubon, N.J., U.S.	208	39.53 N	75.04 W
Audubon, Pa., U.S.	285	40.07 N	75.27 W
Audubon Lake ⊜ 1	198	47.35 N	101.10 W
Audubon Park, Ky., U.S.	218	38.12 N	85.43 W
Audubon Park, N.J., U.S.	285	39.54 N	75.05 W
Audun-le-Roman	56	49.22 N	5.53 E
Aue	54	50.35 N	12.42 E
Aue ≃	52	53.11 N	7.41 E
Auer → Ora	64	46.21 N	11.18 E
Auerbach, Dtsch.	54	50.41 N	12.54 E
Auerbach, Dtsch.	54	50.30 N	12.23 E
Auerbach, Dtsch.	60	48.48 N	13.06 E
Auerbach in der Oberpfalz	60	49.42 N	11.38 E
Auersberg ∧	54	50.27 N	12.39 E
Auerswalde	54	50.54 N	12.55 E
Auezov	86	49.46 N	81.38 E
Auf dem Kreinberge	263	51.27 N	7.36 E
Auffargis	261	48.42 N	1.53 E
Auffay	50	49.43 N	1.06 E
Aufsess	60	49.54 N	11.13 E
Augarten ♠	264b	48.14 N	16.23 E
Augathella	166	25.48 S	146.35 E
Augher	48	54.26 N	7.09 W
Aughnacloy	48	54.25 N	6.58 W
Aughrim	48	52.51 N	6.17 W
Aughton, Eng., U.K.	44	53.22 N	1.18 W
Aughton, Eng., U.K.	262	53.32 N	2.56 W
Aughton Park	262	53.33 N	2.53 W
Aughwick Creek ≃	214	40.22 N	77.50 W
Auglaize □ 6	216	40.34 N	84.12 W
Auglaize ≃	216	41.17 N	84.21 W
Augrabies	158	28.37 S	20.20 E
Augrabies Falls National Park ♠	158	28.35 S	20.19 E
Augrabiesvalle ʟ	158	28.35 S	20.19 E
Au Gres	190	44.02 N	83.41 W
Au Gres ≃	190	44.02 N	83.40 W
Au Gres, East Branch ≃	190	44.05 N	83.41 W
Augsburg	58	48.23 N	10.53 E
Augšlīgatne	76	57.14 N	25.02 E
Augusta, Austl.	162	34.19 S	115.10 E
Augusta, It.	70	37.13 N	15.13 E
Augusta, Ar., U.S.	194	35.16 N	91.21 W
Augusta, Ga., U.S.	192	33.28 N	82.01 W
Augusta, Il., U.S.	194	40.13 N	90.57 W
Augusta, Ks., U.S.	198	37.41 N	97.58 W
Augusta, Ky., U.S.	218	38.46 N	84.00 W
Augusta, Me., U.S.	188	44.18 N	69.46 W
Augusta, Mi., U.S.	216	42.20 N	85.21 W
Augusta, Mo., U.S.	219	38.34 N	90.53 W
Augusta, Mt., U.S.	202	47.29 N	112.23 W
Augusta, N.J., U.S.	210	41.07 N	74.43 W
Augusta, Oh., U.S.	214	40.41 N	81.01 W
Augusta, Wi., U.S.	190	44.40 N	91.07 W
Augusta, Golfo di ⊂	70	37.12 N	15.13 E
Augustdorf	52	51.53 N	8.43 E
Augustenborg	41	54.57 N	9.53 E
Augustine Island I	180	59.22 N	153.28 W
Augusto Severo	250	5.52 S	37.19 W
Augustów	30	53.51 N	22.59 E
Augustowski, Kanał ≊	76	53.54 N	23.26 E
Augustus, Mount ∧	162	24.20 S	116.50 E
Augustusburg	54	50.49 N	13.06 E
Augustus Downs	166	18.33 S	139.52 E
Augustus Island I	164	15.20 S	124.30 E
Auila, Ribeirão ≃	255	12.09 S	53.20 W
Au in der Hallertau	60	48.33 N	11.45 E
Aujon ≃	58	48.09 N	4.48 E
Auki	175e	8.46 S	160.42 E
Aulander	192	36.13 N	77.06 W
Aulanko	26	61.02 N	24.27 E
Auld, Lake ⊜	162	22.32 S	123.44 E
Auldearn	46	57.34 N	3.49 W
Aulendorf	58	47.57 N	9.38 E
Aulestad	26	61.13 N	10.17 E
Auletta	68	40.34 N	15.25 E
Aulla	64	44.12 N	9.58 E
Aulnay	32	46.01 N	0.21 W
Aulnay-sous-Bois	50	48.57 N	2.31 E
Aulnay-sur-Mauldre	261	48.56 N	1.51 E
Aulne ≃	32	48.17 N	4.16 W
Aulneau Peninsula ≻ 1	184	49.23 N	94.29 W
Aulnois-sur-Seille	56	48.52 N	6.19 E
Aulnoye-Aymeries	50	50.12 N	3.50 E
Ault, Fr.	50	50.06 N	1.27 E
Ault, Co., U.S.	200	40.34 N	104.43 W
Ault, Ky., U.S.	218	38.12 N	83.14 W
Aultbea	46	57.50 N	5.35 W
Aultman	214	40.34 N	79.16 W
Aultshire	216	40.13 N	85.19 W
Auma	54	50.42 N	11.54 E
Aumale	50	49.46 N	1.45 E
Auma Point ≻	164	7.55 S	145.25 E
Aumetz	56	49.25 N	5.56 E
Aumont-Aubrac	32	44.43 N	3.17 E
Aumühle	52	53.31 N	10.19 E
Auna	150	10.12 N	4.45 E
Auneau	50	48.27 N	1.46 E
Auneuil	50	49.22 N	2.00 E
Auning	26	56.26 N	10.23 E
Auno	146	11.50 N	12.53 E
Aunuu I	174u	14.17 S	170.33 W
Auob ≃	156	26.25 S	20.35 E
Auponhia	112	1.56 S	125.29 E
Aups	62	43.37 N	6.14 E
Aur, Pulau I	112	2.27 N	104.31 E
Aura	26	60.36 N	22.34 E
Aurach	56	49.15 N	10.25 E
Aurach ≃, Dtsch.	56	49.34 N	10.59 E
Aurach ≃, Dtsch.	56	49.51 N	10.56 E
Aurachmat	85	41.34 N	70.07 E
Auraiya	124	26.28 N	79.31 E
Aurangābād, India	122	19.53 N	75.20 E
Aurangābād, India	124	24.45 N	84.22 E
Auray	32	47.40 N	2.59 W
Aurdal	26	60.56 N	9.24 E
Aure	26	63.16 N	8.32 E
Aurelia	198	42.42 N	95.26 W
Aurelius	216	42.31 N	84.31 W
Aurès, Massif de l' ⋏	148	35.08 N	6.30 E
Auri, Kepulauan II	164	1.59 S	134.42 E
Aurich	52	53.28 N	7.29 E
Auriesville Shrine ♉ 1	210	42.54 N	74.19 W
Auriflama	255	20.41 S	50.34 W

PORTUGUÊS

Nome	Página	Lat.°′	Long.°′ W = Oeste
Aurigny → Alderney I	43b	49.43 N	2.12 W
Aurilândia	255	16.44 S	50.28 W
Aurillac	32	44.56 N	2.26 E
Aurina, Valle V	64	47.00 N	12.00 E
Aurine, Alpi (Zillertaler Alpen) ⋏	64	47.00 N	11.55 E
Aurino ≃	64	46.48 N	11.55 E
Auriol	62	43.23 N	5.38 E
Aurisina	64	45.45 N	13.41 E
Aurlandsfjorden ⊂ 2	26	61.05 N	7.02 E
Aurlandsvangen	26	60.54 N	7.11 E
Aurolzmünster	60	48.15 N	13.27 E
Auron	62	44.14 N	6.56 E
Auronzo di Cadore	64	46.33 N	12.26 E
Aurora, Bra.	250	6.57 S	38.58 W
Aurora, Bra.	287a	22.46 S	43.24 W
Aurora, On., Can.	212	44.00 N	79.28 W
Aurora, S. Afr.	158	32.42 S	18.29 E
Aurora, Co., U.S.	200	39.43 N	104.49 W
Aurora, Il., U.S.	216	41.45 N	88.19 W
Aurora, In., U.S.	218	39.03 N	84.54 W
Aurora, Me., U.S.	188	44.51 N	68.19 W
Aurora, Mn., U.S.	190	47.31 N	92.14 W
Aurora, Mo., U.S.	194	36.58 N	93.43 W
Aurora, Ne., U.S.	198	40.52 N	98.00 W
Aurora, N.Y., U.S.	210	42.45 N	76.42 W
Aurora, N.C., U.S.	192	35.18 N	76.47 W
Aurora, Oh., U.S.	214	41.19 N	81.20 W
Aurora, Or., U.S.	224	45.13 N	122.45 W
Aurora, Ut,. U.S.	200	38.55 N	111.56 W
Aurora, W.V., U.S.	188	39.19 N	79.33 W
Aurora □ 4	116	16.00 N	121.40 E
Aurora ♉	265a	59.57 N	30.21 E
Aurora do Norte	255	12.43 S	46.24 W
Aurora Pond ⊜	279a	41.20 N	81.23 W
Auroux	62	44.45 N	3.44 E
Aursunden ⊜	26	62.40 N	11.40 E
Aurukun	164	13.19 S	141.45 E
Aurukun Aboriginal Land Trust ◆ 4	164	13.45 S	141.45 E
Aurunci, Monti ⋏	66	41.22 N	13.40 E
Aus	156	26.40 S	16.15 E
Ausable ≃, On., Can.	190	43.19 N	81.46 W
Au Sable ≃, Mi., U.S.	190	44.25 N	83.20 W
Au Sable, North Branch ≃	190	44.40 N	84.23 W
Au Sable, South Branch ≃	190	44.40 N	84.23 W
Au Sable Forks	188	44.26 N	73.40 W
Au Sable Point ≻	190	44.20 N	83.20 W
Auschwitz → Oświęcim	30	50.03 N	19.12 E
Ausevik ⊥	26	61.32 N	5.16 E
Auskerry I	46	59.02 N	2.34 W
Ausoni, Monti ⋏	66	41.25 N	13.20 E
Ausserferrera	58	46.33 N	9.26 E
Ausserfragant	64	46.56 N	13.06 E
Aussig → Ústí nad Labem	54	50.40 N	14.02 E
Aussois	62	45.14 N	6.45 E
Aust-Agder □ 6	26	58.50 N	8.00 E
Austerlitz → Slavkov u Brna, Česká Rep.	61	49.09 N	16.52 E
Austerlitz, Ned.	52	52.05 N	5.19 E
Austerlitz, N.Y., U.S.	210	42.19 N	73.28 W
Austerlitz, Gare ◆ 5	261	48.50 N	2.22 E
Austin, Bra.	287a	22.43 S	43.32 W
Austin, Mb., Can.	184	49.57 N	98.56 W
Austin, In., U.S.	218	38.45 N	85.48 W
Austin, Mn., U.S.	190	43.40 N	92.58 W
Austin, Nv., U.S.	204	39.29 N	117.04 W
Austin, Pa., U.S.	214	41.37 N	78.05 W
Austin, Tx., U.S.	222	30.16 N	97.44 W
Austin □ 6	222	29.53 N	96.15 W
Austin ◆ 8	278	41.54 N	87.45 W
Austin, Lake ⊜	162	27.40 S	118.00 E
Austin, Lake ⊜ 1	222	30.19 N	97.46 W
Austin Bayou ≃	222	29.07 N	95.18 W
Austinburg	214	41.46 N	80.51 W
Austin Channel ⊔	176	75.35 N	103.25 W
Austin Lake ⊜	216	42.11 N	85.33 W
Austinmer	170	34.18 S	150.56 E
Austin's Post	158	29.32 S	25.49 E
Austintown	214	41.06 N	80.45 W
Austinville	192	36.51 N	80.54 W
Austnes	26	62.38 N	6.16 E
Austonio	222	31.11 N	95.38 W
Austonley	262	53.34 N	1.50 W
Austral	274a	33.56 S	150.48 E
Australes, Îles II	14	23.00 S	150.00 W
Australia □ 1	160	25.00 S	135.00 E
Australia Mountain ∧	180	63.36 N	138.08 W
Australian Capital Territory □ 8	171b	35.30 S	149.00 E
Australian War Memorial ⊥	171b	35.17 S	149.09 E
Australia Plains	168b	34.06 S	139.09 E
Australie → Australia □ 1	160	25.00 S	135.00 E
Australien → Australia □ 1	160	25.00 S	135.00 E
Australind	168a	33.16 S	115.44 E
Austral Seamounts ✣ 3	14	22.40 S	152.45 W
Austråt	26	63.43 N	9.45 E
Austria (Österreich) □ 1, Europe	22	47.20 N	13.20 E
Austria (Österreich) □ 1, Europe	30	47.20 N	13.20 E
Austvågøya I	24	68.20 N	14.36 E
Autazes	246	3.35 S	59.08 W
Auteuil, Fr.	50	49.21 N	2.05 E
Auteuil, Fr.	261	48.50 N	1.49 E
Autheuil	50	49.06 N	1.17 E
Authie ≃	50	50.21 N	1.38 E
Authon	62	44.14 N	6.08 E
Authon-du-Perche	50	48.12 N	0.55 E
Authon-la-Plaine	50	48.27 N	1.57 E
Auth Village	284c	38.49 N	76.55 W
Autlán de Navarro	234	19.46 N	104.22 W
Autore, Monte ∧	66	41.58 N	13.12 E
Autrey-lès-Gray	58	47.29 N	5.30 E
Autriche → Austria □ 1	30	47.20 N	13.20 E
Autumn Hill	284b	39.16 N	76.48 W
Autun	32	46.57 N	4.18 E
Auve	56	49.02 N	4.42 E
Auvergne	164	15.41 S	130.01 E
Auvergne □ 9	32	45.25 N	2.30 E
Auvernaux	261	48.32 N	2.30 E
Auvers-sur-Oise	50	49.04 N	2.10 E
Auvézère ≃	32	45.12 N	0.51 E
Aux Cayes → Les Cayes	238	18.12 N	73.45 W
Auxerre	50	47.48 N	3.34 E
Auxier	192	37.44 N	82.45 W
Auxi-le-Château	50	50.14 N	2.07 E
Auxon	50	48.06 N	3.55 E
Auxonne	58	47.12 N	5.23 E
Aux Sable Creek ≃	216	41.23 N	88.20 W
Auxvasse	219	39.01 N	91.53 W
Auxvasse Creek ≃	219	38.41 N	91.49 W
Auxy	58	46.57 N	4.24 E
Auyamita, Quebrada ≃	286c	10.30 N	66.46 W
Auyán Tepuy ∧	246	5.55 N	62.32 W
Auzances	32	46.02 N	2.30 E
Auzangate, Nevado ∧	248	13.48 S	71.14 W
Auzon ≃, Fr.	58	48.30 N	4.20 E
Auzon ≃, Fr.	62	44.02 N	4.54 E
Ava, Il., U.S.	194	37.53 N	89.29 W
Ava, Mo., U.S.	194	36.57 N	92.39 W
Avadchara	84	43.31 N	40.39 E
Avadh Plains ⩡	124	26.20 N	82.00 E
Avaí	255	22.08 S	49.22 W
Āvaj	128	35.34 N	49.13 E
Avakubi	154	1.20 N	27.34 E
Aval'	85	40.19 N	71.50 E
Aval, Falaise d' ⩡ 4	50	49.45 N	0.10 E
Avala ⊥	38	44.45 N	20.35 E
Avaldsnes	26	59.21 N	5.16 E
Avallon	50	47.29 N	3.54 E
Avaloirs, Les ∧ 2	32	48.28 N	0.07 W
Avalon, Ca., U.S.	228	33.20 N	118.19 W
Avalon, N.J., U.S.	208	39.06 N	74.43 W
Avalon, Pa., U.S.	214	40.30 N	80.04 W
Avalon, Tx., U.S.	222	32.12 N	96.48 W
Avalon, Wi., U.S.	216	42.38 N	88.52 W
Avalon Peninsula ≻ 1	186	47.30 N	53.30 W
Ávalos	232	28.35 N	106.00 W
Avana ≃	174k	21.14 S	159.43 W
Avanos	130	38.43 N	34.51 E
Avant	196	36.29 N	96.03 W
Avaré	255	23.05 S	48.55 W
Avarskoje Kojsu ≃	84	42.47 N	46.48 E
Avarua	174k	21.12 S	159.46 W
Avarua Harbour ⊂	174k	21.11 S	159.46 W
Avatanak Island I	180	54.03 N	165.19 W
Avatele	174v	19.06 S	169.55 W
Avatele Bay ⊂	174v	19.05 S	169.56 W
Avatiu	174k	21.12 S	159.47 W
Avatiu Harbour ⊂	174k	21.11 S	159.47 W
Avčala	84	41.48 N	44.48 E
Avdiyivka	83	48.08 N	37.46 E
Ave ≃	34	41.20 N	8.45 W
Avebury	42	51.27 N	1.51 W
Avebury Stone Circle ⊥	42	51.28 N	1.51 W
'Avedat, Ḥorvot ⊥	132	30.48 N	34.46 E
Avegbadje ∧	150	7.14 N	0.38 E
Aveiro, Bra.	250	3.15 S	55.10 W
Aveiro, Port.	34	40.38 N	8.39 W
Aveiro, Ria de ≃ 1	34	40.38 N	8.44 W
Avelar	256	22.20 S	43.25 W
Avelengo	64	46.38 N	11.13 E
Aveley	260	51.30 N	0.16 E
Avelgem	50	50.46 N	3.26 E
Avella, It.	68	40.58 N	14.36 E
Avella, Pa., U.S.	214	40.16 N	80.27 W
Avellaneda, Arg.	252	29.07 S	59.40 W
Avellaneda, Arg.	258	34.39 S	58.23 W
Avellaneda □ 5	288	34.40 S	58.20 W
Avellaneda, Estacion ◆ 5	288	34.41 S	58.22 W
Avelle, Île I	275a	45.24 N	74.00 W
Avellino	68	40.54 N	14.47 E
Avellino □ 4	68	41.00 N	15.10 E
Avenal	226	36.00 N	120.07 W
Avenal Creek ≃	226	35.47 N	120.04 W
Aven Armand ⩡ 5	32	44.15 N	3.22 E
Avenas	58	46.12 N	4.37 E
Avenches	58	46.53 N	7.02 E
Avenel	276	40.34 N	74.17 W
Aventureiro, Rio do ≃	256	21.52 S	42.39 W
Avenue	208	38.15 N	76.46 W
Avenwedde	52	51.55 N	8.27 E
Averbode	56	51.02 N	4.59 E
Averbode, Abbaye d' ♉ 1	56	51.02 N	4.59 E
Averill Lake ⊜	206	44.59 N	71.44 W
Averill Park	210	42.38 N	73.33 W
Avern ⊜	40	58.54 N	15.32 E
Avernakø I	41	55.01 N	10.17 E
Avernes	261	49.05 N	1.52 E
Avernes, Ru des ≃	261	49.04 N	2.51 E
Averøya I	26	63.01 N	7.34 E
Aversa	68	40.58 N	14.12 E
Avery, Ca., U.S.	226	38.13 N	120.22 W
Avery, Id., U.S.	202	47.15 N	115.48 W
Avery, Tx., U.S.	194	33.33 N	94.47 W
Avery Island	194	29.54 N	91.54 W
Avesnelles	50	50.07 N	3.57 E
Avesnes-le-Comte	50	50.17 N	2.32 E
Avesnes-lès-Aubert	50	50.12 N	3.23 E
Avesnes-sur-Helpe	50	50.07 N	3.56 E
Avesta	40	60.09 N	16.12 E
Aveto ≃	62	44.42 N	9.23 E
Avetrana	68	40.21 N	17.43 E
Aveyron □ 5	32	44.15 N	2.40 E
Aveyron ≃	32	44.05 N	1.16 E
Avezzano	66	42.02 N	13.25 E
Avgustovka	80	52.16 N	50.44 E
Aviano	64	46.04 N	12.36 E
Avich, Loch ⊜	46	56.16 N	5.20 W
Aviemore	46	57.12 N	3.50 W
Avigliana	62	45.05 N	7.23 E
Avigliano	68	40.44 N	15.44 E
Avignon	62	43.57 N	4.49 E
Ávila	34	40.39 N	4.42 W
Ávila □ 4	34	40.35 N	5.00 W
Ávila, Sierra de ⋏	34	40.35 N	5.08 W
Avila Beach	226	35.10 N	120.43 W
Avilés	34	43.33 N	5.55 W
Avilla	216	41.22 N	85.14 W
Avilley	58	47.26 N	6.16 E
Avinger	222	32.54 N	94.33 W
Avinurme	76	58.59 N	26.51 E
Avio	64	45.44 N	10.56 E
Avion	50	50.24 N	2.50 E
Avioth	56	49.34 N	5.24 E
Avis	210	41.11 N	77.18 W
Avisio ≃	64	46.07 N	11.05 E
Avispa, Cerro ∧	246	1.16 N	65.51 W
Aviston	219	38.36 N	89.36 W
Aviz	34	39.03 N	7.53 W
Avize	50	48.58 N	4.01 E
Avlan Gölü ⊜	130	36.34 N	29.57 E
Avlum	41	56.16 N	8.48 E
Avnbøl	41	54.58 N	9.39 E
Avnik	130	38.39 N	40.20 E
Avoca, Austl.	169	37.05 S	143.28 E
Avoca, Ia., U.S.	198	41.28 N	95.20 W
Avoca, N.Y., U.S.	210	42.24 N	77.25 W
Avoca, Pa., U.S.	210	41.20 N	75.44 W
Avoca ≃, Austl.	166	35.42 S	143.44 E
Avoca ≃, Ire.	48	52.48 N	6.09 W
Avoca, Mount ∧	169	37.07 S	143.21 E
Avoca Beach	170	33.29 S	151.29 E
Avocado Heights	280	34.08 N	117.54 W
Avola, B.C., Can.	182	51.47 N	119.19 W
Avola, It.	70	36.54 N	15.08 E
Avon, Austl.	168b	34.17 S	138.20 E
Avon, Fr.	50	48.24 N	2.43 E
Avon, Ct., U.S.	207	41.48 N	72.49 W
Avon, Il., U.S.	190	40.39 N	90.26 W
Avon, Ma., U.S.	207	42.07 N	71.02 W
Avon, Mn., U.S.	190	45.36 N	94.27 W
Avon, Mt., U.S.	202	46.35 N	112.36 W
Avon, N.Y., U.S.	210	42.54 N	77.44 W
Avon, N.C., U.S.	192	35.21 N	75.30 W
Avon, Oh., U.S.	214	41.27 N	82.02 W
Avon, Pa., U.S.	208	40.22 N	76.23 W
Avon, S.D., U.S.	198	43.00 N	98.03 W
Avon □ 6	42	51.30 N	2.40 W
Avon ≃, Austl.	168a	31.40 S	116.07 E
Avon ≃, N.S., Can.	186	45.10 N	64.15 W
Avon ≃, On., Can.	212	43.18 N	81.11 W
Avon ≃, Eng., U.K.	42	51.30 N	2.43 W
Avon ≃, Eng., U.K.	42	50.17 N	3.52 W
Avon ≃, Eng., U.K.	42	50.43 N	1.46 W
Avon ≃, Eng., U.K.	42	52.25 N	1.31 W
Avon ≃, Eng., U.K.	42	51.59 N	2.10 W
Avon ≃, Scot., U.K.	46	56.01 N	3.40 W
Avon ≃, Scot., U.K.	46	57.25 N	3.23 W
Avon, Ben ∧	46	57.05 N	3.27 W
Avon, Ru d' ≃	261	48.39 N	2.46 E
Avon Basin ⊂	279a	41.30 N	82.03 W
Avon by the Sea	208	40.11 N	74.00 W
Avondale, Az., U.S.	200	33.26 N	112.20 W
Avondale, Co., U.S.	198	38.14 N	104.21 W
Avondale, Md., U.S.	284c	38.56 N	76.59 W
Avondale, Oh., U.S.	214	39.47 N	84.08 W
Avondale Heights	274b	37.46 S	144.51 E
Avon Downs	166	20.05 S	137.30 E
Avondrust	158	34.21 S	21.51 E
Avon Lake	214	41.30 N	82.01 W
Avonlea	184	50.00 N	105.04 W
Avonmore, On., Can.	206	45.10 N	74.58 W
Avonmore, Pa., U.S.	214	40.31 N	79.27 W
Avonmore ≃	48	52.50 N	6.13 W
Avonmouth	42	51.31 N	2.42 W
Avon Park	220	27.35 N	81.30 W
Avon Reservoir ⊜ 1	170	34.24 S	150.40 E
Avontuur	158	33.44 S	23.11 E
Avon Valley National Park ♠	168a	31.41 S	116.06 E
Avon Water ≃	46	55.47 N	4.01 W
Avoudrey	58	47.08 N	6.26 E
Avrainville	261	48.34 N	2.15 E
Avranches	32	48.41 N	1.22 W
Avranlo	84	41.39 N	43.52 E
Avre ≃, Fr.	50	49.53 N	2.20 E
Avre ≃, Fr.	50	48.47 N	1.22 E
Avrieux	62	45.13 N	6.43 E
Avroult	50	50.38 N	2.09 E
Avtatkuul' ≃	180	64.06 N	178.10 E
Avtovo ◆ 8	265a	59.52 N	30.15 E
Avu Avu	175e	9.50 S	160.23 E
Awa, Nihon	96	34.04 N	134.12 E
Awa, Nihon	174m	26.36 N	127.56 E
Awaba	170	33.01 S	151.33 E
A'waj, Nahr al- ≃	132	33.20 N	36.34 E
Awaji	96	34.35 N	135.01 E
Awaji-shima I	96	34.21 N	134.51 E
Awakino	172	38.39 S	174.38 E
'Awālī	128	26.05 N	50.33 E
Awang	115b	8.54 S	116.24 E
Awano	94	36.31 N	139.41 E
Awanui	172	35.03 S	173.15 E
Awar	164	4.09 S	144.51 E
Awara	94	36.13 N	136.12 E
Awarawar, Tanjung ≻	115a	6.45 S	111.56 E
Aware	144	8.15 N	44.10 E
Awarua Point ≻	172	44.15 S	168.03 E
Awasa	144	6.45 N	38.15 E
Awasa, Lake ⊜	144	7.05 N	38.25 E
Awasan Bay ⊂	116	9.56 N	125.36 E
Awash	144	8.59 N	40.10 E
Awash ≃	144	11.45 N	41.05 E
Awa-shima I, Nihon	92	38.27 N	139.14 E
Awa-shima I, Nihon	96	34.16 N	133.38 E
Awash National Park ♠	144	9.05 N	40.00 E
Awaso	150	6.14 N	2.16 W
Awatere ≃	172	41.37 S	174.10 E
Awbārī	146	26.35 N	12.46 E
Awbārī, Ṣaḥrā' ⩡ 8	146	28.00 N	11.30 E
Awdheegle	144	1.59 N	44.50 E
Awe	150	8.09 N	9.07 E
Awe, Loch ⊜	46	56.15 N	5.17 W
Awegyun	110	12.44 N	98.44 E
Awgu	150	6.04 N	7.29 E
Awīsh al-Ḥajar	142	31.01 N	31.19 E
'Awjā', Wādī al- V	132	31.56 N	35.31 E
Awjilah	146	29.09 N	21.15 E
Awka	150	6.12 N	7.05 E
Awlād Mūsā	142	30.48 N	31.44 E
Awled Djellal	148	34.28 N	5.02 E
Awlef	148	26.58 N	1.05 E
Aworo Kit	140	10.59 N	32.38 E
Aworro	164	7.45 S	143.10 E
Awosting	276	41.09 N	74.20 W
Awsīm	273c	30.07 N	31.08 E
Awul	164	6.00 S	151.00 E
Awuna ≃	180	69.04 N	155.30 W
Awwal, Ash-Shallāl al- (First Cataract) ʟ	140	24.01 N	32.52 E
Awwalī, Nahr al- ≃	132	33.35 N	35.23 E
Axamilpa ≃	234	18.35 N	98.11 W
Axams	64	47.14 N	11.18 E
Axat	32	42.48 N	2.14 E
Axbridge	42	51.18 N	2.49 W
Axe ≃, Eng., U.K.	42	51.19 N	2.59 W
Axe ≃, Eng., U.K.	42	50.42 N	3.03 W
Axe Creek ≃	169	36.46 S	144.30 E
Axedale	169	36.47 S	144.30 E
Axe Edge ⋏ 2	262	53.14 N	1.57 W
Axel	52	51.16 N	3.55 E
Axel Heiberg Island I	16	79.45 N	91.00 W
Axim	150	4.52 N	2.14 W
Axinim	246	4.02 S	59.22 W
Axiós (Vardar) ≃	38	40.35 N	22.50 E
Axis	194	30.55 N	88.01 W
Axixá	250	2.51 S	44.04 W
Ax-les-Thermes	32	42.43 N	1.50 E
Axminster	42	50.47 N	3.00 W
Axmouth	42	50.42 N	3.02 W
Axochiapan	234	18.30 N	98.46 W
Axtell, Ks., U.S.	198	39.52 N	96.15 W
Axtell, Ne., U.S.	198	40.28 N	99.07 W
Axtell, Tx., U.S.	222	31.39 N	96.58 W
Aÿ	50	49.03 N	4.00 E
Ayabaca	246	4.38 S	79.43 W
Ayabe	96	35.18 N	135.15 E
Ayachi, Ari n' ∧	148	32.29 N	4.57 W
Ayacucho, Arg.	252	37.09 S	58.29 W
Ayacucho, Bol.	248	17.51 S	63.20 W
Ayacucho, Perú	248	13.07 S	74.13 W
Ayacucho □ 5	248	14.00 S	74.00 W
Ayakkum Hu ⊜	120	37.30 N	89.20 E
Ayamé	150	5.37 N	3.11 W
Ayamiken	152	2.07 N	10.01 E
Ayamonte	34	37.13 N	7.24 W
Āyān	272b	22.43 N	88.09 E
Ayancık	130	41.57 N	34.36 E
Ayangba	150	7.30 N	7.08 E
Ayapel	246	8.19 N	75.09 W
Ayarza, Laguna de ⊜	236	14.25 N	90.08 W
Ayas, It.	62	45.50 N	7.41 E
Ayaş, Tür.	130	40.01 N	32.21 E
Ayase	94	35.26 N	139.26 E
Ayase ≃	268	35.45 N	139.49 E
Ayauta	96	34.13 N	133.53 E
Ayaviri	248	14.52 S	70.35 W
Ayaviri ≃	248	15.01 S	70.22 W
'Aybāl, Jabal ∧	132	32.14 N	35.16 E
Aybastı, Tür.	130	39.42 N	39.02 E
Aybastı, Tür.	130	40.41 N	37.24 E
Aydar ≃	78	48.42 N	39.13 E
Aydar-Mykolayivka	83	48.58 N	38.58 E
Ayden	192	35.28 N	77.24 W
Aydere	128	38.24 N	56.45 E
Aydın	130	37.51 N	27.51 E
Aydın □ 4	130	37.45 N	28.00 E
Aydıncık, Tür.	130	36.08 N	33.19 E
Aydıncık, Tür.	130	40.08 N	35.18 E
Aydın Dağları ⋏	130	38.00 N	28.00 E
Aydınkent	130	37.06 N	31.36 E
Aydıntepe	130	40.24 N	40.09 E
Aydin Ula ∧	86	42.55 N	87.35 E
Aydosdağı ∧	267b	40.56 N	29.15 E
Ayelu ∧	144	10.04 N	40.46 E
Ayer, Schw.	58	46.11 N	7.36 E
Ayer, Ma., U.S.	207	42.33 N	71.35 W
Ayer Baloi	114	1.35 N	103.20 E
Ayer Chawan, Pulau I	271c	1.17 N	103.42 E
Ayer Hitam, Malay.	114	1.55 N	103.11 E
Ayer Hitam, Malay.	114	2.56 N	102.24 E
Ayer Jerneh	114	4.24 N	103.24 E
Ayer Kuning Selatan	114	2.30 N	102.28 E
Ayer Merbau, Pulau I	271c	1.16 N	103.43 E
Ayers Cliff	206	45.10 N	72.03 W
Ayers Rock ∧	162	25.23 S	131.05 E
Ayersville	216	41.14 N	84.17 W
Ayeyarwady □ 8	110	17.00 N	95.00 E
Ayeyarwady (Irrawaddy) ≃	110	15.50 N	95.06 E
Aygün	130	38.26 N	41.17 E
Ayía Marína	38	37.09 N	26.52 E
Ayía Paraskeví, Ellás	38	39.15 N	26.16 E
Ayía Paraskeví, Ellás	267c	38.01 N	23.50 E
Ayiássos	38	39.05 N	26.23 E
Ayía Varvára	267c	37.59 N	23.39 E
Ayina ≃	152	1.48 N	13.10 E
Áyioi Anáryiroi	267c	38.02 N	23.43 E
Áyion Óros □ 8	38	40.15 N	24.15 E
Áyion Óros ≻ 1	38	40.15 N	24.15 E
Áyios Dhimítrios	267c	37.56 N	23.44 E
Áyios Evstrátios I	38	39.31 N	25.00 E
Áyios Ioánnis Réndis	267c	37.58 N	23.40 E
Áyios Kírikos	38	37.37 N	26.14 E
Áyios Nikólaos	38	35.11 N	25.42 E
Ayiou Nikolaou Monastery ♉ 1	267c	37.53 N	23.27 E
Ayíou Órous, Kólpos ⊂	38	40.12 N	24.03 E
Ayl	132	30.13 N	35.32 E
Aylesbury	42	51.50 N	0.50 W
Aylesford	42	51.18 N	0.29 E
Aylesham	42	51.13 N	1.13 E
Aylmer	188	45.26 N	75.50 W
Aylmer, Lake ⊜	206	45.50 N	71.22 W
Aylmer, Mount ∧	182	51.19 N	115.26 W
Aylmer-East	212	45.26 N	75.50 W
Aylmer Lake ⊜	176	64.05 N	108.30 W
Aylmer West	212	42.46 N	80.59 W
Aylsham, Sk., Can.	184	53.11 N	103.49 W
Aylsham, Eng., U.K.	42	52.49 N	1.15 E
'Ayn al-'Arab	130	36.54 N	38.21 E
'Ayn Dār	128	25.59 N	49.23 E
'Ayn Dīwār	130	37.17 N	42.11 E
'Aynīn ⊤ 4	144	20.48 N	41.39 E
Aynor	192	33.59 N	79.11 W
'Aynūnah	128	28.05 N	35.08 E
Ayo	248	15.41 S	72.16 W
Ayo Ayo	248	17.05 S	68.00 W
Ayod	140	8.07 N	31.26 E
Ayodhya	124	26.48 N	82.12 E
Ayo El Chico	234	20.32 N	102.21 W
Ayom	140	7.52 N	28.23 E
Ayorou	150	14.44 N	0.55 E
Ayos	152	3.54 N	12.31 E
'Ayoûn el 'Atroûs	150	16.40 N	9.37 W
Ay-Petri, hora ∧	78	44.27 N	34.03 E
Ayr, Austl.	166	19.35 S	147.24 E
Ayr, On., Can.	212	43.17 N	80.27 W
Ayr, Scot., U.K.	44	55.28 N	4.38 W
Ayr ≃	44	55.29 N	4.28 W
'Ayrah	132	32.37 N	36.32 E
Ayrancı	130	37.22 N	33.42 E
Ayre, Point of ≻	44	54.26 N	4.22 W
Aysgarth	44	54.17 N	2.00 W
Aysha	144	10.46 N	42.37 E
'Aytā al-Fakhkhār	132	33.38 N	35.54 E
'Aytanīt	132	33.34 N	35.40 E
Ayton, Austl.	164	15.56 S	145.22 E
Ayton, On., Can.	212	44.03 N	80.56 W
Ayton, Eng., U.K.	44	54.14 N	0.29 W
Ayu, Kepulauan II	108	0.28 N	131.03 E
Ayubnagar	126	23.46 N	90.23 E
Ayulhai	102	44.36 N	115.36 E
Ayuñgon	116	9.51 N	123.08 E
Ayuquila ≃	234	19.23 N	103.51 W
Ayutla	234	20.07 N	104.22 W
Ayutla de los Libres	234	16.54 N	99.13 W
Ayvacık, Tür.	130	39.36 N	26.24 E
Ayvacık, Tür.	130	41.00 N	36.39 E
Ayvalı	130	38.44 N	37.38 E
Ayvalık	130	39.18 N	26.41 E
Aywaille	56	50.28 N	5.40 E
Azabarabān, Ra's ≻	142	28.51 N	32.43 E
Azacualpa, Hond.	236	14.27 N	86.09 W
Azacualpa, Hond.	236	15.19 N	88.33 W
Azādpur ◆ 8	272a	28.43 N	77.11 E
Azai	94	35.26 N	136.18 E
Azaila	34	41.17 N	0.29 W
Azalea Park	220	28.32 N	81.18 W
Azama	174m	26.11 N	127.49 E
Azamatovo	80	53.18 N	53.28 E
Azambuja	34	39.04 N	8.52 W
Āzamgarh	124	26.04 N	83.11 E
Azamiga-dake ∧	96	34.20 N	131.47 E
Azángaro	248	14.55 S	70.13 W
Azángaro ≃	248	15.17 S	70.10 W
Azanka	86	58.02 N	64.48 E
Azao ∧	148	25.12 N	8.08 E
Azaouâd ◆ 1	150	19.00 N	3.00 W
Azaouagh, Vallée de l' V	150	15.30 N	3.18 E
Azapa, Quebrada de ≃	248	18.30 S	70.17 W
Azar V	150	16.02 N	4.04 E
Azara	150	8.21 N	9.12 E
Āzārbāyjān-e Gharbī □ 4	128	37.40 N	45.00 E
Āzārbāyjān-e Sharqī □ 4	128	38.00 N	47.00 E
Azare	150	11.40 N	10.11 E
Āzar Shahr	128	37.45 N	45.59 E
Azas ≃	88	52.26 N	96.15 E
Azat, gora ∧ 2	86	46.55 N	69.00 E
Azay-le-Rideau	50	47.16 N	0.28 E
Azay-sur-Cher	50	47.21 N	0.51 E
Azay-sur-Indre	50	47.12 N	0.57 E
A'zāz	130	36.35 N	37.03 E
Azazga	148	36.44 N	4.22 E
Azcuénaga	258	34.23 S	59.21 W
Aždaak, gora ∧	84	40.13 N	44.56 E
Azdavay	130	41.39 N	33.18 E
Azeffâl ⩡ 8	148	21.00 N	14.45 W
Azeffoun	148	36.53 N	4.25 E
Azejevo	80	54.41 N	42.02 E
Azemmour	148	33.20 N	8.25 W
Azenhas do Mar	266c	38.50 N	9.28 W
Azennezal, 'Erg V	148	22.50 N	0.25 E
Azerbaidzhan → Azerbaijan □ 1	22	40.30 N	47.30 E
Azerbaijan □ 1, Asia	72	40.30 N	47.30 E
Azerbaijan (Azärbaycan) □ 1, Asia	84	40.30 N	47.30 E
Azerbajdžan → Azerbaijan □ 1	72	40.30 N	47.30 E
Azerbaydzan → Azerbaijan □ 1	72	40.30 N	47.30 E
Azergues ≃	58	45.56 N	4.44 E
Azezo	144	12.35 N	37.28 E
Azgir	80	47.50 N	47.54 E
Azhikode	122	11.59 N	75.21 E
Azilal	148	31.58 N	6.34 W
Azilal □ 4	148	31.55 N	6.30 W
Azile	154	3.32 N	29.52 E
Azincourt	50	50.28 N	2.08 E
Azle	222	32.53 N	97.32 W
Aznakajevo	80	54.53 N	53.04 E
Aznapuquio	286d	11.59 S	77.04 W
Azogues	246	2.44 S	78.50 W
Azoia	266c	38.46 N	9.29 W
Azor	132	32.01 N	34.48 E
Azores → Açores II	148a	38.30 N	28.00 W
Azores-Gibraltar Ridge ✣ 3	10	37.00 N	16.00 W
Azores Plateau ✣ 3	10	39.00 N	30.00 W
Azoum, Bahr (Wādī 'Azūm) V	146	10.53 N	20.15 E
Azov	83	47.07 N	39.25 E
Azov, Sea of ⊤ 2	78	46.00 N	36.00 E
Azovs'ke	78	45.34 N	34.34 E
Azovskij kanal ≊	83	47.07 N	39.27 E
Azoyú	234	16.43 N	98.44 W
Azpeitia	34	43.11 N	2.16 W
Azraq, Al-Baḥr al- → Blue Nile ≃	140	15.38 N	32.31 E
Azraq, Bahr ≃	146	10.52 N	20.35 E
Azraq, Wādī al- V	140	10.33 N	28.40 E
Azraq ash-Shīshān	132	31.50 N	36.48 E
Azrou	148	33.27 N	5.14 W
Aztalan State Park ♠	216	43.04 N	88.51 W
Aztec	200	36.49 N	107.59 W
Azteca, Estadio ♠	286a	19.18 N	99.09 W
Aztec Peak ∧	200	33.48 N	110.55 W
Aztec Ruins National Monument ♠	200	36.51 N	108.10 W
Azua	238	18.27 N	70.44 W
Azuaga	34	38.16 N	5.41 W
Azuay □ 4	246	3.00 S	79.00 W
Azucena	252	37.29 S	59.18 W
Azuchi	94	35.09 N	136.08 E
Azuchi-jō ⊥	94	35.10 N	136.08 E
Azuer ≃	34	39.08 N	3.36 W
Azuero, Península de ≻ 1	246	7.40 N	80.35 W
Azufre, Volcán ∧ 1	252	25.11 S	68.31 W
Azuga	38	45.27 N	25.33 E
Azul	252	36.47 S	59.51 W
Azul, Cerro ∧, C.R.	236	9.54 N	85.14 W

≃	River	Fluß	Río	Rivière	Rio
≊	Canal	Kanal	Canal	Canal	Canal
ʟ	Waterfall, Rapids	Wasserfall, Stromschnellen	Cascada, Rápidos	Chute d'eau, Rapides	Cascata, Rápidos
⊔	Strait	Meeresstraße	Estrecho	Détroit	Estreito
⊂	Bay, Gulf	Bucht, Golf	Bahía, Golfo	Baie, Golfe	Baía, Golfo
⊜	Lake, Lakes	See, Seen	Lago, Lagos	Lac, Lacs	Lago, Lagos
⁝	Swamp	Sumpf	Pantano	Marais	Pântano
⍓	Ice Features, Glacier	Eis- und Gletscherformen	Accidentes Glaciales	Formes glaciaires	Acidentes glaciares
⊤	Other Hydrographic Features	Andere Hydrographische Objekte	Otros Elementos Hidrográficos	Autres données hydrographiques	Outros acidentes hidrográficos

✣	Submarine Features	Untermeerische Objekte	Accidentes Submarinos	Formes de relief sous-marin	Acidentes submarinos
□	Political Unit	Politische Einheit	Unidad Politica	Entité politique	Unidade política
♉	Cultural Institution	Kulturelle Institution	Institución Cultural	Institution culturelle	Instituição cultural
⊥	Historical Site	Historische Stätte	Sitio Histórico	Site historique	Sitio histórico
♠	Recreational Site	Erholungs- und Ferienort	Sitio de Recreo	Centre de loisirs	Area de Lazer
⊠	Airport	Flughafen	Aeropuerto	Aéroport	Aeroporto
■	Military Installation	Militäranlage	Instalación Militar	Installation militaire	Instalação militar
◆	Miscellaneous	Verschiedenes	Misceláneo	Divers	Diversos

Azul, Cerro ∧, Ec. 246a 0.54 S 91.21 W
Azul, Cerro ∧, Hond. 236 14.32 N 88.23 W
Azul, Cordillera ∧ 248 8.30 S 76.10 W
Azul Casa, Cerro ∧ 252 22.29 S 65.20 W
'Azūm, Wādī (Bahr Azoum) V 146 10.53 N 20.15 E
Azuma, Nihon 94 36.31 N 139.19 E
Azuma, Nihon 94 36.33 N 138.54 E
Azuma, Nihon 94 35.56 N 140.28 E
Azuma, Nihon 94 36.36 N 138.20 E
Azumaya-san ∧ 94 36.32 N 138.25 E
Azumazaka 270 34.26 N 135.39 E
Azumi 94 36.11 N 137.47 E
Azur, Côte d' ⌇2 62 43.30 N 7.00 E
Azurduy 248 19.59 S 64.29 W
Azure Clouds, Temple of the ⌖1 271a 40.00 N 116.11 E
Azure Lake ⊜ 182 52.23 N 120.00 W
Azusa 228 34.08 N 117.54 W
Azusa ≃ 94 36.17 N 137.56 E
Ažu-Tajga, gora ∧ 86 51.35 N 88.45 E
Az-Zabābidah 132 32.23 N 35.20 E
Az-Zabadānī 132 33.43 N 36.05 E
Az-Zāb al-Kabīr — Great Zab ≃ 128 36.00 N 43.21 E
Az-Zāb aṣ-Ṣaghīr — Little Zab ≃ 128 35.12 N 43.25 E
Az-Zāhirīyah 132 31.25 N 34.58 E
Az-Zahrān (Dhahran) 128 26.18 N 50.08 E
Az-Zamālik ⌖8 273c 30.04 N 31.13 E
Azzanello 64 45.18 N 9.55 E
Az-Zankalūn 142 30.33 N 31.27 E
Azzano Decimo 64 45.53 N 12.43 E
Az-Zaqāzīq 142 30.35 N 31.31 E
Az-Zarbah 130 36.04 N 36.59 E
Az-Zarqā' 132 32.05 N 36.06 E
Az-Zarqā' ▫8 132 32.00 N 36.45 E
Az-Zawāmil 142 30.21 N 31.26 E
Az-Zāwiyah 146 32.45 N 12.44 E
Az-Zaydāb 140 17.26 N 33.53 E
Az-Zaydīyah 144 15.18 N 43.04 E
Az-Zaytīyah ⌖8 142 29.58 N 32.31 E
Az-Zaytūn ⌖8 273c 30.06 N 31.19 E
Azzel Matti, Sebkha ≃ 148 25.55 N 0.56 E
Az-Zilfī 128 26.18 N 44.48 E
Az-Zrārīyah 132 33.21 N 35.20 E
Az-Zubayr 128 30.23 N 47.43 E
'Azzūn 132 32.11 N 35.03 E
Azzurra, Grotta (Blue Grotto) ⌇5 68 40.35 N 14.14 E

B

Ba ≃, Viet 110 13.02 N 109.03 E
Ba ≃, Zhg. 100 30.25 N 115.02 E
Ba ≃, Zhg. 102 31.03 N 107.08 E
Ba ≃, Zhg. 271a 39.57 N 116.38 E
Ba, Loch ⊜ 46 56.36 N 4.44 W
Baa 112 10.43 S 123.03 E
Baaba, Île I 175f 20.03 S 163.59 E
Baacagaan 102 45.35 N 99.27 E
Baad 58 47.19 N 10.07 E
Baah 112 10.28 S 121.59 E
Baak 263 51.25 N 7.10 E
Baak 56 51.02 N 6.17 E
Baao 116 13.27 N 123.22 E
Baar 58 47.12 N 8.32 E
Baar ⌖1 58 48.00 N 8.30 E
Baarbach ≃ 263 51.27 N 7.39 E
Baardheere (Bardera) 144 2.20 N 42.17 E
Baardskeerdersbos 158 34.34 S 19.35 E
Baargaal 144 11.17 N 51.04 E
Baarle-Hertog 56 51.27 N 4.56 E
Baarle-Nassau 56 51.27 N 4.53 E
Baarlo 52 51.20 N 6.05 E
Baarn 52 52.13 N 5.16 E
Baasrode 50 51.02 N 4.10 E
Baba 246 1.47 S 79.40 W
Baba ≃ 152 6.25 N 17.07 E
Baba Burnu ⟩, Tür. 130 39.29 N 26.04 E
Baba Burnu ⟩, Tür. 130 41.17 N 31.24 E
Babaculândia 250 7.13 S 47.46 W
Babadag, Rom. 38 44.54 N 28.43 E
Babadağ, Tür. 130 37.48 N 28.52 E
Babadağ ∧ 84 41.02 N 48.19 E
Babaeski 130 41.26 N 27.06 E
Babahoyo 246 1.49 S 79.31 W
Babaī (Sarju) ≃ 124 27.42 N 81.16 E
Babailiqiao 100 32.26 N 118.57 E
Babajevo 76 59.23 N 35.56 E
Babajurt 84 43.36 N 46.47 E
Babak 112 7.08 N 125.41 E
Babakin 162 32.07 S 118.01 E
Babana 150 10.26 N 3.50 E
Babanango 158 28.30 S 31.00 E
Babanka 78 48.43 N 30.26 E
Babanūsah 140 11.20 N 27.48 E
Babar, Kepulauan II 164 7.50 S 129.45 E
Babar, Pulau I 164 7.55 S 129.45 E
Babarpur ⌖8 272a 28.41 N 77.17 E
Babat, Indon. 112 2.45 S 103.58 E
Babat, Indon. 115a 7.06 S 112.10 E
Babatag, chrebet ∧ 85 38.15 N 68.20 E
Babati 154 4.13 S 35.45 E
Bābā Valī Sāheb 120 31.40 N 65.40 E
Babaykivka 78 49.01 N 34.32 E
Babb 182 48.51 N 113.26 W
Babbacombe Bay ⊂ 42 50.30 N 3.25 W
Babb Creek ≃ 210 41.33 N 77.23 W
Babbitt, Mn., U.S. 190 47.43 N 91.57 W
Babbitt, Nv., U.S. 204 38.32 N 118.38 W
B'abdā 132 33.50 N 35.32 E
B'abdāt 132 33.53 N 35.40 E
Babel, Mont de ∧ 186 51.27 N 68.42 W
Babelijamun 164 2.04 S 137.43 E
Bab el Mandeb — Mandeb, Bab el ꟸ 144 12.40 N 43.20 E
Babelsberg ⌖8 264a 52.24 N 13.05 E
Babelsberg, Schloss ⌖ 264a 52.24 N 13.05 E
Babelthuap I 175b 7.30 N 134.36 E
Babenhausen, Dtsch. 56 49.57 N 8.56 E
Babenhausen, Dtsch. 58 48.09 N 10.15 E
Babenki 82 55.21 N 37.11 E
Babeyru 154 1.52 N 27.27 E
Babi, Pulau I 114 2.05 N 96.39 E
Babia, Arroyo de la ≃ 196 28.25 N 101.45 W
Babian ≃ 102 22.58 N 101.44 E
Babiči 76 52.17 N 30.00 E
Babil 142 30.41 N 31.00 E
Bābil ≃ 128 32.40 N 44.35 E
Bābil, Atlāl (Babylon) ⌇ 128 32.33 N 44.24 E
Babile 144 9.15 N 42.19 E
Babilônia 256 22.33 S 44.28 W
Babimost 30 52.10 N 15.51 E
Babina 124 25.15 N 78.28 E
Babina Greda 38 45.07 N 18.33 E
Babinda 166 17.20 S 145.55 E
Babine 182 55.19 N 126.37 W
Babine ≃ 182 55.42 N 127.40 W
Babine Lake ⊜ 182 54.45 N 126.00 W
Babine Range ∧ 182 55.00 N 126.25 W
Babino, Ross. 76 56.44 N 34.17 E
Babino, Ross. 76 59.14 N 31.26 E
Babino, Ross. 76 59.50 N 40.49 E
Babino, Ross. 80 57.22 N 48.45 E
Babiogórski Park Narodowy ⌖ 30 49.35 N 19.30 E
Babo 164 2.33 S 133.25 E
Bābol 128 36.34 N 52.42 E
Bābol Sar 128 36.43 N 52.39 E
Baboon Point ⟩ 158 32.19 S 18.20 E
Baboquivari Mountains ∧ 200 31.45 N 111.35 W
Baboquivari Peak ∧ 200 31.46 N 111.35 W
Babor, Djebel ∧ 34 36.30 N 5.28 E
Baborów 30 50.09 N 17.59 E
Babošino 82 54.13 N 37.08 E
Baboua 152 5.48 N 14.49 E
Babrongan Tower ∧2 162 18.36 S 123.33 E
Babson Park, Fl., U.S. 220 27.49 N 81.31 W
Babson Park, Ma., U.S. 283 42.18 N 71.23 W
Babson Reservoir ⊜1 283 42.38 N 70.40 W
Babstovo 89 48.07 N 132.27 E
Bab-Taza 148 35.03 N 5.14 W
Bābu Bheri 272b 22.51 N 88.14 E
Bābūpur, India 126 24.01 N 87.10 E
Bābūpur, India 272a 28.30 N 76.59 E
Babura 150 12.46 N 9.01 E
Bābūsar Pass ꟸ 123 35.09 N 74.03 E
Babuškin 88 51.41 N 105.54 E
Babuškin ⌖8 265b 55.52 N 37.42 E
Babuyan 116 10.00 N 118.54 E
Babuyan Channel ꟸ 116 18.44 N 121.40 E
Babuyan Island I 108 19.32 N 121.57 E
Babuyan Islands II 108 19.15 N 121.40 E
Babylon 210 40.41 N 73.19 W
Babylon — Bābil, Atlāl ⌇ 128 32.33 N 44.24 E
Babynino 76 54.23 N 35.43 E
Bača ≃ 64 46.09 N 13.48 E
Bacaadweeyn 144 7.12 N 47.32 E
Bacabal 250 4.14 S 44.47 W
Bacacay 116 13.18 N 123.47 E
Bacadéhuachi 232 29.44 N 109.10 W
Bacajaí ≃ 250 3.27 S 51.53 W
Bacalhau, Canal do ≃ 287a 23.03 S 43.35 W
Bacalgo 84 42.33 N 44.57 E
Bačalino 86 57.46 N 67.17 E
Bacan, Pulau I 164 0.35 S 127.30 E
Bacao 116 10.27 N 119.48 E
Bacarra 116 18.15 N 120.35 E
Bacatuba 250 5.40 S 43.42 W
Bacău 38 46.34 N 26.55 E
Bacău ▫6 38 46.30 N 26.45 E
Baccalieu Island I 186 48.08 N 52.48 W
Bac Can 110 22.08 N 105.50 E
Baccarat 58 48.27 N 6.45 E
Bacchiglione ≃ 64 45.11 N 12.14 E
Bacchus Marsh 169 37.41 S 144.27 E
Bacchus Marsh 58 46.16 N 8.19 E
Baceno 232 30.18 N 108.50 W
Bacerac 76 53.24 N 29.14 E
Bacevičí 110 21.16 N 106.12 E
Bac Giang 58 47.16 N 10.24 E
Bach 98 40.36 N 122.54 E
Bachagou 246 9.56 N 71.08 W
Bachaquero 56 50.04 N 7.46 E
Bacharach 128 38.26 N 57.25 E
Bachardén 128 38.46 N 58.30 E
Bachardok 116 12.28 N 122.06 E
Bachauan 106 31.05 N 120.40 E
Bache 106 31.27 N 120.52 E
Bacheng 232 28.45 N 107.15 W
Bachi 110 16.12 N 107.52 E
Bachiniva 80 51.06 N 44.46 E
Bach Ma 76 56.22 N 34.03 E
Bachmetjevka 114 6.37 N 101.39 E
Bachmutovo 114 6.04 N 102.24 E
Bacho 85 40.43 N 68.42 E
Bachok 74 62.28 N 89.00 E
Bachta 86 55.45 N 92.26 E
Bachta, Ross. 80 45.43 N 47.38 E
Bachta, Ross. 264a 52.20 N 12.54 E
Bachtemir ≃ 86 46.39 N 82.42 E
Bachten-Berg ∧2 90 39.50 N 78.20 E
Bachty 144 6.48 N 35.53 E
Bachu 176 67.15 N 95.15 W
Bachuma 208 37.06 N 76.17 W
Back ≃, N.T., Can. 38 45.50 N 19.30 E
Back ≃, Va., U.S. 38 45.15 N 19.24 E
Bačka ⌖1 38 45.49 N 19.38 E
Bačka Palanka 283 42.21 N 71.05 W
Bačka Topola 272c 18.56 N 72.49 E
Back Bay ⌖8 208 36.35 N 75.57 W
Back Bay ⊂, India 40 60.37 N 16.37 E
Back Bay ⊂, Va., U.S. 180 63.30 N 129.00 W
Backberg 284c 38.51 N 76.48 W
Backbone Ranges ∧ 276 40.26 N 74.39 W
Back Branch ≃ 279b 40.30 N 80.05 W
Back Channel ≃1 188 38.02 N 79.54 W
Back Creek ≃ 26 63.49 N 16.24 E
Backe 26 58.48 N 12.10 E
Bäckefors 40 60.39 N 15.34 E
Bäckehagen 262 53.15 N 2.54 W
Backford 40 59.10 N 14.11 E
Bäckhammar 38 45.22 N 19.35 E
Bački Petrovac 56 48.56 N 9.25 E
Backnang 208 39.16 N 76.27 W
Back River ≃ 284b 39.18 N 76.26 W
Back River Neck ⟩1
Backstairs Passage ꟸ 168b 35.42 S 138.05 E
Bac Lieu 110 9.17 N 105.44 E
Baccliff 222 29.31 N 94.59 W
Bac Ninh 110 21.11 N 106.03 E
Baco, Mount ∧ 116 12.49 N 121.10 E
Bacoachi 232 30.38 N 109.56 W
Bacoli 68 40.48 N 14.05 E
Bacolod 116 10.40 N 122.57 E
Bacon 116 13.03 N 124.03 E
Baconga ⌖8 273b 4.18 S 15.16 E
Bacon Peak ∧ 224 48.39 N 121.31 W
Bacons Run ≃ 285 40.06 N 74.41 W
Baconton 192 31.22 N 84.09 W
Bacoor 116 14.28 N 120.54 E
Bacoor Bay ⊂ 269f 14.28 N 120.54 E
Bac Phan ▫9 110 22.00 N 105.00 E
Bac Quang 110 22.29 N 104.52 E
Bacqueville-en-Caux 50 49.47 N 1.00 E
Bácsalmás 38 46.08 N 19.20 E
Bács-Kiskun ▫6 30 46.30 N 19.25 E
Bacton 42 52.52 N 1.28 E
Bacu ≃ 38 46.55 N 29.28 E
Bacuag 116 9.37 N 125.38 E
Bacuit Bay ⊂ 116 11.07 N 119.23 E
Bácum 232 27.33 N 110.05 W
Bacup 44 53.43 N 2.12 W
Bacuranao ≃ 286b 23.09 N 82.18 W
Bacuranao, Presa ⊜1 286b 23.07 N 82.13 W
Bacuri, Cachoeira do ≃ 250 5.29 S 54.18 W
Bacuri, Ilha do I 250 2.55 S 49.43 W
Bacuri, Lago do ⊜ 250 3.16 S 42.15 W
Bačurka 24 68.32 N 56.57 E
Bacuyangan 116 9.39 N 122.27 E
Bād 128 33.41 N 52.01 E
Bad ≃, Mi., U.S. 190 43.18 N 84.06 W
Bad ≃, S.D., U.S. 198 44.22 N 100.22 W
Bad ≃, Wi., U.S. 190 46.38 N 90.40 W
Bad', Wādī V 142 29.41 N 32.20 E
Bada 88 51.23 N 109.54 E
Bad Abbach 60 48.56 N 12.03 E
Badagara 122 11.36 N 75.35 E
Badagri 150 6.27 N 3.55 E
Badagri ≃ 273a 6.27 N 3.18 E
Badagri Creek ≃ 273a 6.25 N 3.18 E
Badahl 142 28.56 N 30.54 E
Bad Aibling 64 47.52 N 12.00 E
Bada Jāmda 124 22.09 N 85.23 E
Badajia 100 33.57 N 120.17 E
Badajós ≃ 246 3.15 S 63.02 W
Badajós, Lago ⊜ 246 3.15 S 62.47 W
Badajoz 34 38.53 N 6.58 W
Badajoz ▫4 34 38.40 N 6.00 W
Badakan 54 49.30 N 9.46 E
Badakhshān ▫4 60 47.33 N 13.55 E
Badal Khān Goth 120 26.31 N 67.06 E
Badalona 34 41.27 N 2.15 E
Badalucco 62 43.55 N 7.51 E
Badam 85 42.23 N 69.15 E
Bādāmi 122 15.55 N 75.41 E
Bādāmpahār 124 22.06 N 86.06 E
Badana, Lach V 144 0.50 S 42.04 E
Badanah 128 30.59 N 41.02 E
Badanga 146 11.36 N 17.26 E
Badanganj 126 22.54 N 87.33 E
Badaohao 104 41.47 N 121.57 E
Badaohe, Zhg. 98 40.24 N 118.42 E
Badaohe, Zhg. 98 40.02 N 122.17 E
Badarīnāth 124 30.44 N 79.29 E
Badarma 88 57.46 N 102.36 E
Badas 112 4.36 N 114.27 E
Badas, Kepulauan II 112 0.35 N 107.06 E
Badata, gora ∧ 81 55.51 N 111.35 E
Bad Aussee 64 47.36 N 13.47 E
Bad Axe 190 43.48 N 83.00 W
Badaying 98 41.22 N 117.28 E
Badazhou 102 24.36 N 105.04 E
Bad Bentheim 52 52.19 N 7.10 E
Bad Bergzabern 56 49.07 N 8.00 E
Bad Berka 54 50.54 N 11.17 E
Bad Berleburg 56 51.03 N 8.23 E
Bad Berneck 60 50.03 N 11.40 E
Bad Bertrich 56 50.04 N 7.02 E
Bad Bibra 54 51.12 N 11.35 E
Bad Blankenburg 54 50.41 N 11.16 E
Bad Bramstedt 52 53.55 N 9.53 E
Bad Breisig 56 50.31 N 7.18 E
Bad Brückenau 56 50.18 N 9.47 E
Bad Buchau 58 48.03 N 9.36 E
Bad Camberg 56 50.18 N 8.16 E
Bad Creek ≃ 216 41.25 N 83.57 W
Baddā 132 33.41 N 36.26 E
Badda Rogghie ∧ 144 8.43 N 37.41 E
Baddeck 186 46.07 N 60.45 W
Bad Ditzenbach 56 48.35 N 9.41 E
Baddo ≃ 128 27.59 N 64.21 E
Bad Doberan 54 54.06 N 11.53 E
Baddomalhi 123 31.59 N 74.40 E
Bad Dreibergen 52 53.12 N 8.01 E
Bad Driburg 52 51.44 N 9.01 E
Bad Düben 54 51.36 N 12.34 E
Bad Dürkheim 56 49.28 N 8.10 E
Bad Dürrenberg 54 51.18 N 12.04 E
Bad Dürrheim 58 48.01 N 8.32 E
Badé, Centraf. 152 6.41 N 17.07 E
Bade, Indon. 164 7.10 S 139.35 E
Badeggi 150 9.05 N 6.08 E
Badéguichéri 150 14.30 N 5.22 E
Bad Eilsen 52 52.14 N 9.06 E
Badel 54 52.44 N 11.19 E
Bad Elster 54 50.17 N 12.14 E
Bad Ems 56 50.20 N 7.43 E
Baden, On., Can. 212 43.24 N 80.39 W
Baden, Dtsch. 54 53.00 N 9.04 E
Baden, Erit. 144 17.00 N 38.00 E
Baden, Öst. 61 48.00 N 16.14 E
Baden, Schw. 58 47.29 N 8.18 E
Baden, Pa., U.S. 214 40.38 N 80.13 W
Baden-Baden 56 48.46 N 8.14 E
Bad Endbach 56 50.45 N 8.32 E
Badenoch ▫9 46 56.57 N 4.19 W
Baden-Powell, Mount ∧ 228 34.21 N 117.46 W
Badenweiler 58 47.48 N 7.40 E
Baden-Württemberg ▫3 30 48.30 N 9.00 E
Badenyon 46 57.15 N 3.05 W
Baderna 64 45.12 N 13.45 E
Badersleben 54 51.59 N 10.53 E
Bad Essen 52 52.19 N 8.20 E
Bad Feilnbach 64 47.46 N 12.00 E
Badfish Creek ≃ 216 42.50 N 89.10 W
Bad Frankenhausen 54 51.21 N 11.06 E
Bad Freienwalde 54 52.47 N 14.01 E
Bad Friedrichshall 56 49.14 N 9.11 E
Bad Fusch 64 47.12 N 12.51 E
Badgam 123 34.01 N 74.43 E
Bad Gandersheim 52 51.52 N 10.01 E
Badgastein 64 47.07 N 13.08 E
Badger, Nf., Can. 186 48.59 N 56.02 W
Badger, Mn., U.S. 198 48.46 N 96.00 W
Badger Creek ≃, Co., U.S. 198 40.17 N 103.42 W
Badger Creek ≃, Co., U.S. 200 38.28 N 105.52 W
Badger Creek ≃, Or., U.S. 224 45.16 N 121.11 W
Badger Pass ꟸ 226 37.40 N 119.39 W
Badger's Mount 260 51.20 N 0.09 E
Badgery's Creek 274a 33.53 S 150.44 E
Badgerys Creek ≃ 274a 33.51 S 150.45 E
Bādghīs ▫4 128 35.00 N 63.45 E
Bad Gleichenberg 61 46.52 N 15.54 E
Bad Godesberg 56 50.41 N 7.10 E
Bad Goisern 64 47.38 N 13.37 E
Bad Gottleuba 54 50.51 N 13.56 E
Bad Griesbach 58 48.27 N 8.14 E
Bad Grund 52 51.48 N 10.14 E
Bad Hall 61 48.02 N 14.13 E
Bad Harzburg 54 51.53 N 10.33 E
Bad Heilbrunn 64 47.45 N 11.28 E
Badhela ⌖8 272a 28.38 N 77.04 E
Bad Helmstedt 54 52.14 N 11.03 E
Bad Hersfeld 56 50.52 N 9.42 E
Badhoevedorp 52 52.21 N 4.46 E
Bad Hofgastein 64 47.10 N 13.06 E
Bad Homburg vor der Höhe 56 50.13 N 8.37 E
Bad Honnef 56 50.39 N 7.13 E
Bad Hönningen 56 50.31 N 7.19 E
Badī ≃ 124 27.55 N 83.27 E
Badia (Abtei) 64 46.37 N 11.54 E
Badia, Val V 64 46.40 N 11.53 E
Badia Calavena 64 45.34 N 11.09 E
Badia Polesine 64 45.05 N 11.29 E
Badia Prataglia 66 43.47 N 11.52 E
Badia Tedalda 66 43.42 N 12.11 E
Badile Camuno, Pizzo ∧ 58 46.01 N 10.25 E
Badīn 120 24.39 N 68.50 E
Bādinan 272b 22.54 N 88.14 E
Badinko ≃ 150 13.42 N 9.35 W
Badin Lake ⊜1 192 35.27 N 80.06 W
Badiraguato 232 25.22 N 107.31 W
Bad Ischl 64 47.43 N 13.37 E
Bad Kissingen 56 50.12 N 10.04 E
Bad Kleinen 54 53.46 N 11.28 E
Bad Kleinkirchheim 64 46.49 N 13.49 E
Bad Klosterlausnitz 54 50.55 N 11.52 E
Bad Kohlgrub 64 47.40 N 11.03 E
Bad König 56 49.45 N 9.01 E
Bad Königshofen im Grabfeld 56 50.18 N 10.29 E
Bad Kösen 54 51.08 N 11.43 E
Bad Köstritz 54 50.56 N 12.01 E
Bad Kreuznach 56 49.52 N 7.51 E
Bad Krozingen 58 47.55 N 7.42 E
Badkulla 126 23.17 N 88.32 E
Bad Laasphe 56 50.56 N 8.24 E
Badlands ∧2, U.S. 198 46.45 N 103.30 W
Badlands ∧2, S.D., U.S. 198 43.30 N 102.20 W
Badlands National Park ⌖ 198 43.47 N 102.15 W
Bad Langensalza 54 51.06 N 10.38 E
Bad Lauchstädt 54 51.23 N 11.52 E
Bad Lausick 54 51.08 N 12.39 E
Bad Lauterberg [im Harz] 52 51.38 N 10.28 E
Bad Leonfelden 61 48.33 N 14.19 E
Badli ⌖8 272a 28.45 N 77.09 E
Bad Liebenstein 54 50.49 N 10.21 E
Bad Liebenwerda 54 51.31 N 13.23 E
Bad Liebenzell 56 48.46 N 8.44 E
Bad Lippspringe 52 51.46 N 8.49 E
Bad Meinberg 52 51.53 N 8.59 E
Bad Mergentheim 56 49.30 N 9.46 E
Bad Mitterndorf 60 47.33 N 13.55 E
Bad Mukran 54 54.26 N 13.36 E
Bad Münder 52 52.12 N 9.27 E
Bad Münster am Stein 56 49.49 N 7.51 E
Bad Münstereifel 56 50.33 N 6.46 E
Bad Muskau 54 51.32 N 14.43 E
Bad Nauheim 56 50.22 N 8.44 E
Bad Nenndorf 52 52.20 N 9.23 E
Badnera 122 20.52 N 77.44 E
Badner Lindkogel ∧ 264b 48.01 N 16.11 E
Bad Neuenahr-Ahrweiler 56 50.33 N 7.08 E
Bad Neustadt an der Saale 56 50.19 N 10.13 E
Bad Niedernau 58 48.27 N 8.53 E
Bad Oeynhausen 52 52.12 N 8.48 E
Badogo 150 11.02 N 8.13 W
Badolato 68 38.34 N 16.31 E
Bad Oldesloe 52 53.48 N 10.22 E
Ba Dong, Viet 110 9.40 N 106.34 E
Badong, Zhg. 102 31.02 N 110.20 E
Badonviller 58 48.30 N 6.54 E
Bad Orb 56 50.14 N 9.20 E
Badou, Togo 150 7.35 N 0.36 E
Badou, Zhg. 98 36.27 N 117.55 E
Badouling 100 32.10 N 117.36 E
Badoumbé 150 13.38 N 10.13 W
Bad Peterstal 58 48.26 N 8.12 E
Badplaas 158 25.57 S 30.35 E
Bad Pyrmont 52 51.59 N 9.15 E
Badr 142 30.33 N 30.43 E
Bad Radkersburg 61 46.41 N 15.59 E
Bad Ragaz 58 47.00 N 9.30 E
Bad Rappenau 56 49.14 N 9.06 E
Bad Rehburg 52 52.26 N 9.13 E
Bad Reichenhall 64 47.43 N 12.52 E
Badr Hunayn 128 23.44 N 38.46 E
Bad Rippoldsau 58 48.26 N 8.19 E
Bad River Indian Reservation ⌖4 190 46.33 N 90.40 W
Bad Rothenfelde 52 52.06 N 8.09 E
Bad Saarow-Pieskow 54 52.17 N 14.03 E
Bad Sachsa 54 51.36 N 10.32 E
Bad Säckingen 58 47.33 N 7.56 E
Bad Salzdetfurth 52 52.03 N 10.01 E
Bad Salzig 56 50.12 N 7.38 E
Bad Salzschlirf 56 50.37 N 9.29 E
Bad Salzuflen 52 52.05 N 8.44 E
Bad Salzungen 56 50.48 N 10.13 E
Bad Sankt Leonhard im Lavanttal 61 46.58 N 14.48 E
Bad Sassendorf 52 51.35 N 8.10 E
Bad Schandau 54 50.55 N 14.10 E
Bad Schmiedeberg 54 51.41 N 12.44 E
Bad Schwalbach 56 50.08 N 8.04 E
Bad Schwartau 54 53.55 N 10.40 E
Bad Segeberg 52 53.56 N 10.17 E
Bādshāhpur 124 25.47 N 82.49 E
Bad Soden 56 50.08 N 8.30 E
Bad Soden-Salmünster 56 50.17 N 9.22 E
Bad Sooden-Allendorf 56 51.16 N 9.58 E
Bad Steben 54 50.22 N 11.38 E
Bad Stuer 54 53.22 N 12.19 E
Bad Suderode 54 51.44 N 11.07 E
Bad Sulza 54 51.05 N 11.37 E
Bad Sülze 54 54.06 N 12.38 E
Bad Tatzmannsdorf 61 47.20 N 16.13 E
Bad Teinach 58 48.41 N 8.41 E
Bad Tennstedt 54 51.09 N 10.50 E
Bad Tölz 64 47.46 N 11.34 E
Badu ≃ 287a 22.54 S 43.04 W
Badu, Bra. 100 26.51 N 119.35 E
Badu, Zhg. 100 28.32 N 117.57 E
Badu, Zhg. 102 24.15 N 105.41 E
Badu Island I 164 10.07 S 142.08 E
Badulla 122 6.59 N 81.03 E
Badung, Selat ꟸ 115b 8.40 S 115.22 E
Badupi 120 21.36 N 93.25 E
Bādura 126 22.16 N 90.21 E
Bad Urach 58 48.29 N 9.23 E
Baduria 126 22.44 N 88.47 E
Badvel 122 14.45 N 79.03 E
Bad Vellach 61 46.26 N 14.33 E
Bad Vilbel 56 50.12 N 8.42 E
Bad Vöslau 61 47.57 N 16.16 E
Bad Waldsee 58 47.55 N 9.45 E
Badwater Creek ≃ 202 43.17 N 108.08 W
Bad Westernkotten 52 51.38 N 8.21 E
Bad Wiessee 64 47.43 N 11.43 E
Bad Wildungen 56 51.07 N 9.07 E
Bad Wilsnack 54 52.57 N 11.57 E
Bad Wimpfen 56 49.14 N 9.09 E
Bad Windsheim 56 49.31 N 10.25 E
Bad Wörishofen 58 48.00 N 10.36 E
Bad Wurzach 58 47.54 N 9.54 E
Badžal'skij chrebet ∧ 89 50.40 N 134.50 E
Bad Zwischenahn 52 53.11 N 8.00 E
Baediam 150 15.03 N 11.51 W
Bække 41 55.34 N 9.09 E
Baena 34 37.37 N 4.19 W
Baependi 256 21.57 S 44.53 W
Baependi ≃ 256 21.52 S 45.04 W
Baer Field ꟸ 216 40.59 N 85.11 W
Baerl ⌖8 263 51.29 N 6.41 E
Baesweiler 56 50.54 N 6.11 E
Báez 240p 22.13 N 79.45 W
Baeza, Ec. 246 0.27 S 77.53 W
Baeza, Esp. 34 37.59 N 3.28 W
Baezaeko ≃ 182 53.09 N 123.48 W
Bafang 152 5.09 N 10.11 E
Bafatá 150 12.10 N 14.40 W
Bafelé 150 10.09 N 10.08 W
Baffa 123 34.26 N 73.13 E
Baffin Basin ⌖1 16 73.15 N 67.00 W
Baffin Bay ⊂, N.A. 16 73.00 N 66.00 W
Baffin Bay ⊂, Tx., U.S. 196 27.15 N 97.33 W
Baffin Island I 176 68.00 N 70.00 W
Bafia 152 4.44 N 11.16 E
Bafilo 150 9.21 N 1.16 E
Bafing ≃, Afr. 150 14.02 N 10.51 W
Bafing ≃, Mali 150 12.33 N 10.15 W
Bafing Makana 150 13.48 N 10.50 W
Bafoulabé 150 13.48 N 10.50 W
Bafoussam 152 5.29 N 10.24 E
Bāfq 128 31.35 N 55.24 E
Bafra 130 41.34 N 35.56 E
Bafra Burnu ⟩ 130 41.44 N 35.58 E
Bāft 128 29.14 N 56.38 E
Bafuku 154 1.15 N 27.54 E
Bafwabaka 154 2.07 N 27.40 E
Bafwabalinga 154 0.51 N 27.04 E
Bafwaboli 154 0.39 N 26.10 E
Bafwangbe 154 1.39 N 26.51 E
Bafwapada 154 0.56 N 26.57 E
Bafwasende 154 1.05 N 27.16 E
Bafwasomboli 154 1.27 N 27.01 E
Baga 126 22.26 N 90.28 E
Bagabag 116 16.37 N 121.15 E
Bagabag Island I 164 4.50 S 146.15 E
Baga-Burul 80 46.00 N 44.36 E
Bagac 116 14.36 N 120.23 E
Bagacay Point ⟩ 116 8.58 N 124.48 E
Bagac Bay ⊂ 116 14.36 N 120.22 E
Bagaces 236 10.31 N 85.15 W
Baga Chentej nuruu ∧ 88 48.30 N 107.30 E
Bagage ≃ 254 13.23 N 42.10 E
Bagagem ≃, Bra. 250 11.37 S 48.12 W
Bagagem ≃, Bra. 255 13.58 S 48.21 W
Bagaha 124 27.06 N 84.05 E
Bagahak ∧ 116 5.03 N 118.44 E
Bagajevskij 78 47.19 N 40.23 E
Bagalkot 122 16.11 N 75.42 E
Bagamanoc 116 13.57 N 124.17 E
Bagamoyo 154 6.26 S 38.54 E
Bagan 80 54.06 N 77.40 E
Bagana 80 54.22 N 51.25 E
Bagana, Mount ∧ 175e 6.09 S 155.12 E
Bagan Datoh 114 3.59 N 100.47 E
Bagañga 116 7.35 N 126.34 E
Bagan Serai 114 5.01 N 100.32 E
Bagansiapiapi 114 2.09 N 100.49 E
Bagansinembah 114 1.49 N 100.22 E
Bagansitukang 114 2.38 N 100.15 E
Baganza ≃ 64 44.47 N 10.19 E
Bagar 85 40.55 N 68.26 E
Bagaras 130 37.42 N 27.33 E
Bagaroua 150 14.38 N 4.21 E
Bagasra 120 21.29 N 70.57 E
Bagata 152 3.44 S 17.57 E
Bāgātipāra 126 24.18 N 88.57 E
Bagawi 140 12.19 N 34.21 E
Bagband 52 53.21 N 7.36 E
Bagbe ≃ 150 8.42 N 11.15 W
Bagbele 154 4.21 N 29.17 E
Bagda 126 23.13 N 86.41 E
Bagdad — Baghdād, 'Irāq 128 33.21 N 44.25 E
Bagdad, Az., U.S. 200 34.34 N 113.12 W
Bagdad, Fl., U.S. 194 30.35 N 87.01 W
Bagdad, Ky., U.S. 218 38.15 N 85.03 W
Bagdaha 126 23.13 N 88.53 E
Bagdanga 126 24.02 N 88.32 E
Bagdarin 88 54.26 N 113.36 E
Bagdati 84 42.06 N 42.48 E
Bağdere 130 38.07 N 40.44 E
Bagé 252 31.20 S 54.06 W
Bagehadu 120 35.25 N 84.50 E
Bâgé-le-Châtel 58 46.18 N 4.56 E
Bagenkop 41 54.45 N 10.41 E
Bāgerhāt 124 22.40 N 89.48 E
Bages et de Sigean, Étang de ⊂ 32 43.05 N 3.03 E
Bāgevādi 122 16.35 N 75.58 E
Baggao 116 17.56 N 121.46 E
Baggeryd 24 57.30 N 14.07 E
Baggetorp 40 59.01 N 16.04 E
Baggio ⌖8 266b 45.27 N 9.06 E
Bäggöze 130 37.43 N 41.55 E
Baggs 200 41.02 N 107.39 W
Baggy Point ⟩ 42 51.09 N 4.16 W
Bāgh 123 33.59 N 73.47 E
Baghdād 128 33.21 N 44.25 E
Baghdād ▫4 128 33.30 N 44.30 E
Baghdobā 126 22.08 N 87.54 E
Baghelkhand Plateau ∧1 124 23.45 N 82.20 E
Bāgh-e Malek 128 31.32 N 49.55 E
Bagheria 70 38.05 N 13.30 E
Bāgherpāra 126 23.14 N 89.20 E
Baghia 126 23.27 N 90.29 E
Baghia Bīl ≋ 126 23.07 N 90.03 E
Baghīn 128 30.12 N 56.48 E
Baghlān 120 36.13 N 68.46 E
Baghlān ▫4 120 35.45 N 69.00 E
Bāghmundi 124 23.12 N 86.03 E
Bāghpat 124 28.57 N 77.13 E
Baghrān Khowleh 120 33.01 N 64.58 E
Bagillt 262 53.16 N 3.10 W
Bağırpaşa Dağı ∧ 130 39.30 N 40.06 E
Bağırsak (Sājūr) ≃ 130 36.40 N 38.05 E
Bagkonak 130 38.12 N 31.17 E
Bagley 198 47.31 N 95.23 W
Bāgli 124 22.39 N 76.21 E
Bağlica 130 37.53 N 41.46 E
Bağlum 130 40.03 N 32.51 E
Bāgmāri ⌖8 272b 22.34 N 88.25 E
Bāgmatī ▫8 124 27.45 N 85.30 E
Bāgmatī ≃ 124 25.31 N 86.44 E
Bagn 26 60.49 N 9.34 E
Bagnacavallo 66 44.25 N 12.00 E
Bagnaia 66 42.25 N 12.09 E
Bāgnān 126 22.28 N 87.59 E
Bagnara Calabra 68 38.18 N 15.49 E
Bagnara di Romagna 66 44.23 N 11.49 E
Bag Narin 102 38.57 N 94.08 E
Bagnasco 62 44.18 N 8.02 E
Bagnell Dam ⌖6 194 38.11 N 92.39 W
Bagnères-de-Bigorre 32 43.04 N 0.09 E
Bagnères-de-Luchon 32 42.47 N 0.36 E
Bagnes, Vallée de V 58 46.03 N 7.18 E
Bagneux 261 48.48 N 2.18 E
Bagni Acque Albule 66 41.57 N 12.43 E
Bagni del Masino 58 46.15 N 9.36 E
Bagni di Lucca 66 44.01 N 10.35 E
Bagni di Rabbi 64 46.24 N 10.48 E
Bagno a Ripoli 66 43.45 N 11.19 E
Bagno di Romagna 66 43.50 N 11.57 E
Bagnolet 261 48.52 N 2.25 E
Bagnoli del Trigno 66 41.42 N 14.27 E
Bagnoli di Sopra 64 45.11 N 11.53 E
Bagnoli Irpino 68 40.50 N 15.04 E
Bagnolo in Piano 64 44.46 N 10.40 E
Bagnolo Mella 64 45.26 N 10.10 E
Bagnols-en-Forêt 62 43.32 N 6.42 E
Bagnols-les-Bains 62 44.30 N 3.40 E
Bagnols-sur-Cèze 62 44.10 N 4.37 E
Bagnon 116 13.44 N 122.50 E
Bagnone 64 44.19 N 10.00 E
Bagnoregio 66 42.37 N 12.05 E
Bagno Vignoni 66 43.02 N 11.39 E
Bago (Pegu) 110 17.20 N 96.29 E
Bago ▫8 110 18.00 N 96.00 E
Bago I 41 55.18 N 9.49 E
Bago 116 10.33 N 122.50 E
Bagod 61 46.53 N 16.45 E
Bagodar 124 24.05 N 85.52 E
Bagodo 152 6.25 N 13.23 E
Bagoé ≃ 150 12.36 N 6.34 W
Bagolino 64 45.49 N 10.28 E
Bagoni 146 7.53 N 10.43 E
Bagot ▫6 206 45.40 N 72.45 W
Bagotville, Base des Forces canadiennes ■ 186 48.20 N 70.58 W
Bağpınar 130 37.35 N 38.19 E
Bagrationovsk 76 54.23 N 20.39 E
Bagraula ⌖8 272a 28.34 N 77.04 E
Bagre 250 1.54 S 50.12 W
Bagshot 42 51.22 N 0.42 W
Bag Tal 89 43.20 N 122.16 E
Baguiati 272b 22.37 N 88.25 E
Baguio 116 16.25 N 120.36 E
Bagula 126 23.19 N 88.39 E
Bagumbayan 269f 14.28 N 121.03 E
Bagyrlaj ≃ 80 48.08 N 51.14 E
Bagzane ∧ 150 17.43 N 8.45 E
Bāh 124 26.53 N 78.36 E
Bāhādurābād Ghāt 126 25.09 N 89.42 E
Bāhādurgarh 124 28.41 N 76.56 E
Bāhādurpur 126 23.25 N 88.28 E
Bahaia, Monte ∧ 144 11.20 N 49.45 E
Baha'i Temple ⌖1 278 42.05 N 87.41 W
Bahamas ▫1, N.A. 236 24.15 N 76.00 W
Bahamas ▫1, N.A. 238 24.15 N 76.00 W
Bahār 128 34.54 N 48.26 E
Bahāragora 126 22.17 N 86.43 E
Baharampur 126 24.06 N 88.15 E
Baharpur 126 23.41 N 89.34 E
Bahata Cherneshchyna 78 48.59 N 35.35 E
Bahau 114 2.49 N 102.25 E
Bahau ≃ 112 2.34 N 116.20 E
Bahāwalnagar 123 29.59 N 73.16 E
Bahāwalpur 120 29.24 N 71.41 E
Bahçe 130 37.14 N 36.34 E
Bahçeköy ⌖8 267b 41.11 N 28.59 E
Bahçeköy su kemeri ⌖1 267b 41.03 N 28.59 E
Bahechuan 98 40.59 N 124.49 E
Baheri 124 28.47 N 79.30 E
Baherove 78 45.23 N 36.17 E
Bahi, Pil. 116 13.53 N 123.38 E
Bahi, Tan. 154 5.59 S 35.19 E
Bahia — Salvador 255 12.59 S 38.31 W
Bahia ▫3 250 11.00 S 42.00 W
Bahia, Islas de la II 236 16.20 N 86.30 W
Bahia Azul 236 9.11 N 81.54 W
Bahia Blanca 252 38.43 S 62.17 W
Bahia Bustamante 254 45.08 S 66.32 W
Bahia Erasmo, Parque Nacional ⌖ 254 46.05 S 73.35 W
Bahia Honda 240p 22.54 N 83.10 W
Bahia Honda Key I 220 24.40 N 81.16 W
Bahia Honda Point ⟩ 116 9.24 N 118.07 E
Bahia Kino 232 28.50 N 111.55 W
Bahia Laura 254 48.24 S 66.29 W
Bahij 142 30.56 N 29.35 E
Bahir Dar 144 11.35 N 37.28 E
Bahi Swamp ≋ 154 6.05 S 35.10 E
Bahjoi 124 28.24 N 78.37 E
Bahl 123 28.38 N 75.38 E
Bahlolpur 272a 28.37 N 77.24 E
Bahn 150 7.05 N 8.45 W
Bahnāy 142 30.23 N 31.04 E
Bahnayā 142 30.41 N 31.23 E
Bahrah 144 21.24 N 39.29 E
Bahraich 124 27.35 N 81.36 E
Bahrain (Al-Bahrayn) ▫1, Asia 118 26.00 N 50.30 E
Bahrain (Al-Bahrayn) ▫1, Asia 128 26.00 N 50.30 E
Bahr al-Ghazāl ▫4 140 8.30 N 26.00 E
Bahrām Chāh 128 29.26 N 64.03 E
Bahrānī, Hālat al- I 128 24.23 N 54.14 E
Bahranivtsi 78 49.17 N 27.56 E
Bahrayn, Khalīj al ⊂ 128 25.45 N 50.40 E
Bahrdorf 54 52.23 N 11.00 E
Bahrein — Bahrain ▫1 128 26.00 N 50.30 E
Bahrīyah, Al-Wāḥāt al- ⌖4 140 28.15 N 28.57 E
Bahser 130 37.57 N 39.18 E
Bahtīm 142 30.08 N 31.17 E
Bahṭīt 142 30.29 N 31.38 E
Bāhū Kalāt 128 25.43 N 61.25 E
Bāhū Kalāt ≃ 128 25.11 N 61.31 E
Bahulu, Pulau I 112 3.33 S 122.18 E
Bahu-mbelu 112 2.13 S 121.41 E
Bahūt 142 31.10 N 31.19 E
Bai 150 13.38 N 3.22 W
Bai ≃, Zhg. 102 32.10 N 112.20 E
Bai ≃, Zhg. 105 40.43 N 116.33 E
Baia 68 40.49 N 14.04 E
Baia de Aramă 38 45.00 N 22.49 E
Baía dos Tigres 152 16.36 S 11.43 E
Baía Farta 152 12.40 S 13.11 E
Baia Mare 38 47.40 N 23.35 E
Baiano 68 40.57 N 14.37 E
Baião 250 2.41 S 49.41 W
Baiardo 62 43.54 N 7.43 E
Baia Rica ≃ 248 12.40 S 63.04 W
Baia Sprie 38 47.40 N 23.42 E
Baibao 105 39.04 N 115.31 E
Baibei 100 27.47 N 115.53 E
Baibokoum 146 7.46 N 15.43 E
Baibuting 106 30.33 N 120.46 E
Baicang 120 30.14 N 90.44 E
Baicao 98 41.13 N 116.07 E
Baicaochang 102 32.08 N 103.59 E
Baicao Ling ∧ 102 26.10 N 101.20 E
Baicha 100 29.11 N 115.37 E
Baicheng, Zhg. 89 45.38 N 122.46 E
Baicheng, Zhg. 90 41.46 N 81.52 E
Baidian 106 30.47 N 119.14 E
Baidiao 102 28.07 N 101.28 E
Baidoa — Baydhabo 144 3.07 N 43.39 E
Baidunzi 102 43.11 N 95.19 E
Baidyabāti 126 22.47 N 88.20 E
Baidyanāth 124 24.29 N 86.42 E
Baidyer Bāzār 126 23.39 N 90.37 E
Baie-Comeau 186 49.13 N 68.10 W
Baie-Comeau-Hauterive, Réserve ◆ 186 50.05 N 68.00 W
Baie-des-Ha! Ha! 186 50.56 N 58.56 W
Baie-de-Shawinigan 206 46.34 N 72.45 W
Baie-des-Moutons 186 50.47 N 59.02 W
Baie-du-Renard 186 49.17 N 61.50 W
Baie-d'Urfé 206 45.25 N 73.55 W
Baie-Johan-Beetz 186 50.17 N 62.48 W
Baie-Mahault 241o 16.16 N 61.35 W
Baienfurt 64 47.49 N 9.38 E
Baiersbronn 58 48.30 N 8.22 E
Baiersdorf 60 49.39 N 11.01 E
Baies, Lac des ⊜ 190 47.18 N 77.40 W
Baie-Sainte-Claire 186 49.54 N 64.30 W
Baie-Saint-Paul 186 47.27 N 70.30 W
Baie-Trinité 186 49.25 N 67.18 W
Baie Verte 186 49.56 N 56.11 W
Baieville 206 46.08 N 72.43 W
Baigezhuang 105 39.54 N 118.09 E
Baigneux-les-Juifs 58 47.36 N 4.38 E
Baigong 100 24.18 N 116.14 E
Baigou 105 39.07 N 116.01 E
Baigou ≃ 105 39.06 N 116.00 E
Baiguoshu 106 30.45 N 119.07 E
Baigusi 102 33.10 N 103.52 E
Baihai 105 38.18 N 115.13 E
Baihāli Jot ∧ 123 32.51 N 76.32 E
Baihar 124 22.06 N 80.33 E
Baihe, Zhg. 100 29.12 N 120.55 E
Baihe, Zhg. 102 32.17 N 110.02 E
Baihebu 105 40.39 N 116.10 E
Baihegang 106 31.16 N 121.08 E
Baihekou 102 31.46 N 110.13 E
Baihou 100 24.18 N 116.48 E
Baihua 107 29.07 N 104.37 E
Baihua Shan ∧ 105 39.50 N 115.35 E
Baijala 272b 22.51 N 88.16 E
Baijian 105 39.36 N 115.16 E
Baijiang 100 29.51 N 119.20 E
Baijiawu 105 39.30 N 116.28 E
Baijie 107 29.17 N 106.31 E
Baijietan 107 28.44 N 105.30 E
Baijnāth 124 29.55 N 79.37 E
Baiju 100 33.04 N 120.20 E
Baikal, Lago — Bajkal, ozero ⊜ 88 53.00 N 107.40 E
Baikal, Lake — Bajkal, ozero ⊜ 88 53.00 N 107.40 E
Baikal-See — Bajkal, ozero ⊜ 88 53.00 N 107.40 E
Baikeshu 106 30.26 N 118.55 E
Baikonur — Bajkonyr 86 47.50 N 66.03 E
Baikunthapur 272b 22.59 N 88.13 E
Baikunthpur 124 23.15 N 82.33 E
Bailadores 246 8.15 N 71.50 W
Bailaiqiao 100 32.40 N 118.23 E
Bailang 89 46.57 N 120.05 E
Baildon 44 53.52 N 1.46 W
Baile 39 55.95 N 114.51 E
Baile Átha Luain — Athlone 48 53.25 N 7.56 W
Băile Govora 38 45.05 N 24.11 E
Băile Herculane 38 44.54 N 22.25 E
Băile Olănești 38 45.11 N 24.16 E
Băilești 38 44.02 N 23.21 E
Bailey 192 35.46 N 78.07 W
Bailey Lakes 214 40.57 N 82.21 W
Bailey Run ≃ 279b 40.35 N 79.47 W
Baileys Crossroads 284c 38.51 N 77.08 W
Bail Hongal 122 15.49 N 74.52 E
Bailian 102 24.09 N 112.22 E
Bailicun 105 39.55 N 118.33 E
Bailieborough 48 53.55 N 6.59 W
Bailin, Zhg. 100 27.12 N 120.10 E
Bailin, Zhg. 102 26.20 N 113.18 E
Bailin, Zhg. 107 24.85 N 106.26 E
Bailin, Zhg. 107 29.11 N 105.57 E
Bailingmiao — Darhan Muminggan Lianheqi 102 41.50 N 110.27 E
Bailique 250 0.58 N 50.04 W
Bailique, Ilha I 250 1.02 N 49.58 W
Bailleau-sous-Gallardon 261 48.32 N 1.39 E
Bailleul 50 50.44 N 2.44 E
Ba Illi 146 10.30 N 16.34 E
Baillie ≃ 176 65.10 N 104.24 W
Baillie Islands II 176 70.33 N 128.10 W
Baillif 241o 16.01 N 61.45 W
Bailly-Romainvilliers 261 48.50 N 2.49 E
Bailong ≃ 102 32.18 N 105.42 E
Bailongjiang 106 31.20 N 119.59 E
Bailu ≃ 100 32.25 N 115.54 E
Bailuchang 107 28.56 N 105.57 E
Bailu Hu ⊜ 100 30.03 N 113.06 E
Bailundo 152 12.12 S 15.52 E
Bailuoji 100 29.37 N 113.15 E
Baima, Zhg. 106 31.35 N 119.10 E

Symbols in the index entries represent the broad categories identified in the key at the right. Symbols with superior numbers (∧1) identify subcategories (see complete key on page I · 1).

Symbole im Register stellen die rechts im Schlüssel erklärten Kategorien dar. Symbole mit hochgestellten Ziffern (∧1) bezeichnen Unterabteilungen einer Kategorie (vgl. vollständiger Schlüssel auf Seite I · 1).

Los símbolos incluídos en el texto del índice representan las grandes categorías identificadas con la clave a la derecha. Los símbolos con numeros en su parte superior (∧1) identifican las subcategorías (véase la clave completa en la página I · 1).

Les symboles de l'index représentent les catégories indiquées dans la légende à droite. Les symboles suivis d'un indice (∧1) représentent des sous-catégories (voir légende complète à la page I · 1).

Os símbolos incluídos no texto do índice representam as grandes categorias identificadas com a chave à direita. Os símbolos com números em sua parte superior (∧1) identificam as subcategorias (veja-se a chave completa à página I · 1).

∧ Mountain	Berg	Montaña	Montagne	Montanha
∧ Mountains	Gebirge	Montañas	Montagnes	Montanhas
ꟸ Pass	Paß	Paso	Col	Passo
V Valley, Canyon	Tal, Cañon	Valle, Cañón	Vallée, Canyon	Vale, Canhão
≃ Plain	Ebene	Llano	Plaine	Planície
⟩ Cape	Kap	Cabo	Cap	Cabo
I Island	Insel	Isla	Île	Ilha
II Islands	Inseln	Islas	Îles	Ilhas
⌇ Other Topographic Features	Andere Topographische Objekte	Otros Elementos Topográficos	Autres données topographiques	Outros acidentes topográficos

ESPAÑOL

Nombre	Página	Lat.°′	Long.°′ W = Oeste
Baima, Zhg.	107	30.03 N	103.44 E
Baima, Zhg.	107	29.09 N	104.16 E
Baimachang, Zhg.	102	29.18 N	107.30 E
Baimachang, Zhg.	104	41.59 N	122.30 E
Baimachang, Zhg.	107	29.40 N	103.54 E
Baimaguan	105	40.41 N	116.52 E
Baimakou	102	25.55 N	102.06 E
Baimamiao, Zhg.	102	36.58 N	108.08 E
Baimamiao, Zhg.	107	29.33 N	104.59 E
Baimao, Zhg.	106	31.39 N	120.52 E
Baimao, Zhg.	106	31.35 N	120.54 E
Baima Shan ∧	102	27.12 N	110.32 E
Baimashi	100	29.15 N	118.42 E
Baimazhai	100	28.06 N	115.50 E
Baimiaozi, Zhg.	89	46.18 N	123.35 E
Baimiaozi, Zhg.	98	40.34 N	120.36 E
Baimiaozi, Zhg.	104	41.55 N	122.12 E
Baimiaozi, Zhg.	107	29.47 N	106.29 E
Baimuqiao	106	32.01 N	120.19 E
Baimuru	164	7.30 S	144.49 E
Bain ≃	44	53.05 N	0.12 W
Baïna Bondio	152	5.10 N	16.33 E
Bainang	120	29.11 N	89.12 E
Bainbridge, Ga., U.S.	192	30.54 N	84.34 W
Bainbridge, N.Y., U.S.	210	42.17 N	75.28 W
Bainbridge, Oh., U.S.	218	39.13 N	83.16 W
Bainbridge, Pa., U.S.	208	40.05 N	76.40 W
Bainbridge Island I	224	47.37 N	122.33 W
Bainchi	126	23.07 N	88.14 E
Bainchipota	272b	22.52 N	88.16 E
Bain-de-Bretagne	32	47.50 N	1.41 W
Baing	115b	10.14 S	120.34 E
Bainiqiao	100	29.35 N	114.09 E
Bains-les-Bains	58	48.00 N	6.16 E
Bainville	198	48.08 N	104.13 W
Bainyik	164	3.40 S	143.00 E
Baipeng	102	24.09 N	109.25 E
Baipu	106	32.15 N	120.46 E
Baiqibao	104	41.48 N	122.30 E
Baiqiu	100	32.44 N	112.38 E
Baiquan, Zhg.	89	47.36 N	126.07 E
Baiquan, Zhg.	100	30.06 N	122.08 E
Baiqueyuan	100	31.48 N	115.05 E
Bair, Pa., U.S.	208	39.54 N	76.50 W
Bā'ir, Urd.	132	30.46 N	36.41 E
Bā'ir, Wādī V	132	30.58 N	37.09 E
Bairab Co ◎	120	35.00 N	83.03 E
Baird	196	32.23 N	99.23 W
Baird, Mount ∧	202	43.22 N	111.06 W
Bairdford	214	40.37 N	79.52 W
Baird Inlet c	180	60.45 N	164.00 W
Baird Mountains ⋏	180	67.35 N	161.30 W
Baire	240p	20.19 N	76.20 W
Bairiki	174t	1.20 N	173.01 E
Bairin Zuoqi	90	44.00 N	119.00 E
Bair Island I	282	37.32 N	122.13 W
Bairkum	85	42.05 N	68.11 E
Bairnsdale	166	37.50 S	147.38 E
Bairoil	200	42.14 N	107.33 W
Bairrinho	256	22.36 S	47.06 W
Bairro Alto	256	23.29 S	45.21 W
Bairuopu	100	28.12 N	112.46 E
Bais, Fr.	32	48.15 N	0.22 W
Bais, Pil.	116	9.35 N	123.07 E
Baïse ≃	32	44.17 N	0.18 E
Baisha, Zhg.	100	29.26 N	119.16 E
Baisha, Zhg.	100	25.40 N	118.59 E
Baisha, Zhg.	100	25.24 N	117.16 E
Baisha, Zhg.	100	34.22 N	112.32 E
Baisha, Zhg.	100	26.58 N	115.22 E
Baisha, Zhg.	100	24.39 N	113.31 E
Baisha, Zhg.	100	34.20 N	113.14 E
Baisha, Zhg.	107	28.55 N	105.45 E
Baisha, Zhg.	107	29.04 N	106.07 E
Baisha, Zhg.	110	19.17 N	109.27 E
Baishaba	107	30.03 N	106.21 E
Bai Shan I	106	30.35 N	121.43 E
Baishanji	100	33.48 N	116.40 E
Baishantu	104	42.21 N	122.35 E
Baishapu	100	29.58 N	115.04 E
Baishatan	98	36.52 N	121.38 E
Baishe	100	27.02 N	116.20 E
Baishecun	105	40.10 N	116.18 E
Baishi, Zhg.	100	27.18 N	119.45 E
Baishi, Zhg.	100	26.48 N	119.46 E
Baishi, Zhg.	102	22.36 N	110.55 E
Baishidu	100	25.26 N	113.01 E
Baishiyi	107	29.29 N	106.22 E
Baishizhai	104	40.57 N	122.58 E
Baishui, Zhg.	100	28.42 N	113.04 E
Baishui, Zhg.	106	30.34 N	119.39 E
Baishui, Zhg.	107	30.06 N	105.38 E
Baishuifan	100	30.17 N	115.43 E
Baishuijiang	102	33.29 N	106.01 E
Baishun	100	25.12 N	114.01 E
Baishuxia	100	27.22 N	113.41 E
Baisinga	126	21.39 N	86.54 E
Baisley Pond ◎	276	40.41 N	73.47 W
Baisogala	76	55.38 N	23.43 E
Bāisrasi	126	23.27 N	90.02 E
Baita, India	272b	22.27 N	88.11 E
Baita, Zhg.	106	31.48 N	119.35 E
Baitadī	124	29.32 N	80.26 E
Baital	126	22.57 N	87.28 E
Baitazi	98	42.19 N	120.19 E
Baitazibeigou	104	42.17 N	120.48 E
Bai Thuong	110	19.54 N	105.23 E
Baitings Reservoir ◎[1]	262	53.40 N	1.59 W
Baitou	107	30.37 N	103.36 E
Baitoutan	102	32.30 N	106.56 E
Baitu	106	31.59 N	119.21 E
Baitugang	100	33.28 N	112.22 E
Baiwang	102	24.14 N	108.32 E
Baiwen	102	38.15 N	111.06 E
Baixa da Banheira	266c	38.39 N	9.03 W
Baixa Grande	255	11.57 S	40.11 W
Baixi	107	29.39 N	106.28 E
Baixiang	98	37.32 N	114.34 E
Baixingt	89	43.08 N	121.03 E
Baixio	250	6.44 S	38.43 W
Baixo Longa	152	15.42 S	18.50 E
Baiyan, Zhg.	100	28.04 N	120.02 E
Baiyan, Zhg.	106	31.08 N	119.38 E
Baiyang	100	34.25 N	112.12 E
Baiyang Dian ◎	98	38.53 N	116.00 E
Baiyanghe	86	43.13 N	88.28 E
Baiyan Shan ∧	100	26.05 N	118.25 E
Baiyer River	164	5.35 S	144.10 E
Baiyin	102	36.47 N	104.07 E
Baiyinheshuo	89	44.31 N	119.51 E
Baiyintaohai	89	43.12 N	120.23 E
Baiyü, Zhg.	102	31.18 N	98.49 E
Baiyu, Zhg.	105	40.01 N	115.37 E
Baiyundu	100	26.10 N	118.47 E
Baiyunguan	271a	39.54 N	116.19 E
Baizhongpu	100	33.22 N	114.50 E
Baizi	107	30.06 N	105.43 E
Baja	30	46.11 N	18.57 E
Baja, Punta ›	232	29.58 N	115.49 W
Baja California	200	32.18 N	115.12 W
Baja California □[3]	232	30.00 N	115.00 W
Baja California ›[1]	232	28.00 N	113.30 W
Baja California Seamount Province ✣	16	26.00 N	124.00 W
Baja California Sur □[3]	232	26.00 N	112.00 W
Bajada del Agrio	252	38.23 S	70.02 W
Baján	196	26.32 N	101.15 W
Bajan Adraga	88	48.32 N	111.03 E
Bajan Agt	88	49.02 N	102.05 E
Bajanaul	86	50.47 N	75.42 E
Bajancagaan	102	45.00 N	98.59 E
Bajan Chajrchan	88	49.18 N	96.20 E
Bajanchongor	90	46.08 N	100.43 E
Bajanchongor □[4]	102	45.00 N	99.30 E
Bajancogt	88	45.54 N	106.10 E
Bajandaj	88	53.04 N	105.30 E
Bajandalaj	102	43.28 N	103.28 E
Bajandelger, Mong.	88	47.44 N	108.07 E
Bajandelger, Mong.	102	45.40 N	112.20 E
Bajan Dün	88	49.13 N	113.23 E

FRANÇAIS

Nom	Page	Lat.°′	Long.°′ W = Ouest
Bajandžargalan	102	45.40 N	107.59 E
Bajan Dzürch	88	50.12 N	98.58 E
Bajan-Enger	86	48.25 N	90.50 E
Bajango	88	48.55 N	106.06 E
Bajangol, Ross.	88	50.44 N	103.27 E
Bajan-Gol, Ross.	88	52.49 N	99.54 E
Bajangov'	102	44.44 N	100.24 E
Bajanleg	102	44.33 N	100.50 E
Bajan Nuur	86	48.54 N	91.14 E
Bajanölgij □[4]	86	48.20 N	89.50 E
Bajan-Öndör	102	44.47 N	98.39 E
Bajan-Ovoo, Mong.	88	47.47 N	112.05 E
Bajan-Ovoo, Mong.	102	42.57 N	106.07 E
Bajánsenye	30	46.48 N	16.23 E
Bajan Tümen	88	48.04 N	114.24 E
Bajan Uul, Mong.	88	47.40 N	101.30 E
Bajan Uul, Mong.	88	49.10 N	112.50 E
Bajan Uul, Mong.	88	49.41 N	96.20 E
Bājaur □[9]	123	34.50 N	71.30 E
Baja Verapaz □[5]	236	15.05 N	90.20 W
Bajawa	115b	8.47 S	120.59 E
Bajbičetau ⋏	85	41.12 N	75.15 E
Baj-Chak	88	51.13 N	94.34 E
Bajčunas	80	47.14 N	52.55 E
Bajčurovo	80	51.20 N	42.41 E
Bajdarackaja guba c	72	69.00 N	67.30 E
Bajdonovo	88	54.17 N	104.38 E
Bajdrag ≃	102	45.38 N	99.15 E
Bājegūn, Kūh-e ∧	128	31.28 N	55.51 E
Bājengdoba	124	25.54 N	90.31 E
Bāje Phukura	126	23.09 N	89.45 E
Bajer	88	55.44 N	99.30 E
Bajestān	128	34.31 N	58.10 E
Bajevo	86	53.17 N	80.46 E
Bajgakum	86	44.18 N	66.28 E
Bajganin	86	48.43 N	55.53 E
Bajghera	272a	28.32 N	77.01 E
Bājgīrān	128	37.36 N	58.24 E
Bajgul	80	48.49 N	49.08 E
Bajiaotai	104	41.14 N	121.14 E
Bajiazi, Zhg.	104	42.17 N	122.37 E
Bajiazi, Zhg.	104	42.21 N	121.27 E
Bajiazi, Zhg.	104	41.36 N	123.53 E
Bājil	144	15.04 N	43.16 E
Bajimba, Mount ∧	166	29.18 S	152.07 E
Bajina Bašta	38	43.58 N	19.34 E
Bajkadam	85	43.44 N	69.55 E
Bajkal	88	51.53 N	104.47 E
Bajkal, ozero (Lake Baikal) ◎	88	53.00 N	107.40 E
Bajkalovo, Ross.	86	57.24 N	63.46 E
Bajkalovo, Ross.	86	57.45 N	67.40 E
Bajkal'sk	88	51.33 N	104.05 E
Bajkal'skij chrebet ⋏	88	55.00 N	108.40 E
Bajkal'skij zapovednik ♠	88	51.25 N	105.10 E
Bajkal'skoje	88	55.21 N	109.12 E
Bajkit	74	61.41 N	96.25 E
Bajkonyr	86	47.50 N	66.03 E
Bajkovo	80	54.47 N	44.51 E
Bajmak	86	52.36 N	58.19 E
Bajmok	38	45.58 N	19.25 E
Bajnazar	86	48.32 N	73.42 E
Bajo, Indon.	112	0.27 N	120.48 E
Bajo, Indon.	115b	8.35 S	119.01 E
Bajo, Canal ≍	266a	40.27 N	3.43 W
Bajo Baudó	246	4.58 N	77.22 W
Bajo Boquete	236	8.47 N	82.26 W
Bajool	166	23.39 S	150.39 E
Bajos de Haina	238	18.25 N	70.02 W
Bajos del Balsamar	234	17.34 N	100.48 W
Bajr'aki	80	54.43 N	53.24 E
Bajram-Ali	128	37.37 N	62.10 E
Bajsa	88	53.58 N	113.33 E
Bajseit	85	43.35 N	78.20 E
Baj-Sot	88	51.42 N	95.22 E
Bajsun	85	38.14 N	67.12 E
Bajtajlak	86	45.15 N	75.00 E
Bajulmati	115a	7.56 S	114.23 E
Bajžansaj	85	43.13 N	69.56 E
Bak	61	46.43 N	16.51 E
Bakacak	130	40.12 N	27.06 E
Bakal	86	54.56 N	58.48 E
Bakala	152	6.11 N	20.22 E
Bakaldy	80	55.39 N	44.44 E
Bakali ≃	152	4.34 S	17.06 E
Bakaly	80	55.10 N	53.48 E
Bakambe	152	5.39 S	23.37 E
Bakanas	86	44.50 N	76.15 E
Bakanas ≃	86	47.05 N	79.18 E
Bakap	114	4.26 N	101.04 E
Bakar	116	7.09 N	125.42 E
Bākarganj	124	22.33 N	90.21 E
Bakaruma	124	22.32 N	83.25 E
Bakau, Pulau I	271c	1.16 N	103.43 E
Bakbakty	86	44.35 N	76.40 E
Bakčar	86	57.01 N	82.05 E
Bakčar ≃	86	57.37 N	82.18 E
Bake	112	3.03 S	100.16 E
Bakebe	152	5.35 N	9.33 E
Bakel	150	14.54 N	12.27 W
Bakem	112	1.58 S	105.54 E
Bakenberg ∧[2]	54	54.35 N	13.07 E
Bakenkop	158	28.01 S	23.02 E
Bakeoven Creek ≃	224	45.12 N	121.05 W
Baker, Ca., U.S.	204	35.15 N	116.04 W
Baker, Fl., U.S.	194	30.47 N	86.40 W
Baker, La., U.S.	194	30.35 N	91.10 W
Baker, Mt., U.S.	198	46.22 N	104.17 W
Baker, Or., U.S.	202	44.46 N	117.49 W
Baker ≃, Chile	254	47.49 S	73.37 W
Baker ≃, Wa., U.S.	224	48.38 N	121.41 W
Baker, Canal ʉ	254	48.00 S	74.00 W
Baker, Mount ∧	224	48.47 N	121.49 W
Baker Butte ∧	200	34.27 N	111.22 W
Baker Canyon V	280	33.47 N	117.38 W
Baker Creek ≃, B.C., Can.	182	52.59 N	122.30 W
Baker Creek ≃, Oh., U.S.	279a	41.21 N	81.54 W
Baker Creek ≃, Or., U.S.	224	45.15 N	123.14 W
Baker Island I, Oc.	14	0.15 N	176.27 W
Baker Island I, Ak., U.S.	182	55.20 N	133.36 W
Baker Lake	176	64.15 N	96.00 W
Baker Lake ◎, Austl.	162	26.54 S	126.05 E
Baker Lake ◎, N.T., Can.	176	64.10 N	95.30 W
Baker Lake ◎, Il., U.S.	278	42.08 N	88.07 W
Baker Lake ◎[1]	224	48.43 N	121.37 W
Bakersfield	226	35.22 N	119.01 W
Bakersfield South	228	35.20 N	119.03 W
Bakers Hill	168a	31.45 S	116.27 E
Bakers Island I	283	42.32 N	70.47 W
Bakerstown	214	40.39 N	79.56 W
Baker Street	260	51.30 N	0.21 E
Bakersville, N.C., U.S.	192	36.00 N	82.09 W
Bakersville, Oh., U.S.	214	40.21 N	81.39 W
Bakerville	158	26.00 S	26.06 E
Bakeshu	98	42.26 N	124.37 E
Bâ Kêv	110	13.42 N	107.12 E
Bakewell	44	53.13 N	1.40 W
Bakhchysaray	78	44.45 N	33.51 E
Bakhmach	78	51.13 N	32.46 E
Bakhmut ≃	83	48.56 N	38.03 E
Bakhmutivka	83	48.52 N	39.03 E
Bakhra	126	22.24 N	88.11 E
Bākhrābād	126	23.43 N	90.53 E
Bakhri	124	25.35 N	86.16 E
Bākhtarān (Kermānshāh)	128	34.19 N	47.04 E
Bakhtarān □[4]	128	34.30 N	47.00 E
Bakhtegān, Daryācheh-ye ◎	128	29.20 N	54.05 E
Bakhtiyārpur	124	25.28 N	85.31 E
Bakhuis	250	4.42 N	56.49 W
Bakı (Baku)	84	40.23 N	49.51 E
Bakile	154	13.58 S	35.15 E
Bakino	82	56.20 N	38.59 E
Bakinskaja	78	44.46 N	39.18 E

PORTUGUÊS

Nome	Página	Lat.°′	Long.°′ W = Oeste
Bakır ≃	130	38.55 N	27.00 E
Bakitabu	154	1.29 S	35.34 E
Bakkafjörður	24a	66.04 N	14.45 W
Bakkaflói c	24a	66.10 N	14.45 W
Bakkagerði	24a	65.32 N	13.48 W
Bakkeswar	272b	22.25 N	88.22 E
Bakkeveen	52	53.05 N	6.15 E
Baklan	130	37.58 N	29.36 E
Baklanka	76	58.43 N	40.06 E
Bakloh	123	32.28 N	75.55 E
Bakluši	80	52.07 N	43.22 E
Bako, C. Iv.	150	9.09 N	7.37 W
Bako, Ityo.	144	5.50 N	36.40 E
Bakony ⋏	30	47.15 N	17.50 E
Bakool □[4]	144	4.00 N	44.00 E
Bakoondfontein	158	32.43 S	22.30 E
Bakori	150	11.34 N	7.27 E
Bakou → Bakı	84	40.23 N	49.51 E
Bakouma	152	5.42 N	22.47 E
Bakovka	265b	55.41 N	37.20 E
Bakoy ≃	150	13.49 N	10.50 W
Bakruz'ak	86	52.59 N	58.42 E
Baksan	84	43.40 N	43.32 E
Baksan ≃	84	43.42 N	43.32 E
Bakšejevo, Ross.	80	55.44 N	39.53 E
Bakšejevo, Ross.	86	57.26 N	73.00 E
Baksir Chāndpur	126	23.30 N	89.44 E
Bakšty	76	53.56 N	26.11 E
Baksuk ≃	86	51.50 N	69.30 E
Baku → Bakı	84	40.23 N	49.51 E
Bakulin Point ›	116	8.33 N	126.22 E
Bakum	52	52.45 N	8.11 E
Bakumpai	112	1.26 S	113.05 E
Bakun	120	32.32 N	80.26 E
Bakung, Pulau I	112	0.04 N	104.27 E
Bakungan	114	2.56 N	97.30 E
Bakuriani	84	41.46 N	43.32 E
Bakury	80	52.22 N	44.42 E
Bakwa-Kenge	152	4.51 S	22.04 E
Bakwanga → Mbuji-Mayi	152	6.09 S	23.38 E
Bakyrly	86	44.21 N	67.48 E
Bal ≃	126	21.58 N	89.21 E
Bala, On., Can.	212	45.01 N	79.37 W
Bala, Sén.	150	14.02 N	13.10 W
Balâ, Tür.	130	39.34 N	33.08 E
Bala, Wales, U.K.	42	52.54 N	3.35 W
Balabac	116	7.59 N	117.04 E
Balabac Island I	116	7.57 N	117.01 E
Balabac Strait ʉ	112	7.35 N	117.00 E
Bālā Bāgh	120	34.24 N	70.14 E
Ba'labakk	130	34.00 N	36.12 E
Balabalagan, Kepulauan II	112	2.20 S	117.25 E
Balaban	130	38.28 N	37.36 E
Balabanovo	82	55.11 N	36.40 E
Balabio, Île I	175f	20.07 S	164.11 E
Balabyne	78	47.44 N	35.13 E
Balachčin	86	54.09 N	89.23 E
Balachna	80	56.30 N	43.36 E
Balachta	86	55.24 N	91.37 E
Balachtison, gora ∧	86	54.36 N	93.50 E
Balaci	38	44.21 N	24.55 E
Bala-Cynwyd	285	40.00 N	75.14 W
Balad	128	34.01 N	44.09 E
Baladbandh	272b	22.52 N	88.07 E
Balad'ok	89	53.41 N	133.07 E
Balagansk	88	53.57 N	103.02 E
Bālāghāt	120	21.48 N	80.11 E
Bālāghāt Range ⋏	122	18.45 N	76.30 E
Balagny-sur-Thérain	50	49.18 N	2.20 E
Balaguer	34	41.47 N	0.49 E
Balaikarangan	112	0.50 N	110.26 E
Balaiselasa	112	1.48 S	100.50 E
Balaisepuah	112	0.27 N	111.13 E
Balaj	86	55.52 N	93.59 E
Balaka	152	4.51 S	19.57 E
Balakän	84	41.43 N	46.26 E
Balakété	152	6.56 N	19.54 E
Balakirevo	82	56.30 N	38.51 E
Balaklava, Austl.	168b	34.09 S	138.25 E
Balaklava, Ukr.	78	44.30 N	33.36 E
Balakliya, Ukr.	78	49.14 N	31.44 E
Balakliya, Ukr.	78	49.27 N	36.52 E
Bālākot	123	34.33 N	73.21 E
Balakovo	80	52.02 N	47.47 E
Balal, Laga ≃	154	3.25 N	37.15 E
Balallan	46	58.05 N	6.35 W
Balama, Moç.	154	13.20 S	38.30 E
Bal'amā, Urd.	132	32.14 N	36.05 E
Balamban	116	10.30 N	123.42 E
Balambangan, Pulau I	112	7.15 N	116.55 E
Bālā Morghāb	128	35.35 N	63.20 E
Bālandi	272b	22.58 N	88.32 E
Balanga	116	14.41 N	120.32 E
Balangala	152	0.24 N	19.45 E
Ba Lang An, Mui ›	110	15.14 N	108.56 E
Balangero	62	45.16 N	7.31 E
Balangiga	116	11.07 N	125.23 E
Balāngīr	122	20.43 N	83.29 E
Balanguingui Island I	116	6.01 N	121.41 E
Bālān Şafar 'Ali	128	38.59 N	47.27 E
Balanşūrah	142	27.55 N	30.41 E
Balantak, Gunung ∧	112	0.45 S	123.20 E
Balapulang	115a	7.03 S	109.05 E
Bālāpur	122	20.40 N	76.46 E
Balaqs	273c	30.10 N	31.17 E
Balaqtar	142	31.05 N	30.13 E
Balaraja	115a	6.12 S	106.27 E
Balarāmbāti	272b	22.48 N	88.13 E
Balarāmpota	272b	22.31 N	88.08 E
Balarāmpur	126	23.07 N	86.13 E
Balaruc-le-Vieux	62	43.27 N	3.41 E
Balaši	80	51.24 N	49.55 E
Balašicha	82	55.49 N	37.58 E
Balašov	80	51.32 N	43.08 E
Balassagyarmat	30	48.05 N	19.18 E
Balāṭ	140	25.33 N	29.16 E
Balatan, Indon.	164	6.05 S	134.45 E
Balatan, Pil.	116	13.20 N	123.10 E
Balatina	38	47.42 N	27.21 E
Balaton	198	44.14 N	95.52 W
Balaton ◎	30	46.50 N	17.45 E
Balaurin	112	8.15 S	123.43 E
Balavé	150	12.23 N	4.09 W
Balaxanı	84	40.29 N	49.54 E
Balayan	116	13.57 N	120.44 E
Balayan Bay c	116	13.51 N	120.47 E
Balazote	34	38.53 N	2.08 W
Balbi, Mount ∧[1]	175e	5.55 S	154.59 E
Balbieriškis	76	54.32 N	23.52 E
Balbigny	62	45.49 N	4.11 E
Balbina, Reprêsa ◎[1]	246	1.20 S	59.40 W
Balboa	236	8.57 N	79.34 W
Balbriggan	48	53.37 N	6.11 W
Balcad	144	2.23 N	45.23 E
Balcanoona	166	30.31 S	139.18 E
Balcarce	252	37.50 S	58.15 W
Balcarres	184	50.48 N	103.33 W
Bălceşti	38	44.37 N	23.56 E
Balchaš	86	46.49 N	74.59 E
Balchaš, ozero (Lake Balkhash) ◎	86	46.00 N	74.00 E
Balch Springs	222	32.43 N	96.37 W
Balcı	130	38.43 N	34.06 E
Balčik	38	43.25 N	28.10 E
Balclutha	172	46.14 S	169.44 E
Balcombe	42	51.04 N	0.08 W
Balcones Escarpment ⊥[4]	196	29.30 N	99.15 W
Balde	252	33.20 S	66.38 W
Baldeador	287a	22.53 S	43.02 W
Bald Eagle	214	40.42 N	78.12 W
Bald Eagle Creek ≃	210	41.08 N	77.24 W
Bald Eagle Mountain ∧	214	41.00 N	77.45 W
Bald Eagle State Park ♠	214	41.00 N	77.40 W
Baldegger See ◎	58	47.12 N	8.16 E
Baldeneysee ◎	263	51.24 N	7.03 E
Balderschwang	58	47.28 N	10.06 E
Balderstone	262	53.47 N	2.34 W
Balderton	44	53.03 N	0.47 W
Bald Head ›	162	35.07 S	118.01 E
Bald Hill ∧[2]	166	20.18 S	144.06 E
Bald Hill Branch ≃	284c	18.55 N	76.49 W
Baldhill Creek ≃	198	47.09 N	98.03 W
Bald Hills	171a	27.19 S	153.01 E
Baldichieri d'Asti	62	44.54 N	8.07 E
Baldim	255	19.17 S	43.57 W
Bald Island I	162	34.55 S	118.27 E
Bald Knob	194	35.18 N	91.34 W
Bald Knob ∧, Ca., U.S.	282	37.25 N	122.21 W
Bald Knob ∧, Va., U.S.	192	37.56 N	79.51 W
Bald Knoll ∧	200	42.24 N	110.29 W
Bald Mountain ∧, Ct., U.S.	207	41.59 N	72.25 W
Bald Mountain ∧, Nv., U.S.	226	38.33 N	119.07 W
Bald Mountain ∧, Or., U.S.	202	44.48 N	123.33 W
Bald Mountain ∧, Or., U.S.	202	43.16 N	121.21 W
Bald Mountain ∧, Or., U.S.	202	44.36 N	117.53 W
Bald Mountain ∧, Vt., U.S.	210	42.55 N	73.09 W
Bald Mountain State Recreation Area ♠	216	42.46 N	83.14 W
Baldo, Monte ∧	64	45.47 N	10.48 E
Baldock	42	51.59 N	0.12 W
Baldock Lake ◎	184	56.33 N	97.57 W
Baldone	76	56.45 N	24.24 E
Baldovino, Arroyo ≃	288	34.46 S	58.07 W
Baldoyle	48	53.24 N	6.08 W
Baldpate Pond ◎	283	42.42 N	71.00 W
Balduinstein	56	50.20 N	7.58 E
Baldur	184	49.23 N	99.15 W
Baldwin, Fl., U.S.	192	30.18 N	81.58 W
Baldwin, La., U.S.	194	29.50 N	91.32 W
Baldwin, Mi., U.S.	190	43.54 N	85.51 W
Baldwin, N.Y., U.S.	210	40.39 N	73.36 W
Baldwin, Pa., U.S.	214	40.23 N	79.57 W
Baldwin, Wi., U.S.	190	44.58 N	92.22 W
Baldwin Bay c	276	40.38 N	73.35 W
Baldwin City	198	38.46 N	95.11 W
Baldwin Creek ≃	279a	41.22 N	81.51 W
Baldwin Hills ⋏[2]	280	34.00 N	118.22 W
Baldwin Lake ◎	279a	41.21 N	81.51 W
Baldwin Park	228	34.05 N	117.57 W
Baldwin Peninsula ›[1]	180	66.44 N	162.15 W
Baldwinsville	210	43.09 N	76.19 W
Baldwinville	207	42.36 N	72.04 W
Baldwin-Wallace College ◈[2]	279a	41.23 N	81.51 W
Baldwyn	194	34.31 N	88.38 W
Baldy Mountain ∧, B.C., Can.	182	51.28 N	120.02 W
Baldy Mountain ∧, Mb., Can.	184	51.28 N	100.44 W
Baldy Mountain ∧, Mt., U.S.	202	48.09 N	109.39 W
Baldy Mountain ∧, N.M., U.S.	200	36.38 N	105.13 W
Baldy Peak ∧	200	33.55 N	109.35 W
Bale, Hrv.	64	45.02 N	13.48 E
Bale, India	272c	19.08 N	73.06 E
Bâle → Basel, Schw.	58	47.33 N	7.35 E
Bale □[4]	144	6.20 N	41.30 E
Bale-Akiosi	273a	6.41 N	3.21 E
Balearen → Balears, Illes II	34	39.30 N	3.00 E
Baléares, Îles → Balears, Illes II	34	39.30 N	3.00 E
Balearic Islands → Balears, Illes II	34	39.30 N	3.00 E
Balears □[4]	34	39.30 N	3.00 E
Balears, Illes (Balearic Islands) II	34	39.30 N	3.00 E
Balease, Gunung ∧	112	2.24 S	120.33 E
Balegane	158	26.04 S	31.34 E
Baleh ≃	112	2.01 N	113.01 E
Baleia, Ponta da ›	255	17.40 S	39.07 W
Baleine, Grande rivière de la ≃	176	55.16 N	77.47 W
Baleine, Petite rivière de la ≃	176	56.00 N	76.45 W
Baleine, Rivière à la ≃	176	58.15 N	67.40 W
Balej	88	51.36 N	116.38 E
Balelasberg ⋏	158	27.30 S	30.07 E
Bale Mountains National Park ♠	144	7.00 N	39.40 E
Bâle-Mulhouse, Aéroport ⊠	58	47.35 N	7.32 E
Balen	56	51.10 N	5.09 E
Balena	152	0.55 N	20.00 E
Baleno	116	12.28 N	123.30 E
Baler	116	15.46 N	121.34 E
Baler Bay c	116	15.50 N	121.35 E
Baleshare I	46	57.31 N	7.22 W
Bāleshwar	126	21.30 N	86.56 E
Balesin Island I	116	14.26 N	122.02 E
Balestrand	26	61.12 N	6.32 E
Balestrate	70	38.03 N	13.00 E
Baléya	150	9.15 N	10.29 W
Baléyara	150	13.47 N	2.57 E
Balezino	80	57.58 N	53.00 E
Balfate	236	15.48 N	86.25 W
Balfes Creek	166	20.13 S	145.55 E
Balfour, N.Z.	172	45.50 S	168.35 E
Balfour, S. Afr.	158	26.44 S	28.31 E
Balfour, Scot., U.K.	46	59.01 N	2.55 W
Balfour, N.C., U.S.	192	35.20 N	82.28 W
Balfour Downs	162	22.50 S	120.50 E
Balfour Park ♠	273d	26.08 S	28.06 E
Balfron	46	56.04 N	4.20 W
Balgach	58	47.25 N	9.35 E
Bălgarija → Bulgaria □[1]	38	43.00 N	25.00 E
Balgazyn	88	51.08 N	95.00 E
Balgo	162	20.09 S	127.48 E
Balgowlah	274a	33.48 S	151.16 E
Balguerie, Cap ›	174x	9.45 S	138.47 W
Balhannah	168b	35.00 S	138.50 E
Bāli	120	25.11 N	73.17 E
Bali □[4]	115b	8.30 S	115.00 E
Bali I	115b	8.20 S	115.00 E
Bali, Laut (Bali Sea) ⊤[2]	112	7.45 S	115.30 E
Bali, Selat ʉ	112	8.18 S	114.25 E
Bāliākāndi	126	23.38 N	89.33 E
Baliangao	116	8.40 N	123.36 E
Bāliāpāl	126	21.40 N	87.17 E
Bāliāti	126	23.59 N	90.03 E
Balibago	116	13.37 N	121.18 E
Bali Barat National Park ♠	115b	8.15 S	144.40 E
Baliceaux I	241h	12.57 N	61.08 W
Bāli Chak	126	22.22 N	87.33 E
Balicuatro Islands II	116	12.39 N	124.24 E
Balicuatro Point ›	116	12.35 N	124.16 E
Balidianzi	98	41.13 N	124.49 E
Bālidiha	126	21.58 N	86.38 E
Balige	114	2.20 N	99.04 E
Bālighai	126	21.52 N	87.35 E
Balihan	98	41.29 N	118.41 E
Bālihāti	272b	22.44 N	88.19 E
Balıkesir	130	39.39 N	27.53 E
Balıkesir □[4]	130	39.45 N	27.50 E
Balık Gölü ◎	84	39.47 N	43.34 E
Balīkh ≃	130	35.52 N	39.12 E
Balıklıtohma ≃	130	38.50 N	37.41 E
Balikpapan	112	1.17 S	116.50 E
Balikumbat	152	5.54 N	10.23 E
Balimbing, Indon.	112	5.55 S	104.34 E
Balimbing, Pil.	116	5.05 N	119.58 E
Balimo	164	8.03 S	142.56 E
Balin	89	48.19 N	122.19 E
Balincollig	48	51.53 N	8.35 W
Balindong (Watu)	116	7.55 N	124.12 E
Baling	114	5.40 N	100.55 E
Balingasag	116	8.45 N	124.47 E
Balingen	58	48.16 N	8.51 E
Balingian	112	2.55 N	112.32 E
Balingup	162	33.48 S	115.58 E
Balintang Channel ʉ	108	19.49 N	121.40 E
Balintore	46	57.45 N	3.54 W
Balipu	105	39.53 N	117.48 E
Balışeyh	130	39.56 N	33.43 E
Baliuag	116	14.57 N	120.54 E
Baliung ≃	115a	6.50 S	105.52 E
Baliungan Island I	116	5.09 N	120.12 E
Baliyingzi	104	41.59 N	121.14 E
Baliza	255	16.15 S	52.25 W
Balizhuang, Zhg.	105	39.16 N	116.28 E
Balizhuang, Zhg.	271a	39.52 N	116.28 E
Balk	52	52.54 N	5.34 E
Balkach, Lago → Balchaš, ozero ◎	86	46.00 N	74.00 E
Balkan □[8]	128	39.30 N	55.00 E
Balkan Mountains → Stara Planina ⋏	38	42.45 N	25.00 E
Balkan Peninsula ›[1]	10	44.00 N	23.00 E
Balkaria → Kabardino-Balkarija □[3]	84	43.30 N	43.30 E
Balkašino	86	52.31 N	68.46 E
Balkbrug	52	52.36 N	6.24 E
Balkh	120	36.46 N	66.54 E
Balkh □[4]	120	36.30 N	67.00 E
Balkh ≃	120	36.39 N	66.56 E
Balkhash → Balchaš	86	46.49 N	74.59 E
Balkhash, Lake → Balchaš, ozero ◎	86	46.00 N	74.00 E
Balky	78	47.23 N	34.57 E
Ball	194	31.24 N	92.24 W
Balla	48	53.48 N	9.09 W
Balla Balla	154	20.26 S	29.02 E
Ballabhpur	272b	22.44 N	88.21 E
Ballachulish	46	56.40 N	5.10 W
Balladonia	162	32.27 S	123.51 E
Ballagh	48	52.35 N	7.59 W
Ballaghaderreen	48	53.55 N	8.36 W
Ballālpur	122	19.50 N	79.22 E
Ballan	169	37.36 S	144.14 E
Ballancourt	50	48.31 N	2.23 E
Ballangen	24	68.20 N	16.50 E
Ballantine	202	45.56 N	108.08 W
Ballantrae	44	55.06 N	5.00 W
Ballao	71	39.33 N	9.22 E
Ballarat	169	37.34 S	143.52 E
Ballard, Lake ◎	162	29.27 S	120.55 E
Ballardvale	207	42.37 N	71.09 W
Ballata	70	37.58 N	12.41 E
Ballater	46	57.03 N	3.03 W
Ballaugh	44	54.20 N	4.32 W
Ball Bay c	174c	29.03 S	167.59 E
Ballé	150	15.20 N	8.35 W
Ballen	41	55.49 N	10.39 E
Ballenas, Bahía de c	232	26.45 N	113.26 W
Ballenato, Punta ›	286b	23.06 N	82.30 W
Ballengeich	158	27.52 S	29.59 E
Ballenita, Punta ›	252	25.46 S	70.44 W
Ballenstedt	54	51.43 N	11.14 E
Balleny Basin ✣[1]	9	67.00 S	170.00 E
Balleny Islands II	9	66.35 S	162.50 E
Balleroy	32	49.11 N	0.50 W
Ballerup	41	55.44 N	12.22 E
Ballesteros, Arg.	252	32.33 S	62.59 W
Ballesteros, Pil.	116	18.25 N	121.31 E
Balleza	232	26.57 N	106.21 W
Balleza ≃	232	27.23 N	106.17 W
Ball Ground	192	34.20 N	84.22 W
Ballı	130	40.50 N	27.03 E
Ballia	124	25.45 N	84.10 E
Ballico	226	37.27 N	120.42 W
Ballidu	162	30.36 S	116.46 E
Ballina, Austl.	166	28.52 S	153.33 E
Ballina, Ire.	48	54.07 N	9.09 W
Ballina, Ire.	48	52.49 N	8.26 W
Ballinakill	48	52.53 N	7.18 W
Ballinalack	48	53.37 N	7.28 W
Ballinascarty	48	51.40 N	8.51 W
Ballinasloe	48	53.20 N	8.13 W
Ballinderry ≃	48	54.40 N	6.31 W
Ballindine	48	53.39 N	8.59 W
Ballineen	48	51.44 N	8.56 W
Ballingarry	48	52.29 N	8.52 W
Ballingeary	48	51.49 N	9.13 W
Ballinger	196	31.44 N	99.56 W
Ballingry	46	56.09 N	3.20 W
Ballingslöv	41	56.13 N	13.51 E
Ballinluig	46	56.38 N	3.39 W
Ballino	64	45.58 N	10.48 E
Ballinrobe	48	53.37 N	9.13 W
Ballinskelligs Bay c	48	51.50 N	10.15 W
Ballintoy	48	55.14 N	6.22 W
Ballintra	48	54.35 N	8.08 W
Balloch	46	57.29 N	4.07 W
Ballon	50	48.10 N	0.14 E
Ballona Creek ≃	280	33.58 N	118.27 W
Ballouville	207	41.52 N	71.51 W
Ballsh	38	40.36 N	19.44 E
Balls Pyramid I	160	31.45 S	159.15 E
Ballston	224	45.04 N	123.19 W
Ballston Lake	210	42.54 N	73.52 W
Ballston Spa	210	43.00 N	73.50 W
Ballville	214	41.20 N	83.09 W
Ballwin	219	38.35 N	90.32 W
Bālly, India	272b	22.38 N	88.21 E
Bally, Pa., U.S.	208	40.24 N	75.35 W
Bālly ◆[8]	272b	22.39 N	88.21 E
Ballybay	48	54.08 N	6.54 W
Ballybofey	48	54.48 N	7.47 W
Ballybogy	48	55.07 N	6.34 W
Bālly Bridge ◆[5]	272b	22.39 N	88.21 E
Ballybunnion	48	52.31 N	9.40 W
Ballycanew	48	52.36 N	6.19 W
Ballycastle, Ire.	48	54.16 N	9.23 W
Ballycastle, N. Ire., U.K.	48	55.12 N	6.15 W
Ballyclare	48	54.45 N	6.00 W
Ballyconneely	48	53.26 N	10.02 W
Ballyconnell	48	54.07 N	7.35 W
Ballycotton	48	51.50 N	8.01 W
Ballycroy	48	54.01 N	9.51 W
Ballyduff, Ire.	48	52.09 N	8.03 W
Ballyduff, Ire.	48	52.27 N	9.40 W
Ballyferriter	48	52.09 N	10.26 W
Ballyfinboy ≃	48	53.02 N	8.15 W
Ballygar	48	53.32 N	8.20 W
Ballygawley	48	54.28 N	7.02 W
Ballygorman	48	55.22 N	7.21 W
Ballygowan	48	54.30 N	5.48 W
Ballygunge ◆[8]	272b	22.31 N	88.21 E
Ballyhaise	48	54.03 N	7.19 W
Ballyhalbert	48	54.30 N	5.28 W
Ballyhaunis	48	53.46 N	8.46 W
Ballyhoura Mountains ⋏	48	52.20 N	8.35 W
Ballyjamesduff	48	53.52 N	7.12 W
Ballylongford	48	52.33 N	9.28 W
Ballymacoda	48	51.57 N	7.54 W
Ballymahon	48	53.34 N	7.45 W
Ballymakeery (Ballyvourney)	48	51.55 N	9.09 W
Ballymena	48	54.52 N	6.17 W
Ballymoe	48	53.42 N	8.29 W
Ballymoney	48	55.04 N	6.31 W
Ballymote	48	54.06 N	8.31 W
Ballymurray	48	53.35 N	8.08 W
Ballynahinch	48	54.24 N	5.54 W
Ballyneety	48	52.35 N	8.33 W
Ballynoe	48	52.03 N	8.05 W
Ballyquintin Point ›	48	54.20 N	5.30 W
Ballyragget	48	52.47 N	7.20 W
Ballysadare	48	54.13 N	8.31 W
Ballyshannon	48	54.30 N	8.11 W
Ballyteige Bay c	48	52.11 N	6.39 W
Ballyvaghan	48	53.07 N	9.07 W
Ballyvoy	48	55.12 N	6.12 W
Ballywalter	48	54.33 N	5.30 W
Balm	220	27.45 N	82.15 W
Balmaceda	254	45.55 S	71.41 W
Balmaceda, Cerro ∧	254	51.25 S	73.11 W
Balmain	274a	33.51 S	151.11 E
Balme	62	45.18 N	7.13 E
Balmerino	46	56.24 N	3.02 W
Balmertown	184	51.04 N	93.44 W
Balmhorn ∧	58	46.25 N	7.43 E
Balmoral, Austl.	166	37.15 S	141.51 E
Balmoral, S. Afr.	158	25.52 S	28.59 E
Balmoral Castle ⊥	46	57.02 N	3.14 W
Balmorhea	196	30.59 N	103.45 W
Balmville	210	41.32 N	74.00 W
Balnacra	46	57.28 N	5.23 W
Balnearia	252	31.00 S	62.40 W
Balobanovo	82	55.51 N	38.14 E
Balobe	154	0.05 N	28.00 E
Baloda Bāzār	120	21.40 N	82.10 E
Balombo	152	12.21 S	14.46 E
Balong, Indon.	115a	7.57 S	111.26 E
Balong, Zhg.	102	36.17 N	97.20 E
Balonne ≃	166	28.47 S	147.56 E
Bālotra	120	25.50 N	72.14 E
Baloži	76	56.53 N	24.06 E
Balpahari Reservoir ◎[1]	126	24.04 N	86.28 E
Balrāmpur	124	27.26 N	82.11 E
Balranald	166	34.38 S	143.33 E
Balş	38	44.21 N	24.06 E
Balsam Lake	190	45.27 N	92.27 W
Balsam Lake ◎	212	44.35 N	78.50 W
Bálsamo	255	20.27 S	53.57 W
Balsas	250	7.31 S	46.02 W
Balsas ≃	234	17.55 N	102.10 W
Balsas, Rio das ≃, Bra.	250	7.14 S	44.33 W
Balsas, Rio das ≃, Bra.	250	9.58 S	47.52 W
Balsas Sur	234	17.59 N	99.47 W
Balseiro ≃	250	5.51 S	43.44 W
Balsham	42	52.08 N	0.20 E
Balsorano	66	41.49 N	13.34 E
Bålsta	40	59.35 N	17.30 E
Balsthal	58	47.19 N	7.42 E
Balta	78	47.55 N	29.37 E
Baltaj	80	52.28 N	46.38 E
Baltanás	34	41.56 N	4.15 W
Baltasar Brum	252	30.44 S	57.19 W
Baltasi	80	56.21 N	50.12 E
Baltasound	46a	60.45 N	0.52 W
Baltazar, Arroyo ≃	258	33.47 S	58.58 W
Bălţi	38	47.46 N	27.56 E
Baltic, Ct., U.S.	207	41.37 N	72.05 W
Baltic, Oh., U.S.	214	40.26 N	81.41 W
Baltic Bay c	190	48.22 N	83.43 W
Baltico, Mar → Baltic Sea ⊤[2]	24	57.00 N	19.00 E
Baltic Sea ⊤[2]	24	57.00 N	19.00 E
Baltic Station ◆[5]	265a	59.55 N	30.18 E
Baltijsk	76	54.39 N	19.55 E
Baltijskaja kosa ›[2]	30	54.25 N	19.35 E
Balṭīm	142	31.33 N	31.05 E
Baltimore, Ire.	48	51.29 N	9.22 W
Baltimore, S. Afr.	156	23.15 S	28.20 E
Baltimore, Md., U.S.	208	39.17 N	76.36 W
Baltimore, Md., U.S.	284b	39.17 N	76.36 W
Baltimore, Oh., U.S.	188	39.50 N	82.36 W
Baltimore □[6]	208	39.22 N	76.36 W
Baltimore, University of ◈[2]	284b	39.18 N	76.37 W
Baltimore Airpark ⊠	284b	39.24 N	76.25 W
Baltimore Highlands	284b	39.13 N	76.38 W
Baltimore-Washington International Airport ⊠	208	39.11 N	76.40 W
Baltinglass	48	52.55 N	6.41 W
Baltique, Mer → Baltic Sea ⊤[2]	24	57.00 N	19.00 E
Baltistān ◆[1]	123	35.18 N	75.37 E
Baltit	123	36.20 N	74.40 E
Baltoji-Vokė	76	54.28 N	25.06 E
Baltoro Glacier ⊓	123	35.42 N	76.10 E
Baltra, Isla I	246a	0.26 S	90.16 W
Baltrum I	52	53.44 N	7.23 E
Bālu ≃, Bngl.	126	23.44 N	90.30 E
Ba Lu ≃, Viet	110	14.18 N	107.52 E
Baluarte ≃	234	22.49 N	106.02 W
Baluarte, Arroyo V	196	27.09 N	98.07 W
Baluchistān □[4]	120	29.00 N	67.00 E
Baluchistan □[9]	128	28.00 N	63.00 E
Balud	116	12.02 N	123.12 E
Bālughāta	126	22.05 N	88.01 E
Bāluhāti	272b	22.39 N	88.16 E
Balui ≃	112	2.42 N	113.47 E
Balukbaluk Island I	116	6.40 N	121.43 E
Balupe ≃	76	56.57 N	26.55 E
Bālurghāt	124	25.13 N	88.46 E
Balut Island I	116	5.24 N	125.23 E
Balvano	68	40.39 N	15.31 E
Balve	56	51.20 N	7.51 E
Balvi	76	57.08 N	27.17 E
Balvicar	46	56.14 N	5.38 W
Balwina Aboriginal Reserve ◆[4]	162	20.30 S	128.00 E
Balwyn	274b	37.49 S	145.05 E
Balxuca, Arroyo de la ≃	266d	41.31 N	2.06 E
Balya	130	39.45 N	27.35 E
Balygyčan	74	63.56 N	154.12 E
Balykči	85	40.54 N	71.50 E
Balyksa	86	53.25 N	89.05 E
Balykši	80	47.05 N	51.54 E
Balyktyg-Chem ≃	88	51.15 N	96.54 E
Balyn	78	48.52 N	26.40 E
Balzac	182	51.10 N	114.01 W
Balzar	246	1.22 S	79.54 W
Balzers	58	47.04 N	9.30 E
Bal'zino	88	51.03 N	113.35 E
Balzola	62	45.11 N	8.24 E
Bām, Īrān	128	36.58 N	57.59 E
Bam, Īrān	128	29.06 N	58.21 E
Bama, Nig.	146	11.30 N	13.41 E
Bama, Zhg.	102	24.21 N	107.08 E
Bamaga	164	10.52 S	142.24 E
Bamaji Lake ◎	184	51.09 N	91.25 W
Bamako	150	12.39 N	8.00 W
Bāmangāchi	272b	22.46 N	88.31 E
Bāmangawān	126	24.14 N	86.49 E
Bāmanghāra	272b	22.31 N	88.28 E
Bāmanmura	272b	22.42 N	88.31 E
Bamao	100	29.26 N	120.59 E
Bamata	152	1.00 S	21.06 E
Bamba, Mali	150	17.02 N	1.24 W
Bamba, Zaïre	152	5.45 S	18.23 E
Bambamarca	248	6.41 S	78.32 W
Bambana ≃	236	13.27 N	83.50 W
Bambang	116	16.23 N	121.06 E
Bambannan Island I	116	5.37 N	120.17 E
Bambara Maoundé	150	15.51 N	2.47 W
Bambari	152	5.45 N	20.40 E
Bambaroo	166	18.52 S	146.12 E
Bambāvi	272c	18.58 N	73.03 E
Bamberg, Dtsch.	56	49.53 N	10.53 E
Bamberg, S.C., U.S.	192	33.17 N	81.02 W
Bamber Lake	208	39.54 N	74.19 W
Bamberton	224	48.35 N	123.31 W
Bambesa	154	3.28 N	25.43 E
Bambesi	144	9.45 N	34.38 E
Bambezi	154	20.00 S	28.56 E
Bambili	154	3.39 N	26.07 E
Bambinga	152	3.42 S	18.54 E
Bambio	152	3.54 N	16.59 E
Bamboesberg ⋏	158	31.30 S	26.10 E
Bamboi	150	8.10 N	2.02 W
Bamboo Creek	162	20.56 S	120.13 E
Bamboo Springs	162	22.04 S	119.38 E
Bambouti	154	5.24 N	27.12 E
Bambuí	255	20.01 S	45.58 W
Bambujka	88	55.47 N	115.48 E
Bambula	154	1.17 S	25.38 E
Bamburgh	44	55.36 N	1.42 W

≃	River	Fluß	Río	Rivière	Rio
≍	Canal	Kanal	Canal	Canal	Canal
ʟ	Waterfall, Rapids	Wasserfall, Stromschnellen	Cascada, Rápidos	Chute d'eau, Rapides	Cascata, Rápidos
ʉ	Strait	Meeresstraße	Estrecho	Détroit	Estreito
c	Bay, Gulf	Bucht, Golf	Bahía, Golfo	Baie, Golfe	Baía, Golfo
◎	Lake, Lakes	See, Seen	Lago, Lagos	Lac, Lacs	Lago, Lagos
≣	Swamp	Sumpf	Pantano	Marais	Pântano
⊓	Ice Features, Glacier	Eis- und Gletscherformen	Accidentes Glaciales	Formes glaciaires	Acidentes glaciares
⊤	Other Hydrographic Features	Andere Hydrographische Objekte	Otros Elementos Hidrográficos	Autres données hydrographiques	Outros acidentes hidrográficos

✣	Submarine Features	Untermeerische Objekte	Accidentes Submarinos	Formes de relief sous-marin	Acidentes submarinos
□	Political Unit	Politische Einheit	Unidad Politica	Entité politique	Unidade política
◈	Cultural Institution	Kulturelle Institution	Institución Cultural	Institution culturelle	Institução cultural
⊥	Historical Site	Historische Stätte	Sitio Histórico	Site historique	Sitio histórico
♠	Recreational Site	Erholungs- und Ferienort	Sitio de Recreo	Centre de loisirs	Area de Lazer
⊠	Airport	Flughafen	Aeropuerto	Aéroport	Aeroporto
■	Military Installation	Militäranlage	Instalación Militar	Installation militaire	Instalação militar
◆	Miscellaneous	Verschiedenes	Misceláneo	Divers	Diversos

Bamburral ≃ 248 20.10 S 58.07 W
Bambuto ≃ 200 30.51 N 110.52 W
Bam Co ⊜ 120 31.30 N 91.05 E
Bamencheng 105 39.35 N 117.37 E
Bamenda 152 5.56 N 10.10 E
Bamendjou 152 5.24 N 10.19 E
Bamfield 182 48.50 N 125.08 W
Bamhā 142 29.35 N 31.14 E
Bami 128 38.44 N 56.48 E
Bāmīān 120 34.50 N 67.50 E
Bāmīān □[4] 120 34.45 N 67.15 E
Bamiancheng 89 43.13 N 124.02 E
Bamingui 152 7.34 N 20.11 E
Bamingui ≃ 146 8.33 N 19.05 E
Bamingui-Bangoran □[5] 146 8.15 N 20.15 E
Bamingui-Bangoran, Parc National du ♦ 146 8.00 N 19.40 E
Bam Island I 164 3.35 S 144.50 E
Bāmna 126 22.19 N 90.06 E
Bamndali •[8] 272a 28.33 N 77.03 E
Bamol 164 7.38 S 138.37 E
Bampton, Eng., U.K. 42 51.00 N 3.29 W
Bampton, Eng., U.K. 42 51.44 N 1.33 W
Bampūr 128 27.12 N 60.27 E
Bampūr ≃ 128 27.18 N 59.06 E
Bāmra Hills ⋏[2] 120 21.30 N 84.30 E
Bamu ≃ 164 8.01 S 143.33 E
Bamumo 120 32.30 N 93.15 E
Ban 150 14.05 N 2.27 W
Bana, Malaŵi 154 12.25 S 34.08 E
Ba Na, Viet 110 15.59 N 107.59 E
Banā, Wādī V 144 13.03 N 45.24 E
Banaba (Ocean Island) I 174d 0.52 S 169.35 E
Banabuiú ≃ 250 5.07 S 38.06 W
Banabuiú, Açude ⊜[1] 250 5.20 S 39.05 W
Ban Aen 110 18.02 N 98.37 E
Banagher 48 53.11 N 7.59 W
Banagi 154 2.16 S 34.51 E
Banago 116 7.30 N 124.07 E
Banagrām 126 22.35 N 89.55 E
Banahao, Mount ∧ 116 14.04 N 121.29 E
Banalia 154 1.33 N 25.20 E
Banamba 150 13.33 N 7.27 W
Banana, Austl. 166 24.28 S 150.07 E
Banana, Zaïre 152 6.01 S 12.24 E
Banana Creek ≃ 220 28.36 N 80.38 W
Banana Islands II 150 8.07 N 13.13 W
Bananal 256 22.41 S 44.19 W
Bananal ≃, Bra. 250 8.33 S 49.26 W
Bananal ≃, Bra. 256 22.32 S 44.11 W
Bananal, Ilha do I 250 11.30 S 50.15 W
Banana River ⊂ 220 28.25 N 80.38 W
Bananeiras 250 6.45 S 35.37 W
Bananga 110 6.56 N 93.54 E
Banao, Loma de ∧ 240p 21.51 N 79.36 W
Bānār ≃ 124 24.04 N 90.38 E
Banaras → Vārānasi 124 25.20 N 83.00 E
Banari 71 40.34 N 8.42 E
Bānaripāra 126 22.47 N 90.10 E
Banarlı 130 41.04 N 27.20 E
Banās ≃ 120 25.54 N 76.45 E
Banās, Ra's › 140 23.54 N 35.48 E
Banat □[9] 38 45.20 N 20.40 E
Banate Bay ⊂ 116 10.58 N 122.48 E
Banaue 116 16.55 N 121.04 E
Banavie 46 56.47 N 5.07 W
Banay, Mount ∧ 116 13.42 N 121.10 E
Banaz 130 38.46 N 29.46 E
Ban Baen Phichit 269a 13.50 N 100.40 E
Ban Ban 110 19.38 N 103.34 E
Ban Bang Chan 269a 13.49 N 100.42 E
Ban Bang O 269a 13.53 N 100.36 E
Ban Bang Phli Yai 269a 13.36 N 100.42 E
Ban Bang Phraek 269a 13.53 N 100.26 E
Ban Bang Pu 269a 13.31 N 100.39 E
Banbar 120 30.49 N 94.59 E
Ban Bat 110 13.13 N 108.39 E
Banbidian 271a 39.54 N 116.32 E
Ban Blech 110 13.12 N 108.13 E
Ban Bonèng 110 17.58 N 104.35 E
Ban Bouang-nom 110 15.47 N 106.47 E
Banbridge 48 54.21 N 6.16 W
Ban Bua Chum 110 15.15 N 101.12 E
Banbuji 100 33.34 N 116.44 E
Ban Bung Fang Nok 269a 13.48 N 100.43 E
Ban Bung Na Rang 110 16.11 N 100.09 E
Ban Bungxai 110 15.42 N 106.14 E
Banbury 42 52.04 N 1.20 W
Bancahsaga 114 0.49 N 101.07 E
Bancalan Island I 116 8.14 N 117.06 E
Banc d'Arguin, Parc National du ♦ 150 20.00 N 16.20 W
Ban Chak 110 14.17 N 105.25 E
Ban Cha La 110 17.11 N 106.05 E
Bānchhārāmpur 126 23.46 N 90.48 E
Banchory 46 57.03 N 2.31 W
Banco, Punta › 236 8.23 N 83.09 W
Bancos, Isla → Banks Island I 176 73.15 N 121.30 W
Bancroft, On., Can. 212 45.03 N 77.51 W
Bancroft, Id., U.S. 202 42.43 N 111.53 W
Bancroft, Ia., U.S. 190 43.17 N 94.13 W
Bancroft, Mi., U.S. 216 42.52 N 84.03 W
Bancroft, Ne., U.S. 198 42.00 N 96.34 W
Bancroft → Chililabombwe, Zam. 154 12.18 S 27.43 E
Bancun 106 30.53 N 118.48 E
Banda, India 124 24.03 N 78.57 E
Bānda, India 124 25.29 N 80.20 E
Banda, Zaïre 154 4.11 N 27.04 E
Banda, Kepulauan II 164 4.35 S 129.55 E
Banda, Laut (Banda Sea) ⊤[2] 108 5.00 S 128.00 E
Banda Aceh (Kuturaja) 114 5.34 N 95.20 E
Bandabe 157b 15.31 S 49.04 E
Banda Besar, Pulau I 164 4.34 S 129.55 E
Bānda Dāūd Shāh 123 33.16 N 71.11 E
Banda del Río Salí 252 26.50 S 65.10 W
Banda Elat 164 5.39 S 132.59 E
Bandahara, Gunung ∧ 114 3.45 N 97.47 E
Bandai-Asahi-kokuritsu-kōen ♦ 92 38.16 N 139.57 E
Bandai-san ∧ 92 37.36 N 140.04 E
Bandak ⊜ 26 59.24 N 8.15 E
Bandama ≃ 150 5.10 N 5.00 W
Bandama Blanc ≃ 150 6.54 N 5.31 W
Bandama Rouge ≃ 150 6.54 N 5.31 W
Bandān, Īrān 128 31.23 N 60.44 E
Ban Dan, Thai 110 15.19 N 105.30 E
Bandanaira 164 4.32 S 129.54 E
Bandan'gou 105 39.08 N 115.11 E
Ban Dangtai 110 17.06 N 104.57 E
Ban Dan Lan Hoi 110 17.00 N 99.35 E
Bandar → Machilīpatnam, India 122 16.10 N 81.08 E
Bandar, Indon. 115a 7.02 S 109.47 E
Bandar Baharu 114 5.08 N 100.30 E
Bandar Beheshtī 128 25.18 N 60.37 E
Bandardurian 114 2.21 N 99.44 E
Bandar-e 'Abbās 128 27.11 N 56.17 E
Bandar-e Anzalī (Bandar-e Pahlavī) 128 37.28 N 49.27 E
Bandar-e Būshehr 128 28.59 N 50.50 E
Bandar-e Chārak 128 26.43 N 54.16 E
Bandar-e Deylam 128 30.04 N 50.10 E
Bandar-e Gaz 128 36.47 N 53.59 E
Bandar-e Khomeynī (Bandar-e Shāhpūr) 128 30.25 N 49.05 E
Bandar-e Lengeh 128 26.33 N 54.53 E
Bandar-e Māh Shahr 128 30.33 N 49.12 E
Bandar-e Moghūyeh 128 26.35 N 54.31 E
Bandar-e Rīg 128 29.29 N 50.38 E
Bandar-e Torkeman 128 36.56 N 54.06 E
Bandar Penggaram → Batu Pahat 114 1.51 N 102.56 E
Bandarpulau 114 2.41 N 99.31 E
Bandar Seri Begawan 112 4.56 N 114.55 E
Bandawe 154 11.57 S 34.10 E
Bande 34 42.02 N 7.58 W
Banded Peak ∧ 200 37.06 N 106.38 W
Bandeira, Pico da ∧ 255 20.26 S 41.47 W
Bandeira do Sul 256 21.47 S 46.23 W
Bandeirantes, Bra. 255 13.41 S 50.48 W
Bandeirantes, Bra. 255 19.53 S 54.23 W
Bandeirantes, Bra. 255 23.06 S 50.21 W
Bandeirantes, Palácio dos ♥ 287b 23.36 S 46.43 W
Bandeirantes, Praia dos ⊥[2] 287a 23.01 S 43.25 W
Bandéko 152 1.56 N 17.28 E
Bāndel 272b 22.56 N 88.22 E
Bandeli 157a 12.55 S 45.13 E
Bandelier National Monument ♦ 200 35.45 N 106.20 W
Bandera, Arg. 252 28.54 S 62.16 W
Bandera, Tx., U.S. 196 29.44 N 99.04 W
Bandera, Alto ∧ 238 18.49 N 70.37 W
Banderas 200 31.01 N 105.35 W
Banderas, Bahía de ⊂ 234 20.40 N 105.25 W
Banderilla 234 19.36 N 96.56 W
Bāndhi 120 26.35 N 68.18 E
Bandholm 41 54.50 N 11.29 E
Bandiagara 150 14.21 N 3.37 W
Bandiantaolehai 102 41.41 N 104.06 E
Bāndīkūi 124 27.03 N 76.34 E
Bandipur, India 272b 22.44 N 88.26 E
Bandipur, India 272b 22.51 N 88.10 E
Bandipura 123 34.25 N 74.39 E
Bandırma 130 40.20 N 27.58 E
Bandırma Körfezi ⊂ 130 40.25 N 28.00 E
Bando 152 15.00 S 20.30 E
Bandol 62 43.08 N 5.45 E
Bandon, Ire. 48 51.45 N 8.45 W
Ban Don → Surat Thani, Thai 110 9.08 N 99.19 E
Bandon, Or., U.S. 202 43.07 N 124.24 W
Ban Don, Viet 110 12.53 N 107.48 E
Bandon ≃ 48 51.42 N 8.30 W
Ban Don, Ao ⊂ 110 9.20 N 99.25 E
Ban Donhiang 110 18.05 N 101.48 E
Ban Dônko 110 16.12 N 106.17 E
Ban Don Muang 269a 13.55 N 100.36 E
Bāndra •[8] 272c 19.03 N 72.49 E
Bāndra Point › 272c 19.03 N 72.49 E
Bānduān 126 22.53 N 86.31 E
Bandula 156 19.02 S 33.07 E
Ban Dulad V 144 8.26 N 45.54 E
Bandundu 152 3.18 S 17.20 E
Bandundu □[4] 152 4.30 S 18.30 E
Bandung 115a 6.54 S 107.36 E
Băneasa 38 44.04 N 27.42 E
Banegas 248 17.09 S 62.50 W
Bāneh 128 35.59 N 45.53 E
Banehra 272a 28.44 N 77.23 E
Banes 240p 20.58 N 75.43 W
Banff, Ab., Can. 182 51.10 N 115.34 W
Banff, Scot., U.K. 46 57.40 N 2.33 W
Banff National Park ♦ 182 51.38 N 116.22 W
Banfield •[8] 258 34.44 S 58.23 W
Banfora 150 10.38 N 4.46 W
Banga, India 123 31.11 N 75.59 E
Banga, Pil. 116 11.38 N 122.20 E
Banga, Zaïre 152 5.27 S 20.28 E
Banga ≃ 116 6.44 N 124.34 E
Bañgad 116 12.10 N 123.24 E
Bangaduni Island I 126 21.34 N 88.52 E
Bangala Dam •[6] 154 20.40 S 31.15 E
Bangall 210 41.53 N 73.42 W
Bangalore 122 12.58 N 77.36 E
Bangalur → Bangalore 122 12.58 N 77.36 E
Bangangté 152 5.09 N 10.31 E
Bangaon 126 23.04 N 88.49 E
Bangassou 152 4.50 N 23.07 E
Bangda 102 27.59 N 98.40 E
Bangdag Co ⊜ 120 34.59 N 81.35 E
Bangeluo 120 32.27 N 90.35 E
Bangeswardi 126 23.29 N 89.44 E
Bangeta, Mount ∧ 164 6.15 S 147.04 E
Banggai (Luwuk) 112 1.34 S 123.30 E
Banggai, Kepulauan II 112 1.30 S 123.15 E
Banggai, Pulau I 112 1.37 S 123.33 E
Banggi, Pulau I 116 7.17 N 117.12 E
Banggong Co ⊜ 120 33.45 N 79.30 E
Banghāzī 146 32.07 N 20.04 E
Banghiang ≃ 110 16.03 N 105.15 E
Bangholme 274b 38.02 S 145.11 E
Bangi → Bangui 152 4.22 N 18.35 E
Bangil 115a 7.36 S 112.47 E
Bangjang 140 11.23 N 32.42 E
Bangjun 105 39.59 N 117.16 E
Bangka, Pulau I, Indon. 112 2.15 S 106.00 E
Bangka, Pulau I, Indon. 112 1.48 N 125.09 E
Bangka, Selat ⋓ 112 2.20 S 105.45 E
Bangkalan 115a 7.02 S 112.44 E
Bang Kapi 269a 13.46 N 100.39 E
Bang Kapi, Khlong ≍ 269a 13.45 N 100.36 E
Bangkaru, Pulau I 114 2.04 N 97.07 E
Bang Khen 269a 13.52 N 100.36 E
Bang Khun Thian 269a 13.42 N 100.28 E
Bangkinang 112 0.21 N 101.02 E
Bangkir 112 0.48 N 120.14 E
Bangko 112 2.05 S 102.17 E
Bangkog Co ⊜ 120 31.42 N 89.30 E
Bangkok → Krung Thep 110 13.45 N 100.31 E
Bangkok Station •[5] 269a 13.44 N 100.32 E
Bangkou 106 31.40 N 121.26 E
Bang Krathum 110 16.34 N 100.18 E
Bang Kruai 269a 13.48 N 100.29 E
Bangkulu, Pulau I 112 1.50 S 123.06 E
Bangkulua 115b 8.41 S 118.13 E
Bangladesch → Bangladesh □[1] 120 24.00 N 90.00 E
Bangladesh □[1], Asia 118 24.00 N 90.00 E
Bangladesh □[1], Asia 120 24.00 N 90.00 E
Bang Lamung 110 12.58 N 100.54 E
Bang Mun Nak 110 16.02 N 100.23 E
Ban Gnômmarat Kèo 110 17.36 N 105.10 E
Bangolo 150 7.01 N 7.29 W
Bangor, Ire. 48 54.09 N 9.45 W
Bangor, N. Ire., U.K. 44 54.40 N 5.40 W
Bangor, N. Ire., U.K. 48 54.40 N 5.40 W
Bangor, Wales, U.K. 44 53.13 N 4.08 W
Bangor, Ca., U.S. 226 39.23 N 121.24 W
Bangor, Me., U.S. 188 44.48 N 68.46 W
Bangor, Mi., U.S. 216 42.18 N 86.06 W
Bangor, Pa., U.S. 210 40.51 N 75.12 W
Bangoran ≃ 146 8.42 N 19.06 E
Bang Pa In 110 14.14 N 100.35 E
Bāngra ≃ 126 21.48 N 89.43 E
Bangriposi 126 22.10 N 86.32 E
Bangs 196 31.43 N 99.08 W
Bangs, Mount ∧ 200 36.48 N 113.51 W
Bang Saphan 110 11.12 N 99.31 E
Bangshi 98 40.23 N 122.46 E
Bangs Lake ⊜ 278 42.16 N 88.08 W
Bangsri 115a 6.30 S 110.45 E
Bangu •[8] 256 22.52 S 43.27 W
Bangué 152 3.01 N 15.07 E
Bangued 116 17.36 N 120.37 E
Bangui, Centraf. 152 4.22 N 18.35 E
Bangui, Pil. 116 18.32 N 120.46 E
Bangui Bay ⊂ 116 18.34 N 120.44 E
Bangunpurba 114 3.23 N 98.50 E
Banguru 154 0.27 N 27.17 E
Bangwei 102 23.46 N 107.34 E
Bangweulu, Lake ⊜ 154 11.05 S 29.45 E
Bangweulu Swamps ≡ 154 11.30 S 30.15 E
Bangzhen 106 31.39 N 121.29 E
Banhā 142 30.28 N 31.11 E
Ban Hatgnao 110 14.40 N 106.35 E
Ban Hatkiang 110 18.11 N 102.40 E
Ban Hat Yai → Hat Yai 110 7.01 N 100.28 E
Ban Ha Yaek Pak Kret 269a 13.54 N 100.31 E
Ban Hèt 110 14.44 N 107.29 E
Banhine, Parque Nacional de ♦ 156 22.45 S 32.50 E
Ban Hin Heup 110 18.38 N 102.20 E
Ban Hom 110 15.33 N 98.46 E
Ban Hong 110 18.18 N 98.50 E
Ban Hong Muang 110 17.04 N 105.12 E
Ban Houayxay 110 20.18 N 100.26 E
Ban Huai Yang 110 11.36 N 99.40 E
Ban Hua Lamphu Thong 269a 13.32 N 100.38 E
Bani, Burkina 150 14.02 N 0.02 W
Bani, Centraf. 152 7.07 N 22.49 E
Bani, Pil. 116 16.11 N 119.52 E
Baní, Rep. Dom. 238 18.17 N 70.20 W
Bani ≃ 150 14.30 N 4.12 W
Bani, Jbel ⋏ 148 29.30 N 8.00 W
Bania 152 4.00 N 16.07 E
Baniachang 120 24.31 N 91.22 E
Banī 'Adī al-Bahrīyah 142 27.15 N 30.55 E
Banī 'Adī al-Qiblīyah 142 27.15 N 30.56 E
Banī Ahmad 142 28.03 N 30.46 E
Banī 'Alī 142 28.29 N 30.43 E
Baniara, Indon. 114 2.31 N 98.39 E
Baniara, Pap. N. Gui. 164 9.46 S 149.53 E
Bānibaha 126 23.42 N 89.37 E
Bani Bangou 150 15.03 N 2.42 E
Banie 30 53.08 N 14.38 E
Banifing ≃ 150 12.43 N 6.25 W
Banihāl Pass)(123 33.31 N 75.13 E
Banī Hasan ash-Shurūq 142 27.54 N 30.51 E
Banī Khālid 142 27.50 N 30.44 E
Banikoara 150 11.18 N 2.26 E
Banima 152 5.26 N 23.54 E
Banī Majdūl 273c 30.02 N 31.07 E
Banī Mazār 142 28.30 N 30.48 E
Banī Muhammadīyāt 142 27.17 N 31.05 E
Banī Mūsā 142 29.08 N 31.03 E
Banīnah 146 32.05 N 20.16 E
Banio, Lagune ⊂ 152 3.35 S 11.00 E
Baniou 34 35.25 N 4.21 E
Banī Rāfi' 142 27.22 N 30.53 E
Banī Salāmah 142 30.19 N 30.51 E
Banī Sha'rān 142 27.19 N 30.51 E
Banī Shuqayr 142 27.23 N 30.59 E
Banister ≃ 192 36.42 N 78.48 W
Banī Suhaylah 132 31.20 N 34.20 E
Banī Suwayf 142 29.05 N 31.05 E
Banī Suwayf □[4] 142 29.03 N 31.02 E
Banī 'Ubayd, Misr 142 31.01 N 31.39 E
Banī 'Ubayd, Misr 142 27.57 N 30.46 E
Banī Walīd 146 31.45 N 14.01 E
Bāniyās, Sūrīy. 130 35.11 N 35.57 E
Bāniyās, Sūrīy. 132 33.15 N 35.41 E
Banī Zayd 142 27.13 N 31.09 E
Banja Luka 36 44.46 N 17.11 E
Banjar 115a 7.22 S 108.32 E
Banjarmasin 112 3.20 S 114.35 E
Banjarnegara 115a 7.23 S 109.41 E
Banjin 106 32.19 N 120.24 E
Banjir Kanal ≍ 269e 6.07 S 106.45 E
Banjita 104 41.11 N 120.52 E
Banjščice ⋏[1] 64 46.04 N 13.42 E
Banjuangou 105 40.44 N 115.11 E
Banjul (Bathurst) 150 13.28 N 16.39 W
Bankä, Azer. 84 39.25 N 49.15 E
Bānka, India 124 24.53 N 86.55 E
Ban'ka ≃ 265b 55.49 N 37.22 E
Banka Banka 162 18.48 S 134.01 E
Bānkādāba 126 22.58 N 87.21 E
Bankana 152 4.25 S 16.11 E
Bankas 150 14.04 N 3.31 W
Ban Katèp 110 16.48 N 105.52 E
Ban Kavak 110 17.18 N 105.37 E
Bankberg ⋏ 158 32.22 S 25.26 E
Ban Kèngkabao 110 16.48 N 104.45 E
Ban Kèngkok 110 16.26 N 105.12 E
Ban Kèngtangan 110 16.05 N 105.22 E
Bankeryd 26 57.51 N 14.07 E
Bankfoot 46 56.30 N 3.30 W
Ban Khamphô 110 14.38 N 106.17 E
Ban Khan Na Yao 269a 13.47 N 100.41 E
Bankhari 126 23.44 N 90.03 E
Ban Kheun 110 20.13 N 101.07 E
Ban Khlong Bua Loi 269a 13.41 N 100.41 E
Ban Khlong Kua 110 6.57 N 100.08 E
Ban Khlong Samrong 269a 13.39 N 100.36 E
Ban Khlong Song 269a 13.51 N 100.43 E
Ban Khok Bao Sao 269a 13.52 N 100.39 E
Ban Khuan Mao 110 7.58 N 99.37 E
Bankilaré 150 14.35 N 0.44 E
Bankim 152 6.05 N 11.30 E
Bānkipur 272b 22.48 N 88.14 E
Ban Kota Baru 114 6.27 N 101.21 E
Ban Krang 110 12.52 N 99.18 E
Ban Kruat 110 14.25 N 103.07 E
Banks, Eng., U.K. 44 53.41 N 2.55 W
Banks, Al., U.S. 194 31.48 N 85.50 W
Banks, Or., U.S. 224 45.37 N 123.06 W
Banks, Cape › 274a 34.00 S 151.15 E
Banks, Îles II 175f 13.50 S 167.30 E
Banks, Point › 180 58.36 N 152.18 W
Banksian ≃ 184 53.41 N 94.10 W
Banks Island I, B.C., Can. 182 53.25 N 130.10 W
Banks Island I, N.T., Can. 176 73.15 N 121.30 W
Banks Lake ⊜[1] 202 47.45 N 119.15 W
Banksmeadow 274a 33.58 S 151.13 E
Banks Peninsula ›[1] 172 43.45 S 173.00 E
Banks Strait ⋓ 166 40.40 S 148.07 E
Banks / Torres □[8] 175f 13.50 S 167.20 E
Bankstown 170 33.55 S 151.02 E
Bankstown Aerodrome ⊠ 274a 33.55 S 150.59 E
Banksville 276 41.09 N 73.38 W
Banksville •[8] 279b 40.24 N 80.03 W
Ban Kum Daeng 269a 13.53 N 100.36 E
Bankumuna 152 4.28 S 19.57 E
Bānkura 126 23.15 N 87.04 E
Ban Laem Sing 269a 13.30 N 100.34 E
Banlamen 104 41.51 N 122.27 E
Banlashanzi 104 41.26 N 123.28 E
Ban Lat Phrao 269a 13.47 N 100.36 E
Ban Le Kathe 110 15.49 N 98.53 E
Banliyuan 106 30.50 N 118.58 E
Ban Luk Kho 269a 13.34 N 100.27 E
Ban Mae La Luang 110 18.32 N 97.56 E
Ban Mae Mo 110 18.15 N 99.42 E
Bānmankhi Bazar 124 25.53 N 87.11 E
Banmauk 110 24.24 N 95.51 E
Ban M'diap 110 12.56 N 108.43 E
Ban M'drack 110 12.42 N 108.47 E
Banmian 100 26.02 N 118.06 E
Ban Mit 110 18.51 N 101.55 E
Ban Muangngat 110 19.05 N 104.04 E
Ban Muang Yot 110 19.22 N 100.34 E
Bann ≃ 48 55.10 N 6.46 W
Banna ≃ 62 45.11 N 7.51 E
Ban Nadou 110 15.51 N 105.38 E
Ban Nagnom 110 17.02 N 105.44 E
Ban Nahin 110 18.14 N 104.13 E
Bannaja 88 57.05 N 108.12 E
Ban Nakala 110 16.17 N 105.11 E
Ban Na Kha 110 9.26 N 98.28 E
Ban Nalan 110 15.50 N 106.04 E
Ban Nalè 110 18.42 N 101.34 E
Ban Namcha 110 19.09 N 102.53 E
Ban Nam Chan 110 18.01 N 103.53 E
Ban Namnga 110 20.22 N 102.19 E
Ban Nam Tao 110 17.50 N 101.15 E
Ban Nam Thaeng 110 15.34 N 105.30 E
Ban Naxon 110 18.12 N 103.05 E
Ban Naxouang 110 18.25 N 104.29 E
Bannay 50 47.23 N 2.53 E
Banner Elk 192 36.09 N 81.52 W
Bannerman, Mount ∧[2] 162 19.26 S 127.10 E
Banner Park ♦ 284b 39.19 N 76.42 W
Bannertown 192 36.29 N 80.34 W
Bannesdorf 54 54.28 N 11.13 E
Bannewitz 54 51.00 N 13.43 E
Ban Ngam 110 20.11 N 104.53 E
Bannikovo 86 56.07 N 70.17 E
Banning 228 33.55 N 116.52 W
Banningville → Bandundu 152 3.18 S 17.20 E
Bannister 168a 32.40 S 116.33 E
Bannister ≃ 168a 32.49 S 116.29 E
Bannister Ditch ≍ 279a 41.18 N 82.01 W
Bannock 214 40.06 N 80.59 W
Bannockburn, Austl. 169 38.03 S 144.10 E
Bannockburn, Scot., U.K. 46 56.06 N 3.55 W
Bannockburn, Il., U.S. 278 42.12 N 87.52 W
Bannockburn, Zimb. 154 20.16 S 29.51 E
Bannockburn Battlesite ⊥ 46 56.06 N 3.54 W
Bannock Creek ≃ 202 42.53 N 112.40 W
Bannock Peak ∧ 202 42.36 N 112.42 W
Ban Nong Lumphuk 110 14.40 N 102.43 E
Ban Nong Takhian 110 13.08 N 101.24 E
Bannovka 86 53.45 N 62.57 E
Bannu 123 32.59 N 70.36 E
Bánokszentgyörgy 61 46.33 N 16.47 E
Banon 62 44.02 N 5.38 E
Ban O Pao 269a 13.50 N 100.38 E
Baños, Ec. 246 1.24 S 78.25 W
Baños, Perú 248 10.05 S 76.45 W
Baños de Cerrato 34 41.55 N 4.28 W
Banow 120 35.38 N 69.15 E
Ban Pak Bong 110 18.32 N 98.56 E
Ban Pak Chan 110 10.32 N 98.51 E
Ban Pakha 110 14.38 N 107.24 E
Ban Pakkhop 110 19.49 N 100.36 E
Ban Pak Nam 110 10.26 N 99.15 E
Ban Pakneun 110 19.14 N 101.50 E
Banpās 126 23.24 N 87.45 E
Ban Phai, Thai 110 16.04 N 102.44 E
Ban Phai, Thai 110 17.33 N 103.00 E
Ban Phe 110 12.38 N 101.26 E
Ban Pho 110 13.36 N 101.05 E
Ban Phon 110 15.25 N 106.42 E
Ban Phông Pho 110 14.36 N 105.52 E
Banphot Phisai 110 15.56 N 99.59 E
Ban Phraek Kasa 269a 13.34 N 100.38 E
Ban Phya 110 21.35 N 102.55 E
Ban Pong 110 13.49 N 99.53 E
Banpu 98 34.28 N 119.18 E
Banpura 126 22.27 N 87.22 E
Banqiao, Zhg. 100 30.06 N 120.27 E
Banqiao, Zhg. 100 31.46 N 112.31 E
Banqiao, Zhg. 100 33.21 N 116.41 E
Banqiao, Zhg. 105 39.56 N 115.51 E
Banqiao, Zhg. 106 31.55 N 118.39 E
Banqiao, Zhg. 107 29.31 N 105.59 E
Banqiaochang 107 29.54 N 104.21 E
Banqiaoji 100 32.19 N 116.37 E
Banqiaoxi 107 29.41 N 103.47 E
Banquan 98 35.07 N 118.42 E
Banraeaba 174t 1.20 N 173.02 E
Ban Ron Phibun 110 8.09 N 99.51 E
Ban Sa-ang 110 17.26 N 105.44 E
Ban Saen To 110 16.05 N 99.51 E
Ban Sakhla 269a 13.32 N 100.30 E
Bansalan 116 6.47 N 125.14 E
Ban Salik 110 18.30 N 100.45 E
Ban Samang 110 19.43 N 102.36 E
Ban Sam Phan 110 8.33 N 99.09 E
Ban Sam Pong 110 18.32 N 102.47 E
Ban Samrong 110 14.23 N 102.50 E
Bansang 150 13.26 N 14.39 W
Ban San Xieng La 110 19.27 N 102.26 E
Bansberia 126 22.58 N 88.24 E
Bānsda 120 20.45 N 73.22 E
Bansha 48 52.28 N 8.04 W
Banshadhāra ≃ 122 18.21 N 84.08 E
Banshanpu 100 27.42 N 113.24 E
Banshi 100 25.20 N 115.23 E
Banshigou 104 41.09 N 120.58 E
Bānsi 124 27.11 N 82.56 E
Bansi ≃ 126 23.50 N 90.15 E
Ban Signo 110 17.51 N 105.04 E
Banská Bystrica 30 48.44 N 19.07 E
Banská Štiavnica 30 48.28 N 18.56 E
Bansko 38 41.50 N 23.29 E
Bānskupi 126 24.10 N 86.41 E
Ban Songkhon 110 17.58 N 105.10 E
Ban Song Kong 269a 13.53 N 100.34 E
Ban Sop Huai Hai 110 19.33 N 98.05 E
Ban Sôppheung 110 18.33 N 104.17 E
Banstala 272b 22.32 N 88.25 E
Banstead 42 51.19 N 0.12 W
Bānswāra 120 23.33 N 74.27 E
Banta 226 37.45 N 121.22 W
Banta, Pulau I 115b 8.25 S 119.14 E
Bantaeng 112 5.32 S 119.56 E
Bantaian 114 1.56 N 100.54 E
Bantaji 100 32.41 N 118.35 E
Ban Takhlo 110 15.27 N 100.44 E
Bantam 207 41.43 N 73.14 W
Bantam Lake ⊜ 207 41.42 N 73.13 W
Ban Tamru 269a 13.31 N 100.41 E
Ban Tao Pun 269a 13.53 N 100.41 E
Bantarkawung 115a 7.13 S 108.55 E
Bantayan 116 11.10 N 123.43 E
Bantayan Island I 116 11.13 N 123.44 E
Banteer 48 52.07 N 8.54 W
Banteln 52 52.04 N 9.44 E
Banten 115a 6.03 S 106.09 E
Banten, Teluk ⊂ 115a 6.00 S 106.10 E
Bantenan, Tanjung › 115a 8.47 S 114.33 E
Ban Teung 110 17.54 N 105.29 E
Ban Thabôk 110 18.22 N 103.12 E
Ban Thanoun 110 19.50 N 101.29 E
Ban Thapayi 110 16.19 N 105.41 E
Bantheville 56 49.21 N 5.05 E
Ban Thieng 110 19.08 N 102.12 E
Ban Tian Sa 110 18.43 N 103.14 E
Bantigui Point › 116 13.41 N 121.28 E
Banting 114 2.49 N 101.30 E
Banton (Jones) 116 12.57 N 122.05 E
Ban Tong Khop 110 17.04 N 104.16 E
Banton Island I 116 12.56 N 122.04 E
Bāntra 272b 22.35 N 88.19 E
Bantry 48 51.41 N 9.27 W
Bantry Bay ⊂ 48 51.38 N 9.48 W
Bantul 115a 7.54 S 110.20 E
Bāntva 120 21.29 N 70.05 E
Banūr 124 30.34 N 76.43 E
Ban Van Hom 110 18.44 N 104.01 E
Ban Vat 110 16.54 N 106.25 E
Banwell 42 51.20 N 2.52 W
Banwy ≃ 42 52.42 N 3.16 W
Ban Xènkhalôk 110 19.42 N 101.54 E
Banxiancun 106 30.33 N 119.42 E
Ban Xot 110 18.11 N 104.05 E
Banya, Punta de la › 34 40.34 N 0.38 E
Banyak, Kepulauan II 114 2.10 N 97.15 E
Ban Ya Plong 110 8.53 N 98.35 E
Banyo 152 6.45 N 11.49 E
Banyoles 34 42.07 N 2.46 E
Banyumas 115a 7.31 S 109.17 E
Banyuwangi 115a 8.12 S 114.21 E
Banyuwedang 115b 8.08 S 114.36 E
Banz 164 5.47 S 144.37 E
Banzare Coast ⊥[2] 9 67.00 S 126.00 E
Banzhuyuan 107 28.44 N 106.18 E
Banzi, It. 68 40.52 N 16.01 E
Banzi, Zhg. 100 24.18 N 117.19 E
Bao ≃, Zhg. 100 33.40 N 116.33 E
Bao ≃, Zhg. 105 39.02 N 115.39 E
Bao ≃, Zhg. 105 40.31 N 118.17 E
Bao, Ouadi V 146 16.36 N 23.55 E
Bao'an, Zhg. 100 30.11 N 114.43 E
Baoan → Zhuolu, Zhg. 105 40.22 N 115.12 E
Baoan, Zhg. 106 31.46 N 121.21 E
Baoancun 89 48.13 N 125.52 E
Baochang → Taibus Qi, Zhg. 98 41.56 N 115.22 E
Baochang, Zhg. 106 32.04 N 121.25 E
Baocheng 102 33.08 N 107.09 E
Baode 102 39.06 N 111.11 E
Baodi 105 39.44 N 117.17 E
Baoding 105 38.52 N 115.29 E
Baofeng 100 33.55 N 113.02 E
Baofu 106 30.31 N 119.29 E
Baoguosi 107 29.35 N 103.25 E
Bao Ha 110 22.11 N 104.21 E
Baohekou 105 40.32 N 118.15 E
Baoji, Zhg. 100 33.08 N 118.19 E
Baoji, Zhg. 102 34.23 N 107.09 E
Baojiagou 105 40.05 N 115.22 E
Baojiapu 104 40.51 N 122.14 E
Baojiatou 106 30.11 N 119.48 E
Baojiawazi 104 41.38 N 123.24 E
Baojing 102 28.43 N 109.25 E
Baokang → Horqin Zuoyi Zhongqi 89 44.07 N 123.18 E
Bao Lac, Viet 110 22.57 N 105.40 E
Bao Lac, Viet 110 11.32 N 107.48 E
Baolin 107 30.24 N 105.02 E
Baolizhen 89 42.56 N 123.46 E
Baolunyuan 102 32.22 N 105.40 E
Baomachang 107 29.58 N 104.12 E
Baon 116 6.47 N 126.05 E
Baonian 106 31.55 N 119.21 E
Baoning 102 23.31 N 106.24 E
Baoqing 89 46.21 N 132.14 E
Baoquan 98 36.16 N 119.04 E
Baoro 152 5.40 N 15.58 E
Baoshan, Zhg. 100 32.39 N 113.54 E
Baoshan, Zhg. 102 26.19 N 104.27 E
Baoshan, Zhg. 102 25.09 N 99.09 E
Baoshan, Zhg. 106 31.25 N 121.29 E
Baoting 110 18.42 N 109.45 E
Baotou (Paotow) 102 40.40 N 109.59 E
Baotun 104 42.29 N 122.52 E
Baoulé ≃ 150 13.33 N 9.54 W
Baowei 102 22.39 N 106.50 E
Baoxikou 100 23.16 N 115.14 E
Baoxingchang 107 29.38 N 105.41 E
Baoxinji 100 32.35 N 115.00 E
Baoyi 100 32.13 N 116.42 E
Baoying 100 33.16 N 119.20 E
Baozhuchang 107 29.48 N 104.15 E
Baozidian 105 40.11 N 117.48 E
Bāp 120 27.23 N 72.21 E
Bapanling 104 40.58 N 123.08 E
Bāpatla 122 15.54 N 80.28 E
Bapaume 50 50.06 N 2.51 E
Bapchule 200 33.08 N 111.52 W
Bapsfontein 158 26.08 S 28.25 E
Baptiste Lake ⊜ 212 45.07 N 78.02 W
Baptistown 208 40.31 N 75.00 W
Bāqa el Gharbīya 132 32.25 N 35.03 E
Baqar, Maṣrif Bahr al- ≍ 142 31.05 N 32.08 E
Baqar, Wādī al- V 146 27.49 N 18.37 E
Baqên 120 31.56 N 94.00 E
Baqing 120 32.15 N 93.30 E
B'aqlīn 132 33.41 N 35.33 E
Ba'qūbah 128 33.45 N 44.38 E
Baquedano 252 23.20 S 69.51 W
Ba Queo 269c 10.48 N 106.38 E
Bar, Jugo. 38 42.05 N 19.05 E
Bar, Ross. 88 51.17 N 107.33 E
Bar, Ukr. 78 49.04 N 27.40 E
Bar ≃ 56 49.42 N 4.50 E
Bāra, India 124 25.13 N 87.22 E
Bara, India 272b 22.43 N 88.31 E
Bara, India 272b 22.46 N 88.17 E
Bara, Nig. 146 10.22 N 10.44 E
Baraawe 144 1.06 N 44.03 E
Barabai 112 2.35 S 115.23 E
Bara Bāngurda 126 22.57 N 86.24 E
Bāra Banki 124 26.55 N 81.12 E
Barabanovo 82 54.43 N 38.10 E
Barābhūm 126 23.02 N 86.22 E
Barabinsk 86 55.21 N 78.21 E
Barabinskaja step' ≚ 86 55.00 N 79.00 E
Baraboo 190 43.28 N 89.44 W
Baraboo ≃ 190 43.29 N 89.26 W
Baraboulé 150 14.12 N 1.51 W
Baracaju ≃ 255 12.21 S 51.00 W
Baracaldo 34 43.18 N 2.59 W
Barachit 144 14.39 N 39.27 E
Barachois Pond Provincial Park ♦ 186 48.30 N 58.14 W
Baracoa, Cuba 240p 20.21 N 74.30 W
Baracoa, Hond. 236 15.43 N 87.52 W
Baradā ≃ 132 33.30 N 36.28 E
Baradero 258 33.48 S 59.30 W
Baradero ≃ 258 33.55 S 59.16 W
Baradili 71 39.43 N 8.54 E
Baradine 166 30.56 S 149.04 E
Bara Doāni 126 22.06 N 89.59 E
Baraga 190 46.46 N 88.29 W
Baragaon → Nālanda 124 25.07 N 85.25 E
Baragarh 120 21.20 N 83.37 E
Baragiano 68 40.41 N 15.35 E
Baragoi 154 1.47 N 36.47 E
Baraguá 240p 21.41 N 78.38 W
Baragwanath Aerodrome ⊠ 273d 26.15 S 27.59 E
Baragwanath Military Hospital ♥ 273d 26.16 S 27.56 E
Bārah 140 13.42 N 30.22 E
Barahānuddin 126 22.30 N 90.43 E
Barahona 238 18.12 N 71.06 W
Barāigrām 126 24.19 N 89.10 E
Bara Issa ≃ 150 16.09 N 3.28 W
Barajas, Aeropuerto ⊠ 266a 40.28 N 3.34 W
Barajas de Madrid •[8] 266a 40.28 N 3.35 E
Bara Jorda 126 23.10 N 86.50 E
Barak 130 36.51 N 37.59 E
Barāk ≃ 120 24.52 N 92.30 E
Baraka 154 4.06 S 29.06 E
Baraka (Khawr Barakah) V 144 18.13 N 37.35 E
Barakah 140 10.58 N 27.59 E
Barakah, Khawr (Baraka) V 144 18.13 N 37.35 E
Barākar 126 24.07 N 86.14 E
Barakār ≃ 126 23.42 N 86.48 E
Bara Khunta 126 21.43 N 86.38 E
Baraki 120 33.56 N 68.55 E
Barakkol'skij 86 52.12 N 67.49 E
Bārākpur, Bngl. 126 22.55 N 89.32 E
Bārākpur, India 126 22.46 N 88.21 E
Bārākpur Cantonment 272b 22.46 N 88.22 E
Barakula 166 26.26 S 150.31 E
Barāl 272b 22.27 N 88.22 E
Baral ≃ 126 24.10 N 89.27 E
Baralaba 166 24.11 S 149.49 E
Barām 126 22.57 N 86.18 E
Baram ≃ 112 4.36 N 113.59 E
Baram, Tanjong › 112 4.35 N 113.59 E
Barama ≃ 246 7.40 N 59.15 W
Barāmāria 126 21.42 N 87.04 E
Bārāmati 122 18.09 N 74.35 E
Bāramūla 123 34.12 N 74.21 E
Baran', Bela. 76 54.30 N 28.40 E
Baran', Bela. 76 54.29 N 30.18 E
Bārān, India 124 25.06 N 76.31 E
Baranagar 126 22.38 N 88.22 E
Baranakovo 86 58.08 N 82.58 E
Barancevo 82 55.04 N 37.38 E
Baranello 66 41.32 N 14.34 E
Barangbarang 112 6.24 S 120.28 E
Barangeon ≃ 50 47.12 N 2.10 E
Barani 150 13.10 N 3.53 W
Baraniki 80 46.31 N 41.50 E
Baranivka 78 50.18 N 27.40 E
Baranoa 246 10.48 N 74.55 W
Barano d'Ischia 68 40.42 N 13.55 E
Baranof 180 57.05 N 134.50 W
Baranof Island I 180 57.00 N 135.00 W
Baranoviči 76 53.08 N 26.02 E
Baranovskoje 82 55.25 N 38.45 E
Barany, Ross. 76 57.20 N 29.09 E
Barany, Ross. 80 57.38 N 52.16 E
Baranya □[6] 30 46.05 N 18.15 E
Baranykivka 83 49.10 N 39.50 E
Barão Ataliba Nogueira 256 22.24 S 46.45 W
Barão de Geraldo 256 22.49 S 47.06 W
Barão de Grajaú 250 6.45 S 43.01 W
Barão de Juparanã 256 22.21 S 43.41 W
Barão de Melgaço 248 16.13 S 55.58 W
Barão de Tromaí 250 1.29 S 45.36 W
Baraolt 38 46.05 N 25.36 E
Baraque de Fraiture ∧ 56 50.15 N 5.44 E
Baras 116 13.40 N 124.22 E
Barasāhi 126 21.43 N 86.44 E
Bārāsat, India 126 22.43 N 88.29 E
Bārasat, India 272b 22.51 N 88.22 E
Baraševo 80 54.32 N 42.53 E
Barashi 78 50.43 N 28.01 E
Baraški 24 65.40 N 52.10 E
Barat, Lintasan ⋓ 115a 7.08 S 112.40 E
Baratã 266c 38.48 N 9.19 W
Baratang Island I 110 12.13 N 92.45 E
Barataria 194 29.43 N 90.07 W
Barataria Bay ⊂ 194 29.22 N 89.57 W
Barat Daya, Kepulauan II 108 7.25 S 128.00 E
Barate 112 9.54 S 123.38 E
Bar'atino, Ross. 76 54.19 N 34.31 E
Bar'atino, Ross. 82 54.43 N 36.49 E
Baratolia 126 22.25 N 86.37 E
Baratta 166 31.59 S 139.06 E
Barauana ≃ 246 1.14 N 60.41 W
Baraula 272a 28.34 N 77.22 E
Barauni 124 25.29 N 85.59 E
Baraut 124 29.06 N 77.16 E
Baraya 246 3.10 N 75.04 W
Barbacena 256 21.14 S 43.46 W
Barbacoas 246 1.41 N 78.09 W
Barbades → Barbados □[1] 241g 13.10 N 59.32 W
Barbadillo del Mercado 34 42.02 N 3.21 W
Barbadoes Island I 285 40.07 N 75.22 W
Barbados □[1], N.A. 230 13.10 N 59.32 W
Barbados □[1], N.A. 241g 13.10 N 59.32 W
Barbagia •[1] 71 39.55 N 9.12 E
Barbalha 250 7.19 S 39.17 W
Barbar 140 18.01 N 33.59 E
Barbarano Vicentino 64 45.24 N 11.32 E
Barbarasco 64 44.14 N 9.56 E
Barbareta, Isla I 236 16.26 N 86.09 W
Barbaria, Cap de › 34 38.38 N 1.23 E
Barbaros 130 40.54 N 27.27 E
Barbas, Cap › 148 22.18 N 16.41 W
Barbaši 76 57.42 N 28.24 E
Barbastro 34 42.02 N 0.08 E
Barbate ≃ 34 36.11 N 5.55 W
Barbate de Franco 34 36.12 N 5.55 W
Barbeau Peak ∧ 16 81.54 N 75.01 W
Barbentane 62 43.54 N 4.45 E
Barberà del Vallès 266d 41.31 N 2.08 E
Barber Booth 262 53.22 N 1.50 W
Barberena 236 14.18 N 90.22 W
Barberena ≃ 234 22.34 N 97.52 W
Barberino di Mugello 66 44.00 N 11.15 E
Barberino Val d'Elsa 66 43.32 N 11.10 E
Barbers Point › 229c 21.18 N 158.07 W
Barbers Point Naval Air Station ■ 229c 21.19 N 158.04 W
Barberton, S. Afr. 156 25.48 S 31.03 E
Barberton, Oh., U.S. 214 41.00 N 81.36 W
Barbezieux 32 45.28 N 0.09 W
Bar Bigha 124 25.13 N 85.44 E
Barbil 124 22.06 N 85.20 E
Barbis 54 51.37 N 10.25 E
Barbizon 50 48.27 N 2.36 E
Barbosa, Col. 246 6.26 N 75.20 W
Barbosa, Col. 246 5.57 N 73.37 W
Barboursville 188 38.24 N 82.17 W
Barbourville 192 36.51 N 83.53 W
Barbuda I 238 17.38 N 61.48 W
Barbuise ≃ 50 48.33 N 3.58 E
Barby 54 51.58 N 11.53 E
Bârca 38 43.58 N 23.37 E
Barčadiv 85 38.19 N 72.29 E
Barca Grande ≃ 258 34.09 S 58.23 W
Barcaldine 166 23.33 S 145.17 E
Barcarena 266c 38.44 N 9.17 W
Barcarena, Ribeira de ≃ 266c 38.42 N 9.27 W
Barcarrota 34 38.31 N 6.51 W
Barcău (Berettyó) ≃ 38 46.59 N 21.07 E
Barce → Al-Marj 146 32.30 N 20.54 E
Barcellona Pozzo di Gotto 70 38.09 N 15.13 E
Barcelona, Esp. 34 41.23 N 2.11 E
Barcelona, Esp. 266d 41.23 N 2.11 E
Barcelona, Méx. 232 26.12 N 103.25 W
Barcelona, Pil. 116 12.52 N 124.09 E
Barcelona, Ven. 246 10.08 N 64.42 W
Barcelona □[4] 34 41.40 N 2.00 E
Barcelona •[8] 266a 40.22 N 3.34 E
Barcelona, Aeropuerto Transoceánico de ⊠ 266d 41.18 N 2.05 E
Barcelone → Barcelona 34 41.23 N 2.11 E
Barceloneta 240m 18.27 N 66.32 W
Barcelonnette 62 44.23 N 6.39 E
Barcelos, Bra. 246 0.58 S 62.57 W
Barcelos, Port. 34 41.32 N 8.37 W
Barchaticha 80 57.34 N 45.13 E
Barchyn ≃ 88 48.43 N 110.17 E
Barcillonnette 62 44.26 N 5.55 E
Barcin 30 52.52 N 17.57 E
Barcis 64 46.11 N 12.33 E
Barclay 208 39.08 N 75.51 W
Barclay Brook ≃ 276 40.19 N 74.22 W
Barcoo ≃ 166 25.30 S 142.50 E
Barcroft, Lake ⊜[1] 284c 38.51 N 77.09 W
Barcs 30 45.58 N 17.28 E
Barcy 261 49.01 N 2.53 E
Barczewo 30 53.50 N 20.42 E
Bard 62 45.36 N 7.45 E
Bärdä, Azer. 84 40.23 N 47.08 E
Barda, Ross. 86 56.54 N 55.38 E
Barda del Medio 252 38.43 S 68.10 W
Bardagué, Enneri V 146 22.06 N 16.28 E
Bardai, Sūd. 140 12.43 N 21.53 E
Bardaï, Tchad 146 21.22 N 16.59 E
Bardawīl, Sabkhat al- ≡ 140 31.10 N 33.10 E
Barddhamān 126 23.15 N 87.51 E
Bardejov 30 49.18 N 21.16 E
Bardenas Reales ⋏[1] 34 42.10 N 1.25 W
Bardeskan 128 35.12 N 57.58 E
Bardi 62 44.38 N 9.44 E
Bardīyah 146 31.46 N 25.06 E
Bardız 130 40.26 N 42.20 E
Bardney 44 53.12 N 0.21 W
Bardo 36 36.50 N 10.06 E
Bardoc 162 30.20 S 121.17 E
Bārdoli 120 21.07 N 73.07 E
Bardolino 64 45.33 N 10.43 E
Bardonecchia 62 45.05 N 6.42 E
Bardonia 276 41.07 N 74.00 W
Bardoux, Lac ⊜ 186 51.09 N 67.50 W
Bardowick 52 53.18 N 10.23 E
Bardsey Island I 42 52.45 N 4.45 W
Bardsey Sound ⋓ 42 52.47 N 4.45 W
Bardstown 194 37.48 N 85.28 W
Bardu 24 68.52 N 18.21 E
Bardufoss 24 69.04 N 18.30 E
Bardwell, Ky., U.S. 194 36.52 N 89.00 W
Bardwell, Tx., U.S. 222 32.16 N 96.42 W
Bardwell Lake ⊜[1] 222 32.16 N 96.39 W

Symbols in the index entries represent the broad categories identified in the key at the right. Symbols with superior numbers (⋏[1]) identify subcategories (see complete key on page *I · 1).*

Symbole im Register stellen die rechts im Schlüssel erklärten Kategorien dar. Symbole mit hochgestellten Ziffern (⋏[1]) bezeichnen Unterabteilungen einer Kategorie (vgl. vollständiger Schlüssel auf Seite *I · 1).*

Los símbolos incluídos en el texto del índice representan las grandes categorías identificadas con la clave a la derecha. Los símbolos con numeros en su parte superior (⋏[1]) identifican las subcategorías (véase la clave completa en la página *I · 1).*

Les symboles de l'index représentent les catégories indiquées dans la légende à droite. Les symboles suivis d'un indice (⋏[1]) représentent des sous-catégories (voir légende complète à la page *I · 1).*

Os símbolos incluídos no texto do índice representam as grandes categorias identificadas com a chave à direita. Os símbolos com números em sua parte superior (⋏[1]) identificam as subcategorias (veja-se a chave completa à página *I · 1).*

	English	Deutsch	Español	Français	Português
∧	Mountain	Berg	Montaña	Montagne	Montanha
⋏	Mountains	Gebirge	Montañas	Montagnes	Montanhas
)(	Pass	Paß	Paso	Col	Passo
V	Valley, Canyon	Tal, Cañon	Valle, Cañón	Vallée, Canyon	Vale, Canhão
≚	Plain	Ebene	Llano	Plaine	Planície
›	Cape	Kap	Cabo	Cap	Cabo
I	Island	Insel	Isla	Île	Ilha
II	Islands	Inseln	Islas	Îles	Ilhas
⊥	Other Topographic Features	Andere Topographische Objekte	Otros Elementos Topográficos	Autres données topographiques	Outros acidentes topográficos

ESPAÑOL Nombre / Página / Lat.°′ / Long.°′ W = Oeste
FRANÇAIS Nom / Page / Lat.°′ / Long.°′ W = Ouest
PORTUGUÊS Nome / Página / Lat.°′ / Long.°′ W = Oeste

Bare 144 4.42 N 42.47 E
Bareggio 266b 45.29 N 9.00 E
Barei, Wādī V 140 13.27 N 23.57 E
Bareilly 124 28.21 N 79.25 E
Bareli 124 23.00 N 78.14 E
Barenburg 52 52.37 N 8.47 E
Barendrecht 52 51.51 N 4.32 E
Bärenklau 54 51.56 N 14.34 E
Bärenstein, Dtsch. 54 50.30 N 13.02 E
Bärenstein, Dtsch. 54 50.48 N 13.47 E
Barentin 50 49.33 N 0.57 E
Barents Sea ⇁2 12 74.00 N 36.00 E
Barents Trough ⇁1 12 75.00 N 29.00 E
Barentu 144 15.04 N 37.37 E
Bareo 112 3.45 N 115.27 E
Baresville 208 39.48 N 76.57 W
Bareta 123 29.52 N 75.42 E
Barfleur 32 49.40 N 1.15 W
Barfleur, Pointe de > 32 49.42 N 1.16 W
Barga 64 44.04 N 10.29 E
Bargāchia, India 126 22.39 N 88.07 E
Bargāchia, India 272b 22.48 N 88.27 E
Bargagli 62 44.27 N 9.05 E
Bargaintown 208 39.22 N 70.35 W
Bargara 166 24.49 S 152.27 E
Bargas 34 39.56 N 4.03 W
Barge, It. 62 44.43 N 7.20 E
Barge, Ityo. 144 6.14 N 36.58 E
Barg-e Maṭāl 120 35.40 N 71.21 E
Bargemon 62 43.37 N 6.32 E
Bargen 58 47.48 N 8.37 E
Bargersville 218 39.31 N 86.10 W
Barghanak 128 33.56 N 62.26 E
Barghop 140 9.30 N 28.28 E
Bargo 170 34.18 S 150.35 E
Bargoed 42 51.43 N 3.15 W
Bargteheide 52 53.44 N 10.16 E
Bārguna 126 22.09 N 90.07 E
Barguzin 88 53.37 N 109.37 E
Barguzin ≃ 88 53.27 N 109.00 E
Barguzinskij chrebet ⋀ 88 54.30 N 110.20 E
Barguzinskij zapovednik ♦ 88 54.25 N 109.40 E
Bārh 124 25.29 N 85.43 E
Barhaj 124 26.17 N 83.44 E
Bar Harbor 188 44.23 N 68.12 W
Barharwa 124 24.52 N 87.47 E
Barhau 112 5.19 S 102.10 E
Barhi 124 24.18 N 85.25 E
Bar Hill 42 52.15 N 0.01 E
Barhiya 124 25.17 N 86.02 E
Bāri, India 124 23.03 N 78.05 E
Bāri, India 124 26.39 N 77.36 E
Bari, It. 68 41.07 N 16.52 E
Bari, Zaïre 152 3.19 N 19.23 E
Bari ▫4, It. 68 40.56 N 16.40 E
Bari ▫4, Som. 144 10.00 N 50.00 E
Baria ≃ 246 1.56 N 66.35 W
Baricella 64 44.39 N 11.32 E
Barichara 246 6.38 N 73.14 W
Barīdī, Ra's > 128 24.17 N 37.31 E
Bāri Doāb ⋏1 123 30.25 N 73.00 E
Barī Gāv 120 33.52 N 67.49 E
Barigazzo 64 44.16 N 10.39 E
Barigua, Salina de ≃ 241s 12.08 N 69.59 W
Barika 34 35.23 N 5.22 E
Barika, Oued ≃ 34 35.22 N 5.18 E
Barikiwa 154 9.28 S 37.54 E
Barīkowṭ 120 35.18 N 71.32 E
Barile 68 40.57 N 15.40 E
Barillas 236 15.48 N 91.18 W
Bariloche — San Carlos de Bariloche 254 41.09 S 71.18 W
Barilo-Krepinskaja 83 47.45 N 39.32 E
Barīm (Perim) I 144 12.39 N 43.25 E
Barima ≃ 246 8.33 N 60.25 W
Barima-Waini ▫4 246 7.45 N 59.30 W
Barin 39 39.13 N 44.28 E
Barinas, P.R. 240m 18.01 N 66.51 W
Barinas, Ven. 246 8.38 N 70.12 W
Barinas ▫3 246 8.10 N 69.50 W
Baring 224 47.46 N 121.29 W
Baring, Cape > 176 70.05 N 117.20 W
Baringa, Zaïre 152 0.45 N 20.52 E
Baringa, Zaïre 152 0.38 N 36.05 E
Baringo, Lake ⊜ 154 0.38 N 36.05 E
Båring Vig c 41 55.32 N 9.56 E
Barinitas 246 8.45 N 70.25 W
Bāripada 126 21.56 N 86.43 E
Barirī 255 22.04 S 48.44 W
Bārīs 140 24.40 N 30.36 E
Barisacho 84 42.28 N 44.54 E
Bari Sādri 120 24.25 N 74.28 E
Barisāl 124 22.42 N 90.22 E
Barisan, Pegunungan ⋀ 112 3.00 S 102.15 E
Bari Sardo 71 39.50 N 9.38 E
Barisciano 66 42.19 N 13.35 E
Bariti Bil ⊜ 272b 22.48 N 88.26 E
Barito ≃ 112 3.32 S 114.29 E
Baritú, Parque Nacional ♦ 252 22.30 S 64.35 W
Barjā 132 33.39 N 35.26 E
Barjac 62 44.18 N 4.21 E
Barjols 62 43.33 N 6.00 E
Barjora 126 23.26 N 87.17 E
Barjūj, Wādī V 146 25.57 N 13.12 E
Bark ≃ 216 42.55 N 88.50 W
Barka Kāna 124 23.37 N 85.29 E
Barkal 120 22.44 N 92.23 E
Barkam 102 31.50 N 102.40 E
Barkava 76 56.43 N 26.36 E
Barkelsby 54 54.30 N 9.50 E
Barker, N.Y., U.S. 210 43.19 N 78.33 W
Barker, Ur. 258 34.16 S 57.27 W
Barker Point > 276 40.51 N 73.44 W
Barker Reservoir ⊜1 222 29.44 N 95.44 W
Barkers Brook ≃ 285 40.03 N 74.45 W
Barkerville 182 53.04 N 121.31 W
Barkerville Historic Park ♦ 182 53.04 N 121.30 W
Barkeyville 214 41.12 N 79.58 W
Barkhamsted Reservoir ⊜1 207 41.57 N 72.57 W
Bārkhān 120 29.54 N 69.31 E
Barkhanpur 126 23.50 N 89.33 E
Barking ◆8 42 51.33 N 0.06 E
Barkingside ◆8 260 51.36 N 0.05 E
Barki Saraiya 124 24.10 N 85.53 E
Barkisland 262 53.41 N 1.55 W
Bark Lake ⊜, On., Can. 190 46.54 N 82.28 W
Bark Lake ⊜, On., Can. 212 45.27 N 77.51 W
Barkley, Lake ⊜1 194 36.40 N 87.55 W
Barkley Sound ⪠ 182 48.53 N 125.20 W
Barkly ≃ 169 37.32 S 146.32 E
Barkly, Mount ⋀2 162 21.34 S 132.28 E
Barkly East 158 30.58 S 27.33 E
Barkly Tableland ⋏1 162 18.00 S 136.00 E
Barkly West 158 28.05 S 24.31 E
Barkol 98 43.50 N 93.30 E
Barksdale 196 29.44 N 100.02 W
Barkuhi 124 22.13 N 78.42 E
Barla 130 38.01 N 30.47 E
Bârlad 38 46.14 N 27.40 E
Bârlad ≃ 38 45.36 N 27.31 E
Barlassina 266b 45.39 N 9.08 E
Barlaston 42 52.57 N 2.10 W
Barlby 44 53.48 N 1.03 W
Barleben 54 52.12 N 11.37 E
Bar-le-Duc 56 48.47 N 5.10 E
Barlee, Lake ⊜ 162 29.10 S 119.30 E
Barlee, Mount ⋀2 162 24.37 S 128.06 E
Barlee Range ⋀ 162 23.35 S 116.00 E
Barles 62 44.16 N 6.16 E
Barletta 68 41.19 N 16.17 E
Barlin 50 50.27 N 2.37 E
Barlinek 30 53.00 N 15.12 E
Barling 42 51.35 N 0.47 E
Barlow 194 37.03 N 89.02 W
Barluk 88 54.32 N 101.43 E
Barma 164 1.54 S 133.00 E
Barmancak, ozero ⊜ 80 48.02 N 44.40 E
Barmashove 78 47.07 N 32.26 E
Barmedman 166 34.09 S 147.23 E
Barmen ◆8 263 51.17 N 7.13 E
Bärmer 120 25.45 N 71.23 E
Barmera 166 34.15 S 140.28 E
Barmouth 42 52.43 N 4.03 W
Barmouth Bay c 42 52.42 N 4.08 W
Barmstedt 52 53.47 N 9.46 E
Barnaby Manor Oaks 284c 38.50 N 76.58 W
Barnagar 120 23.03 N 75.22 E
Barnāla 123 30.23 N 75.33 E
Barnard Castle 44 54.33 N 1.55 W
Barnasht 142 29.41 N 31.15 E
Bārnau 60 49.49 N 12.26 E
Barnaul 86 53.22 N 83.45 E
Bārnbach 61 47.05 N 15.06 E
Barn Bluff ⋀ 166 41.43 S 145.56 E
Barneberg 54 52.08 N 11.03 E
Barnegat 208 39.45 N 74.13 W
Barnegat Bay c 208 39.52 N 74.07 W
Barnegat Light 208 39.45 N 74.06 W
Barne Inlet c 9 80.15 S 160.15 E
Barnes 214 41.40 N 79.01 W
Barnes ◆8 260 51.28 N 0.15 W
Barnesboro 214 40.39 N 78.46 W
Barnes Corners 212 43.49 N 75.49 W
Barnes Ice Cap ⊠ 176 70.00 N 73.15 W
Barnes Lake ⊜ 184 56.23 N 98.06 W
Barnes Sound ⪠ 220 25.14 N 80.23 W
Barnesville, Ga., U.S. 192 33.03 N 84.09 W
Barnesville, Mn., U.S. 198 46.39 N 96.25 W
Barnesville, Oh., U.S. 188 39.59 N 81.10 W
Barnet ◆8 42 51.40 N 0.13 W
Barnetby le Wold 44 53.35 N 0.25 W
Barnett 219 39.16 N 89.42 W
Barnetts 208 37.22 N 77.09 W
Barneveld, Ned. 52 52.08 N 5.35 E
Barneveld, N.Y., U.S. 210 43.16 N 75.12 W
Barneville-Carteret 32 49.23 N 1.47 W
Barnhart, Mo., U.S. 219 38.20 N 90.23 W
Barnhart, Tx., U.S. 196 31.08 N 101.10 W
Barnhill 214 40.27 N 81.21 W
Barnim ◆1 54 52.40 N 13.45 E
Barnoldswick 44 53.55 N 2.11 W
Barnowko 54 52.48 N 14.45 E
Barnsboro 285 39.46 N 75.09 W
Barnsdall 196 36.33 N 96.09 W
Barnsley 44 53.34 N 1.28 W
Barnstable 207 41.42 N 70.18 W
Barnstable ▫6 207 41.42 N 70.18 W
Barnstable Harbor c 207 41.43 N 70.18 W
Barnstaple 42 51.05 N 4.04 W
Barnstaple Bay c 42 51.05 N 4.20 W
Barnston 262 53.21 N 3.05 W
Barnstorf 52 52.42 N 8.30 E
Barnt Green 42 52.22 N 1.59 W
Barnton 262 53.16 N 2.33 W
Barntrup 52 51.59 N 9.06 E
Barnum Island 276 40.36 N 73.39 W
Barnwell, Ab., Can. 182 49.46 N 112.15 W
Barnwell, S.C., U.S. 192 33.14 N 81.21 W
Baro 150 8.37 N 6.25 E
Baro ≃ 144 8.26 N 33.13 E
Barobo 116 8.33 N 126.07 E
Baroda — Vadodara, India 122 22.18 N 73.12 E
Baroda, India 124 25.30 N 76.39 E
Baroda, Mi., U.S. 216 41.57 N 86.29 W
Baroe 158 33.13 S 24.33 E
Barometer ⋀ 172 41.50 S 173.39 E
Baron Bluff ≃4 241n 17.47 N 64.47 W
Baronissi 68 40.44 N 14.45 E
Barons 182 50.00 N 113.05 W
Barora Fa Island I 175e 7.30 S 158.20 E
Barora Ite Island I 175e 7.35 S 158.24 E
Barossa Reservoir ⊜1 168b 34.39 S 138.51 E
Barotac Nuevo 116 10.54 N 122.42 E
Barotac Viejo 116 11.03 N 122.51 E
Barouéli 150 13.04 N 6.50 W
Barpathār 120 26.17 N 93.53 E
Barpeta 120 26.19 N 91.00 E
Bar Point > 214 42.03 N 83.06 W
Barqa 120 30.51 N 81.20 E
Barqah (Cyrenaica) ▫9 146 31.00 N 22.30 E
Barqah, Jabal al- ⋀ 140 30.25 N 34.18 E
Barq al-'Izz 142 31.01 N 31.26 E
Barque Canada Reef ⇁2 108 8.12 N 113.19 E
Barques, Pointe aux > 190 44.04 N 82.58 W
Barquisimeto 246 10.04 N 69.19 W
Barr 58 48.24 N 7.27 E
Barra, Bra. 250 11.05 S 43.10 W
Barra, Gam. 150 13.20 N 16.36 W
Barra I 46 56.58 N 7.29 W
Barra, Ponta da > 156 23.47 S 35.32 E
Barra, Sound of ⪠ 46 57.05 N 7.25 W
Barraba 166 30.22 S 150.36 E
Barracas ◆8 288 34.38 S 58.22 W
Barrackpore — Bārākpur 126 22.46 N 88.21 E
Barrackpore Airport ⊠ 272b 22.47 N 88.22 E
Barrackville 188 39.30 N 80.10 W
Barracouta, Cape > 158 34.26 S 21.22 E
Barra da Estiva 255 13.38 S 41.19 W
Barra de Santo Antônio 250 9.24 S 35.30 W
Barra de São Francisco 256 21.58 S 42.42 W
Barra do Bugres 248 15.05 S 57.11 W
Barra do Corda 250 5.30 S 45.15 W
Barra do Cuanza 152 9.09 S 13.08 E
Barra do Dande 152 8.28 S 13.22 E
Barra do Garças 255 15.53 S 52.15 W
Barra do Mendes 255 11.43 S 42.04 W
Barra do Piraí 256 22.28 S 43.49 W
Barra do Ribeiro 252 30.18 S 51.18 W
Barra dos Coqueiros 250 10.54 S 37.03 W
Barra Falsa, Ponta da > 156 22.55 S 35.37 E
Barrafranca 70 37.22 N 14.12 E
Barra Funda ◆8 287b 23.31 S 46.39 W
Barra Head > 46 56.46 N 7.38 W
Barrali 71 39.28 N 9.06 E
Barra Mansa 256 22.32 S 44.11 W
Barranca, Perú 248 10.45 S 77.46 W
Barranca, Perú 248 4.50 S 76.42 W
Barrancabermeja 246 7.03 N 73.52 W
Barrancas, Col. 246 10.57 N 72.50 W
Barrancas, Ven. 246 8.46 N 70.06 W
Barrancas, Ven. 246 8.42 N 62.11 W
Barrancos 34 38.08 N 6.59 W
Barranco Azul 286d 12.09 S 77.02 W
Barranco de Guadalupe 196 29.21 N 104.17 W
Barranco do Velho 34 37.14 N 7.56 W
Barrancos 34 38.08 N 6.59 W
Barrânia 256 21.33 S 46.32 W
Barranqueras 252 27.29 S 58.56 W
Barranquilla 246 10.59 N 74.48 W
Barranquitas 240m 18.11 N 66.18 W
Barras 250 4.15 S 42.18 W
Barrax 34 39.03 N 2.12 W
Barre, Ma., U.S. 207 42.25 N 72.06 W
Barre, Vt., U.S. 188 44.11 N 72.30 W
Barrea 66 41.45 N 13.59 E
Barreal 252 31.38 S 69.28 W
Barreal 214 40.35 N 78.06 W
Barre Falls Dam ◆6 207 42.26 N 72.02 W
Barreirinha 250 2.47 S 57.03 W
Barreirinhas 250 2.45 S 42.50 W
Barreiro 34 38.40 N 9.05 W
Barreiro ≃, Bra. 255 15.43 S 52.18 W
Barreiro ≃, Bra. 287a 22.52 S 43.34 W
Barreiros 250 8.49 S 35.12 W
Barrême 62 43.57 N 6.22 E
Barren ≃ 194 37.11 N 86.37 W
Barren, Nosy II 157b 18.25 S 43.40 E
Barren Island I 110 12.16 N 93.51 E
Barren Islands II 180 58.55 N 152.15 W
Barrenjoey Head > 170 33.34 S 151.20 E
Barren River Lake ⊜1 194 36.45 N 86.02 W
Barren Run ≃ 279b 40.09 N 79.42 W
Barre Plains 207 42.22 N 72.06 W
Barret-le-Bas 62 44.16 N 5.44 E
Barretos 255 20.33 S 48.33 W
Barrett 222 29.53 N 95.04 W
Barrett, Mount ⋀ 162 18.10 S 127.33 E
Barrhead, Ab., Can. 182 54.08 N 114.24 W
Barrhead, Scot., U.K. 46 55.48 N 4.24 W
Barrhill 44 55.07 N 4.46 W
Barrie 212 44.24 N 79.40 W
Barriefield 212 44.14 N 76.28 W
Barrie Island I 190 45.55 N 82.40 W
Barrien 52 52.56 N 8.49 E
Barrier, Cape > 172 36.21 S 175.31 E
Barrière 182 51.11 N 120.07 W
Barrier Range ⋏ 166 31.25 S 141.25 E
Barrier Reef ⇁2 164 11.36 S 153.00 E
Barrigada 174p 13.28 N 144.48 E
Barrilla Draw V 196 31.21 N 103.23 W
Barr Iljās 132 33.46 N 35.54 E
Barrington, N.S., Can. 186 43.34 N 65.34 W
Barrington, Il., U.S. 216 42.09 N 88.08 W
Barrington, N.J., U.S. 285 39.51 N 75.03 W
Barrington, R.I., U.S. 207 41.44 N 71.18 W
Barrington Hills 216 42.07 N 88.09 W
Barrington Lake ⊜ 184 56.55 N 100.15 W
Barrington Tops ⋀ 166 32.00 S 151.28 E
Barrington Woods 278 42.09 N 88.04 W
Barringun 166 29.01 S 145.43 E
Barrio de la Soledad 234 16.48 N 95.15 W
Barrita Vieja 236 13.55 N 90.54 W
Barrīyat al-Uşayfir 142 31.18 N 30.40 E
Barro, Bra. 250 7.11 S 38.47 W
Barro, Gui.-B. 150 12.24 N 15.30 W
Barro Alto 255 15.04 S 48.58 W
Barron 190 45.24 N 91.50 W
Barron Creek ≃ 282 37.27 N 122.05 W
Barron Lake 216 41.51 N 86.11 W
Barrouallie 241h 13.14 N 61.17 W
Barrow, Arg. 252 38.18 S 60.14 W
Barrow, Ak., U.S. 180 71.17 N 156.34 W
Barrow ≃ 48 52.15 N 7.00 W
Barrow, Point > 180 71.23 N 156.30 W
Barrow Bay c 212 44.58 N 81.13 W
Barrow Creek 162 21.33 S 133.53 E
Barrowford 44 53.52 N 2.13 W
Barrow-in-Furness 44 54.07 N 3.14 W
Barrow Island I 162 20.48 S 115.23 E
Barrows 184 52.49 N 101.27 W
Barrow Strait ⪠ 176 74.21 N 94.10 W
Barrowsville 207 41.56 N 71.12 W
Barrow upon Humber 44 53.41 N 0.23 W
Barry, Wales, U.K. 42 51.24 N 3.18 W
Barry, Il., U.S. 219 39.41 N 91.02 W
Barry, Tx., U.S. 222 32.06 N 96.38 W
Barry ▫6 216 42.35 N 85.18 W
Barrydale 158 33.55 S 20.43 E
Barrys Bay 212 45.29 N 77.41 W
Barrys Bay c 212 45.28 N 77.42 W
Barryton 190 43.45 N 85.08 W
Barrytown 210 42.00 N 73.56 W
Barryville 210 41.28 N 74.54 W
Barsakel'mes, ostrov I 86 45.40 N 59.58 E
Barsalpur 120 28.10 N 72.15 E
Baršatas 86 48.13 N 78.21 E
Barsbek 44 55.07 N 11.58 E
Bārsi 122 18.14 N 75.42 E
Baršin 86 49.45 N 69.36 E
Barsinghausen 52 52.18 N 9.27 E
Barskaun 85 42.10 N 77.37 E
Barso I 41 55.07 N 9.34 E
Barßel 52 53.10 N 7.44 E
Barst 56 49.04 N 6.50 E
Barstow, Ca., U.S. 228 34.53 N 117.01 W
Barstow, Tx., U.S. 196 31.28 N 103.24 W
Barsuki 82 54.15 N 37.30 E
Bar-sur-Aube 58 48.14 N 4.43 E
Bar-sur-Seine 50 48.07 N 4.22 E
Bart 208 39.56 N 76.05 W
Bārta ≃ 76 56.24 N 21.03 E
Bartala 272b 22.33 N 88.16 E
Bartang ≃ 120 37.56 N 71.34 E
Bartazuga, Jabal ⋀ 140 21.44 N 33.33 E
Bartelso 219 38.32 N 89.28 W
Bartenheim 58 47.38 N 7.29 E
Bartenstein 58 49.21 N 9.53 E
Barter Island I 180 70.08 N 143.35 W
Barth 54 54.22 N 12.43 E
Barthe ≃ 54 54.22 N 12.41 E
Barthélemy, Deo ⨯ 110 19.26 N 104.06 E
Bartholomew ≃6 218 39.13 N 85.55 W
Bartholomew, Bayou ≃ 194 32.43 N 92.04 W
Bartibougou 150 12.52 N 0.48 E
Bartica 246 6.24 N 58.37 W
Bartın 130 41.38 N 32.21 E
Bartle Frere ⋀ 166 17.23 S 145.49 E
Bartlesville 196 36.44 N 95.58 W
Bartlett, Il., U.S. 216 41.59 N 88.11 W
Bartlett, Ne., U.S. 198 41.53 N 98.33 W
Bartlett, N.H., U.S. 188 44.04 N 71.17 W
Bartlett, Tn., U.S. 194 35.12 N 89.52 W
Bartlett, Tx., U.S. 222 30.48 N 97.26 W
Bartlett Brook ≃ 283 42.42 N 71.13 W
Bartlett Cove 180 58.27 N 135.55 W
Bartlett Reservoir ⊜1 200 33.52 N 111.37 W
Bartletts ⋏2 168a 32.19 S 116.43 E
Bartletts Harbour 186 50.57 N 57.00 W
Bartley 198 40.14 N 100.18 W
Bartolomé Bayre — General Mansilla 258 35.05 S 57.45 W
Bartolomé de las Casas 252 25.24 S 59.34 W
Bartolomeu de Gusmão, Aeroporto ⊠ 256 22.56 S 43.43 W
Bartolomeu Dias 156 21.10 S 35.09 E
Barton, Austl. 162 30.31 S 132.39 E
Barton, N.Y., U.S. 210 42.03 N 76.27 W
Barton, Oh., U.S. 214 40.06 N 80.50 W
Barton, Vt., U.S. 188 44.44 N 72.10 W
Barton Aerodrome ⊠ 262 53.28 N 2.23 W
Barton Creek ≃ 222 30.16 N 97.45 W
Barton Lake 216 42.06 N 85.35 W
Barton Lake ⊜ 184 52.00 N 94.06 W
Barton-le-Clay 42 51.57 N 0.25 W
Barton Mills 42 52.20 N 0.31 E
Barton Park ♦ 274a 33.57 S 151.09 E
Barton Run ≃ 285 39.53 N 74.51 W
Barton-under-Needwood 42 52.45 N 1.43 W
Barton-upon-Humber 44 53.41 N 0.27 W
Bartonville 190 40.39 N 89.39 W
Barton Water Swing Bridge ◆5 262 53.28 N 2.21 W
Bartoszyce 30 54.16 N 20.49 E
Bartow, Fl., U.S. 220 27.53 N 81.50 W
Bartow, Ga., U.S. 192 32.52 N 82.28 W
Baru, Kali ≃ 269e 6.10 S 106.51 E
Barú, Volcán ⋀1 236 8.48 N 82.33 W
Barueri 256 23.31 S 46.53 W
Barugo 116 11.20 N 124.44 E
Bāruipāra 272b 22.58 N 88.26 E
Bāruipur 126 22.21 N 88.27 E
Bārūk, Jabal al- ⋀ 132 33.43 N 35.45 E
Barumini 71 39.42 N 9.00 E
Barumun ≃ 114 2.30 N 100.09 E
Barun Bogd uul ⋀ 90 44.57 N 100.15 E
Barung, Nusa I 115a 8.28 S 113.20 E
Barun Su 102 42.27 N 111.01 E
Barun-Torej, ozero ⊜ 88 50.10 N 115.30 E
Baruntse ⋀ 124 27.51 N 86.59 E
Barus 114 2.02 N 98.24 E
Baruta 286c 10.26 N 66.53 W
Baruth 54 52.03 N 13.30 E
Baruun Bajan-Ulaan 102 45.10 N 101.24 E
Baruun bogd uul ⋀ 102 44.57 N 100.15 E
Baruun-Urt 90 46.42 N 113.15 E
Barva, Volcán ⋀1 236 10.08 N 84.06 W
Barvas 46 58.22 N 6.32 W
Barver 52 52.37 N 8.35 E
Barvicha 265b 55.44 N 37.16 E
Barview 202 43.21 N 124.18 W
Barvinkove 78 48.54 N 37.02 E
Barwa 126 23.51 N 86.26 E
Barwāh 120 22.16 N 76.03 E
Barwāla ◆8 272a 28.46 N 77.04 E
Barwāni 120 22.02 N 74.54 E
Barwa Sāgar 124 25.23 N 78.44 E
Barwell 42 52.32 N 1.21 W
Barwice 30 53.45 N 16.22 E
Barwick 192 30.54 N 83.44 W
Barwidgee 162 27.02 S 120.54 E
Barwon ≃, Austl. 166 30.00 S 148.05 E
Barwon ≃, Austl. 169 38.13 S 144.25 E
Barwon Heads (South Barwon) 169 38.17 S 144.30 E
Barybino, Ross. 82 55.16 N 37.54 E
Barybino, Ross. 82 54.56 N 37.47 E
Barycz ≃ 30 51.42 N 16.15 E
Barykova, mys > 180 63.02 N 179.29 E
Barykovo 82 54.38 N 38.48 E
Barynino 82 55.47 N 36.21 E
Baryš 80 53.39 N 47.08 E
Baryš ≃ 80 54.35 N 46.48 E
Baryševo 86 54.58 N 83.11 E
Baryshivka 78 50.22 N 31.19 E
Baryšniki 80 56.57 N 46.33 E
Barzah 132 33.34 N 36.19 E
Barzas 86 55.43 N 86.19 E
Barzio 58 45.57 N 9.27 E
Bas'a ≃ 76 53.46 N 31.01 E
Basaburua 152 3.37 N 8.54 E
Basai Dārāpur ◆8 272a 28.40 N 77.08 E
Bāsa' Īdū 128 26.39 N 55.17 E
Basail, Arg. 252 27.52 S 59.18 W
Bāsāil, Bngl. 126 24.14 N 90.04 E
Basakin 80 48.11 N 42.18 E
Basāl 123 33.33 N 72.15 E
Basalt ≃ 166 19.38 S 145.52 E
Basalt Island I 271d 22.19 N 114.22 E
Basaluzzo 62 44.46 N 8.42 E
Basandīlah 142 31.12 N 31.26 E
Basankusu 152 1.14 N 19.48 E
Basanta 80 46.05 N 41.56 E
Basanti 126 22.12 N 88.42 E
Basarabeasca 78 46.20 N 28.58 E
Basarabi 38 44.10 N 28.24 E
Basatongwula Shan ⋀ 120 33.05 N 91.30 E
Basavakalyān 122 17.52 N 76.57 E
Basavilbaso 252 32.22 S 58.53 W
Baščelakskij chrebet ⋀ 86 51.15 N 84.30 E
Baschi 66 42.40 N 12.13 E
Basco 108 20.27 N 121.58 E
Bascom 214 41.07 N 83.17 W
Bascuñán, Cabo > 252 28.51 S 71.30 W
Basdahl 52 53.26 N 9.12 E
Basdorf, Dtsch. 54 52.44 N 13.26 E
Basdorf, Dtsch. 56 51.12 N 8.58 E
Basekpio 154 4.44 N 24.40 E
Basel (Bâle) 58 47.33 N 7.35 E
Baselga di Pinè 64 46.08 N 11.14 E
Baselice 68 41.24 N 14.58 E
Basel-Land ▫3 58 47.30 N 7.50 E
Basel-Stadt ▫3 58 47.38 N 7.40 E
Basen ≃ 96 34.48 N 132.51 E
Bas-en-Basset 62 45.18 N 4.06 E
Basentello ≃ 68 40.40 N 16.23 E
Basento ≃ 68 40.21 N 16.50 E
Başeu ≃ 38 47.44 N 27.15 E
Basey 116 11.17 N 125.04 E
Bashaw 182 52.35 N 112.58 W
Basher Kill ≃ 210 41.27 N 74.35 W
Bashi Channel ⪠ 108 22.00 N 121.00 E
Bashikejike 120 37.30 N 85.50 E
Bashiqiao 106 31.40 N 120.22 E
Bashkortostan — Baškirija ▫3 86 54.00 N 56.00 E
Bashtanka 78 47.24 N 32.25 E
Bashtil 273c 30.05 N 31.11 E
Basi, India 123 30.36 N 76.50 E
Basi, India 123 30.41 N 76.24 E
Basiad Bay c 116 14.16 N 122.19 E
Basiano 112 1.16 S 122.50 E
Basibasy 157b 22.10 S 43.40 E
Başibüyük ◆8 267b 40.57 N 29.08 E
Basicò 70 38.04 N 15.04 E
Basiglio 266b 45.21 N 9.09 E
Basilaki Island I 164 10.35 S 151.00 E
Basilan ≃ 116 6.35 N 121.55 E
Basilan Island I 116 6.34 N 122.03 E
Basilan Peak ⋀ 116 6.33 N 122.04 E
Basilan Strait ⪠ 116 6.49 N 122.05 E
Basildon 42 51.35 N 0.25 E
Basildon ▫8 260 51.35 N 0.29 E
Basile 194 30.29 N 92.35 W
Basiliano 64 46.01 N 13.06 E
Basilicata ▫4 68 40.30 N 16.10 E
Basiluzzo, Isola I 70 38.39 N 15.07 E
Basin, Mt., U.S. 202 46.16 N 112.15 W
Basin, Wy., U.S. 202 44.22 N 108.02 W
Bäsingen ⊜ 40 60.09 N 16.20 E
Basinger 220 27.24 N 81.01 W
Basingstoke 42 51.15 N 1.05 W
Basingstoke Canal ≊ 260 51.21 N 0.29 W
Basingwerk Abbey ⊥ 262 53.17 N 3.12 W
Basin Lake ⊜ 184 52.38 N 105.18 W
Basīrhāt 126 22.40 N 88.52 E
Basīrpur 123 30.35 N 73.50 E
Basīţ, Ra's al- > 130 35.51 N 35.48 E
Basiyingzi 104 42.59 N 122.37 E
Basjanovskij 86 58.19 N 60.44 E
Baška 36 44.58 N 14.46 E
Baskahegan Lake ⊜ 188 45.30 N 67.48 W
Baskakovka 76 54.36 N 34.54 E
Başkale 128 38.02 N 44.00 E
Baskatong, Réservoir ⊜1 190 46.48 N 75.50 W
Başkaus ≃ 86 51.09 N 87.43 E
Basket Lake ⊜ 184 49.43 N 92.02 W
Basking Ridge 276 40.42 N 74.32 W
Baškino 82 55.18 N 36.41 E
Baškirija ▫3 86 54.00 N 56.00 E
Baškirskij zapovednik ♦ 86 53.00 N 57.58 E
Baskomutan Milli Parkı ♦ 130 38.50 N 30.05 E
Başköy 84 39.53 N 44.32 E
Baskuduk 85 49.43 N 81.52 E
Baskunčak, ozero ⊜ 80 48.12 N 46.54 E
Baslow 44 53.15 N 1.38 W
Başmakçı 130 37.54 N 30.01 E
Basmakovo 80 53.12 N 43.02 E
Basmat 122 19.19 N 77.10 E
Basna 76 54.22 N 31.08 E
Basoda 124 23.51 N 77.56 E
Basoko 152 1.14 N 23.36 E
Basoli 273b 4.19 S 15.16 E
Basom 210 43.04 N 78.24 W
Basongo 152 4.20 S 20.24 E
Basora, Punt > 241s 12.25 N 69.52 W
Basovizza 64 45.38 N 13.52 E
Başpınar 130 39.12 N 38.42 E
Basque Lands — Euskal Herriko ▫4 34 43.00 N 2.30 W
Basra — Al-Başrah 128 30.30 N 47.47 E
Bas-Rhin ▫5 58 48.35 N 7.40 E
Bass ≃ 169 38.30 S 145.26 E
Bassac ≃ 110 10.15 N 106.20 E
Bassano 182 50.47 N 112.28 W
Bassano del Grappa 64 45.46 N 11.44 E
Bassari 150 9.15 N 0.47 E
Bassas da India ⇁2 138 21.25 S 39.42 E
Bass Creek ≃ 216 42.37 N 89.04 W
Basse-Californie — Baja California ⋏1 232 28.00 N 113.30 W
Bassecourt 58 47.20 N 7.15 E
Bassein — Pathein 110 16.47 N 94.44 E
Bassein ≃1 110 15.56 N 94.18 E
Basse-Kotto ▫5 152 5.00 N 21.30 E
Bassella 34 42.01 N 1.18 E
Bassen 52 53.04 N 9.04 E
Bassendean 168a 31.55 S 115.56 E
Bassenthwaite 44 54.41 N 3.12 W
Bassenthwaite Lake ⊜ 44 54.38 N 3.13 W
Basse-Pointe 240e 14.52 N 61.07 W
Basses, Pointe des > 241o 15.52 N 61.17 W
Basse Santa Su 150 13.19 N 14.13 W
Basse-Terre, Guad. 241o 16.00 N 61.44 W
Basseterre, St. K.-N. 238 17.18 N 62.43 W
Basse Terre, Trin. 241r 10.08 N 61.18 W
Basse-Terre I 241o 16.10 N 61.40 W
Bassett, Ne., U.S. 198 42.35 N 99.32 W
Bassett, Va., U.S. 192 36.45 N 79.59 W
Bassett Creek ≃ 194 31.25 N 87.56 W
Bassett Peak ⋀ 200 32.30 N 110.17 W
Bassfield 194 31.30 N 89.44 W
Bass Harbor 188 44.14 N 68.20 W
Bass Hill 274a 33.54 S 151.00 E
Bassignana 62 45.00 N 8.44 E
Bassikounou 150 15.52 N 5.57 W
Bassila 150 9.01 N 1.40 E
Bassin des Aghlabites ⊥ 36 35.43 N 10.10 E
Bassingbourn 42 52.04 N 0.03 W
Bass Lake, Ca., U.S. 226 37.19 N 119.33 W
Bass Lake, In., U.S. 216 41.12 N 86.36 W
Bass Lake ⊜, On., Can. 212 44.49 N 76.08 W
Bass Lake ⊜, In., U.S. 216 41.13 N 86.36 W
Bass Lake ⊜1 226 37.19 N 119.34 W
Bass Point > 170 34.36 S 150.54 E
Bass River 186 45.25 N 63.47 W
Bass Strait ⪠ 166 39.20 S 145.30 E
Bassum 52 52.51 N 8.43 E
Basswood Lake ⊜, On., Can. 190 46.20 N 83.23 W
Basswood Lake ⊜, N.A. 190 48.06 N 91.40 W
Basta 126 21.41 N 87.03 E
Båstad 26 56.26 N 12.51 E
Bastah 132 30.14 N 35.32 E
Bastak 128 27.14 N 54.22 E
Bastām 128 36.29 N 55.04 E
Bastei ♦ 54 50.58 N 14.04 E
Bastelica 36 42.00 N 9.02 E
Basti 124 26.48 N 82.43 E
Bastia, Fr. 36 42.42 N 9.27 E
Bastia, It. 66 43.04 N 12.33 E
Bastian 192 37.09 N 81.09 W
Bastiglia 64 44.43 N 11.00 E
Bastimentos 236 9.21 N 82.12 W
Bastimentos, Isla I 236 9.18 N 82.08 W
Bastogne 56 50.00 N 5.43 E
Bastrop, La., U.S. 194 32.46 N 91.54 W
Bastrop, Tx., U.S. 222 30.06 N 97.18 W
Bastrop ▫6 222 30.09 N 97.18 W
Bastrop, Lake ⊜1 222 30.09 N 97.18 W
Bastrop Bay c 222 29.06 N 95.11 W
Bastrop State Park ♦ 222 30.07 N 97.17 W
Bastuträsk 26 64.47 N 20.02 E
Basu, Pulau I 112 0.18 S 103.26 E
Basubāti 272b 22.47 N 88.12 E
Bāsudebpur, India 126 21.49 N 87.38 E
Bāsudebpur, India 272b 22.49 N 88.25 E
Basuo — Dongfang 110 19.05 N 108.39 E
Bāsūs 273c 30.08 N 31.13 E
Baswa 126 24.08 N 87.52 E
Basyūn 142 30.57 N 30.49 E
Bas-Zaïre ▫4 152 5.30 S 14.30 E
Bata 152 1.51 N 9.45 E
Bataan ▫4 116 14.40 N 120.25 E
Bataan, Mount ⋀ 116 14.31 N 120.28 E
Bataan Peninsula >1 116 14.40 N 120.25 E
Batabanó 240p 22.43 N 82.17 W
Batabanó, Golfo de c 240p 22.15 N 82.30 W
Batac 116 18.05 N 120.35 E
Batad 116 11.25 N 123.06 E
Batagaj 74 67.38 N 134.38 E
Batagaj-Alyta 74 67.48 N 130.25 E
Batag Island I 116 12.38 N 125.04 E
Bataguaçu 88 52.27 N 100.45 E
Bataguassu 255 21.42 S 52.22 W
Bataiporã 255 22.20 S 53.17 W
Batajsk 83 47.10 N 39.44 E
Batak 38 41.57 N 24.13 E
Batak, Jazovir ⊜1 38 41.59 N 24.11 E
Batakan 112 4.05 S 114.38 E
Batala 123 31.48 N 75.12 E
Batalha, Bra. 250 9.41 S 37.08 W
Batalha, Bra. 250 4.01 S 42.05 W
Batalha, Port. 34 39.39 N 8.50 W
Bataly 86 52.52 N 62.00 E
Batam, Pulau I 114 1.05 N 104.03 E
Batama, Ross. 88 53.53 N 101.36 E
Batama, Zaïre 154 0.56 N 26.39 E
Batamaj 74 63.31 N 129.27 E
Batamšinskij 86 50.36 N 58.16 E
Batan, Pil. 116 11.35 N 122.30 E
Batan, Zhg. 98 34.10 N 120.04 E
Batanagar 272b 22.31 N 88.15 E
Batang, Indon. 115a 6.55 S 109.45 E
Batang, Zhg. 102 30.02 N 99.02 E
Batangafo 152 7.18 N 18.18 E
Batangas 116 13.45 N 121.03 E
Batangas ▫4 116 13.50 N 121.00 E
Batangas Bay c 116 13.43 N 121.00 E
Batangbatangdaya 115a 6.56 S 113.66 E
Batang Berjuntai 114 3.23 N 101.25 E
Batang Kali 114 3.28 N 101.38 E
Batangtoru 114 1.29 N 99.03 E
Batan Island I, Pil. 108 20.26 N 121.58 E
Batan Island I, Pil. 116 13.15 N 124.00 E
Batan Islands II 108 20.30 N 121.50 E
Batanta, Pulau I 164 0.50 S 130.40 E
Batas ≃ 287a 22.44 S 43.24 W
Batas Island I 116 11.10 N 119.36 E
Bátaszék 30 46.12 N 18.44 E
Batatais 255 20.53 S 47.37 W
Batatuba 256 23.04 S 46.25 W
Batavia, Arg. 252 34.47 S 65.41 W
Batavia, Il., U.S. 216 41.51 N 88.18 W
Batavia, Ia., U.S. 190 40.59 N 92.10 W
Batavia, Mi., U.S. 216 41.55 N 85.06 W
Batavia, N.Y., U.S. 210 42.59 N 78.11 W
Batavia, Oh., U.S. 218 39.04 N 84.10 W
Batawa 212 44.10 N 77.36 W
Batbatan Island I 116 11.28 N 121.55 E
Batcengel 88 47.47 N 101.58 E
Batchawana ≃ 190 46.55 N 84.32 W
Batchawana Mountain ⋀ 190 47.04 N 84.24 W
Batchawana Island I 190 46.53 N 84.30 W
Batchelor 164 13.04 S 131.01 E
Bătdâmbâng 110 13.06 N 103.12 E
Bate Bay c 274a 34.03 S 151.12 E
Bateckij 76 58.39 N 30.19 E
Bate Heath 262 53.19 N 2.28 W
Batéké, Plateaux ⋏1 152 3.30 S 15.45 E
Batemans Bay 166 35.43 S 150.11 E
Batenbrock ◆8 263 51.31 N 6.57 E
Batepito ≃ 200 30.48 N 109.11 W
Bates, Mount ⋀ 174c 29.01 S 167.56 E
Batesburg 192 33.54 N 81.32 W
Bates Creek ≃ 200 42.41 N 106.37 W
Bates Range ⋀ 162 27.25 S 121.13 E
Batesville, Ar., U.S. 194 35.46 N 91.38 W
Batesville, In., U.S. 218 39.18 N 85.13 W
Batesville, Ms., U.S. 194 34.18 N 89.56 W
Batesville, Tx., U.S. 196 28.57 N 99.37 W
Bath, N.B., Can. 186 46.31 N 67.36 W
Bath, On., Can. 212 44.11 N 76.47 W
Bath, Eng., U.K. 42 51.23 N 2.22 W
Bath, Il., U.S. 219 40.11 N 90.08 W
Bath, Me., U.S. 188 43.54 N 69.49 W
Bath, Mi., U.S. 216 42.49 N 84.26 W
Bath, N.Y., U.S. 210 42.20 N 77.19 W
Bath, Oh., U.S. 214 41.11 N 81.38 W
Bath, Pa., U.S. 208 40.43 N 75.23 W
Bath ▫6 218 38.14 N 83.48 W
Batha ▫5 146 14.00 N 19.00 E
Batha ≃ 146 12.47 N 17.34 E
Bath Addition 285 40.06 N 74.52 W
Bathgate, Scot., U.K. 46 55.55 N 3.39 W
Bathgate, N.D., U.S. 198 48.52 N 97.28 W
Bathinda 123 30.12 N 74.57 E
Bathsheba 241g 13.13 N 59.31 W
Bathurst, Austl. 166 33.25 S 149.35 E
Bathurst, N.B., Can. 186 47.36 N 65.39 W
Bathurst — Banjul, Gam. 150 13.28 N 16.39 W
Bathurst, S. Afr. 158 33.30 S 26.50 E
Bathurst, Cape > 176 70.35 N 128.00 W
Bathurst, Lake ⊜ 170 35.04 S 149.44 E
Bathurst Inlet 176 66.50 N 108.01 W
Bathurst Inlet c 176 68.10 N 108.50 W
Bathurst Island I, Austl. 164 11.37 S 130.23 E
Bathurst Island I, N.T., Can. 16 76.00 N 100.30 W
Bathurst Island Aboriginal Reserve ◆4 164 11.37 S 130.23 E
Bati 144 11.10 N 40.02 E
Batia 150 10.54 N 1.29 E
Batiāgarh 124 24.07 N 79.21 E
Batié 150 9.53 N 2.55 W
Bātin, Wādī al- V 128 29.35 N 47.00 E
Batina 38 45.51 N 18.51 E
Batiquitos Lagoon c 228 33.05 N 117.18 W
Batīr 132 31.16 N 35.42 E
Batiscan ≃ 206 46.31 N 72.15 W
Batiste Creek ≃ 222 30.04 N 94.28 W
Batkanu 150 9.05 N 12.25 W
Batken 85 40.03 N 70.50 E
Batley 44 53.44 N 1.37 W
Batlow 171b 35.31 S 148.09 E
Batman 130 37.52 N 41.07 E
Batman ▫4 130 38.00 N 41.15 E
Batna 148 35.34 N 6.11 E
Batna ▫5 148 35.30 N 6.10 E
Batn al-Ghūl 132 29.44 N 35.52 E
Batnorov 88 47.55 N 111.30 E
Batō, Nihon 94 36.44 N 140.10 E
Bato, Pil. 116 10.20 N 124.47 E
Ba To, Viet 110 14.46 N 108.44 E
Bato, Lake ⊜ 116 13.19 N 123.21 E
Batobato 152 0.48 N 13.27 E
Batoche Rectory National Historic Site ⊥ 184 52.41 N 106.02 W
Batoka 154 16.47 S 27.15 E
Baton Rouge 194 30.27 N 91.09 W
Bator 123 33.06 N 75.19 E
Batorampon Point > 116 7.07 N 121.54 E
Batouri 152 4.26 N 14.22 E
Batovi 255 15.53 S 53.24 W
Patpajsagyr, peski ◆2 80 47.20 N 48.40 E
Batrā (Petra) ⊥ 132 30.20 N 35.26 E
Batrā', Jibāl al- ⋀ 132 29.53 N 35.38 E
Batrah 142 31.10 N 31.27 E
Ba Tri 110 10.02 N 106.36 E
Batsawul 120 34.15 N 70.52 E
Batson 222 30.15 N 94.37 W
Batsto ≃ 285 39.39 N 74.39 W
Batsto, Skit Branch ≃ 285 39.46 N 74.41 W
Batsto State Historic Site ⊥ 208 39.39 N 74.39 W
Bat Sūmber 88 48.29 N 106.42 E
Battaglia Terme 64 45.17 N 11.47 E
Battambang — Bătdâmbâng 110 13.06 N 103.12 E
Battenberg 56 51.01 N 8.38 E
Batten Kill ≃ 188 43.06 N 73.35 W
Batterie, Pointe de la > 240e 14.44 N 60.54 W
Bätterkinden 58 47.08 N 7.32 E
Battersea ◆8 260 51.28 N 0.10 W
Battersea Park ♦ 260 51.29 N 0.09 W
Batticaloa 122 7.43 N 81.42 E
Battice 56 50.39 N 5.49 E
Battin 224 45.29 N 122.34 W
Battipaglia 68 40.37 N 14.58 E
Battle 42 50.55 N 0.29 E
Battle ≃ 176 52.43 N 108.15 W
Battle Creek, Ia., U.S. 198 42.18 N 95.35 W
Battle Creek, Mi., U.S. 216 42.19 N 85.10 W
Battle Creek, Ne., U.S. 198 41.59 N 97.35 W
Battle Creek ≃, N.A. 202 48.36 N 109.11 W
Battle Creek ≃, Ca., U.S. 204 40.21 N 122.11 W
Battle Creek ≃, Id., U.S. 202 44.14 N 116.32 W
Battle Creek ≃, Mi., U.S. 216 42.19 N 85.12 W
Battle Creek ≃, Tx., U.S. 196 32.50 N 98.58 W
Battle Creek, North Fork ≃ 204 40.26 N 122.00 W
Battle Creek, South Fork ≃ 204 40.26 N 122.00 W
Battlefields 154 18.31 S 29.52 E
Battle Green ⊥ 283 42.27 N 71.14 W
Battle Ground, In., U.S. 216 40.30 N 86.50 W
Battle Ground, Wa., U.S. 224 45.46 N 122.31 W
Battle Harbour 186 52.16 N 55.35 W
Battle Lake 198 46.16 N 95.42 W
Battlement Mesa ⋀ 200 39.20 N 108.00 W
Battle Mountain 204 40.38 N 116.56 W
Battle Mountain ⋀ 204 41.02 N 107.16 W
Battlesbridge 260 51.37 N 0.34 E
Battonya 30 46.17 N 21.01 E
Battuello 266b 45.27 N 8.56 E
Batu 115a 7.52 S 112.31 E
Batu ≃ 144 6.55 N 39.46 E
Batu, Bukit ⋀ 112 2.16 N 113.43 E
Batu, Kepulauan II 112 0.18 S 98.28 E
Batuan 116 12.25 N 123.47 E
Batu Arang 114 3.19 N 101.28 E
Batuata, Pulau I 112 6.12 S 122.42 E
Batuata, Tanjung > 115b 9.37 S 120.29 E
Batu-Batu 112 4.30 S 119.52 E
Batu Berinchang, Gunong ⋀ 114 4.30 N 101.24 E
Batubetumpang 112 2.53 S 106.09 E
Batubrok, Bukit ⋀ 112 1.10 N 114.36 E
Batu Caves 114 3.14 N 101.41 E
Batudaka, Pulau I 112 0.28 S 121.48 E
Batu Enam 114 2.35 N 102.43 E
Batu Gajah 114 4.28 N 101.03 E
Batui 112 1.17 S 122.33 E
Batui, Pegunungan ⋏ 112 1.25 S 122.10 E
Batuidu 112 2.11 S 123.25 E
Batukau, Bukit ⋀ 115b 8.20 S 115.05 E
Batukelau 112 0.48 N 115.01 E
Batu Licin 112 3.27 S 116.00 E
Batumata Point > 164 10.17 S 148.57 E
Batumi 84 41.38 N 41.38 E
Batumundan 114 1.17 N 98.50 E
Batu Pahat (Bandar Penggaram) 114 1.51 N 102.56 E
Batupanjang 114 1.43 N 101.33 E
Batu Puteh, Gunong ⋀ 114 4.15 N 101.27 E
Batuputih 112 1.24 N 118.29 E

≃ River	Fluß	Río	Rivière	Rio	⇁ Submarine Features	Untermeerische Objekte	Accidentes Submarinos / Formes de relief sous-marin / Acidentes submarinos
⪡ Canal	Kanal	Canal	Canal	Canal	▫ Political Unit	Politische Einheit	Unidad Política / Entité politique / Unidade política
⪢ Waterfall, Rapids	Wasserfall, Stromschnellen	Cascada, Rápidos	Chute d'eau, Rapides	Cascata, Rápidos	▫ Cultural Institution	Kulturelle Institution	Institución Cultural / Institution culturelle / Instituição cultural
⪠ Strait	Meeresstraße	Estrecho	Détroit	Estreito	⊥ Historical Site	Historische Stätte	Sitio Histórico / Site historique / Sitio histórico
c Bay, Gulf	Bucht, Golf	Bahía, Golfo	Baie, Golfe	Baía, Golfo	♦ Recreational Site	Erholungs- und Ferienort	Sitio de Recreo / Centre de loisirs / Area de Lazer
⊜ Lake, Lakes	See, Seen	Lago, Lagos	Lac, Lacs	Lago, Lagos	⊠ Airport	Flughafen	Aeropuerto / Aéroport / Aeroporto
≋ Swamp	Sumpf	Pantano	Marais	Pântano	▪ Military Installation	Militäranlage	Instalación Militar / Installation militaire / Instalação militar
⊠ Ice Features, Glacier	Eis- und Gletscherformen	Accidentes Glaciales	Formes glaciaires	Acidentes glaciares	◆ Miscellaneous	Verschiedenes	Misceláneo / Divers / Diversos
⇁ Other Hydrographic Features	Andere Hydrographische Objekte	Otros Elementos Hidrográficos	Autres données hydrographiques	Outros acidentes hidrográficos			

ENGLISH

Name	Page	Lat.°′	Long.°′
Baturaja	112	4.08 S	104.10 E
Batu Rakit	114	5.27 N	103.03 E
Baturetno	115a	7.59 S	110.56 E
Baturino, Ross.	86	57.48 N	85.12 E
Baturino, Ross.	265b	55.35 N	37.31 E
Baturinskaja	78	45.47 N	39.22 E
Baturité	250	4.20 S	38.53 W
Baturotok	115b	8.42 S	117.10 E
Baturusa	112	2.02 S	106.07 E
Baturyn	78	51.21 N	32.51 E
Batusangkar	112	0.27 S	100.35 E
Batutinggi	112	1.55 S	113.19 E
Bat Yam	132	32.01 N	34.45 E
Batyrevo	80	55.04 N	47.38 E
Batyr-Mala, ozero ⊜	80	47.35 N	44.45 E
Bau	112	1.25 N	110.08 E
Baú ≃	250	7.26 S	54.47 W
Bauang	116	16.31 N	120.20 E
Baubašata, gory ⋏	85	41.20 N	72.45 E
Baubau	112	5.28 S	122.38 E
Bauchi	150	10.19 N	9.50 E
Bauchi □[3]	146	10.30 N	10.15 E
Baucina	70	37.55 N	13.32 E
Baud	32	47.52 N	3.01 W
Bauda	120	20.50 N	84.19 E
Baudette	190	48.42 N	94.35 W
Baudó ≃	246	4.57 N	77.22 W
Baudouin Stadium ♦	273b	4.20 S	15.20 E
Baudour	50	50.29 N	3.49 E
Bauernschaft	263	51.34 N	6.33 E
Bauerstown	279b	40.30 N	79.59 W
Baugo Creek ≃	216	41.40 N	86.04 W
Baukau	112	8.27 S	126.27 E
Bauland ◆[1]	56	49.31 N	9.29 E
Bauld, Cape ➤	186	51.38 N	55.25 W
Baulkham Hills	274a	33.46 S	151.00 E
Baulmes	58	46.48 N	6.32 E
Bauma	58	47.23 N	8.53 E
Baumberg	263	51.07 N	6.54 E
Baume ≃	62	44.26 N	4.20 E
Baume-les-Dames	58	47.21 N	6.22 E
Baumholder	56	49.37 N	7.20 E
Baumschulenweg ◆[8]	264a	52.28 N	13.29 E
Baun	112	10.18 S	123.43 E
Baunach	56	49.59 N	10.50 E
Baunach ≃	56	49.59 N	10.51 E
Baunatal	56	51.16 N	9.25 E
Baunei	71	40.02 N	9.40 E
Baunt	88	55.16 N	113.08 E
Baunt, ozero ⊜	88	55.12 N	113.00 E
Bāuphal	126	22.25 N	90.33 E
Baure	150	12.50 N	8.45 E
Baures	248	13.35 S	63.35 W
Baures ≃	248	12.30 S	64.18 W
Bauru	255	22.19 S	49.04 W
Baús	255	18.19 S	53.10 W
Bausendorf	56	50.01 N	6.59 E
Bausenhagen	263	51.31 N	7.48 E
Bauska	76	56.24 N	24.14 E
Bauta	240p	22.59 N	82.33 W
Bauta □[7]	286b	22.59 N	82.33 W
Bautino	84	44.33 N	50.15 E
Bautzen	54	51.11 N	14.26 E
Bauxite	194	34.33 N	92.31 W
Bauya	150	8.11 N	12.34 W
Bavans	58	47.29 N	6.44 E
Bavari	62	44.26 N	9.01 E
Bavaria → Bayern □[3]	30	49.00 N	11.30 E
Bavarian Alps → Bayerische Alpen ⋏	64	47.30 N	11.00 E
Bavay	50	50.18 N	3.47 E
Båven ⊜	40	59.01 N	16.56 E
Baveno	58	45.55 N	8.30 E
Bavilliers	58	47.37 N	6.50 E
Bavispe	232	30.24 N	108.50 W
Bavispe ≃	232	29.15 N	109.11 W
Bavleny	80	56.24 N	39.34 E
Bavly	80	54.25 N	53.17 E
Bavnhöj ʌ[2]	41	55.55 N	10.07 E
Bavtugaj	84	43.11 N	46.49 E
Baw	110	23.19 N	95.50 E
Bāwal	124	28.05 N	76.35 E
Bawal, Pulau I	112	2.44 S	110.06 E
Bāwāli	272b	22.25 N	88.12 E
Bawang	115a	7.06 S	109.55 E
Baw Baw, Mount ʌ	169	37.50 S	146.17 E
Baw Baw National Park ♦	169	37.55 S	146.22 E
Baw Beese Lake ⊜	216	41.54 N	84.36 W
Bawdeswell	42	52.45 N	1.01 E
Bawdwin	110	23.06 N	97.18 E
Bawean, Pulau I	115a	5.46 S	112.40 E
Baweigang	106	31.57 N	120.14 E
Bawku	150	11.05 N	0.14 W
Bawlake	110	19.11 N	97.21 E
Bawmi	110	17.19 N	94.35 E
Bawria	126	22.29 N	88.10 E
Bawtry	44	53.26 N	1.01 W
Baxdo	144	5.46 N	47.15 E
Baxenden	262	53.44 N	2.20 W
Baxian, Zhg.	105	39.06 N	116.23 E
Baxian (Yudongxi), Zhg.	107	29.23 N	106.32 E
Baxley	192	31.46 N	82.20 W
Baxter, Ia., U.S.	190	41.49 N	93.09 W
Baxter, Mn., U.S.	190	46.20 N	94.17 W
Baxter, Tn., U.S.	194	36.09 N	85.38 W
Baxter Estates	276	40.50 N	73.42 W
Baxter Springs	198	37.02 N	94.44 W
Baxter State Park ♦	188	46.00 N	68.58 W
Baxterville	194	31.05 N	89.35 W
Bay	194	35.44 N	90.33 W
Bay □[4]	144	2.30 N	43.30 E
Bay, Laguna de ⊜	116	14.23 N	121.15 E
Baya, Zaïre	152	4.57 N	19.43 E
Baya, Zaïre	154	11.52 S	27.27 E
Bayādah, Wādī al- V	146	26.08 N	18.35 E
Bayāḍ an-Naṣārā	142	29.04 N	31.08 E
Bayag	116	18.16 N	121.02 E
Bayala	158	27.47 S	32.08 E
Bay al-Kabīr, Wādī V	146	31.15 N	15.57 E
Bayambang	116	15.49 N	120.27 E
Bayamo	240p	20.23 N	76.39 W
Bayamo ≃	240p	20.34 N	76.44 W
Bayamón	240m	18.24 N	66.09 W
Bayan, Azer.	84	40.34 N	46.09 E
Bayan, Indon.	115b	8.16 S	116.26 E
Bayan, Zhg.	89	46.05 N	127.24 E
Bayan, Band-e ⋏	120	34.20 N	65.30 E
Bayāna	124	26.54 N	77.17 E
Bayanbayanan	269f	14.39 N	121.06 E
Bayanchagan	89	47.19 N	124.03 E
Bayang	116	7.48 N	124.12 E
Bayanga	152	2.53 N	16.19 E
Bayange	102	39.19 N	107.31 E
Bayan Har Shan ⋏	102	33.48 N	98.10 E
Bayanheshuomiao	89	48.51 N	119.46 E
Bayanjie	89	49.36 N	124.37 E
Bayanluke	89	50.52 N	119.33 E
Bayannaobao	102	39.44 N	107.40 E
Bayano, Lago ⊜[1]	246	9.10 N	78.40 W
Bayan Obo	102	41.58 N	110.02 E
Bayan Tal	89	43.44 N	123.16 E
Bayard, Ia., U.S.	198	41.51 N	94.33 W
Bayard, Ne., U.S.	198	41.45 N	103.19 W
Bayard, N.M., U.S.	200	32.45 N	108.07 W
Bayard, Oh., U.S.	214	40.46 N	81.04 W
Bayard, W.V., U.S.	188	39.16 N	79.21 W
Bayard, Col)(	62	44.37 N	6.05 E
Bayard Cutting Arboretum State Park ♦	276	40.45 N	73.10 W
Bayat, Indon.	112	2.06 S	103.38 E
Bayat, Tür.	130	38.59 N	30.56 E
Bayat, Tür.	130	40.39 N	34.15 E
Bayawan	116	9.22 N	122.48 E
Bayawan ≃	116	9.22 N	122.48 E
Baybay	116	10.41 N	124.48 E
Bayberry	210	43.08 N	76.13 W
Bayble	46	58.12 N	6.13 W
Bayboro	192	35.08 N	76.46 W
Bay Bulls	186	47.19 N	52.49 W
Bayburt	130	40.16 N	40.15 E
Bayburt □[4]	130	40.15 N	40.00 E
Bay Center	224	46.37 N	123.57 W
Bay City, Mi., U.S.	190	43.35 N	83.53 W
Bay City, Or., U.S.	224	45.31 N	123.53 W
Bay City, Tx., U.S.	222	28.58 N	95.58 W
Bay Creek ≃, Il., U.S.	194	37.16 N	88.31 W
Bay Creek ≃, Il., U.S.	219	39.20 N	90.46 W
Baydā', Bi'r ⊤[4]	142	29.45 N	32.13 E
Bay de Verde	186	48.05 N	52.54 W
Baydhabo (Baidoa)	144	3.07 N	43.39 E
Bay du Nord ≃	186	47.44 N	55.25 W
Baye, Cap ➤	175f	20.57 S	165.25 E
Bayel	58	48.12 N	4.47 E
Bayerische Alpen ⋏	64	47.30 N	11.00 E
Bayerisch Eisenstein	60	49.07 N	13.12 E
Bayerischer Wald ⋏	60	49.00 N	12.40 E
Bayerischer Wald, Nationalpark ♦	60	48.56 N	13.28 E
Bayern □[3]	30	49.00 N	11.30 E
Bayeuen	114	4.36 N	97.53 E
Bayeux, Bra.	250	7.08 S	34.56 W
Bayeux, Fr.	32	49.16 N	0.42 W
Bay Farm Island I	282	37.43 N	122.14 W
Bayfield, Co., U.S.	200	37.13 N	107.35 W
Bayfield, Wi., U.S.	190	46.48 N	90.49 W
Bayfield, Île I	186	51.13 N	58.23 W
Bayford	260	51.46 N	0.06 W
'Bayh	132	33.44 N	35.31 E
Bayhān al-Qaṣāb	144	14.48 N	45.43 E
Bay Harbor Islands	220	25.53 N	80.08 W
Bayhead, Scot., U.K.	46	57.33 N	7.24 W
Bay Head, N.J., U.S.	208	40.04 N	74.03 W
Bayiji	98	34.18 N	117.41 E
Bayındır	130	38.13 N	27.40 E
Bayingzi	104	41.28 N	120.46 E
Baykan	130	38.09 N	41.47 E
Baykonur → Bajkonyr	86	47.50 N	66.03 E
Bay Kurt	85	39.58 N	75.33 E
Bay L'Argent	186	47.33 N	54.54 W
Bayley Point ➤	164	16.56 S	139.02 E
Baylis	219	39.44 N	90.54 W
Bay Meadows Race Track ♦	282	37.32 N	122.18 W
Bay Minette	194	30.52 N	87.46 W
Baynūnah ◆[1]	128	23.50 N	52.50 E
Bayo	34	43.09 N	8.58 W
Bayombong	116	16.29 N	121.09 E
Bayon	58	48.29 N	6.19 E
Bayona	34	42.07 N	8.51 W
Bayonne, Fr.	32	43.29 N	1.29 W
Bayonne, N.J., U.S.	210	40.40 N	74.06 W
Bayonne ≃	206	46.05 N	73.10 W
Bayonne Bridge ◆[5]	276	40.38 N	74.09 W
Bayons	62	44.20 N	6.10 E
Bayou Bodcau Reservoir ⊜[1]	194	32.45 N	93.30 W
Bayou Cane	194	29.37 N	90.45 W
Bayou D'Arbonne Lake ⊜[1]	194	32.45 N	92.25 W
Bayou La Batre	194	30.24 N	88.14 W
Bayovar	248	5.50 S	81.03 W
Bay Park	276	40.38 N	73.40 W
Bayport, Fl., U.S.	220	28.33 N	82.39 W
Bay Port, Mi., U.S.	190	43.50 N	83.22 W
Bayport, Mn., U.S.	190	45.01 N	92.46 W
Bayport, N.Y., U.S.	210	40.44 N	73.03 W
Bayramiç	130	39.48 N	26.37 E
Bayramören	130	40.57 N	33.12 E
Bayreuth	60	49.57 N	11.35 E
Bay Ridge	208	38.56 N	76.27 W
Bay Ridge ◆[8]	276	40.37 N	74.02 W
Bay Ridge Channel ≋	276	40.39 N	74.02 W
Bayrischzell	64	47.40 N	12.00 E
Bay Roberts	186	47.36 N	53.16 W
Bayrūt (Beirut)	130	33.53 N	35.30 E
Bayrūt □[4]	132	33.56 N	35.30 E
Bays, Lake of ⊜	212	45.15 N	79.04 W
Bay Saint Louis	194	30.18 N	89.19 W
Bay Shore	210	40.43 N	73.14 W
Bayshore Gardens	220	27.25 N	82.35 W
Bayside, On., Can.	212	44.07 N	77.30 W
Bayside, Ma., U.S.	283	42.18 N	70.53 W
Bayside, Wi., U.S.	216	43.10 N	87.54 W
Bayside ◆[8]	276	40.46 N	73.46 W
Bay Springs	194	31.58 N	89.17 W
Bay Springs Lake ⊜[1]	194	34.35 N	88.20 W
Bayston Hill	42	52.40 N	2.45 W
Bayswater	274b	37.51 S	145.16 E
Bayswater North	274b	37.49 S	145.17 E
Bayt ad-Dīn	132	33.42 N	35.35 E
Bayt al-Faqīh	144	14.32 N	43.20 E
Bayt Hānūn	132	31.32 N	34.33 E
Bayt Jālā	132	31.43 N	35.11 E
Bayt Jinn	132	33.19 N	35.53 E
Bayt Laḥm (Bethlehem)	132	31.43 N	35.12 E
Bayt Mirī	132	33.52 N	35.36 E
Baytown	222	29.44 N	94.58 W
Bayt Sāḥūr	132	31.42 N	35.13 E
Bayt Sīrā	132	31.53 N	35.03 E
Bayunglencir	112	2.03 S	103.41 E
Bayview, Austl.	274a	33.40 S	151.18 E
Bay View, N.Z.	172	39.25 S	176.53 E
Bay View, N.Y., U.S.	210	42.47 N	78.51 W
Bay View, Oh., U.S.	214	41.28 N	82.50 W
Bayview ◆[8]	282	37.44 N	122.23 W
Bay Village	214	41.29 N	81.55 W
Bayville, N.J., U.S.	208	39.54 N	74.09 W
Bayville, N.Y., U.S.	210	40.54 N	73.33 W
Baywater	168a	31.55 S	115.56 E
Baywood Park	226	35.20 N	120.50 W
Bayyāḍah, Ra's al- ➤	132	33.10 N	35.10 E
Bayyā'īyah al-Kabīrah	130	35.42 N	37.09 E
Bayyūḍah ⊤[4]	140	17.32 N	32.07 E
Bayzo	150	13.52 N	4.45 E
Baza	34	37.29 N	2.46 W
Baza, Sierra de ⋏	34	37.15 N	2.45 W
Bazai	100	24.32 N	114.10 E
Bazainville	261	48.48 N	1.40 E
Bazaliya	78	49.43 N	26.27 E
Bazar	88	53.58 N	116.05 E
Bazarčaj	84	39.40 N	45.48 E
Bazardüzü dağ ʌ	84	41.13 N	47.51 E
Bāzār-e Panjvāī	120	31.32 N	65.28 E
Bazargic → Dobrič	38	43.34 N	27.50 E
Bazar-Kurgan	85	41.02 N	72.45 E
Bazarnyje Mataki	80	54.56 N	49.56 E
Bazarnyj Karabulak	80	52.16 N	46.25 E
Bazarnyj Syzgan	80	53.45 N	46.46 E
Bazarovo	82	54.47 N	38.10 E
Bazaršolan	80	49.04 N	51.56 E
Bazartobe	80	49.23 N	51.53 E
Bazaruto, Ilha do I	156	21.40 S	35.28 E
Bazas	32	44.26 N	0.13 W
Bazavluk ≃	78	47.34 N	34.04 E
Bazdār	120	26.21 N	65.03 E
Bazeilles	56	49.40 N	4.59 E
Bazemont	261	48.56 N	1.52 E
Bazetta	214	41.20 N	80.47 W
Bazhong	102	31.51 N	106.39 E
Bazi	100	24.46 N	113.10 E
Baziège	32	43.27 N	1.37 E
Bažigan	84	44.33 N	45.41 E
Bazine	198	38.26 N	99.41 W
Baziqiao	106	32.07 N	119.52 E
Bazkovskaja	80	49.36 N	41.43 E
Bazmān	128	27.49 N	60.12 E
Bazmān, Kūh-e ʌ	128	28.04 N	60.00 E
Bazoches-les-Gallerandes	50	48.10 N	2.03 E
Bazoches-sur-Hoëne	50	48.33 N	0.28 E
Bazoj	86	55.45 N	83.22 E
Bazzano	64	44.30 N	11.05 E
Be ≃	110	11.06 N	106.58 E
Be, Nosy I	157b	13.20 S	48.15 E
Beach, Il., U.S.	216	42.26 N	87.50 W
Beach, N.D., U.S.	198	46.55 N	104.00 W
Beach, Tx., U.S.	222	30.20 N	95.29 W
Beach Channel ≋	276	40.35 N	73.50 W
Beach City	214	40.39 N	81.34 W
Beach City Lake ⊜[1]	214	40.41 N	81.36 W
Beach Glen	276	40.56 N	74.29 W
Beach Haven, N.J., U.S.	208	39.33 N	74.14 W
Beach Haven, Pa., U.S.	210	41.04 N	76.11 W
Beach Haven Terrace	208	39.35 N	74.13 W
Beach Lake	210	41.36 N	75.09 W
Beach Lake ⊜	281	42.33 N	83.43 W
Beach Pond State Park ♦	207	41.35 N	71.45 W
Beachport	166	37.30 S	140.01 E
Beachville	212	43.05 N	80.49 W
Beachwood, N.J., U.S.	208	39.56 N	74.11 W
Beachwood, Oh., U.S.	214	41.27 N	81.30 W
Beachy Head ➤	42	50.44 N	0.16 E
Beacon, Austl.	162	30.26 S	117.51 E
Beacon, N.Y., U.S.	210	41.30 N	73.58 W
Beacon Falls	207	41.26 N	73.03 W
Beacon Heights	284c	38.57 N	76.54 W
Beacon Hill, Austl.	274a	33.45 S	151.15 E
Beacon Hill, Wa., U.S.	224	46.08 N	122.57 W
Beacon Hill ʌ[2], H.K.	271d	22.21 N	114.09 E
Beacon Hill ʌ[2], Wales, U.K.	42	52.23 N	3.12 W
Beacon Rock State Park ♦	224	45.38 N	122.03 W
Beaconsfield, Austl.	166	41.12 S	146.48 E
Beaconsfield, Austl.	274b	38.03 S	145.22 E
Beaconsfield, P.Q., Can.	206	45.26 N	73.50 W
Beaconsfield, Eng., U.K.	42	51.37 N	0.39 W
Beaconsfield □[8]	260	51.34 N	0.35 W
Beadle Lake	216	42.18 N	85.12 W
Beagh, Slieve ʌ[2]	48	54.21 N	7.12 W
Beagle, Canal ≋	254	54.53 S	68.10 W
Beagle Bay	162	16.58 S	122.40 E
Beagle Gulf ⊂	164	12.00 S	130.20 E
Beagle Reef ◆[2]	160	15.20 S	123.29 E
Bealanana	157b	14.33 S	48.44 E
Beale, Cape ➤	182	48.44 N	125.20 W
Beale, Lake ⊜	122	19.45 N	73.44 E
Beale Air Force Base ■	226	39.08 N	121.20 W
Bealiba	169	36.48 S	143.33 E
Bealiba, Mount ʌ[2]	169	36.49 S	143.38 E
Beallsville	214	40.04 N	80.01 W
Beals Creek ≃	196	32.10 N	100.51 W
Beam ≃	260	51.31 N	0.10 E
Beaminster	42	50.49 N	2.45 W
Bean	260	51.25 N	0.17 E
Beanblossom Creek ≃	194	39.20 N	86.39 W
Bean Creek ≃	216	41.35 N	84.19 W
Bear ≃, Sk., Can.	184	54.33 N	103.58 W
Bear ≃, U.S.	200	41.30 N	112.08 W
Bear ≃, Ca., U.S.	226	38.57 N	121.35 W
Bear, Mount ʌ	180	61.17 N	141.09 W
Beara	164	7.30 S	144.52 E
Bear Bay ⊂	176	75.47 N	87.00 W
Bear Branch	218	38.55 N	85.05 W
Bear Brook ≃, On., Can.	212	45.25 N	75.10 W
Bear Brook ≃, N.J., U.S.	276	41.02 N	74.03 W
Bear Brook State Park ♦	188	43.05 N	71.26 W
Bear Butte ʌ	198	44.28 N	103.26 W
Bear Canyon V	280	34.14 N	118.07 W
Bear Cove	182	50.44 N	127.27 W
Bear Creek	210	41.11 N	75.45 W
Bear Creek ≃, On., Can.	214	42.44 N	82.23 W
Bear Creek ≃, U.S.	194	34.46 N	88.05 W
Bear Creek ≃, U.S.	196	37.45 N	101.23 W
Bear Creek ≃, U.S.	216	41.17 N	83.57 W
Bear Creek ≃, Al., U.S.	194	33.11 N	88.05 W
Bear Creek ≃, Ca., U.S.	226	38.56 N	122.20 W
Bear Creek ≃, Ca., U.S.	226	38.02 N	121.18 W
Bear Creek ≃, Ca., U.S.	226	37.17 N	120.50 W
Bear Creek ≃, Ca., U.S.	228	34.10 N	117.01 W
Bear Creek ≃, Ca., U.S.	280	34.14 N	117.53 W
Bear Creek ≃, Co., U.S.	200	39.40 N	105.00 W
Bear Creek ≃, Il., U.S.	219	39.33 N	89.23 W
Bear Creek ≃, Il., U.S.	219	40.07 N	91.29 W
Bear Creek ≃, Md., U.S.	284b	39.13 N	76.30 W
Bear Creek ≃, Mo., U.S.	219	39.03 N	91.14 W
Bear Creek ≃, N.D., U.S.	198	46.10 N	98.06 W
Bear Creek ≃, Oh., U.S.	218	39.39 N	84.17 W
Bear Creek ≃, Or., U.S.	202	44.06 N	120.46 W
Bear Creek ≃, Or., U.S.	202	42.26 N	122.58 W
Bear Creek ≃, Pa., U.S.	214	41.23 N	78.50 W
Bear Creek ≃, Wy., U.S.	198	41.41 N	104.13 W
Bear Creek, South Fork ≃	219	40.09 N	91.18 W
Bear Creek, West Fork ≃	280	34.16 N	117.53 W
Bearden	194	33.43 N	92.36 W
Beardmore	176	49.36 N	87.57 W
Beardmore Glacier ⊠	9	83.45 S	171.00 E
Beardsley Lake ⊜[1]	226	38.13 N	120.03 W
Beardstown, Il., U.S.	219	40.01 N	90.25 W
Beardstown, In., U.S.	216	41.08 N	86.36 W
Beardy and Okemasis Indian Reserves ◆[4]	184	52.48 N	106.20 W
Bearfort Mountain ʌ	276	41.09 N	74.23 W
Bear Head Creek ≃	194	30.18 N	93.35 W
Bear Head Lake ⊜	184	55.33 N	96.10 W
Bear Head Lake State Park ♦	190	47.49 N	92.04 W
Bearhead Mountain ʌ	224	47.02 N	121.53 W
Bear Hill ʌ[2], Ct., U.S.	207	41.39 N	73.24 W
Bear Hill ʌ[2], N.Y., U.S.	210	41.18 N	74.00 W
Bear-in-the-Lodge Creek ≃	198	43.41 N	101.50 W
Bear Island I, Ant.	9	74.30 S	110.45 W
Bear Island I, Mb., Can.	184	54.53 N	98.04 W
Bear Island I, Ire.	48	51.40 N	9.48 W
Bear Island → Bjørnøya I, Sval.	12	74.25 N	19.00 E
Bear Island I, Va., U.S.	284c	38.59 N	77.14 W
Bear Lake, B.C., Can.	182	56.11 N	126.51 W
Bear Lake, Pa., U.S.	214	42.00 N	79.30 W
Bear Lake ⊜, Ab., Can.	182	55.16 N	119.00 W
Bear Lake ⊜, B.C., Can.	182	56.06 N	126.45 W
Bear Lake ⊜, Mb., Can.	184	55.08 N	96.00 W
Bear Lake ⊜, On., Can.	212	45.26 N	79.35 W
Bear Lake ⊜, U.S.	200	42.00 N	111.20 W
Bear Mountain ʌ, Ca., U.S.	228	35.12 N	118.38 W
Bear Mountain ʌ, Ky., U.S.	192	37.32 N	84.16 W
Bear Mountain ʌ, Or., U.S.	202	43.51 N	122.53 W
Bear Mountain ʌ[2]	210	41.18 N	74.01 W
Bear Mountain State Park ♦	210	41.17 N	74.00 W
Béarn □[9]	32	43.20 N	0.45 W
Bear Pond ⊜	276	40.58 N	74.40 W
Bear River	186	44.34 N	65.39 W
Bear River Range ⋏	200	41.50 N	111.30 W
Bear Run ≃	279b	40.33 N	80.04 W
Bearsden	46	55.56 N	4.20 W
Bears Paw Mountains ⋏	202	48.15 N	109.30 W
Bearstead	260	51.16 N	0.35 E
Bearsville	210	42.02 N	74.09 W
Bear Swamp ≃	285	39.54 N	74.47 W
Bear Swamp ≡	285	39.53 N	74.45 W
Bear Swamp Brook ≃	276	41.04 N	74.13 W
Bear Swamp Lake ⊜	276	41.06 N	74.13 W
Beartooth Mountains ⋏	202	45.00 N	109.30 W
Beartooth Pass)(	202	44.58 N	109.28 W
Bear Town	194	31.13 N	90.27 W
Beās	123	31.31 N	75.17 E
Beās ≃	123	31.10 N	74.59 E
Beasain	34	43.03 N	2.11 W
Beas de Segura	34	38.15 N	2.53 W
Beasley	222	29.30 N	95.55 W
Beasley Bay ⊂	208	37.51 N	75.44 W
Beason	219	40.09 N	89.12 W
Beata, Cabo ➤	238	17.36 N	71.25 W
Beata, Isla I	238	17.35 N	71.31 W
Beatenberg	58	46.42 N	7.48 E
Beato ◆[8]	266c	38.44 N	9.06 W
Beaton	182	50.44 N	117.44 W
Beatrice, Al., U.S.	194	31.44 N	87.12 W
Beatrice, Ne., U.S.	198	40.16 N	96.44 W
Beatrice, Zimb.	154	18.15 S	30.55 E
Beatrice, Cape ➤	164	14.15 S	136.59 E
Beattie	198	39.51 N	96.25 W
Beattock	44	55.18 N	3.28 W
Beatton ≃	176	56.10 N	120.25 W
Beatty, Nv., U.S.	204	36.54 N	116.45 W
Beatty, Oh., U.S.	218	39.53 N	83.50 W
Beatty Saugeen ≃	212	44.08 N	81.02 W
Beattyville	192	37.34 N	83.42 W
Beaubru	56	49.46 N	5.05 E
Beaucaire	62	43.48 N	4.38 E
Beauce ◆[1]	50	48.22 N	1.50 E
Beauceville	188	46.12 N	70.46 W
Beauchamp	261	49.01 N	2.12 E
Beauchamp Roding	260	51.46 N	0.18 E
Beauchêne, Lac ⊜	190	46.39 N	78.55 W
Beauchêne Island I	254	52.55 S	59.12 W
Beaucoup Creek ≃, Il., U.S.	194	37.47 N	89.17 W
Beaucoup Creek ≃, Il., U.S.	219	38.13 N	89.20 W
Beaucourt	58	47.29 N	6.55 E
Beaudesert	171a	27.59 S	153.00 E
Beaudette ≃	206	45.12 N	74.19 W
Beaudry, Lac ⊜	190	47.44 N	78.55 W
Beauduc, Pointe de ➤	62	43.22 N	4.34 E
Beaufays	56	50.34 N	5.38 E
Beaufort, Austl.	169	37.26 S	143.23 E
Beaufort, Fr.	58	46.34 N	5.26 E
Beaufort, Fr.	62	45.43 N	6.35 E
Beaufort, Lux.	56	49.51 N	6.18 E
Beaufort, Malay.	112	5.20 N	115.45 E
Beaufort, Mo., U.S.	219	38.26 N	91.12 W
Beaufort, N.C., U.S.	192	34.43 N	76.39 W
Beaufort, S.C., U.S.	192	32.25 N	80.40 W
Beaufort, Cape ➤	162	34.26 S	115.32 E
Beaufort, Massif de ⋏[1]	62	45.44 N	6.35 E
Beaufort Castle → Qal'at ash-Shaqīf ⊥	132	33.19 N	35.32 E
Beaufort Island I	271d	22.11 N	114.15 E
Beaufort Marine Corps Air Station ■	192	32.30 N	80.44 W
Beaufort Sea ⊤[2]	16	73.00 N	140.00 W
Beaufort West	158	32.18 S	22.36 E
Beaugency	50	47.47 N	1.38 E
Beauharnois	206	45.19 N	73.52 W
Beauharnois □[6]	206	45.15 N	74.00 W
Beauharnois, Barrage de ◆[6]	275a	45.19 N	73.55 W
Beauharnois, Canal de ≋	206	45.19 N	73.54 W
Beaujeu	58	46.09 N	4.36 E
Beaujolais □[9]	32	46.05 N	4.10 E
Beaulieu	42	50.49 N	1.27 W
Beaulieu-lès-Loches	50	47.07 N	1.01 E
Beaulieu-sur-Mer	62	43.42 N	7.20 E
Beauly	46	57.29 N	4.29 W
Beauly ≃	46	57.28 N	4.28 W
Beauly Firth ⊂[1]	46	57.30 N	4.23 W
Beaumaris, Austl.	274b	37.59 S	145.02 E
Beaumaris, Wales, U.K.	44	53.16 N	4.05 W
Beaumaris Bay ⊂	274b	38.00 S	145.03 E
Beaumes-de-Venise	62	44.07 N	5.02 E
Beaumesnil	50	49.01 N	0.43 E
Beaumetz-lès-Loges	50	50.14 N	2.39 E
Beaumont, Bel.	50	50.14 N	4.14 E
Beaumont, Nf., Can.	186	49.37 N	55.41 W
Beaumont, Fr.	32	49.40 N	1.51 W
Beaumont, N.Z.	172	45.49 S	169.32 E
Beaumont, Ca., U.S.	228	33.55 N	116.58 W
Beaumont, Ms., U.S.	194	31.10 N	88.55 W
Beaumont, Tx., U.S.	194	30.05 N	94.06 W
Beaumont-du-Gâtinais	50	48.08 N	2.29 E
Beaumont-en-Argonne	56	49.32 N	5.03 E
Beaumont Hill ʌ[2]	166	31.33 S	145.13 E
Beaumont-la-Ronce	50	47.34 N	0.40 E
Beaumont-le-Roger	50	49.05 N	0.47 E
Beaumont Place	222	29.50 N	95.14 W
Beaumont-sur-Oise	50	49.08 N	2.17 E
Beaumont-sur-Sarthe	50	48.13 N	0.08 E
Beaune	58	47.02 N	4.50 E
Beaune-la-Rolande	50	48.04 N	2.26 E
Beauport	206	46.52 N	71.11 W
Beaupré	186	47.03 N	70.54 W
Beaupréau	32	47.12 N	1.00 W
Beaupre Island I	212	44.26 N	76.19 W
Beaupré Lake ⊜	184	54.30 N	107.10 W
Beauraing	56	50.07 N	4.58 E
Beaurepaire	62	45.20 N	5.03 E
Beaurepaire-en-Bresse	58	46.40 N	5.23 E
Beaurières	62	44.35 N	5.33 E
Beaurivage	206	46.25 N	71.14 W
Beaurivage ≃	206	46.42 N	71.16 W
Beauséjour, Mb., Can.	184	50.04 N	96.33 W
Beauséjour, Guad.	241o	16.18 N	61.04 W
Beausoleil	62	43.45 N	7.26 E
Beausoleil Island I	212	44.51 N	79.52 W
Beautor	50	49.39 N	3.20 E
Beauvais, Fr.	50	49.26 N	2.05 E
Beauvais, Fr.	261	48.32 N	2.03 E
Beauvais Creek ≃	202	45.29 N	107.45 W
Beauvais-Tillé, Aéroport ⊠	50	49.28 N	2.07 E
Beauval, Sk., Can.	184	55.09 N	107.37 W
Beauval, Fr.	50	50.06 N	2.20 E
Beauvezer	62	44.09 N	6.36 E
Beauville	32	44.17 N	0.52 E
Beauvoir	261	48.39 N	2.52 E
Beauvoir-sur-Mer	32	46.55 N	2.02 W
Beauvoir-sur-Niort	32	46.11 N	0.28 W
Beaux Arts	224	47.35 N	122.11 W
Beaver, Ak., U.S.	180	66.22 N	147.24 W
Beaver, Ok., U.S.	196	36.48 N	100.31 W
Beaver, Or., U.S.	224	45.16 N	123.49 W
Beaver, Pa., U.S.	214	40.41 N	80.18 W
Beaver, Ut., U.S.	200	38.16 N	112.38 W
Beaver, Wa., U.S.	224	48.03 N	124.19 W
Beaver, W.V., U.S.	192	37.44 N	81.08 W
Beaver □[6]	214	40.40 N	80.25 W
Beaver ≃, Can.	176	59.43 N	124.16 W
Beaver ≃, Can.	184	55.25 N	107.45 W
Beaver ≃, On., Can.	212	44.34 N	80.27 W
Beaver ≃, U.S.	196	36.35 N	99.30 W
Beaver ≃, N.Y., U.S.	188	43.54 N	75.30 W
Beaver ≃, Pa., U.S.	214	40.40 N	80.18 W
Beaver ≃, Ut., U.S.	200	39.10 N	112.57 W
Beaver Brook	210	40.55 N	75.59 W
Beaver Brook ≃, U.S.	207	42.40 N	71.19 W
Beaver Brook ≃, Ma., U.S.	283	42.03 N	70.58 W
Beaver Brook ≃, Ma., U.S.	283	42.36 N	71.21 W
Beaver Brook ≃, Ma., U.S.	283	42.23 N	71.14 W
Beaver Brook ≃, N.J., U.S.	276	40.54 N	74.30 W
Beaver Brook ≃, N.J., U.S.	276	40.58 N	74.35 W
Beaver City	198	40.08 N	99.49 W
Beaver Creek, Yk., Can.	180	62.22 N	140.52 W
Beavercreek, Oh., U.S.	218	39.43 N	84.03 W
Beavercreek, Or., U.S.	224	45.17 N	122.32 W
Beaver Creek ≃, On., Can.	212	44.44 N	76.58 W
Beaver Creek ≃, On., Can.	212	44.30 N	77.42 W
Beaver Creek ≃, On., Can.	275b	43.51 N	79.20 W
Beaver Creek ≃, On., Can.	284a	42.58 N	79.01 W
Beaver Creek ≃, U.S.	198	47.20 N	103.39 W
Beaver Creek ≃, U.S.	198	40.04 N	99.20 W
Beaver Creek ≃, U.S.	198	43.25 N	103.59 W
Beaver Creek ≃, U.S.	216	40.58 N	87.49 W
Beaver Creek ≃, Ak., U.S.	180	66.15 N	147.32 W
Beaver Creek ≃, Ca., U.S.	226	38.12 N	120.19 W
Beaver Creek ≃, Co., U.S.	198	40.20 N	103.33 W
Beaver Creek ≃, Co., U.S.	198	38.22 N	104.58 W
Beaver Creek ≃, Il., U.S.	216	42.16 N	88.56 W
Beaver Creek ≃, Il., U.S.	219	38.33 N	89.30 W
Beaver Creek ≃, Ky., U.S.	218	38.31 N	84.11 W
Beaver Creek ≃, Md., U.S.	208	39.32 N	77.42 W
Beaver Creek ≃, Mo., U.S.	194	36.38 N	93.02 W
Beaver Creek ≃, Mt., U.S.	202	48.29 N	107.24 W
Beaver Creek ≃, Ne., U.S.	198	41.26 N	97.42 W
Beaver Creek ≃, Ne., U.S.	198	40.42 N	97.20 W
Beaver Creek ≃, N.J., U.S.	285	39.45 N	75.23 W
Beaver Creek ≃, N.Y., U.S.	212	44.36 N	75.22 W
Beaver Creek ≃, N.D., U.S.	198	46.15 N	100.29 W
Beaver Creek ≃, Oh., U.S.	216	41.25 N	83.51 W
Beaver Creek ≃, Oh., U.S.	216	40.34 N	84.45 W
Beaver Creek ≃, Oh., U.S.	218	39.57 N	83.46 W
Beaver Creek ≃, Ok., U.S.	196	34.00 N	97.57 W
Beaver Creek ≃, Or., U.S.	224	44.56 N	121.22 W
Beaver Creek ≃, Pa., U.S.	285	40.00 N	75.42 W
Beaver Creek ≃, Tx., U.S.	196	33.53 N	98.49 W
Beaver Creek ≃, Wy., U.S.	202	42.58 N	108.26 W
Beaver Creek State Park ♦	214	40.44 N	80.35 W
Beaver Crossing	198	40.46 N	97.16 W
Beaverdale	214	40.19 N	78.41 W
Beaver Dam, Ky., U.S.	194	37.24 N	86.52 W
Beaverdam, Oh., U.S.	216	40.50 N	83.59 W
Beaver Dam, Wi., U.S.	190	43.27 N	88.50 W
Beaverdam Brook ≃	276	40.26 N	74.28 W
Beaverdam Creek ≃, U.S.	284c	38.55 N	76.57 W
Beaverdam Creek ≃, Md., U.S.	284c	39.01 N	76.54 W
Beaverdam Creek ≃, N.J., U.S.	285	39.56 N	74.45 W
Beaver Dams	210	42.17 N	76.58 W
Beaver Dams Creek ≃	284a	43.06 N	79.11 W
Beaver Dam Wash V	200	36.54 N	114.55 W
Beaverdell	182	49.26 N	119.05 W
Beaver Falls, N.Y., U.S.	212	43.53 N	75.25 W
Beaver Falls, Pa., U.S.	214	40.45 N	80.19 W
Beaverhead ≃	202	45.31 N	112.21 W
Beaverhead Mountains ⋏	202	45.00 N	113.20 W
Beaverhill Lake ⊜, Ab., Can.	182	53.27 N	112.32 W
Beaver Hill Lake ⊜, Mb., Can.	184	54.16 N	94.53 W
Beaverhouse Lake ⊜	190	48.32 N	92.05 W
Beaver Island I	190	45.40 N	85.31 W
Beaver Island State Park ♦	210	42.58 N	78.57 W
Beaver Kill ≃	210	41.59 N	75.08 W
Beaver Lake	210	41.07 N	74.33 W
Beaver Lake ⊜, Ab., Can.	182	54.43 N	111.50 W
Beaver Lake ⊜, On., Can.	212	44.30 N	77.02 W
Beaver Lake ⊜, On., Can.	212	44.44 N	78.17 W
Beaver Lake ⊜, N.J., U.S.	276	41.05 N	74.33 W
Beaver Lake ⊜, N.Y., U.S.	276	40.53 N	73.34 W
Beaver Lake ⊜[1]	194	36.20 N	93.55 W
Beaver Lake Indian Reserve ◆[4]	182	54.39 N	111.54 W
Beaverlodge	182	55.13 N	119.26 W
Beaver Meadow	210	42.40 N	75.41 W
Beaver Meadows	210	40.55 N	75.54 W
Beaver Mountains ⋏	180	62.54 N	156.58 W
Beaver Run ≃, N.J., U.S.	276	41.11 N	74.36 W
Beaver Run ≃, Pa., U.S.	279b	40.34 N	79.33 W
Beaver Run ≃, Pa., U.S.	285	40.10 N	75.40 W
Beaver Run Reservoir ⊜[1]	214	40.29 N	79.33 W
Beavers Bend State Park ♦	194	34.08 N	94.42 W
Beaver Springs	208	40.45 N	77.13 W
Beaver Swamp Brook ≃	276	40.57 N	73.43 W

DEUTSCH

Name	Seite	Breite°′	Länge°′ E = Ost
Beaverton, On., Can.	212	44.26 N	79.09 W
Beaverton, Mi., U.S.	190	43.52 N	84.29 W
Beaverton, Or., U.S.	224	45.29 N	122.48 W
Beaverton ≃	212	44.26 N	79.10 W
Beavertown	210	40.45 N	77.10 W
Beaverville	216	40.57 N	87.39 W
Beāwar	120	26.06 N	74.19 E
Beazley	252	33.45 S	66.39 W
Bebao	157b	17.22 S	44.33 E
Bebar ≃	114	3.07 N	103.27 E
Bebedouro	255	20.56 S	48.28 W
Bebeji	150	11.40 N	8.19 E
Bebek ◆[8]	267b	41.04 N	29.02 E
Bebelevo	82	54.32 N	36.30 E
Bebeli	130	36.41 N	35.27 E
Beberibe	250	4.11 S	38.08 W
Bebertal	54	52.15 N	11.18 E
Bebington	44	53.23 N	3.01 W
Béboto	146	8.16 N	16.56 E
Bebra	56	50.58 N	9.47 E
Becal	232	20.27 N	90.02 W
Bécancour	206	46.20 N	72.26 W
Bécancour ≃	206	46.22 N	72.27 W
Beccar ◆[8]	288	34.28 S	58.31 W
Beccaria	214	40.46 N	78.27 W
Beccles	42	52.28 N	1.34 E
Becconsall	262	53.42 N	2.50 W
Bečej	38	45.37 N	20.03 E
Beceni	38	45.23 N	26.46 E
Becerra Creek ≃	196	28.05 N	98.55 W
Becerreá	34	42.51 N	7.10 W
Becerro, Cayos II	236	15.57 N	83.17 W
Béchar	148	31.37 N	2.13 W
Béchar □[5]	148	29.00 N	3.00 W
Becharof Lake ⊜	180	58.00 N	156.30 W
Bechater	36	37.18 N	9.45 E
Bechem	150	7.05 N	2.02 W
Becher Bay ⊂	224	48.19 N	123.37 W
Becher Point ➤	168a	32.23 S	115.44 E
Bechet	38	43.46 N	23.58 E
Bechevin Bay ⊂	180	55.00 N	163.27 W
Bechhofen	56	49.09 N	10.33 E
Bechtelsville	208	40.22 N	75.38 W
Bechuanaland ◆[1]	158	27.10 S	22.10 E
Bechyně	30	49.18 N	14.29 E
Becke	263	51.24 N	7.47 E
Beckemeyer	219	38.36 N	89.26 W
Beckenham ◆[8]	260	51.24 N	0.02 W
Beckenried	58	46.58 N	8.29 E
Becket	207	42.19 N	73.05 W
Beckhausen ◆[8]	263	51.34 N	7.02 E
Beckingen	56	49.24 N	6.42 E
Beckington	42	51.16 N	2.18 W
Beck Lake ⊜	278	42.04 N	87.52 W
Beckler ≃	224	47.43 N	121.21 W
Beckley	188	37.46 N	81.11 W
Beck Pond ⊜	283	42.36 N	70.49 W
Becks Creek ≃	219	39.08 N	88.56 W
Beckum	52	51.45 N	8.02 E
Beckville	222	32.14 N	94.27 W
Beckwith Island I	212	44.52 N	80.08 W
Becky Peak ʌ	204	39.58 N	114.36 W
Beclean	38	47.11 N	24.10 E
Bečov nad Teplou	54	50.02 N	12.19 E
Becsehely	61	46.27 N	16.48 E
Bedale	44	54.17 N	1.35 W
Bédarieux	32	43.37 N	3.09 E
Bédarrides	62	44.02 N	4.54 E
Bédaya	146	8.55 N	17.52 E
Bedburdyck	56	51.07 N	6.34 E
Bedburg	56	50.59 N	6.35 E
Bedburg-Hau	52	51.45 N	6.10 E
Beddgelert	44	53.01 N	4.06 W
Beddingestrand	41	55.21 N	13.29 E
Beddington ◆[8]	260	51.22 N	0.08 W
Beddome, Mount ʌ	162	25.50 S	134.22 E
Beddouza, Ras ➤	148	32.34 N	9.19 W
Bedele	144	8.33 N	36.23 E
Beden Brook ≃	276	40.25 N	74.38 W
Bedeque Bay ⊂	186	46.22 N	63.53 W
Beder	41	56.04 N	10.13 E
Bederkesa	52	53.38 N	8.50 E
Bederwanak	144	9.34 N	44.23 E
Bedesa	144	8.54 N	40.47 E
Bedford, P.Q., Can.	206	45.07 N	72.59 W
Bedford, S. Afr.	158	32.41 S	26.05 E
Bedford, Eng., U.K.	42	52.08 N	0.29 W
Bedford, In., U.S.	218	38.51 N	86.29 W
Bedford, Ia., U.S.	198	40.40 N	94.43 W
Bedford, Ky., U.S.	218	38.35 N	85.19 W
Bedford, Ma., U.S.	207	42.29 N	71.16 W
Bedford, Mi., U.S.	216	42.23 N	85.13 W
Bedford, N.Y., U.S.	210	41.12 N	73.39 W
Bedford, Oh., U.S.	214	41.23 N	81.32 W
Bedford, Pa., U.S.	188	40.01 N	78.30 W
Bedford, Tx., U.S.	222	32.50 N	97.08 W
Bedford, Va., U.S.	192	37.20 N	79.31 W
Bedford □[6]	214	40.09 N	78.30 W
Bedford, Cape ➤	164	15.14 S	145.21 E
Bedfordale	168a	32.10 S	116.03 E
Bedford Harbour ⊂	162	33.35 S	120.35 E
Bedford Heights	279a	41.25 N	81.31 W
Bedford Hills	210	41.14 N	73.41 W
Bedford Island I	126	21.51 N	88.05 E
Bedford Level ⌣	42	52.27 N	0.02 W
Bedford Park	278	41.46 N	87.49 W
Bedford Park ◆[8]	276	40.52 N	73.53 W
Bedfordshire □[6]	42	52.05 N	0.30 W
Bedford-Stuyvesant ◆[8]	276	40.41 N	73.55 W
Bedi, India	120	22.30 N	70.02 E
Bédi, Tchad	146	11.06 N	18.33 E
Bedias	222	30.46 N	95.57 W
Bedias Creek ≃	222	30.54 N	95.37 W
Bedinggong	112	2.42 S	106.13 E
Bédiondo	146	8.39 N	17.12 E
Bedirli	130	39.35 N	36.38 E
Bedlington	44	55.08 N	1.35 W
Bedminster, N.J., U.S.	276	40.40 N	74.38 W
Bedminster, Pa., U.S.	208	40.26 N	75.11 W
Bedmond	260	51.43 N	0.25 W
Bednodemjanovsk	80	53.56 N	43.10 E
Bedoba	88	58.48 N	97.12 E
Bédoin	62	44.07 N	5.10 E
Bedok	271c	1.19 N	103.57 E
Bedong	114	5.44 N	100.31 E
Bedonia	62	44.30 N	9.38 E
Bedourie	166	24.21 S	139.28 E
Bedum	52	53.17 N	6.36 E
Bedwas	42	51.35 N	3.13 W
Bedworth	42	52.28 N	1.29 W
Beeac	169	38.12 S	143.38 E
Beebe, P.Q., Can.	206	45.01 N	72.09 W
Beebe, Ar., U.S.	194	35.04 N	91.52 W
Beech ≃	194	35.37 N	88.10 W
Beechal Creek ≃	166	27.24 S	145.13 E
Beech Bottom	214	40.13 N	80.39 W
Beech Brook ≃	276	41.08 N	74.18 W
Beech Creek	194	37.10 N	87.03 W
Beech Creek ≃	210	41.04 N	77.34 W
Beechcrest	214	41.05 N	81.20 W
Beecher, Il., U.S.	216	41.20 N	87.37 W
Beecher, Mi., U.S.	216	43.05 N	83.42 W
Beecher City	219	39.11 N	88.47 W
Beecher Falls	206	45.00 N	71.30 W
Beechey Head ➤	224	48.19 N	123.39 W
Beech Forest	169	38.38 S	143.34 E
Beech Fork ≃	194	37.46 N	85.41 W
Beech Grove	218	39.43 N	86.05 W
Beechmont	171a	28.07 S	153.11 E
Beechview ◆[8]	279b	40.25 N	80.02 W
Beechwood, Ky., U.S.	218	38.24 N	84.44 W
Beechwood, Ma., U.S.	283	42.12 N	70.49 W
Beechwood, Mi., U.S.	216	46.09 N	88.46 W
Beechworth	166	36.22 S	146.41 E
Beechy	184	50.51 N	107.25 W
Beeck ◆[8]	263	51.29 N	6.44 E
Beeckerwerth ◆[8]	263	51.29 N	6.41 E
Beecroft	274a	33.45 S	151.04 E
Beecroft Head ➤	170	35.01 S	150.51 E

Symbols in the index entries represent the broad categories identified in the key at the right. Symbols with superior numbers (⋏[1]) identify subcategories (see complete key on page *I · 1*).

Symbole im Register stellen die rechts im Schlüssel erklärten Kategorien dar. Symbole mit hochgestellten Ziffern (⋏[1]) bezeichnen Unterabteilungen einer Kategorie (vgl. vollständiger Schlüssel auf Seite *I · 1*).

Los símbolos incluídos en el texto del índice representan las grandes categorías identificadas con la clave a la derecha. Los símbolos con numeros en su parte superior (⋏[1]) identifican las subcategorías (véase la clave completa en la página *I · 1*).

Les symboles de l'index représentent les catégories indiquées dans la légende à droite. Les symboles suivis d'un indice (⋏[1]) représentent des sous-catégories (voir légende complète à la page *I · 1*).

Os símbolos incluídos no texto do índice representam as grandes categorias identificadas com a chave à direita. Os símbolos com números em sua parte superior (⋏[1]) identificam as subcategorias (veja-se a chave completa à página *I · 1*).

ʌ Mountain	Berg	Montaña	Montagne	Montanha
⋏ Mountains	Gebirge	Montañas	Montagnes	Montanhas
)(Pass	Paß	Paso	Col	Passo
V Valley, Canyon	Tal, Cañon	Valle, Cañón	Vallée, Canyon	Vale, Canhão
⌣ Plain	Ebene	Llano	Plaine	Planície
➤ Cape	Kap	Cabo	Cap	Cabo
I Island	Insel	Isla	Île	Ilha
II Islands	Inseln	Islas	Îles	Ilhas
⊥ Other Topographic Features	Andere Topographische Objekte	Otros Elementos Topográficos	Autres données topographiques	Outros acidentes topográficos

ESPAÑOL: Nombre | Página | Lat.°′ | Long.°′ W = Oeste
FRANÇAIS: Nom | Page | Lat.°′ | Long.°′ W = Ouest
PORTUGUÊS: Nome | Página | Lat.°′ | Long.°′ W = Oeste

Beecroft Peninsula ≻[1] 170 35.02 S 150.50 E
Beedenbostel 52 52.38 N 10.16 E
Beef Island I 240m 18.27 N 64.31 W
Beek, Ned. 52 51.51 N 5.54 E
Beek, Ned. 52 51.32 N 5.38 E
Beek, Ned. 56 50.56 N 5.49 E
Beela ≃ 44 54.13 N 2.47 W
Beeleigh Abbey ⊍[1] 260 51.44 N 0.40 E
Beelen 52 51.55 N 8.07 E
Beelitz 54 52.14 N 12.58 E
Beemer 198 41.55 N 96.48 W
Beemster ✦[1] 52 52.35 N 4.55 E
Beendorf 54 52.14 N 11.05 E
Beenleigh 171a 27.43 S 153.12 E
Beerburrum 171a 26.58 S 152.58 E
Beerfelden 56 49.34 N 8.58 E
Bee Ridge 220 27.17 N 82.28 W
Beeringgnurding Hill ∧[2] 162 29.53 S 117.55 E
Beernem 50 51.09 N 3.20 E
Beerse 56 51.19 N 4.52 E
Beersheba → Be'ér Sheva' 132 31.14 N 34.47 E
Beersheba Springs 194 35.28 N 85.39 W
Be'ér Sheva (Beersheba) 132 31.14 N 34.47 E
Be'er Sheva', Naḥal V 132 31.11 N 34.35 E
Beerta 52 53.10 N 7.05 E
Be'ér Toviyya 132 31.44 N 34.44 E
Beervlei Brak ≃ 158 29.58 S 23.12 E
Beerwah 171a 26.51 S 152.58 E
Beerwah National Park ♠ 171a 26.54 S 152.53 E
Be'er Ya'agov 132 31.56 N 34.50 E
Beesenlaublingen 54 51.42 N 11.41 E
Beeskow 54 52.10 N 14.14 E
Beestekraal 156 25.23 S 27.38 E
Beesten 52 52.26 N 7.30 E
Beeston 42 52.56 N 1.12 W
Beet ≃ 115a 6.16 S 107.15 E
Beethoven Peninsula ≻[1] 9 71.40 S 73.45 W
Beeton 212 44.05 N 79.47 W
Beetsterzwaag 52 53.03 N 6.05 E
Beetz, Lac ⊜ 186 50.34 N 62.42 W
Beetzendorf 54 52.42 N 11.05 E
Beeville 196 28.24 N 97.44 W
Beevor, Mount ∧[2] 168b 34.56 S 139.02 E
Befale 152 0.28 N 20.58 E
Befandriana 157b 15.16 S 48.32 E
Befandriana Atsimo 157b 22.06 S 43.54 E
Befasy 157b 20.33 S 44.23 E
Befori 152 0.06 N 22.17 E
Befotaka, Madag. 157b 13.15 S 48.16 E
Befotaka, Madag. 157b 14.32 S 48.01 E
Befotaka, Madag. 157b 23.49 S 46.59 E
Befotaka, Madag. 157b 21.29 S 44.44 E
Befu ✦[8] 270 34.40 N 135.02 E
Beg, Lough ⊜ 48 54.47 N 6.28 W
Bega 166 36.40 S 149.50 E
Bega (Begej) ≃ 38 45.13 N 20.19 E
Begamganj, Bngl. 124 22.49 N 91.07 E
Begamganj, India 124 23.36 N 78.20 E
Begampur ✦[8] 272a 28.44 N 77.04 E
Beğdeș 130 37.51 N 39.05 E
Begej (Bega) ≃ 38 45.13 N 20.19 E
Beger 102 45.42 N 97.10 E
Beggs 196 35.44 N 96.04 W
Begičevskij 76 53.47 N 38.15 E
Beginsel 158 26.57 S 20.39 E
Beglickaja, kosa ≻[2] 83 47.07 N 38.35 E
Begna ≃ 26 60.10 N 10.16 E
Begoml' 76 54.44 N 28.04 E
Begonias, Presa ⊜[1] 234 20.55 N 100.50 W
Begoro 150 6.23 N 0.23 W
Begovat → Bekabad 85 40.13 N 69.14 E
Begunicy 76 59.35 N 29.19 E
Begur, Cap de ≻ 34 41.57 N 3.14 E
Begusarai 124 25.25 N 86.08 E
Behāla 126 22.31 N 88.19 E
Behague, Pointe ≻ 250 4.40 N 51.54 W
Behbahān 128 30.35 N 50.14 E
Behleg 120 36.47 N 91.41 E
Behm Canal ʊ 182 55.41 N 131.35 W
Beho 56 50.13 N 6.00 E
Béhoust 261 48.50 N 1.43 E
Behrāmpur 272a 28.38 N 77.24 E
Behren-lès-Forbach 56 49.10 N 6.57 E
Behring, Détroit de → Bering Strait ʊ 180 65.30 N 169.00 W
Behringen, Dtsch. 52 53.07 N 9.58 E
Behringen, Dtsch. 54 51.01 N 10.31 E
Behshahr 128 36.43 N 53.34 E
Beht, Oued ≃ 148 34.25 N 6.26 W
Bei ≃ 90 23.09 N 112.48 E
Bei'an 89 48.16 N 126.36 E
Beianhe 105 40.04 N 116.06 E
Beibaihua 105 38.57 N 114.51 E
Beibaozhen 106 31.33 N 121.38 E
Beibei 107 29.49 N 106.26 E
Beicai 106 31.12 N 121.34 E
Beicang 105 39.13 N 117.07 E
Beida → Al-Bayḍā' 146 32.46 N 21.43 E
Beida ≃ 102 40.18 N 99.26 E
Beïda, Chott ⊜ 34 35.56 N 5.49 E
Beidaihe 98 39.54 N 119.29 E
Beidaoqiao 86 44.12 N 89.38 E
Beidouzhen 107 30.02 N 104.26 E
Beidun 100 26.42 N 118.57 E
Beierfeld 54 50.33 N 12.47 E
Beiersdorf 264a 52.42 N 13.47 E
Beifangcun 105 40.20 N 116.42 E
Beifangzi 104 41.22 N 121.03 E
Beigang 100 29.20 N 113.41 E
Beighton 44 53.20 N 1.20 W
Beigi 144 9.20 N 34.29 E
Beiguan Dao I 100 27.10 N 120.32 E
Beiguo 106 31.47 N 120.33 E
Beihai 102 21.29 N 109.05 E
Bei Hai ⊜ 271a 39.56 N 116.22 E
Beihedian 105 39.13 N 115.45 E
Beiheishang'gou 105 39.53 N 118.15 E
Beihuaidian 105 39.16 N 117.33 E
Beijialing 104 41.08 N 124.02 E
Beijiao 100 26.22 N 119.58 E
Beijiean 106 32.15 N 121.12 E
Beijijiazhuang 105 40.01 N 114.51 E
Beijing (Peking), Zhg. 105 39.55 N 116.25 E
Beijing (Peking), Zhg. 271a 39.55 N 116.25 E
Beijing Ji Chang (Capitol Airport) ⊠ 105 40.03 N 116.35 E
Beijing Shi (Peking Shih) □[7] 98 40.15 N 116.30 E
Beiji Shan I 100 27.38 N 121.12 E
Beijuma ≃ 105 39.30 N 115.56 E
Beikan 100 32.23 N 121.21 E
Beilen 52 52.52 N 6.31 E
Beili 110 19.10 N 108.43 E
Beilifang 104 41.59 N 121.57 E
Beiling 100 24.36 N 115.20 E
Beiliu 102 22.42 N 110.22 E
Beiliuwangshui 105 38.57 N 115.03 E
Beilizigu 105 39.30 N 117.28 E
Beilngries 60 49.02 N 11.29 E
Beilong Shan I 100 27.40 N 120.58 E
Beilrode 54 51.35 N 13.03 E
Beilstein, Dtsch. 56 49.02 N 9.18 E
Beilstein, Dtsch. 56 50.36 N 8.14 E
Beilstein, Dtsch. 56 50.06 N 7.14 E
Beimaizhu 105 39.31 N 117.44 E
Beiminjiatun 104 42.38 N 122.43 E
Beimuzhen 107 29.31 N 105.05 E
Beinamar 146 8.40 N 15.23 E
Beine-Nauroy 50 49.15 N 4.13 E
Beinette 62 44.22 N 7.39 E
Beinwil 58 47.22 N 7.35 E
Beinwil am See 58 47.16 N 8.13 E
Beipa 164 8.30 S 146.35 E
Beipan ≃ 102 25.05 N 106.00 E
Beipanxiaozhen 106 31.44 N 121.26 E
Beipiao 104 41.49 N 120.46 E
Beipo 102 21.14 N 109.53 E
Beiqi 98 40.27 N 122.20 E
Beiqiao 106 31.03 N 121.24 E
Beira 156 19.49 S 34.52 E
Beira Baixa □[9] 34 39.45 N 7.30 W
Beira Litoral □[9] 34 40.15 N 8.25 W
Beiru ≃ 100 33.43 N 113.35 E
Beirut → Bayrūt 130 33.53 N 35.30 E
Beirut International Airport ⊠ 132 33.49 N 35.30 E
Beisanjia 98 42.04 N 124.42 E
Beiseker 182 51.23 N 113.32 W
Beishakou 105 39.08 N 116.07 E
Beishan 102 24.28 N 108.35 E
Bei Shan ⋏ 102 41.30 N 96.00 E
Beishangcun 105 39.28 N 116.58 E
Beishipian 105 40.43 N 116.55 E
Beishuangdong 105 40.32 N 117.24 E
Beishuiquan 98 40.05 N 114.40 E
Beisi 102 34.59 N 95.07 E
Beisu 98 38.13 N 114.46 E
Beitaitou 98 37.06 N 118.31 E
Beitang 105 39.07 N 117.42 E
Beitanshiqiao 106 31.05 N 121.38 E
Beitbridge 154 22.13 S 30.00 E
Beith 46 55.45 N 4.38 W
Beitstadfjorden ⊂[2] 26 63.53 N 11.00 E
Beiuș 38 46.40 N 22.21 E
Beiwei 106 32.05 N 121.12 E
Beiwenquan 107 29.51 N 106.24 E
Beiwu 105 40.04 N 116.48 E
Beiwudu 100 33.39 N 113.39 E
Beixiadai 106 32.12 N 120.08 E
Beixiejiadang 105 40.30 N 114.50 E
Beixili 89 51.47 N 125.45 E
Beixin'an 271a 39.55 N 116.08 E
Beixindian 105 39.44 N 116.44 E
Beixing 89 48.29 N 125.40 E
Beixinjing 106 31.13 N 121.22 E
Beixinliu 105 39.16 N 116.31 E
Beixinzhen 106 31.49 N 121.31 E
Beiyan 98 36.33 N 118.42 E
Beiyi ≃ 105 39.19 N 115.39 E
Beiyin 106 31.07 N 120.47 E
Beiyindai 104 42.35 N 122.22 E
Beiyuan 105 40.01 N 116.24 E
Beizhaijiawopeng 104 41.14 N 122.41 E
Beizhen, Zhg. 98 37.22 N 118.01 E
Beizhen (Gaoshanzi), Zhg. 104 41.36 N 121.47 E
Beizhouzhuang 106 31.52 N 120.24 E
Beizifu 98 42.09 N 120.29 E
Beja, Bra. 250 1.36 S 48.47 W
Beja, Port. 34 38.01 N 7.52 W
Beja, Ross. 86 53.03 N 90.54 E
Béja, Tun. 148 36.44 N 9.11 E
Beja □[5] 34 37.50 N 8.00 W
Béja □[8] 148 36.35 N 9.20 E
Bejaïa (Bougie) 148 36.45 N 5.05 E
Bejaïa □[5] 148 36.50 N 4.40 E
Bejaïa, Golfe de ⊂ 34 36.45 N 5.25 E
Béjar 34 40.23 N 5.46 W
Bejhi ≃ 120 29.47 N 67.58 E
Bejneu 86 45.15 N 55.07 E
Bejsug ≃ 78 45.54 N 38.56 E
Bejsugskij liman ⊂ 78 46.07 N 38.25 E
Bejtonovo 89 53.14 N 124.27 E
Bejucal 240p 22.56 N 82.23 W
Bejucal □[7] 286b 22.56 N 82.23 W
Bejuco 236 8.36 N 79.53 W
Bejucos ≃ 234 18.36 N 100.40 W
Bejuma 246 10.11 N 68.16 W
Bek ≃ 152 2.29 N 15.15 E
Béka 146 9.04 N 12.53 E
Bekaa Valley → Al-Biqā' V 128 33.50 N 36.00 E
Bekabad 85 40.13 N 69.14 E
Bekancan 114 3.18 N 98.24 E
Bekasi 115a 6.14 S 106.59 E
Bekasi ≃ 269e 6.10 S 107.02 E
Békásmegyer ✦[8] 264c 47.36 N 19.03 E
Bekasovo 82 55.26 N 36.49 E
Bekdaš 72 41.34 N 52.32 E
Békés 30 46.46 N 21.08 E
Békés □[6] 30 46.46 N 21.08 E
Békéscsaba 30 46.41 N 21.06 E
Beketovo 89 53.13 N 125.01 E
Bekilli 130 38.14 N 29.26 E
Bekily 157b 24.13 S 45.19 E
Bekirhan 130 38.10 N 41.19 E
Bekisopa 157b 21.40 S 45.54 E
Bekitro 157b 24.33 S 45.18 E
Bekkaria 36 35.22 N 8.15 E
Bekkersdal 273d 26.18 S 27.42 E
Bekkevoort 56 50.57 N 4.58 E
Beklemiševo, Ross. 80 53.52 N 47.25 E
Beklemiševo, Ross. 88 52.07 N 112.40 E
Bekodoka 157b 16.58 S 45.07 E
Bekoji 144 7.34 N 39.17 E
Bekok 114 2.18 N 103.08 E
Bekopaka 157b 19.09 S 44.48 E
Bekovo 80 52.28 N 43.43 E
Bektauata, gora ∧ 86 47.30 N 74.50 E
Bektyševo 82 56.34 N 39.14 E
Bekwai 150 6.27 N 1.35 W
Bela, India 124 25.56 N 81.59 E
Bela, Pāk. 120 26.14 N 66.19 E
Bela, Zaïre 154 0.38 N 29.14 E
Bélabo 152 5.00 N 13.20 E
Belabolo 140 8.57 N 25.51 E
Bela Crkva 38 44.54 N 21.26 E
Bela Cruz 250 3.03 S 40.11 W
Belaga 108 2.42 N 113.47 E
Bel'agaš 86 50.48 N 80.44 E
Bel-Air, Fr. 261 48.37 N 2.10 E
Bel Air, Md., U.S. 208 39.32 N 76.20 W
Bel Air, Va., U.S. 284c 38.52 N 77.10 W
Bel Air ✦[8] 280 34.05 N 118.27 W
Bélair, Île I 275a 45.37 N 73.48 W
Bel Aire Estates 207 41.23 N 72.00 W
Belair Recreation Park ♠ 168b 35.01 S 138.39 E
Belaja, Ross. 78 51.03 N 35.43 E
Belaja, Ross. 80 57.59 N 51.42 E
Belaja ≃, Ross. 78 45.04 N 39.23 E
Belaja ≃, Ross. 84 44.45 N 39.50 E
Belaja ≃, Ross. 86 55.54 N 53.33 E
Belaja ≃, Ross. 180 65.45 N 173.20 E
Belaja, gora ∧, Ross. 88 53.10 N 119.50 E
Belaja, gora ∧, Ross. 180 65.50 N 174.40 E
Belaja Ber'ozka 76 52.23 N 33.29 E
Belaja Cholunica 86 58.50 N 50.48 E
Belaja Gora 76 58.31 N 31.45 E
Belaja Kalitva 78 48.11 N 40.46 E
Bel'ajevka, Ross. 86 51.24 N 56.26 E
Bel'ajevka, Ross. 86 57.28 N 55.28 E
Bel'ajevo 76 55.31 N 31.06 E
Belalcázar 34 38.34 N 5.10 W
Bel Alton 208 38.27 N 76.58 W
Belambanganumpu 112 4.54 S 105.03 E
Belampalli 122 19.02 N 79.30 E
Bělá nad Radbuzou 60 49.36 N 12.44 E
Belang 112 0.57 N 124.47 E
Bélanger ≃ 184 53.26 N 97.40 W
Bel'aninovo 265b 55.57 N 37.39 E
Bel'anskij 80 47.45 N 41.33 E
Bela Palanka 38 43.13 N 22.19 E
Bělá pod Bezdězem 54 50.30 N 14.50 E
Belapurpāda 272c 19.01 N 73.02 E
Belarus □[1], Europe 22 53.50 N 28.00 E
Belarus □[1], Europe 76 53.50 N 28.00 E
Belarus Station ✦[5] 265b 55.47 N 37.35 E
Belas 266c 38.47 N 9.16 W
Belau → Palau □[2] 14 5.00 N 137.00 E
Belavenona 157b 24.50 S 47.04 E
Bela Vista, Ang. 152 7.50 S 13.40 E
Bela Vista, Bra. 252 22.06 S 56.31 W
Bela Vista, Moç. 156 26.20 S 32.40 E
Bela Vista ✦[8] 287b 23.33 S 46.38 W
Bela Vista de Goiás 255 16.58 S 48.57 W
Bela Vista do Paraíso 255 23.00 S 51.12 W
Belawan 114 3.47 N 98.41 E
Belaya ∧ 144 11.25 N 36.12 E
Belayan ≃ 112 0.14 S 116.36 E
Belaya Tserkov → Bila Tserkva 78 49.49 N 30.07 E
Belbo ≃ 62 44.54 N 8.31 E
Belbubulo 140 9.57 N 34.04 E
Belbunia 126 23.17 N 87.09 E
Belcamp 208 39.28 N 76.14 W
Belcastro 68 39.02 N 16.47 E
Bełchatów 30 51.22 N 19.21 E
Belchen ∧ 58 47.49 N 7.50 E
Belcher 194 32.44 N 93.49 W
Belcherāgh 120 35.50 N 65.14 E
Belcher Creek ≃ 276 41.08 N 74.23 W
Belcher Islands II 176 56.20 N 79.30 W
Belchertown 207 42.16 N 72.24 W
Belchite 34 41.18 N 0.45 W
Bělčice 60 49.30 N 13.53 E
Belcoo 48 54.17 N 7.52 W
Belcourt 198 48.50 N 99.44 W
Belda 126 22.05 N 87.21 E
Beldānga 126 23.56 N 88.15 E
Bel'd'ažki 76 52.39 N 35.42 E
Belding 216 43.05 N 85.13 W
Bele, ozero ⊜ 86 54.39 N 90.12 E
Belebej 80 54.07 N 54.07 E
Belebelka 76 57.34 N 30.56 E
Belecke 52 51.29 N 8.20 E
Beled Weyne 144 4.45 N 45.12 E
Bélel, Cam. 152 7.03 N 14.26 E
Belel, Nig. 146 9.38 N 13.12 E
Belém, Bra. 250 1.27 S 48.29 W
Belém, Moç. 154 14.13 S 35.58 E
Belém ✦[8] 266c 38.42 N 9.12 W
Belém, Torre de ⊥ 266c 38.42 N 9.13 W
Belém de São Francisco 250 8.46 S 38.58 W
Belén, Arg. 252 27.39 S 67.02 W
Belén, Bol. 248 19.48 S 65.33 W
Belén, Chile 248 18.29 S 69.31 W
Belén, Col. 246 6.00 N 72.55 W
Belén, Nic. 236 11.30 N 85.53 W
Belén, Para. 252 23.30 S 57.06 W
Belen, Tür. 130 36.32 N 36.10 E
Belen, N.M., U.S. 200 34.39 N 106.46 W
Belén, Ur. 252 30.47 S 57.47 W
Belén ≃ 252 28.00 S 66.52 W
Belén de Escobar 258 34.21 S 58.47 W
Belén del Refugio 234 21.31 N 102.25 W
Belene 38 43.39 N 25.07 E
Belenichino 78 50.56 N 36.37 E
Belènzinho ✦[8] 287b 23.32 S 46.35 W
Bélep, Îles II 175f 19.45 S 163.40 E
Beles ≃ 144 11.10 N 36.10 E
Belesar, Embalse de ⊜[1] 34 42.45 N 7.40 W
Belet Uen → Beled Weyne 144 4.45 N 45.12 E
Belews Lake ⊜[1] 192 36.17 N 80.03 W
Belfair 224 47.27 N 122.49 W
Belfast, N.Z. 172 43.27 S 172.38 E
Belfast, S. Afr. 156 25.43 S 30.03 E
Belfast, N. Ire., U.K. 48 54.35 N 5.55 W
Belfast, Me., U.S. 188 44.25 N 69.00 W
Belfast, N.Y., U.S. 210 42.20 N 78.06 W
Belfast, Oh., U.S. 218 39.03 N 83.32 W
Belfast (Aldergrove) Airport ⊠ 48 54.38 N 6.12 W
Belfast Lough ⊂ 48 54.40 N 5.50 W
Belfeld 52 51.19 N 6.06 E
Belfield, Austl. 274a 33.54 S 151.05 E
Belfield, N.D., U.S. 198 46.53 N 103.11 W
Belfiore 64 45.23 N 11.12 E
Belford, Eng., U.K. 44 55.36 N 1.49 W
Belford, N.J., U.S. 276 40.25 N 74.05 W
Belford Roxo 256 22.46 S 43.24 W
Belfort 58 47.38 N 6.52 E
Belfort □[8] 58 47.38 N 6.55 E
Belforte del Chienti 66 43.10 N 13.14 E
Belfry, Ky., U.S. 192 37.37 N 82.16 W
Belfry, Mt., U.S. 202 45.08 N 109.00 W
Belgaum 122 15.52 N 74.31 E
Belgern 54 51.29 N 13.07 E
Bélgica → Belgium □[1] 30 50.50 N 4.00 E
Belgica Mountains ⋏ 9 72.35 S 31.10 E
België → Belgium □[1] 30 50.50 N 4.00 E
Belgien → Belgium □[1] 30 50.50 N 4.00 E
Belgioioso 62 45.10 N 9.19 E
Belgique → Belgium □[1] 30 50.50 N 4.00 E
Belgium □[1], Europe 22 50.50 N 4.00 E
Belgium □[1], Europe 30 50.50 N 4.00 E
Belgodère 36 42.35 N 9.01 E
Belgorod 78 50.36 N 36.35 E
Belgorod Oblast' □[4] 78 50.45 N 37.30 E
Belgrad → Beograd 38 44.50 N 20.30 E
Belgrade → Beograd, Jugo. 38 44.50 N 20.30 E
Belgrade, Mn., U.S. 198 45.27 N 95.00 W
Belgrade, Mt., U.S. 202 45.46 N 111.10 W
Belgrade, Ne., U.S. 198 41.28 N 98.04 W
Belgrado → Beograd 38 44.50 N 20.30 E
Belgrad Ormanı ✦[3] 267b 41.10 N 28.55 E
Belgrano ✦[8] 288 34.34 S 58.28 W
Belgrano ≃ 254 48.15 S 71.12 W
Belgrano, Lago ⊜ 254 47.50 S 72.09 W
Belgrano II ⊍[3] 9 77.46 S 38.11 W
Belgrave 274b 37.55 S 145.21 E
Belhar 124 24.55 N 86.36 E
Belhaven 192 35.32 N 76.37 W
Belhus Park ♠ 260 51.31 N 0.17 E
Beliābera 126 22.17 N 86.55 E
Beliātor 126 23.20 N 87.13 E
Belica, Hrv. 64 46.26 N 16.27 E
Belica, Ross. 78 51.07 N 35.34 E
Belice → Belize City 232 17.30 N 88.12 W
Belice → Belize □[1] 232 17.15 N 88.45 W
Belice ≃ 70 37.35 N 12.52 E
Belichifor 146 6.33 N 33.16 E
Belici ≃ 70 37.31 N 13.50 E
Beličij, ostrov I 84 54.26 N 137.51 E
Belick 78 52.55 N 30.27 E
Beli Drim ≃ 38 42.06 N 20.25 E
Beliling, Gunung ∧ 115b 8.37 S 119.59 E
Beli Manastir 38 45.46 N 18.36 E
Belin 32 44.30 N 0.47 W
Belinga 152 1.13 N 13.12 E
Belington 188 39.01 N 79.56 W
Belinskij 80 52.58 N 43.25 E
Belinyu 112 1.38 S 105.46 E
Belitung I 108 2.50 S 107.55 E
Belize □[1], N.A. 230 17.15 N 88.45 W
Belize □[1], N.A. 232 17.15 N 88.45 W
Belize ≃ 232 17.32 N 88.14 W
Belize City 232 17.30 N 88.12 W
Belize Inlet ⊂ 182 51.08 N 127.35 W
Belknap Crater ▲[6] 202 44.17 N 121.50 W
Belkofski 180 55.05 N 162.02 W
Bel'kovo 82 56.15 N 38.48 E
Bel'kovskij, Ostrov I 74 75.32 N 135.44 E
Bell, Austl. 274b 37.45 S 145.00 E
Bell, S. Afr. 158 33.15 S 27.23 E
Bell, Ca., U.S. 280 33.58 N 118.11 W
Bell □[6] 222 31.03 N 97.27 W
Bell ≃, P.Q., Can. 176 49.48 N 77.38 W
Bell ≃, Yk., Can. 180 67.17 N 137.46 W
Bella 68 40.45 N 15.32 E
Bella Bella 182 52.09 N 128.07 W
Bellac 32 46.07 N 1.02 E
Bella Coola 182 52.22 N 126.46 W
Bella Coola ≃ 182 52.22 N 126.43 W
Bell Acres 279b 40.36 N 80.10 W
Bella Flor 248 11.09 S 67.49 W
Bellagio 58 45.59 N 9.15 E
Bellahy 48 53.58 N 8.48 W
Bellair 192 30.10 N 81.44 W
Bellaire, Mi., U.S. 190 44.58 N 85.12 W
Bellaire, Oh., U.S. 188 40.00 N 80.45 W
Bellaire, Tx., U.S. 222 29.42 N 95.27 W
Bella Isla, Estrecho de → Belle Isle, Strait of ʊ 176 51.35 N 56.30 W
Bella Lake ⊜ 212 45.27 N 79.02 W
Bellambi 170 34.21 S 150.55 E
Bellamy, Al., U.S. 194 32.26 N 88.08 W
Bellamy, Va., U.S. 208 37.24 N 76.34 W
Bellano 58 46.03 N 9.18 E
Bellaria 66 44.09 N 12.28 E
Bellarine 169 38.08 S 144.37 E
Bellarine Peninsula ≻[1] 169 38.13 S 144.35 E
Bellariva 68 41.55 N 15.58 E
Bellary 122 15.09 N 76.56 E
Bellas Artes, Museo de ⊍ 286c 10.30 N 66.53 W
Bellas Artes, Palacio de ⊍ 286a 19.26 N 99.08 W
Bellata 166 29.55 S 149.47 E
Bella Tola ∧ 58 46.15 N 7.39 E
Bella Unión 252 30.15 S 57.35 W
Bella Vista, Arg. 252 28.30 S 59.03 W
Bella Vista, Arg. 252 27.02 S 65.18 W
Bella Vista, Arg. 258 34.33 S 58.41 W
Bellavista, Chile 286e 33.31 S 70.37 W
Bella Vista, Para. 252 22.08 S 56.31 W
Bellavista, Perú 248 4.54 S 80.42 W
Bellavista, Perú 248 7.04 S 76.35 W
Bellavista, Perú 286d 12.04 S 77.08 W
Bellbird 170 32.51 S 151.21 E
Bellbrook, Austl. 166 30.49 S 152.31 E
Bellbrook, Oh., U.S. 218 39.38 N 84.04 W
Bell Brook ≃ 168a 33.01 S 116.15 E
Bell Crags ∧[2] 44 55.03 N 2.22 W
Bell Creek ≃, Ca., U.S. 280 34.12 N 118.36 W
Bell Creek ≃, In., U.S. 218 40.09 N 85.27 W
Bellé, Sén. 150 14.25 N 12.18 W
Belle, Mo., U.S. 219 38.17 N 91.43 W
Belle, W.V., U.S. 188 38.13 N 81.32 W
Belle ≃, On., Can. 214 42.17 N 82.43 W
Belle ≃, Mi., U.S. 214 42.43 N 82.30 W
Belleair 220 27.55 N 82.48 W
Belleau 50 49.06 N 3.18 E
Belle Ayr Mountain ∧ 210 42.07 N 74.29 W
Belle Bay ⊂ 186 47.36 N 55.18 W
Belle Center 216 40.30 N 83.44 W
Belledonne, Chaîne de ⋏ 62 45.18 N 6.08 E
Belle-Église 50 49.12 N 2.13 E
Belleek 48 54.28 N 8.06 W
Belle Farm Estates 208 39.23 N 76.45 W
Bellefontaine, Fr. 58 46.33 N 6.04 E
Bellefontaine, Fr. 261 49.06 N 2.28 E
Bellefontaine, Mart. 240e 14.40 N 61.10 W
Bellefontaine, Oh., U.S. 216 40.21 N 83.45 W
Bellefontaine Neighbors 219 38.44 N 90.13 W
Bellefonte, De., U.S. 208 39.45 N 75.30 W
Bellefonte, Md., U.S. 284c 38.47 N 76.52 W
Bellefonte, Pa., U.S. 214 40.54 N 77.46 W
Belle Fourche 198 44.40 N 103.51 W
Belle Fourche ≃ 198 44.26 N 102.19 W
Belle Fourche Reservoir ⊜[1] 198 44.44 N 103.42 W
Bellegarde, Fr. 58 46.06 N 5.49 E
Bellegarde, Fr. 62 43.45 N 4.31 E
Bellegarde-du-Loiret 50 47.59 N 2.26 E
Bellegem 50 50.47 N 3.16 E
Belle Glade 220 26.41 N 80.40 W
Belle Glade Camp 220 26.40 N 80.41 W
Bellegrove 208 40.22 N 76.33 W
Belle Haven, Va., U.S. 208 37.33 N 75.49 W
Belle Haven, Va., U.S. 284c 38.47 N 77.04 W
Belleherbe 58 47.16 N 6.40 E
Belle Hôtesse ∧ 241o 16.16 N 61.46 W
Belle-Île I 32 47.20 N 3.10 W
Belle Isle 220 28.27 N 81.21 W
Belle Isle I, Nf., Can. 176 51.55 N 55.20 W
Belle Isle I, Mi., U.S. 281 42.20 N 82.58 W
Belle Isle, Strait of ʊ 176 51.35 N 56.30 W
Belle Isle Park ♠ 281 42.20 N 82.59 W
Bellelay 58 47.16 N 7.10 E
Bellême 50 48.22 N 0.34 E
Belle Mead 208 40.28 N 74.39 W
Bellemoor 285 39.43 N 75.35 W
Bellencombre 50 49.42 N 1.14 E
Bellenden Ker National Park ♠ 164 17.15 S 145.53 E
Belleoram 186 47.31 N 55.25 W
Belleplain 208 39.16 N 74.52 W
Belle-Plaine, Sk., Can. 184 50.24 N 105.09 W
Belle Plaine, Ia., U.S. 190 41.53 N 92.16 W
Belle Plaine, Ks., U.S. 198 37.23 N 97.16 W
Belle Plaine, Mn., U.S. 190 44.37 N 93.46 W
Belle Rive 219 38.14 N 88.45 W
Belle River 214 42.18 N 82.43 W
Bellerose 276 40.44 N 73.43 W
Bellerose ✦[8] 276 40.45 N 73.43 W
Bellerose Terrace 276 40.43 N 73.43 W
Belle Terre 276 40.58 N 73.04 W
Bellevaux-Ligneuville 56 50.24 N 6.00 E
Belle Vernon 214 40.07 N 79.52 W
Bellevesvre 58 46.50 N 5.22 E
Belleview, Fl., U.S. 192 29.03 N 82.03 W
Belleview, In., U.S. 218 38.53 N 85.23 W
Belle View, Va., U.S. 208 38.46 N 77.03 W
Belleville, On., Can. 212 44.10 N 77.23 W
Belleville, Fr. 56 48.49 N 6.06 E
Belleville, Il., U.S. 219 38.31 N 89.59 W
Belleville, In., U.S. 218 39.41 N 86.29 W
Belleville, Ks., U.S. 198 39.49 N 97.37 W
Belleville, Mi., U.S. 216 42.12 N 83.29 W
Belleville, N.J., U.S. 210 40.47 N 74.09 W
Belleville, N.Y., U.S. 212 43.47 N 76.07 W
Belleville, Pa., U.S. 214 40.36 N 77.43 W
Belleville, R.I., U.S. 207 41.33 N 71.28 W
Belleville, Wi., U.S. 216 42.51 N 89.32 W
Belleville Lake ⊜ 281 42.12 N 83.29 W
Belleville-sur-Meuse 56 49.11 N 5.23 E
Belleville-sur-Saône 58 46.06 N 4.45 E
Bellevue, Ab., Can. 182 49.35 N 114.22 W
Bellevue, Fr. 50 49.53 N 4.12 E
Bellevue, Id., U.S. 202 43.27 N 114.15 W
Bellevue, Ia., U.S. 190 42.15 N 90.25 W
Bellevue, Ky., U.S. 218 39.06 N 84.28 W
Bellevue, Md., U.S. 208 38.42 N 76.11 W
Bellevue, Mi., U.S. 216 42.26 N 85.01 W
Bellevue, Ne., U.S. 198 41.08 N 95.53 W
Bellevue, Oh., U.S. 214 41.16 N 82.50 W
Bellevue, Pa., U.S. 214 40.29 N 80.03 W
Bellevue, Tx., U.S. 196 33.38 N 98.01 W
Bellevue, Wa., U.S. 224 47.36 N 122.11 W
Bellevue ✦[8] 273d 26.11 S 28.05 E
Belle Vue Zoological Gardens ♠ 262 53.28 N 2.11 W
Bell Ewart 212 44.16 N 79.33 W
Belley 62 45.46 N 5.41 E
Belleydoux 58 46.15 N 5.46 E
Belle Yella 150 7.22 N 10.00 W
Bellflower, Ca., U.S. 228 33.52 N 118.06 W
Bellflower, Il., U.S. 216 40.20 N 88.32 W
Bellflower, Mo., U.S. 219 39.00 N 91.21 W
Bell Gardens 228 33.57 N 118.09 W
Bellheim 56 49.11 N 8.16 E
Bell Hill ∧[2] 210 43.09 N 75.07 W
Bell Homestead ⊥ 212 43.04 N 80.18 W
Bellicourt 50 49.57 N 3.14 E
Bellingdon 260 51.44 N 0.38 W
Bellinge 41 55.20 N 10.20 E
Bellingen 166 30.27 S 152.54 E
Bellingham, Eng., U.K. 44 55.09 N 2.16 W
Bellingham, Ma., U.S. 207 42.05 N 71.28 W
Bellingham, Mn., U.S. 198 45.08 N 96.17 W
Bellingham, Wa., U.S. 224 48.45 N 122.29 W
Bellingham Bay ⊂ 224 48.45 N 122.35 W
Bellingshausen ⊍[3] 9 62.12 S 58.58 W
Bellingshausen Sea ⍑[2] 9 71.00 S 85.00 W
Bellingwolde 52 53.07 N 7.09 E
Bellinzago Novarese 62 45.34 N 8.38 E
Bellinzona 58 46.11 N 9.02 E
Bell Island I, Nf., Can. 186 47.36 N 52.58 W
Bell Island I, Nf., Can. 186 50.44 N 55.35 W
Bell Island Hot Springs 182 55.56 N 131.34 W
Bellmawr 208 39.52 N 75.05 W
Bellmead 222 31.35 N 97.06 W
Bellmore 276 40.40 N 73.31 W
Bell Mountain 228 34.35 N 117.15 W
Bellnhausen 56 50.42 N 8.43 E
Bello, Col. 246 6.20 N 75.33 W
Bello, Cuba 286b 23.07 N 82.24 W
Bello Horizonte → Belo Horizonte 255 19.55 S 43.56 W
Bellona 210 42.46 N 77.01 W
Bellona, Récifs ✢[2] 160 21.30 S 159.00 E
Bellona Plateau ✢[3] 14 20.30 S 158.30 E
Bellone, Cap ≻ 157b 16.14 S 49.51 E
Bellosguardo 68 40.25 N 15.19 E
Bellot Strait ʊ 176 71.58 N 94.45 W
Bellows Falls 188 43.08 N 72.26 W
Belloy-en-France 261 49.05 N 2.22 E
Bellpat 120 28.59 N 68.00 E
Bell Peninsula ≻[1] 176 63.50 N 82.00 W
Bell Point 279b 40.33 N 79.33 W
Bells, Tn., U.S. 194 35.43 N 89.05 W
Bells, Tx., U.S. 196 33.37 N 96.25 W
Bellsbank 44 55.18 N 4.23 W
Bells Bay ⊂ 212 45.30 N 77.51 W
Bells Corners 212 45.19 N 75.50 W
Bellshill 46 55.49 N 4.01 W
Bells Lake 285 39.44 N 75.02 W
Bells Lake ⊜ 285 39.45 N 75.04 W
Belltown, De., U.S. 208 38.44 N 75.10 W
Belltown, Il., U.S. 219 39.23 N 90.25 W
Belluno 64 46.09 N 12.13 E
Belluno □[4] 64 46.15 N 12.08 E
Bellvale 210 41.15 N 74.18 W
Bell Ville, Arg. 252 32.37 S 62.42 W
Bellville, S. Afr. 158 33.53 S 18.36 E
Bellville, Oh., U.S. 214 40.37 N 82.30 W
Bellville, Tx., U.S. 222 29.57 N 96.15 W
Bellwood, Il., U.S. 278 41.52 N 87.52 W
Bellwood, Ne., U.S. 198 41.20 N 97.14 W
Bellwood, Pa., U.S. 214 40.36 N 78.19 W
Bellwood, Lake ⊜ 212 43.46 N 80.20 W
Belly ≃ 182 49.46 N 113.02 W
Bellyk 86 54.32 N 91.17 E
Belm 52 52.18 N 8.08 E
Belmar, Md., U.S. 284b 39.21 N 76.32 W
Belmar, N.J., U.S. 208 40.10 N 74.01 W
Bélmez 34 38.16 N 5.12 W
Belmiro Braga 256 21.57 S 43.25 W
Belmond 190 42.50 N 93.36 W
Belmont, Austl. 169 38.10 S 144.21 E
Belmont, Austl. 170 33.02 S 151.40 E
Belmont, Mb., Can. 184 49.24 N 99.27 W
Belmont, N.S., Can. 186 45.25 N 63.23 W
Belmont, On., Can. 212 42.53 N 81.05 W
Belmont, S. Afr. 158 29.28 S 24.22 E
Belmont, Eng., U.K. 262 53.38 N 2.30 W
Belmont, Ca., U.S. 226 37.31 N 122.16 W
Belmont, Ma., U.S. 283 42.23 N 71.10 W
Belmont, Mi., U.S. 216 43.05 N 85.37 W
Belmont, Ms., U.S. 194 34.30 N 88.12 W
Belmont, N.H., U.S. 188 43.26 N 71.28 W
Belmont, N.Y., U.S. 210 42.13 N 78.02 W
Belmont, Pa., U.S. 214 40.17 N 78.53 W
Belmont, S.C., U.S. 192 34.02 N 81.01 W
Belmont, Tx., U.S. 222 29.31 N 97.41 W
Belmont, Wi., U.S. 190 42.44 N 90.20 W
Belmont □[6] 214 40.05 N 80.54 W
Belmonte, Bra. 255 15.51 S 38.54 W
Belmonte, Esp. 34 43.17 N 6.14 W
Belmonte, Esp. 34 39.34 N 2.42 W
Belmonte, Port. 34 40.21 N 7.21 W
Belmonte Calabro 68 39.09 N 16.05 E
Belmonte Mezzagno 70 38.02 N 13.23 E
Belmont Harbor ⊂ 278 41.57 N 87.38 W
Belmont Lake ⊜, On., Can. 212 44.30 N 77.50 W
Belmont Lake ⊜, N.Y., U.S. 276 40.44 N 73.20 W
Belmont Lake State Park ♠ 276 40.43 N 73.20 W
Belmont Park 214 41.10 N 80.39 W
Belmont Park Race Track ♠ 276 40.43 N 73.43 W
Belmont Reservoir ⊜[1] 262 53.39 N 2.30 W
Belmont Slough ≃ 282 37.33 N 122.14 W
Belmopan 232 17.15 N 88.46 W
Belmore, Austl. 274a 33.55 S 151.05 E
Belmore, Oh., U.S. 216 41.09 N 83.56 W
Belmullet 48 54.14 N 10.00 W
Belmuri 272b 22.57 N 88.09 E
Belo 157b 19.42 S 44.33 E
Belœil, Bel. 50 50.33 N 3.43 E
Beloeil, P.Q., Can. 206 45.34 N 73.12 W
Belœil, Château de ⊍ 50 50.35 N 3.44 E
Beloeil, Ruisseau ≃ 275a 45.39 N 73.12 W
Beloglazovo 86 56.05 N 72.40 E
Belogorje 78 50.30 N 40.01 E
Belogorka 80 50.42 N 53.27 E
Belogornoje 80 52.25 N 47.35 E
Belogorode 82 54.23 N 38.31 E
Belogorsk, Ross. 86 55.05 N 88.28 E
Belogorsk, Ross. 89 50.57 N 128.25 E
Belogorskij 86 49.27 N 83.10 E
Belogorskoje 80 53.35 N 48.12 E
Belogradčik 38 43.38 N 22.41 E
Beloguša 78 51.57 N 26.56 E
Beloha 157b 25.10 S 45.03 E
Belo Horizonte 255 19.55 S 43.56 W
Beloit, Ks., U.S. 198 39.27 N 98.06 W
Beloit, Oh., U.S. 214 40.55 N 80.59 W
Beloit, Wi., U.S. 216 42.30 N 89.01 W
Belo Jardim 250 8.20 S 36.26 W
Belojarsk 86 53.28 N 83.54 E
Beloje, Kaz. 86 48.55 N 82.58 E
Beloje, Ross. 80 58.23 N 39.24 E
Beloje, ozero ⊜ 76 60.11 N 37.37 E
Beloje more (White Sea) ⍑[2] 24 65.30 N 38.00 E
Belokuricha 86 51.59 N 84.59 E
Belomestnaja 76 52.24 N 37.37 E
Belomestnaja Dvojn'a 80 52.42 N 41.03 E
Belomorsk 24 64.32 N 34.48 E
Belomorsko-Baltijskij kanal ≊ 24 62.48 N 34.48 E
Belondo 152 0.16 S 19.31 E
Belonge 152 2.06 S 19.32 E
Belonia 124 23.15 N 91.27 E
Beloomut 76 54.57 N 39.20 E
Beloozersk 76 52.28 N 25.11 E
Belorado 34 42.25 N 3.11 W
Beloreč ensk 78 44.46 N 39.52 E
Beloreck 86 53.58 N 58.24 E
Belören, Tür. 130 40.51 N 33.30 E
Belören, Tür. 130 37.39 N 37.34 E
Belören, Tür. 130 37.12 N 32.33 E
Belorussia → Belarus □[1] 22 53.35 N 28.00 E
Belorussija → Belarus □[1] 72 53.50 N 28.00 E
Belorussiya → Belarus □[1] 72 53.50 N 28.00 E
Belorusskaja gr'ada ∧ 76 53.40 N 27.00 E
Beloščelje 24 64.52 N 46.56 E
Belo-sur-mer 157b 20.44 S 44.00 E
Belot, Lac ⊜ 180 66.55 N 126.18 W
Belousovka 86 50.08 N 82.33 E
Belousovo 82 55.05 N 36.40 E
Bel'ov 76 53.48 N 36.08 E
Belo Vale 255 20.25 S 44.01 W
Beloveżskaja Pušča, zapovednik ♠ 76 52.40 N 23.50 E
Belovo, Ross. 86 52.57 N 82.16 E
Belovo, Ross. 86 54.25 N 86.18 E
Belovodskoje 85 42.50 N 74.06 E
Beloz'orsk 76 60.02 N 37.48 E
Belp 58 46.53 N 7.30 E
Belpāda 272c 19.02 N 73.03 E
Belpasso 70 37.35 N 14.58 E
Belper 44 53.01 N 1.29 W
Belpre 188 39.16 N 81.34 W
Belrose 274a 33.44 S 151.13 E
Belsano 214 40.31 N 78.52 W
Belsele 50 51.09 N 4.05 E
Bel'skoje, Ross. 80 54.44 N 40.22 E
Bel'skoje, Ross. 86 57.49 N 92.09 E
Belson Run ≃ 279b 40.12 N 79.37 W
Belspring 192 37.11 N 80.36 W
Belt 202 47.23 N 110.55 W
Beltana 166 30.48 S 138.25 E
Belt Creek ≃ 202 47.36 N 111.02 W
Belted Range ⋏ 204 37.25 N 116.10 W
Belterra 250 2.38 S 54.57 W
Belthorn 262 53.43 N 2.26 W
Beltinci 61 46.36 N 16.15 E
Belton, Eng., U.K. 42 52.34 N 1.41 E
Belton, Eng., U.K. 44 53.33 N 0.49 W
Belton, Mo., U.S. 194 38.48 N 94.31 W
Belton, S.C., U.S. 192 34.31 N 82.29 W
Belton, Tx., U.S. 222 31.03 N 97.27 W
Belton Lake ⊜[1] 222 31.08 N 97.32 W
Beltra 48 54.13 N 8.37 W
Beltrán 252 27.50 S 64.04 W
Beltsville, Md., U.S. 208 39.02 N 76.54 W
Beltsville, Md., U.S. 284c 39.02 N 76.54 W
Belturbet 48 54.06 N 7.28 W
Beltway Plaza ✦[9] 284c 39.00 N 76.54 W
Bel'tyrskij 86 53.02 N 90.16 E
Beltzville Lake ⊜[1] 210 40.52 N 75.37 W
Beltzville State Park ♠ 210 40.52 N 75.36 W
Belucha, gora ∧ 86 49.48 N 86.40 E
Belucha, ozero ⊜ 80 49.20 N 46.05 E
Belugino 82 54.47 N 37.54 E
Belumut, Gunong ∧ 114 2.02 N 103.34 E
Belūr, India 122 13.10 N 75.52 E
Belur, India 272b 22.38 N 88.18 E
Beluran 112 5.54 N 117.33 E
Belur Math ⊍[1] 272b 22.38 N 88.22 E
Belušje 24 66.54 N 47.31 E
Belvedere, It. 64 45.44 N 13.23 E
Belvedere, Ca., U.S. 226 37.52 N 122.28 W
Belvedere, Va., U.S. 284c 38.50 N 77.10 W
Belvedere ✦[8] 260 51.29 N 0.09 E
Belvedere ⊍ 264b 48.11 N 16.23 E
Belvedere di Spinello 68 39.12 N 16.53 E
Belvedere Homes 220 26.43 N 80.06 W
Belvedere Marittimo 68 39.37 N 15.52 E
Belvedere Ostrense 66 43.34 N 13.09 E
Belvès 32 44.47 N 1.00 E
Belvidere, De., U.S. 208 39.43 N 75.37 W
Belvidere, Il., U.S. 216 42.15 N 88.50 W
Belvidere, N.J., U.S. 210 40.49 N 75.04 W
Belview 198 44.36 N 95.19 W
Belvis 266a 40.33 N 3.33 W
Belvís de la Jara 34 39.45 N 4.57 W
Belvoir → Kokhav HaYarden ⊥ 132 32.36 N 35.31 E
Belvoir, Vale of V 42 52.57 N 0.53 W
Belyando ≃ 166 21.38 S 146.50 E
Belyj 76 55.50 N 32.56 E
Belyj, ostrov I 74 73.10 N 70.45 E
Belyje Berega 76 53.12 N 34.40 E
Belyje Kolodezi 82 54.55 N 38.42 E
Belyje Stolby 82 55.20 N 37.52 E
Belyje Vody 85 42.25 N 69.50 E
Belyj Gorodok 76 56.58 N 37.30 E
Belyj Jar, Ross. 80 53.57 N 48.58 E
Belyj Jar, Ross. 86 53.36 N 91.24 E
Belyj Jar, Ross. 86 58.26 N 85.01 E
Belyj Kalodez' 78 50.02 N 38.40 E
Belyj Luch ≃ 80 57.43 N 43.42 E
Belyj Rast 82 56.08 N 37.26 E
Belyniči 76 53.59 N 29.42 E
Belynkoviči 76 53.15 N 32.08 E
Belz, Fr. 32 47.41 N 3.10 W
Belz, Ukr. 78 50.23 N 24.01 E
Bełżec 30 50.24 N 23.26 E
Belzig 54 52.08 N 12.35 E
Belzoni 194 33.11 N 90.29 W
Bełżyce 30 51.11 N 22.18 E
Bem 219 38.15 N 91.28 W
Bemaraha, Plateau du ⋏[1] 157b 19.15 S 45.00 E
Bemarivo, Madag. 157b 16.56 S 44.21 E
Bemarivo, Madag. 157b 21.45 S 44.45 E
Bemarivo ≃, Madag. 157b 15.27 S 47.40 E
Bemarivo ≃, Madag. 157b 14.09 S 50.09 E
Bemavo 157b 21.37 S 45.24 E
Bembe 152 7.02 S 14.18 E
Bembéréké 150 10.13 N 2.40 E
Bembézar ≃ 34 37.45 N 5.13 W
Bembezi ≃ 154 18.57 S 27.47 E
Bembou Sambayabé 150 10.55 N 13.44 W
Bembridge 42 50.41 N 1.05 W
Bement 194 39.55 N 88.34 W
Bemidji 190 47.28 N 94.52 W
Bemis 194 35.34 N 88.49 W
Bemmel 52 51.54 N 5.54 E
Bemolanga 157b 17.44 S 45.06 E
Bemposta 256 22.09 S 43.07 W
Bemus Point 214 42.09 N 79.23 W
Bemyž 80 56.08 N 51.44 E
Ben, Kinh ≊ 269c 10.43 N 106.37 E
Bena 150 11.18 N 5.55 E
Benaadir □[4] 144 2.07 N 45.24 E
Benāb 128 37.20 N 46.04 E
Benabarre 34 42.07 N 0.29 E
Bena-Dibele 152 4.07 S 22.50 E
Benagaria 126 24.11 N 87.37 E
Benagerie 166 31.25 S 140.24 E
Benahmed 148 33.07 N 7.17 W
Benain ≃ 112 9.39 S 124.59 E
Ben'akoni 76 54.15 N 25.22 E
Bena-Leka 152 5.08 S 22.10 E
Benalla 166 36.33 S 145.59 E
Benamejí 34 37.16 N 4.32 W
Benara ∧ 157a 12.53 S 45.10 E
Benares → Vārānasi 124 25.20 N 83.00 E
Bénat, Cap ≻ 62 43.05 N 6.22 E
Benátky nad Jizerou 54 50.17 N 14.51 E
Bena-Tshadi 152 4.40 S 22.49 E
Benavente, Esp. 34 42.00 N 5.41 W
Benavente, Port. 34 38.59 N 8.48 W
Benavides 196 27.35 N 98.24 W
Benavidez 258 34.25 S 58.42 W
Ben Avon 279b 40.31 N 80.05 W
Ben Avon Heights 279b 40.31 N 80.04 W
Ben Badis 34 34.57 N 0.55 W
Benbane Head ≻ 48 55.15 N 6.28 W
Benbecula I 46 57.26 N 7.21 W
Ben Bolt 196 27.39 N 98.05 W
Benbonyathe Hill ∧ 166 30.24 S 139.11 E
Benbrook 222 32.40 N 97.27 W
Benbrook Lake ⊜[1] 222 32.38 N 97.27 W
Ben Cat 110 11.09 N 106.36 E
Ben Cat, Rach ≃ 269c 10.50 N 106.42 E
Bencha, Khao Phanom ∧ 110 8.17 N 98.56 E
Ben-Chicao, Col de)(34 36.12 N 2.45 E
Bencubbin 162 30.48 S 117.52 E
Bend 202 44.03 N 121.18 W
Benda, Tanjung ≻ 115a 6.37 S 111.29 E
Bendaja 150 7.10 N 11.15 W
Bende 150 5.36 N 7.39 E

Symbol	English	Deutsch	Español	Français	Português
≃	River	Fluß	Río	Rivière	Rio
≊	Canal	Kanal	Canal	Canal	Canal
⌊	Waterfall, Rapids	Wasserfall, Stromschnellen	Cascada, Rápidos	Chute d'eau, Rapides	Cascata, Rápidos
ʊ	Strait	Meeresstraße	Estrecho	Détroit	Estreito
⊂	Bay, Gulf	Bucht, Golf	Bahía, Golfo	Baie, Golfe	Baía, Golfo
⊜	Lake, Lakes	See, Seen	Lago, Lagos	Lac, Lacs	Lago, Lagos
⁂	Swamp	Sumpf	Pantano	Marais	Pântano
⍓	Ice Features, Glacier	Eis- und Gletscherformen	Accidentes Glaciales	Formes glaciaires	Acidentes glaciares
⍑	Other Hydrographic Features	Andere Hydrographische Objekte	Otros Elementos Hidrográficos	Autres données hydrographiques	Outros acidentes hidrográficos

Symbol	English	Deutsch	Español	Français	Português
✢	Submarine Features	Untermeerische Objekte	Accidentes Submarinos	Formes de relief sous-marin	Acidentes submarinos
□	Political Unit	Politische Einheit	Unidad Política	Entité politique	Unidade política
⊍	Cultural Institution	Kulturelle Institution	Institución Cultural	Institution culturelle	Institução cultural
⊥	Historical Site	Historische Stätte	Sitio Histórico	Site historique	Sitio histórico
♠	Recreational Site	Erholungs- und Ferienort	Sitio de Recreo	Centre de loisirs	Area de Lazer
⊠	Airport	Flughafen	Aeropuerto	Aéroport	Aeroporto
■	Military Installation	Militäranlage	Instalación Militar	Installation militaire	Instalação militar
✦	Miscellaneous	Verschiedenes	Misceláneo	Divers	Diversos

ENGLISH — Name, Page, Lat.°′, Long.°′

DEUTSCH — Name, Seite, Breite°′, Länge°′ E = Ost

Name	Page	Lat.°′	Long.°′
Bendel □[3]	**150**	6.00 N	6.00 E
Bendela	**152**	3.18 S	17.36 E
Bendeleben, Mount ∧	**180**	65.10 N	164.03 W
Bendemeer	**166**	30.53 S	151.10 E
Bender Beyla	**144**	9.29 N	50.49 E
Benderge ∧	**158**	31.06 S	27.58 E
Bendersville	**208**	39.59 N	77.15 W
Bendigo	**169**	36.46 S	144.17 E
Bendimahi ≃	**84**	38.56 N	43.38 E
Bendorf	**56**	50.25 N	7.34 E
Bendugu	**150**	9.32 N	10.57 W
Bēne	**76**	56.29 N	23.04 E
Bene Beraq	**132**	32.05 N	34.50 E
Benedict	**208**	38.30 N	76.40 W
Benediktenwand ±[4]	**64**	47.39 N	11.28 E
Beneditinos	**250**	5.27 S	42.22 W
Benedito Leite	**250**	7.13 S	44.34 W
Bénéna	**150**	13.07 N	4.22 W
Benenitra	**157b**	23.27 S	45.05 E
Benepú, Rada ⊤[3]	**174z**	27.10 S	109.25 W
Beneraird ∧[2]	**44**	55.04 N	4.57 W
Benešov	**30**	49.47 N	14.43 E
Benešov nad Ploučnicí	**54**	50.45 N	14.22 E
Bénestroff	**56**	48.55 N	6.45 E
Benetutti	**71**	40.27 N	9.10 E
Beneuvre	**58**	47.42 N	4.57 E
Bene Vagienna	**62**	44.33 N	7.50 E
Bénévent-l'Abbaye	**32**	46.07 N	1.38 E
Benevento	**68**	41.08 N	14.45 E
Benevento □[4]	**68**	41.15 N	14.17 E
Benezett	**214**	41.19 N	78.23 W
Benfeld	**58**	48.22 N	7.36 E
Benfica -•-[8], Bra.	**287a**	22.53 S	43.15 W
Benfica -•-[8], Port.	**266c**	38.45 N	9.12 W
Benfica, Estádio ♦	**266c**	38.45 N	9.11 W
Bèng ≃, Lao	**110**	19.53 N	101.08 E
Beng ≃, Zhg.	**98**	35.05 N	118.24 E
Benga	**154**	13.19 S	34.16 E
Bengābād	**126**	24.18 N	86.21 E
Bengal, Bay of c	**12**	15.00 N	90.00 E
Bengala, Golfo del → Bengal, Bay of c	**12**	15.00 N	90.00 E
Bengalen, Golf von → Bengal, Bay of c	**12**	15.00 N	90.00 E
Bengamisa	**154**	0.57 N	25.10 E
Bengara	**112**	3.11 N	117.12 E
Ben Gardane	**148**	33.08 N	11.13 E
Bengasi → Banghāzī	**146**	32.07 N	20.04 E
Bengbis	**152**	3.27 N	12.27 E
Bengbu	**100**	32.58 N	117.24 E
Benger	**168a**	33.11 S	115.52 E
Benghazi → Banghāzī	**146**	32.07 N	20.04 E
Ben Giang	**110**	15.41 N	107.47 E
Bengkalis	**114**	1.28 N	102.07 E
Bengkalis, Pulau I	**114**	1.30 N	102.15 E
Bengkalis, Selat ⋓	**114**	1.30 N	102.00 E
Bengkayang	**112**	0.50 N	109.29 E
Bengkoka ≃	**116**	6.50 N	117.03 E
Bengkulu	**112**	3.48 S	102.16 E
Bengkulu □[4]	**112**	4.00 S	102.30 E
Bengo □[5]	**152**	8.30 S	13.20 E
Bengo ≃	**152**	8.45 S	13.24 E
Bengo, Baía do c	**152**	8.43 S	13.21 E
Bengoi	**164**	3.01 S	130.12 E
Bengough	**184**	49.24 N	105.08 W
Bengtsfors	**26**	59.02 N	12.13 E
Benguela	**152**	12.35 S	13.25 E
Benguela □[5]	**152**	12.45 S	14.30 E
Benguerir	**148**	32.14 N	7.57 W
Benguet □[4]	**116**	16.30 N	120.40 E
Bengut, Cap ›	**34**	36.55 N	3.54 E
Benha → Banhā	**142**	30.28 N	31.11 E
Benham	**192**	36.57 N	82.56 W
Ben Hur	**222**	31.30 N	96.44 W
Beni, Nig.	**146**	10.27 N	10.24 E
Beni, Zaïre	**154**	0.30 N	29.28 E
Beni □[5]	**248**	14.00 S	65.30 W
Beni ≃	**248**	10.58 S	66.09 W
Béni Abbas	**148**	30.08 N	2.10 W
Benicarló	**34**	40.25 N	0.26 E
Benicia	**226**	38.02 N	122.09 W
Benicia Capitol State Historic Park ♦	**282**	38.03 N	122.09 W
Benicia State Recreation Area ♦	**282**	38.05 N	122.13 W
Benicito ≃	**248**	11.32 S	65.47 W
Benidorm	**34**	38.32 N	0.08 W
Beni-Mellal	**148**	32.22 N	6.29 W
Beni-Mellal □[4]	**148**	32.22 N	6.27 W
Benin (Bénin) □[1], Afr.	**134**	9.30 N	2.15 E
Benin (Bénin) □[1], Afr.	**150**	9.30 N	2.15 E
Benin ≃	**150**	5.45 N	5.04 E
Benin, Bight of c[3]	**150**	5.30 N	3.00 E
Benin City	**150**	6.19 N	5.41 E
Beni Saf	**148**	35.19 N	1.23 W
Benisheikh	**146**	11.49 N	12.29 E
Benissa	**34**	38.34 N	0.03 E
Beni Suef → Banī Suwayf	**142**	29.05 N	31.05 E
Benito	**184**	51.55 N	101.31 W
Benito Juárez, Arg.	**252**	37.40 S	59.48 W
Benito Juárez, Méx.	**234**	19.14 N	100.28 W
Benito Juárez, Méx.	**234**	17.50 N	92.32 W
Benito Juárez, Aeropuerto Internacional ⊠	**286a**	19.26 N	99.04 W
Benito Juárez, Presa ⊜[1]	**234**	16.27 N	95.30 W
Benit Point ›	**116**	9.54 N	125.17 E
Benjamim Constant	**256**	21.57 S	42.53 W
Benjamin	**196**	33.35 N	99.48 W
Benjamín, Isla I	**254**	44.40 S	74.08 W
Benjamín Aceval	**252**	24.58 S	57.34 W
Benjamin Constant	**246**	4.22 S	70.02 W
Benjamin Franklin Bridge -•-[5]	**285**	39.57 N	75.08 W
Benjamín Hill	**232**	30.10 N	111.10 W
Benjamín Zorrilla	**252**	39.06 S	65.29 W
Benkelman	**198**	40.02 N	101.31 W
Benken	**54**	52.10 N	12.28 E
Benkovac	**36**	44.02 N	15.37 E
Benld	**219**	39.05 N	89.48 W
Benllech	**44**	53.19 N	4.13 W
Ben Lomond	**226**	37.05 N	122.05 W
Ben Lomond National Park ♦	**166**	41.34 S	147.11 E
Ben Mehidi	**36**	36.46 N	7.54 E
Benmore, Lake ⊜[1]	**172**	44.25 S	170.15 E
Benndale	**194**	30.52 N	88.48 W
Benndorf	**54**	51.34 N	11.29 E
Benneckenstein	**54**	51.40 N	10.45 E
Bennekom	**52**	52.00 N	5.40 E
Bennet	**198**	40.40 N	96.30 W
Bennett, Lake ⊜	**162**	22.55 S	130.57 E
Bennetta, ostrov I	**74**	76.21 N	148.56 E
Bennett Lake ⊜, Can.	**180**	60.05 N	134.50 W
Bennett Lake ⊜, Mb., Can.	**184**	53.28 N	96.05 W
Bennett Lake ⊜, On., Can.	**212**	44.55 N	76.27 W
Bennett Pass)(	**224**	45.18 N	121.39 W
Bennettsbridge	**48**	52.36 N	7.12 W
Bennetts Creek ≃	**210**	42.16 N	77.35 W
Bennettsville	**192**	34.37 N	79.41 W
Bennettswood	**274b**	37.51 S	145.07 E
Bennigsen	**52**	52.14 N	9.40 E
Benninghofen -•-[8]	**263**	51.29 N	7.31 E
Bennington, In., U.S.	**218**	38.52 N	85.08 W
Bennington, Ks., U.S.	**198**	39.01 N	97.35 W
Bennington, Vt., U.S.	**210**	42.52 N	73.11 W
Bennington □[6]	**207**	42.50 N	73.08 W
Bennington Battle Monument ⊥	**210**	42.53 N	73.13 W
Benniu	**106**	31.52 N	119.48 E
Beno	**152**	3.37 S	17.48 E
Benoa	**115b**	8.46 S	115.13 E
Ben Ohau Range ⋏	**172**	44.00 S	170.00 E
Benoit	**194**	33.39 N	91.00 W
Benom, Gunong ∧	**114**	3.49 N	102.04 E
Benoni	**158**	26.11 S	28.19 E
Benoni □[5]	**273d**	26.08 S	28.22 E
Benoni-Suid	**273d**	26.13 S	28.18 E
Bénoué (Benue) ≃	**134**	7.48 N	6.46 E
Bénoué, Parc National de la ♦	**146**	8.20 N	13.50 E
Benover	**260**	51.13 N	0.26 E
Bénoy	**146**	8.59 N	16.19 E
Benque Viejo del Carmen	**232**	17.05 N	89.08 W
Benrad -•-[8]	**263**	51.20 N	6.30 E
Benrath -•-[8]	**56**	51.10 N	6.51 E
Benrath, Schloss ⊥	**263**	51.10 N	6.52 E
Bensalem	**285**	40.04 N	74.56 W
Bensbach ≃	**164**	9.08 S	141.00 E
Bensberg	**56**	50.58 N	7.09 E
Bensdorf	**54**	52.24 N	12.20 E
Ben Sekka, Rass ›	**36**	37.21 N	9.45 E
Bensenville	**278**	41.57 N	87.56 W
Bensersiel	**52**	53.40 N	7.34 E
Benshausen	**54**	50.38 N	10.35 E
Bensheim	**56**	49.41 N	8.37 E
Bensley	**208**	37.26 N	77.26 W
Ben-Slimane	**148**	33.41 N	7.10 W
Ben-Slimane □[4]	**148**	33.40 N	7.10 W
Ben Smih	**36**	36.23 N	7.31 E
Benson, Eng., U.K.	**42**	51.38 N	1.05 W
Benson, Az., U.S.	**200**	31.58 N	110.17 W
Benson, Md., U.S.	**208**	39.30 N	76.23 W
Benson, Mn., U.S.	**198**	45.18 N	95.35 W
Benson, N.C., U.S.	**192**	35.22 N	78.32 W
Bensonhurst -•-[8]	**276**	40.35 N	73.59 W
Benson Point ›	**174o**	1.56 N	157.29 W
Bens Run ≃	**284b**	39.19 N	76.48 W
Bent	**128**	26.17 N	59.31 E
Benta	**114**	4.01 N	101.58 E
Benteng (Salayar)	**112**	6.08 S	120.27 E
Bentheim, Dtsch.	**52**	52.17 N	7.10 E
Bentheim, Mi., U.S.	**216**	42.42 N	85.55 W
Ben Thuy	**110**	18.39 N	105.42 E
Bentiaba	**152**	14.15 S	12.21 E
Bentiaba ≃	**152**	14.29 S	12.50 E
Bentinck Island I, Austl.	**164**	17.04 S	139.30 E
Bentinck Island I, Mya.	**110**	11.45 N	98.03 E
Bentiu	**140**	9.14 N	29.50 E
Bentleigh	**274b**	37.55 S	145.02 E
Bentley, Ab., Can.	**182**	52.28 N	114.04 W
Bentley, Eng., U.K.	**44**	53.33 N	1.09 W
Bentley College ʊ[2]	**283**	42.23 N	71.13 W
Bentleyville, Oh., U.S.	**279a**	41.25 N	81.26 W
Bentleyville, Pa., U.S.	**214**	40.07 N	80.00 W
Bento Gomes ≃	**248**	16.40 S	57.12 W
Bento Gonçalves	**252**	29.10 S	51.31 W
Bentol	**150**	6.26 N	10.36 W
Benton, Ar., U.S.	**194**	34.33 N	92.35 W
Benton, Il., U.S.	**194**	37.59 N	88.55 W
Benton, In., U.S.	**216**	41.30 N	85.45 W
Benton, Ky., U.S.	**194**	36.51 N	88.21 W
Benton, La., U.S.	**194**	32.41 N	93.44 W
Benton, Ms., U.S.	**194**	32.49 N	90.15 W
Benton, Mo., U.S.	**194**	37.05 N	89.33 W
Benton, Oh., U.S.	**214**	40.36 N	81.51 W
Benton, Pa., U.S.	**210**	41.11 N	76.23 W
Benton, Tn., U.S.	**192**	35.10 N	84.39 W
Benton, Wi., U.S.	**190**	42.34 N	90.22 W
Benton □[6]	**216**	40.37 N	87.19 W
Benton City, Mo., U.S.	**219**	39.08 N	91.45 W
Benton City, Wa., U.S.	**202**	46.15 N	119.29 W
Bentong	**114**	3.32 N	101.55 E
Benton Harbor	**216**	42.07 N	86.26 W
Benton Heights	**216**	42.07 N	86.24 W
Bentonia	**194**	32.38 N	90.21 W
Benton Lake ⊜	**202**	47.40 N	111.20 W
Benton Ridge	**216**	41.00 N	83.47 W
Bentonville, Ar., U.S.	**194**	36.22 N	94.12 W
Bentonville, In., U.S.	**218**	39.45 N	85.15 W
Bentonville, Oh., U.S.	**218**	38.45 N	83.37 W
Ben Tre	**110**	10.14 N	106.23 E
Bent's Old Fort National Historic Site ⊥	**198**	38.05 N	103.28 W
Benua, Pulau I	**112**	0.56 N	107.27 E
Benue □[3]	**150**	7.15 N	8.00 E
Benue (Bénoué) ≃	**134**	7.48 N	6.46 E
Benut	**114**	1.38 N	103.16 E
Benwee ∧	**48**	53.35 N	9.31 W
Benwee Head ›	**48**	54.20 N	9.50 W
Ben Wheeler	**222**	32.27 N	95.42 W
Benxi (Penhsi), Zhg.	**104**	41.18 N	123.45 E
Benxi (Xiaoshi), Zhg.	**104**	41.17 N	124.07 E
Benza	**152**	6.16 S	12.57 E
Beograd (Belgrade)	**38**	44.50 N	20.30 E
Beohāri	**124**	24.03 N	81.23 E
Beonta	**272b**	22.31 N	88.31 E
Béoumi	**150**	7.40 N	5.34 W
Beowawe	**204**	40.35 N	116.28 W
Beppu	**96**	33.17 N	131.30 E
Beppu-wan c	**96**	33.18 N	131.35 E
Bequia I	**241h**	13.01 N	61.13 W
Bequimão	**250**	2.26 S	44.47 W
Bera	**126**	24.05 N	89.37 E
Berābāria	**272b**	22.52 N	88.34 E
Beraberi, India	**272b**	22.46 N	88.27 E
Berāberi, India	**272b**	22.51 N	88.12 E
Beraketa, Madag.	**157b**	24.11 S	45.42 E
Beraketa, Madag.	**157b**	23.07 S	44.25 E
Beramanja	**157b**	13.13 S	48.56 E
Bérandjoko	**152**	3.06 N	17.17 E
Berāsi	**124**	23.36 N	81.51 E
Berasia	**124**	23.38 N	77.26 E
Berat	**38**	40.42 N	19.57 E
Beratzhausen	**60**	49.06 N	11.48 E
Berau	**58**	47.42 N	8.15 E
Berau ≃	**112**	2.10 N	117.42 E
Berau, Teluk c	**164**	2.30 S	132.30 E
Beravina	**157b**	18.10 S	45.14 E
Berazategui	**258**	34.46 S	58.13 W
Berazategui □[5]	**288**	34.50 S	58.10 W
Berbenno di Valtellina	**64**	46.10 N	9.44 E
Berbera	**144**	10.25 N	45.02 E
Berbérati	**152**	4.16 N	15.47 E
Berbice ≃	**246**	6.17 N	57.32 W
Berceto	**64**	44.31 N	9.59 E
Berchem, Bel.	**50**	51.12 N	4.26 E
Berchem, Bel.	**50**	50.47 N	3.30 E
Berchem-Sainte-Agathe	**56**	50.52 N	4.17 E
Berchidda	**71**	40.47 N	9.10 E
Berching	**60**	49.07 N	11.27 E
Berchtesgaden	**64**	47.38 N	13.01 E
Berchtesgaden, Nationalpark ♦	**64**	47.30 N	13.00 E
Berchum -•-[8]	**263**	51.23 N	7.32 E
Berck	**50**	50.24 N	1.34 E
Berclair	**196**	28.32 N	97.36 W
Berčogur	**86**	48.25 N	58.44 E
Bercu	**50**	50.31 N	3.17 E
Berd	**84**	40.53 N	45.23 E
Berda ≃	**78**	46.48 N	36.52 E
Berdaale	**144**	7.04 N	47.51 E
Berdale	**144**	4.56 N	45.02 E
Berd'auš	**86**	55.09 N	59.09 E
Berdigest'ach	**74**	62.06 N	126.40 E
Berdniki	**80**	57.25 N	46.33 E
Berdorf	**56**	49.50 N	6.21 E
Berdsk	**86**	54.47 N	83.02 E
Berd'užje	**86**	55.48 N	68.19 E
Berdyans'k	**78**	46.45 N	36.49 E
Berdyans'ka kosa ›[2]	**78**	46.42 N	36.48 E
Berdyans'ka zatoka c	**78**	46.42 N	36.35 E
Berdychiv	**78**	49.54 N	28.36 E
Béré, Tchad	**146**	9.20 N	16.09 E
Bere, Turk.	**128**	39.47 N	58.06 E
Berea, Ky., U.S.	**192**	37.34 N	84.17 W
Berea, Oh., U.S.	**214**	41.21 N	81.51 W
Berea, S.C., U.S.	**192**	34.53 N	82.27 W
Bere Alston	**42**	50.29 N	4.11 W
Berebei	**164**	9.31 S	147.27 E
Beregajevo	**86**	57.10 N	87.32 E
Beregomet	**78**	48.12 N	25.21 E
Beregovoj	**86**	55.12 N	73.12 E
Bereguardo	**62**	45.15 N	9.01 E
Berehove	**78**	48.13 N	22.39 E
Bereina	**164**	8.40 S	146.30 E
Bereka ≃	**78**	49.12 N	36.59 E
Bereketli	**130**	40.31 N	37.18 E
Bereku	**154**	4.27 S	35.44 E
Berekua	**240d**	15.14 N	61.19 W
Berekum	**150**	7.27 N	2.37 W
Bérem	**152**	7.33 N	13.55 E
Beren, liman ⊜	**80**	46.52 N	44.55 E
Berenda Slough ≃	**226**	37.00 N	120.29 W
Berendejevo	**82**	56.36 N	39.01 E
Berens ≃	**184**	52.21 N	97.02 W
Berens Island I	**184**	52.18 N	97.17 W
Berens River	**184**	52.22 N	97.02 W
Bere Regis	**42**	50.46 N	2.14 W
Beresford, N.B., Can.	**186**	47.42 N	65.42 W
Beresford, S.D., U.S.	**198**	43.04 N	96.46 W
Beresina → Berezina ≃	**76**	52.33 N	30.14 E
Berestechko	**78**	50.23 N	25.07 E
Bereşti	**38**	46.06 N	27.53 E
Berettyó (Barcău) ≃	**38**	46.59 N	21.07 E
Berettyóújfalu	**30**	47.14 N	21.32 E
Berevo, Madag.	**157b**	17.14 S	44.17 E
Berevo, Madag.	**157b**	19.44 S	44.58 E
Berezajka	**76**	57.59 N	33.54 E
Berezan'	**78**	50.19 N	31.30 E
Berezanskaja	**78**	45.43 N	39.34 E
Berezans'kyy lyman c[1]	**78**	46.43 N	31.30 E
Berezdiv	**78**	50.27 N	27.05 E
Bereze	**78**	51.44 N	33.52 E
Berezhany, Ukr.	**78**	51.27 N	26.27 E
Berezhany, Ukr.	**78**	49.27 N	24.56 E
Berezina ≃, Bela.	**76**	52.33 N	30.14 E
Berezina ≃, Bela.	**76**	53.48 N	25.59 E
Berezino, Bela.	**76**	53.49 N	28.59 E
Berezino, Bela.	**76**	54.54 N	28.12 E
Berezino, Kaz.	**80**	50.06 N	48.52 E
Berezinskij zapovednik ♦	**76**	54.40 N	28.15 E
Berezivka, Ukr.	**78**	47.49 N	32.28 E
Berezivka, Ukr.	**78**	45.35 N	33.20 E
Berezivka, Ukr.	**78**	47.12 N	30.55 E
Berezna	**78**	51.34 N	31.47 E
Berezn'agi	**78**	49.59 N	41.06 E
Berezne	**78**	51.00 N	26.45 E
Bereznehuvate	**78**	47.20 N	32.49 E
Bereznik	**24**	62.51 N	42.40 E
Berezniki	**86**	59.24 N	56.46 E
Bereznyaky, Ukr.	**78**	49.09 N	31.57 E
Bereznyaky, Ukr.	**78**	49.51 N	33.01 E
Berezova Rudka	**78**	50.19 N	32.14 E
Berezove	**78**	51.35 N	27.20 E
Berezyne	**78**	46.14 N	29.12 E
Berford Lake ⊜	**212**	44.48 N	81.11 W
Berg, Dtsch.	**64**	47.58 N	11.21 E
Berg, Lux.	**56**	49.49 N	6.05 E
Berg, Nor.	**24**	69.26 N	17.15 E
Berg, Öst.	**64**	46.45 N	13.09 E
Berga, Dtsch.	**54**	50.45 N	12.10 E
Berga, Dtsch.	**54**	51.27 N	11.00 E
Berga, Esp.	**34**	42.06 N	1.51 E
Berga, Sve.	**40**	59.21 N	16.26 E
Bergama	**130**	39.07 N	27.11 E
Bergambacht	**52**	51.56 N	4.46 E
Bergamo	**62**	45.41 N	9.43 E
Bergamo □[4]	**64**	45.50 N	9.48 E
Bergan Point ›	**276**	40.40 N	73.20 W
Bergantín	**246**	10.01 N	64.22 W
Bergantino	**64**	45.05 N	11.15 E
Bergara	**34**	43.07 N	2.25 W
Bergbau Museum ʊ	**263**	51.29 N	7.13 E
Bergby	**26**	60.56 N	17.02 E
Berge, Dtsch.	**52**	52.37 N	7.44 E
Berge, Dtsch.	**54**	53.15 N	11.50 E
Berge, Dtsch.	**263**	51.21 N	7.22 E
Bergedorf -•-[8]	**52**	53.29 N	10.13 E
Bergei ∧[2]	**263**	51.13 N	7.46 E
Bergeijk	**52**	51.19 N	5.22 E
Bergen → Mons, Bel.	**50**	50.27 N	3.56 E
Bergen, Dtsch.	**52**	52.48 N	9.58 E
Bergen, Dtsch.	**54**	52.53 N	10.58 E
Bergen, Dtsch.	**64**	47.48 N	12.35 E
Bergen, Ned.	**52**	52.40 N	4.41 E
Bergen, Nor.	**26**	60.23 N	5.20 E
Bergen, N.Y., U.S.	**210**	43.05 N	77.56 W
Bergen □[6]	**210**	40.53 N	74.03 W
Bergen aan Zee	**52**	52.38 N	4.37 E
Bergen [auf Rügen]	**54**	54.25 N	13.26 E
Bergen Basin c	**276**	40.39 N	73.49 W
Bergen-Belsen-Denkmal ⊥	**52**	52.46 N	9.55 E
Berg en Dal	**250**	5.09 N	55.04 W
Bergenfield	**210**	40.55 N	73.59 W
Bergen Mall -•-[9]	**276**	40.55 N	74.04 W
Bergen op Zoom	**52**	51.30 N	4.17 E
Berger	**219**	38.40 N	91.20 W
Bergerac	**32**	44.51 N	0.29 E
Bergères-lès-Vertus	**50**	48.53 N	4.00 E
Bergerhof	**263**	51.12 N	7.21 E
Bergfelde	**54**	52.40 N	13.19 E
Berggiesshübel	**54**	50.52 N	13.57 E
Berghausen, Dtsch.	**263**	51.18 N	7.17 E
Berghausen, Dtsch.	**263**	51.07 N	6.55 E
Bergheim, Dtsch.	**56**	50.55 N	6.38 E
Bergheim, Fr.	**58**	48.12 N	7.22 E
Bergheim, Öst.	**64**	47.50 N	13.02 E
Berghem	**52**	51.46 N	5.34 E
Berghofen -•-[8]	**263**	51.29 N	7.32 E
Bergholtz	**210**	43.06 N	78.53 W
Bergholtz Creek ≃	**284a**	43.05 N	78.57 W
Bergholz	**214**	40.31 N	80.53 W
Bergholz-Rehbrücke	**54**	52.20 N	13.05 E
Bergisches Land -•-[1]	**56**	51.00 N	7.30 E
Bergisch Gladbach	**56**	50.59 N	7.07 E
Bergkamen	**52**	51.38 N	7.38 E
Bergkvara	**26**	56.23 N	16.05 E
Bergland	**190**	46.35 N	89.34 W
Bergneustadt	**56**	51.01 N	7.39 E
Bergnicourt	**50**	49.25 N	4.15 E
Bergö I	**26**	62.58 N	21.11 E
Bergoo	**188**	38.29 N	80.18 W
Bergplaas	**158**	33.54 S	22.40 E
Bergrheinfeld	**56**	50.00 N	10.10 E
Bergsäng	**40**	60.06 N	13.33 E
Bergsbrunna	**40**	59.49 N	17.43 E
Bergsche Maas ≃	**52**	51.45 N	5.08 E
Bergshamra	**40**	59.38 N	18.37 E
Bergsjö	**26**	61.59 N	17.04 E
Bergslagen -•-[1]	**40**	59.55 N	15.00 E
Bergstrom Air Force Base ■	**222**	30.12 N	97.40 W
Bergtheim	**56**	49.54 N	10.04 E
Berguent	**148**	34.03 N	2.02 W
Bergues	**50**	50.58 N	2.26 E
Bergum	**52**	53.11 N	5.59 E
Bergün	**58**	46.38 N	9.45 E
Bergville	**158**	28.52 S	29.18 E
Bergvreten	**40**	60.31 N	16.26 E
Bergwitz	**54**	51.48 N	12.35 E
Berhala, Selat ⋓	**112**	0.48 S	104.25 E
Beri	**124**	28.42 N	76.35 E
Berici, Monti ⋏	**64**	45.26 N	11.31 E
Berikul'skij	**86**	55.32 N	88.08 E
Beringa, ostrov I	**74**	55.00 N	165.15 E
Beringen	**56**	51.03 N	5.13 E
Bering Glacier ⊓	**180**	60.15 N	143.30 W
Beringhausen	**56**	51.24 N	8.46 E
Beringil	**140**	12.10 N	25.41 E
Beringin	**112**	3.41 S	104.18 E
Beringovskij	**180**	63.03 N	179.19 E
Bering Sea ⊤[2]	**16**	60.00 N	175.00 W
Bering Strait ⋓	**180**	65.30 N	169.00 W
Berinsfield	**42**	51.40 N	1.11 W
Berisso	**258**	34.52 S	57.53 W
Berisso □[5]	**288**	34.55 S	57.53 W
Berja	**34**	36.51 N	2.57 W
Berkåk	**26**	62.50 N	10.00 E
Berkakit	**74**	56.34 N	124.48 E
Berkane	**148**	34.59 N	2.20 W
Berkel ≃	**52**	52.09 N	6.12 E
Berkeley, Eng., U.K.	**42**	51.42 N	2.27 W
Berkeley, Ca., U.S.	**226**	37.52 N	122.16 W
Berkeley, Il., U.S.	**278**	41.53 N	87.54 W
Berkeley, Mo., U.S.	**219**	38.45 N	90.19 W
Berkeley, R.I., U.S.	**207**	41.55 N	71.25 W
Berkeley, Vale of V	**42**	51.43 N	2.25 W
Berkeley Heights	**210**	40.41 N	74.26 W
Berkeley Hills	**279b**	40.32 N	80.00 W
Berkeley Hills ⋏[2]	**282**	37.54 N	122.16 W
Berkeley Plantation ⊥	**208**	37.19 N	77.10 W
Berkeley Springs	**188**	39.37 N	78.13 W
Berkhamsted	**42**	51.46 N	0.35 W
Berkheim	**58**	48.02 N	10.04 E
Berkley, Ma., U.S.	**207**	41.50 N	71.05 W
Berkley, Mi., U.S.	**281**	42.30 N	83.11 W
Berkner Island I	**9**	79.30 S	49.30 W
Berks □[6]	**208**	40.20 N	75.50 W
Berkshire, Ma., U.S.	**207**	42.30 N	73.11 W
Berkshire, N.Y., U.S.	**210**	42.18 N	76.11 W
Berkshire □[6], Eng., U.K.	**42**	51.30 N	1.20 W
Berkshire □[6], Ma., U.S.	**207**	42.27 N	73.15 W
Berkshire Downs ⋏[1]	**42**	51.33 N	1.24 W
Berkshire Hills ⋏[2]	**207**	42.20 N	73.10 W
Berlaar	**56**	51.07 N	4.39 E
Berlaimont	**50**	50.12 N	3.49 E
Berland ≃	**182**	54.01 N	116.50 W
Berlanga de Duero	**34**	41.28 N	2.51 W
Berlenga I	**34**	39.25 N	9.30 W
Berlengas ≃	**250**	5.39 S	42.19 W
Berlevåg	**24**	70.51 N	29.06 E
Berlicum	**52**	51.42 N	5.23 E
Berlikum	**52**	53.15 N	5.39 E
Berlin, Dtsch.	**54**	52.31 N	13.24 E
Berlin, Dtsch.	**264a**	52.31 N	13.24 E
Berlin, S. Afr.	**158**	32.54 S	27.35 E
Berlin, Ct., U.S.	**207**	41.37 N	72.44 W
Berlin, Md., U.S.	**208**	38.19 N	75.13 W
Berlin, Ma., U.S.	**207**	42.22 N	71.38 W
Berlin, N.H., U.S.	**188**	44.28 N	71.11 W
Berlin, N.J., U.S.	**208**	39.47 N	74.55 W
Berlin, N.Y., U.S.	**210**	42.42 N	73.23 W
Berlin, Oh., U.S.	**214**	40.34 N	81.48 W
Berlin, Pa., U.S.	**188**	39.55 N	78.57 W
Berlin, Wi., U.S.	**190**	43.58 N	88.56 W
Berlin □[3]	**264a**	52.33 N	13.30 E
Berlin, Mount ∧	**9**	76.03 S	135.52 W
Berlin Center	**214**	41.01 N	80.57 W
Berlinchen	**54**	53.13 N	12.34 E
Berliner Brücke -•-[5]	**263**	51.27 N	6.47 E
Berlinguet Inlet c	**176**	71.10 N	85.35 W
Berlin Heights	**214**	41.20 N	82.30 W
Berlin-Ichthyosaur State Park ♦	**204**	38.51 N	117.35 W
Berlin Lake ⊜[1]	**214**	41.00 N	81.00 W
Berlin Mountain ∧	**210**	42.42 N	73.17 W
Berlin Park ♦	**285**	39.47 N	74.57 W
Berlin-Schönefeld, Flughafen ⊠	**54**	52.23 N	13.31 E
Berlinsville	**210**	40.47 N	75.35 W
Berlin-Tegel, Flughafen ⊠	**54**	52.34 N	13.18 E
Berlin-Tempelhof, Flughafen ⊠	**54**	52.29 N	13.25 E
Bermagui	**166**	36.25 S	150.04 E
Bermamyt, gora ∧	**84**	43.41 N	42.27 E
Bermejillo	**232**	25.53 N	103.37 W
Bermejito ≃	**252**	25.39 S	60.11 W
Bermejo	**252**	31.37 S	67.39 W
Bermejo ≃, Arg.	**252**	31.52 S	67.22 W
Bermejo ≃, S.A.	**252**	26.51 S	58.23 W
Bermejo, Paso del)(	**252**	32.50 S	70.05 W
Bermen, Lac ⊜	**176**	53.35 N	68.55 W
Bermeo	**34**	43.26 N	2.43 W
Bermillo de Sayago	**34**	41.22 N	6.06 W
Bermo	**124**	23.47 N	85.57 E
Bermondsey -•-[8]	**260**	51.30 N	0.04 W
Bermuda □[2], N.A.	**230**	32.20 N	64.45 W
Bermuda □[2], N.A.	**240a**	32.20 N	64.45 W
Bermuda Rise ⊹[3]	**16**	32.30 N	65.00 W
Bermudes → Bermuda □[2]	**240a**	32.20 N	64.45 W
Bermudian Creek ≃	**208**	40.01 N	76.55 W
Bern (Berne)	**58**	46.57 N	7.26 E
Bern (Berne) □[3]	**58**	46.55 N	7.35 E
Bern, Flughafen ⊠	**58**	46.55 N	7.30 E
Berna → Bern	**58**	46.57 N	7.26 E
Bernabéu, Estadio ♦	**266a**	40.27 N	3.41 W
Bernal -•-[8]	**258**	34.42 S	58.17 W
Bernalda	**68**	40.24 N	16.41 E
Bernalillo	**200**	35.18 N	106.33 W
Bernam ≃	**114**	3.48 N	100.57 E
Bernardo O'Higgins, Parque ♦	**286e**	33.28 S	70.40 W
Bernardston	**207**	42.40 N	72.33 W
Bernardsville	**210**	40.43 N	74.34 W
Bernasconi	**252**	37.54 S	63.43 W
Bernate	**266b**	45.29 N	8.49 E
Bernau am Chiemsee	**64**	47.48 N	12.22 E
Bernau bei Berlin	**54**	52.40 N	13.35 E
Bernauer Heide -•-[3]	**264a**	52.43 N	13.30 E
Bernaville	**50**	50.08 N	2.10 E
Bernay	**50**	49.06 N	0.36 E
Bernbeuren	**58**	47.44 N	10.46 E
Bernburg	**54**	51.48 N	11.44 E
Berndorf	**61**	47.57 N	16.08 E
Berne, Dtsch.	**52**	53.11 N	8.29 E
Berne → Bern, Schw.	**58**	46.57 N	7.26 E
Berne, In., U.S.	**216**	40.39 N	84.57 W
Berne, N.Y., U.S.	**210**	42.38 N	74.08 W
Berneburg	**56**	51.04 N	9.53 E
Berner Alpen ⋏	**58**	46.30 N	7.30 E
Berneray I, Scot., U.K.	**46**	57.43 N	7.12 W
Berneray I, Scot., U.K.	**46**	56.47 N	7.38 W
Berneval-le-Grand	**50**	49.57 N	1.12 E
Berngardovka	**265a**	60.01 N	30.36 E
Bernhardina	**158**	27.53 S	28.40 E
Bernhards Bay	**210**	43.15 N	75.56 W
Bernhardsthal	**61**	48.41 N	16.52 E
Bernice	**194**	32.49 N	92.39 W
Bernie	**194**	36.40 N	89.58 W
Bernier Bay c	**176**	71.00 N	87.30 W
Bernier Island I	**162**	24.52 S	113.08 E
Bernina ⋏	**58**	46.22 N	9.50 E
Bernina, Passo del)(	**58**	46.24 N	10.03 E
Bernina, Piz ∧	**58**	46.21 N	9.51 E
Bernisdale	**46**	57.27 N	6.24 W
Bernkastel-Kues	**56**	49.55 N	7.04 E
Bernried	**64**	47.52 N	11.17 E
Bernsbach	**54**	50.34 N	12.46 E
Bernsdorf	**54**	51.22 N	14.04 E
Bernsfelden	**56**	49.34 N	9.53 E
Bernstadt	**54**	51.03 N	14.50 E
Bernville	**208**	40.26 N	76.07 W
Bero ≃	**152**	15.10 S	12.09 E
Beroga	**114**	2.56 N	101.55 E
Berolzheim	**56**	49.28 N	9.32 E
Beromünster	**58**	47.12 N	8.11 E
Berón de Astrada	**252**	27.33 S	57.32 W
Beror Ḥayil	**132**	31.33 N	34.38 E
Beroroha	**157b**	21.41 S	45.10 E
Ber'ostovica	**76**	53.07 N	23.58 E
Beroun	**30**	49.58 N	14.04 E
Berounka ≃	**30**	50.00 N	14.24 E
Berovo	**38**	41.42 N	22.51 E
Berowra	**170**	33.37 S	151.09 E
Ber'oza	**76**	52.32 N	24.59 E
Ber'ožnoje	**76**	59.55 N	39.17 E
Ber'ozovaja ≃	**80**	48.31 N	41.03 E
Ber'ozovka, Bela.	**76**	53.43 N	25.30 E
Ber'ozovka, Kaz.	**80**	51.11 N	53.16 E
Ber'ozovka, Ross.	**24**	65.00 N	56.26 E
Ber'ozovka, Ross.	**76**	53.26 N	38.53 E
Ber'ozovka, Ross.	**80**	52.06 N	45.07 E
Ber'ozovka, Ross.	**86**	51.51 N	82.58 E
Ber'ozovka, Ross.	**86**	56.03 N	93.07 E
Ber'ozovka, Ross.	**86**	54.02 N	76.35 E
Ber'ozovka, Ross.	**86**	59.24 N	82.38 E
Ber'ozovka, Ross.	**86**	59.35 N	56.02 E
Ber'ozovka, Ross.	**86**	57.37 N	57.18 E
Ber'ozovka, Ross.	**88**	57.46 N	116.09 E
Ber'ozovka, Ross.	**89**	50.35 N	127.52 E
Ber'ozovka, Ross.	**265a**	59.56 N	30.49 E
Ber'ozovo, Ross.	**74**	63.56 N	65.02 E
Ber'ozovo, Ross.	**80**	51.56 N	48.28 E
Ber'ozovo, Ross.	**82**	54.03 N	36.24 E
Ber'ozovo, Ross.	**82**	54.19 N	38.17 E
Ber'ozovskaja	**80**	50.16 N	43.59 E
Ber'ozovskij	**86**	55.39 N	86.16 E
Ber'ozovskij R'adok	**76**	58.06 N	34.29 E
Ber'ozovskoje	**86**	55.50 N	89.36 E
Berra	**64**	44.59 N	11.58 E
Berras, Arroyo los ≃	**288**	34.34 S	58.40 W
Berre ≃	**62**	44.24 N	4.40 E
Berre, Étang de c	**62**	43.27 N	5.08 E
Berrechid	**148**	33.17 N	7.35 W
Berre-des-Alpes	**62**	43.50 N	7.19 E
Berre-l'Étang	**62**	43.28 N	5.11 E
Ber Remad, Oued V	**148**	31.45 N	1.10 E
Berri	**166**	34.17 S	140.36 E
Berridale	**171b**	36.22 S	148.50 E
Berriedale	**46**	58.11 N	3.29 W
Berrien □[6]	**216**	41.59 N	86.30 W
Berrien Springs	**216**	41.56 N	86.20 W
Berrigan	**166**	35.40 S	145.49 E
Berrima	**170**	34.30 S	150.20 E
Berriozábal	**234**	16.48 N	93.16 W
Berriyyane	**148**	32.50 N	3.46 E
Berrouaghia	**34**	36.08 N	2.55 E
Berrugosa Point ›	**116**	10.23 N	125.33 E
Berry, Austl.	**170**	34.47 S	150.42 E
Berry, Al., U.S.	**194**	33.39 N	87.36 W
Berry, Ky., U.S.	**218**	38.31 N	84.23 W
Berry □[9]	**50**	47.20 N	2.10 E
Berry, Canal du ≊	**50**	47.17 N	1.25 E
Berry-au-Bac	**50**	49.24 N	3.54 E
Berry Creek ≃, Ab., Can.	**182**	50.50 N	111.36 W
Berry Creek ≃, Tx., U.S.	**222**	30.40 N	97.36 W
Berryessa, Lake ⊜[1]	**226**	38.35 N	122.14 W
Berryessa Creek ≃	**282**	37.24 N	121.53 W
Berryessa Peak ∧	**226**	38.40 N	122.11 W
Berry Islands II	**238**	25.34 N	77.45 W
Berry Mountain ∧	**208**	40.31 N	77.02 W
Berrysburg	**208**	40.36 N	76.49 W
Berrys Creek ≃	**276**	40.47 N	74.05 W
Berryville	**194**	36.21 N	93.34 W
Berseba	**156**	26.00 S	17.46 E
Bersenbrück	**52**	52.33 N	7.56 E
Bershad'	**78**	48.23 N	29.30 E
Bersut	**80**	55.32 N	50.54 E
Berta ≃	**130**	41.09 N	41.53 E
Bertam	**114**	5.09 N	102.03 E
Berté, Lac ⊜	**186**	50.48 N	68.30 W
Bertha	**198**	46.16 N	95.03 W
Berthåga	**40**	59.52 N	17.35 E
Berthelsdorf	**54**	51.05 N	14.13 E
Berthier □[6]	**206**	46.30 N	73.45 W
Berthierville	**206**	46.05 N	73.10 W
Berthold	**198**	48.18 N	101.44 W
Berthoud	**200**	40.18 N	105.04 W
Berthoud Pass)(	**200**	39.45 N	105.45 W
Bertincourt	**50**	50.05 N	2.59 E
Bertinoro	**66**	44.09 N	12.08 E
Bertioga	**256**	23.51 S	46.09 W
Bertioga, Enseada da c	**256**	23.50 S	46.08 W
Bertkow	**54**	52.43 N	11.54 E
Bertlich	**263**	51.37 N	7.04 E
Bertogne	**56**	50.05 N	5.40 E
Bertolínia	**250**	7.38 S	43.57 W
Bertoua	**152**	4.35 N	13.41 E
Bertram	**196**	30.45 N	98.03 W
Bertrand, Mi., U.S.	**216**	41.46 N	86.15 W
Bertrand, Ne., U.S.	**198**	40.31 N	99.38 W
Bertrix	**56**	49.51 N	5.15 E
Bertry	**50**	50.05 N	3.27 E
Beru I	**14**	1.20 S	176.00 E
Beruas	**114**	4.30 N	100.47 E
Beruri	**246**	3.54 S	61.22 W
Berville	**214**	42.55 N	82.53 W
Berville-sur-Mer	**50**	49.26 N	0.22 E
Berwang	**58**	47.24 N	10.45 E
Berwick, Austl.	**169**	38.02 S	145.21 E
Berwick, N.S., Can.	**186**	45.03 N	64.44 W
Berwick, La., U.S.	**194**	29.41 N	91.13 W
Berwick, Me., U.S.	**188**	43.15 N	70.51 W
Berwick, Pa., U.S.	**210**	41.03 N	76.14 W
Berwick-upon-Tweed	**44**	55.46 N	2.00 W
Berwyn, Il., U.S.	**216**	41.51 N	87.47 W
Berwyn, Pa., U.S.	**208**	40.02 N	75.26 W
Berwyn ⋏	**42**	52.53 N	3.24 W
Berwyn Heights	**284c**	38.59 N	76.54 W
Beryslav	**78**	46.51 N	33.26 E
Bērze ≃	**76**	56.41 N	23.37 E
Berzé-la-Ville	**58**	46.22 N	4.42 E
Berz-Macomb Airport ⊠	**281**	42.40 N	82.58 W
Bès ≃	**62**	44.08 N	6.14 E
Besalampy	**157b**	16.45 S	44.30 E
Besana in Brianza	**62**	45.42 N	9.17 E
Besançon	**58**	47.15 N	6.02 E
Besani	**124**	24.08 N	80.17 E
Besar, Gunong ∧, Malay.	**114**	5.10 N	101.18 E
Besar, Gunong ∧, Malay.	**114**	2.30 N	103.10 E
Besar, Gunung ∧	**112**	2.43 S	115.37 E
Besar, Pulau I	**115b**	8.28 S	122.22 E
Besar Hantu, Gunong ∧	**114**	3.12 N	102.02 E
Besaya ≃	**34**	43.21 N	4.04 W
Besbes	**36**	36.42 N	7.51 E
Besed' ≃	**76**	52.38 N	31.09 E
Besedino	**78**	51.42 N	36.28 E
Besedy	**265b**	55.37 N	37.47 E
Besenfeld	**56**	48.35 N	8.25 E
Bešenkoviči	**76**	55.03 N	29.27 E
Beserah	**114**	3.52 N	103.22 E
Besigheim	**56**	49.00 N	9.08 E
Besikama	**112**	9.36 S	124.57 E
Beşiktaş -•-[8]	**267b**	41.03 N	29.01 E
Beşiri	**130**	37.55 N	41.18 E
Besitang	**114**	4.02 N	98.12 E
Beškent	**128**	38.49 N	65.39 E
Beskid Mountains ⋏	**30**	49.40 N	20.00 E
Beşkonak	**130**	37.08 N	31.12 E
Beskra	**148**	34.51 N	5.44 E
Beskra □[5]	**148**	34.00 N	6.00 E
Beškube	**85**	39.50 N	68.18 E
Beskudnikovo -•-[8]	**265b**	55.52 N	37.34 E
Beslan	**84**	43.12 N	44.33 E
Beslenej	**84**	44.14 N	41.44 E
Besnard Lake ⊜	**184**	55.24 N	106.05 W
Besni	**130**	37.41 N	37.52 E
Besor, Naḥal V	**132**	31.28 N	34.22 E
Besós ≃	**266d**	41.25 N	2.04 E
Besozzo	**62**	45.51 N	8.39 E
Besp'atovo	**82**	54.45 N	38.54 E
Beşpınar, Tür.	**130**	41.09 N	35.14 E
Beşpınar, Tür.	**130**	37.51 N	41.36 E
Besputa ≃	**82**	54.50 N	37.58 E
Bessacarr	**44**	53.30 N	1.04 W
Bessancourt	**261**	49.02 N	2.13 E
Bessans	**62**	45.19 N	7.00 E
Bessarabia □[9]	**38**	47.00 N	28.30 E
Bessarabka	**86**	53.37 N	73.17 E
Bessaz, gora ∧	**85**	43.49 N	68.40 E
Bessbrook	**48**	54.12 N	6.25 W
Besse, Dtsch.	**56**	51.13 N	9.23 E
Besse, Nig.	**150**	11.15 N	4.30 E
Bessèges	**62**	44.17 N	4.06 E
Bessemer, Al., U.S.	**194**	33.24 N	86.57 W
Bessemer, Mi., U.S.	**190**	46.28 N	90.03 W
Bessemer, Pa., U.S.	**214**	40.58 N	80.29 W
Bessemer City	**192**	35.17 N	81.17 W
Besser	**41**	55.52 N	10.39 E
Bessé-sur-Braye	**50**	47.50 N	0.45 E
Bessheim	**26**	61.31 N	8.51 E
Besshiyama	**96**	33.50 N	133.23 E
Bessho	**270**	34.27 N	135.31 E
Bessonovka	**80**	53.18 N	45.03 E
Best	**52**	51.31 N	5.24 E
Best'ach	**74**	61.52 N	129.55 E
Bestamak, Kaz.	**86**	49.43 N	55.07 E
Bestamak, Kaz.	**86**	49.13 N	78.21 E
Beštau, gora ∧	**84**	44.06 N	43.01 E
Besten	**263**	51.39 N	6.54 E
Bestensee	**54**	52.15 N	13.37 E
Bestfield	**285**	39.43 N	75.36 W
Bestobe	**86**	52.30 N	73.05 E
Beštor, gora ∧	**85**	42.03 N	70.50 E
Bestuževo	**24**	61.37 N	43.58 E
Bestwig	**52**	51.22 N	8.24 E
Besuki	**115a**	7.45 S	113.41 E
Besut ≃	**114**	5.48 N	102.35 E
Beswick Aboriginal Reserve -•-[4]	**164**	14.30 S	133.10 E
Betā	**272b**	22.55 N	88.14 E
Betafo	**157b**	19.50 S	46.51 E
Betāgi	**126**	22.25 N	90.11 E
Bet Alfa	**132**	32.31 N	35.26 E
Beta Main Canal ≊	**226**	36.34 N	120.11 W
Betamba	**152**	2.13 S	21.23 E
Betang Melaka	**114**	2.28 N	102.25 E
Betano	**112**	9.10 S	125.43 E
Betanzos, Bol.	**248**	19.34 S	65.27 W
Betanzos, Esp.	**34**	43.17 N	8.12 W
Betanzos, Ría de c[1]	**34**	43.23 N	8.15 W
Betaré Oya	**152**	5.36 N	14.05 E
Betarsjön ⊜	**26**	63.44 N	16.52 E
Bet Bet Creek ≃	**169**	36.52 S	143.52 E
Betbetti	**140**	15.06 N	24.12 E
Betchworth	**260**	51.14 N	0.16 W
Bet Dagan	**132**	32.00 N	34.50 E
Bete Hor	**144**	11.37 N	39.02 E
Betém	**256**	22.52 S	44.17 W
Bétera	**34**	39.35 N	0.27 W
Bétérou	**150**	9.12 N	2.16 E
Bet Guvrin	**132**	31.36 N	34.54 E
Bet Ha'arava	**132**	31.48 N	35.32 E
Bethal	**158**	26.27 S	29.28 E
Bethalto	**219**	38.54 N	90.02 W
Bethanien	**156**	26.32 S	17.11 E
Bethanien □[5]	**156**	26.30 S	17.00 E
Bethany, Ct., U.S.	**207**	41.25 N	72.59 W
Bethany, Il., U.S.	**219**	39.38 N	88.44 W
Bethany, Mo., U.S.	**194**	40.16 N	94.01 W
Bethany, N.Y., U.S.	**210**	42.55 N	78.08 W
Bethany, Ok., U.S.	**196**	35.31 N	97.37 W
Bethany, Pa., U.S.	**210**	41.37 N	75.21 W
Bethany, W.V., U.S.	**214**	40.12 N	80.33 W
Bethany Reservoir ⊜[1]	**226**	37.47 N	121.37 W
Bet HaShitta	**132**	32.33 N	35.26 E
Bethel, Ak., U.S.	**180**	60.48 N	161.46 W
Bethel, Ct., U.S.	**207**	41.22 N	73.24 W
Bethel, De., U.S.	**208**	38.27 N	75.21 W
Bethel, Ky., U.S.	**218**	38.14 N	83.52 W
Bethel, Me., U.S.	**188**	44.24 N	70.47 W
Bethel, Mo., U.S.	**219**	39.52 N	92.01 W
Bethel, N.Y., U.S.	**210**	41.41 N	74.52 W
Bethel, N.C., U.S.	**192**	35.48 N	77.22 W
Bethel, Oh., U.S.	**218**	38.57 N	84.04 W
Bethel, Pa., U.S.	**208**	40.28 N	76.18 W
Bethel, Wa., U.S.	**224**	47.32 N	122.38 W
Bethel Acres	**196**	35.19 N	97.00 W
Bethel Island	**226**	38.01 N	121.39 W
Bethel Manor	**208**	37.06 N	76.25 W
Bethel Park	**214**	40.18 N	80.02 W
Bethelsdorp	**158**	33.52 S	25.34 E
Bethel Springs	**194**	35.14 N	88.36 W
Béthencourt-sur-Mer	**50**	50.05 N	1.30 E
Bethersden	**42**	51.08 N	0.48 E
Bethesda, Wales, U.K.	**44**	53.11 N	4.03 W
Bethesda, Md., U.S.	**208**	38.58 N	77.06 W
Bethesda, Oh., U.S.	**188**	40.00 N	81.04 W
Bethesdaweg	**158**	31.55 S	24.45 E
Bethford	**284a**	42.48 N	78.48 W
Bethgate	**284b**	39.18 N	76.51 W
Béthisy-Saint-Pierre	**50**	49.18 N	2.49 E
Bethlehem, S. Afr.	**158**	28.15 S	28.15 E
Bethlehem, S. Afr.	**158**	27.10 S	24.00 E
Bethlehem, Ct., U.S.	**207**	41.38 N	73.12 W
Bethlehem, In., U.S.	**218**	38.32 N	85.25 W
Bethlehem, Ky., U.S.	**218**	38.24 N	85.04 W
Bethlehem, Pa., U.S.	**210**	40.37 N	75.22 W
Bethlehem, W.V., U.S.	**188**	40.02 N	80.41 W
Bethlehem → Bayt Laḥm, W.B.	**132**	31.43 N	35.12 E
Bethlehem Center	**210**	42.40 N	73.42 W
Bethlehem Steel Corporation ʊ[3], Md., U.S.	**284b**	39.13 N	76.29 W
Bethlehem Steel Corporation (Lackawanna Plant) ʊ[3], N.Y., U.S.	**284a**	42.49 N	78.52 W
Bethnal Green -•-[8]	**260**	51.32 N	0.03 W
Bethoncourt	**58**	47.32 N	6.48 E
Bethpage	**210**	40.44 N	73.28 W
Bethpage State Park ♦	**210**	40.45 N	73.27 W
Bethulie	**158**	30.32 S	25.59 E
Bethune, Sk., Can.	**184**	50.43 N	105.08 W
Béthune, Fr.	**50**	50.32 N	2.38 E
Bethune, S.C., U.S.	**192**	34.24 N	80.20 W
Béthune ≃	**50**	49.53 N	1.09 E
Beticos, Sistemas ⋏	**34**	37.00 N	4.00 W
Betijoque	**246**	9.23 N	70.44 W
Betil	**126**	24.14 N	89.43 E
Betio	**174t**	1.21 N	172.56 E
Betioky	**157b**	23.42 S	44.22 E
Betis ≃	**114**	4.53 N	101.48 E
Betlica	**76**	54.01 N	33.57 E
Betna ≃	**126**	22.34 N	89.12 E
Bet Netofa, Biq'at ≚	**132**	32.49 N	35.19 E
Betnoti	**126**	21.44 N	86.51 E
Beton-Bazoches	**50**	48.42 N	3.15 E
Betong, Malay.	**112**	1.24 N	111.31 E
Betong, Thai	**110**	5.45 N	101.05 E
Betoota	**166**	25.42 S	140.44 E
Bétou	**152**	3.03 N	18.31 E
Betpak-Dala -•-[2]	**86**	46.00 N	70.00 E
Betroka	**157b**	23.16 S	46.06 E
Betsham	**260**	51.25 N	0.19 E
Bet Sh'ean	**132**	32.30 N	35.30 E
Bet She'arim, Ḥorbat ⊥	**132**	32.42 N	35.08 E
Bet Shemesh	**132**	31.45 N	35.00 E
Betsiamites	**186**	48.56 N	68.38 W
Betsiamites ≃	**186**	48.56 N	68.38 W
Betsiamites, Barrage -•-[6]	**186**	49.22 N	69.47 W
Betsiamites, Pointe de ›	**186**	48.55 N	68.37 W
Betsiamites, Réserve indienne de -•-[4]	**186**	49.05 N	68.37 W
Betsiboka ≃	**157b**	16.03 S	46.36 E
Betsie, Point ›	**190**	44.42 N	86.16 W
Betsioky	**157b**	21.31 S	44.28 E
Betsukai	**92a**	43.23 N	145.17 E
Betsy Layne	**192**	37.33 N	82.38 W
Betsy Ross Bridge -•-[5]	**285**	39.59 N	75.04 W
Bette ∧	**146**	22.00 N	19.12 E
Bettembourg	**56**	49.32 N	6.02 E
Bettendorf	**190**	41.31 N	90.30 W
Betterton	**208**	39.21 N	76.03 W
Bettiah	**124**	26.48 N	84.30 E
Bettie	**222**	32.48 N	94.58 W
Bettles Field	**180**	66.55 N	151.30 W
Bettola	**62**	44.47 N	9.36 E
Bettona	**66**	43.01 N	12.29 E

Symbols in the index entries represent the broad categories identified in the key at the right. Symbols with superior numbers (⋏[1]) identify subcategories (see complete key on page *I · 1*).

Symbole im Register stellen die rechts im Schlüssel erklärten Kategorien dar. Symbole mit hochgestellten Ziffern (⋏[1]) bezeichnen Unterabteilungen einer Kategorie (vgl. vollständiger Schlüssel auf Seite *I · 1*).

Los símbolos incluídos en el texto del índice representan las grandes categorías identificadas con la clave a la derecha. Los símbolos con numeros en su parte superior (⋏[1]) identifican las subcategorías (véase la clave completa en la página *I · 1*).

Les symboles de l'index représentent les catégories indiquées dans la légende à droite. Les symboles suivis d'un indice (⋏[1]) représentent des sous-catégories (voir légende complète à la page *I · 1*).

Os símbolos incluídos no texto do índice representam as grandes categorias identificadas com a chave à direita. Os símbolos com números em sua parte superior (⋏[1]) identificam as subcategorias (veja-se a chave completa à página *I · 1*).

∧ Mountain	Berg	Montaña	Montagne	Montanha
⋏ Mountains	Gebirge	Montañas	Montagnes	Montanhas
)(Pass	Paß	Paso	Col	Passo
V Valley, Canyon	Tal, Cañon	Valle, Cañón	Vallée, Canyon	Vale, Canhão
≚ Plain	Ebene	Llano	Plaine	Planície
› Cape	Kap	Cabo	Cap	Cabo
I Island	Insel	Isla	Île	Ilha
II Islands	Inseln	Islas	Îles	Ilhas
± Other Topographic Features	Andere Topographische Objekte	Otros Elementos Topográficos	Autres données topographiques	Outros acidentes topográficos

ESPAÑOL

Nombre	Página	Lat. °′	Long. °′ W = Oeste
Bettrath ◆[8]	263	51.13 N	6.26 E
Bettsville	214	41.14 N	83.14 W
Bettyhill	46	58.32 N	4.14 W
Betty's Bay	158	34.22 S	18.52 E
Betūl	124	21.55 N	77.54 E
Betumbe-Bongo	152	2.11 S	18.46 E
Betung, Indon.	112	1.52 S	103.16 E
Betung, Indon.	112	2.50 S	104.14 E
Betuwe ◆[1]	52	51.55 N	5.30 E
Betwa ≃	124	25.55 N	80.12 E
Betws-y-Coed	44	53.05 N	3.48 W
Betz	50	49.09 N	2.57 E
Betz ≃	50	48.09 N	2.45 E
Betzdorf	56	50.47 N	7.53 E
Betzenstein	60	49.41 N	11.25 E
Béu	152	6.14 S	15.28 E
Beucha	54	51.19 N	12.34 E
Beugneux	50	49.14 N	3.25 E
Beuil	62	44.06 N	6.59 E
Beulah, Austl.	166	35.56 S	142.26 E
Beulah, Co., U.S.	200	38.04 N	104.59 W
Beulah, Mi., U.S.	190	44.37 N	86.05 W
Beulah, Ms., U.S.	194	33.47 N	90.58 W
Beulah, N.D., U.S.	198	47.15 N	101.46 W
Beulah, Lake ⊜	216	42.49 N	88.23 W
Beulah Beach	214	41.25 N	82.22 W
Beulah Reservoir ⊜[1]	202	43.56 N	118.09 W
Beulaville	192	34.55 N	77.46 W
Beult ≃	42	51.14 N	0.25 E
Beure	58	47.12 N	6.00 E
Beureunun	114	5.18 N	95.59 E
Beuron	58	48.03 N	8.58 E
Beuthen → Bytom	30	50.22 N	18.54 E
Beuvron ≃, Fr.	50	47.28 N	3.31 E
Beuvron ≃, Fr.	50	47.29 N	1.15 E
Beuvronne ≃	261	48.56 N	2.44 E
Beuvry	50	50.31 N	2.41 E
Beuzeville	50	49.20 N	0.21 E
Bevagna	66	42.56 N	12.36 E
Bevensen	52	53.05 N	10.34 E
Bever ≃	52	52.01 N	7.46 E
Bevera ≃	62	43.49 N	7.34 E
Beveren	50	51.13 N	4.15 E
B. Everett Jordan Lake ⊜[1]	192	35.45 N	79.00 W
Beverino	62	44.14 N	9.47 E
Beverley, Austl.	168a	32.06 S	116.56 E
Beverley, Eng., U.K.	44	53.52 N	0.26 W
Beverley Minster ʋ[1]	44	53.50 N	0.27 W
Beverley Springs	162	16.43 S	125.28 E
Beverlo	56	51.05 N	5.12 E
Beverly, Ma., U.S.	207	42.33 N	70.52 W
Beverly, N.J., U.S.	208	40.03 N	74.55 W
Beverly, Tx., U.S.	222	31.30 N	97.10 W
Beverly ◆[8]	278	41.43 N	87.41 W
Beverly Farms, Md., U.S.	284c	39.04 N	77.11 W
Beverly Farms, Ma., U.S.	283	42.34 N	70.49 W
Beverly Harbor c	283	42.32 N	70.53 W
Beverly Hills, Austl.	274a	33.57 S	151.05 E
Beverly Hills, Ca., U.S.	228	34.04 N	118.23 W
Beverly Hills, Fl., U.S.	220	28.56 N	82.28 W
Beverly Hills, Mi., U.S.	216	42.31 N	83.13 W
Beverly Lake ⊜	176	64.36 N	100.30 W
Beverly Municipal Airport ⊠	283	42.35 N	70.55 W
Beverly Run ≃	208	37.55 N	77.11 W
Beverly Shores	216	41.41 N	86.58 W
Bevern	52	51.51 N	9.29 E
Beverstausee ⊜[1]	263	51.09 N	7.23 E
Beverstedt	52	53.26 N	8.49 E
Beverungen	52	51.39 N	9.22 E
Beverwijk	52	52.28 N	4.40 E
Bevier	194	39.45 N	92.34 W
Bevin, Lac ⊜	206	45.57 N	74.35 W
Bevoalavo	157b	25.13 S	45.26 E
Bewani	164	3.02 S	141.10 E
Bewani Mountains ⋏	164	3.10 S	141.25 E
Bewār	124	27.13 N	79.18 E
Bewdley, On., Can.	212	44.05 N	78.19 W
Bewdley, Eng., U.K.	42	52.22 N	2.19 W
Bewl Water ⊜[1]	42	51.04 N	0.24 E
Bex	58	46.15 N	7.01 E
Bexhill	42	50.50 N	0.29 E
Bexley, Austl.	274a	33.57 S	151.08 E
Bexley, Oh., U.S.	218	39.58 N	82.56 W
Bexley ◆[8]	42	51.26 N	0.10 E
Beyazköy	130	41.21 N	27.42 E
Beybach ≃	56	50.13 N	7.23 E
Beyçayırı	130	40.15 N	26.55 E
Beycuma	130	41.19 N	31.59 E
Bey Dağları ⋏	130	36.40 N	30.15 E
Beydagları Olimpos Milli Parkı ♦	130	36.40 N	30.25 E
Beydili	130	40.10 N	31.01 E
Beyenburg ◆[8]	263	51.15 N	7.18 E
Beykoz ◆[8]	267b	41.08 N	29.05 E
Beyla	150	8.41 N	8.37 W
Beyläqan	84	39.47 N	47.37 E
Beylerbeyi ◆[8]	267b	41.03 N	29.03 E
Beylikahır	130	39.42 N	31.13 E
Beylul	144	13.10 N	42.26 E
Beynes	261	48.51 N	1.53 E
Beynes-Thiverval, Aérodrome de ⊠	261	48.51 N	1.54 E
Beyoğlu ◆[8]	267b	41.02 N	28.59 E
Beypazarı	130	40.10 N	31.56 E
Beypınarı	130	39.31 N	37.44 E
Beypore	122	11.11 N	75.49 E
Beyra	144	6.57 N	47.19 E
Beyrouth → Bayrūt	130	33.53 N	35.30 E
Beyşehir	130	37.41 N	31.43 E
Beyşehir Gölü ⊜	130	37.40 N	31.30 E
Beytüşşebap	128	37.34 N	43.10 E
Bezaha	157b	23.30 S	44.31 E
Bežanickaja vozvyšennost' ⋏[1]	76	56.54 N	29.20 E
Bežanicy	76	56.58 N	29.53 E
Bezau	58	47.23 N	9.54 E
Bezavona ∧	157b	15.02 S	49.52 E
Bezdež	76	52.19 N	25.18 E
Bezděz ∧	54	50.32 N	14.43 E
Bezděz ⊥	54	50.32 N	14.46 E
Bèze	58	47.28 N	5.16 E
Bežeck	76	57.47 N	36.39 E
Bežeckij Verch ⋏[1]	76	57.36 N	36.54 E
Bezenčuk	80	52.59 N	49.26 E
Bezerra ≃	255	13.16 S	47.31 W
Bezerros	250	8.14 S	35.45 W
Beẓet	132	33.05 N	35.08 E
Béziers	32	43.21 N	3.15 E
Bezimenne	83	47.06 N	37.56 E
Bezmein	128	38.05 N	58.12 E
Bezmenšur	80	56.29 N	51.17 E
Bezno	54	50.22 N	14.48 E
Bezons	261	48.56 N	2.13 E
Bežta	84	42.08 N	46.08 E
Bezwada → Vijayawāda	122	16.31 N	80.37 E
Bezym'anka	80	49.56 N	43.15 E
Bezym'annaja	80	51.20 N	46.26 E
Bezzecca	64	45.55 N	10.43 E
Bezzubovo	82	55.27 N	38.55 E
Bhabānipur, India	272b	22.57 N	88.27 E
Bhabānipur, India	272b	22.56 N	88.13 E
Bhabhua	124	25.03 N	83.37 E
Bhābta	126	23.59 N	88.15 E
Bhadarwāh	123	32.59 N	75.43 E
Bhadaur	123	30.29 N	75.19 E
Bhādgāon → Bhaktapur	124	27.42 N	85.27 E
Bhadohi	124	25.25 N	82.34 E
Bhādra	123	29.07 N	75.10 E
Bhadra ≃[1]	126	22.19 N	89.31 E
Bhadrāchalam	122	17.40 N	80.53 E
Bhadrak	120	21.03 N	86.30 E
Bhadrapur	124	26.32 N	88.06 E
Bhadra Reservoir ⊜[1]	122	13.40 N	75.35 E

FRANÇAIS

Nom	Page	Lat. °′	Long. °′ W = Ouest
Bhadrāvati	122	13.52 N	75.43 E
Bhadreswar	126	22.50 N	88.21 E
Bhādua	272b	22.41 N	88.12 E
Bhāg	120	29.02 N	67.49 E
Bhagaiya	124	25.12 N	87.29 E
Bhāgalpur	124	25.15 N	87.00 E
Bhāgīrathi ≃, India	124	30.08 N	78.35 E
Bhāgīrathi ≃, India	126	23.25 N	88.23 E
Bhagirathpur	126	24.05 N	88.29 E
Bhagwānpur	126	22.07 N	87.45 E
Bhainsa	122	19.06 N	77.58 E
Bhāi Pheru	123	31.12 N	73.57 E
Bhairab ≃[1]	126	22.51 N	89.34 E
Bhairab Bāzār	120	24.04 N	90.58 E
Bhairhawā	124	27.31 N	83.24 E
Bhaironghāti	120	31.01 N	78.53 E
Bhakkar	123	31.38 N	71.04 E
Bhākra Dam ◆[6]	123	31.24 N	76.30 E
Bhaktapur	124	27.42 N	85.27 E
Bhal	272c	19.11 N	73.08 E
Bhālki	122	18.02 N	77.13 E
Bhalswa ◆[8]	272a	28.44 N	77.10 E
Bhalwāl	123	32.16 N	72.54 E
Bhamdūn	132	33.48 N	35.39 E
Bhamo	110	24.16 N	97.14 E
Bhandāra	120	21.10 N	79.39 E
Bhandārdaha	272b	22.37 N	88.13 E
Bhandāria	126	22.29 N	90.04 E
Bhānder	124	25.44 N	78.45 E
Bhander Plateau ⋏[1]	124	24.10 N	80.20 E
Bhāndup ◆[8]	272c	19.09 N	72.57 E
Bhānga	126	23.22 N	89.59 E
Bhāngar	126	22.31 N	88.37 E
Bhāngar Kāta Khāl ≃	272b	22.31 N	88.33 E
Bhanvad	120	21.56 N	69.47 E
Bhārat → India □[1]	118	20.00 N	77.00 E
Bharatpur, India	124	27.13 N	77.29 E
Bharatpur, India	126	23.53 N	88.05 E
Bharatpur, Nepāl	124	27.14 N	84.21 E
Bharthana	124	26.45 N	79.14 E
Bharūch	120	21.42 N	72.58 E
Bhātai	126	23.36 N	89.11 E
Bhātāpāra	120	21.44 N	81.56 E
Bhātār	126	23.25 N	87.54 E
Bhatgaon → Bhaktapur	124	27.42 N	85.27 E
Bhātghar Lake ⊜[1]	122	18.12 N	73.49 E
Bhātiāpāra Ghāt	124	23.13 N	89.42 E
Bhatkal	122	13.58 N	74.34 E
Bhātpāra	126	22.52 N	88.24 E
Bhātpur	272b	22.43 N	88.25 E
Bhātsāla	126	22.33 N	90.30 E
Bhattapratāp	126	22.45 N	89.48 E
Bhattiprolu	122	16.06 N	80.47 E
Bhātua	272b	22.57 N	88.22 E
Bhaun	123	32.52 N	72.45 E
Bhaunja	272a	28.40 N	77.25 E
Bhavāni	122	11.27 N	77.41 E
Bhāvnagar	122	21.46 N	72.09 E
Bhawānīgarh	124	30.16 N	76.02 E
Bhawani Mandi	120	24.25 N	75.50 E
Bhawānipatna	122	19.54 N	83.10 E
Bhedia	126	23.36 N	87.42 E
Bheigeir, Beinn ∧[2]	46	55.44 N	6.05 W
Bhendkhal	272c	18.53 N	72.59 E
Bhera	123	32.29 N	72.55 E
Bheramara	126	24.02 N	88.58 E
Bherī □[8]	124	28.30 N	81.45 E
Bherī ≃	124	28.44 N	81.16 E
Bheula, Beinn ∧	46	56.08 N	4.58 W
Bhīkampur	272a	28.45 N	77.27 E
Bhīkangaon	120	21.52 N	75.57 E
Bhilai	120	21.13 N	81.26 E
Bhilainagar → Bhilai	120	21.13 N	81.26 E
Bhīlwāra	120	25.21 N	74.38 E
Bhīma ≃	122	16.24 N	77.18 E
Bhīmavaram	122	16.32 N	81.32 E
Bhimbar	123	32.59 N	74.04 E
Bhīmphedī	124	27.32 N	85.07 E
Bhīmpur, India	126	22.37 N	87.08 E
Bhimpur, India	272b	22.46 N	88.08 E
Bhind	124	26.34 N	78.48 E
Bhinga	124	27.43 N	81.56 E
Bhīnmāl	120	25.00 N	72.15 E
Bhiwandi	122	19.18 N	73.04 E
Bhiwāni	124	28.47 N	76.08 E
Bhoāgāchi	272b	22.57 N	88.20 E
Bhojpur	124	27.10 N	87.03 E
Bhojudih	126	23.38 N	86.27 E
Bhokardan	122	20.16 N	75.46 E
Bhola	124	22.41 N	90.39 E
Bhola ≃[1]	126	22.04 N	89.49 E
Bhongaon	124	27.15 N	79.11 E
Bhongīr	122	17.31 N	78.53 E
Bhonrāsa	124	22.59 N	76.12 E
Bhopāl	124	23.16 N	77.24 E
Bhopar	272c	19.12 N	73.05 E
Bhopura	272a	28.42 N	77.20 E
Bhoutan → Bhutan □[1]	120	27.30 N	90.30 E
Bhowali	124	29.23 N	79.31 E
Bhuāpur	272a	28.43 N	77.26 E
Bhuban	120	20.53 N	85.50 E
Bhubaneshwar	120	20.14 N	85.50 E
Bhucho	123	30.13 N	75.06 E
Bhuj	120	23.16 N	69.40 E
Bhunarheri	124	30.13 N	76.27 E
Bhunya	158	26.32 S	31.01 E
Bhusāwal	120	21.03 N	75.46 E
Bhūshana	126	23.24 N	89.40 E
Bhutali	272c	19.07 N	73.04 E
Bhutan (Druk-Yul) □[1], Asia	118	27.30 N	90.30 E
Bhutan (Druk-Yul) □[1], Asia	120	27.30 N	90.30 E
Bia ≃, Afr.	150	5.21 N	3.11 W
Biá ≃, Bra.	246	3.28 S	67.23 W
Bia, Phou ∧	110	18.59 N	103.09 E
Bīābānak	128	32.11 N	64.11 E
Biabo ≃	248	6.58 S	76.23 W
Biacesa	64	45.56 N	10.47 E
Biache-Saint-Vaast	50	50.18 N	2.57 E
Biadene	64	45.47 N	12.04 E
Biafra, Bight of c[3]	134	4.00 N	8.00 E
Biak I	164	1.00 S	136.00 E
Biała	30	50.23 N	17.40 E
Biała ≃	30	50.03 N	20.55 E
Biała Piska	30	53.37 N	22.04 E
Biała Podlaska	30	52.02 N	23.06 E
Biała Podlaska □[4]	30	52.00 N	23.00 E
Biała Rawska	30	51.49 N	20.29 E
Białobrzegi	30	51.40 N	20.57 E
Białogard	30	54.01 N	16.00 E
Białowieski Park Narodowy ♦	30	52.40 N	23.50 E
Biały Bór	30	53.54 N	16.51 E
Białystok	30	53.09 N	23.09 E
Białystok □[4]	30	53.00 N	23.00 E
Bian ≃	164	8.07 S	139.56 E
Bian, Bidean nam ∧	46	56.38 N	5.02 W
Biancavilla	70	37.38 N	14.52 E
Bianchi	68	39.06 N	16.24 E
Bianco	68	38.05 N	16.09 E
Bianco, Canale ≊	64	45.02 N	12.05 E
Bianco, Capo ›	70	37.23 N	13.16 E
Bianco, Monte (Mont Blanc) ∧	62	45.50 N	6.52 E
Bian'er	102	31.14 N	101.28 E
Bianga	152	4.51 N	20.25 E
Bian'gezhuang	105	39.28 N	115.53 E
Biankouma	150	7.44 N	7.37 W
Bianlinzhen	98	37.26 N	116.32 E
Bianminchang	107	29.41 N	105.04 E
Bianniulupucun	104	41.30 N	123.42 E
Bianquanwopu	104	41.21 N	120.48 E
Bianzè	62	45.18 N	8.07 E
Biaora	124	23.55 N	76.54 E
Biaro, Pulau I	112	2.05 N	125.20 E
Biarritz	32	43.29 N	1.34 W
Biasca	58	46.22 N	8.58 E
Bias Fortes	256	21.36 S	43.46 W

PORTUGUÊS

Nome	Página	Lat. °′	Long. °′ W = Oeste
Biassono	62	45.37 N	9.16 E
Biaza	86	56.38 N	78.18 E
Bibā	142	28.55 N	30.59 E
Bibai	92a	43.19 N	141.52 E
Bibala	152	14.46 S	13.21 E
Bībān	142	30.47 N	30.40 E
Bibane, Bahiret el c	148	33.16 N	11.19 E
Bibanga	152	6.15 S	23.56 E
Bibban, Khawr V	140	11.00 N	32.41 E
Bibb City	192	32.30 N	84.59 W
Bibbiano	64	44.40 N	10.28 E
Bibbiena	66	43.42 N	11.49 E
Bibbona	66	43.16 N	10.35 E
Bibémi	146	9.19 N	13.53 E
Biberach	58	48.20 N	8.02 E
Biberach an der Riss	58	48.06 N	9.47 E
Biberbach	56	48.31 N	10.48 E
Biberonne ≃	261	48.59 N	2.41 E
Bibert ≃	56	49.27 N	10.59 E
Bibey ≃	34	42.24 N	7.13 W
Bibiani	150	6.28 N	2.20 W
Bībī Chīni	126	22.28 N	90.12 E
Bibione	64	45.38 N	13.00 E
Bibir'ovo	76	54.28 N	33.08 E
Biblián	246	2.42 S	78.52 W
Biblis	56	49.41 N	8.27 E
Bibo	102	29.02 N	99.20 E
Bibrka	78	49.38 N	24.18 E
Bic	186	48.22 N	68.42 W
Biča	86	57.53 N	70.37 E
Bicas	256	21.43 S	43.04 W
Bicaz	38	46.54 N	26.05 E
Biccari	68	41.24 N	15.11 E
Bicester	42	51.54 N	1.09 W
Bičevinka	76	59.44 N	37.40 E
Biche, Lac la ⊜	182	54.50 N	112.03 W
Bichena	144	10.27 N	38.12 E
Bicheno	166	41.53 S	148.18 E
Bichhia	124	22.27 N	80.42 E
Bichl	64	47.43 N	11.24 E
Bichlbach	58	47.25 N	10.47 E
Bichota Canyon V	280	34.16 N	117.48 W
Biči ≃	89	52.10 N	139.50 E
Bičigt	88	47.06 N	95.05 E
Bickerstaffe	262	53.32 N	2.50 W
Bickerton, Cape ›	9	66.20 S	136.56 E
Bickerton Island I	164	13.45 S	136.12 E
Bickle Knob ∧	188	38.56 N	79.44 W
Bickley ◆[8]	260	51.24 N	0.03 E
Bicknacre, Eng., U.K.	42	51.41 N	0.35 E
Bicknacre, Eng., U.K.	260	51.41 N	0.35 E
Bicknell, In., U.S.	194	38.46 N	87.18 W
Bicknell, Ut,. U.S.	200	38.20 N	111.32 W
Bicknor	260	51.18 N	0.40 E
Bicol ≃	116	13.44 N	123.07 E
Bicske	30	47.29 N	18.37 E
Bicudo ≃	255	18.04 S	44.33 W
Bičura	88	50.36 N	107.35 E
Bičurina	86	56.51 N	55.25 E
Bīd	122	18.59 N	75.46 E
Bida, Nig.	146	12.20 N	13.25 E
Bida, Nig.	150	9.05 N	6.01 E
Bīdar	122	17.54 N	77.33 E
Bidde	144	0.58 N	42.37 E
Biddeford	188	43.29 N	70.27 W
Biddenden	42	51.07 N	0.39 E
Biddiyā	132	32.07 N	35.05 E
Biddulph	44	53.08 N	2.10 W
Bideford	42	51.01 N	4.13 W
Bidente ≃	66	44.24 N	12.12 E
Bidford-on-Avon	42	52.10 N	1.51 W
Bidhūna	124	26.49 N	79.31 E
Bidian	100	32.38 N	113.03 E
Bīdokht	128	34.21 N	58.46 E
Bidoni	71	40.07 N	8.56 E
Bidor	114	4.07 N	101.17 E
Bidston	262	53.24 N	3.05 W
Bidwell	188	38.55 N	82.17 W
Bidwell, Mount ∧	204	41.58 N	120.10 W
Bidya ≃[1]	126	21.56 N	88.42 E
Bidyādhari ≃	272b	22.23 N	88.35 E
Bidyādharpur	272b	22.50 N	88.24 E
Bidžan	89	47.58 N	131.58 E
Bidžan ≃	89	47.44 N	132.19 E
Bie	40	59.05 N	16.12 E
Bié □[5]	152	12.30 S	17.15 E
Biebelried	56	49.46 N	10.04 E
Bieber, Dtsch.	56	50.09 N	9.19 E
Bieber, Ca., U.S.	204	41.07 N	121.08 W
Biebrza ≃	30	53.13 N	22.25 E
Biecz	30	49.44 N	21.14 E
Biedenkopf	56	50.55 N	8.32 E
Biederitz	54	52.09 N	11.43 E
Biedermannsdorf	264b	48.05 N	16.21 E
Bieguzhuang	105	39.19 N	116.39 E
Biei	92a	43.35 N	142.28 E
Biel (Bienne)	58	47.10 N	7.12 E
Bielawa	30	50.41 N	16.38 E
Bielawski, Mount ∧	226	37.13 N	122.06 W
Bielefeld	52	52.01 N	8.31 E
Bieler Lake ⊜	176	70.20 N	73.00 W
Bielersee ⊜	58	47.05 N	7.10 E
Bielin	54	52.47 N	14.28 E
Biella	62	45.34 N	8.03 E
Bielsk	30	52.40 N	19.49 E
Bielsko-Biała	30	49.49 N	19.02 E
Bielsko-Biała □[4]	30	49.40 N	19.10 E
Bielsk Podlaski	30	52.47 N	23.12 E
Biemenhorst	52	51.49 N	6.36 E
Bienenbüttel	52	53.08 N	10.29 E
Bienfait	184	49.08 N	102.47 W
Bien Hoa	110	10.57 N	106.49 E
Bienne → Biel	58	47.10 N	7.12 E
Bienne ≃, Fr.	50	48.15 N	0.04 E
Bienne ≃, Fr.	58	46.20 N	5.38 E
Bienno	64	45.56 N	10.18 E
Bientina	66	43.42 N	10.37 E
Bienville	194	32.21 N	92.58 W
Bienville, Lac ⊜	176	55.05 N	72.40 W
Biere, Dtsch.	54	51.58 N	11.39 E
Bière, Schw.	58	46.33 N	6.20 E
Bierné	28	47.49 N	0.32 W
Bieruń Stary	30	50.06 N	19.06 E
Bierutów	30	51.08 N	17.32 E
Bierwart	56	50.34 N	5.01 E
Biesbos ◆[1]	52	51.45 N	4.50 E
Biesdorf ◆[8]	264a	52.31 N	13.33 E
Biese ≃	54	52.45 N	11.37 E
Biesel ◆[8]	263	51.10 N	6.29 E
Biesenthal	54	52.46 N	13.37 E
Bieshan	105	39.58 N	117.29 E
Biesiesvlei	158	26.22 S	25.55 E
Biesles	58	48.05 N	5.18 E
Bieszczadzki Park Narodowy ♦	30	49.05 N	22.45 E
Bieteluobaoluosika	89	48.35 N	119.56 E
Bietigheim	56	48.54 N	8.14 E
Bietigheim-Bissingen	56	48.58 N	9.07 E
Bietschhorn ∧	58	46.24 N	7.51 E
Bièvre	56	49.56 N	5.01 E
Bièvre ≃	261	48.47 N	2.20 E
Bièvres	261	48.45 N	2.13 E
Biferno ≃	66	41.59 N	15.02 E
Bifoun	152	0.22 S	10.23 E
Bifuka	92a	44.29 N	142.21 E
Bifurcación	258	34.19 S	56.48 W
Big ≃, Austl.	169	37.18 S	146.02 E
Big ≃, N.T., Can.	176	72.30 N	125.14 W
Big ≃, Sk., Can.	184	53.50 N	107.02 W
Big ≃, Ak., U.S.	180	63.00 N	154.56 W
Big ≃, Mo., U.S.	219	38.28 N	90.37 W
Biga	130	40.13 N	27.14 E
Bigadiç	130	39.23 N	28.08 E
Big A Mountain ∧	192	37.03 N	82.02 W
Big Annemessex River c	208	38.03 N	75.50 W
Big Antelope Creek ≃	202	42.28 N	117.13 W
Big Bald Mountain ∧, N.B., Can.	186	47.12 N	66.25 W
Big Bald Mountain ∧, Ga., U.S.	192	34.45 N	84.19 W
Big Baldy ∧	202	44.47 N	115.13 W
Big Baldy Mountain ∧	202	46.58 N	110.37 W
Big Bar Creek	182	51.12 N	122.06 W
Big Basin Redwoods State Park ♦	226	37.09 N	122.17 W
Big Bay	190	46.49 N	87.44 W
Big Bay c, N.Z.	172	44.18 S	168.05 E
Big Bay c, Vanuatu	175f	15.06 S	166.54 E
Big Bay De Noc c	190	45.46 N	86.43 W
Big Bay Point ›	212	44.24 N	79.31 W
Big Bear City	228	34.15 N	116.50 W
Big Bear Lake	228	34.15 N	116.53 W
Big Bear Lake ⊜	228	34.15 N	116.55 W
Big Beaver, Sk., Can.	184	49.08 N	105.10 W
Big Beaver, Pa., U.S.	214	40.50 N	80.20 W
Big Beaver Airport ⊠	281	42.33 N	83.06 W
Big Beaver Creek ≃, Mi., U.S.	281	42.32 N	83.01 W
Big Beaver Creek ≃, Oh., U.S.	218	39.01 N	83.03 W
Big Beaver Creek ≃, Wa., U.S.	224	48.40 N	121.08 W
Big Bell	162	27.21 S	117.40 E
Big Belt Mountains ⋏	202	46.40 N	111.25 W
Big Bend, Swaz.	158	26.50 S	31.57 E
Big Bend, Wi., U.S.	216	42.52 N	88.12 W
Big Bend National Park ♦	196	29.12 N	103.12 W
Big Bend Reservoir ⊜[1]	182	52.57 N	115.37 W
Big Black ≃	194	32.00 N	91.05 W
Big Blue ≃, U.S.	198	39.11 N	96.32 W
Big Blue ≃, In., U.S.	218	39.20 N	85.59 W
Big Blue, West Fork ≃	198	40.42 N	96.59 W
Big Bone Lick State Park ♦	218	38.53 N	84.45 W
Big Bonito Creek ≃	200	33.34 N	109.56 W
Big Brook ≃	276	40.19 N	74.10 W
Big Brushy Creek ≃, Tx., U.S.	222	32.32 N	96.20 W
Big Brushy Creek ≃, Tx., U.S.	222	29.12 N	96.55 W
Big Bureau Creek ≃	194	41.17 N	89.21 W
Bigbury Bay c	42	50.16 N	3.48 W
Big Cabin Creek ≃	194	36.26 N	95.08 W
Big Canyon V	196	30.05 N	101.55 W
Big Carlos Pass c	220	26.24 N	81.52 W
Big Cedar Lake ⊜	212	44.37 N	78.10 W
Big Chino Wash V	200	34.52 N	112.28 W
Big Clear Lake ⊜	212	44.43 N	76.55 W
Big Clifty	194	37.32 N	86.09 W
Big Coulee Creek ≃	202	46.17 N	108.56 W
Big Cow Creek ≃	194	30.34 N	93.44 W
Big Creek, B.C., Can.	182	51.44 N	123.03 W
Big Creek, Ca., U.S.	226	37.12 N	119.14 W
Big Creek ≃, B.C., Can.	182	51.40 N	122.50 W
Big Creek ≃, On., Can.	214	42.19 N	82.27 W
Big Creek ≃, On., Can.	214	42.36 N	80.27 W
Big Creek ≃, Ar., U.S.	194	34.21 N	91.03 W
Big Creek ≃, Ca., U.S.	226	37.12 N	119.19 W
Big Creek ≃, Ca., U.S.	226	36.53 N	119.15 W
Big Creek ≃, Id., U.S.	202	45.06 N	114.44 W
Big Creek ≃, Il., U.S.	219	39.07 N	88.52 W
Big Creek ≃, In., U.S.	216	40.38 N	86.46 W
Big Creek ≃, In., U.S.	218	38.48 N	85.39 W
Big Creek ≃, Ks., U.S.	198	38.47 N	98.55 W
Big Creek ≃, La., U.S.	194	32.10 N	91.53 W
Big Creek ≃, Mo., U.S.	194	40.02 N	94.07 W
Big Creek ≃, Mo., U.S.	219	38.52 N	90.50 W
Big Creek ≃, Oh., U.S.	279a	41.27 N	81.41 W
Big Creek ≃, Or., U.S.	224	46.11 N	123.35 W
Big Creek ≃, Tx., U.S.	222	29.22 N	95.34 W
Big Creek ≃, Tx., U.S.	222	31.09 N	96.52 W
Big Creek ≃, Wa., U.S.	224	47.15 N	121.10 W
Big Creek, East Fork ≃	194	40.16 N	94.03 W
Big Creek, West Fork ≃	194	40.16 N	94.03 W
Big Creek Parkway ♦	279a	41.24 N	81.45 W
Big Creek Peak ∧	202	44.28 N	113.32 W
Big Crow Island I	276	40.37 N	73.33 W
Big Cypress Creek ≃	222	33.00 N	94.51 W
Big Cypress Indian Reservation ◆[4]	220	26.14 N	80.49 W
Big Cypress National Preserve ♦	220	25.55 N	81.10 W
Big Cypress Swamp ☷	220	26.10 N	81.38 W
Big Dalton Canyon V	280	34.10 N	117.48 W
Big Dalton Wash V	280	34.04 N	117.58 W
Big Darby Creek ≃	218	39.37 N	82.58 W
Big Delta	180	64.09 N	145.50 W
Big Desert ◆[2]	166	35.40 S	141.00 E
Big Diomede Island → Ratmanova, ostrov I	180	65.46 N	169.02 W
Big Ditch ≊	216	40.13 N	88.22 W
Big Dry Creek ≃	202	47.30 N	106.19 W
Big Dubbo Hill ∧	171b	35.25 S	148.36 E
Big Eau Pleine ≃	190	44.48 N	90.00 W
Big Elk Creek ≃	208	39.35 N	75.52 W
Big Elkhart Creek ≃	222	31.22 N	95.41 W
Big Elm Creek ≃	222	30.53 N	96.56 W
Bigelow Bight c[3]	188	43.15 N	70.30 W
Big Escambia Creek ≃	194	30.58 N	87.14 W
Big Falls	190	48.11 N	93.48 W
Big Flat	194	36.00 N	92.24 W
Big Flat Creek ≃	194	31.33 N	87.31 W
Big Flats	210	42.08 N	76.56 W
Bigfork, Mn., U.S.	190	47.44 N	93.39 W
Bigfork, Mt., U.S.	202	48.04 N	114.04 W
Big Fork ≃	190	48.31 N	93.43 W
Big Four Ditch ≊	216	40.27 N	88.10 W
Big Frog Mountain ∧	192	35.00 N	84.32 W
Biggar, Sk., Can.	184	52.04 N	108.00 W
Biggar, Scot., U.K.	46	55.38 N	3.32 W
Biggarsberg ⋏	158	28.12 S	29.48 E
Bigge	56	51.21 N	8.28 E
Bigge Island I	164	14.35 S	125.10 E
Biggers	194	36.19 N	90.48 W
Biggestausee ⊜[1]	56	51.05 N	7.55 E
Biggin Hill ◆[8]	42	51.18 N	0.04 E
Biggin Hill Aerodrome ⊠	260	51.19 N	0.03 E
Biggleswade	42	52.05 N	0.17 W
Biggs, Ca., U.S.	226	39.24 N	121.42 W
Biggs, Or., U.S.	224	45.40 N	120.50 W
Big Gull Lake ⊜	212	44.50 N	76.58 W
Big Gully Creek ≃	184	53.13 N	109.03 W
Bighāi ≃[1]	126	22.10 N	90.13 E
Big Hawk Lake ⊜	212	45.10 N	78.44 W
Bighead ≃	212	44.36 N	80.35 W
Big Hole ≃	202	45.34 N	112.20 W
Big Hole National Battlefield ⊥	202	45.35 N	113.35 W
Bighorn ≃	202	46.09 N	107.28 W
Bighorn Basin ⌣[1]	202	44.15 N	108.10 W
Bighorn Canyon National Recreation Area ♦	202	45.00 N	108.15 W
Big Horn Lake ⊜[1]	202	45.06 N	108.08 W
Bighorn Mountains ⋏	202	44.00 N	107.30 W
Bight, Head of ›	162	31.30 S	131.10 E
Big Huckleberry Mountain ∧	224	45.51 N	121.47 W
Big Island	192	37.32 N	79.21 W
Big Island I, N.T., Can.	176	62.43 N	70.43 W
Big Island I, On., Can.	184	49.10 N	94.40 W
Big Island I, On., Can.	212	44.33 N	78.30 W
Big Knob ∧	192	36.40 N	82.31 W
Big Koniuji Island I	180	55.06 N	159.33 W
Big Lake, Ak., U.S.	180	61.33 N	149.52 W
Big Lake, Mn., U.S.	190	45.19 N	93.44 W
Big Lake, Tx., U.S.	196	31.11 N	101.27 W
Big Lake, Wa., U.S.	224	48.24 N	122.14 W
Big Lake ⊜, Me., U.S.	188	45.10 N	67.40 W
Big Lake ⊜, Wa., U.S.	224	48.23 N	122.12 W
Bigler	214	40.59 N	78.19 W
Biglerville	208	39.55 N	77.14 W
Big Lick Creek ≃	216	40.22 N	85.27 W
Big Lookout Mountain ∧	202	44.37 N	117.17 W
Big Lost ≃	202	43.50 N	112.44 W
Big Monon Ditch ≊	216	40.52 N	86.46 W
Big Mossy Point ›	184	53.41 N	97.57 W
Big Mountain ∧, B.C., Can.	180	56.53 N	131.31 W
Big Mountain ∧, Nv., U.S.	204	41.17 N	119.04 W
Big Mountain Creek ≃	182	55.04 N	118.39 W
Big Muddy ≃	194	37.35 N	89.31 W
Big Muddy, Casey Fork ≃	194	38.06 N	88.57 W
Big Muddy Creek ≃, Mt., U.S.	198	48.08 N	104.36 W
Big Muddy Creek ≃, N.D., U.S.	198	46.37 N	101.24 W
Big Muddy Lake ⊜	184	49.08 N	104.54 W
Big Muscamoot Bay c	281	42.33 N	82.40 W
Bignasco	58	46.20 N	8.36 E
Big Nasty Creek ≃	198	45.41 N	102.51 W
Big Nemaha, North Fork ≃	198	40.04 N	95.43 W
Bignona	150	12.49 N	16.14 W
Big Oak Flat	226	37.49 N	120.16 W
Bigosovo	76	55.49 N	27.43 E
Bigot, Morne ∧[2]	240e	14.31 N	61.04 W
Big Otter ≃	192	37.07 N	79.23 W
Big Otter Creek ≃	212	42.38 N	80.48 W
Big Ox Creek ≃	218	38.44 N	85.52 W
Big Pine	204	37.09 N	118.17 W
Big Pine Creek ≃	216	40.18 N	87.15 W
Big Pine Key	220	24.40 N	81.21 W
Big Pine Key I	220	24.42 N	81.23 W
Big Pine Mountain ∧	204	34.42 N	119.39 W
Big Piney	200	42.32 N	110.06 W
Big Piney ≃	194	37.53 N	92.04 W
Big Piney Creek ≃	194	35.20 N	93.20 W
Big Pipe Creek ≃	208	39.36 N	77.17 W
Big Plain	218	39.50 N	83.17 W
Big Pocono State Park ♦	210	41.03 N	75.19 W
Bigpoint	194	30.35 N	88.28 W
Big Pond	210	41.53 N	76.43 W
Big Porcupine Creek ≃	202	46.16 N	106.43 W
Big Porcupine Lake ⊜	212	45.27 N	78.36 W
Big Prairie	214	40.40 N	82.06 W
Big Prairie Creek ≃	194	32.35 N	87.45 W
Big Quilcene ≃	224	47.49 N	122.52 W
Big Quill Lake ⊜	184	51.55 N	104.22 W
Big Raccoon Creek ≃	194	39.46 N	87.22 W
Big Rapids	190	43.41 N	85.29 W
Bigras, Île I	275a	45.31 N	73.51 W
Big Rib ≃	190	44.56 N	89.41 W
Big Rideau Lake ⊜	212	44.45 N	76.14 W
Big River	184	53.50 N	107.01 W
Big River Indian Reserve ◆[4]	184	53.33 N	107.10 W
Big Rock	216	41.46 N	88.33 W
Big Rock Creek ≃	216	41.38 N	88.32 W
Big Rocky Creek ≃	222	29.34 N	96.50 W
Big Run	214	40.58 N	78.52 W
Big Sable ≃	190	44.02 N	86.31 W
Big Sable Point ›	190	44.03 N	86.31 W
Big Salmon ≃	180	61.52 N	134.56 W
Big Salmon Range ⋏	180	61.10 N	133.45 W
Big Sand Lake ⊜	176	57.45 N	99.42 W
Big Sandy, Mt., U.S.	202	48.10 N	110.06 W
Big Sandy, Tn., U.S.	194	36.14 N	88.05 W
Big Sandy, Tx., U.S.	222	32.35 N	95.07 W
Big Sandy ≃, U.S.	188	38.25 N	82.36 W
Big Sandy ≃, Az., U.S.	200	34.19 N	113.31 W
Big Sandy ≃, Tn., U.S.	194	36.15 N	88.06 W
Big Sandy ≃, Wy., U.S.	202	41.51 N	109.47 W
Big Sandy Creek ≃, Ca., U.S.	226	35.47 N	120.43 W
Big Sandy Creek ≃, Co., U.S.	198	38.06 N	102.29 W
Big Sandy Creek ≃, Ga., U.S.	192	32.42 N	82.57 W
Big Sandy Creek ≃, Mt., U.S.	202	48.34 N	109.48 W
Big Sandy Creek ≃, Ne., U.S.	198	40.13 N	97.18 W
Big Sandy Creek ≃, Tx., U.S.	196	33.11 N	97.40 W
Big Sandy Creek ≃, Tx., U.S.	222	32.33 N	95.05 W
Big Sandy Creek ≃, Tx., U.S.	222	30.31 N	94.28 W
Big Sandy Lake ⊜, Sk., Can.	184	54.26 N	104.04 W
Big Sandy Lake ⊜, Mn., U.S.	190	46.45 N	93.17 W
Big Sandy Reservoir ⊜[1]	200	42.16 N	109.26 W
Big Satilla Creek ≃	192	31.27 N	82.03 W
Bigsby Island I	184	49.04 N	94.35 W
Big Sewickley Creek ≃	279b	40.35 N	80.13 W
Big Shawnee Creek ≃	216	40.15 N	87.18 W
Big Sheep Mountain ∧	202	47.03 N	105.43 W
Big Signal Peak ∧	204	39.31 N	123.06 W
Big Sinking Creek ≃	194	37.55 N	86.31 W
Big Sioux ≃	198	42.30 N	96.25 W
Big Sixmile Creek ≃	284a	43.02 N	79.01 W
Big Sky	202	45.17 N	111.17 W
Big Slough ≃	192	30.56 N	84.33 W
Big Smoky Valley V	204	38.30 N	117.15 W
Big Snowy Mountains ⋏	202	46.50 N	109.30 W
Big Southern Butte ∧	202	43.23 N	113.01 W
Big Spanish Channel ⋓	220	24.44 N	81.20 W
Bigspring, Mo., U.S.	219	38.38 N	91.28 W
Big Spring, Tx., U.S.	196	32.15 N	101.28 W
Big Springs	198	41.03 N	102.04 W
Big Spruce Knob ∧	188	38.16 N	80.12 W
Big Squaw Mountain ∧	188	45.30 N	69.45 W
Bigstick Lake ⊜	184	50.16 N	109.20 W
Bigstone ≃	184	55.55 N	94.36 W
Big Stone City	198	45.17 N	96.27 W
Big Stone Gap	192	36.52 N	82.44 W
Bigstone Lake ⊜, Mb., Can.	184	53.42 N	95.44 W
Big Stone Lake ⊜, U.S.	198	45.25 N	96.40 W
Big Sunflower ≃	194	32.40 N	90.40 W
Big Sur	226	36.16 N	121.48 W
Big Sur ≃	226	36.17 N	121.51 W
Big Sur ◆[1]	226	35.45 N	121.20 W
Big Swamp Creek ≃	194	32.19 N	86.49 W
Big Swan Creek ≃	194	35.46 N	87.24 W
Big Thicket National Preserve ♦	222	32.35 N	94.40 W
Big Thompson ≃	200	40.21 N	104.45 W
Big Timber	202	45.50 N	109.57 W
Big Timber Creek ≃	285	39.53 N	75.08 W
Big Timber Creek, North Branch ≃	285	39.50 N	75.05 W
Big Timber Creek, South Branch ≃	285	39.50 N	75.05 W
Big Torch Key I	220	24.43 N	81.26 W
Big Tree	210	42.46 N	78.49 W
Big Trout Lake ⊜, On., Can.	176	53.45 N	90.00 W
Big Trout Lake ⊜, On., Can.	212	44.56 N	78.56 W
Big Tujunga Canyon V	228	34.16 N	118.18 W
Big Tujunga Dam ◆[6]	280	34.18 N	118.12 W
Biguaçu	252	27.30 S	48.40 W
Big Valley	182	52.02 N	112.46 W
Bigwa	154	7.13 S	39.09 E
Big Walnut Creek ≃, In., U.S.	194	39.30 N	86.57 W
Big Walnut Creek ≃, Oh., U.S.	218	39.48 N	83.01 W
Big Warrambool ≃	166	30.05 S	147.33 E
Big Water	200	37.05 N	111.41 W
Big Wells	196	28.34 N	99.34 W
Big White Mountain ∧	182	49.42 N	118.58 W
Big Wills Creek ≃	194	33.59 N	86.00 W
Big Wood ≃	202	42.52 N	114.54 W
Bihać	36	44.49 N	15.52 E
Bīhar	124	25.11 N	85.31 E
Bihār □[3]	124	25.00 N	86.00 E
Biharamulo	154	2.38 S	31.20 E
Bihārīganj	124	25.44 N	86.59 E
Bihor □[6]	38	47.00 N	22.15 E
Bihor, Vârful ∧	38	46.27 N	22.42 E
Bihoro	92a	43.49 N	144.07 E
Bihu	100	28.21 N	119.48 E
Bihun	78	51.24 N	28.17 E
Bija ≃	86	52.25 N	85.05 E
Bijagós, Arquipélago dos II	150	11.25 N	16.20 W
Bijainagar	120	25.56 N	74.38 E
Bijaipur	124	26.03 N	77.22 E
Bijaipura	124	24.46 N	77.48 E
Bijāpur	122	16.50 N	75.42 E
Bījār	128	35.52 N	47.36 E
Bijāwar	124	24.38 N	79.30 E
Bijbān Chāh	128	26.54 N	64.42 E
Bījbiāra	123	33.48 N	75.06 E
Bijeljina	38	44.45 N	19.13 E
Bijelo Polje	38	43.02 N	19.44 E
Bijiang	110	26.30 N	98.55 E
Bijia Shan ∧	105	40.17 N	116.50 E
Bijie	102	27.18 N	105.20 E
Bijlikol', ozero ⊜	85	43.03 N	70.41 E
Bijna	272b	22.55 N	88.27 E
Bijni	124	26.31 N	90.40 E
Bijnor	124	29.22 N	78.08 E
Bijōki	268	35.49 N	139.39 E
Bijou Creek ≃	198	40.17 N	103.52 W
Bijpur	126	22.56 N	88.26 E
Bijsk	86	52.34 N	85.15 E
Bijwāsan ◆[8]	272a	28.32 N	77.03 E
Bīkāner	120	28.01 N	73.18 E
Bīkaner Canal ≊	123	30.08 N	73.57 E
Bikar I[1]	14	12.15 N	170.06 E
Bikbulovo	80	55.39 N	53.26 E
Bike	144	9.30 N	41.18 E
Bikeman Island I	174t	1.22 N	173.00 E
Bikenibeu	174t	1.21 N	173.07 E
Bikeqi	102	40.45 N	111.17 E
Bikeru	112	5.15 S	120.07 E
Bikfayyā	132	33.55 N	35.41 E
Bikié	152	3.06 S	13.52 E
Bikin	89	46.48 N	134.16 E
Bikin ≃	89	46.51 N	134.02 E
Bikini I[1]	14	11.35 N	165.23 E
Bikita	154	20.06 S	31.41 E
Bikl'an'	80	55.37 N	52.10 E
Bikoro	152	0.45 S	18.07 E
Bikuar, Parque Nacional do ♦	152	15.12 S	14.42 E
Bila ≃, Indon.	114	2.30 N	100.08 E
Bila ≃, Ukr.	83	49.18 N	38.52 E
Bila ≃, Ukr.	83	48.35 N	39.10 E
Bilaa Point ›	116	9.49 N	125.26 E
Bilac	255	21.24 S	50.28 W
Bilād Zahrān ◆[1]	144	20.16 N	41.14 E
Bílá hora ⊥	54	50.05 N	14.20 E
Bila Krynytsya, Ukr.	78	47.21 N	33.10 E
Bila Krynytsya, Ukr.	78	50.38 N	29.29 E
Bilang, Teluk c	112	1.15 N	121.25 E
Bilanga	150	12.32 N	0.02 E
Bilāra	120	26.10 N	73.42 E
Bilāri	124	28.38 N	78.48 E
Bil'arsk	80	54.58 N	50.22 E
Bilāsipāra	124	26.14 N	90.14 E
Bilāspur, India	123	31.20 N	76.45 E
Bilāspur, India	124	28.53 N	79.16 E
Bilāspur, India	124	22.05 N	82.09 E
Biläsuvar (Pushkino), Azer.	84	39.27 N	48.33 E
Biläsuvar, Azer.	84	39.24 N	48.24 E
Bilatan Island I	116	4.59 N	120.00 E
Bilato	112	0.32 N	122.38 E
Bila Tserkva	78	49.49 N	30.07 E
Bilauktaung Range ⋏	110	13.00 N	99.00 E
Bilbao	34	43.15 N	2.58 W
Bilbays	142	30.25 N	31.34 E
Bilbays Military Base ■	142	30.24 N	31.36 E
Bilbilis ⊥	34	41.25 N	1.39 W
Bil'čir	88	51.02 N	110.34 E
Bile	83	48.31 N	39.04 E
Bileća	38	42.53 N	18.26 E
Bilecik	130	40.09 N	29.59 E
Bilecik □[4]	130	40.10 N	30.10 E
Bilen'ka ≃	83	48.53 N	38.29 E
Bilen'ke, Ukr.	78	47.37 N	35.03 E
Bilen'ke, Ukr.	83	48.46 N	37.38 E
Biles Island I	285	40.10 N	74.45 W
Biłgoraj	30	50.34 N	22.43 E
Bilgrām	124	27.11 N	80.02 E
Bilhorod-Dnistrovs'kyy	78	46.12 N	30.20 E
Bili	154	4.09 N	25.10 E
Bili ≃	136	4.09 N	22.29 E
Bilian	100	28.21 N	120.33 E
Bilifyā	142	29.07 N	31.03 E
Bilimora	120	20.45 N	72.57 E
Bilin	110	17.14 N	97.15 E
Bilin ≃	110	17.05 N	97.08 E
Bílina	54	50.35 N	13.45 E
Bílina ≃	54	50.40 N	14.02 E
Bilioso ≃	68	40.39 N	16.24 E
Biliran Island I	116	11.35 N	124.28 E
Biliran Strait ⋓	116	11.30 N	124.28 E
Biliri	146	9.52 N	11.13 E
Biliu ≃	98	39.30 N	122.36 E
Bilk ◆[8]	263	51.12 N	6.47 E
Bilky	78	50.49 N	28.11 E
Billabong Creek ≃	166	35.06 S	144.02 E
Billeberga	41	55.53 N	13.00 E
Billerbeck	52	51.59 N	7.17 E
Billerica	207	42.33 N	71.16 W
Billericay	42	51.38 N	0.25 E
Billesdon	42	52.37 N	0.55 W
Billesholm	41	56.03 N	13.00 E
Billiat	58	46.04 N	5.47 E
Billigheim	56	49.21 N	9.15 E
Billiluna	162	19.37 S	127.41 E
Billinge, Sve.	41	55.58 N	13.21 E
Billinge, Eng., U.K.	262	53.30 N	2.42 W
Billingen ⋏[2]	26	58.24 N	13.45 E
Billingham	44	54.36 N	1.17 W
Billings, Mo., U.S.	194	37.04 N	93.33 W
Billings, Mt., U.S.	202	45.46 N	108.30 W

≃ River	Fluß	Río	Rivière	Rio
≊ Canal	Kanal	Canal	Canal	Canal
⌊ Waterfall, Rapids	Wasserfall, Stromschnellen	Cascada, Rápidos	Chute d'eau, Rapides	Cascata, Rápidos
⋓ Strait	Meeresstraße	Estrecho	Détroit	Estreito
c Bay, Gulf	Bucht, Golf	Bahía, Golfo	Baie, Golfe	Baía, Golfo
⊜ Lake, Lakes	See, Seen	Lago, Lagos	Lac, Lacs	Lago, Lagos
☷ Swamp	Sumpf	Pantano	Marais	Pântano
⊓ Ice Features, Glacier	Eis- und Gletscherformen	Accidentes Glaciales	Formes glaciaires	Acidentes glaciares
⊤ Other Hydrographic Features	Andere Hydrographische Objekte	Otros Elementos Hidrográficos	Autres données hydrographiques	Outros acidentes hidrográficos

✦ Submarine Features	Untermeerische Objekte	Accidentes Submarinos	Formes de relief sous-marin	Acidentes submarinos
□ Political Unit	Politische Einheit	Unidad Política	Entité politique	Unidade política
ʋ Cultural Institution	Kulturelle Institution	Institución Cultural	Institution culturelle	Instituição cultural
⊥ Historical Site	Historische Stätte	Sitio Histórico	Site historique	Sitio histórico
♦ Recreational Site	Erholungs- und Ferienort	Sitio de Recreo	Centre de loisirs	Area de Lazer
⊠ Airport	Flughafen	Aeropuerto	Aéroport	Aeroporto
■ Military Installation	Militäranlage	Instalación Militar	Installation militaire	Instalação militar
◆ Miscellaneous	Verschiedenes	Misceláneo	Divers	Diversos

ENGLISH — Name / Page / Lat.°′ / Long.°′
DEUTSCH — Name / Seite / Breite°′ / Länge°′ E = Ost

Name	Page	Lat.°′	Long.°′
Billings, Ok., U.S.	196	36.31 N	97.26 W
Billings, Represa ⊜[1]	256	23.47 S	46.37 W
Billingsfors	26	58.59 N	12.15 E
Billings Heights	202	45.50 N	108.32 W
Billingshurst	42	51.01 N	0.28 W
Billmerich	263	51.30 N	7.41 E
Billolo ≃	273b	4.07 S	15.19 E
Billom	32	45.44 N	3.21 E
Billund	41	55.44 N	9.07 E
Bill Williams ≃	200	34.17 N	114.03 W
Bill Williams Mountain ∧	200	35.12 N	112.12 W
Billy Chinook, Lake ⊜[1]	202	44.33 N	121.20 W
Billy-Montigny	50	50.25 N	2.52 E
Bilma	146	18.41 N	12.56 E
Biloela	166	24.24 S	150.30 E
Bilo Gora ⋏	36	46.06 N	16.46 E
Bilohirs'k	78	45.03 N	34.36 E
Bilohir'ya	78	50.01 N	26.25 E
Bilohorivka	83	48.55 N	38.15 E
Bilohorodka	78	50.00 N	26.39 E
Bilokurakine	83	49.33 N	38.44 E
Biloluts'k	83	49.41 N	39.02 E
Bilopillya	78	51.09 N	34.18 E
Bilousivka	78	49.57 N	32.20 E
Bilovods'k	83	49.12 N	39.35 E
Biloxi	194	30.23 N	88.53 W
Biloxi ≃	194	30.26 N	89.00 W
Biloxi Creek ≃	222	31.05 N	94.37 W
Bilozerka	78	46.37 N	32.27 E
Bilozers'ke	78	48.33 N	37.04 E
Bilozir'ya, Ukr.	78	49.29 N	31.35 E
Bilozir'ya, Ukr.	78	49.18 N	31.54 E
Bilpa Morea Claypan ≚	166	25.00 S	140.00 E
Bilpin	170	33.30 S	150.31 E
Bilqās Qism Awwal	142	31.13 N	31.21 E
Bilsārā	126	23.05 N	88.10 E
Bil'sha Kam'yanka ≃	83	48.22 N	40.04 E
Bilshausen	52	51.37 N	10.10 E
Bil'shivtsi	78	49.12 N	24.44 E
Bilsi	124	28.08 N	78.55 E
Bil's'ka Volya	78	51.27 N	25.49 E
Bilston	42	52.34 N	2.04 W
Biltāj	142	31.00 N	30.59 E
Bilthoven	52	52.07 N	5.17 E
Biltine	146	14.32 N	20.55 E
Biltine □[5]	146	15.00 N	21.00 E
Biltmore Forest	192	35.32 N	82.31 W
Bilugyun Island I	110	16.24 N	97.32 E
Bilwaskarma	236	14.45 N	83.53 W
Bilyayivka	78	46.29 N	30.12 E
Bilychi	78	50.29 N	30.19 E
Bilyky	78	49.15 N	34.16 E
Bilyts'ke	83	48.25 N	37.13 E
Bilyy Kolodyaz'	78	50.12 N	37.08 E
Bilzen	56	50.52 N	5.31 E
Bima	115b	8.28 S	118.43 E
Bimbān	140	24.26 N	32.53 E
Bimbe	152	11.49 S	15.49 E
Bimberi Peak ∧	171b	35.40 S	148.47 E
Bimbila	150	8.51 N	0.04 E
Bimbo	152	4.18 N	18.33 E
Bimbowrie	166	32.03 S	140.09 E
Bimé	273b	4.09 S	15.11 E
Bimini Islands II	192	25.42 N	79.15 W
Bin ≃	100	23.40 N	112.58 E
Bina	175e	8.55 S	160.46 E
Bīna-Etāwa	124	24.11 N	78.11 E
Binaiya, Gunung ∧	164	3.11 S	129.26 E
Binalbagan	116	10.12 N	122.50 E
Binalbagan ≃	116	10.12 N	122.51 E
Bin'an	89	45.50 N	127.45 E
Binanga	114	1.24 N	99.46 E
Binangonan	116	14.28 N	121.11 E
Binas	50	47.54 N	1.28 E
Binasco	62	45.20 N	9.06 E
Binau	56	49.22 N	9.04 E
Binche	50	50.24 N	4.10 E
Binchuan	102	25.46 N	100.33 E
Bindal	24	65.06 N	12.30 E
Binder, Mong.	88	48.35 N	110.36 E
Binder, Tchad	146	9.58 N	14.28 E
Bindki	124	26.02 N	80.36 E
Bindlach	60	49.59 N	11.37 E
Bindloss	184	50.52 N	110.16 W
Bindo, Mount ∧	170	33.40 S	150.01 E
Bindow	264a	52.17 N	13.45 E
Bindura	154	17.19 S	31.20 E
Bine-el-Ouidane	148	32.07 N	6.26 W
Binéfar	34	41.51 N	0.18 E
Binford	198	47.33 N	98.20 W
Binga, Pil.	116	10.45 N	119.19 E
Binga, Zaïre	152	2.23 N	20.30 E
Binga, Monte ∧	156	19.45 S	33.04 E
Bingara	166	29.52 S	150.34 E
Bingaram Island I	122	10.56 N	72.17 E
Bingay Point >	116	13.04 N	124.11 E
Bingcha	100	32.30 N	120.52 E
Bingen, Dtsch.	56	49.57 N	7.54 E
Bingen, Wa., U.S.	224	45.42 N	121.27 W
Binger	196	35.18 N	98.20 W
Bingerbrück	56	49.58 N	7.53 E
Bingerville	150	5.21 N	3.54 W
Bingfang	106	32.15 N	121.20 E
Bingham, Eng., U.K.	42	52.57 N	0.57 W
Bingham, Me., U.S.	188	45.03 N	69.52 W
Bingham ≃	168a	33.20 S	116.16 E
Bingham Creek ≃	224	47.09 N	123.24 W
Bingham Farms	281	42.32 N	83.16 W
Binghamton	210	42.05 N	75.55 W
Bin Ghashīr	146	32.41 N	13.11 E
Bin Ghunaymah, Jabal ⋏	146	25.00 N	15.30 E
Bingi	154	0.24 S	29.05 E
Bingley	44	53.51 N	1.50 W
Bingöl	130	38.53 N	40.29 E
Bingöl □[4]	130	39.00 N	40.40 E
Bingöl Dağları ⋏	130	39.20 N	41.20 E
Binhai (Dongkan)	100	34.03 N	119.51 E
Binh Ca	110	21.48 N	105.18 E
Binh Chanh	269c	10.40 N	106.34 E
Binh Gia	110	21.59 N	106.21 E
Binh Hung Hoa	269c	10.49 N	106.37 E
Binh Khe	110	13.57 N	108.51 E
Binh Kieu	110	15.35 N	108.04 E
Bin-Houyé	150	6.47 N	8.19 W
Binh Son	110	15.18 N	108.46 E
Binh Trung	269c	10.47 N	106.46 E
Binigsian Point >	116	9.50 N	122.23 E
Bining	56	49.02 N	7.15 E
Binjai, Indon.	112	3.48 N	108.14 E
Binjai, Indon.	114	3.36 N	98.30 E
Binjohara	114	2.12 N	98.12 E
Bīnlūd, Kūh-e ⋏	128	36.28 N	58.49 E
Binna Burra	171a	28.13 S	153.14 E
Binnah, Ras >	144	11.08 N	51.10 E
Binnaway	166	31.33 S	149.23 E
Binnian, Slieve ∧	48	54.08 N	5.58 W
Binningen	58	47.32 N	7.34 E
Binodepur	126	23.26 N	89.30 E
Binongko, Pulau I	112	5.57 S	124.02 E
Binpur	126	22.36 N	86.55 E
Binscarth	184	50.37 N	101.16 W
Binsheim ✦[8]	263	51.31 N	6.42 E
Bintan, Pulau I	112	1.05 N	104.30 E
Bintang	150	13.10 N	16.08 W
Bintang, Gunong ∧	114	5.25 N	100.52 E
Bintauna	112	0.53 N	123.33 E
Bint Goda	140	13.17 N	31.33 E
Bintimani ∧	150	9.13 N	11.07 W
Bint Jubayl	132	33.07 N	35.26 E
Bintuhan	112	4.48 S	103.22 E
Bintulu	112	3.10 N	113.02 E
Bintuni	164	2.07 S	133.32 E
Bintuni, Teluk ⊂	164	2.20 S	133.30 E
Binxian, Zhg.	89	45.44 N	127.29 E
Binxian, Zhg.	98	37.28 N	117.56 E
Binxian, Zhg.	102	35.00 N	108.08 E
Binyamina	132	32.31 N	34.57 E
Binyang	102	23.18 N	108.46 E
Bin Yauri	150	10.47 N	4.50 E
Binz	54	54.24 N	13.36 E
Binza	273b	4.21 S	15.14 E
Binza ✦[8]	273b	4.20 S	15.14 E
Binza ≃	273b	4.21 S	15.14 E
Bio Addo	144	8.18 N	49.48 E
Bíobío □[4]	252	37.00 S	72.30 W
Bíobío ≃, Chile	252	31.38 S	71.34 W
Biobío ≃, Chile	252	36.49 S	73.10 W
Biodi	154	3.19 N	28.35 E
Biograd	36	43.56 N	15.27 E
Biogradska Gora Nacionalni Park ♦	38	42.57 N	19.40 E
Bioko □[4]	152	3.30 N	8.40 E
Bioko I	152	3.30 N	8.40 E
Biola	226	36.48 N	120.00 W
Bionaz	62	45.52 N	7.25 E
Biondo	154	0.23 S	25.13 E
Biondo Monument ⊥	146	31.25 N	10.15 E
Biot	62	43.38 N	7.06 E
Bipindi	152	3.05 N	10.25 E
Bippus	216	40.56 N	85.37 W
Biqiao	106	31.02 N	119.02 E
Bir, Ras >	144	11.59 N	43.22 E
Bira, India	272b	22.47 N	88.34 E
Bira, Ross.	89	49.15 N	137.16 E
Bira, Ross.	89	49.02 N	132.30 E
Bira ≃	89	48.07 N	133.21 E
Birab	164	6.12 S	138.25 E
Bīraba	126	23.51 N	90.34 E
Birāk	146	27.32 N	14.16 E
Birakan	89	49.01 N	131.42 E
Bi'r 'Alī	144	14.01 N	48.19 E
Bi'r al-Uzam	146	31.54 N	23.58 E
Birandža	89	54.35 N	136.18 E
Birao	146	10.17 N	22.47 E
Birati	272b	22.39 N	88.27 E
Birava	154	2.21 S	28.54 E
Bircao → Buur Gaabo	144	1.12 S	41.51 E
Birch	262	53.34 N	2.13 W
Birch ≃, Ab., Can.	176	58.30 N	112.15 W
Birch ≃, W.V., U.S.	188	38.35 N	80.53 W
Birch Bay	224	48.55 N	122.45 W
Birch Bay ⊂	224	48.53 N	122.47 W
Birch Bay State Park ♦	224	49.54 N	123.47 W
Birch Cliff ✦[8]	275b	43.41 N	79.17 W
Birch Creek ≃, Ak., U.S.	180	66.30 N	146.30 W
Birch Creek ≃, Id., U.S.	202	43.51 N	112.43 W
Birch Creek ≃, Mt., U.S.	202	48.26 N	112.15 W
Birch Creek ≃, Mt., U.S.	202	47.45 N	109.34 W
Birch Hill Dam ✦[6]	207	42.38 N	72.09 W
Birch Hills	184	52.59 N	105.25 W
Birchington	42	51.23 N	1.19 E
Birch Island	182	51.36 N	119.55 W
Birch Island I	184	52.25 N	99.55 W
Birch Lake ⊜, Ab., Can.	182	53.19 N	111.35 W
Birch Lake ⊜, On., Can.	184	51.24 N	92.20 W
Birch Lake ⊜, Sk., Can.	184	53.28 N	108.07 W
Birch Mountains ⋏[2]	176	57.30 N	112.30 W
Bir Chouhada	34	35.53 N	6.18 E
Birch Pond ⊜	283	42.28 N	71.00 W
Birch Reservoir ⊜[1]	196	36.31 N	96.12 W
Birch River	184	52.23 N	101.06 W
Birch Run	190	43.15 N	83.47 W
Birch Run ≃	285	40.09 N	75.37 W
Birchrunville	285	40.08 N	75.39 W
Birch Tree	194	36.59 N	91.29 W
Birch Vale	262	53.23 N	1.57 W
Birchwood, Eng., U.K.	44	53.13 N	0.36 W
Birchwood, Ak., U.S.	180	61.28 N	149.22 W
Birchwood, Wi., U.S.	190	45.39 N	91.33 W
Birchwood City	284c	38.49 N	76.59 W
Birchwood Park, De., U.S.	285	39.22 N	75.39 W
Birchwood Park, N.J., U.S.	208	40.06 N	74.09 W
Birchy Bay	186	49.21 N	54.44 W
Bird City	198	39.45 N	101.31 W
Bird Creek ≃	196	36.13 N	95.44 W
Bird Island	198	44.46 N	94.53 W
Bird Island I, S. Afr.	158	33.51 S	26.18 E
Bird Island I, S. Geor.	244	54.00 S	38.05 W
Bird Island ◉[3]	9	54.00 S	38.03 W
Bird Islet I	160	22.10 S	155.28 E
Bird River ⊂	284b	39.23 N	76.23 W
Birdsall	210	42.23 N	77.55 W
Birdsboro	208	40.15 N	75.48 W
Birds Landing	282	38.08 N	121.52 W
Birdsview	224	48.32 N	121.52 W
Birdsville	166	25.54 S	139.22 E
Birdtail Creek ≃	184	50.16 N	101.12 W
Birdum	164	15.39 S	133.13 E
Birdum Creek ≃	164	15.14 S	133.00 E
Birdwood	168b	34.49 S	138.57 E
Birecik	130	37.02 N	37.58 E
Bire Kpatua Game Reserve ✦[4]	154	5.12 N	27.36 E
Bir el Ater	148	34.44 N	8.03 E
Bir Enzaran	148	23.56 N	14.33 W
Bireuen	114	5.12 N	96.41 E
Bir Ghbalou	34	36.16 N	3.35 E
Birgi	126	22.42 N	86.41 E
Birgi Vecchi	70	37.53 N	12.29 E
Biri	116	12.41 N	124.22 E
Birigui	255	21.18 S	50.19 W
Biri Island I	116	12.40 N	124.22 E
Birikčul'	86	53.20 N	89.56 E
Biril'ussy	86	57.07 N	90.32 E
Birimbāl	142	31.21 N	30.30 E
Birimbāl al-Qadīmah	142	31.10 N	31.44 E
Birimşe	130	38.03 N	38.32 E
Biritiba-Mirim	256	23.35 S	46.02 W
Bīrjand	128	32.53 N	59.13 E
Birkat as-Sab'	142	30.38 N	31.05 E
Birkat Ghiṭās	142	31.07 N	30.16 E
Birkdale	262	53.37 N	3.02 W
Birkeland	26	58.20 N	8.14 E
Birken	182	50.29 N	122.36 W
Birkenfeld, Dtsch.	56	48.52 N	8.38 E
Birkenfeld, Dtsch.	56	49.51 N	9.42 E
Birkenfeld, Dtsch.	56	49.39 N	7.10 E
Birkenfeld, Or., U.S.	224	45.59 N	123.20 W
Birkenhead	44	53.24 N	3.02 W
Birkenhead Park ♦	262	53.24 N	3.02 W
Birkenwerder bei Berlin	54	52.41 N	13.16 E
Birkerød	41	55.50 N	12.26 E
Birkesdorf	56	50.49 N	6.28 E
Birket Fatimé	146	12.54 N	19.05 E
Birkfeld	61	47.21 N	15.42 E
Birkholz	264a	52.38 N	13.34 E
Birkkarspitze ∧	64	47.25 N	11.25 E
Birk-Nack >	41	54.48 N	9.55 E
Birksgate Range ⋏	162	27.10 S	129.45 E
Birky	78	49.42 N	36.02 E
Birla Museum ◉	272b	22.32 N	88.22 E
Birlik, Kaz.	80	47.28 N	50.32 E
Birlik, Kaz.	86	44.05 N	73.31 E
Birling	260	51.19 N	0.25 E
Birling ∧[2]	274a	33.57 S	150.43 E
Birmā	142	30.51 N	30.54 E
Birmania → Myanmar □[1]	110	22.00 N	98.00 E
Birmanie → Myanmar □[1]	110	22.00 N	98.00 E
Birmingham, Eng., U.K.	42	52.28 N	1.55 W
Birmingham, Al., U.S.	194	33.31 N	86.48 W
Birmingham, Ia., U.S.	190	40.52 N	91.56 W
Birmingham, Mi., U.S.	216	42.32 N	83.12 W
Birmingham, N.J., U.S.	285	39.58 N	74.42 W
Birmingham, Oh., U.S.	214	41.20 N	82.21 W
Birmingham, Pa., U.S.	214	40.38 N	78.13 W
Birmingham Airport ⊠	42	52.27 N	1.45 W
Birmitrapur	124	22.24 N	84.46 E
Bîr Mogreïn (Fort-Trinquet)	148	25.14 N	11.35 W
Birnagar	126	23.14 N	88.33 E
Birnamwood	190	44.56 N	89.12 W
Birnbaum	64	46.41 N	12.54 E
Birni	150	10.00 N	1.31 E
Birnie I[1]	14	3.35 S	171.31 W
Birni Ngaouré	150	13.05 N	2.54 E
Birnin Gwari	150	11.01 N	6.48 E
Birnin Kebbi	150	12.32 N	4.12 E
Birni Nkonni	150	13.48 N	5.15 E
Birnin Kudu	150	11.27 N	9.30 E
Birobidžan	89	48.48 N	132.57 E
Birobijan → Jevrej □[3]	89	48.30 N	132.00 E
Birofel'd	89	48.26 N	132.47 E
Birome	222	31.49 N	96.58 W
Birqāsh	142	30.10 N	31.02 E
Birr	48	53.05 N	7.54 W
Birregurra	169	38.20 S	143.48 E
Birrie ≃	166	29.43 S	146.37 E
Birrindudu	162	18.22 S	129.27 E
Birs (Birse) ≃	58	47.22 N	7.22 E
Birsk	86	55.25 N	55.32 E
Birstall	42	52.41 N	1.07 W
Birstein	56	50.21 N	9.19 E
Birštonas	76	54.37 N	24.02 E
Birten	263	51.38 N	6.29 E
Birtle	184	50.25 N	101.03 W
Birtley	44	54.54 N	1.34 W
Biru	120	31.30 N	93.51 E
Bir'učij	83	46.53 N	39.33 E
Bir'učja ≃	83	47.23 N	39.07 E
Birufu	164	5.52 S	138.24 E
Bir'ul'ka	88	53.52 N	106.21 E
Bir'ul'ovo ✦[8]	265b	55.35 N	37.40 E
Birungu, Parc des ♦	154	1.25 S	29.30 E
Birūr	122	13.37 N	75.58 E
Bir'usa	88	57.10 N	96.30 E
Bir'usa (Ona) ≃	88	57.43 N	95.24 E
Bir'usinsk	88	55.57 N	97.49 E
Biryukove	83	47.57 N	39.44 E
Biržai	76	56.12 N	24.45 E
Bîrzava ≃	38	45.16 N	20.49 E
Birżebbuġa	36	35.49 N	14.32 E
Bisa, Pulau I	164	1.15 S	127.28 E
Bisaccia	68	41.01 N	15.22 E
Bisacquino	70	37.42 N	13.15 E
Bisāi, India	126	22.10 N	86.24 E
Bisai, Nihon	94	35.16 N	136.44 E
Bīsalpur	124	28.18 N	79.48 E
Bisamberg	264b	48.20 N	16.22 E
Bisamberg ∧[2]	264b	48.19 N	16.22 E
Bisan-shotō II	96	34.24 N	133.50 E
Bisbee, Az., U.S.	200	31.26 N	109.55 W
Bisbee, N.D., U.S.	198	48.37 N	99.22 W
Biscarrosse	32	44.24 N	1.10 W
Biscarrosse et de Parentis, Lac de ⊂	32	44.20 N	1.10 W
Biscay, Bay of ⊂	32	44.00 N	4.00 W
Biscayne, Key I	220	25.42 N	80.10 W
Biscayne Bay ⊂	220	25.33 N	80.15 W
Biscayne National Park ♦	220	25.25 N	80.12 W
Bisceglie	68	41.14 N	16.31 E
Bischheim	58	48.37 N	7.45 E
Bischofsgrün	60	50.03 N	11.47 E
Bischofsheim, Dtsch.	56	50.24 N	10.01 E
Bischofsheim, Dtsch.	56	49.59 N	8.22 E
Bischofshofen	64	47.25 N	13.13 E
Bischofswerda	54	51.07 N	14.10 E
Bischofswiesen	64	47.39 N	12.57 E
Bischofszell	58	47.29 N	9.15 E
Bischwald, Étang de ⊜	56	49.00 N	6.42 E
Bischwiller	56	48.46 N	7.52 E
Biscoe, Ar., U.S.	194	34.49 N	91.24 W
Biscoe, N.C., U.S.	192	35.21 N	79.46 W
Biscoe Islands II	9	66.00 S	66.30 W
Biscotasi Lake ⊜	190	47.19 N	82.07 W
Biscucuy	246	9.22 N	69.59 W
Bise	174m	26.42 N	127.54 E
Bisei	96	34.41 N	133.33 E
Bisentina, Isola I	66	42.35 N	11.54 E
Bisenzio ≃	66	43.46 N	11.06 E
Biser	86	58.25 N	58.53 E
Biserovo	265b	55.47 N	38.07 E
Biserovskoje, ozero ⊜	265b	55.46 N	38.07 E
Bisert' ≃	86	56.39 N	57.55 E
Bise-zaki >	174m	26.43 N	127.53 E
Bisha	144	15.28 N	37.34 E
Bīshah, Wādī V	144	21.24 N	43.26 E
Bishahari	126	23.10 N	89.01 E
Bishan	107	29.37 N	106.13 E
Bishanga	152	4.31 S	21.02 E
Bishaykhāli	126	23.28 N	89.09 E
Bishkek → Biškek	85	42.54 N	74.36 E
Bishkhāli ≃[1]	126	21.59 N	89.59 E
Bishkin' ≃	83	49.15 N	39.35 E
Bishnāh	123	32.37 N	74.52 E
Bishnupur, India	120	24.38 N	93.46 E
Bishnupur, India	126	22.23 N	88.16 E
Bishnupur, India	126	23.05 N	87.19 E
Bishnupur, India	272b	22.37 N	88.31 E
Bisho	158	32.50 S	27.20 E
Bishop, Ca., U.S.	204	37.21 N	118.23 W
Bishop, Pa., U.S.	279b	40.19 N	80.12 W
Bishop, Tx., U.S.	196	27.35 N	97.47 W
Bishop Airport ⊠	216	42.58 N	83.44 W
Bishop Auckland	44	54.40 N	1.40 W
Bishop Rock I[2]	42a	49.52 N	6.27 W
Bishop's Castle	42	52.29 N	3.00 W
Bishop's Cleeve	42	51.57 N	2.04 W
Bishop's Falls	186	49.01 N	55.30 W
Bishops Frome	42	52.08 N	2.29 W
Bishops Head	208	38.16 N	76.04 W
Bishops Lydeard	42	51.04 N	3.12 W
Bishop's Stortford	42	51.53 N	0.09 E
Bishopsteignton	42	50.34 N	3.31 W
Bishopstoke	42	50.59 N	1.19 W
Bishopston	42	51.35 N	4.03 W
Bishop's Waltham	42	50.58 N	1.12 W
Bishopthorpe	44	53.55 N	1.06 W
Bishopton	206	45.35 N	71.35 W
Bishopville, Md., U.S.	208	38.26 N	75.11 W
Bishopville, S.C., U.S.	192	34.13 N	80.14 W
Bishrah, Ma'ṭan ⊤[4]	146	22.58 N	22.39 E
Bishrī, Jabal ∧	130	35.20 N	39.20 E
Bisignano	68	39.31 N	16.17 E
Bisina, Lake ⊜	154	1.38 N	33.56 E
Bisinadi Game Reserve ✦[4]	154	0.10 N	38.20 E
Bisingen	58	48.18 N	8.55 E
Biskamža	86	53.30 N	89.30 E
Biskaya, Golf von → Biscay, Bay of ⊂	32	44.00 N	4.00 W
Biškek (Frunze)	85	42.54 N	74.36 E
Biskintā	132	33.57 N	35.48 E
Biskupiec	30	53.52 N	20.58 E
Bisley, Eng., U.K.	42	51.45 N	2.08 W
Bisley, Eng., U.K.	260	51.20 N	0.38 W
Bislich	263	51.41 N	6.29 E
Bislig	116	8.13 N	126.19 E
Bislig Bay ⊂	116	8.14 N	126.22 E
Bismarck, Il., U.S.	216	40.16 N	87.37 W
Bismarck, Mo., U.S.	194	37.46 N	90.37 W
Bismarck, N.D., U.S.	198	46.48 N	100.47 W
Bismarck Archipelago II	164	5.00 S	150.00 E
Bismarck Range ⋏	164	5.30 S	144.45 E
Bismarck Sea ⊤[2]	164	4.00 S	148.00 E
Bismark	54	52.39 N	11.32 E
Bismil	130	37.51 N	40.40 E
Bismo	26	61.53 N	8.16 E
Bismuna, Laguna ⊂	236	14.45 N	83.20 W
Biso	154	1.46 N	31.25 E
Bison	198	45.31 N	102.27 W
Bison Peak ∧	200	39.14 N	105.30 W
Bispberg	40	60.22 N	15.47 E
Bispgården	26	63.02 N	16.37 E
Bispingen	52	53.05 N	10.00 E
Bisrakh	272a	28.34 N	77.26 E
Bisrāmpur	124	24.15 N	83.56 E
Bissa, Djebel ∧	34	36.26 N	1.28 E
Bissau	150	11.51 N	15.35 W
Bissaula	146	7.00 N	10.27 E
Bissegem	50	50.49 N	3.13 E
Bissendorf, Dtsch.	52	52.14 N	8.10 E
Bissendorf, Dtsch.	52	52.31 N	9.45 E
Bissett	184	51.02 N	95.40 W
Bissigh, Lach ≃	144	0.45 N	41.33 E
Bissikrima	150	10.51 N	10.56 W
Bissingen	56	48.43 N	10.37 E
Bissingheim ✦[8]	263	51.21 N	7.31 E
Bissorã	150	12.14 N	15.31 W
Bistcho Lake ⊜	176	59.40 N	118.40 W
Bistineau, Lake ⊜[1]	194	32.25 N	93.22 W
Bistra ≃	38	45.29 N	22.11 E
Bistreț	38	43.54 N	23.30 E
Bistrica	61	46.33 N	16.16 E
Bistrița	38	47.08 N	24.30 E
Bistrița ≃	38	46.30 N	26.57 E
Bistrița-Năsăud □[6]	38	47.15 N	24.30 E
Biswān	124	27.30 N	81.00 E
Bisztynek	30	54.06 N	20.55 E
Bitadton	116	11.30 N	122.05 E
Bitam	152	2.05 N	11.29 E
Bitam, Oued ≃	34	35.15 N	5.11 E
Bitatolo ≃	273b	4.09 S	15.19 E
Bitburg	56	49.58 N	6.31 E
Bitca	265b	55.34 N	37.37 E
Bitca ≃	265b	55.34 N	37.37 E
Bitche	56	49.03 N	7.26 E
Bitchū	96	34.47 N	133.27 E
Bitéa, Ouadi V	146	13.11 N	20.10 E
Bitetto	68	41.02 N	16.45 E
Bithia ⊥	71	38.53 N	8.52 E
Bithlo	220	28.33 N	81.06 W
Bithynia □[9]	130	40.10 N	30.15 E
Bitia, Wādī V	140	17.34 N	32.15 E
Bitik	80	50.09 N	50.30 E
Bitkine	146	11.59 N	18.13 E
Bitlis	130	38.22 N	42.06 E
Bitlis □[4]	128	38.30 N	42.10 E
Bitola	38	41.01 N	21.20 E
Bitolj → Bitola	38	41.01 N	21.20 E
Bitonto	68	41.06 N	16.42 E
Bitou	150	11.16 N	0.18 W
Bitra Island I	122	11.33 N	72.09 E
Bitritto	68	41.03 N	16.50 E
Bitschwiller-lès-Thann	58	47.50 N	7.05 E
Bitter Creek ≃, Ut,. U.S.	200	39.58 N	109.25 W
Bitter Creek ≃, Wy., U.S.	200	41.31 N	109.27 W
Bitterfeld	54	51.37 N	12.20 E
Bitterfontein	158	31.00 S	18.32 E
Bitter Lake ⊜	184	50.08 N	109.48 W
Bittermark ✦[8]	263	51.27 N	7.28 E
Bitterness, Mount ∧	172	44.45 S	170.18 E
Bittern Lake ⊜	184	53.55 N	105.50 W
Bitterroot ≃	202	46.52 N	114.06 W
Bitterroot, East Fork ≃	202	45.57 N	114.08 W
Bitterroot, West Fork ≃	202	45.57 N	114.08 W
Bitterroot Range ⋏	202	47.06 N	115.10 W
Bitterwater Creek ≃	226	35.41 N	119.58 W
Bitti	71	40.29 N	9.23 E
Bit'ug ≃	78	50.37 N	39.55 E
Bitung	112	1.27 N	125.11 E
Bitupitá	250	2.54 S	41.16 W
Bituruna	252	26.10 S	51.34 W
Biu	146	10.35 N	12.13 E
Bivalve	208	38.18 N	75.53 W
Bivins	194	33.01 N	94.12 W
Bivio	58	46.28 N	9.38 E
Bivona	70	37.37 N	13.26 E
Bivongi	68	38.28 N	16.27 E
Biwabik	190	47.31 N	92.20 W
Biwa-ko ⊜	94	35.15 N	136.05 E
Biwa-ko-kokutei-kōen ♦	94	35.10 N	136.00 E
Biwa-ko-ōhashi ✦[5]	94	35.08 N	135.56 E
Bixby	196	35.56 N	95.52 W
Biyalā	142	31.10 N	31.13 E
Biyang	100	32.44 N	113.20 E
Biysk → Bijsk	86	52.34 N	85.15 E
Biyuk-Karasu ≃	78	45.27 N	34.47 E
Bi Yun Si (Temple of the Azure Clouds) ◉[1]	105	40.00 N	116.11 E
Biz'aki	80	55.56 N	52.28 E
Bizana	158	30.58 S	29.52 E
Biz'ar	86	57.31 N	56.09 E
Bizard, Île I	275a	45.29 N	73.54 W
Bižbul'ak	80	53.43 N	54.16 E
Bizcocho, Cuchilla del ⋏[2]	258	33.45 S	57.30 W
Bizen	96	34.44 N	134.09 E
Bizerte	148	37.17 N	9.52 E
Bizerte □[8]	148	37.10 N	9.50 E
Bizerte, Lac de ⊜	36	37.12 N	9.52 E
Bīzhanābād	128	27.55 N	58.03 E
Bizkaiko □[4]	34	43.20 N	2.45 W
Bjæverskov	41	55.27 N	12.02 E
Bjala, Blg.	38	43.27 N	25.44 E
Bjala, Blg.	38	42.53 N	27.53 E
Bjala Slatina	38	43.28 N	23.56 E
Bjargtangar >	24a	65.31 N	24.32 W
Bjärnum	41	56.17 N	13.42 E
Bjärred	41	55.43 N	13.01 E
Bjärsjölagård	41	55.44 N	13.41 E
Bjästa	26	63.12 N	18.30 E
Bjelaja → Belaja ≃	72	55.54 N	53.33 E
Bjelovar	36	45.54 N	16.51 E
Bjernede	41	55.27 N	11.38 E
Bjerre Skov ∧[2]	41	55.47 N	9.53 E
Bjerringbro	26	56.23 N	9.40 E
Björbo	40	60.28 N	14.42 E
Bjørkelangen	26	59.53 N	11.34 E
Björklinge	40	60.02 N	17.33 E
Björknäs	40	59.19 N	18.14 E
Björkö I	40	59.53 N	19.00 E
Björköby	26	63.21 N	21.19 E
Björköfjärden ⊂	40	59.53 N	18.56 E
Björkvik	40	58.50 N	16.31 E
Björna	26	63.34 N	18.33 E
Bjørnafjorden ⊂[2]	26	60.06 N	5.22 E
Björndammen	40	59.12 N	16.49 E
Björneborg → Pori, Suomi	26	61.29 N	21.47 E
Björneborg, Sve.	40	59.15 N	14.15 E
Bjornesfjorden ⊜	26	60.10 N	7.41 E
Björnlunda	40	59.04 N	17.09 E
Bjørnøya (Bear Island) I	12	74.25 N	19.00 E
Bjurholm	26	63.56 N	19.13 E
Bjuv	41	56.05 N	12.54 E
Bkāsīn	132	33.34 N	35.35 E
Bla	150	12.57 N	5.46 W
Blaby	42	52.34 N	1.09 W
Blace	38	43.17 N	21.18 E
Black (Lixian) (Da) ≃, Asia	110	21.15 N	105.20 E
Black ≃, Mb., Can.	184	50.49 N	96.20 W
Black ≃, On., Can.	190	48.42 N	80.38 W
Black ≃, On., Can.	190	48.36 N	86.16 W
Black ≃, On., Can.	212	44.32 N	77.22 W
Black ≃, On., Can.	212	44.20 N	79.20 W
Black ≃, On., Can.	212	44.42 N	79.19 W
Black ≃, U.S.	194	35.38 N	91.19 W
Black ≃, Ak., U.S.	180	66.39 N	144.50 W
Black ≃, Az., U.S.	200	33.44 N	110.13 W
Black ≃, La., U.S.	194	31.16 N	91.50 W
Black ≃, Mi., U.S.	190	46.40 N	90.03 W
Black ≃, Mi., U.S.	190	43.00 N	82.25 W
Black ≃, Mi., U.S.	190	45.39 N	84.29 W
Black ≃, Mi., U.S.	214	43.00 N	82.25 W
Black ≃, N.M., U.S.	196	32.14 N	104.03 W
Black ≃, N.Y., U.S.	188	43.59 N	76.04 W
Black ≃, N.C., U.S.	192	34.35 N	78.16 W
Black ≃, Oh., U.S.	214	41.28 N	82.11 W
Black ≃, S.C., U.S.	192	33.24 N	79.15 W
Black ≃, Vt., U.S.	188	43.16 N	72.27 W
Black ≃, Vt., U.S.	188	44.55 N	72.13 W
Black ≃, Wa., U.S.	224	46.49 N	123.13 W
Black ≃, Wi., U.S.	190	43.57 N	91.22 W
Black, East Branch ≃	214	41.22 N	82.07 W
Black, East Fork ≃	190	44.26 N	90.42 W
Black, Middle Branch ≃	216	42.25 N	86.14 W
Black, South Branch ≃	216	42.25 N	86.15 W
Black, West Branch ≃	214	41.22 N	82.07 W
Blackadder Water ≃	46	55.46 N	2.15 W
Blackall	166	24.25 S	145.28 E
Black Bay ⊂	190	48.40 N	88.30 W
Black Bay Peninsula >[1]	190	48.38 N	88.21 W
Black Bear Creek ≃	196	36.25 N	96.38 W
Black Bear Island Lake ⊜	184	55.38 N	105.40 W
Blackberry Creek ≃	216	41.38 N	88.27 W
Blackberry Heights	216	41.45 N	88.23 W
Black Birch Lake ⊜	184	56.54 N	107.45 W
Black Brook ≃, Ma., U.S.	283	41.59 N	71.03 W
Black Brook ≃, Ma., U.S.	283	42.38 N	71.21 W
Black Brook ≃, N.J., U.S.	276	40.42 N	74.31 W
Black Bullock Hill ∧[2]	168b	35.37 S	138.12 E
Blackburn, Austl.	274b	37.49 S	145.09 E
Blackburn, Eng., U.K.	44	53.45 N	2.29 W
Blackburn, Scot., U.K.	46	55.52 N	3.38 W
Blackburn □[8]	262	53.42 N	2.28 W
Blackburn, Mount ∧	180	61.44 N	143.26 W
Blackbutt	171a	26.53 S	152.06 E
Black Butte ∧, Ca., U.S.	228	34.33 N	117.43 W
Black Butte ∧, Mt., U.S.	202	46.47 N	110.56 W
Black Butte ∧, Mt., U.S.	202	44.54 N	111.51 W
Black Butte Lake ⊜[1]	204	39.45 N	122.20 W
Blackbutt Range ⋏	171a	27.00 S	152.00 E
Black Canyon of the Gunnison National Monument ♦	200	38.32 N	107.42 W
Blackcraig Hill ∧	44	55.20 N	4.08 W
Black Creek, B.C., Can.	182	49.50 N	125.08 W
Black Creek, On., Can.	284a	43.00 N	79.01 W
Black Creek, N.Y., U.S.	210	42.17 N	78.14 W
Black Creek ≃, On., Can.	214	42.43 N	82.21 W
Black Creek ≃, On., Can.	275b	43.41 N	79.32 W
Black Creek ≃, On., Can.	284a	42.59 N	79.01 W
Black Creek ≃, Az., U.S.	200	35.16 N	109.14 W
Black Creek ≃, Mi., U.S.	216	41.49 N	83.54 W
Black Creek ≃, Mi., U.S.	216	43.11 N	86.14 W
Black Creek ≃, Ms., U.S.	194	33.01 N	90.21 W
Black Creek ≃, Ms., U.S.	194	30.39 N	88.39 W
Black Creek ≃, Mo., U.S.	219	39.41 N	91.55 W
Black Creek ≃, N.Y., U.S.	210	43.19 N	75.04 W
Black Creek ≃, N.Y., U.S.	210	43.06 N	77.41 W
Black Creek ≃, N.Y., U.S.	284a	43.05 N	78.57 W
Black Creek ≃, N.Y., U.S.	284a	43.03 N	78.42 W
Black Creek ≃, Pa., U.S.	210	41.00 N	76.10 W
Black Creek ≃, S.C., U.S.	192	34.18 N	79.37 W
Black Creek Park ♦	275b	43.46 N	79.31 W
Black Creek Pioneer Village ♦	275b	43.47 N	79.32 W
Black Cypress Creek ≃	222	32.53 N	94.26 W
Blackden Heath	262	53.14 N	2.20 W
Black Devon ≃	46	56.06 N	3.47 W
Black Diamond, Ab., Can.	182	50.42 N	114.14 W
Black Diamond, Wa., U.S.	224	47.18 N	122.00 W
Black Donald Lake ⊜[1]	212	45.13 N	76.55 W
Black Down Hills ⋏[2]	42	50.57 N	3.09 W
Blackdown Tableland National Park ♦	166	23.43 S	149.05 E
Blackduck	190	47.43 N	94.32 W
Black Duck ≃	176	56.51 N	89.02 W
Black Eagle	202	47.31 N	111.16 W
Black Esk ≃	44	55.12 N	3.10 W
Blackfalds	182	52.23 N	113.47 W
Blackfeet Indian Reservation ✦[4]	202	48.40 N	113.00 W
Blackfoot, Id., U.S.	202	43.11 N	112.20 W
Blackfoot, Mt., U.S.	182	48.34 N	112.52 W
Blackfoot ≃, Id., U.S.	202	43.08 N	112.30 W
Blackfoot ≃, Mt., U.S.	202	46.52 N	113.53 W
Blackfoot, North Fork ≃	202	46.59 N	113.07 W
Blackfoot Indian Reserve ✦[4]	182	50.45 N	113.00 W
Blackfoot Reservoir ⊜[1]	202	42.55 N	111.35 W
Blackford	46	56.15 N	3.46 W
Blackford □[6]	216	40.27 N	85.22 W
Black Forest → Schwarzwald ⋏	58	48.00 N	8.15 E
Blackhall Colliery	44	54.44 N	1.14 W
Blackhall Mountain ∧	200	41.02 N	106.41 W
Black Hameldon ∧[2]	262	53.44 N	2.08 W
Black Hawk	184	48.48 N	93.59 W
Black Hawk Creek ≃	190	42.30 N	92.21 W
Black Head >, Ire.	48	53.08 N	9.17 W
Black Head >, Eng., U.K.	42	50.01 N	5.06 W
Blackhead Bay ⊂	186	48.34 N	53.15 W
Blackheath, Austl.	170	33.38 S	150.17 E
Blackheath, S. Afr.	273d	26.08 S	27.58 E
Blackheath, Eng., U.K.	260	51.12 N	0.31 W
Black Hill ∧[2], Eng., U.K.	262	53.20 N	2.01 W
Black Hill ∧[2], Eng., U.K.	262	53.33 N	1.53 W
Black Hills ⋏	198	44.00 N	104.00 W
Black Hills ⋏[2]	282	37.50 N	121.52 W
Blackhope Scar ∧	46	55.44 N	3.05 W
Black Horse, Oh., U.S.	214	41.09 N	81.18 W
Black Horse, Pa., U.S.	285	40.06 N	75.19 W
Black Horse, Pa., U.S.	285	39.55 N	75.25 W
Black Horse Creek ≃	285	40.05 N	75.43 W
Black Island I	184	51.10 N	96.30 W
Black Isle >[1]	46	57.35 N	4.15 W
Black Jack	219	38.47 N	90.16 W
Black Jack Mountain ∧	228	33.23 N	118.24 W
Black-Lake	206	46.03 N	71.21 W
Black Lake ⊜, On., Can.	212	44.46 N	76.18 W
Black Lake ⊜, Sk., Can.	176	59.10 N	105.20 W
Black Lake ⊜, Mi., U.S.	190	45.28 N	84.15 W
Black Lake ⊜, N.Y., U.S.	212	44.31 N	75.35 W
Black Lake ⊜, Wa., U.S.	224	47.00 N	122.58 W
Black Lake Bayou ≃	194	32.01 N	93.09 W
Blacklegs Creek ≃	214	40.30 N	79.27 W
Blackley ✦[8]	262	53.31 N	2.13 W
Black Lick	214	40.28 N	79.11 W
Blacklick Creek ≃	214	40.28 N	79.13 W
Blacklick Creek, North Branch ≃	214	40.29 N	78.55 W
Blacklick Estates	218	39.54 N	83.22 W
Blacklog Mountain ∧	214	40.20 N	77.45 W
Blacklunans	46	56.44 N	3.22 W
Black Mesa ∧, U.S.	196	37.05 N	103.10 W
Black Mesa ∧, Az., U.S.	200	36.35 N	110.20 W
Blackmoor ⋏[1]	42	50.24 N	4.46 W
Blackmoorfoot Reservoir ⊜[1]	262	53.37 N	1.51 W
Blackmoor Vale V	42	50.56 N	2.25 W
Blackmore	260	51.41 N	0.19 E
Blackmore, Mount ∧	202	45.27 N	111.01 W
Black Moshannon State Park ♦	214	40.54 N	78.03 W
Black Mountain	192	35.37 N	82.19 W
Black Mountain ∧, D.Y.	124	27.17 N	90.23 E
Black Mountain ∧, Wales, U.K.	42	51.52 N	3.46 W
Black Mountain ∧, U.S.	192	36.54 N	82.54 W
Black Mountain ∧, Az., U.S.	200	32.46 N	110.57 W
Black Mountain ∧, Ca., U.S.	226	35.24 N	120.21 W
Black Mountain ∧, Ca., U.S.	228	35.08 N	117.14 W
Black Mountain ∧, Ca., U.S.	282	37.19 N	122.09 W
Black Mountain ∧, Id., U.S.	202	46.53 N	115.33 W
Black Mountain ∧, Mt., U.S.	202	46.44 N	112.31 W
Black Mountain ∧, Or., U.S.	202	45.13 N	119.17 W
Black Mountain ∧, Wy., U.S.	202	44.45 N	107.22 W
Black Mountain ∧[2], Austl.	166	21.08 S	139.41 E
Black Mountain ∧[2], Ca., U.S.	228	32.59 N	117.07 W
Black Mountain ∧[2], Tx., U.S.	222	31.09 N	97.44 W
Black Mountains ⋏, Wales, U.K.	42	51.57 N	3.08 W
Black Mountains ⋏, Az., U.S.	200	35.30 N	114.30 W
Black Nossob ≃	156	23.05 S	18.45 E
Black Oak	216	41.33 N	87.23 W
Black Peak ∧	200	34.08 N	114.13 W
Black Pine Peak ∧	202	42.08 N	113.08 W
Black Pipe Creek ≃	198	43.47 N	101.14 W
Black Point	226	38.07 N	122.31 W
Black Point >, Austl.	168b	34.37 S	137.54 E
Black Point >, Austl.	170	34.47 S	150.50 E
Black Point >, Ak., U.S.	180	57.00 N	153.18 W
Blackpool	44	53.50 N	3.03 W
Blackpool □[8]	262	53.47 N	3.02 W
Blackpool (Squire's Gate) Airport ⊠	262	53.47 N	3.02 W
Blackpool Football Ground ♦	262	53.49 N	3.03 W
Blackpool Tower ◉	262	53.49 N	3.03 W
Black Range ⋏	200	33.20 N	107.50 W
Black River, Jam.	241q	18.01 N	77.51 W
Black River, N.Y., U.S.	212	44.00 N	75.47 W
Black River Bay ⊂	212	43.58 N	76.07 W
Black River Falls	190	44.17 N	90.51 W
Black Rock, Austl.	274b	37.59 S	145.01 E
Black Rock, Ar., U.S.	194	36.06 N	91.05 W
Black Rock, Ma., U.S.	283	42.14 N	70.49 W
Black Rock I[2]	48	54.05 N	10.22 W
Black Rock II[1]	244	53.39 S	41.48 W
Black Rock Desert ✦[2]	204	41.10 N	119.00 W
Blackrod	262	53.35 N	2.35 W
Blacksburg, S.C., U.S.	192	35.07 N	81.30 W
Blacksburg, Va., U.S.	192	37.13 N	80.24 W
Blacks Creek ≃	285	40.08 N	74.43 W
Black Sea ⊤[2]	22	43.00 N	35.00 E
Blacks Fork ≃	200	41.24 N	109.38 W
Blacks Harbour	186	45.03 N	66.47 W
Blackshear	192	31.18 N	82.14 W
Blackshear, Lake ⊜[1]	192	31.56 N	83.56 W
Blacksod Bay ⊂	48	54.08 N	10.00 W
Black Springs, Austl.	170	33.52 S	149.42 E
Black Springs, Austl.	274b	37.46 S	145.19 E
Black Springs Hill ∧[2]	274b	37.46 S	145.19 E
Black Star Canyon V	280	33.47 N	117.39 W
Blackstone, Ma., U.S.	207	42.01 N	71.32 W
Blackstone, Va., U.S.	192	37.04 N	77.59 W
Blackstone ≃, Ab., Can.	182	52.50 N	116.07 W
Blackstone ≃, Yk., Can.	180	65.51 N	137.12 W
Blackstone Lake ⊜	212	45.14 N	79.53 W
Black Sugarloaf Mountain ∧	166	31.20 S	151.33 E
Black Thunder Creek ≃	198	43.33 N	104.41 W
Blacktown	170	33.46 S	150.55 E
Blackville	192	33.21 N	81.16 W
Black Volta (Volta Noire) ≃	150	8.41 N	1.33 W
Blackwall Tunnel ✦[5]	260	51.30 N	0.01 E
Blackwalnut Point >	208	38.40 N	76.20 W
Black Warrior ≃	194	32.32 N	87.51 W
Blackwatch Hills	210	43.05 N	77.27 W
Blackwater, Austl.	166	23.35 S	148.53 E
Blackwater, Ire.	48	52.26 N	6.21 W
Blackwater ≃, Europe	48	54.31 N	6.34 W
Blackwater ≃, Ire.	48	53.39 N	6.43 W
Blackwater ≃, Ire.	48	51.51 N	7.50 W
Blackwater ≃, Eng., U.K.	42	51.45 N	1.00 E
Blackwater ≃, U.S.	194	30.36 N	87.02 W
Blackwater ≃, Md., U.S.	208	38.21 N	76.01 W
Blackwater ≃, Mo., U.S.	194	38.56 N	92.51 W
Blackwater ≃, Va., U.S.	208	36.33 N	76.55 W
Blackwater Creek ≃, Austl.	166	25.56 S	144.20 E
Black Water Creek ≃, Fl., U.S.	220	28.51 N	81.24 W
Blackwater Draw V	196	33.35 N	101.50 W
Blackwaterfoot	46	55.30 N	5.19 W
Blackwater Lake ⊜	180	64.00 N	123.05 W
Blackwater Reservoir ⊜[1], Scot., U.K.	46	56.41 N	4.46 W
Blackwater Reservoir ⊜[1], Scot., U.K.	46	56.44 N	3.14 W
Blackwater Sound ⊔	220	25.10 N	80.25 W
Blackwell, Ok., U.S.	196	36.48 N	97.16 W
Blackwell, Tx., U.S.	196	32.05 N	100.19 W
Blackwood, Austl.	168b	35.02 S	138.37 E
Blackwood, Austl.	169	37.29 S	144.19 E

Symbols in the index entries represent the broad categories identified in the key at the right. Symbols with superior numbers (⋏[1]) identify subcategories (see complete key on page *I · 1*).

Symbole im Register stellen die rechts im Schlüssel erklärten Kategorien dar. Symbole mit hochgestellten Ziffern (⋏[1]) bezeichnen Unterabteilungen einer Kategorie (vgl. vollständiger Schlüssel auf Seite *I · 1*).

Los símbolos incluídos en el texto del índice representan las grandes categorías identificadas con la clave a la derecha. Los símbolos con numeros en su parte superior (⋏[1]) identifican las subcategorías (véase la clave completa en la página *I · 1*).

Les symboles de l'index représentent les catégories indiquées dans la légende à droite. Les symboles suivis d'un indice (⋏[1]) représentent des sous-catégories (voir légende complète à la page *I · 1*).

Os símbolos incluídos no texto do índice representam as grandes categorias identificadas com a chave à direita. Os símbolos com números em sua parte superior (⋏[1]) identificam as subcategorias (veja-se a chave completa à página *I · 1*).

∧ Mountain	Berg	Montaña	Montagne	Montanha
⋏ Mountains	Gebirge	Montañas	Montagnes	Montanhas
)(Pass	Paß	Paso	Col	Passo
V Valley, Canyon	Tal, Cañon	Valle, Cañón	Vallée, Canyon	Vale, Canhão
≚ Plain	Ebene	Llano	Plaine	Planície
> Cape	Kap	Cabo	Cap	Cabo
I Island	Insel	Isla	Île	Ilha
II Islands	Inseln	Islas	Îles	Ilhas
⊥ Other Topographic Features	Andere Topographische Objekte	Otros Elementos Topográficos	Autres données topographiques	Outros acidentes topográficos

ESPAÑOL

Nombre	Página	Lat.°′	Long.°′ W = Oeste
Blackwood, N.J., U.S.	285	39.48 N	75.03 W
Blackwood ≃	162	34.19 S	115.11 E
Blackwood, Cape ›	164	7.50 S	144.30 E
Blackwood Terrace	285	39.48 N	75.05 W
Bladel	52	51.23 N	5.13 E
Bladenboro	192	34.32 N	78.47 W
Bladensburg, Md., U.S.	284c	38.56 N	76.56 W
Bladensburg, Oh., U.S.	214	40.17 N	82.17 W
Blades	208	38.38 N	75.36 W
Bladgrond	158	28.52 S	19.57 E
Bladnoch ≃	44	54.51 N	4.25 W
Bladworth	184	51.18 N	106.09 W
Blaenau Ffestiniog	42	52.59 N	3.56 W
Blaenavon	42	51.48 N	3.05 W
Bláfell ∧	24a	64.32 N	19.53 W
Blagaj	36	43.15 N	17.50 E
Blagdon	42	51.20 N	2.43 W
Blagodarnoje	86	47.03 N	82.10 E
Blagodarnyj	72	45.06 N	43.27 E
Blagodatnoje, Kaz.	86	51.18 N	72.49 E
Blagodatnoje, Ross.	78	51.32 N	34.54 E
Blagodatovka	80	52.14 N	50.27 E
Blagoevgrad	38	42.01 N	23.06 E
Blagoveščenka, Kaz.	86	54.22 N	66.58 E
Blagoveščenka, Ross.	80	51.19 N	44.03 E
Blagoveščenka, Ross.	86	52.50 N	79.52 E
Blagoveščensk, Ross.	86	55.01 N	55.59 E
Blagoveščensk, Ross.	89	50.17 N	127.32 E
Blagoveščenskoje, Kaz.	85	43.18 N	74.12 E
Blagoveščenskoje, Ross.	86	58.08 N	62.58 E
Blåhø ∧	26	62.45 N	9.19 E
Blahodatne, Ukr.	83	47.42 N	37.25 E
Blahodatne, Ukr.	83	47.53 N	38.29 E
Blåhøj	41	55.51 N	9.01 E
Blaichach	58	47.34 N	10.15 E
Blaikfjället ∧	26	64.33 N	16.12 E
Blain, Fr.	32	47.29 N	1.46 W
Blain, Pa., U.S.	208	40.20 N	77.31 W
Blaina	42	51.46 N	3.10 W
Blain City	214	40.45 N	78.34 W
Blaine, Mn., U.S.	190	45.09 N	93.14 W
Blaine, Wa., U.S.	224	48.59 N	122.44 W
Blaine Creek ≃	188	38.11 N	82.37 W
Blaine Hill	279b	40.16 N	79.53 W
Blaine Lake	184	52.50 N	106.54 W
Blaineys	224	48.53 N	123.47 W
Blainville	206	45.40 N	73.52 W
Blainville-sur-l'Eau	58	48.33 N	6.24 E
Blair, On., Can.	212	43.23 N	80.23 W
Blair, Ne., U.S.	198	41.32 N	96.07 W
Blair, Ok., U.S.	196	34.46 N	99.20 W
Blair, Wi., U.S.	190	44.18 N	91.14 W
Blair □ [6]	214	40.30 N	78.25 W
Blair Athol	166	22.42 S	147.33 E
Blair Atholl	46	56.46 N	3.51 W
Blairgowrie	46	56.36 N	3.21 W
Blairs Mills	214	40.17 N	77.43 W
Blairstown, Ia., U.S.	190	41.54 N	92.05 W
Blairstown, N.J., U.S.	210	40.59 N	74.57 W
Blairsville, Ga., U.S.	192	34.52 N	83.57 W
Blairsville, Pa., U.S.	214	40.25 N	79.15 W
Blaise ≃, Fr.	50	48.46 N	1.25 E
Blaise ≃, Fr.	58	48.38 N	4.43 E
Blaisy-Bas	58	47.22 N	4.44 E
Blaj	38	46.11 N	23.55 E
Blakehurst	274a	33.59 S	151.07 E
Blakeley Canal ≅	226	36.09 N	119.48 W
Blakely, Ga., U.S.	192	31.22 N	84.56 W
Blakely, Pa., U.S.	210	41.28 N	75.35 W
Blakely Island I	224	48.33 N	122.50 W
Blakeney, Eng., U.K.	42	52.58 N	1.00 E
Blakeney, Eng., U.K.	42	51.46 N	2.29 W
Blake Plateau ✤ [4]	16	31.00 N	79.00 W
Blake Point ›	190	48.12 N	88.25 W
Blake Ridge ✤ [3]	16	29.00 N	73.30 W
Blakes	208	37.30 N	76.22 W
Blakesburg	190	40.57 N	92.38 W
Blakeslee, Oh., U.S.	216	41.31 N	84.44 W
Blakeslee, Pa., U.S.	210	41.06 N	75.36 W
Blalock Island I	202	45.53 N	119.41 W
Blâmont, Fr.	58	48.35 N	6.51 E
Blamont, Fr.	58	47.23 N	6.51 E
Blanc, Cap → Nouâdhibou, Râs ›, Afr.	148	20.46 N	17.03 W
Blanc, Cap ›, Tun.	36	37.20 N	9.51 E
Blanc, Mont ∧, P.Q., Can.	186	48.47 N	66.52 W
Blanc, Mont (Monte Bianco) ∧, Europe	62	45.50 N	6.52 E
Blanca	200	37.27 N	105.31 W
Blanca, Bahía c	252	38.55 S	62.10 W
Blanca, Isla I	248	9.06 S	78.38 W
Blanca, Laguna ⊜	254	52.25 S	71.10 W
Blanca, Punta ›, Arg.	258	34.57 S	57.40 W
Blanca, Punta ›, Chile	252	25.06 S	70.30 W
Blanca, Sierra ∧	200	31.15 N	105.26 W
Blanca Lake ⊜	224	47.53 N	121.21 W
Blanca Peak ∧	200	37.35 N	105.29 W
Blancas, Peñas ⋀	236	13.15 N	85.41 W
Blanc du Cheilon, Mont ∧	58	45.59 N	7.25 E
Blanchard, Ok., U.S.	196	35.08 N	97.39 W
Blanchard, Pa., U.S.	210	41.04 N	77.36 W
Blanchard, Wa., U.S.	224	48.35 N	122.24 W
Blanchard ≃	216	41.02 N	84.18 W
Blanchardville	190	42.48 N	89.51 W
Blanche ≃, On., Can.	190	47.34 N	79.32 W
Blanche ≃, P.Q., Can.	206	46.40 N	72.08 W
Blanche, Cape ›	162	33.01 S	134.09 E
Blanche, Dent ∧	58	46.03 N	7.36 E
Blanche, Lake ⊜, Austl.	162	22.25 S	123.17 E
Blanche, Lake ⊜, Austl.	166	29.15 S	139.39 E
Blanche, Mer → Beloje more ╤ [2]	24	65.30 N	38.00 E
Blanche Channel ʉ	175e	8.30 S	157.30 E
Blancheface	261	48.32 N	2.06 E
Blanche Marie Val ∟	250	4.44 N	56.53 W
Blanchester	218	39.17 N	83.59 W
Blanchisseuse	241r	10.47 N	61.18 W
Blanco, S. Afr.	158	33.57 S	22.24 E
Blanco, Tx., U.S.	196	30.06 N	98.25 W
Blanco ≃, Arg.	252	30.12 S	69.05 W
Blanco ≃, Arg.	254	47.22 S	71.12 W
Blanco ≃, Bol.	248	13.09 S	63.46 W
Blanco ≃, Ec.	246	0.28 N	79.25 W
Blanco ≃, Tx., U.S.	196	29.51 N	97.55 W
Blanco, Cabo → Nouâdhibou, Râs ›, Afr.	148	20.46 N	17.03 W
Blanco, Cabo ›, C.R.	236	9.34 N	85.07 W
Blanco, Cañon V	200	35.20 N	105.05 W
Blanco, Cape ›	202	42.50 N	124.34 W
Blanco, Lago ⊜	254	54.03 S	69.00 W
Blanco, Mar → Beloje more ╤ [2]	24	65.30 N	38.00 E
Blanco, Monte → Blanc, Mont ∧	62	45.50 N	6.52 E
Blanco, Rio ≃	200	37.07 N	107.03 W
Blanco Creek ≃	196	28.19 N	97.19 W
Blanc-Sablon	186	51.25 N	57.07 W
Bland, Mo., U.S.	219	38.18 N	91.37 W
Bland, Va., U.S.	192	37.06 N	81.06 W
Blanda ≃	24a	65.39 N	20.18 W
Blandburg	214	40.41 N	78.24 W
Blandford	207	42.10 N	72.55 W
Blandford Forum	42	50.52 N	2.11 W
Blanding	200	37.37 N	109.28 W
Blandinsville	190	40.33 N	90.51 W
Blandon	208	40.26 N	75.53 W

FRANÇAIS

Nom	Page	Lat.°′	Long.°′ W = Ouest
Blandy	261	48.34 N	2.47 E
Blanes	34	41.41 N	2.48 E
Blangkejeren	114	3.59 N	97.20 E
Blangpidie	114	3.45 N	96.51 E
Blangy-le-Château	50	49.14 N	0.17 E
Blangy-sur-Bresle	50	49.56 N	1.38 E
Blanice ≃	61	49.05 N	14.03 E
Blankenberg	56	50.45 N	7.22 E
Blankenberge	50	51.19 N	3.08 E
Blankenburg	54	51.48 N	10.58 E
Blankenburg ◆ [8]	264a	52.35 N	13.28 E
Blankenese ◆ [8]	52	53.33 N	9.48 E
Blankenfelde	54	52.20 N	13.23 E
Blankenfelde ◆ [8]	264a	52.37 N	13.23 E
Blankenhain	54	50.51 N	11.21 E
Blankenheim, Dtsch.	54	51.31 N	11.25 E
Blankenheim, Dtsch.	56	50.26 N	6.39 E
Blankensee	54	52.14 N	13.08 E
Blankenstein	263	51.24 N	7.14 E
Blanket	196	31.49 N	98.47 W
Blanquilla, Isla I	246	11.51 N	64.37 W
Blansko	30	49.22 N	16.39 E
Blanský Les ◆ [3]	61	48.52 N	14.16 E
Blantyre	154	15.47 S	35.00 E
Blanzac	62	45.07 N	3.51 E
Blanzy	58	46.42 N	4.23 E
Blaricum	52	52.16 N	5.15 E
Blarney	48	51.56 N	8.34 W
Blarney Castle ⊥	48	51.56 N	8.34 W
Blasdell	210	42.47 N	78.49 W
Blasheim	52	52.18 N	8.34 E
Błaszki	30	51.39 N	18.27 E
Blatná	60	49.26 N	13.53 E
Blatten	58	46.25 N	7.50 E
Blatzheim	56	50.51 N	6.38 E
Blau ≃	58	48.23 N	9.49 E
Blaubeuren	58	48.24 N	9.47 E
Blauen ∧	58	47.47 N	7.42 E
Blauer Nil → Blue Nile ≃	140	15.38 N	32.31 E
Blaufelden	56	49.18 N	9.58 E
Blaustein	58	48.25 N	9.53 E
Blauvelt	276	41.03 N	73.57 W
Blauvelt State Park ♦	276	41.04 N	73.56 W
Blawenburg	276	40.24 N	74.42 W
Blawnox	279b	40.29 N	79.51 W
Blaxland	170	33.45 S	150.36 E
Blaxland Creek ≃	274a	33.48 S	150.46 E
Blaydon	44	54.58 N	1.42 W
Blaye-et-Sainte-Luce	32	45.08 N	0.39 W
Blayney	166	33.32 S	149.15 E
Blaze, Point ›	164	12.56 S	130.12 E
Błażowa	30	49.54 N	22.05 E
Bleaker Island I	254	52.13 S	58.53 W
Bleaklow Head ∧	262	53.28 N	1.50 W
Blean	42	51.19 N	1.02 E
Bleckede	54	53.17 N	10.44 E
Bled	36	46.22 N	14.06 E
Bledsoe	196	33.38 N	103.01 W
Bleecker	210	43.07 N	74.22 W
Blefjell ∧	26	59.48 N	9.10 E
Blega	115a	7.08 S	113.03 E
Bleibach	58	48.07 N	8.01 E
Bleiberg ob Villach	64	46.37 N	13.41 E
Bleiburg	61	46.35 N	14.48 E
Bleicherode	54	51.26 N	10.34 E
Blekendorf	54	54.16 N	10.38 E
Blekinge □ [9]	26	56.20 N	15.05 E
Blekinge Län □ [6]	26	56.20 N	15.20 E
Bléneau	50	47.42 N	2.57 E
Blenheim, Austl.	171a	27.39 S	152.20 E
Blenheim, On., Can.	214	42.20 N	82.00 W
Blenheim, N.Z.	172	41.31 S	173.57 E
Blenheim, N.J., U.S.	285	39.48 N	75.05 W
Blenheim Palace ⌂	42	51.47 N	1.21 W
Blenio, Val V	58	46.27 N	8.58 E
Blénod-lès-Pont-à-Mousson	56	48.53 N	6.03 E
Blénod-lès-Toul	58	48.36 N	5.50 E
Bléone ≃	62	44.03 N	6.00 E
Blérancourt	50	49.31 N	3.09 E
Bléré	50	47.20 N	1.00 E
Blerick	52	51.23 N	6.10 E
Blériot-Plage	50	50.57 N	1.50 E
Blesbokspruit ≃	273d	26.14 S	28.29 E
Blessing	222	28.52 N	96.13 W
Blessington	48	53.10 N	6.32 W
Bletchingley	260	51.14 N	0.06 W
Bletchley	42	52.00 N	0.46 W
Bletterans	58	46.45 N	5.27 E
Bleu → Chang ≃	90	31.48 N	121.10 E
Bleue, Mer ≋	212	45.24 N	75.30 W
Bleury	261	48.31 N	1.45 E
Bleus, Monts ⋀	154	1.30 N	30.30 E
Blevio	62	45.50 N	9.05 E
Blewett Falls Lake ⊜ [1]	192	35.03 N	79.54 W
Blexen	52	53.32 N	8.32 E
Blidö I	40	59.37 N	18.54 E
Blidworth	44	53.06 N	1.07 W
Bliedinghausen ◆ [8]	263	51.09 N	7.12 E
Bliersheim ◆ [8]	263	51.23 N	6.43 E
Blies ≃	56	49.07 N	7.04 E
Blieskastel	56	49.14 N	7.16 E
Bligh Sound ʉ	172	44.50 S	167.32 E
Bligh Water ʉ	175g	17.00 S	178.00 E
Bligny	50	49.11 N	3.52 E
Bligny-sur-Ouche	58	47.06 N	4.40 E
Blik, Mount ∧	116	6.58 N	124.15 E
Blina	162	17.46 S	124.32 E
Blind ≃	276	40.57 N	73.42 W
Blind Creek ≃	274b	37.54 S	145.12 E
Blindley Heath	260	51.12 N	0.04 W
Blind River	190	46.10 N	82.58 W
Blinman	166	31.06 S	138.41 E
Blinnenhorn ∧	58	46.26 N	8.19 E
Blinovskij	80	49.23 N	42.19 E
Bliss	210	42.34 N	78.15 W
Blissfield, Mi., U.S.	216	41.49 N	83.51 W
Blissfield, Oh., U.S.	214	40.24 N	81.58 W
Blitar	115a	8.06 S	112.09 E
Blithe ≃	42	52.45 N	1.50 W
Blithfield Reservoir ⊜ [1]	42	52.48 N	1.53 W
Blitta	150	8.19 N	0.59 E
Blocher	218	38.43 N	85.39 W
Block Dam ◆ [6]	212	45.12 N	76.54 W
Block Island	207	41.10 N	71.33 W
Block Island I	207	41.11 N	71.35 W
Block Island Sound ʉ	207	41.10 N	71.45 W
Blockley	42	52.01 N	1.45 W
Blockton	198	40.36 N	94.28 W
Blodgett Mills	210	42.34 N	76.08 W
Bloed ≃	158	28.15 S	30.30 E
Bloedel	182	50.07 N	125.23 W
Bloedrivier, S. Afr.	158	28.06 S	30.33 E
Bloedrivier, S. Afr.	158	27.53 S	30.30 E
Bloekomspruit	158	26.45 S	28.21 E
Bloemendaal	52	52.24 N	4.37 E
Bloemfontein	158	29.12 S	26.07 E
Bloemhof	158	27.38 S	25.32 E
Bloemhofdam ⊜ [1]	158	27.40 S	25.40 E
Blois	50	47.35 N	1.20 E
Blokhus	26	57.15 N	9.35 E
Blokzijl	52	52.44 N	5.57 E
Blombacher Bach ◆ [8]	263	51.15 N	7.14 E
Blombacka	40	59.37 N	13.47 E
Blomberg	52	51.56 N	9.05 E
Blomstermåla	26	56.59 N	16.20 E
Blonay	58	46.28 N	6.54 E
Blönduós	24a	65.39 N	20.15 W
Blongas	115b	8.53 S	116.02 E
Blonville-sur-Mer	50	49.19 N	0.02 E
Blood Indian Creek ≃	184	50.55 N	111.03 W
Blood Indian Reserve ◆ [4]	182	49.30 N	113.10 W
Blood Mountain ∧	192	34.44 N	83.56 W
Blood River ⊥	158	28.20 S	30.35 E
Bloodsworth Island I	208	38.10 N	76.03 W
Bloodvein ≃	184	51.45 N	96.44 W
Bloody Foreland ›	48	55.09 N	8.17 W

PORTUGUÊS

Nome	Página	Lat.°′	Long.°′ W = Oeste
Bloomdale	216	41.10 N	83.33 W
Bloomer	190	45.06 N	91.29 W
Bloomfield, On., Can.	212	43.59 N	77.14 W
Bloomfield, Ct., U.S.	207	41.49 N	72.43 W
Bloomfield, In., U.S.	194	39.01 N	86.56 W
Bloomfield, Ia., U.S.	190	40.45 N	92.24 W
Bloomfield, Ky., U.S.	194	37.54 N	85.19 W
Bloomfield, Mo., U.S.	194	36.53 N	89.55 W
Bloomfield, Ne., U.S.	198	42.35 N	97.38 W
Bloomfield, N.J., U.S.	210	40.48 N	74.11 W
Bloomfield, N.M., U.S.	200	36.42 N	107.59 W
Bloomfield, Oh., U.S.	214	40.03 N	81.44 W
Bloomfield ◆ [8]	279b	40.27 N	79.56 W
Bloomfield Glens	281	42.33 N	83.20 W
Bloomfield Highlands	281	42.36 N	83.16 W
Bloomfield Hills	216	42.35 N	83.14 W
Bloomfield Village	216	42.33 N	83.15 W
Bloomingburg, N.Y., U.S.	210	41.33 N	74.26 W
Bloomingburg, Oh., U.S.	218	39.36 N	83.23 W
Bloomingdale, Il., U.S.	216	41.57 N	88.04 W
Bloomingdale, Mi., U.S.	216	42.22 N	85.57 W
Bloomingdale, N.J., U.S.	210	41.00 N	74.19 W
Bloomingdale, Oh., U.S.	214	40.21 N	80.49 W
Blooming Glen	208	40.22 N	75.15 W
Blooming Grove, In., U.S.	218	39.30 N	85.04 W
Blooming Grove, N.Y., U.S.	210	41.25 N	74.11 W
Blooming Grove, Pa., U.S.	210	41.21 N	75.09 W
Blooming Grove, Tx., U.S.	222	32.06 N	96.43 W
Blooming Prairie	190	43.52 N	93.03 W
Bloomington, Ca., U.S.	228	34.04 N	117.23 W
Bloomington, Il., U.S.	216	40.29 N	88.59 W
Bloomington, In., U.S.	218	39.09 N	86.31 W
Bloomington, Mn., U.S.	190	44.50 N	93.17 W
Bloomington, N.Y., U.S.	210	41.53 N	74.03 W
Bloomington, Tx., U.S.	196	28.38 N	96.53 W
Bloomington, Wi., U.S.	190	42.53 N	90.55 W
Bloomington, Lake ⊜ [1]	216	40.37 N	88.55 W
Blooming Valley	214	41.40 N	80.03 W
Bloomsburg	210	41.00 N	76.27 W
Bloomsbury, Austl.	166	20.43 S	148.35 E
Bloomsbury, N.J., U.S.	210	40.39 N	75.05 W
Bloomsdale Gardens	285	40.07 N	74.52 W
Bloomville, N.Y., U.S.	210	42.20 N	74.48 W
Bloomville, Oh., U.S.	214	41.03 N	83.00 W
Blora	115a	6.57 S	111.25 E
Bloserville	208	40.12 N	77.24 W
Blossburg	210	41.40 N	77.03 W
Blossom	196	33.39 N	95.23 W
Blossom Hill	208	40.05 N	76.19 W
Blötberget	40	60.07 N	15.04 E
Blotzheim	58	47.36 N	7.29 E
Blouberg	156	23.08 S	28.56 E
Blouberg ∧	156	23.01 S	28.59 E
Bloubergstrand	158	33.47 S	18.28 E
Blouin, Lac ⊜	190	48.10 N	77.44 W
Bloumet	148	23.27 N	6.06 E
Blountstown	192	30.26 N	85.02 W
Blountsville	194	34.04 N	86.35 W
Blountville	192	36.31 N	82.19 W
Blovice	60	49.35 N	13.33 E
Blovstrød	41	55.52 N	12.24 E
Blowering Reservoir ⊜ [1]	171b	35.30 S	148.15 E
Blowing Rock	192	36.08 N	81.40 W
Bloxham	42	52.02 N	1.22 W
Bloxom	208	37.49 N	75.37 W
Blšanka ≃	54	50.10 N	13.34 E
Blšany	54	50.10 N	13.29 E
Bludenz	58	47.09 N	9.49 E
Bludnaja ≃	88	51.24 N	110.39 E
Blue ≃, Az., U.S.	200	33.13 N	109.11 W
Blue ≃, Co., U.S.	200	40.03 N	106.24 W
Blue ≃, In., U.S.	216	41.07 N	85.30 W
Blue ≃, In., U.S.	218	38.11 N	86.19 W
Blue ≃, Ok., U.S.	196	33.53 N	95.56 W
Blue, Middle Fork ≃	218	38.33 N	86.07 W
Blue, South Fork ≃	218	38.26 N	86.11 W
Blue, West Fork ≃	218	38.33 N	86.07 W
Blue Anchor	285	39.41 N	74.52 W
Blue Anchor Brook ≃	285	39.42 N	74.49 W
Blue Ash	218	39.13 N	84.22 W
Blue Ball	218	39.29 N	84.21 W
Blue Bell	208	40.09 N	75.16 W
Bluebell Hill	260	51.20 N	0.30 E
Blue Bonnets, Champ de Course ♦	275a	45.29 N	73.39 W
Blue Brook ≃	276	40.40 N	74.25 W
Blue Buck Knob ∧ [2]	194	36.57 N	92.07 W
Bluebush Swamp ≋	162	20.30 S	137.25 E
Blue Creek, Oh., U.S.	218	38.47 N	83.20 W
Blue Creek, Wa., U.S.	182	48.19 N	117.49 W
Blue Creek, Wa., U.S.	202	48.19 N	117.49 W
Blue Creek ≃, Ca., U.S.	226	38.28 N	120.22 W
Blue Creek ≃, Id., U.S.	202	42.02 N	116.08 W
Blue Creek ≃, Ne., U.S.	198	41.19 N	102.10 W
Blue Creek ≃, Oh., U.S.	216	41.07 N	84.26 W
Blue Creek ≃, Ut,. U.S.	200	41.31 N	112.24 W
Blue Cypress Lake ⊜	220	27.44 N	80.45 W
Blue Earth	190	43.38 N	94.06 W
Blue Earth ≃	190	44.09 N	94.02 W
Bluefield, Va., U.S.	192	37.15 N	81.16 W
Bluefield, W.V., U.S.	192	37.16 N	81.13 W
Bluefields	236	12.00 N	83.45 W
Bluefields, Bahía de c	236	12.02 N	83.44 W
Bluefields Bay c	241q	18.10 N	78.03 W
Blue Grass Airport ⊠	218	38.02 N	84.36 W
Blue Grotto → Azzurra, Grotta ⍟ [5]	68	40.35 N	14.14 E
Blue Hill, Me., U.S.	188	44.24 N	68.35 W
Blue Hill, Ne., U.S.	198	40.19 N	98.26 W
Blue Hill Bay c	188	44.15 N	68.30 W
Blue Hills	207	41.40 N	72.56 W
Blue Hills of Couteau ⋀ [2]	186	47.59 N	57.43 W
Blue Hills Reservation ♦	283	42.13 N	71.05 W
Blue Island	216	41.39 N	87.40 W
Blue Jay	228	34.15 N	117.13 W
Bluejoint Lake ⊜	202	42.35 N	119.40 W
Blue Knob ∧	214	40.17 N	78.34 W
Blue Knob State Park ♦	214	40.16 N	78.35 W
Blue Lagoon National Park ♦	154	15.30 S	27.25 E
Blue Lake National Park ♦	171a	27.31 S	153.29 E
Blue Licks Battlefield State Park ♦	218	38.26 N	84.00 W
Blue Marsh Lake ⊜ [1]	208	40.25 N	76.05 W
Blue Mesa Reservoir ⊜ [1]	200	38.27 N	107.10 W
Blue Mosque ⌂ [1]	273c	30.02 N	31.15 E
Blue Mound, Il., U.S.	219	39.42 N	89.07 W
Blue Mound, Ks., U.S.	198	38.05 N	95.00 W
Blue Mound, Tx., U.S.	222	32.51 N	97.19 W
Blue Mountain, Ms., U.S.	194	34.40 N	89.01 W
Blue Mountain, N.Y., U.S.	210	42.07 N	74.01 W
Blue Mountain ∧, N.B., Can.	186	47.49 N	66.19 W
Blue Mountain ∧, Nf., Can.	186	50.24 N	57.10 W
Blue Mountain ∧, Ar., U.S.	194	34.41 N	94.03 W
Blue Mountain ∧, Mt., U.S.	198	47.16 N	104.10 W
Blue Mountain ∧, N.H., U.S.	188	44.47 N	71.28 W
Blue Mountain ∧, Pa., U.S.	188	40.15 N	77.30 W
Blue Mountain ∧ [2], On., Can.	190	48.15 N	80.07 W
Blue Mountain ∧ [2], On., Can.	212	44.40 N	77.58 W
Blue Mountain Peak ∧	241q	18.03 N	76.35 W
Blue Mountains ⋀, Austl.	170	33.37 S	150.17 E
Blue Mountains ⋀, Jam.	241q	18.06 N	76.40 W
Blue Mountains ⋀, U.S.	202	45.30 N	118.15 W
Blue Mountains ⋀, Me., U.S.	188	44.50 N	70.35 W
Blue Mountains National Park ♦	170	33.40 S	150.25 E
Blue Mud Bay c	164	13.26 S	135.56 E
Blue Nile (Al-Baḥr al-Azraq) (Abay) ≃	140	15.38 N	32.31 E
Bluenose Lake ⊜	180	68.25 N	119.45 W
Blue Point	276	40.45 N	73.02 W
Blue Point ›	276	40.44 N	73.02 W
Blue Rapids	198	39.40 N	96.39 W
Blue Ridge, Ab., Can.	182	54.08 N	115.22 W
Blue Ridge, Ga., U.S.	192	34.51 N	84.19 W
Blue Ridge, Il., U.S.	216	40.17 N	88.29 W
Blue Ridge ⋀	178	37.00 N	82.00 W
Blue Ridge Summit	208	39.43 N	77.28 W
Blue River	182	52.05 N	119.17 W
Blue Rock Springs Park ♦	282	38.08 N	122.12 W
Bluesky	182	56.04 N	118.14 W
Blue Springs	198	40.08 N	96.39 W
Blue Stack Mountains ⋀	48	54.45 N	8.05 W
Bluestone ≃	192	37.34 N	80.59 W
Bluestone Dam ◆ [6]	192	37.36 N	80.53 W
Bluestone Lake ⊜ [1]	192	37.30 N	80.50 W
Bluestone State Park ♦	192	37.37 N	80.56 W
Bluewater	200	35.15 N	107.59 W
Blue Water Bridge ◆ [5]	214	43.00 N	82.25 W
Bluff, N.Z.	172	46.36 S	168.20 E
Bluff, Ut,. U.S.	200	37.17 N	109.33 W
Bluff Cape ›	110	18.00 N	94.26 E
Bluff City, Il., U.S.	219	38.57 N	89.02 W
Bluff City, Tn., U.S.	192	36.28 N	82.15 W
Bluff Cove c	280	33.48 N	118.24 W
Bluff Creek ≃, U.S.	196	36.58 N	97.26 W
Bluff Creek ≃, Ks., U.S.	198	37.02 N	99.29 W
Bluff Dale	196	32.21 N	98.01 W
Bluff Head ›	271d	22.11 N	114.12 E
Bluff Island I	271d	22.19 N	114.21 E
Bluff Knoll ∧	162	34.23 S	118.20 E
Bluff Park	194	33.24 N	86.51 W
Bluff Point ›	162	27.50 S	114.06 E
Bluffs	219	39.45 N	90.32 W
Bluff Springs	219	39.59 N	90.21 W
Bluffton, In., U.S.	216	40.44 N	85.10 W
Bluffton, Oh., U.S.	216	40.53 N	83.53 W
Bluffton, S.C., U.S.	192	32.14 N	80.51 W
Bluffy Lake ⊜	184	50.47 N	92.55 W
Bluford	219	38.20 N	88.45 W
Blum	222	32.09 N	97.24 W
Blumberg, Dtsch.	54	52.36 N	13.37 E
Blumberg, Dtsch.	58	47.50 N	8.31 E
Blumenau	252	26.56 S	49.03 W
Blumenhof	184	50.01 N	107.41 W
Blümlisalp ∧	58	46.30 N	7.47 E
Blunt	198	44.30 N	99.59 W
Blup Blup Island I	164	3.30 S	144.37 E
Bly	202	42.23 N	121.02 W
Blying Sound ʉ	180	59.50 N	149.15 W
Blyth, Austl.	168b	33.51 S	138.29 E
Blyth, On., Can.	190	43.44 N	81.26 W
Blyth, Eng., U.K.	44	55.07 N	1.30 W
Blyth ≃, Austl.	164	12.04 S	134.35 E
Blyth ≃, Eng., U.K.	42	52.18 N	1.40 E
Blyth ≃, Eng., U.K.	44	55.08 N	1.31 W
Blyth Bridge	46	55.42 N	3.24 W
Blythe	204	33.36 N	114.35 W
Blythedale	214	40.15 N	79.48 W
Blytheswood	214	42.07 N	82.36 W
Blytheville	194	35.55 N	89.55 W
Blytheville Air Force Base ■	194	35.57 N	89.57 W
Blyth Range ⋀	162	26.50 S	129.00 E
Blyznyuky	78	48.52 N	36.33 E
Bnei Braq → Bene Beraq	132	32.05 N	34.50 E
Bø, Nor.	24	68.37 N	14.33 E
Bø, Nor.	26	59.25 N	9.04 E
Bo, S.L.	150	7.56 N	11.21 W
Boa	154	10.32 S	28.06 E
Boac	116	13.27 N	121.50 E
Boaco	236	12.28 N	85.40 W
Boaco □ [5]	236	12.30 N	85.30 W
Boadilla del Monte	266a	40.24 N	3.53 W
Boa Esperança, Bra.	255	21.05 S	45.34 W
Boa Esperança, Bra.	256	22.48 S	42.34 W
Boa Esperança, Bra.	256	22.24 S	43.05 W
Boa Esperança, Represa ⊜ [1]	250	6.50 S	44.00 W
Bo'ai	102	35.10 N	113.04 E
Boali	152	4.48 N	18.07 E
Boalia	126	23.35 N	88.57 E
Boalsburg	214	40.46 N	77.48 W
Boane	156	26.06 S	32.19 E
Boano, Pulau I	164	2.56 S	127.56 E
Boa Nova	255	14.22 S	40.10 W
Bo'ao	110	19.14 N	110.34 E
Boara Pisani	64	45.08 N	11.47 E
Boara Polesine	64	45.07 N	11.48 E
Board Camp Mountain ∧	204	40.42 N	123.43 W
Boardman	214	41.01 N	80.39 W
Boardman ≃	190	44.46 N	85.38 W
Boarhills	46	56.19 N	2.42 W
Boario Terme	64	45.54 N	10.10 E
Boat Basin	182	49.29 N	126.25 W
Boat Channel ʉ	212	44.10 N	76.31 W
Boath	46	57.44 N	4.23 W
Boat Lake ⊜	212	44.44 N	81.13 W
Boatman	166	27.16 S	146.55 E
Boat of Garten	46	57.20 N	3.44 W
Boa Viagem	250	5.07 S	39.44 W
Boa Vista, Bra.	246	2.49 N	60.40 W
Boa Vista, Bra.	256	21.25 S	45.35 W
Boa Vista I	150a	16.05 N	22.50 W
Boa Vista, Morro ∧ [2]	287a	22.53 S	43.06 W
Boavita	246	6.20 N	72.35 W
Boawai	115b	8.46 S	121.10 E
Boayan Island I	116	10.34 N	119.09 E
Boaz	194	34.12 N	86.09 W
Boba	115b	8.57 S	121.04 E
Bobai	102	22.12 N	109.52 E
Bobbau	54	51.41 N	12.16 E
Bobbili	122	18.34 N	83.22 E
Bobbing	260	51.21 N	0.43 E
Bobbingworth	260	51.44 N	0.13 E
Bobbin Head	274a	33.39 S	151.08 E
Bobbio	62	44.46 N	9.23 E
Bobbio Pellice	62	44.48 N	7.07 E
Bobbys Run ≃	285	39.58 N	74.48 W
Bobcaygeon	212	44.33 N	78.33 W
Bobenheim-Roxheim	56	49.35 N	8.21 E
Bobigny	50	48.54 N	2.27 E
Böbingen, Dtsch.	56	48.49 N	9.54 E
Bobingen, Dtsch.	58	48.16 N	10.50 E
Bobitz	54	53.47 N	11.20 E
Bob Lake ⊜	212	44.55 N	78.47 W
Böblingen	56	48.41 N	9.01 E
Boblo Island Amusement Park ♦	281	42.06 N	83.07 W
Bobo Dioulasso	150	11.12 N	4.18 W
Boboiob, gora ∧	85	40.52 N	70.21 E
Bobo Island I	164	9.08 S	143.14 E
Bobolice	30	53.57 N	16.36 E
Bobonaza ≃	246	2.36 S	76.38 W
Bobonong	156	21.58 S	28.17 E
Bobos ≃	234	20.15 N	96.47 W
Bobotsari	115a	7.18 S	109.22 E
Bobr	76	54.20 N	29.16 E
Bobr ≃, Bela.	76	54.03 N	28.51 E
Bóbr ≃, Pol.	30	52.04 N	15.04 E
Bobrik ≃	76	52.08 N	26.46 E
Bobrov	78	51.06 N	40.02 E
Bobrovytsya	78	50.44 N	31.22 E
Bobrujsk	76	53.09 N	29.14 E
Bobrykove	83	47.56 N	39.13 E
Bobrynets'	78	48.03 N	32.09 E
Bobs Creek ≃	219	38.57 N	90.42 W
Bobs Lake ⊜	212	44.40 N	76.35 W
Bobtown	188	39.45 N	79.58 W
Bobuk	140	11.30 N	34.05 E
Bobures	246	9.15 N	71.11 W
Boby, Pic ∧	157b	22.12 S	46.55 E
Boca ◆ [8]	288	34.38 S	58.21 W
Bôca, Cachoeira da ∟	250	5.27 S	54.24 W
Boca Brava, Isla I	236	8.13 N	82.16 W
Boca Chica	240m	17.59 N	66.32 W
Boca Chica Key I	220	24.34 N	81.42 W
Bôca da Mata	250	9.41 S	36.11 W
Boca del Monte	236	8.21 N	82.07 W
Boca del Río	234	19.06 N	96.06 W
Boca del Rosario	258	34.26 S	57.17 W
Boca de Pozo	246	11.00 N	64.23 W
Boca de Quadra ʉ	182	55.08 N	130.50 W
Boca do Acre	248	8.45 S	67.23 W
Bôca do Jari	250	1.07 S	51.58 W
Bocage, Cap ›	175f	21.12 S	165.35 E
Boca Grande	220	26.44 N	82.15 W
Boca Grande Channel ʉ	220	24.34 N	82.03 W
Boca Grande Key I	220	24.32 N	82.00 W
Bocaina ≃	256	22.40 S	45.00 W
Bocaina, Parque Nacional de ♦	256	23.00 S	44.15 W
Bocaina, Serra da ⋀	256	22.43 S	44.40 W
Bocaina de Minas	256	22.10 S	44.24 W
Bocaiúva	255	17.07 S	43.49 W
Bocanda	150	7.04 N	4.30 W
Bocanegra	286d	12.01 S	77.07 W
Bocaranga	152	6.59 N	15.39 E
Boca Raton	220	26.21 N	80.05 W
Boca Reservoir ⊜ [1]	226	39.24 N	120.06 W
Bocas del Toro	236	9.20 N	82.15 W
Bocas del Toro □ [4]	236	8.50 N	82.10 W
Bocas del Toro, Archipiélago de II	236	9.20 N	82.10 W
Bocaue	116	14.48 N	120.55 E
Bocay	236	14.19 N	85.10 W
Bocay ≃	236	14.20 N	85.10 W
Boccaleone	66	44.39 N	11.48 E
Boccea ◆ [8]	267a	41.58 N	12.19 E
Bocchigliero	68	39.25 N	16.45 E
Bocconi	64	44.01 N	11.46 E
Bočejkovo	76	55.01 N	29.09 E
Bochan	88	53.09 N	103.48 E
Bochil	234	16.59 N	92.55 W
Böch Möron	86	49.40 N	90.20 E
Bochnia	30	49.58 N	20.26 E
Bocholt, Bel.	56	51.10 N	5.35 E
Bocholt, Dtsch.	52	51.50 N	6.36 E
Bocholtz	56	50.49 N	6.00 E
Bochov	54	50.06 N	13.02 E
Bochum, Dtsch.	56	51.28 N	7.13 E
Bochum, Dtsch.	263	51.28 N	7.13 E
Bochum, S. Afr.	156	23.17 S	29.07 E
Bockel	52	53.12 N	9.17 E
Böckel ◆ [8]	263	51.13 N	7.12 E
Bockenem	52	52.00 N	10.07 E
Bockhorn	52	53.23 N	8.01 E
Böckstein	64	47.05 N	13.07 E
Bockum ◆ [8], Dtsch.	263	51.21 N	6.38 E
Bockum ◆ [8], Dtsch.	263	51.20 N	6.44 E
Bockum-Hövel	52	51.42 N	7.46 E
Bocognano	36	42.05 N	9.03 E
Bocón, Caño ≃	246	3.42 N	67.53 W
Boconó	246	9.15 N	70.16 W
Bocq ≃	56	50.20 N	4.53 E
Bocşa	38	45.23 N	21.47 E
Boczów	54	52.19 N	14.58 E
Boda, Centraf.	152	4.19 N	17.28 E
Böda, Sve.	26	57.15 N	17.03 E
Boda, Sve.	26	61.01 N	15.13 E
Bodafors	26	57.30 N	14.42 E
Boda Glasbruk	26	56.44 N	15.40 E
Bodāi	272b	22.48 N	88.29 E
Bodajbo	88	57.51 N	114.10 E
Bodalangi	152	3.14 N	22.14 E
Bodalla	166	36.05 S	150.03 E
Bodallin	162	31.22 S	118.52 E
Bodåsgruvan	40	60.25 N	16.26 E
Bodcau Creek ≃	194	33.01 N	93.31 W
Boddam, Scot., U.K.	46	57.28 N	1.47 W
Boddam, Scot., U.K.	46a	59.55 N	1.17 W
Boddington	168a	32.48 S	116.28 E
Bode	198	42.52 N	94.17 W
Bode ≃	54	51.50 N	11.46 E
Bodega Bay c	204	38.15 N	123.00 W
Bodegraven	52	52.05 N	4.45 E
Bodélé ◆ [1]	146	16.30 N	16.30 E
Bodelschwingh ◆ [8]	263	51.33 N	7.22 E
Boden → Fleres, It.	64	46.58 N	11.21 E
Boden, Sve.	26	65.50 N	21.42 E
Bodenburg	52	52.01 N	10.01 E
Bodenfelde	52	51.38 N	9.33 E
Bodenheim	56	49.56 N	8.18 E
Bodenmais	60	49.04 N	13.06 E
Bodensee (Lake Constance) ⊜	58	47.35 N	9.25 E
Bodenteich	54	52.50 N	10.41 E
Bodenwerder	52	51.59 N	9.31 E
Bodenwies ∧	61	47.45 N	14.34 E
Bodenwöhr	60	49.16 N	12.19 E
Boderg, Lough ⊜	48	53.52 N	7.58 W
Bode Sadu	150	9.00 N	4.47 E
Bodhan	122	18.40 N	77.54 E
Bodh Gaya	124	24.42 N	84.59 E
Bodiam	42	51.00 N	0.33 E
Bodināyakkanūr	122	10.01 N	77.21 E
Bodine, Mount ∧	182	55.37 N	125.49 W
Bodjoki	152	2.59 N	22.18 E
Bodjokola	152	3.54 N	20.17 E
Bodmin	42	50.29 N	4.43 W
Bodmin Moor ◆ [3]	42	50.33 N	4.33 W
Bodø	24	67.17 N	14.23 E
Bodocó	250	7.47 S	39.55 W
Bodoquena, Serra da ⋀ [1]	248	21.00 S	56.50 W
Bodoukpa	152	5.43 N	17.36 E
Bodri ≃	115a	6.52 S	110.10 E
Bodrog ≃	30	48.07 N	21.25 E
Bodrum	130	37.02 N	27.26 E
Bodstedt	54	54.22 N	12.37 E
Bo Duc	110	11.58 N	106.48 E
Bodzentyn	30	50.56 N	20.57 E
Boè, Piz ∧	64	46.31 N	11.48 E
Boëge	58	46.13 N	6.25 E
Boekelo	52	52.13 N	6.47 E
Boele ◆ [8]	263	51.24 N	7.28 E
Boémbé	152	2.54 S	15.39 E
Boende	152	0.13 S	20.52 E
Bœng Lvea	110	12.36 N	105.34 E
Boeni	157a	12.55 S	45.06 E
Boën-sur-Lignon	62	45.44 N	3.59 E
Boeo, Capo ›	70	37.48 N	12.25 E
Boerboonfontein	158	33.43 S	20.32 E
Boerne	196	29.47 N	98.43 W
Boeslunde	41	55.18 N	11.17 E
Boesmanland □ [5]	156	19.30 S	20.00 E
Boesmans ≃, S. Afr.	158	33.42 S	26.39 E
Boesmans ≃, S. Afr.	158	28.46 S	30.09 E
Boesmansriviermond	158	33.42 S	26.39 E
Boetsap	158	27.59 S	24.30 E
Boeuf ≃	194	31.52 N	91.47 W
Boeuf Creek ≃	219	38.36 N	91.09 W
Boffa	150	10.10 N	14.02 W
Boffalora	266b	45.28 N	8.50 E
Boffzen	52	51.45 N	9.23 E
Bofoku	152	0.57 S	20.53 E
Bofors	40	59.20 N	14.32 E
Bofosso	150	8.40 N	9.42 W
Bōfu → Hōfu	96	34.03 N	131.34 E
Boga	154	1.03 N	29.56 E
Bogachiel ≃	224	47.55 N	124.28 W
Bogadjim	164	5.25 S	145.45 E
Bogal, Lagh ≃	154	0.45 N	40.50 E
Bogale	110	16.17 N	95.24 E
Bogalusa	194	30.47 N	89.50 W
Bogan ≃	166	29.57 S	146.21 E
Bogandé	150	12.59 N	0.08 W
Bog and Vly Meadows ≋	276	40.56 N	74.19 W
Bogan Gate	166	33.07 S	147.48 E
Bogangolo	152	5.34 N	18.15 E
Bogantungan	166	23.39 S	147.18 E
Bogart, Mount ∧	182	50.55 N	115.14 W
Bogastow Brook ≃	283	42.12 N	71.22 W
Bogata	196	33.28 N	95.13 W
Bogatiščevo-Jepišino	82	54.47 N	38.25 E
Bogatoje	80	53.04 N	51.24 E
Bogatyje Saby	80	56.01 N	50.27 E
Bogatynia	54	50.53 N	15.00 E
Bogatyr'	80	53.25 N	50.02 E
Bogatyrevo	80	50.22 N	48.46 E
Boğazkale	130	40.02 N	34.37 E
Boğazkaya	130	41.27 N	35.54 E
Boğazköy ◆ [8]	267b	41.11 N	28.46 E
Boğazköy ≃	267b	41.10 N	28.49 E
Boğazlıyan	130	39.12 N	35.15 E
Bogbonga	152	1.35 N	19.25 E
Bogcang ≃	120	31.56 N	87.24 E
Bogd	102	45.11 N	100.43 E
Bogdanovič	86	56.47 N	62.01 E
Bogdanovka, Ross.	80	52.42 N	50.46 E
Bogdanovka, Ross.	80	52.10 N	52.37 E
Bogda Shan ⋀	90	43.30 N	89.45 E
Bogdo Ula ∧	86	43.50 N	88.20 E
Bogel	56	50.11 N	7.48 E
Bogembaj	86	52.29 N	72.20 E
Bogen	60	48.55 N	12.43 E
Bogense	41	55.34 N	10.06 E
Boger City	192	35.29 N	81.12 W
Bogess Creek ≃	282	37.18 N	122.19 W
Boget	80	49.40 N	47.59 E
Boggabilla	166	28.37 S	150.21 E
Boggabri	166	30.42 S	150.02 E
Boggeragh Mountains ⋀	48	52.03 N	8.55 W
Boggola, Mount ∧	162	23.48 S	117.40 E
Boggs Run ≃	279b	40.32 N	80.14 W
Boggstown	218	39.34 N	85.55 W
Boggy Creek ≃	222	31.07 N	95.46 W
Boggy Peak ∧	240c	17.03 N	61.51 W
Bogia	164	4.15 S	144.55 E
Bogie Lake ⊜	281	42.37 N	83.31 W
Bogilima	152	3.34 N	19.16 E
Bogliasco	62	44.23 N	9.04 E
Bognanco Fonti	58	46.07 N	8.12 E
Bognes	24	68.10 N	16.00 E
Bognor Regis	42	50.47 N	0.41 W
Bogny-sur-Meuse	56	49.51 N	4.46 E
Bogo, Cam.	146	10.44 N	14.36 E
Bogo, Pil.	116	11.03 N	124.00 E
Bogø I	41	54.56 N	12.04 E
Bogo Bay c	116	11.05 N	124.01 E
Bogol Manyo	144	4.31 N	41.32 E
Bogol'ubovo, Ross.	76	55.32 N	32.57 E
Bogol'ubovo, Ross.	80	56.13 N	40.31 E
Bogomila	38	41.36 N	21.28 E
Bogong, Mount ∧	166	36.45 S	147.18 E
Bogong Peaks ⋀	171b	35.34 S	148.28 E
Bogor	115a	6.35 S	106.47 E
Bogoria, Lake ⊜	154	0.15 N	36.06 E
Bogoro	154	1.24 N	30.17 E
Bogorodick	76	53.46 N	38.08 E
Bogorodickoje	80	46.20 N	41.10 E
Bogorodsk, Ross.	24	62.16 N	52.28 E
Bogorodsk, Ross.	80	56.06 N	43.31 E
Bogorodskoje, Ross.	80	57.51 N	50.45 E
Bogorodskoje, Ross.	80	46.20 N	43.53 E
Bogorodskoje, Ross.	82	55.02 N	38.29 E
Bogorodskoje, Ross.	82	55.26 N	36.14 E
Bogorodskoje, Ross.	89	52.22 N	140.30 E
Bogorodskoje ◆ [8]	265b	55.49 N	37.44 E
Bogoso	150	5.34 N	2.01 W
Bogosskij chrebet ⋀	84	42.15 N	46.05 E
Bogotá → Santa Fe de Bogotá, Col.	246	4.36 N	74.05 W
Bogota, N.J., U.S.	276	40.52 N	74.01 W
Bogotol	86	56.12 N	89.33 E
Bogou	150	10.39 N	0.11 E
Bogovarovo	24	58.59 N	47.01 E
Bogra	124	24.51 N	89.22 E
Bograd	86	54.13 N	90.51 E
Bogrie Hill ∧ [2]	44	55.08 N	3.55 W
Bogučany	88	58.23 N	97.29 E
Bogučar	78	49.57 N	40.33 E
Bogučar ≃	78	49.57 N	40.39 E
Bogué	150	16.35 N	14.16 W
Bogue Chitto	194	31.26 N	90.27 W
Bogue Chitto ≃	194	30.35 N	89.49 W
Bogue Chitto Creek ≃	194	32.10 N	87.14 W
Bogue Phalia ≃	194	33.15 N	90.44 W
Bogues Bay c	208	37.52 N	75.29 W
Böğürtlen	130	37.10 N	38.04 E
Boguševsk	76	54.51 N	30.13 E
Bogustan	85	41.41 N	70.05 E
Bo Hai (Gulf of Chihli) c	98	38.30 N	120.00 E
Bohai Haixia ʉ	98	38.15 N	121.00 E
Bohain-en-Vermandois	50	49.59 N	3.27 E
Bohai Wan c	98	38.40 N	118.20 E
Bohan	56	49.52 N	4.53 E
Bohannon	208	37.24 N	76.22 W
Böheimkirchen	61	48.12 N	15.46 E
Bohemia	210	40.46 N	73.06 W
Bohemia → Čechy □ [9]	30	49.50 N	14.00 E
Bohemia ≃	208	39.29 N	75.55 W
Bohemia Downs	162	18.53 S	126.14 E
Bohemian Forest ⋀	30	49.15 N	12.45 E
Bohetai	104	42.01 N	123.13 E
Bohicon	150	7.12 N	2.04 E
Bohin	144	11.44 N	51.15 E
Bohinjska Bistrica	36	46.17 N	13.57 E
Bohinjsko Jezero ⊜	64	46.17 N	13.50 E
Böhlen	54	51.12 N	12.23 E
Böhlitz-Ehrenberg ◆ [8]	54	51.21 N	12.17 E
Böhme ≃	52	52.46 N	9.28 E
Böhmen → Čechy □ [9]	30	49.50 N	14.00 E
Böhmenkirch	56	48.41 N	9.55 E
Böhmerwald → Bohemian Forest ⋀	30	49.15 N	12.45 E
Bohmte	52	52.22 N	8.19 E
Bohners Lake	216	42.37 N	88.17 W
Böhnsdorf ◆ [8]	264a	52.24 N	13.33 E

≃	River	Fluß	Río	Rivière	Rio
≅	Canal	Kanal	Canal	Canal	Canal
∟	Waterfall, Rapids	Wasserfall, Stromschnellen	Cascada, Rápidos	Chute d'eau, Rapides	Cascata, Rápidos
ʉ	Strait	Meeresstraße	Estrecho	Détroit	Estreito
c	Bay, Gulf	Bucht, Golf	Bahía, Golfo	Baie, Golfe	Baía, Golfo
⊜	Lake, Lakes	See, Seen	Lago, Lagos	Lac, Lacs	Lago, Lagos
≋	Swamp	Sumpf	Pantano	Marais	Pântano
⁂	Ice Features, Glacier	Eis- und Gletscherformen	Accidentes Glaciales	Formes glaciaires	Acidentes glaciares
╤	Other Hydrographic Features	Andere Hydrographische Objekte	Otros Elementos Hidrográficos	Autres données hydrographiques	Outros acidentes hidrográficos
✤	Submarine Features	Untermeerische Objekte	Accidentes Submarinos	Formes de relief sous-marin	Acidentes submarinos
□	Political Unit	Politische Einheit	Unidad Política	Entité politique	Unidade política
⌂	Cultural Institution	Kulturelle Institution	Institución Cultural	Institution culturelle	Instituição cultural
⊥	Historical Site	Historische Stätte	Sitio Histórico	Site historique	Sitio histórico
♦	Recreational Site	Erholungs- und Ferienort	Sitio de Recreo	Centre de loisirs	Area de Lazer
⊠	Airport	Flughafen	Aeropuerto	Aéroport	Aeroporto
■	Military Installation	Militäranlage	Instalación Militar	Installation militaire	Instalação militar
◆	Miscellaneous	Verschiedenes	Misceláneo	Divers	Diversos

ENGLISH / DEUTSCH

Name	Page	Lat.°′	Long.°′
Bohodou	150	9.46 N	9.04 W
Bohodukhiv	78	50.10 N	35.30 E
Bohol	144	5.45 N	46.09 E
Bohol □[4]	116	9.50 N	124.10 E
Bohol I	116	9.50 N	124.10 E
Bohol Sea ⊤[2]	116	9.10 N	124.25 E
Bohongou	150	12.30 N	0.42 E
Bohorg	152	6.23 N	15.37 E
Bohorodchany	78	48.48 N	24.32 E
Bohorok	114	3.30 N	98.12 E
Bohsdorf	54	51.38 N	14.32 E
Bohuslän □[9]	26	58.15 N	11.50 E
Bohuslav	78	49.33 N	30.53 E
Bohušovice nad Ohří	54	50.29 N	14.07 E
Bohutín	60	49.40 N	13.55 E
Boi	150	9.34 N	9.27 E
Boi, Ponta do >	256	23.58 S	45.15 W
Boiaçu	246	0.27 S	61.46 W
Boiano	66	41.29 N	14.29 E
Boiceville	210	41.59 N	74.15 W
Boiestown	186	46.27 N	66.25 W
Boigu Island I	164	9.16 S	142.12 E
Boila	154	16.10 S	39.50 E
Boiling Springs, N.C., U.S.	192	35.30 N	81.37 W
Boiling Springs, Pa., U.S.	208	40.08 N	77.07 W
Boim	250	2.49 S	55.10 W
Boinville-en-Mantois	261	48.56 N	1.46 E
Boinvilliers	261	48.55 N	1.40 E
Boipeba, Ilha de I	255	13.39 S	38.55 W
Boiro	34	42.39 N	8.54 W
Bois, Lac des ⊜, N.T., Can.	180	66.40 N	125.15 W
Bois, Lac des → Woods, Lake of the ⊜, N.A.	184	49.15 N	94.45 W
Bois, Rio dos ≏	255	18.35 S	50.02 W
Bois Blanc Island I	190	45.45 N	84.28 W
Boisbriand	275a	45.37 N	73.51 W
Bois Brule ≏	190	46.45 N	91.37 W
Boischâtel	206	46.54 N	71.08 W
Bois-Colombes	261	48.55 N	2.16 E
Boisdale, Loch ⊂	46	57.08 N	7.19 W
Bois d'Arc Creek ≏	196	33.50 N	95.50 W
Bois-d'Arcy	261	48.48 N	2.01 E
Bois-des-Filion	206	45.40 N	73.45 W
Bois de Sioux ≏	198	46.16 N	96.36 W
Boise	202	43.36 N	116.12 W
Boise ≏	202	43.49 N	117.01 W
Boise, Middle Fork ≏	202	43.42 N	115.38 W
Boise, North Fork ≏	202	43.42 N	115.38 W
Boise, South Fork ≏	202	43.36 N	115.51 W
Boise City	196	36.43 N	102.30 W
Boisemont	261	49.01 N	2.00 E
Bois-Guillaume	50	49.28 N	1.08 E
Bois-le-Roi	50	48.28 N	2.42 E
Boissettes	261	48.31 N	2.37 E
Boissevain	184	49.14 N	100.03 W
Boissise-la-Bertrand	261	48.32 N	2.35 E
Boissy-l'Aillerie	261	49.05 N	2.02 E
Boissy-Saint-Léger	50	48.45 N	2.31 E
Boissy-sous-Saint-Yon	261	48.34 N	2.13 E
Boistfort Peak ∧	224	46.29 N	123.12 W
Boitzenburg	54	53.15 N	13.37 E
Boizenburg	54	53.22 N	10.43 E
Boja	115a	7.06 S	110.16 E
Bojadła	30	51.57 N	15.50 E
Bojarkino	82	54.57 N	38.31 E
Bojarsk	88	56.19 N	106.04 E
Bojayá ≏	246	6.35 N	76.54 W
Bojeador, Cape >	116	18.30 N	120.34 E
Bojelebung	116	6.31 N	122.11 E
Bojevo	78	51.24 N	39.19 E
Boji Plain ≚	154	1.30 N	39.45 E
Bojizhang	98	41.49 N	117.46 E
Bojnūrd	128	37.28 N	57.19 E
Bojonegoro	115a	7.09 S	111.52 E
Boju	150	7.25 N	7.52 E
Boju Ega	150	7.24 N	8.04 E
Bojuru	252	31.38 S	51.26 W
Bokad	272c	18.53 N	72.58 E
Bokada	152	4.08 N	19.23 E
Bokal	168a	33.29 S	116.54 E
Bokala, Zaïre	152	3.07 S	17.02 E
Bokala, Zaïre	152	2.03 N	18.59 E
Bokani	150	9.26 N	5.13 E
Bokāro Steel City	124	23.45 N	86.07 E
Bokatola	152	0.38 S	18.46 E
Bokchito	196	34.01 N	96.08 W
Boké	150	10.56 N	14.18 W
Bokeelia	220	26.42 N	82.09 W
Bokel	52	53.23 N	8.46 E
Bokela	152	1.08 S	21.56 E
Bokes Creek ≏	188	40.19 N	83.10 W
Bokfontein	158	32.48 S	19.16 E
Bokhara	158	27.57 S	20.30 E
Bokhara ≏	166	29.55 S	146.42 E
Boki	146	8.48 N	13.32 E
Bokino	80	52.38 N	41.26 E
Bokkol ∧	154	1.50 N	37.02 E
Bok Koŭ	110	10.37 N	104.03 E
Böklund	41	54.36 N	9.34 E
Boknafjorden ⊂[2]	26	59.10 N	5.35 E
Boko, Congo	152	4.47 S	14.38 E
Boko, Kaz.	86	49.05 N	81.38 E
Bokod	116	16.30 N	120.50 E
Bokode	152	3.58 N	19.29 E
Bokolako	150	13.36 N	12.33 W
Bokonbajevskoje	85	42.07 N	77.00 E
Bokondji	152	2.22 N	18.42 E
Bokondo	152	0.15 N	22.32 E
Bokong	112	9.58 S	124.04 E
Bokoro	146	12.23 N	17.03 E
Boko Songo	152	4.26 S	13.37 E
Bokota	152	0.51 S	22.18 E
Bokote	152	0.05 S	20.08 E
Bokovo-Antratsit → Antratsyt	83	48.06 N	39.06 E
Bokovskaja	80	49.15 N	41.49 E
Bokpunt >	158	33.34 S	18.19 E
Bokpyin	110	11.16 N	98.46 E
Boksburg	158	26.12 S	28.14 E
Boksburg □[5]	273d	26.12 S	28.14 E
Boksburg-Noord	273d	26.12 S	28.15 E
Boksburg South	273d	26.14 S	28.15 E
Boksburg-West	273d	26.13 S	28.14 E
Boksitogorsk	76	59.28 N	33.51 E
Bokungu	152	0.41 S	22.19 E
Bol, Hrv.	36	43.16 N	16.40 E
Bol, Tchad	146	13.28 N	14.43 E
Bolaang Mongondow	112	0.56 N	124.10 E
Bolama, Gui.-B.	150	11.35 N	15.28 W
Bolama, Zaïre	152	1.57 N	22.58 E
Bolaman	130	41.03 N	37.37 E
Bolān ≏	120	28.38 N	67.42 E
Bolanda, Jabal ∧	140	7.44 N	25.28 E
Bol'andkiik ≏	85	39.11 N	72.17 E
Bolangum	166	36.46 S	142.53 E
Bolaños	234	21.41 N	103.47 W
Bolaños ≏	234	21.14 N	104.08 W
Bolaños de Calatrava	34	38.54 N	3.40 W
Bolān Pass)(	120	29.45 N	67.35 E
Bolans	240c	17.02 N	61.53 W
Bolay I	152	4.20 N	17.21 E
Bolayır	130	40.31 N	26.45 E
Bolbec	50	49.34 N	0.29 E
Bolçalı	84	40.38 N	46.18 E
Bolčary	86	59.49 N	68.48 E
Bolchov	76	53.27 N	36.01 E
Bolchuny	80	47.59 N	46.25 E
Bolda ≏	80	46.10 N	48.14 E
Boldasevo	80	54.43 N	45.33 E
Boldekow	54	53.43 N	13.35 E
Bolderslev	41	54.59 N	9.18 E
Bold Heath	262	53.24 N	2.42 W
Boldon	44	54.57 N	1.27 W
Bol'džuan	85	38.19 N	69.40 E
Bole, Ghana	150	9.02 N	2.29 W
Bole, Zhg.	86	44.53 N	82.05 E
Bolekhiv	78	49.04 N	23.52 E
Boleko	152	1.31 S	19.53 E
Bolero	154	10.59 S	33.45 E
Boles	194	34.46 N	94.02 W
Bolesławiec	30	51.16 N	15.34 E
Boleszkowice	30	52.44 N	14.36 E
Boletice nad Labem	54	50.45 N	14.13 E
Boley	196	35.29 N	96.29 W
Bolgart	162	31.16 S	116.30 E
Bolgatanga	150	10.46 N	0.52 W
Bolhrad	78	45.41 N	28.36 E
Boli, Sūd.	140	6.01 N	28.43 E
Boli, Tchad	146	10.50 N	18.43 E
Boli, Zhg.	89	45.46 N	130.31 E
Bolia	152	1.36 S	18.23 E
Boliden	26	64.52 N	20.23 E
Boligee	194	32.45 N	88.01 W
Boligeqiu	104	42.14 N	121.40 E
Bolíkov	61	49.02 N	15.22 E
Bolinao	116	16.23 N	119.54 E
Bolinas	226	37.54 N	122.42 W
Boling	222	29.15 N	95.56 W
Bolingbrook	216	41.41 N	88.04 W
Bolinger Creek ≏	282	37.47 N	122.00 W
Bolingo	152	3.30 S	21.43 E
Bolishan	89	43.50 N	123.31 E
Bolivar, Austl.	168b	34.46 S	138.36 E
Bolívar, Col.	246	5.50 N	76.01 W
Bolívar, Col.	246	1.50 N	76.58 W
Bolívar, Col.	246	4.21 N	76.10 W
Bolívar, Perú	248	7.18 S	77.48 W
Bolivar, Mo., U.S.	194	37.36 N	93.24 W
Bolivar, N.Y., U.S.	210	42.04 N	78.10 W
Bolivar, Oh., U.S.	214	40.39 N	81.27 W
Bolivar, Pa., U.S.	214	40.23 N	79.09 W
Bolivar, Tn., U.S.	194	35.15 N	88.59 W
Bolívar □[3]	246	6.20 N	63.30 W
Bolívar □[4]	246	1.35 S	79.00 W
Bolívar □[5]	246	9.00 N	74.40 W
Bolívar, Cerro ∧	246	7.28 N	63.25 W
Bolívar, Pico ∧	246	8.30 N	71.02 W
Bolivar Peninsula >[1]	196	29.27 N	94.39 W
Bolivar Run	214	41.59 N	78.39 W
Bolivia □[1], S.A.	242	17.00 S	65.00 W
Bolivia □[1], S.A.	248	17.00 S	65.00 W
Bolivie → Bolivia □[1]	248	17.00 S	65.00 W
Bolivien → Bolivia □[1]	248	17.00 S	65.00 W
Boljarovo	38	42.09 N	26.49 E
Boljoon	116	9.38 N	123.29 E
Bolkar Dağları ⋏	130	37.15 N	34.20 E
Bölkenbusch	263	51.21 N	7.06 E
Boll	56	48.38 N	9.37 E
Bolladello	266b	45.41 N	8.50 E
Bollate	62	45.33 N	9.07 E
Böllberg ∧[2]	263	51.23 N	7.19 E
Bollendorf	56	49.51 N	6.22 E
Bollène	62	44.17 N	4.45 E
Bollensdorf	264a	52.31 N	13.43 E
Bolles Canal ≅	220	26.38 N	80.34 W
Bolles Harbor	216	41.51 N	83.24 W
Bollin ≏	44	53.23 N	2.28 W
Bolling Air Force Base ■	284c	38.51 N	77.02 W
Bollington, Eng., U.K.	44	53.18 N	2.06 W
Bollington, Eng., U.K.	262	53.22 N	2.25 W
Bollnäs	26	61.21 N	16.25 E
Bollon	166	28.05 S	147.15 E
Bollstabruk	26	63.00 N	17.39 E
Bollstanäs	40	59.30 N	17.56 E
Bollullos par del Condado	34	37.20 N	6.32 W
Bollwerk	263	51.10 N	7.35 E
Bolmen ⊜	26	56.55 N	13.40 E
Bolnisi	84	41.28 N	44.33 E
Bolo	144	8.50 N	39.22 E
Bolobo	152	2.10 S	16.14 E
Bolochovo	82	54.05 N	37.50 E
Bologna	64	44.29 N	11.20 E
Bologna □[4]	64	44.28 N	11.26 E
Bologne, Fr.	58	48.12 N	5.08 E
Bologne → Bologna, It.	64	44.29 N	11.20 E
Bolognesi	248	6.35 S	73.10 W
Bolognetta	70	37.58 N	13.27 E
Bolognola	66	42.59 N	13.14 E
Bologoje	76	57.54 N	34.02 E
Bologovo	76	56.54 N	31.42 E
Bololo	152	3.50 S	21.08 E
Bolomba	152	0.29 N	19.12 E
Bolombo	152	3.59 S	21.22 E
Bolombo ≏	152	1.32 N	21.14 E
Bolon'	89	49.55 N	136.07 E
Bolon', ozero ⊜	89	49.51 N	136.22 E
Bolonchén de Rejón	232	20.00 N	89.49 W
Bolondo	152	0.27 N	20.01 E
Bolondrón	240p	22.46 N	81.27 W
Bolong ≏	170	34.15 S	149.36 E
Bolonia → Bologna	64	44.29 N	11.20 E
Bolótana	71	40.20 N	8.57 E
Bolotnoje	86	55.41 N	84.23 E
Boloto	82	54.10 N	36.20 E
Bolotovskoje	86	58.33 N	62.28 E
Bolovens, Plateau des ⋏[1]	110	15.20 N	106.20 E
Bolpur	126	23.40 N	87.43 E
Bolqār (Bolqarçay) ≏	84	39.28 N	48.36 E
Bolqarçay (Bolqār) ≏	84	39.28 N	48.36 E
Bol'šaja	76	59.36 N	41.48 E
Bol'šaja ≏	80	48.36 N	41.00 E
Bol'šaja Atn'a	80	56.15 N	49.27 E
Bol'šaja Balachn'a ≏	74	73.37 N	107.05 E
Bol'šaja Ber'ostovica	76	53.11 N	24.01 E
Bol'šaja Brembola	82	56.45 N	38.55 E
Bol'šaja Bukon'	86	48.53 N	82.43 E
Bol'šaja Čalykla ≏	80	51.51 N	49.34 E
Bol'šaja Černigovka	80	52.07 N	50.52 E
Bol'šaja Chalan'	78	50.56 N	37.26 E
Bol'šaja Cheta ≏	74	69.33 N	84.15 E
Bol'šaja Chobda ≏	86	50.56 N	54.34 E
Bol'šaja Chundala	76	60.04 N	34.18 E
Bol'šaja Čuja ≏	88	58.56 N	112.13 E
Bol'šaja Čurakovka	86	53.03 N	64.20 E
Bol'šaja Damba	80	46.57 N	51.47 E
Bol'šaja Dmitrijevka	80	51.21 N	45.15 E
Bol'šaja Dora	76	59.05 N	37.38 E
Bol'šaja Džalga	80	45.59 N	42.41 E
Bol'šaja Glušica	80	52.24 N	50.28 E
Bol'šaja Ižora	76	59.56 N	29.34 E
Bol'šaja Ižorka ≏	265a	59.48 N	30.36 E
Bol'šaja Kakša ≏	80	57.53 N	45.28 E
Bol'šaja Kamenka	80	53.39 N	50.31 E
Bol'šaja Kandala	80	54.32 N	49.22 E
Bol'šaja Kaskara	86	57.11 N	65.58 E
Bol'šaja Ket'	86	57.39 N	91.45 E
Bol'šaja Kinel' ≏	80	53.14 N	50.30 E
Bol'šaja Kirsanovka	83	47.40 N	38.54 E
Bol'šaja Kokšaga ≏	80	56.08 N	47.47 E
Bol'šaja Konkudera ≏	88	57.34 N	112.30 E
Bol'šaja Kugul'ta ≏	80	45.45 N	41.57 E
Bol'šaja Kuonamka ≏	74	70.45 N	113.24 E
Bol'šaja Laba ≏	84	44.16 N	40.53 E
Bol'šaja Lipovica	80	52.33 N	41.20 E
Bol'šaja Martynovka	80	47.17 N	41.40 E
Bol'šaja Mošanica	76	53.58 N	29.37 E
Bol'šaja Murta	86	56.55 N	93.07 E
Bol'šaja Neva ≏	265a	59.58 N	30.13 E
Bol'šaja Norja	80	56.41 N	52.43 E
Bol'šaja Ochta ◆[8]	265a	59.57 N	30.25 E
Bol'šaja Ol'šanka	80	51.32 N	44.17 E
Bol'šaja Orlovka	80	47.20 N	41.16 E
Bol'šaja Osinovaja ≏	180	66.30 N	174.00 E
Bol'šaja Pas'ma	80	58.38 N	43.53 E
Bol'šaja Rečka	88	51.57 N	104.44 E
Bol'šaja Ržaksa	80	52.08 N	42.13 E
Bol'šaja Sestra ≏	82	56.16 N	35.56 E
Bol'šaja Smedva ≏	82	54.50 N	38.34 E
Bol'šaja Sosnova	80	57.40 N	54.36 E
Bol'šaja Talovaja	78	46.58 N	40.37 E
Bol'šaja Tarel'	88	53.45 N	106.40 E
Bol'šaja Tavoložka	80	52.07 N	49.04 E
Bol'šaja Uča	80	56.37 N	52.05 E
Bol'šaja Usa	86	56.44 N	55.06 E
Bol'šaja Ussurka ≏	89	45.57 N	133.42 E
Bol'šaja Višera	76	58.55 N	32.08 E
Bol'šaja Vladimirovka	86	50.53 N	79.31 E
Bolsa Knolls	226	36.44 N	121.38 W
Bol'šakovo, Ross.	76	54.53 N	21.40 E
Bol'šakovo, Ross.	265b	55.54 N	37.17 E
Bol'šekrepinskaja	83	47.36 N	39.22 E
Bol'šelig	24	62.07 N	52.25 E
Bolsena	66	42.39 N	11.59 E
Bolsena, Lago di ⊜	66	42.36 N	11.56 E
Bol'šenarymskoje	86	49.16 N	84.32 E
Bol'šerečje	86	56.06 N	74.38 E
Bol'šereck	74	52.25 N	156.24 E
Bol'šetroickoje	78	50.33 N	37.17 E
Bol'šeustjikinskoje	86	55.57 N	58.16 E
Bol'ševik, Bela.	76	52.34 N	30.53 E
Bol'ševik, Ross.	74	62.44 N	147.30 E
Bol'ševik, Ross.	265a	59.49 N	30.30 E
Bol'ševik, ostrov I	74	78.40 N	102.30 E
Bol'šezemel'skaja Tundra ◆[1]	72	67.30 N	56.00 E
Bolshoi Theatre v	265b	55.46 N	37.37 E
Bol'šije Algaši	80	55.22 N	46.29 E
Bol'šije Avt'uki	78	52.04 N	29.32 E
Bol'šije Belyniči	82	54.38 N	38.50 E
Bol'šije Berezniki	80	54.11 N	45.58 E
Bol'šije Gorki, Ross.	82	56.28 N	35.51 E
Bol'šije Gorki, Ross.	265a	59.42 N	29.51 E
Bol'šije Kajbicy	80	55.25 N	48.13 E
Bol'šije Kizi, ozero ⊜	89	51.38 N	140.20 E
Bol'šije Kl'uči	80	55.59 N	48.47 E
Bol'šije Kl'učišči	80	54.08 N	48.14 E
Bol'šije Liachvi ≏	84	41.58 N	44.06 E
Bol'šije Michalicyny	80	58.29 N	48.14 E
Bol'šije Ozerki	80	52.36 N	46.33 E
Bol'šije Pom'aly	80	56.42 N	46.40 E
Bol'šije Ručji	82	56.36 N	36.58 E
Bol'šije Saly	83	47.24 N	39.41 E
Bol'šije Tarchany	80	54.42 N	48.34 E
Bol'šije Ugli	88	57.47 N	112.51 E
Bol'šije Uki	86	56.57 N	72.37 E
Bol'šije Ždanovy	80	58.40 N	49.05 E
Bol'šoj	80	50.13 N	43.26 E
Bol'šoj An'uj ≏	74	68.30 N	160.49 E
Bol'šoj Ažbulat, ozero ⊜	86	53.17 N	77.25 E
Bol'šoj Begičev, ostrov I	74	74.20 N	112.30 E
Bol'šoj Bogdo, gora ∧[2]	80	48.08 N	46.52 E
Bol'šoj Boktybaj, gora ∧	86	48.27 N	58.30 E
Bol'šoj Čeremšan ≏	80	54.11 N	49.39 E
Bol'šoj Civil' ≏	80	55.54 N	47.28 E
Bol'šoje, ozero ⊜	265a	60.04 N	30.39 E
Bol'šoje Aksu	86	43.20 N	79.35 E
Bol'šoje Aleksejevskoje	82	55.14 N	38.12 E
Bol'šoje Boldino	80	54.59 N	45.19 E
Bol'šoje Bun'kovo	82	55.51 N	38.37 E
Bol'šoje Goloustnoje	88	52.01 N	105.25 E
Bol'šoje Gorodišče, Ross.	76	57.17 N	30.31 E
Bol'šoje Gorodišče, Ross.	78	50.37 N	37.06 E
Bol'šoje Ignatovo	80	55.02 N	45.34 E
Bol'šoje Jarovoje, ozero ⊜	86	52.53 N	78.36 E
Bol'šoje Jašaltinskoje, ozero ⊜	80	46.17 N	42.27 E
Bol'šoje Kibejevo	80	56.55 N	47.05 E
Bol'šoje Korovino	82	54.30 N	39.02 E
Bol'šoje Manuškino	265a	59.53 N	30.49 E
Bol'šoje Michajlovskoje	82	56.47 N	38.04 E
Bol'šoje Mikuškino	80	53.56 N	51.42 E
Bol'šoje Muraškino	80	55.47 N	44.46 E
Bol'šoje Nagatkino	80	54.31 N	47.58 E
Bol'šoje Nurkejevo	80	55.22 N	52.40 E
Bol'šoje Nyrsy	80	55.44 N	50.19 E
Bol'šoje Ogar'ovo	76	53.33 N	37.43 E
Bol'šoje Pikino	80	56.25 N	44.22 E
Bol'šoje Polpino	76	53.14 N	34.30 E
Bol'šoje Ramenje	76	58.21 N	36.40 E
Bol'šoje Rybuškino	80	55.25 N	45.48 E
Bol'šoje Sazonovo	80	58.06 N	53.21 E
Bol'šoje Selo	76	57.43 N	38.56 E
Bol'šoje Šem'akino	80	55.03 N	48.38 E
Bol'šoje Soldatskoje	78	51.21 N	35.31 E
Bol'šoje Sudačje	80	50.49 N	44.05 E
Bol'šoje Topol'noje, ozero ⊜	86	53.20 N	78.00 E
Bol'šoje Uro	88	53.32 N	109.48 E
Bol'šoje Zagorje	76	57.51 N	28.57 E
Bol'šoje Žokovo	82	54.35 N	38.57 E
Bol'šoj Gašun ≏	80	47.22 N	42.43 E
Bol'šoj Golec, gora ∧	88	51.52 N	119.24 E
Bol'šoj Irgiz ≏	80	52.01 N	47.24 E
Bol'šoj Jenisej (Bij-Chem) ≏	88	51.43 N	94.26 E
Bol'šoj Jugan ≏	86	60.55 N	73.40 E
Bol'šoj Kamen'	89	43.06 N	132.21 E
Bol'šoj Kandarat'	80	54.25 N	47.00 E
Bol'šoj Kanym, gora ∧	86	54.13 N	88.20 E
Bol'šoj Karagaj	86	57.57 N	70.15 E
Bol'šoj Karaman ≏	80	51.40 N	46.38 E
Bol'šoj Ketmen'	86	43.27 N	80.24 E
Bol'šoj Kujaš	86	55.50 N	61.06 E
Bol'šoj Kundyš ≏	80	56.32 N	47.23 E
Bol'šoj Kuvaj	80	54.37 N	47.05 E
Bol'šoj Kymynej, gora ∧	180	66.34 N	172.32 W
Bol'šoj L'achovskij, ostrov I	74	73.35 N	142.00 E
Bol'šoj Lug	88	52.07 N	104.10 E
Bol'šoj Matačynaj, gora ∧	180	66.28 N	179.25 W
Bol'šoj Melik	80	51.38 N	43.18 E
Bol'šoj Nesvetaj ≏	83	47.27 N	39.54 E
Bol'šoj Onguren	88	53.38 N	107.36 E
Bol'šoj Patom ≏	88	59.15 N	113.56 E
Bol'šoj Pit ≏	86	59.01 N	91.44 E
Bol'šoj Porog	86	52.35 N	92.18 E
Bol'šoj Šagan	80	50.57 N	51.08 E
Bol'šoj Sajan ⋏	88	52.00 N	99.30 E
Bol'šoj Šalym ≏	86	60.55 N	70.25 E
Bol'šoj Šantar, ostrov I	89	55.00 N	137.42 E
Bol'šoj Šatan, gora ∧	86	53.41 N	57.36 E
Bol'šoj Simonogont	265a	59.50 N	29.49 E
Bol'šoj Sorokino	86	56.38 N	69.53 E
Bol'šoj Sundyr'	80	56.07 N	46.46 E
Bol'šoj Tal'cy	76	59.13 N	33.00 E
Bol'šoj Tolkaj	80	53.30 N	51.57 E
Bol'šoj T'uters, ostrov I	76	59.51 N	27.13 E
Bol'šoj Uluj	86	56.39 N	90.36 E
Bol'šoj Uran ≏	80	52.24 N	53.15 E
Bol'šoj Uvat, ozero ⊜	86	57.35 N	70.30 E
Bol'šoj Uzen' ≏	80	48.50 N	49.40 E
Bol'šoj Uzigont	265a	59.48 N	29.53 E
Bol'šoj Vjass	80	53.48 N	45.30 E
Bol'šoj Vlasjevo	89	53.24 N	140.55 E
Bol'šoj Zelenčuk ≏	84	44.36 N	41.56 E
Bolsover	44	53.14 N	1.18 W
Bolsward	52	53.03 N	5.31 E
Boltaña	34	42.27 N	0.04 E
Boltigen	58	46.38 N	7.24 E
Boltino	265b	55.58 N	37.41 E
Bolton, On., Can.	212	43.53 N	79.44 W
Bolton, Eng., U.K.	44	53.35 N	2.26 W
Bolton, Ct., U.S.	207	41.46 N	72.26 W
Bolton, Ms., U.S.	194	32.20 N	90.27 W
Bolton, N.C., U.S.	192	34.19 N	78.24 W
Bolton □[8]	262	53.34 N	2.28 W
Bolton Abbey	44	53.59 N	1.53 W
Bolton Abbey v[1]	44	53.59 N	1.54 W
Bolton Center	207	41.47 N	72.26 W
Bolton Creek ≏	212	44.58 N	76.23 W
Bolton Lake ⊜	184	54.16 N	95.47 W
Bolton-le-Sands	44	54.06 N	2.47 W
Bolton upon Dearne	44	53.31 N	1.19 W
Bolton Wanderers Football Ground ♦	262	53.34 N	2.25 W
Bolu	130	40.44 N	31.37 E
Bolu □[4]	130	40.40 N	31.30 E
Bölükyazı	130	38.18 N	42.10 E
Boluntay	120	36.34 N	92.38 E
Boluo, Zhg.	100	23.11 N	114.17 E
Boluo, Zhg.	100	24.27 N	113.03 E
Boluochi	98	41.24 N	119.56 E
Boluokeng	100	24.05 N	113.22 E
Bolus Head >	48	51.46 N	10.21 W
Bolva ≏	76	53.17 N	34.20 E
Bolvadin	130	38.42 N	31.04 E
Bolwarra	166	17.24 S	144.11 E
Bóly	30	45.58 N	18.32 E
Bolyčevo	82	55.46 N	35.43 E
Bolzaneto	62	44.27 N	8.54 E
Bolzano (Bozen)	64	46.31 N	11.22 E
Bolzano □[4]	64	46.43 N	11.30 E
Boma	152	5.51 S	13.03 E
Bomaderry	170	34.51 S	150.37 E
Bomal	56	50.23 N	5.32 E
Bomandjokou	152	0.34 N	14.23 E
Bomaneh	152	1.18 N	23.47 E
Bomarsund	26	60.13 N	20.15 E
Bomate	152	1.10 S	19.41 E
Bomba	66	42.02 N	14.22 E
Bombakabo	152	3.04 N	19.42 E
Bombala	166	36.54 S	149.14 E
Bombarral	34	39.16 N	9.09 W
Bombat	130	38.08 N	42.14 E
Bombay, India	122	18.58 N	72.50 E
Bombay, India	272c	18.58 N	72.50 E
Bombay, N.Y., U.S.	206	44.56 N	74.34 W
Bombay, University of v[2]	272c	18.57 N	72.50 E
Bombay Harbour ⊂	272c	18.57 N	72.53 E
Bomberai, Semenanjung >[1]	164	3.00 S	133.00 E
Bombetoka, Baie de ⊂	157b	15.50 S	46.17 E
Bombimba	152	0.31 N	19.24 E
Bombo	154	0.35 N	32.32 E
Bombo ≏	152	3.58 S	15.59 E
Bombo-Kasanji	152	5.54 S	21.51 E
Bomboma	152	2.25 N	18.54 E
Bombo-Makuka	152	5.26 S	16.19 E
Bombombwa	154	1.21 N	25.30 E
Bombon	261	48.34 N	2.52 E
Bomboyo	146	12.01 N	15.28 E
Bom Conselho	250	9.10 S	36.41 W
Bom Despacho	255	19.43 S	45.15 W
Bomdila	120	27.27 N	92.17 E
Bomei	100	22.57 N	115.46 E
Bömenzien	54	52.59 N	11.31 E
Bom Fim do Bom Jesus	256	23.17 S	47.02 W
Bomhus	40	60.41 N	17.13 E
Bomili	154	1.40 N	27.01 E
Bom Jardim, Ilha do I	287a	23.02 S	43.35 W
Bom Jardim de Goiás	255	16.17 S	52.07 W
Bom Jardim de Minas	256	21.57 S	44.11 W
Bom Jesus, Ang.	152	9.09 S	13.34 E
Bom Jesus, Bra.	250	9.04 S	44.22 W
Bom Jesus da Lapa	255	13.15 S	43.25 W
Bom Jesus de Goiás	255	18.12 S	49.44 W
Bom Jesus dos Perdões	256	23.08 S	46.28 W
Bømlafjorden ⊂[2]	26	59.39 N	5.20 E
Bomlitz	52	52.54 N	9.37 E
Bømlo I	26	59.46 N	5.12 E
Bommerholz	263	51.23 N	7.18 E
Bommern	263	51.25 N	7.20 E
Bomnak	89	54.46 N	128.51 E
Bomokandi ≏	154	3.39 N	26.08 E
Bomongiri	152	1.57 S	21.13 E
Bomongo	152	1.22 N	18.21 E
Bompata	150	6.38 N	1.04 W
Bompensiere	70	37.28 N	13.47 E
Bompietro	70	37.44 N	14.06 E
Bomputu	152	0.20 S	20.06 E
Bom Repouso	256	22.28 S	46.09 W
Bom Retiro	252	27.48 S	49.31 W
Bom Retiro ◆[8]	287b	23.32 S	46.38 W
Bom Sucesso, Bra.	248	15.43 S	56.07 W
Bom Sucesso, Bra.	255	23.42 S	51.45 W
Bom Sucesso, Bra.	256	22.17 S	42.49 W
Bom Sucesso, Bra.	287b	23.25 S	46.24 W
Bomu (Mbomou) ≏	136	4.08 N	22.26 E
Bon, Cap >	36	37.05 N	11.03 E
Bona	40	58.34 N	15.03 E
Bona Bona Island I	164	10.30 S	149.50 E
Bon Accord	158	25.38 S	28.11 E
Bonaduz	58	46.49 N	9.25 E
Bonaero Park	273d	26.07 S	28.16 E
Bonai	114	1.16 N	100.52 E
Bonaigarh	120	21.50 N	84.57 E
Bon Air	208	37.31 N	77.33 W
Bon Aire	214	40.54 N	79.55 W
Bonaire I	241s	12.10 N	68.15 W
Bonampak ⊥	232	16.44 N	91.05 W
Bönan	40	60.44 N	17.18 E
Bonandolok	114	1.47 N	98.48 E
Bonanza, Nic.	236	14.01 N	84.35 W
Bonanza, Or., U.S.	202	42.11 N	121.24 W
Bonanza, Ut,. U.S.	200	40.01 N	109.10 W
Bonanza Peak ∧	224	48.14 N	120.52 W
Bonao	238	18.56 N	70.25 W
Bonaparte	190	40.41 N	91.48 W
Bonaparte ≏	182	50.46 N	121.17 W
Bonaparte, Lake ⊜	212	44.09 N	75.23 W
Bonaparte, Mount ∧	202	48.45 N	119.08 W
Bonaparte Archipelago II	160	14.17 S	125.18 E
Bonaparte Lake ⊜	182	51.16 N	120.35 W
Bonar Bridge	46	57.53 N	4.21 W
Bonarcado	71	40.04 N	8.38 E
Bonasila Dome ∧	180	62.19 N	160.30 W
Bonasse	241r	10.05 N	61.52 W
Bonassola	62	44.11 N	9.35 E
Bonaventure	186	48.03 N	65.29 W
Bonaventure ≏	186	48.02 N	65.28 W
Bonaventure, Île I	186	48.30 N	64.10 W
Bonavista	186	48.39 N	53.07 W
Bonavista, Cape >	186	48.42 N	53.05 W
Bonavista Bay ⊂	186	48.45 N	53.20 W
Bonawe	46	56.26 N	5.13 W
Bonawon	116	9.08 N	122.55 E
Bonbeach	274b	38.04 S	145.08 E
Bonboillon	58	47.20 N	5.42 E
Bon Bon	162	30.26 S	135.28 E
Bonbonon Point >	116	9.03 N	123.08 E
Bonchester Bridge	44	55.24 N	2.40 W
Boncourt	58	47.30 N	6.56 E
Boncuk Dağı ∧	130	36.53 N	29.17 E
Bond	194	30.54 N	89.10 W
Bond □[6]	219	38.53 N	89.25 W
Bondari	80	52.57 N	42.04 E
Bondarivka	83	49.23 N	39.37 E
Bondeno	64	44.53 N	11.25 E
Bondi	274a	33.53 S	151.17 E
Bondo, Zaïre	152	1.22 S	23.53 E
Bondo, Zaïre	152	3.49 N	23.40 E
Bondoc Peninsula >[1]	116	13.30 N	122.30 E
Bondoc Point >	116	13.10 N	122.36 E
Bondorf	58	48.31 N	8.49 E
Bondoufle	261	48.37 N	2.23 E
Bondoukou	150	8.02 N	2.48 W
Bondowoso	115a	7.55 S	113.49 E
Bondsville	207	42.12 N	72.20 W
Bonduel	190	44.44 N	88.26 W
Bondues	50	50.42 N	3.06 E
Bondy	261	48.54 N	2.28 E
Bondy, Forêt de ♦	261	48.55 N	2.35 E
Bône → Annaba, Alg.	148	36.54 N	7.46 E
Bone, Indon.	112	4.46 S	122.52 E
Bone → Watampone, Indon.	112	4.32 S	120.20 E
Bone, Indon.	112	5.09 S	122.37 E
Bone, Teluk ⊂	112	4.00 S	120.40 E
Bonebone	112	2.36 S	120.33 E
Bon Echo Provincial Park ♦	212	44.52 N	77.15 W
Bonefro	66	41.42 N	14.56 E
Bone Island I	212	44.56 N	79.51 W
Bonelipu	112	4.50 S	123.11 E
Bonelohe	112	5.48 S	120.27 E
Bönen	52	51.36 N	7.44 E
Boneogeh	112	7.16 S	120.48 E
Bonerate, Pulau I	112	7.22 S	121.08 E
Bon Espérance, Cap de → Good Hope, Cape of >	158	34.24 S	18.30 E
Bo'ness	46	56.01 N	3.37 W
Bonesteel	198	43.04 N	98.56 W
Bonete, Cerro ∧	252	27.51 S	68.47 W
Bonete Chico, Cerro ∧	252	28.01 S	68.45 W
Bonětice	60	49.41 N	12.49 E
Bonfield	216	41.09 N	88.03 W
Bonfinópolis de Minas	255	16.28 S	45.59 W
Bonfol	58	47.29 N	7.09 E
Bonga	144	7.17 N	36.15 E
Bongabon	116	15.38 N	121.08 E
Bongabon ≏	116	12.40 N	121.33 E
Bongabong	116	12.45 N	121.29 E
Bongaigaon	124	26.28 N	90.34 E
Bongak	140	7.27 N	33.14 E
Bongandanga	152	1.30 N	21.03 E
Bongao Island I	116	5.01 N	119.46 E
Bongaree	171a	27.05 S	153.10 E
Bonggaw	116	5.02 N	119.46 E
Bongka	112	0.58 S	121.27 E
Bongka ≏	112	0.59 S	121.05 E
Bong Mieu	110	15.25 N	108.24 E
Bongo, Ang.	152	8.48 S	17.49 E
Bongo, Gabon	152	2.10 S	10.12 E
Bongo, Massif des ⋏	146	8.40 N	22.25 E
Bongo I	152	3.01 N	20.06 E
Bongo II	152	1.47 S	17.41 E
Bongo Island I	116	7.20 N	124.02 E
Bongolu	152	2.48 N	22.29 E
Bongon	112	6.35 N	116.52 E
Bongor	146	10.17 N	15.22 E
Bongou ≏	140	6.42 N	22.04 E
Bongouanou	150	6.39 N	4.12 W
Bong Range ⋏	150	6.50 N	10.00 W
Bong Son	110	14.26 N	109.01 E
Bonham	196	33.34 N	96.10 W
Bonheiden	56	51.02 N	4.32 E
Bonhomme, Col du)(	58	48.10 N	7.06 E
Bonhomme, Morne ∧	238	19.05 N	72.18 W
Bonhomme Island I	219	38.42 N	90.36 W
Bonifacio, Fr.	36	41.23 N	9.10 E
Bonifacio, Pil.	116	8.03 N	123.37 E
Bonifacio, Strait of ⊔	36	41.20 N	9.15 E
Bonifacio Monument ⊥	269f	14.39 N	120.59 E
Bonifati	68	39.35 N	15.54 E
Bonifati, Capo >	68	39.35 N	15.52 E
Bonifay	194	30.47 N	85.40 W
Bonifica del Volturno ≚	68	41.01 N	14.00 E
Bonilla Island I	182	53.29 N	130.36 W
Bonin Islands → Ogasawara-guntō II	14	27.00 N	142.10 E
Bonita	194	32.55 N	91.40 W
Bonita, Point >	282	37.49 N	122.32 W
Bonita Springs	220	26.20 N	81.46 W
Bonito, Bra.	248	21.08 S	56.28 W
Bonito, Bra.	250	8.29 S	35.44 W
Bonito, It.	68	41.06 N	15.00 E
Bonito ≏, Bra.	255	16.31 S	51.23 W
Bonito ≏, Bra.	256	22.12 S	43.02 W
Bonito ≏, Bra.	256	22.09 S	43.40 W
Bonito, Pico ∧	236	15.38 N	86.55 W
Bonito, Rio ≏	200	33.23 N	105.16 W
Bonito de Santa Fé	250	7.19 S	38.31 W
Bonjol	112	0.01 S	100.13 E
Bonkoukou	150	14.01 N	3.13 E
Bon Meade	279b	40.33 N	80.14 W
Bonn	56	50.44 N	7.05 E
Bonnanaro	71	40.32 N	8.45 E
Bonndorf im Schwarzwald	58	47.49 N	8.20 E
Bonneauville	208	39.46 N	77.10 W
Bonne Bay (Woody Point)	186	49.30 N	57.56 W
Bonne Bay ⊂	186	49.33 N	57.55 W
Bonnebosq	50	49.12 N	0.05 E
Bonnechere ≏	190	45.31 N	76.33 W
Bonneia	144	5.41 N	37.45 E
Bonnelles	261	48.37 N	2.02 E
Bonner	202	46.52 N	113.51 W
Bonners Ferry	202	48.41 N	116.18 W
Bonne-sur-Ménoge	58	46.10 N	6.20 E
Bonnet, Lac du ⊜	184	50.22 N	95.55 W
Bonnétable	50	48.11 N	0.26 E
Bonne Terre	194	37.55 N	90.33 W
Bonnet Plume ≏	180	65.55 N	134.58 W
Bonneuil-sur-Marne	261	48.46 N	2.29 E
Bonneval	50	48.11 N	1.24 E
Bonneval-sur-Arc	62	45.22 N	7.03 E
Bonnevaux	58	46.18 N	6.40 E
Bonneville, Fr.	58	46.05 N	6.25 E
Bonneville, Or., U.S.	224	45.38 N	121.57 W
Bonneville Dam ◆[6]	224	45.39 N	121.56 W
Bonneville Peak ∧	202	42.46 N	112.08 W
Bonneville Salt Flats ≚	200	40.45 N	113.52 W
Bonney, Lake ⊜	166	37.48 S	140.22 E
Bonney Lake	224	47.10 N	122.11 W
Bonnie Doone	192	35.05 N	78.57 W
Bonnières	50	49.02 N	1.35 E
Bonnie Rock	162	30.32 S	118.21 E
Bonnieux	62	43.49 N	5.18 E
Bonnievale	158	33.57 S	20.06 E
Bönninghardt	263	51.35 N	6.28 E
Bonnots Mill	219	38.34 N	91.58 W
Bonny	150	4.27 N	7.10 E
Bonny ≏[1]	150	4.20 N	7.10 E
Bonnyrigg, Austl.	274a	33.54 S	150.54 E
Bonnyrigg, Scot., U.K.	46	55.52 N	3.08 W
Bonny-sur-Loire	50	47.34 N	2.50 E
Bonnyville	182	54.16 N	110.44 W
Bono, It.	71	40.25 N	9.02 E
Bono, Ar., U.S.	194	35.54 N	90.48 W
Bono, Oh., U.S.	214	41.38 N	83.16 W
Bonoi	164	1.51 S	137.48 E
Bonorva	71	40.25 N	8.46 E
Bonoua	150	5.16 N	3.36 W
Bonpas Creek ≏	194	38.16 N	87.59 W
Bonriki	174t	1.23 N	173.09 E
Bonriki Airport ⊠	174t	1.22 N	173.10 E
Bons	58	46.16 N	6.23 E
Bonsall	228	33.17 N	117.13 W
Bonsari	272c	19.04 N	73.02 E
Bon Secour	194	30.18 N	87.43 W
Bon-Secours, Bel.	50	50.30 N	3.36 E
Bonsecours, Fr.	50	49.26 N	1.08 E
Bonshaw	186	46.12 N	63.21 W
Bonsucesso ◆[8]	287a	22.52 S	43.15 W
Bontang	112	0.08 N	117.30 E
Bontberg ∧	158	32.21 S	21.04 E
Bontebok National Park ♦	158	34.07 S	20.23 E
Bonthe	150	7.32 N	12.30 W
Bontoc	116	17.05 N	120.58 E
Bon Wier	194	30.44 N	93.39 W
Bonyhád	30	46.19 N	18.32 E
Boo, Kepulauan II	164	1.12 S	129.24 E
Booby Point >	284b	39.17 N	76.23 W
Boock	54	53.29 N	14.15 E
Boody	219	39.46 N	89.03 W
Boogardie	162	28.02 S	117.47 E
Booischot	56	51.03 N	4.46 E
Bookabie	162	31.50 S	132.41 E
Bookaloo	166	31.55 S	137.22 E
Book Cliffs ⊥[4]	200	39.20 N	109.00 W
Booke	152	2.33 S	22.00 E
Booker	196	36.27 N	100.32 W
Booker T. Washington National Monument ♦	192	37.01 N	79.45 W
Bookwalter	218	39.42 N	83.32 W
Boola	150	8.22 N	8.43 W
Boolaloo	162	22.35 S	115.51 E
Booleroo Centre	166	32.53 S	138.21 E
Booligal	166	33.52 S	144.53 E
Boologooro	162	24.21 S	114.02 E
Boom	50	51.05 N	4.22 E
Boomarra	166	19.33 S	140.20 E
Boomer	188	38.09 N	81.17 W
Boomi	166	28.44 S	149.35 E
Boomrivier	158	29.33 S	20.27 E
Boonah	171a	28.00 S	152.41 E
Böön cagaan nuur ⊜	102	45.35 N	99.09 E
Boone, Ia., U.S.	190	42.03 N	93.52 W
Boone, N.C., U.S.	192	36.13 N	81.40 W
Boone □[6], Il., U.S.	216	42.15 N	88.50 W
Boone □[6], In., U.S.	218	40.03 N	86.28 W
Boone □[6], Ky., U.S.	218	38.57 N	84.45 W
Boone □[6], Mo., U.S.	219	38.55 N	92.15 W
Boone ≏	190	42.19 N	93.56 W
Boone Draw V	196	33.51 N	103.42 W
Boone Grove	216	41.21 N	87.08 W
Boone Lake ⊜[1]	192	36.25 N	82.25 W
Boone Reservoir ⊜[1]	279b	40.15 N	80.08 W
Boones Mill	192	37.06 N	79.57 W
Booneville, Ar., U.S.	194	35.08 N	93.55 W
Booneville, Ky., U.S.	192	37.28 N	83.40 W
Booneville, Ms., U.S.	194	34.39 N	88.34 W
Boon Point >	240c	17.10 N	61.50 W
Boons	158	25.59 S	27.13 E
Boonsboro	208	39.30 N	77.39 W
Boonsville	222	33.04 N	97.52 W
Boonton	210	40.54 N	74.24 W
Boonton Reservoir ⊜[1]	276	40.53 N	74.25 W
Boonville, Ca., U.S.	204	39.00 N	123.21 W
Boonville, In., U.S.	194	38.02 N	87.16 W
Boonville, Mo., U.S.	194	38.58 N	92.44 W
Boonville, N.Y., U.S.	212	43.29 N	75.20 W
Boopi ≏	248	15.41 S	67.15 W
Boorabbin National Park ♦	162	31.13 S	120.10 E
Boorama	144	9.56 N	43.11 E
Boorindal	166	30.21 S	146.08 E
Booroorban	166	34.56 S	144.46 E
Boorowa	166	34.26 S	148.43 E
Boos	50	49.23 N	1.12 E
Boosaaso	144	11.17 N	49.11 E
Boossen	54	52.22 N	14.29 E
Boot	44	54.24 N	3.17 W
Bootahnie Indian Reserve ◆[4]	182	50.24 N	121.31 W
Booth	194	32.30 N	86.34 W
Booth, Lac ⊜	190	46.45 N	78.34 W
Boothbay Harbor	188	43.51 N	69.37 W
Boothby, Cape >	9	66.34 S	57.16 E
Booth Corner	285	39.51 N	75.29 W
Boothia, Gulf of ⊂	176	71.00 N	91.00 W
Boothia Peninsula >[1]	176	70.30 N	95.00 W
Boothstown	262	53.30 N	2.25 W
Boothville	194	29.20 N	89.25 W
Booth Wood Reservoir ⊜[1]	262	53.38 N	1.58 W
Boothwyn	285	39.49 N	75.26 W
Bootle	44	53.28 N	3.00 W
Boot Reefs ✦[2]	164	10.00 S	144.40 E
Booué	152	0.06 S	11.56 E
Booysens ◆[8]	273d	26.14 S	28.01 E
Booze Creek ≏	284c	38.59 N	77.07 W
Bopfingen	56	48.51 N	10.21 E
Bo Phloi	110	14.19 N	99.31 E
Bophuthatswana □[9]	156	26.00 S	25.35 E
Boping	98	36.36 N	116.07 E
Boping Ling ⋏	100	25.00 N	117.00 E
Bopo	150	7.37 N	7.52 E
Bopolu	150	7.03 N	10.32 W
Boppard	56	50.14 N	7.35 E
Boqér, Har ∧	132	30.52 N	34.43 E
Boqueirão, Ilha do I	287a	22.46 S	43.09 W
Boqueirão, Serra do ⋏[2]	250	11.30 S	43.45 W
Boquerón	236	8.30 N	82.34 W
Boquerón □[5]	252	21.30 S	60.00 W
Boquerón, Bahía de ⊂	240m	18.01 N	67.12 W
Boquerón, Túnel ◆[5]	286c	10.34 N	67.00 W
Boquet	279b	40.23 N	79.36 W
Boquilla, Presa de la ⊜[1]	232	27.30 N	105.30 W
Boquilla del Refugio	196	25.33 N	102.28 W
Boquillas del Carmen	232	29.17 N	102.53 W
Boquim	250	11.09 S	37.37 W
Bor, Česká Rep.	60	49.43 N	12.47 E
Bor, Jugo.	38	44.05 N	22.07 E
Bor, Ross.	24	63.00 N	42.38 E
Bor, Ross.	80	56.22 N	44.05 E
Bor, Sūd.	140	6.12 N	31.33 E
Bor, Tür.	130	37.54 N	34.34 E
Bor, Lak ≏	154	1.18 N	40.40 E
Bora-Bora I	14	16.30 S	151.45 W
Borabu	110	16.02 N	103.07 E
Boracay Island I	116	11.59 N	121.55 E
Boraha, Nosy I	157b	16.50 S	49.55 E
Borah Peak ∧	202	44.08 N	113.48 W
Boraldaj ≏	85	42.33 N	69.07 E
Borale	144	9.10 N	42.35 E
Borambola	171b	35.12 S	147.41 E
Borang, Tanjung >	164	5.16 S	133.07 E
Borås	26	57.43 N	12.55 E
Borāzjān	128	29.16 N	51.12 E
Borba, Bra.	246	4.24 S	59.35 W
Borba, Port.	34	38.48 N	7.27 W
Borbeck ◆[8]	263	51.29 N	6.57 E
Borbera ≏	62	44.42 N	8.52 E
Borca di Cadore	64	46.26 N	12.13 E
Borcea, Brațul ≏	38	44.40 N	27.53 E
Borchen	52	51.39 N	8.44 E
Borçka	130	41.22 N	41.40 E
Borculo, Ned.	52	52.07 N	6.31 E
Borculo, Mi., U.S.	216	42.53 N	86.01 W
Borda, Cape >	166	35.45 S	136.34 E
Borda da Mata	256	22.16 S	46.10 W
Bordeaux, Fr.	32	44.50 N	0.34 W
Bordeaux, S. Afr.	273d	26.06 S	28.01 E
Bordeaux ◆[8]	275a	45.33 N	73.41 W
Bordeaux Mountain ∧[2]	240m	18.20 N	64.44 W
Borden, Austl.	162	34.05 S	118.16 E
Borden, Sk., Can.	184	52.25 N	107.13 W
Borden, Eng., U.K.	260	51.20 N	0.42 E
Borden, In., U.S.	218	38.28 N	85.57 W
Borden, Canadian Forces Base ■	212	44.17 N	79.55 W
Borden Lake ⊜	190	47.50 N	83.18 W
Borden Peninsula >[1]	176	73.00 N	83.00 W
Bordentown	208	40.08 N	74.42 W
Border Mountains ⋏	164	3.40 S	141.05 E
Borders □[4]	46	55.37 N	3.15 W
Bordertown	166	36.19 S	140.47 E
Bordesholm	30	54.11 N	10.01 E
Borđeyri	24a	65.15 N	21.10 W
Bordighera	62	43.46 N	7.39 E
Bording	41	56.12 N	9.17 E
Bording Kirkeby	41	56.10 N	9.15 E
Bordino, Fiume di ≏	70	37.53 N	12.37 E
Bordj Bou Arreridj	148	36.04 N	4.46 E
Bordj Bounaama	34	35.51 N	1.36 E
Bordj Menaïel	148	36.44 N	3.43 E
Bordj Omar Idriss	148	28.09 N	6.43 E
Bordj Sidi Toui	148	32.44 N	11.22 E
Bordunskij	85	42.40 N	75.37 E
Bore, It.	62	44.43 N	9.47 E

DEUTSCH: Name · Seite · Breite°′ · Länge°′ E = Ost

Symbols in the index entries represent the broad categories identified in the key at the right. Symbols with superior numbers (⋏[1]) identify subcategories (see complete key on page *I · 1).*

Symbole im Register stellen die rechts im Schlüssel erklärten Kategorien dar. Symbole mit hochgestellten Ziffern (⋏[1]) bezeichnen Unterabteilungen einer Kategorie (vgl. vollständiger Schlüssel auf Seite *I · 1).*

Los símbolos incluídos en el texto del índice representan las grandes categorías identificadas con la clave a la derecha. Los símbolos con numeros en su parte superior (⋏[1]) identifican las subcategorías (véase la clave completa en la página *I · 1).*

Les symboles de l'index représentent les catégories indiquées dans la légende à droite. Les symboles suivis d'un indice (⋏[1]) représentent des sous-catégories (voir légende complète à la page *I · 1).*

Os símbolos incluídos no texto do índice representam as grandes categorias identificadas com a chave à direita. Os símbolos com números em sua parte superior (⋏[1]) identificam as subcategorias (veja-se a chave completa à página *I · 1).*

English	Deutsch	Español	Français	Português
∧ Mountain	Berg	Montaña	Montagne	Montanha
⋏ Mountains	Gebirge	Montañas	Montagnes	Montanhas
)(Pass	Paß	Paso	Col	Passo
V Valley, Canyon	Tal, Cañon	Valle, Cañón	Vallée, Canyon	Vale, Canhão
≚ Plain	Ebene	Llano	Plaine	Planície
> Cape	Kap	Cabo	Cap	Cabo
I Island	Insel	Isla	Île	Ilha
II Islands	Inseln	Islas	Îles	Ilhas
⊥ Other Topographic Features	Andere Topographische Objekte	Otros Elementos Topográficos	Autres données topographiques	Outros acidentes topográficos

ESPAÑOL — Nombre | Página | Lat.°' | Long.°' W = Oeste

FRANÇAIS — Nom | Page | Lat.°' | Long.°' W = Ouest

PORTUGUÊS — Nome | Página | Lat.°' | Long.°' W = Oeste

Bore, Ityo. 144 4.40 N 37.40 E
Boré, Mali 150 15.08 N 3.29 W
Boreda 144 6.32 N 37.48 E
Boreham 260 51.46 N 0.33 E
Borehamwood 42 51.40 N 0.16 W
Borel Hill ∧ 282 37.19 N 122.12 W
Borello 66 44.03 N 12.11 E
Borensberg 26 58.34 N 15.17 E
Boreray I 46 57.42 N 7.18 W
Boretto 64 44.54 N 10.33 E
Borgå → Porvoo 26 60.24 N 25.40 E
Borgallo, Galleria del ◆[5] 62 44.25 N 9.53 E
Borgarnes 24a 64.35 N 21.53 W
Borgata Costiera 70 37.43 N 12.39 E
Børgefjell Nasjonalpark ♦ 24 65.10 N 14.00 E
Borgentreich 52 51.34 N 9.14 E
Börger, Dtsch. 52 52.54 N 7.32 E
Borger, Ned. 52 52.55 N 6.46 E
Borger, Tx., U.S. 196 35.40 N 101.23 W
Borgerhout 50 51.13 N 4.26 E
Borgetto 70 38.03 N 13.08 E
Borggård 40 58.44 N 15.32 E
Borghetto 64 45.41 N 10.56 E
Borghetto di Vara 62 44.13 N 9.43 E
Borghetto Lodigiano 62 45.13 N 9.30 E
Borghetto Santo Spirito 62 44.06 N 8.14 E
Borgholm 26 56.53 N 16.39 E
Borghorst 52 52.07 N 7.23 E
Borgia 68 38.49 N 16.30 E
Borgio-Verezzi 62 44.10 N 8.18 E
Borgloon 56 50.48 N 5.20 E
Borg Mountain ∧ 9 72.42 S 3.30 W
Borgne, Lake c 194 30.05 N 89.40 W
Borgnesse, Pointe ≻ 240e 14.27 N 60.54 W
Borgo 64 46.03 N 11.27 E
Borgo alla Collina 66 43.45 N 11.43 E
Borgo a Mozzano 66 43.59 N 10.33 E
Borgo Cerreto 66 42.49 N 12.54 E
Borgo d'Ale 62 45.21 N 8.03 E
Borgoforte 64 45.03 N 10.45 E
Borgofranco d'Ivrea 62 45.30 N 7.51 E
Borgolavezzaro 62 45.19 N 8.42 E
Borgomanero 62 45.42 N 8.28 E
Borgomaro 62 43.58 N 7.56 E
Borgonovo Val Tidone 62 45.01 N 9.26 E
Borgo Pace 66 43.39 N 12.17 E
Borgoricco 64 45.32 N 11.58 E
Borgorose 66 42.11 N 13.13 E
Borgo San Dalmazzo 62 44.20 N 7.30 E
Borgo San Giacomo 64 45.21 N 9.58 E
Borgo San Lorenzo 66 43.57 N 11.23 E
Borgosatollo 64 45.28 N 10.14 E
Borgosesia 62 45.43 N 8.16 E
Borgo Tossignano 66 44.16 N 11.35 E
Borgou □[5] 150 10.30 N 2.50 E
Borgo Val di Taro 62 44.29 N 9.46 E
Borgo Vercelli 62 45.21 N 8.28 E
Borgsdorf 54 52.42 N 13.14 E
Borgsdorf, Forst ◆[3] 264a 52.42 N 13.19 E
Borgu Game Reserve ◆[4] 150 10.15 N 4.10 E
Borgund v[1] 26 61.03 N 7.49 E
Bori 150 4.42 N 7.21 E
Borig Delijn els ◆[2] 88 50.00 N 94.00 E
Borikhan 110 18.33 N 103.43 E
Borilovo 76 53.22 N 35.58 E
Borinage □[9] 50 50.30 N 4.00 E
Boring, Md., U.S. 208 39.31 N 76.49 W
Boring, Or., U.S. 224 45.25 N 122.22 W
Borinskoje 76 52.27 N 39.22 E
Borisoglebsk 80 51.23 N 42.06 E
Borisoglebskij 80 57.16 N 39.09 E
Borisov 76 54.15 N 28.30 E
Borisovka, Ross. 76 52.50 N 39.58 E
Borisovka, Ross. 78 50.36 N 36.01 E
Borisovo 82 55.25 N 36.03 E
Borisovo ◆[8] 265b 55.38 N 37.45 E
Borisovo-Sudskoje 76 59.54 N 36.01 E
Borisovskaja 76 60.12 N 39.48 E
Borivs'ke 83 48.51 N 38.34 E
Borja, Esp. 34 41.50 N 1.32 W
Borja, Perú 246 4.26 S 77.33 W
Bork 52 51.40 N 7.28 E
Borken, Dtsch. 52 51.51 N 6.51 E
Borken, Dtsch. 56 51.03 N 9.16 E
Borkenwirthe 52 51.53 N 6.50 E
Borki 86 59.08 N 82.15 E
Borkoldoj, chrebet ⋀ 85 41.25 N 77.50 E
Børkop 41 55.39 N 9.39 E
Borkou ◆[1] 146 18.15 N 18.50 E
Borkou-Ennedi-Tibesti □[5] 146 18.15 N 18.50 E
Borkoviči 76 55.40 N 28.20 E
Borkum 52 53.35 N 6.40 E
Borkum I 52 53.35 N 6.41 E
Borland Manor 279b 40.15 N 80.09 W
Borlänge 40 60.29 N 15.25 E
Borle ◆[8] 272c 19.02 N 72.55 E
Borlu 130 38.44 N 28.27 E
Bormes-les-Mimosas 62 43.09 N 6.20 E
Bormida ≏ 62 44.56 N 8.40 E
Bormida di Millesimo ≏ 62 44.40 N 8.20 E
Bormida di Spigno ≏ 62 44.40 N 8.20 E
Bormio 64 46.28 N 10.22 E
Born, Dtsch. 54 52.22 N 11.28 E
Born, Dtsch. 54 54.23 N 12.32 E
Borna, Dtsch. 54 51.19 N 13.11 E
Borna, Dtsch. 54 51.07 N 12.30 E
Borndiep c 52 53.25 N 5.35 E
Borne 52 52.18 N 6.45 E
Borne ≏ 62 45.03 N 3.54 E
Borneo (Kalimantan) I 112 0.30 N 114.00 E
Bornheim 56 50.46 N 6.59 E
Bornholm I 26 55.10 N 15.00 E
Bornholte 52 51.52 N 8.29 E
Bornhöved 54 54.04 N 10.16 E
Börnicke, Dtsch. 54 52.41 N 12.56 E
Börnicke, Dtsch. 264a 52.40 N 13.38 E
Börnig ◆[8] 263 51.33 N 7.16 E
Bornim ◆[8] 264a 52.26 N 13.00 E
Borno 64 45.56 N 10.12 E
Bornos, Embalse de ⊜[1] 34 36.50 N 5.30 W
Bornsdorf 54 51.46 N 13.41 E
Bornstedt ◆[8] 264a 52.25 N 13.02 E
Bornu □[3] 146 12.00 N 12.45 E
Boro ≏ 140 8.52 N 26.11 E
Borobudur ⊥ 115a 7.36 S 110.12 E
Borodarou 150 10.59 N 2.53 E
Borodino, Ross. 82 55.32 N 35.50 E
Borodino, Ross. 82 56.53 N 37.00 E
Borodino, Ross. 88 55.55 N 94.55 E
Borodino, Ukr. 78 46.18 N 29.13 E
Borodulicha 86 50.43 N 80.55 E
Borodulino 80 57.59 N 54.20 E
Borodyanka 78 50.39 N 29.56 E
Borogoncy 74 62.42 N 131.08 E
Borohoro Shan ⋀ 86 44.06 N 83.10 E
Boroko 112 0.55 N 123.16 E
Boromlya 78 50.37 N 34.59 E
Boromo 150 11.45 N 2.56 W
Boron, Mali 150 14.01 N 7.30 W
Boron, Ca., U.S. 228 34.59 N 117.38 W
Boronga Islands II 110 19.58 N 93.06 E
Borongan 116 11.37 N 125.26 E
Boronia 274b 37.52 S 145.17 E
Boron'ki 76 53.09 N 32.08 E
Borore 71 40.13 N 8.48 E
Borotou 150 8.44 N 7.30 W
Boroughbridge 44 54.06 N 1.23 W
Borough Green 42 51.17 N 0.19 E
Borough Park ◆[8] 276 40.38 N 74.00 W
Borova, Ukr. 78 50.12 N 30.07 E
Borova, Ukr. 83 49.24 N 37.40 E
Borova ≏ 83 48.58 N 38.24 E
Borovan 38 43.26 N 23.45 E
Borovany 61 48.54 N 14.39 E
Borove 78 51.06 N 27.13 E
Boroviči 76 58.24 N 33.55 E
Borovka ≏ 80 52.54 N 52.00 E
Borovl'anka 86 52.38 N 84.29 E
Borovoj 24 59.55 N 51.38 E
Borovoje 86 53.04 N 70.19 E
Borovsk 82 55.12 N 36.30 E
Borovskaja 24 60.46 N 41.06 E
Borovskij 86 57.03 N 65.44 E
Borovskoj 86 53.48 N 64.12 E
Borovskoje 86 52.39 N 82.08 E
Borovucha 76 55.36 N 28.37 E
Borovy 60 49.33 N 13.18 E
Borovyk ≏ 83 49.11 N 38.33 E
Borozdino 82 54.07 N 38.22 E
Borraan 144 10.14 N 48.44 E
Borrachudo ≏ 255 18.12 S 45.16 W
Borrazópolis 255 23.56 S 51.36 W
Borrby 26 55.27 N 14.10 E
Borre 41 55.00 N 12.28 E
Borre ⊥ 26 59.23 N 10.28 E
Borreby 41 55.14 N 11.19 E
Borriana, Esp. 34 39.53 N 0.05 W
Borriana, It. 62 45.30 N 8.02 E
Borris 48 52.35 N 6.55 W
Borrisokane 48 52.59 N 8.07 W
Borrisoleigh 48 52.45 N 7.57 W
Borroloola 164 16.04 S 136.17 E
Borroloola Aboriginal Reserve ◆[4] 164 16.00 S 136.15 E
Borrowdale 44 54.31 N 3.10 W
Börry 52 52.01 N 9.27 E
Borș 38 47.07 N 21.49 E
Borșa, Rom. 38 47.39 N 24.40 E
Borșa, Rom. 38 46.56 N 23.40 E
Borsad 120 22.25 N 72.54 E
Borsano 266b 45.35 N 8.51 E
Borschemich 263 51.04 N 6.25 E
Borščovo 82 56.30 N 36.51 E
Borščovočnyj chrebet ⋀ 88 52.00 N 117.00 E
Borsdorf 54 51.21 N 12.32 E
Borshchiv 78 48.48 N 26.03 E
Borskoje 80 53.02 N 51.43 E
Borsod-Abaúj-Zemplén □[6] 30 48.15 N 21.00 E
Börssum 54 52.04 N 10.35 E
Borstendorf 54 50.46 N 13.10 E
Bortala ≏ 86 44.50 N 82.45 E
Borth, Dtsch. 52 51.36 N 6.33 E
Borth, Wales, U.K. 42 52.29 N 4.03 W
Borthwick Water ≏ 44 55.24 N 2.50 W
Bortigali 71 40.17 N 8.50 E
Bortigiadas 71 40.53 N 9.02 E
Bort-les-Orgues 32 45.24 N 2.30 E
Bortnychi 78 50.22 N 30.41 E
Borto 88 53.35 N 111.53 E
Bortondale 285 39.54 N 79.24 W
Boru 164 10.14 S 148.50 E
Boruca 236 9.00 N 83.20 W
Borūjen 128 31.59 N 51.18 E
Borūjerd 128 33.54 N 48.46 E
Bor Ul Shan ⋀ 102 41.20 N 98.55 E
Borve 46 56.58 N 7.32 W
Borysiv 78 50.11 N 26.31 E
Boryslav 78 49.16 N 23.27 E
Boryspil' 78 50.21 N 30.57 E
Borz'a 88 50.24 N 116.31 E
Borz'a ≏ 88 50.38 N 115.38 E
Borzna 78 51.15 N 32.25 E
Boržomi 84 41.50 N 43.21 E
Boržomskij zapovednik ♦ 84 41.50 N 43.10 E
Borzonasca 62 44.25 N 9.23 E
Borzyszkowy 30 54.03 N 17.22 E
Bosa 71 40.18 N 8.30 E
Bosaga 86 47.55 N 72.58 E
Bosambi 152 2.24 N 22.39 E
Bosanska Dubica 36 45.11 N 16.49 E
Bosanska Gradiška 36 45.09 N 17.15 E
Bosanska Krupa 36 44.53 N 16.10 E
Bosanski Novi 36 45.03 N 16.23 E
Bosanski Petrovac 36 44.33 N 16.22 E
Bosanski Šamac 38 45.03 N 18.28 E
Bosansko Grahovo 36 44.11 N 16.22 E
Bősárkány 61 47.41 N 17.14 E
Bosau 54 54.06 N 10.25 E
Bosavi, Mount ∧ 164 6.35 S 142.50 E
Boscastle 42 50.41 N 4.42 W
Bosco, It. 66 44.53 N 12.14 E
Bosco, It. 66 43.08 N 12.28 E
Boscobel 190 43.08 N 90.42 W
Bosco Chiesanuova 64 45.37 N 11.02 E
Bosco Marengo 62 44.49 N 8.41 E
Boscoreale 68 40.46 N 14.28 E
Bose 102 23.54 N 106.37 E
Bösel 52 53.00 N 7.58 E
Bosencheve, Parque Nacional ♦ 234 19.36 N 100.15 W
Bosenge 152 1.18 N 22.19 E
Bósforo, Estrecho del → İstanbul Boğazı ⊔ 130 41.06 N 29.04 E
Bosham 42 50.49 N 0.52 W
Boshan 98 36.29 N 117.50 E
Boshkung Lake ⊜ 212 45.04 N 78.44 W
Boshoek 156 25.30 S 27.09 E
Boshof 158 28.34 S 25.04 E
Boshrūyeh 128 33.53 N 57.26 E
Bosilegrad 38 42.29 N 22.28 E
Bösingen 58 48.14 N 8.34 E
Bosjökloster 41 55.54 N 13.31 E
Boškajnar 85 38.13 N 68.51 E
Boskop 158 26.34 S 27.08 E
Boskop ∧ 273d 26.05 S 27.57 E
Boskovice 30 49.29 N 16.40 E
Boskuil 158 27.23 S 25.51 E
Bosman 164 4.10 S 144.40 E
Bosna 272b 22.37 N 88.30 E
Bosna ≏ 36 45.04 N 18.29 E
Bosna-Hercegovina → Bosnia and Herzegovina □[1] 36 44.15 N 17.30 E
Bošn'akovo 89 49.38 N 142.10 E
Bosnia and Herzegovina □[1], Europe 22 44.15 N 17.30 E
Bosnia and Herzegovina (Bosna-Hercegovina) □[1], Europe 36 44.15 N 17.30 E
Bosnik 164 1.10 S 136.14 E
Boso 272b 22.58 N 88.08 E
Bosobolo 152 4.11 N 19.54 E
Boso-Djafo 152 1.06 N 19.14 E
Bosogo 85 41.09 N 76.25 E
Bōsō-hantō ≻[1] 94 35.18 N 140.10 E
Bōsō-kyūryō ⋀[2] 268 35.08 N 139.56 E
Bososama 152 4.18 N 20.00 E
Bösperde 263 51.28 N 7.46 E
Bosphore, Détroit du → İstanbul Boğazı ⊔ 130 41.06 N 29.04 E
Bosporus → İstanbul Boğazı ⊔ 130 41.06 N 29.04 E
Bosque □[6] 222 31.55 N 97.35 W
Bosque, Paseo del ♦ 288 34.55 S 57.56 W
Bosque Farms 200 34.53 N 106.40 W
Bosques 288 34.49 S 58.14 W
Bosques Petrificados, Monumento Natural ♦ 254 47.39 S 68.07 W
Bosqueville 222 31.38 N 97.13 W
Bossangoa 152 6.29 N 17.27 E
Bossdorf 54 51.59 N 12.40 E
Bossé Bangou 150 13.21 N 1.18 E
Bossembélé 152 5.16 N 17.39 E
Bossentele 152 5.41 N 16.38 E
Bossert Estates 285 40.09 N 74.44 W
Bossier City 194 32.30 N 93.43 W
Bossley Park 274a 33.52 S 150.54 E
Bosso 146 13.42 N 13.19 E
Bosso, Dallol V 150 12.25 N 2.50 E
Bossolasco 62 44.32 N 8.02 E
Bossut, Cape ≻ 162 18.43 S 121.38 E
Bostān, Īrān 128 31.43 N 48.00 E
Bostān, Pāk. 120 30.26 N 67.02 E
Bostancı ◆[8] 267b 40.57 N 29.05 E
Bostandyk 80 49.38 N 48.54 E
Bosten Hu ⊜ 90 42.00 N 87.00 E
Bostock Green 262 53.13 N 2.30 W
Boston, Pil. 116 7.52 N 126.22 E
Boston, Eng., U.K. 44 52.59 N 0.01 W
Boston, Ga., U.S. 192 30.47 N 83.47 W
Boston, In., U.S. 218 39.44 N 84.51 W
Boston, Ma., U.S. 207 42.21 N 71.03 W
Boston, Ma., U.S. 283 42.21 N 71.03 W
Boston, N.Y., U.S. 210 42.38 N 78.44 W
Boston, Pa., U.S. 279b 40.18 N 79.49 W
Boston Bar 182 49.52 N 121.26 W
Boston Bay c 283 42.22 N 70.54 W
Boston Brook ≏ 283 42.37 N 71.00 W
Boston College v[2] 283 42.20 N 71.10 W
Boston Common ♦ 283 42.21 N 71.05 W
Boston Corners 210 42.03 N 73.31 W
Boston Creek ≏ 212 43.02 N 79.56 W
Boston Harbor 224 47.08 N 122.54 W
Boston Harbor c 283 42.20 N 70.58 W
Boston Heights 214 41.15 N 81.30 W
Boston Mill 214 41.16 N 81.34 W
Boston Mountains ⋀ 194 35.50 N 93.20 W
Boston Spa 44 53.54 N 1.21 W
Boston University v[2] 283 42.21 N 71.07 W
Bosumtwi, Lake ⊜ 150 6.30 N 1.25 W
Bosut ≏ 38 44.57 N 19.22 E
Boswell, In., U.S. 216 40.31 N 87.22 W
Boswell, Ok., U.S. 196 34.01 N 95.52 W
Boswell, Pa., U.S. 214 40.09 N 79.01 W
Boswell Bay 180 60.24 N 146.08 W
Bosworth 194 39.28 N 93.20 W
Bosworth Airport ⊠ 279a 41.26 N 82.00 W
Bosworth Field ⊥ 42 52.36 N 1.25 W
Botād 120 22.10 N 71.40 E
Botafogo ◆[8] 287a 22.57 S 43.11 W
Botafogo, Enseada de c 287a 22.57 S 43.10 W
Botany 274a 33.57 S 151.12 E
Botany Bay ◆[8] 260 51.41 N 0.07 W
Botany Bay c 170 33.59 S 151.12 E
Botelhos 256 21.39 S 46.24 W
Botera 152 11.37 S 14.17 E
Botersleegte 158 30.35 S 21.22 E
Botesdale 42 52.20 N 1.01 E
Boteti ≏ 156 20.08 S 23.23 E
Botev ∧ 38 42.43 N 24.55 E
Botevgrad 38 42.54 N 23.47 E
Botha's Hill 158 29.45 S 30.45 E
Bothaville 158 27.27 S 26.36 E
Bothell 224 47.45 N 122.12 W
Bothe-Napa Valley State Park ♦ 226 38.32 N 122.32 W
Bothnia, Gulf of c 26 63.00 N 20.00 E
Bothwell, Austl. 166 42.23 S 147.00 E
Bothwell, On., Can. 214 42.38 N 81.52 W
Boticas 34 41.41 N 7.40 W
Botija, Ilha da I 246 3.58 S 62.53 W
Botija, Isla I 258 33.52 S 59.02 W
Botiyeve 78 46.41 N 35.52 E
Botkins 216 40.28 N 84.10 W
Botkul', ozero ⊜ 80 48.46 N 46.40 E
Botkyrka 40 59.14 N 17.49 E
Botlich 84 42.39 N 46.14 E
Bot Makak 152 4.00 N 10.55 E
Botnia, Golfo de → Bothnia, Gulf of c 26 63.00 N 20.00 E
Botola 152 1.17 S 18.13 E
Botolan 116 15.17 N 120.01 E
Botoșani 38 47.45 N 26.40 E
Botoșani □[6] 38 48.00 N 26.45 E
Botoșanița 38 47.53 N 26.07 E
Botou 150 12.40 N 2.03 E
Botovo 82 56.03 N 38.26 E
Bo Trach 110 17.35 N 106.32 E
Botrange ∧ 56 50.30 N 6.08 E
Botricello 68 38.56 N 16.51 E
Botro 150 7.51 N 5.19 W
Botsford 210 41.21 N 73.15 W
Botswana □[1], Afr. 138 22.00 S 24.00 E
Botswana □[1], Afr. 156 22.00 S 24.00 E
Botte Donato, Monte ∧ 68 39.17 N 16.26 E
Bottenhavet (Selkämeri) c 26 62.00 N 20.00 E
Bottenviken (Perämeri) c 26 65.00 N 23.00 E
Bottesford 42 52.56 N 0.48 W
Bottineau 198 48.49 N 100.26 W
Bottisham 42 52.13 N 0.16 E
Bottnischer Meerbusen → Bothnia, Gulf of c 26 63.00 N 20.00 E
Bottoms Reservoir ⊜[1] 262 53.28 N 1.58 W
Bottrop 52 51.31 N 6.55 E
Botucatu 255 22.52 S 48.26 W
Botwood 186 49.09 N 55.21 W
Boty 88 52.24 N 118.32 E
Bötzingen 58 48.04 N 7.44 E
Bötzow 54 52.39 N 13.08 E
Bötzsee ⊜ 264a 52.34 N 13.50 E
Bouaflé, C. Iv. 150 6.59 N 5.45 W
Bouafle, Fr. 261 48.58 N 1.54 E
Bou Ahmed 148 35.25 N 5.00 W
Bouaké 150 7.41 N 5.02 W
Bou Ali, Oued V 148 31.14 N 4.16 E
Bouânane 148 32.03 N 3.03 W
Bouandougou 150 8.13 N 5.40 W
Bouar 152 5.57 N 15.36 E
Bou Arada 36 36.20 N 9.38 E
Bou Areg, Sebkha c 34 35.10 N 2.45 W
Bouârfa 148 32.30 N 1.59 W
Bouaye 32 47.09 N 1.42 W
Boubandjidah, Parc National de ♦ 146 8.45 N 14.45 E
Bou Bernous 148 27.18 N 2.59 W
Boubín ∧ 60 48.59 N 13.51 E
Bouca 152 6.30 N 18.17 E
Bouchain 50 50.17 N 3.19 E
Bouchegouf 36 36.28 N 7.44 E
Boucher ≏ 186 49.10 N 69.06 W
Boucher, Lac ⊜ 186 51.07 N 59.35 W
Boucherville 206 45.36 N 73.27 W
Boucherville, Îles de II 275a 45.37 N 73.28 W
Bouches-du-Rhône □[5] 62 43.30 N 5.00 E
Bouchoir 50 49.45 N 2.41 E
Bouclans 58 47.14 N 6.15 E
Boucle du Baoulé, Parc National de la ♦ 150 13.50 N 9.00 W
Bouddi National Park ♦ 170 33.31 S 131.24 E
Boudjellil 34 36.20 N 4.21 E
Boudnib 148 31.57 N 4.38 W
Boudouaou 34 36.43 N 3.25 E
Boudry 58 46.57 N 6.50 E
Boué 50 50.01 N 3.42 E
Bouenza □[5] 152 4.00 S 13.45 E
Boufarik 148 36.34 N 2.55 E
Bouffémont 261 49.03 N 2.18 E
Bou Ficha 36 36.18 N 10.29 E
Bougaa 34 36.20 N 5.05 E
Bougainville □[5] 175e 6.00 S 155.00 E
Bougainville I 175e 6.00 S 155.00 E
Bougainville, Cape ≻ 164 13.54 S 126.06 E
Bougainville, Détroit de ⊔ 175f 15.50 S 167.10 E
Bougainville Reef ✦[2] 164 15.30 S 147.06 E
Bougainville Strait ⊔ 175e 6.40 S 156.10 E
Bougar'oûn, Cap ≻ 34 37.06 N 6.28 E
Bough Beech Reservoir ⊜[1] 260 51.13 N 0.08 E
Boughton 44 53.12 N 1.00 W
Boughton Green 260 51.14 N 0.32 E
Boughton Malherbe 260 51.13 N 0.42 E
Boughton Place v 260 51.13 N 0.32 E
Bougie → Bejaïa 148 36.45 N 5.05 E
Bougou 152 3.45 S 11.12 E
Bougouni 150 11.25 N 7.29 W
Bougouriba ≏ 150 10.42 N 2.56 W
Bougzoul 34 35.42 N 2.51 E
Bou Hadjar 36 36.30 N 8.06 E
Bou Hajar 36 35.42 N 10.48 E
Bouillante 241o 16.06 N 61.45 W
Bouillon 56 49.48 N 5.04 E
Bouilly 50 48.12 N 4.00 E
Bouïra 148 36.23 N 3.54 E
Bouïra □[5] 148 36.00 N 4.00 E
Bouisy, Ru de ≏ 261 48.34 N 2.45 E
Bou Izakarn 148 29.09 N 9.44 W
Boujad 148 32.48 N 6.26 W
Boujailles 58 46.53 N 6.05 E
Boujdour, Cap ≻ 148 26.08 N 14.30 W
Bouka ≏ 150 11.00 N 10.50 W
Bou Kadir 148 36.04 N 1.07 E
Bou Khadra 36 35.45 N 8.02 E
Boukiéro 273b 4.12 S 15.18 E
Boukiéro, Mont ∧[2] 273b 4.11 S 15.17 E
Boukombé 150 10.11 N 1.06 E
Boula Ibib 146 9.34 N 13.46 E
Boulaide 56 49.54 N 5.49 E
Boularderie Island I 186 46.15 N 60.30 W
Boulay-Moselle 56 49.11 N 6.30 E
Boulbon 62 43.52 N 4.41 E
Boulder, Co., U.S. 200 40.00 N 105.16 W
Boulder, Mt., U.S. 202 46.14 N 112.07 W
Boulder ≏ 202 45.52 N 111.57 W
Boulder City 204 35.58 N 114.49 W
Boulder Creek 226 37.07 N 122.07 W
Boulder Creek ≏ 200 37.47 N 111.22 W
Boulder Hill 216 41.41 N 88.25 W
Bouleaux, Lac des ⊜ 275a 45.33 N 73.19 W
Bouli ≏ 150 13.15 N 0.03 E
Boulia 166 22.54 S 139.54 E
Bouligny 56 49.17 N 5.45 E
Boullay-les-Troux 261 48.41 N 2.03 E
Boulmane 148 33.22 N 4.45 W
Boulmane □[4] 148 33.00 N 4.00 W
Boulogne ◆[8] 258 34.31 S 58.34 W
Boulogne, Bois de ♦ 261 48.50 N 2.15 E
Boulogne-Billancourt 50 48.50 N 2.15 E
Boulogne-sur-Gesse 32 43.18 N 0.39 E
Boulogne-sur-Mer 50 50.43 N 1.37 E
Bouloire 50 47.58 N 0.33 E
Boulouli 150 15.34 N 9.21 W
Bouloupari 175f 21.52 S 166.04 E
Boulouris-sur-Mer 62 43.25 N 6.48 E
Boulsa 150 12.39 N 0.34 W
Boulsworth Hill ∧ 44 53.48 N 2.06 W
Bouly 150 15.19 N 11.48 W
Bou Maad, Djebel ∧ 34 36.26 N 2.08 E
Boumalne 148 31.32 N 5.27 W
Boumba ≏ 152 2.02 N 15.12 E
Boumbé I ≏ 152 4.04 N 15.23 E
Boumbé II ≏ 152 4.08 N 15.08 E
Boumboum 150 15.01 N 1.42 W
Boûmdeïd 150 17.26 N 9.50 W
Bou Medfaa 34 36.22 N 2.28 E
Boumentana 152 6.59 N 16.56 E
Boumnyebe 152 3.52 N 10.49 E
Boumou 146 9.02 N 16.26 E
Bouna 150 9.16 N 3.00 W
Boundary 180 64.04 N 141.06 W
Boundary Bay c 224 49.00 N 122.58 W
Boundary Peak ∧ 204 37.51 N 118.21 W
Boundary Ranges ⋀ 180 59.00 N 134.00 W
Bound Brook 210 40.34 N 74.32 W
Bound Brook ≏, Ma., U.S. 283 42.13 N 70.47 W
Bound Brook ≏, N.J., U.S. 276 40.35 N 74.30 W
Boundiali 150 9.31 N 6.29 W
Boun Nua 110 21.38 N 101.54 E
Bountiful 200 40.53 N 111.52 W
Bounty Bay c 174e 25.04 S 130.05 W
Bounty Islands II 14 47.42 S 179.04 E
Bounty Trough ✦[1] 14 46.00 S 178.00 E
Bouqteb 148 34.02 N 0.05 E
Bouquet Reservoir ⊜[1] 228 34.35 N 118.24 W
Bouqueval 261 49.01 N 2.26 E
Boura 150 12.25 N 4.33 W
Bouradière 62 43.58 N 5.19 E
Bourail 175f 21.34 S 165.30 E
Bouray-sur-Juine 261 48.31 N 2.18 E
Bourbeuse ≏ 194 38.24 N 90.53 W
Bourbeuse, Dry Fork ≏ 194 38.16 N 91.26 W
Bourbon, In., U.S. 216 41.17 N 86.06 W
Bourbon, Mo., U.S. 194 38.09 N 91.14 W
Bourbon □[6] 218 38.14 N 84.14 W
Bourbon ≏ 206 46.17 N 71.55 W
Bourbon-Lancy 32 46.38 N 3.46 E
Bourbonnais 216 41.08 N 87.52 W
Bourbonnais □[9] 32 46.20 N 3.00 E
Bourbonne-les-Bains 58 47.57 N 5.45 E
Bourbourg 50 50.57 N 2.12 E
Bourbre ≏ 62 45.47 N 5.11 E
Bourdeaux 62 44.35 N 5.08 E
Bourdon, Île I 275a 45.43 N 73.29 W
Bourdon, Réservoir du ⊜[1] 50 47.36 N 3.07 E
Bourdonné 261 48.45 N 1.40 E
Bou Regreg, Oued ≏ 148 34.03 N 6.50 W
Bourem 150 16.57 N 0.21 W
Bourg 194 29.33 N 90.36 W
Bourg-Achard 50 49.21 N 0.49 E
Bourganeuf 32 45.57 N 1.46 E
Bourg-Argental 62 45.18 N 4.33 E
Bourg-de-Péage 62 45.02 N 5.03 E
Bourg-en-Bresse 58 46.12 N 5.13 E
Bourges 32 47.05 N 2.24 E
Bourget 206 45.26 N 75.09 W
Bourget, Lac du ⊜ 62 45.44 N 5.52 E
Bourg-la-Reine 261 48.47 N 2.19 E
Bourg-Lastic 32 45.39 N 2.33 E
Bourg-lès-Valence 62 44.57 N 4.53 E
Bourgneuf 261 48.36 N 2.00 E
Bourgneuf-en-Retz 32 47.02 N 1.57 W
Bourgogne 50 49.21 N 4.04 E
Bourgogne (Burgundy) □[9] 32 47.00 N 4.30 E
Bourgogne, Canal de ≚ 32 47.58 N 3.30 E
Bourgoin-Jallieu 62 45.35 N 5.17 E
Bourg-Saint-Andéol 62 44.22 N 4.39 E
Bourg-Saint-Maurice 62 45.37 N 6.46 E
Bourg-Saint-Pierre 58 45.57 N 7.12 E
Bourgtheroulde 50 49.18 N 0.53 E
Bourgueil 50 47.17 N 0.10 E
Bou Rjeïmât ⫪[4] 150 19.04 N 15.08 W
Bourke 166 30.05 S 145.56 E
Bourmont 58 48.12 N 5.35 E
Bourne 42 52.46 N 0.23 W
Bourne ≏, Fr. 62 45.04 N 5.15 E
Bourne ≏, Eng., U.K. 42 51.02 N 1.47 W
Bournebridge 260 51.38 N 0.11 E
Bourne End 260 51.45 N 0.32 W
Bournemouth 42 50.43 N 1.54 W
Bourneville, Fr. 50 49.23 N 0.37 E
Bourneville, Oh., U.S. 218 39.17 N 83.09 W
Bourn Vincent Memorial Park ♦ 48 52.01 N 9.30 W
Bouroum 150 13.37 N 0.39 W
Bourron-Marlotte 50 48.20 N 2.42 E
Bourscheid 56 49.55 N 6.04 E
Bourtange 52 53.00 N 7.11 E
Bourtanger Moor ◆[3] 52 52.50 N 7.06 E
Bourton-on-the-Water 42 51.53 N 1.45 W
Bourzanga 150 13.41 N 1.33 W
Bou Saâda 148 35.12 N 4.11 E
Bou Salem 36 36.36 N 8.59 E
Bousbecque 50 50.46 N 3.05 E
Bouse 200 33.55 N 114.00 W
Bou Sellam, Oued ≏ 34 36.26 N 4.34 E
Bouse Wash V 200 34.02 N 114.20 W
Bou Smail 148 36.38 N 2.41 E
Boussac 32 46.21 N 2.13 E
Boussé, Burkina 150 12.39 N 1.53 W
Bousse, Fr. 56 49.17 N 6.12 E
Boussières 58 47.09 N 5.54 E
Bousso 146 10.29 N 16.43 E
Boussois 50 50.17 N 4.03 E
Boussouma 150 12.55 N 1.05 W
Boussu 50 50.26 N 3.48 E
Boussy-Saint-Antoine 261 48.41 N 2.32 E
Bout, Pointe du ≻ 240e 14.34 N 61.03 W
Bouteille, Lac de la ⊜ 206 46.42 N 73.41 W
Bouteldja 36 36.47 N 8.12 E
Bou Temezguida ∧ 148 29.21 N 9.55 W
Boutilimit 150 17.33 N 14.42 W
Bouttencourt 50 49.56 N 1.38 E
Bouvard, Cape ≻ 168a 32.41 S 115.37 E
Bouvetøya I 9 54.26 S 3.24 E
Bouvier Bay c 281 42.39 N 82.38 W
Bouvières 62 44.30 N 5.13 E
Bouxières-aux-Dames 56 48.45 N 6.10 E
Bouxwiller 56 48.49 N 7.29 E
Bouyon 62 43.50 N 7.07 E
Bouza 150 14.25 N 6.02 E
Bou Zadjar 34 35.35 N 1.09 W
Bouzonville 56 49.18 N 6.32 E
Bov 41 54.50 N 9.23 E
Bova 68 38.00 N 15.56 E
Bøvågen 26 60.40 N 4.58 E
Bovalino Marina 68 38.10 N 16.11 E
Bova Marina 68 37.56 N 15.55 E
Bovard 279b 40.19 N 79.30 W
Bovec 36 46.20 N 13.33 E
Bovegno 64 45.48 N 10.16 E
Bovenden 52 51.35 N 9.55 E
Bovenkarspel 52 52.42 N 5.15 E
Bøverdal 26 61.43 N 8.21 E
Boves, Fr. 50 49.51 N 2.23 E
Boves, It. 62 44.19 N 7.33 E
Bovey 190 47.17 N 93.25 W
Bovey ≏ 42 50.34 N 3.37 W
Bovey Tracey 42 50.36 N 3.40 W
Bovill 202 46.51 N 116.23 W
Boville Ernica 66 41.38 N 13.28 E
Bovina 196 34.31 N 102.53 W
Bovina Center 210 42.16 N 74.47 W
Bovingdon 42 51.44 N 0.32 W
Bövinghausen ◆[8] 263 51.31 N 7.19 E
Bovington Camp 42 50.42 N 2.14 W
Bovino 68 41.15 N 15.20 E
Bovisio Masciago 266b 45.37 N 9.09 E
Bovolenta 64 45.16 N 11.56 E
Bovolone 64 45.15 N 11.07 E
Bovril 252 31.21 S 59.26 W
Bovrup 41 54.59 N 9.36 E
Bow 224 48.33 N 122.23 W
Bow ≏, Austl. 162 16.32 S 128.39 E
Bow ≏, Ab., Can. 182 49.56 N 111.42 W
Bow ≏, Sk., Can. 184 54.56 N 105.13 W
Bo-Wadrif 158 32.26 S 20.07 E
Bowang 106 31.34 N 118.50 E
Bowbells 198 48.48 N 102.14 W
Bow Brook ≏ 42 52.04 N 2.07 W
Bowburn 44 54.43 N 1.31 W
Bow Creek ≏ 198 39.35 N 99.14 W
Bowden 182 51.55 N 114.02 W
Bowdle 198 45.27 N 99.39 W
Bowdoin, Lake ⊜ 202 48.24 N 107.41 W
Bowdon, Eng., U.K. 262 53.23 N 2.22 W
Bowdon, Ga., U.S. 192 33.32 N 85.15 W
Bowdon, N.D., U.S. 198 47.28 N 99.42 W
Bowelling 168a 33.25 S 116.29 E
Bowen, Arg. 252 35.00 S 67.31 W
Bowen, Austl. 166 20.01 S 148.15 E
Bowen, Il., U.S. 194 40.14 N 91.04 W
Bowen ≏ 166 20.24 S 147.21 E
Bowenfels 170 33.31 S 150.07 E
Bowens Creek ≏ 170 33.21 S 150.35 E
Bowers 208 39.15 N 75.36 W
Bowers Gifford 260 51.34 N 0.32 E
Bowers Mansion ⊥ 226 39.17 N 119.50 W
Bowers Marshes ≋ 260 51.33 N 0.32 E
Bowers Ridge ✦[3] 16 54.00 N 179.00 E
Bowerston 214 40.25 N 81.11 W
Bowersville 218 39.34 N 83.43 W
Bowgreave 44 53.52 N 2.45 W
Bowie, Az., U.S. 200 32.19 N 109.29 W
Bowie, Md., U.S. 208 39.00 N 76.46 W
Bowie, Tx., U.S. 196 33.33 N 97.50 W
Bowie Creek ≏ 194 31.26 N 89.24 W
Bow Island 184 49.52 N 111.22 W
Bowland, Forest of ◆[3] 44 53.58 N 2.32 W
Bowles Creek ≏ 222 32.02 N 94.59 W
Bowley Bar ≻[2] 284b 39.18 N 76.23 W
Bowleys Quarters 284b 39.19 N 76.24 W
Bowling Green, Fl., U.S. 220 27.38 N 81.49 W
Bowling Green, Ky., U.S. 194 36.59 N 86.26 W
Bowling Green, Mo., U.S. 219 39.20 N 91.11 W
Bowling Green, Oh., U.S. 216 41.22 N 83.39 W
Bowling Green, Pa., U.S. 285 39.55 N 75.23 W
Bowling Green, Va., U.S. 208 38.02 N 77.20 W
Bowling Green, Cape ≻ 166 19.19 S 147.25 E
Bowling Green Bay National Park ♦ 166 19.28 S 147.14 E
Bowman, Ca., U.S. 226 38.57 N 121.03 W
Bowman, Ga., U.S. 192 34.12 N 83.01 W
Bowman, N.D., U.S. 198 46.10 N 103.23 W
Bowman, S.C., U.S. 192 33.20 N 80.40 W
Bowman, Mount ∧ 182 51.10 N 121.55 W
Bowman Creek ≏, Pa., U.S. 210 41.31 N 75.58 W
Bowman Creek ≏, Wa., U.S. 224 45.50 N 121.03 W
Bowman-Haley Lake ⊜[1] 198 46.00 N 103.20 W
Bowman Island I 9 65.17 S 103.08 E
Bowman Lake ⊜[1] 226 39.27 N 120.38 W
Bowmans 168b 34.09 S 138.16 E
Bowmansdale 208 40.10 N 76.59 W
Bowmanstown 208 40.48 N 75.40 W
Bowmansville, N.Y., U.S. 212 42.56 N 78.41 W
Bowmansville, Pa., U.S. 208 40.10 N 76.04 W
Bowmanville 212 43.55 N 78.41 W
Bowmanville Creek ≏ 212 43.53 N 78.40 W
Bowmont Water ≏ 44 55.34 N 2.09 W
Bowmore 46 55.45 N 6.17 W
Bowness-on-Windermere 44 54.22 N 2.55 W
Bowokan, Kepulauan II 112 2.05 S 123.35 E
Bowral 170 34.28 S 150.25 E
Bowraville 166 30.39 S 152.51 E
Bowron ≏ 182 54.04 N 121.48 W
Bowron Lake Provincial Park ♦ 182 53.10 N 121.06 W
Bowsman 184 52.14 N 101.14 W
Bowwood 154 17.07 S 26.17 E
Box 42 51.26 N 2.15 W
Boxberg 56 49.29 N 9.38 E
Box Butte Creek ≏ 198 42.28 N 102.37 W
Box Creek ≏, Tx., U.S. 222 31.33 N 95.43 W
Box Creek ≏, Tx., U.S. 222 31.35 N 95.10 W
Box Elder 202 48.19 N 110.00 W
Boxelder Creek ≏, U.S. 198 45.59 N 103.57 W
Boxelder Creek ≏, Co., U.S. 198 40.33 N 105.00 W
Box Elder Creek ≏, Co., U.S. 198 40.23 N 104.28 W
Box Elder Creek ≏, Mt., U.S. 202 46.57 N 108.04 W
Boxelder Creek ≏, S.D., U.S. 198 44.01 N 102.27 W
Boxey 186 47.25 N 55.34 W
Boxey Point ≻ 186 47.24 N 55.35 W
Boxford 207 42.39 N 70.59 W
Boxford State Forest ♦ 283 42.39 N 71.02 W
Box Grove 275b 43.51 N 79.14 W
Box Hill 169 37.49 S 145.08 E
Boxholm 26 58.12 N 15.03 E
Boxian 100 33.53 N 115.45 E
Boxing 98 37.08 N 118.07 E
Boxley 260 51.18 N 0.33 E
Boxmeer 52 51.39 N 5.57 E
Boxmoor 260 51.45 N 0.29 W
Boxodoi 98 42.34 N 115.18 E
Boxtel 52 51.35 N 5.20 E
Boyabat 130 41.28 N 34.47 E
Boyabo 152 3.43 N 18.46 E
Boyacá □[5] 246 5.30 N 73.30 W
Boyacıköy ◆[8] 267b 41.06 N 29.02 E
Boyalı 130 41.02 N 33.19 E
Boyalık 130 41.15 N 28.37 E
Boyang 100 28.59 N 116.40 E
Boyanup 168a 33.29 S 115.44 E
Boyarka 78 50.19 N 30.19 E
Boyasengese 152 3.29 N 20.33 E
Boyce 194 31.23 N 92.40 W
Boyceville 190 45.02 N 92.02 W
Boyd, Mn., U.S. 198 44.50 N 95.54 W
Boyd, Tx., U.S. 222 33.05 N 97.34 W
Boyd ≏ 166 29.51 S 152.35 E
Boyd's Cove 186 49.27 N 54.39 W
Boydton 192 36.40 N 78.23 W
Boyenge 152 0.25 N 18.51 E
Boyer ≏ 198 41.28 N 95.55 W
Boyera 152 0.38 S 19.25 E
Boyer Aḥmadī va Kohkīlūyeh □[4] 128 30.40 N 50.40 E
Boyer Run ≏ 279b 40.13 N 79.32 W
Boyers 214 41.06 N 79.54 W
Boyer's Creek ≏ 284a 43.00 N 79.02 W
Boyertown 208 40.20 N 75.38 W
Boyes Hot Springs 226 38.19 N 122.29 W
Boykins 208 36.34 N 77.12 W
Boyle, Ab., Can. 182 54.35 N 112.49 W
Boyle, Ire. 48 53.58 N 8.18 W
Boyle, Ms., U.S. 194 33.42 N 90.50 W
Boyle Drain ≏ 212 43.42 N 81.06 W
Boyle Heights ◆[8] 280 34.02 N 118.13 W
Boylston, Al., U.S. 194 32.26 N 86.17 W
Boylston, Ma., U.S. 207 42.23 N 71.42 W
Boyne 275b 43.29 N 79.50 W
Boyne ≏, Austl. 166 23.56 S 151.21 E
Boyne ≏, Mb., Can. 184 49.34 N 97.52 W
Boyne ≏, On., Can. 212 44.10 N 79.49 W
Boyne ≏, Ire. 48 53.43 N 6.15 W
Boyne Battlesite ⊥ 48 53.42 N 6.23 W
Boyne City 190 45.12 N 85.00 W
Boynton 196 35.38 N 95.39 W
Boynton Beach 220 26.31 N 80.04 W
Boyo 152 5.43 N 21.33 E
Boyolali 115a 7.32 S 110.35 E
Boysen Reservoir ⊜[1] 202 43.19 N 108.11 W
Boysen State Park ♦ 202 43.23 N 108.07 W
Boys Ranch 196 35.32 N 102.15 W
Boyuibe 248 20.25 S 63.17 W
Böyük Hinaldağ ∧ 84 40.20 N 45.57 E
Böyük Kirs dağ ∧ 84 39.41 N 46.44 E
Boyup Brook 162 33.50 S 116.24 E
Bozburun 130 36.41 N 28.04 E
Boz Burun ≻ 130 40.32 N 28.46 E
Bozburun Yarımadası ≻[1] 130 36.40 N 28.10 E
Bozcaada 130 39.50 N 26.04 E
Boz Dağ ∧, Tür. 130 37.18 N 29.12 E
Boz Dağ ∧, Tür. 130 38.19 N 28.08 E
Bozdağ ∧, Tür. 130 36.50 N 36.22 E
Boz Dağlar ⋀ 130 38.20 N 27.45 E
Bozdoğan 130 37.40 N 28.19 E
Bozel 62 45.27 N 6.39 E
Bozeman 202 45.40 N 111.02 W
Bozen → Bolzano 64 46.31 N 11.22 E
Bozene 152 2.56 N 19.12 E
Bozhen 98 38.07 N 116.32 E
Boží Dar 54 50.24 N 12.55 E
Bozkır 130 37.11 N 32.15 E
Bozkurt, Tür. 130 37.49 N 29.37 E
Bozkurt, Tür. 130 41.57 N 34.01 E
Bozman 208 38.46 N 76.16 W
Bozoğlak 130 39.38 N 38.49 E
Bozok 130 37.18 N 40.22 E
Bozoum 152 6.19 N 16.23 E
Bozova, Tür. 130 37.22 N 38.31 E
Bozova, Tür. 130 37.13 N 30.18 E
Bozovici 38 44.55 N 21.59 E
Bozšakol' 86 51.50 N 74.20 E
Bozum 52 53.05 N 5.42 E
Bozüyük 130 39.54 N 30.03 E
Bozzolo 64 45.06 N 10.29 E
Bra 62 44.42 N 7.51 E
Braan ≏ 46 56.33 N 3.35 W
Braås 26 57.04 N 15.03 E
Brabant □[4] 56 50.45 N 4.30 E
Brabante, Isla de → Brabant Island I 9 64.15 S 62.20 W
Brabant Island I 9 64.15 S 62.20 W
Brabant Lake ⊜ 184 56.00 N 103.43 W
Brabrand 41 56.09 N 10.07 E
Brač, Otok I 36 43.20 N 16.40 E
Bracadale, Loch c 46 57.19 N 6.30 W
Bracciano 66 42.06 N 12.10 E
Bracciano, Lago di ⊜ 66 42.07 N 12.14 E
Bracco, Passo del)(62 44.15 N 9.34 E
Bracebridge 212 45.02 N 79.19 W
Bracebridge Heath 44 53.13 N 0.33 W
Braceville, Il., U.S. 216 41.14 N 88.16 W
Braceville, Oh., U.S. 214 41.14 N 80.58 W
Brachfield 222 32.03 N 94.39 W
Bracieux 50 47.33 N 1.33 E
Bracigliano 68 40.49 N 14.42 E
Bracigovo 38 42.01 N 24.22 E
Bräcke 26 62.43 N 15.27 E
Brackel ◆[8] 263 51.32 N 7.33 E
Bracken □[6] 218 38.40 N 84.06 W
Brackendale 182 49.46 N 123.09 W
Brackenheim 56 49.05 N 9.03 E
Brackenhurst 273d 26.19 S 28.06 E
Bracken Lake ⊜ 184 53.37 N 99.50 W
Brackenridge 214 40.36 N 79.44 W
Brackett Field ⊠ 280 34.05 N 117.47 W
Brackettville 196 29.18 N 100.25 W
Brački Kanal ⊔ 36 43.24 N 16.40 E
Brackley 42 52.02 N 1.09 W
Bracknell 42 51.26 N 0.45 W
Bracktown 218 38.04 N 84.31 W
Brackwede 52 51.59 N 8.31 E
Braco 46 56.15 N 3.53 W
Braço do Norte 252 28.17 S 49.11 W
Bracuí ≏ 256 22.57 S 44.24 W
Brad 38 46.08 N 22.47 E
Bradano ≏ 68 40.23 N 16.51 E
Bradbury 280 34.08 N 117.59 W
Bradbury Heights 284c 38.52 N 76.56 W
Braddock, N.J., U.S. 285 39.42 N 74.53 W
Braddock, Pa., U.S. 214 40.24 N 79.52 W
Braddock Acres 284c 38.49 N 77.10 W
Braddock Heights, Md., U.S. 208 39.25 N 77.30 W
Braddock Heights, N.Y., U.S. 210 43.19 N 77.42 W
Braddock Hills 279b 40.25 N 79.51 W
Braddock Point ≻ 210 43.19 N 77.43 W
Braddocks Millpond ⊜ 285 39.49 N 74.51 W
Braden ≏ 220 27.30 N 82.32 W
Bradenton 220 27.29 N 82.34 W
Bradenton Beach 220 27.28 N 82.42 W

≏	River	Fluß	Río	Rivière	Rio
≚	Canal	Kanal	Canal	Canal	Canal
ʟ	Waterfall, Rapids	Wasserfall, Stromschnellen	Cascada, Rápidos	Chute d'eau, Rapides	Cascata, Rápidos
⊔	Strait	Meeresstraße	Estrecho	Détroit	Estreito
c	Bay, Gulf	Bucht, Golf	Bahía, Golfo	Baie, Golfe	Baía, Golfo
⊜	Lake, Lakes	See, Seen	Lago, Lagos	Lac, Lacs	Lago, Lagos
≋	Swamp	Sumpf	Pantano	Marais	Pântano
⊓	Ice Features, Glacier	Eis- und Gletscherformen	Accidentes Glaciales	Formes glaciaires	Acidentes glaciares
⫪	Other Hydrographic Features	Andere Hydrographische Objekte	Otros Elementos Hidrográficos	Autres données hydrographiques	Outros acidentes hidrográficos
✦	Submarine Features	Untermeerische Objekte	Accidentes Submarinos	Formes de relief sous-marin	Acidentes submarinos
□	Political Unit	Politische Einheit	Unidad Politica	Entité politique	Unidade política
v	Cultural Institution	Kulturelle Institution	Institución Cultural	Institution culturelle	Instituição cultural
⊥	Historical Site	Historische Stätte	Sitio Histórico	Site historique	Sitio histórico
♦	Recreational Site	Erholungs- und Ferienort	Sitio de Recreo	Centre de loisirs	Area de Lazer
⊠	Airport	Flughafen	Aeropuerto	Aéroport	Aeroporto
■	Military Installation	Militäranlage	Instalación Militar	Installation militaire	Instalação militar
◆	Miscellaneous	Verschiedenes	Misceláneo	Divers	Diversos

Bradenville 214 40.19 N 79.20 W
Braderup 41 54.50 N 8.53 E
Bradford, On., Can. 212 44.07 N 79.34 W
Bradford, Eng., U.K. 44 53.48 N 1.45 W
Bradford, Ar., U.S. 194 35.25 N 91.27 W
Bradford, Il., U.S. 190 41.10 N 89.39 W
Bradford, N.Y., U.S. 210 42.22 N 77.07 W
Bradford, Oh., U.S. 218 40.08 N 84.26 W
Bradford, Pa., U.S. 214 41.57 N 78.38 W
Bradford, R.I., U.S. 207 41.23 N 71.44 W
Bradford, Tn., U.S. 194 36.04 N 88.48 W
Bradford, Vt., U.S. 188 43.59 N 72.09 W
Bradford □[6] 210 41.56 N 78.40 W
Bradford □[8] 262 53.47 N 1.52 W
Bradford Hills 285 40.01 N 75.39 W
Bradford Mountain ∧ 207 41.59 N 73.18 W
Bradford-on-Avon 42 51.20 N 2.15 W
Bradford Regional Airport ⊠ 214 41.48 N 78.38 W
Bradfordwoods 214 40.38 N 80.05 W
Brading 42 50.41 N 1.09 W
Bradley, Ar., U.S. 194 33.05 N 93.39 W
Bradley, Ca., U.S. 226 35.51 N 120.47 W
Bradley, Fl., U.S. 220 27.48 N 81.59 W
Bradley, Il., U.S. 216 41.08 N 87.51 W
Bradley, Mi., U.S. 216 42.38 N 85.39 W
Bradley, S.D., U.S. 198 45.05 N 97.38 W
Bradley Beach 208 40.12 N 74.01 W
Bradley Farms 284c 39.00 N 77.11 W
Bradley Gardens 276 40.34 N 74.39 W
Bradley Institute 154 17.02 S 31.27 E
Bradley International Airport ⊠ 207 41.55 N 72.40 W
Bradley Reefs ✧[2] 175e 6.52 S 160.48 E
Bradley Woods Reservation ♦ 279a 41.25 N 81.58 W
Bradley W. Palmer State Park ♦ 283 42.39 N 70.54 W
Bradner, B.C., Can. 224 49.06 N 122.25 W
Bradner, Oh., U.S. 214 41.19 N 83.26 W
Bradninch 42 50.50 N 3.25 W
Bradore-Bay 186 51.28 N 57.14 W
Bradshaw, Eng., U.K. 262 53.36 N 2.24 W
Bradshaw, Md., U.S. 208 39.25 N 76.22 W
Bradshaw, Ne., U.S. 198 40.53 N 97.44 W
Bradshaw, W.V., U.S. 192 37.21 N 81.47 W
Bradwell-on-Sea 42 51.44 N 0.54 E
Bradworthy 42 50.54 N 4.22 W
Brady, Mt., U.S. 202 48.02 N 111.50 W
Brady, Ne., U.S. 198 41.01 N 100.22 W
Brady, Tx., U.S. 196 31.08 N 99.20 W
Brady Creek ≃ 196 31.07 N 98.59 W
Brady Lake 214 41.09 N 81.19 W
Brady Mountains ⋏[2] 196 31.20 N 99.40 W
Brae 46a 60.23 N 1.21 W
Brædstrup 41 55.58 N 9.37 E
Braemar 46 57.01 N 3.23 W
Braeside, Austl. 162 21.12 S 121.01 E
Braeside, Austl. 274b 37.59 S 145.07 E
Braeside, On., Can. 212 45.28 N 76.24 W
Braga 34 41.33 N 8.26 W
Bragado 252 35.08 S 60.30 W
Bragança, Bra. 250 1.03 S 46.46 W
Braganca, Bra. 256 23.18 S 45.38 W
Bragança, Port. 34 41.49 N 6.45 W
Bragança Paulista 256 22.57 S 46.34 W
Bragar 46 58.24 N 6.40 W
Bragin 78 51.47 N 30.14 E
Braginka ≃ 78 51.22 N 30.24 E
Braham 190 45.43 N 93.10 W
Brahetrolleborg ⊥ 41 55.09 N 10.22 E
Brahma Island I 220 27.52 N 81.15 W
Brāhmanbāria 120 23.59 N 91.07 E
Brāhmani ≃, India 120 20.39 N 86.46 E
Brāhmani ≃, India 126 24.09 N 88.01 E
Brahmapur, India 122 19.19 N 84.47 E
Brahmapur, India 272b 22.28 N 88.22 E
Brahmaputra (Yarlung) ≃ 120 24.02 N 90.59 E
Brāhmaur 123 32.27 N 76.32 E
Brahynivka 78 48.29 N 36.21 E
Braich y Pwll › 42 52.48 N 4.36 W
Braidwood, Austl. 166 35.27 S 149.48 E
Braidwood, Il., U.S. 216 41.15 N 88.12 W
Braies (Prags) 64 46.42 N 12.08 E
Brăila 38 45.16 N 27.58 E
Brăila □[6] 38 45.00 N 27.40 E
Brain ≃ 42 51.48 N 0.39 E
Brainard, Ne., U.S. 198 41.11 N 97.00 W
Brainard, N.Y., U.S. 210 42.30 N 73.31 W
Braine 50 49.20 N 3.32 E
Braine-l'Alleud 50 50.41 N 4.22 E
Braine-le-Château 50 50.41 N 4.16 E
Braine-le-Comte 50 50.36 N 4.08 E
Brainerd 190 46.21 N 94.12 W
Braint ≃ 44 53.08 N 4.19 W
Braintree, Eng., U.K. 42 51.53 N 0.32 E
Braintree, Ma., U.S. 207 42.13 N 71.00 W
Braintree □[8] 260 51.47 N 0.36 E
Brak ≃, S. Afr. 158 31.32 S 21.33 E
Brak ≃, S. Afr. 158 29.35 S 22.55 E
Brake, Dtsch. 52 53.19 N 8.28 E
Brake, Dtsch. 52 52.04 N 8.35 E
Brake, Dtsch. 52 52.01 N 8.55 E
Brakel, Bel. 50 50.48 N 3.46 E
Brakel, Dtsch. 52 51.43 N 9.10 E
Brakna □[4] 150 17.30 N 13.30 W
Brakpan 158 26.14 S 28.22 E
Brakpan □[5] 273d 26.16 S 28.21 E
Brakpoort 158 31.20 S 23.22 E
Brakputs 158 29.29 S 18.24 E
Brakwater 156 22.24 S 17.06 E
Brålanda 26 58.34 N 12.22 E
Bralorne 182 50.47 N 122.49 W
Bramalea 212 43.44 N 79.43 W
Bramall Hall ⊥ 262 53.23 N 2.09 W
Braman 196 36.55 N 97.20 W
Brambauer 263 51.35 N 7.27 E
Bramberg am Wildkogel 64 47.16 N 12.21 E
Bramble Bay c 171a 27.17 S 153.05 E
Bramble Cay I 164 9.08 S 143.52 E
Bramdrupdam 41 55.31 N 9.28 E
Bramey-Lenningsen 263 51.34 N 7.46 E
Bramfeld ◆[8] 52 53.37 N 10.04 E
Bramford 42 52.04 N 1.06 E
Bramhall 262 53.22 N 2.10 W
Bramhope 44 53.53 N 1.37 W
Bramley 260 51.12 N 0.34 W
Bramley ◆[8] 273d 26.08 S 28.05 E
Bramley Mountain ∧ 210 42.18 N 74.49 W
Bramming 41 55.28 N 8.42 E
Brampton, On., Can. 212 43.41 N 79.46 W
Brampton, Eng., U.K. 42 52.19 N 0.14 W
Brampton, Eng., U.K. 44 54.57 N 2.43 W
Brampton Airfield ⊠ 275b 43.40 N 79.47 W
Bramsche 52 52.24 N 7.58 E
Bramsöfjärden ⊜ 40 60.20 N 17.10 E
Bramstedt 52 53.22 N 8.41 E
Brancaleone Marina 68 37.58 N 16.06 E
Brancaster 42 52.58 N 0.39 E
Brancaster Roads ⊤[3] 42 53.00 N 0.41 E
Branch 186 46.53 N 53.57 W
Branch □[6] 216 41.55 N 85.03 W
Branch Brook Park ♦ 276 40.46 N 74.10 W
Branch Dale 208 40.41 N 76.20 W
Branchport 210 42.36 N 77.09 W
Branchville, Ct., U.S. 207 41.16 N 73.26 W
Branchville, N.J., U.S. 210 41.08 N 74.45 W
Branchville, S.C., U.S. 192 33.15 N 80.48 W
Branchville, Va., U.S. 208 36.34 N 77.14 W
Branco 152 12.30 S 20.32 E
Branco ≃, Bra. 246 1.24 S 61.51 W
Branco ≃, Bra. 248 10.03 S 67.51 W
Branco ≃, Bra. 248 7.44 S 61.46 W
Branco ≃, Bra. 248 9.12 S 64.22 W
Branco ≃, Bra. 248 9.37 S 60.33 W
Branco ≃, Bra. 248 21.00 S 57.48 W
Branco ≃, Bra. 250 7.01 S 51.42 W
Branco ≃, Bra. 250 12.00 S 44.56 W
Branco, Ilhéu I 150a 16.39 N 24.41 W
Brand, Dtsch. 56 50.43 N 6.09 E
Brand, Öst. 58 47.06 N 9.44 E
Brandamore 208 40.03 N 75.50 W
Brandaris ∧[2] 241s 12.17 N 68.24 W
Brandberg ∧ 156 21.10 S 14.33 E
Brandbu 26 60.28 N 10.30 E
Brande 41 55.57 N 9.07 E
Brandebourg → Brandenburg 54 52.24 N 12.32 E
Brandeis University ᵾ[2] 283 42.22 N 71.16 W
Brandenberg 64 47.29 N 11.53 E
Brandenberg ∧[2] 263 51.20 N 7.37 E
Brandenburg, Dtsch. 54 52.24 N 12.32 E
Brandenburg, Ky., U.S. 194 38.00 N 86.10 W
Brandenburg □[3] 54 52.30 N 13.30 E
Brandenburger Tor ⊥ 264a 52.31 N 13.23 E
Brand-Erbisdorf 54 50.52 N 13.19 E
Brandfort 158 28.47 S 26.30 E
Br'andino 80 54.23 N 49.23 E
Brandis, Dtsch. 54 51.48 N 13.10 E
Brandis, Dtsch. 54 51.20 N 12.36 E
Brandizzo 62 45.11 N 7.51 E
Brandkop 158 31.13 S 19.13 E
Brandon, Mb., Can. 184 49.50 N 99.57 W
Brandon, Eng., U.K. 42 52.27 N 0.37 E
Brandon, Eng., U.K. 44 54.46 N 1.39 W
Brandon, Fl., U.S. 220 27.56 N 82.17 W
Brandon, Ms., U.S. 194 32.16 N 89.59 W
Brandon, S.D., U.S. 198 43.35 N 96.34 W
Brandon, Tx., U.S. 222 32.03 N 96.58 W
Brandon, Vt., U.S. 188 43.47 N 73.05 W
Brandon, Wi., U.S. 190 43.44 N 88.46 W
Brandon Bay c 48 52.15 N 10.05 W
Brandon Head › 48 52.16 N 10.14 W
Brandon Mountain ∧ 48 52.14 N 10.15 W
Brandon Road Lock and Dam ◆[5] 278 41.30 N 88.06 W
Brandonville 210 40.52 N 76.10 W
Brand Park ♦ 280 34.11 N 118.16 W
Brandsen 258 35.10 S 58.14 W
Brands Hatch Motor Race Circuit ♦ 260 51.22 N 0.16 E
Brandsø I 41 55.21 N 9.43 E
Brandt 218 39.54 N 84.05 W
Brandvlei 158 30.25 S 20.30 E
Brandy Camp 214 41.19 N 78.41 W
Brandy Peak ∧ 202 42.36 N 123.53 W
Brandýsek 54 50.10 N 14.10 E
Brandýs nad Labem 54 50.10 N 14.41 E
Brandywine Battlefield ⊥ 208 39.53 N 75.35 W
Brandywine Creek ≃, U.S. 285 39.44 N 75.32 W
Brandywine Creek ≃, In., U.S. 218 39.31 N 85.52 W
Brandywine Creek ≃, Oh., U.S. 279a 41.17 N 81.34 W
Brandywine Creek, East Branch ≃ 208 39.55 N 75.39 W
Brandywine Creek, West Branch ≃ 208 39.55 N 75.39 W
Brandywine Creek State Park ♦ 285 39.48 N 75.35 W
Brandywine Park ♦ 285 39.45 N 75.33 W
Brandywine Springs Park ♦ 285 39.45 N 75.38 W
Branford, Ct., U.S. 207 41.16 N 72.48 W
Branford, Fl., U.S. 192 29.57 N 82.55 W
Brani, Pulau I 271c 1.15 N 103.50 E
Braniewo 30 54.24 N 19.50 E
Branka, Česká Rep. 60 49.50 N 12.33 E
Br'anka, Ross. 86 59.08 N 93.27 E
Branlin ≃ 50 47.51 N 3.06 E
Brannenburg 64 47.44 N 12.05 E
Branquinho ≃ 248 5.45 S 71.27 W
Bransby 166 28.14 S 142.04 E
Bransfield Strait ʯ 9 63.00 S 59.00 W
Bransgore 42 50.47 N 1.44 W
Brańsk, Pol. 30 52.45 N 22.51 E
Br'ansk, Ross. 76 53.15 N 34.22 E
Br'anskaja Kosa, mys › 84 44.22 N 47.00 E
Br'ansk Oblast' □[4] 76 53.00 N 34.00 E
Branson 194 36.38 N 93.13 W
Brant 210 42.35 N 79.01 W
Brant □[6] 212 43.10 N 80.20 W
Brant ≃ 44 53.09 N 0.35 W
Br'anta ≃ 89 54.27 N 127.42 E
Brantas ≃ 115a 7.28 S 112.25 E
Brantford 212 43.08 N 80.16 W
Brantingham Lake ⊜ 212 43.42 N 75.17 W
Brant Lake 188 43.40 N 73.45 W
Brantley 194 31.34 N 86.15 W
Brantôme 32 45.22 N 0.39 E
Brant Rock 283 42.05 N 70.38 W
Brantville 186 47.22 N 64.58 W
Branxholme 166 37.51 S 141.47 E
Branxton 170 32.39 S 151.22 E
Branzi 64 46.00 N 9.46 E
Brás ◆[8] 287b 23.32 S 46.36 W
Brás Cubas 256 23.32 S 46.13 W
Bras d'Or Lake ⊜ 186 45.52 N 60.50 W
Brashear 222 33.07 N 95.44 W
Brasil → Brazil □[1] 242 10.00 S 55.00 W
Brasilândia ◆[8] 287b 23.28 S 46.41 W
Brasiléia 248 11.00 S 68.44 W
Brasília 255 15.47 S 47.55 W
Brasília, Parque Nacional de ♦ 255 15.36 S 48.08 W
Brasília de Minas 255 16.12 S 44.26 W
Brasília Legal 250 3.49 S 55.36 W
Brasilien → Brazil □[1] 242 10.00 S 55.00 W
Braslav 76 55.38 N 27.02 E
Brasopolis 256 22.28 S 45.37 W
Brașov 38 45.39 N 25.37 E
Brașov □[6] 38 45.45 N 25.15 E
Brass 150 4.19 N 6.14 E
Brass Castle 210 40.47 N 74.58 W
Brasschaat 50 51.17 N 4.27 E
Brassert 263 51.40 N 7.05 E
Brassey, Banjaran ⋏ 112 4.54 N 117.30 E
Brassey, Mount ∧ 162 23.05 S 134.38 E
Brass Islands II 240m 18.24 N 64.58 W
Brassó → Brașov 38 45.39 N 25.37 E
Brasstown Bald ∧ 192 34.52 N 83.48 W
Brastad 26 58.23 N 11.29 E
Brasted 260 51.16 N 0.06 E
Brasted Chart 260 51.16 N 0.06 E
Břasy 60 49.50 N 13.35 E
Bratca 38 46.56 N 22.37 E
Bratcevo ◆[8] 265b 55.51 N 37.24 E
Bratejevo ◆[8] 265b 55.38 N 37.45 E
Bratenahl 279a 41.32 N 81.37 W
Brateș, Lacul ⊜ 38 45.30 N 28.05 E
Bratislava 30 48.09 N 17.07 E
Bratol'ubovka 86 51.13 N 66.46 E
Bratsk 88 56.05 N 101.48 E
Bratskaja Kada 88 55.02 N 102.06 E
Brats'ke 78 47.52 N 31.34 E
Bratskoje vodochranilišče ⊜[1] 88 56.10 N 102.10 E
Bratslav 78 48.50 N 28.55 E
Brattfors 40 59.40 N 14.01 E
Brattleboro 207 42.51 N 72.33 W
Bratto 64 45.55 N 10.04 E
Brattvåg 26 62.36 N 6.27 E
Braubach 56 50.16 N 7.40 E
Braulio Carrillo, Parque Nacional ♦ 236 10.10 N 84.00 W
Braúnas 255 19.04 S 42.43 W
Braunau am Inn 60 48.15 N 13.02 E
Braunfels 56 50.31 N 8.23 E
Braunlage 54 51.44 N 10.37 E
Bräunlingen 58 47.55 N 8.26 E
Braunsbedra 54 51.15 N 11.49 E
Braunschweig, Dtsch. 52 52.16 N 10.31 E
Braunschweig, S. Afr. 158 32.48 S 27.22 E
Braunschweig □[5] 52 52.00 N 10.20 E
Braunston 42 52.17 N 1.12 W
Braunton 42 51.07 N 4.10 W
Braunwald 58 46.56 N 9.00 E
Brava I 150a 14.52 N 24.43 W
Brava, Costa ≗[2] 34 41.45 N 3.04 E
Brava, Laguna ⊜ 252 28.22 S 68.50 W
Brava, Punta › 258 34.56 S 56.10 W
Brave 188 39.44 N 80.16 W
Bravicea 38 47.22 N 28.26 E
Bråviken c 40 58.38 N 16.32 E
Bravo, Cerro ∧, Bol. 248 17.40 S 64.35 W
Bravo, Cerro ∧, Perú 248 5.32 S 79.15 W
Bravo del Norte (Rio Grande) ≃ 178 25.55 N 97.09 W
Brawley 204 32.58 N 115.31 W
Brawley Peaks ⋏ 204 38.15 N 118.55 W
Brawley Wash V 200 32.34 N 111.26 W
Bray, Bel. 50 50.26 N 4.06 E
Bray, Ire. 48 53.12 N 6.06 W
Bray ≃ 42 50.59 N 3.53 W
Bray, Pays de ◆[1] 50 49.46 N 1.26 E
Braybrook 274b 37.47 S 144.51 E
Bray-Dunes 50 51.05 N 2.31 E
Braye ≃ 50 47.45 N 0.42 E
Bray Head › 48 51.53 N 10.26 W
Brayiliv 78 49.06 N 28.09 E
Bray Island I 176 69.20 N 76.45 W
Braymer 194 39.35 N 93.47 W
Braysur-Seine 50 48.25 N 3.14 E
Bray-sur-Somme 50 49.56 N 2.43 E
Brayton 44 53.46 N 1.05 W
Brazeau ≃ 182 52.55 N 115.15 W
Brazeau, Mount ∧ 182 52.33 N 117.21 W
Brazeau Dam ◆[6] 182 52.45 N 115.30 W
Brazen Head › 158 31.43 S 29.25 E
Brazey-en-Plaine 58 47.08 N 5.13 E
Brazil 194 39.31 N 87.07 W
Brazil (Brasil) □[1] 242 10.00 S 55.00 W
Brazil Basin ✧[1] 8 15.00 S 25.00 W
Brazo Chico, Arroyo ≃ 258 33.45 S 58.32 W
Brazo Largo, Arroyo ≃ 258 33.47 S 58.36 W
Brazoria 222 29.02 N 95.34 W
Brazoria □[6] 222 29.12 N 95.25 W
Brazoria Reservoir ⊜[1] 222 29.05 N 95.01 W
Brazos □[6] 222 30.40 N 96.18 W
Brazos ≃ 196 28.53 N 95.23 W
Brazos, Clear Fork ≃ 196 33.01 N 98.40 W
Brazos, Double Mountain Fork ≃ 196 33.15 N 100.00 W
Brazos, Salt Fork ≃ 196 33.15 N 100.00 W
Brazo Sur [del Rio Coig] ≃ 254 51.32 S 70.04 W
Brazzaville, Congo 152 4.16 S 15.17 E
Brazzaville, Congo 273b 4.16 S 15.17 E
Brazzaville (Maya Maya) Airport ⊠ 273b 4.15 S 15.15 E
Brčko 38 44.53 N 18.48 E
Brda ≃ 30 53.07 N 18.08 E
Brdy ⋏ 60 49.40 N 13.50 E
Bré → Bray 48 53.12 N 6.06 W
Brea 228 33.55 N 117.53 W
Brea, Punta › 240m 17.56 N 66.55 W
Brea Canyon V 280 33.55 N 117.55 W
Brea Creek ≃ 280 33.53 N 117.59 W
Breadalbane 166 23.49 S 139.35 E
Brea Dam ◆[6] 280 33.54 N 117.56 W
Breaden Bluff ∧[2] 162 26.56 S 124.32 E
Breadysville 285 40.13 N 75.04 W
Breakenridge, Mount ∧ 182 49.43 N 121.56 W
Breakheart Reservation ♦ 283 42.29 N 71.02 W
Breaksea Sound ʯ 172 45.35 S 166.40 E
Breaks Interstate Park ♦ 192 37.17 N 82.18 W
Bream 42 51.45 N 2.34 W
Bream Bay c 172 35.55 S 174.30 E
Bream Head › 172 35.51 S 174.35 E
Breamish ≃ 44 55.31 N 1.56 W
Bream Tail › 172 36.03 S 174.35 E
Brea Pozo 252 28.15 S 63.57 W
Breaston 44 52.54 N 1.19 W
Bréau 261 48.34 N 2.53 E
Breaux Bridge 194 30.16 N 91.53 W
Breaza 38 45.11 N 25.40 E
Brebes 115a 6.53 S 109.03 E
Brécey 32 48.44 N 1.10 W
Brechen 56 50.20 N 8.14 E
Brechfa 42 51.57 N 4.09 W
Brechin 46 56.44 N 2.40 W
Brecht 56 51.21 N 4.38 E
Brechten ◆[8] 263 51.35 N 7.28 E
Breckenridge, Co., U.S. 200 39.28 N 106.02 W
Breckenridge, Mi., U.S. 190 43.24 N 84.28 W
Breckenridge, Mn., U.S. 198 46.15 N 96.35 W
Breckenridge, Mo., U.S. 194 39.45 N 93.48 W
Breckenridge, Tx., U.S. 196 32.45 N 98.54 W
Breckerfeld 56 51.16 N 7.28 E
Breckland ◆[1] 42 52.28 N 0.37 E
Brecknock → Brecon 42 51.57 N 3.24 W
Brecknock, Península ›[1] 254 54.35 S 71.50 W
Brecksville 214 41.19 N 81.37 W
Břeclav 30 48.46 N 16.53 E
Brecon 42 51.57 N 3.24 W
Brecon Beacons ∧ 42 51.53 N 3.31 W
Brecon Beacons National Park ♦ 42 51.52 N 3.25 W
Bred 41 55.22 N 10.07 E
Breda, Ned. 52 51.35 N 4.46 E
Breda, Ia., U.S. 198 42.10 N 94.58 W
Bredaryd 26 57.10 N 13.44 E
Bredasdorp 158 34.32 S 20.02 E
Bredbo 171b 35.57 S 149.10 E
Bredbo ≃ 171b 35.58 S 149.08 E
Bredbury 262 53.25 N 2.06 W
Bredbyn 26 63.27 N 18.06 E
Breddin 54 52.52 N 12.13 E
Brede ≃ 41 55.09 N 8.42 E
Bredebro 41 55.03 N 8.49 E
Bredell 273d 26.05 S 28.17 E
Bredenbeck 52 52.15 N 9.37 E
Bredenbruch 263 51.21 N 7.45 E
Bredenbury 184 50.57 N 102.03 W
Bredene 50 51.14 N 2.58 E
Bredeney ◆[8] 263 51.24 N 6.59 E
Bredenscheid-Stüter 263 51.22 N 7.11 E
Bredereiche 54 53.08 N 13.14 E
Bredgar 260 51.18 N 0.42 E
Bredhurst 260 51.20 N 0.35 E
Bredon Hill ∧[2] 42 52.06 N 2.03 W
Bredsjö 40 59.50 N 14.44 E
Bredsjön ⊜ 40 60.13 N 13.55 E
Bredstedt 41 54.37 N 8.59 E
Bredsten 41 55.42 N 9.24 E
Bredy 86 52.26 N 60.21 E
Bree 56 51.08 N 5.36 E
Breë ≃ 158 34.24 S 20.50 E
Breeches, Lac ⊜ 206 45.54 N 71.28 W
Breedoge ≃ 48 53.55 N 8.27 W
Breeds Pond ⊜ 283 42.28 N 70.59 W
Breedsville 216 42.21 N 86.08 W
Breese 219 38.36 N 89.31 W
Breesport 210 42.10 N 76.44 W
Breeza Plains 164 14.50 S 144.07 E
Breezewood 279b 40.34 N 80.03 W
Breg ≃ 58 47.57 N 8.31 E
Bregalnica ≃ 38 41.43 N 22.09 E
Breganze 64 45.42 N 11.34 E
Bregenz 58 47.30 N 9.46 E
Bregenzer Wald ⋏ 58 47.20 N 10.00 E
Bregninge, Dan. 41 55.41 N 11.19 E
Bregninge, Dan. 41 55.01 N 10.37 E
Bregovo 38 44.09 N 22.39 E
Breguzzo 64 46.00 N 10.42 E
Brégy 261 49.05 N 2.52 E
Bréhal 32 48.54 N 1.31 W
Brehna 54 51.33 N 12.12 E
Breiðafjörður c 24a 65.15 N 23.15 W
Breidbach 158 32.54 S 27.27 E
Breidenbach 56 49.08 N 7.25 E
Breidenstein 56 50.55 N 8.28 E
Breil-sur-Roya 62 43.56 N 7.30 E
Breinizer 214 40.24 N 79.16 W
Breisach 58 48.01 N 7.40 E
Breisgau □[9] 58 47.45 N 7.45 E
Breitenbrunn 54 50.29 N 12.46 E
Breitenfelde 52 53.36 N 10.38 E
Breitenfurt bei Wien 61 48.08 N 16.08 E
Breitengüssbach 56 49.58 N 10.53 E
Breitenlee ◆[8] 264b 48.15 N 16.30 E
Breitenstein 54 51.37 N 10.56 E
Breitenworbis 54 51.24 N 10.25 E
Breithorn ∧ 58 45.56 N 7.45 E
Breitlingsee ⊜ 54 52.23 N 12.28 E
Breitscheid, Dtsch. 56 50.41 N 8.11 E
Breitscheid, Dtsch. 56 51.22 N 6.52 E
Breitsetten 61 48.12 N 16.42 E
Breitungen 54 50.45 N 10.20 E
Brejinho de Nazaré 250 11.01 S 48.34 W
Brejo 250 3.41 S 42.47 W
Brejões 255 13.06 S 39.48 W
Brejo Grande 250 10.26 S 36.28 W
Brejo Santo 250 7.29 S 39.00 W
Brejtovo 76 58.18 N 37.52 E
Brekken 26 62.39 N 11.53 E
Brekstad 26 63.41 N 9.41 E
Breloh 52 53.01 N 10.04 E
Bremangerlandet I 26 61.51 N 5.02 E
Brembio 62 45.13 N 9.34 E
Brembo ≃ 62 45.35 N 9.32 E
Brême → Bremen 52 53.04 N 8.49 E
Bremelau 58 48.20 N 9.32 E
Bremen, Dtsch. 52 53.04 N 8.49 E
Bremen, Ga., U.S. 192 33.43 N 85.08 W
Bremen, In., U.S. 216 41.26 N 86.08 W
Bremen, Oh., U.S. 188 39.42 N 82.25 W
Bremen □[3] 52 53.05 N 8.50 E
Bremen, Flughafen ⊠ 52 53.03 N 8.46 E
Bremer ≃, Austl. 168b 35.23 S 139.02 E
Bremer ≃, Austl. 171a 27.39 S 152.45 E
Bremer Bay 162 34.24 S 119.22 E
Bremer Bay c 162 34.23 S 119.25 E
Bremerhaven 52 53.33 N 8.34 E
Bremerton 224 47.34 N 122.37 W
Bremerton East 224 47.35 N 122.38 W
Bremervörde 52 53.29 N 9.08 E
Bremgarten 58 47.21 N 8.21 E
Bremke, Dtsch. 52 52.07 N 9.06 E
Bremke, Dtsch. 56 51.15 N 8.12 E
Bremke, Dtsch. 263 51.23 N 7.41 E
Bremner ≃ 190 48.41 N 85.31 W
Bremond 222 31.09 N 96.40 W
Brem River 182 50.26 N 124.39 W
Breña 286d 12.04 S 77.04 W
Brendel Lake ⊜ 281 42.38 N 83.30 W
Brenderup 41 55.29 N 9.59 E
Brendlorenzen 56 50.20 N 10.13 E
Brendon Hills ⋏[2] 42 51.07 N 3.25 W
Brenham 222 30.10 N 96.23 W
Brenig, Llyn ⊜[1] 44 53.05 N 3.32 W
Brenish 46 58.08 N 7.08 W
Brenish, Aird › 46 58.08 N 7.08 W
Bren Mar Park 284c 38.48 N 77.09 W
Brenne ≃, Fr. 50 47.38 N 4.16 E
Brenne ≃, Fr. 50 47.24 N 0.51 E
Brennero (Brenner) 64 47.00 N 11.30 E
Brennero, Passo del → Brenner Pass)(64 47.00 N 11.30 E
Brenner Pass)(64 47.00 N 11.30 E
Breno, It. 64 45.57 N 10.18 E
Breno, Schw. 58 46.02 N 8.53 E
Brénod 58 46.04 N 5.36 E
Brent, Al., U.S. 194 32.56 N 87.09 W
Brent, Fl., U.S. 194 30.28 N 87.14 W
Brent ◆[8] 42 51.34 N 0.17 W
Brent ≃ 260 51.28 N 0.18 W
Brenta ≃ 64 45.11 N 12.18 E
Brenta, Gruppo di ⋏ 64 46.11 N 10.54 E
Brentford ◆[8] 260 51.29 N 0.18 W
Brenthurst 273d 26.16 S 28.23 E
Brentino 64 45.40 N 10.55 E
Brentonico 64 45.49 N 10.57 E
Brent Reservoir ⊜[1] 260 51.35 N 0.15 W
Brentwood, Eng., U.K. 42 51.38 N 0.18 E
Brentwood, Eng., U.K. 260 51.38 N 0.18 E
Brentwood, Ca., U.S. 226 37.55 N 121.41 W
Brentwood, Md., U.S. 208 38.56 N 76.57 W
Brentwood, N.Y., U.S. 210 40.46 N 73.14 W
Brentwood, Oh., U.S. 218 39.13 N 84.31 W
Brentwood, Pa., U.S. 214 40.22 N 79.58 W
Brentwood, Tn., U.S. 194 36.01 N 86.46 W
Brentwood □[8] 260 51.37 N 0.20 E
Brentwood Bay 224 48.35 N 123.28 W
Brentwood Estates 214 40.25 N 80.45 W
Brentwood Heights ◆[8] 280 34.04 N 118.30 W
Brentwood Lake 214 41.19 N 82.05 W
Brentwood Park 273d 26.08 S 28.18 E
Brenz ≃ 56 48.34 N 10.24 E
Breo 62 44.23 N 7.49 E
Bréon, Ruisseu du ≃ 261 48.40 N 2.49 E
Brera, Palazzo di ᵾ 266b 45.28 N 9.11 E
Brereton Park 158 26.55 S 30.30 E
Brescello 64 44.54 N 10.31 E
Brescia 64 45.33 N 10.15 E
Brescia □[4] 64 45.38 N 10.18 E
Bresewitz 54 54.24 N 12.40 E
Brésil → Brazil □[1] 242 10.00 S 55.00 W
Breskens 52 51.24 N 3.34 E
Breslau, On., Can. 212 43.28 N 80.25 W
Breslau → Wrocław, Pol. 30 51.06 N 17.00 E
Breslau, Tx., U.S. 222 29.31 N 97.00 W
Bresle ≃ 50 50.04 N 1.22 E
Bresles 50 49.25 N 2.15 E
Bresnahan, Mount ∧ 162 23.50 S 117.55 E
Bressanone (Brixen) 64 46.43 N 11.39 E
Bressay I 46a 60.08 N 1.05 W
Bressay Sound ʯ 46a 60.07 N 1.09 W
Bresse ◆[1] 58 46.30 N 5.15 E
Bresso 266b 45.32 N 9.11 E
Bressuire 32 46.51 N 0.30 W
Brest, Blg. 38 43.38 N 24.35 E
Brest, Bela. 76 52.06 N 23.42 E
Brest, Fr. 32 48.24 N 4.29 W
Brest □[8] 76 52.30 N 25.30 E
Brestanica 36 45.59 N 15.29 E
Bretagne (Brittany) □[9] 32 48.00 N 3.00 W
Bretenoux 32 44.55 N 1.50 E
Breteuil 50 49.38 N 2.18 E
Breteuil-sur-Iton 50 48.50 N 0.55 E
Bréthencourt 261 48.30 N 1.55 E
Bretherton 262 53.41 N 2.48 W
Brétigny ■ 261 48.35 N 2.20 E
Brétigny-sur-Orge 50 48.37 N 2.19 E
Bretnig 54 51.08 N 14.04 E
Breton 182 53.07 N 114.28 W
Bretón, Canal de ʯ 240p 21.10 N 79.30 W
Breton, Pertuis ʯ 32 46.25 N 1.20 W
Breton Bay c 208 38.16 N 76.39 W
Breton Islands II 194 29.28 N 89.11 W
Breton Sound ʯ 194 29.30 N 89.30 W
Breton Woods 208 40.02 N 74.06 W
Brett ≃ 42 51.58 N 0.58 E
Brett, Cape › 172 35.10 S 174.20 E
Bretten 56 49.02 N 8.42 E
Breu, Rio do ≃ 246 3.29 S 66.20 W
Breueh, Pulau I 110 5.41 N 95.05 E

ENGLISH

Name Page Lat.°' Long.°'

Breuil-Bois-Robert 261 48.57 N 1.43 E
Breuil-Cervinia 58 45.56 N 7.38 E
Breuillet 261 48.34 N 2.10 E
Breuilpont 50 48.58 N 1.26 E
Breukelen 52 52.10 N 5.00 E
Breux 261 48.34 N 2.11 E
Brevard 192 35.14 N 82.44 W
Brevard □[6] 220 28.18 N 80.42 W
Brévenne ≃ 62 45.51 N 4.40 E
Brevens bruk 40 59.01 N 15.35 E
Breves 250 1.40 S 50.29 W
Brevig Mission 180 65.20 N 166.29 W
Brevik, Nor. 26 59.04 N 9.42 E
Brevik, Sve. 40 59.21 N 18.12 E
Brevoort Island I 176 63.30 N 64.20 W
Brewarrina 166 29.57 S 146.52 E
Brewer 188 44.47 N 68.45 W
Brewer Island I 282 37.33 N 122.16 W
Brewersville 218 39.05 N 85.37 W
Brewerton 210 43.14 N 76.08 W
Brewerville 150 6.26 N 10.47 W
Brewongle 170 33.29 S 149.43 E
Brewood 42 52.41 N 2.10 W
Brewster, Ks., U.S. 198 39.22 N 101.22 W
Brewster, Ma., U.S. 207 41.45 N 70.05 W
Brewster, Mn., U.S. 198 43.41 N 95.28 W
Brewster, Ne., U.S. 198 41.56 N 99.51 W
Brewster, N.Y., U.S. 210 41.23 N 73.37 W
Brewster, Oh., U.S. 214 40.42 N 81.35 W
Brewster, Wa., U.S. 202 48.05 N 119.46 W
Brewster, Kap › 16 70.19 N 22.05 W
Brewster, Lake ⊜ 166 33.28 S 146.00 E
Brewster, Mount ∧ 172 44.04 S 169.27 E
Brewton 194 31.06 N 87.04 W
Breyten 158 26.16 S 30.00 E
Břežany 61 48.52 N 16.20 E
Brežice 36 45.54 N 15.36 E
Brézina 148 33.04 N 1.14 E
Brézins 62 45.21 N 5.19 E
Březnice 60 49.33 N 13.57 E
Breznik 38 42.44 N 22.54 E
Březno, Česká Rep. 54 50.24 N 13.26 E
Brezno, Slvk. 30 48.50 N 19.39 E
Brézolles 50 48.41 N 1.04 E
Březová 54 50.06 N 12.39 E
Březové Hory 60 49.41 N 13.58 E
Bria 152 6.32 N 21.59 E
Brian Boru Peak ∧ 182 55.05 N 127.35 W
Briançon 62 44.54 N 6.39 E
Brian Head ∧ 200 37.41 N 112.50 W
Brianza □[9] 62 45.40 N 9.10 E
Briar 222 33.00 N 97.34 W
Briarcliff Manor 210 41.08 N 73.49 W
Briar Creek 210 40.10 N 76.46 W
Briar Creek ≃ 222 32.06 N 96.22 W
Briare 50 47.38 N 2.44 E
Briare, Canal de ≅ 50 48.02 N 2.43 E
Briarres-sur-Essonne 50 48.14 N 2.25 E
Briarwood Beach 214 41.06 N 81.54 W
Briarwood Center ◆[9] 281 42.14 N 83.45 W
Briatico 68 38.43 N 16.02 E
Bribano 64 46.06 N 12.05 E
Bribie Island I 171a 27.00 S 153.07 E
Bricelyn 190 43.33 N 93.48 W
Briceni 38 48.22 N 27.04 E
Brice Run ≃ 284b 39.19 N 76.50 W
Brices Cross Roads National Battlefield Site ⊥ 194 34.31 N 88.41 W
Briceville 192 36.10 N 84.11 W
Bricherasio 62 44.49 N 7.18 E
Bricht 263 51.41 N 6.51 E
Brickebacken 40 59.15 N 15.15 E
Brick Lake ⊜ 220 28.10 N 81.12 W
Brick Township 208 40.04 N 74.08 W
Briçonnet, Lac ⊜ 186 51.27 N 60.11 W
Bricquebec 32 49.28 N 1.38 W
Bridal Veil 224 45.33 N 122.10 W
Bridalveil Fall ⌊ 226 37.43 N 119.39 W
Bride 44 54.22 N 4.22 W
Bride ≃ 48 52.04 N 7.52 W
Bridesburg ◆[8] 285 40.00 N 75.04 W
Brides-les-Bains 62 45.27 N 6.34 E
Bridge 42 51.14 N 1.07 E
Bridge ≃ 182 50.45 N 121.55 W
Bridge City 194 30.01 N 93.50 W
Bridge Creek ≃ 224 48.26 N 120.52 W
Bridgehampton 207 40.56 N 72.18 W
Bridge Lake 182 51.29 N 120.43 W
Bridgend, Scot., U.K. 46 55.48 N 6.16 W
Bridgend, Scot., U.K. 46 56.48 N 2.45 W
Bridgend, Wales, U.K. 42 51.31 N 3.35 W
Bridgenorth 212 44.23 N 78.23 W
Bridge of Allan 46 56.09 N 3.57 W
Bridge of Gaur 46 56.41 N 4.27 W
Bridge of Orchy 46 56.30 N 4.46 W
Bridge of Weir 46 55.52 N 4.35 W
Bridgeport, On., Can. 212 43.29 N 80.29 W
Bridgeport, Al., U.S. 194 34.56 N 85.42 W
Bridgeport, Ca., U.S. 226 38.10 N 119.13 W
Bridgeport, Ct., U.S. 207 41.10 N 73.12 W
Bridgeport, Il., U.S. 194 38.42 N 87.45 W
Bridgeport, Mi., U.S. 190 43.21 N 83.52 W
Bridgeport, Ne., U.S. 198 41.39 N 103.05 W
Bridgeport, N.J., U.S. 285 39.48 N 75.20 W
Bridgeport, N.Y., U.S. 210 43.09 N 75.58 W
Bridgeport, Oh., U.S. 214 40.04 N 80.44 W
Bridgeport, Pa., U.S. 285 40.06 N 75.21 W
Bridgeport, Tx., U.S. 222 33.12 N 97.45 W
Bridgeport, Wa., U.S. 202 48.00 N 119.40 W
Bridgeport, W.V., U.S. 188 39.17 N 80.15 W
Bridgeport ◆[8] 278 41.51 N 87.39 W
Bridgeport, Lake ⊜[1] 222 33.13 N 97.48 W
Bridgeport, University of ᵾ[2] 276 41.10 N 73.12 W
Bridgeport Airport ⊠ 285 39.47 N 75.20 W
Bridgeport Harbor c 276 41.10 N 73.11 W
Bridgeport Municipal Airport ⊠ 276 41.10 N 73.08 W
Bridgeport Reservoir ⊜[1] 226 38.22 N 119.14 W
Bridger 202 45.17 N 108.54 W
Bridge River Indian Reserve ◆[4] 182 50.45 N 122.00 W
Bridger Peak ∧ 200 41.12 N 107.02 W
Bridges Point › 174o 1.58 N 157.28 W
Bridgeton, Mo., U.S. 219 38.44 N 90.24 W
Bridgeton, N.J., U.S. 208 39.25 N 75.14 W
Bridgetown, Austl. 162 33.57 S 116.08 E
Bridgetown, Barb. 241g 13.06 N 59.37 W
Bridgetown, N.S., Can. 186 44.51 N 65.18 W
Bridgetown, Oh., U.S. 218 39.09 N 84.38 W
Bridge Trafford 262 53.14 N 2.49 W
Bridgeview 278 41.45 N 87.48 W
Bridgeville, De., U.S. 208 38.44 N 75.36 W
Bridgeville, Pa., U.S. 214 40.21 N 80.06 W
Bridgewater, Austl. 166 42.44 S 147.14 E
Bridgewater, Austl. 168b 35.02 S 138.47 E
Bridgewater, N.S., Can. 186 44.23 N 64.31 W
Bridgewater, Ct., U.S. 210 41.32 N 73.22 W
Bridgewater, Me., U.S. 186 46.25 N 67.50 W
Bridgewater, Ma., U.S. 207 41.59 N 70.58 W
Bridgewater, N.Y., U.S. 210 42.58 N 75.15 W
Bridgewater, Pa., U.S. 285 40.05 N 74.55 W
Bridgewater, S.D., U.S. 198 43.33 N 97.30 W
Bridgewater, Va., U.S. 188 38.22 N 78.58 W
Bridgewater Canal ≅ 262 53.20 N 2.45 W
Bridgewater State College ᵾ[2] 283 41.59 N 70.58 W
Bridgman 216 41.57 N 86.33 W

DEUTSCH

Name Seite Breite°' Länge°' E = Ost

Bridgnorth 42 52.33 N 2.25 W
Bridgton 188 44.03 N 70.42 W
Bridgwater 42 51.08 N 3.00 W
Bridgwater Bay c 42 51.16 N 3.12 W
Bridlington 44 54.05 N 0.12 W
Bridlington Bay c 44 54.04 N 0.08 W
Bridport 42 50.44 N 2.46 W
Brie ◆[1] 50 48.40 N 3.20 E
Briec 32 48.06 N 4.00 W
Brie-Comte-Robert 50 48.41 N 2.37 E
Brie Française ◆[1] 261 48.48 N 2.46 E
Brieg → Brzeg 30 50.52 N 17.27 E
Brielle, Ned. 52 51.54 N 4.10 E
Brielle, N.J., U.S. 208 40.06 N 74.03 W
Brienne-le-Château 58 48.24 N 4.32 E
Brienne-sur-Aisne 50 49.26 N 4.03 E
Brienno 58 45.55 N 9.07 E
Brienon-sur-Armançon 50 48.00 N 3.37 E
Brien Run ≃ 284b 39.20 N 76.28 W
Brienz 58 46.46 N 8.03 E
Brienza 68 40.29 N 15.37 E
Brienzer Rothorn ∧ 58 46.48 N 8.04 E
Brienzersee ⊜ 58 46.43 N 7.57 E
Brier Creek ≃ 192 32.47 N 81.26 W
Brierfield 44 53.50 N 2.14 W
Brier Hill 212 44.32 N 75.40 W
Brier Island I 186 44.16 N 66.22 W
Brierley Hill 42 52.29 N 2.07 W
Brier Mountain ∧ 210 41.37 N 77.02 W
Briese 264a 52.42 N 13.18 E
Briese ≃ 264a 52.41 N 13.15 E
Brieselang 54 52.35 N 13.00 E
Briesen 54 52.20 N 14.16 E
Brieske 54 51.29 N 13.57 E
Brieskow-Finkenheerd 54 52.16 N 14.35 E
Briest 54 52.31 N 12.08 E
Briey 56 49.15 N 5.56 E
Brig 58 46.19 N 8.00 E
Brigach ≃ 58 47.58 N 8.30 E
Brigantine 208 39.24 N 74.21 W
Brig Bay 186 51.04 N 56.55 W
Brigden 214 42.49 N 82.17 W
Brigg 44 53.34 N 0.30 W
Briggs 196 30.53 N 97.56 W
Brigham City 200 41.30 N 112.00 W
Brighouse 44 53.42 N 1.47 W
Brighstone 42 50.38 N 1.24 W
Bright 166 36.44 S 146.58 E
Brightlingsea 42 51.49 N 1.02 E
Brightmoor ◆[8] 281 42.24 N 83.14 W
Brighton, Austl. 168b 35.01 S 138.31 E
Brighton, Austl. 169 37.55 S 145.00 E
Brighton, On., Can. 212 44.02 N 77.44 W
Brighton, N.Z. 172 45.57 S 170.20 E
Brighton, Eng., U.K. 42 50.50 N 0.08 W
Brighton, Co., U.S. 200 39.59 N 104.49 W
Brighton, Fl., U.S. 220 27.14 N 81.06 W
Brighton, Il., U.S. 219 39.02 N 90.08 W
Brighton, Ia., U.S. 190 41.10 N 91.49 W
Brighton, Md., U.S. 284b 39.21 N 76.43 W
Brighton, Mi., U.S. 216 42.31 N 83.46 W
Brighton, N.Y., U.S. 210 43.08 N 77.33 W
Brighton ◆[8] 283 42.21 N 71.08 W
Brighton Airport ⊠ 281 42.34 N 83.47 W
Brighton Downs 166 23.22 S 141.34 E
Brighton Indian Reservation ◆[4] 220 27.04 N 81.05 W
Brighton-Le-Sands 274a 33.58 S 151.09 E
Brighton Park ◆[8] 278 41.49 N 87.42 W
Brighton State Recreation Area ♦ 216 42.30 N 83.48 W
Brightsand Lake ⊜ 184 53.36 N 108.52 W
Brightwater 172 41.23 S 173.07 E
Brightwaters 276 40.43 N 73.16 W
Brightwood 224 45.23 N 122.01 W
Brightwood ◆[8] 284c 38.58 N 77.02 W
Brigittenau ◆[8] 264b 48.14 N 16.22 E
Brignoles 62 43.24 N 6.04 E
Brignoud 62 45.15 N 5.54 E
Brig o'Turk 46 56.13 N 4.22 W
Brigstock 42 52.27 N 0.36 W
Brigus 186 47.32 N 53.13 W
Brihuega 34 40.45 N 2.52 W
Briis-sous-Forges 261 48.38 N 2.07 E
Brijuni (Brioni) 64 44.55 N 13.46 E
Brijuni I 64 44.55 N 13.46 E
Brikama 150 13.15 N 16.39 W
Brilhante ≃ 255 21.58 S 54.18 W
Brill 42 51.49 N 1.03 W
Brilliant, B.C., Can. 182 49.19 N 117.38 W
Brilliant, Al., U.S. 194 34.01 N 87.45 W
Brilliant, Oh., U.S. 214 40.15 N 80.37 W
Brillion 190 44.10 N 88.03 W
Brilon 56 51.24 N 8.34 E
Brilyn Park 284c 38.54 N 77.10 W
Brimfield, Eng., U.K. 42 52.18 N 2.42 W
Brimfield, In., U.S. 216 41.27 N 85.24 W
Brimfield, Ma., U.S. 207 42.07 N 72.12 W
Brimfield, Oh., U.S. 214 41.06 N 81.21 W
Brimington 44 53.16 N 1.23 W
Brindabella 171b 35.23 S 148.45 E
Brindisi 68 40.38 N 17.56 E
Brindisi □[4] 68 40.35 N 17.40 E
Brindisi Montagna 68 40.37 N 15.57 E
Brindle 262 53.43 N 2.36 W
Bringelly 170 33.56 S 150.44 E
Bringelly Creek ≃ 274a 33.58 S 150.38 E
Brinje 36 45.00 N 15.08 E
Brinkerton 279b 40.13 N 79.32 W
Brinkhaven 214 40.28 N 82.12 W
Brinkleigh 284b 39.18 N 76.50 W
Brinkley, Austl. 168b 35.14 S 139.13 E
Brinkley, Ar., U.S. 194 34.53 N 91.11 W
Brinkum 52 53.00 N 8.47 E
Brinkworth 166 33.42 S 138.24 E
Brinnon 224 47.40 N 122.53 W
Brinon-sur-Beuvron 50 47.17 N 3.30 E
Brins, Ābār al- ⊤[4] 142 30.29 N 30.05 E
Brinscall 262 53.41 N 2.34 W
Brinyan 46 59.07 N 2.59 W
Brion, Île I 186 47.48 N 61.28 W
Brione 58 46.18 N 8.47 E
Briones Hills ⋏[2] 282 37.56 N 122.08 W
Briones Regional Park ♦ 282 37.56 N 122.08 W
Briones Reservoir ⊜[1] 282 37.55 N 122.12 W
Brionne 50 49.12 N 0.43 E
Brion-sur-Ource 58 47.55 N 4.39 E
Brioude 32 45.18 N 3.23 E
Briouze 32 48.42 N 0.22 W
Brisbane, Austl. 171a 27.28 S 153.02 E
Brisbane, Ca., U.S. 226 37.41 N 122.24 W
Brisbane ≃ 171a 27.24 S 153.09 E
Brisbane, Mount ∧ 171a 27.05 S 152.32 E
Brisbane International Airport ⊠ 171a 27.27 S 153.11 E
Brisbane Ranges National Park ♦ 169 37.52 S 144.14 E
Brisbane Water c 170 33.28 S 151.20 E
Brisbane Water National Park ♦ 170 33.30 S 151.15 E
Brisben 210 42.22 N 75.41 W
Brisbin 214 40.50 N 78.21 W
Briseñas 234 20.16 N 102.33 W
Brisighella 66 44.13 N 11.46 E
Brissac 62 43.52 N 3.42 E
Brissago 58 46.07 N 8.43 E
Bristol, Eng., U.K. 42 51.27 N 2.35 W
Bristol, Ct., U.S. 207 41.41 N 72.57 W
Bristol, Fl., U.S. 192 30.25 N 84.58 W
Bristol, Il., U.S. 216 41.39 N 88.27 W
Bristol, In., U.S. 216 41.43 N 85.49 W
Bristol, N.H., U.S. 188 43.35 N 71.44 W
Bristol, Pa., U.S. 208 40.06 N 74.51 W
Bristol, R.I., U.S. 207 41.40 N 71.16 W
Bristol, S.D., U.S. 198 45.20 N 97.44 W
Bristol, Tn., U.S. 192 36.35 N 82.11 W
Bristol, Vt., U.S. 188 44.08 N 73.04 W
Bristol, Va., U.S. 192 36.35 N 82.11 W
Bristol, Wi., U.S. 216 42.33 N 88.02 W

Symbols in the index entries represent the broad categories identified in the key at the right. Symbols with superior numbers (⋏[1]) identify subcategories (see complete key on page *I · 1)*.

Symbole im Register stellen die rechts im Schlüssel erklärten Kategorien dar. Symbole mit hochgestellten Ziffern (⋏[1]) bezeichnen Unterabteilungen einer Kategorie (vgl. vollständiger Schlüssel auf Seite *I · 1)*.

Los símbolos incluídos en el texto del índice representan las grandes categorías identificadas con la clave a la derecha. Los símbolos con numeros en su parte superior (⋏[1]) identifican las subcategorías (véase la clave completa en la página *I · 1)*.

Les symboles de l'index représentent les catégories indiquées dans la légende à droite. Les symboles suivis d'un indice (⋏[1]) représentent des sous-catégories (voir légende complète à la page *I · 1)*.

Os símbolos incluídos no texto do índice representam as grandes categorias identificadas com a chave à direita. Os símbolos com números em sua parte superior (⋏[1]) identificam as subcategorias (veja-se a chave completa à página *I · 1)*.

∧	Mountain	Berg	Montaña	Montagne	Montanha
⋏	Mountains	Gebirge	Montañas	Montagnes	Montanhas
)(	Pass	Paß	Paso	Col	Passo
V	Valley, Canyon	Tal, Cañon	Valle, Cañón	Vallée, Canyon	Vale, Canhão
≃	Plain	Ebene	Llano	Plaine	Planície
›	Cape	Kap	Cabo	Cap	Cabo
I	Island	Insel	Isla	Île	Ilha
II	Islands	Inseln	Islas	Îles	Ilhas
≗	Other Topographic Features	Andere Topographische Objekte	Otros Elementos Topográficos	Autres données topographiques	Outros acidentes topográficos

ESPAÑOL

Nombre	Página	Lat.°′	Long.°′ W = Oeste
Bristol □[6], Ma., U.S.	207	41.54 N	71.06 W
Bristol □[6], R.I., U.S.	207	41.42 N	71.18 W
Bristol (Lulsgate) Airport ⊠	42	51.23 N	2.43 W
Bristol Bay c	180	58.00 N	159.00 W
Bristol-Blake Reservation ♠	283	42.06 N	71.19 W
Bristol Center	210	42.49 N	77.23 W
Bristol Channel ʊ	42	51.20 N	4.00 W
Bristol Lake ⊜	204	34.28 N	115.41 W
Bristolville	214	41.23 N	80.52 W
Bristow	196	35.49 N	96.23 W
Britânia	255	15.14 S	51.09 W
Británicas, Islas → British Isles II	4	54.00 N	4.00 W
Britannia, On., Can.	275b	43.37 N	79.41 W
Britannia, Eng., U.K.	262	53.41 N	2.11 W
Britannia Beach	182	49.38 N	123.12 W
Britische Jungfern-Inseln → British Virgin Islands □[2]	240m	18.30 N	64.30 W
Britisches Antarktis-Territorium → British Antarctic Territory □[2]	9	60.00 S	45.00 W
British Antarctic Territory □[2]	9	60.00 S	45.00 W
British Columbia □[4], Can.	176	54.00 N	125.00 W
British Columbia □[4], Can.	182	54.00 N	125.00 W
British Honduras → Belize □[1]	232	17.15 N	88.45 W
British Indian Ocean Territory □[2]	12	7.00 S	72.00 E
British Isles II	4	54.00 N	4.00 W
British Mountains ⋀	180	69.00 N	140.20 W
British Museum ⊽	260	51.31 N	0.08 W
British Solomon Islands → Solomon Islands □[1]	175e	8.00 S	159.00 E
British Virgin Islands □[2], N.A.	230	18.30 N	64.30 W
British Virgin Islands □[2], N.A.	240m	18.30 N	64.30 W
Britland Edge Hill ∧[2]	262	53.31 N	1.50 W
Briton Ferry	42	51.38 N	3.49 W
Brits	158	25.42 S	27.45 E
Britstown	158	30.37 S	23.30 E
Britt	190	43.05 N	93.48 W
Brittany → Bretagne □[9]	32	48.00 N	3.00 W
Brittas	48	53.14 N	6.27 W
Britten	158	27.42 S	25.17 E
Brittingham	196	25.45 N	103.24 W
Britton, Mi., U.S.	216	41.59 N	83.49 W
Britton, S.D., U.S.	198	45.47 N	97.45 W
Britton, Tx., U.S.	222	32.33 N	97.04 W
Britton, Mount ∧[2]	162	26.31 S	134.43 E
Britz	54	52.53 N	13.49 E
Britz ◆[8]	264a	52.27 N	13.26 E
Brive-la-Gaillarde	32	45.10 N	1.32 E
Brives-Charensac	62	45.03 N	3.56 E
Briviesca	34	42.33 N	3.19 W
Brivio	62	45.44 N	9.27 E
Brixen im Thale	64	47.27 N	12.15 E
Brixham	42	50.24 N	3.30 W
Brixlegg	64	47.25 N	11.53 E
Brixton	166	23.32 S	144.57 E
Brixworth	42	52.20 N	0.54 W
Brlik	85	43.40 N	73.49 E
Brloh	61	48.56 N	14.13 E
Brno	30	49.12 N	16.37 E
Bro	40	59.31 N	17.38 E
Broa, Ensenada de la c	240p	22.35 N	82.00 W
Broad ≃, U.S.	192	34.00 N	81.04 W
Broad ≃, Fl., U.S.	220	25.28 N	81.09 W
Broad ≃, Ga., U.S.	192	33.59 N	82.39 W
Broadalbin	210	43.03 N	74.11 W
Broad Arrow	162	30.20 S	121.27 E
Broad Axe	285	40.10 N	75.15 W
Broadback ≃	176	51.21 N	78.52 W
Broad Bay c	46	58.15 N	6.15 W
Broadbottom	262	53.26 N	2.01 W
Broad Brook	207	41.54 N	72.32 W
Broad Chalke	42	51.02 N	1.57 W
Broadclyst	42	50.46 N	3.26 W
Broad Creek c	208	38.45 N	76.15 W
Broad Creek ≃	208	39.42 N	76.14 W
Broadford, Austl.	169	37.13 S	145.03 E
Broadford, Scot., U.K.	46	57.14 N	5.54 W
Broad Haven c	48	54.18 N	9.55 W
Broadheath	262	53.24 N	2.21 W
Broadhurst Range ⋀	162	22.23 S	122.09 E
Broadkill ≃	208	38.47 N	75.10 W
Broad Law ∧	46	55.30 N	3.22 W
Broadley Common	260	51.45 N	0.04 E
Broadmeadows	169	37.40 S	144.54 E
Broadmoor	226	37.41 N	122.29 W
Broad Neck >[1]	208	39.03 N	76.27 W
Broad Oak	42	50.57 N	0.36 E
Broad Pass)(	180	63.18 N	149.09 W
Broad Run ≃, Pa., U.S.	285	39.56 N	75.41 W
Broad Run ≃, Pa., U.S.	285	39.59 N	75.40 W
Broad Run ≃, Va., U.S.	208	38.41 N	77.29 W
Broad Sound ʊ, Austl.	166	22.10 S	149.45 E
Broad Sound ʊ, Ma., U.S.	283	42.25 N	70.58 W
Broad Sound Channel ʊ	166	22.05 S	150.20 E
Broadstairs	42	51.22 N	1.27 E
Broad Street	260	51.17 N	0.38 E
Broad Top	214	40.12 N	78.08 W
Broadus	198	45.26 N	105.24 W
Broadview, Sk., Can.	184	50.20 N	102.30 W
Broadview, Il., U.S.	216	41.51 N	87.51 W
Broadview, In., U.S.	218	39.10 N	87.33 W
Broadview Heights	214	41.18 N	81.41 W
Broadwater	198	41.35 N	102.51 W
Broadway, Eng., U.K.	42	52.02 N	1.51 W
Broadway, Oh., U.S.	214	40.20 N	83.24 W
Broadway, Va., U.S.	188	38.38 N	78.46 W
Broadwell	219	40.04 N	89.27 W
Broadwindsor	42	50.49 N	2.48 W
Broadwood	172	35.16 S	173.23 E
Broager	41	54.53 N	9.41 E
Brobo	150	7.43 N	4.42 W
Broby	26	56.15 N	14.05 E
Brobyværk	41	55.14 N	10.15 E
Broc	58	46.36 N	7.06 E
Brocēni	76	56.42 N	22.35 E
Brochel	46	57.26 N	6.01 W
Brochet	176	57.53 N	101.40 W
Brochet, Lac au ⊜	186	49.40 N	69.37 W
Brochterbeck	52	52.13 N	7.44 E
Brock	184	51.27 N	108.42 W
Brock ≃	44	53.52 N	2.47 W
Brock Creek ≃	285	40.15 N	74.50 W
Brocken ∧	54	51.48 N	10.36 E
Brockenhurst	42	50.49 N	1.34 W
Brockenscheidt	263	51.38 N	7.25 E
Brockhagen	52	51.59 N	8.20 E
Brockham	260	51.14 N	0.17 W
Brockman ≃	168a	31.41 S	116.07 E
Brockman, Mount ∧	162	22.28 S	117.18 E
Brock Monument ⊥	284a	43.09 N	79.04 W
Brockport, N.Y., U.S.	210	43.12 N	77.56 W
Brockport, Pa., U.S.	214	41.16 N	78.44 W
Brocks Beach	212	44.27 N	80.06 W
Brocks Creek	164	13.28 S	131.25 E
Brockton, Ma., U.S.	207	42.05 N	71.01 W
Brockton, Mt., U.S.	198	48.09 N	104.54 W
Brockton, Pa., U.S.	208	40.45 N	76.04 W
Brockton Reservoir ⊜[1]	283	42.07 N	71.03 W

FRANÇAIS

Nom	Page	Lat.°′	Long.°′ W = Ouest
Brock University ⊽[2]	284a	43.07 N	79.15 W
Brockville	212	44.35 N	75.41 W
Brockway	214	41.15 N	78.47 W
Brockworth	42	51.51 N	2.09 W
Brocoió, Ilha de I	287a	22.45 S	43.07 W
Brocton	214	42.23 N	79.26 W
Brod, Česká Rep.	60	49.51 N	12.45 E
Brod, Mak.	38	41.31 N	21.12 E
Broddbo	40	59.59 N	16.28 E
Brodenbach	56	50.14 N	7.26 E
Broderick	226	38.35 N	121.30 W
Brodeur Peninsula >[1]	176	73.00 N	88.00 W
Brodhead, Ky., U.S.	192	37.24 N	84.24 W
Brodhead, Wi., U.S.	190	42.37 N	89.22 W
Brodhead Creek ≃	210	40.59 N	75.08 W
Brodheadsville	210	40.55 N	75.24 W
Brodick	46	55.35 N	5.09 W
Brodnax	192	36.42 N	78.01 W
Brodnica	30	53.16 N	19.23 E
Brodokalmak	86	55.35 N	62.06 E
Brody, Pol.	30	51.45 N	14.45 E
Brody, Ukr.	78	50.06 N	25.10 E
Broedersput	158	26.49 S	25.08 E
Broek [op Langendijk]	52	52.40 N	4.48 E
Brogan	202	44.14 N	117.30 W
Broglie	50	49.01 N	0.32 E
Brohlbach ≃	56	50.29 N	7.20 E
Broich ◆[8]	263	51.25 N	6.51 E
Broichweiden	56	50.49 N	6.09 E
Brok	30	52.43 N	21.52 E
Brok ∧	123	34.32 N	76.35 E
Brokdorf	52	53.52 N	9.19 E
Broke	170	32.45 S	151.06 E
Broke Inlet c	162	34.55 S	116.25 E
Broken ≃	169	36.41 S	146.00 E
Broken Arrow	196	36.03 N	95.47 W
Broken Bay c	170	33.34 S	151.18 E
Broken Bow, Ne., U.S.	198	41.24 N	99.38 W
Broken Bow, Ok., U.S.	194	34.01 N	94.44 W
Broken Bow Lake ⊜[1]	194	34.10 N	94.40 W
Broken Cross, Eng., U.K.	262	53.15 N	2.29 W
Broken Cross, Eng., U.K.	262	53.15 N	2.10 W
Brokenhead ≃	184	50.25 N	96.40 W
Broken Hill, Austl.	166	31.57 S	141.27 E
Broken Hill → Kabwe, Zam.	154	14.27 S	28.27 E
Broken Ridge ✢[3]	12	31.30 S	95.00 E
Brokenstraw Creek ≃	214	41.51 N	79.09 W
Broken Sword Creek ≃	214	40.46 N	83.11 W
Brokopondo	250	5.04 N	54.58 W
Brokopondo □[5]	250	4.40 N	55.00 W
Brokopondo Stuwmeer ⊜[1]	250	4.45 N	55.00 W
Brölbach ≃	56	50.47 N	7.18 E
Brolo	70	38.09 N	14.50 E
Bromberg → Bydgoszcz	30	53.08 N	18.00 E
Bromborough	262	53.19 N	2.59 W
Brome, P.Q., Can.	206	45.12 N	72.34 W
Brome, Dtsch.	54	52.36 N	10.56 E
Brome □[6]	206	45.10 N	72.30 W
Brome, Lac ⊜	206	45.15 N	72.30 W
Brome, Mont ∧	206	45.17 N	72.38 W
Bromham	42	52.09 N	0.31 W
Bromley ◆[8]	42	51.24 N	0.02 E
Bromley Common ◆[8]	260	51.22 N	0.03 E
Bromley Plateau ✢[3]	18	32.00 S	35.00 W
Bromma ◆[8]	40	59.21 N	17.55 E
Bromma flygplats ⊠	40	59.21 N	17.55 E
Brommö I	40	58.50 N	13.41 E
Bromo, Gunung ∧	115a	7.57 S	112.57 E
Bromölla	26	56.04 N	14.28 E
Brompton, Eng., U.K.	44	54.22 N	1.25 W
Brompton, Eng., U.K.	260	51.23 N	0.33 E
Brompton, Lac ⊜	206	45.27 N	72.09 W
Bromptonville	206	45.28 N	71.57 W
Bromsgrove	42	52.20 N	2.03 W
Bromyard	42	52.11 N	2.30 W
Bron	62	45.44 N	4.55 E
Brønderslev	26	57.16 N	9.58 E
Bronevskaja	24	61.43 N	39.10 E
Brong-Ahafo □[4]	150	7.45 N	1.30 W
Broni	62	45.04 N	9.16 E
Bronkhorstspruit	158	25.48 S	28.44 E
Bronkhorstspruitdam ⊜[1]	158	25.55 S	28.42 E
Bronkow	54	51.40 N	13.55 E
Bronllys	42	52.01 N	3.16 W
Bronlund Peak ∧	176	57.26 N	126.38 W
Bronn	60	49.44 N	11.28 E
Bronnicy	82	55.25 N	38.16 E
Bronnikovo	86	58.32 N	68.25 E
Bronnoje	76	52.19 N	30.29 E
Brønnøysund	24	65.30 N	12.10 E
Bronnzell	56	50.31 N	9.41 E
Brøns	41	55.11 N	8.44 E
Bronson, Fl., U.S.	192	29.26 N	82.38 W
Bronson, Ks., U.S.	198	37.54 N	95.04 W
Bronson, Mi., U.S.	216	41.52 N	85.11 W
Bronson, Tx., U.S.	194	31.21 N	94.01 W
Bronson Lake ⊜	184	53.52 N	109.43 W
Bronte, It.	70	37.47 N	14.50 E
Bronte, Tx., U.S.	196	31.53 N	100.18 W
Bronte Creek ≃	212	43.23 N	79.43 W
Bronwood	192	31.49 N	84.21 W
Bronx □[6]	210	40.49 N	73.56 W
Bronx ◆[8]	276	40.49 N	73.56 W
Bronx ≃	276	40.49 N	73.52 W
Bronx Park ♠	276	40.52 N	73.53 W
Bronxville	276	40.56 N	73.49 W
Bronx-Whitestone Bridge ◆[5]	276	40.48 N	73.50 W
Bronx Zoo ♠	276	40.51 N	73.53 W
Bronyts'ka Huta	78	50.56 N	27.19 E
Bronzolo (Branzoll)	64	46.24 N	11.19 E
Brooch, Lac ⊜	186	50.44 N	67.58 W
Broodsnyersplaas	158	26.03 S	29.29 E
Brook	216	40.51 N	87.21 W
Brookdale	226	37.06 N	122.06 W
Brooke	208	38.23 N	77.22 W
Brooke □[6]	214	40.18 N	80.33 W
Brookeborough	48	54.19 N	7.24 W
Brookeland	194	31.09 N	94.00 W
Brooker	192	29.53 N	82.19 W
Brooke's Point	116	8.47 N	117.50 E
Brookfield, N.S., Can.	186	45.15 N	63.17 W
Brookfield, Ct., U.S.	207	41.28 N	73.24 W
Brookfield, Il., U.S.	216	41.49 N	87.51 W
Brookfield, Ma., U.S.	207	42.12 N	72.06 W
Brookfield, Mi., U.S.	216	42.27 N	84.47 W
Brookfield, Mo., U.S.	194	39.47 N	93.04 W
Brookfield, N.Y., U.S.	210	42.48 N	75.19 W
Brookfield, Oh., U.S.	214	41.14 N	80.34 W
Brookfield, Wi., U.S.	216	43.03 N	88.06 W
Brookfield Center	207	41.27 N	73.23 W
Brookfield Zoo ♠	278	41.50 N	87.50 W
Brookford	192	35.42 N	81.20 W
Brookhaven, De., U.S.	285	39.42 N	75.41 W
Brookhaven, Ms., U.S.	194	31.34 N	90.26 W
Brookhaven, Pa., U.S.	285	39.52 N	75.22 W
Brookhaven National Laboratory ⊽[3]	207	40.54 N	72.52 W
Brookings, Or., U.S.	202	42.03 N	124.16 W
Brookings, S.D., U.S.	198	44.18 N	96.47 W
Brookland, Eng., U.K.	42	50.59 N	0.50 E
Brookland, Ar., U.S.	194	35.54 N	90.34 W
Brookland ◆[8]	284c	38.56 N	76.59 W
Brooklands	214	42.38 N	83.06 W
Brookland Terrace	285	39.44 N	75.37 W
Brooklandville	284b	39.25 N	76.40 W
Brooklawn	285	39.52 N	75.07 W
Brooklet	192	32.22 N	81.39 W

PORTUGUÊS

Nome	Página	Lat.°′	Long.°′ W = Oeste
Brooklin	212	43.57 N	78.57 W
Brookline, Ma., U.S.	207	42.21 N	71.07 W
Brookline, N.H., U.S.	207	42.44 N	71.39 W
Brooklyn, N.S., Can.	186	44.03 N	64.42 W
Brooklyn, Ct., U.S.	207	41.47 N	71.57 W
Brooklyn, Il., U.S.	219	40.14 N	90.46 W
Brooklyn, In., U.S.	218	39.32 N	86.22 W
Brooklyn, Ia., U.S.	190	41.44 N	92.26 W
Brooklyn, Mi., U.S.	216	42.06 N	84.14 W
Brooklyn, Ms., U.S.	194	31.03 N	89.11 W
Brooklyn, Oh., U.S.	214	41.26 N	81.44 W
Brooklyn, Pa., U.S.	210	41.45 N	75.48 W
Brooklyn, Wa., U.S.	224	46.47 N	123.31 W
Brooklyn, Wi., U.S.	216	42.51 N	89.22 W
Brooklyn ◆[8], Md., U.S.	284b	39.14 N	76.36 W
Brooklyn ◆[8], N.Y., U.S.	210	40.42 N	74.00 W
Brooklyn Battery Tunnel ◆[5]	276	40.42 N	74.01 W
Brooklyn Bridge ◆[5]	276	40.42 N	74.00 W
Brooklyn Center	190	45.04 N	93.19 W
Brooklyn Heights	279a	41.24 N	81.40 W
Brooklyn Marine Park ♠	276	40.35 N	73.55 W
Brooklyn Museum ⊽	276	40.40 N	73.58 W
Brookmans Park	260	51.43 N	0.12 W
Brookmere	182	49.49 N	120.53 W
Brookmont	284c	38.57 N	77.07 W
Brookneal	192	37.03 N	78.56 W
Brook Park	214	41.23 N	81.48 W
Brookport	194	37.07 N	88.37 W
Brooks, Ab., Can.	182	50.35 N	111.53 W
Brooks, Ca., U.S.	226	38.45 N	122.09 W
Brooks, Me., U.S.	188	44.33 N	69.07 W
Brooks, Or., U.S.	224	45.02 N	122.57 W
Brooks, Mount ∧	180	63.11 N	150.40 W
Brooks Air Force Base ■	196	29.21 N	98.25 W
Brooks Bay c	182	50.13 N	127.55 W
Brooksburg	218	38.44 N	85.15 W
Brookshire	222	29.47 N	95.57 W
Brookside, De., U.S.	285	39.40 N	75.43 W
Brookside, N.J., U.S.	276	40.48 N	74.34 W
Brookside, Pa., U.S.	214	42.08 N	80.00 W
Brookside, Tx., U.S.	222	29.35 N	95.18 W
Brookside Park ♠	279a	41.27 N	81.43 W
Brooks Island I	282	37.54 N	122.21 W
Brooks Mountain ∧	180	65.33 N	167.09 W
Brooks Place	283	42.02 N	71.01 W
Brooks Range ⋀	180	68.00 N	154.00 W
Brookston	216	40.36 N	86.52 W
Brook Street	260	51.37 N	0.17 E
Brooksville, Fl., U.S.	220	28.33 N	82.23 W
Brooksville, Ky., U.S.	218	38.40 N	84.03 W
Brooksville, Ms., U.S.	194	33.14 N	88.34 W
Brookton	162	32.22 S	117.01 E
Brooktondale	210	42.23 N	76.24 W
Brookvale	274a	33.46 S	151.17 E
Brookview	210	42.32 N	73.43 W
Brookville, In., U.S.	218	39.25 N	85.00 W
Brookville, Ma., U.S.	207	42.07 N	71.00 W
Brookville, N.Y., U.S.	276	40.48 N	73.34 W
Brookville, Oh., U.S.	218	39.50 N	84.24 W
Brookville, Pa., U.S.	214	41.09 N	79.05 W
Brookville Lake ⊜[1]	218	39.30 N	85.00 W
Brookwood	260	51.18 N	0.38 W
Brooloo	166	26.29 S	152.42 E
Broom, Little Loch c	46	57.54 N	5.22 W
Broom, Loch c	46	57.52 N	5.08 W
Broomall	285	39.58 N	75.21 W
Broome	162	17.58 S	122.14 E
Broome □[6]	210	42.08 N	75.54 W
Broome County Airport ⊠	210	42.13 N	75.59 W
Broomes Island	208	38.25 N	76.32 W
Broomfield, Eng., U.K.	260	51.46 N	0.28 E
Broomfield, Eng., U.K.	260	51.14 N	0.38 E
Broomfield, Co., U.S.	200	39.55 N	105.05 W
Broons	32	48.19 N	2.16 W
Brooten	198	45.30 N	95.07 W
Brophy, Mount ∧[2]	162	19.11 S	128.51 E
Brora	46	58.01 N	3.51 W
Brora ≃	46	58.01 N	3.52 W
Brørup	41	55.29 N	9.01 E
Broseley	42	52.37 N	2.29 W
Brosewere Bay c	276	40.37 N	73.42 W
Broshniv-Osada	78	49.00 N	24.13 E
Brosna ≃	48	53.13 N	7.58 W
Brossac	32	45.20 N	0.03 W
Brossard	206	45.26 N	73.29 W
Brossasco	62	44.34 N	7.21 E
Brosso	62	45.30 N	7.48 E
Brotas de Macaúbas	255	12.00 S	42.38 W
Brothers Brook ≃	276	41.02 N	73.36 W
Brötjärna	40	60.30 N	15.01 E
Broto	34	42.36 N	0.06 W
Brotterode	54	50.49 N	10.26 E
Brotton	44	54.34 N	0.56 W
Brou	50	48.13 N	1.11 E
Brough, Eng., U.K.	44	54.32 N	2.19 W
Brough, Eng., U.K.	44	53.44 N	0.35 W
Brough, Scot., U.K.	46	58.39 N	3.20 W
Brougham	212	43.55 N	79.06 W
Brough Head >	46	59.08 N	3.17 W
Broughshane	48	54.54 N	6.12 W
Broughton, Eng., U.K.	42	52.23 N	0.46 W
Broughton, Eng., U.K.	44	53.49 N	2.44 W
Broughton, Eng., U.K.	44	53.34 N	0.33 W
Broughton, Eng., U.K.	262	53.49 N	2.44 W
Broughton, Scot., U.K.	46	55.37 N	3.25 W
Broughton, Wales, U.K.	44	53.10 N	2.59 W
Broughton, Pa., U.S.	214	40.21 N	79.59 W
Broughton in Furness	44	54.17 N	3.12 W
Broughton Island I	176	67.35 N	63.50 W
Broughtown	46	59.15 N	2.36 W
Broughty Ferry	46	56.28 N	2.53 W
Broumov	30	50.35 N	16.20 E
Brousseval	58	48.29 N	4.58 E
Brou-sur-Chantereine	261	48.53 N	2.38 E
Brouvelieures	58	48.14 N	6.44 E
Brouwersdam ◆[6]	52	51.46 N	3.51 E
Brouwershaven	52	51.44 N	3.54 E
Brovary	78	50.31 N	30.46 E
Brovst	26	57.06 N	9.32 E
Broward □[6]	220	26.09 N	80.29 W
Browerville	198	46.05 N	94.51 W
Brown □[6], Il., U.S.	219	39.59 N	90.45 W
Brown □[6], In., U.S.	218	39.12 N	86.15 W
Brown □[6], Oh., U.S.	218	38.52 N	83.54 W
Brown, Mount ∧	202	48.52 N	111.09 W
Brown, Point >	224	46.56 N	124.10 W
Brownbacks	285	40.11 N	75.37 W
Brown City	190	43.12 N	82.59 W
Brown Clee Hill ∧[2]	42	52.28 N	2.35 W
Brown County State Park ♠	218	39.09 N	86.14 W
Brown Creek ≃	276	40.43 N	73.04 W
Browndale	210	41.40 N	75.27 W
Brown Deer	216	43.09 N	87.57 W
Browne Bay c	176	73.08 N	97.30 W
Brownfield	196	33.10 N	102.16 W
Brown Gelly ∧[2]	42	50.32 N	4.32 W
Brownhills	42	52.39 N	1.55 W
Browning, Il., U.S.	219	40.08 N	90.22 W
Browning, Mo., U.S.	194	40.02 N	93.09 W
Browning, Mt., U.S.	202	48.33 N	113.00 W
Browning Entrance c	182	53.41 N	130.30 W
Browning Island I	212	45.00 N	79.25 W
Brown Lake ⊜	176	65.55 N	91.15 W
Brownlee Park	216	42.18 N	85.05 W
Brownlee Reservoir ⊜[1]	202	44.40 N	117.05 W
Brown Mountain ∧, Ca., U.S.	204	35.41 N	117.01 W

Brown Mountain ∧, Ca., U.S.	280	34.14 N	118.08 W
Brown Mountain ∧[2]	222	31.51 N	97.39 W
Brown Point >	276	40.43 N	73.04 W
Brownsberg, Natuurpark ♠	250	4.50 N	55.10 W
Brownsboro	222	32.18 N	95.37 W
Browns Brook ≃	276	41.09 N	73.17 W
Brownsburg, P.Q., Can.	206	45.41 N	74.25 W
Brownsburg, In., U.S.	218	39.50 N	86.23 W
Browns Canyon V	280	34.18 N	118.35 W
Brownsdale	190	43.44 N	92.52 W
Browns Island I	282	38.02 N	121.52 W
Browns Lake	216	42.42 N	88.14 W
Brownsmead	224	46.13 N	123.32 W
Browns Mills	208	39.58 N	74.35 W
Browns Point	224	47.18 N	122.21 W
Browns Town, Jam.	241q	18.24 N	77.22 W
Brownstown, Il., U.S.	219	38.59 N	88.57 W
Brownstown, In., U.S.	218	38.52 N	86.02 W
Brownstown, Pa., U.S.	208	40.08 N	76.13 W
Brownstown Creek ≃	281	42.06 N	83.13 W
Browns Valley, Ca., U.S.	226	39.15 N	121.23 W
Browns Valley, Mn., U.S.	198	45.35 N	96.49 W
Brownsville, On., Can.	212	42.52 N	80.50 W
Brownsville, Ca., U.S.	226	39.28 N	121.16 W
Brownsville, Fl., U.S.	220	25.50 N	80.17 W
Brownsville, In., U.S.	218	39.39 N	85.00 W
Brownsville, Ky., U.S.	194	37.11 N	86.16 W
Brownsville, La., U.S.	194	32.30 N	92.10 W
Brownsville, Or., U.S.	202	44.23 N	122.59 W
Brownsville, Pa., U.S.	188	40.01 N	79.53 W
Brownsville, Tn., U.S.	194	35.35 N	89.15 W
Brownsville, Tx., U.S.	196	25.54 N	97.29 W
Brownton	190	44.43 N	94.21 W
Browntown	276	40.24 N	74.19 W
Brownvale	182	56.08 N	117.53 W
Brownville, Al., U.S.	194	33.23 N	87.45 W
Brownville, Me., U.S.	188	45.18 N	69.02 W
Brownville, Ne., U.S.	198	40.23 N	95.39 W
Brownville, N.Y., U.S.	212	44.00 N	75.59 W
Brownville Junction	188	45.21 N	69.03 W
Brown Willy ∧[2]	42	50.35 N	4.36 W
Brownwood	196	31.42 N	98.59 W
Brownwood, Lake ⊜[1]	196	31.51 N	99.02 W
Browse Island I	160	14.07 S	123.33 E
Broxbourne	260	51.45 N	0.01 W
Broxbourne □[8]	260	51.44 N	0.04 W
Broxton	192	31.37 N	82.53 W
Broye ≃	58	46.55 N	7.02 E
Broyhill Park	284c	38.51 N	77.11 W
Broža	76	52.57 N	29.07 E
Brozas	34	39.37 N	6.46 W
Brozzo	64	45.43 N	10.14 E
Brtonigla	64	45.23 N	13.38 E
Brû	58	48.21 N	6.41 E
Bruay-en-Artois	50	50.29 N	2.33 E
Bruay-sur-l'Escaut	50	50.23 N	3.32 E
Bruce, Ms., U.S.	194	33.59 N	89.20 W
Bruce, S.D., U.S.	198	44.26 N	96.53 W
Bruce, Wi., U.S.	190	45.27 N	91.16 W
Bruce □[6]	212	44.30 N	81.15 W
Bruce, Mount ∧	162	22.36 S	118.08 E
Bruce Bay	172	43.35 S	169.41 E
Bruce Creek ≃	275b	43.52 N	79.18 W
Bruce Lake	184	50.48 N	93.24 W
Bruce Lake ⊜	184	50.49 N	93.20 W
Bruce Mines	190	46.18 N	83.48 W
Bruce Museum ⊽	276	41.01 N	73.37 W
Bruce Peninsula >[1]	190	44.50 N	81.20 W
Bruce Peninsula National Park ♠	190	45.12 N	81.40 W
Bruce Rock	162	31.53 S	118.09 E
Bruceville	222	31.19 N	97.14 W
Bruchberg ∧	54	51.47 N	10.29 E
Bruche ≃	58	48.34 N	7.43 E
Bruchhausen	56	51.26 N	8.01 E
Bruchhausen-Vilsen	52	52.50 N	9.00 E
Bruchmühlbach-Miesau	56	49.24 N	7.26 E
Bruchmühle	264a	52.33 N	13.47 E
Br'uchoveckaja	78	45.48 N	38.59 E
Bruchsal	56	49.07 N	8.35 E
Brück, Dtsch.	54	52.12 N	12.46 E
Bruck, Öst.	64	47.17 N	12.49 E
Bruck an der Leitha	61	48.02 N	16.47 E
Bruck an der Mur	61	47.25 N	15.16 E
Bruckhausen ◆[8]	263	51.29 N	6.44 E
Bruck in der Oberpfalz	60	49.15 N	12.18 E
Brückl	61	46.45 N	14.32 E
Bruckmühl	64	47.53 N	11.54 E
Brucoli ◆[8]	70	37.17 N	15.11 E
Brudager	41	55.07 N	10.41 E
Bruderheim	182	53.47 N	112.56 W
Brue ≃	42	51.13 N	3.00 W
Brue-Auriac	62	43.32 N	5.57 E
Brueil-en-Vexin	261	49.02 N	1.49 E
Brüel	54	53.44 N	11.43 E
Bruff	48	52.29 N	8.33 W
Bruges → Brugge	50	51.13 N	3.14 E
Brugg	58	47.29 N	8.12 E
Brugge (Bruges), Bel.	50	51.13 N	3.14 E
Brügge, Dtsch.	263	51.13 N	7.34 E
Brüggen	56	51.14 N	6.11 E
Brugherio	62	45.33 N	9.18 E
Brugnato	62	44.14 N	9.43 E
Brühl	56	50.48 N	6.54 E
Bruin, Ky., U.S.	218	38.11 N	83.01 W
Bruin, Pa., U.S.	214	41.04 N	79.44 W
Bruinisse	52	51.40 N	4.06 E
Bruin Point ∧	200	39.39 N	110.22 W
Bruit, Pulau I	112	2.35 N	111.20 E
Bruja, Cerro ∧	236	9.29 N	79.34 W
Brule	198	41.05 N	101.53 W
Brule ≃	190	45.57 N	88.12 W
Brûlé, Lac ⊜, Can.	176	52.17 N	63.52 W
Brûlé, Lac ⊜, P.Q., Can.	190	46.57 N	77.12 W
Brule Lake ⊜	212	45.03 N	77.04 W
Brûly	50	49.58 N	4.31 E
Brumadinho	255	20.08 S	44.13 W
Brumado	255	14.13 S	41.40 W
Brumath	56	48.44 N	7.43 E
Brumby Creek ≃	162	24.09 S	118.39 E
Brummen	52	52.05 N	6.09 E
Brumunddal	26	60.53 N	10.56 E
Bruna ≃	66	42.45 N	10.53 E
Brunate	62	45.49 N	9.06 E
Brunau	54	52.45 N	11.28 E
Brundall	42	52.37 N	1.26 E
Brundby	41	55.49 N	10.37 E
Brundidge	194	31.43 N	85.48 W
Brune ≃	50	49.45 N	3.47 E
Bruneau	202	42.52 N	115.47 W
Bruneau ≃	202	42.57 N	115.58 W
Brunei → Bandar Seri Begawan	112	4.56 N	114.55 E
Brunei □[1], Asia	108	4.30 N	114.40 E
Brunei □[1], Asia	112	4.30 N	114.40 E
Brunei, Teluk c	112	5.05 N	115.18 E
Brünen	52	51.43 N	6.39 E
Brunette Creek ≃	162	18.47 S	135.41 E
Brunette Downs	162	18.38 S	135.57 E
Brunette Island I	186	47.16 N	55.54 W
Brunflo	26	63.05 N	14.49 E
Brungle	171b	35.10 S	148.14 E
Brunico (Bruneck)	64	46.48 N	11.56 E
Brünigpass)(	58	46.46 N	8.09 E
Brüninghausen	263	51.13 N	7.41 E
Brunkeberg	26	59.26 N	8.29 E
Brünn → Brno, Česká Rep.	30	49.12 N	16.37 E

Brünn, Dtsch.	54	50.27 N	10.51 E
Brunn, Dtsch.	54	53.40 N	13.22 E
Brunna	40	59.51 N	17.26 E
Brunn am Gebirge	61	48.07 N	16.17 E
Brunnen, Dtsch.	60	48.38 N	11.18 E
Brunnen, Schw.	58	47.00 N	8.36 E
Brunner, Lake ⊜	172	42.37 S	171.27 E
Brunnerville	208	40.11 N	76.17 W
Brunni	58	47.03 N	8.42 E
Brunnsvik	40	60.12 N	15.08 E
Bruno	184	52.15 N	105.30 W
Brunot Island I	279b	40.28 N	80.03 W
Brunow	264a	52.44 N	13.52 E
Brunoy	50	48.42 N	2.30 E
Brunsbüttel	52	53.54 N	9.07 E
Brunsbüttelkoog	52	53.54 N	9.08 E
Brunson	192	32.55 N	81.11 W
Brunssum	56	50.56 N	5.59 E
Brunswick, Austl.	274b	37.46 S	144.58 E
Brunswick → Braunschweig, Dtsch.	52	52.16 N	10.31 E
Brunswick, Ga., U.S.	192	31.08 N	81.29 W
Brunswick, Me., U.S.	188	43.54 N	69.57 W
Brunswick, Md., U.S.	208	39.18 N	77.37 W
Brunswick, Mo., U.S.	194	39.25 N	93.07 W
Brunswick, Oh., U.S.	214	41.14 N	81.50 W
Brunswick ≃	168a	33.15 S	115.45 E
Brunswick, Península >[1]	254	53.30 S	71.25 W
Brunswick Junction	168a	33.15 S	115.51 E
Brunswick Lake ⊜	190	49.00 N	83.23 W
Brunswick Naval Air Station ■	188	43.54 N	69.56 W
Brunswick Square ◆[9]	276	40.25 N	74.23 W
Bruntál	30	49.59 N	17.28 E
Bruree	48	52.26 N	8.36 W
Brus, Laguna de c	236	15.50 N	84.35 W
Brus'any	80	53.13 N	49.24 E
Brusasco	62	45.09 N	8.04 E
Bruselas → Bruxelles	50	50.50 N	4.20 E
Brusendorf	264a	52.19 N	13.31 E
Brush	198	40.15 N	103.37 W
Brush Creek ≃, Oh., U.S.	216	41.26 N	84.24 W
Brush Creek ≃, Pa., U.S.	279b	40.23 N	79.46 W
Brush Run ≃, Pa., U.S.	279b	40.18 N	80.07 W
Brush Run ≃, Pa., U.S.	279b	40.16 N	80.10 W
Brush Valley	214	40.32 N	79.04 W
Brushy Creek ≃, Austl.	274b	37.43 S	145.17 E
Brushy Creek ≃, Ok., U.S.	196	34.55 N	95.34 W
Brushy Creek ≃, Tx., U.S.	222	32.59 N	96.12 W
Brushy Creek ≃, Tx., U.S.	222	30.48 N	95.09 W
Brushy Creek ≃, Tx., U.S.	222	31.55 N	95.26 W
Brushy Creek ≃, Tx., U.S.	222	30.43 N	97.03 W
Brushy Creek ≃, Tx., U.S.	222	29.04 N	96.34 W
Brusio	58	46.14 N	10.07 E
Brus Laguna	236	15.47 N	84.35 W
Brusovo	76	57.51 N	35.24 E
Brusque	252	27.06 S	48.56 W
Brussel → Bruxelles	50	50.50 N	4.20 E
Brussels → Bruxelles, Bel.	50	50.50 N	4.20 E
Brussels, On., Can.	212	43.44 N	81.15 W
Brussels, Il., U.S.	219	38.57 N	90.36 W
Brusson	62	45.45 N	7.44 E
Brüssow	54	53.24 N	14.07 E
Brusy	30	53.53 N	17.45 E
Brusyliv	78	50.17 N	29.32 E
Brutelles	50	50.08 N	1.31 E
Bruthen	166	37.43 S	147.48 E
Bruton	42	51.07 N	2.27 W
Brüx → Most	54	50.32 N	13.39 E
Bruxelles (Brussels) (Brussel)	56	50.50 N	4.20 E
Bruxelles National, Aéroport ⊠	50	50.54 N	4.30 E
Bruyères	58	48.12 N	6.43 E
Bruyères-le-Châtel	261	48.36 N	2.11 E
Bruzual	246	8.03 N	69.19 W
Bruzzano Zeffirio	68	38.02 N	16.05 E
Brwinów	30	52.09 N	20.43 E
Bryan, Oh., U.S.	216	41.28 N	84.33 W
Bryan, Tx., U.S.	222	30.40 N	96.22 W
Bryan, Mount ∧	166	33.26 S	138.59 E
Bryan Coast ≐[2]	9	73.45 S	82.00 W
Bryanka	83	48.29 N	38.39 E
Bryansk → Br'ansk	76	53.15 N	34.22 E
Bryans Road	208	38.37 N	77.04 W
Bryant, Ar., U.S.	194	34.35 N	92.29 W
Bryant, In., U.S.	216	40.32 N	84.58 W
Bryant, S.D., U.S.	198	44.35 N	97.28 W
Bryant Creek ≃	194	36.36 N	92.17 W
Bryant Mountain ∧	207	42.28 N	72.58 W
Bryantville	207	42.02 N	70.50 W
Bryas, Lac ⊜	206	46.44 N	73.05 W
Bryce Canyon National Park ♠	200	37.29 N	112.12 W
Bryher I	42a	49.57 N	6.20 W
Brykalansk	24	65.30 N	54.12 E
Brykovka	80	52.32 N	48.35 E
Bryli	76	53.54 N	30.33 E
Brymbo	44	53.06 N	3.04 W
Bryn	262	53.30 N	2.39 W
Brynamman	42	51.49 N	3.52 W
Bryn Athyn	285	40.08 N	75.04 W
Bryn Brawd ∧[2]	42	52.09 N	3.54 W
Bryncethin	42	51.33 N	3.34 W
Bryne	26	58.44 N	5.39 E
Brynford	262	53.16 N	3.14 W
Bryn Gates	262	53.30 N	2.37 W
Bryn'kovskaja	78	46.02 N	38.35 E
Brynmawr, Wales, U.K.	42	51.49 N	3.11 W
Bryn Mawr, Ca., U.S.	228	34.03 N	117.14 W
Bryn Mawr, Pa., U.S.	208	40.01 N	75.18 W
Bryn Mawr College ⊽[2]	285	40.02 N	75.19 W
Bryrup	41	56.01 N	9.31 E
Bryson, P.Q., Can.	188	45.41 N	76.37 W
Bryson, Tx., U.S.	196	33.10 N	98.23 W
Bryson City	192	35.25 N	83.26 W
Bryte	226	38.36 N	121.33 W
Brza Palanka	38	44.28 N	22.27 E
Brzeg	30	50.52 N	17.27 E
Brześć Kujawski	30	52.37 N	18.55 E
Brześć nad Bugiem → Brest	76	52.06 N	23.42 E
Brzesko	30	49.59 N	20.36 E
Brzeszcze	30	49.59 N	19.08 E
Brzeziny	30	51.48 N	19.46 E
Brzozów	30	49.42 N	22.02 E
Bsharrī	130	34.15 N	36.01 E
Bua ≃	154	12.42 S	34.13 E
Bu'aale	144	1.05 N	42.35 E
Buada Lagoon c	174b	0.31 S	166.55 E
Buad Island I	116	11.40 N	124.51 E
Buagan ≃	269e	6.17 S	106.55 E
Buala	175e	8.08 S	159.35 E
Bū al-Ḥīdān, Wādī V	146	27.25 N	19.22 E
Buangor, Mount ∧	169	37.18 S	143.13 E
Buapinang	112	4.46 S	121.34 E
Buariki	174t	1.36 N	172.58 E
Buatan	114	0.44 N	101.51 E
Bua Yai	110	15.35 N	102.25 E
Buayan ≃	116	6.06 N	125.14 E
Bu'ayrāt al-Ḥasūn	146	31.24 N	15.44 E
Buba	150	11.36 N	14.55 W

Bubai	268	35.40 N	139.29 E
Bū Bānī, Jabal ∧	140	22.38 N	25.00 E
Bubanza	154	3.06 S	29.23 E
Bubaque	150	11.17 N	15.50 W
Bubendorf	58	47.27 N	7.44 E
Bubia	164	6.40 S	146.55 E
Būbiyān I	128	29.45 N	48.15 E
Bubu ≃	154	6.03 S	35.19 E
Bubu, Gunong ∧	114	4.42 N	100.47 E
Bubuan Island I, Pil.	116	6.21 N	121.58 E
Bubuan Island I, Pil.	116	6.11 N	120.58 E
Bubuduo	120	30.06 N	84.38 E
Buburu	152	1.26 N	18.03 E
Bubye ≃	154	22.20 S	31.07 E
Buc	261	48.46 N	2.08 E
Bucak	130	37.28 N	30.36 E
Bucakkışla	130	36.57 N	33.02 E
Bucaramanga	246	7.08 N	73.09 W
Bucarest → București	38	44.26 N	26.06 E
Bucas Grande Island I	116	9.40 N	125.57 E
Buccaneer Archipelago II	160	16.17 S	123.20 E
Buccheri	70	37.08 N	14.51 E
Bucchianico	66	42.18 N	14.11 E
Buccinasco	266b	45.24 N	9.07 E
Buccino	68	40.37 N	15.23 E
Buccurale	144	4.31 N	42.01 E
Bucelas	266c	38.54 N	9.07 W
Bucelas ∧[2]	266c	38.53 N	9.07 W
Buch ◆[8]	264a	52.38 N	13.30 E
Buchach	78	49.04 N	25.23 E
Buchanan, Arg.	258	34.58 S	58.13 W
Buchanan, Sk., Can.	184	51.43 N	102.45 W
Buchanan, Liber.	150	5.57 N	10.02 W
Buchanan, Ga., U.S.	192	33.48 N	85.11 W
Buchanan, Mi., U.S.	216	41.49 N	86.21 W
Buchanan, N.Y., U.S.	210	41.16 N	73.56 W
Buchanan, Va., U.S.	192	37.31 N	79.40 W
Buchanan, Lake ⊜	166	21.28 S	145.52 E
Buchanan, Lake ⊜[1]	196	30.48 N	98.25 W
Buchanan Creek ≃	162	19.11 S	136.16 E
Buchanan Field ⊠	282	37.59 N	122.03 W
Buchanan Hills ⋀[2]	162	18.53 S	131.02 E
Buchan Ness >	46	57.28 N	1.45 W
Buchans	186	48.49 N	56.52 W
Buchara	128	39.48 N	64.25 E
Buchara □[8]	128	40.00 N	64.00 E
Bucharest → București	38	44.26 N	26.06 E
Buchbach	60	48.19 N	12.17 E
Buchelay	261	48.59 N	1.40 E
Büchen, Dtsch.	52	53.29 N	10.36 E
Buchen, Dtsch.	56	49.32 N	9.17 E
Buchenberg	58	47.42 N	10.14 E
Büchenbeuren	56	49.55 N	7.16 E
Buchenwald-Denkmal ⊥	54	51.01 N	11.15 E
Buchholz, Dtsch.	54	52.10 N	12.55 E
Buchholz, Dtsch.	56	50.41 N	7.23 E
Buchholz, Dtsch.	263	51.23 N	7.15 E
Buchholz, Dtsch.	264a	52.35 N	13.47 E
Buchholz ◆[8], Dtsch.	263	51.23 N	6.46 E
Buchholz ◆[8], Dtsch.	264a	52.36 N	13.26 E
Buchholz in der Nordheide	52	53.20 N	9.52 E
Büchlberg	60	48.40 N	13.30 E
Buchloe	58	48.02 N	10.44 E
Buchmany	78	51.04 N	28.04 E
Bucholt	263	51.39 N	6.43 E
Buchon, Point >	226	35.15 N	120.54 W
Buchow-Karpzow	264a	52.31 N	12.57 E
Buchs, Schw.	58	47.23 N	8.04 E
Buchs, Schw.	58	47.10 N	9.28 E
Buchufontein	158	30.18 S	19.36 E
Buchy	50	49.35 N	1.22 E
Bučina	60	48.58 N	13.36 E
Bucine	66	43.29 N	11.37 E
Buck, Lake ⊜	162	19.38 S	130.21 E
Buckatunna	194	31.32 N	88.31 W
Buckatunna Creek ≃	194	31.30 N	88.32 W
Buck Branch ≃	284b	39.01 N	77.10 W
Buck Creek	216	40.29 N	86.46 W
Buck Creek ≃, U.S.	196	34.35 N	99.58 W
Buck Creek ≃, In., U.S.	218	39.37 N	85.56 W
Buck Creek ≃, In., U.S.	218	40.11 N	85.30 W
Buck Creek ≃, Ky., U.S.	192	36.59 N	84.29 W
Buck Creek ≃, Oh., U.S.	218	39.56 N	83.51 W
Buck Creek ≃, Pa., U.S.	285	40.15 N	74.50 W
Buckden, Eng., U.K.	42	52.17 N	0.16 W
Buckden, Eng., U.K.	44	54.12 N	2.05 W
Bückeburg	52	52.16 N	9.02 E
Bücken	52	52.46 N	9.07 E
Buckeye	200	33.22 N	112.34 W
Buckeye Creek ≃	226	38.54 N	121.55 W
Buckeye Lake	188	39.56 N	82.28 W
Buckeystown	208	39.20 N	77.25 W
Buckfastleigh	42	50.29 N	3.46 W
Buckhannon	188	38.59 N	80.13 W
Buckhaven	46	56.11 N	3.03 W
Buck Hill Falls	210	41.11 N	75.15 W
Buck Hollow ≃	224	45.10 N	120.50 W
Buckholts	222	30.52 N	97.08 W
Buckhorn ≃	180	66.13 N	161.10 W
Buckhorn Draw V	196	30.39 N	100.52 W
Buckhorn Island State Park ♠	284a	43.03 N	78.59 W
Buckhorn Lake ⊜, On., Can.	212	44.28 N	78.23 W
Buckhorn Lake ⊜, Ca., U.S.	228	34.50 N	117.59 W
Buckie	46	57.40 N	2.58 W
Buckingham, Austl.	168a	33.24 S	116.19 E
Buckingham, P.Q., Can.	188	45.35 N	75.25 W
Buckingham, Eng., U.K.	42	52.00 N	1.00 W
Buckingham, Pa., U.S.	208	40.18 N	75.01 W
Buckingham, Va., U.S.	192	37.32 N	78.37 W
Buckingham Bay c	164	12.10 S	135.46 E
Buckingham Palace ⊽	260	51.30 N	0.08 W
Buckinghamshire □[6]	42	51.45 N	0.48 W
Buck Island I	241n	17.48 N	64.37 W
Buck Island Reef National Monument ♠	241n	17.48 N	64.37 W
Buck Lake ⊜, Ab., Can.	182	53.00 N	114.45 W
Buck Lake ⊜, On., Can.	212	45.25 N	79.24 W
Buckland, Austl.	166	42.37 S	147.43 E
Buckland, Eng., U.K.	260	51.15 N	0.15 W
Buckland, Ak., U.S.	180	65.59 N	161.07 W
Buckland, Ma., U.S.	207	42.35 N	72.47 W
Buckland, Oh., U.S.	216	40.37 N	84.16 W
Buckland Brewer	42	50.57 N	4.14 W
Buckland Common	260	51.45 N	0.39 W
Bucklands	158	29.03 S	23.44 E
Buckleboo	166	32.55 S	136.12 E
Buckley, Wales, U.K.	44	53.09 N	3.04 W
Buckley, Il., U.S.	216	40.36 N	88.02 W
Buckley, Wa., U.S.	224	47.09 N	122.01 W
Buckley ≃	166	20.22 S	137.57 E
Buckley Bay c	9	68.16 S	148.12 E
Bucklin, Ks., U.S.	198	37.32 N	99.38 W
Bucklin, Mo., U.S.	194	39.46 N	92.53 W
Buck Lodge	284c	39.01 N	76.58 W
Buck Mountain ∧, Va., U.S.	192	36.40 N	81.15 W
Buck Mountain ∧, Wa., U.S.	202	48.26 N	119.50 W
Bucknell Heights	284c	38.46 N	77.04 W
Bucknell Manor	208	38.46 N	77.04 W
Buckner	218	38.23 N	85.26 W
Buckner Creek ≃	198	38.11 N	99.34 W

≃	River	Fluß	Río	Rivière	Rio
≅	Canal	Kanal	Canal	Canal	Canal
⌊	Waterfall, Rapids	Wasserfall, Stromschnellen	Cascada, Rápidos	Chute d'eau, Rapides	Cascata, Rápidos
ʊ	Strait	Meeresstraße	Estrecho	Détroit	Estreito
c	Bay, Gulf	Bucht, Golf	Bahía, Golfo	Baie, Golfe	Baía, Golfo
⊜	Lake, Lakes	See, Seen	Lago, Lagos	Lac, Lacs	Lago, Lagos
⩸	Swamp	Sumpf	Pantano	Marais	Pântano
⊓	Ice Features, Glacier	Eis- und Gletscherformen	Accidentes Glaciales	Formes glaciaires	Acidentes glaciares
⫪	Other Hydrographic Features	Andere Hydrographische Objekte	Otros Elementos Hidrográficos	Autres données hydrographiques	Outros acidentes hidrográficos
✢	Submarine Features	Untermeerische Objekte	Accidentes Submarinos	Formes de relief sous-marin	Acidentes submarinos
□	Political Unit	Politische Einheit	Unidad Politica	Entité politique	Unidade política
⊽	Cultural Institution	Kulturelle Institution	Institución Cultural	Institution culturelle	Instituição cultural
⊥	Historical Site	Historische Stätte	Sitio Histórico	Site historique	Sitio histórico
♠	Recreational Site	Erholungs- und Ferienort	Sitio de Recreo	Centre de loisirs	Area de Lazer
⊠	Airport	Flughafen	Aeropuerto	Aéroport	Aeroporto
■	Military Installation	Militäranlage	Instalación Militar	Installation militaire	Instalação militar
◆	Miscellaneous	Verschiedenes	Misceláneo	Divers	Diversos

Buckners Creek ≃ 222 29.53 N 96.53 W
Buckow 54 52.34 N 14.04 E
Buckow ✦ [8] 264a 52.25 N 13.26 E
Bucks □ [6] 208 40.19 N 75.08 W
Bucksburn 46 57.12 N 2.18 W
Buckshot Lake ⊜ 212 45.00 N 77.04 W
Buckskin Creek ≃ 218 39.14 N 83.17 W
Buckskin Gulch V 200 37.01 N 111.52 W
Bucks Knob ʌ 224 46.41 N 123.20 W
Bucksport 188 44.34 N 68.47 W
Bucktown 285 40.10 N 75.43 W
Bückwitz 54 52.52 N 12.29 E
Buc-Louis-Blériot, Aérodrome de ⊠ 261 48.45 N 2.05 E
Bucoda 224 46.47 N 122.52 W
Bucovăț 38 47.13 N 28.27 E
Buco Zau 152 4.46 S 12.33 E
Bucquoy 50 50.08 N 2.42 E
Buctouche 186 46.28 N 64.43 W
Bucun 98 36.37 N 117.27 E
București (Bucharest) 38 44.26 N 26.06 E
București □ [7] 38 44.30 N 26.15 E
Bucutua Island I 116 6.09 N 121.49 E
Bucy-lès-Pierrepont 50 49.39 N 3.54 E
Bucyrus 214 40.48 N 82.58 W
Bud 26 62.55 N 6.55 E
Buda, Il., U.S. 190 41.19 N 89.40 W
Buda, Tx., U.S. 196 30.05 N 97.51 W
Buda ✦ [8] 264c 47.30 N 19.02 E
Buda Castle ⊥ 264c 47.30 N 19.02 E
Budafok ✦ [8] 264c 47.26 N 19.02 E
Budagovo 88 54.38 N 100.08 E
Budai-hegység ⋏ 264c 47.31 N 18.58 E
Budakalász 264c 47.37 N 19.03 E
Budakeszi 264c 47.31 N 18.56 E
Buda-Kosel'ovo 76 52.43 N 30.34 E
Budalin 110 22.22 N 95.08 E
Budaörs 264c 47.27 N 18.58 E
Budapest, Magy. 30 47.30 N 19.05 E
Budapest, Magy. 264c 47.30 N 19.05 E
Budapest □ [7] 264c 47.30 N 19.05 E
Búðardalur 24a 65.10 N 21.42 W
Budarin 80 47.54 N 42.36 E
Budarino 80 50.31 N 51.04 E
Budatétény ✦ [8] 264c 47.25 N 19.01 E
Budaun 124 28.03 N 79.07 E
Budawang National Park ♠ 170 35.26 S 150.02 E
Budawang Range ⋏ 170 35.20 S 150.03 E
Budayuan 98 40.56 N 125.19 E
Budberg 263 51.32 N 6.38 E
Budbud 144 4.11 N 46.28 E
Budd Coast ≛ [2] 9 66.30 S 113.00 E
Buddh Gaya → Bodh Gaya 124 24.42 N 84.59 E
Budd Inlet ⊂ 224 47.06 N 122.54 W
Budd Lake 210 40.52 N 74.44 W
Buddtown 285 39.56 N 74.42 W
Buddu 140 11.54 N 24.08 E
Buddusò 71 40.35 N 9.15 E
Bude, Eng., U.K. 42 50.50 N 4.33 W
Bude, Ms., U.S. 194 31.27 N 90.51 W
Bude Bay ⊂ 42 50.50 N 4.37 W
Budel 52 51.17 N 5.35 E
Budelli, Isola I 71 41.17 N 9.21 E
Büdelsdorf 41 54.18 N 9.40 E
Büderich 52 51.37 N 6.34 E
Budești 38 44.14 N 26.28 E
Budge Budge 126 22.27 N 88.10 E
Buḍhāthum 124 28.04 N 84.50 E
Budhhāta 126 22.36 N 89.10 E
Budhī Gaṇḍakī ≃ 124 27.48 N 84.45 E
Budhlāda 123 29.56 N 75.34 E
Budi 152 3.04 S 23.56 E
Büdingen 56 50.17 N 9.07 E
Búðir 24a 64.56 N 13.58 W
Budišov nad Budišovkou 30 49.47 N 17.38 E
Budjala 152 2.39 N 19.42 E
Budkov 61 49.03 N 15.39 E
Budleigh Salterton 42 50.38 N 3.20 W
Budogošč' 76 59.17 N 32.27 E
Budogovišči 76 53.36 N 36.18 E
Budoni 71 40.43 N 9.42 E
Bud'onnovka 80 50.52 N 52.48 E
Bud'onnovsk 84 44.46 N 44.09 E
Bud'onnovskaja 80 46.56 N 41.33 E
Bud'onnyj, Kyrg. 85 42.30 N 72.35 E
Bud'onnyj, Ross. 83 47.27 N 39.46 E
Budrio 64 44.32 N 11.32 E
Budslav 76 54.47 N 27.27 E
Budweis → České Budějovice 30 48.59 N 14.28 E
Budworth Mere ⊜ 262 53.17 N 2.31 W
Budy 78 49.53 N 36.02 E
Budylka 78 50.30 N 34.26 E
Budyně nad Ohří 54 50.22 N 14.09 E
Budzhak ⋏ [1] 78 46.10 N 29.00 E
Buea 152 4.09 N 9.14 E
Buëch ≃ 62 44.12 N 5.57 E
Buechel 218 38.11 N 85.39 W
Buehl Airport ⊠ 285 40.11 N 74.54 W
Bueil 50 48.56 N 1.27 E
Buela 152 5.55 S 14.33 E
Buell 219 39.02 N 91.27 W
Bue Marino, Grotta del ≛ [5] 71 40.15 N 9.38 E
Buena 208 39.30 N 74.55 W
Buena Esperanza 252 34.45 S 65.15 W
Buena Esperanza, Cabo de → Good Hope, Cape of ≻ 158 34.24 S 18.30 E
Buena Park, Ca., U.S. 228 33.52 N 117.59 W
Buena Park, Wi., U.S. 216 42.48 N 88.14 W
Buenaventura, Col. 246 3.53 N 77.04 W
Buenaventura, Méx. 232 29.51 N 107.29 W
Buena Vista, Bol. 248 17.27 S 63.40 W
Buena Vista, Méx. 204 32.32 N 116.44 W
Buenavista, Méx. 234 22.36 N 100.09 W
Buena Vista, Para. 252 26.08 S 56.03 W
Buenavista, Pil. 116 8.59 N 125.24 E
Buenavista, Pil. 116 13.15 N 121.57 E
Buenavista, Pil. 116 10.04 N 118.49 E
Buenavista, Pil. 116 7.15 N 122.16 E
Buena Vista, Co., U.S. 200 38.50 N 106.07 W
Buena Vista, Fl., U.S. 220 28.11 N 82.44 W
Buena Vista, Ga., U.S. 192 32.19 N 84.31 W
Buena Vista, Md., U.S. 284c 38.57 N 76.50 W
Buena Vista, Ms., U.S. 194 33.53 N 88.50 W
Buena Vista, Pa., U.S. 279b 40.17 N 79.48 W
Buena Vista, Va., U.S. 192 37.44 N 79.21 W
Buena Vista, Bahía de ⊂ 240p 22.30 N 79.08 W
Buena Vista Canal ≍ 228 35.21 N 119.06 W
Buenavista de Cuéllar 234 18.27 N 99.25 W
Buena Vista Lake Bed ⊜ 204 35.11 N 119.17 W
Buenavista Tomatlán 234 19.12 N 102.36 W
Buen Día 196 26.21 N 104.32 W
Buendia, Embalse de ⊜ [1] 34 40.25 N 2.43 W
Buenga ≃ 152 6.07 S 15.58 E
Bueno ≃ 254 40.13 S 73.43 W
Bueno Brandão 256 22.27 S 46.21 W
Buenópolis 255 17.54 S 44.11 W
Buenos Aires, Arg. 258 34.36 S 58.27 W
Buenos Aires, Arg. 288 34.36 S 58.27 W
Buenos Aires, Col. 246 3.02 N 76.38 W
Buenos Aires, C.R. 236 9.10 N 83.20 W
Buenos Aires □ [4] 252 36.00 S 60.00 W
Buenos Aires, Lago (Lago General Carrera) ⊜ 254 46.35 S 72.00 W
Buen Pasto 254 45.05 S 69.28 W
Buer ✦ [8] 263 51.36 N 7.03 E
Buerarema 255 14.57 S 39.19 W
Buerāt, Bi'r ⊤ [4] 142 28.59 N 32.10 E
Buertuokai 85 39.35 N 74.58 E
Buesaco 246 1.23 N 77.09 W
Buescher State Park ♠ 222 30.02 N 97.09 W
Buet, Le ʌ 58 46.02 N 6.52 E
Buey ≃ 240p 20.28 N 77.05 W
Bufalotta, Fosso della ≃ 267a 41.59 N 12.30 E
Buffalo, Il., U.S. 219 39.51 N 89.25 W
Buffalo, In., U.S. 216 40.53 N 86.45 W
Buffalo, Ks., U.S. 198 37.42 N 95.41 W
Buffalo, Mn., U.S. 190 45.10 N 93.52 W
Buffalo, Mo., U.S. 194 37.38 N 93.05 W
Buffalo, N.Y., U.S. 210 42.53 N 78.52 W
Buffalo, N.Y., U.S. 284a 42.53 N 78.52 W
Buffalo, Oh., U.S. 188 39.54 N 81.31 W
Buffalo, Ok., U.S. 196 36.50 N 99.37 W
Buffalo, S.C., U.S. 192 34.43 N 81.41 W
Buffalo, S.D., U.S. 198 45.35 N 103.32 W
Buffalo, Tx., U.S. 222 31.28 N 96.04 W
Buffalo, Wy., U.S. 202 44.20 N 106.41 W
Buffalo ≃, Can. 176 60.55 N 115.00 W
Buffalo ≃, S. Afr. 158 28.43 S 30.37 E
Buffalo ≃, Ar., U.S. 194 36.10 N 92.26 W
Buffalo ≃, Mn., U.S. 198 47.06 N 96.49 W
Buffalo ≃, Ms., U.S. 194 31.04 N 91.34 W
Buffalo ≃, N.Y., U.S. 284a 42.53 N 78.53 W
Buffalo ≃, Tn., U.S. 194 36.00 N 87.50 W
Buffalo ≃, Wi., U.S. 190 44.22 N 91.55 W
Buffalo, State University College at ✱ [2] 284a 42.56 N 78.53 W
Buffalo Airpark ⊠ 284a 42.52 N 78.43 W
Buffalo Bayou ≃ 222 29.46 N 95.05 W
Buffalo Bill Ranch State Historical Park ♠ 198 41.10 N 100.48 W
Buffalo Bill Reservoir ⊜ [1] 202 44.29 N 109.13 W
Buffalo Bill State Park ♠ 202 44.30 N 109.14 W
Buffalo Center 190 43.23 N 93.56 W
Buffalo Coast Guard Base ■ 284a 42.52 N 78.54 W
Buffalo Creek ≃, U.S. 198 45.57 N 102.56 W
Buffalo Creek ≃, U.S. 214 40.16 N 80.37 W
Buffalo Creek ≃, Il., U.S. 278 42.08 N 87.55 W
Buffalo Creek ≃, Ia., U.S. 190 42.06 N 91.18 W
Buffalo Creek ≃, Ks., U.S. 198 39.35 N 97.43 W
Buffalo Creek ≃, Ky., U.S. 218 38.28 N 83.03 W
Buffalo Creek ≃, Mn., U.S. 198 44.51 N 94.00 W
Buffalo Creek ≃, N.Y., U.S. 210 42.52 N 78.47 W
Buffalo Creek ≃, Ok., U.S. 196 36.47 N 99.15 W
Buffalo Creek ≃, Pa., U.S. 208 40.29 N 77.08 W
Buffalo Creek ≃, Pa., U.S. 210 40.58 N 76.53 W
Buffalo Creek ≃, Pa., U.S. 214 40.40 N 79.41 W
Buffalo Grove 216 42.09 N 87.57 W
Buffalo Harbor ⊂ 284a 42.51 N 78.52 W
Buffalo Lake 198 44.44 N 94.37 W
Buffalo Lake ⊜, Ab., Can. 182 52.27 N 112.54 W
Buffalo Lake ⊜, N.T., Can. 176 60.10 N 115.30 W
Buffalo Lake ⊜ [1] 196 34.54 N 102.07 W
Buffalo Museum of Science ✱ 284a 42.54 N 78.51 W
Buffalo Narrows 184 55.51 N 108.30 W
Buffalo National River ♠ 194 35.58 N 92.53 W
Buffalo Pound Lake ⊜ 184 50.39 N 105.30 W
Buffalo Pound Provincial Park ♠ 184 50.36 N 105.30 W
Buffalo Run ≃ 279b 40.12 N 79.37 W
Buffalo Zoo ♠ 284a 42.56 N 78.51 W
Buffels ≃, S. Afr. 156 29.41 S 17.03 E
Buffels ≃, S. Afr. 158 33.45 S 21.11 E
Buffington Harbor ⊂ 278 41.38 N 87.25 W
Buffum, Lake ⊜ 220 27.48 N 81.40 W
Buford, Ga., U.S. 192 34.07 N 84.00 W
Buford, Oh., U.S. 218 39.04 N 83.50 W
Buford, Wy., U.S. 200 41.07 N 105.18 W
Buford Dam ✦ [6] 192 34.11 N 84.03 W
Buftea 38 44.34 N 25.57 E
Bug ≃ 22 52.31 N 21.05 E
Buga, Col. 246 3.54 N 76.17 W
Buga, Nig. 150 8.30 N 7.21 E
Bugajevka 83 49.39 N 39.42 E
Bugalagrande 246 4.11 N 76.09 W
Bugala Island I 154 0.40 S 32.20 E
Bugallon 116 15.57 N 120.13 E
Buganga 154 0.03 S 31.59 E
Bugasong 116 11.03 N 122.04 E
Bugat, Mong. 86 48.59 N 90.10 E
Bugat, Mong. 88 47.55 N 101.16 E
Bugbrooke 42 52.12 N 1.01 W
Bug Catooti 144 10.44 N 50.35 E
Buğdaylı 130 40.13 N 27.46 E
Bugeat 32 45.35 N 1.59 E
Bugel, Ujung ≻ 115a 6.26 S 111.03 E
Bugene 154 1.35 S 31.08 E
Bugey ✦ [1] 58 45.55 N 5.30 E
Buggenhout 50 51.01 N 4.12 E
Buggerru 71 39.24 N 8.24 E
Bugio I 266c 38.39 N 9.18 W
Bugiri 154 0.34 N 33.45 E
Bugle 42 50.24 N 4.47 W
Bug Méridional → Pivdennyy Buh ≃ 78 46.59 N 31.58 E
Bugojno 36 44.03 N 17.27 E
Bugøynes 24 69.58 N 29.39 E
Bugrino 24 68.48 N 49.09 E
Bugry, Ross. 76 58.46 N 35.15 E
Bugry, Ross. 265a 60.04 N 30.24 E
Bugsanga ≃ 116 12.26 N 120.59 E
Bugsuk Island I 116 8.15 N 117.18 E
Bugt, Zhg. 89 48.46 N 121.57 E
Bugt, Zhg. 98 42.20 N 120.43 E
Buguba 164 3.41 S 137.30 E
Buguey 116 18.17 N 121.50 E
Bugui Point ≻ 116 12.36 N 123.14 E
Bugul'dejka 88 52.33 N 106.05 E
Bugul'ma 80 54.33 N 52.48 E
Bugul'minsko-Belebejevskaja vozvyšennost' ⋏ [1] 80 54.54 N 52.42 E
Bugun' ≃ 85 42.58 N 68.35 E
Bugun'skoje vodochranilišče ⊜ [1] 85 42.45 N 69.05 E
Buguruslan 80 53.39 N 52.26 E
Buh ≃ 102 36.58 N 99.48 E
Buhanhua 104 42.39 N 122.46 E
Bū Hashīshah, Thamad ⊤ [4] 146 26.23 N 18.47 E
Buhayivka 83 49.28 N 37.23 E
Buḥayrah, Rayyāḥ al- ≍ 142 30.43 N 30.45 E
Buḥaythān, Jabal al- ʌ 132 30.55 N 35.53 E
Buhera 154 19.18 S 31.29 E
Buhi 116 13.26 N 123.31 E
Buhi, Lake ⊜ 116 13.26 N 123.31 E
Bühl, Dtsch. 56 48.42 N 8.08 E
Buhl, Fr. 58 47.56 N 7.11 E
Buhl, Id., U.S. 202 42.35 N 114.45 W
Buhl, Mn., U.S. 190 47.29 N 92.46 W
Buhler 198 38.08 N 97.46 W
Bühler ≃ 56 49.10 N 9.47 E
Bühlertal 56 48.41 N 8.10 E
Buhuai 120 33.22 N 80.36 E
Buhuși 38 46.43 N 26.41 E
Bui Dam ✦ [6] 150 8.22 N 2.10 W
Buie, Loch ⊂ 46 56.20 N 5.52 W
Buile Hill Park ♠ 262 53.29 N 2.18 W
Builth Wells 42 52.09 N 3.24 W
Buin, Chile 252 33.44 S 70.45 W
Buin, Pap. N. Gui. 175e 6.50 S 155.44 E
Buin, Piz ʌ 58 46.50 N 10.08 E
Buinen 52 52.55 N 6.50 E
Buinsk, Ross. 80 55.12 N 47.03 E
Buinsk, Ross. 80 54.57 N 48.17 E
Buíque 250 8.37 S 37.09 W
Buis-les-Baronnies 62 44.16 N 5.16 E
Buitenpost 52 53.15 N 6.09 E
Buj 80 58.30 N 41.30 E
Buj ≃ 80 56.13 N 54.12 E
Bujaki 24 59.03 N 48.40 E
Bujalance 34 37.54 N 4.22 W
Bujant, Mong. 86 48.33 N 89.34 E
Bujant, Mong. 86 48.10 N 91.55 E
Bujant ≃ 88 47.08 N 97.38 E
Bujant-Ovoo 102 44.58 N 107.05 E
Bujaraloz 34 41.30 N 0.09 W
Buje 36 45.24 N 13.40 E
Buji 102 33.58 N 95.22 E
Bujnaksk 84 42.49 N 47.07 E
Bujnoviči 78 51.52 N 28.33 E
Bujr nuur ⊜ 88 47.48 N 117.42 E
Bujukly 89 49.30 N 142.47 E
Bujumbura 154 3.23 S 29.22 E
Bük, Magy. 61 47.23 N 16.45 E
Buk, Pol. 30 52.22 N 16.31 E
Buka 85 40.48 N 69.11 E
Bukačača 88 52.59 N 116.55 E
Bukachivtsi 78 49.15 N 24.29 E
Buka Island I 175e 5.15 S 154.35 E
Bukama 154 9.12 S 25.51 E
Būkān, Īrān 128 36.31 N 46.12 E
Bukan', Ross. 76 53.55 N 34.42 E
Bukanovskaja 80 49.42 N 42.18 E
Buka Passage)(175e 5.25 S 154.41 E
Bukarest → București 38 44.26 N 26.06 E
Bukarevo 82 55.57 N 36.44 E
Bukavu 154 2.30 S 28.52 E
Bukene 154 4.14 S 32.53 E
Bukhara → Buchara 128 39.48 N 64.25 E
Bukhayt, Bi'r ⊤ [4] 142 29.13 N 32.17 E
Bukide, Pulau I 112 3.47 N 125.36 E
Bukidnon □ [4] 116 8.00 N 125.00 E
Bukima 154 1.48 S 33.25 E
Bukit Baharu 114 2.13 N 102.16 E
Bukitbatu 114 1.27 N 102.00 E
Bukit Betong 114 4.15 N 101.56 E
Bukit Fraser 114 3.43 N 101.45 E
Bukit Kachi 114 6.24 N 100.32 E
Bukit Mandai 271c 1.25 N 103.45 E
Bukit Mertajam 114 5.22 N 100.28 E
Bukit Panjang 271c 1.23 N 103.46 E
Bukit Serok 114 2.55 N 102.50 E
Bukit Timah 271c 1.20 N 103.47 E
Bukit Timah Race Course ✱ 271c 1.20 N 103.48 E
Bukittinggi 112 0.19 S 100.22 E
Bükk ⋏ 30 48.05 N 20.30 E
Bukoba 154 1.20 S 31.49 E
Bukombe 154 3.31 S 32.03 E
Bukovica ✦ [1] 36 44.10 N 15.40 E
Bukovina □ [9] 78 48.00 N 25.30 E
Bukrino 82 54.48 N 36.14 E
Bukuka 88 51.11 N 116.39 E
Bukukun 88 49.27 N 111.08 E
Bukum, Pulau I 271c 1.14 N 103.47 E
Bukumbirwa 154 0.46 S 28.44 E
Bukum Kechil, Pulau I 271c 1.14 N 103.46 E
Bukunga 154 7.41 S 25.56 E
Bukuru 150 9.48 N 8.51 E
Bukuya 154 0.41 N 31.50 E
Bula 164 3.06 S 130.30 E
Bula ≃ 80 55.12 N 48.23 E
Bula Atumba 152 8.40 S 14.48 E
Bulacan □ [4] 116 15.00 N 121.05 E
Bulacaue Point ≻ 116 11.36 N 123.09 E
Bülach 58 47.31 N 8.32 E
Bulajevo 86 54.54 N 70.26 E
Bulak 88 51.02 N 115.21 E
Bulaka ≃ 164 8.06 S 139.12 E
Bulak Gölü ⊜ 130 38.32 N 32.55 E
Bulalacao 116 12.20 N 121.20 E
Bulalacao Island I 116 11.45 N 120.10 E
Bulalaqui Point ≻ 116 11.17 N 124.03 E
Bulan, Pil. 116 12.40 N 123.52 E
Bulan, Pil. 116 6.44 N 124.47 E
Bulan, Ky., U.S. 192 37.18 N 83.09 W
Bulanaš 86 57.16 N 62.00 E
Bulancak 130 40.57 N 38.14 E
Bulandshahr 124 28.24 N 77.51 E
Bulanicha 86 52.48 N 84.57 E
Bulanık 130 39.05 N 42.15 E
Bulan Island I 116 6.08 N 121.50 E
Bulanovo 86 52.27 N 55.10 E
Būlāq 140 25.12 N 30.32 E
Būlāq ✦ [8] 273c 30.04 N 31.14 E
Būlāq ad-Dakrūr 273c 30.02 N 31.11 E
Bulava 89 51.55 N 140.25 E
Bulawa, Gunung ʌ 112 0.30 N 123.34 E
Bulawayo 154 20.09 S 28.36 E
Bulbjerg ʌ [2] 26 57.09 N 9.02 E
Bulbul 130 36.46 N 36.49 E
Bulbul, Wādī V 140 10.59 N 24.33 E
Bulcherry Island I 126 21.33 N 88.31 E
Buldan 130 38.03 N 28.51 E
Buldāna 122 20.32 N 76.11 E
Buldern 52 51.52 N 7.22 E
Buldibuyo 248 8.07 S 77.22 W
Buldir Island I 181a 52.21 N 175.54 E
Buldon 116 7.33 N 124.25 E
Buldurtinskij 80 50.05 N 53.11 E
Buldyrty ≃ 80 49.48 N 52.34 E
Bulembu 158 25.56 S 31.06 E
Bulga 170 32.39 S 151.01 E
Bulgakovo 76 55.14 N 32.08 E
Bulgan, Mong. 86 46.53 N 91.05 E
Bulgan, Mong. 88 48.45 N 103.34 E
Bulgan, Mong. 102 44.05 N 103.32 E
Bulgan □ [4] 88 49.00 N 103.30 E
Bulgar 80 54.57 N 49.05 E
Bulgaria (Bǎlgarija) □ [1], Europe 22 43.00 N 25.00 E
Bulgaria (Bǎlgarija) □ [1], Europe 38 43.00 N 25.00 E
Bulgarie → Bulgaria □ [1] 38 43.00 N 25.00 E
Bulgarien → Bulgaria □ [1] 38 43.00 N 25.00 E
Bulger 214 40.23 N 80.20 W
Bulgnéville 58 48.13 N 5.50 E
Bulgroo 166 25.48 S 143.59 E
Bulhale 144 5.20 N 46.29 E
Buliluyan 116 8.20 N 117.12 E
Buliluyan, Cape ≻ 116 8.20 N 117.11 E
Bulim 271c 1.22 N 103.43 E
Bulimba 171a 27.25 S 153.04 E
Bulki 144 6.10 N 36.40 E
Bulkington 42 52.29 N 1.25 W
Bulkley ≃ 182 55.13 N 127.40 W
Bulkley Ranges ⋏ 182 54.30 N 127.30 W
Bull ≃ 182 49.28 N 115.26 W
Bullabulling 162 31.01 S 120.32 E
Bullaque ≃ 34 38.59 N 4.17 W
Bullara 162 22.40 S 114.03 E
Bullard 222 32.08 N 95.19 W
Bulla Regia ⊥ 36 36.34 N 8.46 E
Bullas 34 38.03 N 1.40 W
Bullaxaar 144 10.23 N 44.25 E
Bullay 56 50.03 N 7.08 E
Bull Creek ≃, Nv., U.S. 204 38.43 N 115.34 W
Bull Creek ≃, N.Y., U.S. 284a 43.03 N 78.50 W
Bull Creek ≃, Oh., U.S. 214 40.42 N 80.32 W
Bull Creek ≃, S.D., U.S. 198 43.41 N 99.28 W
Bull Creek ≃, S.D., U.S. 198 45.40 N 103.18 W
Bull Creek ≃, Tx., U.S. 196 32.36 N 101.10 W
Bulldog 164 7.45 S 146.25 E
Bulle 58 46.37 N 7.04 E
Buller ≃ 172 41.44 S 171.35 E
Buller, Mount ʌ 169 37.09 S 146.26 E
Bullfinch 162 30.59 S 119.06 E
Bullfrog Creek ≃ 200 37.19 N 110.44 W
Bull Harbour 182 50.54 N 127.55 W
Bullhead 198 45.45 N 101.04 W
Bullhead City 204 35.08 N 114.34 W
Bull Hide Creek ≃ 222 31.23 N 97.01 W
Bull Hill ʌ [2] 262 53.40 N 2.21 W
Bulli 170 34.20 S 150.55 E
Bullicame ⊥ 66 42.22 N 12.04 E
Büllingen 56 50.25 N 6.16 E
Bullioh 171b 36.12 S 147.20 E
Bullion 261 48.37 N 2.00 E
Bull Lake ⊜ [1] 202 43.11 N 109.07 W
Bull Lake Creek ≃ 202 43.14 N 109.02 W
Bull Mountain ʌ 202 46.05 N 112.04 W
Bullock 192 36.30 N 78.33 W
Bullock Creek 166 17.43 S 144.31 E
Bullock Creek ≃ 166 21.40 S 145.09 E
Bulloo ≃ 166 28.43 S 142.30 E
Bulloo Downs 166 28.31 S 142.57 E
Bulloo Lake ⊜ 166 28.43 S 142.25 E
Bulloo River Overflow ≚ 166 28.50 S 142.40 E
Bullpound Creek ≃ 182 51.05 N 111.58 W
Bull Run ≃, Or., U.S. 224 45.26 N 122.15 W
Bull Run ≃, Va., U.S. 208 38.43 N 77.23 W
Bull Run Lake ⊜ 224 45.27 N 121.50 W
Bull Run Reservoir Number 1 ⊜ [1], Or., U.S. 224 45.30 N 122.04 W
Bull Run Reservoir Number 2 ⊜ [1], Or., U.S. 224 45.28 N 122.10 W
Bullrun Rock ʌ 202 44.21 N 118.17 W
Bulls 172 40.10 S 175.23 E
Bulls Bay ⊂ 192 32.59 N 79.33 W
Bullsbrook 168a 31.40 S 116.01 E
Bulls Gap 192 36.15 N 83.05 W
Bull Shoals 194 36.23 N 92.34 W
Bull Shoals Lake ⊜ [1] 194 36.30 N 92.50 W
Bullskin Creek ≃ 218 38.10 N 85.19 W
Bullville 210 41.33 N 74.22 W
Bully Creek ≃ 202 43.58 N 117.15 W
Bully Hill 214 41.22 N 79.50 W
Bully-les-Mines 50 50.26 N 2.43 E
Bulmke-Hüllen ✦ [8] 263 51.31 N 7.06 E
Bulnaj nuruu ⋏ 88 49.05 N 98.30 E
Bulnes 252 36.44 S 72.18 W
Bulo Ghedudo 144 2.52 N 43.01 E
Bulolo 164 7.10 S 146.40 E
Bulpham 260 51.33 N 0.22 E
Bulpitt 219 39.35 N 89.26 W
Bulsār 122 20.38 N 72.56 E
Bulstrode ≃ 206 46.02 N 72.15 W
Bultei 71 40.27 N 9.03 E
Bultfontein 158 28.20 S 26.05 E
Buluan 116 6.44 N 124.47 E
Buluan ≃ 116 6.47 N 124.47 E
Buluan, Lake ⊜ 116 6.40 N 124.49 E
Buluduku 114 2.20 N 98.14 E
Bulugansk 88 52.24 N 110.23 E
Bulukumba 112 5.33 S 120.11 E
Bulukuto 152 0.12 S 21.42 E
Bululawang 115a 8.05 S 112.38 E
Bulungu, Zaïre 152 6.04 S 21.54 E
Bulungu, Zaïre 152 4.33 S 18.36 E
Bulupayung 114 1.38 N 99.11 E
Bulusan 116 12.45 N 124.08 E
Bulusan Volcano ʌ 116 12.46 N 124.03 E
Bulwater 158 32.29 S 21.48 E
Bulwer 158 29.46 S 29.47 E
Bulyčevo 82 55.06 N 37.15 E
Bulyee 162 32.22 S 117.31 E
Bumba 152 2.11 N 22.28 E
Bumbah, Khalīj al- ⊂ 146 32.20 N 23.10 E
Bumbire Island I 154 1.40 S 31.53 E
Bumbles Green 260 51.44 N 0.02 E
Bumbo 152 6.55 S 19.16 E
Bumbu ≃ 273b 4.23 S 15.18 E
Bumbulan 112 0.29 N 122.04 E
Bumbun, Pulau I 112 4.27 N 118.40 E
Bumbuna 150 9.03 N 11.44 W
Bumbunga Lake ⊜ 168b 33.54 S 138.11 E
Bumiayu 115a 7.15 S 109.00 E
Bumijawa 115a 7.10 S 109.07 E
Bumkin Island I 283 42.17 N 70.54 W
Bumping ≃ 224 46.59 N 121.06 W
Bumping Lake ⊜ 224 46.52 N 121.19 W
Bumpus, Mount ʌ [2] 176 69.33 N 112.40 W
Bumtang ≃ 124 26.56 N 90.51 E
Bumu Hu ⊜ 120 31.15 N 91.10 E
Buna, Kenya 154 2.47 N 39.31 E
Buna, Pap. N. Gui. 164 8.40 S 148.25 E
Buna, Tx., U.S. 194 30.26 N 93.58 W
Buna, Zaïre 152 3.15 S 18.59 E
Bunagāti 126 23.19 N 89.25 E
Bunai 164 2.11 S 147.14 E
Bunaj 85 38.26 N 71.32 E
Bun'atino 82 56.24 N 37.15 E
Bunavista 196 35.39 N 101.28 W
Bunawan 116 8.12 N 125.57 E
Bunazi 154 1.13 S 31.24 E
Bunbeg 48 55.03 N 8.18 W
Bunbury 168a 33.19 S 115.38 E
Bunceton 194 38.47 N 92.47 W
Bunclody 48 52.38 N 6.40 W
Buncrana 48 55.08 N 7.27 W
Bundaberg 166 24.52 S 152.21 E
Bundanoon 170 34.39 S 150.18 E
Bundarra 166 30.10 S 151.05 E
Bunde, Dtsch. 52 53.11 N 7.16 E
Bünde, Dtsch. 52 52.12 N 8.35 E
Bunde, Ned. 56 50.54 N 5.45 E
Bundeena 274a 34.05 S 151.09 E
Bundenthal 56 49.06 N 7.48 E
Bundey ≃ 162 21.46 S 135.37 E
Bündheim 54 51.53 N 10.32 E
Būndi, India 120 25.27 N 75.39 E
Bundi, Pap. N. Gui. 164 5.40 S 145.15 E
Bundick Creek ≃ 194 30.36 N 92.57 W
Bundoora 274b 37.42 S 145.04 E
Bundoran 48 54.28 N 8.17 W
Būndu, India 124 23.11 N 85.35 E
Bundu, S. Afr. 158 29.45 S 22.02 E
Bunduqiyah 154 5.06 N 30.53 E
Bund'ur 86 57.32 N 82.01 E
Buner □ [9] 123 34.35 N 72.35 E
Bunessan 46 56.19 N 6.14 W
Bunga 150 11.04 N 9.38 E
Bunga ≃ 150 11.23 N 9.56 E
Bungamas 112 3.42 S 102.23 E
Bungay 42 52.28 N 1.26 E
Bungbulang 115a 7.27 S 107.35 E
Bunge 26 57.51 N 19.01 E
Bungegep 164 7.48 S 139.52 E
Bungendore 171b 35.15 S 149.27 E
Bunger Hills ⋏ [2] 9 66.17 S 100.47 E
Bung Kan 110 18.23 N 103.37 E
Bungku 112 2.33 S 121.58 E
Bungo 152 7.26 S 15.23 E
Bungoma 154 0.34 N 34.34 E
Bungonia 170 34.51 S 149.57 E
Bungo-suidō)(92 33.00 N 132.13 E
Bungo-takada 96 33.33 N 131.27 E
Bungsberg ʌ [2] 54 54.12 N 10.43 E
Bungtlang 120 22.20 N 92.46 E
Bungu 154 7.38 S 39.03 E
Buni ≃ 115a 7.26 S 106.47 E
Bunia 154 1.34 N 30.15 E

ENGLISH

Name	Page	Lat.°′	Long.°′

Bunianga 152 3.34 S 20.06 E
Būnīken, Kūh-e ʌ 128 26.46 N 58.12 E
Buninyong 169 37.39 S 143.53 E
Buninyong, Mount ʌ 169 37.39 S 143.56 E
Bunji 123 35.40 N 74.36 E
Bunkeflo strand 41 55.33 N 12.57 E
Bunker 194 37.27 N 91.12 W
Bunker Group II 166 23.48 S 152.20 E
Bunker Hill, Il., U.S. 219 39.02 N 89.57 W
Bunker Hill, In., U.S. 216 40.40 N 86.06 W
Bunker Hill, Or., U.S. 202 43.21 N 124.12 W
Bunker Hill, Tx., U.S. 222 29.46 N 95.32 W
Bunker Hill ʌ 204 39.15 N 117.08 W
Bunker Hill Monument ⊥ 283 42.22 N 71.04 W
Bunkeya 154 10.07 S 27.17 E
Bunkie 194 30.57 N 92.10 W
Bunkyō ✦ [8] 268 35.43 N 139.45 E
Bunnahowen 48 54.11 N 9.54 W
Bunnell 192 29.27 N 81.15 W
Bunnik 52 52.04 N 5.12 E
Bünningstedt 52 53.41 N 10.13 E
Bunola 214 40.14 N 79.56 W
Bun Plains ≚ 154 0.44 N 40.42 E
Bunratty Castle ⊥ 48 52.42 N 8.48 W
Bunschoten 52 52.14 N 5.22 E
Bunsuru ≃ 150 13.21 N 6.23 E
Bunta 112 0.48 S 122.10 E
Buntine 162 29.59 S 116.34 E
Buntingford 42 51.57 N 0.01 W
Buntok 112 1.42 S 114.48 E
Bununu Dass 150 10.00 N 9.31 E
Bunut 112 0.46 N 112.30 E
Bunyambili 154 2.21 S 29.25 E
Bünyan 130 38.51 N 35.52 E
Bunyip 169 38.06 S 145.43 E
Bunyip ≃ 169 38.13 S 145.27 E
Bunyolo 34 39.25 N 0.47 W
Bunyrevo 82 54.34 N 37.09 E
Bunyu, Pulau I 112 3.30 N 117.50 E
Bunza 150 12.08 N 4.00 E
Buochs 58 46.58 N 8.22 E
Buol 112 1.10 N 121.26 E
Buolkalach 74 72.56 N 119.50 E
Buonalbergo 68 41.13 N 14.59 E
Buona Vista 271c 1.16 N 103.47 E
Buon Bu N'jang 110 12.06 N 107.40 E
Buonconvento 66 43.08 N 11.29 E
Buon Me Thuot 110 12.40 N 108.03 E
Buon Mrong 110 12.48 N 108.28 E
Buon Ngo 110 12.30 N 108.28 E
Buon Thach Hom 110 12.17 N 108.48 E
Buon Ya Soup 110 13.05 N 107.52 E
Buor-Chaja, guba ⊂ 74 71.30 N 131.00 E
Buor-Chaja, mys ≻ 74 71.56 N 132.40 E
Bupul 164 7.31 S 140.52 E
Buqayʿāwīyah, Qāʿ al- ≚ 132 32.03 N 37.07 E
Buqayq 128 25.56 N 49.40 E
Buqda Koosaar 144 4.31 N 44.49 E
Buqde Caqable 144 4.04 N 45.15 E
Buquira ≃ 256 23.10 S 45.54 W
Buquirivu ≃ 287b 23.28 S 46.28 W
Buqūm, Ḥarrat al- ≛ [9] 144 20.54 N 42.00 E
Bur 88 58.47 N 107.01 E
Bura, Kenya 154 3.30 S 38.18 E
Bura, Kenya 154 1.06 S 39.57 E
Bura Gaurānga ≃ [1] 126 22.00 N 90.33 E
Burakin 162 30.31 S 117.10 E
Buraly 80 55.04 N 52.52 E
Buram 140 10.49 N 25.10 E
Buran 86 48.04 N 85.15 E
Burangulovo 86 53.26 N 58.23 E
Buranhém ≃ 255 16.27 S 39.04 W
Burankol' 86 46.14 N 54.12 E
Burannoje 86 50.59 N 54.28 E
Burano ≃ 66 43.37 N 12.40 E
Burao Kibir 144 8.42 N 45.29 E
Burāq 132 33.10 N 36.29 E
Burāri ✦ [8] 272a 28.46 N 77.12 E
Buras 194 29.21 N 89.31 W
Buraševo 82 56.44 N 35.52 E
Burauen 116 10.58 N 124.53 E
Burayd, Bi'r ⊤ [4] 142 29.08 N 32.07 E
Buraydah 128 26.20 N 43.59 E
Burayk 146 26.33 N 13.08 E
Buraykah 132 32.50 N 36.34 E
Burbach 56 50.45 N 8.05 E
Burbage, Eng., U.K. 42 51.20 N 1.40 W
Burbage, Eng., U.K. 262 53.15 N 1.56 W
Burbank, Ca., U.S. 226 37.19 N 121.55 W
Burbank, Ca., U.S. 228 34.10 N 118.18 W
Burbank, Il., U.S. 216 41.45 N 87.45 W
Burbank, Il., U.S. 278 41.45 N 87.46 W
Burbank, Oh., U.S. 214 40.59 N 81.59 W
Burbank, Wa., U.S. 202 46.12 N 119.00 W
Burbank Studios ✱ [3] 280 34.09 N 118.21 W
Burbure 50 50.32 N 2.28 E
Burç 130 37.02 N 37.10 E
Burcei 71 39.21 N 9.21 E
Burcevo 82 55.02 N 38.09 E
Burcher 166 33.32 S 147.18 E
Burcin 62 45.26 N 5.26 E
Burco 144 9.31 N 45.34 E
Burda 124 25.50 N 77.35 E
Burdalyk 128 38.25 N 64.20 E
Burdekin ≃ 166 19.39 S 147.30 E
Burdekin Falls ↓ 166 20.39 S 147.09 E
Burden 198 37.18 N 96.45 W
Burdeos → Bordeaux, Fr. 32 44.50 N 0.34 W
Burdeos, Pil. 116 14.51 N 121.58 E
Burdeos Bay ⊂ 116 14.44 N 122.06 E
Burdett, Ab., Can. 182 49.50 N 111.32 W
Burdett, Ks., U.S. 198 38.11 N 99.31 W
Burdett, N.Y., U.S. 210 42.25 N 76.50 W
Burdul 272c 19.07 N 73.07 E
Burdur 130 37.43 N 30.17 E
Burdur □ [4] 130 37.30 N 30.00 E
Burdur Gölü ⊜ 130 37.44 N 30.12 E
Burdwood Bank ⤊ [3] 18 54.15 S 59.00 W
Bure, Ityo. 144 8.15 N 35.09 E
Bure, Ityo. 144 10.47 N 37.06 E
Bure ≃ 42 52.37 N 1.43 E
Bure, Pic de ʌ 62 44.38 N 5.56 E
Bureå 26 64.37 N 21.12 E
Bureälven ≃ 26 64.37 N 21.13 E
Bureg Changaj 88 48.14 N 103.57 E
Bureinskij chrebet ⋏ 89 50.35 N 133.35 E
Bureja 89 49.52 N 129.48 E
Bureja ≃ 89 49.25 N 129.35 E
Burekup 168a 33.19 S 115.49 E
Büren, Dtsch. 52 51.33 N 8.33 E
Büren, Mong. 88 47.13 N 95.54 E
Büren an der Aare 58 47.08 N 7.23 E
Büren Chaan 88 49.29 N 99.14 E
Bürengijn nuruu ⋏ 88 49.15 N 104.30 E
Bures 261 48.57 N 1.58 E
Bures-sur-Yvette 261 48.42 N 2.10 E
Burey-en-Vaux 58 48.34 N 5.40 E
Burfjord 24 69.56 N 22.00 E
Burford, On., Can. 212 43.06 N 80.26 W
Burford, Eng., U.K. 42 51.49 N 1.38 W
Būr Fu'ād ✦ [8] 142 31.15 N 32.19 E
Burg, Dtsch. 54 51.49 N 14.08 E
Burg, Dtsch. 54 52.16 N 11.51 E
Burg, Dtsch. 56 50.42 N 8.19 E
Burg ✦ [8] 263 51.08 N 7.09 E
Burg, Schloss ⊥ 263 51.08 N 7.10 E
Burga 76 58.45 N 32.29 E
Burgas 38 42.30 N 27.28 E
Burgas □ [4], Blg. 38 42.36 N 26.41 E
Burgas □ [4], Blg. 130 42.10 N 27.00 E
Burgaski Zaliv ⊂ 38 42.30 N 27.33 E
Burgau 58 48.26 N 10.25 E
Burg [auf Fehmarn] 54 54.26 N 11.12 E
Burgaw 192 34.33 N 77.55 W
Burgaz ✦ [8] 267b 40.53 N 29.03 E
Burgaz Adası I 267b 40.53 N 29.04 E
Burgbernheim 56 49.27 N 10.19 E
Burgdorf, Dtsch. 52 52.27 N 10.00 E
Burgdorf, Schw. 58 47.04 N 7.37 E
Burgebrach 56 49.50 N 10.44 E

DEUTSCH

Name	Seite	Breite°′	Länge°′ E = Ost

Bürgel 54 50.56 N 11.45 E
Burgenland □ [3] 61 47.30 N 16.20 E
Burgeo 186 47.37 N 57.37 W
Burgersdorp 158 31.00 S 26.20 E
Burger Township 273d 26.05 S 27.46 E
Burges, Mount ʌ [2] 162 30.50 S 121.06 E
Burgess 208 37.53 N 76.21 W
Burgess Hill 42 50.57 N 0.07 W
Burgessville 212 43.01 N 80.39 W
Burgettstown 214 40.22 N 80.23 W
Burggrafenberg ʌ [2] 263 51.13 N 7.07 E
Burghausen 60 48.09 N 12.49 E
Burghead 46 57.42 N 3.30 W
Burgheim 60 48.42 N 11.01 E
Burgh Heath 260 51.18 N 0.13 W
Burghill 214 41.22 N 80.34 W
Burgh le Marsh 44 53.09 N 0.15 E
Burghūth, Sabkhat al- ⊜ 130 34.58 N 41.06 E
Burgin 194 37.45 N 84.46 W
Burgio 70 37.36 N 13.17 E
Burgjoss 56 50.12 N 9.29 E
Burgkirchen 60 48.12 N 13.06 E
Burgkunstadt 54 50.08 N 11.14 E
Bürglen, Schw. 58 46.53 N 8.40 E
Bürglen, Schw. 58 47.33 N 9.09 E
Burglengenfeld 60 49.13 N 12.03 E
Burgoon 214 41.16 N 83.15 W
Burgos, Esp. 34 42.21 N 3.42 W
Burgos, It. 71 40.23 N 8.59 E
Burgos, Méx. 232 24.57 N 98.47 W
Burgos, Pil. 116 16.04 N 119.52 E
Burgos, Pil. 116 15.30 N 120.24 E
Burgos □ [4] 34 42.20 N 3.40 W
Burgsinn 56 50.09 N 9.38 E
Burgstädt 54 50.55 N 12.49 E
Burgstall, Dtsch. 54 52.24 N 11.41 E
Burgstall → Postal, It. 64 46.36 N 11.11 E
Burg Stargard 54 53.29 N 13.18 E
Burgsvik 26 57.03 N 18.16 E
Burgueño, Arroyo ≃ 288 34.24 S 58.47 W
Burgund → Bourgogne □ [9] 32 47.00 N 4.30 E
Burgundy → Bourgogne □ [9] 32 47.00 N 4.30 E
Burgusio (Burgeis) 64 46.42 N 10.31 E
Burgwedel 52 52.29 N 9.51 E
Burgwindheim 56 49.49 N 10.35 E
Burhābalang ≃ 126 21.28 N 87.04 E
Burham 260 51.20 N 0.29 E
Burhan Budai Shan ⋏ 102 36.00 N 96.00 E
Burhaniye, Tür. 130 37.57 N 28.45 E
Burhaniye, Tür. 130 39.30 N 26.58 E
Burhānpur 120 21.18 N 76.14 E
Burhar 124 23.13 N 81.32 E
Burhave 52 53.34 N 8.21 E
Burholme ✦ [8] 285 40.03 N 75.05 W
Buri 255 23.48 S 48.35 W
Burias Island I 116 12.57 N 123.08 E
Burias Pass)(116 13.00 N 123.15 E
Buribaj 86 51.57 N 58.11 E
Būr Ibrāhīm ✦ [8] 142 29.57 N 32.34 E
Burica, Punta ≻ 236 8.03 N 82.53 W
Burien 224 47.28 N 122.20 W
Burigi, Lake ⊜ 154 2.05 S 31.15 E
Burila Mare 38 44.27 N 22.34 E
Burin 186 47.02 N 55.10 W
Burin Peninsula ≻ [1] 186 47.00 N 55.40 W
Buri Ram 110 15.00 N 103.07 E
Buriswar ≃ [1] 126 21.58 N 90.02 E
Buritama 255 21.03 S 50.08 W
Buriti, Bra. 250 3.55 S 42.57 W
Buriti, Bra. 255 16.27 S 53.27 W
Buriti ≃ 248 12.50 S 58.28 W
Buriti Alegre 255 18.09 S 49.03 W
Buriti Bravo 250 5.50 S 43.50 W
Buriticupu ≃ 250 4.13 S 46.33 W
Buriti dos Lopes 250 3.10 S 41.52 W
Buritizeiro 255 17.21 S 44.58 W
Būriya 124 30.09 N 77.21 E
Burj al-ʿArab 140 30.55 N 29.32 E
Burjassot 34 39.31 N 0.25 W
Burjatija □ [3] 88 53.00 N 109.00 E
Burji 144 5.20 N 37.57 E
Burj Islām 130 35.41 N 35.48 E
Burj Mughayzil 142 31.27 N 30.23 E
Burkan ≃ 85 41.43 N 76.46 E
Burkau 54 51.10 N 14.10 E
Burkburnett 196 34.05 N 98.34 W
Burke, S.D., U.S. 198 43.10 N 99.17 W
Burke, Tx., U.S. 222 31.14 N 94.46 W
Burke, Va., U.S. 284c 38.47 N 77.16 W
Burke ≃ 166 23.12 S 139.33 E
Burke Channel)(182 52.07 N 127.38 W
Burke Island I 9 73.15 S 104.35 W
Burke Lake ⊜ [1] 284c 38.46 N 77.18 W
Burke Lake County Park ♠ 284c 38.45 N 77.18 W
Burke Lakefront Airport ⊠ 279a 41.31 N 81.41 W
Burkesville 194 36.47 N 85.22 W
Burket 216 41.09 N 85.58 W
Burketown 166 17.43 S 139.34 E
Burkett Gardens 226 37.57 N 121.15 W
Burkettsville 216 40.21 N 84.39 W
Burkhardtsdorf 54 50.44 N 12.55 E
Burkina Faso □ [1], Afr. 134 13.00 N 1.30 W
Burkina Faso □ [1], Afr. 150 13.00 N 1.30 W
Burkit 80 47.03 N 50.42 E
Burksville 219 38.16 N 90.09 W
Burla 86 53.19 N 78.21 E
Burla ≃ 86 53.20 N 78.02 E
Burladingen 58 48.17 N 9.07 E
Burleigh 208 39.02 N 74.51 W
Burleigh Falls 212 44.34 N 78.13 W
Burleigh Heads 171a 28.06 S 153.27 E
Burleson 222 32.32 N 97.19 W
Burleson □ [6] 222 30.30 N 96.43 W
Burley, Id., U.S. 202 42.32 N 113.47 W
Burley, Wa., U.S. 224 47.25 N 122.37 W
Burley Griffin, Lake ⊜ 171b 35.13 S 149.05 E
Burli, Kaz. 80 51.25 N 52.44 E
Burli, Kaz. 86 53.36 N 61.55 E
Burlingame, Ca., U.S. 226 37.35 N 122.21 W
Burlingame, Ks., U.S. 198 38.45 N 95.00 W
Burlingame State Park ♠ 207 41.22 N 71.43 W
Burlington, Nf., Can. 186 49.45 N 56.02 W
Burlington, On., Can. 212 43.19 N 79.47 W
Burlington, Co., U.S. 198 39.18 N 102.16 W
Burlington, Ct., U.S. 207 41.46 N 72.57 W
Burlington, Il., U.S. 216 42.03 N 88.33 W
Burlington, In., U.S. 216 40.29 N 86.24 W
Burlington, Ia., U.S. 190 40.48 N 91.06 W
Burlington, Ks., U.S. 198 38.11 N 95.44 W
Burlington, Ky., U.S. 218 39.01 N 84.43 W
Burlington, Ma., U.S. 207 42.30 N 71.11 W
Burlington, Mi., U.S. 216 42.06 N 85.05 W
Burlington, N.J., U.S. 208 40.04 N 74.51 W
Burlington, N.C., U.S. 192 36.05 N 79.26 W
Burlington, N.D., U.S. 198 48.16 N 101.25 W
Burlington, Pa., U.S. 210 41.47 N 76.37 W
Burlington, Tx., U.S. 222 31.01 N 96.60 W
Burlington, Vt., U.S. 188 44.28 N 73.12 W
Burlington, Wa., U.S. 224 48.28 N 122.19 W
Burlington, Wi., U.S. 216 42.40 N 88.16 W
Burlington, Wy., U.S. 202 44.26 N 108.25 W
Burlington □ [6] 208 39.50 N 74.47 W
Burlington Beach 216 41.30 N 87.03 W
Burlington County Airpark ⊠ 285 39.56 N 74.50 W
Burlington Island I 285 40.05 N 74.51 W
Burlington Junction 194 40.26 N 95.03 W
Burlington Mall ✦ [9] 283 42.29 N 71.13 W
Burlit 89 46.33 N 134.14 E
Burluk 80 50.34 N 44.33 E
Burma → Myanmar □ [1] 110 22.00 N 98.00 E
Burmā, Tall ʌ 132 30.38 N 35.50 E
Burmakino 80 57.27 N 40.20 E
Burn ≃ 44 54.12 N 1.38 W
Burnaby 224 49.15 N 122.57 W

Symbols in the index entries represent the broad categories identified in the key at the right. Symbols with superior numbers (⋏ [1]) identify subcategories (see complete key on page *I · 1).*

Symbole im Register stellen die rechts im Schlüssel erklärten Kategorien dar. Symbole mit hochgestellten Ziffern (⋏ [1]) bezeichnen Unterabteilungen einer Kategorie (vgl. vollständiger Schlüssel auf Seite *I · 1).*

Los símbolos incluídos en el texto del índice representan las grandes categorías identificadas con la clave a la derecha. Los símbolos con numeros en su parte superior (⋏ [1]) identifican las subcategorías (véase la clave completa en la página *I · 1).*

Les symboles de l'index représentent les catégories indiquées dans la légende à droite. Les symboles suivis d'un indice (⋏ [1]) représentent des sous-catégories (voir légende complète à la page *I · 1).*

Os símbolos incluídos no texto do índice representam as grandes categorias identificadas com a chave à direita. Os símbolos com números em sua parte superior (⋏ [1]) identificam as subcategorias (veja-se a chave completa à página *I · 1).*

ʌ Mountain	Berg	Montaña	Montagne	Montanha
⋏ Mountains	Gebirge	Montañas	Montagnes	Montanhas
)(Pass	Paß	Paso	Col	Passo
V Valley, Canyon	Tal, Cañon	Valle, Cañón	Vallée, Canyon	Vale, Canhão
≚ Plain	Ebene	Llano	Plaine	Planície
≻ Cape	Kap	Cabo	Cap	Cabo
I Island	Insel	Isla	Île	Ilha
II Islands	Inseln	Islas	Îles	Ilhas
✱ Other Topographic Features	Andere Topographische Objekte	Otros Elementos Topográficos	Autres données topographiques	Outros acidentes topográficos

ESPAÑOL — Nombre | Página | Lat.°′ | Long.°′ W = Oeste
FRANÇAIS — Nom | Page | Lat.°′ | Long.°′ W = Ouest
PORTUGUÊS — Nome | Página | Lat.°′ | Long.°′ W = Oeste

Burnaby Island I 182 52.24 N 131.20 W
Burnage 262 53.26 N 2.12 W
Burnas, ozero ⊜ 78 45.52 N 30.08 E
Burnet 196 30.45 N 98.13 W
Burnett ≃ 166 24.46 S 152.25 E
Burnett Bay ⊂ 176 73.53 N 124.00 W
Burnett Brook ≃ 276 40.46 N 74.38 W
Burnett Heads 166 24.46 S 152.25 E
Burnettsville 216 40.46 N 86.36 W
Burney, Ca., U.S. 204 40.52 N 121.39 W
Burney, In., U.S. 218 39.19 N 85.38 W
Burnham, Eng., U.K. 42 51.33 N 0.39 W
Burnham, Il., U.S. 278 41.39 N 87.34 W
Burnham, Pa., U.S. 208 40.38 N 77.34 W
Burnham Beeches ◂[3] 260 51.34 N 0.38 W
Burnham Market 42 52.57 N 0.44 E
Burnham-on-Crouch 42 51.38 N 0.49 E
Burnham-on-Sea 42 51.15 N 3.00 W
Burnhamthorpe 275b 43.37 N 79.36 W
Burnhaven 46 57.29 N 1.47 W
Burnie 166 41.04 S 145.54 E
Burning Tree Estates 284c 39.01 N 77.12 W
Burnips 216 42.44 N 85.50 W
Burniston 44 54.19 N 0.26 W
Burnley 44 53.48 N 2.14 W
Burnley □[8] 262 53.46 N 2.15 W
Burnley Creek ≃ 212 44.13 N 77.51 W
Burnley Football Ground ♠ 262 53.48 N 2.14 W
Burnmouth 46 55.50 N 2.04 W
Burnoje 85 42.37 N 70.46 E
Burno-Okt'abr'skoje 85 42.42 N 70.49 E
Burnpur 126 23.40 N 86.57 E
Burns, Ks., U.S. 198 38.05 N 96.53 W
Burns, Or., U.S. 202 43.35 N 119.03 W
Burns, Tn., U.S. 194 36.03 N 87.18 W
Burns, Wy., U.S. 198 41.11 N 104.21 W
Burns Creek ≃ 198 47.22 N 104.25 W
Burns Flat 196 35.20 N 99.10 W
Burns Harbor 216 41.37 N 87.10 W
Burnside, Austl. 168b 34.57 S 138.40 E
Burnside, Ky., U.S. 192 36.59 N 84.36 W
Burnside, Pa., U.S. 214 40.49 N 78.47 W
Burnside ≃ 176 66.51 N 108.04 W
Burnside, Lake ⊜ 162 25.33 S 123.02 E
Burns Lake 182 54.14 N 125.46 W
Burnsville, Al., U.S. 194 32.28 N 86.53 W
Burnsville, Ms., U.S. 194 34.50 N 88.18 W
Burnsville, N.C., U.S. 192 35.55 N 82.18 W
Burnsville, W.V., U.S. 188 38.51 N 80.39 W
Burnt ≃, On., Can. 212 44.35 N 78.46 W
Burnt ≃, Or., U.S. 202 44.22 N 117.14 W
Burnt Cabins 214 40.05 N 77.54 W
Burnt Corn Creek ≃ 194 31.06 N 87.04 W
Burnt Hills 210 42.54 N 73.53 W
Burnt Island, Nf., Can. 186 47.36 N 58.53 W
Burntisland, Scot., U.K. 46 56.03 N 3.15 W
Burnt Meadow Brook ≃ 276 41.05 N 74.18 W
Burnt Mills, Lake ⊜ 208 36.50 N 76.38 W
Burnt Mills Hills 284c 39.02 N 77.00 W
Burnt Mills Manor 284c 39.02 N 77.00 W
Burnt Mountain ʌ 228 33.12 N 117.04 W
Burntop 158 26.49 S 30.54 E
Burnt Pine 174c 29.02 S 167.56 E
Burnt Pond ⊜ 186 48.11 N 57.24 W
Burntwick Island I 260 51.25 N 0.41 E
Burntwood 42 52.41 N 1.56 W
Burntwood ≃ 184 56.08 N 96.30 W
Burntwood Lake ⊜ 184 55.29 N 100.07 W
Burnyj, porog ∟ 86 57.43 N 95.18 E
Buro 144 11.28 N 49.41 E
Buron 84 42.48 N 44.03 E
Buronzo 62 45.29 N 8.16 E
Burow 54 53.46 N 13.16 E
Burpengary 171a 27.10 S 152.57 E
Burpham 260 51.15 N 0.33 W
Burqin 86 47.43 N 86.53 E
Burqin ≃ 86 47.40 N 86.55 E
Burra 166 33.40 S 138.56 E
Burra Burra Creek ≃ 170 34.10 S 149.38 E
Burracoppin 162 31.23 S 118.29 E
Burra Creek ≃ 168b 33.51 S 139.18 E
Burrage 283 42.02 N 70.51 W
Burrage Pond ⊜ 283 42.01 N 70.52 W
Burragorang, Lake ⊜[1] 170 33.57 S 150.26 E
Burramurra 166 20.30 S 137.20 E
Burravoe 46a 60.32 N 1.28 W
Burrawang 170 34.36 S 150.31 E
Burray I 46 58.51 N 2.54 W
Burrel, Shq. 38 41.37 N 20.00 E
Burrel, Ca., U.S. 226 36.30 N 119.59 W
Burrendong Reservoir ⊜[1] 166 32.39 S 149.15 E
Burren Junction 166 30.06 S 148.58 E
Burrill Lake ⊂ 170 35.23 S 150.27 E
Burrinjuck Reservoir ⊜[1] 166 35.00 S 148.45 E
Burro, Serranías del ʌʌ 196 29.10 N 102.05 W
Burr Oak, In., U.S. 216 41.15 N 86.25 W
Burr Oak, Ks., U.S. 198 39.51 N 98.18 W
Burr Oak, Mi., U.S. 216 41.50 N 85.19 W
Burro Burro ≃ 246 4.48 N 58.51 W
Burro Creek ≃ 200 34.32 N 113.35 W
Burro Peak ʌ 200 32.35 N 108.26 W
Burrowa, Mount ʌ 171b 36.05 S 147.42 E
Burrowa-Pine Mountain National Park ♠ 171b 36.06 S 147.44 E
Burrow Head ≻ 44 54.41 N 4.24 W
Burrowhill 260 51.21 N 0.36 W
Burrows 216 40.40 N 86.30 W
Burrows Island I 224 48.29 N 122.42 W
Burr Ridge 278 41.46 N 87.55 W
Burrs Mill Brook ≃ 285 39.53 N 74.42 W
Burrton 198 38.01 N 97.40 W
Burrumbeet, Lake ⊜ 169 37.30 S 143.39 E
Burrundie 164 13.32 S 131.42 E
Burruyacú 252 26.30 S 64.45 W
Burrwood 194 28.58 N 89.22 W
Burry Holms I 42 51.37 N 4.18 W
Burry Port 42 51.42 N 4.15 W
Bürs 58 47.09 N 9.48 E
Bursa 130 40.11 N 29.04 E
Bursa □[4] 130 40.10 N 29.00 E
Būr Safājah 140 26.44 N 33.56 E
Būr Sa'īd (Port Said) 142 31.16 N 32.18 E
Būr Sa'īd □[4] 142 30.36 N 32.15 E
Burscheid 56 51.05 N 7.06 E
Burscough 262 53.35 N 2.51 W
Burscough Bridge 44 53.36 N 2.52 W
Bursey, Mount ʌ 9 76.00 S 132.40 W
Burshtyn 78 49.17 N 24.37 E
Bursol' 86 53.11 N 78.27 E
Bürstadt 56 49.38 N 8.27 E
Burstall 184 50.40 N 109.54 W
Būr Sūdān (Port Sudan) 140 19.37 N 37.14 E
Burt, Ia., U.S. 190 43.11 N 94.13 W
Burt, N.Y., U.S. 210 43.19 N 78.43 W
Būr Tawfīq ◂[8] 128 29.57 N 32.34 E
Burtenbach 58 48.20 N 10.26 E
Burt Lake ⊜ 190 45.27 N 84.40 W
Burtnieks ezers ⊜ 76 57.45 N 25.16 E
Burton, B.C., Can. 182 49.59 N 117.54 W
Burton, Eng., U.K. 42 50.44 N 1.45 W
Burton, Eng., U.K. 262 53.16 N 3.01 W
Burton, Il., U.S. 219 39.55 N 91.15 W
Burton, Mi., U.S. 216 43.01 N 84.16 W
Burton, Mi., U.S. 216 43.02 N 83.36 W
Burton, Oh., U.S. 214 41.28 N 81.08 W
Burton, Tx., U.S. 222 30.11 N 96.36 W
Burton, Wa., U.S. 224 47.23 N 122.27 W
Burton, Lake ⊜[1] 192 34.50 N 83.33 W
Burton Fleming 44 54.08 N 0.20 W
Burton Latimer 42 52.23 N 0.41 W
Burtons Bridge 216 42.17 N 88.14 W
Burton Seamount ✢[3] 14 32.00 S 171.45 W
Burtonsville 208 39.07 N 76.56 W
Burton upon Stather 44 53.39 N 0.41 W
Burton upon Trent 42 52.49 N 1.36 W
Burtonwood 262 53.26 N 2.39 W
Burtonwood Airfield ⊠ 262 53.24 N 2.39 W
Burträsk 26 64.31 N 20.39 E
Burtundy 166 33.44 S 142.16 E
Burṭus 142 30.09 N 31.08 E
Buru I 108 3.24 S 126.40 E
Buruanga 116 11.51 N 121.53 E
Burukan 89 53.02 N 136.03 E
Buruldaj 85 42.48 N 75.52 E
Burullus, Buḥayrat al- ⊜ 142 31.30 N 30.50 E
Burūm 144 14.22 N 48.57 E
Burundaj 85 43.23 N 76.51 E
Burundi □[1], Afr. 138 3.15 S 30.00 E
Burundi □[1], Afr. 154 3.15 S 30.00 E
Burundučicha 80 58.21 N 46.07 E
Burun-Šibertuj, gora ʌ 88 49.42 N 109.59 E
Bururi 154 3.57 S 29.37 E
Burutu 150 5.21 N 5.31 E
Buruz Bāgān 126 23.03 N 89.00 E
Burwash 190 46.19 N 80.48 W
Burwash Landing 180 61.21 N 139.00 W
Burwell, Eng., U.K. 42 52.16 N 0.19 E
Burwell, Ne., U.S. 198 41.46 N 99.07 W
Burwell Bay ⊂ 208 37.04 N 76.38 W
Burwick 46 58.44 N 2.57 W
Burwood, Austl. 274a 33.53 S 151.06 E
Burwood, Austl. 274b 37.51 S 145.06 E
Bury, P.Q., Can. 206 45.28 N 71.30 W
Bury, Eng., U.K. 42 50.54 N 0.34 W
Bury, Eng., U.K. 44 53.36 N 2.17 W
Bury □[8] 262 53.35 N 2.19 W
Buryatia → Burjatija □[3] 88 53.00 N 109.00 E
Buryn' 78 51.13 N 33.49 E
Bury Saint Edmunds 42 52.15 N 0.43 E
Burzaco 258 34.49 S 58.24 W
Burzet 62 44.44 N 4.15 E
Burzil 123 34.52 N 75.07 E
Burzil Pass)(123 34.54 N 75.06 E
Būṣ, Ghubbat al- ⊂ 142 29.36 N 32.22 E
Busa, Mount ʌ 116 6.08 N 124.39 E
Busachi 71 40.02 N 8.54 E
Busalla 62 44.34 N 8.57 E
Busambra, Rocca ʌ 70 37.51 N 13.24 E
Busan → Pusan 98 35.06 N 129.03 E
Busana 64 44.22 N 10.19 E
Busanga 152 0.51 S 22.04 E
Busanga Swamp ≡ 154 14.10 S 25.50 E
Busangu 154 8.32 S 25.31 E
Buṣayrah 130 35.09 N 40.26 E
Busby, Austl. 274a 33.54 S 150.53 E
Busby, Mt., U.S. 202 45.32 N 106.57 W
Busca 62 44.31 N 7.29 E
Buscate 266b 45.32 N 8.49 E
Buscbusc ≃ 144 1.08 S 41.49 E
Buschberg ʌ[2] 61 48.34 N 16.23 E
Busche 64 46.02 N 11.59 E
Busch Gardens ♠ 280 34.13 N 118.28 W
Buschhausen ◂[8] 263 51.30 N 6.51 E
Busdorf 41 54.29 N 9.32 E
Buseck 56 50.36 N 8.47 E
Buseto Palizzolo 70 38.01 N 12.43 E
Būsh 142 29.09 N 31.08 E
Bush ≃, N. Ire., U.K. 44 55.13 N 6.32 W
Bush ≃, S.C., U.S. 192 34.08 N 81.36 W
Būshehr □[4] 128 28.50 N 51.20 E
Bushenyi 154 0.32 S 30.11 E
Bushey 42 51.39 N 0.22 W
Bushey Heath 260 51.38 N 0.20 W
Bushi 268 35.50 N 139.22 E
Bushimaie ≃ 152 6.02 S 23.45 E
Bushiribana 241s 12.33 N 69.58 W
Bushkill 210 41.06 N 75.00 W
Bush Kill ≃ 210 41.05 N 74.59 W
Bushkill Falls ∟ 210 41.09 N 75.01 W
Bushland 196 35.11 N 102.04 W
Bush Lot 246 6.12 N 57.16 W
Bushman Land □[9] 158 29.15 S 20.00 E
Bushmills 48 55.12 N 6.32 W
Bushnell, Fl., U.S. 220 28.39 N 82.06 W
Bushnell, Il., U.S. 190 40.33 N 90.30 W
Bush River ≃ 208 39.21 N 76.14 W
Bushton 198 38.30 N 98.23 W
Bushtyna 78 48.04 N 23.27 E
Bū Shubayrim, Wādī V 146 27.07 N 19.30 E
Bushwick ◂[8] 276 40.42 N 73.55 W
Bushy Park 166 21.16 S 139.43 E
Bushy Park ♠ 260 51.25 N 0.20 W
Bushy Run ≃ 279b 40.20 N 79.40 W
Bushy Run Battlefield ⊥ 279b 40.21 N 79.38 W
Busia 154 0.28 N 34.05 E
Busigny 50 50.02 N 3.28 E
Busing, Pulau I 271c 1.14 N 103.45 E
Businga 152 3.20 N 20.53 E
Büsingen 58 47.42 N 8.41 E
Busira ≃ 152 0.15 S 18.59 E
Busjön ⊜, Sve. 40 60.06 N 13.28 E
Busjön ⊜, Sve. 40 60.31 N 13.58 E
Bus'k 78 49.58 N 24.37 E
Buskerud □[6] 26 60.25 N 9.12 E
Buskhyttan 40 58.40 N 16.56 E
Busko Zdrój 30 50.28 N 20.44 E
Buskul' 86 53.45 N 61.12 E
Busle 144 5.28 N 44.25 E
Busoga □[5] 154 0.40 N 33.30 E
Busovača 36 44.06 N 17.53 E
Buṣrā al-Ḥarīrī (Bosor) 132 32.50 N 36.20 E
Buṣrá ash-Shām 132 32.31 N 36.29 E
Bussana 62 43.49 N 7.51 E
Bussang 58 47.53 N 6.51 E
Bussang, Col de)(58 47.54 N 6.54 E
Busselton 162 33.39 S 115.20 E
Busseri ≃ 140 7.41 N 28.03 E
Busseto 64 44.59 N 10.02 E
Bussey 190 41.12 N 92.52 W
Bussières 62 45.50 N 4.16 E
Bussi sul Tirino 66 42.12 N 13.49 E
Busskoje 84 43.50 N 44.37 E
Bussolengo 64 45.28 N 10.51 E
Bussoleno 62 45.08 N 7.09 E
Bussum 52 52.16 N 5.10 E
Bussy-Rabutin, Château de ⊥ 58 47.35 N 4.31 E
Bussy-Saint-Georges 261 48.51 N 2.42 E
Bustamante, Méx. 232 26.33 N 100.30 W
Bustamante, Méx. 234 23.26 N 99.47 W
Bustān, Wādī al- V 142 28.24 N 30.49 E
Buštěhrad 54 50.09 N 14.10 E
Bușteni 38 45.25 N 25.32 E
Busti 214 42.02 N 79.17 W
Bustleton ◂[8] 285 40.05 N 75.02 W
Busto Arsizio 62 45.37 N 8.51 E
Busto Garolfo 62 45.33 N 8.53 E
Buston, Taj. 85 40.31 N 69.19 E
Buston, Uzb. 128 40.04 N 64.49 E
Busu-Adula 152 2.05 N 21.40 E
Busuanga 116 12.10 N 119.55 E
Busuanga Island I 116 12.05 N 120.05 E
Busu-Djanoa 152 1.43 N 21.23 E
Bušuicha 76 59.02 N 40.26 E
Bušulej 88 52.45 N 117.13 E
Büsum 30 54.08 N 8.51 E
Busu-Melo 152 1.48 N 20.15 E
Bū Sunbul, Jabal ʌʌ[2] 146 23.10 N 22.21 E
Buta, Ross. 80 55.02 N 51.57 E
Buta, Zaïre 154 2.48 N 24.44 E
Butag 116 12.38 N 123.56 E
Butajira 144 8.07 N 38.22 E
Butala 164 6.42 S 147.37 E
Butan 38 43.39 N 23.45 E
Bután → Bhutan □[1] 120 27.30 N 90.30 E
Butand State Park ♠ 226 37.13 N 122.20 W
Butantã ◂[8] 287b 23.34 S 46.43 W
Butantã, Instituto ⊍[3] 287b 23.34 S 46.43 W
Buta Ranquil 252 37.03 S 69.50 W
Butare 154 2.36 S 29.44 E
Butaritari I[1] 14 3.07 N 172.48 E
Butarque, Arroyo de ≃ 266a 40.19 N 3.39 W
Butauanan Island I 116 14.07 N 123.17 E
Butchart Gardens ♠ 224 48.33 N 123.28 W
Butcher Island (Dia Deva) I 272c 18.58 N 72.54 E
Bute 168b 33.52 S 138.01 E
Bute, Island of I 46 55.50 N 5.06 W
Bute, Kyles of ʊ 46 55.53 N 5.13 W
Bute, Sound of ʊ 46 55.44 N 5.12 W
Büteelijn nuruu ʌʌ 88 50.00 N 104.50 E
Bute Giarti 144 4.33 N 37.45 E
Bute Inlet ⊂ 182 50.37 N 124.53 W
Butemba 154 1.09 N 31.36 E
Butembo 154 0.09 N 29.17 E
Butera 70 37.11 N 14.11 E
Butere 154 0.13 N 34.30 E
Bütgenbach 56 50.26 N 6.12 E
Butha Buthe 158 28.45 S 28.15 E
Butha Qi (Zalantun) 89 48.02 N 122.43 E
Buthidaung 110 20.52 N 92.32 E
Buthier ≃ 62 45.44 N 7.22 E
Buthroton ⊥ 38 39.46 N 20.00 E
Buti 66 43.44 N 10.35 E
Butiá 252 30.07 S 51.58 W
Butiaba 154 1.49 N 31.19 E
Butig Mountains ʌʌ 116 7.39 N 124.20 E
Butka 86 56.47 N 63.47 E
Butler, Al., U.S. 194 32.05 N 88.13 W
Butler, Ga., U.S. 192 32.33 N 84.14 W
Butler, Il., U.S. 219 39.12 N 89.32 W
Butler, In., U.S. 216 41.25 N 84.52 W
Butler, Ky., U.S. 218 38.47 N 84.22 W
Butler, Mo., U.S. 194 38.15 N 94.19 W
Butler, N.J., U.S. 210 41.00 N 74.20 W
Butler, Oh., U.S. 214 40.35 N 82.25 W
Butler, Ok., U.S. 196 35.38 N 99.11 W
Butler, Pa., U.S. 214 40.51 N 79.53 W
Butler, Tx., U.S. 222 30.19 N 97.18 W
Butler, Wi., U.S. 216 43.06 N 88.04 W
Butler □[6], Oh., U.S. 218 39.26 N 84.30 W
Butler □[6], Pa., U.S. 214 40.52 N 79.54 W
Butler, Lake ⊜ 220 28.28 N 81.33 W
Butler Lake ⊜ 278 42.17 N 87.58 W
Butler Point ≻ 207 41.40 N 70.43 W
Butler Reservoir ⊜[1] 276 40.59 N 74.23 W
Butlers Bridge 48 54.02 N 7.22 W
Butlerville 218 39.02 N 85.30 W
Butmīyah 132 32.56 N 35.53 E
Butnau Lake ⊜ 184 56.13 N 95.20 W
Butner 192 36.07 N 78.45 W
Buto 152 15.46 S 15.09 E
Buton, Pulau I 112 5.00 S 122.55 E
Butong 112 1.06 S 114.50 E
Butru 166 21.30 S 139.43 E
Butsha 154 0.57 N 29.13 E
Buttapietra 64 45.20 N 11.00 E
Butte, Mt., U.S. 202 46.00 N 112.32 W
Butte, Ne., U.S. 198 42.54 N 98.50 W
Butte □[6] 226 39.27 N 121.30 W
Butte City 226 39.28 N 121.59 W
Butte Creek ≃, Ca., U.S. 204 39.12 N 121.56 W
Butte Creek ≃, Or., U.S. 224 45.09 N 122.46 W
Butte du Lion ⊥ 50 50.40 N 4.24 E
Butte Falls 202 42.32 N 122.33 W
Buttelstedt 54 51.05 N 11.20 E
Butte Mountains ʌʌ 204 39.50 N 115.05 W
Butten 56 48.58 N 7.13 E
Butter Brook ≃ 283 42.31 N 71.24 W
Butter Creek ≃ 202 45.52 N 119.19 W
Butterfield, Il., U.S. 278 41.50 N 88.02 W
Butterfield, Mn., U.S. 198 43.57 N 94.47 W
Butterfield Creek ≃ 278 41.33 N 87.37 W
Butterfield Lake ⊜ 212 44.19 N 75.46 W
Butterley Reservoir ⊜[1] 262 53.35 N 1.56 W
Buttermere 44 54.33 N 3.17 W
Butternut 190 46.00 N 90.29 W
Butternut Creek ≃, N.Y., U.S. 210 42.25 N 75.22 W
Butternut Creek ≃, N.Y., U.S. 210 43.06 N 76.00 W
Butterwick 44 52.59 N 0.05 E
Butterworth, Malay. 114 5.25 N 100.24 E
Butterworth, S. Afr. 158 32.23 S 28.04 E
Buttevant 48 52.14 N 8.40 W
Büttgen 56 51.12 N 6.36 E
Buttlar 56 50.45 N 9.57 E
Buttle Lake ⊜ 182 49.46 N 125.36 W
Button Islands II 176 60.35 N 64.45 W
Buttonville 275b 43.52 N 79.22 W
Buttonville Airfield ⊠ 275b 43.52 N 79.23 W
Buttonwillow 226 35.24 N 119.28 W
Buttrio 64 46.01 N 13.20 E
Buttstädt 54 51.07 N 11.25 E
Butty Head ≻ 162 33.54 S 121.38 E
Buttzville 210 40.49 N 75.00 W
Butuan 116 8.57 N 125.33 E
Butuan Bay ⊂ 116 9.06 N 125.20 E
Butuj 88 53.27 N 112.22 E
Bū Tumayyim, Wādī V 146 26.56 N 19.13 E
Buṭūris 142 31.00 N 30.15 E
Buturlino, Ross. 80 55.34 N 44.55 E
Buturlino, Ross. 82 54.55 N 37.29 E
Buturlinovka 78 50.50 N 40.36 E
Buṭwal 124 27.42 N 83.27 E
Butylicy 80 55.32 N 41.31 E
Butzbach 56 50.26 N 8.40 E
Bützfleth 52 53.39 N 9.28 E
Bützow 54 53.50 N 11.59 E
Bützsee ⊜ 54 52.49 N 12.53 E
Butztown 208 40.39 N 75.22 W
Buuhoodle 144 8.15 N 46.20 E
Buulo Berde 144 3.51 N 45.34 E
Buur Gaabo 144 1.12 S 41.51 E
Buurgplaatz ʌ 56 50.10 N 6.01 E
Buur Hakaba 144 2.47 N 44.05 E
Buur Haybe 144 3.57 N 45.07 E
Buwarah, Sabkhat al- ≡ 130 35.09 N 41.12 E
Buwayḍān 132 33.12 N 36.26 E
Buxar 124 25.35 N 83.59 E
Buxtehude 52 53.28 N 9.41 E
Buxton, Guy. 246 6.47 N 58.02 W
Buxton, S. Afr. 158 27.38 S 24.42 E
Buxton, Eng., U.K. 44 53.15 N 1.55 W
Buxton, N.C., U.S. 192 35.16 N 75.32 W
Buxton, N.D., U.S. 198 47.36 N 97.05 W
Buxton, Or., U.S. 224 45.41 N 123.11 W
Buxton, Mount ʌ 182 51.35 N 127.55 W
Buxy 58 46.43 N 4.41 E
Buye 154 4.38 N 27.30 E
Buyiqiao 106 31.47 N 119.48 E
Buyo 150 6.16 N 7.03 W
Buyo, Barrage de ◂[6] 150 6.15 N 7.05 W
Buyuan ≃ 102 21.51 N 101.13 E
Büyükada 130 40.52 N 29.07 E
Büyükada I 267b 40.52 N 29.07 E
Büyükarmutlu 130 39.35 N 38.26 E
Büyükbakkal ◂[8] 267b 40.59 N 29.11 E
Büyükçeçeli 130 39.43 N 33.52 E
Büyükçekmece 130 41.01 N 28.34 E
Büyükdere ◂[8] 267b 41.09 N 29.02 E
Büyükeceli 130 36.11 N 33.40 E
Büyükkale 130 38.01 N 27.34 E
Büyükkarıştıran 130 41.18 N 27.32 E
Büyükkemikli Burnu ≻ 130 40.18 N 26.14 E
Büyükmenderes ≃ 130 37.28 N 27.11 E
Büyükzap → Great Zab ≃ 128 36.00 N 43.21 E
Buyun Shan ʌ 98 40.06 N 122.42 E
Buyun Uzun 128 39.13 N 63.19 E
Buzan ≃ 80 46.18 N 49.06 E
Buzanaj, peski ◂[2] 80 47.30 N 49.50 E
Buzançais 32 46.53 N 1.25 E
Buzancy 56 49.25 N 4.57 E
Bužaninovo 82 56.23 N 38.18 E
Bužarovo 82 55.59 N 36.47 E
Buzău 38 45.09 N 26.49 E
Buzău □[6] 38 45.15 N 26.45 E
Buzău ≃ 38 45.26 N 27.44 E
Buzen 96 33.37 N 131.08 E
Búzi ≃ 156 19.50 S 34.43 E
Buziaș 38 45.39 N 21.36 E
Buziji 100 33.49 N 118.14 E
Buzinovka 80 48.32 N 43.53 E
Búzios, Ilha dos I 256 23.48 S 45.08 W
Búzios, Ponta dos ≻ 255 22.44 S 41.53 W
Buz'kyy lyman ⊂[1] 78 46.45 N 31.55 E
Buzlanovo 265b 55.46 N 37.13 E
Buzovna 84 40.31 N 50.04 E
Buzuluk, Kaz. 86 51.55 N 66.16 E
Buzuluk, Ross. 80 52.47 N 52.15 E
Buzuluk ≃, Ross. 80 50.13 N 42.12 E
Buzuluk ≃, Ross. 80 52.47 N 52.16 E
Buzzards Bay 207 41.44 N 70.37 W
Buzzards Bay ⊂ 207 41.33 N 70.47 W
Bwana Mkubwa 154 13.01 S 28.42 E
Bwasa 152 3.53 S 18.25 E
Bwendi 154 4.01 N 26.41 E
Bwlch 42 51.54 N 3.15 W
By 40 60.12 N 16.28 E
Byādgi 122 14.41 N 75.29 E
Byam Channel ʊ 176 75.20 N 105.20 W
Byam Martin Channel ʊ 176 75.45 N 104.00 W
Byam Martin Island I 176 75.15 N 104.00 W
Byberry Creek ≃ 285 40.04 N 74.59 W
Byblos → Jubayl 130 34.07 N 35.39 E
Bychawa 30 51.01 N 22.32 E
Bychok ≃ 83 48.26 N 37.47 E
Bychov 76 53.32 N 30.12 E
Byčicha 76 55.41 N 29.58 E
Byčki, Ross. 76 54.15 N 34.39 E
Byčki, Ross. 80 53.38 N 40.54 E
Byculla ◂[8] 272c 18.58 N 72.49 E
Byczyna 30 51.07 N 18.11 E
Bydalen 26 63.06 N 13.47 E
Bydgoszcz 30 53.08 N 18.00 E
Bydgoszcz □[4] 30 53.15 N 18.00 E
Byelorussia → Belarus □[1] 72 53.50 N 28.00 E
Byers, Pa., U.S. 285 40.05 N 75.41 W
Byers, Tx., U.S. 196 34.04 N 98.11 W
Byersdale 279b 40.37 N 80.13 W
Byers Run ≃ 279b 40.24 N 79.42 W
Byesville 188 39.58 N 81.32 W
Byfang ◂[8] 263 51.24 N 7.06 E
Byfield, Eng., U.K. 42 52.11 N 1.14 W
Byfield, Ma., U.S. 207 42.45 N 70.56 W
Byfleet 42 51.20 N 0.29 W
Byford 168a 32.13 S 116.00 E
Byforde 284c 39.01 N 77.05 W
Bygdeå 26 64.04 N 20.51 E
Bygdeträsket ⊜ 26 64.26 N 20.32 E
Bygdin 26 61.20 N 8.48 E
Bygdin ⊜ 26 61.21 N 8.36 E
Bygi 80 57.13 N 53.44 E
Byglandsfjord 26 58.41 N 7.48 E
Byglandsfjorden ⊜ 26 58.48 N 7.50 E
Byhalia 194 34.52 N 89.41 W
Bykivka 78 50.17 N 27.58 E
Bykle 26 59.21 N 7.20 E
Bykov 89 47.21 N 142.32 E
Bykovka 82 55.29 N 37.40 E
Bykovo, Ross. 80 49.47 N 45.22 E
Bykovo, Ross. 82 54.01 N 37.54 E
Bykovo, Ross. 82 55.37 N 38.04 E
Bykovo Airport ⊠ 265b 55.36 N 38.05 E
Bylas 200 33.08 N 110.07 W
Bylbasivka 83 48.51 N 37.30 E
Bylderup 41 54.57 N 9.07 E
Byley 262 53.13 N 2.25 W
Bylkyldak 86 48.38 N 75.16 E
Bylnice 30 49.04 N 18.01 E
Bylot Island I 176 73.13 N 78.34 W
Byng Inlet 190 45.46 N 80.33 W
Bynum, Mt., U.S. 182 47.58 N 112.18 W
Bynum, N.C., U.S. 192 35.46 N 79.08 W
Bynum, Tx., U.S. 222 31.58 N 97.00 W
Byōdōin Temple ⊍[1] 270 34.53 N 135.48 E
Byram ≃ 276 40.59 N 73.39 W
Byramgore Reef ✢[2] 122 11.54 N 71.49 E
Byram Lake Reservoir ⊜[1] 276 41.10 N 73.41 W
Byrd, Lac ⊜ 190 47.01 N 76.56 W
Byrdstown 194 36.34 N 85.07 W
Byrka 88 50.39 N 118.31 E
Byrne Arena ♠ 276 40.49 N 74.05 W
Byrnedale 214 41.17 N 78.30 W
Byro 162 26.05 S 116.09 E
Byrock 166 30.40 S 146.24 E
Byron, Ca., U.S. 226 37.52 N 121.38 W
Byron, Ga., U.S. 192 32.39 N 83.45 W
Byron, Il., U.S. 190 42.07 N 89.15 W
Byron, Mi., U.S. 216 42.49 N 83.57 W
Byron, N.Y., U.S. 210 43.04 N 78.03 W
Byron, Wy., U.S. 202 44.47 N 108.30 W
Byron, Cape ≻ 166 28.39 S 153.38 E
Byron, Isla I 254 47.47 S 75.12 W
Byron Bay 166 28.39 S 153.37 E
Byron Center 216 42.49 N 85.42 W
Byrranga, gory ʌʌ 74 75.00 N 104.00 E
Byryuchyy Ostriv, kosa ≻[2] 78 46.08 N 35.05 E
Byšice-Liblice 54 50.19 N 14.38 E
Bysjön ⊜ 40 60.23 N 14.30 E
Byske 26 64.57 N 21.12 E
Byskeälven ≃ 26 64.57 N 21.13 E
Bystraja ≃ 80 47.58 N 41.00 E
Bystřany 54 50.38 N 13.51 E
Bystrica ≃ 80 58.38 N 49.05 E
Bystřice 30 49.45 N 14.41 E
Bystřice pod Hostýnem 30 49.24 N 17.40 E
Bystrij Tanyp ≃ 86 55.46 N 54.35 E
Bystrovka 85 42.47 N 75.43 E
Bystryj 86 57.50 N 73.58 E
Bystryj Istok 86 52.23 N 84.24 E
Bystrzyca Kłodzka 30 50.18 N 16.38 E
Bytantaj ≃ 74 68.46 N 134.20 E
Bytča, Bela. 76 54.18 N 28.24 E
Bytča, Slvk. 30 49.14 N 18.36 E
Byten' 76 52.54 N 25.29 E
Bytkiv 78 48.38 N 24.26 E
Bytom (Beuthen) 30 50.22 N 18.54 E
Bytoš' 76 53.50 N 34.06 E
Bytów 30 54.11 N 17.30 E
Byumba 154 1.35 S 30.04 E
Byvalki 78 51.51 N 30.37 E
Byxelkrok 26 57.20 N 17.00 E
Bzyb' ≃ 84 43.12 N 40.18 E
Bzybskij chrebet ʌʌ 84 43.18 N 40.41 E

C

Ça ≃ 110 18.46 N 105.47 E
Čaa-Chol' 86 51.32 N 92.23 E
Çaacupé 252 25.23 S 57.09 W
Čaadajevka 80 53.09 N 45.56 E
Čaadajevo 80 55.40 N 42.02 E
Caaguazú 252 25.26 S 56.02 W
Caaguazú □[5] 252 25.00 S 55.45 W
Caála 152 12.51 S 15.33 E
Caamaño Sound ʊ 182 52.49 N 129.28 W
Caapiranga 246 3.18 S 61.13 W
Caapucú 252 26.13 S 57.12 W
Caarapó 255 22.38 S 54.48 W
Caatinga 255 17.10 S 45.53 W
Caazapá 252 26.09 S 56.24 W
Caazapá □[5] 252 26.10 S 56.00 W
Cabaçal ≃ 248 16.00 S 57.42 W
Cabadbaran 116 9.10 N 125.38 E
Cabadiangan Plateau ʌʌ[1] 116 9.50 N 122.36 E
Cabagan 116 17.26 N 121.46 E
Cabaiguán 240p 22.05 N 79.30 W
Cabalete Island I 116 14.17 N 121.50 E
Cabalian 116 10.16 N 125.10 E
Cabaliana, Lago ⊜ 246 3.20 S 60.50 W
Cabalian Bay ⊂ 116 10.13 N 125.10 E
Cabalian Point ≻ 116 12.06 N 122.01 E
Caballero Creek ≃ 280 34.11 N 118.32 W
Caballito ◂[8] 288 34.37 S 58.27 W
Caballones, Cayo I 240p 20.52 N 79.00 W
Caballo Reservoir ⊜[1] 200 32.58 N 107.18 W
Cabana 248 8.24 S 78.02 W
Cabanaconde 248 15.37 S 71.59 W
Cabañas 240p 22.58 N 82.55 W
Cabanatuan 116 15.29 N 120.58 E
Cabangan 116 15.10 N 120.03 E
Cabano 186 47.41 N 68.53 W
Cabarroguis 116 16.33 N 121.32 E
Cabarruyan Island I 116 16.18 N 119.59 E
Cabaun Island I 116 12.34 N 124.30 E
Cabeceiras 255 15.48 S 46.59 W
Cabeço de Montachique 266c 38.54 N 9.11 W
Cabellera, Sierra de la ʌʌ 200 30.55 N 109.07 W
Cabery 216 41.00 N 88.12 W
Cabeza del Buey 34 38.43 N 5.13 W
Cabeza de Tigre 286c 10.28 N 66.46 W
Cabezas 248 18.46 S 63.24 W
Cabiao 116 15.15 N 120.51 E
Cabiate 266b 45.40 N 9.10 E
Cabildo, Arg. 252 38.29 S 61.54 W
Cabildo, Chile 252 32.26 S 71.05 W
Cabimas 246 10.23 N 71.28 W
Cabin Branch ≃, Md., U.S. 284b 39.13 N 76.35 W
Cabin Branch ≃, Md., U.S. 284c 38.51 N 76.48 W
Cabin Creek ≃ 198 46.55 N 104.52 W
Cabinda 152 5.33 S 12.12 E
Cabinda □[5] 152 5.00 S 12.30 E
Cabinet Mountains ʌʌ 202 48.20 N 116.00 W
Cabingaan Island I 116 5.41 N 121.03 E
Cabin John 208 38.58 N 77.09 W
Cabin John Creek ≃ 284b 38.58 N 77.09 W
Cabin John Creek Park ♠ 284c 38.59 N 77.09 W
Cabin John Regional Park ♠ 284c 39.02 N 77.09 W
Cabiri 152 8.52 S 13.39 E
Cabixi ≃ 248 13.41 S 60.44 W
Cable 190 46.12 N 91.17 W
Cable Airport ⊠ 280 34.08 N 117.41 W
Cables 162 27.59 S 123.23 E
Cabo 250 8.17 S 35.02 W
Cabo Blanco 254 47.12 S 65.45 W
Cabo de Hornos, Parque Nacional ♠ 250 55.45 S 67.25 W
Cabo Delgado □[5] 154 12.35 S 39.00 E
Cabo Frio 255 22.53 S 42.01 W
Cabo Gracias a Dios 236 14.59 N 83.10 W
Cabo Ledo 152 9.39 S 13.17 E
Cabonga, Réservoir ⊜[1] 190 47.20 N 76.35 W
Cabool 194 37.07 N 92.06 W
Caboolture 166 27.05 S 152.57 E
Cabo Orange, Parque Nacional do ♠ 250 3.00 N 51.00 W
Cabora Bassa 154 15.35 S 32.48 E
Cabora Bassa Dam ◂[6] 154 15.35 S 32.42 E
Cabo Raso 254 44.21 S 65.14 W
Caborca 232 30.37 N 112.06 W
Cabo Rojo 240m 18.05 N 67.09 W
Cabot, Ar., U.S. 194 34.58 N 92.00 W
Cabot, Pa., U.S. 214 40.46 N 79.46 W
Cabot, Mount ʌ 188 44.31 N 71.24 W
Cabot Head ≻ 212 45.14 N 81.17 W
Cabot Strait ʊ 186 47.20 N 59.30 W
Cabo Verde 256 21.28 S 46.24 W
Cabo Verde → Cape Verde □[1] 150a 16.00 N 24.00 W
Cabo Verde ≃ 256 21.28 S 46.17 W
Cabra 34 37.28 N 4.27 W
Cabra Corral, Embalse ⊜[1] 252 25.15 S 65.25 W
Cabra Island I 116 13.53 N 120.02 E
Cabramatta 274a 33.54 S 150.56 E
Cabramatta Creek ≃ 274a 33.54 S 150.57 E
Cabramurra 171b 35.58 S 148.23 E
Cabras 71 39.56 N 8.32 E
Cabras, Stagno di ⊜ 71 39.57 N 8.29 E
Cabras Island I 174p 13.27 N 144.40 E
Cabrayıl 84 39.23 N 47.02 E
Cabrel 234 20.06 N 105.14 W
Cabrera ≃, Col. 246 3.26 N 75.07 W
Cabrera ≃, Esp. 34 42.25 N 6.49 W
Cabrera, Illa de I 34 39.09 N 2.56 E
Cabrera, Sierra de la ʌʌ 34 42.12 N 6.40 W
Cabrera de Mar 266d 41.32 N 2.24 E
Cabreúva 256 23.18 S 47.08 W
Cabri 184 50.37 N 108.28 W
Cabria 64 45.54 N 13.35 E
Cabriel ≃ 34 39.14 N 1.03 W
Cabrillo National Monument ♠ 228 32.41 N 117.15 W
Cabrils 266d 41.32 N 2.22 E
Cabrobó 250 8.31 S 39.19 W
Cabruta 246 7.38 N 66.15 W
Cabucgayan 116 11.29 N 124.34 E
Cabuçu 256 22.50 S 42.55 W
Cabuçu ≃, Bra. 287a 22.59 S 43.37 W
Cabuçu ≃, Bra. 287a 22.48 S 43.37 W
Cabuçu de Cima ≃ 287b 23.31 S 46.33 W
Cabugao 116 17.48 N 120.27 E
Cabulauan Island I 116 11.23 N 120.06 E
Cabullónes, Punta ≻ 240m 17.58 N 66.35 W
Cabulo 152 10.15 S 16.40 E
Cabure 246 11.08 N 69.38 W
Cabuta 152 9.50 S 14.48 E
Cabuya 236 9.36 N 85.06 W
Cabuyal 236 10.40 N 85.40 W
Cabuyaro 246 4.18 N 72.49 W
Caca 80 48.11 N 44.40 E
Çaçador 252 26.47 S 51.00 W
Čačak 38 43.53 N 20.21 E
Cacaohatán 236 14.59 N 92.10 W
Cacaoui, Lac ⊜ 186 50.53 N 66.58 W
Caçapava 256 23.06 S 45.42 W
Caçapava do Sul 252 30.30 S 53.30 W
Caçapava Velha 256 23.07 S 45.39 W
Cacapon ≃ 188 39.37 N 78.16 W
Cacapon State Park ♠ 188 39.32 N 78.23 W
Cacas 130 38.23 N 41.17 E
Caccamo 70 37.56 N 13.40 E
Caccia, Capo ≻ 71 40.34 N 8.09 E
Çaccuri 68 39.14 N 16.47 E
Čačenka ≃ 265b 55.46 N 37.18 E
Cacequi 252 29.53 S 54.49 W
Cáceres, Bra. 248 16.04 S 57.41 W
Cáceres, Col. 246 7.35 N 75.20 W
Cáceres, Esp. 34 39.29 N 6.22 W
Cáceres □[4] 34 39.40 N 6.05 E
Cachan 261 48.48 N 2.20 E
Cacharí 252 36.24 S 59.32 W
Cache 196 34.37 N 98.37 W
Cache ≃, Ar., U.S. 194 34.42 N 91.20 W
Cache ≃, Il., U.S. 194 37.04 N 89.10 W
Caché, Lac ⊜ 206 46.21 N 74.39 W
Cache Creek 182 50.48 N 121.19 W
Cache Creek ≃, Ca., U.S. 226 38.42 N 121.42 W
Cache Creek ≃, Ca., U.S. 228 35.06 N 117.58 W
Cache Creek, North Fork ≃ 226 38.59 N 122.30 W
Cache la Poudre ≃ 200 40.25 N 104.36 W
Cache la Poudre, North Fork ≃ 198 40.54 N 105.22 W
Cache Mountain ʌ 180 65.31 N 147.20 W
Cache Peak ʌ, Ca., U.S. 228 35.13 N 118.15 W
Cache Peak ʌ, Id., U.S. 202 42.11 N 113.40 W
Cache Slough ≃ 226 38.11 N 121.40 W
Cacheu 150 12.16 N 16.10 W
Cacheu ⊂[1] 150 12.10 N 16.21 W
Cachí 252 25.06 S 66.11 W
Cachimbo 250 9.24 S 54.56 W
Cachimbo, Serra do ʌʌ 250 8.30 S 55.50 W
Cachimo 152 8.21 S 21.20 E
Cachingues 152 13.05 S 16.43 E
Cachir 88 48.06 N 98.52 E
Cachkadzor 84 40.33 N 44.43 E
Cachoeira ≃ 256 23.06 S 46.29 W
Cachoeira, Reservatório ⊜[1] 256 23.03 S 46.15 W
Cachoeira, Rio da ≃ 287a 23.00 S 43.18 W
Cachoeira Alta 255 18.48 S 50.58 W
Cachoeira de Goiás 255 16.44 S 50.38 W
Cachoeira de Manteiga 255 16.39 S 45.16 W
Cachoeira de Minas 256 22.21 S 45.47 W
Cachoeira do Arari 250 1.01 S 48.58 W
Cachoeira do Sul 252 30.02 S 52.54 W
Cachoeira Grande, Alto da ʌ 256 21.54 S 44.06 W
Cachoeira Paulista 256 22.40 S 45.01 W
Cachoeiras 287a 22.39 S 43.28 W
Cachoeiras de Macacu 256 22.28 S 42.39 W
Cachoeirinha 250 8.29 S 36.14 W
Cachoeiro de Itapemirim 255 20.51 S 41.06 W
Cachos, Punta ≻ 252 27.39 S 71.02 W
Çachos, Rio dos ≃ 287b 23.36 S 46.26 W
Čachrov 60 49.16 N 13.18 E
Cachuela Esperanza 248 10.32 S 65.38 W
Cachuma, Lake ⊜[1] 204 34.35 N 119.55 W
Cacilhas 266c 38.41 N 9.09 W
Cacine 150 11.08 N 14.57 W
Caciporé ≃ 250 3.51 N 51.08 W
Caciporé, Cabo ≻ 250 3.55 N 51.07 W
Căciulați 38 44.38 N 26.10 E
Cacnipa Island I 116 10.30 N 119.04 E
Cacocum 240p 20.44 N 76.23 W
Cacólo 152 10.07 S 19.17 E
Caconda 152 13.43 S 15.06 E
Caconde 256 21.33 S 46.38 W
Cacra 248 12.48 S 75.48 W
Cactus 196 36.04 N 102.00 W
Cactus Flat ≚ 204 37.45 N 116.45 W
Cactus Peak ʌ 204 37.47 N 116.53 W
Caçu 255 18.37 S 51.04 W
Cacuaco 152 8.47 S 13.22 E
Cacula 152 14.29 S 14.10 E
Caculé 255 14.30 S 42.13 W
Caculuvar ≃ 152 16.46 S 14.36 E
Cacuri, Ang. 152 8.14 S 18.20 E
Cacuri, Ven. 246 4.48 N 65.21 W
Cacuso 152 9.26 S 15.43 E
Çadale 144 2.45 N 46.19 E
Čadan 86 51.17 N 91.35 E
Cadaqués 34 42.17 N 3.17 E
Çadariri ≃ 248 6.20 S 57.46 W
Čadca 30 49.26 N 18.48 E
Caddington 42 51.51 N 0.27 W
Caddo, Ok., U.S. 196 34.07 N 96.15 W
Caddo, Tx., U.S. 196 32.38 N 98.40 W
Caddo ≃ 194 34.10 N 93.03 W
Caddo Creek ≃ 196 34.14 N 96.59 W
Caddo Lake ⊜[1] 194 32.42 N 94.01 W
Caddo Mills 222 33.04 N 96.14 W
Caddo Peak ʌ 222 32.29 N 97.24 W
Caddy Vista 216 42.50 N 87.54 W
Cadell ≃ 166 22.51 S 141.55 E
Cadena, Arroyo de la ≃ 196 26.17 N 104.00 W
Cadena, Cerro ʌ 196 25.50 N 104.04 W
Cadena, Punta ≻ 240m 18.18 N 67.14 W
Cadenberge 52 53.46 N 9.04 E
Cadenet 62 43.44 N 5.22 E
Cadeo 62 44.58 N 9.48 E
Cadereyta de Jiménez 232 25.36 N 100.00 W
Cader Idris ʌ 42 52.42 N 3.54 W
Cadibarrawirracanna, Lake ⊜ 162 28.52 S 135.27 E
Cadig, Mount ʌ 116 14.09 N 122.27 E
Cadillac, Sk., Can. 184 49.44 N 107.43 W
Cadillac, Fr. 32 44.38 N 0.19 W
Cadillac, Mi., U.S. 190 44.15 N 85.24 W
Cadipietra (Steinhaus) 64 46.59 N 11.59 E
Cadishead 262 53.25 N 2.26 W
Cadix → Cádiz 34 36.32 N 6.18 W
Cádiz, Esp. 34 36.32 N 6.18 W
Cadiz, Pil. 116 10.57 N 123.18 E
Cadiz, In., U.S. 218 39.57 N 85.30 W
Cadiz, Ky., U.S. 194 36.51 N 87.50 W
Cadiz, Oh., U.S. 214 40.16 N 80.59 W
Cádiz □[4] 34 36.35 N 5.50 W
Cádiz, Bahía de ⊂ 34 36.32 N 6.16 W
Cádiz, Golfo de ⊂ 34 36.50 N 7.10 W
Cadiz Lake ⊜ 204 34.18 N 115.24 W
Cadlao Island I 116 11.13 N 119.21 E
Çadnam 42 50.55 N 1.35 W
Čadobec 88 58.40 N 98.51 E
Čadobec ≃ 88 58.40 N 98.50 E
Cadogan 214 40.45 N 79.34 W
Cadomin 182 53.02 N 117.20 W
Cadoneghe 64 45.26 N 11.55 E
Cadore ◂[1] 64 46.30 N 12.20 E
Cadosia 210 41.58 N 75.16 W
Cadott 190 44.56 N 91.09 W
Cadoux 162 30.47 S 117.08 E
Caduruan Point ≻ 116 11.45 N 124.05 E
Caduta, Fosso delle ≃ 267a 41.56 N 12.12 E
Cadwell 192 32.20 N 83.02 W
Cady Marsh Ditch ≅ 278 41.33 N 87.29 W
Cady Mountain ʌ[2] 224 48.33 N 123.07 W
Cadzand 52 51.22 N 3.25 E
Caen 32 49.11 N 0.21 W
Caengo (Kwenge) ≃ 152 4.50 S 18.42 E
Caerano di San Marco 64 45.47 N 12.00 E
Caere ⊥ 66 42.02 N 12.07 E
Caergwrle 44 53.07 N 3.03 W
Caerleon 42 51.37 N 2.57 W
Caernarfon 44 53.08 N 4.16 W
Caernarfon Bay ⊂ 44 53.05 N 4.30 W
Caernarfon Castle ⊥ 44 53.08 N 4.16 W
Caerphilly 42 51.35 N 3.14 W
Caerphilly Castle ⊥ 42 51.34 N 3.14 W
Caersws 42 52.31 N 3.25 W
Caesar Creek ≃ 218 39.29 N 84.06 W
Caesar Creek, Anderson Fork ≃ 218 39.33 N 83.58 W
Caesar Creek Lake ⊜[1] 218 39.30 N 84.00 W
Cæsarea → Qesari, Horbat ⊥ 132 32.30 N 34.53 E
Caetanópolis 255 19.18 S 44.24 W
Caeté 255 19.54 S 43.40 W
Caeté ≃ 248 9.03 S 68.39 W
Caeté, Morro ʌ[2] 287a 23.03 S 43.31 W
Caetité 255 14.04 S 42.29 W
Cafayate 252 26.05 S 65.58 W
Cafelândia do Leste 255 16.40 S 53.25 W
Cafima 152 16.39 S 16.27 E
Cafu 152 16.27 S 15.14 E
Cafuini ≃ 246 1.17 N 57.11 W
Cagaan Chajrchan 88 49.25 N 94.15 E
Cagaan Gol 86 48.57 N 89.07 E
Cagaan Nuur, Mong. 86 49.32 N 89.42 E
Cagaannuur, Mong. 88 50.20 N 105.03 E
Cagaan-Ovoo 102 45.51 N 105.17 E

≃ River — Fluß — Río — Rivière — Rio
≅ Canal — Kanal — Canal — Canal — Canal
∟ Waterfall, Rapids — Wasserfall, Stromschnellen — Cascada, Rápidos — Chute d'eau, Rapides — Cascata, Rápidos
ʊ Strait — Meeresstraße — Estrecho — Détroit — Estreito
⊂ Bay, Gulf — Bucht, Golf — Bahía, Golfo — Baie, Golfe — Baía, Golfo
⊜ Lake, Lakes — See, Seen — Lago, Lagos — Lac, Lacs — Lago, Lagos
≡ Swamp — Sumpf — Pantano — Marais — Pântano
⍓ Ice Features, Glacier — Eis- und Gletscherformen — Accidentes Glaciales — Formes glaciaires — Acidentes glaciares
⍑ Other Hydrographic Features — Andere Hydrographische Objekte — Otros Elementos Hidrográficos — Autres données hydrographiques — Outros acidentes hidrográficos

✢ Submarine Features — Untermeerische Objekte — Accidentes Submarinos — Formes de relief sous-marin — Acidentes submarinos
□ Political Unit — Politische Einheit — Unidad Politica — Entité politique — Unidade política
⊍ Cultural Institution — Kulturelle Institution — Institución Cultural — Institution culturelle — Institução cultural
⊥ Historical Site — Historische Stätte — Sitio Histórico — Site historique — Sitio histórico
♠ Recreational Site — Erholungs- und Ferienort — Sitio de Recreo — Centre de loisirs — Area de Lazer
⊠ Airport — Flughafen — Aeropuerto — Aéroport — Aeroporto
▪ Military Installation — Militäranlage — Instalación Militar — Installation militaire — Instalação militar
◂ Miscellaneous — Verschiedenes — Misceláneo — Divers — Diversos

ENGLISH / DEUTSCH

Name	Page	Lat.°′	Long.°′
Cagaan Uul	88	49.28 N	98.30 E
Cagaan-Üür	88	50.32 N	101.30 E
Çagado ≃	256	22.02 S	43.09 W
Čagan ≃	80	51.12 N	51.20 E
Čagan-Aman	80	47.34 N	46.43 E
Cagan-Churtej, chrebet ⋏	88	51.32 N	110.00 E
Cagarras, Ilhas ıı	287a	23.02 S	43.12 W
Cagayan □[4]	116	18.00 N	121.50 E
Cagayan ≃	116	18.22 N	121.37 E
Cagayancillo	116	9.34 N	121.12 E
Cagayan de Oro	116	8.29 N	124.39 E
Cagayan de Tawi-Tawi	116	7.01 N	118.30 E
Cagayan Island ı	116	9.36 N	121.14 E
Cagayan Islands ıı	116	9.40 N	121.16 E
Cagayan Sulu Island ı	116	7.01 N	118.30 E
Čagda	74	58.45 N	130.37 E
Cageri	84	42.39 N	42.45 E
Caggiano	68	40.34 N	15.29 E
Çağış	130	39.30 N	28.01 E
Çağlarca	130	39.05 N	39.10 E
Cagli	66	43.33 N	12.39 E
Cagliari	71	39.13 N	9.07 E
Cagliari □[4]	71	39.30 N	8.45 E
Cagliari, Golfo di c	71	39.08 N	9.11 E
Cagliari, Stagno di ⊜	71	39.13 N	9.02 E
Čaglinka ≃	86	53.59 N	69.47 E
Cagnano Varano	68	41.49 N	15.47 E
Cagnes-sur-Mer	62	43.40 N	7.09 E
Čagoda	76	59.10 N	35.17 E
Čagoda ≃	76	59.05 N	35.18 E
Čagodošča ≃	76	58.57 N	36.35 E
Čagojan	89	52.08 N	128.15 E
Čagra ≃	80	52.37 N	48.15 E
Cagraray Island ı	116	13.18 N	123.52 E
Cagua	246	10.11 N	67.27 W
Caguán ≃	246	0.08 S	74.18 W
Caguas	240m	18.14 N	66.02 W
Cagveri	84	41.48 N	43.29 E
Cagwait	116	8.55 N	126.18 E
Cahaba ≃	194	32.20 N	87.05 W
Cahabón	236	15.34 N	89.49 W
Cahabón ≃	236	15.25 N	89.36 W
Cahama	152	16.17 S	14.19 E
Caha Mountains ⋏	48	51.45 N	9.45 W
Caher	48	52.21 N	7.56 W
Caherdaniel	48	51.45 N	10.05 W
Cahersiveen	48	51.57 N	10.13 W
Cahokia	219	38.34 N	90.11 W
Cahokia Creek ≃	219	38.47 N	90.01 W
Cahokia Mounds State Park ♦	219	38.39 N	90.03 W
Cahoon Creek ≃	279a	41.29 N	81.55 W
Cahoon Park ♦	279a	41.29 N	81.56 W
Cahonzie	210	41.26 N	74.43 W
Cahore Point >	48	52.34 N	6.11 W
Cahors	32	44.27 N	1.26 E
Cahto Peak ∧	204	39.41 N	123.35 W
Cahuilla Indian Reservation ✦[4]	204	33.30 N	116.43 W
Cahuinari ≃	246	1.21 S	70.44 W
Cahuita, Punta >	236	9.45 N	82.49 W
Cahul	38	45.54 N	28.11 E
Caí ≃	252	29.56 S	51.16 W
Caia ≃	34	38.50 N	7.05 W
Caianda	152	11.02 S	23.31 E
Caiapó ≃, Bra.	250	8.52 S	49.36 W
Caiapó ≃, Bra.	255	15.49 S	51.53 W
Caiapó, Serra do ⋏	255	17.00 S	52.00 W
Caiapônia	255	16.57 S	51.49 W
Caiazzo	68	41.11 N	14.22 E
Caibarién	240p	22.31 N	79.28 W
Cai Bau, Dao ı	110	21.10 N	107.27 E
Caibiran	116	11.34 N	124.35 E
Caiçara, Bra.	250	6.36 S	35.29 W
Caiçara, Bra.	255	15.34 S	50.12 W
Caicara, Caño ≃	246	7.44 N	69.04 W
Caicara de Maturín	246	9.49 N	63.36 W
Caicara de Orinoco	246	7.37 N	66.10 W
Caicedonia	246	4.20 N	75.50 W
Caicó	250	6.27 S	37.06 W
Caicos Bank ✦[4]	238	21.35 N	71.55 W
Caicos Islands ıı	238	21.56 N	71.58 W
Caicos Passage Ʉ	238	22.00 N	72.30 W
Caieiras	256	23.22 S	46.44 W
Caieiras □[7]	287b	23.23 S	46.41 W
Caigou	100	33.16 N	114.32 E
Caiguna	162	32.17 S	125.25 E
Caihuaping	100	26.54 N	113.23 E
Caijiachang	107	29.44 N	106.29 E
Caijiagang	107	28.55 N	106.21 E
Caijialou	104	41.24 N	121.06 E
Caijiapo	102	34.17 N	107.39 E
Caijiazhuang	105	40.48 N	114.44 E
Caille	62	43.46 N	6.44 E
Cailloma	248	15.12 S	71.46 W
Caillou Bay c	194	29.06 N	90.56 W
Caima Bay c	116	13.42 N	122.48 E
Caimán, Islas — Cayman Islands □[2]	238	19.30 N	80.40 W
Caimanera	240p	19.59 N	75.09 W
Caïmanes — Cayman Islands □[2]	238	19.30 N	80.40 W
Caiman Point >	116	15.55 N	119.46 E
Caimbambo	152	12.58 S	14.01 E
Cain ≃	42	52.46 N	3.08 W
Cain Creek ≃	198	44.17 N	98.10 W
Cainde	152	15.42 S	12.05 E
Caine ≃	248	18.23 S	65.21 W
Caino	64	45.38 N	10.18 E
Cains ≃	186	46.40 N	65.47 W
Cainsdorf	54	50.41 N	12.29 E
Cainsville	194	40.28 N	93.59 W
Cainta	269f	14.35 N	121.07 E
Cai Nuoc	110	8.56 N	105.01 E
Cairano	68	40.54 N	15.22 E
Cairari	250	2.33 S	49.07 W
Caird Coast ±[2]	9	76.00 S	24.30 W
Caire, Le — Al-Qāhirah	142	30.03 N	31.15 E
Cairnbrook	214	40.07 N	78.49 W
Cairn Curran Reservoir ⊜[1]	169	37.04 S	143.59 E
Cairndow	46	56.15 N	4.56 W
Cairngorm Mountains ⋏	46	57.04 N	3.50 W
Cairn Mountain ∧	180	61.10 N	155.20 W
Cairnryan	44	54.58 N	5.02 W
Cairns	166	16.55 S	145.46 E
Cairns Lake ⊜	184	51.42 N	94.30 W
Cairnsmore of Carsphairn ∧	44	55.15 N	4.12 W
Cairnsmore of Fleet ∧	44	54.59 N	4.20 W
Cairn Table ∧	44	55.29 N	4.02 W
Cairn Water ≃	44	55.07 N	3.45 W
Cairo — Al-Qāhirah, Miṣr	142	30.03 N	31.15 E
Cairo, Ga., U.S.	192	30.52 N	84.12 W
Cairo, Il., U.S.	194	37.00 N	89.10 W
Cairo, Ne., U.S.	198	41.00 N	98.36 W
Cairo, N.Y., U.S.	210	42.17 N	73.59 W
Cairo, Oh., U.S.	216	40.49 N	84.05 W
Cairo, W.V., U.S.	188	39.12 N	81.09 W
Cairo (Almaza) Airport ✈, Miṣr	273c	30.06 N	31.22 E
Cairo (Imbābah) Airport ✈, Miṣr	273c	30.04 N	31.12 E
Cairo, University of ⊻[2]	273c	30.02 N	31.12 E
Cairoçu, Pico do ∧	256	23.18 S	44.36 W
Cairofa	152	14.05 S	12.54 E
Cairo International Airport ✈	142	30.08 N	31.24 E
Cairo Main Station ✦[5]	273c	30.04 N	31.15 E
Cairo Montenotte	62	44.24 N	8.16 E
Cairu	255	13.30 S	39.03 W
Caister-on-Sea	42	52.39 N	1.44 E
Caistor	44	53.30 N	0.20 W
Caitingqiao	105	39.54 N	117.39 E
Caitou	152	14.28 S	13.06 E
Caiundo	152	15.46 S	17.28 E
Caivano	68	40.57 N	14.18 E
Caiwan	102	25.50 N	110.50 E
Caixi	100	25.15 N	116.28 E
Caiyu	105	39.39 N	116.37 E
Caizhuang	98	34.17 N	114.08 E
Çaizi Hu ⊜	100	30.48 N	117.05 E
Čaja ≃, Ross.	86	58.08 N	82.57 E
Čaja ≃, Ross.	88	58.15 N	109.35 E
Cajabamba, Ec.	246	1.42 S	78.45 W
Cajabamba, Perú	248	7.37 S	78.03 W
Cajacay	248	10.10 S	77.26 W
Caja de Muertos, Isla ı	240m	17.54 N	66.32 W
Cajamar	256	23.21 S	46.53 W
Cajamarca	248	7.10 S	78.31 W
Cajamarca □[5]	248	6.15 S	78.50 W
Čajan	85	43.02 N	69.23 E
Čajan ≃	85	42.52 N	68.56 E
Cajapió	250	2.58 S	44.48 W
Cajarc	32	44.29 N	1.50 E
Cajari	250	3.20 S	45.01 W
Cajari ≃	250	0.48 S	51.43 W
Cajatambo	248	10.29 S	77.02 W
Čajatyn, chrebet ⋏	89	52.25 N	138.25 E
Cajàzeiras	250	6.54 S	38.34 W
Čajek	85	41.56 N	74.30 E
Čajkovskij	80	56.47 N	54.09 E
Čajniče	38	43.33 N	19.04 E
Cajones ≃	234	17.45 N	95.55 W
Cajones, Cayos ✦[2]	236	16.05 N	83.12 W
Cajon Mountain ∧	228	34.16 N	117.25 W
Cajon Pass)(	228	34.19 N	117.26 W
Cajon Summit)(	228	34.21 N	117.27 W
Caju ✦[8]	287a	22.53 S	43.13 W
Cajuru	255	21.17 S	47.18 W
Čaka	102	36.48 N	99.19 E
Čaka Yanhu ⊜	102	36.40 N	99.20 E
Čakčar, chrebet ⋏	85	38.35 N	67.28 E
Čakeri	152	17.48 S	19.27 E
Cakir	88	50.27 N	103.35 E
Çakıralan	130	41.10 N	35.47 E
Çakırgöl Dağı ∧	130	40.34 N	39.42 E
Çakırhüyük	130	37.34 N	37.50 E
Çakmak	130	37.37 N	34.19 E
Çakmak Dağı ∧	130	39.46 N	42.12 E
Čakovec	61	46.23 N	16.26 E
Čakovice ✦[8]	54	50.08 N	14.31 E
Çakung ≃	269e	6.06 S	106.56 E
Çal	130	38.05 N	29.24 E
Cala, S. Afr.	158	31.30 S	27.37 E
Cala, Tür.	84	41.05 N	43.21 E
Cala, Embalse de ⊜[1]	34	37.50 N	6.00 W
Calabacillas	234	23.13 N	99.45 W
Calabanga	116	13.42 N	123.12 E
Calabar	150	4.57 N	8.19 E
Calabasas, Arroyo ≃	280	34.12 N	118.36 W
Calabazar ✦[8]	286b	23.01 N	82.22 W
Calabazas Creek ≃	282	37.25 N	121.58 W
Calabernardo	70	36.52 N	15.08 E
Calabogie	212	45.18 N	76.43 W
Calabogie Lake ⊜	212	45.16 N	76.45 W
Calabozo	246	8.56 N	67.26 W
Calabozo, Ensenada de c	246	11.30 N	71.45 W
Calabria □[4]	68	39.00 N	16.30 E
Calabria, Parco Nazionale di ♦	68	38.09 N	15.54 E
Calabritto	68	40.47 N	15.13 E
Calabro ≃	70	37.53 N	14.11 E
Calabugdong Island ı	116	11.06 N	119.41 E
Calaca	116	13.56 N	120.49 E
Calacuccia	36	42.20 N	9.03 E
Caladang, Mount ∧	116	14.49 N	121.21 E
Caladesi Island ı	220	28.02 N	82.49 W
Caladesi Island State Park ♦	220	28.02 N	82.48 W
Cala d'Oliva	71	41.05 N	8.20 E
Calafat	38	43.59 N	22.56 E
Calafquén, Lago ⊜	254	39.31 S	72.10 W
Calagnaan Island ı	116	11.29 N	123.13 E
Cala Gonone	71	40.18 N	9.38 E
Calagua Islands ıı	116	14.27 N	122.55 E
Calahorra	34	42.18 N	1.58 W
Calais, Fr.	50	50.57 N	1.50 E
Calais, Me., U.S.	188	45.11 N	67.16 W
Calais, Canal de ≡	50	50.57 N	1.51 E
Calais, Pas de (Strait of Dover) Ʉ	50	51.00 N	1.30 E
Calala	152	12.59 S	23.30 E
Calalaste, Sierra de ⋏	252	25.30 S	67.30 W
Calalzo di Cadore	64	46.27 N	12.23 E
Calama	252	22.28 S	68.56 W
Calamar, Col.	246	10.15 N	74.55 W
Calamar, Col.	246	1.58 N	72.41 W
Calamarca	248	16.55 S	68.09 W
Calamba, Pil.	116	14.13 N	121.10 E
Calamba, Pil.	116	8.35 N	123.39 E
Calamian Group ıı	116	12.00 N	120.00 E
Calamity Creek ≃	226	29.41 N	103.42 W
Calamocha	34	40.55 N	1.18 W
Calamonaci	70	37.31 N	13.17 E
Calamus ≃	198	41.48 N	99.09 W
Calañas	34	37.39 N	6.53 W
Calanca, Val V	58	46.22 N	9.07 E
Calanda	34	40.56 N	0.14 W
Calandagan Island ı	116	10.39 N	120.15 E
Calang	114	4.38 N	95.34 E
Calangianus	71	40.55 N	9.11 E
Calanna	68	38.11 N	15.43 E
Calapan	116	13.25 N	121.10 E
Calape	116	9.54 N	123.52 E
Calapooia ≃	202	44.38 N	123.08 W
Calapooya Mountains ⋏	202	43.30 N	122.50 W
Călăraşi, Mol.	38	47.16 N	28.19 E
Călăraşi, Rom.	38	44.11 N	27.20 E
Călăraşi □[6]	38	44.20 N	27.10 E
Calarcá	246	4.31 N	75.38 W
Calascibetta	70	37.35 N	14.16 E
Calasetta	71	39.07 N	8.22 E
Calatabiano	70	37.49 N	15.14 E
Calatafimi	70	37.55 N	12.52 E
Calatagan	116	13.50 N	120.38 E
Calatayud	34	41.21 N	1.38 W
Calau	54	51.45 N	13.56 E
Calauag Bay c	116	14.02 N	122.13 E
Calavà, Capo >	70	38.11 N	14.55 E
Calaveras □[6]	226	38.12 N	120.41 W
Calaveras ≃	226	37.58 N	121.22 W
Calaveras, North Fork ≃	226	38.12 N	120.43 W
Calaveras Big Trees State Park ♦	226	38.16 N	120.19 W
Calaveras Point >	282	37.28 N	122.03 W
Calaveras Reservoir ⊜[1]	226	37.28 N	121.49 W
Calaveritas Creek ≃	226	38.10 N	120.40 W
Calavino	64	46.03 N	10.59 E
Calavite, Cape >	116	13.27 N	120.18 E
Calavite, Mount ∧	116	13.29 N	120.24 E
Calavite Passage Ʉ	116	13.26 N	120.25 E
Calavon ≃	62	43.52 N	5.35 E
Calawah ≃	224	47.56 N	124.27 W
Calawah, North Fork ≃	224	47.58 N	124.20 W
Calawah, South Fork ≃	224	47.58 N	124.23 W
Calayan	116	19.16 N	121.28 E
Calayan Island ı	116	19.20 N	121.27 E
Calba	89	52.43 N	131.27 E
Calbayog	116	12.04 N	124.36 E
Calbe	54	51.54 N	11.46 E
Calbiga	116	11.38 N	125.01 E
Calbuco	254	41.46 S	73.08 W
Calca	248	13.20 S	71.57 W
Calçado ≃	256	22.05 S	43.04 W
Calcasieu ≃	194	30.05 N	93.20 W
Calcasieu Lake ⊜	194	29.50 N	93.17 W
Calceta	246	0.51 S	80.10 W
Calcha	248	21.06 S	67.31 W
Calchaquí	252	29.54 S	60.18 W
Calchaquí ≃	252	26.03 S	65.50 W
Calciano	68	40.35 N	16.11 E
Calcinaia	66	43.41 N	10.37 E
Calcinato	62	45.27 N	10.24 E
Calcio	62	45.30 N	9.50 E
Calcium	212	44.01 N	75.51 W
Calçoene	250	2.30 N	50.57 W
Calçoene ≃	250	2.30 N	50.50 W
Calcutta, India	126	22.32 N	88.22 E
Calcutta, India	272b	22.32 N	88.22 E
Calcutta, Oh., U.S.	214	40.40 N	80.34 W
Calcutta University ⊻[2]	272b	22.35 N	88.22 E
Caldaro (Kaltern)	64	46.25 N	11.14 E
Caldarola	66	43.08 N	13.13 E
Caldas, Bra.	256	21.56 S	46.23 W
Caldas, Col.	246	6.05 N	75.38 W
Caldas □[5]	246	5.15 N	75.30 W
Caldas da Rainha	34	39.24 N	9.08 W
Caldas de Reyes	34	42.36 N	8.38 W
Caldas Novas	255	17.45 S	48.38 W
Caldè	58	45.57 N	8.38 E
Caldecott Tunnel ✦[8]	282	37.52 N	122.12 W
Calder ≃, Eng., U.K.	44	53.44 N	1.21 W
Calder ≃, Eng., U.K.	262	53.49 N	2.24 W
Calder, Loch ⊜	46	58.31 N	3.36 W
Caldera	252	27.04 S	70.50 W
Caldera de Taburiente, Parque Nacional de la ♦	148	28.48 N	17.52 W
Calder and Hebble Navigation Canal ≡	262	53.43 N	1.54 W
Calder Bridge	44	54.27 N	3.29 W
Calderbrook	262	53.39 N	2.05 W
Calderdale □[8]	262	53.44 N	2.00 W
Calderstones Park ♦	262	53.23 N	2.54 W
Caldes	64	46.22 N	10.56 E
Caldes ≃	266d	41.31 N	2.13 E
Caldew ≃	44	54.54 N	2.56 W
Caldey Island ı	42	51.38 N	4.41 W
Caldicot	42	51.36 N	2.45 W
Caldiero	64	45.22 N	11.11 E
Caldiran	84	39.09 N	43.55 E
Caldonazzo	64	45.59 N	11.16 E
Caldonazzo, Lago di ⊜	64	46.01 N	11.15 E
Čaldonka	88	53.47 N	119.12 E
Caldwell, Id., U.S.	202	43.39 N	116.41 W
Caldwell, Ks., U.S.	198	37.01 N	97.36 W
Caldwell, N.J., U.S.	276	40.51 N	74.17 W
Caldwell, Oh., U.S.	188	39.44 N	81.31 W
Caldwell, Tx., U.S.	222	30.31 N	96.41 W
Caldwell □[6]	222	29.50 N	97.40 W
Caldwell Creek ≃	214	41.37 N	79.37 W
Caldwell-Wright Airport ✈	276	40.53 N	74.17 W
Caldy	262	53.21 N	3.10 W
Cale ≃	42	50.59 N	2.20 W
Caledon, On., Can.	212	43.52 N	80.00 W
Caledon, S. Afr.	158	34.12 S	19.23 E
Caledon (Mohokare) ≃	158	30.31 S	26.05 E
Caledon East	212	43.52 N	79.52 W
Caledonia, Belize	232	18.14 N	88.29 W
Caledonia, N.S., Can.	186	44.22 N	65.02 W
Caledonia, On., Can.	212	43.04 N	79.56 W
Caledonia, Il., U.S.	216	42.22 N	88.53 W
Caledonia, Mi., U.S.	216	42.47 N	85.31 W
Caledonia, Mn., U.S.	190	43.38 N	91.29 W
Caledonia, Ms., U.S.	194	33.40 N	88.19 W
Caledonia, N.Y., U.S.	210	42.58 N	77.51 W
Caledonia, Oh., U.S.	214	40.38 N	82.58 W
Caledonia, Pa., U.S.	214	41.17 N	78.27 W
Caledonian Canal ≡	46	56.50 N	5.06 W
Caledonia State Park ♦	208	39.56 N	77.29 W
Calego	152	12.10 S	23.36 E
Calella	34	41.37 N	2.40 E
Calemba	152	16.05 S	15.44 E
Calen	166	20.54 S	148.46 E
Calendžicha	84	42.37 N	42.04 E
Calenzano	66	43.51 N	11.09 E
Calera, Al., U.S.	194	33.06 N	86.45 W
Calera, Ok., U.S.	196	33.56 N	96.25 W
Calera Creek ≃	282	37.27 N	121.54 W
Caleta, Punta >	240p	20.04 N	74.18 W
Caleta Olivia	254	46.26 S	67.32 W
Caleufú	252	35.35 S	64.33 W
Calexico	204	32.40 N	115.29 W
Calf Island ı	283	42.20 N	70.54 W
Calf Islands ıı	276	40.59 N	73.38 W
Calfkiller ≃	194	35.49 N	85.29 W
Calf of Man ı	44	54.03 N	4.48 W
Calfpasture ≃	188	37.58 N	79.28 W
Calf Pasture Point >	276	41.05 N	73.24 W
Calgary	182	51.03 N	114.05 W
Calhan	198	39.02 N	104.17 W
Calharis ✦[8]	266c	38.44 N	9.12 W
Calhoun, Al., U.S.	194	32.03 N	86.32 W
Calhoun, Ga., U.S.	192	34.30 N	84.57 W
Calhoun, Ky., U.S.	194	37.32 N	87.15 W
Calhoun, Mo., U.S.	194	38.28 N	93.37 W
Calhoun, Tn., U.S.	192	35.17 N	84.44 W
Calhoun □[6], Il., U.S.	219	39.09 N	90.37 W
Calhoun □[6], Mi., U.S.	216	42.14 N	85.00 W
Calhoun City	194	33.51 N	89.18 W
Calhoun Falls	192	34.05 N	82.35 W
Cali, Col.	246	3.27 N	76.31 W
Çalı, Tür.	130	40.10 N	28.54 E
Calian Point >	116	6.07 N	125.42 E
Calicoan Island ı	116	10.59 N	125.48 E
Calico Ghost Town ±	228	34.57 N	116.52 W
Calico Rock	194	36.07 N	92.08 W
Calicut	122	11.15 N	75.46 E
Caliente, Ca., U.S.	228	35.17 N	118.37 W
Caliente, Nv., U.S.	204	37.36 N	114.30 W
Caliente Creek ≃	228	35.17 N	118.48 W
Califon	210	40.43 N	74.50 W
California, Mo., U.S.	194	38.37 N	92.33 W
California, Pa., U.S.	214	40.03 N	79.53 W
California □[3], U.S.	178	37.30 N	119.30 W
California □[3], U.S.	204	37.30 N	119.30 W
California, Golfo de c	232	28.00 N	112.00 W
California, University of ⊻[2]	282	37.52 N	122.15 W
California Aqueduct ≡[1]	204	33.52 N	117.12 W
California City	228	35.08 N	117.58 W
California Creek ≃	226	33.05 N	99.33 W
California Institute of Technology ⊻[2]	280	34.08 N	118.08 W
California Institution for Men ⊻	280	33.59 N	117.40 W
California Institution for Women ⊻	280	33.57 N	117.38 W
California-Los Angeles, University of (U.C.L.A.) ⊻[2]	280	34.04 N	118.26 W
California State Polytechnic University ⊻[2]	280	34.04 N	117.49 W
California State University (Northridge) ⊻[2], Ca., U.S.	280	34.14 N	118.32 W
California State University (Los Angeles) ⊻[2], Ca., U.S.	280	34.04 N	118.10 W
California State University (Fullerton) ⊻[2], Ca., U.S.	280	33.53 N	117.53 W
California State University (Long Beach) ⊻[2], Ca., U.S.	280	33.47 N	118.06 W
California State University (Dominguez Hills) ⊻[2], Ca., U.S.	280	33.52 N	118.17 W
California State University (Hayward) ⊻[2], Ca., U.S.	282	37.39 N	122.04 W
Calihualá	234	17.35 N	98.10 W
Cälilabad	84	39.14 N	48.31 E
Calilegua	252	23.47 S	64.47 W
Calilegua, Parque Nacional ♦	252	23.40 S	64.50 W
Călimăneşti	38	45.14 N	24.20 E
Călimani, Munţii ⋏	38	47.07 N	25.03 E
Calimera	68	40.15 N	18.17 E
Calimere, Point >	122	10.18 N	79.52 E
Calimesa	228	34.00 N	117.03 W
Calindó ≃	255	14.26 S	43.51 W
Calingasta	252	31.19 S	69.25 W
Calingiri	162	31.06 S	116.27 E
Calinog	116	11.07 N	122.32 E
Calintaan	116	12.35 N	120.56 E
Calion	194	33.19 N	92.32 W
Calipatria	204	33.07 N	115.30 W
Calispell Peak ∧	202	48.26 N	117.30 W
Calistoga	226	38.34 N	122.34 W
Calitri	68	40.54 N	15.27 E
Calitzdorp	158	33.33 S	21.42 E
Calizzano	62	44.14 N	8.07 E
Calka	84	41.37 N	44.05 E
Calkinskoje vodochranilišče ⊜[1]	84	41.38 N	44.03 E
Čalkojdy	85	40.44 N	73.39 E
Calla	226	37.46 N	121.11 W
Callabonna, Lake ⊜	166	29.45 S	140.04 E
Callabonna Creek ≃	166	29.38 S	140.08 E
Callac	32	48.24 N	3.26 W
Callaghan, Mount ∧	204	39.42 N	116.57 W
Callahan	192	30.33 N	81.49 W
Callahan, Mount ∧	200	39.26 N	108.07 W
Callahans	276	40.58 N	74.37 W
Callan	48	52.33 N	7.23 W
Callander, On., Can.	190	46.13 N	79.23 W
Callander, Scot., U.K.	46	56.15 N	4.14 W
Callang	116	17.02 N	121.38 E
Callanish	46	58.12 N	6.43 W
Callanmarca	248	12.52 S	74.38 W
Callanna	166	29.38 S	137.55 E
Callantsoog	52	52.49 N	4.41 E
Callao, Perú	248	12.04 S	77.09 W
Callao, Va., U.S.	208	37.58 N	76.33 W
Callao □[4]	286d	12.04 S	77.09 W
Callaquén, Volcán ∧[1]	252	37.54 S	71.26 W
Callas	62	43.35 N	6.32 E
Callaway	198	41.17 N	99.55 W
Callaway □[6]	219	38.50 N	91.52 W
Callaway Gardens ♦	192	32.51 N	84.52 W
Calle	56	51.20 N	8.13 E
Callensburg	214	41.08 N	79.33 W
Callery	214	40.45 N	80.02 W
Call Hill ∧[2]	210	42.13 N	77.40 W
Calliano, It.	62	45.00 N	8.15 E
Calliano, It.	64	45.56 N	11.05 E
Calliaqua	241h	13.08 N	61.12 W
Callicoon	210	41.46 N	75.03 W
Callicoon Center	210	41.50 N	74.57 W
Calliham	196	28.29 N	98.21 W
Calling Lake	182	55.15 N	113.15 W
Calling Lake ⊜	182	55.13 N	113.15 W
Callington, Austl.	168b	35.07 S	139.02 E
Callington, Eng., U.K.	42	50.30 N	4.18 W
Calliope	166	24.00 S	151.12 E
Callosa d'En Sarrià	34	38.39 N	0.07 W
Callosa de Segura	34	38.08 N	0.52 W
Calloway Canal ≡	226	35.24 N	119.01 W
Calmar, Ab., Can.	182	53.16 N	113.49 W
Calmar — Kalmar, Sve.	26	56.40 N	16.22 E
Calmar, Ia., U.S.	190	43.11 N	91.51 W
Călmăţui ≃	38	44.50 N	27.50 E
Calmazzo	66	43.40 N	12.46 E
Calmbach	56	48.46 N	8.35 E
Calm Lake ⊜	190	48.46 N	92.04 W
Čal'mny-Varre	24	67.10 N	37.33 E
Čalna	24	61.55 N	34.01 E
Calnali	234	20.55 N	98.35 W
Calne	42	51.27 N	2.00 W
Calobre	236	8.19 N	80.51 W
Calola	152	16.30 S	17.51 E
Calolbon	116	13.36 N	124.06 E
Calólo	152	10.00 S	14.53 E
Calolziocorte	62	45.48 N	9.26 E
Calonne-Ricouart	50	50.29 N	2.29 E
Caloocan	116	14.39 N	120.58 E
Caloosahatchee ≃	220	26.31 N	82.01 W
Caloosahatchee Canal ≡	220	26.46 N	81.27 W
Caloote	168b	34.58 S	139.16 E
Calore ≃, It.	68	41.11 N	14.28 E
Calore ≃, It.	68	40.31 N	15.01 E
Caloundra	166	26.48 S	153.09 E
Calouste-Gulbenkian, Museu de ⊻	266c	38.44 N	9.08 W
Caloveto	68	39.30 N	16.45 E
Calp	34	38.39 N	0.03 E
Calpulalpan	234	19.35 N	98.35 W
Čalpy	80	55.05 N	53.06 E
Calshot	42	50.49 N	1.19 W
Calstock	42	50.30 N	4.12 W
Caltabellotta	70	37.34 N	13.13 E
Caltagirone	70	37.14 N	14.31 E
Caltagirone ≃	70	37.21 N	14.42 E
Caltanissetta	70	37.29 N	14.04 E
Caltanissetta □[4]	70	37.29 N	14.04 E
Caltavuturo	70	37.49 N	13.53 E
Çaltıbük	130	39.57 N	28.36 E
Caltra	48	53.26 N	8.25 W
Čaltyr'	83	47.17 N	39.30 E
Caluango	152	8.21 S	19.40 E
Calubian	116	11.27 N	124.26 E
Calucinga	152	11.18 S	16.12 E
Călugăreni	38	44.07 N	26.01 E
Caluire-et-Cuire	62	45.48 N	4.51 E
Calumbolaca	152	11.41 S	14.40 E
Calumet, Mi., U.S.	190	47.14 N	88.27 W
Calumet, Mn., U.S.	190	47.19 N	93.16 W
Calumet, Pa., U.S.	214	40.13 N	79.28 W
Calumet □[6]	190	44.05 N	88.15 W
Calumet ≃	278	41.44 N	87.32 W
Calumet, Lake ⊜	278	41.41 N	87.35 W
Calumet City	278	41.36 N	87.31 W
Calumet Harbor c	278	41.44 N	87.32 W
Calumet Park	278	41.39 N	87.39 W
Calumet Park ♦	278	41.43 N	87.32 W
Calumet Sag Channel ≡	278	41.42 N	87.57 W
Calumpit	116	14.55 N	120.46 E
Calunda	152	12.06 S	23.23 E
Caluquembe	152	13.47 S	14.44 E
Calusa Island ı	116	9.37 N	121.01 E
Caluso	62	45.18 N	7.53 E
Caluula	144	11.58 N	50.45 E
Caluula, Raasiga >	144	11.58 N	50.47 E
Calvados □[5]	32	49.10 N	0.30 W
Calvello	68	40.28 N	15.51 E
Calver	44	53.16 N	1.38 W
Calvera	68	40.09 N	16.09 E
Calvert, Al., U.S.	194	31.09 N	88.01 W
Calvert, Tx., U.S.	222	30.58 N	96.40 W
Calvert □[6]	208	38.30 N	76.35 W
Calvert ≃	164	16.17 S	137.44 E
Calvert, Lough ⊜	169	38.11 S	143.42 E
Calvert City	194	37.02 N	88.21 W
Calvert Hills	166	17.15 S	137.20 E
Calvert Island ı	182	51.35 N	128.00 W
Calverton, Eng., U.K.	44	53.02 N	1.05 W
Calverton, Md., U.S.	284c	39.03 N	76.56 W
Calverton, N.Y., U.S.	207	40.55 N	72.45 W
Calvi	36	42.34 N	8.45 E
Calvi, Monte ∧	66	43.05 N	10.37 E
Calvia	34	39.34 N	2.31 E
Calvi dell'Umbria	66	42.24 N	12.34 E
Calvillo	234	21.51 N	102.43 W
Calvin, Ok., U.S.	196	34.58 N	96.14 W
Calvin, Pa., U.S.	214	40.20 N	78.02 W
Calvinia	158	31.25 S	19.45 E
Calvisano	64	45.20 N	10.20 E
Calvo, Monte ∧	68	41.44 N	15.46 E
Calvörde	54	52.23 N	11.17 E
Calw	56	48.43 N	8.44 E
Calwa	226	36.42 N	119.45 W
Calypso	192	35.09 N	78.06 W
Calzada	248	6.02 S	77.02 W
Cam ≃	42	52.21 N	0.15 E
Camabatela	152	8.11 S	15.22 E
Camaçã ≃	248	6.35 S	66.27 W
Camaçari	255	12.41 S	38.18 W
Camachigama, Lac ⊜	190	47.50 N	76.19 W
Camacupa	152	12.03 S	17.30 E
Camaguán	246	8.06 N	67.36 W
Camagüey	240p	21.23 N	77.55 W
Camagüey □[4]	240p	21.30 N	78.00 W
Camagüey, Archipiélago de ıı	240p	22.30 N	78.10 W
Camaiore	64	43.56 N	10.18 E
Camaiú ≃	248	5.30 S	59.42 W
Camajuaní	240p	22.28 N	79.44 W
Camaldoli, Eremo di ⊻[1]	66	43.46 N	11.47 E
Camamu	255	13.57 S	39.07 W
Camaná	248	16.37 S	72.42 W
Camaná ≃	248	16.39 S	72.46 W
Camanaú ≃	246	1.51 S	61.14 W
Camanche	190	41.47 N	90.15 W
Camanche Reservoir ⊜[1]	226	38.13 N	120.58 W
Camandag Island ı	116	11.59 N	124.25 E
Camanducaia	256	22.46 S	46.09 W
Camanducaia ≃, Bra.	256	22.39 S	46.58 W
Camanducaia ≃, Bra.	256	22.55 S	46.25 W
Camano Island ı	224	48.10 N	122.30 W
Camaoi ≃	250	3.12 S	48.04 W
Camapuã	255	19.30 S	54.05 W
Camaquã	252	30.51 S	51.49 W
Camaquã ≃	252	31.17 S	51.47 W
Camará	246	3.55 S	62.44 W
Camarajibe	250	8.01 S	34.58 W
Camararé ≃	248	12.15 S	58.55 W
Camarat, Cap >	62	43.12 N	6.41 E
Camarda	66	42.23 N	13.29 E
Çamardı	130	37.50 N	35.00 E
Camarès	32	43.49 N	2.53 E
Camargo, Bol.	248	20.39 S	65.13 W
Camargo, Méx.	232	27.40 N	105.10 W
Camargos, Represa de ⊜[1]	256	21.25 S	44.30 W
Camargue ✦[1]	62	43.34 N	4.34 E
Camargue, Parc Naturel Regional de ♦	62	43.30 N	4.28 E
Camarillo	228	34.12 N	119.02 W
Camarillo Heights	228	34.14 N	119.02 W
Camarina ±	70	36.52 N	14.27 E
Camariñas	34	43.07 N	9.10 W
Camarines Norte □[4]	116	14.10 N	122.40 E
Camarines Sur □[4]	116	13.35 N	123.20 E
Camarón, Arroyo ≃	196	27.08 N	100.00 W
Camarón, Cabo >	236	16.00 N	85.05 W
Camarones	254	44.48 S	65.42 W
Camarones, Bahía c	254	44.45 S	65.34 W
Camas, Esp.	34	37.24 N	6.02 W
Çamaş, Tür.	130	40.55 N	37.32 E
Camas, Wa., U.S.	224	45.35 N	122.23 W
Camas Creek ≃, Id., U.S.	202	44.53 N	114.44 W
Camas Creek ≃, Id., U.S.	202	43.53 N	112.21 W
Camas Creek ≃, Id., U.S.	202	43.20 N	114.24 W
Camas Creek ≃, Or., U.S.	202	45.01 N	118.59 W
Camastra	70	37.15 N	13.47 E
Camatagua, Embalse de ⊜[1]	246	9.50 N	67.00 W
Camatambo	152	6.30 S	15.18 E
Ca Mau	110	9.11 N	105.08 E
Ca Mau, Mui >	110	8.38 N	104.44 E
Camaxilo	152	8.21 S	18.56 E
Camba	112	4.54 S	119.50 E
Camba Cassai	152	9.40 S	19.18 E
Cambados	34	42.30 N	8.48 W
Cambará	255	23.03 S	50.05 W
Čambarak	84	40.36 N	45.21 E
Camberley	42	51.21 N	0.45 W
Camberwell	169	37.50 S	145.04 E
Camberwell ✦[8]	260	51.28 N	0.05 W
Cambiano	62	44.58 N	7.47 E
Cambo	44	55.10 N	1.57 W
Cambo ≃	152	7.40 S	17.17 E
Cambodia (Kâmpŭchéa) □[1], Asia	108	13.00 N	105.00 E
Cambodia (Kâmpŭchéa) □[1], Asia	110	13.00 N	105.00 E
Cambois	44	55.10 N	1.31 W
Cambonda, Serra ⋏	152	12.06 S	14.00 E
Camboon	166	25.03 S	150.26 E
Cambooya	171a	27.42 S	151.52 E
Camboriú	252	27.01 S	48.38 W
Camborne	42	50.12 N	5.19 W
Cambra	210	41.11 N	76.18 W
Cambrai, Austl.	168b	34.39 S	139.17 E
Cambrai, Fr.	50	50.10 N	3.14 E
Cambremer	50	49.09 N	0.03 E
Cambria, Ca., U.S.	226	35.33 N	121.04 W
Cambria, In., U.S.	216	40.22 N	86.33 W
Cambria, Mi., U.S.	216	41.49 N	84.39 W
Cambria, Wi., U.S.	190	43.32 N	89.06 W
Cambria □[6]	214	40.25 N	78.40 W
Cambria Ice Field ⊜	182	55.55 N	129.30 W
Cambrian Mountains ⋏	28	52.35 N	3.35 W
Cambrian Park	282	37.15 N	121.55 W
Cambridge (Galt), On., Can.	212	43.22 N	80.19 W
Cambridge, N.Z.	172	37.53 S	175.28 E
Cambridge, Eng., U.K.	42	52.13 N	0.08 E
Cambridge, Id., U.S.	202	44.34 N	116.41 W
Cambridge, Il., U.S.	190	41.18 N	90.11 W
Cambridge, Ia., U.S.	190	41.53 N	93.31 W
Cambridge, Md., U.S.	208	38.33 N	76.04 W
Cambridge, Ma., U.S.	207	42.22 N	71.06 W
Cambridge, Mn., U.S.	190	45.34 N	93.13 W
Cambridge, Ne., U.S.	198	40.16 N	100.09 W
Cambridge, N.Y., U.S.	210	43.01 N	73.22 W
Cambridge, Oh., U.S.	188	40.02 N	81.35 W
Cambridge, Wi., U.S.	216	43.00 N	89.01 W
Cambridge Bay	176	69.03 N	105.05 W
Cambridge City	218	39.48 N	85.10 W
Cambridge Fiord c[2]	176	71.20 N	74.44 W
Cambridge Gulf c	164	14.55 S	128.15 E
Cambridge Park	274a	33.45 S	150.43 E
Cambridge Reservoir ⊜[1]	283	42.24 N	71.16 W
Cambridgeshire □[6]	42	52.20 N	0.05 E
Cambridge Springs	214	41.48 N	80.03 W
Cambrils	34	41.04 N	1.03 E
Cambriú, Ponta de >	252	25.10 S	47.55 W
Cambuci ✦[8]	287b	23.34 S	46.37 W
Cambuí	256	22.37 S	46.04 W
Cambulo	152	7.48 S	21.14 E
Cambundi-Catembo	152	10.09 S	17.31 E
Cambuquira	256	21.51 S	45.18 W
Cambural	286c	10.26 N	66.59 W
Camburg	54	51.03 N	11.42 E
Camburú ≃	256	23.41 S	45.28 W
Çamby	218	39.40 N	86.19 W
Čamčakly	128	37.56 N	63.06 E
Camden, Austl.	170	34.03 S	150.42 E
Camden, S. Afr.	158	26.38 S	30.07 E
Camden, Al., U.S.	194	31.59 N	87.17 W
Camden, Ar., U.S.	194	33.35 N	92.50 W
Camden, De., U.S.	208	39.06 N	75.32 W
Camden, Il., U.S.	219	40.09 N	90.46 W
Camden, In., U.S.	216	40.36 N	86.32 W
Camden, Me., U.S.	188	44.12 N	69.03 W
Camden, Mi., U.S.	216	41.45 N	84.45 W
Camden, Ms., U.S.	194	32.46 N	89.50 W
Camden, N.J., U.S.	208	39.55 N	75.07 W
Camden, N.Y., U.S.	210	43.20 N	75.44 W
Camden, N.C., U.S.	192	36.19 N	76.10 W
Camden, Oh., U.S.	218	39.37 N	84.38 W
Camden, S.C., U.S.	192	34.14 N	80.36 W
Camden, Tn., U.S.	194	36.03 N	88.05 W
Camden, Tx., U.S.	222	30.55 N	94.44 W
Camden □[6], N.J., U.S.	208	39.57 N	75.07 W
Camden □[6], N.C., U.S.	208	36.28 N	76.21 W
Camden ✦[8]	260	51.33 N	0.10 W
Camden, Grupo ıı	254	54.40 S	71.58 W
Camden Aerodrome ✈	274a	34.03 S	150.41 E
Camden Bay c	180	70.00 N	145.00 W
Camden Hills State Park ♦	188	44.17 N	69.05 W
Camden Lake ⊜	212	44.25 N	76.52 W
Camden Station ✦[5]	284b	39.17 N	76.37 W
Camdenton	194	38.00 N	92.44 W
Camedo	58	46.09 N	8.37 E
Cameia, Parque Nacional da ♦	152	11.45 S	21.20 E
Camel ≃	42	50.33 N	4.55 W
Camel, Mount ∧[2]	169	36.45 S	144.43 E
Camelback Mountain ∧, Ak., U.S.	180	62.33 N	157.20 W
Camelback Mountain ∧, Pa., U.S.	210	41.03 N	75.21 W
Camelford	42	50.37 N	4.41 W
Çameli	130	37.05 N	29.20 E
Camels Hump ∧	188	44.19 N	72.53 W
Camenca	38	48.03 N	28.42 E
Cameo Acres	282	37.51 N	121.58 W
Camerano	66	43.32 N	13.33 E
Cameri	62	45.30 N	8.39 E
Cameri, Aeroporto di ✈	266b	45.32 N	8.40 E
Camerino	66	43.08 N	13.04 E
Cameron, Ca., U.S.	226	38.39 N	120.56 W
Cameron, La., U.S.	194	29.47 N	93.19 W
Cameron, Mo., U.S.	194	39.44 N	94.14 W
Cameron, N.Y., U.S.	210	42.12 N	77.24 W
Cameron, Pa., U.S.	214	41.27 N	78.10 W
Cameron, S.C., U.S.	192	33.33 N	80.42 W
Cameron, Tx., U.S.	222	30.51 N	96.58 W
Cameron, W.V., U.S.	188	39.49 N	80.34 W
Cameron, Wi., U.S.	190	45.24 N	91.44 W
Cameron □[6]	214	41.31 N	78.14 W
Cameron ≃	224	49.17 N	124.38 W
Cameron, Lac ⊜	206	46.06 N	74.50 W
Cameron Highlands	114	4.29 N	101.27 E
Cameron Hills ⋏[2]	176	59.48 N	118.00 W
Cameron Lake ⊜, B.C., Can.	224	49.17 N	124.37 W
Cameron Lake ⊜, On., Can.	212	44.34 N	78.45 W
Cameron Mills	210	42.11 N	77.22 W
Cameron Mountains ⋏	172	46.00 S	167.00 E
Cameron Run ≃	284c	38.48 N	77.04 W
Cameroon (Cameroun) □[1]	134	6.00 N	12.00 E
Cameroon Mountain ∧	152	4.12 N	9.11 E
Camerota	68	40.02 N	15.23 E
Cameroun — Cameroon □[1]	134	6.00 N	12.00 E
Camerún — Cameroon □[1]	134	6.00 N	12.00 E
Cametá	250	2.15 S	49.30 W
Camfield	164	17.09 S	131.21 E
Çamiçi Gölü ⊜	130	37.30 N	27.25 E
Camiguin □[4]	116	9.15 N	124.40 E
Camiguin Island ı, Pil.	116	18.56 N	121.55 E
Camiguin Island ı, Pil.	116	9.11 N	124.42 E
Camiling	116	15.42 N	120.24 E
Camilla	192	31.13 N	84.12 W
Camillus	210	43.02 N	76.19 W
Camin	54	53.27 N	10.58 E
Camiña	248	19.18 S	69.26 W
Caminha	34	41.52 N	8.50 W
Camino	226	38.44 N	120.40 W
Camiranga	250	1.48 S	46.17 W
Camiri	248	20.03 S	63.31 W
Camisano Vicentino	64	45.31 N	11.43 E
Camisea ≃	248	11.35 S	72.58 W
Camissombo	152	8.10 S	20.39 E
Camlad ≃	42	52.36 N	3.10 W
Çamlibel	130	40.05 N	36.29 E
Çamlıdere, Tür.	130	37.08 N	29.03 E
Çamlıdere, Tür.	130	40.30 N	32.29 E
Çamlıyayla	130	37.09 N	34.36 E
Çam Lo	110	16.49 N	106.59 E
Čamlyk ≃	84	44.45 N	40.45 E
Cammal	210	41.24 N	77.28 W
Cammarata	70	37.38 N	13.38 E
Cammarta, Monte ∧	70	37.37 N	13.36 E
Camoapa	236	12.23 N	85.31 W
Camocim	250	2.54 S	40.50 W
Camogli	62	44.21 N	9.09 E
Çamoluk	130	40.08 N	38.45 E
Čamonica, Val V	64	46.00 N	10.20 E
Camooweal	166	19.55 S	138.07 E
Camopi ≃	250	3.11 N	52.20 W
Camorim ≃	287a	22.59 S	43.25 W
Camorim, Reprêsa do ⊜[1]	287a	22.58 S	43.27 W
Camorta Island ı	110	8.08 N	93.30 E
Camote, Cerro ∧	286d	11.57 S	77.06 W
Camotes Islands ıı	116	10.40 N	124.24 E
Camotes Sea ≂[2]	116	10.30 N	124.15 E
Camotlán ≃	234	22.01 N	104.15 W
Camowen ≃	48	54.36 N	7.18 W
Camp □[6]	222	33.00 N	94.58 W
Campagna	68	40.40 N	15.08 E
Campagna di Roma ✦[1]	66	41.50 N	12.35 E
Campagna Lupia	64	45.21 N	12.06 E
Campagnano di Roma	66	42.08 N	12.23 E
Campagnatico	66	42.53 N	11.16 E
Campagne-lès-Hesdin	50	50.24 N	1.52 E
Campaign	194	35.46 N	85.37 W
Campamento	236	14.33 N	86.42 W
Campana, Arg.	258	34.10 S	58.57 W
Campana, It.	68	39.24 N	16.50 E
Campana, Isla ı	254	48.20 S	75.15 W
Campanario	34	38.52 N	5.37 W
Campanario, Cerro de ∧	248	5.57 S	77.31 W
Campanella, Punta >	68	40.34 N	14.19 E
Campanero, Cerro ∧	246	5.54 N	65.12 W
Campanha	256	21.50 S	45.24 W
Campania □[4]	68	40.55 N	14.50 E
Campania Island ı	182	53.05 N	129.30 W
Camparada	266b	45.39 N	9.19 E
Campaspe ≃, Austl.	166	21.00 S	146.24 E
Campaspe ≃, Austl.	169	36.41 S	144.31 E
Campbell, S. Afr.	158	28.48 S	23.44 E
Campbell, Ca., U.S.	226	37.17 N	121.56 W
Campbell, Mn., U.S.	198	46.05 N	96.24 W
Campbell, Mo., U.S.	194	36.29 N	90.04 W
Campbell, Ne., U.S.	198	40.18 N	98.44 W
Campbell, N.Y., U.S.	210	42.13 N	77.11 W
Campbell, Oh., U.S.	214	41.04 N	80.35 W
Campbell, Tx., U.S.	222	33.09 N	95.57 W
Campbell □[6]	218	38.55 N	84.20 W
Campbell, Cape >	172	41.44 S	174.17 E
Campbell Airport ✈	279b	40.21 N	80.11 W
Campbellfield	274b	37.41 S	144.57 E
Campbellford	212	44.18 N	77.48 W
Campbell Hall	210	41.27 N	74.16 W
Campbell Hill ∧[2]	216	40.22 N	83.43 W
Campbell Island	182	52.10 N	128.09 W
Campbell Island ı	9	52.30 S	169.05 E
Campbell Lake ⊜	182	50.01 N	125.27 W
Campbell Plateau ✦[3]	9	51.00 S	170.00 E
Campbell Point >	171a	27.22 S	153.55 E
Campbellpore	123	33.46 N	72.22 E

(German column headings: Name, Seite, Breite°′, Länge°′ E = Ost)

Symbols in the index entries represent the broad categories identified in the key at the right. Symbols with superior numbers (∧[1]) identify subcategories (see complete key on page I · 1).

Symbole im Register stellen die rechts im Schlüssel erklärten Kategorien dar. Symbole mit hochgestellten Ziffern (∧[1]) bezeichnen Unterabteilungen einer Kategorie (vgl. vollständiger Schlüssel auf Seite I · 1).

Los símbolos incluídos en el texto del índice representan las grandes categorías identificadas con la clave a la derecha. Los símbolos con numeros en su parte superior (∧[1]) identifican las subcategorías (véase la clave completa en la página I · 1).

Les symboles de l'index représentent les catégories indiquées dans la légende à droite. Les symboles suivis d'un indice (∧[1]) représentent des sous-catégories (voir légende complète à la page I · 1).

Os símbolos incluídos no texto do índice representam as grandes categorias identificadas com a chave à direita. Os símbolos com números em sua parte superior (∧[1]) identificam as subcategorias (veja-se a chave completa à página I · 1).

Symbol	English	Deutsch	Español	Français	Português
∧	Mountain	Berg	Montaña	Montagne	Montanha
⋏	Mountains	Gebirge	Montañas	Montagnes	Montanhas
)(	Pass	Paß	Paso	Col	Passo
V	Valley, Canyon	Tal, Cañon	Valle, Cañón	Vallée, Canyon	Vale, Canhão
≡	Plain	Ebene	Llano	Plaine	Planície
>	Cape	Kap	Cabo	Cap	Cabo
ı	Island	Insel	Isla	Île	Ilha
ıı	Islands	Inseln	Islas	Îles	Ilhas
±	Other Topographic Features	Andere Topographische Objekte	Otros Elementos Topográficos	Autres données topographiques	Outros acidentes topográficos

ESPAÑOL · FRANÇAIS · PORTUGUÊS

Nombre / Nom / Nome	Página / Page	Lat. °′	Long. °′ W = Oeste / W = Ouest
Campbell Range ⋏	180	61.08 N	129.45 W
Campbell River	182	50.01 N	125.15 W
Campbells ≃	170	33.42 S	149.37 E
Campbell's Airport ⊠	278	42.20 N	88.04 W
Campbell's-Bay	188	45.44 N	76.36 W
Campbellsburg, In., U.S.	218	38.39 N	86.15 W
Campbellsburg, Ky., U.S.	218	38.31 N	85.12 W
Campbell Slough ≃	226	39.22 N	121.51 W
Campbellsport	190	43.35 N	88.16 W
Campbells River	170	33.54 S	149.37 E
Campbells Run ≃	279b	40.24 N	80.05 W
Campbellsville	194	37.20 N	85.20 W
Campbellton, N.B., Can.	186	48.00 N	66.40 W
Campbellton, Nf., Can.	186	49.17 N	54.56 W
Campbellton, P.E., Can.	186	46.47 N	64.18 W
Campbellton, Fl., U.S.	192	30.56 N	85.24 W
Campbell Town, Austl.	166	41.56 S	147.29 E
Campbelltown, Austl.	168b	34.53 S	138.40 E
Campbelltown, Austl.	170	34.04 S	150.49 E
Campbelltown, Pa., U.S.	208	40.17 N	76.35 W
Campbellville	212	43.29 N	79.59 W
Campbeltown	46	55.26 N	5.36 W
Camp Creek ≃, Ca., U.S.	226	38.38 N	120.40 W
Camp Creek ≃, Mo., U.S.	219	39.02 N	91.12 W
Camp Creek Lake ⊜[1]	222	31.03 N	96.19 W
Camp David ⊕	208	39.38 N	77.28 W
Camp de Frileuse ■	261	48.52 N	1.55 E
Camp de Satory ■	261	48.47 N	2.06 E
Camp Dix	218	38.29 N	83.17 W
Camp Douglas	190	43.55 N	90.16 W
Campeche	232	19.51 N	90.32 W
Campeche □[3], Méx.	232	19.00 N	90.30 W
Campeche □[3], Méx.	232	19.00 N	90.30 W
Campeche, Bahía de c	232	20.00 N	94.00 W
Campeche Bank ✧[4]	16	22.00 N	90.00 W
Campechuela	240p	20.14 N	77.17 W
Campegine	64	44.45 N	10.32 E
Campello Monti	58	45.56 N	8.15 E
Câmpeni	38	46.22 N	23.03 E
Camperdown, Austl.	169	38.14 S	143.09 E
Camperdown, S. Afr.	158	29.42 S	30.33 E
Camperville	184	51.59 N	100.09 W
Campestre	256	21.43 S	46.15 W
Cam Pha	110	21.01 N	107.19 E
Camp Hill, Al., U.S.	194	32.48 N	85.39 W
Camp Hill, Pa., U.S.	208	40.14 N	76.55 W
Câmpia Turzii	38	46.33 N	23.54 E
Campi Bisenzio	66	43.49 N	11.08 E
Campidano ◂[1]	71	39.30 N	8.47 E
Campiglia dei Fosci	66	43.27 N	11.03 E
Campiglia Marittima	66	43.03 N	10.37 E
Campillo de Llerena	34	38.30 N	5.50 W
Campillos	34	37.03 N	4.51 W
Câmpina	38	45.08 N	25.44 E
Campina ◂[1]	34	37.45 N	4.45 W
Campina Grande	250	7.13 S	35.53 W
Campinas	256	22.54 S	47.05 W
Campina Verde	255	19.31 S	49.28 W
Campinho, Rio do ≃	287a	22.52 S	43.37 W
Campione	58	45.58 N	8.58 E
Campione del Garda	64	45.45 N	10.45 E
Campi Salentina	68	40.24 N	18.01 E
Campitello	64	46.28 N	11.44 E
Camp King	150	4.55 N	7.58 W
Camp Lake	216	42.32 N	88.09 W
Camp Lake ⊜	212	45.27 N	78.54 W
Camp Leger ■	261	48.34 N	2.34 E
Camp Lejeune Marine Corps Base ■	192	34.40 N	77.21 W
Campli	66	42.43 N	13.41 E
Camplong	112	10.02 S	123.55 E
Campo, Cam.	152	2.22 N	9.49 E
Campo, Moç.	156	17.44 S	36.21 E
Campo, Co., U.S.	198	37.06 N	102.34 W
Campo, Réserve de ◂[4]	152	2.35 N	9.57 E
Campoalegre	246	2.41 N	75.20 W
Campo Alegre ≃	250	9.19 S	50.06 W
Campo Alegre de Goiás	255	17.39 S	47.45 W
Campobasso	66	41.34 N	14.39 E
Campobasso □[4]	66	41.38 N	14.35 E
Campobello di Licata	70	37.15 N	13.55 E
Campobello di Mazara	70	37.38 N	12.45 E
Campobello Island I	186	44.53 N	66.55 W
Campo Belo	255	20.53 S	45.16 W
Campo Blenio	58	46.34 N	8.56 E
Campocologno	58	46.13 N	10.08 E
Campodarsego	64	45.30 N	11.54 E
Campo de Criptana	34	39.24 N	3.07 W
Campo de la Cruz	246	10.23 N	74.53 W
Campo de Marte ♦	286d	12.04 S	77.03 W
Campo de Marte ■	287b	23.30 S	46.37 W
Campo de Mayo ■	288	34.32 S	58.38 W
Campo di Giove	66	42.01 N	14.03 E
Campo di Trens (Trens)	64	46.52 N	11.29 E
Campo do Coelho	256	22.15 S	42.39 W
Campodolcino	58	46.24 N	9.21 E
Campo Erê	252	26.23 S	53.03 W
Campofelice di Fitalia	70	37.50 N	13.29 E
Campofelice di Roccella	70	37.59 N	13.53 E
Campofiorito	70	37.45 N	13.16 E
Campo Florido	255	19.47 S	48.35 W
Campoformido	64	46.01 N	13.09 E
Campo Formoso	250	10.31 S	40.20 W
Campofranco	70	37.30 N	13.43 E
Campogalliano	64	44.41 N	10.50 E
Campo Gallo	252	26.35 S	62.51 W
Campo Grande, Arg.	252	27.13 S	54.58 W
Campo Grande, Bra.	255	20.27 S	54.37 W
Campo Grande ◂[8], Bra.	256	22.54 S	43.34 W
Campo Grande ◂[8], Port.	266c	38.45 N	9.09 W
Campo Indian Reservation ◂[4]	204	32.40 N	116.20 W
Campo Largo, Arg.	252	26.48 S	60.50 W
Campo Largo, Bra.	252	25.26 S	49.32 W
Campolaro	64	45.55 N	10.20 E
Campolasta (Astfeld)	64	46.40 N	11.22 E
Campolato, Capo ›	70	37.17 N	15.12 E
Campo Libertad ■	286b	23.05 N	82.26 W
Campolide	256	21.36 S	43.53 W
Campolieto	66	41.38 N	14.46 E
Campo Ligure	62	44.32 N	8.42 E
Campo Limpo Paulista	256	23.12 S	46.48 W
Campo Maior, Bra.	250	4.49 S	42.10 W
Campo Maior, Port.	34	39.01 N	7.04 W
Campomarino	66	41.57 N	15.02 E
Campo Militar Número Uno ■	286a	19.27 N	99.14 W
Campomorone	62	44.30 N	8.53 E
Campo Mourão	255	24.03 S	52.22 W
Campo Novo	252	27.42 S	53.48 W
Campo Pequeno ♦	266c	38.44 N	9.08 W
Campo Quijano	252	24.55 S	65.39 W
Campora	68	40.19 N	15.17 E
Camporeale	70	37.54 N	13.06 E
Camporgiano	64	44.09 N	10.20 E
Camporredondo	248	6.07 S	78.21 W
Campos	255	21.45 S	41.18 W
Campos Altos	255	19.41 S	46.10 W
Camposampiero	64	45.34 N	11.56 E
Campo Santo, Arg.	252	24.40 S	65.06 W
Camposanto, It.	64	44.47 N	11.08 E
Campos Belos	255	13.03 S	46.53 W
Campos de Cunha	256	22.55 S	44.49 W
Campos do Jordão	256	22.44 S	45.35 W
Campos Elisios	256	22.42 S	43.17 W
Campos Gerais	256	21.14 S	45.46 W
Campos Novos	252	27.24 S	51.12 W
Campos Sales	250	7.04 S	40.23 W
Campo Tencia, Pizzo ∧	58	46.26 N	8.43 E
Campotosto	66	42.33 N	13.22 E
Campotosto, Lago di ⊜	66	42.32 N	13.22 E
Campo Tures (Sand in Taufers)	64	46.55 N	11.57 E
Campovalano	66	42.44 N	13.40 E
Camp Parks Communications Annex ■	282	37.44 N	121.54 W
Camp Pendleton Marine Corps Base ■	228	33.19 N	117.18 W
Camp Point	219	40.02 N	91.04 W
Camp Ruby	222	30.42 N	94.45 W
Campsie	274a	33.55 S	151.06 E
Campsie Fells ⋏[2]	46	56.02 N	4.12 W
Camp Springs	208	38.48 N	76.54 W
Campti	194	31.53 N	93.07 W
Campton	192	37.44 N	83.32 W
Camptonville	226	39.27 N	121.03 W
Camptown	210	41.43 N	76.14 W
Câmpulung	38	45.16 N	25.03 E
Câmpulung Moldovenesc	38	47.31 N	25.34 E
Campus	216	41.01 N	88.18 W
Campuya ≃	246	1.43 S	73.30 W
Camp Verde	200	34.33 N	111.51 W
Campville	210	42.06 N	76.09 W
Camp Wood	196	29.40 N	100.01 W
Cam Ranh	110	11.54 N	109.09 E
Cam Ranh, Vinh c	110	11.53 N	109.10 E
Camrose, Ab., Can.	182	53.01 N	112.50 W
Camrose, Wales, U.K.	42	51.51 N	5.01 W
Camsell ≃	176	65.40 N	118.07 W
Camu ≃	250	1.15 N	57.09 W
Camucia	66	43.16 N	11.58 E
Camucuio	152	14.12 S	13.20 E
Camurí Chiquito, Quebrada ≃	286c	10.37 N	66.52 W
Çamurlu Dağ ∧	130	40.21 N	42.26 E
Camuy	240m	18.29 N	66.51 W
Çam Xuyen	110	18.15 N	106.00 E
Çamyndy	85	41.37 N	74.20 E
Čamzinka	80	54.24 N	45.47 E
Çan, Tür.	130	40.02 N	27.03 E
Çan, Tür.	130	39.09 N	40.13 E
Čan ≃	42	51.44 N	0.28 E
Canaan, Ct., U.S.	207	42.01 N	73.19 W
Canaan, Fl., U.S.	220	28.48 N	81.14 W
Canaan, In., U.S.	218	38.52 N	85.25 W
Canaan, N.Y., U.S.	210	42.25 N	73.27 W
Canaan, Vt., U.S.	206	44.59 N	71.32 W
Canaan ≃	186	45.55 N	65.47 W
Canaan Lake ⊜	276	40.47 N	73.01 W
Canaan Valley State Park ♦	188	39.02 N	79.32 W
Cana-brava ≃, Bra.	255	13.11 S	48.11 W
Cana-brava ≃, Bra.	255	12.12 S	48.40 W
Cañacao Bay c	269f	14.29 N	120.55 E
Canaçari, Lago ⊜	250	2.57 S	58.15 W
Canada □[1]	176	60.00 N	95.00 W
Cañada, Loma la ∧[2]	240p	21.41 N	82.57 W
Canada Bay c	186	50.43 N	56.10 W
Cañada de Caracheo	234	20.22 N	100.57 W
Cañada de Gómez	252	32.49 S	61.24 W
Cañada Honda	252	31.59 S	68.33 W
Canada Lake ⊜	210	43.10 N	74.32 W
Cañada Nieto	258	33.43 S	58.05 W
Canadarago Lake ⊜	210	42.48 N	75.01 W
Canada's Wonderland ♦	275b	43.51 N	79.33 W
Cañada Verde → Villa Huidobro	252	34.50 S	64.35 W
Canadaway Creek ≃	214	42.28 N	79.22 W
Canadensis	210	41.11 N	75.15 W
Canadian	196	35.54 N	100.22 W
Canadian ≃, U.S.	196	35.27 N	95.03 W
Canadian ≃, Co., U.S.	200	40.53 N	106.20 W
Canadian, Deep Fork ≃	196	35.28 N	95.50 W
Canadian Forces Base Trenton ■	212	44.07 N	77.33 W
Canadice Lake ⊜	210	42.43 N	77.34 W
Cañadón Seco	254	46.33 S	67.35 W
Canaguá ≃	246	7.57 N	69.36 W
Canaima	246	6.14 N	62.52 W
Canaima, Parque Nacional ♦	246	4.27 N	62.00 W
Canajoharie	210	42.54 N	74.34 W
Çanakkale	130	40.09 N	26.24 E
Çanakkale □[4]	130	40.10 N	26.45 E
Çanakkale Boğazı (Dardanelles) ⋓	130	40.15 N	26.25 E
Canal, Islas del → Channel Islands II	28	49.20 N	2.20 W
Canala	175f	21.32 S	165.57 E
Canale	62	44.48 N	8.00 E
Canale, Val ∨	64	46.29 N	13.30 E
Canalejas	234	19.57 N	99.39 W
Canal Flats	182	50.09 N	115.48 W
Canal Fulton	214	40.53 N	81.35 W
Canal Lake ⊜	212	44.34 N	79.03 W
Canal Lewisville	214	40.18 N	81.50 W
Canal Point	220	26.51 N	80.38 W
Canals	252	33.33 S	62.53 W
Canal Winchester	188	39.51 N	82.48 W
Canamã ≃	248	8.45 S	59.15 W
Canandaigua	210	42.52 N	77.20 W
Canandaigua Lake ⊜	210	42.49 N	77.16 W
Canandaigua Outlet ≃	210	43.04 N	77.00 W
Cananea	232	30.57 N	110.18 W
Cananéia	252	25.01 S	47.57 W
Canan Station	214	40.28 N	78.26 W
Canapine, Forca)(	66	42.45 N	13.12 E
Canápolis	255	18.44 S	49.13 W
Canapville	50	49.19 N	0.08 E
Cañar	246	2.33 S	78.56 W
Cañar □[4]	246	2.30 S	79.00 W
Canard ≃	214	42.09 N	83.06 W
Canard, Lac au ⊜	206	45.48 N	71.31 W
Canarias, Islas (Canary Islands) II	148	28.00 N	15.30 W
Canaries	241f	13.55 N	61.04 W
Canaro	64	44.56 N	11.40 E
Canarreos, Archipiélago de los II	240p	21.50 N	82.30 W
Canarsie ◂[8]	276	40.38 N	73.53 W
Canarsie Park ♦	276	40.38 N	73.53 W
Canarsie Polder I	276	40.37 N	73.52 W
Canary Basin ✧[1]	10	30.00 N	25.00 W
Canary Islands → Canarias, Islas II	148	28.00 N	15.30 W
Cañas	236	10.25 N	85.07 W
Canaseraga	210	42.27 N	77.46 W
Canaseraga Creek ≃	210	42.45 N	77.50 W
Cañasgordas	246	6.45 N	76.01 W
Canastota	210	43.04 N	75.45 W
Canatlán	232	24.31 N	104.47 W
Canaveral, Cape ›	220	28.27 N	80.32 W
Canaveral Bight c[3]	220	28.26 N	80.33 W
Canaveral National Seashore ♦	220	28.45 N	80.45 W
Canaveral Peninsula ›[1]	220	28.28 N	80.34 W
Cañaveras	34	40.22 N	2.24 W
Canavese □[9]	62	45.20 N	7.40 E
Canavieiras	255	15.39 S	38.57 W
Cañazas	236	8.19 N	81.13 W
Canazei	64	46.28 N	11.46 E
Canbelego	166	31.33 S	146.19 E
Canberra	171b	35.17 S	149.08 E
Canberra Wildlife Gardens ♦	171b	35.20 S	149.09 E
Canby, Ca., U.S.	204	41.26 N	120.52 W
Canby, Mn., U.S.	198	44.42 N	96.16 W
Canby, Or., U.S.	224	45.15 N	122.41 W
Cancajanang, Mount ∧	116	11.04 N	124.47 E
Cancale	32	48.41 N	1.51 W
Cancano, Lago di ⊜	64	46.31 N	10.18 E
Cance ≃	62	45.12 N	4.48 E
Cancellara	68	40.44 N	15.56 E
Cancello e Arnone	68	41.04 N	14.03 E
Canchaque	248	5.24 S	79.36 W
Canche ≃	50	50.31 N	1.39 E
Cancon	32	44.32 N	0.38 E
Cancún	232	21.05 N	86.46 W
Čančur	88	53.49 N	106.59 E
Canda	64	45.03 N	11.30 E
Candala → Qandala	144	11.28 N	49.52 E
Candarave	248	17.16 S	70.15 W
Çandarlı	130	38.56 N	26.56 E
Çandarlı Körfezi c	130	38.52 N	26.55 E
Candás	34	43.35 N	5.46 W
Candé	32	47.34 N	1.02 W
Candeias, Bra.	255	12.40 S	38.33 W
Candeias, Bra.	255	20.47 S	45.16 W
Candeias ≃	248	8.39 S	63.31 W
Candela, It.	68	41.08 N	15.31 E
Candela, Méx.	232	26.50 N	100.40 W
Candela, Río de ≃	196	27.16 N	100.18 W
Candelaria, Arg.	252	27.28 S	55.44 W
Candelaria, Arg.	252	32.04 S	65.49 W
Candelária, Bra.	252	29.40 S	52.48 W
Candelaria, Col.	246	3.25 N	76.20 W
Candelaria, Cuba	240p	22.44 N	82.58 W
Candelaria, Pil.	116	15.38 N	119.56 E
Candelaria ≃	232	18.37 N	91.14 W
Candelaria Loxicha	234	15.54 N	96.31 W
Candelaro ≃	68	41.34 N	15.53 E
Candeleda	34	40.09 N	5.14 W
Candelo, Austl.	166	36.46 S	149.42 E
Candelo, It.	62	45.33 N	8.07 E
Candia → Iráklion	38	35.20 N	25.09 E
Candiac	206	45.23 N	73.31 W
Candia Canavese	62	45.20 N	7.53 E
Candia Lomellina	62	45.11 N	8.36 E
Cándido Aguilar	232	25.30 N	98.02 W
Cândido de Abreu	252	24.35 S	51.20 W
Cândido Mendes	250	1.27 S	45.43 W
Candies Creek ≃	192	35.18 N	84.51 W
Candijay	116	9.49 N	124.30 E
Çandır, Tür.	130	40.16 N	33.29 E
Çandır, Tür.	130	39.15 N	35.32 E
Candle	180	65.55 N	161.56 W
Candle Lake ⊜	184	53.50 N	105.18 W
Candlemas Islands II	18	57.03 S	26.40 W
Candlestick	194	32.15 N	90.20 W
Candlestick Park ♦	282	37.43 N	122.23 W
Candlewood, Lake ⊜	207	41.32 N	73.27 W
Candlewood Isle	207	41.28 N	73.27 W
Candlewood Knolls	207	41.28 N	73.27 W
Candlewood Shores	207	41.28 N	73.26 W
Čandman', Mong.	86	50.02 N	92.03 E
Čandman', Mong.	102	45.20 N	97.59 E
Cando, Ang.	152	16.30 S	18.19 E
Cando, Sk., Can.	184	52.23 N	108.14 W
Cando, N.D., U.S.	198	48.29 N	99.12 W
Candombé ≃	152	16.54 S	21.52 E
Candon	116	17.12 N	120.27 E
Candon Point ›	116	17.13 N	120.24 E
Candor, N.Y., U.S.	210	42.13 N	76.20 W
Candor, N.C., U.S.	192	35.17 N	79.44 W
Candover	158	27.28 S	31.57 E
Cane ≃, Austl.	162	21.33 S	115.23 E
Cane ≃, La., U.S.	194	31.31 N	92.43 W
Cane ≃, N.C., U.S.	192	36.00 N	82.16 W
Canea → Khaniá	38	35.31 N	24.02 E
Caneadea	210	42.23 N	78.09 W
Caneças	266c	38.49 N	9.14 W
Cane Creek ≃	194	36.29 N	90.28 W
Canegrate	266b	45.34 N	8.56 E
Canela	252	29.22 S	50.50 W
Canelas	232	25.06 N	106.34 W
Canelles, Embalse de ⊜[1]	34	42.10 N	0.30 E
Canelli	62	44.43 N	8.17 E
Canelones	258	34.32 S	56.17 W
Canelones □[5]	258	34.35 S	56.15 W
Canelón Grande, Arroyo ≃	258	34.30 S	56.24 W
Cane Run ≃	218	38.13 N	84.37 W
Cañete, Chile	252	37.48 S	73.24 W
Cañete, Esp.	34	40.03 N	1.35 W
Caneva	64	45.58 N	12.26 E
Caney	198	37.00 N	95.56 W
Caney ≃	196	36.20 N	95.42 W
Caney Brook ≃	276	41.07 N	73.50 W
Caney Creek ≃, Ar., U.S.	194	33.46 N	93.07 W
Caney Creek ≃, Tx., U.S.	196	28.46 N	95.39 W
Caney Creek ≃, Tx., U.S.	222	32.48 N	95.33 W
Caney Creek ≃, Tx., U.S.	222	30.28 N	95.38 W
Caney Creek ≃, Tx., U.S.	222	30.04 N	96.08 W
Caney Creek ≃, Tx., U.S.	222	31.52 N	96.13 W
Caney Creek ≃, Tx., U.S.	222	31.03 N	94.33 W
Caney Creek ≃, Tx., U.S.	222	30.53 N	95.48 W
Caney Creek ≃, Tx., U.S.	222	30.07 N	95.10 W
Canfield	214	41.01 N	80.45 W
Canfield Island I	276	41.06 N	73.23 W
Canfranc	34	42.43 N	0.31 W
Cangaíba ◂[8]	287b	23.30 S	46.31 W
Cangallo	248	13.33 S	74.12 W
Cangamba	152	13.40 S	19.54 E
Cangandala	152	9.45 S	16.33 E
Cangandala, Parque Nacional da ♦	152	9.45 S	16.50 E
Cangas, Bra.	248	16.05 S	56.33 W
Cangas, Esp.	34	42.16 N	8.47 W
Cangas de Narcea	34	43.11 N	6.33 W
Cangas de Onís	34	43.21 N	5.07 W
Cangbu	100	30.49 N	114.35 E
Can Gioc ≃	269c	10.42 N	106.37 E
Cangkuang, Tanjung ›	115a	6.51 S	105.15 E
Cangniutun	105	39.23 N	115.54 E
Cango Caves ⊥[5]	158	33.23 S	22.14 E
Cangola	152	7.58 S	15.52 E
Cangombe	152	14.24 S	19.59 E
Cangongo	152	9.24 S	17.30 E
Cangqian, Zhg.	106	30.17 N	120.25 E
Cangqian, Zhg.	106	30.18 N	120.00 E
Cangshangtun	105	40.03 N	117.32 E
Canguaretama	250	6.24 S	35.08 W
Canguçu	252	31.24 S	52.41 W
Canguera	256	23.36 S	47.09 W
Cangumbe	152	12.00 S	19.17 E
Cangwu	102	23.22 N	111.13 E
Çangxi	102	31.48 N	105.57 E
Čangyrtas	85	40.53 N	72.50 E
Cangyuan	102	23.12 N	99.16 E
Cangzhou	98	38.19 N	116.51 E
Canhoca	152	9.15 S	14.41 E
Canhotinho	250	8.53 S	36.12 W
Caniapiscau ≃	176	57.40 N	69.30 W
Caniapiscau, Lac ⊜	176	54.10 N	69.55 W
Canicanian	116	14.46 N	122.01 E
Canicattì	70	37.21 N	13.51 E
Canicattini Bagni	70	37.02 N	15.04 E
Canigao Channel ⋓	116	10.15 N	124.42 E
Canigou, Pic du ∧	32	42.31 N	2.27 E
Canillas ◂[8]	266a	40.28 N	3.38 W
Canillejas ◂[8]	266a	40.27 N	3.37 W
Canim Lake	182	51.46 N	120.54 W
Canim Lake ⊜	182	51.52 N	120.45 W
Canim Lake Indian Reserve ◂[4]	182	51.47 N	121.00 W
Canindé	250	4.22 S	39.19 W
Canindé ≃	250	6.15 S	42.52 W
Canindeyú □[5]	252	24.15 S	55.15 W
Canino	66	42.28 N	11.45 E
Canipaan	116	8.35 N	117.16 E
Canipo Island I	116	10.59 N	120.57 E
Canisius College ⊕[2]	284a	42.55 N	78.52 W
Canisp ∧	46	58.07 N	5.03 W
Canistear Reservoir ⊜[1]	276	41.08 N	74.29 W
Canisteo	210	42.16 N	77.36 W
Canisteo ≃	210	42.07 N	77.08 W
Canistota	198	43.35 N	97.17 W
Cañitas de Felipe Pescador	234	23.36 N	102.43 W
Canjáyar	34	37.00 N	2.44 W
Canjinge	152	10.12 S	21.17 E
Cankhor	144	10.46 N	46.13 E
Çankırı	130	40.36 N	33.37 E
Çankırı □[4]	130	40.45 N	33.25 E
Canlaon	116	10.22 N	123.12 E
Canlaon Volcano ∧[1]	116	10.25 N	123.08 E
Canley Vale	274a	33.53 S	150.57 E
Canmore	182	51.05 N	115.21 W
Canna	68	40.05 N	16.30 E
Canna I	46	57.04 N	6.34 W
Canna, Sound of ⋓	46	57.03 N	6.25 W
Cannanore	122	11.51 N	75.22 E
Cannara	66	43.00 N	12.35 E
Canne ⊥	68	41.18 N	16.09 E
Cannel City	192	37.47 N	83.16 W
Cannelton	194	37.54 N	86.44 W
Canner ≃	56	49.24 N	6.16 E
Cannero-Riviera	58	46.01 N	8.41 E
Cannes	62	43.33 N	7.01 E
Cannes, Bayou des ≃	194	30.12 N	92.35 W
Canneto, It.	66	43.12 N	10.44 E
Canneto, It.	70	38.29 N	14.58 E
Canneto sull'Oglio	64	45.09 N	10.25 E
Cannich	46	57.21 N	4.46 W
Cannich ≃	46	57.21 N	4.44 W
Cannifton	212	44.12 N	77.23 W
Canning, Arg.	288	34.53 S	58.30 W
Canning, Austl.	168a	32.02 S	115.56 E
Canning, N.S., Can.	186	45.09 N	64.25 W
Canning ≃, Austl.	168a	32.01 S	115.51 E
Canning ≃, Ak., U.S.	180	70.05 N	145.30 W
Canning Hill ∧[2]	162	28.50 S	117.49 E
Canning Lake ⊜	212	44.56 N	78.38 W
Canning Reservoir ⊜[1]	168a	32.10 S	116.09 E
Cannington, On., Can.	212	44.21 N	79.02 W
Cannington, Eng., U.K.	42	51.09 N	3.04 W
Cannobio	58	46.04 N	8.42 E
Cannock	42	52.42 N	2.09 W
Cannock Chase ◂[1]	42	52.43 N	2.00 W
Cannon ≃	190	44.35 N	92.33 W
Cannon Air Force Base ■	196	34.23 N	103.18 W
Cannon Ball	198	46.23 N	100.35 W
Cannonball ≃	198	46.26 N	100.38 W
Cannon Beach	224	45.53 N	123.57 W
Cannondale	207	41.12 N	73.25 W
Cannon Falls	190	44.30 N	92.54 W
Cannonsburg	216	43.03 N	85.28 W
Cannonsville Reservoir ⊜[1]	210	42.08 N	75.19 W
Cannonvale	166	20.17 S	148.42 E
Cann River	166	37.34 S	149.10 E
Caño, Isla del I	236	8.44 N	83.53 W
Canoas	252	29.56 S	51.11 W
Canoas ≃, Bra.	252	27.36 S	51.25 W
Canoas ≃, Bra.	256	21.30 S	47.09 W
Canobie Lake	283	42.48 N	71.14 W
Canobie Lake ⊜	283	42.49 N	71.15 W
Canobie Lake Park ♦	283	42.48 N	71.15 W
Canoe	182	50.45 N	119.13 W
Canoe ≃, B.C., Can.	182	52.09 N	118.27 W
Canoe ≃, Ma., U.S.	283	41.58 N	71.08 W
Canoe Brook ≃	276	40.45 N	74.22 W
Canoe Brook Reservoirs ⊜[1]	276	40.45 N	74.21 W
Canoe Creek Indian Reserve ◂[4]	182	51.32 N	122.15 W
Canoe Lake ⊜	184	55.11 N	108.15 W
Canoe Lake Indian Reserve ◂[4]	184	55.08 N	108.12 W
Canoga Park ◂[8]	280	34.12 N	118.35 W
Canoinhas	252	26.10 S	50.24 W
Canol	180	65.14 N	126.56 W
Canon	192	34.21 N	83.07 W
Canon ≃	224	46.36 N	123.53 W
Canonbie	44	55.05 N	2.57 W
Canon City	200	38.24 N	105.13 W
Cañón del Sumidero, Parque Nacional ♦	234	16.45 N	93.05 W
Caño Negro	236	10.54 N	84.44 W
Canonsburg	214	40.15 N	80.11 W
Canonsburg Lake ⊜	279b	40.16 N	80.07 W
Canoochee ≃	192	31.59 N	81.18 W
Canoole Cise	144	2.02 N	42.19 E
Canopus ⊥	142	31.18 N	30.03 E
Canora	184	51.37 N	102.26 W
Canosa di Puglia	68	41.13 N	16.04 E
Canossa ⊥	64	44.35 N	10.27 E
Canot, Pointe ›	241o	16.12 N	61.28 W
Canouan I	238	12.43 N	61.20 W
Canova	198	43.52 N	97.30 W
Canova Beach	220	28.08 N	80.34 W
Cañovanas	240m	18.23 N	65.54 W
Cánoves ≃	266d	41.37 N	2.22 E
Canow	54	53.12 N	12.54 E
Canowindra	166	33.34 S	148.38 E
Can Quer, Torrente de ≃	266d	41.31 N	2.11 E
Cansado	148	20.51 N	17.02 W
Cansanção	250	10.41 S	39.31 W
Canso	186	45.20 N	61.00 W
Canso, Strait of ⋓	186	45.37 N	61.25 W
Canta	248	11.25 S	76.38 W
Cantabria	234	19.50 N	101.44 W
Cantabria (Santander) □[4], Esp.	34	43.15 N	4.00 W
Cantabria □[4], Esp.	34	43.15 N	4.00 W
Cantábrica, Cordillera ⋏	34	43.00 N	5.00 W
Cantabriques → Cantábrica, Cordillera ⋏	34	43.00 N	5.00 W
Cantagalo	255	21.58 S	42.22 W
Cantagalo, Cachoeira ∟	250	7.18 S	54.52 W
Cantal □[5]	32	45.05 N	2.45 E
Cantalejo	34	41.15 N	3.55 W
Cantalupo in Sabina	66	42.18 N	12.39 E
Çantalupo nel Sannio	66	41.31 N	14.24 E
Čantal'vejergyn ≃	180	67.38 N	179.22 W
Cantanhede, Bra.	250	3.39 S	44.24 W
Cantanhede, Port.	34	40.21 N	8.36 W
Cantareira ◂[8]	287b	23.27 S	46.37 W
Cantareira, Serra da ∧	287b	23.25 S	46.39 W
Cantaura	246	9.19 N	64.21 W
Cant Clough Reservoir ⊜[1]	262	53.46 N	2.09 W
Canteleu	50	49.27 N	1.02 E
Canterbury, Austl.	274a	33.55 S	151.07 E
Canterbury, Austl.	274b	37.49 S	145.05 E
Canterbury, N.B., Can.	186	45.53 N	67.29 W
Canterbury, Eng., U.K.	42	51.17 N	1.05 E
Canterbury Bight c[3]	172	44.15 S	171.38 E
Canterbury Cathedral ⊕[1]	42	51.17 N	1.05 E
Canterbury Park Racecourse ♦	274a	33.54 S	151.07 E
Canterbury Plains ≅	172	44.00 S	171.45 E
Canterbury Woods	284c	38.49 N	77.15 W
Can Tho	110	10.02 N	105.47 E
Cantiano	66	43.28 N	12.38 E
Cantil	228	35.18 N	117.58 W
Cantiles, Cayo I	240p	21.36 N	82.02 W
Cantin Lake ⊜	184	53.27 N	95.10 W
Canto do Buriti	250	8.07 S	42.58 W
Canto do Pontes	287a	22.58 S	43.04 W
Canto Grande, Quebrada ∨	286d	11.59 S	77.01 W
Cantoira	62	45.21 N	7.23 E
Canton, Ct., U.S.	207	41.49 N	72.53 W
Canton, Ga., U.S.	192	34.14 N	84.29 W
Canton, Il., U.S.	190	40.33 N	90.02 W
Canton, Ks., U.S.	198	38.23 N	97.25 W
Canton, Ma., U.S.	207	42.09 N	71.08 W
Canton, Mn., U.S.	190	43.31 N	91.55 W
Canton, Ms., U.S.	194	32.36 N	90.02 W
Canton, Mo., U.S.	219	40.07 N	91.37 W
Canton, N.J., U.S.	208	39.28 N	75.24 W
Canton, N.Y., U.S.	188	44.35 N	75.10 W
Canton, N.C., U.S.	192	35.31 N	82.50 W
Canton, Oh., U.S.	214	40.47 N	81.22 W
Canton, Ok., U.S.	196	36.03 N	98.35 W
Canton, Pa., U.S.	210	41.39 N	76.51 W
Canton, S.D., U.S.	198	43.18 N	96.35 W
Canton, Tx., U.S.	222	32.33 N	95.51 W
Canton → Guangzhou, Zhg.	100	23.06 N	113.16 E
Canton → Kanton I	174h	2.50 S	171.40 W
Canton Airport ⊠	174h	2.46 S	171.43 W
Canton Lake ⊜[1]	196	36.08 N	98.36 W
Canton Lake State Recreational Area ♦	196	36.08 N	98.39 W
Cantonment	194	30.36 N	87.20 W
Cantorbéry → Canterbury	42	51.17 N	1.05 E
Cantrall	219	39.56 N	89.41 W
Cantribana	266c	38.53 N	9.25 W
Cantù	62	45.44 N	9.08 E
Cantu ≃	252	24.46 S	52.54 W
Cantua Creek	226	36.30 N	120.19 W
Cantua Creek ≃	226	36.28 N	120.17 W
Cantwell	180	63.23 N	148.57 W
Cañuelas	258	35.03 S	58.44 W
Cañuelas □[5]	288	34.56 S	58.41 W
Cañuelas, Arroyo ≃	258	34.55 S	58.38 W
Canumã	246	4.02 S	59.04 W
Canumã ≃	246	3.55 S	59.10 W
Canungra	171a	28.01 S	153.10 E
Canungra Creek ≃	171a	27.55 S	153.06 E
Canungra Jungle Training Ground ■	171a	28.02 S	153.10 E
Canutama	248	6.32 S	64.20 W
Canutillo	200	31.54 N	106.35 W
Canvastown	172	41.18 S	173.40 E
Canvey Island	42	51.32 N	0.36 E
Çanvey Island I	42	51.33 N	0.34 E
Čany	86	55.19 N	76.46 E
Čany, ozero ⊜	86	54.50 N	77.30 E
Cany-Barville	50	49.47 N	0.38 E
Canyon, Yk., Can.	180	60.52 N	137.02 W
Canyon, Ca., U.S.	282	37.49 N	122.09 W
Canyon, Tx., U.S.	196	34.58 N	101.55 W
Canyon City	202	44.23 N	118.56 W
Canyon Country	228	34.25 N	118.28 W
Canyon Creek	182	55.22 N	115.05 W
Canyon Creek ≃, Az., U.S.	200	33.49 N	110.40 W
Canyon Creek ≃, Ca., U.S.	226	39.22 N	120.45 W
Canyon Creek ≃, Id., U.S.	202	42.59 N	115.59 W
Canyon Creek ≃, Wa., U.S.	224	45.57 N	122.22 W
Canyon Creek ≃, Wa., U.S.	224	48.43 N	120.55 W
Canyon de Chelly National Monument ♦	200	36.01 N	109.26 W
Canyon Ferry Lake ⊜[1]	202	46.33 N	111.37 W
Canyon Lake ⊜[1]	196	29.52 N	98.16 W
Canyonlands National Park ♦	200	38.10 N	110.00 W
Canyonville	202	42.55 N	123.16 W
Canzar	152	7.38 S	21.32 E
Canzo	62	45.51 N	9.16 E
Cao ≃, Zhg.	98	40.29 N	124.08 E
Cao ≃, Zhg.	105	38.52 N	115.46 E
Cao Bang	110	22.40 N	106.15 E
Caochi	107	30.19 N	104.24 E
Caocun	106	31.42 N	118.56 E
Caodian, Zhg.	100	28.39 N	120.23 E
Caodian, Zhg.	100	33.21 N	112.39 E
Caodian, Zhg.	102	32.32 N	111.11 E
Cao'e	100	30.01 N	120.52 E
Cao'e ≃	100	30.06 N	120.46 E
Caofang	100	26.04 N	116.35 E
Caogezhai	105	40.09 N	117.50 E
Caohe, Zhg.	105	38.57 N	115.32 E
Caohe, Zhg.	269b	31.09 N	121.25 E
Caohecheng	104	40.46 N	124.02 E
Caohekou	104	40.54 N	123.53 E
Caohezhang	104	41.04 N	124.03 E
Caojian	102	25.38 N	99.07 E
Caojiawopeng	104	42.00 N	122.20 E
Caojiawopu	104	42.37 N	122.19 E
Caojiawu	105	39.24 N	116.31 E
Caojiazhen	106	31.55 N	121.38 E
Caojiezi	107	29.53 N	106.24 E
Caojing	106	30.47 N	121.24 E
Caojun	100	29.41 N	116.17 E
Cao Lanh	110	10.27 N	105.38 E
Caolaoji	100	33.06 N	117.22 E
Caolisport, Loch c	46	55.54 N	5.37 W
Caomaji	98	34.52 N	116.17 E
Caombo	152	8.43 S	16.51 E
Caonao ≃	240p	22.05 N	78.05 W
Caonian	100	32.56 N	120.20 E
Caonillas, Lago ⊜	240m	18.16 N	66.39 W
Caopeng	106	31.44 N	121.17 E
Caoping	100	28.48 N	118.22 E
Caopu	98	34.34 N	118.52 E
Caoqiao	106	31.32 N	119.59 E
Caorle	64	45.36 N	12.53 E
Caorso	62	45.03 N	9.52 E
Caoshi, Zhg.	98	42.17 N	125.16 E
Caoshi, Zhg.	100	33.32 N	116.29 E
Caota	100	29.42 N	120.08 E
Caotang	106	31.16 N	118.59 E
Caoxi	100	28.42 N	117.18 E
Caoxian	98	34.53 N	115.33 E
Caoyangxi	100	26.34 N	118.47 E
Cap, Le → Cape Town	158	33.55 S	18.22 E
Cap, Pointe du ›	241f	14.07 N	60.57 W
Capac	190	43.00 N	82.55 W
Capaccio	68	40.25 N	15.05 E
Capacciotti, Lago di ⊜[1]	68	41.10 N	15.47 E
Capaci	70	38.10 N	13.14 E
Çapage	152	13.21 S	21.05 E
Čapajev	80	50.12 N	51.10 E
Čapajevka	82	54.38 N	35.50 E
Čapajevka ≃	80	53.08 N	49.37 E
Čapajevsk	80	52.58 N	49.41 E
Capala	152	13.37 S	14.45 E
Capalbio	66	42.27 N	11.25 E
Capalonga	116	14.20 N	122.30 E
Capanaparo ≃	246	7.01 N	67.07 W
Capanema, Bra.	250	1.12 S	47.11 W
Capanema, Bra.	252	25.40 S	53.48 W
Capangombe	152	15.05 S	13.08 E
Capanne, Monte ∧	66	42.46 N	10.10 E
Capannoli	66	43.35 N	10.41 E
Capannori	66	43.50 N	10.34 E
Capão Bonito	255	24.01 S	48.20 W
Capão Doce, Morro do ∧	252	26.43 S	51.25 W
Capão Redondo ◂[8]	287b	23.40 S	46.46 W
Capaotigamau, Lac ⊜	186	50.18 N	68.14 W
Caparaó, Parque Nacional do ♦	255	20.33 S	41.45 W
Caparica	266c	38.40 N	9.12 W
Caparo Viejo ≃	246	7.46 N	70.23 W
Capas	116	15.20 N	120.35 E
Capatárida	246	11.11 N	70.37 W
Cap-aux-Meules (Grindstone Island)	186	47.23 N	61.52 W
Cap aux Meules, Île du I	186	47.23 N	61.54 W
Capay	226	38.32 N	122.03 W
Cap-Chat	186	49.06 N	66.42 W
Cap-de-la-Madeleine	206	46.22 N	72.31 W
Cape ≃	166	20.49 S	146.51 E
Cape Arid National Park ♦	162	33.40 S	123.25 E
Cape Barren Island I	166	40.25 S	148.12 E
Cape Basin ✧[1]	8	37.00 S	7.00 E
Cape Bougainville Aboriginal Reserve ◂[4]	164	14.10 S	126.30 E
Cape Breton Highlands National Park ♦	186	46.45 N	60.45 W
Cape Breton Island I	186	46.00 N	60.30 W
Cape Broyle	186	47.06 N	52.57 W
Cape Canaveral	220	28.24 N	80.36 W
Cape Canaveral Air Force Station ■	220	28.29 N	80.35 W
Cape Charles	208	37.16 N	76.01 W
Cape Coast	150	5.05 N	1.15 W
Cape Cod Bay c	207	41.52 N	70.22 W
Cape Cod Canal ≅	207	41.47 N	70.30 W
Cape Cod National Seashore ♦	207	41.56 N	70.00 W
Cape Comorin → Kanniyākumari	122	8.05 N	77.34 E
Cape Coral	220	26.33 N	81.56 W
Cape Croker Indian Reserve ◂[4]	212	44.55 N	81.01 W
Cape Dorset	176	64.14 N	76.32 W
Cape Elizabeth	188	43.33 N	70.12 W
Cape Fear ≃	192	33.53 N	78.00 W
Cape Girardeau	194	37.18 N	89.31 W
Cape Hatteras National Seashore ♦	192	35.30 N	76.35 W
Cape Henlopen State Park ♦	208	38.45 N	75.06 W
Cape Jervis	168b	35.36 S	138.06 E
Cape Johnson Tablemount ✧[3]	14	17.08 N	177.15 W
Cape Krusenstern National Monument ♦	180	67.30 N	163.40 W
Capela	250	10.30 S	37.04 W
Cape LaHave Island I	186	44.12 N	64.22 W
Cape la Hune	186	47.33 N	56.52 W
Capel Curig	44	53.06 N	3.54 W
Capelengue	152	9.12 S	19.43 E
Capelinha	255	17.42 S	42.31 W
Capelinha do Embirazal	256	22.02 S	45.26 W
Cape Lisburne	180	68.52 N	166.05 W
Capel'ka	76	58.03 N	28.59 E
Capella	166	23.05 S	148.02 E
Capella ∧	164	5.00 S	141.05 E
Capelle [aan de IJssel]	52	51.55 N	4.35 E
Capellen	56	49.38 N	5.59 E
Capelongo	152	14.54 S	15.08 E
Cape Lookout National Seashore ♦	192	34.40 N	76.23 W
Cape Lookout State Park ♦	224	45.21 N	123.59 W
Capel Saint Mary	42	52.00 N	1.04 E
Cape May	208	38.56 N	74.54 W
Cape May □[6]	208	38.56 N	74.55 W
Cape May Coast Guard Air Station ■	208	38.57 N	74.53 W
Cape May Court House	208	39.04 N	74.49 W
Cape May Point	208	39.09 N	74.46 W
Capembé ≃	152	16.10 S	21.00 E
Cape Melville National Park ♦	164	14.20 S	144.30 E
Capenda Camulemba	152	9.24 S	18.27 E
Capenga ≃	287a	22.49 S	43.37 W
Capenhurst	262	53.15 N	2.57 W
Cape of Good Hope Nature Reserve ◂[4]	158	34.18 S	18.26 E
Cape Pole	180	55.58 N	133.48 W
Cape Pond ⊜	283	42.38 N	70.38 W
Cape Porpoise	188	43.22 N	70.26 W
Cape Range National Park ♦	162	22.10 S	113.55 E
Cape Rise ✧[3]	8	42.00 S	15.00 E
Capernaum → Kefar Naḥum ⊥	132	32.53 N	35.34 E
Cape Romanzof	180	61.49 N	165.56 W
Capertee	170	33.09 S	149.59 E
Capertee ≃	170	33.12 S	150.28 E
Cape Sable Island I	186	43.25 N	65.37 W
Cape Scott Provincial Park ♦	182	50.45 N	128.20 W
Capesterre	241o	15.54 N	61.13 W
Capesterre, Pointe de la ›	241o	16.03 N	61.33 W
Capesterre-Belle-Eau	241o	16.03 N	61.34 W
Capesthorne Hall ⊥	262	53.15 N	2.14 W
Capestrano	66	42.16 N	13.46 E
Capetinga ≃	256	22.04 S	47.14 W
Cape Tormentine	186	46.08 N	63.47 W
Cape Town (Kaapstad)	158	33.55 S	18.22 E
Cape Verde (Cabo Verde) □[1], Afr.	134	16.00 N	24.00 W
Cape Verde (Cabo Verde) □[1], Afr.	150a	16.00 N	24.00 W
Cape Verde Basin ✧[1]	8	15.00 N	30.00 W
Cape Verde Islands → Cape Verde □[1]	150a	16.00 N	24.00 W
Cape Verde Terrace ✧[3]	10	18.00 N	20.00 W
Capeville	208	37.12 N	75.57 W
Cape Vincent	212	44.07 N	76.19 W
Cape Yakataga	180	60.04 N	142.26 W
Cape York Peninsula ›[1]	164	14.00 S	142.30 E
Cap-Haïtien	238	19.45 N	72.12 W
Capilla de Farruco	252	32.53 S	55.25 W
Capilla del Monte	252	30.51 S	64.31 W
Capilla del Señor	258	34.18 S	59.06 W
Capim ≃	250	1.40 S	47.47 W
Capim Melado, Morro do ∧	287a	22.50 S	43.29 W
Capinas Point ›	116	11.05 N	125.14 E
Capinópolis	255	18.41 S	49.35 W
Capinota	248	17.43 S	66.14 W
Capinzal	252	27.20 S	51.36 W
Capira	236	8.45 N	79.53 W
Cap Island I	116	5.57 N	120.06 E
Capistrano, Bra.	250	4.28 S	38.55 W
Capistrano, It.	68	38.41 N	16.17 E
Capistrano Beach	228	33.27 N	117.40 W
Capistrello	66	41.57 N	13.23 E
Capitachouane ≃	190	47.36 N	76.54 W
Capitachouane, Lac ⊜	190	48.05 N	75.55 W
Capital Airport ⊠	219	39.51 N	89.41 W
Capital Centre ♦	284c	38.54 N	76.51 W
Capital City Airport ⊠	216	42.47 N	84.35 W
Capitan	200	33.32 N	105.34 W
Capitán Aracena, Isla I	254	54.10 S	71.20 W

	English	Deutsch	Español	Français	Português
≃	River	Fluß	Río	Rivière	Rio
≅	Canal	Kanal	Canal	Canal	Canal
∟	Waterfall, Rapids	Wasserfall, Stromschnellen	Cascada, Rápidos	Chute d'eau, Rapides	Cascata, Rápidos
⋓	Strait	Meeresstraße	Estrecho	Détroit	Estreito
c	Bay, Gulf	Bucht, Golf	Bahía, Golfo	Baie, Golfe	Baía, Golfo
⊜	Lake, Lakes	See, Seen	Lago, Lagos	Lac, Lacs	Lago, Lagos
⩸	Swamp	Sumpf	Pantano	Marais	Pântano
⩀	Ice Features, Glacier	Eis- und Gletscherformen	Accidentes Glaciales	Formes glaciaires	Acidentes glaciares
⫪	Other Hydrographic Features	Andere Hydrographische Objekte	Otros Elementos Hidrográficos	Autres données hydrographiques	Outros acidentes hidrográficos

	English	Deutsch	Español	Français	Português
✧	Submarine Features	Untermeerische Objekte	Accidentes Submarinos	Formes de relief sous-marin	Acidentes submarinos
□	Political Unit	Politische Einheit	Unidad Política	Entité politique	Unidade política
⊕	Cultural Institution	Kulturelle Institution	Institución Cultural	Institution culturelle	Instituição cultural
⊥	Historical Site	Historische Stätte	Sitio Histórico	Site historique	Sitio histórico
♦	Recreational Site	Erholungs- und Ferienort	Sitio de Recreo	Centre de loisirs	Area de Lazer
⊠	Airport	Flughafen	Aeropuerto	Aéroport	Aeroporto
■	Military Installation	Militäranlage	Instalación Militar	Installation militaire	Instalação militar
◂	Miscellaneous	Verschiedenes	Misceláneo	Divers	Diversos

ENGLISH | DEUTSCH

Name / Name	Page / Seite	Lat.°′ / Breite°′	Long.°′ / Länge°′ E = Ost
Capitán Arturo Prat ☉[3]	9	62.30 S	59.41 W
Capitán Bado	255	23.16 S	55.32 W
Capitán Bermúdez	252	32.49 S	60.43 W
Capitán Meza	252	26.55 S	55.15 W
Capitan Peak ∧	200	33.36 N	105.16 W
Capitán Sarmiento	252	34.10 S	59.48 W
Capitão de Campos	250	4.28 S	41.57 W
Capitão Enéas	255	16.21 S	43.43 W
Capitola	226	36.58 N	121.57 W
Capitol Heights	208	38.53 N	76.54 W
Capitol Park	208	39.08 N	75.30 W
Capitol Peak ∧	204	41.50 N	117.18 W
Capitol Reef National Park ♦	200	38.11 N	111.20 W
Capitol View	192	33.57 N	80.56 W
Capivari	255	23.00 S	47.31 W
Capivari ≃, Bra.	248	19.16 S	57.10 W
Capivari ≃, Bra.	255	12.30 S	39.55 W
Capivari ≃, Bra.	256	24.09 S	46.48 W
Capivari ≃, Bra.	256	22.14 S	44.57 W
Capivari ≃, Bra.	256	21.53 S	46.15 W
Capivari ≃, Bra.	256	22.26 S	45.47 W
Capivari ≃, Bra.	256	22.56 S	47.16 W
Capivari ≃, Bra.	256	21.30 S	44.20 W
Capivari ≃, Bra.	256	21.12 S	44.52 W
Capivari, Canal ≡	287a	22.42 S	43.21 W
Capiz → Roxas	116	11.35 N	122.45 E
Capiz □[4]	116	11.30 N	122.30 E
Capizzi	70	37.51 N	14.29 E
Caplan	186	48.06 N	65.41 W
Caplen	222	29.29 N	94.33 W
Caples Lake ⊜[1]	226	38.42 N	120.03 W
Çaplina ≃	248	18.14 S	70.33 W
Čaplino	180	64.25 N	172.15 W
Čapljina	36	43.07 N	17.42 E
Çaplone, Monte ∧	64	45.48 N	10.38 E
Čaplygin	76	53.14 N	39.58 E
Cap Mountain ∧	180	63.25 N	123.29 W
Capnoyan Island I	116	10.44 N	120.54 E
Capoche ≃	154	15.23 S	32.53 E
Capodichino, Aeroporto di ⊠	68	40.50 N	14.17 E
Capodimonte	66	42.33 N	11.55 E
Capo di Ponte	64	46.02 N	10.21 E
Capo d'Orlando	70	38.10 N	14.53 E
Capoeira, Corredeira ⌊	250	6.48 S	58.21 W
Capolago	58	45.55 N	8.59 E
Capoliveri	66	42.45 N	10.22 E
Caporolo ≃	152	12.56 S	13.00 E
Caposele	68	40.49 N	15.13 E
Capostrada	66	43.57 N	10.54 E
Capot ≃	240e	14.51 N	61.05 W
Capoterra	71	39.11 N	8.58 E
Capoti-an, Mount ∧	116	11.45 N	125.15 E
Capotoan, Mount ∧	116	12.09 N	124.57 E
Cappadocia □[9]	130	38.30 N	36.00 E
Cappamore	48	52.37 N	8.20 W
Cap-Pelé	186	46.13 N	64.18 W
Cappella Islands II	240m	18.17 N	64.54 W
Cappelle	66	42.03 N	13.22 E
Cappelle sul Tavo	66	42.28 N	14.06 E
Cappeln	52	52.48 N	8.07 E
Cappenberg	263	51.39 N	7.32 E
Cappenberg, Schloss ⊥	263	51.39 N	7.32 E
Cappercleuch	44	55.29 N	3.12 W
Cappoquin	48	52.08 N	7.50 W
Capracotta	66	41.50 N	14.16 E
Capraia	66	43.03 N	9.50 E
Capraia, Isola I	66	42.08 N	15.31 E
Capraia, Isola di I	66	43.02 N	9.49 E
Capranica	66	42.15 N	12.11 E
Caprara, Punta ›	71	41.07 N	8.19 E
Caprarola	66	42.19 N	12.14 E
Capreol	190	46.43 N	80.56 W
Caprera, Isola I	71	41.12 N	9.28 E
Caprese Michelangelo	66	43.39 N	11.59 E
Capri	68	40.33 N	14.14 E
Capri, Isola di I	68	40.33 N	14.13 E
Capriati a Volturno	68	41.28 N	14.08 E
Capricorn, Cape ›	166	23.30 S	151.13 E
Capricorn Channel ʮ	166	23.00 S	152.20 E
Capricorn Group II	166	23.28 S	152.00 E
Capri Leone	70	38.05 N	14.44 E
Caprino Veronese	64	45.36 N	10.47 E
Caprivi Oss □[5]	156	17.45 S	24.00 E
Caprivi Zipfel (Caprivi Strip) □[9]	156	17.59 S	23.00 E
Caprolace, Lago di ⊜	66	41.21 N	12.58 E
Capron, Il., U.S.	216	42.24 N	88.44 W
Capron, Va., U.S.	208	36.42 N	77.12 W
Cap Saint Jacques → Vung Tau	110	10.21 N	107.04 E
Cap-Santé	206	46.40 N	71.47 W
Capstone	260	51.21 N	0.34 E
Captain Anthony Meldahl Dam ◆[6]	218	38.48 N	84.11 W
Captain Cook	229d	19.29 N	155.55 W
Captain Cook Bridge ◆[5]	274a	34.00 S	151.08 E
Captain Cook Landing Place Park ♦	274a	34.00 S	151.14 E
Captain Cook Monument ⊥	174c	29.00 S	167.56 E
Captain Daniel Wright Woods ♦	278	42.13 N	87.56 W
Captain Harbor ⊂	276	41.00 N	73.36 W
Captain Pond ⊜	283	42.48 N	71.10 W
Captains Flat	171b	35.35 S	149.27 E
Captieux	32	44.18 N	0.16 W
Captina Creek ≃	188	39.52 N	80.48 W
Captiva	220	26.31 N	82.11 W
Captiva Island I	220	26.31 N	82.11 W
Captree Island I	276	40.39 N	73.16 W
Captree State Park ♦	276	40.39 N	73.16 W
Capua	68	41.06 N	14.12 E
Capual Island I	116	6.02 N	121.24 E
Capuáva	287b	23.39 S	46.29 W
Capuça I	152	17.22 S	21.18 E
Capucapu ≃	246	1.45 S	58.35 W
Capucin ›	240d	15.38 N	61.28 W
Capul	116	12.25 N	124.11 E
Capulín, Río del ≃	196	27.31 N	101.33 W
Capulin Mountain National Monument ♦	196	36.48 N	103.55 W
Capul Island I	116	12.26 N	124.10 E
Capuna	152	15.38 S	19.43 E
Capunda	152	14.57 S	14.03 E
Capurro	258	34.25 S	56.28 W
Capurso	68	41.03 N	16.55 E
Caputh	54	52.21 N	13.00 E
Cap-Vert → Cape Verde □[1]	150a	16.00 N	24.00 W
Caquende	256	21.20 S	44.33 W
Caquetá □[8]	246	1.00 N	74.00 W
Caquetá (Japurá) ≃	246	3.08 S	64.46 W
Çaquiaviri	248	17.03 S	68.38 W
Čar ≃	86	50.22 N	80.55 E
Çara, Ityo.	144	5.52 N	37.12 E
Çara, Ross.	88	56.54 N	118.12 E
Čara ≃	74	60.22 N	120.50 E
Cará, Ilha do I	250	0.01 S	50.50 W
Caraballeda	286c	10.37 N	66.50 W
Caraballeda, Punta ›	286c	10.37 N	66.50 W
Carabanchel Alto ◆[8]	266a	40.22 N	3.45 W
Carabanchel Bajo ◆[8]	266a	40.23 N	3.47 W
Carabao Island I	116	12.04 N	121.56 E
Carabaya ≃	248	14.43 S	70.17 W
Carabaya, Cordillera de ⋏	248	13.50 S	70.45 W
Carabayllo	286d	11.52 S	77.02 W
Carabelas Grande ≃	258	34.15 S	58.43 W
Carabinani ≃	246	1.58 S	61.31 W
Carabobo □[3]	246	10.10 N	68.05 W
Carabost	171b	35.36 S	147.44 E
Caracal	38	44.07 N	24.21 E
Caracalla, Terme di ⊥	267a	41.53 N	12.29 E
Caracaraí	246	1.50 N	61.08 W
Caracas, Ven.	246	10.30 N	66.56 W
Çaracas, Ven.	286c	10.30 N	66.56 W
Čarach	86	59.03 N	62.15 E
Carache	246	9.38 N	70.14 W
Caracol, Bra.	250	9.17 S	43.20 W
Caracol, Bra.	252	22.01 S	57.02 W
Caracollo	248	17.39 S	67.10 W
Caracorum → Karakoram Range ⋏	120	35.30 N	77.00 E
Carácuaro de Morelos	234	18.46 N	101.02 W
Caradoc Indian Reserve ◆[4]	214	42.48 N	81.29 W
Caraffa di Catanzaro	68	38.53 N	16.29 E
Caraga	116	7.20 N	126.34 E
Caraga ≃	116	7.20 N	126.34 E
Caragh, Lough ⊜	48	52.03 N	9.52 W
Caraghnan Mountain ∧	166	31.20 S	149.03 E
Caraglio	62	44.25 N	7.26 E
Caraguata, Arroyo ≃	288	34.24 S	58.38 W
Caraguatatuba	256	23.37 S	45.25 W
Caraguatatuba, Enseada de ⊂	256	23.40 S	45.20 W
Caraguatay	252	25.14 S	56.52 W
Caraí	255	17.12 S	41.42 W
Caraibamba	248	14.24 S	73.09 W
Caraïbes, Îles des → West Indies II	230	19.00 N	70.00 W
Caraïbes, Mer des → Caribbean Sea ∓[2]	230	15.00 N	73.00 W
Caraigres, Cerro ∧	236	9.43 N	84.05 W
Caraíva ≃	255	16.48 S	39.08 W
Carajari ≃	250	4.45 S	54.20 W
Carajás	250	6.06 S	50.23 W
Carajás, Serra dos ⋏	250	5.50 S	51.20 W
Caralue Bluff ∧[2]	166	33.26 S	136.16 E
Caramagna-Piemonte	62	44.46 N	7.44 E
Caramanico Terme	66	42.09 N	14.00 E
Caramay	116	10.11 N	119.14 E
Caramoan	116	13.46 N	123.52 E
Caramoan Peninsula ›[1]	116	13.48 N	123.40 E
Caramoran	116	13.59 N	124.08 E
Caramy ≃	62	43.26 N	6.12 E
Caranavi	248	15.46 S	67.36 W
Carandaí	255	20.57 S	43.48 W
Carandayti	248	20.45 S	63.04 W
Carangola	255	20.44 S	42.02 W
Carano	64	46.16 N	11.27 E
Caransebeş	38	45.25 N	22.13 E
Carapá ≃	252	24.30 S	54.20 W
Carapachay ≃[1]	288	34.25 S	58.35 W
Carapajó	250	2.16 S	49.22 W
Cara-Paraná ≃	246	1.45 S	73.13 W
Carapeguá	252	25.48 S	57.14 W
Carapelle ≃	68	41.30 N	15.55 E
Carapicuíba	256	23.31 S	46.50 W
Carapicuíba □[7]	287b	23.31 S	46.53 W
Carapo ≃	246	7.30 N	64.02 W
Caraquet	186	47.48 N	64.57 W
Caráquez	246	0.36 S	80.25 W
Carare ≃	246	6.48 N	74.06 W
Carasco	62	44.21 N	9.21 E
Caraş-Severin □[6]	38	45.00 N	22.00 E
Caratasca, Laguna de ⊂	236	15.23 N	83.55 W
Carate Brianza	62	45.41 N	9.14 E
Caratinga	255	19.47 S	42.08 W
Carauari	246	4.52 S	66.54 W
Caraúbas	250	5.47 S	37.34 W
Caravaca	34	38.06 N	1.51 W
Caravaggio	62	45.30 N	9.38 E
Caravela, Ilha I	150	11.30 N	16.20 W
Caravelas	255	17.45 S	39.15 W
Caravelí	248	15.46 S	73.22 W
Caravelle, Presqu'île de la ›[1]	240e	14.45 N	60.55 W
Caravius, Monte is ∧	71	39.09 N	8.49 E
Caraway	194	35.45 N	90.19 W
Carayaó	252	25.10 S	56.26 W
Caraz	248	9.03 S	77.45 W
Caraza ◆[8]	288	34.42 S	58.26 W
Carazinho	252	28.18 S	52.48 W
Carazo □[5]	236	11.45 N	86.15 W
Carballiño	34	42.26 N	8.04 W
Carballo	34	43.13 N	8.41 W
Carberry	184	49.52 N	99.20 W
Carbet, Pitons du ⋏	240e	14.42 N	61.07 W
Carbo	232	29.42 N	110.58 W
Carbol ≃	70	37.32 N	12.59 E
Carbon, Ab., Can.	182	51.29 N	113.09 W
Carbon, Pa., U.S.	279b	40.17 N	79.34 W
Carbon, Tx., U.S.	196	32.16 N	98.50 W
Carbon □[6]	210	40.52 N	75.45 W
Carbon ≃	224	47.07 N	122.13 W
Carbon, Cap ›	34	36.47 N	5.06 E
Carbonado	224	47.04 N	122.03 W
Carbonara, Capo ›	71	39.06 N	9.31 E
Carbonara, Pizzo ∧	70	37.54 N	14.02 E
Carbonare	64	45.56 N	11.13 E
Carbonate	266b	45.41 N	8.56 E
Carbon-Blanc	32	44.53 N	0.31 W
Carbon Canyon Dam ◆[6]	280	33.55 N	117.50 W
Carbon Creek ≃	280	33.49 N	118.04 W
Carbondale, Co., U.S.	200	39.24 N	107.12 W
Carbondale, Il., U.S.	194	37.43 N	89.13 W
Carbondale, Ks., U.S.	198	38.49 N	95.41 W
Carbondale, Pa., U.S.	210	41.34 N	75.30 W
Carbone	68	40.09 N	16.05 E
Carbonear	186	47.45 N	53.13 W
Carboneras de Guadazaon	34	39.53 N	1.48 W
Carbon Hill	194	33.53 N	87.31 W
Carbonia	71	39.10 N	8.31 E
Carbonin (Schluderbach)	64	46.37 N	12.13 E
Carbost	46	57.18 N	6.22 W
Carcaixent	34	39.08 N	0.27 W
Carcajou ≃	180	65.37 N	128.43 W
Carcalgong Hill ∧	170	32.52 S	149.41 E
Carcans, Lac de ⊂	32	45.08 N	1.08 W
Carcar	116	10.06 N	123.38 E
Carcarañá	252	32.51 S	61.09 W
Carcarañá ≃	252	32.27 S	60.48 W
Carcare	62	44.21 N	8.18 E
Carcar Point ›	116	10.05 N	123.41 E
Carcassonne	32	43.13 N	2.21 E
Carcastillo	34	42.23 N	1.26 W
Carcavelos, Port.	266c	38.41 N	9.20 W
Carcavelos, Port.	266c	38.53 N	9.14 W
Carceri, Eremo delle ☉[1]	66	43.05 N	12.42 E
Carcès	62	43.28 N	6.11 E
Carchi □[4]	246	0.45 N	78.00 W
Carcroft	44	53.34 N	1.11 W
Carcross	180	60.10 N	134.42 W
Cardabia	162	23.06 S	113.48 E
Çardak, Tür.	130	38.06 N	36.49 E
Čardak, Uzb.	85	41.37 N	69.56 E
Cardal	258	34.18 S	56.24 W
Çardano al Campo	266b	45.39 N	8.47 E
Čardara	85	41.17 N	67.55 E
Čardara, step' ⋏[1]	85	42.00 N	68.00 E
Čardarinskoje vodochranilišče ⊜[1]	85	41.10 N	68.15 E
Cardeña	34	38.13 N	4.19 W
Cárdenas, Cuba	240p	23.02 N	81.12 W
Cárdenas, Méx.	234	22.00 N	99.40 W
Cárdenas, Méx.	234	17.59 N	93.22 W
Cárdenas, Nic.	236	11.12 N	85.31 W
Cárdenas, Bahía de ⊂	240p	23.05 N	81.10 W
Cardener ≃	34	41.41 N	1.51 E
Carderock Springs	284c	38.59 N	77.10 W
Cardiel, Lago ⊜	254	48.55 S	71.15 W
Cardiff, Austl.	170	32.57 S	151.41 E
Cardiff, Wales, U.K.	42	51.29 N	3.13 W
Cardiff, Md., U.S.	208	39.43 N	76.20 W
Cardiff, N.J., U.S.	208	39.24 N	74.35 W
Cardiff by the Sea	228	33.01 N	117.16 W
Cardigan, P.E., Can.	186	46.14 N	62.37 W
Cardigan, Wales, U.K.	42	52.06 N	4.40 W
Cardigan Bay ⊂, P.E., Can.	186	46.10 N	62.30 W
Cardigan Bay ⊂, Wales, U.K.	42	52.30 N	4.20 W
Cardigan Island I	42	52.08 N	4.41 W
Cardigan State Park ♦	188	43.38 N	71.54 W
Cardinal	212	44.47 N	75.23 W
Cardinale	68	38.38 N	16.23 E
Cardinal Heights	212	45.27 N	75.37 W
Cardinal Lake ⊜	182	56.14 N	117.44 W
Cardington, S. Afr.	158	27.11 S	23.30 E
Cardington, Oh., U.S.	214	40.30 N	82.53 W
Cardinia Creek ≃	274b	38.12 S	145.23 E
Cardinia Reservoir ⊜[1]	169	37.58 S	145.25 E
Cardona	258	33.53 S	57.23 W
Cardonal, Punta ›	232	28.28 N	111.45 W
Cardoso	255	20.04 S	49.54 W
Cardozo	252	32.38 S	56.21 W
Card Sound ʮ	220	25.20 N	80.18 W
Cardston	182	49.12 N	113.18 W
Cardwell, Austl.	166	18.16 S	146.02 E
Cardwell, Mo., U.S.	194	36.02 N	90.17 W
Çardwell Mountain ∧	194	35.41 N	85.41 W
Čardžou	128	39.06 N	63.34 E
Čardžou □[8]	128	38.51 N	63.34 E
Careaçu	256	22.02 S	45.42 W
Careen Lake ⊜	184	57.00 N	108.10 W
Carega, Cima ∧	64	45.44 N	11.08 E
Carei	38	47.42 N	22.28 E
Careiro	246	3.12 S	59.45 W
Careiro, Ilha do I	246	3.10 S	59.44 W
Çarén	252	30.51 S	70.47 W
Čarencavan	84	40.24 N	44.38 E
Carencro	194	30.19 N	92.02 W
Carentan	32	49.18 N	1.14 W
Careri	68	38.10 N	16.07 E
Cares ≃	34	43.19 N	4.36 W
Caresana	62	45.13 N	8.30 E
Caretta	192	37.20 N	81.40 W
Careviščina	80	52.27 N	46.43 E
Carey	214	40.57 N	83.22 W
Carey, Lake ⊜	162	29.05 S	122.15 E
Carey Downs	162	25.38 S	115.27 E
Careysburg	150	6.30 N	10.32 W
Cargados Carajos Shoals II	12	16.38 S	59.38 E
Cargill	46	56.30 N	3.22 W
Carhaix-Plouguer	32	48.17 N	3.35 W
Carhuamayo	248	10.55 S	76.02 W
Carhuanca	248	13.45 S	73.48 W
Carhuaz	248	9.16 S	77.38 W
Carhué	252	37.11 S	62.44 W
Caria □[9]	130	37.30 N	28.00 E
Cariacica	255	20.16 S	40.25 W
Cariaco	246	10.29 N	63.33 W
Cariaco, Golfo de ⊂	246	10.30 N	64.00 W
Cariamanga	246	4.20 S	79.35 W
Cariango	152	10.37 S	15.20 E
Cariati	68	39.30 N	16.56 E
Caribana, Punta ›	246	8.37 N	76.52 W
Caribbean Sea ∓[2]	230	15.00 N	73.00 W
Caribe, Mar → Caribbean Sea ∓[2]	230	15.00 N	73.00 W
Cariboo ≃	182	52.40 N	121.40 W
Cariboo Mountains ⋏	182	53.00 N	121.00 W
Caribou, N.S., Can.	186	45.44 N	62.42 W
Caribou, Me., U.S.	186	46.51 N	68.00 W
Caribou ≃	176	59.20 N	94.44 W
Caribou, Lac du ⊜	206	46.56 N	72.50 W
Caribou Island I	190	47.22 N	85.49 W
Caribou Mountain ∧, Id., U.S.	202	43.06 N	111.18 W
Caribou Mountain ∧, Me., U.S.	188	45.26 N	70.38 W
Caribou Mountains ⋏	176	59.12 N	115.40 W
Caribou Range ⋏	202	43.05 N	111.15 W
Carichic	232	27.56 N	107.03 W
Caricuao	286c	10.27 N	66.59 W
Caricuao, Quebrada ≃	286c	10.26 N	66.59 W
Caricyn → Volgograd	80	48.44 N	44.25 E
Caridad, Pil.	116	10.50 N	124.45 E
Caridad, Pil.	269f	14.29 N	120.53 E
Caridade	250	4.13 S	39.12 W
Carife	68	41.01 N	15.12 E
Carigara	116	11.18 N	124.41 E
Carigara Bay ⊂	116	11.24 N	124.40 E
Carignan, P.Q., Can.	275a	45.27 N	73.18 W
Carignan, Fr.	56	49.38 N	5.10 E
Carignano, It.	62	44.55 N	7.40 E
Carignano, It.	66	43.49 N	12.56 E
Cari Laufquen Grande, Lago ⊜	254	41.07 S	69.30 W
Carinda	166	30.28 S	147.41 E
Cariñena	34	41.20 N	1.13 W
Caringbah	274a	34.03 S	151.08 E
Carinhanha	255	14.18 S	43.47 W
Carinhanha ≃	255	14.20 S	43.47 W
Carini	70	38.08 N	13.11 E
Carini, Golfo di ⊂	70	38.12 N	13.22 E
Carinish	46	57.31 N	7.18 W
Carinola	68	41.11 N	13.58 E
Carioca, Serra da ∧	256	22.47 S	44.18 W
Caripe	246	10.12 N	63.29 W
Caripi ≃	250	3.56 N	51.27 W
Caripito	246	10.08 N	63.06 W
Carira	250	10.21 S	37.42 W
Cariré	250	3.57 S	40.27 W
Caririaçu	250	7.02 S	39.17 W
Carisbrook	169	37.02 S	143.49 E
Carisbrooke	42	50.41 N	1.19 W
Carisolo	64	46.10 N	10.45 E
Carite	286c	10.24 N	67.01 W
Carite, Lago ⊜	240m	18.04 N	66.06 W
Çariús	250	6.32 S	39.30 W
Čarkesar	85	41.02 N	70.53 E
Carlentini	70	37.16 N	15.01 E
Carle Place	276	40.45 N	73.36 W
Carles	116	11.34 N	123.08 E
Carlet	34	39.14 N	0.31 W
Carleton, Mi., U.S.	216	42.03 N	83.23 W
Carleton, Ne., U.S.	198	40.18 N	97.40 W
Carleton, Mount ∧	186	47.23 N	66.53 W
Carleton Place	212	45.08 N	76.09 W
Carletonville	158	26.23 S	27.22 E
Cârlibaba	38	47.35 N	25.07 E
Carlin	204	40.42 N	116.06 W
Carling	56	49.10 N	6.43 E
Carlingford	274a	33.47 S	151.03 E
Carlingford Lough ⊂	48	54.04 N	6.10 W
Carlinville	219	39.16 N	89.52 W
Carlinville, Lake ⊜[1]	219	39.14 N	89.51 W
Carlisle, On., Can.	212	43.23 N	79.59 W
Carlisle, Eng., U.K.	44	54.54 N	2.55 W
Carlisle, Ar., U.S.	194	34.46 N	91.44 W
Carlisle, In., U.S.	194	38.58 N	87.24 W
Carlisle, Ia., U.S.	190	41.30 N	93.29 W
Carlisle, Ky., U.S.	218	38.18 N	84.01 W
Carlisle, Ma., U.S.	283	42.31 N	71.21 W
Carlisle, N.Y., U.S.	210	42.45 N	74.27 W
Carlisle, Oh., U.S.	218	39.35 N	84.20 W
Carlisle, Pa., U.S.	208	40.12 N	77.11 W
Carlisle Barracks ■	208	40.13 N	77.11 W
Carlisle Bay ⊂	241g	13.05 N	59.37 W
Carlisle Gardens	210	43.11 N	78.39 W
Carlisle Island I	180	52.52 N	170.02 W
Carlisle Springs	208	40.16 N	77.10 W
Carl Junction	194	37.10 N	94.33 W
Carlls ≃	276	40.41 N	73.20 W
Carloforte	71	39.08 N	8.18 E
Carlopoli	68	39.03 N	16.27 E
Carlópolis	255	23.25 S	49.41 W
Carlos, Isla I	254	54.03 S	73.20 W
Carlos Alves	256	21.37 S	43.07 W
Carlos Barbosa	252	29.18 S	51.30 W
Carlos Beguerie	258	35.29 S	59.06 W
Carlos Casares	252	35.38 S	61.21 W
Carlos Chagas	255	17.43 S	40.45 W
Carlos City	218	40.02 N	85.02 W
Carlos Forseca Amador	236	11.59 N	86.31 W
Carlos Keen	258	34.29 S	59.14 W
Carlos Manuel de Céspedes	240p	21.35 N	78.17 W
Carlos Pellegrini	252	32.03 S	61.48 W
Carlos Reyles	252	33.03 S	56.29 W
Carlos Sampaio	287a	22.42 S	43.31 W
Carlos Tejedor	252	35.23 S	62.25 W
Carlow	48	52.50 N	6.55 W
Carlow □[6]	48	52.40 N	6.50 W
Carloway	46	58.17 N	6.48 W
Carl Sandburg Home National Historic Site ⊥	192	35.16 N	82.27 W
Carlsbad → Karlovy Vary, Česká Rep.	54	50.11 N	12.52 E
Carlsbad, Ca., U.S.	228	33.09 N	117.20 W
Carlsbad, N.M., U.S.	196	32.25 N	104.13 W
Carlsbad, Tx., U.S.	196	31.36 N	100.38 W
Carlsbad Caverns National Park ♦	196	32.08 N	104.35 W
Carlsberg Ridge ✦[3]	12	6.00 N	61.00 E
Carlsborg	224	48.05 N	123.10 W
Carlsfeld	54	50.26 N	12.35 E
Carlstadt	276	40.50 N	74.05 W
Carlton, Austl.	274a	33.58 S	151.08 E
Carlton, Eng., U.K.	42	52.58 N	1.05 W
Carlton, Eng., U.K.	44	53.42 N	1.01 W
Carlton, Mn., U.S.	190	46.39 N	92.25 W
Carlton, Or., U.S.	224	45.18 N	123.11 W
Carlton, Tx., U.S.	196	31.55 N	98.10 W
Carlton Gardens ♦	274b	37.48 S	144.59 E
Carlton Lake ⊜	224	45.18 N	123.11 W
Carluke	46	55.45 N	3.51 W
Carlyle, Sk., Can.	184	49.38 N	102.16 W
Carlyle, Il., U.S.	219	38.36 N	89.22 W
Carlyle Lake ⊜[1]	219	38.40 N	89.18 W
Carmacks	180	62.05 N	136.18 W
Carmagnola	62	44.51 N	7.43 E
Carman	184	49.32 N	98.00 W
Carmanah Creek ≃	224	48.37 N	124.44 W
Carmangay	182	50.08 N	113.07 W
Carmanville	186	49.24 N	54.17 W
Carmarthen	42	51.52 N	4.19 W
Carmarthen Bay ⊂	42	51.40 N	4.30 W
Carmaux	32	44.03 N	2.09 E
Carmel, Wales, U.K.	262	53.17 N	3.15 W
Carmel, Ca., U.S.	226	36.33 N	121.55 W
Carmel, In., U.S.	218	39.58 N	86.07 W
Carmel, N.J., U.S.	208	39.26 N	75.07 W
Carmel, N.Y., U.S.	210	41.26 N	73.41 W
Carmel ≃	226	36.32 N	121.56 W
Carmel, Mount ∧, Ca., U.S.	226	36.23 N	121.47 W
Carmel, Mount → Karmel, Har ∧, Yis.	132	32.44 N	35.02 E
Carmel Bay ⊂	226	36.33 N	121.57 W
Carmel Head ›	44	53.24 N	4.34 W
Carmel Highlands	226	36.30 N	121.56 W
Carmel Hills	226	36.32 N	121.53 W
Carmel Mountain ∧[2]	228	32.55 N	117.13 W
Carmelo	258	34.00 S	58.17 W
Carmel Point	226	36.31 N	122.55 W
Carmel Valley	226	36.29 N	121.43 W
Carmel Woods	226	36.34 N	121.54 W
Carmen → Ciudad del Carmen, Méx.	232	18.38 N	91.50 W
Carmen, Pil.	116	8.59 N	125.17 E
Carmen, Pil.	116	9.50 N	124.12 E
Carmen, Pil.	116	10.35 N	124.01 E
Carmen, Pil.	116	12.37 N	122.07 E
Carmen, Ok., U.S.	196	36.34 N	98.27 W
Carmen, Ur.	252	33.15 S	56.01 W
Carmen, Isla I	232	25.57 N	111.12 W
Carmen, Isla del I	232	18.42 N	91.40 W
Carmen, Río del ≃	252	28.45 S	70.30 W
Carmen Alto	252	23.11 S	69.40 W
Carmen de Apicalá	246	4.09 N	74.44 W
Carmen de Areco	252	34.22 S	59.49 W
Carmen de Huechuraba	286e	33.21 S	70.40 W
Carmen de Patagones	254	40.48 S	62.59 W
Carmer Hill ∧[2]	214	41.54 N	77.58 W
Carmi	194	38.05 N	88.09 W
Carmi, Lake ⊜	206	44.58 N	72.53 W
Carmiano	68	40.21 N	18.03 E
Carmichael	226	38.37 N	121.19 W
Carmignano di Brenta	64	45.38 N	11.42 E
Carmila	166	21.55 S	149.25 E
Carmine	222	30.09 N	96.41 W
Carmo	256	21.56 S	42.37 W
Carmo, Monte ∧	62	44.11 N	8.11 E
Carmo, Ribeirão do ≃	256	21.20 S	45.10 W
Carmo, Rio do ≃	250	5.02 S	37.12 W
Carmo da Cachoeira	256	21.28 S	45.13 W
Carmo de Minas	256	22.07 S	45.08 W
Carmo do Paranaíba	255	18.59 S	46.21 W
Carmo do Rio Verde	255	15.21 S	49.42 W
Carmody Hills	284c	38.54 N	76.54 W
Carmona, Esp.	34	37.28 N	5.38 W
Carmona, Pil.	116	14.19 N	121.03 E
Carmópolis de Minas	255	20.33 S	44.38 W
Carmzow	54	53.23 N	14.02 E
Carnaíba	250	7.48 S	37.49 W
Carnamah	162	29.42 S	115.53 E
Carnarvon, Austl.	162	24.53 S	113.40 E
Carnarvon, S. Afr.	158	30.56 S	22.08 E
Carnarvon → Caernarfon, Wales, U.K.	44	53.08 N	4.16 W
Carnarvon National Park ♦	166	25.00 S	148.00 E
Carnatic □[9]	118	12.30 N	78.15 E
Carnation	224	47.38 N	121.54 W
Carnaval, Arroyo ≃	288	34.52 S	58.02 W
Carnaxide	266c	38.43 N	9.15 W
Carncastle	48	54.54 N	5.53 W
Carndonagh	48	55.15 N	7.15 W
Carnduff	184	49.10 N	101.50 W
Carnedd Llewelyn ∧	44	53.10 N	3.58 W
Carnedd Wen ∧	42	52.41 N	3.35 W
Carnegie, Austl.	162	25.43 S	122.59 E
Carnegie, N.Y., U.S.	210	42.45 N	78.51 W
Carnegie, Ok., U.S.	196	35.06 N	98.36 W
Carnegie, Pa., U.S.	214	40.24 N	80.05 W
Carnegie, Lake ⊜	162	26.10 S	122.30 E
Carnegie Institute ☉[2]	279b	40.27 N	79.57 W
Carnegie-Mellon University ☉[2]	279b	40.27 N	79.57 W
Carnegie Ridge ✦[3]	18	1.00 S	85.00 W
Carnelian Bay	226	39.14 N	120.05 W
Carnetin	261	48.54 N	2.42 E
Carnew	48	52.43 N	6.30 W
Carneys Point	208	39.42 N	75.28 W
Carnforth	44	54.08 N	2.46 W
Carnia	64	46.22 N	13.08 E
Carnia ◆[1]	64	46.25 N	13.00 E
Carniche, Alpi (Karnische Alpen) ⋏	64	46.40 N	13.00 E
Car Nicobar Island I	110	9.10 N	92.47 E
Carnide ◆[8]	266c	38.46 N	9.11 W
Carnières	50	50.10 N	3.21 E
Carniques → Karnische Alpen ⋏	64	46.40 N	13.00 E
Carnlough	48	54.59 N	6.00 W
Carno	42	52.33 N	3.31 W
Carnon-Plage	62	43.32 N	3.59 E
Carnot, Centraf.	152	4.56 N	15.52 E
Carnot, Pa., U.S.	214	40.31 N	80.13 W
Carnot, Cape ›	166	34.57 S	135.38 E
Carnoules	62	43.18 N	6.11 E
Carnoustie	46	56.30 N	2.44 W
Carnsore Point ›	48	52.10 N	6.22 W
Carnwath	46	55.43 N	3.38 W
Carnwath ≃	180	68.26 N	128.50 W
Caro	190	43.29 N	83.23 W
Caroga Creek ≃	210	42.58 N	74.38 W
Caroga Lake	210	43.08 N	74.29 W
Carol Beach Estates	216	42.31 N	87.49 W
Carol City	220	25.56 N	80.14 W
Carole Acres	284c	39.04 N	77.00 W
Caroleen	192	35.16 N	81.47 W
Carole Highlands	284c	38.58 N	76.59 W
Carolei	68	39.15 N	16.13 E
Carolina, Bra.	250	7.20 S	47.28 W
Carolina, Col.	246	6.43 N	75.17 W
Carolina, El Sal.	236	13.51 N	88.19 W
Carolina, P.R.	240m	18.23 N	65.57 W
Carolina, S. Afr.	158	26.05 S	30.06 E
Carolina, R.I., U.S.	207	41.27 N	71.39 W
Carolina Beach	192	34.02 N	77.53 W
Carolinas, Puntan ›	174n	14.55 N	145.38 E
Caroline □[6], Md., U.S.	208	38.53 N	75.50 W
Caroline □[6], Va., U.S.	208	38.00 N	77.20 W
Caroline I[1]	14	9.58 S	150.13 W
Caroline du Nord → North Carolina □[3]	192	35.30 N	80.00 W
Caroline du Sud → South Carolina □[3]	192	34.00 N	81.00 W
Caroline Islands II	14	8.00 N	147.00 E
Caroline Livermore, Mount ∧[2]	282	37.52 N	122.26 W
Caroline Peak ∧	172	45.56 S	167.13 E
Carol Stream	278	41.54 N	88.08 W
Caron	184	50.28 N	105.52 W
Caron, Lac ⊜	190	48.00 N	78.53 W
Çarona	64	46.01 N	9.47 E
Čaronda	76	60.34 N	38.59 E
Caroní ≃	246	8.21 N	62.43 W
Caronia	70	38.01 N	14.26 E
Caronia ≃	70	38.03 N	14.26 E
Caronno Pertusella	266b	45.36 N	9.03 E
Carora	246	10.11 N	70.05 W
Carosino	68	40.27 N	17.23 E
Carouge	58	46.11 N	6.09 E
Car'ov	80	48.40 N	45.22 E
Carovigno	68	40.42 N	17.39 E
Carovilli	66	41.43 N	14.17 E
Çar'ovščina	80	53.37 N	44.45 E
Čarozero	76	60.28 N	38.39 E
Carp	212	45.21 N	76.02 W
Carp ≃, On., Can.	212	45.29 N	76.14 W
Carp ≃, Mi., U.S.	190	46.02 N	84.42 W
Carpaneto Piacentino	62	44.55 N	9.47 E
Carpanzano	68	39.09 N	16.18 E
Carpates → Carpathian Mountains ⋏	22	48.00 N	24.00 E
Carpathian Mountains ⋏	22	48.00 N	24.00 E
Carpații Meridionali ⋏	38	45.30 N	24.15 E
Cárpatos → Carpathian Mountains ⋏	22	48.00 N	24.00 E
Carpegna	66	43.47 N	12.20 E
Carpenedolo	64	45.22 N	10.26 E
Carpentaria, Gulf of ⊂	164	14.00 S	139.00 E
Carpenter	198	41.02 N	104.21 W
Carpenter Creek ≃	216	40.54 N	87.12 W
Carpenter Lake ⊜	182	50.50 N	122.30 W
Carpentersville	216	42.07 N	88.15 W
Carpentertown	279b	40.11 N	79.31 W
Carpentras	62	44.03 N	5.03 E
Carpet Museum ☉	267d	35.43 N	51.24 E
Carpi	64	44.47 N	10.53 E
Carpignano Sesia	62	45.32 N	8.25 E
Carpina	250	7.51 S	35.15 W
Cărpineni	38	46.47 N	28.22 E
Carpineti	64	44.28 N	10.31 E
Carpineto Romano	66	41.36 N	13.05 E
Carpino	68	41.51 N	15.51 E
Carpinone	66	41.35 N	14.19 E
Carpinteria	204	34.23 N	119.31 W
Carpio	198	48.26 N	101.42 W
Carp Lake ⊜	182	54.45 N	123.20 W
Carpolac	166	36.44 S	141.19 E
Carquefou	32	47.18 N	1.30 W
Carqueiranne	62	43.05 N	6.05 E
Carquinez Bridge ◆[5]	282	38.04 N	122.14 W
Carquinez Strait ʮ	282	38.02 N	122.12 W
Carra, Lough ⊜	48	53.42 N	9.16 W
Carrabelle	192	29.51 N	84.39 W
Carradale	46	55.35 N	5.28 W
Carramar	274a	33.53 S	150.58 E
Carrancas	256	21.30 S	44.39 W
Carr and Craggs Moor ◆[3]	262	53.43 N	2.09 W
Carranglan	116	15.58 N	121.04 E
Carranza, Cabo ›	252	35.36 S	72.38 W
Carrao ≃	246	6.17 N	62.51 W
Carrara	64	44.05 N	10.06 E
Carrascal	116	9.22 N	125.56 E
Carrasco ◆[8]	258	34.54 S	56.05 W
Carrasco, Aeropuerto Nacional de ⊠	258	34.52 S	56.02 W
Carrathool	166	34.24 S	145.26 E
Carrauntoohil ∧	48	51.59 N	9.45 W
Carrazedo	250	1.36 S	51.54 W
Carrboro	192	35.54 N	79.04 W
Carr Bridge	46	57.17 N	3.49 W
Carrcroft	285	39.47 N	75.30 W
Carrcroft Crest	285	39.47 N	75.30 W
Carrefour Pompadour ♦	261	48.46 N	2.26 E
Carregueira, Serra da ⋏[2]	266c	38.48 N	9.15 W
Carreria	252	21.59 S	58.35 W
Carreta, Punta ›	248	14.13 S	76.18 W
Carreta Quemada, Arroyo ≃	258	34.21 S	56.41 W
Carriacou I	238	12.30 N	61.27 W
Carrick ◆[8]	279b	40.23 N	79.59 W
Carrick ◆[1]	44	55.12 N	4.38 W
Carrickart	48	55.10 N	7.47 W
Carrickfergus	48	54.43 N	5.49 W
Carrickmacross	48	53.58 N	6.43 W
Carrick on Shannon	48	53.57 N	8.05 W
Carrick on Suir	48	52.21 N	7.25 W
Carrie, Mount ∧	224	47.53 N	123.39 W
Carriere	194	30.37 N	89.39 W
Carrière, Lac ⊜	190	47.14 N	77.12 W
Carrières, Pointe aux ›	275a	45.31 N	73.54 W
Carrières-sous-Bois	261	48.57 N	2.07 E
Carrières-sous-Poissy	261	48.57 N	2.03 E
Carrières-sur-Seine	261	48.55 N	2.11 E
Carriers Mills	194	37.41 N	88.38 W
Carrieton	166	32.26 S	138.32 E
Carrigahorig	48	53.04 N	8.09 W
Carrigaline	48	51.48 N	8.24 W
Carrigallen	48	53.59 N	7.39 W
Carrillo, C.R.	236	9.52 N	85.30 W
Carrillo, Méx.	232	26.54 N	103.55 W
Carrington, Eng., U.K.	262	53.26 N	2.24 W
Carrington, N.D., U.S.	198	47.26 N	99.07 W
Carrington Island I	202	41.00 N	112.37 W
Carrington Moss ◆[3]	262	53.25 N	2.23 W
Carr Inlet ⊂	224	47.17 N	122.42 W
Carrión ≃	34	41.53 N	4.32 W
Carrión de los Condes	34	42.20 N	4.36 W
Carrizal ≃	234	23.03 N	97.46 W
Carrizal, Cerro ∧	196	26.43 N	100.36 W
Carrizal Bajo	252	28.05 S	71.10 W
Carrizo	34	42.35 N	5.50 W
Carrizo Creek ≃, U.S.	196	36.05 N	102.36 W
Carrizo Creek ≃, N.M., U.S.	196	35.40 N	103.43 W
Carrizo Mountain ∧	200	33.41 N	105.42 W
Carrizo Mountains ⋏	200	36.45 N	109.10 W
Carrizo Plain ≚	226	35.25 N	120.00 W
Carrizo Springs	196	28.31 N	99.51 W
Carrizo Wash V, U.S.	200	34.36 N	109.26 W
Carrizo Wash V, Ca., U.S.	204	33.05 N	115.56 W
Carrizozo	200	33.38 N	105.52 W
Carro	62	43.20 N	5.02 E
Carrodano	62	44.14 N	9.39 E
Carroll, Ia., U.S.	198	42.03 N	94.52 W
Carroll, Ne., U.S.	198	42.16 N	97.11 W
Carroll □[6], In., U.S.	216	40.36 N	86.41 W
Carroll □[6], Ky., U.S.	218	38.39 N	85.06 W
Carroll □[6], Md., U.S.	208	39.35 N	77.00 W
Carroll □[6], Oh., U.S.	214	40.34 N	81.05 W
Carroll Lake ⊜	184	51.07 N	95.05 W
Carroll Park ♦	284b	39.17 N	76.39 W
Carrolls	224	46.05 N	122.52 W
Carrollton, Al., U.S.	194	33.10 N	88.06 W
Carrollton, Ga., U.S.	192	33.35 N	85.05 W
Carrollton, Il., U.S.	219	39.18 N	90.24 W
Carrollton, Ky., U.S.	218	38.40 N	85.10 W
Carrollton, Mi., U.S.	190	43.27 N	83.55 W
Carrollton, Ms., U.S.	194	33.30 N	89.55 W
Carrollton, Mo., U.S.	194	39.21 N	93.29 W
Carrollton, Oh., U.S.	214	40.34 N	81.05 W
Carrollton, Tx., U.S.	222	32.57 N	96.53 W
Carrollton Manor	208	39.05 N	76.35 W
Carrolltown	214	40.36 N	78.43 W
Carrollwood	284b	39.20 N	76.23 W
Carron ≃, Austl.	166	17.42 S	141.06 E
Carron ≃, Scot., U.K.	46	57.53 N	4.21 W
Carron ≃, Scot., U.K.	46	57.25 N	5.27 W
Carron ≃, Scot., U.K.	46	56.02 N	3.44 W
Carron, Loch ⊂	46	57.22 N	5.31 W
Carronbridge	44	55.16 N	3.48 W
Carron Valley Reservoir ⊜[1]	46	56.02 N	4.05 W
Carros	62	43.48 N	7.11 E
Carrot ≃	184	53.50 N	101.17 W
Carrot River	184	53.17 N	103.35 W
Carrouges	28	48.34 N	0.09 W
Carrowmore Lake ⊜	48	54.12 N	9.47 W
Carrsville	208	36.43 N	76.50 W
Carrù	62	44.29 N	7.52 E
Carrum	169	38.05 S	145.08 E
Carrum Downs	274b	38.06 S	145.11 E
Carrum North	274b	38.03 S	145.09 E
Carrville	194	32.32 N	85.52 W
Carryduff	48	54.31 N	5.53 W
Carry Falls Reservoir ⊜[1]	188	44.25 N	74.45 W
Carry-le-Rouet	62	43.20 N	5.09 E
Carsaig	46	56.17 N	6.00 W
Çarşamba	130	41.12 N	36.44 E
Čaršanga	128	37.30 N	66.01 E
Carseland	182	50.51 N	113.28 W
Çarshalton ◆[8]	260	51.22 N	0.10 W
Čarsk	86	49.35 N	81.05 E
Carsoli	66	42.06 N	13.05 E
Carson, Ca., U.S.	228	33.49 N	118.16 W
Carson, N.D., U.S.	198	46.25 N	101.33 W
Carson, Va., U.S.	208	37.02 N	77.23 W
Carson, Wa., U.S.	224	45.43 N	121.49 W
Carson ≃	204	39.45 N	118.40 W
Carson, East Fork ≃	226	38.59 N	119.49 W
Carson, West Fork ≃	226	38.59 N	119.49 W
Carson City, Mi., U.S.	190	43.10 N	84.50 W
Carson City, Nv., U.S.	226	39.10 N	119.46 W
Carsondale	284c	38.57 N	76.50 W
Carson Lake ⊜, On., Can.	212	45.31 N	77.46 W
Carson Lake ⊜, Nv., U.S.	204	39.19 N	118.43 W
Carson Range ⋏	226	39.15 N	119.50 W
Carson Sink ⊜	204	39.45 N	118.30 W
Carson Valley V	226	39.00 N	119.48 W
Carstairs, Ab., Can.	182	51.34 N	114.06 W
Carstairs, Scot., U.K.	46	55.42 N	3.42 W
Carstensz-Toppen → Jaya, Puncak ∧	164	4.05 S	137.11 E
Carswell Air Force Base ■	222	32.47 N	97.26 W
Cartagena, Chile	252	33.33 S	71.37 W
Cartagena, Col.	246	10.25 N	75.32 W
Cartagena, Esp.	34	37.36 N	0.59 W
Cartago, Col.	246	4.45 N	75.55 W
Cartago, C.R.	236	9.52 N	83.55 W
Çartago □[4]	236	9.50 N	83.45 W
Čartak	85	41.05 N	71.50 E
Cartaxo	34	39.09 N	8.47 W
Cartaxos ∧[2]	266c	38.54 N	9.20 W
Cartaya	34	37.17 N	7.09 W
Carter	196	35.13 N	99.30 W
Carter □[6]	218	38.20 N	83.05 W
Carter Bridge ◆[5]	273a	6.28 N	3.23 E
Carter Caves State Resort Park ♦	218	38.22 N	83.10 W
Carteret	210	40.34 N	74.13 W
Carter Lake	198	41.17 N	95.55 W
Carter Mountain ∧	202	44.12 N	109.25 W
Carters Lake ⊜[1]	192	34.35 N	84.35 W
Cartersville	192	34.09 N	84.48 W
Carterton, N.Z.	172	41.02 S	175.31 E
Carterton, Eng., U.K.	42	51.45 N	1.35 W
Carterville	194	37.45 N	89.04 W
Carthage, Tun.	148	36.51 N	10.21 E
Carthage, Ar., U.S.	194	34.04 N	92.33 W
Carthage, Il., U.S.	190	40.24 N	91.08 W
Carthage, In., U.S.	218	39.44 N	85.34 W
Carthage, Ms., U.S.	194	32.43 N	89.32 W
Carthage, Mo., U.S.	194	37.10 N	94.18 W
Carthage, N.Y., U.S.	212	43.58 N	75.36 W
Carthage, N.C., U.S.	192	35.20 N	79.25 W
Carthage, S.D., U.S.	198	44.10 N	97.42 W
Carthage, Tn., U.S.	194	36.15 N	85.57 W
Carthage, Tx., U.S.	194	32.09 N	94.20 W
Carthage ⊥	36	36.52 N	10.20 E
Cartier Islands II	160	12.32 S	123.32 E
Cartierville ◆[8]	275a	45.32 N	73.42 W
Cartierville, Aéroport de ⊠	275a	45.31 N	73.43 W
Cartridge Hill ∧[2]	262	53.41 N	2.30 W
Cartura	64	45.16 N	11.50 E
Cartwright, Mb., Can.	184	49.06 N	99.20 W
Cartwright, Nf., Can.	176	53.42 N	57.01 W
Caruaru	250	8.17 S	35.58 W
Caruban	115a	7.33 S	111.39 E
Çarumas	248	16.49 S	70.43 W
Čarüngol	88	49.14 N	106.29 E
Carunjamba ≃	152	13.57 S	12.25 E
Carúpano	246	10.40 N	63.14 W
Caruray	116	10.20 N	119.00 E
Carutapera	250	1.13 S	46.01 W
Caruthers	226	36.32 N	119.50 W
Caruthersville	194	36.11 N	89.39 W
Carutu ≃	246	5.05 N	63.28 W
Carvalhopolis	256	21.47 S	46.51 W
Carvalhos	256	22.00 S	44.28 W
Carver	207	41.53 N	70.45 W
Carversville	208	40.23 N	75.04 W
Carvin	50	50.29 N	2.58 E
Carvoeiro	246	1.24 S	61.59 W
Carvoeiro, Cabo ›	34	39.21 N	9.24 W
Carwitzer See ⊜	54	53.18 N	13.28 E
Cary, Il., U.S.	216	42.12 N	88.14 W
Cary, Ms., U.S.	194	32.48 N	90.55 W
Cary, N.C., U.S.	192	35.47 N	78.46 W
Cary ≃	42	51.09 N	2.59 W
Caryčelekskij zapovednik ♦	85	41.50 N	71.55 E
Çaryk, ozero ⊜	80	46.13 N	42.43 E
Çarymovo	86	58.31 N	77.42 E
Çaryn	86	43.46 N	79.24 E
Čaryš ≃	86	52.22 N	83.45 E
Čaryšskoje	86	51.24 N	83.35 E
Caryville, Fl., U.S.	194	30.46 N	85.48 W

Symbols in the index entries represent the broad categories identified in the key at the right. Symbols with superior numbers (⋏[1]) identify subcategories (see complete key on page *I · 1*).

Symbole im Register stellen die rechts im Schlüssel erklärten Kategorien dar. Symbole mit hochgestellten Ziffern (⋏[1]) bezeichnen Unterabteilungen einer Kategorie (vgl. vollständiger Schlüssel auf Seite *I · 1*).

Los símbolos incluídos en el texto del índice representan las grandes categorías identificadas con la clave a la derecha. Los símbolos con numeros en su parte superior (⋏[1]) identifican las subcategorías (véase la clave completa en la página *I · 1*).

Les symboles de l'index représentent les catégories indiquées dans la légende à droite. Les symboles suivis d'un indice (⋏[1]) représentent des sous-catégories (voir légende complète à la page *I · 1*).

Os símbolos incluídos no texto do índice representam as grandes categorias identificadas com a chave à direita. Os símbolos com números em sua parte superior (⋏[1]) identificam as subcategorias (veja-se a chave completa à página *I · 1*).

∧ Mountain	Berg	Montaña	Montagne	Montanha
⋏ Mountains	Gebirge	Montañas	Montagnes	Montanhas
)(Pass	Paß	Paso	Col	Passo
V Valley, Canyon	Tal, Cañon	Valle, Cañón	Vallée, Canyon	Vale, Canhão
≚ Plain	Ebene	Llano	Plaine	Planície
› Cape	Kap	Cabo	Cap	Cabo
I Island	Insel	Isla	Île	Ilha
II Islands	Inseln	Islas	Îles	Ilhas
⊥ Other Topographic Features	Andere Topographische Objekte	Otros Elementos Topográficos	Autres données topographiques	Outros acidentes topográficos

ESPAÑOL

Nombre	Página	Lat.°′	Long.°′ W = Oeste
Caryville, Tn., U.S.	192	36.17 N	84.13 W
Casablanca (Dar-el-Beida)	148	33.39 N	7.35 W
Casablanca □[4]	148	33.35 N	7.30 W
Casablanca ●[8]	286b	23.09 N	82.20 W
Casabona	68	39.15 N	16.57 E
Casa Branca	256	21.46 S	47.04 W
Casacalenda	68	41.44 N	14.51 E
Casa de la Torrecilla	266a	40.19 N	3.37 W
Casa del Campo ♠	266a	40.32 N	3.47 W
Casa de Piedra, Embalse ◎[1]	252	38.15 S	67.20 W
Casa Grande	200	32.52 N	111.45 W
Casa Grande National Monument ♠	200	32.59 N	111.32 W
Casainhos	266c	38.53 N	9.10 W
Casalanguida	66	42.03 N	14.30 E
Casalattico	66	41.37 N	13.43 E
Casalbordino	66	42.09 N	14.35 E
Casalbuono	68	40.13 N	15.41 E
Casalbuttano	64	45.15 N	9.58 E
Casal di Principe	68	41.00 N	14.08 E
Casale Abbruciato ●[8]	267a	41.44 N	12.33 E
Casalecchio di Reno	64	44.28 N	11.16 E
Casale Monferrato	62	45.08 N	8.27 E
Casale sul Sile	64	45.36 N	12.19 E
Casaletto Spartano	68	40.09 N	15.37 E
Casalmaggiore	64	44.59 N	10.26 E
Casalmorano	62	45.17 N	9.54 E
Casalnuovo Monterotaro	68	41.37 N	15.06 E
Casa Loma ♜	275b	43.41 N	79.25 W
Casalone ●[8]	267a	41.56 N	12.41 E
Casalotti ●[8]	267a	41.55 N	12.22 E
Casalpusterlengo	62	45.11 N	9.39 E
Casal Velino	68	40.11 N	15.06 E
Casalvieri	66	41.38 N	13.43 E
Casamance ≃	150	12.33 N	16.46 W
Casamari, Abbazia di ♜[1]	66	41.41 N	13.29 E
Casamassima	68	40.57 N	16.55 E
Casamicciola Terme	68	40.45 N	13.54 E
Casanare □[3]	246	5.45 N	72.00 W
Casanare ≃	246	6.02 N	69.51 W
Casanay	246	10.30 N	63.25 W
Casa Nova	250	9.07 S	40.58 W
Casarano	68	40.00 N	18.10 E
Casar de Cáceres	34	39.34 N	6.25 W
Casarsa della Delizia	64	45.57 N	12.50 E
Casas	234	23.44 N	98.45 W
Casas Adobes	200	32.19 N	110.59 W
Casas Grandes ≃	232	31.22 N	107.31 W
Casas Ibáñez	34	39.17 N	1.28 W
Casasimarro	34	39.22 N	2.02 W
Casauman ≃	116	7.16 N	126.31 E
Casa Verde ●[8]	287b	23.30 S	46.39 W
Casavieja	34	40.17 N	4.46 W
Casbas	252	36.45 S	62.30 W
Casca	252	28.34 S	51.59 W
Casca, Rio da ≃	248	14.52 S	55.52 W
Cascadas Basaseachic, Parque Nacional ♠	232	28.10 N	108.22 W
Cascade, B.C., Can.	182	49.01 N	118.13 W
Cascade, Id., U.S.	202	44.30 N	116.02 W
Cascade, Ia., U.S.	190	42.17 N	91.00 W
Cascade, Mi., U.S.	216	42.55 N	85.30 W
Cascade, Mt., U.S.	202	47.16 N	111.41 W
Cascade, Wi., U.S.	190	43.39 N	88.00 W
Cascade ≃, N.Z.	172	44.02 S	168.22 E
Cascade ≃, Wa., U.S.	224	48.32 N	121.26 W
Cascade Bay c	174c	29.01 S	167.58 E
Cascade Locks	224	45.40 N	121.53 W
Cascade Mountains (Cascade Range) ⋀	202	45.00 N	121.30 W
Cascade Park ♠	279a	41.23 N	82.06 W
Cascade Point ›	172	44.00 S	168.22 E
Cascade Range ⋀	178	45.00 N	121.30 W
Cascade Reservoir ◎[1]	202	44.35 N	116.06 W
Cascade Tunnel ●[5]	224	47.40 N	121.03 W
Cascadura ●[8]	287a	22.53 S	43.20 W
Cascais	34	38.42 N	9.25 W
Cascalho Rico	255	18.34 S	47.52 W
Cascapédia ≃	186	48.11 N	65.54 W
Cascatinha	256	22.29 S	43.09 W
Cascavel, Bra.	250	4.07 S	38.14 W
Cascavel, Bra.	252	24.57 S	53.28 W
Cascia	66	42.43 N	13.01 E
Casciana Terme	66	43.31 N	10.32 E
Cascina	66	43.41 N	10.33 E
Casco Bay c	188	43.40 N	70.00 W
Cascumpec Bay c	186	46.45 N	64.03 W
Čascy	82	55.37 N	36.52 E
Casei Gerola	62	45.00 N	8.55 E
Case Inlet c	224	47.19 N	122.53 W
Casekow	54	53.12 N	14.12 E
Casella	62	44.32 N	9.00 E
Caselle, Aeroporto di ⊠	62	45.13 N	7.40 E
Caselle in Pittari	68	40.10 N	15.33 E
Caselle Torinese	62	45.10 N	7.39 E
Cà Selva, Lago di ◎[1]	64	46.16 N	12.40 E
Casenove	66	42.58 N	12.50 E
Casentino V	66	43.40 N	11.50 E
Casenuove	266b	45.38 N	8.42 E
Case-Pilote	240e	14.38 N	61.08 W
Caseros	258	34.36 S	58.33 W
Caserta	68	41.04 N	14.20 E
Caserta □[4]	68	41.14 N	14.10 E
Caseville	190	43.56 N	83.16 W
Case Western Reserve University ♜[2]	279a	41.30 N	81.36 W
Casey, Il., U.S.	194	39.17 N	87.59 W
Casey, Ia., U.S.	198	41.30 N	94.31 W
Casey ♜[3]	9	66.17 S	110.32 E
Casey, Mount ∧	202	48.26 N	116.42 W
Casey Bay c	9	67.20 S	48.00 E
Casey Key I	220	27.10 N	82.29 W
Caseyr ›	144	11.49 N	51.15 E
Caseyville	219	38.38 N	90.02 W
Cash	222	32.59 N	96.07 W
Cashel, Ire.	48	53.25 N	9.48 W
Cashel, Ire.	48	52.31 N	7.53 W
Cashie ≃	192	35.53 N	76.49 W
Cashiers	192	35.06 N	83.05 W
Cashmere	202	47.31 N	120.28 W
Cashmere Downs	162	28.58 S	119.35 E
Cashton	190	43.44 N	90.46 W
Cashtown	208	39.53 N	77.22 W
Casigua	246	8.46 N	72.30 W
Casiguran, Pil.	116	16.17 N	122.07 E
Casiguran, Pil.	116	12.52 N	124.00 E
Casiguran Sound Ⴎ	116	16.06 N	121.58 E
Casilda, Arg.	252	33.03 S	61.10 W
Casilda, Cuba	240p	21.46 N	79.59 W
Casimcea	38	44.43 N	28.23 E
Casimiro Castillo	234	19.38 N	104.28 W
Casina	64	44.30 N	10.30 E
Casino	166	28.52 S	153.03 E
Casiquiare ≃	246	2.01 N	67.07 W
Casita	200	31.00 N	110.53 W
Casitas Springs	228	34.22 N	119.18 W
Čáslav	30	49.54 N	15.23 E
Casma	248	9.28 S	78.19 W
Čašniki	76	54.52 N	29.08 E
Čašnikovo	265b	55.59 N	37.25 E
Časnočor, gora ∧	24	67.45 N	33.25 E
Casola in Lunigiana	64	44.14 N	10.10 E
Casola Valsenio	66	44.13 N	11.37 E
Casole d'Elsa	66	43.20 N	11.02 E
Casoli	66	42.07 N	14.18 E
Cason	222	33.02 N	94.49 W
Casorate Primo	62	45.19 N	9.01 E
Casorate Sempione	62	45.40 N	8.44 E
Casorezzo	266b	45.31 N	8.54 E
Casoria	68	40.54 N	14.17 E
Časovo	24	62.01 N	50.36 E
Caspe	34	41.14 N	0.02 W

FRANÇAIS

Nom	Page	Lat.°′	Long.°′ W = Ouest
Casper	200	42.52 N	106.18 W
Casper Creek, Middle Fork ≃	200	43.01 N	106.29 W
Caspian	190	46.03 N	88.37 W
Caspian Sea ⫪[2]	72	42.00 N	50.30 E
Caspienne, Mer → Caspian Sea ⫪[2]	72	42.00 N	50.30 E
Caspio, Depresión del → Prikaspijskaja nizmennost' ≚	80	48.00 N	52.00 E
Caspio, Mar → Caspian Sea ⫪[2]	72	42.00 N	50.30 E
Caspoggio	64	46.16 N	9.52 E
Cass □[6], Il., U.S.	219	39.57 N	90.13 W
Cass □[6], In., U.S.	216	40.45 N	86.21 W
Cass □[6], Mi., U.S.	216	41.55 N	86.01 W
Cass □[6], Tx., U.S.	222	33.05 N	94.32 W
Cass ≃	190	43.23 N	83.59 W
Cassadaga	214	42.20 N	79.18 W
Cassadaga Creek ≃	214	42.05 N	79.08 W
Cassadaga Lakes ◎	214	42.21 N	79.19 W
Cassaday Point ›	284a	42.52 N	79.13 W
Cassagnas	62	44.16 N	3.45 E
Cassai	152	10.33 S	21.59 E
Cassai (Kasai) ≃	152	3.02 S	16.57 E
Cassamba	152	13.06 S	20.18 E
Cassandra	214	40.24 N	78.38 W
Cassanje ≃	248	17.06 S	57.23 W
Cassano allo Ionio	68	39.47 N	16.20 E
Cassano d'Adda	62	45.32 N	9.31 E
Cassano delle Murge	68	40.53 N	16.46 E
Cassano Magnago	62	45.41 N	8.50 E
Cassaro	70	37.07 N	14.56 E
Cass Benton Parkway ♠	281	42.25 N	83.28 W
Cass City	190	43.36 N	83.10 W
Cassel	50	50.48 N	2.29 E
Casselberry	220	28.40 N	81.19 W
Cassella	216	40.25 N	84.34 W
Casselman	206	45.19 N	75.05 W
Casselton	198	46.54 N	97.12 W
Cássia, Bra.	255	20.36 S	46.56 W
Cassia, Fl., U.S.	220	28.53 N	81.28 W
Cássia dos Coqueiros	256	21.17 S	47.10 W
Cassiar	180	59.16 N	129.40 W
Cassiar Mountains ⋀	176	59.00 N	129.00 W
Cassibile ≃	70	36.57 N	15.11 E
Cassidy	224	49.04 N	123.53 W
Cassidy Airfield ⊠	174o	1.57 N	157.18 W
Cassilândia	255	19.09 S	51.45 W
Cassimbazar	126	24.07 N	88.16 E
Cassine	62	44.45 N	8.31 E
Cassinetta di Lugagnano	266b	45.25 N	8.54 E
Cassinga	152	15.08 S	16.05 E
Cassino, Bra.	252	32.11 S	52.10 W
Cassino, It.	66	41.30 N	13.49 E
Cassio	64	44.35 N	10.02 E
Cassipore ●[8]	272b	22.37 N	88.22 E
Cassis	62	43.13 N	5.32 E
Cass Lake	190	47.22 N	94.36 W
Cass Lake ◎, Mi., U.S.	281	42.36 N	83.22 W
Cass Lake ◎, Mn., U.S.	190	47.25 N	94.32 W
Cassley ≃	46	57.58 N	4.35 W
Cassoalala	152	9.30 S	14.22 E
Cassoango	152	13.42 S	20.56 E
Cassolnovo	62	45.22 N	8.48 E
Cassone	64	45.44 N	10.46 E
Cassongue	152	11.51 S	15.03 E
Cassopolis	216	41.54 N	86.00 W
Casstown	218	40.03 N	84.07 W
Cassumba, Ilha I	255	17.46 S	39.17 W
Cassunda	152	10.57 S	21.03 E
Cassununga	255	16.03 S	53.38 W
Cassville, In., U.S.	216	40.33 N	86.08 W
Cassville, Mo., U.S.	194	36.40 N	93.52 W
Cassville, N.Y., U.S.	210	42.57 N	75.15 W
Cassville, Pa., U.S.	214	40.18 N	78.02 W
Cassville, Wi., U.S.	190	42.42 N	90.59 W
Castac Lake ◎	228	34.50 N	118.51 W
Castagnaro	64	45.07 N	11.24 E
Castagneto Carducci	66	43.10 N	10.36 E
Castaic	228	34.30 N	118.37 W
Castaic Creek ≃	228	34.25 N	118.37 W
Castaic Lake ◎[1]	228	34.32 N	118.37 W
Castalia	214	41.24 N	82.48 W
Castanea	210	41.07 N	77.25 W
Castanhal	250	1.18 S	47.55 W
Castanheira de Pêra	34	40.00 N	8.13 W
Castaños	196	26.47 N	101.25 W
Castañones, Punta ›	236	12.28 N	87.11 W
Castano Primo	62	45.33 N	8.47 E
Casteggio	62	45.00 N	9.07 E
Castel	43b	49.28 N	2.34 W
Castelar	258	34.40 S	58.40 W
Castel Baronia	68	41.03 N	15.11 E
Castel Bolognese	66	44.19 N	11.48 E
Castelbuono	70	37.56 N	14.05 E
Castelcivita	68	40.30 N	15.15 E
Casteldaccia	70	38.03 N	13.32 E
Castel d'Ario	64	45.11 N	10.58 E
Casteldarne (Ehrenburg)	64	46.48 N	11.50 E
Casteldelfino	62	44.35 N	7.04 E
Castel del Monte	66	42.22 N	13.43 E
Castel del Piano	66	42.53 N	11.32 E
Castel del Rio	66	44.12 N	11.30 E
Castel di Decima ●[8]	267a	41.45 N	12.26 E
Castel di Guido ●[8]	267a	41.54 N	12.17 E
Castel di Ieri	66	42.06 N	13.44 E
Castel di Iudica	70	37.30 N	14.38 E
Castel di Leva ●[8]	267a	41.47 N	12.32 E
Castel di Lucio	70	37.53 N	14.19 E
Castel di Sangro	66	41.47 N	14.06 E
Castel di Tora	66	42.13 N	12.58 E
Castelfidardo	66	43.28 N	13.33 E
Castelfiorentino	66	43.36 N	10.58 E
Castelfondo	64	46.27 N	11.07 E
Castelforte	66	41.18 N	13.49 E
Castelfranco Emilia	64	44.37 N	11.03 E
Castelfranco in Miscano	68	41.18 N	15.05 E
Castelfranco Veneto	64	45.40 N	11.55 E
Castel Frentano	66	42.12 N	14.22 E
Castel Fusano ●[8]	267a	41.44 N	12.19 E
Castel Gandolfo	66	41.45 N	12.39 E
Castel Giorgio	66	42.42 N	11.59 E
Castelgrande	68	40.47 N	15.26 E
Castelhanos, Baía de c	256	23.51 S	45.15 W
Castelhanos, Ponta dos ›	256	23.10 S	44.06 W
Castellabate	68	40.17 N	14.57 E
Castell'Alfero	62	44.59 N	8.13 E
Castellalto	66	42.40 N	13.49 E
Castellammare, Golfo di c	70	38.08 N	12.54 E
Castellammare del Golfo	70	38.01 N	12.53 E
Castellammare di Stabia	68	40.42 N	14.29 E
Castellamonte	62	45.23 N	7.42 E
Castellana, Grotte di ⏏[5]	68	40.53 N	17.07 E
Castellana Grotte	68	40.53 N	17.11 E
Castellana Sicula	70	37.47 N	14.02 E
Castellane	62	43.51 N	6.31 E
Castellaneta	68	40.37 N	16.57 E
Castellanza	62	45.37 N	8.54 E
Castellarano	64	44.30 N	10.44 E
Castell'Arquato	62	44.51 N	9.52 E
Castell'Azzara	66	42.46 N	11.42 E
Castellazzo Bormida	62	44.51 N	8.34 E
Castellbisbal	266d	41.29 N	1.59 E
Castelldefels	266d	41.17 N	1.59 E
Castelleone	62	45.18 N	9.46 E
Castelletto	266b	45.30 N	8.48 E
Castelletto di Brenzone	64	45.41 N	10.45 E

PORTUGUÊS

Nome	Página	Lat.°′	Long.°′ W = Oeste
Castelli, Arg.	252	36.06 S	57.47 W
Castelli, It.	66	42.29 N	13.43 E
Castellina in Chianti	66	43.28 N	11.17 E
Castellina Marittima	66	43.25 N	10.35 E
Castelli Romani ●[1]	267a	41.48 N	12.42 E
Castelló □[4]	34	40.10 N	0.10 W
Castello, Monte ∧[2]	66	43.03 N	9.49 E
Castello d'Annone	62	44.53 N	8.19 E
Castelló de la Plana	34	39.59 N	0.02 W
Castello di Fiemme	64	46.17 N	11.26 E
Castello Lavazzo	64	46.17 N	12.18 E
Castellote	34	40.48 N	0.19 W
Castello Tesino	64	46.04 N	11.38 E
Castellucchio	64	45.09 N	10.39 E
Castelluccio	68	40.00 N	15.58 E
Castell'Umberto	70	38.05 N	14.48 E
Castelluzzo	70	38.06 N	12.44 E
Castel Madama	66	41.58 N	12.52 E
Castel Maggiore	64	44.34 N	11.22 E
Castelmagno	62	44.24 N	7.13 E
Castelmassa	64	45.01 N	11.18 E
Castelmauro	66	41.50 N	14.43 E
Castelmezzano	68	40.32 N	16.03 E
Castelmoron-sur-Lot	32	44.24 N	0.30 E
Castelnaudary	32	43.19 N	1.57 E
Castelnau-Montratier	32	44.16 N	1.21 E
Castelnovo di Sotto	64	44.49 N	10.34 E
Castelnovo ne'Monti	64	44.26 N	10.24 E
Castelnuovo	64	45.26 N	10.47 E
Castelnuovo Berardenga	66	43.21 N	11.30 E
Castelnuovo dell'Abate	66	43.00 N	11.31 E
Castelnuovo della Daunia	68	41.35 N	15.07 E
Castelnuovo di Garfagnana	64	44.06 N	10.24 E
Castelnuovo di Porto	66	42.07 N	12.30 E
Castelnuovo di Val di Cecina	66	43.12 N	10.59 E
Castelnuovo Don Bosco	62	45.03 N	7.58 E
Castelnuovo Nigra	62	45.26 N	7.41 E
Castelnuovo Rangone	64	44.33 N	10.56 E
Castelnuovo Scrivia	62	44.59 N	8.53 E
Castelo	255	20.36 S	41.12 W
Castelo Branco	34	39.49 N	7.30 W
Castelo do Piauí	250	5.20 S	41.33 W
Castel Pagano	68	41.24 N	14.48 E
Castel Porziano ●[8]	267a	41.44 N	12.24 E
Castelraimondo	66	43.12 N	13.04 E
Castel Romano ●[8]	267a	41.44 N	12.27 E
Castel San Gimignano	66	43.24 N	11.00 E
Castel San Giorgio	68	40.47 N	14.42 E
Castel San Giovanni	62	45.04 N	9.26 E
Castel San Lorenzo	68	40.25 N	15.14 E
Castel San Pietro Terme	66	44.24 N	11.35 E
Castel Sant'Elia	66	42.15 N	12.22 E
Castelsaraceno	68	40.10 N	16.00 E
Castelsardo	71	40.55 N	8.43 E
Castelsarrasin	32	44.02 N	1.06 E
Castelsilano	68	39.16 N	16.46 E
Casteltermini	70	37.32 N	13.39 E
Castelvecchio Subequo	66	42.08 N	13.44 E
Castelvetere in Val Fortore	68	41.27 N	14.56 E
Castelvetrano	70	37.41 N	12.47 E
Castelvetro di Modena	64	44.30 N	10.57 E
Castelvetro Piacentino	64	45.05 N	9.59 E
Castel Viscardo	66	42.45 N	12.00 E
Castel Volturno	68	41.02 N	13.56 E
Castenaso	64	44.30 N	11.28 E
Castenedolo	64	45.28 N	10.18 E
Casterton	166	37.35 S	141.24 E
Castets	32	43.53 N	1.09 W
Castiglioncello	66	43.24 N	10.24 E
Castiglione Chiavarese	62	44.16 N	9.21 E
Castiglione d'Adda	62	45.13 N	9.41 E
Castiglione dei Pepoli	66	44.08 N	11.09 E
Castiglione del Lago	66	43.07 N	12.03 E
Castiglione della Pescaia	66	42.46 N	10.53 E
Castiglione delle Stiviere	64	45.23 N	10.29 E
Castiglione di Sicilia	70	37.53 N	15.07 E
Castiglione d'Orcia	66	43.00 N	11.37 E
Castiglione d'Ossola	58	46.03 N	8.13 E
Castiglione Messer Marino	66	41.52 N	14.27 E
Castiglione Olona	62	45.46 N	8.52 E
Castiglion Fibocchi	66	43.32 N	11.46 E
Castiglion Fiorentino	66	43.20 N	11.55 E
Castile	210	42.37 N	78.03 W
Castilho	255	20.52 S	51.29 W
Castilla	248	5.12 S	80.38 W
Castilla, Playa de ⏏[2]	34	37.00 N	6.33 W
Castilla-La Mancha □[4]	34	39.30 N	3.00 W
Castilla la Nueva □[9]	34	40.00 N	3.45 W
Castilla la Vieja □[9]	34	41.30 N	4.00 W
Castilla-León □[4]	34	41.30 N	5.00 W
Castillo	258	33.53 S	57.40 W
Castillo, Cerro ∧	254	43.03 S	71.57 W
Castillo, Pampa del ≚	254	45.58 S	68.24 W
Castillo de San Marcos National Monument ♠	192	29.44 N	81.20 W
Castillo Incaico de Ingapirca ⊥	246	2.34 S	78.50 W
Castillon-la-Bataille	32	44.51 N	0.03 W
Castillos	252	34.12 S	53.50 W
Castillos, Laguna de ◎	252	34.20 S	53.54 W
Castine	188	44.23 N	68.48 W
Castione della Presolana	64	45.54 N	10.04 E
Castions di Strada	64	45.54 N	13.11 E
Castle Acre	42	52.42 N	0.41 E
Castle Air Force Base ■	226	37.22 N	120.34 W
Castlebar	48	53.52 N	9.17 W
Castlebay	46	56.57 N	7.28 W
Castlebellingham	48	53.54 N	6.23 W
Castleberry	194	31.17 N	87.01 W
Castleblayney	48	54.07 N	6.44 W
Castle Bruce	240d	15.26 N	61.16 W
Castle Cape ›	180	56.15 N	158.06 W
Castle Cary	42	51.06 N	2.31 W
Castlecliff	172	39.57 S	174.59 E
Castlecomer	48	52.48 N	7.12 W
Castleconnell	48	52.43 N	8.30 W
Castlecrag	274a	33.48 S	151.13 E
Castle Crags State Park ♠	204	41.10 N	122.20 W
Castle Creek	210	42.14 N	75.55 W
Castle Creek ≃, Austl.	169	36.41 S	145.29 E
Castle Creek ≃, Id., U.S.	202	43.06 N	116.16 W
Castle Dale	200	39.23 N	110.27 W
Castledawson	48	54.47 N	6.33 W
Castlederg	48	54.42 N	7.36 W
Castledermot	48	52.55 N	6.50 W
Castle Dome Peak ∧	200	33.05 N	114.08 W
Castle Donington	42	52.51 N	1.19 W
Castle Douglas	44	54.57 N	3.56 W
Castlefinn	48	54.47 N	7.35 W
Castleford	44	53.44 N	1.21 W
Castlegar	182	49.19 N	117.40 W
Castle Harbour c	240a	32.21 N	64.40 W
Castle Hill	274a	33.44 S	151.00 E
Castle Hills, De., U.S.	208	39.41 N	75.33 W
Castle Hills, Tx., U.S.	196	29.32 N	98.31 W
Castleisland	48	52.14 N	9.27 W
Castlemaine, Austl.	169	37.04 S	144.13 E
Castlemaine, Ire.	48	52.09 N	9.43 W
Castlemartyr	48	51.55 N	8.03 W
Castlemore	275b	43.47 N	79.41 W
Castle Mountain ∧, Ab., Can.	182	51.18 N	115.55 W
Castle Mountain ∧, Yk., Can.	180	64.32 N	135.25 W
Castle Mountain ∧, Ca., U.S.	226	35.56 N	120.20 W
Castle Neck ›[1]	283	42.41 N	70.45 W
Castle Neck ≃	283	42.40 N	70.44 W
Castle Park	228	32.36 N	117.04 W
Castle Peak ∧, Co., U.S.	200	39.01 N	106.52 W
Castle Peak ∧, Id., U.S.	202	44.02 N	114.35 W
Castle Peak ∧, Wa., U.S.	224	48.58 N	120.51 W
Castlepoint	172	40.54 S	176.13 E
Castle Point □[8]	260	51.33 N	0.35 E
Castlepollard	48	53.40 N	7.17 W
Castlerea	48	53.46 N	8.29 W
Castlereagh ≃	166	30.12 S	147.32 E
Castle Rock, Co., U.S.	200	39.22 N	104.51 W
Castle Rock, Pa., U.S.	285	39.58 N	75.26 W
Castle Rock, Wa., U.S.	224	46.16 N	122.54 W
Castle Rock ∧, Or., U.S.	202	44.02 N	118.11 W
Castle Rock ∧, Va., U.S.	192	37.57 N	78.44 W
Castle Rock Butte ∧	198	45.00 N	103.27 W
Castle Rock Lake ◎[1]	190	43.56 N	89.58 W
Castle Shannon	279b	40.21 N	80.01 W
Castleshaw Moor ●[3]	262	53.36 N	2.00 W
Castleside	44	54.50 N	1.52 W
Castleton, Eng., U.K.	44	53.21 N	1.46 W
Castleton, Eng., U.K.	44	54.28 N	0.56 W
Castleton, Eng., U.K.	262	53.35 N	2.11 W
Castleton, In., U.S.	218	39.54 N	86.03 W
Castleton, Vt., U.S.	188	43.36 N	73.10 W
Castleton on Hudson	210	42.32 N	73.45 W
Castletown, I. of Man	44	54.04 N	4.40 W
Castletown, Scot., U.K.	46	58.35 N	3.23 W
Castletown Bearhaven (Castletown Bere)	48	51.39 N	9.55 W
Castletown Bere → Castletown Bearhaven	48	51.39 N	9.55 W
Castletown Geoghegan	48	53.26 N	7.38 W
Castletownroche	48	52.10 N	8.28 W
Castletownshend	48	51.32 N	9.11 W
Castlewellan	48	54.16 N	5.57 W
Castlewood, Ky., U.S.	218	38.04 N	84.27 W
Castlewood, S.D., U.S.	198	44.43 N	97.01 W
Castlewood, Va., U.S.	192	36.53 N	82.16 W
Častoje	82	54.11 N	37.47 E
Častooz'ornoje	86	55.34 N	67.53 E
Castor	182	52.13 N	111.53 W
Castor ≃, On., Can.	212	45.18 N	75.10 W
Castor ≃, Mo., U.S.	194	36.51 N	89.44 W
Castorano	66	42.54 N	13.43 E
Castor Creek ≃	194	31.47 N	92.22 W
Castorland	212	43.53 N	75.30 W
Castra Vetera ⊥	263	51.39 N	6.28 E
Castres	32	43.36 N	2.15 E
Castricum	52	52.33 N	4.39 E
Castries, Fr.	62	43.40 N	3.59 E
Castries, St. Luc.	241f	14.01 N	61.00 W
Castries, Port c	241f	14.01 N	61.01 W
Castro, Bra.	252	24.47 S	50.00 W
Castro, Chile	254	42.29 S	73.46 W
Castro, It.	64	45.48 N	10.04 E
Castro, Arroyo de ≃	258	33.37 S	56.10 W
Castro, Punta ›	254	43.22 S	65.03 W
Castro Barros	252	30.35 S	65.44 W
Castrocaro Terme	66	44.10 N	11.57 E
Castrocielo	66	41.32 N	13.42 E
Castro Daire	34	40.54 N	7.56 W
Castro dei Volsci	66	41.30 N	13.24 E
Castro del Río	34	37.41 N	4.28 W
Castrofilippo	70	37.21 N	13.46 E
Castrojeriz	34	42.17 N	4.08 W
Castro Marim	34	37.13 N	7.26 W
Castronuño	34	41.23 N	5.16 W
Castronuovo di Sant'Andrea	68	40.11 N	16.11 E
Castronuovo di Sicilia	70	37.41 N	13.36 E
Castropol	34	43.32 N	7.02 W
Castrop-Rauxel	52	51.34 N	7.18 E
Castroreale	70	38.06 N	15.12 E
Castro-Urdiales	34	43.23 N	3.13 W
Castro Valley	226	37.41 N	122.05 W
Castro Verde	34	37.42 N	8.05 W
Castrovillari	68	39.49 N	16.13 E
Castroville, Ca., U.S.	226	36.45 N	121.45 W
Castroville, Tx., U.S.	196	29.21 N	98.52 W
Castrovirreyna	248	13.16 S	75.19 W
Castuera	34	38.43 N	5.33 W
Ċast uul ∧	86	48.40 N	90.45 E
Častyje	80	57.19 N	54.59 E
Casummit Lake	184	51.28 N	92.24 W
Casupá	252	34.07 S	55.39 W
Caswell Sound Ⴎ	172	45.00 S	167.10 E
Çat	130	39.40 N	41.00 E
Cat ≃	184	51.07 N	91.25 W
Catabola	152	12.09 S	17.16 E
Cataby	162	30.43 S	115.31 E
Catacamas	236	14.48 N	85.54 W
Catacaos	248	5.16 S	80.41 W
Catacocha	246	4.04 S	79.38 W
Cataguarino	256	21.18 S	42.43 W
Cataguases	256	21.24 S	42.41 W
Catahoula Lake ◎	194	31.30 N	92.06 W
Çatak	128	38.01 N	43.07 E
Çatakköprü	130	38.09 N	41.12 E
Catalaban Island I	116	11.51 N	125.28 E
Çatalan	130	37.14 N	35.16 E
Catalão	255	18.10 S	47.57 W
Catalão, Ponta do ›	287a	22.51 S	43.13 W
Çatalca	130	41.09 N	28.27 E
Çatalçam	130	40.00 N	38.51 E
Catalfaro ≃	70	37.22 N	14.43 E
Catalina, Nf., Can.	186	48.31 N	53.05 W
Catalina, Chile	252	25.13 S	69.43 W
Catalina → Santa Catalina Island I	228	33.23 N	118.24 W
Catalina, Punta ›	254	52.32 S	68.47 W
Catalonia → Catalunya □[4]	34	41.40 N	1.30 E
Catalunya □[4]	34	41.40 N	1.30 E
Catalzeytin	130	41.57 N	34.13 E
Catamarca □[4]	252	27.00 S	67.00 W
Catamare	286c	10.36 N	67.02 W
Catamayo	246	3.59 S	79.21 W
Catamayo ≃	246	4.18 S	80.09 W
Catanauan	116	13.36 N	122.19 E
Catanduanes □[4]	116	13.47 N	124.16 E
Catanduanes Island I	116	13.45 N	124.15 E
Catanduva	255	21.08 S	48.58 W
Catane → Catania	70	37.30 N	15.06 E
Catania	70	37.30 N	15.06 E
Catania □[4]	70	37.23 N	14.40 E
Catania, Golfo di c	70	37.24 N	15.09 E
Catania, Piana di ≚	70	37.25 N	14.51 E
Cataño	240m	18.27 N	66.07 W
Catanzaro	68	38.54 N	16.36 E
Catanzaro □[4]	68	38.54 N	16.36 E
Catanzaro Lido	68	38.49 N	16.36 E
Cataonia □[9]	130	38.00 N	35.00 E
Catára ≃	152	13.34 S	12.35 E
Cataract Canyon V	200	36.03 N	112.35 W
Cataract Reservoir ◎[1]	170	34.16 S	150.48 E
Catarama	246	1.35 S	79.28 W
Cataraqui	212	44.16 N	76.32 W
Cataraqui ≃	212	44.13 N	76.28 W
Catarina	250	6.12 S	39.54 W
Catarman, Pil.	116	9.08 N	124.40 E
Catarman, Pil.	116	12.30 N	124.38 E
Catarroja	34	39.24 N	0.24 W
Catasauqua	208	40.39 N	75.29 W
Catatumbo ≃	246	9.22 N	71.45 W
Catawba	218	40.00 N	83.37 W
Catawba ≃	192	34.36 N	80.54 W
Catawba Island	214	41.35 N	82.50 W
Catawissa, Mo., U.S.	219	38.25 N	90.47 W
Catawissa, Pa., U.S.	210	40.57 N	76.27 W
Catawissa Creek ≃	210	40.57 N	76.28 W
Cataxa	154	15.58 S	33.12 E
Cat Ba, Dao I	110	20.50 N	107.00 E
Catbalogan	116	11.46 N	124.53 E
Catchabutan, Punta ›	236	15.50 N	86.32 W
Catchacoma Lake ◎	212	44.45 N	78.20 W
Cateco Cangola	152	8.27 S	15.48 E
Catedral, Cerro ∧[2]	252	34.23 S	54.40 W
Cateel	116	7.48 N	126.27 E
Cateel ≃	116	7.47 N	126.27 E
Cateel Bay c	116	7.54 N	126.25 E
Catemaco	234	18.25 N	95.07 W
Catemaco, Laguna ◎	234	18.25 N	95.05 W
Catembe	156	26.00 S	32.33 E
Catenanuova	70	37.34 N	14.41 E
Caterham	42	51.17 N	0.04 W
Caterino Rodriguez	232	24.51 N	100.19 W
Catete	152	9.06 S	13.43 E
Catete ●[8]	287a	22.55 S	43.10 W
Catete ≃	250	6.04 S	54.09 W
Catfish Creek ≃, On., Can.	212	42.39 N	81.01 W
Catfish Creek ≃, N.Y., U.S.	212	43.31 N	76.19 W
Catfish Creek ≃, Tx., U.S.	222	31.47 N	95.56 W
Catford ●[8]	260	51.27 N	0.01 W
Catharine Creek ≃	210	42.21 N	76.51 W
Cathcart	158	32.18 S	27.09 E
Cathead Mountain ∧	210	43.17 N	74.17 W
Cathedral City	204	33.46 N	116.27 W
Cathedral Gorge State Park ♠	204	37.50 N	114.30 W
Cathedral Mountain ∧	196	30.10 N	103.40 W
Cathedral of the Pines ♜[1]	207	42.47 N	71.58 W
Cathedral Provincial Park ♠	202	49.05 N	120.10 W
Cathedral Range ⋀	226	37.47 N	119.21 W
Catherines Peak ∧	241q	18.04 N	76.42 W
Catheys Valley	226	37.25 N	120.06 W
Cathlamet	224	46.12 N	123.22 W
Catholic University ♜[2]	284c	38.56 N	77.00 W
Catia ●[8]	286c	10.31 N	66.57 W
Catia La Mar	286c	10.36 N	67.02 W
Ca' Tiepolo	66	44.56 N	12.22 E
Catignano	66	42.21 N	13.57 E
Catió	150	11.13 N	15.10 W
Catirina, Punta ∧	71	40.29 N	9.32 E
Cat Island I, Ba.	238	24.27 N	75.30 W
Cat Island I, Ma., U.S.	283	42.31 N	70.49 W
Cat Island I, Ms., U.S.	194	30.13 N	89.06 W
Čatkal ≃	85	41.38 N	70.01 E
Čatkal'skij chrebet ⋀	85	41.40 N	71.05 E
Cat Lake ◎	184	51.40 N	91.50 W
Catlettsburg	188	38.24 N	82.36 W
Catlin	194	40.03 N	87.42 W
Catlins ≃	172	46.29 S	169.43 E
Catlodge	46	57.00 N	4.15 W
Catnip Mountain ∧	204	41.52 N	119.23 W
Cato	210	43.10 N	76.34 W
Catoche, Cabo ›	232	21.35 N	87.05 W
Catoctin Creek ≃	208	39.18 N	77.33 W
Catoctin Mountain ∧	208	39.26 N	77.31 W
Cato Island I	166	23.15 S	155.32 E
Catolé do Rocha	250	6.21 S	37.45 W
Católica, Universidad ♜[2], Chile	286e	33.27 S	70.39 W
Católica, Universidad ♜[2], Perú	286d	12.04 S	77.05 W
Caton	44	54.04 N	2.43 W
Catonsville	208	39.16 N	76.43 W
Catonsville Manor	284b	39.18 N	76.44 W
Catoosa	196	36.11 N	95.44 W
Catorce	234	23.42 N	100.54 W
Catorce, Sierra de ⋀	234	23.36 N	100.52 W
Catota	152	13.52 S	17.15 E
Catria, Monte ∧	66	43.28 N	12.42 E
Catriló	252	36.26 S	63.24 W
Catrimani ≃	246	0.28 N	61.44 W
Catrine	46	55.30 N	4.20 W
Cats, Mont des ∧[2]	50	50.47 N	2.40 E
Catshill	42	52.22 N	2.03 W
Catskill	210	42.13 N	73.51 W
Catskill Aqueduct ≃	276	41.11 N	73.48 W
Catskill Creek ≃	210	42.12 N	73.51 W
Catskill Game Farm ♠	210	42.15 N	74.01 W
Catskill Mountains ⋀	210	42.10 N	74.30 W
Catskill Park ♠	210	42.00 N	74.30 W
Cat Spring	222	29.51 N	96.20 W
Catt, Mount ∧	182	54.21 N	128.47 W
Cattai Creek ≃	274a	33.40 S	150.56 E
Cattaraugus	210	42.19 N	78.52 W
Cattaraugus □[6]	214	42.15 N	78.45 W
Cattaraugus Creek ≃	214	42.35 N	79.10 W
Cattaraugus Creek, South Branch ≃	214	42.26 N	78.53 W
Cattaraugus Indian Reservation ●[4]	210	42.33 N	78.56 W
Cattenom	56	49.25 N	6.15 E
Catterick	44	54.22 N	1.38 W
Catterick Garrison	44	54.22 N	1.43 W
Cattle Canyon V	280	34.14 N	117.46 W
Cattolica	66	43.58 N	12.44 E
Cattolica del Sacro Cuore, Università ♜[2]	266b	45.27 N	9.11 E
Cattolica Eraclea	70	37.26 N	13.24 E
Catton	44	54.55 N	2.15 W
Catu	255	12.21 S	38.23 W
Catuala	152	16.29 S	19.03 E
Catuane	156	26.48 S	32.18 E
Catubig	116	12.24 N	125.03 E
Catubig ≃	116	12.34 N	125.01 E
Catuçaba	256	23.15 S	45.12 W
Catumbela	152	12.25 S	13.34 E
Catumbela ≃	152	12.27 S	13.29 E
Catur	154	13.45 S	35.30 E
Catus	32	44.34 N	1.20 E
Çatwick, Îles II	110	10.00 N	109.00 E
Čatyrk'ol', ozero ◎	85	40.38 N	75.17 E
Čatyrtaš	85	40.55 N	76.26 E
Cau ≃	110	21.07 N	106.18 E
Cau, Rach ≃	269c	10.51 N	106.49 E
Cauaburi ≃	246	0.17 S	65.56 W
Cauayan, Pil.	116	16.56 N	121.46 E
Cauayan, Pil.	116	9.58 N	122.37 E
Caubvick, Mount (Mont d'Iberville) ∧	176	58.53 N	63.43 W
Cauca □[5]	246	2.30 N	76.50 W
Cauca ≃	246	8.54 N	74.28 W
Caucaia	250	3.42 S	38.39 W
Caucaia do Alto	256	23.41 S	47.02 W
Caucase, Monts du → Caucasus ⋀	84	42.30 N	45.00 E
Caucasia	246	8.00 N	75.12 W
Caucaso → Caucasus ⋀	84	42.30 N	45.00 E
Caucasus (Bol'šoj Kavkaz) ⋀	84	42.30 N	45.00 E
Caucete	252	31.39 S	68.17 W
Cauchari, Salar de ≚	252	23.50 S	66.50 W
Cauchon Lake ◎	184	55.25 N	96.30 W
Caudebec-en-Caux	50	49.32 N	0.44 E
Caudebec-lés-Elbeuf	50	49.17 N	1.02 E
Caudry	50	50.08 N	3.25 E
Caughdenoy	210	43.16 N	76.12 W
Caughnawaga	275a	45.25 N	73.41 W
Caughnawaga Indian Reserve ●[4]	206	45.23 N	73.41 W
Cauitan, Mount ∧	116	17.16 N	121.00 E
Cauit Point ›, Pil.	116	12.16 N	122.38 E
Cauit Point ›, Pil.	116	9.18 N	126.12 E
Cauldcleuch Head ∧	44	55.18 N	2.51 W
Caulfield	169	37.53 S	145.03 E
Caulfield Racecourse ♠	274b	37.53 S	145.02 E
Caulkerbush	44	54.54 N	3.40 W
Caulonia	68	38.23 N	16.25 E
Caumont-sur-Durance	62	43.54 N	4.57 E
Caumsett State Park ♠	276	40.55 N	73.28 W
Caúngula	152	8.25 S	18.40 E
Čaunskaja guba c	74	69.20 N	170.00 E
Cauquenes	252	35.58 S	72.21 W
Caura ≃	246	7.38 N	64.53 W
Caurés ≃	246	1.21 S	62.20 W
Caurimare ≃	286c	10.28 N	66.48 W
Căuşani	38	46.38 N	29.25 E
Causapscal	186	48.22 N	67.14 W
Čausovo	82	54.49 N	36.55 E
Caussade	32	44.10 N	1.32 E
Čausy	76	53.48 N	30.58 E
Cautário ≃	248	12.13 S	64.34 W
Caution, Cape ›	182	51.10 N	127.47 W
Cauto ≃	240p	20.33 N	77.14 W
Čauvaj	85	40.08 N	72.13 E
Caux, Pays de ●[1]	50	49.40 N	0.40 E
Cava	256	22.41 S	43.26 W
Cava de' Tirreni	68	40.42 N	14.42 E
Cávado ≃	34	41.32 N	8.48 W
Cavaglià	62	45.24 N	8.05 E
Cavaillon	62	43.50 N	5.02 E
Cavalaire-sur-Mer	62	43.10 N	6.32 E
Cavalcante	255	13.48 S	47.30 W
Cavalese	64	46.17 N	11.27 E
Cavalheiro	255	17.15 S	48.02 W
Cavalier	198	48.47 N	97.37 W
Cavalière	62	43.09 N	6.26 E
Cavalla (Cavally) ≃	150	4.22 N	7.32 W
Cavalleria, Cap de ›	34	40.05 N	4.05 E
Cavallermaggiore	62	44.43 N	7.41 E
Cavalli Islands II	172	35.02 S	173.58 E
Cavallino, Litorale di ⏏[2]	64	45.27 N	12.30 E
Cavallo, Île I	71	41.21 N	9.16 E
Cavallo, Monte ∧	64	46.08 N	12.30 E
Cavally (Cavalla) ≃	150	4.22 N	7.32 W
Cavalos, Ribeirão dos ≃	256	21.29 S	44.13 W
Cava Manara	62	45.08 N	9.07 E
Cavan	48	54.00 N	7.21 W
Cavan □[6]	48	53.55 N	7.15 W
Cavanaugh, Lake ◎	224	48.23 N	122.00 W
Čavan'ga	24	66.06 N	37.47 E
Cavarzere	64	45.08 N	12.05 E
Cavaso del Tomba	64	45.51 N	11.52 E
Çavdır	130	37.09 N	29.42 E
Cave, It.	66	41.49 N	12.56 E
Cave, N.Z.	172	44.19 S	170.57 E
Cave City, Ar., U.S.	194	35.56 N	91.32 W
Cave City, Ky., U.S.	194	37.08 N	85.57 W
Cave Creek ≃	200	33.34 N	112.07 W
Cave del Predil	64	46.26 N	13.34 E
Cavedine	64	45.59 N	10.59 E
Cave In Rock	194	37.29 N	88.10 W
Caveiras ≃	252	27.35 S	50.56 W
Cavelo	152	17.33 S	19.21 E
Cavendish	166	37.31 S	142.02 E
Cavernago	62	45.38 N	9.46 E
Cavertitz	54	51.23 N	13.08 E
Cave Run Lake ◎[1]	188	38.03 N	83.30 W
Cave Spring	192	34.14 N	85.20 W
Cavettsville	279b	40.22 N	79.46 W
Cavezzo	64	44.50 N	11.02 E
Cavi	62	44.17 N	9.22 E
Caviana de Fora, Ilha I	250	0.10 N	50.10 W
Cavili Island I	116	9.17 N	120.50 E
Cavinzas, Isla I	286d	12.07 S	77.13 W
Cavite	116	14.29 N	120.55 E
Cavite □[4]	116	14.15 N	120.50 E
Čavka	84	41.44 N	41.45 E
Čavlisaj	85	41.08 N	69.44 E
Cavo, Monte ∧	267a	41.45 N	12.42 E
Cavoli, Isola dei I	71	39.05 N	9.33 E
Cavonne ≃	68	40.17 N	16.47 E
Cavour	62	44.47 N	7.22 E
Cavour, Canale ≊	62	45.11 N	7.54 E
Cavriago	64	44.42 N	10.31 E
Cavriana	64	45.21 N	10.36 E
Cavtat	38	42.35 N	18.13 E
Çavuş	130	37.36 N	31.56 E
Çavuşbaşı ≃	267b	40.58 N	28.51 E
Çavuşçu Gölü ◎	130	38.25 N	31.53 E
Cawatose, Lac ◎	190	47.20 N	77.07 W
Cawayan	116	11.56 N	123.46 E
Cawdor	46	57.31 N	3.56 W
Cawker City	198	39.30 N	98.26 W
Cawnpore → Kānpur	124	26.28 N	80.21 E
Cawood, Eng., U.K.	44	53.50 N	1.07 W
Cawood, Ky., U.S.	192	36.47 N	83.13 W
Cawston, B.C., Can.	182	49.11 N	119.45 W
Cawston, Eng., U.K.	42	52.46 N	1.10 E
Cawthon	222	30.25 N	96.14 W
Caxambu	256	21.59 S	44.56 W
Caxias, Bra.	250	4.50 S	43.21 W
Caxias, Port.	266c	38.42 N	9.16 W
Caxias do Sul	252	29.10 S	51.11 W
Caxinas, Punta ›	236	16.01 N	86.02 W
Caxito	152	8.33 S	13.36 E
Caxiuana, Baía de c	250	1.45 S	51.20 W
Caxopa	152	11.52 S	20.52 E
Çay	130	38.35 N	31.02 E
Cayacal, Punta ›	234	17.56 N	102.11 W
Çayağzı ●[8]	267b	41.13 N	29.12 E
Çayağzı ≃	267b	41.14 N	29.12 E
Cayambe	246	0.03 N	78.08 W
Cayambe ∧[1]	246	0.00	77.59 W
Cayapoñga	116	5.48 N	125.33 E
Çaybaşı	130	41.02 N	37.06 E
Cayce	192	33.57 N	81.04 W
Çaycuma	130	41.25 N	32.05 E
Caycuse	224	48.53 N	124.22 W
Caycuse ≃	224	48.48 N	124.41 W
Cay Duong, Vinh c	110	10.10 N	104.45 E
Cayenne	250	4.56 N	52.20 W
Cayenne □[8]	250	4.00 N	52.30 W
Cayes → Les Cayes	238	18.12 N	73.45 W
Cayeux-sur-Mer	50	50.11 N	1.29 E
Cayey	240m	18.07 N	66.10 W
Cayey, Sierra de ⋀	240m	18.07 N	66.02 W
Çayıralan	130	39.18 N	35.40 E
Çayırbaşı	130	40.53 N	42.36 E
Çayırhan	130	40.06 N	31.37 E
Çayırlı	130	39.48 N	40.01 E
Çaylarbası	130	37.41 N	39.00 E
Caylus	32	44.14 N	1.46 E
Cayman Brac I	238	19.43 N	79.49 W
Cayman Islands □[2], N.A.	230	19.30 N	80.40 W
Cayman Islands □[2], N.A.	238	19.30 N	80.40 W
Cayman Trench ✣[1]	16	19.00 N	80.00 W
Cayna	248	10.11 S	76.20 W
Caynabo	144	8.57 N	46.26 E
Cayo Agua, Isla I	236	9.09 N	82.02 W
Çayözü	130	39.36 N	38.11 E
Cay Point ›	240b	24.59 N	77.25 W
Çayra	130	40.41 N	39.06 E
Cayres	62	44.55 N	3.48 E
Cay Sal Bank ✣[2]	238	23.45 N	80.00 W
Çaytepe	130	38.48 N	40.41 E
Cayucos	226	35.27 N	120.54 W
Cayuga, In., U.S.	194	39.56 N	87.27 W
Cayuga, N.Y., U.S.	210	42.55 N	76.44 W
Cayuga, N.D., U.S.	198	46.04 N	97.23 W

≃	River	Fluß	Río	Rivière	Rio
≊	Canal	Kanal	Canal	Canal	Canal
⌊	Waterfall, Rapids	Wasserfall, Stromschnellen	Cascada, Rápidos	Chute d'eau, Rapides	Cascata, Rápidos
Ⴎ	Strait	Meeresstraße	Estrecho	Détroit	Estreito
c	Bay, Gulf	Bucht, Golf	Bahía, Golfo	Baie, Golfe	Baía, Golfo
◎	Lake, Lakes	See, Seen	Lago, Lagos	Lac, Lacs	Lago, Lagos
☷	Swamp	Sumpf	Pantano	Marais	Pântano
⍓	Ice Features, Glacier	Eis- und Gletscherformen	Accidentes Glaciales	Formes glaciaires	Acidentes glaciares
⫪	Other Hydrographic Features	Andere Hydrographische Objekte	Otros Elementos Hidrográficos	Autres données hydrographiques	Outros acidentes hidrográficos
✣	Submarine Features	Untermeerische Objekte	Accidentes Submarinos	Formes de relief sous-marin	Acidentes submarinos
□	Political Unit	Politische Einheit	Unidad Politica	Entité politique	Unidade política
♜	Cultural Institution	Kulturelle Institution	Institución Cultural	Institution culturelle	Instituição cultural
⊥	Historical Site	Historische Stätte	Sitio Histórico	Site historique	Sitio histórico
♠	Recreational Site	Erholungs- und Ferienort	Sitio de Recreo	Centre de loisirs	Area de Lazer
⊠	Airport	Flughafen	Aeropuerto	Aéroport	Aeroporto
■	Military Installation	Militäranlage	Instalación Militar	Installation militaire	Instalação militar
●	Miscellaneous	Verschiedenes	Misceláneo	Divers	Diversos

ENGLISH — DEUTSCH

Name	Page	Lat.°′	Long.°′
Cayuga, Tx., U.S.	222	31.57 N	95.57 W
Cayuga □[6]	210	42.56 N	76.34 W
Cayuga and Seneca Canal ≅	210	42.56 N	76.44 W
Cayuga Creek ≃, N.Y., U.S.	210	42.52 N	78.47 W
Cayuga Creek ≃, N.Y., U.S.	284a	43.04 N	78.57 W
Cayuga Heights	210	42.27 N	76.29 W
Cayuga Lake ⊜	210	42.45 N	76.45 W
Cayuta	210	42.17 N	76.42 W
Cayuta Creek ≃	210	41.59 N	76.30 W
Cazaclia	38	46.00 N	28.37 E
Cazage	152	11.02 S	20.45 E
Cazalla de la Sierra	34	37.56 N	5.45 W
Căzănești	38	44.37 N	27.01 E
Cazaux et de Sanguinet, Lac de ⊂	32	44.30 N	1.10 W
Cazenovia	210	42.55 N	75.51 W
Cazenovia Creek ≃	210	42.52 N	78.50 W
Cazenovia Creek, East Branch ≃	210	42.46 N	78.38 W
Cazenovia Creek, West Branch ≃	210	42.46 N	78.39 W
Cazenovia Lake ⊜	210	42.57 N	75.53 W
Cazenovia Park ♦	284a	42.51 N	78.48 W
Cazères	32	43.13 N	1.05 E
Cazhai	269b	31.12 N	121.34 E
Cazin	36	44.58 N	15.57 E
Čazis	58	46.43 N	9.25 E
Čazma	36	45.45 N	16.37 E
Cazombo	152	11.54 S	22.52 E
Cazones ≃	234	20.44 N	97.12 W
Cazones, Golfo de ⊂	240p	21.55 N	81.20 W
Cazorla, Esp.	34	37.55 N	3.00 W
Cazorla, Ven.	246	8.01 N	67.00 W
Cazula	154	15.25 S	33.40 E
Ccapi	248	13.52 S	72.05 W
Cchaltubo	84	42.20 N	42.35 E
Cchenisckali ≃	84	42.07 N	42.18 E
Cchinvali	84	42.13 N	43.56 E
Cchorocku	84	42.32 N	42.07 E
Cchunkuri	84	42.23 N	42.34 E
Cea ≃	34	42.00 N	5.36 W
Ceanannus Mór (Kells)	48	53.44 N	6.53 W
Ceará → Fortaleza	250	3.43 S	38.30 W
Ceará □[3]	250	5.00 S	40.00 W
Ceará-Mirim	250	5.38 S	35.26 W
Ceará-Mirim ≃	250	5.40 S	35.13 W
Ceatharlach → Carlow	48	52.50 N	6.55 W
Cebaco, Isla De I	246	7.32 N	81.09 W
Ceballos	232	26.32 N	104.09 W
Čebarkul'	86	54.58 N	60.25 E
Çebeci ◆[8]	267b	41.07 N	28.52 E
Čeboksarskoje vodochranilišče ⊜[1]	24	56.10 N	46.00 E
Čeboksary	80	56.09 N	47.15 E
Cebolla Creek ≃	200	38.29 N	107.13 W
Cebollar	252	29.06 S	66.33 W
Cebollas	234	23.23 N	104.50 W
Cebollatí	252	33.16 S	53.47 W
Cebollatí ≃	252	33.09 S	53.38 W
Cebollita Peak ∧	200	34.43 N	107.51 W
Céboruco, Volcán ∧[1]	234	21.09 N	104.30 W
Čebotovka, Ross.	83	48.42 N	39.51 E
Čebotovka, Ross.	83	48.41 N	40.00 E
Cebreros	34	40.27 N	4.28 W
Čebsara	76	59.12 N	38.50 E
Cebu	116	10.18 N	123.54 E
Cebu □[4]	116	10.20 N	123.45 E
Cebu I	116	10.20 N	123.45 E
Čeburgol'	78	45.34 N	38.07 E
Cebu Strait ⋈	116	9.45 N	123.40 E
Ceccano	66	41.34 N	13.20 E
Cecchignola ◆[8]	267a	41.49 N	12.29 E
Čeceda	196	26.04 N	103.25 W
Čečen', ostrov I	84	43.58 N	47.45 E
Cecer Chaan → Öndörchaan	88	47.19 N	110.39 E
Cecerleg, Mong.	88	48.52 N	101.14 E
Cecerleg, Mong.	88	47.30 N	101.27 E
Cecerleg, Mong.	88	49.30 N	97.36 E
Čečersk	76	52.55 N	30.55 E
Čečeviči	76	53.31 N	29.51 E
Cecheng	105	39.06 N	116.48 E
Čechov, Ross.	82	55.09 N	37.27 E
Čechov, Ross.	89	47.28 N	141.59 E
Čechova, gora ∧	89	47.03 N	142.50 E
Čechtice	30	49.37 N	15.03 E
Čechy □[9]	30	49.50 N	14.00 E
Cecil, Ga., U.S.	192	31.02 N	83.23 W
Cecil, Oh., U.S.	216	41.13 N	84.35 W
Cecil, Pa., U.S.	214	40.19 N	80.10 W
Cecil □[6]	208	39.36 N	75.50 W
Cecil Field Naval Air Station ■	192	30.12 N	81.52 W
Cecilia	194	37.39 N	85.57 W
Cecilia, Mount ∧[2]	162	20.45 S	120.55 E
Cecil Park	274a	33.52 S	150.51 E
Cecil Plains	166	27.32 S	151.12 E
Cecil Rhodes, Mount ∧	162	25.26 S	121.26 E
Cecilton	208	39.24 N	75.52 W
Cecina	66	43.19 N	10.31 E
Cecina ≃	66	43.18 N	10.29 E
Cecita, Lago di ⊜	68	39.24 N	16.30 E
Čečnja-Ingušetija □[3]	84	43.15 N	45.40 E
Čečuj ≃	88	58.12 N	109.18 E
Čečujsk	88	58.05 N	108.42 E
Cedar ≃, U.S.	190	41.17 N	91.21 W
Cedar ≃, Mi., U.S.	190	43.53 N	84.29 W
Cedar ≃, Mi., U.S.	190	45.25 N	87.21 W
Cedar ≃, Ne., U.S.	198	41.22 N	97.57 W
Cedar ≃, N.Y., U.S.	188	43.51 N	74.11 W
Cedar ≃, Wa., U.S.	224	47.30 N	122.12 W
Cedar, Middle Branch ≃	216	42.38 N	84.05 W
Cedar, West Branch ≃	216	42.41 N	84.09 W
Cedar, West Fork ≃	190	42.37 N	92.29 W
Cedar Bayou ≃	222	29.41 N	94.56 W
Cedar Beach	284b	39.17 N	76.25 W
Cedar Bluff Reservoir ⊜[1]	198	38.47 N	99.47 W
Cedar Bluffs	198	41.23 N	96.36 W
Cedar Breaks National Monument ♦	200	37.29 N	112.53 W
Cedar Brook	208	39.42 N	74.54 W
Cedar Brook ≃, N.J., U.S.	276	40.19 N	74.33 W
Cedar Brook ≃, N.J., U.S.	276	40.23 N	74.23 W
Cedar Brook ≃, N.J., U.S.	285	39.40 N	74.43 W
Cedar Brook Park ♦	275b	43.45 N	79.14 W
Cedarburg	190	43.17 N	87.59 W
Cedar City, Mo., U.S.	219	38.35 N	92.10 W
Cedar City, Ut,. U.S.	200	37.40 N	113.03 W
Cedar Creek	222	30.05 N	97.30 W
Cedar Creek ≃, Al., U.S.	194	32.13 N	87.06 W
Cedar Creek ≃, Az., U.S.	200	33.48 N	110.18 W
Cedar Creek ≃, Ct., U.S.	276	41.09 N	73.13 W
Cedar Creek ≃, De., U.S.	208	38.55 N	75.20 W
Cedar Creek ≃, Ga., U.S.	194	34.08 N	85.19 W
Cedar Creek ≃, Id., U.S.	202	42.24 N	114.49 W
Cedar Creek ≃, In., U.S.	216	41.12 N	85.02 W
Cedar Creek ≃, Ia., U.S.	190	40.58 N	91.40 W
Cedar Creek ≃, Ia., U.S.	198	42.24 N	94.59 W
Cedar Creek ≃, Ky., U.S.	218	38.25 N	84.53 W
Cedar Creek ≃, Mo., U.S.	219	38.38 N	92.13 W
Cedar Creek ≃, N.D., U.S.	198	46.07 N	101.18 W
Cedar Creek ≃, Oh., U.S.	214	41.38 N	83.17 W
Cedar Creek ≃, Pa., U.S.	279b	40.10 N	79.47 W
Cedar Creek ≃, Tx., U.S.	196	32.53 N	98.37 W
Cedar Creek ≃, Tx., U.S.	222	30.51 N	96.12 W
Cedar Creek ≃, Tx., U.S.	222	32.04 N	96.05 W
Cedar Creek ≃, Tx., U.S.	222	30.02 N	97.17 W
Cedar Creek ≃, Wa., U.S.	224	45.56 N	122.37 W
Cedar Creek Reservoir ⊜[1]	222	32.20 N	96.10 W
Cedar Crest Manor	285	39.41 N	75.28 W
Cedaredge	200	38.54 N	107.55 W
Cedar Falls	190	42.31 N	92.26 W
Cedar Grove, On., Can.	275b	43.52 N	79.12 W
Cedar Grove, In., U.S.	218	39.21 N	84.56 W
Cedar Grove, N.J., U.S.	276	40.51 N	74.13 W
Cedar Grove, W.V., U.S.	188	38.13 N	81.25 W
Cedar Grove, Wi., U.S.	190	43.34 N	87.49 W
Cedar Grove Reservoir ⊜[1]	276	40.52 N	74.13 W
Cedar Heights, Md., U.S.	284c	38.54 N	76.54 W
Cedar Heights, Pa., U.S.	285	40.05 N	75.17 W
Cedar Hill, Mo., U.S.	219	38.21 N	90.39 W
Cedar Hill, N.Y., U.S.	210	42.33 N	73.47 W
Cedar Hill, Tn., U.S.	194	36.33 N	86.59 W
Cedar Hill, Tx., U.S.	222	32.35 N	96.57 W
Cedar Hills	224	45.30 N	122.47 W
Cedar Hollow	285	40.04 N	75.31 W
Cedarhurst, Md., U.S.	208	39.07 N	76.41 W
Cedarhurst, N.Y., U.S.	276	40.37 N	73.43 W
Cedar Island I, Md., U.S.	208	37.56 N	75.52 W
Cedar Island I, N.Y., U.S.	276	40.38 N	73.21 W
Cedar Island I, Va., U.S.	208	37.39 N	75.36 W
Cedar Island Lake ⊜	281	42.38 N	83.28 W
Cedar Key	192	29.08 N	83.02 W
Cedar Knolls	276	40.49 N	74.26 W
Cedar Lake, In., U.S.	216	41.21 N	87.26 W
Cedar Lake, Tx., U.S.	222	28.54 N	95.35 W
Cedar Lake ⊜, On., Can.	190	46.02 N	78.30 W
Cedar Lake ⊜, In., U.S.	216	41.22 N	87.26 W
Cedar Lake ⊜, N.J., U.S.	276	40.55 N	74.28 W
Cedar Lake ⊜, Tx., U.S.	196	32.49 N	102.17 W
Cedar Lake ⊜[1]	184	53.15 N	100.10 W
Cedar Lake Creek ≃	222	28.50 N	95.35 W
Cedar Lane	222	28.54 N	95.38 W
Cedar Mill	224	45.32 N	122.51 W
Cedarmont	158	26.50 S	29.01 E
Cedar Mountain ∧	204	41.36 N	120.16 W
Cedar Point	216	41.16 N	89.08 W
Cedar Point ›, Ct., U.S.	276	41.06 N	73.22 W
Cedar Point ›, Oh., U.S.	214	41.42 N	83.20 W
Cedar Point ›, Oh., U.S.	214	41.30 N	82.41 W
Cedar Pond ⊜	276	41.07 N	74.06 W
Cedar Rapids, Ia., U.S.	190	41.59 N	91.40 W
Cedar Rapids, Ne., U.S.	198	41.34 N	98.09 W
Cedar Ridge	226	39.12 N	121.01 W
Cedar Run ≃	208	38.41 N	77.29 W
Cedars	285	40.13 N	75.22 W
Cedars of Lebanon → Arz Lubnān ◆[3]	130	34.14 N	36.03 E
Cedar Springs, On., Can.	214	42.17 N	82.02 W
Cedar Springs, Mi., U.S.	190	43.13 N	85.33 W
Cedar Swamp ≡, Ma., U.S.	283	42.33 N	71.05 W
Cedar Swamp ≡, N.J., U.S.	285	39.48 N	75.20 W
Cedartown	192	34.03 N	85.15 W
Cedarvale, B.C., Can.	182	55.01 N	128.20 W
Cedar Vale, Ks., U.S.	198	37.06 N	96.30 W
Cedarville, S. Afr.	158	30.23 S	29.03 E
Cedarville, Ca., U.S.	204	41.31 N	120.10 W
Cedarville, In., U.S.	216	41.12 N	85.01 W
Cedarville, Ma., U.S.	207	41.48 N	70.33 W
Cedarville, Mi., U.S.	190	46.00 N	84.22 W
Cedarville, N.J., U.S.	208	39.19 N	75.12 W
Cedarville, N.Y., U.S.	210	42.56 N	75.07 W
Cedarville, Oh., U.S.	218	39.44 N	83.48 W
Cedarville, Pa., U.S.	285	40.14 N	75.40 W
Cedarville Reservoir ⊜[1]	216	41.12 N	85.01 W
Cedar Wash V	200	35.53 N	111.25 W
Cedarwood Park	208	40.03 N	74.08 W
Cedegolo	64	46.05 N	10.21 E
Cedeira	34	43.39 N	8.03 W
Čeder	88	51.25 N	94.45 E
Cedillo, Embalse de ⊜[1]	34	39.40 N	7.25 W
Cedral	234	23.48 N	100.44 W
Cedrino ≃	71	40.23 N	9.44 E
Cedro	250	6.36 S	39.03 W
Cedro, Cerro ∧	234	18.35 N	99.42 W
Cedros, Hond.	236	14.35 N	87.08 W
Cedros, Méx.	232	24.41 N	101.47 W
Cedros, Isla I	232	28.12 N	115.15 W
Ceduna	162	32.07 S	133.40 E
Cedynia	30	52.50 N	14.14 E
Ceel	102	45.36 N	95.51 E
Ceelaayo	144	11.15 N	48.54 E
Ceel Afweyne	144	9.55 N	47.15 E
Ceel Berdaale	144	3.14 N	43.11 E
Ceel Berde	144	4.50 N	43.39 E
Ceel Buur	144	4.40 N	46.37 E
Ceel Dhaab	144	8.56 N	46.30 E
Ceel Dheere, Som.	144	3.51 N	47.12 E
Ceeldheere, Som.	144	5.22 N	46.11 E
Ceel Doofaar	144	10.38 N	49.02 E
Ceel Waaq	144	2.44 N	41.01 E
Ceel Xamurre	144	7.13 N	48.54 E
Ceemadle	144	5.14 N	46.56 E
Ceepeecee	182	49.52 N	126.43 W
Ceerigaabo	144	10.37 N	47.22 E
Cefalà Diana	70	37.54 N	13.28 E
Cefalonia → Kefallinía I	38	38.15 N	20.35 E
Cefalù	70	38.02 N	14.01 E
Cefni ≃	44	53.12 N	4.23 W
Cefn-mawr	42	52.58 N	3.04 W
Ceg	144	8.58 N	45.20 E
Cega ≃	34	41.33 N	4.46 W
Čeganly	80	53.54 N	53.34 E
Čegdomyn	89	51.07 N	133.05 E
Čegem ≃	84	43.38 N	43.48 E
Čegem Pervyj	84	43.34 N	43.35 E
Čegitun'	180	66.34 N	171.06 W
Cegléd	30	47.10 N	19.48 E
Ceglie Messapico	68	40.39 N	17.31 E
Cehegín	34	38.06 N	1.48 W
Ceheng	102	25.10 N	105.48 E
Cehnice	60	49.12 N	14.02 E
Cehu Silvaniei	38	47.25 N	23.11 E
Ceiba	240m	18.16 N	65.39 W
Ceibo ≃	258	33.57 S	58.27 W
Ceilán → Sri Lanka □[1]	122	7.00 N	81.00 E
Ceiriog ≃	42	52.57 N	3.02 W
Ceirw ≃	44	52.59 N	3.27 W
Čejč	61	48.57 N	16.57 E
Čekalin	82	54.06 N	36.15 E
Čekan	80	54.51 N	53.34 E
Čekanovskij	88	56.13 N	101.25 E
Çekerek	130	40.04 N	35.31 E
Çekerek ≃	130	40.34 N	35.46 E
Čekmaguš	86	55.08 N	54.40 E
Çekme ◆[8]	267b	41.03 N	29.10 E
Čekšino	76	59.39 N	40.33 E
Čekujevo	24	63.34 N	38.56 E
Čekunda	89	50.48 N	132.10 E
Čel'abinsk	86	55.10 N	61.24 E
Čel'abinsk Oblast' □[4]	86	54.30 N	60.30 E
Čelákovice	54	50.10 N	14.46 E
Celâlli	130	39.42 N	37.26 E
Celano	66	42.05 N	13.33 E
Celanova	34	42.09 N	7.58 W
Celaya	234	20.31 N	100.49 W
Čelbas ≃	78	46.06 N	38.59 E
Čelbasskaja	78	45.59 N	39.22 E
Celbridge	48	53.20 N	6.33 W
Celebes → Sulawesi I	112	2.00 S	121.00 E
Celebes Basin ✣[1]	14	4.00 N	122.00 E
Celebes Sea ⊤[2]	112	3.00 N	122.00 E
Čeleken	128	39.26 N	53.07 E
Celendín	248	6.52 S	78.09 W
Celenza sul Trigno	66	41.52 N	14.35 E
Celenza Valfortore	68	41.34 N	14.58 E
Celerina	58	46.31 N	9.51 E
Celeryville	214	41.02 N	82.45 W
Celeste	196	33.18 N	96.12 W
Celestún	232	20.52 N	90.24 W
Celica	246	4.07 S	79.59 W
Celico	68	39.19 N	16.20 E
Çelikhan	130	38.02 N	38.15 E
Čelina, Ross.	80	46.32 N	41.02 E
Celina, Oh., U.S.	216	40.32 N	84.34 W
Celina, Tn., U.S.	194	36.33 N	85.30 W
Celina, Tx., U.S.	196	33.19 N	96.47 W
Celinnoje, Ross.	86	53.04 N	85.40 E
Celinnoje, Ross.	86	54.31 N	63.39 E
Celinnyj	80	46.40 N	44.32 E
Celinograd	86	51.10 N	71.30 E
Celinograd □[8]	86	51.00 N	70.00 E
Celje	36	46.14 N	15.16 E
Čelkar	86	47.50 N	59.36 E
Cellar Head ›	46	58.26 N	6.10 W
Celldömölk	30	47.16 N	17.09 E
Celle	52	52.37 N	10.05 E
Celle, Ruisseau la ≃	261	48.35 N	2.01 E
Celle Ligure	62	44.20 N	8.33 E
Celles	56	50.14 N	5.01 E
Celles-sur-Plaine	58	48.28 N	6.57 E
Cellettes	50	47.32 N	1.23 E
Cellina ≃	64	46.02 N	12.47 E
Cellino Attanasio	66	42.36 N	13.52 E
Cellino San Marco	68	40.28 N	17.58 E
Čelmozero	24	64.18 N	31.48 E
Čelno-Veršiny	80	54.26 N	51.06 E
Čelobitjevo	265b	55.55 N	37.40 E
Celone ≃	68	41.36 N	15.41 E
Celorico da Beira	34	40.38 N	7.23 W
Celoron	214	42.06 N	79.17 W
Celtic Sea ⊤[2]	28	51.00 N	6.30 W
Celtic Shelf ✣[4]	10	49.15 N	7.00 W
Çeltikçi, Tür.	130	40.20 N	32.28 E
Çeltikçi, Tür.	130	37.32 N	30.29 E
Čel'uš	86	51.32 N	87.46 E
Čel'uskin, mys ›	74	77.45 N	104.20 E
Čel'uskincev park ♦	265a	60.01 N	30.19 E
Cemaes Head ›	42	52.07 N	4.44 W
Čemal	86	51.25 N	86.01 E
Čembilej	80	55.19 N	45.43 E
Cembra	64	46.10 N	11.13 E
Cembra, Val di V	64	46.10 N	11.13 E
Cement	196	34.55 N	98.08 W
Cement City	216	42.04 N	84.19 W
Cementon, N.Y., U.S.	210	42.09 N	73.55 W
Cementon, Pa., U.S.	208	40.41 N	75.30 W
Čemerisy	78	51.42 N	30.24 E
Čemerno	36	43.11 N	18.37 E
Cemesskaja buchta ⊂	78	44.40 N	37.50 E
Cemilbey	130	40.21 N	35.04 E
Çemişkezek	130	39.04 N	38.55 E
Cemmaes	42	52.37 N	3.42 W
Čemolgan	85	43.23 N	76.37 E
Cempi, Teluk ⊂	115b	8.44 S	118.25 E
Čenča	88	55.57 N	110.59 E
Cencenighe	64	46.21 N	11.58 E
Čenchermandal	88	47.37 N	109.05 E
Čency	82	56.03 N	36.01 E
Cenderawasih, Teluk ⊂	164	2.30 S	135.20 E
Cendras	62	44.09 N	4.04 E
Cene	62	45.47 N	9.49 E
Cenepa ≃	246	4.35 S	78.12 W
Čengel	86	48.56 N	89.10 E
Čengel'dy, Kaz.	85	43.59 N	77.26 E
Čengel'dy, Kaz.	85	41.51 N	68.59 E
Çengelköy ◆[8]	267b	41.03 N	29.03 E
Čengerli	130	39.48 N	38.52 E
Cengles, Croda di ∧	64	46.34 N	10.38 E
Ceno ≃	36	44.41 N	10.05 E
Cenovo	38	43.32 N	25.39 E
Cenrana	112	3.18 S	118.50 E
Censeau	58	46.49 N	6.04 E
Centallo	62	44.30 N	7.35 E
Centenario	252	38.48 S	68.08 W
Centenário do Sul	255	22.48 S	51.37 W
Centennial Lake ⊜	285	39.50 N	74.51 W
Centennial Lake ⊜[1]	212	45.10 N	72.05 W
Centennial Mountains ⋏	202	44.35 N	111.55 W
Centennial Park ♦, Austl.	274a	33.54 S	151.14 E
Centennial Park ♦, On., Can.	275b	43.39 N	79.35 W
Centennial Wash V	200	33.14 N	112.46 W
Centeno	66	42.48 N	11.49 E
Center, Co., U.S.	200	37.45 N	106.06 W
Center, In., U.S.	216	40.26 N	86.04 W
Center, Mo., U.S.	219	39.30 N	91.31 W
Center, Ne., U.S.	198	42.36 N	97.52 W
Center, N.D., U.S.	198	47.06 N	101.17 W
Center, Tx., U.S.	194	31.47 N	94.10 W
Centerbrook	207	41.21 N	72.24 W
Center Brunswick	210	42.45 N	73.37 W
Centerburg	214	40.18 N	82.41 W
Center City	190	45.23 N	92.48 W
Center Cross	208	37.48 N	76.46 W
Centereach	210	40.51 N	73.06 W
Centerfield	218	38.21 N	83.24 W
Center Hill	220	28.38 N	81.59 W
Center Hill Lake ⊜[1]	194	36.00 N	85.45 W
Center Line	214	42.29 N	83.01 W
Center Moriches	188	40.48 N	72.47 W
Center Mountain ∧	202	45.06 N	115.13 W
Center Point, Al., U.S.	194	33.37 N	86.41 W
Center Point, Ia., U.S.	190	42.11 N	91.47 W
Center Point, Tx., U.S.	196	29.57 N	99.02 W
Centerport, N.Y., U.S.	210	40.54 N	73.22 W
Centerport, Pa., U.S.	208	40.29 N	76.01 W
Center Square, N.J., U.S.	285	39.46 N	75.23 W
Center Square, Pa., U.S.	208	40.10 N	75.18 W
Centerton, In., U.S.	218	39.30 N	86.23 W
Centerton, N.J., U.S.	285	39.31 N	75.10 W
Center Valley	208	40.32 N	75.24 W
Centerville, De., U.S.	285	39.49 N	75.37 W
Centerville, In., U.S.	218	39.49 N	84.59 W
Centerville, Ia., U.S.	190	40.43 N	92.52 W
Centerville, Ma., U.S.	207	41.38 N	70.20 W
Centerville, Mo., U.S.	194	37.26 N	90.57 W
Centerville, N.Y., U.S.	210	42.29 N	78.15 W
Centerville, Oh., U.S.	218	39.37 N	84.09 W
Centerville, Pa., U.S.	188	40.02 N	79.58 W
Centerville, S.D., U.S.	198	43.07 N	96.57 W
Centerville, Tn., U.S.	194	35.46 N	87.28 W
Centerville, Tx., U.S.	222	31.15 N	95.58 W
Centerville, Ut,. U.S.	200	40.55 N	111.52 W
Centerville, Wa., U.S.	224	45.45 N	120.54 W
Centinela	196	28.47 N	100.34 W
Cento	64	44.43 N	11.17 E
Centocelle ◆[8]	267a	41.53 N	12.34 E
Cento Croci, Passo di)(	62	44.25 N	9.37 E
Centola	68	40.04 N	15.19 E
Central, Bra.	250	11.08 S	42.08 W
Central, Ak., U.S.	180	65.34 N	144.48 W
Central, Az., U.S.	200	32.52 N	109.47 W
Central, N.M., U.S.	200	32.46 N	108.08 W
Central, S.C., U.S.	192	34.43 N	82.46 W
Central, Tx., U.S.	222	31.26 N	94.49 W
Central □[4], Ghana	150	5.30 N	1.00 W
Central □[4], Kenya	154	0.45 S	37.00 E
Central □[4], Malaŵi	154	13.00 S	34.00 E
Central □[4], Sol.Is.	175e	9.10 S	159.50 E
Central □[4], Scot., U.K.	46	56.05 N	4.20 W
Central □[4], Zam.	154	14.30 S	29.00 E
Central □[5], Bots.	156	21.30 S	26.00 E
Central □[5], Pap. N. Gui.	164	9.00 S	147.00 E
Central □[5], Para.	252	25.30 S	57.30 W
Central □[5], Ug.	154	0.10 N	32.00 E
Central, Cordillera ⋏, Col.	246	5.00 N	75.00 W
Central, Cordillera ⋏, C.R.	236	10.10 N	84.05 W
Central, Cordillera ⋏, Pan.	236	8.30 N	81.30 W
Central, Cordillera ⋏, Perú	248	8.00 S	77.00 W
Central, Cordillera ⋏, Pil.	116	17.20 N	120.57 E
Central, Cordillera ⋏, P.R.	240m	18.10 N	66.35 W
Central, Macizo → Central, Massif ⋏	32	45.00 N	3.10 E
Central, Massif ⋏	32	45.00 N	3.10 E
Central, Planalto ⋏[1]	242	18.00 S	47.00 W
Central, Sistema ⋏	34	40.30 N	5.00 W
Central African Republic □[1]	136	7.00 N	21.00 E
Central Aguirre	240m	17.57 N	66.13 W
Central Barren	218	38.22 N	86.06 W
Central Brāhui Range ⋏	120	29.20 N	66.55 E
Central Bridge	210	42.42 N	74.20 W
Central Butte	184	50.47 N	106.30 W
Central City, Il., U.S.	219	38.32 N	89.07 W
Central City, Ia., U.S.	190	42.12 N	91.31 W
Central City, Ky., U.S.	194	37.17 N	87.07 W
Central City, Ne., U.S.	198	41.06 N	98.00 W
Central City, Pa., U.S.	214	40.06 N	78.48 W
Central Division □[5]	175g	18.05 S	178.30 E
Centrale, Stazione ◆[5]	266b	45.29 N	9.12 E
Central Falls	207	41.53 N	71.23 W
Central Heights	200	33.24 N	110.48 W
Central Highlands	279b	40.16 N	79.50 W
Centralia, Il., U.S.	219	38.31 N	89.08 W
Centralia, Ks., U.S.	198	39.43 N	96.07 W
Centralia, Mo., U.S.	219	39.12 N	92.08 W
Centralia, Tx., U.S.	222	31.16 N	95.02 W
Centralia, Wa., U.S.	224	46.42 N	122.57 W
Centralia, Lake ⊜	219	38.32 N	88.59 W
Centralia Draw V	196	31.27 N	101.16 W
Centralia Reservoir ⊜[1]	219	38.32 N	89.08 W
Centralina	255	18.34 S	49.13 W
Central Intelligence Agency ☼	284c	38.57 N	77.09 W
Central Island I	154	3.30 N	36.03 E
Central Islip	210	40.47 N	73.12 W
Central Kalahari Game Reserve ◆[4]	156	22.15 S	23.45 E
Central Lake	190	45.04 N	85.15 W
Central Makrān Range ⋏	128	26.40 N	64.30 E
Central'nolesnoj zapovednik ◆[4]	76	56.32 N	32.50 E
Central Nyack	276	41.06 N	73.57 W
Central'nyj, Ross.	76	53.41 N	39.38 E
Central'nyj, Ross.	86	55.12 N	87.40 E
Central'nyj, Ross.	86	58.45 N	84.28 E
Central'nyj, Ross.	86	57.41 N	80.57 E
Central'nyj, Ross.	265b	55.53 N	37.52 E
Central'nyje Karakumy ◆[2]	128	39.00 N	60.00 E
Central Pacific Basin ✣[1]	14	5.00 N	175.00 W
Central Park, N.J., U.S.	276	40.26 N	74.18 W
Central Park, Wa., U.S.	224	46.58 N	123.41 W
Central Park ♦	276	40.47 N	73.58 W
Central Point	202	42.22 N	122.54 W
Central Railroad Station ◆[5]	272c	18.58 N	72.50 E
Central Range ⋏, Leso.	158	29.35 S	28.35 E
Central Range ⋏, Pap. N. Gui.	164	5.00 S	142.30 E
Central Square	210	43.17 N	76.08 W
Central Utah Canal ≅	200	39.35 N	112.12 W
Central Valley, Ca., U.S.	204	40.40 N	122.22 W
Central Valley, N.Y., U.S.	210	41.19 N	74.07 W
Central Village	207	41.43 N	71.54 W
Centre	194	34.09 N	85.40 W
Centre □[6]	210	40.55 N	77.47 W
Centre, Canal du ≅	32	46.27 N	4.07 E
Centre Atomique de Marcoule ☼[3]	62	44.08 N	4.42 E
Centre City	285	39.46 N	75.10 W
Centre d'Énergie de Pierrelatte ☼[3]	62	44.21 N	4.44 E
Centre Hall	214	40.50 N	77.41 W
Centre Island	276	40.54 N	73.32 W
Centre Island I	172	46.28 S	167.51 E
Centre Island Park ♦	275b	43.37 N	79.23 W
Centre Lake ⊜	212	44.36 N	75.51 W
Centre Peak ∧	182	55.41 N	126.26 W
Centre-Sud □[4]	152	4.10 N	12.00 E
Centreville, Al., U.S.	194	32.56 N	87.08 W
Centreville, Il., U.S.	219	38.35 N	90.07 W
Centreville, Ky., U.S.	218	38.13 N	84.24 W
Centreville, Md., U.S.	208	39.02 N	76.04 W
Centreville, Mi., U.S.	216	41.55 N	85.31 W
Centreville, Ms., U.S.	194	31.05 N	91.04 W
Centreville, Va., U.S.	208	38.50 N	77.25 W
Centro Puntas	240m	18.22 N	67.16 W
Centro Simón Bolívar ◆[9]	286c	10.30 N	66.55 W
Centuripe	70	37.37 N	14.44 E
Century, Fl., U.S.	194	30.58 N	87.15 W
Century, W.V., U.S.	188	39.05 N	80.11 W
Century City ◆[8]	280	34.03 N	118.26 W
Century III Mall ◆[9]	279b	40.21 N	79.57 W
Century Village	220	26.42 N	80.05 W
Cenxi	102	22.59 N	111.00 E
Čepca	80	57.54 N	53.25 E
Čepca ≃	80	58.36 N	50.04 E
Čepeckij	80	58.29 N	51.12 E
Čepelare	38	41.44 N	24.41 E
Čepel'ovo	82	55.11 N	37.30 E
Čepovan	64	46.03 N	13.47 E
Cepoy	50	48.03 N	2.44 E
Ceprano	66	41.33 N	13.31 E
Čepřovice	60	49.10 N	13.59 E
Ceptia	152	12.56 S	17.35 E
Cepu	115a	7.09 S	111.35 E
Ceraino	64	45.35 N	10.50 E
Ceram → Seram I	164	3.00 S	129.00 E
Cerami	70	37.49 N	14.30 E
Cerami ≃	70	37.42 N	14.29 E
Ceram Sea → Seram, Laut ⊤[2]	108	2.30 S	128.00 E
Cerano, It.	62	45.25 N	8.47 E
Cerano, Méx.	234	20.07 N	101.23 W
Ceraso	68	40.11 N	15.15 E
Cerbicale, Îles II	71	41.34 N	9.24 E
Čerčany	30	49.51 N	14.43 E
Cerchiara di Calabria	68	39.51 N	16.23 E
Čerchov ∧	60	49.23 N	12.47 E
Cercié	58	46.07 N	4.40 E
Cerco, Alto do ∧	256	22.38 S	45.22 W
Cerda	70	37.54 N	13.49 E
Čerdakly	80	54.23 N	48.51 E
Cerdanyola del Vallès	266d	41.30 N	2.09 E
Cerdas	248	20.48 S	66.29 W
Cerdeña, Isla de → Sardegna I	71	40.00 N	9.00 E
Čerdojak	86	48.48 N	84.00 E
Cerdon, Fr.	50	47.38 N	2.22 E
Cerdon, Fr.	58	46.05 N	5.28 E
Čerdyn'	24	60.23 N	56.24 E
Cère ≃	32	44.55 N	1.53 E
Cerea	64	45.12 N	11.13 E
Cereal	184	51.25 N	110.48 W
Cereales	252	36.49 S	63.51 W
Čerecha ≃	76	57.46 N	28.21 E
Cereglio	64	44.18 N	11.04 E
Čereja	76	54.37 N	29.17 E
Čerek ≃	84	43.42 N	44.03 E
Čeremchovo	88	53.09 N	103.05 E
Čeremisinovo	78	51.54 N	37.15 E
Čeremšan, Ross.	80	55.15 N	48.07 E
Čeremšan, Ross.	80	54.40 N	51.30 E
Čeremšanka, Ross.	86	59.10 N	76.51 E
Čeremšanka, Ross.	86	56.07 N	60.19 E
Čeremšany	89	44.42 N	135.43 E
Cerenti	112	0.30 S	101.52 E
Čerepanovka	80	57.07 N	54.10 E
Čerepanovo	86	54.13 N	83.22 E
Čerepaška, ostrov I	83	47.11 N	38.59 E
Čerepet'	82	54.07 N	36.23 E
Čerepkovo ◆[8]	265b	55.46 N	37.23 E
Čerepovec	76	59.08 N	37.54 E
Ceres, Arg.	252	29.53 S	61.57 W
Ceres, Bra.	255	15.17 S	49.35 W
Ceres, It.	62	45.19 N	7.23 E
Ceres, S. Afr.	158	33.21 S	19.18 E
Ceres, Ca., U.S.	226	37.35 N	120.57 W
Ceres, N.Y., U.S.	210	42.00 N	78.16 W
Ceresco, Mi., U.S.	216	42.16 N	85.04 W
Ceresco, Ne., U.S.	198	41.03 N	96.38 W
Ceresole Reale	62	45.26 N	7.15 E
Céreste	62	43.51 N	5.35 E
Céret	32	42.29 N	2.45 E
Čereté	246	8.53 N	75.48 W
Čerevkovo	24	61.46 N	45.12 E
Cereweh	115b	8.52 S	116.51 E
Cerf Island I	138	9.32 S	50.59 E
Čerga	86	51.35 N	85.38 E
Cergy	261	49.02 N	2.04 E
Ceri ≃	42	52.03 N	4.29 W
Ceriale	62	44.06 N	8.14 E
Ceriana	62	43.53 N	7.46 E
Ceriano	266b	45.38 N	9.05 E
Cerignola	68	41.16 N	15.54 E
Čerikov	76	53.34 N	31.23 E
Cérilly	32	46.37 N	2.49 E
Cerisano	68	39.16 N	16.11 E
Cerisiers	50	48.08 N	3.29 E
Čerkašina	88	58.37 N	108.30 E
Čerkasovo	82	54.33 N	36.48 E
Čerkasskoje	80	52.26 N	47.13 E
Čerkassy	76	52.41 N	38.43 E
Çerkeş	130	40.50 N	32.54 E
Čerkesovskij	80	50.41 N	42.34 E
Čerkessk	84	44.14 N	42.04 E
Çerkezköy	130	41.17 N	28.00 E
Čerkizovo, Ross.	82	55.12 N	38.45 E
Čerkizovo, Ross.	265b	55.58 N	37.48 E
Čerkizovo, Ross.	265b	55.57 N	37.22 E
Cerknica	36	45.48 N	14.22 E
Čerkovišče	76	55.54 N	30.51 E
Čerlak	86	54.09 N	74.48 E
Čerlakskij	86	53.47 N	74.31 E
Čermei	38	46.33 N	21.51 E
Čermen	84	43.11 N	44.42 E
Cermignano	66	42.35 N	13.47 E
Çermik	130	38.09 N	39.27 E
Čermoz	86	58.53 N	56.08 E
Čern'	76	53.27 N	36.55 E
Cerna, Hrv.	38	45.11 N	18.42 E
Cerna, Rom.	38	45.04 N	28.18 E
Čern'achovsk (Insterburg)	76	54.38 N	21.49 E
Černá hora ∧	60	48.58 N	13.48 E
Čern'ajevo	89	52.45 N	126.00 E
Černak	85	43.24 N	68.02 E
Čern'anka	78	50.55 N	37.49 E
Cernăuți → Chernivtsi	78	48.18 N	25.56 E
Černava	76	53.37 N	39.09 E
Černavčicy	76	52.13 N	23.44 E
Černavka, Ross.	80	52.18 N	47.14 E
Černavka, Ross.	80	52.11 N	42.25 E
Cernavodă	38	44.21 N	28.01 E
Černá v Pošumaví	61	48.44 N	14.07 E
Cernay	58	47.49 N	7.10 E
Cernay-la-Ville	50	48.40 N	1.58 E
Cerne Abbas	42	50.49 N	2.29 W
Černeckoje	82	55.15 N	37.20 E
Cernei, Munții ⋏	38	45.02 N	22.31 E
Černigovka, Kaz.	86	50.28 N	71.27 E
Černigovka, Ross.	89	49.37 N	129.57 E
Černigovka, Ross.	89	44.21 N	132.33 E
Černigovskaja	78	44.41 N	39.40 E
Cerni Vrăh ∧	38	42.34 N	23.17 E
Cernobbio	62	45.50 N	9.04 E
Černogolovka	82	56.00 N	38.22 E
Černogorsk	86	53.49 N	91.18 E
Černokol'skaja	86	56.42 N	72.49 E
Černorečenskoje	85	43.00 N	74.55 E
Černorečje	84	43.15 N	45.41 E
Černošín	60	49.49 N	12.53 E
Černovice	60	49.49 N	13.06 E
Černovka, Ross.	86	56.47 N	76.28 E
Černovka, Ross.	89	51.43 N	128.12 E
Čern'ovo, Ross.	76	58.39 N	28.14 E
Čern'ovo, Ross.	82	54.43 N	38.36 E
Čern'ovo, Ross.	265b	55.50 N	37.18 E
Černovskije Kopi	88	52.00 N	113.15 E
Černovskoje, Ross.	80	58.42 N	47.23 E
Černovskoje, Ross.	80	57.29 N	54.36 E
Černucha	80	55.36 N	43.46 E
Cernusco sul Naviglio	62	45.31 N	9.19 E
Černuška, Ross.	86	56.29 N	56.03 E
Černuška, Ross.	88	52.58 N	101.55 E
Cerny-en-Laonnois	50	49.27 N	3.40 E
Černyševsk	88	52.35 N	117.00 E
Černyševskij	74	63.00 N	112.15 E
Černyškovskij	80	48.27 N	42.14 E
Černyšova, gr'ada ⋏	24	66.30 N	59.00 E
Čer'omuchova	80	54.57 N	51.09 E
Čer'omuski ◆[8]	265b	55.41 N	37.35 E
Cerralvo	232	26.06 N	99.37 W
Cerralvo, Isla I	232	24.15 N	109.55 W
Cerreto, Passo del)(	64	44.18 N	10.13 E
Cerreto d'Esi	66	43.19 N	12.59 E
Cerreto Guidi	66	43.45 N	10.53 E
Cerreto Sannita	68	41.17 N	14.33 E
Cerrigydrudion	44	53.02 N	3.33 W
Cërrik	38	41.02 N	19.57 E
Name	**Seite**	**Breite°′**	**Länge°′ E = Ost**
Cerrillos, Arg.	252	24.54 S	65.29 W
Cerrillos, Chile	286e	33.30 S	70.43 W
Cerrillos, N.M., U.S.	200	35.26 N	106.07 W
Cerrina	62	45.07 N	8.13 E
Cerritos, Méx.	234	22.26 N	100.17 W
Cerritos, Ca., U.S.	280	33.52 N	118.05 W
Cerro	58	45.54 N	8.36 E
Cerro, Forca di)(	66	42.45 N	12.47 E
Cerro Azul, Arg.	252	27.38 S	55.29 W
Cerro Azul, Bra.	252	24.50 S	49.15 W
Cerro Azul, Méx.	234	21.12 N	97.44 W
Cerro Azul, Perú	248	13.02 S	76.30 W
Cerro Chato	252	33.06 S	55.08 W
Cerro Colorado	252	33.52 S	55.33 W
Cerro Corá	250	6.03 S	36.21 W
Cerro de las Mesas ⊥	234	18.47 N	96.05 W
Cerro de los Angeles ☼[1]	266a	40.19 N	3.41 W
Cerro de Pasco	248	10.41 S	76.16 W
Cerro Gordo	219	39.53 N	88.43 W
Cerro Grande ≃	286c	10.37 N	66.49 W
Cerro Largo	252	28.09 S	54.45 W
Cerro Maggiore	266b	45.36 N	8.58 E
Cerro Moreno	252	23.28 S	70.25 W
Cerrón, Cerro ∧	246	10.19 N	70.39 W
Cerro Navia	286e	33.25 S	70.43 W
Cerrón Grande, Embalse ⊜[1]	236	14.00 N	89.00 W
Cerro Prieto	204	32.27 N	115.17 W
Cerros Colorados, Embalse ⊜[1]	252	38.35 S	68.40 W
Cerros de Amotape, Parque Nacional ♦	246	4.10 S	80.30 W
Cerro Tololo, Observatorio ☼[3]	252	30.05 S	71.00 W
Cerro Vera	252	33.11 S	57.28 W
Čerskij	74	68.45 N	161.45 E
Čerskogo, chrebet ⋏, Ross.	74	65.00 N	144.00 E
Čerskogo, chrebet ⋏, Ross.	88	52.00 N	114.00 E
Čerskogo, gora ∧	88	55.05 N	108.40 E
Cersosimo	68	40.03 N	16.21 E
Certaldo	66	43.33 N	11.02 E
Čertanovka ≃	265b	55.38 N	37.47 E
Čertanovo ◆[8]	265b	55.38 N	37.37 E
Čertkovo	83	49.23 N	40.10 E
Čertolino	76	56.12 N	33.54 E
Certosa (Karthaus)	64	46.42 N	10.54 E
Certosa di Pavia	62	45.15 N	9.09 E
Čerusti	76	55.33 N	40.01 E
Červ'anka	88	57.41 N	99.33 E
Cervantes, Austl.	162	30.30 S	115.04 E
Cervantes, Pil.	116	16.59 N	120.44 E
Cervarezza	64	44.23 N	10.20 E
Cervaro	66	41.29 N	13.54 E
Cervaro ≃	68	41.30 N	15.52 E
Cervati, Monte ∧	68	40.17 N	15.29 E
Cervelló	266d	41.24 N	1.57 E
Cervello, Cozzo ∧	68	39.24 N	16.05 E
Cervelló, Riera de ≃	266d	41.24 N	2.01 E
Červen'	76	53.42 N	28.26 E
Červen Brjag	38	43.16 N	24.06 E
Červený Kostelec	30	50.29 N	16.06 E
Cervera	34	41.40 N	1.17 E
Cervera del Río Alhama	34	42.01 N	1.57 W
Cervera de Pisuerga	34	42.52 N	4.30 W
Cerveteri	66	42.00 N	12.06 E
Cervi, Monte dei ∧	70	37.53 N	13.58 E
Cervia	66	44.15 N	12.22 E
Cervialto, Monte ∧	68	40.47 N	15.08 E
Cervignano del Friuli	64	45.49 N	13.20 E
Cervin, Mont → Matterhorn ∧	58	45.59 N	7.43 E
Cervinara	68	41.01 N	14.37 E
Cervino (Matterhorn) ∧	58	45.59 N	7.43 E
Cervione	36	42.20 N	9.31 E
Červl'onnaja	84	43.30 N	45.54 E
Cervo, Esp.	34	43.40 N	7.25 W
Cervo, It.	62	43.55 N	8.07 E
Cervo ≃	62	45.22 N	8.24 E
Cervo, Capo ›	62	43.55 N	8.08 E
Cervo, Rio do ≃, Bra.	256	22.07 S	45.49 W
Cervo, Rio do ≃, Bra.	256	21.12 S	45.10 W
Cervo, Serra do ∧	256	22.06 S	46.07 W
Červonoje, ozero ⊜	76	52.24 N	27.57 E
Cesana Torinese	62	44.57 N	6.47 E
Cesano, It.	66	43.45 N	13.10 E
Cesano, It.	66	42.07 N	12.21 E
Cesano ≃	66	43.45 N	13.10 E
Cesano Boscone	266b	45.27 N	9.06 E
Cesano Maderno	62	45.38 N	9.08 E
Cesar □[5]	246	9.20 N	73.30 W
Cesar ≃	246	9.00 N	73.58 W
Cesarò	70	37.50 N	14.43 E
Cesate	266b	45.36 N	9.05 E
Cesena	66	44.08 N	12.15 E
Cesenatico	66	44.12 N	12.24 E
Cesi, Poggio ∧[2]	267a	42.02 N	12.44 E
Cesiomaggiore	64	46.05 N	11.59 E
Cēsis	76	57.18 N	25.15 E
Česká Kamenice	54	50.47 N	14.26 E
Česká Kublice	60	49.22 N	12.52 E
Česká Lípa	54	50.42 N	14.32 E
Česká Třebová	30	49.54 N	16.27 E
České Budějovice	61	48.59 N	14.28 E
České středohoří ⋏	54	50.35 N	14.09 E
Českomoravská vrchovina ⋏[1]	30	49.20 N	15.30 E
Český Brod	54	50.02 N	14.58 E
Český Krumlov	61	48.49 N	14.19 E
Česma	86	53.50 N	60.40 E
Çeşme	130	38.18 N	26.19 E
Cessalto	64	45.42 N	12.36 E
Češskaja guba ⊂	24	67.30 N	46.30 E
Cessnock	170	32.50 S	151.21 E
Cesson	261	48.34 N	2.36 E
Cestos ≃	150	5.40 N	9.10 W
Cesvaine	76	56.58 N	26.19 E
Čet' ≃	86	56.51 N	86.48 E
Cetara	68	40.39 N	14.42 E
Cetate	38	44.06 N	23.03 E
Cetatea Albă → Bilhorod-Dnistrovs'kyy	78	46.12 N	30.20 E
Četbulak	85	41.17 N	73.58 E
Cetian	100	25.44 N	116.22 E
Cetina ≃	36	43.26 N	16.42 E
Cetinje	38	42.23 N	18.55 E
Çetinkaya	130	39.15 N	37.38 E
Cetona	66	42.58 N	11.54 E
Cetona, Monte ∧	66	42.56 N	11.52 E
Cetraro	68	39.31 N	15.56 E
Cetronia	208	40.35 N	75.31 W
Céüse, Montagne de ∧	62	44.31 N	5.57 E
Ceuta	34	35.53 N	5.19 W
Ceva	62	44.23 N	8.02 E
Cevedale, Monte (Zufallspitze) ∧	64	46.27 N	10.37 E
Cevennen → Cévennes ◆[1]	32	44.00 N	3.30 E
Cévennes ◆[1]	32	44.00 N	3.30 E
Cévennes, Parc National des ♦	32	44.15 N	3.40 E
Cevins	62	45.35 N	6.28 E
Cevio	58	46.19 N	8.36 E
Cevizli	130	37.12 N	31.45 E
Ceyhan	130	37.04 N	35.47 E
Ceyhan ≃	130	36.45 N	35.41 E
Ceylanpınar	130	36.51 N	40.02 E
Çeyldağ	84	40.17 N	49.18 E
Ceylon, Sk., Can.	184	49.28 N	104.36 W
Ceylon, Mn., U.S.	198	43.32 N	94.37 W
Ceylon → Sri Lanka □[1]	122	7.00 N	81.00 E
Ceyzériat	58	46.10 N	5.19 E
Cèze ≃	62	44.06 N	4.42 E
Chaam, Ned.	52	51.31 N	4.52 E

Symbols in the index entries represent the broad categories identified in the key at the right. Symbols with superior numbers (⋏[1]) identify subcategories (see complete key on page *I · 1)*.

Symbole im Register stellen die rechts im Schlüssel erklärten Kategorien dar. Symbole mit hochgestellten Ziffern (⋏[1]) bezeichnen Unterabteilungen einer Kategorie (vgl. vollständiger Schlüssel auf Seite *I · 1)*.

Los símbolos incluídos en el texto del índice representan las grandes categorías identificadas con la clave a la derecha. Los símbolos con numeros en su parte superior (⋏[1]) identifican las subcategorías (véase la clave completa en la página *I · 1)*.

Les symboles de l'index représentent les catégories indiquées dans la légende à droite. Les symboles suivis d'un indice (⋏[1]) représentent des sous-catégories (voir légende complète à la page *I · 1)*.

Os símbolos incluídos no texto do índice representam as grandes categorias identificadas com a chave à direita. Os símbolos com números em sua parte superior (⋏[1]) identificam as subcategorias (veja-se a chave completa à página *I · 1)*.

Symbol	English	Deutsch	Español	Français	Português
∧	Mountain	Berg	Montaña	Montagne	Montanha
⋏	Mountains	Gebirge	Montañas	Montagnes	Montanhas
)(	Pass	Paß	Paso	Col	Passo
V	Valley, Canyon	Tal, Cañon	Valle, Cañón	Vallée, Canyon	Vale, Canhão
≚	Plain	Ebene	Llano	Plaine	Planície
›	Cape	Kap	Cabo	Cap	Cabo
I	Island	Insel	Isla	Île	Ilha
II	Islands	Inseln	Islas	Îles	Ilhas
⊥	Other Topographic Features	Andere Topographische Objekte	Otros Elementos Topográficos	Autres données topographiques	Outros acidentes topográficos

ESPAÑOL

Nombre	Página	Lat.°′	Long.°′ W = Oeste
Cha-am, Thai	110	12.48 N	99.58 E
Chaanling	100	29.39 N	113.49 E
Chaatl Island I	182	53.00 N	132.25 W
Chabanais	32	45.52 N	0.43 E
Chabang Tiga	114	5.19 N	103.08 E
Chabaricha	24	65.50 N	52.16 E
Chabařovice	54	50.40 N	13.56 E
Chabarovo	72	69.39 N	60.24 E
Chabarovsk	89	48.27 N	135.06 E
Chabarovsk Kraj □[8]	89	52.00 N	138.00 E
Chabarowsk → Chabarovsk	89	48.27 N	135.06 E
Chabary	86	53.37 N	79.33 E
Chabás	252	33.15 S	61.22 W
Chabeuil	62	44.54 N	5.01 E
Chabez	84	44.02 N	41.47 E
Chābi	124	22.49 N	80.41 E
Chabjuwardoo Bay ⊂	162	22.57 S	113.48 E
Chablais ◆[1]	58	46.18 N	6.39 E
Chablis	50	47.49 N	3.48 E
Chabogongba	120	31.47 N	81.14 E
Chaboje	265a	59.53 N	30.46 E
Chabot, Lake ⊜, Ca., U.S.	282	38.08 N	122.14 W
Chabot, Lake ⊜, Ca., U.S.	282	37.43 N	122.07 W
Chabris	50	47.15 N	1.39 E
Chabuchaer	86	43.42 N	81.04 E
Chabu-Rabot, pereval)(	85	38.40 N	70.43 E
Chacabuco	252	34.38 S	60.29 W
Chacaito, Quebrada ≃	286c	10.29 N	66.52 W
Chacaltianguis	234	18.20 N	95.50 W
Chacao	286c	10.30 N	66.51 W
Chácara	256	21.41 S	43.13 W
Chacarita, Cementerio de la ◆	288	34.33 S	58.28 W
Chacarrão, Cachoeira do ⌞	250	6.32 S	58.12 W
Chacayán	248	10.24 S	76.25 W
Chachani, Nevado ∧	248	16.12 S	71.33 W
Chachapoyas, Perú	242	6.13 S	77.51 W
Chachapoyas, Perú	248	6.13 S	77.51 W
Chachas	248	15.30 S	72.16 W
Chachoengsao	110	13.42 N	101.05 E
Chāchora	124	24.10 N	76.59 E
Chāchro	120	25.07 N	70.15 E
Chachu	120	33.16 N	81.41 E
Chaclacyo	248	11.59 S	76.46 W
Chaco □[4]	252	26.25 S	60.30 W
Chaco □[5]	248	20.00 S	60.30 W
Chaco ≃	200	36.46 N	108.39 W
Chaco Austral ◆[1]	252	26.30 S	61.30 W
Chaco Boreal ◆[1]	252	23.00 S	60.00 W
Chaco Central ◆[1]	252	25.00 S	59.45 W
Chaco Culture National Historical Park ♠	200	36.06 N	108.00 W
Chaco Mesa ∧	200	35.47 N	107.35 W
Chacón, Arroyo ≃	288	34.53 S	58.39 W
Chacon, Cape ›	182	54.42 N	132.00 W
Chacra Cerro	286d	11.55 S	77.04 W
Chacuaco Creek ≃	196	37.34 N	103.38 W
Chad (Tchad) □[1], Afr.	136	15.00 N	19.00 E
Chad (Tchad) □[1], Afr.	146	15.00 N	19.00 E
Chad, Lake (Lac Tchad) ⊜	146	13.20 N	14.00 E
Chada-Bulak	88	50.38 N	116.18 E
Chadbourn	192	34.19 N	78.49 W
Chadderton	44	53.33 N	2.08 W
Chadds Ford	285	39.52 N	75.35 W
Chādegān	128	32.46 N	50.39 E
Chadian, Zhg.	102	26.48 N	105.48 E
Chadian, Zhg.	105	39.14 N	117.45 E
Chadian, Zhg.	107	30.14 N	105.56 E
Chadianzi	107	30.31 N	104.22 E
Chadiza	154	14.05 S	32.28 E
Chadron	198	42.49 N	103.00 W
Chadstone	274b	37.53 S	145.05 E
Chadwell Saint Mary	260	51.29 N	0.22 E
Chadwick	190	42.01 N	89.53 W
Chadwick Manor	284b	39.19 N	76.46 W
Chadwick Pond ⊜	283	42.44 N	71.05 W
Chadwicks	210	43.01 N	75.16 W
Chadyžensk	78	44.25 N	39.33 E
Chadžalmachi	84	42.26 N	47.13 E
Chae Hom	110	18.43 N	99.35 E
Chaem ≃	110	18.11 N	98.38 E
Chaersen	89	46.19 N	121.54 E
Chaeryŏng	98	38.24 N	125.36 E
Chafarinas, Islas II	34	35.11 N	2.26 W
Chafe	150	11.56 N	6.55 E
Chaffee	194	37.10 N	89.39 W
Chaffins	207	42.21 N	71.51 W
Chāgai	128	29.18 N	64.42 E
Chāgai Hills ⋏[2]	128	29.30 N	64.15 E
Chagandianlisu	102	41.47 N	103.29 E
Chagang Do □[4]	98	40.50 N	126.30 E
'Chaghcharān	120	34.32 N	65.15 E
Chagny	58	46.55 N	4.45 E
Chagos Archipelago II	12	6.00 S	72.00 E
Chagos-Laccadive Plateau ✥[3]	12	3.00 N	73.00 E
Chagrin ≃	214	41.40 N	81.27 W
Chagrin, Aurora Branch ≃	279a	41.25 N	81.25 W
Chagrin Falls	214	41.26 N	81.24 W
Chagrin Falls Park	214	41.21 N	81.32 W
Chagrin Valley Parkway ♠	279a	41.26 N	81.25 W
Chaguanas	241r	10.31 N	61.25 W
Chaguaramas	246	9.20 N	66.16 W
Chahaignes	50	47.44 N	0.31 E
Chāhak	128	33.17 N	58.54 E
Chahal	236	15.45 N	89.34 W
Chahancheluo	98	41.39 N	114.22 E
Chahanwusu → Dulan	102	36.16 N	98.28 E
Chahār Borjak	128	30.17 N	62.03 E
Chahār Deh-ye Ghowrband	120	34.59 N	68.44 E
Chahār Maḥāl va Bakhtīārī □[4]	128	32.00 N	51.00 E
Chahayang	89	48.24 N	124.15 E
Chahe, Zhg.	100	33.16 N	119.02 E
Chahe, Zhg.	102	33.48 N	97.22 E
Chahe, Zhg.	105	39.50 N	115.21 E
Chāh Gheybī, Hāmūn-e ⩳	128	28.06 N	60.50 E
Chahuamiao	100	33.00 N	115.56 E
Chahuites	234	16.17 N	94.11 W
Chai ≃	104	42.20 N	123.52 E
Chai Badan	110	15.04 N	101.05 E
Chāībāsa	124	22.34 N	85.49 E
Chaigou	98	36.15 N	119.36 E
Chaihe	89	44.47 N	129.42 E
Chaijiawan	100	29.10 N	113.06 E
Chaillé-les-Marais	32	46.24 N	1.01 W
Chailley	50	48.05 N	3.42 E
Chailly-en-Bière	50	48.28 N	2.35 E
Chai Nat	110	15.11 N	100.08 E
Chainhurst	260	51.12 N	0.29 E
Chain O'Lakes State Park ♠, Il., U.S.	216	42.27 N	88.11 W
Chain O'Lakes State Park ♠, In., U.S.	216	41.20 N	85.26 W
Chainpur	124	23.08 N	84.15 E
Chaipudyrskaja guba ⊂	24	68.30 N	59.30 E
Chaiqiao	100	29.51 N	121.56 E
Chairel, Laguna de ⊂	234	22.17 N	97.57 W
Chaishudian	105	40.46 N	116.30 E
Chaiši	84	42.57 N	42.12 E
Chait	85	39.11 N	70.53 E
Chaital	126	22.31 N	88.47 E
Chaitén	254	42.55 S	72.43 W
Chaiwopu	86	43.33 N	87.59 E
Chaiya	110	9.23 N	99.14 E
Chaiyaphum	110	15.48 N	102.02 E
Chajarí	252	30.46 S	57.59 W

FRANÇAIS

Nom	Page	Lat.°′	Long.°′ W = Ouest
Chajdarken	85	39.57 N	71.21 E
Chajia	107	29.37 N	104.27 E
Chajian	100	32.40 N	118.46 E
Chajianling	98	39.14 N	114.36 E
Chajiaqiao	100	34.00 N	120.07 E
Chajrchan	88	48.35 N	101.56 E
Chajrchandulaan	102	45.57 N	102.03 E
Chajul	236	15.30 N	91.02 W
Chaka	154	4.49 N	31.14 E
Chakachamna Lake ⊜	180	61.13 N	152.35 W
Chakāltor	126	23.14 N	86.22 E
Chak Amru	123	32.22 N	75.11 E
Chakari	154	18.05 S	29.51 E
Chakaria	120	21.45 N	92.05 E
Chakarnaba	146	14.13 N	20.51 E
Chakasija □[3]	86	53.00 N	90.00 E
Chākdaha, India	126	23.05 N	88.31 E
Chākdaha, India	272b	22.20 N	88.20 E
Chake Chake	154	5.15 S	39.46 E
Chakhānsūr	128	31.10 N	62.04 E
Chākia	124	26.25 N	85.03 E
Chakkarat	110	15.00 N	102.16 E
Chakou, Zhg.	98	38.03 N	113.36 E
Chakou, Zhg.	105	38.53 N	116.41 E
Chakradharpur	124	22.42 N	85.38 E
Chakrāta	120	30.42 N	77.51 E
Chāksu	120	26.36 N	75.57 E
Chākulia	126	22.29 N	86.43 E
Chakwadām	102	27.29 N	98.31 E
Chakwāl	123	32.56 N	72.52 E
Chal	272c	19.06 N	73.08 E
Chala	248	15.52 S	74.16 W
Chalabesa	154	11.22 S	31.01 E
Chalais	32	45.16 N	0.02 E
Chālakuda	122	10.18 N	76.20 E
Chalamont	58	46.00 N	5.10 E
Chalampé	58	47.49 N	7.33 E
Chalan Kanoa	174n	15.08 N	145.43 E
Chalatenango	236	14.03 N	88.56 W
Chalaua	154	16.06 S	39.11 E
Chalaux ≃	50	47.23 N	3.54 E
Chalaxung	102	34.10 N	97.44 E
Chalbi Desert ◆[2]	154	3.00 N	37.20 E
Chalchgol	88	48.11 N	114.54 E
Chalchihuites	234	23.29 N	103.53 W
Chalchis Terara ∧	144	9.08 N	36.44 E
Chalchuapa	236	13.59 N	89.41 W
Chalchyn ≃	88	47.55 N	117.47 E
Chalcis → Khalkís	38	38.28 N	23.36 E
Chalco ≃	286a	19.19 N	99.08 W
Chaldon	260	51.17 N	0.07 W
Chaleine	261	48.36 N	1.43 E
Chalengkou	120	38.02 N	93.54 E
Châlette-sur-Loing	50	48.01 N	2.44 E
Chaleur Bay ⊂	186	48.00 N	65.45 W
Chalfant	279b	40.25 N	79.52 W
Chalfant Run ≃	279b	40.25 N	79.48 W
Chalfont	208	40.17 N	75.13 W
Chalfont Common	260	51.38 N	0.33 W
Chalfonte	285	39.49 N	75.32 W
Chalfont Saint Giles	260	51.38 N	0.34 W
Chalfont Saint Peter	42	51.37 N	0.33 W
Chalford	42	51.45 N	2.09 W
Chalhuanca	248	14.17 S	73.15 W
Chalía ≃	254	49.35 S	69.34 W
Chalifert	261	48.53 N	2.46 E
Chalilovo	86	51.24 N	58.04 E
Chalindrey	58	47.48 N	5.26 E
Chaling	100	26.47 N	113.33 E
Chālisgaon	122	20.28 N	75.01 E
Chalisi	102	32.55 N	102.04 E
Chaliun	88	48.50 N	103.59 E
Chalk	260	51.26 N	0.25 E
Chalkabad	86	42.42 N	59.43 E
Chalk Draw V	196	29.36 N	103.15 W
Chalk River	190	46.01 N	77.27 W
Chalkyitsik	180	66.39 N	143.43 W
Challakere	122	14.19 N	76.39 E
Challans	32	46.51 N	1.53 W
Challapata	248	18.54 S	66.47 W
Challenge	226	39.29 N	121.13 W
Challenger, Mount ∧	224	48.50 N	121.20 W
Challenger Deep ✥[1]	14	11.21 N	142.12 E
Challes-les-Eaux	62	45.33 N	5.59 E
Challis	202	44.30 N	114.13 W
Challviri, Salar de ⩳	248	22.32 S	67.34 W
Chal'mer-Ju	24	67.58 N	64.50 E
Chalmers	216	40.39 N	86.52 W
Chalmette	194	29.56 N	89.57 W
Chalone Creek ≃	226	36.21 N	121.14 W
Chalonnes-sur-Loire	32	47.21 N	0.46 W
Châlons-sur-Marne	50	48.57 N	4.22 E
Chalon-sur-Saône	58	46.47 N	4.51 E
Chalosse ◆[1]	32	43.45 N	0.30 W
Chalt	123	36.15 N	74.20 E
Chaltel, Cerro (Monte Fitzroy) ∧	254	49.17 S	73.05 W
Chaluhe	89	43.43 N	126.00 E
Châlus, Fr.	32	45.39 N	0.59 E
Chālūs, Īrān	128	36.38 N	51.26 E
Cham, Dtsch.	60	49.13 N	12.41 E
Cham, Schw.	58	47.11 N	8.28 E
Chama	200	36.54 N	106.34 W
Chama ≃	246	9.03 N	71.40 W
Chama, Rio ≃	200	36.03 N	106.05 W
Chamah, Gunong ∧	114	5.13 N	101.33 E
Chamaicó	252	35.03 S	64.58 W
Chamama	154	12.55 S	33.43 E
Chamamat'urt	84	43.36 N	46.30 E
Chaman	120	30.55 N	66.27 E
Chamangonge	152	11.16 S	20.24 E
Chamao, Khao ∧	110	12.57 N	101.45 E
Chamarande	261	48.31 N	2.13 E
Chamar-Daban, chrebet ⋏	88	51.15 N	105.00 E
Chāmārpāra	272b	22.35 N	88.08 E
Chamaya ≃	248	5.44 S	78.39 W
Chamb ≃	60	49.13 N	12.42 E
Chamba, India	123	32.34 N	76.08 E
Chamba, Moç.	154	12.07 S	36.57 E
Chamba, Tan.	154	11.35 S	36.58 E
Chambal ≃	120	26.30 N	79.15 E
Chambaran, Plateau de ⋏[1]	62	45.15 N	5.15 E
Chambas	240p	22.12 N	78.55 W
Chamberlain, Sk., Can.	184	50.50 N	105.34 W
Chamberlain, S.D., U.S.	198	43.48 N	99.19 W
Chamberlain ≃	164	15.08 S	128.06 E
Chamberlain Lake ⊜	186	46.17 N	69.20 W
Chamberlin, Mount ∧	180	69.16 N	144.55 W
Chamberry, Ruisseau ≃	275a	45.20 N	73.58 W
Chambers, Az., U.S.	200	35.11 N	109.25 W
Chambers, Ne., U.S.	198	42.12 N	98.44 W
Chambers, N.Y., U.S.	210	42.16 N	76.57 W
Chambers □[6]	222	29.42 N	94.40 W
Chambers Brook ≃	276	40.35 N	74.41 W
Chambersburg, Il., U.S.	219	39.49 N	90.39 W
Chambersburg, In., U.S.	218	38.31 N	86.24 W
Chambersburg, Pa., U.S.	208	39.56 N	77.39 W
Chambers Corner	285	40.01 N	74.44 W
Chambers Creek ≃	222	31.58 N	96.10 W
Chambers Creek, North Fork ≃	222	32.16 N	96.58 W
Chambers Creek, South Fork ≃	222	32.16 N	96.58 W
Chambers Island I	190	45.11 N	87.21 W
Chambéry	62	45.34 N	5.56 E
Chambeshi ≃	154	11.21 S	30.37 E
Chambi, Jebel ∧	148	35.11 N	8.42 E
Chambira ≃, Perú	246	3.55 S	73.45 W
Chambira ≃, Perú	246	4.28 S	74.50 W
Chamblee	192	33.53 N	84.17 W
Chambley-Bussières	56	49.03 N	5.54 E
Chambly, P.Q., Can.	206	45.27 N	73.17 W
Chambly, Fr.	50	49.10 N	2.15 E

PORTUGUÊS

Nome	Página	Lat.°′	Long.°′ W = Oeste
Chambly □[6]	206	45.30 N	73.20 W
Chambly, Bassin de ⊜	206	45.27 N	73.17 W
Chambly, Canal de ≊	275a	45.25 N	73.15 W
Chambois	50	48.48 N	0.07 E
Chambon-sur-Dolore	62	45.30 N	3.37 E
Chambon-sur-Voueize	32	46.11 N	2.25 E
Chambord, Château de ⊥	50	47.37 N	1.31 E
Chambourcy	261	48.54 N	2.03 E
Chambri Lake ⊜	164	4.16 S	143.08 E
Chambry	261	49.00 N	2.54 E
Chamburi Kalāt	128	26.09 N	64.43 E
Chamdo → Qamdo	102	31.11 N	97.15 E
Chāme, Nepāl	124	28.33 N	84.15 E
Chame, Pan.	236	8.35 N	79.53 W
Chame, Punta ›	236	8.39 N	79.42 W
Chamela	234	19.32 N	105.05 W
Chamelecón	236	15.24 N	88.01 W
Chamelecón ≃	236	15.51 N	87.49 W
Chamical	252	30.21 S	66.19 W
Chamizo	258	34.10 S	56.41 W
Chamizo, Arroyo ≃	258	34.15 S	56.44 W
Chamkanī	120	33.48 N	69.49 E
Chāmlūjā ≃	124	29.38 N	80.24 E
Chamo, Lake ⊜	144	5.50 N	37.33 E
Chamois, It.	62	45.50 N	7.37 E
Chamois, Mo., U.S.	219	38.40 N	91.46 W
Chamojie	89	49.25 N	124.45 E
Chamoli	124	30.24 N	79.21 E
Chamonix-Mont-Blanc	58	45.55 N	6.52 E
Chamousset	62	45.33 N	6.12 E
Chamoux-sur-Gelon	62	45.32 N	6.13 E
Chāmpa	124	22.03 N	82.39 E
Champagne, Yk., Can.	180	60.47 N	136.29 W
Champagne, Fr.	62	45.16 N	4.48 E
Champagne □[9]	32	49.00 N	4.30 E
Champagne Castle ∧	158	29.06 S	29.20 E
Champagne-en-Valromay	58	45.54 N	5.41 E
Champagner-Berg ∧[2]	264a	52.31 N	13.05 E
Champagne-sur-Seine	50	48.24 N	2.48 E
Champagney	58	47.42 N	6.41 E
Champagnole	58	46.45 N	5.55 E
Champagny	62	45.27 N	6.42 E
Chāmpāhāti	126	22.23 N	88.29 E
Champaign	194	40.06 N	88.14 W
Champaign □[6], Il., U.S.	216	40.07 N	88.12 W
Champaign □[6], Oh., U.S.	218	40.07 N	83.45 W
Champapur	126	24.02 N	86.31 E
Champaquí, Cerro ∧	252	31.59 S	64.56 W
Champasak	110	14.53 N	105.52 E
Champāwat	124	29.20 N	80.06 E
Champcueil	261	48.31 N	2.27 E
Champdāni	126	22.48 N	88.21 E
Champdeniers	32	46.29 N	0.24 W
Champdepraz	62	45.41 N	7.39 E
Champdeuil	261	48.37 N	2.44 E
Champdor	58	46.01 N	5.36 E
Champdoré, Lac ⊜	176	55.55 N	65.49 W
Champeaux	50	48.35 N	2.48 E
Champeix	32	45.36 N	3.08 E
Champerico	236	14.18 N	91.55 W
Champéry	58	46.10 N	6.52 E
Champex	58	46.02 N	7.07 E
Champier	62	45.27 N	5.17 E
Champigneulles	56	48.44 N	6.10 E
Champigny-sur-Marne	261	48.49 N	2.31 E
Champion, Ab., Can.	182	50.14 N	113.09 W
Champion, Mi., U.S.	190	46.30 N	87.57 W
Champion, Oh., U.S.	214	41.17 N	80.51 W
Champion, Pa., U.S.	214	40.05 N	79.21 W
Champions	222	29.59 N	95.31 W
Champlain	206	44.59 N	73.26 W
Champlain □[6]	206	46.45 N	72.35 W
Champlain ≃	206	46.27 N	72.17 W
Champlain, Lake ⊜	188	44.45 N	73.15 W
Champlain, Pont ◆[5]	206	45.28 N	73.32 W
Champlain Canal ≊	210	43.20 N	73.34 W
Champlan	261	48.43 N	2.16 E
Champlin Creek ≃	276	40.43 N	73.12 W
Champlitte-et-le-Prélot	58	47.37 N	5.31 E
Champlon	56	50.07 N	5.28 E
Champoluc	62	45.50 N	7.44 E
Champotón	232	19.21 N	90.43 W
Champrond-en-Gâtine	50	48.24 N	1.05 E
Champs	50	47.44 N	3.36 E
Champs-sur-Marne	261	48.51 N	2.36 E
Chāmpua	124	22.05 N	85.40 E
Champvans	58	47.06 N	5.26 E
Chāmrāil	272b	22.38 N	88.18 E
Chāmrājnagar Rāmasamudram	122	11.55 N	76.57 E
Chamrousse	62	45.08 N	5.52 E
Chamsara ≃	88	52.42 N	95.46 E
Chamusca	34	39.21 N	8.29 W
Chamza Chakimzada	85	40.26 N	71.30 E
Chana	110	6.55 N	100.44 E
Chanabadskij	85	40.49 N	72.58 E
Chanakyapuri □[9]	272a	28.36 N	77.11 E
Chañar	252	30.32 S	65.58 W
Chañaral	252	26.21 S	70.37 W
Chañaral, Isla I	252	29.02 S	71.35 W
Chanas	62	45.18 N	4.49 E
Chānasma	120	23.43 N	72.07 E
Chanbogd	102	43.12 N	107.10 E
Chancay	248	11.35 S	77.16 W
Chancay ≃	248	11.37 S	77.15 W
Chance	208	38.10 N	75.56 W
Chanceaux	58	47.31 N	4.42 E
Chanceaux-sur-Choisille	50	47.28 N	0.42 E
Chanch	88	51.30 N	100.40 E
Chanchelulla Peak ∧	204	40.28 N	122.59 W
Chanchiang → Zhanjiang	102	21.16 N	110.28 E
Chanchöchij uul ⋏	88	49.30 N	94.30 E
Chanchongor	102	43.50 N	104.25 E
Chanco	252	35.44 S	72.32 W
Chancy	58	46.08 N	6.00 E
Chanda → Chandrapur, India	122	19.57 N	79.18 E
Chanda, Ross.	88	55.00 N	107.14 E
Chanda ≃	88	55.00 N	107.14 E
Chāndābila	126	22.05 N	87.00 E
Chandagajty	86	50.44 N	92.03 E
Chandalar	180	67.30 N	148.30 W
Chandalar ≃	180	66.36 N	145.48 W
Chandalar, East Fork ≃	180	67.05 N	147.16 W
Chandalar, Middle Fork ≃	180	67.10 N	148.19 W
Chandalar, North Fork ≃	180	67.10 N	148.19 W
Chandan Chauki	124	28.33 N	80.47 E
Chandankiāri	126	23.34 N	86.22 E
Chandannagar	126	22.51 N	88.21 E
Chandanpratāp	126	23.33 N	89.24 E
Chāndar	126	23.54 N	89.58 E
Chandausi	124	28.27 N	78.46 E
Chāndbāli	120	20.47 N	86.46 E
Chandeleur Islands II	194	29.48 N	88.51 W
Chandeleur Sound ⊎	194	29.55 N	89.10 W
Chanderi	124	24.43 N	78.08 E
Chandernagore → Chandannagar	126	22.51 N	88.21 E
Chandīgarh	123	30.44 N	76.55 E
Chandīgarh □[8]	123	30.45 N	76.50 E
Chāndil	124	22.58 N	86.03 E
Chandīpur	126	23.59 N	89.01 E
Chanditala	272b	22.41 N	88.16 E
Chandla	124	25.05 N	80.12 E
Chandler, P.Q., Can.	186	48.21 N	64.41 W
Chandler, Az., U.S.	200	33.18 N	111.50 W
Chandler, In., U.S.	194	38.02 N	87.22 W
Chandler, Ok., U.S.	196	35.42 N	96.52 W
Chandler, Tx., U.S.	222	32.18 N	95.29 W
Chandler ≃	180	69.27 N	151.30 W
Chandler, Mount ∧[2]	162	27.00 S	133.20 E
Chandler Lake ⊜	180	68.15 N	152.43 W
Chandler Park ♠	281	42.24 N	82.58 W
Chandler's Cross	260	51.40 N	0.27 W
Chandler's Ford	42	50.59 N	1.23 W
Chandlers Valley	214	41.56 N	79.18 W
Chandlerville	219	40.02 N	90.09 W
Chandless ≃	248	9.08 S	69.51 W
Chāndor Hills ⋏[2]	122	20.30 N	74.00 E
Chandos Lake ⊜	212	44.49 N	78.00 W
Chāndpara	126	22.58 N	88.47 E
Chāndpur, Bngl.	120	22.08 N	91.55 E
Chāndpur, Bngl.	124	23.13 N	90.39 E
Chāndpur, India	124	29.09 N	78.16 E
Chāndpur ◆[8]	272a	28.45 N	77.01 E
Chāndra	126	22.28 N	87.09 E
Chandrabhāga ≃	123	32.59 N	76.25 E
Chandra Dighalia	126	23.04 N	89.46 E
Chandrakona	126	22.44 N	87.31 E
Chandrakona Road	126	22.44 N	87.21 E
Chandrapur	122	19.57 N	79.18 E
Chāndvad	122	20.20 N	74.15 E
Chandyga	74	62.40 N	135.36 E
Chanfang	105	39.56 N	115.55 E
Chang (Yangtze) ≃, Zhg.	90	31.48 N	121.10 E
Chang ≃, Zhg.	100	26.53 N	119.41 E
Chang ≃, Zhg.	100	28.59 N	116.42 E
Chang, Ko I	110	12.05 N	102.20 E
Changa	84	44.27 N	50.36 E
Changaj	88	47.52 N	99.28 E
Changajn nuruu ⋏	90	47.30 N	100.00 E
Changal	88	49.19 N	104.24 E
Changalane	156	26.17 S	32.11 E
Chang'an, Zhg.	102	26.00 N	109.34 E
Changan → Xi'an, Zhg.	102	34.15 N	108.52 E
Changanācheri	122	9.28 N	76.33 E
Changane ≃	156	24.43 S	33.32 E
Chang'anzhen	106	30.28 N	120.27 E
Changara	154	16.54 S	33.14 E
Changarul'skij chrebet ⋏	88	51.10 N	103.00 E
Changbai	98	41.26 N	128.11 E
Changbai Shan ⋏	98	41.40 N	128.00 E
Changbu	100	23.48 N	115.26 E
Changcaocun	105	39.49 N	115.47 E
Changchaoling	106	31.00 N	119.40 E
Changcheng, Zhg.	100	31.49 N	116.54 E
Changcheng, Zhg.	110	19.24 N	108.42 E
Chang Cheng (Great Wall) ⊥	98	40.30 N	116.30 E
Chang Chenmo ≃	120	34.17 N	78.19 E
Changchiak'ou → Zhangjiakou	105	40.50 N	114.53 E
Ch'angchih → Changzhi	102	36.11 N	113.08 E
Changchou → Zhangzhou	100	24.33 N	117.39 E
Changchow → Changzhou	106	31.47 N	119.57 E
Changchun	89	43.53 N	125.19 E
Changchunling	89	45.22 N	125.28 E
Changdan	98	37.56 N	126.45 E
Changdang Hu ⊜	106	31.35 N	119.35 E
Changdao (Sihou)	98	37.56 N	120.42 E
Changde	102	29.02 N	111.41 E
Changdian	105	40.01 N	116.32 E
Ch'angdo	98	38.30 N	127.40 E
Ch'ang-dong	98	39.03 N	126.34 E
Change Islands	186	49.40 N	54.25 W
Changeon ≃	50	47.16 N	0.05 E
Changfeng	100	32.27 N	117.09 E
Changgang	100	24.38 N	113.05 E
Changgangzi	104	41.26 N	122.41 E
Changge	100	34.15 N	113.50 E
Changgi-ap ›	98	36.05 N	129.34 E
Changgi-li	271b	37.35 N	126.44 E
Changgi-ri	271b	37.38 N	126.41 E
Changgou	105	39.34 N	115.53 E
Changgouyu	105	39.44 N	115.52 E
Changguandian	100	32.58 N	115.16 E
Changguowei	100	29.15 N	121.56 E
Changgye-ri	98	34.33 N	126.49 E
Changgyong Palace ♉	271b	37.36 N	127.00 E
Changhai, Zhg.	98	39.18 N	122.35 E
Chang-hai → Shanghai, Zhg.	106	31.14 N	121.28 E
Changhang	98	36.01 N	126.40 E
Changhe	106	30.11 N	120.11 E
Changhowŏn	98	37.08 N	127.39 E
Chang Hu ⊜	100	30.15 N	112.35 E
Changhua, T'aiwan	100	24.05 N	120.32 E
Changhua, Zhg.	100	30.11 N	119.13 E
Changhŭng	98	34.41 N	126.52 E
Changhŭng-ni	98	40.24 N	128.19 E
Changi	271c	1.23 N	103.59 E
Changi, Tanjong ›	271c	1.23 N	104.00 E
Changi International Airport ⊠	271c	1.22 N	103.59 E
Changi Prison ♉	271c	1.22 N	103.58 E
Changji	86	44.01 N	87.19 E
Changjiang, Zhg.	100	25.19 N	113.56 E
Changjiang, Zhg.	110	19.17 N	109.02 E
Changjiangbu	100	30.52 N	113.43 E
Changjiapuzi	104	40.51 N	123.43 E
Changjiazhuang	105	40.35 N	115.24 E
Changjie	100	29.16 N	121.40 E
Changjing	106	31.45 N	120.29 E
Changjin-gang ≃	98	41.24 N	127.45 E
Changjin-ŭp	98	40.23 N	127.15 E
Changkai	100	28.04 N	116.18 E
Changkalajier	85	40.09 N	76.59 E
Changkeng	106	30.19 N	121.57 E
Changkiakow → Zhangjiakou	105	40.50 N	114.53 E
Changlapod Pass)(	124	30.08 N	87.06 E
Changle, Zhg.	98	36.42 N	118.49 E
Changle, Zhg.	100	29.25 N	120.37 E
Changle, Zhg.	100	26.00 N	119.31 E
Changlejie	100	28.52 N	113.19 E
Changleqiao	106	30.21 N	119.51 E
Changlezhen	106	31.56 N	121.15 E
Changli, Zhg.	98	39.43 N	119.11 E
Changli, Zhg.	98	36.57 N	119.45 E
Changling	89	44.15 N	123.58 E
Changlingfeng	105	40.11 N	118.24 E
Changlingji	100	32.30 N	114.54 E
Changlingzi, Zhg.	98	39.47 N	122.43 E
Changlingzi, Zhg.	98	39.33 N	121.19 E
Changlinhe	100	31.40 N	117.29 E
Changlun	114	6.26 N	100.26 E
Changmar	120	34.15 N	79.45 E
Changmong-ni	98	34.58 N	128.41 E
Changning, Zhg.	102	26.19 N	112.21 E
Changning, Zhg.	102	24.55 N	99.35 E
Changning (Anningqiao), Zhg.	102	28.21 N	104.53 E
Changning, Zhg.	105	39.59 N	114.55 E
Ch'angnyŏng	98	35.33 N	128.29 E
Changnyŏn-ni	98	38.37 N	125.16 E
Changokurt	72	61.58 N	64.18 E
Ch'angpin	100	23.19 N	121.27 E
Changping	105	40.14 N	116.14 E
Changputong	102	28.05 N	98.29 E
Ch'angp'yŏng-dong	98	41.27 N	127.31 E
Changqiao, Zhg.	100	24.15 N	117.39 E
Changqiao, Zhg.	100	26.49 N	118.50 E
Changqing	98	36.34 N	116.43 E
Changsa	102	19.51 N	110.53 E
Changsan-got ›	98	38.08 N	124.39 E
Changsha, Zhg.	100	28.12 N	112.58 E
Changsha, Zhg.	100	24.13 N	116.07 E
Changshaba Shuiku ⊜[1]	107	29.42 N	104.40 E
Changshageng	107	30.00 N	104.35 E
Changshan, Zhg.	98	36.54 N	117.50 E
Changshan, Zhg.	100	28.55 N	118.30 E
Changshan, Zhg.	107	29.30 N	104.13 E
Changshan ≃	100	28.57 N	118.50 E
Changshan Qundao II	98	39.00 N	122.45 E
Changsheng	100	26.16 N	116.01 E
Changshengqiao	107	29.31 N	106.39 E
Changshitai	104	42.33 N	120.43 E
Changshitou	102	35.03 N	99.11 E
Changshou	102	29.51 N	107.06 E
Changshoudian	100	31.26 N	112.35 E
Changshoujie	100	28.44 N	113.57 E
Changshu	106	31.39 N	120.45 E
Changshui	102	34.21 N	111.29 E
Changsŏng	98	35.20 N	126.49 E
Changsŏng-ni	98	40.58 N	127.04 E
Changsu	98	35.40 N	127.32 E
Changtai, Zhg.	100	24.40 N	117.46 E
Changtai, Zhg.	100	28.34 N	118.37 E
Changtai, Zhg.	104	41.34 N	122.00 E
Changtancun	104	41.33 N	123.02 E
Ch'angte → Changde	102	29.02 N	111.41 E
Changteh → Anyang	98	36.06 N	114.21 E
Changting, Zhg.	89	44.32 N	128.47 E
Changting, Zhg.	100	25.52 N	116.20 E
Changtumiao	102	43.30 N	114.34 E
Changuinola	236	9.25 N	82.32 W
Changuinola ≃	236	9.28 N	82.27 W
Changwu, Zhg.	89	46.00 N	125.36 E
Changwu, Zhg.	102	35.09 N	107.42 E
Changxindianzhen	105	39.49 N	116.12 E
Changxing	106	31.01 N	119.54 E
Changxing Dao I, Zhg.	98	39.34 N	121.23 E
Changxing Dao I, Zhg.	106	31.24 N	121.42 E
Changxingdian, Zhg.	104	41.27 N	121.44 E
Changxingdian, Zhg.	104	41.33 N	123.23 E
Changxingzhen	104	41.40 N	122.14 E
Changxuanling	100	31.08 N	114.20 E
Changyi	98	36.51 N	119.23 E
Changyŏn	98	38.15 N	125.06 E
Changyuan	98	35.13 N	114.39 E
Changyukou	105	40.46 N	115.08 E
Changzhi	102	36.11 N	113.08 E
Changzhou (Changchow)	106	31.47 N	119.57 E
Chanhanga	152	16.04 S	14.07 E
Chanh Hung	269c	10.44 N	106.41 E
Chani	88	57.05 N	120.58 E
Chani ≃	88	57.02 N	120.59 E
Chanino	76	54.13 N	36.37 E
Chanka, ozero (Xingkai Hu) ⊜	89	45.00 N	132.24 E
Chankiang → Zhanjiang	102	21.16 N	110.28 E
Chankou	102	35.52 N	104.27 E
Channagiri	122	14.02 N	75.56 E
Channahon	216	41.26 N	88.14 W
Channapatna	122	12.39 N	77.13 E
Channel Country ◆[1]	166	24.45 S	141.00 E
Channel Islands II, Europe	43b	49.20 N	2.20 W
Channel Islands II, Ca., U.S.	204	33.30 N	119.15 W
Channel Islands National Park ♠	204	33.28 N	119.02 W
Channel Lake	216	42.29 N	88.08 W
Channel-Port-aux-Basques	186	47.34 N	59.09 W
Channel Tunnel ◆[5]	50	51.00 N	1.35 E
Channelview	222	29.46 N	95.06 W
Channing, Mi., U.S.	190	46.08 N	88.05 W
Channing, Tx., U.S.	196	35.41 N	102.20 W
Chānpādānga	126	22.50 N	87.58 E
Chantada	34	42.37 N	7.46 W
Chantajskoje, ozero ⊜	74	68.20 N	91.00 E
Chantajskoje vodochranilišče ⊜[1]	72	68.00 N	88.00 E
Chantang	100	33.41 N	117.37 E
Chantau	86	44.13 N	73.51 E
Chanteloup	261	48.51 N	2.44 E
Chanteloup-les-Vignes	261	48.59 N	2.02 E
Chanthaburi	110	12.36 N	102.09 E
Chantilly	50	49.12 N	2.28 E
Chantraine	58	48.10 N	6.26 E
Chantrans	58	47.03 N	6.09 E
Chantrey Inlet ⊂	176	67.48 N	96.20 W
Chanty-Mansijsk	74	61.00 N	69.06 E
Chanty-Mansijskij Avtonomnyj Okrug □[8]	86	60.15 N	70.45 E
Chanujn ≃	88	49.22 N	102.22 E
Chanumla	110	8.19 N	93.05 E
Chanute	198	37.40 N	95.27 W
Chanute Air Force Base ■	216	40.18 N	88.09 W
Chanuwāla	123	32.44 N	73.08 E
Chao ≃	105	40.36 N	117.08 E
Chao, Isla I	248	8.45 S	78.47 W
Chao'an	100	23.41 N	116.38 E
Chaobai ≃	105	39.48 N	117.08 E
Chaobai Xinhe ≃	105	39.37 N	117.26 E
Chaocheng	98	36.05 N	115.35 E
Ch'aochou, T'aiwan	100	22.33 N	120.32 E
Ch'aochou → Chao'an, Zhg.	100	23.41 N	116.38 E
Chao Hu ⊜	100	31.31 N	117.33 E
Chaomidian	105	39.04 N	117.01 E
Chao Phraya ≃	110	13.32 N	100.36 E
Chaor ≃	89	46.48 N	123.37 E
Chaoshui, Zhg.	89	49.44 N	127.21 E
Chaoshui, Zhg.	98	37.42 N	120.55 E
Chaouen	148	35.10 N	5.16 W
Chaouen □[4]	148	35.15 N	5.00 W
Chaource	50	48.04 N	4.08 E
Chaoxian	100	31.36 N	117.52 E
Chaoyang, Zhg.	89	44.34 N	126.20 E
Chaoyang, Zhg.	100	23.17 N	116.37 E
Chaoyang, Zhg.	104	41.35 N	120.28 E
Chaoyangchuan	98	42.54 N	129.21 E
Chaoyangcun	89	50.02 N	124.16 E
Chaoyanggou	104	42.07 N	121.04 E
Chaoyangpo	89	43.37 N	124.42 E
Chaoyangshan	89	43.02 N	125.40 E
Chaozhuang	98	34.18 N	114.56 E
Chapada dos Guimarães	248	15.26 S	55.45 W
Chapada dos Veadeiros, Parque Nacional da ♠	255	13.58 S	47.30 W
Chapadinha	250	3.44 S	43.21 W
Chapala	234	20.18 N	103.12 W
Chapala, Laguna de ⊜	234	20.15 N	103.00 W
Chapare ≃, Bol.	248	15.58 S	64.42 W
Chapare ≃, Bol.	248	16.25 S	64.35 W
Chapareillan	62	45.28 N	5.58 E
Chāparmukh	120	26.12 N	92.32 E
Chaparra, Bahía de ⊂	240p	21.13 N	76.31 W
Chaparral	246	3.43 N	75.28 W
Chapayeve	78	49.21 N	35.54 E
Chapayevka, Ukr.	78	49.33 N	32.06 E
Chapayevka, Ukr.	78	47.29 N	36.20 E
Chapčeranga	88	49.42 N	112.24 E
Chapeauroux	62	44.50 N	3.44 E
Chapecó	252	27.06 S	52.36 W
Chapel-en-le-Frith	44	53.20 N	1.54 W
Chapelfell Top ∧	44	54.41 N	2.13 W
Chapelhall	46	55.50 N	3.56 W
Chapel Hill, De., U.S.	285	39.42 N	75.44 W
Chapel Hill, N.C., U.S.	192	35.54 N	79.03 W
Chapel Hill, Tn., U.S.	194	35.37 N	86.41 W
Chapel Hill Channel ⊎	276	40.32 N	74.02 W
Chapelle Creek ≃	198	44.16 N	99.55 W
Chapellerie	261	49.02 N	2.26 E
Chapel Oaks	284c	38.54 N	76.55 W
Chapel Point ›	42	50.16 N	4.46 W
Chapel Saint Leonards	44	53.13 N	0.19 E
Chapelton	241q	18.05 N	77.16 W
Chapeltown, Eng., U.K.	44	53.28 N	1.28 W
Chapeltown, Eng., U.K.	262	53.38 N	2.24 W
Chapet	261	48.58 N	1.56 E
Chapéu, Morro do ∧	255	14.55 S	42.31 W
Chapéu, Ribeirão do ≃	256	23.14 S	45.18 W
Chapicuy	252	31.39 S	57.54 W
Chapimarca	248	13.58 S	73.04 W
Chapin	219	39.46 N	90.24 W
Chapin, Lake ⊜	216	41.56 N	86.21 W
Chaplain, Lake ⊜[1]	224	47.57 N	121.51 W
Chapleau	190	47.50 N	83.24 W
Chapleau ≃	190	48.29 N	82.57 W
Chapleau, Lac ⊜	206	46.14 N	74.57 W
Chaplin, Sk., Can.	184	50.28 N	106.40 W
Chaplin, Ct., U.S.	207	41.47 N	72.07 W
Chaplin ≃	194	37.50 N	85.11 W
Chaplin Lake ⊜	184	50.18 N	106.35 W
Chapliyivka	78	51.43 N	33.12 E
Chaplyne	78	48.09 N	36.14 E
Chaplynka	78	46.23 N	33.32 E
Chapman, Ks., U.S.	198	38.58 N	97.01 W
Chapman, Ne., U.S.	198	41.01 N	98.09 W
Chapman, Pa., U.S.	208	40.46 N	75.24 W
Chapman, Cape ›	176	69.12 N	88.59 W
Chapman, Mount ∧	182	51.50 N	118.20 W
Chapman College ♉[2]	280	33.47 N	117.51 W
Chapman Creek ≃	198	38.58 N	97.00 W
Chapman Lake ⊜	184	56.58 N	98.12 W
Chapman's (Okwa) ≃	156	22.30 S	23.00 E
Chapmanville	188	37.58 N	82.01 W
Chapman Woods	280	34.08 N	118.05 W
Chapo	196	29.17 N	104.20 W
Chaponval	261	49.04 N	2.09 E
Chappaqua	210	41.09 N	73.45 W
Chappell	198	41.05 N	102.28 W
Chappell Hill	222	30.09 N	96.16 W
Chāpra	126	23.32 N	88.33 E
Chapry	83	47.14 N	39.31 E
Chaptico Bay ⊂	208	38.21 N	76.49 W
Chapultepec, Méx.	204	31.50 N	116.38 W
Chapultepec, Méx.	204	32.22 N	115.05 W
Chapultepec, Bosque de ♠	286a	19.25 N	99.12 W
Chapultepec, Castillo de ⊥	286a	19.25 N	99.11 W
Chá Pungana	152	13.44 S	18.39 E
Chaqui	248	19.36 S	65.32 W
Chaquiago	252	27.32 S	66.21 W
Char ≃	42	50.44 N	2.53 W
Char ⫪[4]	148	21.31 N	12.51 W
Charaa ≃	88	49.38 N	105.49 E
Charabali	80	47.24 N	47.16 E
Chara-Chužar	88	52.30 N	99.39 E
Charadai	252	27.38 S	59.54 W
Charagauli	84	42.01 N	43.12 E
Charagua	248	19.48 S	63.13 W
Charagun	88	51.36 N	111.05 E
Char-Ajrag	102	45.49 N	109.17 E
Charal	88	51.58 N	96.39 E
Charalá	246	6.17 N	73.10 W
Charām	128	30.45 N	50.44 E
Charaña	248	17.36 S	69.28 W
Charanor	88	50.05 N	116.40 E
Charanpur	126	23.45 N	87.02 E
Charapán	234	19.41 N	102.06 W
Charapucu, Ilha I	250	0.18 S	50.48 W
Charata	252	27.13 S	61.12 W
Charauz	88	52.16 N	106.17 E
Charavines-les-Bains	62	45.26 N	5.31 E
Charazani → Amarete	248	15.14 S	68.58 W
Charazargaj	88	52.57 N	104.41 E
Charbala	74	64.07 N	120.19 E
Char Bansi	126	22.59 N	90.43 E
Charbatovo	88	53.46 N	106.00 E
Charbon	170	32.54 S	149.58 E
Charcana	248	15.15 S	73.04 W
Charcas	234	23.08 N	101.07 W
Charco Azul, Bahía de ⊂	236	8.15 N	82.45 W
Charco Hondo	240m	18.25 N	66.43 W
Charcos de Figueroa	232	27.45 N	102.11 W
Charcos de Risa	232	26.15 N	103.10 W
Charcot Island I	9	69.45 S	75.15 W
Chard	42	50.53 N	2.58 W
Chardon	214	41.36 N	81.08 W
Charduār	120	26.52 N	92.46 E
Chardzhou → Čardžou	128	39.06 N	63.34 E
Charef, Oued V	148	34.07 N	2.05 W
Charente □[5]	32	45.40 N	0.10 E
Charente ≃	32	45.57 N	1.05 W
Charente-Maritime □[5]	32	45.30 N	0.45 W
Charenton-du-Cher	32	46.44 N	2.38 E
Charenton-le-Pont	261	48.49 N	2.25 E
Charentonne ≃	50	49.07 N	0.44 E
Charest ≃	206	46.36 N	72.14 W
Chārghāt	126	24.17 N	88.45 E
Char Hāim	126	23.04 N	90.38 E
Chari ≃	146	12.58 N	14.31 E
Chariāl Canal ≊	272b	22.28 N	88.11 E
Chari-Baguirmi □[5]	146	11.30 N	16.30 E
Charik	88	54.15 N	101.39 E
Chārīkār	120	35.01 N	69.11 E
Charing	42	51.13 N	0.48 E
Charing Cross	214	42.20 N	82.06 W
Charino, Ross.	76	59.57 N	43.44 E
Charino, Ross.	82	54.33 N	37.52 E
Charistvala	84	42.26 N	43.02 E
Chariton	190	41.00 N	93.18 W
Chariton ≃	194	39.19 N	92.57 W
Chariton, Mussel Fork ≃	194	39.24 N	92.55 W
Charitonovo, Ross.	24	61.27 N	47.28 E
Charitonovo, Ross.	82	56.52 N	36.44 E
Charity	246	7.24 N	58.36 W
Charkhāri	124	25.24 N	79.45 E
Charkhi Dādri	124	28.37 N	76.16 E
Char'kin	80	48.46 N	51.49 E
Charkop ◆[8]	272c	19.13 N	72.49 E
Charkow → Kharkiv	78	50.00 N	36.15 E
Char Lākhpur	126	24.04 N	90.40 E
Charland, Lac ⊜	206	46.52 N	74.11 W
Charlbury	42	51.53 N	1.29 W
Charl Cilliers	158	26.39 S	29.12 E
Charlemagne	206	45.43 N	73.29 W
Charlemont	207	42.37 N	72.52 W
Charleroi, Bel.	50	50.25 N	4.26 E
Charleroi, Pa., U.S.	214	40.08 N	79.53 W
Charleroi à Bruxelles, Canal de ≊	50	50.51 N	4.19 E
Charles □[6]	208	38.32 N	76.59 W
Charles ≃	207	42.22 N	71.03 W
Charles, Cape ›	208	37.08 N	75.58 W
Charles, Lake ⊜	278	42.15 N	87.58 W
Charles, Peak ∧	162	32.52 S	121.11 E
Charlesbourg	206	46.51 N	71.16 W
Charles Branch ≃	284c	38.47 N	76.48 W
Charles City, Ia., U.S.	190	43.03 N	92.40 W
Charles City, Va., U.S.	208	37.20 N	77.04 W
Charles City □[6]	208	37.20 N	77.02 W
Charles de Gaulle, Aéroport ⊠	50	49.01 N	2.33 E
Charles Island I	176	62.40 N	74.15 W
Charles Lee Tilden Regional Park ♠	282	37.54 N	122.15 W
Charles Mill Lake ⊜[1]	214	40.45 N	82.22 W
Charles Mound ∧[2]	190	42.30 N	90.14 W
Charles Point ›	164	12.23 S	130.36 E
Charles Sound ⊎	172	45.02 S	167.04 E
Charleston, Austl.	168b	34.55 S	138.54 E
Charleston, N.Z.	172	41.54 S	171.26 E
Charleston, Ar., U.S.	194	35.17 N	94.02 W
Charleston, Il., U.S.	194	39.29 N	88.10 W
Charleston, Ms., U.S.	194	34.00 N	90.03 W
Charleston, Mo., U.S.	194	36.55 N	89.21 W

≃	River	Fluß	Río	Rivière	Rio
≊	Canal	Kanal	Canal	Canal	Canal
⌞	Waterfall, Rapids	Wasserfall, Stromschnellen	Cascada, Rápidos	Chute d'eau, Rapides	Cascata, Rápidos
⊎	Strait	Meeresstraße	Estrecho	Détroit	Estreito
⊂	Bay, Gulf	Bucht, Golf	Bahía, Golfo	Baie, Golfe	Baía, Golfo
⊜	Lake, Lakes	See, Seen	Lago, Lagos	Lac, Lacs	Lago, Lagos
⩳	Swamp	Sumpf	Pantano	Marais	Pântano
⌂	Ice Features, Glacier	Eis- und Gletscherformen	Accidentes Glaciales	Formes glaciaires	Acidentes glaciares
⫪	Other Hydrographic Features	Andere Hydrographische Objekte	Otros Elementos Hidrográficos	Autres données hydrographiques	Outros acidentes hidrográficos
✥	Submarine Features	Untermeerische Objekte	Accidentes Submarinos	Formes de relief sous-marin	Acidentes submarinos
□	Political Unit	Politische Einheit	Unidad Politica	Entité politique	Unidade política
♉	Cultural Institution	Kulturelle Institution	Institución Cultural	Institution culturelle	Instituição cultural
⊥	Historical Site	Historische Stätte	Sitio Histórico	Site historique	Sitio histórico
♠	Recreational Site	Erholungs- und Ferienort	Sitio de Recreo	Centre de loisirs	Area de Lazer
⊠	Airport	Flughafen	Aeropuerto	Aéroport	Aeroporto
■	Military Installation	Militäranlage	Instalación Militar	Installation militaire	Instalação militar
◆	Miscellaneous	Verschiedenes	Misceláneo	Divers	Diversos

Name	Page	Lat.°′	Long.°′
Charleston, S.C., U.S.	192	32.46 N	79.55 W
Charleston, W.V., U.S.	188	38.20 N	81.37 W
Charleston Air Force Base ■	192	32.55 N	80.03 W
Charleston Lake ⊜	212	44.32 N	76.00 W
Charleston Peak ∧	204	36.16 N	115.42 W
Charlestown, Austl.	170	32.58 S	151.42 E
Charlestown, Ire.	48	53.57 N	8.49 W
Charlestown, St. K.-N.	238	17.08 N	62.37 W
Charlestown, S. Afr.	158	27.30 S	29.55 E
Charlestown, In., U.S.	218	38.27 N	85.40 W
Charlestown, Md., U.S.	208	39.34 N	75.58 W
Charlestown, N.H., U.S.	188	43.14 N	72.25 W
Charlestown, Pa., U.S.	285	40.06 N	75.33 W
Charlestown, R.I., U.S.	207	41.22 N	71.38 W
Charles Town, W.V., U.S.	188	39.17 N	77.51 W
Charlestown ◆[8]	283	42.23 N	71.04 W
Charlestown of Aberlour	46	57.28 N	3.14 W
Charlesworth	262	53.26 N	1.59 W
Charleville, Austl.	166	26.24 S	146.15 E
Charleville → Ráth Luirc, Ire.	48	52.21 N	8.41 W
Charleville-Mézières	56	49.46 N	4.43 E
Charlevoix	190	45.19 N	85.15 W
Charlevoix, Lake ⊜	190	45.15 N	85.08 W
Charley ≃	180	65.20 N	142.49 W
Charlie Bluff	216	42.50 N	88.58 W
Charlie Creek ≃	220	27.21 N	81.49 W
Charlie Lake	182	56.16 N	120.57 W
Charlieu	32	46.10 N	4.10 E
Charlotte, Mi., U.S.	216	42.33 N	84.50 W
Charlotte, N.C., U.S.	192	35.13 N	80.50 W
Charlotte, Tn., U.S.	194	36.10 N	87.20 W
Charlotte, Tx., U.S.	196	28.51 N	98.42 W
Charlotte □[6]	220	26.54 N	81.58 W
Charlotte Amalie	240m	18.21 N	64.56 W
Charlotte Court House	192	37.03 N	78.39 W
Charlotte Creek ≃	210	42.27 N	75.01 W
Charlotte Harbor	220	26.57 N	82.04 W
Charlotte Harbor ⊂	220	26.45 N	82.12 W
Charlotte Lake ⊜	182	52.11 N	125.20 W
Charlottenberg	26	59.53 N	12.17 E
Charlottenburg ◆[8]	264a	52.31 N	13.16 E
Charlottenburg, Schloss ⊥	264a	52.31 N	13.14 E
Charlottesburg Reservoir ⊜[1]	276	41.02 N	74.26 W
Charlottes Pass ♦	171b	36.25 S	145.20 E
Charlottesville, In., U.S.	218	39.47 N	85.36 W
Charlottesville, Va., U.S.	192	38.01 N	78.28 W
Charlottetown	186	46.14 N	63.08 W
Charlotteville	210	42.33 N	74.40 W
Charlovka	24	68.47 N	37.15 E
Charlton, Austl.	166	36.16 S	143.21 E
Charlton, Ma., U.S.	207	42.08 N	71.58 W
Charlton ◆[8]	260	51.29 N	0.02 E
Charlton City	207	42.08 N	71.59 W
Charlton Island I	176	52.00 N	79.30 W
Charlton Kings	42	51.53 N	2.03 W
Charlu	24	61.48 N	30.52 E
Charly-sur-Marne	50	48.58 N	3.17 E
Charm	214	40.30 N	81.47 W
Charmentray	261	48.57 N	2.47 E
Charmes	58	48.22 N	6.17 E
Charmes-sur-Rhône	62	44.52 N	4.50 E
Charmey	58	46.38 N	7.10 E
Charminster	42	50.43 N	2.28 W
Charmois-l'Orgueilleux	58	48.06 N	6.16 E
Charmont-en-Beauce	50	48.14 N	2.06 E
Charmouth	42	50.45 N	2.55 W
Charnay-lès-Mâcon	58	46.18 N	4.47 E
Charneca	266c	38.44 N	9.27 W
Charneca ◆[8]	266c	38.47 N	9.08 W
Charnley ≃	164	16.25 S	124.57 E
Charnock Richard	262	53.38 N	2.41 W
Char nuur ⊜, Mong.	88	48.06 N	93.12 E
Char nuur ⊜, Mong.	88	48.20 N	96.05 E
Charnwood Forest ◆[3]	42	52.43 N	1.15 W
Charny, P.Q., Can.	206	46.43 N	71.16 W
Charny, Fr.	50	47.53 N	3.06 E
Charny, Fr.	261	48.58 N	2.46 E
Charny-sur-Meuse	56	49.12 N	5.22 E
Charo	234	19.45 N	101.03 W
Charolles	32	46.26 N	4.17 E
Charouine	148	29.01 N	0.16 W
Charovsk	76	59.59 N	40.11 E
Charpi ≃	89	49.40 N	136.10 E
Charquemont	58	47.13 N	6.49 E
Charred Oak Estates	284c	39.00 N	77.10 W
Charrette Creek ≃	219	38.37 N	91.03 W
Charron Lake ⊜	184	52.45 N	95.15 W
Charroux	32	46.09 N	0.24 E
Chars	50	49.10 N	1.56 E
Chārsadda	123	34.09 N	71.44 E
Charter Oak, Ca., U.S.	280	34.06 N	117.52 W
Charter Oak, Ia., U.S.	198	42.04 N	95.35 W
Charters Towers	166	20.05 S	146.16 E
Charterwood	279b	40.33 N	80.00 W
Chartiers Creek ≃	214	40.28 N	80.03 W
Chartiers Run ≃, Pa., U.S.	279b	40.36 N	79.43 W
Chartiers Run ≃, Pa., U.S.	279b	40.15 N	80.12 W
Chartley	207	41.56 N	71.13 W
Chartres	50	48.27 N	1.30 E
Chartrettes	50	48.29 N	2.42 E
Chartridge	260	51.44 N	0.39 W
Chart Sutton	260	51.13 N	0.35 E
Chartwell ⊥	260	51.14 N	0.05 E
Char Us nuur ⊜	90	48.00 N	92.10 E
Charutajuvom	24	66.49 N	59.30 E
Chās	126	23.38 N	86.10 E
Chasav'urt	84	43.15 N	46.37 E
Chascomús	258	35.34 S	58.01 W
Chascomús, Laguna ⊜	258	35.36 S	58.01 W
Chašdala	85	39.42 N	67.07 E
Chase, B.C., Can.	182	50.49 N	119.41 W
Chase, Ak., U.S.	180	62.27 N	150.07 W
Chase, Ks., U.S.	198	38.21 N	98.20 W
Chase, Md., U.S.	208	39.21 N	76.22 W
Chase, Mount ∧	188	46.07 N	68.29 W
Chase Brook ≃	283	42.48 N	71.27 W
Chase City	192	36.47 N	78.27 W
Chase Field Naval Air Station ■	196	28.21 N	97.40 W
Chasefu	154	11.55 S	33.08 E
Chase Lake	212	43.46 N	75.19 W
Chase River	224	49.08 N	123.55 W
Chashma Barrage ◆[6]	123	32.26 N	71.23 E
Chasicó	254	40.18 S	68.58 W
Chasidaba	104	42.19 N	121.19 E
Chasiv Yar	83	48.35 N	37.50 E
Chaska	190	44.47 N	93.36 W
Chaslands Mistake ›	172	46.38 S	169.22 E
Chasŏng	98	41.27 N	126.37 E
Chasŏngganggu	98	41.34 N	126.36 E
Chassahowitzka	220	28.43 N	82.34 W
Chassahowitzka Bay ⊂	220	28.41 N	82.40 W
Chassahowitzka Swamp ≡	220	28.38 N	82.37 W
Chasseron, Mont ∧	58	46.51 N	6.33 E
Chasse-sur-Rhône	62	45.34 N	4.49 E
Chassezac ≃	62	44.26 N	4.19 E
Chašuri	84	42.00 N	43.36 E
Chasurta	88	52.17 N	108.52 E
Chasuta	248	6.35 S	76.11 W
Chāt	128	37.59 N	55.16 E
Chatanbulag	102	43.09 N	109.08 E
Chatanga	74	71.58 N	102.30 E
Chatanga ≃	74	72.55 N	106.00 E
Chatangskij zaliv ⊂	74	73.30 N	109.00 E
Chatanika	180	65.07 N	147.31 W
Chatanika ≃	180	65.04 N	149.18 W
Château-Arnoux	62	44.06 N	6.00 E
Chateaubelair	241h	13.17 N	61.15 W
Châteaubriant	32	47.43 N	1.23 W
Château-Chinon	32	47.04 N	3.56 E
Château d'Oex	58	46.28 N	7.08 E
Château-du-Loir	50	47.42 N	0.25 E
Châteaudun	50	48.05 N	1.20 E
Châteaufort	261	48.44 N	2.06 E
Chateaugay	206	44.55 N	74.04 W
Château-Gontier	32	47.50 N	0.42 W
Châteauguay	206	45.23 N	73.45 W
Châteauguay □[6]	206	45.15 N	73.45 W
Châteauguay ≃	188	45.24 N	73.45 W
Châteauguay-Centre	206	45.21 N	73.45 W
Châteauguay Heights	275a	45.23 N	73.44 W
Château-Landon	50	48.09 N	2.42 E
Château-la-Vallière	50	47.33 N	0.19 E
Châteaulin	32	48.12 N	4.05 W
Châteaumeillant	32	46.34 N	2.12 E
Châteauneuf	62	43.23 N	5.10 E
Châteauneuf-de-Randon	62	44.39 N	3.40 E
Châteauneuf-du-Pape	62	44.03 N	4.50 E
Châteauneuf-du-Rhône	62	44.29 N	4.43 E
Châteauneuf-en-Thymerais	50	48.35 N	1.15 E
Châteauneuf-sur-Charente	32	45.36 N	0.03 W
Châteauneuf-sur-Loire	50	47.52 N	2.14 E
Châteauneuf-sur-Sarthe	32	47.41 N	0.30 W
Châteauneuf-Val-de-Bargis	50	47.17 N	3.14 E
Château-Porcien	50	49.32 N	4.15 E
Château-Queyras	62	44.45 N	6.47 E
Châteauredon	62	44.01 N	6.13 E
Châteaurenard, Fr.	50	47.56 N	2.56 E
Châteaurenard, Fr.	62	43.53 N	4.51 E
Château-Renault	50	47.35 N	0.55 E
Château-Richer	186	46.58 N	71.01 W
Châteauroux	32	46.49 N	1.42 E
Château-Salins	56	48.49 N	6.30 E
Château-Thierry	50	49.03 N	3.24 E
Châteauvillain	58	48.02 N	4.55 E
Châtel	58	46.17 N	6.50 E
Châtel-Censoir	50	47.31 N	3.38 E
Châtelet	50	50.24 N	4.31 E
Châtelineau	56	50.25 N	4.31 E
Châtellerault	32	46.49 N	0.33 E
Châtel-Saint-Denis	58	46.32 N	6.54 E
Châtel-sur-Moselle	58	48.18 N	6.24 E
Châtelus-Malvaleix	32	46.18 N	2.01 E
Châtenay-en-France	261	49.04 N	2.27 E
Châtenay-Malabry	261	48.46 N	2.17 E
Châtenois, Fr.	58	48.18 N	5.50 E
Châtenois, Fr.	58	48.16 N	7.24 E
Châtenois-les-Forges	58	47.34 N	6.51 E
Chater ≃	42	52.38 N	0.32 W
Chatfield, Mn., U.S.	190	43.50 N	92.11 W
Chatfield, Oh., U.S.	214	40.57 N	82.56 W
Chatgal	88	50.26 N	100.09 E
Chatham, N.B., Can.	186	47.02 N	65.28 W
Chatham, On., Can.	214	42.24 N	82.11 W
Chatham, Eng., U.K.	42	51.23 N	0.32 E
Chatham, Il., U.S.	219	39.40 N	89.42 W
Chatham, La., U.S.	194	32.18 N	92.27 W
Chatham, Ma., U.S.	207	41.40 N	69.57 W
Chatham, N.J., U.S.	210	40.44 N	74.23 W
Chatham, N.Y., U.S.	210	42.21 N	73.35 W
Chatham, Oh., U.S.	214	41.06 N	82.01 W
Chatham, Pa., U.S.	208	39.51 N	75.49 W
Chatham, Va., U.S.	192	36.49 N	79.23 W
Chatham ◆[8]	278	41.45 N	87.37 W
Chatham ≃	220	25.42 N	81.17 W
Chatham, Isla I	254	50.40 S	74.20 W
Chatham Head	186	47.00 N	65.33 W
Chatham Islands II	14	43.55 S	176.30 W
Chatham Rise ✦[3]	14	43.30 S	178.00 W
Chatham Sound ⊔	182	54.32 N	130.35 W
Chatham Strait ⊔	180	57.30 N	134.45 W
Chatian	100	27.54 N	118.58 E
Châtillon, Fr.	261	48.48 N	2.17 E
Châtillon, It.	62	45.45 N	7.37 E
Châtillon-Coligny	50	47.50 N	2.51 E
Châtillon-en-Bazois	32	47.03 N	3.40 E
Châtillon-en-Diois	62	44.41 N	5.28 E
Châtillon-la-Borde	261	48.33 N	2.49 E
Châtillon-sur-Chalaronne	58	46.07 N	4.58 E
Châtillon-sur-Indre	32	46.59 N	1.11 E
Châtillon-sur-Loire	50	47.35 N	2.45 E
Châtillon-sur-Marne	50	49.06 N	3.45 E
Châtillon-sur-Seine	58	47.51 N	4.33 E
Chating	106	31.21 N	119.25 E
Chātmohar	126	24.13 N	89.15 E
Chat Moss ◆[3]	262	53.27 N	2.27 W
Chato, Cerro ∧	254	42.29 S	72.01 W
Chatom	194	31.27 N	88.15 W
Chatonville	261	48.33 N	1.52 E
Chatou	261	48.54 N	2.09 E
Chatpur ◆[8]	272b	22.36 N	88.22 E
Chatra, India	124	24.13 N	84.52 E
Chatra, India	272b	22.46 N	88.20 E
Châtres	261	48.43 N	2.49 E
Chats, Lac des ⊜	212	45.28 N	76.23 W
Chatsquot Mountain ∧	182	53.08 N	127.30 W
Chatswood	274a	33.48 S	151.12 E
Chatsworth, Austl.	166	21.58 S	140.19 E
Chatsworth, On., Can.	212	44.27 N	80.54 W
Chatsworth, Ga., U.S.	192	34.45 N	84.46 W
Chatsworth, Il., U.S.	216	40.45 N	88.17 W
Chatsworth, N.J., U.S.	208	39.49 N	74.32 W
Chatsworth, Zimb.	154	19.38 S	31.13 E
Chatsworth ◆[8]	280	34.15 N	118.36 W
Chatsworth House ⊍	44	53.13 N	1.36 W
Chatsworth Reservoir ⊜[1]	228	34.14 N	118.37 W
Chattahoochee	192	30.42 N	84.50 W
Chattahoochee ≃	192	30.52 N	84.57 W
Chattanooga, Oh., U.S.	216	40.38 N	84.47 W
Chattanooga, Tn., U.S.	194	35.02 N	85.18 W
Chattaroy	192	37.42 N	82.16 W
Chattenden	260	51.25 N	0.32 E
Chatteris	42	52.27 N	0.03 E
Châttillon-de-Michaille	58	46.08 N	5.47 E
Chattolanee	284b	39.24 N	76.45 W
Chatton	44	55.33 N	1.55 W
Chatun'	82	55.00 N	37.50 E
Chaturat	110	15.34 N	101.51 E
Chatwood	208	39.58 N	75.35 W
Chatyrka	74	62.03 N	175.15 E
Chaubaria	126	22.59 N	88.40 E
Chaubourg, Mount ∧[2]	241f	14.02 N	60.57 W
Chauconin	261	48.58 N	2.51 E
Chaudes-Aigues	32	44.51 N	3.00 E
Chaudfontaine	56	50.35 N	5.38 E
Chaudière ≃	186	46.45 N	71.17 W
Chau Doc	110	10.42 N	105.07 E
Chauekuktuli, Lake ⊜	180	60.03 N	158.45 W
Chauffayer	62	44.45 N	6.01 E
Chaugācha, Bngl.	126	23.16 N	89.01 E
Chaugācha, Bngl.	126	23.16 N	89.01 E
Chauhtan	120	25.29 N	71.04 E
Chauk	110	20.54 N	94.50 E
Chaukhandi	272a	28.37 N	77.24 E
Chaullay	248	12.57 S	72.39 W
Chaulnes	50	49.49 N	2.48 E
Chaumergy	58	46.51 N	5.29 E
Chaumes-en-Brie	261	48.40 N	2.51 E
Chaumont, Fr.	58	48.07 N	5.08 E
Chaumont, N.Y., U.S.	212	44.04 N	76.07 W
Chaumont ≃	212	44.04 N	76.08 W
Chaumont Bay ⊂	212	44.02 N	76.13 W
Chaumont-en-Vexin	50	49.16 N	1.53 E
Chaumont-Porcien	50	49.39 N	4.15 E
Chaumont-sur-Aire	56	48.56 N	5.15 E
Chaumont-sur-Loire	50	47.29 N	1.11 E
Chaumont-sur-Tharonne	50	47.37 N	1.54 E
Chaumua	272b	22.39 N	88.33 E
Chauncey	188	39.23 N	82.07 W
Chaŭn-do I	98	34.53 N	126.03 E
Chaungwabyin	110	13.41 N	98.22 E
Chaungzon	110	16.22 N	97.32 E
Chauny	50	49.37 N	3.13 E
Chaupāran	124	24.23 N	85.15 E
Chaussin	58	46.58 N	5.25 E
Chausu-yama ∧	94	35.14 N	137.39 E
Chausuyama-kofun ⊥	94	36.25 N	139.50 E
Chautārā	124	27.46 N	85.42 E
Chautauqua	214	42.12 N	79.28 W
Chautauqua □[6]	214	42.15 N	79.30 W
Chautauqua Creek ≃	214	42.20 N	79.36 W
Chautauqua Lake ⊜	214	42.12 N	79.27 W
Chautengo, Laguna ⊂	234	16.37 N	99.07 W
Chauvigny	32	46.34 N	0.39 E
Chauvin, Ab., Can.	184	52.42 N	110.07 W
Chauvin, La., U.S.	194	29.26 N	90.35 W
Chauvirey-le-Châtel	58	47.47 N	5.45 E
Chauvry	261	49.03 N	2.16 E
Chavakkad	122	10.32 N	76.06 E
Chaval	250	3.02 S	41.15 W
Chavanges	58	48.31 N	4.34 E
Chavannes, Lac ⊜	190	46.51 N	77.10 W
Chavarría, Arg.	252	28.57 S	58.35 W
Chavarría, Perú	286d	12.01 S	77.05 W
Chavast	85	40.13 N	68.50 E
Chavenay	261	48.51 N	1.59 E
Chavenay-Villepreux, Aérodrome de ⊠	261	48.51 N	1.58 E
Chavertovo	82	54.17 N	39.12 E
Chaves, Bra.	250	0.10 S	49.55 W
Chaves, Port.	34	41.44 N	7.28 W
Chaville	261	48.48 N	2.10 E
Chaviña	248	14.59 S	73.50 W
Cháviva	246	4.22 N	72.20 W
Chavki	82	54.20 N	38.13 E
Chavornay	58	46.43 N	6.34 E
Chavuma	152	13.05 S	22.40 E
Chawa'nanake	120	31.36 N	89.41 E
Chawang	110	8.25 N	99.30 E
Chawinda	123	32.21 N	74.42 E
Chay ≃	110	21.39 N	105.12 E
Chayanta	248	18.27 S	66.30 W
Chayuan, Zhg.	100	29.20 N	121.34 E
Chayuan, Zhg.	100	27.40 N	112.57 E
Chayue	106	30.49 N	119.21 E
Chazay-d'Azergues	62	45.53 N	4.37 E
Chazelles-sur-Lyon	62	45.38 N	4.23 E
Chazratišoch, chrebet ⋏	85	38.30 N	70.15 E
Chazy	188	44.53 N	73.26 W
Chbar ≃	110	13.19 N	107.05 E
Cheadle, Eng., U.K.	42	52.59 N	1.59 W
Cheadle, Eng., U.K.	44	53.24 N	2.13 W
Cheadle Hulme	262	53.22 N	2.12 W
Cheaha Mountain ∧	194	33.30 N	85.47 W
Cheakamus Indian Reserve ◆[4]	182	49.48 N	123.11 W
Cheam ◆[8]	260	51.21 N	0.13 W
Cheam View	224	49.15 N	121.41 W
Cheapside	222	29.17 N	97.24 W
Cheat ≃	188	39.45 N	79.54 W
Cheat, Shavers Fork ≃	188	39.06 N	79.33 W
Cheb	54	50.01 N	12.25 E
Chebacco Lake ⊜	283	42.37 N	70.48 W
Chebanse	216	41.00 N	87.54 W
Chebba	148	35.14 N	10.02 E
Chebeigou	89	43.28 N	127.04 E
Chebogue Point ›	186	43.45 N	66.07 W
Cheboksary → Čeboksary	80	56.09 N	47.15 E
Cheboygan	190	45.38 N	84.28 W
Chech, Erg ◆[2]	148	25.00 N	2.15 W
Chechel'nyk	78	48.14 N	29.21 E
Ch'ech'eng	100	22.05 N	120.42 E
Chechnia → Čečnja-Ingušetija □[3]	84	43.15 N	45.40 E
Chech'on	98	37.08 N	128.12 E
Chęciny	30	50.48 N	20.28 E
Checleset Bay ⊂	182	50.03 N	127.40 W
Checotah	196	35.28 N	95.31 W
Chedabucto Bay ⊂	186	45.23 N	61.10 W
Chedaoyu	105	40.22 N	117.57 E
Cheddar	42	51.17 N	2.46 W
Cheddleton	44	53.04 N	2.02 W
Cheduba Island I	110	18.48 N	93.38 E
Cheduba Strait ⊔	110	18.56 N	93.45 E
Chedun	100	24.09 N	117.19 E
Chée ≃	56	48.45 N	4.39 E
Cheektowaga	210	42.55 N	78.46 W
Cheepie	166	26.39 S	145.01 E
Cheesequake	276	40.25 N	74.17 W
Cheesequake Creek ≃	276	40.28 N	74.16 W
Cheesequake State Park ♦	276	40.26 N	74.16 W
Cheetham Hill ◆[8]	262	53.31 N	2.15 W
Chefang, Zhg.	104	41.35 N	121.26 E
Chefang, Zhg.	106	31.15 N	120.45 E
Chef-Boutonne	32	46.07 N	0.04 W
Chefoo → Yantai	98	37.33 N	121.20 E
Chefornak	180	60.13 N	164.12 W
Chefumage ≃	152	12.15 S	22.19 E
Chefuzwe	156	17.38 S	24.30 E
Chegar Perah	114	4.25 N	101.56 E
Chegga ⊤[4]	148	25.30 N	5.46 W
Chegutu	154	18.10 S	30.14 E
Chehalis	224	46.39 N	122.57 W
Chehalis ≃	224	46.57 N	123.50 W
Chehalis, South Fork ≃	224	46.40 N	123.15 W
Chehalis Indian Reservation ◆[4]	224	46.49 N	123.13 W
Chehe	102	25.00 N	107.38 E
Chehel Dokhtarān	128	35.06 N	62.19 E
Cheheqiao	105	40.21 N	118.16 E
Cheil, Ras el ›	144	7.44 N	49.50 E
Cheine	54	52.52 N	11.04 E
Cheiron, Cime du ∧	62	43.49 N	6.58 E
Chejiatun	104	41.57 N	123.01 E
Chejiawopeng	104	42.29 N	123.07 E
Cheju	90	33.31 N	126.32 E
Cheju-do I	90	33.20 N	126.30 E
Chekiang → Zhejiang □[4]	100	29.00 N	120.00 E
Chek Jawa, Tanjong ›	271c	1.24 N	104.00 E
Chek Kang	271d	22.26 N	114.21 E
Chela, Serra da ∧	152	16.00 S	13.10 E
Chelan	202	47.50 N	120.00 W
Chelan □[6]	224	47.56 N	120.52 W
Chelan, Lake ⊜	202	48.05 N	120.30 W
Chelas ◆[8]	266c	38.45 N	9.07 W
Cheleiros	266c	38.53 N	9.20 W
Cheleiros, Ribeira de ≃	266c	38.54 N	9.22 W
Chelelektu	144	6.00 N	38.09 E
Chelford	262	53.16 N	2.16 W
Chelforó	252	39.04 S	66.32 W
Chelghoum el Aïd	148	36.10 N	6.10 E
Chéliff, Oued ≃	148	36.01 N	0.07 E
Chelīk-e Yās Khān	120	37.05 N	66.14 E
Chellaston	42	52.53 N	1.27 W
Chelles	50	48.53 N	2.36 E
Chelles-le-Pin, Aérodrome de ⊠	261	48.55 N	2.35 E
Chełm	30	51.10 N	23.28 E
Chełm □[4]	30	51.20 N	23.20 E
Chelmer ≃	42	51.44 N	0.42 E
Chelmer and Blackwater Navigation ≡	260	51.44 N	0.43 E
Chełmno	30	53.22 N	18.26 E
Chelmorton	262	53.13 N	1.50 W
Chelmsford, On., Can.	190	46.35 N	81.12 W
Chelmsford, Eng., U.K.	42	51.44 N	0.28 E
Chelmsford, Ma., U.S.	207	42.35 N	71.21 W
Chelmsford □[8]	260	51.44 N	0.30 E
Chelmsford Dam ⊜[1]	158	28.02 S	29.52 E
Chełmża	30	53.12 N	18.37 E
Chelsea, Austl.	169	38.03 S	145.07 E
Chelsea, Ia., U.S.	190	41.55 N	92.23 W
Chelsea, Ma., U.S.	207	42.23 N	71.02 W
Chelsea, Mi., U.S.	216	42.19 N	84.01 W
Chelsea, Ok., U.S.	196	36.32 N	95.25 W
Chelsea, Pa., U.S.	285	39.52 N	75.28 W
Chelsea, Vt., U.S.	188	43.59 N	72.26 W
Chelsea Estates	208	39.41 N	75.36 W
Chelsea Park	224	47.28 N	122.21 W
Chelsfield ◆[8]	260	51.21 N	0.08 E
Cheltenham, Austl.	274a	33.46 S	151.05 E
Cheltenham, Austl.	274b	37.58 S	145.03 E
Cheltenham, Eng., U.K.	42	51.54 N	2.04 W
Cheltenham, Md., U.S.	208	38.44 N	76.49 W
Cheltenham, Pa., U.S.	208	40.03 N	75.05 W
Chel'ul'ja	26	61.44 N	30.41 E
Chelvand	128	38.18 N	48.50 E
Chelyabinsk → Čel'abinsk	86	55.10 N	61.24 E
Chelyāma	126	23.37 N	86.33 E
Chelyan	188	38.11 N	81.29 W
Chemaïa	148	32.05 N	8.37 W
Chemainus	224	48.55 N	123.43 W
Chemainus ⊜	224	48.53 N	123.41 W
Chemaogang	106	31.33 N	121.52 E
Chemax	232	20.39 N	87.56 W
Chemba	154	17.08 S	34.52 E
Chembūr ◆[8]	272c	19.04 N	72.54 E
Chemchâm, Sebkhet ⊜	148	21.05 N	12.05 W
Chemčik ≃	86	51.47 N	92.00 E
Chemehuevi Indian Reservation ◆[4]	204	34.30 N	114.23 W
Chemer	78	51.07 N	31.13 E
Chemerivtsi	78	49.01 N	26.21 E
Chemillé	32	47.13 N	0.44 W
Chemin	58	46.59 N	5.19 E
Cheminis, Colline ∧[2]	190	48.08 N	79.31 W
Chemnitz	54	50.50 N	12.55 E
Chemnitz ≃	54	50.59 N	12.47 E
Chemor	114	4.43 N	101.07 E
Chemulpo → Inch'ŏn	98	37.28 N	126.38 E
Chemult	202	43.13 N	121.46 W
Chemung, Il., U.S.	216	42.25 N	88.40 W
Chemung, N.Y., U.S.	210	42.01 N	76.37 W
Chemung □[6]	210	42.06 N	76.49 W
Chemung ≃	210	41.55 N	76.31 W
Chemung County Airport ⊠	210	42.10 N	76.53 W
Chemung Lake ⊜	212	44.25 N	78.22 W
Chena, Cerro ∧	286e	33.36 S	70.45 W
Chenāb ≃	123	29.23 N	71.02 E
Chenachane	148	26.00 N	4.15 W
Chenail Ecarté ≃[1]	214	42.28 N	82.29 W
Chenango □[6]	210	42.32 N	75.31 W
Chenango ≃	210	42.05 N	75.55 W
Chenango Bridge	210	42.10 N	75.51 W
Chenango Forks	210	42.14 N	75.50 W
Chenango Valley State Park ♦	210	42.14 N	75.50 W
Chenārān	128	36.39 N	59.06 E
Chenaut	258	34.15 S	59.13 W
Chen Barag Qi	89	49.21 N	119.31 E
Chenbofang	98	37.27 N	115.18 E
Chencai	100	29.37 N	120.22 E
Chenchiang → Zhenjiang	106	32.13 N	119.26 E
Chencun	100	22.58 N	113.13 E
Chendai	100	23.48 N	117.24 E
Chendauli ◆[8]	272c	19.07 N	72.54 E
Chenderiang	114	4.16 N	101.14 E
Chenderoh, Tasek ⊜	114	4.58 N	100.57 E
Chêne, Rivière du ≃, P.Q., Can.	206	46.34 N	72.00 W
Chêne, Rivière du ≃, P.Q., Can.	206	45.33 N	73.54 W
Chenele	152	12.54 S	23.54 E
Chenequa	216	43.06 N	88.23 W
Chénéville	206	45.53 N	75.03 W
Cheney, Ks., U.S.	198	37.37 N	97.46 W
Cheney, Wa., U.S.	202	47.29 N	117.34 W
Cheney Reservoir ⊜[1]	198	37.45 N	97.50 W
Cheneys Point	214	42.08 N	79.24 W
Cheneyville	194	31.00 N	92.17 W
Chenfang	100	28.01 N	117.32 E
Cheng'an	98	36.27 N	114.41 E
Chengannūr	122	9.20 N	76.38 E
Chengbu	102	26.18 N	110.13 E
Chengchow → Zhengzhou	102	34.48 N	113.39 E
Chengde (Xiabancheng), Zhg.	105	40.47 N	118.08 E
Chengde, Zhg.	105	40.58 N	117.53 E
Chengdu (Chengtu)	107	30.39 N	104.04 E
Chengele	120	28.47 N	96.16 E
Chenggang	100	26.32 N	115.26 E
Chenggu	102	33.10 N	107.22 E
Chenghai	100	23.30 N	116.46 E
Cheng Hu ⊜	106	31.13 N	120.49 E
Chenghuang	102	22.32 N	109.39 E
Chengjia	100	24.50 N	112.50 E
Chengjiahe	100	32.18 N	112.27 E
Chengjiang	102	24.45 N	102.54 E
Chengjiangzhen	107	29.52 N	106.23 E
Chengjiazhen	107	29.24 N	104.36 E
Chengkou	102	31.54 N	108.41 E
Chenglingji	100	29.26 N	113.09 E
Chenglong	100	24.51 N	114.41 E
Chengmai	110	19.48 N	110.02 E
Chengmao	106	31.10 N	120.53 E
Chengpu	100	25.46 N	118.48 E
Chengqian	98	35.21 N	117.21 E
Chengqianwei	100	28.09 N	116.13 E
Chengshan Jiao ›	98	37.24 N	122.42 E
Chengteh → Chengde	105	40.58 N	117.53 E
Chengtu → Chengdu	107	30.39 N	104.04 E
Ch'engtzuliao	269d	25.06 N	121.27 E
Chengwu	98	34.58 N	115.52 E
Chengxian	102	33.43 N	105.41 E
Chengxi Hu ⊜	100	32.24 N	116.15 E
Chengyang, Zhg.	98	36.18 N	120.22 E
Chengyang, Zhg.	100	29.59 N	119.44 E
Chengzi, Zhg.	98	41.57 N	117.16 E
Chengzi, Zhg.	105	39.58 N	116.02 E
Chengzitan	98	39.30 N	122.30 E
Ch'enhsien → Chenxian	100	25.48 N	112.59 E
Chen Hu ⊜	100	30.29 N	113.22 E
Chenies	260	51.41 N	0.32 W
Chenil, Lac ⊜	186	51.51 N	59.41 W
Cheniménil	58	48.08 N	6.36 E
Chenji	100	33.50 N	119.11 E
Chenjiachang, Zhg.	107	29.35 N	104.52 E
Chenjiachang, Zhg.	107	30.04 N	105.15 E
Chenjiagang	98	34.25 N	119.49 E
Chenjiahe	102	29.28 N	109.59 E
Chenjiaji	100	30.42 N	114.21 E
Chenjiapang	106	31.14 N	119.42 E
Chenjiapu	105	40.31 N	115.37 E
Chenjiaqiao	106	31.27 N	121.16 E
Chenjiatun, Zhg.	104	42.20 N	124.06 E
Chenjiatun, Zhg.	104	40.57 N	121.01 E
Chenjiawan	106	31.02 N	120.35 E
Chenjiaxiang	100	31.29 N	113.45 E
Chenjiazhen	106	31.30 N	121.48 E
Chenjiazui	105	39.17 N	116.59 E
Chenkeng	100	25.06 N	116.15 E
Chenlingjiao	106	30.23 N	118.47 E
Chenliu	98	34.43 N	114.31 E
Chenlong	269b	31.17 N	121.25 E
Chennevières	261	49.00 N	2.07 E
Chennevières-lès-Louvres	261	49.03 N	2.33 E
Chenoa	216	40.44 N	88.43 W
Chenonceaux	50	47.20 N	1.04 E
Chenonceaux, Château de ⊥	50	47.20 N	1.04 E
Chenôve	58	47.17 N	5.00 E
Chenoweth	224	45.37 N	121.13 W
Chenqiao	98	34.58 N	114.32 E
Chenquingqiao	89	49.08 N	127.16 E
Chenshanzhuang	105	39.43 N	117.30 E
Chenshichang	107	29.17 N	106.00 E
Chens-sur-Léman	58	46.20 N	6.16 E
Chentang	102	23.54 N	110.39 E
Chentejn nuruu ⋏	88	48.30 N	108.30 E
Chentij	88	48.05 N	109.45 E
Chentij □[4]	88	48.00 N	110.30 E
Chenxi	102	27.51 N	109.59 E
Chenxian	100	25.48 N	112.59 E
Chenxiangtun	104	41.36 N	123.30 E
Chenyang, Zhg.	100	33.47 N	120.10 E
Chenyang → Shenyang, Zhg.	104	41.48 N	123.27 E
Cheonan → Ch'ŏnan	98	36.48 N	127.09 E
Cheongju → Ch'ŏngju	98	36.39 N	127.31 E
Cheo Reo	110	13.24 N	108.27 E
Chepachet	207	41.54 N	71.40 W
Chepaúa	152	12.58 S	22.43 E
Chepén	248	7.13 S	79.27 W
Chépénéhé	175f	20.47 S	167.09 E
Chepes	252	31.21 S	66.36 W
Chepil'	78	49.19 N	36.55 E
Chepkotet ∧	154	1.15 N	35.26 E
Chepo	246	9.10 N	79.06 W
Chepstow	42	51.39 N	2.41 W
Cheptainville	261	48.33 N	2.16 E
Cher □[5]	32	47.05 N	2.30 E
Cher ≃	32	47.21 N	0.29 E
Cheradi, Isole II	68	40.27 N	17.10 E
Cherain	56	50.11 N	5.52 E
Cherán	234	19.41 N	101.57 W
Chéran ≃	62	45.53 N	5.56 E
Cheranchi	150	12.40 N	7.42 E
Cherangany Hills ⋏[2]	154	1.15 N	35.27 E
Cherasco	62	44.39 N	7.51 E
Cherāt	123	33.49 N	71.53 E
Cheraw	192	34.41 N	79.53 W
Cheraw State Park ♦	192	34.36 N	79.55 W
Cherbaniani Reef ✦[2]	122	12.18 N	71.53 E
Cherbourg	32	49.39 N	1.39 W
Cherchell	148	36.36 N	2.12 E
Cheremkhovo → Čeremchovo	88	53.09 N	103.05 E
Cheremosh ≃	78	48.23 N	25.37 E
Chérence	261	49.05 N	1.41 E
Chereponi	150	10.09 N	0.17 E
Cherepovets → Čerepovec	76	59.08 N	37.54 E
Chergui, Chott ech ⊜	148	34.21 N	0.30 E
Chergui, Île I	148	34.44 N	11.14 E
Chergui, Zahrez ⊜	148	35.12 N	3.32 E
Cheribon → Cirebon	115a	6.44 S	108.34 E
Cherio ≃	64	45.34 N	9.51 E
Cherita, Sebkhet ⊜	36	35.21 N	10.19 E
Cheriton	208	37.17 N	75.58 W
Cheriyam Island I	122	10.09 N	73.40 E
Cherkas'ke, Ukr.	78	48.44 N	35.22 E
Cherkas'ke, Ukr.	83	48.50 N	37.23 E
Cherkasy	78	49.26 N	32.04 E
Cherkasy □[4]	78	49.30 N	31.30 E
Cherkessia → Karačajevo-Čerkesija □[3]	84	44.00 N	42.00 E
Cherkessk → Čerkessk	84	44.14 N	42.04 E
Cherlen → Kerulen ≃	90	48.48 N	117.00 E
Chermside	171a	27.23 S	153.02 E
Chernelytsya	78	48.48 N	25.26 E
Chernigov → Chernihiv	78	51.30 N	31.18 E
Chernihiv	78	51.30 N	31.18 E
Chernihiv □[4]	78	51.15 N	32.00 E
Chernihivka	78	47.13 N	36.14 E
Chernivtsi, Ukr.	78	48.18 N	25.56 E
Chernivtsi, Ukr.	78	48.33 N	28.09 E
Chernivtsi □[8]	78	43.30 N	26.00 E
Chernobyl → Chornobyl'	78	51.16 N	30.14 E
Chernofski	180	53.24 N	167.33 W
Chernogorsk → Černogorsk	86	53.49 N	91.18 E
Chernovtsy → Chernivtsi	78	48.18 N	25.56 E
Chernyakhiv	78	50.27 N	28.39 E
Chero ≃	62	45.03 N	9.51 E
Cherokee, Al., U.S.	194	34.45 N	87.58 W
Cherokee, Ia., U.S.	198	42.44 N	95.33 W
Cherokee, Ks., U.S.	198	37.20 N	94.48 W
Cherokee, Ok., U.S.	196	36.45 N	98.21 W
Cherokee, Tx., U.S.	196	30.59 N	98.43 W
Cherokee □[6]	222	31.48 N	95.10 W
Cherokee, Lake ⊜[1]	222	32.21 N	94.39 W
Cherokee Canal ≡	226	39.18 N	121.55 W
Cherokee Lake ⊜[1]	192	36.16 N	83.20 W
Cherokee Point ›	192	26.16 N	77.03 W
Cherokee Ranch	208	40.25 N	75.55 W
Cherokees, Lake O' The ⊜[1]	194	36.39 N	94.49 W
Cherokee Village	194	36.17 N	91.30 W
Chéroy	50	48.12 N	3.00 E
Cherpuči	89	53.01 N	138.52 E
Cherquenco	252	38.41 S	72.00 W
Cherrabun	162	18.29 S	125.19 E
Cherrapunji	120	25.18 N	91.42 E
Cherry Brook ≃, Ma., U.S.	283	42.23 N	71.17 W
Cherry Brook ≃, N.J., U.S.	276	41.01 N	74.00 W
Cherry City	279b	40.29 N	79.58 W
Cherry Creek, B.C., Can.	224	49.17 N	124.47 W
Cherry Creek, N.Y., U.S.	214	42.17 N	79.06 W
Cherry Creek ≃, Az., U.S.	200	33.41 N	110.49 W
Cherry Creek ≃, Ca., U.S.	226	37.53 N	119.58 W
Cherry Creek ≃, Co., U.S.	198	39.45 N	105.01 W
Cherry Creek ≃, Mt., U.S.	198	46.48 N	105.15 W
Cherry Creek ≃, N.D., U.S.	198	47.41 N	103.02 W
Cherry Creek ≃, S.D., U.S.	198	44.36 N	101.30 W
Cherry Creek ≃, Tx., U.S.	196	31.13 N	103.34 W
Cherry Creek, East Fork ≃	226	38.06 N	119.47 W
Cherry Creek, West Fork ≃	226	38.04 N	119.54 W
Cherry Fork	218	38.53 N	83.37 W
Cherry Grove, N.Y., U.S.	210	40.39 N	73.06 W
Cherry Grove, Or., U.S.	224	45.26 N	123.14 W
Cherry Hill, Il., U.S.	278	41.32 N	88.02 W
Cherry Hill, N.J., U.S.	208	39.56 N	75.01 W
Cherry Hill ◆[8]	284b	39.15 N	76.38 W
Cherry Hill Mall ◆[9]	285	39.56 N	75.02 W
Cherry Island I	285	39.43 N	75.31 W
Cherry Lake ⊜[1]	226	38.00 N	119.54 W
Cherryland	226	37.41 N	122.06 W
Cherry Lane	279b	40.34 N	79.33 W
Cherryplain	210	42.38 N	73.22 W
Cherry Point Marine Corps Air Station ■	192	34.54 N	76.54 W
Cherryvale	198	37.16 N	95.33 W
Cherry Valley, Ar., U.S.	194	35.24 N	90.45 W
Cherry Valley, Ca., U.S.	228	33.57 N	116.53 W
Cherry Valley, Il., U.S.	216	42.14 N	88.56 W
Cherry Valley, Ma., U.S.	207	42.14 N	71.52 W
Cherry Valley, N.Y., U.S.	210	42.47 N	74.45 W
Cherry Valley, Pa., U.S.	214	41.10 N	79.48 W
Cherry Valley Creek ≃	210	42.35 N	74.56 W
Cherryville, N.C., U.S.	192	35.22 N	81.22 W
Cherryville, Pa., U.S.	208	40.45 N	75.33 W
Cherrywood	275b	43.52 N	79.08 W
Chertsey	42	51.24 N	0.30 W
Chervona Kam'yanka	78	48.38 N	33.26 E
Chervonapopivka	83	49.08 N	38.09 E
Chervone, Ukr.	78	51.46 N	34.04 E
Chervone, Ukr.	78	49.57 N	28.53 E
Chervonoarmiys'k, Ukr.	78	50.28 N	28.14 E
Chervonoarmiys'k, Ukr.	78	50.08 N	25.16 E
Chervonohrad	78	50.24 N	24.14 E
Chervonooskils'ke vodoskhovyshche ⊜[1]	83	49.17 N	37.37 E
Chervonopartyzans'k	83	48.04 N	39.50 E
Chervonyy Donets'	78	49.29 N	36.34 E
Chervonyy Oskil	83	49.11 N	37.26 E
Chervonyy Zhovten'	83	48.56 N	39.23 E
Cherwell ≃	42	51.44 N	1.15 W
Chesaco Park	284b	39.19 N	76.30 W
Chesaning	190	43.11 N	84.06 W
Chesapeake	208	36.49 N	76.16 W
Chesapeake and Delaware Canal ≡	208	39.32 N	75.51 W
Chesapeake and Ohio Canal National Historical Park ♦	208	39.03 N	77.16 W
Chesapeake Bay ⊂	208	38.40 N	76.25 W
Chesapeake Bay Bridge-Tunnel ◆[5]	208	37.00 N	76.02 W
Chesapeake Beach	208	38.41 N	76.32 W
Chesaw	182	48.56 N	119.03 W
Chesdin, Lake ⊜[1]	208	37.15 N	77.33 W
Cheseaux	58	46.35 N	6.36 E
Chesham	42	51.43 N	0.38 W
Chesham Bois	260	51.41 N	0.37 W
Cheshire, Ct., U.S.	207	41.29 N	72.54 W
Cheshire, Ma., U.S.	207	42.33 N	73.09 W
Cheshire, N.Y., U.S.	210	42.49 N	77.20 W
Cheshire □[6], Eng., U.K.	44	53.23 N	2.30 W
Cheshire □[6], N.H., U.S.	207	42.50 N	72.15 W
Cheshire Plain ≚	44	53.17 N	2.40 W
Cheshire Reservoir ⊜[1]	207	42.32 N	73.11 W
Chesht-e Sharīf	128	34.21 N	63.44 E
Cheshunt	42	51.43 N	0.02 W
Chesil Beach ⊻[2]	42	50.38 N	2.33 W
Chesilhurst	285	39.43 N	74.52 W
Cheslatta Lake ⊜	182	53.44 N	125.18 W
Chesley	212	44.17 N	81.05 W
Chesnee	192	35.08 N	81.51 W
Chess ≃	260	51.38 N	0.27 W
Chessington ◆[8]	260	51.21 N	0.18 W
Chessy	261	48.53 N	2.46 E
Chest Creek ≃	214	40.53 N	78.44 W
Chester, Eng., U.K.	44	53.12 N	2.54 W
Chester, Ca., U.S.	204	40.18 N	121.13 W
Chester, Ct., U.S.	207	41.24 N	72.27 W
Chester, Il., U.S.	194	37.54 N	89.49 W
Chester, Md., U.S.	208	38.58 N	76.17 W
Chester, Ma., U.S.	207	42.16 N	72.58 W
Chester, Mt., U.S.	202	48.30 N	110.58 W
Chester, Ne., U.S.	198	40.00 N	97.37 W
Chester, N.J., U.S.	210	40.47 N	74.41 W
Chester, Ok., U.S.	196	36.12 N	98.55 W
Chester, Pa., U.S.	208	39.50 N	75.21 W
Chester, S.C., U.S.	192	34.42 N	81.12 W
Chester, Tx., U.S.	222	30.55 N	94.36 W
Chester, Vt., U.S.	188	43.15 N	72.35 W
Chester, Va., U.S.	208	37.21 N	77.26 W
Chester, W.V., U.S.	214	40.36 N	80.33 W
Chester □[6]	208	39.58 N	75.36 W
Chester □[8]	262	53.16 N	2.52 W
Chester ≃	208	39.00 N	76.10 W
Chester Basin	186	44.34 N	64.19 W
Chesterbrook	284c	38.55 N	77.09 W
Chester Brook ≃	283	42.23 N	71.14 W
Chesterbrook Woods	284c	38.56 N	77.08 W
Chester Creek ≃	208	39.50 N	75.22 W
Chester Creek, East Branch ≃	285	39.56 N	75.32 W
Chester Creek, West Branch ≃	285	39.54 N	75.27 W
Chesterfield, Eng., U.K.	44	53.15 N	1.25 W
Chesterfield, Ct., U.S.	207	41.24 N	72.11 W
Chesterfield, Il., U.S.	219	39.15 N	90.04 W
Chesterfield, In., U.S.	218	40.06 N	85.35 W
Chesterfield, Ma., U.S.	207	42.23 N	72.50 W
Chesterfield, S.C., U.S.	192	34.44 N	80.05 W
Chesterfield, Va., U.S.	192	37.22 N	77.30 W
Chesterfield □[6]	208	37.20 N	77.25 W
Chesterfield, Îles II	160	19.30 S	158.00 E
Chesterfield, Nosy I	157b	16.20 S	43.58 E
Chesterfield Inlet	176	63.21 N	90.42 W
Chesterfield Inlet ⊂	176	63.25 N	90.45 W
Chester Heights	285	39.53 N	75.28 W
Chester Hill, Austl.	274a	33.53 S	151.00 E
Chesterhill, Oh., U.S.	188	39.29 N	81.51 W
Chester Hill, Pa., U.S.	214	40.53 N	78.14 W
Chester Island I	285	39.50 N	75.21 W
Chesterland	214	41.31 N	81.21 W
Chester-le-Street	44	54.52 N	1.34 W
Chester Morse Lake ⊜[1]	224	47.23 N	121.42 W
Chesters	44	55.23 N	2.36 W
Chester Springs	285	40.06 N	75.37 W
Chesterton	216	41.36 N	87.03 W
Chesterton Range ⋏	166	25.30 S	147.27 E
Chestertown	208	39.12 N	76.04 W
Chesterville, On., Can.	212	45.06 N	75.14 W
Chesterville, Oh., U.S.	214	40.29 N	82.41 W
Chestnut	219	40.03 N	89.11 W
Chestnut Hill, Ma., U.S.	283	42.20 N	71.10 W
Chestnut Hill, Pa., U.S.	210	40.04 N	75.12 W
Chestnut Hill ◆[8]	285	40.04 N	75.13 W
Chestnut Hill ∧[2]	285	40.13 N	75.45 W
Chestnut Hill Estates	285	39.41 N	75.42 W
Chestnut Hill Reservoir ⊜[1]	283	42.20 N	71.10 W
Chestnut Ridge ∧	214	40.09 N	79.24 W

Symbols in the index entries represent the broad categories identified in the key at the right. Symbols with superior numbers (⋏[1]) identify subcategories (see complete key on page *I · 1).*

Symbole im Register stellen die rechts im Schlüssel erklärten Kategorien dar. Symbole mit hochgestellten Ziffern (⋏[1]) bezeichnen Unterabteilungen einer Kategorie (vgl. vollständiger Schlüssel auf Seite *I · 1).*

Los símbolos incluídos en el texto del índice representan las grandes categorías identificadas con la clave a la derecha. Los símbolos con numeros en su parte superior (⋏[1]) identifican las subcategorías (véase la clave completa en la página *I · 1).*

Les symboles de l'index représentent les catégories indiquées dans la légende à droite. Les symboles suivis d'un indice (⋏[1]) représentent des sous-catégories (voir légende complète à la page *I · 1).*

Os símbolos incluídos no texto do índice representam as grandes categorias identificadas com a chave à direita. Os símbolos com números em sua parte superior (⋏[1]) identificam as subcategorias (veja-se a chave completa à página *I · 1).*

English	Deutsch	Español	Français	Português
∧ Mountain	Berg	Montaña	Montagne	Montanha
⋏ Mountains	Gebirge	Montañas	Montagnes	Montanhas
)(Pass	Paß	Paso	Col	Passo
V Valley, Canyon	Tal, Cañon	Valle, Cañón	Vallée, Canyon	Vale, Canhão
≚ Plain	Ebene	Llano	Plaine	Planície
› Cape	Kap	Cabo	Cap	Cabo
I Island	Insel	Isla	Île	Ilha
II Islands	Inseln	Islas	Îles	Ilhas
⊻ Other Topographic Features	Andere Topographische Objekte	Otros Elementos Topográficos	Autres données topographiques	Outros acidentes topográficos

ESPAÑOL

Nombre	Página	Lat.°′	Long.°′ W = Oeste
Chestnut Ridge Park ♠	284a	42.43 N	78.46 W
Chest Peak ∧	172	43.06 S	172.01 E
Chesuncook Lake ⊜	188	46.00 N	69.20 W
Cheswick	214	40.32 N	79.47 W
Cheswold	208	39.13 N	75.35 W
Chet ≃	42	52.33 N	1.32 E
Cheta ≃	74	71.54 N	102.06 E
Chetaibi	36	37.04 N	7.23 E
Chetco ≃	202	42.03 N	124.16 W
Chetek	190	45.18 N	91.39 W
Chéticamp	186	46.38 N	61.01 W
Chet Iter, Oued ∨	148	21.39 N	2.30 E
Chetopa	198	37.02 N	95.05 W
Chettlatt Island I	122	11.42 N	72.42 E
Chetumal	232	18.30 N	88.18 W
Chetumal, Bahía ⊂	232	18.20 N	88.05 W
Chetwynd	182	55.42 N	121.40 W
Cheung Chau I	271d	22.12 N	114.01 E
Cheung Shue Tan	271d	22.26 N	114.12 E
Chevak	180	61.39 N	165.17 W
Cheval Blanc, Sommet du ∧	62	44.07 N	6.26 E
Chevannes	261	48.32 N	2.27 E
Chevelon Creek ≃	200	34.57 N	110.31 W
Chevening	260	51.18 N	0.08 E
Chevenoz	58	46.20 N	6.39 E
Cheverly	284c	38.55 N	76.54 W
Cheverny	50	47.30 N	1.28 E
Chevillon	58	48.32 N	5.08 E
Chevilly-Larue	261	48.46 N	2.21 E
Cheviot, N.Z.	172	42.49 S	173.16 E
Cheviot, Oh., U.S.	218	39.09 N	84.36 W
Cheviot Hills ⩕[2]	44	55.22 N	2.22 W
Chevreuse	50	48.42 N	2.03 E
Chèvreville	261	49.07 N	2.51 E
Chevril, Lac du ⊜	62	45.29 N	6.56 E
Chevry-Cossigny	261	48.43 N	2.40 E
Chevy Chase	284c	38.58 N	77.04 W
Chevy Chase Heights	214	40.36 N	79.08 W
Chevy Chase View	284c	39.01 N	77.05 W
Chewaucan ≃	202	42.30 N	120.18 W
Chew Bahir (Lake Stefanie) ⊜	144	4.40 N	36.50 E
Chewelah	202	48.16 N	117.42 W
Chew Magna	42	51.22 N	2.35 W
Chew Reservoir ⊜[1]	262	53.31 N	1.56 W
Chews Landing	285	39.50 N	75.04 W
Chewton, Austl.	169	37.05 S	144.16 E
Chewton, Pa., U.S.	214	40.53 N	80.20 W
Chexbres	58	46.29 N	6.47 E
Cheyenne, Ok., U.S.	196	35.36 N	99.40 W
Cheyenne, Wy., U.S.	200	41.08 N	104.49 W
Cheyenne ≃	198	44.40 N	101.15 W
Cheyenne, Dry Fork ≃	198	43.25 N	105.23 W
Cheyenne River Indian Reservation ◆[4]	198	45.00 N	100.40 W
Cheyenne Wells	198	38.49 N	102.21 W
Cheyne Bay ⊂	162	34.35 S	118.50 E
Cheyne Point ›	162	33.58 S	122.34 E
Cheyney	285	39.56 N	75.31 W
Cheyney University of Pennsylvania ᵾ[2]	285	39.56 N	75.32 W
Chezhen	98	37.54 N	117.37 E
Chhabra	124	24.40 N	76.50 E
Chhachhrauli	124	30.15 N	77.22 E
Chhajārsi	272a	28.38 N	77.23 E
Chhalera Bāngar	272a	28.33 N	77.20 E
Chhanka	126	23.59 N	89.55 E
Chhapra	124	25.46 N	84.45 E
Chhātak	120	25.02 N	91.40 E
Chhatarpur, India	124	24.23 N	84.11 E
Chhatarpur, India	124	24.55 N	79.36 E
Chhātna	126	23.18 N	86.58 E
Chhatrapur	122	19.21 N	84.59 E
Chhattīsgarh ≍	122	21.15 N	82.00 E
Chhay Arêng ≃	110	11.31 N	103.25 E
Chhêb Kândal	110	13.45 N	105.24 E
Chhibrāmau	124	27.09 N	79.31 E
Chhināmor	272b	22.48 N	88.18 E
Chhindwāra	124	22.04 N	78.56 E
Chhiruti	126	24.01 N	88.11 E
Chhitauni	124	27.09 N	83.58 E
Chhlong ≃	110	12.15 N	105.58 E
Chhota Bāisdia	126	22.00 N	90.27 E
Chhota-Chhindwāra	124	23.03 N	79.29 E
Chhota Udepur	120	22.19 N	74.01 E
Chhukha Dzong	124	27.09 N	89.36 E
Chi ≃, Thai	110	15.11 N	104.43 E
Chi ≃, Thai	110	15.18 N	103.31 E
Chi ≃, Zhg.	100	32.51 N	117.59 E
Chía	246	4.52 N	74.04 W
Chia, Laguna ⊜	234	22.10 N	98.02 W
Chiador	256	22.01 S	43.03 W
Chiahsien	100	23.05 N	120.35 E
Chiahsing → Jiaxing	106	30.46 N	120.45 E
Chiai	100	23.29 N	120.27 E
Chialamberto	62	45.22 N	7.21 E
Chiali	100	23.10 N	120.10 E
Chiambala ≃	152	16.22 S	11.49 E
Chiampo	64	45.33 N	11.17 E
Chiampo ≃	64	45.20 N	11.16 E
Chiamussu → Jiamusi	89	46.50 N	130.21 E
Chian → Ji'an	100	27.07 N	114.58 E
Chiana, Val di ∨	66	43.15 N	11.50 E
Chianciano Terme	66	43.03 N	11.50 E
Chiang Dao	110	19.22 N	98.58 E
Chiange	152	15.45 S	13.48 E
Chiang Kham	110	19.32 N	100.18 E
Chiang Khan	110	17.52 N	101.36 E
Chiang Khian	110	19.37 N	100.00 E
Chiang Mai	110	18.47 N	98.59 E
Chiangmen → Jiangmen	100	22.35 N	113.05 E
Chiang Rai	110	19.54 N	99.50 E
Chiang Saen	110	20.16 N	100.05 E
Chiangtu → Yangzhou	100	32.24 N	119.26 E
Chiangyin → Jiangyin	106	31.55 N	120.16 E
Chiani ≃	66	42.44 N	12.07 E
Chianni	66	43.29 N	10.38 E
Chianti □[9]	66	43.25 N	11.20 E
Chianti, Monti del ⩕	66	43.32 N	11.25 E
Chiaohsi	100	24.49 N	121.46 E
Chiaohsien → Jiaoxian	98	36.18 N	119.58 E
Chiaopan	100	24.50 N	121.21 E
Chiaotso → Jiaozuo	102	35.15 N	113.13 E
Chiao-Tung Normal University ᵾ[2]	269b	31.14 N	121.24 E
Chiapa	248	19.32 S	69.13 W
Chiapa de Corzo	234	16.42 N	93.00 W
Chiapaot'ai	100	24.11 N	121.00 E
Chiapas □[3]	232	16.30 N	92.30 W
Chiaramonte Gulfi	70	37.02 N	14.42 E
Chiaramonti	71	40.45 N	8.49 E
Chiaravalle	66	43.36 N	13.19 E
Chiaravalle Centrale	68	38.41 N	16.25 E
Chiareggio	64	46.19 N	9.47 E
Chiari	62	45.32 N	9.56 E
Chiaromonte	68	40.07 N	16.13 E
Chiasso	58	45.50 N	9.01 E
Chiautla de Tapia	234	18.17 N	98.36 W
Chiavari	62	44.19 N	9.19 E
Chiavenna	58	46.19 N	9.24 E
Chiawelo	273d	26.17 S	27.52 E
Chiba	94	35.36 N	140.07 E
Chiba □[5]	94	35.30 N	140.20 E
Chibabava	156	20.19 S	33.39 E
Chiba-kō ⊂	268	35.35 N	140.06 E
Chibakou	100	29.36 N	113.01 E
Chibango	152	13.38 S	21.56 E
Chiba University ᵾ[2]	268	35.38 N	140.06 E
Chibemba	152	15.45 S	14.05 E
Chibi	154	20.19 S	30.30 E
Chibia	152	15.11 S	13.41 E

FRANÇAIS

Nom	Page	Lat.°′	Long.°′ W = Ouest
Chibouet ≃	206	45.47 N	72.52 W
Chibougamau	176	49.55 N	74.22 W
Chibuto	156	24.44 S	33.33 E
Chibuzhangchu Hu ⊜	120	33.25 N	90.15 E
Chibwe	154	14.12 S	28.31 E
Chicago, Il., U.S.	216	41.51 N	87.39 W
Chicago, Il., U.S.	278	41.51 N	87.39 W
Chicago, North Branch ≃	216	41.53 N	87.38 W
Chicago, North Branch, West Fork ≃	278	42.03 N	87.54 W
Chicago, South Branch ≃	278	41.53 N	87.38 W
Chicago, University of ᵾ[2]	278	41.47 N	87.36 W
Chicago Botanic Garden ♠	278	42.09 N	87.47 W
Chicago Harbor ⊂	278	41.53 N	87.37 W
Chicago Heights	216	41.30 N	87.38 W
Chicago-Hinsdale Airport ⊠	278	41.46 N	87.56 W
Chicago Lawn ◆[8]	278	41.47 N	87.41 W
Chicago-Midway Airport ⊠	216	41.47 N	87.45 W
Chicago-O'Hare International Airport ⊠	278	41.59 N	87.54 W
Chicago Park	226	39.09 N	120.58 W
Chicago Portage National Historic Site ⊥	278	41.48 N	87.49 W
Chicago Ridge	216	41.42 N	87.46 W
Chicago Sanitary and Ship Canal ≍	216	41.32 N	88.05 W
Chicago Stadium ♠	278	41.53 N	87.40 W
Chicama ≃	248	7.56 S	79.17 W
Chicamacomico ≃	208	38.26 N	75.59 W
Chicamba, Barragem de ◆[6]	156	19.08 S	33.00 E
Chicapa ≃	152	6.26 S	20.47 E
Chicayán ≃	234	21.59 N	94.06 W
Chic-Chocs, Monts ⩕	186	48.55 N	66.00 W
Chichagof Island I	180	57.30 N	135.30 W
Chichas, Cordillera de ⩕	248	21.00 S	66.20 W
Chīchāwatni	123	30.32 N	72.42 E
Chiché ≃	250	8.15 S	53.30 W
Chicheng	98	40.54 N	115.46 E
Chichén Itzá ⊥	232	20.40 N	88.35 W
Chichester, Eng., U.K.	42	50.50 N	0.48 W
Chichester, N.Y., U.S.	210	42.06 N	74.19 W
Chichester Range ⩕	162	22.00 S	118.50 E
Chichi	100	23.50 N	120.47 E
Chichibu	94	35.59 N	139.05 E
Chichibu-Tama-kokuritsu-kōen ♠	94	35.52 N	139.00 E
Chichica	236	8.22 N	81.40 W
Chichicastenango	236	14.56 N	91.07 W
Chichigalpa	236	12.34 N	87.02 W
Chichigapa	234	17.47 N	94.25 W
Ch'ich'ihaerh → Qiqihar	89	47.19 N	123.55 E
Chichihualco	234	17.41 N	99.39 W
Chichijima-rettō II	14	27.06 N	142.12 E
Chichimilá	232	20.37 N	88.13 W
Chichiriviche	246	10.56 N	68.16 W
Chicholi	124	22.01 N	77.40 E
Chichra	126	22.19 N	86.53 E
Chickahominy ≃	208	37.14 N	76.53 W
Chickaloon	180	61.48 N	148.28 W
Chickamauga	192	34.52 N	85.17 W
Chickamauga Lake ⊜[1]	192	35.22 N	85.02 W
Chickamin ≃	182	55.47 N	130.58 W
Chickasaw, Al., U.S.	194	30.45 N	88.04 W
Chickasaw, Oh., U.S.	216	40.26 N	84.30 W
Chickasaw Bogue ≃	194	32.17 N	87.55 W
Chickasawhatchie Creek ≃	192	31.19 N	84.29 W
Chickasawhay ≃	194	31.00 N	88.45 W
Chickasaw National Recreation Area ♠	196	34.25 N	96.59 W
Chickasha	196	35.03 N	97.56 W
Chicken	180	64.04 N	141.56 W
Chicken Brook ≃	283	42.08 N	71.25 W
Chickerell	42	50.37 N	2.30 W
Chickies Creek ≃	208	40.03 N	76.32 W
Chiclana de la Frontera	34	36.25 N	6.08 W
Chiclayo	248	6.46 S	79.51 W
Chico, Ca., U.S.	204	39.43 N	121.50 W
Chico, Tx., U.S.	196	33.17 N	97.47 W
Chico, Wa., U.S.	224	47.36 N	122.42 W
Chico ≃, Arg.	254	43.48 S	66.25 W
Chico ≃, Arg.	254	42.25 S	70.30 W
Chico ≃, Arg.	254	49.56 S	68.32 W
Chico ≃, Cuba	286b	23.02 N	82.17 W
Chico ≃, Pan.	236	8.20 N	80.28 W
Chico ≃, Pil.	116	17.58 N	121.36 E
Chico ≃, S.A.	254	51.40 S	69.09 W
Chicoasén, Presa ⊜[1]	234	16.55 N	93.05 W
Chicobi, Lac ⊜	190	48.53 N	78.30 W
Chico Creek ≃	198	38.15 N	104.20 W
Chicolete Creek ≃	222	29.05 N	96.49 W
Chicomba	152	14.09 S	14.57 E
Chicomo	156	24.31 S	34.17 E
Chicomuselo	232	15.46 N	92.16 W
Chiconautla, Cerro ∧	286a	19.39 N	98.58 W
Chicunono	154	12.56 S	35.43 E
Chicontepec de Tejeda	234	20.58 N	98.10 W
Chicopee, Ga., U.S.	192	34.15 N	83.50 W
Chicopee, Ma., U.S.	207	42.08 N	72.36 W
Chicopee ≃	207	42.09 N	72.37 W
Chicora	214	40.56 N	79.44 W
Chicot, Lake ⊜	194	33.20 N	91.14 W
Chicot, Rivière du ≃	275a	45.35 N	73.51 W
Chicot State Park ♠	194	30.47 N	92.19 W
Chicoutimi	186	48.26 N	71.04 W
Chicoutimi ≃	186	48.26 N	71.05 W
Chicoutimi, Réserve ♠	186	48.30 N	70.15 W
Chicú, Cerro ∧	236	8.35 N	80.51 W
Chicualoque	234	20.23 N	97.39 W
Chicuma	152	13.23 S	14.51 E
Chicxulub	232	21.08 N	89.31 W
Chidambaram	122	11.24 N	79.42 E
Chiddingfold	42	51.06 N	0.37 W
Chiddingstone Causeway	260	51.12 N	0.10 E
Chidenguele	156	24.54 S	34.13 E
Chidlow	168a	31.52 S	116.14 E
Chi-do I	98	35.04 N	126.13 E
Chidralada Palace ᵾ	269a	13.46 N	100.32 E
Chief	222	32.33 N	96.10 W
Chief Justice William Cushing Memorial State Park ♠	283	42.10 N	70.45 W
Chiefland	192	29.28 N	82.51 W
Chiefs Point ›	212	44.42 N	81.18 W
Chief's Point Indian Reserve ◆[4]	212	44.41 N	81.17 W
Chiehyang → Jieyang	100	23.35 N	116.21 E
Chiemgauer Alpen ⩕	64	47.40 N	12.30 E
Chiemsee ⊜	64	47.54 N	12.29 E
Chien, Bayou de ≃	194	36.35 N	89.11 W
Chienes (Kiens)	64	46.48 N	11.50 E
Chiengi	154	8.39 S	29.10 E
Chiengo	152	13.20 S	21.55 E
Chiens, Rivière aux ≃	275a	45.39 N	73.46 W
Chienti ≃	66	43.18 N	13.45 E
Chieo Lan Reservoir ⊜[1]	110	9.00 N	98.45 E
Chieri	62	45.01 N	7.49 E
Chiers ≃	56	49.39 N	5.00 E
Chiesa in Valmalenco	64	46.16 N	9.51 E
Chiese ≃	64	45.08 N	10.25 E
Chieti	66	42.21 N	14.10 E
Chieti □[4]	66	42.07 N	14.21 E

PORTUGUÊS

Nome	Página	Lat.°′	Long.°′ W = Oeste
Chietla	234	18.31 N	98.35 W
Chieuti	68	41.51 N	15.10 E
Chieveley	42	51.27 N	1.19 W
Chièvres	50	50.35 N	3.48 E
Chifeng (Ulanhad)	98	42.18 N	119.00 E
Chigasaki	94	35.19 N	139.24 E
Chiginagak, Mount ∧	180	57.08 N	156.59 W
Chigmit Mountains ⩕	180	60.00 N	153.00 W
Chignahuapan	234	19.50 N	98.02 W
Chignall Saint James	260	51.46 N	0.25 E
Chignall Smealy	260	51.47 N	0.25 E
Chignecto, Cape ›	186	45.20 N	64.57 W
Chignecto Bay ⊂	186	45.35 N	64.45 W
Chignik	180	56.18 N	158.23 W
Chignik Bay ⊂	180	56.22 N	158.15 W
Chignik Lagoon	180	56.21 N	158.31 W
Chignik Lake	180	56.15 N	158.45 W
Chignolo Po	62	45.09 N	9.29 E
Chigombe ≃	156	23.26 S	33.19 E
Chigorodó	246	7.41 N	76.42 W
Chigu	100	27.34 N	114.40 E
Chigubo	156	22.50 S	33.34 E
Chigu Co ⊜	120	28.40 N	91.45 E
Chigwell	42	51.38 N	0.05 E
Chigwell Row	260	51.37 N	0.07 E
Chigyŏng	98	39.51 N	127.26 E
Chihaya-akasaka	270	34.24 N	135.38 E
Chihaya Castle ⊥	270	34.24 N	135.40 E
Chihe	100	32.32 N	117.58 E
Ch'ihfeng → Chifeng	98	42.18 N	119.00 E
Chihli, Gulf of → Bo Hai ⊂	98	38.30 N	120.00 E
Chihpen	100	22.42 N	121.02 E
Ch'ihshang	100	23.07 N	121.12 E
Chihsi → Jixi	89	45.17 N	130.59 E
Ch'ihsing Shan ∧, T'aiwan	100	25.10 N	121.33 E
Ch'ihsing Shan ∧, T'aiwan	269d	25.10 N	121.33 E
Ch'ihsing Yen I	100	21.46 N	120.49 E
Chihtungtsun	100	22.44 N	120.14 E
Chihu	100	24.07 N	117.51 E
Chihuahua	232	28.38 N	106.05 W
Chihuahua □[3]	232	28.30 N	106.00 W
Chihuahuan Desert ◆[2]	16	35.00 N	106.00 W
Chii-san ∧	98	35.20 N	127.44 E
Chii-san Kukrip Kongwŏn ♠	98	35.20 N	127.39 E
Chiitola	26	61.16 N	29.38 E
Chikaskia ≃	196	36.37 N	97.15 W
Chik Ballāpur	122	13.28 N	77.44 E
Chikhli	122	20.21 N	76.15 E
Chikindzonot	232	20.20 N	88.29 W
Chikmagalūr	122	13.19 N	75.47 E
Chiknai ≃	126	24.06 N	89.17 E
Chiknāyakanhalli	122	13.26 N	76.37 E
Chikoa	154	13.24 S	32.07 E
Chikodi	122	16.26 N	74.36 E
Chikou	100	30.44 N	117.32 E
Chikrêng ≃	110	12.51 N	104.14 E
Ch'iku	100	23.08 N	120.07 E
Chikugo	96	33.12 N	130.30 E
Chikugo ≃	92	33.09 N	130.21 E
Chikujō-kichi, Kōkū-jieitai- ■	96	33.41 N	131.03 E
Chikuma ≃	94	36.59 N	138.35 E
Chikuminuk Lake ⊜	180	60.14 N	159.00 W
Chikura	94	34.57 N	139.57 E
Chikusa	96	35.09 N	134.26 E
Chikusa ≃	96	34.44 N	134.24 E
Chikushino	96	33.29 N	130.31 E
Chikwawa	154	16.03 S	34.48 E
Chi-kyaw	110	20.17 N	93.54 E
Chikyu-misaki ›	92a	42.18 N	141.00 E
Chila	152	12.04 S	14.29 E
Chilacachapa	234	18.17 N	99.43 W
Chilakalūrupet	122	16.05 N	80.10 E
Chilako ≃	182	53.54 N	122.59 W
Chilam Chauki	123	35.03 N	75.07 E
Chilanga	154	15.34 S	28.17 E
Chilanko Forks	182	52.06 N	124.10 W
Chilapa de Álvarez	234	17.36 N	99.10 W
Chilās	123	35.26 N	74.05 E
Chilaw	122	7.34 N	79.47 E
Chilca, Perú	248	12.32 S	76.44 W
Chilca, Perú	248	12.09 S	75.11 W
Chilca, Punta ›	248	12.27 S	76.48 W
Chilchota	234	19.51 N	102.08 W
Chilcotin ≃	182	51.45 N	122.24 W
Chilcott Island I	166	16.58 S	149.58 E
Childers	166	25.14 S	152.17 E
Childersburg	194	33.16 N	86.21 W
Childer Thornton	262	53.17 N	2.57 W
Childress	196	34.25 N	100.12 W
Childs	210	41.34 N	75.32 W
Chile □[1]	244	30.00 S	71.00 W
Chile, Hipódromo ♠	286e	33.24 S	70.41 W
Chile, Universidad de ᵾ[2]	286e	33.27 S	70.40 W
Chile Basin ✣[1]	18	33.00 S	80.00 W
Chile Chico	254	46.33 S	71.44 W
Chilecito, Arg.	252	29.10 S	67.30 W
Chilecito, Arg.	252	33.53 S	69.03 W
Chilengue, Serra do ⩕	152	13.10 S	15.18 E
Chileno, Arroyo ≃, Ur.	258	33.55 S	58.08 W
Chileno, Arroyo ≃, Ur.	288	34.22 S	57.54 W
Chile Rise ✣[3]	18	40.00 S	90.00 W
Chilete	248	7.14 S	78.51 W
Chilham	42	51.15 N	0.57 E
Chilhowie	192	36.47 N	81.40 W
Chili	216	40.52 N	86.02 W
Chili → Chile □[1]	244	30.00 S	71.00 W
Chili ≃	248	16.23 S	71.46 W
Chili, Ouadi ∨	146	16.44 N	20.53 E
Chilia, Brațul ≃[1]	78	45.18 N	29.40 E
Chili Center	210	43.06 N	77.44 W
Chilika Lake ⊜	122	19.45 N	85.25 E
Chililabombwe (Bancroft)	154	12.18 S	27.43 E
Chilin → Jilin	89	43.51 N	126.33 E
Chilingchang	107	28.58 N	105.31 E
Chilivani	71	40.36 N	8.56 E
Chilkat Pass)(	180	59.43 N	136.35 W
Chilko ≃	182	52.08 N	123.30 W
Chilko Lake ⊜	182	51.20 N	124.05 W
Chilko Lake Indian Reserve ◆[4]	182	51.25 N	124.07 W
Chillagoe	166	17.09 S	144.32 E
Chillán	252	36.36 S	72.07 W
Chillar	252	37.18 S	59.59 W
Chilla Saroda ◆[8]	272a	28.36 N	77.18 E
Chillicothe, Il., U.S.	190	40.55 N	89.29 W
Chillicothe, Mo., U.S.	194	39.47 N	93.33 W
Chillicothe, Oh., U.S.	218	39.19 N	82.58 W
Chillicothe, Tx., U.S.	196	34.15 N	99.30 W
Chilliwack	224	49.10 N	121.57 W
Chilliwack ≃	224	49.05 N	121.57 W
Chilliwack Lake ⊜	224	49.03 N	121.25 W
Chillón	286d	11.55 S	77.05 W
Chillón ≃	248	11.57 S	77.09 W
Chillon, Château de ⊥	58	46.25 N	6.56 E
Chillum	284c	38.58 N	76.59 W
Chilly-Mazarin	261	48.42 N	2.19 E
Chilmāri	124	25.33 N	89.43 E
Chilmark	207	41.20 N	70.44 W
Chilo	218	38.48 N	84.08 W
Chiloane, Ilha I	156	20.40 S	34.55 E
Chiloé, Isla Grande de I	254	42.30 S	73.55 W
Chilok	88	51.21 N	110.28 E
Chilok ≃	88	51.19 N	106.59 E
Chilón	232	17.14 N	92.25 W
Chilonga	154	12.03 S	31.21 E
Chilongo	152	13.55 S	16.35 E
Chiloquin	202	42.34 N	121.51 W

Chilovo	76	57.46 N	29.23 E
Chilpancingo de los Bravo	234	17.33 N	99.30 W
Chilpi	124	22.15 N	81.33 E
Chilston Park ♠	260	51.12 N	0.42 E
Chiltern □[8]	260	51.40 N	0.37 W
Chiltern Hills ⩕[2]	42	51.42 N	0.48 W
Chilton, Eng., U.K.	44	54.39 N	1.33 W
Chilton, Tx., U.S.	222	31.16 N	97.03 W
Chilton, Wi., U.S.	190	44.01 N	88.09 W
Chiluage	152	9.30 S	21.47 E
Chilubula Mission	154	10.09 S	31.00 E
Chilumba	154	10.28 S	34.12 E
Chilung	100	25.08 N	121.44 E
Chilung ≃	269d	25.07 N	121.27 E
Chilung Kang ⊂	269d	25.09 N	121.45 E
Chilung Shih □[7]	269d	25.08 N	121.45 E
Chiluvya	154	12.18 S	34.01 E
Chilwa, Lake ⊜	154	15.12 S	35.50 E
Chilwell	169	38.10 S	144.21 E
Chimaco	152	15.12 S	21.56 E
Chimacum	224	48.00 N	122.46 W
Chimacum Creek ≃	224	48.03 N	122.45 W
Chimakela	152	15.24 S	16.58 E
Chimaltenango	236	14.40 N	90.49 W
Chimaltenango □[5]	236	14.40 N	90.55 W
Chimaltitán	234	21.46 N	103.50 W
Chimán	246	8.42 N	78.37 W
Chimanimani National Park ♠	154	19.48 S	33.56 E
Chimay	50	50.03 N	4.19 E
Chimayo	200	36.00 N	105.55 W
Chimbarongo	252	34.42 S	71.03 W
Chimbas	252	31.29 S	68.32 W
Chimborazo □[4]	246	2.00 S	78.40 W
Chimborazo ∧	236	13.05 N	85.58 W
Chimborazo ∧[1]	246	1.28 S	78.48 W
Chimbote	248	9.05 S	78.36 W
Chimbu □[5]	164	6.05 S	145.00 E
Chimbua	152	16.32 S	15.08 E
Ch'imei Yü I	100	23.13 N	119.26 E
Chimichagua	246	9.15 N	73.49 W
Chimkent → Čimkent	85	42.18 N	69.36 E
Chimki	82	55.54 N	37.26 E
Chimki-Chovrino ◆[8]	265b	55.51 N	37.30 E
Chimkinskoje vodochranilišče ⊜[1]	265b	55.51 N	37.28 E
Chimney Reservoir ⊜[1]	204	41.25 N	117.10 W
Chimney Rock National Historic Site ⊥	198	41.39 N	103.20 W
Chimoio	156	19.08 S	33.29 E
Chimon Island I	276	41.04 N	73.23 W
Chimpay	252	39.10 S	66.09 W
Chimpembe	154	9.31 S	29.33 E
Chimpôro ≃	152	17.20 S	17.17 E
Chin □[8]	110	22.00 N	93.30 E
China, Méx.	232	25.42 N	99.14 W
Chinā, Nihon	174m	26.24 N	127.46 E
China (Zhongguo) □[1]	90	35.00 N	105.00 E
China, Tanjong ›	271c	1.14 N	103.51 E
Chinácota	246	7.37 N	72.36 W
China Grove	192	35.34 N	80.34 W
China Lake ⊜	204	35.46 N	117.39 W
China Lake Naval Weapons Center ■	204	35.35 N	117.10 W
Chinameca	236	13.30 N	88.21 W
China Meridional, Mar de → South China Sea ⊤[2]	108	10.00 N	113.00 E
Chinan, Taehan	98	35.48 N	127.25 E
Chinan → Jinan, Zhg.	98	36.40 N	116.57 E
Chinandega	236	12.37 N	87.09 W
Chinandega □[5]	236	12.45 N	87.05 W
China Spring	222	31.39 N	97.18 W
Chinati Peak ∧	196	29.57 N	104.29 W
Chinatown ◆[8]	282	37.48 N	122.26 W
Chincha Alta	248	13.27 S	76.08 W
Chinchaga ≃	176	58.50 N	118.20 W
Chincheros	248	13.27 S	73.44 W
Chinchiang → Quanzhou	100	24.54 N	118.35 E
Chinchilla, Austl.	166	26.45 S	150.38 E
Chinchilla, Pa., U.S.	210	41.28 N	75.41 W
Chinchiná	246	4.58 N	75.36 W
Chincholi	272c	19.10 N	73.08 E
Chinchón, Esp.	34	40.08 N	3.25 W
Chinch'ŏn, Taehan	98	36.52 N	127.26 E
Chinchorro, Banco ✣[4]	232	18.35 N	87.22 W
Chinchou → Jinzhou	104	41.07 N	121.08 E
Chincilla de Monte Aragón	34	38.55 N	1.43 W
Chincolco	252	32.13 S	70.50 W
Chincoteague	208	37.55 N	75.22 W
Chincoteague Bay ⊂	208	38.06 N	75.15 W
Chincoteague Inlet ⊂	208	37.53 N	75.25 W
Chinde	156	18.37 S	36.24 E
Chindo	98	34.28 N	126.15 E
Chin-do I	98	34.25 N	126.15 E
Chindong	98	35.07 N	128.29 E
Chindwinn ≃	110	21.26 N	95.15 E
Chine (la République populaire de) → China □[1], Asia	90	35.00 N	105.00 E
Chine (nationaliste) → Taiwan □[1], Asia	100	23.30 N	121.00 E
Chinen	174m	26.09 N	127.49 E
Chineni	123	33.02 N	75.17 E
Chine Orientale, Mer de → East China Sea ⊤[2]	90	30.00 N	126.00 E
Chinese Camp	226	37.52 N	120.26 W
Chinese Cemetery ◆	269f	14.38 N	120.59 E
Chinese University ᵾ[2]	271d	22.26 N	114.12 E
Chingamba	152	12.49 S	18.20 E
Chingansk	89	49.07 N	131.11 E
Chingarora Creek ≃	276	40.27 N	74.12 W
Ch'ingchiang → Qingjiang	100	33.35 N	119.02 E
Chingford ◆[8]	260	51.38 N	0.01 E
Chingleput	122	12.42 N	79.59 E
Chingmei ◆[8]	269d	24.59 N	121.32 E
Chingola	154	12.32 S	27.52 E
Chingoni	157a	12.48 S	45.08 E
Chingoroi	152	13.37 S	14.01 E
Chingshih → Jinshi	102	29.39 N	111.52 E
Ch'ingtao → Qingdao	98	36.06 N	120.19 E
Chingtechen → Jingdezhen	100	29.16 N	117.11 E
Ch'ingt'ung	269d	25.02 N	121.43 E
Chinguar	152	12.36 S	16.20 E
Chinguetti	150	20.27 N	12.22 W
Chingune	156	20.38 S	34.55 E
Chinhae	98	35.09 N	128.40 E
Chinhae-man ⊂	98	35.01 N	128.34 E
Chin Hills ⩕[2]	110	22.30 N	93.30 E
Chinhoyi	154	17.22 S	30.12 E
Chinhsien → Jinxian	98	39.04 N	121.40 E
Chinhua → Jinhua	100	29.07 N	119.39 E
Ch'inhuangtao → Qinhuangdao	98	39.56 N	119.36 E
Chīni	120	31.32 N	78.15 E
Chiniak, Cape ›	180	57.36 N	152.08 W
Chining → Jining, Zhg.	98	35.25 N	116.36 E
Chining → Jining, Zhg.	102	40.57 N	113.02 E
Chiniot	123	31.43 N	72.59 E
Chinit ≃	110	12.55 N	105.35 E
Chinitna Point ›	180	59.43 N	153.02 W
Chinizíua	156	19.00 S	35.09 E
Chinjan	120	30.34 N	67.58 E

Chinju	98	35.11 N	128.05 E
Chinkiang → Zhenjiang	106	32.13 N	119.26 E
Chinko ≃	136	4.50 N	23.53 E
Chinkuashih	100	25.07 N	121.51 E
Chin Lakes ⊜	182	49.37 N	112.13 W
Chinle	200	36.09 N	109.33 W
Chinle Creek ≃	200	37.12 N	109.43 W
Chinle Wash ∨	200	36.54 N	109.45 W
Chinley	262	53.20 N	1.56 W
Chinley Churn ∧[2]	262	53.21 N	1.57 W
Chinmen	100	24.27 N	118.21 E
Chinmen Tao I	100	24.27 N	118.23 E
Chinnampo → Namp'o	98	38.45 N	125.23 E
Chinnor	42	51.43 N	0.56 W
Chino, Nihon	94	35.59 N	138.09 E
Chino, Ca., U.S.	228	34.00 N	117.41 W
Chino Airport ⊠	280	33.59 N	117.38 W
Chino Creek ≃	280	33.53 N	117.38 W
Chino Hills ⩕[2]	280	33.56 N	117.45 W
Chinon	50	47.10 N	0.15 E
Chinook, Ab., Can.	184	51.27 N	110.56 W
Chinook, Mt., U.S.	202	48.35 N	109.13 W
Chinook, Wa., U.S.	224	46.16 N	123.56 W
Chinook Cove	182	51.14 N	120.10 W
Chino Valley	200	34.45 N	112.27 W
Chinowths Corner	226	36.20 N	119.19 W
Chinpāi	126	23.50 N	87.28 E
Chinquapin	192	34.49 N	77.49 W
Chinsali	154	10.34 S	32.03 E
Chinshan	100	25.13 N	121.38 E
Chinshui	100	24.36 N	120.53 E
Chintāmani	122	13.24 N	78.04 E
Chintembwe	154	13.25 S	33.59 E
Chintheche	154	11.52 S	34.09 E
Chinú	246	9.06 N	75.24 W
Chinunje	154	11.19 S	37.19 E
Chinwangtao → Qinhuangdao	98	39.56 N	119.36 E
Chiny	56	49.44 N	5.20 E
Chinyama Litapi	152	13.31 S	22.21 E
Chioco	154	16.25 S	32.50 E
Chioggia	64	45.13 N	12.17 E
Chiomonte	62	45.07 N	6.59 E
Chios → Khíos	38	38.22 N	26.08 E
Chios → Khíos I	38	38.22 N	26.00 E
Chipamanu (Xipamanu) ≃	248	10.43 S	67.50 W
Chipao	248	14.15 S	73.57 W
Chipata (Fort Jameson)	154	13.39 S	32.40 E
Chipei Tao I	100	23.45 N	119.37 E
Chipera	154	15.28 S	32.30 E
Chiperceni	38	47.32 N	28.50 E
Chiperone ∧	154	16.28 S	35.12 E
Chipili	154	10.44 S	29.04 E
Chiping	98	36.37 N	116.16 E
Chipinge	154	20.12 S	32.38 E
Chip Lake ⊜	182	53.40 N	115.20 W
Chipley	194	30.46 N	85.32 W
Chiplūn	122	17.32 N	73.31 E
Chipman	186	46.11 N	65.53 W
Chipogolo	154	6.52 S	36.02 E
Chipoka	154	14.00 S	34.31 E
Chipola ≃	192	30.01 N	85.05 W
Chippawa ◆[8]	284a	43.04 N	79.03 W
Chippawa Channel ≃[1]	284a	43.04 N	79.01 W
Chippego Lake ⊜	212	44.34 N	76.49 W
Chippenham	42	51.28 N	2.07 W
Chipperfield	260	51.42 N	0.29 W
Chippewa ≃, Mi., U.S.	190	43.35 N	84.17 W
Chippewa ≃, Mn., U.S.	198	44.56 N	95.44 W
Chippewa ≃, Wi., U.S.	190	44.25 N	92.10 W
Chippewa, East Branch ≃	198	45.20 N	95.36 W
Chippewa, East Fork ≃	190	45.53 N	91.05 W
Chippewa, Lake ⊜	190	45.56 N	91.13 W
Chippewa Bay ⊂	212	44.27 N	75.47 W
Chippewa Creek ≃	212	44.27 N	75.46 W
Chippewa Falls	190	44.56 N	91.23 W
Chippewa Lake	214	41.04 N	81.54 W
Chippewanuck Creek ≃	216	41.07 N	86.12 W
Chipping Campden	42	52.03 N	1.46 W
Chipping Norton	42	51.56 N	1.32 W
Chipping Ongar	42	51.43 N	0.15 E
Chipping Sodbury	42	51.33 N	2.24 W
Chippis	58	46.17 N	7.33 E
Chippokes Plantation State Park ♠	208	37.08 N	76.44 W
Chipps Island I	282	38.03 N	121.55 W
Chipre → Cyprus □[1]	130	35.00 N	33.00 E
Chipstead, Eng., U.K.	260	51.17 N	0.09 E
Chipstead, Eng., U.K.	260	51.18 N	0.10 W
Chipuriro	154	16.39 S	30.42 E
Chiquelequele	152	16.40 S	19.06 E
Chiquián	248	10.09 S	77.11 W
Chiquihuitlán	234	17.59 N	96.48 W
Chiquimula	236	14.48 N	89.33 W
Chiquimula □[5]	236	14.40 N	89.25 W
Chiquimulilla	236	14.05 N	90.23 W
Chiquinquirá	246	5.37 N	73.50 W
Chiquintirca	248	13.09 S	73.41 W
Chiquita	152	8.38 S	17.05 E
Chiquito ≃	234	18.29 N	101.07 W
Chiquito Creek ≃	226	37.20 N	119.20 W
Chira ≃	246	4.54 S	81.08 W
Chira, Isla I	236	10.06 N	85.09 W
Chirad	272c	19.09 N	73.07 E
Chiradzulu	154	15.42 S	35.10 E
Chirāgh Delhi ◆[8]	272a	28.32 N	77.14 E
Chīrāla	122	15.49 N	80.21 E
Chiramba	154	16.55 S	34.39 E
Chirape	156	21.18 S	33.33 E
Chirāwa	120	28.15 N	75.38 E
Chirchik → Čirčik	85	41.29 N	69.35 E
Chire (Shire) ≃	154	17.42 S	35.19 E
Chiredzi	154	21.03 S	31.45 E
Chireno	194	31.30 N	94.21 W
Chirens	62	45.25 N	5.33 E
Chirfa	146	20.57 N	12.21 E
Chīrgaon	124	25.35 N	78.49 E
Chiriaco ≃	248	5.05 S	78.19 W
Chiricahua Mountains ⩕	200	31.50 N	109.15 W
Chiricahua National Monument ♠	200	32.02 N	109.19 W
Chiricahua Peak ∧	200	31.52 N	109.20 W
Chiriguaná	246	9.22 N	73.36 W
Chirikof Island I	180	55.50 N	155.35 W
Chirilagua	236	13.13 N	88.08 W
Chirinos	248	5.16 S	78.52 W
Chiriquí	236	8.24 N	82.19 W
Chiriquí □[4]	236	8.30 N	82.00 W
Chiriquí, Golfo de ⊂	246	8.00 N	82.20 W
Chiriquí, Laguna de ⊂	236	9.03 N	82.00 W
Chiriquí Grande	236	8.57 N	82.07 W
Chiriquí Viejo ≃	236	8.20 N	82.41 W
Chirk	42	52.56 N	3.03 W
Chirki	126	24.03 N	86.09 E
Chirle	272c	18.56 N	73.02 E
Chirmiri	124	23.12 N	82.21 E
Chirnside	46	55.48 N	2.13 W
Chiromo	154	16.33 S	35.08 E
Chirovo	76	58.56 N	33.24 E
Chirripó ≃	236	10.41 N	83.41 W
Chirripó, Cerro ∧	236	9.29 N	83.30 W
Chirripó, Parque Nacional ♠	236	9.30 N	83.30 W
Chirsa	84	41.31 N	46.06 E
Chirundu	154	15.59 S	28.54 E
Chirvosti	265a	59.57 N	30.37 E
Chiryū	94	35.00 N	137.02 E

Chisago City	190	45.22 N	92.53 W
Chisamba	154	14.58 S	28.23 E
Chisana	180	62.09 N	142.10 W
Chisasibi	176	53.50 N	79.00 W
Chiscas	246	6.33 N	72.29 W
Chisec	236	15.49 N	90.17 W
Chiseldon	42	51.31 N	1.44 W
Chisenga	154	9.56 S	33.26 E
Chisep'o	98	34.50 N	128.42 E
Ch'ishan	100	22.53 N	120.28 E
Chishanji	98	36.56 N	122.23 E
Chishi	100	27.42 N	117.58 E
Chishisi	100	25.32 N	113.11 E
Chisholm, Al., U.S.	194	32.25 N	86.15 W
Chisholm, Me., U.S.	188	44.28 N	70.12 W
Chisholm, Mn., U.S.	190	47.29 N	92.53 W
Chisholm, Tx., U.S.	222	32.51 N	96.22 W
Chisholm Mills	182	54.55 N	114.08 W
Chishtiān Mandi	123	29.48 N	72.52 E
Chishui	102	28.29 N	105.38 E
Chishui ≃, Zhg.	102	28.53 N	105.48 E
Chishui ≃, Zhg.	107	28.49 N	105.50 E
Chishuihe	102	27.50 N	105.32 E
Chišig-Öndör	88	48.19 N	103.25 E
Chisimaio → Kismaayo	144	0.22 N	42.32 E
Chișinău (Kishinev)	38	47.00 N	28.50 E
Chișineu-Criș	38	46.31 N	21.31 E
Chislaviči	76	54.11 N	32.10 E
Chislehurst ◆[8]	260	51.25 N	0.04 E
Chisone ≃	62	44.49 N	7.25 E
Chisone, Valle del ∨	62	45.01 N	7.07 E
Chisos Mountains ⩕	196	29.15 N	103.20 W
Chisseaux	50	47.20 N	1.05 E
Chissengue	152	9.14 S	20.42 E
Chissilo	152	13.34 S	16.30 E
Chistochina	180	62.34 N	144.40 W
Chistopol → Čistopol'	80	55.21 N	50.37 E
Chiswellgreen	260	51.44 N	0.22 W
Chiswick ◆[8]	260	51.29 N	0.16 W
Chita, Bol.	248	20.06 S	66.57 W
Chita, Col.	246	6.11 N	72.28 W
Chita, Nihon	94	35.00 N	136.51 E
Chita → Čita, Ross.	88	52.03 N	113.30 E
Chitado	152	17.20 S	13.54 E
Chitagá	246	7.09 N	72.40 W
Chita-hantō ›[1]	94	34.50 N	136.53 E
Chitambo	154	12.55 S	30.39 E
Chitanda ≃	152	16.01 S	15.12 E
Chitarda	126	21.50 N	86.57 E
Chitata	152	13.47 S	15.43 E
Chitato	152	7.20 S	20.47 E
Chita-wan ⊂	94	34.47 N	136.58 E
Chițcani	38	46.47 N	29.36 E
Chitek ≃	184	54.06 N	108.16 W
Chitek Lake ⊜, Mb., Can.	184	52.26 N	99.25 W
Chitek Lake ⊜, Sk., Can.	184	53.44 N	107.47 W
Chitembo	152	13.34 S	16.40 E
Chitina	180	61.31 N	144.27 W
Chitina ≃	180	61.30 N	144.28 W
Chitipa	154	9.43 S	33.16 E
Chitokoloki	152	13.50 S	23.13 E
Chitose	92a	42.49 N	141.39 E
Chitose-chūtonchi, Rikujō-jieitai- ■	92a	42.46 N	141.40 E
Chitou Shan I	100	27.40 N	120.50 E
Chitra ≃[1]	126	22.53 N	89.40 E
Chitradurga	122	14.14 N	76.24 E
Chitrakūt Dham	124	25.11 N	80.52 E
Chitrāl	123	35.51 N	71.47 E
Chitrasāli	272b	22.52 N	88.09 E
Chitrāvati ≃	122	14.48 N	78.14 E
Chitré	236	7.58 N	80.26 W
Chittagong	120	22.20 N	91.50 E
Chittagong □[5]	120	23.00 N	91.00 E
Chīttāpur	122	17.07 N	77.05 E
Chittaranjan	126	23.52 N	86.52 E
Chittaurgarh	120	24.53 N	74.38 E
Chittenango	210	43.02 N	75.52 W
Chittenango Creek ≃	210	43.11 N	76.00 W
Chittenango Falls	210	42.59 N	75.50 W
Chittering	162	31.29 S	116.06 E
Chittoor	122	13.12 N	79.07 E
Chittūr	122	10.42 N	76.45 E
Chitu, Ityo.	144	8.36 N	37.59 E
Ch'itu, T'aiwan	269d	25.06 N	121.43 E
Chitungwiza	154	17.45 S	31.16 E
Chiuchiang → Jiujiang	100	29.44 N	115.59 E
Chíuchíu	252	22.21 S	68.39 W
Chiuduno	62	45.40 N	9.51 E
Chiumbe	152	12.29 S	16.08 E
Chiumbe ≃	152	7.00 S	21.12 E
Chiúme	152	15.03 S	21.14 E
Chiuppano	64	45.46 N	11.28 E
Chiuro	64	46.10 N	9.59 E
Chiusa (Klausen)	64	46.38 N	11.34 E
Chiusa di Pesio	62	44.19 N	7.40 E
Chiusa di San Michele	62	45.06 N	7.19 E
Chiusaforte	64	46.24 N	13.18 E
Chiusa Sclafani	70	37.41 N	13.16 E
Chiusella ≃	62	45.24 N	7.55 E
Chiusi	66	43.01 N	11.57 E
Chiusi, Lago di ⊜	66	43.03 N	11.58 E
Chiúta	154	15.34 S	33.17 E
Chiuta, Lake ⊜	154	14.55 S	35.50 E
Chiv	84	41.46 N	47.54 E
Chiva	72	41.24 N	60.22 E
Chivacoa	246	10.10 N	68.54 W
Chivasso	62	45.11 N	7.53 E
Chivato, Punta ›	232	27.05 N	111.59 W
Chivay	248	15.40 S	71.35 W
Chivhu	154	19.01 S	30.53 E
Chivilcoy	252	34.53 S	60.01 W
Chivirira Falls └	154	21.14 S	32.20 E
Chiwanda	154	11.22 S	34.54 E
Chiwawa ≃	224	47.47 N	120.40 W
Chixi	100	28.22 N	116.22 E
Chixoy (Salinas) ≃	232	16.28 N	90.33 W
Chixoy, Embalse ⊜[1]	236	15.15 N	90.30 W
Chiyoda, Nihon	94	36.12 N	139.26 E
Chiyoda, Nihon	94	36.11 N	140.14 E
Chiyoda, Nihon	96	34.41 N	132.32 E
Chiyoda ◆[8]	268	35.41 N	139.44 E
Chizarira National Park ♠	154	17.45 S	28.00 E
Chizhen	100	31.55 N	118.12 E
Chizizhen	100	32.22 N	115.11 E
Chizu	96	35.16 N	134.14 E
Chjargas	88	49.32 N	93.48 E
Chjargas nuur ⊜	88	49.12 N	93.24 E
Chkalov → Orenburg	86	51.54 N	55.06 E
Chkalove	78	46.28 N	34.11 E
Chlebnikovo, Ross.	80	56.38 N	49.56 E
Chlebnikovo, Ross.	265b	55.58 N	37.31 E
Chlebodarnyj	80	46.41 N	40.50 E
Chlevnoje	76	52.12 N	39.05 E
Chloride	200	35.24 N	114.11 W
Chlum	60	48.52 N	13.55 E
Chlum ∧	61	48.42 N	14.04 E
Chmelevicy	80	57.45 N	46.22 E
Chmelevo	82	56.09 N	39.08 E
Chmelita	76	55.25 N	33.53 E
Chmel'niki, Ross.	82	56.52 N	38.13 E
Chmel'niki, Ross.	82	56.53 N	38.39 E
Chmielnik	30	50.37 N	20.46 E
Chmost' ≃	76	54.45 N	32.34 E
Choa Chu Kang	271c	1.22 N	103.41 E
Choāli	272b	22.24 N	88.24 E
Chŏâm Khsant	110	14.13 N	104.56 E
Choba	154	2.26 N	38.03 E
Chobe □[5]	156	18.30 S	25.00 E
Chobe ≃	156	17.50 S	25.05 E
Chobeju	24	64.53 N	60.10 E
Chobe National Park ♠	156	18.45 S	24.15 E
Chobham	260	51.21 N	0.36 W

≃	River	Fluß	Río	Rivière	Rio
≍	Canal	Kanal	Canal	Canal	Canal
└	Waterfall, Rapids	Wasserfall, Stromschnellen	Cascada, Rápidos	Chute d'eau, Rapides	Cascata, Rápidos
)(	Strait	Meeresstraße	Estrecho	Détroit	Estreito
⊂	Bay, Gulf	Bucht, Golf	Bahía, Golfo	Baie, Golfe	Baía, Golfo
⊜	Lake, Lakes	See, Seen	Lago, Lagos	Lac, Lacs	Lago, Lagos
☷	Swamp	Sumpf	Pantano	Marais	Pântano
⊡	Ice Features, Glacier	Eis- und Gletscherformen	Accidentes Glaciales	Formes glaciaires	Acidentes glaciares
⊤	Other Hydrographic Features	Andere Hydrographische Objekte	Otros Elementos Hidrográficos	Autres données hydrographiques	Outros acidentes hidrográficos

✣	Submarine Features	Untermeerische Objekte	Accidentes Submarinos	Formes de relief sous-marin	Acidentes submarinos
□	Political Unit	Politische Einheit	Unidad Politica	Entité politique	Unidade política
ᵾ	Cultural Institution	Kulturelle Institution	Institución Cultural	Institution culturelle	Instituição cultural
⊥	Historical Site	Historische Stätte	Sitio Histórico	Site historique	Sitio histórico
♠	Recreational Site	Erholungs- und Ferienort	Sitio de Recreo	Centre de loisirs	Area de Lazer
⊠	Airport	Flughafen	Aeropuerto	Aéroport	Aeroporto
■	Military Installation	Militäranlage	Instalación Militar	Installation militaire	Instalação militar
◆	Miscellaneous	Verschiedenes	Misceláneo	Divers	Diversos

Chobham Common ♦ 260 51.23 N 0.37 W
Chobi 84 42.21 N 41.53 E
Chocamán 234 18.59 N 97.01 W
Choccolocco Creek ≐ 194 33.33 N 86.11 W
Choceň 30 50.00 N 16.13 E
Chocenice 60 49.33 N 13.31 E
Chochis, Cerro ∧ 248 18.04 S 60.03 W
Choch'iwŏn 98 36.37 N 127.18 E
Chochloma 80 56.58 N 43.54 E
Chŏchmor't 88 47.21 N 94.33 E
Chochol'skij 78 51.34 N 38.45 E
Cho Chu 110 21.54 N 105.39 E
Chocianów 30 51.25 N 15.55 E
Chociwel 30 53.28 N 15.19 E
Chocó □[5] 246 6.00 N 77.00 W
Chocolate Bay ⊂ 222 29.11 N 95.09 W
Chocolate Bayou ≐ 222 29.13 N 95.13 W
Chocolate Mountains ⋏ 204 33.20 N 115.15 W
Chocontá 246 5.09 N 73.41 W
Chocope 248 7.47 S 79.13 W
Choctawhatchee, East Fork ≐ 194 31.21 N 85.33 W
Choctawhatchee, West Fork ≐ 194 31.21 N 85.33 W
Choctawhatchee Bay ⊂ 194 30.25 N 86.21 W
Choctaw Lake ⊜[1] 218 39.58 N 83.29 W
Chodarus 88 52.36 N 99.19 E
Chodavaram 122 17.50 N 82.57 E
Chodecz 30 52.24 N 19.01 E
Ch'o-do I, C.M.I.K. 98 38.32 N 124.50 E
Ch'o-do I, Taehan 98 34.14 N 127.15 E
Chodoi 114 2.50 N 101.27 E
Chodosy 76 53.56 N 31.29 E
Chodov 54 50.11 N 12.43 E
Chodovaja Griva 80 57.08 N 50.16 E
Chodovaricha 24 68.57 N 53.40 E
Chodz' ≐ 84 44.43 N 40.45 E
Chodžaimetk 85 39.37 N 69.14 E
Chodžakala 128 38.43 N 56.20 E
Chodžejli 72 42.48 N 59.25 E
Chodzież 30 52.59 N 16.56 E
Choele-Choel 252 39.16 S 65.41 W
Chofombo 154 14.35 S 31.50 E
Chōfu 94 35.39 N 139.33 E
Chofu Airport ✈ 268 35.40 N 139.32 E
Chogo Lungma Glacier ⊓ 123 35.52 N 75.19 E
Chogot 88 53.15 N 105.52 E
Choiceland 184 53.27 N 104.25 W
Choichuff, Laga ≐ 154 1.34 N 39.24 E
Choire, Loch ⊜ 46 58.13 N 4.21 W
Choisel 261 48.41 N 2.01 E
Choiseul 241f 13.47 N 61.03 W
Choiseul I 175e 7.05 S 157.00 E
Choiseul Sound 𝔘 254 51.57 S 58.35 W
Choisy 58 45.59 N 6.03 E
Choisy-le-Roi 261 48.46 N 2.25 E
Choix 232 26.43 N 108.17 W
Chojna 30 52.58 N 14.28 E
Chojnice 30 53.42 N 17.34 E
Chojniki 78 51.53 N 29.56 E
Chojnów 30 51.17 N 15.56 E
Chōkai-san ∧ 92 39.06 N 140.03 E
Choke ⋏ 144 10.45 N 37.35 E
Choke Canyon Lake ⊜[1] 196 28.30 N 98.20 W
Chokio 198 45.34 N 96.10 W
Chokoloskee 220 25.48 N 81.21 W
Chokwé 156 24.36 S 33.00 E
Cholame 226 35.43 N 120.17 W
Cholame Creek ≐ 226 35.39 N 120.22 W
Cholame Hills ⋏[2] 226 35.45 N 120.30 W
Cholbon 88 51.53 N 116.15 E
Choldarkipčak 85 39.51 N 68.52 E
Cholet 32 47.04 N 0.53 W
Cholila 254 42.31 S 71.27 W
Chŏlla Namdo □[4] 98 34.45 N 127.00 E
Chŏlla Pukdo □[4] 98 35.45 N 127.15 E
Cholm 76 57.09 N 31.11 E
Cholmeč', Bela. 78 52.09 N 30.37 E
Cholmec, Ross. 76 56.21 N 33.21 E
Cholmogorovka 86 44.25 N 78.31 E
Cholmogorskaja 24 63.49 N 40.39 E
Cholmogory 24 64.15 N 41.40 E
Cholmsk 89 47.03 N 142.03 E
Cholmskij 78 44.52 N 38.24 E
Cholmy 82 54.56 N 38.33 E
Cholm-Žirkovskij 76 55.31 N 33.29 E
Choloj ≐ 88 53.12 N 112.47 E
Choloma 236 15.34 N 87.56 W
Chölönbujr 88 47.55 N 112.57 E
Cholopeniči 76 54.31 N 28.58 E
Ch'ŏlsan 98 39.46 N 124.40 E
Cholsey 42 51.34 N 1.10 W
Choltobino 82 54.11 N 38.28 E
Choltoson 88 50.20 N 103.20 E
Choluj, Ross. 80 56.34 N 41.53 E
Choluj, Ross. 80 56.04 N 42.08 E
Cholula [de Rivadabia] 234 19.04 N 98.18 W
Choluteca 236 13.18 N 87.12 W
Choluteca □[5] 236 13.20 N 87.10 W
Choluteca ≐ 236 13.07 N 87.19 W
Choma 154 16.48 S 26.59 E
Chomedey ✦[8] 275a 45.32 N 73.44 W
Chomen Swamp ≡ 144 9.25 N 37.20 E
Chomérac 62 44.42 N 4.39 E
Chomičev 80 48.11 N 45.01 E
Chomiomo ∧ 124 28.01 N 88.31 E
Cho Moi, Viet 110 10.33 N 105.24 E
Cho Moi, Viet 269c 10.51 N 106.38 E
Chomo Lhāri ∧ 124 27.50 N 89.15 E
Chom Thong 110 18.25 N 98.41 E
Chomūm 120 27.10 N 75.44 E
Chomutov 54 50.28 N 13.26 E
Chomutovka 78 51.56 N 34.33 E
Chomutovka ≐ 54 50.11 N 13.37 E
Chomutovo, Ross. 76 52.51 N 37.27 E
Chomutovo, Ross. 88 52.28 N 104.25 E
Chomutovskaja 83 47.03 N 40.04 E
Chōnan, Nihon 94 35.24 N 140.14 E
Ch'ŏnan, Taehan 98 36.48 N 127.09 E
Chon'atino 82 55.11 N 38.07 E
Chon Buri 110 13.22 N 100.59 E
Chonchi 254 42.38 S 73.47 W
Choncholoj 88 51.08 N 108.14 E
Chon Daen 110 16.11 N 100.51 E
Chone 246 0.41 S 80.06 W
Chone ≐ 246 0.35 S 80.25 W
Chong'an 100 27.45 N 118.02 E
Ch'ŏngch'ŏn-gang ≐ 98 39.35 N 125.28 E
Ch'ŏngdan 98 37.58 N 125.56 E
Chongde 106 30.32 N 120.26 E
Ch'ŏngdo 98 35.38 N 128.43 E
Chonggu 106 31.12 N 121.10 E
Ch'ŏngha 98 36.13 N 129.20 E
Ch'onghak-ni 271b 37.43 N 127.05 E
Chonghe 89 44.43 N 127.45 E
Ch'ŏngjin 98 41.47 N 129.50 E
Chŏngju, C.M.I.K. 98 39.41 N 125.13 E
Ch'ŏngju, Taehan 98 36.39 N 127.31 E
Chŏng Kal 110 13.57 N 103.35 E
Chongkanzhen 107 30.09 N 105.37 E
Chongli (Xiwanzi) 98 40.54 N 115.16 E
Chongming 106 31.37 N 121.24 E
Chongming Dao I 106 31.36 N 121.33 E
Chongoene 156 25.00 S 33.47 E
Chongor 102 45.59 N 112.45 E
Chongos Bajo 248 12.07 S 75.16 W
Chongoyape 248 6.39 S 79.24 W
Chong Pang 271c 1.26 N 103.50 E
Chŏngp'yŏng-chŏsuji ⊜[1] 98 37.40 N 127.30 E
Chongqing, Zhg. 107 30.39 N 103.41 E
Chongqing (Chungking), Zhg. 107 29.34 N 106.35 E
Chongren, Zhg. 100 29.37 N 120.43 E
Chongren, Zhg. 100 27.46 N 116.01 E
Chongru 100 27.01 N 120.10 E
Ch'ŏngsan 98 36.22 N 127.46 E
Ch'ŏngsan-do I 98 34.11 N 126.54 E
Chongshi 100 25.24 N 115.28 E
Chŏngsŏn 98 37.22 N 128.38 E
Ch'ŏngsong 98 41.47 N 129.48 E
Chŏngŭp 98 35.36 N 126.51 E
Chongwe ≐ 154 15.43 S 29.20 E
Chongwu 100 24.53 N 118.55 E
Chongxi 98 42.07 N 128.59 E
Chongxin 102 35.13 N 107.29 E
Ch'ŏngyang, Taehan 98 36.27 N 126.48 E
Chongyang, Zhg. 100 29.33 N 114.00 E
Chongyang ≐ 100 27.18 N 118.08 E
Chongyi 100 25.44 N 114.18 E
Chongzuo 102 22.21 N 107.26 E
Choni 84 42.20 N 42.25 E
Chŏnju 98 35.49 N 127.08 E
Chonkham 120 27.48 N 96.02 E
Ch'ŏnma 98 40.03 N 125.01 E
Chonobad 85 40.48 N 72.58 E
Chonos, Archipiélago de los II 254 45.00 S 74.00 W
Ch'ŏnsu-ri 98 41.43 N 128.45 E
Chontaleña, Cordillera ⋏ 236 11.50 N 84.50 W
Chontales □[5] 236 12.05 N 85.10 W
Chon Thanh 110 11.24 N 106.36 E
Chŏnŭi 98 36.42 N 127.11 E
Chonuu 74 66.27 N 143.06 E
Chonzie, Ben ∧ 46 56.27 N 3.59 W
Cho Oyu → Chopu ∧ 124 28.06 N 86.39 E
Chop 78 48.26 N 22.10 E
Chopda 120 21.15 N 75.18 E
Cho Phuoc Hai 110 10.26 N 107.18 E
Chopim ≐ 252 25.35 S 53.05 W
Chopinzinho 252 25.51 S 52.30 W
Chopon 124 24.31 N 83.02 E
Chop'or ≐ 80 49.36 N 42.19 E
Chop'orskij zapovednik ✦[4] 80 51.15 N 41.48 E
Chopovychi 78 50.49 N 27.58 E
Choptank ≐ 208 38.38 N 76.13 W
Chopu ∧ 124 28.06 N 86.39 E
Chopwell 44 54.55 N 1.49 W
Chor 89 47.53 N 134.58 E
Chor ≐ 89 47.48 N 134.43 E
Chora Saādatpur 272a 28.36 N 77.21 E
Chordil sar'dag ⋏ 88 50.50 N 99.40 E
Chorejver 24 67.25 N 58.03 E
Chorges 62 44.33 N 6.17 E
Chorin ⊥ 54 52.54 N 13.52 E
Chorinsk 88 52.10 N 109.46 E
Chorley 44 53.39 N 2.39 W
Chorley □[8] 262 53.38 N 2.38 W
Chorleywood 260 51.39 N 0.31 W
Chorlovo 82 55.20 N 38.49 E
Chorlton-cum-Hardy ✦[8] 262 53.27 N 2.17 W
Chorna 78 47.37 N 29.20 E
Chornobay 78 49.41 N 32.19 E
Chornobayivka 78 46.42 N 32.32 E
Chornobyl' 78 51.16 N 30.14 E
Chornomors'ke, Ukr. 78 45.30 N 32.42 E
Chornomors'ke, Ukr. 78 45.03 N 35.58 E
Chornukhy 78 50.16 N 32.57 E
Chornukhyne 83 48.19 N 38.30 E
Chornyy Ostriv 78 49.32 N 26.46 E
Chornyy Tashlyk ≐ 78 48.11 N 30.51 E
Chorog 120 37.31 N 71.33 E
Chorol' 89 44.25 N 132.04 E
Chorolque, Cerro ∧ 248 20.56 S 66.01 W
Choros, Isla I 252 29.16 S 71.33 W
Chorošovo 82 55.08 N 38.47 E
Chorošovo ✦[8] 265b 55.47 N 37.28 E
Choroszcz 30 53.09 N 22.59 E
Chorreras 232 28.50 N 105.18 W
Chorrillos 286d 12.10 S 77.02 W
Chorrochó 250 8.59 S 39.06 W
Chorro Creek ≐ 226 35.20 N 120.50 W
Chort'ak, gora ∧ 88 53.15 N 110.45 E
Chortkiv 78 49.01 N 25.48 E
Chortomlyk 78 47.37 N 34.09 E
Ch'ŏrwŏn 98 38.16 N 127.12 E
Chorzele 30 53.16 N 20.55 E
Ch'osan 98 40.50 N 125.47 E
Chosanch'am 98 40.22 N 126.11 E
Chosedachard 24 67.02 N 59.22 E
Chosen 220 26.42 N 80.41 W
Chošeutovo 80 47.02 N 47.50 E
Chōshi 94 35.44 N 140.50 E
Choshi-ōhashi ✦[5] 94 35.44 N 140.50 E
Chōshi-zuka-kofun ⊥ 94 34.42 N 137.50 E
Choshui ≐ 100 24.03 N 120.24 E
Chosica 248 11.54 S 76.42 W
Chos Malal 252 37.23 S 70.16 W
Chosŏn Minjujuŭi In'min Konghwaguk → Korea, North □[1] 98 40.00 N 127.00 E
Chosrech 84 41.59 N 47.18 E
Chosta 84 43.33 N 39.53 E
Choszczno 30 53.10 N 15.26 E
Chota 248 6.33 S 78.39 W
Chotanāgpur Plateau ⋏[1] 124 23.30 N 84.30 E
Chotča ≐ 82 56.54 N 37.35 E
Choteau 202 47.48 N 112.10 W
Choteau Creek ≐ 198 42.51 N 98.09 W
Chotěboř 30 49.43 N 15.40 E
Chotěšov 60 49.39 N 13.12 E
Chotila 120 22.25 N 71.11 E
Chotilovo 76 57.44 N 34.05 E
Chotimsk 76 53.26 N 32.35 E
Chotisino 82 54.24 N 36.33 E
Chot'kovo, Ross. 76 53.46 N 35.14 E
Chot'kovo, Ross. 76 52.56 N 35.23 E
Chot'kovo, Ross. 82 56.15 N 38.00 E
Chotovn'a 76 53.17 N 30.32 E
Chotuš' 82 54.32 N 37.44 E
Chotynec 76 53.08 N 35.24 E
Chotyniči 76 52.38 N 26.18 E
Chotyrboky 78 50.02 N 27.01 E
Chouchiak'ou → Shangshui 100 33.33 N 114.34 E
Chouk'ou → Shangshui 100 33.33 N 114.34 E
Choûm 148 21.18 N 13.01 W
Chouteau 196 36.11 N 95.20 W
Chovaling 85 38.21 N 69.58 E
Chovd, Mong. 86 48.08 N 91.23 E
Chovd, Mong. 86 48.01 N 91.38 E
Chovd, Mong. 86 49.16 N 90.55 E
Chovd, Mong. 102 44.42 N 102.24 E
Chovd □[4] 86 48.00 N 91.30 E
Chovd ≐ 90 48.06 N 92.11 E
Chövsgöl 102 43.36 N 109.39 E
Chövsgöl □[4] 88 50.00 N 100.00 E
Chövsgöl nuur ⊜ 88 51.00 N 100.30 E
Chovu-Aksy 88 51.11 N 93.53 E
Chowan ≐ 192 36.00 N 76.40 W
Chowchilla 226 37.07 N 120.15 W
Chowchilla ≐ 226 37.07 N 120.32 W
Chowchilla, East Fork ≐ 226 37.20 N 119.50 W
Chowchilla, West Fork ≐ 226 37.20 N 119.50 W
Chowkay 123 34.41 N 70.56 E
Chown, Mount ∧ 182 53.24 N 119.22 W
Ch'owŏn-ni 98 39.40 N 127.17 E
Choya 252 28.30 S 64.52 W
Choyak-to I 98 34.22 N 126.54 E
Chrapun' 78 51.42 N 27.29 E
Chr'aščevka 80 53.48 N 49.06 E
Chrást 60 49.48 N 13.29 E
Chrebtovo 82 56.35 N 38.16 E
Chrenovoje 80 51.07 N 40.17 E
Chreščatij 83 49.37 N 39.42 E
Chřibská 54 50.50 N 14.29 E
Chříč 60 49.57 N 13.39 E
Chriesman 222 30.36 N 96.46 W
Chrisman 194 39.48 N 87.40 W
Chrissiesmeer 158 26.16 S 30.13 E
Chrissiesmeer ⊜ 158 26.19 S 30.13 E
Christanshåb (Qasigiannguit) 176 68.50 N 51.12 W
Christchurch, N.Z. 172 43.32 S 172.38 E
Christchurch, Eng., U.K. 42 50.44 N 1.45 W
Christ Church Cathedral ✝[1] 273a 6.27 N 3.23 E
Christian □[6] 219 39.33 N 89.18 W
Christian ≐ 180 66.36 N 145.49 W
Christian, Cape ⊳ 176 70.31 N 68.18 W
Christian, Point ⊳ 174e 25.04 S 130.07 W
Christiana, Jam. 241q 18.10 N 77.29 W
Christiana, S. Afr. 158 27.52 S 25.08 E
Christiana, De., U.S. 285 39.39 N 75.39 W
Christiana, Pa., U.S. 208 39.57 N 75.59 W
Christiana Creek ≐ 216 41.41 N 85.59 W
Christianburg 218 38.17 N 85.06 W
Christian Channel 𝔘 212 44.47 N 80.08 W
Christian Island I 212 44.50 N 80.13 W
Christian Island Indian Reserve ✦[4] 212 44.50 N 80.10 W
Christiansburg, Oh., U.S. 218 40.03 N 84.01 W
Christiansburg, Va., U.S. 192 37.07 N 80.24 W
Christiansfeld 41 55.21 N 9.29 E
Christiansø I 26 55.19 N 15.12 E
Christian Sound 𝔘 180 55.56 N 134.40 W
Christiansted 241n 17.45 N 64.42 W
Christie, Mount ∧ 180 63.01 N 129.40 W
Christie, Mount ∧[2] 216 42.53 N 83.20 W
Christie Bay ⊂ 176 62.32 N 111.10 W
Christie Lake ⊜, Mb., Can. 184 56.54 N 96.56 W
Christie Lake ⊜, On., Can. 212 44.48 N 76.26 W
Christina ≐, Ab., Can. 184 56.40 N 111.03 W
Christina ≐, De., U.S. 285 39.43 N 75.31 W
Christina Lake ⊜, Ab., Can. 182 55.38 N 110.55 W
Christina Lake ⊜, B.C., Can. 182 49.05 N 118.14 W
Christmas 220 28.32 N 81.01 W
Christmas Bay ⊂ 222 29.03 N 95.11 W
Christmas Creek 162 18.53 S 125.55 E
Christmas Creek ≐ 162 18.29 S 125.23 E
Christmas Island □[2], Oc. 108 10.30 S 105.40 E
Christmas Island □[2], Oc. 112 10.30 S 105.40 E
Christmas Island → Kiritimati I[1] 174o 1.52 N 157.20 W
Christmas Mountain ∧ 180 64.34 N 160.34 W
Christmas Ridge ✦[3] 14 5.00 N 160.00 W
Christoforovo 24 60.53 N 47.13 E
Christ of the Andes → Cristo Redentor ⊥ 252 32.50 S 70.05 W
Christoph Columbus-Spitze → Cristóbal Colón, Pico ∧ 246 10.50 N 73.41 W
Christopher 194 37.58 N 89.03 W
Christopher, Lake ⊜ 162 24.49 S 127.42 E
Christoval 196 31.12 N 100.30 W
Chroma ≐ 74 71.36 N 144.49 E
Chromtau 86 50.17 N 58.27 E
Chrudim 30 49.57 N 15.48 E
Chrustal'nyj 89 44.24 N 135.06 E
Chrzanów 30 50.09 N 19.24 E
Chu (Xam) ≐, Asia 110 19.53 N 105.45 E
Chu ≐, Zhg. 100 32.08 N 118.43 E
Chu ≐, Zhg. 106 32.15 N 119.03 E
Chuādanga 124 23.38 N 88.51 E
Chualar 226 36.34 N 121.31 W
Chuanbu 106 31.17 N 119.49 E
Chuanchang ≡ 100 33.46 N 119.51 E
Chuanergu 105 39.20 N 117.43 E
Chuan'gang 106 31.57 N 121.04 E
Chuangjiapuzi 104 40.50 N 124.06 E
Chuanliao 100 28.17 N 120.13 E
Chuansha 106 31.12 N 121.42 E
Chuanshan 100 29.53 N 121.57 E
Chuanxindian 104 41.25 N 120.30 E
Chuanyao Gang ⊂ 106 32.12 N 121.25 E
Chuathbaluk 180 61.40 N 159.15 W
Chubbuck 202 42.55 N 112.27 W
Chūbu-Sangaku-kokuritsu-kōen ♦ 94 36.30 N 137.41 E
Chubut □[4] 254 44.00 S 69.00 W
Chubut ≐ 254 43.20 S 65.03 W
Ch'üchiang → Shaoguan 100 24.50 N 113.37 E
Chuchi Lake ⊜ 182 55.10 N 124.33 W
Chuchou → Zhuzhou 100 27.50 N 113.09 E
Chu Chua 182 51.21 N 120.10 W
Chuchuwayha Indian Reserve ✦[4] 182 49.21 N 120.06 W
Chuckatuck 208 36.52 N 76.35 W
Chučni 84 41.57 N 47.55 E
Chucuito 248 15.53 S 69.53 W
Chucun 100 33.04 N 116.32 E
Chucunaque ≐ 246 8.09 N 77.44 W
Chudan ≐ 88 52.08 N 109.40 E
Chudanskij chrebet ⋏ 88 52.00 N 110.00 E
Chudeč 60 49.58 N 13.05 E
Chudleigh 42 50.36 N 3.38 W
Chudniv 78 50.04 N 28.06 E
Chudojelan' 88 54.42 N 99.37 E
Chudžand (Leninabad) 85 40.17 N 69.37 E
Chudžand □[4] 85 39.15 N 69.30 E
Chudzirt 86 47.05 N 91.10 E
Chuen Lung 271d 22.24 N 114.06 E
Chugach Islands II 180 59.06 N 151.42 W
Chugach Mountains ⋏ 180 61.00 N 145.00 W
Chuginadak Island I 180 52.49 N 169.50 W
Chūgoku-sanchi ⋏ 96 34.58 N 132.57 E
Chugwater 200 41.45 N 104.49 W
Chugwater Creek ≐ 198 42.07 N 104.51 W
Chugyn-ri 271b 37.39 N 126.50 E
Chūhar Kāna 123 31.45 N 73.48 E
Chuhe 100 34.03 N 113.35 E
Chuhuichupa 232 29.38 N 108.22 W
Chuhuyiv 78 49.50 N 36.41 E
Chuhynka 83 48.55 N 39.39 E
Chuí 252 33.41 S 53.27 W
Chuius Mountain ∧ 182 54.51 N 124.30 W
Chukai 114 4.15 N 103.25 E
Chukchi Sea ⊤[2] 16 69.00 N 171.00 W
Chuke Hu ⊜ 120 31.40 N 88.00 E
Chukou 100 25.44 N 113.22 E
Chulalongkorn University ✝[2] 269a 13.44 N 100.33 E
Chula Vista 228 32.38 N 117.05 W
Chuld 102 45.04 N 105.35 E
Chulga ≐ 24 64.20 N 61.00 E
Chullora 274a 33.54 S 151.04 E
Chulmleigh 42 50.55 N 3.52 W
Chulo 84 41.41 N 42.18 E
Chulp'o 98 35.37 N 126.40 E
Chulucanas 248 5.06 S 80.10 W
Chulumani 248 16.24 S 67.31 W
Chuluota 220 28.38 N 81.10 W
Chuma 248 15.24 S 68.56 W
Chumalag 84 43.14 N 44.28 E
Chumbicha 252 28.52 S 66.14 W
Chummi, ozero ⊜ 89 50.18 N 137.17 E
Chum Phae 110 16.32 N 102.06 E
Chumphon 110 10.30 N 99.10 E
Chumphon Buri 110 15.21 N 103.24 E
Chumpi 248 15.06 S 73.46 W
Chum Saeng 110 15.54 N 100.19 E
Chumunjin 98 37.54 N 128.49 E
Chunal 262 53.25 N 1.57 W
Chunan, T'aiwan 100 24.41 N 120.52 E
Chun'an, Zhg. 100 29.35 N 118.58 E
Chunār 124 25.08 N 82.54 E
Chuncheon → Ch'unch'ŏn 98 37.52 N 127.43 E
Chunchi, Ec. 246 2.17 S 78.55 W
Chunchi, Zhg. 100 27.22 N 119.20 E
Ch'unch'ŏn 98 37.52 N 127.43 E
Chunchula 194 30.55 N 88.12 W
Chūnd 123 31.26 N 72.16 E
Chung-ang University ✝[2] 271b 37.30 N 126.58 E
Chungari ≐ 89 50.04 N 136.55 E
Ch'ungch'ŏng Namdo □[4] 98 36.30 N 127.00 E
Ch'ungch'ŏng Pukdo □[4] 98 36.45 N 128.00 E
Chunggang-ni 98 40.52 N 127.20 E
Chung Hau 271d 22.16 N 114.00 E
Chungho 269d 25.00 N 121.30 E
Chung Hsing Bridge ✦[5] 269d 25.03 N 121.29 E
Chunghwa 98 38.52 N 125.47 E
Ch'ungju 98 36.58 N 127.58 E
Chungking → Chongqing 107 29.34 N 106.35 E
Chungli 100 24.57 N 121.13 E
Chungliao 100 22.41 N 121.28 E
Ch'ungmu 98 34.51 N 128.25 E
Chungp'u 100 23.25 N 120.31 E
Chungp'yŏngjang 98 41.11 N 128.03 E
Chungsam-ni 98 38.34 N 127.09 E
Chŭngsan 98 39.06 N 125.22 E
Chŭngsanha-ri ✦[8] 271b 37.35 N 126.54 E
Chungshan → Zhongshan 100 22.31 N 113.22 E
Chungshan Bridge ✦[5] 269d 25.05 N 121.31 E
Chunguj ≐ 88 48.51 N 93.32 E
Chungyang Shanmo ⋏ 100 23.30 N 121.00 E
Chunheji 100 32.12 N 115.22 E
Chunhua, Zhg. 102 34.50 N 108.31 E
Chunhua, Zhg. 106 31.56 N 118.56 E
Chunhuhux 232 19.12 N 88.55 W
Chūniān 123 30.58 N 73.59 E
Chuntuquí 232 17.31 N 90.09 W
Chünüj ≐ 88 48.48 N 102.00 E
Chunya 154 8.32 S 33.25 E
Ch'unyang, Taehan 98 36.56 N 128.54 E
Chunyang, Zhg. 89 43.43 N 129.28 E
Chunzach 84 42.33 N 46.43 E
Chūō 96 35.00 N 133.58 E
Chūō ✦[8], Nihon 268 35.40 N 139.47 E
Chūō ✦[8], Nihon 270 34.42 N 135.11 E
Chuŏr Phnum Krâvanh ⋏ 110 12.00 N 103.15 E
Chuosijia 102 31.53 N 101.59 E
Chupaca 248 12.04 S 75.19 W
Chupadera Arroyo V 200 33.47 N 106.37 W
Chupadero, Cerro ∧ 200 31.01 N 111.37 W
Chupakhivka 78 50.23 N 34.36 E
Chupara Point ⊳ 241r 10.48 N 61.22 W
Chuquibamba 248 15.50 S 72.39 W
Chuquibambilla 248 14.07 S 72.43 W
Chuquicamata 252 22.19 S 68.56 W
Chuquisaca □[5] 248 20.00 S 64.20 W
Chuquitanta 286d 11.58 S 77.06 W
Chur 58 46.51 N 9.32 E
Churach ≐ 88 48.37 N 110.42 E
Churāchāndpur 120 24.20 N 93.40 E
Churāmankāti 126 23.14 N 89.09 E
Churcampa 248 12.42 S 74.24 W
Church 262 53.45 N 2.24 W
Churchdown 42 51.53 N 2.10 W
Church Hill 192 36.31 N 82.42 W
Churchill, Mb., Can. 176 58.46 N 94.10 W
Churchill, Oh., U.S. 214 41.09 N 80.39 W
Churchill, Pa., U.S. 279b 40.27 N 79.51 W
Churchill, Va., U.S. 284c 38.54 N 77.10 W
Churchill ≐, Can. 176 58.47 N 94.12 W
Churchill ≐, Nf., Can. 176 53.30 N 60.10 W
Churchill, Cape ⊳ 176 58.46 N 93.12 W
Churchill, Mount ∧, B.C., Can. 182 49.58 N 123.51 W
Churchill, Mount ∧, Ak., U.S. 180 61.25 N 141.43 W
Churchill Downs ♦ 218 38.12 N 85.46 W
Churchill Falls ⊥ 176 53.35 N 64.27 W
Churchill Lake ⊜ 184 55.55 N 108.20 W
Churchill National Park ♦ 169 37.58 S 145.17 E
Church Point 194 30.24 N 92.12 W
Church Rock 200 35.32 N 108.35 W
Church Street 260 51.26 N 0.28 E
Church Stretton 42 52.32 N 2.49 W
Churchton 208 38.48 N 76.32 W
Churchtown, Eng., U.K. 262 53.40 N 2.58 W
Churchtown, Pa., U.S. 208 40.08 N 75.58 W
Church View 208 37.41 N 76.41 W
Churchville, On., Can. 275b 43.38 N 79.45 W
Churchville, Md., U.S. 208 39.33 N 76.14 W
Churchville, N.Y., U.S. 210 43.06 N 77.53 W
Churchville, Pa., U.S. 285 40.11 N 75.01 W
Churdan 198 42.09 N 94.28 W
Churen Himāl ∧ 124 28.44 N 83.12 E
Chure Śringklā ⋏ 124 27.40 N 83.40 E
Churfirsten ⋏ 58 47.08 N 9.17 E
Chürmen 102 43.20 N 104.05 E
Churmuli 89 51.00 N 136.50 E
Churn ≐ 42 51.38 N 1.53 W
Churn Creek ≐ 182 51.30 N 122.17 W
Churnet ≐ 44 52.55 N 1.50 W
Churni ≐[1] 126 23.08 N 88.30 E
Chursdorf 54 50.46 N 12.15 E
Chūru 120 28.18 N 74.57 E
Churubusco, In., U.S. 216 41.13 N 85.19 W
Churubusco, N.Y., U.S. 206 44.57 N 73.56 W
Churuguara 246 10.49 N 69.32 W
Churumuco de Morelos 234 18.37 N 101.38 W
Churwalden 58 46.47 N 9.33 E
Chušenga 88 51.27 N 110.55 E
Chushan 100 23.45 N 120.40 E
Chushul 120 33.36 N 78.39 E
Chuska Mountains ⋏ 200 36.15 N 108.50 W
Chuska Peak ∧ 200 35.53 N 108.50 W
Chusovoy → Čusovoj 86 58.17 N 57.49 E
Chusuut uul ∧ 88 47.45 N 105.45 E
Chūta 174m 26.32 N 127.58 E
Chutag 88 49.23 N 102.43 E
Chutag Uul 102 43.23 N 110.13 E
Chute-à-Blondeau 206 45.35 N 74.29 W
Chute-Panet 206 46.51 N 71.51 W
Chutorskoj 80 46.52 N 42.59 E
Chutove 78 49.43 N 35.10 E
Chutu ≐ 89 49.27 N 140.02 E
Chutung 100 24.44 N 121.05 E
Chuŭl 98 41.33 N 129.34 E
Chuvashia → Čuvašija □[3] 80 55.30 N 47.00 E
Chuwang 98 36.02 N 114.52 E
Chuwang-san Kukrip Kongwŏn ♦ 98 36.26 N 129.10 E
Chuwei 269d 25.08 N 121.27 E
Chuxian 100 32.19 N 118.17 E
Chuxiong 102 25.02 N 101.30 E
Chuy 252 33.41 S 53.27 W
Chuzenji-ko ⊜ 94 36.44 N 139.29 E
Chuzhai 100 33.22 N 113.37 E
Chužir 88 53.11 N 107.20 E
Chūzu 94 35.06 N 136.00 E
Chvalynsk 80 52.30 N 48.07 E
Chvančkara 84 42.34 N 43.01 E
Chvastoviči 76 53.28 N 35.06 E
Chvatovka 80 52.21 N 46.34 E
Chvojnaja 76 58.54 N 34.32 E
Chvorost'anka 80 52.36 N 48.59 E
Chvostovo 92a 46.08 N 142.14 E
Chwefru ≐ 42 52.09 N 3.25 W
Ch'wiya-ri 98 38.03 N 125.32 E

ENGLISH

Name	Page	Lat.°′	Long.°′
Chychykliya ≐	78	47.23 N	31.34 E
Chyhyryn	78	49.04 N	32.40 E
Chynadiyeve	78	48.30 N	22.50 E
Chypre → Cyprus □[1]	130	35.00 N	33.00 E
Chystovodivka	83	49.24 N	37.20 E
Ci ≐, Zhg.	98	38.19 N	115.23 E
Ci ≐, Zhg.	100	33.27 N	115.31 E
Ciadâr Lunga	38	46.03 N	28.47 E
Ciago	64	46.12 N	12.46 E
Ciagola, Monte ∧	68	39.54 N	15.53 E
Ciales	240m	18.20 N	66.28 W
Ciamis	115a	7.20 S	108.21 E
Ciampino	66	41.48 N	12.36 E
Ciampino, Aeroporto di ✈	267a	41.48 N	12.36 E
Cianciana	70	37.31 N	13.26 E
Ciandur	115a	6.24 S	105.59 E
Cianjur	115a	6.49 S	107.08 E
Ciano d'Enza	64	44.36 N	10.24 E
Cianorte	255	23.37 S	52.37 W
Çians, Gorges du V	62	43.57 N	6.59 E
Čiatura	84	42.17 N	43.17 E
Ciavolo	70	37.46 N	12.33 E
Ciawi, Indon.	115a	7.10 S	108.09 E
Ciawi, Indon.	115a	6.40 S	106.50 E
Ciawigebang	115a	6.58 S	108.34 E
Ciba	107	29.07 N	105.55 E
Cibadak	115a	6.53 S	106.46 E
Cibaliung	115a	6.46 S	105.51 E
Čibargata	85	41.08 N	69.48 E
Cibatu	115a	7.06 S	107.59 E
Cibeber	115a	6.56 S	107.07 E
Cibecue	200	34.02 N	110.29 W
Cibiana	64	46.23 N	12.17 E
Cibinong	115a	6.27 S	106.51 E
Čibisovka	78	50.47 N	40.05 E
Čibižek	86	54.27 N	93.40 E
Cibolo Creek ≐, Tx., U.S.	196	28.57 N	97.53 W
Cibolo Creek ≐, Tx., U.S.	196	29.34 N	104.24 W
Cibolo Creek ≐, Tx., U.S.	196	28.27 N	98.54 W
Cibuta	200	31.04 N	110.54 W
Cicagna	62	44.25 N	9.14 E
Cicala	68	39.01 N	16.29 E
Cicalengka	115a	6.59 S	107.50 E
Ćićarija ⋏	36	45.30 N	13.54 E
Čičatka	89	54.03 N	121.18 E
Cicciano	68	40.58 N	14.32 E
Cicero, Il., U.S.	216	41.50 N	87.45 W
Cicero, In., U.S.	218	40.07 N	86.00 W
Cicero, N.Y., U.S.	210	43.10 N	76.07 W
Cicero Creek ≐	194	40.01 N	86.01 W
Cícero Dantas	250	10.36 S	38.23 W
Čichačovo, Ross.	76	57.17 N	29.54 E
Čichačovo, Ross.	89	51.50 N	141.07 E
Čichareši	84	42.48 N	43.03 E
Ciche, Sgurr na ∧	46	57.01 N	5.27 W
Cicheng	100	30.00 N	121.22 E
Čičkajul ≐	86	57.34 N	85.44 E
Cicladas, Islas → Kikládhes II	38	37.30 N	25.00 E
Cicolano ✦[1]	66	42.12 N	13.12 E
Cicurug	115a	6.47 S	106.47 E
Cidacos ≐	34	42.19 N	1.55 W
Cidade, Rio da ≐	256	22.25 S	43.09 W
Cidade Universitária ✝[2], Bra.	287a	22.52 S	43.14 W
Cidade Universitária ✝[2], Bra.	287b	23.33 S	46.43 W
Cide	130	41.54 N	33.00 E
Cidra	240m	18.11 N	66.10 W
Cidra, Lago de ⊜[1]	240m	18.12 N	66.08 W
Ciechanów	30	52.53 N	20.38 E
Ciechanów □[4]	30	53.00 N	20.20 E
Ciechanowiec	30	52.42 N	22.31 E
Ciechocinek	30	52.52 N	18.49 E
Ciego de Ávila	240p	21.51 N	78.46 W
Ciego de Ávila □[4]	240p	22.00 N	78.40 W
Ciempozuelos	34	40.10 N	3.37 W
Ciénaga	246	11.01 N	74.15 W
Ciénaga de Oro	246	8.53 N	75.37 W
Ciénega de Flores	196	25.57 N	100.11 W
Cienfuegos	240p	22.09 N	80.27 W
Cienfuegos □[4]	240p	22.10 N	80.25 W
Cienfuegos, Bahía de ⊂	240p	22.07 N	80.29 W
Čierna [nad Tisou]	30	48.25 N	22.05 E
Čierny Balog	30	48.45 N	19.40 E
Cies, Islas II	34	42.13 N	8.54 W
Cieszanów	30	50.16 N	23.08 E
Cieszyn	30	49.45 N	18.38 E
Cieza	34	38.14 N	1.25 W
Çiftalan ✦[8]	267b	41.15 N	28.54 E
Çiftehan	130	37.31 N	34.46 E
Çifteler	130	39.22 N	31.03 E
Çiftlik	130	38.11 N	34.30 E
Cifuentes, Cuba	240p	22.39 N	80.03 W
Cifuentes, Esp.	34	40.47 N	2.37 W
Čiganak, Kaz.	86	45.06 N	73.58 E
Čiganak, Ross.	80	51.47 N	43.18 E
Čiganaki	80	47.57 N	43.05 E
Cigliano	62	45.18 N	8.01 E
Čigorak	80	51.26 N	42.09 E
Cigou	100	33.51 N	113.35 E
Cigüela ≐	34	39.08 N	3.44 W
Cihanbeyli	130	38.40 N	32.56 E
Cihara	115a	6.52 S	106.06 E
Cihuatlán	234	19.14 N	104.35 W
Čiili	86	44.10 N	66.45 E
Cijara, Embalse de ⊜[1]	34	39.18 N	4.52 W
Čijen	85	43.08 N	75.55 E
Cijiawu	105	39.48 N	115.59 E
Čijirčik, pereval)(	85	40.15 N	73.20 E
Čijli ≐	85	40.17 N	72.38 E
Cijulang	115a	7.44 S	108.27 E
Čik	86	55.01 N	82.27 E
Cikajang	115a	7.22 S	107.47 E
Cikalong-kulon	115a	6.42 S	107.12 E
Cikampek	115a	6.24 S	107.27 E
Čikan	88	54.54 N	105.39 E
Cikarang	115a	6.15 S	107.09 E
Cikatomas	115a	7.37 S	108.15 E
Čikišl'ar	128	37.34 N	53.55 E
Čikoj	88	50.16 N	106.54 E
Čikoj ≐	88	51.02 N	106.39 E
Čikola	84	43.12 N	43.55 E
Cikou	100	29.42 N	114.46 E
Cıksı	130	38.30 N	40.55 E
Cilacap	115a	7.44 S	109.00 E
Cilamaya	115a	6.15 S	107.35 E
Cilavegna	62	45.19 N	8.44 E
Çıldır	84	41.08 N	43.07 E
Çıldır Gölü ⊜	84	41.04 N	43.15 E
Ciledug	115a	6.54 S	108.44 E
Cilegon	115a	6.01 S	106.03 E
Čilekovo	80	47.50 N	43.30 E
Cilento ✦[1]	68	40.15 N	15.15 E
Čil'gazi	85	40.10 N	70.39 E
Cili	102	29.17 N	111.00 E
Cilicia □[9]	130	36.40 N	34.20 E
Čilik, Kaz.	85	43.36 N	78.15 E
Čilik, Kaz.	86	51.07 N	54.07 E
Čilik ≐	85	43.05 N	78.28 E
Cililin	115a	6.56 S	107.26 E
Cilimus	115a	6.52 S	108.29 E
Cilincing ✦[8]	269e	6.06 S	106.56 E
Cill Airne → Killarney	48	52.03 N	9.30 W
Cill Chainnigh → Kilkenny	48	52.39 N	7.15 W
Cilleruelo de Bezana	34	42.58 N	3.51 W
Cil'ma ≐	24	65.27 N	52.06 E
Čilov ada I	84	40.19 N	50.36 E
Cimabanche (Schluderbach)	64	46.37 N	12.11 E
Cima Gogna	64	46.31 N	12.28 E
Cimahi	115a	6.53 S	107.32 E
Cimalaka	115a	6.49 S	107.56 E
Cimalmotto	58	46.17 N	8.29 E

DEUTSCH

Name	Seite	Breite°′	Länge°′ E = Ost
Cimarron, Ks., U.S.	198	37.48 N	100.20 W
Cimarron, N.M., U.S.	200	36.30 N	104.54 W
Cimarron ≐, U.S.	196	36.10 N	96.17 W
Cimarron ≐, N.M., U.S.	196	36.20 N	104.31 W
Cimarron, North Fork ≐	196	37.25 N	101.13 W
Čimbaj	86	42.57 N	59.47 E
Čimčinej, gora ∧[2]	180	63.37 N	178.04 E
Cimini, Monti ⋏	66	42.20 N	12.10 E
Ciminna	70	37.54 N	13.34 E
Cimino, Monte ∧	66	42.24 N	12.12 E
Čimion	85	40.16 N	71.31 E
Cimișlia	38	46.32 N	28.44 E
Cimitile	68	40.56 N	14.31 E
Čimkent	85	42.18 N	69.36 E
Čimkent □[4]	85	42.30 N	68.30 E
Čimkorgon	85	42.50 N	75.30 E
Cimla ≐	80	48.01 N	42.24 E
Ciml'ansk	80	47.38 N	42.04 E
Ciml'anskoje vodochranilišče ⊜[1]	80	48.00 N	43.00 E
Cimolais	64	46.17 N	12.26 E
Cimone, Monte ∧	64	44.12 N	10.42 E
Cimpu	112	3.25 S	120.22 E
Čimtarga, gora ∧	85	39.12 N	68.10 E
Čina ≐	88	54.20 N	112.24 E
Cina, Tanjung ⊳	112	5.56 S	104.45 E
Činabad	85	40.52 N	71.58 E
Cinandali	84	41.53 N	45.34 E
Çınar	130	37.44 N	40.25 E
Çınarcık	130	40.39 N	29.06 E
Cinaruco ≐	246	6.41 N	67.07 W
Činaz	85	40.56 N	68.45 E
Cinca ≐	34	41.26 N	0.21 E
Cincar ∧	36	43.54 N	17.04 E
Cincinnati, Ia., U.S.	190	40.37 N	92.55 W
Cincinnati, Oh., U.S.	218	39.09 N	84.27 W
Cincinnatus	210	42.32 N	75.53 W
Cinco, Canal Numero ≡	252	37.35 S	57.20 W
Cinco Balas, Cayos II	240p	21.06 N	79.20 W
Cinco de Mayo	196	25.46 N	104.19 W
Cinco Pinos	236	13.14 N	86.52 W
Cinco Saltos	252	38.49 S	68.04 W
Cinderella	273d	26.15 S	28.16 E
Cinderella Dam ⊜[1]	273d	26.15 S	28.14 E
Cinderford	42	51.50 N	2.29 W
Cinder Island I	276	40.36 N	73.36 W
Çine	130	37.36 N	28.04 E
Cinebar	224	46.36 N	122.32 W
Cinecittà ✝[3]	267a	41.51 N	12.34 E
Cinema	182	53.14 N	122.27 W
Ciney	56	50.18 N	5.06 E
Cinfães	34	41.04 N	8.05 W
Čingaly	86	60.13 N	69.45 E
Čingis	86	54.08 N	81.41 E
Čingistaj	86	49.13 N	85.55 E
Cingoli	66	43.22 N	13.13 E
Cinigiano	66	42.53 N	11.24 E
Cinisello Balsamo	62	45.33 N	9.13 E
Cinișeuți	38	47.42 N	28.52 E
Cinisi	70	38.09 N	13.06 E
Činja-Voryk	24	63.13 N	52.38 E
Cinkota ✦[8]	264c	47.31 N	19.14 E
Cinnaminson	285	40.00 N	74.59 W
Cínovec	54	50.43 N	13.45 E
Cinq, Lac des ⊜	206	46.51 N	72.59 W
Cinq Doigts, Lac ⊜	206	46.36 N	74.32 W
Cinquefrondi	68	38.25 N	16.06 E
Cinquemiglia, Piano delle ≐	66	41.50 N	14.00 E
Cinqueterre □[9]	62	44.10 N	9.45 E
Cintalapa	234	16.44 N	93.43 W
Cinto, Monte ∧	36	42.23 N	8.56 E
Cinto Euganeo	64	45.16 N	11.40 E
Cintra → Sintra	34	38.48 N	9.23 W
Cintra, Golfe de ⊂	148	23.00 N	16.20 W
Ciocănești	38	44.12 N	27.04 E
Ciociaria ✦[1]	66	41.45 N	13.15 E
Ciomas	115a	6.12 S	106.01 E
Čiovo, Otok I	36	43.30 N	16.20 E
Cipa ≐	88	55.23 N	115.55 E
Ciparay	115a	7.03 S	107.43 E
Cipatujah	115a	7.45 S	108.00 E
Cipikan	88	54.55 N	113.21 E
Cipikan ≐	88	55.14 N	113.05 E
Cipó	250	11.06 S	38.31 W
Cipó ≐	255	18.40 S	43.59 W
Cipolândia	255	20.08 S	55.24 W
Cipolletti	252	38.56 S	67.59 W
Ciqikou	107	29.35 N	106.26 E
Čir	80	48.29 N	43.10 E
Čir ≐	80	48.35 N	42.51 E
Ciraadhame	144	10.30 N	49.22 E
Čirachčaj ≐	84	41.40 N	48.11 E
Čiragidzor	84	40.27 N	46.19 E
Ciranjang	115a	6.49 S	107.14 E
Circeo, Monte ∧	66	41.14 N	13.03 E
Circeo, Parco Nazionale del ♦	66	41.17 N	13.05 E
Čirčik	85	41.29 N	69.35 E
Čirčik ≐	85	40.54 N	68.41 E
Çırçır	130	40.04 N	36.48 E
Circle, Ak., U.S.	180	65.50 N	144.04 W
Circle, Mt., U.S.	202	47.20 N	105.35 W
Circle Hot Springs	180	65.28 N	144.39 W
Circleville, N.Y., U.S.	210	41.31 N	75.23 W
Circleville, Oh., U.S.	218	39.36 N	82.56 W
Circleville, Pa., U.S.	279b	40.20 N	79.44 W
Circleville, Ut,. U.S.	200	38.10 N	112.16 W
Circleville Mountain ∧	200	38.12 N	112.24 W
Circular Reef ✦[2]	164	3.25 S	147.47 E
Circus World ♦	220	28.14 N	81.38 W
Cirebon	115a	6.44 S	108.34 E
Cireglio	66	43.59 N	10.51 E
Ciremay, Gunung ∧	115a	6.54 S	108.24 E
Cirencester	42	51.44 N	1.59 W
Cirey-sur-Vezouze	58	48.35 N	6.57 E
Čirgalandy	88	50.36 N	97.20 E
Ciriè	62	45.14 N	7.36 E
Cirigliano	68	40.24 N	16.10 E
Čirikovo	82	55.23 N	37.14 E
Ciriquiri ≐	248	8.05 S	65.18 W
Čirk, gora ∧	180	64.33 N	175.25 E
Cirò	68	39.23 N	17.04 E
Cirò Marina	68	39.22 N	17.08 E
Ciro Redondo	240p	22.01 N	78.43 W
Čirpan	38	42.12 N	25.20 E
Ciruas	115a	6.06 S	106.13 E
Cisa, Passo della)(	64	44.28 N	9.55 E
Cisano	64	45.32 N	10.43 E
Cisarua	115a	6.40 S	106.59 E
Cisco, Il., U.S.	219	40.01 N	88.43 W
Cisco, Tx., U.S.	196	32.23 N	98.58 W
Cishan	98	36.37 N	114.07 E
Cishangang	106	30.55 N	119.31 E
Ciskei □[9]	158	32.50 S	27.00 E
Cislago	62	45.39 N	8.58 E
Cisliano	266b	45.27 N	8.59 E
Cismar	54	54.11 N	10.59 E
Čismena	82	56.02 N	36.13 E
Cismon ≐	64	45.55 N	11.43 E
Cismon del Grappa	64	45.55 N	11.44 E
Čišmy	86	54.35 N	55.20 E
Cisnădie	38	45.43 N	24.09 E
Cisne	194	38.31 N	88.26 W
Cisneros	246	6.33 N	75.04 W
Cisnes ≐	254	44.45 S	72.42 W
Cisolok	115a	6.57 S	106.26 E
Cison di Valmarino	64	45.58 N	12.10 E
Cispus ≐	224	46.25 N	122.10 W
Cisse ≐	50	47.25 N	0.47 E
Cissna Park	216	40.33 N	87.53 W
Čistá, Česká Rep.	54	50.06 N	12.44 E
Čistá, Česká Rep.	60	50.02 N	13.35 E
Cisterna di Latina	66	41.35 N	12.49 E
Cisternino	68	40.44 N	17.25 E
Cistern Point ⊳	238	23.43 N	77.35 W
Cistierna	34	42.48 N	5.07 W
Čistoje	80	56.32 N	43.02 E
Čistooz'ornoje	86	54.43 N	76.33 E

Symbols in the index entries represent the broad categories identified in the key at the right. Symbols with superior numbers (⋏[1]) identify subcategories (see complete key on page I · 1).

Symbole im Register stellen die rechts im Schlüssel erklärten Kategorien dar. Symbole mit hochgestellten Ziffern (⋏[1]) bezeichnen Unterabteilungen einer Kategorie (vgl. vollständiger Schlüssel auf Seite I · 1).

Los símbolos incluídos en el texto del índice representan las grandes categorías identificadas con la clave a la derecha. Los símbolos con numeros en su parte superior (⋏[1]) identifican las subcategorías (véase la clave completa en la página I · 1).

Les symboles de l'index représentent les catégories indiquées dans la légende à droite. Les symboles suivis d'un indice (⋏[1]) représentent des sous-catégories (voir légende complète à la page I · 1).

Os símbolos incluídos no texto do índice representam as grandes categorias identificadas com a chave à direita. Os símbolos com números em sua parte superior (⋏[1]) identificam as subcategorias (veja-se a chave completa à página I · 1).

∧ Mountain	Berg	Montaña	Montagne	Montanha
⋏ Mountains	Gebirge	Montañas	Montagnes	Montanhas
)(Pass	Paß	Paso	Col	Passo
V Valley, Canyon	Tal, Cañon	Valle, Cañón	Vallée, Canyon	Vale, Canhão
≐ Plain	Ebene	Llano	Plaine	Planície
⊳ Cape	Kap	Cabo	Cap	Cabo
I Island	Insel	Isla	Île	Ilha
II Islands	Inseln	Islas	Îles	Ilhas
⊥ Other Topographic Features	Andere Topographische Objekte	Otros Elementos Topográficos	Autres données topographiques	Outros acidentes topográficos

ESPAÑOL

Nombre	Página	Lat.°′	Long.°′ W = Oeste
Čistopol'	80	55.21 N	50.37 E
Čistopolje, Kaz.	86	52.34 N	67.15 E
Čistopolje, Ross.	83	47.31 N	39.27 E
Čita	88	52.03 N	113.30 E
Čita ≃	88	52.00 N	113.30 E
Çitac, Nevado ∧	248	12.48 S	75.14 W
Čita Oblast' □[4]	88	52.00 N	117.00 E
Citaré ≃	250	1.11 N	54.41 W
Cité Universitaire ⚲[2]	261	48.49 N	2.20 E
Citlaltépetl, Volcán → Orizaba, Pico de ∧[1]	234	19.01 N	97.16 E
Citra	192	29.24 N	82.06 W
Citronelle	194	31.05 N	88.13 W
Citrus □[6]	220	28.52 N	82.28 W
Citrusdal	158	32.36 S	19.00 E
Citrus Heights	226	38.42 N	121.16 W
Citrus Springs	220	29.00 N	82.27 W
Citrus Tower ⚲	220	28.33 N	81.44 W
Cittadella	64	45.39 N	11.47 E
Città della Pieve	66	42.57 N	12.00 E
Città del Vaticano → Vatican City □[1]	66	41.54 N	12.27 E
Città di Castello	66	43.27 N	12.14 E
Cittaducale	66	42.23 N	12.57 E
Cittanova	68	38.21 N	16.05 E
Cittareale	66	42.37 N	13.10 E
Città Sant'Angelo	66	42.31 N	14.03 E
Città Universitaria ⚲[2]	267a	41.55 N	12.31 E
City Beach	168a	31.56 S	115.45 E
City Bell ◆[8]	258	34.52 S	58.05 W
City Island ◆[8]	276	40.51 N	73.47 W
City Mills	283	42.06 N	71.21 W
City of Hope National Medical Center ⚲	280	34.08 N	117.58 W
City Of Industry	280	34.01 N	117.57 W
City of London ◆[8]	260	51.31 N	0.05 W
City of Refuge → Pu'uhonua o Honaunau National Historic Site ⊥	229d	19.25 N	155.54 W
City of Sunrise	220	26.08 N	80.14 W
City Point	220	28.24 N	80.45 W
City University of New York Brooklyn College ⚲[2]	276	40.38 N	73.57 W
City University of New York City College ⚲[2]	276	40.49 N	73.57 W
City University of New York Queens College ⚲[2]	276	40.44 N	73.49 W
City University of New York York College ⚲[2]	276	40.42 N	73.48 W
Ciucaș, Vârful ∧	38	45.31 N	25.55 E
Ciuciuleni	38	47.02 N	28.22 E
Ciudad Acuña	232	29.18 N	100.55 W
Ciudad Altamirano	234	18.20 N	100.40 W
Ciudad Barrios	236	13.46 N	88.16 W
Ciudad Bolívar	246	8.08 N	63.33 W
Ciudad Bolivia	246	8.21 N	70.34 W
Ciudad Camargo	232	26.19 N	98.50 W
Ciudad Constitución	232	24.59 N	111.39 W
Ciudad Cortés	236	8.58 N	83.32 W
Ciudad Cuauhtémoc	234	22.28 N	102.20 W
Ciudad Darío	236	12.43 N	86.08 W
Ciudad de Carangas	248	17.53 S	66.11 W
Ciudad de Guayana → Ciudad Guayana	246	8.22 N	62.40 W
Ciudad de la Habana □[4]	240p	23.08 N	82.22 W
Ciudad del Cabo → Cape Town	158	33.55 S	18.22 E
Ciudad del Carmen	232	18.38 N	91.50 W
Ciudad del Este	252	25.30 S	54.36 W
Ciudad del Maíz	234	22.24 N	99.36 W
Ciudad de los Deportes ♠	286a	19.23 N	99.11 W
Ciudad del Vaticano → Vatican City □[1]	66	41.54 N	12.27 E
Ciudad de México (Mexico City), Méx.	234	19.24 N	99.09 W
Ciudad de México (Mexico City), Méx.	286a	19.24 N	99.09 W
Ciudad de Nutrias	246	8.05 N	69.18 W
Ciudad Deportiva ♠, Cuba	286b	23.07 N	82.22 W
Ciudad Deportiva ♠, Méx.	286a	19.24 N	99.06 W
Ciudadela, Parque de la ♠	266d	41.23 N	2.11 E
Ciudad General Belgrano	288	34.43 S	58.32 W
Ciudad Guayana	246	8.22 N	62.40 W
Ciudad Guzmán	234	19.41 N	103.29 W
Ciudad Hidalgo, Méx.	234	19.41 N	100.34 W
Ciudad Hidalgo, Méx.	236	14.41 N	92.09 W
Ciudad Juárez	232	31.44 N	106.29 W
Ciudad Lerdo	196	25.32 N	103.32 W
Ciudad Lerdo de Tejada	234	18.37 N	95.31 W
Ciudad Lineal ◆[8]	266a	40.27 N	3.40 W
Ciudad López Mateos	286a	19.33 N	99.15 W
Ciudad Madero	234	22.16 N	97.50 W
Ciudad Mante	234	22.44 N	98.57 W
Ciudad Manuel Doblado	234	20.44 N	101.56 W
Ciudad Mendoza	234	18.48 N	97.11 W
Ciudad Miguel Alemán	232	26.23 N	99.01 W
Ciudad Morelos	232	32.38 N	114.52 W
Ciudad Obregón	232	27.29 N	109.56 W
Ciudad Ojeda (Lagunillas)	246	10.12 N	71.19 W
Ciudad Piar	246	7.27 N	63.19 W
Ciudad Real	34	38.59 N	3.56 W
Ciudad Real □[4]	34	38.50 N	3.45 W
Ciudad Rodrigo	34	40.36 N	6.32 W
Ciudad Sahagún	234	19.47 N	98.33 W
Ciudad Sandino	236	13.43 N	86.08 W
Ciudad Serdán	234	18.59 N	97.27 W
Ciudad Tecún Umán	236	14.40 N	92.09 W
Ciudad Trujillo → Santo Domingo	238	18.28 N	69.54 W
Ciudad Universitaria ◆[8]	266a	40.27 N	3.44 W
Ciudad Universitaria ⚲[2], Esp.	266a	40.27 N	3.43 W
Ciudad Universitaria ⚲[2], Méx.	286a	19.20 N	99.11 W
Ciudad Universitaria ⚲[2], Ven.	286c	10.29 N	66.53 W
Ciudad Valles	234	21.59 N	99.01 W
Ciudad Victoria, Méx.	204	32.20 N	115.06 W
Ciudad Victoria, Méx.	234	23.44 N	99.08 W
Ciudad Vieja	236	14.31 N	90.46 W
Ciuma	152	13.14 S	15.40 E
Ciutadella	34	40.02 N	3.50 E
Civa Burnu ›	130	41.22 N	36.35 E
Civate	62	45.50 N	9.21 E
Civenna	58	45.56 N	9.16 E
Civetta, Monte ∧	64	46.23 N	12.03 E
Civezzano	64	46.05 N	11.11 E
Cividale del Friuli	64	46.06 N	13.25 E
Cividate al Piano	62	45.33 N	9.50 E
Cividate Camuno	64	45.57 N	10.17 E
Civil' ≃	80	56.08 N	47.35 E
Civil'sk	80	55.53 N	47.29 E
Civita	68	39.49 N	16.18 E
Civitacampomarano	66	41.47 N	14.41 E
Civita Castellana	66	42.17 N	12.25 E
Civita di Bagno	66	42.18 N	13.26 E
Civitanova Alta	66	43.19 N	13.40 E
Civitanova del Sannio	66	41.40 N	14.24 E
Civitanova Marche	66	43.18 N	13.44 E
Civitaquana	66	42.19 N	13.54 E
Civitavecchia	66	42.06 N	11.48 E
Civitella del Tronto	66	42.46 N	13.40 E
Civitella di Romagna	66	44.00 N	11.56 E
Civitella in Val di Chiana	66	43.25 N	11.43 E

FRANÇAIS

Nom	Page	Lat.°′	Long.°′ W = Ouest
Civitella Marittima	66	43.00 N	11.17 E
Civitella Roveto	66	41.54 N	13.25 E
Civray	32	46.09 N	0.18 E
Çivril	130	38.18 N	29.45 E
Ciwidey	115a	7.06 S	107.27 E
Cixerri ≃	71	39.17 N	8.59 E
Cixi	100	30.11 N	121.15 E
Cixian	98	36.22 N	114.23 E
Ciyutuo	104	41.31 N	122.53 E
Čiža	24	67.06 N	44.19 E
Čižapka ≃	86	59.01 N	79.36 E
Čiža Vtoraja	80	50.52 N	49.40 E
Cize	58	46.12 N	5.26 E
Cizhuping	107	29.11 N	103.36 E
Čižinskije razlivy ≡	80	50.25 N	49.40 E
Cizre	130	37.20 N	42.12 E
C.J. Strike Reservoir ⊜[1]	202	42.57 N	115.53 W
Čkalov → Orenburg	86	51.54 N	55.06 E
Čkalovo	86	53.38 N	70.24 E
Čkalovsk, Kaz.	85	41.15 N	68.00 E
Čkalovsk, Ross.	80	56.46 N	43.16 E
Čkalovsk, Taj.	85	40.13 N	69.50 E
Čkalovskij	265b	55.54 N	38.04 E
Ç K Creek ≃	202	47.36 N	108.29 W
Čkyně	60	49.07 N	13.49 E
Čl'a, ozero ⊜	89	53.27 N	140.03 E
Clachan	46	55.45 N	5.34 W
Clackamas	224	45.24 N	122.34 W
Clackamas □[6]	224	45.10 N	122.16 W
Clackamas ≃	224	45.22 N	122.36 W
Clackamas, Oak Grove Fork ≃	224	45.05 N	122.03 W
Clackamas Heights	224	45.23 N	122.34 W
Clackline	168a	31.43 S	116.31 E
Clackmannan	46	56.06 N	3.46 W
Clacton-on-Sea	42	51.48 N	1.09 E
Cladich	46	56.21 N	5.05 W
Claerwen ≃	42	52.16 N	3.35 W
Claerwen Reservoir ⊜[1]	42	52.17 N	3.43 W
Claflin	198	38.31 N	98.32 W
Claiborne	194	31.32 N	87.31 W
Clain ≃	32	46.47 N	0.32 E
Claire, Lake ⊜	176	58.35 N	112.05 W
Claire, Pointe ›	275a	45.25 N	73.50 W
Clairefontaine-en-Yvelines	50	48.37 N	1.55 E
Clair Engle Lake ⊜[1]	204	40.52 N	122.43 W
Claireville	275b	43.45 N	79.38 W
Claireville Reservoir ⊜[1]	275b	43.44 N	79.39 W
Clairis ≃	50	48.07 N	2.45 E
Clairmarais	50	50.46 N	2.18 E
Clairmont	182	55.16 N	118.47 W
Clairton	214	40.17 N	79.52 W
Clairvaux-les-Lacs	58	46.34 N	5.45 E
Claix	62	45.07 N	5.40 E
Clallam □[6]	224	48.10 N	123.49 W
Clallam Bay	224	48.15 N	124.15 W
Clam ≃, Mi., U.S.	190	44.05 N	85.00 W
Clam ≃, Wi., U.S.	190	45.57 N	92.33 W
Clam, North Fork ≃	190	45.46 N	92.18 W
Clamart	261	48.48 N	2.16 E
Clamecy	50	47.27 N	3.31 E
Clam Gulch	180	60.15 N	151.22 W
Clam Lake ⊜	184	55.19 N	105.43 W
Clampton	162	29.56 S	119.06 E
Clan Alpine Mountains ⋏	204	39.40 N	117.55 W
Clandonald	182	53.34 N	110.44 W
Clandon Park ♠	260	51.15 N	0.30 W
Clandulla	170	32.55 S	149.57 E
Clane	48	53.18 N	6.41 W
Clans	62	44.00 N	7.09 E
Clanton	194	32.50 N	86.37 W
Clanwilliam	158	32.11 S	18.54 E
Claonaig	46	55.46 N	5.22 W
Clapham	42	52.09 N	0.29 W
Clapier, Mont ∧	62	44.07 N	7.25 E
Clapperton Island I	190	46.02 N	82.13 W
Clapp Farm	214	41.24 N	79.32 W
Clàr, Loch nan ⊜	46	58.17 N	4.08 W
Clara, Arg.	252	31.50 S	58.49 W
Clara, Ire.	48	53.20 N	7.36 W
Clara, Ms., U.S.	194	31.34 N	88.41 W
Clara ≃	166	18.30 S	141.18 E
Clara City	198	44.57 N	95.21 W
Clara Island I	110	10.54 N	97.55 E
Claraz	252	37.54 S	59.17 W
Clare, Austl.	166	33.25 S	143.55 E
Clare, Austl.	168b	33.50 S	138.36 E
Clare, Eng., U.K.	42	52.05 N	0.35 E
Clare, Mi., U.S.	190	43.49 N	84.46 W
Clare □[6]	48	52.50 N	9.00 W
Clare ≃, On., Can.	212	44.28 N	77.17 W
Clare ≃, Ire.	48	53.20 N	9.03 W
Clarecastle	48	52.49 N	8.57 W
Claregalway	48	53.21 N	8.57 W
Clare Island I	48	53.48 N	10.00 W
Claremont, On., Can.	212	43.58 N	79.07 W
Claremont, Eng., U.K.	260	51.21 N	0.22 W
Claremont, Ca., U.S.	228	34.05 N	117.43 W
Claremont, N.H., U.S.	188	43.22 N	72.20 W
Claremont, S.D., U.S.	198	45.40 N	98.00 W
Claremont, Va., U.S.	208	37.13 N	76.57 W
Claremont ∧	204	39.53 N	120.57 W
Claremore	196	36.18 N	95.36 W
Claremorris	48	53.44 N	9.00 W
Clarence, N.Z.	172	42.10 S	173.56 E
Clarence, Il., U.S.	216	40.28 N	87.58 W
Clarence, Ia., U.S.	190	41.53 N	91.03 W
Clarence, Mo., U.S.	219	39.44 N	92.15 W
Clarence, N.Y., U.S.	210	42.59 N	78.35 W
Clarence, Pa., U.S.	214	41.03 N	77.56 W
Clarence ≃, Austl.	166	29.25 S	153.22 E
Clarence ≃, N.Z.	172	42.10 S	173.57 E
Clarence, Isla I	254	54.10 S	71.50 W
Clarence, Port ⊂	180	65.15 N	166.40 W
Clarence Cannon Dam ◆[6]	219	39.31 N	91.39 W
Clarence Center	210	43.00 N	78.35 W
Clarence Creek	206	45.30 N	75.13 W
Clarence Fahnestock Memorial State Park ♠	210	41.26 N	73.50 W
Clarence Island I	9	61.09 S	54.06 W
Clarence J. Brown Reservoir ⊜[1]	218	39.58 N	83.44 W
Clarence Strait ⊔, Austl.	164	12.00 S	131.00 E
Clarence Strait ⊔, Ak., U.S.	180	55.25 N	132.00 W
Clarence Town, Austl.	170	32.35 S	151.47 E
Clarence Town, Ba.	238	23.06 N	74.59 W
Clarenceville, P.Q., Can.	206	45.04 N	73.15 W
Clarenceville, Mi., U.S.	281	42.27 N	83.19 W
Clarendon, Austl.	168b	35.07 S	138.38 E
Clarendon, Ar., U.S.	194	34.41 N	91.18 W
Clarendon, N.Y., U.S.	210	43.11 N	78.04 W
Clarendon, Pa., U.S.	214	41.46 N	79.05 W
Clarendon, Tx., U.S.	196	34.56 N	100.53 W
Clarendon Hills	278	41.47 N	87.57 W
Clarens	158	28.30 S	28.29 E
Clarenville	186	48.10 N	53.58 W
Claresholm	182	50.02 N	113.35 W
Claret	62	43.52 N	3.54 E
Clarholz	52	51.54 N	8.11 E
Claridge	214	40.21 N	79.37 W
Clarie Coast ⊥[2]	9	66.30 S	133.00 E
Clarin	116	9.58 N	124.01 E
Clarinda	198	40.44 N	95.02 W
Clarines	246	9.56 N	65.10 W
Clarington	214	41.20 N	79.07 W
Clarion, Ia., U.S.	190	42.43 N	93.43 W
Clarion, Pa., U.S.	214	41.12 N	79.23 W
Clarion □[6]	214	41.13 N	79.24 W
Clarion ≃	214	41.07 N	79.41 W
Clarión, Isla I	232	18.22 N	114.44 W

PORTUGUÊS

Nome	Página	Lat.°′	Long.°′ W = Oeste
Clarion, West Branch ≃	214	41.29 N	78.41 W
Clarion Fracture Zone ✦	16	18.00 N	122.00 W
Clarissa	198	46.07 N	94.56 W
Clark, N.J., U.S.	276	40.38 N	74.18 W
Clark, Oh., U.S.	214	40.27 N	81.54 W
Clark, S.D., U.S.	198	44.52 N	97.43 W
Clark, Tx., U.S.	222	30.23 N	94.46 W
Clark □[6], In., U.S.	218	38.17 N	85.44 W
Clark □[6], Oh., U.S.	218	39.56 N	83.49 W
Clark □[6], Wa., U.S.	224	45.48 N	122.31 W
Clark, Lake ⊜	180	60.15 N	154.15 W
Clark, Mount ∧	180	64.25 N	124.12 W
Clark, Point ›	190	44.04 N	81.45 W
Clark Air Base (U.S.) ■	116	15.11 N	120.32 E
Clark Branch ≃	285	39.43 N	74.45 W
Clark Canyon Reservoir ⊜[1]	202	44.58 N	112.51 W
Clark Creek ≃	208	40.22 N	76.58 W
Clarkdale	200	34.46 N	112.03 W
Clarke ≃	166	19.12 S	145.30 E
Clarke City	186	50.12 N	66.38 W
Clarke Island I	166	40.33 S	148.10 E
Clarke Lake ⊜	184	54.25 N	106.51 W
Clarke Range ⋏	166	20.50 S	148.33 E
Clarkesville	192	34.36 N	83.31 W
Clarkfield	198	44.47 N	95.48 W
Clark Fork	202	48.08 N	116.10 W
Clark Fork ≃	202	48.09 N	116.15 W
Clark Hill	218	38.18 N	83.12 W
Clarklake	216	42.04 N	84.21 W
Clark Lake ⊜	216	42.07 N	84.19 W
Clark Mills	210	43.06 N	75.22 W
Clark Mountain ∧, Ca., U.S.	204	35.32 N	115.35 W
Clark Mountain ∧, Wa., U.S.	224	48.03 N	120.57 W
Clarks, La., U.S.	194	32.01 N	92.08 W
Clarks, Ne., U.S.	198	41.12 N	97.50 W
Clarks ≃	194	37.03 N	88.33 W
Clarks, West Fork ≃	194	36.59 N	88.31 W
Clarksboro	285	39.47 N	75.13 W
Clarksburg, On., Can.	212	44.43 N	80.27 W
Clarksburg, Ca., U.S.	226	38.25 N	121.32 W
Clarksburg, Il., U.S.	219	39.20 N	88.44 W
Clarksburg, In., U.S.	218	39.26 N	85.20 W
Clarksburg, Md., U.S.	208	39.14 N	77.16 W
Clarksburg, N.J., U.S.	208	40.11 N	74.26 W
Clarksburg, Oh., U.S.	218	39.30 N	83.09 W
Clarksburg, W.V., U.S.	188	39.16 N	80.20 W
Clarksburg State Park ♠	207	42.43 N	73.06 W
Clarks Creek ≃, Ks., U.S.	198	39.05 N	96.42 W
Clarks Creek ≃, Ky., U.S.	218	38.40 N	84.44 W
Clarksdale	194	34.12 N	90.34 W
Clarks Green	210	41.30 N	75.42 W
Clark's Harbour	186	43.26 N	65.38 W
Clarks Hill	216	40.14 N	86.43 W
Clarks Hill Lake ⊜[1]	192	33.50 N	82.20 W
Clarks Island I	283	42.01 N	70.38 W
Clarks Mills	214	41.24 N	80.11 W
Clarkson, On., Can.	275b	43.31 N	79.37 W
Clarkson, Ky., U.S.	194	37.29 N	86.13 W
Clarkson, Ne., U.S.	198	41.43 N	97.07 W
Clarkson, N.Y., U.S.	210	43.14 N	77.56 W
Clarks Point	180	58.51 N	158.30 W
Clarks Summit	210	41.29 N	75.42 W
Clarkston, Mi., U.S.	216	42.44 N	83.25 W
Clarkston, Wa., U.S.	202	46.24 N	117.02 W
Clark's Town	241q	18.25 N	77.34 W
Clarksville, Ar., U.S.	194	35.28 N	93.27 W
Clarksville, De., U.S.	208	38.32 N	75.08 W
Clarksville, In., U.S.	218	38.15 N	85.47 W
Clarksville, Ia., U.S.	190	42.47 N	92.40 W
Clarksville, Md., U.S.	208	39.12 N	76.56 W
Clarksville, Mi., U.S.	216	42.50 N	85.14 W
Clarksville, Mo., U.S.	219	39.22 N	90.54 W
Clarksville, N.Y., U.S.	210	42.35 N	73.58 W
Clarksville, Oh., U.S.	218	39.24 N	83.58 W
Clarksville, Tn., U.S.	194	36.31 N	87.21 W
Clarksville, Tx., U.S.	196	33.36 N	95.03 W
Clarksville, Va., U.S.	192	36.37 N	78.33 W
Clarksville City	222	32.32 N	94.34 W
Clarkton, Mo., U.S.	194	36.27 N	89.58 W
Clarkton, N.C., U.S.	192	34.29 N	78.39 W
Claro ≃, Bra.	248	13.25 S	56.35 W
Claro ≃, Bra.	255	15.28 S	51.43 W
Claro ≃, Bra.	255	19.06 S	47.52 W
Claro ≃, Bra.	255	19.08 S	50.40 W
Claro, Arroyo ≃	288	34.25 S	58.41 W
Claro, Ribeirão ≃	287b	23.40 S	46.17 W
Clary	50	50.05 N	3.24 E
Claryville	210	41.55 N	74.34 W
Clashmore	48	52.00 N	7.48 W
Clatskanie	224	46.06 N	123.12 W
Clatskanie ≃	224	46.08 N	123.14 W
Clatsop □[6]	224	46.01 N	123.41 W
Clatsop Spit ›[2]	224	46.13 N	124.01 W
Clatteringshaws Lake ⊜	44	55.05 N	4.17 W
Claude	196	35.07 N	101.22 W
Claudy	48	54.54 N	7.09 W
Claughton	44	54.06 N	2.40 W
Claussnitz	54	50.56 N	12.53 E
Clausthal-Zellerfeld	52	51.48 N	10.20 E
Claver	116	9.35 N	125.44 E
Claverack	210	42.13 N	73.44 W
Claveria, Pil.	116	18.37 N	121.05 E
Claveria, Pil.	116	8.38 N	124.55 E
Clavet	184	52.00 N	106.23 W
Clavey ≃	226	37.52 N	120.07 W
Clawit, Mount ∧	116	16.58 N	120.58 E
Clawson, Mi., U.S.	281	42.32 N	83.08 W
Clawson, Tx., U.S.	222	31.24 N	94.47 W
Claxton	192	32.09 N	81.54 W
Clay, Ky., U.S.	194	37.28 N	87.49 W
Clay, Tx., U.S.	222	30.23 N	96.21 W
Clay, W.V., U.S.	188	38.27 N	81.05 W
Clay □[6]	219	38.45 N	88.40 W
Claybank Creek ≃	194	31.10 N	85.44 W
Clay Center, Ks., U.S.	198	39.22 N	97.07 W
Clay Center, Ne., U.S.	198	40.31 N	98.03 W
Clay Center, Oh., U.S.	214	41.33 N	83.21 W
Clay City, Il., U.S.	194	38.41 N	88.21 W
Clay City, In., U.S.	194	39.16 N	87.06 W
Clay City, Ky., U.S.	192	37.51 N	83.55 W
Clay Creek ≃	198	38.06 N	102.31 W
Clay Cross	44	53.10 N	1.24 W
Claydon	42	52.06 N	1.07 E
Claye-Souilly	50	48.57 N	2.42 E
Claygate	260	51.22 N	0.20 W
Claygate Cross	260	51.16 N	0.19 E
Clayhole Wash V	200	36.59 N	113.17 W
Clayhurst	182	56.15 N	120.01 W
Claymont	208	39.48 N	75.27 W
Clayoquot Sound ⊔	182	49.11 N	126.08 W
Claypole	288	34.48 S	58.20 W
Claypool, Az., U.S.	200	33.24 N	110.50 W
Claypool, In., U.S.	216	41.07 N	85.52 W
Claysburg	214	40.17 N	78.27 W
Clay Springs	200	34.21 N	110.17 W
Claysville	214	40.07 N	80.24 W
Clayton, Austl.	274b	37.56 S	145.07 E
Clayton, Eng., U.K.	262	53.47 N	1.50 W
Clayton, Al., U.S.	194	31.52 N	85.26 W
Clayton, Ca., U.S.	282	37.57 N	121.56 W
Clayton, De., U.S.	208	39.17 N	75.38 W
Clayton, Ga., U.S.	192	34.52 N	83.24 W
Clayton, Il., U.S.	219	40.01 N	90.57 W
Clayton, In., U.S.	218	39.41 N	86.31 W
Clayton, La., U.S.	194	31.43 N	91.32 W
Clayton, Mi., U.S.	216	41.52 N	84.14 W
Clayton, Mo., U.S.	219	38.38 N	90.19 W
Clayton, N.J., U.S.	208	39.39 N	75.05 W
Clayton, N.M., U.S.	196	36.27 N	103.11 W
Clayton, N.Y., U.S.	212	44.14 N	76.05 W
Clayton, N.C., U.S.	192	35.39 N	78.27 W
Clayton, Ok., U.S.	196	34.35 N	95.21 W
Clayton, Tx., U.S.	222	32.06 N	94.28 W
Clayton, Wa., U.S.	182	48.00 N	117.33 W
Clayton ≃	166	29.06 S	138.05 E
Claytonia	214	41.00 N	79.58 W
Clayton-le-Moors	262	53.47 N	2.23 W
Clayton-le-Woods	262	53.41 N	2.38 W
Clayton Park ♠	285	39.52 N	75.29 W
Clayton Valley V	282	37.58 N	121.58 W
Claytonville	216	40.34 N	87.49 W
Clay Village	218	38.11 N	85.07 W
Clayville	210	42.59 N	75.15 W
Clear ≃	182	56.11 N	119.42 W
Clear, Cape ›, Ire.	48	51.24 N	9.30 W
Clear, Cape ›, Ak., U.S.	180	59.48 N	147.54 W
Clear, Lake ⊜	212	45.26 N	77.12 W
Clear, Mount ∧	171b	35.52 S	149.04 E
Clear Boggy Creek ≃	196	34.03 N	95.47 W
Clearbrook, B.C., Can.	224	49.08 N	122.26 W
Clearbrook, Mn., U.S.	198	47.41 N	95.25 W
Clear Creek	218	39.07 N	86.32 W
Clear Creek ≃, Al., U.S.	194	34.00 N	87.19 W
Clear Creek ≃, Az., U.S.	200	34.59 N	110.38 W
Clear Creek ≃, Ca., U.S.	204	40.31 N	122.22 W
Clear Creek ≃, Ca., U.S.	280	34.17 N	118.12 W
Clear Creek ≃, Ca., U.S.	282	37.20 N	122.21 W
Clear Creek ≃, Ky., U.S.	218	38.10 N	85.17 W
Clear Creek ≃, Mo., U.S.	194	38.00 N	93.56 W
Clear Creek ≃, Mt., U.S.	202	48.46 N	109.25 W
Clear Creek ≃, Ne., U.S.	198	41.08 N	99.06 W
Clear Creek ≃, Oh., U.S.	218	39.33 N	84.20 W
Clear Creek ≃, Or., U.S.	224	45.23 N	122.29 W
Clear Creek ≃, Or., U.S.	224	45.09 N	121.31 W
Clear Creek ≃, Tn., U.S.	192	36.05 N	84.42 W
Clear Creek ≃, Tx., U.S.	196	33.16 N	97.03 W
Clear Creek ≃, Tx., U.S.	222	29.33 N	95.05 W
Clear Creek ≃, Tx., U.S.	222	29.09 N	97.23 W
Clear Creek ≃, Wa., U.S.	224	46.07 N	122.00 W
Clear Creek ≃, Wy., U.S.	202	44.53 N	106.04 W
Clear Creek State Park ♠	214	41.20 N	79.05 W
Clearfield, Ia., U.S.	198	40.48 N	94.28 W
Clearfield, Ky., U.S.	218	38.09 N	83.25 W
Clearfield, Pa., U.S.	214	41.01 N	78.26 W
Clearfield, Ut,. U.S.	200	41.06 N	112.01 W
Clearfield □[6]	214	41.02 N	78.27 W
Clearfield Creek ≃	214	41.02 N	78.24 W
Clear Fork Reservoir ⊜[1]	214	40.42 N	82.38 W
Clearing ◆[8]	278	41.47 N	87.47 W
Clear Island I	48	51.26 N	9.30 W
Clearlake, Ca., U.S.	226	38.57 N	122.38 W
Clear Lake, Ia., U.S.	190	43.08 N	93.22 W
Clear Lake, S.D., U.S.	198	44.44 N	96.40 W
Clearlake, Wa., U.S.	224	48.28 N	122.14 W
Clear Lake, Wi., U.S.	190	45.15 N	92.16 W
Clear Lake ⊜, Mb., Can.	184	50.42 N	100.00 W
Clear Lake ⊜, On., Can.	212	44.59 N	79.33 W
Clear Lake ⊜, On., Can.	212	45.14 N	79.57 W
Clear Lake ⊜, On., Can.	212	44.30 N	78.13 W
Clear Lake ⊜, In., U.S.	216	41.44 N	84.50 W
Clear Lake ⊜[1], Ca., U.S.	204	39.02 N	122.50 W
Clear Lake ⊜[1], La., U.S.	194	31.55 N	93.05 W
Clearlake Oaks	226	39.07 N	122.40 W
Clearlake Park	226	38.58 N	122.39 W
Clear Lake Reservoir ⊜[1]	204	41.52 N	121.08 W
Clear Lake Shores	222	29.33 N	95.02 W
Clearmont	202	44.38 N	106.22 W
Clear Run	214	41.08 N	78.45 W
Clear Site	180	64.19 N	149.11 W
Clearview, Oh., U.S.	214	41.25 N	82.10 W
Clearview, Wa., U.S.	224	47.45 N	122.06 W
Clearview, W.V., U.S.	214	40.09 N	80.41 W
Clearview Estates	279b	40.34 N	80.16 W
Clearwater, B.C., Can.	182	51.38 N	120.02 W
Clearwater, Mb., Can.	184	49.08 N	99.01 W
Clearwater, Fl., U.S.	220	27.57 N	82.48 W
Clearwater, Ks., U.S.	198	37.30 N	97.30 W
Clearwater, Ne., U.S.	198	42.10 N	98.11 W
Clearwater, S.C., U.S.	192	33.29 N	81.53 W
Clearwater, Wa., U.S.	224	47.34 N	124.17 W
Clearwater ≃, Can.	184	56.44 N	111.23 W
Clearwater ≃, Ab., Can.	182	52.23 N	114.50 W
Clearwater ≃, B.C., Can.	182	51.42 N	120.00 W
Clearwater ≃, Id., U.S.	202	46.25 N	117.02 W
Clearwater ≃, Mn., U.S.	198	47.54 N	96.16 W
Clearwater ≃, Mt., U.S.	202	46.58 N	113.23 W
Clearwater ≃, Wa., U.S.	224	47.33 N	124.21 W
Clearwater, Middle Fork ≃	202	46.09 N	115.59 W
Clearwater, North Fork ≃	202	46.30 N	116.19 W
Clearwater, South Fork ≃	202	46.09 N	115.59 W
Clear Water Bay ⊂	271d	22.17 N	114.18 E
Clearwater Beach Island I	220	27.59 N	82.49 W
Clearwater Lake ⊜, B.C., Can.	182	52.15 N	120.13 W
Clearwater Lake ⊜, Mb., Can.	184	54.05 N	101.00 W
Clearwater Lake Provincial Park ♠	184	54.03 N	101.10 W
Clearwater Mountains ⋏	202	46.00 N	115.30 W
Cleator Moor	44	54.31 N	3.30 W
Clebit	196	34.21 N	94.52 W
Cleburne	222	32.20 N	97.23 W
Cleckheaton	44	53.43 N	1.43 W
Cle Elum	224	47.11 N	120.56 W
Cle Elum ≃	224	47.11 N	121.01 W
Cle Elum Lake ⊜[1]	224	47.18 N	121.06 W
Cleethorpes	44	53.34 N	0.02 W
Cleeve Cloud ∧[2]	42	51.54 N	2.00 W
Clefmont	58	48.06 N	5.31 E
Cleggan	48	53.33 N	10.09 W
Cleland Conservation Park ♠	168b	34.59 S	138.44 E
Cleland Heights	285	39.44 N	75.34 W
Clelles	62	44.50 N	5.37 E
Clementon	285	39.48 N	74.59 W
Clementsport	186	44.40 N	65.37 W
Clemson	192	34.41 N	82.50 W
Clemville	222	29.00 N	96.08 W
Clendenin	188	38.29 N	81.20 W
Clendening Lake ⊜[1]	214	40.16 N	81.13 W
Clenze	54	52.56 N	10.58 E
Cleobury Mortimer	42	52.23 N	2.29 W
Cleona	208	40.20 N	76.28 W
Cléon-d'Andran	62	44.37 N	4.56 E
Cleopatra Needle ∧	116	10.07 N	118.58 E
Clères	50	49.36 N	1.07 E
Clerke Rocks II[1]	244	55.01 S	34.41 W
Clermont, Austl.	166	22.49 S	147.39 E
Clermont, P.Q., Can.	186	47.41 N	70.14 W
Clermont, Fr.	50	49.23 N	2.24 E
Clermont, Fl., U.S.	220	28.32 N	81.46 W
Clermont, N.J., U.S.	285	39.59 N	74.48 W
Clermont, Pa., U.S.	214	41.41 N	78.29 W
Clermont □[6]	218	39.05 N	84.11 W
Clermont-en-Argonne	56	49.06 N	5.04 E
Clermont-Ferrand	32	45.47 N	3.05 E
Clermont State Park ♠	210	42.05 N	73.55 W
Clerval	58	47.24 N	6.30 E
Clervaux	56	50.04 N	6.01 E
Cléry-Saint-André	50	47.49 N	1.45 E
Cles	64	46.22 N	11.02 E
Cleve	166	33.42 S	136.30 E
Clevedon	42	51.27 N	2.51 W
Cleveland, Austl.	171a	27.32 S	153.17 E
Cleveland, Al., U.S.	194	33.59 N	86.34 W
Cleveland, Fl., U.S.	220	26.57 N	82.00 W
Cleveland, Ga., U.S.	192	34.35 N	83.45 W
Cleveland, Ms., U.S.	194	33.44 N	90.43 W
Cleveland, N.Y., U.S.	210	43.14 N	75.53 W
Cleveland, N.C., U.S.	192	35.43 N	80.40 W
Cleveland, Oh., U.S.	214	41.29 N	81.41 W
Cleveland, Oh., U.S.	279a	41.29 N	81.41 W
Cleveland, Ok., U.S.	196	36.18 N	96.27 W
Cleveland, Tn., U.S.	194	35.09 N	84.52 W
Cleveland, Tx., U.S.	222	30.20 N	95.05 W
Cleveland, Va., U.S.	192	36.56 N	82.09 W
Cleveland □[6]	44	54.35 N	1.15 W
Cleveland, Cape ›	166	19.11 S	147.01 E
Cleveland, Mount ∧, Austl.	166	41.25 S	145.23 E
Cleveland, Mount ∧, Mt., U.S.	202	48.56 N	113.51 W
Cleveland Heights	214	41.31 N	81.33 W
Cleveland Hills ⋏[2]	44	54.23 N	1.05 W
Cleveland-Hopkins International Airport ⊠	279a	41.25 N	81.51 W
Clevelândia	252	26.24 S	52.21 W
Clevelândia do Norte	250	3.49 N	51.52 W
Cleveland Museum of Art ⚲	279a	41.31 N	81.37 W
Cleveland National Forest ♠	280	33.47 N	117.38 W
Cleveland Park ◆[8]	284c	38.56 N	77.04 W
Cleveland Peninsula ›[1]	182	55.45 N	132.00 W
Cleveland Pond ⊜	283	42.07 N	70.58 W
Cleveland State University ⚲[2]	279a	41.30 N	81.40 W
Cleveland Zoo ♠	279a	41.27 N	81.43 W
Cleveleys	44	53.53 N	3.03 W
Cleversburg	208	40.02 N	77.28 W
Cleves → Kleve, Dtsch.	52	51.48 N	6.09 E
Cleves, Oh., U.S.	218	39.10 N	84.45 W
Clew Bay ⊂	48	53.50 N	9.50 W
Clewer	158	25.55 S	29.07 E
Clewiston	220	26.45 N	80.56 W
Cley next the Sea	42	52.58 N	1.03 E
Clichy	50	48.54 N	2.18 E
Clichy-sous-Bois	261	48.55 N	2.33 E
Clifden	48	53.29 N	10.01 W
Clifden Bay ⊂	48	53.28 N	10.05 W
Cliffdale Creek ≃	166	16.56 S	138.48 E
Cliffdell	224	46.44 N	120.42 W
Cliffe	42	51.28 N	0.30 E
Cliffe Marshes ≡	260	51.28 N	0.30 E
Cliffe Woods	260	51.26 N	0.30 E
Clifford, On., Can.	212	43.58 N	80.58 W
Clifford, S. Afr.	158	31.04 S	27.28 E
Clifford, In., U.S.	218	39.16 N	85.52 W
Clifford, Pa., U.S.	210	41.39 N	75.36 W
Clifford Park ♠	274b	37.43 S	145.16 E
Cliffside	210	42.31 N	74.59 W
Cliffside Park	276	40.58 N	73.57 W
Cliffwood	276	40.26 N	74.14 W
Cliffwood Beach	276	40.26 N	74.13 W
Clifton, Austl.	171a	27.56 S	151.54 E
Clifton, Eng., U.K.	262	53.46 N	2.49 W
Clifton, Az., U.S.	200	33.03 N	109.17 W
Clifton, Il., U.S.	216	40.56 N	87.56 W
Clifton, Ks., U.S.	198	39.34 N	97.16 W
Clifton, N.J., U.S.	210	40.51 N	74.09 W
Clifton, N.Y., U.S.	210	43.03 N	77.49 W
Clifton, Or., U.S.	224	46.12 N	123.27 W
Clifton, Tn., U.S.	194	35.23 N	87.59 W
Clifton, Tx., U.S.	222	31.46 N	97.34 W
Clifton, Lake ⊜	168a	32.49 S	115.41 E
Clifton Court Forebay ⊜[1]	226	37.50 N	121.35 W
Clifton Forge	192	37.48 N	79.49 W
Clifton Gorge V	42	51.28 N	2.37 W
Clifton Heights, N.Y., U.S.	284a	42.44 N	78.56 W
Clifton Heights, Pa., U.S.	285	39.55 N	75.17 W
Clifton Hills	166	26.52 S	138.50 E
Clifton Knolls	210	42.52 N	73.46 W
Clifton Park ♠	284b	39.19 N	76.35 W
Clifton Point ›	240b	25.01 N	77.34 W
Clifton Springs	210	42.57 N	77.08 W
Clifty, Mount ∧	224	47.07 N	121.10 W
Clifty Creek ≃	218	39.09 N	85.54 W
Clifty Falls State Park ♠	218	38.45 N	85.26 W
Clignon ≃	50	49.07 N	3.04 E
Climax, Sk., Can.	184	49.13 N	108.23 W
Climax, Co., U.S.	200	39.22 N	106.10 W
Climax, Ga., U.S.	192	30.52 N	84.25 W
Climax, Mi., U.S.	216	42.14 N	85.20 W
Climax, Pa., U.S.	214	40.59 N	79.23 W
Clinch ≃	192	35.53 N	84.29 W
Clinchco	192	37.09 N	82.21 W
Clingen	54	51.14 N	10.55 E
Clingmans Dome ∧	192	35.35 N	83.30 W
Clinton, B.C., Can.	182	51.05 N	121.35 W
Clinton, On., Can.	190	43.37 N	81.32 W
Clinton, N.Z.	172	46.12 S	169.22 E
Clinton, Al., U.S.	194	32.55 N	88.00 W
Clinton, Ar., U.S.	194	35.35 N	92.27 W
Clinton, Ct., U.S.	207	41.16 N	72.31 W
Clinton, Il., U.S.	219	40.09 N	88.57 W
Clinton, In., U.S.	194	39.39 N	87.23 W
Clinton, Ia., U.S.	190	41.50 N	90.11 W
Clinton, Ky., U.S.	194	36.40 N	88.59 W
Clinton, La., U.S.	194	30.51 N	91.00 W
Clinton, Me., U.S.	188	44.38 N	69.30 W
Clinton, Md., U.S.	208	38.45 N	76.53 W
Clinton, Ma., U.S.	207	42.25 N	71.41 W
Clinton, Mi., U.S.	216	42.04 N	83.58 W
Clinton, Mn., U.S.	198	45.27 N	96.26 W
Clinton, Ms., U.S.	194	32.20 N	90.19 W
Clinton, Mo., U.S.	194	38.22 N	93.46 W
Clinton, N.J., U.S.	210	40.38 N	74.54 W
Clinton, N.Y., U.S.	210	43.02 N	75.22 W
Clinton, N.C., U.S.	192	34.59 N	78.19 W
Clinton, Oh., U.S.	214	40.56 N	81.42 W
Clinton, Ok., U.S.	196	35.30 N	98.58 W
Clinton, Pa., U.S.	214	40.29 N	80.18 W
Clinton, S.C., U.S.	192	34.28 N	81.52 W
Clinton, Tn., U.S.	192	36.06 N	84.07 W
Clinton, Tx., U.S.	222	33.06 N	96.14 W
Clinton, Wa., U.S.	224	47.58 N	122.21 W
Clinton, Wi., U.S.	216	42.33 N	88.51 W
Clinton □[6], Il., U.S.	219	38.37 N	89.22 W
Clinton □[6], In., U.S.	216	40.17 N	86.31 W
Clinton □[6], Mi., U.S.	216	42.56 N	84.36 W
Clinton □[6], N.Y., U.S.	206	44.57 N	73.42 W
Clinton □[6], Oh., U.S.	218	39.27 N	83.50 W
Clinton □[6], Pa., U.S.	210	41.08 N	71.26 W
Clinton ≃	214	42.36 N	82.48 W
Clinton, Cape ›	166	22.32 S	150.47 E
Clinton, Lake ⊜[1]	194	40.10 N	88.50 W
Clinton, Middle Branch ≃	281	42.36 N	82.54 W
Clinton, North Branch ≃	214	42.36 N	82.54 W
Clinton-Colden Lake ⊜	176	63.58 N	107.27 W
Clintondale	210	41.01 N	77.29 W
Clinton Lake ⊜[1]	198	38.55 N	95.25 W
Clinton Park	210	42.36 N	73.43 W
Clinton Reservoir ⊜[1]	276	41.05 N	74.27 W
Clinton Township	214	42.33 N	82.53 W
Clintonville, Mi., U.S.	281	42.43 N	83.22 W
Clintonville, Pa., U.S.	214	41.12 N	79.53 W
Clintonville, Wi., U.S.	190	44.37 N	88.45 W
Clintwood	192	37.09 N	82.27 W
Clio, Al., U.S.	194	31.42 N	85.36 W
Clio, Mi., U.S.	190	43.10 N	83.44 W
Clio, S.C., U.S.	192	34.34 N	79.32 W
Clipperton, Île I[1]	230	10.17 N	109.13 W
Clipperton Fracture Zone ✦	16	10.00 N	115.00 W
Clisham ∧	46	57.57 N	6.49 W
Clisson	32	47.05 N	1.17 W
Clitheroe	44	53.53 N	2.23 W
Clitunno ≃	66	42.56 N	12.37 E
Clive	172	39.35 S	176.55 E
Cloates, Point ›	162	22.43 S	113.40 E
Clock Face	262	53.25 N	2.43 W
Clocolan	158	29.00 S	27.30 E
Clodomira	252	27.35 S	64.08 W
Cloe	214	40.56 N	78.56 W
Cloete	196	27.55 N	101.10 W
Cloghan, Ire.	48	53.13 N	7.53 W
Cloghan, Ire.	48	54.51 N	7.56 W
Cloghane	48	52.13 N	10.12 W
Clogheen	48	52.16 N	8.00 W
Clogher	48	54.25 N	7.12 W
Clogher Head ›	48	53.48 N	6.12 W
Cloghjordan	48	52.57 N	8.02 W
Clonakilty	48	51.37 N	8.54 W
Clonakilty Bay ⊂	48	51.35 N	8.50 W
Cloncurry	166	20.42 S	140.30 E
Cloncurry ≃	166	18.37 S	140.40 E
Clondalkin	48	53.19 N	6.24 W
Clonee	48	53.25 N	6.26 W
Clones	48	54.11 N	7.15 W
Clonfert	48	53.14 N	8.05 W
Clonmacnois ⊥	48	53.20 N	7.59 W
Clonmany	48	55.14 N	7.25 W
Clonmel	48	52.21 N	7.42 W
Clonroche	48	52.27 N	6.43 W
Clontarf	274a	33.48 S	151.16 E
Cloone	48	53.57 N	7.46 W
Clo-oose	224	48.40 N	124.49 W
Cloppenburg	52	52.50 N	8.02 E
Cloquallum Creek ≃	224	46.58 N	123.24 W
Cloquet	190	46.43 N	92.27 W
Cloquet ≃	190	46.52 N	92.35 W
Clorinda	252	25.17 S	57.43 W
Closter	276	40.58 N	73.57 W
Cloudcroft	200	32.57 N	105.44 W
Cloud Peak ∧, Ak., U.S.	180	68.24 N	148.26 W
Cloud Peak ∧, Wy., U.S.	202	44.25 N	107.10 W
Cloudy Bay ⊂	172	41.27 S	174.10 E
Cloudy Mountain ∧	180	63.11 N	156.05 W
Clough	48	54.18 N	5.50 W
Clough Foot	262	53.43 N	2.08 W
Clova	46	56.50 N	3.06 W
Clova, Glen V	46	56.49 N	3.04 W
Clove Lakes Park ♠	276	40.37 N	74.07 W
Clovelly, Austl.	274a	33.55 S	151.16 E
Clovelly, Eng., U.K.	42	51.00 N	4.24 W
Clover	192	35.06 N	81.13 W
Clover Bank	210	42.45 N	78.53 W
Clover Creek ≃, Id., U.S.	202	42.34 N	115.38 W
Clover Creek ≃, Id., U.S.	202	43.00 N	115.11 W
Cloverdale, B.C., Can.	224	49.06 N	122.44 W
Cloverdale, Al., U.S.	194	34.56 N	87.46 W
Cloverdale, Ca., U.S.	204	38.48 N	123.00 W
Cloverdale, Il., U.S.	278	41.56 N	88.07 W
Cloverdale, In., U.S.	194	39.30 N	86.47 W
Cloverdale, Ky., U.S.	218	38.10 N	84.53 W
Cloverdale, Mi., U.S.	216	42.32 N	85.23 W
Cloverdale, Oh., U.S.	216	41.01 N	84.18 W
Cloverdale, Or., U.S.	224	45.12 N	123.53 W
Cloverdale Mall ◆[9]	275b	43.38 N	79.34 W
Cloverdene	273d	26.09 S	28.22 E
Cloverleaf	222	29.46 N	95.10 W
Clover Pass	182	55.28 N	131.47 W
Cloverport	194	37.50 N	86.37 W
Cloverville	216	43.11 N	86.10 W
Clovis, Ca., U.S.	226	36.49 N	119.42 W
Clovis, N.M., U.S.	196	34.24 N	103.12 W
Clowbridge Reservoir ⊜[1]	262	53.45 N	2.16 W
Clowne	44	53.18 N	1.16 W
Cloyes-sur-le-Loir	50	48.00 N	1.14 E
Cloyne	48	51.51 N	8.08 W
Cluain Meala → Clonmel	48	52.21 N	7.42 W
Cluanie, Loch ⊜	46	57.07 N	5.05 W
Cluj □[6]	38	46.45 N	23.45 E
Cluj-Napoca	38	46.47 N	23.36 E
Clun	42	52.26 N	3.00 W
Clun ≃	42	52.22 N	2.53 W
Clune	214	40.34 N	79.18 W
Clunes	169	37.18 S	143.47 E
Clun Forest ◆[3]	42	52.28 N	3.07 W
Clunie Water ≃	46	57.00 N	3.24 W
Cluny, Austl.	166	24.31 S	139.35 E
Cluny, Fr.	58	46.26 N	4.39 E
Cluses	58	46.04 N	6.36 E
Clusone	64	45.53 N	9.57 E
Clute	222	29.01 N	95.23 W
Clutha ≃	172	46.21 S	169.48 E
Clwyd □[6]	44	53.05 N	3.20 W
Clwyd ≃	44	53.20 N	3.30 W
Clwyd, Vale of V	44	53.12 N	3.24 W
Clwydian Range ⋏	44	53.10 N	3.20 W
Clydach	42	51.43 N	3.50 W
Clyde, Austl.	274a	33.50 S	151.00 E
Clyde, Ab., Can.	182	54.09 N	113.39 W
Clyde, N.Z.	172	45.11 S	169.19 E
Clyde, Ca., U.S.	226	38.02 N	122.02 W
Clyde, Ks., U.S.	198	39.35 N	97.23 W
Clyde, Mi., U.S.	281	42.41 N	83.37 W
Clyde, N.Y., U.S.	210	43.05 N	76.52 W
Clyde, N.C., U.S.	192	35.32 N	82.54 W
Clyde, Oh., U.S.	214	41.18 N	82.58 W
Clyde, Tx., U.S.	196	32.24 N	99.30 W
Clyde ≃, Austl.	170	35.23 S	150.15 E
Clyde ≃, N.S., Can.	186	43.35 N	65.25 W
Clyde ≃, On., Can.	212	44.58 N	76.22 W
Clyde ≃, Scot., U.K.	46	55.44 N	4.55 W
Clyde ≃, N.Y., U.S.	210	43.04 N	77.00 W
Clyde ≃, Vt., U.S.	188	44.56 N	72.12 W
Clyde, Firth of ⊂[1]	46	55.42 N	5.00 W
Clydebank	46	55.54 N	4.24 W
Clydegale Lake ⊜	212	45.25 N	78.23 W
Clyde Lake ⊜	182	55.18 N	111.28 W
Clyde No. 3	214	39.59 N	80.03 W
Clyde Park	202	45.53 N	110.36 W
Clyde Potts Reservoir ⊜[1]	276	40.48 N	74.35 W
Clyde River	176	70.25 N	68.30 W
Clydesdale	158	26.54 S	27.55 E
Clydesdale V	46	55.42 N	3.50 W
Clymer, N.Y., U.S.	214	42.01 N	79.37 W
Clymer, Pa., U.S.	214	40.40 N	79.00 W
Clynnog-fawr	44	53.01 N	4.23 W
Clywedog ≃	42	52.27 N	3.32 W
Ćmielów	30	50.53 N	21.31 E
Cna ≃, Bela.	76	52.10 N	27.03 E

≃ River	Fluß	Río	Rivière	Rio
≍ Canal	Kanal	Canal	Canal	Canal
⌊ Waterfall, Rapids	Wasserfall, Stromschnellen	Cascada, Rápidos	Chute d'eau, Rapides	Cascata, Rápidos
⊔ Strait	Meeresstraße	Estrecho	Détroit	Estreito
⊂ Bay, Gulf	Bucht, Golf	Bahía, Golfo	Baie, Golfe	Baía, Golfo
⊜ Lake, Lakes	See, Seen	Lago, Lagos	Lac, Lacs	Lago, Lagos
≡ Swamp	Sumpf	Pantano	Marais	Pântano
⊠ Ice Features, Glacier	Eis- und Gletscherformen	Accidentes Glaciales	Formes glaciaires	Acidentes glaciares
⊤ Other Hydrographic Features	Andere Hydrographische Objekte	Otros Elementos Hidrográficos	Autres données hydrographiques	Outros acidentes hidrográficos

✦ Submarine Features	Untermeerische Objekte	Accidentes Submarinos	Formes de relief sous-marin	Acidentes submarinos
□ Political Unit	Politische Einheit	Unidad Politica	Entité politique	Unidade política
⚲ Cultural Institution	Kulturelle Institution	Institución Cultural	Institution culturelle	Institução cultural
⊥ Historical Site	Historische Stätte	Sitio Histórico	Site historique	Sitio histórico
♠ Recreational Site	Erholungs- und Ferienort	Sitio de Recreo	Centre de loisirs	Area de Lazer
⊠ Airport	Flughafen	Aeropuerto	Aéroport	Aeroporto
■ Military Installation	Militäranlage	Instalación Militar	Installation militaire	Instalação militar
◆ Miscellaneous	Verschiedenes	Misceláneo	Divers	Diversos

ENGLISH — DEUTSCH

Name	Page (Seite)	Lat.°′ (Breite°′)	Long.°′ (Länge°′ E = Ost)
Cna ≃, Ross.	76	57.33 N	34.36 E
Cna ≃, Ross.	80	54.32 N	42.05 E
Cna ≃, Ross.	82	55.03 N	39.09 E
Cnori	84	41.37 N	45.59 E
Cnossus → Knossós ⊥	38	35.20 N	25.10 E
Côa ≃	34	41.05 N	7.06 W
Coacalco	286a	19.37 N	99.05 W
Coachella	204	33.40 N	116.10 W
Coachella Canal ≅	204	33.34 N	116.00 W
Coachford	48	51.53 N	8.48 W
Coacoyole	232	24.31 N	106.34 W
Coacuilco	234	21.07 N	98.35 W
Coahoma	196	32.18 N	101.18 W
Coahuayana	234	18.44 N	103.41 W
Coahuayutla de Guerrero	234	18.19 N	101.49 W
Coahuila	200	32.12 N	114.59 W
Coahuila □[3]	232	27.20 N	102.00 W
Coal ≃	180	59.39 N	126.57 W
Coalbrook	158	26.51 S	27.53 E
Coalbrookdale	42	52.38 N	2.30 W
Coalburg	214	41.11 N	80.36 W
Coalburn	46	55.36 N	3.54 W
Coal City	216	41.17 N	88.17 W
Coalcomán ≃	234	18.11 N	103.08 W
Coalcomán de Matamoros	234	18.47 N	103.09 W
Coal Creek	180	65.22 N	143.10 W
Coal Creek ≃, Co., U.S.	198	40.30 N	104.26 W
Coal Creek ≃, In., U.S.	194	39.57 N	87.25 W
Coal Creek ≃, Wa., U.S.	202	47.19 N	118.36 W
Coal Creek Flat	172	45.29 S	169.18 E
Coaldale, Ab., Can.	182	49.43 N	112.37 W
Coaldale, Pa., U.S.	210	40.49 N	75.54 W
Coal Fire Creek ≃	194	33.15 N	88.18 W
Coal Fork	188	38.19 N	81.32 W
Coalgate, N.Z.	172	43.29 S	171.58 E
Coalgate, Ok., U.S.	196	34.32 N	96.13 W
Coal Grove	188	38.30 N	82.38 W
Coal Harbour	182	50.36 N	127.35 W
Coal Hill	194	35.26 N	93.40 W
Coal Hill Park ♠	271a	39.56 N	116.23 E
Coalhurst	182	49.45 N	112.56 W
Coalinga	226	36.08 N	120.21 W
Coalisland	48	54.33 N	6.42 W
Coal Island I	172	46.07 S	166.38 E
Coalmont	182	49.31 N	120.41 W
Coalpit Heath	42	51.32 N	2.28 W
Coalport	214	40.44 N	78.32 W
Coal River	180	59.45 N	126.55 W
Coal Run ≃	279b	40.21 N	80.07 W
Coalspur	182	53.11 N	117.01 W
Coalton	219	39.17 N	89.19 W
Coaltown	214	41.02 N	80.20 W
Coal Valley ∨	204	38.00 N	115.05 W
Coalville, S. Afr.	158	26.01 S	29.10 E
Coalville, Eng., U.K.	42	52.44 N	1.20 W
Coalville, Ut,. U.S.	200	40.55 N	111.23 W
Coamo	240m	18.05 N	66.22 W
Coamo, Lago ⊜[1]	240m	18.01 N	66.23 W
Coapilla	234	17.08 N	93.10 W
Coaraci	255	14.38 S	39.32 W
Coari	246	4.05 S	63.08 W
Coari ≃	246	4.30 S	63.33 W
Coari, Lago de ⊜	246	4.15 S	63.22 W
Coarsegold	226	37.16 N	119.42 W
Coast □[4]	154	3.00 S	39.30 E
Coast Mountains ⋏	176	55.00 N	129.00 W
Coast Ranges ⋏	178	41.00 N	123.30 W
Coatán ≃	236	14.48 N	92.31 W
Coatbridge	46	55.52 N	4.01 W
Coatepec	234	19.27 N	96.58 W
Coatepec Harinas	234	18.54 N	99.43 W
Coatepeque	236	14.42 N	91.52 W
Coatepeque, Lago de ⊜	236	13.52 N	89.33 W
Coates Creek ≃	212	44.24 N	79.54 W
Coatesville	208	39.58 N	75.49 W
Coaticook	206	45.08 N	71.48 W
Coaticook ≃	206	45.20 N	71.53 W
Coatsburg	219	40.02 N	91.10 W
Coats Island I	176	62.30 N	83.00 W
Coats Land ◆[1]	9	77.00 S	28.00 W
Coatzacoalcos	234	18.09 N	94.25 W
Coatzacoalcos ≃	234	18.10 N	94.27 W
Coatzintla	234	20.29 N	97.27 W
Coayllo	248	12.44 S	76.28 W
Coazze	62	45.03 N	7.18 E
Cobá ⊥	232	20.36 N	87.35 W
Cobadin	38	44.04 N	28.13 E
Coballo Cocha	246	3.54 S	70.32 W
Cobalt, On., Can.	190	47.24 N	79.41 W
Cobalt, Ct., U.S.	207	41.33 N	72.33 W
Cobán	236	15.29 N	90.19 W
Çobanlar	130	38.41 N	30.47 E
Cobar	166	31.30 S	145.49 E
Cobargo	166	36.23 S	149.53 E
Cobb	226	38.49 N	122.43 W
Cobb Creek ≃	196	35.05 N	98.25 W
Cobberas, Mount ∧	166	36.52 S	148.10 E
Cobbetts Pond ⊜	283	42.48 N	71.17 W
Cobbin's Brook ≃	260	51.41 N	0.01 W
Cobb Island	208	38.16 N	76.51 W
Cobb Island I, Md., U.S.	208	38.16 N	76.51 W
Cobb Island I, Va., U.S.	208	37.20 N	75.44 W
Cobbitty	274a	34.01 S	150.41 E
Cobbitty ∧[2]	274a	33.59 S	150.42 E
Cobble Hill	224	48.41 N	123.36 W
Cobble Mountain Reservoir ⊜[1]	207	42.08 N	72.55 W
Cobblestone Mountain ∧	228	34.37 N	118.52 W
Cobb Neck ›[1]	208	38.20 N	76.55 W
Cobbs Creek ≃	285	39.54 N	75.15 W
Cobbs Creek Park ♠	285	39.58 N	75.16 W
Cobb Seamount ✣[3]	16	46.46 N	130.49 W
Cobden, Austl.	169	38.20 S	143.05 E
Cobden, On., Can.	190	45.38 N	76.53 W
Cobden, Il., U.S.	194	37.31 N	89.15 W
Cobeña	266a	40.34 N	3.30 W
Cobequid Bay ⊂	186	45.21 N	63.45 W
Cobequid Mountains ⋏	186	45.31 N	64.05 W
Cobh	48	51.51 N	8.17 W
Cobham, Eng., U.K.	42	51.20 N	0.25 W
Cobham, Eng., U.K.	260	51.23 N	0.24 E
Cobham ≃	184	53.15 N	93.58 W
Cobham Hall ⊥	260	51.23 N	0.25 E
Cobija, Bol.	248	11.02 S	68.44 W
Cobija, Chile	252	22.33 S	70.16 W
Coblenz → Koblenz	56	50.21 N	7.35 E
Cobleskill	210	42.40 N	74.29 W
Cobleskill Creek ≃	210	42.43 N	74.20 W
Coboconk	212	44.39 N	78.48 W
Cobo Hall ⌂	281	42.19 N	83.03 W
Cobolgo, gora ∧	84	42.50 N	46.23 E
Çoboto, Cerro ∧	200	31.29 N	112.05 W
Čoboty	265b	55.39 N	37.21 E
Cobourg	212	43.58 N	78.10 W
Cobourg Peninsula ›[1]	164	11.20 S	132.15 E
Cobquecura	252	36.08 S	72.47 W
Cobram	166	35.55 S	145.39 E
Cobras, Ilha das I	287a	22.54 S	43.10 W
Cobras, Ribeirão das ≃	256	23.08 S	46.05 W
Cobre ≃	236	8.01 N	81.18 W
Cobre, Barranca del ∨	232	27.28 N	107.50 W
Cóbuè	154	12.04 S	34.50 E
Coburg, Austl.	169	37.45 S	144.58 E
Coburg, Dtsch.	56	50.15 N	10.58 E
Coburg Island I	176	76.00 N	79.25 W
Coburn	210	40.52 N	77.28 W
Coburn Mountain ∧	188	45.28 N	70.06 W
Coca ≃	246	0.29 S	76.58 W
Coca, Laguna ⊜	286b	22.57 N	82.27 W
Coca, Pizzo di ∧	64	46.04 N	10.01 E
Cocachacra	248	17.06 S	71.46 W
Cocais, Ribeirão dos ≃	256	21.59 S	47.15 W
Cocal	250	3.28 S	41.34 W
Cocalico Creek ≃	208	40.07 N	76.14 W
Coccaglio	64	45.34 N	9.58 E
Cocconato	62	45.05 N	8.02 E
Cocentaina	34	38.45 N	0.26 W
Cochabamba	248	17.24 S	66.09 W
Çochabamba □[5]	248	17.30 S	65.40 W
Čochatauri	84	42.01 N	42.15 E
Cochato ≃	283	42.10 N	71.01 W
Coche, Isla I	246	10.45 N	63.55 W
Cochem	56	50.11 N	7.09 E
Cochesett	283	42.01 N	71.02 W
Cochetopa Creek ≃	200	38.31 N	106.47 W
Cochichewick, Lake ⊜	283	42.42 N	71.06 W
Cochin	122	9.58 N	76.14 E
Cochin China → Nam Phan □[9]	110	11.00 N	107.00 E
Cochinos, Bahía de (Bay of Pigs) ⊂	240p	22.07 N	81.10 W
Cochinos, Cayos II	236	15.57 N	86.33 W
Cochise Head ∧	200	32.03 N	109.18 W
Cochiti Indian Reservation ◆[4]	200	35.37 N	106.20 W
Cochituate	207	42.19 N	71.21 W
Cochituate, Lake ⊜	283	42.17 N	71.22 W
Cochituate State Park ♠	207	42.20 N	71.22 W
Cochran	192	32.23 N	83.21 W
Cochrane, Ab., Can.	182	51.11 N	114.28 W
Cochrane, On., Can.	176	49.04 N	81.01 W
Cochrane, Chile	254	47.16 S	72.33 W
Cochrane, Wi., U.S.	190	44.13 N	91.50 W
Cochrane ≃	176	57.52 N	101.38 W
Cochrane, Cerro (Monte San Lorenzo) ∧	254	47.37 S	72.19 W
Cochrane, Lago (Lago Pueyrredón) ⊜	254	47.20 S	72.00 W
Cochranton	214	41.31 N	80.02 W
Cochranville	208	39.53 N	75.55 W
Cochstedt	54	51.53 N	11.24 E
Cockatoo-Inseln → Buccaneer Archipelago II	160	16.17 S	123.20 E
Cock Bridge	46	57.09 N	3.14 W
Cockburn	166	32.05 S	141.00 E
Cockburn, Canal ⊔	254	54.20 S	71.30 W
Cockburn, Cape ›	164	11.20 S	132.52 E
Cockburn, Mount ∧	162	22.46 S	130.36 E
Cockburn Island I	190	45.55 N	83.22 W
Cockburn Sound ⊔	168a	32.12 S	115.42 E
Cockburnspath	46	55.56 N	2.21 W
Cock Clarks	260	51.42 N	0.37 E
Cockenoe Island I	276	41.05 N	73.21 W
Cockenzie	46	55.58 N	2.58 W
Cocker ≃	44	54.39 N	3.22 W
Cockerham	44	53.59 N	2.50 W
Cockermouth	44	54.40 N	3.21 W
Cockeysville	208	39.28 N	76.38 W
Cockfield	44	54.37 N	1.48 W
Cockfosters ◆[8]	260	51.39 N	0.09 W
Cocklebiddy	162	32.02 S	126.06 E
Cockpit Country ◆[1]	241q	18.18 N	77.43 W
Cockrell Hill	222	32.44 N	96.53 W
Cockroach Island I	240m	18.24 N	65.04 W
Cockscomb Point ›	174u	14.14 S	170.40 W
Coclé □[4]	236	8.30 N	80.15 W
Coclé del Norte ≃	236	9.05 N	80.35 W
Coclois	50	48.28 N	4.20 E
Coco ≃	236	15.00 N	83.10 W
Coco, Cayo I	240p	22.30 N	78.28 W
Coco, Isla del I	230	5.32 N	87.04 W
Côco, Rio do ≃	250	9.27 S	50.02 W
Cocoa	220	28.23 N	80.44 W
Cocoa Beach	220	28.19 N	80.36 W
Cocobeach	152	0.59 N	9.36 E
Coco Channel ⊔	110	13.45 N	93.00 E
Cococi	250	6.25 S	40.30 W
Cocodrie Lake ⊜[1]	194	30.58 N	92.25 W
Coco Islands II	110	14.05 N	93.18 E
Coconino Plateau ⋏[1]	200	35.50 N	112.30 W
Cocorocuma, Cayos ✣[2]	236	15.45 N	83.00 W
Cocos	255	14.10 S	44.33 W
Cocos (Keeling) Islands □[2]	14	12.10 S	96.55 E
Cocos Bay ⊂	241r	10.27 N	61.00 W
Cocos Island I	174p	13.14 N	144.39 E
Cocos Lagoon ⊂	174p	13.14 N	144.38 E
Cocos Ridge ✣[3]	16	5.30 N	86.00 W
Cocotá ◆[8]	287a	22.49 S	43.11 W
Cocuiza ≃	246	10.59 N	71.17 W
Cocula, Méx.	234	18.14 N	99.40 W
Cocula, Méx.	234	20.23 N	103.50 W
Cod ≃	44	54.10 N	1.22 W
Cod, Cape ›[1]	207	41.42 N	70.15 W
Codăeşti	38	46.52 N	27.46 E
Codajás	246	3.50 S	62.05 W
Codaruina	71	40.56 N	8.49 E
Coddenham	42	52.09 N	1.07 E
Codera, Cabo ›	246	10.35 N	66.05 W
Coderre	184	50.10 N	106.23 W
Coderre, Ruisseau ≃	275a	45.43 N	73.19 W
Codesa	182	55.45 N	118.04 W
Codfish Island I	172	46.47 S	167.38 E
Codigoro	66	44.49 N	12.08 E
Cod Island I	176	57.45 N	61.50 W
Codlea	38	45.42 N	25.27 E
Codnor	44	53.03 N	1.23 W
Codó	250	4.29 S	43.53 W
Codogno	62	45.09 N	9.42 E
Codorus	208	39.48 N	76.52 W
Codorus Creek ≃	208	40.03 N	76.38 W
Codorus State Park ♠	208	39.48 N	76.54 W
Codòzinho	250	4.46 S	44.10 W
Codpa	248	18.50 S	69.44 W
Çodrii ⋏[2]	38	47.10 N	28.25 E
Čodro	86	50.50 N	88.34 E
Codroipo	64	45.58 N	12.59 E
Codrongianos	71	40.39 N	8.41 E
Codroy	186	47.53 N	59.24 W
Codroy Pond	186	48.04 N	58.52 W
Codru-Moma, Munții ⋏	38	46.30 N	22.20 E
Codsall	42	52.38 N	2.12 W
Cody, Ne., U.S.	198	42.56 N	101.14 W
Cody, Wy., U.S.	202	44.31 N	109.03 W
Coeburn	192	36.56 N	82.27 W
Coelemu	252	36.29 S	72.42 W
Coelho da Rocha	256	22.47 S	43.23 W
Coelho Neto	250	4.15 S	43.00 W
Coemba	152	12.08 S	18.05 E
Coen	164	13.56 S	143.12 E
Coen ≃, Austl.	164	13.56 S	142.02 E
Coén ≃, C.R.	236	9.34 N	82.58 W
Coeneo [de la Libertad]	234	19.49 N	101.35 W
Coeroeni ≃	250	3.21 N	57.31 W
Coesfeld	52	51.56 N	7.10 E
Coetivy Island I	138	7.08 S	56.16 E
Coeur d'Alene	202	47.40 N	116.46 W
Coeur d'Alene ≃	202	47.28 N	116.48 W
Coeur d'Alene Indian Reservation ◆[4]	202	47.18 N	116.45 W
Coeur d'Alene Lake ⊜	202	47.32 N	116.48 W
Coeur d'Alene Mountains ⋏	202	47.50 N	116.05 W
Coevorden	52	52.40 N	6.45 E
Coeymans	210	42.28 N	73.48 W
Coffeen	219	39.05 N	89.24 W
Coffeen Lake ⊜[1]	219	39.03 N	89.20 W
Coffeeville	194	33.58 N	89.40 W
Coffeyville	198	37.02 N	95.36 W
Coffin Bay	162	34.37 S	135.29 E
Coffin Bay ⊂	162	34.27 S	135.19 E
Coffin Bay Peninsula ›[1]	162	34.32 S	135.15 E
Coffs Harbour	166	30.18 S	153.08 E
Cofimvaba	158	32.00 S	27.35 E
Cofradía	236	15.24 N	88.09 W
Cofre de Perote, Cerro ∧	234	19.29 N	97.08 W
Cofre de Perote, Parque Nacional ♠	234	19.32 N	97.10 W
Cofrents	34	39.14 N	1.04 W
Cogâlnic (Kohyl'nyk) ≃	78	45.51 N	29.38 E
Coggeshall	42	51.52 N	0.41 E
Coggiola	62	45.41 N	8.11 E
Coggon	190	42.16 N	91.31 W
Coghill, Mount ∧	170	35.10 S	149.44 E
Coghinas ≃	71	40.56 N	8.48 E
Coghinas, Lago del ⊜	71	40.45 N	9.02 E
Coglians, Monte (Hohe Warte) ∧	64	46.37 N	12.53 E
Cogliate	266b	45.39 N	9.05 E
Cognac	32	45.42 N	0.20 W
Cogne	62	45.37 N	7.21 E
Cognin	62	45.34 N	5.54 E
Cogo	152	1.05 N	9.42 E
Cogoleto	62	44.23 N	8.39 E
Cogolin	62	43.15 N	6.32 E
Cogollo del Cengio	64	45.47 N	11.25 E
Cogolludo	34	40.57 N	3.05 W
Cogolo	64	46.21 N	10.41 E
Çogoon ≃	166	27.19 S	148.50 E
Čograjuskoje vodochranilišče ⊜[1]	80	45.30 N	44.25 E
Cogswell	198	46.06 N	97.46 W
Cogswell Reservoir ⊜[1]	280	34.14 N	117.58 W
Cogt	102	45.20 N	96.38 E
Cogtoandman'	102	45.50 N	104.28 E
Cogton Bay ⊂	116	9.51 N	124.33 E
Cogt-Ovoo	102	44.25 N	105.20 E
Çoğun	130	39.20 N	34.08 E
Cohansey ≃	208	39.21 N	75.22 W
Cohasset	207	42.14 N	70.48 W
Cohasset Harbor ⊂	283	42.15 N	70.47 W
Cohengu ≃	248	10.17 S	73.57 W
Cohoctah	216	42.46 N	83.57 W
Cohocton	210	42.30 N	77.30 W
Cohocton ≃	210	42.09 N	77.05 W
Cohoe	180	60.23 N	151.18 W
Cohoes	210	42.46 N	73.42 W
Cohoon, Lake ⊜[1]	208	36.45 N	76.38 W
Cohuna	166	35.49 S	144.13 E
Coiba, Isla de I	246	7.27 N	81.45 W
Coig ≃	254	50.58 S	69.11 W
Coigeach, Rubha ›	46	58.06 N	5.26 W
Coignières	261	48.45 N	1.55 E
Coihaique	254	45.34 S	72.04 W
Coils Creek ≃	204	39.32 N	116.16 W
Coimbatore	122	11.00 N	76.58 E
Coimbra, Bra.	248	19.55 S	57.47 W
Coimbra, Bra.	255	20.52 S	42.48 W
Coimbra, Port.	34	40.12 N	8.25 W
Coín, Esp.	34	36.40 N	4.45 W
Coin, Ia., U.S.	198	40.39 N	95.13 W
Coina ≃	266c	38.38 N	9.03 W
Coipasa, Lago ⊜	248	19.12 S	68.07 W
Coipasa, Salar de ≍	248	19.26 S	68.09 W
Coire → Chur	58	46.51 N	9.32 E
Čojbalsan, Mong.	88	48.25 N	114.52 E
Čojbalsan, Mong.	88	48.04 N	114.30 E
Čojbalsan uul ∧	88	47.49 N	107.00 E
Cojedes	246	9.37 N	68.55 W
Cojedes □[3]	246	9.20 N	68.20 W
Cojímar ◆[8]	286b	23.10 N	82.18 W
Cojímar ≃	286b	23.10 N	82.17 W
Cojudo Blanco, Cerro ∧	254	47.05 S	69.20 W
Cojumatlán de Régules	234	20.07 N	102.50 W
Cojutepeque	236	13.43 N	88.56 W
Çokak	130	37.45 N	36.19 E
Čokato	190	45.04 N	94.11 W
Cokeburg	214	40.06 N	80.04 W
Coker	273a	6.29 N	3.20 E
Çokeville	200	42.04 N	110.57 W
Čoktal	85	42.36 N	76.44 E
Čokurdach	74	70.38 N	147.55 E
Colāba ◆[8]	272c	18.54 N	72.48 E
Colāba Point ›	272c	18.53 N	72.48 E
Colac	169	38.20 S	143.35 E
Colac, Lake ⊜	169	38.18 S	143.35 E
Çolaklı	130	38.22 N	38.33 E
Čolalao del Valle	252	26.22 S	65.57 W
Colapsin Point ›	116	6.38 N	125.25 E
Colares, Bra.	250	0.56 S	48.17 W
Colares, Port.	266c	38.48 N	9.27 W
Colares, Ribeira de ≃	266c	38.49 N	9.28 W
Colatina	255	19.32 S	40.37 W
Cölbe	56	50.51 N	8.48 E
Colbeck, Cape ›	9	77.06 S	157.48 W
Colberry Park	281	42.36 N	83.16 W
Colbert	196	33.51 N	96.30 W
Colbinabbin	166	36.35 S	144.49 E
Colbitz	54	52.19 N	11.36 E
Colbitz-Letzlinger Heide ◆[3]	54	52.27 N	11.35 E
Colborne, On., Can.	212	42.51 N	80.19 W
Colborne, On., Can.	212	44.00 N	77.53 W
Colbún	252	35.42 S	71.25 W
Colbún, Embalse ⊜[1]	252	35.40 S	71.20 W
Colburn, Eng., U.K.	44	54.23 N	1.41 W
Colburn, In., U.S.	216	40.31 N	86.42 W
Colby, Ks., U.S.	198	39.23 N	101.03 W
Colby, Wi., U.S.	190	44.54 N	90.18 W
Colca	248	12.18 S	75.13 W
Colca ≃	248	15.51 S	72.26 W
Colcamar	248	6.16 S	77.55 W
Colchester, On., Can.	214	41.59 N	82.56 W
Colchester, Eng., U.K.	42	51.54 N	0.54 E
Colchester, Ct., U.S.	207	41.34 N	72.19 W
Colchester, Il., U.S.	190	40.25 N	90.47 W
Coldbackie	46	58.31 N	4.23 W
Cold Bay	180	55.11 N	162.30 W
Cold Bay ⊂	180	55.13 N	162.33 W
Coldblow ◆[8]	260	51.26 N	0.10 E
Cold Brook	210	43.15 N	75.03 W
Cold Creek ≃	212	44.12 N	77.36 W
Colden	210	42.39 N	78.41 W
Cold Fell ∧	44	54.54 N	2.36 W
Cold Harbor Battlefield ⊥	208	37.36 N	77.20 W
Coldingham	46	55.53 N	2.10 W
Colditz	54	51.07 N	12.48 E
Cold Lake	184	54.27 N	110.10 W
Cold Lake ⊜	184	54.33 N	110.05 W
Cold Lake, Canadian Forces Base ■	184	54.25 N	110.17 W
Cold Lake Indian Reserve ◆[4]	184	54.33 N	110.10 W
Cold Norton	260	51.40 N	0.40 E
Coldrano	64	46.38 N	10.50 E
Cold Spring, Ky., U.S.	218	39.01 N	84.26 W
Cold Spring, Mn., U.S.	190	45.27 N	94.25 W
Cold Spring, N.J., U.S.	208	38.58 N	74.55 W
Cold Spring, N.Y., U.S.	210	41.25 N	73.57 W
Coldspring, Tx., U.S.	222	30.36 N	95.08 W
Cold Spring Harbor	276	40.52 N	73.27 W
Cold Spring Harbor ⊂	276	40.53 N	73.28 W
Coldsprings, On., Can.	212	44.17 N	78.18 W
Cold Springs, N.Y., U.S.	210	43.08 N	76.15 W
Cold Spring Terrace	276	40.50 N	73.26 W
Coldstream, Austl.	169	37.44 S	145.23 E
Coldstream, Scot., U.K.	46	55.39 N	2.15 W
Cold Stream ≃	226	39.35 N	120.22 W
Coldwater, On., Can.	212	44.42 N	79.40 W
Coldwater, Ks., U.S.	198	37.16 N	99.19 W
Coldwater, Mi., U.S.	216	41.56 N	85.00 W
Coldwater, Ms., U.S.	194	34.41 N	89.58 W
Coldwater, Oh., U.S.	216	40.28 N	84.37 W
Coldwater ≃, On., Can.	212	44.44 N	79.39 W
Coldwater ≃, Mi., U.S.	216	42.04 N	85.08 W
Coldwater ≃, Ms., U.S.	194	34.11 N	90.13 W
Coldwater Canyon ∨	280	34.14 N	117.44 W
Coldwater Creek ≃	196	36.40 N	101.08 W
Coldwater Indian Reserve ◆[4]	182	50.04 N	120.48 W
Coldwater Lake ⊜	216	41.49 N	84.58 W
Cole □[6]	219	38.30 N	92.13 W
Cole ≃, Ang.	152	9.07 S	15.50 E
Cole ≃, Eng., U.K.	42	51.42 N	1.42 W
Coleambally	166	34.49 S	145.52 E
Colebrook, N.H., U.S.	188	44.53 N	71.29 W
Colebrook, Oh., U.S.	214	41.32 N	80.46 W
Colebrook River Lake ⊜[1]	207	42.03 N	73.04 W
Cole Camp	194	38.27 N	93.12 W
Coledale	170	34.17 S	150.57 E
Coleen ≃	180	67.05 N	142.31 W
Coleford, Eng., U.K.	42	51.48 N	2.36 W
Coleford, Eng., U.K.	42	51.14 N	2.27 W
Colégio, Morro do ∧	287b	23.38 S	46.21 W
Coleman, Ab., Can.	182	49.38 N	114.30 W
Coleman, Fl., U.S.	220	28.47 N	82.04 W
Coleman, Md., U.S.	208	39.20 N	76.04 W
Coleman, Mi., U.S.	190	43.45 N	84.35 W
Coleman, Tx., U.S.	196	31.49 N	99.25 W
Coleman, Wi., U.S.	190	45.03 N	88.02 W
Coleman ≃	164	15.06 S	141.38 E
Coleman, Lake ⊜[1]	196	32.02 N	99.30 W
Colembert	50	50.45 N	1.50 E
Colen Lakes ⊜	184	54.33 N	95.25 W
Colenso	158	28.50 S	29.44 E
Colerain	214	40.07 N	80.49 W
Coleraine, Austl.	166	37.36 S	141.42 E
Coleraine, N. Ire., U.K.	48	55.08 N	6.40 W
Coleraine, Mn., U.S.	190	47.17 N	93.25 W
Coleridge	198	42.30 N	97.12 W
Coleridge, Lake ⊜	172	43.17 S	171.30 E
Coles	194	31.16 N	91.01 W
Coles, Punta ›	248	17.42 S	71.23 W
Colesberg	158	30.45 S	25.05 E
Coles Brook ≃	276	40.55 N	74.02 W
Coleshill, Eng., U.K.	42	52.30 N	1.42 W
Coleshill, Eng., U.K.	260	51.39 N	0.38 W
Coles Point	208	38.09 N	76.38 W
Colesville, Md., U.S.	284c	39.05 N	77.00 W
Colesville, N.J., U.S.	210	41.15 N	74.39 W
Coleto Creek ≃	196	28.41 N	97.01 W
Coleville, Sk., Can.	184	51.43 N	109.16 W
Coleville, Ca., U.S.	226	38.33 N	119.30 W
Colfax, Ca., U.S.	226	39.06 N	120.57 W
Colfax, Il., U.S.	216	40.34 N	88.36 W
Colfax, In., U.S.	194	40.11 N	86.40 W
Colfax, Ia., U.S.	190	41.40 N	93.14 W
Colfax, La., U.S.	194	31.31 N	92.42 W
Colfax, Wa., U.S.	202	46.52 N	117.21 W
Colfax, Wi., U.S.	190	44.59 N	91.43 W
Colfiorito	66	43.02 N	12.55 E
Colgate	216	43.12 N	88.12 W
Colgate Creek ≃	284b	39.15 N	76.32 W
Colgong	124	25.16 N	87.13 E
Colgrave Sound ⊔	46a	60.37 N	0.58 W
Colhué Huapi, Lago ⊜	254	45.30 S	68.48 W
Coliban ≃	169	36.56 S	144.33 E
Colibris, Pointe des ›, Guad.	241o	16.15 N	61.11 W
Colibris, Pointe des ›, Guad.	241o	16.17 N	61.06 W
Colico	58	46.08 N	9.22 E
Coligny, Fr.	58	46.23 N	5.21 E
Coligny, S. Afr.	158	26.17 S	26.15 E
Colijnsplaat	52	51.46 N	3.51 E
Colima, Méx.	200	32.25 N	115.05 W
Colima, Méx.	234	19.14 N	103.43 W
Colima □[3]	234	19.10 N	104.00 W
Colima, Nevado de ∧	234	19.33 N	103.38 W
Colimes ≃	246	1.32 S	80.00 W
Colin ≃	50	47.08 N	2.32 E
Colina	252	33.12 S	70.41 W
Colinas, Bra.	250	6.02 S	44.14 W
Colinas, Bra.	255	14.12 S	48.03 W
Colinet	186	47.13 N	53.33 W
Colinton, Austl.	171b	35.51 S	149.09 E
Colinton, Ab., Can.	182	54.37 N	113.15 W
Coliseum → Colosseo ⊥	267a	41.54 N	12.29 E
Coll I	46	56.38 N	6.34 W
Colla	258	34.04 S	57.21 W
Colla, Arroyo ≃	258	34.19 S	57.20 W
Collagna	64	44.21 N	10.16 E
Collalbo (Klobenstein)	64	46.32 N	11.28 E
Collalto Sabino	66	42.08 N	13.02 E
Collamer	210	43.06 N	76.04 W
Collarenebri	166	29.33 S	148.35 E
Collarmele	66	42.03 N	13.38 E
Collaroy	274a	33.44 S	151.18 E
Collazzone	66	42.54 N	12.26 E
Collbran	200	39.14 N	107.57 W
Collecchio	64	44.45 N	10.13 E
Collecorvino	66	42.27 N	14.01 E
Colle di Tora	66	42.13 N	12.57 E
Colle di Val d'Elsa	66	43.25 N	11.07 E
Colleen Bawn	154	21.00 S	29.13 E
Colleferro	66	41.44 N	12.59 E
College	180	64.51 N	147.47 W
College City	226	39.00 N	122.00 W
College Corner	218	39.30 N	84.36 W
Collegedale	194	35.04 N	85.03 W
College Meadows	218	39.56 N	86.07 W
College Park, Ga., U.S.	192	33.39 N	84.26 W
College Park, Md., U.S.	208	38.58 N	76.56 W
College Park Airport ⊠	284c	38.58 N	76.55 W
College Place	202	46.02 N	118.23 W
College Point ◆[8]	276	40.47 N	73.51 W
College Station, Ar., U.S.	194	34.43 N	92.13 W
College Station, Tx., U.S.	222	30.37 N	96.20 W
Collegeville, In., U.S.	216	40.54 N	87.09 W
Collegeville, Pa., U.S.	208	40.11 N	75.27 W
Collégien	261	48.50 N	2.40 E
Collegno	62	45.05 N	7.34 E
Colle Isarco (Gossensass)	64	46.56 N	11.26 E
Collepardo	66	41.46 N	13.22 E
Collepasso	68	40.04 N	18.10 E
Collepietro	66	42.13 N	13.46 E
Collerina	166	29.41 S	146.38 E
Collesalvetti	66	43.35 N	10.28 E
Colle Sannita	68	41.22 N	14.50 E
Collesano	70	37.55 N	13.56 E
Colletorto	66	41.40 N	14.58 E
Colleymount	182	54.01 N	126.09 W
Colleyville	222	32.52 N	97.09 W
Colliano	68	40.43 N	15.17 E
Colli a Volturno	66	41.36 N	14.06 E
Colli del Tronto	66	42.52 N	13.44 E
Colli di Monte Bove	66	42.06 N	13.09 E
Collie	168a	33.21 S	116.09 E
Collie ≃	168a	33.18 S	115.44 E
Collie East ≃	168a	33.18 S	116.10 E
Collier □[6]	220	26.10 N	81.22 W
Collier Bay ⊂	160	16.10 S	124.15 E
Collier Bridge ◆[5]	220	26.57 N	82.04 W
Collier City	220	26.14 N	80.09 W
Collier Law ∧[2]	44	54.46 N	1.58 W
Collier Range ⋏	162	24.43 S	119.12 E
Collier Range National Park ♠	162	24.40 S	119.15 E
Collier Row ◆[8]	260	51.36 N	0.10 E
Colliers	214	40.22 N	80.32 W
Collier-Seminole State Park ♠	220	25.59 N	81.36 W
Colliersville	210	42.29 N	74.59 W
Collierville	194	35.02 N	89.39 W
Collie South ≃	168a	33.18 S	116.10 E
Collieston	46	57.21 N	1.56 W
Colliford Lake Reservoir ⊜[1]	42	50.32 N	4.33 W
Colligan ≃	48	52.06 N	7.38 W
Collin □[6]	222	33.07 N	96.35 W
Collingbourne Kingston	42	51.18 N	1.40 W
Collingdale	208	39.54 N	75.16 W
Collingham	44	53.54 N	1.24 W
Collingswood	285	39.55 N	75.04 W
Collingwood, Austl.	274b	37.48 S	145.00 E
Collingwood, On., Can.	212	44.29 N	80.13 W
Collingwood, N.Z.	172	40.40 S	172.41 E
Collingwood Bay ⊂	164	9.20 S	149.30 E
Collins, Ga., U.S.	192	32.10 N	82.06 W
Collins, Ia., U.S.	190	41.54 N	93.18 W
Collins, Ms., U.S.	194	31.38 N	89.33 W
Collins, N.Y., U.S.	210	42.30 N	78.55 W
Collins, Oh., U.S.	214	41.16 N	82.30 W
Collins ≃	194	35.48 N	85.37 W
Collins, Mount ∧[2]	190	47.51 N	80.59 W
Collins Bay	212	44.15 N	76.36 W
Collinsburg	214	40.13 N	79.46 W
Collins Center	210	42.30 N	78.51 W
Collins Lake ⊜	212	44.22 N	76.27 W
Collins Park	208	39.41 N	75.33 W
Collinston	194	32.41 N	91.52 W
Collinsville, Austl.	166	20.34 S	147.51 E
Collinsville, Al., U.S.	194	34.15 N	85.51 W
Collinsville, Ca., U.S.	282	38.05 N	121.51 W
Collinsville, Ct., U.S.	207	41.48 N	72.55 W
Collinsville, Il., U.S.	219	38.40 N	89.59 W
Collinsville, Ms., U.S.	194	32.29 N	88.50 W
Collinsville, N.J., U.S.	276	40.49 N	74.28 W
Collinsville, Ok., U.S.	196	36.21 N	95.50 W
Collinsville, Tx., U.S.	196	33.32 N	96.54 W
Collinwood	194	35.10 N	87.44 W
Collio	64	45.48 N	10.20 E
Collipulli	252	37.57 S	72.26 W
Collister	202	43.38 N	116.15 W
Collobrières	62	43.14 N	6.18 E
Collombey	58	46.16 N	6.57 E
Collomsville	210	41.09 N	77.09 W
Collon	48	53.47 N	6.29 W
Collonges	58	46.08 N	5.54 E
Collooney	48	54.11 N	8.29 W
Collserola, Serra de ⋏	266d	41.26 N	2.07 E
Colma	226	37.41 N	122.28 W
Colma Creek ≃	282	37.38 N	122.23 W
Colman	198	43.58 N	96.48 W
Colmar	58	48.05 N	7.22 E
Colmar Manor	284c	38.55 N	76.56 W
Colmars	62	44.11 N	6.38 E
Colmenar	34	36.54 N	4.20 W
Colmenar de Oreja	34	40.06 N	3.23 W
Colmenar Viejo	34	40.40 N	3.46 W
Colmeneros	234	18.06 N	101.40 W
Colmesneil	194	30.54 N	94.25 W
Colmnitz	54	50.54 N	13.31 E
Colmonell	44	55.08 N	4.55 W
Coln ≃	42	51.42 N	1.42 W
Colnbrook	260	51.29 N	0.31 W
Colne	44	53.52 N	2.09 W
Colne ≃, Eng., U.K.	42	51.48 N	1.01 E
Colne ≃, Eng., U.K.	260	51.26 N	0.30 W
Colney Heath	260	51.44 N	0.15 W
Colney Street	260	51.42 N	0.20 W
Colo	190	42.01 N	93.18 W
Colo ≃	170	33.26 S	150.53 E
Colobraro	68	40.11 N	16.25 E
Cologna Veneta	64	45.18 N	11.23 E
Cologne → Köln, Dtsch.	56	50.56 N	6.59 E
Cologne, Mn., U.S.	190	44.46 N	93.46 W
Cologne, N.J., U.S.	208	39.30 N	74.36 W
Cologno al Serio	62	45.37 N	9.42 E
Cologno Monzese	266b	45.32 N	9.17 E
Cololo, Nevado ∧	248	14.53 S	69.06 W
Coloma, Ca., U.S.	226	38.48 N	120.53 W
Coloma, Mi., U.S.	216	42.11 N	86.18 W
Coloma, Wi., U.S.	190	44.02 N	89.31 W
Colomb-Béchar → Béchar	148	31.37 N	2.13 W
Colombes	50	48.55 N	2.15 E
Colombey-les-Belles	58	48.32 N	5.54 E
Colombey-les-Deux-Églises	58	48.13 N	4.53 E
Colômbia, Bra.	255	20.30 S	48.37 W
Colombia, Col.	246	3.24 N	74.49 W
Colombia, Cuba	240p	20.59 N	77.25 W
Colombia, Méx.	196	27.42 N	99.45 W
Colombia □[1], S.A.	242	4.00 N	72.00 W
Colombia □[1], S.A.	246	4.00 N	72.00 W
Colombian Basin ✣[1]	16	13.00 N	76.00 W
Colombie → Colombia □[1]	246	4.00 N	72.00 W
Colombie-Britannique → British Columbia □[4]	182	54.00 N	125.00 W
Colombier	58	46.58 N	6.52 E
Colombo, Bra.	252	25.17 S	49.14 W
Colombo, S. Lan.	122	6.56 N	79.51 E
Colome	198	43.15 N	99.42 W
Colomiers	32	43.37 N	1.20 E
Colón, Arg.	252	33.53 S	61.07 W
Colón, Arg.	252	32.13 S	58.08 W
Colón, Cuba	240p	22.43 N	80.54 W
Colón, Méx.	234	20.48 N	100.03 W
Colón, Pan.	236	9.22 N	79.54 W
Colon, Mi., U.S.	216	41.57 N	85.19 W
Colón, Ur.	252	33.53 S	54.43 W
Colón, Ur.	258	34.48 S	56.14 W
Colón □[4]	236	9.00 N	80.20 W
Colón □[5]	236	15.40 N	85.30 W
Colón, Archipiélago de (Galapagos Islands) II	246a	0.30 S	90.30 W
Colón, Cementerio ◆	286b	23.08 N	82.23 W
Colón, Isla I	236	9.24 N	82.17 W
Colón, Montañas de ⋏	236	14.55 N	84.45 W
Colón, Teatro ♠	288	34.36 S	58.23 W
Colona	162	31.38 S	132.05 E
Colonard-Corubert	50	48.25 N	0.39 E
Colonarie ≃	241h	13.14 N	61.06 W
Colonel Danforth Park ♠	275b	43.47 N	79.10 W
Colonelganj	124	27.08 N	81.42 E
Coloneşti	38	46.34 N	27.18 E
Colonet	204	31.05 N	116.10 W
Colonet, Cabo ›	204	30.58 N	116.19 W
Colongulac, Lake ⊜	169	38.10 S	143.11 E
Colonia → Köln, Dtsch.	56	50.56 N	6.59 E
Colonia, Micron.	174q	9.31 N	138.08 E
Colonia, N.J., U.S.	210	40.34 N	74.18 W
Colonia □[5]	258	34.10 S	57.30 W
Colônia ≃	255	15.11 S	39.45 W
Colonia, Aeropuerto ⊠	258	34.28 S	57.49 W
Colonia, Cuchilla de la ⋏[2]	258	34.15 S	57.35 W
Colonia Alvear	252	35.00 S	67.40 W
Colonia Caroya	252	31.02 S	64.05 W
Colonia del Sacramento	258	34.28 S	57.51 W
Colonia Dora	252	28.36 S	62.57 W
Colonia Elisa	252	26.56 S	59.32 W
Colonia Guadalupe	204	32.04 N	116.37 W
Colonia Hogar Ricardo Gutiérrez	288	34.51 S	58.51 W
Colonia José Mármol	252	26.59 S	60.44 W
Colonial Acres	208	39.31 N	76.20 W
Colonia Lavalleja	252	31.06 S	57.01 W
Colonial Beach	208	38.15 N	76.57 W
Colonial Crest	208	40.20 N	76.50 W
Colônia Leopoldina	250	8.57 S	35.39 W
Colonial Heights	208	37.14 N	77.24 W
Colonial Manor	285	39.51 N	75.09 W
Colonial National Historical Park ♠	208	37.12 N	76.45 W
Colonial Park	208	40.18 N	76.48 W
Colonial Village, N.Y., U.S.	210	43.08 N	78.58 W
Colonial Village, Pa., U.S.	285	40.04 N	75.24 W
Colonial Village Airport ⊠	284a	43.08 N	78.58 W
Colonial Williamsburg ⊥	208	37.16 N	76.42 W
Colonia Morelos	200	30.50 N	109.10 W
Colonia Nicolich	258	34.50 S	56.02 W
Colonia Progreso	204	32.35 N	115.37 W
Colonia Providencia	240m	17.59 N	66.00 W
Colonias Unidas	252	26.42 S	59.38 W
Colonia Valdense	258	34.20 S	57.14 W
Colonia Vicente Guerrero	232	30.45 N	116.00 W
Colonia Villafañe	252	26.12 S	59.05 W
Colonie	210	42.43 N	73.50 W
Colon Koret	152	0.34 N	23.28 E
Colonna	267a	41.50 N	12.45 E
Colonna, Capo ›	68	39.02 N	17.11 E
Colonnata	64	44.05 N	10.10 E
Colón Ridge ✣[3]	18	2.00 N	96.00 W
Colonsay	184	51.59 N	105.53 W
Colonsay I	46	56.04 N	6.13 W
Colony	198	38.04 N	95.21 W
Colora	208	39.40 N	76.06 W
Colorada, Laguna ≡	254	44.50 S	68.15 W
Colorada, Punta ›	288	34.45 S	58.06 W
Coloradas, Lomas ⋏[2]	254	43.24 S	67.24 W
Colorado, C.R.	236	10.46 N	83.35 W
Colorado, Hond.	236	15.47 N	87.19 W
Colorado, Ak., U.S.	180	63.09 N	149.26 W
Colorado □[6]	222	29.40 N	96.30 W
Colorado □[3]	178	39.00 N	105.30 W
Colorado ≃, Arg.	244	39.50 S	62.08 W
Colorado ≃, Bra.	248	13.03 S	62.20 W
Colorado ≃, Méx.	234	16.30 N	97.31 W
Colorado ≃, N.A.	200	31.54 N	114.57 W
Colorado ≃, Tx., U.S.	196	28.36 N	95.58 W
Colorado, Canal do ≅	287a	23.00 S	43.25 W
Colorado, Cerro ∧, Arg.	254	45.02 S	69.38 W
Colorado, Cerro ∧, Chile	286e	33.24 S	70.45 W
Colorado, Cerro ∧, Perú	286d	12.07 S	76.55 W
Colorado, Williams Fork ≃	200	40.03 N	106.11 W
Colorado City, Az., U.S.	200	36.59 N	112.58 W
Colorado City, Co., U.S.	200	37.56 N	104.50 W
Colorado City, Tx., U.S.	196	32.23 N	100.51 W
Colorado de Abajo	196	26.28 N	99.54 W
Colorado Grande, Salina ≍	252	38.15 S	63.47 W
Colorado National Monument ♠	200	39.04 N	108.25 W
Colorado Plateau ⋏[1]	200	36.30 N	108.00 W
Colorado River Aqueduct ≅[1]	204	33.50 N	117.23 W
Colorado River Indian Reservation ◆[4]	200	34.00 N	114.25 W
Colorados, Archipiélago de los II	240p	22.36 N	84.20 W
Colorado Springs	200	38.50 N	104.49 W
Colorines	234	19.07 N	100.12 W
Colorno	64	44.56 N	10.23 E
Colosimi	68	39.07 N	16.24 E
Colosseo ⊥	267a	41.54 N	12.29 E
Colotepec ≃	234	15.47 N	97.03 W
Colotlán	234	22.06 N	103.16 W
Colotlán ≃	234	22.06 N	103.42 W
Colotlipa	234	17.25 N	99.09 W
Çolo Vale	170	34.24 S	150.29 E
Čolpon	85	42.12 N	75.28 E
Čolpon-Ata	85	42.40 N	77.06 E
Colpoys Bay ⊂	212	44.47 N	81.05 W
Colquechaca	248	18.40 S	66.01 W
Colquencha	248	17.00 S	68.17 W
Colquiri	248	17.25 S	67.08 W
Colquitt	192	31.10 N	84.44 W
Colsterworth	42	52.48 N	0.37 W
Colstrip	202	45.53 N	106.37 W
Colt	194	35.07 N	90.48 W
Colta	248	15.10 S	73.18 W
Coltauco	252	34.18 S	71.06 W
Coltishall	42	52.44 N	1.22 E
Colton, Austl.	162	33.29 S	134.56 E
Colton, Ca., U.S.	228	34.04 N	117.18 W
Colton, Oh., U.S.	216	41.28 N	83.57 W
Colton, Or., U.S.	224	45.10 N	122.26 W
Colton, S.D., U.S.	198	43.47 N	96.55 W
Coltons Point	208	38.13 N	76.45 W
Colts Neck	208	40.17 N	74.10 W
Coltsville Center	214	41.05 N	80.34 W
Columbia, Al., U.S.	192	31.17 N	85.06 W
Columbia, Ca., U.S.	226	38.02 N	120.24 W
Columbia, Ct., U.S.	207	41.42 N	72.18 W
Columbia, Il., U.S.	219	38.26 N	90.12 W
Columbia, In., U.S.	218	39.35 N	85.12 W
Columbia, Ky., U.S.	194	37.06 N	85.18 W
Columbia, La., U.S.	194	32.06 N	92.04 W
Columbia, Md., U.S.	208	39.14 N	76.50 W
Columbia, Ms., U.S.	194	31.15 N	89.50 W
Columbia, Mo., U.S.	219	38.57 N	92.20 W
Columbia, N.J., U.S.	210	40.55 N	75.05 W
Columbia, N.C., U.S.	192	35.55 N	76.15 W
Columbia, Pa., U.S.	208	40.02 N	76.30 W
Columbia, S.C., U.S.	192	34.00 N	81.02 W
Columbia, Tn., U.S.	194	35.36 N	87.02 W
Columbia □[6], N.Y., U.S.	210	42.15 N	73.47 W
Columbia □[6], Or., U.S.	224	45.57 N	123.03 W
Columbia □[6], Pa., U.S.	210	41.00 N	76.28 W
Columbia ≃	176	46.15 N	124.05 W
Columbia, Cape ›	16	83.08 N	70.35 W
Columbia, Lake ⊜[1]	216	42.05 N	84.18 W
Columbia, Mount ∧	182	52.09 N	117.25 W
Columbia Airport ⊠	279a	41.19 N	81.58 W
Columbia Basin ≍[1]	202	46.45 N	119.05 W
Columbia Center	279a	41.19 N	81.56 W
Columbia City, In., U.S.	216	41.09 N	85.29 W
Columbia City, Or., U.S.	224	45.53 N	122.48 W
Columbia Cross Roads	210	41.50 N	76.48 W
Columbia Falls, Me., U.S.	188	44.39 N	67.43 W
Columbia Falls, Mt., U.S.	202	48.22 N	114.10 W
Columbia Heights	224	46.09 N	122.58 W
Columbia Hills	284b	39.15 N	76.50 W
Columbia Icefield ⊓	182	52.10 N	117.30 W
Columbia Lake ⊜	182	50.15 N	115.57 W
Columbia Lake Indian Reserve ◆[4]	182	50.25 N	115.57 W
Columbia Mountains ⋏	182	52.00 N	119.00 W
Columbiana, Al., U.S.	194	33.10 N	86.36 W
Columbiana, Oh., U.S.	214	40.53 N	80.41 W
Columbiana □[6]	214	40.47 N	80.46 W
Columbia Plateau ⋏[1]	202	44.00 N	117.30 W
Columbia Regional Airport ⊠	219	38.50 N	92.13 W
Columbia Road Reservoir ⊜[1]	198	45.45 N	98.15 W
Columbia State Historical Park ♠	226	38.02 N	120.25 W

Symbols in the index entries represent the broad categories identified in the key at the right. Symbols with superior numbers (⋏[1]) identify subcategories (see complete key on page *I · 1).*

Symbole im Register stellen die rechts im Schlüssel erklärten Kategorien dar. Symbole mit hochgestellten Ziffern (⋏[1]) bezeichnen Unterabteilungen einer Kategorie (vgl. vollständiger Schlüssel auf Seite *I · 1).*

Los símbolos incluídos en el texto del índice representan las grandes categorías identificadas con la clave a la derecha. Los símbolos con numeros en su parte superior (⋏[1]) identifican las subcategorías (véase la clave completa en la página *I · 1).*

Les symboles de l'index représentent les catégories indiquées dans la légende à droite. Les symboles suivis d'un indice (⋏[1]) représentent des sous-catégories (voir légende complète à la page *I · 1).*

Os símbolos incluídos no texto do índice representam as grandes categorias identificadas com a chave à direita. Os símbolos com números em sua parte superior (⋏[1]) identificam as subcategorias (veja-se a chave completa à página *I · 1).*

	English	Deutsch	Español	Français	Português
∧	Mountain	Berg	Montaña	Montagne	Montanha
⋏	Mountains	Gebirge	Montañas	Montagnes	Montanhas
)(	Pass	Paß	Paso	Col	Passo
∨	Valley, Canyon	Tal, Cañon	Valle, Cañón	Vallée, Canyon	Vale, Canhão
≍	Plain	Ebene	Llano	Plaine	Planície
›	Cape	Kap	Cabo	Cap	Cabo
I	Island	Insel	Isla	Île	Ilha
II	Islands	Inseln	Islas	Îles	Ilhas
⊥	Other Topographic Features	Andere Topographische Objekte	Otros Elementos Topográficos	Autres données topographiques	Outros acidentes topográficos

ESPAÑOL / FRANÇAIS / PORTUGUÊS

Nombre / Nom / Nome	Página / Page / Página	Lat.°′	Long.°′ W = Oeste / W = Ouest / W = Oeste
Columbia Station	214	41.20 N	81.57 W
Columbia University ⛉[2]	276	40.48 N	73.58 W
Columbiaville, Mi., U.S.	190	43.09 N	83.24 W
Columbiaville, N.Y., U.S.	210	42.19 N	73.45 W
Columbine, Cape ›	158	32.47 S	17.52 E
Columbrets, Illes II	34	39.52 N	0.40 E
Columbus, Ga., U.S.	192	32.29 N	84.59 W
Columbus, In., U.S.	218	39.12 N	85.55 W
Columbus, Ks., U.S.	198	37.10 N	94.50 W
Columbus, Ms., U.S.	194	33.29 N	88.25 W
Columbus, Mt., U.S.	202	45.38 N	109.15 W
Columbus, Ne., U.S.	198	41.25 N	97.22 W
Columbus, N.J., U.S.	208	40.04 N	74.43 W
Columbus, N.M., U.S.	200	31.49 N	107.38 W
Columbus, N.C., U.S.	192	35.15 N	82.11 W
Columbus, N.D., U.S.	198	48.54 N	102.46 W
Columbus, Oh., U.S.	214	39.57 N	82.59 W
Columbus, Pa., U.S.	214	41.56 N	79.35 W
Columbus, Tx., U.S.	222	29.42 N	96.32 W
Columbus, Wi., U.S.	190	43.20 N	89.00 W
Columbus Air Force Base ■	194	33.38 N	88.26 W
Columbus Grove	216	40.55 N	84.03 W
Columbus Junction	190	41.16 N	91.21 W
Columbus Lake ⊜[1]	194	33.35 N	88.30 W
Columbus Park ♠	278	41.53 N	87.47 W
Columbus Point ›, Ba.	238	24.08 N	75.16 W
Columbus Point ›, Trin.	241r	11.08 N	60.48 W
Columbus Salt Marsh ≡	204	38.04 N	117.58 W
Coluna	255	18.14 S	42.50 W
Colusa	226	39.12 N	122.00 W
Colusa □[6]	226	39.13 N	122.01 W
Colusa Trough ≊	226	39.02 N	121.59 W
Colver	214	40.32 N	78.47 W
Colville, N.Z.	172	36.38 S	175.28 E
Colville, Wa., U.S.	202	48.32 N	117.54 W
Colville ≏, Ak., U.S.	180	70.25 N	150.30 W
Colville ≏, Wa., U.S.	202	48.37 N	118.05 W
Colville, Cape ›	172	36.28 S	175.21 E
Colville Channel ʯ	172	36.23 S	175.24 E
Colville Indian Reservation ◆[4]	202	48.15 N	119.00 W
Colville Lake ⊜	180	67.10 N	126.00 W
Colvin Run	284c	38.58 N	77.18 W
Colwell	44	55.04 N	2.04 W
Colwood	224	48.26 N	123.29 W
Colwyn	285	39.55 N	75.15 W
Colwyn Bay	44	53.18 N	3.43 W
Colyton, Austl.	274a	33.47 S	150.48 E
Colyton, Eng., U.K.	42	50.44 N	3.04 W
Comacchio	66	44.42 N	12.11 E
Comacchio, Valli di ᑕ	66	44.38 N	12.06 E
Comal	115a	6.55 S	109.31 E
Comala	234	19.19 N	103.45 W
Comalapa, Guat.	236	14.44 N	90.53 W
Comalapa, Nic.	236	12.17 N	85.31 W
Comalcalco	234	18.16 N	93.13 W
Comallo, Arroyo ≏	254	40.29 S	70.12 W
Coman, Mount ʌ	9	74.02 S	65.04 W
Comana	38	43.54 N	28.19 E
Comanche, Ok., U.S.	196	34.22 N	97.57 W
Comanche, Tx., U.S.	196	31.53 N	98.36 W
Comanche Creek ≏, Co., U.S.	198	39.53 N	104.19 W
Comanche Creek ≏, Tx., U.S.	196	31.06 N	102.24 W
Comandante Ferraz ⛉[3]	9	62.05 S	58.23 W
Comandante Fontana	252	25.20 S	59.41 W
Comandante Leal	252	30.53 S	65.47 W
Comandante Luis Piedrabuena	254	49.59 S	68.54 W
Comandante Nicanor Otamendi	252	38.07 S	57.51 W
Comănești	38	46.25 N	26.26 E
Comanjá de Corona	234	21.19 N	101.42 W
Comarapa	248	17.54 S	64.29 W
Comar Gambon	144	3.10 N	45.47 E
Comas, Perú	248	11.46 S	75.02 W
Comas, Perú	286d	11.57 S	77.04 W
Comayagua	236	14.25 N	87.37 W
Comayagua □[5]	236	14.30 N	87.40 W
Comayagua, Montañas de ʌʌ	236	14.23 N	87.26 W
Combahee ≏	192	32.30 N	80.31 W
Combarbalá	252	31.11 S	71.02 W
Combault	261	48.48 N	2.36 E
Combeaufontaine	58	47.43 N	5.53 E
Combe Bank ✣[3]	14	12.32 S	177.35 W
Combe Martin	42	51.13 N	4.02 W
Comber, On., Can.	214	42.14 N	82.33 W
Comber, N. Ire., U.K.	48	54.33 N	5.45 W
Comberbach	262	53.17 N	2.32 W
Combermere Bay ᑕ	110	19.37 N	93.34 E
Comberton	42	52.11 N	0.02 E
Combie, Lake ⊜[1]	226	39.01 N	121.02 W
Comblain-au-Pont	56	50.28 N	5.35 E
Combles	50	50.01 N	2.52 E
Combloux	62	45.54 N	6.39 E
Combourg	32	48.25 N	1.45 W
Comboyne	166	31.36 S	152.29 E
Comboyuro Point ›	171a	27.04 S	153.24 E
Combres	50	48.19 N	1.04 E
Combronde	32	45.59 N	3.05 E
Combs	262	53.18 N	1.57 W
Combs-la-Ville	50	48.40 N	2.34 E
Combs Reservoir ⊜[1]	262	53.19 N	1.57 W
Comburg ⛉[1]	56	49.06 N	9.44 E
Comb Wash V	200	37.13 N	109.42 W
Come by Chance	186	47.51 N	53.58 W
Comeglians	64	46.31 N	12.52 E
Comelico Superiore	64	46.35 N	12.30 E
Comendado Levy Gasparain	256	22.01 S	43.12 W
Comendador	238	18.53 N	71.42 W
Comendador Gomes	255	19.41 S	49.05 W
Comer	192	34.03 N	83.07 W
Comercinho	255	16.19 S	41.47 W
Comerío	240m	18.13 N	66.14 W
Comet	166	23.37 S	148.33 E
Comet ≏	166	23.34 S	148.32 E
Cometela	156	21.51 S	34.29 E
Comfort, N.C., U.S.	192	35.00 N	77.30 W
Comfort, Tx., U.S.	196	29.58 N	98.54 W
Comfort, Cape ›	176	65.08 N	83.21 W
Comfort, Point ›	276	40.27 N	74.08 W
Comfrey	198	44.06 N	94.54 W
Comilla	124	23.27 N	91.12 E
Comines	50	50.46 N	3.01 E
Comino → Kemmuna I	36	36.00 N	14.20 E
Comino, Capo ›	71	40.32 N	9.49 E
Comiskey Park ♠	278	41.50 N	87.38 W
Comiso	70	36.56 N	14.36 E
Comitan de Dominguez	232	16.15 N	92.08 W
Comitini	70	37.24 N	13.39 E
Comloșu Mare	38	45.54 N	20.38 E
Commack	210	40.50 N	73.17 W
Commagene □[9]	130	37.50 N	38.00 E
Commencement Bay ᑕ	224	47.17 N	122.28 W
Commentry	32	46.17 N	2.44 E
Commerce, Ca., U.S.	280	34.00 N	118.09 W
Commerce, Ga., U.S.	192	34.12 N	83.27 W
Commerce, Mi., U.S.	216	42.34 N	83.30 W
Commerce, Ok., U.S.	196	36.56 N	94.52 W
Commerce, Tx., U.S.	196	33.14 N	95.53 W
Commerce City	198	39.49 N	104.56 W
Commerciale Luigi Bocconi, Università ⛉[2]	266b	45.26 N	9.11 E
Commercial Point	218	39.46 N	83.04 W
Commercy	56	48.45 N	5.35 E
Commewijne □[5]	250	5.50 N	55.00 W
Comminges ◆[1]	32	43.15 N	0.45 E
Committee Bay ᑕ	176	68.30 N	86.30 W
Commodore	214	40.43 N	78.57 W
Commodore Barry Bridge ◆[5]	285	39.49 N	75.22 W
Commondale	158	27.20 S	30.56 E
Common Edge	262	53.47 N	3.02 W
Commonwealth Bay ᑕ	9	66.54 S	142.40 E
Commonwealth Range ʌʌ	9	84.15 S	172.20 E
Commoron Creek ≏	166	28.22 S	150.08 E
Community Center	228	34.16 N	118.44 W
Como, Austl.	274a	34.00 S	151.04 E
Como, It.	62	45.47 N	9.05 E
Como, Ms., U.S.	194	34.30 N	89.56 W
Como, N.C., U.S.	208	36.30 N	77.00 W
Como, Tx., U.S.	222	33.03 N	95.28 W
Como, Wi., U.S.	216	42.37 N	88.28 W
Como □[4]	58	45.59 N	9.13 E
Como, Lago di ⊜	58	46.00 N	9.20 E
Como, Lake ⊜	216	42.36 N	88.29 W
Como, Mount ʌ	226	39.02 N	119.28 W
Comodoro Rivadavia	254	45.52 S	67.30 W
Como Lake ⊜	190	47.55 N	83.30 W
Comologno	58	46.12 N	8.34 E
Comonfort	234	20.43 N	100.46 W
Comoras → Comoros □[1]	157a	12.10 S	44.15 E
Comores → Comoros □[1]	157a	12.10 S	44.15 E
Comores, Archipel des II	157a	12.10 S	44.15 E
Comorin, Cape ›	122	8.06 N	77.33 E
Comoros (Comores) □[1], Afr.	138	12.10 S	44.15 E
Comoros (Comores) □[1], Afr.	157a	12.10 S	44.15 E
Comox	182	49.40 N	124.55 W
Comox, Canadian Forces Base ■	182	49.43 N	124.54 W
Companhia Siderúrgica Nacional ⛉[3]	256	22.31 S	44.07 W
Compans	261	49.00 N	2.40 E
Compatsch	58	46.58 N	10.25 E
Compiègne	50	49.25 N	2.50 E
Compo Cove ᑕ	276	41.07 N	73.21 W
Compostela, Méx.	234	21.15 N	104.53 W
Compostela, Pil.	116	7.40 N	126.02 E
Comprida, Ilha I, Bra.	252	24.50 S	47.42 W
Comprida, Ilha I, Bra.	287a	23.02 S	43.12 W
Comps-sur-Artuby	62	43.43 N	6.30 E
Compstall	262	53.25 N	2.03 W
Compton, Eng., U.K.	260	51.13 N	0.38 W
Compton, Ca., U.S.	228	33.53 N	118.13 W
Compton, Il., U.S.	216	41.42 N	89.05 W
Compton □[6]	206	45.20 N	71.25 W
Compton Airport ⊠	280	33.53 N	118.15 W
Compton Creek ≏, Ca., U.S.	280	33.50 N	118.12 W
Compton Creek ≏, N.J., U.S.	276	40.26 N	74.05 W
Comptonville	273d	26.17 S	27.58 E
Comrat	38	46.18 N	28.38 E
Comrie	46	56.22 N	4.00 W
Comstock, Mi., U.S.	216	42.17 N	85.30 W
Comstock, Ne., U.S.	198	41.33 N	99.15 W
Comstock, Tx., U.S.	196	29.41 N	101.11 W
Comstock Park	216	43.02 N	85.40 W
Comunanza	66	42.57 N	13.25 E
Con ≏, Ross.	76	52.54 N	36.00 E
Çon ≏, Viet	110	19.02 N	104.58 E
Čona ≏, Ross.	74	62.54 N	111.06 E
Cona ≏, Scot., U.K.	46	56.46 N	5.14 W
Co Nag ⊜	120	32.00 N	91.15 E
Conakry	150	9.31 N	13.43 W
Conambo ≏	246	2.07 S	76.03 W
Conanicut Island I	207	41.32 N	71.21 W
Cona Niyeo	254	41.53 S	67.00 W
Conara Junction	166	41.50 S	147.26 E
Conasauga ≏	192	34.33 N	84.55 W
Conaskonk Point ›	276	40.27 N	74.11 W
Conca ≏	66	43.58 N	12.43 E
Concarán	252	32.34 S	65.15 W
Concarneau	32	47.52 N	3.55 W
Conceição, Bra.	248	7.24 S	58.05 W
Conceição, Bra.	250	7.33 S	38.31 W
Conceição, Moç.	156	18.45 S	36.10 E
Conceição, Cachoeira ᒪ	248	9.34 S	64.22 W
Conceição, Ilha da I	287a	22.52 S	43.07 W
Conceição da Barra	255	18.35 S	39.45 W
Conceição da Pedra	256	22.09 S	45.27 W
Conceição das Alagoas	255	19.55 S	48.23 W
Conceição de Ipanema	255	19.55 S	41.41 W
Conceição de Jacareí	256	23.02 S	44.09 W
Conceição do Almeida	255	12.48 S	39.12 W
Conceição do Araguaia	250	8.15 S	49.17 W
Conceição do Canindé	250	7.54 S	41.34 W
Conceição do Coité	250	11.33 S	39.16 W
Conceição do Formoso	256	21.25 S	43.21 W
Conceição do Mato Dentro	255	19.01 S	43.25 W
Conceição do Maú	246	3.35 N	59.53 W
Conceição do Norte	255	12.13 S	47.18 W
Conceição do Rio Verde	256	21.53 S	45.05 W
Conceição dos Ouros	256	22.25 S	45.47 W
Concepción, Arg.	252	28.23 S	57.53 W
Concepción, Arg.	252	27.20 S	65.35 W
Concepción, Bol.	248	11.29 S	66.31 W
Concepción, Bol.	248	16.15 S	62.04 W
Concepción, Chile	252	36.50 S	73.03 W
Concepción, Col.	246	6.46 N	72.42 W
Concepción, Para.	252	23.25 S	57.17 W
Concepción, Perú	248	11.55 S	75.17 W
Concepcion, Pil.	116	11.13 N	123.06 E
Concepcion, Pil.	116	10.42 N	123.03 E
Concepcion, Pil.	116	12.24 N	122.06 E
Concepcion, Pil.	116	15.19 N	120.39 E
Concepción □[5]	252	23.00 S	57.00 W
Concepción, Bahía ᑕ	232	26.39 N	111.48 W
Concepción, Canal ʯ	254	50.30 S	74.55 W
Concepción, Laguna ⊜	248	17.29 S	61.25 W
Concepción, Volcán ʌ[1]	236	11.34 N	85.37 W
Concepcion Bay ᑕ	116	11.15 N	123.07 E
Concepción de Ataco	236	13.52 N	89.51 W
Concepción de Buenos Aires	234	19.58 N	103.16 W
Concepción de la Sierra	252	27.59 S	55.31 W
Concepcíon del Oro	232	24.38 N	101.25 W
Concepción del Uruguay	252	32.29 S	58.14 W
Concepción Huista	236	15.37 N	91.41 W
Concepción Quezaltepeque	236	14.06 N	88.58 W
Conception, Point ›	204	34.27 N	120.27 W
Conception Bay ᑕ, Nf., Can.	186	47.45 N	53.00 W
Conception Bay ᑕ, Namibia	156	23.53 S	14.28 E
Concession	154	17.22 S	30.57 E
Conchagua	236	13.19 N	87.52 W
Conchagua, Volcán ʌ[1]	236	13.14 N	87.46 W
Conchal	256	22.20 S	47.10 W
Conchalí	286e	33.24 S	70.39 W
Conchalí, Cerros de ʌʌ	286e	33.20 S	70.38 W
Conchas ≏	196	35.23 N	104.18 W
Conchas Dam	196	35.22 N	104.11 W
Conchas Lake ⊜[1]	196	35.25 N	104.14 W
Conche	186	50.53 N	55.54 W
Conches-en-Ouche	50	48.58 N	0.56 E
Conchi	252	22.02 S	68.38 W
Conchillas	258	34.15 S	58.04 W
Conchitas, Arroyo ≏	288	34.45 S	58.09 W
Concho	200	34.28 N	109.36 W
Concho ≏	196	31.34 N	99.43 W
Conchos ≏, Méx.	232	29.35 N	104.25 W
Conchos ≏, Méx.	232	24.55 N	97.40 W
Concise	58	46.51 N	6.43 E
Conco	64	45.48 N	11.36 E
Concón	252	32.55 S	71.31 W
Concononongon Point ›	116	12.14 N	120.13 E
Conconully	182	48.33 N	119.44 W
Concord, Austl.	274a	33.52 S	151.06 E
Concord, On., Can.	275b	43.48 N	79.29 W
Concord, Ca., U.S.	226	37.58 N	122.01 W
Concord, Ga., U.S.	192	33.05 N	84.26 W
Concord, Il., U.S.	219	39.49 N	90.22 W
Concord, Ky., U.S.	218	38.41 N	83.29 W
Concord, Ma., U.S.	207	42.27 N	71.20 W
Concord, Mi., U.S.	216	42.10 N	84.38 W
Concord, Mo., U.S.	219	38.31 N	90.23 W
Concord, N.H., U.S.	188	43.12 N	71.32 W
Concord, N.C., U.S.	192	35.24 N	80.34 W
Concord, Pa., U.S.	214	40.15 N	77.42 W
Concord, Tx., U.S.	222	31.16 N	96.09 W
Concord ≏	283	42.39 N	71.18 W
Concord Battleground ⊥	283	42.28 N	71.21 W
Concordia, Arg.	252	31.24 S	58.02 W
Concórdia, Bra.	246	4.35 S	66.35 W
Concórdia, Bra.	252	27.14 S	52.01 W
Concordia, Méx.	234	23.17 N	106.04 W
Concordia, Perú	246	4.30 S	74.55 W
Concordia, Ks., U.S.	198	39.34 N	97.39 W
Concordia, Mo., U.S.	194	38.59 N	93.34 W
Concordia Gardens	216	41.09 N	85.08 W
Concordia Sagittaria ⊥	64	45.45 N	12.51 E
Concordia sulla Secchia	64	44.55 N	10.59 E
Concord Naval Weapons Station ■	282	38.03 N	122.02 W
Concordville	285	39.53 N	75.31 W
Concord West	274a	33.51 S	151.05 E
Concorezzo	62	45.35 N	9.20 E
Concrete	224	48.32 N	121.44 W
Con Cuong	110	19.02 N	104.54 E
Conda	152	11.06 S	14.20 E
Condamine	166	26.56 S	150.08 E
Condamine ≏	166	27.07 S	149.48 E
Condé, Ang.	152	10.50 S	14.37 E
Conde, Bra.	255	11.49 S	37.37 W
Condé, Fr.	32	48.51 N	0.33 W
Conde, S.D., U.S.	198	45.09 N	98.05 W
Condécourt	261	49.02 N	1.57 E
Condé-en-Brie	50	49.00 N	3.33 E
Condega	236	13.21 N	86.24 W
Condeixa	250	0.54 S	48.36 W
Condé-sur-l'Escaut	50	50.27 N	3.35 E
Condè-sur-Vesgre	261	48.45 N	1.40 E
Condeúba	255	14.53 S	41.59 W
Condevilla	286d	12.02 S	77.05 W
Condino	64	45.53 N	10.36 E
Condobolin	166	33.05 S	147.09 E
Condom	32	43.58 N	0.22 E
Condon	202	45.14 N	120.11 W
Condoto	246	5.06 N	76.37 W
Condove	62	45.07 N	7.18 E
Condrieu	62	45.27 N	4.46 E
Condroz □[9]	56	50.25 N	5.00 E
Cone	196	33.48 N	101.23 W
Conecuh ≏	194	30.58 N	87.14 W
Conegliano	64	45.53 N	12.18 E
Conejos	200	37.05 N	106.01 W
Conejos ≏	200	37.18 N	105.44 W
Conemaugh	214	40.24 N	78.52 W
Conemaugh ≏	214	40.28 N	79.27 W
Conemaugh River Lake ⊜[1]	214	40.28 N	79.17 W
Conembaro, Cerro ʌ	234	18.40 N	102.06 W
Cone Mountain ʌ	180	66.12 N	156.03 W
Conero, Monte ʌ	66	43.33 N	13.36 E
Conestoga	208	39.57 N	76.21 W
Conestoga Creek ≏	208	39.56 N	76.23 W
Conestogo	212	43.32 N	80.30 W
Conestogo ≏	212	43.32 N	80.29 W
Conestogo Lake ⊜	212	43.44 N	80.44 W
Conesus	210	42.43 N	77.41 W
Conesus Lake ⊜	210	42.47 N	77.43 W
Conesville	214	40.11 N	81.53 W
Conewago Creek ≏	208	40.07 N	76.42 W
Conewago Lake ⊜	208	40.06 N	76.52 W
Conewango Creek ≏	214	41.50 N	79.09 W
Coney Island ◆[8]	276	40.34 N	74.00 W
Confederation Lake ⊜	184	51.05 N	92.44 W
Configni	66	42.25 N	12.38 E
Conflans-en-Jarnisy	56	49.10 N	5.51 E
Conflans-Sainte-Honorine	50	48.59 N	2.06 E
Conflenti	68	39.04 N	16.17 E
Conflict Group II	164	10.45 S	151.45 E
Confluence	188	39.48 N	79.21 W
Confolens	32	46.01 N	0.41 E
Confraternidad, Parque ♠	286d	12.09 S	77.02 W
Confusion Bay ᑕ	186	49.58 N	55.47 W
Confuso ≏	252	25.09 S	57.34 W
Cong	48	53.32 N	9.19 W
Congamond	207	42.01 N	72.46 W
Congaree ≏	192	33.45 N	80.37 W
Congaz	38	46.07 N	28.33 E
Congelin	168a	32.50 S	116.54 E
Congers	210	41.09 N	73.56 W
Congers Lake ⊜	276	41.09 N	73.57 W
Cong Hoa Stadium ♠	269c	10.45 N	106.40 E
Conghua	100	23.32 N	113.32 E
Congjiang	102	25.41 N	108.47 E
Congleton	44	53.10 N	2.13 W
Congo □[1], Afr.	138	1.00 S	15.00 E
Congo □[1], Afr.	152	1.00 S	15.00 E
Congo (Zaire) (Zaïre) ≏	138	6.04 S	12.24 E
Congo, Democratic Republic of the → Zaire □[1]	138	4.00 S	25.00 E
Congo, République démocratique du → Zaire □[1]	138	4.00 S	25.00 E
Congo, république du → Congo □[1]	152	1.00 S	15.00 E
Congo, Serra do ʌʌ	152	6.30 S	13.43 E
Congo Basin ≚[1]	10	0.00	20.00 E
Congonhal	256	22.09 S	46.02 W
Congonhas, Aeroporto de ⊠	256	23.38 S	46.38 W
Congost ≏	266d	41.33 N	2.15 E
Congresbury	42	51.23 N	2.48 W
Congress, Sk., Can.	184	49.46 N	106.00 W
Congress, Oh., U.S.	214	40.55 N	82.03 W
Conie ≏	50	48.06 N	1.21 E
Conigli, Isola dei I	70a	35.30 N	12.33 E
Coningsby	44	53.07 N	0.10 W
Conisbrough	44	53.29 N	1.13 W
Coniston, On., Can.	190	46.29 N	80.51 W
Coniston, Eng., U.K.	44	54.22 N	3.05 W
Coniston Water ⊜	44	54.20 N	3.04 W
Conitaca	232	24.10 N	106.43 W
Conjeeveram → Kānchipuram	122	12.50 N	79.43 E
Conjola	170	35.13 S	150.27 E
Çonjola Lake ᑕ	170	35.16 S	150.27 E
Čon-Kemin ≏	85	42.42 N	75.54 E
Conklin, Ab., Can.	182	55.38 N	111.05 W
Conklin, N.Y., U.S.	210	42.02 N	75.48 W
Conklingville Dam ◆[6]	210	43.17 N	74.02 W
Conklin Point ›	276	40.41 N	73.17 W
Conkouati	152	4.00 S	11.13 E
Conliège	58	46.39 N	5.36 E
Conlin, Lake ⊜	220	28.14 N	81.07 W
Conn, Lough ⊜	48	54.04 N	9.20 W
Connah's Quay	44	53.13 N	3.03 W
Connaught □[9]	48	53.45 N	9.00 W
Connaughton	285	40.05 N	75.19 W
Connaughton, Mount ʌ[2]	162	22.42 S	122.40 E
Connaught Place ♠	272a	28.38 N	77.12 E
Connaux	62	44.05 N	4.36 E
Conneaut	214	41.56 N	80.33 W
Conneaut Creek ≏	214	41.58 N	80.33 W
Conneaut Lake	214	41.36 N	80.19 W
Conneaut Lake ⊜	214	41.37 N	80.18 W
Conneaut Outlet ≏	214	41.33 N	80.06 W
Conneautville	214	41.45 N	80.22 W
Connecticut □[3], U.S.	178	41.45 N	72.45 W
Connecticut □[3], U.S.	207	41.45 N	72.45 W
Connecticut ≏	188	41.17 N	72.21 W
Connell	202	46.39 N	118.51 W
Connell, Mount ʌ	182	49.18 N	115.38 W
Connellsville	188	40.01 N	79.35 W
Connelly	210	41.55 N	73.59 W
Connel Park	44	55.23 N	4.12 W
Connemara	166	24.13 S	142.17 E
Connemara ◆[1]	48	53.25 N	9.45 W
Conner	116	17.48 N	121.19 E
Conner, Mount ʌ	162	25.23 S	131.54 E
Connerré	50	48.03 N	0.30 E
Connersville, Fl., U.S.	220	27.54 N	81.47 W
Connersville, In., U.S.	218	39.38 N	85.08 W
Connetquot ≏	276	40.43 N	73.08 W
Connetquot Brook ≏	276	40.45 N	73.09 W
Connetquot River State Park ♠	210	40.46 N	73.09 W
Connewarre, Lake ⊜	169	38.14 S	144.27 E
Conn Island I	284c	39.00 N	77.16 W
Conn Lake ⊜	176	70.34 N	73.30 W
Connoquenessing	214	40.49 N	80.59 W
Connoquenessing Creek ≏	214	40.51 N	80.19 W
Connors Range ʌʌ	166	21.40 S	149.10 E
Conodoguinet Creek ≏	208	40.17 N	76.55 W
Conon ≏	46	57.34 N	4.26 W
Cononaco ≏	246	1.32 S	75.35 W
Cononbridge	46	57.34 N	4.26 W
Conorochite ≏	246	2.41 N	67.29 W
Conotton Creek ≏	214	40.34 N	81.23 W
Conover	192	35.42 N	81.13 W
Conowingo	208	39.40 N	76.09 W
Conowingo ◆[6]	208	39.33 N	76.04 W
Conowingo Creek ≏	208	39.41 N	76.12 W
Conowingo Dam ◆[6]	208	39.39 N	76.10 W
Conquest	184	51.32 N	107.17 W
Conquista	255	19.56 S	47.33 W
Conrad, Ia., U.S.	190	42.13 N	92.52 W
Conrad, Mt., U.S.	202	48.10 N	111.56 W
Conrado	256	22.32 S	43.33 W
Conroe	222	30.18 N	95.27 W
Conroe, Lake ⊜[1]	222	30.25 N	95.37 W
Çonsandolo	66	44.39 N	11.46 E
Čon-Saryoj	85	42.37 N	76.53 E
Conscience Bay ᑕ	276	40.57 N	73.07 W
Consdorf	56	49.46 N	6.20 E
Consecon	212	44.00 N	77.31 W
Conselheiro Lafaiete	255	20.40 S	43.48 W
Conselheiro Paulino	256	22.13 S	42.31 W
Conselheiro Pena	255	19.10 S	41.30 W
Conselice	66	44.31 N	11.49 E
Conselve	64	45.14 N	11.52 E
Conservatória	256	22.18 S	43.57 W
Consett	44	54.51 N	1.49 W
Conshohocken	208	40.04 N	75.18 W
Consolação	256	22.33 S	45.55 W
Consolação ◆[8]	287b	23.33 S	46.39 W
Consolación del Sur	240p	22.30 N	83.31 W
Consolidated Main Reef Mines ◆[7]	273d	26.11 S	27.56 E
Con Son II	110	8.43 N	106.36 E
Consort	184	52.01 N	110.46 W
Constable	206	44.56 N	74.18 W
Constableville	212	43.34 N	75.25 W
Constance → Konstanz	58	47.40 N	9.10 E
Constance, Lake → Bodensee ⊜	58	47.35 N	9.25 E
Constance Lake ⊜	212	45.25 N	75.58 W
Constância	34	39.28 N	8.20 W
Constanța	38	44.11 N	28.39 E
Constanța □[6]	38	44.20 N	28.20 E
Constant Creek ≏	212	45.17 N	76.46 W
Constantia	210	43.14 N	76.00 W
Constantina	34	37.52 N	5.37 W
Constantine → Qacentina, Alg.	148	36.22 N	6.37 E
Constantine, Mi., U.S.	216	41.50 N	85.40 W
Constantine, Cape ›	180	58.25 N	158.50 W
Constantinople → İstanbul	130	41.01 N	28.58 E
Constant Lake ⊜	212	45.24 N	77.00 W
Constitución, Chile	252	35.20 S	72.25 W
Constitución, Ur.	252	31.05 S	57.50 W
Constitución ◆[8]	288	34.37 S	58.23 W
Constitución de 1857, Parque Nacional ♠	204	32.05 N	115.55 W
Constitution, Mount ʌ	224	48.40 N	122.50 W
Consuegra	34	39.28 N	3.36 W
Consul	184	49.21 N	109.30 W
Consuma	66	43.47 N	11.35 E
Consuma, Passo della)(	66	43.47 N	11.36 E
Contai	126	21.47 N	87.45 E
Contamana	248	7.15 S	74.54 W
Contarina	64	45.00 N	12.13 E
Contas, Rio de ≏	255	14.17 S	39.01 W
Contee	208	39.05 N	76.52 W
Contendas do Sincorá	255	13.45 S	41.02 W
Contentnea Creek ≏	192	35.21 N	77.23 W
Contes	62	43.49 N	7.19 E
Contessa Entellina	70	37.44 N	13.11 E
Contigliano	66	42.24 N	12.46 E
Continental	216	41.06 N	84.15 W
Continental Peak ʌ	200	42.16 N	108.43 W
Contoocook Lake ⊜	207	42.47 N	72.01 W
Contraalmirante Cordero	252	38.44 S	68.10 W
Contra Costa □[6]	226	37.55 N	121.55 W
Contra Costa Canal ≊	282	38.02 N	121.58 W
Contra Loma Reservoir ⊜[1]	282	37.58 N	121.49 W
Contramaestre	240p	20.18 N	76.15 W
Contramaestre ≏	240p	20.31 N	76.18 W
Contratación	246	6.18 N	73.29 W
Contrecoeur	206	45.51 N	73.14 W
Contre Island ›[1]	276	40.54 N	73.32 W
Contreras, Embalse de ⊜[1]	34	39.32 N	1.30 W
Contreras, Isla I	254	51.55 S	74.55 W
Contres	50	47.25 N	1.26 E
Contrexéville	58	48.11 N	5.54 E
Contrisson	56	48.48 N	4.57 E
Controller Bay ᑕ	180	60.07 N	144.15 W
Contumazá	248	7.22 S	78.49 W
Contursi	68	40.39 N	15.14 E
Contwoyto Lake ⊜	176	65.42 N	110.50 W
Conty	50	49.44 N	2.09 E
Contz-les-Bains	56	49.27 N	6.21 E
Convención	246	8.28 N	73.21 W
Convent	194	30.01 N	90.49 W
Convento	236	9.21 N	83.30 W
Convent Station	276	40.47 N	74.26 W
Conversano	68	40.58 N	17.08 E
Converse	216	40.34 N	85.52 W
Converse Lake ⊜	276	41.08 N	73.39 W
Converse Pond Brook ≏	276	41.03 N	73.40 W
Convoy	216	40.55 N	84.42 W
Conway, P.E., Can.	186	46.40 N	63.59 W
Conway, S. Afr.	158	31.43 S	25.16 E
Conway, Ar., U.S.	194	35.05 N	92.26 W
Conway, Fl., U.S.	220	28.30 N	81.19 W
Conway, Ma., U.S.	207	42.30 N	72.42 W
Conway, Mo., U.S.	194	37.30 N	92.49 W
Conway, N.H., U.S.	188	43.58 N	71.07 W
Conway, N.C., U.S.	192	36.26 N	77.13 W
Conway, Pa., U.S.	214	40.39 N	80.14 W
Conway, S.C., U.S.	192	33.50 N	79.02 W
Conway, Wa., U.S.	224	48.21 N	122.21 W
Conway, Cape ›	166	20.32 S	148.56 E
Conway, Lake ⊜	162	28.17 S	135.35 E
Conway, Lake ⊜[1]	194	35.00 N	92.25 W
Conway, Mount ʌ	162	23.45 S	133.25 E
Conway National Park ♠	166	20.22 S	148.51 E
Conway Springs	198	37.23 N	97.38 W
Conwy	44	53.17 N	3.50 W
Conwy ≏	44	53.17 N	3.50 W
Conwy, Vale of V	44	53.12 N	3.48 W
Conwy Bay ᑕ	44	53.18 N	3.55 W
Conyers	192	33.40 N	84.01 W
Conyngham	210	40.59 N	76.03 W
Coo	56	50.24 N	5.52 E
Coober Pedy	162	29.01 S	134.43 E
Coogee, Austl.	168a	32.07 S	115.46 E
Coogee, Austl.	274a	33.55 S	151.16 E
Coogee Bay ᑕ	274a	33.55 S	151.16 E
Cook, Austl.	162	30.37 S	130.25 E
Cook, In., U.S.	216	41.22 N	87.26 W
Cook, Mn., U.S.	190	47.51 N	92.41 W
Cook, Ne., U.S.	198	40.30 N	96.09 W
Cook, Wa., U.S.	224	45.43 N	121.40 W
Cook □[6]	216	41.53 N	87.45 W
Cook, Bahía ᑕ	254	55.10 S	70.10 W
Cook, Baie de ᑕ	174s	17.29 S	149.49 W
Cook, Cape ›	182	50.08 N	127.55 W
Cook, Mount ʌ	172	43.36 S	170.10 E
Cook, Point ›	274b	37.55 S	144.48 E
Cook, Récif de ✣[2]	175f	19.25 S	163.50 E
Cookardinia	171b	35.34 S	147.14 E
Cook Bay ᑕ	212	44.15 N	79.30 W
Cook Creek ≏	224	47.17 N	124.05 W
Cooke, Mount ʌ	168a	32.25 S	116.18 E
Cookernup	168a	33.00 S	115.54 E
Cookes Peak ʌ	200	32.32 N	107.44 W
Cookeville	194	36.09 N	85.30 W
Cook Forest State Park ♠	214	41.22 N	79.12 W
Cookham	42	51.34 N	0.43 W
Cookhouse	158	32.45 S	25.49 E
Cook Ice Shelf ⊓	9	68.40 S	152.30 E
Cooking Lake ⊜	182	53.25 N	113.02 W
Cook Inlet ᑕ	180	60.30 N	152.00 W
Cook-Inseln → Cook Islands □[2]	14	20.00 S	158.00 W
Cook Island I	174o	1.57 N	157.28 W
Cook Islands □[2]	14	20.00 S	158.00 W
Cooks ≏	274a	33.56 S	151.10 E
Cooksburg	214	41.20 N	79.12 W
Cooks Falls	210	41.57 N	74.59 W
Cook's Harbour	186	51.36 N	55.52 W
Cookshire	206	45.25 N	71.38 W
Cooksmill Green	260	51.44 N	0.22 E
Cooks Mills	284a	43.00 N	79.11 W
Cookstown, On., Can.	212	44.11 N	79.42 W
Cookstown, N. Ire., U.K.	48	54.39 N	6.45 W
Cook Strait ʯ	172	41.15 S	174.30 E
Cooksville, Il., U.S.	216	40.33 N	88.43 W
Cooksville, Md., U.S.	208	39.19 N	77.01 W
Cooksville, Wi., U.S.	216	42.50 N	89.14 W
Cooksville Creek ≏	275b	43.34 N	79.34 W
Cooktown	164	15.28 S	145.15 E
Cookville	222	33.11 N	94.51 W
Coolabah	166	31.02 S	146.43 E
Cooladdi	166	26.39 S	145.28 E
Coolah	166	31.50 S	149.42 E
Coolamon	166	34.49 S	147.12 E
Coolaney	48	54.10 N	8.36 W
Coolangatta	171a	28.10 S	153.32 E
Coolawanyah	162	21.47 S	117.48 E
Coole ≏	50	48.56 N	4.21 E
Cooleemee	192	35.48 N	80.33 W
Cooley Lake ⊜	281	42.37 N	83.27 W
Coolgardie	162	30.57 S	121.10 E
Coolidge, Az., U.S.	200	32.58 N	111.31 W
Coolidge, Ga., U.S.	192	31.00 N	83.51 W
Coolidge, Tx., U.S.	222	31.45 N	96.38 W
Coolidge, Mount ʌ	198	43.44 N	103.29 W
Coolidge Dam ◆[6]	200	33.00 N	110.20 W
Coolidge Point ›	283	42.34 N	70.44 W
Coolin	202	48.28 N	116.50 W
Cooling	260	51.27 N	0.32 E
Cooloola National Park ♠	166	26.05 S	153.00 E
Cooloongup, Lake ⊜	168a	32.18 S	115.47 E
Coolspring	214	41.02 N	79.05 W
Coolumburra Hill ʌ	170	35.01 S	150.10 E
Coolup	168a	32.44 S	115.53 E
Cooma	171b	36.14 S	149.08 E
Cooma Creek ≏	171b	36.07 S	149.11 E
Coombe Cottage ⊥	274b	37.43 S	145.23 E
Coomberdale	162	30.28 S	116.02 E
Coomera	171a	27.52 S	153.19 E
Coomera ≏	171a	27.53 S	153.24 E
Coominya	171a	27.23 S	152.30 E
Coonabarabran	166	31.16 S	149.17 E
Coonalpyn	166	35.42 S	139.51 E
Coonamble	166	30.57 S	148.23 E
Coonana	162	31.01 S	123.07 E
Coon Creek ≏, Ca., U.S.	226	38.51 N	121.34 W
Coon Creek ≏, Il., U.S.	216	42.15 N	88.48 W
Coon Creek ≏, Tx., U.S.	222	31.59 N	95.52 W
Coon Creek Lake ⊜[1]	222	32.04 N	95.52 W
Coondambo	166	31.04 S	135.52 E
Coongan ≏	162	20.53 S	119.47 E
Coonoor	122	11.21 N	76.49 E
Coon Rapids, Ia., U.S.	198	41.52 N	94.41 W
Coon Rapids, Mn., U.S.	190	45.10 N	93.19 W
Coontown	276	40.37 N	74.31 W
Coon Valley	190	43.42 N	91.00 W
Cooper	196	33.22 N	95.41 W
Cooper ≏, N.J., U.S.	285	39.57 N	75.07 W
Cooper ≏, Wa., U.S.	224	47.23 N	121.23 W
Cooper, Mount ʌ, Austl.	162	26.11 S	127.56 E
Cooper, Mount ʌ, B.C., Can.	182	50.11 N	117.12 W
Cooper, North Branch ≏	285	39.55 N	75.02 W
Cooper Center	216	42.23 N	85.37 W
Cooper Creek ≏	166	28.29 S	137.46 E
Cooper Island I	240m	18.22 N	64.30 W
Cooper Landing	180	60.29 N	149.51 W
Cooper Mountain ʌ	180	60.23 N	149.51 W
Cooper River Parkway ♠	285	39.55 N	75.03 W
Cooper Road	194	32.26 N	93.48 W
Coopers	194	32.46 N	86.33 W
Coopersale Common	260	51.42 N	0.08 E
Coopersburg	208	40.30 N	75.23 W
Coopers Plains, Austl.	171a	27.34 S	153.02 E
Coopers Plains, N.Y., U.S.	210	42.11 N	77.08 W
Cooperstown, N.Y., U.S.	210	42.42 N	74.55 W
Cooperstown, N.D., U.S.	198	47.26 N	98.07 W
Cooperstown, Pa., U.S.	214	40.43 N	79.57 W
Cooperstown, Pa., U.S.	214	41.30 N	79.52 W
Coopersville	216	43.03 N	85.56 W
Coorabie	162	31.54 S	132.18 E
Cooranbong	170	33.04 S	151.27 E
Coorong National Park ♠	166	36.01 S	139.32 E
Coorow	162	29.53 S	116.01 E
Cooroy	166	26.25 S	152.55 E
Coorparoo	171a	27.30 S	153.03 E
Coos □[6]	206	45.04 N	71.20 W
Coosa ≏	194	32.30 N	86.16 W
Coosawhatchie ≏	192	32.32 N	80.52 W
Coos Bay	202	43.22 N	124.12 W
Coos Bay ᑕ	202	43.23 N	124.16 W
Cootamundra	166	34.39 S	148.02 E
Cootehill	48	54.04 N	7.05 W
Cooyar	171a	26.59 S	151.50 E
Cooyar Creek ≏	171a	26.50 S	152.04 E
Cooyar Mountain ʌ	171a	26.57 S	151.47 E
Copacabana, Arg.	252	28.12 S	67.29 W
Copacabana, Bol.	248	16.10 S	69.05 W
Copacabana, Col.	246	6.20 N	75.30 W
Copacabana ◆[8]	287a	22.58 S	43.11 W
Copacabana, Forte de ⊥	287a	22.59 S	43.11 W
Copainalá	234	17.05 N	93.12 W
Copake	210	42.06 N	73.33 W
Copake Falls	210	42.07 N	73.31 W
Copala	234	16.37 N	98.58 W
Copalillo	234	18.02 N	99.07 W
Copalis ≏	224	47.07 N	124.13 W
Copalis Beach	224	47.06 N	124.10 W
Copalita ≏	234	15.46 N	96.03 W
Copán, Hond.	236	14.50 N	89.09 W
Copan, Ok., U.S.	196	36.53 N	95.55 W
Copán □[5]	236	14.50 N	89.00 W
Copán ⊥	236	14.50 N	89.09 W
Copanatoyac	234	17.15 N	98.45 W
Copándaro	234	19.53 N	101.13 W
Copan Lake ⊜[1]	196	36.55 N	95.56 W
Copano Bay ᑕ	196	28.05 N	97.05 W
Copatana	246	2.48 S	67.04 W
Cope	198	39.39 N	102.51 W
Copeá, Paraná ≏[1]	246	3.52 S	63.20 W
Copeau ≏	184	52.45 N	103.00 W
Copeland	220	25.57 N	81.21 W
Copeland Island I	48	54.41 N	5.32 W
Copenhagen → København, Dan.	41	55.40 N	12.35 E
Copenhagen, N.Y., U.S.	212	43.53 N	75.40 W
Copenhague → København	41	55.40 N	12.35 E
Copenhaver	284c	39.04 N	77.11 W
Copertino	68	40.16 N	18.03 E
Copetonas	252	38.43 S	60.27 W
Copeville	222	33.05 N	96.25 W
Copiague	210	40.40 N	73.24 W
Copiague Neck ›[1]	276	40.40 N	73.22 W
Copiapó	252	27.22 S	70.20 W
Copiapó ≏	252	27.19 S	70.56 W
Copinsay I	46	58.54 N	2.40 W
Coplay	208	40.40 N	75.29 W
Copley, Austl.	166	30.32 S	138.25 E
Copley, Oh., U.S.	214	41.06 N	81.39 W
Copmanthorpe	44	53.55 N	1.08 W
Copoas, Mount ʌ	116	10.48 N	119.17 E
Copolo	152	10.22 S	14.07 E
Copparo	64	44.54 N	11.49 E
Coppell	222	32.57 N	97.01 W
Coppename ≏	250	5.48 N	55.55 W
Coppenbrügge	52	52.07 N	9.32 E
Copper ≏	180	60.30 N	144.50 W
Copperas Cove	196	31.07 N	97.54 W
Copperas Mountain ʌ	276	41.02 N	74.28 W
Copperbelt □[4]	154	13.00 S	28.00 E
Copper Butte ʌ	202	48.42 N	118.28 W
Copper Canyon → Cobre, Barranca del V	232	27.28 N	107.50 W
Copper Center	180	61.58 N	145.19 W
Copper Cliff	190	46.28 N	81.04 W
Copper Creek ≏	192	36.40 N	82.45 W
Copper Harbor	190	47.27 N	87.53 W
Coppermine	176	67.50 N	115.05 W
Coppermine ≏	176	67.49 N	115.04 W
Copper Mine Point ›, Br. Vir. Is.	240m	18.26 N	64.25 W
Coppermine Point ›, On., Can.	190	46.59 N	84.47 W
Copper Mountain	182	49.20 N	120.33 W
Copper Mountain ʌ, Ak., U.S.	182	55.14 N	132.36 W
Copper Mountain ʌ, Wy., U.S.	200	43.27 N	107.57 W
Copperopolis	226	37.59 N	120.38 W
Coppet	58	46.19 N	6.12 E
Coppin State College ⛉[2]	284b	39.19 N	76.40 W
Copplestone	42	50.49 N	3.45 W
Coppull	262	53.37 N	2.40 W
Copster Green	262	53.48 N	2.30 W
Coptic Museum ⛉	273c	30.00 N	31.13 E
Copton Creek ≏	182	54.16 N	119.15 W
Copton Point ›	116	10.00 N	123.22 E
Coqên	120	31.20 N	85.25 E
Coquet ≏	44	55.22 N	1.37 W
Coquet Dale V	44	55.16 N	1.50 W
Coquí	240m	17.59 N	66.14 W
Coquilhatville → Mbandaka	152	0.04 N	18.16 E
Coquille	202	43.10 N	124.11 W
Coquille ≏	202	43.07 N	124.26 W
Coquille, East Fork ≏	202	43.06 N	124.04 W
Coquille, Middle Fork ≏	202	43.05 N	124.09 W
Coquille, South Fork ≏	202	43.02 N	124.07 W
Coquimatlán	234	19.12 N	103.48 W
Coquimbo	252	29.58 S	71.21 W
Coquimbo □[4]	252	30.45 S	71.00 W
Coquina Key I	220	27.44 N	82.38 W
Corabia	38	43.46 N	24.30 E
Coração de Jesus	255	16.42 S	44.22 W
Coração de Maria	255	12.14 S	38.45 W
Corace ≏	68	38.49 N	16.37 E
Coracora	248	15.02 S	73.47 W
Corail, Mer de → Coral Sea ⍑[2]	14	20.00 S	158.00 E
Coral	214	40.29 N	79.10 W
Coral Bay ᑕ, Pil.	116	8.25 N	117.20 E
Coral Bay ᑕ, Vir. Is., U.S.	240m	18.20 N	64.41 W
Coral Gables	220	25.43 N	80.16 W
Coral Harbour	176	64.08 N	83.10 W
Coral Hills	284c	38.52 N	76.55 W
Coralque ≏	248	16.26 S	70.45 W
Coral Sea ⍑[2]	14	20.00 S	158.00 E
Coral Sea Basin ✣[1]	14	14.00 S	152.00 E
Coral Sea Islands Territory □[8]	166	18.30 S	152.00 E
Coral Springs	220	26.16 N	80.13 W
Coralville	190	41.40 N	91.34 W
Coralville Lake ⊜[1]	190	41.47 N	91.48 W
Coram, Mt., U.S.	202	48.25 N	114.02 W
Coram, N.Y., U.S.	210	40.52 N	73.00 W
Corangamite, Lake ⊜	169	38.10 S	143.25 E
Corantijn (Corentyne) ≏	250	5.55 N	57.05 W
Coraopolis	214	40.31 N	80.10 W
Coraopolis Heights	279b	40.29 N	80.10 W
Corato	68	41.09 N	16.25 E
Corbara, Lago di ⊜[1]	66	42.43 N	12.15 E
Corbeil-Essonnes	50	48.36 N	2.29 E
Corbenay	58	47.54 N	6.20 E
Corbeny	50	49.28 N	3.49 E
Corbera, Riera de ≏	266d	41.27 N	1.59 E
Corberon	58	47.01 N	4.59 E
Corbett	210	42.03 N	75.02 W
Corbetta	62	45.28 N	8.55 E
Corbett National Park ♠	124	29.40 N	78.45 E
Corbettsville	210	42.01 N	75.48 W
Corbie	50	49.55 N	2.30 E
Corbière Point ›	43b	49.11 N	2.15 W
Corbières ʌʌ	32	42.55 N	2.38 E
Corbigny	50	47.15 N	3.40 E
Corbin	192	36.56 N	84.05 W
Corbion	56	49.48 N	5.00 E
Corbola	64	45.00 N	12.05 E

Symbol	English	Deutsch	Español	Français	Português
≏	River	Fluß	Río	Rivière	Rio
≊	Canal	Kanal	Canal	Canal	Canal
ᒪ	Waterfall, Rapids	Wasserfall, Stromschnellen	Cascada, Rápidos	Chute d'eau, Rapides	Cascata, Rápidos
ʯ	Strait	Meeresstraße	Estrecho	Détroit	Estreito
ᑕ	Bay, Gulf	Bucht, Golf	Bahía, Golfo	Baie, Golfe	Baía, Golfo
⊜	Lake, Lakes	See, Seen	Lago, Lagos	Lac, Lacs	Lago, Lagos
≡	Swamp	Sumpf	Pantano	Marais	Pântano
⊓	Ice Features, Glacier	Eis- und Gletscherformen	Accidentes Glaciales	Formes glaciaires	Acidentes glaciares
⍑	Other Hydrographic Features	Andere Hydrographische Objekte	Otros Elementos Hidrográficos	Autres données hydrographiques	Outros acidentes hidrográficos
✣	Submarine Features	Untermeerische Objekte	Accidentes Submarinos	Formes de relief sous-marin	Acidentes submarinos
□	Political Unit	Politische Einheit	Unidad Politica	Entité politique	Unidade política
⛉	Cultural Institution	Kulturelle Institution	Institución Cultural	Institution culturelle	Instituição cultural
⊥	Historical Site	Historische Stätte	Sitio Histórico	Site historique	Sitio histórico
♠	Recreational Site	Erholungs- und Ferienort	Sitio de Recreo	Centre de loisirs	Area de Lazer
⊠	Airport	Flughafen	Aeropuerto	Aéroport	Aeroporto
■	Military Installation	Militäranlage	Instalación Militar	Installation militaire	Instalação militar
◆	Miscellaneous	Verschiedenes	Misceláneo	Divers	Diversos

Corbones ≏ 34 37.36 N 5.39 W
Corbridge 44 54.58 N 2.01 W
Corbu 38 44.29 N 24.43 E
Corby 42 52.29 N 0.40 W
Corcaigh → Cork 48 51.54 N 8.28 W
Córcega 240m 18.19 N 67.15 W
Córcega, Isla de → Corse I 36 42.00 N 9.00 E
Corciano 66 43.08 N 12.17 E
Corcieux 58 48.10 N 6.53 E
Corcolle • 8 267a 41.55 N 12.46 E
Corcoran 226 36.05 N 119.33 W
Corcovado, Golfo c 254 43.30 S 73.30 W
Corcovado, Morro do ∧ 287a 22.57 S 43.13 W
Corcovado, Parque Nacional ♦ 236 8.35 N 83.40 W
Corcovado, Volcán ∧ 1 254 43.12 S 72.48 W
Corcubión 34 42.57 N 9.11 W
Cordeaux Reservoir ◎ 1 170 34.22 S 150.45 E
Cordeiro 255 22.02 S 42.22 W
Cordele, Ga., U.S. 192 31.57 N 83.46 W
Cordele, Tx., U.S. 222 29.08 N 96.38 W
Cordell 196 35.17 N 98.59 W
Cordell Hull Reservoir ◎ 1 194 36.25 N 85.40 W
Cordenons 64 45.59 N 12.42 E
Corder 194 39.05 N 93.38 W
Cordes 32 44.04 N 1.57 E
Cordevole ≏ 64 46.05 N 12.04 E
Cordignano 64 45.57 N 12.25 E
Cordillera □ 5 252 25.15 S 57.00 W
Cordillera de los Picachos, Parque Nacional ♦ 246 3.00 N 74.30 W
Cordillo Downs 166 26.43 S 140.38 E
Cordisburgo 255 19.07 S 44.21 W
Cordislândia 256 21.48 S 45.43 W
Córdoba, Arg. 252 31.24 S 64.11 W
Córdoba, Esp. 34 37.53 N 4.46 W
Córdoba, Méx. 234 18.53 N 96.56 W
Córdoba □ 4, Arg. 252 32.00 S 64.00 W
Córdoba □ 4, Esp. 34 38.00 N 4.50 W
Córdoba □ 5 246 8.20 N 75.40 W
Córdoba, Península ≻ 1 254 53.20 S 72.50 W
Cordon 116 16.40 N 121.28 E
Cordova → Córdoba, Esp. 34 37.53 N 4.46 W
Córdova, Perú 248 14.04 S 75.03 W
Cordova, Al., U.S. 194 33.45 N 87.11 W
Cordova, Ak., U.S. 180 60.33 N 145.46 W
Cordova, Il., U.S. 190 41.41 N 90.19 W
Cordova, Md., U.S. 208 38.52 N 75.59 W
Cordova Bay c 182 54.55 N 132.35 W
Cordova Lake ◎ 212 44.35 N 77.49 W
Cordova Peak ∧ 180 60.51 N 145.16 W
Corea, Estrecho de → Korea Strait ⊍ 90 34.00 N 129.00 E
Corea del Norte → Korea, North □ 1 98 40.00 N 127.00 E
Corea del Sur → Korea, South □ 1 98 36.30 N 128.00 E
Coreaú 250 3.33 S 40.39 W
Coreaú ≏ 250 2.54 S 40.50 W
Core Creek ≏ 285 40.11 N 74.55 W
Corée, Détroit de → Korea Strait ⊍ 90 34.00 N 129.00 E
Coree, Mount ∧ 171b 35.18 S 148.48 E
Corée du Nord → Korea, North □ 1 98 40.00 N 127.00 E
Corée du Sud → Korea, South □ 1 98 36.30 N 128.00 E
Coreglia Antelminelli 64 44.04 N 10.31 E
Coreinbob 171b 35.13 S 147.38 E
Coremas 250 7.01 S 37.58 W
Corentyne (Corantijn) ≏ 250 5.55 N 57.05 W
Corerepe 232 25.40 N 108.40 W
Corese Terra 66 42.10 N 12.42 E
Corey Lake ◎ 216 41.55 N 85.45 W
Corfe Castle 42 50.38 N 2.04 W
Corfield 166 21.43 S 143.22 E
Corfu → Kérkira, Ellás 38 39.36 N 19.56 E
Corfu, N.Y., U.S. 210 42.57 N 78.24 W
Corfu → Kérkira I 38 39.40 N 19.45 E
Corhanwarrabul Creek ≏ 274b 37.55 S 145.12 E
Cori 66 41.39 N 12.55 E
Coria 34 39.59 N 6.32 W
Coria del Río 34 37.16 N 6.03 W
Coribe 255 13.50 S 44.28 W
Coricudgy, Mount ∧ 170 32.50 S 150.22 E
Corigliano Calabro 68 39.36 N 16.31 E
Corigliano d'Otranto 68 40.09 N 18.15 E
Corinaldo 66 43.39 N 13.03 E
Corinda 166 17.53 S 138.35 E
Corinne, Pa., U.S. 285 39.54 N 75.40 W
Corinne, Ut,. U.S. 200 41.33 N 112.06 W
Corinne, W.V., U.S. 192 37.34 N 81.21 W
Corinth → Kórinthos, Ellás 38 37.56 N 22.56 E
Corinth, Ky., U.S. 218 38.29 N 84.33 W
Corinth, Ms., U.S. 194 34.56 N 88.31 W
Corinth, N.Y., U.S. 210 43.14 N 73.49 W
Corinth, Gulf of → Korinthiakós Kólpos c 38 38.19 N 22.04 E
Corinth Canal → Korínthou, Dhiórix ≋ 38 37.57 N 22.56 E
Corinto, Bra. 255 18.21 S 44.27 W
Corinto, El Sal. 236 13.49 N 87.58 W
Corinto, Nic. 236 12.29 N 87.10 W
Corio 169 38.04 S 144.23 E
Corio Bay c 169 38.07 S 144.24 E
Coripata 248 16.18 S 67.36 W
Corire 248 16.14 S 72.28 W
Coris 248 9.50 S 77.45 W
Corisco, Isla de I 152 0.53 N 9.20 E
Corixo Grande (Curiche Grande) ≏ 248 17.43 S 57.43 W
Corjeuți 38 48.13 N 27.02 E
Cork (Corcaigh) 48 51.54 N 8.28 W
Cork □ 6 48 51.58 N 8.35 W
Cork Airport ⊠ 48 51.51 N 8.29 W
Cork Harbour c 48 51.45 N 8.15 W
Corkscrew 220 26.28 N 81.33 W
Corkscrew Swamp ≡ 220 26.25 N 81.34 W
Čorku 85 39.58 N 70.33 E
Corlay 32 48.19 N 3.03 W
Corleone 70 37.49 N 13.18 E
Corleto Perticara 68 40.23 N 16.03 E
Çorlu 130 41.09 N 27.48 E
Cormainville 50 48.08 N 1.36 E
Cormano 266b 45.33 N 9.10 E
Cormatin 58 46.33 N 4.41 E
Cormeilles 50 49.15 N 0.23 E
Cormeilles-en-Parisis 50 48.59 N 2.12 E
Cormery 50 47.16 N 0.51 E
Cormons 64 45.58 N 13.28 E
Cormoran Reef ⊹ 2 175b 7.50 N 134.32 E
Cormorant 184 54.14 N 100.35 W
Cormorant Lake ◎ 184 54.13 N 100.47 W
Çorna 64 45.53 N 10.10 E
Čornaja, Ross. 24 68.35 N 56.30 E
Čornaja, Ross. 82 55.45 N 38.04 E
Čornaja ≏, Ross. 265a 59.47 N 30.10 E
Čornaja ≏, Ross. 265a 59.50 N 30.00 E
Čornaja ≏, Ross. 265a 60.01 N 30.10 E
Čornaja ≏, Ross. 265a 59.55 N 30.59 E
Čornaja ≏, Ross. 265b 55.41 N 37.58 E
Čornaja Cholunica 86 58.51 N 51.42 E
Čornaja Gr'az', Ross. 82 54.31 N 35.52 E
Čornaja Gr'az', Ross. 82 54.58 N 36.48 E
Čornaja Gr'az', Ross. 265b 55.58 N 37.19 E
Čornaja Rečka 265a 59.56 N 30.58 E
Čornaja rečka ≏, Ross. 265a 59.46 N 30.45 E
Čornaja rečka ≏, Ross. 265a 59.55 N 30.22 E
Čornaja Sloboda 24 60.48 N 37.46 E
Cornaredo 266b 45.30 N 9.02 E
Cornas 62 44.58 N 4.51 E
Cornedo Vicentino 64 45.37 N 11.20 E
Cornelia, S. Afr. 158 27.13 S 28.52 E
Cornelia, Ga., U.S. 192 34.30 N 83.31 W
Cornélio Procópio 255 23.08 S 50.39 W
Cornelius, N.C., U.S. 192 35.29 N 80.51 W
Cornelius, Or., U.S. 224 45.31 N 123.03 W
Cornelius Grinnell Bay c 176 63.20 N 64.50 W
Cornell, Il., U.S. 216 41.00 N 88.44 W
Cornell, Wi., U.S. 190 45.10 N 91.08 W
Cornellà de Llobregat 266d 41.21 N 2.05 E
Corner Brook 186 48.57 N 57.57 W
Corner Inlet c 169 38.43 S 146.20 E
Corner Store 285 40.07 N 75.30 W
Cornersville 194 35.21 N 86.50 W
Cornes, Lac des ◎ 206 46.43 N 75.09 W
Cornești 38 47.22 N 27.59 E
Corneta, Punta ≻ 234 15.39 N 96.34 W
Cornforth 44 54.42 N 1.31 W
Cornhill 46 57.36 N 2.42 W
Cornholme 262 53.44 N 2.08 W
Cornia ≏ 66 42.57 N 10.33 E
Corniglia 62 44.07 N 9.42 E
Corniglio 64 44.28 N 10.05 E
Corning, Ar., U.S. 194 36.24 N 90.34 W
Corning, Ca., U.S. 204 39.55 N 122.10 W
Corning, Ia., U.S. 198 40.59 N 94.44 W
Corning, Ks., U.S. 198 39.39 N 96.01 W
Corning, N.Y., U.S. 210 42.08 N 77.03 W
Corning, Oh., U.S. 188 39.36 N 82.05 W
Cornish 188 43.48 N 70.48 W
Cornish, Mount ∧ 162 20.13 S 126.28 E
Cornland 219 39.56 N 89.24 W
Corno ≏ 66 42.49 N 12.55 E
Corno Grande ∧ 66 42.28 N 13.34 E
Čornoje, Kaz. 86 51.44 N 77.34 E
Čornoje, Ross. 80 57.32 N 46.25 E
Čornolesskoje 84 44.42 N 43.42 E
Čornomorskij 78 44.51 N 38.29 E
Čornoreck 86 52.45 N 76.40 E
Cornuda 64 45.50 N 12.00 E
Cornwall, On., Can. 206 45.02 N 74.44 W
Cornwall, N.Y., U.S. 210 41.26 N 74.01 W
Cornwall, Pa., U.S. 208 40.16 N 76.24 W
Cornwall □ 6 42 50.30 N 4.40 W
Cornwall Bridge 207 41.49 N 73.22 W
Cornwallis Island I 176 75.15 N 94.30 W
Cornwall on Hudson 210 41.27 N 74.00 W
Cornwell 220 27.23 N 81.05 W
Čornyj Jar 80 48.04 N 46.08 E
Čornyj Mys, Ross. 24 68.20 N 38.37 E
Čornyj Mys, Ross. 86 55.33 N 80.04 E
Čornyj Otrog 86 51.55 N 55.59 E
Corny Point 166 34.55 S 137.03 E
Coro 246 11.25 N 69.41 W
Coro, Golfete de c 241s 11.30 N 69.55 W
Coroaci 255 18.35 S 42.17 W
Coroa Grande 256 22.54 S 43.52 W
Coroatá 250 4.08 S 44.08 W
Çoroca ≏ 152 15.43 S 11.55 E
Čoroch (Çoruh) ≏ 130 41.36 N 41.35 E
Corocoro 248 17.12 S 68.29 W
Corocoro Island I 246 8.30 N 60.10 W
Coroico 248 16.10 S 67.44 W
Coroico ≏ 248 15.27 S 67.50 W
Coromandel, Bra. 255 18.28 S 47.13 W
Coromandel, N.Z. 172 36.46 S 175.30 E
Coromandel Coast ≗ 2 122 13.30 N 80.30 E
Coromandel Peninsula ≻ 1 172 36.50 S 175.35 E
Coromandel Range ⋏ 172 37.00 S 175.40 E
Coron 116 12.00 N 120.12 E
Corona, Ca., U.S. 228 33.52 N 117.33 W
Corona, N.M., U.S. 200 34.15 N 105.36 W
Corona • 8 276 40.45 N 73.52 W
Coronación, Golfo de la → Coronation Gulf c 176 68.25 N 110.00 W
Coronación, Isla de la → Coronation Island I 9 60.37 S 45.30 W
Corona del Mar • 8 228 33.36 N 117.52 W
Coronado, Méx. 234 22.55 N 100.56 W
Coronado, Ca., U.S. 228 32.41 N 117.10 W
Coronado, Bahía de c 236 9.00 N 83.50 W
Coronado National Memorial ⊥ 200 31.10 N 110.29 W
Coronado Naval Amphibious Base ■ 228 32.40 N 117.10 W
Coronados, Golfo c 254 41.40 S 74.00 W
Coronation 182 52.05 N 111.27 W
Coronation Gardens ♦ 275b 43.41 N 79.29 W
Coronation Gulf c 176 68.25 N 110.00 W
Coronation Island I, Ant. 9 60.37 S 45.30 W
Coronation Island I, Ak., U.S. 180 55.52 N 134.15 W
Coronation Park ♦ 273d 26.06 S 27.47 E
Coron Bay c 116 11.54 N 120.08 E
Coronda 252 31.58 S 60.55 W
Coronel 252 37.01 S 73.08 W
Coronel Bogado 252 27.11 S 56.18 W
Coronel Dorrego 252 38.42 S 61.17 W
Coronel Du Graty 252 27.40 S 60.56 W
Coronel Eugenio del Busto 252 38.57 S 64.15 W
Coronel Fabriciano 255 19.31 S 42.38 W
Coronel Moldes, Arg. 252 25.16 S 65.29 W
Coronel Moldes, Arg. 252 33.38 S 64.36 W
Coronel Murta 255 16.37 S 42.11 W
Coronel Oviedo 252 25.25 S 56.27 W
Coronel Pacheco 256 21.35 S 43.16 W
Coronel Ponce 255 15.34 S 55.01 W
Coronel Pringles 252 37.58 S 61.22 W
Coronel Sapucaia 255 23.15 S 55.31 W
Coronel Suárez 252 37.28 S 61.55 W
Coronel Vidal 252 37.27 S 57.43 W
Coronel Vivida 252 25.58 S 52.34 W
Corongo 248 8.35 S 77.55 W
Corongoros 234 19.17 N 102.48 W
Coronie □ 5 250 5.50 N 56.20 W
Coron Island I 116 11.55 N 120.14 E
Coronita 228 33.52 N 117.36 W
Coropuna, Nevado ∧ 248 15.31 S 72.42 W
Çorovodë 38 40.30 N 20.13 E
Corowa 166 36.02 S 146.23 E
Corozal, Belize 232 18.24 N 88.24 W
Corozal, Col. 246 9.19 N 75.18 W
Corozal, Hond. 236 15.48 N 86.43 W
Corozal, P.R. 240m 18.21 N 66.17 W
Corps 62 44.49 N 5.57 E
Corpus 252 27.07 S 55.31 W
Corpus Christi 196 27.48 N 97.23 W
Corpus Christi, Lake ◎ 1 196 28.10 N 97.53 W
Corpus Christi Bay c 196 27.48 N 97.20 W
Corpus Christi Naval Air Station ■ 196 27.42 N 97.16 W
Corque 248 18.21 S 67.42 W
Corquín 236 14.34 N 88.52 W
Corral 254 39.52 S 73.26 W
Corral de Almaguer 34 39.46 N 3.11 W
Corral de Bustos 252 33.17 S 62.12 W
Corralero, Laguna c 234 16.12 N 98.07 W
Corralillo 240p 22.59 N 80.35 W
Corralito 252 32.03 S 64.12 W
Corralito, Arroyo del ≏ 258 33.39 S 58.03 W
Corralito, Cuchilla del ⋏ 2 258 33.40 S 57.44 W
Corralitos, Méx. 196 26.57 N 104.39 W
Corralitos, Ca., U.S. 226 36.59 N 121.48 W
Corran 46 56.43 N 5.14 W
Corraun Peninsula ≻ 1 48 53.54 N 9.53 W
Correas, Arroyo ≏ 288 34.24 S 58.32 W
Correboi, Arcu)(71 40.05 N 9.21 E
Correctionville 198 42.28 N 95.47 W
Corredor 287b 23.27 S 46.19 W
Correggio 64 44.46 N 10.47 E
Corregidor Island I 116 14.23 N 120.35 E
Corrego do Bom Jesus 256 22.38 S 46.02 W
Córrego do Ouro 256 21.22 S 45.47 W
Córrego Rico 255 15.14 S 47.48 W
Correia de Almeida 256 21.17 S 43.38 W
Corrente 250 10.27 S 45.10 W
Corrente ≏, Bra. 255 19.19 S 50.50 W
Corrente ≏, Bra. 255 13.08 S 43.28 W
Correntes 250 9.08 S 36.19 W
Correntes ≏ 248 17.21 S 55.37 W
Correntes, Cabo das ≻ 156 24.11 S 35.34 E
Correnti, Isola delle I 70 36.38 N 15.05 E
Correntina 255 13.20 S 44.39 W
Corrèze □ 5 32 45.20 N 1.50 E
Correzzana 266b 45.40 N 9.18 E
Corrib, Lough ◎ 48 53.26 N 9.14 W
Corridonia 66 43.15 N 13.30 E
Corrientes 252 27.28 S 58.50 W
Corrientes □ 4 252 29.00 S 58.00 W
Corrientes ≏, Arg. 252 30.21 S 59.33 W
Corrientes ≏, S.A. 246 3.43 S 74.35 W
Corrientes, Bahía de c 240p 21.51 N 84.36 W
Corrientes, Cabo ≻, Arg. 252 38.01 S 57.32 W
Corrientes, Cabo ≻, Col. 246 5.30 N 77.34 W
Corrientes, Cabo ≻, Cuba 240p 21.45 N 84.31 W
Corrientes, Cabo ≻, Méx. 234 20.25 N 105.42 W
Corrigan 222 30.59 N 94.49 W
Corrigin 162 32.21 S 117.52 E
Corrimal 170 34.22 S 150.54 E
Corringham 260 51.31 N 0.28 E
Corriverton 246 5.53 N 57.08 W
Corrofin 48 52.56 N 9.03 W
Corroios 266c 38.38 N 9.09 W
Corropoli 66 42.49 N 13.50 E
Corrumpa Creek ≏ 196 36.36 N 102.52 W
Corry 214 41.55 N 79.38 W
Corryong 171b 36.12 S 147.54 E
Corryong Creek ≏ 171b 36.06 S 147.59 E
Corryvreckan, Gulf of ⊍ 46 56.09 N 5.44 W
Corsano 68 39.53 N 18.22 E
Corse (Corsica) I 36 42.00 N 9.00 E
Corse, Cap ≻ 36 43.00 N 9.25 E
Corse-du-Sud □ 5 36 41.50 N 9.00 E
Corserine ∧ 44 55.09 N 4.22 W
Corsham 42 51.26 N 2.11 W
Corsica, Pa., U.S. 214 41.10 N 79.12 W
Corsica, S.D., U.S. 198 43.25 N 98.24 W
Corsica → Corse I 36 42.00 N 9.00 E
Corsicana 222 32.05 N 96.28 W
Corsica River c 208 39.05 N 76.08 W
Corsico 62 45.26 N 9.07 E
Corsock 44 55.04 N 3.57 W
Corson Inlet c 208 39.12 N 74.39 W
Cortaccia (Kurtatsch) 64 46.19 N 11.13 E
Cortachy 46 56.43 N 2.58 W
Cort Adelaer, Kap ≻ 176 62.00 N 42.00 W
Cortale 68 38.50 N 16.25 E
Cortazar 234 20.29 N 100.56 W
Corte 36 42.18 N 9.08 E
Corte Alto 254 40.57 S 73.10 W
Cortegana 34 37.55 N 6.49 W
Corte Madera 226 37.55 N 122.31 W
Corte Madera Creek ≏ 282 37.23 N 122.14 W
Cortemaggiore 64 44.59 N 9.56 E
Cortemilia 62 44.35 N 8.12 E
Corteno Golgi 64 46.10 N 10.15 E
Cortes 116 9.17 N 126.11 E
Cortés □ 5 236 15.30 N 88.00 W
Cortes ʊ 266a 40.25 N 3.41 W
Cortés, Bahía de c 240p 22.05 N 83.52 W
Cortez, Co., U.S. 200 37.20 N 108.35 W
Cortez, Fl., U.S. 220 27.28 N 82.41 W
Cortez, Sea of → California, Golfo de c 232 28.00 N 112.00 W
Cortez Mountains ⋏ 204 40.20 N 116.20 W
Cortina Creek ≏ 226 39.06 N 122.02 W
Cortina d'Ampezzo 64 46.32 N 12.08 E
Cortines 258 34.34 S 59.13 W
Cortland, Il., U.S. 216 41.55 N 88.41 W
Cortland, In., U.S. 218 38.58 N 85.58 W
Cortland, Ne., U.S. 198 40.30 N 96.42 W
Cortland, N.Y., U.S. 210 42.36 N 76.10 W
Cortland, Oh., U.S. 214 41.19 N 80.43 W
Cortland □ 6 210 42.36 N 76.11 W
Corton 42 52.32 N 1.44 E
Cortona 66 43.16 N 11.59 E
Çorubal (Koliba) ≏ 150 11.57 N 15.06 W
Čoruch-Dajron 85 40.24 N 69.40 E
Coruche 34 38.57 N 8.31 W
Çoruh (Čoroch) ≏ 130 41.36 N 41.35 E
Çorum, Tür. 130 39.14 N 28.27 E
Çorum, Tür. 130 40.33 N 34.58 E
Çorum □ 4 130 40.30 N 34.40 E
Corumbá 248 19.01 S 57.39 W
Corumbá ≏ 255 18.19 S 48.55 W
Corumbá de Goiás 255 15.55 S 48.48 W
Corumbaíba 255 18.09 S 48.34 W
Corumbataí ≏ 252 23.55 S 51.57 W
Corumbaú, Ponta do ≻ 255 16.53 S 39.06 W
Corumbiara ≏ 248 13.13 S 62.06 W
Corumo ≏ 246 6.49 N 60.52 W
Corund 38 46.28 N 25.11 E
Corunna, On., Can. 214 42.53 N 82.26 W
Corunna → La Coruña, Esp. 34 43.22 N 8.23 W
Corunna, In., U.S. 216 41.26 N 85.08 W
Corunna, Mi., U.S. 216 42.58 N 84.07 W
Corunna Downs 162 21.28 S 119.51 E
Coruripe 250 10.08 S 36.10 W
Corvallis, Mt., U.S. 202 46.18 N 114.06 W
Corvallis, Or., U.S. 202 44.33 N 123.15 W
Corvara in Badia 64 46.33 N 11.52 E
Corve Dale V 42 52.30 N 2.40 W
Corvey, Kloster ʊ 1 52 51.46 N 9.25 E
Corviale • 8 267a 41.52 N 12.25 E
Corvo I 148a 39.42 N 31.06 W
Corwen 42 52.59 N 3.22 W
Corwin, Cape ≻ 180 59.54 N 165.41 W
Corwith 190 42.59 N 93.57 W
Corydon, In., U.S. 218 38.12 N 86.07 W
Corydon, Ia., U.S. 190 40.45 N 93.19 W
Corydon, Ky., U.S. 194 37.44 N 87.42 W
Coryell 222 31.33 N 97.37 W
Coryell □ 6 222 31.25 N 97.40 W
Coryell Creek ≏ 222 31.23 N 97.35 W
Coryton 260 51.31 N 0.31 E
Coryville 214 41.53 N 78.24 W
Corzu 38 44.28 N 23.10 E
Corzuela 252 26.57 S 60.58 W
Cos → Kos I 38 36.50 N 27.10 E
Cosa (Ansedonia) ⊥ 66 42.25 N 11.18 E
Cosamaloapan [de Carpio] 232 18.22 N 95.48 W
Cosapa 248 18.11 S 68.40 W
Coscile ≏ 68 39.42 N 16.28 E
Cos Cob 276 41.02 N 73.36 W
Cos Cob Harbor c 276 41.01 N 73.36 W
Coscomatepec [de Bravo] 234 19.04 N 97.02 W
Coseley 42 52.33 N 2.06 W
Cosenza 68 39.17 N 16.15 E
Cosenza □ 4 68 39.28 N 16.25 E
Cosgroves Creek ≏ 274a 33.50 S 150.46 E
Coshocton 214 40.16 N 81.51 W
Coshocton □ 6 214 40.16 N 81.51 W
Cosigüina, Punta ≻ 236 12.54 N 87.41 W
Cosigüina, Volcán ∧ 1 236 12.59 N 87.34 W
Coslada 266a 40.26 N 3.34 W
Cosmo • 8 256 22.54 S 43.37 W
Cosmoledo Island I 138 9.43 S 47.35 E
Cosmópolis, Bra. 256 22.38 S 47.12 W
Cosmopolis, Wa., U.S. 224 46.57 N 123.46 W
Cosmos 198 44.56 N 94.41 W
Cosmos • 8 287a 22.55 S 44.37 W
Cosne-Cours-sur-Loire 50 47.24 N 2.55 E
Cosoleacaque 234 18.00 N 94.37 W
Cospán 248 7.26 S 78.33 W
Cosquín 252 31.15 S 64.29 W
Cossato 62 45.34 N 8.10 E
Cossatot ≏ 194 33.48 N 94.09 W
Cossayuna 210 43.11 N 73.26 W
Cossayuna Lake ◎ 210 43.12 N 73.25 W
Cossebaude 54 51.05 N 13.38 E
Cossé-le-Vivien 28 47.57 N 0.55 W
Cossoine 71 40.27 N 8.43 E
Cosson ≏ 50 47.30 N 1.15 E
Cossonay 58 46.37 N 6.31 E
Cost 222 29.26 N 97.32 W
Costa, Cayo I 220 26.41 N 82.15 W
Costa, Cordillera de la ⋏ 286c 10.33 N 66.52 W
Costa, Sierra de la → Coast Ranges ⋏ 178 41.00 N 123.30 W
Costacciaro 66 43.21 N 12.42 E
Costa de Caparica 266c 38.38 N 9.14 W
Costa del Marfil → Cote d'Ivoire □ 1 150 8.00 N 5.00 W
Costa de San José 258 33.51 S 56.53 W
Costa di Rovigo 64 45.03 N 11.42 E
Costa Mesa 228 33.38 N 117.55 W
Costanera, Cadena → Coast Mountains ⋏ 176 55.00 N 129.00 W
Costanera Sur, Parque Natural ♦ 288 34.37 S 58.21 W
Costanero, Canal de ≋ 288 34.28 S 58.28 W
Costa Rica 232 24.32 N 107.18 W
Costa Rica □ 1, N.A. 230 10.00 N 84.00 W
Costa Rica □ 1, N.A. 236 10.00 N 84.00 W
Costaros 62 44.54 N 3.50 E
Costas 256 22.39 S 45.56 W
Costello 214 41.36 N 78.03 W
Costelloe 48 53.17 N 9.32 W
Costermansville → Bukavu 154 2.30 S 28.52 E
Costessey 42 52.40 N 1.11 E
Costești, Mol. 38 46.52 N 28.44 E
Costești, Rom. 38 44.40 N 24.53 E
Costiera, Catena ⋏ 68 39.20 N 16.05 E
Costigan Lake ◎ 184 56.56 N 105.55 W
Costigliole d'Asti 62 44.47 N 8.11 E
Costigliole Saluzzo 62 44.34 N 7.29 E
Costilla 200 36.58 N 105.31 W
Costilla Creek ≏ 200 36.59 N 105.43 W
Cosumnes ≏ 226 38.16 N 121.26 W
Cosumnes, Middle Fork ≏ 226 38.33 N 120.51 W
Cosumnes, North Fork ≏ 226 38.33 N 120.51 W
Cosumnes, South Fork ≏ 226 38.33 N 120.49 W
Coswig, Dtsch. 54 51.07 N 13.34 E
Coswig, Dtsch. 54 51.53 N 12.26 E
Cotabambas 248 13.45 S 72.21 W
Cotabato 116 7.13 N 124.15 E
Cotacajes ≏ 248 16.00 S 67.01 W
Cotagaita 248 20.50 S 65.41 W
Cotagaita ≏ 248 21.01 S 65.23 W
Cotahuasi 248 15.12 S 72.56 W
Cotão ∧ 2 266c 38.45 N 9.18 W
Cotati 226 38.20 N 122.42 W
Coteau-Landing 206 45.15 N 74.13 W
Coteau-Station 206 45.17 N 74.14 W
Coteaux 238 18.12 N 74.02 W
Cote d'Ivoire (Ivory Coast) □ 1, Afr. 134 8.00 N 5.00 W
Cote d'Ivoire □ 1, Afr. 150 8.00 N 5.00 W
Côte-d'Or □ 5 32 47.30 N 4.50 E
Cotegipe 255 12.02 S 44.15 W
Cote Indian Reserve • 4 184 51.38 N 101.53 W
Cotentin ≻ 1 32 49.30 N 1.30 W
Côte-Saint-Luc 275a 45.28 N 73.40 W
Côtes-d'Armor □ 5 32 48.25 N 2.40 W
Côte Visitation • 8 275a 45.33 N 73.36 W
Cothi ≏ 42 51.52 N 4.10 W
Coti ≏ 248 8.36 S 65.33 W
Cotia 256 23.37 S 46.56 W
Cotia □ 7 287b 23.38 S 46.56 W
Cotia ≏ 256 23.31 S 46.51 W
Cotia, Reprêsa de ◎ 1 287b 23.44 S 46.57 W
Cotignac 62 43.32 N 6.09 E
Cotignola 66 44.23 N 11.56 E
Cotija de la Paz 234 19.49 N 102.43 W
Cotingo ≏ 246 3.55 N 60.30 W
Cotis, Laguna ◎ 258 35.11 S 59.16 W
Cotiujeni 38 47.51 N 28.36 E
Cotmeana ≏ 38 44.24 N 24.45 E
Cotoca 248 17.49 S 63.03 W
Cotonou 150 6.21 N 2.26 E
Cotopaxi □ 4 246 0.55 S 78.55 W
Cotopaxi ∧ 1 246 0.40 S 78.26 W
Cotopaxi, Parque Nacional ♦ 246 0.15 S 78.25 W
Cotorra, Isla I 241r 10.02 N 62.16 W
Cotorro • 8 286b 23.03 N 82.16 W
Cotronei 68 39.09 N 16.47 E
Cotswold Hills ⋏ 2 42 51.45 N 2.10 W
Cottage Grove, In., U.S. 218 39.36 N 84.52 W
Cottage Grove, Or., U.S. 202 43.47 N 123.03 W
Cottage Grove, Wi., U.S. 216 43.05 N 89.12 W
Cottage Hills 219 38.55 N 90.04 W
Cottageville 192 32.56 N 80.28 W
Cottam, On., Can. 214 42.08 N 82.45 W
Cottam, Eng., U.K. 262 53.47 N 2.46 W
Cottanello 66 42.24 N 12.41 E
Cottbus 54 51.45 N 14.19 E
Cottekill 210 41.51 N 74.06 W
Cottel Island I 186 48.51 N 53.42 W
Cottenham 42 52.18 N 0.09 E
Cotter 194 36.16 N 92.32 W
Cotter ≏ 171b 35.19 S 148.57 E
Cottesloe 168a 31.59 S 115.45 E
Cottiennes, Alpes (Alpi Cozie) ⋏ 62 44.45 N 7.00 E
Cottingham 44 53.47 N 0.24 W
Cottleville 219 38.44 N 90.39 W
Cottondale, Al., U.S. 194 33.11 N 87.27 W
Cottondale, Fl., U.S. 192 30.47 N 85.22 W
Cotton Lake ◎, Mb., Can. 184 55.05 N 96.50 W
Cotton Lake ◎, Tx., U.S. 222 29.48 N 94.48 W
Cotton Plant 194 35.00 N 91.15 W
Cottonport 194 30.59 N 92.03 W
Cotton Valley 194 32.49 N 93.25 W
Cottonwood, Az., U.S. 200 34.44 N 112.00 W
Cottonwood, Ca., U.S. 204 40.23 N 122.16 W
Cottonwood, Id., U.S. 202 46.02 N 116.20 W
Cottonwood, Mn., U.S. 198 44.36 N 95.40 W
Cottonwood ≏, Ks., U.S. 198 38.23 N 96.03 W
Cottonwood ≏, Mn., U.S. 198 44.17 N 94.25 W
Cottonwood Creek ≏, Ca., U.S. 226 36.27 N 119.20 W
Cottonwood Creek ≏, Ca., U.S. 226 36.52 N 120.12 W
Cottonwood Creek ≏, Mt., U.S. 202 48.33 N 107.45 W
Cottonwood Creek ≏, N.D., U.S. 198 46.16 N 98.15 W
Cottonwood Creek ≏, Ok., U.S. 196 35.54 N 97.27 W
Cottonwood Creek ≏, Or., U.S. 202 43.53 N 117.43 W
Cottonwood Creek ≏, Tx., U.S. 196 31.23 N 103.46 W
Cottonwood Creek ≏, Tx., U.S. 196 32.48 N 100.21 W
Cottonwood Creek ≏, Ut,. U.S. 200 39.09 N 110.55 W
Cottonwood Creek ≏, Wy., U.S. 202 43.51 N 108.09 W
Cottonwood Creek, Middle Fork ≏ 204 40.23 N 122.20 W
Cottonwood Creek, South Fork ≏ 204 40.23 N 122.20 W
Cottonwood Falls 198 38.22 N 96.32 W
Cottonwood Wash V, Az., U.S. 200 36.19 N 113.59 W
Cottonwood Wash V, Az., U.S. 200 35.00 N 110.39 W
Cotubandê 287a 22.51 S 43.01 W
Cotuhé ≏ 246 2.53 S 69.44 W
Cotui 238 19.03 N 70.09 W
Cotuit 207 41.37 N 70.26 W
Cotulla 196 28.26 N 99.14 W
Cotunduba, Ilha de I 287a 22.58 S 43.09 W
Coubert 261 48.40 N 2.42 E
Coubre, Pointe de la ≻ 32 45.41 N 1.13 W
Coubron 261 48.55 N 2.35 E
Couches-les-Mines 58 46.52 N 4.34 E
Couchiching, Lake ◎ 212 44.40 N 79.23 W
Coucouron 62 44.48 N 3.58 E
Coucy-le-Château-Auffrique 50 49.31 N 3.19 E
Coudekerque-Branche 50 51.02 N 2.24 E
Coudersport 214 41.46 N 78.01 W
Coudres, Île aux I 186 47.24 N 70.23 W
Couesnon ≏ 32 48.37 N 1.31 W
Cougar 224 46.03 N 122.17 W
Cougar Reservoir ◎ 1 202 44.06 N 122.12 W
Couhé 32 46.18 N 0.11 E
Couillet 50 50.23 N 4.27 E
Couilly-Pont-aux-Dames 261 48.53 N 2.52 E
Coulanges-la-Vineuse 50 47.42 N 3.35 E
Coulanges-sur-Yonne 50 47.31 N 3.32 E
Coulee City 202 47.36 N 119.17 W
Coulee Dam 202 47.57 N 118.58 W
Coulee Dam National Recreation Area ♦ 202 48.10 N 118.15 W
Coulihaut 240d 15.30 N 61.29 W
Coulman Island I 9 73.27 S 169.40 E
Coulmier-le-Sec 58 47.45 N 4.29 E
Coulogne 50 50.55 N 1.53 E
Coulomby 50 50.42 N 2.00 E
Coulommiers 50 48.49 N 3.05 E
Coulon ≏ 62 43.51 N 5.00 E
Coulonge ≏ 190 45.51 N 76.46 W
Coulonge Est ≏ 190 46.06 N 76.44 W
Coulsdon • 8 260 51.19 N 0.08 W
Coulta 166 34.23 S 135.29 E
Coulters 279b 40.18 N 79.48 W
Coulterville, Ca., U.S. 226 37.42 N 120.11 W
Coulterville, Il., U.S. 194 38.11 N 89.36 W
Counce 194 35.02 N 88.16 W
Council 202 44.44 N 116.26 W
Council Bluffs 198 41.15 N 95.51 W
Council Grove 198 38.39 N 96.29 W
Council Grove Lake ◎ 1 198 38.42 N 96.31 W
Coundon 44 54.40 N 1.39 W
Countegany 171b 36.11 S 149.27 E
Countesthorpe 42 52.33 N 1.08 W
Country Campus 222 30.49 N 95.26 W
Country Club Estates 220 28.03 N 81.57 W
Country Club Hills 278 41.34 N 87.43 W
Country Club View 284c 38.49 N 77.19 W
Country Hills 279b 40.19 N 79.42 W
Country Homes 202 47.44 N 117.24 W
Country Ridge Estates 276 41.02 N 73.41 W
Countryside 278 41.46 N 87.52 W
Countryside Lake ◎ 278 42.15 N 88.03 W
Countryside Manor 278 42.18 N 87.56 W
Coupar Angus 46 56.33 N 3.17 W
Coupeville 224 48.13 N 122.41 W
Coupland 222 30.28 N 97.24 W
Coupon 214 40.32 N 78.31 W
Coupvray 261 48.54 N 2.48 E
Courbevoie 50 48.54 N 2.15 E
Courbons 62 44.06 N 6.12 E
Courçay 50 47.15 N 0.52 E
Courcelle 261 48.42 N 2.06 E
Courcelles, Bel. 50 50.28 N 4.22 E
Courcelles, Fr. 261 49.07 N 2.18 E
Courcelles-Chaussy 56 49.07 N 6.24 E
Courcelles-sur-Nied 56 49.04 N 6.18 E
Courchevel 62 45.25 N 6.38 E
Cour-Cheverny 50 47.30 N 1.27 E
Courcibo ≏ 250 4.53 N 53.00 W
Courçon 32 46.15 N 0.49 W
Courcouronnes 261 48.37 N 2.24 E
Courdimanche 261 49.02 N 2.00 E
Cour-et-Buis 62 45.26 N 5.00 E
Courgent, Fr. 261 48.54 N 1.40 E
Courgent, Fr. 261 49.04 N 1.35 E
Courland → Kurzeme □ 9 76 56.50 N 22.30 E
Courmayeur 62 45.47 N 6.58 E
Couronne, Cap ≻ 62 43.19 N 5.03 E
Couronnement, Île du → Coronation Island I 9 60.37 S 45.30 W
Courpière 62 45.45 N 3.33 E
Courquetaine 261 48.41 N 2.45 E
Course Brook ≏ 283 42.17 N 71.22 W
Courseulles 28 49.20 N 0.27 W
Courson-les-Carrières 50 47.36 N 3.30 E
Court 58 47.14 N 7.20 E
Courtacon 50 48.42 N 3.17 E
Courtalain 50 48.05 N 1.09 E
Courteilles 50 48.58 N 0.29 E
Courtenay, B.C., Can. 182 49.41 N 125.00 W
Courtenay, Fr. 50 48.02 N 3.03 E
Courthézon 62 44.05 N 4.53 E
Courtice 212 43.55 N 78.46 W
Courtisols 56 48.59 N 4.31 E
Courtland, On., Can. 212 42.51 N 80.38 W
Courtland, Al., U.S. 194 34.40 N 87.18 W
Courtland, Ca., U.S. 226 38.20 N 121.34 W
Courtland, Va., U.S. 208 36.42 N 77.04 W
Courtleigh 284b 39.22 N 76.46 W
Courtmacsherry 48 51.38 N 8.43 W
Courtmacsherry Bay c 48 51.35 N 8.40 W
Courtney, Pa., U.S. 279b 40.13 N 79.58 W
Courtney, Tx., U.S. 222 30.16 N 96.04 W
Courtney Creek ≏ 196 31.16 N 102.50 W
Courtomer, Fr. 50 48.38 N 0.22 E
Courtomer, Fr. 261 48.39 N 2.54 E
Courtown 48 52.38 N 6.13 W
Courtrai → Kortrijk 50 50.50 N 3.16 E
Courtright 214 42.49 N 82.28 W
Courtry, Fr. 261 48.33 N 2.46 E
Courtry, Fr. 261 48.55 N 2.36 E
Court-Saint-Étienne 50 50.39 N 4.34 E
Courville-sur-Eure 50 48.27 N 1.15 E
Coushatta 194 32.00 N 93.20 W
Cousin ≏ 50 47.32 N 3.46 E
Cousiño Macul, Parque ♦ 286e 33.30 S 70.35 W
Cousolre 50 50.15 N 4.09 E
Coussegrey 50 47.57 N 4.01 E
Coussey 58 48.25 N 5.41 E
Coustellet 62 43.53 N 5.11 E
Coutances 32 49.03 N 1.26 W
Coutevroult 261 48.52 N 2.51 E
Couto do Magalhães 250 8.17 S 49.16 W
Couto Magalhães ≏ 255 13.37 S 53.09 W
Coutras 32 45.02 N 0.08 W
Coutts 182 49.00 N 111.57 W
Couture, Lac ◎ 176 60.07 N 75.20 W
Couture-sur-Loir 50 47.45 N 0.41 E
Couves, Ilha das I 256 23.25 S 44.52 W
Couvet 58 46.56 N 6.38 E
Couvin 50 50.03 N 4.29 E
Cova da Piedade 266c 38.40 N 9.10 W
Covane 156 21.22 S 33.56 E
Covasna 38 45.51 N 26.11 E
Covasna □ 6 38 46.00 N 26.00 E
Cove, Scot., U.K. 46 57.51 N 5.42 W
Cove, Or., U.S. 202 45.17 N 117.48 W
Cove Bay 46 57.06 N 2.04 W
Covedale 218 39.07 N 84.36 W
Cove Harbor c 276 41.03 N 73.30 W
Cove Island I 190 45.17 N 81.44 W
Covelo, Ang. 152 12.06 S 13.55 E
Covelo, Ca., U.S. 204 39.47 N 123.14 W
Cove Neck 276 40.53 N 73.31 W
Cove Neck ≻ 1 276 40.53 N 73.30 W
Coventry, Eng., U.K. 42 52.25 N 1.30 W
Coventry, Ct., U.S. 207 41.46 N 72.18 W
Coventry, De., U.S. 285 39.40 N 75.38 W
Coventry, R.I., U.S. 207 41.41 N 71.34 W
Coventry Cathedral ʊ 1 42 52.25 N 1.30 W
Coventryville 285 40.10 N 75.41 W
Cove Palisades State Park ♦ 202 44.34 N 121.15 W
Cove Point 208 38.22 N 76.23 W
Cove Point ≻ 208 38.23 N 76.23 W
Cover ≏ 44 54.17 N 1.46 W
Covered Wells 200 31.48 N 111.59 W
Covert 216 42.17 N 86.15 W
Covigliaio 66 44.08 N 11.18 E
Covilhã 34 40.17 N 7.30 W
Covina 228 34.05 N 117.53 W
Covington, Ga., U.S. 192 33.35 N 83.51 W
Covington, In., U.S. 194 40.08 N 87.23 W
Covington, Ky., U.S. 218 39.05 N 84.30 W
Covington, La., U.S. 194 30.28 N 90.06 W
Covington, Oh., U.S. 218 40.07 N 84.21 W
Covington, Ok., U.S. 196 36.18 N 97.35 W
Covington, Pa., U.S. 210 41.45 N 77.05 W
Covington, Tn., U.S. 194 35.33 N 89.38 W
Covington, Tx., U.S. 222 32.11 N 97.16 W
Covington, Va., U.S. 192 37.47 N 79.59 W
Covões 266c 38.50 N 9.20 W
Covunco, Arroyo ≏ 252 38.29 S 69.32 W
Cow ≏ 190 47.23 N 83.59 W
Cowal ≻ 1 46 56.05 N 5.08 W
Cowal, Lake ◎ 166 33.35 S 147.25 E
Cowan, Ky., U.S. 218 38.24 N 83.54 W
Cowan, Tn., U.S. 194 35.09 N 86.00 W
Cowan, Lake ◎ 162 31.50 S 121.50 E
Cowan Creek ≏ 274a 33.40 S 151.10 E
Cowanesque 210 41.56 N 77.30 W
Cowanesque ≏ 210 42.00 N 77.07 W
Cowan Heights 280 33.47 N 117.47 W
Cowan Lake ◎, Sk., Can. 184 54.00 N 107.15 W
Cowan Lake ◎, Oh., U.S. 218 39.23 N 83.54 W
Cowan Lake State Park ♦ 218 39.23 N 83.53 W
Cowansburg 279b 40.15 N 79.46 W
Cowanshannock Creek ≏ 214 40.51 N 79.30 W
Cowansville, P.Q., Can. 206 45.12 N 72.45 W
Cowansville, Pa., U.S. 214 40.53 N 79.36 W
Cowaramup 162 33.52 S 115.05 E
Coward 192 33.58 N 79.44 W
Coward Springs 166 29.24 S 136.49 E
Cowarie 166 27.43 S 138.20 E
Cow Bayou ≏ 222 31.19 N 97.00 W
Cowbridge 42 51.28 N 3.27 W
Cowburn Tunnel • 5 262 53.21 N 1.52 W
Cow Canyon V 280 34.01 N 120.06 W
Cowcowing Lakes ◎ 162 31.01 S 117.18 E
Cow Creek ≏, Ks., U.S. 198 38.02 N 97.56 W
Cow Creek ≏, Mt., U.S. 202 47.47 N 108.56 W
Cow Creek ≏, Ok., U.S. 196 34.10 N 98.00 W
Cow Creek ≏, Or., U.S. 202 42.57 N 123.20 W
Cow Creek ≏, Wa., U.S. 202 46.45 N 118.09 W
Cowden, Il., U.S. 219 39.15 N 88.52 W
Cowden, Pa., U.S. 279b 40.19 N 80.13 W
Cowdenbeath 46 56.07 N 3.21 W
Coweeman ≏ 224 46.06 N 122.52 W
Cowell 166 33.41 S 136.55 E
Cowen 188 38.24 N 80.33 W
Cowen, Mount ∧ 202 45.23 N 110.29 W
Cowes, Austl. 169 38.27 S 145.14 E
Cowes, Eng., U.K. 42 50.45 N 1.18 W
Cowessess Indian Reserve • 4 184 50.31 N 102.42 W
Coweta 196 35.57 N 95.39 W
Cow Green Reservoir ◎ 1 44 54.40 N 2.18 W
Cow Gulch ≏ 202 46.02 N 107.52 W
Cow Head 186 49.55 N 57.48 W
Cowhouse Creek ≏ 222 31.10 N 97.35 W
Cowichan ≏ 224 48.46 N 123.38 W
Cowichan Bay 224 48.44 N 123.40 W
Cowichan Lake ◎ 224 48.54 N 124.20 W
Cowiche Creek, North Fork ≏ 224 46.38 N 120.41 W
Cowiche Creek, South Fork ≏ 224 46.38 N 120.41 W
Cowie Water ≏ 46 56.58 N 2.12 W
Cowles Dam ◎ 1 273d 26.13 S 28.28 E
Cowlesville 210 42.51 N 78.28 W
Cowley, Austl. 166 26.54 S 144.49 E
Cowley, Ab., Can. 182 49.34 N 114.05 W
Cowley, Eng., U.K. 42 51.43 N 1.12 W
Cowley, Wy., U.S. 202 44.53 N 108.28 W
Cowley • 8 260 51.32 N 0.29 W
Cowley, Mount ∧ 169 38.33 S 143.52 E
Cowlitz □ 6 224 46.07 N 122.43 W
Cowlitz ≏ 224 46.05 N 122.53 W
Cowm Reservoir ◎ 1 262 53.40 N 2.11 W
Cow Palace ʊ 282 37.42 N 122.25 W
Cowpasture ≏ 188 37.48 N 79.45 W
Cowpens 192 35.01 N 81.48 W
Cowpens National Battlefield ♦ 192 35.06 N 81.46 W
Cowra 166 33.50 S 148.41 E
Cox ≏ 164 15.19 S 135.25 E
Cox, Mount ∧ 2 162 24.55 S 125.36 E
Coxá ≏ 255 14.16 S 44.11 W
Cox Creek ≏ 212 43.35 N 80.29 W
Coxheath 42 51.14 N 0.30 E
Coxim 255 18.30 S 54.45 W
Coxim ≏ 255 18.34 S 54.46 W
Coxipi, Lac ◎ 186 51.33 N 58.25 W
Coxquihui 234 20.11 N 97.35 W
Cox River Aboriginal Reserve • 4 164 15.40 S 134.45 E
Coxs ≏ 170 33.57 S 150.25 E
Coxsackie 210 42.21 N 73.48 W
Cox's Bāzār 120 21.26 N 91.59 E
Cox's Cove 186 49.07 N 58.05 W
Coyaguaima, Cerro ∧ 252 22.55 S 66.35 W
Coyah 150 9.43 N 13.23 W
Coyame 232 29.28 N 105.06 W
Coyanosa Draw V 196 31.18 N 103.06 W
Coya Sur 252 22.25 S 69.38 W
Coyle, Water of ≏ 44 55.28 N 4.32 W
Coyoacán • 8 286a 19.20 N 99.10 W

Symbols in the index entries represent the broad categories identified in the key at the right. Symbols with superior numbers (⋏ 1) identify subcategories (see complete key on page *I · 1*).

Symbole im Register stellen die rechts im Schlüssel erklärten Kategorien dar. Symbole mit hochgestellten Ziffern (⋏ 1) bezeichnen Unterabteilungen einer Kategorie (vgl. vollständiger Schlüssel auf Seite *I · 1*).

Los símbolos incluídos en el texto del índice representan las grandes categorías identificadas con la clave a la derecha. Los símbolos con numeros en su parte superior (⋏ 1) identifican las subcategorías (véase la clave completa en la página *I · 1*).

Les symboles de l'index représentent les catégories indiquées dans la légende à droite. Les symboles suivis d'un indice (⋏ 1) représentent des sous-catégories (voir légende complète à la page *I · 1*).

Os símbolos incluídos no texto do índice representam as grandes categorias identificadas com a chave à direita. Os símbolos com números em sua parte superior (⋏ 1) identificam as subcategorias (veja-se a chave completa à página *I · 1*).

∧	Mountain	Berg	Montaña	Montagne	Montanha
⋏	Mountains	Gebirge	Montañas	Montagnes	Montanhas
)(	Pass	Paß	Paso	Col	Passo
V	Valley, Canyon	Tal, Cañon	Valle, Cañón	Vallée, Canyon	Vale, Canhão
≚	Plain	Ebene	Llano	Plaine	Planície
≻	Cape	Kap	Cabo	Cap	Cabo
I	Island	Insel	Isla	Île	Ilha
II	Islands	Inseln	Islas	Îles	Ilhas
≗	Other Topographic Features	Andere Topographische Objekte	Otros Elementos Topográficos	Autres données topographiques	Outros acidentes topográficos

ESPAÑOL

Nombre	Página	Lat.°′	Long.°′ W = Oeste
Coyote	226	37.13 N	121.44 W
Coyote Creek ≃, Ca., U.S.	204	33.13 N	116.13 W
Coyote Creek ≃, Ca., U.S.	226	37.28 N	122.03 W
Coyote Creek ≃, Ca., U.S.	280	33.47 N	118.05 W
Coyote Creek, East Fork ≃	226	37.10 N	121.30 W
Coyote Creek, Middle Fork ≃	226	37.10 N	121.30 W
Coyote Hills ⋏[2]	282	37.33 N	122.05 W
Coyote Hills Regional Park ♦	282	37.33 N	122.06 W
Coyote Lake ⊜	204	35.04 N	116.45 W
Coyote Lake ⊜[1]	226	37.06 N	121.32 W
Coyotepec	234	19.46 N	99.12 W
Coyote Point ›	282	37.35 N	122.19 W
Coyote Wash V, Az., U.S.	200	32.40 N	114.08 W
Coyote Wash V, N.M., U.S.	200	36.11 N	108.33 W
Coy Pond ⊜	283	42.36 N	70.49 W
Coyuca de Benítez	234	17.02 N	100.04 W
Coyuca de Catalán	234	18.20 N	100.39 W
Coyutla	234	20.15 N	97.39 W
Cozad	198	40.51 N	99.59 W
Cozes	32	45.35 N	0.50 W
Cozie, Alpi (Alpes Cottiennes) ⋏	62	44.45 N	7.00 E
Cozoyoapan	234	16.46 N	98.15 W
Cozumel	232	20.31 N	86.55 W
Cozumel, Isla I	232	20.25 N	86.55 W
Cozy Lake	276	41.01 N	74.30 W
Crab Alley Bay ⊂	208	38.55 N	76.17 W
Crab Creek ≃	202	46.49 N	119.55 W
Crab Meadow ≡	276	40.55 N	73.20 W
Crab Orchard, Ky., U.S.	192	37.27 N	84.30 W
Crab Orchard, Tn., U.S.	192	35.54 N	84.52 W
Crab Orchard Lake ⊜[1]	194	37.43 N	89.05 W
Crabtree	214	40.21 N	79.28 W
Crabtree Creek ≃	279b	40.21 N	79.30 W
Crabtree Mills	206	45.58 N	73.28 W
Craches	261	48.34 N	1.49 E
Crackenback ≃	171b	36.21 S	148.36 E
Craco	68	40.23 N	16.26 E
Cracovie → Kraków	30	50.03 N	19.58 E
Cradle Mountain-Lake Saint Clair National Park ♦	166	42.00 S	146.00 E
Cradock, Austl.	166	32.04 S	138.30 E
Cradock, S. Afr.	158	32.08 S	25.36 E
Cradock Channel ⊔	172	36.11 S	175.15 E
Crafers	168b	35.01 S	138.47 E
Crafton	214	40.26 N	80.03 W
Crafts Creek ≃	285	40.07 N	74.46 W
Cragg Vale	262	53.42 N	2.00 W
Cragsmoor	210	41.40 N	74.23 W
Crai	42	51.55 N	3.36 W
Craig, B.C., Can.	224	49.18 N	124.15 W
Craig, Ak., U.S.	182	55.29 N	133.09 W
Craig, Co., U.S.	200	40.30 N	107.32 W
Craig, Mo., U.S.	194	40.11 N	95.22 W
Craig, Ne., U.S.	198	41.47 N	96.21 W
Craig, Point ∧	162	26.51 S	126.19 E
Craigavon	48	54.27 N	6.24 W
Craig Beach	214	41.07 N	81.01 W
Craig Creek ≃	192	37.39 N	79.49 W
Craigellachie	182	50.59 N	118.43 W
Craighall ◆[8]	273d	26.07 S	28.02 E
Craighall Park ◆[8]	273d	26.08 S	28.01 E
Craighouse	46	55.51 N	5.57 W
Craigmont	202	46.14 N	116.27 W
Craigmyle	182	51.40 N	112.15 W
Craignish Point ›	46	56.07 N	5.37 W
Craignure	46	56.28 N	5.42 W
Craigsville, Pa., U.S.	214	40.51 N	79.39 W
Craigsville, Va., U.S.	192	38.04 N	79.23 W
Craigville	216	40.47 N	85.06 W
Craik	184	51.03 N	105.49 W
Crail	46	56.16 N	2.38 W
Crailsheim	56	49.08 N	10.04 E
Craiova	38	44.19 N	23.48 E
Crake ≃	44	54.14 N	3.03 W
Craley	208	39.57 N	76.31 W
Cramant	50	48.59 N	3.59 E
Cramlington	44	55.05 N	1.36 W
Cranage	262	53.12 N	2.22 W
Cranberry	214	41.21 N	79.43 W
Cranberry Brook ≃	283	42.11 N	71.01 W
Cranberry Creek	210	43.09 N	74.14 W
Cranberry Island I	212	44.44 N	81.18 W
Cranberry Lake	210	40.57 N	74.44 W
Cranberry Lake ⊜, On., Can.	212	44.26 N	76.19 W
Cranberry Lake ⊜, On., Can.	212	44.47 N	75.50 W
Cranberry Lake ⊜, N.Y., U.S.	188	44.10 N	74.50 W
Cranberry Lake ⊜, Wa., U.S.	224	47.17 N	123.05 W
Cranberry Mountain ∧	182	50.42 N	118.12 W
Cranberry Pond ⊜	276	41.08 N	74.12 W
Cranberry Portage	184	54.35 N	101.23 W
Cranborne Chase ◆[3]	42	50.55 N	2.05 W
Cranbourne	169	38.06 S	145.17 E
Cranbrook, Austl.	162	34.18 S	117.32 E
Cranbrook, B.C., Can.	182	49.31 N	115.46 W
Cranbrook, Eng., U.K.	42	51.06 N	0.33 E
Cranbrook Academy of Art ⊻	281	42.34 N	83.14 W
Cranbury	276	40.18 N	74.30 W
Cranbury Brook ≃	276	40.19 N	74.37 W
Crandall	222	32.37 N	96.27 W
Crandon	190	45.34 N	88.54 W
Crandon Lakes	210	41.07 N	74.50 W
Crane, Az., U.S.	204	32.42 N	114.40 W
Crane, In., U.S.	194	38.53 N	86.54 W
Crane, Mo., U.S.	194	36.54 N	93.34 W
Crane, Tx., U.S.	196	31.23 N	102.20 W
Crane Beach ⍛[2]	283	42.41 N	70.46 W
Cranebrook	274a	33.43 S	150.42 E
Crane Creek ≃	190	43.01 N	91.58 W
Crane Lake ⊜, On., Can.	212	45.13 N	79.57 W
Crane Lake ⊜, Sk., Can.	184	50.06 N	109.06 W
Crane Mountain ∧	202	42.04 N	120.13 W
Crane Neck Point ›	210	40.58 N	73.10 W
Crane River Indian Reserve ◆[4]	184	51.30 N	99.14 W
Cranesville	214	41.54 N	80.21 W
Cranfield	42	52.05 N	0.35 W
Cranfills Gap	222	31.46 N	97.50 W
Cranford	210	40.39 N	74.19 W
Crange ◆[8]	263	51.32 N	7.11 E
Crângeni	38	44.01 N	24.47 E
Cran-Gévrier	58	45.54 N	6.06 E
Crank	262	53.29 N	2.45 W
Cranleigh	42	51.09 N	0.30 W
Crans	58	46.19 N	7.28 E
Cranston	207	41.46 N	71.26 W
Cranston Heights	285	39.38 N	75.38 W
Craon	32	47.51 N	0.57 W
Craonne	50	49.26 N	3.47 E
Craponne, Fr.	62	45.44 N	4.43 E
Craponne, Fr.	62	45.20 N	3.51 E
Craponne, Canal de ≅	62	43.40 N	4.39 E
Craryville	210	42.11 N	73.35 W
Crasna, Rom.	38	46.31 N	27.51 E
Crasna, Rom.	38	45.36 N	26.08 E
Crasna (Kraszna) ≃	38	48.09 N	22.20 E
Crasnoe	38	46.38 N	29.50 E
Crassier	58	46.22 N	6.11 E
Crater Lake ⊜	202	42.56 N	122.06 W

FRANÇAIS

Nom	Page	Lat.°′	Long.°′ W = Ouest
Crater Lake National Park ♦	202	42.49 N	122.08 W
Crater Mount ∧	164	6.30 S	145.10 E
Crater Point ›	164	5.22 S	152.09 E
Craters of the Moon National Monument ♦	202	43.20 N	113.35 W
Crateús	250	5.10 S	40.40 W
Crathie	46	57.02 N	3.12 W
Crati ≃	68	39.43 N	16.31 E
Crato	250	7.14 S	39.23 W
Crau ◆[1]	62	43.36 N	4.50 E
Crauford, Cape ›	176	73.43 N	84.50 W
Craughwell	48	53.13 N	8.43 W
Cravant	50	47.41 N	3.41 E
Cravari ≃	248	12.06 S	58.03 W
Cravat	219	38.25 N	89.06 W
Craven	184	50.39 N	104.50 W
Craven Arms	42	52.26 N	2.50 W
Cravensville	171b	36.24 S	147.34 E
Cravo Norte	246	6.18 N	70.12 W
Cravo Norte ≃	246	6.18 N	70.12 W
Cravo Sur ≃	246	4.42 N	71.36 W
Crawfish ≃	216	43.00 N	88.49 W
Crawford, Scot., U.K.	44	55.28 N	3.40 W
Crawford, Co., U.S.	200	38.42 N	107.36 W
Crawford, Ms., U.S.	194	33.18 N	88.36 W
Crawford, Ne., U.S.	198	42.40 N	103.24 W
Crawford, Tx., U.S.	222	31.32 N	97.27 W
Crawford □[6], In., U.S.	218	38.20 N	86.28 W
Crawford □[6], Oh., U.S.	214	40.48 N	82.58 W
Crawford □[6], Pa., U.S.	214	41.39 N	80.10 W
Crawford Bay	182	49.42 N	116.48 W
Crawford Countryside	278	41.32 N	87.43 W
Crawford Notch State Park ♦	188	44.13 N	71.25 W
Crawfordsville, Ar., U.S.	194	35.13 N	90.19 W
Crawfordsville, In., U.S.	194	40.02 N	86.52 W
Crawfordville, Fl., U.S.	192	30.10 N	84.22 W
Crawfordville, Ga., U.S.	192	33.33 N	82.53 W
Crawinkel	54	50.47 N	10.47 E
Crawley	42	51.07 N	0.12 W
Crawshawbooth	262	53.43 N	2.17 W
Crayford ◆[8]	260	51.27 N	0.11 E
Crays Hill	260	51.36 N	0.28 E
Crazy Mountains ⋏	202	46.08 N	110.20 W
Crazy Peak ∧	202	46.01 N	110.16 W
Crazy Woman Creek ≃	202	44.29 N	106.08 W
Creagan	46	56.33 N	5.17 W
Creagorry	46	57.26 N	7.19 W
Creal Springs	194	37.37 N	88.50 W
Creamery	285	40.13 N	75.25 W
Crean Lake ⊜	184	54.05 N	106.10 W
Crêches-sur-Saône	58	46.15 N	4.47 E
Crécy, Forêt de ♦	261	48.48 N	2.53 E
Crécy-en-Brie	50	48.51 N	2.55 E
Crécy-en-Ponthieu	50	50.15 N	1.53 E
Crécy-sur-Serre	50	49.42 N	3.37 E
Credenhill	42	52.06 N	2.48 W
Credit ≃	212	43.33 N	79.35 W
Crediton	42	50.47 N	3.39 W
Cree ≃, Sk., Can.	176	59.00 N	105.47 W
Cree ≃, Scot., U.K.	44	54.52 N	4.20 W
Creede	200	37.50 N	106.55 W
Creedmoor	192	36.07 N	78.41 W
Creedmore	222	30.12 N	97.43 W
Creegh	48	52.44 N	9.26 W
Creek Brook ≃	283	42.47 N	71.08 W
Creek Locks	210	41.52 N	74.03 W
Creekmouth ◆[8]	260	51.31 N	0.06 E
Creekside	214	40.40 N	79.11 W
Creekwood	278	41.39 N	87.59 W
Creel	232	27.45 N	107.38 W
Cree Lake ⊜	176	57.30 N	106.30 W
Creemore	212	44.19 N	80.06 W
Creetown	44	54.54 N	4.23 W
Cregganbaun	48	53.42 N	9.51 W
Creglingen	56	49.28 N	10.01 E
Crégy-lès-Meaux	261	48.58 N	2.52 E
Créhange	56	49.03 N	6.35 E
Creighton, Sk., Can.	184	54.45 N	101.54 W
Creighton, S. Afr.	158	30.01 S	29.51 E
Creighton, Ne., U.S.	198	42.28 N	97.54 W
Creighton, Pa., U.S.	214	40.35 N	79.46 W
Creighton Mine	190	46.28 N	81.11 W
Creightons Creek ≃	169	36.43 S	145.22 E
Creil, Fr.	50	49.16 N	2.29 E
Creil, Ned.	52	52.45 N	5.40 E
Crema	62	45.22 N	9.41 E
Cremia	58	46.05 N	9.16 E
Crémieu	62	45.43 N	5.15 E
Cremlingen	54	52.15 N	10.39 E
Cremona, Ab., Can.	182	51.33 N	114.29 W
Cremona, It.	64	45.07 N	10.02 E
Cremona □[4]	64	45.12 N	10.00 E
Crenshaw, Ms., U.S.	194	34.30 N	90.12 W
Crenshaw, Pa., U.S.	214	41.15 N	78.46 W
Crep Nudo ∧	64	46.13 N	12.24 E
Crepori ≃	250	5.42 S	57.08 W
Crépy-en-Laonnois	50	49.36 N	3.31 E
Crépy-en-Valois	50	49.14 N	2.54 E
Créquy	50	50.29 N	2.03 E
Creran, Loch ⊜	46	56.31 N	5.20 W
Cres	36	44.58 N	14.25 E
Cres, Otok I	36	44.50 N	14.25 E
Cresaptown	188	39.35 N	78.50 W
Crescent, N.Y., U.S.	210	42.49 N	73.43 W
Crescent, Ok., U.S.	196	35.57 N	97.35 W
Crescent, Or., U.S.	202	43.27 N	121.41 W
Crescent, Lake ⊜	224	48.05 N	123.50 W
Crescent Beach, B.C., Can.	224	49.04 N	122.53 W
Crescent Beach, Fl., U.S.	220	27.15 N	82.32 W
Crescent City, Ca., U.S.	204	41.45 N	124.12 W
Crescent City, Fl., U.S.	192	29.25 N	81.30 W
Crescent City, Il., U.S.	216	40.46 N	87.51 W
Crescent Ditch ≅	226	36.29 N	120.07 W
Crescent Heights, N.J., U.S.	285	39.58 N	74.43 W
Crescent Heights, Tx., U.S.	222	32.11 N	95.56 W
Crescent Lake ⊜, Fl., U.S.	192	29.28 N	81.30 W
Crescent Lake ⊜, Or., U.S.	202	43.29 N	121.59 W
Crescent Lake Estates	281	42.38 N	83.25 W
Crescent Spur	182	53.35 N	120.41 W
Crescentville ◆[8]	285	40.02 N	75.05 W
Crescenzago ◆[8]	266b	45.30 N	9.15 E
Cresco, Ia., U.S.	190	43.22 N	92.06 W
Cresco, Pa., U.S.	210	41.09 N	75.17 W
Crespano del Grappa	64	45.49 N	11.50 E
Crespian	62	43.53 N	4.06 E
Crespières	261	48.53 N	1.55 E
Crespin	50	50.25 N	3.39 E
Crespino	64	44.59 N	11.53 E
Crespo	252	32.02 S	60.19 W
Cressbrook Creek ≃	171a	27.05 S	152.27 E
Cressely	261	48.43 N	2.05 E
Cressey	226	37.25 N	120.40 W
Cresskill	276	40.56 N	73.57 W
Cresskill Brook ≃	276	40.57 N	73.58 W
Cresson, Pa., U.S.	214	40.27 N	78.35 W
Cresson, Tx., U.S.	222	32.32 N	97.37 W
Cressona	208	40.37 N	76.11 W
Cressy	169	38.02 S	143.38 E
Crest	62	44.44 N	5.02 E
Cresta	58	46.28 N	9.31 E
Crested Butte	200	38.52 N	106.59 W

PORTUGUÊS

Nome	Página	Lat.°′	Long.°′ W = Oeste
Cresthaven	220	26.03 N	80.08 W
Crest Hill	216	41.33 N	88.05 W
Crestline, Ca., U.S.	228	34.14 N	117.17 W
Crestline, Oh., U.S.	214	40.47 N	82.44 W
Creston, B.C., Can.	182	49.06 N	116.31 W
Creston, Nf., Can.	186	47.09 N	55.11 W
Creston, Ca., U.S.	226	35.31 N	120.31 W
Creston, Il., U.S.	216	41.56 N	88.58 W
Creston, Ia., U.S.	198	41.03 N	94.21 W
Creston, Oh., U.S.	214	40.59 N	81.53 W
Crestone Peak ∧	200	37.58 N	105.36 W
Crestview, Fl., U.S.	194	30.45 N	86.34 W
Crestview, Wi., U.S.	216	42.49 N	87.49 W
Crestview Heights	210	42.05 N	76.07 W
Crestwood, Il., U.S.	278	41.39 N	87.45 W
Crestwood, Ky., U.S.	218	38.19 N	85.28 W
Crestwood, Mo., U.S.	219	38.33 N	90.22 W
Crestwood Hills	192	35.56 N	84.05 W
Creswell, Eng., U.K.	44	53.16 N	1.12 W
Creswell, Or., U.S.	202	43.55 N	123.01 W
Creswell Bay ⊂	176	72.35 N	93.25 W
Creswell Creek ≃	162	18.10 S	135.11 E
Creswell Downs	162	17.57 S	135.55 E
Creswick	169	37.26 S	143.54 E
Creta → Kríti I	38	35.15 N	25.00 E
Crete, Il., U.S.	216	41.27 N	87.38 W
Crete, Ne., U.S.	198	40.37 N	96.57 W
Crete → Kríti I	38	35.15 N	25.00 E
Crete, Sea of → Kritikón Pélagos ⊤[2]	38	35.46 N	23.54 E
Créteil	50	48.48 N	2.28 E
Crétéville	36	36.40 N	10.20 E
Cretin, Cape ›	164	6.40 S	147.52 E
Creus, Cap de ›	34	42.19 N	3.19 E
Creuse □[5]	32	46.05 N	2.00 E
Creuse ≃	32	47.00 N	0.34 E
Creussen	60	49.51 N	11.37 E
Creutzwald	56	49.12 N	6.41 E
Creuzburg	56	51.03 N	10.15 E
Crevacuore	62	45.41 N	8.15 E
Crevalcore	64	44.43 N	11.09 E
Creve Coeur, Il., U.S.	190	40.38 N	89.35 W
Creve Coeur, Mo., U.S.	219	38.39 N	90.25 W
Crèvecœur-en-Auge	50	49.07 N	0.01 E
Crèvecœur-en-Brie	261	48.45 N	2.55 E
Crèvecœur-le-Grand	50	49.36 N	2.05 E
Crevillent	34	38.15 N	0.48 W
Crevoladossola	58	46.09 N	8.18 E
Crewe, Eng., U.K.	44	53.05 N	2.27 W
Crewe, Va., U.S.	192	37.10 N	78.07 W
Crewkerne	42	50.53 N	2.48 W
Crews Lake ⊜	220	28.23 N	82.31 W
Crewsville	220	27.16 N	81.36 W
Crianlarich	46	56.23 N	4.36 W
Crib Point	169	38.22 S	145.12 E
Cricamola ≃	236	8.59 N	81.54 W
Cricaré ≃	255	18.37 S	40.05 W
Criccieth	42	52.55 N	4.14 W
Crichi	68	38.57 N	16.38 E
Criciúma	252	28.40 S	49.23 W
Crick	42	52.21 N	1.07 W
Cricket	192	36.10 N	81.11 W
Crickhowell	42	51.53 N	3.07 W
Cricklade	42	51.39 N	1.51 W
Cridersville	216	40.39 N	84.09 W
Crieff	46	56.23 N	3.52 W
Criel-sur-Mer	50	50.01 N	1.19 E
Criffell ∧	44	54.57 N	3.38 W
Crikvenica	36	45.11 N	14.42 E
Crillon, Mount ∧	180	58.40 N	137.10 W
Crimean Peninsula → Kryms'kyy pivostriv ›[1]	78	45.00 N	34.00 E
Crimmitschau	54	50.49 N	12.23 E
Crimond	46	57.36 N	1.54 W
Crinan	46	56.05 N	5.35 W
Cringila	170	34.28 S	150.53 E
Cripple Creek	200	38.44 N	105.10 W
Criquetot l'Esneval	50	49.39 N	0.16 E
Crirninoso, Monte ∧	256	21.32 S	43.25 W
Crisenoy	261	48.36 N	2.45 E
Crisfield	208	37.59 N	75.51 W
Crisólia	256	22.15 S	46.25 W
Crisóstomo, Ribeirão ≃	250	10.19 S	50.26 W
Crispiano	68	40.36 N	17.14 E
Criss Creek	182	51.03 N	120.44 W
Crissiumal	252	27.30 S	54.07 W
Cristal, Monts de ⋏	152	0.30 N	10.30 E
Cristal, Sierra del ⋏	240p	20.33 N	75.31 W
Cristalândia	250	10.36 S	49.11 W
Cristália	255	16.43 S	42.52 W
Cristalina	255	16.45 S	47.36 W
Cristalino ≃	255	12.38 S	50.40 W
Cristallo ∧	64	46.34 N	12.12 E
Cristianópolis	255	17.13 S	48.45 W
Cristina	256	22.13 S	45.16 W
Cristinápolis	250	11.29 S	37.46 W
Cristino Castro	250	8.49 S	44.13 W
Cristóbal	236	9.21 N	79.55 W
Cristóbal Colón, Pico ∧	246	10.50 N	73.41 W
Cristóbal Obregón	234	16.20 N	93.30 W
Cristoforo Colombo, Aeroporto di ⊠	62	44.25 N	8.49 E
Cristo Redentor ⊥	252	32.50 S	70.05 W
Cristo Redentor, Estatua do ⊻[1]	287a	22.57 S	43.13 W
Cristuru Secuiesc	38	46.17 N	25.02 E
Crișul Alb ≃	38	46.42 N	21.17 E
Crișul Negru ≃	38	46.42 N	21.16 E
Crișul Repede (Sebes Körös) ≃	38	46.55 N	20.59 E
Crittenden	218	38.46 N	84.36 W
Criuleni	38	47.13 N	29.09 E
Crivitz, Dtsch.	54	53.35 N	11.38 E
Crivitz, Wi., U.S.	190	45.13 N	88.00 W
Crixalândia	255	15.18 S	47.15 W
Crixás	255	14.27 S	49.58 W
Crixás ≃	250	11.02 S	48.34 W
Crixás-Açu ≃	255	13.19 S	50.36 W
Crixás-Mirim ≃	255	13.30 S	50.30 W
Črna	61	46.28 N	14.51 E
Crna ≃	38	41.35 N	21.59 E
Crna Gora □[3]	38	42.30 N	19.18 E
Črni vrh ∧	61	46.29 N	15.14 E
Črnomelj	36	45.34 N	15.11 E
Croachy	46	57.19 N	4.14 W
Croagh Patrick ∧	48	53.46 N	9.40 W
Croajingolong National Park ♦	166	37.40 S	149.30 E
Croal ≃	262	53.33 N	2.23 W
Croatia □[1], Europe	22	45.10 N	15.30 E
Croatia (Hrvatska) □[1], Europe	36	45.10 N	15.30 E
Croce dello Scrivano, Passo)(	68	40.34 N	15.50 E
Croce Domini, Passo di)(	64	45.54 N	10.24 E
Crocefieschi	62	44.35 N	9.01 E
Crocetta del Montello	64	45.50 N	12.02 E
Crocheron	208	38.14 N	76.03 W
Crockenhill	260	51.23 N	0.10 E
Crocker	194	37.56 N	92.15 W
Crocker, Banjaran ⋏	112	5.40 N	116.14 E
Crockery Creek ≃	216	43.02 N	86.05 W
Crocketford	44	55.02 N	3.50 W
Crockett, Ca., U.S.	226	38.03 N	122.12 W
Crockett, Tx., U.S.	222	31.19 N	95.27 W
Crockham Hill	260	51.14 N	0.04 E
Crocus Hill → The Valley	238	18.13 N	63.04 W
Croft	262	53.26 N	2.33 W
Crofton, B.C., Can.	224	48.52 N	123.38 W
Crofton, Ky., U.S.	194	37.02 N	87.29 W
Crofton, Md., U.S.	208	39.00 N	76.41 W
Crofton, Ne., U.S.	198	42.43 N	97.29 W
Croft State Park ♦	192	34.49 N	81.52 W
Croggan	46	56.22 N	5.42 W
Croghan	212	43.53 N	75.23 W
Croglin	44	54.49 N	2.39 W
Croick	46	57.53 N	4.35 W
Croil Islands II	206	44.58 N	74.58 W
Croisette, Cap ›	62	43.13 N	5.20 E
Croisilles	50	50.12 N	2.53 E
Croissy-Beaubourg	261	48.50 N	2.40 E
Croissy-sur-Seine	261	48.53 N	2.09 E
Croix	50	50.40 N	3.09 E
Croix, Lac à la ⊜	186	51.16 N	70.13 W
Croix, Lac la ⊜	190	48.21 N	92.05 W
Croker, Cape ›, Austl.	164	10.58 S	132.35 E
Croker, Cape ›, On., Can.	212	44.58 N	80.59 W
Croker Island I	164	11.12 S	132.32 E
Crolles	62	45.17 N	5.53 E
Cromarty	46	57.40 N	4.02 W
Cromarty Firth ⊂[1]	46	57.41 N	4.07 W
Cromby	285	40.09 N	75.32 W
Cromer, Austl.	274a	33.44 S	151.17 E
Cromer, Eng., U.K.	42	52.56 N	1.18 E
Cromford	44	53.06 N	1.34 W
Cromínia	255	17.17 S	49.21 W
Cromore	46	58.09 N	6.29 W
Crompton Point ›	240d	15.35 N	61.19 W
Cromwell, N.Z.	172	45.03 S	169.12 E
Cromwell, Al., U.S.	194	32.13 N	88.16 W
Cromwell, Ct., U.S.	207	41.35 N	72.38 W
Cromwell, In., U.S.	216	41.24 N	85.36 W
Cromwell Park ♦	279a	41.28 N	82.08 W
Cronadun	172	42.02 S	171.52 E
Cronenberg ◆[8]	263	51.12 N	7.08 E
Cronin, Mount ∧	182	54.54 N	126.52 W
Cronton	262	53.23 N	2.46 W
Cronulla	170	34.03 S	151.09 E
Cronulla Beach ⍛[2]	274a	34.02 S	151.11 E
Croob, Slieve ∧[2]	48	54.20 N	5.58 W
Crook, Eng., U.K.	44	54.43 N	1.44 W
Crook, Co., U.S.	198	40.51 N	102.48 W
Crooked ≃, B.C., Can.	182	54.50 N	122.54 W
Crooked ≃, Mo., U.S.	194	39.13 N	93.49 W
Crooked ≃, Or., U.S.	202	44.34 N	121.16 W
Crooked Creek	180	61.52 N	158.08 W
Crooked Creek ≃, U.S.	196	36.57 N	100.06 W
Crooked Creek ≃, Ar., U.S.	194	36.14 N	92.29 W
Crooked Creek ≃, Il., U.S.	219	38.30 N	89.25 W
Crooked Creek ≃, In., U.S.	216	40.45 N	86.30 W
Crooked Creek ≃, Mo., U.S.	219	39.34 N	91.55 W
Crooked Creek ≃, Pa., U.S.	210	41.55 N	77.08 W
Crooked Creek ≃, Pa., U.S.	214	40.45 N	79.33 W
Crooked Creek Lake ⊜[1]	214	40.42 N	79.30 W
Crooked Island I	238	22.45 N	74.13 W
Crooked Island Passage ⊔	238	22.55 N	74.35 W
Crooked Lake, In., U.S.	216	41.41 N	85.02 W
Crooked Lake, Mi., U.S.	216	42.29 N	85.25 W
Crooked Lake ⊜, Nf., Can.	186	48.24 N	56.17 W
Crooked Lake ⊜, Sk., Can.	184	50.36 N	102.45 W
Crooked Lake ⊜, N.A.	190	48.13 N	91.50 W
Crooked Lake ⊜, Fl., U.S.	220	27.48 N	81.35 W
Crooked Lake ⊜, In., U.S.	216	41.40 N	85.03 W
Crooked River	184	52.51 N	103.44 W
Crookes Point ›	276	40.32 N	74.08 W
Crookham	279b	40.12 N	79.59 W
Crookston	198	47.46 N	96.36 W
Crookstown	48	51.50 N	8.50 W
Crooksville	188	39.46 N	82.05 W
Crookwell	166	34.28 S	149.28 E
Croom	48	52.31 N	8.42 W
Cropalati	68	39.31 N	16.43 E
Cropani	68	38.58 N	16.47 E
Cropper	218	38.18 N	85.06 W
Crosby, Eng., U.K.	44	53.30 N	3.02 W
Crosby, Mn., U.S.	190	46.28 N	93.57 W
Crosby, Ms., U.S.	194	31.17 N	91.03 W
Crosby, N.D., U.S.	198	48.54 N	103.17 W
Crosby, Pa., U.S.	214	41.45 N	78.24 W
Crosby, Tx., U.S.	222	29.55 N	95.04 W
Crosby, Mount ∧	202	43.53 N	109.20 W
Crosby Lake ⊜	212	44.45 N	76.26 W
Crosbyton	196	33.39 N	101.14 W
Crosia	68	39.34 N	16.46 E
Crosne	261	48.43 N	2.28 E
Cross ≃	152	4.42 N	8.21 E
Cross Banks II	283	42.43 N	70.49 W
Cross Bay ⊂	184	53.15 N	99.25 W
Cross Bay Bridge ◆[5]	276	40.35 N	73.49 W
Crossbost	46	58.08 N	6.23 W
Cross City	192	29.38 N	83.07 W
Cross County Center ◆[9]	276	40.56 N	73.51 W
Cross Creek ≃, Ca., U.S.	226	36.08 N	119.38 W
Cross Creek ≃, Oh., U.S.	214	40.18 N	80.36 W
Crossen	54	50.45 N	12.29 E
Crossens	262	53.41 N	2.57 W
Crossett	194	33.07 N	91.57 W
Cross Fell ∧	44	54.42 N	2.29 W
Crossfield	182	51.26 N	114.02 W
Crossgar	48	54.24 N	5.45 W
Cross Hands	42	51.48 N	4.04 W
Crosshaven	48	51.48 N	8.17 W
Crosshill	44	55.19 N	4.39 W
Crossinsee ⊜	264a	52.22 N	13.41 E
Cross Island I	272c	18.57 N	72.51 E
Cross Keys	285	39.42 N	75.01 W
Cross Keys Airfield ⊠	285	39.42 N	75.02 W
Cross Lake	184	54.37 N	97.47 W
Cross Lake ⊜, Mb., Can.	184	54.45 N	97.30 W
Cross Lake ⊜, On., Can.	190	46.53 N	79.57 W
Cross Lake ⊜, N.Y., U.S.	210	43.08 N	76.29 W
Crossley, Mount ∧	172	42.50 S	172.04 E
Crossmaglen	48	54.05 N	6.37 W
Crossman	168a	32.47 S	116.36 E
Crossman ≃	168a	32.47 S	116.32 E
Crossman Peak ∧	200	34.32 N	114.07 W
Crossmolina	48	54.06 N	9.20 W
Cross Plains, In., U.S.	218	38.57 N	85.12 W
Cross Plains, Tx., U.S.	196	32.08 N	99.11 W
Cross Plains, Wi., U.S.	190	43.06 N	89.39 W
Cross River □[3]	150	5.50 N	8.30 E
Cross Roads	222	32.03 N	95.58 W
Cross Sound ⊔	180	58.10 N	136.30 W
Crossville, Il., U.S.	194	38.09 N	88.03 W
Crossville, Tn., U.S.	194	35.56 N	85.01 W
Crosswicks	285	40.09 N	74.38 W
Crosswicks Creek ≃	208	40.09 N	74.43 W
Crostolo ≃	64	44.55 N	10.38 E
Croston	44	53.39 N	2.46 W
Croswell	190	43.16 N	82.37 W
Crotch Lake ⊜	212	44.55 N	76.48 W
Crotenay	58	46.45 N	5.49 E
Crothersville	218	38.48 N	85.50 W
Croton	214	40.14 N	82.41 W
Crotona Park ♦	276	40.50 N	73.54 W
Croton Creek ≃	196	33.18 N	100.25 W
Crotone	68	39.05 N	17.07 E
Croton Falls	210	41.21 N	73.40 W
Croton-on-Hudson	210	41.12 N	73.53 W
Croton Point ›	276	41.10 N	73.54 W
Crottendorf	54	50.30 N	12.56 E
Crouch ≃	42	51.37 N	0.57 E
Crouse Run ≃	279b	40.35 N	79.58 W
Crouy	50	49.24 N	3.22 E
Crow ≃	190	45.15 N	93.31 W
Crow, North Fork ≃	190	45.05 N	93.45 W
Crow, South Fork ≃	190	45.05 N	93.45 W
Crow Agency	202	45.36 N	107.27 W
Crowborough	42	51.03 N	0.09 E
Crow Creek ≃, U.S.	198	40.23 N	104.29 W
Crow Creek ≃, Ca., U.S.	282	37.42 N	122.03 W
Crow Creek ≃, Il., U.S.	194	40.56 N	89.27 W
Crow Creek ≃, Mt., U.S.	198	45.45 N	105.06 W
Crow Creek ≃, Mt., U.S.	202	46.11 N	111.29 W
Crow Creek ≃, S.D., U.S.	198	43.57 N	99.15 W
Crow Creek ≃, Wy., U.S.	202	43.19 N	109.09 W
Crow Creek Indian Reservation ◆[4]	198	44.11 N	99.30 W
Crowder, Ms., U.S.	194	34.10 N	90.08 W
Crowder, Ok., U.S.	196	35.07 N	95.40 W
Crowduck Lake ⊜	184	50.08 N	95.15 W
Crowdy Head ›	166	31.50 S	152.45 E
Crowe ≃	212	44.22 N	77.46 W
Crowe Lake ⊜	212	44.29 N	77.46 W
Crowell	196	33.59 N	99.43 W
Crowfoot, Mount ∧	172	45.33 S	167.03 E
Crow Hill ∧[2]	262	53.42 N	1.58 W
Crowhurst	260	51.12 N	0.01 W
Crow Indian Reservation ◆[4]	202	45.27 N	108.00 W
Crow Lake	184	49.12 N	93.57 W
Crow Lake ⊜	212	44.43 N	76.37 W
Crowland	42	52.41 N	0.11 W
Crowle	44	53.37 N	0.49 W
Crowley, Ca., U.S.	226	36.21 N	119.17 W
Crowley, La., U.S.	194	30.12 N	92.22 W
Crowley, Tx., U.S.	222	32.34 N	97.21 W
Crowley, Lake ⊜[1]	204	37.37 N	118.44 W
Crowleys Ridge ∧	194	35.45 N	90.45 W
Crowlin Islands II	46	57.20 N	5.44 W
Crown	214	41.23 N	79.16 W
Crown Hill	212	44.26 N	79.39 W
Crown Island I	164	5.05 S	146.55 E
Crown Memorial Beach ♦	282	37.46 N	122.16 W
Crown Mines ◆[7]	273d	26.13 S	28.00 E
Crown Mountain ∧	240m	18.21 N	64.58 W
Crown Point, In., U.S.	216	41.25 N	87.21 W
Crownpoint, N.M., U.S.	200	35.40 N	108.09 W
Crown Point, N.Y., U.S.	188	43.57 N	73.26 W
Crown Point State Park ♦	224	45.32 N	122.15 W
Crown Prince Frederik Island I	176	70.02 N	86.50 W
Crown Village	276	40.40 N	73.27 W
Crow Peak ∧	202	46.18 N	111.54 W
Crow Rock Creek ≃	202	47.06 N	106.15 W
Crows Fork Creek ≃	219	38.47 N	91.52 W
Crows Landing	226	37.24 N	121.04 W
Crows Nest, Austl.	171a	27.16 S	152.03 E
Crows Nest, Austl.	274a	33.50 S	151.12 E
Crowsnest, Ab., Can.	182	49.38 N	114.41 W
Crows Nest Falls National Park ♦	171a	27.16 S	152.08 E
Crowsnest Pass	182	49.36 N	114.26 W
Crowsnest Pass)(	182	49.39 N	114.45 W
Crows Nest Peak ∧	198	44.03 N	103.58 W
Crowthorne	42	51.23 N	0.49 W
Crowton	262	53.16 N	2.38 W
Crow Wing ≃	198	46.19 N	94.20 W
Croxley Green	42	51.39 N	0.27 W
Croxteth Park ♦	262	53.26 N	2.53 W
Croy	46	57.31 N	4.02 W
Croyde	42	51.07 N	4.13 W
Croydon, Austl.	166	18.12 S	142.14 E
Croydon, Austl.	169	37.48 S	145.17 E
Croydon, Austl.	274a	33.53 S	151.07 E
Croydon, Pa., U.S.	208	40.05 N	74.54 W
Croydon ◆[8]	42	51.23 N	0.06 W
Croydon Park	274a	33.54 S	151.07 E
Croydon Peak ∧	188	43.28 N	72.13 W
Croydon Station	182	53.05 N	119.44 W
Crozet	192	38.04 N	78.42 W
Crozet, Archipel II	6	46.00 S	52.00 E
Crozet Basin ✣[1]	6	39.00 S	60.00 E
Crozon	32	48.15 N	4.29 W
Cruachan, Ben ∧	46	56.25 N	5.08 W
Cruas	62	44.39 N	4.46 E
Crucea	38	44.32 N	28.14 E
Crucero	248	14.21 S	70.00 W
Cruces, Cuba	240p	22.21 N	80.16 W
Cruces, Méx.	232	29.26 N	107.24 W
Crucoli	68	39.25 N	17.00 E
Cruden Bay	46	57.25 N	1.50 W
Crudgington	42	52.46 N	2.33 W
Crudine Creek ≃	170	33.05 S	149.40 E
Cruger	194	33.19 N	90.13 W
Cruillas	232	24.45 N	98.31 W
Crum Creek ≃	285	39.51 N	75.19 W
Crumhorn Mountain ∧	210	42.33 N	74.55 W
Crumlin, On., Can.	212	43.01 N	81.09 W
Crumlin, N. Ire., U.K.	48	54.37 N	6.14 W
Crum Lynne	285	39.52 N	75.20 W
Crummock Water ⊜	44	54.34 N	3.18 W
Crump Lake ⊜	202	42.17 N	119.50 W
Crumpton	208	39.14 N	75.55 W
Crumstown	216	41.38 N	86.25 W
Crupet	56	50.21 N	4.48 E
Cruseilles	58	46.02 N	6.07 E
Cruser Brook ≃	276	40.27 N	74.39 W
Crusheen	48	52.58 N	8.53 W
Crusnes	56	49.26 N	5.55 E
Crusnes ≃	56	49.27 N	5.36 E
Crustepec, Cerro ∧	234	21.15 N	97.53 W
Cruz, Arroyo de la ≃, Ca., U.S.	226	35.42 N	121.09 W
Cruz, Arroyo de la ≃, Ur.	258	34.00 S	56.08 W
Cruz, Cabo ›	240p	19.51 N	77.44 W
Cruz, Cañada de la ≃	258	34.09 S	58.58 W
Cruz, Cayo I	240p	22.15 N	77.49 W
Cruz, Pico de la ∧	148	28.44 N	17.52 W
Cruz Alta, Arg.	252	33.01 S	61.49 W
Cruz Alta, Bra.	252	28.39 S	53.36 W
Cruz Bay	240m	18.20 N	64.48 W
Cruz de Elorza	234	23.49 N	100.29 W
Cruz del Eje	252	30.44 S	64.48 W
Cruz del Marquez, Cerro ∧	286a	19.12 N	99.15 W
Cruzeiro	256	22.34 S	44.58 W
Cruzeiro do Oeste	255	23.46 S	53.04 W
Cruzeiro do Sul	248	7.38 S	72.36 W
Cruzeta	250	6.25 S	36.47 W
Cruz Grande, Chile	252	29.25 S	71.18 W
Cruz Grande, Méx.	234	16.44 N	99.08 W
Cruzília	256	21.50 S	44.48 W
Cruz Machado	252	26.01 S	51.21 W
Cruzy-le-Châtel	50	47.51 N	4.12 E
Crvenka	38	45.39 N	19.28 E
Crymych	42	51.59 N	4.40 W
Crynant	42	51.43 N	3.45 W
Crysler	188	45.13 N	75.09 W
Crystal, Mn., U.S.	190	45.01 N	93.21 W
Crystal, N.D., U.S.	198	48.35 N	97.40 W
Crystal ≃	200	39.25 N	107.14 W
Crystal Bay	226	39.13 N	120.00 W
Crystal Bay ⊂	220	28.55 N	82.43 W
Crystal Beach, On., Can.	284a	42.52 N	79.04 W
Crystal Beach, Fl., U.S.	220	28.05 N	82.46 W
Crystal Beach, Tx., U.S.	222	29.27 N	94.38 W
Crystal Brook	166	33.21 S	138.13 E
Crystal Cave ⍛[5]	208	40.32 N	75.51 W
Crystal City, Mb., Can.	184	49.09 N	98.56 W
Crystal City, Mo., U.S.	219	38.13 N	90.22 W
Crystal City, Tx., U.S.	196	28.40 N	99.49 W
Crystal Creek ≃	278	41.58 N	87.51 W
Crystal Falls	190	46.05 N	88.20 W
Crystal Gardens	216	42.14 N	88.23 W
Crystal Lake, Il., U.S.	216	42.14 N	88.18 W
Crystal Lake, N.Y., U.S.	210	42.31 N	74.12 W
Crystal Lake, N.Y., U.S.	210	42.28 N	78.20 W
Crystal Lake ⊜, On., Can.	212	44.45 N	78.30 W
Crystal Lake ⊜, Ma., U.S.	283	42.29 N	71.05 W
Crystal Lake ⊜, Ma., U.S.	283	42.48 N	71.09 W
Crystal Lake ⊜, Mi., U.S.	190	44.40 N	86.10 W
Crystal Lake ⊜, N.J., U.S.	276	41.02 N	74.15 W
Crystal Lakes	218	39.52 N	84.04 W
Crystal Lawns	216	41.34 N	88.09 W
Crystal Manor	216	42.14 N	88.17 W
Crystal Palace Stadium and Motor Race Track ♦	260	51.25 N	0.04 W
Crystal River	192	28.54 N	82.35 W
Crystal Spring Lake ⊜	285	39.43 N	75.01 W
Crystal Springs, Fl., U.S.	220	28.10 N	82.09 W
Crystal Springs, Ms., U.S.	194	31.59 N	90.21 W
Crystal Springs Dam ◆[6]	282	37.32 N	122.22 W
Crystal Vista	216	42.14 N	88.24 W
Csepel ◆[8]	264c	47.24 N	19.14 E
Csepel-sziget I	30	47.15 N	18.57 E
Csepreg	61	47.24 N	16.43 E
Cserhát ⋏	30	47.55 N	19.30 E
Cserta ≃	61	46.35 N	16.36 E
Csesznek ⊥	30	47.16 N	17.53 E
Csesztreg	61	46.43 N	16.31 E
Csobánka	264c	47.38 N	18.58 E
Csomád	264c	47.40 N	19.15 E
Csömodér	61	46.37 N	16.39 E
Csömör	264c	47.33 N	19.14 E
Csömöri-patak ≃	264c	47.36 N	19.07 E
Csongrád	30	46.43 N	20.09 E
Csongrád □[6]	30	46.25 N	20.15 E
Csorna	30	47.37 N	17.16 E
Csurgó	30	46.16 N	17.06 E
Ču	85	43.36 N	73.45 E
Ču □[4]	85	42.30 N	74.30 E
Ču ≃	86	45.00 N	67.44 E
Cúa	246	10.10 N	66.54 W
Cuacnopalan	234	18.49 N	97.30 W
Cuácua ≃	154	17.54 S	36.48 E
Cuajimalpa ◆[8]	286a	19.21 N	99.18 W
Cuajinicuilapa	234	16.28 N	98.25 W
Cuajone	248	17.00 S	70.43 W
Cuále	152	8.06 S	16.03 E
Cua Lo	110	18.49 N	105.43 E
Cuamato	152	17.05 S	15.09 E
Cuamba	154	14.49 S	36.33 E
Cuambog	116	7.20 N	125.52 E
Cuanavale ≃	152	15.07 S	19.14 E
Cuando	152	16.32 S	22.07 E
Cuando (Kwando) ≃	152	18.27 S	23.32 E
Cuando Cubango □[5]	152	16.00 S	20.00 E
Cuangar	152	17.36 S	18.39 E
Cuango, Ang.	152	14.30 S	18.59 E
Cuango, Ang.	152	9.10 S	17.58 E
Cuango, Ang.	152	6.17 S	16.41 E
Cuango (Kwango) ≃	152	3.14 S	17.23 E
Cuanza ≃	152	9.19 S	13.08 E
Cuanza Norte □[5]	152	8.50 S	14.30 E
Cuanza Sul □[5]	152	10.50 S	14.50 E
Cuao ≃	246	4.55 N	67.40 W
Cuapiaxtla	234	19.18 N	97.46 W
Cuareim (Quaraí) ≃	252	30.12 S	57.36 W
Cuaró	252	30.37 S	56.54 W
Cuartillo, Arroyo ≃	258	33.45 S	59.06 W
Cuarto ≃	252	33.25 S	62.56 W
Cuatir ≃	152	17.01 S	18.09 E
Cuatro Caminos	286b	22.54 N	82.23 W
Cuatro Ciénegas [de Carranza]	196	26.59 N	102.05 W
Cuatro Islands II	116	10.31 N	124.39 E
Cuauhtémoc, Méx.	232	28.25 N	106.52 W
Cuauhtémoc, Méx.	234	22.38 N	98.08 W
Cuauhtémoc, Méx.	234	19.20 N	103.36 W
Cuautepec el Alto ◆[8]	286a	19.34 N	99.08 W
Cuautitlán	234	19.26 N	104.23 W
Cuautitlán ≃	286a	19.41 N	99.13 W
Cuautitlán [de Romero Rubio]	234	19.40 N	99.11 W
Cuautitlán Izcalli	286a	19.39 N	99.13 W
Cuautla, Méx.	234	20.11 N	104.21 W
Cuautla, Méx.	234	18.48 N	98.57 W
Cuautzin, Volcán ∧[1]	286a	19.09 N	99.06 W
Cuba, Port.	34	38.10 N	7.53 W
Cuba, Al., U.S.	194	32.25 N	88.22 W
Cuba, Il., U.S.	190	40.29 N	90.11 W
Cuba, Ks., U.S.	198	39.48 N	97.27 W
Cuba, Mo., U.S.	194	38.03 N	91.24 W
Cuba, N.M., U.S.	200	36.01 N	106.57 W
Cuba, N.Y., U.S.	210	42.13 N	78.16 W
Cuba □[1], N.A.	230	21.30 N	80.00 W
Cuba □[1], N.A.	240p	21.30 N	80.00 W
Cubabi, Cerro ∧	200	31.42 N	112.46 W
Cubadak	112	0.19 N	100.00 E
Cubagua, Isla I	246	10.48 N	64.10 W
Cuba Island I	276	40.38 N	73.32 W
Cubal	152	13.02 S	14.19 E
Cubal ≃, Ang.	152	15.22 S	12.39 E
Cubal ≃, Ang.	152	12.42 S	13.56 E
Cubal ≃, Ang.	152	11.19 S	13.48 E
Cuba Lake ⊜	210	42.15 N	78.18 W
Cubanea	254	41.02 S	70.16 W
Cubango (Okavango) ≃	138	18.50 S	22.25 E
Çubangui ≃	152	14.22 S	19.58 E
Čubaricha	86	57.37 N	68.22 E
Čubarovo	82	55.12 N	36.56 E
Cubatão	256	23.53 S	46.25 W
Cubatão, Serra do ⍛[4]	256	23.52 S	46.28 W
Cubati	250	6.51 S	36.21 W
Cub Hills ⋏[2]	184	54.20 N	104.30 W
Çubia ≃	152	16.01 S	21.50 E
Čublas	24	64.44 N	45.00 E
Cub Run ≃	208	38.48 N	77.28 W
Çubuk	130	40.15 N	33.02 E
Čuc ≃	250	1.22 N	53.33 W
Cucamonga	228	34.06 N	117.35 W
Cucamonga Creek ≃	280	33.57 N	117.37 W
Cucamonga Peak ∧	228	34.14 N	117.36 W
Cuccaro Vetere	68	40.09 N	15.18 E
Çucco, Monte ∧	66	43.22 N	12.45 E
Čučeviči	76	52.35 N	26.52 E
Cucharas ≃	198	37.55 N	104.32 W
Cucharas, Sierra ⋏	234	22.20 N	98.55 W
Cuchi	152	14.36 S	16.58 E
Cuchi ≃	152	15.28 S	17.21 E
Cuchibi ≃	152	15.00 S	20.45 E
Cuchilla Alta, Cerro ∧	236	15.10 N	88.12 W
Cuchillo-Có	252	38.20 S	64.37 W
Cuchillo Negro Creek ≃	200	33.08 N	107.14 W
Çuchivero ≃	246	7.40 N	65.57 W
Čuchloma	76	58.45 N	42.41 E

Symbol	English	Deutsch	Español	Français	Português
≃	River	Fluß	Río	Rivière	Rio
≅	Canal	Kanal	Canal	Canal	Canal
⌊	Waterfall, Rapids	Wasserfall, Stromschnellen	Cascada, Rápidos	Chute d'eau, Rapides	Cascata, Rápidos
⊔	Strait	Meeresstraße	Estrecho	Détroit	Estreito
⊂	Bay, Gulf	Bucht, Golf	Bahía, Golfo	Baie, Golfe	Baía, Golfo
⊜	Lake, Lakes	See, Seen	Lago, Lagos	Lac, Lacs	Lago, Lagos
≡	Swamp	Sumpf	Pantano	Marais	Pântano
⊓	Ice Features, Glacier	Eis- und Gletscherformen	Accidentes Glaciales	Formes glaciaires	Acidentes glaciares
⊤	Other Hydrographic Features	Andere Hydrographische Objekte	Otros Elementos Hidrográficos	Autres données hydrographiques	Outros acidentes hidrográficos
✣	Submarine Features	Untermeerische Objekte	Accidentes Submarinos	Formes de relief sous-marin	Acidentes submarinos
□	Political Unit	Politische Einheit	Unidad Politica	Entité politique	Unidade política
⊻	Cultural Institution	Kulturelle Institution	Institución Cultural	Institution culturelle	Institução cultural
⊥	Historical Site	Historische Stätte	Sitio Histórico	Site historique	Sitio histórico
♦	Recreational Site	Erholungs- und Ferienort	Sitio de Recreo	Centre de loisirs	Area de Lazer
⊠	Airport	Flughafen	Aeropuerto	Aéroport	Aeroporto
■	Military Installation	Militäranlage	Instalación Militar	Installation militaire	Instalação militar
◆	Miscellaneous	Verschiedenes	Misceláneo	Divers	Diversos

Čuchlomskoje, ozero ⊜ 76 58.46 N 42.35 E
Cuchumatanes, Sierra los ⋏ 236 15.35 N 91.25 W
Cuckels Brook ≃ 276 40.33 N 74.33 W
Cuckfield 42 51.00 N 0.09 W
Cuckney 44 53.15 N 1.08 W
Cuckold Point > 284b 39.14 N 76.24 W
Čučkovo, Ross. 76 59.36 N 41.14 E
Čučkovo, Ross. 80 54.17 N 41.26 E
Cucuí 246 1.12 N 66.50 W
Cucumbi 152 10.17 S 19.05 E
Cucuron 62 43.47 N 5.26 E
Cucurpe 232 30.20 N 110.43 W
Cúcuta 246 7.54 N 72.31 W
Cudachar 84 42.21 N 47.11 E
Cudahy, Ca., U.S. 280 33.57 N 118.11 W
Cudahy, Wi., U.S. 216 42.57 N 87.51 W
Cuddalore 122 11.45 N 79.45 E
Cuddapah 122 14.28 N 78.49 E
Cuddeback Lake ⊜ 228 35.18 N 117.28 W
Cuddebackville 210 41.28 N 74.36 W
Cuddia ≃ 70 37.53 N 12.37 E
Cuddington 44 53.14 N 2.36 W
Cuddle Lake ⊜ 184 55.25 N 95.47 W
Cuddy 279b 40.21 N 80.09 W
Cuddy Mountain ∧ 202 44.46 N 116.47 W
Cudgegong 170 32.48 S 149.49 E
Cudgegong ≃ 170 32.37 S 149.43 E
Cudgewa 171b 36.12 S 147.46 E
Cudgewa Creek ≃ 171b 36.03 S 147.55 E
Cudham ◆[8] 260 51.19 N 0.05 E
Cudia Park ♦ 275b 43.43 N 79.13 W
Čudin 76 52.44 N 26.59 E
Cudjoe Key I 220 24.40 N 81.30 W
Čudovo 76 59.07 N 31.41 E
Čudskoje ozero (Peipsi järv) ⊜ 76 58.45 N 27.30 E
Cudworth, Sk., Can. 184 52.30 N 105.45 W
Cudworth, Eng., U.K. 44 53.35 N 1.25 W
Cue 162 27.25 S 117.54 E
Cuebe ≃ 152 15.48 S 17.30 E
Cueio ≃, Ang. 152 15.27 S 21.21 E
Cueio ≃, Ang. 152 16.17 S 17.46 E
Cuelei ≃ 152 15.33 S 17.21 E
Cuéllar 34 41.24 N 4.19 W
Cuenca, Ec. 246 2.53 S 78.59 W
Cuenca, Esp. 34 40.04 N 2.08 W
Cuenca □[4] 34 39.55 N 2.10 W
Cuencamé [de Ceniceros] 232 24.53 N 103.42 W
Cuerámaro 234 20.37 N 101.43 W
Cuernavaca 234 18.55 N 99.15 W
Cuero 222 29.05 N 97.17 W
Cuers 62 43.14 N 6.04 E
Cuervos 204 32.38 N 114.52 W
Cuesmes 50 50.26 N 3.55 E
Cuesta Pass)(226 35.21 N 120.38 W
Cueto 240p 20.39 N 75.56 W
Cuetzala del Progreso 234 18.07 N 99.50 W
Cuetzalan del Progreso 234 20.02 N 97.31 W
Cuevas del Almanzora 34 37.18 N 1.53 W
Cuevo 248 20.27 S 63.32 W
Čufarovo 80 54.06 N 47.19 E
Cuffley 42 51.42 N 0.07 W
Cufra — Al-Kufrah ⊤[4] 146 24.20 N 23.15 E
Cufré 258 34.12 S 57.06 W
Cufré, Arroyo ≃ 258 34.27 S 57.09 W
Cuggiono 62 45.31 N 8.49 E
Cugir 38 45.50 N 23.22 E
Cuglieri 71 40.11 N 8.34 E
Cugo ≃ 152 7.18 S 16.39 E
Čugujevka 89 44.08 N 133.53 E
Čugunaš 86 52.52 N 87.46 E
Čuguš, gora ∧ 84 43.47 N 40.16 E
Cuiabá 248 15.35 S 56.05 W
Cuiabá ≃ 248 17.53 S 57.27 W
Cuiari 246 1.30 N 68.11 W
Cuiari ≃ 246 1.30 N 68.11 W
Cuicatlán 234 17.48 N 96.58 W
Cuichapa 234 17.59 N 94.15 W
Cuieiras ≃ 246 2.50 S 60.31 W
Cuigezhuang, Zhg. 105 40.01 N 116.28 E
Cuigezhuang, Zhg. 105 40.02 N 117.54 E
Cuihuangkou 105 39.32 N 117.11 E
Cuijiatun 104 40.57 N 121.09 E
Cuijiazhuang 104 40.57 N 122.44 E
Cuilapa 236 14.17 N 90.18 W
Cuilcagh ∧ 48 54.10 N 7.48 W
Cuilco 236 15.24 N 91.58 W
Cuillin Hills ⋏[2] 46 57.15 N 6.15 W
Cuilo (Kwilu) ≃, Afr. 152 3.22 S 17.22 E
Cuilo ≃, Afr. 152 5.52 S 16.35 E
Cuilo Futa 152 6.25 S 15.44 E
Cuimba 152 6.08 S 14.38 E
Cuio 152 12.58 S 12.58 E
Cuiqiao 98 34.12 N 114.36 E
Cuiseaux 58 46.30 N 5.24 E
Cuisery 58 46.33 N 5.00 E
Cuisy 261 49.01 N 2.46 E
Cuité 250 6.29 S 36.09 W
Cuitláhuac 234 18.49 N 96.43 W
Cuíto ≃ 152 18.01 S 20.48 E
Cuíto-Cuanavale 152 15.10 S 19.10 E
Cuitzeo, Laguna de ⊜ 234 19.55 N 101.05 W
Cuitzeo del Porvenir 234 19.59 N 101.09 W
Cuiuni ≃ 246 0.45 S 63.07 W
Cuivre ≃ 219 38.56 N 90.42 W
Cuivre, North Fork ≃ 219 39.02 N 90.59 W
Cuivre, West Fork ≃ 219 39.02 N 90.59 W
Cuivre River State Park ♦ 219 39.02 N 90.57 W
Čuja 88 59.12 N 112.25 E
Čuja ≃, Ross. 86 50.24 N 86.39 E
Čuja ≃, Ross. 88 59.17 N 112.24 E
Cují 286c 10.28 N 67.02 W
Čukas 112 0.25 S 104.18 E
Čukčagirskoje ozero ⊜ 89 52.00 N 136.36 E
Čukotskaja Avtonomnaja Oblast' □[8] 180 66.00 N 178.00 E
Čukotskij, mys > 180 64.14 N 173.10 W
Čukotskij poluostrov >[1] 180 66.00 N 175.00 W
Çukurca 128 37.15 N 43.37 E
Čukurčak 85 41.47 N 71.07 E
Culaba 116 11.40 N 124.32 E
Čulak-Kurgan 85 43.46 N 69.12 E
Culaman 116 5.58 N 125.40 E
Culari ≃ 250 1.27 N 53.42 W
Culasi, Pil. 116 11.26 N 122.03 E
Culasi, Pil. 116 10.43 N 125.43 E
Culasian 116 8.51 N 117.29 E
Culasi Point > 116 11.37 N 122.42 E
Culbertson, Mt., U.S. 198 48.08 N 104.30 W
Culbertson, Ne., U.S. 198 40.13 N 100.50 W
Culbertson Run ≃ 285 40.03 N 75.45 W
Culbin 168a 33.10 S 116.50 E
Culburra 170 34.57 S 150.47 E
Culcairn 166 35.40 S 147.03 E
Culcheth 262 53.27 N 2.32 W
Culdaff 48 55.18 N 7.11 W
Culdaff Bay c 48 55.17 N 7.10 W
Culebra 240m 18.18 N 65.18 W
Culebra, Isla de I 240m 18.19 N 65.17 W
Culebra, Sierra de la ⋏ 34 41.54 N 6.20 W
Culebra Peak ∧ 200 37.07 N 105.11 W
Culebrinas ≃ 240m 18.24 N 67.11 W
Culebrita, Isla I 240m 18.19 N 65.14 W
Culebro, Arroyo del ≃ 266a 40.19 N 3.34 W
Culemborg 52 51.56 N 5.13 E
Culfa 84 38.58 N 45.38 E
Culgoa ≃ 166 29.56 S 146.20 E
Culham Inlet c 162 33.55 S 120.04 E
Culiacán, Méx. 232 24.04 N 107.05 W
Culiacán, Méx. 232 24.48 N 107.24 W
Culiacán, Cerro ∧ 234 20.20 N 100.58 W
Culiacancito 232 24.50 N 107.32 W
Culijón, Nevado ∧ 248 14.38 S 69.14 W
Culion 116 11.53 N 120.01 E
Culion Island I 116 11.50 N 119.55 E
Cúllar de Baza 34 37.35 N 2.34 W
Cull Creek ≃ 282 37.42 N 122.03 W
Cullen, Scot., U.K. 46 57.41 N 2.49 W
Cullen, La., U.S. 194 32.58 N 93.27 W
Cullen Bullen 170 33.18 S 150.01 E
Cullen Point > 164 11.57 S 141.54 E
Culleoka, Tn., U.S. 194 35.28 N 86.58 W
Culleoka, Tx., U.S. 222 33.08 N 96.29 W
Cullera 34 39.10 N 0.15 W
Cullicudden 46 57.39 N 4.13 W
Cullin, Lough ⊜ 48 53.57 N 9.12 W
Cullinan 158 25.40 S 28.31 E
Cullman 194 34.10 N 86.50 W
Culloden Battlesite ⊥ 46 57.28 N 4.05 W
Cullom 216 40.53 N 88.16 W
Cullompton 42 50.52 N 3.24 W
Cullowhee 192 35.18 N 83.10 W
Cully 58 46.29 N 6.44 E
Cullybackey 48 54.53 N 6.21 W
Culm ≃ 42 50.46 N 3.31 W
Čul'man 74 56.52 N 124.52 E
Cülmen 130 37.19 N 38.48 E
Culmore 284c 38.51 N 77.08 W
Culoz 62 45.51 N 5.47 E
Culpeper 188 38.28 N 77.59 W
Culpina 248 20.50 S 64.58 W
Culrain 46 57.55 N 4.24 W
Cults 46 57.07 N 2.10 W
Cultus Lake 224 49.04 N 121.58 W
Cultus Lake ⊜ 224 49.03 N 121.58 W
Cultus Lake Provincial Park ♦ 224 49.03 N 121.58 W
Culú-Culú, Arroyo ≃ 258 35.19 S 58.57 W
Culú-Culú, Laguna ⊜ 258 35.20 S 58.59 W
Culuene ≃ 255 12.56 S 52.51 W
Čuluunchoroot 88 49.41 N 114.15 E
Čuluut 102 45.48 N 107.05 E
Čuluutyn ≃ 88 49.11 N 100.41 E
Culvain ∧ 46 56.56 N 5.17 W
Culver, In., U.S. 216 41.13 N 86.25 W
Culver, Or., U.S. 202 44.31 N 121.12 W
Culver, Point > 162 32.54 S 124.43 E
Culver City 228 34.01 N 118.23 W
Culverden 172 42.46 S 172.51 E
Culvers Lake 210 41.10 N 74.48 W
Culverstone Green 260 51.20 N 0.21 E
Čulym 86 55.06 N 80.58 E
Čulym ≃, Ross. 86 57.43 N 83.51 E
Čulym ≃, Ross. 86 54.38 N 78.16 E
Čulyšman ≃ 86 51.20 N 87.45 E
Čum 24 67.06 N 63.07 E
Cuma 152 12.52 S 15.05 E
Cuma (Cumae) ⊥ 68 40.50 N 14.06 E
Čumakovo 86 55.41 N 79.02 E
Cumalı 130 36.42 N 27.27 E
Cumaná 246 10.28 N 64.10 W
Cumanacoa 246 10.15 N 63.55 W
Cumanayagua 240p 22.09 N 80.12 W
Cumaovası 130 38.15 N 27.09 E
Cumare, Cerro ∧[2] 246 0.28 N 73.52 W
Cumari 255 18.16 S 48.11 W
Cumbal 246 0.54 N 77.47 W
Cumbal, Nevado ∧ 246 0.57 N 77.52 W
Cumbe 250 10.21 S 37.14 W
Cumbee 220 28.04 N 81.55 W
Cumberland, B.C., Can. 182 49.37 N 125.01 W
Cumberland, Ia., U.S. 198 41.16 N 94.52 W
Cumberland, Ky., U.S. 192 36.58 N 82.59 W
Cumberland, Md., U.S. 188 39.39 N 78.45 W
Cumberland, Va., U.S. 192 37.29 N 78.14 W
Cumberland, Wa., U.S. 224 47.16 N 121.55 W
Cumberland, Wi., U.S. 190 45.31 N 92.01 W
Cumberland □[6], N.J., U.S. 208 39.26 N 75.14 W
Cumberland □[6], Pa., U.S. 208 40.12 N 77.12 W
Cumberland ≃ 178 37.09 N 88.25 W
Cumberland, Lake ⊜[1] 194 36.57 N 84.55 W
Cumberland, South Fork ≃ 192 36.58 N 84.36 W
Cumberland City 194 36.23 N 87.38 W
Cumberland Falls State Resort Park ♦ 192 36.50 N 84.20 W
Cumberland Gap)(192 36.36 N 83.41 W
Cumberland Gap National Historical Park ♦ 192 36.36 N 83.40 W
Cumberland Hill 207 41.58 N 71.27 W
Cumberland House 184 53.58 N 102.16 W
Cumberland Indian Reserve ◆[4] 184 53.04 N 104.50 W
Cumberland Island National Seashore ♦ 192 30.50 N 81.27 W
Cumberland Islands II 166 20.40 S 149.09 E
Cumberland Lake ⊜ 184 54.02 N 102.17 W
Cumberland Peninsula >[1] 176 66.50 N 64.00 W
Cumberland Plateau ⋏[1] 192 36.20 N 84.30 W
Cumberland Sound ⊻ 176 65.10 N 65.30 W
Cumbernauld 46 55.58 N 3.59 W
Cumborah 166 29.44 S 147.46 E
Cumbria □[6] 44 54.30 N 3.00 W
Cumbrian Mountains ⋏ 44 54.30 N 3.05 W
Čumbur-Kosa 83 46.57 N 38.53 E
Cumby 222 33.08 N 95.50 W
Cumeral Nuevo 200 30.54 N 110.51 W
Cumiana 62 44.59 N 7.22 E
Čumikan 89 54.42 N 135.19 E
Cuminá — Paru de Oeste ≃ 250 1.30 S 56.00 W
Cuminapanema ≃ 250 1.09 S 54.54 W
Cuminestown 46 57.32 N 2.20 W
Cumming 192 34.12 N 84.08 W
Cummings Mountain ∧ 228 35.03 N 118.34 W
Cummington 207 42.27 N 72.53 W
Cummins 166 34.16 S 135.44 E
Cummins, Mount ∧ 182 52.03 N 118.15 W
Cummins Creek ≃ 222 29.43 N 96.31 W
Cummins Range ⋏ 162 19.05 S 127.10 E
Cumnock 44 55.27 N 4.16 W
Cumnor 42 51.44 N 1.20 W
Cumpas 232 30.02 N 109.48 W
Çumra 130 37.34 N 32.48 E
Cumshewa Inlet c 182 53.03 N 131.45 W
Cumuripa 232 28.08 N 109.53 W
Cumwhinton 44 54.52 N 2.51 W
Čumyš ≃ 86 53.31 N 83.10 E
Čun'a ≃, Ross. 74 61.36 N 96.30 E
Čuna ≃, Ross. 88 57.47 N 95.26 E
Cunani 250 2.52 N 51.06 W
Cunauaru ≃ 246 3.10 S 63.01 W
Cunaviche 246 7.22 N 67.25 W
Cunco 252 38.55 S 72.02 W
Cuncumén 252 31.53 S 70.38 W
Cundeelee Reserve ◆[4] 162 30.30 S 123.25 E
Cunderdin 162 31.39 S 117.15 E
Cundinamarca □[5] 246 5.00 N 74.00 W
Cunduacán 234 18.04 N 93.10 W
Čundža 86 43.32 N 79.28 E
Cunene □[5] 152 16.30 S 15.30 E
Cunene (Kunene) ≃ 152 17.20 S 11.50 E
Cuneo 62 44.23 N 7.32 E
Cuneo □[4] 62 44.31 N 7.34 E
Cunewalde 54 51.06 N 14.30 E
Cuney 222 32.02 N 95.25 W
Cung Hau, Cua ≃[1] 110 9.46 N 106.34 E
Cung Son 110 13.02 N 108.58 E
Çüngüş 130 38.13 N 39.17 E
Cunha 256 23.05 S 44.58 W
Cunhambebe 256 23.00 S 44.20 W
Cunha Porã 252 26.54 S 53.09 W
Cunhinga 152 12.11 S 16.47 E
Cunhinga ≃ 152 10.38 S 16.48 E
Cunhuã, Igarapé ≃ 248 5.46 S 64.36 W
Cunlhat 62 45.38 N 3.35 E
Cunliffe 168b 34.05 S 137.45 E
Cunnamulla 166 28.04 S 145.41 E
Cunningham, Austl. 171a 28.09 S 151.51 E
Cunningham, Ks., U.S. 198 37.38 N 98.25 W
Cunningham, Lake ⊜ 240b 25.04 N 77.26 W
Cunninghame □[9] 46 55.40 N 4.30 W
Cunningham Falls State Park ♦ 208 39.35 N 77.27 W
Cunningham Park ♦, Ma., U.S. 283 42.15 N 71.03 W
Cunningham Park ♦, N.Y., U.S. 276 40.44 N 73.46 W
Čunojar 88 57.27 N 97.18 E
Cunqian 100 28.30 N 115.10 E
Čunskij, Ross. 88 56.05 N 99.41 E
Čunskij, Ross. 88 57.26 N 97.31 E
Cuntan 107 29.37 N 106.36 E
Cunucunuma ≃ 246 3.13 N 65.58 W
Čuny 76 59.39 N 36.04 E
Čuokkarašša ∧ 24 69.57 N 24.32 E
Cuorgnè 62 45.23 N 7.39 E
Čupa 24 66.16 N 33.00 E
Čupalejka 80 55.11 N 42.33 E
Cupar, Sk., Can. 184 50.57 N 104.12 W
Cupar, Scot., U.K. 46 56.19 N 3.01 W
Cupecê, Ribeirão ≃ 287b 23.37 S 46.42 W
Cupello 66 42.04 N 14.40 E
Cuperly 50 49.04 N 4.26 E
Cupertino 226 37.19 N 122.01 W
Cupica, Golfo de c 246 6.35 N 77.25 W
Cupins 255 19.51 S 51.03 W
Cupra Marittima 66 43.01 N 13.51 E
Cupramontana 66 43.27 N 13.07 E
Ćuprija 38 43.56 N 21.23 E
Čuprovo 24 64.14 N 46.36 E
Cupsaw Lake ⊜ 276 41.07 N 74.15 W
Cuqiao 107 30.36 N 103.59 E
Cuquema ≃ 152 12.03 S 17.40 E
Cuquenán ≃ 246 4.45 N 61.30 W
Cuquío 234 20.55 N 103.02 W
Čur 80 57.07 N 52.58 E
Curaçá 250 8.59 S 39.54 W
Curaçao I 241s 12.11 N 69.00 W
Curacautín 252 38.26 S 71.53 W
Curacaví 252 33.24 S 71.09 W
Čuračiki 80 55.44 N 47.26 E
Curaglia 58 46.41 N 8.51 E
Cural Novo, Ribeirão ≃ 256 21.17 S 43.51 W
Curanilahue 252 37.28 S 73.21 W
Curanipe 252 35.50 S 72.38 W
Curanja ≃ 248 9.58 S 70.58 W
Čurapča 74 62.00 N 132.24 E
Curapi ≃ 250 1.25 N 53.49 W
Curaray ≃ 246 2.20 S 74.05 W
Čurbek 85 39.59 N 69.56 E
Curcani 38 44.12 N 26.35 E
Curdies ≃ 169 38.30 S 142.55 E
Cure ≃ 50 47.40 N 3.41 E
Curecanti National Recreation Area ♦ 200 38.24 N 107.25 W
Curepipe 157c 20.19 S 57.31 E
Curepto 252 35.05 S 72.01 W
Curequetê ≃ 248 8.20 S 65.40 W
Curiapo 246 8.33 N 61.00 W
Curib 84 42.14 N 46.49 E
Curiche Grande (Corixo Grande) ≃ 248 17.43 S 57.43 W
Curicó 252 34.59 S 71.14 W
Curicuriari ≃ 246 0.14 S 66.48 W
Curières, Lac ⊜ 206 46.41 N 74.51 W
Curimatá 250 10.02 S 44.17 W
Curimeo 234 20.01 N 101.42 W
Curinga 68 38.49 N 16.19 E
Curious, Mount ∧ 162 27.28 S 114.20 E
Curisevo ≃ 255 12.14 S 53.17 W
Curitiba 252 25.25 S 49.15 W
Curitibanos 252 27.18 S 50.36 W
Curiuaú ≃ 246 1.51 S 61.14 W
Curiúva 255 24.02 S 50.27 W
Curl Curl 274a 33.46 S 151.18 E
Curlew 182 48.53 N 118.35 W
Curlewis 166 31.07 S 150.16 E
Curnamona 166 31.39 S 139.32 E
Curoca Norte 152 16.18 S 12.58 E
Curone ≃ 62 45.03 N 8.54 E
Curon Venosta (Graun) 64 46.49 N 10.32 E
Čurovići 78 52.10 N 32.01 E
Currais Novos 250 6.15 S 36.31 W
Curralinho 250 1.48 S 49.47 W
Curramulka 168b 34.42 S 137.42 E
Curran 219 39.44 N 89.46 W
Currant Creek ≃, Co., U.S. 200 38.29 N 105.24 W
Currant Creek ≃, Mt., U.S. 202 46.22 N 108.39 W
Currant Mountain ∧ 204 38.55 N 115.25 W
Currarong 170 35.01 S 150.49 E
Currency Creek 168b 35.28 S 138.46 E
Current ≃, On., Can. 190 48.27 N 89.11 W
Current ≃, U.S. 194 36.16 N 90.57 W
Current Islands II 192 25.22 N 76.49 W
Currie, Austl. 166 39.56 S 143.52 E
Currie, Scot., U.K. 46 55.54 N 3.20 W
Currie, Mn., U.S. 198 44.04 N 95.39 W
Currituck 192 36.26 N 76.00 W
Currituck □[6] 208 36.28 N 76.03 W
Currituck Seamount ◆[3] 14 30.00 S 173.30 W
Currituck Sound ⊻ 192 36.20 N 75.52 W
Curry 180 62.37 N 150.01 W
Curry, Lake ⊜[1] 226 38.22 N 122.08 W
Curry Rivel 42 51.02 N 2.52 W
Curryville, Mo., U.S. 219 39.20 N 91.20 W
Curryville, Pa., U.S. 214 40.17 N 78.20 W
Cursi 68 40.09 N 18.18 E
Curslack ◆[8] 52 53.27 N 10.13 E
Curtarolo 64 45.31 N 11.50 E
Curtea de Argeș 38 45.08 N 24.41 E
Curtice 214 41.29 N 82.49 W
Curtina 252 32.09 S 56.07 W
Curtin Springs 162 25.20 S 131.45 E
Curtis, Esp. 34 43.07 N 8.03 W
Curtis, Ar., U.S. 194 33.59 N 93.06 W
Curtis, Ne., U.S. 198 40.37 N 100.30 W
Curtis, Port ⊤[3] 166 24.00 S 151.30 E
Curtis Bay c 284b 39.13 N 76.35 W
Curtis Channel ⊻ 166 23.30 S 151.45 E
Curtis Creek c 284b 39.12 N 76.35 W
Curtis Island I, Austl. 166 23.38 S 151.09 E
Curtis Island I, N.Z. 14 30.30 S 178.34 W
Curtis Lake ⊜ 176 66.38 N 89.02 W
Curtisville 214 40.38 N 79.51 W
Curu ≃ 250 3.22 S 39.04 W
Curuá ≃, Bra. 250 5.23 S 54.22 W
Curuá ≃, Bra. 250 1.55 S 55.07 W
Curuá ≃, Bra. 255 13.51 S 51.38 W
Curuá, Ilha do I 250 0.48 N 50.10 W
Curuaés ≃ 250 7.30 S 54.45 W
Curuan 116 7.13 N 122.14 E
Curuá-Una ≃ 250 2.24 S 54.05 W
Curubandé 236 10.43 N 85.26 W
Curuçá 250 0.43 S 47.50 W
Curuçá ◆[8] 287b 23.30 S 46.25 W
Curuçá ≃ 246 4.27 S 71.23 W
Curuçambaba 250 2.08 S 49.18 W
Curug, Indon. 115a 6.15 S 106.33 E
Čurug, Jugo. 38 45.29 N 20.04 E
Curuguaty 252 24.31 S 55.42 W
Curumo 286c 10.27 N 66.52 W
Curumu 250 1.01 S 51.03 W
Curunga 152 12.51 S 21.12 E
Curup 112 3.28 S 102.32 E
Curupá 250 9.54 S 45.54 W
Curupayty, Riacho ≃ 248 22.03 S 58.00 W
Cururu ≃, Bra. 248 7.12 S 58.03 W
Cururu ≃, Bra. 250 0.39 S 50.11 W
Cururu-Açu ≃ 250 8.58 S 57.13 W
Cururupu 250 1.50 S 44.52 W
Curuzú Cuatiá 252 29.47 S 58.03 W
Curva Grande 250 2.37 S 45.27 W
Curvelo 255 18.45 S 44.25 W
Curwensville 214 40.58 N 78.31 W
Curwensville Lake ⊜[1] 214 40.55 N 78.37 W
Curwensville State Park ♦ 214 40.55 N 78.34 W
Cusago 266b 45.27 N 9.02 E
Cusano Milanino 62 45.33 N 9.11 E
Cusano Mutri 68 41.20 N 14.30 E
Cusco 248 13.31 S 71.59 W
Cusco □[5] 248 12.30 S 72.30 W
Cuscuzeiro, Pico do ∧ 256 23.18 S 44.47 W
Cushabatay ≃ 248 7.09 S 75.08 W
Cushendall 48 55.06 N 6.04 W
Cushendun 48 55.07 N 6.03 W
Cushina ≃ 48 53.11 N 7.05 W
Cushing, Ok., U.S. 196 35.59 N 96.46 W
Cushing, Tx., U.S. 222 31.43 N 94.50 W
Cushing Memorial State Park ♦ 283 42.10 N 70.45 W
Cushman 194 35.52 N 91.45 W
Cushman, Lake ⊜[1] 224 47.28 N 123.14 W
Cusiana ≃ 246 4.33 N 71.51 W
Cusick 202 48.20 N 117.17 W
Cusihuiriáchic 232 28.14 N 106.50 W
Cusna, Monte ∧ 64 44.17 N 10.23 E
Čusovaja ≃ 86 58.13 N 56.22 E
Čusovoj 86 58.17 N 57.49 E
Cusset 32 46.08 N 3.28 E
Cusseta 192 32.18 N 84.46 W
Cussewago Creek ≃ 214 41.38 N 80.11 W
Cussey-sur-l'Ognon 58 47.20 N 5.56 E
Cusso ≃ 152 14.16 S 15.36 E
Cust, N.Z. 172 43.19 S 172.22 E
Čust, Uzb. 85 41.00 N 71.15 E
Custar 216 41.17 N 83.51 W
Custer, Mi., U.S. 190 43.57 N 86.13 W
Custer, Mt., U.S. 202 46.07 N 107.33 W
Custer, Ok., U.S. 196 35.40 N 98.53 W
Custer, S.D., U.S. 198 43.46 N 103.35 W
Custer, Wa., U.S. 224 48.55 N 122.38 W
Custer Battlefield National Monument ♦ 202 45.32 N 107.20 W
Custer City 214 41.54 N 78.39 W
Custer Creek ≃ 198 46.42 N 105.29 W
Custer State Park ♦ 198 43.43 N 103.23 W
Custines 56 48.48 N 6.09 E
Custódia 250 8.07 S 37.39 W
Custonaci 70 38.04 N 12.41 E
Cut, Nuhu I 164 5.35 S 133.00 E
Cut and Shoot 222 30.19 N 95.25 W
Cutato ≃ 152 10.33 S 16.48 E
Cut Bank 202 48.37 N 112.19 W
Cutbank ≃ 182 54.44 N 118.31 W
Cut Bank Creek ≃, N.A. 198 48.35 N 100.52 W
Cut Bank Creek ≃, Mt., U.S. 202 48.29 N 112.14 W
Cut Beaver Lake ⊜ 184 53.47 N 102.38 W
Čutejevo 80 55.16 N 47.47 E
Cutervo 248 6.22 S 78.51 W
Cutervo, Parque Nacional ♦ 248 6.10 S 78.45 W
Cuthand Creek ≃ 194 33.23 N 94.57 W
Cuthbert 192 31.46 N 84.47 W
Cut Knife 184 52.44 N 109.01 W
Cutler, Ca., U.S. 226 36.31 N 119.17 W
Cutler, Me., U.S. 188 44.39 N 67.12 W
Cutler Ridge 220 25.34 N 80.20 W
Cutlerville 216 42.50 N 85.39 W
Cutral-Có 252 38.56 S 69.14 W
Cutro 68 39.02 N 16.59 E
Cutrofiano 68 40.07 N 18.12 E
Cuttack 120 20.30 N 85.50 E
Cuttyhunk Island I 207 41.25 N 70.56 W
Čutyr' 80 57.24 N 53.17 E
Cutzamala ≃ 234 18.22 N 100.39 W
Cutzamala de Pinzón 234 18.28 N 100.34 W
Cutzio 234 18.39 N 100.54 W
Čuvašija □[3] 80 55.30 N 47.00 E
Cuvette □[5] 152 0.30 S 16.00 E
Cuvier, Cape > 162 24.05 S 113.22 E
Cuvilly 50 49.33 N 2.42 E
Cuvo ≃ 152 10.50 S 13.47 E
Cuxhaven 52 53.52 N 8.42 E
Cuxton 260 51.22 N 0.27 E
Cuyabá — Cuiabá 248 15.35 S 56.05 W
Cuyaguateje ≃ 240p 22.05 N 83.58 W
Cuyahoga □[6] 214 41.30 N 81.41 W
Cuyahoga ≃ 214 41.30 N 81.42 W
Cuyahoga County Airport ⊠ 279a 41.34 N 81.29 W
Cuyahoga Falls 214 41.08 N 81.29 W
Cuyahoga Heights 279a 41.26 N 81.39 W
Cuyahoga Valley National Recreation Area ♦ 214 41.20 N 81.35 W
Cuyama ≃ 204 34.54 N 120.18 W
Cuyamaca Peak ∧ 204 32.57 N 116.36 W
Cuyamaca Rancho State Park ♦ 204 32.58 N 116.32 W
Cuyamel 236 15.38 N 88.12 W
Cuyapo 116 15.46 N 120.40 E
Cuyk 52 51.44 N 5.52 E
Cuyler 210 42.44 N 75.57 W
Cuylerville 210 42.47 N 77.52 W
Cuyo 116 10.51 N 121.00 E
Cuyo East Pass ⊻ 116 11.00 N 121.28 E
Cuyo Island I 116 10.51 N 121.02 E
Cuyo Islands II 116 11.04 N 120.57 E
Cuyo West Pass ⊻ 116 11.00 N 120.30 E
Cuyubini ≃ 246 8.20 N 60.20 W
Cuyuni ≃ 246 6.23 N 58.41 W
Cuyuni-Mazaruni □[4] 246 6.00 N 60.00 W
Cuyutlán, Laguna c 234 19.00 N 104.10 W
Cuzco — Cusco 248 13.31 S 71.59 W
Čuzik ≃ 86 58.03 N 80.37 E
Cuzna ≃ 34 38.04 N 4.41 W
Cuzzago 58 46.00 N 8.22 E
Cvetnogorsk 86 54.14 N 90.27 E
Cvikov 54 50.48 N 14.40 E
Cwmbran 42 51.39 N 3.00 W
Cyangugu 154 2.29 S 28.54 E
Cybinka 30 52.12 N 14.48 E
Cyclades — Kikládhes II 38 37.30 N 25.00 E
Cyclone 214 41.50 N 78.35 W
Cygnet 216 41.14 N 83.38 W
Cygnet Bay c 162 16.35 S 123.05 E
Cygnet Lake ⊜ 184 56.47 N 94.54 W
Cygnet River 168b 35.42 S 137.31 E
Cylburn Park ♦ 284b 39.21 N 76.39 W
Cynin ≃ 42 51.48 N 4.29 W
Cynthiana, Ky., U.S. 218 38.23 N 84.17 W
Cynthiana, Oh., U.S. 218 39.10 N 83.21 W
Cynwyl Elfed 42 51.55 N 4.22 W
Cypern — Cyprus □[1] 130 35.00 N 33.00 E
Cypress, Ca., U.S. 280 33.49 N 118.02 W
Cypress, La., U.S. 194 31.36 N 93.02 W
Cypress, Tx., U.S. 222 29.58 N 95.42 W
Cypress Bayou ≃ 194 35.03 N 91.42 W
Cypress Creek ≃, Fl., U.S. 220 28.05 N 82.24 W
Cypress Creek ≃, Tx., U.S. 194 30.19 N 93.45 W
Cypress Creek ≃, Tx., U.S. 222 30.02 N 95.19 W
Cypress Gardens ♦ 220 28.00 N 81.42 W

ENGLISH

Name | Page | Lat.°′ | Long.°′

Cypress Hills ⋏[2] 184 49.40 N 109.30 W
Cypress Hills Provincial Park ♦, Ab., Can. 184 49.39 N 110.10 W
Cypress Hills Provincial Park ♦, Sk., Can. 184 49.39 N 109.30 W
Cypress Island I 224 48.35 N 122.42 W
Cypress Lake ⊜, Sk., Can. 184 49.28 N 109.29 W
Cypress Lake ⊜, Fl., U.S. 220 28.05 N 81.19 W
Cypress Point > 226 36.35 N 121.59 W
Cypress Quarters 220 27.15 N 80.48 W
Cypress River 184 49.34 N 99.05 W
Cypress Swamp ≃ 208 37.02 N 76.53 W
Cypress Swamp ≡ 208 38.30 N 75.17 W
Cyprus □[1], Asia 22 35.00 N 33.00 E
Cyprus □[1], Asia 130 35.00 N 33.00 E
Cyprus, North (Kuzey Kıbrıs) □[1], Asia 22 35.15 N 33.40 E
Cyprus, North (Kuzey Kıbrıs) □[1], Asia 130 35.15 N 33.40 E
Cyrenaica — Barqah □[9] 146 31.00 N 22.30 E
Cyrene 219 39.17 N 91.06 W
Cyrene ⊥ 146 32.49 N 21.52 E
Cyril 196 34.53 N 98.12 W
Cyrildene ◆[8] 273d 26.11 S 28.06 E
Cyrus Field Bay c 176 62.50 N 64.55 W
Cysoing 50 50.34 N 3.13 E
Cythera — Kíthira I 38 36.20 N 22.58 E
Czaplinek 30 53.34 N 16.14 E
Czarna Białostocka 30 53.19 N 23.16 E
Czarna Woda 30 53.51 N 18.06 E
Czarne 30 53.42 N 16.57 E
Czarnków 30 52.55 N 16.34 E
Czech Republic (Česká Republika) □[1], Europe 22 49.40 N 15.10 E
Czech Republic (Česká Republika) □[1], Europe 30 49.40 N 15.10 E
Czempiń 30 52.10 N 16.47 E
Czerniejewo 30 52.26 N 17.30 E
Czernowitz — Chernivtsi 78 48.18 N 25.56 E
Czersk 30 53.48 N 18.00 E
Czerwieńsk 30 52.01 N 15.25 E
Częstochowa 30 50.49 N 19.06 E
Częstochowa □[4] 30 50.40 N 19.15 E
Człopa 30 53.06 N 16.08 E
Człuchów 30 53.41 N 17.21 E
Czudec 30 49.57 N 21.50 E

D

Da — Black ≃, Asia 110 21.15 N 105.20 E
Da ≃, Zhg. 100 28.10 N 120.14 E
Daaden 56 50.44 N 7.58 E
Da'an, Zhg. 89 45.28 N 124.18 E
Da'an, Zhg. 100 23.05 N 115.37 E
Da'an, Zhg. 107 29.23 N 106.01 E
Da'an, Zhg. 110 23.19 N 110.34 E
Daanbantayan 116 11.14 N 124.00 E
Daba 104 42.06 N 122.00 E
Ḍabāb, Jabal aḍ- ∧ 132 31.02 N 35.38 E
Dabagou 104 42.27 N 122.00 E
Ḍab'ah, Ra's aḍ- > 140 31.05 N 28.26 E
Dabai 150 11.31 N 5.11 E
Dabaizhuang 105 39.27 N 117.23 E
Dabajuro 246 11.02 N 70.40 W
Dabakala 150 8.22 N 4.26 W
Dabali 104 41.51 N 120.37 E
Daba Ling ∧ 100 24.28 N 113.17 E
Dabancheng 86 43.21 N 88.19 E
Dabangdian 100 31.37 N 113.41 E
Dabaojiagangzi 104 42.09 N 123.33 E
Dabaozhuang 105 40.18 N 116.58 E
Dabaozi 105 40.11 N 115.10 E
Daba Shan ⋏ 102 31.55 N 109.05 E
Dabasi 107 28.55 N 105.09 E
Dabat 144 12.58 N 37.48 E
Dabayingzi 104 42.11 N 121.35 E
Dabbāgh, Jabal ∧ 128 27.52 N 35.45 E
Dabbūriya 132 32.41 N 35.22 E
Dabegabis 158 28.07 S 18.36 E
Dabeiba 246 7.01 N 76.16 W
Dabeiwa 105 40.48 N 117.31 E
Dabeiyingzi 104 42.05 N 122.08 E
Dabendorf 54 52.14 N 13.26 E
Daberas 156 25.38 S 18.29 E
Daberg ◆[8] 263 51.40 N 7.47 E
Dabhoi 120 22.11 N 73.26 E
Dābhol 122 17.36 N 73.10 E
Ḍab'ī, Wādī aḍ- V 132 31.42 N 36.42 E
Dąbie 30 52.06 N 18.49 E
Dąbie ◆[8] 54 53.24 N 14.40 E
Dąbie, Jezioro ⊜ 54 53.27 N 14.40 E
Dabie Shan ⋏ 100 31.00 N 115.40 E
Dabilda 146 12.46 N 14.34 E
Ḍablān 130 34.52 N 40.34 E
Ďáblice ◆[8] 54 50.08 N 14.29 E
Dabnou 150 14.09 N 5.22 E
Dabo 58 48.39 N 7.14 E
Dabob Bay c 224 47.47 N 122.50 W
Dabobeizhuang 105 39.18 N 117.59 E
Dabola 150 10.45 N 11.07 W
Dabong 114 5.23 N 102.01 E
Daborow 144 6.21 N 48.43 E
Dabou 150 5.19 N 4.23 W
Daboya 150 9.32 N 1.23 W
Dabra 124 25.54 N 78.20 E
Dābri ◆[8] 272a 28.37 N 77.05 E
Dabringhausen 52 51.05 N 7.11 E
Dąbrowa Białostocka 30 53.39 N 23.20 E
Dąbrowa Tarnowska 30 50.11 N 21.00 E
Dabsan Hu ⊜ 102 36.58 N 94.55 E
Dabu, Zhg. 100 24.19 N 116.43 E
Dabu, Zhg. 100 23.52 N 116.54 E
Dabu, Zhg. 100 24.20 N 114.35 E
Dabus ≃ 144 10.48 N 35.10 E
Dabusutu-Ula, gora ∧ 86 50.44 N 92.40 E
Dacaitun 104 41.38 N 121.18 E
Dacangzigou 104 40.59 N 121.01 E
Dacaocun 105 40.34 N 117.07 E
Dacca — Dhaka 126 23.43 N 90.25 E
Dachakou 100 29.38 N 118.18 E
Dachang, Zhg. 105 39.53 N 116.59 E
Dachang, Zhg. 106 32.12 N 118.45 E
Dachang, Zhg. 106 31.18 N 121.25 E
Dachang Airport ⊠ 269b 31.18 N 121.25 E
Dachangshan Dao I 98 39.10 N 122.34 E
Dachau 60 48.15 N 11.27 E
Dachauer Moos ≡ 60 48.12 N 11.25 E
Dacheng 100 28.34 N 115.31 E
Dachengji 100 33.52 N 119.26 E
Dachenjiabao 106 32.11 N 120.22 E
Dachen Shan I 106 30.21 N 121.52 E
Dachixu 100 25.10 N 116.46 E
Dachongyu 105 40.23 N 117.41 E
Dachsberg ∧[2] 263 51.30 N 6.30 E
Dachsteinhöhlen ⊥[5] 64 47.32 N 13.43 E
Dačice 61 49.05 N 15.26 E
Dac Lac, Cao Nguyen ⋏[1] 110 12.50 N 108.05 E
Dačnoje ◆[8] 265a 59.50 N 30.16 E
Dacoma 196 36.39 N 98.33 W
Dacorum □[8] 260 51.45 N 0.30 W
Dac To 110 14.42 N 107.51 E
Dacun, Zhg. 102 27.55 N 101.08 E
Dacun, Zhg. 106 31.12 N 119.40 E
Dadal 88 49.01 N 111.37 E
Dadanawa 246 2.50 N 59.30 W
Dadaolizhuang 105 39.59 N 116.59 E
Dadaotun 104 41.46 N 122.13 E
Dadar ◆[8] 272c 19.01 N 72.50 E
Daday 130 41.28 N 33.28 E

DEUTSCH

Name | Seite | Breite°′ | Länge°′ E = Ost

Dadayungou 104 41.23 N 123.25 E
Daddys Creek ≃ 192 36.05 N 84.47 W
Dade □[6] 220 25.33 N 80.32 W
Dade Battlefield Historic Memorial ⊥ 220 28.38 N 82.09 W
Dade City 220 28.21 N 82.11 W
Daḍeldhurā 124 29.18 N 80.35 E
Dadès, Oued ≃ 148 30.55 N 6.47 W
Dadeville 194 32.49 N 85.45 W
Dādhar 120 29.28 N 67.39 E
Dadian 100 33.36 N 117.16 E
Dadiangas — General Santos 116 6.07 N 125.11 E
Dadianzi 104 42.11 N 124.02 E
Dadingjiawopu 104 41.13 N 122.16 E
D'adino 88 55.44 N 105.45 E
Dadiya 146 9.37 N 11.26 E
Dadle 144 5.20 N 46.58 E
Ḍadnah 128 25.33 N 56.21 E
Dadonggejiang 105 39.51 N 116.48 E
Dadongzhou 104 41.44 N 124.00 E
Dadou ≃ 32 43.44 N 1.49 E
Dādpur, India 272b 22.42 N 88.33 E
Dādpur, India 272b 22.54 N 88.31 E
Dādra and Nagar Haveli □[8] 122 20.05 N 73.00 E
Dādu 120 26.44 N 67.47 E
Dadu ≃ 102 29.33 N 103.45 E
Dadugang 102 22.23 N 100.55 E
Dadukou, Zhg. 100 25.44 N 119.05 E
Dadukou, Zhg. 107 28.45 N 105.13 E
Dadukou, Zhg. 107 29.28 N 106.29 E
Daegu — Taegu 98 35.52 N 128.35 E
Daejeon — Taejŏn 98 36.20 N 127.26 E
Daerhanwangfu 89 44.19 N 122.15 E
Da'erhao 98 41.45 N 116.01 E
Daet 116 14.05 N 122.55 E
Daf' 146 28.03 N 19.57 E
Dafan, Zhg. 100 29.41 N 114.40 E
Dafan, Zhg. 104 42.38 N 122.11 E
Dafang 102 27.04 N 105.31 E
Dafangshen, Zhg. 104 42.25 N 123.14 E
Dafangshen, Zhg. 104 42.34 N 123.28 E
Dafangshen, Zhg. 104 42.36 N 123.04 E
Dafanhe 104 42.13 N 123.43 E
Dafanpuzi 104 41.37 N 122.50 E
Dafeng 100 33.12 N 120.30 E
Dafna 132 33.14 N 35.38 E
Dafoe 184 51.46 N 104.32 W
Dafoe ≃ 184 55.55 N 94.48 W
Dafoe Lake ⊜ 184 55.43 N 96.15 W
Da Fo Si (Great Buddha Temple) ⊌[1] 106 30.16 N 120.09 E
Dafoutuo 105 40.24 N 115.58 E
Dafu 100 29.55 N 118.35 E
Dafu ≃ 100 30.52 N 113.32 E
Dāfūr al-Janūbīyah □[4] 140 11.45 N 25.25 E
Dagā ≃ 110 16.56 N 94.45 E
Daga Medo 144 7.59 N 43.01 E
Dagana 150 16.31 N 15.30 W
Dagang, Zhg. 100 33.12 N 120.07 E
Dagang, Zhg. 100 22.49 N 113.23 E
Dagang, Zhg. 106 32.12 N 119.39 E
Dagangtou 100 28.18 N 119.44 E
Daganwangzhai 104 40.49 N 122.33 E
Daganzo de Arriba 266a 40.33 N 3.27 W
Dagaokan 104 40.46 N 122.22 E
Dagaolifangcun 104 41.10 N 122.28 E
Dagaolitun 104 42.26 N 123.53 E
Dagaoyang 106 30.35 N 120.26 E
Daga Post 140 9.12 N 33.58 E
Dağardı 130 39.26 N 29.00 E
Dagash 140 19.22 N 33.24 E
Dağbeli 130 37.12 N 30.31 E
Dagcanglhamo 102 34.02 N 102.30 E
Dagda 76 56.06 N 27.32 E
Dageløkke 41 55.04 N 10.53 E
Dagenham ◆[8] 260 51.32 N 0.10 E
Dagestan □[3], Ross. 72 43.00 N 47.00 E
Dagestanskije Ogni 84 42.07 N 48.12 E
Daggafontein 273d 26.18 S 28.28 E
Daggafontein Mines ◆[7] 273d 26.18 S 28.29 E
Daggett 228 34.51 N 116.53 W
Dagg Sound ⊻ 172 45.23 S 166.46 E
Daghfalī 140 19.17 N 32.30 E
Dağkızılca 130 38.18 N 27.24 E
Daglung 120 28.54 N 90.33 E
Dagmersellen 58 47.13 N 7.59 E
Dagö — Hiiumaa I 76 58.52 N 22.40 E
Dagomys 84 43.40 N 39.41 E
Dagongtun 89 42.48 N 121.58 E
Dagoretti 154 1.18 S 36.46 E
Dagsboro 208 38.32 N 75.14 W
Dagshai 123 30.53 N 77.03 E
Dagu 105 38.59 N 117.41 E
Dagu ≃ 98 36.15 N 120.06 E
Dagua 164 3.25 S 143.20 E
Daguan, Zhg. 100 31.14 N 117.01 E
Daguan, Zhg. 102 27.44 N 104.16 E
Daguan Hu ⊜ 100 30.00 N 116.24 E
Daguao 240m 18.14 N 65.41 W
Dagufen'gou 105 40.41 N 116.20 E
D'Aguilar, Cape > 271d 22.14 N 114.15 E
D'Aguilar, Mount ∧ 171a 27.19 S 152.47 E
D'Aguilar Range ⋏ 171a 27.10 S 152.45 E
Dagujia 98 42.22 N 124.52 E
Dagujiazi 104 42.20 N 123.20 E
Da Guokui Shan ∧ 89 45.17 N 129.30 E
Dagupan 116 16.03 N 120.20 E
Daguragu Aboriginal Reserve ◆[4] 162 17.35 S 130.30 E
Dagushan 104 41.03 N 123.02 E
Dagus Mines 214 41.21 N 78.36 W
Dagutang 100 29.38 N 116.06 E
Dagwin 110 18.04 N 97.41 E
Dagzê Co ⊜ 120 31.55 N 87.35 E
Dahabān 144 21.55 N 39.04 E
Dahalac National Park ♦ 144 15.40 N 40.05 E
Dahanchang 105 39.29 N 117.05 E
Dahaneh-ye Ghowrī 120 35.54 N 68.30 E
Dahaneh-ye Kāshār 120 35.09 N 66.14 E
Dahan-e Qowmghī 120 34.28 N 66.31 E
Dahantun 104 42.10 N 122.41 E
Dahasah, Wādī V 142 28.08 N 31.00 E
Dahḍāh, Tall ∧[2] 132 32.36 N 36.03 E
Dahe 106 31.42 N 120.37 E
Dahebei 105 39.10 N 117.39 E
Dahei 120 21.42 N 72.35 E
Daheiding Shan ∧ 89 47.58 N 129.07 E
Daheiyugou 104 41.21 N 121.55 E
Dahekou 106 32.16 N 119.05 E
Dahengdu 100 29.03 N 121.30 E
Dahenqin Dao I 100 22.06 N 113.30 E
Daheqiao 100 29.25 N 115.16 E
Dahijuri 126 22.31 N 86.59 E
Da Hinggan Ling ⋏ 90 49.00 N 122.00 E
Dahīrpur ◆[8] 272a 28.43 N 77.12 E
Dahl 56 51.18 N 7.31 E
Dahlak Archipelago II 144 15.45 N 40.30 E
Dahle 263 51.18 N 7.45 E
Dahlem 56 50.23 N 6.33 E
Dahlem ◆[8] 264a 52.28 N 13.17 E
Dahlem, Museum ⊌ 264a 52.27 N 13.18 E
Dahlen 54 51.22 N 12.59 E
Dahlenburg 54 53.11 N 10.44 E
Dahlerau 263 51.13 N 7.19 E
Dahlewitz 54 52.19 N 13.26 E
Dahlgren, Il., U.S. 194 38.12 N 88.41 W
Dahlgren, Va., U.S. 208 38.19 N 77.03 W
Dahlhausen 54 53.03 N 12.20 E
Dahlia 154 18.35 S 27.08 E
Dahlonega 192 34.31 N 83.59 W
Dahlonega Plateau ⋏[1] 192 34.10 N 84.20 W
Dahlwitz 264a 52.30 N 13.38 E
Dahlwitz-Hoppegarten 54 52.30 N 13.38 E
Dahmani 36 35.57 N 8.50 E

Symbols in the index entries represent the broad categories identified in the key at the right. Symbols with superior numbers (⋏[1]) identify subcategories (see complete key on page *I · 1).*

Symbole im Register stellen die rechts im Schlüssel erklärten Kategorien dar. Symbole mit hochgestellten Ziffern (⋏[1]) bezeichnen Unterabteilungen einer Kategorie (vgl. vollständiger Schlüssel auf Seite *I · 1).*

Los símbolos incluídos en el texto del índice representan las grandes categorías identificadas con la clave a la derecha. Los símbolos con numeros en su parte superior (⋏[1]) identifican las subcategorías (véase la clave completa en la página *I · 1).*

Les symboles de l'index représentent les catégories indiquées dans la légende à droite. Les symboles suivis d'un indice (⋏[1]) représentent des sous-catégories (voir légende complète à la page *I · 1).*

Os símbolos incluídos no texto do índice representam as grandes categorias identificadas com a chave à direita. Os símbolos com números em sua parte superior (⋏[1]) identificam as subcategorias (veja-se a chave completa à página *I · 1).*

∧	Mountain	Berg	Montaña	Montagne	Montanha
⋏	Mountains	Gebirge	Montañas	Montagnes	Montanhas
)(	Pass	Paß	Paso	Col	Passo
V	Valley, Canyon	Tal, Cañon	Valle, Cañón	Vallée, Canyon	Vale, Canhão
≐	Plain	Ebene	Llano	Plaine	Planície
>	Cape	Kap	Cabo	Cap	Cabo
I	Island	Insel	Isla	Île	Ilha
II	Islands	Inseln	Islas	Îles	Ilhas
◆	Other Topographic Features	Andere Topographische Objekte	Otros Elementos Topográficos	Autres données topographiques	Outros acidentes topográficos

ESPAÑOL
Nombre | Página | Lat.°′ | Long.°′ W = Oeste

Dahmarū 142 28.41 N 30.49 E
Dahme, Dtsch. 54 51.52 N 13.25 E
Dahme, Dtsch. 54 54.13 N 11.04 E
Dahme ≃ 54 52.25 N 13.35 E
Dahn 56 49.09 N 7.47 E
Dāhod 120 22.50 N 74.16 E
Dahomey
— Benin ◻[1] 150 9.30 N 2.15 E
Dahong 106 31.53 N 121.17 E
Dahongmen 105 39.50 N 116.25 E
Dahongqi 104 41.52 N 122.36 E
Dahong Shan ⩘ 100 31.30 N 113.00 E
Dahongtaizi 104 41.41 N 121.23 E
Dahoucun 105 38.51 N 115.37 E
Dahra 146 29.34 N 17.50 E
Dahra ⩘ 34 36.25 N 1.00 E
Dähre 54 52.48 N 10.54 E
Dahsah, Wādī ad- V 142 27.19 N 31.26 E
Dahshūr 142 29.45 N 31.14 E
Dahu, Zhg. 100 26.22 N 119.06 E
Dahu, Zhg. 100 26.04 N 117.19 E
Dahua 102 23.44 N 107.59 E
Dahuan 100 22.33 N 113.29 E
Dahuangdi 104 42.08 N 122.27 E
Dahuangji 98 35.06 N 115.15 E
Dahuangpu 105 39.26 N 117.16 E
Dahuangshanpu 104 41.16 N 121.23 E
Dahuashan 105 40.17 N 117.04 E
Dahuasi 107 30.05 N 104.08 E
Dahujiang 100 26.10 N 114.57 E
Dahūk 128 36.52 N 43.00 E
Dahūk ◻[4] 128 37.00 N 43.00 E
Dahuni 164 10.31 S 149.55 E
Dahuofang Shuiku ⊜[1] 98 41.55 N 124.15 E
Dahushan 104 41.37 N 122.09 E
Dahy, Nafūd ad- ◆[2] 118 22.20 N 45.35 E
Dai I 175e 7.57 S 160.37 E
Dai ≃ 100 26.14 N 119.40 E
Dai, Pulau I 164 7.33 S 129.41 E
Daia 38 44.00 N 25.59 E
Daian 94 35.05 N 136.33 E
Daibosatsu-rei ▲ 94 35.45 N 138.51 E
Daibu, Zhg. 100 32.19 N 117.12 E
Daibu, Zhg. 106 31.18 N 119.30 E
Daibutsu ⊍[1] 94 35.19 N 139.32 E
Daiei 96 35.29 N 133.45 E
Daifang 100 27.32 N 115.41 E
Daigo 94 36.46 N 140.21 E
Daigo ◆[8] 270 34.57 N 135.50 E
Daiguantun 105 39.57 N 117.50 E
Dai Hai ⊜ 102 40.31 N 112.43 E
Daihaiyingzi 104 42.30 N 121.26 E
Daiji 100 33.48 N 115.03 E
Daijiagou 107 30.00 N 106.33 E
Daijiayao 100 32.56 N 120.19 E
Daikanbō ▲ 96 33.00 N 131.04 E
Daik-u 110 17.47 N 96.40 E
Dā'il 132 32.45 N 36.08 E
Dailekh 124 28.50 N 81.44 E
Dailing 89 47.01 N 129.02 E
Dailly 44 55.16 N 4.43 W
Daimanji-san ▲ 92 36.15 N 133.19 E
Daimiel 34 39.04 N 3.37 W
Daimon, Nihon 94 36.44 N 137.03 E
Daimon, Nihon 268 35.53 N 139.44 E
Daimuken-zan ▲ 94 35.15 N 138.10 E
Dainan 100 32.43 N 120.06 E
Daingean 48 53.18 N 7.17 W
Daingerfield 222 33.01 N 94.43 W
Dainhāt 126 23.37 N 88.04 E
Dainichiga-take ▲ 94 36.00 N 136.50 E
Dainkog 102 32.31 N 97.59 E
Daintree 164 16.15 S 145.19 E
Daintree National Park ♦ 164 16.15 S 145.10 E
Daiō-zaki › 92 34.17 N 136.54 E
Dāira Dīn Panāh 123 30.34 N 70.56 E
Dairago 266b 45.34 N 8.52 E
Daireaux 252 36.36 S 61.45 W
Dairen
— Dalian 98 38.53 N 121.35 E
Dairsie 46 56.20 N 2.56 W
Dairy City
— Cypress 280 33.50 N 118.01 W
Dairy Creek, East Fork ≃ 224 45.34 N 123.09 W
Dairy Creek, West Fork ≃ 224 45.34 N 123.09 W
Dairyland
— La Palma, Ca., U.S. 280 33.51 N 118.02 W
Dairyland, N.Y., U.S. 210 41.45 N 74.33 W
Dairyland Reservoir ⊜[1] 190 45.30 N 91.00 W
Dairy Valley
— Cerritos 280 33.51 N 118.05 W
Dai-sen ▲ 96 35.22 N 133.33 E
Daisen-oki-kokuritsu-kōen ♦ 96 35.20 N 133.35 E
Daisen-zan ▲ 96 34.07 N 133.56 E
Daisetsu-zan-kokuritsu-kōen ♦ 92a 43.30 N 142.57 E
Daisetta 222 30.06 N 94.38 W
Daishan 100 30.14 N 122.12 E
Daishin 94 37.12 N 140.15 E
Daishōji ≃ 94 36.18 N 136.15 E
Daisizhen 107 29.14 N 105.09 E
Daitō, Nihon 96 34.42 N 135.38 E
Daitō, Nihon 96 35.19 N 132.58 E
Daiwa, Nihon 96 34.32 N 132.57 E
Daiwa, Nihon 96 34.57 N 132.39 E
Daixi 106 30.40 N 120.01 E
Daixian 102 39.08 N 113.01 E
Daixiqiao 106 31.36 N 120.04 E
Daiya ≃ 94 36.45 N 139.46 E
Daiyun Shan ⩘ 100 25.46 N 118.16 E
Dajabón 238 19.33 N 71.42 W
Dājal 120 29.33 N 70.23 E
Da'jānīyah, Jabal ad- ▲ 132 30.34 N 35.43 E
Dajarra 166 21.41 S 139.31 E
Dajian Shan ▲ 102 26.42 N 103.34 E
Dajidian 105 38.50 N 115.26 E
Dajindian 100 34.24 N 112.58 E
Dajing, Zhg. 100 28.24 N 121.07 E
Dajing, Zhg. 100 28.59 N 113.19 E
Dajin Shan II 106 30.41 N 121.26 E
Dajishan 100 24.38 N 114.26 E
Dajitai 104 42.20 N 121.11 E
Dajiuba 120 36.50 N 89.35 E
Daji Yang ʊ 100 30.54 N 122.18 E
Daju 105 39.12 N 115.31 E
Da Juh 102 36.36 N 94.04 E
Dak ⊜ 128 32.48 N 61.14 E
Daka ≃ 150 8.19 N 0.13 W
Dakangpu 104 41.32 N 121.06 E
Dakanzi 104 40.52 N 122.53 E
Dakar 150 14.40 N 17.26 W
Dakar ◻[4] 150 14.45 N 17.25 W
Dākātia ≃[1] 126 22.57 N 90.42 E
Dakeng 100 26.18 N 115.32 E
Dakengkou 100 24.33 N 113.37 E
Daketa ≃ 144 7.16 N 42.13 E
Dak Gle 110 15.11 N 107.48 E
Dakhal, Bi'r ad- ⊤[4] 142 28.40 N 32.24 E
Dakhal, Wādī ad- V 142 28.49 N 32.45 E
Dākhilah, Al-Wāḥāt ad- ⊤[4] 140 25.30 N 29.05 E
Dakhin Shāhbāzpur Island I 126 22.30 N 90.45 E
Dakhla 148 23.43 N 15.57 W
Dakhlet Nouâdhibou ◻[4] 148 20.40 N 16.00 W
Dakingari 150 11.37 N 4.01 E
Dakka
— Dhaka 124 23.43 N 90.25 E
Dākoānk 110 7.02 N 93.43 E
Dakongcheng 105 39.30 N 117.09 E
Dakongwan 104 40.51 N 122.19 E
Dakoro 150 14.31 N 6.46 E
Dakota City, Ia., U.S. 190 42.43 N 94.12 W

FRANÇAIS
Nom | Page | Lat.°′ | Long.°′ W = Ouest

Dakota City, Ne., U.S. 198 42.24 N 96.25 W
Dakou 100 34.27 N 112.44 E
Dakoutun 105 39.35 N 117.14 E
Đakovica 38 42.23 N 20.25 E
Đakovo 38 45.19 N 18.25 E
Dakshin Gangotri ⊍[3] 9 70.05 S 12.00 E
Dakshingram 126 24.03 N 87.48 E
Dakumu 89 48.51 N 124.18 E
Dakunlun 98 36.34 N 117.52 E
Dakwa 154 4.00 N 26.26 E
Dakwah, Tall ad- ▲[2] 132 33.25 N 36.56 E
Dala, Ang. 152 11.03 S 20.17 E
Dala, Ang. 152 8.05 S 15.50 E
Dala, Sol.Is. 175e 8.35 S 160.40 E
Dalaas 58 47.07 N 10.00 E
Dalaba 150 10.42 N 12.15 W
Dalabani 150 10.28 N 9.27 W
Dala Cachibo 152 10.28 S 14.39 E
Dalad Qi 102 40.28 N 110.02 E
Dala-Floda 40 60.31 N 14.47 E
Dalaguete 116 9.46 N 123.32 E
Dalahan (Shiqizhan) 89 52.06 N 125.46 E
Dala-Husby 40 60.21 N 16.00 E
Dala-Järna 26 60.33 N 14.21 E
Dalajchöl 86 47.59 N 90.47 E
Dalaji 89 51.38 N 120.06 E
Dalälven ≃ 40 60.38 N 17.27 E
Dalama 130 37.47 N 28.04 E
Dalaman ≃ 130 36.40 N 28.45 E
Dalāmī 140 11.52 N 30.28 E
Dalan 100 23.19 N 114.47 E
Dalan Dzadgad 102 43.37 N 104.29 E
Dalandžargalan 102 45.55 N 109.05 E
Dalane ◆[1] 26 58.35 N 6.20 E
Dalang 100 22.57 N 113.56 E
Dalantuozi 104 41.28 N 122.47 E
Dalao 150 11.29 N 13.40 W
Dalarna ◻[9] 26 61.01 N 14.04 E
Dalarö 40 59.08 N 18.24 E
Dalat, Malay. 112 2.44 N 111.56 E
Da Lat, Viet 110 11.56 N 108.25 E
Dalayaozi 105 40.49 N 117.41 E
Dālbandin 128 28.53 N 64.25 E
Dalbeattie 44 54.56 N 3.49 W
D'Albertis Dome ▲ 164 5.00 S 142.05 E
Dalbosjön ⊂ 26 58.45 N 12.48 E
Dalby, Austl. 166 27.11 S 151.16 E
Dalby, Sve. 41 55.40 N 13.20 E
Dalby Söderskogs Nationalpark ♦ 41 55.43 N 13.17 E
Dalcahue 254 42.23 S 73.40 W
Dalch ≃ 42 50.52 N 3.47 W
Dale, Nor. 26 61.22 N 5.25 E
Dale, Nor. 26 60.35 N 5.49 E
Dale, Wales, U.K. 42 51.43 N 5.11 W
Dale, In., U.S. 194 38.10 N 86.59 W
Dale, Pa., U.S. 214 40.18 N 78.54 W
Dale, Tx., U.S. 222 29.56 N 97.34 W
Dale ≃ 168a 32.10 S 116.49 E
Dale, Mount ▲ 168a 32.08 S 116.18 E
Dale Bridge 168a 32.05 S 116.49 E
Dalecarlia
— Dalarna ◻[9] 26 61.01 N 14.04 E
Dale City 208 38.38 N 77.18 W
Dale Hollow Lake ⊜[1] 192 36.36 N 85.19 W
Dale Lake ⊜ 204 34.08 N 115.42 W
Dalen 26 59.27 N 8.00 E
Dalengtu 98 41.11 N 113.45 E
Dalešice, údolní nádrž ⊜[1] 61 49.09 N 16.05 E
Daleside 158 26.30 S 28.04 E
Dale South ≃ 168a 32.16 S 116.47 E
Dalesville 206 45.42 N 74.24 W
Dalesville ≃ 206 45.40 N 74.24 W
Daleszyce 30 50.48 N 20.48 E
Dalet 110 19.59 N 93.51 E
Daleville, Al., U.S. 194 31.18 N 85.42 W
Daleville, In., U.S. 218 40.07 N 85.33 W
Daleville, Pa., U.S. 210 41.18 N 75.31 W
Dalfsen 52 52.30 N 6.16 E
Dalgaranga 162 27.46 S 117.02 E
Dalgaranger ▲ 162 27.51 S 117.06 E
Dalgety 171b 36.30 S 148.50 E
Dalgety Bay 46 56.02 N 3.20 W
Dalgety Brook ≃ 162 25.07 S 115.47 E
Dalgety Downs 162 25.17 S 116.15 E
Dalgomai 124 26.06 N 90.47 E
Dalhalvaig 46 58.28 N 3.54 W
Dalhart 196 36.03 N 102.30 W
Dalhausen 52 51.37 N 9.17 E
Dalhousie, N.B., Can. 186 48.04 N 66.23 W
Dalhousie, India 123 32.32 N 75.59 E
Dalhousie, Cape › 180 70.14 N 129.42 W
Dalhousie Island I 126 21.35 N 88.45 E
Dalhousie Lake ⊜ 212 44.58 N 76.35 W
Dalhousie Square ♦ 272b 22.33 N 88.22 E
Dali, Zhg. 102 34.47 N 109.57 E
Dali, Zhg. 102 25.38 N 100.09 E
Dalian (Dairen) 98 38.53 N 121.35 E
Dalian Dao I 100 25.40 N 119.42 E
Daliangdi 98 41.54 N 115.45 E
Daliang Shan ⩘ 102 28.00 N 103.00 E
Dalianhe 104 40.57 N 123.15 E
Daliankeng 105 40.54 N 117.45 E
Dalian Wan ⊂ 98 38.57 N 121.45 E
Dalianwukou 106 30.17 N 119.00 E
Daliao ≃ 104 40.42 N 122.08 E
Dalías 34 36.49 N 2.52 W
Dälidağ ▲ 84 39.55 N 46.02 E
Dalikou 100 26.52 N 118.00 E
Dälimämmadli 84 40.42 N 46.34 E
Dalin, Zhg. 89 43.43 N 122.45 E
Dalin, Zhg. 107 30.17 N 104.07 E
Daling 104 41.27 N 121.15 E
Daling ≃ 98 40.56 N 121.43 E
Dalingbeigou 104 40.42 N 123.08 E
Dalipe Point › 116 10.46 N 121.55 E
Daliushugou 104 40.46 N 122.14 E
Daliutai 104 41.25 N 121.55 E
Daliutun 104 42.14 N 122.46 E
Daliuzhen 105 38.51 N 116.19 E
Daliuzhuang 100 33.04 N 114.03 E
Daliyat et Karmil 132 32.42 N 35.03 E
Daliyya 132 32.35 N 35.04 E
Dalizi 98 41.45 N 126.49 E
Dalj 38 45.29 N 18.59 E
Daljā' 142 27.39 N 30.42 E
Dalkarlsberg 40 59.26 N 14.51 E
Dalkeith 46 55.54 N 3.04 W
Dālkola 124 25.52 N 87.51 E
Dall, Mount ▲ 180 62.35 N 152.18 W
Dāllah, 'Ayn ⊤[4] 140 27.19 N 27.20 E
Dallardsville 222 30.38 N 94.38 W
Dallas, Scot., U.K. 46 57.33 N 3.28 W
Dallas, Al., U.S. 194 33.50 N 86.39 W
Dallas, Ga., U.S. 192 33.55 N 84.50 W
Dallas, N.C., U.S. 192 35.18 N 81.10 W
Dallas, Or., U.S. 202 44.55 N 123.18 W
Dallas, Pa., U.S. 210 41.20 N 75.57 W
Dallas, Tx., U.S. 222 32.46 N 96.47 W
Dallas, Wi., U.S. 190 45.15 N 91.48 W
Dallas ◻[6] 222 32.17 N 96.47 W
Dallas Center 190 41.41 N 93.57 W
Dallas City 190 40.38 N 91.10 W
Dallas-Fort Worth Regional Airport ⊠ 222 32.54 N 97.01 W
Dallas Naval Air Station ■ 222 32.44 N 96.59 W
Dallastown 208 39.53 N 76.38 W
Dallgow 54 52.32 N 13.05 E
Dallıbahçe 130 39.09 N 39.53 E
Dalli Rājhara 122 20.35 N 81.04 E
Dall Island I 182 54.50 N 132.55 W
Dall Lake ⊜ 180 60.18 N 163.35 W
Dalmā I 128 24.30 N 52.20 E
Dalmacija ◻[9] 36 43.00 N 17.00 E
Dalmacio Vélez Sarsfield 252 32.36 S 63.35 W
Dalmally 46 56.24 N 4.58 W
Dalmatia 208 40.39 N 76.54 W
Dalmatia
— Dalmacija ◻[9] 36 43.00 N 17.00 E

PORTUGUÊS
Nome | Página | Lat.°′ | Long.°′ W = Oeste

Dalmatovo 86 56.16 N 62.56 E
Dalmau 124 26.04 N 81.02 E
Dalmellington 44 55.19 N 4.24 W
Dalmeny 184 52.20 N 106.46 W
Dalmine 62 45.39 N 9.36 E
Dalmose 41 55.18 N 11.26 E
Dal'n'aja 89 45.56 N 142.04 E
Dal'n'aja Muja 88 54.21 N 103.37 E
Dalnaspidal 46 56.50 N 4.14 W
Dal'negorsk 89 44.35 N 135.35 E
Dal'neje-Konstantinovo 80 55.49 N 44.06 E
Dal'nerečensk 89 45.55 N 133.43 E
Dal'ne-Rusanovo 82 54.15 N 36.45 E
Dal'nyk 78 46.28 N 30.34 E
Daloa 150 6.53 N 6.27 W
Dalongchang 105 39.50 N 116.06 E
Dalonghua 105 39.18 N 115.18 E
Dalongtian 100 24.14 N 115.44 E
Dalovice 54 50.11 N 12.55 E
Dalqū 140 20.07 N 30.37 E
Dalroy 182 51.07 N 113.39 W
Dalry, Scot., U.K. 44 55.07 N 4.10 W
Dalry, Scot., U.K. 46 55.43 N 4.44 W
Dalrymple 44 55.23 N 4.35 W
Dalrymple, Mount ▲ 166 21.02 S 148.38 E
Dalrymple Creek ≃ 171a 27.59 S 151.46 E
Dalrymple Lake ⊜ 212 44.38 N 79.07 W
Dalsbruk (Taalintehdas) 26 60.02 N 22.31 E
Dalsingpara 124 26.47 N 89.22 E
Dalsing Sarai 124 25.40 N 85.50 E
Dalsjöfors 26 57.43 N 13.05 E
Dalsland ◻[9] 26 58.30 N 12.50 E
Dals-Långed 26 58.55 N 12.18 E
Dal'stroja 180 68.19 N 177.39 W
Dāltenganj 124 24.02 N 84.04 E
Dalton, S. Afr. 158 29.20 S 30.40 E
Dalton, Eng., U.K. 262 53.34 N 2.46 W
Dalton, Ga., U.S. 192 34.47 N 84.58 W
Dalton, Ma., U.S. 207 42.28 N 73.10 W
Dalton, Ne., U.S. 198 41.24 N 102.58 W
Dalton, N.Y., U.S. 210 42.32 N 77.57 W
Dalton, Oh., U.S. 214 40.47 N 81.41 W
Dalton, Pa., U.S. 210 41.32 N 75.44 W
Dalton City 219 39.43 N 88.48 W
Dalton Gardens 202 47.43 N 116.46 W
Dalton-in-Furness 44 54.09 N 3.11 W
Dalu 104 41.27 N 123.19 E
Dalubeikou 105 38.59 N 117.12 E
Daludalu 114 1.05 N 100.15 E
Dalu Dao I 98 39.44 N 123.45 E
Daluis, Gorges de V 62 44.04 N 6.49 E
Dalum, Dan. 41 55.22 N 10.22 E
Dalum, Dtsch. 52 52.35 N 7.14 E
Daluojiazhuang 106 32.09 N 120.08 E
Daluotaozi 104 41.17 N 122.52 E
Daluoxi 100 25.14 N 118.36 E
Daluping 100 26.11 N 114.30 E
Dalupiri Island I, Pil. 116 19.05 N 121.14 E
Dalupiri Island I, Pil. 116 12.25 N 124.16 E
Daluxi 100 24.28 N 117.01 E
Dalview 273d 26.15 S 28.21 E
Dalvík 24a 65.59 N 18.32 W
Dalwallinu 162 30.17 S 116.40 E
Dalwhinnie 46 56.56 N 4.14 W
Dalworthington Gardens 222 32.42 N 97.10 W
Daly ≃ 164 13.20 S 130.19 E
Daly Bay ⊂ 176 64.00 N 89.40 W
Daly City 226 37.43 N 122.31 W
Daly Lake ⊜ 184 56.33 N 105.40 W
Daly Point › 212 44.53 N 80.14 W
Daly River 164 13.45 S 130.50 E
Daly River Aboriginal Reserve ◆[4] 164 14.20 S 130.00 E
Daly Waters 164 16.15 S 133.22 E
Dam ≃ 120 33.56 N 92.41 E
Dāmā, Sūrīy. 132 32.57 N 36.25 E
Dama, Zhg. 100 32.03 N 118.02 E
Damagum 146 11.41 N 11.20 E
Damān 122 20.25 N 72.51 E
Damān ◻[8] 122 20.10 N 73.00 E
Damanhār Shubra 273c 30.07 N 31.14 E
Damanhūr 142 31.02 N 30.28 E
Damanling 105 40.36 N 115.08 E
Damaopu 104 41.16 N 121.07 E
Damar 130 41.15 N 41.34 E
Damar, Pulau I, Indon. 164 1.00 S 128.24 E
Damar, Pulau I, Indon. 164 7.09 S 128.40 E
Damara 152 4.58 N 18.42 E
Damaraland ◻[5] 156 21.00 S 14.20 E
Damaraland ◻[9] 156 22.34 S 17.06 E
Damāṣ, Miṣr 142 30.48 N 31.20 E
Damas
— Dimashq, Sūrīy. 132 33.30 N 36.18 E
Damasco
— Dimashq 132 33.30 N 36.18 E
Damascus
— Dimashq, Sūrīy. 132 33.30 N 36.18 E
Damascus, Ar., U.S. 194 35.22 N 92.24 W
Damascus, Ga., U.S. 192 34.33 N 84.56 W
Damascus, Md., U.S. 208 39.17 N 77.12 W
Damascus, Oh., U.S. 214 40.54 N 80.58 W
Damascus, Pa., U.S. 210 41.42 N 75.04 W
Damascus, Va., U.S. 192 36.38 N 81.47 W
Damascus International Airport ⊠ 132 33.29 N 36.13 E
Damaskus
— Dimashq 132 33.30 N 36.18 E
Damāṭ 142 30.57 N 30.57 E
Damaturu 146 11.45 N 11.58 E
Damāvand 128 35.43 N 52.04 E
Damāvand, Qolleh-ye ▲ 128 35.56 N 52.08 E
Damba 152 6.41 S 15.08 E
Dambach-la-Ville 58 48.20 N 7.26 E
Dambarta 150 12.26 N 8.31 E
Dambeck 54 52.48 N 11.09 E
Dâmbovița ◻[6] 38 45.00 N 25.30 E
Dâmbovița ≃ 38 44.14 N 26.27 E
Dambuki 89 54.21 N 127.38 E
Dam Doi 110 8.50 N 105.15 E
Damelevières 58 48.33 N 6.23 E
Damen Dao I 100 27.58 N 121.06 E
Damengjialazi 104 41.04 N 120.53 E
Damengzhuang 105 39.32 N 116.59 E
Damergou ◆[1] 150 15.00 N 8.55 E
Damerham 42 50.57 N 1.52 W
Dämeritzsee ⊜ 264a 52.25 N 13.45 E
Damery 50 49.04 N 3.53 E
Dames Quarter 208 38.11 N 75.53 W
Dam Gamad 140 13.17 N 27.28 E
Dāmghān 128 36.09 N 54.22 E
Damianópolis 255 14.33 S 46.10 W
Damianzhen 107 30.36 N 104.10 E
Damiao, Zhg. 98 42.26 N 118.22 E
Damiao, Zhg. 98 34.20 N 117.23 E
Damiao, Zhg. 102 37.18 N 104.39 E
Damiao, Zhg. 104 42.33 N 122.18 E
Damiaochang 107 29.39 N 106.05 E
Damiaogou 104 41.06 N 123.52 E
Damiaojiang 106 31.00 N 120.28 E
Damiaoshang 105 39.56 N 115.12 E
Dămienești 38 46.44 N 26.59 E
Damietta
— Dumyāṭ 142 31.25 N 31.48 E
Damietta Branch
— Dumyāṭ, Far' ≃ 142 31.32 N 31.51 E
Damietta Mouth
— Dumyāṭ, Maṣabb ≃[1] 142 31.32 N 31.51 E
Damin 100 28.56 N 120.29 E
Daming 98 36.19 N 115.06 E
Damingzhen 104 42.34 N 123.36 E
Damintun 104 41.52 N 122.56 E
Dāmiyā 132 32.06 N 35.33 E
Damlacık 130 37.56 N 38.39 E
Damm 263 51.40 N 6.48 E
Dammai Island I 116 5.47 N 120.25 E

Dammarie 50 48.21 N 1.30 E
Dammarie-lès-Lys 50 48.31 N 2.39 E
Dammartin-en-Goële 50 49.03 N 2.41 E
Dammartin-en-Serve 50 48.54 N 1.37 E
Dammastock ▲ 58 46.39 N 8.25 E
Damme, Bel. 50 51.15 N 3.17 E
Damme, Dtsch. 54 53.17 N 14.01 E
Dammer Berge ⩘[2] 52 52.32 N 8.10 E
Dāmodar ≃ 124 22.17 N 88.05 E
Dāmodar Main Canal ≋ 126 23.01 N 87.53 E
Damoh, India 118 23.50 N 79.27 E
Damoh, India 124 23.50 N 79.27 E
Damon 222 29.17 N 95.45 W
Damongo 150 9.05 N 1.49 W
Damotapāda 272c 19.03 N 73.04 E
Damous 34 36.33 N 1.42 E
Damozhuang 105 39.53 N 115.40 E
Dampar, Tasek ⊜ 114 3.02 N 102.43 E
Dampelas
— Sabang 112 0.11 N 119.51 E
Dampier 162 20.39 S 116.45 E
Dampier, Cape › 164 6.02 S 151.02 E
Dampier, Selat ʊ 164 0.40 S 130.40 E
Dampier Archipelago II 162 20.35 S 116.35 E
Dampier Land ›[1] 162 17.30 S 122.55 E
Dampierre, Fr. 50 48.42 N 1.59 E
Dampierre, Fr. 58 47.09 N 5.45 E
Dampierre, Château de ⊥ 261 48.42 N 1.59 E
Dampierre-en-Burly 50 47.46 N 2.31 E
Dampierre-sur-Linotte 58 47.31 N 6.14 E
Dampierre-sur-Salon 58 47.33 N 5.41 E
Dampier Strait ʊ 164 5.36 S 148.12 E
Dampit 115a 8.13 S 112.45 E
Dampmart 261 48.53 N 2.44 E
Damprichard 58 47.15 N 6.53 E
Dâmrei, Chuŏr Phnum ⩘ 110 11.00 N 104.05 E
Damují ≃ 240p 22.11 N 80.33 W
Damüls 58 47.17 N 9.53 E
Dāmurhuda 126 23.36 N 88.47 E
Damutougou 98 42.28 N 118.56 E
Damville 50 48.52 N 1.04 E
Damvillers 56 49.20 N 5.24 E
Damxung 120 30.31 N 91.08 E
Dan 132 33.14 N 35.39 E
Dan ≃, U.S. 192 36.42 N 78.45 W
Dan ≃, Zhg. 102 33.02 N 111.20 E
Dana, Cam. 146 10.14 N 15.18 E
Dana, In., U.S. 194 39.48 N 87.29 W
Dana, Mount ▲ 226 37.54 N 119.13 W
Dana, Pulau I 112 10.50 S 121.16 E
Danahu 102 42.28 N 93.32 E
Danai 112 0.29 N 103.26 E
Danajon Bank ✣[4] 116 10.16 N 124.17 E
Danakil
— Denakil ◆[1] 144 13.00 N 41.00 E
Danakil National Park ♦ 144 10.50 N 40.45 E
Danané 150 7.16 N 8.09 W
Da Nang 110 16.04 N 108.13 E
Danan'gou 105 40.32 N 117.49 E
Danao, Pil. 116 10.32 N 124.02 E
Danao, Pil. 116 12.29 N 122.39 E
Dana Point 228 33.29 N 117.44 W
Dana Point › 228 33.28 N 117.43 W
Dānāpur 124 25.38 N 85.03 E
Danba 102 31.00 N 101.50 E
Danboro 208 40.21 N 75.08 W
Danbury, Eng., U.K. 42 51.44 N 0.33 E
Danbury, Ct., U.S. 207 41.23 N 73.27 W
Danbury, Ia., U.S. 198 42.14 N 95.43 W
Danbury, Ne., U.S. 198 40.02 N 100.24 W
Danbury, N.C., U.S. 192 36.24 N 80.12 W
Danbury, Tx., U.S. 222 29.14 N 95.21 W
Danby Lake ⊜ 204 34.14 N 115.07 W
Dancheng 100 33.39 N 115.11 E
Danchengji 100 33.47 N 116.17 E
Dancug 144 10.58 N 49.04 E
Dand 120 31.37 N 65.41 E
Dandaragan 162 30.40 S 115.42 E
Dande ≃ 152 8.28 S 13.21 E
Dandeli 122 15.15 N 74.37 E
Dandenong 169 37.59 S 145.12 E
Dandenong, Mount ▲ 274b 37.50 S 145.21 E
Dandenong Creek ≃ 274b 38.01 S 145.05 E
Dandenong Ranges National Park ♦ 169 37.53 S 145.20 E
Danderyd 40 59.25 N 18.01 E
Dandīl 142 29.10 N 31.02 E
Dandong 98 40.08 N 124.20 E
Dandot 123 32.39 N 72.58 E
Dandridge 192 36.00 N 83.24 W
Dan Dume 150 11.27 N 7.10 E
Dane ◻[6] 216 43.04 N 89.15 W
Dane ≃ 44 53.15 N 2.31 W
Dane County Regional Airport-Truax Field ⊠ 216 43.08 N 89.20 W
Dänemark
— Denmark ◻[1] 26 56.00 N 10.00 E
Dänemark-Strasse
— Denmark Strait ʊ 10 67.00 N 25.00 W
Danevang 222 29.03 N 96.13 W
Danewitz 264a 52.44 N 13.40 E
Danfeng 102 33.40 N 110.17 E
Danfengzhen 102 24.50 N 103.56 E
Danforth, Il., U.S. 216 40.49 N 87.59 W
Danforth, Me., U.S. 188 45.39 N 67.52 W
Danforth Hills ⩘ 200 40.15 N 108.00 W
Dang ≃ 102 40.30 N 94.42 E
Dānga, Bngl. 126 23.54 N 90.36 E
Dānga, India 272b 22.47 N 88.28 E
Danga ≃ 271c 1.27 N 103.43 E
Dangādiha 126 21.30 N 86.19 E
Dangan Liedao II 100 22.00 N 114.14 E
Dangara, Taj. 85 38.06 N 69.22 E
Dangara, Uzb. 85 40.35 N 70.54 E
Dangba 98 40.46 N 118.32 E
Dangchang 102 34.03 N 104.23 E
Dangcheng 98 38.46 N 114.34 E
Dange, Ang. 152 8.09 S 14.46 E
Dange, Ang. 152 7.56 S 15.02 E
Dange, Nig. 150 12.52 N 5.21 E
Dange-Iá-Menha 152 9.32 S 14.39 E
Danger, Point › 171a 28.10 S 153.33 E
Danger Point › 158 34.40 S 19.17 E
Danggali Conservation Park ♦ 166 33.20 S 140.40 E
Danghe Nanshan ⩘ 102 38.53 N 96.11 E
Danghui 105 40.03 N 117.04 E
Dangila 144 11.16 N 36.50 E
Dangkou 106 31.32 N 120.34 E
Dango 140 10.00 N 24.45 E
Dan Gora 150 11.30 N 8.09 E
Dāngori 120 27.40 N 95.32 E
Dangriga 232 16.58 N 88.13 W
Dangshan 98 34.26 N 116.21 E
Dangtu 100 31.34 N 118.30 E
Dan Gulbi 150 11.38 N 6.16 E
Dangyang 102 30.50 N 111.38 E
Dangyu 105 40.00 N 118.01 E
Dani 150 13.43 N 0.10 W
Dania 220 26.03 N 80.08 W
Daniel 200 42.51 N 110.04 W
Daniel, Mount ▲ 224 47.34 N 121.11 W
Daniel Boone Home ⊥ 219 38.39 N 90.52 W
Daniel Boone Homestead State Historic Site ⊥ 208 40.21 N 75.49 W
Daniel-Johnson, Barrage ◆[6] 186 50.39 N 68.44 W
Daniels 284b 39.26 N 77.03 W
Daniel's Harbour 186 50.14 N 57.35 W
Danielskuil 158 28.11 S 23.33 E
Danielson 207 41.48 N 71.53 W
Daniels Pass)(200 40.18 N 111.15 W
Daniels Run ≃ 284c 38.51 N 77.17 W

Danielsville, Ga., U.S. 192 34.07 N 83.13 W
Danielsville, Pa., U.S. 208 40.48 N 75.32 W
Danilov 80 58.12 N 40.12 E
Danilovka, Kaz. 86 52.23 N 70.39 E
Danilovka, Ross. 80 52.33 N 45.23 E
Danilovka, Ross. 80 50.21 N 44.06 E
Danilovo 82 55.40 N 38.46 E
Danilovskaja vozvyšennost' ⩘[1] 80 58.12 N 40.16 E
Danilovskoje 82 56.48 N 35.45 E
Daning, Zhg. 102 24.39 N 111.51 E
Daning, Zhg. 102 36.33 N 110.38 E
Daningbashi 85 38.45 N 75.04 E
Dänisch Nienhof 54 54.28 N 10.07 E
Daniupucun 104 41.23 N 122.37 E
Dänizkänarı 84 40.13 N 49.33 E
Danja 150 11.21 N 7.31 E
Danjiangkou Shuiku ⊜[1] 102 32.37 N 111.30 E
Danjo-guntō II 92 32.02 N 128.23 E
Danjoutin 58 47.37 N 6.52 E
Dank 128 23.33 N 56.17 E
Dankama 150 13.20 N 7.44 E
Dankersen 52 52.17 N 8.58 E
Danki 82 54.55 N 37.34 E
Dankov 76 53.15 N 39.08 E
Dankova, Pik ▲ 85 41.05 N 77.38 E
Danleng, Zhg. 102 29.58 N 103.31 E
Danleng, Zhg. 102 29.18 N 103.10 E
Danleng, Zhg. 107 30.01 N 103.30 E
Danlí 236 14.00 N 86.35 W
Danmark
— Denmark ◻[1] 26 56.00 N 10.00 E
Dannebrog 198 41.07 N 98.32 W
Dannemare 41 54.45 N 11.12 E
Dannemarie 58 47.38 N 7.08 E
Dannemora, Sve. 40 60.11 N 17.49 E
Dannemora, N.Y., U.S. 188 44.43 N 73.43 W
Dannenberg 54 53.06 N 11.05 E
Dannenreich 264a 52.19 N 13.45 E
Dannenwalde 54 53.04 N 13.11 E
Dannevirke 172 40.12 S 176.07 E
Dannewerk 41 54.29 N 9.31 E
Dannhauser 158 28.04 S 30.04 E
Dano 150 11.09 N 3.04 W
Danompari 112 0.09 N 115.02 E
Dañoso, Cabo › 254 48.50 S 67.13 W
Dan Ryan Woods ♦ 278 41.45 N 87.39 W
Dan Sai 110 17.17 N 101.09 E
Danshan 107 30.06 N 104.54 E
Danshui 100 22.49 N 114.27 E
Dansville, Mi., U.S. 216 42.34 N 84.18 W
Dansville, N.Y., U.S. 210 42.33 N 77.41 W
Dāntan 126 21.57 N 87.16 E
Dante 192 36.58 N 82.17 W
Dantewāra 122 18.54 N 81.21 E
Dantuzhen 106 32.12 N 119.31 E
Danube ≃ 22 45.20 N 29.40 E
Danube, Mouths of the ≃[1] 38 45.10 N 29.50 E
Danubio
— Danube ≃ 22 45.20 N 29.40 E
Danubyu 110 17.15 N 95.35 E
Danvers, Il., U.S. 190 40.31 N 89.10 W
Danvers, Ma., U.S. 207 42.34 N 70.55 W
Danvers ≃ 283 42.32 N 70.53 W
Danville, P.Q., Can. 206 45.47 N 72.01 W
Danville, Ar., U.S. 194 35.03 N 93.23 W
Danville, Ca., U.S. 226 37.49 N 121.59 W
Danville, Ga., U.S. 192 32.36 N 83.14 W
Danville, Il., U.S. 194 40.07 N 87.37 W
Danville, In., U.S. 218 39.45 N 86.31 W
Danville, Ky., U.S. 194 37.42 N 84.46 W
Danville, Mo., U.S. 219 38.54 N 91.32 W
Danville, Oh., U.S. 214 40.26 N 82.15 W
Danville, Pa., U.S. 210 40.57 N 76.36 W
Danville, Vt., U.S. 188 44.25 N 72.07 W
Danville, Va., U.S. 192 36.35 N 79.23 W
Danville, Wa., U.S. 182 48.59 N 118.30 W
Danxian (Nada) 110 19.35 N 109.17 E
Danyang, Zhg. 100 26.22 N 119.30 E
Danyang, Zhg. 106 32.00 N 119.35 E
Danylivka 83 49.08 N 39.38 E
Danzig
— Gdańsk 30 54.23 N 18.40 E
Dao 116 10.31 N 121.57 E
Dâo ≃, Port. 34 40.20 N 8.11 W
Dao ≃, Zhg. 100 30.44 N 114.39 E
Daocheng 102 29.06 N 100.38 E
Daodemiao 89 43.41 N 120.19 E
Daodi 105 39.32 N 118.11 E
Daoguanhe 100 30.54 N 114.57 E
Daohu 100 29.42 N 117.29 E
Daolazui 105 40.06 N 115.06 E
Daoliban 104 41.52 N 121.37 E
Daolin 100 27.59 N 112.42 E
Daolinggang 98 34.02 N 114.34 E
Daoliupu 107 30.12 N 105.09 E
Daomaguan 98 39.07 N 114.38 E
Daosa 124 26.53 N 76.20 E
Daoshiwu 106 30.18 N 118.57 E
Daoshuqiao 106 31.51 N 119.41 E
Daotiandi 89 48.53 N 130.03 E
Dao Timmi 146 20.32 N 13.33 E
Daotou 98 37.14 N 120.20 E
Daoukro 150 7.03 N 3.58 W
Daoulas 32 48.22 N 4.15 W
Daoura, Oued V 148 28.15 N 3.30 W
Daoxian 102 25.35 N 111.27 E
Daozhen 102 28.42 N 107.56 E
Daozi 89 45.00 N 123.43 E
Dapa 116 9.46 N 126.03 E
Dapango 150 10.52 N 0.12 E
Dapanzhuang 98 37.20 N 115.28 E
Dapaozi 89 45.27 N 122.07 E
Dapchi 146 12.28 N 11.32 E
Dapdap 116 14.14 N 122.15 E
Dapeng 100 22.34 N 114.29 E
Daphne 194 30.36 N 87.54 W
Dapiak, Mount ▲ 116 8.15 N 123.28 E
Daping, Zhg. 100 23.11 N 115.49 E
Daping, Zhg. 100 24.24 N 115.58 E
Dapingshan 102 25.30 N 109.39 E
Dapishi 100 26.30 N 112.54 E
Dapitan 116 8.39 N 123.25 E
Dapitan ≃ 116 8.38 N 123.25 E
Dapitan Bay ⊂ 116 8.40 N 123.23 E
Dapto 170 34.30 S 150.47 E
Dapu, Zhg. 98 40.34 N 124.12 E
Dapu, Zhg. 100 23.16 N 113.32 E
Dapu, Zhg. 106 31.19 N 119.56 E
Dapujie 100 27.01 N 112.46 E
Da Qaidam 102 37.53 N 95.07 E
Da Qaidam Hu ⊜ 102 37.50 N 95.00 E
Daqian 106 30.55 N 120.11 E
Daqiangmen 106 31.29 N 120.27 E
Daqiangzi 104 42.21 N 120.29 E
Daqiao, Zhg. 100 29.39 N 121.26 E
Daqiao, Zhg. 100 26.38 N 118.54 E
Daqiao, Zhg. 100 28.11 N 114.16 E
Daqiao, Zhg. 100 32.21 N 119.41 E
Daqiao, Zhg. 100 24.56 N 113.09 E
Daqiao, Zhg. 106 30.59 N 121.14 E
Daqiao, Zhg. 107 28.52 N 105.40 E
Daqiaojie 106 30.46 N 119.14 E
Daqiaokou 100 27.06 N 113.38 E
Daqiaotou 106 30.47 N 120.52 E
Daqiaozhai 102 25.21 N 106.15 E
Daqing 98 39.13 N 118.51 E
Daqing ≃ 105 39.04 N 116.55 E
Daqinggou, Zhg. 98 41.16 N 114.10 E
Daqinggou, Zhg. 98 41.12 N 125.07 E
Daqing Shan ▲, Zhg. 89 45.35 N 127.51 E
Daqing Shan ▲, Zhg. 104 42.03 N 123.45 E
Daqing Shan ▲, Zhg. 104 41.47 N 121.15 E
Daqiu 100 25.24 N 119.39 E
Daqqāq 140 12.56 N 26.58 E
Daquan 102 41.21 N 95.17 E
Daquanshan 98 40.14 N 113.47 E
Daquantou 105 39.31 N 114.46 E
Daquanyan 104 42.37 N 123.32 E
Dāqūf 142 28.24 N 30.38 E

Daqu Shan I 100 30.27 N 122.20 E
Dara, Sén. 150 15.21 N 15.29 W
Dar'ā, Sūrīy. 132 32.37 N 36.06 E
Dar'ā ◻[8] 132 33.00 N 36.10 E
Dārāb 128 28.45 N 54.34 E
Darāban 120 31.44 N 70.20 E
Darabani 38 48.11 N 26.35 E
Darāfisah 140 13.23 N 31.59 E
Daraga 116 11.54 N 123.52 E
Daragodleh 144 10.10 N 44.51 E
Daraina 157b 13.12 S 49.40 E
Darājīl 142 30.39 N 30.52 E
Daram Island I 116 11.38 N 124.47 E
Dārān 128 32.59 N 50.24 E
Daraoli ◆[8] 272c 19.11 N 72.48 E
Darap 112 1.13 S 112.03 E
Dār as-Salām 273c 29.59 N 31.13 E
Darasun 88 51.40 N 114.00 E
Daraut-Kurgan 85 39.33 N 72.13 E
Darave 272c 19.02 N 73.01 E
Darāw 140 24.25 N 32.56 E
Darawah 142 30.13 N 31.06 E
Dārayyā 132 33.27 N 36.15 E
Darazo 146 11.00 N 10.24 E
Darb Al-Ḥājj 142 30.10 N 31.33 E
Darb al-Ḥajj, Jabal ▲ 132 30.05 N 35.26 E
Darband 123 34.20 N 72.52 E
Darbāsīyah 130 37.04 N 40.39 E
Darbaza 85 41.35 N 69.02 E
Darbėnai 76 56.01 N 21.15 E
Dar-Beni-Kriche-Bahri 34 35.30 N 5.20 W
Darbhanga 124 26.10 N 85.54 E
Darbod (Taikang) 89 46.52 N 124.27 E
D'Arbonne, Bayou ≃ 194 32.34 N 92.09 W
Darburruk 144 9.44 N 44.31 E
Darby, Mt., U.S. 202 46.01 N 114.10 W
Darby, Pa., U.S. 208 39.55 N 75.15 W
Darby, Cape › 180 64.20 N 162.22 W
Darby Creek ≃ 285 39.52 N 75.18 W
Darbydale 218 39.51 N 83.11 W
Darčeli 84 42.27 N 41.42 E
Darchan 88 49.29 N 105.55 E
D'Archiac, Mount ▲ 172 43.28 S 170.35 E
D'Arcy 182 50.33 N 122.29 W
D'Arcy Island I 224 48.34 N 123.17 W
Darda 38 45.37 N 18.41 E
Dardadine 168a 33.14 S 116.50 E
Dardanelle, Ar., U.S. 194 35.13 N 93.09 W
Dardanelle, Ca., U.S. 226 38.20 N 119.50 W
Dardanelle Lake ⊜[1] 194 35.25 N 93.20 W
Dardanelles
— Çanakkale Boğazı ʊ 130 40.15 N 26.25 E
Dardanup 168a 33.24 S 115.45 E
Dardara 34 35.08 N 5.15 W
Dardenelles Cone ▲ 226 38.25 N 119.53 W
Dardenne Creek ≃ 219 38.52 N 90.32 W
Dardesheim 54 51.59 N 10.49 E
Dardistān ◻[9] 123 35.30 N 74.00 E
Dare 208 37.10 N 76.26 W
Darebin Creek ≃ 274b 37.47 S 145.02 E
Dareda 154 4.13 S 35.33 E
Dar-el-Beida
— Casablanca 148 33.39 N 7.35 W
Darende 130 38.34 N 37.30 E
Darent ≃ 42 51.28 N 0.13 E
Daresbury 262 53.21 N 2.38 W
Dar es Salaam 154 6.48 S 39.17 E
Dar es Salaam ◻[4] 154 6.30 S 39.25 E
Daressalam
— Dar es Salaam 154 6.48 S 39.17 E
Darfeld 52 52.01 N 7.16 E
Darfo 64 45.53 N 10.11 E
Dārfūr ash-Shamālīyah ◻[4] 140 16.00 N 25.25 E
Dargai 123 34.30 N 71.54 E
Dargan-Ata 72 40.29 N 62.10 E
Dargaville 172 35.56 S 173.53 E
Dargeçit 130 37.33 N 41.44 E
Dargol 150 13.55 N 1.15 E
Dargol ≃ 150 13.53 N 1.33 E
Dargun 54 53.54 N 12.51 E
Darhan Muminggan Lianheqi 102 41.50 N 110.27 E
Dari 140 5.48 N 30.21 E
Dāriāpur 126 23.36 N 89.27 E
Darıca 130 40.45 N 29.23 E
Darie Hills ⩘ 144 8.21 N 47.16 E
Darién, Col. 246 3.56 N 76.31 W
Darien, Ct., U.S. 207 41.04 N 73.28 W
Darien, Ga., U.S. 192 31.22 N 81.26 W
Darien, Il., U.S. 278 41.45 N 87.58 W
Darien, N.Y., U.S. 210 42.54 N 78.21 W
Darien, Wi., U.S. 216 42.36 N 88.42 W
Darien, Parque Nacional ♦ 246 7.40 N 77.40 W
Darién, Serranía del ⩘ 246 8.20 N 77.22 W
Darien Center 210 42.54 N 78.23 W
Darien Lakes State Park ♦ 210 42.55 N 78.25 W
Dariense, Cordillera ⩘ 236 12.55 N 85.30 W
Dariganga 102 45.18 N 113.52 E
Darigayos Point › 116 16.50 N 120.20 E
Dariv 88 46.57 N 93.38 E
Darjevka 83 47.42 N 39.41 E
Dārjiling 124 27.02 N 88.16 E
Darjinskij 86 49.04 N 72.56 E
Darjinskoje 80 51.20 N 51.44 E
Darkan 168a 33.20 S 116.44 E
Darke ◻[6] 218 40.06 N 84.38 W
Darke Peak 166 33.28 S 136.12 E
Darkhāna 123 30.39 N 72.11 E
Dar Khazīneh 128 31.54 N 48.59 E
Dark Head › 241h 13.17 N 61.16 W
Darkin ≃ 168a 32.00 S 116.14 E
Darkūsh 130 35.59 N 36.23 E
Darlag 102 33.48 N 99.52 E
Darley Woods 285 39.49 N 75.28 W
Darling, S. Afr. 158 33.23 S 18.23 E
Darling, Ms., U.S. 194 34.21 N 90.16 W
Darling ≃ 166 34.07 S 141.55 E
Darling, Lake ⊜[1] 198 48.35 N 101.40 W
Darling Downs ◆[1] 166 27.30 S 150.30 E
Darlingford 184 49.12 N 98.22 W
Darling Range ⩘ 162 31.25 S 116.00 E
Darlington, Austl. 169 38.00 S 143.03 E
Darlington, Eng., U.K. 44 54.31 N 1.34 W
Darlington, Md., U.S. 208 39.38 N 76.12 W
Darlington, Pa., U.S. 214 40.49 N 80.26 W
Darlington, Pa., U.S. 285 39.54 N 75.28 W
Darlington, S.C., U.S. 192 34.17 N 79.52 W
Darlington, Wi., U.S. 190 42.40 N 90.07 W
Darlington Brook ≃ 276 41.05 N 74.11 W
Darlington Corners 285 39.55 N 75.34 W
Darlington Range ⩘ 171a 27.50 S 153.15 E
Darlot, Lake ⊜ 162 27.48 S 121.35 E
Darłowo 30 54.26 N 16.23 E
Darmagī, Kūh-e ▲ 128 26.35 N 58.54 E
Darmstadt 56 49.53 N 8.40 E
Darmstadt ◻[5] 56 49.45 N 8.40 E
Darnah 146 32.46 N 22.39 E
Darnall 158 29.23 S 31.18 E
Darnétal 50 49.27 N 1.09 E
Darney 58 48.05 N 6.03 E
Darnick 166 32.51 S 143.37 E
Darnley, Cape › 9 67.43 S 69.30 E
Darnley Bay ⊂ 176 69.35 N 123.30 W
Daroca 34 41.07 N 1.25 W
Darodih 126 23.14 N 86.27 E
Daror 144 8.14 N 44.42 E
Dar-Ould-Zidouh 148 32.22 N 6.49 W
Darou Mousti 150 15.03 N 16.03 W
Darovoje 82 54.34 N 38.22 E
Darr ≃ 166 23.39 S 143.50 E
Darra 171a 27.34 S 152.58 E
Darragh 279b 40.16 N 79.41 W
Darrah, Mount ▲ 182 49.28 N 114.35 W
Darregueira 252 37.42 S 63.10 W
Darreh Gaz 128 37.27 N 59.07 E
Darrington 224 48.15 N 121.36 W
Darrouzett 196 36.27 N 100.20 W
Darryl Gardens 284b 39.25 N 76.25 W
Dārsana 126 23.32 N 88.52 E

Symbol	English	Deutsch	Español	Français	Português
≃	River	Fluß	Río	Rivière	Rio
≋	Canal	Kanal	Canal	Canal	Canal
⌊	Waterfall, Rapids	Wasserfall, Stromschnellen	Cascada, Rápidos	Chute d'eau, Rapides	Cascata, Rápidos
ʊ	Strait	Meeresstraße	Estrecho	Détroit	Estreito
⊂	Bay, Gulf	Bucht, Golf	Bahía, Golfo	Baie, Golfe	Baía, Golfo
⊜	Lake, Lakes	See, Seen	Lago, Lagos	Lac, Lacs	Lago, Lagos
⩩	Swamp	Sumpf	Pantano	Marais	Pântano
⍽	Ice Features, Glacier	Eis- und Gletscherformen	Accidentes Glaciales	Formes glaciaires	Acidentes glaciares
⊤	Other Hydrographic Features	Andere Hydrographische Objekte	Otros Elementos Hidrográficos	Autres données hydrographiques	Outros acidentes hidrográficos

Symbol	English	Deutsch	Español	Français	Português
✣	Submarine Features	Untermeerische Objekte	Accidentes Submarinos	Formes de relief sous-marin	Acidentes submarinos
◻	Political Unit	Politische Einheit	Unidad Política	Entité politique	Unidade política
⊍	Cultural Institution	Kulturelle Institution	Institución Cultural	Institution culturelle	Instituição cultural
⊥	Historical Site	Historische Stätte	Sitio Histórico	Site historique	Sitio histórico
♦	Recreational Site	Erholungs- und Ferienort	Sitio de Recreo	Centre de loisirs	Area de Lazer
⊠	Airport	Flughafen	Aeropuerto	Aéroport	Aeroporto
■	Military Installation	Militäranlage	Instalación Militar	Installation militaire	Instalação militar
◆	Miscellaneous	Verschiedenes	Misceláneo	Divers	Diversos

Darscheid 56 50.12 N 6.53 E
Darss ›¹ 54 54.25 N 12.31 E
Darsser Ort › 54 54.29 N 12.31 E
Dart ≐ 42 50.20 N 3.33 W
Dart, Cape › 9 73.06 S 126.20 W
Dār Ta'izzah 130 36.17 N 36.51 E
Dartford 42 51.27 N 0.14 E
Dartford □⁸ 260 51.26 N 0.15 E
Dartford Tunnel ◆⁵ 260 51.28 N 0.16 E
Dartmoor 166 37.55 S 141.17 E
Dartmoor ◆³ 42 50.35 N 3.55 W
Dartmoor National Park ♦ 42 50.37 N 3.52 W
Dartmouth, N.S., Can. 186 44.40 N 63.34 W
Dartmouth, Eng., U.K. 42 50.21 N 3.35 W
Dartmouth ≐ 186 48.53 N 64.34 W
Dartmouth, Lake ⊜ 166 26.04 S 145.18 E
Dartmouth Woods 285 39.50 N 75.31 W
Darton 44 53.36 N 1.32 W
Daru, Pap. N. Gui. 164 9.04 S 143.21 E
Daru, S.L. 150 7.59 N 10.50 W
Daruvar 36 45.36 N 17.13 E
Darvaza 128 40.11 N 58.24 E
Darvazskij chrebet ⋏ 85 38.30 N 71.15 E
Darvel 46 55.37 N 4.18 W
Darvinskij zapovednik ◆⁴ 76 58.50 N 37.40 E
Darwāzahgêy 120 31.48 N 67.44 E
Darwen 44 53.42 N 2.28 W
Darwen ≐ 262 53.45 N 2.41 W
Darwendale 154 17.43 S 30.33 E
Dārwha 122 20.19 N 77.46 E
Darwin, Arg. 254 39.12 S 65.46 W
Darwin, Austl. 164 12.28 S 130.50 E
Darwin, Bahía c 254 45.27 S 74.40 W
Darwin, Cordillera ⋏ 254 54.40 S 70.00 W
Darwin, Isla I 246a 1.39 N 92.00 W
Darwin, Volcán ∧¹ 246a 0.10 S 91.18 W
Darwin River 164 12.49 S 130.58 E
Daryābād 124 26.53 N 81.33 E
Darya Khān 123 31.48 N 71.06 E
Daryāpur 120 20.56 N 77.20 E
Darzāb 120 35.58 N 65.22 E
Darzo 64 45.51 N 10.33 E
Dār Zubi 140 13.07 N 23.40 E
Dās 123 35.05 N 75.05 E
Dās I 128 25.09 N 52.53 E
Dasanjiazi 104 42.31 N 122.54 E
Daš Balbar 88 49.31 N 114.21 E
Dasburg 56 50.03 N 6.07 E
Dase → Dese 144 11.05 N 39.41 E
Dasha ≐ 98 38.20 N 115.22 E
Dashafa 105 39.19 N 116.19 E
Dashalitu 104 42.31 N 122.30 E
Dashan 98 38.02 N 117.39 E
Dashankou 105 40.17 N 115.49 E
Dashanpu 107 29.25 N 104.49 E
Dashaping 100 29.24 N 113.51 E
Dashava 78 49.16 N 24.01 E
Dashengfenchang 106 31.53 N 121.34 E
Dashengpu 104 41.13 N 121.02 E
Dashentang 105 39.13 N 117.56 E
Dashetai 102 40.58 N 109.19 E
Dashi 107 30.39 N 105.37 E
Dashi ≐ 105 39.35 N 116.05 E
Dashields Dam ◆⁶ 214 40.33 N 80.12 W
Dashiqiao, Zhg. 100 33.57 N 113.53 E
Dashiqiao, Zhg. 104 41.52 N 123.17 E
Dashiqiao, Zhg. 107 30.07 N 106.12 E
Dashiqiao, Zhg. 107 30.28 N 106.29 E
Dashitou, Zhg. 89 43.19 N 128.28 E
Dashitou, Zhg. 102 42.49 N 95.19 E
Dashiv 78 49.00 N 29.26 E
Dashizhai 89 46.16 N 121.25 E
Dashlūṭ 142 27.34 N 30.42 E
Dash Point 224 47.19 N 122.26 W
Dasht ≐ 128 25.10 N 61.40 E
Dashu 106 31.13 N 120.56 E
Dashun 100 28.06 N 119.52 E
Dashutang 102 23.00 N 103.55 E
Dashuwan 105 40.37 N 117.19 E
Dasi (Huangfansi) 102 38.15 N 100.22 E
Dasiji 100 33.48 N 115.55 E
Dašinčilen 88 47.51 N 104.03 E
Dasing 60 48.23 N 11.03 E
Dasizhan 89 45.53 N 130.24 E
Daska 123 32.20 N 74.21 E
Daşkäsän 84 40.30 N 46.04 E
Daskop 158 33.44 S 22.43 E
Daškovka 76 53.44 N 30.13 E
Dasmina 126 22.17 N 90.35 E
Dasol 116 15.59 N 119.52 E
Dasol Bay c 116 15.53 N 119.51 E
Dassalan Island I 116 6.45 N 121.28 E
Dassel, Dtsch. 52 51.48 N 9.41 E
Dassel, Mn., U.S. 190 45.04 N 94.18 W
Dasseneiland I 158 33.26 S 18.04 E
Dasserat, Lac ⊜ 190 48.16 N 79.25 W
Dassiefontein 158 31.35 S 24.25 E
Dassow 54 53.50 N 10.59 E
Dasswang 60 49.09 N 11.40 E
Dastakert 84 39.23 N 46.02 E
Dastgardān 128 34.19 N 56.51 E
Daštidžum 85 38.01 N 70.12 E
Daštioburdon 85 39.24 N 69.04 E
Dastjerd 128 34.33 N 50.15 E
Dasūa 123 31.49 N 75.38 E
Dāsuria 126 24.07 N 89.08 E
Datachang 107 28.55 N 104.21 E
Datagenoyang 112 2.03 N 115.10 E
Datai 105 39.58 N 115.54 E
Dataizi 104 41.17 N 121.46 E
Datan, Zhg. 98 41.35 N 116.00 E
Datan, Zhg. 98 39.31 N 122.11 E
Datang, Zhg. 100 24.47 N 113.43 E
Datang, Zhg. 100 25.17 N 114.56 E
Datang, Zhg. 102 22.23 N 108.23 E
Datang, Zhg. 102 24.11 N 109.00 E
Datça 130 36.45 N 27.40 E
Datchet 260 51.29 N 0.34 W
Datchet Reservoir ⊜¹ 260 51.29 N 0.33 W
Date 92a 42.27 N 140.51 E
Date Creek ≐ 200 34.13 N 113.29 W
Datia 124 25.40 N 78.28 E
Datian, Zhg. 100 25.42 N 117.49 E
Datian, Zhg. 100 24.06 N 116.19 E
Datian Ding ∧ 102 22.17 N 111.13 E
Datianwei 100 25.54 N 115.10 E
Dativli 272c 19.11 N 73.03 E
D'at'kovo 76 53.36 N 34.20 E
D'atloviči 76 52.20 N 26.50 E
D'atlovo, Bela. 76 53.28 N 25.24 E
D'atlovo, Ross. 82 56.14 N 36.16 E
Datong, Zhg. 89 46.03 N 124.50 E
Datong, Zhg. 100 30.48 N 117.45 E
Datong, Zhg. 100 32.50 N 118.52 E
Datong, Zhg. 102 37.03 N 101.45 E
Datong, Zhg. 102 40.05 N 113.18 E
Datong ≐ 102 36.20 N 102.55 E
Datong Shan ⋏ 102 38.00 N 99.30 E
Datongzhen 106 32.12 N 121.19 E
Datoushan 98 41.50 N 117.08 E
Dātra 272b 22.58 N 88.16 E
Datta 89 49.18 N 140.22 E
Dattapāra 126 23.01 N 90.53 E
Dattapukur 126 22.45 N 88.33 E
Dattapulia 126 23.14 N 88.43 E
Datteln 52 51.40 N 7.23 E
Datteln-Hamm-Kanal ≋ 263 51.39 N 7.21 E
Dattilo 70 37.58 N 12.39 E
Datu, Tanjung › 112 2.05 N 109.39 E
Datuan 106 30.58 N 121.44 E
Datumakuta 112 2.32 N 117.51 E
Datun, Zhg. 89 43.49 N 125.12 E
Datun, Zhg. 98 40.37 N 119.57 E
Datun, Zhg. 104 40.59 N 122.55 E
Datuopu 100 28.03 N 112.58 E
Datu Piang 116 7.01 N 124.30 E
Daua (Dawa) ≐ 144 4.11 N 42.06 E
Daudkāndi 126 23.32 N 90.43 E
Dāud Khel 123 32.53 N 71.34 E
Daudnagar 124 25.02 N 84.24 E
Daugai 76 54.22 N 24.20 E
Daugård 41 55.44 N 9.43 E
Daugava (Zapadnaja Dvina) ≐ 76 57.04 N 24.03 E
Daugavpils 76 55.53 N 26.32 E
Dauin 116 9.12 N 123.16 E
Daulatabad 126 24.08 N 88.22 E
Daulatkhān 126 22.38 N 90.49 E
Daulatpur, Bngl. 126 24.00 N 88.52 E
Daulatpur, Bngl. 126 22.53 N 89.31 E
Daulatpur, Bngl. 126 23.58 N 89.50 E
Daulatpur, India 272b 22.26 N 88.18 E
Daulatpur, Pāk. 120 26.30 N 67.58 E
Daulatpur ◆⁸ 272a 28.44 N 77.06 E
Daule, Ec. 246 0.24 N 80.00 W
Daule, Ec. 246 1.50 S 79.56 W
Daule, India 272c 19.10 N 73.03 E
Daule ≐ 246 2.10 S 79.52 W
Daultāla 123 33.12 N 73.09 E
Daulton Creek ≐ 226 37.04 N 119.59 W
Daun 56 50.11 N 6.50 E
Daund 122 18.28 N 74.36 E
Daung Kyun I 110 12.14 N 98.05 E
Dauphin, Mb., Can. 184 51.09 N 100.03 W
Dauphin, Pa., U.S. 208 40.22 N 76.55 W
Dauphin □⁶ 208 40.15 N 76.52 W
Dauphin ≐ 184 51.58 N 98.04 W
Dauphiné □⁹ 62 44.50 N 6.00 E
Dauphin Island 194 30.15 N 88.07 W
Dauphin Island I 194 30.14 N 88.12 W
Dauphin Lake ⊜ 184 51.17 N 99.48 W
Daura 150 13.02 N 8.21 E
Daurija 88 49.56 N 116.52 E
Daurskoje 86 55.14 N 92.05 E
Dausenau 56 50.20 N 7.45 E
D'Auteuil, Lac ⊜ 186 50.38 N 61.17 W
Dautphetal 56 50.51 N 8.32 E
Däväçi 84 41.12 N 48.59 E
Dāvangere 122 14.28 N 75.55 E
Davant 194 29.37 N 89.51 W
Davao 116 7.04 N 125.36 E
Davao □⁴ 116 7.40 N 125.50 E
Davao ≐ 116 7.04 N 125.37 E
Davao del Sur □⁴ 116 6.50 N 125.20 E
Davao Gulf c 116 6.40 N 125.55 E
Davao Oriental □⁴ 116 7.30 N 126.30 E
Dāvar Panāh 128 27.21 N 62.21 E
Dāvarzan 128 36.23 N 56.50 E
Davegoriale 144 8.45 N 44.50 E
Davel 158 26.24 S 29.40 E
Daveluyville 206 46.12 N 72.08 W
Davenda 88 53.33 N 119.18 E
Davenham 262 53.14 N 2.31 W
Davenport, Ca., U.S. 226 37.00 N 122.11 W
Davenport, Fl., U.S. 220 28.09 N 81.36 W
Davenport, Ia., U.S. 190 41.31 N 90.34 W
Davenport, Ne., U.S. 198 40.18 N 97.48 W
Davenport, N.Y., U.S. 210 42.28 N 74.51 W
Davenport, Ok., U.S. 196 35.42 N 96.45 W
Davenport, Wa., U.S. 202 47.39 N 118.08 W
Davenport, Mount ∧ 162 22.23 S 130.51 E
Davenport Downs 166 24.08 S 141.07 E
Davenport Range ⋏ 162 20.47 S 134.48 E
Daventry 42 52.16 N 1.09 W
Davey, Port c 166 43.19 S 145.55 E
Daveyton 273d 26.09 S 28.25 E
David 236 8.26 N 82.26 W
David City 198 41.15 N 97.07 W
David-Gorodok 78 52.03 N 27.14 E
Davids Island I 276 40.53 N 73.46 W
Davidson, Sk., Can. 184 51.16 N 105.59 W
Davidson, N.C., U.S. 192 35.29 N 80.50 W
Davidson, Ok., U.S. 196 34.14 N 99.04 W
Davidson, Mount ∧ 170 33.09 S 150.07 E
Davidson Creek ≐ 222 30.21 N 96.27 W
Davidson Heights 214 40.35 N 80.15 W
Davidson Lake ⊜ 184 53.47 N 99.37 W
Davidson Mountains ⋏ 180 68.45 N 142.10 W
Davidson Park ♦ 274a 33.45 S 151.12 E
Davidsville 214 40.14 N 78.56 W
Davie 220 26.03 N 80.13 W
Davies, Mount ∧ 162 26.14 S 129.16 E
Davignab 158 27.32 S 19.48 E
Davila 116 18.29 N 120.35 E
Davilla 222 30.47 N 97.17 W
Davington 44 55.18 N 3.12 W
Davin Lake ⊜ 184 56.50 N 103.40 W
Davinópolis 255 15.58 S 50.08 W
Daviot 46 57.25 N 4.08 W
Davis, Ca., U.S. 226 38.32 N 121.44 W
Davis, N.C., U.S. 192 34.47 N 76.27 W
Davis, Ok., U.S. 196 34.30 N 97.07 W
Davis, W.V., U.S. 188 39.07 N 79.27 W
Davis ≐ 162 21.42 S 121.05 E
Davis ʊ³ 9 68.35 S 77.58 E
Davis, Mount ∧ 188 39.47 N 79.10 W
Davis Bay c 9 66.08 S 134.05 E
Davisboro 192 32.58 N 82.36 W
Davisburg 216 42.45 N 83.33 W
Davis City 190 40.38 N 93.48 W
Davis Cove 186 47.40 N 54.18 W
Davis Creek ≐, Mi., U.S. 281 42.27 N 83.43 W
Davis Creek ≐, Mo., U.S. 219 39.12 N 91.53 W
Davis Dam 200 35.10 N 114.33 W
Davis Dam ◆⁶ 200 35.11 N 114.21 W
Davis Island I 279b 40.29 N 80.05 W
Davis Lake ⊜ 278 42.16 N 88.05 W
Davis-Monthan Air Force Base ■ 200 32.11 N 110.53 W
Davis Mountains ⋏ 196 30.35 N 104.00 W
Davison 216 43.02 N 83.31 W
Davis Park 210 40.42 N 72.59 W
Davis Point › 282 38.03 N 122.15 W
Davis Sea ⊤² 9 66.00 S 92.00 E
Davis Strait ɰ 176 67.00 N 57.00 W
Davlekanovo 86 54.13 N 55.03 E
Davo ≐ 150 5.00 N 6.08 W
Davoli 68 38.39 N 16.29 E
Davos 58 46.48 N 9.50 E
Davron 261 48.52 N 1.57 E
Davst 86 50.36 N 92.28 E
Davulga 130 38.58 N 31.23 E
Davutlar 130 37.43 N 27.17 E
Davy 192 37.28 N 81.39 W
Davydiv Brid 78 47.14 N 33.12 E
Davydkovo, Ross. 82 56.17 N 36.49 E
Davydkovo, Ross. 265b 55.35 N 37.12 E
Davydov, gora ∧ 88 52.34 N 107.25 E
Davydovka 78 51.10 N 39.25 E
Davydovo 82 55.37 N 38.52 E
Davydovskoje 82 55.52 N 36.48 E
Davyhulme 262 53.27 N 2.22 W
Dawa, Zhg. 104 41.00 N 122.03 E
Dawa, Zhg. 104 41.54 N 123.32 E
Dawa (Daua) ≐ 144 4.11 N 42.06 E
Dawaki 150 12.06 N 8.20 E
Dawan 102 23.52 N 109.29 E
Dawang 98 36.58 N 118.31 E
Dawangcun 106 30.45 N 118.59 E
Dawangdian 105 39.04 N 115.26 E
Dawangdong 105 38.53 N 116.21 E
Dawangjia Dao I 98 39.27 N 123.07 E
Dawangsangou 104 41.43 N 121.36 E
Dawangzhai 269b 31.22 N 121.25 E
Dawangzhuang, Zhg. 105 39.23 N 116.28 E
Dawangzhuang, Zhg. 105 38.59 N 115.56 E
Dawāsir, Wādī ad- V 144 20.24 N 46.29 E
Dawatun 104 41.05 N 121.01 E
Dawei (Tavoy) 110 14.05 N 98.12 E
Daweizhuang 105 39.34 N 116.53 E
Daweizigou 104 42.38 N 123.09 E
Dawen ≐ 98 35.38 N 116.24 E
Dawenkou 98 35.59 N 117.07 E
Dawera, Pulau I 164 7.44 S 130.00 E
Dawes Park ♦ 278 42.03 N 87.40 W
Dawlan 110 16.44 N 98.01 E
Dawlish 42 50.35 N 3.28 W
Dawn 208 37.50 N 77.22 W
Dawna Range ⋏ 110 16.50 N 98.15 E
Dawqah 144 19.36 N 40.54 E
Dawrah 140 12.22 N 24.19 E
Daws Heath 260 51.34 N 0.37 E
Dawson, Yk., Can. 180 64.04 N 139.25 W
Dawson, Ga., U.S. 192 31.46 N 84.26 W
Dawson, Il., U.S. 219 39.51 N 89.28 W
Dawson, Mn., U.S. 198 44.55 N 96.03 W
Dawson, Ne., U.S. 198 40.07 N 95.49 W
Dawson, Tx., U.S. 222 31.53 N 96.42 W
Dawson ≐ 166 23.38 S 149.46 E
Dawson, Isla I 254 53.55 S 70.45 W
Dawson, Mount ∧ 182 51.09 N 117.25 W
Dawson Bay c 184 52.55 N 100.50 W
Dawson Creek 182 55.46 N 120.14 W
Dawson Inlet c 176 61.50 N 93.25 W
Dawson Range ⋏, Austl. 166 24.20 S 149.45 E
Dawson Range ⋏, Yk., Can. 180 62.40 N 139.00 W
Dawson Ridge 214 40.42 N 80.22 W
Dawson Springs 194 37.10 N 87.41 W
Dawsonville 192 34.25 N 84.07 W
Dawu, Zhg. 100 31.34 N 114.06 E
Dawu, Zhg. 102 31.07 N 101.08 E
Dawudapu 104 41.36 N 123.03 E
Dawuji 271a 39.51 N 116.30 E
Dawujiawopeng 104 41.55 N 122.29 E
Dawujiazi 104 42.16 N 121.52 E
Dawulaba 104 42.13 N 122.23 E
Dawulah 104 41.56 N 121.05 E
Dax 32 43.43 N 1.03 W
Daxian 102 31.18 N 107.30 E
Daxin, Zhg. 100 33.54 N 118.30 E
Daxin, Zhg. 102 22.50 N 107.26 E
Daxing, Zhg. 98 39.44 N 116.20 E
Daxing (Huangcun), Zhg. 105 39.44 N 116.20 E
Daxing, Zhg. 106 31.50 N 121.40 E
Daxingchang 107 30.17 N 103.26 E
Daxingcun 106 31.45 N 121.40 E
Daxingzhai 102 23.13 N 102.21 E
Daxinji 100 34.03 N 119.28 E
Daxinzhuang, Zhg. 105 40.23 N 116.44 E
Daxinzhuang, Zhg. 105 39.26 N 118.20 E
Daxiyang 106 30.21 N 121.58 E
Daxu, Zhg. 100 29.32 N 121.52 E
Daxu, Zhg. 102 25.09 N 110.21 E
Daxue Shan ⋏ 102 30.10 N 101.50 E
Daxujia 98 34.18 N 117.34 E
Dayakou 102 22.46 N 100.18 E
Dayanchi 102 27.41 N 101.55 E
Dayang, Zhg. 98 36.04 N 116.31 E
Dayang, Zhg. 100 25.56 N 118.48 E
Dayang ≐ 98 39.54 N 123.40 E
Dayang Bunting, Pulau I 114 6.14 N 99.48 E
Dayangcha 98 42.04 N 126.43 E
Dayanggou 104 41.14 N 123.51 E
Dayang Shan I 106 30.35 N 122.00 E
Dayangshu 89 49.45 N 124.35 E
Dayao, Zhg. 100 27.59 N 113.42 E
Dayao, Zhg. 102 25.43 N 101.13 E
Dayaoshan 102 24.05 N 110.17 E
Daya Wan c 100 22.37 N 114.40 E
Dayboro 171a 27.11 S 152.50 E
Daye 100 30.06 N 114.57 E
Dayghar 272c 19.09 N 73.03 E
Day Heights 218 39.11 N 84.14 W
Dayi 107 30.37 N 103.31 E
Dayiji 100 32.32 N 119.14 E
Daying, Zhg. 98 34.27 N 113.59 E
Daying, Zhg. 98 37.19 N 115.43 E
Daying, Zhg. 98 39.53 N 123.07 E
Daying, Zhg. 98 39.19 N 113.46 E
Daying, Zhg. 100 33.59 N 112.51 E
Daying, Zhg. 105 39.05 N 116.06 E
Daying (Taping) ≐ 102 24.17 N 97.14 E
Dayingzi, Zhg. 98 41.19 N 118.19 E
Dayingzi, Zhg. 98 41.28 N 120.21 E
Dayingzi, Zhg. 104 41.08 N 122.50 E
Dayiqiao 106 31.44 N 120.45 E
Day Island 224 47.15 N 122.33 W
Day Lake ⊜ 224 48.23 N 121.58 W
Daylesford 169 37.21 S 144.09 E
Daymán ≐ 252 31.30 S 58.02 W
Daym Zubayr 140 7.43 N 26.13 E
Dayong, Zhg. 100 22.28 N 113.16 E
Dayong, Zhg. 102 29.06 N 110.29 E
Dayou 98 34.12 N 119.52 E
Dayr, Jabal ad- ∧ 140 12.27 N 30.42 E
Dayr Abū Sa'īd 132 32.30 N 35.41 E
Dayr al-Balaḥ 132 31.25 N 34.21 E
Dayr al-Ghuṣūn 132 32.21 N 35.05 E
Dayr 'Alī 132 33.17 N 36.18 E
Dayr 'Allā 132 32.12 N 35.37 E
Dayr 'Aṭīyah 130 34.06 N 36.46 E
Dayr az-Zawr 130 35.20 N 40.09 E
Dayr az-Zawr □⁸ 130 35.00 N 40.30 E
Dayr Dibwān 132 31.55 N 35.16 E
Dayr Ḥāfir 130 36.09 N 37.42 E
Dayr Jabal Aṭ-Ṭayr 142 28.17 N 30.45 E
Dayr Mawās 142 27.38 N 30.51 E
Dayr Qānūn 132 33.36 N 36.08 E
Dayr Sharaf 132 32.15 N 35.11 E
Dayrūṭ, Miṣr 142 27.33 N 30.49 E
Dayrūṭ, Miṣr 142 31.13 N 30.30 E
Dayrūṭ ash-Sharīf 142 27.35 N 30.49 E
Days Island I 284b 39.24 N 76.22 W
Daysland 182 52.52 N 112.15 W
Day Star Indian Reserve ◆⁴ 184 51.43 N 104.14 W
Dayton, Il., U.S. 216 41.23 N 88.47 W
Dayton, In., U.S. 216 40.22 N 86.46 W
Dayton, Ia., U.S. 190 42.15 N 94.04 W
Dayton, Ky., U.S. 218 39.06 N 84.28 W
Dayton, Mi., U.S. 216 41.48 N 86.26 W
Dayton, Nv., U.S. 226 39.14 N 119.35 W
Dayton, N.J., U.S. 276 40.22 N 74.30 W
Dayton, N.Y., U.S. 210 42.25 N 78.58 W
Dayton, Oh., U.S. 218 39.45 N 84.11 W
Dayton, Or., U.S. 224 45.13 N 123.04 W
Dayton, Pa., U.S. 214 40.52 N 79.14 W
Dayton, Tn., U.S. 194 35.29 N 85.00 W
Dayton, Tx., U.S. 222 30.02 N 94.53 W
Dayton, Va., U.S. 188 38.24 N 78.56 W
Dayton, Wa., U.S. 202 46.19 N 117.58 W
Dayton, Wy., U.S. 202 44.52 N 107.15 W
Daytona Beach 192 29.12 N 81.01 W
Dayton Municipal Airport ⊠ 218 39.54 N 84.13 W
Dayu, Indon. 112 1.59 S 115.04 E
Dayu, Zhg. 100 25.24 N 114.22 E
Dayuba 107 29.15 N 103.34 E
Dayu Ling ⋏ 100 25.20 N 114.16 E
Da Yunhe (Grand Canal) ≋ 90 32.12 N 119.31 E
Dayu Shan I, Zhg. 100 26.57 N 120.21 E
Dayu Shan I, Zhg. 106 30.19 N 121.58 E
Dayushupu 104 41.32 N 121.24 E
Dayville, Ct., U.S. 207 41.50 N 71.53 W
Dayville, Or., U.S. 202 44.28 N 119.32 W
Dazaifu ⊥ 96 33.31 N 130.31 E
Dazaoliyingzi 104 42.07 N 121.20 E
Dazaomiao 106 32.06 N 121.29 E
Dazhang ≐ 100 25.56 N 119.12 E
Dazhangzi 98 40.38 N 118.07 E
Dazhaotai 104 41.14 N 123.03 E
Dazhengjiatun 98 39.37 N 122.52 E
Dazhengzhuangzi 105 39.16 N 116.46 E
Dazhi 100 34.29 N 113.17 E
Dazhiba 102 27.09 N 99.52 E
Dazhifang 104 41.21 N 123.12 E
Dazhou 100 28.53 N 118.58 E
Dazhu 102 30.48 N 107.12 E
Dazhuangke 105 40.32 N 115.42 E
Dazhubao 107 28.59 N 103.38 E
Dazhuyuan 100 23.43 N 115.57 E
Dazifangshen 104 42.27 N 124.12 E
Daziling 104 41.21 N 121.26 E
Daziying 104 41.42 N 123.36 E
Dazkırı 130 37.55 N 29.52 E
Dazu 107 29.43 N 105.42 E
Dazui 100 30.16 N 114.02 E
De Aar 158 30.39 S 24.00 E
Dead ≐, Me., U.S. 188 45.20 N 69.58 W
Dead ≐, Mi., U.S. 190 46.34 N 87.24 W
Dead ≐, N.J., U.S. 276 40.39 N 74.31 W
Deadhorse 180 70.11 N 148.27 W
Dead Horse Point State Park ♦ 200 38.28 N 109.44 W
Deadman ≐ 182 50.45 N 120.55 W
Deadman Brook ≐ 276 41.08 N 73.22 W
Deadman Creek ≐ 226 37.12 N 120.42 W
Deadman Hill ∧ 162 23.48 S 119.25 E
Deadman's Cay 238 23.14 N 75.14 W
Deadmans Creek ≐ 274a 33.58 S 151.00 E
Deadman's Creek Indian Reserve ◆⁴ 182 50.49 N 121.00 W
Dead Run ≐ 284c 38.57 N 77.11 W
Dead Sea (Al-Baḥr al-Mayyit) (Yam HaMelaḥ) ⊜ 132 31.30 N 35.30 E
Deadwood 198 44.22 N 103.43 W
Deadwood ≐ 202 44.05 N 115.40 W
Deagan Island I 116 12.15 N 123.51 E
Deakin 162 30.46 S 128.58 E
Deakin, Mount ∧² 162 17.38 S 130.48 E
Deakin Bay c 9 68.23 S 150.10 E
Deal, Eng., U.K. 42 51.14 N 1.24 E
Deal, N.J., U.S. 208 40.15 N 74.00 W
Deale 208 38.46 N 76.33 W
Dealesville 158 28.40 S 25.37 E
Deal Island 208 38.09 N 75.56 W
Deal Island I 208 38.09 N 75.56 W
Deam Lake ⊜¹ 218 38.28 N 85.51 W
De'an 100 29.20 N 115.46 E
Dean ≐, B.C., Can. 182 52.50 N 126.57 W
Dean ≐, Eng., U.K. 262 53.20 N 2.14 W
Dean, Forest of ◆³ 42 51.48 N 2.30 W
Dean Channel ɰ 182 52.33 N 127.13 W
Deane 262 53.34 N 2.28 W
Deán Funes 252 30.26 S 64.21 W
Dean Row 262 53.20 N 2.11 W
Deans 276 40.24 N 74.30 W
Deansboro 210 43.00 N 75.26 W
Deans Dundas Bay c 176 72.15 N 118.25 W
Deanville 222 30.26 N 96.46 W
Dearborn 216 42.18 N 83.10 W
Dearborn □⁶ 218 39.06 N 84.51 W
Dearborn ≐ 202 47.07 N 111.55 W
Dearborn Heights 216 42.20 N 83.16 W
Dearg, Beinn ∧ 46 57.47 N 4.56 W
Dearham 44 54.42 N 3.26 W
Dearne ≐ 44 53.30 N 1.16 W
Dear Reservoir ⊜¹ 44 55.20 N 3.37 W
Dease ≐ 180 59.54 N 128.30 W
Dease Arm c 180 66.52 N 119.37 W
Dease Lake ⊜ 180 58.35 N 130.02 W
Dease Strait ɰ 176 68.40 N 108.00 W
Death Valley 204 36.18 N 116.25 W
Death Valley V 204 36.30 N 117.00 W
Death Valley National Monument ♦ 204 36.30 N 117.00 W
Deatsville 194 32.36 N 86.23 W
Deauville 50 49.22 N 0.04 E
Deba 146 10.20 N 11.54 E
Debagrām 126 23.41 N 88.18 E
Debal'tseve 83 48.20 N 38.24 E
Debānāndapur 272b 22.56 N 88.22 E
Debao 102 23.21 N 106.31 E
Debar 38 41.31 N 20.30 E
De Bary 220 28.52 N 81.18 W
Debauch Mountain ∧ 180 64.31 N 159.52 W
Débé 241r 10.12 N 61.27 W
Debed ≐ 84 41.22 N 44.58 E
Deben ≐ 42 51.58 N 1.24 E
Debenham 42 52.13 N 1.11 E
De Beque 200 39.20 N 108.12 W
De Berry 194 32.18 N 94.10 W
Debesy 80 57.39 N 53.49 E
Debhāta 124 22.33 N 88.58 E
Dębica 30 50.04 N 21.24 E
De Bilt 52 52.06 N 5.10 E
Debipur 126 24.14 N 88.38 E
Debīr Char 126 22.24 N 90.41 E
Dęblin 30 51.35 N 21.50 E
Dębno 30 52.45 N 14.40 E
Débo, Lac ⊜ 150 15.18 N 4.09 W
Deborah, Mount ∧ 180 63.38 N 147.15 W
Deborah West, Lake ⊜ 162 30.45 S 119.07 E
Deboyne Islands II 164 10.45 S 152.25 E
Debra 126 22.24 N 87.33 E
Debra Sina 144 9.51 N 39.50 E
Debre Birhan 144 9.40 N 39.33 E
Debrecen 30 47.32 N 21.38 E
Debre Markos 144 10.20 N 37.45 E
Debre May 144 11.19 N 37.30 E
Debre Tabor 144 11.50 N 38.05 E
Debre Zebit 144 11.50 N 38.40 E
Debre Zeyit 144 8.45 N 38.59 E
Debrzno 30 53.33 N 17.14 E
Debstedt 52 53.37 N 8.38 E
Decatur, Al., U.S. 194 34.36 N 86.59 W
Decatur, Ga., U.S. 192 33.46 N 84.17 W
Decatur, Il., U.S. 219 39.50 N 88.57 W
Decatur, In., U.S. 216 40.50 N 84.56 W
Decatur, Mi., U.S. 216 42.06 N 85.58 W
Decatur, Ms., U.S. 194 32.26 N 89.06 W
Decatur, Ne., U.S. 198 42.00 N 96.14 W
Decatur, Oh., U.S. 218 38.49 N 83.42 W
Decatur, Tn., U.S. 192 35.30 N 84.47 W
Decatur, Tx., U.S. 222 33.14 N 97.35 W
Decatur □⁶ 218 39.20 N 85.29 W
Decatur, Lake ⊜¹ 219 39.51 N 88.52 W
Decatur Island I 224 48.31 N 122.50 W
Decatur Municipal Airport ⊠ 219 39.50 N 88.52 W
Decaturville 194 35.35 N 88.07 W
Decazeville 32 44.34 N 2.15 E
Deccan ⋏¹ 122 17.00 N 78.00 E
Decelles, Réservoir ⊜¹ 190 47.42 N 78.08 W
Deception ≐ 156 21.04 S 24.25 E
Deception, Mount ∧ 224 47.49 N 123.14 W
Deception Bay c 171a 27.07 S 153.05 E
Deception Island I 9 62.57 S 60.38 W
Deception Lake ⊜ 184 56.33 N 104.15 W
Deception Pass ≋ 224 48.24 N 122.38 W
Deception Pass State Park ♦ 224 48.24 N 122.39 W
Dechang 102 27.24 N 102.10 E
Dechêne, Lac ⊜ 186 51.15 N 67.51 W
Dechenhöhle ⩞⁵ 263 51.22 N 7.39 E
Decherd 194 35.12 N 86.04 W
Dechhu 120 26.47 N 72.20 E
Déchy 50 50.21 N 3.07 E
Decimomannu 71 39.19 N 8.58 E
Decimoputzu 71 39.20 N 8.55 E
Děčín 54 50.48 N 14.13 E
Děčínské stěny ⋏ 54 50.50 N 14.12 E
Decize 32 46.50 N 3.27 E
Decker Lake 182 54.17 N 125.50 W
Decker Lake ⊜¹ 222 30.18 N 97.36 W
Deckers Point 214 40.46 N 78.59 W
Deckerville 190 43.31 N 82.44 W
De Cocksdorp 52 53.08 N 4.52 E
Decollatura 68 39.03 N 16.21 E
Decorah 190 43.18 N 91.47 W
Decs 30 46.17 N 18.46 E
Deda 38 46.57 N 24.53 E
Dedaye 110 16.24 N 95.53 E
Deddington 42 51.59 N 1.19 W
Dededo 174p 13.31 N 144.49 E
Dedegöl Dağları ⋏ 130 37.47 N 31.13 E
Dedegöl Tepesi ∧ 130 37.39 N 31.17 E
Dedeleben 54 52.02 N 10.54 E
Dedeli 84 39.11 N 43.05 E
Dedelow 54 53.22 N 13.48 E
Dedemsvaart 52 52.36 N 6.28 E
Dedenevo 82 56.15 N 37.31 E
Deder 144 9.22 N 41.26 E
Dedesdorf 52 53.27 N 8.30 E
Dedham 207 42.14 N 71.10 W
Dedilovskije Vyselki 82 54.20 N 38.03 E
Dedinovo 82 55.03 N 39.07 E
Dedo, Cerro ∧ 254 44.49 S 71.52 W
Dedo de Deus, Pico ∧ 256 22.30 S 43.03 W
De Doorns 158 33.28 S 19.41 E
Dedoplis Ckaro 84 41.28 N 46.07 E
Dédougou 150 12.28 N 3.28 W
Dedoviči 76 57.32 N 29.56 E
Dedovsk 82 55.52 N 37.07 E
Dedu 89 48.31 N 126.14 E
Deduru ≐ 122 7.36 N 79.48 E
Dedza 154 14.22 S 34.20 E
Dee ≐, Ire. 48 53.52 N 6.21 W
Dee ≐, U.K. 44 53.20 N 3.12 W
Dee ≐, Eng., U.K. 44 54.18 N 2.32 W
Dee ≐, Scot., U.K. 44 54.50 N 4.03 W
Dee ≐, Scot., U.K. 46 57.09 N 2.07 W
Dee, Loch ⊜ 44 55.05 N 4.24 W
Deedsville 216 40.55 N 86.06 W
De Efteling ♦ 52 51.39 N 5.02 E
Deeg 124 27.28 N 77.20 E
Deelfontein 158 30.59 S 23.48 E
Deelpan 158 26.19 S 25.36 E
Deenwood 192 31.14 N 82.23 W
Deep ≐, In., U.S. 216 41.34 N 87.17 W
Deep ≐, N.C., U.S. 192 35.36 N 79.03 W
Deepavaal Brook ≐ 276 40.53 N 74.16 W
Deep Bay c 184 56.25 N 103.00 W
Deep Brook ≐, Ma., U.S. 283 42.38 N 71.22 W
Deep Brook ≐, N.J., U.S. 276 40.58 N 74.09 W
Deep Creek ≐, Austl. 169 37.37 S 144.48 E
Deep Creek ≐, U.S. 200 41.44 N 113.00 W
Deep Creek ≐, Ca., U.S. 228 34.20 N 117.14 W
Deep Creek ≐, De., U.S. 208 38.38 N 75.37 W
Deep Creek ≐, Id., U.S. 202 42.15 N 116.40 W
Deep Creek ≐, Md., U.S. 284b 39.17 N 76.28 W
Deep Creek ≐, Tx., U.S. 196 32.31 N 100.55 W
Deep Creek ≐, Tx., U.S. 196 32.45 N 99.10 W
Deep Creek ≐, Ut,. U.S. 200 40.10 N 113.50 W
Deep Creek Conservation Park ♦ 168b 35.39 S 138.12 E
Deep Creek Indian Reserve ◆⁴ 182 52.16 N 122.07 W
Deeping Fen ≡ 42 52.44 N 0.13 W
Deep Red Creek ≐ 196 34.17 N 98.39 W
Deep River, On., Can. 190 46.06 N 77.30 W
Deep River, Ct., U.S. 207 41.23 N 72.26 W
Deep River, Ia., U.S. 190 41.34 N 92.22 W
Deep River, Wa., U.S. 224 46.21 N 123.41 W
Deep Run ≐, Md., U.S. 284b 39.13 N 76.42 W
Deep Run ≐, Md., U.S. 284b 39.25 N 76.40 W
Deep Run ≐, N.J., U.S. 276 40.26 N 74.22 W
Deep Run ≐, N.J., U.S. 285 39.44 N 74.41 W
Deepwater, Austl. 166 29.27 S 151.51 E
Deepwater, Mo., U.S. 194 38.15 N 93.46 W
Deep Water, N.J., U.S. 208 39.41 N 75.29 W
Deep Well 162 24.25 S 134.05 E
Deer ≐, N.Y., U.S. 188 44.55 N 74.43 W
Deer ≐, N.Y., U.S. 212 43.56 N 75.34 W
Deer Creek, In., U.S. 216 40.37 N 86.23 W
Deer Creek, Mn., U.S. 198 46.23 N 95.19 W
Deer Creek ≐, U.S. 208 39.37 N 76.09 W
Deer Creek ≐, Ca., U.S. 204 39.56 N 122.04 W
Deer Creek ≐, Ca., U.S. 226 39.13 N 121.17 W
Deer Creek ≐, Ca., U.S. 226 35.56 N 119.28 W
Deer Creek ≐, Ca., U.S. 226 38.22 N 121.21 W
Deer Creek ≐, Ca., U.S. 282 37.24 N 122.09 W
Deer Creek ≐, Il., U.S. 278 41.32 N 87.37 W
Deer Creek ≐, In., U.S. 216 40.34 N 86.41 W
Deer Creek ≐, Ks., U.S. 198 39.40 N 99.06 W
Deer Creek ≐, Ms., U.S. 194 32.33 N 90.47 W
Deer Creek ≐, Ne., U.S. 198 40.28 N 100.00 W
Deer Creek ≐, Oh., U.S. 218 39.27 N 83.00 W
Deer Creek ≐, Ok., U.S. 196 35.38 N 98.28 W
Deer Creek ≐, Or., U.S. 224 45.08 N 123.15 W
Deer Creek ≐, Pa., U.S. 279b 40.32 N 79.51 W
Deer Creek ≐, Wa., U.S. 224 48.16 N 121.55 W
Deer Creek ≐, Wy., U.S. 200 42.52 N 105.52 W
Deer Creek ≐, Wy., U.S. 202 43.09 N 107.42 W
Deer Creek Indian Reservation ◆⁴ 190 47.50 N 93.25 W
Deer Creek Lake ⊜¹ 218 39.40 N 83.15 W
Deerfield, Il., U.S. 216 42.10 N 87.50 W
Deerfield, In., U.S. 216 40.17 N 84.59 W
Deerfield, Ks., U.S. 198 37.58 N 101.07 W
Deerfield, Ma., U.S. 207 42.32 N 72.36 W
Deerfield, Mi., U.S. 216 41.53 N 83.46 W
Deerfield, Oh., U.S. 214 41.01 N 81.03 W
Deerfield, Wi., U.S. 216 43.03 N 89.04 W
Deerfield ≐ 207 42.35 N 72.35 W
Deerfield Beach 220 26.19 N 80.06 W
Deerfield Street 208 39.31 N 75.14 W
Deer Grove ♦ 278 42.09 N 88.04 W
Deer Harbor 224 48.37 N 123.00 W
Deering 180 66.05 N 162.43 W
Deering, Mount ∧² 162 24.53 S 129.04 E
Deer Island ›¹ 283 42.21 N 70.58 W
Deer Island I, N.B., Can. 186 45.00 N 66.57 W
Deer Island I, Ak., U.S. 180 54.53 N 162.25 W
Deer Island I, Or., U.S. 224 45.58 N 122.50 W
Deer Isle 188 44.13 N 68.40 W
Deer Lake, Nf., Can. 186 49.10 N 57.26 W
Deer Lake, Pa., U.S. 208 40.37 N 76.03 W
Deer Lake ⊜, Nf., Can. 186 49.07 N 57.35 W
Deer Lake ⊜, On., Can. 184 52.40 N 94.30 W
Deer Lakes Regional Park ♦ 279b 40.38 N 79.49 W
Deerlijk 50 50.51 N 3.21 E
Deer Lodge 202 46.23 N 112.44 W
Deer Mountain ∧ 188 45.01 N 70.56 W
Deer Park, Austl. 274b 37.47 S 144.47 E
Deer Park, Al., U.S. 194 31.13 N 88.19 W
Deer Park, Ca., U.S. 226 38.32 N 122.28 W
Deer Park, Il., U.S. 278 42.09 N 88.04 W
Deer Park, N.Y., U.S. 210 40.45 N 73.19 W
Deer Park, Oh., U.S. 218 39.12 N 84.23 W
Deer Park, Tx., U.S. 222 29.42 N 95.07 W
Deer Park, Wa., U.S. 202 47.57 N 117.28 W
Deer Park ♦ 272a 28.33 N 77.11 E
Deer Park Airport ⊠ 276 40.46 N 73.19 W
Deerpass Bay c 180 65.56 N 122.25 W
Deer Pond ⊜, Nf., Can. 186 48.30 N 54.45 W
Deer Pond ⊜, N.J., U.S. 276 40.57 N 74.24 W
Deer River, Mn., U.S. 190 47.19 N 93.47 W
Deer River, N.Y., U.S. 212 43.56 N 75.36 W
Deer Sound ɰ 46 58.58 N 2.48 W
Deersville 214 40.19 N 81.11 W
Deer Trail 198 39.36 N 104.02 W
Deerwood 190 46.28 N 93.53 W
Dee Why 170 33.45 S 151.17 E
Dee Why Head › 274a 33.46 S 151.19 E
Dee Why Lagoon c 274a 33.45 S 151.18 E
Deex Nugaaleed V 144 7.58 N 49.51 E
Defengzhuang 98 41.02 N 113.16 E
Defereggen V 64 46.55 N 12.25 E
Defereggen Alpen ⋏ 64 46.52 N 12.20 E
Deferiet 212 44.02 N 75.41 W
Defiance, Ia., U.S. 198 41.49 N 95.20 W
Defiance, Oh., U.S. 216 41.17 N 84.21 W
Defiance, Pa., U.S. 214 40.10 N 78.14 W
Defiance □⁶ 216 41.19 N 84.30 W
Defiance, Mount ∧ 224 45.38 N 121.43 W
Defiance Plateau ⋏¹ 200 36.00 N 109.15 W
De Forest 190 43.14 N 89.20 W
De Forest Lake ⊜ 276 41.08 N 73.58 W
Defu 271c 1.21 N 103.54 E
De Funiak Springs 194 30.43 N 86.06 W
Deganga 126 22.40 N 88.39 E
Deganwy 44 53.17 N 3.50 W
Deganya 132 32.42 N 35.35 E
Dêgê 102 31.50 N 98.40 E
Degeberga 26 55.50 N 14.05 E
Degeh Bur 144 8.13 N 43.34 E
Dégelis (Sainte-Rose-du-Dégelis) 186 47.33 N 68.39 W
Degema 150 4.45 N 6.47 E
Degerby 26 60.02 N 20.23 E
Degeres 85 43.14 N 75.49 E
Degerfors 40 59.14 N 14.26 E
Degerhamn 26 56.21 N 16.24 E
Degerndorf 64 47.44 N 12.06 E
Deggendorf 60 48.51 N 12.59 E
Deggingen 56 48.36 N 9.43 E
Degh ≐ 123 31.36 N 74.09 E
Değirmendere 130 38.07 N 27.09 E
Değirmenlik 130 35.15 N 33.29 E
Deglunden ⊜ 40 60.05 N 13.49 E
Dego 62 44.27 N 8.19 E
Degollado 234 20.28 N 102.09 W
Degoma 144 12.28 N 37.37 E
Degong 114 4.05 N 101.08 E
De Graafschap ◆¹ 52 52.00 N 6.30 E
De Graff 216 40.18 N 83.54 W
De Gray Lake ⊜¹ 194 34.15 N 93.15 W
De Grey 162 20.10 S 119.12 E
De Grey ≐ 162 20.12 S 119.11 E
Degt'arka ≐ 265a 59.57 N 30.52 E
Degunino ◆⁸ 265b 55.52 N 37.33 E
De Haan 50 51.16 N 3.02 E
Dehak ≐ 128 32.01 N 58.35 E
Dehalak Deset I 144 15.40 N 40.05 E
Deharda 126 21.40 N 87.25 E
De Hart Reservoir ⊜¹ 208 40.28 N 76.45 W
Deh Bālā 123 34.04 N 70.29 E
Deh Bīd 128 30.38 N 53.13 E
Dehdez 128 31.43 N 50.17 E
Deh-e Salm 128 31.12 N 59.19 E
Dehgolān 128 35.17 N 47.25 E
Dehibat 148 32.01 N 10.42 E
Dehiwala-Mount Lavinia 122 6.51 N 79.52 E
Deh Kord 128 33.49 N 48.53 E
Dehlorān 128 32.41 N 47.16 E
De Hoek 158 32.57 S 18.46 E
Dehpehk I 174r 6.57 N 158.18 E
Dehra Dūn 124 30.19 N 78.02 E
Dehri 124 24.52 N 84.11 E
Dehrn 56 50.25 N 8.05 E
Dehu 122 18.35 N 73.51 E
Dehua 100 25.32 N 118.15 E
Dehuang 98 35.12 N 114.25 E
Dehui 89 44.34 N 125.43 E
Deidesheim 56 49.24 N 8.11 E
Deilbach ≐ 263 51.23 N 7.05 E
Deilinghofen 56 51.22 N 7.47 E
Deining 60 49.13 N 11.32 E
Deinze 50 50.59 N 3.32 E
Deir el Asad 132 32.56 N 35.16 E
Deister ⋏ 52 52.15 N 9.30 E
Deiva Marina 62 44.13 N 9.30 E
Dej 38 47.09 N 23.52 E
Deje 40 59.36 N 13.28 E
Dejima 94 36.05 N 140.20 E
Dejnau 128 39.15 N 63.11 E
De Jongs, Tanjong › 164 6.56 S 138.32 E
Deka ≐ 154 18.04 S 26.42 E
De Kalb, Il., U.S. 216 41.55 N 88.45 W
De Kalb, Ms., U.S. 194 32.46 N 88.39 W
De Kalb, Tx., U.S. 194 33.30 N 94.36 W
De Kalb □⁶, Il., U.S. 216 41.59 N 88.41 W
De Kalb □⁶, In., U.S. 216 41.22 N 85.04 W
De Kalb Junction 212 44.30 N 75.16 W
Dekan, Hochland von → Deccan ⋏¹ 122 17.00 N 78.00 E
De-Kastri 89 51.28 N 140.47 E
Dekehtik I 174r 7.00 N 158.12 E
Dekemhare 144 15.05 N 39.02 E
Dekese 152 3.27 S 21.24 E
Deke Sokehs I 174r 6.59 N 158.11 E
Dekhgila Military Base ■ 142 31.08 N 29.48 E
Dekina 150 7.39 N 7.02 E
Dékoa 152 6.19 N 19.04 E
De Koog 52 53.05 N 4.45 E
De Krim 52 52.38 N 6.38 E
De La Blanche, Lac ⊜ 186 50.05 N 69.29 W
Delabole 42 50.37 N 4.42 W
Delafield 216 43.03 N 88.24 W
Del Aire 280 33.55 N 118.21 W
Delamere, Austl. 164 15.45 S 131.33 E
Delamere, Austl. 168b 35.35 S 138.11 E
Delamere, Eng., U.K. 262 53.13 N 2.39 W
Delamere Forest ◆³ 44 53.14 N 2.38 W
Delami Mayal, Jabal ∧ 140 11.38 N 30.23 E
Del Amo Fashion Center ◆⁹ 280 33.50 N 118.21 W
De Lancey, N.Y., U.S. 210 42.12 N 74.58 W
De Lancey, Pa., U.S. 214 40.59 N 78.58 W
Delanco 208 40.03 N 74.57 W
De Land 220 29.01 N 81.18 W
Delanggu 115a 7.37 S 110.41 E
Delano, Ca., U.S. 226 35.46 N 119.14 W
Delano, Mn., U.S. 190 45.02 N 93.47 W
Delano, Pa., U.S. 210 40.50 N 76.04 W
Delano Peak ∧ 200 38.22 N 112.23 W
Delanson 210 42.44 N 74.11 W
Delaport Point › 240b 25.05 N 77.27 W
Delapu 120 31.35 N 90.35 E
Delārām 128 32.11 N 63.25 E
Delareyville 158 26.44 S 25.29 E
Delarof Islands II 181a 51.30 N 178.45 W
Delaronde Lake ⊜ 184 54.05 N 107.05 W
Del'atiči 76 53.47 N 25.59 E
Delatite ≐ 169 37.10 S 146.00 E
Delavan, Il., U.S. 194 40.22 N 89.32 W
Delavan, Wi., U.S. 216 42.37 N 88.38 W
Delavan Lake 216 42.35 N 88.37 W
Delavan Lake ⊜ 216 42.37 N 88.38 W
Delaware, On., Can. 214 42.55 N 81.25 W
Delaware, N.J., U.S. 210 40.53 N 75.03 W
Delaware, Oh., U.S. 214 40.17 N 83.04 W
Delaware, Ok., U.S. 196 36.46 N 95.38 W
Delaware □⁶, In., U.S. 216 40.18 N 85.23 W
Delaware □⁶, N.Y., U.S. 210 42.17 N 74.55 W
Delaware □⁶, Oh., U.S. 214 40.18 N 83.04 W

Symbols in the index entries represent the broad categories identified in the key at the right. Symbols with superior numbers (⋏¹) identify subcategories (see complete key on page *I · 1*).

Symbole im Register stellen die rechts im Schlüssel erklärten Kategorien dar. Symbole mit hochgestellten Ziffern (⋏¹) bezeichnen Unterabteilungen einer Kategorie (vgl. vollständiger Schlüssel auf Seite *I · 1*).

Los símbolos incluídos en el texto del índice representan las grandes categorías identificadas con la clave a la derecha. Los símbolos con numeros en su parte superior (⋏¹) identifican las subcategorías (véase la clave completa en la página *I · 1*).

Les symboles de l'index représentent les catégories indiquées dans la légende à droite. Les symboles suivis d'un indice (⋏¹) représentent des sous-catégories (voir légende complète à la page *I · 1*).

Os símbolos incluídos no texto do índice representam as grandes categorias identificadas com a chave à direita. Os símbolos com números em sua parte superior (⋏¹) identificam as subcategorias (veja-se a chave completa à página *I · 1*).

∧ Mountain	Berg	Montaña	Montagne	Montanha
⋏ Mountains	Gebirge	Montañas	Montagnes	Montanhas
)(Pass	Paß	Paso	Col	Passo
V Valley, Canyon	Tal, Cañon	Valle, Cañón	Vallée, Canyon	Vale, Canhão
≚ Plain	Ebene	Llano	Plaine	Planície
› Cape	Kap	Cabo	Cap	Cabo
I Island	Insel	Isla	Île	Ilha
II Islands	Inseln	Islas	Îles	Ilhas
⩞ Other Topographic Features	Andere Topographische Objekte	Otros Elementos Topográficos	Autres données topographiques	Outros acidentes topográficos

ESPAÑOL | FRANÇAIS | PORTUGUÊS

Nombre / Nom / Nome	Página / Page / Página	Lat.°′	Long.°′ W = Oeste / W = Ouest / W = Oeste
Delaware □[6], Pa., U.S.	208	39.55 N	75.23 W
Delaware □[3], U.S.	178	39.10 N	75.30 W
Delaware □[3], U.S.	208	39.10 N	75.30 W
Delaware ≃, U.S.	188	39.20 N	75.25 W
Delaware ≃, U.S.	196	32.02 N	104.01 W
Delaware ≃, Ks., U.S.	198	39.03 N	95.24 W
Delaware, East Branch ≃	210	41.55 N	75.17 W
Delaware, University of ⚘[2]	285	39.41 N	75.45 W
Delaware, West Branch ≃	210	41.56 N	75.17 W
Delaware and Raritan Canal ≊	208	40.29 N	74.26 W
Delaware Aqueduct ≊[1]	210	42.05 N	74.54 W
Delaware Bay ⊂	208	39.05 N	75.15 W
Delaware City	208	39.34 N	75.35 W
Delaware Lake ⊜[1]	214	40.20 N	83.00 W
Delaware Memorial Bridge ◆[5]	285	40.07 N	74.50 W
Delaware Memorial Bridges ◆[5]	208	39.41 N	75.31 W
Delaware Mountains ⋀	196	31.35 N	104.40 W
Delaware Museum of Natural History ⚘	285	39.47 N	75.36 W
Delaware Park	210	40.43 N	75.11 W
Delaware Park ♠	284a	42.56 N	78.52 W
Delaware Park Race Track ♠	285	39.42 N	75.40 W
Delaware Seashore State Park ♠	208	38.38 N	75.04 W
Delaware State Park ♠	214	40.23 N	83.04 W
Delaware Water Gap	210	40.59 N	75.09 W
Delaware Water Gap National Recreation Area ♠	210	41.08 N	74.55 W
Delbrück	52	51.46 N	8.33 E
Delburne	182	52.12 N	113.14 W
Delcambre	194	29.57 N	91.59 W
Del Campillo	252	34.22 S	64.29 W
Del Carril	258	35.31 S	59.30 W
Del City	196	35.26 N	97.26 W
Delcommune, Lac ⊜[1]	154	10.45 S	25.45 E
Del Dios	228	33.04 N	117.08 W
Delegate	166	37.03 S	148.58 E
Délembé	146	9.53 N	22.37 E
Delémont	58	47.22 N	7.21 E
De Leon	196	32.06 N	98.32 W
De Leon Springs	192	29.07 N	81.21 W
Delet ⋓	26	60.15 N	20.35 E
Delevan	210	42.29 N	78.28 W
Delfim Moreira	256	22.30 S	45.17 W
Delfinópolis	255	20.20 S	46.51 W
Delft	52	52.00 N	4.21 E
Delft Island I	122	9.30 N	79.42 E
Delfzijl	52	53.19 N	6.46 E
Delgada, Punta ≻	254	42.46 S	63.38 W
Delgado	236	13.43 N	89.10 W
Delgado, Cabo ≻	154	10.40 S	40.35 E
Del Gallego	116	13.56 N	122.36 E
Delgany	48	53.08 N	6.05 W
Delger ≃	88	49.17 N	100.40 E
Delger chaan uul ∧	88	50.00 N	106.22 E
Delgerchangaj	102	45.15 N	104.50 E
Delgerchet	102	45.52 N	110.26 E
Delgercogt	102	46.08 N	106.23 E
Delgerech	102	45.48 N	111.12 E
Del Haven	208	39.03 N	74.56 W
Delhi, On., Can.	212	42.51 N	80.30 W
Delhi, India	124	28.40 N	77.13 E
Delhi, India	272a	28.40 N	77.13 E
Delhi, Ca., U.S.	226	37.26 N	120.46 W
Delhi, Il., U.S.	219	39.03 N	90.15 W
Delhi, Ia., U.S.	190	42.25 N	91.19 W
Delhi, La., U.S.	194	32.27 N	91.29 W
Delhi, N.Y., U.S.	210	42.16 N	74.54 W
Delhi □[8]	124	28.37 N	77.10 E
Delhi Cantonment	272a	28.36 N	77.08 E
Delhi Hills	218	39.05 N	84.36 W
Delhi Railroad Station ◆[5]	272a	28.40 N	77.13 E
Delhi Tail Distributary ≊	272a	28.41 N	77.10 E
Delhi University ⚘[2]	272a	28.42 N	77.13 E
Deli, Pulau I	115a	7.00 S	105.32 E
Delia, Ab., Can.	182	51.38 N	112.23 W
Delia, It.	70	37.21 N	13.55 E
Delia ≃	70	37.38 N	12.37 E
Delianuova	68	38.14 N	15.55 E
Deliblato	38	44.50 N	21.03 E
Delice	130	39.58 N	34.02 E
Delice ≃	130	40.28 N	34.10 E
Delices	240d	15.17 N	61.16 W
Deliceto	68	41.13 N	15.23 E
Delicias, Cuba	240p	21.11 N	76.34 W
Delicias, Méx.	232	28.13 N	105.28 W
De Lier	52	51.57 N	4.15 E
Delight	194	34.01 N	93.30 W
Delightful	214	41.18 N	80.57 W
Deliilyas	130	39.20 N	36.48 E
Delījān	128	33.59 N	50.40 E
Deliktaş	130	39.21 N	37.13 E
Delingde	74	70.08 N	114.00 E
Delingha	102	37.14 N	97.11 E
Dēliņkalns ∧[2]	76	57.30 N	26.58 E
Déli Pályaudvar ◆[5]	264c	47.30 N	19.01 E
Delisle	184	51.55 N	107.08 W
Delisle ≃	206	45.17 N	74.11 W
Delitua	114	3.30 N	98.41 E
Delitzsch	54	51.31 N	12.20 E
Delkern	228	35.21 N	119.01 W
Dell	46	58.30 N	6.20 W
Dellach	64	46.40 N	13.05 E
Dell City	200	31.56 N	105.12 W
Delle	58	47.30 N	7.00 E
Dellenbaugh, Mount ∧	200	36.07 N	113.32 W
Dellensjöarna ⊜	26	61.54 N	16.41 E
Delles	148	36.55 N	3.55 E
Delligsen	52	51.57 N	9.48 E
Dello	64	45.25 N	10.04 E
Dell Rapids	198	43.50 N	96.43 W
Dellroy	214	40.33 N	81.11 W
Dellwig	263	51.29 N	7.41 E
Dellwig ◆[8]	263	51.29 N	6.56 E
Dellwood	219	38.44 N	90.17 W
Dellwood Highlands	278	41.34 N	88.03 W
Del Mar, Ca., U.S.	228	32.57 N	117.15 W
Delmar, De., U.S.	208	38.27 N	75.34 W
Delmar, Ia., U.S.	190	42.00 N	90.36 W
Delmar, Md., U.S.	208	38.27 N	75.34 W
Delmar, N.Y., U.S.	210	42.37 N	73.49 W
Del Mar Hills	196	27.37 N	99.26 W
Delmarva Peninsula ≻[1]	208	38.30 N	75.30 W
Del Mar Woods	278	42.12 N	87.51 W
Delmas, Sk., Can.	184	52.55 N	108.36 W
Delmas, S. Afr.	158	26.08 S	28.43 E
Delmas □[5]	273d	26.10 S	28.33 E
Delme	56	48.53 N	6.24 E
Delme ≃	52	53.05 N	8.40 E
Delmenhorst	52	53.03 N	8.38 E
Delmiro Gouveia	250	9.23 S	37.59 W
Delmont, N.J., U.S.	208	39.12 N	74.57 W
Delmont, Pa., U.S.	214	40.25 N	79.34 W
Delmont, S.D., U.S.	198	43.16 N	98.09 W
Del Monte Heights	226	36.36 N	121.50 W
Del Monte Park	226	36.36 N	121.56 W
Delnice	36	45.24 N	14.48 E
Del Norte	200	37.40 N	106.21 W
Del Norte Coast Redwood State Park ♠	204	41.38 N	124.05 W
De-Longa, ostrova II	74	76.30 N	153.00 E
De Long Mountains ⋀	180	68.20 N	162.00 W
De-Long-Strasse → Longa, proliv ⋓	74	70.20 N	178.00 E
Deloraine, Austl.	166	41.31 S	146.39 E
Deloraine, Mb., Can.	184	49.12 N	100.29 W
Delorme, Lac ⊜	176	54.31 N	69.52 W
Deloro	212	44.31 N	77.37 W
Delos → Dhílos ⟂	38	37.26 N	25.16 E
Delph	44	53.34 N	2.01 W
Delphi	216	40.35 N	86.40 W
Delphi → Dhelfoí ⟂	38	38.30 N	22.29 E
Delphi Falls	210	42.53 N	75.55 W
Delphos, Ks., U.S.	198	39.16 N	97.46 W
Delphos, Oh., U.S.	216	40.50 N	84.20 W
Delph Reservoir ⊜[1]	262	53.38 N	2.27 W
Delportshoop	158	28.22 S	24.20 E
Del Puerto Creek ≃	226	37.32 N	121.07 W
Delran	285	40.01 N	74.57 W
Delrath	263	51.08 N	6.47 E
Delray ◆[8]	281	42.18 N	83.08 W
Delray Beach	220	26.27 N	80.04 W
Del Rey	226	36.40 N	119.36 W
Del Rey Oaks	226	36.36 N	121.50 W
Del Rio, Fl., U.S.	220	28.03 N	82.26 W
Del Rio, Tx., U.S.	196	29.21 N	100.53 W
Del Rosa	228	34.08 N	117.15 W
Delsbo	26	61.48 N	16.35 E
Delson	206	45.22 N	73.33 W
Delstern ◆[8]	263	51.20 N	7.31 E
Delta, On., Can.	212	44.37 N	76.08 W
Delta, Méx.	200	32.22 N	115.12 W
Delta, Co., U.S.	200	38.44 N	108.04 W
Delta, Mo., U.S.	194	37.11 N	89.44 W
Delta, Oh., U.S.	216	41.34 N	84.00 W
Delta, Pa., U.S.	208	39.43 N	76.19 W
Delta, Ut,. U.S.	200	39.21 N	112.34 W
Delta □[9]	194	33.30 N	90.45 W
Delta ≃	180	64.09 N	146.18 W
Delta Amacuro □[8]	246	8.30 N	61.30 W
Delta Barrage ◆[6]	142	30.11 N	31.07 E
Delta Beach	184	50.11 N	98.19 W
Delta City	194	33.04 N	90.47 W
Delta Downs	166	17.00 S	141.18 E
Delta Junction	180	64.02 N	145.41 W
Delta Mendota Canal ≊	226	37.49 N	121.34 W
Delta Peak ∧	180	56.39 N	129.34 W
Delta Reservoir ⊜[1]	210	43.17 N	75.26 W
Deltaville	208	37.33 N	76.20 W
Delton	216	42.29 N	85.24 W
Deltona	220	28.54 N	81.15 W
Delungra	166	29.39 S	150.50 E
Del'un-Uranskij chrebet ⋀	88	56.30 N	114.00 E
Delüün	86	47.42 N	90.59 E
De Luz Creek ≃	228	33.22 N	117.19 W
Del Valle	222	30.12 N	97.40 W
Del Valle, Lake ⊜[1]	226	37.35 N	121.43 W
Del Verme Falls ∟	144	5.27 N	40.17 E
Delvin	48	53.36 N	7.05 W
Delvinë	38	39.57 N	20.06 E
Del Viso	258	34.27 S	58.48 W
Delyatyn	78	48.32 N	24.37 E
Delyn □[8]	262	53.16 N	3.11 W
Demak	115a	6.53 S	110.38 E
Demaki	80	58.26 N	51.43 E
Dem'ansk	76	57.38 N	32.28 E
Demarcation Point ≻	180	69.40 N	141.15 W
Demarest	276	40.57 N	73.57 W
Demarest Brook ≃	276	40.57 N	73.58 W
Demavend, Mount → Damāvand, Qolleh-ye ∧	128	35.56 N	52.08 E
Demba	152	5.30 S	22.16 E
Demba Chio	152	9.41 S	13.41 E
Dembecha	144	10.35 N	37.30 E
Dembéni	157a	11.50 S	43.24 E
Dembi	144	8.05 N	36.27 E
Dembia, Centraf.	154	5.07 N	24.25 E
Dembia, Zaïre	154	3.31 N	25.50 E
Dembi Dolo	144	8.32 N	34.48 E
Dembo	152	3.56 S	12.35 E
Dême ≃	50	47.43 N	0.29 E
Demer ≃	56	50.58 N	4.42 E
Demerara ≃	246	6.48 N	58.10 W
Demerara-Mahaica □[4]	246	6.40 N	58.00 W
Demerthin	54	52.58 N	12.17 E
Demidov	76	55.16 N	31.31 E
Demidovo	76	59.17 N	38.17 E
Deming, N.M., U.S.	200	32.16 N	107.45 W
Deming, Wa., U.S.	224	48.49 N	122.12 W
Demini ≃	246	0.46 S	62.56 W
Demirci	130	39.03 N	28.40 E
Demirköprü Barajı ⊜[1]	130	38.40 N	28.20 E
Demirköy	130	41.49 N	27.45 E
Demirtaş	130	40.16 N	29.06 E
Demitz-Thumitz	54	51.09 N	14.14 E
Demjanka ≃	86	59.34 N	69.20 E
Demjanovo	24	60.22 N	47.03 E
Demjanskoje	86	59.36 N	69.18 E
Demjas	80	51.13 N	49.08 E
Demmeltrath ◆[8]	263	51.11 N	7.03 E
Demmin	54	53.54 N	13.02 E
Demmitt	182	55.26 N	119.54 W
Demnate	148	31.44 N	6.59 W
Democracy Monument ⟂	269a	13.45 N	100.30 E
Democrat Point ≻	276	40.37 N	73.18 W
Demoiselles, Grotte des ⟂[5]	62	43.55 N	3.45 E
Demone, Val ◆[1]	70	37.58 N	14.35 E
Demonte	62	44.19 N	7.17 E
De Montigny, Lac ⊜	190	48.08 N	77.54 W
Demopolis	194	32.31 N	87.50 W
Demorest	192	34.33 N	83.32 W
De Mossville	218	38.48 N	84.25 W
Demotte	216	41.12 N	87.12 W
Dempo, Gunung ∧	112	4.02 S	103.09 E
Dempster, Point ≻	162	33.39 S	123.52 E
Demsa	146	9.32 N	13.14 E
Demta	164	2.20 S	140.08 E
Demuryne	78	48.10 N	36.29 E
Demydivka	78	50.25 N	25.20 E
De Naauwte	158	30.08 S	21.42 E
Denain	50	50.20 N	3.23 E
Denair	226	37.32 N	120.47 W
Denakil ◆[1]	144	13.00 N	41.00 E
Denali	180	63.11 N	147.28 W
Denali National Park	180	63.44 N	148.54 W
Denali National Park ♠	180	63.15 N	150.30 W
Denan	144	6.30 N	43.30 E
Denare Beach	184	54.40 N	102.05 W
Denau	85	38.16 N	67.54 E
Denbigh, On., Can.	212	45.08 N	77.16 W
Denbigh, Wales, U.K.	44	53.11 N	3.25 W
Denbigh, Cape ≻	180	64.23 N	161.31 W
Den Burg	52	53.03 N	4.48 E
Denby Dale	44	53.35 N	1.38 W
Den Chai	110	17.59 N	100.04 E
Dendang	112	3.05 S	107.54 E
Dender (Dendre) ≃	50	51.02 N	4.06 E
Denderleeuw	50	50.53 N	4.04 E
Dendermonde	50	51.02 N	4.07 E
Dendre (Dender) ≃	50	51.02 N	4.06 E
Dendron, S. Afr.	156	23.25 S	29.11 E
Dendron, Va., U.S.	208	37.02 N	76.56 W
Dendy Park ♠	274b	37.56 S	145.00 E
Deneba	144	9.50 N	39.09 E
Denekamp	52	52.23 N	7.00 E
Denenchōfu ◆[8]	268	35.35 N	139.41 E
Deneysville	158	26.53 S	28.06 E
Denezhnykove	83	49.02 N	38.57 E
Deneżnikovo	82	55.26 N	38.07 E
Dengcheng	100	33.41 N	114.27 E
Deng Deng	152	5.12 N	13.31 E
Denge	154	3.34 N	28.14 E
Denge Marsh ⠿	42	50.57 N	0.55 E
Dengfeng	100	34.29 N	113.04 E
Denggongchang	107	30.24 N	103.49 E
Dengguanzhen	107	29.10 N	104.56 E
Dengkou	102	40.20 N	106.59 E
Denglongshu	98	41.20 N	115.15 E
Dengmingsi	98	37.53 N	116.42 E
Dêngqên	102	31.32 N	95.27 E
Dengshahe	98	39.13 N	122.04 E
Dengta	100	24.01 N	114.49 E
Denguiro	152	5.38 N	23.02 E
Dengxian	102	32.42 N	112.01 E
Dengyoufang	98	41.34 N	114.32 E
Den Haag → 's-Gravenhage	52	52.06 N	4.18 E
Denham, Austl.	162	25.55 S	113.32 E
Denham, Eng., U.K.	260	51.34 N	0.30 W
Denham, In., U.S.	216	41.09 N	86.43 W
Denham, Mount ∧	241q	18.13 N	77.32 W
Denham Aerodrome ⊠	260	51.36 N	0.31 W
Denham Island I	166	16.43 S	139.09 E
Denham Place ⚘	260	51.34 N	0.30 W
Denham Range ⋀	166	21.55 S	147.46 E
Denham Sound ⋓	162	25.40 S	113.15 E
Denham Springs	194	30.29 N	90.57 W
Den Helder	52	52.54 N	4.45 E
Denholme	262	53.48 N	1.54 W
Dénia	34	38.51 N	0.07 E
Denial Bay	162	32.06 S	133.32 E
Dénié	150	11.14 N	7.29 W
Deniliquin	166	35.32 S	144.58 E
Deniskoviči, Bela.	76	52.44 N	26.41 E
Deniskoviči, Ross.	76	52.19 N	31.43 E
Denison, Ia., U.S.	198	42.01 N	95.21 W
Denison, Tx., U.S.	196	33.45 N	96.32 W
Denison, Mount ∧	180	58.25 N	154.27 W
Denison Dam ◆[6]	196	33.50 N	96.34 W
Denisovka	24	66.14 N	55.20 E
Denisōvo	82	54.28 N	37.51 E
Denisy	261	48.33 N	1.56 E
Denizli	130	37.46 N	29.06 E
Denizli □[4]	130	37.40 N	29.15 E
Denkanikota	122	12.32 N	77.48 E
Denkendorf	60	48.56 N	11.27 E
Denkingen	58	47.53 N	9.19 E
Denklingen, Dtsch.	56	50.55 N	7.39 E
Denklingen, Dtsch.	58	47.55 N	10.51 E
Den'kovo	82	56.01 N	36.21 E
Denmark, Austl.	162	34.57 S	117.21 E
Denmark, S.C., U.S.	192	33.19 N	81.08 W
Denmark, Wi., U.S.	190	44.20 N	87.49 W
Denmark (Danmark) □[1], Europe	22	56.00 N	10.00 E
Denmark (Danmark) □[1], Europe	26	56.00 N	10.00 E
Denmark, Lake ⊜	276	40.58 N	74.31 W
Denmark Bay ⊂	176	70.33 N	103.20 W
Denmark Strait ⋓	10	67.00 N	25.00 W
Denmead	42	50.54 N	1.04 W
Dennemont	261	49.01 N	1.42 E
Dennery	241f	13.55 N	60.54 W
Dennis	207	41.44 N	70.11 W
Dennis Head ≻	46	59.23 N	2.23 W
Dennison	214	40.23 N	81.20 W
Dennis Port	207	41.39 N	70.07 W
Denniston	172	41.44 S	171.48 E
Denniston Creek ≃	282	37.30 N	122.28 W
Dennisville	208	39.11 N	74.49 W
Denny	46	56.02 N	3.55 W
Den Oever	52	52.56 N	5.02 E
Denouval	261	48.58 N	2.03 E
Denpasar	115b	8.39 S	115.13 E
Denshaw	262	53.35 N	2.02 W
Dent Ditch ≊	279a	41.18 N	82.08 W
Denton, Eng., U.K.	44	53.27 N	2.07 W
Denton, Md., U.S.	208	38.53 N	75.49 W
Denton, Mi., U.S.	281	42.20 N	83.03 W
Denton, Mt., U.S.	202	47.19 N	109.56 W
Denton, N.C., U.S.	192	35.38 N	80.06 W
Denton, Tx., U.S.	222	33.12 N	97.07 W
Denton □[6]	222	33.07 N	97.10 W
Denton Creek ≃	196	32.58 N	96.57 W
Dentonia Park ♠	275b	43.42 N	79.17 W
D'Entrecasteaux, Point ≻	162	34.50 S	116.00 E
D'Entrecasteaux Islands II	164	9.30 S	150.40 E
D'Entrecasteaux National Park ♠	162	34.41 S	115.58 E
Dents du Midi ⋀	58	46.10 N	6.56 E
Denver, Co., U.S.	200	39.44 N	104.59 W
Denver, In., U.S.	216	40.51 N	86.04 W
Denver, Ia., U.S.	190	42.40 N	92.20 W
Denver, Pa., U.S.	208	40.13 N	76.08 W
Denver City	196	32.57 N	102.49 W
Denville	210	40.53 N	74.28 W
Denzlingen	58	48.04 N	7.52 E
Deoband	124	29.42 N	77.41 E
Deocha	126	24.03 N	87.35 E
Deodoro ◆[8]	287a	22.51 S	43.23 W
Deogarh, India	120	25.32 N	73.54 E
Deogarh, India	122	21.32 N	84.44 E
Deogarh, India	124	24.33 N	78.15 E
Deogarh ∧	124	23.32 N	82.16 E
Deogarh Hills ⋀[2]	124	23.35 N	82.30 E
Deoghar	124	24.29 N	86.42 E
Deogsu Palace ⚘	271b	37.35 N	126.58 E
Deolāli	122	19.57 N	73.50 E
Deoli	126	22.03 N	86.49 E
Deoli ◆[8]	272a	28.30 N	77.14 E
Deongwar, Mount ∧	171a	27.12 S	152.16 E
Deopāra	126	22.55 N	90.15 E
Deori, India	124	23.08 N	78.41 E
Deori, India	124	23.24 N	79.01 E
Deoria	124	26.31 N	83.47 E
Deosai Mountains ⋀	123	35.20 N	75.12 E
Deosil	124	23.42 N	82.15 E
Dep ≃	89	52.54 N	127.45 E
Depāl	126	21.44 N	87.33 E
De Panne	50	51.06 N	2.35 E
Depāra	272b	22.53 N	88.34 E
Departure Bay	224	49.12 N	123.58 W
DePaul University ⚘[2]	278	41.56 N	87.39 W
Depauville	212	44.08 N	76.04 W
Depauw	218	38.20 N	86.13 W
De Peel ⠿	52	51.25 N	6.00 E
De Pere	190	44.26 N	88.03 W
Depew, N.Y., U.S.	210	42.54 N	78.41 W
Depew, Ok., U.S.	196	35.48 N	96.30 W
Deping	98	37.28 N	116.57 E
De Pinte	50	51.00 N	3.39 E
Depoe Bay	202	44.48 N	124.03 W
Depok	115a	6.24 S	106.50 E
Deport	196	33.32 N	95.19 W
Deposit	210	42.03 N	75.25 W
Deptford	285	39.50 N	75.07 W
Deptford ◆[8]	260	51.28 N	0.02 W
Deptford Mall ◆[9]	285	39.50 N	75.06 W
Deptford Terrace	285	39.48 N	75.09 W
Depuch Island I	162	20.38 S	117.43 E
Depue	190	41.19 N	89.18 W
Deputy	218	38.48 N	85.39 W
Dêqên	102	28.38 N	98.52 E
Deqing, Zhg.	102	23.09 N	111.45 E
Deqing, Zhg.	106	30.33 N	120.05 E
De Queen	194	34.02 N	94.20 W
De Quincy	194	30.27 N	93.25 W
Dera ≃	264c	47.39 N	19.05 E
Dera, Lach (Lak Dera) V	144	0.35 N	41.50 E
Dera Bugti	120	29.02 N	69.09 E
Dera Ghāzi Khān	123	30.03 N	70.38 E
Dera Gopipur	123	31.54 N	76.13 E
Dera Ismāīl Khān	123	31.50 N	70.54 E
Derakht-e Yaḩyá	120	31.50 N	68.08 E
Dera Nānak	123	32.02 N	75.01 E
Dera Nawāb	123	29.06 N	71.16 E
Derāwar Fort	123	28.46 N	71.20 E
Derazhnya	78	49.16 N	27.26 E
Derbent	84	42.03 N	48.18 E
Derbeškinskij	80	55.52 N	53.30 E
Derbetovka	80	45.48 N	43.05 E
Der Bodden ⋓	54	54.16 N	13.12 E
Derby, Austl.	162	17.18 S	123.38 E
Derby, Austl.	166	41.09 S	147.47 E
Derby, S. Afr.	158	25.55 S	27.02 E
Derby, Eng., U.K.	42	52.55 N	1.29 W
Derby, Ct., U.S.	207	41.19 N	73.05 W
Derby, Ks., U.S.	198	37.32 N	97.16 W
Derby, Me., U.S.	188	45.14 N	68.58 W
Derby, N.Y., U.S.	210	42.40 N	78.58 W
Derby, Oh., U.S.	218	39.46 N	83.12 W
Derby, Vt., U.S.	206	44.57 N	72.08 W
Derby Acres	226	35.15 N	119.35 W
Derby Line	206	45.00 N	72.05 W
Derbyshire □[6]	44	53.00 N	1.33 W
Der-Chantecoq, Lac du ⊜[1]	58	48.35 N	4.46 E
Derdepoort	156	24.42 S	26.20 E
Dere	130	39.00 N	39.18 E
Derečin	76	53.15 N	24.55 E
Derecske	30	47.21 N	21.34 E
Dereköy, Tür.	130	39.16 N	27.19 E
Dereköy, Tür.	130	40.08 N	37.47 E
Dereköy, Tür.	130	41.56 N	27.21 E
Dereli	130	40.45 N	38.27 E
Derenburg	54	51.52 N	10.54 E
Derendorf ◆[8]	263	51.15 N	6.48 E
Derenwu	105	39.40 N	116.46 E
Dereseki ◆[8]	267b	41.08 N	29.08 E
Derev'anka	24	61.34 N	34.27 E
Derg ≃	48	54.44 N	7.25 W
Derg, Lough ⊜, Ire.	48	52.57 N	8.19 W
Derg, Lough ⊜, Ire.	48	54.36 N	7.53 W
Dergači	80	51.14 N	48.46 E
Dergaon	120	26.42 N	93.58 E
Der Grabow ⊂	54	54.23 N	12.50 E
Derhachi	78	50.07 N	36.07 E
De Ridder	194	30.50 N	93.17 W
De Rijp	52	52.34 N	4.50 E
Derik	130	37.22 N	40.17 E
Derinkuyu	130	38.23 N	34.45 E
Der Kanal → English Channel ⋓	28	50.20 N	1.00 W
Derkul	80	51.16 N	51.18 E
Derkul ≃	83	48.35 N	39.41 E
Dermbach	56	50.43 N	10.06 E
Dermott	194	33.31 N	91.26 W
Dermulo	64	46.20 N	11.04 E
Derne	263	51.35 N	7.41 E
Derne ◆[8]	263	51.34 N	7.31 E
Dernieres, Isles II	194	29.02 N	90.47 W
Dernoviči	78	51.36 N	29.43 E
Deroche	224	49.11 N	122.04 W
Dero Eri	144	9.01 N	46.43 E
Dêrong	102	28.47 N	99.14 E
Déroute, Passage de la ⋓	32	49.25 N	2.00 W
Derrame	196	26.19 N	104.23 W
Derravaragh, Lough ⊜	48	53.40 N	7.24 W
Derre	154	16.56 S	36.11 E
Derrick City	214	41.58 N	78.34 W
Derrinallum	169	37.57 S	143.13 E
Derry → Londonderry, N. Ire., U.K.	48	54.59 N	7.20 W
Derry, N.H., U.S.	188	42.52 N	71.19 W
Derry, Pa., U.S.	214	40.20 N	79.18 W
Derrybrien	48	53.04 N	8.36 W
Derrykeighan	48	55.08 N	6.29 W
Derryveagh Mountains ⋀	48	55.00 N	8.05 W
Derry West	275b	43.39 N	79.42 W
Der Sārāi ◆[8]	272a	28.33 N	77.11 E
Dersau	54	54.07 N	10.20 E
Dersingham	42	52.51 N	0.30 E
Derudeb	140	17.32 N	36.06 E
De Rust	158	33.30 S	22.32 E
Deruta	66	42.59 N	12.25 E
De Ruyter	210	42.45 N	75.53 W
DeRuyter Reservoir ⊜[1]	210	42.49 N	75.53 W
Der'uzino	82	56.18 N	38.16 E
Derval	32	47.40 N	1.40 W
Derventa	38	44.58 N	17.55 E
Derwent	182	53.39 N	110.58 W
Derwent ≃, Austl.	166	43.03 S	147.22 E
Derwent ≃, Eng., U.K.	44	53.45 N	0.57 W
Derwent ≃, Eng., U.K.	44	54.57 N	1.41 W
Derwent ≃, Eng., U.K.	44	54.38 N	3.34 W
Derwent ≃, Eng., U.K.	44	52.53 N	1.17 W
Derwent Bridge	166	42.08 S	146.13 E
Derwent Reservoir ⊜[1]	44	54.50 N	2.00 W
Derwent Water ⊜	44	54.34 N	3.08 W
Deržavino	80	53.13 N	52.22 E
Deržavinsk	86	51.03 N	66.19 E
Desaguadero ≃, Arg.	252	34.13 S	66.47 W
Desaguadero ≃, Bol.	248	18.24 S	67.05 W
Desagüe, Canal de ≊	286a	19.29 N	99.05 W
Des Allemands	194	29.49 N	90.28 W
Desamparados	236	9.54 N	84.04 W
Désappointement, Îles du II	14	14.10 S	141.20 W
Des Arc	194	34.58 N	91.29 W
Desborough	42	52.27 N	0.49 W
Descabezado Grande, Volcán ∧[1]	252	35.36 S	70.45 W
Descanso, Bra.	252	26.50 S	53.35 W
Descanso, Ca., U.S.	204	32.51 N	116.37 W
Descanso, Punta ≻	204	32.16 N	117.03 W
Descanso Gardens ♠	280	34.12 N	118.13 W
Descartes	32	46.58 N	0.42 E
Deschaillons	206	46.32 N	72.07 W
Deschambault	206	46.39 N	71.56 W
Deschambault Lake	184	54.55 N	103.22 W
Deschambault Lake ⊜	184	54.40 N	103.35 W
Descharme Lake ⊜	184	57.05 N	109.13 W
Deschênes	212	45.23 N	75.48 W
Deschênes, Lac ⊜	212	45.22 N	75.51 W
Deschutes ≃, Or., U.S.	202	45.38 N	120.54 W
Deschutes ≃, Wa., U.S.	224	47.02 N	122.54 W
Descoberto	256	21.27 S	42.58 W
Desdunes	238	19.17 N	72.39 W
Dese	144	11.05 N	39.41 E
Deseado ≃	254	47.45 S	65.54 W
Deseado, Cabo ≻	254	52.44 S	74.44 W
Desembarco de los 33 Orientales, Monumento ⟂	258	33.48 S	58.25 W
Desengaño, Punta ≻	254	49.15 S	67.37 W
Desenzano del Garda	64	45.28 N	10.32 E
Deseret Peak ∧	200	40.28 N	112.38 W
Deseronto	212	44.12 N	77.03 W
Désert ≃	190	46.23 N	75.58 W
Désert, Lac ⊜	190	46.35 N	76.19 W
Desertas, Ilhas II	148	32.30 N	16.30 W
Desert Creek ≃	226	38.48 N	119.19 W
Desert Hot Springs	204	33.57 N	116.30 W
Desert Lake ⊜, On., Can.	212	44.32 N	76.35 W
Desert Lake ⊜, Nv., U.S.	204	36.58 N	115.05 W
Desert Mountains ⋀	226	39.16 N	119.00 W
Desert Peak ∧	200	41.11 N	113.22 W
Desert Valley V	204	41.15 N	118.20 W
Desert View Highlands	228	34.37 N	118.13 W
Desford	42	52.39 N	1.17 W
Desha	194	35.44 N	91.40 W
Deshaies	241o	16.18 N	61.48 W
Desheng	102	24.45 N	108.28 E
Deshengchang	107	29.06 N	105.25 E
Deshengpo	102	26.58 N	103.59 E
Deshengtai	104	42.14 N	123.45 E
Deshengyingzi	104	41.44 N	123.14 E
Deshler, Ne., U.S.	198	40.08 N	97.43 W
Deshler, Oh., U.S.	216	41.12 N	83.53 W
Deshnok	120	27.48 N	73.21 E
Deshon Manor	214	40.52 N	79.57 W
Deshu	128	30.26 N	63.19 E
Deshun	106	31.58 N	120.29 E
Desiderio Tello	252	31.13 S	66.19 W
Desio	62	45.37 N	9.13 E
Des Lacs ≃	198	48.17 N	101.25 W
Deslinde, Arroyo ≃	258	33.44 S	58.52 W
Desloge	194	37.52 N	90.31 W
Desmarais	182	55.56 N	113.49 W
De Smet	198	44.23 N	97.33 W
De Smet, Lake ⊜[1]	202	44.29 N	106.45 W
Des Moines, Ia., U.S.	190	41.36 N	93.36 W
Des Moines, N.M., U.S.	196	36.45 N	103.50 W
Des Moines, Wa., U.S.	224	47.24 N	122.19 W
Des Moines ≃	178	40.22 N	91.26 W
Des Moines, East Fork ≃	198	42.41 N	94.12 W
Dešná, Česká Rep.	61	48.58 N	15.33 E
Desna, Ukr.	78	50.56 N	30.46 E
Desna ≃, Europe	78	50.33 N	30.32 E
Desna ≃, Ross.	82	55.26 N	37.30 E
Desolación, Isla I	254	53.00 S	74.10 W
Désolation, Cap de la → Disappointment, Cape ≻	244	54.53 S	36.07 W
Desolation Point ≻	116	10.28 N	125.39 E
Desor, Mount ∧[2]	190	47.58 N	89.01 W
De Soto, Il., U.S.	194	37.49 N	89.13 W
De Soto, In., U.S.	216	40.15 N	85.17 W
De Soto, Mo., U.S.	194	38.08 N	90.33 W
De Soto, Tx., U.S.	222	32.35 N	96.51 W
De Soto □[6]	220	27.11 N	81.48 W
De Soto City	220	27.26 N	81.24 W
De Soto National Memorial ⟂	220	27.31 N	82.40 W
De Soto State Park ♠	194	34.28 N	85.36 W
Despatch	158	33.46 S	25.30 E
Despeñaperros, Desfiladero de)(	34	38.24 N	3.30 W
Des Plaines	216	42.02 N	87.53 W
Des Plaines ≃	216	41.24 N	88.16 W
Despotovac	38	44.05 N	21.33 E
Despujols	116	12.31 N	122.01 E
Desroches, Île I	138	5.41 S	53.41 E
Desruisseaux	241f	13.47 N	60.56 W
Dessau	54	51.50 N	12.14 E
Dessel	56	51.14 N	5.07 E
Deşt	130	39.10 N	39.22 E
Destacado Island I	116	12.16 N	124.06 E
De Steeg	52	52.02 N	6.04 E
Destek	130	40.51 N	36.12 E
Destelbergen	50	51.03 N	3.48 E
Desterro	250	7.17 S	37.06 W
Destin	194	30.23 N	86.29 W
Destruction, Mount ∧[2]	162	24.35 S	127.59 E
Destruction Bay	180	61.15 N	138.48 W
Destruction Island I	224	47.40 N	124.30 W
Desulo	71	40.01 N	9.14 E
Desvres	50	50.40 N	1.50 E
Deta	38	45.24 N	21.13 E
Detčino	82	54.49 N	36.19 E
Dete	154	18.38 S	26.50 E
Dethlingen	52	52.57 N	10.07 E
Detling	260	51.18 N	0.34 E
Detmold	52	51.56 N	8.52 E
Detmold □[5]	52	52.00 N	8.45 E
Detour, Point ≻	190	45.36 N	86.37 W
De Tour Village	190	46.00 N	83.54 W
Detrital Wash V	200	36.02 N	114.28 W
Detroit, Il., U.S.	219	39.37 N	90.40 W
Detroit, Mi., U.S.	216	42.20 N	83.03 W
Detroit, Mi., U.S.	281	42.20 N	83.03 W
Detroit, Or., U.S.	202	44.44 N	122.08 W
Detroit, Tx., U.S.	196	33.40 N	95.16 W
Detroit ≃	214	42.06 N	83.08 W
Detroit Beach	216	41.55 N	83.20 W
Detroit City Airport ⊠	281	42.25 N	83.01 W
Detroit Institute of Arts ⚘	281	42.22 N	83.04 W
Detroit Lake ⊜[1]	202	44.42 N	122.10 W
Detroit Lakes	198	46.48 N	95.50 W
Detroit Mercy, University Of ⚘[2]	281	42.25 N	83.08 W
Detroit Metropolitan-Wayne County Airport ⊠	281	42.13 N	83.22 W
Detroit Race Course ♠	281	42.23 N	83.19 W
Detroit-Windsor Tunnel ◆[5]	281	42.20 N	83.02 W
Detroit Zoological Park ♠	281	42.29 N	83.09 W
Detskosel'skij	265a	59.44 N	30.28 E
Dettelbach	56	49.48 N	10.09 E
Dettifoss ∟	24a	65.50 N	16.20 W
Dettingen an der Erms	56	48.32 N	9.20 E
Dettwiller	56	48.45 N	7.28 E
Det Udom	110	14.54 N	105.05 E
Detva	30	48.31 N	19.28 E
Deua National Park ♠	166	36.00 S	149.45 E
Deuben	54	51.06 N	12.04 E
Deuels Corners	284a	42.45 N	78.45 W
Deuil-la-Barre	261	48.59 N	2.20 E
Deūlgaon Rāja	122	20.01 N	76.02 E
Deulpur	272b	22.36 N	88.10 E
Deulti	126	22.26 N	87.56 E
Deurne, Bel.	50	51.13 N	4.28 E
Deurne, Ned.	52	51.28 N	5.47 E
Deusen ◆[8]	263	51.33 N	7.26 E
Deutsche Bucht ⊂	30	54.30 N	7.30 E
Deutsch Eylau → Iława	30	53.37 N	19.33 E
Deutschfeistritz	61	47.11 N	15.20 E
Deutschkreutz	61	47.36 N	16.38 E
Deutsch Krone → Wałcz	30	53.17 N	16.28 E
Deutschland → Germany □[1]	30	51.00 N	10.00 E
Deutschlandsberg	61	46.49 N	15.13 E
Deutsch-Neudorf	54	50.38 N	13.27 E
Deutsch Wagram	61	48.18 N	16.34 E
Deutsch Wusterhausen	264a	52.18 N	13.35 E
Deutzen	54	51.06 N	12.26 E
Deux-Montagnes	206	45.32 N	73.53 W
Deux-Montagnes □[6]	206	45.35 N	74.05 W
Deux Montagnes, Lac des ⊜	206	45.28 N	73.59 W
Deux-Sèvres □[5]	32	46.30 N	0.20 W
Deva	38	45.53 N	22.55 E
Devakottai	122	9.57 N	78.49 E
De Valls Bluff	194	34.47 N	91.27 W
Devaprayāg	124	30.09 N	78.37 E
Dev'atern'a	80	56.12 N	53.24 E
Dev'atiny	24	60.56 N	36.46 E
Devault	285	40.05 N	75.32 W
Dévaványa	30	47.02 N	20.58 E
Devecikonağı	130	39.55 N	28.34 E
Devecser	30	47.06 N	17.26 E
Devedağı Tepesi ∧	130	40.34 N	41.21 E
Devegeçidi Barajı ⊜[1]	130	38.05 N	39.55 E
Develi	130	38.23 N	35.30 E
Deventer	52	52.15 N	6.10 E
Deveron ≃	46	57.40 N	2.31 W
Devers	222	30.02 N	94.36 W
Devers Canal, West Branch ≊	222	29.57 N	94.46 W
Deversoir Military Base ■	142	30.25 N	32.20 E
Devès, Monts du ⋀	32	45.00 N	3.45 E
Devgadh Bāriva	120	22.42 N	73.54 E
De View, Bayou ≃	194	34.48 N	91.18 W
Devīkot	120	26.42 N	71.12 E
Devil Lake ⊜	212	44.35 N	76.27 W
Deville	56	49.53 N	4.42 E
Déville-lès-Rouen	50	49.28 N	1.02 E
Devil Peak ∧	226	37.32 N	119.44 W
Devil River Peak ∧	172	40.58 S	172.39 E
Devils ≃	196	29.39 N	100.58 W
Devil's Bridge	42	52.23 N	3.51 W
Devils Brook ≃	276	40.20 N	74.37 W
Devils Canyon V	280	34.16 N	117.58 W
Devil's Den State Park ♠	194	35.46 N	94.16 W
Devils Hole Rapids ∟	284a	43.08 N	79.03 W
Devils Hopyard State Park ♠	207	41.28 N	72.22 W
Devils Island → Diable, Île du I	250	5.17 N	52.35 W
Devils Lake	198	48.06 N	98.51 W
Devils Lake ⊜, Mi., U.S.	216	41.58 N	84.17 W
Devils Lake ⊜, N.D., U.S.	198	48.01 N	98.52 W
Devils Lake State Park ♠	190	43.24 N	89.44 W
Devils Marbles ♠	162	20.30 S	134.14 E
Devils Paw ∧	180	58.44 N	133.50 W
Devils Postpile National Monument ♠	226	37.37 N	119.05 W
Devils Tower ∧	198	44.31 N	104.57 W
Devils Tower National Monument ♠	198	44.31 N	104.57 W
Devil's Water ≃	44	54.58 N	2.02 W
Devin	38	41.45 N	24.24 E
Devine, B.C., Can.	182	50.32 N	122.30 W
Devine, Tx., U.S.	196	29.08 N	98.54 W
Devizes	42	51.22 N	1.59 W
Devladove	78	48.07 N	33.45 E
Devli	120	25.45 N	75.23 E
De Voe Lake ⊜	276	40.23 N	74.23 W
Devoll ≃	38	40.49 N	19.51 E
Dévoluy ⋀	62	44.39 N	5.53 E
Devon, Ab., Can.	182	53.22 N	113.44 W
Devon, S. Afr.	158	26.21 S	28.48 E
Devon, Pa., U.S.	285	40.02 N	75.25 W
Devon □[6]	42	50.45 N	3.50 W
Devon ≃, Eng., U.K.	42	53.04 N	0.43 W
Devon ≃, Scot., U.K.	46	56.07 N	3.51 W
Devon Island I	16	75.00 N	87.00 W
Devonport, Austl.	166	41.11 S	146.21 E
Devonport, N.Z.	172	36.49 S	174.48 E
Devonport, Eng., U.K.	42	50.22 N	4.10 W
Devonshire	285	39.49 N	75.32 W
Devonshire Plaza ◆[9]	281	42.17 N	83.00 W
Devore	228	34.13 N	117.25 W
Devoto	252	31.24 S	62.19 W
Devrek	130	41.13 N	31.57 E
Devrekâni	130	41.36 N	33.51 E
Devres ≃	130	41.06 N	34.25 E
Devure ≃	154	20.00 S	32.20 E
Dewa, Ujung ≻	114	2.55 N	95.48 E
Dewakang-lompo, Pulau I	112	5.24 S	118.25 E
Dewar	196	35.27 N	95.56 W
Dewart	210	41.07 N	76.53 W
Dewart Lake ⊜	216	41.22 N	85.47 W
Dewās	120	22.58 N	76.04 E
Dewa-sanchi ⋀[2]	92	39.05 N	140.10 E
Dewdney	224	49.10 N	122.12 W
Dewetsdorp	158	29.33 S	26.34 E
Dewey, Il., U.S.	216	40.19 N	88.17 W
Dewey, Ok., U.S.	196	36.47 N	95.56 W
Dewey, Wa., U.S.	224	48.25 N	122.37 W
Dewey Beach	208	38.41 N	75.04 W
Deweyville	194	30.18 N	93.45 W
De Witt, Ar., U.S.	194	34.17 N	91.20 W
Dewitt, Il., U.S.	219	40.11 N	88.47 W
De Witt, Ia., U.S.	190	41.49 N	90.32 W
De Witt, Mi., U.S.	216	42.50 N	84.34 W
De Witt, Ne., U.S.	198	40.23 N	96.55 W
De Witt, N.Y., U.S.	210	43.02 N	76.03 W
De Witt □[6], Il., U.S.	216	40.12 N	88.55 W
De Witt □[6], Tx., U.S.	222	29.07 N	97.20 W
Dewittville	214	42.14 N	79.27 W
Dewsbury	44	53.42 N	1.37 W
Dexing	100	28.54 N	117.36 E
Dexingjie	98	39.54 N	122.50 E
Dexter, Me., U.S.	188	45.01 N	69.17 W
Dexter, Mi., U.S.	216	42.20 N	83.53 W
Dexter, Mo., U.S.	194	36.47 N	89.57 W
Dexter, N.M., U.S.	196	33.11 N	104.22 W
Dexter, N.Y., U.S.	212	44.00 N	76.02 W
Dexterity Fiord ⊂[2]	176	71.11 N	73.03 W
Deyang	102	31.14 N	104.22 E
Dey-Dey, Lake ⊜	162	29.12 S	131.04 E
Deyhūk	128	33.17 N	57.30 E
Deyyer	128	27.50 N	51.55 E
Dez ≃	128	31.39 N	48.52 E
Dezfūl	128	32.23 N	48.24 E
Dez Gerd	128	30.45 N	51.57 E
Dezhou	98	37.27 N	116.18 E
Dežneva, mys ≻	180	66.06 N	169.45 W
Dezong	120	32.09 N	90.20 E
Dezzo di Scalve	64	45.59 N	10.05 E
Dgâmcha, Sebkhet te-n- ⊜	150	18.45 N	15.48 W
Dhabān Singh	123	31.44 N	73.34 E
Dhāding	124	27.52 N	84.55 E
Dhādkā	126	22.47 N	86.30 E
Dháfna ∧	267c	38.07 N	23.38 E
Dháfni, Ellás	38	37.48 N	22.01 E
Dháfni, Ellás	267c	38.01 N	23.38 E
Dhafnion Monastery ⚘[1]	267c	38.01 N	23.38 E
Dhahab	140	28.29 N	34.32 E
Dhahab, Wādī adh- V	132	32.44 N	35.54 E
Dhahran → Aẓ-Ẓahrān	128	26.18 N	50.08 E
Dhaka (Dacca), Bngl.	126	23.43 N	90.25 E
Dhāka, India	124	26.41 N	85.10 E
Dhaka □[5]	120	24.15 N	90.15 E
Dhākauli	124	24.45 N	77.51 E
Dhakuria Lake ⊜	272b	22.31 N	88.22 E
Dhaleswari ≃	126	23.32 N	90.34 E
Dháli	130	35.01 N	33.25 E
Dhamār	144	14.46 N	44.23 E
Dhāmpur	124	29.19 N	78.31 E
Dhāmrai	126	23.55 N	90.13 E
Dhamtari	122	20.41 N	81.34 E
Dhāmura	126	22.53 N	90.12 E
Dhanaula	123	30.17 N	75.35 E
Dhanaura	124	28.58 N	78.15 E
Dhanbād	126	23.48 N	86.27 E
Dhandhuka	120	22.22 N	71.59 E
Dhanera	126	23.25 N	86.39 E
Dhaneswargāti	126	23.25 N	89.20 E
Dhangadhī	124	28.41 N	80.36 E
Dhaniakhāli	126	22.58 N	88.06 E
D'Hanis	196	29.20 N	99.17 W
Dhankuṭa	124	26.59 N	87.20 E
Dhansar	272c	19.07 N	73.05 E
Dhānyahānā	272b	22.48 N	88.11 E
Dhār	120	22.36 N	75.18 E
Dharampur	122	20.32 N	73.11 E
Dharān	124	26.49 N	87.17 E
Dharangaon	120	21.01 N	75.16 E
Dhārāpuram	122	10.44 N	77.31 E
Dhāri	120	21.20 N	71.01 E
Dhārīwāl	123	31.57 N	75.19 E
Dharmābād	122	18.54 N	77.51 E
Dharmapuri	122	12.08 N	78.10 E
Dharmavaram	122	14.26 N	77.43 E
Dharmjaygarh	124	22.28 N	83.13 E
Dharmkot	123	30.57 N	75.14 E
Dharmshāla	123	32.13 N	76.19 E
Dharoor, Tog V	144	10.20 N	50.30 E
Dharug National Park ♠	170	33.25 S	151.05 E
Dhasān ≃	124	25.48 N	79.24 E
Dhātrigrām	126	23.15 N	88.20 E
Dhaulpur	124	26.42 N	77.54 E
Dhawalāgiri □[8]	124	28.30 N	83.30 E
Dhawalāgiri ∧	124	28.42 N	83.30 E
Dhebar Lake ⊜	120	24.16 N	74.00 E
Dhelfoí ⟂	38	38.30 N	22.29 E
Dhenkānāl	120	20.40 N	85.36 E
Dhenoúsa I	38	37.06 N	25.49 E
Dherínia	130	35.03 N	33.57 E
Dhërmiu ⚘[1]	38	40.08 N	19.42 E
Dherue, Loch an ⊜	46	58.25 N	4.27 W
Dheskáti	38	39.55 N	21.49 E
Dheune ≃	58	46.54 N	5.00 E
Dhiavolítsion	38	37.18 N	21.58 E

≃ River	Fluß	Río	Rivière	Rio
≊ Canal	Kanal	Canal	Canal	Canal
∟ Waterfall, Rapids	Wasserfall, Stromschnellen	Cascada, Rápidos	Chute d'eau, Rapides	Cascata, Rápidos
⋓ Strait	Meeresstraße	Estrecho	Détroit	Estreito
⊂ Bay, Gulf	Bucht, Golf	Bahía, Golfo	Baie, Golfe	Baía, Golfo
⊜ Lake, Lakes	See, Seen	Lago, Lagos	Lac, Lacs	Lago, Lagos
⠿ Swamp	Sumpf	Pantano	Marais	Pântano
⩍ Ice Features, Glacier	Eis- und Gletscherformen	Accidentes Glaciales	Formes glaciaires	Acidentes glaciares
⍑ Other Hydrographic Features	Andere Hydrographische Objekte	Otros Elementos Hidrográficos	Autres données hydrographiques	Outros acidentes hidrográficos

⟡ Submarine Features	Untermeerische Objekte	Accidentes Submarinos	Formes de relief sous-marin	Acidentes submarinos
□ Political Unit	Politische Einheit	Unidad Politica	Entité politique	Unidade política
⚘ Cultural Institution	Kulturelle Institution	Institución Cultural	Institution culturelle	Institução cultural
⟂ Historical Site	Historische Stätte	Sitio Histórico	Site historique	Sitio histórico
♠ Recreational Site	Erholungs- und Ferienort	Sitio de Recreo	Centre de loisirs	Area de Lazer
⊠ Airport	Flughafen	Aeropuerto	Aéroport	Aeroporto
■ Military Installation	Militäranlage	Instalación Militar	Installation militaire	Instalação militar
◆ Miscellaneous	Verschiedenes	Misceláneo	Divers	Diversos

Name / Name	Page / Seite	Lat.°′ / Breite°′	Long.°′ / Länge°′ E = Ost
Dhībān	132	31.30 N	35.47 E
Dhidhimótikhon	38	41.21 N	26.30 E
Dhiinsoor	144	2.24 N	42.59 E
Dhíkti ʌ	38	35.08 N	25.30 E
Dhílos ı	38	37.26 N	25.16 E
Dhimitsána	38	37.37 N	22.03 E
Dhiónisos	267c	38.06 N	23.53 E
Dhī Qār □[4]	128	31.00 N	46.15 E
Dhirāsrām	126	23.57 N	90.25 E
Dhirwah, Wādī adh- V	132	31.18 N	36.56 E
Dhodhekánisos (Dodecanese) ıı	38	36.30 N	27.00 E
Dhodhóni ı	38	39.34 N	20.47 E
Dhofar → Ẓufār ◆[1]	118	17.00 N	54.10 E
Dhokra	272b	22.40 N	88.34 E
Dholka	120	22.43 N	72.28 E
Dhomhnuill, Sgurr ʌ	46	56.45 N	5.27 W
Dhone	122	15.25 N	77.53 E
Dhopākhola	126	23.08 N	89.10 E
Dhorāji	120	21.44 N	70.27 E
Dhosha	126	22.15 N	88.33 E
Dhowa	126	24.03 N	86.54 E
Dhoxáton	38	41.05 N	24.14 E
Dhrāngadhra	120	22.59 N	71.28 E
Dhrapetsóna	267c	37.57 N	23.37 E
Dhrol	120	22.34 N	70.25 E
Dhron ≃	56	49.52 N	6.54 E
Dhubāb	144	12.56 N	43.25 E
Dhuburi	124	26.01 N	89.59 E
Dhudiāl	123	33.04 N	72.58 E
Dhulāgarh	272b	22.35 N	88.11 E
Dhule	120	20.54 N	74.47 E
Dhulia → Dhule	120	20.54 N	74.47 E
Dhuliān	124	24.41 N	87.58 E
Dhulikhel	124	27.37 N	85.33 E
Dhūlsīrās ◆[8]	272a	28.33 N	77.02 E
Dhünn	56	51.06 N	7.16 E
Dhünn-Stausee ⊜[1]	263	51.05 N	7.16 E
Dhupgāri	124	26.36 N	89.01 E
Dhurbo	144	11.37 N	50.20 E
Dhūri	124	30.22 N	75.52 E
Dhutumkhar ≃	272c	18.54 N	73.00 E
Dhuudo	144	9.20 N	50.12 E
Dhuudo V	144	9.14 N	50.39 E
Dhuusa Mareeb	144	5.31 N	46.24 E
Dhytikí Ellás □[4]	38	38.00 N	21.30 E
Dhytikí Makedhonía □[4]	38	40.30 N	21.30 E
Día ı	38	35.27 N	25.13 E
Diabaig	46	57.34 N	5.40 W
Diabakania	150	10.38 N	10.58 W
Diable, Île du (Devils Island) ı	250	5.17 N	52.35 W
Diable, Lac du ⊜	206	46.31 N	74.20 W
Diable, Pointe du >	240e	14.47 N	60.54 W
Diable, Rivière du ≃	206	46.03 N	74.38 W
Diables, Morne aux ʌ	240d	15.37 N	61.27 W
Diablo, Ca., U.S.	226	37.50 N	121.58 W
Diablo, Wa., U.S.	224	48.43 N	121.09 W
Diablo, Canyon V	200	35.18 N	110.59 W
Diablo, Isla del → Diable, Île du ı	250	5.17 N	52.35 W
Diablo, Mount ʌ	226	37.53 N	121.55 W
Diablo, Pico del ʌ	232	30.59 N	115.45 W
Diablo, Sierra del ʎ	196	27.20 N	104.05 W
Diablo Lake ⊜[1]	224	48.43 N	121.08 W
Diablo Plateau ʎ[1]	200	31.30 N	105.30 W
Diablo Range ʎ	226	37.00 N	121.20 W
Diablotins, Morne ʌ	240d	15.30 N	61.24 W
Diabo	150	7.47 N	5.11 W
Diaca	154	11.30 S	39.59 E
Diadema	256	23.42 S	46.37 W
Diadema □[7]	287b	23.42 S	46.36 W
Diafarabé	150	14.09 N	5.01 W
Diagonal	198	40.48 N	94.20 W
Diaka ≃[1]	150	15.13 N	4.14 W
Dialakoto	150	13.19 N	13.18 W
Dialassagou	150	13.45 N	3.37 W
Diamant, Pointe du >	240e	14.27 N	61.03 W
Diamante, Arg.	252	32.04 S	60.39 W
Diamante, It.	68	39.41 N	15.49 E
Diamante ≃	252	34.31 S	66.56 W
Diamante, Punta >	234	16.47 N	99.52 W
Diamante de Ubá	256	21.12 S	42.55 W
Diamantina	255	18.15 S	43.36 W
Diamantina ≃	166	26.45 S	139.10 E
Diamantina Fracture Zone ✧	14	36.00 S	105.00 E
Diamantina Lakes	166	23.46 S	141.09 E
Diamantino	248	14.25 S	56.27 W
Diamantino ≃	255	16.08 S	52.28 W
Diamond, Il., U.S.	216	41.17 N	88.15 W
Diamond, Mo., U.S.	194	37.00 N	94.19 W
Diamond, Oh., U.S.	214	41.06 N	81.01 W
Diamond Bar	228	34.01 N	117.48 W
Diamond Brook ≃	276	40.56 N	74.08 W
Diamond Creek	274b	37.41 S	145.09 E
Diamond Creek ≃	169	37.44 S	145.09 E
Diamond Harbour	126	22.12 N	88.12 E
Diamond Head ±[6]	229c	21.16 N	157.49 W
Diamond Hill	207	41.59 N	71.24 W
Diamond Hill Reservoir ⊜[1]	283	42.00 N	71.24 W
Diamond Hill State Park ♦	283	42.00 N	71.26 W
Diamond Islets ıı	166	17.25 S	150.58 E
Diamond Lake	216	42.15 N	88.00 W
Diamond Lake ⊜, On., Can.	212	45.04 N	78.02 W
Diamond Lake ⊜, Il., U.S.	278	42.15 N	88.00 W
Diamond Lake ⊜, Mi., U.S.	216	41.54 N	85.59 W
Diamond Lake ⊜, Or., U.S.	202	43.10 N	122.09 W
Diamond Peak ʌ, Id., U.S.	202	44.09 N	113.05 W
Diamond Peak ʌ, Or., U.S.	202	43.33 N	122.09 W
Diamond Peak ʌ, Wa., U.S.	202	46.07 N	117.32 W
Diamond Springs	226	38.41 N	120.48 W
Diamondville	200	41.46 N	110.32 W
Diana	222	32.43 N	94.45 W
Diana Bay c	176	60.50 N	69.50 W
Dianalund	41	55.32 N	11.30 E
Dianbai	102	21.30 N	111.01 E
Dian Chi ⊜	102	24.50 N	102.42 E
Diancun	105	39.55 N	116.14 E
Dianfangba	102	32.54 N	103.35 E
Diangounté Kamara	150	14.33 N	9.31 W
Dianhu	100	33.58 N	119.38 E
Dianji	98	36.32 N	120.27 E
Dianjiang	102	30.21 N	107.23 E
Diano, Vallo di V	68	40.21 N	15.36 E
Diano Marina	62	43.54 N	8.05 E
Dianópolis	250	11.38 S	46.50 W
Dianqianhe	100	30.44 N	116.02 E
Dianra	150	8.45 N	6.14 W
Dianshang	106	31.10 N	118.51 E
Dianshan Hu ⊜	106	31.08 N	120.55 E
Diantou	100	27.18 N	120.11 E
Dianzi	104	41.37 N	122.05 E
Diaobingshan	104	42.28 N	123.33 E
Diao'ecun	105	40.43 N	115.49 E
Diaohetou	105	39.17 N	116.41 E
Diaopu	100	32.22 N	119.54 E
Diaoshuilouzi	104	40.59 N	122.22 E
Diaotai	100	29.40 N	119.39 E
Diaowo	105	39.30 N	116.04 E
Diapaga	150	12.04 N	1.47 E
Diapangou	150	12.07 N	0.11 E
Diapblo, Puntan >	174n	15.00 N	145.35 E
Dias	256	22.28 S	45.34 W
Diascund Creek Reservoir ⊜[1]	208	37.27 N	76.54 W
Diawala	150	10.07 N	5.28 W
Diaz	194	35.38 N	91.15 W
Diaz Point >	156	26.38 S	15.05 E
Dibai	124	28.13 N	78.15 E
Dibāng ≃	120	27.50 N	95.32 E
Dibay → Dubayy	128	25.18 N	55.18 E
Dibaya	152	6.30 S	22.57 E
Dibbīn	132	32.26 N	36.34 E
Dibeng	158	27.35 S	22.54 E
D'Iberville	194	30.25 N	88.53 W
Dibete	156	23.45 S	26.26 E
Dibi	144	4.13 N	41.56 E
Dibo	144	6.31 N	41.52 E
Diboll	222	31.11 N	94.46 W
Dibrugarh	120	27.29 N	94.54 E
Dibs	140	12.34 N	24.14 E
Dibs, Bi'r ╤[4]	140	22.12 N	29.32 E
Dichāon Kalān ◆[8]	272a	28.39 N	76.59 E
Dick, Mount ʌ[2]	168a	31.35 S	116.42 E
Dickelsbach ≃	263	51.24 N	6.45 E
Dickens	196	33.37 N	100.50 W
Dickerson	208	39.13 N	77.25 W
Dickey ≃	224	47.55 N	124.37 W
Dickey Lake ⊜, On., Can.	212	44.47 N	77.44 W
Dickey Lake ⊜, Wa., U.S.	224	48.06 N	124.31 W
Dickinson, N.D., U.S.	198	46.52 N	102.47 W
Dickinson, Pa., U.S.	208	40.07 N	77.20 W
Dickinson, Tx., U.S.	222	29.27 N	95.03 W
Dickinson Bayou ≃	222	29.28 N	94.58 W
Dickinson Island ı	281	42.37 N	82.38 W
Dickins Seamount ✧[3]	16	54.30 N	137.00 W
Dicks	158	27.43 S	30.10 E
Dickson, Ok., U.S.	196	34.11 N	96.59 W
Dickson, Tn., U.S.	194	36.04 N	87.23 W
Dickson City	210	41.28 N	75.36 W
Dicle, Tür.	130	38.22 N	40.04 E
Dicle, Tür.	130	37.18 N	42.04 E
Dicle → Tigris ≃	128	31.00 N	47.25 E
Dicomano	66	43.53 N	11.31 E
Diculom	116	7.54 N	122.14 E
Dicun	100	33.46 N	117.32 E
Didam	52	51.56 N	6.08 E
Didao	89	45.22 N	130.51 E
Didbiran	89	51.58 N	139.20 E
Didcot	42	51.37 N	1.15 W
Didesa ≃	144	9.56 N	35.45 E
Didiéni	150	13.53 N	8.06 W
Didimbo	152	17.30 S	21.45 E
Didinga Hills ʎ	154	4.20 N	33.35 E
Didsbury	182	51.40 N	114.08 W
Didsbury ◆[8]	262	53.25 N	2.14 W
Diduyon ≃	116	16.36 N	121.42 E
Dīdwāna	120	27.24 N	74.34 E
Didy	157b	18.07 S	48.32 E
Die	62	44.45 N	5.22 E
Die Aue ◆[1]	263	51.40 N	6.35 E
Die Berg ʌ	156	25.12 S	30.09 E
Die Boss	158	31.59 S	19.44 E
Diébougou	150	10.58 N	3.15 W
Dieburg	56	49.54 N	8.50 E
Dieciocho de Julio	252	33.41 S	53.33 W
Diecke	150	7.21 N	8.58 W
Diedenhofen → Thionville	56	49.22 N	6.10 E
Diedersdorf	264a	52.20 N	13.21 E
Die Erpe ≃	264a	52.27 N	13.38 E
Diefenbaker, Lake ⊜[1]	184	51.00 N	106.55 W
Diego de Almagro	252	26.23 S	70.03 W
Diego de Almagro, Isla ı	254	51.25 S	75.10 W
Diego de Ocampo, Pico ʌ	238	19.35 N	70.45 W
Diego Garcia ı	12	7.20 S	72.25 E
Diego Gaynor	258	34.17 S	59.14 W
Diego Pérez, Cayería de ıı	240p	22.05 N	81.40 W
Diego Ramírez, Islas ıı	244	56.30 S	68.44 W
Die Haard ◆[1]	263	51.41 N	7.15 E
Diekirch	56	49.53 N	6.10 E
Dieksee ⊜	54	54.10 N	10.30 E
Dieleemu	86	46.22 N	88.43 E
Dielingen	52	52.26 N	8.20 E
Dielsdorf	58	47.29 N	8.27 E
Diéma	150	14.32 N	9.12 W
Diemansputs	158	29.54 S	21.33 E
Diembéring	150	12.28 N	16.47 W
Diemel ≃	52	51.39 N	9.27 E
Diemel-Talsperre ◆[6]	56	51.22 N	8.43 E
Diemen	52	52.20 N	4.58 E
Diemuchuoke	120	32.42 N	79.29 E
Dien Bien Phu	110	21.23 N	103.01 E
Dien Khanh	110	12.15 N	109.06 E
Diepenau	52	52.25 N	8.44 E
Diepenbeek	56	50.54 N	5.24 E
Diepenheim	52	52.12 N	6.33 E
Diepensee	264a	52.22 N	13.31 E
Diepenveen	52	52.18 N	6.08 E
Diepholz	52	52.35 N	8.21 E
Diepoldsau	58	47.23 N	9.38 E
Dieppe, N.B., Can.	186	46.06 N	64.45 W
Dieppe, Fr.	50	49.56 N	1.05 E
Dierbao	98	40.20 N	114.32 E
Dierdorf	56	50.33 N	7.39 E
Dieren	52	52.03 N	6.06 E
Dierks	194	34.07 N	94.00 W
Diersbach	60	48.25 N	13.34 E
Di'er Songhua ≃	89	45.26 N	124.39 E
Diesdorf	54	52.45 N	10.52 E
Dieskau	54	51.26 N	12.02 E
Diessem ◆[8]	263	51.20 N	6.35 E
Diessen	64	47.56 N	11.06 E
Diessenhofen	58	47.41 N	8.45 E
Diest	56	50.59 N	5.03 E
Dietenheim	58	48.12 N	10.04 E
Dietersburg	60	48.30 N	12.55 E
Dietersdorf	56	50.13 N	10.49 E
Dietfurt	56	48.57 N	10.56 E
Dietfurt an der Altmühl	60	49.02 N	11.35 E
Dietikon	58	47.24 N	8.24 E
Dietmannsried	58	47.49 N	10.17 E
Dietrich	202	42.54 N	114.15 W
Dietzenbach	56	50.01 N	8.47 E
Dietzhölztal	56	50.50 N	8.19 E
Dieue-sur-Meuse	56	49.04 N	5.25 E
Dieulefit	62	44.31 N	5.04 E
Dieulouard	56	48.51 N	6.04 E
Dieuze	56	48.49 N	6.43 E
Dieveniškės	76	54.12 N	25.37 E
Diever	52	52.52 N	6.19 E
Die Ville ʎ[2]	56	50.40 N	6.55 E
Die Wurzen (Koren))(	64	46.31 N	13.45 E
Diez	56	50.22 N	8.01 E
Diez de Octubre	232	24.44 N	104.39 W
Dif	144	0.59 N	40.57 E
Difang	98	35.23 N	117.52 E
Diffa	146	13.19 N	12.37 E
Diffa □[5]	146	16.00 N	13.30 E
Differdange	56	49.32 N	5.52 E
Difficult Run ≃	284c	38.58 N	77.14 W
Diffun	116	16.34 N	121.33 E
Difuri ı	122	5.24 N	73.38 E
Digambar Jain Temple ᴗ[1]	272b	22.36 N	88.23 E
Digambarpur	126	21.57 N	88.22 E
Digba	154	4.24 N	25.47 E
Digboi	120	27.23 N	95.38 E
Digby	186	44.37 N	65.46 W
Digby Neck >[1]	186	44.30 N	66.10 W
Dige	98	34.22 N	114.28 E
Digerberget ʌ[2]	40	60.35 N	13.25 E
Digges Islands ıı	176	62.35 N	77.50 W
Diggle	262	53.34 N	1.59 W
Dighalia	126	23.07 N	89.39 E
Dighipāra	126	21.58 N	88.17 E
Dighode	272c	18.54 N	73.02 E
Dighra	272b	22.47 N	88.32 E
Dighton, Ks., U.S.	198	38.28 N	100.28 W
Dighton, Ma., U.S.	207	41.48 N	71.07 W
Di Giorgio	228	35.15 N	118.51 W
Dīglūr	122	18.33 N	77.36 E
Digmoor	262	53.32 N	2.45 W
Dīgnagar	126	23.27 N	87.41 E
Dignano	64	46.05 N	12.56 E
Digne	62	44.06 N	6.14 E
Digoin	32	46.29 N	3.59 E
Digomi	84	41.47 N	44.44 E
Digong	104	42.11 N	122.03 E
Digor	84	40.23 N	43.24 E
Digora	84	43.10 N	44.09 E
Digos	116	6.45 N	125.20 E
Digra	272b	22.50 N	88.20 E
Digras	122	20.07 N	77.43 E
Digri	120	25.10 N	69.07 E
Digui	152	5.28 N	20.50 E
Digul ≃	164	7.07 S	138.42 E
Dihaer	86	42.35 N	89.49 E
Dihtyari	78	50.35 N	32.45 E
Dihun	144	7.18 N	42.42 E
Diirmentobe	86	45.44 N	63.37 E
Dijag	24	65.48 N	57.39 E
Dijlah → Tigris ≃	128	31.00 N	47.25 E
Dijlah, Wādī V	142	29.58 N	31.18 E
Dijle (Dyle) ≃	56	51.04 N	4.25 E
Dijohan Point >	116	16.19 N	122.14 E
Dijon	58	47.19 N	5.01 E
Dik	146	9.58 N	17.31 E
Dikaja	76	59.15 N	39.30 E
Dikala	154	4.41 N	31.23 E
Dikbıyık	130	41.13 N	36.38 E
Dike	190	42.27 N	92.37 W
Dikhil	144	11.06 N	42.22 E
Dikili	130	39.04 N	26.53 E
Dikirnis	142	31.05 N	31.35 E
Dikli	76	57.35 N	25.06 E
Diklosmta, gora ʌ	84	42.29 N	45.47 E
Dikmen	130	39.53 N	32.50 E
Dikodougou	150	9.04 N	5.46 W
Diksmuide (Dixmude)	50	51.02 N	2.52 E
Dikson	74	73.30 N	80.35 E
Dikwa	146	12.02 N	13.56 E
Dila	144	6.21 N	38.17 E
Dilektepe	130	38.04 N	41.49 E
Dile Point >	116	17.34 N	120.20 E
Dilerpur	272b	22.51 N	88.10 E
Dili	112	8.33 S	125.35 E
Dilia V	146	16.53 N	11.00 E
Diligent Strait ʊ	110	12.11 N	92.57 E
Di Linh	110	11.35 N	108.04 E
Diližan	84	40.45 N	44.52 E
Diližanskij zapovednik ♦	84	40.40 N	45.00 E
Dill ≃	56	50.33 N	8.29 E
Dill City	196	35.16 N	99.08 W
Dillenburg	56	50.44 N	8.17 E
Diller	198	40.06 N	96.56 W
Dilley, Or., U.S.	224	45.29 N	123.07 W
Dilley, Tx., U.S.	196	28.40 N	99.10 W
Dilling	140	12.03 N	29.39 E
Dillingen	56	49.21 N	6.44 E
Dillingen an der Donau	56	48.34 N	10.29 E
Dillingham	180	59.02 N	158.29 W
Dillon, Co., U.S.	200	39.37 N	106.02 W
Dillon, Mt., U.S.	202	45.12 N	112.38 W
Dillon, S.C., U.S.	192	34.24 N	79.22 W
Dillon ≃	184	55.56 N	108.57 W
Dillon Cone ʌ	172	42.16 S	173.13 E
Dillon Lake ⊜	184	55.45 N	109.30 W
Dillon Lake ⊜[1]	188	40.02 N	82.10 W
Dillon Mountain ʌ	200	33.51 N	108.48 W
Dillon Reservoir ⊜[1]	200	39.35 N	106.02 W
Dillon State Park ♦	188	40.03 N	82.08 W
Dillonvale	214	40.11 N	80.46 W
Dillsboro	218	39.01 N	85.03 W
Dillsburg	208	40.06 N	77.02 W
Dilltown	214	40.29 N	79.00 W
Dillwyn	192	37.32 N	78.27 W
Dilly	150	15.01 N	7.40 W
Dilolo	152	10.42 S	22.20 E
Dilsen	56	51.02 N	5.44 E
Dilworth	198	46.52 N	96.42 W
Dilworthtown	285	39.54 N	75.34 W
Dima, Ang.	152	15.27 S	20.10 E
Dima, Indon.	114	1.20 N	97.20 E
Dimāpur	120	25.54 N	93.44 E
Dimaro	64	46.20 N	10.52 E
Dimasalang	116	12.12 N	123.51 E
Dimashq (Damascus)	132	33.30 N	36.18 E
Dimashq □[8]	132	33.30 N	37.00 E
Dimass, Rass >	36	35.37 N	11.03 E
Dimataling	116	7.32 N	123.22 E
Dimbelenge	152	5.33 S	23.07 E
Dimbokro	150	6.39 N	4.42 W
Dimboola	166	36.27 S	142.02 E
Dimbulah	166	17.09 S	145.07 E
Dime	144	6.16 N	36.20 E
Dime Box	222	30.21 N	96.50 W
Dimitrovgrad, Blg.	38	42.03 N	25.36 E
Dimitrovgrad, Jugo.	38	43.01 N	22.47 E
Dimitrovgrad, Ross.	80	54.14 N	49.39 E
Dimitrovo → Pernik	38	42.36 N	23.02 E
Dimitrovskoje	85	40.16 N	69.03 E
Dimlang ʌ	146	8.24 N	11.47 E
Dimmitt	196	34.33 N	102.18 W
Dimo	154	5.19 N	29.10 E
Dimock	210	41.45 N	75.32 W
Dimona	132	31.04 N	35.02 E
Dimondale	216	42.38 N	84.38 W
Dina	123	33.02 N	73.36 E
Dinach	144	9.15 N	50.37 E
Dinagat	116	9.59 N	125.35 E
Dinagat Island ı	116	10.12 N	125.35 E
Dinagat Sound ʊ	116	9.59 N	125.50 E
Dinahican Point >	116	14.42 N	121.44 E
Dinājpur	124	25.38 N	88.38 E
Dinalupihan	116	14.52 N	120.28 E
Dinamarca → Denmark □[1]	26	56.00 N	10.00 E
Dinamarca, Estrecho de → Denmark Strait ʊ	10	67.00 N	25.00 W
Dinami	68	38.31 N	16.09 E
Dinamita	196	25.43 N	103.38 W
Dinamo	80	50.15 N	41.38 E
Dinan	32	48.27 N	2.02 W
Dīnānagar	123	32.09 N	75.28 E
Dinant	56	50.16 N	4.55 E
Dinar	130	38.04 N	30.10 E
Dinara (Dinaric Alps) ʎ	36	43.50 N	16.35 E
Dinard	32	48.38 N	2.04 W
Dinaric Alps → Dinara ʎ	36	43.50 N	16.35 E
Dinarische Alpen → Dinara ʎ	36	43.50 N	16.35 E
Dinas, Pil.	116	7.38 N	123.20 E
Dinas, Wales, U.K.	42	52.00 N	4.54 W
Dinas Head >	42	52.02 N	4.55 W
Dinas Powys	42	51.26 N	3.14 W
Dindanko	150	14.08 N	9.30 W
Dindar, Nahr ad- (Dinder) ≃	140	14.06 N	33.40 E
Dīndārpur ◆[8]	272a	28.36 N	76.59 E
Dinde	152	14.12 S	13.44 E
Dinder (Nahr ad-Dindar) ≃	140	14.06 N	33.40 E
Dinder National Park ♦	140	12.40 N	35.20 E
Dindi ≃	122	16.21 N	79.13 E
Dindigul	122	10.21 N	77.57 E
Dindima	150	10.18 N	10.12 E
Dindori	124	22.57 N	81.05 E
Dineksaray	130	37.23 N	32.37 E
Dinga, Pāk.	120	25.26 N	67.10 E
Dinga, Pāk.	123	32.38 N	73.43 E
Dinga, Zaïre	152	5.19 S	16.34 E
Dingalan Bay c	116	15.18 N	121.25 E
Ding'an	110	19.44 N	110.21 E
Dingba	154	3.24 N	27.55 E
Dingbian	102	37.40 N	107.41 E
Dingbianji	102	36.37 N	108.41 E
Dingbu	106	31.18 N	119.10 E
Dingden	52	51.46 N	6.37 E
Dinge	152	4.58 S	12.22 E
Dingelsdorf	58	47.44 N	9.09 E
Dingelstädt	54	51.18 N	10.19 E
Dingelstedt	54	51.58 N	10.58 E
Dingeryu	105	39.37 N	114.55 E
Dingfeng	106	31.20 N	121.45 E
Dinggou	100	32.34 N	119.39 E
Dinggyê	124	28.29 N	88.06 E
Dinghai	100	30.02 N	122.06 E
Dingila	154	3.39 N	26.22 E
Dingjia	107	29.24 N	106.09 E
Dingjiagou	104	40.40 N	122.35 E
Dingjiandian	106	32.06 N	120.52 E
Dingjiasuo	100	32.32 N	120.40 E
Dingjiazhuang	106	32.11 N	120.16 E
Dingkouzhen	102	39.55 N	106.40 E
Dingle	48	52.08 N	10.15 W
Dingle ◆[8]	262	53.23 N	2.57 W
Dingle Bay c	48	52.05 N	10.15 W
Dingley	274b	37.58 S	145.07 E
Dinglingen	58	48.20 N	7.50 E
Dingman Creek ≃	212	42.55 N	81.25 W
Dingmans Ferry	210	41.14 N	74.53 W
Dingnan	100	24.48 N	114.59 E
Dingnan ≃	100	24.28 N	115.26 E
Dingo	166	23.39 S	149.20 E
Dingolfing	60	48.38 N	12.31 E
Dingras	116	18.06 N	120.42 E
Dingshuzhen	106	31.17 N	119.50 E
Dingtao	98	35.04 N	115.34 E
Dingtuna	40	59.34 N	16.22 E
Dinguira	150	14.11 N	11.16 W
Dinguiraye	150	11.18 N	10.43 W
Dingwall, N.S., Can.	186	46.54 N	60.28 W
Dingwall, Scot., U.K.	46	57.35 N	4.29 W
Dingxi	102	35.33 N	104.32 E
Dingxian	98	38.32 N	114.59 E
Dingxiang	102	38.30 N	113.00 E
Dingxiao	102	25.13 N	105.07 E
Dingxing	105	39.17 N	115.46 E
Dingyan	100	32.23 N	120.45 E
Dingyuan	100	32.32 N	117.40 E
Dingzhouying	105	40.20 N	115.43 E
Dingzichang	107	28.54 N	106.08 E
Dingzi Gang c	98	36.37 N	120.50 E
Dinh, Mui >	110	11.22 N	109.01 E
Dinhāta	124	26.08 N	89.28 E
Dinh Ca	110	21.45 N	106.03 E
Dinh Lap	110	21.33 N	107.06 E
Dinin ≃	48	52.43 N	7.18 W
Dinkel ≃	52	52.30 N	6.58 E
Dinkelsbühl	56	49.04 N	10.19 E
Dinkelscherben	58	48.21 N	10.35 E
Dinkey Creek ≃	226	36.54 N	119.07 W
Dinklage	52	52.40 N	8.07 E
Dinnebito Wash V	200	35.29 N	111.14 W
Dinner Point >	220	28.28 N	82.41 W
Dinnet	46	57.03 N	2.54 W
Dinnington	44	53.22 N	1.12 W
Dinokwe	156	23.24 S	26.40 E
Dinorwic	184	49.41 N	92.30 W
Dinorwic Lake ⊜	184	49.37 N	92.33 W
Dinosaur	200	40.14 N	109.00 W
Dinosaur Lake ⊜[1]	182	55.57 N	122.07 W
Dinosaur National Monument ♦	200	40.32 N	108.58 W
Dinosaur Provincial Park ♦	182	50.45 N	111.30 W
Dinskaja	78	45.13 N	39.14 E
Dinslaken	52	51.34 N	6.44 E
Dinslakener Bruch	263	51.35 N	6.43 E
Dinslaken-Schwarze Heide, Flughafen ⊠	263	51.37 N	6.51 E
Dinsmore	184	51.20 N	107.26 W
Dintel ≃	52	51.39 N	4.22 E
Dinteloord	52	51.37 N	4.22 E
Dinuba	226	36.32 N	119.23 W
Dinwiddie, S. Afr.	273d	26.16 S	28.10 E
Dinwiddie, Va., U.S.	208	37.04 N	77.35 W
Dinwiddie □[6]	208	37.10 N	77.20 W
Dinxperlo	52	51.52 N	6.29 E
Diö	26	56.38 N	14.13 E
Diobo	152	2.16 N	20.29 E
Dioïla	150	12.29 N	6.48 W
Diois ◆[1]	62	44.40 N	5.20 E
Diomede	180	65.47 N	169.00 W
Dion ≃	150	10.12 N	8.39 W
Dionísio	255	19.49 S	42.45 W
Dionísio Cerqueira	252	26.15 S	53.38 W
Dionne, Lac ⊜	186	49.26 N	67.55 W
Dions	62	43.56 N	4.19 E
Diorama	255	16.21 S	51.14 W
Dios	175e	5.33 S	154.58 E
Dios, Cayos de ıı	240p	21.39 N	81.09 W
Diósd	264c	47.25 N	18.57 E
Diouloulou	150	13.03 N	16.36 W
Dioumanténé	150	10.32 N	5.55 W
Dioundiou	150	12.37 N	3.33 E
Dioungani	150	14.19 N	2.44 W
Dioura	150	14.50 N	5.15 W
Diourbel	150	14.40 N	16.15 W
Diourbel □[4]	150	14.45 N	16.30 W
Dipaculao	116	15.51 N	121.32 E
Dipai	100	23.50 N	114.06 E
Dīpālpur	123	30.40 N	73.39 E
Dipignano	68	39.15 N	16.15 E
Dipilo, Pizzo ʌ	70	37.57 N	13.59 E
Dipkarpaz	130	35.36 N	34.23 E
Diplo	120	24.28 N	69.35 E
Dipolog	116	8.35 N	123.20 E
Dippoldiswalde	54	50.54 N	13.40 E
Dipton	172	45.54 S	168.22 E
Dipu	106	30.38 N	119.41 E
Diqiyingzi	104	42.11 N	121.29 E
Dique Florentino Ameghino	254	43.40 S	66.25 W
Dīr	123	35.12 N	71.53 E
Dira, Djebel ʌ	34	36.05 N	3.38 E
Diré	150	16.16 N	3.24 W
Direction, Cape >	164	12.51 S	143.32 E
Dire Dawa	144	9.37 N	41.52 E
Direkli	130	39.43 N	36.40 E
Diriamba	236	11.51 N	86.14 W
Dirico	152	17.58 S	20.47 E
Dirillo, Lago ⊜	70	37.08 N	14.42 E
Diriomo	236	11.52 N	86.03 W
Dirj	146	30.09 N	10.26 E
Dirk Hartog Island ı	162	25.48 S	113.00 E
Dirkiesdorp	158	27.10 S	30.25 E
Dirkou	146	19.01 N	12.53 E
Dirkshorn	52	52.45 N	4.45 E
Dirksland	52	51.44 N	4.06 E
Dirnaich	60	48.27 N	12.30 E
Dirrah	140	13.37 N	26.06 E
Dirranbandi	166	28.35 S	148.14 E
Dirri	144	4.20 N	46.37 E
Dirs	144	18.32 N	42.05 E
Dirschau → Tczew	30	54.06 N	18.47 E
Dirty Devil ≃	200	37.53 N	110.24 W
Dīsa	120	24.15 N	72.10 E
Dīsah	140	12.02 N	34.19 E
Disappointment, Cape >, S. Geor.	244	54.53 S	36.07 W
Disappointment, Cape >, Wa., U.S.	224	46.18 N	124.03 W
Disappointment, Lake ⊜	162	23.30 S	122.50 E
Disappointment, Mount ʌ	169	37.25 S	145.18 E
Disappointment Creek ≃	200	38.01 N	108.51 W
Disaster Bay c	166	37.17 S	150.00 E
Disautel	182	48.22 N	119.14 W
Disbrow Drain ≊	281	42.06 N	83.27 W
Disco	214	42.41 N	83.02 W
Discovery	273d	26.10 S	27.54 E
Discovery Bay c, Austl.	166	38.12 S	141.07 E
Discovery Bay c, H.K.	271d	22.18 N	114.01 E
Discovery Bay c, Wa., U.S.	224	48.05 N	122.52 W
Discovery Island ı	224	48.25 N	123.15 W
Discovery Passage ʊ	182	50.00 N	125.15 W
Discovery Tablemount ✧[3]	8	42.00 S	0.10 E
Disentis	58	46.43 N	8.51 E
Dishāshah	142	28.59 N	30.51 E
Dishergarh	126	23.41 N	86.50 E
Dishman	202	47.39 N	117.16 W
Dishnā	140	26.07 N	32.28 E
Dishna ≃	180	63.37 N	157.18 W
Disihao	89	50.28 N	124.35 E
Disko	216	41.00 N	85.57 W
Disko ı	176	69.50 N	53.30 W
Disko Bugt c	176	69.15 N	52.00 W
Disley	262	53.21 N	2.02 W
Disley Tunnel ◆[5]	262	53.22 N	2.03 W
Dismal ≃	198	41.50 N	100.05 W
Dismal Lakes ⊜	176	67.26 N	117.07 W
Dismal Swamp Canal ≊	208	36.45 N	76.20 W
Disna	76	55.33 N	28.10 E
Disna ≃	76	55.34 N	28.12 E
Disney	196	36.28 N	95.00 W
Disneyland ♦	228	33.48 N	117.55 W
Disneyworld ♦	220	28.27 N	81.28 W
Diso	68	40.00 N	18.23 E
Dispur	120	26.08 N	91.47 E
Disputanta	208	37.07 N	77.13 W
Disraeli	206	45.54 N	71.21 W
Diss	42	52.23 N	1.07 E
Dissen	52	52.07 N	8.12 E
Dissimieux, Lac ⊜	186	49.51 N	69.48 W
Distant	214	40.58 N	79.21 W
Disteghil Sār ʌ	123	36.19 N	75.12 E
Disteln	263	51.36 N	7.09 E
Distington	44	54.36 N	3.32 W
District Heights	284c	38.51 N	76.53 W
District of Columbia □[3]	208	38.54 N	77.01 W
Distrito Especial □[5]	246	4.15 N	74.15 W
Distrito Federal □[5], Arg.	258	34.36 S	58.26 W
Distrito Federal □[5], Bra.	255	15.45 S	47.45 W
Distrito Federal □[5], Méx.	234	19.15 N	99.10 W
Distrito Federal □[5], Ven.	246	10.30 N	66.55 W
Distroff	56	49.20 N	6.16 E
Disūq	142	31.08 N	30.39 E
Ditfurt	54	51.50 N	11.11 E
Dithmarschen ◆[1]	30	54.05 N	9.00 E
Dit Island ı	116	11.15 N	120.56 E
Dittáino ≃	70	37.25 N	15.00 E
Ditton, Eng., U.K.	260	51.18 N	0.27 E
Ditton, Eng., U.K.	262	53.22 N	2.45 W
Ditton ≃	206	45.23 N	71.12 W
Ditton Priors	42	52.30 N	2.35 W
Ditzingen	56	48.49 N	9.03 E
Ditzum	52	53.18 N	7.16 E
Diu	120	20.42 N	70.59 E
Diu □[8]	120	20.42 N	70.59 E
Diuata Mountains ʎ	116	9.10 N	125.47 E
Diuata Point >	116	9.05 N	125.12 E
Dīva	272c	19.09 N	72.59 E
Divalá	236	8.25 N	82.43 W
Dīvāndarreh	128	35.55 N	47.02 E
Dívčice	61	49.06 N	14.19 E
Dive	272c	19.11 N	73.02 E
Divejevo	80	55.03 N	43.15 E
Divenié	152	2.41 S	12.05 E
Divenskaja	76	59.12 N	30.01 E
Diveria ≃	58	46.09 N	8.19 E
Divernon	219	39.33 N	89.39 W
Dives ≃	32	49.19 N	0.05 W
Dividing Creek	208	39.16 N	75.06 W
Dividing Creek ≃	208	38.05 N	75.32 W
Dividing Ridge ʌ	219	39.07 N	90.39 W
Divignano	266b	45.40 N	8.36 E
Divilacan Bay c	116	17.25 N	122.19 E
Divin	76	51.58 N	24.35 E
Divine Corners	210	41.48 N	74.40 W
Divinhe	156	20.40 S	34.49 E
Divino	255	20.37 S	42.09 W
Divinolândia	256	21.40 S	46.45 W
Divinópolis	255	20.09 S	44.54 W
Divi Point >	122	15.58 N	81.09 E
Divis ʌ[2]	48	54.37 N	6.01 W
Divisa Nova	256	21.31 S	46.12 W
Divisor, Serra do (Cordillera Ultraoriental) ʎ[1]	248	8.20 S	73.30 W
Divnogorsk	86	55.58 N	92.22 E
Divnoje	80	45.55 N	43.22 E
Divo	150	5.50 N	5.22 W
Divodar	120	24.06 N	71.47 E
Divonne-les-Bains	58	46.22 N	6.08 E
Divriği	130	39.23 N	38.07 E
Dīwāl Qol	120	34.19 N	67.54 E
Dix, Il., U.S.	219	38.27 N	88.56 W
Dix, Ne., U.S.	198	41.14 N	103.29 W
Dix ≃	192	37.49 N	84.43 W
Dix, Lac des ⊜	58	46.03 N	7.24 E
Dixboro	216	42.19 N	83.39 W
Dixfield	188	44.32 N	70.27 W
Dix Hills	276	40.49 N	73.22 W
Dixie	275b	43.36 N	79.36 W
Dixie Valley V	204	39.50 N	117.55 W
Dix Milles, Lac ⊜	190	46.46 N	77.45 W
Dixmoor	278	41.38 N	87.40 W
Dixmude → Diksmuide	50	51.02 N	2.52 E
Dixon, Ca., U.S.	226	38.19 N	121.49 W
Dixon, Il., U.S.	190	41.50 N	89.28 W
Dixon, Ky., U.S.	194	37.31 N	87.41 W
Dixon, Mo., U.S.	194	37.59 N	92.05 W
Dixon, N.M., U.S.	200	36.11 N	105.53 W
Dixon, Oh., U.S.	216	40.57 N	84.48 W
Dixon Entrance ʊ	182	54.25 N	132.30 W
Dixons Mills	194	32.04 N	87.47 W
Dixons Pond ⊜	276	40.56 N	74.27 W
Dixonville	214	40.42 N	79.00 W
Dixville	206	45.04 N	71.46 W
Diyā al-Kawm	142	30.38 N	31.05 E
Diyadin	84	39.33 N	43.41 E
Diyālā □[4]	128	34.00 N	45.00 E
Diyālā (Sīrvān) ≃	128	33.14 N	44.31 E
Diyanga	152	1.29 S	11.52 E
Diyarbakır	130	37.55 N	40.14 E
Diyarbakır □[4]	130	38.05 N	40.15 E
Diyarb Najm	142	30.45 N	31.26 E
Diyu al-Wasta	142	30.54 N	31.30 E
Dizangsi	104	41.26 N	120.57 E
Dizhou	102	23.00 N	106.20 E
Dizy	50	49.04 N	3.58 E
Dizzard Point >	42	50.45 N	4.38 W
Dja ≃	152	2.02 N	15.12 E
Dja, Réserve du ◆[4]	152	3.05 N	13.00 E
Djabalpur → Jabalpur	124	23.10 N	79.57 E
Djabir	152	0.32 N	24.05 E
Djadié ≃	152	0.46 N	12.58 E
Djado	146	21.01 N	12.18 E
Djado, Plateau du ʎ[1]	146	21.45 N	12.50 E
Djaipur → Jaipur	120	26.55 N	75.49 E
Djakarta → Jakarta	269e	6.10 S	106.48 E
Djakonovo	82	54.34 N	38.20 E
Djakovka	80	50.43 N	46.46 E
Djakovo ◆[8]	265b	55.39 N	37.40 E
Djamâa	148	33.32 N	6.00 E
Djamba, Ang.	152	16.46 S	13.59 E
Djamba, Zaïre	152	9.49 S	22.07 E
Djambala	152	2.33 S	14.45 E
Djamschedpur → Jamshedpur	126	22.48 N	86.11 E
Djanet	148	24.34 N	9.29 E
Djaouro Mbali	152	5.52 N	13.29 E
Djaret, Oued V	148	26.32 N	1.30 E
Djebobo ʌ	150	8.20 N	0.35 E
Djébrène	146	11.14 N	19.01 E
Djédaa	146	13.31 N	18.34 E
Djedda → Jiddah	144	21.30 N	39.12 E
Djedi, Oued V	148	34.28 N	6.05 E
Djéké Djéké	146	8.25 N	18.12 E
Djelo-Binza	273b	4.23 S	15.16 E
Djema	140	6.03 N	25.19 E
Djember → Jember, Indon.	115a	8.10 S	113.42 E
Djember, Tchad	146	10.25 N	17.50 E
Djemila ı	34	36.25 N	5.44 E
Djénné	150	13.54 N	4.33 W
Djenoun, Garet el ʌ	148	25.05 N	5.25 E
Djérem ≃	152	5.20 N	13.24 E
Djibasso	150	13.07 N	4.10 W
Djibo	150	14.06 N	1.38 W
Djibouti	144	11.36 N	43.09 E
Djibouti □[1], Afr.	136	11.30 N	43.00 E
Djibouti □[1], Afr.	144	11.30 N	43.00 E
Djibrouïa	150	13.13 N	11.14 W
Djiri	273b	4.08 S	15.19 E
Djiri ≃	273b	4.11 S	15.20 E
Djohong	152	6.50 N	14.42 E
Djokjakarta → Yogyakarta	115a	7.48 S	110.22 E
Djokoumatombi	152	0.47 N	15.22 E
Djokupunda	152	5.27 S	20.58 E
Djolu	152	0.37 N	22.21 E
Djombo	152	1.21 N	20.22 E
Djoua ≃	152	1.13 N	13.12 E
Djouari ≃	273b	4.13 S	15.08 E
Djoubissi	152	6.12 N	20.45 E
Djoué ≃	273b	4.19 S	15.14 E
Djougou	150	9.42 N	1.40 E
Djoum	152	2.40 N	12.40 E
Djouna	146	10.27 N	20.04 E
Djourab, Erg du ±[8]	146	16.40 N	18.50 E
Djugu	154	1.55 N	30.30 E
Djúpivogur	24a	64.40 N	14.10 W
Djura	40	60.37 N	15.00 E
Djurås	40	60.33 N	15.08 E
Djurmo	40	60.33 N	15.10 E
Djurö	40	59.19 N	18.41 E
Djurö ı	26	58.52 N	13.28 E
Djursholm	40	59.24 N	18.05 E
Dlouhá Ves	60	49.12 N	13.31 E
Dmanisi	84	41.22 N	44.12 E
Dmitr'ašovka	76	52.09 N	39.04 E
Dmitrija Lapteva, proliv ʊ	74	73.00 N	142.00 E
Dmitrijevka, Kaz.	85	43.30 N	77.02 E
Dmitrijevka, Ross.	76	52.53 N	40.47 E
Dmitrijevka, Ross.	86	55.10 N	75.36 E
Dmitrijev-L'govskij	78	52.08 N	35.05 E
Dmitrijevskij	86	49.08 N	57.50 E
Dmitrijevskoje, Ross.	80	45.48 N	41.54 E
Dmitrijevskoje, Ross.	82	54.40 N	37.38 E
Dmitrijev Usad, Ross.	76	54.08 N	43.08 E
Dmitrijev Usad, Ross.	80	54.14 N	43.18 E
Dmitrijevy Gory	80	55.12 N	41.47 E
Dmitrivka	78	45.29 N	35.04 E
Dmitrov	82	56.21 N	37.31 E
Dmitrovcy	82	55.16 N	38.55 E
Dmitroviči	76	53.59 N	29.06 E
Dmitrovskij Pogost	76	55.19 N	39.49 E
Dmitrovsk-Orlovskij	76	52.30 N	35.09 E
Dmukhaylivka	78	49.03 N	34.46 E
Dmytrivka, Ukr.	78	48.48 N	32.44 E
Dmytrivka, Ukr.	78	46.51 N	36.35 E
Dmytrivka, Ukr.	78	50.56 N	32.58 E
Dmytrivka, Ukr.	83	48.55 N	39.10 E
Dmytriyivka	83	47.56 N	38.56 E
Dnepropetrovsk → Dnipropetrovs'k	78	48.27 N	34.59 E
Dneprovsko-Bugskij kanal ≊	76	52.03 N	25.35 E
Dneprovskoje	76	55.40 N	33.55 E
Dnieper (Dnipro) ≃	78	46.30 N	32.18 E
Dniepropetrovsk → Dnipropetrovs'k	78	48.27 N	34.59 E
Dniester → Dnister ≃	78	46.18 N	30.17 E
Dniprodzerzhyns'k	78	48.30 N	34.37 E
Dniprodzerzhyns'ke vodoskhovyshche ⊜[1]	78	48.45 N	34.00 E
Dnipropetrovs'k	78	48.27 N	34.59 E
Dnipropetrovs'k □[4]	78	48.30 N	35.00 E
Dniprovka	78	47.26 N	34.38 E
Dniprovs'kyy lyman c[1]	78	46.35 N	31.55 E
Dnipryany	78	46.44 N	33.16 E
Dnister (Nistru) ≃	78	46.18 N	30.17 E
Dnistrovs'ke vodoskhovyshche ⊜[1]	78	48.30 N	26.45 E
Dnistrovs'kyy lyman ⊜	78	46.15 N	30.17 E
Dno	76	57.50 N	29.59 E
Do, Lac ⊜	150	15.54 N	2.45 W
Doa	154	16.44 S	34.32 E
Do Āb-e Mīkh-e Zarrīn	120	35.16 N	68.00 E
Doaktown	186	46.33 N	66.08 W
Doangdoangan-Besar, Pulau ı	112	5.24 S	117.55 E
Doany	157b	14.22 S	49.31 E
Doba	146	8.39 N	16.51 E
Dobane	140	6.24 N	24.42 E
Dobbertin	54	53.37 N	12.04 E
Dobbiaco (Toblach)	64	46.44 N	12.14 E
Dobbin	222	30.22 N	95.46 W
Dobbins	226	39.22 N	121.12 W
Dobbins Air Force Base ■	192	33.54 N	84.31 W
Dobbs Ferry	210	41.00 N	73.52 W
Dobczyce	30	49.54 N	20.06 E
Dobel	56	48.48 N	8.29 E
Dobele	76	56.37 N	23.16 E
Döbeln	54	51.07 N	13.07 E
Doberai, Jazirah (Vogelkop) >[1]	164	1.30 S	132.30 E
Döberitz	264a	52.33 N	13.03 E
Doberlug-Kirchhain	54	51.38 N	13.34 E
Döbern	54	51.37 N	14.36 E
Dobiegniew	30	52.59 N	15.47 E
Döbling ◆[8]	264b	48.15 N	16.22 E
Dobo	164	5.46 S	134.13 E
Doboj	38	44.44 N	18.06 E
Dobra, Pol.	30	51.54 N	18.37 E
Dobra, Pol.	30	53.35 N	15.18 E
Dobra ≃	36	45.33 N	15.31 E
Dobr'anka	86	58.27 N	56.24 E
Dobřany	60	49.40 N	13.18 E
Dobra Stausee ⊜[1]	61	48.35 N	15.20 E
Dobre Miasto	30	53.59 N	20.25 E
Döbriach	64	46.47 N	13.39 E
Dobrič	38	43.34 N	27.50 E
Dobrich → Dobrič	38	43.34 N	27.50 E
Dobrinka, Ross.	80	52.09 N	40.29 E
Dobrinka, Ross.	80	48.49 N	42.58 E
Dobrinka, Ross.	80	50.49 N	41.51 E
Dobříš	30	49.47 N	14.11 E
Dobritz	54	52.01 N	12.13 E
Dobrodzień	30	50.44 N	18.27 E
Dobroje, Ross.	76	57.06 N	32.02 E
Dobroje, Ross.	76	52.52 N	39.48 E
Dobroměřice	54	50.23 N	13.46 E
Dobromyl'	78	49.34 N	22.47 E
Dobropillya	78	48.28 N	37.05 E
Dobroslavka	76	52.24 N	26.15 E
Dobroteasa	38	44.47 N	24.23 E
Dobrotvir	78	50.14 N	24.22 E
Dobrovelychkivka	78	48.23 N	31.11 E
Dobrovillya	78	48.41 N	36.37 E
Dobrovol'sk	76	54.46 N	22.31 E
Dobrudžansko plato ʎ[1]	38	43.32 N	27.50 E
Dobruja □[9]	38	44.00 N	28.00 E

Symbols in the index entries represent the broad categories identified in the key at the right. Symbols with superior numbers (ʎ[1]) identify subcategories (see complete key on page *I · 1*).

Symbole im Register stellen die rechts im Schlüssel erklärten Kategorien dar. Symbole mit hochgestellten Ziffern (ʎ[1]) bezeichnen Unterabteilungen einer Kategorie (vgl. vollständiger Schlüssel auf Seite *I · 1*).

Los símbolos incluídos en el texto del índice representan las grandes categorías identificadas con la clave a la derecha. Los símbolos con numeros en su parte superior (ʎ[1]) identifican las subcategorías (véase la clave completa en la página *I · 1*).

Les symboles de l'index représentent les catégories indiquées dans la légende à droite. Les symboles suivis d'un indice (ʎ[1]) représentent des sous-catégories (voir légende complète à la page *I · 1*).

Os símbolos incluídos no texto do índice representam as grandes categorias identificadas com a chave à direita. Os símbolos com números em sua parte superior (ʎ[1]) identificam as subcategorias (veja-se a chave completa à página *I · 1*).

Symbol	English	Deutsch	Español	Français	Português
ʌ	Mountain	Berg	Montaña	Montagne	Montanha
ʎ	Mountains	Gebirge	Montañas	Montagnes	Montanhas
)(	Pass	Paß	Paso	Col	Passo
V	Valley, Canyon	Tal, Cañon	Valle, Cañón	Vallée, Canyon	Vale, Canhão
≃	Plain	Ebene	Llano	Plaine	Planície
>	Cape	Kap	Cabo	Cap	Cabo
ı	Island	Insel	Isla	Île	Ilha
ıı	Islands	Inseln	Islas	Îles	Ilhas
±	Other Topographic Features	Andere Topographische Objekte	Otros Elementos Topográficos	Autres données topographiques	Outros acidentes topográficos

ESPAÑOL — Nombre | Página | Lat.°′ | Long.°′ W = Oeste

Dobruš 76 52.25 N 31.19 E
Dobruška 30 50.17 N 16.10 E
Dobryanka, Ukr. 78 52.04 N 31.11 E
Dobryanka, Ukr. 78 48.21 N 30.54 E
Dobryn' 78 51.46 N 29.12 E
Dobrzany 30 53.22 N 15.25 E
Dobrzyń nad Wisłą 30 52.38 N 19.20 E
Dobšiná 30 48.49 N 20.23 E
Dobson 192 36.23 N 80.43 W
Dobzha 120 28.28 N 88.14 E
Doce ≃, Bra. 255 19.37 S 39.49 W
Doce ≃, Bra. 255 18.28 S 51.05 W
Doce de Octubre 196 25.38 N 97.47 W
Dochart ≃ 46 56.28 N 4.20 W
Döčin ≃ 88 49.39 N 114.48 E
Docker River 162 24.52 S 129.05 E
Docking 42 52.55 N 0.38 E
Dock Junction 192 31.11 N 81.31 W
Dockton 224 47.22 N 122.27 W
Dockweiler 56 50.15 N 6.46 E
Dockweiler Beach State Park ♠ 280 33.55 N 118.26 W
Doctor Arroyo 234 23.40 N 100.11 W
Doctor Cecilio Báez 252 25.03 S 56.19 W
Doctor Coss 196 25.55 N 99.11 W
Doctor Edmund A. Babler Memorial State Park ♠ 219 38.36 N 90.43 W
Doctor Hicks Range ⋏ 162 28.40 S 124.20 E
Doctor Pedro P. Peña 252 22.26 S 62.22 W
Doctors Creek ≃ 208 40.11 N 74.41 W
Doda 123 33.08 N 75.34 E
Dod Ballāpur 122 13.18 N 77.32 E
Doddinghurst 42 51.40 N 0.18 E
Doddridge 194 33.05 N 93.54 W
Dodds Island I 219 38.35 N 91.59 W
Doddsville 194 33.39 N 90.31 W
Dodecanese → Dhodhekánisos II 38 36.30 N 27.00 E
Dodéo 152 7.29 N 12.04 E
Dodge, Ne., U.S. 198 41.43 N 96.52 W
Dodge, Tx., U.S. 222 30.45 N 95.24 W
Dodge □[6] 216 43.14 N 88.40 W
Dodge Brothers State Park Number 4♠, Mi., U.S. 281 42.37 N 83.22 W
Dodge Brothers State Park Number 8♠, Mi., U.S. 281 42.36 N 83.01 W
Dodge Center 190 44.01 N 92.51 W
Dodge City 198 37.45 N 100.01 W
Dodge Park 284c 38.56 N 76.53 W
Dodger Stadium ♠ 280 34.04 N 118.14 W
Dodgeville 190 42.57 N 90.07 W
Dodman Point ≻ 42 50.13 N 4.48 W
Dodo Goei 140 5.57 N 29.26 E
Dodola 144 7.02 N 39.07 E
Dodoma 154 6.11 S 35.45 E
Dodoma □[4] 154 6.00 S 36.00 E
Dodori ≃ 154 1.52 S 41.02 E
Dodsland 184 51.48 N 108.49 W
Dodson, La., U.S. 194 32.04 N 92.39 W
Dodson, Mt., U.S. 202 48.23 N 108.14 W
Dodson, Tx., U.S. 196 34.46 N 100.02 W
Dodurga 130 39.48 N 29.55 E
Doe Lake ⊜ 212 45.32 N 79.25 W
Doe River 182 56.00 N 120.05 W
Doerun 192 31.19 N 83.55 W
Doesburg 52 52.01 N 6.09 E
Doetinchem 52 51.58 N 6.17 E
Dog ≃ 190 48.51 N 89.37 W
Dogāchia 272b 22.58 N 88.31 E
Dogai Coring ⊜ 120 34.30 N 89.15 E
Dōga-mori ∧ 96 33.09 N 132.53 E
Doğanbey, Tür. 130 37.37 N 27.11 E
Doğanbey, Tür. 130 38.04 N 26.53 E
Doğanbey, Tür. 130 37.48 N 31.54 E
Doğanca 130 37.49 N 42.20 E
Doğançay 130 40.37 N 30.20 E
Doganella 66 41.34 N 12.56 E
Doğanhisar 130 38.09 N 31.41 E
Doğankent, Tür. 130 36.52 N 35.18 E
Doğankent, Tür. 130 40.48 N 38.56 E
Doğanşehir 130 38.06 N 37.53 E
Doğanyol 130 38.19 N 39.03 E
Doğanyurt, Tür. 130 42.00 N 33.27 E
Doğanyurt, Tür. 130 40.41 N 36.43 E
Dog Creek 182 51.35 N 122.15 W
Dog Creek ≃, B.C., Can. 182 51.35 N 122.17 W
Dog Creek ≃, Mt., U.S. 202 47.44 N 109.36 W
Dog Creek ≃, Oh., U.S. 216 41.03 N 84.23 W
Dog Ear Creek ≃ 198 43.42 N 99.59 W
Dog Island I, Anguilla 238 18.17 N 63.16 W
Dog Island I, Fl., U.S. 192 29.48 N 84.35 W
Dog Islands II 240m 18.29 N 64.28 W
Dog Lake ⊜, Mb., Can. 184 51.02 N 98.30 W
Dog Lake ⊜, On., Can. 190 48.46 N 89.32 W
Dog Lake ⊜, On., Can. 190 48.18 N 84.10 W
Dog Lake ⊜, On., Can. 212 44.27 N 76.20 W
Dogliani 62 44.32 N 7.56 E
Dogna 64 46.27 N 13.19 E
Dōgo I 92 36.15 N 133.16 E
Do Gonbadān 128 30.21 N 50.48 E
Dogondoutchi 150 13.38 N 4.02 E
Doğonşar 130 40.14 N 37.33 E
Dōgo-yama ∧ 96 35.04 N 133.14 E
Dogpound Creek ≃ 182 51.50 N 114.24 W
Dogs, Isle of I 260 51.29 N 0.01 W
D'ogtevo, Ross. 78 49.10 N 40.39 E
D'ogtevo, Ross. 80 49.11 N 40.39 E
Doğubayazıt 84 39.32 N 44.08 E
Doguéraoua 150 13.58 N 5.35 E
Doğu Karadeniz Dağları ⋏ 130 40.30 N 40.30 E
Dogura 164 10.05 S 150.05 E
Doha → Ad-Dawḥah 128 25.17 N 51.32 E
Dohār 126 23.35 N 90.09 E
Dohhi 124 24.32 N 84.54 E
Dohna 54 50.57 N 13.51 E
Dohrgaul 263 51.06 N 7.27 E
Dohrīghāt 124 26.16 N 83.31 E
Doi 96 33.57 N 133.26 E
Doi, Kinh ≊ 269c 10.43 N 106.37 E
Doilungdêqên 124 29.48 N 90.47 E
Doiran, Lake ⊜ 38 41.13 N 22.44 E
Doiras, Embalse de ⊜[1] 34 43.10 N 6.45 W
Dois de Novembro, Cachoeira ⌊ 248 8.52 S 62.16 W
Dois Irmãos, Pico ∧ 287a 22.59 S 43.14 W
Dois Irmãos de Goiás 250 9.16 S 49.05 W
Doi Suthep-Pui National Park ♠ 110 18.50 N 98.50 E
Dōjō 268 35.51 N 139.37 E
Dōjō ◆[8] 270 34.52 N 135.14 E
Doka, Indon. 164 6.39 S 134.15 E
Doka, Sūd. 140 13.31 N 35.46 E
Doki ≃ 96 34.18 N 133.48 E
Dokka 26 60.50 N 10.05 E
Dokkum 52 53.19 N 6.00 E
Dökmetepe 130 40.19 N 36.18 E
Dokri 120 27.23 N 68.06 E
Dokšicy 76 54.54 N 27.46 E
Dokská pahorkatina ⋏[2] 54 50.30 N 14.45 E
Doksy 54 50.35 N 14.38 E
Dokuchayevs'k 83 47.44 N 37.40 E
Dola 216 40.47 N 83.42 W
Dolak ≃ 164 7.48 S 139.00 E
Doland 198 44.53 N 98.06 W
Dolany 60 49.27 N 13.15 E
Dolavon 254 43.18 S 65.42 W

FRANÇAIS — Nom | Page | Lat.°′ | Long.°′ W = Ouest

Dolayoba 267b 40.54 N 29.15 E
Dolbeau 176 48.53 N 72.14 W
Dolberg 52 51.42 N 7.55 E
Dolceacqua 62 43.51 N 7.37 E
Dolcedorme, Serra ∧ 68 39.53 N 16.13 E
Dol-de-Bretagne 32 48.33 N 1.45 W
Dole 58 47.06 N 5.30 E
Dolega 236 8.34 N 82.25 W
Dolen 222 30.26 N 94.54 W
Dolgaja 86 55.49 N 64.15 E
Dolgaja, kosa ≻[2] 78 46.43 N 37.41 E
Dolgarrog 44 53.11 N 3.51 W
Dolgelin 54 52.29 N 14.24 E
Dolgellau 42 52.44 N 3.53 W
Dolgeville 210 43.06 N 74.46 W
Dolgij, ostrov I 24 69.15 N 59.04 E
Dolgij Most 88 56.45 N 96.48 E
Dolginovo 76 54.39 N 27.29 E
Dolgoi Island I 180 55.10 N 161.45 W
Dolgoje 78 52.04 N 37.34 E
Dolgoprudnyj 82 55.56 N 37.31 E
Dolgorukovo 76 52.19 N 38.21 E
Dolgoščelje 24 66.03 N 43.24 E
Dolianova 71 39.22 N 9.10 E
Dolinnyj 80 51.16 N 52.11 E
Dolinsk 89 47.21 N 142.48 E
Dolisie 152 4.12 S 12.41 E
Dolj □[6] 38 44.15 N 23.45 E
Döllach 64 46.58 N 12.54 E
Dollar 46 56.09 N 3.40 W
Dollard C 52 53.17 N 7.10 E
Dollard-des-Ormeaux 206 45.29 N 73.49 W
Dollar Law ∧ 46 55.33 N 3.17 W
Döllbach 56 50.26 N 9.44 E
Dolle 54 52.25 N 11.37 E
Dollern 52 53.32 N 9.32 E
Dollerup 41 54.46 N 9.40 E
Döllnitz 54 51.24 N 12.01 E
Dollnstein 60 48.52 N 11.04 E
Döllstädt 54 51.05 N 10.49 E
Dolmabahce Palace ♜ 267b 41.02 N 29.00 E
Dolmativka 78 46.13 N 32.26 E
Dolmatovskij 80 57.29 N 42.18 E
Dolni Dăbnik 38 43.24 N 24.26 E
Dolní Dvořiště 61 48.39 N 14.27 E
Dolní Jiřetín 54 50.35 N 13.33 E
Dolni Lom 38 43.31 N 22.47 E
Dolni Žandov 60 50.02 N 12.34 E
Dolný Kubín 30 49.12 N 19.17 E
Dolo 64 45.25 N 12.05 E
Dolohmwar ∧ 174r 6.52 N 158.14 E
Dolokmerawan 114 3.10 N 99.08 E
Dolokparibuan 114 3.01 N 98.39 E
Dolomites → Dolomiti ⋏ 64 46.25 N 11.50 E
Dolomiti (Dolomiten) ⋏ 64 46.25 N 11.50 E
Dolon' 86 50.40 N 79.18 E
Dolon ≃ 62 45.18 N 4.46 E
Dolon, pereval)(85 41.52 N 75.45 E
Dolores, Arg. 252 36.20 S 57.40 W
Dolores, Col. 246 3.33 N 74.54 W
Dolores, Guat. 232 16.31 N 89.25 W
Dolores, Méx. 196 26.20 N 101.29 W
Dolores, Co., U.S. 200 37.28 N 108.30 W
Dolores, Ur. 252 33.33 S 58.13 W
Dolores, Ven. 246 8.18 N 69.34 W
Dolores ≃, Pil. 116 12.02 N 125.29 E
Dolores ≃, U.S. 200 38.49 N 109.17 W
Dolores, Mission ♜[1] 282 37.46 N 122.26 W
Dolores Hidalgo 234 21.10 N 100.56 W
Dolphin, Cape ≻ 254 51.15 S 58.57 W
Dolphin and Union Strait U 176 69.05 N 114.45 W
Dolphin Head ∧ 241q 18.22 N 78.10 W
Dölsach 64 46.49 N 12.51 E
Dolsk 30 52.00 N 17.03 E
Dol'skoje 82 54.47 N 36.26 E
Dolton, Eng., U.K. 42 50.53 N 4.01 W
Dolton, Il., U.S. 216 41.38 N 87.36 W
Dolwyddelan 44 53.03 N 3.53 W
Dolyna, Ukr. 78 48.58 N 24.01 E
Dolyna, Ukr. 83 48.59 N 37.27 E
Dolyns'ka 78 48.07 N 32.44 E
Dolžanskaja 78 46.37 N 37.48 E
Dolzhak 78 48.41 N 26.32 E
Dolžicy, Ross. 76 58.00 N 29.51 E
Dolžicy, Ross. 76 58.31 N 29.08 E
Dom ∧ 58 46.06 N 7.50 E
Dom, Gunung ∧ 164 2.40 S 136.53 E
D'oma ≃ 86 54.42 N 55.57 E
Domacha 76 52.28 N 34.58 E
Domačovo 78 51.44 N 23.37 E
Domadare 144 1.50 N 41.13 E
Domaine, Pointe du ≻ 275a 45.23 N 73.54 W
Domaniči 76 53.02 N 33.25 E
Domanico 68 39.13 N 16.12 E
Domanivka 78 47.37 N 30.58 E
Dom Aquino 255 15.48 S 54.53 W
Domar, Enneri V 146 18.11 N 18.04 E
Domariāganj 124 27.13 N 82.40 E
Domart-en-Ponthieu 50 50.04 N 2.07 E
Domasi 154 15.18 S 35.20 E
Domaška 80 53.00 N 50.47 E
Domaso 58 46.09 N 9.19 E
Domat/Ems 58 46.50 N 9.28 E
Domažlice 60 49.27 N 12.56 E
Dombaj 84 43.17 N 41.37 E
Dombaj-Ul'gen, gora ∧ 84 43.14 N 41.41 E
Dombarovskij 86 50.46 N 59.32 E
Dombås 26 62.05 N 9.08 E
Dombasle-sur-Meurthe 58 48.38 N 6.21 E
Dombe 156 19.59 S 33.25 E
Dombe Grande 152 12.58 S 13.11 E
Dombes ◆[1] 58 46.00 N 5.03 E
Dombóvár 30 46.23 N 18.08 E
Dombrád 30 48.14 N 21.56 E
Dombresson 58 47.04 N 6.58 E
Domburg 52 51.34 N 3.30 E
Dom Cavati 255 19.23 S 42.06 W
Dôme, Puy de ∧ 32 45.47 N 2.58 E
Dome Creek 182 53.44 N 121.01 W
Domegge di Cadore 64 46.27 N 12.25 E
Domène 62 45.12 N 5.50 E
Dome Peak ∧, Pil. 116 5.37 N 125.20 E
Dome Peak ∧, Wa., U.S. 224 48.18 N 121.02 W
Domett 172 42.51 S 173.13 E
Domèvre-en-Haye 56 48.49 N 5.55 E
Domeyko 252 28.57 S 70.54 W
Domeyko, Cordillera ⋏ 252 24.30 S 69.00 W
Domfront 32 48.36 N 0.39 W
Domiciano Ribeiro 255 16.56 S 47.46 W
Domíngo M. Irala 252 25.54 S 54.43 W
Domingos Martins 255 20.22 S 40.40 W
Dominguez 280 33.50 N 118.13 W
Dominguez Channel U 280 38.47 N 118.15 W
Dominguez Hills ⋏[2] 280 33.52 N 118.14 W
Dominica □[1], N.A. 230 15.30 N 61.20 W
Dominica □[1], N.A. 240d 15.30 N 61.20 W
Dominicain (république) → Dominican Republic □[1] 238 19.00 N 70.40 W
Dominical 236 9.13 N 83.51 W
Dominicana, República → Dominican Republic □[1] 238 19.00 N 70.40 W
Dominican Republic (República Dominicana) □[1], N.A. 230 19.00 N 70.40 W
Dominican Republic (República Dominicana) □[1], N.A. 238 19.00 N 70.40 W
Dominica Passage U 238 15.45 N 61.30 W

PORTUGUÊS — Nome | Página | Lat.°′ | Long.°′ W = Oeste

Dominikanische Republik → Dominican Republic □[1] 238 19.00 N 70.40 W
Dominion 186 46.13 N 60.01 W
Dominion, Cape ≻ 176 66.13 N 74.28 W
Dominion Astrophysical Observatory ♜[3] 224 48.31 N 123.25 W
Dominion City 184 49.08 N 97.09 W
Dominique → Dominica □[1] 240d 15.30 N 61.20 W
Domiongo 152 4.37 S 21.15 E
Domitilla, Catacombe di ⊥ 267a 41.52 N 12.31 E
Dömitz 54 53.08 N 11.14 E
Dom Joaquim 255 18.57 S 43.16 W
Domleschg V 58 46.44 N 9.28 E
Dommartin-lès-Toul 58 48.40 N 5.54 E
Dommartin-Varimont 56 48.58 N 4.46 E
Dommary-Baroncourt 56 49.17 N 5.42 E
Dommel ≃ 52 51.40 N 5.20 E
Dommitzsch 54 51.38 N 12.53 E
Domnarvet 40 60.30 N 15.27 E
Domnești 38 44.25 N 25.56 E
Domnino 82 54.10 N 38.11 E
Dom Noi ≃ 110 15.17 N 105.28 E
Domo 144 7.54 N 46.52 E
Domodedovo 82 55.26 N 37.46 E
Domodossola 58 46.07 N 8.17 E
Domohani 124 26.35 N 88.48 E
Domoni 157a 12.15 S 44.32 E
Domont 261 49.02 N 2.20 E
Dompaire 58 48.13 N 6.13 E
Dom Pedrito 252 30.59 S 54.40 W
Dom Pedro 250 4.29 S 44.27 W
Dom Pedro II, Estação ◆[5] 287a 23.54 S 43.12 W
Dompu 115b 8.32 S 118.28 E
Domremy 184 52.47 N 105.44 W
Domrémy-la-Pucelle 58 48.27 N 5.41 E
Domselaar 258 35.04 S 58.18 W
Dom Silvério 255 20.09 S 42.58 W
Domsjö 26 63.15 N 18.43 E
Domus de Maria 71 38.57 N 8.52 E
Domusnovas 71 39.19 N 8.39 E
Domuyo, Volcán ∧[1] 252 36.38 S 70.26 W
Domvast 50 50.12 N 1.55 E
Dom Viçoso 256 22.13 S 45.09 W
Dom Yai ≃ 110 15.18 N 105.10 E
Domžale 36 46.08 N 14.36 E
Don ≃, On., Can. 212 43.39 N 79.21 W
Don ≃, India 122 16.17 N 76.27 E
Don ≃, Lao 110 15.07 N 105.48 E
Don ≃, Ross. 72 47.04 N 39.18 E
Don ≃, Eng., U.K. 44 53.39 N 0.59 W
Don ≃, Eng., U.K. 262 53.47 N 2.14 W
Don ≃, Scot., U.K. 46 57.08 N 2.05 W
Don, East Branch ≃, On., Can. 212 43.42 N 79.20 W
Don, East Branch ≃, On., Can. 275b 43.43 N 79.20 W
Don, West Branch ≃ 275b 43.43 N 79.20 W
Dona Ana, Moç. 154 17.25 S 35.07 E
Dona Ana, N.M., U.S. 200 32.23 N 106.48 W
Donada 64 45.02 N 12.12 E
Donadeu 252 26.43 S 62.44 W
Dona Euzébia 256 21.18 S 42.48 W
Donaghadee 48 54.39 N 5.33 W
Donaghmore 48 54.32 N 6.49 W
Donahoe Creek ≃ 222 30.49 N 97.12 W
Donald 166 36.22 S 143.00 E
Donalda 182 52.35 N 112.34 W
Donaldson, Ar., U.S. 194 34.14 N 92.55 W
Donaldson, In., U.S. 216 41.22 N 86.27 W
Donaldson, Pa., U.S. 208 40.38 N 76.24 W
Donaldson Crossroads 279b 40.16 N 80.07 W
Donaldson Dam ⊜[1] 273d 26.17 S 27.41 E
Donaldsonville 194 30.06 N 90.59 W
Donalsonville 192 31.02 N 84.52 W
Doñana, Parque Nacional de ♠ 34 37.00 N 6.30 W
Donard, Slieve ∧ 48 54.11 N 5.55 W
Donau → Danube ≃ 22 45.20 N 29.40 E
Donaueschingen 58 47.57 N 8.29 E
Donaufeld ◆[8] 264b 48.15 N 16.25 E
Donaukanal ≊ 264b 48.10 N 16.30 E
Donaumoos ≡, Dtsch. 58 48.30 N 10.15 E
Donaumoos ≡, Dtsch. 60 48.40 N 11.15 E
Donaupark ♠ 264b 48.14 N 16.25 E
Donauried ◆[1] 56 48.35 N 10.40 E
Donaustadt ◆[8] 264b 48.13 N 16.30 E
Donaustauf 60 49.02 N 12.13 E
Donauturm ♜ 264b 48.14 N 16.25 E
Donauwörth 56 48.43 N 10.46 E
Don Benito 34 38.57 N 5.52 W
Dönberg ◆[8] 263 51.18 N 7.10 E
Don Bosco ◆[8] 258 34.42 S 58.18 W
Doncaster, Austl. 274b 37.47 S 145.08 E
Doncaster, On., Can. 275b 43.48 N 79.25 W
Doncaster, Eng., U.K. 44 53.32 N 1.07 W
Doncaster ≃ 206 45.58 N 74.06 W
Doncaster East 274b 37.47 S 145.10 E
Doncaster Indian Reserve ◆[4] 206 46.09 N 74.07 W
Donchêry 56 49.42 N 4.52 E
Dondaicha 120 21.20 N 74.34 E
Dondo, Ang. 152 9.38 S 14.25 E
Dondo, Moç. 156 19.36 S 34.44 E
Dondo, Teluk C 112 0.55 N 120.30 E
Dondra Head ≻ 122 5.55 N 80.35 E
Donduşeni 38 48.15 N 27.37 E
Doneck 83 48.21 N 40.02 E
Donegal, Ire. 48 54.39 N 8.07 W
Donegal, S. Afr. 158 26.10 S 23.58 E
Donegal, Pa., U.S. 214 40.07 N 79.23 W
Donegal □[6] 48 54.50 N 8.00 W
Donegal Bay C 48 54.30 N 8.30 W
Doneraile, Ire. 48 52.13 N 8.35 W
Doneraile, S.C., U.S. 192 34.19 N 79.53 W
Donets'k 83 48.00 N 37.48 E
Donets'k □[4] 78 48.00 N 37.30 E
Donets'kyy ◆[8] 83 48.42 N 38.41 E
Donets'kyy kryazh ∧ 83 48.15 N 38.45 E
Dong ≃, Zhg. 100 23.06 N 114.00 E
Dong ≃, Zhg. 100 25.00 N 118.27 E
Dong ≃, Zhg. 100 23.42 N 117.13 E
Dong ≃, Zhg. 102 42.10 N 101.00 E
Donga ≃ 146 8.19 N 9.58 E
Dong'an, Zhg. 89 47.20 N 134.10 E
Dongan → Mishan, Zhg. 89 45.33 N 131.52 E
Dong'an, Zhg. 100 33.24 N 114.24 E
Dong'an, Zhg. 102 26.17 N 111.07 E
Dong'an, Zhg. 106 30.30 N 118.48 E
Dong'an, Zhg. 106 31.35 N 119.44 E
Dongao 100 29.12 N 121.25 E
Dongara 162 29.15 S 114.56 E
Dongargarh 120 21.12 N 80.44 E
Dongba, Zhg. 105 39.58 N 116.32 E
Dongba, Zhg. 106 31.18 N 119.03 E
Dongbahe 105 39.58 N 116.27 E
Dongbaimiao 105 40.34 N 116.05 E
Dongbei 100 27.15 N 116.06 E
Dongbeicha 98 41.43 N 127.23 E
Dongbeijipo 98 36.06 N 117.08 E
Dongchan 107 30.20 N 105.20 E
Dongchang 106 31.52 N 121.38 E
Dongchangjie 106 32.04 N 119.18 E
Dongcheng 100 28.56 N 121.16 E
Dongchong 100 26.35 N 119.52 E
Dongchuan (Xincun) 102 26.10 N 103.01 E
Dongcun 106 30.57 N 121.46 E
Dongdaoan 98 38.21 N 117.12 E
Dong Dian ≡ 105 39.03 N 116.35 E
Dongduluo 105 39.04 N 115.15 E
Dong'e (Tongcheng) 98 36.14 N 116.16 E
Dongen 52 51.37 N 4.56 E
Dong'ezhen 98 36.11 N 116.16 E
Dongfang (Basuo) 110 19.05 N 108.39 E
Dongfeng, Zhg. 98 42.40 N 125.28 E

Dongfeng, Zhg. 100 27.20 N 118.53 E
Dongfengtai 105 39.34 N 117.45 E
Donggala 112 0.40 S 119.44 E
Donggang 100 22.58 N 115.57 E
Donggangzi 89 45.53 N 129.49 E
Donggi 112 1.33 S 122.15 E
Donggi Cona ⊜ 102 37.10 N 96.55 E
Donggong Shan ⋏ 100 27.36 N 119.26 E
Donggongsuo 106 32.07 N 121.25 E
Donggou, Zhg. 98 39.54 N 124.09 E
Donggou, Zhg. 100 33.38 N 119.40 E
Donggou, Zhg. 106 32.17 N 118.59 E
Donggu 100 26.46 N 115.22 E
Dongguan, Zhg. 100 27.49 N 116.25 E
Dongguan, Zhg. 100 23.03 N 113.46 E
Dongguan, Zhg. 106 30.22 N 119.28 E
Dongguan, Zhg. 107 30.47 N 106.16 E
Dongguang 98 37.53 N 116.30 E
Dongguanpu 106 31.13 N 120.43 E
Dongguanyingzi 104 41.55 N 120.38 E
Donggugang 105 39.10 N 116.49 E
Dong Hai, Viet 110 12.34 N 109.14 E
Donghai (Niushan), Zhg. 98 34.30 N 118.47 E
Dong Hai → East China Sea ⚲[2] 90 30.00 N 126.00 E
Donghai Dao I 102 21.02 N 110.25 E
Dongheng ≊ 106 31.54 N 120.17 E
Donghezhen 106 31.08 N 120.17 E
Dong Hoi 110 17.29 N 106.36 E
Donghu 100 26.28 N 113.07 E
Dong Hu ⊜ 120 32.10 N 84.40 E
Donghuanggou 104 40.43 N 123.29 E
Dongi 112 2.02 S 121.28 E
Dongio 58 46.27 N 8.58 E
Dongjia 98 37.18 N 118.24 E
Dongjiangkou 102 33.37 N 108.49 E
Dongjie 100 25.53 N 116.22 E
Dongjielang 100 31.03 N 115.57 E
Dongjingcheng 89 44.07 N 129.09 E
Dongjingji 98 40.02 N 114.01 E
Dongjingling 104 41.18 N 123.15 E
Dongjug 120 29.58 N 94.53 E
Dongkaihecheng 104 41.04 N 122.38 E
Dongkalang 112 0.10 N 120.06 E
Dongkeng, Zhg. 100 27.48 N 119.42 E
Dongkeng, Zhg. 100 24.59 N 114.54 E
Dong Khe 110 22.26 N 106.27 E
Dongkou 98 35.29 N 115.20 E
Donglan 102 24.40 N 107.18 E
Donglaohuyu 104 42.28 N 124.17 E
Donglaojunpu 104 41.24 N 121.22 E
Dongli 102 20.50 N 110.20 E
Dongliang 104 42.00 N 121.25 E
Dongliangjia 105 40.52 N 118.17 E
Donglidian 98 36.02 N 118.23 E
Donglinchang 107 29.39 N 104.07 E
Dongling 104 41.50 N 123.35 E
Dongliu, Zhg. 100 30.14 N 116.53 E
Dongliu, Zhg. 106 32.06 N 118.58 E
Dongliujiazi 104 42.21 N 122.44 E
Donglizhuang 105 39.21 N 116.47 E
Donglong 100 23.36 N 116.50 E
Donglucun 89 49.28 N 128.50 E
Dongmen 100 28.29 N 114.02 E
Dongming 98 35.18 N 115.08 E
Dong Nai ≃ 110 10.45 N 106.46 E
Dongnangou 104 41.25 N 122.02 E
Dong Nhien, Rach ≃ 269c 10.49 N 106.46 E
Dongning 89 44.04 N 131.07 E
Dongo, Ang. 152 14.36 S 15.48 E
Dongo, It. 58 46.07 N 9.17 E
Dongo, Zaïre 152 2.43 N 18.24 E
Dongobe 152 4.37 N 23.12 E
Dongobesh 154 4.04 S 35.23 E
Dongola → Dunqulah 140 19.10 N 30.29 E
Dongon Point ≻ 116 12.44 N 120.48 E
Dongou 152 2.02 N 18.04 E
Dongping, Zhg. 98 35.55 N 116.18 E
Dongping, Zhg. 100 27.24 N 118.39 E
Dongping, Zhg. 102 21.43 N 112.15 E
Dongping Hu ⊜ 98 36.00 N 116.12 E
Dongpu 100 30.03 N 120.34 E
Dongqian 106 30.52 N 120.23 E
Dongqiao 100 31.12 N 112.48 E
Dongqing 106 31.49 N 120.03 E
Dongqingduizi 104 41.02 N 122.08 E
Dongsanjiazi 104 41.54 N 122.48 E
Dongsanlintang 106 31.09 N 121.31 E
Dongsanpu 100 33.38 N 117.09 E
Dongsha ≃ 104 41.07 N 121.50 E
Dongshaer 120 28.41 N 89.09 E
Dongshajiao 100 30.19 N 122.09 E
Dongshan, Zhg. 100 23.42 N 117.24 E
Dongshan, Zhg. 102 19.50 N 110.14 E
Dongshan, Zhg. 106 31.04 N 120.24 E
Dongshan Dao I 100 23.40 N 117.25 E
Dongshanqiao 106 31.52 N 118.46 E
Dongshe 106 32.07 N 121.12 E
Dongsheng 102 39.49 N 109.59 E
Dongsheshanzi 104 42.15 N 123.09 E
Dongshi, Zhg. 100 24.42 N 118.27 E
Dongshi, Zhg. 100 24.43 N 115.59 E
Dongshi, Zhg. 271a 39.49 N 116.34 E
Dongshuiyan 105 39.15 N 115.23 E
Dongtai 100 32.51 N 120.20 E
Dongtai Hu C 106 31.05 N 120.30 E
Dongtaipingzhen 89 45.18 N 122.05 E
Dongtangou 105 39.23 N 118.22 E
Dongtianmu Shan ∧ 106 30.22 N 119.31 E
Dongtiao ≃ 106 30.51 N 120.06 E
Dongting 98 38.29 N 115.08 E
Dongtinghu 106 30.53 N 119.30 E
Dongting Hu ⊜ 102 29.20 N 112.54 E
Dongtingxi 102 28.34 N 110.36 E
Dongtou 100 27.50 N 121.09 E
Dongtou Shan I 100 27.50 N 121.08 E
Dong Trieu 110 21.05 N 106.31 E
Dongtuhulu 104 41.55 N 121.33 E
Dongtuoshanzi 104 42.10 N 123.08 E
Dongtuozi 104 41.17 N 121.53 E
Dong Van 110 23.16 N 105.22 E
Dongwangfu 89 44.47 N 120.53 E
Dongwangzhuang 106 32.16 N 120.32 E
Dongwe ≃ 152 13.58 S 23.53 E
Dongwuquan 105 39.20 N 115.43 E
Dongxi, Zhg. 100 28.35 N 120.02 E
Dongxi, Zhg. 102 28.47 N 106.39 E
Dongxi, Zhg. 107 30.24 N 104.33 E
Dongxia 106 31.11 N 119.05 E
Dongxiagaogao 104 42.36 N 122.30 E
Dongxiang 100 28.13 N 116.35 E
Dongxiang Dao I 100 25.36 N 119.48 E
Dongxing 89 46.23 N 127.52 E
Dongxingchang, Zhg. 107 29.16 N 103.55 E
Dongxingchang, Zhg. 107 29.36 N 105.04 E
Dongxinghe 105 39.46 N 114.49 E
Dongxinpu 104 41.00 N 123.18 E
Dongxinzhen 106 31.57 N 121.42 E
Dongyang, Zhg. 89 48.03 N 124.17 E
Dongyang, Zhg. 100 29.16 N 120.14 E
Dongyangqiao 106 30.52 N 120.34 E
Dongyao 98 35.56 N 113.58 E
Dongyian 105 39.22 N 115.46 E
Dongyin ≃ 105 39.09 N 117.43 E
Dongyou 100 27.10 N 118.37 E
Dongyuemiao 106 31.36 N 119.14 E
Dongyuezhen 107 30.24 N 103.32 E
Dongzhang 100 25.44 N 119.17 E
Dongzhaocun 105 40.02 N 116.46 E
Dongzhaozhuang 105 39.57 N 118.24 E
Dongzhenbeng 106 30.59 N 121.01 E
Dongzhi 100 30.07 N 116.59 E
Dongzhizhuang 105 40.25 N 116.50 E
Dongzhuangpu 105 40.34 N 115.42 E
Dongziya 105 38.50 N 116.44 E
Donie 222 31.29 N 96.13 W
Doninga 150 10.37 N 1.26 W
Donington 42 52.55 N 0.12 W
Doniphan, Mo., U.S. 194 36.37 N 90.49 W
Doniphan, Ne., U.S. 198 40.46 N 98.22 W

Don Islands II 116 11.05 N 123.38 E
Donja Stubica 36 45.59 N 15.58 E
Donjek ≃ 180 62.35 N 140.00 W
Donjezk → Donets'k 83 48.00 N 37.48 E
Donji Vakuf 36 44.09 N 17.25 E
Donk 52 51.33 N 5.37 E
Donkerpoort 158 30.32 S 25.30 E
Donkey Creek ≃ 198 44.12 N 104.58 W
Donkey Town 260 51.20 N 0.39 W
Donmānick Islands II 126 22.00 N 90.37 E
Don Martín 196 27.32 N 100.37 W
Don Matías 246 6.30 N 75.22 W
Don Mills ◆[8] 275b 43.44 N 79.20 W
Don Mills Centre ◆[9] 275b 43.44 N 79.21 W
Don Muang Airport ⊠ 269a 13.56 N 100.37 E
Donna 196 26.10 N 98.03 W
Donna, Punta sa ∧ 71 40.35 N 9.25 E
Donna Buang, Mount ∧ 169 37.43 S 145.40 E
Donnacona 206 46.40 N 71.47 W
Donnalucata 70 36.45 N 14.38 E
Donnaz 62 45.36 N 7.46 E
Donnell Lake ⊜[1] 226 38.20 N 119.56 W
Donnellson 219 39.02 N 89.29 W
Donnelly, Ab., Can. 182 55.44 N 117.06 W
Donnelly, Ak., U.S. 180 63.41 N 145.53 W
Donnelly, Id., U.S. 202 44.43 N 116.04 W
Donnellys Crossing 172 35.43 S 173.37 E
Donnemarie-Dontilly 50 48.29 N 3.08 E
Donner 194 29.41 N 90.56 W
Donner Lake ⊜[1] 226 39.20 N 120.16 W
Donner Memorial State Park ♠ 226 39.18 N 120.16 W
Donner Pass)(226 39.19 N 120.20 W
Donnersberg ∧ 56 49.38 N 7.55 E
Donner und Blitzen ≃ 202 43.17 N 118.49 W
Donnybrook, Austl. 162 33.35 S 115.49 E
Donnybrook, S. Afr. 158 30.00 S 29.48 E
Donora 214 40.10 N 79.51 W
Donostia (San Sebastián) 34 43.19 N 1.59 W
Donovan 216 40.53 N 87.37 W
Don Pedro Reservoir ⊜[1] 226 37.43 N 120.23 W
Don Peninsula ≻[1] 182 52.30 N 128.10 W
Donque 152 15.28 S 14.06 E
Donskaja gr'ada ⋏[2] 80 49.30 N 42.00 E
Dons'ke 83 47.31 N 37.33 E
Donskoj, Ross. 76 53.58 N 38.20 E
Donskoj, Ross. 83 48.49 N 40.06 E
Donskoj, Ross. 83 47.25 N 40.14 E
Donskoje, Ross. 76 52.37 N 39.00 E
Donskoje, Ross. 80 45.21 N 41.59 E
Donskoje belogorje ⋏[1] 78 50.30 N 39.45 E
Donsol 116 12.54 N 123.36 E
Don Torcuato 288 34.30 S 58.38 W
Don Torcuato, Aeródromo ⊠ 288 34.30 S 58.36 W
Dontsivka 83 49.35 N 39.16 E
Donuzlav, ozero ⊜ 78 45.23 N 33.05 E
Donyztau ⋏ 86 46.25 N 57.00 E
Donzdorf 56 48.41 N 9.48 E
Donzère 62 44.27 N 4.43 E
Donzy 50 47.22 N 3.08 E
Dooagh 48 53.59 N 10.09 W
Dood nuur ⊜ 88 51.20 N 99.20 E
Doogort 48 54.01 N 10.01 W
Doolow 144 4.10 N 42.05 E
Doomadgee 166 17.56 S 138.49 E
Doomadgee Aboriginal Reserve ◆[4] 166 17.43 S 138.36 E
Doon, On., Can. 212 43.23 N 80.26 W
Doon, Ia., U.S. 198 43.16 N 96.13 W
Doon ≃ 44 55.26 N 4.38 W
Doon, Loch ⊜ 44 55.15 N 4.22 W
Doonbeg 48 52.44 N 9.32 W
Doonbeg ≃ 48 52.44 N 9.34 W
Doon Doon Aboriginal Reserve ◆[4] 164 16.15 S 128.15 E
Doonerak, Mount ∧ 180 67.56 N 150.37 W
Doonside 274a 33.46 S 150.52 E
Dooralong 170 33.12 S 151.22 E
Doorn 52 52.03 N 5.21 E
Doorndam 158 28.03 S 21.03 E
Doornik → Tournai 50 50.36 N 3.23 E
Door Peninsula ≻[1] 190 44.55 N 87.20 W
Dopping Brook ≃ 283 42.12 N 71.23 W
Do Qal'eh 128 32.18 N 61.31 E
Dor 132 32.37 N 34.55 E
Dora 194 33.43 N 87.05 W
Dora, Lake ⊜, Austl. 162 22.05 S 122.55 E
Dora, Lake ⊜, Fl., U.S. 220 29.00 N 81.37 W
Dora Baltea ≃ 62 45.11 N 8.05 E
Dora di Rhêmes ≃ 62 45.42 N 7.11 E
Dorado 240m 18.28 N 66.15 W
Dorāha 123 30.49 N 76.01 E
Dorāh Ān)(123 36.07 N 71.15 E
Dorain, Beinn ∧ 46 56.30 N 4.42 W
Dorândia 256 22.27 S 43.57 W
Dora Riparia ≃ 62 45.05 N 7.44 E
Doraville 192 33.53 N 84.17 W
Dorback Burn ≃ 46 57.31 N 3.40 W
Dorcheat, Bayou ≃ 194 32.30 N 93.21 W
Dorchester, N.B., Can. 186 45.54 N 64.31 W
Dorchester, On., Can. 212 42.59 N 81.04 W
Dorchester, Eng., U.K. 42 50.43 N 2.26 W
Dorchester, Eng., U.K. 42 51.39 N 1.10 W
Dorchester, Il., U.S. 219 39.05 N 89.53 W
Dorchester, Ne., U.S. 198 40.38 N 97.06 W
Dorchester, N.J., U.S. 208 39.16 N 74.58 W
Dorchester, Wi., U.S. 190 45.00 N 90.20 W
Dorchester □[6] 208 38.34 N 76.04 W
Dorchester ◆[8] 283 42.17 N 71.04 W
Dorchester, Cape ≻ 176 65.29 N 77.30 W
Dorchester Bay C 283 42.19 N 71.02 W
Dorchester Crossing 186 46.10 N 64.34 W
Dorchester Estates 284c 38.47 N 76.55 W
Dorchester Heights National Historic Site ⊥ 283 42.20 N 71.03 W
Dorchheim 56 50.30 N 8.04 E
Dordabis 156 22.52 S 17.38 E
Dordives 50 48.09 N 2.46 E
Dordogne □[5] 32 45.10 N 0.45 E
Dordogne ≃ 32 45.02 N 0.35 W
Dordon 42 52.36 N 1.37 W
Dordrecht, Ned. 52 51.49 N 4.40 E
Dordrecht, S. Afr. 158 31.20 S 27.03 E
Doré ≃, Sk., Can. 184 54.56 N 107.45 W
Dore ≃, Fr. 62 45.50 N 3.35 E
Dore ≃, Eng., U.K. 42 51.57 N 2.52 W
Dore, Monts ⋏ 32 45.30 N 2.45 E
Doreissou 146 10.33 N 15.08 E
Doré Lake 184 54.38 N 107.24 W
Doré Lake ⊜ 184 54.46 N 107.17 W
Dorena 202 43.43 N 122.51 W
Dörentrup 52 52.03 N 8.59 E
Dores 46 57.22 N 4.15 W
Dores do Indaiá 255 19.27 S 45.36 W
Dores do Paraibuna 256 21.31 S 43.39 W
Dorfen 60 48.17 N 12.08 E
Dorfgastein 64 47.15 N 13.06 E
Dorfmark 52 52.54 N 9.46 E
Dorgali 71 40.17 N 9.35 E
Dörgön nuur ⊜ 88 47.40 N 93.30 E
Doring ≃ 158 31.54 S 18.39 E
Doringbaai 158 31.48 S 18.15 E
Doringkop ∧ 273d 26.15 S 27.50 E
Dorino 82 56.28 N 36.09 E
Dorion-Vaudreuil 206 45.23 N 74.01 W
Dorje Lāpka ∧ 124 28.11 N 85.47 E
Dorking 42 51.14 N 0.20 W

Dorloo 210 42.43 N 74.37 W
Dormaa Ahenkro 150 7.17 N 2.53 W
Dormagen 56 51.05 N 6.50 E
Dormans 50 49.04 N 3.38 E
Dormidontovka 89 47.45 N 134.57 E
Dormont 279b 40.23 N 80.02 W
Dornach 58 47.29 N 7.37 E
Dornap ◆[8] 263 51.15 N 7.04 E
Dornbach ◆[8] 264b 48.14 N 16.18 E
Dornbirn 58 47.25 N 9.44 E
Dornburg 56 50.30 N 8.07 E
Dorndorf, Dtsch. 54 51.00 N 11.40 E
Dorndorf, Dtsch. 56 50.50 N 10.05 E
Dornecy 50 47.26 N 3.35 E
Dorney 260 51.30 N 0.40 W
Dornhan 58 48.21 N 8.30 E
Dornie 46 57.17 N 5.31 W
Dorno 62 45.09 N 8.57 E
Dornoch 46 57.52 N 4.02 W
Dornoch Firth C[1] 46 57.53 N 4.00 W
Dornod □[4] 88 48.00 N 115.00 E
Dornogov' □[4] 102 44.30 N 110.00 E
Dornsife 208 40.45 N 76.47 W
Dornstadt 58 48.28 N 9.56 E
Dornstetten 58 48.28 N 8.30 E
Dornumersiel 52 53.40 N 7.28 E
Doro, Indon. 115a 7.02 S 109.41 E
Doro, Mali 150 16.09 N 0.51 W
Dorochovo 82 55.33 N 36.23 E
Dorog 30 47.43 N 18.44 E
Dorogobuž 76 54.55 N 33.18 E
Doroḥ 128 32.17 N 60.30 E
Dorohoi 38 47.57 N 26.24 E
Dorokempo 115b 8.33 S 118.15 E
Doromata 115b 8.46 S 118.13 E
Doromo 154 3.49 N 26.17 E
Dorošata 80 57.21 N 51.08 E
Dorošicha 82 56.52 N 35.50 E
Dorotea 26 64.16 N 16.24 E
Dorothy 208 39.24 N 74.49 W
Dorothy, Lake ⊜ 224 47.34 N 121.22 W
Dorotockeys Run ≃ 276 40.59 N 73.58 W
Dorpat → Tartu 76 58.23 N 26.43 E
Dörpen 52 52.57 N 7.20 E
Dorr 216 42.43 N 85.43 W
Dorrance 198 38.50 N 98.35 W
Dorre Island I 162 25.09 S 113.07 E
Dorrigo 166 30.21 S 152.43 E
Dorris 204 41.58 N 121.55 W
Dorsale ⋏ 36 36.00 N 9.50 E
Dorset, Oh., U.S. 214 41.41 N 80.40 W
Dorset, Vt., U.S. 210 43.15 N 73.05 W
Dorset □[6] 42 50.47 N 2.20 W
Dorset Peak ∧ 188 43.19 N 73.02 W
Dorsey Run ≃ 284b 39.11 N 76.48 W
Dorseyville 279b 40.35 N 79.53 W
Dorsten 52 51.39 N 6.58 E
Dorstfeld ◆[8] 263 51.31 N 7.25 E
Dort → Dordrecht 52 51.49 N 4.40 E
Dortan 58 46.19 N 5.40 E
Dörtdivan 130 40.43 N 32.04 E
Dortmund, Dtsch. 52 51.31 N 7.28 E
Dortmund, Dtsch. 263 51.31 N 7.28 E
Dortmund-Ems-Kanal ≊ 52 51.32 N 7.27 E
Dortmunder Rieselfelder ◆[1] 263 51.39 N 7.25 E
Dortmund-Wickede, Flughafen ⊠ 263 51.32 N 7.35 E
Dorton 192 37.16 N 82.34 W
Dörtyol 130 36.52 N 36.12 E
Do Rūd 128 33.28 N 49.04 E
Dorum 52 53.41 N 8.34 E
Doruma 154 4.44 N 27.42 E
Dorval 206 45.27 N 73.44 W
Dorval, Île I 275a 45.26 N 73.45 W
Dorval Gardens Centre ◆[9] 275a 45.27 N 73.44 W
Dörverden 52 52.51 N 9.13 E
Dörvöldžin 88 48.08 N 93.58 E
Dörzbach 56 49.23 N 9.42 E
Dos, Canal Numero ≊ 252 36.21 S 56.54 W
Dosara 150 12.32 N 6.09 E
Do Sārī 128 28.25 N 57.59 E
Dos Arroyos 234 17.02 N 99.40 W
Dosatuj 88 50.23 N 118.38 E
Dos Bahías, Cabo ≻ 254 44.55 S 65.32 W
Dos Bocas 240m 18.20 N 66.40 W
Dos Bocas, Lago ⊜[1] 240m 18.19 N 66.40 W
Doščatoje 80 55.23 N 42.07 E
Döşemealtı 130 37.04 N 30.36 E
Dosewallips ≃ 224 47.42 N 122.53 W
Dos Hermanas 34 37.17 N 5.55 W
Dos Hermanas, Islas II 258 34.05 S 58.17 W
Dōshi 94 35.32 N 139.02 E
Dōshi ≃ 94 35.36 N 139.14 E
Doshisha University ♜[2] 270 35.02 N 135.46 E
Dosi 164 5.56 S 134.34 E
Dösjebro 41 55.49 N 13.01 E
Do Son 110 20.42 N 106.47 E
Dosoris Island ≻[1] 276 40.53 N 73.38 W
Dosoris Pond ⊜ 276 40.54 N 73.38 W
Dos Palos 226 36.59 N 120.37 W
Dos Pos 241s 12.15 N 68.20 W
Dos Quebradas 246 4.51 N 75.40 W
Dos Reyes, Punta ≻ 252 24.33 S 70.35 W
Dosse ≃ 54 53.13 N 12.20 E
Dosséo, Bahr ≃ 146 9.01 N 19.38 E
Dossin Great Lakes Museum ♜ 281 42.20 N 82.59 W
Dosso 150 13.03 N 3.12 E
Dosso □[5] 150 13.00 N 3.00 E
Dossor 80 47.32 N 53.01 E
Doster 216 42.27 N 85.33 W
Doswell 208 37.51 N 77.27 W
Dothan 194 31.13 N 85.23 W
Doting Cove 186 49.27 N 53.57 W
Dot Lake 180 63.40 N 144.04 W
Dotnuva 76 55.21 N 23.54 E
Dotson 222 32.01 N 94.31 W
Döttingen 58 47.34 N 8.16 E
Doty 224 46.38 N 123.16 W
Dou ≃ 105 39.13 N 118.03 E
Douai 50 50.22 N 3.04 E
Douala 152 4.03 N 9.42 E
Douala-Edéa, Réserve de ◆[4] 152 4.30 S 9.50 E
Douarnenez 32 48.06 N 4.20 W
Doubabougou 150 14.13 N 7.59 W
Double, Lac ⊜ 186 50.46 N 70.23 W
Doublé, Pointe ≻ 241o 16.20 N 61.00 W
Double Bayou 222 29.41 N 94.39 W
Double Cone ∧ 172 45.04 S 168.48 E
Double Island Point ≻ 166 25.56 S 153.11 E
Double Mountain ∧ 228 35.02 N 118.29 W
Double Point ≻ 166 17.39 S 146.09 E
Double Springs 194 34.08 N 87.24 W
Doubletop Peak ∧ 200 43.21 N 110.17 W
Doubs 58 46.56 N 6.21 E
Doubs □[5] 58 47.10 N 6.25 E
Doubs ≃ 58 46.54 N 5.02 E
Doubs, Saut de ⌊ 58 47.05 N 6.43 E
Doubtful Sound U 172 45.17 S 166.51 E
Doubtless Bay C 172 34.55 S 173.25 E
Douchy 50 47.57 N 3.03 E
Douchy-les-Mines 50 50.18 N 3.23 E
Doudeville 50 49.43 N 0.48 E
Doudian 105 39.39 N 116.03 E
Doué ≃[1] 150 16.38 N 15.02 W
Douentza 150 15.00 N 2.57 W
Dougga ⊥ 36 36.25 N 9.13 E
Doughboy 170 35.15 S 149.39 E
Doughboy Bay C 172 47.02 S 167.41 E
Douglas, Austl. 164 16.29 S 145.28 E
Douglas, Mb., Can. 184 49.53 N 99.42 W
Douglas, On., Can. 212 45.31 N 76.56 W
Douglas, I. of Man 44 54.09 N 4.28 W
Douglas, S. Afr. 158 29.04 S 23.46 E

Symbol	English	Deutsch	Español	Français	Português
≃	River	Fluß	Río	Rivière	Rio
≊	Canal	Kanal	Canal	Canal	Canal
⌊	Waterfall, Rapids	Wasserfall, Stromschnellen	Cascada, Rápidos	Chute d'eau, Rapides	Cascata, Rápidos
U	Strait	Meeresstraße	Estrecho	Détroit	Estreito
C	Bay, Gulf	Bucht, Golf	Bahía, Golfo	Baie, Golfe	Baía, Golfo
⊜	Lake, Lakes	See, Seen	Lago, Lagos	Lac, Lacs	Lago, Lagos
≡	Swamp	Sumpf	Pantano	Marais	Pântano
⩯	Ice Features, Glacier	Eis- und Gletscherformen	Accidentes Glaciales	Formes glaciaires	Acidentes glaciares
⚲	Other Hydrographic Features	Andere Hydrographische Objekte	Otros Elementos Hidrográficos	Autres données hydrographiques	Outros acidentes hidrográficos

Symbol	English	Deutsch	Español	Français	Português
⧫	Submarine Features	Untermeerische Objekte	Accidentes Submarinos	Formes de relief sous-marin	Acidentes submarinos
□	Political Unit	Politische Einheit	Unidad Política	Entité politique	Unidade política
♜	Cultural Institution	Kulturelle Institution	Institución Cultural	Institution culturelle	Instituição cultural
⊥	Historical Site	Historische Stätte	Sitio Histórico	Site historique	Sitio histórico
♠	Recreational Site	Erholungs- und Ferienort	Sitio de Recreo	Centre de loisirs	Area de Lazer
⊠	Airport	Flughafen	Aeropuerto	Aéroport	Aeroporto
■	Military Installation	Militäranlage	Instalación Militar	Installation militaire	Instalação militar
◆	Miscellaneous	Verschiedenes	Misceláneo	Divers	Diversos

Name	Page	Lat.°'	Long.°'
Douglas, Scot., U.K.	46	55.33 N	3.51 W
Douglas, Ak., U.S.	180	58.16 N	134.22 W
Douglas, Az., U.S.	200	31.20 N	109.32 W
Douglas, Ga., U.S.	192	31.30 N	82.51 W
Douglas, Mi., U.S.	216	42.38 N	86.12 W
Douglas, N.D., U.S.	198	47.51 N	101.30 W
Douglas, Wy., U.S.	200	42.45 N	105.22 W
Douglas □[6]	226	38.55 N	119.39 W
Douglas ≐	44	53.43 N	2.50 W
Douglas, Cape >	180	58.52 N	153.18 W
Douglas, Mount ∧	180	58.52 N	153.31 W
Douglas, Mount ∧[2]	162	28.39 S	123.53 E
Douglas Aircraft Company ♦[3]	280	33.50 N	118.09 W
Douglas Channel)(	182	53.30 N	129.12 W
Douglas Creek ≐	200	40.06 N	108.46 W
Douglas Lake	182	50.10 N	120.12 W
Douglas Lake ⊜[1]	192	36.00 N	83.22 W
Douglas Lake Indian Reserve •[4]	182	50.10 N	120.49 W
Douglas Park	170	34.11 S	150.43 E
Douglas Park ♠	278	41.52 N	87.42 W
Douglass, Ks., U.S.	198	37.31 N	97.01 W
Douglass, Tx., U.S.	222	31.40 N	94.53 W
Douglass Run ≐	279b	40.15 N	79.48 W
Douglassville	208	40.15 N	75.44 W
Douglasville	192	33.45 N	84.44 W
Douglas Water ≐	46	55.38 N	3.46 W
Dougouzi, Zhg.	89	49.57 N	127.01 E
Dougouzi, Zhg.	104	41.16 N	122.34 E
Douhutun	98	42.06 N	124.50 E
Douigny	152	3.11 S	10.45 E
Doujiapu	104	41.05 N	122.12 E
Doujiazhuang	105	40.22 N	116.59 E
Doukkane, Djebel ∧	36	35.23 N	8.00 E
Doulaincourt	58	48.19 N	5.12 E
Doulevant-le-Château	58	48.23 N	4.55 E
Doullens	50	50.09 N	2.21 E
Doumanaba	150	11.40 N	5.56 W
Doumanga	152	2.41 S	12.40 E
Doumba Bélo	152	5.05 N	14.18 E
Doumdégué	152	7.29 N	18.58 E
Doumé, Cam.	152	4.14 N	13.27 E
Doumé, Cam.	152	5.32 N	12.19 E
Doumé ≐	152	4.06 N	14.34 E
Doumen, Zhg.	100	22.12 N	113.16 E
Doumen, Zhg.	105	39.18 N	115.53 E
Douna	150	14.39 N	1.44 W
Doune	46	56.12 N	4.05 W
Doune Castle ⊥	46	56.11 N	4.03 W
Dounguila	152	2.53 S	11.58 E
Doupov	54	50.10 N	13.08 E
Doupovské hory ⋏	54	50.13 N	13.08 E
Dour	50	50.24 N	3.47 E
Doura	150	13.14 N	5.55 W
Dourada, Serra ⋏[1]	255	13.10 S	48.45 W
Douradinho	256	21.45 S	45.46 W
Dourado ≐	256	21.43 S	45.44 W
Dourados	255	22.13 S	54.48 W
Dourados ≐	255	21.58 S	54.18 W
Dourbali	146	11.49 N	15.52 E
Dourdan	50	48.32 N	2.01 E
Dourdou ≐	32	44.00 N	2.41 E
Dourges	50	50.26 N	2.59 E
Dourkoulé	146	14.27 N	22.13 E
Douro ≐, Bra.	287a	22.42 S	43.35 W
Douro (Duero) ≐, Europe	34	41.08 N	8.40 W
Doushanhe	100	31.38 N	114.42 E
Dousman	216	43.00 N	88.28 W
Douthat State Park ♠	192	37.55 N	79.50 W
Douvaine	58	46.19 N	6.18 E
Douvres → Dover	42	51.08 N	1.19 E
Douvres, Falaises de ⊥[4]	273b	4.06 S	15.25 E
Douvrin	50	50.31 N	2.50 E
Doux ≐	62	45.04 N	4.50 E
Douy-la-Ramée	261	49.04 N	2.53 E
Douyu	98	37.53 N	114.30 E
Douz	148	33.28 N	9.01 E
Douze ≐	32	43.54 N	0.30 W
Douzhangzhuang	105	39.23 N	116.55 E
Douzishan	107	29.04 N	104.57 E
Douziyu	105	40.18 N	117.19 E
Douzy	56	49.40 N	5.03 E
Dovadola	66	44.07 N	11.53 E
Dovbysh	78	50.22 N	27.59 E
Dove ≐, Eng., U.K.	44	52.50 N	1.35 W
Dove ≐, Eng., U.K.	44	54.12 N	0.54 W
Dove Creek	200	37.45 N	108.54 W
Dove Creek ≐, Tx., U.S.	196	31.20 N	100.36 W
Dove Creek ≐, Ut,. U.S.	200	41.37 N	113.15 W
Dove Holes	262	53.18 N	1.53 W
Dove Holes Tunnel •[5]	262	53.18 N	1.53 W
Dover, Austl.	166	43.19 S	147.01 E
Dover, S. Afr.	158	27.02 S	27.46 E
Dover, Eng., U.K.	42	51.08 N	1.19 E
Dover, Ar., U.S.	194	35.24 N	93.06 W
Dover, De., U.S.	208	39.09 N	75.31 W
Dover, Fl., U.S.	220	27.59 N	82.13 W
Dover, Id., U.S.	202	48.15 N	116.36 W
Dover, Ky., U.S.	218	38.45 N	83.52 W
Dover, Ma., U.S.	283	42.14 N	71.17 W
Dover, N.H., U.S.	188	43.11 N	70.52 W
Dover, N.J., U.S.	210	40.53 N	74.34 W
Dover, N.C., U.S.	192	35.12 N	77.26 W
Dover, Oh., U.S.	214	40.31 N	81.28 W
Dover, Ok., U.S.	196	35.58 N	97.54 W
Dover, Pa., U.S.	208	40.00 N	76.51 W
Dover, Tn., U.S.	194	36.29 N	87.50 W
Dover, Point >	162	32.32 S	125.32 E
Dover, Strait of (Pas de Calais))(	50	51.00 N	1.30 E
Dover Air Force Base ■	208	39.08 N	75.28 W
Dover-Foxcroft	188	45.11 N	69.13 W
Dover Heights	274a	33.53 S	151.17 E
Dover Hills	276	40.52 N	74.33 W
Dover Plains	210	41.44 N	73.35 W
Dovers Hills ⋏[2]	162	23.10 S	128.45 E
Dove Stone Reservoir ⊜[1]	262	53.32 N	1.58 W
Doveton	274b	38.00 S	145.14 E
Dovey Valley V	42	52.35 N	3.50 W
Dovhen'ke	83	49.01 N	37.19 E
Dovol'noje	86	54.30 N	79.40 E
Dovre	26	61.59 N	9.15 E
Dovrefjell ⋏	26	62.06 N	9.25 E
Dovrefjell Nasjonalpark ♠	26	62.18 N	9.36 E
Dovsk	76	53.09 N	30.28 E
Dovzhyk	78	50.13 N	35.55 E
Dowa	154	13.40 S	33.58 E
Dowagiac	216	41.59 N	86.06 W
Dowagiac ≐	216	41.51 N	86.16 W
Dowagiac Creek ≐	216	41.49 N	86.10 W
Dowally	46	56.36 N	3.37 W
Dow City	198	41.55 N	95.29 W
Dowden Terrace	284c	38.50 N	77.08 W
Dowell	208	38.20 N	76.27 W
Dowerin	162	31.12 S	117.02 E
Dowi, Tanjung >	114	1.31 N	97.25 E
Dowker, Île I	275a	45.24 N	73.54 W
Dowlatābād, Afg.	120	36.59 N	66.50 E
Dowlatābād, Afg.	120	36.26 N	64.55 E
Dowlatābād, Īrān	128	28.18 N	56.40 E
Dowlat Yār	120	34.33 N	65.47 E
Dowling Lake ⊜	182	51.44 N	112.00 W
Downderry	42	50.22 N	4.22 W
Downe •[8]	260	51.20 N	0.03 E
Down East	285	40.03 N	75.32 W
Downers Grove	216	41.48 N	88.00 W
Downey, Ca., U.S.	228	33.56 N	118.07 W
Downey, Id., U.S.	202	42.25 N	112.07 W
Downey Creek ≐	224	48.16 N	121.14 W
Downham, Eng., U.K.	42	52.26 N	0.15 E
Downham, Eng., U.K.	260	51.38 N	0.30 E
Downham Market	42	52.36 N	0.23 E
Down House ⊥	260	51.20 N	0.03 E
Downieville	226	39.33 N	120.49 W
Downing	194	40.29 N	92.22 W
Downingtown	208	40.00 N	75.42 W
Downingtown Airport ⊠	285	39.59 N	75.45 W
Downpatrick	48	54.20 N	5.43 W
Downpatrick Head >	48	54.20 N	9.20 W
Downs, Il., U.S.	216	40.24 N	88.52 W
Downs, Ks., U.S.	198	39.30 N	98.32 W
Downs Mountain ∧	200	43.18 N	109.40 W
Downsview Dells Park ♠	275b	43.44 N	79.30 W
Downsville	210	42.04 N	74.59 W
Downsville Dam •[6]	210	42.05 N	74.58 W
Downton	42	51.00 N	1.44 W
Downton, Mount ∧	182	52.42 N	124.51 W
Downton Lake ⊜	182	50.51 N	123.00 W
Downwind Acres Airfield ⊠	281	42.09 N	83.34 W
Dows	190	42.39 N	93.30 W
Dowshī	120	35.37 N	68.41 E
Doygaab	144	0.59 N	43.32 E
Doyle	204	40.01 N	120.06 W
Doyles	186	47.50 N	59.12 W
Doylesburg	214	40.13 N	77.42 W
Doylestown, Oh., U.S.	214	40.58 N	81.41 W
Doylestown, Pa., U.S.	208	40.18 N	75.07 W
Doyline	194	32.32 N	93.25 W
Dōzan ≐	96	33.58 N	133.47 E
Dōzen II	92	36.05 N	133.05 E
Dozier	194	31.29 N	86.21 W
Dozois, Réservoir ⊜[1]	190	47.30 N	77.05 W
Dozza	66	44.22 N	11.37 E
Drâa, Cap >	148	28.44 N	11.08 W
Dra'a, Hamada du •[2]	148	29.00 N	6.45 W
Drâa, Oued V	148	28.43 N	11.09 W
Draa el Mizan	34	36.32 N	3.50 E
Drabble → José Enrique Rodó	258	33.41 S	57.34 W
Drabenderhöhe	56	50.57 N	7.27 E
Drabiv	78	49.58 N	32.08 E
Drac ≐	62	45.13 N	5.41 E
Dracena	255	21.32 S	51.29 W
Drachenfels ⊥	56	50.40 N	7.12 E
Drachten	52	53.06 N	6.05 E
Dracut	207	42.40 N	71.18 W
Dragalina	38	44.26 N	27.20 E
Drăgănești-Olt	38	44.10 N	24.32 E
Drăgănești-Vlașca	38	44.06 N	25.36 E
Drăgășani	38	44.40 N	24.16 E
Drag Lake ⊜	212	45.05 N	78.24 W
Dragone ≐	64	44.23 N	10.37 E
Dragonera I	34	39.35 N	2.19 E
Dragoni	68	41.16 N	14.18 E
Dragonja ≐	64	45.28 N	13.37 E
Dragons Mouths)(	241r	10.45 N	61.46 W
Dragon Swamp ≐	208	37.33 N	76.34 W
Dragoon	200	32.01 N	110.02 W
Dragør	41	55.36 N	12.41 E
Draguignan	62	43.32 N	6.28 E
Drain	202	43.39 N	123.19 W
Drake, Mo., U.S.	219	38.28 N	91.28 W
Drake, N.D., U.S.	198	47.55 N	100.22 W
Drakenburg	52	52.41 N	9.13 E
Drakensberg ⋏	156	27.00 S	30.00 E
Drake Passage)(	18	58.00 S	70.00 W
Drake Peak ∧	202	42.19 N	120.07 W
Drakesboro	194	37.13 N	87.02 W
Drakes Branch	192	36.59 N	78.36 W
Drakes Brook ≐	276	40.49 N	74.43 W
Drake Well Museum ♦	214	41.36 N	79.39 W
Drakino	82	54.52 N	37.17 E
Dráma	38	41.09 N	24.08 E
Drammen	26	59.44 N	10.15 E
Dran	110	11.51 N	108.35 E
Drancy	50	48.56 N	2.27 E
Dranda	84	42.53 N	41.09 E
Drang ≐	110	13.19 N	107.21 E
Drangajökull ⩍	24a	66.11 N	22.15 W
Drangstedt	52	53.36 N	8.44 E
Dranov, Ostrovul I	38	44.52 N	29.15 E
Dransfeld	52	51.30 N	9.45 E
Dranske	54	54.38 N	13.14 E
Drap	62	43.45 N	7.19 E
Draper, N.C., U.S.	192	36.31 N	79.41 W
Draper, Ut,. U.S.	200	40.31 N	111.51 W
Draperstown	48	54.48 N	6.47 W
Drās	123	34.27 N	75.46 E
Drās ≐	123	34.37 N	75.59 E
Drau (Drava) (Dráva) ≐	36	45.33 N	18.55 E
Drava (Drau) (Dráva) ≐	36	45.33 N	18.55 E
Draveil	50	48.41 N	2.25 E
Dravinja ≐	36	46.22 N	15.57 E
Dravograd	61	46.35 N	15.02 E
Dravosburg	279b	40.21 N	79.51 W
Drawno	30	53.13 N	15.45 E
Drawsko Pomorskie	30	53.32 N	15.48 E
Drayton, On., Can.	212	43.46 N	80.40 W
Drayton, Eng., U.K.	42	51.38 N	1.18 W
Drayton, N.D., U.S.	198	48.34 N	97.10 W
Drayton, S.C., U.S.	192	34.58 N	81.54 W
Drayton Plains	216	42.41 N	83.22 W
Drayton Valley	182	53.13 N	114.59 W
Draženov	60	49.28 N	12.52 E
Drean	36	36.41 N	7.46 E
Drebkau	54	51.39 N	14.13 E
Dreieich	56	50.01 N	8.41 E
Dreifelder Weiher ⊜	56	50.36 N	7.49 E
Dreihausen	56	50.43 N	8.50 E
Dreiherrnspitze (Picco dei Tre Signori) ∧	64	47.04 N	12.15 E
Dreikikir	164	3.35 S	142.45 E
Drejø I	41	54.58 N	10.25 E
Dremsel, Mount ∧	164	2.10 S	146.55 E
Drena	64	45.58 N	10.56 E
Drenovec	38	43.42 N	22.59 E
Drensteinfurt	52	51.48 N	7.44 E
Drenthe □[4]	52	52.45 N	6.30 E
Dresde → Dresden	54	51.03 N	13.44 E
Dresden, On., Can.	214	42.35 N	82.11 W
Dresden, Dtsch.	54	51.03 N	13.44 E
Dresden, N.Y., U.S.	210	42.41 N	76.58 W
Dresden, Oh., U.S.	214	40.07 N	82.00 W
Dresden, Tn., U.S.	194	36.17 N	88.42 W
Dresher	285	40.08 N	75.10 W
Dretun	76	55.41 N	29.13 E
Dreux	50	48.44 N	1.22 E
Drevenack	263	51.40 N	6.45 E
Drew	194	33.48 N	90.31 W
Drewer	263	51.40 N	7.07 E
Drewitz, Dtsch.	54	52.22 N	13.07 E
Drewitz, Dtsch.	54	52.12 N	12.10 E
Drewitz •[8]	264a	52.22 N	13.08 E
Drewryville	208	36.42 N	77.18 W
Drews Reservoir ⊜[1]	202	42.10 N	120.40 W
Drew University ♦[2]	276	40.46 N	74.25 W
Drexel	218	39.44 N	84.17 W
Drexel Gardens	218	39.44 N	86.15 W
Drexel Hill	285	39.56 N	75.17 W
Drexel University ♦[2]	285	39.57 N	75.11 W
Drezdenko	30	52.51 N	15.50 E
Drezna	82	55.44 N	38.51 E
Dribin	76	54.08 N	31.06 E
Driebergen	52	52.03 N	5.16 E
Drienov	30	48.53 N	21.17 E
Drifton	210	41.00 N	75.54 W
Driftpile ≐	182	55.23 N	115.40 W
Drift Pile River Indian Reserve •[4]	182	55.18 N	115.45 W
Driftwood, B.C., Can.	182	55.49 N	126.25 W
Driftwood, Pa., U.S.	214	41.20 N	78.08 W
Driftwood ≐, B.C., Can.	182	55.43 N	126.15 W
Driftwood ≐, In., U.S.	218	39.12 N	85.56 W
Driftwood Creek ≐	198	40.11 N	100.39 W
Driggs	202	43.43 N	111.06 W
Drimnin	46	56.36 N	6.00 W
Drimoleague	48	51.38 N	9.14 W
Drin ≐	38	41.45 N	19.34 E
Drina ≐	38	44.53 N	19.21 E
Dringenberg	52	51.40 N	9.02 E
Drini i Zi ≐	38	42.00 N	20.21 E
Drinit, Gjiri i C	38	41.45 N	19.28 E
Driorejo	115a	7.21 S	112.37 E
Driscoll	196	27.40 N	97.45 W
Driskill Mountain ∧[2]	194	32.25 N	92.54 W
Drissa ≐	76	55.47 N	27.55 E
Drisv'aty, ozero ⊜	76	55.38 N	26.35 E
Driver	208	36.49 N	76.30 W
Drizzle Lake ⊜	212	45.20 N	78.10 W
Drjanovo	38	42.58 N	25.27 E
Drnholec	61	48.52 N	16.29 E
Drniš	36	43.51 N	16.09 E
Dro	64	45.58 N	10.54 E
Drøbak	26	59.39 N	10.39 E
Drobeta-Turnu Severin	38	44.38 N	22.39 E
Drobylevo	82	55.44 N	35.53 E
Drobysheve	83	49.02 N	37.44 E
Drobyšovo	86	53.58 N	74.40 E
Drochia	38	48.03 N	27.48 E
Drochtersen	52	53.42 N	9.23 E
Drocourt	261	49.03 N	1.46 E
Droë Harts ≐	158	27.35 S	24.41 E
Drogheda (Droichead Átha)	48	53.43 N	6.21 W
Drogičin	76	52.11 N	25.09 E
Drohiczyn	30	52.24 N	22.41 E
Drohobych	78	49.21 N	23.30 E
Drohobycz → Drohobych	78	49.21 N	23.30 E
Droichead Átha → Drogheda	48	53.43 N	6.21 W
Droichead Nua	48	53.11 N	6.48 W
Droitwich	42	52.16 N	2.09 W
Drolshagen	56	51.01 N	7.46 E
Dromahair	48	54.14 N	8.19 W
Dromana	169	38.21 S	144.58 E
Dromara	48	54.23 N	6.01 W
Dromcolliher	48	52.20 N	8.54 W
Drôme □[5]	62	44.35 N	5.10 E
Drôme ≐	62	44.46 N	4.46 E
Drömling •[1]	54	52.29 N	11.04 E
Dromod	48	53.51 N	7.55 W
Dromore, N. Ire., U.K.	48	54.31 N	7.28 W
Dromore, N. Ire., U.K.	48	54.25 N	6.09 W
Dromore West	48	54.15 N	8.53 W
Dronero	62	44.28 N	7.22 E
Dronfield	44	53.19 N	1.27 W
Drongan	44	55.26 N	4.27 W
Drongen	50	51.03 N	3.40 E
Dronne ≐	32	45.02 N	0.09 W
Dronninglund	26	57.09 N	10.18 E
Dronrijp	52	53.11 N	5.38 E
Dröschede	263	51.22 N	7.39 E
Drosendorf Stadt	61	48.52 N	15.37 E
Drosiá	267c	38.07 N	23.52 E
Drösing	61	48.32 N	16.54 E
Droskovo	76	52.31 N	37.05 E
Drottningholm slott ⊥	40	59.19 N	17.53 E
Droué	50	48.02 N	1.05 E
Droue-sur-Drouette	261	48.36 N	1.42 E
Drouette ≐	261	48.37 N	1.37 E
Drouin	169	38.08 S	145.51 E
Drov'anaja	88	51.35 N	113.02 E
Droylsden	262	53.29 N	2.10 W
Droyssig	54	51.02 N	12.01 E
Druid Hill Park ♠	284b	39.19 N	76.39 W
Druja	76	55.47 N	27.27 E
Druk-Yul → Bhutan □[1]	120	27.30 N	90.30 E
Drulingen	56	48.52 N	7.11 E
Drum, Mount ∧	180	62.07 N	144.35 W
Drumbeg	46	58.14 N	5.12 W
Drumbo	212	43.14 N	80.33 W
Drumcliff	48	54.20 N	8.30 W
Drumheller	182	51.28 N	112.42 W
Drumlish	48	53.48 N	7.46 W
Drummond, N.Z.	172	46.09 S	168.09 E
Drummond, Mt., U.S.	202	46.40 N	113.08 W
Drummond, Wi., U.S.	190	46.20 N	91.15 W
Drummond □[6]	206	45.50 N	72.20 W
Drummond, Lake ⊜	208	36.36 N	76.28 W
Drummond Island I	190	46.00 N	83.40 W
Drummond Range ⋏	166	23.30 S	147.15 E
Drummondville	206	45.53 N	72.29 W
Drummore	44	54.42 N	4.54 W
Drummoyne	274a	33.51 S	151.09 E
Drumquin	48	54.37 N	7.30 W
Drumright	196	35.59 N	96.36 W
Drumshanbo	48	54.02 N	8.02 W
Drunen	52	51.42 N	5.08 E
Drusenheim	56	48.46 N	7.57 E
Druskininkai	76	54.01 N	23.58 E
Drut' ≐	76	53.03 N	30.42 E
Druten	52	51.54 N	5.36 E
Druyes-les-Belles-Fontaines	50	47.33 N	3.25 E
Družba, Kaz.	86	45.15 N	82.26 E
Družba, Ross.	265b	55.53 N	37.45 E
Druzhba	78	52.03 N	33.56 E
Druzhkivka	83	48.37 N	37.33 E
Družina	74	68.14 N	145.18 E
Družnaja Gorka	76	59.17 N	30.08 E
Drvar	36	44.22 N	16.24 E
Drwęca ≐	30	53.00 N	18.42 E
Dry ≐	164	14.54 S	132.24 E
Dry Arm C	202	47.45 N	106.20 W
Dry Bay C	180	59.08 N	138.25 W
Dryberry Lake ⊜	184	49.33 N	93.53 W
Dryburgh Abbey ♦[1]	46	55.34 N	2.40 W
Dry Cimarron ≐	196	36.54 N	102.59 W
Dry Creek ≐, Ca., U.S.	204	38.35 N	122.51 W
Dry Creek ≐, Ca., U.S.	226	37.27 N	120.37 W
Dry Creek ≐, Ca., U.S.	226	38.39 N	121.28 W
Dry Creek ≐, Ca., U.S.	226	38.22 N	122.18 W
Dry Creek ≐, Ca., U.S.	226	38.58 N	121.32 W
Dry Creek ≐, Ca., U.S.	226	39.13 N	121.25 W
Dry Creek ≐, Ca., U.S.	226	38.14 N	121.24 W
Dry Creek ≐, Ca., U.S.	226	36.58 N	120.13 W
Dry Creek ≐, Ca., U.S.	226	36.47 N	119.46 W
Dry Creek ≐, Ca., U.S.	282	37.22 N	122.23 W
Dry Creek ≐, Or., U.S.	202	43.34 N	117.21 W
Dry Creek ≐, Or., U.S.	224	45.30 N	121.03 W
Dry Creek ≐, Tx., U.S.	222	32.46 N	95.28 W
Dry Creek ≐, Wy., U.S.	202	43.13 N	108.54 W
Dry Creek ≐, Wy., U.S.	202	44.30 N	108.03 W
Dry Creek Mountain ∧	204	41.22 N	116.22 W
Dryden, On., Can.	184	49.47 N	92.50 W
Dryden, N.Y., U.S.	210	42.29 N	76.17 W
Dryden, Wa., U.S.	224	47.32 N	120.33 W
Dry Devils ≐, Tx., U.S.	196	29.47 N	100.59 W
Dry Devils ≐, Tx., U.S.	196	30.20 N	100.57 W
Dryfe Water ≐	44	55.08 N	3.26 W
Dry Fork ≐	194	37.58 N	91.31 W
Dry Frio ≐	196	29.17 N	99.39 W
Drygalski Island I	9	65.45 S	92.30 E
Dry Lake ⊜	198	48.15 N	98.58 W
Drymen	46	56.04 N	4.27 W
Dry Prong	194	31.34 N	92.31 W
Dry Ridge	218	38.40 N	84.35 W
Dry Run	214	40.10 N	77.45 W
Drysdale	169	38.11 S	144.34 E
Drysdale ≐	164	13.59 S	126.51 E
Drysdale River National Park ♠	164	15.00 S	127.00 E
Dry Tortugas II	220	24.38 N	82.55 W
Drzewica	30	51.27 N	20.28 E
Drzewice	54	52.38 N	14.38 E
Dschang	152	5.27 N	10.04 E
Dschidda → Jiddah	144	21.30 N	39.12 E
Dschuba → Jubba ≐	144	0.15 S	42.38 E
Du	150	10.30 N	0.59 W
Du ≐	102	32.48 N	110.38 E
Dua ≐	152	3.20 N	20.53 E
Duabo	150	5.40 N	8.05 W
Duāigaon	126	24.14 N	90.51 E
Duala → Douala	152	4.03 N	9.42 E
Dualchi	71	40.13 N	8.54 E
Du'an	102	24.06 N	108.10 E
Duancun	105	38.52 N	115.56 E
Duane L. Bliss State Park ♠	226	38.59 N	120.06 W
Duanesburg	210	42.46 N	74.08 W
Duanjialing	105	39.59 N	117.09 E
Duaringa	166	23.43 S	149.40 E
Duarte	228	34.08 N	117.58 W
Duarte, Pico ∧	238	19.02 N	70.59 W
Duartina	255	22.24 S	49.25 W
Duas Barras	256	22.02 S	42.32 W
Duayaw Nkwanta	150	7.10 N	2.06 W
Ḍubā, Ar. Su.	128	27.21 N	35.40 E
Dubá, Česká Rep.	54	50.34 N	14.33 E
Dubach	194	32.41 N	92.39 W
Dubai → Dubayy	128	25.18 N	55.18 E
Dubăsari (Dubesar')	38	47.16 N	29.08 E
Dubăsari, Lacul ⊜[1]	38	47.35 N	29.00 E
Dubawnt ≐	176	64.33 N	100.06 W
Dubawnt Lake ⊜	176	63.08 N	101.30 W
Dubayy	128	25.18 N	55.18 E
Dubbeldam	52	51.47 N	4.42 E
Dubbo	166	32.15 S	148.36 E
Dube ≐	150	5.45 N	8.00 W
Dubele	154	2.54 N	29.33 E
Dübendorf	58	47.25 N	8.38 E
Dübener Heide •[3]	54	51.40 N	12.40 E
Dubenskij	86	51.27 N	56.38 E
Dubh Artach II[1]	46	56.08 N	6.40 W
Dubí	54	50.42 N	13.45 E
Dubi Bheri	272b	22.53 N	88.17 E
Dubica	36	45.11 N	16.48 E
Dubie	154	8.33 S	28.32 E
Dubinino	82	56.09 N	37.01 E
Dubino	58	46.09 N	9.27 E
Dubjazy	80	56.08 N	49.13 E
Dubki, Ross.	265a	60.00 N	30.00 E
Dubki, Ross.	265b	55.41 N	37.14 E
Dublin, Austl.	168b	34.27 S	138.21 E
Dublin, On., Can.	212	43.31 N	81.17 W
Dublin (Baile Átha Cliath), Ire.	48	53.20 N	6.15 W
Dublin, Ca., U.S.	226	37.42 N	121.56 W
Dublin, Ga., U.S.	192	32.32 N	82.54 W
Dublin, In., U.S.	218	39.48 N	85.12 W
Dublin, Md., U.S.	208	39.39 N	76.16 W
Dublin, Oh., U.S.	214	40.06 N	83.07 W
Dublin, Pa., U.S.	208	40.22 N	75.12 W
Dublin, Tx., U.S.	196	32.05 N	98.20 W
Dublin, Va., U.S.	192	37.06 N	80.41 W
Dublin □[6]	48	53.20 N	6.15 W
Dublin (Collinstown) Airport ⊠	48	53.26 N	6.15 W
Dublin Bay C	48	53.20 N	6.06 W
Dublin Canyon V	282	37.42 N	121.59 W
Dublon I	175c	7.23 N	151.53 E
Dubna, Ross.	82	54.09 N	36.58 E
Dubna, Ross.	82	56.44 N	37.10 E
Dubna ≐, Lat.	76	56.22 N	26.10 E
Dubna ≐, Ross.	82	56.47 N	37.15 E
Dubňany	30	48.55 N	17.06 E
Dubnevo	82	55.06 N	38.08 E
Dubnica nad Váhom	30	48.58 N	18.09 E
Dubno	78	50.26 N	25.44 E
Dubois, Id., U.S.	202	44.10 N	112.13 W
Dubois, Il., U.S.	219	38.13 N	89.13 W
Dubois, In., U.S.	194	38.26 N	86.48 W
Du Bois, Ne., U.S.	198	40.02 N	96.02 W
Du Bois, Pa., U.S.	214	41.07 N	78.45 W
Dubois, Wy., U.S.	200	43.32 N	109.37 W
Du Bois Reservoir ⊜[1]	214	41.06 N	78.38 W
Duboistown	210	41.13 N	77.02 W
Dub'onki	80	54.27 N	46.18 E
Dubovaja Rošča	76	53.11 N	36.04 E
Dubovka, Ross.	78	51.26 N	41.25 E
Dubovka, Ross.	80	49.03 N	44.50 E
Dubovoje	76	53.08 N	40.05 E
Dubovskij	80	56.21 N	46.48 E
Dubovskoje	80	47.25 N	42.46 E
Dubov'yazivka	78	51.08 N	33.22 E
Dubovychi	78	51.38 N	33.35 E
Dubovyj Ovrag	80	48.20 N	44.37 E
Dubovyj Umet	80	52.59 N	50.17 E
Duboweitun	89	50.42 N	120.14 E
Dubra	126	23.32 N	86.31 E
Dubrājpur	126	23.48 N	87.23 E
Dübrar dağ ∧	84	40.55 N	48.50 E
Dubréka	150	9.48 N	13.31 W
Dubrova, Bela.	76	52.25 N	29.58 E
Dubrova, Bela.	78	51.47 N	28.13 E
Dubrova, Ross.	80	56.59 N	54.33 E
Dubrova, Ross.	80	57.42 N	55.01 E
Dubroviči	80	54.39 N	39.56 E
Dubrovicy	82	56.46 N	39.10 E
Dubrovino	86	55.28 N	83.17 E
Dubrovka, Ross.	76	59.13 N	36.13 E
Dubrovka, Ross.	76	53.42 N	33.30 E
Dubrovka, Ross.	76	59.51 N	30.56 E
Dubrovka, Ross.	82	54.44 N	36.21 E
Dubrovki	80	53.49 N	43.19 E
Dubrovnik	38	42.38 N	18.07 E
Dubrovno	76	54.35 N	30.41 E
Dubrovnoje, Kaz.	86	54.49 N	68.06 E
Dubrovnoje, Ross.	86	57.58 N	69.25 E
Dubrovo	76	59.51 N	33.34 E
Dubrovskoje	88	58.45 N	111.10 E
Dubrovytsya	78	51.34 N	26.34 E
Dubunskaja	86	43.46 N	80.13 E
Dubuque	190	42.30 N	90.39 W
Dubysa ≐	76	55.05 N	23.26 E
Duchana	85	38.02 N	68.13 E
Duchang	100	29.15 N	116.13 E
Duchcov	54	50.37 N	13.45 E
Ducherow	54	53.46 N	13.46 E
Duchesne	200	40.09 N	110.24 W
Duchesne ≐	200	40.05 N	109.41 W
Duchess	166	21.22 S	139.52 E
Duchovnickoje	80	52.28 N	48.15 E
Duchovščina	76	55.12 N	32.25 E
Duck ≐, Austl.	274a	33.50 S	151.02 E
Duck ≐, Tn., U.S.	194	36.02 N	87.52 W
Duckabush ≐	224	47.38 N	122.56 W
Duck Bay	184	52.10 N	100.09 W
Duck Creek ≐, On., Can.	281	42.18 N	82.41 W
Duck Creek ≐, Ca., U.S.	226	37.55 N	121.16 W
Duck Creek ≐, In., U.S.	218	40.08 N	85.57 W
Duck Creek ≐, Nv., U.S.	204	40.06 N	114.43 W
Duck Creek ≐, N.D., U.S.	198	46.03 N	102.14 W
Duck Creek ≐, Tx., U.S.	196	33.14 N	100.42 W
Duck Creek ≐, Tx., U.S.	222	32.48 N	96.31 W
Duck Creek ≐, Tx., U.S.	222	31.06 N	96.17 W
Duck Creek ≐, Wi., U.S.	190	44.33 N	88.02 W
Duck Hill	194	33.37 N	89.42 W
Duck Island Harbor C	276	40.55 N	73.23 W
Duck Key I	220	24.46 N	80.56 W
Duck Lake, Sk., Can.	184	52.47 N	106.13 W
Duck Lake, Mi., U.S.	216	42.24 N	84.47 W
Duck Lake ⊜, Mb., Can.	184	54.52 N	98.11 W
Duck Lake ⊜, Mi., U.S.	216	42.23 N	84.47 W
Duck Lake ⊜, Mi., U.S.	281	42.40 N	83.35 W
Duck Mountain ∧	184	51.35 N	101.00 W
Duck Mountain Provincial Park ♠, Mb., Can.	184	51.36 N	100.55 W
Duck Mountain Provincial Park ♠, Sk., Can.	184	51.38 N	101.53 W
Duck Valley Indian Reservation •[4]	204	42.00 N	116.10 W
Duckwall Mountain ∧	226	37.58 N	120.07 W
Duclair	50	49.29 N	0.53 E
Ducos	240e	14.34 N	60.58 W
Du Couedic, Cape >	166	36.04 S	136.42 E
Ducun	106	31.07 N	120.27 E
Duda ≐	246	2.33 N	74.02 W
Dudačkino	76	59.57 N	32.53 E
Dudchany	78	47.12 N	33.46 E
Duddington	42	52.36 N	0.32 W
Duddon ≐	44	54.15 N	3.13 W
Dudelange	56	49.28 N	6.05 E
Dudergofka ≐	265a	59.52 N	30.12 E
Duderstadt	52	51.31 N	10.16 E
Dūdhi	124	24.13 N	83.15 E
Dudhkośī ≐	124	27.08 N	86.26 E
Dudhnai	124	25.59 N	90.44 E
Dudinka	74	69.25 N	86.15 E
Dudkin	78	47.53 N	40.32 E
Dudley, Eng., U.K.	42	52.30 N	2.05 W
Dudley, Eng., U.K.	44	55.03 N	1.35 W
Dudley, Ma., U.S.	207	42.02 N	71.55 W
Dudley, Pa., U.S.	214	40.12 N	78.10 W
Dudley Pond ⊜	283	42.20 N	71.22 W
Dudleyville	200	32.58 N	110.47 W
Dudna ≐	122	19.07 N	76.54 E
Dudorovskij	76	53.40 N	35.22 E
Dūḍuwā Śringklā ⋏	124	27.45 N	82.30 E
Dudwa National Park ♠	124	28.30 N	80.40 E
Dudweiler	56	49.17 N	7.02 E
Dudzele	50	51.17 N	3.14 E
Due	89	50.50 N	142.06 E
Duékoué	150	6.45 N	7.21 W
Dueré	250	11.20 S	49.17 W
Dueré ≐	250	10.59 S	49.48 W
Duerji	89	45.39 N	121.49 E
Duerna ≐	34	42.19 N	5.54 W
Duero (Douro) ≐	34	41.08 N	8.40 W
Dueville	64	45.38 N	11.32 E
Due West	192	34.20 N	82.23 W
Dufault, Lac ⊜	190	48.19 N	79.00 W
Duff Dunbar	123	32.15 N	77.12 E
Duffel	50	51.06 N	4.31 E
Dufferin □[6]	212	44.05 N	80.15 W
Duffer Peak ∧	204	41.40 N	118.44 W
Duffield, Austl.	162	25.50 S	134.40 E
Duffield, Eng., U.K.	44	52.58 N	1.29 W
Duffins Creek ≐	212	43.49 N	79.02 W
Dufftown	46	57.26 N	3.08 W
Dufourspitze ∧	58	45.55 N	7.52 E
Dufresne ≐	206	46.16 N	73.59 W
Dufur	224	45.27 N	121.07 W
Dugadda	124	29.48 N	78.37 E
Duga Resa	36	45.27 N	15.30 E
Duga-Zapadnaja, mys >	74	59.09 N	145.59 E
Dugdemona ≐	194	31.47 N	92.22 W
Dugede	120	30.54 N	90.48 E
Dugger	194	39.04 N	87.16 W
Dugino	83	47.09 N	39.27 E
Dugi Otok I	36	44.00 N	15.04 E
Dugna	82	54.25 N	36.51 E
Dugny-sur-Meuse	56	49.06 N	5.23 E
Dug Pond ⊜	283	42.17 N	71.22 W
Du Gué ≐	176	57.21 N	70.45 W
Dugui Qarag	102	39.38 N	108.40 E
Dugway Proving Ground ■	200	40.10 N	113.15 W
Duhernal Lake ⊜	276	40.24 N	74.22 W
Duhi	140	7.07 N	28.45 E
Duhnen	52	53.53 N	8.38 E
Duhu	100	22.04 N	112.56 E
Ḍuhūr ash-Shuwayr	132	33.55 N	35.43 E
Duich, Loch C	46	57.14 N	5.30 W
Duida, Cerro ∧	246	3.25 N	65.40 W
Duifken Point >	164	12.33 S	141.38 E
Duingen	52	52.00 N	9.42 E
Duingt	62	45.50 N	6.12 E
Duino	64	45.46 N	13.36 E
Duirinish	46	57.19 N	5.41 W
Duisburg, Dtsch.	56	51.25 N	6.46 E
Duisburg, Dtsch.	263	51.25 N	6.46 E
Duissern •[8]	263	51.26 N	6.47 E
Duitama	246	5.50 N	73.02 W
Duitsland → Germany □[1]	30	51.00 N	10.00 E
Duiveland I	52	51.38 N	4.00 E
Duiwelskloof	156	23.42 S	30.06 E
Duji, Zhg.	98	37.44 N	116.50 E
Duji, Zhg.	98	34.11 N	115.48 E
Dujiahang	106	31.03 N	121.29 E
Dujuuma	144	1.15 N	42.34 E
Dukambiya	144	14.47 N	37.28 E
Dukana ⩗[4]	154	3.59 N	37.16 E
Dukazi	120	30.54 N	92.52 E
Duke	196	34.39 N	99.34 W
Duke Center	214	41.57 N	78.28 W
Duke Island I	182	54.56 N	131.20 W
Duke of York Bay C	176	65.25 N	84.50 W
Duke of York Island I	164	4.10 S	152.26 E
Dukes □[6]	207	41.23 N	70.31 W
Dukes Brook ≐	276	40.33 N	74.37 W
Duk Fadiat	140	7.45 N	31.25 E
Duk Faiwil	140	7.30 N	31.29 E
Dukhān	128	25.25 N	50.48 E
Dukhmays	142	31.07 N	31.04 E
Duki	120	30.09 N	68.34 E
Dukinfield	262	53.29 N	2.05 W
Dukla	30	49.34 N	21.41 E
Dukla Pass)(	30	49.25 N	21.43 E
Dukou	102	26.40 N	101.39 E
Dūkštas	76	55.32 N	26.20 E
Duku, Nig.	146	10.49 N	10.46 E
Duku, Nig.	150	11.10 N	4.55 E
Dula	152	4.41 N	20.22 E
Dūlāb •[8]	267d	35.39 N	51.27 E
Dulag	116	10.57 N	125.02 E
Dulāi	124	23.57 N	89.31 E
Dulais ≐	42	51.41 N	3.47 W
Dulan (Chahanwusu)	102	36.16 N	98.28 E
Dul'apino	80	57.15 N	40.49 E
Dulas ≐	42	52.36 N	3.50 W
Dulas Bay C	44	53.23 N	4.15 W
Dulata	86	43.26 N	80.50 E
Dulayb, Khawr V	140	11.45 N	32.47 E
Dulaym	146	25.58 N	14.03 E
Dulce	200	36.56 N	106.59 W
Dulce ≐	252	30.31 S	62.32 W
Dulce, Arroyo ≐	258	35.28 S	57.41 W
Dulce, Golfo C	236	8.32 N	83.14 W
Dulce Grande	234	22.59 N	102.14 W
Dulce Nombre de Culmí	236	15.09 N	85.37 W
Dul'durga	88	50.41 N	113.36 E
Duleek	48	53.39 N	6.25 W
Dulgalach ≐	74	67.44 N	133.12 E
Dulin	98	38.22 N	116.43 E
Duliu, Zhg.	105	39.13 N	116.16 E
Duliu, Zhg.	105	39.01 N	116.54 E
Duliu Jianhe ≐	105	38.51 N	117.20 E
Duljo Point >	116	9.35 N	123.43 E
Dulkaninna	166	29.01 S	138.27 E
Dülken	56	51.15 N	6.20 E
Dulles International Airport ⊠	208	38.58 N	77.28 W
Dullstroom	156	25.27 S	30.07 E
Dülmen	52	51.51 N	7.16 E
Dulnain Bridge	46	57.16 N	3.41 W
Dulnan ≐	46	57.18 N	3.40 W
Dulovka	76	57.32 N	28.20 E
Dulovo	38	43.49 N	27.09 E
Dulq Maghār	130	36.22 N	38.39 E
D'ul'tydag, gora ∧	84	41.58 N	46.56 E
Dulung ≐	126	22.08 N	87.05 E
Dulunguin Point >	116	7.45 N	122.05 E
Duluth, Ga., U.S.	192	34.00 N	84.08 W
Duluth, Mn., U.S.	190	46.45 N	92.07 W
Dulverton	42	51.03 N	3.33 W
Dulwich •[8]	260	51.26 N	0.05 W
Duma, Bots.	156	18.45 S	22.46 E
Dūmā, Lubnān	130	34.12 N	35.50 E
Dūmā, Sūrīy.	132	33.35 N	36.24 E
Duma, Zaïre	154	4.57 N	27.19 E
Dumaguete	116	9.18 N	123.18 E
Dumai	114	1.41 N	101.27 E
Dumalag	116	11.18 N	122.37 E
Dumalinao	116	7.49 N	123.23 E
Dumali Point >	116	13.07 N	121.33 E
Dumanjug	116	10.04 N	123.26 E
Dumanlıdağ ∧	84	40.31 N	43.25 E
Dumanquilas Bay C	116	7.34 N	123.04 E
Dumaran Channel)(	116	10.25 N	119.45 E
Dumaran Island I	116	10.33 N	119.51 E
Dumaresq ≐	166	28.40 S	150.28 E
Dumaring	112	1.36 N	118.12 E
Dumas, Ar., U.S.	194	33.53 N	91.29 W
Dumas, Tx., U.S.	196	35.51 N	101.58 W
Ḍumayr	132	33.38 N	36.40 E
Dumbarton	46	55.57 N	4.35 W
Dumbarton Bridge •[5]	282	37.31 N	122.07 W
Dumbarton Point >	282	37.30 N	122.06 W
Ďumbier ∧	30	48.57 N	19.37 E
Dumbleyung	162	33.19 S	117.44 E
Dumbo	152	14.06 S	17.24 E
Dumboa	146	11.10 N	12.45 E
Dumbrăveni	38	46.14 N	24.35 E
Dum Dum	126	22.35 N	88.24 E
Dum Dum International Airport ⊠	126	22.38 N	88.25 E
Dume, Point >	228	34.00 N	118.48 W
Dumei	100	24.47 N	117.21 E
Dumfries, Scot., U.K.	44	55.04 N	3.37 W
Dumfries, Va., U.S.	208	38.34 N	77.19 W
Dumfries and Galloway □[4]	44	55.00 N	4.00 W
Duminiči	76	53.55 N	35.06 E
Dumjor	272b	22.38 N	88.13 E
Dumka	126	24.16 N	87.15 E
Dumlupınar	130	38.52 N	30.00 E
Dummar	132	33.32 N	36.14 E
Dümmer ⊜	52	52.31 N	8.19 E
Dummer Range ⋏	162	20.11 S	125.59 E
Dumoga-Bone National Park ♠	112	0.30 N	123.25 E
Dumoga Kecil	112	0.31 N	123.55 E
Dumoine ≐	190	46.13 N	77.51 W
Dumoine, Lac ⊜	190	46.53 N	77.54 W
Dumont, Ia., U.S.	190	42.45 N	92.58 W
Dumont, N.J., U.S.	210	40.56 N	73.59 W
Dumont, Lac ⊜	190	46.04 N	76.27 W
Dumont d'Urville ♦[3]	9	66.35 S	140.00 E
Dümpelfeld	56	50.27 N	6.56 E
Dümpten •[8]	263	51.27 N	6.54 E
Dumpu	164	5.50 S	145.45 E
Dumra	124	26.34 N	85.31 E
Dumraon	124	25.33 N	84.09 E
Dumuria, Bngl.	126	22.47 N	89.26 E
Dumuriā, India	126	22.11 N	86.20 E
Dumyāṭ (Damietta)	142	31.25 N	31.48 E
Dumyāṭ □[4]	142	31.20 N	31.45 E
Dumyāṭ, Far' (Damietta Branch) ≐	142	31.32 N	31.51 E
Dumyāṭ, Maṣabb (Damietta Mouth) ≐[1]	142	31.32 N	31.51 E
Dün ∧	54	51.21 N	10.30 E
Duna → Danube ≐	22	45.20 N	29.40 E
Dünaburg → Daugavpils	76	55.53 N	26.32 E
Dunaff Head >	48	55.17 N	7.33 W
Dunaföldvár	30	46.48 N	18.55 E
Dunaharaszti	30	47.21 N	19.05 E
Dunaj, Ross.	89	42.52 N	132.22 E
Dunaj, Ross.	265a	59.58 N	30.56 E
Dunaj → Danube ≐	22	45.20 N	29.40 E
Dunaj, ostrova II	74	73.52 N	124.29 E
Dunajec ≐	30	50.14 N	20.44 E
Dunajevo	88	52.05 N	117.02 E
Dunajská Streda	30	48.01 N	17.35 E
Dunakeszi	30	47.38 N	19.08 E
Dunany Point >	48	53.52 N	6.14 W
Dunărea → Danube ≐	22	45.20 N	29.40 E
Dunărea Veche, Bratul ≐	38	45.17 N	28.02 E
Duna-Tisza-csatorna ≊	264c	47.21 N	19.05 E
Dunaújváros	30	46.58 N	18.57 E
Dunav → Danube ≐	22	45.20 N	29.40 E
Dunavățu de Sus	38	44.59 N	29.13 E
Duna-Völgyi-főcsatorna ≊	30	46.12 N	18.56 E
Dunayivtsi	78	48.54 N	26.51 E
Dunback	172	45.23 S	170.38 E
Dunbar, Scot., U.K.	46	56.00 N	2.31 W
Dunbar, W.V., U.S.	188	38.21 N	81.44 W
Dunbarton	275b	43.49 N	79.06 W
Dunbeath	46	58.15 N	3.25 W
Dunblane, Sk., Can.	184	51.11 N	106.52 W
Dunblane, Scot., U.K.	46	56.12 N	3.59 W
Dunboyne	48	53.24 N	6.28 W
Duncan, B.C., Can.	224	48.47 N	123.42 W
Duncan, Az., U.S.	200	32.43 N	109.06 W
Duncan, Ms., U.S.	194	34.02 N	90.44 W
Duncan, Ok., U.S.	196	34.30 N	97.57 W
Duncan ≐	182	50.11 N	116.57 W
Duncan Lake ⊜[1]	182	50.20 N	117.00 W
Duncannon	208	40.23 N	77.01 W
Duncan Passage)(	110	11.00 N	92.30 E
Duncans	241q	18.28 N	77.32 W
Duncansby Head >	46	58.39 N	3.02 W
Duncans Creek ≐	274a	33.53 S	150.39 E
Duncansville	214	40.25 N	78.26 W
Duncanville	222	32.39 N	96.54 W
Dunchurch	42	52.20 N	1.16 W
Duncormick	48	52.14 N	6.39 W
Dundaga	76	57.31 N	22.21 E
Dundāhera	272a	28.38 N	77.26 E
Dundalk, On., Can.	212	44.10 N	80.24 W
Dundalk (Dún Dealgan), Ire.	48	54.01 N	6.25 W
Dundalk, Md., U.S.	208	39.15 N	76.31 W
Dundalk Bay C	48	53.57 N	6.17 W
Dundas, Austl.	274a	33.48 S	151.02 E
Dundas, On., Can.	212	43.16 N	79.58 W
Dundas, Mn., U.S.	190	44.25 N	93.12 W
Dundas, Cape >	212	44.57 N	81.07 W
Dundas, Lake ⊜	162	32.35 S	121.50 E
Dundas Island I	182	54.33 N	130.55 W
Dundas Peninsula >[1]	176	74.50 N	111.30 W
Dundas Strait)(	164	11.20 S	131.35 E
Dún Dealgan → Dundalk	48	54.01 N	6.25 W
Dundee, S. Afr.	158	28.12 S	30.16 E
Dundee, Scot., U.K.	46	56.28 N	2.58 W
Dundee, Fl., U.S.	220	28.01 N	81.37 W

Symbols in the index entries represent the broad categories identified in the key at the right. Symbols with superior numbers (⋏[1]) identify subcategories (see complete key on page *I · 1*).

Symbole im Register stellen die rechts im Schlüssel erklärten Kategorien dar. Symbole mit hochgestellten Ziffern (⋏[1]) bezeichnen Unterabteilungen einer Kategorie (vgl. vollständiger Schlüssel auf Seite *I · 1*).

Los símbolos incluídos en el texto del índice representan las grandes categorías identificadas con la clave a la derecha. Los símbolos con numeros en su parte superior (⋏[1]) identifican las subcategorías (véase la clave completa en la página *I · 1*).

Les symboles de l'index représentent les catégories indiquées dans la légende à droite. Les symboles suivis d'un indice (⋏[1]) représentent des sous-catégories (voir légende complète à la page *I · 1*).

Os símbolos incluídos no texto do índice representam as grandes categorias identificadas com a chave à direita. Os símbolos com números em sua parte superior (⋏[1]) identificam as subcategorias (veja-se a chave completa à página *I · 1*).

∧	Mountain	Berg	Montaña	Montagne	Montanha
⋏	Mountains	Gebirge	Montañas	Montagnes	Montanhas
)(	Pass	Paß	Paso	Col	Passo
V	Valley, Canyon	Tal, Cañon	Valle, Cañón	Vallée, Canyon	Vale, Canhão
⩦	Plain	Ebene	Llano	Plaine	Planície
>	Cape	Kap	Cabo	Cap	Cabo
I	Island	Insel	Isla	Île	Ilha
II	Islands	Inseln	Islas	Îles	Ilhas
⊥	Other Topographic Features	Andere Topographische Objekte	Otros Elementos Topográficos	Autres données topographiques	Outros acidentes topográficos

ESPAÑOL — Nombre, Página, Lat.°′, Long.°′ W = Oeste
FRANÇAIS — Nom, Page, Lat.°′, Long.°′ W = Ouest
PORTUGUÊS — Nome, Página, Lat.°′, Long.°′ W = Oeste

Nombre	Página	Lat.°′	Long.°′ W = Oeste
Dundee, Il., U.S.	216	42.06 N	88.17 W
Dundee, Mi., U.S.	216	41.57 N	83.39 W
Dundee, Ms., U.S.	194	34.31 N	90.27 W
Dundee, N.Y., U.S.	210	42.31 N	76.58 W
Dundee, Oh., U.S.	214	40.35 N	81.37 W
Dundee, Or., U.S.	224	45.16 N	123.00 W
Dundee Creek c	284b	39.21 N	76.22 W
Dundgov′ □[4]	102	45.30 N	106.30 E
Dundīṭ	142	30.41 N	31.18 E
Dundonald	46	55.34 N	4.35 W
Dundoo	166	27.39 S	144.39 E
Dundrum, Ire.	48	52.33 N	8.03 W
Dundrum, N. Ire., U.K.	48	54.16 N	5.51 W
Dundrum Bay c	48	54.13 N	5.45 W
Dundurn	184	51.49 N	106.30 W
Duneaton Water ≏	46	55.32 N	3.42 W
Dunedin, N.Z.	172	45.52 S	170.30 E
Dunedin, Fl., U.S.	220	28.01 N	82.46 W
Dunedoo	166	32.01 S	149.24 E
Duneland Beach	216	41.35 N	86.50 W
Dunellen	276	40.35 N	74.28 W
Dunewood	276	40.38 N	73.11 W
Dunfanaghy	48	55.11 N	7.59 W
Dunfermline	46	56.04 N	3.29 W
Du Ngae, Khao ∧	110	15.10 N	98.47 E
Dungannon, N. Ire., U.K.	48	54.31 N	6.46 W
Dungannon, Va., U.S.	192	36.49 N	82.28 W
Dūngarpur	120	23.50 N	73.43 E
Dungarvan	48	52.05 N	7.37 W
Dungarvan Harbour c	48	52.10 N	7.35 W
Dungas	150	13.04 N	9.20 E
Dungau ◆[1]	60	48.50 N	12.40 E
Dungeness ›	42	50.55 N	0.58 E
Dungeness ≏	224	48.08 N	123.06 W
Dungeness, Punta ›	254	52.23 S	68.25 W
Dungeness Bay c	224	48.10 N	123.07 W
Dungeness Spit ›[2]	224	48.10 N	123.09 W
Dungiven	48	54.55 N	6.55 W
Dunglow	48	54.57 N	8.22 W
Dungo, Lagoa do ◎	152	17.20 S	18.58 E
Dungog	166	32.24 S	151.46 E
Dungu	154	3.37 N	28.34 E
Dungu ≏	154	3.37 N	28.34 E
Dungun	114	4.47 N	103.26 E
Dungun ≏	114	4.47 N	103.23 E
Dunham	206	45.08 N	72.48 W
Dunham Lake ◎	281	42.39 N	83.41 W
Dunham-on-the-Hill	262	53.15 N	2.47 W
Dunham Park ♠	262	53.23 N	2.24 W
Dunham Town	262	53.23 N	2.24 W
Dunheved, Austl.	274a	33.45 S	150.47 E
Dunheved → Launceston, Eng., U.K.	42	50.38 N	4.21 W
Dunholme	44	53.18 N	0.28 W
Dunhou	100	27.02 N	114.58 E
Dunhua	89	43.21 N	128.13 E
Dunhuang	102	40.12 N	94.41 E
Dunières	62	45.13 N	4.20 E
Dunilovo, Ross.	76	57.46 N	38.55 E
Dunilovo, Ross.	80	57.00 N	41.27 E
Dunkeld	46	56.34 N	3.35 W
Dunkeld ◆[8]	273d	26.09 S	28.03 E
Dunkellin ≏	48	53.12 N	8.54 W
Dunkelsteinerwald ◆[3]	61	48.15 N	15.29 E
Dunkern ◎	40	59.09 N	16.52 E
Dunkerque	50	51.03 N	2.22 E
Dunkerrin	48	52.55 N	7.55 W
Dunkery Hill ∧[2]	42	51.11 N	3.35 W
Dunkineely	48	54.38 N	8.23 W
Dunkinsville	218	38.51 N	83.30 W
Dunkirk → Dunkerque, Fr.	50	51.03 N	2.22 E
Dunkirk, Eng., U.K.	42	51.17 N	0.59 E
Dunkirk, In., U.S.	216	40.22 N	85.12 W
Dunkirk, N.Y., U.S.	214	42.28 N	79.20 W
Dunkirk, Oh., U.S.	216	40.47 N	83.38 W
Dunk's Green	260	51.15 N	0.19 E
Dunkuj	140	12.50 N	32.49 E
Dunkwa, Ghana	150	5.58 N	1.46 W
Dunkwa, Ghana	150	5.22 N	1.12 W
Dún Laoghaire	48	53.17 N	6.08 W
Dunlap, In., U.S.	216	41.38 N	85.55 W
Dunlap, Ia., U.S.	198	41.51 N	95.36 W
Dunlap, Tn., U.S.	194	35.22 N	85.23 W
Dunlap Acres	228	34.03 N	117.06 W
Dunlavin	48	53.02 N	6.41 W
Dunleary → Dún Laoghaire	48	53.17 N	6.08 W
Dunleer	48	53.50 N	6.24 W
Dunleith	285	39.42 N	75.33 W
Dun-le-Palestel	32	46.18 N	1.40 E
Dunlo	214	40.17 N	78.43 W
Dunlop	46	55.43 N	4.32 W
Dunloy	48	55.01 N	6.25 W
Dunmanus Bay c	48	51.35 N	9.45 W
Dunmanway	48	51.43 N	9.06 W
Dunmarra	164	16.42 S	133.25 E
Dunmore, Ire.	48	53.36 N	8.46 W
Dunmore, Pa., U.S.	210	41.25 N	75.37 W
Dunmore Cave ±[5]	48	52.44 N	7.15 W
Dunmore East	48	52.09 N	7.00 W
Dunmore Town	238	25.30 N	76.39 W
Dunmurry	48	54.33 N	6.01 W
Dunn	192	35.18 N	78.36 W
Dunnamanagh	48	54.52 N	7.18 W
Dünnbach ≏	56	50.10 N	7.18 E
Dunnellon	220	29.02 N	82.27 W
Dunnet	46	58.37 N	3.20 W
Dunnet Bay c	46	58.37 N	3.24 W
Dunnet Head ›	46	58.40 N	3.24 W
Dunnigan	226	38.53 N	121.58 W
Dunning	198	41.49 N	100.06 W
Dunning Creek ≏	214	40.02 N	78.28 W
Dunnington	44	53.57 N	0.59 W
Dunningtown	279b	40.25 N	79.35 W
Dunn Loring	284c	38.53 N	77.14 W
Dunn Loring Woods	284c	38.52 N	77.14 W
Dunnockshaw	262	53.45 N	2.17 W
Dunnottar Castle ⊥	46	56.57 N	2.11 W
Dunns Bridge	216	41.13 N	86.59 W
Dunnville	212	42.54 N	79.36 W
Dunolly	169	36.52 S	143.44 E
Dunoon	46	55.57 N	4.56 W
Dunqul ⍑[4]	140	23.26 N	31.37 E
Dunqulah	140	19.10 N	30.29 E
Dunqulah al-Qadīmah	140	18.13 N	30.45 E
Dunqunāb	140	21.06 N	37.05 E
Dunqunāb, Khalīj c	140	21.05 N	37.08 E
Dunrea	184	49.25 N	99.44 W
Dun Rig ∧	46	55.34 N	3.10 W
Duns	46	55.47 N	2.20 W
Dunsandel	172	43.40 S	172.11 E
Dunsborough	162	33.36 S	115.06 E
Dunseith	198	48.48 N	100.03 W
Dunsford	42	50.41 N	3.40 W
Dunsmuir	204	41.13 N	122.16 W
Dunstable, Eng., U.K.	42	51.53 N	0.32 W
Dunstable, Ma., U.S.	207	42.40 N	71.29 W
Dunstaffnage Castle ⊥	46	56.26 N	5.32 W
Dunstan Mountains ⋏	172	44.57 S	169.32 E
Dunster, B.C., Can.	182	53.08 N	119.50 W
Dunster, Eng., U.K.	42	51.12 N	3.27 W
Dun-sur-Auron	32	46.53 N	2.34 E
Dun-sur-Meuse	56	49.23 N	5.11 E
Duntelchaig, Loch ◎	46	57.20 N	4.18 W
Dunton Green	42	51.18 N	0.11 E
Dunton Wayletts	260	51.35 N	0.24 E
Duntou	100	29.21 N	119.46 E
Duntroon	172	44.52 S	170.41 E
Dunvegan, S. Afr.	273d	26.09 S	28.09 E
Dunvegan, Scot., U.K.	46	57.26 N	6.35 W
Dunvegan, Loch c	46	57.28 N	6.40 W
Dunvegan Castle ⊥	46	57.26 N	6.35 W
Dunvegan Head ›	46	57.31 N	6.43 W
Dunville	186	47.16 N	53.54 W
Dunwich	171a	27.31 S	153.23 E
Dunyāpur	123	29.48 N	71.44 E
Duobukur ≏	89	49.56 N	125.12 E
Duogu'nao	102	31.32 N	103.14 E
Duojundian	105	39.22 N	117.31 E
Duolun (Dolonnur)	98	42.15 N	116.18 E
Duolundabohuer	120	33.25 N	93.54 E
Duomo ʊ[1]	266b	45.27 N	9.11 E
Duomula	120	34.07 N	82.30 E
Duoyuezhen	107	30.11 N	103.42 E
Duozhu	100	22.59 N	114.43 E
Duozhuang	98	35.35 N	118.12 E
Du Page □[6]	216	41.52 N	88.06 W
Du Page ≏	216	41.25 N	88.14 W
Du Page, East Branch ≏	278	41.42 N	88.09 W
Dupang Ling ⋏	102	25.32 N	111.11 E
Duparquet, Lac ◎	190	48.28 N	79.16 W
Dupax	116	16.17 N	121.05 E
Duping	102	27.11 N	108.20 E
Dupl'atka	80	51.07 N	42.20 E
Dupli	82	54.21 N	36.54 E
Dupnica	38	42.16 N	23.07 E
Dupo	219	38.31 N	90.13 W
Dupont, In., U.S.	218	38.53 N	85.31 W
Dupont, Oh., U.S.	216	41.03 N	84.18 W
Dupont, Pa., U.S.	210	41.19 N	75.44 W
Du Pont, Wa., U.S.	224	47.05 N	122.37 W
Dupont Research Center ʊ[3]	285	39.46 N	75.34 W
Düppel, Berliner Forst ◆[3]	264a	52.25 N	13.08 E
Dupree	198	45.02 N	101.36 W
Duque Bacelar	250	4.09 S	42.57 W
Duque de Caxias	256	22.47 S	43.18 W
Duque de Caxias □[7]	287a	22.45 S	43.16 W
Duque de York, Isla I	254	50.40 S	75.20 W
Duquesne	214	40.22 N	79.51 W
Duquesne University ʊ[2]	279b	40.26 N	79.59 W
DuQuoin	194	37.59 N	89.15 W
Dūrā	132	31.30 N	35.02 E
Durack ≏	164	15.33 S	127.52 E
Durack Ranges ⋏	160	17.00 S	128.00 E
Durağan	130	41.25 N	35.04 E
Durak	130	39.42 N	28.17 E
Durak Dağı ∧	84	39.47 N	43.42 E
Dural	170	33.41 S	151.02 E
Duran	200	34.28 N	105.23 W
Durance ≏	62	43.55 N	4.44 E
Durand, Il., U.S.	190	42.26 N	89.19 W
Durand, Mi., U.S.	216	42.54 N	83.59 W
Durand, Wi., U.S.	190	44.37 N	91.57 W
Durand Reef ✣[2]	175f	22.03 S	168.39 E
Duran Durat I	271c	1.15 N	103.51 E
Durango, Esp.	34	43.10 N	2.37 W
Durango, Méx.	234	24.02 N	104.40 W
Durango, Co., U.S.	200	37.16 N	107.52 W
Durango □[3]	232	24.50 N	104.50 W
Duranillin	168a	33.31 S	116.48 E
Durant, Ia., U.S.	190	41.35 N	90.54 W
Durant, Ms., U.S.	194	33.04 N	89.51 W
Durant, Ok., U.S.	196	33.59 N	96.22 W
Duras	32	44.41 N	0.11 E
Duratón ≏	34	41.37 N	4.07 W
Duraur V	144	10.33 N	49.07 E
Durazno	252	33.22 S	56.31 W
Durazzo → Durrës	38	41.19 N	19.26 E
Durbādānga	126	22.57 N	89.15 E
Durban	158	29.55 S	30.56 E
Durban Roodepoort Deep Gold Mines ◆[7]	273d	26.10 S	27.51 E
Durbanville	158	33.50 S	18.39 E
Durbe	76	56.35 N	21.21 E
D'urbel'džin	85	41.16 N	74.57 E
Durbet-Daba, pereval)(	86	49.37 N	89.25 E
Durbin	188	38.32 N	79.49 W
Durbuy	56	50.21 N	5.28 E
Durchholz	263	51.23 N	7.17 E
Durdent ≏	50	49.51 N	0.36 E
Đurđevac	36	46.03 N	17.04 E
Durdur V	144	10.34 N	43.58 E
Dureji	120	25.53 N	67.18 E
Düren	56	50.48 N	6.28 E
Durg	120	21.11 N	81.17 E
Durgāpur	126	23.29 N	87.20 E
Durham, On., Can.	212	44.10 N	80.49 W
Durham, Eng., U.K.	44	54.47 N	1.34 W
Durham, Ca., U.S.	204	39.38 N	121.47 W
Durham, Ct., U.S.	207	41.28 N	72.40 W
Durham, Mo., U.S.	219	39.58 N	91.40 W
Durham, N.H., U.S.	188	43.08 N	70.55 W
Durham, N.C., U.S.	192	35.59 N	78.53 W
Durham, Or., U.S.	224	45.25 N	122.46 W
Durham □[6], On., Can.	212	43.56 N	78.53 W
Durham □[6], Eng., U.K.	44	54.45 N	1.45 W
Durham Cathedral ʊ[1]	44	54.46 N	1.36 W
Durham Downs	166	27.05 S	141.54 E
Durham Heights ∧	176	71.08 N	122.56 W
Durham Pond ◎	276	41.00 N	74.27 W
Durhamville	210	43.07 N	75.40 W
Durian ≏	115a	6.01 S	106.24 E
Durian, Selat ʯ	114	0.42 N	103.42 E
Duriansebatang	112	0.47 S	109.56 E
Durian Tipus	114	3.07 N	102.13 E
D'urinskije razlivy ☷	80	50.25 N	50.20 E
Durlabhpur	272b	22.47 N	88.29 E
Durlach ◆[8]	56	49.00 N	8.28 E
Durlești	38	47.02 N	28.45 E
Durmersheim	56	48.56 N	8.16 E
Durmitor ∧	38	43.08 N	19.01 E
Durness	46	58.33 N	4.45 W
Durness, Kyle of c	46	58.34 N	4.49 W
Durneva, ostrova II	80	45.25 N	52.50 E
Durnikino	80	51.39 N	42.49 E
Dürnkrut	61	48.28 N	16.51 E
Dürnstein ⊥	61	48.24 N	15.32 E
Duro ∧	144	5.31 N	37.12 E
Durón	34	40.38 N	2.43 W
Duross Heights	285	39.40 N	75.37 W
Dürre Liesing ≏	264b	48.08 N	16.16 E
Durrell	186	49.40 N	54.44 W
Dürrenboden	58	46.57 N	8.50 E
Durrës	38	41.19 N	19.26 E
Durrie	166	25.38 S	140.16 E
Durrington	42	51.13 N	1.45 W
Dürröhrsdorf	54	51.01 N	14.00 E
Durrow	48	52.50 N	7.22 W
Durrus	48	51.36 N	9.31 W
Dursey Head ›	48	51.35 N	10.14 W
Dursey Island I	48	51.36 N	10.12 W
Dursley	42	51.42 N	2.21 W
Dursunbey	130	39.35 N	28.38 E
D'urt'uli	86	55.29 N	54.52 E
Duru	154	4.14 N	28.45 E
Duru Gölü ◎	130	41.20 N	28.35 E
Durulova	130	38.17 N	38.01 E
Durunkah	142	27.08 N	31.10 E
Durūz, Jabal ad- ⋏	132	32.40 N	36.44 E
D'Urville, Tanjung ›	164	1.28 S	137.54 E
D'Urville Island I	172	40.50 S	173.52 E
Duryea	210	41.20 N	75.44 W
Dury Voe c	46a	60.20 N	1.08 W
Dušak	128	37.13 N	60.02 E
Dušanbe	85	38.35 N	68.48 E
Dušekan	74	60.39 N	109.03 E
Dušeti	84	42.06 N	44.42 E
Dusetos	76	55.45 N	25.51 E
Dushan, Zhg.	100	31.36 N	116.14 E
Dushan, Zhg.	102	25.53 N	107.30 E
Du Shan ∧	98	40.30 N	118.45 E
Dushanbe → Dušanbe	85	38.35 N	68.48 E
Dushan Hu ◎	98	35.06 N	116.52 E
Dushantou	106	30.46 N	119.47 E
Dushanzi	86	44.20 N	84.51 E
Dusheng	98	38.23 N	116.33 E
Dushichang	107	29.10 N	106.31 E
Dushikou	98	41.17 N	115.38 E
Dushore	210	41.31 N	76.24 W
Düshorn	52	52.49 N	9.37 E
Dushu	100	33.21 N	113.09 E
Dushu Hu ◎	106	31.17 N	120.42 E
Dusios ežeras ◎	76	54.18 N	23.42 E
Dusky Sound ʯ	172	45.47 S	166.28 E
Dušocha, gora ∧	85	39.10 N	70.01 E
Duson	194	30.14 N	92.11 W
Dušonovo	82	56.04 N	38.18 E
Düssel	263	51.16 N	7.03 E
Düssel ≏	263	51.13 N	6.45 E
Düsseldorf, Dtsch.	56	51.12 N	6.47 E
Düsseldorf, Dtsch.	263	51.12 N	6.47 E
Düsseldorf □[5]	52	51.15 N	7.00 E
Düsseldorf, Flughafen ⊠	56	51.17 N	6.47 E
Düsseldorf, Universität ʊ[2]	263	51.12 N	6.48 E
Dusslingen	58	48.27 N	9.03 E
Dussnang	58	47.26 N	8.58 E
Dustin	196	35.16 N	96.01 W
Dutch Creek ≏, B.C., Can.	182	50.20 N	115.52 W
Dutch Creek ≏, Ar., U.S.	194	35.03 N	93.24 W
Dutchess □[6]	210	41.42 N	73.56 W
Dutch Harbor	180	53.53 N	166.32 W
Dutch John	200	40.55 N	109.23 W
Dutchman Creek ≏	226	37.11 N	120.28 W
Dutianjie	102	24.38 N	101.31 E
Dutluca	130	39.09 N	38.37 E
Dutlwe	156	23.55 S	23.47 E
Dutoitspiek ∧	158	33.46 S	19.12 E
Dutou, Zhg.	100	22.54 N	115.12 E
Dutou, Zhg.	106	31.19 N	120.54 E
Dutovlje	64	45.46 N	13.50 E
Dutovo	24	63.47 N	56.35 E
Dutsen Wai	150	10.50 N	8.12 E
Dutton, Austl.	168b	34.22 S	139.08 E
Dutton, On., Can.	214	42.39 N	81.30 W
Dutton, Eng., U.K.	262	53.19 N	2.38 W
Dutton, Mi., U.S.	216	42.50 N	85.35 W
Dutton, Mt., U.S.	202	47.50 N	111.42 W
Dutton ≏	166	20.45 S	143.12 E
Dutton, Mount ∧, Ak., U.S.	180	55.10 N	162.15 W
Dutton, Mount ∧, Ut,. U.S.	200	38.01 N	112.13 W
Dutun	105	39.46 N	117.02 E
Dutzow	219	38.37 N	90.59 W
Duut	86	47.30 N	91.40 E
Duval, Lac ◎	190	46.19 N	76.55 W
Duvall	224	47.44 N	121.59 W
Duvan	86	55.42 N	57.54 E
Duvanka ≏	83	49.35 N	38.10 E
Duved	26	63.24 N	12.52 E
Duvernay ◆[8]	275a	45.35 N	73.40 W
Duvno	36	43.43 N	17.14 E
Duwamish	224	47.32 N	122.19 W
Duwaydār, Bi'r ad- ⍑[4]	142	30.55 N	32.31 E
Duxbury	207	42.02 N	70.40 W
Duxbury Bay c	207	42.02 N	70.39 W
Duxbury Beach ±[2]	283	42.03 N	70.38 W
Duxun	100	23.55 N	117.37 E
Duyagan Point ›	116	12.36 N	121.33 E
Duyun	102	26.12 N	107.31 E
Düzce	130	40.50 N	31.10 E
Duze	100	29.07 N	118.56 E
Dve Mogili	38	43.36 N	25.52 E
Dvina Occidental → Zapadnaja Dvina ≏	76	57.04 N	24.03 E
Dvina Septentrional → Severnaja Dvina ≏	24	64.32 N	40.30 E
Dvinje, ozero ◎	76	56.08 N	31.12 E
Dvinsk → Daugavpils	76	55.53 N	26.32 E
Dvinskaja guba c	24	65.00 N	39.45 E
Dvojnovskij	80	51.03 N	42.27 E
Dvorcy	82	54.37 N	36.00 E
Dvorec	88	58.23 N	99.56 E
Dvorichna	78	49.52 N	37.40 E
Dvoriši	76	58.12 N	35.13 E
Dvornikovo	82	55.30 N	38.38 E
Dvuch Cirkov, gora ∧	74	67.35 N	168.07 E
Dvugorbaja, gora ∧	180	68.30 N	179.20 E
Dvulučnoje	78	50.02 N	38.02 E
Dvůr Králové [nad Labem]	30	50.26 N	15.48 E
Dwangwa ≏	154	12.33 S	34.12 E
Dwarbasini	272b	22.59 N	88.14 E
Dwārka	120	22.14 N	68.58 E
Dwārka ≏	126	23.44 N	88.11 E
Dwārkeswar ≏	126	23.06 N	87.21 E
Dwarli	272c	19.12 N	73.08 E
Dwars Kill ≏	276	40.58 N	73.58 W
Dwellingup	168a	32.43 S	116.02 E
D.W. Field Park ♠	283	42.06 N	71.03 W
Dwight	216	41.05 N	88.25 W
Dwight D. Eisenhower Lock ◆[5]	206	45.00 N	74.45 W
Dwina-Bucht → Dvinskaja guba c	24	65.00 N	39.45 E
Dwingeloo	52	52.50 N	6.21 E
Dworshak Reservoir ◎[1]	202	46.40 N	116.00 W
Dwyfor ≏	44	52.55 N	4.17 W
Dwyka	158	33.02 S	21.30 E
Dwyka ≏	158	33.18 S	21.39 E
Dyakove	83	47.57 N	39.09 E
Dyaul Island I	164	2.56 S	150.55 E
Dybbøl	41	54.55 N	9.45 E
Dyberry Creek ≏	210	41.35 N	75.15 W
Dyce	46	57.12 N	2.11 W
Dyche Stadium ♠	278	42.04 N	87.41 W
Dychtau, gora ∧	84	43.03 N	43.08 E
Dyck, Schloss ⊥	263	51.09 N	6.34 E
Dyer, In., U.S.	216	41.29 N	87.31 W
Dyer, Tn., U.S.	194	36.04 N	88.59 W
Dyer, Cape ›	176	66.37 N	61.18 W
Dyer Bay c	212	45.10 N	81.18 W
Dyer Island I	158	34.41 S	19.25 E
Dyero	150	12.50 N	6.30 W
Dyersburg	194	36.02 N	89.23 W
Dyersville	190	42.29 N	91.07 W
Dyess Air Force Base ■	196	32.25 N	99.51 W
Dyfed □[6]	42	52.00 N	4.30 W
Dyfi ≏	42	52.32 N	4.03 W
Dyje (Thaya) ≏	61	48.37 N	16.56 E
Dykan'ka	78	49.49 N	34.32 E
Dyke	46	57.36 N	3.41 W
Dyke Ackland Bay c	164	9.00 S	148.45 E
Dyken Pond ◎	210	42.43 N	73.26 W
Dykes Pond ◎	283	42.36 N	70.44 W
Dyle (Dijle) ≏	56	51.04 N	4.25 E
Dyleň ∧	60	49.58 N	12.30 E
Dylym	84	43.04 N	46.38 E
Dymchurch	42	51.02 N	1.00 E
Dyment	184	49.37 N	92.19 W
Dymer	78	50.47 N	30.18 E
Dymock	42	51.59 N	2.26 W
Dymytrov	83	48.15 N	37.18 E
Dymytrove	78	48.36 N	33.01 E
Dynamo Stadium ♠	265b	55.48 N	37.34 E
Dynów	30	49.49 N	22.14 E
Dyreborg	41	55.04 N	10.13 E
Dyrnesvågen	26	63.26 N	7.51 E
Dyrotz	264a	52.33 N	12.58 E
Dysart, Austl.	166	22.27 S	148.20 E
Dysart, Sk., Can.	184	50.56 N	104.02 W
Dysart, Scot., U.K.	46	56.08 N	3.08 W
Dysart, Ia., U.S.	190	42.10 N	92.18 W
Dysart, Pa., U.S.	214	40.36 N	78.31 W
Dýšina	60	49.46 N	13.29 E
Dysnų ežeras ◎	76	55.29 N	26.20 E
Dysselsdorp	158	33.34 S	22.28 E
Dysynni ≏	42	52.36 N	4.05 W
Dyviziya	78	45.57 N	29.59 E
Dzaamar	88	48.10 N	104.50 E
Dzaamaryn uul ∧	88	48.10 N	104.30 E
Džabžur	84	40.54 N	43.58 E
Dzachuj	102	44.59 N	96.37 E
Džagdy, chrebet ⋏	89	53.40 N	131.00 E
Džalagaš	86	45.05 N	64.40 E
Džalal-Abad	85	40.56 N	73.00 E
Džalal-Abad □[4]	85	41.30 N	72.30 E
Džalinda	89	53.29 N	123.54 E
Džamantau, gory ⋏	85	40.55 N	74.40 E
Džamašuj	85	40.52 N	71.28 E
Džambejty	80	50.16 N	52.35 E
Džambul, Kaz.	80	47.34 N	50.12 E
Džambul, Kaz.	85	42.54 N	71.22 E
Džambul, Kaz.	86	47.12 N	71.42 E
Džambul □[4]	85	43.30 N	72.30 E
Džambul, gora ∧	86	44.46 N	73.08 E
Džanga	128	40.00 N	53.03 E
Džangi-Džol	85	41.36 N	72.08 E
Džansugurov	86	45.24 N	79.29 E
Džanybek	80	49.25 N	46.51 E
Dzaoudzi	157a	12.47 S	45.17 E
Džardžan	74	68.43 N	124.02 E
Džargalant → Chovd, Mong.	86	48.01 N	91.39 E
Džargalant, Mong.	88	48.40 N	100.43 E
Džargalant, Mong.	88	46.57 N	115.15 E
Džargalant, Mong.	88	48.33 N	99.20 E
Džargaltchaan	88	47.28 N	109.30 E
Dzaudzhikau → Vladikavkaz	84	43.03 N	44.40 E
Džaur	89	50.02 N	138.30 E
Džava	84	42.24 N	43.54 E
Dzavchan	88	48.48 N	93.07 E
Dzavchan □[4]	88	48.00 N	96.00 E
Dzavchan ≏	88	48.54 N	93.23 E
Dzavchan Mandal	88	48.19 N	95.07 E
Džavchlant → Uliastaj	88	47.45 N	96.49 E
Džazator	86	49.45 N	87.23 E
Džbán ∧	54	50.12 N	13.45 E
Džebel	128	39.38 N	54.14 E
Dzelter ≏	88	50.30 N	105.06 E
Dzemul	232	21.12 N	89.18 W
Dzeng	152	3.45 N	12.00 E
Dženretlen, mys ›	180	67.07 N	173.45 W
Džergetal	85	41.30 N	75.47 E
Džermuk	84	39.51 N	45.41 E
Dzerzhinsk → Dzeržinsk	80	56.15 N	43.24 E
Dzerzhyns'k, Ukr.	78	50.09 N	27.56 E
Dzerzhyns'k, Ukr.	83	48.26 N	37.50 E
Dzeržinsk, Bela.	76	53.41 N	27.08 E
Dzeržinsk, Ross.	80	56.15 N	43.24 E
Dzeržinskaja, gora ∧[2]	76	53.51 N	27.03 E
Dzeržinskij	82	55.38 N	37.50 E
Dzeržinskoje, Kaz.	86	45.50 N	81.07 E
Dzeržinskoje, Ross.	86	56.49 N	95.18 E
Džetim, chrebet ⋏	85	41.35 N	77.05 E
Džetygara	86	52.11 N	61.12 E
Džetyoguz	85	42.27 N	78.14 E
Džetyoguzskij zapovednik ♠	85	42.15 N	78.20 E
Džetysaj	85	40.47 N	68.16 E
Džezdy	86	48.04 N	67.05 E
Džezkazgan, Kaz.	86	47.53 N	67.27 E
Džezkazgan, Kaz.	86	47.47 N	67.46 E
Džezkazgan □[8]	86	47.30 N	70.00 E
Dzhambul → Džambul	85	42.54 N	71.22 E
Dzhankoy	78	45.43 N	34.24 E
Dzharylhach, ostriv I	78	46.02 N	32.55 E
Dzharylhats'ka zatoka c	78	46.05 N	32.50 E
Dzhuryn	78	48.41 N	28.18 E
Działdowo	30	53.15 N	20.10 E
Działoszyce	30	50.22 N	20.21 E
Dzibalchén	232	19.31 N	89.45 W
Dzibilchaltun ⊥	232	21.05 N	89.36 W
Džida ≏	88	50.37 N	106.14 E
Džidinskij chrebet ⋏	88	50.10 N	102.00 E
Dzierzgoń	30	53.56 N	19.21 E
Dzierżoniów (Reichenbach)	30	50.44 N	16.39 E
Dzilam González	232	21.17 N	88.56 W
Džilav	85	39.19 N	67.45 E
Džilga	85	41.43 N	69.01 E
Džinst	102	45.24 N	100.35 E
Dzioua	148	33.14 N	5.14 E
Džirgatal'	85	39.13 N	71.12 E
Dzitás	232	20.51 N	88.31 W
Dzitbalché	232	20.19 N	90.03 W
Dziwna ≏[1]	54	54.01 N	14.44 E
Dziwnów	30	54.03 N	14.45 E
Džizak	85	40.06 N	67.50 E
Džizak □[4]	85	40.30 N	67.45 E
Dzodze	150	6.14 N	1.00 E
Džubga	78	44.20 N	38.43 E
Džugdžur, chrebet ⋏	74	58.00 N	136.00 E
Džūkste	76	56.47 N	23.15 E
Džumabazar	85	39.31 N	67.13 E
Džumgoltau, chrebet ⋏	85	42.18 N	74.32 E
Dzungarian Basin → Junggar Pendi ≚[1]	86	45.00 N	88.00 E
Dzungarian Gate (Džungarskije vorota))(	86	45.25 N	82.25 E
Džungarskij Alatau, chrebet ⋏	86	45.00 N	81.00 E
Džungarskije vorota → Dzungarian Gate)(	86	45.25 N	82.25 E
Džurak-Sal ≏	80	47.18 N	43.36 E
Dzürch	88	48.55 N	100.10 E
Džurun	86	49.15 N	57.37 E
Džusaly	86	45.28 N	64.05 E
Dzüün Changaj	88	49.17 N	95.14 E
Dzüün Charaa	88	48.52 N	106.28 E
Dzüün Gov	88	49.55 N	93.47 E
Dzuunmod	88	47.45 N	106.55 E
Džvari	84	42.43 N	42.04 E
Dzyhivka	78	48.22 N	28.19 E
E			
Eads	198	38.28 N	102.46 W
Eagar	200	34.06 N	109.17 W
Eagle, Ak., U.S.	180	64.46 N	141.16 W
Eagle, Co., U.S.	200	39.39 N	106.49 W
Eagle, N.Y., U.S.	210	42.33 N	78.18 W
Eagle, Wi., U.S.	216	42.52 N	88.28 W
Eagle ≏, Nf., Can.	176	53.35 N	57.25 W
Eagle ≏, Yk., Can.	180	67.20 N	137.10 W
Eagle ≏, Co., U.S.	200	39.39 N	107.04 W
Eagle, Mount ∧[2]	241n	17.46 N	64.49 W
Eagle Bay	182	50.56 N	119.12 W
Eagle Bend	198	46.09 N	95.02 W
Eagle Bridge	210	42.57 N	73.24 W
Eagle Butte	198	45.00 N	101.14 W
Eagle Chief Creek ≏	196	36.22 N	98.27 W
Eagle Creek	224	45.21 N	122.21 W
Eagle Creek ≏, Sk., Can.	184	52.22 N	107.24 W
Eagle Creek ≏, Az., U.S.	200	32.58 N	109.25 W
Eagle Creek ≏, In., U.S.	218	39.43 N	86.12 W
Eagle Creek ≏, Ky., U.S.	218	38.36 N	85.04 W
Eagle Creek ≏, Mt., U.S.	202	48.12 N	111.11 W
Eagle Creek ≏, N.M., U.S.	196	32.47 N	104.20 W
Eagle Creek ≏, Oh., U.S.	214	41.18 N	80.53 W
Eagle Creek ≏, Oh., U.S.	218	38.43 N	83.51 W
Eagle Creek ≏, Or., U.S.	202	44.45 N	117.10 W
Eagle Creek ≏, Or., U.S.	224	45.21 N	122.23 W
Eagle Creek, East Fork ≏	218	38.47 N	83.43 W
Eagle Creek, West Fork ≏	218	38.47 N	83.43 W
Eagle Creek Reservoir ◎[1]	218	39.50 N	86.18 W
Eagledale	224	47.37 N	122.32 W
Eagle Grove	190	42.39 N	93.54 W
Eagle Harbor	210	43.15 N	78.15 W
Eaglehawk	169	36.43 S	144.15 E
Eagle Hill ≏	283	42.42 N	70.49 W
Eagle Key I	220	25.09 N	80.36 W
Eagle Lake, Fl., U.S.	220	27.59 N	81.45 W
Eagle Lake, Me., U.S.	186	47.02 N	68.35 W
Eagle Lake, Mi., U.S.	216	41.48 N	86.02 W
Eagle Lake, Tx., U.S.	222	29.35 N	96.20 W
Eagle Lake ◎, B.C., Can.	182	51.55 N	124.25 W
Eagle Lake ◎, On., Can.	184	50.39 N	94.54 W
Eagle Lake ◎, On., Can.	184	49.42 N	93.13 W
Eagle Lake ◎, On., Can.	212	44.41 N	76.43 W
Eagle Lake ◎, On., Can.	212	45.08 N	78.29 W
Eagle Lake ◎, Ca., U.S.	204	40.39 N	120.44 W
Eagle Lake ◎, Me., U.S.	186	46.20 N	69.20 W
Eagle Lake ◎, Mi., U.S.	216	41.48 N	86.02 W
Eagle Lake ◎, Tx., U.S.	222	29.34 N	96.21 W
Eagle Lake ◎, Wi., U.S.	216	42.42 N	88.07 W
Eagle Mountain, Ca., U.S.	204	33.49 N	115.27 W
Eagle Mountain, Tx., U.S.	222	32.52 N	97.30 W
Eagle Mountain ∧	202	46.20 N	115.07 W
Eagle Mountain ∧[2]	190	47.54 N	90.33 W
Eagle Mountain Lake ◎[1]	222	32.55 N	97.30 W
Eagle Nest Butte ∧	198	43.27 N	101.39 W
Eagle Nest Lake ◎	222	29.13 N	95.37 W
Eagle Pass	196	28.42 N	100.29 W
Eagle Peak ∧, Ca., U.S.	204	41.17 N	120.12 W
Eagle Peak ∧, Ca., U.S.	228	35.15 N	118.28 W
Eagle Peak ∧, Ca., U.S.	282	37.54 N	121.54 W
Eagle River, Mi., U.S.	190	47.24 N	88.18 W
Eagle River, Wi., U.S.	190	45.55 N	89.14 W
Eagle Rock	192	37.38 N	79.48 W
Eagle Rock ◆[8]	280	34.09 N	118.12 W
Eagle Rock Reservation ♠	276	40.49 N	74.14 W
Eaglesfield	44	55.03 N	3.12 W
Eaglesham, Ab., Can.	182	55.47 N	117.53 W
Eaglesham, Scot., U.K.	46	55.44 N	4.18 W
Eagles Mere	210	41.25 N	76.35 W
Eagleton Village	192	35.46 N	83.56 W
Eagletown	194	34.02 N	94.34 W
Eagle Village	180	64.47 N	141.07 W
Eagleville, Ct., U.S.	207	41.47 N	72.16 W
Eagleville, Pa., U.S.	285	40.10 N	75.24 W
Eagleville, Wi., U.S.	216	42.52 N	88.26 W
Ealing ◆[8]	42	51.31 N	0.20 W
Eamont ≏	44	54.40 N	2.39 W
Earaheedy	162	25.34 S	121.39 E
Earby	44	53.56 N	2.08 W
Earcroft	262	53.43 N	2.29 W
Eardisley	42	52.08 N	2.59 W
Eardley Lake ◎	184	52.32 N	96.05 W
Ear Falls	184	50.38 N	93.13 W
Earle	194	35.16 N	90.28 W
Earlestown	262	53.27 N	2.39 W
Earl Grey	184	50.56 N	104.45 W
Earlham	194	41.29 N	94.07 W
Earlimart	226	35.53 N	119.16 W
Earlington	194	37.16 N	87.30 W
Earlish	46	57.34 N	6.23 W
Earl Park	216	40.40 N	87.24 W
Earl Rowe Provincial Park ♠	212	44.10 N	79.54 W
Earls Barton	42	52.15 N	0.45 W
Earls Colne	42	51.56 N	0.42 E
Earlsferry	46	56.11 N	2.50 W
Earl Shilton	42	52.35 N	1.20 W
Earl Soham	42	52.14 N	1.16 E
Earlston	46	55.39 N	2.40 W
Earlton	210	42.21 N	73.54 W
Earlville, Il., U.S.	216	41.35 N	88.55 W
Earlville, N.Y., U.S.	210	42.44 N	75.33 W
Earlville, Pa., U.S.	208	40.19 N	75.44 W
Earlwood	274a	33.56 S	151.08 E
Early, Ia., U.S.	198	42.27 N	95.09 W
Early, Tx., U.S.	196	31.45 N	98.54 W
Early Winters Creek ≏	224	48.35 N	120.35 W
Earn ≏	46	56.21 N	3.19 W
Earn, Loch ◎	46	56.23 N	4.14 W
Earnslaw, Mount ∧	172	44.37 S	168.24 E
Earth	196	34.14 N	102.24 W
Eas	175f	16.22 S	168.12 E
Easington, Eng., U.K.	44	53.40 N	0.07 E
Easington, Eng., U.K.	44	54.47 N	1.19 W
Easingwold	44	54.07 N	1.11 W
Easky	48	54.18 N	8.58 W
Easley	192	34.49 N	82.36 W
East ≏, On., Can.	190	45.20 N	79.17 W
East ≏, Co., U.S.	200	38.40 N	106.51 W
East ≏, N.Y., U.S.	276	40.48 N	73.48 W
East, University of the ʊ[2]	269f	14.36 N	120.59 E
East Acton	283	42.28 N	71.24 W
East Allen ≏	44	54.55 N	2.19 W
East Alliance	214	40.55 N	81.04 W
East Alligator ≏	164	12.08 S	132.42 E
East Alton	219	38.52 N	90.06 W
East Amherst	210	43.01 N	78.42 W
East-Angus	206	45.29 N	71.40 W
East Arlington	210	43.03 N	73.08 W
East Atlantic Beach	276	40.35 N	73.43 W
East Aurora	210	42.46 N	78.36 W
East Avon	210	42.55 N	77.42 W
East Baines ≏	164	15.38 S	129.58 E
East Bangor	210	40.52 N	75.11 W
East Barming	260	51.16 N	0.28 E
East Barnet ◆[8]	260	51.38 N	0.09 W
East Basin c	279a	41.32 N	81.40 W
East Bay c, Fl., U.S.	194	30.05 N	85.32 W
East Bay c, N.Y., U.S.	210	40.38 N	73.32 W
East Bay c, Tx., U.S.	222	29.30 N	94.35 W
East Bedfont ◆[8]	260	51.27 N	0.26 W
East Bend	192	36.12 N	80.30 W
East Berbice-Corentyne □[4]	246	4.00 N	58.15 W
East Berkshire	206	44.56 N	72.42 W
East Berlin, Ct., U.S.	207	41.37 N	72.42 W
East Berlin, N.J., U.S.	285	39.48 N	74.55 W
East Berlin, Pa., U.S.	208	39.56 N	76.58 W
East Bernard	222	29.32 N	96.04 W
East Bernstadt	192	37.11 N	84.07 W
East Berwick	210	41.03 N	76.13 W
East Bethany	210	42.56 N	78.06 W
East Bhāgīrath Plain ≚	126	23.30 N	88.30 E
East Bijou Creek ≏	198	39.51 N	104.08 W
East Billerica	283	42.34 N	71.14 W
East Blackstone	207	42.02 N	71.31 W
East Bloomfield	210	42.54 N	77.26 W
East Boston ◆[8]	283	42.23 N	71.02 W
Eastbourne, N.Z.	172	41.18 S	174.54 E
Eastbourne, Eng., U.K.	42	50.46 N	0.17 E
East Brady	214	40.59 N	79.36 W
East Braintree	184	49.37 N	95.38 W
East Branch	210	41.59 N	75.08 W
East Branch Lake ◎[1]	214	41.35 N	78.35 W
East Brewster	207	41.46 N	70.03 W
East Brewton	194	31.05 N	87.03 W
East Bridgewater	207	42.02 N	70.58 W
East Brimfield Lake ◎[1]	207	42.06 N	72.10 W
East Brookfield	207	42.13 N	72.02 W
East Brooklyn	207	41.47 N	71.53 W
East Brother I	271d	22.20 N	113.58 E
East Brunswick	208	40.25 N	74.23 W
East Bucas Island I	116	9.43 N	126.02 E
East Burwood	274b	37.51 S	145.09 E
Eastbury	260	51.37 N	0.25 W
East Butler	214	40.53 N	79.51 W
East Cache Creek ≏	196	34.08 N	98.16 W
East Caicos I	238	21.41 N	71.30 W
East Calder	46	55.54 N	3.27 W
East Canaan	207	42.00 N	73.17 W
East Canada Creek ≏	210	43.00 N	74.45 W
East Canton	214	40.47 N	81.17 W
East Cape ›, N.Z.	172	37.41 S	178.33 E
East Cape ›, Ak., U.S.	181a	51.21 N	179.29 E
East Cape ›, Fl., U.S.	220	25.07 N	81.05 W
East Carancahua Creek ≏	222	28.51 N	96.19 W
East Carbon	200	39.32 N	110.24 W
East Carlisle	214	41.19 N	82.05 W
East Caroline Basin ✣[1]	14	4.00 N	146.45 E
East Castor ≏	212	45.16 N	75.17 W
East Catfish Creek ≏	212	42.47 N	81.04 W
East Channel ≏[1]	180	69.20 N	134.00 W
East Chatham	210	42.25 N	73.32 W
East Chelmsford	207	42.36 N	71.18 W
Eastchester	210	40.57 N	73.49 W
Eastchester Bay c	276	40.51 N	73.48 W
East Chicago	216	41.38 N	87.27 W
East Chicago Heights	278	41.30 N	87.35 W
East China Sea ⍑[2]	90	30.00 N	126.00 E
Eastchurch	42	51.25 N	0.52 E
East Clandon	260	51.15 N	0.29 W
East Claridon	214	41.32 N	81.07 W
East Cleddau ≏	42	51.46 N	4.52 W
East Cleveland	214	41.31 N	81.34 W
East Coast Bays	172	36.45 S	174.46 E
East Concord	210	42.33 N	78.38 W
Eastcote ◆[8]	260	51.35 N	0.24 W
East Cote Blanche Bay c	194	29.35 N	91.40 W
East Coulee	182	51.20 N	112.29 W
East Creek ≏	276	40.27 N	74.09 W
East Cross Creek ≏	212	44.17 N	78.44 W
East Dean	42	50.45 N	0.12 E
East Delaware Aqueduct ≊[1]	210	41.52 N	74.31 W
East Dennis	207	41.44 N	70.09 W
East Dereham	42	52.41 N	0.56 E
East Detroit	214	42.28 N	82.57 W
East Dismal Swamp ☷	192	35.45 N	76.35 W
East Ditch ≊	276	40.56 N	74.19 W
East Douglas	207	42.04 N	71.42 W
East Dublin	192	32.32 N	82.52 W
East Dubuque	190	42.29 N	90.38 W
East Dundee	216	42.06 N	88.16 W
East Durham	210	42.22 N	74.06 W
East Ely	204	39.15 N	114.53 W
Eastend, Sk., Can.	184	49.31 N	108.48 W
East End, Vir. Is., U.S.	240m	18.21 N	64.40 W
East End Point ›	240b	25.03 N	77.16 W
East Enterprise	218	38.52 N	84.59 W
Easter Island → Pascua, Isla de I	174z	27.07 S	109.22 W
Easterly	222	31.06 N	96.23 W
Eastern □[4], Ghana	150	6.30 N	0.30 W
Eastern □[4], Kenya	154	0.05 N	38.00 E
Eastern □[4], S.L.	150	8.15 N	11.00 W
Eastern □[4], Zam.	154	13.00 S	32.15 E
Eastern □[5]	154	1.25 N	33.50 E
Eastern Bay c	208	38.51 N	76.19 W
Eastern Cape □[4]	158	32.30 S	26.30 E
Eastern Channel → Tsushima-kaikyō ʯ	92	34.00 N	129.00 E
Eastern Cherokee Indian Reservation ◆[4]	192	35.25 N	83.24 W
Eastern Cove c	168b	35.46 S	137.50 E
Eastern Creek ≏, Austl.	166	20.10 S	141.08 E
Eastern Creek ≏, Austl.	274a	33.39 S	150.51 E
Eastern Division □[5]	175g	19.00 S	180.00 E
Eastern Fields ✣[2]	164	10.20 S	145.45 E
Eastern Ghāts ⋏	122	14.00 N	78.50 E
Eastern Highlands □[5]	164	6.30 S	145.15 E
Eastern Island I	174g	28.12 N	177.20 W
Eastern Isles II	42a	49.57 N	6.15 W
Eastern Michigan University ʊ[2]	281	42.15 N	83.37 W
Eastern Neck Island I	208	39.02 N	76.13 W
Eastern Point ›	283	42.35 N	70.40 W
Eastern Samar □[4]	116	12.00 N	125.00 E
Eastern Sayans → Vostočnyj Sajan ⋏	88	53.00 N	97.00 E
Eastern Shore ◆[1]	208	38.40 N	75.50 W
Eastern Transvaal □[4]	156	26.00 S	30.30 E
Eastern Yamuna Canal ≊	272a	28.40 N	77.15 E
East Falkland I	254	51.55 S	59.00 W
East Falls ◆[8]	285	40.01 N	75.11 W
East Falmouth	207	41.34 N	70.33 W
East Farleigh	260	51.15 N	0.29 E
East Farmingdale	276	40.44 N	73.26 W
East Faxon	210	41.15 N	76.58 W
East Fayetteville	192	35.05 N	78.51 W
Eastfield	44	54.14 N	0.24 W
East Flat Rock	192	35.16 N	82.25 W
Eastford	207	41.54 N	72.04 W
East Foxboro	283	42.03 N	71.12 W
East Freedom	214	40.21 N	78.26 W
East Freetown	207	41.46 N	70.57 W
East Frisian Islands → Ostfriesische Inseln II	52	53.44 N	7.25 E
East Gaffney	192	35.04 N	81.37 W
East Gallatin ≏	202	45.53 N	111.20 W
Eastgate	224	47.34 N	122.09 W
East Ghor Canal → Ghawr ash-Sharqīyah, Qanāt al- ≊	132	32.41 N	35.38 E
East Glacier Park	202	48.26 N	113.13 W
East Glenville	210	42.53 N	73.55 W
East Granby	207	41.56 N	72.43 W
East Grand Forks	198	47.55 N	97.01 W
East Grand Rapids	216	42.56 N	85.36 W
East Greenbush	210	42.35 N	73.42 W
East Greenville, Oh., U.S.	214	40.48 N	81.36 W
East Greenville, Pa., U.S.	208	40.24 N	75.30 W
East Greenwich, N.Y., U.S.	210	43.09 N	73.24 W
East Greenwich, R.I., U.S.	207	41.39 N	71.27 W
East Grinstead	42	51.08 N	0.01 W
East Gwillimbury	212	44.08 N	79.25 W
East Haddam	207	41.27 N	72.27 W
East Half Hollow Hills	276	40.57 N	72.11 W
Eastham, Eng., U.K.	262	53.19 N	2.58 W
Eastham, Ma., U.S.	207	41.49 N	69.58 W
East Ham ◆[8]	260	51.32 N	0.03 E

Symbol	English	Deutsch	Español	Français	Português
≏	River	Fluß	Río	Rivière	Rio
≊	Canal	Kanal	Canal	Canal	Canal
⌊	Waterfall, Rapids	Wasserfall, Stromschnellen	Cascada, Rápidos	Chute d'eau, Rapides	Cascata, Rápidos
ʯ	Strait	Meeresstraße	Estrecho	Détroit	Estreito
c	Bay, Gulf	Bucht, Golf	Bahía, Golfo	Baie, Golfe	Baía, Golfo
◎	Lake, Lakes	See, Seen	Lago, Lagos	Lac, Lacs	Lago, Lagos
☷	Swamp	Sumpf	Pantano	Marais	Pântano
⍓	Ice Features, Glacier	Eis- und Gletscherformen	Accidentes Glaciales	Formes glaciaires	Acidentes glaciares
⍑	Other Hydrographic Features	Andere Hydrographische Objekte	Otros Elementos Hidrográficos	Autres données hydrographiques	Outros acidentes hidrográficos
✣	Submarine Features	Untermeerische Objekte	Accidentes Submarinos	Formes de relief sous-marin	Acidentes submarinos
□	Political Unit	Politische Einheit	Unidad Politica	Entité politique	Unidade política
ʊ	Cultural Institution	Kulturelle Institution	Institución Cultural	Institution culturelle	Institução cultural
⊥	Historical Site	Historische Stätte	Sitio Histórico	Site historique	Sitio histórico
♠	Recreational Site	Erholungs- und Ferienort	Sitio de Recreo	Centre de loisirs	Area de Lazer
⊠	Airport	Flughafen	Aeropuerto	Aéroport	Aeroporto
■	Military Installation	Militäranlage	Instalación Militar	Installation militaire	Instalação militar
◆	Miscellaneous	Verschiedenes	Misceláneo	Divers	Diversos

ENGLISH — Name · Page · Lat.°′ · Long.°′
DEUTSCH — Name · Seite · Breite°′ · Länge°′ E = Ost

Name	Page	Lat.°′	Long.°′
East Hampton, Ct., U.S.	207	41.34 N	72.30 W
Easthampton, Ma., U.S.	207	42.16 N	72.40 W
East Hampton, N.Y., U.S.	207	40.57 N	72.11 W
East Hanningfield	260	51.41 N	0.34 E
East Hanover	276	40.48 N	74.22 W
East Harbor State Park ♦	214	41.32 N	82.49 W
East Harling	42	52.26 N	0.55 E
East Hartford	207	41.46 N	72.36 W
East Hartland	207	41.59 N	72.54 W
East Harwich	207	41.43 N	70.02 W
East Haven	207	41.16 N	72.52 W
East Hazel Crest	278	41.35 N	87.39 W
East Helena	202	46.35 N	111.54 W
East Hemet	228	33.45 N	116.57 W
East Herkimer	210	43.02 N	74.58 W
East Hertfordshire □[8]	260	51.46 N	0.02 W
East Hickory	214	41.35 N	79.24 W
East Highland Park	208	37.36 N	77.25 W
East Hills, Austl.	274a	33.58 S	150.59 E
East Hills, N.Y., U.S.	276	40.47 N	73.37 W
East Hoathly	42	50.55 N	0.10 E
East Horsley	42	51.15 N	0.26 W
East Humber ≃	212	43.47 N	79.35 W
East Huntington	276	40.52 N	73.24 W
East Ilsley	42	51.32 N	1.17 W
East Irvington	276	41.03 N	73.51 W
East Island ›[1]	276	40.54 N	73.38 W
East Islip	276	40.43 N	73.11 W
East Jewett	210	42.14 N	74.09 W
East Jordan	190	45.09 N	85.07 W
East Keansburg	276	40.26 N	74.07 W
East Kelowna	182	49.51 N	119.25 W
East Kilbride	46	55.46 N	4.10 W
East Killingly	207	41.50 N	71.49 W
East Kingston	210	41.57 N	73.58 W
Eastlake, Mi., U.S.	190	44.15 N	86.18 W
Eastlake, Oh., U.S.	214	41.39 N	81.27 W
East Lake ⊜, On., Can.	184	53.42 N	93.10 W
East Lake ⊜, On., Can.	212	43.55 N	77.12 W
East Lake ⊜, N.J., U.S.	276	40.58 N	74.21 W
East Lake Tohopekaliga ⊜	220	28.18 N	81.17 W
East Lamma Channel ʮ	271d	22.14 N	114.09 E
Eastland	196	32.24 N	98.49 W
Eastland Center •[9]	281	42.27 N	82.56 W
Eastland Shopping Plaza •[9]	279b	40.22 N	79.50 W
East Lansdowne	285	39.56 N	75.16 W
East Lansing	216	42.44 N	84.29 W
East Laurinburg	192	34.46 N	79.26 W
East Leake	42	52.49 N	1.10 W
Eastleigh	42	50.58 N	1.22 W
East Lewistown	214	40.57 N	80.42 W
East Liberty	216	40.19 N	83.34 W
East Liberty •[8]	279b	40.27 N	79.55 W
East Licking Creek ≃	208	40.32 N	77.24 W
East Lindfield	274a	33.46 S	151.11 E
East Linton	46	55.59 N	2.39 W
East Liverpool	214	40.37 N	80.34 W
East London (Oos-Londen)	158	33.00 S	27.55 E
East Longmeadow	207	42.03 N	72.30 W
East Los Angeles	228	34.01 N	118.10 W
East Lyme	207	41.22 N	72.13 W
East Lynn	216	40.28 N	87.48 W
East Lynn Lake ⊜[1]	188	38.05 N	82.20 W
Eastmain	176	52.15 N	78.30 W
Eastmain ≃	176	52.15 N	78.35 W
Eastmain-Opinaca, Réservoir ⊜[1]	176	52.25 N	76.35 W
East Malling	260	51.17 N	0.26 E
Eastman, P.Q., Can.	206	45.18 N	72.19 W
Eastman, Ga., U.S.	192	32.11 N	83.10 W
Eastman Lake ⊜[1]	226	37.14 N	119.58 W
East Mansfield	283	42.01 N	71.10 W
East Mariana Basin ⊹[1]	14	12.00 N	153.00 E
East Marin Island I	282	37.58 N	122.27 W
East Markham	44	53.15 N	0.54 W
East McKeesport	279b	40.23 N	79.48 W
East Meadow	210	40.43 N	73.33 W
East Meadow ≃	283	42.47 N	71.02 W
East Meadow Brook ≃	276	40.39 N	73.34 W
East Meadowview	216	41.08 N	87.52 W
East Mecca	214	41.24 N	80.45 W
East Meredith	210	42.25 N	74.53 W
East Midlands Airport ⊠	42	52.50 N	1.20 W
East Millbury	207	42.13 N	71.44 W
East Mill Creek ≃	222	29.55 N	96.17 W
East Millinocket	188	45.37 N	68.34 W
East Millstone	276	40.30 N	74.35 W
East Missoula	202	46.52 N	113.58 W
East Molesey	260	51.24 N	0.21 W
East Moline	190	41.30 N	90.26 W
East Monongahela	279b	40.12 N	79.55 W
East Mountain	222	32.35 N	94.51 W
East Mustang Creek ≃	222	29.03 N	96.27 W
East Naples	220	26.06 N	81.44 W
East Nassau	210	42.30 N	73.30 W
East Newark	276	40.48 N	73.59 W
East New Britain □[5]	164	6.00 S	152.00 E
East New Market	208	38.35 N	75.55 W
East New York •[8]	276	40.40 N	73.53 W
East Nishnabotna ≃	198	40.39 N	95.37 W
East Nodaway ≃	194	40.38 N	95.01 W
East Norriton	208	40.09 N	75.18 W
East Northfield	207	42.43 N	72.27 W
East Northport	210	40.52 N	73.19 W
East Norwich	210	40.50 N	73.32 W
East Novaya Zemlya Trough ⊹[1]	12	73.30 N	61.00 E
East Olympia	224	46.58 N	122.50 W
Easton, Eng., U.K.	42	50.32 N	2.26 W
Easton, Ca., U.S.	226	36.39 N	119.47 W
Easton, Ct., U.S.	207	41.15 N	73.17 W
Easton, Il., U.S.	219	40.14 N	89.50 W
Easton, Md., U.S.	208	38.46 N	76.04 W
Easton, Ma., U.S.	283	42.02 N	71.06 W
Easton, Pa., U.S.	208	40.41 N	75.13 W
Easton, Tx., U.S.	222	32.23 N	94.35 W
Easton, Wa., U.S.	224	47.14 N	121.10 W
Eastondale	283	42.02 N	71.04 W
Easton Reservoir ⊜[1]	207	41.16 N	73.16 W
East Orange	210	40.46 N	74.12 W
East Orleans	207	41.47 N	69.58 W
East Otto	210	42.23 N	78.45 W
Eastover	192	33.52 N	80.41 W
East Pacific Rise ⊹[3]	6	20.00 S	115.00 W
East Pakistan → Bangladesh □[1]	118	24.00 N	90.00 E
East Palatka	192	29.39 N	81.35 W
East Palestine	214	40.50 N	80.32 W
East Palo Alto	226	37.28 N	122.08 W
East Park Reservoir ⊜[1]	226	39.21 N	122.30 W
East Parkrose	224	45.33 N	122.32 W
East Peak ∧	116	11.13 N	119.29 E
East Peckham	42	51.15 N	0.23 E
East Pecos	200	35.34 N	105.39 W
East Pembroke, Ma., U.S.	283	42.05 N	70.46 W
East Pembroke, N.Y., U.S.	210	42.59 N	78.18 W
East Peoria	190	40.39 N	89.34 W
East Pepperell	207	42.39 N	71.34 W
East Petersburg	208	40.06 N	76.21 W
East Pharsalia	210	42.34 N	75.43 W
East Pine	182	55.43 N	121.13 W
East Pines	284c	38.57 N	76.55 W
East Pittsburgh	279b	40.23 N	79.50 W
Eastpoint, Fl., U.S.	192	29.44 N	84.52 W
East Point, Ga., U.S.	192	33.40 N	84.26 W
East Point ›, P.E., Can.	186	46.27 N	61.58 W
East Point ›, Ma., U.S.	207	42.25 N	70.54 W
East Point ›, Vir. Is., U.S.	241n	17.45 N	64.34 W
Eastpoint •[9]	284b	39.18 N	76.31 W
Eastport, Nf., Can.	186	48.39 N	53.45 W
Eastport, Id., U.S.	202	49.00 N	116.10 W
Eastport, Me., U.S.	188	44.54 N	66.59 W
Eastport, N.Y., U.S.	207	40.49 N	72.44 W
East Porterville	204	36.04 N	118.56 W
East Potomac Park ♦	284c	38.52 N	77.01 W
East Prairie	194	36.46 N	89.23 W
East Prairie ≃	182	55.34 N	116.25 W
East Prospect	208	39.58 N	76.31 W
East Providence	207	41.48 N	71.22 W
East Pryor Mountain ∧	202	45.11 N	108.20 W
East Quogue	207	40.51 N	72.35 W
East Rājasthān Uplands ⋏[1]	124	26.40 N	76.35 E
East Randolph	210	42.10 N	78.56 W
East Retford	44	53.19 N	0.56 W
East Richmond	226	37.57 N	122.19 W
Eastridge Center •[9]	282	37.20 N	121.49 W
East Rigaud ≃	206	45.27 N	74.22 W
Eastriggs	44	54.59 N	3.10 W
East River ⊂	208	37.24 N	76.21 W
East Rochester, N.Y., U.S.	210	43.06 N	77.29 W
East Rochester, Oh., U.S.	214	40.45 N	81.02 W
East Rockaway	276	40.38 N	73.40 W
East Rockingham	192	34.55 N	79.45 W
East Rockwood	216	42.03 N	83.13 W
East Rosebud Creek ≃	202	45.29 N	109.27 W
East Rudolf National Park ♦	154	3.55 N	36.20 E
East Rutherford	276	40.50 N	74.05 W
Eastry	42	51.15 N	1.18 E
East Saint Louis	219	38.38 N	90.09 W
East Salem	208	40.37 N	77.14 W
East Salt Creek ≃	200	39.13 N	108.54 W
East Sandwich	207	41.44 N	70.27 W
East Sandy Creek ≃	214	41.22 N	79.51 W
East Schodack	210	42.34 N	73.38 W
East Scotia Basin ⊹[1]	9	57.00 S	35.00 W
East Sepik □[5]	164	4.00 S	143.30 E
East Setauket	210	40.57 N	73.06 W
East Shoal Lake ⊜	184	50.23 N	97.37 W
East Siberian Sea → Vostočno-Sibirskoje more ▾[2]	12	74.00 N	166.00 E
East Side	210	41.04 N	75.46 W
Eastside Bypass ≅	226	37.05 N	120.28 W
East Side Canal ≅, Ca., U.S.	226	37.21 N	120.55 W
East Side Canal ≅, Ca., U.S.	226	35.33 N	119.33 W
East Sixteen Mile Creek ≃	275b	43.28 N	79.48 W
East Smethport	214	41.49 N	78.26 W
East Smithfield	210	41.52 N	76.38 W
East Sooke	224	48.22 N	123.43 W
Eastsound	224	48.41 N	122.54 W
East Sound ʮ	224	48.39 N	122.53 W
East Sparta	214	40.40 N	81.21 W
East Spencer	192	35.40 N	80.25 W
East Springbrook	284c	39.04 N	77.00 W
East Springfield, Oh., U.S.	214	40.27 N	80.52 W
East Springfield, Pa., U.S.	214	41.57 N	80.28 W
East Stony Creek ≃	210	43.15 N	74.12 W
East Stour ≃	42	51.08 N	0.53 E
East Stroudsburg	210	40.59 N	75.10 W
East Sudbury	283	42.24 N	71.24 W
East Sussex □[6]	42	50.55 N	0.15 E
East Syracuse	210	43.04 N	76.05 W
East Tawas	190	44.16 N	83.29 W
East Templeton	207	42.33 N	72.02 W
East Texas	210	40.33 N	75.33 W
East Thompson	207	42.00 N	71.48 W
East Tilbury	260	51.28 N	0.26 E
East Troy	216	42.47 N	88.24 W
East Tustin	280	33.46 N	117.49 W
Eastvale	214	40.46 N	80.19 W
East Vandergrift	214	40.36 N	79.34 W
Eastview	218	40.19 N	80.38 W
Eastville	208	37.21 N	75.56 W
East Walker ≃	204	38.53 N	119.10 W
East Walpole	207	42.09 N	71.12 W
East Wareham	207	41.45 N	70.40 W
East Washington	214	40.10 N	80.14 W
East Waterford	208	40.22 N	77.36 W
East Wemyss	46	56.09 N	3.04 W
East Wenatchee	202	47.24 N	120.17 W
East Wenonah	285	39.47 N	75.08 W
East White Plains	276	41.03 N	73.47 W
Eastwick •[8]	285	39.55 N	75.14 W
East Wickham •[8]	260	51.28 N	0.07 E
East Williamson	210	43.14 N	77.09 W
East Williston	276	40.46 N	73.38 W
East Wilmington	192	34.13 N	77.53 W
East Wittering	42	50.41 N	0.53 W
Eastwood, Austl.	274a	33.48 S	151.05 E
Eastwood, Eng., U.K.	44	53.01 N	1.18 W
Eastwood, Eng., U.K.	260	51.34 N	0.40 E
Eastwood, Eng., U.K.	262	53.43 N	2.03 W
Eastwood, Mi., U.S.	216	42.18 N	85.33 W
Eastwood, Pa., U.S.	279b	40.17 N	79.31 W
East Worcester	210	42.37 N	74.40 W
East Yegua Creek ≃	222	30.19 N	96.45 W
East Yellow Creek ≃	194	39.38 N	93.04 W
East York, On., Can.	212	43.41 N	79.20 W
East York, Pa., U.S.	208	39.58 N	76.43 W
Eaton, Austl.	168a	33.19 S	115.43 E
Eaton, Co., U.S.	200	40.31 N	104.42 W
Eaton, In., U.S.	216	40.20 N	85.21 W
Eaton, N.Y., U.S.	210	42.51 N	75.37 W
Eaton, Oh., U.S.	218	39.44 N	84.38 W
Eaton ≃	206	45.28 N	71.39 W
Eaton Estates	214	41.19 N	82.01 W
Eatonia	184	51.13 N	109.23 W
Eaton Nord ≃	206	45.24 N	71.35 W
Eaton Park	220	28.00 N	81.54 W
Eaton Rapids	216	42.30 N	84.39 W
Eatons Neck	276	40.56 N	73.24 W
Eatons Neck ›[1]	276	40.57 N	73.23 W
Eatons Neck Point ›	210	40.57 N	73.24 W
Eaton Socon	42	52.13 N	0.18 W
Eatonton	192	33.19 N	83.23 W
Eatontown	208	40.17 N	74.03 W
Eatonville	224	46.52 N	122.15 W
Eaton Wash V	280	34.04 N	118.03 W
Eaton Wash Dam •[6]	280	34.10 N	118.06 W
Eau ≃	44	53.31 N	0.44 W
Eaubonne	261	49.00 N	2.17 E
Eau Claire, Mi., U.S.	216	41.59 N	86.17 W
Eau Claire, Pa., U.S.	214	41.08 N	79.48 W
Eau Claire, Wi., U.S.	190	44.48 N	91.29 W
Eau Claire ≃, Wi., U.S.	190	44.49 N	91.31 W
Eau Claire ≃, Wi., U.S.	190	44.55 N	89.37 W
Eau Claire, Lac à l' ⊜, P.Q., Can.	176	56.10 N	74.25 W
Eau Claire, Lac à l' ⊜, P.Q., Can.	206	46.33 N	73.04 W
Eau d'Heure ≃	56	50.18 N	4.24 E
Eau Galle ≃	190	44.37 N	92.00 W
Eau Gallie	220	28.08 N	80.38 W
Eaulne ≃	50	49.54 N	1.07 E
Eauripik I[1]	108	6.42 N	143.03 E
Eauripik Rise ⊹[3]	14	3.00 N	142.00 E
Eauze	32	43.52 N	0.06 E
Ebabaka	152	2.30 S	18.19 E
Eban	150	9.44 N	4.56 E
Ebanga	152	12.44 S	14.44 E
Ebangalakata	152	0.29 S	21.29 E
Ebano	234	22.13 N	98.22 W
Ebb and Flow Indian Reserve •[4]	184	51.05 N	99.05 W
Ebb and Flow Lake ⊜	184	51.05 N	98.56 W
Ebbegebirge ⋏	56	51.08 N	7.46 E
Ebben Creek ≃	283	42.38 N	70.45 W
Ebberup	41	55.15 N	9.59 E
Ebbetts Pass)(	226	38.33 N	119.48 W
Ebbs	64	47.38 N	12.13 E
Ebbw ≃	42	51.33 N	2.59 W
Ebbw Vale	42	51.47 N	3.12 W
Ebebiyín	152	2.09 N	11.20 E
Ebeji (El Beïd) ≃	146	12.32 N	14.11 E
Ebejty, ozero ⊜	86	54.38 N	71.44 E
Ebeleben	54	51.17 N	10.43 E
Ebeltoft	41	56.12 N	10.41 E
Ebeltoft Vig ⊂	41	56.10 N	10.36 E
Ebenau	64	47.47 N	13.11 E
Ebendorf	54	52.11 N	11.34 E
Ebene Reichenau	64	46.51 N	13.54 E
Ebenezer	275b	43.46 N	79.40 W
Ebenezer Ridge ∧	218	39.06 N	84.55 W
Eben Junction	190	46.21 N	86.58 W
Ebensburg	214	40.29 N	78.43 W
Ebensee	64	47.48 N	13.46 E
Ebensfeld	56	50.04 N	10.58 E
Eberbach	56	49.28 N	8.59 E
Ebergassing	264b	48.03 N	16.31 E
Eber Gölü ⊜	130	38.38 N	31.12 E
Ebergötzen	52	51.34 N	10.06 E
Ebermannstadt	60	49.43 N	11.13 E
Ebern	56	50.05 N	10.47 E
Eberndorf	61	46.35 N	14.38 E
Ebersbach, Dtsch.	54	51.00 N	14.35 E
Ebersbach, Dtsch.	56	48.43 N	9.31 E
Ebersberg	60	48.05 N	11.58 E
Eberschwang	60	48.09 N	13.34 E
Ebersdorf	52	53.31 N	9.03 E
Ebersdorf bei Coburg	56	50.13 N	11.04 E
Eberstein	61	46.48 N	14.34 E
Eberswalde	54	52.50 N	13.49 E
Ebetsu	92a	43.07 N	141.34 E
Ebian	102	29.10 N	103.20 E
Ebina	94	35.26 N	139.25 E
Ebino	92	32.03 N	130.50 E
Ebinur Hu ⊜	86	44.55 N	82.55 E
Ebi-Sekigahara-Yōrō-kokutei-kōen ♦	94	35.30 N	136.30 E
Ebnat	58	47.15 N	9.08 E
Ebo	152	11.02 S	14.41 E
Ebola ≃	152	3.20 N	20.57 E
Eboli	68	40.37 N	15.04 E
Ebolowa	152	2.54 N	11.09 E
Ebon I[1]	14	4.35 N	168.44 E
Ebonda	152	2.12 N	22.21 E
Ebony	156	22.05 S	15.15 E
Eboshi-yama ∧	96	35.04 N	133.04 E
Eboué Stadium ♦	273b	4.17 S	15.18 E
Ebrach	56	49.50 N	10.29 E
Ebre, Delta de l' ≚[2]	34	40.43 N	0.54 E
Ebreichsdorf	61	47.58 N	16.24 E
Ébrié, Lagune ⊂	150	5.14 N	4.26 W
Ebro (Ebre) ≃	34	40.43 N	0.54 E
Ebro, Embalse del ⊜[1]	34	43.00 N	3.58 W
Ebstorf	52	53.01 N	10.25 E
Ebute-Ikorodu	273a	6.37 N	3.30 E
Ebute-Metta •[8]	273a	6.29 N	3.23 E
Ecatepec	286a	19.35 N	99.04 W
Écaussinnes-d'Enghen	50	50.34 N	4.10 E
Ecclefechan	44	55.03 N	3.17 W
Eccles, Eng., U.K.	44	53.29 N	2.21 W
Eccles, Eng., U.K.	260	51.19 N	0.29 E
Eccles, W.V., U.S.	192	37.46 N	81.15 W
Eccleshall	42	52.52 N	2.15 W
Eccleston, Eng., U.K.	44	53.38 N	2.43 W
Eccleston, Eng., U.K.	262	53.27 N	2.47 W
Eccleston, Md., U.S.	284b	39.24 N	76.44 W
Eceabat	130	40.11 N	26.21 E
Echabi	89	53.30 N	142.59 E
Echague	116	16.42 N	121.40 E
Echallens	58	46.38 N	6.38 E
Echaporã	255	22.26 S	50.12 W
Echarcon	261	48.34 N	2.24 E
Échauffour	50	48.44 N	0.23 E
Ech Cheliff (Orléansville)	148	36.10 N	1.20 E
Ech Cheliff □[5]	148	36.20 N	1.50 E
Echeconnee Creek ≃	192	32.39 N	83.36 W
Echelon Mall •[9]	285	39.51 N	75.00 W
Echeng	100	30.24 N	114.51 E
Échenoz-la-Méline	58	47.36 N	6.08 E
Echi ≃	94	35.13 N	136.07 E
Echigawa	94	35.10 N	136.12 E
Echigo-sammyaku ⋏	92	37.50 N	139.50 E
Echimamish ≃	184	54.20 N	97.27 W
Eching	60	48.18 N	11.37 E
Echizen	94	35.54 N	136.00 E
Echizen-Kaga-kaigan-kokutei-kōen ♦	94	36.08 N	136.05 E
Echizen-misaki ›	94	35.59 N	135.57 E
Echo	198	44.37 N	95.25 W
Echo Bay	176	66.05 N	118.02 W
Echo Bay ⊂	276	40.54 N	73.46 W
Echoing ≃	184	55.51 N	92.05 W
Echoing Lake ⊜	184	54.31 N	92.15 W
Echo Lake ⊜, Il., U.S.	278	42.13 N	88.05 W
Echo Lake ⊜, N.J., U.S.	276	41.04 N	74.25 W
Echo Summit ∧	226	38.50 N	120.02 W
Echouani, Lac ⊜	190	47.46 N	75.42 W
Echt, Ned.	52	51.06 N	5.52 E
Echt, Scot., U.K.	46	57.08 N	2.26 W
Echternach	56	49.48 N	6.26 E
Echternacherbrück	56	49.49 N	6.25 E
Echuca	166	36.08 S	144.46 E
Echunga	168b	35.07 S	138.48 E
Écija	34	37.32 N	5.05 W
Ecilda Paullier	258	34.22 S	57.04 W
Eck, Loch ⊜	46	56.05 N	5.00 W
Eckartsberga	54	51.07 N	11.34 E
Eckbolsheim	58	48.35 N	7.41 E
Eckernförde	41	54.28 N	9.50 E
Eckernförder Bucht ⊂	41	54.30 N	10.02 E
Eckerö I	26	60.14 N	19.35 E
Eckington	44	53.19 N	1.21 W
Eckley	210	40.59 N	75.51 W
Eckville	182	52.21 N	114.22 W
Eckwarderhörne	52	53.31 N	8.14 E
Eclectic	194	32.38 N	86.02 W
Ecleto	222	29.03 N	97.45 W
Ecleto Creek ≃	196	28.52 N	97.45 W
Eclipse Sound ʮ	176	72.38 N	79.00 W
Ečmiadzin	84	40.10 N	44.18 E
Ecola State Park ♦	224	45.57 N	123.58 W
Ècole ≃	261	48.32 N	2.33 E
École Militaire (Saint-Cyr) ■	261	48.48 N	2.04 E
Écommoy	50	47.50 N	0.16 E
Econfina ≃	192	30.02 N	83.55 W
Econlockhatchee ≃	220	28.42 N	81.02 W
Economy, In., U.S.	218	39.58 N	85.05 W
Economy, Pa., U.S.	214	40.39 N	80.14 W
Economy Park ♦	279b	40.37 N	80.12 W
Ecoporanga	255	18.23 S	40.50 W
Écorce, Lac de l' ⊜[1]	190	47.05 N	76.24 W
Écorces, Lac des ⊜	206	46.00 N	74.32 W
Ecorse	216	42.14 N	83.08 W
Ecorse ≃	281	42.14 N	83.09 W
Ecorse, South Branch ≃	281	42.14 N	83.09 W
Écos	50	49.10 N	1.39 E
Écosse → Scotland □[8]	28	57.00 N	4.00 W
Écouen	50	49.01 N	2.23 E
Écouen, Château d' ⊥	261	49.01 N	2.23 E
Écouis	50	49.19 N	1.26 E
Ecoute, Ru d' ≃	261	48.39 N	2.26 E
Ecquevilly	261	48.57 N	1.55 E
Écrins, Barre des ∧	62	44.55 N	6.22 E
Écrins, Massif des ⋏[1]	62	44.55 N	6.20 E
Écrins, Parc National des ♦	62	44.50 N	6.15 E
Écrosnes	261	48.33 N	1.44 E
Ecru	194	34.21 N	89.01 W
Ecser	264c	47.27 N	19.20 E
Ecstall ≃	182	54.09 N	129.56 W
Ecuador □[1], S.A.	242	2.00 S	77.30 W
Ecuador □[1], S.A.	246	2.00 S	77.30 W
Ecuandureo	234	20.10 N	102.11 W
Écueillé	32	47.05 N	1.21 E
Écuisses	58	46.45 N	4.32 E
Ecum Secum	186	44.58 N	62.08 W
Écury-sur-Coole	50	48.54 N	4.20 E
Ed, Erit.	144	13.52 N	41.40 E
Ed, Sve.	26	58.55 N	11.55 E
Eda •[8]	268	35.34 N	139.34 E
Edah	162	28.17 S	117.10 E
Edam, Sk., Can.	184	53.12 N	108.46 W
Edam, Ned.	52	52.31 N	5.03 E
Eday I	46	59.11 N	2.47 W
Edderton	46	57.50 N	4.10 W
Eddington Gardens	285	40.06 N	74.57 W
Eddleston	46	55.43 N	3.13 W
Eddrachillis Bay ⊂	46	58.18 N	5.15 W
Eddy	222	31.18 N	97.15 W
Eddystone	208	39.51 N	75.20 W
Eddystone Point ›	166	41.00 S	148.21 E
Eddystone Rocks II[1]	42	50.12 N	4.15 W
Eddyville, Ia., U.S.	190	41.09 N	92.38 W
Eddyville, Ky., U.S.	194	37.05 N	88.04 W
Eddyville, N.Y., U.S.	210	41.54 N	74.02 W
Ede, Ned.	52	52.03 N	5.40 E
Ede, Nig.	150	7.44 N	4.27 E
Edéa	152	3.48 N	10.08 E
Edebäck	40	60.04 N	13.33 E
Edebo	40	60.01 N	18.34 E
Edegem	52	51.09 N	4.27 E
Edehon Lake ⊜	176	60.25 N	97.15 W
Edéia	255	17.18 S	49.55 W
Edelény	30	48.18 N	20.44 E
Edelsfeld	60	49.34 N	11.42 E
Edelshausen	60	48.37 N	11.17 E
Edelweiss	273d	26.16 S	28.28 E
Edelweiss Spitze ∧	64	47.07 N	12.50 E
Edemissen	52	52.23 N	10.16 E
Eden, Austl.	166	37.04 S	149.54 E
Éden, Bra.	287a	22.48 S	43.24 W
Eden, N. Ire., U.K.	48	54.44 N	5.47 W
Eden, Mi., U.S.	216	42.32 N	84.26 W
Eden, Ms., U.S.	194	32.59 N	90.19 W
Eden, N.Y., U.S.	210	42.39 N	78.53 W
Eden, Tx., U.S.	196	31.12 N	99.50 W
Eden, Wy., U.S.	200	42.03 N	109.26 W
Eden ≃, Eng., U.K.	42	51.10 N	0.11 E
Eden ≃, Eng., U.K.	44	54.57 N	3.01 W
Eden ≃, Scot., U.K.	46	56.22 N	2.50 W
Eden ≃, Wales, U.K.	42	52.48 N	3.53 W
Edenbridge	42	51.12 N	0.04 E
Edenburg	158	29.45 S	25.56 E
Eden Canyon V	282	37.42 N	122.01 W
Edendale, N.Z.	172	46.19 S	168.47 E
Edendale, S. Afr.	158	29.39 S	30.18 E
Edendale, S. Afr.	273d	26.09 S	28.09 E
Edenderry	48	53.20 N	7.03 W
Edenfield	262	53.40 N	2.18 W
Eden Hill ∧[2]	207	41.20 N	73.19 W
Edenkoben	56	49.17 N	8.07 E
Eden Lake ⊜	184	56.38 N	100.15 W
Eden Mills	212	43.35 N	80.09 W
Eden Park •[8]	260	51.23 N	0.02 W
Edenside V	44	54.40 N	2.35 W
Edenton	192	36.03 N	76.36 W
Edenvale	273d	26.08 S	28.09 E
Eden Valley, Austl.	168b	34.39 S	139.06 E
Eden Valley, Mn., U.S.	190	45.19 N	94.32 W
Edenville	158	27.37 S	27.34 E
Edeowie	166	31.27 S	138.27 E
Eder ≃	56	51.13 N	9.27 E
Ederkopf ∧	56	50.56 N	8.12 E
Ederny	48	54.32 N	7.39 W
Edersee ⊜[1]	56	51.11 N	9.00 E
Eder-Talsperre •[6]	56	51.11 N	9.02 E
Edesheim	56	49.16 N	8.08 E
Edessa → Édhessa	38	40.48 N	22.03 E
Edewecht	52	53.07 N	8.02 E
Edfu → Idfū	140	24.58 N	32.52 E
Edgar, Ne., U.S.	198	40.22 N	97.58 W
Edgar, Wi., U.S.	190	44.55 N	89.57 W
Edgard	194	30.03 N	90.34 W
Edgar Ranges ⋏	162	18.43 S	123.25 E
Edgars Creek ≃	274b	37.44 S	144.58 E
Edgartown	207	41.23 N	70.30 W
Edgartown Harbor ⊂	207	41.24 N	70.30 W
Edgecliff	222	32.39 N	97.22 W
Edgecumbe	172	37.59 S	176.50 E
Edgefield	192	33.47 N	81.55 W
Edge Hill •[8]	262	53.24 N	2.57 W
Edge Hill ∧	42	52.08 N	1.27 W
Edgeley, On., Can.	275b	43.48 N	79.31 W
Edgeley, N.D., U.S.	198	46.21 N	98.42 W
Edgely	285	40.07 N	74.50 W
Edgemere	208	39.14 N	76.26 W
Edgemont, Ca., U.S.	228	33.53 N	117.18 W
Edgemont, Pa., U.S.	285	39.57 N	75.27 W
Edgemont, S.D., U.S.	198	43.18 N	103.49 W
Edgemont Park	216	42.44 N	84.36 W
Edgemoor	285	39.45 N	75.30 W
Edge Mountain ∧	180	58.12 N	152.06 W
Edgeøya I	12	77.45 N	22.30 E
Edgeroi	166	30.07 S	149.48 E
Edgerton, Ab., Can.	184	52.45 N	110.27 W
Edgerton, In., U.S.	216	41.05 N	84.49 W
Edgerton, Mn., U.S.	198	43.52 N	96.07 W
Edgerton, Oh., U.S.	216	41.26 N	84.44 W
Edgerton, Wi., U.S.	216	42.50 N	89.04 W
Edgerton, Wy., U.S.	200	43.24 N	106.14 W
Edgewater, Al., U.S.	194	33.31 N	86.57 W
Edgewater, Fl., U.S.	220	28.59 N	80.54 W
Edgewater, N.J., U.S.	276	40.50 N	73.58 W
Edgewater Park	285	40.04 N	74.54 W
Edgewater Park ♦	279a	41.29 N	81.43 W
Edgewater Point ›	276	40.55 N	73.44 W
Edgewood, B.C., Can.	182	49.47 N	118.08 W
Edgewood, Fl., U.S.	220	28.29 N	81.22 W
Edgewood, Il., U.S.	219	38.55 N	88.40 W
Edgewood, In., U.S.	218	40.06 N	85.44 W
Edgewood, Ia., U.S.	190	42.38 N	91.24 W
Edgewood, Md., U.S.	208	39.25 N	76.17 W
Edgewood, Oh., U.S.	214	41.52 N	80.46 W
Edgewood, Pa., U.S.	279b	40.25 N	79.52 W
Edgewood, Tx., U.S.	222	32.42 N	95.53 W
Edgeworth	214	40.33 N	80.11 W
Edgeworthstown → Mostrim	48	53.42 N	7.36 W
Edgware •[8]	260	51.37 N	0.17 W
Edgworth	262	53.39 N	2.24 W
Édhessa	38	40.48 N	22.03 E
Ediger	56	50.06 N	7.09 E
Edimbourg → Edinburgh	46	55.57 N	3.13 W
Edimburgo → Edinburgh	46	55.57 N	3.13 W
Edina, Liber.	150	6.01 N	10.10 W
Edina, Mn., U.S.	190	44.53 N	93.20 W
Edina, Mo., U.S.	219	40.10 N	92.10 W
Edinboro	214	41.52 N	80.07 W
Edinboro Lake ⊜	214	41.53 N	80.08 W
Edinburg, Il., U.S.	219	39.39 N	89.23 W
Edinburg, In., U.S.	218	39.21 N	85.58 W
Edinburg, Ms., U.S.	194	32.47 N	89.20 W
Edinburg, N.Y., U.S.	210	43.13 N	74.07 W
Edinburg, N.D., U.S.	198	48.29 N	97.51 W
Edinburg, Oh., U.S.	214	41.06 N	81.09 W
Edinburg, Tx., U.S.	196	26.18 N	98.09 W
Edinburg, Va., U.S.	188	38.49 N	78.33 W
Edinburgh	46	55.57 N	3.13 W
Edinburgh (Turnhouse) Airport ⊠	46	55.57 N	3.21 W
Edinburgh, Arrecife ⊹[2]	236	14.50 N	82.39 W
Edinburgh Castle ⊥	46	55.56 N	3.14 W
Edinburgh Channel ʮ	236	14.45 N	82.40 W
Edinburgh Mountain ∧	224	48.38 N	124.24 W
Edincik	130	40.20 N	27.51 E
Edineț	38	48.10 N	27.19 E
Edingen → Enghien	50	50.42 N	4.02 E
Edirne	130	41.40 N	26.34 E
Edirne □[4]	130	41.20 N	26.40 E
Edison, Ga., U.S.	192	31.33 N	84.44 W
Edison, N.J., U.S.	210	40.27 N	74.18 W
Edison, Oh., U.S.	214	40.33 N	82.51 W
Edison, Pa., U.S.	208	40.17 N	75.07 W
Edison Bridge •[5]	214	41.27 N	82.49 W
Edison National Historic Site ⊥	276	40.47 N	74.14 W
Edison Park •[8]	278	42.01 N	87.49 W
Edisseja	84	44.03 N	44.33 E
Edisto ≃	192	32.39 N	80.24 W
Edisto, North Fork ≃	192	33.16 N	80.53 W
Edisto, South Fork ≃	192	33.16 N	80.53 W
Edisto Island I	192	32.35 N	80.20 W
Edith	170	33.48 S	149.55 E
Edith, Mount ∧	202	46.26 N	111.11 W
Edithburgh	168b	35.06 S	137.44 E
Edith Cavell, Mount ∧	182	52.40 N	118.03 W
Edith River	164	14.11 S	132.02 E
Edithvale	274b	38.02 S	145.07 E
Edith Weston	42	52.37 N	0.37 W
Edjejou, Oued i-n- V	148	22.46 N	4.05 E
Edjeleh	148	27.38 N	9.50 E
Edjerir ≃	150	18.06 N	0.50 E
Edjudina	162	29.48 S	122.23 E
Edmeston	210	42.41 N	75.14 W
Edmond	196	35.39 N	97.28 W
Edmondbyers	44	54.51 N	1.58 W
Edmonds	224	47.48 N	122.22 W
Edmondson Heights	284b	39.18 N	76.43 W
Edmonston	284c	38.57 N	76.56 W
Edmonton, Austl.	166	17.01 S	145.45 E
Edmonton, Ab., Can.	182	53.33 N	113.28 W
Edmonton, Ky., U.S.	194	36.58 N	85.36 W
Edmonton •[8]	260	51.37 N	0.04 W
Edmore, Mi., U.S.	190	43.24 N	85.02 W
Edmore, N.D., U.S.	198	48.24 N	98.27 W
Edmund	162	23.46 S	116.02 E
Edmund Lake ⊜	184	54.45 N	93.15 W
Edmundson Acres	228	35.14 N	118.49 W
Edmundston	186	47.22 N	68.20 W
Edna, Ks., U.S.	198	37.03 N	95.21 W
Edna, Pa., U.S.	279b	40.19 N	79.39 W
Edna, Tx., U.S.	222	28.58 N	96.38 W
Edna Bay	180	55.57 N	133.40 W
Ednor	208	39.09 N	76.59 W
Edo ≃	94	35.37 N	139.53 E
Edogawa •[8]	268	35.42 N	139.52 E
Edolo	64	46.11 N	10.20 E
Edom	222	32.22 N	95.37 W
Edon	216	41.33 N	84.46 W
Edosaki	94	35.57 N	140.19 E
Edremit	130	39.35 N	27.01 E
Edremit Körfezi ⊂	130	39.30 N	26.45 E
Edrengijn nuruu ⋏	102	44.15 N	97.45 E
Edsall Park	284c	38.48 N	77.11 W
Edsbro	40	59.54 N	18.29 E
Edsbruk	26	58.02 N	16.28 E
Edsbyn	26	61.23 N	15.49 E
Edsgatan	40	59.26 N	13.33 E
Edson	182	53.35 N	116.26 W
Edson Butte ∧	202	42.52 N	124.20 W
Eduardo Castex	252	35.54 S	64.18 W
Eduardo VII, Península → Edward VII Peninsula ›[1]	9	77.40 S	155.00 W
Eduni, Mount ∧	180	64.15 N	128.04 W
Edward ≃, Austl.	164	14.44 S	141.35 E
Edward ≃, Austl.	166	35.33 S	144.58 E
Edward, Lake ⊜	154	0.25 S	29.30 E
Edward, Mount ∧	162	23.22 S	131.55 E
Edwardes Park ♦	274b	37.43 S	145.00 E
Edward Island I	190	48.24 N	88.36 W
Edward River Aboriginal Reserve •[4]	164	14.30 S	141.45 E
Edwards, Ca., U.S.	228	34.54 N	117.53 W
Edwards, Ms., U.S.	194	32.19 N	90.36 W
Edwards, N.Y., U.S.	212	44.19 N	75.15 W
Edwards ≃	190	41.09 N	90.59 W
Edwards Air Force Base ■	228	34.54 N	117.52 W
Edwards Airport ⊠	276	40.45 N	73.03 W
Edwardsburg	216	41.47 N	86.04 W
Edwards Butte ∧	224	45.23 N	123.41 W
Edwards Gardens ♦	275b	43.44 N	79.22 W
Edwards Plateau ⋏[1]	196	31.20 N	101.00 W
Edwards Point ›	169	38.13 S	144.42 E
Edwards Run ≃	285	39.48 N	75.12 W
Edwardsville, Il., U.S.	219	38.48 N	89.57 W
Edwardsville, In., U.S.	218	38.16 N	85.55 W
Edwardsville, Pa., U.S.	210	41.16 N	75.55 W
Edward VIII Bay ⊂	9	66.50 S	57.00 E
Edward VII Peninsula ›[1]	9	77.40 S	155.00 W
Edwinstowe	44	53.12 N	1.04 W
Edzell	46	56.48 N	2.39 W
Edziza, Mount ∧	180	57.40 N	130.36 W
Eede	52	51.15 N	3.28 E
Eefde	52	52.10 N	6.14 E
Eek	180	60.12 N	162.15 W
Eek ≃	180	60.12 N	162.15 W
Eeklo	50	51.11 N	3.34 E
Eel ≃, Ca., U.S.	204	40.40 N	124.20 W
Eel ≃, In., U.S.	194	39.07 N	86.57 W
Eel ≃, In., U.S.	216	40.45 N	86.22 W
Eel, Middle Fork ≃	204	39.42 N	123.21 W
Eel, North Fork ≃	204	39.57 N	123.26 W
Eel, South Fork ≃	204	40.22 N	123.55 W
Eel Bay ⊂	212	44.19 N	76.02 W
Eelde	52	53.07 N	6.35 E
Eels Creek ≃	212	44.35 N	78.03 W
Eels Lake ⊜	212	44.54 N	78.08 W
Eemskanaal ≅	52	53.15 N	6.45 E
Eerbeek	52	52.07 N	6.04 E
Eersel	52	51.22 N	5.19 E
Eesti → Estonia □[1]	22	59.00 N	26.00 E
Eexta	52	53.10 N	6.59 E
Efate □[8]	175f	17.45 S	168.20 E
Éfaté I	175f	17.40 S	168.25 E
Eferding	61	48.18 N	14.02 E
Efes (Ephesus) ⊥	130	37.55 N	27.17 E
Effigy Mounds National Monument ♦	190	43.06 N	91.13 W
Effingham, Eng., U.K.	260	51.16 N	0.24 W
Effingham, Il., U.S.	194	39.07 N	88.32 W
Effingham, Ks., U.S.	198	39.31 N	95.24 W
Effingham □[6]	219	39.07 N	88.33 W
Effingham Lake ⊜	212	44.59 N	77.22 W
Effort	210	40.56 N	75.26 W
Efiduasi	150	6.51 N	1.24 W
Efkere	130	38.47 N	35.40 E
Eflâni	130	41.26 N	32.57 E
Eforie Nord	38	44.06 N	28.38 E
Eforie Sud	38	44.03 N	28.38 E
Efringen-Kirchen	58	47.39 N	7.34 E
Ega ≃	34	42.19 N	1.55 W
Egadi, Isole II	70	37.58 N	12.16 E
Egan	222	32.28 N	97.17 W
Egaña	252	36.59 S	59.06 W
Egan Range ⋏	204	39.10 N	114.55 W
Eganville	190	45.32 N	77.06 W
Egau ≃	56	48.36 N	10.34 E
Egba □[8]	273a	6.41 N	3.23 E
Egbe, Nig.	150	8.16 N	5.31 E
Egbe, Nig.	273a	6.33 N	3.17 E
Egbunda	154	2.44 N	27.12 E
Egedesminde (Aasiaat)	176	68.42 N	52.45 W
Égée, Mer → Aegean Sea ▾[2]	38	38.30 N	25.00 E
Egegik	180	58.13 N	157.22 W
Egeln	54	51.56 N	11.25 E
Egeo, Mar → Aegean Sea ▾[2]	38	38.30 N	25.00 E
Eger → Cheb, Česká Rep.	54	50.01 N	12.25 E
Eger, Magy.	30	47.54 N	20.23 E
Eger ≃, Dtsch.	56	48.50 N	10.37 E
Eger (Ohře) ≃, Europe	54	50.32 N	14.08 E
Egeria Mountain ∧	182	53.55 N	130.22 W
Egernsund	41	54.54 N	9.37 E
Egerpohl	263	51.07 N	7.27 E
Egersund	26	58.27 N	6.00 E
Egerton	262	53.38 N	2.26 W
Egerton, Mount ∧	9	80.50 S	158.50 E
Egeskov ⊥	41	55.10 N	10.30 E
Egestorf	52	53.11 N	10.04 E
Egestorf [am Süntel]	52	52.17 N	9.31 E
Egg	58	47.26 N	9.54 E
Egg Creek ≃	198	48.22 N	100.47 W
Egge ⋏	52	51.40 N	8.55 E
Eggebek	41	54.37 N	9.22 E
Eggelsberg	60	48.05 N	13.00 E
Eggenberg, Schloss ⊥	61	47.05 N	15.25 E
Eggenburg	61	48.39 N	15.50 E
Eggenfelden	60	48.25 N	12.46 E
Eggenstein-Leopoldshafen	56	49.04 N	8.23 E
Eggerscheid	263	51.19 N	6.53 E
Eggersdorf	54	52.32 N	13.49 E
Eggesin	54	53.41 N	14.05 E
Egg Harbor City	208	39.31 N	74.38 W
Egg Island Point ›	208	39.11 N	75.08 W
Egg Lagoon	166	39.39 S	143.58 E
Egg Lake ⊜, Mb., Can.	184	54.21 N	101.26 W
Egg Lake ⊜, Sk., Can.	184	55.05 N	105.30 W
Egglestone Abbey ψ[1]	44	54.32 N	1.54 W
Egglham	60	48.32 N	13.04 E
Egglkofen	60	48.24 N	12.27 E
Eggmühl	60	48.51 N	12.11 E
Egham	42	51.26 N	0.34 W
Egherta	144	2.04 N	43.11 E
Éghezée	56	50.36 N	4.54 E
Egijn ≃	88	49.24 N	103.36 E
Eğil	130	38.15 N	40.05 E
Egilsay I	46	59.09 N	2.56 W
Egilsstaðir	24a	65.16 N	14.18 W
Eging	60	48.43 N	13.16 E
Egipto → Egypt □[1]	140	27.00 N	30.00 E
Égletons	32	45.24 N	2.03 E
Eglin Air Force Base ■	194	30.29 N	86.30 W
Eglinton	48	55.02 N	7.11 W
Eglisau	58	47.34 N	8.32 E
Egloskerry	42	50.39 N	4.27 W
Égly	261	48.35 N	2.13 E
Egmond aan Zee	52	52.36 N	4.37 E
Egmond-Binnen	52	52.35 N	4.39 E
Egmont, Cape ›	172	39.17 S	173.45 E
Egmont, Mount → Taranaki, Mount ∧	172	39.18 S	174.04 E
Egmont Bay ⊂	186	46.35 N	64.12 W
Egmont Channel ʮ	220	27.36 N	82.45 W
Egmont Key I	220	27.35 N	82.46 W
Egmont National Park ♦	172	39.15 S	174.05 E
Egna (Neumarkt)	64	46.19 N	11.16 E
Egnach	58	47.33 N	9.23 E
Egnazia ⊥	68	40.53 N	17.24 E
Egoryevsk → Jegorjevsk	82	55.23 N	39.02 E
Egota •[8]	268	35.43 N	139.40 E
Egra	126	21.54 N	87.32 E
Egremont, Ab., Can.	182	54.02 N	113.08 W
Egremont, Eng., U.K.	44	54.29 N	3.33 W
Égreville	50	48.10 N	2.52 E
Eğridir	130	37.52 N	30.51 E
Eğridir Gölü ⊜	130	38.02 N	30.53 E
Eğriköy	130	38.44 N	27.21 E
Egrisskij chrebet ⋏	84	42.49 N	42.24 E
Egton	44	54.26 N	0.45 W
Egtved	41	55.37 N	9.18 E
Éguas, Rio das ≃	255	13.26 S	44.14 W
Éguilles	62	43.34 N	5.22 E
Eguisheim	58	48.03 N	7.18 E
Egum Atoll I[1]	164	9.25 S	151.55 E
Egvekinot	180	66.19 N	179.10 W
Egyházasrádóc	61	47.05 N	16.37 E
Egypt, Ma., U.S.	207	42.12 N	70.45 W
Egypt, Pa., U.S.	208	40.41 N	75.32 W
Egypt, Tx., U.S.	222	29.24 N	96.14 W
Egypt (Miṣr) □[1], Afr.	136	27.00 N	30.00 E
Egypt (Miṣr) □[1], Afr.	140	27.00 N	30.00 E
Egypt, Lake of ⊜[1]	194	37.35 N	88.55 W
Égypte → Egypt □[1]	140	27.00 N	30.00 E
Egyptian Museum ψ	273c	30.03 N	31.14 E
Eha-Amufu	150	6.40 N	7.46 E
Ehekirchen	60	48.38 N	11.06 E
Ehen ≃	44	54.25 N	3.30 W
Ehime □[5]	96	33.40 N	132.50 E
Ehingen	58	48.17 N	9.43 E
Ehingen •[8]	263	51.22 N	6.42 E
Ehle ≃	54	52.12 N	11.44 E
Ehmen	54	52.24 N	10.41 E
Ehra-Lessien	54	52.34 N	10.46 E
Ehrang	56	49.49 N	6.41 E
Ehrenberg	200	33.36 N	114.31 W
Ehrenberg Range ⋏	162	23.18 S	130.20 E
Ehrenbreitstein, Feste ⊥	56	50.21 N	7.37 E
Ehrenburg ⊥	56	50.12 N	7.27 E
Ehrenfeld	214	40.22 N	78.46 W
Ehrenfriedersdorf	54	50.38 N	12.58 E
Ehrenhausen	61	46.43 N	15.35 E
Ehreshoven	56	50.58 N	7.20 E
Ehrhardt	192	33.05 N	81.00 W
Ehrhorn	52	53.10 N	9.53 E
Ehringhausen	263	51.11 N	7.33 E
Ehringhausen •[8]	263	51.09 N	7.11 E
Ehrwald	64	47.24 N	10.55 E
Ehwa Women's University ψ[2]	271b	37.34 N	126.56 E
Ei	92	31.12 N	130.30 E
Eibar	34	43.11 N	2.28 W
Eibau	54	50.58 N	14.40 E
Eibelstadt	56	49.43 N	10.00 E
Eibenstock	54	50.29 N	12.35 E
Eibergen	52	52.06 N	6.39 E
Eibiswald	61	46.41 N	15.15 E
Eibsee ⊜	64	47.27 N	10.58 E
Eicha	54	50.21 N	10.34 E
Eich-Berg ∧[2]	264a	52.39 N	13.50 E
Eiche, Dtsch.	264a	52.34 N	13.36 E
Eiche, Dtsch.	264a	52.25 N	12.58 E
Eichenbarleben	54	52.10 N	11.24 E
Eichenbrandt	264a	52.38 N	13.51 E
Eichendorf	60	48.38 N	12.51 E
Eichgraben	61	48.10 N	15.59 E
Eichlinghofen •[8]	263	51.29 N	7.24 E
Eichsfeld •[1]	56	51.20 N	10.10 E
Eichstädt	264a	52.42 N	13.07 E
Eichstätt	60	48.54 N	11.12 E
Eichstetten	58	48.05 N	7.44 E
Eichtersheim	56	49.14 N	8.46 E
Eichwalde	54	52.22 N	13.37 E
Eickelborn	52	51.39 N	8.13 E
Eicken •[8]	263	51.13 N	6.26 E
Eickerend	263	51.13 N	6.34 E
Eickerkopf ∧[2]	263	51.21 N	7.42 E
Eicklingen	52	52.33 N	10.10 E
Eide	26	62.55 N	7.26 E
Eidelstedt •[8]	52	53.36 N	9.53 E
Eider ≃	41	54.19 N	8.58 E

Symbols in the index entries represent the broad categories identified in the key at the right. Symbols with superior numbers (⋏[1]) identify subcategories (see complete key on page *I · 1*).

Symbole im Register stellen die rechts im Schlüssel erklärten Kategorien dar. Symbole mit hochgestellten Ziffern (⋏[1]) bezeichnen Unterabteilungen einer Kategorie (vgl. vollständiger Schlüssel auf Seite *I · 1*).

Los símbolos incluídos en el texto del índice representan las grandes categorías identificadas con la clave a la derecha. Los símbolos con numeros en su parte superior (⋏[1]) identifican las subcategorías (véase la clave completa en la página *I · 1*).

Les symboles de l'index représentent les catégories indiquées dans la légende à droite. Les symboles suivis d'un indice (⋏[1]) représentent des sous-catégories (voir légende complète à la page *I · 1*).

Os símbolos incluídos no texto do índice representam as grandes categorias identificadas com a chave à direita. Os símbolos com números em sua parte superior (⋏[1]) identificam as subcategorias (veja-se a chave completa à página *I · 1*).

	English	Deutsch	Español	Français	Português
∧	Mountain	Berg	Montaña	Montagne	Montanha
⋏	Mountains	Gebirge	Montañas	Montagnes	Montanhas
)(	Pass	Paß	Paso	Col	Passo
V	Valley, Canyon	Tal, Cañon	Valle, Cañón	Vallée, Canyon	Vale, Canhão
≚	Plain	Ebene	Llano	Plaine	Planície
›	Cape	Kap	Cabo	Cap	Cabo
I	Island	Insel	Isla	Île	Ilha
II	Islands	Inseln	Islas	Îles	Ilhas
⊥	Other Topographic Features	Andere Topographische Objekte	Otros Elementos Topográficos	Autres données topographiques	Outros acidentes topográficos

ESPAÑOL — Nombre | Página | Lat.°′ | Long.°′ W = Oeste

FRANÇAIS — Nom | Page | Lat.°′ | Long.°′ W = Ouest

PORTUGUÊS — Nome | Página | Lat.°′ | Long.°′ W = Oeste

Eiderstedt ›[1]	41	54.22 N	8.50 E
Eidfjord	26	60.28 N	7.05 E
Eidsvåg, Nor.	26	60.27 N	5.21 E
Eidsvåg, Nor.	26	62.47 N	8.03 E
Eidsvold	166	25.22 S	151.07 E
Eidsvoll	26	60.19 N	11.14 E
Eifa	56	50.58 N	8.34 E
Eifel ⩘	56	50.15 N	6.45 E
Eiffel, Tour ⊥	261	48.51 N	2.18 E
Eiffel Flats	154	18.15 S	29.59 E
Eifgenbach ≃	263	51.05 N	7.09 E
Eige, Carn ∧	46	57.17 N	5.07 W
Eigen ◆[8]	263	51.33 N	6.57 E
Eigenji	94	35.04 N	136.18 E
Eigenrieden	54	51.11 N	10.22 E
Eiger ∧	58	46.35 N	8.00 E
Eigg I	46	56.54 N	6.10 W
Eigg, Sound of ⊎	46	56.51 N	6.13 W
Eight Degree Channel ⊎	122	8.00 N	73.00 E
Eighteenmile Creek ≃, N.Y., U.S.	210	43.21 N	78.43 W
Eighteenmile Creek ≃, N.Y., U.S.	210	42.43 N	78.58 W
Eight Mile Creek ≃, On., Can.	284a	43.14 N	79.11 W
Eightmile Creek ≃, In., U.S.	216	40.57 N	85.22 W
Eightmile Creek ≃, Or., U.S.	224	45.36 N	121.05 W
Eights Coast ⩦[2]	9	73.30 S	93.00 W
Eighty Four	279b	40.11 N	80.08 W
Eighty Mile Beach ⩦[2]	162	19.45 S	121.00 E
Eiheiji	94	36.05 N	136.20 E
Eijerlandsche Gat ⊂	52	53.12 N	4.50 E
Eijsden	56	50.47 N	5.43 E
Eikeren ⊜	26	59.38 N	9.58 E
Eikisdalsvatnet ⊜	26	62.34 N	8.11 E
Eildon	169	37.14 S	145.56 E
Eildon, Lake ⊜[1]	169	37.11 S	145.55 E
Eilean Gowan Island I	212	45.02 N	79.25 W
Eileen	216	41.17 N	88.15 W
Eilenburg	54	51.27 N	12.37 E
Eil Malk I	175b	7.09 N	134.22 E
Eilsleben	54	52.09 N	11.13 E
Eimbeckhausen	52	52.14 N	9.25 E
Eimke	52	52.58 N	10.19 E
Eina	26	60.38 N	10.36 E
Einasleigh	166	18.31 S	144.05 E
Einasleigh ≃	166	17.30 S	142.17 E
Einbeck	52	51.49 N	9.52 E
Eindhoven	52	51.26 N	5.28 E
Eine	50	50.52 N	3.37 E
Einme	110	16.54 N	95.11 E
Einöd	56	49.16 N	7.19 E
Einödriegel ∧	60	48.56 N	13.02 E
Einruhr	56	50.35 N	6.22 E
Einsiedel	54	50.46 N	12.58 E
Einsiedeln	58	47.08 N	8.45 E
Einville-au-Jard	58	48.39 N	6.30 E
Eirauli	272c	19.10 N	72.59 E
Éire → Ireland □[1]	48	53.00 N	8.00 W
Eiru ≃	248	6.42 S	69.52 W
Eirunepé	248	6.40 S	69.52 W
Eisbach ≃	56	49.38 N	8.22 E
Eisch ≃	56	49.45 N	6.07 E
Eiseb ≃	156	20.33 S	20.59 E
Eisenach	54	50.59 N	10.19 E
Eisenberg, Dtsch.	54	50.58 N	11.53 E
Eisenberg, Dtsch.	56	49.38 N	8.05 E
Eisenberg ∧[2]	61	47.12 N	16.24 E
Eisenerz	61	47.33 N	14.53 E
Eisenerzer Alpen ⩘	61	47.28 N	14.45 E
Eisenhower Center ▿	198	38.54 N	97.12 W
Eisenhower Memorial Park ♠	276	40.44 N	73.34 W
Eisenhüttenstadt	54	52.10 N	14.39 E
Eisenkappel	61	46.29 N	14.35 E
Eisenschmitt	56	50.03 N	6.43 E
Eisenstadt	61	47.51 N	16.32 E
Eisfeld	54	50.26 N	10.54 E
Eisgarn	61	48.54 N	15.06 E
Eishken	46	58.01 N	6.32 W
Eishort, Loch ⊂	46	57.10 N	5.59 W
Eišiškės	76	54.10 N	25.00 E
Eisk → Jejsk	78	46.42 N	38.16 E
Eisleben	54	51.31 N	11.32 E
Eislingen	56	48.42 N	9.42 E
Eisriesenwelt ⩦[5]	64	47.32 N	13.10 E
Eita	174t	1.21 N	173.05 E
Eitorf	56	50.46 N	7.26 E
Eivissa	34	38.54 N	1.26 E
Eivissa (Ibiza) I	34	39.00 N	1.25 E
Ejasi → Eyasi, Lake ⊜	154	3.40 S	35.05 E
Ejby, Dan.	41	55.30 N	12.07 E
Ejby, Dan.	41	55.26 N	9.57 E
Ejea de los Caballeros	34	42.08 N	1.08 W
Ejeda	157b	24.20 S	44.31 E
Ejército Rebelde, Presa ⊜[1]	286b	23.01 N	82.20 W
Ejido	246	8.33 N	71.14 W
Ejido Jaboncillos	232	28.57 N	102.39 W
Ejigbo	273a	6.33 N	3.18 E
Ejin Horo Qi	102	39.27 N	109.40 E
Ejin Qi	102	41.50 N	100.50 E
Ejstrup	41	55.59 N	9.17 E
Ejura	150	7.23 N	1.22 W
Ejutla de Crespo	234	16.34 N	96.44 W
Ekalaka	198	45.53 N	104.33 W
Ekáli	267c	38.07 N	23.50 E
Ekanga	152	2.23 S	23.14 E
Ekas	115b	8.53 S	116.27 E
Ekaterinburg → Jekaterinburg	86	56.51 N	60.36 E
Ekaterinodar → Krasnodar	78	45.02 N	39.00 E
Ekaterinoslav → Dnipropetrovs'k	78	48.27 N	34.59 E
Ekeby	41	56.00 N	12.58 E
Ekenäs (Taamisaari)	26	59.58 N	23.26 E
Ekenässjön	26	57.30 N	15.00 E
Ekerö I	40	59.18 N	17.43 E
Eket, Nig.	150	4.39 N	7.56 E
Eket, Sve.	41	56.15 N	13.11 E
Eketahuna	172	40.39 S	175.42 E
Ekhínos	38	41.17 N	24.59 E
Ekiatapskij chrebet ⩘	74	68.30 N	179.00 E
Ekibastuz	86	51.42 N	75.22 E
Ekimčan	89	53.04 N	132.58 E
Ekitykskij chrebet ⩘	180	67.45 N	179.00 E
Eko → Lagos	150	6.27 N	3.24 E
Ekoli	152	0.23 S	24.16 E
Ekoln ⊜	40	59.45 N	17.37 E
Ekolsund	40	59.37 N	17.22 E
Ekolsundsviken ⊂	40	59.35 N	17.24 E
Ekombe	152	1.16 N	21.36 E
Ekonda	74	65.47 N	105.17 E
Ekoungounou	152	0.33 S	15.38 E
Ekovamou	152	0.07 N	16.31 E
Ekpoma	150	6.46 N	6.08 E
Eksāra	272b	22.38 N	88.17 E
Eksel	56	51.09 N	5.23 E
Eksjö	26	57.40 N	14.57 E
Ekuk	180	58.49 N	158.34 W
Ekuku	152	0.42 S	21.38 E
Ekuta	152	2.59 N	18.42 E
Ekwan ≃	176	53.14 N	82.13 W
Ekwata	152	0.13 S	9.18 E
Ekwendeni	154	11.23 S	33.50 E
Ekwok	180	59.22 N	157.30 W
El- → Ad-, Al-, An-, Ar-, As-, Ash-, At-, Az-			
Ela	110	19.37 N	96.13 E
El Aaiún (La'youn)	148	27.09 N	13.12 W
El Abiadh Sidi Cheikh	148	32.56 N	0.42 E
El 'Açâba □[4]	150	16.10 N	11.30 W
El 'Açâba ⩘[1]	150	16.00 N	12.00 W
El Adde	144	2.35 N	46.09 E
El Adeb Larache	148	27.22 N	8.52 E
El Adelanto	236	14.10 N	89.50 W
El Affroun	34	36.30 N	2.38 E
El Agreb	148	30.48 N	5.30 E
El Aguacate	286c	10.28 N	66.59 W
El Aguacate ≃	234	18.16 N	100.40 W
El Aguilar	252	23.12 S	65.42 W
El Agustino	286d	12.03 S	76.59 W
El Agustino, Cerro ∧[2]	286d	12.04 S	77.00 W
Elaine	194	34.18 N	90.51 W
El Alamein → Al-'Alamayn	140	30.49 N	28.57 E
El Álamo, Méx.	196	27.32 N	100.52 W
El Álamo, Méx.	196	26.29 N	99.46 W
El Álamo, Méx.	204	31.34 N	116.02 W
El Alia	36	37.10 N	10.03 E
El Alto, Arg.	252	28.18 S	65.22 W
El Alto, Perú	246	4.18 S	81.07 W
Elam	285	39.51 N	75.32 W
Elamanchili	122	17.33 N	82.52 E
El Amparo de Apure	246	7.06 N	70.45 W
Elan ≃, Rom.	38	46.07 N	28.04 E
Elan ≃, Wales, U.K.	42	52.17 N	3.31 W
Élancourt	261	48.47 N	1.58 E
Elands ≃, S. Afr.	156	25.10 S	29.10 E
Elands ≃, S. Afr.	158	25.31 S	26.39 E
Elandsbaai	158	32.19 S	18.21 E
Elandsfontein	273d	26.10 S	28.12 E
Elandsvlei	158	32.19 S	19.33 E
El Angel	246	0.37 N	77.56 W
Elanora Heights	274a	33.42 S	151.17 E
El Aouinet	36	35.52 N	7.54 E
El Arahal	34	37.16 N	5.33 W
El Arba	34	36.37 N	3.13 E
El Arco	232	28.00 N	113.25 W
El Arenal	234	20.47 N	103.42 W
El Aricha	148	34.09 N	1.10 W
El Aroussa	36	36.22 N	9.28 E
El Arrayán	286e	33.21 S	70.28 W
Elassón	38	39.54 N	22.11 E
Elat	132	29.33 N	34.57 E
Elat, Gulf of → Aqaba, Gulf of ⊂	128	29.00 N	34.40 E
Elat, Sede Te'ufa ⊠	132	29.34 N	34.55 E
El Avagi	144	3.36 N	46.57 E
El Ávila, Cerro ∧	286c	10.33 N	66.52 W
El Ávila, Parque Nacional ♠	246	10.35 N	66.48 W
Elazığ	130	38.41 N	39.14 E
Elazığ □[4]	130	38.35 N	39.30 E
El Azúcar, Presa de ⊜[1]	196	26.10 N	99.00 W
El Azul, Sierra ⩘	234	23.25 N	100.30 W
Elba, Al., U.S.	194	31.24 N	86.04 W
Elba, Mi., U.S.	216	43.02 N	83.26 W
Elba, N.Y., U.S.	210	43.04 N	78.11 W
Elba → Elbe ≃	30	53.50 N	9.00 E
Elba, Isola d' I	66	42.46 N	10.17 E
El'ban	89	50.06 N	136.31 E
El Banco	246	9.00 N	73.58 W
El Barco de Avila	34	40.21 N	5.31 W
El Barco de Valdeorras	34	42.25 N	6.59 W
El Barreal	200	31.17 N	107.10 W
El Barril	234	23.02 N	102.08 W
Elbasan	38	41.06 N	20.05 E
Elbaşı	130	38.41 N	35.59 E
El Baúl	246	8.57 N	68.17 W
El Baúl, Cerro ∧, Méx.	234	16.36 N	94.13 W
El Baúl, Cerro ∧, Méx.	234	17.38 N	100.19 W
Elbe	224	46.45 N	121.49 W
Elbe (Labe) ≃	30	53.50 N	9.00 E
Elbe, Île d' → Elba, Isola di I	66	42.46 N	10.17 E
Elbe-Havel-Kanal ≊	54	52.24 N	12.23 E
El Beïd (Ebeji) ≃	146	12.32 N	14.11 E
El-Beida → Al-Bayḍā'	146	32.46 N	21.43 E
Elbe-Lübeck-Kanal ≊	54	53.50 N	10.36 E
Elberfeld ◆[8]	263	51.16 N	7.08 E
Elbert	198	39.13 N	104.32 W
Elbert, Mount ∧	200	39.07 N	106.27 W
Elberta	190	44.37 N	86.13 W
Elberton	192	34.06 N	82.52 W
Elbeuf	50	49.17 N	1.00 E
Elbeyli	130	36.41 N	37.26 E
El Beyyadh	148	33.40 N	1.01 E
Elbing → Elbląg	30	54.10 N	19.25 E
Elbingerode	54	51.45 N	10.46 E
Elbistan	130	38.13 N	37.12 E
Elbląg (Elbing)	30	54.10 N	19.25 E
Elbląg □[4]	30	54.00 N	19.30 E
El Bluff	236	11.59 N	83.40 W
El Bolsón	254	41.58 S	71.31 W
El Bonillo	34	38.57 N	2.32 W
El-Borj	34	35.43 N	5.40 W
El-Borouj	148	32.30 N	7.10 W
El Bosque, Chile	286e	33.34 S	70.41 W
El Bosque, Méx.	234	17.04 N	92.44 W
El Boulaïda	148	36.28 N	2.50 E
El Boulaïda □[5]	148	36.20 N	2.20 E
Elbow	184	51.07 N	106.35 W
Elbow ≃	182	51.03 N	114.02 W
Elbow Cay I	238	23.57 N	80.29 W
Elbow Lake	198	45.59 N	95.58 W
Elbow Lake ⊜	184	54.50 N	100.53 W
Elbridge	210	43.02 N	76.27 W
El'brus, gora (Mount Elbrus) ∧	84	43.21 N	42.26 E
Elbrus, Mount → El'brus, gora ∧	84	43.21 N	42.26 E
El'brusskij	84	43.38 N	42.10 E
Elbsandsteingebirge ⩘	54	50.50 N	14.20 E
Elburg	52	52.26 N	5.50 E
El Burgo de Osma	34	41.35 N	3.04 W
Elburn	216	41.53 N	88.28 W
Elburz Mountains → Alborz, Reshteh-ye Kūhhā-ye ⩘	128	36.00 N	53.00 E
El'buzd	83	46.53 N	39.41 E
El'buzd ≃	83	46.53 N	39.43 E
El Cabezo, Arrecife ✣[2]	234	19.04 N	95.51 W
El Caburé	252	26.01 S	62.22 W
El Caimanero, Laguna ⊂	234	23.00 N	106.07 W
El Cajon	228	32.47 N	116.57 W
El Cajón, Embalse ⊜[1]	236	15.00 N	87.35 W
El Calafate	254	50.20 S	72.18 W
El Callao	246	7.21 N	61.49 W
El Calvario, Col.	246	4.22 N	73.40 W
El Calvario, Ven.	246	8.59 N	67.00 W
El Calvario ◆[8]	286b	23.05 N	82.20 W
El Campamento	240m	18.22 N	66.28 W
El Campamento ◆[8]	266a	40.24 N	3.46 W
El Campo	222	29.11 N	96.16 W
El Capitan ∧, Ca., U.S.	226	37.43 N	119.38 W
El Capitan ∧, Mt., U.S.	202	46.01 N	114.23 W
El Caracol Depósito de Evaporación Solar ▿[3]	286a	19.35 N	99.00 W
El Caribe	286c	10.37 N	66.50 W
El Carmen, Arg.	252	24.23 S	65.16 W
El Cármen, Bol.	248	18.49 S	58.33 W
El Carmen, Chile	286e	33.21 S	70.43 W
El Carmen, Col.	246	8.30 N	73.27 W
El Carmen, Méx.	234	15.35 N	93.05 W
El Carmen, Perú	248	13.30 S	76.04 W
El Carmen, Ven.	286c	10.24 N	67.01 W
El Carmen, Ven.	286c	10.24 N	66.50 W
El Carmen ≃	232	30.42 N	106.29 W
El Carmen, Canal ≊	286e	33.18 S	70.41 W
El Carmen, Laguna ⊂	234	18.17 N	93.48 W
El Carmen de Bolívar	246	9.43 N	75.08 W
El Carricito	232	28.24 N	103.23 W
El Carril	252	25.05 S	65.28 W
El Casco	196	25.34 N	104.35 W
El Castillo de La Concepción	236	11.01 N	84.24 W
El Cedral	236	16.26 N	90.03 W
El Cedrito	232	29.11 N	101.59 W
El Cenajo, Embalse de ⊜[1]	34	38.25 N	2.00 W
El Centinela	204	32.38 N	115.40 W
El Centinela, Cerro ∧	234	19.13 N	104.17 W
El Centro	204	32.47 N	115.33 W
El Cerrito, Col.	246	3.42 N	76.19 W
El Cerrito, Ca., U.S.	226	37.54 N	122.18 W
El Cerrito, Ca., U.S.	228	37.54 N	122.18 W
El Cerro, Bol.	248	17.31 S	61.34 W
El Cerro, Ur.	258	34.00 S	58.15 W
El Cerro Del Aripo ∧	241r	10.43 N	61.15 W
El Chamal	234	23.56 N	97.54 W
El Chante	234	19.41 N	104.10 W
Elche → Elx	34	38.15 N	0.42 W
Elche de la Sierra	34	38.27 N	2.03 W
El Chichonal, Volcán ∧[1]	234	17.22 N	93.14 W
El Chile, Montaña ∧	236	14.22 N	86.51 W
El'chkakvun ≃	180	68.42 N	171.00 E
Elcho	190	45.26 N	89.11 W
Elcho Island I	164	11.55 S	135.45 E
El Chorrillo	252	33.18 S	66.16 W
El Ciprés	204	31.50 N	116.38 W
El Cobre	240p	20.03 N	75.57 W
El Cocuy	246	6.25 N	72.27 W
El Cojo	286c	10.37 N	66.53 W
El Cojo, Quebrada ≃	286c	10.37 N	66.53 W
El Colorado	252	26.18 S	59.22 W
El Cóndor, Cerro ∧	252	26.38 S	68.22 W
El Congo	236	13.54 N	89.30 W
El Corazón	246	1.12 S	79.06 W
El Corcovado	254	43.32 S	71.36 W
El Corozo	286c	10.35 N	66.58 W
El Corpus	236	13.16 N	87.03 W
El Corte ≃	234	17.03 N	94.54 W
El Corte de Madera Creek ≃	282	37.19 N	122.20 W
El Cortijo	286e	33.22 S	70.42 W
El Coto	240m	18.28 N	66.44 W
El Coyote	200	30.50 N	112.40 W
El Coyote ≃	232	30.32 N	113.02 W
El Coyote, Laguna ⊜	196	27.14 N	103.18 W
El Cozón	232	31.18 N	112.29 W
El Cristo	240p	20.07 N	75.45 W
El Cubo → Casigua	246	8.46 N	72.30 W
El Cuco	236	13.10 N	88.07 W
El Cuervo, Laguna ⊜	232	29.17 N	105.57 W
El Cuidado	234	22.20 N	103.07 W
El Cuy	254	39.56 S	68.20 W
Elda	34	38.29 N	0.47 W
Eldagsen	52	52.10 N	9.40 E
El Dambahaddo	144	3.17 N	46.40 E
El Dátil	232	30.07 N	112.15 W
Elde ≃	54	53.14 N	11.27 E
Eldekanal ≊	54	53.24 N	11.36 E
Eldena, Dtsch.	54	53.13 N	11.25 E
Eldena, Dtsch.	54	54.05 N	13.26 E
El Der ∨	144	8.49 N	47.28 E
El Dere	144	5.07 N	43.10 E
Elder Island I	276	40.38 N	73.23 W
Elder Mills	275b	43.49 N	79.38 W
Eldersville	214	40.21 N	80.29 W
Elderton	214	40.42 N	79.21 W
El Descanso	204	32.12 N	116.55 W
El Desemboque, Méx.	232	29.30 N	112.27 W
El Desemboque, Méx.	232	30.30 N	112.59 W
Eldforsen	40	60.26 N	14.13 E
El'dikan	74	60.48 N	135.11 E
Eldingen	52	52.41 N	10.21 E
Eld Inlet ⊂	224	47.04 N	123.01 W
Eldivan	130	40.32 N	33.31 E
El Diviso	246	1.22 N	78.14 W
El Djazaïr (Algiers)	148	36.47 N	3.03 E
El Djazaïr □[5]	148	36.50 N	3.00 E
El Djelfa	148	34.40 N	3.15 E
El Djelfa □[5]	148	35.20 N	3.50 E
El Doce	234	17.13 N	94.03 W
Eldon, Ia., U.S.	190	40.55 N	92.13 W
Eldon, Mo., U.S.	194	38.20 N	92.34 W
Eldon Hazlet State Park ♠	219	38.39 N	89.22 W
Eldora, Ia., U.S.	190	42.21 N	93.05 W
Eldora, Pa., U.S.	279b	40.10 N	79.53 W
Eldorado, Arg.	252	26.24 S	54.38 W
Eldorado, Bra.	252	24.32 S	48.06 W
El Dorado, Méx.	232	24.17 N	107.21 W
El Dorado, Ar., U.S.	194	33.12 N	92.39 W
El Dorado, Ca., U.S.	226	38.41 N	120.51 W
Eldorado, Il., U.S.	194	37.48 N	88.26 W
El Dorado, Ks., U.S.	198	37.49 N	96.51 W
Eldorado, Oh., U.S.	218	39.54 N	84.40 W
Eldorado, Ok., U.S.	196	34.28 N	99.38 W
Eldorado, Tx., U.S.	196	30.51 N	100.36 W
El Dorado, Ven.	246	6.44 N	61.38 W
El Dorado □[6]	226	38.43 N	120.48 W
Eldorado Hills	226	38.37 N	120.27 W
Eldoradopark	273d	26.18 S	27.53 E
El Dorado Park ♠	280	33.49 N	118.05 W
Eldorado Peak ∧	224	48.32 N	121.08 W
El Dorado Springs	194	37.52 N	94.01 W
Eldoret	154	0.31 N	35.17 E
Eldred, Il., U.S.	219	39.17 N	90.33 W
Eldred, N.Y., U.S.	210	41.32 N	74.53 W
Eldred, Pa., U.S.	214	41.57 N	78.23 W
Eldridge	190	41.39 N	90.35 W
Eldridge, Mount ∧	180	64.46 N	141.48 W
Eldridges Hill	285	39.40 N	75.18 W
El Dudu	144	2.37 N	41.46 E
El Durazno, Arroyo ≃	258	34.41 S	58.52 W
Eleanor	188	38.32 N	81.55 W
Eleanor, Lake ⊜[1]	226	37.59 N	119.51 W
Eleasar	158	26.40 S	26.53 E
Electra	196	34.01 N	98.55 W
Electric City	202	47.56 N	119.02 W
Eleele	229b	21.55 N	159.35 W
Elefante, Isla del → Elephant Island I	9	61.10 S	55.14 W
Elefantes, Estero ⊂[2]	254	46.10 S	73.41 W
Elefantes, Rio dos (Olifants) ≃	156	24.10 S	32.40 E
Elegest ≃	88	51.32 N	94.05 E
El Eglab ◆[2]	148	26.25 N	5.00 W
Elei, Wādī ∨	140	22.04 N	34.27 E
Eleja	76	56.26 N	23.42 E
Elektrogorsk	82	55.53 N	38.47 E
Elektrostal'	82	55.47 N	38.28 E
Elektrougli	82	55.43 N	38.13 E
Elektrozavod	80	52.34 N	54.01 E
Elele	150	5.07 N	6.48 E
Elena	38	42.56 N	25.53 E
El Encantado	286c	10.27 N	66.47 W
El Encanto, Col.	246	1.37 S	73.14 W
El Encanto, Guat.	232	17.17 N	89.34 W
Elend	54	51.44 N	10.41 E
Elepete	273a	6.41 N	3.28 E
Elephant, Mount ∧[2]	169	37.58 S	143.12 E
Elephanta Caves ⩦[5]	272c	18.58 N	72.56 E
Elephanta Island (Ghārāpuri) I	272c	18.57 N	72.55 E
Elephant Butte Lake State Park ♠	200	33.11 N	107.14 W
Elephant Butte Reservoir ⊜[1]	200	33.19 N	107.10 W
Elephant Island I	9	61.10 S	55.14 W
Elephant Lake ⊜	212	45.08 N	78.07 W
Elephant Mountain ∧	188	44.46 N	70.46 W
Elesbão Veloso	250	6.13 S	42.08 W
Eleşkirt	130	39.48 N	42.42 E
El Espinal	234	16.29 N	95.03 W
El Estor	236	15.32 N	89.21 W
Elets → Jelec	76	52.37 N	38.30 E
El Eulma	148	36.08 N	5.40 E
Eleusis → Elevsís	38	38.02 N	23.32 E
Eleutério	256	22.19 S	46.43 W
Eleutero ≃	70	38.06 N	13.29 E
Eleuthera I	238	25.10 N	76.14 W
Eleuthera Point ›	238	24.40 N	76.11 W
Eleva	190	44.34 N	91.28 W
Eleven Point ≃	194	36.09 N	91.05 W
Elevsínos, Kólpos ⊂	267c	38.02 N	23.34 E
Elevsís	38	38.02 N	23.32 E
Elevtheroúpolis	38	40.55 N	24.16 E
El Fahs	36	36.22 N	9.55 E
El Faro	240m	18.00 N	66.47 W
Elfenbeinküste → Cote d'Ivoire □[1]	150	8.00 N	5.00 W
El Ferrol del Caudillo	34	43.29 N	8.14 W
Elfers	220	28.13 N	82.43 W
Elfgen	263	51.05 N	6.32 E
Elfin Cove	180	58.12 N	136.20 W
Elfrida	200	31.41 N	109.41 W
Elfros	184	51.43 N	103.52 W
El Fud	144	7.20 N	42.50 E
El Fuerte	232	26.25 N	108.39 W
El Galpón	252	25.23 S	64.38 W
Elgershausen	56	51.16 N	9.22 E
El Ghazawet	148	35.06 N	1.51 W
Elgin, Austl.	168a	33.31 S	115.37 E
Elgin, On., Can.	212	44.36 N	76.13 W
Elgin, Scot., U.K.	46	57.39 N	3.20 W
Elgin, Il., U.S.	216	42.02 N	88.16 W
Elgin, Ia., U.S.	190	42.57 N	91.37 W
Elgin, Mn., U.S.	190	44.07 N	92.15 W
Elgin, Ne., U.S.	198	41.59 N	98.05 W
Elgin, N.D., U.S.	198	46.24 N	101.50 W
Elgin, Oh., U.S.	216	40.44 N	84.28 W
Elgin, Ok., U.S.	196	34.46 N	98.17 W
Elgin, Or., U.S.	202	45.33 N	117.54 W
Elgin, Pa., U.S.	214	41.54 N	79.45 W
Elgin, Tx., U.S.	222	30.20 N	97.22 W
Elgin □[6]	214	42.42 N	81.15 W
Elgin, Lake ⊜	206	45.45 N	71.20 W
Elgol	46	57.09 N	6.06 W
El Golfete ⊜	236	15.44 N	88.53 W
El Goloso ◆[8]	266a	40.33 N	3.42 W
Elgon, Mount ∧	154	1.08 N	34.33 E
Elgoras, gora ∧	24	68.06 N	31.30 E
El Granada	226	37.30 N	122.28 W
El Grara	148	32.46 N	4.34 E
El Grove	34	42.30 N	8.52 W
El Grullo	234	19.48 N	104.13 W
El Guaje	232	27.52 N	103.18 W
El Guaje, Laguna ⊜	232	28.00 N	103.13 W
El Guamo	246	10.02 N	74.59 W
El Guanábano	286c	10.24 N	67.01 W
El Guapo	246	10.09 N	65.58 W
El Guarapo	286c	10.36 N	66.58 W
El Guayabo de Abajo	232	26.00 N	107.26 W
El Guayaneco, Parque Nacional ♠	254	48.15 S	75.30 W
El'gygytgyn, ozero ⊜	180	67.30 N	172.00 E
El Hadjar	36	36.48 N	7.45 E
Elham	42	51.10 N	1.07 E
El Ḥammâmi ◆[1]	148	23.03 N	11.30 W
El Hank ⩦[4]	148	24.30 N	7.00 W
El Haouaria	36	37.03 N	11.02 E
El Hatillo	286c	10.26 N	66.49 W
El Hatillo, Quebrada ≃	286c	10.27 N	66.47 W
El Havre → Le Havre	50	49.30 N	0.08 E
El Higo	234	21.46 N	98.28 W
Elhovo	38	42.10 N	26.34 E
El Huecú	252	37.37 S	70.36 W
El Huisache	234	22.55 N	100.25 W
Eliase	164	8.21 S	130.47 E
Elías Romero	258	34.46 S	58.52 W
Eliasville	196	32.57 N	98.46 W
Elida, N.M., U.S.	196	33.56 N	103.39 W
Elida, Oh., U.S.	216	40.47 N	84.12 W
El Ídolo, Isla I	234	21.25 N	97.27 W
El Idrissia	148	34.30 N	2.37 E
Elila	154	2.43 S	25.53 E
Elila ≃	154	2.45 S	25.53 E
Elim, Namibia	156	17.48 S	15.31 E
Elim, S. Afr.	158	34.35 S	19.45 E
Elim, Ak., U.S.	180	64.37 N	162.15 W
Elimsport	210	41.08 N	77.02 W
El Infiernillo, Canal ⊎	232	29.09 N	112.15 W
Elingampangu	152	2.03 S	24.02 E
Elin Pelin	38	42.40 N	23.36 E
Eliot	188	43.09 N	70.48 W
Elipa	152	0.53 S	24.34 E
Elisabeth-Sophien-Koog	41	54.30 N	8.53 E
Élisabethville, Fr.	261	48.58 N	1.51 E
Élisabethville → Lubumbashi, Zaïre	154	11.40 S	27.28 E
Elisenvaara	24	61.25 N	29.46 E
Eliseu Martins	250	8.13 S	43.42 W
Elista	80	46.16 N	44.14 E
Elizabeth, Austl.	168b	34.43 S	138.40 E
Elizabeth, Co., U.S.	200	39.21 N	104.35 W
Elizabeth, Il., U.S.	190	42.19 N	90.13 W
Elizabeth, La., U.S.	194	30.52 N	92.47 W
Elizabeth, N.J., U.S.	210	40.39 N	74.12 W
Elizabeth, Pa., U.S.	214	40.16 N	79.53 W
Elizabeth, W.V., U.S.	188	39.03 N	81.23 W
Elizabeth ≃, N.J., U.S.	276	40.38 N	74.12 W
Elizabeth ≃, Va., U.S.	208	36.54 N	76.20 W
Elizabeth, Bahía ⊂	246a	0.38 S	91.27 W
Elizabeth, Cape ›	224	47.22 N	124.22 W
Elizabeth, Lake ⊜[1]	282	37.33 N	121.58 W
Elizabeth, West Branch ≃	276	40.42 N	74.14 W
Elizabeth Bay ⊂	156	27.04 S	15.11 E
Elizabeth City	192	36.18 N	76.13 W
Elizabeth Creek ≃	222	33.02 N	97.14 W
Elizabeth Islands II	207	41.27 N	70.47 W
Elizabeth Lake ⊜	281	42.38 N	83.23 W
Elizabeth Lake Estates	281	42.38 N	83.22 W
Elizabeth Park ♠	281	42.07 N	83.11 W
Elizabeth Reef I[1]	160	29.56 S	159.04 E
Elizabethton	192	36.20 N	82.12 W
Elizabethtown, Il., U.S.	194	37.26 N	88.18 W
Elizabethtown, In., U.S.	218	39.08 N	85.48 W
Elizabethtown, Ky., U.S.	194	37.41 N	85.51 W
Elizabethtown, N.Y., U.S.	188	44.12 N	73.35 W
Elizabethtown, N.C., U.S.	192	34.37 N	78.36 W
Elizabethtown, Pa., U.S.	208	40.09 N	76.36 W
Elizabethville	208	40.32 N	76.48 W
Eliza Howell Park ♠	281	42.24 N	83.16 W
Elizaville, In., U.S.	218	40.08 N	86.24 W
Elizaville, N.Y., U.S.	210	42.03 N	73.48 W
El-Jadida (Mazagan)	148	33.16 N	8.30 W
El-Jadida □[4]	148	33.00 N	8.40 W
El Jaralito	232	26.07 N	104.10 W
El Jebel	200	39.23 N	107.05 W
El-Jebha	34	35.13 N	4.38 W
El Jem	148	35.18 N	10.43 E
El Jícaro ≃	236	13.31 N	86.00 W
El Jobean	220	26.58 N	82.13 W
El Juile	234	17.45 N	94.59 W
Ełk	30	53.50 N	22.22 E
Elk □[6]	214	41.26 N	78.43 W
Elk ≃, Ab., Can.	182	52.55 N	115.40 W
Elk ≃, B.C., Can.	182	49.10 N	115.14 W
Ełk ≃, Pol.	30	53.31 N	22.47 E
Elk ≃, U.S.	194	34.46 N	87.16 W
Elk ≃, Co., U.S.	200	40.29 N	106.58 W
Elk ≃, Ks., U.S.	198	37.15 N	95.41 W
Elk ≃, Mn., U.S.	190	45.18 N	93.34 W
Elk ≃, Mo., U.S.	194	36.38 N	94.38 W
Elk ≃, W.V., U.S.	188	38.21 N	81.38 W
Elk ≃, Wi., U.S.	190	45.42 N	90.37 W
Elkader	190	42.51 N	91.24 W
El Kantara	148	33.41 N	10.55 E
El-Karafab	140	18.10 N	31.36 E
Elk Bayou ≃	226	36.06 N	119.24 W
Elk City	196	35.24 N	99.24 W
Elk City Lake ⊜[1]	198	37.15 N	95.55 W
Elk Creek	204	39.36 N	122.32 W
Elk Creek ≃, Ok., U.S.	196	34.48 N	99.09 W
Elk Creek ≃, Or., U.S.	202	43.38 N	123.34 W
Elk Creek ≃, Pa., U.S.	214	42.01 N	80.22 W
Elk Creek ≃, S.D., U.S.	198	44.15 N	102.22 W
Elk Creek ≃, Wa., U.S.	224	46.38 N	123.17 W
Elkedra ≃	162	21.08 S	136.22 E
El Kef	148	36.11 N	8.43 E
El Kef □[8]	148	36.00 N	9.00 E
El-Kelâa-des-Srarhna	148	32.02 N	7.23 W
El-Kelâa-des-Srarhna □[4]	148	32.05 N	7.30 W
El Kere	144	5.51 N	42.06 E
El Kerma	34	35.36 N	0.35 W
Elk Grove	226	38.24 N	121.22 W
Elk Grove Village	278	42.00 N	87.58 W
Elkhart, Il., U.S.	219	40.01 N	89.29 W
Elkhart, In., U.S.	216	41.40 N	85.58 W
Elkhart, Ks., U.S.	198	37.00 N	101.53 W
Elkhart, Tx., U.S.	222	31.38 N	95.35 W
Elkhart □[6]	216	41.35 N	85.50 W
Elkhart ≃	216	41.41 N	85.58 W
Elkhart Lake	190	43.50 N	88.01 W
El Khaṭṭ ⩦[4]	148	22.40 N	10.05 W
Elkhead Creek ≃	200	40.31 N	107.26 W
Elkhead Mountains ⩘	200	40.50 N	107.05 W
Elk Hills ⩘[2]	226	35.15 N	119.25 W
El Khnâchîch ⩦[4]	148	21.50 N	3.45 W
Elkhorn, Mb., Can.	184	49.58 N	101.14 W
Elk Horn, Ia., U.S.	198	41.35 N	95.03 W
Elkhorn, Wi., U.S.	216	42.40 N	88.32 W
Elkhorn ≃	198	41.07 N	96.19 W
Elkhorn City	192	37.18 N	82.21 W
Elkhorn Creek ≃, Ky., U.S.	218	38.19 N	84.52 W
Elkhorn Creek ≃, Mo., U.S.	219	39.05 N	91.20 W
Elkhorn Mountain ∧	182	49.48 N	125.50 W
Elkin	192	36.14 N	80.50 W
Elkins	188	38.55 N	79.50 W
Elkins Park	208	40.04 N	75.07 W
Elk Island I	184	50.45 N	96.32 W
Elk Island National Park ♠	182	53.37 N	112.45 W
Elkland	210	41.59 N	77.18 W
Elk Mills	208	39.39 N	75.49 W
Elk Mountain	200	41.41 N	106.24 W
Elk Mountain ∧, Wa., U.S.	224	46.08 N	122.28 W
Elk Mountain ∧, Wy., U.S.	200	41.38 N	106.32 W
Elk Neck ›[1]	208	39.35 N	75.55 W
Elk Neck State Park ♠	208	39.30 N	75.58 W
Elko, B.C., Can.	182	49.18 N	115.07 W
Elko, Nv., U.S.	204	40.49 N	115.45 W
El Kouif	36	35.29 N	8.19 E
Elk Peak ∧	202	46.27 N	110.46 W
Elk Plain	224	47.04 N	122.24 W
Elk Point, Ab., Can.	182	53.54 N	110.54 W
Elk Point, S.D., U.S.	198	42.41 N	96.41 W
Elk Rapids	190	44.53 N	85.24 W
El Krib	36	36.19 N	9.09 E
Elkridge	284b	39.12 N	76.42 W
Elk River, Id., U.S.	202	46.47 N	116.10 W
Elk River, Mn., U.S.	190	45.18 N	93.35 W
Elk River ⊂	208	39.31 N	75.55 W
El Kseur	34	36.46 N	4.49 E
Elk State Park ♠	214	41.38 N	78.34 W
Elkton, Ky., U.S.	194	36.48 N	87.09 W
Elkton, Md., U.S.	208	39.36 N	75.50 W
Elkton, Mi., U.S.	190	43.49 N	83.10 W
Elkton, Oh., U.S.	214	40.46 N	80.42 W
Elkton, S.D., U.S.	198	44.14 N	96.28 W
Elkton, Va., U.S.	188	38.24 N	78.37 W
El Kure	144	5.41 N	42.21 E
Elkville	194	37.54 N	89.14 W
Ell, Lake ⊜	162	29.13 S	127.46 E
Ellamar	180	60.54 N	146.42 W
Elland	44	53.41 N	1.50 W
Ellard Lake ⊜	184	54.33 N	91.55 W
Ellás → Greece □[1]	38	39.00 N	22.00 E
Ellavalla	162	25.05 S	114.22 E
Ellaville	192	32.14 N	84.18 W
Ellefeld	54	50.29 N	12.23 E
Ellef Ringnes Island I	16	78.30 N	104.00 W
El Leh	144	3.48 N	39.48 E
Elleker	162	35.00 S	117.43 E
Ellemandsbjerg ∧[2]	41	56.07 N	10.32 E
Ellen ≃	44	54.43 N	3.30 W
Ellen, Mount ∧	200	38.07 N	110.49 W
Ellen Brook ≃	168a	31.48 S	116.00 E
Ellendale, Austl.	162	17.56 S	124.48 E
Ellendale, De., U.S.	208	38.48 N	75.25 W
Ellendale, Mn., U.S.	190	43.52 N	93.18 W
Ellendale, N.D., U.S.	198	46.00 N	98.31 W
Ellensburg	202	46.59 N	120.32 W
Ellenton, Fl., U.S.	220	27.31 N	82.31 W
Ellenton, Ga., U.S.	192	31.10 N	83.35 W
Ellenville	210	41.43 N	74.23 W
Eller ◆[8]	263	51.12 N	6.51 E
Ellerbe	192	35.04 N	79.46 W
Ellero ≃	62	44.27 N	7.54 E
Ellerspring ∧[2]	56	49.55 N	7.37 E
Ellès	36	35.57 N	9.06 E
Ellesmere	42	52.54 N	2.54 W
Ellesmere, Lake ⊂	172	43.48 S	172.25 E
Ellesmere Island I	16	81.00 N	80.00 W
Ellesmere Park	262	53.29 N	2.20 W
Ellesmere Port	44	53.17 N	2.54 W
Ellesmere Port □[8]	262	53.18 N	2.47 W
Ellettsville	194	39.14 N	86.37 W
Ellewoutsdijk	52	51.24 N	3.49 E
Ellezelles	50	50.44 N	3.41 E
Ellice ≃	176	68.02 N	103.26 W
Ellice Islands → Tuvalu □[1]	14	8.00 S	178.00 E
Ellichpur → Achalpur	120	21.16 N	77.31 E
Ellicott City	208	39.16 N	76.47 W
Ellicott Creek ≃	210	43.01 N	78.53 W
Ellicott Creek Park ♠	284a	43.01 N	78.50 W
Ellicottville	210	42.16 N	78.40 W
Ellijay	192	34.41 N	84.28 W
El Limón, Méx.	234	18.05 N	101.59 W
El Limón, Méx.	234	19.49 N	104.11 W
El Limoncito	286c	10.29 N	66.47 W
El Limón de Teachi	232	24.43 N	107.08 W
Ellingen	56	49.04 N	10.58 E
Ellinger	222	29.50 N	96.44 W
Ellinghorst ◆[8]	263	51.34 N	6.57 E
Ellington, Eng., U.K.	44	55.13 N	1.34 W
Ellington, Ct., U.S.	207	41.54 N	72.28 W
Ellington, Mo., U.S.	194	37.14 N	90.58 W
Ellington, N.Y., U.S.	214	42.13 N	79.07 W
Elliniko International Airport ⊠	267c	37.54 N	23.44 E
Ellinikón	267c	37.53 N	23.44 E
Ellinwood	198	38.21 N	98.34 W
Elliot	158	31.18 S	27.50 E
Elliot, Mount ∧	166	19.29 S	146.58 E
Elliotdale	158	31.55 S	28.38 E
Elliotganj	126	23.31 N	90.52 E
Elliot Lake	190	46.23 N	82.39 W
Elliot Lake ⊜	184	52.55 N	95.20 W
Elliott, Austl.	162	17.33 S	133.32 E
Elliott, Il., U.S.	216	40.28 N	88.16 W
Elliott, Ia., U.S.	198	41.09 N	95.10 W
Elliott, Ms., U.S.	194	33.36 N	89.45 W
Elliott □[6]	218	38.13 N	83.10 W
Elliott, Mount ∧	162	20.29 S	126.37 E
Elliott Bay ⊂	224	47.36 N	122.22 W
Elliott Key I	220	25.27 N	80.11 W
Elliottville	218	38.11 N	83.16 W
Ellis	198	38.56 N	99.33 W
Ellis □[6]	222	32.20 N	96.48 W
Ellisburg	212	43.44 N	76.08 W
Ellis Island I	276	40.42 N	74.02 W
Ellis Mountain ∧	224	48.10 N	124.19 W
Ellison Creek Reservoir ⊜[1]	222	32.56 N	94.43 W
Ellisport	224	47.25 N	122.26 W
Ellisras	156	23.40 S	27.46 E
Elliston, Austl.	162	33.39 S	134.55 E
Elliston, Nf., Can.	186	48.38 N	53.03 W
Elliston, Mt., U.S.	202	46.33 N	112.25 W
Ellisville, Ms., U.S.	194	31.36 N	89.11 W
Ellisville, Mo., U.S.	219	38.35 N	90.35 W
Ellmau	64	47.31 N	12.18 E
Ellmauer Halt ∧	64	47.34 N	12.18 E
Ellon	46	57.22 N	2.05 W
Ellora	122	20.01 N	75.10 E
Ellore → Elūru	122	16.42 N	81.06 E
Elloree	192	33.31 N	80.34 W
Ellport	214	40.51 N	80.15 W
Ellrich	54	51.35 N	10.40 E
Ellsworth, Il., U.S.	216	40.27 N	88.43 W
Ellsworth, Ks., U.S.	198	38.43 N	98.13 W
Ellsworth, Me., U.S.	188	44.32 N	68.25 W
Ellsworth, Mi., U.S.	190	45.09 N	85.14 W
Ellsworth, Mn., U.S.	198	43.31 N	96.01 W
Ellsworth, Oh., U.S.	214	41.01 N	80.52 W
Ellsworth, Pa., U.S.	214	40.06 N	80.01 W
Ellsworth, Wa., U.S.	224	45.37 N	122.36 W
Ellsworth, Wi., U.S.	190	44.43 N	92.29 W
Ellsworth Air Force Base ■	198	44.08 N	103.05 W
Ellsworth Land ◆[1]	9	75.30 S	80.00 W
Ellsworth Mountains ⩘	9	79.00 S	85.00 W
El Lucero	196	25.53 N	103.25 W
Ellwangen	56	48.57 N	10.07 E
Ellwanger Berge ⩘[2]	56	49.00 N	10.01 E
Ellwood City	214	40.51 N	80.17 W
Elm, Dtsch.	52	53.31 N	9.12 E
Elm, Schw.	58	46.55 N	9.11 E
Elm, Eng., U.K.	42	52.38 N	0.10 E
Elm ∧	64	47.40 N	13.57 E
Elm ⩘[2]	54	52.09 N	10.53 E
Elm ≃, U.S.	198	45.36 N	98.19 W
Elm ≃, Il., U.S.	194	38.24 N	88.14 W
Elm ≃, N.D., U.S.	198	47.15 N	96.50 W
Elma, Ia., U.S.	190	43.14 N	92.26 W
Elma, N.Y., U.S.	210	42.51 N	78.38 W
Elma, Wa., U.S.	224	47.00 N	123.24 W
El Macero	226	38.33 N	121.41 W
El Machorro, Punta ›	200	31.03 N	114.51 W
Elmadağ (Küçükyozgat)	130	39.55 N	33.15 E
Elmadağ ∧	130	39.49 N	33.00 E
El Mahia ◆[1]	148	22.30 N	2.30 W
El Maitén	254	42.03 S	71.10 W
El Malah	34	35.24 N	1.05 W
Elmalı	130	36.44 N	29.56 E
Elmalı Bendi ◆[6]	267b	41.04 N	29.06 E
El Maneadero	232	31.45 N	116.35 W
El Manteco	246	7.27 N	62.32 W
El Marsa el Kebir	148	35.45 N	0.43 W
Elmas	71	39.16 N	9.03 E
Elmas, Aeroporto di ⊠	71	39.14 N	9.03 E
Elmas Burnu ›	267b	41.13 N	29.13 E
El Masnou	266d	41.29 N	2.19 E
Elmaton	222	28.53 N	96.09 W
El Mayoco	254	42.39 S	70.59 W
Elmbridge □[8]	260	51.22 N	0.23 W
Elm Brook ≃	283	42.29 N	71.16 W
Elm City	192	35.48 N	77.51 W
Elm Creek, Mb., Can.	184	49.41 N	98.00 W
Elm Creek, Ne., U.S.	198	40.43 N	99.22 W
Elm Creek ≃, Mn., U.S.	198	43.45 N	94.11 W
Elm Creek ≃, S.D., U.S.	198	44.21 N	102.42 W
Elm Creek ≃, Tx., U.S.	196	28.54 N	100.12 W
Elm Creek ≃, Tx., U.S.	196	32.40 N	99.41 W
Elm Creek ≃, Tx., U.S.	196	33.12 N	98.50 W
Elm Creek ≃, Tx., U.S.	222	29.15 N	97.32 W
El Meco	234	22.35 N	99.20 W
El Médano	232	24.25 N	111.30 W
Elmen	58	47.20 N	10.32 E
El Menia	148	30.30 N	2.50 E
Elmer	208	39.35 N	75.10 W
El Mghayyar	148	33.55 N	5.58 E
Elm Grove	216	43.02 N	88.04 W
Elmhurst, Austl.	169	37.11 S	143.15 E
Elmhurst, Il., U.S.	216	41.53 N	87.56 W
Elmhurst, Pa., U.S.	210	41.22 N	75.32 W
Elmhurst ◆[8]	276	40.44 N	73.53 W
El Mijao	286c	10.23 N	66.48 W
El Milagro	252	31.01 S	65.59 W
El Miliyya	148	36.48 N	6.14 E
El Mimbre	196	25.40 N	102.20 W
Elmina	150	5.05 N	1.21 W
El Minao	240m	18.22 N	66.05 W
Elmira, On., Can.	212	43.36 N	80.33 W
Elmira, P.E., Can.	186	46.27 N	62.04 W
Elmira, Ca., U.S.	226	38.21 N	121.55 W
Elmira, N.Y., U.S.	210	42.05 N	76.48 W
El Mirador ∧	234	19.25 N	98.42 W
El Mirage	200	33.36 N	112.19 W
El Mirage Lake ⊜	228	34.38 N	117.35 W
Elmira Heights	210	42.07 N	76.49 W
Elm Mott	222	31.40 N	97.06 W
Elmo, Mt., U.S.	182	47.49 N	114.20 W
Elmo, Tx., U.S.	222	32.43 N	96.10 W
El Mochito	236	14.49 N	88.06 W
El Mohammadia	148	35.33 N	0.03 E
El Molinillo	34	39.28 N	4.13 W
Elmont, N.Y., U.S.	276	40.42 N	73.42 W
Elmont, Va., U.S.	208	37.42 N	77.29 W
El Monte, Chile	252	33.41 S	71.01 W
El Monte, Ca., U.S.	228	34.04 N	118.01 W
El Monte Airport ⊠	280	34.06 N	118.02 W
Elmora	214	40.36 N	78.45 W
El Moral	196	28.51 N	100.39 W
Elmore, Austl.	166	36.30 S	144.37 E
Elmore, Mn., U.S.	190	43.30 N	94.05 W
Elmore, Oh., U.S.	214	41.28 N	83.17 W
Elmore City	196	34.37 N	97.23 W
El Morro ⊥	240m	18.28 N	66.07 W
El Morro National Monument ♠	200	35.05 N	108.22 W
Elm Point ›	276	40.49 N	73.46 W
Elmpt	56	51.13 N	6.10 E
El Mreiti ⫪[4]	148	23.29 N	7.52 W
El Mreyyé ◆[1]	150	19.30 N	7.00 W
Elmschenhagen ◆[8]	54	54.18 N	10.12 E
Elmsdale	186	44.58 N	63.30 W
Elmsford	210	41.03 N	73.49 W
Elmshorn	52	53.45 N	9.39 E
Elm Springs	194	36.12 N	94.14 W
Elmsta	26	59.58 N	18.48 E
Elmstein	56	49.21 N	7.56 E
Elmswell	42	52.15 N	0.53 E
El Mulato	196	29.22 N	104.10 W
El Multe	232	17.41 N	91.24 W
Elmvale	212	44.35 N	79.52 W
Elmville	218	38.20 N	84.46 W
Elmwood, On., Can.	212	44.14 N	81.03 W
Elmwood, Il., U.S.	190	40.46 N	89.57 W
Elmwood, Md., U.S.	284b	39.21 N	76.32 W
Elmwood, Ma., U.S.	283	42.00 N	70.57 W
Elmwood, Ne., U.S.	198	40.50 N	96.17 W

≃ River	Fluß	Río	Rivière	Rio
≊ Canal	Kanal	Canal	Canal	Canal
∟ Waterfall, Rapids	Wasserfall, Stromschnellen	Cascada, Rápidos	Chute d'eau, Rapides	Cascata, Rápidos
⊎ Strait	Meeresstraße	Estrecho	Détroit	Estreito
⊂ Bay, Gulf	Bucht, Golf	Bahía, Golfo	Baie, Golfe	Baía, Golfo
⊜ Lake, Lakes	See, Seen	Lago, Lagos	Lac, Lacs	Lago, Lagos
≡ Swamp	Sumpf	Pantano	Marais	Pântano
⊞ Ice Features, Glacier	Eis- und Gletscherformen	Accidentes Glaciales	Formes glaciaires	Acidentes glaciares
⫪ Other Hydrographic Features	Andere Hydrographische Objekte	Otros Elementos Hidrográficos	Autres données hydrographiques	Outros acidentes hidrográficos

✣ Submarine Features	Untermeerische Objekte	Accidentes Submarinos	Formes de relief sous-marin	Acidentes submarinos
□ Political Unit	Politische Einheit	Unidad Politica	Entité politique	Unidade política
▿ Cultural Institution	Kulturelle Institution	Institución Cultural	Institution culturelle	Instituição cultural
⊥ Historical Site	Historische Stätte	Sitio Histórico	Site historique	Sitio histórico
♠ Recreational Site	Erholungs- und Ferienort	Sitio de Recreo	Centre de loisirs	Area de Lazer
⊠ Airport	Flughafen	Aeropuerto	Aéroport	Aeroporto
■ Military Installation	Militäranlage	Instalación Militar	Installation militaire	Instalação militar
◆ Miscellaneous	Verschiedenes	Misceláneo	Divers	Diversos

Name	Page	Lat.°′	Long.°′
Elmwood, Wi., U.S.	190	44.46 N	92.08 W
Elmwood -•- [8]	285	39.56 N	75.14 W
Elmwood Park, Il., U.S.	216	41.55 N	87.48 W
Elmwood Park, N.J., U.S.	276	40.54 N	74.07 W
Elmwood Park, Wi., U.S.	216	42.41 N	87.50 W
Elmwood Park ♦	285	40.08 N	75.21 W
El Naranjo ≃	234	18.41 N	103.45 W
El Naranjo de Chila	234	18.55 N	102.28 W
Elne	32	42.36 N	2.58 E
El Negralejo	266a	40.24 N	3.31 W
El Negrito	236	15.16 N	87.41 W
El Nido, Pil.	116	11.11 N	119.23 E
El Nido, Ca., U.S.	226	37.08 N	120.29 W
El Nihuil	252	35.02 S	68.40 W
El Niybo	144	4.32 N	39.59 E
El Nopal, Cerro ∧	232	28.15 N	107.36 W
Elnora, Ab., Can.	182	51.59 N	113.12 W
Elnora, In., U.S.	194	38.52 N	87.05 W
El Oasis	286c	10.35 N	66.59 W
El-Obeid → Al-Ubayyiḍ	140	13.11 N	30.13 E
Elobey, Islas II	152	0.59 N	9.30 E
El Ocote, Cerro ∧	232	25.58 N	106.08 W
Elogbatindi	152	3.27 N	10.08 E
Eloida, Lake ⊜	212	44.40 N	75.58 W
Elói Mendes	256	21.37 S	45.34 W
Eloise	220	27.59 N	81.44 W
Elora, On., Can.	212	43.41 N	80.26 W
Elora, Tn., U.S.	194	35.00 N	86.21 W
El Oro □ [4]	246	3.30 S	79.50 W
Elortondo	252	33.42 S	61.37 W
Elorza	246	7.03 N	69.31 W
El Otro Lado	286c	10.24 N	66.49 W
Eloy	200	32.45 N	111.33 W
Eloy Alfaro	246	2.12 S	79.50 W
Éloyes	58	48.06 N	6.37 E
El Pacayal	232	15.37 N	92.02 W
El Palmar, Bol.	248	21.54 S	63.39 W
El Palmar, Ven.	246	7.58 N	61.53 W
El Palmar, Ven.	286c	10.38 N	66.52 W
El Palomar	288	34.36 S	58.36 W
El Palomar, Base Aérea Militar ■	288	34.37 S	58.37 W
El Palqui	252	30.45 S	70.59 W
El Pantanoso, Arroyo ≃	288	34.47 S	58.40 W
El Pao, Ven.	246	8.01 N	62.38 W
El Pao, Ven.	246	9.38 N	68.08 W
El Papiol	266d	41.26 N	2.01 E
El Paraíso, Hond.	236	13.51 N	86.34 W
El Paraíso, Méx.	234	17.25 N	100.15 W
El Paraíso □ [5]	236	14.10 N	86.30 W
El Pardo -•- [8]	266a	40.31 N	3.47 W
El Pardo, Embalse de ⊜ [1]	266a	40.33 N	3.48 W
El Pardo, Monte de ⋏ [2]	266a	40.33 N	3.48 W
El Paso, Il., U.S.	216	40.44 N	89.00 W
El Paso, Tx., U.S.	200	31.45 N	106.29 W
El Paso Creek ≃	228	35.02 N	118.51 W
El Paso de Robles → Paso Robles	226	35.38 N	120.41 W
El Paso Peaks ⋏	204	35.28 N	117.43 W
El Paují	286c	10.26 N	66.49 W
El Pedregal -•- [8]	286c	10.30 N	66.51 W
El Peñón Blanco, Cerro ∧	234	22.31 N	101.40 W
El Peñuelo	232	24.34 N	100.46 W
El Peral	286e	33.35 S	70.34 W
El Perú	246	7.19 N	61.49 W
El Pescadero, Laguna ⊂	234	22.12 N	105.20 W
El Pescado, Arroyo ≃	258	34.54 S	57.47 W
Elphin	48	53.51 N	8.12 W
Elphinstone	184	50.33 N	100.19 W
El Picacho, Cerro ∧	234	20.40 N	100.43 W
El Pilar	246	10.32 N	63.09 W
El Pinar, Parque Nacional ♦	286c	10.29 N	66.56 W
El Piñón	246	10.24 N	74.50 W
El Pintado	252	24.38 S	61.27 W
El Piojo, Arroyo ≃	288	34.50 S	58.45 W
El Piquete	252	24.13 S	64.39 W
El Pital, Cerro ∧	236	14.23 N	89.08 W
El Placer	234	23.33 N	106.10 W
El Planchón, Volcán ∧ [1]	252	35.13 S	70.34 W
El Plantío -•- [8]	266a	40.28 N	3.49 W
El Plomo	200	31.15 N	112.04 W
El Polvorín	240m	18.26 N	66.17 W
El Pont de Segur	34	42.24 N	0.45 E
El Porcal	266a	40.18 N	3.32 W
El Portal, Ca., U.S.	226	37.40 N	119.46 W
El Portal, Fl., U.S.	220	25.51 N	80.11 W
El Port de Pollença	34	39.55 N	3.05 E
El Porvenir, Méx.	196	27.33 N	104.57 W
El Porvenir, Méx.	234	15.44 N	93.22 W
El Porvenir, Perú	248	8.05 S	79.00 W
El Potosí, Punta >	234	17.32 N	101.28 W
El Potrero	196	26.23 N	100.27 W
El Prat de Llobregat	34	41.20 N	2.06 E
El Progreso, Ec.	246a	0.54 S	89.33 W
El Progreso, Guat.	236	14.21 N	89.51 W
El Progreso, Hond.	236	15.21 N	87.49 W
El Progreso □ [5]	236	14.50 N	90.00 W
El Puente del Arzobispo	34	39.48 N	5.10 W
El Puerto de Santa María	34	36.36 N	6.13 W
El Puesto	252	27.57 S	67.38 W
El Qala	148	36.50 N	8.30 E
El Qoll	148	37.00 N	6.34 E
El Quebrachal	252	25.17 S	64.04 W
El Quelite	234	23.32 N	106.28 W
Elquera Bushland ♦	274a	33.42 S	151.04 E
Elqui ≃	252	29.54 S	71.17 W
Elrama	214	40.15 N	79.55 W
El Ranchito	234	18.40 N	103.41 W
El Rastro	246	9.03 N	67.27 W
El Real de Santa María	246	8.08 N	77.43 W
El Recreo -•- [8]	286c	10.30 N	66.53 W
El Refugio	234	21.57 N	100.02 W
El Remolino	196	28.44 N	101.07 W
El Reno	196	35.31 N	97.57 W
El Rey, Parque Nacional ♦	252	25.00 S	64.40 W
El Rio	228	34.13 N	119.10 W
El Rito	200	36.20 N	106.11 W
El Rito ≃	200	36.12 N	106.14 W
El Roba	154	3.57 N	40.01 E
El Roble, Mesa ∧	232	31.31 N	115.31 W
El Rom	132	33.11 N	35.46 E
El Rosario, Laguna ⊜	234	17.52 N	93.48 W
El Rosarito	232	28.38 N	114.04 W
Elrose	184	51.13 N	108.01 W
Elroy	190	43.44 N	90.16 W
El Rucio	234	23.23 N	102.05 W
Elsa, Yk., Can.	180	63.55 N	135.28 W
Elsa, Tx., U.S.	196	26.17 N	97.59 W
Elsa ≃	66	43.43 N	10.52 E
Elsah	219	38.57 N	90.22 W
El Sahuaro	200	31.05 N	112.55 W
El Salado	252	26.25 S	70.19 W
El Salado, Parque Nacional ♦	246	2.12 S	80.00 W
El Salitre	246	1.50 S	79.48 W
El Salto, Méx.	234	23.47 N	105.22 W
El Salto, Méx.	234	20.32 N	103.11 W
El Salvador, Chile	252	26.17 S	69.43 W
El Salvador, Pil.	116	8.34 N	124.32 E
El Salvador □ [1], N.A.	230	13.50 N	88.55 W
El Salvador □ [1], N.A.	236	13.50 N	88.55 W
El Samán de Apure	246	7.55 N	68.44 W
El Santo	240p	22.42 N	79.41 W
Elsass → Alsace □ [9]	32	48.30 N	7.30 E
El Sauce, Laguna ⊜	258	35.20 S	58.16 W
El Sauz	232	29.02 N	106.16 W
El Sauzal	232	31.54 N	116.41 W
Elsberry	219	39.10 N	90.46 W
Elsbethen	64	47.45 N	13.05 E
Elsburg	273d	26.15 S	28.12 E
Elsdorf, Dtsch.	52	53.14 N	9.20 E
Elsdorf, Dtsch.	56	50.54 N	6.34 E
El Seco, Laguna ⊜	258	35.31 S	58.42 W
El Segundo	228	33.55 N	118.24 W
El Seibo	238	18.46 N	69.02 W
Elsen	52	51.44 N	8.39 E
Elsenham	42	51.55 N	0.14 E
Elsen Nur ⊜	120	35.11 N	92.15 E
Elsenz ≃	56	49.24 N	8.48 E
Elsfleth	52	53.14 N	8.28 E
El Siasgo, Arroyo ≃	258	35.33 S	58.33 W
Elsie, Mi., U.S.	216	43.05 N	84.23 W
Elsie, Or., U.S.	224	45.52 N	123.35 W
Elsinore → Helsingør, Dan.	41	56.02 N	12.37 E
Elsinore, Ut,. U.S.	200	38.40 N	112.08 W
Elsinore, Lake ⊜ [1]	228	33.39 N	117.21 W
El Sitio	286c	10.28 N	66.46 W
Elsmere, De., U.S.	208	39.44 N	75.35 W
Elsmere, Ky., U.S.	218	39.00 N	84.36 W
Elsmere, N.Y., U.S.	210	42.37 N	73.49 W
El Sobrante	226	37.58 N	122.17 W
El Socorro	246	8.59 N	65.44 W
El Sombrero	246	9.23 N	67.03 W
Elspark	273d	26.16 S	28.14 E
Elspeet	52	52.17 N	5.46 E
Elst	52	51.55 N	5.50 E
Elstal	54	52.32 N	12.59 E
Elstead	42	51.11 N	0.43 W
Elster	54	51.50 N	12.49 E
Elsterberg	54	50.36 N	12.10 E
Elstergebirge ⋏	54	50.15 N	12.20 E
Elsterwerda	54	51.28 N	13.31 E
Elston, In., U.S.	216	40.22 N	86.55 W
Elston, Mo., U.S.	219	38.37 N	92.19 W
Elstra	54	51.13 N	14.08 E
Elstree	42	51.39 N	0.16 W
Elstree Aerodrome ⊠	260	51.39 N	0.19 W
El Sueco	232	29.54 N	106.24 W
El Tagarete, Cerro ∧	232	26.31 N	105.56 W
El Tajín ⊥	234	20.27 N	97.23 W
El Tala	252	26.07 S	65.17 W
El Talar	258	34.27 S	58.39 W
El Tamarindo	236	13.11 N	87.54 W
El Tambo, Col.	246	1.26 N	77.23 W
El Tambo, Perú	248	12.04 S	75.13 W
El Tanque	196	26.28 N	99.38 W
El Tapextle	234	23.52 N	105.33 W
El Tarf	36	36.45 N	8.20 E
El Tecuán	232	25.29 N	107.00 W
El Tejocote, Cerro ∧	234	18.48 N	103.03 W
Elten	52	51.52 N	6.10 E
El Terrero	234	18.58 N	102.28 W
Eltham, Austl.	169	37.44 S	145.09 E
Eltham, N.Z.	172	39.26 S	174.18 E
Eltham -•- [8]	260	51.27 N	0.04 E
Eltham Palace ʊ	260	51.27 N	0.03 E
El Tigre	246	8.55 N	64.15 W
El Tigre, Isla I	236	13.16 N	87.38 W
El Tigrito → San José de Guanipa	246	8.54 N	64.09 W
El Timbiriche	234	18.38 N	101.31 W
Eltmann	56	49.58 N	10.40 E
El Tocuyo	246	9.47 N	69.48 W
El Tofo	252	29.27 S	71.15 W
El'ton, Ross.	80	49.08 N	46.50 E
Elton, Eng., U.K.	262	53.16 N	2.49 W
Elton, La., U.S.	194	30.28 N	92.41 W
Elton, Pa., U.S.	214	40.17 N	78.48 W
El'ton, ozero ⊜	80	49.16 N	46.35 E
El Toreo ♦	286a	19.27 N	99.13 W
El Toro	228	33.37 N	117.41 W
El Toro ∧	240m	18.16 N	65.49 W
El Toro, Isla I	234	21.26 N	97.31 W
El Toro Marine Corps Air Station ■	228	33.41 N	117.44 W
El Tranco, Embalse de ⊜ [1]	34	38.10 N	2.45 W
El Tránsito, Chile	252	28.52 S	70.17 W
El Tránsito, El Sal.	236	13.22 N	88.21 W
El Trébol	252	32.12 S	61.42 W
El Triunfo, Hond.	236	13.06 N	87.00 W
El Triunfo, Méx.	232	23.47 N	110.08 W
El Triunfo, Cerro ∧	234	15.40 N	92.49 W
El Triunfo de la Cruz	236	15.46 N	87.26 W
El Tuito	234	20.19 N	105.22 W
El Tulillo	234	22.30 N	104.05 W
El Tunal	252	25.15 S	64.27 W
El Turbio	254	51.41 S	72.05 W
Eltville	56	50.02 N	8.07 E
Eltz, Burg ⊥	56	50.12 N	7.20 E
El-Uarre	144	3.41 N	45.20 E
Elura → Ellora	122	20.01 N	75.10 E
Elūru	122	16.42 N	81.06 E
Elva	76	58.13 N	26.25 E
El Valle	236	8.36 N	80.08 W
El Valle -•- [8]	286c	10.27 N	66.55 W
Elvas	34	38.53 N	7.10 W
Elvas ≃	256	21.12 S	44.08 W
Elven	32	47.44 N	2.35 W
El Vendrell	34	41.13 N	1.32 E
El Verano	226	38.18 N	122.29 W
El Verde	234	23.21 N	106.09 W
Elverdissen	52	52.05 N	8.38 E
Elverlingsen	263	51.17 N	7.42 E
Elverta	226	38.43 N	121.28 W
Elverum	26	60.53 N	11.34 E
El Viejo	236	12.40 N	87.10 W
El Vigía	246	8.38 N	71.39 W
El Vigía, Cerro ∧	234	21.19 N	104.03 W
Elvins	194	37.50 N	90.31 W
Elvira	258	35.14 S	59.29 W
Elvo ≃	62	45.23 N	8.21 E
El Volcán	252	33.49 S	70.11 W
El Wad	148	33.20 N	6.58 E
El Wak	154	2.49 N	40.56 E
El Walamo	234	23.07 N	106.15 W
El Wanza	148	35.57 N	8.04 E
Elwell, Lake ⊜ [1]	202	48.22 N	111.17 W
Elwha ≃	224	48.10 N	123.35 W
Elwood, Austl.	274b	37.53 S	144.59 E
Elwood, Il., U.S.	216	41.24 N	88.07 W
Elwood, In., U.S.	216	40.16 N	85.50 W
Elwood, Ks., U.S.	198	39.45 N	94.52 W
Elwood, Ne., U.S.	198	40.35 N	99.51 W
Elwood, N.J., U.S.	208	39.35 N	74.43 W
Elwood, N.Y., U.S.	207	40.50 N	73.20 W
Elwood Park, Fl., U.S.	220	27.28 N	82.30 W
Elwood Park, Pa., U.S.	279b	40.10 N	80.17 W
Elwy ≃	44	53.16 N	3.26 W
Elwyn	285	39.54 N	75.24 W
Elx	34	38.15 N	0.42 W
Elxleben	54	51.02 N	10.56 E
Ely, Eng., U.K.	42	52.24 N	0.16 E
Ely, Mn., U.S.	190	47.54 N	91.52 W
Ely, Mo., U.S.	219	39.41 N	91.39 W
Ely, Nv., U.S.	204	39.14 N	114.53 W
Ely, Isle of -•- [1]	42	52.24 N	0.10 E
El Yagual	246	7.29 N	68.25 W
Ely Cathedral ʊ [1]	42	52.24 N	0.16 E
Elyria	214	41.22 N	82.06 W
Elyria Airport ⊠	279a	41.20 N	82.06 W
Elysburg	210	40.51 N	76.33 W
Elysian Park ♦	280	34.05 N	118.14 W
El Yunque ∧	240m	18.19 N	65.48 W
Elywood Park ♦	279a	41.23 N	82.06 W
Elz	56	50.25 N	8.02 E
Elz ≃	58	48.21 N	7.45 E
Elzach	58	48.10 N	8.04 E
El Zamural	286c	10.27 N	67.00 W
El Zapotal	234	15.27 N	93.10 W
Elzbach ≃	56	50.12 N	7.22 E
Elze, Dtsch.	52	52.35 N	9.44 E
Elze, Dtsch.	52	52.07 N	9.44 E
El Zig-Zag	286c	10.33 N	66.58 W
Émaé I	175f	17.04 S	168.24 E
Emajõgi ≃	76	58.26 N	27.15 E
Emali	154	2.05 S	37.38 E
Emam Khomeyni Mosque ʊ [1]	267d	35.40 N	51.25 E
Emāmshahr (Shāhrūd)	128	36.25 N	55.01 E
Emån ≃	26	57.08 N	16.30 E
Émancé	261	48.35 N	1.44 E
Emas, Parque Nacional das ♦	255	18.08 S	52.48 W
Emba	86	48.50 N	58.08 E
Emba ≃	80	46.38 N	53.14 E
Embarcación	252	23.13 S	64.06 W
Embarras ≃, Ab., Can.	182	53.27 N	116.37 W
Embarras ≃, Il., U.S.	194	38.39 N	87.37 W
Embarras, North Fork ≃	194	38.55 N	87.59 W
Embarrass	190	44.39 N	88.42 W
Embarrass ≃, Mn., U.S.	190	47.24 N	92.25 W
Embarrass ≃, Wi., U.S.	190	44.23 N	88.45 W
Embetsu	92a	44.44 N	141.47 E
Embid	34	40.58 N	1.43 W
Embleton	44	55.30 N	1.37 W
Embo	46	57.54 N	3.59 W
Emboabas	256	21.18 S	44.08 W
Embondo	152	0.15 N	19.38 E
Emborcação, Reprêsa ⊜ [1]	255	18.30 S	47.50 W
Embrach	58	47.30 N	8.36 E
Embreeville, Pa., U.S.	285	39.56 N	75.44 W
Embreeville, Tn., U.S.	192	36.10 N	82.27 W
Embro	212	43.09 N	80.54 W
Embrun, On., Can.	212	45.16 N	75.17 W
Embrun, Fr.	62	44.34 N	6.30 E
Embry	50	50.29 N	1.58 E
Embsay	44	53.58 N	1.59 W
Embu, Bra.	256	23.39 S	46.51 W
Embu, Kenya	154	0.32 S	37.27 E
Embu □ [7]	287b	23.40 S	46.50 W
Embu-Guaçu	256	23.49 S	46.48 W
Embu-Guaçu □ [7]	287b	23.48 S	46.48 W
Embu-mirim ≃	287b	23.39 S	46.51 W
Emden, Dtsch.	52	53.22 N	7.12 E
Emden, Il., U.S.	194	40.18 N	89.29 W
Emden, Mo., U.S.	219	39.48 N	91.52 W
Emei	107	29.36 N	103.31 E
Emeigh	214	40.42 N	78.47 W
Emel' (Emin) ≃	86	46.20 N	81.46 E
Emelle	194	32.43 N	88.18 W
Emerado	198	47.55 N	97.21 W
Émerainville	261	48.49 N	2.37 E
Emerald, Austl.	166	23.32 S	148.10 E
Emerald, Austl.	169	37.56 S	145.26 E
Emerald Bay State Park ♦	226	38.57 N	120.05 W
Emerald Lake	226	37.28 N	122.16 W
Emerson, Mb., Can.	184	49.00 N	97.12 W
Emerson, Ar., U.S.	194	33.05 N	93.11 W
Emerson, Ga., U.S.	192	34.07 N	84.45 W
Emerson, Ia., U.S.	198	41.01 N	95.24 W
Emerson, Mo., U.S.	219	39.53 N	91.42 W
Emerson, Ne., U.S.	198	42.17 N	96.44 W
Emerson, N.J., U.S.	276	40.58 N	74.01 W
Emery, S.D., U.S.	198	43.36 N	97.37 W
Emery, Ut,. U.S.	200	38.55 N	111.14 W
Emeryville, On., Can.	214	42.18 N	82.45 W
Emeryville, Ca., U.S.	226	37.50 N	122.17 W
Emet	130	39.20 N	29.15 E
Emgayet	146	29.04 N	12.58 E
Emhouse	222	32.09 N	96.35 W
Emi	88	50.36 N	97.49 E
Emigrant Gap	226	39.17 N	120.40 W
Emigrant Gap)(	226	39.18 N	120.40 W
Emigsville	208	40.01 N	76.44 W
Emiliano Mitre, Canal ⋓	288	34.36 S	58.18 W
Emiliano Zapata, Méx.	232	17.45 N	91.46 W
Emiliano Zapata, Méx.	234	16.10 N	94.01 W
Emiliano Zapata, Bahía ⊂	232	19.40 N	87.30 W
Emilia-Romagna □ [4]	36	44.35 N	11.00 E
Emílio de Carvalho	152	5.55 S	12.57 E
Emily Provincial Park ♦	212	44.21 N	78.31 W
Emin	86	46.32 N	83.39 E
Emin (Emel') ≃	86	46.20 N	81.46 E
Eminābād	123	32.02 N	74.16 E
Emine, nos >	38	42.42 N	27.51 E
Eminence, Ky., U.S.	218	38.22 N	85.10 W
Eminence, Mo., U.S.	194	37.09 N	91.21 W
Emiralem	130	38.36 N	27.09 E
Emiratos Arabes Unidos → United Arab Emirates □ [1]	128	24.00 N	54.00 E
Emirau Island I	164	1.40 S	150.00 E
Emirdağ	130	39.01 N	31.10 E
Emır Dağları ⋏	130	38.50 N	31.15 E
Emirhan	130	39.42 N	37.46 E
Emir Pasha Gulf ⊂	154	2.32 S	31.52 E
Emissi, Tarso ∧	146	21.13 N	18.32 E
Emita	166	40.00 S	147.54 E
Emlembe ∧	158	25.57 S	31.11 E
Emlenton	214	41.11 N	79.43 W
Emlichheim	52	52.36 N	6.50 E
Emmaån ≃	40	58.44 N	15.35 E
Emmaboda	26	56.38 N	15.32 E
Emmaste	76	58.42 N	22.36 E
Emmaus, Ross.	82	56.47 N	36.07 E
Emmaus, Pa., U.S.	208	40.32 N	75.29 W
Emmaville	166	29.26 S	151.36 E
Emme ≃	58	47.13 N	7.34 E
Emmeline Lake ⊜	184	55.00 N	106.22 W
Emmeloord	52	52.43 N	5.45 E
Emmen	52	52.47 N	6.54 E
Emmenbrücke	58	47.04 N	8.17 E
Emmendingen	58	48.07 N	7.50 E
Emmental V	58	46.56 N	7.45 E
Emmer ≃	52	52.03 N	9.23 E
Emmer-Compascuum	52	52.48 N	7.02 E
Emmer-Erfscheidenveen	52	52.48 N	7.01 E
Emmerich	52	51.50 N	6.15 E
Emmerstedt	54	52.15 N	10.58 E
Emmerthal	52	52.03 N	9.23 E
Emmet, Austl.	166	24.40 S	144.28 E
Emmet, Ar., U.S.	194	33.43 N	93.28 W
Emmetsburg	198	43.06 N	94.40 W
Emmett, Id., U.S.	202	43.52 N	116.29 W
Emmett, Mi., U.S.	214	42.59 N	82.45 W
Emmiganūru	122	15.44 N	77.29 E
Emmitsburg	208	39.42 N	77.20 W
Emmonak	180	62.46 N	164.30 W
Emneth	42	52.38 N	0.11 E
Emo	190	48.38 N	93.50 W
Emőd	30	47.56 N	20.49 E
Emory	222	32.52 N	95.46 W
Emory ≃	192	35.56 N	84.29 W
Emory Peak ∧	196	29.13 N	103.17 W
Empalme	232	27.58 N	110.51 W
Empalme Escobedo	234	20.41 N	100.44 W
Empalme Purísima	234	23.55 N	105.05 W
Empalme San Vicente	258	34.58 S	58.22 W
Empangeni	158	28.50 S	31.48 E
Empedrado, Arg.	252	27.57 S	58.48 W
Empedrado, Chile	252	35.36 S	72.17 W
Emperor Jimmu, Tomb of ⊥	270	34.29 N	135.47 E
Emperor Nintoku, Tomb of ⊥	270	34.34 N	135.29 E
Emperor Range ⋏	175e	5.45 S	154.55 E
Emperor Seamounts ⊹ [3]	6	42.00 N	170.00 E
Emperor Tenchi, Tomb of ⊥	270	34.59 N	135.48 E
Empfingen	58	48.24 N	8.42 E
Empire, Ca., U.S.	226	37.38 N	120.54 W
Empire, La., U.S.	194	29.23 N	89.35 W
Empire, Nv., U.S.	204	40.34 N	119.20 W
Empire, Oh., U.S.	214	40.30 N	80.37 W
Empoli	66	43.43 N	10.57 E
Emporia, Ks., U.S.	198	38.24 N	96.10 W
Emporia, Va., U.S.	208	36.41 N	77.32 W
Emporium	214	41.30 N	78.14 W
Empress	184	50.57 N	110.00 W
Empress Augusta Bay ⊂	175e	6.25 S	155.05 E
Emptinne	56	50.19 N	5.07 E
Empty Quarter → Ar-Rub' al-Khālī -•- [2]	118	20.00 N	51.00 E
Ems ≃	52	53.20 N	7.06 E
Emscher ≃	263	51.34 N	6.42 E
Emscherbruch -•- [1]	263	51.34 N	7.09 E
Emsdetten	52	52.10 N	7.31 E
Ems-Jade-Kanal ≅	52	53.19 N	7.10 E
Emskirchen	56	49.33 N	10.43 E
Emsland -•- [1]	52	52.50 N	7.20 E
Emst -•- [8]	263	51.21 N	7.30 E
Emstek	52	52.50 N	8.09 E
Emsworth, Eng., U.K.	42	50.51 N	0.56 W
Emsworth, Pa., U.S.	214	40.30 N	80.05 W
Emsworth Dam -•- [6]	279b	40.30 N	80.05 W
Emu	89	43.45 N	128.10 E
Emu, Mount ∧ [2]	169	37.35 S	143.27 E
Emu Creek ≃	171a	26.56 S	152.19 E
Emu Downs	168b	33.54 S	138.59 E
Emukae	92	33.18 N	129.38 E
Emu Park	166	23.15 S	150.50 E
Emu Plains	274a	33.45 S	150.41 E
Emur ≃	89	53.24 N	124.00 E
Emuren	273a	6.40 N	3.31 E
Emyvale	48	54.20 N	6.59 W
En (Inn) ≃, Europe	32	48.35 N	13.28 E
En ≃, Zhg.	100	27.12 N	115.08 E
Ena	94	35.27 N	137.25 E
Enana	156	17.29 S	16.19 E
Enånger	26	61.32 N	17.00 E
Enard Bay ⊂	46	58.05 N	5.20 W
Enarotali	164	3.55 S	136.21 E
Ena-san ∧	94	35.26 N	137.36 E
Ena-san Tunnel -•- [5]	94	35.30 N	137.40 E
Enbacka	40	60.25 N	15.36 E
Enborne ≃	42	51.24 N	1.06 W
Encampment	200	41.12 N	106.47 W
Encampment ≃	200	41.18 N	106.43 W
Encantado	252	29.15 S	51.53 W
Encantado -•- [8]	287a	22.54 S	43.18 W
Encanto, Cape >	116	15.44 N	121.37 E
Encarnação -•- [8]	266c	38.47 N	9.06 W
Encarnación	252	27.20 S	55.54 W
Encarnación de Díaz	234	21.31 N	102.14 W
Encha	98	37.25 N	115.42 E
Enchenberg	56	49.01 N	7.20 E
Enchi	150	5.49 N	2.49 W
Enchilayas	200	30.50 N	112.50 W
Enchovas, Enseada das ⊂	256	23.57 S	45.18 W
Enciastraia, Monte ∧	62	44.22 N	6.53 E
Encinal	196	28.02 N	99.21 W
Encinitas	228	33.02 N	117.17 W
Encino, N.M., U.S.	200	34.39 N	105.27 W
Encino, Tx., U.S.	196	26.57 N	98.08 W
Encino -•- [8]	280	34.09 N	118.30 W
Encino Reservoir ⊜ [1]	280	34.05 N	118.31 W
Encontrados	246	9.03 N	72.14 W
Encounter Bay ⊂	168b	35.35 S	138.44 E
Encrucijada, Cuba	240p	22.37 N	79.52 W
Encrucijada, Méx.	234	18.18 N	93.29 W
Encruzilhada	255	15.31 S	40.54 W
Encruzilhada do Sul	252	30.32 S	52.31 W
Encs	30	48.20 N	21.08 E
Endako	182	54.05 N	125.02 W
Endako ≃	182	54.05 N	124.55 W
Endau ≃	114	2.39 N	103.38 E
Ende	115b	8.50 S	121.39 E
Ende, Pulau I	115b	8.53 S	121.32 E
Ende, Teluk ⊂	115b	8.52 S	121.30 E
Endeavor, Pa., U.S.	214	41.35 N	79.23 W
Endeavor, Wi., U.S.	190	43.42 N	89.27 W
Endeavour	184	52.08 N	102.40 W
Endeavour Strait ⋓	164	10.50 S	142.15 E
Endelave I	41	55.46 N	10.17 E
Enderbury I [1]	14	3.08 S	171.05 W
Enderby, B.C., Can.	182	50.33 N	119.08 W
Enderby, Eng., U.K.	42	52.36 N	1.12 W
Enderby Land -•- [1]	9	67.30 S	53.00 E
Enderlin	198	46.37 N	97.36 W
Endicott, N.Y., U.S.	210	42.05 N	76.02 W
Endicott, Wa., U.S.	202	46.55 N	117.40 W
Endicott Mountains ⋏	180	67.50 N	152.00 W
Endimari ≃	248	8.46 S	66.07 W
Endine	64	45.46 N	9.59 E
Endine Gaiano	64	45.48 N	9.59 E
Endingen	58	48.09 N	7.42 E
Endja, Oued ≃	34	36.31 N	6.15 E
Endō	268	35.23 N	139.27 E
Endola	156	17.37 S	15.50 E
'En Dor	132	32.39 N	35.25 E
Endorf in Oberbayern	64	47.54 N	12.18 E
Endre ≃	62	43.28 N	6.36 E
Endrick ∧	170	35.12 S	150.12 E
Endrick ≃	170	35.01 S	150.03 E
Endwell	210	42.06 N	76.01 W
Ene ≃	248	11.09 S	74.19 W
Eneabba	162	29.50 S	115.20 E
Enemonzo	64	46.25 N	12.53 E
Enewetak I [1]	14	11.30 N	162.15 E
Enez	130	40.44 N	26.04 E
Enfida	36	36.07 N	10.23 E
Enfield, Austl.	168b	34.53 S	138.35 E
Enfield, Austl.	274a	33.53 S	151.06 E
Enfield, N.Z.	172	45.03 S	170.52 E
Enfield, Ct., U.S.	207	41.58 N	72.35 W
Enfield, N.H., U.S.	188	43.38 N	72.08 W
Enfield, N.C., U.S.	192	36.10 N	77.40 W
Enfield, Va., U.S.	208	37.43 N	77.12 W
Enfield -•- [8]	42	51.40 N	0.05 W
Enga □ [5]	164	5.30 S	143.30 E
Engadine	170	34.04 S	151.01 E
Engaño, Cabo >	238	18.37 N	68.20 W
Engaru	92a	44.03 N	143.31 E
Engažimo	88	57.51 N	114.56 E
Engcobo	158	31.37 S	28.00 E
'En Gedi	132	31.27 N	35.23 E
Engelberg	58	46.49 N	8.25 E
Engelhard	192	35.30 N	75.59 W
Engelhartszell	60	48.31 N	13.44 E
Engel's	80	51.30 N	46.07 E
Engelsdorf	54	51.20 N	12.29 E
Engelskirchen	56	50.59 N	7.24 E
Engelsmanplaat I	52	53.28 N	6.02 E
Engen, B.C., Can.	182	54.02 N	124.18 W
Engen, Dtsch.	58	47.51 N	8.46 E
Engenheiro Navarro	255	17.17 S	43.57 W
Engenheiro Passos	256	22.30 S	44.41 W
Engenheiro Paulo de Frontin	256	22.33 S	43.41 W
Engenho	248	15.10 S	56.25 W
Engenho, Ilha do I	287a	22.50 S	43.07 W
Engenho de Dentro -•- [8]	287a	22.54 S	43.18 W
Engenho do Mato	287a	22.52 S	43.01 W
Engenho Novo	256	21.49 S	43.00 W
Engenho Nôvo -•- [8]	287a	22.55 S	43.17 W
Enger	52	52.08 N	8.34 E
Engestofte	41	54.46 N	11.34 E
Engesvang	41	56.10 N	9.21 E
'En Gev	132	32.47 N	35.38 E
Enggano, Pulau I	112	5.24 S	102.16 E
Enghershatu ∧	144	16.40 N	38.20 E
Enghien (Edingen)	50	50.42 N	4.02 E
Enghien-les-Bains	261	48.58 N	2.19 E
Enghien-Moisselles, Aéroport d' ⊠	261	49.02 N	2.21 E
Engiadina Bassa V	58	46.50 N	10.20 E
Engis	56	50.35 N	5.25 E
Engizek Dağı ∧	130	37.50 N	37.10 E
Engjan	26	63.09 N	8.32 E
England	194	34.32 N	91.58 W
England □ [8]	28	52.30 N	1.30 W
England Air Force Base ■	194	31.20 N	92.33 W
Englebright Lake ⊜ [1]	226	39.15 N	121.15 W
Englee	186	50.44 N	56.06 W
Englefield, Cape >	176	69.51 N	85.39 W
Englefield Green	260	51.26 N	0.35 W
Englefontaine	50	50.11 N	3.39 E
Englehart	190	47.49 N	79.52 W
Englehart ≃	190	47.51 N	79.50 W
Engleside	208	38.43 N	77.05 W
Englewood, B.C., Can.	182	50.33 N	126.53 W
Englewood, Co., U.S.	200	39.38 N	104.59 W
Englewood, Fl., U.S.	220	26.57 N	82.21 W
Englewood, In., U.S.	218	38.50 N	86.31 W
Englewood, Ks., U.S.	198	37.02 N	99.58 W
Englewood, N.J., U.S.	210	40.53 N	73.58 W
Englewood, Oh., U.S.	218	39.52 N	84.18 W
Englewood, Tn., U.S.	192	35.25 N	84.29 W
Englewood -•- [8]	278	41.47 N	87.39 W
Englewood Cliffs	276	40.53 N	73.57 W
Englewood Dam -•- [6]	218	39.52 N	84.17 W
English, In., U.S.	218	38.20 N	86.27 W
English, Ky., U.S.	218	38.37 N	85.08 W
English ≃, On., Can.	176	50.12 N	95.00 W
English (Rivière des Anglais) ≃, N.A.	206	45.13 N	73.50 W
English ≃, Ia., U.S.	190	41.29 N	91.30 W
English Bay	180	59.22 N	151.55 W
English Bāzār → Ingrāj Bāzār	124	25.00 N	88.09 E
English Center	210	41.26 N	77.17 W
English Channel (La Manche) ⋓	28	50.20 N	1.00 W
English Coast ⊥ [2]	9	73.45 S	73.00 W
English Harbour West	186	47.28 N	55.29 W
Englishman ≃	224	49.22 N	124.18 W
Englishtown	208	40.17 N	74.21 W
Engong	152	0.36 N	10.06 E
Engter	52	52.23 N	8.04 E
Énguera	34	38.59 N	0.41 W
Engum	41	55.44 N	9.40 E
Engure	76	57.10 N	23.13 E
Engures ezers ⊜	76	57.16 N	23.06 E
Engwilen	58	47.37 N	9.05 E
'En Harod	132	32.33 N	35.23 E
'En HaShofét	132	32.35 N	35.06 E
Enid	196	36.23 N	97.52 W
Enid Lake ⊜ [1]	194	34.10 N	89.50 W
Enilda	182	55.25 N	116.18 W
Eningen unter Achalm	58	48.29 N	9.16 E
Eniwa	92a	42.45 N	141.33 E
Eniwetok → Enewetak I [1]	14	11.30 N	162.15 E
eNjesuthi ∧	158	29.09 S	29.23 E
Enka	192	35.32 N	82.39 W
Enkenbach	56	49.29 N	7.54 E
Enkhuizen	52	52.42 N	5.17 E
Enkirch	56	49.59 N	7.07 E
Enköping	40	59.38 N	17.04 E
Enle	102	24.00 N	101.07 E
Enmedio	196	29.04 N	103.29 W
Enmedio, Cerro de ∧	234	19.48 N	100.36 W
Enmelen	180	65.01 N	175.54 W
Enna	70	37.34 N	14.16 E
Enna □ [4]	70	37.35 N	14.26 E
Ennadai Lake ⊜	176	60.53 N	101.15 W
Enné, Ouadi V	146	14.24 N	18.45 E
Ennedi ⋏ [1]	146	17.15 N	22.00 E
Ennell, Lough ⊜	48	53.28 N	7.24 W
Ennenda	58	47.01 N	9.05 E
Ennepe ≃	263	51.22 N	7.27 E
Ennepestausee ⊜ [1]	263	51.14 N	7.25 E
Ennepetal	56	51.18 N	7.22 E
Ennerdale Water ⊜	44	54.31 N	3.23 W
Ennery	261	49.05 N	2.06 E
Enngonia	166	29.19 S	145.51 E
Enniger	52	51.50 N	7.56 E
Ennigerloh	52	51.50 N	8.02 E
Ennigloh	52	52.12 N	8.34 E
Ennis, Ire.	48	52.50 N	8.59 W
Ennis, Mt., U.S.	202	45.20 N	111.43 W
Ennis, Tx., U.S.	222	32.19 N	96.37 W
Enniscorthy	48	52.30 N	6.34 W
Enniskillen	48	54.21 N	7.38 W
Ennis Lake ⊜ [1]	202	45.26 N	111.41 W
Ennistimon	48	52.57 N	9.15 W
Enns	61	48.13 N	14.29 E
Enns ≃	61	48.14 N	14.32 E
Ennstaler Alpen ⋏	61	47.37 N	14.35 E
Eno	26	62.48 N	30.09 E
Enø I	41	55.10 N	11.40 E
Eno ≃	96	34.53 N	132.41 E
Enochs	196	33.52 N	102.46 W
Enogera Military Camp ■	171a	27.25 S	152.58 E
Enola	208	40.17 N	76.56 W
Enon	218	39.53 N	83.56 W
Enontekiö	24	68.23 N	23.38 E
Enon Valley	214	40.51 N	80.28 W
Enoree ≃	192	34.26 N	81.25 W
Enosburg Falls	188	44.54 N	72.48 W
Eno-shima I	94	35.18 N	139.29 E
Enping	102	22.11 N	112.17 E
Enrekang	112	3.34 S	119.47 E
Enrile	116	17.34 N	121.42 E
Enrique Fynn	258	34.50 S	59.08 W
Enrique Urien	252	27.34 S	60.32 W
Enriquillo	238	17.54 N	71.14 W
Enriquillo, Lago ⊜	238	18.27 N	71.39 W
Ens	52	52.38 N	5.50 E
Ensay I	46	57.46 N	7.05 W
Enschede	52	52.12 N	6.53 E
Ensdorf	60	49.21 N	11.56 E
Ensenada, Arg.	258	34.51 S	57.55 W
Ensenada, Méx.	232	31.52 N	116.37 W
Ensenada, P.R.	240m	17.58 N	66.56 W
Ensenada □ [5]	288	34.50 S	58.00 W
Enshi	102	30.17 N	109.19 E
Enshū-nada ⊹ [2]	92	34.27 N	137.38 E
Ensisheim	58	47.52 N	7.21 E
Enstaberga	40	58.45 N	16.51 E
Entebbe	154	0.04 N	32.28 E
Entenbühl ∧	60	49.46 N	12.24 E
Enter	52	52.18 N	6.34 E
Enterprise, Guy.	246	6.56 N	58.24 W
Enterprise, Al., U.S.	194	31.18 N	85.51 W
Enterprise, Ca., U.S.	204	39.32 N	121.22 W
Enterprise, Ks., U.S.	198	38.54 N	97.07 W
Enterprise, Ms., U.S.	194	32.10 N	88.49 W
Enterprise, Or., U.S.	202	45.25 N	117.16 W
Enterprise, Ut,. U.S.	200	37.34 N	113.43 W
Entiat ≃	202	47.40 N	120.14 W
Entiat, Lake ⊜ [1]	202	47.40 N	120.12 W
Entiat Mountains ⋏	224	48.00 N	120.42 W
Entinas, Punta de las >	34	36.41 N	2.46 W
Entlebuch	58	47.00 N	8.04 E
Entlebuch V	58	46.58 N	8.00 E
Entracque	62	44.14 N	7.24 E
Entraigues-sur-Sorgue	62	44.00 N	4.55 E
Entrains-sur-Nohain	50	47.27 N	3.15 E
Entrance, Cape >	164	2.21 S	150.12 E
Entraunes	62	44.11 N	6.45 E
Entraygues	32	44.39 N	2.34 E
Entrechaux	62	44.13 N	5.08 E
Entrée, Île d' I	186	47.17 N	61.42 W
Entremont-le-Vieux	62	45.26 N	5.53 E
Entrepeñas, Embalse de ⊜ [1]	34	40.34 N	2.42 W
Entre Rios, Bol.	248	21.32 S	64.12 W
Entre Rios, Bra.	255	11.56 S	38.05 W
Entre Ríos □ [4]	252	32.00 S	59.00 W
Entre Ríos, Cordillera ⋏	236	14.05 N	85.37 W
Entre-Rios de Minas	255	20.41 S	44.04 W
Entrevaux	62	43.57 N	6.49 E
Entrèves	62	45.49 N	6.57 E
Entriken	214	40.20 N	78.12 W
Entroncamento	34	39.28 N	8.28 W
Entupido	256	22.30 S	44.51 W
Entwistle	182	53.36 N	115.00 W
Enu, Pulau I	164	7.05 S	134.30 E
Enugu	150	6.27 N	7.27 E
Enumclaw	224	47.12 N	121.59 W
Enurmino	180	66.57 N	171.49 W
Envalira, Port d')(	34	42.35 N	1.45 E
Envermeu	50	49.54 N	1.16 E
Envies, Rivière des ≃	206	46.37 N	72.24 W
Envigado	246	6.10 N	75.35 W
Envira	248	7.18 S	70.13 W
Envira ≃	248	6.42 S	69.46 W
'En Yahav	132	30.38 N	35.11 E
Enyamba	154	3.40 S	24.58 E
Enyang	102	31.48 N	106.31 E
Enyellé	152	2.49 N	18.06 E
Enys, Mount ∧	172	43.14 S	171.38 E
Enz ≃	56	49.01 N	9.07 E
Enza ≃	64	44.54 N	10.31 E
Enzan	94	35.42 N	138.44 E
Enzbach ≃	56	49.54 N	6.25 E
Enzenkirchen	60	48.23 N	13.39 E
Enzesfeld	61	47.55 N	16.10 E
Enzklösterle	56	48.40 N	8.28 E
Eo ≃	34	43.28 N	7.03 W
Eolia	219	39.14 N	91.00 W
Eolie o Lipari, Isole II	70	38.30 N	14.50 E
Epanomí	38	40.26 N	22.56 E
Épars, Bois de l' ♦	261	48.45 N	1.45 E
Epe, Dtsch.	52	52.11 N	7.02 E
Epe, Ned.	52	52.21 N	6.00 E
Epe, Nig.	150	6.37 N	3.59 E
Epecuén, Lago ⊜	252	37.10 S	62.54 W
Épéhy	50	50.02 N	3.10 E
Epéna	152	1.22 N	17.29 E
Épernay	50	49.03 N	3.57 E
Épernon	50	48.37 N	1.41 E
Epes	194	32.41 N	88.07 W
Ephesus → Efes ⊥	130	37.55 N	27.17 E
Ephraim	200	39.21 N	111.35 W
Ephrata, Pa., U.S.	208	40.10 N	76.10 W
Ephrata, Wa., U.S.	202	47.19 N	119.33 W
Ephrata Cloister ⊥	208	40.12 N	76.09 W
Ephratah	210	43.00 N	74.32 W
Epi □ [8]	175f	16.42 S	168.15 E
Épi I	175f	16.43 S	168.15 E
Épiais-lès-Louvres	261	49.02 N	2.33 E
Épila	34	41.36 N	1.17 W
Épinac-les-Mines	58	46.59 N	4.31 E
Épinal	58	48.11 N	6.27 E
Épinay-sous-Sénart	261	48.42 N	2.31 E
Épinay-sur-Orge	261	48.40 N	2.20 E
Épinay-sur-Seine	261	48.57 N	2.19 E
Epirus → Ípeiros □ [9]	38	39.40 N	20.50 E
Episcopia	68	40.04 N	16.06 E
Episkopí	130	34.40 N	32.54 E
Époisses	50	47.30 N	4.10 E
Epokiro	156	21.41 S	19.08 E
Epomeo, Monte ∧	68	40.44 N	13.54 E
Épône	261	48.57 N	1.49 E
Eport, Loch ⊂	46	57.33 N	7.11 W
Eppalock, Lake ⊜ [1]	169	36.52 S	144.31 E
Eppelborn	56	49.24 N	6.58 E
Eppendorf -•- [8]	263	51.27 N	7.11 E
Eppenhausen -•- [8]	263	51.21 N	7.31 E
Eppeville	50	49.44 N	3.03 E
Epping, Austl.	169	37.39 S	145.02 E
Epping, Austl.	274a	33.46 S	151.05 E
Epping, Eng., U.K.	42	51.43 N	0.07 E
Epping, N.H., U.S.	188	43.02 N	71.04 W
Eppingen	56	49.08 N	8.54 E
Epping Forest □ [8]	260	51.43 N	0.10 E
Epping Forest -•- [3]	42	51.40 N	0.03 E
Epping Green, Eng., U.K.	260	51.44 N	0.05 E
Epping Green, Eng., U.K.	260	51.45 N	0.07 W
Epping Upland	260	51.43 N	0.06 E
Epsom	42	51.20 N	0.16 W
Epsom and Ewell □ [8]	260	51.20 N	0.16 W
Epsom Downs Race Course ♦	260	51.19 N	0.15 W
Epte ≃	50	49.04 N	1.37 E
Épuisay	50	47.54 N	0.56 E
Epukiro ≃	156	20.45 S	21.05 E
Epupa Falls L	152	16.55 S	13.10 E
Epuyén	254	42.14 S	71.21 W
Epworth	44	53.32 N	0.49 W
Eqlīd	128	30.55 N	52.39 E
Equality	194	37.44 N	88.20 W
Équateur □ [4]	152	1.00 N	20.30 E
Équateur → Ecuador □ [1]	246	2.00 S	77.30 W
Equatorial Guinea (Guinea Ecuatorial) □ [1]	152	2.00 N	9.00 E
Équihen-Plage	50	50.41 N	1.34 E
Equimina ≃	152	13.11 S	12.47 E
Equinox Mountain ∧	210	43.10 N	73.08 W
Equinunk	210	41.51 N	75.14 W
Equi Terme	64	44.09 N	10.10 E
Era ≃, It.	66	43.40 N	10.38 E
Era ≃, Pap. N. Gui.	164	7.35 S	144.41 E
Erac Creek ≃	166	26.56 S	145.48 E
Eraclea	64	45.35 N	12.40 E
Eraclea ⊥	68	40.13 N	16.40 E
Eraclea Minoa ⊥	70	37.23 N	13.17 E
Eradu	162	28.41 S	115.02 E
Éragny	261	49.01 N	2.06 E
Eramosa ≃	212	43.32 N	80.14 W
Eran Bay ⊂	116	9.06 N	117.43 E
Eranga	152	1.52 S	18.56 E
Erangal -•- [8]	272c	19.10 N	72.47 E
Erap	164	6.35 S	146.40 E
Erath	194	29.57 N	92.02 W
Erave	164	6.40 S	143.50 E
Erave ≃	164	6.40 S	143.55 E
Erba	62	45.48 N	9.15 E
Erba, Jabal ∧, Sūd.	140	19.04 N	36.46 E
Erba, Jabal ∧, Sūd.	140	20.45 N	36.50 E
Erbaa	130	40.42 N	36.36 E
Erbach, Dtsch.	56	49.40 N	8.59 E
Erbach, Dtsch.	58	48.20 N	9.53 E
Erbendorf	60	49.50 N	12.03 E
Erbeskopf ∧	56	49.44 N	7.05 E
Erchie	68	40.26 N	17.44 E
Erciş	84	39.02 N	43.22 E
Erciyes Dağı ∧	130	38.32 N	35.28 E
Ercolano	68	40.48 N	14.21 E
Ercolano (Herculaneum) ⊥	68	40.46 N	14.20 E
Érd	30	47.23 N	18.56 E
Erdao ≃, Zhg.	98	42.39 N	127.35 E
Erdao ≃, Zhg.	104	42.16 N	122.20 E
Erdao Bai ≃	98	42.34 N	128.08 E
Erdaobaihe	98	42.22 N	128.07 E
Erdaofang, Zhg.	104	41.54 N	123.57 E
Erdaofang, Zhg.	104	41.37 N	122.34 E
Erdaofangshen	104	42.09 N	123.17 E
Erdaogangzi, Zhg.	104	41.57 N	122.09 E
Erdaogangzi, Zhg.	104	42.04 N	123.06 E
Erdaohe	89	43.37 N	127.35 E
Erdaohezi, Zhg.	89	45.07 N	127.16 E
Erdaohezi, Zhg.	89	45.08 N	129.39 E
Erdaojingzi	104	41.49 N	122.20 E
Erdaoliangzi, Zhg.	98	40.50 N	119.04 E
Erdaoliangzi, Zhg.	105	40.31 N	118.03 E
Erdaowan	89	47.58 N	124.33 E
Erdek	130	40.24 N	27.48 E
Erdemli	130	36.37 N	34.18 E
Erdene, Mong.	88	47.48 N	107.55 E
Erdene, Mong.	102	45.08 N	97.45 E
Erdene, Mong.	102	44.15 N	111.14 E
Erdene Bulgan	88	50.07 N	101.35 E
Erdene-Büren	86	48.26 N	91.27 E
Erdenedalaj	102	46.02 N	104.55 E
Erdene Mandal	88	48.30 N	101.21 E
Erdenheim	285	40.05 N	75.12 W

Symbols in the index entries represent the broad categories identified in the key at the right. Symbols with superior numbers (⋏ [1]) identify subcategories (see complete key on page *I · 1).*

Symbole im Register stellen die rechts im Schlüssel erklärten Kategorien dar. Symbole mit hochgestellten Ziffern (⋏ [1]) bezeichnen Unterabteilungen einer Kategorie (vgl. vollständiger Schlüssel auf Seite *I · 1).*

Los símbolos incluídos en el texto del índice representan las grandes categorías identificadas con la clave a la derecha. Los símbolos con numeros en su parte superior (⋏ [1]) identifican las subcategorías (véase la clave completa en la página *I · 1).*

Les symboles de l'index représentent les catégories indiquées dans la légende à droite. Les symboles suivis d'un indice (⋏ [1]) représentent des sous-catégories (voir légende complète à la page *I · 1).*

Os símbolos incluídos no texto do índice representam as grandes categorias identificadas com a chave à direita. Os símbolos com números em sua parte superior (⋏ [1]) identificam as subcategorias (veja-se a chave completa à página *I · 1).*

∧	Mountain	Berg	Montaña	Montagne	Montanha
⋏	Mountains	Gebirge	Montañas	Montagnes	Montanhas
)(	Pass	Paß	Paso	Col	Passo
V	Valley, Canyon	Tal, Cañon	Valle, Cañón	Vallée, Canyon	Vale, Canhão
≃	Plain	Ebene	Llano	Plaine	Planície
>	Cape	Kap	Cabo	Cap	Cabo
I	Island	Insel	Isla	Île	Ilha
II	Islands	Inseln	Islas	Îles	Ilhas
⊥	Other Topographic Features	Andere Topographische Objekte	Otros Elementos Topográficos	Autres données topographiques	Outros acidentes topográficos

ESPAÑOL

Nombre	Página	Lat.°′	Long.°′ W = Oeste
Erdevik	38	45.07 N	19.25 E
Erdiao	106	32.12 N	121.12 E
Erding	60	48.18 N	11.54 E
Erdinger Moos ≣	60	48.22 N	11.52 E
Erdnijevskij	80	46.52 N	46.17 E
Erebato ≃	246	5.54 N	64.16 W
Erebus, Mount ∧	9	77.32 S	167.09 E
Ereğli, Tür.	130	37.31 N	34.04 E
Ereğli, Tür.	130	41.17 N	31.25 E
Eregun	273a	6.36 N	3.22 E
Erei, Monti ⋏	70	37.27 N	14.19 E
Erenas	116	12.25 N	124.19 E
Erenhot	102	43.46 N	112.05 E
Erenköy ◆[8]	267b	40.58 N	29.04 E
Erepecuru, Lago do ⊜	250	1.20 S	56.35 W
Eresma ≃	34	41.26 N	4.45 W
Eressós	38	39.10 N	25.56 E
Erétria	38	38.24 N	23.48 E
Erexim	252	27.38 S	52.17 W
Erez	132	31.34 N	34.34 E
Érezée	56	50.18 N	5.33 E
Erfa ≃	56	49.43 N	9.15 E
Erfde	41	54.19 N	9.19 E
Erfelek	130	41.53 N	34.55 E
Erfenisdam ⊜[1]	158	28.33 S	26.50 E
Erfoud	148	31.28 N	4.10 W
Erft ≃	56	51.11 N	6.44 E
Erftstadt	56	50.48 N	6.46 E
Erfurt	54	50.58 N	11.01 E
Ergak-Targak-Tajga, chrebet ⋏	88	53.25 N	95.30 E
Ergani	130	38.17 N	39.46 E
Ergene ≃	130	41.01 N	26.22 E
Ergenzingen	58	48.29 N	8.48 E
Erges (Erjas) ≃	34	39.40 N	7.01 W
Ērgļi	76	56.54 N	25.38 E
Ergolding	60	48.35 N	12.10 E
Ergoldsbach	60	48.41 N	12.12 E
Ergste	56	51.25 N	7.34 E
Erguig, Bahr ≃	146	11.22 N	15.24 E
Ergun (Argun') ≃	74	53.20 N	121.28 E
Ergun Youqi	89	50.14 N	120.10 E
Ergun Zuoqi	89	50.47 N	121.31 E
Erguvejem ≃	180	65.20 N	176.00 W
Er Hai ⊜	102	25.48 N	100.11 E
Erhlin	100	23.54 N	120.22 E
Erhshui	100	23.49 N	120.36 E
Erhulai	98	41.23 N	125.08 E
Eria ≃	34	42.03 N	5.44 W
Erial	208	39.46 N	75.00 W
Eriba	140	16.37 N	36.04 E
Eriboll	46	58.28 N	4.41 W
Eriboll, Loch ⊂	46	58.31 N	4.41 W
Erica, Austl.	169	37.59 S	146.22 E
Erica, Ned.	52	52.43 N	6.55 E
Erice	70	38.02 N	12.35 E
Ericeira	34	38.59 N	9.25 W
Erichsen Lake ⊜	176	70.38 N	80.21 W
Erichshagen	52	52.40 N	9.14 E
Ericht, Loch ⊜	46	56.48 N	4.24 W
Erick	196	35.12 N	99.51 W
Erickson, B.C., Can.	182	49.05 N	116.28 W
Erickson, Mb., Can.	184	50.30 N	99.55 W
Ericson	198	41.46 N	98.40 W
Erie, Co., U.S.	200	40.03 N	105.03 W
Erie, Il., U.S.	190	41.39 N	90.04 W
Erie, Ks., U.S.	198	37.34 N	95.14 W
Erie, Mi., U.S.	216	41.47 N	83.29 W
Erie, Pa., U.S.	214	42.07 N	80.05 W
Erie □[6], N.Y., U.S.	210	42.54 N	78.53 W
Erie □[6], Oh., U.S.	214	41.27 N	82.42 W
Erie □[6], Pa., U.S.	214	42.08 N	80.04 W
Erie, Lake ⊜	214	42.15 N	81.00 W
Erieau	214	42.16 N	81.56 W
Erie Basin ⊂	276	40.40 N	74.01 W
Erie Beach, On., Can.	214	42.16 N	82.00 W
Erie Beach, On., Can.	284a	42.53 N	78.57 W
Erie Canal → New York State Barge Canal ≍	210	43.05 N	78.43 W
Erie County Fairgrounds ♠	284a	42.45 N	78.49 W
Erie International Airport ⊠	214	42.05 N	80.11 W
Eriksberg ⊥	40	58.56 N	16.22 E
Eriksdale	184	50.52 N	98.06 W
Erímanthos ∧	38	37.59 N	21.51 E
Erimo	92a	42.01 N	143.09 E
Erimo-misaki ›	92a	41.55 N	143.15 E
Erin, On., Can.	212	43.45 N	80.07 W
Erin, N.Y., U.S.	210	42.11 N	76.40 W
Erin, Tn., U.S.	194	36.19 N	87.41 W
Erindale	275b	43.32 N	79.39 W
Ering	60	48.18 N	13.09 E
Eriskay I	46	57.04 N	7.18 W
Erisort, Loch ⊂	46	58.07 N	6.24 W
Eriswil	58	47.05 N	7.51 E
Erith ◆[8]	260	51.29 N	0.10 E
Erithraí	38	38.13 N	23.19 E
Eritrea □[1], Afr.	136	15.20 N	39.00 E
Eritrea □[1], Afr.	144	15.20 N	39.00 E
Erivan → Jerevan	84	40.11 N	44.30 E
Erjas (Erges) ≃	34	39.40 N	7.01 W
Erjiazhen	106	32.02 N	121.13 E
Erkelenz	56	51.05 N	6.19 E
Erken ⊜	40	59.51 N	18.34 E
Erken-Jurt	84	44.27 N	41.54 E
Erkheim	58	48.02 N	10.20 E
Erkilet	130	38.49 N	35.27 E
Erkina ≃	48	52.51 N	7.23 W
Erkner	54	52.25 N	13.45 E
Erkner, Forst ◆[3]	264a	52.22 N	13.47 E
Erkowit	140	18.46 N	37.07 E
Erkrath	56	51.13 N	6.55 E
Erl	64	47.41 N	12.11 E
Erlach, Öst.	61	47.43 N	16.13 E
Erlach, Schw.	58	47.03 N	7.06 E
Erlands Point	224	47.36 N	122.42 W
Erlangen	60	49.36 N	11.01 E
Erlanger	218	39.01 N	84.36 W
Erlanghe	100	30.19 N	116.04 E
Erlangmiao	100	33.46 N	112.23 E
Erlau ≃	60	48.34 N	13.36 E
Erlauf ≃	61	48.12 N	15.11 E
Erlbach	54	50.18 N	12.22 E
Erldunda	162	25.14 S	133.12 E
Erle ◆[8]	263	51.33 N	7.05 E
Erli	62	44.08 N	8.06 E
Erling	106	31.53 N	119.36 E
Erling, Lake ⊜[1]	194	33.05 N	93.35 W
Erlistoun	162	28.20 S	122.08 E
Erlongshan, Zhg.	89	47.20 N	132.28 E
Erlongshan, Zhg.	89	50.04 N	126.47 E
Erlongshantun	89	48.28 N	126.31 E
Erlsbach	64	46.55 N	12.15 E
Erma	208	38.58 N	74.54 W
Ermana, chrebet ⋏	88	50.00 N	113.30 E
Ermatingen	58	47.41 N	9.06 E
Erme ≃	42	50.18 N	3.56 W
Ermelindo Matarazo ◆[8]	287b	23.29 S	46.29 W
Ermelo, Ned.	52	52.17 N	5.37 E
Ermelo, S. Afr.	158	26.34 S	29.58 E
Ermendegou	104	42.02 N	121.56 E
Ermenek	130	36.38 N	32.54 E
Ermenek ≃	130	36.35 N	33.23 E
Ermenonville	50	49.08 N	2.42 E
Ermidas	34	38.00 N	8.23 W
Ermil Post	140	13.37 N	27.36 E
Ermineskin Indian Reserve ◆[4]	182	52.52 N	113.30 W
Ermington	274a	33.48 S	151.04 E
Ermita de Guadalupe	234	22.36 N	103.03 W
Ermita de los Correas	234	22.54 N	103.01 W
Ermont	50	48.59 N	2.16 E
Ermoúpolis	38	37.26 N	24.56 E
Ermsleben	54	51.44 N	11.21 E
Ernaballa	162	26.17 S	132.07 E
Erndtebrück	56	50.59 N	8.15 E
Erne ≃	48	54.30 N	8.16 W

FRANÇAIS

Nom	Page	Lat.°′	Long.°′ W = Ouest
Erne, Lower Lough ⊜	48	54.26 N	7.46 W
Erne, Upper Lough ⊜	48	54.14 N	7.32 W
Ernée	32	48.18 N	0.56 W
Ernest	214	40.41 N	79.10 W
Ernestina	258	35.16 S	59.34 W
Ernest Sound ⊔	182	55.52 N	132.10 W
Ernici, Monti ⋏	66	41.48 N	13.22 E
Ernstbrunn	61	48.32 N	16.22 E
Ernst Thälmann, Pioneerpark ♠	264a	52.28 N	13.33 E
Ernst-Thälmann-Stadion ♠	264a	52.23 N	13.05 E
Ernz Blanche ≃	56	49.52 N	6.16 E
Erode	122	11.21 N	77.44 E
Eromanga	166	26.40 S	143.16 E
Erongo	156	21.44 S	15.53 E
Erongo ⋏	156	21.45 S	15.37 E
Erota	144	16.14 N	37.55 E
Erp	56	50.46 N	6.43 E
Erpuzi	105	40.29 N	115.33 E
Erquelinnes	50	50.18 N	4.07 E
Err, Piz d' ∧	58	46.33 N	9.41 E
Errabiddy	162	25.28 S	117.07 E
Er-Rachidia	148	31.58 N	4.25 W
Er-Rachidia □[4]	148	31.15 N	4.05 W
Errego	154	16.02 S	37.14 E
Errer ≃	144	7.32 N	42.05 E
Er-Riad → Ar-Riyāḍ	128	24.38 N	46.43 E
Errigal Mountain ∧	48	55.02 N	8.07 W
Errington	224	49.17 N	124.22 W
Erris Head ›	48	54.19 N	10.00 W
Errochty, Loch ⊜	46	56.45 N	4.12 W
Errogie	46	57.16 N	4.22 W
Errol Heights	224	45.28 N	122.36 W
Erromango I	175f	18.45 S	169.05 E
Ersekë	38	40.20 N	20.41 E
Ershijiazi	104	41.17 N	120.32 E
Ershilipu	105	40.07 N	117.24 E
Ershiqizhan	89	53.23 N	123.16 E
Ershiwuzhan	89	53.22 N	123.55 E
Erskine	198	47.40 N	96.00 W
Erskine, Lake ⊜	276	41.06 N	74.15 W
Erskine Inlet ⊂	176	76.15 N	102.20 W
Erskine Park	274a	33.49 S	150.47 E
Erstein	58	48.26 N	7.40 E
Erste Wiener Hochquellenleitung ≍[1]	61	48.10 N	16.17 E
Erstfeld	58	46.49 N	8.39 E
Ertai, Zhg.	86	46.07 N	90.06 E
Ertai, Zhg.	86	44.14 N	80.52 E
Ertaizi, Zhg.	104	41.52 N	121.56 E
Ertaizi, Zhg.	104	42.05 N	123.35 E
Ertaizi, Zhg.	104	42.35 N	124.00 E
Ertaizi, Zhg.	104	40.47 N	120.54 E
Ertil'	78	51.51 N	40.49 E
Ertingen	58	48.06 N	9.28 E
Ertix (Irtyš) ≃	74	61.04 N	68.52 E
Erto	64	46.16 N	12.22 E
Ertuğrul	130	39.34 N	27.43 E
Ertvelde	50	51.11 N	3.45 E
Eruar	126	23.28 N	87.52 E
Erudina	166	31.28 S	139.23 E
Eruh	130	37.46 N	42.11 E
Erundu	156	20.36 S	16.25 E
Erunkan	273a	6.37 N	3.24 E
Erva, Ponta da ›	266c	38.50 N	8.58 W
Erval	252	32.02 S	53.24 W
Erval d'Oeste	252	27.13 S	51.34 W
Ervalla	40	59.22 N	15.15 E
Erving	207	42.36 N	72.23 W
Ervy-le-Châtel	50	48.02 N	3.55 E
Erwin, N.C., U.S.	192	35.19 N	78.40 W
Erwin, Tn., U.S.	192	36.08 N	82.25 W
Erwitte	52	51.37 N	8.20 E
Erwood	184	52.50 N	102.10 W
Erxleben	54	52.13 N	11.14 E
Érythrée → Eritrea □[1]	144	15.20 N	39.00 E
Eryuan	102	26.06 N	99.55 E
Erzaohang	106	31.05 N	121.49 E
Erzberg ◆[7]	61	47.32 N	14.54 E
Erzgebirge (Krušné hory) ⋏	54	50.30 N	13.10 E
Erzhan	89	43.58 N	128.44 E
Erzhuang	105	39.24 N	117.22 E
Erzin	88	50.15 N	95.10 E
Erzincan	130	39.44 N	39.29 E
Erzincan □[4]	130	39.40 N	39.30 E
Erzingen	58	47.39 N	8.25 E
Erzurum	130	39.55 N	41.17 E
Erzurum □[4]	130	40.00 N	41.30 E
Esa'ala	164	9.44 S	150.49 E
Esambo	152	3.40 S	23.24 E
Esan-misaki ›	92a	41.49 N	141.11 E
Esashi, Nihon	92	41.52 N	140.07 E
Esashi, Nihon	92	39.12 N	141.09 E
Esashi, Nihon	92a	44.56 N	142.35 E
Esbiye	130	40.57 N	38.44 E
Esbjerg	26	55.28 N	8.27 E
Esbly	261	48.54 N	2.49 E
Esbo → Espoo	26	60.13 N	24.40 E
Esborn	263	51.23 N	7.20 E
Esca ≃	34	42.37 N	1.03 W
Escada	250	8.22 S	35.14 W
Escalada	258	34.10 S	59.07 W
Escalante, Pil.	116	10.50 N	123.33 E
Escalante, Ut,. U.S.	200	37.46 N	111.36 W
Escalante ≃, Ut,. U.S.	200	37.17 N	110.53 W
Escalante ≃, Ven.	246	9.15 N	71.50 W
Escalante Desert ◆[2]	200	37.50 N	113.30 W
Escalaplano	71	39.37 N	9.21 E
Escalón, Méx.	232	26.45 N	104.20 W
Escalon, Ca., U.S.	226	37.47 N	120.59 W
Escalona	34	40.10 N	4.24 W
Escambia ≃	194	30.32 N	87.11 W
Escanaba	190	45.44 N	87.04 W
Escanaba ≃	190	45.47 N	87.04 W
Escandón, Puerto)(	34	40.17 N	1.00 W
Escárcega	232	18.37 N	90.43 W
Escarpada Point ›	116	18.31 N	122.13 E
Escarpado Peak ∧	116	8.36 N	117.22 E
Escarpment	284a	43.10 N	79.00 W
Escatawpa ≃	194	30.25 N	88.35 W
Escaudain	50	50.20 N	3.21 E
Escaut (Schelde) ≃	50	51.22 N	4.15 E
Eschach	58	47.44 N	9.36 E
Eschau	58	48.29 N	7.43 E
Esche ≃	56	48.54 N	6.04 E
Eschebrügge	52	52.37 N	6.46 E
Eschede	52	52.44 N	10.14 E
Eschen	58	47.13 N	9.31 E
Eschenau	60	49.34 N	11.12 E
Eschenbach	60	49.45 N	11.49 E
Eschenburg	56	50.49 N	8.20 E
Eschenlohe	64	47.36 N	11.11 E
Eschershausen	52	51.56 N	9.38 E
Eschlkam	60	49.18 N	12.55 E
Escholzmatt	58	46.55 N	7.56 E
Eschscholtz Bay ⊂	180	66.18 N	161.25 W
Esch-sur-Alzette	56	49.30 N	5.59 E
Esch-sur-Sûre	56	49.55 N	5.55 E
Eschwege	56	51.11 N	10.04 E
Eschweiler	56	50.49 N	6.16 E
Esclave, Grand Lac de l' → Great Slave Lake ⊜	176	61.30 N	114.00 W
Esclavo, Gran Lago del → Great Slave Lake ⊜	176	61.30 N	114.00 W
Escobal	236	9.09 N	79.58 W
Escobar □[5]	288	34.23 S	58.46 W
Escobar, Arroyo ≃	288	34.21 S	58.44 W
Escobedo, Méx.	196	27.13 N	101.21 W
Escobedo, Méx.	232	29.05 N	102.19 W
Escocesa, Bahía ⊂	238	19.25 N	69.45 W
Escoheag	207	41.36 N	71.45 W
Escondido	228	33.07 N	117.05 W

PORTUGUÊS

Nome	Página	Lat.°′	Long.°′ W = Oeste
Escondido ≃, Méx.	196	28.39 N	100.34 W
Escondido ≃, Nic.	236	12.04 N	83.45 W
Escondido Creek ≃	228	33.01 N	117.15 W
Escorial → San Lorenzo de El Escorial	34	40.35 N	4.09 W
Escoutay ≃	62	44.29 N	4.42 E
Escravos ≃[1]	150	5.35 N	5.10 E
Escrick	44	53.53 N	1.02 W
Escuadrón 201 ◆[8]	286a	19.22 N	99.06 W
Escudero, Arroyo ≃	258	34.20 S	57.05 W
Escudo de Veraguas, Isla I	236	9.06 N	81.33 W
Escuinapa de Hidalgo	234	22.51 N	105.48 W
Escuintla, Guat.	236	14.18 N	90.47 W
Escuintla, Méx.	232	15.20 N	92.38 W
Escuintla □[5]	236	14.10 N	91.00 W
Escuminac, Point ›	186	47.04 N	64.46 W
Esebi	154	2.57 N	30.39 E
Eséka	152	3.39 N	10.46 E
Eşen	130	36.27 N	29.16 E
Eşen ≃	130	36.16 N	29.15 E
Esenler ◆[8]	267b	41.02 N	28.51 E
Esens	52	53.39 N	7.37 E
Esera ≃	34	42.06 N	0.15 E
Esesi	130	39.49 N	39.19 E
Eşfahān (Isfahan)	128	32.40 N	51.38 E
Eşfahān □[4]	128	33.00 N	52.00 E
Esfandaqeh	128	28.38 N	57.12 E
Esfarāyen	128	37.02 N	57.27 E
Esgueva ≃	34	41.40 N	4.43 W
Eshan	102	24.11 N	102.22 E
Esher ◆[8]	42	51.23 N	0.22 W
Eshkāshem	123	36.42 N	71.34 E
Eshowe	158	28.58 S	31.29 E
Esh-Sham → Dimashq	132	33.30 N	36.18 E
Eshta'ol	132	31.47 N	35.00 E
Esh Winning	44	54.47 N	1.43 W
Esiama	150	4.56 N	2.21 W
Esigodini	154	20.18 S	28.56 E
Esine	64	45.55 N	10.15 E
Esino ≃	66	43.39 N	13.22 E
Esira	157b	24.20 S	46.42 E
Esk	171a	27.15 S	152.25 E
Esk ≃, N.Z.	172	43.06 S	171.57 E
Esk ≃, U.K.	44	54.58 N	3.04 W
Esk ≃, Eng., U.K.	44	54.29 N	0.37 W
Esk ≃, Eng., U.K.	44	54.21 N	3.23 W
Esk ≃, Scot., U.K.	46	55.57 N	3.03 W
Eskdale, N.Z.	172	39.24 S	176.50 E
Eskdale, W.V., U.S.	188	38.05 N	81.26 W
Eskdale ∨	44	55.10 N	3.00 W
Eske, Lough ⊜	48	54.41 N	8.03 W
Eski Dzhumaya → Târgovište	38	43.15 N	26.34 E
Eskifjörður	24a	65.04 N	13.59 W
Eskiikan	85	43.12 N	68.31 E
Eskilstrup	41	54.51 N	11.54 E
Eskilstuna	40	59.22 N	16.30 E
Eskimalatya	130	38.26 N	38.23 E
Eskimo Lakes ⊜	180	69.15 N	132.17 W
Eskimo Point	176	61.07 N	94.03 W
Eskipazar	130	40.58 N	32.33 E
Eskişehir	130	39.46 N	30.32 E
Eskişehir □[4]	130	39.35 N	31.10 E
Eskridge	198	38.51 N	96.06 W
Esla ≃	34	41.29 N	6.03 W
Eslāmābād	128	34.06 N	46.31 E
Eslām Qal'eh	128	34.40 N	61.04 E
Eslāmshahr	128	35.40 N	51.10 E
Eslarn	60	49.35 N	12.32 E
Eslohe	56	51.15 N	8.09 E
Eslöv	41	55.50 N	13.20 E
Eşme	130	38.24 N	28.59 E
Esmeralda, Austl.	166	18.50 S	142.34 E
Esmeralda, Cuba	240p	21.51 N	78.07 W
Esmeralda, Méx.	196	25.40 N	103.30 W
Esmeralda, Isla I	254	48.57 S	75.25 W
Esmeraldas	246	0.59 N	79.42 W
Esmeraldas □[4]	246	0.40 N	79.30 W
Esmeraldas ≃	246	0.58 N	79.38 W
Esmirna → İzmir	130	38.25 N	27.09 E
Esmond, N.D., U.S.	198	48.02 N	99.45 W
Esmond, R.I., U.S.	207	41.52 N	71.29 W
Esnagi Lake ⊜	190	48.38 N	84.32 W
Esneux	56	50.32 N	5.34 E
Esong	152	2.09 N	10.58 E
Esopus Creek ≃	210	42.04 N	73.56 W
Espada, Punta ›	246	12.05 N	71.07 W
Espagne → Spain □[1]	34	40.00 N	4.00 W
Espalion	32	44.31 N	2.46 E
Espaly-Saint-Marcel	62	45.03 N	3.52 E
España → Spain □[1]	34	40.00 N	4.00 W
Espanola, On., Can.	190	46.15 N	81.46 W
Espanola, N.M., U.S.	200	35.59 N	106.04 W
Española, Isla I	246a	1.25 S	89.42 W
Esparto	226	38.41 N	122.00 W
Esparza	236	9.59 N	84.40 W
Espasingen	58	47.49 N	9.00 E
Espe, Dan.	41	55.12 N	10.25 E
Espe, Kaz.	85	43.52 N	74.10 E
Espejo	34	37.41 N	4.33 W
Espelkamp	52	52.25 N	8.36 E
Espenberg, Cape ›	180	66.33 N	163.36 W
Espenhain	54	51.11 N	12.29 E
Espera, Arroyo ≃[1]	288	34.24 S	58.36 W
Espera Feliz	255	20.39 S	41.55 W
Esperança, Bra.	246	4.24 S	69.52 W
Esperança, Bra.	250	7.01 S	35.51 W
Esperance, Austl.	162	33.51 S	121.53 E
Esperance, N.Y., U.S.	210	42.46 N	74.15 W
Esperance Bay ⊂	162	33.51 S	121.53 E
Esperantina	250	3.54 S	42.14 W
Esperantinópolis	250	4.53 S	44.53 W
Esperanza, Arg.	252	31.27 S	60.56 W
Esperanza, Cuba	240p	22.27 N	80.06 W
Esperanza, Méx.	232	27.35 N	109.56 W
Esperanza, Méx.	234	18.52 N	97.24 W
Esperanza, Pil.	116	8.43 N	125.36 E
Esperanza, Pil.	116	11.44 N	124.03 E
Esperanza, P.R.	240m	18.06 N	65.28 W
Esperanza, S. Afr.	158	30.21 S	30.40 E
Esperanza ⊽[3]	9	63.24 S	56.59 W
Esperanza Inlet ⊂	182	49.48 N	126.50 W
Espergærde	41	56.00 N	12.34 E
Esperia	66	41.23 N	13.41 E
Esperito, Arroyo ≃[1]	288	34.23 S	58.36 W
Espevær	26	59.36 N	5.10 E
Espichel, Cabo ›	34	38.25 N	9.13 W
Espinal	246	4.09 N	74.53 W
Espinazo	196	26.16 N	101.06 W
Espinazo, Sierra del → Espinhaço, Serra do ⋏	255	17.30 S	43.30 W
Espingarda ≃	250	10.03 S	47.13 W
Espinhaço, Serra do ⋏	255	17.30 S	43.30 W
Espinho	34	41.00 N	8.39 W
Espinillo	252	24.58 S	58.34 W
Espinillo, Arroyo ≃	258	34.59 S	57.36 W
Espinillo, Punta del ›	258	34.50 S	56.26 W
Espino	246	8.34 N	66.01 W
Espinosa	255	14.56 S	42.50 W
Espírito Santo → Vila Velha	250	3.13 N	51.13 W
Espírito Santo □[3]	255	19.30 S	40.30 W
Espírito Santo do Dourado	256	22.03 S	45.58 W
Espiritu Santo I	175f	15.15 S	166.50 E
Espíritu Santo, Isla I	232	24.30 N	110.22 W
Espita	232	21.01 N	88.19 W
Espoir, Bay d' ⊂	186	47.50 N	55.51 W
Espoo (Esbo)	26	60.13 N	24.40 E
Esposende	34	41.32 N	8.47 W
Esposizione Universale di Roma ♠	267a	41.50 N	12.28 E

Espugues de Llobregat	266d	41.22 N	2.05 E
Espumoso	252	28.44 S	52.51 W
Espungabera	156	20.29 S	32.48 E
Espy	210	41.00 N	76.24 W
Espyville Station	214	41.36 N	80.29 W
Esquatzel Coulee ∨	202	46.17 N	119.07 W
Esquel	254	42.54 S	71.19 W
Esquimalt	224	48.26 N	123.24 W
Esquina	252	30.01 S	59.32 W
Esquina Negra	258	35.02 S	58.03 W
Esquipulas, Guat.	236	14.34 N	89.21 W
Esquipulas, Nic.	236	12.40 N	85.47 W
Esquiú	252	29.23 S	65.17 W
Esrum Sø ⊜	41	56.00 N	12.24 E
Essa ≃	76	54.53 N	28.40 E
Essaoui Mellene, Oued ∨	148	27.26 N	6.40 E
Essaouira (Mogador)	148	31.30 N	9.47 W
Essaouira □[4]	148	31.25 N	9.30 W
Essarts	261	48.30 N	1.46 E
Essé	152	4.05 N	11.53 E
Esse ≃	66	43.16 N	11.54 E
Esseg → Osijek	38	45.33 N	18.41 E
Es-Sekhira	148	34.17 N	10.06 E
Essen, Bel.	50	51.28 N	4.28 E
Essen, Dtsch.	52	52.43 N	7.57 E
Essen, Dtsch.	56	51.28 N	7.01 E
Essen, Dtsch.	263	51.28 N	7.01 E
Essenbach	60	48.37 N	12.13 E
Essenberg ◆[8]	263	51.26 N	6.42 E
Essendon, Austl.	169	37.46 S	144.55 E
Essendon, Eng., U.K.	260	51.46 N	0.09 W
Essendon, Mount ∧	162	24.59 S	120.28 E
Essendon Airport ⊠	169	37.43 S	144.53 E
Essen-Mülheim, Flughafen ⊠	263	51.24 N	6.58 E
Essentuki → Jessentuki	84	44.03 N	42.51 E
Essequibo ≃	246	6.59 N	58.23 W
Essequibo Islands-West Demerara □[4]	246	6.40 N	58.30 W
Es Sers	36	36.04 N	9.02 E
Essex, On., Can.	214	42.10 N	82.49 W
Essex, Ct., U.S.	207	41.21 N	72.23 W
Essex, Il., U.S.	216	41.11 N	88.11 W
Essex, Ia., U.S.	198	40.50 N	95.18 W
Essex, Md., U.S.	208	39.18 N	76.28 W
Essex, Ma., U.S.	207	42.37 N	70.47 W
Essex, Mo., U.S.	194	36.48 N	89.51 W
Essex, Mt., U.S.	182	48.16 N	113.36 W
Essex □[6], On., Can.	214	42.10 N	82.50 W
Essex □[6], Eng., U.K.	42	51.48 N	0.40 E
Essex □[6], Ma., U.S.	207	42.40 N	70.55 W
Essex □[6], N.J., U.S.	210	40.48 N	74.12 W
Essex □[6], Vt., U.S.	206	44.57 N	71.43 W
Essex □[6], Va., U.S.	208	37.55 N	76.55 W
Essex ≃	283	42.39 N	70.46 W
Essex Bay ⊂	283	42.39 N	70.44 W
Essex Fells	276	40.49 N	74.17 W
Essex Junction	188	44.29 N	73.06 W
Essex Skypark ⊠	284b	39.18 N	76.28 W
Essexville	190	43.36 N	83.50 W
Essing	60	48.56 N	11.47 E
Essington	285	39.52 N	75.18 W
Essling ◆[8]	264b	48.13 N	16.32 E
Esslingen	56	48.45 N	9.16 E
Es Smala es Souassi	36	35.21 N	10.33 E
Esson Lake ⊜	212	45.02 N	78.16 W
Essonne □[5]	50	48.36 N	2.20 E
Essonne ≃	50	48.37 N	2.29 E
Essoyes	58	48.04 N	4.32 E
Es-Suki	140	13.20 N	33.54 E
Essvik	26	62.19 N	17.24 E
Est □[4]	152	4.00 N	14.00 E
Est, Canal de l' ≍	56	48.45 N	5.35 E
Est, Cap ›	157b	15.16 S	50.29 E
Est, Gare ◆[5]	261	48.53 N	2.22 E
Est, Île de l' I	186	47.37 N	61.26 W
Est, Pointe de l' ›	186	49.08 N	61.41 W
Estacada	224	45.17 N	122.19 W
Estaca de Bares, Punta de la ›	34	43.46 N	7.42 W
Estacado, Llano ≚	196	33.30 N	102.40 W
Estación La Colorado	234	23.52 N	102.26 W
Estado, Parque do ♠	287b	23.39 S	46.37 W
Estados, Isla de los (Staten Island) I	254	54.47 S	64.15 W
Estados Unidos → United States □[1]	178	38.00 N	97.00 W
Eṣṭahbān	128	29.08 N	54.04 E
Estaires	50	50.38 N	2.43 E
Estambul → İstanbul	130	41.01 N	28.58 E
Estância, Bra.	250	11.16 S	37.26 W
Estancia, Pil.	116	11.28 N	123.09 E
Estancia, S. Afr.	158	26.17 S	29.52 E
Estancia, N.M., U.S.	200	34.45 N	106.03 W
Estancia Los López	234	20.53 N	104.31 W
Estanislao del Campo	252	25.03 S	60.06 W
Estanzuelas	236	13.38 N	88.30 W
Estarreja	34	40.45 N	8.34 W
Estats, Pique d' ∧	34	42.40 N	1.24 E
Estavayer-le-Lac	58	46.51 N	6.50 E
Estcourt	158	29.01 S	29.52 E
Este	64	45.14 N	11.39 E
Este ≃	52	53.32 N	9.47 E
Este, Parque Nacional del ♠	286c	10.30 N	66.50 W
Este, Punta ›	240m	18.08 N	65.16 W
Esteban Echeverría	258	34.50 S	58.28 W
Esteban Echeverría □[5]	288	34.51 S	58.32 W
Estefanía, Lago → Stefanie, Lake ⊜	144	4.40 N	36.50 E
Esteio	252	29.51 S	51.10 W
Estelí	236	13.05 N	86.23 W
Estelí □[5]	236	13.10 N	86.20 W
Estella	34	42.40 N	2.02 W
Estelline, S.D., U.S.	198	44.34 N	96.54 W
Estelline, Tx., U.S.	196	34.33 N	100.26 W
Estell Manor	208	39.24 N	74.44 W
Estèng	62	44.14 N	6.45 E
Estepa	34	37.18 N	4.54 W
Estepas de Kirguises → Kirgizskij chrebet ⋏	85	42.30 N	74.00 E
Estepona	34	36.26 N	5.08 W
Ester	180	64.51 N	148.01 W
Esterel ⋏	62	43.30 N	6.50 E
Esterhazy	184	50.40 N	102.08 W
Esterhazy, Schloss ⊥	61	47.51 N	16.32 E
Estérias, Cap ›	152	0.37 N	9.20 E
Esternay	50	48.44 N	3.34 E
Estero	220	26.26 N	81.49 W
Estero Bay ⊂, Ca., U.S.	226	35.24 N	120.53 W
Estero Bay ⊂, Fl., U.S.	220	26.25 N	81.52 W
Estero Island I	220	26.26 N	81.56 W
Estéron ≃	62	43.49 N	7.11 E
Esteros	252	26.37 S	63.39 W
Esterwegen	52	52.59 N	7.38 E
Estes Park	200	40.22 N	105.31 W
Este Sudeste, Cayos del II	236	12.26 N	81.27 W
Estevan	184	49.08 N	102.59 W
Estevan Group II	182	53.05 N	129.40 W
Estevan Point	182	49.23 N	126.33 W
Esther Island I	180	60.50 N	148.05 W
Estherville	198	43.24 N	94.49 W
Estill	192	32.45 N	81.14 W
Estissac	50	48.16 N	3.49 E
Estiva	256	22.28 S	46.02 W
Estiva, Ribeirão da ≃	287b	23.44 S	46.23 W
Estiva, Rio da ≃	255	12.23 S	45.05 W
Estling, Lake ⊜	276	40.53 N	74.30 W
Estocolmo → Stockholm	40	59.20 N	18.03 E
Eston, Sk., Can.	184	51.10 N	108.46 W

Eston, Eng., U.K.	44	54.34 N	1.07 W
Estonia (Eesti) □[1], Europe	22	59.00 N	26.00 E
Estonia (Eesti) □[1], Europe	76	59.00 N	26.00 E
Estoril	34	38.42 N	9.23 W
Estrasburgo → Strasbourg	58	48.35 N	7.45 E
Estrées-Saint-Denis	50	49.26 N	2.39 E
Estrela	252	29.29 S	51.58 W
Estrela ∧	34	40.19 N	7.37 W
Estrela ≃	287a	22.43 S	43.13 W
Estrela, Serra da ⋏	34	40.20 N	7.38 W
Estrela do Norte	255	13.49 S	49.04 W
Estrela do Sul	255	18.46 S	47.42 W
Estrella ≃	226	35.45 N	120.41 W
Estremadura □[9]	34	39.15 N	9.10 W
Estremoz	34	38.51 N	7.35 W
Estribo	234	22.26 N	99.17 W
Estrondo, Serra do ⋏[1]	250	9.00 S	48.45 W
Estuaire □[4]	152	0.15 N	10.00 E
Estuary	184	50.56 N	109.46 W
Esumba, Île I	152	2.00 N	21.12 E
Eszék → Osijek	38	45.33 N	18.41 E
Esztergom	30	47.48 N	18.45 E
Étables	32	48.38 N	2.50 W
Etadunna	166	28.43 S	138.38 E
Etah, India	124	27.38 N	78.40 E
Etah, Kal. Nun.	16	78.19 N	72.38 W
Étain	56	49.13 N	5.38 E
Etajima	96	34.15 N	132.30 E
Eta-jima I	96	34.15 N	132.28 E
Étalle	56	49.41 N	5.36 E
Étamaniou ≃	186	50.17 N	59.58 W
Étampes	50	48.26 N	2.09 E
Etamunbanie, Lake ⊜	166	26.15 S	139.44 E
Étaples	50	50.31 N	1.39 E
États-Unis → United States □[1]	178	38.00 N	97.00 W
Etāwah	124	26.46 N	79.02 E
Etchemin ≃	186	46.46 N	71.14 W
Etchojoa	232	26.55 N	109.38 W
Etéké	152	1.29 S	11.35 E
Etembue	152	1.17 N	9.25 E
Etendard, Pic de l' ∧	62	45.09 N	6.09 E
Ethan	198	43.32 N	97.59 W
Ethel	194	33.07 N	89.27 W
Ethel ≃	162	24.09 S	118.26 E
Ethel, Mount ∧	200	40.39 N	106.41 W
Ethelbert	184	51.31 N	100.22 W
Ethel Creek	162	22.54 S	120.09 E
Ethel Lake ⊜	180	63.21 N	136.00 W
Etherow ≃	262	53.24 N	2.03 W
Ethiopia (Ityopiya) □[1], Afr.	136	9.00 N	39.00 E
Ethiopia (Ityopiya) □[1], Afr.	144	9.00 N	39.00 E
Ethiopian Plateau ⋏[1]	144	9.00 N	38.00 E
Ethiopie → Ethiopia □[1]	144	9.00 N	39.00 E
Ethridge, Mt., U.S.	202	48.33 N	112.07 W
Ethridge, Tn., U.S.	194	35.19 N	87.18 W
Eticoga	150	11.09 N	16.08 W
Eticuera Creek ≃	226	38.41 N	122.16 W
Etigo-heiya ≚	92	37.45 N	139.00 E
Etili	130	39.59 N	26.54 E
Étiolles	261	48.38 N	2.29 E
Etiopía → Ethiopia □[1]	144	9.00 N	39.00 E
Etive, Loch ⊜	46	56.29 N	5.09 W
Etiwanda	228	34.08 N	117.31 W
Etjo ∧	156	21.09 S	16.30 E
Etna, Ca., U.S.	204	41.27 N	122.53 W
Etna, N.Y., U.S.	210	42.29 N	76.23 W
Etna, Pa., U.S.	214	40.30 N	79.56 W
Etna, Wy., U.S.	200	43.02 N	111.00 W
Etna, Monte (Mongibello) ∧[1]	70	37.46 N	15.00 E
Etna Green	216	41.17 N	86.03 W
Etne	26	59.40 N	5.56 E
Etobicoke	212	43.42 N	79.32 W
Etobicoke Creek ≃	212	43.35 N	79.32 W
Etoile	154	11.38 S	27.34 E
Étoile, Chaîne de l' ⋏	62	43.22 N	5.30 E
Etoka	152	0.10 N	23.23 E
Etolin Island I	180	56.08 N	132.26 W
Etolin Strait ⊔	180	60.20 N	165.15 W
Etomami ≃	184	52.48 N	102.33 W
Eton, Austl.	166	21.16 S	148.58 E
Eton, Eng., U.K.	42	51.30 N	0.36 W
Eton College ⊽[2]	260	51.30 N	0.36 W
Etondo	152	7.46 S	23.36 E
Etorofu-tō → Iturup, ostrov I	92a	44.54 N	147.30 E
Etosha National Park ♠	156	19.00 S	15.50 E
Etosha Pan ≚	156	18.45 S	16.15 E
Etoumbi	152	0.01 S	14.57 E
Etowah	192	35.19 N	84.31 W
Etowah ≃	192	34.15 N	85.11 W
Étréchy	50	48.30 N	2.12 E
Étrépagny	50	49.18 N	1.37 E
Étretat	50	49.42 N	0.12 E
Etrotroka	157b	22.53 S	47.36 E
Etroubles	62	45.49 N	7.14 E
Etrusca, Necropoli ⊥	66	42.15 N	11.47 E
Etsch → Adige ≃	64	45.10 N	12.20 E
Ettal	64	47.34 N	11.05 E
Ettalong	170	33.31 S	151.21 E
Ettelbruck	56	49.52 N	6.05 E
Ettenheim	58	48.15 N	7.49 E
Etten-Leur	52	51.34 N	4.38 E
Etterbeek	56	50.50 N	4.23 E
Etters	208	40.09 N	76.45 W
Et Tîdra I	150	19.44 N	16.24 W
Ettington	42	52.09 N	1.36 W
Ettlingen	56	48.56 N	8.24 E
Ettrema Creek ≃	170	34.50 S	150.22 E
Ettrick	208	37.14 N	77.25 W
Ettrick Forest ◆[3]	46	55.30 N	3.00 W
Ettrick Pen ∧	44	55.22 N	3.16 W
Ettrick Water ≃	46	55.31 N	2.55 W
Ettringen, Dtsch.	56	50.21 N	7.13 E
Ettringen, Dtsch.	58	48.06 N	10.39 E
Etuku	154	3.43 S	25.44 E
Etyka	88	51.00 N	116.50 E
Etzatlán	234	20.46 N	104.05 W
Etzikom Coulee ≃	184	49.25 N	111.10 W
Etzná ⊥	232	19.35 N	90.15 W
Eu	50	50.03 N	1.25 E
Eua I	14	21.22 S	174.56 W
Eua Iki I	174w	21.07 S	174.59 W
Eubank Acres	222	30.23 N	97.42 W
Euboea → Évvoia I	38	38.34 N	23.50 E
Eucalyptus Hills	228	32.56 N	116.56 W
Euchiniko ≃	182	53.14 N	123.30 W
Eucla	162	31.43 S	128.52 E
Euclid, Oh., U.S.	214	41.35 N	81.31 W
Euclid, Pa., U.S.	214	41.00 N	79.56 W
Euclid Center	216	42.08 N	86.24 W
Euclid Creek ≃	279a	41.35 N	81.35 W
Euclid Creek Reservation ♠	279a	41.33 N	81.32 W
Euclides da Cunha	250	10.31 S	39.01 W
Eucumbene	171b	36.07 S	148.38 E
Eucumbene ≃	171b	36.21 S	148.38 E
Eucumbene, Lake ⊜[1]	171b	36.05 S	148.45 E
Eudistes, Lac des ⊜	186	50.30 N	65.15 W
Eudora, Ar., U.S.	194	33.06 N	91.15 W
Eudora, Ks., U.S.	198	38.56 N	95.05 W
Eudunda	168b	34.11 S	139.04 E
Eufaula, Al., U.S.	194	31.53 N	85.08 W
Eufaula, Ok., U.S.	196	35.17 N	95.34 W
Eufaula Lake ⊜[1]	196	35.17 N	95.31 W
Eufrates → Euphrates ≃	128	31.00 N	47.25 E
Euganei, Colli ⋏[2]	64	45.19 N	11.40 E
Eugendorf	64	47.52 N	13.07 E

Eugene	202	44.03 N	123.05 W
Eugenia, Punta ›	232	27.50 N	115.05 W
Eugenia Lake ⊜	212	44.20 N	80.30 W
Eugenio Bustos	252	33.46 S	69.04 W
Eugênio de Melo	256	23.09 S	45.47 W
Eugmo I	26	63.49 N	22.45 E
Eugowra	166	33.26 S	148.23 E
Euijeongbu → Ŭijŏngbu	98	37.44 N	127.03 E
Euless	222	32.50 N	97.04 W
Eulo	166	28.10 S	145.03 E
Eume ≃	34	43.25 N	8.08 W
Eumemmerring Creek ≃	274b	38.03 S	145.10 E
Eumungerie	166	31.57 S	148.37 E
Eunápolis	255	16.22 S	39.35 W
Eungella National Park ♠	166	21.00 S	148.30 E
Eunice, La., U.S.	194	30.29 N	92.25 W
Eunice, N.M., U.S.	196	32.26 N	103.09 W
Eupen	56	50.38 N	6.02 E
Euphrat → Euphrates ≃	128	31.00 N	47.25 E
Euphrates (Fırat) (Nahr al-Furāt) ≃	128	31.00 N	47.25 E
Eupora	194	33.32 N	89.16 W
Eure	208	36.25 N	76.51 W
Eure □[5]	50	49.10 N	1.00 E
Eure ≃	50	49.18 N	1.12 E
Eure-et-Loir □[5]	50	48.30 N	1.30 E
Eureka, Ak., U.S.	180	61.56 N	147.10 W
Eureka, Ca., U.S.	204	40.48 N	124.09 W
Eureka, Il., U.S.	190	40.43 N	89.16 W
Eureka, Ks., U.S.	198	37.49 N	96.17 W
Eureka, Mo., U.S.	219	38.30 N	90.37 W
Eureka, Mt., U.S.	202	48.52 N	115.03 W
Eureka, Nv., U.S.	204	39.30 N	115.57 W
Eureka, Pa., U.S.	214	40.15 N	78.46 W
Eureka, S.C., U.S.	192	34.42 N	81.11 W
Eureka, S.D., U.S.	198	45.46 N	99.37 W
Eureka, Tx., U.S.	222	32.01 N	96.18 W
Eureka, Ut,. U.S.	200	39.57 N	112.07 W
Eureka, Mount ∧	162	26.34 S	121.32 E
Eureka Springs	194	36.24 N	93.44 W
Eurialo, Castello ⊥	70	37.06 N	15.14 E
Eurinilla Creek ≃	166	30.50 S	140.01 E
Euroa	169	36.45 S	145.35 E
Euro Disney, Parc ♠	261	48.51 N	2.47 E
Europa, Île I	138	22.20 S	40.22 E
Europa, Picos de ⋏	34	43.12 N	4.48 W
Europabrücke ◆[5]	64	47.11 N	11.23 E
Europa Point ›	34	36.10 N	5.22 W
Europe ✢[1]	4	50.00 N	28.00 E
Europe ✢[1]	10	50.00 N	28.00 E
Europoort ◆[5]	52	51.57 N	4.07 E
Eursinge	52	52.46 N	6.28 E
Eurville	58	48.35 N	5.02 E
Euseigne	58	46.10 N	7.25 E
Euskal Herriko □[4]	34	43.00 N	2.30 W
Euskirchen	56	50.39 N	6.47 E
Eustace	222	32.18 N	96.01 W
Eustis, Fl., U.S.	220	28.51 N	81.41 W
Eustis, Ne., U.S.	198	40.39 N	100.09 W
Eustis, Lake ⊜	220	28.50 N	81.44 W
Euston	166	34.35 S	142.44 E
Euston Station ◆[5]	260	51.32 N	0.08 W
Eutaw	194	32.50 N	87.53 W
Eutin	54	54.08 N	10.37 E
Eutingen	56	48.55 N	8.45 E
Eutsuk Lake ⊜	182	53.20 N	126.44 W
Eutzsch	54	51.49 N	12.38 E
Euxton	44	53.39 N	2.40 W
Euzet-les-Bains	62	44.04 N	4.14 E
Eva	194	34.20 N	86.46 W
Evadale	194	30.21 N	94.04 W
Eva Downs	162	18.01 S	134.52 E
Evale	152	16.33 S	15.44 E
Evällen ⊜	40	60.03 N	18.20 E
Evançon ≃	62	45.40 N	7.41 E
Evandale	166	41.34 S	147.14 E
Evans	200	40.22 N	104.41 W
Evans, Lac ⊜	176	50.55 N	77.00 W
Evans, Mount ∧	200	39.35 N	105.38 W
Evansburg, Ab., Can.	182	53.36 N	115.01 W
Evansburg, Pa., U.S.	285	40.11 N	75.26 W
Evans Center	210	42.39 N	79.02 W
Evans City	214	40.46 N	80.03 W
Evans Creek ≃	202	42.25 N	123.11 W
Evansdale	190	42.28 N	92.16 W
Evans Head ›	166	29.07 S	153.26 E
Evans Mills	212	44.05 N	75.48 W
Evansport	216	41.25 N	84.24 W
Evans Strait ⊔	176	63.15 N	82.00 W
Evanston, Il., U.S.	216	42.02 N	87.41 W
Evanston, Pa., U.S.	279b	40.16 N	79.41 W
Evanston, Wy., U.S.	200	41.16 N	110.57 W
Evansville, Il., U.S.	194	38.05 N	89.56 W
Evansville, In., U.S.	194	37.58 N	87.33 W
Evansville, Mn., U.S.	198	46.00 N	95.40 W
Evansville, Wi., U.S.	216	42.46 N	89.17 W
Evansville, Wy., U.S.	200	42.51 N	106.16 W
Evant	196	31.29 N	98.09 W
Evanton	46	57.40 N	4.20 W
Eva Perón → La Plata	258	34.55 S	57.57 W
Evart	190	43.54 N	85.15 W
Evarts	192	36.51 N	83.11 W
Evaz	128	27.46 N	53.59 E
Ève	261	49.05 N	2.42 E
Evecquemont	261	49.02 N	1.57 E
Eveking	263	51.14 N	7.44 E
Eveleth	190	47.27 N	92.32 W
Evelyn, Mount ∧[2]	164	13.36 S	132.53 E
Evening Shade	194	36.04 N	91.37 W
Evenkamp	263	51.40 N	7.39 E
Evenlode ≃	42	51.47 N	1.21 W
Evensk	74	61.57 N	159.14 E
Evenwood	44	54.37 N	1.46 W
Even Yehuda	132	32.16 N	34.53 E
Everard, Lake ⊜	162	31.25 S	135.05 E
Everard, Mount ∧, Austl.	162	26.16 S	132.04 E
Everard, Mount ∧, B.C., Can.	182	51.05 N	125.45 W
Everard Ranges ⋏	162	27.05 S	132.28 E
Evercreech	42	51.09 N	2.30 W
Evere	56	50.52 N	4.24 E
Everest	198	39.40 N	95.25 W
Everest, Mount (Qomolangma Feng) ∧	124	27.59 N	86.56 E
Everett, On., Can.	212	44.11 N	79.57 W
Everett, Ma., U.S.	207	42.24 N	71.03 W
Everett, N.J., U.S.	276	40.21 N	74.09 W
Everett, Pa., U.S.	188	40.00 N	78.22 W
Everett, Wa., U.S.	224	47.58 N	122.12 W
Everett, Mount ∧	207	42.06 N	73.25 W
Evergem	50	51.07 N	3.42 E
Everglades, The ≣	220	26.00 N	80.40 W
Everglades City	220	25.52 N	81.23 W
Everglades National Park ♠	220	25.27 N	80.53 W
Evergreen, Al., U.S.	194	31.26 N	86.57 W
Evergreen, Ca., U.S.	204	35.54 N	120.26 W
Evergreen, Mt., U.S.	202	48.13 N	114.18 W
Evergreen, Tx., U.S.	222	30.33 N	95.14 W
Evergreen Lake ⊜[1]	216	40.40 N	89.02 W
Evergreen Park	216	41.43 N	87.42 W
Evergreen Plaza ◆[9]	278	41.43 N	87.41 W
Everly	198	43.09 N	95.19 W
Everman	222	32.37 N	97.17 W
Everman, Volcán ∧[1]	232	18.48 N	110.59 W
Everöd	26	55.54 N	14.06 E
Eversael	263	51.33 N	6.39 E
Eversberg	56	51.21 N	8.20 E
Eversen	52	52.45 N	10.02 E
Everson, Pa., U.S.	214	40.05 N	79.35 W
Everson, Wa., U.S.	224	48.55 N	122.20 W
Everswinkel	52	51.55 N	7.50 E
Everton	218	39.34 N	85.05 W
Everton ◆[8]	262	53.25 N	2.58 W
Everton Football Ground ♠	262	53.26 N	2.58 W

≃ River	Fluß	Río	Rivière	Rio	
≍ Canal	Kanal	Canal	Canal	Canal	
∟ Waterfall, Rapids	Wasserfall, Stromschnellen	Cascada, Rápidos	Chute d'eau, Rapides	Cascata, Rápidos	
⊔ Strait	Meeresstraße	Estrecho	Détroit	Estreito	
⊂ Bay, Gulf	Bucht, Golf	Bahía, Golfo	Baie, Golfe	Baía, Golfo	
⊜ Lake, Lakes	See, Seen	Lago, Lagos	Lac, Lacs	Lago, Lagos	
≣ Swamp	Sumpf	Pantano	Marais	Pântano	
⊓ Ice Features, Glacier	Eis- und Gletscherformen	Accidentes Glaciales	Formes glaciaires	Acidentes glaciares	
⊤ Other Hydrographic Features	Andere Hydrographische Objekte	Otros Elementos Hidrográficos	Autres données hydrographiques	Outros acidentes hidrográficos	

✢ Submarine Features	Untermeerische Objekte	Accidentes Submarinos	Formes de relief sous-marin	Acidentes submarinos
□ Political Unit	Politische Einheit	Unidad Politica	Entité politique	Unidade política
⊽ Cultural Institution	Kulturelle Institution	Institución Cultural	Institution culturelle	Institução cultural
⊥ Historical Site	Historische Stätte	Sitio Histórico	Site historique	Sitio histórico
♠ Recreational Site	Erholungs- und Ferienort	Sitio de Recreo	Centre de loisirs	Area de Lazer
⊠ Airport	Flughafen	Aeropuerto	Aéroport	Aeroporto
■ Military Installation	Militäranlage	Instalación Militar	Installation militaire	Instalação militar
◆ Miscellaneous	Verschiedenes	Misceláneo	Divers	Diversos

ENGLISH — DEUTSCH

Name / Page / Lat.°′ / Long.°′ — Name / Seite / Breite°′ / Länge°′ E = Ost

Evesen **52** 52.17 N 8.59 E
Evesham, Sk., Can. **184** 52.24 N 109.50 W
Evesham, Eng., U.K. **42** 52.06 N 1.56 W
Evesham, Vale of ∨ **42** 52.06 N 1.50 W
Évian-les-Bains **58** 46.23 N 6.35 E
Evijärvi **26** 63.22 N 23.29 E
Evinayong **152** 1.27 N 10.34 E
Eving ⊸[8] **263** 51.33 N 7.29 E
Evingsen **263** 51.18 N 7.44 E
Evionnaz **58** 46.11 N 7.01 E
Evisa **36** 42.15 N 8.47 E
Evje **26** 58.36 N 7.51 E
Evolène **58** 46.07 N 7.30 E
Évora **34** 38.34 N 7.54 W
Evoron, ozero ⊜ **89** 51.28 N 136.30 E
Evpatoria
— Yevpatoriya **78** 45.12 N 33.22 E
Évrange **56** 49.30 N 6.12 E
Évreux **50** 49.01 N 1.09 E
Evrieu **62** 45.35 N 5.34 E
ʿEvron **132** 32.59 N 35.06 E
Évros (Marica) (Meriç) ≃ **38** 40.52 N 26.12 E
Evrótas ≃ **38** 36.48 N 22.40 E
Évry **50** 48.38 N 2.27 E
Évry-les-Châteaux **261** 48.39 N 2.38 E
E. V. Spence Reservoir ⊜[1] **196** 31.55 N 100.35 W
Evungu **154** 4.27 S 25.12 E
Évvoia I **38** 38.34 N 23.50 E
Évzonos ∧ **267c** 37.57 N 23.49 E
Ewa **229c** 21.20 N 158.02 W
Ewa Beach **229c** 21.18 N 158.00 W
Ewan **285** 39.42 N 75.11 W
Ewaninga **162** 23.58 S 133.58 E
Ewan Lake ⊜ **285** 39.42 N 75.11 W
Ewansville **285** 39.59 N 74.44 W
Ewbank **158** 26.14 S 23.35 E
Ewbank da Câmara **256** 21.31 S 43.33 W
Ewe, Loch ⊂ **46** 57.48 N 5.40 W
Ewell, Eng., U.K. **260** 51.21 N 0.15 W
Ewell, Md., U.S. **208** 37.59 N 76.02 W
Ewen **190** 46.32 N 89.16 W
Ewenkiku Zizhiqi **89** 49.07 N 119.40 E
Ewes Water ≃ **44** 55.08 N 3.00 W
Ewing, Ky., U.S. **218** 38.25 N 83.51 W
Ewing, Mo., U.S. **219** 40.00 N 91.42 W
Ewing, Ne., U.S. **198** 42.15 N 98.20 W
Ewing, Va., U.S. **192** 36.38 N 83.25 W
Ewingsville **279b** 40.24 N 80.06 W
Ewing Township **208** 40.16 N 74.46 W
Ewo **152** 0.53 S 14.49 E
Ewu **273a** 6.33 N 3.19 E
Exaltación **248** 13.16 S 65.15 W
Excelda **158** 32.16 S 22.08 E
Excello **218** 39.29 N 84.25 W
Excelsior **158** 28.56 S 27.06 E
Excelsior Mountain ∧ **226** 38.02 N 119.18 W
Excelsior Park ◆ **274a** 33.45 S 151.01 E
Excelsior Springs **194** 39.20 N 94.13 W
Excenevex **58** 46.21 N 6.21 E
Exchange **210** 41.07 N 76.41 W
Exchange Station ⊸[5] **262** 53.25 N 2.59 W
Excursion Inlet **180** 58.25 N 135.27 W
Exe ≃ **42** 50.37 N 3.25 W
Executive Committee Range ⋏ **9** 76.50 S 126.00 W
Exeter, Austl. **170** 34.38 S 150.19 E
Exeter, On., Can. **190** 43.21 N 81.29 W
Exeter, Eng., U.K. **42** 50.43 N 3.31 W
Exeter, Ca., U.S. **226** 36.17 N 119.08 W
Exeter, Ne., U.S. **198** 40.38 N 97.27 W
Exeter, N.H., U.S. **188** 42.58 N 70.56 W
Exeter, Pa., U.S. **210** 41.19 N 75.49 W
Exeter, R.I., U.S. **207** 41.34 N 71.32 W
Exeter ≃ **188** 43.02 N 70.55 W
Exeter Sound ʮ **176** 66.14 N 62.00 W
Exford **42** 51.08 N 3.38 W
Exhibition of Economic Achievements ᴗ **265b** 55.50 N 37.37 E
Exhibition Park ◆ **275b** 43.38 N 79.25 W
Exhibition Stadium ◆ **275b** 43.38 N 79.25 W
Exincourt **58** 47.30 N 6.50 E
Exira **198** 41.35 N 94.52 W
Exline Slough ≃ **216** 41.05 N 87.47 W
Exmes **50** 48.46 N 0.11 E
Exminster **42** 50.41 N 3.29 W
Exmoor ⋏[1] **42** 51.10 N 3.45 W
Exmoor National Park ◆ **42** 51.12 N 3.46 W
Exmore **208** 37.31 N 75.49 W
Exmouth, Austl. **162** 21.56 S 114.07 E
Exmouth, Eng., U.K. **42** 50.37 N 3.25 W
Exmouth Gulf ⊂ **162** 22.00 S 114.20 E
Exmouth Plateau ✧[3] **14** 19.00 S 114.00 E
Exning **42** 52.16 N 0.21 E
Expedition Range ⋏ **166** 24.30 S 149.05 E
Experiment **192** 33.15 N 84.16 W
Exploits ≃ **186** 49.05 N 55.20 W
Exploits, Bay of ⊂ **186** 49.24 N 55.00 W
Exploits Dam ⊸[6] **186** 48.45 N 56.30 W
Expo Memorial Park ◆ **270** 34.48 N 135.32 E
Export **214** 40.25 N 79.37 W
Exposition Park ◆ **280** 34.01 N 118.17 W
Exshaw **182** 51.03 N 115.09 W
Extension **224** 49.06 N 123.57 W
Exter **52** 52.08 N 8.46 E
Externsteine ⊥ **52** 51.52 N 8.55 E
Extertal **52** 52.04 N 9.07 E
Exton **208** 40.02 N 75.37 W
Extoraz ≃ **234** 21.06 N 99.23 W
Extrema **256** 22.51 S 46.19 W
Extremadura □[4] **34** 39.15 N 6.15 W
Exu **250** 7.31 S 39.43 W
Exuma Cays II **238** 24.15 N 76.30 W
Exuma Sound ʮ **238** 24.15 N 76.00 W
Eyak **180** 60.32 N 145.36 W
Eyam **44** 53.17 N 1.41 W
Eyasi, Lake ⊜ **154** 3.40 S 35.05 E
Eydehavn **26** 58.31 N 8.53 E
Eye, Eng., U.K. **42** 52.19 N 1.09 E
Eye, Eng., U.K. **42** 52.35 N 0.10 W
Eyebrow **184** 50.47 N 106.09 W
Eyehill Creek ≃ **184** 52.40 N 109.39 W
Eyemouth **46** 55.52 N 2.06 W
Eye Peninsula ›[1] **46** 58.13 N 6.13 W
Eyers Grove **210** 41.05 N 76.31 W
Eye Water ≃ **46** 55.53 N 2.06 W
Eygalières **62** 43.45 N 4.57 E
Eyguières **62** 43.42 N 5.02 E
Eyhorne Street **260** 51.16 N 0.38 E
Eyjafjörður ⊂[2] **24a** 65.54 N 18.15 W
Eyl **144** 7.59 N 49.49 E
Eylar Mountain ∧ **204** 37.28 N 121.33 W
Eymet **32** 44.40 N 0.24 E
Eymir **130** 40.02 N 35.14 E
Eymoutiers **32** 45.44 N 1.44 E
Eynesil **130** 41.03 N 39.08 E
Eynhallow Sound ʮ **46** 59.08 N 3.06 W
Eynort, Loch ⊂ **46** 57.13 N 7.18 W
Eynsford **260** 51.22 N 0.13 E
Eynsham **42** 51.48 N 1.22 W
Eyota **190** 43.59 N 92.13 W
Eyrarbakki **24a** 63.53 N 21.05 W
Eyre **162** 32.15 S 126.18 E
Eyrecourt **48** 53.11 N 8.07 W
Eyre Creek ≃ **166** 26.40 S 139.00 E
Eyre Mountains ⋏ **172** 45.20 S 168.30 E
Eyre North, Lake ⊜ **166** 28.40 S 137.10 E
Eyre Peninsula ›[1] **162** 34.00 S 135.45 E
Eyre South, Lake ⊜ **166** 29.30 S 137.20 E
Eyrieux ≃ **62** 44.48 N 4.48 E
Eystrup **52** 52.46 N 9.13 E
Eythorne **42** 51.11 N 1.17 E
Eythra **54** 51.14 N 12.17 E
Eyüp ⊸[8] **267b** 41.03 N 28.55 E
Eyvānekey **128** 35.20 N 52.04 E
Eyzaguirre, Canal ≖ **286e** 33.36 S 70.41 W
Ézanville **261** 49.02 N 2.22 E
Ezbekīyah ⊸[8] **273c** 30.03 N 31.15 E
Ezeiza, Aeropuerto Internacional de ⊠ **288** 34.49 S 58.32 W
Ezequiel Ramos Mexía, Embalse ⊜[1] **254** 39.30 S 69.00 W
Ezere **76** 56.26 N 22.22 E
Ežerėlis **76** 54.53 N 23.37 E
Ezeriș **38** 45.24 N 21.53 E
Ezine **130** 39.47 N 26.20 E
Ezinepazarı **130** 40.34 N 36.09 E
Ezop, chrebet ⋏ **89** 52.36 N 133.37 E
Ežva **24** 61.47 N 50.40 E
Ézy-sur-Eure **50** 48.52 N 1.25 E
Ezzell **222** 29.17 N 96.58 W

F

Faaa Airport ⊠ **174s** 17.33 S 149.36 W
Faafaxdhuun **144** 2.13 N 41.37 E
Faal **174q** 9.37 N 138.10 E
Faaone **174s** 17.40 S 149.18 W
Fabala **150** 9.44 N 9.05 W
Fabbrico **64** 44.52 N 10.50 E
Fabens **200** 31.30 N 106.09 W
Fåberg **26** 61.10 N 10.24 E
Faber Lake ⊜ **176** 63.56 N 117.15 W
Fabert Seamount ✧[3] **14** 24.07 S 158.33 W
Fabius **210** 42.50 N 75.59 W
Fåborg **41** 55.06 N 10.15 E
Fábrega, Cerro ∧ **236** 9.07 N 82.52 W
Fabrègues **62** 43.33 N 3.46 E
Fabreville ⊸[8] **275a** 45.34 N 73.50 W
Fabriano **66** 43.20 N 12.54 E
Fabrica di Roma **66** 42.20 N 12.18 E
Fabričnyj **85** 43.11 N 76.24 E
Fabrizia **68** 38.29 N 16.18 E
Facatativá **246** 4.49 N 74.22 W
Facha **146** 29.27 N 17.18 E
Faches-Thumesnil **50** 50.35 N 3.04 E
Fachi **146** 18.06 N 11.34 E
Facpi Point › **174p** 13.20 N 144.38 E
Factoryville **210** 41.34 N 75.47 W
Facundo **254** 45.18 S 69.58 W
Fada **146** 17.14 N 21.33 E
Fada, Lochan ⊜ **46** 57.41 N 5.18 W
Fadalto **64** 46.05 N 12.20 E
Fada Ngourma **150** 12.04 N 0.21 E
Fadd **30** 46.28 N 18.50 E
Faddeja, zaliv ⊂ **74** 76.40 N 107.20 E
Faddejevskij, ostrov I **74** 75.30 N 144.00 E
Faddoi **140** 8.07 N 32.07 E
Fadian Point › **174p** 13.26 N 144.49 E
Fadiffolu Atoll I[1] **122** 5.25 N 73.30 E
Fadit **140** 9.58 N 32.13 E
Faedis **64** 46.10 N 13.20 E
Fænø I **41** 55.29 N 9.42 E
Faenza **66** 44.17 N 11.53 E
Faeroe Islands □[2] **22** 62.00 N 7.00 W
Faeröerne
— Faeroe Islands □[2] **22** 62.00 N 7.00 W
Faete, Monte ∧ **267a** 41.45 N 12.44 E
Fafa **150** 15.20 N 0.43 E
Fafa ≃ **152** 7.18 N 18.16 E
Fafakourou **150** 13.04 N 14.34 W
Fafe **34** 41.27 N 8.10 W
Fafen ≃ **144** 5.59 N 44.25 E
Faga ≃ **150** 13.15 N 0.55 E
Fagaitua **174u** 14.16 S 170.37 W
Fagamalo **175a** 13.25 S 172.21 W
Făgăraș **38** 45.51 N 24.58 E
Făgărașului, Munții ⋏ **38** 45.35 N 25.00 E
Fagasa **174u** 14.17 S 170.43 W
Fagatogo **174u** 14.17 S 170.41 W
Fagernes **26** 60.59 N 9.15 E
Fagersta **40** 60.00 N 15.47 E
Fagertärn ⊸[4] **40** 58.46 N 14.42 E
Fagerviken **40** 60.33 N 17.45 E
Făget **38** 45.51 N 22.10 E
Faggen Bach ≃ **64** 47.05 N 10.40 E
Faggo **150** 11.23 N 9.57 E
Fagnano, Lago ⊜ **254** 54.35 S 68.00 W
Fagnano Castello **68** 39.34 N 16.03 E
Fagnano Olona **62** 45.40 N 8.52 E
Fagnières **50** 48.58 N 4.19 E
Faguibine, Lac ⊜ **150** 16.45 N 3.54 W
Fagundes, Rio do ≃ **256** 22.12 S 43.11 W
Fagurhólsmýri **24a** 63.54 N 16.38 W
Fagwir **140** 9.33 N 30.25 E
Fahan **48** 55.05 N 7.28 W
Fahl, Oued el ∨ **148** 31.15 N 4.41 E
Fahraj **128** 28.58 N 58.52 E
Fährdorf **54** 53.58 N 11.28 E
Fahrland **54** 52.28 N 13.01 E
Fahrlander See ⊜ **264a** 52.27 N 13.01 E
Fahrnau **58** 47.39 N 7.50 E
Fahuaqiao **106** 30.52 N 121.25 E
Faial I **148a** 38.34 N 28.42 W
Faichuk II **175c** 7.23 N 151.40 E
Fā'id **142** 30.19 N 32.19 E
Fā'id Military Base ■ **142** 30.20 N 32.16 E
Faido **58** 46.29 N 8.48 E
Faillon, Lac ⊜ **190** 48.21 N 76.38 W
Failsworth **44** 53.31 N 2.09 W
Fains-les-Sources **56** 48.47 N 5.08 E
Fairbairn Airport ⊠ **171b** 35.18 S 149.15 E
Fairbairn Park ◆ **274b** 37.47 S 144.55 E
Fairbairn Reservoir ⊜[1] **166** 23.45 S 148.00 E
Fairbank **190** 42.38 N 92.02 W
Fairbanks, Ak., U.S. **180** 64.51 N 147.43 W
Fairbanks, La., U.S. **194** 30.00 N 92.02 W
Fair Bluff **192** 34.18 N 79.02 W
Fairborn **218** 39.49 N 84.01 W
Fairbourne **42** 52.41 N 4.03 W
Fairburn **192** 33.34 N 84.34 W
Fairbury, Il., U.S. **216** 40.44 N 88.30 W
Fairbury, Ne., U.S. **198** 40.08 N 97.10 W
Fairchance **188** 39.49 N 79.45 W
Fairchild **190** 44.36 N 90.57 W
Fairchild Air Force Base ■ **202** 47.38 N 117.38 W
Fairchild Creek ≃ **212** 43.07 N 80.07 W
Fairdale **216** 42.06 N 88.56 W
Faire **116** 17.53 N 121.34 E
Fairfax, Al., U.S. **194** 32.47 N 85.11 W
Fairfax, Ca., U.S. **226** 37.59 N 122.35 W
Fairfax, De., U.S. **285** 39.47 N 75.32 W
Fairfax, Mn., U.S. **198** 44.31 N 94.43 W
Fairfax, Mo., U.S. **194** 40.20 N 95.23 W
Fairfax, Ok., U.S. **196** 36.34 N 96.42 W
Fairfax, S.C., U.S. **192** 32.57 N 81.14 W
Fairfax, S.D., U.S. **198** 43.01 N 98.53 W
Fairfax, Vt., U.S. **188** 44.39 N 73.00 W
Fairfax, Va., U.S. **208** 38.50 N 77.18 W
Fairfax □[6] **208** 38.45 N 77.15 W
Fairfax Forest **284c** 38.52 N 77.15 W
Fairfax Park **284c** 38.47 N 77.14 W
Fairfax State Recreation Area ◆ **218** 39.02 N 86.29 W
Fairfax Station **284c** 38.48 N 77.19 W
Fairfield, Austl. **170** 33.52 S 150.57 E
Fairfield, Al., U.S. **194** 33.33 N 86.47 W
Fairfield, Ca., U.S. **226** 38.14 N 122.02 W
Fairfield, Ct., U.S. **210** 41.08 N 73.15 W
Fairfield, Id., U.S. **202** 43.20 N 114.47 W
Fairfield, Il., U.S. **194** 38.22 N 88.21 W
Fairfield, Ia., U.S. **190** 41.00 N 91.57 W
Fairfield, Me., U.S. **188** 44.35 N 69.35 W
Fairfield, Mt., U.S. **202** 47.36 N 111.58 W
Fairfield, Ne., U.S. **198** 40.25 N 98.06 W
Fairfield, N.J., U.S. **276** 40.53 N 74.16 W
Fairfield, N.Y., U.S. **210** 43.08 N 74.55 W
Fairfield, Oh., U.S. **218** 39.20 N 84.33 W
Fairfield, Pa., U.S. **214** 39.47 N 77.22 W
Fairfield, Tx., U.S. **222** 31.43 N 96.09 W
Fairfield □[6] **207** 41.15 N 73.20 W
Fairfield Lake ⊜[1] **222** 31.50 N 96.05 W
Fairfield University ᴗ[2] **276** 41.09 N 73.15 W
Fairford **42** 51.44 N 1.47 W
Fairgrove **190** 43.31 N 83.32 W
Fair Harbor **210** 40.38 N 73.11 W
Fairhaven, Ma., U.S. **207** 41.38 N 70.54 W
Fair Haven, Mi., U.S. **214** 42.40 N 82.39 W
Fair Haven, N.J., U.S. **208** 40.21 N 74.02 W
Fair Haven, N.Y., U.S. **210** 43.18 N 76.42 W
Fairhaven, Oh., U.S. **218** 39.38 N 84.47 W
Fair Haven, Vt., U.S. **188** 43.35 N 73.15 W
Fair Haven, Va., U.S. **284c** 38.47 N 77.05 W
Fairhaven Bay ⊜ **283** 42.26 N 71.21 W
Fair Haven Beach State Park ◆, N.Y., U.S. **210** 43.21 N 76.41 W
Fair Haven Beach State Park ◆, N.Y., U.S. **212** 43.21 N 76.41 W
Fair Head › **48** 55.13 N 6.09 W
Fairhope, Al., U.S. **194** 30.31 N 87.54 W
Fairhope, Oh., U.S. **214** 40.51 N 81.19 W
Fairhope, Pa., U.S. **214** 40.07 N 79.50 W
Fair Isle I **46** 59.32 N 1.39 W
Fairknoll **284c** 39.05 N 76.59 W
Fairland, In., U.S. **218** 39.35 N 85.51 W
Fairland, Md., U.S. **284c** 39.05 N 76.58 W
Fairland, Ok., U.S. **196** 36.45 N 94.50 W
Fairlane Town Center ⊸[9] **281** 42.19 N 83.13 W
Fair Lawn, N.J., U.S. **210** 40.56 N 74.07 W
Fairlawn, Oh., U.S. **214** 41.07 N 81.36 W
Fairlee **284c** 38.52 N 77.16 W
Fairleigh Dickinson University (Florham-Madison) ᴗ[2], N.J., U.S. **276** 40.46 N 74.26 W
Fairleigh Dickinson University (Teaneck) ᴗ[2], N.J., U.S. **276** 40.53 N 74.02 W
Fairleigh Dickinson University ᴗ[2], N.J., U.S. **276** 40.50 N 74.07 W
Fairless Hills **208** 40.10 N 74.51 W
Fairlie, N.Z. **172** 44.06 S 170.50 E
Fairlie, Scot., U.K. **46** 55.46 N 4.51 W
Fairlight **42** 50.53 N 0.40 E
Fairmont, Il., U.S. **216** 41.33 N 88.03 W
Fairmont, Mn., U.S. **198** 43.39 N 94.27 W
Fairmont, Ne., U.S. **198** 40.38 N 97.35 W
Fairmont, N.C., U.S. **192** 34.29 N 79.06 W
Fairmont, Pa., U.S. **279b** 40.19 N 79.43 W
Fairmont, Wa., U.S. **224** 48.54 N 122.16 W
Fairmont, W.V., U.S. **188** 39.29 N 80.08 W
Fairmont City **219** 38.40 N 90.06 W
Fairmont Hot Springs **182** 50.19 N 115.53 W
Fairmont Reservoir ⊜[1] **228** 34.43 N 118.26 W
Fairmont Terrace **282** 37.43 N 122.07 W
Fairmount, Ga., U.S. **192** 34.26 N 84.42 W
Fairmount, Il., U.S. **194** 40.03 N 87.56 W
Fairmount, In., U.S. **216** 40.24 N 85.39 W
Fairmount, N.Y., U.S. **210** 43.02 N 76.14 W
Fairmount, N.D., U.S. **198** 46.03 N 96.36 W
Fairmount City **214** 41.01 N 79.19 W
Fairmount Heights **208** 38.54 N 76.54 W
Fairmount Park ◆ **285** 40.00 N 75.12 W
Fair Ness › **176** 63.24 N 72.05 W
Fair Oaks, Ca., U.S. **226** 38.38 N 121.16 W
Fair Oaks, Ga., U.S. **192** 33.54 N 84.32 W
Fair Oaks, In., U.S. **216** 41.05 N 87.16 W
Fairoaks, Pa., U.S. **279b** 40.34 N 80.13 W
Fairoaks Airport ⊠ **260** 51.21 N 0.32 W
Fair Plain **216** 42.05 N 86.27 W
Fairplains **192** 36.13 N 81.10 W
Fairplay **200** 39.13 N 106.00 W
Fairpoint **214** 40.07 N 80.55 W
Fairport, On., Can. **275b** 43.49 N 79.05 W
Fairport, N.Y., U.S. **210** 43.05 N 77.26 W
Fairport Beach **275b** 43.48 N 79.06 W
Fairport Harbor **214** 41.44 N 81.16 W
Fairseat **260** 51.20 N 0.20 E
Fairton **208** 39.22 N 75.13 W
Fairview, Austl. **164** 15.33 S 144.19 E
Fairview, Ab., Can. **182** 56.04 N 118.23 W
Fairview, Ga., U.S. **192** 34.56 N 85.17 W
Fairview, Il., U.S. **190** 40.38 N 90.10 W
Fairview, In., U.S. **216** 40.18 N 85.11 W
Fairview, Ks., U.S. **198** 39.50 N 95.43 W
Fairview, Md., U.S. **208** 39.09 N 76.29 W
Fairview, Mi., U.S. **190** 44.43 N 84.03 W
Fairview, Mt., U.S. **198** 47.51 N 104.02 W
Fairview, N.J., U.S. **276** 40.51 N 73.58 W
Fairview, N.Y., U.S. **210** 41.43 N 73.55 W
Fairview, Oh., U.S. **214** 40.03 N 81.14 W
Fairview, Ok., U.S. **196** 36.16 N 98.28 W
Fairview, Pa., U.S. **214** 42.01 N 80.15 W
Fairview, Tn., U.S. **194** 35.58 N 87.07 W
Fairview, Ut,. U.S. **200** 39.37 N 111.26 W
Fairview, W.V., U.S. **188** 39.35 N 80.14 W
Fairview Heights **219** 38.10 N 90.00 W
Fairview Lanes **214** 41.23 N 82.40 W
Fairview Mall ⊸[9] **275b** 43.47 N 79.21 W
Fairview Park, In., U.S. **194** 39.40 N 87.25 W
Fairview Park, Oh., U.S. **214** 41.26 N 81.51 W
Fairview Park, Pa., U.S. **210** 41.10 N 75.53 W
Fairview Peak ∧, Nv., U.S. **204** 39.14 N 118.08 W
Fairview Peak ∧, Or., U.S. **202** 43.35 N 122.39 W
Fairview Pointe Claire Centre ⊸[9] **275a** 45.28 N 73.50 W
Fairview Shores **220** 28.35 N 81.23 W
Fairview Village **285** 40.10 N 75.23 W
Fairvilla **220** 28.35 N 81.24 W
Fairville **285** 39.51 N 75.38 W
Fairweather Mountain ∧ **180** 58.54 N 137.32 W
Fairy Lake ⊜ **212** 45.20 N 79.11 W
Fairy Meadow **170** 34.23 S 150.54 E
Fairy Stone State Park ◆ **192** 36.48 N 80.06 W
Fairy Water ≃ **48** 54.37 N 7.20 W
Fais I **108** 9.46 N 140.31 E
Faisalabad (Lyallpur) **123** 31.25 N 73.05 E
Faison **192** 35.06 N 78.08 W
Faistós ⊥ **38** 35.01 N 24.48 E
Faith **198** 45.01 N 102.02 W
Faiyum
— Al-Fayyūm **142** 29.19 N 30.50 E
Faizābād **124** 26.47 N 82.08 E
Fajansovyj **76** 54.04 N 34.24 E
Fajardo **240m** 18.20 N 65.39 W
Fajou, Îlet à I **241o** 16.21 N 61.35 W
Fajr, Wādī ∨ **128** 30.06 N 38.18 E
Fajzabad **85** 38.34 N 69.19 E
Fakahatchee Strand ⩩ **220** 26.10 N 81.35 W
Fakaofo I[1] **14** 9.22 S 171.14 W
Fakarava I[1] **14** 16.20 S 145.37 W
Fakejev **80** 48.57 N 49.56 E
Fakel **80** 57.38 N 53.02 E
Fakenham **42** 52.50 N 0.51 E
Fakfak **164** 2.55 S 132.18 E
Fakılı **130** 39.13 N 35.00 E
Fakīrganj **124** 25.58 N 90.02 E
Fakī Şādiq **140** 12.08 N 23.55 E
Fakrinkotti **140** 18.01 N 31.20 E
Fakse **41** 55.15 N 12.08 E
Fakse Bugt ⊂ **41** 55.10 N 12.15 E
Fakse Ladeplads **41** 55.13 N 12.11 E
Faku **104** 42.30 N 123.24 E
Fal ≃ **42** 50.08 N 5.02 W
Falaba **150** 9.51 N 11.19 W
Faladyé **150** 13.08 N 8.20 W
Falaise **32** 48.54 N 0.12 W
Fālākāta **124** 26.32 N 89.12 E
Falam **110** 22.55 N 93.40 E
Falāvarjān **128** 32.33 N 51.30 E
Falcade **64** 46.21 N 11.51 E
Falcão **256** 22.17 S 44.16 W
Fălciu **38** 46.18 N 28.08 E
Falck **56** 49.14 N 6.38 E
Falcognana di Sotto ⊸[8] **267a** 41.45 N 12.33 E
Falcón □[3] **246** 11.00 N 69.50 W
Falcon, Cap › **34** 35.46 N 0.48 W
Falcon, Cape › **224** 45.46 N 123.59 W
Falcón, Presa (Falcon Reservoir) ⊜[1] **196** 26.37 N 99.11 W
Falconara Albanese **68** 39.16 N 16.05 E
Falconara Alta **66** 43.37 N 13.24 E
Falconara Marittima **66** 43.37 N 13.24 E
Falconbridge **190** 46.35 N 80.48 W
Falconcrest **285** 39.58 N 75.33 W
Falcone **70** 38.07 N 15.05 E
Falcone, Capo del › **71** 40.58 N 8.12 E
Falconer **214** 42.07 N 79.11 W
Falcon Heights **202** 42.08 N 121.45 W
Falcon Reservoir (Presa Falcón) ⊜[1] **196** 26.37 N 99.11 W
Falconwood **210** 43.00 N 78.57 W
Faldsled **41** 55.09 N 10.09 E
Faléa **150** 12.16 N 11.17 W
Faleasao **174y** 14.13 S 169.32 W
Falelatai **175a** 13.55 S 171.59 W
Falelima **175a** 13.32 S 172.41 W
Falémé ≃ **150** 14.46 N 12.14 W
Falenki **80** 58.22 N 51.35 E
Falerii Novi ⊥ **66** 42.16 N 12.20 E
Falerna **68** 39.00 N 16.10 E
Falerone **66** 43.06 N 13.28 E
Fălești **38** 47.34 N 27.43 E
Falfurrias **196** 27.13 N 98.08 W
Falher **182** 55.44 N 117.12 W
Falicon **62** 43.45 N 7.17 E
Fálirou, Órmos ⊂ **267c** 37.56 N 23.40 E
Falkenberg, Dtsch. **54** 51.35 N 13.14 E
Falkenberg, Dtsch. **54** 52.48 N 13.58 E
Falkenberg, Dtsch. **60** 49.52 N 12.14 E
Falkenberg, Dtsch. **60** 48.28 N 12.43 E
Falkenberg, Sve. **26** 56.54 N 12.28 E
Falkenberg ⊸[8] **264a** 52.34 N 13.33 E
Falkenhagen, Dtsch. **54** 53.12 N 12.12 E
Falkenhagen, Dtsch. **54** 52.26 N 14.19 E
Falkenhagener See ⊜ **264a** 52.34 N 13.08 E
Falkenrehde **264a** 52.30 N 12.56 E
Falkensee **54** 52.33 N 13.04 E
Falkenstein **54** 50.29 N 12.22 E
Falkenthal **54** 52.54 N 13.17 E
Falkirk **46** 56.00 N 3.48 W
Falkland, B.C., Can. **182** 50.30 N 119.33 W
Falkland, Scot., U.K. **46** 56.15 N 3.12 W
Falkland-Inseln
— Falkland Islands □[2] **254** 51.45 S 59.00 W
Falkland Islands □[2], S.A. **244** 51.45 S 59.00 W
Falkland Islands □[2], S.A. **254** 51.45 S 59.00 W
Falkland Plateau ✧[3] **18** 51.00 S 50.00 W
Falkland Sound ʮ **254** 51.45 S 59.25 W
Falköping **26** 58.10 N 13.31 E
Falkville **194** 34.22 N 86.54 W
Fall ≃, On., Can. **212** 44.59 N 76.22 W
Fall ≃, Ks., U.S. **198** 37.24 N 95.40 W
Fall ≃, Wa., U.S. **224** 46.47 N 123.30 W
Falla **40** 58.41 N 15.45 E
Fallais **56** 50.37 N 5.10 E
Fallbach **61** 48.39 N 16.25 E
Fallbrook **228** 33.22 N 117.15 W
Fallbrook Square ⊸[9] **280** 34.12 N 118.38 W
Fall City **224** 47.34 N 121.53 W
Fall Creek **190** 44.45 N 91.16 W
Fall Creek ≃, In., U.S. **218** 39.47 N 86.11 W
Fall Creek ≃, N.Y., U.S. **210** 42.28 N 76.31 W
Fall Creek Falls State Park ◆, Tn., U.S. **192** 35.39 N 85.25 W
Fall Creek Falls State Park ◆, Tn., U.S. **194** 35.39 N 85.25 W
Fallen Jerusalem I **240m** 18.25 N 64.27 W
Fallen Leaf **226** 38.53 N 120.04 W
Fallen Leaf Reservoir ⊜[1] **226** 38.54 N 120.03 W
Fallentimber **214** 40.41 N 78.30 W
Fallentimber Creek ≃ **182** 51.45 N 114.39 W
Fallen Timbers State Memorial ⊥ **216** 41.33 N 83.42 W
Fallersleben **54** 52.25 N 10.43 E
Fallin **46** 56.06 N 3.52 W
Falling ≃ **192** 37.01 N 78.55 W
Fallingbostel **52** 52.52 N 9.41 E
Falling Creek ≃ **208** 37.26 N 77.26 W
Fallon, Mt., U.S. **198** 46.50 N 105.07 W
Fallon, Nv., U.S. **204** 39.28 N 118.46 W
Fall River, Ks., U.S. **198** 37.36 N 96.01 W
Fall River, Ma., U.S. **207** 41.42 N 71.09 W
Fall River, Wi., U.S. **190** 43.23 N 89.02 W
Fall River Lake ⊜[1] **198** 37.42 N 96.08 W
Fall River Mills **204** 41.00 N 121.26 W
Falls **210** 41.28 N 75.51 W
Falls □[6] **222** 31.17 N 96.55 W
Fallsburg **210** 41.44 N 74.36 W
Falls Church **208** 38.53 N 77.11 W
Falls City, Ne., U.S. **198** 40.03 N 95.36 W
Falls City, Or., U.S. **202** 44.51 N 123.26 W
Falls Creek, Austl. **170** 34.59 S 150.36 E
Falls Creek, Pa., U.S. **214** 41.09 N 78.48 W
Falls Creek ≃ **226** 37.57 N 119.46 W
Fallsington **208** 40.12 N 74.48 W
Falls Lake ⊜[1] **192** 36.00 N 78.45 W
Falls Pond ⊜ **283** 41.58 N 71.20 W
Falls Run ≃ **284b** 39.22 N 76.52 W
Fallston **208** 39.31 N 76.25 W
Falls Village **207** 41.57 N 73.21 W
Falmer **42** 50.51 N 0.04 W
Falmey **150** 12.36 N 2.51 E
Falmouth, Jam. **241q** 18.30 N 77.39 W
Falmouth, Eng., U.K. **42** 50.08 N 5.04 W
Falmouth, Ky., U.S. **218** 38.40 N 84.19 W
Falmouth, Me., U.S. **188** 43.43 N 70.14 W
Falmouth, Ma., U.S. **207** 41.33 N 70.36 W
Falmouth, Va., U.S. **208** 38.19 N 77.28 W
Falmouth Bay ⊂ **42** 50.05 N 5.01 W
Falmouth Heights **207** 41.33 N 70.36 W
False Cape ›, Fl., U.S. **220** 28.35 N 80.34 W
False Cape ›, Va., U.S. **208** 36.39 N 76.51 W
False Divi Point › **122** 15.43 N 80.49 E
False Ducks Islands II **212** 43.57 N 76.49 W
False Pass **180** 54.52 N 163.24 W
Falset **34** 41.08 N 0.49 E
Falsino ≃ **250** 0.56 N 51.35 W
Fal'šivyj Gelendžik **78** 44.31 N 38.09 E
Falso, Cabo ›, Hond. **236** 15.12 N 83.20 W
Falso, Cabo ›, Rep. Dom. **238** 17.47 N 71.41 W
Falso Cabo de Hornos › **254** 55.43 S 68.05 W
Falster I **41** 54.48 N 11.58 E
Falsterbo **41** 55.24 N 12.50 E
Falstone **44** 55.11 N 2.25 W
Fălticeni **38** 47.28 N 26.18 E
Falun, Sve. **40** 60.36 N 15.38 E
Falun, Zhg. **107** 29.58 N 104.29 E
Falzarego, Passo di)(**64** 46.31 N 12.00 E
Fam, Kepulauan II **164** 0.40 S 130.15 E
Fama **256** 21.25 S 46.51 W
Fama, Ouadi ∨ **146** 15.22 N 20.34 E
Famagusta
— Gazimağusa **130** 35.07 N 33.57 E
Famaillá **252** 27.03 S 65.24 W
Famatina **252** 28.55 S 67.31 W
Famatina, Sierra de ⋏ **252** 29.00 S 67.51 W
Fambach **54** 50.44 N 10.22 E
Fameck **56** 49.18 N 6.07 E
Famenne ⊸[1] **56** 50.10 N 5.15 E
Familleureux **50** 50.31 N 4.12 E
Family Lake ⊜ **184** 51.54 N 95.30 W
Fan ≃ **104** 42.16 N 123.40 E
Fana **150** 12.47 N 6.57 W
Fanaco, Lago ⊜ **70** 37.39 N 13.33 E
Fanad Head › **48** 55.16 N 7.38 W
Fanado ≃ **255** 17.10 S 42.40 W
Fanambana **157b** 13.34 S 50.00 E
Fanan I **175c** 7.11 N 151.59 E
Fanano **64** 44.12 N 10.47 E
Fanārah **142** 30.17 N 32.21 E
Fanchang **100** 31.07 N 118.12 E
Fanch'eng
— Xiangfan **102** 32.03 N 112.01 E
Fancher, Il., U.S. **219** 39.16 N 88.47 W
Fancher, N.Y., U.S. **210** 43.15 N 66.06 W
Fanchon, Pointe › **238** 18.26 N 74.29 W
Fanchuan **100** 32.40 N 119.42 E
Fancy **241h** 13.22 N 61.11 W
Fancy Creek ≃ **198** 39.28 N 96.45 W
Fancy Prairie **219** 39.59 N 89.36 W
Fandriana **157b** 20.14 S 47.23 E
Fane ≃ **48** 53.57 N 6.22 W
Fanepura **123** 31.29 N 72.54 E
Faneromenis Monastery ᴗ[1] **267c** 37.59 N 23.26 E
Fang **110** 19.55 N 99.13 E
Fangaga ∧ **144** 17.30 N 38.01 E
Fangak **140** 9.04 N 30.53 E
Fangbian **106** 31.42 N 119.06 E
Fangcheng, Zhg. **100** 33.16 N 112.59 E
Fangcheng, Zhg. **102** 21.49 N 108.22 E
Fangcheng, Zhg. **105** 39.16 N 115.28 E
Fangcun, Zhg. **100** 29.04 N 118.36 E
Fangcun, Zhg. **100** 26.50 N 118.15 E
Fangdao **100** 27.01 N 118.06 E
Fängersee ⊜ **264a** 52.35 N 13.50 E
Fangguan **105** 39.20 N 115.58 E
Fangji **100** 31.54 N 115.35 E
Fangjiachang **107** 30.05 N 104.16 E
Fangjiazhuang **106** 30.45 N 119.53 E
Fangliao **100** 22.22 N 120.35 E
Fangmutun **98** 42.34 N 124.34 E
Fangniu **102** 27.40 N 100.25 E
Fangshan, T'aiwan **100** 22.16 N 120.39 E
Fangshan, Zhg. **98** 39.42 N 115.58 E
Fang Shan ∧ **106** 31.40 N 119.16 E
Fang Shan ∧[2] **106** 31.29 N 119.09 E
Fangshanzhen **104** 41.54 N 122.05 E
Fangshen **104** 42.02 N 124.04 E
Fangshengpu **107** 30.20 N 104.54 E
Fangsi **98** 36.56 N 116.29 E
Fangtai **106** 31.19 N 121.12 E
Fangxi **100** 28.23 N 114.38 E
Fangxian **102** 32.02 N 110.45 E
Fangxianzhen **106** 32.00 N 119.44 E
Fangzheng **89** 45.50 N 128.50 E
Fangzi **98** 36.36 N 119.07 E
Fanhões **266c** 38.53 N 9.09 W
Fanipol' **76** 53.45 N 27.20 E
Fanjakana **157b** 21.10 S 46.53 E
Fanjiadai **106** 32.04 N 120.15 E
Fanjiadian **104** 41.41 N 121.50 E
Fanjiatun **89** 43.43 N 125.06 E
Fanjiazhuang **105** 39.12 N 117.20 E
Fannaråki ∧ **26** 61.31 N 7.55 E
Fannettsburg **214** 40.04 N 77.50 W
Fannich, Loch ⊜ **46** 57.38 N 5.00 W
Fannrem **26** 63.16 N 9.50 E
Fanny, Mount ∧ **202** 45.20 N 117.41 W
Fanny Bay **182** 49.30 N 124.50 W
Fano **66** 43.50 N 13.01 E
Fanø I **26** 55.25 N 8.25 E
Fanqiao **100** 28.48 N 121.10 E
Fans, Col des)(**62** 44.56 N 4.47 E
Fanshan, Zhg. **100** 27.21 N 120.24 E
Fanshan, Zhg. **105** 40.13 N 115.25 E
Fanshang **106** 31.40 N 120.01 E
Fanshawe Lake ⊜ **212** 43.05 N 81.10 W
Fansher Creek ≃ **214** 42.37 N 82.01 W
Fanshui **100** 33.07 N 119.25 E
Fan Si Pan ∧ **110** 22.15 N 103.46 E
Fantasy Island ◆ **284a** 43.02 N 78.58 W
Fanthyttan **40** 59.40 N 15.06 E
Fanwood **276** 40.38 N 74.23 W
Fanxian **98** 35.57 N 115.38 E
Fanzhen **98** 36.14 N 117.21 E
Faoileann, Bàgh nam ⊂ **46** 57.23 N 7.17 W
Faqīrah, Wādī ∨ **142** 28.52 N 30.57 E
Faqqūʿah **132** 32.30 N 35.24 E
Fāqūs **142** 30.44 N 31.48 E
Farab **85** 39.14 N 67.28 E
Faraday ᴗ[3] **9** 65.15 S 64.16 W
Faraday, Mount ∧ **172** 42.02 S 171.34 E
Faradje **154** 3.44 N 29.43 E
Faradofay **157b** 25.02 S 47.00 E
Farafangana **157b** 22.49 S 47.50 E
Farāfirah, Al-Wāḥat al- ⚲[4] **140** 27.15 N 28.10 E
Farāh **128** 32.22 N 62.07 E
Farāh □[4] **128** 33.00 N 62.30 E
Farāh ≃ **128** 31.29 N 61.24 E
Farahābād **267d** 35.42 N 51.30 E
Farahalana **157b** 14.26 S 50.10 E
Farā'id, Jabal al- ∧ **140** 23.31 N 35.20 E
Fara in Sabina **66** 42.12 N 12.43 E
Farallón, Paso del ʮ **288** 34.41 S 57.57 W
Farallon de Medinilla I **108** 16.01 N 146.04 E
Farallon de Pajaros I **108** 20.32 N 144.54 E
Farallon Islands II **204** 37.43 N 123.03 W
Faramana **150** 12.03 N 4.40 W
Faranah **150** 10.02 N 10.44 W
Farángi Samariás (Samaria Gorge) ∨ **38** 35.18 N 24.00 E
Fara Novarese **62** 45.33 N 8.27 E
Farasān, Jazā'ir II **144** 16.48 N 41.54 E
Farasān al-Kabīr I **144** 16.42 N 42.00 E
Faratsiho **157b** 19.24 S 46.57 E
Faraulep I[1] **108** 8.36 N 144.33 E
Farber **219** 39.16 N 91.34 W
Farbovane **78** 50.09 N 31.51 E
Farcău, Vârful ∧ **38** 47.56 N 24.27 E
Farchant **64** 47.32 N 11.06 E
Farcy **261** 48.31 N 2.37 E
Fardes ≃ **34** 37.35 N 3.00 W
Fare ≃ **50** 47.39 N 0.14 E
Fareara, Pointe › **174s** 17.52 S 149.39 W
Fareham **42** 50.51 N 1.10 W
Fårevejle **41** 55.48 N 11.27 E
Farewell **180** 62.31 N 153.53 W
Farewell, Cape › **172** 40.30 S 172.41 E
Farewell Spit ›[2] **172** 40.31 S 172.52 E
Färgelanda **26** 58.34 N 11.59 E
Fargniers **50** 49.39 N 3.19 E
Fargo **198** 46.52 N 96.47 W
Far Hills **276** 40.41 N 74.38 W
Faria ≃ **287a** 22.53 S 43.15 W
Fāriʿah, Wādī al- ∨ **132** 32.06 N 35.31 E
Faribault **190** 44.17 N 93.16 W
Faribault, Lac ⊜ **176** 59.00 N 72.00 W
Farīdābad **124** 28.26 N 77.19 E
Farīdganj **126** 23.08 N 90.45 E
Farīdkot **123** 30.40 N 74.45 E
Farīdnagar **124** 28.46 N 77.37 E
Farīdpur, Bngl. **126** 24.10 N 89.26 E
Farīdpur, Bngl. **126** 23.36 N 89.50 E
Farīdpur, India **124** 28.13 N 79.33 E
Farié Haoussa **150** 13.48 N 1.38 E
Fārigh, Wādī al- ∨ **146** 29.59 N 19.25 E
Färila **26** 61.48 N 15.51 E
Farilhões II **34** 39.28 N 9.34 W
Farim **150** 12.27 N 15.17 W
Farīmān **128** 35.43 N 59.53 E
Farina **219** 38.50 N 88.46 W
Faringdon **42** 51.40 N 1.35 W
Farington **262** 53.43 N 2.42 W
Farinha ≃ **250** 6.51 S 47.30 W
Farini d'Olmo **62** 44.43 N 9.34 E
Fariš **85** 40.35 N 66.52 E
Fariske **130** 36.37 N 32.38 E
Fāriskūr **142** 31.20 N 31.43 E
Farit, Amba ∧ **144** 10.56 N 38.58 E
Färjestaden **26** 56.39 N 16.27 E
Farkwa **154** 5.24 S 35.36 E
Farleigh **260** 51.19 N 0.02 W
Farley **190** 42.26 N 91.00 W
Farley Green **260** 51.12 N 0.29 W
Farmahīn **128** 34.30 N 49.41 E
Farmer City **216** 40.14 N 88.38 W
Farmers Branch **222** 32.55 N 96.53 W
Farmersburg **194** 39.14 N 87.22 W
Farmers Fork **208** 38.02 N 76.45 W
Farmer's Museum ᴗ **210** 42.42 N 74.57 W
Farmers Retreat **218** 38.58 N 85.06 W
Farmersville, Ca., U.S. **226** 36.17 N 119.12 W
Farmersville, Il., U.S. **219** 39.26 N 89.39 W
Farmersville, Pa., U.S. **208** 40.08 N 76.10 W
Farmersville, Tx., U.S. **222** 33.09 N 96.21 W
Farmersville Station **210** 42.26 N 78.22 W
Farmerville **194** 32.46 N 92.24 W
Farmingdale, N.J., U.S. **208** 40.11 N 74.10 W
Farmingdale, N.Y., U.S. **276** 40.43 N 73.26 W
Farmington, Ca., U.S. **226** 37.56 N 120.59 W
Farmington, Ct., U.S. **207** 41.43 N 72.49 W
Farmington, De., U.S. **208** 38.52 N 75.34 W
Farmington, Il., U.S. **190** 40.41 N 90.00 W
Farmington, Ia., U.S. **190** 40.38 N 91.44 W
Farmington, Me., U.S. **188** 44.40 N 70.09 W
Farmington, Mi., U.S. **216** 42.27 N 83.22 W
Farmington, Mn., U.S. **190** 44.38 N 93.08 W
Farmington, Mo., U.S. **194** 37.47 N 90.25 W
Farmington, Mt., U.S. **182** 47.54 N 112.11 W
Farmington, N.H., U.S. **188** 43.23 N 71.03 W
Farmington, N.M., U.S. **200** 36.43 N 108.13 W
Farmington, Ut,. U.S. **200** 40.58 N 111.53 W
Farmington ≃ **207** 41.51 N 72.38 W
Farmington, West Branch ≃ **207** 41.52 N 72.57 W
Farmington Flood Control Basin ⊜[1] **226** 37.55 N 120.55 W
Farmington Hills **281** 42.28 N 83.23 W
Farmingville **210** 40.49 N 73.01 W
Farmland **218** 40.11 N 85.07 W
Far Mountain ∧ **182** 52.46 N 125.17 W
Farm Pond ⊜, Ma., U.S. **283** 42.17 N 71.26 W
Farm Pond ⊜, Ma., U.S. **283** 42.14 N 71.21 W
Farmville, N.C., U.S. **192** 35.35 N 77.35 W
Farmville, Va., U.S. **192** 37.18 N 78.23 W
Färna **40** 59.47 N 15.51 E
Farnam **198** 40.42 N 100.12 W
Farnawā **142** 30.59 N 30.39 E
Farnborough **42** 51.17 N 0.46 W
Farnborough ⊸[8] **260** 51.21 N 0.04 E
Farncombe **260** 51.12 N 0.36 W
Farndon **44** 53.05 N 0.51 W
Färnebofjärden ⊜ **40** 60.14 N 16.47 E
Farne Islands II **44** 55.38 N 1.38 W
Farnham, P.Q., Can. **206** 45.17 N 72.59 W
Farnham, Eng., U.K. **42** 51.13 N 0.49 W
Farnham, N.Y., U.S. **214** 42.36 N 79.05 W
Farnham, Va., U.S. **208** 37.53 N 76.37 W
Farnham, Mount ∧ **182** 50.29 N 116.30 W
Farnham Common **260** 51.33 N 0.37 W
Farnham Royal **260** 51.32 N 0.37 W
Farnhamville **198** 42.16 N 94.24 W
Farningham **260** 51.23 N 0.13 E
Farnroda **54** 50.56 N 10.23 E
Farnworth, Eng., U.K. **44** 53.33 N 2.24 W
Farnworth, Eng., U.K. **262** 53.23 N 2.44 W
Faro, Bra. **250** 2.11 S 56.44 W
Faro, Port. **34** 37.01 N 7.56 W
Faro □[5] **34** 37.15 N 8.00 W
Faro ≃ **146** 9.21 N 12.55 E
Faro, Punta del › **70** 38.16 N 15.39 E
Faro, Réserve du ⊸[4] **146** 8.10 N 12.35 E
Färöer
— Faeroe Islands □[2] **22** 62.00 N 7.00 W
Fårön I **26** 57.56 N 19.08 E
Fårösund **26** 57.52 N 19.03 E
Farquhar, Cape › **162** 23.37 S 113.37 E
Farquhar Group II **138** 10.10 S 51.10 E
Farr **46** 57.21 N 4.12 W
Farra d'Isonzo **64** 45.56 N 13.31 E
Farragut **198** 40.43 N 95.28 W
Farragut State Recreation Area ◆ **202** 47.55 N 116.35 W
Farrandsville **210** 41.10 N 77.31 W
Farrar ≃ **46** 57.24 N 4.50 W
Farrar Pond ⊜ **283** 42.25 N 71.21 W
Farrars Creek ≃ **166** 25.35 S 140.43 E
Farrāshband **128** 28.53 N 52.06 E
Farrell **214** 41.12 N 80.29 W
Farrell Flat **168b** 33.50 S 138.47 E
Farrer Park ◆ **271c** 1.19 N 103.51 E
Farrington Lake ⊜ **276** 40.26 N 74.28 W
Farrington Lake Heights **276** 40.26 N 74.27 W
Far Rockaway ⊸[8] **276** 40.36 N 73.45 W
Farrukhābād **124** 27.24 N 79.34 E
Farrukhnagar, India **124** 28.27 N 76.49 E
Farrukhnagar, India **272a** 28.43 N 77.23 E
Fārs □[4] **128** 29.00 N 53.00 E
Fársala **38** 39.18 N 22.23 E
Farschviller **56** 49.06 N 6.54 E
Fārsī **128** 33.47 N 63.15 E
Fārsī, Jazīreh-ye I **128** 27.58 N 50.11 E
Farsīs **142** 30.40 N 31.14 E
Farsø **26** 56.47 N 9.21 E
Farsta **40** 59.14 N 18.04 E
Farsund **26** 58.05 N 6.48 E
Fartak, Ra's › **118** 15.38 N 52.15 E
Farukolu I **122** 6.12 N 73.16 E
Farum **41** 55.48 N 12.22 E
Fårvang **41** 56.16 N 9.44 E
Farvel, Kap › **176** 59.45 N 44.00 W
Farwell, Mi., U.S. **190** 43.50 N 84.52 W
Farwell, Tx., U.S. **196** 30.15 N 103.15 W
Fāryāb □[4] **128** 36.00 N 65.00 E
Fasā **128** 28.56 N 53.42 E
Fasano **68** 40.50 N 17.22 E
Fashchivka **83** 48.16 N 38.37 E
Fashkhah, ʿAyn ⚲[4] **132** 31.43 N 35.27 E
Fåsjön ⊜ **40** 59.36 N 14.58 E
Fassa **150** 13.26 N 8.15 W
Fassberg **52** 52.54 N 10.10 E
Fasterholt **41** 56.01 N 9.07 E
Fastiv **78** 50.06 N 29.55 E
Fastnet Rock I[2] **48** 51.24 N 9.35 W
Fastoveckaja **78** 45.56 N 40.09 E
Fatagar Tuting, Tanjung › **164** 2.46 S 131.57 E
Fataki **154** 4.46 S 28.11 E
Fatala ≃ **150** 10.13 N 14.00 W
Fat Deer Key I **220** 24.44 N 81.00 W
Fate **222** 32.56 N 96.23 W
Fatehābād, India **123** 29.31 N 75.27 E
Fatehābād, India **124** 27.01 N 78.19 E
Fatehgarh, India **124** 27.22 N 79.38 E
Fatehgarh, India **124** 24.48 N 76.58 E
Fatehgarh Chūriān **123** 31.52 N 74.58 E
Fatehjang **123** 33.34 N 72.39 E
Fatehpur, India **120** 27.59 N 74.57 E
Fatehpur, India **124** 25.56 N 80.48 E
Fatehpur, India **124** 27.10 N 81.13 E
Fatehpur, India **126** 22.17 N 88.14 E
Fatehpur, India **126** 24.05 N 87.44 E
Fatehpur, Pāk. **123** 31.09 N 71.13 E
Fatehpur Sīkri **124** 27.06 N 77.40 E
Fathai **140** 8.05 N 31.48 E
Fathom Five National Marine Park ◆ **190** 45.15 N 81.40 W
Fatick **150** 14.20 N 16.25 W
Fatick □[4] **150** 14.00 N 16.30 W
Fatigue, Mount ∧ **169** 38.34 S 146.18 E
Fatima, Arg. **258** 34.26 S 59.00 W
Fátima, Port. **34** 39.37 N 8.39 W
Fatima do Sol **255** 22.16 S 54.25 W

Symbols in the index entries represent the broad categories identified in the key at the right. Symbols with superior numbers (⋏[1]) identify subcategories (see complete key on page *I* · *1*).

Symbole im Register stellen die rechts im Schlüssel erklärten Kategorien dar. Symbole mit hochgestellten Ziffern (⋏[1]) bezeichnen Unterabteilungen einer Kategorie (vgl. vollständiger Schlüssel auf Seite *I* · *1*).

Los símbolos incluídos en el texto del índice representan las grandes categorías identificadas con la clave a la derecha. Los símbolos con numeros en su parte superior (⋏[1]) identifican las subcategorías (véase la clave completa en la página *I* · *1*).

Les symboles de l'index représentent les catégories indiquées dans la légende à droite. Les symboles suivis d'un indice (⋏[1]) représentent des sous-catégories (voir légende complète à la page *I* · *1*).

Os símbolos incluídos no texto do índice representam as grandes categorias identificadas com a chave à direita. Os símbolos com números em sua parte superior (⋏[1]) identificam as subcategorias (veja-se a chave completa à página *I* · *1*).

∧ Mountain	Berg	Montaña	Montagne	Montanha
⋏ Mountains	Gebirge	Montañas	Montagnes	Montanhas
)(Pass	Paß	Paso	Col	Passo
∨ Valley, Canyon	Tal, Cañon	Valle, Cañón	Vallée, Canyon	Vale, Canhão
≚ Plain	Ebene	Llano	Plaine	Planície
› Cape	Kap	Cabo	Cap	Cabo
I Island	Insel	Isla	Île	Ilha
II Islands	Inseln	Islas	Îles	Ilhas
⊥ Other Topographic Features	Andere Topographische Objekte	Otros Elementos Topográficos	Autres données topographiques	Outros acidentes topográficos

ESPAÑOL

Nombre	Página	Lat.°′	Long.°′ W = Oeste
Fatima do Sul	252	22.16 S	54.22 W
Fāṭimah, Wādī V	144	21.27 N	39.09 E
Fatoto	150	13.26 N	13.52 W
Fat'ož	78	52.07 N	35.52 E
Fatsa	130	41.02 N	37.31 E
Fatshan → Foshan	100	23.03 N	113.09 E
Fat Tong Point ›	271d	22.16 N	114.15 E
Fatu-Berlio	112	8.56 S	125.52 E
Fatulla	126	23.38 N	90.29 E
Fatumu	174w	21.13 S	175.07 W
Fatunda	152	4.08 S	17.13 E
Fatwā	124	25.31 N	85.19 E
Fauabu	175e	8.34 S	160.43 E
Faucigny	58	46.07 N	6.22 E
Faucille, Col de la)(	58	46.22 N	6.02 E
Faucilles, Monts ⋏	58	48.07 N	6.16 E
Faucogney	58	47.51 N	6.34 E
Faucon-de-Barcelonnette	62	44.24 N	6.41 E
Fauglia	66	43.34 N	10.31 E
Fauldhouse	46	55.50 N	3.37 W
Faulkton	198	45.02 N	99.07 W
Faulquemont	56	49.03 N	6.36 E
Fauquembergues	50	50.36 N	2.05 E
Fauquier	182	49.53 N	118.05 W
Fauquier □[6]	208	38.35 N	77.35 W
Făurei	38	45.06 N	27.14 E
Faure Island I	162	25.51 S	113.52 E
Fauresmith	158	29.42 S	25.21 E
Fauro Island I	175e	6.55 S	156.04 E
Fauske	24	67.15 N	15.24 E
Faust	182	55.19 N	115.38 W
Faustovo	82	55.26 N	38.29 E
Fauville-en-Caux	50	49.39 N	0.35 E
Fauvillers	56	49.51 N	5.40 E
Faux-Cap	157b	25.33 S	45.32 E
Fåvang	26	61.27 N	10.11 E
Favara	70	37.19 N	13.39 E
Faverges	62	45.45 N	6.18 E
Faverney	58	47.46 N	6.06 E
Faversham	42	51.20 N	0.53 E
Favières	261	48.46 N	2.47 E
Favignana	70	37.56 N	12.20 E
Favignana, Isola I	70	37.56 N	12.19 E
Favoriten ◆[8]	264b	48.11 N	16.23 E
Favourable Lake ⊜	184	52.53 N	93.56 W
Favrieux	261	48.57 N	1.39 E
Fawcett	182	54.32 N	114.05 W
Fawcett Lake ⊜	182	55.19 N	113.57 W
Fawkham Green	260	51.22 N	0.17 E
Fawkner	274b	37.43 S	144.58 E
Fawkner Park ♠	274b	37.50 S	144.59 E
Fawley	42	50.49 N	1.20 W
Fawn ≃, On., Can.	176	55.22 N	88.20 W
Fawn ≃, U.S.	216	41.51 N	85.40 W
Fawn Grove	208	39.44 N	76.27 W
Fawnie Nose ∧	182	53.16 N	125.08 W
Fawnie Range ⋏	182	53.10 N	125.00 W
Fawsett Farms	284c	38.59 N	77.14 W
Faxaflói c	24a	64.25 N	23.00 W
Faxälven ≃	26	63.13 N	17.13 E
Faxinal	255	23.59 S	51.22 W
Faxinal do Soturno	252	29.37 S	53.26 W
Faxon	210	41.15 N	76.58 W
Faya	146	17.55 N	19.07 E
Fayd	128	27.07 N	42.27 E
Fayence	62	43.37 N	6.41 E
Fayerweather Island I	276	41.08 N	73.13 W
Fayette, Al., U.S.	194	33.41 N	87.49 W
Fayette, Ia., U.S.	190	42.50 N	91.48 W
Fayette, Ms., U.S.	194	31.42 N	91.03 W
Fayette, Mo., U.S.	194	39.08 N	92.41 W
Fayette, N.Y., U.S.	210	42.49 N	76.49 W
Fayette, Oh., U.S.	216	41.40 N	84.19 W
Fayette □[6], Il., U.S.	219	38.58 N	89.06 W
Fayette □[6], In., U.S.	218	39.39 N	85.08 W
Fayette □[6], Ky., U.S.	218	38.07 N	84.30 W
Fayette □[6], Oh., U.S.	218	39.32 N	83.26 W
Fayette □[6], Pa., U.S.	214	40.05 N	79.39 W
Fayette □[6], Tx., U.S.	222	29.50 N	96.57 W
Fayette, Lake ⊜[1]	222	29.56 N	96.44 W
Fayette City	214	40.06 N	79.50 W
Fayetteville, Ar., U.S.	194	36.03 N	94.09 W
Fayetteville, Ga., U.S.	192	33.26 N	84.27 W
Fayetteville, Il., U.S.	219	38.22 N	89.48 W
Fayetteville, N.Y., U.S.	210	43.02 N	76.00 W
Fayetteville, N.C., U.S.	192	35.03 N	78.52 W
Fayetteville, Oh., U.S.	218	39.11 N	83.55 W
Fayetteville, Pa., U.S.	208	39.54 N	77.33 W
Fayetteville, Tn., U.S.	194	35.09 N	86.34 W
Fayetteville, Tx., U.S.	222	29.54 N	96.41 W
Fayetteville, W.V., U.S.	188	38.03 N	81.06 W
Faylakah I	128	29.27 N	48.20 E
Fayl-Billot	58	47.47 N	5.36 E
Fayrā	144	13.17 N	43.25 E
Fay-sur-Lignon	62	44.59 N	4.14 E
Fayville	207	42.17 N	71.30 W
Fayyum → Al-Fayyūm	142	29.19 N	30.50 E
Fažana	64	44.55 N	13.49 E
Fazao	150	8.42 N	0.46 E
Fazao, Parc National du ♠	150	8.40 N	0.42 E
Fazeley	42	52.37 N	1.42 W
Fazenda de Cima	248	15.56 S	56.37 W
Fazenda Libongo	152	8.24 S	13.24 E
Fazenda Nova	255	16.11 S	50.48 W
Fāzilka	123	30.24 N	74.02 E
Fāzilpur	120	29.18 N	70.27 E
Fazzān (Fezzan) □[9]	146	26.00 N	14.00 E
Fdérik	148	22.41 N	12.43 W
Feale ≃	48	52.28 N	9.40 W
Fear, Cape ›	192	33.50 N	77.58 W
Fearnhead	262	53.25 N	2.33 W
Feasterville	208	40.08 N	75.00 W
Feather ≃	204	38.47 N	121.36 W
Feather, Middle Fork ≃	204	39.34 N	121.26 W
Feather, North Fork ≃	204	39.34 N	121.28 W
Feather, North Fork, East Branch ≃	204	40.01 N	121.13 W
Feather, South Fork ≃	204	39.33 N	121.28 W
Featherbed Top ∧	262	53.26 N	1.52 W
Featherly Regional Park ♠	280	33.52 N	117.42 W
Featherston	172	41.07 S	175.20 E
Featherstone, Eng., U.K.	44	53.41 N	1.21 W
Featherstone, Zimb.	154	18.42 S	30.49 E
Feathertop, Mount ∧	166	36.54 S	147.08 E
Fécamp	50	49.45 N	0.22 E
Fedala → Mohammedia	148	33.44 N	7.24 W
Fedderwardergroden	52	53.35 N	8.05 E
Feddet ›[1]	41	55.09 N	12.07 E
Federación	252	31.00 S	57.54 W
Federal, Arg.	252	30.57 S	58.48 W
Federal, Pa., U.S.	279b	40.23 N	80.09 W
Federal Capital Territory □[3]	150	9.00 N	7.15 E
Federalsburg	208	38.41 N	75.46 W
Federal Territory □[8]	273a	6.29 N	3.25 E
Federal Way	224	47.19 N	122.18 W
Federation Forest State Park ♠	224	47.09 N	121.40 W
Federsee ⊜	58	48.05 N	9.38 E
Fedeshk	128	32.45 N	58.50 E
Fedje	26	60.47 N	4.42 E
Fedorino	82	55.08 N	36.06 E
Fedorivka, Ukr.	78	47.33 N	36.33 E
Fedorivka, Ukr.	78	49.23 N	35.07 E
Fedosejevka	80	46.53 N	44.00 E
Fedosejevskaja	24	62.07 N	40.42 E
Fedosicha	86	54.47 N	81.54 E
Fedosjino	82	55.08 N	38.30 E
Fedotovo	82	55.41 N	39.12 E
Feeagh, Lough ⊜	48	53.55 N	9.36 W

FRANÇAIS

Nom	Page	Lat.°′	Long.°′ W = Ouest
Feeding Hills	207	42.04 N	72.40 W
Feerfeer	144	8.30 N	47.55 E
Feesburg	218	38.52 N	83.58 W
Fefan I	175c	7.21 N	151.51 E
Fehérgyarmat	30	47.58 N	22.32 E
Fehmarn I	54	54.28 N	11.08 E
Fehmarnbelt (Femer Bælt))(	41	54.35 N	11.15 E
Fehmarnsund)(	54	54.24 N	11.07 E
Fehrbellin	54	52.49 N	12.46 E
Fehring	61	46.56 N	16.01 E
Feia, Lagoa c	255	22.00 S	41.20 W
Feicheng	98	36.15 N	116.46 E
Feichten	58	47.02 N	10.44 E
Feidong	100	31.52 N	117.29 E
Feignies	50	50.18 N	3.55 E
Feigumfossen ʟ	26	61.23 N	7.26 E
Feiheji	100	33.36 N	115.36 E
Fei Huang ≃	100	33.35 N	119.02 E
Feijó	248	8.09 S	70.21 W
Feiketu	89	45.46 N	127.09 E
Feilding	172	40.13 S	175.34 E
Feiler ∧	64	47.07 N	10.52 E
Feiliqiao	106	31.05 N	119.05 E
Feilitzsch	54	50.22 N	11.56 E
Feilong, Zhg.	107	30.25 N	106.20 E
Feilong, Zhg.	107	30.36 N	105.54 E
Feilongguan	107	28.57 N	105.05 E
Feiluan	100	26.35 N	119.35 E
Feira	154	15.37 S	30.25 E
Feira de Santana	255	12.15 S	38.57 W
Feistritz ≃	61	47.01 N	16.08 E
Feistritz an der Gail	64	46.34 N	13.36 E
Feistritzer Spitze ∧	61	46.31 N	14.45 E
Feixi	100	31.42 N	117.10 E
Feixian	98	35.18 N	117.57 E
Feixiang	98	36.34 N	114.49 E
Feiyun ≃	100	27.48 N	120.36 E
Fejaj, Chott ≡	148	33.55 N	9.10 E
Fejér □[6]	30	47.10 N	18.35 E
Fejø I	41	54.57 N	11.26 E
Feke	130	37.53 N	35.58 E
Feklistova, ostrov I	89	55.02 N	136.55 E
Felâhiye	130	39.06 N	35.35 E
Felanitx	34	39.28 N	3.08 E
Felbertauerntunnel ◆[5]	64	47.08 N	12.31 E
Felda	220	26.33 N	81.26 W
Felda ≃, Dtsch.	56	50.51 N	10.05 E
Felda ≃, Dtsch.	56	50.42 N	9.03 E
Feldafing	64	47.57 N	11.17 E
Feldaist ≃	61	48.19 N	14.34 E
Feld am See	64	46.47 N	13.45 E
Feldbach	61	46.57 N	15.54 E
Feldberg, Dtsch.	54	53.20 N	13.26 E
Feldberg, Dtsch.	58	47.51 N	8.02 E
Feldberg ∧	58	47.52 N	8.00 E
Felderbach ≃	263	51.22 N	7.08 E
Feldhausen ◆[8]	263	51.37 N	6.59 E
Feldis	58	46.48 N	9.26 E
Feldkirch	58	47.14 N	9.36 E
Feldkirchen an der Donau	61	48.21 N	14.03 E
Feldkirchen bei Graz	61	47.01 N	15.27 E
Feldkirchen in Kärnten	61	46.43 N	14.05 E
Feldmark	263	51.41 N	6.38 E
Feldstetten	58	48.28 N	9.37 E
Felhit	144	16.43 N	38.02 E
Feliciano, Méx.	234	18.01 N	101.58 W
Feliciano, P.R.	240m	18.28 N	67.08 W
Feliciano, Arroyo ≃	252	31.06 S	59.54 W
Felicity	218	38.50 N	84.05 W
Felina	64	44.27 N	10.27 E
Felino	64	44.42 N	10.15 E
Felipe Carrillo Puerto, Méx.	234	19.08 N	102.42 W
Felipe Carrillo Puerto, Méx.	234	21.09 N	104.52 W
Felix, Cape ›	176	69.54 N	97.50 W
Felix, Rio ≃	196	33.08 N	104.19 W
Felixburg	154	19.29 S	30.51 E
Felixdorf	61	47.53 N	16.15 E
Felixlândia	255	18.47 S	44.55 W
Felixstowe	42	51.58 N	1.20 E
Felixton	158	28.50 S	31.53 E
Félix U. Gómez	232	29.50 N	111.30 W
Felizzano	62	44.54 N	8.26 E
Fella ≃	64	46.21 N	13.07 E
Fellbach	56	48.48 N	9.15 E
Felletin	32	45.53 N	2.10 E
Felling	44	54.57 N	1.33 W
Fellingsbro	40	59.26 N	15.35 E
Fellows	226	35.11 N	119.32 W
Fellows Creek ≃	281	42.17 N	83.26 W
Fellowship	285	39.55 N	74.58 W
Fellsburg	214	40.11 N	79.49 W
Fellsmere	220	27.46 N	80.36 W
Fellwick	285	40.08 N	75.11 W
Felpham	42	50.47 N	0.39 W
Felsberg	56	51.08 N	9.25 E
Felső-Válicka ≃	61	46.52 N	16.53 E
Feltham ◆[8]	260	51.27 N	0.24 W
Felt Lake ⊜	282	37.23 N	122.11 W
Felton, Ca., U.S.	226	37.03 N	122.04 W
Felton, De., U.S.	208	39.00 N	75.34 W
Felton, Pa., U.S.	208	39.51 N	76.34 W
Feltre	64	46.01 N	11.54 E
Felts Mills	212	44.01 N	75.46 W
Feltwell	42	52.29 N	0.32 E
Femer Bælt (Fehmarnbelt))(	41	54.35 N	11.15 E
Femme Osage Creek ≃	219	38.39 N	90.44 W
Femmøller	41	56.14 N	10.35 E
Femø I	41	54.58 N	11.33 E
Femund ⊜	26	62.12 N	11.52 E
Femundsenden	26	61.55 N	11.55 E
Femundsmarka Nasjonalpark ♠	26	62.20 N	12.07 E
Fen ≃	102	35.36 N	110.42 E
Fena Valley Reservoir ⊜[1]	174p	13.21 N	144.42 E
Fendaozi	104	41.35 N	120.51 E
Fenelon Falls	212	44.32 N	78.45 W
Fenelton	214	40.52 N	79.44 W
Fener ◆[8]	267b	41.02 N	28.56 E
Fenerbahce Stadium ♠	267b	40.59 N	29.02 E
Fener Burnu ›	130	41.07 N	39.25 E
Fener Tepesi ∧[2]	267b	41.09 N	28.47 E
Fenestrelle	62	45.02 N	7.03 E
Fénétrange	56	48.51 N	7.01 E
Feng ≃	105	39.25 N	116.57 E
Fengcheng, Zhg.	98	40.27 N	124.02 E
Fengcheng, Zhg.	100	28.10 N	115.46 E
Fengcheng, Zhg.	102	38.32 N	101.50 E
Fengcheng, Zhg.	106	30.55 N	121.38 E
Fengdengwu	105	39.42 N	117.55 E
Fengdian	107	30.41 N	104.51 E
Fengdu	102	29.58 N	107.41 E
Fengfeng	98	36.28 N	114.14 E
Fenggang, Zhg.	100	28.34 N	116.34 E
Fenggang, Zhg.	102	27.58 N	107.47 E
Fenggaopu	107	29.24 N	105.41 E
Fenghua	100	29.40 N	121.24 E
Fenghuang, Zhg.	100	23.58 N	116.44 E
Fenghuang, Zhg.	102	24.25 N	107.17 E
Fenghuang, Zhg.	102	27.58 N	109.19 E
Fenghuang, Zhg.	106	31.21 N	121.44 E
Fenghuangchang	107	29.44 N	106.19 E
Fenghuang Shan ∧	107	28.54 N	106.35 E
Fenghuanjing	100	31.11 N	117.49 E
Fenghui	100	29.56 N	120.58 E
Fengjia, Zhg.	98	37.03 N	121.42 E
Fengjia, Zhg.	104	42.35 N	122.30 E
Fengjiabao	102	36.12 N	104.49 E
Fengjiakou	98	38.11 N	116.44 E
Fengjianjiao	106	30.41 N	120.51 E
Fengjiatun	104	41.14 N	122.00 E
Fengjiawopeng	104	42.19 N	123.40 E
Fengjiaxiang	106	30.56 N	121.06 E
Fengjie	102	31.03 N	109.31 E

PORTUGUÊS

Nome	Página	Lat.°′	Long.°′ W = Oeste
Fengjing	106	30.53 N	121.01 E
Fengkou	100	30.05 N	113.18 E
Fengle, Zhg.	89	45.47 N	125.26 E
Fengle, Zhg.	100	27.13 N	118.11 E
Fenglezhen	98	36.14 N	114.18 E
Fengliang	100	23.59 N	116.14 E
Fenglin, T'aiwan	100	23.45 N	121.26 E
Fenglin, Zhg.	100	28.19 N	120.46 E
Fengling Guan)(	100	28.14 N	118.29 E
Fenglingtou	100	28.26 N	117.50 E
Fengman	89	43.46 N	126.41 E
Fengnan (Xugezhuang)	105	39.34 N	118.06 E
Fengning (Dagezhen)	98	41.12 N	116.32 E
Fengpin	100	23.36 N	121.31 E
Fengpingzi	102	32.46 N	105.12 E
Fengqiao, Zhg.	100	29.46 N	120.26 E
Fengqiao, Zhg.	106	31.19 N	120.33 E
Fengqing	102	24.46 N	99.52 E
Fengqiu	98	35.05 N	114.25 E
Fengrun	105	39.50 N	118.07 E
Fengshan, Zhg.	89	46.22 N	128.30 E
Fengshan, Zhg.	98	41.14 N	117.05 E
Fengshan, Zhg.	102	22.01 N	109.59 E
Fengshi	100	24.42 N	116.34 E
Fengshun	100	23.48 N	116.11 E
Fengtai, Zhg.	100	32.44 N	116.43 E
Fengtai, Zhg.	105	39.51 N	116.16 E
Fengtian, Zhg.	100	25.46 N	115.30 E
Fengtian, Zhg.	100	27.24 N	114.43 E
Fengtien → Shenyang	104	41.48 N	123.27 E
Fengting	100	25.16 N	118.54 E
Fengwan	100	24.48 N	113.50 E
Fengxi	102	31.48 N	109.50 E
Fengxian, Zhg.	98	34.42 N	116.34 E
Fengxian, Zhg.	102	33.57 N	106.44 E
Fengxian, Zhg.	106	30.55 N	121.27 E
Fengxiang	102	34.29 N	107.29 E
Fengxin	100	28.43 N	115.23 E
Fengyang, Zhg.	100	32.52 N	117.34 E
Fengyang, Zhg.	100	24.49 N	117.53 E
Fengyi	102	31.44 N	103.53 E
Fengyu	100	26.31 N	119.18 E
Fengyüan	100	24.15 N	120.43 E
Fengzhen	102	40.24 N	113.09 E
Fengzhou	100	25.41 N	113.52 E
Fengzhuangtou	106	31.00 N	118.39 E
Fenholloway ≃	192	29.59 N	83.47 W
Fen Hu ⊜	106	31.00 N	120.47 E
Feni	124	23.00 N	91.24 E
Fenicia Moncata ⊥	70	37.33 N	14.57 E
Feni Islands II	14	4.05 S	153.42 E
Fenimore Pass)(	180	52.00 N	175.35 W
Fenino	265b	55.44 N	37.57 E
Fenis	62	45.44 N	7.29 E
Feniscowles	262	53.43 N	2.32 W
Fenjie	106	32.17 N	120.20 E
Fennimore	190	42.59 N	90.39 W
Fennville	216	42.35 N	86.06 W
Fenny Compton	42	52.09 N	1.20 W
Fenny Stratford	42	52.00 N	0.43 W
Feno, Capo di ›, Fr.	36	41.57 N	8.36 E
Feno, Capo di ›, Fr.	71	41.23 N	9.06 E
Fenoarivo, Madag.	157b	20.52 S	46.53 E
Fenoarivo, Madag.	157b	18.26 S	46.34 E
Fenoarivo, Madag.	157b	21.43 S	46.24 E
Fenoarivo Atsinanana	157b	17.22 S	49.25 E
Fensfjorden c[2]	26	60.51 N	4.50 E
Fenshui	104	40.41 N	122.32 E
Fenshui ≃	100	29.49 N	119.41 E
Fenshui'ao	100	25.20 N	114.43 E
Fenshuidunshen	106	31.30 N	120.01 E
Fenshuiling, Zhg.	107	28.51 N	105.35 E
Fenshuiling, Zhg.	107	30.20 N	105.15 E
Fenshuipu	107	30.05 N	104.05 E
Fenshuizhen	107	29.44 N	103.55 E
Fenshuizui	100	30.35 N	113.38 E
Fensmark	41	55.17 N	11.49 E
Fenstanton	42	52.18 N	0.04 W
Fenton, Mi., U.S.	216	42.47 N	83.42 W
Fenton, Mo., U.S.	219	38.32 N	90.22 W
Fenton, Lake ⊜	216	42.50 N	83.43 W
Fentou	105	38.53 N	116.32 E
Fentress	222	29.45 N	97.47 W
Fenway Park ♠	283	42.21 N	71.06 W
Fenwick	188	38.13 N	80.34 W
Fenwick Island ›[1]	208	38.25 N	75.03 W
Fenyang	102	37.17 N	111.48 E
Fenyi	100	27.47 N	114.42 E
Feodosiya	78	45.02 N	35.23 E
Feodosiys'ka zatoka c	78	45.05 N	35.35 E
Fépin	56	50.01 N	4.44 E
Fer, Cap de ›	148	37.05 N	7.10 E
Ferbane	48	53.15 N	7.49 W
Ferbitz	264a	52.30 N	13.01 E
Ferch	264a	52.19 N	12.56 E
Fercher Berge ∧[2]	264a	52.19 N	12.57 E
Ferchland	54	52.26 N	12.00 E
Ferdig	182	48.45 N	111.46 W
Ferdinand	194	38.13 N	86.51 W
Ferdinandshof	54	53.39 N	13.53 E
Ferdows	128	34.00 N	58.09 E
Fère-Champenoise	50	48.45 N	3.59 E
Fère-en-Tardenois	50	49.12 N	3.31 E
Ferencváros ◆[8]	264c	47.28 N	19.06 E
Ferentillo	66	42.37 N	12.47 E
Ferentino	66	41.42 N	13.15 E
Fergana	85	40.23 N	71.46 E
Fergana □[4]	85	40.30 N	71.20 E
Ferganskaja dolina V	85	40.50 N	71.30 E
Ferganskij chrebet ⋏	85	41.00 N	74.00 E
Fergus	212	43.42 N	80.22 W
Fergus Falls	198	46.16 N	96.04 W
Ferguson, Austl.	168a	33.26 S	115.51 E
Ferguson, B.C., Can.	182	50.41 N	117.28 W
Ferguson, Ky., U.S.	192	37.04 N	84.36 W
Ferguson, Mo., U.S.	219	38.44 N	90.18 W
Ferguson ≃	168a	33.21 S	115.40 E
Fergusonville	285	40.07 N	74.54 W
Fergusson Island I	164	9.30 S	150.40 E
Fériana	148	34.57 N	8.34 E
Ferihegyi Airport ⊠	264c	47.26 N	19.15 E
Ferkéssédougou	150	9.36 N	5.12 W
Ferla	70	37.07 N	14.56 E
Ferlach	61	46.31 N	14.18 E
Ferleiten	64	47.10 N	12.49 E
Ferlo ◆[1]	150	0.15 N	0.14 W
Ferlo, Vallée du V	150	15.42 N	15.30 W
Fermiers, Île aux I	275a	45.40 N	73.27 W
Fermignano	66	43.40 N	12.39 E
Fermin, Point ›	228	33.42 N	118.18 W
Fermi National Accelerator Laboratory ʊ[3]	216	41.50 N	88.15 W
Fermo	66	43.09 N	13.43 E
Fermont	176	52.47 N	67.05 W
Fermoselle	34	41.19 N	6.23 W
Fermoy	48	52.08 N	8.16 W
Fernández	252	27.55 S	63.54 W
Fernández Leal	200	30.51 N	108.17 W
Fernandina, Isla I	246a	0.25 S	91.30 W
Fernandina Beach	192	30.40 N	81.27 W
Fernando de la Mora	252	25.19 S	57.36 W
Fernando de Noronha, Ilha I	250	3.51 S	32.25 W
Fernandópolis	255	20.16 S	50.14 W
Fernando Póo → Bioko I	152	3.30 N	8.40 E
Fernán-Núñez	34	37.40 N	4.43 W
Fernão Veloso, Baía de c	154	14.20 S	40.45 E
Ferndale, S. Afr.	273d	26.05 S	27.59 E
Ferndale, Ca., U.S.	204	40.34 N	124.15 W
Ferndale, Fl., U.S.	220	28.37 N	81.42 W
Ferndale, Md., U.S.	208	39.10 N	76.38 W
Ferndale, Mi., U.S.	216	42.27 N	83.08 W
Ferndale, N.Y., U.S.	210	41.46 N	74.44 W
Ferndale, Pa., U.S.	214	40.17 N	78.54 W
Ferndale, Wa., U.S.	202	48.50 N	122.35 W
Ferndale Lake ⊜	222	32.57 N	95.05 W
Ferndown	42	50.48 N	1.55 W

Nome	Página	Lat.°′	Long.°′ W = Oeste
Ferney-Voltaire	58	46.15 N	6.07 E
Fern Glen	210	40.57 N	76.10 W
Fernhill Heath	42	52.14 N	2.12 W
Fernie	182	49.30 N	115.03 W
Fernilee	262	53.18 N	1.58 W
Fernilee Reservoir ⊜[1]	262	53.17 N	1.59 W
Fernley	204	39.36 N	119.15 W
Ferno	266b	45.37 N	8.45 E
Fernow, Mount ∧	224	47.45 N	121.14 W
Fern Park	220	28.41 N	81.20 W
Fernpass)(	58	47.22 N	10.50 E
Fern Ridge Lake ⊜[1]	202	44.05 N	123.18 W
Ferns	48	52.35 N	6.31 W
Fernvale	171a	27.27 S	152.39 E
Fernway	214	40.41 N	80.07 W
Fernwood, Id., U.S.	202	47.06 N	116.23 W
Fernwood, N.Y., U.S.	210	43.16 N	73.40 W
Fernwood, Pa., U.S.	285	39.57 N	75.15 W
Ferny Creek	274b	37.53 S	145.21 E
Feroé, Islas → Faeroe Islands □[2]	22	62.00 N	7.00 W
Feroës → Faeroe Islands □[2]	22	62.00 N	7.00 W
Ferokh	122	11.11 N	75.51 E
Feroleto Antico	68	38.58 N	16.23 E
Feroleto della Chiesa	68	38.28 N	16.04 E
Ferolle Point ›	186	51.05 N	57.07 W
Ferozepore → Fīrozpur	123	30.55 N	74.36 E
Ferrandina	68	40.29 N	16.28 E
Ferrara	64	44.50 N	11.35 E
Ferrara □[4]	64	44.48 N	11.50 E
Ferrat, Cap ›	34	35.54 N	0.23 W
Ferrato, Capo ›	71	39.18 N	9.38 E
Ferraz de Vasconcelos	256	23.32 S	46.22 W
Ferraz de Vasconcelos □[7]	287b	23.33 S	46.21 W
Ferrazzano	66	41.32 N	14.40 E
Ferré, Cap ›	240e	14.28 N	60.49 W
Ferreira, Ang.	152	12.53 S	22.48 E
Ferreira, S. Afr.	158	29.13 S	26.10 E
Ferreira do Alentejo	34	38.03 N	8.07 W
Ferreira Gomes	250	0.48 N	51.08 W
Ferreiros	256	22.25 S	43.34 W
Ferrell	285	39.41 N	75.12 W
Ferrell's Bridge Dam ◆[6]	222	32.45 N	94.30 W
Ferreñafe	248	6.38 S	79.45 W
Ferrera Erbognone	62	45.07 N	8.52 E
Ferret	58	45.55 N	7.06 E
Ferret, Cap ›	32	44.37 N	1.15 W
Ferreyra	252	31.28 S	64.08 W
Ferriday	194	31.37 N	91.33 W
Ferriere	62	44.38 N	9.30 E
Ferrière-la-Grande	50	50.15 N	4.00 E
Ferrières	50	48.05 N	2.47 E
Ferrières-en-Brie	50	48.49 N	2.43 E
Ferris	222	32.32 N	96.39 W
Ferritslev	41	55.18 N	10.36 E
Ferro ≃	255	12.27 S	54.31 W
Ferro, Canale del V	64	46.21 N	13.07 E
Ferrol → El Ferrol del Caudillo	34	43.29 N	8.14 W
Ferrol, Península de ›[1]	248	9.10 S	78.37 W
Ferron	200	39.05 N	111.08 W
Ferron Creek ≃	200	39.09 N	110.55 W
Ferros	255	19.14 S	43.02 W
Ferru, Monte ∧, It.	71	40.08 N	8.36 E
Ferru, Monte ∧, It.	71	39.44 N	9.38 E
Ferruzzano	68	38.02 N	16.05 E
Ferry, Pointe ›	241o	16.17 N	61.49 W
Ferryhill	44	54.41 N	1.33 W
Ferryland	186	47.02 N	52.53 W
Ferry Point Park ♠	276	40.49 N	73.50 W
Ferrysburg	216	43.05 N	86.13 W
Ferry Village	284a	43.58 N	78.57 W
Ferryville → Menzel Bourguiba	148	37.10 N	9.48 E
Feršampenuaz	86	53.32 N	59.51 E
Fertile	198	47.32 N	96.16 W
Fertilia, Aeroporto di ⊠	71	40.37 N	8.15 E
Fertő (Neusiedler See) ⊜	61	47.50 N	16.45 E
Fertőd ⊥	61	47.37 N	16.53 E
Fertőrákos	61	47.43 N	16.39 E
Fertőújlak	61	47.40 N	16.51 E
Ferulargiu, Monte ∧	71	40.31 N	9.34 E
Ferzikovo	82	54.32 N	36.45 E
Fès	148	34.05 N	4.57 W
Fès □[4]	148	33.55 N	4.57 W
Feshi	152	6.07 S	18.10 E
Feshie ≃	46	57.08 N	3.55 W
Fessenden	198	47.38 N	99.37 W
Festus	219	38.13 N	90.23 W
Fetcham	42	51.17 N	0.22 W
Fet Dom, Tanjung ›	164	1.53 S	129.43 E
Fété Bowé	150	14.56 N	13.30 W
Fetești	38	44.23 N	27.50 E
Fethaland, Point of ›	46a	60.38 N	1.18 W
Fethard	48	52.27 N	7.41 W
Fethiye	130	36.37 N	29.07 E
Fethiye Körfezi c	130	36.40 N	29.00 E
Fetisovo	72	42.46 N	52.38 E
Fetlar I	46a	60.37 N	0.52 W
Fetsund	26	59.56 N	11.10 E
Fetterangus	46	57.33 N	2.01 W
Fettercairn	46	56.51 N	2.34 W
Feucherolles	261	48.52 N	1.58 E
Feucht	60	49.22 N	11.13 E
Feuchtwangen	56	49.10 N	10.20 E
Feudingen	56	50.56 N	8.19 E
Feuerland → Tierra del Fuego, Isla Grande de I	254	54.00 S	69.00 W
Feuet	146	24.57 N	10.04 E
Feuilles, Baie aux c	176	58.55 N	69.20 W
Feuilles, Rivière aux ≃	176	58.47 N	70.04 W
Feuquières-en-Vimeu	50	50.04 N	1.36 E
Feura Bush	210	42.35 N	73.53 W
Feurs	62	45.45 N	4.14 E
Fevik	26	58.23 N	8.42 E
Fevzipaşa	130	37.07 N	36.37 E
Féy	56	49.02 N	6.06 E
Feyẕābād, Afg.	120	37.06 N	70.34 E
Feyẕābād, Īrān	128	35.01 N	58.46 E
Feyzin	62	45.40 N	4.51 E
Fez → Fès	148	34.05 N	4.57 W
Fezzan → Fazzān □[9]	146	26.00 N	14.00 E
Ffestiniog	42	52.58 N	3.55 W
Fforest Fawr ◆[1]	42	51.52 N	3.36 W
F. Gilbert Hills State Forest ♠	283	42.03 N	71.17 W
Fhada, Beinn ∧	46	57.13 N	5.18 W
Fiambalá	252	27.41 S	67.38 W
Fiamignano	66	42.16 N	13.07 E
Fian	150	10.23 N	2.29 W
Fianarantsoa	157b	21.26 S	47.05 E
Fianarantsoa □[4]	157b	22.00 S	47.00 E
Fianga	146	9.55 N	15.09 E
Fiano	62	45.13 N	7.31 E
Fiantsonana	157b	19.09 S	46.12 E
Fiastra, Abbazia di ʊ[1]	66	43.13 N	13.25 E
Fiavè	64	46.00 N	10.50 E
Ficarazzi	70	38.05 N	13.28 E
Ficarolo	64	44.57 N	11.26 E
Ficarra	70	38.06 N	14.50 E
Fiche	144	9.52 N	38.46 E
Fichtelberg	60	50.01 N	11.51 E
Fichtelberg ∧	54	50.26 N	12.57 E
Fichtelgebirge ⋏	30	50.00 N	11.55 E
Fichtenau	264a	52.27 N	13.42 E

Nome	Página	Lat.°′	Long.°′ W = Oeste
Ficksburg	158	28.57 S	27.50 E
Ficulle	66	42.50 N	12.04 E
Ficuzza ≃	70	37.00 N	14.20 E
Fidalgo ≃	250	7.28 S	42.32 W
Fidalgo Island I	224	48.25 N	122.35 W
Fidān, Wādī al- V	132	30.46 N	35.18 E
Fiddlers Hamlet	260	51.41 N	0.08 E
Fiddletown	226	38.30 N	120.46 W
Fiddyment Creek ≃	278	41.36 N	88.03 W
Fidelity	219	39.09 N	90.10 W
Fidenza	64	44.52 N	10.03 E
Fidīmīn	142	29.23 N	30.46 E
Fiditi	150	7.45 N	3.53 E
Fidji → Fiji □[1]	175g	18.00 S	178.00 E
Fidler Lake ⊜	184	57.11 N	96.57 W
Fidschi → Fiji □[1]	175g	18.00 S	178.00 E
Fiè (Völs)	64	46.31 N	11.30 E
Fieberbrunn	64	47.29 N	12.33 E
Field	182	51.24 N	116.29 W
Fieldale	192	36.42 N	79.56 W
Field Museum ʊ	278	41.53 N	87.37 W
Fieldon	219	39.07 N	90.30 W
Fieldsboro	285	40.08 N	74.43 W
Fieldstone	276	40.44 N	74.33 W
Fiemme, Val di V	64	46.20 N	11.35 E
Fiener Bruch ≡	54	52.19 N	12.10 E
Fienvillers	50	50.07 N	2.14 E
Fier	38	40.43 N	19.34 E
Fier ≃	58	45.56 N	5.50 E
Fiéra Campionaria ♠	266b	45.28 N	9.09 E
Fiera di Primiero	64	46.10 N	11.49 E
Fierenana	157b	18.29 S	48.24 E
Fiery Creek ≃, Austl.	166	18.23 S	139.52 E
Fiery Creek ≃, Austl.	169	37.44 S	142.56 E
Fiery Range ⋏	171b	35.30 S	148.40 E
Fierzës, Liqeni i ⊜[1]	38	42.10 N	20.15 E
Fiesch	58	46.20 N	8.10 E
Fiesole	66	43.48 N	11.17 E
Fiesso d'Artico	64	45.24 N	12.02 E
Fiesso Umbertiano	64	44.56 N	11.36 E
Fife	224	47.14 N	122.22 W
Fife □[4]	46	56.13 N	3.02 W
Fife Lake, Sk., Can.	184	49.12 N	105.43 W
Fife Lake, Mi., U.S.	190	44.34 N	85.21 W
Fife Lake ⊜	184	49.14 N	105.53 W
Fife Ness ›	46	56.17 N	2.36 W
Fifield	190	45.52 N	90.25 W
Fifteenmile Creek ≃, Or., U.S.	224	45.37 N	121.07 W
Fifteenmile Creek ≃, Wy., U.S.	202	44.01 N	108.01 W
Fifth Cataract → Khāmis, Ash-Shallāl al- ʟ	140	18.23 N	33.47 E
Fifth Depot Lake ⊜	212	44.36 N	76.52 W
Figeac	32	44.37 N	2.02 E
Figeholm	26	57.22 N	16.33 E
Fig Garden	226	36.48 N	119.47 W
Fighting Island I	281	42.13 N	83.07 W
Figline Valdarno	66	43.37 N	11.28 E
Figtree	154	20.24 S	28.21 E
Figueira → Governador Valadares, Bra.	255	18.51 S	41.56 W
Figueira, Bra.	287a	22.42 S	43.27 W
Figueira, Cachoeira ʟ	250	9.49 S	58.13 W
Figueira da Foz	34	40.09 N	8.52 W
Figueres	34	42.16 N	2.58 E
Figuig	148	32.10 N	1.15 W
Figuig □[4]	148	32.40 N	2.15 W
Fihaonana	157b	18.36 S	47.12 E
Fiherenana ≃	157b	23.19 S	43.37 E
Fiji □[1], Oc.	14	18.00 S	178.00 E
Fiji □[1], Oc.	175g	18.00 S	178.00 E
Fiji Islands II	14	18.00 S	178.00 E
Fijnaart	52	51.37 N	4.31 E
Fik	144	8.10 N	42.18 E
Fika	146	11.17 N	11.18 E
Fiktūriyā, Bi'r ⊤[4]	142	30.24 N	30.36 E
Filabusi	154	20.34 S	29.20 E
Filadélfia, Bra.	250	7.21 S	47.30 W
Filadelfia, C.R.	236	10.26 N	85.34 W
Filadelfia, It.	68	38.48 N	16.18 E
Filadelfia → Philadelphia, Pa., U.S.	208	39.57 N	75.07 W
Fil'akovo	30	48.17 N	19.51 E
Filandari	68	38.37 N	16.02 E
Filatova Gora	76	57.40 N	28.10 E
Filchner Ice Shelf ⊓	9	79.00 S	40.00 W
Filderstadt	56	48.41 N	9.13 E
File Lake ⊜	184	54.53 N	100.20 W
Filettino	66	41.53 N	13.19 E
Filey	44	54.12 N	0.17 W
Filey Bay c	44	54.12 N	0.16 W
Fili ◆[8]	265b	55.45 N	37.31 E
Filí ⊥	38	38.06 N	23.40 E
Filiano	68	40.49 N	15.42 E
Filiași	38	44.33 N	23.31 E
Filiatrá	38	37.10 N	21.35 E
Filicudi, Isola I	70	38.34 N	14.34 E
Filimonovo	86	56.12 N	95.28 E
Filingué	150	14.21 N	3.19 E
Filipinas → Philippines □[1]	116	13.00 N	122.00 E
Filipinas, Mar de → Philippine Sea ⊤[2]	14	20.00 N	135.00 E
Filipino Cemetery and Memorial ◆	269f	14.31 N	121.02 E
Fílippoi ⊥	38	41.00 N	24.16 E
Filippovka	80	53.59 N	49.46 E
Filippovo	80	58.18 N	50.30 E
Filippovskoje, Ross.	82	56.06 N	38.37 E
Filippovskoje, Ross.	82	56.48 N	39.07 E
Filipstad	40	59.43 N	14.10 E
Filisola	234	17.50 N	94.19 W
Fillmore, Sk., Can.	184	49.50 N	103.25 W
Fillmore, Ca., U.S.	228	34.23 N	118.55 W
Fillmore, Il., U.S.	219	39.07 N	89.17 W
Fillmore, N.Y., U.S.	210	42.27 N	78.06 W
Fillmore, Ut,. U.S.	200	38.58 N	112.19 W
Fillmore Glen State Park ♠	210	42.42 N	76.20 W
Filogaso	68	38.41 N	16.14 E
Filomeno Mata	234	20.12 N	97.42 W
Filonovskaja	80	50.34 N	42.46 E
Filottrano	66	43.26 N	13.21 E
Fils ≃	56	48.42 N	9.25 E
Filskov	41	55.48 N	9.02 E
Filton	42	51.31 N	2.35 W
Filtu	144	5.07 N	40.39 E
Filzbach	58	47.07 N	9.08 E
Fimi ≃	152	3.01 S	16.58 E
Fina, Réserve de ◆[4]	150	12.50 N	8.30 W
Finale Emilia	64	44.50 N	11.17 E
Finale Ligure	62	44.10 N	8.20 E
Finarwa	144	13.06 N	39.01 E
Fincastle	192	37.29 N	79.52 W
Finch	206	45.11 N	75.07 W
Fincham	42	52.37 N	0.30 E
Finchley ◆[8]	260	51.36 N	0.10 W
Finderne	276	40.34 N	74.35 W
Findhorn	46	57.39 N	3.36 W
Findhorn ≃	46	57.38 N	3.38 W
Fındık	130	37.31 N	41.58 E
Findlay, Il., U.S.	219	39.31 N	88.45 W
Findlay, Oh., U.S.	216	41.02 N	83.39 W
Findlay, Mount ∧	182	50.04 N	116.28 W
Findley Lake	214	42.07 N	79.44 W
Findley Lake ⊜	214	42.06 N	79.43 W
Findochty	46	57.41 N	2.54 W
Fine Arts, Museum of ʊ	283	42.20 N	71.06 W
Finedon	42	52.20 N	0.39 W
Finejevo	82	56.02 N	38.53 E
Finesville	210	40.36 N	75.10 W
Fingal, On., Can.	214	42.43 N	81.19 W
Fingal, N.D., U.S.	198	46.45 N	97.47 W
Finger Lake ⊜	184	53.09 N	93.30 W
Fíngoè	154	15.12 S	31.50 E

Nome	Página	Lat.°′	Long.°′ W = Oeste
Finike	130	36.18 N	30.09 E
Finike Körfezi c	130	36.17 N	30.16 E
Finisk ≃	48	52.07 N	7.50 W
Finistère □[5]	32	48.20 N	4.00 W
Finisterre	196	25.59 N	103.15 W
Finisterre → Land's End ›	42	50.03 N	5.44 W
Finisterre, Cabo de ›	34	42.53 N	9.16 W
Finisterre Range ⋏	164	5.50 S	146.05 E
Finja	41	56.10 N	13.41 E
Finjasjön ⊜	41	56.08 N	13.42 E
Finke	162	25.34 S	134.35 E
Finke ≃	162	26.20 S	136.00 E
Finke, Mount ∧[2]	162	30.55 S	134.02 E
Finke Gorge National Park ♠	162	24.15 S	132.50 E
Finkenkrug	264a	52.34 N	13.03 E
Finkenwerder ◆[8]	52	53.31 N	9.52 E
Finksburg	208	39.29 N	76.53 W
Finland (Suomi) □[1], Europe	22	64.00 N	26.00 E
Finland (Suomi) □[1], Europe	24	64.00 N	26.00 E
Finland, Gulf of (Suomenlahti) (Finskij zaliv) c	26	60.00 N	27.00 E
Finlande → Finland □[1]	24	64.00 N	26.00 E
Finlandia → Finland □[1]	24	64.00 N	26.00 E
Finlandia, Golfo de → Finland, Gulf of c	26	60.00 N	27.00 E
Finland Station ◆[5]	265a	59.57 N	30.22 E
Finlas, Loch ⊜	44	55.15 N	4.25 W
Finlay ≃	176	56.54 N	124.57 W
Finley, Austl.	166	35.39 S	145.35 E
Finley, N.D., U.S.	198	47.30 N	97.50 W
Finley Creek ≃	194	36.58 N	93.22 W
Finleyville, Pa., U.S.	214	40.09 N	78.11 W
Finleyville, Pa., U.S.	214	40.15 N	80.00 W
Finleyville Airport ⊠	279b	40.15 N	80.01 W
Finmoore	182	53.59 N	123.37 W
Finn ≃	48	54.50 N	7.29 W
Finne ◆[1]	54	51.13 N	11.19 E
Finnegan	182	51.07 N	112.04 W
Finnentrop	56	51.09 N	7.58 E
Finnerödja	40	58.56 N	14.26 E
Finney Creek ≃	224	48.31 N	121.51 W
Finnhamn	40	59.28 N	18.50 E
Finnigan, Mount ∧	164	15.49 S	145.17 E
Finnis, Cape ›	162	33.38 S	134.51 E
Finnischer Meerbusen → Finland, Gulf of c	26	60.00 N	27.00 E
Finniss	168b	35.24 S	138.49 E
Finniss ≃	168b	35.30 S	138.53 E
Finnland → Finland □[1]	24	64.00 N	26.00 E
Finnmark □[6]	24	70.00 N	25.00 E
Finn Mountain ∧	180	60.37 N	157.11 W
Finno ∧[2]	154	3.27 N	41.32 E
Finnskogen ◆[3]	26	60.40 N	12.40 E
Finnsnes	24	69.14 N	17.59 E
Finocchio ◆[8]	267a	41.53 N	12.41 E
Finow	54	52.50 N	13.43 E
Finowfurt	54	52.51 N	13.41 E
Finowkanal ≍	54	52.51 N	13.24 E
Fins, Fr.	50	50.02 N	3.03 E
Fins, 'Umān	128	22.56 N	59.13 E
Finsbury	273d	26.13 S	27.39 E
Finschhafen	164	6.35 S	147.50 E
Finse	26	60.36 N	7.30 E
Finskij zaliv → Finland, Gulf of c	26	60.00 N	27.00 E
Finspång	40	58.43 N	15.47 E
Finsta	40	59.44 N	18.30 E
Finsteraarhorn ∧	58	46.32 N	8.08 E
Finsterwalde	54	51.38 N	13.42 E
Finsterwolde	52	53.12 N	7.04 E
Fintel	52	53.10 N	9.40 E
Fintona	48	54.30 N	7.19 W
Fintown	48	54.52 N	8.08 W
Finvoy	48	55.00 N	6.30 W
Fionn Loch ⊜	46	57.46 N	5.29 W
Fiora ≃	66	42.20 N	11.34 E
Fiorano Modenese	64	44.32 N	10.49 E
Fiordland National Park ♠	172	45.30 S	167.20 E
Fiorenzuola d'Arda	62	44.56 N	9.55 E
Fiorenzuola di Focara	66	43.57 N	12.48 E
Fiorito ◆[8]	288	34.42 S	58.27 W
Fīq	132	32.47 N	35.42 E
Fırat → Euphrates ≃	128	31.00 N	47.25 E
Firavitoba	246	5.40 N	73.00 W
Fircrest	224	47.14 N	122.30 W
Fire ≃	190	48.52 N	83.21 W
Firebaugh	226	36.51 N	120.27 W
Firebrick	218	38.41 N	83.03 W
Fire Island I	210	40.42 N	73.00 W
Fire Island Inlet c	276	40.38 N	73.16 W
Fire Island National Seashore ♠	188	40.38 N	73.08 W
Fire Island Pines	276	40.40 N	73.04 W
Fire Islands II	276	40.40 N	73.11 W
Firenze (Florence)	66	43.46 N	11.15 E
Firenze □[4]	66	43.50 N	11.20 E
Firenzuola	66	44.07 N	11.23 E
Firesteel Creek ≃	198	43.43 N	97.58 W
Firgrove	262	53.37 N	2.08 W
Firmat	252	33.27 S	61.29 W
Firminópolis	255	16.40 S	50.19 W
Firminy	62	45.23 N	4.18 E
Firmo	68	39.43 N	16.10 E
Firovo	76	57.29 N	33.40 E
Fīrozābād	124	27.09 N	78.25 E
Fīrozpur	123	30.55 N	74.36 E
Firozpur Jhirka	124	27.48 N	76.57 E
Firsanovka	265b	55.57 N	37.15 E
Firsovo	88	52.20 N	118.06 E
First Broad ≃	192	35.11 N	81.37 W
First Cataract → Awwal, Ash-Shallāl al- ʟ	140	24.01 N	32.52 E
First Cliff ⊥[4]	283	42.12 N	70.43 W
First Connecticut Lake ⊜	206	45.05 N	71.15 W
First Han-gang Bridge ◆[5]	271b	37.32 N	126.56 E
First Herring Brook ≃	283	42.11 N	70.45 W
First Watchung Mountain ∧	276	40.55 N	74.10 W
Firth	198	40.31 N	96.36 W
Firth ≃	180	69.32 N	139.22 W
Fir'uza	128	37.56 N	58.04 E
Fīrūzābād	128	28.50 N	52.36 E
Fīrūz Kūh	128	35.45 N	52.47 E
Fischa ≃	61	48.07 N	16.41 E
Fischamend	61	48.07 N	16.37 E
Fischbach, Dtsch.	56	49.44 N	7.23 E
Fischbach, Dtsch.	60	49.25 N	11.12 E
Fischbachau	64	47.43 N	11.57 E
Fischbacher Alpen ⋏	61	47.28 N	15.30 E
Fischbeck, Dtsch.	52	52.09 N	9.17 E
Fischbeck, Dtsch.	54	52.32 N	12.01 E
Fischeln ◆[8]	263	51.18 N	6.35 E
Fischen	58	47.28 N	10.16 E
Fischhausen → Primorsk	76	54.44 N	20.01 E
Fischland ⊥[2]	54	54.22 N	12.25 E
Fish ≃, Austl.	170	33.29 S	149.37 E
Fish (Vis) ≃, Namibia	156	28.07 S	17.45 E
Fish ≃, Al., U.S.	194	30.25 N	87.50 W
Fish ≃, Me., U.S.	186	47.15 N	68.36 W
Fishbourne	42	50.44 N	1.12 W
Fish Brook ≃, Ma., U.S.	283	42.38 N	70.58 W
Fish Brook ≃, Ma., U.S.	283	42.42 N	71.13 W
Fish Camp	226	37.29 N	119.38 W

≃ River	Fluß	Río	Rivière	Rio
≍ Canal	Kanal	Canal	Canal	Canal
ʟ Waterfall, Rapids	Wasserfall, Stromschnellen	Cascada, Rápidos	Chute d'eau, Rapides	Cascata, Rápidos
)(Strait	Meeresstraße	Estrecho	Détroit	Estreito
c Bay, Gulf	Bucht, Golf	Bahía, Golfo	Baie, Golfe	Baía, Golfo
⊜ Lake, Lakes	See, Seen	Lago, Lagos	Lac, Lacs	Lago, Lagos
≡ Swamp	Sumpf	Pantano	Marais	Pântano
⊓ Ice Features, Glacier	Eis- und Gletscherformen	Accidentes Glaciales	Formes glaciaires	Acidentes glaciares
⊤ Other Hydrographic Features	Andere Hydrographische Objekte	Otros Elementos Hidrográficos	Autres données hydrographiques	Outros acidentes hidrográficos

✦ Submarine Features	Untermeerische Objekte	Accidentes Submarinos	Formes de relief sous-marin	Acidentes submarinos
□ Political Unit	Politische Einheit	Unidad Politica	Entité politique	Unidade política
ʊ Cultural Institution	Kulturelle Institution	Institución Cultural	Institution culturelle	Instituição cultural
⊥ Historical Site	Historische Stätte	Sitio Histórico	Site historique	Sítio histórico
♠ Recreational Site	Erholungs- und Ferienort	Sitio de Recreo	Centre de loisirs	Area de Lazer
⊠ Airport	Flughafen	Aeropuerto	Aéroport	Aeroporto
■ Military Installation	Militäranlage	Instalación Militar	Installation militaire	Instalação militar
◆ Miscellaneous	Verschiedenes	Misceláneo	Divers	Diversos

Fish Canyon V 280 34.11 N 117.55 W
Fish Creek ≃, On., Can. 212 43.13 N 81.13 W
Fish Creek ≃, U.S. 216 41.28 N 84.45 W
Fish Creek ≃, Mi., U.S. 190 43.04 N 84.51 W
Fish Creek ≃, Mt., U.S. 202 46.17 N 109.13 W
Fish Creek ≃, N.Y., U.S. 212 43.12 N 75.43 W
Fish Creek ≃, Or., U.S. 224 45.09 N 122.09 W
Fish Creek, East Branch ≃ 212 43.16 N 75.38 W
Fish Creek, West Branch ≃ 212 43.16 N 75.38 W
Fish Creek Mountain ∧ 224 45.05 N 122.08 W
Fisheating Creek ≃ 220 26.57 N 81.07 W
Fisher, Austl. 162 30.33 S 130.58 E
Fisher, Ar., U.S. 194 35.29 N 90.58 W
Fisher, Il., U.S. 216 40.18 N 88.21 W
Fisher, La., U.S. 194 31.29 N 93.27 W
Fisher, Pa., U.S. 214 41.16 N 79.15 W
Fisher ≃, Mb., Can. 184 51.26 N 97.18 W
Fisher ≃, Mt., U.S. 202 48.22 N 115.19 W
Fisher Bay c, Mb., Can. 184 51.30 N 97.16 W
Fisher Bay c, Mi., U.S. 281 42.36 N 82.39 W
Fisher Branch 184 51.05 N 97.37 W
Fisher Channel ⵡ 182 52.10 N 127.42 W
Fisher Heights 279b 40.10 N 79.54 W
Fishermans Island I 208 37.06 N 75.58 W
Fisherman's Wharf ⊥ 282 37.48 N 122.25 W
Fisher Peak ∧ 192 36.33 N 80.50 W
Fisher River Indian Reserve ◆[4] 184 51.26 N 97.20 W
Fishers, In., U.S. 218 39.57 N 86.00 W
Fishers, N.Y., U.S. 210 43.00 N 77.28 W
Fishers Island I 207 41.16 N 72.00 W
Fishers Peak ∧ 196 37.06 N 104.28 W
Fisher Strait ⵡ 176 63.15 N 83.30 W
Fishertown 214 40.08 N 78.35 W
Fisherville 275b 43.47 N 79.28 W
Fishguard 42 51.59 N 4.59 W
Fishhook 219 39.48 N 90.53 W
Fish House 210 43.08 N 74.08 W
Fishing Bay c 208 38.18 N 76.01 W
Fishing Creek 208 38.20 N 76.14 W
Fishing Creek ≃, Ky., U.S. 192 37.06 N 84.41 W
Fishing Creek ≃, N.C., U.S. 192 35.57 N 77.31 W
Fishing Creek ≃, Pa., U.S. 210 40.58 N 76.28 W
Fishing Creek ≃, Pa., U.S. 210 41.07 N 77.29 W
Fishing Creek ≃, S.C., U.S. 192 34.36 N 80.54 W
Fishing Islands II 212 44.45 N 81.20 W
Fishing Lake ⊜, Mb., Can. 184 52.07 N 95.25 W
Fishing Lake ⊜, Sk., Can. 184 51.50 N 103.32 W
Fishkill 210 41.32 N 73.53 W
Fishkill Creek ≃ 210 41.29 N 73.59 W
Fish Lake 216 41.34 N 86.33 W
Fish Lake ⊜, On., Can. 212 44.06 N 77.11 W
Fish Lake ⊜, Mi., U.S. 216 42.03 N 85.52 W
Fish Lake ⊜, Wa., U.S. 224 47.50 N 120.42 W
Fishmoor Reservoir ⊜[1] 262 53.44 N 2.28 W
Fish Point > 214 41.43 N 82.40 W
Fishpool 262 53.35 N 2.17 W
Fish River 166 17.55 S 137.45 E
Fishs Eddy 210 41.58 N 75.10 W
Fisk 194 36.46 N 90.12 W
Fiskárdhon 38 38.27 N 20.35 E
Fiskdale 207 42.06 N 72.06 W
Fiskebäckskil 26 58.15 N 11.27 E
Fismes 50 49.18 N 3.41 E
Fišt, gora ∧ 84 43.58 N 39.54 E
Fitchburg, Ma., U.S. 207 42.35 N 71.48 W
Fitchburg, Wi., U.S. 216 42.57 N 89.28 W
Fitchville, Ct., U.S. 207 41.33 N 72.09 W
Fitchville, Oh., U.S. 214 41.06 N 82.29 W
Fitful Head > 46a 59.54 N 1.23 W
Fitiuta 174y 14.13 S 169.27 W
Fito, Mount ∧ 175a 13.55 S 171.44 W
Fitri, Lac ⊜ 146 12.50 N 17.28 E
Fittja 40 59.15 N 17.52 E
Fittleworth 42 50.58 N 0.35 W
Fitzgerald 192 31.42 N 83.15 W
Fitzgerald River National Park ◆ 162 34.00 S 119.30 E
Fitz Henry 279b 40.10 N 79.45 W
Fitz Hugh Sound ⵡ 182 51.40 N 127.57 W
Fitzmaurice ≃ 164 14.50 S 129.44 E
Fitz Roy, Arg. 254 47.02 S 67.15 W
Fitzroy, Austl. 274b 37.48 S 144.59 E
Fitzroy ≃, Austl. 162 17.31 S 123.35 E
Fitzroy ≃, Austl. 166 23.32 S 150.52 E
Fitzroy, Monte (Cerro Chaltel) ∧ 254 49.17 S 73.05 W
Fitzroy Crossing 162 18.11 S 125.35 E
Fitzroy Falls Reservoir ⊜[1] 170 34.38 S 150.30 E
Fitzwilliam 207 42.46 N 72.08 W
Fitzwilliam Island I 190 45.30 N 81.45 W
Fiuggi 66 41.48 N 13.13 E
Fiumalbo 64 44.11 N 10.39 E
Fiume — Rijeka 36 45.20 N 14.27 E
Fiumedinisi 70 38.02 N 15.23 E
Fiumefreddo Bruzio 68 39.14 N 16.04 E
Fiumefreddo di Sicilia 70 37.47 N 15.12 E
Fiumesino 66 43.38 N 13.22 E
Fiume Veneto 64 45.56 N 12.44 E
Fiumicino ◆[8] 66 41.46 N 12.14 E
Five Corners 283 42.01 N 71.07 W
Five Cowrie Creek ≃[1] 273a 6.27 N 3.27 E
Five Dock 274a 33.52 S 151.08 E
Five Forks 284c 38.47 N 77.16 W
Five Islands 186 45.25 N 64.02 W
Five Islands Harbour c 240c 17.06 N 61.54 W
Fivemile ≃ 276 41.03 N 73.27 W
Fivemile Creek ≃, N.Y., U.S. 210 42.22 N 77.22 W
Fivemile Creek ≃, Or., U.S. 224 45.36 N 121.05 W
Fivemile Creek ≃, Wy., U.S. 202 43.14 N 108.12 W
Fivemile Point 210 42.06 N 75.48 W
Fivemiletown 48 54.23 N 7.18 W
Five Penny Borve 46 58.25 N 6.25 W
Five Points, Ca., U.S. 226 36.26 N 120.06 W
Five Points, In., U.S. 218 39.35 N 86.20 W
Five Points, N.M., U.S. 200 35.03 N 106.39 W
Five Points, Oh., U.S. 218 39.41 N 83.12 W
Five Points, Pa., U.S. 214 40.34 N 80.15 W
Five Points, Pa., U.S. 285 39.50 N 75.42 W
Fivizzano 64 44.14 N 10.08 E
Fiwila Mission 154 13.58 S 29.36 E
Fixin 58 47.15 N 4.58 E
Fix-Saint-Geneys 62 45.08 N 3.40 E
Fizi 154 4.18 S 28.57 E
Fjællebroen 41 55.03 N 10.24 E
Fjærlandsfjorden c[2] 26 61.17 N 6.40 E
Fjällåsen 24 67.29 N 20.10 E
Fjällbacka 26 58.36 N 11.17 E
Fjällsjöälven ≃ 26 63.29 N 16.50 E
Fjärdhundra 40 59.47 N 16.56 E
Fjärdhundra □9 40 59.47 N 16.55 E
Fjenneslev 41 55.26 N 11.40 E
Fjerritslev 26 57.05 N 9.16 E
Fjugesta 40 59.10 N 14.52 E
Fkih-Ben-Salah 148 32.32 N 6.40 W
Flacksta 40 59.23 N 16.27 E
Fladnitz im Raabtal 61 46.59 N 15.47 E
Fladså ≃ 41 55.19 N 8.54 E
Fladungen 56 50.31 N 10.08 E
Flag Creek ≃ 278 41.43 N 87.55 W
Flagler 198 39.17 N 103.04 W
Flagler Beach 192 29.28 N 81.07 W
Flagstaff, S. Afr. 158 31.05 S 29.29 E
Flagstaff, Az., U.S. 200 35.11 N 111.39 W
Flagstaff Lake ⊜[1] 188 45.10 N 70.15 W
Flagtown 276 40.31 N 74.41 W
Flaken-See ⊜ 264a 52.25 N 13.46 E
Flåm 26 60.50 N 7.07 E
Flambeau ≃ 190 45.18 N 91.15 W
Flambeau, South Fork ≃ 190 45.39 N 90.48 W
Flamborough, On., Can. 212 43.20 N 79.53 W
Flamborough, Eng., U.K. 44 54.06 N 0.07 W
Flamborough Head > 44 54.07 N 0.04 W
Fläming ◆[1] 54 52.00 N 12.30 E
Flaming Gorge National Recreation Area ◆ 200 41.30 N 109.30 W
Flaming Gorge Reservoir ⊜[1] 200 41.15 N 109.30 W
Flamingo 220 25.09 N 80.56 W
Flamingo, Teluk c 164 5.33 S 138.00 E
Flanagan 216 40.52 N 88.51 W
Flanagan ≃ 184 52.50 N 93.28 W
Flanagan Passage ⵡ 240m 18.18 N 64.39 W
Flanders, On., Can. 190 48.44 N 92.05 W
Flanders, N.J., U.S. 276 40.50 N 74.41 W
Flanders, N.Y., U.S. 207 40.49 N 72.36 W
Flanders (Flandre) □9 50 51.00 N 3.00 E
Flanders Airport ⊠ 276 40.50 N 74.41 W
Flandes 246 4.18 N 74.49 W
Flandorf 264b 48.21 N 16.23 E
Flandre — Flanders □9 50 51.00 N 3.00 E
Flandreau 198 44.02 N 96.35 W
Flannan Islands II 46 58.18 N 7.36 W
Flåren ⊜ 26 57.02 N 14.06 E
Flasher 198 46.27 N 101.13 W
Flåsjön ⊜ 26 64.06 N 15.51 E
Flat, Ak., U.S. 180 62.27 N 158.01 W
Flat, Tx., U.S. 222 31.19 N 97.38 W
Flat ≃, N.T., Can. 180 61.33 N 125.18 W
Flat ≃, Mi., U.S. 190 42.56 N 85.20 W
Flat ≃, N.C., U.S. 192 36.05 N 78.49 W
Flat Bay 186 48.24 N 58.36 W
Flat Branch ≃ 219 39.33 N 89.16 W
Flatbush ◆[8] 276 40.39 N 73.56 W
Flat Creek ≃, Ky., U.S. 218 38.17 N 83.48 W
Flat Creek ≃, Mo., U.S. 194 36.45 N 93.31 W
Flat Creek ≃, Mt., U.S. 202 47.43 N 109.50 W
Flat Creek ≃, N.J., U.S. 276 40.27 N 74.10 W
Flat Creek Reservoir ⊜[1] 222 32.14 N 95.45 W
Flatey 24a 65.19 N 23.07 W
Flateyri 24a 65.59 N 23.42 W
Flathead ≃ 202 47.22 N 114.47 W
Flathead, Middle Fork ≃ 202 48.28 N 114.04 W
Flathead, North Fork ≃ 202 48.28 N 114.04 W
Flathead, South Fork ≃ 202 48.23 N 114.04 W
Flathead Indian Reservation ◆[4] 202 47.30 N 114.25 W
Flathead Lake ⊜ 202 47.52 N 114.08 W
Flat Holm I 42 51.23 N 3.08 W
Flat Lake ⊜ 182 54.39 N 112.55 W
Flat Lick 192 36.49 N 83.46 W
Flatonia 222 29.41 N 97.06 W
Flatow 264a 52.44 N 12.57 E
Flat River, P.E., Can. 186 46.01 N 62.52 W
Flat River, Mo., U.S. 194 37.51 N 90.31 W
Flat River Reservoir ⊜[1] 207 41.42 N 71.37 W
Flat Rock, Al., U.S. 194 34.46 N 85.42 W
Flat Rock, Il., U.S. 194 38.54 N 87.40 W
Flat Rock, In., U.S. 218 39.22 N 85.50 W
Flat Rock, Mi., U.S. 216 42.05 N 83.17 W
Flat Rock, Oh., U.S. 214 41.14 N 82.51 W
Flatrock ≃ 218 39.12 N 85.56 W
Flatrock Creek ≃ 216 41.10 N 84.27 W
Flatrock Lake ⊜ 184 55.37 N 100.47 W
Flatruet ⋏[2] 26 62.45 N 12.50 E
Flats 222 32.50 N 95.53 W
Flattery, Cape >, Austl. 164 14.58 S 145.21 E
Flattery, Cape >, Wa., U.S. 224 48.23 N 124.43 W
Flatts 240a 32.19 N 64.44 W
Flatwillow Creek ≃ 202 46.56 N 107.55 W
Flatwood 194 32.27 N 86.15 W
Flatwoods 188 38.31 N 82.43 W
Flaugherty Run ≃ 279b 40.33 N 80.13 W
Flaunden 260 51.42 N 0.32 W
Flavigny-sur-Moselle 58 48.34 N 6.11 E
Flavigny-sur-Ozerain 58 47.30 N 4.32 E
Flavy-le-Martel 50 49.43 N 3.12 E
Flawil 58 47.24 N 9.12 E
Flaxcombe 184 51.29 N 109.36 W
Flaxman Island I 180 70.13 N 146.00 W
Flax Pond ⊜, Ma., U.S. 283 42.29 N 70.57 W
Flax Pond ⊜, N.Y., U.S. 276 40.58 N 73.08 W
Flaxton 198 48.53 N 102.23 W
Flaxville 198 48.48 N 105.10 W
Flechas Point > 116 10.22 N 119.34 E
Flechtingen 54 52.20 N 11.14 E
Fleckeby 41 54.29 N 9.41 E
Flecken Zechlin 54 53.09 N 12.46 E
Fleesensee ⊜ 54 53.30 N 12.29 E
Fleet 42 51.16 N 0.50 W
Fleet ≃ 46 57.57 N 4.05 W
Fleets Bay c 208 37.40 N 76.19 W
Fleetville 210 41.36 N 75.43 W
Fleetwing Estates 285 40.07 N 74.51 W
Fleetwood, Eng., U.K. 44 53.56 N 3.01 W
Fleetwood, Pa., U.S. 208 40.27 N 75.49 W
Flehe ◆[8] 263 51.12 N 6.47 E
Flehingen 56 49.05 N 8.46 E
Fleischmanns 210 42.09 N 74.31 W
Fleischman Village 284c 38.51 N 76.57 W
Flekkefjord 26 58.17 N 6.41 E
Fleming, Co., U.S. 198 40.40 N 102.50 W
Fleming, Pa., U.S. 214 40.55 N 77.52 W
Fleming □6 218 38.21 N 83.42 W
Fleming Creek ≃, On., Can. 214 42.38 N 81.47 W
Fleming Creek ≃, Ky., U.S. 218 38.22 N 83.57 W
Fleming Creek ≃, Mi., U.S. 281 42.16 N 83.40 W
Fleming-Neon 192 37.11 N 82.42 W
Flemingsburg 218 38.25 N 83.44 W
Flemington, N.J., U.S. 210 40.30 N 74.51 W
Flemington, Pa., U.S. 210 41.07 N 77.28 W
Flemington Racecourse ◆ 274b 37.47 S 144.55 E
Flemish Cap ◆[4] 16 47.00 N 45.00 W
Flemsdorf 54 53.03 N 14.13 E
Flen 40 59.04 N 16.35 E
Flensburg 41 54.47 N 9.26 E
Flensburger Förde c 41 54.49 N 9.45 E
Fleres (Boden) 64 46.58 N 11.21 E
Flers 32 48.45 N 0.34 W
Flers-sur-Noye 50 49.44 N 2.15 E
Flesherton 212 44.16 N 80.33 W
Flesko, Tanjung > 112 0.29 N 124.30 E
Fletcher, On., Can. 214 42.18 N 82.18 W
Fletcher, N.C., U.S. 192 35.25 N 82.30 W
Fletcher, Oh., U.S. 218 40.08 N 84.06 W
Fletcher, Ok., U.S. 196 34.49 N 98.14 W
Fletcher Islands II 9 72.40 S 94.10 W
Fletcher Moss Museum ⊎ 262 53.25 N 2.14 W
Fletcher Pond ⊜[1] 190 44.58 N 83.52 W
Fletchers Creek ≃ 275b 43.38 N 79.42 W
Fleurance 32 43.50 N 0.40 E
Fleur-de-Lys 186 50.07 N 56.08 W
Fleurier 58 46.54 N 6.35 E
Fleurieu Peninsula >[1] 168b 35.30 S 138.30 E
Fleurus 56 50.29 N 4.33 E
Fleurville 58 46.27 N 4.53 E
Fleury-les-Aubrais 50 47.56 N 1.55 E
Fleury-Mérogis 261 48.38 N 2.22 E
Fleury-sur-Andelle 50 49.22 N 1.22 E
Fleuth ≃ 263 51.32 N 6.26 E
Flevoland □4 52 52.30 N 5.30 E
Flexanville 261 48.51 N 1.44 E
Flexenpass ẋ 58 47.09 N 10.10 E
Fley ◆[8] 263 51.23 N 7.30 E
Flieden 56 50.25 N 9.33 E
Flierich 263 51.35 N 7.48 E
Flight Locks ⊎[3] 284a 43.08 N 79.12 W
Flimby 44 54.41 N 3.31 W
Flims 58 46.50 N 9.17 E
Flinders 169 38.28 S 145.01 E
Flinders ≃ 166 17.36 S 140.36 E
Flinders Bay c 162 34.23 S 115.19 E
Flinders Chase National Park ◆ 166 36.00 S 136.45 E
Flinders Island I, Austl. 162 33.44 S 134.31 E
Flinders Island I, Austl. 166 40.00 S 148.00 E
Flinders Peak ∧ 171a 27.49 S 152.49 E
Flinders Peak ∧[2] 169 37.51 S 144.24 E
Flinders Ranges National Park ◆ 166 31.20 S 138.45 E
Flinders Reefs ◆[2] 166 17.37 S 148.31 E
Flinders Street Station ◆[5] 274b 37.49 S 144.58 E
Flinesjön ⊜ 40 60.23 N 16.06 E
Flines-lez-Râches 50 50.25 N 3.11 E
Flin Flon 184 54.46 N 101.53 W
Flingern ◆[8] 263 51.14 N 6.49 E
Flins-sur-Seine 261 48.58 N 1.52 E
Flint, Wales, U.K. 44 53.15 N 3.07 W
Flint, Mi., U.S. 216 43.00 N 83.41 W
Flint, Tx., U.S. 222 32.12 N 95.21 W
Flint I 14 11.26 S 151.48 W
Flint ≃, U.S. 194 34.30 N 86.31 W
Flint ≃, Ga., U.S. 192 30.52 N 84.38 W
Flint ≃, Mi., U.S. 190 43.21 N 84.03 W
Flint, South Branch ≃ 216 43.10 N 83.23 W
Flint Castle ⊥ 262 53.16 N 3.07 W
Flint Creek ≃, Al., U.S. 194 34.30 N 86.57 W
Flint Creek ≃, Mt., U.S. 202 46.39 N 113.08 W
Flint Creek ≃, N.Y., U.S. 210 42.57 N 77.03 W
Flint Creek Range ⋏ 202 46.20 N 113.05 W
Flinthill 219 38.53 N 90.52 W
Flint Hills ⋏[2] 198 37.50 N 96.40 W
Flint Lake ⊜, N.T., Can. 176 69.10 N 74.20 W
Flint Lake ⊜, In., U.S. 216 41.31 N 87.03 W
Flinton, Austl. 166 27.54 S 149.34 E
Flinton, Pa., U.S. 214 40.43 N 78.31 W
Flint Peak ∧ 280 34.10 N 118.12 W
Flint Pond ⊜ 283 42.40 N 71.26 W
Flinträrinnan ⵡ 41 55.34 N 12.50 E
Flintridge 280 34.11 N 118.11 W
Flints Pond ⊜ 283 42.26 N 71.19 W
Flintville 194 35.03 N 86.25 W
Flipper Point > 174a 19.18 N 166.35 E
Flippin 194 36.16 N 92.35 W
Flirey 56 48.53 N 5.50 E
Flirsch 58 47.09 N 10.24 E
Flisa 26 60.34 N 12.06 E
Flitwick 42 52.00 N 0.29 W
Flix, Pantà de ⊜[1] 34 41.15 N 0.25 E
Flixecourt 50 50.01 N 2.05 E
Flize 56 49.42 N 4.46 E
Flobecq (Vloesberg) 50 50.44 N 3.44 E
Floby 26 58.08 N 13.20 E
Floda, Sve. 26 57.48 N 12.22 E
Floda, Sve. 40 59.04 N 16.21 E
Flodden 44 55.38 N 2.10 W
Flodden Field Battlesite ⊥ 44 55.38 N 2.13 W
Flogny 50 47.57 N 3.52 E
Flöha 54 50.51 N 13.04 E
Flöha ≃ 54 50.51 N 13.04 E
Floing 56 49.43 N 4.56 E
Flomaton 194 31.00 N 87.15 W
Flomborn 56 49.41 N 8.08 E
Flomot 196 34.14 N 100.59 W
Floodwood 190 46.55 N 92.55 W
Flora, Il., U.S. 194 38.40 N 88.29 W
Flora, In., U.S. 216 40.32 N 86.31 W
Flora, Ms., U.S. 194 32.32 N 90.18 W
Florac 62 44.19 N 3.36 E
Florala 194 31.00 N 86.19 W
Floral City 220 28.45 N 82.17 W
Floral Park, Mt., U.S. 202 45.57 N 112.26 W
Floral Park, N.Y., U.S. 210 40.43 N 73.42 W
Florange 56 49.20 N 6.07 E
Florânia 250 6.08 S 36.49 W
Flora Vista 200 36.47 N 108.04 W
Flore, Piton ∧ 241f 13.58 N 60.57 W
Floreffe 56 50.26 N 4.45 E
Florence — Firenze, It. 66 43.46 N 11.15 E
Florence, Al., U.S. 194 34.47 N 87.40 W
Florence, Az., U.S. 200 33.02 N 111.23 W
Florence, Ca., U.S. 228 33.58 N 118.14 W
Florence, Co., U.S. 200 38.23 N 105.07 W
Florence, Ks., U.S. 198 38.14 N 96.55 W
Florence, Ky., U.S. 218 38.59 N 84.37 W
Florence, N.J., U.S. 285 40.07 N 74.49 W
Florence, Or., U.S. 202 43.58 N 124.05 W
Florence, Pa., U.S. 214 40.26 N 80.26 W
Florence, S.C., U.S. 192 34.11 N 79.45 W
Florence, Tx., U.S. 222 30.51 N 97.48 W
Florence, Wi., U.S. 190 45.55 N 88.15 W
Florencia, Col. 246 1.36 N 75.36 W
Florencia — Firenze, It. 66 43.46 N 11.15 E
Florencio Sánchez 258 33.53 S 57.24 W
Florencio Varela 258 34.49 S 58.17 W
Florencio Varela □5 288 34.52 S 58.15 W
Florennes 56 50.15 N 4.37 E
Florentia 273d 26.16 S 28.08 E
Florentino Ameghino, Embalse ⊜[1] 254 43.55 S 66.20 W
Florenville 56 49.42 N 5.18 E
Florenz — Firenze 66 43.46 N 11.15 E
Flores 250 7.51 S 37.59 W
Flores □5 258 33.48 S 56.50 W
Flores ◆[8] 288 34.38 S 58.28 W
Flores I, Indon. 115b 8.30 S 121.00 E
Flores I, Port. 148a 39.26 N 31.13 W
Flores, Laut (Flores Sea) ᗐ2 112 8.00 S 120.00 E
Flores, Río das ≃ 256 22.05 S 43.34 W
Flores, Selat ⵡ 115b 8.25 S 122.55 E
Flores da Cunha 252 29.02 S 51.11 W
Flores de Goiás 255 14.34 S 47.04 W
Flores Island I 182 49.20 N 126.10 W
Flores Sea — Flores, Laut ᗐ2 112 8.00 S 120.00 E
Floresta, Bra. 250 8.36 S 38.34 W
Floresta, It. 70 37.59 N 14.55 E
Floresta ◆[8] 288 34.38 S 58.29 W
Floresta Azul 255 14.51 S 39.41 W
Florestal de Monsanto, Parque ◆ 266c 38.43 N 9.11 W
Florești 38 47.53 N 28.17 E
Floresville 196 29.08 N 98.09 W
Florham Park 210 40.47 N 74.23 W
Floriano, Bra. 250 6.47 S 43.01 W
Floriano, Bra. 256 22.27 S 44.18 W
Floriano Peixoto 248 9.03 S 67.24 W
Florianópolis 252 27.35 S 48.34 W
Florida, Col. 246 3.21 N 76.15 W
Florida, Cuba 240p 21.32 N 78.14 W
Florida, Hond. 236 15.01 N 88.50 W
Florida, Perú 248 5.50 S 77.55 W
Florida, P.R. 240m 18.22 N 66.34 W
Florida, P.R. 240m 18.14 N 65.47 W
Florida, S. Afr. 273d 26.11 S 27.55 E
Florida, In., U.S. 218 40.10 N 85.42 W
Florida, N.Y., U.S. 210 41.19 N 74.21 W
Florida, Oh., U.S. 216 41.20 N 84.12 W
Florida, Ur. 258 34.06 S 56.13 W
Florida □5 258 34.00 S 56.15 W
Florida ◆[8] 288 34.32 S 58.30 W
Florida □3, U.S. 178 28.00 N 82.00 W
Florida □3, U.S. 192 28.00 N 82.00 W
Florida ≃ 200 37.03 N 107.52 W
Florida, Cape > 220 25.40 N 80.09 W
Florida, Straits of ⵡ 238 25.00 N 79.45 W
Florida Bay c 220 25.00 N 80.45 W
Floridablanca 246 7.04 N 73.06 W
Florida Caverns State Park ◆ 192 30.50 N 85.18 W
Florida City 220 25.26 N 80.28 W
Florida Islands II 175e 9.00 S 160.10 E
Florida Keys II 220 24.45 N 81.00 W
Florida Lake ⊜[1] 273d 26.11 S 27.54 E
Florida Ridge 220 27.35 N 80.23 W
Floridia 70 37.05 N 15.09 E
Florido ≃ 232 27.43 N 105.10 W
Floridsdorf ◆[8] 264b 48.16 N 16.24 E
Floridsdorfer Brücke ◆[5] 264b 48.14 N 16.23 E
Florien 194 31.26 N 93.27 W
Florin 226 38.29 N 121.24 W
Florina 38 40.47 N 21.24 E
Florisbad 158 28.46 S 26.06 E
Florissant 219 38.47 N 90.19 W
Florissant Fossil Beds National Monument ◆ 200 38.54 N 105.16 W
Floriston 226 39.24 N 120.01 W
Florø 26 61.36 N 5.00 E
Flörsheim 56 50.01 N 8.26 E
Florvåg 26 60.25 N 5.14 E
Flosaille 62 45.39 N 5.18 E
Floss 60 49.44 N 12.17 E
Flossach ≃ 58 48.24 N 10.25 E
Flossenbürg 60 49.44 N 12.21 E
Flossmoor 216 41.32 N 87.41 W
Flotantes, Jardines ◆ 286a 19.16 N 99.06 W
Flöthbach ≃ 263 51.17 N 6.26 E
Flotta I 46 58.50 N 3.07 W
Flotte, Cap de > 175f 21.10 S 167.25 E
Flotten Lake ⊜ 184 54.38 N 108.30 W
Flourtown 285 40.06 N 75.12 W
Flower Hill 276 40.48 N 73.40 W
Flower Mound 222 33.02 N 97.04 W
Flower's Cove 186 51.18 N 56.44 W
Flowery Branch 192 34.11 N 83.55 W
Floyd, N.M., U.S. 196 34.13 N 103.35 W
Floyd, Tx., U.S. 222 33.09 N 96.15 W
Floyd, Va., U.S. 192 36.54 N 80.19 W
Floyd □6 218 38.18 N 85.49 W
Floyd ≃ 198 42.29 N 96.23 W
Floydada 196 33.59 N 101.20 W
Floyds Fork ≃ 194 38.00 N 85.41 W
Fluchthorn ∧ 58 46.53 N 10.13 E
Flüela Pass ẋ 58 46.45 N 9.57 E
Flüelen 58 46.54 N 8.38 E
Fluessen ⊜ 52 52.57 N 5.30 E
Flühli 58 46.53 N 8.01 E
Flumen ≃ 34 41.43 N 0.09 W
Flumendosa ≃ 71 39.26 N 9.37 E
Flumendosa, Lago Alto del ⊜ 71 39.56 N 9.26 E
Flumendosa, Lago del ⊜[1] 71 39.40 N 9.17 E
Flumeri 68 41.05 N 15.09 E
Flumet 62 45.49 N 6.30 E
Fluminimaggiore 71 39.26 N 8.30 E
Flums 58 47.05 N 9.20 E
Flüren 263 51.41 N 6.33 E
Flushing — Vlissingen, Ned. 52 51.26 N 3.35 E
Flushing, Mi., U.S. 216 43.03 N 83.51 W
Flushing, Oh., U.S. 214 40.08 N 81.04 W
Flushing ◆[8] 276 40.45 N 73.49 W
Flushing Airport ⊠ 276 40.47 N 73.50 W
Flushing Bay c 276 40.47 N 73.51 W
Flushing Meadow-Corona Park ◆ 276 40.45 N 73.51 W
Fluvanna, N.Y., U.S. 214 42.07 N 79.18 W
Fluvanna, Tx., U.S. 196 32.53 N 101.09 W
Fluvià ≃ 34 42.12 N 3.07 E
Fly ≃ 164 8.30 S 143.41 E
Fly Creek 210 42.43 N 74.59 W
Fly Creek ≃ 202 45.59 N 107.59 W
Flyinge 41 55.45 N 13.21 E
Flying Fish Cove 112 10.25 S 105.43 E
Flynn 222 31.09 N 96.08 W
Foam Lake 184 51.39 N 103.33 W
Fobbing 260 51.32 N 0.29 E
Fobello 62 45.53 N 8.10 E
Foča, Bos. 38 43.31 N 18.47 E
Foça, Tür. 130 38.39 N 26.46 E
Focene ◆[8] 267a 41.48 N 12.14 E
Fochabers 46 57.37 N 3.05 W
Fochville 158 26.30 S 27.30 E
Fockbek 41 54.18 N 9.36 E
Focșani 38 45.41 N 27.11 E
Fodda, Oued ≃ 34 36.14 N 1.33 E
Fodé 152 5.29 N 23.18 E
Fodécontea 150 10.50 N 14.22 W
Foding Shan ∧ 102 27.08 N 108.02 E
F'odorovka, Kaz. 80 51.09 N 51.59 E
F'odorovka, Kaz. 86 53.38 N 62.42 E
F'odorovka, Ross. 86 53.22 N 76.18 E
F'odorovka, Ross. 80 53.28 N 49.38 E
F'odorovka, Ross. 82 52.21 N 52.55 E
F'odorovka, Ross. 82 56.15 N 37.14 E
F'odorovka, Ross. 83 47.20 N 38.06 E
F'odorovka, Ross. 86 56.05 N 78.49 E
F'odorovka, Ross. 86 53.11 N 55.11 E
F'odorovka, Ross. 86 56.44 N 36.58 E
F'odorovskoje, Ross. 82 56.08 N 38.04 E
F'odorovskoje, Ross. 82 56.07 N 38.52 E
Foëcy 50 47.10 N 2.10 E
Foelsche ≃ 164 16.03 S 136.50 E
Foeni 38 45.30 N 20.53 E
Fogang (Shijiao) 100 23.52 N 113.32 E
Fogdön ≃[1] 40 59.25 N 16.52 E
Fogelevo 85 42.03 N 69.32 E
Fogelsville 208 40.35 N 75.38 W
Foggaret el Arab 148 27.03 N 2.59 E
Foggaret ez Zoua 148 27.20 N 3.00 E
Foggia 68 41.27 N 15.34 E
Foggia □4 68 41.30 N 15.30 E
Foggy Island Bay c 180 70.15 N 147.30 W
Foglia ≃ 66 43.55 N 12.54 E
Foglianise 68 41.10 N 14.40 E
Fogliano, Lago di c 66 41.24 N 12.54 E
Foglizzo 62 45.16 N 7.49 E
Fogo 186 49.43 N 54.17 W
Fogo I 150a 14.55 N 24.25 W
Fogo, Cape > 186 49.39 N 54.00 W
Fogo Island I 186 49.40 N 54.13 W
Fogolawa 150 11.19 N 8.41 E
Fogueteiro 266c 38.37 N 9.07 W
Fohnsdorf 61 47.13 N 14.41 E
Föhr I 41 54.43 N 8.30 E
Foia ∧ 34 37.19 N 8.36 W
Foiano della Chiana 66 43.15 N 11.49 E
Foiano di Val Fortore 68 41.21 N 14.59 E

ENGLISH — Name Page Lat.°′ Long.°′ | DEUTSCH — Name Seite Breite°′ Länge°′ E = Ost

Foinaven ∧ 46 58.25 N 4.53 W
Foins, Lac aux ⊜ 190 47.05 N 78.11 W
Foivre ≃ 56 49.30 N 4.32 E
Foix 32 42.58 N 1.36 E
Foix □9 32 43.00 N 1.40 E
Fojnica 36 43.58 N 17.54 E
Foki 80 56.42 N 54.21 E
Fokino 76 53.27 N 34.24 E
Fokku 150 11.40 N 4.31 E
Folakara 157b 18.20 S 45.02 E
Folamasi 104 41.56 N 121.27 E
Folarskardnuten ∧ 26 60.37 N 7.45 E
Folcroft 208 39.53 N 75.17 W
Folda c[2] 24 67.36 N 14.50 E
Foldingbro 41 55.26 N 9.01 E
Folégandros I 38 36.38 N 24.54 E
Folembray 50 49.33 N 3.17 E
Foley, Al., U.S. 194 30.24 N 87.41 W
Foley, Mn., U.S. 190 45.39 N 93.54 W
Foley, Mo., U.S. 219 39.02 N 90.44 W
Foleyet 190 48.15 N 82.27 W
Foley Island I 176 68.35 N 75.10 W
Folgaria 64 45.55 N 11.10 E
Folgefonni ⩔ 26 60.00 N 6.20 E
Folger Hill ∧[2] 207 41.17 N 70.01 W
Foligno 66 42.57 N 12.42 E
Folk 219 38.26 N 92.06 W
Folkärna 40 60.09 N 16.19 E
Folkestone 42 51.05 N 1.11 E
Folkingham 42 52.54 N 0.24 W
Folkston 192 30.49 N 82.00 W
Folkwangmuseum ⊎ 263 51.27 N 7.00 E
Follafoss 26 63.59 N 11.06 E
Follainville-Dennemont 261 49.01 N 1.43 E
Follansbee 214 40.19 N 80.35 W
Folldal 26 62.08 N 10.03 E
Folle Anse, Pointe de > 241o 15.57 N 61.20 W
Follebu 26 61.14 N 10.17 E
Follets Island I 222 29.02 N 95.10 W
Follett 196 36.26 N 100.08 W
Follina 64 45.57 N 12.07 E
Föllinge 26 63.40 N 14.37 E
Follonica 66 42.55 N 10.45 E
Follonica, Golfo di c 66 42.54 N 10.43 E
Folly Branch ≃ 284b 38.56 N 76.49 W
Folmhusen 52 53.10 N 7.28 E
Folschviller 56 49.04 N 6.41 E
Folsom, Ca., U.S. 226 38.40 N 121.10 W
Folsom, N.J., U.S. 208 39.36 N 74.50 W
Folsom, Pa., U.S. 285 39.53 N 75.19 W
Folsom Lake ⊜[1] 226 38.43 N 121.08 W
Folsom Lake State Recreation Area ◆ 226 38.46 N 121.06 W
Fomboni 157a 12.16 S 43.45 E
Fomento, Cuba 240p 22.06 N 79.43 W
Fomento, Ur. 258 34.26 S 57.14 W
Fomin 80 46.58 N 43.38 E
Fominiči 76 54.07 N 34.41 E
Fominki 80 55.57 N 42.22 E
Fominskaja 24 61.17 N 48.40 E
Fominskoje, Ross. 24 59.43 N 42.05 E
Fominskoje, Ross. 76 58.59 N 39.06 E
Fomkino 80 54.25 N 50.30 E
Foncine-le-Bas 58 46.38 N 6.03 E
Fonda, Ia., U.S. 198 42.34 N 94.50 W
Fonda, N.Y., U.S. 210 42.57 N 74.22 W
Fondachelli 70 37.58 N 15.11 E
Fond du Lac, Sk., Can. 176 59.19 N 107.10 W
Fond du Lac, Wi., U.S. 190 43.46 N 88.26 W
Fond du Lac ≃ 176 59.17 N 106.00 W
Fond du Lac Indian Reservation ◆[4] 190 46.45 N 92.37 W
Fondi 66 41.21 N 13.25 E
Fondi, Lago di c 66 41.19 N 13.20 E
Fondo 64 46.26 N 11.08 E
Fondouk el Aouareb 36 35.34 N 9.46 E
Fongfong 140 12.56 N 23.14 E
Fonni 71 40.07 N 9.15 E
Fonsagrada 34 43.08 N 7.04 W
Fonseca 246 10.54 N 72.51 W
Fonseca, Golfo de c 236 13.10 N 87.40 W
Fons-Outre-Gardon 62 43.54 N 4.11 E
Font ≃ 44 55.10 N 1.44 W
Fontaine, Fr. 58 47.40 N 7.00 E
Fontaine, Fr. 58 45.11 N 5.40 E
Fontainebleau, Fr. 50 48.24 N 2.42 E
Fontainebleau, S. Afr. 273d 26.07 S 27.59 E
Fontaine-Française 58 47.31 N 5.22 E
Fontaine-le-Dun 50 49.49 N 0.51 E
Fontaine-lès-Dijon 58 47.21 N 5.01 E
Fontaine-lès-Grès 50 48.25 N 3.54 E
Fontaine-lès-Luxeuil 58 47.51 N 6.20 E
Fontaines 58 46.51 N 4.46 E
Fontaines-sur-Saône 62 45.50 N 4.51 E
Fontan 62 44.00 N 7.33 E
Fontana, Arg. 252 27.25 S 59.02 W
Fontana, Ca., U.S. 228 34.05 N 117.26 W
Fontana, Wi., U.S. 216 42.33 N 88.34 W
Fontana, Lago ⊜ 254 44.56 S 71.30 W
Fontanafredda 64 45.58 N 12.34 E
Fontana Lake ⊜[1] 192 35.26 N 83.38 W
Fontanarosa 68 41.01 N 15.01 E
Fontanarossa, Aeroporto di ⊠ 70 37.29 N 15.03 E
Fontanelas 266c 38.51 N 9.26 W
Fontanelice 64 44.15 N 11.33 E
Fontanella 64 45.27 N 9.48 E
Fontanellato 64 44.53 N 10.10 E
Fontanelle 198 41.17 N 94.33 W
Fontanetto Po 62 45.12 N 8.11 E
Fontanigorda 62 44.33 N 9.19 E
Fontarabie, Lac ⊜ 186 51.10 N 66.25 W
Fontas ≃ 176 58.20 N 121.50 W
Fonte, Bra. 287b 23.25 S 46.21 W
Fonte, It. 64 45.47 N 11.53 E
Fonte, It. 66 41.46 N 13.13 E
Fonte Avellana, Monastero di ⊎[1] 66 43.29 N 12.45 E
Fonte Blanda 66 42.34 N 11.10 E
Fonte Boa 246 2.32 S 66.01 W
Fonte Colombo, Convento di ⊎[1] 66 42.23 N 12.50 E
Fontenay, Abbaye de ⊎[1] 58 47.39 N 4.24 E
Fontenay-aux-Roses 261 48.47 N 2.17 E
Fontenay-en-Parisis 261 49.03 N 2.27 E
Fontenay-le-Comte 32 46.28 N 0.48 W
Fontenay-le-Fleury 261 48.49 N 2.03 E
Fontenay-lès-Briis 261 48.37 N 2.09 E
Fontenay-le-Vicomte 261 48.33 N 2.24 E
Fontenay-Saint-Père 261 49.02 N 1.45 E
Fontenay-sous-Bois 261 48.51 N 2.29 E
Fontenay-Trésigny 50 48.42 N 2.52 E
Fonteneau, Lac ⊜ 186 51.55 N 61.30 W
Fontenelle 186 48.53 N 64.33 W
Fontenelle Creek ≃ 200 42.05 N 110.08 W
Fontenelle Reservoir ⊜[1] 200 42.05 N 110.06 W
Fontespina 66 43.17 N 13.45 E
Fontevivo 64 44.51 N 10.10 E
Font Hill Manor 284b 39.17 N 76.52 W
Fonti del Clitunno ᗐ[4] 66 42.49 N 12.46 E
Fontoy 56 49.21 N 6.00 E
Fontur > 24a 66.23 N 14.30 W
Fontvieille 62 43.43 N 4.43 E
Fonyód 30 46.44 N 17.34 E
Fonzaso 64 46.01 N 11.48 E
Foochow — Fuzhou 100 26.06 N 119.17 E
Foot Creek ≃ 198 45.26 N 98.29 W
Foothill Farms 226 38.40 N 121.20 W
Foothills 182 53.04 N 116.48 W
Footprint Lake ⊜ 184 55.47 N 98.53 W
Footscray 169 37.48 S 144.54 E
Footville 216 42.40 N 89.12 W
Foping 102 33.21 N 107.59 E
Foppolo 64 46.03 N 9.45 E
Fora, Ponta de > 287a 22.57 S 43.07 W
Foraker, Mount ∧ 180 62.56 N 151.26 W
Forari 175f 17.39 S 168.32 E
Forbach, Dtsch. 56 48.41 N 8.21 E
Forbach, Fr. 56 49.11 N 6.54 E
Forbes 166 33.23 S 148.01 E
Forbes, Lac ⊜ 206 46.31 N 74.12 W
Forbes, Mount ∧ 182 51.52 N 116.56 W
Forbesganj 124 26.18 N 87.15 E
Forbes Reef 158 26.10 S 31.05 E
Forbes Road 214 40.21 N 79.32 W
Forbestown 226 39.31 N 121.16 W
Forcados 150 5.22 N 5.24 E
Forcados ≃[1] 150 5.25 N 5.19 E
Forcalquier 62 43.58 N 5.47 E
Force 214 41.15 N 78.30 W
Forchheim, Dtsch. 54 50.43 N 13.16 E
Forchheim, Dtsch. 60 49.43 N 11.04 E
Forclaz, Col de la ẋ 58 46.04 N 7.00 E
Ford, Scot., U.K. 46 56.10 N 5.26 W
Ford, Ks., U.S. 198 37.38 N 99.45 W
Ford □6 216 40.27 N 88.06 W
Ford ≃ 190 45.40 N 87.09 W
Ford, Cape > 164 13.26 S 129.52 E
Ford City, Ca., U.S. 226 35.09 N 119.27 W
Ford City, Pa., U.S. 214 40.46 N 79.31 W
Ford City ◆[9] 278 41.46 N 87.44 W
Ford Cliff 214 40.45 N 79.32 W
Ford Dam ◆[6] 281 42.13 N 83.33 W
Ford Dry Lake ⊜ 204 33.38 N 115.00 W
Førde, Nor. 26 59.36 N 5.29 E
Førde, Nor. 26 61.27 N 5.52 E
Førdefjorden c[2] 26 61.28 N 5.39 E
Forden 42 52.36 N 3.08 W
Förderstedt 54 51.54 N 11.38 E
Fordham University ⊎[2] 276 40.51 N 73.53 W
Fordingbridge 42 50.56 N 1.47 W
Ford Lake ⊜ 281 42.13 N 83.36 W
Ford Mansion ⊥ 276 40.48 N 74.28 W
Ford Motor Company (River Rouge Plant) ⊎[3] 281 42.18 N 83.10 W
Ford Museum ⊎ 281 42.18 N 83.14 W
Fordongianus 71 39.59 N 8.48 E
Ford Ranges ⋏ 9 77.00 S 145.00 W
Fords 276 40.31 N 74.18 W
Fords Bridge 166 29.45 S 145.26 E
Fordsburg ◆[8] 273d 26.13 S 28.02 E
Fords Prairie 224 46.44 N 122.59 W
Fordsville 194 37.38 N 86.43 W
Fordville 198 48.13 N 97.47 W
Fordyce 194 33.48 N 92.24 W
Fordyce Lake ⊜[1] 226 39.23 N 120.28 W
Foré 150 13.08 N 10.42 W
Forécariah 150 9.26 N 13.06 W
Forel, Mont ∧ 176 67.00 N 37.00 W
Foreland Point > 42 51.16 N 3.47 W
Foreman 194 33.43 N 94.23 W
Foremost 184 49.29 N 111.25 W
Forenza 68 40.51 N 15.51 E
Forepaugh Airport ⊠ 279a 41.21 N 81.30 W
Foresman 216 40.52 N 87.18 W
Forest, Bel. 50 50.48 N 4.19 E
Forest, On., Can. 190 43.06 N 82.00 W
Forest, In., U.S. 216 40.22 N 86.19 W
Forest, Ms., U.S. 194 32.21 N 89.28 W
Forest, Oh., U.S. 216 40.48 N 83.30 W
Forest □6 214 41.29 N 79.27 W
Forest, Middle Branch ≃ 198 48.13 N 97.48 W
Forest Acres 192 34.01 N 80.59 W
Forestburg 182 52.35 N 112.04 W
Forest City, Ia., U.S. 190 43.15 N 93.38 W
Forest City, N.C., U.S. 192 35.20 N 81.51 W
Forest City, Pa., U.S. 210 41.39 N 75.28 W
Forest Creek ≃ 226 38.23 N 120.28 W
Forest Gate ◆[8] 260 51.33 N 0.02 E
Forest Glade 221 31.39 N 96.31 W
Forest Grove, B.C., Can. 182 51.46 N 121.06 W
Forest Grove, Or., U.S. 224 45.31 N 123.06 W
Forest Grove, Pa., U.S. 279b 40.30 N 80.04 W
Forest Heights 284c 38.49 N 77.00 W
Forest Hill, Austl. 171a 27.35 S 152.22 E
Forest Hill, Austl. 171b 35.09 S 147.27 E
Forest Hill, Austl. 274b 37.50 S 145.11 E
Foresthill, Ca., U.S. 226 39.01 N 120.49 W
Forest Hill, Md., U.S. 208 39.35 N 76.23 W
Forest Hill, Tx., U.S. 222 32.40 N 97.16 W
Forest Hill ◆[8] 275b 43.42 N 79.24 W
Forest Hill Park ◆ 279a 41.31 N 81.35 W
Forest Hill Parkway ◆ 279a 41.33 N 81.36 W
Forest Hills 279b 40.25 N 79.51 W
Forest Hills ◆[8] 276 40.42 N 73.51 W
Forest Home 194 31.52 N 86.50 W
Forestier Peninsula >[1] 166 42.57 S 147.55 E
Forest Knolls 284c 39.02 N 77.01 W
Forest Lake, Il., U.S. 216 42.13 N 88.03 W
Forest Lake, Mn., U.S. 190 45.16 N 92.59 W
Forest Lake ⊜, Il., U.S. 278 42.13 N 88.03 W
Forest Lake ⊜, Ma., U.S. 283 42.43 N 71.15 W
Forest Lawn Memorial Park ◆ 280 34.09 N 118.19 W
Forest Manor 284c 38.50 N 76.53 W
Forest Park, Ga., U.S. 192 33.37 N 84.22 W
Forest Park, Il., U.S. 278 41.52 N 87.48 W
Forest Park, Oh., U.S. 218 39.16 N 84.34 W
Forest Park ◆[8] 284b 39.19 N 76.41 W
Forest Park ◆ 276 40.42 N 73.51 W
Forest River 278 42.05 N 87.54 W
Forest Row 42 51.06 N 0.02 E
Forest View 278 41.49 N 87.47 W
Forestville, Austl. 274a 33.46 S 151.13 E
Forestville, P.Q., Can. 186 48.45 N 69.06 W
Forestville, Md., U.S. 284c 38.50 N 76.52 W
Forestville, N.Y., U.S. 214 42.28 N 79.10 W
Forestville, Pa., U.S. 214 41.06 N 80.00 W
Forestville, Wi., U.S. 190 44.41 N 87.28 W
Forêt l'Orient, Lac de la ⊜[1] 50 48.17 N 4.20 E
Forêt-Noire — Schwarzwald ⋏ 58 48.00 N 8.15 E
Forez, Monts du ⋏ 32 45.35 N 3.48 E
Forfar 46 56.38 N 2.54 W
Forfry 261 49.03 N 2.51 E
Forgan 196 36.54 N 100.32 W
Forgaria 64 46.13 N 12.58 E
Forge Acres 284b 39.25 N 76.27 W
Forge Heights 284b 39.25 N 76.25 W
Forges-les-Bains 261 48.38 N 2.06 E
Forges-les-Eaux 50 49.37 N 1.33 E
Forget, Pointe > 275a 45.27 N 73.58 W
Forge Village 207 42.34 N 71.29 W
Forggensee ⊜ 58 47.36 N 10.44 E
Forillon, Parc National de ◆ 186 48.55 N 64.12 W
Forino 68 40.52 N 14.44 E
Foristell 219 38.49 N 90.57 W
Fork 208 39.28 N 76.27 W
Forked Creek ≃ 216 41.19 N 88.09 W
Forked Deer ≃ 194 35.56 N 89.35 W
Forked Deer, Middle Fork ≃ 194 36.01 N 89.13 W
Forked Deer, North Fork ≃ 194 36.00 N 89.20 W
Forked Deer, South Fork ≃ 194 36.00 N 89.26 W
Forked River 208 39.50 N 74.11 W
Forks 224 47.57 N 124.23 W
Forkston 210 41.31 N 76.07 W
Forksville 210 41.29 N 76.36 W
Forleti, Arroyo ≃ 288 34.35 S 58.41 W
Forlì 66 44.13 N 12.03 E
Forlì □4 64 44.05 N 12.02 E
Forlimpopoli 66 44.11 N 12.07 E

Symbols in the index entries represent the broad categories identified in the key at the right. Symbols with superior numbers (⋏[1]) identify subcategories (see complete key on page I · 1).

Symbole im Register stellen die rechts im Schlüssel erklärten Kategorien dar. Symbole mit hochgestellten Ziffern (⋏[1]) bezeichnen Unterabteilungen einer Kategorie (vgl. vollständiger Schlüssel auf Seite I · 1).

Los símbolos incluidos en el texto del índice representan las grandes categorías identificadas con la clave a la derecha. Los símbolos con numeros en su parte superior (⋏[1]) identifican las subcategorías (véase la clave completa en la página I · 1).

Les symboles de l'index représentent les catégories indiquées dans la légende à droite. Les symboles suivis d'un indice (⋏[1]) représentent des sous-catégories (voir légende complète à la page I · 1).

Os símbolos incluídos no texto do índice representam as grandes categorias identificadas com a chave à direita. Os símbolos com números em sua parte superior (⋏[1]) identificam as subcategorias (veja-se a chave completa à página I · 1).

∧ Mountain	Berg	Montaña	Montagne	Montanha
⋏ Mountains	Gebirge	Montañas	Montagnes	Montanhas
ẋ Pass	Paß	Paso	Col	Passo
V Valley, Canyon	Tal, Cañon	Valle, Cañón	Vallée, Canyon	Vale, Canhão
= Plain	Ebene	Llano	Plaine	Planície
> Cape	Kap	Cabo	Cap	Cabo
I Island	Insel	Isla	Île	Ilha
II Islands	Inseln	Islas	Îles	Ilhas
⊥ Other Topographic Features	Andere Topographische Objekte	Otros Elementos Topográficos	Autres données topographiques	Outros acidentes topográficos

ESPAÑOL — Nombre | Página | Lat.°′ | Long.°′ W = Oeste
FRANÇAIS — Nom | Page | Lat.°′ | Long.°′ W = Ouest
PORTUGUÊS — Nome | Página | Lat.°′ | Long.°′ W = Oeste

Forman 198 46.06 N 97.38 W
Formazza 58 46.22 N 8.26 E
Formby 44 53.34 N 3.05 W
Formby Hills ⋏² 262 53.34 N 3.06 W
Formby Point > 44 53.33 N 3.06 W
Formentera I 34 38.42 N 1.28 E
Formentor, Cap de > 34 39.58 N 3.12 E
Formerie 50 49.39 N 1.44 E
Formia 66 41.15 N 13.37 E
Formiga 255 20.27 S 45.25 W
Formiga ≃ 250 11.15 S 48.27 W
Formigine 64 44.34 N 10.51 E
Formignana 64 44.50 N 11.51 E
Formosa, Arg. 252 26.11 S 58.11 W
Formosa, Bra. 255 15.32 S 47.20 W
Formosa □⁴ 252 25.00 S 60.00 W
Formosa
— Taiwan □¹ 100 23.30 N 121.00 E
Formosa, Ilha I 150 11.29 N 15.58 W
Formosa, Serra ⋏¹ 250 12.00 S 55.00 W
Formosa Strait
— Taiwan Strait ʉ 100 24.00 N 119.00 E
Formoso ≃, Bra. 250 10.34 S 49.56 W
Formoso ≃, Bra. 255 13.26 S 44.14 W
Formoso ≃, Bra. 255 18.25 S 52.28 W
Formoso ≃, Bra. 256 21.20 S 43.10 W
Fornaes > 26 56.27 N 10.58 E
Forncelle 66 43.55 N 11.06 E
Fornelli 71 41.00 N 8.14 E
Forney 222 32.44 N 96.28 W
Forni Avoltri 64 46.35 N 12.46 E
Forni di sopra 64 46.25 N 12.35 E
Forni di sotto 64 46.23 N 12.40 E
Forni di Val d'Astico 64 45.51 N 11.22 E
Forno 64 46.21 N 11.37 E
Forno Alpi Graie 62 45.22 N 7.13 E
Forno di Zoldo 64 46.21 N 12.11 E
Fornosovo 76 59.35 N 30.35 E
Fornovo di Taro 64 44.42 N 10.06 E
Foro Romano ⊥ 267a 41.54 N 12.29 E
Føroyar
— Faeroe Islands □² 22 62.00 N 7.00 W
Forpost 86 56.47 N 72.10 E
Forres, Arg. 252 27.53 S 63.58 W
Forres, Scot., U.K. 46 57.37 N 3.38 W
Forrest, Austl. 162 30.51 S 128.06 E
Forrest, Austl. 169 38.31 S 143.43 E
Forrest, Il., U.S. 216 40.45 N 88.24 W
Forrest ≃ 164 15.18 S 128.04 E
Forrest, Mount ∧ 162 24.48 S 127.45 E
Forrestal Research Center ᵾ³ 276 40.21 N 74.37 W
Forrest City 194 35.00 N 90.47 W
Forrester Island I 182 54.48 N 133.32 W
Forrest Lakes ⊜ 162 29.12 S 128.46 E
Forreston, Il., U.S. 190 42.07 N 89.34 W
Forreston, Tx., U.S. 222 32.16 N 96.52 W
Forrest River Aboriginal Reserve ⊸⁴ 164 15.00 S 127.40 E
Fors 40 60.13 N 16.18 E
Forsan 196 32.07 N 101.22 W
Forsayth 166 18.35 S 143.36 E
Forsbacka 40 60.37 N 16.53 E
Forsby 26 60.30 N 25.56 E
Forserum 26 57.42 N 14.28 E
Forshaga 40 59.32 N 13.28 E
Forsmark 40 60.22 N 18.09 E
Forssa 26 60.49 N 23.38 E
Forst 54 51.44 N 14.39 E
Förste 52 51.44 N 10.10 E
Forster 166 32.11 S 152.31 E
Forstwald ⊸⁸ 263 51.18 N 6.30 E
Forsyth, Ga., U.S. 192 33.02 N 83.56 W
Forsyth, Il., U.S. 219 39.56 N 88.57 W
Forsyth, Mo., U.S. 194 36.41 N 93.07 W
Forsyth, Mt., U.S. 202 46.15 N 106.40 W
Forsyth Island I 164 16.50 S 139.06 E
Forsyth Range ⋏ 166 22.45 S 143.15 E
Fort ⊸⁸ 272c 18.56 N 72.50 E
Fort Abbās 123 29.12 N 72.52 E
Fort Adams 194 31.05 N 91.32 W
Fort Albany 176 52.15 N 81.37 W
Fort Alexander Indian Reserve ⊸⁴ 184 50.27 N 96.15 W
Fortaleza 250 3.43 S 38.30 W
Fortaleza ≃ 248 10.40 S 77.52 W
Fortaleza de Santa Teresa ⊥ 252 33.59 S 53.32 W
Fortaleza do Ituxi 248 7.29 S 66.20 W
Fortaleza dos Nogueiras 250 6.54 S 46.09 W
Fort Amherst National Historic Park ♦ 186 46.12 N 63.09 W
Fort Ancient State Memorial ⊥ 218 39.24 N 84.06 W
Fort Anne National Historic Park ♦ 186 44.44 N 65.26 W
Fort Apache Indian Reservation ⊸⁴ 200 34.01 N 110.28 W
Fort-Archambault
— Sarh 146 9.09 N 18.23 E
Fort Assiniboine 182 54.20 N 114.46 W
Fort Atkinson 216 42.55 N 88.50 W
Fort Augusta ⊥ 210 40.53 N 76.46 W
Fort Augustus 46 57.09 N 4.41 W
Fort Baker ■ 282 37.50 N 122.29 W
Fort Battleford National Historic Park ♦ 184 52.42 N 108.15 W
Fort Bayard
— Zhanjiang 102 21.16 N 110.28 E
Fort Beaufort 158 32.46 S 26.40 E
Fort Beauséjour National Historic Park ♦ 186 45.51 N 64.18 W
Fort Belknap Agency 202 48.28 N 108.45 W
Fort Belknap Indian Reservation ⊸⁴ 202 48.16 N 108.38 W
Fort Belvoir ■ 208 38.44 N 77.10 W
Fort Bend □⁶ 222 29.32 N 95.47 W
Fort Benjamin Harrison ■ 218 39.52 N 86.01 W
Fort Benning ■ 192 32.22 N 84.50 W
Fort Benton 202 47.49 N 110.40 W
Fort Berthold Indian Reservation ⊸⁴ 198 47.40 N 102.25 W
Fort Bidwell 204 41.51 N 120.09 W
Fort Bliss ■ 200 32.15 N 106.00 W
Fort Bowie National Historic Site ⊥ 200 32.09 N 109.24 W
Fort Bragg 204 39.26 N 123.48 W
Fort Bragg ■ 192 35.09 N 78.59 W
Fort Branch 194 38.15 N 87.34 W
Fort Bridger 200 41.19 N 110.23 W
Fort Calhoun 198 41.27 N 96.01 W
Fort Campbell ■ 194 36.39 N 87.29 W
Fort Canby State Park ♦ 224 46.17 N 124.04 W
Fort-Carnot 157b 21.53 S 47.28 E
Fort Caroline National Memorial ⊥ 192 30.20 N 81.30 W
Fort Carson ■ 200 38.44 N 104.48 W
Fort Casey Historical State Park ♦ 224 48.10 N 122.40 W
Fort Chambly National Historic Park ♦ 206 45.27 N 73.17 W
Fort Chipewyan 176 58.42 N 111.08 W
Fort Churchill Historic State Monument ⊥ 226 39.18 N 119.17 W
Fort Clatsop National Memorial ⊥ 224 46.08 N 123.54 W
Fort Cobb 196 35.05 N 98.26 W
Fort Cobb Reservoir ⊜¹ 196 35.12 N 98.29 W
Fort Collins 200 40.35 N 105.05 W
Fort Columbia Historical State Park ♦ 224 46.15 N 123.56 W
Fort Constantine 166 20.28 S 140.37 E
Fort-Coulonge 188 45.51 N 76.44 W
Fort Covington 206 44.59 N 74.29 W
Fort Custer State Recreation Area ♦ 216 42.18 N 85.20 W
Fort Davis, Al., U.S. 194 32.14 N 85.42 W
Fort Davis, Tx., U.S. 196 30.35 N 103.53 W
Fort Davis National Historic Site ⊥ 196 30.33 N 103.53 W
Fort de Douaumont ⊥ 56 49.13 N 5.25 E
Fort Defiance 200 35.44 N 109.04 W
Fort-de-France 240e 14.36 N 61.05 W
Fort-de-France, Baie de ⊂ 240e 14.34 N 61.04 W
Fort-de-France-Lamentin, Aérodrome de ✈ 240e 14.35 N 61.00 W
Fort Deposit 194 31.59 N 86.34 W
Fort Detrick ■ 208 39.27 N 77.26 W
Fort de Vaux ⊥ 56 49.12 N 5.28 E
Fort Devens ■ 207 42.32 N 71.37 W
Fort Dix ■ 208 40.00 N 74.33 W
Fort Dodge 190 42.29 N 94.10 W
Fort Donelson National Military Park ♦ 194 36.26 N 87.49 W
Fort Duchesne 200 40.17 N 109.51 W
Fort Dupont Park ♦ 284c 38.53 N 76.57 W
Forte, Monte ∧² 71 40.43 N 8.15 E
Forteau 186 51.28 N 56.58 W
Forte dei Marmi 64 43.57 N 10.10 E
Forte de Magoito 266c 38.52 N 9.27 W
Fort Edward 210 43.16 N 73.35 W
Forte República 152 7.45 S 16.23 E
Fort Erie 212 42.54 N 78.56 W
Fort Erie Race Track ♦ 284a 42.55 N 78.56 W
Fortescue ≃ 162 21.00 S 116.06 E
Fort Eustis ■ 208 37.09 N 76.35 W
Fortevoit 46 56.20 N 3.32 W
Fortezza (Franzensfeste) 64 46.47 N 11.37 E
Fort Fairfield 186 46.46 N 67.50 W
Fort Fitzgerald 176 59.53 N 111.37 W
Fort Foote Village 284c 38.46 N 77.01 W
Fort-Foureau 146 12.05 N 15.02 E
Fort Frances 190 48.36 N 93.24 W
Fort Franklin 180 65.11 N 123.46 W
Fort Fraser 182 54.04 N 124.33 W
Fort Frederica National Monument ♦ 192 31.12 N 81.26 W
Fort Gaines 192 31.36 N 85.02 W
Fort Garland 200 37.25 N 105.26 W
Fort Gay 188 38.06 N 82.35 W
Fort George ⊥ 284a 43.15 N 79.04 W
Fort George G. Meade ■ 208 39.05 N 76.50 W
Fort Gibson 196 35.47 N 95.15 W
Fort Gibson Lake ⊜¹ 196 36.00 N 95.18 W
Fort Good Hope 180 66.15 N 128.38 W
Fort Gordon ■ 192 33.25 N 82.11 W
Fort-Gouraud
— Fdérik 148 22.41 N 12.43 W
Fort Green 220 27.36 N 81.56 W
Forth 46 55.47 N 3.41 W
Forth ≃ 46 56.03 N 3.44 W
Forth, Carse of V 46 56.08 N 4.05 W
Forth, Firth of ⊂ 46 56.10 N 2.45 W
Förtha 56 50.56 N 10.14 E
Fort Hall 202 43.02 N 112.26 W
Fort Hall Indian Reservation ⊸⁴ 202 43.10 N 112.10 W
Fort Hamilton ■ 276 40.37 N 74.02 W
Forth Bridge ⊸⁵ 46 56.00 N 3.25 W
Fort Hertz
— Putao 102 27.21 N 97.24 E
Fort Hill
— Chitipa 154 9.43 S 33.16 E
Fort Hill ♦ 188 38.04 N 77.19 W
Fort Hill State Memorial ⊥ 218 39.07 N 83.25 W
Fort Hood ■ 222 31.08 N 97.46 W
Fort Howard 208 39.12 N 76.27 W
Fort Huachuca ■ 200 31.33 N 110.20 W
Fort Hunter 210 42.57 N 74.17 W
Fort Hunter Liggett ■ 226 35.55 N 121.15 W
Fortierville 206 46.29 N 72.02 W
Fortín 234 18.54 N 97.00 W
Fortin, Lac ⊜ 186 50.50 N 67.46 W
Fortín Ayacucho 248 19.58 S 59.47 W
Fortín Coroneles Sánchez 248 19.20 S 59.58 W
Fortine 182 48.45 N 114.54 W
Fortín Florida 248 20.45 S 59.17 W
Fortín Garrapatal 248 21.27 S 61.30 W
Fortín Teniente Montania 252 22.04 S 59.57 W
Fortín Uno 252 38.51 S 65.17 W
Fort Jackson ■ 192 34.01 N 80.57 W
Fort Jameson
— Chipata 154 13.39 S 32.40 E
Fort Jefferson National Monument ♦ 220 24.37 N 82.54 W
Fort Jennings 216 40.54 N 84.17 W
Fort Jeudy, Point of > 241k 12.00 N 61.42 W
Fort Johnson 210 42.57 N 74.14 W
Fort Johnston
— Mangochi 154 14.28 S 35.16 E
Fort Jones 204 41.36 N 122.50 W
Fort Kent 186 47.15 N 68.35 W
Fort Klamath 202 42.42 N 121.59 W
Fort Knox ■ 194 37.54 N 85.57 W
Fort-Lamy
— N'Djamena 146 12.07 N 15.03 E
Fort Langley 224 49.10 N 122.35 W
Fort Langley National Historic Park ♦ 224 49.10 N 122.35 W
Fort Laramie 200 42.12 N 104.31 W
Fort Laramie National Historic Site ⊥ 198 42.09 N 104.41 W
Fort Larned National Historic Site ⊥ 198 38.10 N 99.12 W
Fort Lauderdale 220 26.07 N 80.08 W
Fort Lauderdale-Hollywood International Airport ✈ 220 26.04 N 80.09 W
Fort Laurens State Memorial ⊥ 214 40.38 N 81.27 W
Fort Leavenworth ■ 198 39.21 N 94.55 W
Fort Le Boeuf ⊥ 214 41.56 N 79.59 W
Fort Lee 210 40.51 N 73.58 W
Fort Lee ■ 208 37.14 N 77.20 W
Fort Lennox National Historic Park ♦ 206 45.06 N 73.16 W
Fort Leonard Wood ■ 194 37.45 N 92.07 W
Fort Lewis ■ 224 47.05 N 122.37 W
Fort Liard 176 60.15 N 123.28 W
Fort-Liberté 238 19.39 N 71.49 W
Fort Lincoln State Park ♦ 198 46.45 N 100.52 W
Fort Littleton 214 40.04 N 77.58 W
Fort Loramie 216 40.21 N 84.22 W
Fort Loudoun Lake ⊜¹ 192 35.45 N 84.10 W
Fort Lupton 200 40.05 N 104.48 W
Fort Lyon Canal ≡ 198 38.11 N 102.31 W
Fort Macleod 182 49.43 N 113.25 W
Fort Madison 190 40.37 N 91.18 W
Fort-Mahon-Plage 50 50.21 N 1.34 E
Fort Malden National Historic Park ♦ 281 42.06 N 83.07 W
Fort Matanzas National Monument ♦ 192 29.40 N 81.18 W
Fort McClellan ■ 194 33.43 N 85.47 W
Fort McDermitt Indian Reservation ⊸⁴ 202 42.00 N 117.32 W
Fort McDowell Indian Reservation ⊸⁴ 200 33.38 N 111.41 W
Fort McHenry National Monument and Historic Shrine ♦ 208 39.16 N 76.35 W
Fort Mckinley 218 39.47 N 84.15 W
Fort McMurray 184 56.44 N 111.23 W
Fort McNair ■ 284c 38.52 N 77.04 W
Fort McPherson 180 67.27 N 134.53 W
Fort Meade 220 27.45 N 81.48 W
Fort Mill 192 35.00 N 80.56 W
Fort Miller 210 43.10 N 73.35 W
Fort Mitchell, Al., U.S. 192 32.21 N 85.01 W
Fort Mitchell, Ky., U.S. 218 39.03 N 84.32 W
Fort Mojave Indian Reservation ⊸⁴ 200 34.55 N 114.35 W
Fort Monmouth ■ 208 40.19 N 74.02 W
Fort Monroe ■ 208 37.00 N 76.18 W
Fort Montgomery 210 41.20 N 73.59 W
Fort Morgan 198 40.15 N 103.47 W
Fort Myer ■ 284c 38.53 N 77.05 W
Fort Myers 220 26.38 N 81.52 W
Fort Myers Beach 220 26.27 N 81.56 W
Fort Myers Shores 220 26.43 N 81.45 W
Fort Myers Villas 220 26.34 N 81.52 W
Fort Necessity National Battlefield ⊥ 188 39.47 N 79.39 W
Fort Neck >¹ 276 40.39 N 73.28 W
Fort Nelson 176 58.49 N 122.43 W
Fort Nelson ≃ 176 59.30 N 124.00 W
Fort Niagara Beach 284a 43.16 N 79.03 W
Fort Niagara State Park ♦, N.Y., U.S. 210 43.16 N 79.03 W
Fort Niagara State Park ♦, N.Y., U.S. 284a 43.16 N 79.03 W
Fort Nonsense ⊥ 276 40.48 N 74.29 W
Fort Norman 180 64.54 N 125.34 W
Fort Nottingham 158 29.25 S 29.55 E
Fort Ogden 220 27.05 N 81.57 W
Fort Ord ■ 226 36.40 N 121.48 W
Fortore ≃ 68 41.55 N 15.17 E
Fort Parker State Park ♦ 222 31.36 N 96.33 W
Fort Payne 194 34.26 N 85.43 W
Fort Peck 202 48.00 N 106.26 W
Fort Peck Dam ⊸⁶ 202 47.52 N 106.38 W
Fort Peck Indian Reservation ⊸⁴ 202 48.22 N 105.40 W
Fort Peck Lake ⊜¹ 202 47.45 N 106.50 W
Fort Pierce 220 27.26 N 80.19 W
Fort Pierce Inlet ⊂ 220 27.28 N 80.18 W
Fort Pierre 198 44.21 N 100.22 W
Fort Pitt Tunnels ⊸⁵ 279b 40.25 N 80.00 W
Fort Plain 210 42.55 N 74.37 W
Fort Point National Historic Site ⊥ 282 37.48 N 122.28 W
Fort Polk ■ 194 31.04 N 93.11 W
Fort Portal 154 0.40 N 30.17 E
Fort Providence 176 61.21 N 117.39 W
Fort Pulaski National Monument ♦ 192 32.01 N 80.59 W
Fort Qu'Appelle 184 50.46 N 103.48 W
Fort Raleigh National Historic Site ⊥ 192 35.55 N 75.40 W
Fort Randall Dam ⊸⁶ 198 42.48 N 98.35 W
Fort Recovery 216 40.24 N 84.46 W
Fort Resolution 176 61.10 N 113.40 W
Fortress Mountain ∧ 202 44.20 N 109.47 W
Fortress of Louisbourg National Historic Park ♦ 186 45.56 N 59.57 W
Fort Riley ■ 198 39.04 N 96.47 W
Fort Ritchie ■ 208 39.43 N 77.30 W
Fort Rixon 154 20.01 S 29.18 E
Fort Robinson State Park ♦ 198 42.41 N 103.30 W
Fort Rodd Hill National Historic Park ♦ 224 48.26 N 123.28 W
Fortrose, N.Z. 172 46.34 S 168.48 E
Fortrose, Scot., U.K. 46 57.34 N 4.09 W
Fort Rosebery
— Mansa 154 11.12 S 28.53 E
Fort Rucker ■ 194 31.20 N 85.42 W
Fort Saint James 182 54.26 N 124.15 W
Fort Saint John 182 56.15 N 120.51 W
Fort Salonga 276 40.55 N 73.18 W
Fort Sam Houston ■ 196 29.27 N 98.27 W
Fort Saskatchewan 182 53.43 N 113.13 W
Fort Scott 198 37.50 N 94.42 W
Fort Seneca 214 41.13 N 83.10 W
Fort-Ševčenko 84 44.31 N 50.16 E
Fort Severn 176 56.00 N 87.38 W
Fort Shawnee 216 40.41 N 84.08 W
Fort Sheridan ■ 216 42.13 N 87.48 W
Fort Sill ■ 196 34.40 N 98.25 W
Fort Simcoe Historical State Park ♦ 224 46.21 N 120.50 W
Fort Simpson 176 61.52 N 121.23 W
Fort Sisseton State Park ♦ 198 45.39 N 97.32 W
Fort Smith, N.T., Can. 176 60.00 N 111.53 W
Fort Smith, Ar., U.S. 194 35.23 N 94.23 W
Fort Steele 182 49.37 N 115.38 W
Fort Stevens State Park ♦ 224 46.10 N 124.00 W
Fort Stewart ■ 192 31.52 N 81.37 W
Fort Stockton 196 30.53 N 102.52 W
Fort Sumner 196 34.28 N 104.14 W
Fort Sumter National Monument ♦ 192 32.44 N 79.46 W
Fort Supply 196 36.34 N 99.34 W
Fort Tejon State Historical Park ♦ 228 34.52 N 118.53 W
Fort Thomas, Az., U.S. 200 33.02 N 109.57 W
Fort Thomas, Ky., U.S. 218 39.04 N 84.26 W
Fort Thompson 198 44.04 N 99.26 W
Fort Tilden ■ 276 40.33 N 73.53 W
Fort Totten 198 47.58 N 98.59 W
Fort Totten Indian Reservation ⊸⁴ 198 47.53 N 98.50 W
Fort Totten Park ♦ 284c 38.57 N 77.00 W
Fort Towson 196 34.01 N 95.15 W
Fort-Trinquet
— Bîr Mogreïn 148 25.14 N 11.35 W
Fortuna, Arg. 252 35.07 S 65.23 W
Fortuna, C.R. 236 10.30 N 84.35 W
Fortuna, Ca., U.S. 204 40.35 N 124.09 W
Fortuna, Rio de la ≃ 248 16.36 S 58.46 W
Fortuna Ledge (Marshall) 180 61.53 N 162.05 W
Fortune 186 47.04 N 55.50 W
Fortune Bay ⊂ 186 47.25 N 55.25 W
Fortune Ditch ≡ 279a 41.20 N 82.03 W
Fortune Harbour 186 49.31 N 55.15 W
Fortuneswell 42 50.34 N 2.27 W
Fort Union National Monument ♦ 200 35.55 N 105.01 W
Fort Union Trading Post National Historic Site ⊥ 198 48.00 N 104.03 W
Fort Valley 192 32.33 N 83.53 W
Fort Vancouver National Historic Site ⊥ 224 45.38 N 122.37 W
Fort Vermilion 176 58.24 N 116.00 W
Fortville 218 39.55 N 85.50 W
Fort Walton Beach 194 30.24 N 86.37 W
Fort Washakie 200 43.00 N 108.52 W
Fort Washington 284c 38.44 N 77.01 W
Fort Washington Forest 208 38.43 N 76.59 W
Fort Washington State Park ♦ 285 40.07 N 75.14 W
Fort Wayne 216 41.07 N 85.07 W
Fort Wayne Military Museum ᵾ 281 42.18 N 83.06 W
Fort Wellington 246 6.24 N 57.36 W
Fort Wellington National Historic Park ♦ 212 44.44 N 75.31 W
Fort White 192 29.55 N 82.42 W
Fort William
— Thunder Bay, On., Can. 190 48.23 N 89.15 W
Fort William, Scot., U.K. 46 56.49 N 5.07 W
Fort Worth 222 32.43 N 97.19 W
Fort Yates 198 46.05 N 100.37 W
Forty Foot Drain ≡ 42 52.28 N 0.05 W
Forty Fort 210 41.16 N 75.52 W
Fortymile ≃ 180 64.26 N 140.32 W
Fort Yukon 180 66.34 N 145.17 W
Fort Yuma Indian Reservation ⊸⁴ 204 32.48 N 114.34 W
Forum ♦ 275a 45.29 N 73.35 W
Forūr, Jazīreh-ye I 128 26.17 N 54.32 E
Forza d'Agrò 70 37.55 N 15.20 E
Foscagno, Passo di)(64 46.30 N 10.08 E
Fosdinovo 64 44.08 N 10.01 E
Fosforescente, Bahía ⊂ 240m 17.59 N 67.01 W
Fosforitnyj 82 55.19 N 38.54 E
Foshan 100 23.03 N 113.09 E
Fosna >¹, Nor. 24 64.00 N 10.30 E
Fosna >¹, Nor. 26 63.45 N 10.25 E
Fosnavåg 26 62.21 N 5.39 E
Foso 150 5.42 N 1.17 W
Foss 46 56.41 N 3.58 W
Foss ≃, Eng., U.K. 44 53.57 N 1.06 W
Foss ≃, Wa., U.S. 224 47.43 N 121.18 W
Fossacesia 66 42.15 N 14.29 E
Fossacesia Marina 66 42.15 N 14.30 E
Fossa Eugeniana ≡ 263 51.33 N 6.36 E
Fossano 62 44.33 N 7.43 E
Fossato, Colle di)(66 43.19 N 12.47 E
Fossé 56 49.27 N 5.00 E
Fosse-Martin 261 49.05 N 2.54 E
Fosses 261 49.06 N 2.29 E
Fosses-la-Ville 56 50.24 N 4.42 E
Fossil 202 44.59 N 120.12 W
Fossil Butte National Monument ♦ 202 41.50 N 110.40 W
Fossil Downs 162 18.08 S 125.38 E
Fossil Lake ⊜ 202 43.18 N 120.15 W
Fossombrone 66 43.41 N 12.48 E
Fosston 198 47.34 N 95.45 W
Fos-sur-Mer 62 43.26 N 4.57 E
Foster, Austl. 169 38.39 S 146.12 E
Foster, Ky., U.S. 218 38.47 N 84.12 W
Foster, R.I., U.S. 207 41.51 N 71.45 W
Foster ≃ 184 55.47 N 105.49 W
Foster, Mount ∧ 180 59.48 N 135.29 W
Foster Brook 214 41.59 N 78.37 W
Foster City 226 37.33 N 122.16 W
Foster Creek ≃ 198 44.34 N 98.12 W
Fosterdale 210 41.42 N 74.58 W
Foster Joseph Sayers Reservoir ⊜¹ 214 41.02 N 77.40 W
Foster Park 228 34.21 N 119.18 W
Fosters 194 33.05 N 87.41 W
Fosters Pond ⊜ 283 42.37 N 71.08 W
Foster Street 260 51.46 N 0.09 E
Foster Village 229c 21.21 N 157.55 W
Fostoria 214 41.09 N 83.25 W
Fót 264c 47.37 N 19.12 E
Fotadrevo 157b 24.03 S 45.01 E
Fotan 100 24.12 N 117.53 E
Fóti-Somlyó ∧² 264c 47.38 N 19.13 E
Foucarmont 50 49.51 N 1.34 E
Fou-Chouen
— Fushun 104 41.52 N 123.53 E
Fouesnant 32 47.54 N 4.01 W
Foug 56 48.41 N 5.47 E
Fougamou 152 1.13 S 10.36 E
Fougères 32 48.21 N 1.12 W
Fougères-sur-Bièvre 50 47.27 N 1.21 E
Fougerolles 58 47.53 N 6.24 E
Fou-hsin
— Fuxin 104 42.03 N 121.46 E
Fouju 261 48.35 N 2.47 E
Fouke 194 33.16 N 93.53 W
Foula I 46a 60.08 N 2.05 W
Foulain 58 48.02 N 5.13 E
Foulalaba 150 10.41 N 7.22 W
Foula Mori 150 12.10 N 13.51 W
Foulatari 146 13.41 N 12.03 E
Foul Bay ⊂ 140 23.30 N 35.39 E
Fouling
— Fuling 102 29.42 N 107.21 E
Foulness ≃ 44 53.47 N 0.43 W
Foulness Island I 42 51.36 N 0.55 E
Foulness Point > 42 51.38 N 0.57 E
Foulpointe 157b 17.41 S 49.31 E
Foulsham 42 52.48 N 1.01 E
Foulwind, Cape > 172 41.45 S 171.28 E
Foumban 152 5.43 N 10.55 E
Foumbot 152 5.30 N 10.38 E
Foumbouni 157a 11.50 S 43.30 E
Foum-el-Hisn 148 28.59 N 8.55 W
Foum-Zguid 148 30.04 N 6.54 W
Foundiougne 150 14.08 N 16.28 W
Fountain, Co., U.S. 198 38.40 N 104.42 W
Fountain, Fl., U.S. 194 30.29 N 85.25 W
Fountain □⁶ 216 40.17 N 87.13 W
Fountain City, In., U.S. 218 39.57 N 84.55 W
Fountain City, Wi., U.S. 190 44.07 N 91.43 W
Fountain Creek ≃, Co., U.S. 198 38.15 N 104.35 W
Fountain Creek ≃, Il., U.S. 219 38.20 N 90.22 W
Fountain Green 200 39.37 N 111.38 W
Fountain Hill 208 40.36 N 75.23 W
Fountain Inn 192 34.41 N 82.11 W
Fountain Park 216 41.50 N 84.32 W
Fountain Peak ∧ 204 34.57 N 115.32 W
Fountain Place 194 30.31 N 91.09 W
Fountains Abbey ᵾ¹ 44 54.07 N 1.34 W
Fountains Creek ≃ 208 36.33 N 77.21 W
Fountaintown 218 39.41 N 85.47 W
Fountain Valley 228 33.42 N 117.57 W
Fourche LaFave ≃ 194 34.58 N 92.35 W
Fourche Maline ≃ 194 34.55 N 94.55 W
Fourchu 186 45.43 N 60.15 W
Four Corners 202 44.55 N 122.58 W
Four Elms 260 51.13 N 0.06 E
Four Hole Swamp ≚ 192 33.03 N 80.24 W
Fouriesburg 158 28.38 S 28.14 E
Fourmies 50 50.00 N 4.03 E
Four Mile Creek ≃, N.Y., U.S. 284a 43.15 N 79.08 W
Fourmile Creek ≃, On., Can. 284a 43.17 N 79.00 W
Four Mile Creek ≃, Oh., U.S. 218 39.26 N 84.32 W
Four Mile Creek State Park ♦ 284a 43.16 N 79.00 W
Fourmile Draw V 196 32.40 N 104.18 W
Four Mile Lake ⊜ 212 44.40 N 78.44 W
Four Mile Run ≃ 284c 38.50 N 77.02 W
Four Mountains, Islands of II 180 52.50 N 170.00 W
Fournaise, Piton de la ∧ 157c 21.14 S 55.43 E
Fourneau, Pointe à > 275a 45.22 N 73.51 W
Fourneaux, Fr. 50 47.53 N 1.48 E
Fourneaux, Fr. 62 45.11 N 6.39 E
Fournier, Lac ⊜ 186 51.33 N 65.25 W
Fournière, Lac ⊜ 190 48.04 N 78.03 W
Fournoi I 38 37.34 N 26.30 E
Four Oaks 192 35.26 N 78.25 W
Fourqueux 261 48.53 N 2.04 E
Fours 32 46.49 N 3.43 E
Fourteenmile Creek ≃ 218 38.26 N 85.37 W
Fourth Cataract
— Rābiʻ, Ash-Shallāl ar- ʟ 140 18.47 N 32.03 E
Fourth Cliff ⋏⁴ 283 42.09 N 70.42 W
Four Towns 281 42.37 N 83.25 W
Fous, Pointe des > 240d 15.12 N 61.20 W
Foussard ≃ 50 48.16 N 1.17 E
Fouta Djalon ⊸¹ 150 11.30 N 12.30 W
Fou-Tcheou
— Fuzhou 100 26.06 N 119.17 E
Foux, Cap à > 238 19.41 N 73.27 W
Fouyang
— Fuyang 100 32.54 N 115.49 E
Fouzon ≃ 50 47.16 N 1.27 E
Foveaux Strait ʉ 172 46.35 S 168.00 E
Foveran 46 57.18 N 2.02 W
Fowey 42 50.20 N 4.38 W
Fowler, Ca., U.S. 226 36.37 N 119.40 W
Fowler, Co., U.S. 198 38.07 N 104.01 W
Fowler, In., U.S. 216 40.37 N 87.19 W
Fowler, Ks., U.S. 198 37.23 N 100.11 W
Fowler, Mi., U.S. 216 43.00 N 84.44 W
Fowler, Oh., U.S. 214 41.19 N 80.40 W
Fowler, Lake ⊜ 168b 35.06 S 137.37 E
Fowler, Point > 162 32.02 S 132.29 E
Fowler Creek ≃ 281 42.17 N 83.30 W
Fowlers Bay 162 31.59 S 132.27 E
Fowlerton 196 28.28 N 98.48 W
Fowlerville 216 42.39 N 84.04 W
Fowling
— Jingdezhen 100 29.16 N 117.11 E
Fowman 128 37.13 N 49.19 E
Fox 180 64.51 N 147.46 W
Fox ≃, Mb., Can. 184 56.03 N 93.18 W
Fox ≃, U.S. 194 40.18 N 91.30 W
Fox ≃, U.S. 216 41.21 N 88.50 W
Fox ≃, Il., U.S. 218 38.32 N 88.08 W
Fox ≃, Wi., U.S. 190 44.32 N 88.01 W
Fox, Cape > 182 54.47 N 130.51 W
Foxboro, On., Can. 212 44.15 N 77.26 W
Foxboro, Ma., U.S. 207 42.03 N 71.15 W
Foxboro Raceway ♦ 283 42.06 N 71.16 W
Foxboro Stadium ♦ 283 42.05 N 71.16 W
Fox Brook ≃ 276 41.03 N 74.13 W
Foxburg 214 41.09 N 79.41 W
Fox Chapel 279b 40.30 N 79.55 W
Fox Chase ⊸⁸ 285 40.04 N 75.05 W
Fox Chase Manor 285 40.05 N 75.06 W
Fox Creek ≃, Ky., U.S. 218 38.16 N 83.41 W
Fox Creek ≃, N.Y., U.S. 210 42.41 N 74.18 W
Foxe Basin ⊂ 176 68.25 N 77.00 W
Foxe-Becken
— Foxe Basin ⊂ 176 68.25 N 77.00 W
Foxe Channel ʉ 176 64.30 N 80.00 W
Foxen ⊜ 26 59.23 N 11.52 E
Foxe Peninsula >¹ 176 65.00 N 76.00 W
Foxford 48 53.58 N 9.08 W
Fox Glacier 172 43.28 S 170.00 E
Foxhall 284c 39.04 N 77.03 W
Fox Harbour 186 47.19 N 53.55 W
Fox Hills 284c 39.02 N 77.11 W
Foxhole 42 50.21 N 4.52 W
Foxholes 44 54.08 N 0.28 W
Fox Hollow Lake ⊜ 276 41.02 N 74.40 W
Fox Island I, On., Can. 212 44.28 N 78.24 W
Fox Island I, Wa., U.S. 224 47.16 N 122.37 W
Fox Islands II 180 53.30 N 168.00 W
Fox Lake, Il., U.S. 216 42.23 N 88.11 W
Fox Lake, Wi., U.S. 190 43.33 N 88.54 W
Fox Lake ⊜ 216 42.25 N 88.09 W
Fox Mountain ∧ 180 61.55 N 133.22 W
Foxpark 200 41.05 N 106.09 W
Fox Point 216 43.09 N 87.54 W
Fox Point > 276 40.54 N 73.35 W
Fox River Estates 216 41.58 N 88.20 W
Fox River Grove 216 42.12 N 88.12 W
Foxton 172 40.28 S 175.18 E
Foxton Beach 172 40.28 S 175.13 E
Foxvale 283 42.02 N 71.14 W
Fox Valley, Austl. 274a 33.45 S 151.06 E
Fox Valley, Sk., Can. 184 50.29 N 109.28 W
Foxwells 208 37.38 N 76.18 W
Foxwist Green 262 53.12 N 2.34 W
Foxworth 194 31.14 N 89.52 W
Foyedong 98 40.41 N 119.12 E
Foyers 46 57.14 N 4.29 W
Foyle ≃ 48 54.59 N 7.18 W
Foyle, Lough ⊂ 48 55.06 N 7.08 W
Foynes 48 52.37 N 9.06 W
Foza 64 45.54 N 11.38 E
Foz do Areia, Represa de ⊜¹ 252 26.00 S 51.35 W
Foz do Cunene 152 17.16 S 11.50 E
Foz do Iguaçu 252 25.33 S 54.35 W
Foz do Jordão 248 9.23 S 71.56 W
Foz Giraldo 34 40.00 N 7.43 W
Foziling 100 31.20 N 116.17 E
Frabosa Soprana 62 44.17 N 7.48 E
Frackville 208 40.47 N 76.13 W
Fraction Run ≃ 214 41.34 N 88.04 W
Fraga, Arg. 252 33.30 S 65.48 W
Fraga, Esp. 34 41.31 N 0.21 E
Fragagnano 68 40.26 N 17.28 E
Fragneto Monforte 68 41.15 N 14.46 E
Fragoso, Cayo I 240p 22.44 N 79.30 W
Fragrant Hills Park ♦ 271a 39.59 N 116.11 E
Fragua, Sierra de la ∧ 196 26.41 N 102.13 W
Fraile Muerto 252 32.31 S 54.32 W
Fraîn, Chott el ⊜ 34 35.57 N 5.38 E
Fraire 50 50.16 N 4.30 E
Fraisans 58 47.09 N 5.46 E
Fraisse 62 45.23 N 4.15 E
Fraize 58 48.11 N 7.00 E
Fram 61 46.27 N 15.38 E
Frameries 50 50.24 N 3.54 E
Framingham 207 42.16 N 71.25 W
Framingham State College ᵾ² 283 42.18 N 71.26 W
Framlingham 42 52.13 N 1.21 E
Frammersbach 56 50.04 N 9.28 E
Framnes Mountains ⋏ 9 67.50 S 62.35 E
Frampol 30 50.41 N 22.40 E
Frampton Cotterell 42 51.32 N 2.29 W
Frampton on Severn 42 51.46 N 2.22 W
França, Bra. 250 11.13 S 40.36 W
Franca, Bra. 255 20.32 S 47.24 W
Franca-Iosifa, Zeml'a (Franz Josef Land) II 12 81.00 N 55.00 E
Français, Récif des ⊸² 175f 19.40 S 163.20 E
Francavilla al Mare 66 42.25 N 14.17 E
Francavilla Angitola 68 38.46 N 16.16 E
Francavilla d'Ete 66 43.11 N 13.32 E
Francavilla di Sicilia 70 37.54 N 15.08 E
Francavilla Fontana 68 40.31 N 17.35 E
Francavilla in Sinni 68 40.05 N 16.12 E
Francavilla Marittima 68 39.49 N 16.23 E
France □¹, Europe 22 46.00 N 2.00 E
France □¹, Europe 32 46.00 N 2.00 E
Frances ≃ 180 60.12 N 129.02 W
Francés, Cabo >, Cuba 240p 21.54 N 84.02 W
Frances, Cabo >, Cuba 240p 21.38 N 83.12 W
Frances Creek 164 13.35 S 131.52 E
Francês dos Carvalhos 256 22.05 S 44.29 W
Frances Lake ⊜ 180 61.25 N 129.30 W
Francés Viejo, Cabo > 238 19.39 N 69.55 W
Francesville 216 40.59 N 86.52 W
Franceville 152 1.38 S 13.35 E
Francfort-sur-Main
— Frankfurt am Main 56 50.07 N 8.40 E
Franche-Comté □⁹ 58 47.00 N 6.00 E
Franchère, Lac ⊜ 206 46.47 N 74.58 W
Franches-Montagnes ⋏ 58 47.12 N 7.00 E
Francia 252 32.33 S 56.37 W
Francia
— France □¹ 32 46.00 N 2.00 E
Francia, Estación de ⊸⁵ 266d 41.23 N 2.11 E
Francia, Peña de ∧ 34 42.35 N 8.02 W
Francis 184 50.05 N 103.55 W
Francis, Lake ⊜ 206 45.02 N 71.20 W
Francis Case, Lake ⊜¹ 198 43.15 N 99.00 W
Francisco A. Berra 258 35.23 S 58.51 W
Francisco Álvarez 258 34.38 S 58.52 W
Francisco Beltrão 252 26.05 S 53.04 W
Francisco I. Madero, Méx. 232 25.45 N 103.21 W
Francisco I. Madero, Méx. 232 24.32 N 104.22 W
Francisco I. Madero, Méx. 234 21.36 N 104.49 W
Francisco José, Tierra
— Franca-Iosifa, Zeml'a II 12 81.00 N 55.00 E
Francisco Morato 256 23.16 S 46.45 W
Francisco Morazán □⁵ 236 14.15 N 87.15 W
Francisco Murguía 234 24.00 N 103.01 W
Francisco Perito Moreno, Parque Nacional ♦ 254 47.50 S 72.08 W
Francisco Sá 255 16.28 S 43.30 W
Francisco Zarco 204 32.06 N 116.30 W
Francis E. Warren Air Force Base ■ 198 41.09 N 104.52 W
Francistown 156 21.11 S 27.32 E
Francitas 222 28.52 N 96.20 W
Franco da Rocha 256 23.20 S 46.43 W
Francofonte 70 37.14 N 14.53 E
François 186 47.35 N 56.45 W
François, Lacs à ⊜ 186 51.40 N 65.49 W
François-Joseph, Îles du
— Franca-Iosifa, Zeml'a II 12 81.00 N 55.00 E
François Lake 182 54.04 N 125.44 W
François Lake ⊜ 182 54.00 N 125.40 W
Francolise 68 41.11 N 14.03 E
Franconia Notch State Park ♦ 188 44.06 N 71.43 W
Franconville 261 48.59 N 2.14 E
Francs Peak ∧ 202 43.58 N 109.20 W
Francueil 50 47.19 N 1.05 E
Franeker 52 53.11 N 5.32 E
Frangy 58 46.01 N 5.56 E
Frank 279b 40.16 N 79.48 W
Frank and Poet Drain ≡ 281 42.06 N 83.12 W
Frankby 262 53.22 N 3.08 W
Frankel City 196 32.23 N 102.47 W
Franken □⁹ 30 50.00 N 10.00 E
Frankenau 56 51.05 N 8.56 E
Frankenbach 56 50.40 N 8.34 E
Frankenberg 54 50.54 N 13.01 E
Frankenberg-Eder 56 51.03 N 8.48 E
Frankenburg 60 48.05 N 13.30 E
Frankenheim 56 50.32 N 10.04 E
Frankenhöhe ⋏ 56 49.15 N 10.15 E
Frankenmarkt 64 47.59 N 13.25 E
Frankenmuth 190 43.19 N 83.44 W
Frankenstein 56 49.26 N 7.58 E
Frankenthal 56 49.32 N 8.21 E
Frankenwald ⋏ 54 50.18 N 11.36 E
Frankfield 241q 18.09 N 77.22 W
Frankford, On., Can. 212 44.12 N 77.36 W
Frankford, De., U.S. 208 38.31 N 75.14 W
Frankford, Mo., U.S. 219 39.29 N 91.19 W
Frankford ⊸⁸ 285 40.01 N 75.05 W
Frankford Arsenal ■ 285 40.00 N 75.04 W
Frankfort, S. Afr. 158 32.44 S 27.28 E
Frankfort, S. Afr. 158 27.17 S 28.30 E
Frankfort, Il., U.S. 216 41.29 N 87.50 W
Frankfort, In., U.S. 216 40.16 N 86.30 W
Frankfort, Ks., U.S. 198 39.42 N 96.25 W
Frankfort, Ky., U.S. 218 38.12 N 84.52 W
Frankfort, Mi., U.S. 190 44.38 N 86.14 W
Frankfort, N.Y., U.S. 210 43.02 N 75.04 W
Frankfort, Oh., U.S. 218 39.24 N 83.10 W
Frankfort, S.D., U.S. 198 44.52 N 98.18 W
Frankfort Springs 214 40.30 N 80.25 W
Frankfurt am Main 56 50.07 N 8.40 E
Frankfurt am Main, Flughafen ✈ 56 50.02 N 8.33 E
Frankfurt an der Oder 54 52.20 N 14.33 E
Frank G. Bonelli Regional County Park ♦ 280 34.05 N 117.49 W
Frank Hann National Park ♦ 162 32.50 S 120.25 E
Fränkische Alb ⋏² 60 49.20 N 11.30 E
Fränkische Rezat ≃ 56 49.11 N 11.01 E
Fränkische Saale ≃ 56 50.03 N 9.42 E
Fränkische Schweiz ⋏¹ 60 49.45 N 11.25 E
Frank Key I 220 25.07 N 80.54 W
Frankland ≃ 162 34.58 S 116.49 E
Frankleben 54 51.18 N 11.56 E
Franklin, S. Afr. 158 30.18 S 29.30 E
Franklin, Az., U.S. 200 32.40 N 109.04 W
Franklin, Ga., U.S. 192 33.16 N 85.05 W
Franklin, Id., U.S. 202 42.00 N 111.48 W
Franklin, Il., U.S. 219 39.37 N 90.03 W
Franklin, In., U.S. 218 39.28 N 86.03 W
Franklin, Ky., U.S. 194 36.43 N 86.34 W
Franklin, La., U.S. 194 29.47 N 91.30 W
Franklin, Me., U.S. 188 44.35 N 68.13 W
Franklin, Ma., U.S. 207 42.05 N 71.23 W
Franklin, Mi., U.S. 281 42.31 N 83.18 W
Franklin, Mn., U.S. 198 44.31 N 94.52 W
Franklin, Ne., U.S. 198 40.05 N 98.57 W
Franklin, N.H., U.S. 188 43.26 N 71.38 W
Franklin, N.J., U.S. 210 41.07 N 74.34 W
Franklin, N.Y., U.S. 210 42.20 N 75.09 W
Franklin, N.C., U.S. 192 35.10 N 83.22 W
Franklin, Oh., U.S. 218 39.33 N 84.18 W
Franklin, Pa., U.S. 214 41.24 N 79.50 W
Franklin, Tn., U.S. 194 35.55 N 86.52 W
Franklin, Tx., U.S. 222 31.01 N 96.29 W
Franklin, Vt., U.S. 206 44.58 N 72.55 W
Franklin, Va., U.S. 208 36.40 N 76.55 W
Franklin, W.V., U.S. 188 38.39 N 79.20 W
Franklin, Wi., U.S. 216 42.54 N 88.03 W
Franklin □⁶, In., U.S. 218 39.25 N 85.01 W
Franklin □⁶, Ky., U.S. 218 38.14 N 84.52 W
Franklin □⁶, Mo., U.S. 219 38.25 N 91.03 W
Franklin □⁶, N.Y., U.S. 206 44.57 N 74.18 W
Franklin □⁶, Oh., U.S. 218 39.57 N 83.00 W
Franklin □⁶, Pa., U.S. 208 39.56 N 77.40 W
Franklin □⁶, Va., U.S. 208 37.00 N 79.52 W
Franklin □⁶, Vt., U.S. 206 44.57 N 72.52 W
Franklin, Mount ∧ 171b 35.29 S 148.47 E
Franklin, Point > 180 70.54 N 158.48 W
Franklin Bay ⊂ 176 69.45 N 126.00 W
Franklin Canyon Reservoir ⊜¹ 280 34.06 N 118.25 W
Franklin Delano Roosevelt National Historic Site ⊥ 210 41.46 N 73.56 W
Franklin Delano Roosevelt Park ♦ 285 39.54 N 75.11 W
Franklin D. Roosevelt Lake ⊜¹ 202 48.20 N 118.10 W
Franklin Farms 279b 40.10 N 80.16 W
Franklin Grove 190 41.50 N 89.18 W
Franklin Harbor ⊂ 166 33.42 S 136.56 E
Franklin Institute ᵾ 285 39.57 N 75.10 W
Franklin Island I 212 45.24 N 80.20 W

≃ River — Fluß — Río — Rivière — Rio
≡ Canal — Kanal — Canal — Canal — Canal
ʟ Waterfall, Rapids — Wasserfall, Stromschnellen — Cascada, Rápidos — Chute d'eau, Rapides — Cascata, Rápidos
ʉ Strait — Meeresstraße — Estrecho — Détroit — Estreito
⊂ Bay, Gulf — Bucht, Golf — Bahía, Golfo — Baie, Golfe — Baía, Golfo
⊜ Lake, Lakes — See, Seen — Lago, Lagos — Lac, Lacs — Lago, Lagos
≚ Swamp — Sumpf — Pantano — Marais — Pântano
✱ Ice Features, Glacier — Eis- und Gletscherformen — Accidentes Glaciales — Formes glaciaires — Acidentes glaciares
⫪ Other Hydrographic Features — Andere Hydrographische Objekte — Otros Elementos Hidrográficos — Autres données hydrographiques — Outros acidentes hidrográficos

⊸ Submarine Features — Untermeerische Objekte — Accidentes Submarinos — Formes de relief sous-marin — Acidentes submarinos
□ Political Unit — Politische Einheit — Unidad Política — Entité politique — Unidade política
ᵾ Cultural Institution — Kulturelle Institution — Institución Cultural — Institution culturelle — Instituição cultural
⊥ Historical Site — Historische Stätte — Sitio Histórico — Site historique — Sitio histórico
♦ Recreational Site — Erholungs- und Ferienort — Sitio de Recreo — Centre de loisirs — Area de Lazer
✈ Airport — Flughafen — Aeropuerto — Aéroport — Aeroporto
■ Military Installation — Militäranlage — Instalación Militar — Installation militaire — Instalação militar
⊸ Miscellaneous — Verschiedenes — Misceláneo — Divers — Diversos

ENGLISH — Name, Page, Lat.°′, Long.°′ | DEUTSCH — Name, Seite, Breite°′, Länge°′ E = Ost

Name	Page	Lat.°′	Long.°′
Franklin Lake ⊜, N.T., Can.	176	66.56 N	96.03 W
Franklin Lake ⊜, Nv., U.S.	204	40.24 N	115.12 W
Franklin Lake ⊜, N.J., U.S.	276	40.59 N	74.13 W
Franklin Lakes	276	41.01 N	74.12 W
Franklin-Lower Gordon Wild Rivers National Park ♠	166	42.46 S	145.45 E
Franklin Mountains ⩘, N.T., Can.	180	63.00 N	123.50 W
Franklin Mountains ⩘, N.Z.	172	44.55 S	167.45 E
Franklin Park, Il., U.S.	216	41.56 N	87.51 W
Franklin Park, Md., U.S.	284c	39.03 N	77.06 W
Franklin Park, N.J., U.S.	276	40.26 N	74.32 W
Franklin Park, N.Y., U.S.	210	43.05 N	76.05 W
Franklin Park, Pa., U.S.	279b	40.35 N	80.06 W
Franklin Park, Va., U.S.	284c	38.55 N	77.09 W
Franklin Park ♠	283	42.18 N	71.06 W
Franklin Pond ⊜	276	41.06 N	74.35 W
Franklin Ridge ∧	282	38.00 N	122.10 W
Franklin River	224	49.06 N	124.49 W
Franklin Roosevelt Park ◆[8]	273d	26.09 S	27.59 E
Franklin Springs	210	43.02 N	75.24 W
Franklin Square	210	40.42 N	73.40 W
Franklin State Forest ♠	283	42.04 N	71.26 W
Franklin Strait ⊍	176	72.00 N	96.00 W
Franklinton, La., U.S.	194	30.50 N	90.09 W
Franklinton, N.C., U.S.	192	36.06 N	78.27 W
Franklintown	208	40.05 N	77.02 W
Franklinville, N.J., U.S.	208	39.37 N	75.04 W
Franklinville, N.Y., U.S.	210	42.20 N	78.27 W
Frankreich → France □[1]	32	46.00 N	2.00 E
Frankston, Austl.	169	38.08 S	145.07 E
Frankston, Tx., U.S.	222	32.03 N	95.30 W
Franksville	216	42.45 N	87.54 W
Frankton	216	40.13 N	85.46 W
Frankville	194	31.38 N	88.08 W
Frånö	26	62.54 N	17.50 E
Fr'anovo	82	56.08 N	38.27 E
Franschhoek	158	33.55 S	19.09 E
Fransfontein	156	20.12 S	15.01 E
Fränsta	26	62.30 N	16.09 E
Františkovy Lázně	54	50.04 N	12.21 E
Franvillers	50	49.58 N	2.30 E
Franzburg	54	54.11 N	12.52 E
Franzensburg ⊥	264b	48.04 N	16.22 E
Franzensfeste → Fortezza	64	46.47 N	11.37 E
Franz Josef	172	43.24 S	170.11 E
Franz Josef Land → Franca Iosifa, Zeml'a II	12	81.00 N	55.00 E
Franz-Josefs-Bahnhof ◆[5]	264b	48.13 N	16.21 E
Franz-Josefs-Höhe ♠	64	47.04 N	12.45 E
Französische Süd- und Antarktis-Gebiete → French Southern and Antarctic Ter □[2]	6	49.30 S	69.30 E
Französisch-Polynesien → French Polynesia □[2]	14	15.00 S	140.00 W
Frasca, Capo della ›	71	39.46 N	8.27 E
Frascati	66	41.48 N	12.41 E
Frascineto	68	39.50 N	16.16 E
Frasdorf	64	47.48 N	12.16 E
Fraser, Co., U.S.	200	39.56 N	105.49 W
Fraser, Mi., U.S.	281	42.32 N	82.56 W
Fraser ≃, B.C., Can.	182	49.09 N	123.12 W
Fraser ≃, Nf., Can.	176	56.35 N	61.55 W
Fraser ≃, Co., U.S.	200	40.06 N	105.58 W
Fraser, Mount ∧	162	25.39 S	118.23 E
Fraserburg	158	31.55 S	21.30 E
Fraserburgh	46	57.42 N	2.00 W
Fraser Island I	166	25.15 S	153.10 E
Fraser Lake	182	54.04 N	124.51 W
Fraser Lake ⊜	182	54.05 N	124.35 W
Fraser Mills	224	49.14 N	122.52 W
Fraser National Park ♠	169	37.10 S	145.50 E
Fraser Plateau ⩘[1]	182	52.00 N	123.00 W
Fraser Range	162	32.03 S	122.48 E
Frasertown	172	38.58 S	177.24 E
Frasne	58	46.51 N	6.10 E
Frasnes-lez-Anvaing	50	50.40 N	3.36 E
Frassine ≃	64	45.18 N	11.37 E
Frassinoro	64	44.18 N	10.34 E
Frati, Monte dei ∧	66	43.40 N	12.10 E
Fratres	61	48.59 N	15.21 E
Frattamaggiore	68	40.57 N	14.16 E
Frattócchie	267a	41.46 N	12.37 E
Frauenfeld	58	47.34 N	8.54 E
Frauenkirchen	61	47.50 N	16.56 E
Frauenstein	54	50.48 N	13.32 E
Frauental an der Lassnitz	61	46.48 N	15.14 E
Frauenwald	54	50.35 N	10.51 E
Fray Bentos	252	33.08 S	58.18 W
Fray Jorge, Parque Nacional ♠	252	30.40 S	71.45 W
Fray Luis Beltrán	252	39.19 S	65.46 W
Fray Marcos	252	34.11 S	55.44 W
Frazee	198	46.43 N	95.42 W
Frazer, Mt., U.S.	202	48.03 N	106.02 W
Frazer, Pa., U.S.	208	40.02 N	75.33 W
Frazeysburg	214	40.07 N	82.07 W
Frazier Mountain ∧	228	34.47 N	118.58 W
Frazier Park	228	34.49 N	118.56 W
Fr'azino	82	55.58 N	38.04 E
Frazzanò	70	38.04 N	14.44 E
Frechen	56	50.54 N	6.49 E
Frechilla	34	42.08 N	4.50 W
Freckenhorst	52	51.55 N	7.58 E
Freckleton	262	53.45 N	2.52 W
Freddo ≃	70	38.01 N	12.54 E
Fredeburg	56	51.11 N	8.18 E
Freden	52	51.56 N	9.54 E
Fredensborg	41	55.58 N	12.24 E
Fredensborg ⊥	41	55.58 N	12.23 E
Frederic	190	45.39 N	92.28 W
Frederica	208	39.00 N	75.27 W
Fredericia	41	55.35 N	9.46 E
Frederick, Il., U.S.	219	40.04 N	90.26 W
Frederick, Md., U.S.	208	39.24 N	77.24 W
Frederick, Ok., U.S.	196	34.23 N	99.01 W
Frederick, S.D., U.S.	198	45.49 N	98.30 W
Frederick □[6]	208	39.25 N	77.25 W
Frederick Hills ⩘[2]	164	12.41 S	136.00 E
Frederick House ≃	190	49.06 N	81.10 W
Frederick House Lake ⊜	190	48.40 N	80.55 W
Frederick Island I	162	34.04 S	122.00 E
Frederick Reef ✢[2]	166	20.58 S	154.23 E
Fredericksburg, In., U.S.	218	38.26 N	86.11 W
Fredericksburg, Ia., U.S.	190	42.57 N	92.11 W
Fredericksburg, Oh., U.S.	214	40.40 N	81.52 W
Fredericksburg, Pa., U.S.	214	40.27 N	76.26 W
Fredericksburg, Tx., U.S.	196	30.16 N	98.52 W
Fredericksburg, Va., U.S.	208	38.18 N	77.27 W
Fredericksburg Battlefield ⊥	208	38.17 N	77.28 W
Frederick Sound ⊍	180	57.00 N	133.00 W
Fredericktown, Mo., U.S.	194	37.33 N	90.17 W
Fredericktown, Oh., U.S.	214	40.28 N	82.32 W
Frederico Westphalen	252	27.22 S	53.24 W
Fredericton	186	45.58 N	66.39 W
Fredericton Junction	186	45.40 N	66.37 W
Frederik Hendrikeiland → Yos Sudarso, Pulau I	164	7.50 S	138.30 E
Frederiksberg, Dan.	41	55.25 N	11.34 E
Frederiksberg, Dan.	41	55.41 N	12.32 E
Frederiksborg □[6]	41	55.56 N	12.18 E
Frederiksborg ⊥	41	55.56 N	12.19 E
Frederikshåb (Paamiut)	176	62.00 N	49.43 W
Frederikshavn	26	57.26 N	10.32 E
Frederikssund	41	55.50 N	12.04 E
Frederiksted	241n	17.43 N	64.53 W
Frederiksværk	41	55.58 N	12.02 E
Frederik Willem IV Vallen ∟	250	3.28 N	57.37 W
Fredersdorf bei Berlin	54	52.31 N	13.44 E
Fredonia, Col.	246	5.55 N	75.41 W
Fredonia, Az., U.S.	200	36.03 N	112.08 W
Fredonia, Ks., U.S.	198	37.32 N	95.49 W
Fredonia, N.Y., U.S.	214	42.26 N	79.19 W
Fredonia, N.D., U.S.	198	46.19 N	99.05 W
Fredonia, Pa., U.S.	214	41.20 N	80.14 W
Fredrika	26	64.05 N	18.24 E
Fredriksberg	40	60.08 N	14.23 E
Fredrikstad	26	59.13 N	10.57 E
Freeburg, Il., U.S.	219	38.25 N	89.54 W
Freeburg, Mo., U.S.	219	38.18 N	91.55 W
Freeburg, Pa., U.S.	208	40.46 N	76.57 W
Freedom, Ca., U.S.	226	36.56 N	121.46 W
Freedom, Pa., U.S.	214	40.40 N	80.14 W
Freehold, N.J., U.S.	208	40.15 N	74.16 W
Freehold, N.Y., U.S.	210	42.22 N	74.03 W
Freeland, Mi., U.S.	190	43.31 N	84.07 W
Freeland, Pa., U.S.	210	41.01 N	75.53 W
Freeland, Wa., U.S.	224	48.01 N	122.32 W
Freeland Park	216	40.37 N	87.30 W
Freeling, Mount ∧	162	22.35 S	133.06 E
Freel Peak ∧	226	38.52 N	119.54 W
Freels, Cape ›, Nf., Can.	186	49.15 N	53.28 W
Freels, Cape ›, Nf., Can.	186	46.37 N	53.33 W
Freeman	198	43.21 N	97.26 W
Freeman ≃	182	54.20 N	114.47 W
Freeman, Lake ⊜	216	40.42 N	86.45 W
Freemansburg	210	40.37 N	75.20 W
Freemount	48	52.16 N	8.53 W
Freeport, Ba.	238	26.30 N	78.45 W
Freeport, N.S., Can.	186	44.17 N	66.19 W
Freeport, On., Can.	212	43.25 N	80.25 W
Freeport, Fl., U.S.	194	30.29 N	86.08 W
Freeport, Il., U.S.	190	42.17 N	89.37 W
Freeport, Me., U.S.	188	43.51 N	70.06 W
Freeport, Mi., U.S.	216	42.45 N	85.18 W
Freeport, N.Y., U.S.	210	40.39 N	73.35 W
Freeport, Oh., U.S.	214	40.12 N	81.15 W
Freeport, Pa., U.S.	210	40.40 N	79.41 W
Freeport, Tx., U.S.	222	28.57 N	95.21 W
Freer	196	27.52 N	98.37 W
Freest	54	54.08 N	13.43 E
Freeston	222	31.32 N	96.15 W
Freestone	171a	28.08 S	152.08 E
Freestone □[6]	222	31.44 N	96.10 W
Freetown, Antig.	240c	17.03 N	61.42 W
Freetown, S.L.	150	8.30 N	13.15 W
Freetown, In., U.S.	218	38.58 N	86.07 W
Freetown, N.Y., U.S.	207	40.58 N	72.11 W
Freeville	210	42.30 N	76.20 W
Freewood Acres	208	40.10 N	74.15 W
Freezeout Lake ⊜	202	47.40 N	112.03 W
Fregenal de la Sierra	34	38.10 N	6.39 W
Fregene ◆[8]	66	41.51 N	12.12 E
Freiberg	54	50.54 N	13.20 E
Freiberger Mulde ≃	54	51.10 N	12.48 E
Freiburg → Fribourg	58	46.48 N	7.09 E
Freiburg □[5]	58	48.00 N	8.25 E
Freiburg an der Elbe	52	53.49 N	9.17 E
Freiburg im Breisgau	58	47.59 N	7.51 E
Freienbach	58	47.12 N	8.45 E
Freienhufen	54	51.35 N	13.58 E
Freie Universität ʊ[2]	264a	52.26 N	13.16 E
Freigericht	56	50.08 N	9.07 E
Freihung	60	49.37 N	11.55 E
Freiland	61	47.58 N	15.34 E
Freilassing	64	47.50 N	12.59 E
Freilingen	56	50.33 N	7.50 E
Freinberg	60	48.34 N	13.31 E
Freinsheim	56	49.30 N	8.13 E
Freirina	252	28.30 S	71.06 W
Freisen	56	49.33 N	7.14 E
Freisenbruch ◆[8]	263	51.27 N	7.06 E
Freising	60	48.23 N	11.44 E
Freistadt	61	48.31 N	14.31 E
Freital	54	51.00 N	13.39 E
Freiwalde	54	51.58 N	13.44 E
Freixial	266c	38.54 N	9.09 W
Fréjus	62	43.26 N	6.44 E
Fréjus, Tunnel du ◆[5]	62	45.08 N	6.40 E
Frémainville	261	49.04 N	1.52 E
Fremantle	168a	32.03 S	115.45 E
Fremdingen	56	48.58 N	10.27 E
Fremington	42	51.04 N	4.07 W
Fremont, Ca., U.S.	226	37.32 N	121.59 W
Fremont, In., U.S.	216	41.43 N	84.55 W
Fremont, Ia., U.S.	190	41.12 N	92.26 W
Fremont, Mi., U.S.	190	43.28 N	85.56 W
Fremont, Ne., U.S.	198	41.26 N	96.29 W
Fremont, N.C., U.S.	192	35.32 N	77.58 W
Fremont, Oh., U.S.	214	41.21 N	83.07 W
Fremont, Wi., U.S.	190	44.15 N	88.51 W
Fremont ≃	200	38.24 N	110.42 W
Fremont Canyon V	280	33.48 N	117.42 W
Fremont Island I	200	41.09 N	112.20 W
Fremont Lake ⊜	202	42.57 N	109.49 W
Fremont Peak ∧, Ca., U.S.	226	36.46 N	121.30 W
Fremont Peak ∧, Ca., U.S.	228	35.12 N	117.27 W
Fremont Valley V	228	35.10 N	118.00 W
French ≃	190	45.56 N	80.54 W
French Broad ≃	192	35.57 N	83.51 W
Frenchburg	192	37.57 N	83.37 W
French Camp	226	37.53 N	121.16 W
Frenchcap Cay I	240m	18.14 N	64.51 W
French Creek ≃, Mb., Can.	184	57.02 N	92.12 W
French Creek ≃, U.S.	214	41.25 N	79.50 W
French Creek ≃, Oh., U.S.	279a	41.27 N	82.07 W
French Creek ≃, Pa., U.S.	208	40.08 N	75.31 W
French Creek ≃, S.D., U.S.	198	43.38 N	102.55 W
French Creek, South Branch ≃, Pa., U.S.	214	41.54 N	79.54 W
French Creek, South Branch ≃, Pa., U.S.	285	40.10 N	75.42 W
French Creek, West Branch ≃	214	41.58 N	79.52 W
French Creek State Park ♠	208	40.13 N	75.47 W
French Frigate Shoals ✢[2]	14	23.45 N	166.10 W
French Guiana (Guyane français) □[2], S.A.	242	4.00 N	53.00 W
French Guiana (Guyane français) □[2], S.A.	250	4.00 N	53.00 W
French Island I	169	38.21 S	145.21 E
French Lick	194	38.32 N	86.37 W
Frenchman (Frenchman Creek) ≃	202	48.24 N	107.05 W
Frenchman Bay ⊂	188	44.25 N	68.10 W
Frenchman Butte	184	53.35 N	109.38 W
Frenchman Creek (Frenchman) ≃, N.A.	202	48.24 N	107.05 W
Frenchman Creek ≃, U.S.	198	40.13 N	100.50 W
Frenchman Lake ⊜	204	36.48 N	116.56 W
Frenchman Point ›	212	44.35 N	81.18 W
Frenchman's Bay ⊂	275b	43.49 N	79.05 W
Frenchmans Cap ∧	166	42.16 S	145.50 E
Frenchman's Creek ≃, On., Can.	284a	42.56 N	78.56 W
Frenchmans Creek ≃, Ca., U.S.	282	37.29 N	122.27 W
French Meadows Reservoir ⊜[1]	226	39.07 N	120.25 W
Frenchpark	48	53.52 N	8.26 W
French Pass	172	40.56 S	173.50 E
French Polynesia □[2]	14	15.00 S	140.00 W
Frenchs Forest	274a	33.45 S	151.14 E
French Southern and Antarctic Territories □[2]	6	49.30 S	69.30 E
French Stream ≃	283	42.07 N	70.53 W
Frenchtown	210	40.31 N	75.03 W
Frenda	148	35.02 N	1.01 E
Freneuse	261	49.03 N	1.36 E
Frensdorferhaar	52	52.25 N	7.03 E
Frenštát pod Radhoštěm	30	49.33 N	18.14 E
Frentani, Monti dei ⩘	66	41.54 N	14.37 E
Frépillon	261	49.03 N	2.12 E
Frere	158	28.52 S	29.47 E
Freren	52	52.29 N	7.32 E
Fresco	150	5.05 N	5.34 W
Fresco ≃	250	6.39 S	51.59 W
Freshfield	262	53.34 N	3.04 W
Freshfield, Mount ∧	182	51.44 N	116.57 W
Freshford	48	52.43 N	7.24 W
Fresh Meadows ◆[8]	276	40.44 N	73.48 W
Fresh Pond ⊜, Ma., U.S.	283	42.23 N	71.09 W
Fresh Pond ⊜, N.Y., U.S.	276	40.55 N	73.18 W
Freshwater	42	50.40 N	1.30 W
Freshwater Creek ≃	226	39.12 N	122.04 W
Fresia	254	41.09 S	73.27 W
Fresnes	261	48.45 N	2.19 E
Fresne-Saint-Mamès	58	47.33 N	5.52 E
Fresnes-en-Woëvre	56	49.08 N	5.39 E
Fresnes-sur-Escaut	50	50.26 N	3.35 E
Fresnes-sur-Marne	261	48.56 N	2.45 E
Fresnillo	234	23.10 N	102.53 W
Fresno, Col.	246	5.09 N	75.01 W
Fresno, Ca., U.S.	226	36.44 N	119.46 W
Fresno, Oh., U.S.	214	40.20 N	81.44 W
Fresno, Tx., U.S.	222	29.32 N	95.27 W
Fresno □[6]	226	36.38 N	119.45 W
Fresno ≃	226	37.05 N	120.33 W
Fresno, Lewis Fork ≃	226	37.20 N	119.39 W
Fresno Air Terminal ⊠	226	36.46 N	119.43 W
Fresno Reservoir ⊜[1]	202	48.41 N	109.57 W
Fresno Slough ≃	226	36.47 N	120.22 W
Fresnoy-Folny	50	49.53 N	1.26 E
Fresnoy-le-Grand	50	49.57 N	3.25 E
Fressenneville	50	50.04 N	1.34 E
Fressin	50	50.27 N	2.03 E
Freswick	46	58.35 N	3.05 W
Fréteval	50	47.53 N	1.13 E
Frétigney-et-Velloreille	58	47.29 N	5.56 E
Fretin	50	50.33 N	3.08 E
Frettes	58	47.41 N	5.34 E
Freu, Cap des ›	34	39.45 N	3.27 E
Freudenberg, Dtsch.	56	49.44 N	9.19 E
Freudenberg, Dtsch.	56	50.54 N	7.52 E
Freudenberg, Dtsch.	264a	52.42 N	13.49 E
Freudenstadt	58	48.28 N	8.25 E
Frévent	50	50.16 N	2.17 E
Frew ≃	162	20.00 S	135.38 E
Frewena	162	19.25 S	135.25 E
Frewsburg	214	42.03 N	79.09 W
Freyburg	54	51.13 N	11.46 E
Freycinet, Cape ›	162	34.06 S	114.59 E
Freycinet Estuary ⊂[1]	162	26.25 S	113.45 E
Freycinet National Park ♠	166	42.10 S	148.20 E
Freycinet Peninsula ›[1]	166	42.13 S	148.18 E
Freyenstein	54	53.17 N	12.20 E
Freyming-Merlebach	56	49.09 N	6.48 E
Freyre	252	31.10 S	62.06 W
Freystadt	60	49.12 N	11.20 E
Freyung	60	48.48 N	13.33 E
Fria	150	10.05 N	13.32 W
Fria, Cape ›	152	18.30 S	12.01 E
Friant	226	36.59 N	119.42 W
Friant Dam ◆[6]	226	37.00 N	119.43 W
Friant-Kern Canal ≚	226	35.22 N	119.06 W
Friars Point	194	34.22 N	90.38 W
Frías, Arg.	252	28.39 S	65.09 W
Frías, Perú	248	4.52 S	79.57 W
Fribourg (Freiburg)	58	46.48 N	7.09 E
Fribourg (Freiburg) □[3]	58	46.45 N	7.05 E
Frick	58	47.31 N	8.01 E
Frick Park ♠	279b	40.26 N	79.54 W
Friday	222	31.07 N	95.15 W
Friday Harbor	224	48.32 N	123.00 W
Fridaythorpe	44	54.01 N	0.40 W
Fridingen an der Donau	58	48.01 N	8.56 E
Fridley	190	45.05 N	93.15 W
Fridolfing	60	48.00 N	12.49 E
Fridtjof Nansen, Mount ∧	9	85.21 S	167.33 W
Friedberg, Dtsch.	56	50.20 N	8.45 E
Friedberg, Dtsch.	58	48.21 N	10.58 E
Friedberg, Öst.	61	47.27 N	16.03 E
Friedeburg [/Saale]	54	51.37 N	11.44 E
Friedenau ◆[8]	264a	52.28 N	13.20 E
Friedens	214	40.03 N	79.00 W
Friedensburg	208	40.36 N	76.14 W
Friedersdorf, Dtsch.	54	52.17 N	13.47 E
Friedersdorf, Dtsch.	54	51.01 N	14.34 E
Friedersdorf, Dtsch.	54	51.39 N	12.21 E
Friedesheim	158	27.55 S	26.43 E
Friedland, Dtsch.	54	52.06 N	14.16 E
Friedland, Dtsch.	54	53.40 N	13.33 E
Friedland, Dtsch.	56	51.25 N	9.55 E
Friedrich-Ebert-Brücke ◆[5]	263	51.28 N	6.43 E
Friedrich Krupp-Aktiengesellschaft ʊ[3]	263	51.28 N	7.00 E
Friedrichroda	54	50.52 N	10.34 E
Friedrichsbrunn	54	51.41 N	11.02 E
Friedrichsdorf	56	50.15 N	8.38 E
Friedrichsfeld	263	51.38 N	6.39 E
Friedrichsfelde ◆[8]	264a	52.31 N	13.31 E
Friedrichshafen	58	47.39 N	9.28 E
Friedrichshagen ◆[8]	264a	52.27 N	13.38 E
Friedrichshain ◆[8]	264a	52.31 N	13.25 E
Friedrichshof	264a	52.19 N	13.46 E
Friedrichsort ◆[8]	54	54.24 N	10.11 E
Friedrichsruh, Schloss ⊥	52	53.32 N	10.20 E
Friedrichsruhe	54	53.31 N	11.45 E
Friedrichstadt	41	54.22 N	9.05 E
Friedrichsthal, Dtsch.	54	52.48 N	13.16 E
Friedrichsthal, Dtsch.	56	49.19 N	7.06 E
Friedrichstrasse, Bahnhof ◆[5]	264a	52.31 N	13.24 E
Friedrichswalde	54	53.02 N	13.42 E
Frielas	266c	38.49 N	9.09 W
Frielendorf	56	50.58 N	9.19 E
Friemersheim ◆[8]	263	51.23 N	6.42 E
Friend, Ne., U.S.	198	40.39 N	97.17 W
Friend, Or., U.S.	224	45.21 N	121.16 W
Friends Colony ◆[8]	272a	28.34 N	77.16 E
Friendship, N.Y., U.S.	210	42.12 N	78.08 W
Friendship, Tn., U.S.	194	35.54 N	89.14 W
Friendship, Wi., U.S.	190	43.58 N	89.49 W
Friendship Creek ≃	285	39.55 N	74.43 W
Friendship Shoal ✢[2]	112	5.58 N	112.31 E
Friends Meeting House State Memorial ⊥	214	40.09 N	80.47 W
Friendswood	222	29.31 N	95.12 W
Friern Barnet ◆[8]	260	51.37 N	0.10 W
Fries	192	36.42 N	80.58 W
Friesach	61	46.57 N	14.24 E
Friesack	54	52.44 N	12.34 E
Friesenheim	58	48.22 N	7.53 E
Friesenhofen	58	47.45 N	10.04 E
Friesenried	58	47.52 N	10.31 E
Friesland □[4]	52	53.03 N	5.45 E
Friesland □[9]	30	53.00 N	5.40 E
Fries Mills	285	39.39 N	75.03 W
Friesoythe	52	53.01 N	7.51 E
Frigate Point ›	174g	28.11 N	177.24 W
Frigento	68	41.01 N	15.06 E
Frignano	68	41.00 N	14.10 E
Frignano ◆[1]	64	44.20 N	10.51 E
Friguia	150	12.03 N	10.56 W
Friitala	26	61.26 N	21.52 E
Frillendorf ◆[8]	263	51.28 N	7.05 E
Frindsbury	260	51.24 N	0.30 E
Frinsted	260	51.17 N	0.43 E
Frinton-on-Sea	42	51.50 N	1.14 E
Frintrop ◆[8]	263	51.29 N	6.55 E
Frío ≃, N.A.	236	11.08 N	84.46 W
Frio ≃, Tx., U.S.	196	28.30 N	98.10 W
Frio, Cabo ›	255	22.53 S	42.00 W
Friockheim	46	56.38 N	2.38 W
Frio Draw V	196	34.50 N	102.19 W
Friona	196	34.38 N	102.43 W
Frisa, Loch ⊜	46	56.34 N	6.05 W
Frisange	56	49.32 N	6.12 E
Frisches Haff → Vislinskij zaliv ⊂	30	54.27 N	19.40 E
Frisco, Pa., U.S.	214	40.51 N	80.16 W
Frisco, Tx., U.S.	222	33.09 N	96.49 W
Frisco City	194	31.26 N	87.24 W
Frisco Creek ≃	196	36.34 N	101.23 W
Frisian Islands II	30	53.35 N	6.40 E
Friskney	44	53.04 N	0.11 E
Fristad	26	57.50 N	13.01 E
Fritch	196	35.38 N	101.36 W
Fritsla	26	57.33 N	12.47 E
Fritzlar	56	51.08 N	9.16 E
Friuli □[9]	64	46.00 N	13.00 E
Friuli-Venezia Giulia □[4]	64	46.00 N	13.00 E
Friza, proliv ⊍	74	45.30 N	149.10 E
Frizington	44	54.32 N	3.30 W
Frobisher	184	49.12 N	102.26 W
Frobisher Bay ⊂	176	62.30 N	66.00 W
Frobisher Lake ⊜	184	56.25 N	108.20 W
Frodsham, Eng., U.K.	44	53.18 N	2.44 W
Frodsham, Eng., U.K.	262	53.18 N	2.44 W
Frog Lake ⊜	184	53.55 N	110.18 W
Frohavet ⊍	24	63.52 N	9.26 E
Frohburg	54	51.03 N	12.33 E
Frohlinde ◆[8]	263	51.32 N	7.21 E
Frohnau ◆[8]	264a	52.38 N	13.18 E
Frohnhausen	263	51.29 N	7.48 E
Frohnhausen ◆[8]	263	51.27 N	6.58 E
Frohnleiten	61	47.16 N	15.20 E
Frohse	54	52.02 N	11.43 E
Froid	198	48.20 N	104.30 W
Froid, Lac ⊜	206	46.40 N	74.32 W
Froid, Ruisseau ≃	206	46.23 N	74.46 W
Froidmont-Cohartille	50	49.41 N	3.42 E
Froidos	56	49.03 N	5.07 E
Froissy	50	49.34 N	2.13 E
Froitzheim	56	50.42 N	6.34 E
Frolišči, Ross.	80	56.25 N	42.39 E
Frolišči, Ross.	82	56.18 N	39.13 E
Frolovo	80	49.47 N	43.39 E
Froman Run ≃	279b	40.12 N	80.00 W
Fromberg	202	45.23 N	108.54 W
Frombork	30	54.22 N	19.41 E
Frome	42	51.14 N	2.20 W
Frome ≃, Austl.	166	29.06 S	137.52 E
Frome ≃, Eng., U.K.	42	52.03 N	2.38 W
Frome ≃, Eng., U.K.	42	50.41 N	2.04 W
Frome, Lake ⊜	166	30.48 S	139.48 E
Frome Downs	166	31.13 S	139.46 E
Fromelennes	56	50.08 N	4.52 E
Fromentières	50	48.54 N	3.43 E
Frömern	263	51.30 N	7.44 E
Frommern	58	48.15 N	8.52 E
Fröndenberg	56	51.28 N	7.46 E
Frönsberg	263	51.21 N	7.46 E
Fronteiras	250	7.05 S	40.37 W
Frontenac, Fl., U.S.	220	28.27 N	80.46 W
Frontenac, Ks., U.S.	198	37.27 N	94.41 W
Frontenac □[6], On., Can.	212	44.40 N	76.45 W
Frontenac □[6], P.Q., Can.	206	45.42 N	71.15 W
Frontenard	58	46.55 N	5.10 E
Frontenex-Villard-Rosset	62	45.38 N	6.19 E
Frontera, Méx.	232	26.56 N	101.27 W
Frontera, Méx.	234	18.32 N	92.38 W
Fronteras	200	30.56 N	109.31 W
Frontier, Sk., Can.	184	49.12 N	108.34 W
Frontier, Mi., U.S.	216	41.47 N	84.36 W
Frontier, Wy., U.S.	200	41.48 N	110.32 W
Frontignan	62	43.27 N	3.45 E
Frontino	246	6.46 N	76.08 W
Frontino, Páramo ∧	246	6.28 N	76.04 W
Frontón, Isla I	286d	12.07 S	77.11 W
Front Range ⩘, Leso.	158	29.05 S	28.20 E
Front Range ⩘, Co., U.S.	200	39.45 N	105.45 W
Front Royal	188	38.55 N	78.11 W
Frose	54	51.48 N	11.23 E
Frosinone	66	41.38 N	13.19 E
Frosinone □[4]	66	41.37 N	13.27 E
Frosolone	66	41.36 N	14.27 E
Frösön	26	63.11 N	14.32 E
Frost	222	32.05 N	96.48 W
Frostavallen	41	55.58 N	13.30 E
Frostburg	188	39.39 N	78.55 W
Frostproof	220	27.44 N	81.31 W
Frotheim	52	52.21 N	8.40 E
Frouard	56	48.46 N	6.08 E
Frövi	40	59.28 N	15.22 E
Frøya I	24	63.43 N	8.42 E
Fruges	50	50.31 N	2.08 E
Fruita	200	39.09 N	108.43 W
Fruitdale, Al., U.S.	194	31.20 N	88.24 W
Fruitdale, Or., U.S.	202	42.24 N	123.20 W
Fruithurst	194	33.43 N	85.26 W
Fruitland, Id., U.S.	202	44.00 N	116.54 W
Fruitland, Md., U.S.	208	38.19 N	75.37 W
Fruitland Park	220	28.51 N	81.54 W
Fruitport	216	43.07 N	86.09 W
Fruitvale, B.C., Can.	182	49.07 N	117.33 W
Fruitvale, Tx., U.S.	222	32.41 N	95.48 W
Fruitvale, Wa., U.S.	202	46.37 N	120.33 W
Fruitville	192	27.19 N	82.27 W
Frumușița	38	45.40 N	28.04 E
Frunze → Biškek, Kyrg.	85	42.54 N	74.36 E
Frunze, Kyrg.	85	40.07 N	71.44 E
Frunze, Ukr.	78	46.16 N	34.52 E
Frunze, Ukr.	83	48.40 N	38.45 E
Frunzivka	78	47.20 N	29.44 E
Frutal	255	20.02 S	48.55 W
Frutigen	58	46.35 N	7.39 E
Frutillar	254	41.07 S	73.03 W
Fryburg	214	41.21 N	79.26 W
Frýdek-Místek	30	49.41 N	18.22 E
Frýdlant	30	50.56 N	15.05 E
Frye	279b	40.11 N	79.56 W
Fryeburg	188	44.00 N	70.58 W
Fryerning	260	51.41 N	0.22 E
Fryingpan ≃	200	39.22 N	107.02 W
Fu ≃, Zhg.	100	29.52 N	115.28 E
Fu ≃, Zhg.	100	28.36 N	116.04 E
Fu ≃, Zhg.	102	29.59 N	106.16 E
Fua'amotu	174w	21.16 S	175.08 W
Fua'amotu International Airport ⊠	174w	21.17 S	175.08 W
Fu'an, Zhg.	100	27.08 N	119.40 E
Fu'an, Zhg.	100	32.41 N	120.41 E
Fuanjie	100	25.29 N	117.53 E
Fubao	107	28.47 N	106.05 E
Fubine	62	44.58 N	8.26 E
Fucecchio	66	43.44 N	10.48 E
Fuchang	100	30.06 N	113.08 E
Fucheng	98	37.52 N	116.07 E
Fuchikou	100	29.51 N	115.27 E
Fuchow → Fuzhou	100	28.01 N	116.20 E
Fuchs-Berg ∧[2]	264a	52.27 N	13.51 E
Fuchskaute ∧	56	50.40 N	8.06 E
Füchtorf	52	52.03 N	8.02 E
Fuchū, Nihon	94	35.40 N	139.29 E
Fuchū, Nihon	94	36.39 N	137.10 E
Fuchū, Nihon	96	34.24 N	132.30 E
Fuchū, Nihon	96	34.34 N	133.14 E
Fuchun ≃	106	30.10 N	120.09 E
Fucine	64	46.18 N	10.44 E
Fucino, Conca del ≚	66	42.01 N	13.31 E
Fudan University ʊ[2]	269b	31.17 N	121.29 E
Fuday I	46	57.03 N	7.23 W
Fuding	100	27.21 N	120.12 E
Fudu ≃	107	29.52 N	106.10 E
Fuefuki ≃	94	35.33 N	138.28 E
Fuego, Volcán de ∧[1]	236	14.29 N	90.53 W
Fuelbeckestausee ⊜[1]	263	51.15 N	7.40 E
Fuencaliente	34	38.24 N	4.18 W
Fuencarral ◆[8]	266a	40.30 N	3.41 W
Fuenlabrada	266a	40.17 N	3.48 W
Fuensalida	34	40.03 N	4.12 W
Fuensanta, Embalse de ⊜[1]	34	38.23 N	2.13 W
Fuente	196	28.40 N	100.32 W
Fuente de Cantos	34	38.15 N	6.18 W
Fuente de Oro	246	3.28 N	73.37 W
Fuenteobejuna	34	38.16 N	5.25 W
Fuentesaúco	34	41.14 N	5.30 W
Fuentes de Ebro	34	41.31 N	0.38 W
Fuerli	105	39.40 N	116.41 E
Fuerte ≃	232	25.54 N	109.22 W
Fuerte Olimpo	248	21.02 S	57.54 W
Fuerteventura I	148	28.20 N	14.00 W
Fuerza, Castillo de la ⊥	286b	23.09 N	82.21 W
Fufeng	102	34.20 N	107.51 E
Fuga Island I	116	18.52 N	121.22 E
Fugama, Wādī V	140	14.43 N	24.36 E
Fügen	64	47.21 N	11.51 E
Fuglebjerg	41	55.18 N	11.34 E
Fugløysund ⊍	24	70.12 N	20.20 E
Fugong	102	27.09 N	98.52 E
Fugou	98	34.04 N	114.24 E
Fuhai	86	47.06 N	87.23 E
Fuhe	100	23.22 N	113.37 E
Fuhlenbrock ◆[8]	263	51.32 N	6.54 E
Fuhrberg	52	52.34 N	9.50 E
Fuhse ≃	52	52.37 N	10.03 E
Fuhsien → Fuxian	98	39.37 N	122.01 E
Fuhu	100	29.11 N	118.04 E
Fuji, Nihon	94	35.09 N	138.39 E
Fuji, Zhg.	98	34.24 N	114.48 E
Fuji, Zhg.	107	29.09 N	105.23 E
Fuji ≃	94	35.07 N	138.39 E
Fuji, Mount → Fuji-san ∧[1]	94	35.22 N	138.44 E
Fujiafeng	105	39.11 N	117.32 E
Fujian (Fukien) □[4]	100	26.00 N	118.00 E
Fujiatun	104	41.42 N	123.44 E
Fujiawopu	104	40.58 N	122.14 E
Fujiazhen	107	29.57 N	104.18 E
Fujiazhuangcun	104	41.15 N	122.20 E
Fujie	106	31.09 N	119.27 E
Fujieda	94	34.52 N	138.16 E
Fuji-Hakone-Izu-kokuritsu-kōen ♠	94	35.21 N	138.44 E
Fujiidera	96	34.34 N	135.36 E
Fujikawa	94	35.08 N	138.37 E
Fujikubo	268	35.50 N	139.32 E
Fujimi, Nihon	94	36.27 N	139.05 E
Fujimi, Nihon	94	35.55 N	138.15 E
Fujimi, Nihon	94	35.51 N	139.33 E
Fujin	89	47.14 N	132.00 E
Fujino	94	35.37 N	139.10 E
Fujinomiya	94	35.12 N	138.38 E
Fujioka, Nihon	94	35.12 N	137.12 E
Fujioka, Nihon	94	36.15 N	139.05 E
Fujioka, Nihon	94	36.15 N	139.39 E
Fuji-san ∧[1]	94	35.22 N	138.44 E
Fujisawa	94	35.21 N	139.29 E
Fujishiro	94	35.55 N	140.07 E
Fujiwara, Nihon	94	35.09 N	136.30 E
Fujiwara, Nihon	94	36.51 N	139.44 E
Fujiwara-dam ◆[6]	94	36.49 N	139.02 E
Fujiyama → Fuji-san ∧[1]	94	35.22 N	138.44 E
Fuji-yoshida	94	35.29 N	138.48 E
Fukagawa	92a	43.43 N	142.03 E
Fukagawa ◆[8]	268	35.40 N	139.48 E
Fukami	268	35.28 N	139.28 E
Fukane I	174w	21.05 S	175.02 W
Fukang	86	44.10 N	87.59 E
Fukasaka-tunnel ◆[5]	94	35.35 N	136.10 E
Fuka Shan ∧	89	47.55 N	120.53 E
Fukaya	94	36.12 N	139.17 E
Fukiage	94	36.06 N	139.27 E
Fukiai ◆[8]	270	34.42 N	135.12 E
Fukien → Fujian □[4]	100	26.00 N	118.00 E
Fukou, Zhg.	100	25.45 N	118.28 E
Fukou, Zhg.	100	26.28 N	117.40 E
Fukube	96	35.33 N	134.18 E
Fukuchiyama	96	35.18 N	135.07 E
Fukude	94	34.40 N	137.53 E
Fukue	92	32.41 N	128.50 E
Fukuei Chiao ›	100	25.18 N	121.32 E
Fukue-jima I	92	32.40 N	128.45 E
Fukui, Nihon	94	36.04 N	136.13 E
Fukui, Nihon	270	34.51 N	135.34 E
Fukui □[5]	92	36.00 N	136.15 E
Fukuma	96	33.46 N	130.28 E
Fukumitsu	94	36.33 N	136.52 E
Fukuno	94	36.35 N	136.55 E
Fukuoka, Nihon	94	35.34 N	137.27 E
Fukuoka, Nihon	94	36.42 N	136.56 E
Fukuoka, Nihon	96	33.35 N	130.24 E
Fukuoka □[5]	96	33.45 N	130.30 E
Fukuoka-chūtonchi, Rikujō-jieitai- ■	96	33.32 N	130.28 E
Fukuroda-no-taki ∟	94	36.46 N	140.25 E
Fukuroi	94	34.45 N	137.55 E
Fukushima, Nihon	92	37.45 N	140.28 E
Fukushima, Nihon	92a	41.29 N	140.15 E
Fukushima □[5]	94	37.08 N	140.00 E
Fukushima ◆[8]	270	34.42 N	135.29 E
Fukusumi	270	34.37 N	135.56 E
Fukutani ◆[8]	270	34.43 N	135.02 E
Fukuyama	96	34.29 N	133.22 E
Fukuzaki	96	34.57 N	134.45 E
Fulacunda	150	11.44 N	15.03 W
Fūlādī, Kūh-e ∧	120	34.38 N	67.32 E
Fūlād Maḥalleh	128	36.02 N	53.44 E
Fulanga Island I	175g	19.08 S	178.34 W
Fulanga Passage ⊍	175g	19.00 S	178.40 W
Fulbourn	42	52.11 N	0.13 E
Fulda, Dtsch.	56	50.33 N	9.41 E
Fulda, Mn., U.S.	198	43.52 N	95.36 W
Fulda ≃	30	51.25 N	9.39 E
Fuldatal	56	51.22 N	9.31 E
Fuldera	58	46.37 N	10.22 E
Fule	102	25.27 N	104.19 E
Fulerum ◆[8]	263	51.26 N	6.57 E
Fulford Harbour	224	48.46 N	123.27 W
Fulgatore	70	37.57 N	12.42 E
Fulham ◆[8]	260	51.29 N	0.12 W
Fuli	100	23.11 N	121.14 E
Fuliji	100	33.46 N	116.58 E
Fuling	102	29.42 N	107.21 E
Fulitun	89	46.42 N	131.10 E
Fullarton ≃	166	20.15 S	141.10 E
Fullen ⊜	40	60.31 N	16.09 E
Fuller Springs	222	31.18 N	94.41 W
Fullerton, Ca., U.S.	228	33.52 N	117.55 W
Fullerton, Ky., U.S.	218	38.43 N	82.58 W
Fullerton, Md., U.S.	284b	39.22 N	76.31 W
Fullerton, Ne., U.S.	198	41.21 N	97.58 W
Fullerton, Pa., U.S.	208	40.38 N	75.28 W
Fullerton Municipal Airport ⊠	280	33.52 N	117.59 W
Fullerton Point ›	240c	17.06 N	61.54 W
Fulmer	260	51.33 N	0.34 W
Fulong	102	22.57 N	107.41 E
Fulongchang	107	30.03 N	103.38 E
Fulongquan	89	44.22 N	124.36 E
Fulpmes	64	47.10 N	11.21 E
Fulshear	222	29.41 N	95.54 W
Fulton, Al., U.S.	194	31.47 N	87.43 W
Fulton, Ar., U.S.	194	33.36 N	93.48 W
Fulton, Il., U.S.	190	41.52 N	90.09 W
Fulton, In., U.S.	216	40.56 N	86.15 W
Fulton, Ks., U.S.	198	38.00 N	94.43 W
Fulton, Ky., U.S.	194	36.30 N	88.52 W
Fulton, Md., U.S.	208	39.09 N	76.55 W
Fulton, Mi., U.S.	216	47.17 N	88.21 W
Fulton, Ms., U.S.	194	34.16 N	88.24 W
Fulton, Mo., U.S.	219	38.50 N	91.56 W
Fulton, N.Y., U.S.	210	43.19 N	76.25 W
Fulton, Oh., U.S.	214	40.27 N	82.49 W
Fulton, Tx., U.S.	196	28.04 N	97.02 W
Fulton □[6], Il., U.S.	219	40.13 N	90.17 W
Fulton □[6], In., U.S.	216	41.04 N	86.13 W
Fulton □[6], N.Y., U.S.	210	43.00 N	74.22 W
Fulton □[6], Oh., U.S.	216	41.33 N	84.09 W
Fulton □[6], Pa., U.S.	214	40.06 N	78.04 W
Fulton ≃	182	54.48 N	126.07 W
Fultondale	194	33.36 N	86.47 W
Fultonham	210	42.31 N	75.03 W
Fultonville	210	42.57 N	74.22 W
Fuluchang	107	29.38 N	106.08 E
Fulufjället ∧	26	61.33 N	12.43 E
Fuluzhen	107	29.18 N	103.40 E
Fulwood	44	53.47 N	2.41 W
Fumaça	256	22.17 S	44.19 W
Fumahashi	94	36.42 N	137.19 E
Fumane	156	24.29 S	33.58 E
Fumay	56	49.59 N	4.42 E
Fumel	32	44.29 N	0.57 E
Fumin, Zhg.	102	25.16 N	102.26 E
Fumin, Zhg.	106	31.54 N	121.10 E
Fumintun	98	42.29 N	126.22 E
Fuminzhen	106	31.37 N	121.39 E
Funa ≃	273b	4.23 S	15.19 E
Funabashi	94	35.42 N	139.59 E
Funafuti I	14	8.31 S	179.13 E
Funagawa → Oga	92	39.53 N	139.51 E
Funakuyā	175d	24.30 N	124.17 E
Funan	100	32.39 N	115.32 E
Funan Gaba	144	4.25 N	37.57 E
Funaoka	96	35.23 N	134.14 E
Funasaka	270	34.48 N	135.17 E
Funäsdalen	26	62.32 N	12.33 E
Funchal	148	32.38 N	16.54 W
Funchal □[5]	148	32.40 N	16.55 W
Fundación	246	10.31 N	74.11 W
Fundão	34	40.08 N	7.30 W
Fundão, Ilha do I	287a	22.51 S	43.14 W
Funde	272c	18.54 N	72.58 E
Fundo ≃	250	10.12 S	44.39 W
Fundo, Arroio ≃	287a	22.58 S	43.22 W
Fundy, Bay of ⊂	186	45.00 N	66.00 W
Fundy National Park ♠	186	45.38 N	65.00 W
Fünfkirchen → Pécs	30	46.05 N	18.13 E
Funhalouro	156	23.03 S	34.25 E
Funil, Represa do ⊜[1]	256	22.33 S	44.35 W
Funil, Ribeirão do ≃	256	22.02 S	43.46 W
Funil, Rio do ≃	256	22.58 S	44.34 W
Funing, Zhg.	98	39.54 N	119.14 E
Funing, Zhg.	100	33.47 N	119.48 E
Funing, Zhg.	102	23.33 N	105.35 E
Funiuchang	107	29.03 N	106.33 E
Funiu Shan ⩘	100	33.40 N	112.30 E
Funk Island I	186	49.46 N	53.10 W
Funks Creek ≃	226	39.19 N	122.11 W
Funkturm ʊ	264a	52.31 N	13.16 E
Funne ≃	263	51.42 N	7.36 E
Funnel Creek ≃	166	22.18 S	148.57 E
Funnel Hill ∧[2]	272c	18.54 N	73.07 E
Funo	96	34.53 N	132.47 E
Funshinagh, Lough ⊜	48	53.31 N	8.07 W
Funsi	150	10.17 N	1.58 W
Funtana Coberta ⊥	71	39.34 N	9.21 E
Funtua	150	11.31 N	7.17 E
Funza	246	4.40 N	74.09 W
Fuorn, Pass dal (Ofenpass))(	58	46.37 N	10.15 E
Fuping	102	34.47 N	109.07 E
Fuqiao	106	31.36 N	121.12 E
Fuqikou	100	29.44 N	117.48 E
Fuqing	100	25.44 N	119.22 E
Fuquay-Varina	192	35.35 N	78.48 W
Füramoos	58	48.00 N	9.53 E
Furancungo	154	14.55 S	33.35 E
Furano	92a	43.21 N	142.24 E
Furāt, Nahr al- → Euphrates ≃	128	31.00 N	47.25 E
Furci Siculo	70	37.57 N	15.23 E
Furculești	38	43.52 N	25.09 E
Fures	62	45.19 N	5.30 E
Fūrg	128	28.18 N	55.13 E
Furkapass)(	58	46.34 N	8.25 E
Furka-Tunnel ◆[5]	58	46.33 N	8.26 E
Furlong	208	40.18 N	75.05 W
Furmanov	80	57.15 N	41.07 E
Furmanovka	86	44.17 N	72.57 E
Furmanovo	80	49.42 N	49.28 E
Furn, Wādī al- V	142	30.13 N	31.40 E
Furnace	46	56.09 N	5.10 W
Furnace Brook ≃	283	42.06 N	70.43 W
Furnace Creek ≃	284b	39.11 N	76.35 W
Furnace Pond ⊜	283	42.03 N	70.49 W
Furnari	70	38.07 N	15.08 E
Furnas, Represa de ⊜[1]	255	20.45 S	46.00 W
Furn ash-Shubbāk	132	33.52 N	35.31 E
Furneaux Group II	166	40.10 S	148.05 E
Furnes → Veurne	50	51.04 N	2.40 E
Furness Abbey ʊ[1]	44	54.07 N	3.12 W
Furness Fells ⩘[2]	44	54.18 N	3.07 W
Furong Shan ∧	100	27.30 N	115.52 E
Furqlus	130	34.36 N	37.05 E
Fürstenau, Dtsch.	52	52.31 N	7.40 E
Fürstenau, Dtsch.	52	51.50 N	9.19 E
Fürstenberg, Dtsch.	52	51.44 N	9.24 E
Fürstenberg, Dtsch.	54	52.09 N	14.40 E
Fürstenberg/Havel	54	53.11 N	13.08 E
Fürstenfeld	61	47.03 N	16.05 E
Fürstenfeldbruck	60	48.10 N	11.15 E
Fürstenhagen	56	51.12 N	9.41 E
Fürstenstein	60	48.43 N	13.20 E
Fürstenwalde	54	52.21 N	14.04 E
Fürstenwerder	54	53.24 N	13.34 E
Fürstenzell	60	48.32 N	13.19 E
Furtei	71	39.34 N	8.57 E
Fürth, Dtsch.	56	49.28 N	10.59 E
Fürth, Dtsch.	56	49.39 N	8.47 E
Furth im Wald	60	49.18 N	12.51 E
Furtwangen	58	48.03 N	8.12 E
Furuba ≃	256	23.21 S	44.57 W
Furubō-san ∧[2]	270	34.53 N	135.19 E
Furudal	26	61.10 N	15.08 E
Furudono	94	37.05 N	140.34 E

Symbols in the index entries represent the broad categories identified in the key at the right. Symbols with superior numbers (⩘[1]) identify subcategories (see complete key on page *I · 1).*

Symbole im Register stellen die rechts im Schlüssel erklärten Kategorien dar. Symbole mit hochgestellten Ziffern (⩘[1]) bezeichnen Unterabteilungen einer Kategorie (vgl. vollständiger Schlüssel auf Seite *I · 1).*

Los símbolos incluídos en el texto del índice representan las grandes categorías identificadas con la clave a la derecha. Los símbolos con numeros en su parte superior (⩘[1]) identifican las subcategorías (véase la clave completa en la página *I · 1).*

Les symboles de l'index représentent les catégories indiquées dans la légende à droite. Les symboles suivis d'un indice (⩘[1]) représentent des sous-catégories (voir légende complète à la page *I · 1).*

Os símbolos incluídos no texto do índice representam as grandes categorias identificadas com a chave à direita. Os símbolos com números em sua parte superior (⩘[1]) identificam as subcategorias (veja-se a chave completa à página *I · 1).*

	English	Deutsch	Español	Français	Português
∧	Mountain	Berg	Montaña	Montagne	Montanha
⩘	Mountains	Gebirge	Montañas	Montagnes	Montanhas
)(	Pass	Paß	Paso	Col	Passo
V	Valley, Canyon	Tal, Cañon	Valle, Cañón	Vallée, Canyon	Vale, Canhão
≚	Plain	Ebene	Llano	Plaine	Planície
›	Cape	Kap	Cabo	Cap	Cabo
I	Island	Insel	Isla	Île	Ilha
II	Islands	Inseln	Islas	Îles	Ilhas
⊥	Other Topographic Features	Andere Topographische Objekte	Otros Elementos Topográficos	Autres données topographiques	Outros acidentes topográficos

ESPAÑOL — Nombre / Página / Lat.°′ / Long.°′ W = Oeste
FRANÇAIS — Nom / Page / Lat.°′ / Long.°′ W = Ouest
PORTUGUÊS — Nome / Página / Lat.°′ / Long.°′ W = Oeste

Furukawa, Nihon 92 38.34 N 140.58 E
Furukawa, Nihon 94 36.14 N 137.11 E
Furulund 41 55.46 N 13.04 E
Furusund 40 59.40 N 18.55 E
Furu-tone ≐ 94 35.48 N 139.51 E
Furuvik 40 60.39 N 17.20 E
Furuyakami 268 35.55 N 139.32 E
Fürwiggestausee ◎[1] 263 51.09 N 7.41 E
Fury and Hecla Strait ⊭ 176 69.56 N 84.00 W
Fusagasugá 246 4.21 N 74.22 W
Fusain ≐ 50 48.09 N 2.45 E
Fusan
— Pusan 98 35.06 N 129.03 E
Fuscaldo 68 39.25 N 16.02 E
Fusch 64 47.13 N 12.49 E
Fuschl am See 64 47.48 N 13.18 E
Fuschun
— Fushun 104 41.52 N 123.53 E
Fuse
— Higashiōsaka, Nihon 96 34.39 N 135.35 E
Fuse, Nihon 268 35.53 N 140.00 E
Fushan, Zhg. 98 37.29 N 121.16 E
Fushan, Zhg. 102 35.58 N 111.51 E
Fushan, Zhg. 106 31.49 N 120.46 E
Fushimi ✦[8] 270 34.55 N 135.46 E
Fushino ≐ 96 34.03 N 131.24 E
Fushuigang 100 31.21 N 113.40 E
Fushun (Funan), Zhg. 104 41.52 N 123.53 E
Fushun, Zhg. 107 29.11 N 105.00 E
Fushuncheng 104 41.53 N 123.51 E
Fusignano 66 44.28 N 11.57 E
Fusilier 184 51.51 N 109.46 W
Fusin
— Fuxin 104 42.03 N 121.46 E
Fusine in Valromana 64 46.30 N 13.39 E
Fusio 58 46.27 N 8.40 E
Fusō 94 35.21 N 136.55 E
Fusong 98 42.18 N 127.20 E
Fussa 94 35.45 N 139.20 E
Füssen 64 47.34 N 10.42 E
Fuste, Picacho del ∧ 196 27.35 N 102.47 W
Fusui 102 22.32 N 107.56 E
Futa, Passo della)(66 44.05 N 11.17 E
Futaba 94 35.41 N 138.30 E
Futago-san ∧ 96 33.35 N 131.36 E
Futamata
— Tenryū 94 34.52 N 137.49 E
Futamatagawa ✦[8] 268 35.28 N 139.33 E
Futami, Nihon 94 34.30 N 136.47 E
Futami, Nihon 96 33.41 N 132.38 E
Futang, Zhg. 102 24.26 N 112.09 E
Futang, Zhg. 106 30.40 N 119.35 E
Futaoi-jima I 96 34.06 N 130.47 E
Futatabi-yama ∧ 270 34.43 N 135.11 E
Futatsubashi ✦[8] 268 35.28 N 139.30 E
Futatsu-ne I[2] 174f 24.46 N 141.18 E
Fu Tau Pun Chau I 271d 22.21 N 114.22 E
Futian 100 27.26 N 114.56 E
Futianhe 100 31.30 N 115.05 E
Futianpu 100 27.22 N 112.47 E
Futjāni ≐ 126 24.06 N 90.09 E
Futschou
— Fuzhou 100 26.06 N 119.17 E
Futtsu, Nihon 94 35.19 N 139.49 E
Futtsu, Nihon 94 35.13 N 139.52 E
Futtsu-misaki > 268 35.19 N 139.46 E
Futun ≐ 100 26.51 N 117.46 E
Futuna I 175f 19.32 S 170.14 E
Futuna, Île I 14 14.15 S 178.09 W
Futuyu 105 39.18 N 114.50 E
Fuveau 62 43.27 N 5.34 E
Fuwah 142 31.12 N 30.33 E
Fuwen 86 47.13 N 89.39 E
Fuxi, Zhg. 100 27.14 N 119.50 E
Fuxi, Zhg. 100 25.14 N 113.52 E
Fuxi ≐ 107 29.09 N 104.57 E
Fuxian (Wafangdian), Zhg. 98 39.37 N 122.01 E
Fuxian, Zhg. 102 36.02 N 109.13 E
Fuxian Hu ◎ 102 24.30 N 102.55 E
Fuxin, Zhg. 104 42.03 N 121.46 E
Fuxin, Zhg. 104 42.08 N 121.45 E
Fuxing, Zhg. 107 30.27 N 106.04 E
Fuxing, Zhg. 107 30.24 N 104.53 E
Fuxing, Zhg. 107 29.54 N 105.43 E
Fuxingchang 107 29.40 N 105.13 E
Fuxing Dao I 269b 31.17 N 121.23 E
Fuxinghao 104 42.35 N 120.32 E
Fuyang, Zhg. 100 32.54 N 115.49 E
Fuyang, Zhg. 100 30.03 N 119.57 E
Fuyang, Zhg. 100 23.36 N 116.37 E
Fuyang ≐ 98 38.14 N 116.05 E
Fuyouertuo Shan ∧ 89 45.52 N 119.48 E
Fuyu, Zhg. 89 47.49 N 124.27 E
Fuyu, Zhg. 89 45.10 N 124.50 E
Fuyuan, Zhg. 89 48.21 N 134.18 E
Fuyuan, Zhg. 102 25.39 N 104.12 E
Fuzhai 100 29.32 N 120.02 E
Fuzhong 102 24.28 N 111.22 E
Fuzhou, Zhg. 100 28.01 N 116.20 E
Fuzhou (Foochow), Zhg. 100 26.06 N 119.17 E
Fuzhoucheng 98 39.45 N 121.47 E
Fuzhuang 98 34.57 N 118.17 E
Fuzhuangyi 98 38.02 N 116.08 E
Füzuli 84 39.37 N 47.08 E
Fyfield 42 51.45 N 0.16 E
Fylde □[8] 262 53.46 N 2.53 W
Fylde > 44 53.47 N 2.56 W
Fyn □[6] 41 55.20 N 10.25 E
Fyn I 41 55.20 N 10.30 E
Fyne, Loch c 46 56.00 N 5.24 W
Fyns Hoved > 41 55.37 N 10.36 E
Fyresvatn ◎ 26 59.06 N 8.12 E
Fyrisån ≐ 40 59.47 N 17.39 E
Fysingen ◎ 40 59.34 N 17.55 E
Fyvie 46 57.25 N 2.23 W
Fzâra, Garaʾet ◎ 36 36.47 N 7.30 E

G

Ga 150 9.47 N 2.30 W
Gaaden 264b 48.03 N 16.12 E
Gaalkacyo 144 6.47 N 47.26 E
Gaanderen 52 51.56 N 6.21 E
Gabah 144 8.08 N 50.02 E
Gabai 146 11.05 N 11.39 E
Gabaldón 116 15.28 N 121.19 E
Gabare 38 43.19 N 23.55 E
Gabarus 186 45.50 N 60.09 W
Gabarus Bay c 186 45.51 N 60.07 W
Gabas ≐ 32 43.46 N 0.42 W
Gabbs 204 38.52 N 117.55 W
Gabby Heights 214 40.09 N 80.15 W
Gabela 152 10.48 S 14.20 E
Gaberones
— Gaborone 156 24.45 S 25.55 E
Gabès 148 33.53 N 10.07 E
Gabès □[8] 148 33.15 N 9.00 E
Gabès, Golfe de c 148 34.00 N 10.25 E
Gabia 152 4.34 S 17.07 E
Gabiarra 255 16.15 S 39.41 W
Gabicce Mare 66 43.58 N 12.46 E
Gabii ⊥ 267a 41.54 N 12.43 E
Gabil 146 11.09 N 18.12 E
Gabilan Creek ≐ 226 36.41 N 121.38 W
Gabilan Range ∧ 226 36.30 N 121.15 W
Gabin 30 52.25 N 19.44 E
Gabir 140 8.35 N 24.40 E
Gable Mountain ∧ 182 54.30 N 121.40 W
Gablenz 54 51.41 N 14.31 E
Gablingen 58 48.27 N 10.49 E
Gablitz 61 48.14 N 16.09 E
Gablonz
— Jablonec nad Nisou 30 50.44 N 15.10 E
Gabon □[1], Afr. 138 1.00 S 11.45 E
Gabon □[1], Afr. 152 1.00 S 11.45 E
Gabon, Estuaire du c[1] 152 0.25 N 9.20 E
Gaborone 156 24.45 S 25.55 E
Gabras 140 10.16 N 26.14 E
Gabria 64 45.52 N 13.34 E
Gabriel 250 11.14 S 41.53 W
Gabriel Strait ⊭ 176 61.45 N 65.30 W
Gabriel y Galan, Embalse de ◎[1] 34 40.15 N 6.15 W
Gabriel Zamora 234 19.05 N 102.05 W
Gābrīk 128 25.44 N 58.28 E
Gabriola 224 49.12 N 123.50 W
Gabriola Island I 224 49.10 N 123.47 W
Gabrovo 38 42.52 N 25.19 E
Gabun
— Gabon □[1] 152 1.00 S 11.45 E
Gaby 62 45.43 N 7.53 E
Gacé 50 48.48 N 0.18 E
Gachetá 246 4.49 N 73.36 W
Gachpar 174q 9.33 N 138.10 E
Gachsārān 128 30.12 N 50.47 E
Gackle 198 46.37 N 99.08 W
Gacko 38 43.10 N 18.32 E
Gädäbäy 84 40.34 N 45.49 E
Gadag 122 15.25 N 75.37 E
Gadamai 140 17.09 N 36.06 E
Gādarwāra 124 22.55 N 78.47 E
Gadbjerg 41 55.46 N 9.20 E
Gäddede 26 64.30 N 14.09 E
Gadderbaum 52 52.00 N 8.31 E
Gade ≐ 260 51.38 N 0.28 W
Gadebusch 54 53.42 N 11.07 E
Gadein 140 8.11 N 28.44 E
Gadera ≐ 64 46.47 N 11.54 E
Gadevang 41 55.58 N 12.18 E
Gadilovići 76 53.05 N 30.16 E
Gadis ≐ 114 1.03 N 98.55 E
Gadmen 58 46.44 N 8.21 E
Gado Bravo, Ilha do I 250 10.54 S 42.52 W
Gádor 34 36.57 N 2.29 W
Gadra 120 25.40 N 70.37 E
Gadsden, Al., U.S. 194 34.00 N 86.00 W
Gadsden, Az., U.S. 200 32.33 N 114.47 W
Gadwāl 122 16.14 N 77.48 E
Gadzi 152 4.47 N 16.42 E
Gaerwen 44 53.13 N 4.16 W
Găești 38 44.43 N 25.19 E
Gaeta 66 41.12 N 13.35 E
Gaeta, Golfo di c 66 41.06 N 13.30 E
Gaferut I 108 9.14 N 145.23 E
Gaffney 192 35.04 N 81.39 W
Gafour 36 36.18 N 9.19 E
Gafsa 148 34.25 N 8.48 E
Gafsa □[8] 148 34.15 N 8.25 E
Gafurov 85 40.14 N 69.44 E
Gag, Pulau I 164 0.27 S 129.52 E
Gagal 146 9.01 N 15.08 E
Gagarawa 150 12.25 N 9.32 E
Gagarin 76 55.33 N 35.00 E
Gage 196 36.18 N 99.45 W
Gagere ≐ 150 13.21 N 6.23 E
Gages Lake 278 42.21 N 87.59 W
Gages Lake ◎ 278 42.21 N 88.00 W
Gagetown 186 45.47 N 66.09 W
Gagetown, Canadian Forces Base ■ 186 45.43 N 66.15 W
Gaggenau 56 48.48 N 8.19 E
Gaggi 70 37.51 N 15.13 E
Gaggiano 62 45.24 N 9.02 E
Gaghamni 140 11.41 N 28.19 E
Gagil Tamil I 174q 9.32 N 138.10 E
Gagino 80 55.14 N 45.02 E
Gagliano Castelferrato 70 37.43 N 14.32 E
Gagliano del Capo 68 39.50 N 18.22 E
Gagnef 40 60.35 N 15.04 E
Gagnia 152 1.28 S 16.02 E
Gagnoa 150 6.08 N 5.56 W
Gagnon 176 51.53 N 68.10 W
Gagnon, Lac ◎ 206 46.07 N 75.07 W
Gagny 261 48.53 N 2.32 E
Gagra 84 43.20 N 40.15 E
Gagret 123 31.40 N 76.04 E
Gahanna 218 40.01 N 82.52 W
Gahlen 52 51.40 N 6.52 E
Gaiarine 64 45.52 N 12.29 E
Gaibandha 124 25.19 N 89.33 E
Gaichtpass)(58 47.27 N 10.37 E
Gaigalava 76 56.40 N 27.18 E
Gaighāta 126 22.56 N 88.44 E
Gaijiatun 104 40.50 N 122.37 E
Gail 196 32.46 N 101.27 W
Gail ≐ 64 46.36 N 13.53 E
Gailberg Sattel)(64 46.43 N 12.58 E
Gail Creek ≐ 222 31.07 N 95.23 W
Gaildorf 56 49.00 N 9.46 E
Gaillac 32 43.54 N 1.55 E
Gaillard, Château ⊥ 50 49.13 N 1.25 E
Gaillard, Lac ◎ 186 50.06 N 68.47 W
Gaillard, Lake ◎ 207 41.21 N 72.46 W
Gaillefontaine 50 49.39 N 1.37 E
Gaillimh
— Galway 48 53.16 N 9.03 W
Gaillon, Fr. 50 49.10 N 1.20 E
Gaillon, Fr. 261 49.02 N 1.54 E
Gailtaler Alpen ∧ 64 46.42 N 13.00 E
Gaima 164 8.20 S 142.55 E
Gaimán 254 43.17 S 65.29 W
Gaimersheim 60 48.49 N 11.22 E
Gaines, Mi., U.S. 216 42.52 N 83.54 W
Gaines, Pa., U.S. 210 41.45 N 77.34 W
Gainesboro 194 36.21 N 85.39 W
Gainesville, Fl., U.S. 192 29.39 N 82.19 W
Gainesville, Ga., U.S. 192 34.17 N 83.49 W
Gainesville, Mo., U.S. 194 36.36 N 92.25 W
Gainesville, N.Y., U.S. 210 42.38 N 78.08 W
Gainesville, Tx., U.S. 196 33.37 N 97.07 W
Gainford 44 54.32 N 1.44 W
Gainsborough, Sk., Can. 184 49.10 N 101.26 W
Gainsborough, Eng., U.K. 44 53.24 N 0.46 W
Gainsborough Creek ≐ 184 49.10 N 101.02 W
Gaiole in Chianti 66 43.28 N 11.26 E
Gairatganj 124 23.24 N 78.13 E
Gairdner ≐ 162 34.17 S 119.28 E
Gairdner, Lake ◎ 162 31.35 S 136.00 E
Gairloch 46 57.42 N 5.40 W
Gairloch, Loch c 46 57.44 N 5.44 W
Gairn ≐ 46 57.03 N 3.05 W
Gais, It. 64 46.50 N 11.57 E
Gais, Schw. 58 47.22 N 9.27 E
Gaisberg ∧ 64 47.48 N 13.07 E
Gaisbeuren 58 47.54 N 9.43 E
Gaital, Cerro ∧ 236 8.37 N 80.07 W
Gaither 208 39.21 N 76.59 W
Gaithersburg 208 39.08 N 77.12 W
Gaixian 104 40.24 N 122.22 E
Gaizina Kalns ∧[2] 76 56.52 N 25.57 E
Gaj, Hrv. 36 45.29 N 17.02 E
Gaj, Ross. 86 51.27 N 58.27 E
Gajā 272b 22.52 N 88.10 E
Gajahmungkur, Waduk ◎[1] 115a 7.55 S 110.55 E
Gajendragarh 122 15.44 N 75.58 E
Gajiram 146 12.30 N 13.12 E
Gajny 24 60.15 N 54.15 E
Gajol 124 25.13 N 88.12 E
Gajsinghpur 123 29.40 N 73.27 E
Gajuapara ≐ 250 4.17 S 47.25 W
Gajutino 76 58.42 N 38.32 E
Gakarosa ∧ 158 27.54 S 23.33 E
Gakona 180 62.18 N 145.18 W
Gākuch 123 36.10 N 73.45 E
Gakugsa 24 61.34 N 36.26 E
Gāla, Bngl. 126 24.18 N 89.44 E
Gala, Zhg. 124 28.16 N 89.23 E
Galaassija 128 39.52 N 64.27 E
Galāchipa 126 22.10 N 90.25 E
Galahad 182 52.31 N 111.56 W
Galamares 266c 38.48 N 9.25 W
Galán, Cerro ∧ 252 25.55 S 66.52 W
Galana ≐ 154 3.09 S 40.08 E
Galangue 152 13.48 S 16.09 E
Galanovo 80 56.09 N 54.07 E
Galanta 30 48.12 N 17.43 E
Galápagos □[4] 246a 0.30 S 90.30 W
Galápagos, Parque Nacional de ◆ 246a 0.15 S 90.15 W
Galapagos Islands
— Colón, Archipiélago de II 246a 0.30 S 90.30 W
Galaroza 34 37.55 N 6.42 W
Galas ≐ 114 5.31 N 102.12 E
Galashiels 46 55.37 N 2.49 W
Galata ✦[8] 267b 41.01 N 28.58 E
Galata Köprüsü ✦[5] 267b 41.01 N 28.58 E
Galata Tower ᵿ 267b 41.01 N 28.58 E
Galatea 172 38.25 S 176.45 E
Galați 38 45.26 N 28.03 E
Galați □[6] 38 45.45 N 27.45 E
Galatia 194 37.50 N 88.36 W
Galatia □[9] 130 39.30 N 32.40 E
Galatina 68 40.10 N 18.10 E
Galatone 68 40.09 N 18.04 E
Galatro 68 38.28 N 16.06 E
Galátsion 267c 38.01 N 23.45 E
Galatz
— Galați 38 45.26 N 28.03 E
Galaure ≐ 62 45.11 N 4.49 E
Gala Water ≐ 46 55.37 N 2.48 W
Galax 192 36.39 N 80.55 W
Galaxídhion 38 38.22 N 22.23 E
Galbyn gov' ✦[2] 102 42.30 N 107.00 E
Galdhøpiggen ∧ 26 61.37 N 8.17 E
Gale, Lac ◎ 190 46.46 N 76.51 W
Galeairy Lake ◎ 212 45.29 N 78.17 W
Galeana, Méx. 232 30.07 N 107.38 W
Galeana, Méx. 232 24.50 N 100.04 W
Galeão, Aeroporto do ✈ 256 22.50 S 43.15 W
Galeata 66 44.00 N 11.55 E
Galegu 140 12.36 N 35.02 E
Galeh Dār 128 27.38 N 52.42 E
Galela 108 1.50 N 127.50 E
Galena, Austl. 162 27.50 S 114.41 E
Galena, Ak., U.S. 180 64.44 N 156.57 W
Galena, Il., U.S. 190 42.25 N 90.25 W
Galena, In., U.S. 218 38.21 N 85.56 W
Galena, Ks., U.S. 198 37.04 N 94.38 W
Galena, Md., U.S. 208 39.20 N 75.52 W
Galena, Mo., U.S. 194 36.48 N 93.27 W
Galena, Oh., U.S. 214 40.12 N 82.52 W
Galena Park 222 29.43 N 95.13 W
Galenbecker See ◎ 54 53.38 N 13.43 E
Galeota Point > 241r 10.08 N 60.59 W
Galera ≐ 248 14.25 S 60.07 W
Galera, Punta >, Chile 254 39.59 S 73.43 W
Galera, Punta >, Ec. 246 0.49 N 80.03 W
Galera, Punta de > 34 39.06 N 1.31 E
Galera Point > 241r 10.49 N 60.55 W
Galeras, Volcán ∧[1] 246 1.13 N 77.22 W
Galeria ⊥ 267a 42.02 N 12.18 E
Galeria, Fosso la ≐ 267a 41.48 N 12.21 E
Galesburg, Il., U.S. 190 40.56 N 90.22 W
Galesburg, Mi., U.S. 216 42.17 N 85.25 W
Gales Creek 224 45.35 N 123.12 W
Gales Creek ≐ 224 45.29 N 123.06 W
Gales Ferry 207 41.25 N 72.04 W
Gales Point > 283 42.33 N 70.47 W
Galesville, Md., U.S. 208 38.50 N 76.32 W
Galesville, Wi., U.S. 190 44.04 N 91.20 W
Galeton 214 41.43 N 77.38 W
Galeville 210 43.05 N 76.10 W
Galgasc 144 0.11 N 41.38 E
Galgate 44 54.00 N 2.47 W
Galguduud □[4] 144 5.00 N 46.30 E
Galheiros 255 13.18 S 46.25 W
Gali 84 42.38 N 41.44 E
Gali, Torrente de ≐ 266d 41.28 N 2.00 E
Galiano 224 48.52 N 123.21 W
Galiano Island I 224 48.56 N 123.29 W
Galibier, Col du)(62 45.04 N 6.24 E
Galič 80 58.23 N 42.21 E
Galicia □[4] 34 42.45 N 8.00 W
Galicia □[9] 22 49.00 N 22.00 E
Galičskaja vozvyšennost' ✦[2] 24 58.25 N 42.20 E
Galičskoje, ozero ◎ 80 58.24 N 42.18 E
Galien 216 41.47 N 86.29 W
Galien ≐ 216 41.48 N 86.45 W
Galilee 207 41.22 N 71.30 W
Galilee
— HaGalil □[9] 132 32.54 N 35.20 E
Galilee, Lake ◎ 166 22.21 S 145.48 E
Galilee, Sea of
— Kinneret, Yam ◎ 132 32.48 N 35.35 E
Galiléia 255 19.00 S 41.33 W
Galim 152 7.06 N 12.29 E
Galina Point > 241q 18.24 N 76.53 W
Galindo Creek ≐ 282 37.58 N 122.02 W
Galion 214 40.44 N 82.47 W
Galion, Baie du c 240e 14.44 N 60.57 W
Galis 115a 7.08 S 113.33 E
Galisteo Creek ≐ 200 35.31 N 106.22 W
Galite, Canal de la ⊭ 36 37.20 N 9.00 E
Galiuro Mountains ∧ 200 32.40 N 110.20 W
Galiwinku 164 12.02 S 135.34 E
Galižana 64 44.56 N 13.52 E
Galka'yo 144 6.47 N 47.26 E
Galkhausen 263 51.05 N 6.58 E
Galkino, Kaz. 86 52.14 N 78.20 E
Galkino, Ross. 82 54.46 N 35.49 E
Galkino, Ross. 86 55.36 N 62.55 E
Gall'aaral 85 40.02 N 67.35 E
Gallan Head > 46 58.14 N 7.03 W
Gallarate 62 45.40 N 8.47 E
Gallardon 50 48.32 N 1.42 E
Gallatin, Mo., U.S. 194 39.54 N 93.57 W
Gallatin, Pa., U.S. 279b 40.12 N 79.53 W
Gallatin, Tn., U.S. 194 36.23 N 86.26 W
Gallatin, Tx., U.S. 222 31.54 N 95.09 W
Gallatin □[6] 218 38.45 N 84.51 W
Gallatin ≐ 202 45.56 N 111.29 W
Gallatin Range ∧ 202 45.15 N 111.05 W
Galle 122 6.02 N 80.13 E
Gallego 232 29.49 N 106.22 W
Gállego ≐ 34 41.39 N 0.51 W
Gallegos ≐ 254 51.35 S 68.59 W
Galles
— Wales □[8] 28 52.30 N 3.30 W
Galleyend 260 51.42 N 0.29 E
Galley Head > 48 51.30 N 8.57 W
Galleywood 260 51.42 N 0.28 E
Galliano 194 29.26 N 90.17 W
Galliate 62 45.29 N 8.42 E
Gallicano 64 44.04 N 10.26 E
Gallicano nel Lazio 267a 41.52 N 12.49 E
Gallicchio 68 40.17 N 16.08 E
Gallico 68 38.10 N 15.41 E
Galliera Veneta 64 45.39 N 11.49 E
Gallinara I 62 44.02 N 8.14 E
Gallinas ≐ 196 35.10 N 104.35 W
Gallinas, Punta > 246 12.28 N 71.40 W
Gallinas Creek ≐ 282 38.01 N 122.30 W
Gallinas Peak ∧ 200 34.14 N 105.45 W
Gallio 64 45.53 N 11.33 E
Gallipoli, Austl. 166 19.10 S 137.55 E
Gallipoli, It. 68 40.03 N 17.58 E
Gallipoli
— Gelibolu, Tür. 130 40.24 N 26.40 E
Gallipoli Peninsula
— Gelibolu Yarımadası >[1] 130 40.20 N 26.30 E
Gallipolis 188 38.48 N 82.12 W
Gallitzin 214 40.28 N 78.33 W
Gallivaggio 58 46.21 N 9.21 E
Gällivare 24 67.07 N 20.45 E
Gallneukirchen 61 48.21 N 14.25 E
Gällö 26 62.55 N 15.14 E
Gallo, Capo > 70 38.13 N 13.19 E
Gallo, Lago del ◎[1] 64 46.37 N 10.10 E
Gallo, Lago di ◎[1] 58 46.37 N 10.10 E
Gallo, Laguna ◎ 258 35.30 S 58.28 W
Gallo Arroyo V 200 33.55 N 105.00 W
Galloo Island I 212 43.54 N 76.25 W
Galloupes Point > 283 42.28 N 70.53 W
Galloway □[9] 44 55.00 N 4.25 W
Galloway, Mull of > 44 54.38 N 4.50 W
Galloway Creek ≐, Md., U.S. 284b 39.18 N 76.23 W
Galloway Creek ≐, Mi., U.S. 281 42.39 N 83.12 W
Galluis 261 48.48 N 1.48 E
Gallup 200 35.31 N 108.44 W
Gallupville 210 42.40 N 74.14 W
Gallur 34 41.52 N 1.19 W
Gallura ✦[1] 71 41.00 N 9.13 E
Gally, Ru de ≐ 261 48.53 N 1.53 E
Gålnan ≐ 40 59.31 N 18.45 E
Gålö I 40 59.05 N 18.17 E
Galop Island I 212 44.46 N 75.24 W
Galoppo, Ippodromo del ✦ 266b 45.28 N 9.07 E
Galougo 150 13.50 N 11.04 W
Galsi 126 23.20 N 87.42 E
Galston 46 55.36 N 4.24 W
Galt, Mong. 88 48.46 N 99.53 E
Galt, Ca., U.S. 226 38.15 N 121.17 W
Gal Tardo 144 3.34 N 45.58 E
Galtat Zemmour 148 25.15 N 12.20 W
Galtelli 71 40.23 N 9.37 E
Galten 41 56.09 N 9.55 E
Galten c 40 59.27 N 16.09 E
Galtür 58 46.58 N 10.11 E
Galtymore Mountain ∧ 48 52.22 N 8.10 W
Galty Mountains ∧ 48 52.25 N 8.10 W
Galūgāh-e Āsīyeh 128 34.01 N 59.55 E
Galugur 114 2.34 N 99.39 E
Galula 154 8.36 S 33.02 E
Galunggung, Gunung ∧ 115a 7.15 S 108.03 E
Galuut 88 48.33 N 113.12 E
Galva, Il., U.S. 190 41.10 N 90.02 W
Galva, Ia., U.S. 198 42.30 N 95.25 W
Galva, Ks., U.S. 198 38.22 N 97.32 W
Galvarino 252 38.24 S 72.47 W
Galveston, In., U.S. 216 40.34 N 86.11 W
Galveston, Tx., U.S. 222 29.17 N 94.47 W
Galveston □[6] 222 29.20 N 94.53 W
Galveston Bay c 222 29.36 N 94.57 W
Galveston Island I 222 29.13 N 94.55 W
Gálvez 252 32.02 S 61.13 W
Gálvez ≐ 248 5.12 S 72.53 W
Galvin, Austl. 274b 37.51 S 144.49 E
Galvin, Wa., U.S. 224 46.44 N 123.01 W
Galway (Gaillimh), Ire. 48 53.16 N 9.03 W
Galway, N.Y., U.S. 210 43.01 N 74.02 W
Galway □[6] 48 53.20 N 9.00 W
Galway Bay c 48 53.10 N 9.15 W
Gam (Jin) ≐ 110 21.55 N 105.12 E
Gam, Pulau I 164 0.27 S 130.36 E
Gama, Isla I 254 40.29 S 62.12 W
Gamaches 50 49.59 N 1.33 E
Gamagōri 94 34.50 N 137.14 E
Gamalejevka 80 52.16 N 53.26 E
Gamaliel 194 36.38 N 85.47 W
Ga-Mankoeng 156 23.57 S 29.42 E
Gamare, Lake ◎ 144 11.30 N 41.40 E
Gamarra 246 8.20 N 73.45 W
Gamawa 146 12.08 N 10.32 E
Gamay 116 12.23 N 125.18 E
Gamay Bay c 116 12.21 N 125.21 E
Gamba 120 28.17 N 88.32 E
Gambach 56 50.28 N 8.44 E
Gambaga 150 10.32 N 0.26 W
Gambais 261 48.46 N 1.40 E
Gambaiseuil 261 48.45 N 1.44 E
Gambang 114 3.43 N 103.06 E
Gambara, It. 62 45.15 N 10.18 E
Gámbara, Méx. 234 18.55 N 102.05 W
Gambarie 68 38.10 N 15.50 E
Gambassi 66 43.32 N 10.57 E
Gambatesa 66 41.30 N 14.54 E
Gambela 144 8.18 N 34.37 E
Gambell 180 63.46 N 171.46 W
Gambellara 64 45.28 N 11.20 E
Gamber 208 39.27 N 76.58 W
Gambia □[1], Afr. 134 13.30 N 15.30 W
Gambia □[1], Afr. 150 13.30 N 15.30 W
Gambia (Gambie) ≐ 150 13.28 N 16.34 W
Gambi Atrash 140 10.03 N 33.47 E
Gambie
— Gambia □[1] 150 13.30 N 15.30 W
Gambie (Gambia) ≐ 150 13.28 N 16.34 W
Gambier 214 40.22 N 82.23 W
Gambier, Îles II 6 21.20 S 136.30 W
Gamble Mansion State Historic Site ⊥ 220 27.32 N 82.32 W
Gambo, Nf., Can. 186 48.46 N 54.13 W
Gambo, Centraf. 152 4.39 N 22.16 E
Gamboa 236 9.07 N 79.42 W
Gamboli 120 29.50 N 68.26 E
Gambolò 62 45.15 N 8.51 E
Gamboma 152 1.53 S 15.51 E
Gamboula 152 4.08 N 15.09 E
Gambrill State Park ◆ 208 39.30 N 77.30 W
Gamchab ≐ 156 28.15 S 17.26 E
Gamé 150 6.44 N 1.11 E
Game Creek ≐ 285 39.41 N 75.28 W
Gamensee ◎ 264a 52.40 N 13.51 E
Gaming 61 47.56 N 15.06 E
Gamış dağ ∧ 84 40.18 N 46.23 E
Gamka ≐ 158 33.18 S 21.39 E
Gamlakarleby
— Kokkola 26 63.50 N 23.07 E
Gamla Uppsala 40 59.54 N 17.38 E
Gamleby 26 57.54 N 16.24 E
Gamlitz 61 46.43 N 15.33 E
Gammel Estrup ⊥ 41 56.26 N 10.21 E
Gammelstad ᵿ[1] 26 65.38 N 22.01 E
Gammertingen 58 48.15 N 9.13 E
Gammon, Point > 207 41.36 N 70.16 W
Gammon Ranges National Park ◆ 166 30.29 S 139.10 E
Gamō, Nihon 94 35.03 N 136.11 E
Gamō, Nihon 268 35.52 N 139.48 E
Gamoep 158 29.55 S 18.25 E
Ga-Mogara ≐ 158 27.07 S 22.57 E
Gamo Gofa □[4] 144 5.45 N 37.00 E
Gamon 150 13.20 N 12.55 W
Gamova, mys > 89 42.35 N 131.12 E
Gamph, Slieve ∧ 48 54.05 N 9.00 W
Gampoko 273b 4.16 S 15.10 E
Gampola 122 7.10 N 80.34 E
Gampongbatak 114 4.48 N 97.39 E
Gampoui 273b 4.08 S 15.22 E
Gams 58 47.12 N 9.28 E
Gamsfeld ∧ 64 47.37 N 13.29 E
Gamtoos ≐ 158 33.58 S 25.01 E
Gamud ∧ 144 4.05 N 38.03 E
Gan ≐, Zhg. 89 49.12 N 125.14 E
Gan ≐, Zhg. 100 29.12 N 116.00 E
Ganado, Az., U.S. 200 35.42 N 109.32 W
Ganado, Tx., U.S. 222 29.02 N 96.31 W
Ganano ≐ 116 16.45 N 121.44 E
Gananoque 212 44.20 N 76.10 W
Gananoque ≐ 212 44.19 N 76.09 W
Gananoque Lake ◎ 212 44.27 N 76.09 W
Ganaraska ≐ 212 43.57 N 78.18 W
Ganargua Creek ≐ 210 43.04 N 77.00 W
Ganassi 116 7.49 N 124.06 E
Ganāveh 128 29.34 N 50.31 E
Gäncä 84 40.40 N 46.22 E
Gäncäçay ≐ 84 40.54 N 46.28 E
Gancevići 76 52.45 N 26.26 E
Ganchangba 107 28.52 N 103.41 E
Gančī 85 39.58 N 69.08 E
Gand
— Gent 50 51.03 N 3.43 E
Ganda, Ang. 152 13.02 S 14.40 E
Ganda, Zaïre 152 4.05 N 23.32 E
Gandadiwata, Bulu ∧ 112 2.42 S 119.27 E
Gandajika 152 6.45 S 23.57 E
Gandak (Nārāyani) ≐ 124 25.39 N 85.13 E
Gandakī □[8] 124 28.15 N 84.15 E
Gandara 258 35.26 S 58.06 W
Ganda Singhwāla 123 31.02 N 74.31 E
Gandāva 120 28.37 N 67.29 E
Gandavaroyi Falls ⊾ 154 17.17 S 29.07 E
Gānde 126 24.10 N 86.26 E
Gander 186 48.57 N 54.37 W
Gander ≐ 186 49.15 N 54.30 W
Gander Bay 186 49.18 N 54.29 W
Gander Bay c 186 49.25 N 54.28 W
Ganderkesee 52 53.02 N 8.32 E
Gander Lake ◎ 186 48.55 N 54.40 W
Gandesa 34 41.03 N 0.26 E
Găndeşti 38 47.53 N 28.23 E
Gandevi 120 20.49 N 72.59 E
Gāndhinagar 120 23.12 N 72.40 E
Gāndhi Sāgar ◎[1] 120 24.18 N 75.21 E
Gandi 150 12.55 N 5.49 E
Gandi, Wādī V 140 11.23 N 24.31 E
Gandia 34 38.58 N 0.11 W
Gandino 62 45.49 N 9.54 E
Gando 152 12.30 S 17.25 E
Gandole 146 8.26 N 11.34 E
Gandou 152 2.24 N 17.27 E
Gandrange 56 49.16 N 6.08 E
Gandria 58 46.01 N 9.00 E
Gandu 255 13.45 S 39.30 W
Gandy Bridge ✦[5] 220 27.53 N 82.34 W
Ganfang 100 28.40 N 114.51 E
Ganfosi 107 29.36 N 104.03 E
Ganga
— Ganges ≐ 124 23.22 N 90.32 E
Gangādharpur 272b 22.36 N 88.11 E
Gangafani 150 14.23 N 2.24 W
Gangājalghāti 126 23.25 N 87.07 E
Gangala-Na-Bodio 154 3.41 N 29.08 E
Gangalingolo 273b 4.20 S 15.09 E
Gan Gan 254 42.30 S 68.16 W
Gangānagar 123 29.55 N 73.53 E
Gangāpur, India 120 25.13 N 74.16 E
Gangāpur, India 122 19.41 N 75.01 E
Gangāpur, India 124 26.29 N 76.43 E
Gangara, Niger 150 14.36 N 8.30 E
Gangara, Niger 150 13.33 N 7.14 E
Gangārāmpur 124 25.24 N 88.31 E
Ganga Sāgar 126 21.38 N 88.05 E
Gangaw 110 22.11 N 94.07 E
Gangāwati 122 15.26 N 76.32 E
Gangaw Range ∧ 110 24.50 N 96.40 E
Ganga-Yamuna Doāb ∧[1] 124 26.40 N 79.30 E
Gangcheng 98 35.52 N 116.52 E
Gangdāba, Tchabal ∧ 152 7.44 N 12.45 E
Gangdhār 120 23.57 N 75.37 E
Gangdisê Shan ∧ 120 31.00 N 82.00 E
Gangelt 56 50.59 N 5.59 E
Ganges, B.C., Can. 224 48.51 N 123.30 W
Ganges, Fr. 62 43.56 N 3.42 E
Ganges (Ganga) (Padma) ≐ 124 23.22 N 90.32 E
Ganges, Mouths of the ≐[1] 120 22.00 N 89.00 E
Ganges Delta ≡[2] 124 23.00 N 89.00 E
Ganghu 120 32.05 N 86.45 E
Gangi 70 37.49 N 14.13 E
Gangkofen 60 48.26 N 12.34 E
Gangkou, Zhg. 100 29.21 N 117.58 E
Gangkou, Zhg. 100 22.38 N 113.22 E
Gangkou, Zhg. 100 22.36 N 114.54 E
Gangkou, Zhg. 100 29.12 N 113.19 E
Gangkou, Zhg. 106 30.44 N 118.54 E
Gangkou, Zhg. 106 31.45 N 120.40 E
Gangkouzhen 106 29.45 N 115.44 E
Gangmar Co ◎ 120 33.46 N 84.15 E
Gang Mills 210 42.08 N 77.07 W
Gangnāpur 126 23.09 N 88.38 E
Gangneung
— Kangnŭng 98 37.45 N 128.54 E
Gango ≐ 152 9.48 S 15.40 E
Gangoa 102 37.15 N 100.28 E
Gangoh 124 29.46 N 77.15 E
Gangotri, India 120 30.56 N 79.02 E
Gangotri, India 120 31.01 N 78.27 E
Gangou 98 40.30 N 119.27 E
Gangoumen 98 41.40 N 116.35 E
Gangouyi 102 36.01 N 105.03 E
Gangqiao 107 30.13 N 105.22 E
Gang Ranch 182 51.33 N 122.00 W
Gangshangji 100 28.06 N 116.30 E
Gangtok 124 27.20 N 88.37 E
Gangtou 98 38.04 N 113.56 E
Gangtouli 106 31.42 N 119.02 E
Gangu 102 34.45 N 105.20 E
Gangwa, Zaïre 152 3.30 S 20.55 E
Gangwa, Zhg. 105 39.48 N 116.10 E
Gangwei 100 24.20 N 118.01 E
Ganhezi 86 44.08 N 88.32 E
Ganhu 102 44.33 N 94.09 E
Gani 164 0.47 S 128.13 E
Ganišob 85 39.03 N 70.47 E
Ganj Dundwara 124 27.44 N 78.57 E
Ganjiang 107 29.42 N 103.38 E
Ganlan Shan ∧ 124 29.54 N 90.02 E
Ganlu 106 31.32 N 120.35 E
Ganluchang 107 29.54 N 104.47 E
Ganluo 102 29.03 N 102.59 E
Gannahoek 158 26.44 S 24.08 E
Gannan 89 47.54 N 123.30 E
Gannano, Lago di ◎ 68 40.19 N 16.26 E
Gannapan 158 30.23 S 22.12 E
Gannat 32 46.06 N 3.12 E
Gannett Peak ∧ 200 43.11 N 109.39 W
Gannvalley 198 44.02 N 98.59 W
Ganpingsi 102 35.13 N 102.30 E
Ganpu 106 30.24 N 120.53 E
Ganq 120 37.25 N 92.15 E
Ganquan 102 36.25 N 109.16 E
Gansbaai 158 34.35 S 19.22 E
Gänsbrunnen 58 47.16 N 7.28 E
Gänserndorf 61 48.20 N 16.43 E
Gansevoort 210 43.12 N 73.39 W
Ganshoren 56 50.52 N 4.18 E
Ganspan 158 27.57 S 24.47 E
Gansu (Kansu) □[4] 102 37.00 N 103.00 E
Ganta 150 7.15 N 8.59 W
Gantan 100 29.37 N 119.34 E
Gantang, Zhg. 100 26.56 N 119.40 E
Gantang, Zhg. 102 22.58 N 109.00 E
Gantao ≐ 98 38.01 N 114.07 E
Gante
— Gent 50 51.03 N 3.43 E
Gantheaume, Cape > 166 36.05 S 137.27 E
Gantheaume Bay c 162 27.44 S 114.07 E
Gantheaume Point > 162 17.59 S 122.10 E
Gantiadi 84 43.24 N 40.06 E
Gantian 100 27.30 N 113.10 E
Gantt 194 31.24 N 86.29 W
Gantung 112 2.58 S 108.09 E
Gantung, Mount ∧ 116 8.57 N 117.48 E
Gan'uškino 80 46.36 N 49.16 E
Ganwo 150 11.13 N 4.42 E
Ganxi, Zhg. 100 28.08 N 118.06 E
Ganxi, Zhg. 102 29.02 N 109.32 E
Ganyanchi 102 36.39 N 105.18 E
Ganyesa 158 26.35 S 24.10 E
Ganyu (Qing Kou) 98 34.52 N 119.10 E
Ganzê 102 31.40 N 100.01 E
Ganzhenyi 100 30.33 N 113.21 E
Ganzhou, Zhg. 100 25.54 N 114.55 E
Ganzhou, Zhg. 100 28.49 N 115.25 E
Ganzhou
— Zhangye, Zhg. 102 38.56 N 100.27 E
Ganzhuermiao 88 48.24 N 118.08 E
Ganzlin 54 53.23 N 12.15 E
Ganzo Azul 248 8.51 S 74.44 W
Gao 150 16.16 N 0.03 W
Gao □[4] 150 18.00 N 1.30 E
Gao'an 100 28.25 N 115.22 E
Gaobaita 271a 39.53 N 116.30 E
Gaobei 100 26.37 N 114.38 E
Gaobeidian 271a 39.54 N 116.33 E
Gaobu 100 27.48 N 117.01 E
Gaochang 107 28.49 N 104.24 E
Gaocheng, Zhg. 98 38.04 N 114.49 E
Gaocheng, Zhg. 100 31.57 N 113.25 E
Gaocheng, Zhg. 106 31.28 N 119.48 E
Gaochengzhai 104 41.24 N 123.43 E
Gaochun 106 31.20 N 118.52 E
Gaocun 98 37.05 N 122.12 E
Gaodianzi 102 30.40 N 110.01 E
Gao Feng ∧ 106 30.34 N 118.40 E
Gaogongmiao 100 33.25 N 115.53 E
Gaogou 100 34.03 N 119.15 E
Gaohe 100 22.47 N 112.57 E
Gaohebu 100 30.44 N 116.50 E
Gaoil, Sliabh ∧ 46 55.55 N 5.28 W
Gaojiabu 102 38.30 N 110.11 E
Gaojiadi 98 41.33 N 114.58 E
Gaojiadian 98 42.40 N 124.28 E
Gaojian 100 29.04 N 121.14 E
Gaojiapuzi 104 41.22 N 123.36 E
Gaojiaqiao 106 30.43 N 120.38 E
Gaojiatun 104 41.06 N 121.19 E
Gaojiawopeng 104 41.28 N 122.10 E
Gaojiawopu 104 41.50 N 122.47 E
Gaojiazhai 269b 31.23 N 121.33 E
Gaojiazhen 102 30.05 N 107.51 E
Gaokan 104 40.46 N 122.23 E
Gaokeng 100 27.40 N 113.58 E
Gaolan 102 36.25 N 103.56 E
Gaolan Dao I 100 21.55 N 113.15 E
Gaolao 104 41.54 N 120.59 E
Gaoli 105 39.17 N 115.38 E
Gaoliang 107 29.45 N 105.15 E
Gaoliban 104 41.39 N 121.58 E
Gaolifangshen 104 42.27 N 123.21 E
Gaolimen 98 40.22 N 124.02 E
Gaoling 105 40.32 N 117.01 E
Gaolinying 105 39.06 N 115.38 E
Gaoliying 105 40.10 N 116.29 E
Gaoliyingzi 104 41.56 N 124.17 E
Gaolong 100 26.56 N 113.45 E
Gaolou 105 39.59 N 116.50 E
Gaolouchang, Zhg. 107 29.51 N 104.41 E
Gaolouchang, Zhg. 107 30.03 N 105.58 E
Gaoluo 98 37.27 N 113.55 E
Gaomi 98 36.23 N 119.44 E
Gaona 252 25.12 S 64.05 W
Gaopi 100 24.14 N 116.39 E
Gaoping, Zhg. 102 35.48 N 112.52 E
Gaoping, Zhg. 107 30.28 N 105.45 E
Gaopingba 107 30.47 N 106.06 E
Gaoqiao, Zhg. 100 30.08 N 119.56 E
Gaoqiao, Zhg. 100 26.36 N 117.46 E
Gaoqiao, Zhg. 102 28.06 N 106.36 E
Gaoqiao, Zhg. 106 32.14 N 119.38 E
Gaoqiao, Zhg. 106 31.21 N 121.34 E
Gaoqiaomen 106 32.01 N 118.51 E
Gaoqiaozhen 104 40.55 N 121.00 E
Gaoqing (Tianzhen) 98 37.11 N 117.47 E
Gaoqipu 104 41.32 N 121.40 E
Gaosha 100 26.27 N 117.56 E
Gaoshaling 105 38.51 N 117.36 E
Gaoshan, Zhg. 100 25.29 N 119.34 E
Gaoshan, Zhg. 107 29.26 N 104.28 E
Gaoshanbao 105 40.40 N 117.29 E
Gaoshangbao 98 39.11 N 118.30 E
Gaoshanpu 102 27.10 N 105.14 E
Gaoshantai 104 42.22 N 122.28 E
Gaoshanzi 104 41.34 N 122.02 E
Gaoshengchang 107 29.59 N 105.31 E
Gaoshengzhen 104 41.20 N 122.12 E
Gaoshi 107 29.36 N 104.44 E
Gaoshikan 107 29.12 N 105.04 E
Gaosichang 107 30.17 N 104.52 E
Gaotai 102 39.20 N 99.58 E
Gaotaishan 104 42.02 N 122.52 E
Gaotan, Zhg. 100 30.23 N 117.23 E
Gaotan, Zhg. 100 23.12 N 115.22 E
Gaotan, Zhg. 102 32.22 N 108.36 E
Gaotang 98 36.54 N 116.14 E
Gaotangji 100 32.24 N 116.01 E
Gaotingsi 100 26.05 N 112.53 E
Gaotuozi 104 41.08 N 122.40 E
Gaoua 150 10.20 N 3.11 W
Gaoual 150 11.45 N 13.12 W
Gaoxian 102 28.20 N 104.38 E
Gaoxingru 100 26.28 N 115.14 E
Gaoxinji 98 34.11 N 115.33 E
Gaoya 98 36.22 N 118.49 E
Gaoyang 98 34.30 N 114.40 E
Gaoyapu 107 29.14 N 106.19 E
Gaoyi 98 37.36 N 114.36 E
Gaoyou, Zhg. 100 32.47 N 119.27 E
Gaoyou, Zhg. 100 28.25 N 115.31 E
Gaoyou Hu ◎ 100 32.50 N 119.20 E
Gaozhangjia 102 36.06 N 107.18 E
Gaozhou 102 21.55 N 110.50 E
Gaozi 106 32.11 N 119.18 E
Gaoziba 107 29.01 N 106.00 E
Gaozuo 100 33.57 N 118.03 E
Gap, Fr. 62 44.34 N 6.05 E
Gap, Pa., U.S. 208 39.59 N 76.01 W
Gapālnagar 272b 22.49 N 88.08 E
Gapan 116 15.19 N 120.57 E
Gapeau ≐ 62 43.07 N 6.11 E
Gapern ◎ 40 59.31 N 13.40 E
Gar 120 32.11 N 79.59 E
Gar ≐ 120 32.28 N 79.44 E
Gara, Lough ◎ 48 53.55 N 8.25 W
Garacad 144 6.57 N 49.19 E
Garachiné 246 8.04 N 78.22 W
Garadag 144 9.26 N 46.52 E
Gārādāha 126 24.14 N 89.34 E
Garagoa 246 5.05 N 73.21 W
Garaguso 68 40.33 N 16.14 E
Garah 166 29.04 S 149.38 E
Garai ≐[1] 126 23.32 N 89.31 E
Garaina 164 7.50 S 147.10 E
Gārākhola Madhukhāli 126 23.33 N 89.38 E
Garamba ≐ 154 3.53 N 29.12 E
Garamba, Parc National de la ◆ 154 4.10 N 29.30 E
Gara Muleta ∧ 144 9.17 N 41.47 E
Garānberia 272b 22.24 N 88.34 E
Garancières 261 48.49 N 1.46 E
Garango 150 11.48 N 0.34 W
Garanhuns 250 8.54 S 36.29 W
Garapan 174n 15.12 N 145.43 E
Garara 164 8.37 S 148.17 E
Garautha 124 25.34 N 79.18 E
Garba 146 9.12 N 20.30 E
Garbagna 266b 45.23 N 8.39 E
Garbagnate Milanese 266b 45.35 N 9.05 E
Garbahaarrey 144 3.19 N 42.13 E
Garbatella ✦[8] 267a 41.52 N 12.29 E
Garba Tula 154 0.32 N 38.31 E
Garber 196 36.26 N 97.35 W
Garberville 204 40.06 N 123.47 W
Garbokaraj 88 54.09 N 99.52 E
Garboldisham 42 52.24 N 0.56 E
Gârbova 38 46.50 N 29.21 E
Gârbovu 38 44.44 N 23.21 E
Garbsen 52 52.25 N 9.34 E
Garça 255 22.14 S 49.37 W
Garças, Rio das ≐ 255 15.54 S 52.16 W
Garcevo 76 52.45 N 32.59 E
Garches 261 48.51 N 2.11 E
Garching 60 48.15 N 11.39 E

Symbol	English	Deutsch	Español	Français	Português
≐	River	Fluß	Río	Rivière	Rio
⊏	Canal	Kanal	Canal	Canal	Canal
⊾	Waterfall, Rapids	Wasserfall, Stromschnellen	Cascada, Rápidos	Chute d'eau, Rapides	Cascata, Rápidos
⊭	Strait	Meeresstraße	Estrecho	Détroit	Estreito
c	Bay, Gulf	Bucht, Golf	Bahía, Golfo	Baie, Golfe	Baía, Golfo
◎	Lake, Lakes	See, Seen	Lago, Lagos	Lac, Lacs	Lago, Lagos
⩩	Swamp	Sumpf	Pantano	Marais	Pântano
≡	Ice Features, Glacier	Eis- und Gletscherformen	Accidentes Glaciales	Formes glaciaires	Acidentes glaciares
⫯	Other Hydrographic Features	Andere Hydrographische Objekte	Otros Elementos Hidrográficos	Autres données hydrographiques	Outros acidentes hidrográficos
✦	Submarine Features	Untermeerische Objekte	Accidentes Submarinos	Formes de relief sous-marin	Acidentes submarinos
□	Political Unit	Politische Einheit	Unidad Politica	Entité politique	Unidade política
ᵿ	Cultural Institution	Kulturelle Institution	Institución Cultural	Institution culturelle	Institução cultural
⊥	Historical Site	Historische Stätte	Sitio Histórico	Site historique	Sitio histórico
◆	Recreational Site	Erholungs- und Ferienort	Sitio de Recreo	Centre de loisirs	Area de Lazer
✈	Airport	Flughafen	Aeropuerto	Aéroport	Aeroporto
■	Military Installation	Militäranlage	Instalación Militar	Installation militaire	Instalação militar
✦	Miscellaneous	Verschiedenes	Misceláneo	Divers	Diversos

Garching an der Alz 60 48.08 N 12.34 E
Garchitorena 116 13.52 N 123.40 E
García 232 29.59 N 108.20 W
García, Laguna ⊜ 288 34.58 S 58.09 W
García de la Cadena 234 21.09 N 103.28 W
García de Sola, Embalse de ⊜1 34 39.15 N 5.05 W
Garcia Hernandez 116 9.37 N 124.18 E
Garcias 255 20.34 S 52.13 W
Garcitas Creek ≃ 222 28.51 N 96.46 W
Gard ⊡5 32 44.00 N 4.00 E
Gard ≃ 62 43.51 N 4.37 E
Gard, Pont du ◆5 62 43.56 N 4.36 E
Garda 64 45.34 N 10.42 E
Garda, Lago di ⊜ 64 45.40 N 10.41 E
Gardabani 84 41.28 N 45.06 E
Gardanne 62 43.27 N 5.28 E
Garde, Lac la ⊜ 190 46.46 N 78.14 W
Gardelegen 54 52.31 N 11.23 E
Garden ≃ 190 46.32 N 84.09 W
Gardena 228 33.53 N 118.18 W
Gardena, Val V 64 46.35 N 11.35 E
Garden Acres 226 37.58 N 121.13 W
Garden City, Ga., U.S. 192 32.06 N 81.09 W
Garden City, Ks., U.S. 198 37.58 N 100.52 W
Garden City, Mi., U.S. 216 42.19 N 83.19 W
Garden City, Mo., U.S. 194 38.33 N 94.11 W
Garden City, N.Y., U.S. 210 40.43 N 73.38 W
Garden City, Tx., U.S. 196 31.52 N 101.29 W
Garden City — Qasr al-Dubārā ◆8 273c 30.02 N 31.14 E
Garden City Park 276 40.44 N 73.39 W
Garden City Raceway ◆ 284a 43.09 N 79.11 W
Gardendale 194 33.39 N 86.48 W
Garden Farms 226 35.24 N 120.07 W
Garden Gate Village 282 37.20 N 122.02 W
Garden Grove, Ca., U.S. 228 33.46 N 117.56 W
Garden Grove, Ia., U.S. 190 40.50 N 93.36 W
Garden Home 224 45.27 N 122.45 W
Garden Island I, Austl. 168a 32.13 S 115.41 E
Garden Island I, Mi., U.S. 190 45.49 N 85.30 W
Garden Lakes 192 34.17 N 85.16 W
Garden Peninsula ›1 190 45.45 N 86.35 W
Garden Plain 198 37.39 N 97.41 W
Garden Prairie 216 42.15 N 88.44 W
Garden Reach 126 22.33 N 88.17 E
Gardenside 218 38.03 N 84.33 W
Garden State Arts Center ◆ 276 40.24 N 74.11 W
Garden State Park Race Track ◆, N.J., U.S. 285 39.55 N 75.02 W
Garden State Park Race Track ◆, Pa., U.S. 285 39.55 N 75.02 W
Garden State Plaza ◆9 276 40.55 N 74.05 W
Gardenton 184 49.05 N 96.40 W
Garden Valley 226 38.51 N 120.51 W
Garden View 210 41.16 N 77.03 W
Gardenville 208 40.22 N 75.07 W
Gardermoen 26 60.13 N 11.06 E
Gardey 252 37.17 S 59.21 W
Gardeyz 120 33.37 N 69.07 E
Gardinas — Grodno 76 53.41 N 23.50 E
Gardiner, Me., U.S. 188 44.13 N 69.46 W
Gardiner, Mt., U.S. 202 45.01 N 110.42 W
Gardiner, N.Y., U.S. 210 41.41 N 74.09 W
Gardiner, Or., U.S. 202 43.43 N 124.06 W
Gardiner, Wa., U.S. 224 48.03 N 122.55 W
Gardiner Dam ◆6 184 51.17 N 106.51 W
Gardiner Range ∧ 162 23.50 S 131.46 E
Gardiners Bay c 207 41.08 N 72.10 W
Gardiners Creek ≃ 274b 37.50 S 145.02 E
Gardiners Island I 207 41.05 N 72.07 W
Garding 41 54.20 N 8.46 E
Gardner, Il., U.S. 216 41.11 N 88.18 W
Gardner, Ks., U.S. 198 38.48 N 94.55 W
Gardner, Ma., U.S. 207 42.34 N 71.59 W
Gardner Canal c 182 53.28 N 128.15 W
Gardner Lake ⊜ 207 41.31 N 72.13 W
Gardner Pinnacles II1 14 25.00 N 167.55 W
Gardnersville 218 38.46 N 84.30 W
Gardnertown 210 41.32 N 74.04 W
Gardnerville 226 38.56 N 119.44 W
Gardno 54 53.15 N 14.38 E
Gardolo 64 46.07 N 11.05 E
Gardon d'Alès ≃ 62 44.02 N 4.08 E
Gardon d'Anduze ≃ 62 44.02 N 4.08 E
Gardone Riviera 64 45.37 N 10.34 E
Gardone Val Trompia 64 45.41 N 10.11 E
Gårdsjö 40 58.52 N 14.19 E
Gårdskär 40 60.37 N 17.35 E
Gare Loch c 46 56.01 N 4.48 W
Garelochhead 46 56.05 N 4.50 W
Gareloi Island I 181a 51.47 N 178.48 W
Garenfeld ◆8 263 51.24 N 7.31 E
Garenin 46 58.21 N 6.50 W
Gare Simon 273b 4.15 S 15.11 E
Garešnica 36 45.35 N 16.56 E
Garessio 62 44.12 N 8.02 E
Garet, Mont ∧1 175f 14.16 S 167.30 E
Garfield, Ks., U.S. 198 38.04 N 99.14 W
Garfield, N.J., U.S. 210 40.52 N 74.06 W
Garfield, N.M., U.S. 200 32.45 N 107.15 W
Garfield, Wa., U.S. 202 47.00 N 117.08 W
Garfield Heights 214 41.25 N 81.36 W
Garfield Mountain ∧ 202 44.31 N 112.37 W
Garfield Park 208 39.42 N 75.33 W
Garfield Park ◆, Il., U.S. 278 41.53 N 87.43 W
Garfield Park ◆, Oh., U.S. 279a 41.26 N 81.36 W
Garfield Peak ∧ 200 42.47 N 107.18 W
Garforth 44 53.48 N 1.22 W
Garga 88 54.26 N 110.33 E
Gargaliánoi 38 37.04 N 21.39 E
Gargano, Promontorio del › 68 41.50 N 16.00 E
Gargano, Testa del › 68 41.49 N 16.12 E
Gargantua, Cape › 190 47.36 N 85.02 W
Garga Sarali 152 5.11 N 14.00 E
Gargazzone (Gargazon) 64 46.35 N 11.12 E
Gargellen 58 46.58 N 9.56 E
Gargenville 261 49.00 N 1.49 E
Garges-lès-Gonesse 261 48.58 N 2.25 E
Gargnano 64 45.41 N 10.40 E
Gargouna 150 15.56 N 0.13 E
Gargrave 44 53.59 N 2.06 W
Gargždai 76 55.43 N 21.24 E
Garhākota 124 23.46 N 79.09 E
Garhbeta 126 22.51 N 87.19 E
Garhdīwāla 123 31.44 N 75.45 E
Garhi Habībullāh Khān 123 34.24 N 73.23 E
Garhi Jasaya 272a 28.46 N 77.16 E
Garhi Katiya 272a 28.45 N 77.11 E
Garhi Khairo 120 28.04 N 67.59 E
Garhi Malehra 124 25.02 N 79.40 E
Garhjāt Hills ∧2 126 21.47 N 86.20 E
Garhmuktesar 124 28.48 N 78.06 E
Garhshankar 123 31.13 N 76.08 E
Garhwa 124 24.11 N 83.49 E
Gari 86 59.26 N 62.21 E
Garibaldi, Bra. 252 29.15 S 51.32 W
Garibaldi, B.C., Can. 182 49.58 N 123.09 W
Garibaldi, Or., U.S. 224 45.34 N 123.55 W
Garibaldi, Casa di ⊥ 71 41.13 N 9.27 E
Garibaldi, Mount ∧ 182 49.51 N 123.01 W
Garibaldi Provincial Park ◆ 182 50.00 N 122.50 W
Garies 158 30.30 S 18.00 E
Garigliano ≃ 66 41.13 N 13.45 E
Gariglione, Monte ∧ 68 39.09 N 16.41 E
Garin 258 34.26 S 58.44 W
Garín, Arroyo ≃ 288 34.23 S 58.43 W
Garin Regional Park ◆ 282 37.38 N 122.03 W
Garipçe Burnu › 267b 41.13 N 29.07 E
Garissa 154 0.28 S 39.38 E
Garita Palmera 236 13.44 N 90.05 W
Gariya 272b 22.28 N 88.23 E
Gārji 272b 22.51 N 88.19 E
Garkida 146 10.25 N 12.36 E
Garko 150 11.38 N 8.48 E
Garland, Al., U.S. 194 31.33 N 86.49 W
Garland, Md., U.S. 284b 39.11 N 76.39 W
Garland, Pa., U.S. 214 41.49 N 79.27 W
Garland, Tx., U.S. 222 32.54 N 96.38 W
Garland, Ut., U.S. 200 41.44 N 112.09 W
Garland Park ◆ 275b 43.44 N 79.35 W
Garland Peak ∧ 224 48.01 N 120.43 W
Garlasco 62 45.12 N 8.55 E
Garlate 62 45.49 N 9.23 E
Garlate, Lago di ⊜ 58 45.49 N 9.24 E
Garliava 76 54.49 N 23.52 E
Garlieston 44 54.48 N 4.22 W
Garlin 32 43.34 N 0.15 W
Garm 85 39.02 N 70.22 E
Garm Āb 120 32.14 N 65.01 E
Garmal 144 8.35 N 50.19 E
Garmersdorf 60 49.26 N 11.54 E
Garmī 128 39.01 N 48.03 E
Garmisch-Partenkirchen 64 47.29 N 11.05 E
Garmouth 46 57.40 N 3.07 W
Garmsār 128 35.20 N 52.13 E
Garnavillo 190 42.52 N 91.14 W
Garne 261 48.41 N 1.58 E
Garner, Ia., U.S. 190 43.06 N 93.36 W
Garner, N.C., U.S. 192 35.42 N 78.36 W
Garnet Range ∧ 202 46.45 N 113.15 W
Garnett 198 38.16 N 95.14 W
Garnijskij zapovednik ◆ 84 40.00 N 44.55 E
Garnish 186 47.14 N 55.22 W
Garnock ≃ 46 55.38 N 4.42 W
Garnpung, Lake ⊜ 166 33.30 S 143.12 E
Gāro Hills ∧2 124 25.30 N 90.30 E
Garona — Garonne ≃ 32 45.02 N 0.36 W
Garonne ≃ 32 45.02 N 0.36 W
Garoowe 144 8.24 N 48.29 E
Garou, Lac ⊜ 150 16.04 N 2.45 W
Garoua, Cam. 146 9.18 N 13.24 E
Garoua, Niger 146 13.53 N 13.11 E
Garoua Boulaï 152 5.53 N 14.33 E
Garove Island I 164 4.40 S 149.30 E
Garpenberg 40 60.19 N 16.12 E
Garphyttan 40 59.19 N 14.56 E
Garphyttans Nationalpark ◆ 40 59.17 N 14.51 E
Garqu Yan, Zhg. 118 34.29 N 92.35 E
Garqu Yan, Zhg. 120 33.50 N 92.28 E
Garraf, Costa de ⊥2 266d 41.16 N 2.02 E
Garrattsville 210 42.39 N 75.10 W
Garrel 52 52.57 N 8.01 E
Garret Mountain Reservation ◆ 276 40.54 N 74.11 W
Garretson 198 43.43 N 96.30 W
Garrett, In., U.S. 216 41.20 N 85.08 W
Garrett, Ky., U.S. 192 37.28 N 82.49 W
Garrett Creek ≃ 222 32.57 N 95.44 W
Garrett Park 208 39.02 N 77.05 W
Garrett Park Estates 284c 39.02 N 77.06 W
Garrettsville 214 41.17 N 81.06 W
Garrison, N. Ire., U.K. 48 54.25 N 8.05 W
Garrison, Ky., U.S. 218 38.36 N 83.10 W
Garrison, Md., U.S. 208 39.24 N 76.45 W
Garrison, Mt., U.S. 202 46.31 N 112.48 W
Garrison, N.Y., U.S. 210 41.23 N 73.56 W
Garrison, N.D., U.S. 198 47.39 N 101.24 W
Garrison, Tx., U.S. 222 31.49 N 94.30 W
Garrison Dam ◆6 198 47.22 N 101.25 W
Garron Point › 48 55.03 N 5.57 W
Garros 46 57.37 N 6.11 W
Garrovillas 34 39.43 N 6.33 W
Garry ≃ 46 56.43 N 3.47 W
Garry, Loch ⊜ 206 45.15 N 74.43 W
Garry Bay c 176 68.55 N 85.05 W
Garry Lake ⊜ 176 66.00 N 100.00 W
Gars am Kamp 61 48.36 N 15.40 E
Garsdale Head 44 54.19 N 2.20 W
Garsen 154 2.16 S 40.07 E
Garskolk 158 30.41 S 22.02 E
Gårslev 41 55.38 N 9.43 E
Garson 190 46.34 N 80.52 W
Garson Lake ⊜ 184 56.19 N 110.02 W
Garstang 44 53.55 N 2.47 W
Garstedt 52 53.41 N 9.58 E
Garstedterheide ◆3 52 53.17 N 8.43 E
Garsten 61 48.01 N 14.24 E
Garston 260 51.41 N 0.23 W
Garston ◆8 262 53.21 N 2.53 W
Garswood 262 53.29 N 2.40 W
Gartempe ≃ 32 46.48 N 0.50 E
Gartenstadt ◆8 263 51.30 N 7.26 E
Garthby Station (Beaulac) 206 45.50 N 71.23 W
Gartow 54 53.02 N 11.29 E
Gartrop-Bühl 263 51.40 N 6.49 E
Gartz 54 53.12 N 14.23 E
Garu 150 10.51 N 0.11 W
Garub 156 26.33 S 16.00 E
Garubhāsa 124 26.33 N 90.22 E
Gārulia 126 22.49 N 88.22 E
Garut 115a 7.13 S 107.54 E
Garve 46 57.37 N 4.42 W
Garvellachs II 46 56.14 N 5.47 W
Garvey Reservoir ⊜1 280 34.13 N 118.07 W
Garvie Mountains ∧ 172 45.30 S 168.50 E
Garwin 190 42.05 N 92.40 W
Garwolin 30 51.54 N 21.37 E
Garwood, N.J., U.S. 276 40.39 N 74.19 W
Garwood, Tx., U.S. 222 29.27 N 96.24 W
Gary, In., U.S. 216 41.35 N 87.20 W
Gary, S.D., U.S. 198 44.47 N 96.27 W
Gary, Tx., U.S. 194 32.07 N 94.22 W
Gary, W.V., U.S. 192 37.21 N 81.33 W
Garyarsa 120 31.44 N 80.21 E
Gary Harbor c 278 41.38 N 87.20 W
Garyi 120 30.54 N 98.56 E
Gary Municipal Airport ≋ 278 41.37 N 87.25 W
Garysburg 208 36.27 N 77.33 W
Garz 54 54.19 N 13.20 E
Garza 252 28.09 S 63.32 W
Garza Ayala 196 26.29 N 100.02 W
Garza García 196 25.40 N 100.24 W
Garzas Creek ≃ 226 37.13 N 120.57 W
Garzeno 58 46.08 N 9.15 E
Garzón, Col. 246 2.12 N 75.38 W
Garzón, Ur. 252 34.36 S 54.33 W
Gas 261 48.34 N 1.40 E
Gasan 116 13.19 N 121.51 E
Gasan-Kuli 128 37.27 N 53.59 E
Gas City 216 40.29 N 85.36 W
Gascogne ⊡9 32 44.00 N 0.05 E
Gascogne, Golfe de — Biscay, Bay of c 32 44.00 N 4.00 W
Gasconade 219 38.40 N 91.33 W
Gasconade ⊡6 219 38.27 N 91.30 W
Gasconade ≃ 194 38.40 N 91.33 W
Gasconade, Osage Fork ≃ 194 37.45 N 92.26 W
Gascoyne ≃ 162 24.52 S 113.37 E
Gascoyne, Mount ∧ 162 24.58 S 116.38 E
Gascoyne Junction 162 25.03 S 115.12 E
Gash (Nahr al-Qāsh) ≃ 140 16.48 N 35.51 E
Gashaka 146 7.21 N 11.27 E
Gasherbrum I ∧ 123 35.43 N 76.43 E
Gas Hu ⊜ 120 38.10 N 90.42 E
Gashua 146 12.54 N 11.00 E
Gasline 284a 42.53 N 79.11 W
Gasny 50 49.05 N 1.36 E
Gaspar 252 26.56 S 48.58 W
Gaspard Creek ≃ 182 51.34 N 122.17 W
Gasparilla Island I 220 26.46 N 82.16 W
Gasparilla Sound ⫯ 220 26.48 N 82.15 W
Gaspé 186 48.50 N 64.29 W
Gaspé, Baie de c 186 48.46 N 64.17 W
Gaspé, Cap › 186 48.45 N 64.10 W
Gaspé Peninsula — Gaspésie, Péninsule de la ›1 186 48.30 N 65.00 W
Gaspereau Lake ⊜ 186 44.57 N 64.34 W
Gasperina 68 38.44 N 16.30 E
Gaspésie, Parc Provincial de la ◆ 186 48.55 N 66.00 W
Gaspésie, Péninsule de la ›1 186 48.30 N 65.00 W
Gaspoltshofen 60 48.08 N 13.46 E
Gasport 210 43.11 N 78.34 W
Gassan 150 12.49 N 3.12 W
Gas-san ∧ 92 38.32 N 140.01 E
Gassaway 188 38.40 N 80.46 W
Gasse 64 47.23 N 11.09 E
Gasselte 52 52.57 N 6.46 E
Gassin 62 43.13 N 6.35 E
Gassino Torinese 62 45.08 N 7.49 E
Gassol 146 8.32 N 10.28 E
Gastein — Badgastein 64 47.07 N 13.08 E
Gasteiner Tal V 64 47.11 N 13.06 E
Gasteiz — Vitoria 34 42.51 N 2.40 W
Gastello 89 49.07 N 142.58 E
Gaston, In., U.S. 216 40.18 N 85.30 W
Gaston, N.C., U.S. 192 36.30 N 77.38 W
Gaston, Or., U.S. 224 45.26 N 123.08 W
Gaston, S.C., U.S. 192 33.49 N 81.05 W
Gaston, Lake ⊜1 192 36.35 N 78.00 W
Gastonia, N.C., U.S. 192 35.15 N 81.11 W
Gastonia, Tx., U.S. 222 32.37 N 96.24 W
Gastonville 279b 40.15 N 79.59 W
Gastoúni 38 37.51 N 21.16 E
Gastre 254 42.17 S 69.14 W
Gästrikland ⊡9 40 60.30 N 16.27 E
Gat 132 31.37 N 34.47 E
Gata, Cabo de › 34 36.43 N 2.12 W
Gata, Sierra de ∧ 34 40.14 N 6.45 W
Gătaia 38 45.26 N 21.26 E
Gatas, Akrotírion › 130 34.34 N 33.02 E
Gatčina 76 59.34 N 30.08 E
Gate 196 36.51 N 100.03 W
Gateacre ◆8 262 53.23 N 2.51 W
Gate City 192 36.38 N 82.34 W
Gatehouse of Fleet 44 54.53 N 4.11 W
Gatersleben 54 51.49 N 11.17 E
Gates, N.Y., U.S. 210 43.09 N 77.41 W
Gates, N.C., U.S. 208 36.30 N 76.46 W
Gates ⊡6 208 36.28 N 76.43 W
Gateshead 44 54.58 N 1.37 W
Gateshead Island I 176 70.22 N 100.27 W
Gates Mills 279a 41.31 N 81.24 W
Gates of the Arctic National Park ◆ 180 67.45 N 153.30 W
Gatesville, N.C., U.S. 192 36.24 N 76.45 W
Gatesville, Tx., U.S. 222 31.26 N 97.44 W
Gateway 200 38.40 N 108.58 W
Gateway Arch ◆ 219 38.37 N 90.12 W
Gateway National Recreation Area ◆ 276 40.34 N 74.06 W
Gateway of India ⊥ 272c 18.55 N 72.50 E
Gateway Stadium ◆ 279a 41.30 N 81.41 W
Gaths Mine 154 20.00 S 30.31 E
Gathurst 262 53.34 N 2.42 W
Gatié Loumo 150 10.28 N 4.37 W
Gatineau 212 45.29 N 75.38 W
Gatineau ⊡6 212 45.25 N 75.45 W
Gatineau ≃ 176 45.27 N 75.40 W
Gatineau, Parc de la ◆ 188 45.30 N 76.05 W
Gatley 262 53.23 N 2.14 W
Gatlinburg 192 35.42 N 83.30 W
Gato, Arroyo del ≃, Arg. 288 34.55 S 58.37 W
Gato, Arroyo del ≃, Arg. 288 34.51 S 57.56 W
Ga'ton 132 33.00 N 35.13 E
Gato Negro 286c 10.33 N 66.57 W
Gatow ◆5 264a 52.29 N 13.11 E
Gatow, Flugplatz ≋ 264a 52.28 N 13.08 E
Gattendorf 61 48.01 N 16.59 E
Gattières 62 43.46 N 7.11 E
Gattinara 62 45.37 N 8.22 E
Gatton 171a 27.33 S 152.17 E
Gattorna 62 44.26 N 9.11 E
Gatún, Esclusas de ◆5 236 9.16 N 79.55 W
Gatún, Lago ⊜1 236 9.12 N 79.55 W
Gatvand 128 32.15 N 48.50 E
Gau-Algesheim 56 49.57 N 8.01 E
Gauchy 50 49.49 N 3.16 E
Gaucín 34 36.31 N 5.19 W
Gauer Lake ⊜ 184 57.00 N 97.50 W
Gauhāti 124 26.11 N 91.44 E
Gauja ≃ 76 57.09 N 24.16 E
Gaujiena 76 57.30 N 26.40 E
Gaukler Point › 281 42.27 N 82.52 W
Gaula ≃ 26 63.21 N 10.14 E
Gauley ≃ 188 38.10 N 81.12 W
Gauley Bridge 188 38.10 N 81.11 W
Gaultois 186 47.36 N 55.54 W
Gaunless ≃ 44 54.40 N 1.41 W
Gau-Odernheim 56 49.47 N 8.11 E
Gaur 124 26.46 N 85.17 E
Gaurain-Ramecroix 50 50.35 N 3.29 E
Gaurambha 126 22.39 N 89.34 E
Gaurela 124 22.45 N 81.54 E
Gaurhāti 126 22.46 N 87.48 E
Gauribaradia 126 23.45 N 89.52 E
Gauribidanūr 122 13.37 N 77.31 E
Gauri Phanta 124 28.41 N 80.33 E
Gaurīpur 124 26.05 N 89.58 E
Gaurīsankar ∧ 124 27.57 N 86.21 E
Gaurnadi 126 22.58 N 90.14 E
Gause 222 30.47 N 96.43 W
Gausta ∧ 26 59.50 N 8.35 E
Gauthiot, Chutes ⊑ 146 9.43 N 14.34 E
Gauting 60 48.04 N 11.23 E
Gavà 34 41.18 N 2.01 E
Gāvanpāda 272c 18.57 N 73.01 E
Gavardo 64 45.35 N 10.26 E
Gávdhos I 38 34.50 N 24.06 E
Gávea ◆8 287a 22.58 S 43.14 W
Gávea, Hipódromo da ◆ 287a 22.58 S 43.13 W
Gávea, Pedra da ∧ 287a 23.00 S 43.17 W
Gävel-Långsjön ⊜ 40 59.50 N 18.18 E
Gavello 64 45.01 N 11.55 E
Gavet 62 45.04 N 5.52 E
Gavi 62 44.41 N 8.49 E
Gavia, Arroyo de la ≃ 266a 40.21 N 3.40 W
Gavião ≃ 255 14.06 S 41.01 W
Gavião, Pico do ∧ 256 21.37 S 44.50 W
Gavien 164 3.54 S 144.07 E
Gavilán 286c 10.24 N 66.51 W
Gavinana 66 44.03 N 10.55 E
Gavins Point Dam ◆6 198 42.48 N 97.40 W
Gaviões 256 22.34 S 42.33 W
Gavirate 62 45.50 N 8.43 E
Gavja ≃ 76 53.49 N 25.35 E
Gāv Khūnī, Bātlāq-e ⊞ 128 32.10 N 52.50 E
Gävle 40 60.40 N 17.10 E
Gävleborgs Län ⊡6 26 61.30 N 16.15 E
Gävlebukten c 40 60.42 N 17.20 E
Gavnø 41 55.11 N 11.44 E
Gavoi 71 40.10 N 9.12 E
Gavorrano 66 42.55 N 10.54 E
Gavrilov-Jam 80 57.18 N 39.51 E
Gavrilovka Vtoraja 80 52.53 N 42.46 E
Gavrilov Posad 80 56.33 N 40.07 E
Gávrion 38 37.52 N 24.46 E
Gavry 76 56.55 N 27.53 E
Gawachab 156 27.03 S 17.50 E
Gāwān 124 24.37 N 85.55 E
Gaweinstal 61 48.28 N 16.35 E
Gāwīlgarh Hills ∧2 122 21.20 N 77.00 E
Gawler 168b 34.37 S 138.44 E
Gawler ≃ 168b 34.41 S 138.27 E
Gawler Ranges ∧ 162 32.30 S 136.00 E
Gawso 150 6.48 N 2.31 W
Gawsworth 262 53.13 N 2.10 W
Gawthorpe Hall ⊥ 262 53.48 N 2.18 W
Gaxun Nur (Juyanhai) ⊜ 102 42.22 N 100.34 E
Gaya, India 124 24.47 N 85.00 E
Gaya, Niger 150 11.53 N 3.27 E
Gaya, Nig. 150 11.53 N 9.02 E
Gay City State Park ◆ 207 41.42 N 72.28 W
Gayéri 150 12.39 N 0.29 E
Gay Head 207 41.20 N 70.48 W
Gay Hill 222 30.16 N 96.30 W
Gaylord, Mi., U.S. 190 45.01 N 84.40 W
Gaylord, Mn., U.S. 190 44.33 N 94.13 W
Gaylordsville 207 41.38 N 73.29 W
Gayndah 166 25.37 S 151.36 E
Gays Mills 190 43.19 N 90.50 W
Gayton, Eng., U.K. 42 52.45 N 0.34 E
Gayton, Eng., U.K. 262 53.19 N 3.06 W
Gaza — Ghazzah 132 31.30 N 34.28 E
Gaza ⊡5 156 23.30 S 32.45 E
Gazalkent 85 41.33 N 69.47 E
Gazaoua 150 13.32 N 7.55 E
Gaza Strip ⊡9 132 31.25 N 34.20 E
Gazelle Channel ⫯ 164 2.50 S 150.55 E
Gazelle Peninsula ›1 164 4.40 S 152.00 E
Gazeran 261 48.38 N 1.46 E
Gazeran, Bois de ◆ 261 48.40 N 1.45 E
Gazi, Kenya 154 4.25 S 39.30 E
Gazi, Zaïre 154 1.04 N 24.31 E
Gaziantep 130 37.05 N 37.22 E
Gaziantep ⊡4 130 37.00 N 37.20 E
Gazimağusa (Famagusta) 130 35.07 N 33.57 E
Gazimağusa Körfezi c 130 35.15 N 34.10 E
Gazimur ≃ 88 52.57 N 120.22 E
Gazimurskij Zavod 88 51.33 N 118.22 E
Gazipaşa 130 36.17 N 32.20 E
Gazira Sporting Club ◆ 273c 30.04 N 31.13 E
Gazivoda Jezero ⊜1 38 42.55 N 20.40 E
Gaznau 85 40.10 N 71.02 E
Gazoldo degli Ippoliti 64 45.12 N 10.35 E
Gazos Creek ≃ 226 37.10 N 122.22 W
Gazzada 62 45.47 N 8.51 E
Gazzaniga 62 45.48 N 9.50 E
Gazzuolo 64 45.04 N 10.35 E
Gbangbatok 150 7.48 N 12.23 W
Gbanhala ≃ 150 10.14 N 8.38 W
Gbaoui Bodanga 152 5.33 N 16.45 E
Gbarnga 150 7.00 N 9.29 W
Gbogbo 273a 6.36 N 3.31 E
Gboko 150 7.20 N 8.57 E
Gbon 150 9.50 N 6.27 W
Gbwado 152 3.54 N 20.46 E
Gcoverega 156 19.08 S 24.15 E
Gdańsk (Danzig) 30 54.23 N 18.40 E
Gdańsk ⊡4 30 54.15 N 18.25 E
Gdansk, Gulf of c 30 54.40 N 19.15 E
Gden' 78 51.20 N 30.25 E
Gdov 76 58.44 N 27.48 E
Gdyel 34 35.48 N 0.26 W
Gdynia 30 54.32 N 18.33 E
Gearhart 224 46.01 N 123.54 W
Gearhart Mountain ∧ 202 42.30 N 120.53 W
Gearhartville 214 40.53 N 78.15 W
Geary, N.B., Can. 186 45.46 N 66.29 W
Geary, Ok., U.S. 196 35.43 N 98.22 W
Geauga ⊡6 214 41.35 N 81.12 W
Geauga Lake Park ◆ 279a 41.21 N 81.23 W
Geba ≃ 150 11.46 N 15.36 W
Gebaberg ∧ 56 50.36 N 10.16 E
Gebe, Pulau I 164 0.05 S 129.20 E
Gebeit Mine 140 21.03 N 36.19 E
Gebenbach 60 49.32 N 11.53 E
Gebesee 54 51.07 N 10.56 E
Gebi 84 42.46 N 43.30 E
Gebilu 144 10.35 N 41.28 E
Gebiz 130 37.06 N 30.56 E
Gebra 54 51.24 N 10.35 E
Gebweiler — Guebwiller 58 47.55 N 7.12 E
Gebze 130 40.48 N 29.25 E
Gecha 144 7.31 N 35.22 E
Gechang 106 31.05 N 119.27 E
Geçitkale 130 35.15 N 33.45 E
Gecun 106 32.10 N 119.37 E
Geddes, Mi., U.S. 281 42.16 N 83.40 W
Geddes, S.D., U.S. 198 43.15 N 98.41 W
Gede, Gunung ∧ 115a 6.47 S 106.59 E
Gedera 132 31.49 N 34.46 E
Gedern 56 50.25 N 9.12 E
Gedian 100 30.32 N 114.38 E
Gedikler 130 39.06 N 38.49 E
Gediksaray 130 40.27 N 35.38 E
Gedi National Monument ◆ 154 3.19 S 40.03 E
Gedinne 56 49.59 N 4.56 E
Gediz 130 39.02 N 29.25 E
Gediz ≃ 130 38.35 N 26.48 E
Gedlegube 144 6.52 N 45.02 E
Gedo 144 8.58 N 37.27 E
Gedo ⊡4 144 3.00 N 42.00 E
Gedongdalem 112 5.04 S 105.25 E
Gedongtataan 115a 5.23 S 105.05 E
Gedser 41 54.35 N 11.57 E
Gedser Odde › 41 54.34 N 11.59 E
Geduld 273d 26.15 S 28.25 E
Gedun 100 27.39 N 118.26 E
Geebung 171a 27.22 S 153.03 E
Gee Cross 262 53.26 N 2.04 W
Geehi 171b 36.24 S 148.11 E
Geehi ≃ 171b 36.11 S 148.02 E
Geel 56 51.10 N 5.00 E
Geelong 169 38.08 S 144.21 E
Geelong West 169 38.08 S 144.20 E
Geelvink Channel ⫯ 162 28.30 S 114.10 E
Geer ≃ 56 50.51 N 5.42 E
Geeste ≃ 52 53.32 N 8.35 E
Geesthacht 52 53.26 N 10.22 E
Geeveston 166 43.10 S 146.55 E
Gefell 54 50.26 N 11.52 E
Gefle — Gävle 40 60.40 N 17.10 E
Gefrees 54 50.06 N 11.44 E
Gegang 100 30.04 N 117.38 E
Gegenmiao 89 45.58 N 122.15 E
Gegong 100 30.05 N 117.11 E
Gegou 98 35.24 N 118.32 E
Gegu 105 38.59 N 117.30 E
Gehackte Berge ∧2 264a 52.41 N 13.30 E
Gehrden 52 52.18 N 9.36 E
Gehren 54 50.39 N 10.59 E
Gehu 100 27.46 N 119.16 E
Ge Hu ⊜ 106 31.36 N 119.51 E
Gehua 106 30.20 N 120.25 E
Geidam 146 12.57 N 11.57 E
Geiger 194 32.52 N 88.18 W
Geigertown 208 40.13 N 75.50 W
Geihoku 96 34.44 N 132.17 E
Geikie ≃ 176 57.45 N 103.52 W

ENGLISH

Name — Page — Lat.°′ — Long.°′

Geilenkirchen 56 50.57 N 6.07 E
Geilo 26 60.31 N 8.12 E
Geinō 94 34.48 N 136.25 E
Geiranger 26 62.06 N 7.12 E
Geisa 56 50.43 N 9.57 E
Geisberg ∧ 60 49.53 N 11.03 E
Geisecke 263 51.27 N 7.37 E
Geisei 96 33.31 N 133.49 E
Geiselhöring 60 48.50 N 12.23 E
Geisenfeld 60 48.41 N 11.37 E
Geisenhausen 60 48.28 N 12.15 E
Geisenheim 56 49.59 N 7.58 E
Geisingen 58 47.55 N 8.38 E
Geislingen an der Steige 56 48.36 N 9.50 E
Geismar 52 51.31 N 9.57 E
Geispolsheim 58 48.31 N 7.39 E
Geisstein ∧ 64 47.20 N 12.30 E
Geistenbeck ◆8 263 51.09 N 6.27 E
Geistown 214 40.17 N 78.52 W
Geist Reservoir ⊜1, In., U.S. 218 39.56 N 85.56 W
Geist Reservoir ⊜1, Pa., U.S. 285 39.57 N 75.24 W
Geisweid 56 50.55 N 8.01 E
Geita 154 2.52 S 32.10 E
Geithain 54 51.03 N 12.41 E
Geiyō-shotō II 96 34.10 N 132.45 E
Gejah 272a 28.31 N 77.23 E
Gejiatun 98 40.27 N 119.55 E
Gejiu (Kokiu) 102 23.22 N 103.06 E
Geka, mys › 180 64.26 N 178.10 E
Gela 70 37.04 N 14.15 E
Gela ≃ 70 37.03 N 14.15 E
Gela, Golfo di c 70 37.03 N 14.10 E
Geladandong ∧ 120 33.16 N 91.27 E
Geladi 144 6.57 N 46.25 E
Gelai ∧1 154 2.33 S 36.05 E
Gelan 102 30.03 N 107.04 E
Gelang, Tanjong › 114 3.58 N 103.26 E
Gelaochang 107 29.36 N 103.39 E
Gelasa, Selat ⫯ 112 2.40 S 107.15 E
Gelber Fluss — Huang ≃ 90 37.32 N 118.19 E
Gelbes Meer — Yellow Sea ᐁ2 90 36.00 N 123.00 E
Gelderland ⊡4 52 52.10 N 5.50 E
Geldermalsen 52 51.53 N 5.17 E
Geldern 52 51.31 N 6.20 E
Geldrop 52 51.25 N 5.33 E
Geleen 56 50.58 N 5.52 E
Gelembe 130 39.10 N 27.50 E
Gelemso 144 8.48 N 40.35 E
Gelenau 54 50.42 N 12.58 E
Gelendost 130 38.07 N 31.01 E
Gelendžik 78 44.33 N 38.06 E
Gelfingen 58 47.13 N 8.16 E
Gelgaudiškis 76 55.05 N 23.00 E
Gelib — Jilib 144 0.29 N 42.46 E
Gelibolu 130 40.24 N 26.40 E
Gelibolu Yarımadası (Gallipoli Peninsula) ›1 130 40.20 N 26.30 E
Gelibolu Yarımadası Milli Parkı ◆ 130 40.05 N 26.10 E
Gelinden 56 50.46 N 5.15 E
Gélise ≃ 32 44.11 N 0.17 E
Geliting 115b 8.39 S 122.18 E
Geliting, Teluk c 115b 8.36 S 122.17 E
Gellénháza 61 46.46 N 16.47 E
Gellenstrom ⫯ 54 54.28 N 13.03 E
Gellep-Stratum ◆8 263 51.20 N 6.41 E
Gellibrand ≃ 169 38.41 S 143.09 E
Gellibrand, Mount ∧2 169 38.14 S 143.48 E
Gellibrand, Point › 274b 37.52 S 144.54 E
Gellibrand River 169 38.32 S 143.32 E
Gellingen — Ghislenghien 50 50.39 N 3.52 E
Gellinsoor 144 6.26 N 46.42 E
Gelnhausen 56 50.11 N 9.11 E
Gelså ≃ 41 55.19 N 8.54 E
Gelsdorf 56 50.35 N 7.02 E
Gelsenkirchen 52 51.31 N 7.07 E
Gelsenkirchen-Horst, Galopprennbahn ◆ 263 51.32 N 7.02 E
Gelsted 41 55.24 N 9.59 E
Gelt ≃ 44 54.56 N 2.47 W
Geltendorf 60 48.07 N 11.01 E
Gelterkinden 58 47.28 N 7.51 E
Gelting 41 54.45 N 9.53 E
Geltow 54 52.22 N 12.58 E
Geltsa 144 6.14 N 37.05 E
Geluji 98 37.08 N 121.50 E
Geluksburg 158 28.30 S 29.33 E
Geluwe 50 50.48 N 3.04 E
Gemas 114 2.35 N 102.37 E
Gembloux 56 50.34 N 4.41 E
Gembrook 169 37.57 S 145.33 E
Gemen 52 51.51 N 6.52 E
Gemena 152 3.15 N 19.46 E
Géménos 62 43.18 N 5.38 E
Gemerek 130 39.11 N 36.05 E
Gemert 52 51.34 N 5.40 E
Gemla 26 56.52 N 14.38 E
Gemlik 130 40.26 N 29.09 E
Gemlik Körfezi c 130 40.25 N 28.55 E
Gemolong 115a 7.24 S 110.50 E
Gemona del Friuli 64 46.16 N 13.09 E
Gemonio 62 45.53 N 8.40 E
Gemsbok National Park ◆ 156 25.15 S 21.10 E
Gemünd 56 50.34 N 6.30 E
Gemünden, Dtsch. 56 50.03 N 9.41 E
Gemünden, Dtsch. 56 50.58 N 8.58 E
Gemünden, Dtsch. 56 49.54 N 7.28 E
Gen ≃ 89 50.16 N 119.22 E
Genadendal 158 34.02 S 19.33 E
Genalbashi 268 35.21 N 140.04 E
Genale (Jubba) ≃ 144 0.15 S 42.38 E
Genappe 50 50.36 N 4.27 E
Genarp 41 55.36 N 13.23 E
Genazzano 66 41.50 N 12.58 E
Genç 130 38.46 N 40.35 E
Gençay 32 46.23 N 0.24 E
Gencek 130 37.27 N 31.33 E
Gencsapáti 61 47.17 N 16.36 E
Gending 115a 7.48 S 113.18 E
Gendrey 58 47.12 N 5.41 E
Gendringen 52 51.52 N 6.22 E
Gendt 52 51.53 N 5.59 E
Genegantslet Creek ≃ 210 42.18 N 75.48 W
Genemuiden 52 52.37 N 6.07 E
General ≃ 236 8.59 N 83.11 W
General Acha 252 37.23 S 64.36 W
General Alvear, Arg. 252 36.03 S 60.01 W
General Alvear, Arg. 252 34.58 S 67.42 W
General Aquino 252 24.26 S 56.42 W
General Arenales 252 34.18 S 61.18 W
General Belgrano 252 35.46 S 58.30 W
General Bernardo O'Higgins ◆3 9 63.19 S 57.54 W
General Bravo 232 25.48 N 99.10 W
General Butler State Resort Park ◆ 218 38.40 N 85.10 W
General Cabrera 252 32.48 S 63.52 W
General Campos 252 31.32 S 58.24 W
General Carneiro 255 15.42 S 52.45 W
General Carrera, Lago (Lago Buenos Aires) ⊜ 254 46.35 S 72.00 W
General Cepeda 232 25.23 N 101.27 W
General Conesa, Arg. 252 36.30 S 57.20 W
General Conesa, Arg. 254 40.06 S 64.26 W
General Daniel Cerri 252 38.42 S 62.24 W
General del Sur, Cementerio ◆ 286c 10.28 N 66.55 W
General Elizardo Aquino 252 26.53 S 56.17 W

DEUTSCH

Name — Seite — Breite°′ — Länge°′ E = Ost

General Enrique Martínez 252 33.12 S 53.48 W
General Enrique Mosconi 252 22.36 S 63.49 W
General Escobedo, Méx. 196 25.49 N 100.20 W
General Escobedo, Méx. 232 25.30 N 105.15 W
General Eugenio A. Garay, Para. 248 20.31 S 62.08 W
General Eugenio A. Garay, Para. 252 25.55 S 56.11 W
General Galarza 252 32.43 S 59.24 W
General Güemes 252 24.40 S 65.03 W
General Guido 252 36.40 S 57.46 W
General Hornos 258 34.53 S 58.56 W
General Island I 116 9.25 N 126.00 E
General José de San Martín 252 26.33 S 59.21 W
General Juan José Ríos 232 25.40 N 108.40 W
General Juan Madariaga 252 37.00 S 57.09 W
General La Madrid 252 37.16 S 61.17 W
General Las Heras 258 34.56 S 58.57 W
General Las Heras ⊡5 288 34.56 S 58.51 W
General Lavalle 252 36.24 S 56.58 W
General Leonidas Plaza Gutiérrez 246 2.58 S 78.25 W
General Levalle 252 34.01 S 63.56 W
General Lorenzo Vintter 254 40.44 S 64.29 W
General Luna 116 9.47 N 126.09 E
General MacArthur (Pambuhan Sur) 116 11.15 N 125.32 E
General Mansilla (Bartolomé Bavio) 258 35.05 S 57.45 W
General Manuel Belgrano, Cerro ∧ 252 29.01 S 67.49 W
General Mitchell Field ≋ 216 42.57 N 87.54 W
General Motors Corporation (Pontiac Division) ◆3 281 42.49 N 83.17 W
General Motors Proving Grounds ◆3 281 42.35 N 83.41 W
General Motors Technical Center ◆3 281 42.31 N 83.02 W
General'nyj ≃ 265a 60.00 N 30.32 E
General O'Brien 252 34.54 S 60.45 W
General Pacheco 288 34.28 S 58.38 W
General Pánfilo Natera 234 22.40 N 102.06 W
General Paz 258 35.31 S 58.19 W
General Pico 252 35.40 S 63.44 W
General Pinedo 252 27.19 S 61.17 W
General Pinto 252 34.46 S 61.53 W
General Pizarro 252 24.13 S 64.01 W
General Roca 252 39.02 S 67.35 W
General Rodríguez 258 34.36 S 58.57 W
General San Martín, Arg. 252 37.59 S 63.34 W
General San Martín, Arg. 258 34.34 S 58.32 W
General San Martín ⊡5 288 34.34 S 58.34 W
General Santos (Dadiangas) 116 6.07 N 125.11 E
General Sarmiento 258 34.33 S 58.43 W
General Sarmiento ⊡5 288 34.32 S 58.43 W
General'skoje 83 47.28 N 39.35 E
General Terán 232 25.16 N 99.41 W
General Tinio 116 15.21 N 121.03 E
General Toševo 38 43.42 N 28.02 E
General Treviño 196 26.14 N 99.29 W
General Viamonte (Los Toldos) 252 35.01 S 61.01 W
General Villegas 252 35.02 S 63.01 W
General Vintter, Lago (Lago Palena) ⊜ 254 43.55 S 71.40 W
General Warren Village 285 40.02 N 75.32 W
General Zuazua 196 25.54 N 100.07 W
Gênes — Genova 62 44.25 N 8.57 E
Genesee, Id., U.S. 202 46.33 N 116.55 W
Genesee, Pa., U.S. 214 41.59 N 77.52 W
Genesee, Wi., U.S. 216 42.58 N 88.21 W
Genesee ⊡6, Mi., U.S. 216 42.56 N 83.41 W
Genesee ⊡6, N.Y., U.S. 210 43.00 N 78.11 W
Genesee ≃ 210 43.16 N 77.36 W
Geneseo, Il., U.S. 190 41.26 N 90.09 W
Geneseo, Ks., U.S. 198 38.30 N 98.09 W
Geneseo, N.Y., U.S. 210 42.47 N 77.49 W
Geneva — Genève, Schw. 58 46.12 N 6.09 E
Geneva, S. Afr. 158 27.50 S 27.08 E
Geneva, Al., U.S. 194 31.01 N 85.51 W
Geneva, Fl., U.S. 220 28.44 N 81.07 W
Geneva, Il., U.S. 216 41.53 N 88.18 W
Geneva, In., U.S. 216 40.35 N 84.57 W
Geneva, Ne., U.S. 198 40.31 N 97.35 W
Geneva, N.Y., U.S. 210 42.52 N 77.00 W
Geneva, Oh., U.S. 214 41.48 N 80.56 W
Geneva, Pa., U.S. 214 41.35 N 80.14 W
Geneva, Wa., U.S. 224 48.45 N 122.24 W
Geneva, Lake (Lac Léman) (Lac de Genève) ⊜, Europe 58 46.25 N 6.30 E
Geneva, Lake ⊜, Wi., U.S. 216 42.34 N 88.30 W
Geneva-on-the-Lake 214 41.52 N 80.57 W
Genève (Geneva) 58 46.12 N 6.09 E
Genève ⊡3 58 46.15 N 6.10 E
Genève, Lac de — Geneva, Lake ⊜ 58 46.25 N 6.30 E
Genève-Cointrin, Aéroport ≋ 58 46.14 N 6.06 E
Genevois ◆1 58 46.03 N 6.14 E
Genévriers, Île des I 186 51.15 N 58.26 W
Genf — Genève 58 46.12 N 6.09 E
Genga 66 43.26 N 12.56 E
Gengenbach 58 48.24 N 8.01 E
Genghis Khan, Wall of ⊥, Asia 88 49.00 N 115.00 E
Genghis Khan, Wall of ⊥, Mong. 88 49.00 N 116.00 E
Gengji 100 33.47 N 112.47 E
Gengma 102 23.34 N 99.06 E
Gengputou 106 31.12 N 119.55 E
Gengzhuang 104 40.59 N 122.42 E
Génicourt 261 49.05 N 2.04 E
Génicourt-sur-Meuse 56 49.02 N 5.26 E
Genil ≃ 34 37.42 N 5.19 W
Génissiat 58 46.03 N 5.47 E
Genk 56 50.58 N 5.30 E
Genkai 96 33.51 N 130.30 E
Genkai-kokutei-kōen ◆ 96 33.54 N 130.31 E
Genkai-nada ᐁ2 92 34.00 N 130.00 E
Genkanyj, chrebet ∧ 180 66.15 N 172.00 W
Genlis 58 47.14 N 5.13 E
Gennach ≃ 58 48.10 N 10.43 E
Gennargentu, Monti del ∧ 71 40.01 N 9.19 E
Gennebreck 263 51.19 N 7.12 E
Gennep 52 51.42 N 5.58 E
Genner 41 55.07 N 9.26 E
Gennes 32 47.20 N 0.14 W
Gennevilliers 261 48.56 N 2.18 E
Genoa, Austl. 166 37.29 S 149.35 E
Genoa — Genova, It. 62 44.25 N 8.57 E
Genoa, Il., U.S. 216 42.05 N 88.41 W
Genoa, Ne., U.S. 198 41.26 N 97.43 W

Symbols in the index entries represent the broad categories identified in the key at the right. Symbols with superior numbers (∧1) identify subcategories (see complete key on page I · 1).

Symbole im Register stellen die rechts im Schlüssel erklärten Kategorien dar. Symbole mit hochgestellten Ziffern (∧1) bezeichnen Unterabteilungen einer Kategorie (vgl. vollständiger Schlüssel auf Seite I · 1).

Los símbolos incluidos en el texto del índice representan las grandes categorías identificadas con la clave a la derecha. Los símbolos con numeros en su parte superior (∧1) identifican las subcategorías (véase la clave completa en la página I · 1).

Les symboles de l'index représentent les catégories indiquées dans la légende à droite. Les symboles suivis d'un indice (∧1) représentent des sous-catégories (voir légende complète à la page I · 1).

Os símbolos incluídos no texto do índice representam as grandes categorias identificadas com a chave à direita. Os símbolos com números em sua parte superior (∧1) identificam as subcategorias (veja-se a chave completa à página I · 1).

∧ Mountain	Berg	Montaña	Montagne	Montanha	
∧ Mountains	Gebirge	Montañas	Montagnes	Montanhas	
x Pass	Paß	Paso	Col	Passo	
V Valley, Canyon	Tal, Cañon	Valle, Cañón	Vallée, Canyon	Vale, Canhão	
= Plain	Ebene	Llano	Plaine	Planície	
› Cape	Kap	Cabo	Cap	Cabo	
I Island	Insel	Isla	Île	Ilha	
II Islands	Inseln	Islas	Îles	Ilhas	
⊥ Other Topographic Features	Andere Topographische Objekte	Otros Elementos Topográficos	Autres données topographiques	Outros acidentes topográficos	

ESPAÑOL

Nombre	Página	Lat.°′	Long.°′ W = Oeste
Genoa, Nv., U.S.	226	39.00 N	119.50 W
Genoa, N.Y., U.S.	210	42.40 N	76.32 W
Genoa, Oh., U.S.	214	41.31 N	83.21 W
Genoa, Wi., U.S.	190	43.34 N	91.13 W
Genoa, Arroyo ≃	254	44.58 S	70.06 W
Genoa City	216	42.29 N	88.19 W
Genoa Peak ∧	226	39.03 N	119.53 W
Genola	62	44.35 N	7.39 E
Génolhac	62	44.21 N	3.57 E
Genova (Genoa)	62	44.25 N	8.57 E
Genova □[4]	62	44.30 N	9.04 E
Genova, Golfo di ⊂	62	44.10 N	8.55 E
Genova, Val V	64	46.11 N	10.40 E
Genovesa, Isla I	246a	0.20 N	89.58 W
Genrijetty, ostrov I	74	77.06 N	156.30 E
Gensan → Wŏnsan	98	39.09 N	127.25 E
Gens de Terre ≃	190	46.53 N	76.00 W
Genshagen	264a	52.19 N	13.19 E
Genshagener Heide ◆[3]	264a	52.20 N	13.18 E
Genshiryoku-kenkyūsho ɤ[3]	94	36.27 N	140.36 E
Gensingen	56	49.53 N	7.55 E
Gensungen	56	51.08 N	9.26 E
Gent (Gand)	50	51.03 N	3.43 E
Gentbrugge	50	51.03 N	3.45 E
Gent-Brugge, Kanaal ≍	50	51.03 N	3.43 E
Genteng	115a	8.22 S	114.09 E
Genteng, Gili I	115a	7.12 S	113.54 E
Genteng, Tanjung ›	115a	7.23 S	106.24 E
Genthin	54	52.24 N	12.09 E
Gentilly	261	48.49 N	2.21 E
Gentilly ≃	206	46.24 N	72.21 W
Genting	114	3.42 N	98.10 E
Gentio do Ouro	250	11.25 S	42.30 W
Gentioux	32	45.47 N	1.59 E
Gentofte	41	55.45 N	12.33 E
Gentry	194	36.16 N	94.29 W
Gentry, Lake ⊜	220	28.08 N	81.15 W
Genua → Genova	62	44.25 N	8.57 E
Genuang	114	2.29 N	102.53 E
Genval	50	50.43 N	4.29 E
Genyem	164	2.46 S	140.12 E
Genzano di Lucania	68	40.51 N	16.02 E
Genzano di Roma	66	41.42 N	12.41 E
Geographe Bay ⊂	162	33.35 S	115.15 E
Geographe Channel ⊔	162	24.40 S	113.20 E
Geok-Tepe	128	38.09 N	57.58 E
Geonkhāli	126	22.12 N	88.03 E
George, S. Afr.	158	33.58 S	22.24 E
George, Ia., U.S.	198	43.20 N	96.00 W
George, Tx., U.S.	222	30.59 N	96.07 W
George ≃, Austl.	162	20.50 S	117.28 E
George ≃, P.Q., Can.	176	58.49 N	66.10 W
George, Cape ›	186	45.53 N	61.53 W
George, Lake ⊜, Austl.	162	22.37 S	123.38 E
George, Lake ⊜, Austl.	166	35.05 S	149.25 E
George, Lake ⊜, N.A.	190	46.28 N	84.10 W
George, Lake ⊜, Ug.	154	0.02 N	30.12 E
George, Lake ⊜, U.S.	216	41.45 N	85.00 W
George, Lake ⊜, Fl., U.S.	192	29.17 N	81.36 W
George, Lake ⊜, In., U.S.	216	41.40 N	87.30 W
George, Lake ⊜, N.Y., U.S.	188	43.35 N	73.35 W
George Air Force Base ■	228	34.35 N	117.22 W
George B. Stevenson Dam ◆[6]	214	41.25 N	78.01 W
George Gill Range ⋏	162	24.15 S	131.36 E
George H. Crosby Manitou State Park ♦	190	47.29 N	91.10 W
George Island I	254	52.19 S	59.45 W
George Mason University ɤ[2]	284c	38.50 N	77.17 W
Georgensgmünd	56	49.11 N	11.00 E
Georgenthal	54	50.49 N	10.40 E
Georges ≃	170	33.57 S	150.58 E
Georges Bank ✢[4]	16	41.15 N	67.30 W
Georges Island I	283	42.19 N	70.56 W
George Sound ⊔	172	44.50 S	167.23 E
Georges River Bridge ◆[5]	274a	34.00 S	151.07 E
Georges Run	214	40.21 N	80.37 W
Georges Run ≃	279b	40.23 N	80.06 W
Georgetown, Austl.	166	18.18 S	143.33 E
George Town, Austl.	166	41.06 S	146.50 E
Georgetown → Halton Hills, On., Can.	190	43.37 N	79.56 W
Georgetown, P.E., Can.	186	46.11 N	62.32 W
George Town, Cay. Is.	238	19.18 N	81.23 W
Georgetown, Gam.	150	13.30 N	14.47 W
Georgetown, Guy.	246	6.48 N	58.10 W
George Town (Pinang), Malay.	114	5.25 N	100.20 E
Georgetown, St. Vin.	241h	13.16 N	61.08 W
Georgetown, Ca., U.S.	226	38.54 N	120.50 W
Georgetown, Co., U.S.	200	39.42 N	105.41 W
Georgetown, Ct., U.S.	207	41.15 N	73.26 W
Georgetown, De., U.S.	208	38.41 N	75.23 W
Georgetown, Fl., U.S.	192	29.23 N	81.38 W
Georgetown, Ga., U.S.	192	31.53 N	85.06 W
Georgetown, Id., U.S.	202	42.29 N	111.22 W
Georgetown, Il., U.S.	194	39.58 N	87.38 W
Georgetown, In., U.S.	218	38.17 N	85.58 W
Georgetown, Ky., U.S.	218	38.12 N	84.33 W
Georgetown, Ma., U.S.	207	42.43 N	70.59 W
Georgetown, Ms., U.S.	194	31.52 N	90.09 W
Georgetown, N.J., U.S.	285	40.04 N	74.39 W
Georgetown, N.Y., U.S.	210	42.46 N	75.44 W
Georgetown, Oh., U.S.	218	38.51 N	83.54 W
Georgetown, Pa., U.S.	214	40.39 N	80.30 W
Georgetown, S.C., U.S.	192	33.22 N	79.17 W
Georgetown, Tx., U.S.	222	30.37 N	97.40 W
Georgetown ◆[8]	284c	38.54 N	77.03 W
Georgetown, Lake ⊜[1]	222	30.40 N	97.45 W
Georgetown Lake ⊜	202	46.11 N	113.17 W
Georgetown Rowley State Forest ♦	283	42.42 N	70.58 W
Georgetown University ɤ[2]	284c	38.54 N	77.04 W
George V Coast ⩡[2]	9	68.30 S	147.30 E
George VI Sound ⊔	9	71.00 S	68.00 W
George Washington Birthplace National Monument ♦	208	38.11 N	76.56 W
George Washington Bridge ◆[5]	276	40.51 N	73.57 W
George Washington Carver National Monument ♦	194	37.00 N	94.19 W
George West	196	28.19 N	98.07 W
Georg Forster ɤ[3]	9	70.47 S	11.51 E
Georgia □[1], Asia	72	42.00 N	44.00 E

FRANÇAIS

Nom	Page	Lat.°′	Long.°′ W = Ouest
Georgia □[1], Asia	84	42.00 N	44.00 E
Georgia □[3], U.S.	178	32.50 N	83.15 W
Georgia □[3], U.S.	192	32.50 N	83.15 W
Georgia, Strait of ⊔	182	49.20 N	124.00 W
Georgia del Sur, Isla de → South Georgia I	244	54.15 S	36.45 W
Georgiana	194	31.38 N	86.44 W
Georgian Bay ⊂	190	45.15 N	80.50 W
Georgian Bay Islands National Park ♦	190	44.54 N	79.52 W
Géorgie du Sud → South Georgia I	244	54.15 S	36.45 W
Georgijevka, Kaz.	85	43.03 N	74.43 E
Georgijevka, Kaz.	85	42.11 N	70.00 E
Georgijevka, Kaz.	86	49.19 N	81.35 E
Georgijevka, Ross.	80	53.18 N	51.01 E
Georgijevsk	84	44.09 N	43.28 E
Georgina ≃	166	23.30 S	139.47 E
Georgina Island I	212	44.23 N	79.17 W
Georgina Island Indian Reserve ◆[4]	212	44.22 N	79.19 W
Georgsmarienhütte	52	52.12 N	8.02 E
Georg von Neumayer ɤ[3]	9	70.37 S	8.22 W
Gera	54	50.52 N	12.04 E
Gera ≃	54	51.08 N	10.56 E
Geraardsbergen	50	50.46 N	3.52 E
Geraberg	54	50.43 N	10.50 E
Gerabronn	56	49.15 N	9.55 E
Gerace	68	38.16 N	16.13 E
Geraci Siculo	70	37.51 N	14.09 E
Geral, Serra ⩡[4], Bra.	250	11.15 S	46.30 W
Geral, Serra ⩡[4], Bra.	252	26.30 S	50.30 W
Gerald	219	38.23 N	91.19 W
Geral de Goiás, Serra ⩡[4]	242	13.00 S	46.15 W
Geraldine, N.Z.	172	44.05 S	171.14 E
Geraldine, Mt., U.S.	202	47.36 N	110.15 W
Geraldton, Austl.	162	28.46 S	114.36 E
Geraldton, On., Can.	176	49.44 N	86.57 W
Gerar, Naḥal V	132	31.24 N	34.26 E
Gerard, Lake ⊜	276	41.06 N	74.33 W
Gerard, Mount ∧	162	27.13 S	122.41 E
Gérardmer	58	48.04 N	6.53 E
Geras	61	48.48 N	15.40 E
Gerasa ⊥	132	32.17 N	35.53 E
Gerasdorf	61	48.18 N	16.28 E
Gerasimovka	86	58.37 N	71.53 E
Gerber	204	40.03 N	122.08 W
Gerber Reservoir ⊜[1]	202	42.12 N	121.06 W
Gerbéviller	58	48.30 N	6.31 E
Gerblingerode	52	51.29 N	10.15 E
Gerbstedt	54	51.38 N	11.37 E
Gerchsheim	56	49.42 N	9.47 E
Gercüş	130	37.34 N	41.23 E
Gerdau	158	26.28 S	26.06 E
Gerdine, Mount ∧	180	61.35 N	152.26 W
Gerdview	273d	26.10 S	28.11 E
Gère ≃	62	45.32 N	4.54 E
Gerede	130	40.48 N	32.12 E
Gereja Cathedral ɤ[1]	269e	6.10 S	106.49 E
Gerenzano	266b	45.38 N	9.00 E
Gereshk	120	31.48 N	64.34 E
Geretsried	64	47.51 N	11.28 E
Gérgal	34	37.07 N	2.33 W
Gerge'bil	84	42.31 N	47.05 E
Gerger	130	37.57 N	39.01 E
Geria Nij	126	23.56 N	86.55 E
Gerik	114	5.25 N	101.08 E
Gering	198	41.49 N	103.39 W
Geringswalde	54	51.04 N	12.54 E
Geriş	130	36.58 N	31.44 E
Gerlachovský štít ∧	30	49.12 N	20.08 E
Gerlafingen	58	47.10 N	7.34 E
Gerli ◆[8]	288	34.41 S	58.23 W
Gerlingen	56	48.48 N	9.03 E
Gerlos	64	47.14 N	12.02 E
Gerlospass)(	64	47.14 N	12.08 E
Gerlova Hut'	60	49.10 N	13.17 E
Germa (Jarmah) ⊥	146	26.33 N	13.04 E
Germagnano	62	45.15 N	7.28 E
Germain, Grand lac ⊜	186	51.12 N	66.41 W
Germania	214	41.39 N	77.40 W
Germano	214	40.25 N	80.57 W
Germanoviči	76	55.25 N	27.44 E
Germansen, Mount ∧	182	55.37 N	124.50 W
Germansen Lake ⊜	182	55.41 N	124.53 W
Germansen Landing	182	55.47 N	124.43 W
Germansville	208	40.42 N	75.42 W
Germantown, Il., U.S.	219	38.33 N	89.32 W
Germantown, Ky., U.S.	218	38.39 N	83.57 W
Germantown, N.Y., U.S.	210	42.08 N	73.54 W
Germantown, Oh., U.S.	218	39.37 N	84.22 W
Germantown, Tn., U.S.	194	35.05 N	89.48 W
Germantown, Wi., U.S.	216	43.13 N	88.06 W
Germantown ◆[8]	285	40.03 N	75.11 W
Germantown Dam ◆[6]	218	39.38 N	84.24 W
Germany (Deutschland) □[1], Europe	22	51.00 N	10.00 E
Germany (Deutschland) □[1], Europe	30	51.00 N	10.00 E
Germany Flats ≚	276	41.05 N	74.39 W
Germay	58	48.25 N	5.21 E
Germencik	130	37.51 N	27.37 E
Germendorf	54	52.45 N	13.10 E
Germering	60	48.08 N	11.22 E
Germersheim	56	49.13 N	8.22 E
Germfask	190	46.14 N	85.55 W
Germiston	158	26.13 S	28.11 E
Germiston □[5]	273d	26.15 S	28.10 E
Germiston South	273d	26.15 S	28.10 E
Gernika-Lumo (Guernica y Luno)	34	43.19 N	2.41 W
Gernrode	54	51.43 N	11.08 E
Gernsbach	56	48.46 N	8.19 E
Gernsheim	56	49.44 N	8.29 E
Gero	94	35.48 N	137.14 E
Geroda	56	50.17 N	9.53 E
Gerola Alta	58	46.03 N	9.32 E
Geroldsgrün	54	50.20 N	11.35 E
Geroldstein	56	50.06 N	7.56 E
Gerolsbach	60	48.30 N	11.22 E
Gerolstein	56	50.13 N	6.40 E
Gerolzhofen	56	49.54 N	10.21 E
Gerona → Girona, Esp.	34	41.59 N	2.49 E
Gerona, Pil.	116	15.36 N	120.36 E
Geronimo	196	34.28 N	98.22 W
Gerpinnes	50	50.20 N	4.31 E
Gerrards Cross	260	51.35 N	0.34 W
Gerrei ◆[1]	71	39.28 N	9.17 E
Gerresheim ◆[8]	263	51.14 N	6.52 E
Gerringong	170	34.45 S	150.50 E
Gerry	214	42.12 N	79.15 W
Gers □[5]	32	43.40 N	0.30 E
Gers ≃	32	44.09 N	0.39 E
Gersau	58	47.00 N	8.32 E
Gersdorf	54	50.45 N	12.42 E
Gersfeld	56	50.27 N	9.55 E
Gershøj	41	55.43 N	11.59 E
Gersprenz ≃	56	49.59 N	9.04 E
Gerstetten	56	48.37 N	10.01 E
Gersthofen	58	48.25 N	10.53 E
Gerstungen	56	50.58 N	10.04 E
Gertak Sanggul, Tanjong ›	114	5.15 N	100.11 E
Gerthe ◆[8]	263	51.31 N	7.17 E
Gerufa	156	19.17 S	26.02 E
Gervais	224	45.06 N	122.53 W
Gerwisch	54	52.10 N	11.44 E
Gerza	142	29.26 N	31.11 E

PORTUGUÊS

Nome	Página	Lat.°′	Long.°′ W = Oeste
Gerze, Tür.	130	41.48 N	35.12 E
Gêrzê, Zhg.	120	32.16 N	84.12 E
Gerzen	60	48.31 N	12.25 E
Gerzensee	58	46.51 N	7.33 E
Gescher	52	51.57 N	6.59 E
Geschriebenstein (Írottkő) ∧	61	47.21 N	16.26 E
Geschwenda	54	50.44 N	10.49 E
Gesees	60	49.54 N	11.32 E
Geseke	52	51.38 N	8.31 E
Geser	164	3.53 S	130.54 E
Gesher HaZiw	132	33.02 N	35.06 E
Gesi	115a	7.20 S	111.01 E
Gesoa	164	8.25 S	143.35 E
Gespunsart	56	49.49 N	4.50 E
Gessertshausen	58	48.20 N	10.44 E
Gesso ≃	62	44.24 N	7.33 E
Gessopalena	66	42.03 N	14.16 E
Gesten	41	55.31 N	9.12 E
Gesualdo	68	41.00 N	15.04 E
Geta	26	60.23 N	19.50 E
Getafe	34	40.18 N	3.43 W
Getafe, Aeropuerto ⊠	266a	40.18 N	3.43 W
Gete ≃	56	50.57 N	5.07 E
Gethaoli	272c	19.08 N	73.01 E
Geti	154	1.13 N	30.12 E
Getinge	26	56.49 N	12.44 E
Gettorf	41	54.24 N	9.58 E
Gettysburg, Oh., U.S.	218	40.06 N	84.29 W
Gettysburg, Pa., U.S.	208	39.49 N	77.13 W
Gettysburg, S.D., U.S.	198	45.00 N	99.57 W
Gettysburg National Military Park ♦	208	39.49 N	77.15 W
Getulândia	256	22.40 S	44.06 W
Getulina	255	21.49 S	49.55 W
Getuiio	116	10.45 N	122.40 E
Getúlio Vargas	252	27.50 S	52.16 W
Getz Ice Shelf ⩃	9	75.00 S	129.00 W
Getzville	210	43.01 N	78.46 W
Geumpang	114	4.48 N	96.09 E
Geureudong, Gunung ∧	114	4.48 N	96.48 E
Gevān	128	26.03 N	57.17 E
Gevaş	128	38.16 N	43.07 E
Gevelsberg	56	51.19 N	7.20 E
Gevgelija	38	41.08 N	22.30 E
Gévora ≃	34	38.53 N	6.57 W
Gevrey-Chambertin	58	47.14 N	4.57 E
Gewane	144	10.10 N	40.39 E
Geweke ◆[8]	263	51.22 N	7.25 E
Gex	58	46.20 N	6.04 E
Geyer	54	50.37 N	12.55 E
Geyer Ditch ≍	216	41.36 N	86.25 W
Geyikli	130	39.48 N	26.12 E
Geysdorp	158	26.32 S	25.18 E
Geyser	202	47.15 N	110.29 W
Geyserville	204	38.42 N	122.54 W
Geyshtasar, Kūh-e ∧	84	38.51 N	47.14 E
Geyuan	100	28.31 N	117.44 E
Geyve	130	40.30 N	30.18 E
Gézenti	146	21.41 N	18.18 E
Gezer	132	31.52 N	34.55 E
Gföhl	61	48.31 N	15.30 E
Ghaapplato ⋏[1]	158	27.30 S	24.00 E
Ghabāghib	132	33.10 N	36.13 E
Ghābat al-ʿArab	140	9.02 N	29.29 E
Ghadaf, Wādī al- V	132	31.46 N	36.50 E
Ghadāmis	146	30.08 N	9.30 E
Ghaddūwah	146	26.26 N	14.18 E
Ghafe	272c	19.05 N	73.07 E
Ghagghar ≃	123	29.30 N	74.53 E
Ghāghara ≃	124	25.47 N	84.37 E
Ghaghar Reservoir ⊜[1]	124	24.38 N	83.11 E
Ghāghra	124	23.17 N	84.33 E
Ghakhar	123	32.18 N	74.09 E
Ghallah, Wādī al- V	140	10.25 N	27.32 E
Ghammāzah al-Kubrā	142	29.43 N	31.18 E
Ghamrīn	142	30.30 N	30.55 E
Ghana □[1], Afr.	134	8.00 N	1.00 W
Ghana □[1], Afr.	150	8.00 N	1.00 W
Ghansoli	272c	19.08 N	72.59 E
Ghanzi	156	21.38 S	21.45 E
Ghanzi □[5]	156	22.00 S	23.00 E
Ghārāpuri	272c	18.54 N	72.56 E
Gharaunda	124	29.33 N	76.58 E
Gharbah, Wādī V	142	29.40 N	31.58 E
Gharbi, Chott ⊜	148	33.50 N	1.30 W
Gharbi, Oued el V	148	31.50 N	0.51 E
Gharbīyah, Aṣ-Ṣaḥrā' al- (Western Desert) ◆[2]	140	27.00 N	27.00 E
Ghardaïa	148	32.31 N	3.37 E
Ghardimaou	36	36.26 N	8.27 E
Gharghoda	124	22.10 N	83.21 E
Gharībwāl	123	32.41 N	73.10 E
Gharīfah	132	33.38 N	35.33 E
Gharig	140	10.47 N	27.33 E
Ghārīyat al-Gharbīyah	132	32.41 N	36.13 E
Ghārīyat ash-Sharqīyah	132	32.40 N	36.16 E
Gharo	120	24.44 N	67.35 E
Gharrāf, Shaṭṭ al- ≃	128	32.30 N	45.48 E
Gharroli ◆[8]	272a	28.37 N	77.20 E
Gharsa, Chott el ⊜	148	34.06 N	7.50 E
Gharw, Jazīrat I	142	31.21 N	30.06 E
Gharyān	146	32.10 N	13.01 E
Ghaṣm	132	32.33 N	36.22 E
Ghāt	146	24.58 N	10.11 E
Ghātāl	126	22.40 N	87.43 E
Ghatampur	272b	22.54 N	88.10 E
Ghatere, Mount ∧	175e	7.49 S	158.54 E
Ghates Occidentales → Western Ghāts ⋏	122	14.00 N	75.00 E
Ghates Orientales → Eastern Ghāts ⋏	122	14.00 N	78.50 E
Ghātkopar ◆[8]	272c	19.05 N	72.54 E
Ghātprabha ≃	122	16.20 N	75.48 E
Ghātsīla	126	22.36 N	86.29 E
Għawdex (Gozo) I	36	36.03 N	14.15 E
Ghawr ash-Sharqīyah, Qanāt al- (East Ghor Canal) ≍	132	32.41 N	35.38 E
Ghaylah ∧[1]	132	33.11 N	37.05 E
Ghayl Bā Wazīr	144	14.48 N	49.21 E
Ghayl Bin Yumayn ⍑[4]	144	15.33 N	49.23 E
Ghayth, Wādī V	132	30.59 N	36.00 E
Ghazāl, Baḥr al- ≃	140	9.31 N	30.25 E
Ghazal, Bahr el V	146	13.01 N	15.28 E
Ghazālat al-Khīs	142	30.34 N	31.34 E
Ghāziābād	123	28.40 N	77.26 E
Ghāzīpur, India	124	25.35 N	83.34 E
Ghazipur, India	272b	22.36 N	88.34 E
Ghāzipur ◆[8]	272a	28.38 N	77.19 E
Ghazīr	130	34.01 N	35.40 E
Ghazlūna	120	31.24 N	67.49 E
Ghaznī	120	33.33 N	68.26 E
Ghaznī □[4]	120	33.15 N	67.45 E
Ghaznī ≃	120	32.35 N	67.58 E
Ghazni Khel	123	32.33 N	70.44 E
Ghazzah (Gaza), Gaza	132	31.30 N	34.28 E
Ghazzah, Lubnān	132	33.40 N	35.49 E
Gheā ≃	272b	22.52 N	88.19 E
Ghedi	64	45.24 N	10.16 E
Ghemme	62	45.37 N	8.25 E
Ghennes Heights	279b	40.09 N	79.56 W
Ghent → Gent, Bel.	50	51.03 N	3.43 E
Ghent, Ky., U.S.	218	38.44 N	85.03 W
Ghent, N.Y., U.S.	210	42.19 N	73.36 W
Ghent, Oh., U.S.	214	41.09 N	81.38 W
Gheora ◆[8]	272a	28.42 N	77.01 E
Gheorgheni	38	46.43 N	25.36 E
Gherla	38	47.02 N	23.55 E
Ghesar	272c	19.09 N	73.05 E
Ghigo	62	44.53 N	7.03 E
Ghilarza	71	40.07 N	8.50 E
Ghilizane	148	35.44 N	0.30 E
Ghīn, Tall ∧	132	32.39 N	36.43 E
Ghior	126	23.54 N	89.53 E
Ghislenghien (Gellingen)	50	50.39 N	3.52 E
Ghisonaccia	36	42.00 N	9.25 E
Ghizar ≃	123	36.15 N	73.25 E
Ghizunabeana Islands II	175e	7.31 S	158.42 E
Ghlin	50	50.28 N	3.53 E
Ghlò, Beinn a' ∧	46	56.50 N	3.43 W
Ghogha	120	21.41 N	72.17 E
Gholson	222	31.43 N	97.12 W
Ghonda ◆[8]	272a	28.41 N	77.16 E
Ghondi ◆[8]	272a	28.42 N	77.16 E
Ghorāsahan	124	26.50 N	85.08 E
Ghoshpur, Bngl.	126	23.27 N	89.39 E
Ghoshpur, India	272b	22.23 N	88.29 E
Ghotki	120	28.01 N	69.19 E
Ghowr □[4]	128	34.00 N	65.00 E
Ghubaysh	140	12.09 N	27.21 E
Ghudāf, Wādī al- V	128	32.56 N	43.30 E
Ghulayfiqah	144	14.27 N	43.02 E
Ghunthur	130	34.23 N	37.09 E
Ghurāb, Jabal ∧[2]	142	28.58 N	31.16 E
Ghurayrah	144	18.37 N	42.41 E
Ghūrīān	128	34.21 N	61.30 E
Ghushuri	272b	22.37 N	88.22 E
Ghuwaybah, Wādī V	142	29.36 N	32.20 E
Ghuwayr, ʿAyn al- ⍑[4]	132	31.37 N	35.25 E
Ghuzzayil, Sabkhat ⊜	146	29.50 N	19.35 E
Giaginskaja	78	44.53 N	40.05 E
Gianh ≃	110	17.40 N	106.30 E
Giannutri, Isola di I	66	42.15 N	11.06 E
Giano, Monte ∧	66	42.25 N	13.06 E
Giano dell'Umbria	66	42.50 N	12.35 E
Giant City State Park ♦	194	37.39 N	89.12 W
Giant Mountain ∧	188	44.10 N	73.44 W
Giant's Castle ∧	158	29.21 S	29.27 E
Giant's Castle Game Reserve ◆[4]	158	29.16 S	29.30 E
Giant's Causeway ♦	48	55.14 N	6.30 W
Giants Neck	207	41.18 N	72.13 W
Giants Stadium ♦	276	40.49 N	74.05 W
Giants Tomb Island I	212	44.55 N	80.00 W
Gianyar	115b	8.32 S	115.20 E
Gia Rai	110	9.14 N	105.28 E
Giardinello	70	38.05 N	13.09 E
Giardinetto	68	41.19 N	15.24 E
Giardini	70	37.50 N	15.17 E
Giarratana	70	37.03 N	14.48 E
Giarre	70	37.43 N	15.11 E
Giaveno	62	45.02 N	7.21 E
Giazza	64	45.39 N	11.07 E
Giba	71	39.04 N	8.38 E
Gibara	240p	21.07 N	76.08 W
Gibbon, Mn., U.S.	190	44.32 N	94.31 W
Gibbon, Ne., U.S.	198	40.44 N	98.50 W
Gibbons	182	53.50 N	113.20 W
Gibbonsville	202	45.33 N	113.55 W
Gibb River	164	16.25 S	126.22 E
Gibbs, Mount ∧	162	32.55 S	120.00 E
Gibbsboro	285	39.50 N	74.58 W
Gibbstown	208	39.49 N	75.17 W
Gibellina	70	37.47 N	12.58 E
Gibeon	156	25.09 S	17.43 E
Gibilmanna, Santuario di ɤ[1]	70	37.59 N	14.02 E
Gibraleón	34	37.23 N	6.58 W
Gibraltar, Gib.	34	36.08 N	5.21 W
Gibraltar, Mi., U.S.	216	42.06 N	83.12 W
Gibraltar, Pa., U.S.	208	40.17 N	75.52 W
Gibraltar □[2], Europe	22	36.08 N	5.21 W
Gibraltar □[2], Europe	34	36.08 N	5.21 W
Gibraltar, Strait of (Estrecho de Gibraltar) ⊔	34	35.57 N	5.36 W
Gibraltar Point ›, On., Can.	275b	43.36 N	79.23 W
Gibraltar Point ›, Eng., U.K.	44	53.05 N	0.19 E
Gibsland	194	32.32 N	93.03 W
Gibson, Austl.	162	33.39 S	121.48 E
Gibson, Ga., U.S.	192	33.14 N	82.35 W
Gibson, N.Y., U.S.	210	42.08 N	76.59 W
Gibson, Pa., U.S.	210	41.44 N	75.38 W
Gibson ≃	212	44.58 N	79.51 W
Gibson, Lake ⊜[1]	284a	43.06 N	79.14 W
Gibsonburg	214	41.23 N	83.19 W
Gibson City	216	40.27 N	88.22 W
Gibson Desert ◆[2]	162	24.30 S	126.00 E
Gibson Hill ∧[2]	214	41.51 N	80.10 W
Gibsonia, Fl., U.S.	220	28.06 N	81.58 W
Gibsonia, Pa., U.S.	214	40.38 N	79.59 W
Gibson Indian Reserve ◆[4]	212	45.01 N	79.44 W
Gibson Island I	208	39.05 N	76.26 W
Gibsons	182	49.24 N	123.30 W
Gibsonton	220	27.51 N	82.22 W
Gicäki dağ ∧	84	40.25 N	49.01 E
Gidajevo	24	59.57 N	52.22 E
Gidami	144	9.58 N	34.37 E
Gidda	144	9.34 N	35.23 E
Giddalūr	122	15.21 N	78.55 E
Giddarbāha	123	30.12 N	74.40 E
Giddings	222	30.10 N	96.56 W
Gideälven ≃	26	63.20 N	19.08 E
Gidea Park ◆[8]	260	51.35 N	0.12 E
Gideåvallen	26	63.29 N	18.58 E
Gideon	194	36.27 N	89.55 W
Gidgee	162	27.16 S	119.22 E
Gidgi, Lake ⊜	162	29.16 S	126.03 E
Gidhni	126	22.29 N	86.51 E
Gidole	144	5.38 N	37.30 E
Gidrotorf	80	56.28 N	43.33 E
Giebelstadt	56	49.39 N	9.56 E
Gieboldehausen	52	51.36 N	10.13 E
Giedraičiai	76	55.05 N	25.15 E
Gielow	54	53.42 N	12.44 E
Gielsdorf	264a	52.36 N	13.52 E
Gien	50	47.42 N	2.38 E
Giengen	56	48.37 N	10.14 E
Giens	62	43.02 N	6.08 E
Gier ≃	62	45.35 N	4.46 E
Gierath	263	51.07 N	6.33 E
Gierle	56	51.16 N	4.51 E
Gieselwerder	52	51.36 N	9.33 E
Giesenkirchen ◆[8]	263	51.09 N	6.30 E
Giessbachfälle ⌞	58	46.42 N	8.03 E
Giessen	56	50.35 N	8.40 E
Giessen □[5]	56	50.40 N	8.40 E
Gieten	52	53.00 N	6.46 E
Giethoorn	52	52.43 N	6.05 E
Gièvres	50	47.16 N	1.40 E
Giez	62	45.45 N	6.15 E
Giffone	68	38.27 N	16.10 E
Gifford, Scot., U.K.	46	55.54 N	2.45 W
Gifford, Fl., U.S.	220	27.40 N	80.24 W
Gifford, Il., U.S.	216	40.18 N	88.01 W
Gifford, In., U.S.	216	41.06 N	87.01 W
Gifford, Pa., U.S.	214	41.51 N	78.36 W
Gifford ≃	176	70.21 N	83.05 W
Gifford Creek	162	24.05 S	116.11 E
Gifford Pinchot State Park ♦	208	40.04 N	76.53 W
Giffre ≃	58	46.05 N	6.30 E
Gifhorn	52	52.29 N	10.33 E
Giflitz	56	51.09 N	9.07 E
Gif-sur-Yvette	261	48.42 N	2.08 E
Gifu	94	35.25 N	136.45 E
Gifu □[5]	94	35.45 N	137.00 E
Gigant	80	46.30 N	41.20 E
Giganta, Sierra de la ⋏	232	26.00 N	111.30 W
Gigante	246	2.23 N	75.33 W
Gigante Islands II	116	11.36 N	123.20 E
Gigen	38	43.42 N	24.29 E
Gigena → Alcira	252	32.45 S	64.20 W
Giggleswick	44	54.04 N	2.17 W
Gigha, Sound of ⊔	46	55.41 N	5.42 W
Gigha Island I	46	55.41 N	5.46 W
Gig Harbor	224	47.19 N	122.34 W
Giglio, Isola del I	66	42.21 N	10.54 E
Giglio Castello	66	42.22 N	10.54 E
Gigliola	66	44.51 N	12.14 E
Giglio Porto	66	42.22 N	10.55 E
Gigmoto	116	13.47 N	124.23 E
Gignod	62	45.46 N	7.17 E
Gihu → Gifu	94	35.25 N	136.45 E
Gijón	34	43.32 N	5.40 W
Gikongoro	154	2.29 S	29.34 E
Gila ≃	200	32.43 N	114.33 W
Gila, Middle Fork ≃	200	33.14 N	108.14 W
Gila Bend	200	32.56 N	112.42 W
Gila Bend Indian Reservation ◆[4]	200	33.00 N	112.46 W
Gila Bend Mountains ⋏	200	33.10 N	113.10 W
Gila Cliff Dwellings National Monument ♦	200	33.02 N	108.16 W
Gila Mountains ⋏	200	33.05 N	109.50 W
Gīlān □[4]	128	37.15 N	49.30 E
Gīlān-e Gharb	128	34.08 N	45.55 E
Gila River Indian Reservation ◆[4]	200	33.12 N	112.00 W
Gilātala	126	22.36 N	89.41 E
Giläzi Dili burnu ›	84	40.50 N	49.33 E
Gilberdyke	44	53.45 N	0.44 W
Gilbert, La., U.S.	194	32.02 N	91.39 W
Gilbert, Mn., U.S.	190	47.29 N	92.27 W
Gilbert ≃, Austl.	166	16.35 S	141.15 E
Gilbert ≃, Austl.	168b	34.22 S	138.40 E
Gilbert, Mount ∧	182	50.51 N	124.20 W
Gilbert Airport ⊠	279a	41.22 N	81.58 W
Gilbert Island I	219	39.35 N	91.11 W
Gilbert Islands → Kiribati □[1]	14	5.00 S	170.00 W
Gilbert Lake ⊜	281	42.34 N	83.17 W
Gilbert Lake State Park ♦	210	42.36 N	75.08 W
Gilberton	210	40.48 N	76.13 W
Gilbertown	194	31.52 N	88.19 W
Gilbert Peak ∧	224	46.30 N	121.25 W
Gilbert Plains	184	51.09 N	100.29 W
Gilbert River	166	18.09 S	142.52 E
Gilberts	216	42.06 N	88.23 W
Gilbert Seamount ✢[3]	16	52.50 N	150.10 W
Gilbertsville, N.Y., U.S.	210	42.28 N	75.19 W
Gilbertsville, Pa., U.S.	208	40.19 N	75.37 W
Gilbertville	207	42.18 N	72.12 W
Gilbjerg Hoved ›	41	56.08 N	12.17 E
Gilboa	216	41.01 N	83.55 W
Gilboaʿ, Haré ⋏[2]	132	32.30 N	35.23 E
Gilbués	250	9.50 S	45.21 W
Gilching	60	48.07 N	11.17 E
Gildehaus	52	52.18 N	7.06 E
Gildford	202	48.34 N	110.17 W
Gilead	216	41.48 N	85.09 W
Giles, Arroyo de ≃	258	34.20 S	59.23 W
Giles Meteorological Station ɤ[3]	162	25.02 S	128.18 E
Giles Point ›	168b	35.03 S	137.45 E
Gilette	62	43.51 N	7.10 E
Gilford	48	54.23 N	6.22 W
Gilford Island I	182	50.45 N	126.25 W
Gilford Park	208	39.58 N	74.08 W
Gilgai	162	31.15 S	119.56 E
Gilgandra	166	31.42 S	148.39 E
Gilgil	154	0.30 S	36.19 E
Gil Gil Creek ≃	166	29.10 S	148.51 E
Gilgit	123	35.55 N	74.18 E
Gilgit ≃	123	35.44 N	74.38 E
Gilgo Island I	276	40.38 N	73.25 W
Gilgo State Park ♦	276	40.38 N	73.22 W
Gilima	154	3.55 N	28.22 E
Gilimanuk	115a	8.10 S	114.26 E
Gilirang	112	3.55 S	120.09 E
Gil Island I	182	53.13 N	129.15 W
Gill, Lough ⊜	48	54.16 N	8.24 W
Gillam	184	56.21 N	94.43 W
Gilleland Creek ≃	222	30.13 N	97.32 W
Gilleleje	41	56.07 N	12.19 E
Gillen, Lake ⊜	162	26.11 S	124.38 E
Gilles, Lake ⊜	166	32.50 S	136.45 E
Gillespie	219	39.07 N	89.49 W
Gillespies Point ›	172	43.24 S	169.50 E
Gillett, Ar., U.S.	194	34.07 N	91.22 W
Gillett, Pa., U.S.	210	41.57 N	76.48 W
Gillett, Wi., U.S.	190	44.53 N	88.18 W
Gillette, N.J., U.S.	276	40.41 N	74.28 W
Gillette, Wy., U.S.	198	44.17 N	105.30 W
Gillette Castle State Park ♦	207	41.26 N	72.25 W
Gillian, Lake ⊜	176	69.32 N	75.23 W
Gillingham, Eng., U.K.	42	51.24 N	0.33 E
Gillingham, Eng., U.K.	42	51.02 N	2.17 W
Gillingham □[8]	260	51.22 N	0.35 E
Gills Rock	190	45.17 N	87.01 W
Gilman, Ct., U.S.	207	41.34 N	72.11 W
Gilman, Il., U.S.	216	40.46 N	87.59 W
Gilman, Ia., U.S.	190	41.52 N	92.47 W
Gilman, Wi., U.S.	190	45.10 N	90.48 W
Gilman Hot Springs	228	33.50 N	116.59 W
Gilman Lake	285	39.41 N	75.11 W
Gilmer, Il., U.S.	278	42.14 N	88.02 W
Gilmer, Tx., U.S.	222	32.43 N	94.56 W
Gilmer Park	216	41.36 N	86.15 W
Gilmore	171b	35.20 S	148.11 E
Gilmore City	198	42.44 N	94.27 W
Gilmore Creek ≃	171b	35.18 S	148.13 E
Gilo ≃	144	8.10 N	33.15 E
Gilroy	226	37.00 N	121.34 W
Gilserberg	56	50.57 N	9.04 E
Gilsizer Slough ≃	226	38.58 N	121.44 W
Gilston Park ♦	260	51.48 N	0.04 E
Giltner	198	40.46 N	98.09 W
Gil'uj ≃	89	53.58 N	127.30 E
Giluwe, Mount ∧	164	6.05 S	143.50 E
Gilwern	42	51.51 N	3.06 W
Gilze	52	51.33 N	4.57 E
Gimån ≃	26	62.28 N	16.20 E
Gimbi	144	9.10 N	35.42 E
Gimborn	52	51.03 N	7.28 E
Gimcheon → Kimch'ŏn	98	36.07 N	128.05 E
Gimie, Mount ∧	241f	13.52 N	61.01 W
Gimigliano	68	38.58 N	16.32 E
Gimlet	218	38.13 N	83.09 W
Gimli	184	50.38 N	96.59 W
Gimo	40	60.11 N	18.11 E
Gimoly	24	63.03 N	32.19 E
Gimone ≃	32	44.00 N	1.06 E
Gimont	32	43.38 N	0.53 E
Gimpu	112	1.36 S	120.02 E
Ginderich	263	51.39 N	6.32 E
Ginebra → Genève	58	46.12 N	6.09 E
Gineste, Col de la)(	62	43.15 N	5.27 E
Gingell	216	42.43 N	83.17 W
Gingera, Mount ∧	171b	35.35 S	148.47 E
Ginger Hill	279b	40.12 N	80.00 W
Ginger Island I	240m	18.24 N	64.28 W
Gingin, Austl.	162	31.21 S	115.42 E
Gin Gin, Austl.	166	25.00 S	151.58 E
Gingindlovu	158	29.02 S	31.30 E
Gingoog	116	8.50 N	125.07 E
Gingoog Bay ⊂	116	8.59 N	125.05 E
Gingst	54	54.27 N	13.16 E
Ginir	144	7.07 N	40.46 E
Ginkakuji Temple ɤ[1]	270	35.03 N	135.47 E
Ginkgo State Park ♦	202	46.59 N	120.01 W
Ginnosar	132	32.51 N	35.31 E
Ginosa	68	40.35 N	16.46 E
Ginostra	70	38.47 N	15.11 E
Ginowan	174m	26.17 N	127.46 E
Ginoza	174m	26.28 N	127.57 E
Ginter	214	40.46 N	78.23 W
Ginza ◆[8]	268	35.40 N	139.47 E
Gioi	68	40.17 N	15.13 E
Gioia, Golfo di ⊂	68	38.30 N	15.45 E
Gioia dei Marsi	66	41.57 N	13.42 E
Gioia del Colle	68	40.48 N	16.56 E
Gioia Tauro	68	38.26 N	15.54 E
Gioia Vecchio	66	41.54 N	13.44 E
Gioiosa Ionica	68	38.20 N	16.18 E
Gioiosa Marea	70	38.10 N	14.54 E
Giong Rieng	110	9.55 N	105.19 E
Giornico	58	46.24 N	8.52 E
Giovi, Passo dei)(	62	44.33 N	8.57 E
Giovinazzo	68	41.11 N	16.40 E
Giporlos	116	11.07 N	125.27 E
Gipping ≃	42	52.04 N	1.10 E
Gipsy	214	40.48 N	78.53 W
Gipuzkoako □[4]	34	43.10 N	2.10 W
Giraglia, Île de la I	62	43.02 N	9.24 E
Giralia	162	22.41 S	114.21 E
Giraltovce	30	49.07 N	21.31 E
Girard, Il., U.S.	219	39.26 N	89.46 W
Girard, Ks., U.S.	198	37.30 N	94.50 W
Girard, Mi., U.S.	216	42.02 N	85.00 W
Girard, Oh., U.S.	214	41.09 N	80.42 W
Girard, Pa., U.S.	214	42.00 N	80.19 W
Girard, Tx., U.S.	196	33.22 N	100.40 W
Girardot	246	4.18 N	74.48 W
Girardville	208	40.47 N	76.17 W
Giraud, Pointe ›	240d	15.19 N	61.15 W
Giraul ≃	152	15.04 S	12.08 E
Giraumont	56	49.10 N	5.55 E
Girdletree	208	38.05 N	75.23 W
Giresun	130	40.55 N	38.24 E
Giresun □[4]	130	40.30 N	38.30 E
Giresun Dağları ⋏	130	40.30 N	39.00 E
Girgarre	166	36.24 S	144.59 E
Girgaum ◆[8]	272c	18.57 N	72.48 E
Girgenti → Agrigento	70	37.18 N	13.35 E
Girgir, Cape ›	164	3.50 S	144.34 E
Giri ≃	152	0.28 N	17.59 E
Girīdīh	126	24.11 N	86.18 E
Girifalco	68	38.49 N	16.25 E
Girilambone	166	31.15 S	146.54 E
Girmeli	130	37.07 N	41.26 E
Girna ≃	122	21.08 N	75.19 E
Gir National Park ♦	120	21.00 N	70.50 E
Girne (Kyrenia)	130	35.20 N	33.19 E
Giro, Nig.	150	11.06 N	4.46 E
Giro, Zaïre	154	3.08 N	29.15 E
Giromagny	58	47.45 N	6.50 E
Girón, Ec.	246	3.10 S	79.08 W
Giron, Fr.	58	46.14 N	5.46 E
Girona	34	41.59 N	2.49 E
Girona □[4]	34	42.00 N	2.40 E
Gironde □[5]	32	44.45 N	0.35 W
Gironde ⊂[1]	32	45.20 N	0.45 W
Gironville-sous-les-Côtes	56	48.48 N	5.40 E
Girou ≃	32	43.46 N	1.23 E
Girouxville	182	55.45 N	117.20 W
Gīr Range ⋏	120	21.18 N	71.00 E
Girton	42	52.14 N	0.05 E
Girtys Run ≃	279b	40.28 N	79.58 W
Giru	166	19.31 S	147.06 E
Giruá	252	28.02 S	54.21 W
Girvan	44	55.15 N	4.51 W
Girvan, Water of ≃	44	55.15 N	4.51 W
Girvas	24	62.30 N	33.40 E
Gisborne, Austl.	169	37.29 S	144.35 E
Gisborne, N.Z.	172	38.40 S	178.01 E
Gisborne Lake ⊜	186	47.48 N	54.50 W
Giscome	182	54.04 N	122.22 W
Gisenyi	154	1.42 S	29.15 E
Gishyita	154	2.11 S	29.18 E
Gislaved	26	57.18 N	13.32 E
Gislev	41	55.13 N	10.37 E
Gislinge	41	55.44 N	11.33 E
Gislövs läge	41	55.21 N	13.14 E
Gisors	50	49.17 N	1.47 E
Gissar	85	38.33 N	68.35 E
Gissarskij chrebet ⋏	85	39.00 N	68.40 E
Gisselfeld	41	55.18 N	11.59 E
Gissi	66	42.01 N	14.33 E
Gisslarbo	40	59.38 N	15.49 E
Gistel	50	51.10 N	2.57 E
Giswil	58	46.50 N	8.11 E
Gitambo	154	4.21 N	24.45 E
Gitarama	154	2.07 S	29.45 E
Gitega	154	3.26 S	29.56 E
Gittelde	52	51.48 N	10.10 E
Giuba, Isole II	144	0.45 S	42.19 E
Giudicarie, Valli V	64	45.58 N	10.45 E
Giugliano in Campania	68	40.56 N	14.12 E
Giuliana	70	37.40 N	13.14 E
Giulianova	66	42.45 N	13.57 E
Giulie, Alpi → Julian Alps ⋏	36	46.00 N	14.00 E
Giumbo → Jumboo	144	0.15 S	42.38 E
Giurgiu	38	43.53 N	25.57 E
Giurgiu □[6]	38	44.10 N	26.00 E
Giussano	62	45.42 N	9.14 E
Giuvala, Pasul)(	38	45.26 N	25.17 E
Givʿatayim	132	32.04 N	34.48 E
Givʿat Brenner	132	31.52 N	34.48 E
Give	41	55.51 N	9.15 E
Giverny	50	49.04 N	1.32 E
Givet	56	50.08 N	4.50 E
Givors	62	45.35 N	4.46 E
Givrine, Col de la)(	58	46.27 N	6.05 E
Givry	58	46.47 N	4.45 E
Givry-en-Argonne	56	48.57 N	4.53 E
Givry Island I	175c	7.07 N	151.53 E
Giyon	144	8.30 N	38.00 E
Giza → Al-Jīzah	142	30.01 N	31.13 E
Gīzāb	120	33.23 N	66.16 E
Giždduvan	128	40.06 N	64.41 E
Gizen	140	10.49 N	34.48 E
Gizeux	50	47.24 N	0.12 E
Gižiga	74	62.03 N	160.30 E
Gižiginskaja guba ⊂	74	61.30 N	158.00 E
Gizo	175e	8.06 S	156.51 E
Gizo Island I	175e	8.04 S	156.48 E
Giżycko	30	54.03 N	21.47 E
Gizzeria	68	38.59 N	16.12 E
Gjedved	41	55.56 N	9.51 E
Gjern	41	56.14 N	9.45 E
Gjirokastër	38	40.05 N	20.10 E
Gjoa Haven	176	68.38 N	95.57 W
Gjøvik	26	60.48 N	10.42 E
Gjuesevo	38	42.14 N	22.28 E
Gjuhëzës, Kep i ›	38	40.25 N	19.18 E
Glace Bay	186	46.12 N	59.57 W
Glacier, B.C., Can.	182	51.16 N	117.31 W
Glacier, Wa., U.S.	224	48.53 N	121.56 W
Glacier Bay ⊂	180	58.40 N	136.00 W
Glacier Bay National Park ♦	180	58.45 N	136.30 W
Glacier Hills	276	40.51 N	74.28 W
Glacier National Park ♦, B.C., Can.	182	51.15 N	117.35 W
Glacier National Park ♦, Mt., U.S.	202	48.35 N	113.40 W
Glacier Peak ∧	224	48.07 N	121.07 W
Glad'	76	59.07 N	32.06 E
Gl'ad'anskoje	86	54.54 N	65.06 E
Gladbach → Mönchengladbach	56	51.12 N	6.28 E
Gladbeck	52	51.34 N	6.59 E
Gladbrook	190	42.11 N	92.42 W
Gladden	279b	40.21 N	80.11 W

English	Deutsch	Español	Français	Português
≃ River	Fluß	Río	Rivière	Rio
≍ Canal	Kanal	Canal	Canal	Canal
⌞ Waterfall, Rapids	Wasserfall, Stromschnellen	Cascada, Rápidos	Chute d'eau, Rapides	Cascata, Rápidos
⊔ Strait	Meeresstraße	Estrecho	Détroit	Estreito
⊂ Bay, Gulf	Bucht, Golf	Bahía, Golfo	Baie, Golfe	Baía, Golfo
⊜ Lake, Lakes	See, Seen	Lago, Lagos	Lac, Lacs	Lago, Lagos
≚ Swamp	Sumpf	Pantano	Marais	Pântano
⩃ Ice Features, Glacier	Eis- und Gletscherformen	Accidentes Glaciales	Formes glaciaires	Acidentes glaciares
⍑ Other Hydrographic Features	Andere Hydrographische Objekte	Otros Elementos Hidrográficos	Autres données hydrographiques	Outros acidentes hidrográficos
✢ Submarine Features	Untermeerische Objekte	Accidentes Submarinos	Formes de relief sous-marin	Acidentes submarinos
□ Political Unit	Politische Einheit	Unidad Politica	Entité politique	Unidade política
ɤ Cultural Institution	Kulturelle Institution	Institución Cultural	Institution culturelle	Instituição cultural
⊥ Historical Site	Historische Stätte	Sitio Histórico	Site historique	Sitio histórico
♦ Recreational Site	Erholungs- und Ferienort	Sitio de Recreo	Centre de loisirs	Area de Lazer
⊠ Airport	Flughafen	Aeropuerto	Aéroport	Aeroporto
■ Military Installation	Militäranlage	Instalación Militar	Installation militaire	Instalação militar
◆ Miscellaneous	Verschiedenes	Misceláneo	Divers	Diversos

Gladden Heights 279b 40.22 N 80.15 W
Glade Creek ≃ 202 45.54 N 119.42 W
Gladenbach 56 50.46 N 8.34 E
Glades □[6] 220 26.59 N 81.12 W
Glade Spring 192 36.47 N 81.46 W
Gladesville 274a 33.50 S 151.08 E
Gladewater 222 32.32 N 94.56 W
Gladewater, Lake ⊜[1] 222 32.35 N 94.57 W
Gladsakse 41 55.44 N 12.29 E
Gladstone, Austl. 166 23.51 S 151.16 E
Gladstone, Austl. 166 33.17 S 138.22 E
Gladstone, Mb., Can. 184 50.13 N 98.57 W
Gladstone, Mi., U.S. 190 45.51 N 87.01 W
Gladstone, Mo., U.S. 194 39.12 N 94.33 W
Gladstone, N.J., U.S. 210 40.43 N 74.39 W
Gladstone, Or., U.S. 224 45.22 N 122.35 W
Gladstone Brook ≃ 276 40.43 N 74.40 W
Gladwin 190 43.58 N 84.29 W
Gladwyne 285 40.02 N 75.17 W
Gladys Lake ⊜ 180 59.55 N 132.55 W
Glænø I 41 55.12 N 11.28 E
Glafsfjorden ⊜ 26 59.34 N 12.37 E
Glåma ≃ 26 59.12 N 10.57 E
Glamis 46 56.36 N 3.00 W
Glamis Castle ⊥ 46 56.37 N 3.00 W
Glamoč 36 44.03 N 16.51 E
Glamor Lake ⊜ 212 44.58 N 78.23 W
Glamsbjerg 41 55.16 N 10.07 E
Glan 116 5.49 N 125.10 E
Glan ⊜ 40 58.37 N 15.58 E
Glan ≃, Dtsch. 56 49.47 N 7.43 E
Glan ≃, Öst. 61 46.36 N 14.25 E
Glan ≃, Pil. 116 5.50 N 125.12 E
Glanamman 42 51.48 N 3.54 W
Gland 58 46.26 N 6.16 E
Gland ≃ 50 49.55 N 4.52 E
Glandon, Col du)(62 45.14 N 6.11 E
Glandorf, Dtsch. 52 52.05 N 7.59 E
Glandorf, Oh., U.S. 216 41.01 N 84.04 W
Glâne ≃ 58 46.47 N 7.08 E
Glanegg 61 46.44 N 14.11 E
Glanerbrug 52 52.13 N 6.58 E
Glanmire 48 51.55 N 8.24 W
Glanshammar 40 59.19 N 15.24 E
Glanum ⊥ 62 43.49 N 4.47 E
Glan-y-Don 262 53.19 N 3.15 W
Glaris
— Glarus 58 47.02 N 9.04 E
Glarner Alpen ⋏ 58 46.55 N 9.00 E
Glärnisch ⋏ 58 47.00 N 9.00 E
Glarus 58 47.02 N 9.04 E
Glarus □[3] 58 47.00 N 9.03 E
Glascarnoch, Loch ⊜ 46 57.40 N 4.50 W
Glasco, Ks., U.S. 198 39.21 N 97.50 W
Glasco, N.Y., U.S. 210 42.02 N 73.56 W
Glasgow, Scot., U.K. 46 55.53 N 4.15 W
Glasgow, Il., U.S. 219 39.33 N 90.29 W
Glasgow, Ky., U.S. 194 36.59 N 85.54 W
Glasgow, Mo., U.S. 194 39.13 N 92.50 W
Glasgow, Mt., U.S. 202 48.11 N 106.38 W
Glasgow, Pa., U.S. 214 40.42 N 78.27 W
Glasgow, Va., U.S. 192 37.38 N 79.27 W
Glasgow (Abbotsinch) Airport ⊠ 46 55.52 N 4.26 W
Glashütte, Dtsch. 54 53.41 N 10.02 E
Glashütte, Dtsch. 54 50.51 N 13.47 E
Glashütte ◆[8] 263 51.13 N 6.52 E
Glaslyn 184 53.21 N 108.22 W
Glaslyn ≃ 42 52.56 N 4.06 W
Glas Maol ∧ 46 56.52 N 3.22 W
Glasow 54 52.20 N 13.28 E
Glass, Loch ⊜ 46 57.43 N 4.30 W
Glassan 48 53.28 N 7.52 W
Glassboro 208 39.42 N 75.06 W
Glassboro State College ⊌[2] 285 39.42 N 75.07 W
Glass House Mountains 171a 26.53 S 152.58 E
Glassmanor 284c 38.49 N 76.59 W
Glass Mountains ⋏ 196 30.25 N 103.15 W
Glassport 214 40.19 N 79.53 W
Glastonbury, Eng., U.K. 42 51.06 N 2.43 W
Glastonbury, Ct., U.S. 207 41.42 N 72.36 W
Glatt ≃ 58 47.34 N 8.28 E
Glatten 58 48.26 N 8.31 E
Glattfelden 58 47.33 N 8.30 E
Glatz
— Kłodzko 30 50.27 N 16.39 E
Glaubitz 54 51.19 N 13.22 E
Glauchau 54 50.49 N 12.32 E
Glaven ≃ 42 52.58 N 1.03 E
Glaze Brook ≃ 262 53.25 N 2.27 W
Glazebury 262 53.28 N 2.30 W
Glazevo 76 59.41 N 32.05 E
Glazok 80 53.06 N 40.42 E
Glazov 80 58.09 N 52.40 E
Glazovo, Ross. 82 54.57 N 37.22 E
Glazovo, Ross. 82 54.47 N 37.34 E
Glazovo, Ross. 82 55.38 N 35.46 E
Glazunovka 76 52.30 N 36.19 E
Glazunovskaja 80 49.50 N 42.51 E
Gleason 194 36.12 N 88.36 W
Glebovka 78 46.38 N 39.59 E
Glebovo, Ross. 82 56.54 N 37.43 E
Glebovo, Ross. 82 56.39 N 38.42 E
Gleed 224 46.40 N 120.37 W
Glehn 263 51.10 N 6.35 E
Gleichen 182 50.52 N 113.03 W
Gleidingen 52 52.16 N 9.50 E
Gleinalpe ⋏ 61 47.15 N 15.03 E
Gleisdorf 61 47.06 N 15.44 E
Gleiwitz
— Gliwice 30 50.17 N 18.40 E
Glejbjerg 41 55.33 N 8.50 E
Glemsford 42 52.06 N 0.41 E
Glen ≃, Ire. 48 54.38 N 8.40 W
Glen ≃, Eng., U.K. 42 52.51 N 0.06 W
Glen Acres 285 39.58 N 75.34 W
Glen Afton 172 37.37 S 175.02 E
Glen Alice 170 33.02 S 150.13 E
Glen Allen 208 37.39 N 77.30 W
Glen Alpine 192 35.43 N 81.46 W
Glenamoy 48 54.14 N 9.42 W
Glenarchy 275b 43.29 N 79.46 W
Glenarden 208 38.56 N 76.52 W
Glenarm, N. Ire., U.K. 48 54.58 N 5.57 W
Glen Arm, Md., U.S. 284b 39.27 N 76.30 W
Glen Ashton Farms 285 40.06 N 74.55 W
Glen Aubrey 210 42.15 N 76.01 W
Glenavon, Sk., Can. 184 50.10 N 103.10 W
Glen Avon, S. Afr. 158 31.43 S 26.12 E
Glen Avon, Ca., U.S. 228 34.01 N 117.29 W
Glenavy, N.Z. 172 44.55 S 171.06 E
Glenavy, N. Ire., U.K. 48 54.36 N 6.13 W
Glenboro 184 49.32 N 99.15 W
Glenbrook 170 33.46 S 150.37 E
Glenbrook Heights 226 39.15 N 121.02 W
Glenburn, N.D., U.S. 198 48.30 N 101.13 W
Glenburn, Pa., U.S. 210 41.31 N 75.44 W
Glen Burnie 208 39.09 N 76.37 W
Glen Burnie Park 208 39.09 N 76.38 W
Glen Campbell 214 40.49 N 78.50 W
Glen Canyon V 200 37.10 N 110.50 W
Glen Canyon Dam ◆[6] 200 36.48 N 111.13 W
Glen Canyon National Recreation Area ♦ 200 37.00 N 111.20 W
Glen Carbon 219 38.44 N 89.58 W
Glencoe, Austl. 166 37.42 S 140.37 E
Glencoe, On., Can. 214 42.45 N 81.43 W
Glencoe, S. Afr. 158 28.12 S 30.07 E
Glencoe, Al., U.S. 194 33.57 N 85.55 W
Glencoe, Il., U.S. 216 42.08 N 87.45 W
Glencoe, Ky., U.S. 218 38.42 N 84.49 W
Glencoe, Md., U.S. 208 39.32 N 76.38 W
Glencoe, Mn., U.S. 190 44.46 N 94.09 W
Glencolumbkille 48 54.43 N 8.45 W
Glencoul, Loch c 46 58.14 N 4.58 W
Glencova 154 19.59 S 31.26 E
Glen Cove 210 40.51 N 73.38 W
Glendale, Az., U.S. 200 33.32 N 112.11 W
Glendale, Ca., U.S. 228 34.08 N 118.15 W
Glendale, Ma., U.S. 207 42.17 N 73.20 W
Glendale, Ms., U.S. 194 31.21 N 89.18 W
Glendale, Mo., U.S. 219 38.35 N 90.22 W
Glendale, Or., U.S. 202 42.44 N 123.25 W
Glendale, R.I., U.S. 207 41.58 N 71.37 W
Glendale, Tx., U.S. 222 31.01 N 95.18 W
Glendale, Ut., U.S. 200 37.19 N 112.35 W
Glendale, Wi., U.S. 216 43.08 N 87.56 W
Glendale, Zimb. 154 17.21 S 31.04 E
Glendale Heights, Il., U.S. 278 41.54 N 88.04 W
Glendale Heights, Md., U.S. 284c 38.59 N 76.49 W
Glendale Lake ⊜ 214 40.41 N 78.32 W
Glendalough ⊥ 48 53.01 N 6.26 W
Glen Davis 170 33.08 S 150.17 E
Glendive 198 47.06 N 104.42 W
Glendo 198 42.30 N 105.01 W
Glendoe Forest ◆[3] 46 57.06 N 4.37 W
Glendon, Ab., Can. 182 54.15 N 111.10 W
Glendon, Pa., U.S. 208 40.40 N 75.14 W
Glendora, Ca., U.S. 228 34.08 N 117.51 W
Glendora, N.J., U.S. 285 39.50 N 75.04 W
Glendo Reservoir ⊜[1] 198 42.31 N 104.58 W
Glendo State Park ♦ 198 42.33 N 104.58 W
Glendowan 48 54.58 N 7.57 W
Glen Eagle, Austl. 168a 32.17 S 116.11 E
Gleneagle, Austl. 171a 27.57 S 152.59 E
Glen Echo 284c 38.58 N 77.08 W
Glen Echo Amusement Park ♦ 284c 38.58 N 77.08 W
Glen Echo Heights 284c 38.58 N 77.08 W
Gleneden Beach 202 44.53 N 124.02 W
Glen Elder 198 39.29 N 98.18 W
Glenelg, Austl. 168b 34.59 S 138.31 E
Glenelg, Scot., U.K. 46 57.13 N 5.38 W
Glenelg ≃ 166 38.03 S 141.00 E
Glen Ellen 226 38.22 N 122.31 W
Glenelly ≃ 48 54.44 N 7.18 W
Glen Ellyn 278 41.52 N 88.04 W
Glen Ellyn Countryside 278 41.55 N 88.04 W
Glenfarg 46 56.16 N 3.24 W
Glenfarne 48 54.17 N 7.59 W
Glenfield, Austl. 274a 33.58 S 150.54 E
Glenfield, Eng., U.K. 42 52.39 N 1.12 W
Glenfield, N.Y., U.S. 212 43.43 N 75.24 W
Glenfield, Pa., U.S. 279b 40.31 N 80.08 W
Glenfinnan 46 56.52 N 5.27 W
Glen Flora 222 29.21 N 96.12 W
Glen Florrie 162 22.55 S 115.59 E
Glenford 210 42.00 N 74.07 W
Glen Forest 168a 31.54 S 116.06 E
Glengallan Creek ≃ 171a 28.09 S 151.53 E
Glen Gardner 210 40.41 N 74.56 W
Glengarriff 48 51.45 N 9.33 W
Glengarry Range ⋏ 162 26.13 S 118.59 E
Glengyle 166 24.48 S 139.37 E
Glenham 210 41.31 N 73.55 W
Glenhaven 274a 33.42 S 151.00 E
Glen Head 276 40.50 N 73.37 W
Glen Helen 162 23.43 S 132.40 E
Glen Hills 208 39.04 N 77.12 W
Glenhope 172 41.39 S 172.39 E
Glenhuntly 274b 37.54 S 145.03 E
Glen Innes 166 29.44 S 151.44 E
Glen Island I 276 40.53 N 73.47 W
Glen Lake 224 48.26 N 123.31 W
Glenluce 44 54.53 N 4.49 W
Glenluce Abbey ⊌[1] 44 54.53 N 4.50 W
Glen Lyon 210 41.10 N 76.04 W
Glen Miller 212 44.08 N 77.35 W
Glen Mills 285 39.55 N 75.30 W
Glenmont, N.Y., U.S. 210 42.36 N 73.46 W
Glenmont, Oh., U.S. 214 40.31 N 82.06 W
Glenmoor 214 40.40 N 80.37 W
Glenmoore, Pa., U.S. 208 40.05 N 75.46 W
Glen Moore, Pa., U.S. 208 40.03 N 76.18 W
Glenmora 194 30.58 N 92.35 W
Glenmore 284b 39.11 N 76.36 W
Glenmorgan 166 27.15 S 149.41 E
Glenn, Ca., U.S. 226 39.31 N 122.01 W
Glenn, Mi., U.S. 216 42.31 N 86.13 W
Glenn □[6] 226 39.29 N 122.18 W
Glennallen 180 62.07 N 145.33 W
Glennamaddy 48 53.37 N 8.35 W
Glenn-Colusa Canal ≡ 226 39.07 N 122.08 W
Glenn Dale 284c 38.59 N 76.49 W
Glenns Creek ≃ 218 38.09 N 84.52 W
Glenns Ferry 202 42.57 N 115.18 W
Glenn Shoals, Lake ⊜[1] 219 39.13 N 89.28 W
Glennville 192 31.56 N 81.55 W
Glen Oak 278 41.53 N 88.02 W
Glenolden 285 39.54 N 75.17 W
Glenoma 224 46.30 N 122.09 W
Glenorchy 172 44.51 S 168.23 E
Glenore Grove 171a 27.32 S 152.24 E
Glenorie 274a 33.36 S 151.00 E
Glenormiston 166 22.55 S 138.48 E
Glen Park 212 44.00 N 75.57 W
Glenreagh 166 30.03 S 152.59 E
Glen Richey 214 40.57 N 78.29 W
Glen Riddle 285 39.54 N 75.26 W
Glenridge, Ma., U.S. 283 42.14 N 71.19 W
Glen Ridge, N.J., U.S. 276 40.48 N 74.12 W
Glen Robertson 206 45.21 N 74.30 W
Glen Rock, N.J., U.S. 276 40.57 N 74.08 W
Glen Rock, Pa., U.S. 208 39.47 N 76.43 W
Glenrock, Wy., U.S. 200 42.52 N 105.52 W
Glen Rose 222 32.14 N 97.45 W
Glen Ross 212 44.16 N 77.36 W
Glenrothes 46 56.12 N 3.10 W
Glenroy, Austl. 162 21.46 S 114.49 E
Glenroy, Austl. 162 17.22 S 126.06 E
Glenroy, Austl. 274b 37.42 S 144.55 E
Glenroy ≃ 172 42.00 S 172.20 E
Glen Roy ≃ 46 56.56 N 4.45 W
Glens Falls 210 43.18 N 73.38 W
Glenshaw 214 40.31 N 79.58 W
Glenshee V 46 56.48 N 3.30 W
Glenside, S. Afr. 158 29.25 S 30.47 E
Glenside, N.J., U.S. 208 39.40 N 75.29 W
Glenside, Pa., U.S. 285 40.06 N 75.09 W
Glen Spey 210 41.29 N 74.49 W
Glen Stewart Park ♦ 275b 43.41 N 79.18 W
Glenties 48 54.47 N 8.17 W
Glen Ullin 198 46.48 N 101.49 W
Glenview 278 42.04 N 87.47 W
Glenview Countryside 278 42.04 N 87.50 W
Glenview Naval Air Station ■ 216 42.05 N 87.50 W
Glenville, Ire. 48 52.03 N 8.26 W
Glenville, Mn., U.S. 190 43.34 N 93.16 W
Glenville, N.Y., U.S. 276 41.04 N 73.50 W
Glenville, W.V., U.S. 188 38.56 N 80.50 W
Glenvista 273d 26.17 S 28.13 E
Glen Waverley 274b 37.53 S 145.10 E
Glen White 192 37.44 N 81.16 W
Glen Wild 210 41.29 N 74.36 W
Glen Wild Lake ⊜ 276 41.02 N 74.20 W
Glenwillard 214 40.34 N 80.13 W
Glen Williams 212 43.40 N 79.55 W
Glenwillow 214 41.22 N 81.28 W
Glenwood, Ab., Can. 182 49.22 N 113.31 W
Glenwood, Nf., Can. 186 48.59 N 54.52 W
Glenwood, Al., U.S. 194 31.39 N 86.10 W
Glenwood, Ar., U.S. 194 34.19 N 93.33 W
Glenwood, Ga., U.S. 192 32.10 N 82.40 W
Glenwood, Il., U.S. 278 41.32 N 87.36 W
Glenwood, In., U.S. 218 39.37 N 85.18 W
Glenwood, Ia., U.S. 198 41.02 N 95.44 W
Glenwood, Mn., U.S. 198 45.39 N 95.23 W
Glenwood, Mo., U.S. 194 40.31 N 92.34 W
Glenwood, N.J., U.S. 210 41.15 N 74.29 W
Glenwood, N.M., U.S. 200 33.19 N 108.52 W
Glenwood, N.Y., U.S. 210 42.37 N 78.39 W
Glenwood, Or., U.S. 224 45.38 N 123.16 W
Glenwood, Tx., U.S. 222 32.39 N 94.51 W
Glenwood, Ut., U.S. 200 38.45 N 111.59 W
Glenwood, Va., U.S. 192 36.35 N 79.21 W
Glenwood, Wa., U.S. 224a 46.01 N 121.17 W
Glenwood City 190 45.03 N 92.10 W
Glenwood Landing 276 40.50 N 73.39 W
Glenwood Park 284c 38.58 N 76.50 W
Glenwood Springs 200 39.33 N 107.19 W
Gleschendorf 54 54.02 N 10.40 E
Glesien 54 51.27 N 12.13 E
Gletsch 58 46.34 N 8.22 E
Gleussen 56 50.08 N 10.53 E
Glew 258 34.53 S 58.23 W
Glidden, Ia., U.S. 198 42.03 N 94.43 W
Glidden, Tx., U.S. 222 29.42 N 96.35 W
Glidden, Wi., U.S. 190 46.08 N 90.34 W
Glide 202 43.18 N 123.06 W
Gliener Berg ∧[2] 264a 52.42 N 13.00 E
Glienicke, Dtsch. 54 52.13 N 14.05 E
Glienicke, Dtsch. 54 52.37 N 13.19 E
Glifa 38 38.57 N 22.58 E
Glifádha 267c 37.52 N 23.45 E
Glimåkra 26 56.18 N 14.08 E
Glimmingehus 26 55.30 N 14.13 E
Glin 48 52.34 N 9.17 W
Glina 36 45.20 N 16.06 E
Glina ≃ 36 45.26 N 16.07 E
Glinde 52 53.32 N 10.13 E
Glindow 54 52.21 N 12.54 E
Glindowsee ⊜ 264a 52.21 N 12.56 E
Glinka 76 54.39 N 32.52 E
Glinkovo 85 42.55 N 69.40 E
Glittertinden ∧ 26 61.39 N 8.33 E
Gliwice (Gleiwitz) 30 50.17 N 18.40 E
G. L. Martin State Airport ⊠ 284b 39.20 N 76.25 W
Globe, Az., U.S. 200 33.23 N 110.47 W
Globe, Ky., U.S. 218 38.17 N 83.14 W
Glodeanu-Siliştea 38 44.50 N 26.48 E
Glodeni 38 47.47 N 27.31 E
Glödok ◆[8] 269e 6.08 S 106.48 E
Glogau
— Głogów 30 51.40 N 16.05 E
Gloggnitz 61 47.40 N 15.57 E
Glogn ≃ 58 46.46 N 9.12 E
Głogów, Pol. 30 51.40 N 16.05 E
Głogów, Pol. 30 50.10 N 21.58 E
Głogówek 30 50.22 N 17.51 E
Glommersträsk 26 65.16 N 19.38 E
Glonn 64 47.59 N 11.52 E
Glonn ≃ 60 48.26 N 11.36 E
Glorenza (Glurns) 64 46.40 N 10.33 E
Glória 250 9.11 S 38.18 W
Gloria, Bahía de la c 240p 21.50 N 77.40 W
Glória de Dourados 255 22.21 S 54.13 W
Gloria Glens Park 214 41.03 N 81.54 W
Glorieta 200 35.34 N 105.46 W
Glorieuses, Îles II 138 11.30 S 47.20 E
Glörstausee ⊜[1] 263 51.14 N 7.29 E
Glos-la-Ferrière 50 48.51 N 0.36 E
Glossop 44 53.27 N 1.57 W
Glossopteris, Mount ∧ 9 84.44 S 113.51 W
Gloster 194 31.11 N 91.01 W
Glostrup 41 55.40 N 12.24 E
Glotovka 80 53.57 N 46.42 E
Glotovo 24 63.30 N 49.23 E
Gloucester, Austl. 166 31.59 S 151.58 E
Gloucester, On., Can. 212 45.22 N 75.35 W
Gloucester, Eng., U.K. 42 51.53 N 2.14 W
Gloucester, Ma., U.S. 207 42.36 N 70.39 W
Gloucester, Va., U.S. 208 37.24 N 76.31 W
Gloucester □[6], N.J., U.S. 208 39.50 N 75.10 W
Gloucester □[6], Va., U.S. 208 37.25 N 76.30 W
Gloucester, Cape ≻ 164 5.27 S 148.25 E
Gloucester, Vale of V 42 51.55 N 2.10 W
Gloucester City 285 39.53 N 75.07 W
Gloucester Fisherman ⊥ 283 42.36 N 70.40 W
Gloucester Harbor c 207 42.36 N 70.40 W
Gloucester Island I 166 20.01 S 148.27 E
Gloucester Point 208 37.15 N 76.29 W
Gloucester Pool ⊜ 212 44.51 N 79.43 W
Gloucestershire □[6] 42 51.47 N 2.15 W
Glouster 188 39.30 N 82.05 W
Glover-Archbold Park ♦ 284c 38.55 N 77.05 W
Glover Creek ≃ 194 34.02 N 94.56 W
Glover Island I 186 48.44 N 57.45 W
Glovers Reef ◆[2] 232 16.49 N 87.48 W
Gloversville 210 43.03 N 74.20 W
Glovertown 186 48.41 N 54.02 W
Glowe 54 54.35 N 13.28 E
Glöwen 54 52.55 N 12.05 E
Głowno 30 51.58 N 19.44 E
Głubczyce 30 50.13 N 17.49 E
Glubokij, Ross. 80 48.31 N 40.19 E
Glubokij, Ross. 80 47.01 N 42.47 E
Glubokij, Ross. 89 52.53 N 129.44 E
Glubokoje, Bela. 76 55.08 N 27.41 E
Glubokoje, Kaz. 86 50.06 N 82.19 E
Glubokoje, Ross. 82 54.32 N 38.32 E
Głuchołazy 30 50.20 N 17.22 E
Gluchovo 265b 55.46 N 37.16 E
Glückauf-Kampfbahn ♦ 263 51.32 N 7.05 E
Glücksburg 41 54.50 N 9.33 E
Glückstadt, Dtsch. 52 53.47 N 9.25 E
Gluckstadt, S. Afr. 158 27.57 S 31.02 E
Glucomanka, gora ∧ 89 45.10 N 135.48 E
Glud 41 55.49 N 10.00 E
Glumslöv 41 55.56 N 12.48 E
Glumsø 41 55.21 N 11.42 E
Gluša 76 53.05 N 28.52 E
Glusburn 44 53.54 N 1.59 W
Glusk 76 52.54 N 28.41 E
Gluškeviči 78 51.34 N 27.47 E
Gluškovo 76 51.22 N 34.38 E
Glyde ≃, Austl. 164 12.15 S 135.03 E
Glyde ≃, Ire. 48 53.52 N 6.21 W
Glyder Fawr ∧ 44 53.06 N 4.01 W
Glyme ≃ 42 51.49 N 1.22 W
Glyndebourne 42 50.52 N 0.04 E
Glyndon, Md., U.S. 208 39.28 N 76.48 W
Glyndon, Mn., U.S. 198 46.52 N 96.34 W
Glyngøre 26 56.46 N 8.52 E
Glyn-Neath 42 51.46 N 3.38 W
Gmelinka 80 50.24 N 46.54 E
Gmünd, Öst. 61 48.47 N 15.00 E
Gmünd, Öst. 64 46.54 N 13.32 E
Gmund am Tegernsee 64 47.45 N 11.44 E
Gmunden 64 47.55 N 13.48 E
Gnadenhutten 214 40.21 N 81.26 W
Gnadenhutten Monument ⊥ 214 40.21 N 81.25 W
Gnalta 166 31.03 S 142.20 E
Gnaraloo 162 23.51 S 113.31 E
Gnarp 26 62.03 N 17.16 E
Gnarpurt, Lake ⊜ 169 38.03 S 143.24 E
Gnarrenburg 52 53.22 N 9.00 E
Gnaw Bone 218 39.12 N 86.09 W
Gnesen
— Gniezno 30 52.31 N 17.37 E
Gnesta 40 59.03 N 17.18 E
Gnezdovo 76 54.47 N 31.47 E
Gniben ≻ 41 56.01 N 11.18 E
Gniew 30 53.51 N 18.49 E
Gniewkowo 30 52.54 N 18.25 E
Gniezno 30 52.31 N 17.37 E
Gnilec 76 52.22 N 36.01 E
Gnjilane 38 42.28 N 21.29 E
Gnoien 54 53.58 N 12.42 E
Gnosall 42 52.47 N 2.15 W
Gnosjö 26 57.22 N 13.44 E
Gnowangerup 162 33.56 S 117.59 E
Gō ≃ 96 35.02 N 132.13 E
Goa 116 13.42 N 123.29 E
Goa □[3] 122 15.20 N 74.00 E
Goageb 156 26.44 S 17.15 E
Goalen Head ≻ 166 36.40 S 150.05 E
Goāliar ≃ 126 24.07 N 90.18 E
Goālpāra 124 26.11 N 90.37 E
Goāltor 126 22.43 N 87.10 E
Goan 150 13.14 N 5.09 W
Goascorán 236 13.36 N 87.45 W
Goascorán ≃ 236 13.25 N 87.48 W
Goat Fell ∧ 46 55.38 N 5.12 W
Goathland 44 54.23 N 0.44 W
Goat Island I 284a 43.05 N 79.04 W
Goat Mountain ∧ 202 47.21 N 113.21 W
Goat Peak ∧ 224 46.56 N 121.16 W
Goba, Ityo. 144 7.02 N 40.00 E
Goba, Moç. 156 26.12 S 32.08 E
Gobabis 156 22.30 S 18.58 E
Gobabis □[5] 156 22.30 S 19.00 E
Gobai ≃ 126 23.37 N 86.28 E
Gobardānga 126 22.53 N 88.45 E
Göbel 130 40.00 N 28.09 E
Gobernador Andonaegui 258 34.10 S 59.19 W
Gobernador Costa 254 44.03 S 70.35 W
Gobernador Gregores 254 48.46 S 70.15 W
Gobernador Ingeniero Valentín Virasoro 252 28.03 S 56.02 W
Gobernador Juan E. Martínez 252 28.55 S 58.56 W
Gobernador Monteverde 288 34.48 S 58.16 W
Gobernador Racedo 252 31.34 S 60.04 W
Gobernador Udaondo 258 35.18 S 58.36 W
Gobi ◆[2] 102 43.00 N 105.00 E
Gobindapur, India 126 23.16 N 87.58 E
Gobindapur, India 272b 22.23 N 88.25 E
Gobindapur, India 272b 22.55 N 88.12 E
Gobindgarh 123 30.41 N 76.18 E
Gobindpur 126 23.50 N 86.31 E
Göbberg ∧ 60 48.06 N 13.32 E
Gobles 216 42.21 N 85.52 W
Gobō 96 33.53 N 135.10 E
Gobowen 42 52.53 N 3.02 W
Gobra 126 23.45 N 89.12 E
Gobur 154 4.20 N 31.04 E
Gobza ≃ 76 55.16 N 31.31 E
Göçbeyli 130 39.13 N 27.25 E
Goceano, Catena del ⋏ 71 40.28 N 9.02 E
Goce Delčev 38 41.34 N 23.44 E
Goch 52 51.41 N 6.10 E
Gochas 156 24.55 S 18.55 E
Gochsheim 56 50.01 N 10.16 E
Go Cong 269c 10.50 N 106.50 E
Göcsej ⋏[2] 61 46.43 N 16.42 E
Godafoss ∟ 24a 65.40 N 17.30 W
Godalming 42 51.11 N 0.37 W
Godar 144 4.28 N 43.24 E
Godār ≃ 128 28.10 N 63.14 E
Godāvari ≃ 122 17.00 N 81.45 E
Godāvari, Mouths of the ≃[1] 122 16.25 N 82.00 E
Godbout 186 49.19 N 67.36 W
Godbout ≃ 186 49.19 N 67.37 W
Godda 124 24.50 N 87.13 E
Goddard 218 38.22 N 83.37 W
Goddard Space Flight Center ⊌ 284c 39.00 N 76.52 W
Godeffroy 210 41.27 N 74.37 W
Godega di Sant'Urbano 64 45.56 N 12.24 E
Godegård 40 58.44 N 15.09 E
Godelheim 52 51.44 N 9.22 E
Godere 144 5.05 N 43.50 E
Goderich 190 43.45 N 81.43 W
Goderville 50 49.39 N 0.22 E
Godfrey 219 38.57 N 90.11 W
Godhavn (Qeqertarsuaq) 176 69.15 N 53.33 W
Godhra 120 22.45 N 73.38 E
Godinlabe 144 5.54 N 46.38 E
Godinne 56 50.21 N 4.52 E
Godley 222 32.27 N 97.32 W
Godmanchester 42 52.19 N 0.11 W
Godo, Indon. 115b 8.33 S 118.40 E
Gōdo, Nihon 94 35.25 N 136.36 E
Gōdo, Nihon 268 35.51 N 139.44 E
Gödöllö 264c 47.36 N 19.22 E
Gödöllői Dombság ⋏[2] 264c 47.37 N 19.16 E
Godong 115a 7.02 S 110.46 E
Godoy Cruz 252 32.55 S 68.50 W
Godramstein 56 49.12 N 8.05 E
Godrano 70 37.54 N 13.26 E
Gods ≃ 184 56.22 N 92.51 W
Godshill 42 50.38 N 1.14 W
Godshorn 52 52.26 N 9.43 E
Gods Lake 184 54.40 N 94.09 W
Gods Lake ⊜ 184 54.40 N 94.20 W
Gods Mercy, Bay of c 176 63.30 N 86.10 W
Godstone 42 51.15 N 0.04 W
Godthåb (Nuuk) 176 64.11 N 51.44 W
Godunovo 82 56.29 N 39.02 E
Godwin Austen
— K2 ∧ 123 35.53 N 76.30 E
Goéland, Lac au ⊜ 176 49.47 N 76.48 W
Goélands, Lac aux ⊜ 176 55.27 N 64.17 W
Goeree I 52 51.50 N 3.55 E
Goes 52 51.30 N 3.54 E
Goetzenbruck 56 48.59 N 7.23 E
Goff, Som. 144 2.39 N 41.00 E
Goff, Ks., U.S. 198 39.39 N 95.55 W
Goff Creek ≃ 196 36.43 N 101.29 W
Goffle Brook ≃ 276 40.56 N 74.08 W
Goff's Oak 260 51.43 N 0.05 W
Goffstown 188 43.01 N 71.36 W
Gogama 190 47.40 N 81.43 W
Gogebic, Lake ⊜ 190 46.30 N 89.35 W
Gogebic Range ⋏[2] 190 46.30 N 89.50 W
Gogeldrie 166 34.38 S 146.17 E
Göggingen 58 48.20 N 10.52 E
Gogland, ostrov I 76 60.04 N 27.00 E
Goglio 58 46.18 N 8.16 E
Gogoi 156 20.17 S 33.08 E
Gogonou 150 10.50 N 2.50 E
Gogo-shima I 96 33.54 N 132.41 E
Gogrial 140 8.32 N 28.07 E
Gohad 124 26.26 N 78.27 E
Gohāla 126 23.15 N 89.59 E
Gohāla ≃ 126 24.08 N 89.35 E
Gohāna 124 29.08 N 76.42 E
Gohfeld 52 52.12 N 8.45 E
Gohitafla 150 7.30 N 5.53 W
Göhl 54 54.17 N 10.56 E
Gohoku 96 33.39 N 133.21 E
Go Home Lake ⊜ 212 45.00 N 79.51 W
Gohpur 120 26.53 N 93.38 E
Gohr 263 51.06 N 6.43 E
Göhrde 54 53.08 N 10.52 E
Göhren 54 54.20 N 13.44 E
Goiana, Bra. 250 7.33 S 34.59 W
Goianá, Bra. 256 21.32 S 43.12 W
Goianápolis 255 16.30 S 49.01 W
Goiandira 255 18.08 S 48.06 W
Goianésia 255 15.18 S 49.07 W
Goiânia 255 16.40 S 49.16 W
Goianinha 250 6.16 S 35.12 W
Goiás 255 15.56 S 50.08 W
Goiás □[3] 255 16.00 S 50.00 W
Goiatuba 255 18.01 S 49.22 W
Goichran 120 31.04 N 78.07 E
Goil, Loch c 46 56.08 N 4.52 W
Goio-Erê 252 24.12 S 53.01 W
Gôio-Erê ≃ 252 24.14 S 53.21 W
Goirle 52 51.32 N 5.04 E
Góis 34 40.09 N 8.07 W
Goito 64 45.15 N 10.40 E
Gojam □[4] 144 11.00 N 37.00 E
Gojeb ≃ 144 7.20 N 37.21 E
Gojō 96 34.21 N 135.42 E

ENGLISH
Name Page Lat.°' Long.°'

Gojōme 92 39.56 N 140.07 E
Gojra 123 31.09 N 72.41 E
Gojtchskij, pereval)(84 44.18 N 39.18 E
Gök ≃ 130 41.24 N 35.08 E
Gokāk 122 16.10 N 74.50 E
Gokarna 126 24.03 N 88.07 E
Gokase ≃ 92 32.35 N 131.42 E
Gökçeada I 130 40.10 N 25.50 E
Gökçebey 130 41.19 N 32.08 E
Gökçedağ 130 39.33 N 28.56 E
Gökçekent 130 40.19 N 38.07 E
Gökçeli 130 40.35 N 36.44 E
Gökçen 130 38.07 N 27.53 E
Gökçesu 130 40.54 N 31.58 E
Gökdere, Tür. 130 40.29 N 36.47 E
Gökdere, Tür. 130 38.44 N 40.13 E
Gokōmutsumi 268 35.48 N 139.59 E
Gökova Körfezi c 130 36.50 N 28.00 E
Göksholm 40 59.16 N 15.33 E
Göksu ≃, Tür. 84 39.19 N 42.17 E
Göksu ≃, Tür. 130 36.19 N 34.02 E
Göksu ≃, Tür. 130 37.37 N 35.35 E
Göksu ≃, Tür. 267b 41.06 N 29.03 E
Göksun 130 38.03 N 36.30 E
Göktaş 130 41.17 N 41.46 E
Göktepe 130 37.15 N 28.36 E
Göktürk ◆[8] 267b 41.11 N 28.53 E
Gokwe 154 18.07 S 28.58 E
Gol 26 60.42 N 8.57 E
Gol, Khawr V 140 6.55 N 30.16 E
Golabāri 272b 22.36 N 88.20 E
Golāghāt 120 26.31 N 93.58 E
Gola Gokarannāth 124 28.05 N 80.28 E
Gola Island I 48 55.05 N 8.22 W
Gołańcz 30 52.57 N 17.18 E
Golan Heights ⊥[4] 132 32.55 N 35.42 E
Golāshkerd 128 27.59 N 57.16 E
Golbāf 128 29.51 N 57.44 E
Gölbaşı, Tür. 130 37.50 N 37.40 E
Gölbaşı, Tür. 130 39.48 N 32.49 E
Golborne 262 53.29 N 2.36 W
Golcar 262 53.39 N 1.51 W
Gol'čicha 74 71.43 N 83.36 E
Golconda, Il., U.S. 194 37.22 N 88.29 W
Golconda, Nv., U.S. 204 40.57 N 117.29 W
Gölcük, Tür. 130 39.18 N 27.59 E
Gölcük, Tür. 130 40.44 N 29.48 E
Golczewo 54 53.49 N 14.59 E
Gołdap 30 54.19 N 22.19 E
Goldau 58 47.03 N 8.33 E
Gold Bar 224 47.51 N 121.41 W
Gold Beach 202 42.24 N 124.25 W
Goldbeck 54 52.43 N 11.52 E
Goldberg 54 53.35 N 12.05 E
Goldberger See ⊜ 54 53.36 N 12.07 E
Goldbergtunnel ◆[5] 263 51.21 N 7.28 E
Goldbey 58 48.12 N 6.26 E
Goldboro 186 45.11 N 61.39 W
Gold Bridge 182 50.51 N 122.50 W
Gold Coast
— Southport 171a 27.58 S 153.25 E
Gold Coast ⊥[2] 150 5.20 N 0.45 W
Gold Creek 180 62.46 N 149.41 W
Gold Creek ≃ 182 49.04 N 115.12 W
Golden, B.C., Can. 182 51.18 N 116.58 W
Golden, Ire. 48 52.29 N 7.58 W
Golden, Co., U.S. 200 39.45 N 105.13 W
Golden, Il., U.S. 219 40.07 N 91.01 W
Golden Bay c 172 40.40 S 172.50 E
Golden Beach 220 25.57 N 80.07 W
Golden Brook ≃ 283 42.44 N 71.19 W
Golden City 194 37.23 N 94.05 W
Goldendale 224 45.49 N 120.49 W
Golden Ears Provincial Park ♦ 182 49.30 N 122.25 W
Goldene Aue V 54 51.25 N 11.00 E
Golden Gate 220 26.09 N 81.43 W
Golden Gate ⊻ 226 37.49 N 122.29 W
Golden Gate Bridge ◆[5] 282 37.49 N 122.28 W
Golden Gate Fields Race Track ♦ 282 37.53 N 122.19 W
Golden Gate Highlands National Park ♦ 158 28.30 S 28.40 E
Golden Gate National Recreation Area ♦ 282 37.49 N 122.31 W
Golden Gate Park ♦ 282 37.46 N 122.28 W
Golden Green 260 51.12 N 0.21 E
Golden Hill Creek ≃ 210 43.22 N 78.28 W
Golden Hinde ∧ 182 49.40 N 125.45 W
Golden Horn
— Haliç c 267b 41.02 N 28.58 E
Golden Lake ⊜ 212 45.35 N 77.20 W
Golden Meadow 194 29.22 N 90.15 W
Golden Prairie 184 50.14 N 109.38 W
Golden Ring Mall ◆[9] 284b 39.20 N 76.29 W
Golden Rock 122 10.48 N 78.44 E
Goldenrod 220 28.37 N 81.18 W
Golden Spike National Historic Site ⊥ 202 41.38 N 112.35 W
Goldenstedt 52 52.48 N 8.25 E
Golden Valley V 42 52.02 N 2.56 W
Golders Green ◆[8] 260 51.35 N 0.12 W
Goldfield, Ia., U.S. 190 42.44 N 93.55 W
Goldfield, Nv., U.S. 204 37.42 N 117.14 W
Gold Lake ⊜ 212 44.43 N 78.17 W
Goldlauter 54 50.38 N 10.44 E
Gold Mountain ∧ 204 37.15 N 117.18 W
Goldney 258 34.37 S 59.18 W
Goldonna 194 32.01 N 92.54 W
Goldpan Peak ∧ 180 61.12 N 153.22 W
Gold River 182 49.41 N 126.08 W
Gold Rock 184 49.27 N 92.43 W
Gold Run 226 39.10 N 120.52 W
Goldsand Lake ⊜ 184 57.02 N 101.08 W
Goldsboro, Md., U.S. 208 39.02 N 75.47 W
Goldsboro, N.C., U.S. 192 35.23 N 77.59 W
Goldsmith, In., U.S. 216 40.17 N 86.08 W
Goldsmith, Tx., U.S. 196 31.58 N 102.36 W
Goldsmith, Lake ⊜ 169 37.32 S 143.21 E
Goldston 192 35.35 N 79.19 W
Goldstone Lake ⊜ 228 35.22 N 116.54 W
Goldstream Provincial Park ♦ 224 48.29 N 123.33 W
Goldsworthy 162 20.20 S 119.30 E
Goldsworthy, Mount ∧[2] 162 20.21 S 119.32 E
Goldthwaite 196 31.26 N 98.34 W
Göle 130 40.48 N 42.36 E
Golec, gora ∧ 88 58.39 N 94.10 E
Goleen 48 51.28 N 9.43 W
Golela 158 27.20 S 31.55 E
Goleniów 30 53.36 N 14.50 E
Golestan Palace ⊌ 267d 35.41 N 51.25 E
Goleta 204 34.26 N 119.49 W
Golf, Fl., U.S. 220 26.31 N 80.06 W
Golf, Il., U.S. 278 42.03 N 87.48 W
Golfcrest 216 41.57 N 83.22 W
Golfe-Juan 62 43.34 N 7.05 E
Golfito 236 8.38 N 83.11 W
Golf Manor 285 39.42 N 75.28 W
Golf Mill ◆[9] 278 42.03 N 87.50 W
Golfo Aranci 71 40.59 N 9.38 E
Golfo de Santa Clara 232 31.42 N 114.30 W
Golfside 281 42.15 N 83.41 W
Golf View 208 39.43 N 75.28 W
Golfview Hills 278 41.47 N 87.56 W
Gölhisar 130 37.10 N 29.30 E
Goliad 196 28.40 N 97.23 W
Goliad □[6] 222 28.52 N 97.22 W
Golicyno, Ross. 80 53.38 N 44.07 E
Golicyno, Ross. 80 55.58 N 40.26 E
Golicyno, Ross. 82 55.37 N 36.59 E
Golina 30 52.16 N 18.05 E
Golin Baixing 89 44.53 N 121.58 E
Golinda 222 31.25 N 97.05 W
Goljama Kamčija ≃ 38 43.03 N 27.29 E
Goljam Perelik ∧ 38 41.36 N 24.34 E
Goljanovo ◆[8] 265b 55.49 N 37.48 E

DEUTSCH
Name Seite Breite°' Länge°' E = Ost

Goljevo 265b 55.48 N 37.19 E
Gölköy 130 40.42 N 37.38 E
Gollach ≃ 56 49.31 N 10.00 E
Göllersbach ≃ 61 48.22 N 16.11 E
Göllet 130 40.45 N 42.18 E
Golling an der Salzach 64 47.36 N 13.10 E
Golm 264a 52.24 N 12.58 E
Gölmarmara 130 38.42 N 27.56 E
Golmberg ∧[2] 54 52.01 N 13.21 E
Golmud 102 36.22 N 94.55 E
Golmud ≃ 102 36.54 N 95.11 E
Golo ≃ 36 42.31 N 9.32 E
Golodnaja Guba, ozero ⊜ 24 67.52 N 52.48 E
Golo Island I 116 13.40 N 120.22 E
Golok (Kolok) ≃ 114 6.15 N 102.05 E
Golongoso 146 9.00 N 19.09 E
Gölören 130 37.48 N 33.52 E
Gölova 130 40.04 N 38.37 E
Golovačovka 85 42.52 N 71.13 E
Golovanovo 80 54.55 N 40.27 E
Golovčin 76 54.04 N 29.55 E
Golovčino 78 50.32 N 35.47 E
Golovin 180 64.33 N 163.02 W
Golovinka 84 43.48 N 39.28 E
Golovino, Ross. 76 55.58 N 40.26 E
Golovino, Ross. 82 56.01 N 39.11 E
Golovinščino 80 53.18 N 43.59 E
Golovinskaja 88 53.26 N 102.43 E
Golovnino 82 54.23 N 36.10 E
Golovskoje 88 55.30 N 105.32 E
Golpāyegān 128 33.27 N 50.18 E
Gölpazarı 130 40.15 N 30.19 E
Golra 123 33.42 N 72.58 E
Golrān 128 35.06 N 61.41 E
Gols 61 47.54 N 16.55 E
Gol'šany 76 54.15 N 26.01 E
Gölsdorf 54 51.57 N 12.58 E
Golspie, Austl. 170 34.17 S 149.40 E
Golspie, Scot., U.K. 46 57.58 N 3.58 W
Golssen 54 51.58 N 13.36 E
Gol't'ajevo 82 55.13 N 36.02 E
Gol't'avino 88 58.26 N 98.27 E
Golub-Dobrzyń 30 53.08 N 19.02 E
Golubi 76 59.28 N 41.39 E
Golubinskij 80 48.52 N 43.34 E
Golubovka 86 53.09 N 74.12 E
Golumet' 88 53.03 N 102.21 E
Golungo Alto 152 9.08 S 14.46 E
Golva 198 46.44 N 103.59 W
Golweyn 144 1.40 N 44.35 E
Gölyaka 130 40.47 N 30.59 E
Golynki 76 54.52 N 31.23 E
Golyšmanovo, Ross. 86 56.23 N 68.23 E
Golyšmanovo, Ross. 86 56.28 N 68.38 E
Golzheim ◆[8] 263 51.15 N 6.46 E
Golzow, Dtsch. 54 52.34 N 14.29 E
Golzow, Dtsch. 54 52.16 N 12.36 E
Goma 154 1.41 S 29.14 E
Gomadan-zan ∧ 96 34.03 N 135.34 E
Gomagoi 64 46.35 N 10.32 E
Gomang Co ⊜ 120 31.15 N 89.15 E
Gomaringen 58 48.27 N 9.05 E
Gomas, Sierra de ⋏ 196 26.23 N 100.32 W
Gomati ≃ 124 25.32 N 83.10 E
Gomati Plain ≚ 124 26.30 N 81.10 E
Goma Tsétsé 273b 4.14 S 15.08 E
Gombari 154 2.43 N 29.04 E
Gombe, Nig. 146 10.19 N 11.02 E
Gombe, Zaïre 152 0.42 S 17.35 E
Gombe Stream National Park ♦ 154 4.30 S 29.42 E
Gombi 146 10.10 N 12.45 E
Gomboro 150 13.29 N 2.46 W
Gomel' 76 52.25 N 31.00 E
Gomel' □[8] 76 52.30 N 30.00 E
Gomer 216 40.51 N 84.11 W
Gomera I 148 28.06 N 17.08 W
Gometra I 46 56.29 N 6.17 W
Gometz-la-Ville 261 48.40 N 2.08 E
Gometz-le-Châtel 261 48.41 N 2.08 E
Gomez 220 27.06 N 80.09 W
Gómez Farías, Méx. 232 29.18 N 107.40 W
Gómez Farías, Méx. 234 19.47 N 103.29 W
Gómez Palacio 232 25.34 N 103.30 W
Gómez Plata 246 6.41 N 75.12 W
Gomīshān 128 37.04 N 54.06 E
Gommécourt 261 49.05 N 1.36 E
Gommern 54 52.04 N 11.50 E
Gomo Co ⊜ 120 33.47 N 85.30 E
Gomogomo 164 6.40 S 134.43 E
Gomoh 126 23.52 N 86.10 E
Gompa 123 35.02 N 77.20 E
Goms V 58 46.27 N 8.15 E
Gomshall 260 51.13 N 0.27 W
Gomumu, Pulau I 164 1.49 S 127.38 E
Gonābād 128 34.20 N 58.42 E
Gonaïves 238 19.27 N 72.41 W
Gonaka 152 2.56 S 13.14 E
Gonam 74 57.21 N 131.12 E
Gonam ≃ 74 57.21 N 131.14 E
Gonarezhou National Park ♦ 154 21.30 S 32.00 E
Gonars 64 45.53 N 13.13 E
Gonäs 40 60.09 N 15.06 E
Gonâve, Golfe de la c 238 19.00 N 73.30 W
Gonâve, Île de la I 238 18.51 N 73.03 W
Gonbad-e Qābūs 128 37.17 N 55.17 E
Gonçalves 256 22.40 S 45.51 W
Gonçalves Dias 250 4.57 S 44.14 W
Gončarovka 78 50.32 N 39.28 E
Goncelin 62 45.20 N 5.59 E
Gonda 124 27.08 N 81.56 E
Gondal 120 21.58 N 70.48 E
Gondang 115a 7.24 S 111.06 E
Gondar
— Gonder 144 12.40 N 37.30 E
Gondarbal 123 34.14 N 74.47 E
Gonder 144 12.40 N 37.30 E
Gonder □[4] 144 13.10 N 37.00 E
Gondey 146 9.09 N 19.19 E
Gondia 120 21.27 N 80.12 E
Gondola 156 19.10 S 33.40 E
Gondomar 34 41.09 N 8.32 W
Gondrecourt-le-Château 58 48.31 N 5.30 E
Gondreville 58 48.42 N 5.58 E
Gondrexange, Étang de ⊜ 56 48.42 N 6.54 E
Goneāna 123 30.19 N 74.54 E
Gönen, Tür. 130 40.06 N 27.39 E
Gonén, Yis. 132 33.08 N 35.39 E
Gonesse 50 48.59 N 2.27 E
Gonfaron 62 43.19 N 6.17 E
Gong ≃ 100 26.00 N 115.22 E
Gong'an 102 30.02 N 112.04 E
Gonganbao 86 44.59 N 86.18 E
Gonganpucun 104 41.19 N 123.27 E
Gongbuchang 105 40.17 N 116.15 E
Gongchangling 104 41.06 N 123.30 E
Gongcheng 102 24.49 N 110.46 E
Gongchenqiao 106 30.20 N 120.08 E
Gongchuan, Zhg. 100 26.06 N 117.24 E
Gongchuan, Zhg. 102 23.40 N 107.50 E
Gongcun 105 39.28 N 116.10 E
Gongdaoqiao 100 32.36 N 119.22 E
Gongdian 100 28.06 N 116.56 E
Gongen-yama ∧ 94 35.40 N 139.01 E
Gongfang 100 27.36 N 115.34 E
Gonggar 120 29.17 N 90.46 E
Gongga Shan (Minya Konka) ∧ 102 29.35 N 101.51 E
Gonghe 102 36.20 N 100.48 E
Gonghui 98 41.12 N 114.37 E
Gongjialu 106 31.17 N 121.40 E
Gongjiatun 104 40.55 N 120.37 E
Gongjiazhai 104 41.57 N 124.01 E
Gongjing 107 29.21 N 104.43 E
Gongjingying 105 39.12 N 116.11 E

Symbols in the index entries represent the broad categories identified in the key at the right. Symbols with superior numbers (⋏[1]) identify subcategories (see complete key on page *I · 1*).

Symbole im Register stellen die rechts im Schlüssel erklärten Kategorien dar. Symbole mit hochgestellten Ziffern (⋏[1]) bezeichnen Unterabteilungen einer Kategorie (vgl. vollständiger Schlüssel auf Seite *I · 1*).

Los símbolos incluidos en el texto del índice representan las grandes categorías identificadas con la clave a la derecha. Los símbolos con numeros en su parte superior (⋏[1]) identifican las subcategorías (véase la clave completa en la página *I · 1*).

Les symboles de l'index représentent les catégories indiquées dans la légende à droite. Les symboles suivis d'un indice (⋏[1]) représentent des sous-catégories (voir légende complète à la page *I · 1*).

Os símbolos incluídos no texto do índice representam as grandes categorias identificadas com a chave à direita. Os símbolos com números em sua parte superior (⋏[1]) identificam as subcategorias (veja-se a chave completa à página *I · 1*).

∧ Mountain	Berg	Montaña	Montagne	Montanha
⋏ Mountains	Gebirge	Montañas	Montagnes	Montanhas
)(Pass	Paß	Paso	Col	Passo
V Valley, Canyon	Tal, Cañon	Valle, Cañón	Vallée, Canyon	Vale, Canhão
≚ Plain	Ebene	Llano	Plaine	Planície
≻ Cape	Kap	Cabo	Cap	Cabo
I Island	Insel	Isla	Île	Ilha
II Islands	Inseln	Islas	Îles	Ilhas
⊥ Other Topographic Features	Andere Topographische Objekte	Otros Elementos Topográficos	Autres données topographiques	Outros acidentes topográficos

ESPAÑOL / FRANÇAIS / PORTUGUÊS

Nombre / Nom / Nome	Página / Page	Lat.°′	Long.°′ W = Oeste / W = Ouest
Gongkou	98	35.38 N	119.47 E
Gongli	98	35.55 N	117.24 E
Gongling	100	26.18 N	119.40 E
Gongliu	86	43.30 N	82.15 E
Gonglu Shan ∧	106	30.39 N	119.18 E
Gongo	146	9.00 N	18.56 E
Gongola □[3]	146	9.00 N	11.40 E
Gongola ≃	146	9.30 N	12.04 E
Gongoué	152	0.32 S	9.12 E
Gongo-Yembe	152	1.58 S	18.40 E
Gongpengzi	89	45.09 N	125.39 E
Gongping	100	23.05 N	115.24 E
Gongpingxu	100	26.12 N	112.51 E
Gongshan	102	25.50 N	103.13 E
Gongshiya	120	31.25 N	84.37 E
Gongsizhen	106	31.41 N	121.48 E
Gongtangtou	106	31.48 N	118.42 E
Gongxi	100	27.38 N	115.52 E
Gongxian	102	34.48 N	113.03 E
Gongyefu	98	42.16 N	118.32 E
Gongyemiao	89	43.40 N	121.06 E
Gongyingzi	98	40.54 N	119.41 E
Gongzhutun	104	42.10 N	123.00 E
Gongzui	107	29.19 N	103.28 E
Goni, It.	71	39.34 N	9.17 E
Goñi, Ur.	252	33.31 S	56.24 W
Goniądz	30	53.30 N	22.45 E
Gonini ≃	250	4.10 N	54.24 W
Goniri	146	11.30 N	12.20 E
Gonjo	102	30.43 N	98.19 E
Gonnesa	71	39.16 N	8.28 E
Gonnesa, Golfo di c	71	39.17 N	8.23 E
Gonnosfanadiga	71	39.29 N	8.39 E
Gonnostramatza	71	39.41 N	8.50 E
Gonochovo	86	52.57 N	81.20 E
Gōnoura	92	33.45 N	129.41 E
Gonubie Mouth	158	32.57 S	28.01 E
Gonža	89	53.36 N	125.19 E
Gonzaga, It.	64	44.57 N	10.49 E
Gonzaga, Pil.	116	18.16 N	122.00 E
Gonzales, Ca., U.S.	226	36.30 N	121.26 W
Gonzales, La., U.S.	194	30.14 N	90.55 W
Gonzales, Tx., U.S.	222	29.30 N	97.27 W
Gonzales □[6]	222	29.28 N	97.30 W
González, Méx.	234	22.50 N	98.27 W
González, Ur.	258	34.14 S	56.52 W
González, Riacho ≃	252	22.48 S	57.54 W
González Catán	258	34.46 S	58.39 W
González Chaves	252	38.02 S	60.06 W
González Moreno	252	35.33 S	63.22 W
González Ortega, Méx.	204	32.40 N	115.23 W
González Ortega, Méx.	234	23.59 N	103.27 W
González Ortega, Méx.	234	23.11 N	102.29 W
González Risos	258	34.52 S	59.13 W
Gonzanamá	246	4.15 S	79.27 W
Goobarragandra ≃	171b	35.20 S	148.15 E
Goochland	192	37.41 N	77.53 W
Good Easter	260	51.47 N	0.21 E
Goodells	214	42.59 N	82.40 W
Goode Mountain ∧	224	48.29 N	120.55 W
Goodenough, Mount ∧	180	67.56 N	135.31 W
Goodenough Bay c	164	9.55 S	150.00 E
Goodenough Island I	164	9.20 S	150.15 E
Gooderham	212	44.54 N	78.23 W
Goodeve	184	51.04 N	103.10 W
Goodfellow Air Force Base ■	196	31.26 N	100.25 W
Good Hope, S. Afr.	158	31.51 S	21.55 E
Good Hope, Oh., U.S.	218	39.26 N	83.21 W
Good Hope, Cape of (Kaap die Gooie Hoop) ›	158	34.24 S	18.30 E
Goodhope Bay c	180	66.10 N	163.45 W
Good Hope Mountain ∧	182	51.09 N	124.10 W
Goodhouse	158	28.57 S	18.13 E
Goodhue	190	44.24 N	92.37 W
Gooding	202	42.56 N	114.42 W
Goodison	214	42.44 N	83.10 W
Goodland, Fl., U.S.	220	25.55 N	81.38 W
Goodland, In., U.S.	216	40.45 N	87.17 W
Goodland, Ks., U.S.	198	39.21 N	101.42 W
Goodlands	184	49.05 N	100.35 W
Goodlow Park	222	32.07 N	96.14 W
Goodman, Ms., U.S.	194	32.58 N	89.54 W
Goodman, Wi., U.S.	190	45.37 N	88.21 W
Goodna	171a	27.37 S	152.54 E
Goodnews Bay	180	59.07 N	161.35 W
Goodnight	200	38.14 N	104.43 W
Goodooga	166	29.07 S	147.27 E
Goodradigbee ≃	171b	35.08 S	148.41 E
Goodrich, Mi., U.S.	216	42.55 N	83.30 W
Goodrich, N.D., U.S.	198	47.28 N	100.07 W
Goodrich, Tx., U.S.	222	30.36 N	94.57 W
Good Spirit Lake ⊜	184	51.34 N	102.40 W
Good Spirit Lake Provincial Park ♠	184	51.36 N	102.45 W
Good Thunder	190	44.00 N	94.03 W
Goodview	190	44.03 N	91.41 W
Goodville	208	40.08 N	76.00 W
Goodwater	194	33.03 N	86.03 W
Goodwell	196	36.35 N	101.38 W
Goodwick	42	52.00 N	5.00 W
Goodwin, Lake ⊜	224	48.08 N	122.18 W
Goodwives ≃	276	41.04 N	73.28 W
Goodwood	212	44.02 N	79.12 W
Goodyear	200	33.26 N	112.21 W
Goof, Webi ≃	144	1.10 N	43.43 E
Googong Reservoir ⊜[1]	171b	35.27 S	149.16 E
Gooie Hoop, Kaap die → Good Hope, Cape of ›	158	34.24 S	18.30 E
Goole	44	53.42 N	0.52 W
Goolgowi	166	33.59 S	145.42 E
Goolwa	168b	35.31 S	138.47 E
Goomalling	162	31.19 S	116.49 E
Goombalie	166	29.59 S	145.23 E
Goombungee	171a	27.18 S	151.51 E
Goomburra	171a	28.03 S	152.07 E
Goonda	156	19.51 S	34.00 E
Goondiwindi	166	28.32 S	150.19 E
Goongarrie	162	30.03 S	121.09 E
Goongarrie National Park ♠	162	29.58 S	121.34 E
Goonyella	166	21.45 S	147.55 E
Goor	52	52.14 N	6.35 E
Goose ≃, Ab., Can.	182	54.58 N	117.11 W
Goose ≃, N.D., U.S.	198	47.28 N	96.52 W
Goose Bay → Happy Valley-Goose Bay	176	53.20 N	60.25 W
Goose Bay c	281	42.35 N	82.41 W
Gooseberry Creek ≃	202	43.55 N	108.04 W
Goose Creek	192	32.58 N	80.01 W
Goose Creek ≃, U.S.	202	42.33 N	113.46 W
Goose Creek ≃, Ne., U.S.	198	42.02 N	100.03 W
Goose Creek ≃, N.Y., U.S.	214	42.06 N	79.22 W
Goose Creek ≃, Va., U.S.	208	39.06 N	77.29 W
Goose Island I	182	51.55 N	128.25 W
Goose Lake ⊜, Mb., Can.	184	54.26 N	101.30 W
Goose Lake ⊜, On., Can.	184	51.46 N	93.00 W
Goose Lake ⊜, On., Can.	212	44.25 N	78.52 W
Goose Lake ⊜, On., Can.	214	42.31 N	82.31 W
Goose Lake ⊜, Sk., Can.	184	51.45 N	107.23 W
Goose Lake ⊜, U.S.	204	41.57 N	120.25 W
Goose Lake Canal ≊	226	35.50 N	119.37 W
Goose Lake Prairie State Park ♠	216	41.21 N	88.18 W
Gooseprairie	224	46.54 N	121.15 W
Goostrey	262	53.13 N	2.20 W
Gooty	122	15.07 N	77.38 E
Gopālganj, Bngl.	124	23.01 N	89.50 E
Gopālganj, India	124	26.28 N	84.26 E
Gopālnagar, India	126	23.03 N	88.45 E
Gopālnagar, India	272b	22.50 N	88.14 E
Gopālpur, Bngl.	124	24.33 N	89.56 E
Gopālpur, India	272b	22.38 N	88.27 E
Gopeng	114	4.28 N	101.10 E
Göpfritz an der Wild	61	48.43 N	15.24 E
Gopiballabhpur	126	22.13 N	86.54 E
Gopichettipālaiyam	122	11.28 N	77.27 E
Gopinagar	272b	22.50 N	88.07 E
Goppenstein	58	46.22 N	7.45 E
Göppingen	56	48.42 N	9.40 E
Goqên	102	29.15 N	96.59 E
Go Quao	110	9.43 N	105.17 E
Gor	123	35.32 N	74.31 E
Góra, Pol.	30	51.40 N	16.33 E
Gora, Ross.	76	60.02 N	41.43 E
Gor'ačegorsk	86	55.24 N	88.55 E
Gor'ačij Kl'uč	84	44.37 N	39.07 E
Gor'ačinsk	88	52.59 N	108.18 E
Goradit	144	11.25 N	38.25 E
Góra Kalwaria	30	51.59 N	21.12 E
Gorakhpur	124	26.45 N	83.22 E
Goranboy	84	40.36 N	46.47 E
Gor'any	76	55.25 N	29.02 E
Goras	124	25.32 N	76.56 E
Goražde	38	43.40 N	18.56 E
Gorbatov	80	56.08 N	43.04 E
Gorbatovka	80	56.15 N	43.45 E
Gorbica	88	53.06 N	119.13 E
Gorboviči	76	53.49 N	30.41 E
Gorčucha	80	57.43 N	43.43 E
Gorda, Punta ›, Chile	248	19.18 S	70.18 W
Gorda, Punta ›, Cuba	240p	22.24 N	82.10 W
Gorda, Punta ›, Nic.	236	11.26 N	83.48 W
Gorda, Punta ›, Nic.	236	14.21 N	83.12 W
Gorda, Punta ›, Ca., U.S.	204	40.16 N	124.22 W
Gordejevka	76	52.59 N	31.58 E
Gordes, Fr.	62	43.54 N	5.12 E
Gördes, Tür.	130	38.54 N	28.18 E
Gordil	146	9.44 N	21.35 E
Gørding	41	55.29 N	8.48 E
Gordion ⊥	130	39.41 N	32.01 E
Gordo	194	33.19 N	87.54 W
Gordo, Cerro ∧	234	20.46 N	102.35 W
Gordola	58	46.11 N	8.52 E
Gordon, Scot., U.K.	46	55.41 N	2.34 W
Gordon, Ga., U.S.	192	32.52 N	83.19 W
Gordon, Ne., U.S.	198	42.48 N	102.12 W
Gordon, Oh., U.S.	218	39.56 N	84.31 W
Gordon, Pa., U.S.	208	40.45 N	76.21 W
Gordon, Wi., U.S.	190	46.14 N	91.47 W
Gordon ≃	224	48.35 N	124.24 W
Gordon, Isla I	254	54.58 S	69.35 W
Gordon, Lake ⊜[1]	166	42.42 S	146.12 E
Gordon Creek ≃	198	42.49 N	100.40 W
Gordon Downs	162	18.44 S	128.35 E
Gordon Heights	207	40.51 N	72.58 W
Gordon Horne Peak ∧	182	51.46 N	118.50 W
Gordon Indian Reserve ◆[4]	184	51.16 N	104.16 W
Gordon Lake ⊜, Ab., Can.	184	56.30 N	110.25 W
Gordon Lake ⊜, Sk., Can.	184	55.50 N	106.26 W
Gordon Lakes	276	41.03 N	74.22 W
Gordon Pass c	220	26.06 N	81.48 W
Gordon River	224	48.47 N	124.21 W
Gordon's Bay	158	34.10 S	18.52 E
Gordonsville	188	38.08 N	78.11 W
Gordonton	172	37.40 S	175.18 E
Gordonvale	166	17.05 S	145.47 E
Gordonville	220	27.57 N	81.49 W
Gore, Austl.	166	28.17 S	151.29 E
Gore, N.S., Can.	186	45.07 N	63.43 W
Gore, Ityo.	144	8.08 N	35.33 E
Gore, N.Z.	172	46.06 S	168.58 E
Goré, Tchad	146	7.53 N	16.40 E
Gore Bay	190	45.55 N	82.28 W
Gorebridge	46	55.51 N	3.02 W
Goreda	164	3.39 S	134.58 E
Goree	196	33.28 N	99.31 W
Gore Hill	274a	33.49 S	151.11 E
Görele	130	41.02 N	39.00 E
Gorelki	82	54.15 N	37.37 E
Goreloje	80	52.57 N	41.28 E
Gorelovo	265a	59.47 N	30.08 E
Gorelovo Airport ⊠	265a	59.47 N	30.05 E
Gorelyj ≃	265a	59.58 N	30.28 E
Göreme Milli Parkı ♠	130	38.26 N	34.54 E
Gore Mountain ∧	188	44.55 N	71.48 W
Gorenki	265b	55.48 N	37.55 E
Gore Point ›, Austl.	166	17.38 S	139.56 E
Gore Point ›, Ak., U.S.	180	59.12 N	151.00 W
Gore Range ⩘	200	40.00 N	106.30 W
Goretovka ≃	265b	55.56 N	37.20 E
Goreville	194	37.33 N	88.58 W
Gorey, Ire.	48	52.40 N	6.18 W
Gorey, Jersey	43b	49.12 N	2.02 W
Gorfoundurei	144	4.30 N	46.41 E
Gorgān	128	36.50 N	54.29 E
Gorgān ≃	128	36.59 N	54.00 E
Gorge Lake ⊜[1]	224	48.42 N	121.13 W
Görgeshausen	56	50.24 N	7.56 E
Gorgoglione	68	40.23 N	16.09 E
Gorgol □[4]	150	16.00 N	13.00 W
Gorgol el Abiod ≃	150	16.14 N	12.58 W
Gorgol el Akhdar ≃	150	16.13 N	12.58 W
Gorgona, Isla I	246	2.59 N	78.12 W
Gorgona, Isola di I	36	43.26 N	9.54 E
Gorgonzola	62	45.32 N	9.24 E
Gorgor	248	10.35 S	77.02 W
Gorgora	144	12.13 N	37.16 E
Gorgoram	146	12.38 N	10.43 E
Gorgota	38	44.47 N	26.05 E
Gorgova	38	45.11 N	29.10 E
Gorham, Me., U.S.	188	43.40 N	70.26 W
Gorham, N.H., U.S.	188	44.23 N	71.10 W
Gorham, N.Y., U.S.	210	42.47 N	77.07 W
Gorhambury House ⊥	260	51.47 N	0.24 W
Gori	84	41.58 N	44.07 E
Goria	272b	22.24 N	88.29 E
Gorica → Gorizia	64	45.57 N	13.38 E
Goričan	61	46.23 N	16.41 E
Goricy	76	57.09 N	36.44 E
Gorinchem	52	51.50 N	5.00 E
Goring	42	51.32 N	1.09 W
Goring-by-Sea	42	50.49 N	0.25 W
Goring Gap V	42	51.32 N	1.08 W
Goris	84	39.31 N	46.23 E
Göritz	54	53.24 N	13.54 E
Göritzhain	54	50.58 N	12.47 E
Gorizia	64	45.57 N	13.38 E
Gorizia □[4]	64	45.55 N	13.30 E
Gorj □[6]	38	45.00 N	23.20 E
Gorjani	38	45.24 N	18.21 E
Gor'kaja Balka	84	44.17 N	43.59 E
Gor'kaja balka ≃	84	44.38 N	45.00 E
Görke	54	53.51 N	13.38 E
Gorkhā	124	28.00 N	84.37 E
Gorki, Bela.	76	54.17 N	30.59 E
Gorki → Nižnij Novgorod, Ross.	80	56.20 N	44.00 E
Gorki, Ross.	80	57.38 N	45.05 E
Gorki, Ross.	82	54.18 N	36.08 E
Gorki, Ross.	82	55.32 N	37.45 E
Gorki, Ross.	82	56.54 N	38.51 E
Gorki, Ross.	265b	55.57 N	37.55 E
Gor'kij → Nižnij Novgorod	80	56.20 N	44.00 E
Gorki Vtoryje	265b	55.44 N	37.11 E
Gor'koje, ozero ⊜	86	52.30 N	81.20 E
Gor'kovskoje	86	55.22 N	74.24 E
Gor'kovskoje vodochranilišče ⊜[1]	80	57.00 N	43.10 E
Gorky → Nižnij Novgorod	80	56.20 N	44.00 E
Gorky Park ♠	265b	55.44 N	37.36 E
Gorlago	62	45.40 N	9.49 E
Gorla Maggiore	266b	45.40 N	8.53 E
Gorla Minore	266b	45.39 N	8.54 E
Gorleston on Sea	42	52.36 N	1.43 E
Gørlev	41	55.32 N	11.14 E
Gorlice	30	49.40 N	21.10 E
Görlitz	54	51.09 N	14.59 E
Gorlosen	54	53.11 N	11.27 E
Gorlovka, Sak.	84	41.14 N	43.42 E
Gorlovka → Horlivka, Ukr.	83	48.18 N	38.03 E
Gorlovo	76	53.50 N	39.02 E
Gorm, Loch ⊜	46	55.48 N	6.25 W
Gorman, Ca., U.S.	228	34.48 N	118.51 W
Gorman, Tx., U.S.	196	32.12 N	98.40 W
Gorman Creek ≃	228	34.38 N	118.45 W
Görmin	54	53.59 N	13.16 E
Gorn'ackij, Ross.	24	67.32 N	64.03 E
Gorn'ackij, Ross.	78	48.17 N	40.55 E
Gorna Dzhumaya → Blagoevgrad	38	42.01 N	23.06 E
Gornaja Prolejka	80	49.24 N	44.59 E
Gorn'ak, Ross.	76	53.36 N	39.29 E
Gorn'ak, Ross.	86	51.00 N	81.29 E
Gornalunga ≃	70	37.24 N	15.03 E
Gorna Orjahovica	38	43.07 N	25.41 E
Gornergrat ♠	58	45.59 N	7.47 E
Gornja Radgona	36	46.41 N	16.00 E
Gornji Grad	36	46.18 N	14.49 E
Gornji Milanovac	38	44.01 N	20.27 E
Gornji Vakuf	36	43.56 N	17.35 E
Gorno-Altajsk	86	51.58 N	85.58 E
Gorno-Altay → Altaj □[3]	86	51.00 N	86.00 E
Gorno-Badachšanskaja Avtonomnaja Respublika □[3]	85	38.30 N	73.00 E
Gornoje	86	48.29 N	85.00 E
Gorno-Lesnoj zapovednik ♠	85	41.10 N	69.55 E
Gornopravdinsk	86	60.07 N	69.54 E
Gorno-Vod'anoje	80	49.16 N	44.56 E
Gornovodnoje	89	43.42 N	134.44 E
Gornozavodsk, Ross.	86	58.20 N	58.32 E
Gornozavodsk, Ross.	89	46.34 N	141.49 E
Gornyj, Ross.	80	51.46 N	48.34 E
Gornyj, Ross.	89	50.48 N	136.29 E
Gornyj, Ross.	89	44.57 N	133.59 E
Gornyj Balyklej	80	49.34 N	45.04 E
Gornyje Kl'uči	89	45.12 N	133.31 E
Goro, Ityo.	144	6.56 N	40.32 E
Goro, N. Cal.	175f	22.16 S	167.02 E
Gorochan ∧	144	9.22 N	37.04 E
Gorochovec	80	56.12 N	42.40 E
Gorochovje	76	56.31 N	30.29 E
Gorodec, Bela.	76	52.12 N	24.40 E
Gorodec, Bela.	76	52.58 N	30.21 E
Gorodec, Bela.	76	53.33 N	30.02 E
Gorodec, Ross.	76	58.32 N	29.47 E
Gorodec, Ross.	80	56.38 N	43.30 E
Gorodeja	76	53.19 N	26.32 E
Gorodišče, Bela.	76	53.19 N	26.00 E
Gorodišče, Bela.	76	53.44 N	29.48 E
Gorodišče, Ross.	76	59.38 N	32.08 E
Gorodišče, Ross.	78	51.09 N	38.04 E
Gorodišče, Ross.	80	53.17 N	45.42 E
Gorodišče, Ross.	80	48.48 N	44.29 E
Gorodišče, Ross.	82	54.53 N	38.13 E
Gorodišče, Ross.	82	56.47 N	38.52 E
Gorodišči	82	55.52 N	39.05 E
Gorodn'a, Ross.	82	54.57 N	38.49 E
Gorodn'a, Ross.	82	56.43 N	36.19 E
Gorodn'a ≃	265b	55.38 N	37.48 E
Gorodno	76	57.32 N	29.35 E
Gorodok	76	55.28 N	29.59 E
Goroka	164	6.05 S	145.25 E
Gorokan	170	33.16 S	151.30 E
Gorom-Gorom	150	14.26 N	0.14 W
Gorong, Pulau I	164	3.59 S	131.25 E
Gorongosa, Parque Nacional da ♠	156	18.45 S	34.15 E
Gorongosa, Serra da ∧	154	18.30 S	34.03 E
Gorongose ≃	156	20.30 S	34.40 E
Gorontalo	112	0.33 N	123.03 E
Goronyo	150	13.29 N	5.39 E
Goroubi ≃	150	12.54 N	2.23 E
Gorouol ≃	150	14.42 N	0.53 E
Górowo Iławeckie	30	54.17 N	20.30 E
Gorple Reservoirs ⊜[1]	262	53.47 N	2.06 W
Gorran ⊜	40	59.43 N	17.32 E
Gorredijk	52	53.00 N	6.05 E
Gorron	28	48.25 N	0.49 W
Görsdorf	54	51.54 N	13.29 E
Goršečnoje	78	51.32 N	38.02 E
Gorsedd	262	53.17 N	3.16 W
Gorseinon	42	51.40 N	4.02 W
Gorskaja	265a	60.03 N	29.59 E
Gorškovo	82	54.26 N	37.59 E
Gorst	224	47.32 N	122.42 W
Gort	48	53.04 N	8.50 W
Gortahork	48	55.08 N	8.09 W
Gorton ◆[8]	262	53.27 N	2.10 W
Görtschitz ≃	61	46.45 N	14.32 E
Goru, Vârful ∧	38	45.48 N	26.25 E
Görükle	130	40.14 N	28.50 E
Gorumna Island I	48	53.14 N	9.40 W
Gor'un ≃	89	50.45 N	137.50 E
Gorutuba ≃	255	14.57 S	43.33 W
Görwihl	58	47.39 N	8.04 E
Gory, Bela.	76	54.16 N	31.13 E
Gory, Kaz.	80	48.38 N	51.46 E
Goryn' (Horyn') ≃	78	52.08 N	27.17 E
Görz → Gorizia	64	45.57 N	13.38 E
Gorzano, Monte ∧	66	42.37 N	13.24 E
Gorze	56	49.03 N	6.00 E
Görzig	54	51.40 N	12.00 E
Görzke	54	52.10 N	12.22 E
Górzno	30	53.13 N	19.38 E
Gorzów Śląski	30	51.02 N	18.24 E
Gorzów Wielkopolski (Landsberg an der Warthe)	30	52.44 N	15.15 E
Gorzów Wielkopolski □[4]	30	52.45 N	15.20 E
Górzyca	54	52.29 N	14.40 E
Gosāba	126	22.10 N	88.48 E
Gosairhāt	126	23.05 N	90.26 E
Gosaldo	64	46.13 N	11.58 E
Gosau	64	47.34 N	13.31 E
Gosauseen ⊜	64	47.32 N	13.31 E
Gosberton	42	52.51 N	0.09 W
Göschenen	58	46.40 N	8.35 E
Goschen Strait Ц	164	10.09 S	150.56 E
Gose	96	34.27 N	135.44 E
Gosen, Dtsch.	264a	52.24 N	13.43 E
Gosen, Nihon	92	37.44 N	139.11 E
Gosford	170	33.26 S	151.21 E
Gosforth, Eng., U.K.	44	55.01 N	1.37 W
Gosforth, Eng., U.K.	44	54.26 N	3.27 W
Gosforth Park ♠	273d	26.14 S	28.10 E
Gosforth Park Race Course ♠	273d	26.14 S	28.08 E
Goshabi	140	17.58 N	31.06 E
Goshen, N.S., Can.	186	45.23 N	61.59 W
Goshen, Ca., U.S.	226	36.21 N	119.25 W
Goshen, Ct., U.S.	207	41.49 N	73.13 W
Goshen, In., U.S.	216	41.34 N	85.50 W
Goshen, Ma., U.S.	207	42.26 N	72.48 W
Goshen, N.J., U.S.	208	39.08 N	74.51 W
Goshen, N.Y., U.S.	210	41.24 N	74.19 W
Goshen, Oh., U.S.	218	39.14 N	84.10 W
Goshiki	96	34.24 N	134.47 E
Goshogawara	92	40.48 N	140.27 E
Goshute Indian Reservation ◆[4]	200	39.53 N	114.08 W
Goshute Lake ⊜	204	40.08 N	114.38 W
Goshute Valley V	204	40.40 N	114.30 W
Goslar	52	51.54 N	10.25 E
Gosnells	168a	32.04 S	116.00 E
Gospić	36	44.33 N	15.23 E
Gosport, Eng., U.K.	42	50.48 N	1.08 W
Gosport, In., U.S.	194	39.21 N	86.40 W
Gossa	54	51.40 N	12.26 E
Gossas	150	14.30 N	16.04 W
Gossau	58	47.25 N	9.15 E
Gosse ◆[8]	263	51.08 N	7.01 E
Gosse Bluff ∧	162	23.49 S	132.19 E
Gosselies	56	50.28 N	4.25 E
Gössenheim	56	50.01 N	9.46 E
Gossensass → Colle Isarco	64	46.56 N	11.26 E
Gosser Hill	279b	40.37 N	79.37 W
Gossi	150	15.49 N	1.17 W
Gossinga	140	8.39 N	25.59 E
Gössnitz	54	50.53 N	12.26 E
Gossolengo	62	44.59 N	9.37 E
Gössweinstein	60	49.46 N	11.20 E
Gostagajevskaja	78	45.01 N	37.30 E
Gostilovo	82	55.18 N	38.36 E
Gostiščevo	78	50.47 N	36.39 E
Gostivar	38	41.47 N	20.54 E
Göstling an der Ybbs	61	47.48 N	14.55 E
Gostyń	30	51.53 N	17.00 E
Gostynin	30	52.26 N	19.29 E
Göta älv ≃	26	57.42 N	11.52 E
Göta kanal ≊	40	58.50 N	13.58 E
Gotchen Creek ≃	224	46.00 N	121.30 W
Got Creek ≃	284a	43.03 N	78.42 W
Gotebo	196	35.04 N	98.52 W
Göteborg (Gothenburg)	26	57.43 N	11.58 E
Göteborgs och Bohus län □[6]	26	58.30 N	11.30 E
Gotel Mountains ⩘	152	6.55 N	11.15 E
Gotemba	94	35.18 N	138.56 E
Götene	26	58.32 N	13.29 E
Gotești	38	46.09 N	28.10 E
Gotha, Dtsch.	54	50.57 N	10.41 E
Gotha, Fl., U.S.	220	28.32 N	81.31 W
Gothem	26	57.35 N	18.43 E
Gothenburg → Göteborg, Sve.	26	57.43 N	11.58 E
Gothenburg, Ne., U.S.	198	40.55 N	100.09 W
Gothèye	150	13.52 N	1.34 E
Gotland I	26	57.30 N	18.33 E
Gotlands Län □[6]	26	57.30 N	18.30 E
Gotoputovo	86	56.46 N	70.10 E
Gotō-rettō II	92	32.50 N	129.00 E
Gotska Sandön I	26	58.23 N	19.16 E
Gōtsu	96	35.00 N	132.14 E
Gottenheim	58	48.03 N	7.44 E
Götterswickerhamm	263	51.35 N	6.40 E
Gottesbrücke	264a	52.25 N	13.49 E
Gotthard Tunnel ◆[5]	58	46.35 N	8.35 E
Göttin	264a	52.27 N	12.54 E
Göttingen, Dtsch.	52	51.32 N	9.55 E
Göttingen, Dtsch.	56	50.52 N	8.46 E
Göttin See ⊜	264a	52.28 N	12.54 E
Gottmadingen	58	47.44 N	8.47 E
Gottolengo	64	45.17 N	10.16 E
Gottorf, Schloss ⊥	41	54.30 N	9.32 E
Gottsbüren	52	51.35 N	9.30 E
Gottvaterkapelle ⊍[1]	60	49.42 N	11.41 E
Götzendorf	264b	48.01 N	16.35 E
Gőtzis	58	47.20 N	9.38 E
Gouarec	32	48.13 N	3.11 W
Goubangzi	104	41.22 N	121.46 E
Goubone	146	20.43 N	17.08 E
Gouda, Ned.	52	52.01 N	4.43 E
Gouda, S. Afr.	158	33.19 S	19.04 E
Goudet	62	44.53 N	3.55 E
Goudge	252	34.40 S	68.08 W
Goudhurst	42	51.07 N	0.28 E
Goudiry	150	14.11 N	12.43 W
Goudoumaria	146	13.42 N	11.10 E
Goudswaard	52	51.47 N	4.16 E
Gouéké	150	8.02 N	8.43 W
Goûfi, Djebel el ∧	34	36.57 N	6.27 E
Gougezhuang	105	38.53 N	116.11 E
Gough Island I	10	40.20 S	10.00 W
Gough Lake ⊜	182	52.02 N	112.28 W
Gouin, Réservoir ⊜[1]	176	48.38 N	74.54 W
Goujiaozhen	107	30.36 N	106.33 E
Goukou	89	48.39 N	122.06 E
Goulais ≃	190	46.43 N	84.27 W
Goulburn	170	34.45 S	149.43 E
Goulburn ≃	169	36.41 S	145.12 E
Goulburn Islands II	164	11.33 S	133.26 E
Goulburn Weir ⊜[1]	169	36.45 S	145.08 E
Gould	194	33.59 N	91.33 W
Gould City	190	46.05 N	85.41 W
Gould Park	214	40.04 N	82.53 W
Goulds	220	25.33 N	80.22 W
Gouldsboro	210	41.44 N	75.28 W
Gouldsboro State Park ♠	210	41.13 N	75.28 W
Goulet Lake ⊜	184	55.23 N	96.18 W
Goulia	150	10.01 N	7.11 W
Goulicun	106	31.40 N	120.00 E
Goulimime	148	28.56 N	10.04 W
Goulimine □[4]	148	28.30 N	9.45 W
Goulmima	148	31.02 N	5.00 W
Goumbati ∧[2]	150	13.08 N	12.06 W
Goumbou	150	14.59 N	7.27 W
Gouménissa	38	40.57 N	22.27 E
Goumois	58	47.16 N	6.57 E
Gouna	146	8.32 N	13.34 E
Gounda ≃	146	9.25 N	20.57 E
Goundam	150	16.25 N	3.40 W
Goundi	146	9.22 N	17.22 E
Gounou-Gaya	146	9.38 N	15.31 E
Gouougang, Mount ∧	170	33.53 S	150.07 E
Goupillières	261	48.53 N	1.46 E
Gouraya	34	36.34 N	1.55 E
Gourbassi	150	13.24 N	11.38 W
Gourbeyre	241o	16.00 N	61.42 W
Gourcy	150	13.13 N	2.21 W
Gourdhead Run ≃	279b	40.33 N	79.57 W
Gourdon, Fr.	32	44.44 N	1.23 E
Gourdon, Fr.	62	43.43 N	6.59 E
Gouré	150	13.58 N	10.18 E
Gouri ⊥	124	24.53 N	88.07 E
Gourin	32	48.08 N	3.36 W
Gouripur	124	24.46 N	90.34 E
Gourits ≃	158	34.21 S	21.52 E
Gourlay Lake ⊜	190	48.52 N	84.54 W
Gourma Rharous	150	16.53 N	1.55 W
Gournay-en-Bray	50	49.29 N	1.44 E
Gournay-sur-Marne	261	48.52 N	2.34 E
Gouro	146	19.33 N	19.33 E
Gourock	46	55.58 N	4.49 W
Goussainville	50	49.01 N	2.28 E
Goussonville	261	48.55 N	1.46 E
Goutou	105	39.49 N	117.11 E
Gouveia, Bra.	255	18.27 S	43.44 W
Gouveia, Port.	266c	38.50 N	9.26 W
Gouverneur	212	44.20 N	75.27 W
Gouyadong	100	25.10 N	112.55 E
Gouyave	241k	12.10 N	61.44 W
Gov'altaj □[4]	102	45.30 N	96.00 E
Govan	184	51.18 N	105.00 W
Go Vap	269c	10.49 N	106.41 E
Govardhan	124	27.30 N	77.28 E
Gove	198	38.57 N	100.29 W
Govea ≃	286b	22.56 N	82.30 W
Govena, mys ›	74	59.48 N	166.06 E
Govenlock	184	49.15 N	109.48 W
Gove Peninsula ›[1]	164	12.20 S	136.50 E
Governador, Ilha do I	287a	22.48 S	43.12 W
Governador Portela	256	22.29 S	43.30 W
Governador Valadares	255	18.51 S	41.56 W
Government Camp	224	45.18 N	121.45 W
Governor Bond Lake ⊜[1]	219	38.56 N	89.23 W
Governor Dodge State Park ♠	190	43.00 N	90.07 W
Governor Generoso	116	6.39 N	126.05 E
Governor Head ›	170	35.07 S	150.46 E
Governor Nice Memorial Bridge ◆[5]	208	38.22 N	77.00 W
Governor Printz Park ♠	285	39.52 N	75.18 W
Governor's Harbour	238	25.10 N	76.14 W
Governors Island I	276	40.41 N	74.01 W
Govind Ballabh Pant Sāgar ⊜[1]	124	24.05 N	82.50 E
Govindgarh	124	24.23 N	81.18 E
Govind Sāgar ⊜[1]	123	31.20 N	76.45 E
Gov'-Ugtaal	102	46.04 N	107.30 E
Gowan ≃	184	55.49 N	94.08 W
Gowanda	210	42.27 N	78.56 W
Gowan Range ⩘	166	25.00 S	145.00 E
Gowen City	208	40.45 N	76.32 W
Gower	194	39.36 N	94.35 W
Gower ›[1]	42	51.36 N	4.10 W
Gowerton	42	51.39 N	4.01 W
Gowienica ≃	54	53.40 N	14.38 E
Gowmal (Gumal) ≃	120	31.56 N	70.22 E
Gowmal Kalay	120	32.29 N	68.55 E
Gowna, Lough ⊜	48	53.51 N	7.34 W
Gowrie	198	42.16 N	94.17 W
Gowy ≃	44	53.17 N	2.51 W
Goya	252	29.08 S	59.16 W
Goyania → Goiânia	255	16.40 S	49.16 W
Goyatz	54	52.01 N	14.09 E
Goyave	241o	16.08 N	61.34 W
Goyaves, Grande Rivière à ≃	241o	16.18 N	61.37 W
Goyaves, Îlets à II	241o	16.10 N	61.48 W
Göyçay	84	40.39 N	47.44 E
Göyçay ≃	84	40.39 N	47.45 E
Goyder ≃	164	12.38 S	135.11 E
Goyder Creek ≃	162	25.39 S	134.47 E
Goyelle, Lac ⊜	186	50.47 N	60.45 W
Goyeneche	258	35.20 S	58.43 W
Goyer, Île I	275a	45.29 N	73.17 W
Goyerkāta	124	26.42 N	89.02 E
Göynücek	130	40.24 N	35.32 E
Göynük, Tür.	130	40.24 N	30.47 E
Göynük, Tür.	130	39.08 N	40.53 E
Göynük ≃, Tür.	130	40.20 N	30.05 E
Göynük ≃, Tür.	130	38.53 N	40.34 E
Goyt ≃	262	53.24 N	2.09 W
Göytäpä	84	39.08 N	48.36 E
Goz-Beïda	146	12.13 N	21.25 E
Gozdnica	30	51.26 N	15.06 E
Gozdowice	54	52.45 N	14.18 E
Göze Dağı ∧	130	41.24 N	42.30 E
Gözeli	130	38.25 N	39.04 E
Gozen-yama	94	36.32 N	140.20 E
Gozha Co ⊜	120	34.59 N	81.06 E
Gözne	130	36.59 N	34.34 E
Gozo → Għawdex I	36	36.03 N	14.15 E
Göz Tepe ∧[2]	267b	41.06 N	29.06 E
Gozzano	62	45.45 N	8.26 E
Graaff-Reinet	158	32.14 S	24.32 E
Graafwater	158	32.00 S	18.37 E
Graauw	52	51.20 N	4.05 E
Grabc'ovo	82	54.34 N	36.22 E
Graben-Neudorf	56	49.09 N	8.29 E
Grabenstätt	64	47.51 N	12.32 E
Grabill	216	41.12 N	84.58 W
Grabo	150	4.55 N	7.30 W
Grabouw	158	34.09 S	19.02 E
Grabovo	86	53.07 N	74.52 E
Grabow	54	53.16 N	11.34 E
Grabowiec	30	50.50 N	23.33 E
Grabów nad Prosną	30	51.31 N	18.06 E
Gračac	36	44.18 N	15.51 E
Gračanica	38	44.42 N	18.19 E
Gračanica, Manastir ⊍[1]	38	42.36 N	21.09 E
Graçay	50	47.08 N	1.51 E
Grace	202	42.34 N	111.43 W
Gracefield	188	46.06 N	76.03 W
Graceham	208	39.36 N	77.22 W
Graceton	214	40.30 N	79.10 W
Graceville, Fl., U.S.	192	30.57 N	85.31 W
Graceville, Mn., U.S.	198	45.34 N	96.26 W
Gračevka	82	55.06 N	36.49 E
Grächen	58	46.12 N	7.50 E
Grachovo	80	56.04 N	51.58 E
Grači	80	49.49 N	43.33 E
Gracia ◆[8]	266d	41.23 N	2.09 E
Gracias	236	14.35 N	88.35 W
Gracias a Dios □[5]	236	15.10 N	84.20 W
Gracias a Dios, Cabo ›	236	15.00 N	83.10 W
Gračiki ≃	83	48.30 N	39.52 E
Graciosa I	148a	39.04 N	28.00 W
Graciosa, Isla I	148	29.15 N	13.30 W
Gračov	80	49.26 N	41.32 E
Gračovka, Ross.	80	52.07 N	40.01 E
Gračovka, Ross.	80	52.57 N	52.52 E
Gračov Kust	80	51.59 N	49.50 E
Gradačac	38	44.53 N	18.26 E
Gradara	66	43.57 N	12.46 E
Gradaús	250	7.43 S	51.11 W
Gr'adcy	76	56.24 N	31.55 E
Gräddö	40	59.46 N	19.02 E
Gradisca d'Isonzo	64	45.53 N	13.30 E
Grado, Esp.	34	43.23 N	6.04 W
Grado, It.	64	45.40 N	13.23 E
Grado, Laguna di c	64	45.43 N	13.20 E
Gradoli	66	42.39 N	11.51 E
Grad Sofija □[4]	38	42.41 N	23.19 E
Grady, Ar., U.S.	194	34.04 N	91.42 W
Grady, N.M., U.S.	196	34.49 N	103.19 W
Gradyville	285	39.57 N	75.28 W
Graemsay I	46	58.56 N	3.17 W
Græsted	41	56.04 N	12.17 E
Graettinger	198	43.14 N	94.45 W
Gräfelfing	60	48.07 N	11.25 E
Grafenau	60	48.52 N	13.25 E
Gräfenberg	60	49.39 N	11.15 E
Grafenberg ◆[8]	263	51.14 N	6.50 E
Gräfenhainichen	54	51.44 N	12.27 E
Gräfenroda	54	50.45 N	10.48 E
Gräfenthal	54	50.31 N	11.18 E
Gräfentonna	54	51.05 N	10.44 E
Grafenwöhr	60	49.43 N	11.54 E
Graffignano	66	42.34 N	12.12 E
Grafham Water ⊜	42	52.17 N	0.20 W
Gräfinau-Angstedt	54	50.42 N	11.01 E
Grafing bei München	60	48.02 N	11.59 E
Gråfjell ∧	26	60.16 N	9.29 E
Graford	196	32.56 N	98.14 W
Gräfrath ◆[8]	263	51.13 N	7.04 E
Grafschaft Bentheim □[9]	52	52.30 N	7.00 E
Grafton, Austl.	166	29.41 S	152.56 E
Grafton, On., Can.	212	44.00 N	78.01 W
Grafton, Il., U.S.	219	38.58 N	90.25 W
Grafton, Ma., U.S.	207	42.12 N	71.41 W
Grafton, N.Y., U.S.	210	42.46 N	73.27 W
Grafton, N.D., U.S.	198	48.24 N	97.24 W
Grafton, Oh., U.S.	214	41.16 N	82.03 W
Grafton, W.V., U.S.	188	39.20 N	80.01 W
Grafton, Wi., U.S.	190	43.19 N	87.57 W
Grafton, Cape ›	164	16.52 S	145.55 E
Grafton Lakes State Park ♠	210	42.48 N	73.28 W
Grafty Green	260	51.12 N	0.41 E
Graglia	62	45.33 N	7.59 E
Gragnano	68	40.41 N	14.31 E
Gragnano Trebbiense	62	45.01 N	9.34 E
Graham, Ca., U.S.	280	34.15 N	118.31 W
Graham, N.C., U.S.	192	36.04 N	79.24 W
Graham, Tx., U.S.	196	33.06 N	98.35 W
Graham, Wa., U.S.	224	47.03 N	122.17 W
Graham, Mount ∧	200	32.42 N	109.52 W
Graham Cave State Park ♠	219	38.55 N	91.32 W
Graham Creek ≃	218	38.49 N	85.39 W
Graham Hill County Park ♠	276	41.07 N	73.48 W
Graham Island I	182	53.40 N	132.30 W
Graham Lake ⊜, On., Can.	212	44.34 N	75.53 W
Graham Lake ⊜, Me., U.S.	188	44.40 N	68.25 W
Graham Land ◆[1]	9	66.00 S	63.30 W
Graham Memorial Park ♠	284b	39.25 N	76.30 W
Graham Moore, Cape ›	176	72.52 N	76.04 W
Graham Moore Bay c	176	75.26 N	101.25 W
Grahamstad → Grahamstown	158	33.19 S	26.31 E
Grahamstown	158	33.19 S	26.31 E
Grahamsville	210	41.51 N	74.33 W
Grahn	218	38.17 N	83.04 W
Graie, Alpi (Alpes Grées) ⩘	62	45.30 N	7.10 E
Graiguenarmanagh	48	52.32 N	6.57 W
Grain	42	51.28 N	0.43 E
Grain, Isle of I	42	51.27 N	0.41 E
Grain Coast ⊥[2]	150	5.00 N	9.00 W
Grainfield	198	39.06 N	100.27 W
Grajagan	115a	8.35 S	114.13 E
Grajagan, Teluk c	115a	8.40 S	114.18 E
Grajaú	250	5.49 S	46.08 W
Grajaú ≃	250	3.41 S	44.48 W
Grajewo	30	53.39 N	22.27 E
Grajvoron	78	50.28 N	35.39 E
Gram	41	55.17 N	9.04 E
Gramacho	287a	22.44 S	43.18 W
Gramada	38	43.50 N	22.39 E
Gramado	252	29.24 S	50.54 W
Gramalote	246	7.53 N	72.48 W
Gramastetten	61	48.23 N	14.12 E
Gramat	32	44.47 N	1.43 E
Gramatneusiedl	264b	48.02 N	16.29 E
Grambling	194	32.31 N	92.42 W
Gramilla	252	27.18 S	64.37 W
Gramínea	256	22.10 S	46.38 W
Graminha, Represa ⊜[1]	256	21.40 S	46.35 W
Grammer	218	39.09 N	85.43 W
Grammichele	70	37.13 N	14.38 E
Grammont → Geraardsbergen	50	50.46 N	3.52 E
Gramoteino	86	54.31 N	86.22 E
Grampian	214	40.57 N	78.36 W
Grampian □[4]	46	57.15 N	2.45 W
Grampian Mountains ⩘	46	56.55 N	4.00 W
Grampians National Park ♠	166	37.20 S	142.30 E
Gramschatz	56	49.56 N	9.58 E
Gramsh	38	40.52 N	20.11 E
Gramzow	54	53.12 N	14.00 E
Gran → Esztergom	30	47.48 N	18.45 E
Grana ≃	62	44.25 N	7.27 E
Granaatboskolk	158	30.02 S	19.51 E
Granada, Col.	246	3.34 N	73.45 W
Granada, Esp.	34	37.13 N	3.41 W
Granada, Nic.	236	11.56 N	85.57 W
Granada, Pil.	116	10.40 N	123.02 E
Granada, Co., U.S.	198	38.03 N	102.18 W
Granada, Mn., U.S.	190	43.41 N	94.20 W
Granada □[4]	34	37.15 N	3.15 W
Granada □[5]	236	11.50 N	86.00 W
Granada → Grenada □[1]	241k	12.07 N	61.40 W
Granada Hills ◆[8]	280	34.16 N	118.31 W
Granado	286d	12.04 S	76.57 W
Granaglione	66	44.07 N	10.58 E
Gran Altiplanicie Central ⩘[1]	254	48.55 S	69.45 W
Granard	48	53.47 N	7.30 W
Granarolo dell'Emilia	64	44.33 N	11.27 E
Granatello	70	37.53 N	12.32 E
Gran Bahía Australiana → Great Australian Bight c[3]	162	35.00 S	135.00 E
Gran Bajo de San Julián V	254	49.30 S	68.30 W
Gran Barrera de Arrecifes → Great Barrier Reef ✧[2]	160	18.00 S	145.50 E
Granbergsdal	40	59.24 N	14.35 E
Granbury	222	32.26 N	97.47 W
Granbury, Lake ⊜[1]	222	32.25 N	97.45 W
Granby, P.Q., Can.	206	45.24 N	72.44 W
Granby, Co., U.S.	200	40.05 N	105.56 W
Granby, Ct., U.S.	207	41.57 N	72.47 W
Granby, Ma., U.S.	207	42.15 N	72.31 W
Granby, Mo., U.S.	194	36.55 N	94.15 W
Granby ≃	182	49.03 N	118.25 W
Granby, Lake ⊜[1]	200	40.09 N	105.50 W
Gran Canaria I	148	28.00 N	15.36 W
Grancey-le-Château	58	47.40 N	5.02 E
Gran Chaco ≡	18	23.00 S	60.00 W
Grand	58	48.23 N	5.29 E
Grand ≃, On., Can.	212	42.51 N	79.34 W
Grand ≃, U.S.	194	39.23 N	93.06 W
Grand ≃, Mi., U.S.	216	43.04 N	86.15 W
Grand ≃, Oh., U.S.	214	41.46 N	81.17 W
Grand ≃, S.D., U.S.	198	45.40 N	100.32 W
Grand ≃, Wi., U.S.	190	43.45 N	89.16 W
Grand, East Fork ≃	194	40.12 N	94.21 W
Grand, Lac ⊜	190	47.10 N	76.57 W
Grand, North Fork ≃	198	45.47 N	102.16 W
Grand, South Fork ≃	198	45.43 N	102.17 W
Grandas	34	43.13 N	6.52 W
Grand Bahama I	238	26.38 N	78.25 W
Grand Ballon ∧	58	47.55 N	7.08 E
Grand Bank	186	47.06 N	55.46 W
Grand Banks of Newfoundland ✧[4]	16	45.00 N	53.00 W
Grand-Bassam	150	5.12 N	3.44 W
Grand Bay, N.B., Can.	186	45.18 N	66.12 W
Grand Bay, Al., U.S.	194	30.28 N	88.20 W
Grand Beach	184	50.35 N	96.40 W
Grand Bend	190	43.15 N	81.45 W
Grand Béréby	150	4.38 N	6.55 W
Grand Blanc	216	42.55 N	83.37 W
Grand-Bourg	241o	15.53 N	61.19 W
Grand Bruit	186	47.41 N	58.13 W
Grand Caille Point ›	241f	13.52 N	61.05 W
Grand Calumet ≃	278	41.38 N	87.34 W
Grand Calumet, Île du I	190	45.44 N	76.41 W
Grand Canal ≊, Ire.	48	53.21 N	6.14 W
Grand Canal → Da Yunhe ≊, Zhg.	90	32.12 N	119.31 E
Grand Cane	194	32.05 N	93.48 W
Grand Cañon du Verdon ♠	62	43.47 N	6.27 E
Grand Canyon	200	36.03 N	112.08 W
Grand Canyon V	200	36.10 N	112.45 W
Grand Canyon National Park ♠	200	36.15 N	112.58 W
Grand Canyon of Pennsylvania ♠	210	41.43 N	77.28 W
Grand Cayman I	238	19.20 N	81.15 W

≃ River	Fluß	Río	Rivière	Rio
≊ Canal	Kanal	Canal	Canal	Canal
∟ Waterfall, Rapids	Wasserfall, Stromschnellen	Cascada, Rápidos	Chute d'eau, Rapides	Cascata, Rápidos
Ц Strait	Meeresstraße	Estrecho	Détroit	Estreito
c Bay, Gulf	Bucht, Golf	Bahía, Golfo	Baie, Golfe	Baía, Golfo
⊜ Lake, Lakes	See, Seen	Lago, Lagos	Lac, Lacs	Lago, Lagos
≡ Swamp	Sumpf	Pantano	Marais	Pântano
⊓ Ice Features, Glacier	Eis- und Gletscherformen	Accidentes Glaciales	Formes glaciaires	Acidentes glaciares
⊤ Other Hydrographic Features	Andere Hydrographische Objekte	Otros Elementos Hidrográficos	Autres données hydrographiques	Outros acidentes hidrográficos
✧ Submarine Features	Untermeerische Objekte	Accidentes Submarinos	Formes de relief sous-marin	Acidentes submarinos
□ Political Unit	Politische Einheit	Unidad Politica	Entité politique	Unidade política
⊍ Cultural Institution	Kulturelle Institution	Institución Cultural	Institution culturelle	Institução cultural
⊥ Historical Site	Historische Stätte	Sitio Histórico	Site historique	Sitio histórico
♠ Recreational Site	Erholungs- und Ferienort	Sitio de Recreo	Centre de loisirs	Area de Lazer
⊠ Airport	Flughafen	Aeropuerto	Aéroport	Aeroporto
■ Military Installation	Militäranlage	Instalación Militar	Installation militaire	Instalação militar
◆ Miscellaneous	Verschiedenes	Misceláneo	Divers	Diversos

Grand Central Terminal ✦[5] 276 40.45 N 73.59 W
Grand Centre 174 54.25 N 110.13 W
Grand Cess 150 4.36 N 8.10 W
Grandchamp, Fr. 58 47.43 N 5.27 E
Grandchamp, Fr. 261 48.43 N 1.37 E
Grand-Charmont 58 47.32 N 6.50 E
Grand Chenier 194 29.46 N 92.58 W
Grand Combin ∧ 58 45.56 N 7.18 E
Grand Coulee 202 47.56 N 119.00 W
Grand Coulee V 202 47.45 N 119.15 W
Grand Coulee Dam ✦[6] 202 47.57 N 118.59 W
Grand-Couronne 50 49.21 N 1.00 E
Grand Cul-de-Sac Marin c 241o 16.20 N 61.35 W
Grande ≃, Arg. 252 36.52 S 69.45 W
Grande ≃, Arg. 252 24.12 S 64.42 W
Grande ≃, Bol. 248 15.51 S 64.39 W
Grande ≃, Bra. 242 11.05 S 43.09 W
Grande ≃, Bra. 252 20.06 S 51.04 W
Grande ≃, Bra. 287a 22.55 S 43.25 W
Grande ≃, Bra. 287b 23.45 S 46.22 W
Grande ≃, Chile 252 30.35 S 71.11 W
Grande ≃, Esp. 34 39.07 N 0.44 W
Grande ≃, It. 70 37.55 N 13.13 E
Grande ≃, Méx. 234 17.43 N 96.56 W
Grande ≃, Méx. 234 18.50 N 102.05 W
Grande ≃, Nic. 236 12.28 N 86.21 W
Grande ≃, Pan. 236 8.18 N 80.24 W
Grande ≃, Perú 248 14.59 S 75.29 W
Grande ≃, S.A. 254 53.48 S 67.40 W
Grande ≃, Ven. 246 8.39 N 60.59 W
Grande, Arroyo ≃, Arg. 258 34.37 S 59.25 W
Grande, Arroyo ≃, Arg. 288 34.45 S 58.08 W
Grande, Arroyo ≃, Méx. 234 23.55 N 98.44 W
Grande, Arroyo ≃, Ur. 252 33.08 S 57.09 W
Grande, Arroyo ≃, Ur. 258 33.37 S 57.09 W
Grande, Bahía c[3] 254 50.45 S 68.45 W
Grande, Boca c 220 26.43 N 82.16 W
Grande, Boca ≃[1] 246 8.38 N 60.30 W
Grande, Cañada ≃, Arg. 258 35.15 S 59.23 W
Grande, Cañada ≃, Arg. 258 35.19 S 57.48 W
Grande, Cayo I 240p 20.59 N 79.09 W
Grande, Cerro ∧, Méx. 232 28.46 N 107.32 W
Grande, Cerro ∧, Méx. 234 23.22 N 103.35 W
Grande, Cerro ∧, Méx. 234 21.45 N 103.05 W
Grande, Cerro ∧, Méx. 234 20.43 N 101.12 W
Grande, Cerro ∧, Méx. 234 23.39 N 100.51 W
Grande, Corixa (Curiche Grande) ≡ 248 17.10 S 58.20 W
Grande, Cuchilla ∧ 252 33.15 S 55.07 W
Grande, Curiche (Corixa Grande) ≃ 248 17.10 S 58.20 W
Grande, Igarapé ≃ 250 3.37 S 48.53 W
Grande, Ilha I, Bra. 252 23.45 S 54.03 W
Grande, Ilha I, Bra. 256 23.09 S 44.14 W
Grande, Isola I 70 37.53 N 12.26 E
Grande, Lago ⊜, Arg. 254 47.44 S 68.04 W
Grande, Lago ⊜, Bra. 250 2.16 S 54.17 W
Grande, Laguna ⊜, Arg. 258 34.14 S 58.53 W
Grande, Laguna ⊜, Méx. 234 20.06 N 96.40 W
Grande, Mare c 68 40.27 N 17.12 E
Grande, Naviglio ≡ 266b 45.35 N 8.42 E
Grande, Ponta > 255 16.22 S 39.01 W
Grande, Praia ≍[2] 256 24.05 S 46.30 W
Grande, Punta > 252 21.54 S 70.12 W
Grande, Ribeirão ≃ 256 21.24 S 44.29 W
Grande, Rio (Bravo del Norte) ≃ 178 25.55 N 97.09 W
Grande, Salina ≡ 68 40.26 N 17.18 E
Grande, Serra ⋌ 250 6.00 S 40.52 W
Grande, Sierra ⋌ 196 29.40 N 104.55 W
Grande-Anse 186 47.48 N 65.11 W
Grande Anse, La c 275a 45.23 N 73.53 W
Grande Anse Bay c 241k 12.02 N 61.45 W
Grande Baie, La c 275a 45.29 N 74.00 W
Grande Cache 182 53.53 N 119.08 W
Grande Casse, Pointe de la ∧ 62 45.24 N 6.50 E
Grande Cayemite I 238 18.37 N 73.45 W
Grande Chartreuse, Couvent de la ✦[1] 62 45.22 N 5.50 E
Grande de Añasco ≃ 240m 18.16 N 67.11 W
Grande de Arecibo ≃ 240m 18.29 N 66.42 W
Grande de Jutaí, Ilha I 250 3.15 S 49.37 W
Grande de Lipez ≃ 248 20.47 S 67.14 W
Grande de Loíza ≃ 240m 18.27 N 65.53 W
Grande de Manacapuru, Lago ⊜ 246 3.04 S 61.25 W
Grande de Manatí ≃ 240m 18.29 N 66.32 W
Grande de Matagalpa ≃ 236 12.54 N 83.32 W
Grande de Santiago ≃ 234 21.36 N 105.26 W
Grande de Tarija ≃ 248 22.53 S 64.21 W
Grande de Térraba ≃ 236 8.59 N 83.37 W
Grande do Curuai, Lago ⊜ 250 2.15 S 55.20 W
Grande do Gurupá, Ilha I 250 1.00 S 51.30 W
Grande do Tapará, Ilha I 250 2.14 S 54.39 W
Grande Île de Criques I 273b 4.20 S 15.25 E
Grande Inferior, Cuchilla ⋌[2] 258 33.50 S 56.27 W
Grand-Entrée 186 47.33 N 61.34 W
Grande-Prairie 182 55.10 N 118.48 W
Grand Erg de Bilma ✦[2] 146 18.30 N 14.00 E
Grand Erg Occidental ✦[2] 148 30.30 N 0.30 E
Grand Erg Oriental ✦[2] 148 30.30 N 7.00 E
Grande-Rivière 186 48.24 N 64.30 W
Grande Rivière, La ≃ 176 53.50 N 79.00 W
Grande Ronde ≃ 202 46.05 N 116.59 W
Grandes, Salinas ≡, Arg. 252 30.05 S 65.05 W
Grandes, Salinas ≡, Arg. 252 23.43 S 66.00 W
Grandes Antillas, Islas — Greater Antilles II 238 20.00 N 74.00 W
Grandes Antilles, Îles — Greater Antilles II 238 20.00 N 74.00 W
Grande Sassière, Aiguille de la ∧ 62 45.30 N 7.00 E
Grande Sauldre ≃ 50 47.26 N 2.05 E
Gran Desierto de Arena — Great Sandy Desert ✦[2] 162 21.30 S 125.00 E
Gran Desierto Victoria — Great Victoria Desert ✦[2] 162 28.30 S 127.45 E
Grandes-Piles 206 46.41 N 72.44 W
Grande-Synthe 50 51.01 N 2.19 E
Grand-Étang 186 46.33 N 61.02 W
Grande-Terre I 241o 16.20 N 61.25 W
Grande Vigie, Pointe de la > 241o 16.31 N 61.28 W
Grand Eyvia ≃ 62 45.42 N 7.14 E
Grand Falls, N.B., Can. 186 47.03 N 67.44 W
Grand Falls, Nf., Can. 186 48.56 N 55.40 W
Grandfalls, Tx., U.S. 196 31.20 N 102.51 W
Grandfather Mountain ∧ 192 36.07 N 81.48 W
Grandfield 196 34.13 N 98.41 W
Grand Forks, B.C., Can. 182 49.02 N 118.27 W
Grand Forks, N.D., U.S. 198 47.55 N 97.01 W
Grand Forks Air Force Base ■ 198 47.57 N 97.25 W
Grand-Fort-Philippe 50 51.00 N 2.06 E
Grand-Fougeray 32 47.44 N 1.44 W
Grand-Gallargues 62 43.43 N 4.10 E
Grand Gorge 210 42.21 N 74.29 W
Grand-Halleux 56 50.19 N 5.54 E
Grand Haven 216 43.03 N 86.13 W
Grand Haven State Park ✦ 216 43.02 N 86.13 W
Grand Hers ≃ 32 43.47 N 1.20 E
Grandiči 76 53.43 N 23.49 E
Grandin, Lac ⊜ 176 63.59 N 119.00 W
Grandioznyj, pik ∧ 88 53.50 N 96.11 E
Grand Island, Fl., U.S. 220 28.53 N 81.44 W
Grand Island, Ne., U.S. 198 40.55 N 98.20 W
Grand Island, N.Y., U.S. 212 43.01 N 78.58 W
Grand Island I, On., Can. 212 44.34 N 78.50 W
Grand Island I, Mi., U.S. 190 46.30 N 86.40 W
Grand Island I, N.Y., U.S. 210 43.02 N 78.58 W
Grand Isle 194 29.14 N 89.59 W
Grand Isle □[6] 206 44.57 N 73.17 W
Grand Junction, Co., U.S. 200 39.03 N 108.33 W
Grand Junction, Ia., U.S. 198 42.01 N 94.14 W
Grand Junction, Mi., U.S. 216 42.24 N 86.04 W
Grand Junction, Tn., U.S. 194 35.02 N 89.11 W
Grand Lac Salé — Great Salt Lake ⊜ 200 41.10 N 112.30 W
Grand lac Victoria ⊜ 190 47.31 N 77.30 W
Grand-Lahou 150 5.08 N 5.01 W
Grand Lake 200 40.15 N 105.49 W
Grand Lake ⊜, N.B., Can. 186 45.55 N 66.05 W
Grand Lake ⊜, Nf., Can. 186 49.00 N 57.25 W
Grand Lake ⊜, N.A. 186 45.43 N 67.50 W
Grand Lake ⊜, La., U.S. 194 29.55 N 91.25 W
Grand Lake ⊜, La., U.S. 194 29.55 N 92.47 W
Grand Lake ⊜, Mi., U.S. 190 45.18 N 83.30 W
Grand Lake ⊜, Oh., U.S. 216 40.30 N 84.32 W
Grand Lake Saint Marys State Park ✦ 216 40.33 N 84.27 W
Grand Ledge 216 42.45 N 84.44 W
Grand Lieu, Lac de ⊜ 32 47.06 N 1.40 W
Grand'Maison, Barrage de ✦[6] 62 45.12 N 6.07 E
Grand Manan Channel ≋ 186 44.45 N 66.52 W
Grand Manan Island I 186 44.40 N 66.50 W
Grand Marais, Mi., U.S. 190 46.40 N 85.59 W
Grand Marais, Mn., U.S. 190 47.45 N 90.20 W
Grand Meadow 198 43.42 N 92.34 W
Grand-Mère 206 46.37 N 72.41 W
Grand Mesa ∧ 200 39.00 N 108.00 W
Grandmesnil, Lac ⊜ 186 51.19 N 67.33 W
Grand Morin ≃ 50 48.54 N 2.50 E
Grand Muveran ∧ 58 46.14 N 7.08 E
Grandola, It. 58 46.02 N 9.13 E
Grândola, Port. 34 38.10 N 8.34 W
Grand Pabos, Rivière du ≃ 186 48.21 N 64.43 W
Grand Palace ✦ 269a 13.45 N 100.30 E
Grand Passage ≋ 175f 18.45 S 163.10 E
Grand-Popo 150 6.17 N 1.50 E
Grand Portage 190 47.57 N 89.41 W
Grand Portage Indian Reservation ✦[4] 190 47.55 N 89.45 W
Grand Portage National Monument ✦ 190 48.02 N 89.38 W
Grand Prairie 222 32.44 N 96.59 W
Grandpré 56 49.20 N 4.52 E
Grand Pré National Historic Park ✦ 186 45.08 N 64.18 W
Grand Prix Airport ⊠ 281 42.33 N 83.11 W
Grand Rapids, Mb., Can. 184 53.08 N 99.20 W
Grand Rapids, Mi., U.S. 216 42.58 N 85.40 W
Grand Rapids, Mn., U.S. 190 47.14 N 93.31 W
Grand Rapids, Oh., U.S. 216 41.24 N 83.51 W
Grand Rhône ≃ 62 43.20 N 4.50 E
Grand Ridge 216 41.14 N 88.50 W
Grandrieu, Bel. 50 50.12 N 4.10 E
Grandrieu, Fr. 62 44.47 N 3.38 E
Grand River 214 41.44 N 81.17 W
Grand' Rivière 240e 14.52 N 61.11 W
Grand Ronde 224 45.03 N 123.36 W
Grand Roy 241k 12.08 N 61.45 W
Grand Ruisseau, Le ≃ 275a 45.39 N 73.12 W
Grand-Saint-Bernard, Col du)(58 45.50 N 7.10 E
Grand-Saint-Bernard, Tunnel du ✦[5] 58 45.51 N 7.11 E
Grand Saline 222 32.40 N 95.42 W
Grand Saline Creek ≃ 222 32.41 N 95.36 W
Grand-Santi 250 4.19 N 54.24 W
Grandson 58 46.49 N 6.38 E
Grand Terrace 228 34.02 N 117.18 W
Grand Teton ∧ 202 43.44 N 110.48 W
Grand Teton National Park ✦ 202 43.30 N 110.45 W
Grand Tower 194 37.37 N 89.29 W
Grand Traverse Bay c 190 45.02 N 85.30 W
Grand Traverse Bay, East Arm c 190 44.52 N 85.28 W
Grand Traverse Bay, West Arm c 190 44.52 N 85.35 W
Grandtully 46 56.39 N 3.46 W
Grand Turk 238 21.28 N 71.08 W
Grand Union Canal ≡ 260 51.30 N 0.02 W
Grand Valley, On., Can. 212 43.54 N 80.19 W
Grand Valley, Pa., U.S. 214 41.43 N 79.32 W
Grandview, Mb., Can. 184 51.10 N 100.42 W
Grandview, Il., U.S. 219 42.06 N 89.50 W
Grandview, Mo., U.S. 194 38.53 N 94.31 W
Grandview, Pa., U.S. 279b 40.10 N 79.52 W
Grandview, Tx., U.S. 222 32.16 N 97.11 W
Grandview, Wa., U.S. 202 46.15 N 119.54 W
Grand View, Wi., U.S. 190 46.22 N 91.06 W
Grandview Beach 216 41.50 N 83.24 W
Grandview Heights, Oh., U.S. 218 39.58 N 83.02 W
Grandview Heights, Pa., U.S. 208 40.03 N 76.17 W
Grandview Homes 216 40.44 N 84.04 W
Grand View-on-Hudson 276 41.04 N 73.55 W
Grandvillars 58 47.33 N 6.58 E
Grandville 216 42.54 N 85.45 W
Grandvilliers 50 49.40 N 1.56 E
Grand Wash Cliffs ✦[4] 200 35.40 N 113.50 W
Grandyle Village 210 43.00 N 78.57 W
Grâne 62 44.44 N 4.55 E
Grañén 34 41.56 N 0.22 W
Graneros 252 34.04 S 70.44 W
Granetalsperre ✦[6] 52 51.48 N 10.27 E
Graney, Lough ⊜ 48 52.59 N 8.40 W
Grangärde 40 60.16 N 14.59 E
Grange, Austl. 168b 34.54 S 138.30 E
Grange, Eng., U.K. 262 53.23 N 3.09 W
Grange, Bois de la ✦ 261 48.45 N 2.30 E
Grange-Bléneau, Château de la ⊥ 50 48.41 N 2.55 E
Grange Hill 260 51.37 N 0.05 E
Grangemouth 46 56.02 N 3.45 W
Grängen ⊜ 40 59.45 N 14.47 E
Grangent, Lac de ⊜[1] 62 45.25 N 4.15 E
Grange-over-Sands 44 54.12 N 2.55 W
Granger, Tx., U.S. 222 30.43 N 97.26 W
Granger, Wa., U.S. 202 46.20 N 120.11 W
Granger, Wy., U.S. 200 41.35 N 109.58 W
Granger Draw V 196 30.20 N 100.57 W
Granger Lake ⊜[1] 222 30.42 N 97.22 W
Granges — Grenchen 58 47.11 N 7.24 E
Grängesberg 40 60.05 N 14.59 E
Granges-sur-Vologne 58 48.09 N 6.47 E
Grangeville, Id., U.S. 202 45.55 N 116.07 W
Grangeville, Pa., U.S. 208 39.47 N 76.58 W
Grangousier Hill ∧[2] 190 47.35 N 84.56 W
Gran Guardia 252 25.52 S 58.53 W
Granite, Md., U.S. 284b 39.21 N 76.51 W
Granite, Ok., U.S. 196 34.57 N 99.22 W
Granite City 219 38.42 N 90.08 W
Granite Creek ≃ 224 48.43 N 120.55 W
Granite Dome ∧ 226 38.13 N 119.44 W
Granite Downs 162 26.57 S 133.30 E
Granite Falls, Mn., U.S. 198 44.48 N 95.32 W
Granite Falls, N.C., U.S. 192 35.47 N 81.25 W
Granite Falls, Wa., U.S. 224 48.05 N 121.58 W
Granite Lake ⊜[1] 186 48.08 N 57.05 W
Granite Mountain ∧, Austl. 171b 35.44 S 148.13 E
Granite Mountain ∧, Ak., U.S. 180 65.26 N 161.14 W
Granite Mountain ∧, Ak., U.S. 182 55.30 N 132.35 W
Granite Mountains ⋌ 202 42.35 N 107.30 W
Granite Pass)(202 44.38 N 107.30 W
Granite Peak 162 25.38 S 121.21 E
Granite Peak ∧, Mt., U.S. 202 45.10 N 109.48 W
Granite Peak ∧, Mt., U.S. 202 45.34 N 112.02 W
Granite Peak ∧, Nv., U.S. 204 41.40 N 117.35 W
Granite Peak ∧, Nv., U.S. 204 40.48 N 119.25 W
Granite Range ⋌ 204 41.00 N 119.35 W
Graniteville, Ma., U.S. 207 42.35 N 71.27 W
Graniteville, S.C., U.S. 192 33.33 N 81.48 W
Graniteville, Vt., U.S. 188 44.09 N 72.29 W
Graniti 70 37.53 N 15.14 E
Granitogorsk 85 42.44 N 73.27 E
Granitola, Capo > 70 37.34 N 12.41 E
Granitola Torretta 70 37.34 N 12.40 E
Granity 172 41.38 S 171.51 E
Granitzenbach ≃ 61 47.11 N 14.48 E
Granja, Bra. 250 3.06 S 40.50 W
Granja, Port. 266c 38.51 N 9.06 W
Gran Khingan — Da Hinggan Ling ⋌ 90 49.00 N 122.00 E
Granki 76 54.51 N 31.27 E
Grankulla (Kauniainen) 26 60.13 N 24.45 E
Gran Lago Salado — Great Salt Lake ⊜ 200 41.10 N 112.30 W
Gran Laguna Salada ⊜ 254 44.24 S 67.23 W
Granma □[4] 240p 20.10 N 76.50 W
Gränna 26 58.01 N 14.28 E
Grannoch, Loch ⊜ 44 55.00 N 4.17 W
Granollers 34 41.37 N 2.18 E
Granön 26 64.15 N 19.19 E
Gran Pajonal ⋌ 248 10.45 S 74.30 W
Gran Paradiso ∧ 62 45.32 N 7.16 E
Gran Paradiso, Parco Nazionale del ✦ 62 45.34 N 7.18 E
Gran Pilastro (Hochfeiler) ∧ 64 46.58 N 11.44 E
Gran Rio ≃ 250 4.01 N 55.31 W
Gran Sasso d'Italia ⋌ 66 42.27 N 13.42 E
Gransee 54 53.00 N 13.09 E
Grant, Fl., U.S. 220 27.55 N 80.31 W
Grant, Mi., U.S. 190 43.20 N 85.48 W
Grant, Ne., U.S. 198 40.50 N 101.43 W
Grant □[6], In., U.S. 216 40.33 N 85.40 W
Grant □[6], Ky., U.S. 218 38.39 N 84.39 W
Grant ≃ 190 42.40 N 90.45 W
Grant, Lake ⊜ 218 39.00 N 83.53 W
Grant, Mount ∧ 204 38.34 N 118.48 W
Grant, Point > 169 38.31 S 145.07 E
Granta ≃ 42 52.10 N 0.06 E
Grant Birthplace ⊥ 218 38.54 N 84.14 W
Grant City 194 40.29 N 94.24 W
Grantham, Austl. 171a 27.34 S 152.12 E
Grantham, Eng., U.K. 42 52.55 N 0.39 W
Grantham, Pa., U.S. 208 40.09 N 77.00 W
Grant-Kohrs Ranch National Historic Site ⊥ 202 46.25 N 112.40 W
Grant Lake ⊜[1] 226 37.50 N 119.07 W
Grantley Adams International Airport ⊠ 241g 13.04 N 59.29 W
Grant Mills 283 41.57 N 71.26 W
Granton 46 55.59 N 3.14 W
Grantorto 64 45.36 N 11.43 E
Grantown-on-Spey 46 57.19 N 3.37 W
Grant Park 216 41.14 N 87.39 W
Grant Park ✦ 278 41.52 N 87.37 W
Grant Point > 176 68.19 N 98.53 W
Grant Range ⋌ 204 38.25 N 115.30 W
Grants 200 35.09 N 107.50 W
Grantsburg, In., U.S. 218 38.17 N 86.28 W
Grantsburg, Wi., U.S. 190 45.46 N 92.40 W
Grantshouse 46 55.53 N 2.19 W
Grants Pass 202 42.26 N 123.19 W
Grants Patch 162 30.27 S 121.07 E
Grant-Suttie Bay c 176 69.47 N 77.15 W
Grantsville, Ut., U.S. 200 40.36 N 112.27 W
Grantsville, W.V., U.S. 188 38.55 N 81.05 W
Grantville, Ga., U.S. 192 33.14 N 84.50 W
Grantville, Pa., U.S. 208 40.23 N 76.39 W
Granum 182 49.52 N 113.30 W
Granville, Austl. 274a 33.50 S 151.01 E
Granville, Fr. 32 48.50 N 1.36 W
Granville, Il., U.S. 190 41.15 N 89.13 W
Granville, Ma., U.S. 207 42.04 N 72.51 W
Granville, Mo., U.S. 219 39.34 N 92.06 W
Granville, N.Y., U.S. 188 43.24 N 73.15 W
Granville, N.D., U.S. 198 48.16 N 100.50 W
Granville, Oh., U.S. 214 40.04 N 82.31 W
Granville, Pa., U.S. 208 40.33 N 77.38 W
Granville, W.V., U.S. 188 39.38 N 79.59 W
Granville Lake ⊜ 184 56.18 N 100.30 W
Granvin 26 60.33 N 6.43 E
Granzin, Dtsch. 54 53.25 N 12.53 E
Granzin, Dtsch. 54 53.30 N 11.56 E
Grão Mogol 255 16.34 S 42.54 W
Grão-Mogol ≍ 256 21.46 S 43.40 W
Grape Creek ≃ 200 38.26 N 105.18 W
Grape Island I 283 42.16 N 70.55 W
Grapeland 222 31.29 N 95.28 W
Grapeview 224 47.19 N 122.50 W
Grapeville 214 40.19 N 79.36 W
Grapevine 222 32.56 N 97.04 W
Grapevine Lake ⊜[1] 222 32.59 N 97.06 W
Grapevine Peak ∧ 204 36.57 N 117.09 W
Grappa, Monte ∧ 64 45.52 N 11.48 E
Grappenhall 262 53.22 N 2.32 W
Grarem 34 36.31 N 6.19 E
Gras, Lac de ⊜ 176 64.30 N 110.30 W
Grasbult 158 30.52 S 21.47 E
Grasdorf 52 52.06 N 10.09 E
Graskop 156 24.58 S 30.49 E
Grasleben 54 52.18 N 11.01 E
Grasmere, S. Afr. 158 26.26 S 27.52 E
Grasmere, Eng., U.K. 44 54.28 N 3.02 W
Grasmere Lake ⊜ 276 40.36 N 74.05 W
Gräsö 40 60.21 N 18.28 E
Gräsö I 40 60.24 N 18.25 E
Grasonville 208 38.57 N 76.12 W
Grass ≃, Mb., Can. 184 56.03 N 96.33 W
Grass ≃, N.Y., U.S. 188 44.59 N 74.46 W
Grass, North Branch ≃ 188 44.25 N 75.06 W
Grass, South Branch ≃ 188 44.22 N 75.05 W
Grassano 68 40.38 N 16.18 E
Grassau 64 47.47 N 12.27 E
Grass Creek 202 43.56 N 108.39 W
Grass Creek ≃ 202 43.52 N 108.22 W
Grasscroft 262 53.32 N 2.02 W
Grasse 62 43.40 N 6.55 E
Grassendale ✦[8] 262 53.21 N 2.54 W
Grassflat 214 41.00 N 78.07 W
Grass Hassock Channel ≋ 276 40.36 N 73.48 W
Grasshopper Creek ≃ 202 45.06 N 112.47 W
Grassington 44 54.04 N 2.00 W
Grass Island I 276 40.39 N 73.18 W
Grässjön ⊜ 40 59.52 N 13.43 E
Grass Lake 216 42.15 N 84.13 W
Grass Lake ⊜ 216 42.27 N 88.10 W
Grassmere, Lake ⊜ 172 41.44 S 174.10 E
Grass Patch 162 33.14 S 121.43 E
Grass Range 202 47.01 N 108.48 W
Grassridge Dam ⊜[1] 158 31.45 S 25.29 E
Grass River Provincial Park ✦ 184 54.40 N 100.50 W
Grass Valley, Austl. 168a 31.38 S 116.48 E
Grass Valley, Ca., U.S. 226 39.13 N 121.03 W
Grass Valley, Or., U.S. 224 45.21 N 120.47 W
Grassy 166 40.03 S 144.04 E
Grassy ≃ 190 48.22 N 81.27 W
Grassy Bay c 276 40.38 N 73.48 W
Grassy Brook ≃ 284a 43.03 N 79.07 W
Grassy Creek ≃, In., U.S. 216 40.55 N 86.30 W
Grassy Creek ≃, Mo., U.S. 219 39.54 N 91.37 W
Grassy Hill ∧ 271d 22.25 N 114.09 E
Grassy Island I 276 41.04 N 73.23 W
Grassy Island Lake ⊜ 184 51.50 N 110.20 W
Grassy Key I 220 24.46 N 80.57 W
Grassy Lake 182 49.49 N 111.43 W
Grassy Lake ⊜ 220 27.13 N 81.20 W
Grassy Plains 182 53.57 N 125.54 W
Grassy Sprain Reservoir ⊜[1] 276 40.58 N 73.51 W
Grästen 41 54.55 N 9.36 E
Grästorp 26 58.20 N 12.40 E
Graterford 285 40.13 N 75.27 W
Graterford State Correctional Institution ✦ 285 40.14 N 75.26 W
Grates Point > 186 48.10 N 52.57 W
Gratiot □[6] 218 39.38 N 84.31 W
Gratitunon 115a 7.43 S 113.00 E
Gratkorn 61 47.08 N 15.21 E
Gratwein 61 47.07 N 15.19 E
Gratz, Ky., U.S. 218 38.28 N 84.57 W
Gratz, Pa., U.S. 208 40.37 N 76.43 W
Gratztown 279b 40.14 N 79.47 W
Graubünden (Grischun) □[3] 58 46.45 N 9.30 E
Graudenz — Grudziądz 30 53.29 N 18.45 E
Graue Hörner ∧ 58 46.57 N 9.23 E
Graukogel ∧ 64 47.06 N 13.10 E
Graulhet 32 43.46 N 2.00 E
Graulinster 56 49.45 N 6.18 E
Graun — Curon Venosta 64 46.49 N 10.32 E
Graupa 54 51.00 N 13.54 E
Gravatá 250 8.12 S 35.34 W
Gravataí ≃ 255 16.53 S 42.10 W
Grave 52 51.45 N 5.44 E
Grave Creek ≃ 202 42.39 N 123.35 W
Gravedona 58 46.09 N 9.18 E
Gravelbourg 184 49.53 N 106.34 W
Gravelines 50 50.59 N 2.07 E
Gravellona-Toce 58 45.55 N 8.26 E
Gravell Point > 176 67.10 N 76.43 W
Gravelly Bay c 284a 42.52 N 79.15 W
Gravelly Brook ≃ 276 40.25 N 74.13 W
Gravelly Pond ⊜ 283 42.36 N 70.48 W
Gravelotte, Fr. 56 49.07 N 6.01 E
Gravelotte, S. Afr. 156 23.56 S 30.34 E
Gravenhurst 212 44.55 N 79.22 W
Grävenwiesbach 56 50.23 N 8.27 E
Grave Peak ∧ 202 46.24 N 114.44 W
Gravesend, Austl. 166 29.35 S 150.19 E
Gravesend, Eng., U.K. 42 51.27 N 0.24 E
Gravesend Bay c 276 40.36 N 74.01 W
Gravesham □[8] 260 51.25 N 0.24 E
Gravette 194 36.25 N 94.27 W
Gravigny 50 49.03 N 1.10 E
Gravina 70 37.34 N 15.03 E
Gravina di Matera ≃ 68 40.29 N 16.43 E
Gravina in Puglia 68 40.49 N 16.25 E
Gravina Island I 182 55.17 N 131.45 W
Gray, Fr. 58 47.27 N 5.35 E
Gray, Ga., U.S. 192 33.00 N 83.32 W
Gray, Ky., U.S. 192 36.56 N 84.00 W
Gray, Pa., U.S. 214 40.08 N 79.05 W
Grayback Mountain ∧, Ak., U.S. 180 57.08 N 153.54 W
Grayback Mountain ∧, Or., U.S. 202 42.07 N 123.18 W
Grayland 224 46.48 N 124.05 W
Grayling, Ak., U.S. 180 62.57 N 160.03 W
Grayling, Mi., U.S. 190 44.39 N 84.42 W
Graylyn Crest 285 39.48 N 75.31 W
Grays 42 51.29 N 0.20 E
Grays ≃ 224 46.18 N 123.41 W
Grays Harbor □[6] 224 47.09 N 123.45 W
Grays Harbor c 224 46.56 N 124.05 W
Grayshott 42 51.11 N 0.45 W
Grayslake 216 42.21 N 88.03 W
Grays Lake ⊜ 278 42.21 N 88.03 W
Grays Lake ≡ 202 43.04 N 111.26 W
Grays Lake Outlet ≃ 202 43.22 N 111.46 W
Grayson, Sk., Can. 184 50.44 N 102.40 W
Grayson, Al., U.S. 194 34.16 N 87.19 W
Grayson, Ca., U.S. 226 37.33 N 121.10 W
Grayson, Ky., U.S. 218 38.19 N 82.56 W
Grayson, La., U.S. 194 32.02 N 92.06 W
Grayson Lake ⊜[1] 218 38.13 N 83.00 W
Grayson Lake State Park ✦ 218 38.13 N 83.02 W
Grays Peak ∧ 200 39.37 N 105.45 W
Grays Point 274a 34.04 S 151.05 E
Grays River 224 46.21 N 123.36 W
Gray Summit 219 38.29 N 90.49 W
Graysville 194 35.26 N 85.05 W
Graytown 214 41.33 N 83.16 W
Grayville 194 37.57 N 88.10 W
Gray Wolf ≃ 224 47.55 N 123.07 W
Graz 61 47.05 N 15.27 E
Grazalema 34 36.46 N 5.22 W
Graždanka ✦[8] 265a 60.00 N 30.24 E
Gr'azeva ≃ 265b 55.51 N 37.08 E
Gr'azi 80 52.29 N 39.57 E
Grazierville 214 40.40 N 78.16 W
Gr'aznoje 82 54.02 N 39.07 E
Gr'aznovo, Ross. 82 54.18 N 36.49 E
Gr'aznovo, Ross. 265b 55.57 N 37.34 E
Gr'aznyj Irtek 80 51.56 N 53.11 E
Gr'azovec 76 58.53 N 40.14 E
Grdelica 38 42.54 N 22.04 E
Greåker 26 59.16 N 11.02 E
Greasby 262 53.23 N 3.07 W
Great ≃ 241k 12.08 N 61.36 W
Great Adventure ✦ 208 40.09 N 74.27 W
Great Altcar 262 53.33 N 3.01 W
Great America ✦ 282 37.24 N 121.59 W
Great Amwell 260 51.48 N 0.01 W
Great Artesian Basin ≍[1] 166 25.00 S 143.00 E
Great Australian Bight c[3] 162 35.00 S 130.00 E
Great Ayton 44 54.30 N 1.08 W
Great Baddow 42 51.43 N 0.29 E
Great Bahama Bank ✦[4] 238 23.15 N 78.00 W
Great Barford 42 52.09 N 0.21 W
Great Barrier Island I 172 36.10 S 175.25 E
Great Barrier Reef ✦[2] 160 18.00 S 146.50 E
Great Barrier Reef Marine Park ✦ 166 21.00 S 151.00 E
Great Barrington 207 42.11 N 73.21 W
Great Barrow 262 53.12 N 2.48 W
Great Basin ≍[1] 178 40.00 N 117.00 W
Great Basin National Park ✦ 204 38.55 N 114.14 W
Great Bay c 208 39.30 N 74.23 W
Great Bear ≃ 180 64.54 N 125.35 W
Great Bear Lake ⊜ 176 66.00 N 120.00 W
Great Beaver Lake ⊜ 182 54.25 N 123.45 W
Great Belt — Storebælt ≋ 41 55.30 N 11.00 E
Great Bend, Ks., U.S. 198 38.21 N 98.45 W
Great Bend, N.Y., U.S. 212 44.02 N 75.43 W
Great Bend, Pa., U.S. 210 41.58 N 75.44 W
Great Bernera I 46 58.13 N 6.49 W
Great Bitter Lake — Murrah al-Kubrā, Al-Buhayrah al- ⊜ 142 30.20 N 32.23 E
Great Blasket Island I 48 52.05 N 10.32 W
Great Blue Hill ∧[2] 207 42.13 N 71.07 W
Great Bookham 260 51.16 N 0.22 W
Great Braxted 260 51.48 N 0.42 E
Great Brewster Island I 283 42.20 N 70.53 W
Great Britain I 22 54.00 N 2.00 W
Great Brook ≃ 276 40.42 N 74.31 W
Great Buddha ✦[1] 268 35.19 N 139.32 E
Great Budworth 262 53.18 N 2.30 W
Great Burnt Lake ⊜ 186 48.20 N 56.13 W
Great Burstead 260 51.36 N 0.25 E
Great Camanoe I 240m 18.29 N 64.32 W
Great Captain Island I 276 40.59 N 73.38 W
Great Central 182 49.19 N 124.59 W
Great Central Lake ⊜ 182 49.27 N 125.12 W
Great Channel ≋ 110 6.25 N 94.20 E
Great Chazy ≃ 188 44.56 N 73.23 W
Great Clifton 44 54.39 N 3.29 W
Great Coco Island I 110 14.05 N 93.24 E
Great Coharie Creek ≃ 192 34.50 N 78.22 W
Great Cove c 276 40.43 N 73.14 W
Great Crosby 262 53.29 N 3.01 W
Great Crossing 218 38.08 N 84.38 W
Great Cumbrae Island I 46 55.46 N 4.55 W
Great Dismal Swamp ≡ 192 36.30 N 76.30 W
Great Ditch ≡ 276 40.24 N 74.31 W
Great Divide Basin ≍[1] 202 42.00 N 108.10 W
Great Dividing Range ⋌ 160 25.00 S 147.00 E
Great Driffield 44 54.00 N 0.27 W
Great Duck Island I 190 45.40 N 82.58 W
Great Dunmow 42 51.53 N 0.22 E
Great Eau ≃ 44 53.25 N 0.13 E
Great Egg Harbor ≃ 208 39.18 N 74.40 W
Great Egg Harbor Bay c 208 39.18 N 74.37 W
Great Egg Harbor Inlet c 208 39.20 N 74.34 W
Greater Antilles II 238 20.00 N 74.00 W
Greater Buffalo International Airport ⊠ 210 42.56 N 78.44 W
Greater Cincinnati Airport ⊠ 218 39.03 N 84.40 W
Greater Khingan Range — Da Hinggan Ling ⋌ 90 49.00 N 122.00 E
Greater London □[6] 42 51.30 N 0.10 W
Greater Manchester □[6] 44 53.30 N 2.20 W
Greater Pittsburgh International Airport ⊠ 214 40.29 N 80.14 W
Greater Sunda Islands II 108 2.00 S 110.00 E
Greater Wilmington Airport ⊠ 208 39.41 N 75.36 W
Greater Wollongong — Wollongong 170 34.25 S 150.54 E
Great Escape ✦ 210 43.22 N 73.42 W
Great Exuma I 238 23.32 N 75.50 W
Great Falls, Mb., Can. 184 50.27 N 96.02 W
Great Falls, Mt., U.S. 202 47.30 N 111.17 W
Great Falls, S.C., U.S. 192 34.34 N 80.54 W
Great Falls, Va., U.S. 284c 39.00 N 77.17 W
Great Falls ∟ 284c 39.00 N 77.16 W
Great Falls Park ✦ 284c 39.00 N 77.15 W
Great Fish Point > 158 33.30 S 27.10 E
Great Gable ∧ 44 54.28 N 3.12 W
Great Gaddesden 260 51.47 N 0.30 W
Great Grimsby — Grimsby 44 53.35 N 0.05 W
Great Guana Cay I 238 24.00 N 76.20 W
Great Hameldon ∧[2] 262 53.45 N 2.19 W
Great Harwood 44 53.48 N 2.24 W
Great Haywood 42 52.48 N 2.00 W
Great Himalaya Range ⋌ 120 29.00 N 83.00 E
Greathouse Peak ∧ 202 46.46 N 109.21 W
Great Inagua I 238 21.05 N 73.18 W
Great Indian Desert (Thar Desert) ✦[2] 120 27.00 N 71.00 E
Great Island I, Ire. 48 51.52 N 8.17 W
Great Island I, N.Y., U.S. 276 40.38 N 73.30 W
Great Island I, N.Y., U.S. 276 41.05 N 73.44 W
Great Karroo (Groot Karroo) ⋌[1] 158 32.25 S 22.40 E
Great Kills ✦[8] 276 40.33 N 74.10 W
Great Kills Harbor c 276 40.32 N 74.08 W
Great Kills Park ✦ 276 40.33 N 74.08 W
Great La Cloche Island I 190 46.01 N 81.52 W
Great Lake ⊜ 166 41.52 S 146.45 E
Great Lakes Naval Training Center ■ 216 42.18 N 87.50 W
Great Lakes Steel Works ✦[3] 281 42.15 N 83.08 W
Great Machipongo Inlet c 208 37.22 N 75.43 W
Great Malvern 42 52.07 N 2.19 W
Great Marsh ≡ 208 36.32 N 75.57 W
Great Marton 262 53.48 N 3.02 W
Great Massingham 42 52.46 N 0.40 E
Great Meadows 210 40.52 N 74.54 W
Great Meadows National Wildlife Refuge ✦[4] 283 42.29 N 71.20 W
Great Mercury Island I 172 36.37 S 175.48 E
Great Meteor Tablemount ✦[3] 18 30.00 N 28.30 W
Great Miami ≃ 188 39.06 N 84.49 W
Great Mills 208 38.14 N 76.30 W
Great Misery Island I 283 42.33 N 70.48 W
Great Missenden 42 51.43 N 0.43 W
Great Mis Tor ∧ 42 50.34 N 4.01 W
Great Mosque ✦[1] 146 32.46 N 22.40 E
Great Namaqualand □[9] 156 25.00 S 17.00 E
Great Neck 276 40.48 N 73.43 W
Great Neck >[1], Ma., U.S. 283 42.42 N 70.48 W
Great Neck >[1], N.Y., U.S. 276 40.50 N 73.45 W
Great Neck Estates 276 40.47 N 73.44 W
Great Nicobar I 110 7.00 N 93.50 E
Great North East Channel ≋ 164 9.30 S 143.25 E
Great Notch Reservoir ⊜[1] 276 40.53 N 74.12 W
Great Ormes Head > 44 53.21 N 3.52 W
Great Ouse ≃ 42 52.47 N 0.22 E
Great Oxney Green 260 51.44 N 0.25 E
Great Palm Island I 166 18.43 S 146.37 E
Great Parndon 260 51.45 N 0.05 E
Great Patchogue Lake ⊜ 276 40.46 N 73.01 W
Great Peconic Bay c 207 40.56 N 72.30 W
Great Pee Dee ≃ 192 33.21 N 79.16 W
Great Piece Meadows ≡ 276 40.54 N 74.19 W
Great Plain of the Koukdjuak ≍ 176 66.00 N 73.00 W
Great Plains ≍ 16 42.00 N 100.00 W
Great Point > 207 41.23 N 70.03 W
Great Pubnico Lake ⊜ 186 43.42 N 65.43 W
Great Quittacas Pond ⊜ 207 41.48 N 70.54 W
Great River 276 40.45 N 73.10 W
Great Ruaha ≃ 154 7.56 S 37.52 E
Great Sacandaga Lake ⊜ 210 43.08 N 74.10 W
Great Saint Bernard Pass — Grand-Saint-Bernard, Col du)(58 45.50 N 7.10 E
Great Sale Cay I 192 27.00 N 78.12 W
Great Salt Lake ⊜ 200 41.10 N 112.30 W
Great Salt Lake Desert ✦[2] 200 40.40 N 113.30 W
Great Salt Plains Lake ⊜[1] 196 36.44 N 98.12 W
Great Sand Dunes National Monument ✦ 200 37.43 N 105.36 W
Great Sand Hills ⋌[2] 184 50.35 N 109.05 W
Great Sandy Desert ✦[2] 162 21.30 S 125.00 E
Great Sandy National Park ✦ 166 24.59 S 153.17 E
Great Sankey 44 53.23 N 2.37 W
Great Santa Cruz Island I 116 6.52 N 122.03 E
Great Scarcies (Kolenté) ≃ 150 8.55 N 13.08 W
Great Sea Reef ✦[2] 175g 16.15 S 179.00 E
Great Seneca Creek ≃ 208 39.08 N 77.20 W
Great Shelford 42 52.09 N 0.09 E
Great Sitkin Island I 180 52.03 N 176.07 W
Great Slave Lake ⊜ 176 61.30 N 114.00 W
Great Smoky Mountains ⋌ 192 35.35 N 83.30 W
Great Smoky Mountains National Park ✦ 192 35.39 N 83.30 W
Great Sound ≋, Ber. 240a 32.17 N 64.51 W
Great Sound ≋, N.J., U.S. 208 39.06 N 74.47 W
Great South Bay c 210 40.40 N 73.17 W
Great Stour ≃ 42 51.19 N 1.15 E
Great Sutton 262 53.17 N 2.56 W
Great Swamp ≡ 276 40.43 N 74.28 W
Great Swamp National Wildlife Refuge ✦[4] 276 40.43 N 74.28 W
Great Tenasserim ≃ 110 12.24 N 98.37 E
Great Tobago I 240m 18.27 N 64.48 W
Great Torrington 42 50.57 N 4.08 W
Great Totham 260 51.47 N 0.43 E
Great Usutu (Maputo) (Lusutfu) ≃ 158 26.11 S 32.42 E
Great Valley 210 42.13 N 78.38 W
Great Victoria Desert ✦[2] 162 28.30 S 127.45 E
Great Wall ✦[3] 9 62.13 S 58.58 W
Great Wall — Chang Cheng ⊥ 98 40.30 N 116.30 E
Great Waltham 260 51.48 N 0.28 E
Great Warley 260 51.35 N 0.17 E
Great Western Forum ✦ 280 33.57 N 118.20 W
Great Whernside ∧ 44 54.09 N 1.59 W
Great Wicomico ≃ 208 37.48 N 76.18 W
Great Wyrley 42 52.41 N 2.01 W
Great Yarmouth 42 52.37 N 1.44 E
Great Zab (Büyükzap) (Az-Zāb al-Kabīr) ≃ 128 36.00 N 43.21 E
Great Zimbabwe Ruins National Park ✦ 154 20.17 S 30.57 E
Grebbestad 26 58.42 N 11.15 E
Grebenhain 56 50.29 N 9.19 E
Grebenstein 56 51.26 N 9.24 E
Grebnevo 265b 55.58 N 38.05 E
Gréboun ∧ 150 20.00 N 8.35 E
Grèce — Greece □[1] 38 39.00 N 22.00 E
Grecia 236 10.05 N 84.18 W
Grecia — Greece □[1] 38 39.00 N 22.00 E
Grecken ⊜ 40 59.35 N 14.44 E
Greco 252 32.48 S 57.03 W
Greco ✦[8] 266b 45.30 N 9.13 E
Greco, Monte ∧ 66 41.48 N 14.00 E
Greco Island I 282 37.31 N 122.11 W
Greding 60 49.03 N 11.21 E
Gredos, Sierra de ⋌ 34 40.18 N 5.05 W
Gredstedbro 41 55.24 N 8.45 E
Greece 210 43.12 N 77.41 W
Greece (Ellás) □[1], Europe 22 39.00 N 22.00 E
Greece (Ellás) □[1], Europe 38 39.00 N 22.00 E
Greeley, Co., U.S. 200 40.25 N 104.42 W
Greeley, Ks., U.S. 198 38.19 N 95.26 W
Greeley, Ne., U.S. 198 41.33 N 98.32 W

Symbols in the index entries represent the broad categories identified in the key at the right. Symbols with superior numbers (⋌[1]) identify subcategories (see complete key on page *I · 1*).

Symbole im Register stellen die rechts im Schlüssel erklärten Kategorien dar. Symbole mit hochgestellten Ziffern (⋌[1]) bezeichnen Unterabteilungen einer Kategorie (vgl. vollständiger Schlüssel auf Seite *I · 1*).

Los símbolos incluídos en el texto del índice representan las grandes categorías identificadas con la clave a la derecha. Los símbolos con numeros en su parte superior (⋌[1]) identifican las subcategorías (véase la clave completa en la página *I · 1*).

Les symboles de l'index représentent les catégories indiquées dans la légende à droite. Les symboles suivis d'un indice (⋌[1]) représentent des sous-catégories (voir légende complète à la page *I · 1*).

Os símbolos incluídos no texto do índice representam as grandes categorias identificadas com a chave à direita. Os símbolos com números em sua parte superior (⋌[1]) identificam as subcategorias (veja-se a chave completa à página *I · 1*).

∧ Mountain	Berg	Montaña	Montagne	Montanha
⋌ Mountains	Gebirge	Montañas	Montagnes	Montanhas
)(Pass	Paß	Paso	Col	Passo
V Valley, Canyon	Tal, Cañon	Valle, Cañón	Vallée, Canyon	Vale, Canhão
≍ Plain	Ebene	Llano	Plaine	Planície
> Cape	Kap	Cabo	Cap	Cabo
I Island	Insel	Isla	Île	Ilha
II Islands	Inseln	Islas	Îles	Ilhas
✦ Other Topographic Features	Andere Topographische Objekte	Otros Elementos Topográficos	Autres données topographiques	Outros acidentes topográficos

ESPAÑOL Nombre	Página	Lat.°′	Long.°′ W = Oeste
Greeley, Pa., U.S.	210	41.25 N	75.00 W
Greeleyville	192	33.34 N	79.59 W
Green □6	216	42.48 N	89.25 W
Green ≃, N.B., Can.	186	47.18 N	68.09 W
Green ≃, U.S.	200	38.11 N	109.53 W
Green ≃, U.S.	207	42.35 N	72.36 W
Green ≃, U.S.	207	42.10 N	73.22 W
Green ≃, Il., U.S.	190	41.28 N	90.23 W
Green ≃, Il., U.S.	216	41.46 N	89.10 W
Green ≃, Ky., U.S.	194	37.55 N	87.30 W
Green ≃, N.D., U.S.	198	46.52 N	102.35 W
Green ≃, Vt., U.S.	210	43.06 N	73.13 W
Green ≃, Wa., U.S.	224	47.33 N	122.20 W
Green ≃, Wa., U.S.	224	46.20 N	122.34 W
Greenacres, Ca., U.S.	226	35.23 N	119.07 W
Green Acres, De., U.S.	285	39.47 N	75.30 W
Greenacres, Wa., U.S.	202	47.39 N	117.06 W
Green Acres ✦9	276	40.40 N	73.43 W
Greenacres City	220	26.37 N	80.07 W
Greenbackville	208	38.00 N	75.23 W
Greenbank	224	48.06 N	122.34 W
Green Bay	190	44.31 N	88.01 W
Green Bay c, Nf., Can.	186	49.43 N	55.58 W
Green Bay c, On., Can.	212	44.38 N	76.36 W
Green Bay c, U.S.	190	45.00 N	87.30 W
Greenbelt	284c	39.00 N	76.52 W
Greenbelt Park ♦	284c	38.59 N	76.54 W
Greenbo Lake ⊜	218	38.29 N	82.54 W
Greenbo Lake State Resort Park ♦	218	38.29 N	82.54 W
Greenbooth Reservoir ⊜1	262	53.38 N	2.13 W
Greenbrae	226	37.57 N	122.31 W
Greenbrier, Ar., U.S.	194	35.14 N	92.23 W
Green Brier, Tn., U.S.	194	36.25 N	86.48 W
Greenbrier ≃	192	37.39 N	80.53 W
Greenbrier State Park ♦	208	39.33 N	77.38 W
Green Brook	276	40.36 N	74.27 W
Green Brook ≃	276	40.33 N	74.32 W
Greenburg	194	30.51 N	90.40 W
Greenbush, Ma., U.S.	207	42.11 N	70.45 W
Greenbush, Mn., U.S.	198	48.42 N	96.10 W
Greenbush, Va., U.S.	208	37.45 N	75.41 W
Greenbushes	162	33.51 S	116.03 E
Green Camp	214	40.31 N	83.12 W
Green Cape >	166	37.15 S	150.03 E
Greencastle, Ire.	48	55.12 N	6.59 W
Greencastle, In., U.S.	194	39.38 N	86.51 W
Greencastle, Pa., U.S.	188	39.47 N	77.43 W
Green City	194	40.16 N	92.57 W
Green Cove Springs	192	29.59 N	81.40 W
Green Creek	208	39.02 N	74.54 W
Green Creek ≃, Oh., U.S.	214	41.26 N	83.01 W
Green Creek ≃, Pa., U.S.	285	39.53 N	75.28 W
Greencrest Park	214	41.23 N	80.24 W
Greendale, Austl.	274a	33.55 S	150.39 E
Greendale, In., U.S.	218	39.06 N	84.51 W
Greendale, Wi., U.S.	216	42.56 N	87.59 W
Greene, Dtsch.	52	51.52 N	9.56 E
Greene, Ia., U.S.	190	42.53 N	92.48 W
Greene, N.Y., U.S.	210	42.19 N	75.46 W
Greene, R.I., U.S.	207	41.41 N	71.44 W
Greene □6, Il., U.S.	219	39.18 N	90.24 W
Greene □6, N.Y., U.S.	210	42.13 N	73.52 W
Greene □6, Oh., U.S.	218	39.41 N	83.56 W
Greeneville	192	36.06 N	82.42 W
Greenfield, Eng., U.K.	262	53.32 N	2.01 W
Greenfield, Wales, U.K.	44	53.18 N	3.13 W
Greenfield, Ca., U.S.	226	36.19 N	121.14 W
Greenfield, Il., U.S.	219	39.20 N	90.12 W
Greenfield, In., U.S.	218	39.47 N	85.46 W
Greenfield, Ia., U.S.	198	41.18 N	94.27 W
Greenfield, Ma., U.S.	207	42.35 N	72.36 W
Greenfield, Mo., U.S.	194	37.24 N	93.50 W
Greenfield, Oh., U.S.	218	39.21 N	83.22 W
Greenfield, Tn., U.S.	194	36.09 N	88.48 W
Greenfield, Wi., U.S.	216	42.58 N	88.02 W
Greenfield-Park, P.Q., Can.	275a	45.29 N	73.29 W
Greenfield Park, N.Y., U.S.	210	41.44 N	74.29 W
Greenfields Village	285	75.10 N	39.49 W
Greenfield Village ⊥	281	42.18 N	83.14 W
Greenford ✦8	260	51.32 N	0.21 W
Green Forest	194	36.20 N	93.26 W
Green Harbor	207	42.04 N	70.39 W
Green Harbor ≃	283	42.05 N	70.39 W
Green Head >	162	30.05 S	114.58 E
Green Hill	285	39.59 N	75.36 W
Greenhill ✦8	260	51.35 N	0.20 W
Greenhills, S. Afr.	273d	26.10 S	27.40 E
Greenhills, Oh., U.S.	218	39.16 N	84.31 W
Greenhithe	260	51.27 N	0.17 E
Greenhorn Creek ≃	198	38.08 N	104.38 W
Greenhurst	214	42.07 N	79.19 W
Green Hut Park	276	40.50 N	74.39 W
Green Island, N.Z.	172	45.54 S	170.26 E
Greenisland, N. Ire., U.K.	48	54.42 N	5.52 W
Green Island, N.Y., U.S.	210	42.44 N	73.41 W
Green Island I	241k	12.14 N	61.35 W
Green Island Bay c	116	10.12 N	119.22 E
Green Islands II	14	4.30 S	154.10 E
Green Knoll	276	40.36 N	74.36 W
Green Lake, Sk., Can.	184	54.17 N	107.47 W
Green Lake, Wi., U.S.	190	43.50 N	88.57 W
Green Lake ⊜, B.C., Can.	182	51.24 N	121.15 W
Green Lake ⊜, Sk., Can.	184	54.10 N	107.43 W
Green Lake ⊜, Mi., U.S.	281	42.36 N	83.25 W
Green Lake ⊜, N.Y., U.S.	284a	42.45 N	78.45 W
Green Lake ⊜, Wi., U.S.	190	43.41 N	88.57 W
Green Lakes State Park ♦	212	43.03 N	75.58 W
Greenlal (Saint-Grégoire-de-Greenlay)	206	45.34 N	72.01 W
Greenland, Ar., U.S.	194	35.59 N	94.10 W
Greenland, Mi., U.S.	190	46.46 N	89.06 W
Greenland (Kalaallit Nunaat) □2	16	70.00 N	40.00 W
Greenland Basin ✧1	16	73.30 N	5.00 W
Greenland-Iceland Rise ✧3	10	67.00 N	27.00 W
Greenlands	158	27.07 S	27.40 E
Greenland Sea ╤2	16	77.00 N	1.00 W
Green Lane	208	40.20 N	75.28 W
Green Lane Reservoir ⊜1	208	40.22 N	75.29 W
Greenlaw	46	55.43 N	2.28 W
Greenlawn	276	40.52 N	73.21 W
Greenlawn Park	285	40.07 N	74.51 W
Greenleaf	198	39.43 N	96.58 W
Green Lookout Mountain ∧	224	45.52 N	122.08 W
Green Manorville	207	42.00 N	72.32 W
Green Meadows	284c	38.58 N	76.57 W
Greenmount, Austl.	171a	27.47 S	151.54 E
Greenmount, Eng., U.K.	262	53.37 N	2.20 W
Greenmount, Md., U.S.	208	39.37 N	76.51 W
Green Mountains ⋏	188	43.45 N	72.45 W

FRANÇAIS Nom	Page	Lat.°′	Long.°′ W = Ouest
Green Oak Lake ⊜	281	42.27 N	83.43 W
Green Oaks	278	42.18 N	87.55 W
Greenock, Austl.	168b	34.27 S	138.55 E
Greenock, Scot., U.K.	46	55.57 N	4.45 W
Greenock, Pa., U.S.	279b	40.19 N	79.48 W
Greenodd	44	54.14 N	3.04 W
Greenore Point >	48	52.15 N	6.18 W
Greenough	162	28.57 S	114.44 E
Greenough ≃	162	28.51 S	114.38 E
Greenough, Mount ∧	180	69.10 N	141.35 W
Green Park	208	40.23 N	77.19 W
Green Peter Lake ⊜1	202	44.28 N	122.30 W
Green Point >	276	40.43 N	73.06 W
Green Pond, Al., U.S.	194	33.13 N	87.07 W
Green Pond, N.J., U.S.	276	41.01 N	74.29 W
Green Pond ⊜	276	41.00 N	74.30 W
Green Pond Brook ≃	276	40.53 N	74.34 W
Greenport	207	41.06 N	72.21 W
Green Ridge	285	39.51 N	75.25 W
Green River, Pap. N. Gui.	164	3.55 S	141.10 E
Green River, Ut,. U.S.	200	38.59 N	110.09 W
Green River, Wy., U.S.	200	41.31 N	109.27 W
Green River Lake ⊜1	194	37.15 N	85.15 W
Greensboro, Al., U.S.	194	32.42 N	87.35 W
Greensboro, Fl., U.S.	192	30.34 N	84.44 W
Greensboro, Ga., U.S.	192	33.34 N	83.10 W
Greensboro, Md., U.S.	208	38.58 N	75.48 W
Greensboro, N.C., U.S.	192	36.04 N	79.47 W
Greensborough	274b	37.42 S	145.06 E
Greensburg, In., U.S.	218	39.20 N	85.29 W
Greensburg, Ks., U.S.	198	37.36 N	99.17 W
Greensburg, Ky., U.S.	194	37.15 N	85.29 W
Greensburg, Oh., U.S.	214	40.56 N	81.28 W
Greensburg, Pa., U.S.	214	40.18 N	79.32 W
Greens Farms	276	41.07 N	73.19 W
Greens Fork	218	39.53 N	85.02 W
Greens Fork ≃	218	39.45 N	85.07 W
Greenside ✦8	273d	26.09 S	28.01 E
Greens Lake c	222	29.16 N	94.59 W
Greens Peak ∧	200	34.07 N	109.35 W
Greenspond	186	49.04 N	53.34 W
Green Springs	214	41.15 N	83.03 W
Greenstead	260	51.42 N	0.14 E
Greenstone	208	39.45 N	77.27 W
Greenstone Point >	46	57.55 N	5.38 W
Green Street	260	51.40 N	0.16 W
Green Street Green ✦8	260	51.21 N	0.04 E
Greensville □6	208	36.40 N	77.30 W
Green Swamp ≡, Fl., U.S.	220	28.20 N	81.48 W
Green Swamp ≡, N.C., U.S.	192	34.10 N	78.20 W
Greentown, In., U.S.	216	40.28 N	85.58 W
Greentown, Oh., U.S.	214	40.56 N	81.28 W
Greentown, Pa., U.S.	210	41.19 N	75.18 W
Green Tree	279b	40.24 N	80.02 W
Greenup, Il., U.S.	194	39.14 N	88.09 W
Greenup, Ky., U.S.	218	38.34 N	82.49 W
Greenup □6	218	38.33 N	83.00 W
Greenup Dam ✦6	218	38.39 N	82.52 W
Greenvale, Austl.	166	18.59 S	145.07 E
Greenvale, N.Y., U.S.	276	40.49 N	73.38 W
Green Valley, On., Can.	206	45.16 N	74.36 W
Green Valley, Az., U.S.	200	31.52 N	110.59 W
Green Valley, Il., U.S.	190	40.24 N	89.38 W
Green Valley Creek ≃	226	38.13 N	122.08 W
Greenview	219	40.04 N	89.44 W
Green Village, N.J., U.S.	276	40.44 N	74.27 W
Greenvillage, Pa., U.S.	208	40.00 N	77.36 W
Greenville, Liber.	150	5.01 N	9.03 W
Greenville, Al., U.S.	194	31.49 N	86.37 W
Greenville, Ca., U.S.	204	40.08 N	120.57 W
Greenville, Fl., U.S.	192	30.28 N	83.37 W
Greenville, Ga., U.S.	192	33.01 N	84.42 W
Greenville, Il., U.S.	219	38.53 N	89.24 W
Greenville, In., U.S.	218	38.22 N	85.59 W
Greenville, Ky., U.S.	194	37.12 N	87.10 W
Greenville, Me., U.S.	188	45.28 N	69.35 W
Greenville, Mi., U.S.	190	43.10 N	85.15 W
Greenville, Ms., U.S.	194	33.24 N	91.03 W
Greenville, Mo., U.S.	194	37.08 N	90.27 W
Greenville, N.H., U.S.	207	42.46 N	71.48 W
Greenville, N.Y., U.S.	210	40.59 N	73.49 W
Greenville, N.Y., U.S.	276	40.59 N	73.49 W
Greenville, N.C., U.S.	192	35.36 N	77.22 W
Greenville, Oh., U.S.	218	40.06 N	84.37 W
Greenville, Pa., U.S.	214	41.24 N	80.23 W
Greenville, R.I., U.S.	207	41.52 N	71.33 W
Greenville, S.C., U.S.	192	34.51 N	82.23 W
Greenville, Tx., U.S.	222	33.08 N	96.06 W
Greenville Creek ≃	218	40.07 N	84.22 W
Greenville Place	285	39.46 N	75.36 W
Greenwater ≃	224	47.09 N	121.39 W
Greenwater Lake ⊜	190	48.34 N	90.26 W
Greenwater Lake Provincial Park ♦	184	52.33 N	103.33 W
Greenwell Point	170	34.55 S	150.44 E
Greenwich, Austl.	274a	33.50 S	151.11 E
Greenwich, Ct., U.S.	207	41.01 N	73.37 W
Greenwich, N.J., U.S.	208	39.23 N	75.20 W
Greenwich, N.Y., U.S.	210	43.05 N	73.29 W
Greenwich, Oh., U.S.	214	41.01 N	82.30 W
Greenwich ✦8	42	51.28 N	0.02 E
Greenwich Cove c	276	41.01 N	73.35 W
Greenwich Creek ≃	276	41.02 N	73.37 W
Greenwich Observatory ⊽3	260	51.28 N	0.00
Greenwich Point >	276	41.00 N	73.34 W
Greenwich Village ✦8	276	40.44 N	74.00 W
Greenwood, B.C., Can.	182	49.05 N	118.41 W
Greenwood, Ar., U.S.	194	35.12 N	94.15 W
Greenwood, Ca., U.S.	226	38.54 N	120.55 W
Greenwood, De., U.S.	208	38.48 N	75.35 W
Greenwood, In., U.S.	218	39.36 N	86.06 W
Greenwood, Ma., U.S.	283	42.29 N	71.04 W
Greenwood, Ms., U.S.	194	33.30 N	90.10 W
Greenwood, Ne., U.S.	198	40.57 N	96.26 W
Greenwood, N.Y., U.S.	210	42.08 N	77.38 W
Greenwood, Pa., U.S.	214	40.32 N	78.21 W
Greenwood, S.C., U.S.	192	34.11 N	82.09 W
Greenwood, Wi., U.S.	190	44.46 N	90.35 W
Greenwood, Lake ⊜1	192	34.15 N	82.02 W
Greenwood Cemetery ✦	276	40.39 N	73.59 W
Greenwood Lake	210	41.13 N	74.17 W
Greenwood Lake ⊜, U.S.	210	41.11 N	74.19 W
Greenwood Lake ⊜, Ma., U.S.	283	42.00 N	71.17 W
Greenwood Race Track ♦	275b	43.40 N	79.19 W
Greer, Oh., U.S.	214	40.31 N	82.13 W

PORTUGUÊS Nome	Página	Lat.°′	Long.°′ W = Oeste
Greer, S.C., U.S.	192	34.56 N	82.13 W
Greers Ferry Lake ⊜1	194	35.30 N	92.10 W
Greerton	172	37.43 S	176.08 E
Grées, Alpes (Alpi Graie) ⋏	62	45.30 N	7.10 E
Greeson, Lake ⊜1	194	34.10 N	93.45 W
Greet ≃	44	53.03 N	0.53 W
Greetland	262	53.41 N	1.52 W
Greetsiel	52	53.30 N	7.05 E
Greffiers	261	48.37 N	1.51 E
Grefrath, Dtsch.	56	51.20 N	6.20 E
Grefrath, Dtsch.	263	51.10 N	6.38 E
Gregadoo	171b	35.14 S	147.27 E
Gregbe	150	6.48 N	6.43 W
Gregg	279b	40.24 N	80.10 W
Gregg □6	222	32.30 N	94.50 W
Greggio	62	45.27 N	8.23 E
Greg Greg	171b	36.03 S	148.02 E
Gregoire Lake Indian Reserve ✦4	184	56.28 N	111.10 W
Gregório ≃	248	6.50 S	70.46 W
Gregory, Mi., U.S.	216	42.27 N	84.05 W
Gregory, S.D., U.S.	198	43.13 N	99.25 W
Gregory, Tx., U.S.	196	27.55 N	97.17 W
Gregory ≃	166	17.53 S	139.17 E
Gregory, Lake ⊜, Austl.	162	20.10 S	127.20 E
Gregory, Lake ⊜, Austl.	162	25.38 S	119.58 E
Gregory, Lake ⊜, Austl.	166	28.55 S	139.00 E
Gregory National Park ♦	164	16.30 S	130.30 E
Gregory Range ⋏	166	19.00 S	143.05 E
Grégy-sur-Yerre	261	48.40 N	2.37 E
Greifenburg	64	46.45 N	13.11 E
Greifendorf	54	51.01 N	13.06 E
Greifensee	58	47.22 N	8.41 E
Greifensee ⊜	58	47.21 N	8.41 E
Greifenstein	264b	48.21 N	16.15 E
Greiffenberg	54	53.05 N	13.58 E
Greiffenburg ⊥	263	51.20 N	6.38 E
Greifswald	54	54.05 N	13.23 E
Greifswalder Bodden c	54	54.15 N	13.35 E
Greifswalder Oie I	54	54.14 N	13.55 E
Greim ∧	61	47.15 N	14.09 E
Grein	61	48.14 N	14.51 E
Greiz	54	50.39 N	12.12 E
Grejdernoje	80	46.53 N	45.01 E
Grejsdal	41	55.45 N	9.32 E
Grekov	80	47.24 N	43.41 E
Grekovo	83	48.54 N	40.14 E
Grem'ačevo	82	54.14 N	36.15 E
Grem'ačij	88	57.01 N	108.12 E
Grem'ačinsk, Ross.	86	58.34 N	57.51 E
Grem'ačinsk, Ross.	88	52.48 N	107.57 E
Grem'ačje	78	51.29 N	39.00 E
Gremersdorf	54	54.20 N	10.55 E
Gremicha	24	68.03 N	39.27 E
Grenå	26	56.25 N	10.53 E
Grenada	194	33.46 N	89.48 W
Grenada □1, N.A.	230	12.07 N	61.40 W
Grenada □1, N.A.	241k	12.07 N	61.40 W
Grenada Lake ⊜1	194	33.50 N	89.40 W
Grenade → Grenada □1	241k	12.07 N	61.40 W
Grenadier Island I	212	44.03 N	76.22 W
Grenadier Pond ⊜	275b	43.38 N	79.28 W
Grenadines II	238	12.40 N	61.15 W
Grenagh	48	52.00 N	8.37 W
Grenay	50	50.27 N	2.44 E
Grenchen	58	47.11 N	7.24 E
Grenell	212	44.16 N	76.04 W
Grenen >2	26	57.44 N	10.40 E
Grenfell, Austl.	166	33.54 S	148.10 E
Grenfell, Sk., Can.	184	50.25 N	102.56 W
Grenloch	285	39.47 N	75.03 W
Grenoble	62	45.10 N	5.43 E
Grenola	198	37.20 N	96.27 W
Grenora	198	48.37 N	103.56 W
Grenville, P.Q., Can.	206	45.37 N	74.36 W
Grenville, Gren.	241k	12.07 N	61.37 W
Grenville, Cape >	164	11.58 S	143.14 E
Grenville Bay	206	45.38 N	74.36 W
Grenville Bay c	241k	12.07 N	61.36 W
Grenville Channel ʊ	182	53.40 N	129.40 W
Grenzaa ≃	52	52.39 N	6.45 E
Grenz-Berge ∧2	264a	52.27 N	13.44 E
Grenzlandring ♦	56	51.11 N	6.17 E
Gréolières	62	43.48 N	6.57 E
Gréoux-les-Bains	62	43.45 N	5.53 E
Greppin	54	51.39 N	12.18 E
Gresenhorst	54	54.09 N	12.26 E
Gresham	224	45.29 N	122.25 W
Gresham Park	192	33.42 N	84.19 W
Gresik, Indon.	112	2.18 S	103.57 E
Gresik, Indon.	115a	7.09 S	112.38 E
Gressåmoen Nasjonalpark ♦	26	64.15 N	13.08 E
Gresse-en-Vercors	62	44.54 N	5.34 E
Gressey	261	48.50 N	1.37 E
Gressitt	208	37.29 N	76.43 W
Gressk	76	53.10 N	27.29 E
Gressoney, Val di V	62	45.47 N	7.49 E
Gressoney-la-Trinité	62	45.50 N	7.49 E
Gressoney-Saint-Jean	62	45.47 N	7.49 E
Gressy	261	48.58 N	2.41 E
Gresten	61	48.00 N	15.02 E
Grésy-sur-Aix	62	45.43 N	5.57 E
Grésy-sur-Isère	62	45.36 N	6.15 E
Greta	170	32.41 S	151.24 E
Greta ≃, Eng., U.K.	44	54.32 N	1.53 W
Greta ≃, Eng., U.K.	44	54.36 N	3.10 W
Greta ≃, Eng., U.K.	44	54.09 N	2.36 W
Gretna, Mb., Can.	184	49.02 N	97.35 W
Gretna, Scot., U.K.	44	54.59 N	3.04 W
Gretna, La., U.S.	194	29.54 N	90.03 W
Gretna, Va., U.S.	192	36.57 N	79.21 W
Gretz-Armainvilliers	50	48.44 N	2.44 E
Greussen	54	51.14 N	10.57 E
Greve, Dan.	41	55.36 N	12.15 E
Greve, It.	66	43.35 N	11.19 E
Greve ≃	66	43.46 N	11.13 E
Grevel ✦8	263	51.34 N	7.33 E
Grevelingen ʊ	52	51.45 N	4.00 E
Grevelingendam ✦5	52	51.40 N	4.10 E
Greven	52	52.05 N	7.36 E
Grevená	38	40.05 N	21.25 E
Grevenbroich	56	51.05 N	6.35 E
Greven-Granzin	54	53.29 N	10.48 E
Grevenmacher	56	49.42 N	6.20 E
Grevesmühlen	54	53.51 N	11.10 E
Greve Strand	41	55.35 N	12.14 E
Greville Bay c	186	45.22 N	64.38 W
Grevinge	41	55.48 N	11.34 E
Grey □6	212	44.20 N	80.45 W
Grey ≃, Nf., Can.	186	47.38 N	57.05 W
Grey ≃, N.Z.	172	42.27 S	171.12 E
Grey, Cape >	164	13.00 S	136.40 E
Grey, Point >, Austl.	169	38.34 S	143.59 E
Grey, Point >, B.C., Can.	224	49.16 N	123.16 W
Greyabbey	48	54.32 N	5.33 W
Greybull	202	44.29 N	108.03 W
Greybull ≃	202	44.28 N	108.03 W
Grey Eagle	190	45.49 N	94.44 W
Grey Islands II	186	50.50 N	55.37 W
Greylingstad	158	26.44 S	28.45 E
Greylock, Mount ∧	207	42.38 N	73.10 W
Greymouth	172	42.28 S	171.12 E
Grey Range ⋏	166	27.00 S	143.35 E
Grey River	186	47.35 N	57.06 W
Greys ≃	202	43.10 N	111.00 W
Greystanes	274a	33.49 S	150.55 E
Greystoke	44	54.40 N	2.52 W
Greystones	48	53.09 N	6.04 W
Greyton	158	34.04 S	19.38 E
Greytown, N.Z.	172	41.05 S	175.27 E

Nome	Página	Lat.°′	Long.°′
Greytown → San Juan del Norte, Nic.	236	10.55 N	83.42 W
Greytown, S. Afr.	158	29.07 S	30.30 E
Grez-Doiceau	56	50.44 N	4.42 E
Grez-sur-Loing	50	48.19 N	2.42 E
Grezzana	64	45.31 N	11.01 E
Gribanovskij	80	51.27 N	41.58 E
Gribbel Island I	182	53.25 N	129.00 W
Gribbin Head >	42	50.19 N	4.40 W
Gribingui □5	152	7.00 N	19.15 E
Gribingui ≃	146	8.33 N	19.05 E
Gribingui-Bamingui, Réserve de Faune du ✦4	146	8.00 N	19.10 E
Gribovka	82	54.19 N	38.27 E
Gridley, Ca., U.S.	226	39.21 N	121.41 W
Gridley, Il., U.S.	216	40.44 N	88.52 W
Griebnitz See ⊜	264a	52.24 N	13.06 E
Griechenland → Greece □1	38	39.00 N	22.00 E
Griekwastad	158	28.49 S	23.15 E
Grier City	210	40.50 N	76.04 W
Gries am Brenner	64	47.03 N	11.29 E
Griesbach im Rottal	60	48.28 N	13.11 E
Griesen	64	47.29 N	10.56 E
Griesheim	56	49.50 N	8.34 E
Gries im Sellrain	64	47.12 N	11.09 E
Grieskirchen	60	48.14 N	13.50 E
Griessem	52	52.00 N	9.12 E
Griesspitzen ∧	64	47.22 N	10.58 E
Griffen	61	46.42 N	14.44 E
Griffin, Sk., Can.	184	49.40 N	103.26 W
Griffin, Ga., U.S.	192	33.14 N	84.15 W
Griffin, Lake ⊜	220	28.52 N	81.51 W
Griffin Bay c	224	48.30 N	122.58 W
Griffiss Air Force Base ■	210	43.14 N	75.26 W
Griffith, Austl.	166	34.17 S	146.03 E
Griffith, In., U.S.	216	41.31 N	87.25 W
Griffith Airport ⊠	278	41.31 N	87.23 W
Griffith Island I, N.T., Can.	176	74.35 N	95.30 W
Griffith Island I, On., Can.	212	44.51 N	80.54 W
Griffith Park ♦	280	34.09 N	118.17 W
Grifton	192	35.22 N	77.26 W
Griggs Drain ≍	281	42.11 N	83.26 W
Griggs Reservoir ⊜1	214	40.03 N	83.06 W
Griggstown	276	40.26 N	74.36 W
Griggsville	219	39.42 N	90.43 W
Grignan	62	44.25 N	4.54 E
Grignano	64	45.42 N	13.43 E
Grignasco	62	45.41 N	8.20 E
Grigno	64	46.01 N	11.38 E
Grignols	32	44.23 N	0.03 W
Grignon	261	48.51 N	1.57 E
Grigny, Fr.	62	45.37 N	4.47 E
Grigny, Fr.	261	48.40 N	2.24 E
Grigoriopol	38	47.10 N	29.18 E
Grigorjevka, Kyrg.	85	42.43 N	77.30 E
Grigorjevka, Ross.	83	47.27 N	38.23 E
Grigorjevskoje, Ross.	82	54.49 N	37.59 E
Grigorjevskoje, Ross.	82	54.48 N	39.15 E
Grigorovka	82	54.38 N	36.20 E
Grigorovo	82	56.42 N	37.35 E
Grigorovskoje	82	54.17 N	36.21 E
Grijalva ≃, Méx.	232	18.36 N	92.39 W
Grijalva (Cuilco) ≃, N.A.	232	17.01 N	93.22 W
Grijpskerk	52	53.15 N	6.18 E
Grillby	40	59.37 N	17.15 E
Grillenburg	54	50.57 N	13.31 E
Grim, Cape >	166	40.41 S	144.41 E
Grima	152	3.59 N	17.06 E
Grimaldi	68	39.08 N	16.14 E
Grimari	152	5.44 N	20.03 E
Grimaud	62	43.16 N	6.31 E
Grimbergen	50	50.56 N	4.23 E
Grimeford Village	262	53.36 N	2.34 W
Grimes	226	39.04 N	121.54 W
Grimes □6	222	30.35 N	96.00 W
Grimlinghausen	263	51.10 N	6.44 E
Grimma	54	51.14 N	12.43 E
Grimmen	54	54.07 N	13.02 E
Grimmenstein	61	47.38 N	16.06 E
Grimmialp	58	46.34 N	7.29 E
Grimnitzsee ⊜	54	52.58 N	13.47 E
Grimsargh	262	53.48 N	2.38 W
Grimsby, On., Can.	212	43.12 N	79.34 W
Grimsby, Eng., U.K.	44	53.35 N	0.05 W
Grimselpass)(	58	46.34 N	8.21 E
Grimselsee ⊜	58	46.34 N	8.18 E
Grímsey I	24a	66.34 N	18.00 W
Grimshaw	182	56.11 N	117.36 W
Grímsstaðir	24a	65.40 N	16.01 W
Grimstad	26	58.20 N	8.36 E
Grimstead	208	37.30 N	76.18 W
Grímsvötn ∧	24a	64.24 N	17.22 W
Grindavík	24a	63.52 N	22.27 W
Grindelwald	58	46.37 N	8.02 E
Grindsted	41	55.45 N	8.56 E
Grindstone Island → Cap-aux-Meules	186	47.23 N	61.52 W
Grindstone Island I	212	44.16 N	76.07 W
Grinnell	190	41.44 N	92.43 W
Grinnell, Lake ⊜	276	41.06 N	74.38 W
Grinnell Peninsula >1	176	76.40 N	95.00 W
Grin'ovo	76	52.35 N	33.04 E
Grintavec ∧	61	46.21 N	14.32 E
Grinzing ✦8	264b	48.15 N	16.21 E
Grip	26	63.14 N	7.37 E
Gripsholm slott ⊥	40	59.15 N	17.13 E
Gripsholmsviken c	40	59.17 N	17.20 E
Griqualand East □9	158	30.30 S	29.00 E
Griqualand West □9	158	28.20 S	23.30 E
Grisdale	224	47.22 N	123.37 W
Grisee → Gresik	115a	7.09 S	112.38 E
Grišino	82	56.13 N	37.40 E
Gris-Nez, Cap >	50	50.52 N	1.35 E
Grisolia	68	39.43 N	15.51 E
Grisons → Graubünden □3	58	46.45 N	9.30 E
Grisslehamn	40	60.06 N	18.50 E
Grissom Air Force Base ■	216	40.40 N	86.08 W
Gristow	54	54.10 N	13.20 E
Griswold, Mb., Can.	184	49.45 N	100.25 W
Griswold, Ia., U.S.	198	41.14 N	95.08 W
Griswold Creek ≃	279a	41.27 N	81.23 W
Griswoldville	207	42.39 N	72.42 W
Grisy-Suisnes	261	48.41 N	2.40 E
Grivaï Pamia	152	7.03 N	19.26 E
Grivenskaja	78	45.38 N	38.09 E
Grizzana	64	44.15 N	11.09 E
Grizzly Bay c	226	38.07 N	122.01 W
Grizzly Bear Mountain ∧	176	65.22 N	121.00 W
Grizzly Bear's Head and Lead Man Indian Reserve ✦4	184	52.33 N	108.16 W
Grizzly Creek ≃	282	37.52 N	122.06 W
Grizzly Flats	226	38.38 N	120.31 W
Grizzly Island I	282	38.08 N	121.58 W
Grizzly Mountain ∧, Id., U.S.	202	47.43 N	116.06 W
Grizzly Mountain ∧, Or., U.S.	202	44.26 N	120.57 W
Grizzly Mountain ∧, Wa., U.S.	202	48.25 N	118.30 W
Grizzly Slough ≃	282	38.06 N	121.53 W
Grmeč ⋏	36	44.40 N	16.30 E
Groaíras	250	3.53 S	40.23 W
Groais Island I	186	50.57 N	55.35 W
Grobbendonk	56	51.12 N	4.43 E
Gröben	264a	52.17 N	13.10 E
Gröbener-See ⊜	264a	52.17 N	13.11 E
Gröbenzell	60	48.11 N	11.22 E
Grobiņa	76	56.33 N	21.10 E
Groblersdal	156	25.15 S	29.25 E
Groblershoop	158	28.55 S	20.59 E
Gröbming	64	47.26 N	13.54 E
Grobogan	115a	7.01 S	110.55 E
Gröbzig	54	51.41 N	11.52 E
Grodekovo	85	42.49 N	71.29 E
Grödig	64	47.44 N	13.02 E
Gröditsch	54	52.03 N	13.59 E
Gröditz	54	51.24 N	13.27 E
Grodków	30	50.43 N	17.22 E
Grodno	76	53.41 N	23.50 E
Grodno □8	76	53.30 N	25.00 E
Grodz'anka	76	53.33 N	28.45 E
Grodzisk Mazowiecki	30	52.07 N	20.37 E
Grodzisk [Wielkopolski]	30	52.14 N	16.22 E
Groede	52	51.23 N	3.30 E
Groen ≃, S. Afr.	158	30.40 S	23.17 E
Groen ≃, S. Afr.	158	29.00 S	22.10 E
Groënland → Greenland □2	16	70.00 N	40.00 W
Groenlandia → Greenland □2	16	70.00 N	40.00 W
Groenlo	52	52.03 N	6.38 E
Groenvlei	158	27.27 S	30.13 E
Groesbeck, Oh., U.S.	218	39.13 N	84.35 W
Groesbeck, Tx., U.S.	222	31.31 N	96.32 W
Groesbeek	52	51.47 N	5.55 E
Grofa, hora ∧	78	48.37 N	23.56 E
Grogol, Kali ≃	269e	6.10 S	106.47 E
Grogol-hilir ✦8	269e	6.13 S	106.47 E
Grohnde	52	52.01 N	9.25 E
Groitzsch	54	51.09 N	12.16 E
Groix	32	47.38 N	3.28 W
Groix, Île de I	32	47.38 N	3.27 W
Grójec	30	51.52 N	20.52 E
Grokgak	115a	8.11 S	114.47 E
Grolley	58	46.50 N	7.05 E
Grombalia	148	36.36 N	10.30 E
Grömitz	54	54.09 N	10.58 E
Gromo	64	45.58 N	9.56 E
Gromoslavka	80	48.12 N	43.37 E
Gronau, Dtsch.	52	52.13 N	7.00 E
Gronau, Dtsch.	52	52.05 N	9.46 E
Grondines (Saint-Charles-des-Grondines)	206	46.36 N	72.03 W
Grondneus	158	28.06 S	20.48 E
Grone	52	51.32 N	9.53 E
Grönenbach	58	47.52 N	10.13 E
Grong	24	64.28 N	12.18 E
Gröningen, Dtsch.	54	51.56 N	11.13 E
Groningen, Ned.	52	53.13 N	6.33 E
Groningen, Sur.	250	5.48 N	55.28 W
Groningen □4	52	53.15 N	6.45 E
Grønland → Greenland □2	16	70.00 N	40.00 W
Gronlid	184	53.06 N	104.28 W
Grønsund ʊ	41	54.53 N	12.08 E
Grönwohld	52	53.39 N	10.25 E
Groom	196	35.12 N	101.06 W
Groom Lake ⊜	204	37.15 N	115.48 W
Groot ≃, S. Afr.	158	33.54 S	21.39 E
Groot ≃, S. Afr.	158	33.45 S	24.36 E
Groot-Berg ≃	158	32.47 S	18.08 E
Groot-Brakrivier	158	34.02 S	22.14 E
Grootdraaidam ⊜1	158	26.56 S	29.20 E
Grootebroek	52	52.43 N	5.13 E
Groote Eylandt I	164	14.00 S	136.40 E
Groote Eylandt Aboriginal Reserve ✦4	164	14.00 S	136.40 E
Grootfontein	156	19.32 S	18.05 E
Groot Karasberge ⋏	158	27.20 S	18.40 E
Groot Karroo → Great Karroo ⋏1	158	32.25 S	22.40 E
Groot-Kei ≃	158	32.41 S	28.22 E
Groot Laagte ≃	156	20.37 S	21.37 E
Groot-Letaba ≃	156	23.58 S	31.50 E
Groot-Marico	156	25.37 S	26.26 E
Grootpan	158	25.58 S	26.33 E
Groot-Swartberge ⋏	158	33.22 S	22.20 E
Groot-Vis ≃	158	33.30 S	27.08 E
Grootvlei	158	26.44 S	28.32 E
Grootvloer ≚	158	30.00 S	20.40 E
Gröpelingen ✦8	52	53.07 N	8.46 E
Gropello Cairoli	62	45.11 N	9.00 E
Gropeni	38	45.04 N	27.53 E
Grosbliederstroff	56	49.09 N	7.01 E
Gros Bois, Parc de ♦	261	48.44 N	2.32 E
Groscavallo	62	45.22 N	7.15 E
Grose ≃	170	33.36 S	150.41 E
Grosio	64	46.18 N	10.16 E
Gros Islet	241f	14.05 N	60.58 W
Groslay	261	48.59 N	2.21 E
Gros Mécatina, Cap du >	186	50.45 N	59.00 W
Gros-Morne	240e	14.43 N	61.01 W
Gros Morne ∧	186	49.36 N	57.48 W
Gros Morne National Park ♦	186	49.40 N	57.45 W
Grosne ≃	58	46.42 N	4.56 E
Grosnez Point >	43b	49.16 N	2.15 W
Grosotto	64	46.17 N	10.15 E
Gros Piton ∧	241f	13.49 N	61.04 W
Grosrouvre	261	48.47 N	1.46 E
Grossa, Ponta >, Bra.	256	23.35 S	45.13 W
Grossa, Ponta >, Bra.	287a	22.47 S	43.11 W
Grossache (Tiroler Ache) ≃	60	47.51 N	12.30 E
Grossaitingen	58	48.14 N	10.47 E
Grossalmerode	56	51.15 N	9.46 E
Grossalsleben	54	51.59 N	11.13 E
Gross Ammensleben	54	52.14 N	11.31 E
Grossarl	64	47.14 N	13.12 E
Gross-Beeren	54	52.21 N	13.18 E
Gross Berkel	52	52.04 N	9.19 E
Grossbodungen	54	51.28 N	10.28 E
Gross Börnecke	54	51.50 N	11.29 E
Grossbothen	54	51.11 N	12.44 E
Grossbottwar	56	49.00 N	9.17 E
Grossbreitenbach	54	50.35 N	11.02 E
Grossdeuben	54	51.14 N	12.23 E
Grossdubrau	54	51.15 N	14.28 E
Gross Düngen	52	52.06 N	10.01 E
Grosse Antillen → Greater Antilles II	238	20.00 N	74.00 W
Grosse Aue ≃	52	52.37 N	9.10 E
Grosse Australische Bucht → Great Australian Bight c3	162	35.00 S	135.00 E
Grossebersdorf	54	50.47 N	11.57 E
Grosse Ebene → Great Plains ≚	16	42.00 N	100.00 W
Grossefehn	52	53.24 N	7.36 E
Grosse Herrenwiese ≡	264a	52.17 N	13.20 E
Grosse Ile	216	42.08 N	83.09 W
Grosse Ile I	216	42.08 N	83.09 W
Grosse Île, La I	186	47.37 N	61.31 W
Grosse Laber ≃	60	48.56 N	12.30 E
Grosse Mühl ≃	61	48.25 N	13.59 E
Grossenbaum ✦8	263	51.22 N	6.47 E
Grossenbrode	54	54.22 N	11.05 E
Grossengottern	54	51.09 N	10.34 E
Grossengstingen	58	48.23 N	9.17 E
Grossenhain	54	51.17 N	13.31 E
Grossenkneten	52	52.56 N	8.16 E
Grossen-Linden	56	50.31 N	8.39 E
Grossenlüder	56	50.35 N	9.32 E
Grossenritte	56	51.15 N	9.23 E
Grossenwiehe	41	54.43 N	9.15 E
Gross-Enzersdorf	61	48.12 N	16.33 E
Grosse Pointe	214	42.23 N	82.54 W
Grosse Pointe >	241o	16.01 N	61.16 W
Grosse Pointe Farms	214	42.25 N	82.53 W
Grosse Pointe Park	214	42.22 N	82.56 W
Grosse Pointe Shores	214	42.26 N	82.53 W
Grosse Pointe Woods	214	42.26 N	82.54 W
Grosser Arber ∧	60	49.07 N	13.07 E
Grosser Bären-See → Great Bear Lake ⊜	176	66.00 N	120.00 W
Grosser Beerberg ∧	54	50.37 N	10.44 E
Grosser Bösenstein ∧	61	47.26 N	14.24 E
Grosser Buchstein ∧	61	47.36 N	14.35 E
Grosser Chingan → Da Hinggan Ling ⋏	90	49.00 N	122.00 E
Grosser Feldberg ∧	56	50.14 N	8.26 E
Grosser Galtenberg ∧	64	47.20 N	11.58 E
Grosser Gleichberg ∧	54	50.23 N	10.35 E
Grosser Heuberg ⋏1	58	48.06 N	8.55 E
Grosser Inselsberg ∧	54	50.52 N	10.28 E
Grosser Jasmunder Bodden c	54	54.31 N	13.29 E
Grosser Knallstein ∧	61	47.19 N	13.58 E
Grosser Königstuhl ∧	64	46.57 N	13.47 E
Grosser Müggelsee ⊜	54	52.26 N	13.39 E
Grosse Röder ≃	54	51.30 N	13.25 E
Grosser oder Kaiser-Kanal → Da Yunhe ≍	90	32.12 N	119.31 E
Grosse Rodl ≃	61	48.20 N	14.09 E
Grosser Peilstein ∧	61	48.18 N	15.06 E
Grosser Plessower See ⊜	264a	52.23 N	12.54 E
Grosser Plöner See ⊜	54	54.06 N	10.25 E
Grosser Priel ∧	61	47.43 N	14.04 E
Grosser Rachel ∧	60	48.59 N	13.24 E
Grosser Ravens-Berg ∧2	264a	52.21 N	13.04 E
Grosser Salz-See → Great Salt Lake ⊜	200	41.10 N	112.30 W
Grosser Seddiner See ⊜	264a	52.17 N	13.02 E
Grosser Selchower See ⊜	54	52.14 N	13.53 E
Grosser Sklaven-See → Great Slave Lake ⊜	176	61.30 N	114.00 W
Grosser Speikkogel ∧	61	46.47 N	14.58 E
Grosser Walfisch-Fluss → Baleine, Grande rivière de la ≃	176	55.16 N	77.47 W
Grosser Wannsee ⊜	264a	52.26 N	13.11 E
Grosser Winterberg ∧2	54	50.54 N	14.16 E
Grosser Zern-See ⊜	264a	52.24 N	12.56 E
Grosse Sandspitze ∧	64	46.46 N	12.49 E
Grosse Sandwüste → Great Sandy Desert ✦2	162	21.30 S	125.00 E
Grosses Barrier-Riff → Great Barrier Reef ✧2	160	18.00 S	145.50 E
Grosses Meer ⊜	52	53.25 N	7.17 E
Grosses Moor ✦3, Dtsch.	52	52.35 N	8.45 E
Grosses Moor ✦3, Dtsch.	52	52.40 N	8.20 E
Grosses Schulerloch ♦	60	48.55 N	11.48 E
Grosse Sundainseln → Greater Sunda Islands II	108	2.00 S	110.00 E
Grosses Walsertal V	58	47.14 N	9.56 E
Grosse Syrte → Surt, Khalīj c	146	31.30 N	18.00 E
Grosseto	66	42.46 N	11.08 E
Grosseto □4	66	42.50 N	11.15 E
Grosseto, Formiche di I	66	42.39 N	10.53 E
Grosse Tulln ≃	61	48.20 N	16.02 E
Grossevići	89	47.59 N	139.30 E
Grosse Windgällen ∧	58	46.49 N	8.44 E
Gross-Gerau	56	49.55 N	8.29 E
Gross-Gerungs	61	48.34 N	14.57 E
Gross Gleidingen	54	52.14 N	10.25 E
Gross Glienicke	264a	52.28 N	13.07 E
Gross-Glienicker See ⊜	264a	52.28 N	13.06 E
Grossglockner ∧	64	47.04 N	12.42 E
Grossgmain	64	47.43 N	12.55 E
Grossgörschen	54	51.13 N	12.11 E
Gross Grönau	54	53.46 N	10.44 E
Grosshansdorf	52	53.40 N	10.17 E
Grosshartmannsdorf	54	50.48 N	13.19 E
Gross-Hehlen	52	52.39 N	10.03 E
Grossheide	52	53.35 N	7.20 E
Grosshennersdorf	54	50.59 N	14.47 E
Grosshöchstetten	58	46.55 N	7.38 E
Grossholzleute	58	47.41 N	10.05 E
Grossjedlersdorf ✦8	264b	48.17 N	16.25 E
Grosskayna	54	51.17 N	11.56 E
Gross Kienitz	264a	52.19 N	13.28 E
Gross-Kollmar	52	53.44 N	9.30 E
Grosskorbetha	54	51.16 N	12.01 E
Gross Kreutz	54	52.24 N	12.46 E
Grosskrut	61	48.38 N	16.43 E
Grosslehna	54	51.18 N	12.10 E
Gross Leine	54	52.00 N	14.03 E
Grosslittgen	56	50.02 N	6.47 E
Gross-Machnow	264a	52.16 N	13.28 E
Grossmehring	60	48.46 N	11.32 E
Grossmont	228	32.47 N	116.59 W
Gross Muckrow	54	52.04 N	14.26 E
Gross Oesingen	52	52.38 N	10.29 E
Grossörner	54	51.37 N	11.29 E
Grossos	250	4.59 S	37.09 W
Grossostheim	56	49.55 N	9.04 E
Grosspetersdorf	61	47.14 N	16.19 E
Grosspostwitz	54	51.07 N	14.26 E
Grossquenstedt	54	51.56 N	11.07 E
Grossraming	61	47.53 N	14.33 E
Grossräschen	54	51.35 N	14.00 E
Gross Rhüden	52	51.56 N	10.07 E
Grossrinderfeld	56	49.39 N	9.44 E
Gross Rodensleben	54	52.08 N	11.25 E
Grossröhrsdorf	54	51.08 N	14.01 E
Gross Rosenburg	54	51.55 N	11.53 E
Grossrückerswalde	54	50.38 N	13.07 E
Grossrudestedt	54	51.05 N	11.06 E
Gross Sankt Florian	61	46.49 N	15.19 E
Gross-Sarau	54	53.45 N	10.44 E
Grossschirma	54	50.58 N	13.17 E
Grossschönau	54	50.54 N	14.40 E
Gross Schönebeck	54	52.54 N	13.32 E
Gross-Schulzendorf	264a	52.16 N	13.21 E
Gross-Siegharts	61	48.48 N	15.24 E
Grosssölk	64	47.25 N	13.58 E
Gross-Umstadt	56	49.52 N	8.55 E
Grossvenediger ∧	64	47.06 N	12.21 E
Grosswardein → Oradea	38	47.03 N	21.57 E
Grossweil	64	47.41 N	11.18 E
Grossweissenbach	61	48.33 N	15.10 E
Gross Wittensee	41	54.24 N	9.46 E
Gross Ziethen, Dtsch.	264a	52.24 N	13.27 E
Gross Ziethen, Dtsch.	264a	52.44 N	13.01 E
Gross-Zimmern	56	49.52 N	8.50 E
Grostenquin	56	48.59 N	6.44 E
Grosvenor, Lake ⊜	180	58.40 N	155.15 W
Grosvenor Dale	207	41.58 N	71.53 W
Gros Ventre ≃	202	43.33 N	110.46 W
Groswater Bay c	176	54.20 N	57.30 W
Grote Nete ≃	56	51.07 N	4.34 E
Groton, Ct., U.S.	207	41.21 N	72.04 W
Groton, Ma., U.S.	207	42.36 N	71.34 W
Groton, N.Y., U.S.	210	42.35 N	76.22 W

Symbol	English	Deutsch	Español	Français	Português
≃	River	Fluß	Río	Rivière	Rio
≍	Canal	Kanal	Canal	Canal	Canal
L	Waterfall, Rapids	Wasserfall, Stromschnellen	Cascada, Rápidos	Chute d'eau, Rapides	Cascata, Rápidos
ʊ	Strait	Meeresstraße	Estrecho	Détroit	Estreito
c	Bay, Gulf	Bucht, Golf	Bahía, Golfo	Baie, Golfe	Baía, Golfo
⊜	Lake, Lakes	See, Seen	Lago, Lagos	Lac, Lacs	Lago, Lagos
≡	Swamp	Sumpf	Pantano	Marais	Pântano
≚	Ice Features, Glacier	Eis- und Gletscherformen	Accidentes Glaciales	Formes glaciaires	Acidentes glaciares
╤	Other Hydrographic Features	Andere Hydrographische Objekte	Otros Elementos Hidrográficos	Autres données hydrographiques	Outros acidentes hidrográficos

Symbol	English	Deutsch	Español	Français	Português
✧	Submarine Features	Untermeerische Objekte	Accidentes Submarinos	Formes de relief sous-marin	Acidentes submarinos
□	Political Unit	Politische Einheit	Unidad Política	Entité politique	Unidade política
⊽	Cultural Institution	Kulturelle Institution	Institución Cultural	Institution culturelle	Instituição cultural
⊥	Historical Site	Historische Stätte	Sitio Histórico	Site historique	Sítio histórico
♦	Recreational Site	Erholungs- und Ferienort	Sitio de Recreo	Centre de loisirs	Área de Lazer
⊠	Airport	Flughafen	Aeropuerto	Aéroport	Aeroporto
■	Military Installation	Militäranlage	Instalación Militar	Installation militaire	Instalação militar
✦	Miscellaneous	Verschiedenes	Misceláneo	Divers	Diversos

ENGLISH | DEUTSCH

Name	Page	Lat.°′	Long.°′
Groton, S.D., U.S.	**198**	45.26 N	98.05 W
Grottaferrata	**66**	41.47 N	12.40 E
Grottaglie	**68**	40.32 N	17.26 E
Grottaminarda	**68**	41.04 N	15.02 E
Grottammare	**66**	42.59 N	13.52 E
Grotte	**70**	37.24 N	13.42 E
Grotte di Castro	**66**	42.40 N	11.52 E
Grotteria	**68**	38.22 N	16.17 E
Grottoes	**188**	38.16 N	78.49 W
Grottole	**68**	40.36 N	16.23 E
Grou, Oued V	**148**	33.56 N	6.45 W
Grouard Mission	**182**	55.31 N	116.09 W
Groundbirch	**182**	55.47 N	120.55 W
Groundhog ≃	**176**	49.43 N	81.58 W
Grouse Creek ≃, Ks., U.S.	**198**	37.00 N	96.55 W
Grouse Creek ≃, Ut., U.S.	**200**	41.22 N	113.55 W
Grouse Creek Mountain ∧	**202**	44.22 N	113.54 W
Grouw	**52**	53.05 N	5.45 E
Grove, Eng., U.K.	**42**	51.36 N	1.25 W
Grove, Ok., U.S.	**196**	36.35 N	94.46 W
Grove, Pa., U.S.	**285**	40.01 N	75.38 W
Grove City, Fl., U.S.	**220**	26.54 N	82.19 W
Grove City, Mn., U.S.	**198**	45.09 N	94.40 W
Grove City, Oh., U.S.	**218**	39.52 N	83.05 W
Grove City, Pa., U.S.	**214**	41.09 N	80.05 W
Grove Hill	**194**	31.42 N	87.46 W
Groveland, Ca., U.S.	**226**	37.50 N	120.13 W
Groveland, Fl., U.S.	**220**	28.33 N	81.51 W
Groveland, Ma., U.S.	**207**	42.45 N	71.01 W
Groveland, N.Y., U.S.	**210**	42.39 N	77.46 W
Grovely Ridge ∧	**42**	51.08 N	2.04 W
Grove Mountains ⋏	**9**	72.53 S	74.53 E
Grove Park ◆[8]	**260**	51.26 N	0.01 E
Groveport	**218**	39.52 N	82.53 W
Grover	**210**	41.37 N	76.52 W
Grover City	**204**	35.07 N	120.37 W
Grover Cleveland Birthplace ⊥	**276**	40.50 N	74.16 W
Grover Cleveland Park ♦	**284a**	42.57 N	78.49 W
Grover Hill	**216**	41.01 N	84.28 W
Grovers Mills	**276**	40.19 N	74.37 W
Groves	**194**	29.56 N	93.55 W
Groveton, N.H., U.S.	**188**	44.35 N	71.30 W
Groveton, Pa., U.S.	**279b**	40.30 N	80.06 W
Groveton, Tx., U.S.	**222**	31.03 N	95.07 W
Groveton, Va., U.S.	**284c**	38.46 N	77.05 W
Grovetown	**192**	33.27 N	82.11 W
Groveville	**208**	40.10 N	74.40 W
Growa Point >	**150**	4.21 N	7.37 W
Growler Peak ∧	**200**	32.24 N	113.07 W
Growler Wash V	**200**	32.35 N	113.30 W
Groznoje	**85**	42.36 N	71.12 E
Groznyj	**84**	43.20 N	45.42 E
Groznyy → Groznyj	**84**	43.20 N	45.42 E
Grube, Dtsch.	**54**	54.14 N	11.01 E
Grube, Dtsch.	**264a**	52.26 N	12.57 E
Grubišno Polje	**36**	45.42 N	17.10 E
Grubweg	**60**	48.35 N	13.29 E
Grudziądz	**30**	53.29 N	18.45 E
Gruesa, Punta >	**248**	20.22 S	70.11 W
Gruetli-Laager	**194**	35.22 N	85.40 W
Grugapark ♦	**263**	51.26 N	7.00 E
Grugliasco	**62**	45.04 N	7.35 E
Gruia	**38**	44.16 N	22.42 E
Gruinard Bay ⊂	**46**	57.53 N	5.31 W
Gruinart, Loch ⊂	**46**	55.52 N	6.20 W
Gruiten	**56**	51.14 N	7.01 E
Gruitrode	**56**	51.05 N	5.35 E
Grulla	**196**	26.16 N	98.39 W
Grumello del Monte	**62**	45.38 N	9.52 E
Grumento Nova	**68**	40.17 N	15.53 E
Grumentum ⊥	**68**	40.17 N	15.55 E
Grumman-Bethpage Airport ⊠	**276**	40.45 N	73.29 W
Grumman Corporation ʊ[3]	**276**	40.45 N	73.30 W
Grumme ◆[8]	**263**	51.30 N	7.14 E
Grumo Appula	**68**	41.01 N	16.42 E
Grums	**26**	59.21 N	13.06 E
Grüna	**54**	50.49 N	12.47 E
Grünau	**156**	27.44 S	18.23 E
Grünau ◆[8]	**264a**	52.25 N	13.34 E
Grünau im Almtal	**64**	47.51 N	13.57 E
Grunavat, Loch ⊜	**46**	58.10 N	6.55 W
Grünbach	**54**	50.26 N	12.22 E
Grünberg, Dtsch.	**56**	50.35 N	8.58 E
Grünberg → Zielona Góra, Pol.	**30**	51.56 N	15.31 E
Grünburg	**61**	47.57 N	14.15 E
Grundlsee ⊜	**64**	47.38 N	13.52 E
Grundy	**192**	37.16 N	82.05 W
Grundy □[6]	**216**	41.22 N	88.26 W
Grundy Center	**190**	42.21 N	92.46 W
Grundy Lake Provincial Park ♦	**190**	45.48 N	80.34 W
Grünefeld	**264a**	52.41 N	12.58 E
Grünenplan	**52**	51.57 N	9.44 E
Grünewald, Dtsch.	**54**	51.24 N	14.00 E
Grünewald, Dtsch.	**263**	51.13 N	7.37 E
Grunewald ◆[8]	**264a**	52.30 N	13.17 E
Grunewald, Berliner Forst ◆[3]	**264a**	52.28 N	13.13 E
Grunewald, Jagdschloss ⊥	**264a**	52.28 N	13.16 E
Grünhain	**54**	50.35 N	12.48 E
Grünhainichen	**54**	50.46 N	13.08 E
Grünheide	**54**	52.25 N	13.49 E
Grünsfeld	**56**	49.36 N	9.44 E
Grünstadt	**56**	49.34 N	8.10 E
Grüntal	**264a**	52.45 N	13.44 E
Grunthal	**184**	49.25 N	96.52 W
Grünwald	**60**	48.02 N	11.31 E
Gruševka	**78**	47.55 N	40.40 E
Gruševka ≃	**83**	47.26 N	40.00 E
Gruševskaja	**83**	47.26 N	39.57 E
Grušino	**76**	59.27 N	44.09 E
Gruting	**46a**	60.14 N	1.30 W
Gruver	**196**	36.16 N	101.24 W
Gruyère, Lac de la ⊜	**58**	46.38 N	7.06 E
Gruyères	**58**	46.35 N	7.05 E
Gruzdžiai	**76**	56.06 N	23.16 E
Gruzija → Georgia □[1]	**72**	42.00 N	44.00 E
Gruziya → Georgia □[1]	**72**	42.00 N	44.00 E
Gruznovka	**88**	55.09 N	105.12 E
Gruzskaja Balka	**78**	46.25 N	40.19 E
Grybów	**30**	49.38 N	20.56 E
Grycken ⊜	**40**	60.27 N	16.13 E
Gryfice	**30**	53.56 N	15.12 E
Gryfino	**30**	53.12 N	14.30 E
Grytgöl	**40**	58.48 N	15.33 E
Grythyttan	**40**	59.42 N	14.32 E
Gschnitz	**64**	47.03 N	11.22 E
Gschütt, Pass)(	**64**	47.35 N	13.30 E
Gschwend	**56**	48.56 N	9.44 E
Gstaad	**58**	46.28 N	7.17 E
Gsteig	**58**	46.23 N	7.16 E
Gu ≃	**100**	27.02 N	115.03 E
Gua	**124**	22.12 N	85.23 E
Guabaria ≃[1]	**126**	22.10 N	90.30 E
Guabito	**236**	9.30 N	82.37 W
Guabu	**106**	32.16 N	118.53 E
Guacanayabo, Golfo de ⊂	**240p**	20.28 N	77.30 W
Guacara	**246**	10.14 N	67.53 W
Guacarí	**246**	3.46 N	76.20 W
Gu Achi	**200**	32.19 N	112.02 W
Guachinango	**234**	20.32 N	104.24 W
Guachiría ≃	**246**	5.27 N	70.36 W
Guachochi	**232**	26.51 N	107.05 W
Guaçuí	**255**	20.46 S	41.41 W
Guadajira ≃	**34**	38.52 N	6.41 W
Guadajoz ≃	**34**	37.50 N	4.51 W
Guadalajara, Esp.	**34**	40.38 N	3.10 W
Guadalajara, Méx.	**234**	20.40 N	103.20 W
Guadalajara □[4]	**34**	40.50 N	2.30 W
Guadalaviar ≃	**34**	40.21 N	1.08 W
Guadalcanal	**34**	38.06 N	5.49 W
Guadalcanal □[4]	**175e**	9.50 S	160.00 E
Guadalcanal I	**175e**	9.32 S	160.12 E
Guadalcázar	**234**	22.37 N	100.24 W
Guadalén ≃	**34**	38.05 N	3.32 W
Guadalén, Embalse de ⊜[1]	**34**	38.25 N	3.15 W
Guadalentin ≃	**34**	37.59 N	1.04 W
Guadalete ≃	**34**	36.35 N	6.13 W
Guadalhorce ≃	**34**	36.41 N	4.27 W
Guadalimar ≃	**34**	38.05 N	3.06 W
Guadalmena ≃	**34**	38.19 N	2.56 W
Guadalmez ≃	**34**	38.46 N	5.04 W
Guadalope ≃	**34**	41.15 N	0.03 W
Guadalquivir ≃	**34**	36.47 N	6.22 W
Guadalupe, Bol.	**248**	18.33 S	64.05 W
Guadalupe, Col.	**246**	2.01 N	75.45 W
Guadalupe, C.R.	**236**	9.57 N	84.03 W
Guadalupe, Méx.	**196**	28.09 N	100.36 W
Guadalupe, Méx.	**232**	25.41 N	100.15 W
Guadalupe, Méx.	**234**	22.45 N	102.31 W
Guadalupe, Perú	**248**	7.15 S	79.29 W
Guadalupe, Ca., U.S.	**204**	34.58 N	120.34 W
Guadalupe □[6]	**222**	29.37 N	97.45 W
Guadalupe ◆[8]	**287a**	22.50 S	43.23 W
Guadalupe → Guadeloupe □[2]	**241o**	16.15 N	61.35 W
Guadalupe ≃, Méx.	**204**	32.05 N	116.53 W
Guadalupe ≃, Ca., U.S.	**282**	37.25 N	121.58 W
Guadalupe ≃, Tx., U.S.	**196**	28.30 N	96.53 W
Guadalupe, Basílica de ʊ[1]	**286a**	19.29 N	99.07 W
Guadalupe, Isla I	**178**	29.00 N	118.16 W
Guadalupe, Presa de ⊜[1]	**286a**	19.37 N	99.16 W
Guadalupe, Sierra de ⋏, Esp.	**34**	39.26 N	5.25 W
Guadalupe, Sierra de ⋏, Méx.	**286a**	19.35 N	99.08 W
Guadalupe [Bravos]	**232**	31.23 N	106.07 W
Guadalupe del Norte ≚	**286a**	19.34 N	99.01 W
Guadalupe de Ramírez	**234**	17.45 N	98.10 W
Guadalupe Mountains ⋏	**196**	32.20 N	105.00 W
Guadalupe Mountains National Park ♦	**196**	31.55 N	104.55 W
Guadalupe Peak ∧	**196**	31.50 N	104.52 W
Guadalupe Seamount ✤[3]	**14**	27.50 N	168.45 E
Guadalupe Slough ≃	**282**	37.27 N	122.02 W
Guadalupe Victoria, Méx.	**196**	27.47 N	101.04 W
Guadalupe Victoria, Méx.	**232**	24.27 N	104.07 W
Guadalupe Victoria, Méx.	**234**	19.17 N	97.21 W
Guadalupe Victoria, Presa ⊜[1]	**234**	23.50 N	104.46 W
Guadalupita	**200**	36.08 N	105.14 W
Guadarrama, Puerto de)(	**34**	40.43 N	4.10 W
Guadarrama, Sierra de ⋏	**34**	40.55 N	4.00 W
Guadazaón ≃	**34**	39.42 N	1.36 W
Guadeloupe □[2], N.A.	**230**	16.15 N	61.35 W
Guadeloupe □[2], N.A.	**241o**	16.15 N	61.35 W
Guadeloupe Passage ꟷ	**238**	16.45 N	61.30 W
Guadiana ≃	**34**	37.14 N	7.22 W
Guadiana, Bahía de ⊂	**240p**	22.05 N	84.24 W
Guadiana Menor ≃	**34**	37.56 N	3.15 W
Guadiaro ≃	**34**	36.17 N	5.17 W
Guadiato ≃	**34**	38.20 N	5.22 W
Guadiela ≃	**34**	40.22 N	2.49 W
Guadix	**34**	37.18 N	3.08 W
Guafo, Isla I	**254**	43.36 S	74.43 W
Guagnano	**68**	40.24 N	17.57 E
Guagua	**116**	14.58 N	120.38 E
Guahe	**105**	39.12 N	115.00 E
Guaianases ◆[8]	**287b**	23.33 S	46.25 W
Guaíba	**252**	30.06 S	51.19 W
Guaíba ⊂[1]	**252**	30.15 S	51.12 W
Guaicaipuro □[5]	**286c**	10.25 N	66.57 W
Guaihe	**100**	33.28 N	112.59 E
Guaimaca	**236**	14.32 N	86.51 W
Guáimaro	**240p**	21.03 N	77.21 W
Guaimoreto, Laguna de ⊂	**236**	15.58 N	85.55 W
Guaimozi	**98**	41.31 N	125.26 E
Guainía □[5]	**246**	2.30 N	69.00 W
Guainía ≃	**246**	2.01 N	67.07 W
Guaió ≃	**287b**	23.31 S	46.19 W
Guaipava	**256**	21.40 S	45.43 W
Guaiquinima, Cerro ∧	**246**	5.49 N	63.40 W
Guaíra, Bra.	**252**	24.04 S	54.15 W
Guaíra, Bra.	**255**	20.19 S	48.18 W
Guairá □[5]	**252**	25.45 S	56.30 W
Guaire ≃	**286c**	10.25 N	66.46 W
Guáitara ≃	**246**	1.34 N	77.27 W
Guaitecas, Archipiélago de las II	**254**	43.57 S	73.50 W
Guajaba, Cayo I	**240p**	21.50 N	77.30 W
Guajará ≃	**250**	1.48 S	53.02 W
Guajará-Açu	**250**	1.38 S	48.07 W
Guajará-Miri	**250**	1.29 S	48.17 W
Guajará-Mirim	**248**	10.48 S	65.22 W
Guajataca ≃	**240m**	18.29 N	66.57 W
Guajataca, Lago de ⊜[1]	**240m**	18.23 N	66.55 W
Guajiasi	**104**	41.15 N	120.54 E
Gualaca	**236**	8.32 N	82.18 W
Gualaceo	**246**	2.54 S	78.47 W
Gualala	**204**	38.45 N	123.31 W
Gualán	**236**	15.08 N	89.22 W
Gualaquiza	**246**	3.24 S	78.33 W
Gualdo Tadino	**66**	43.14 N	12.47 E
Gualeguay	**252**	33.09 S	59.20 W
Gualeguay ≃	**252**	33.19 S	59.39 W
Gualeguaychú	**252**	33.01 S	58.31 W
Gualicho, Salina del ≚	**254**	40.24 S	65.15 W
Gualjaina	**254**	42.42 S	70.30 W
Gualtieri	**64**	44.54 N	10.38 E
Guam □[2], Oc.	**14**	13.28 N	144.47 E
Guam □[2], Oc.	**174p**	13.28 N	144.47 E
Guamá ≃, Bra.	**250**	1.29 S	48.30 W
Guamá ≃, Cuba	**240p**	22.11 N	83.41 W
Guamal, Col.	**246**	9.09 N	74.14 W
Guamal, Col.	**246**	3.52 N	73.44 W
Guamal, Quebrada ≃	**286c**	10.31 N	66.59 W
Guamblín, Isla I	**254**	44.51 S	75.05 W
Guaminí	**252**	37.02 S	62.25 W
Guam International Airport ⊠	**174p**	13.29 N	144.48 E
Guamo	**246**	4.02 N	74.58 W
Guamo Embarcadero	**240p**	20.37 N	76.58 W
Guamote	**246**	1.56 S	78.43 W
Guamúchil, Méx.	**232**	25.28 N	108.06 W
Guamúchil, Méx.	**234**	25.28 N	108.06 W
Guamués ≃	**246**	0.32 N	76.33 W
Gua Musang	**114**	4.53 N	101.58 E
Gu'an	**105**	39.26 N	116.18 E
Guan ≃, Zhg.	**100**	32.16 N	115.42 E
Guan ≃, Zhg.	**100**	34.29 N	119.49 E
Guanábana	**240m**	18.01 N	67.07 W
Guanabara, Baía de ⊂	**287a**	22.50 S	43.10 W
Guanabara, Palácio ʊ	**287a**	22.56 S	43.11 W
Guanacaste □[4]	**236**	10.30 N	85.15 W
Guanacaste, Cordillera de ⋏	**236**	10.45 N	85.05 W
Guanacaste, Parque Nacional ♦	**236**	10.50 N	85.30 W
Guanacaure, Cerro ∧	**236**	13.14 N	87.07 W
Guanaceví	**232**	25.56 N	105.57 W
Guanache ≃	**248**	5.53 S	74.21 W
Guanahacabibes, Golfo de ⊂	**240p**	22.08 N	84.35 W
Guanahacabibes, Península de >[1]	**240p**	21.57 N	84.35 W
Guana Island I	**240m**	18.29 N	64.34 W
Guanaja	**236**	16.27 N	85.54 W
Guanaja, Isla de I	**236**	16.30 N	85.55 W
Guanajay	**240p**	22.55 N	82.42 W
Guanajibo ≃	**240m**	18.10 N	67.11 W
Guanajibo, Punta >	**240m**	18.10 N	67.11 W
Guanajuato	**234**	21.01 N	101.15 W
Guanajuato □[3]	**234**	21.00 N	101.00 W
Guanambi	**255**	14.13 S	42.47 W
Guanaparo, Caño ≃	**246**	8.19 N	68.10 W
Guañape, Islas II	**248**	8.33 S	78.57 W
Guanare	**246**	9.03 N	69.45 W
Guanare ≃	**246**	8.13 N	67.46 W
Guanarito	**246**	8.42 N	69.12 W
Guanay	**248**	15.28 S	67.52 W
Guanay, Cerro ∧	**246**	5.51 N	66.18 W
Guanay, Cerro ∧[2]	**286d**	12.07 S	77.13 W
Guanbuqiao	**100**	29.56 N	114.21 E
Guanchao	**100**	26.41 N	114.58 E
Guancheng, Zhg.	**100**	30.11 N	121.25 E
Guancheng, Zhg.	**107**	30.01 N	103.54 E
Guancun	**106**	31.30 N	119.43 E
Guandacol	**252**	29.31 S	68.32 W
Guandanghu	**100**	30.06 N	113.37 E
Guandi, Zhg.	**98**	41.48 N	116.52 E
Guandi, Zhg.	**98**	42.37 N	118.27 E
Guandian	**100**	32.40 N	118.04 E
Guandu, Zhg.	**100**	24.17 N	113.53 E
Guandu, Zhg.	**107**	30.04 N	106.25 E
Guane	**240p**	22.12 N	84.05 W
Guang'an	**107**	30.28 N	106.39 E
Guang'anmen Station ◆[5]	**271a**	39.53 N	116.20 E
Guangchang	**100**	26.50 N	116.14 E
Guangde	**106**	30.54 N	119.26 E
Guangdong (Kwangtung) □[4]	**90**	23.00 N	113.00 E
Guangfeng	**100**	28.25 N	118.11 E
Guangfu, Zhg.	**106**	31.18 N	120.23 E
Guangfu, Zhg.	**107**	30.13 N	104.41 E
Guangfu, Zhg.	**269b**	31.21 N	121.19 E
Guangfuyingzi	**104**	42.14 N	120.58 E
Guanghua	**102**	32.25 N	111.36 E
Guangji	**100**	29.52 N	115.34 E
Guangling, Zhg.	**98**	39.47 N	114.17 E
Guangling, Zhg.	**106**	32.06 N	120.13 E
Guanglu Dao I	**98**	39.09 N	122.21 E
Guangmao Shan ∧	**102**	27.02 N	100.58 E
Guangming Ding ∧	**100**	30.07 N	118.10 E
Guangnan	**102**	24.10 N	105.06 E
Guangningsi, Zhg.	**98**	40.27 N	118.31 E
Guangningsi, Zhg.	**98**	39.08 N	121.45 E
Guangping	**98**	36.30 N	114.57 E
Guangrao	**98**	37.02 N	118.25 E
Guangsbunchang	**107**	29.22 N	105.31 E
Guangshan	**100**	32.02 N	114.52 E
Guangshui	**100**	31.40 N	114.00 E
Guangxing	**107**	29.04 N	106.33 E
Guangxi Zhuangzu Zizhiqu (Kwangsi Chuang) □[4]	**102**	24.00 N	109.00 E
Guangyuan	**102**	32.26 N	105.52 E
Guangyuanzhen	**107**	30.37 N	104.47 E
Guangze	**100**	27.32 N	117.20 E
Guangzhen	**106**	30.45 N	121.07 E
Guangzhou (Canton)	**100**	23.06 N	113.16 E
Guangzong	**98**	37.06 N	115.08 E
Guanhães	**255**	18.46 S	42.53 W
Guanhu	**98**	34.26 N	117.59 E
Guánica	**240m**	17.58 N	66.55 W
Guánica, Laguna de ⊜	**240m**	18.00 N	66.56 W
Guaniguanico, Cordillera de ⋏	**240p**	22.35 N	83.45 W
Guanipa ≃	**246**	9.56 N	62.26 W
Guanjian	**107**	29.59 N	105.59 E
Guanjian ≃	**107**	30.00 N	106.01 E
Guankou, Zhg.	**100**	30.35 N	115.20 E
Guankou, Zhg.	**107**	30.39 N	103.26 E
Guanlin	**106**	31.32 N	119.42 E
Guanling	**102**	25.57 N	105.29 E
Guanlipu	**104**	41.37 N	123.18 E
Guanmenshan	**89**	47.23 N	122.20 E
Guannan (Xin'anzhen)	**98**	34.07 N	119.23 E
Guano	**246**	1.35 S	78.38 W
Guano Creek ≃	**202**	42.12 N	119.31 W
Guanputou	**105**	38.58 N	117.04 E
Guanqian, Zhg.	**100**	30.42 N	117.39 E
Guanqian, Zhg.	**100**	27.48 N	118.31 E
Guanqian, Zhg.	**100**	25.57 N	116.33 E
Guanqian, Zhg.	**100**	26.12 N	117.57 E
Guanqiao, Zhg.	**98**	34.58 N	117.14 E
Guanqiao, Zhg.	**100**	25.03 N	118.06 E
Guanqiaopu	**100**	31.08 N	112.54 E
Guanshanchang	**107**	28.46 N	103.42 E
Guanshi	**100**	26.43 N	112.53 E
Guanshui	**98**	40.55 N	124.33 E
Guanta	**246**	10.14 N	64.36 W
Guantánamo	**240p**	20.08 N	75.12 W
Guantánamo □[4]	**240p**	20.20 N	75.00 W
Guantánamo ≃	**240p**	19.55 N	75.12 W
Guantánamo, Bahía de ⊂	**240p**	20.00 N	75.08 W
Guantanamo Bay Naval Station ■	**240p**	19.55 N	75.10 W
Guantang	**106**	31.37 N	119.06 E
Guantangqiao	**106**	32.09 N	119.27 E
Guantao (Nanguantao)	**98**	36.35 N	115.19 E
Guanting, Zhg.	**100**	34.19 N	113.47 E
Guanting, Zhg.	**105**	40.13 N	115.37 E
Guanting Shuiku ⊜[1]	**105**	40.20 N	115.38 E
Guantou, Zhg.	**100**	28.03 N	120.41 E
Guantou, Zhg.	**100**	26.08 N	119.33 E
Guantunpu	**98**	40.28 N	113.24 E
Guanxian, Zhg.	**98**	36.30 N	115.27 E
Guanxian, Zhg.	**102**	31.00 N	103.40 E
Guanxun	**100**	24.19 N	117.45 E
Guanyin	**107**	30.16 N	103.51 E
Guanyinchang, Zhg.	**107**	29.15 N	104.02 E
Guanyinchang, Zhg.	**107**	30.28 N	105.16 E
Guanyingzicun	**104**	41.52 N	121.53 E
Guanyinpu	**107**	28.58 N	104.53 E
Guanyinqiao, Zhg.	**107**	29.05 N	104.46 E
Guanyinqiao, Zhg.	**107**	29.46 N	104.12 E
Guanyinshan	**106**	32.01 N	120.58 E
Guanyinsi	**106**	31.48 N	118.57 E
Guanyintan	**107**	29.35 N	105.14 E
Guanyintang, Zhg.	**100**	31.01 N	112.35 E
Guanyintang, Zhg.	**105**	39.52 N	116.31 E
Guanyintang, Zhg.	**106**	32.09 N	121.09 E
Guanyinzhen	**107**	29.06 N	104.24 E
Guanyinzhou	**100**	29.30 N	113.09 E
Guanyun (Dayishan)	**98**	34.20 N	119.17 E
Guanzhuang, Zhg.	**98**	37.12 N	114.30 E
Guanzhuang, Zhg.	**100**	32.49 N	114.16 E
Guanzhuang, Zhg.	**100**	28.58 N	117.24 E
Guapí	**246**	2.36 N	77.54 W
Guapiaçu ≃	**256**	22.40 S	42.55 W
Guapiara	**255**	24.10 S	48.32 W
Guápiles	**236**	10.13 N	83.46 W
Guapimirim	**256**	22.32 S	42.59 W
Guapimirim ≃	**256**	22.40 S	42.58 W
Guapo Bay ⊂	**241r**	10.12 N	61.40 W
Guaporé	**252**	28.51 S	51.54 W
Guaporé (Itenes) ≃	**248**	11.54 S	65.01 W
Guaqui	**248**	16.35 S	68.51 W
Guará ≃	**255**	12.59 S	44.49 W
Guara, Sierra de ⋏	**34**	42.17 N	0.10 W
Guarabira	**250**	6.51 S	35.29 W
Guaraçaí	**255**	21.02 S	51.11 W
Guaracarumbo	**286c**	10.34 N	66.59 W
Guaraci	**255**	20.29 S	48.57 W
Guaraciaba do Norte	**250**	4.10 S	40.46 W
Guaraciana	**255**	17.03 S	43.41 W
Guaraguara, Punta >	**241r**	10.31 N	62.19 W
Guaraí ≃	**287a**	22.42 S	43.02 W
Guaramirim	**252**	26.27 S	49.00 W
Guaranda	**246**	1.36 S	79.00 W
Guaranésia	**256**	21.18 S	46.48 W
Guarani	**256**	21.22 S	43.03 W
Guaraniaçu	**252**	25.06 S	52.52 W
Guarani das Missões	**252**	28.08 S	54.34 W
Guarani de Goiás	**255**	13.59 S	46.31 W
Guarapari	**255**	20.40 S	40.30 W
Guarapiranga, Represa ⊜[1]	**256**	23.44 S	46.44 W
Guarapuava	**252**	25.23 S	51.27 W
Guaraqueçaba	**252**	25.17 S	48.21 W
Guarará	**256**	21.43 S	43.02 W
Guarará ≃	**287b**	23.39 S	46.30 W
Guararé	**246**	7.49 N	80.17 W
Guararema	**256**	23.25 S	46.02 W
Guaratiba, Morro de ∧	**287a**	23.04 S	43.33 W
Guaratinga	**255**	16.34 S	39.34 W
Guaratinguetá	**256**	22.49 S	45.13 W
Guaratinguetá ≃	**256**	22.49 S	45.13 W
Guaratuba	**252**	25.54 S	48.34 W
Guar Chempedak	**114**	5.52 N	100.28 E
Guarcino	**66**	41.48 N	13.19 E
Guarda	**34**	40.32 N	7.16 W
Guardado de Abajo	**196**	26.22 N	98.57 W
Guardafui, Cape → Caseyr >	**144**	11.49 N	51.15 E
Guardavalle	**68**	38.30 N	16.30 E
Guardea	**66**	42.37 N	12.18 E
Guardia Escolta	**252**	28.59 S	62.08 W
Guardiagrele	**66**	42.11 N	14.13 E
Guardia Lombardi	**68**	40.57 N	15.12 E
Guardia Mitre	**254**	40.26 S	63.41 W
Guardia Sanframondi	**68**	41.15 N	14.36 E
Guardo	**34**	42.47 N	4.50 W
Guareña	**34**	38.51 N	6.06 W
Guareña ≃	**34**	41.29 N	5.23 W
Guarenas	**246**	10.28 N	66.37 W
Guarenas ≃	**286c**	10.30 N	66.45 W
Guariba ≃	**248**	7.41 S	60.18 W
Guarico	**246**	9.32 N	69.48 W
Guárico □[3]	**246**	8.40 N	66.35 W
Guárico ≃	**246**	7.55 N	67.23 W
Guárico, Embalse del ⊜[1]	**246**	9.05 N	67.25 W
Guarico, Punta >	**240p**	20.37 N	74.44 W
Guariquito ≃	**246**	7.40 N	66.18 W
Guarizama	**236**	14.55 N	86.20 W
Guarujá	**256**	24.00 S	46.16 W
Guarulhos	**256**	23.28 S	46.32 W
Guarulhos □[7]	**287b**	23.26 S	46.29 W
Guasare ≃	**246**	11.03 N	72.02 W
Guasave	**232**	25.34 N	108.27 W
Guasdualito	**246**	7.15 N	70.44 W
Guasila	**71**	39.34 N	9.03 E
Guasipati	**246**	7.28 N	61.54 W
Guastalla	**64**	44.55 N	10.39 E
Guastatoya	**236**	14.51 N	90.04 W
Guāsuba ≃[1]	**126**	21.38 N	88.53 E
Guatajiagua	**236**	13.40 N	88.13 W
Guatemala, Cuba	**240p**	20.46 N	75.39 W
Guatemala, Guat.	**236**	14.38 N	90.31 W
Guatemala □[5]	**236**	14.40 N	90.30 W
Guatemala □[1], N.A.	**230**	15.30 N	90.15 W
Guatemala □[1], N.A.	**236**	15.30 N	90.15 W
Guatemala Basin ✤[1]	**16**	11.00 N	95.00 W
Guateque	**246**	5.00 N	73.28 W
Guatimozín	**252**	33.27 S	62.27 W
Guatopo, Parque Nacional ♦	**246**	10.05 N	66.25 W
Guatraché	**252**	37.40 S	63.32 W
Guatuaro Point >	**241r**	10.20 N	60.59 W
Guaugurina	**164**	10.37 S	150.28 E
Guavi ≃	**164**	7.49 S	143.15 E
Guaviare □[8]	**246**	2.00 N	72.00 W
Guaviare ≃	**246**	4.03 N	67.44 W
Guaxindiba ≃	**287a**	22.44 S	43.02 W
Guaxupé	**256**	21.18 S	46.42 W
Guayabal, Cuba	**240p**	20.42 N	77.36 W
Guayabal, Ven.	**246**	8.00 N	67.24 W
Guayabal, Lago ⊜[1]	**240m**	18.06 N	66.30 W
Guayabero ≃	**246**	2.36 N	72.47 W
Guayacán	**252**	29.58 S	71.22 W
Guayaguayare	**241r**	10.08 N	61.02 W
Guayalejo ≃	**234**	22.27 N	98.29 W
Guayama	**240m**	17.59 N	66.07 W
Guayambre ≃	**236**	14.26 N	86.02 W
Guayameo	**234**	18.12 N	101.19 W
Guayana → Ciudad Guayana	**246**	8.22 N	62.40 W
Guayana → Guyana □[1]	**246**	5.00 N	59.00 W
Guayaneco, Archipiélago II	**254**	47.45 S	75.10 W
Guayanés, Punta >	**240m**	18.04 N	65.48 W
Guayanilla	**240m**	18.01 N	66.47 W
Guayanilla, Bahía de ⊂	**240m**	18.00 N	66.46 W
Guayape	**236**	14.45 N	86.52 W
Guayape ≃	**236**	14.26 N	85.58 W
Guayapo ≃	**246**	4.30 N	67.35 W
Guayaquil	**246**	2.10 S	79.50 W
Guayaquil, Golfo de ⊂	**246**	3.00 S	80.30 W
Guayaramerín	**248**	10.48 S	65.23 W
Guayas □[4]	**246**	2.00 S	80.00 W
Guayas ≃, Col.	**246**	1.23 N	74.50 W
Guayas ≃, Ec.	**246**	2.36 S	79.52 W
Guayatayoc, Laguna de ⊜	**252**	23.25 S	65.51 W
Guaycora	**232**	28.50 N	109.21 W
Guaycurú, Arroyo ≃	**258**	34.00 S	56.50 W
Guaymas	**232**	27.56 N	110.54 W
Guaynabo	**240m**	18.22 N	66.07 W
Guayquiraró ≃	**252**	30.10 S	58.34 W
Guayuriba ≃	**246**	3.55 N	73.05 W
Guazacapán	**236**	14.04 N	90.25 W
Guazapares	**232**	27.22 N	108.15 W
Guazárachi	**232**	26.57 N	106.43 W
Guazhou	**106**	32.15 N	119.23 E
Guazunamby, Arroyo ≃	**288**	34.24 S	58.38 W
Guba, Ityo.	**144**	10.16 N	35.17 E
Guba, Zaïre	**154**	10.40 S	26.26 E
Gubacha	**86**	58.52 N	57.36 E
Gubam	**164**	8.40 S	141.55 E
Gubany	**76**	56.37 N	30.40 E
Gubari	**80**	51.32 N	42.33 E
Gubat	**116**	12.55 N	124.07 E
Gubavica ⌞	**36**	43.26 N	16.54 E
Gubbi	**122**	13.19 N	76.56 E
Gubbio	**66**	43.21 N	12.35 E
Gubeikou	**105**	40.42 N	117.09 E
Guben	**54**	51.57 N	14.43 E
Gubentaoligai	**104**	42.16 N	122.13 E
Gubin	**30**	51.56 N	14.45 E
Gubino, Ross.	**80**	53.19 N	48.44 E
Gubino, Ross.	**82**	55.42 N	39.07 E
Gubio	**146**	12.29 N	12.48 E
Gubkin	**78**	51.18 N	37.32 E
Gubug	**115a**	7.03 S	110.40 E
Gucheng (Zhengjiakou), Zhg.	**98**	37.22 N	115.56 E
Gucheng, Zhg.	**100**	33.59 N	117.29 E
Gucheng, Zhg.	**100**	25.53 N	116.11 E
Gucheng, Zhg.	**100**	32.46 N	118.32 E
Gucheng, Zhg.	**102**	32.18 N	111.35 E
Gucheng, Zhg.	**105**	40.32 N	116.02 E
Gucheng, Zhg.	**105**	39.08 N	115.42 E
Gucheng, Zhg.	**106**	30.29 N	119.46 E
Guchengcang	**100**	32.34 N	115.20 E
Gucheng Hu ⊜	**106**	31.17 N	118.54 E
Guchengzi, Zhg.	**104**	42.33 N	123.45 E
Guchengzi, Zhg.	**104**	40.58 N	122.36 E
Guchengzi, Zhg.	**104**	40.40 N	120.31 E
Guchengzi, Zhg.	**104**	41.44 N	123.35 E
Gučin-Us	**102**	45.27 N	102.25 E
Gücük	**130**	38.12 N	37.29 E
Gūdalūr	**122**	9.41 N	77.16 E
Gúdar, Sierra de ⋏	**34**	40.27 N	0.42 W
Gudauta	**84**	43.06 N	40.37 E
Gudbrandsdalen V	**26**	61.30 N	10.00 E
Gudenå ≃	**26**	56.29 N	10.13 E
Gudensberg	**56**	51.10 N	9.22 E
Gudermes	**84**	43.20 N	46.08 E
Guderup	**41**	54.59 N	9.53 E
Gudgenby ≃	**171b**	35.39 S	149.04 E
Gudhjem	**26**	55.13 N	14.59 E
Gudianzi	**100**	31.49 N	116.05 E
Gudivāda	**122**	16.27 N	80.59 E
Gudiyāttam	**122**	12.57 N	78.52 E
Gudme	**41**	55.09 N	10.43 E
Gudow	**54**	53.33 N	10.46 E
Güdül	**130**	40.13 N	32.15 E
Gūdūr	**122**	14.08 N	79.51 E
Gudvangen	**26**	60.52 N	6.50 E
Guebwiller (Gebweiler)	**58**	47.55 N	7.12 E
Guéckédou	**150**	8.33 N	10.09 W
Gué-de-Longroi	**261**	48.30 N	1.43 E
Gué-d'Hossus	**50**	49.57 N	4.32 E
Guédi, Mont ∧	**146**	12.14 N	18.58 E
Guéguen, Lac ⊜	**190**	48.06 N	77.13 W
Guéherville	**261**	48.32 N	1.53 E
Güejar ≃	**246**	2.55 N	73.14 W
Guélendeng	**146**	10.56 N	15.32 E
Guelma	**148**	36.28 N	7.26 E
Guelma □[5]	**148**	36.10 N	7.50 E
Guelph	**212**	43.33 N	80.15 W
Guémené-sur-Scorff	**32**	48.04 N	3.12 W
Güemes	**234**	23.56 N	99.00 W
Guemes Island I	**224**	48.33 N	122.37 W
Guené	**150**	11.44 N	3.13 E
Guenguel ≃	**254**	45.41 S	70.20 W
Guer	**32**	47.54 N	2.07 W
Guéra □[5]	**146**	11.30 N	18.30 E
Guéra, Massif de ∧	**146**	11.55 N	18.12 E
Guérande	**32**	47.20 N	2.26 W
Guercif	**148**	34.15 N	3.21 W
Guerdjoumane, Djebel ∧	**34**	36.25 N	2.51 E
Güere ≃	**246**	9.50 N	65.08 W
Guéréda	**146**	14.31 N	22.05 E
Guéret	**32**	46.10 N	1.52 E
Guérin Kouka	**150**	9.41 N	0.37 E
Guerla Mandata Shan ∧	**120**	30.26 N	81.20 E
Guermantes	**261**	48.51 N	2.42 E
Guerne	**214**	40.46 N	81.54 W
Guernes	**261**	49.01 N	1.38 E
Guerneville	**204**	38.30 N	123.00 W
Guernica, Arg.	**258**	34.56 S	58.25 W
Guernica → Gernika-Lumo, Esp.	**34**	43.19 N	2.41 W
Guernsey	**200**	42.16 N	104.44 W
Guernsey □[6]	**214**	40.08 N	81.30 W
Guernsey □[2], Europe	**22**	49.28 N	2.35 W
Guernsey □[2], Europe	**43b**	49.28 N	2.35 W
Guernsey Reservoir ⊜[1]	**198**	42.19 N	104.48 W
Guernsey State Park ♦	**198**	42.20 N	104.50 W
Guerrero, Méx.	**196**	28.20 N	100.23 W
Guerrero, Méx.	**232**	28.33 N	107.30 W
Guerrero □[3]	**234**	17.40 N	100.00 W
Guerrero Negro	**232**	27.56 N	114.08 W
Guerville	**261**	48.57 N	1.44 E
Guerzim	**148**	29.45 N	1.47 W
Guesle ≃	**261**	48.36 N	1.40 E
Guessou-Sud	**150**	10.03 N	2.38 E
Guest Peninsula >[1]	**9**	76.18 S	148.00 W
Gueydan	**194**	30.01 N	92.30 W
Guéyo	**150**	5.49 N	6.36 W
Gufang	**100**	29.04 N	119.32 E
Guffin Bay ⊂	**212**	44.01 N	76.09 W
Guga	**89**	52.43 N	137.35 E
Gugang	**100**	28.17 N	113.46 E
Guge ∧	**144**	6.10 N	37.26 E
Gugera	**123**	30.58 N	73.19 E
Gugging	**264b**	48.19 N	16.15 E
Güglia, Pass dal)(	**58**	46.28 N	9.44 E
Güglingen	**56**	49.04 N	9.00 E
Guglionesi	**66**	41.55 N	14.55 E
Gugu ∧	**144**	8.12 N	39.58 E
Guguan	**102**	40.27 N	99.13 E
Guguan I	**108**	17.19 N	145.51 E
Guhe	**100**	31.54 N	117.58 E
Gui ≃	**102**	23.28 N	111.18 E
Guia	**248**	15.22 S	56.14 W
Guia de Pacobaíba	**256**	22.43 S	43.10 W
Guia Lopes da Laguna	**248**	21.26 S	56.07 W
Guiana Basin ✤[1]	**18**	11.00 N	52.00 W
Guiana Island I	**240c**	17.07 N	61.44 W
Guibéroua	**150**	6.14 N	6.10 W
Guibes	**156**	26.41 S	16.42 E
Güicán	**246**	6.28 N	72.25 W
Guichen	**32**	47.58 N	1.48 W
Guichi	**100**	30.40 N	117.28 E
Guichón	**252**	32.21 S	57.12 W
Guicun	**100**	33.37 N	114.11 E
Guidan Roumji	**150**	13.40 N	6.42 E
Guidari	**146**	9.17 N	16.40 E
Guide	**102**	36.03 N	101.28 E
Guide, Mount ∧[2]	**162**	22.36 S	136.54 E
Guide Post	**44**	55.10 N	1.35 W
Guider	**146**	9.56 N	13.57 E
Guide Rock	**198**	40.04 N	98.19 W
Guidexiang	**107**	29.51 N	104.47 E
Guidigri	**146**	13.40 N	9.51 E
Guidimaka □[4]	**150**	15.30 N	12.10 W
Guidimouni	**150**	13.42 N	9.30 E
Guiding	**102**	26.34 N	107.14 E
Guidizzolo	**64**	45.19 N	10.35 E
Guidong	**100**	26.05 N	113.57 E
Guidonia	**66**	42.01 N	12.45 E
Guidouma	**152**	1.37 S	10.41 E
Guiers ≃	**62**	45.37 N	5.37 E
Guiers, Lac de ⊜	**150**	16.12 N	15.50 W
Guifujie	**100**	27.20 N	120.01 E
Guiglia	**64**	44.26 N	10.58 E
Guiglo	**150**	6.33 N	7.29 W
Guignes-Rabutin	**50**	48.38 N	2.48 E
Guihuayuan	**107**	30.37 N	105.25 E
Guihulngan	**116**	10.07 N	123.16 E
Güija, Lago de ⊜	**236**	14.17 N	89.31 W
Guijalo	**116**	13.44 N	123.52 E
Guiji	**100**	32.51 N	116.33 E
Guijingqiao	**106**	31.21 N	119.40 E
Guijuelo	**34**	40.33 N	5.40 W
Guil ≃	**62**	44.40 N	6.36 E
Guilarte, Monte ∧	**240m**	18.09 N	66.46 W
Guilderland	**210**	42.42 N	73.54 W
Guildford, Austl.	**274a**	33.51 S	150.59 E
Guildford, Eng., U.K.	**42**	51.14 N	0.35 W
Guildford □[8]	**260**	51.16 N	0.32 W
Guildford Cathedral ʊ[1]	**260**	51.14 N	0.35 W
Guildhall	**188**	44.33 N	71.33 W
Guildtown	**46**	56.28 N	3.24 W
Guiler	**89**	46.11 N	121.45 E
Guilford, Ct., U.S.	**207**	41.17 N	72.40 W
Guilford, In., U.S.	**218**	39.10 N	84.55 W
Guilford, Me., U.S.	**188**	45.10 N	69.23 W
Guilford, N.Y., U.S.	**210**	42.24 N	75.29 W
Guilford Courthouse National Military Park ♦	**192**	36.01 N	79.45 W
Guilherand	**62**	44.56 N	4.52 E
Guilin (Kweilin)	**102**	25.17 N	110.17 E
Guilinchang	**107**	30.13 N	105.50 E
Guilinzhen	**107**	30.15 N	104.53 E
Guillaume-Delisle, Lac ⊜	**176**	56.15 N	76.17 W
Guillaumes	**62**	44.05 N	6.51 E
Guillermo E. Hudson	**288**	34.47 S	58.10 W
Guillestre	**62**	44.40 N	6.39 E
Guillon	**50**	47.31 N	4.06 E
Guilsfield	**42**	52.42 N	3.09 W
Guilvinec	**32**	47.47 N	4.17 W
Guimarães, Bra.	**250**	2.08 S	44.36 W
Guimarães, Port.	**34**	41.27 N	8.18 W
Guimaras Island I	**116**	10.35 N	122.37 E
Guimaras Strait ꟷ	**116**	10.30 N	122.44 E
Guimba	**116**	15.40 N	120.46 E
Guimbal	**116**	10.40 N	122.19 E
Guimeishan	**100**	24.44 N	114.52 E
Guimu Zhang ∧	**100**	24.40 N	116.48 E
Guin	**194**	33.57 N	87.54 W
Guinan	**102**	35.24 N	100.57 E
Guinayang	**269f**	14.42 N	121.08 E
Guinayangan	**116**	13.54 N	122.27 E
Guinda	**226**	38.50 N	122.12 W
Guindulman	**116**	9.46 N	124.29 E
Guindulman Bay ⊂	**116**	9.44 N	124.29 E
Guiné → Guinea-Bissau □[1]	**150**	12.00 N	15.00 W
Guinea	**208**	38.08 N	77.26 W
Guinea (Guinée) □[1], Afr.	**134**	11.00 N	10.00 W
Guinea (Guinée) □[1], Afr.	**150**	11.00 N	10.00 W
Guinea, Gulf of ⊂	**10**	2.00 N	2.30 E
Guinea Basin ✤[1]	**10**	0.00	5.00 W
Guinea-Bissau (Guiné-Bissau) □[1], Afr.	**134**	12.00 N	15.00 W
Guinea-Bissau (Guiné-Bissau) □[1], Afr.	**150**	12.00 N	15.00 W
Guineacor Creek ≃	**170**	34.21 S	150.05 E
Guinea Ecuatorial → Equatorial Guinea □[1]	**152**	2.00 N	9.00 E
Guinea Rise ✤[3]	**10**	8.00 S	0.00
Guiné-Bissau → Guinea-Bissau □[1]	**150**	12.00 N	15.00 W
Guinecourt, Lac ⊜	**186**	50.55 N	69.16 W
Guinée → Guinea □[1]	**150**	11.00 N	10.00 W
Guinée-Bissau → Guinea-Bissau □[1]	**150**	12.00 N	15.00 W
Guinée équitoriale → Equatorial Guinea □[1]	**152**	2.00 N	9.00 E
Güines, Cuba	**240p**	22.50 N	82.02 W
Guînes, Fr.	**50**	50.52 N	1.52 E
Guingamp	**32**	48.33 N	3.11 W
Guinguinéo	**150**	14.16 N	15.57 W
Guinobatan	**116**	13.11 N	123.36 E
Güinope	**236**	13.51 N	86.55 W
Guintacan Island I	**116**	11.19 N	123.54 E
Guintinguintin, Mount ∧	**116**	12.25 N	122.24 E
Guintinua Island I	**116**	14.26 N	122.51 E
Guiones, Punta >	**236**	9.54 N	85.41 W
Guiong	**116**	6.25 N	122.01 E
Guiperreux	**261**	48.40 N	1.42 E
Guiperreux, Étang de ⊜	**261**	48.40 N	1.43 E
Guiping	**102**	23.20 N	110.09 E
Guir, Hammada du ◆[2]	**148**	30.45 N	3.15 W
Guir, Oued V	**148**	30.29 N	2.17 W
Güira de Melena	**240p**	22.48 N	82.30 W
Guiraí ≃	**255**	22.40 S	53.34 W
Guiratinga	**255**	16.21 S	53.45 W
Guiren	**100**	33.42 N	118.12 E
Güiria	**246**	10.34 N	62.18 W
Guiricema	**255**	21.00 S	42.43 W
Guisachan Forest ◆[3]	**46**	57.17 N	4.55 W
Guisanbourg	**250**	4.25 N	51.56 W
Guisborough	**44**	54.32 N	1.04 W
Guiscard	**50**	49.39 N	3.03 E
Guise	**50**	49.54 N	3.38 E
Guiseley	**44**	53.53 N	1.42 W
Guisijan	**116**	11.05 N	122.03 E
Güisisil ∧	**236**	12.37 N	86.13 W
Guist Creek ≃	**218**	38.09 N	85.13 W
Guitiriz	**34**	43.11 N	7.54 W
Guitou	**100**	24.58 N	113.25 E
Guitrancourt	**261**	49.01 N	1.47 E
Guîtres	**32**	45.03 N	0.11 W
Guitry	**150**	5.31 N	5.14 W
Guiuan	**116**	11.02 N	125.43 E
Guixi	**100**	28.16 N	117.10 E
Guixian	**102**	23.06 N	109.39 E
Guiyang, Zhg.	**100**	25.46 N	112.43 E
Guiyang (Kweiyang), Zhg.	**102**	26.35 N	106.43 E
Güiza ≃	**246**	1.22 N	78.36 W
Guizhou (Kweichow) □[4]	**102**	27.00 N	107.00 E
Gujarāt □[3]	**118**	22.00 N	72.00 E
Gūjar Khān	**123**	33.16 N	73.19 E
Gujba	**146**	11.30 N	11.55 E
Gujiabeng	**106**	30.45 N	120.59 E
Gujiang	**100**	27.11 N	114.49 E
Gujiatun	**104**	40.39 N	124.08 E
Gujiatuo	**107**	29.14 N	106.12 E
Gujiazhai	**269b**	31.22 N	121.28 E
Gujiazi, Zhg.	**104**	42.02 N	123.01 E
Gujiazi, Zhg.	**104**	41.44 N	124.11 E
Gujrānwāla	**123**	32.09 N	74.11 E
Gujrāt	**123**	32.34 N	74.05 E
Gukas'an	**84**	41.03 N	43.52 E
Gukou	**100**	26.27 N	118.38 E
Gukovo	**83**	48.03 N	39.56 E
Gul, Tanjong >	**271c**	1.17 N	103.39 E
Gul'a	**88**	54.41 N	121.01 E
Gul'aj-Borisovka	**78**	46.38 N	40.13 E
Gul'ajevskije Koški, ostrova II	**24**	68.55 N	55.10 E
Gulang	**102**	37.36 N	102.58 E
Gulaothi	**124**	28.36 N	77.47 E
Gulargambone	**166**	31.20 S	148.28 E
Gulbarga	**122**	17.20 N	76.50 E
Gulbene	**76**	57.11 N	26.45 E
Gul'ča	**85**	40.19 N	73.26 E
Gul'ča ≃	**85**	40.20 N	73.26 E
Guldasteh	**267d**	35.36 N	51.16 E
Guldborg	**41**	54.52 N	11.45 E
Guldborg Sund ꟷ	**41**	54.48 N	11.48 E
Guldsmedshyttan	**40**	59.42 N	15.06 E
Güldüzü	**130**	36.52 N	37.07 E
Gülebağdı	**130**	39.52 N	39.50 E
Guledagudda	**122**	16.03 N	75.48 E
Guleitou	**100**	23.47 N	117.36 E
Gülek Boğazı)(	**130**	37.16 N	34.48 E
Gulf □[5]	**164**	7.00 S	145.00 E
Gulf Gate Estates	**220**	27.15 N	82.31 W
Gulf Hammock	**192**	29.15 N	82.43 W
Gulf Harbors	**220**	28.14 N	82.45 W
Gulf Islands National Seashore ♦	**194**	30.14 N	88.42 W
Gulf of Alaska Seamount Province ✤	**16**	56.00 N	147.00 W
Gulfport, Fl., U.S.	**220**	27.45 N	82.40 W
Gulfport, Ms., U.S.	**194**	30.22 N	89.05 W
Gulf Shores	**194**	30.14 N	87.42 W
Gulf State Park ♦	**194**	30.16 N	87.40 W
Gulf Stream ≃	**212**	43.51 N	75.56 W
Gulgong	**166**	32.22 S	149.32 E
Guli	**106**	31.38 N	120.50 E
Gulian	**89**	52.55 N	122.19 E
Gulicun	**106**	31.52 N	118.41 E
Gul Imām	**123**	32.16 N	70.32 E
Gulistān, Pāk.	**120**	30.36 N	66.35 E
Gulistan, Uzb.	**85**	40.30 N	68.46 E
Guliya Shan ∧	**89**	49.48 N	122.25 E
Guljanci	**38**	43.38 N	24.42 E
Gulkana	**180**	62.16 N	145.23 W
Gull ≃	**212**	44.37 N	78.49 W
Gulland Rock II[1]	**42**	50.34 N	4.59 W

Symbols in the index entries represent the broad categories identified in the key at the right. Symbols with superior numbers (⋏[1]) identify subcategories (see complete key on page *I · 1).*

Symbole im Register stellen die rechts im Schlüssel erklärten Kategorien dar. Symbole mit hochgestellten Ziffern (⋏[1]) bezeichnen Unterabteilungen einer Kategorie (vgl. vollständiger Schlüssel auf Seite *I · 1).*

Los símbolos incluídos en el texto del índice representan las grandes categorías identificadas con la clave a la derecha. Los símbolos con numeros en su parte superior (⋏[1]) identifican las subcategorías (véase la clave completa en la página *I · 1).*

Les symboles de l'index représentent les catégories indiquées dans la légende à droite. Les symboles suivis d'un indice (⋏[1]) représentent des sous-catégories (voir légende complète à la page *I · 1).*

Os símbolos incluídos no texto do índice representam as grandes categorias identificadas com a chave à direita. Os símbolos com números em sua parte superior (⋏[1]) identificam as subcategorias (veja-se a chave completa à página *I · 1).*

∧ Mountain	Berg	Montaña	Montagne	Montanha
⋏ Mountains	Gebirge	Montañas	Montagnes	Montanhas
)(Pass	Paß	Paso	Col	Passo
V Valley, Canyon	Tal, Cañon	Valle, Cañón	Vallée, Canyon	Vale, Canhão
≚ Plain	Ebene	Llano	Plaine	Planície
> Cape	Kap	Cabo	Cap	Cabo
I Island	Insel	Isla	Île	Ilha
II Islands	Inseln	Islas	Îles	Ilhas
◆ Other Topographic Features	Andere Topographische Objekte	Otros Elementos Topográficos	Autres données topographiques	Outros acidentes topográficos

ESPAÑOL — Nombre / Página / Lat.°′ / Long.°′ W = Oeste
FRANÇAIS — Nom / Page / Lat.°′ / Long.°′ W = Ouest
PORTUGUÊS — Nome / Página / Lat.°′ / Long.°′ W = Oeste

Gullane 46 56.02 N 2.50 W
Gullfoss ⌞ 24a 64.24 N 20.08 W
Gullholmen 26 58.11 N 11.24 E
Gullion, Slieve ∧² 48 54.08 N 6.27 W
Gull Island I 281 42.32 N 82.41 W
Gullivan Bay ⊂ 220 25.52 N 81.38 W
Gull Lake 184 50.08 N 108.27 W
Gull Lake ⊜, Ab., Can. 182 52.35 N 114.00 W
Gull Lake ⊜, On., Can. 184 51.18 N 91.58 W
Gull Lake ⊜, On., Can. 212 44.51 N 78.47 W
Gull Lake ⊜, Mi., U.S. 216 42.24 N 85.25 W
Gull Lake ⊜, Mn., U.S. 190 46.25 N 94.20 W
Gullrock Lake ⊜ 184 50.58 N 93.40 W
Gullspång 40 58.59 N 14.06 E
Güllük 130 37.14 N 27.36 E
Güllük Körfezi ⊂ 130 37.12 N 27.20 E
Gulmarg 123 34.03 N 74.23 E
Gulnam 140 6.55 N 29.30 E
Gülnar 130 36.20 N 33.25 E
Gulong 89 45.51 N 124.14 E
Gulpen 56 50.48 N 5.54 E
Gülper See ⊜ 54 52.44 N 12.14 E
Gulph Mills 285 40.04 N 75.21 W
Gülpınar 130 39.32 N 26.07 E
Gul'ripš 84 42.57 N 41.06 E
Gul'šad 86 46.39 N 74.24 E
Gülşehir 130 38.45 N 34.38 E
Gulshan 126 23.49 N 90.27 E
Gulsvik 26 60.23 N 9.35 E
Gulu, Ug. 154 2.47 N 32.18 E
Gulu, Zhg. 120 28.06 N 89.17 E
Gulukguluk 115a 7.04 S 113.40 E
Guluogongba 120 34.20 N 84.50 E
Guluy 144 14.44 N 36.43 E
Gulwe 154 6.30 S 36.29 E
Gumaca 116 13.55 N 122.06 E
Gumahang 116 12.35 N 123.16 E
Gumal (Gowmal) ≃ 120 31.56 N 70.22 E
Gumare 156 19.21 S 22.12 E
Gumba, Ang. 152 11.40 S 16.34 E
Gumba, Zaïre 152 2.57 N 21.26 E
Gumbinnen → Gusev 76 54.36 N 22.12 E
Gumbiro 154 10.16 S 35.39 E
Gumel 150 12.39 N 9.22 E
Gumeracha 168b 34.49 S 138.53 E
Gumiao 100 32.26 N 113.16 E
Gumieńce ✦⁸ 54 53.25 N 14.30 E
Gumistskij zapovednik ♦ 84 43.15 N 41.05 E
Gumla 124 23.03 N 84.33 E
Gumma □⁵ 94 36.30 N 139.00 E
Gummersbach 56 51.02 N 7.34 E
Gummi 150 12.09 N 5.09 E
Gumpas Pond ⊜ 283 42.44 N 71.22 W
Gumpas Pond Brook ≃ 283 42.42 N 71.21 W
Gumpoldskirchen 264b 48.03 N 16.17 E
Gum Swamp Creek ≃ 192 32.08 N 82.55 W
Gumti ≃ 126 23.32 N 90.43 E
Gümüşçay 130 40.16 N 27.17 E
Gümüşhacıköy 130 40.53 N 35.14 E
Gümüşhane 130 40.27 N 39.29 E
Gümüşhane □⁴ 130 40.15 N 39.45 E
Gümüşkent 130 38.50 N 34.32 E
Gümüşköy ✦⁸ 267b 41.14 N 28.58 E
Gümüşova 130 40.51 N 30.57 E
Gümüşsü 130 38.14 N 30.01 E
Gun ≃ 216 42.28 N 85.40 W
Guna, India 124 24.39 N 77.19 E
Guna, Ityo. 144 8.19 N 39.51 E
Guna ∧ 144 11.42 N 38.12 E
Gunbar 166 34.01 S 145.25 E
Gun Barrel City 222 32.20 N 96.10 W
Gun Creek ≃ 284a 43.03 N 78.55 W
Gunda 88 52.47 N 111.44 E
Gundagai 166 35.04 S 148.07 E
Gundelfingen 56 48.33 N 10.22 E
Gundelsheim 56 49.17 N 9.09 E
Gundik 115a 7.12 S 110.54 E
Gundji 152 2.05 N 21.27 E
Gundlakamma ≃ 122 15.32 N 80.14 E
Gundlupet 122 11.48 N 76.41 E
Gündoğdu 130 40.15 N 27.07 E
Gündoğmuş 130 36.48 N 32.01 E
Guneh Ghar ∧ 123 35.19 N 71.47 E
Güney 130 38.09 N 29.05 E
Gungartan ∧ 171b 36.18 S 148.24 E
Gungi 152 6.21 S 19.15 E
Gungo 152 11.48 S 14.08 E
Güngören ✦⁸ 267b 41.01 N 28.53 E
Gungu 152 5.44 S 19.19 E
Gunib 84 42.25 N 46.57 E
Gunisao ≃ 184 53.54 N 97.58 W
Gunisao Lake ⊜ 184 53.33 N 96.15 W
Gunjrauliya 124 26.35 N 84.34 E
Gun Lake ⊜ 216 42.37 N 85.32 W
Gunma 94 36.24 N 139.00 E
Gunnar 176 59.23 N 108.53 W
Günnarijn 102 45.38 N 102.01 E
Gunnarn 26 65.00 N 17.40 E
Gunnbjørn Fjeld ∧ 16 68.55 N 29.53 W
Gunnebo 26 57.43 N 16.32 E
Gunnedah 166 30.59 S 150.15 E
Gunning Island I 276 40.22 N 73.59 W
Gunnislake 42 50.31 N 4.12 W
Gunnison, Co., U.S. 200 38.32 N 106.55 W
Gunnison, Ut,. U.S. 200 39.09 N 111.49 W
Gunnison ≃ 200 39.03 N 108.35 W
Gunnison, Lake Fork ≃ 200 38.28 N 107.19 W
Gunnison, North Fork ≃ 200 38.47 N 107.50 W
Gunn Peak ∧ 224 47.49 N 121.27 W
Gunong Mulu National Park ♦ 112 4.10 N 114.55 E
Gunpowder Creek ≃, Austl. 166 19.14 S 139.58 E
Gunpowder Creek ≃, Ky., U.S. 218 38.53 N 84.47 W
Gunpowder Falls ≃ 208 39.24 N 76.22 W
Gunpowder Falls State Park ♦ 208 39.37 N 76.40 W
Gunpowder River ⊂ 208 39.22 N 76.22 W
Gunsan → Kunsan 98 35.58 N 126.41 E
Gunskirchen 60 48.08 N 13.57 E
Gunston Cove ⊂ 208 38.40 N 77.09 W
Guntakal 122 15.10 N 77.23 E
Güntersberge 54 51.38 N 10.59 E
Guntersblum 56 49.47 N 8.21 E
Guntersdorf 61 48.39 N 16.03 E
Guntersville 194 34.21 N 86.17 W
Guntersville Dam ✦⁶ 194 34.13 N 86.23 W
Guntersville Lake ⊜¹ 194 34.45 N 86.03 W
Guntingsaga 114 2.33 N 99.39 E
Guntramsdorf 61 48.03 N 16.19 E
Guntung 114 1.38 N 101.34 E
Guntūr 122 16.18 N 80.27 E
Gunungkencana 115a 6.34 S 106.04 E
Gunungmegang 112 3.27 S 103.52 E
Gunungsahilan 112 0.06 N 101.18 E
Gunungsitoli 114 1.17 N 97.37 E
Gunungtua 114 1.30 N 99.37 E
Gunupur 122 19.05 N 83.49 E
Gunyidi 162 30.08 S 116.04 E
Günyüzü 130 39.24 N 31.50 E
Günz ≃ 58 48.27 N 10.16 E
Gunza ≃ 152 11.10 S 13.50 E
Günzburg 58 48.27 N 10.16 E
Gunzenhausen 56 49.07 N 10.45 E
Gunzigou 104 41.31 N 123.58 E
Guo ≃ 100 32.57 N 117.14 E
Guobei 107 29.33 N 105.08 E
Guodian 106 30.27 N 120.33 E
Guoji 100 32.59 N 113.06 E
Guojiadian 104 41.51 N 121.30 E
Guojiajiang 106 32.17 N 120.50 E
Guojiatun, Zhg. 98 41.31 N 117.02 E
Guojiatun, Zhg. 104 42.00 N 122.51 E
Guojiatun, Zhg. 104 40.52 N 122.04 E
Guojiawopeng 104 42.03 N 122.46 E
Guojiayao 105 40.37 N 115.39 E
Guojiayuan 106 32.10 N 120.35 E
Guojiga 86 43.47 N 80.48 E
Guoleizhuang 98 40.44 N 114.36 E
Guolutan 100 32.04 N 115.40 E
Guosu 98 38.24 N 114.00 E
Guoyang 100 33.32 N 116.12 E
Guoyangzhen 102 38.54 N 112.50 E
Guozhuang 98 35.25 N 117.10 E
Guozhuangmiao 106 31.49 N 119.01 E
Gupei 98 34.09 N 117.54 E
Gupis 123 36.14 N 73.26 E
Gura 80 57.18 N 51.25 E
Gura, Wādī V 140 17.28 N 35.10 E
Gurabo 240m 18.16 N 65.58 W
Guraferda 144 6.51 N 35.04 E
Gura Galbehei 38 46.43 N 28.42 E
Gurage ∧ 144 8.24 N 38.24 E
Gurahonț 38 46.16 N 22.21 E
Gura Humorului 38 47.33 N 25.54 E
Gurais 123 34.38 N 74.50 E
Guran 88 54.46 N 100.38 E
Gurara ≃ 150 8.12 N 6.41 E
Gurban Anggir 102 37.45 N 97.30 E
Gurban Obo 102 43.14 N 112.28 E
Gurdāspur 123 32.02 N 75.31 E
Gurdon 194 33.55 N 93.09 W
Gurdžaani 84 41.43 N 45.48 E
Güre 130 38.39 N 29.10 E
Gurejev 80 47.21 N 43.16 E
Gürgan 84 40.23 N 50.19 E
Gurgaon 124 28.28 N 77.02 E
Gurgei, Jabal ∧ 140 13.50 N 24.19 E
Gurghiului, Munții ✧ 38 46.41 N 25.12 E
Gurgó ∧² 61 46.31 N 16.50 E
Gurgueia ≃ 250 6.50 S 43.24 W
Gurgur 144 7.48 N 41.32 E
Gurha 120 25.11 N 71.40 E
Guri 144 7.27 N 40.36 E
Guri, Embalse de ⊜¹ 246 7.30 N 62.50 W
Gurig National Park ♦ 164 11.25 S 132.15 E
Gurjevo 82 54.42 N 36.28 E
Gurjevsk, Ross. 76 54.47 N 20.38 E
Gurjevsk, Ross. 86 54.17 N 85.56 E
Gurk 61 46.52 N 14.18 E
Gurk ≃ 61 46.36 N 14.31 E
Gurk ⚲¹ 61 46.52 N 14.15 E
Gurktaler Alpen ✧ 64 46.55 N 14.00 E
Gūr Kūh ∧ 128 26.06 N 58.28 E
Gurla Mandhata → Guerla Mandata Shan ∧ 120 30.26 N 81.20 E
Gurlevo 76 59.28 N 28.54 E
Gurnee 216 42.22 N 87.54 W
Gurnet Point ≻ 283 42.01 N 70.34 W
Gürpınar 128 38.18 N 43.25 E
Gurror 174q 9.27 N 138.04 E
Gursarai 124 25.37 N 79.11 E
Gurskoje 89 50.21 N 138.12 E
Gurskøy I 26 62.15 N 5.41 E
Gürsu 130 40.13 N 29.12 E
Gurué 154 15.25 S 36.58 E
Guru Har Sahāi 123 30.43 N 74.25 E
Gurumeti ≃ 154 2.05 S 33.57 E
Gurun, Malay. 114 5.49 N 100.29 E
Gürün, Tür. 130 38.43 N 37.17 E
Gurupá 250 1.25 S 51.39 W
Gurupi 250 11.43 S 49.04 W
Gurupi ≃ 250 1.13 S 46.06 W
Guru Sikhar ∧ 120 24.39 N 72.46 E
Gurvanbulag 88 47.38 N 103.31 E
Gurvansajchan 102 45.32 N 107.00 E
Gurvan Sajchan uul ✧ 102 43.50 N 103.30 E
Gurvantes 102 43.26 N 101.36 E
Gus' ≃ 80 55.00 N 41.11 E
Gusar 85 39.28 N 67.50 E
Gušari 85 38.55 N 68.51 E
Gusau 150 12.12 N 6.40 E
Gus'-Chrustal'nyj 80 55.37 N 40.40 E
Guselka 80 50.27 N 45.09 E
Güsen 54 52.21 N 11.59 E
Gusen ≃ 61 48.15 N 14.30 E
Gusev, Ross. 76 54.36 N 22.12 E
Gusev, Ross. 78 48.27 N 40.32 E
Gusevo 76 56.06 N 33.21 E
Gusevskij 80 55.40 N 40.34 E
Gushan, Zhg. 98 39.53 N 123.36 E
Gushan, Zhg. 98 36.30 N 116.53 E
Gushan, Zhg. 106 31.44 N 120.33 E
Gu Shan ∧, Zhg. 100 26.05 N 119.22 E
Gu Shan ∧, Zhg. 104 41.18 N 120.35 E
Gushanbeizifu 104 42.10 N 120.30 E
Gushankou 105 39.38 N 115.49 E
Gushantun 89 48.18 N 123.47 E
Gushanzi, Zhg. 98 40.22 N 120.03 E
Gushanzi, Zhg. 104 41.03 N 123.03 E
Gushi, Zhg. 100 28.34 N 119.24 E
Gushi, Zhg. 100 32.12 N 115.41 E
Gushiago 150 9.55 N 0.12 W
Gushikami 174m 26.07 N 127.45 E
Gushikawa 174m 26.21 N 127.52 E
Gushu, Zhg. 104 42.36 N 123.26 E
Gushu, Zhg. 105 39.55 N 117.35 E
Gushuji 98 34.15 N 115.48 E
Gusi 112 6.07 N 117.08 E
Gusino 76 54.44 N 31.22 E
Gusinoje, ozero ⊜ 88 51.12 N 106.24 E
Gusinoje Ozero 88 51.09 N 106.10 E
Gusinoozersk 88 51.17 N 106.30 E
Guskef 85 39.02 N 69.20 E
Guskhara 126 23.30 N 87.45 E
Gus'-Khrustal'nyy → Gus'-Chrustal'nyj 80 55.37 N 40.40 E
Guskube 175d 24.45 N 125.26 E
Gusong 102 28.18 N 105.14 E
Guspini 71 39.32 N 8.37 E
Gussago 64 45.35 N 10.09 E
Gusselby 40 59.39 N 15.14 E
Güssing 61 47.04 N 16.20 E
Gussola 64 45.00 N 10.20 E
Gusswerk 61 47.45 N 15.18 E
Gustav Holm, Kap ≻ 176 67.00 N 34.00 W
Gustavo A. Madero ✦⁸ 286a 19.29 N 99.07 W
Gustavo Díaz Ordaz 234 17.44 N 94.23 W
Gustavsberg 40 59.19 N 18.23 E
Gustavus 180 58.25 N 135.44 W
Güsten 54 51.49 N 11.35 E
Gustia 272b 22.59 N 88.26 E
Gustine, Ca., U.S. 226 37.15 N 120.59 W
Gustine, Tx., U.S. 196 31.51 N 98.24 W
Gustorf 56 51.04 N 6.34 E
Güstrow 54 53.48 N 12.10 E
Gusum 26 58.16 N 16.29 E
Gus'-Železnyj 80 55.03 N 41.10 E
Gutach 58 48.15 N 8.13 E
Gutaj 88 49.59 N 108.12 E
Gutanggou 104 42.02 N 124.10 E
Gutara ≃ 88 54.50 N 97.23 E
Gutarskij chrebet ✧ 88 54.30 N 97.40 E
Gutau 61 48.25 N 14.37 E
Gutcher 46a 60.40 N 1.00 W
Gutenfels, Burg ⊥ 56 50.07 N 7.46 E
Guten Hoffnung, Kap der → Good Hope, Cape of ≻ 158 34.24 S 18.30 E
Güterfelde 264a 52.22 N 13.12 E
Gütersloh 52 51.54 N 8.23 E
Guthrie, In., U.S. 218 38.59 N 86.31 W
Guthrie, Ky., U.S. 194 36.38 N 87.09 W
Guthrie, Ok., U.S. 196 35.52 N 97.25 W
Guthrie, Tx., U.S. 196 33.37 N 100.19 W
Guthrie Center 198 41.40 N 94.30 W
Guthrie Lake ⊜ 184 55.17 N 100.38 W
Gutian, Zhg. 100 26.36 N 118.46 E
Gutian, Zhg. 100 25.15 N 116.46 E
Gutian, Zhg. 100 25.43 N 116.57 E
Gutian ≃ 100 26.22 N 118.42 E
Gutierrez 248 19.25 S 63.34 W
Gutiérrez Zamora 234 20.27 N 97.05 W
Gutland ✦¹ 56 49.40 N 6.10 E
Gutob Bay ⊂ 116 12.09 N 119.54 E
Guton, gora ∧ 84 41.51 N 46.45 E
Gutorfölde 61 46.39 N 16.44 E
Guttannen 58 46.39 N 8.18 E
Guttau 54 51.15 N 14.34 E
Guttenberg, Ia., U.S. 190 42.47 N 91.05 W
Guttenberg, N.J., U.S. 276 40.47 N 74.00 W
Gutu 154 19.38 S 31.10 E
Gutujevskij, ostrov I 265a 59.54 N 30.14 E
Gutulia Nasjonalpark ♦ 26 62.02 N 12.12 E
Gützkow 54 53.56 N 13.24 E
Güvem 130 40.36 N 32.40 E
Guwāhāti 120 26.10 N 91.45 E
Guxhagen 56 51.12 N 9.28 E
Guxi 107 30.18 N 105.52 E
Guxian, Zhg. 98 37.35 N 121.09 E
Guxian, Zhg. 100 32.26 N 113.37 E
Guxian, Zhg. 100 27.09 N 115.31 E
Guxiandu 100 29.06 N 116.50 E
Guxiansi 100 32.01 N 116.20 E
Guxiong 106 31.55 N 118.38 E
Guy 222 29.21 N 95.47 W
Guyana □¹, S.A. 242 5.00 N 59.00 W
Guyana □¹, S.A. 246 5.00 N 59.00 W
Guyancourt 261 48.46 N 2.04 E
Guyancourt, Aéroport de ⊠ 261 48.45 N 2.05 E
Guyandotte ≃ 188 38.26 N 82.23 W
Guyane → Guyana □¹ 246 5.00 N 59.00 W
Guyane française → French Guiana □² 250 4.00 N 53.00 W
Guyang, Zhg. 98 34.58 N 114.58 E
Guyang, Zhg. 102 41.03 N 110.03 E
Guye 105 39.44 N 118.25 E
Guy Fawkes River National Park ♦ 166 30.02 S 152.18 E
Guyi, Zhg. 100 25.38 N 118.47 E
Guyi, Zhg. 107 30.22 N 103.33 E
Guyin 102 23.58 N 105.47 E
Guymon 196 36.40 N 101.28 W
Guyonne, Ruisseau la ≃ 261 48.49 N 1.52 E
Guyot, Mount ∧ 192 35.42 N 83.15 W
Guyra 166 30.14 S 151.40 E
Guysborough 186 45.23 N 61.30 W
Guys Mills 214 41.38 N 79.59 W
Guyton 192 32.20 N 81.23 W
Guyuan (Pingdingbu), Zhg. 98 41.40 N 115.41 E
Guyuan, Zhg. 102 36.01 N 106.17 E
Guzar 72 38.36 N 66.15 E
Güzel ≃ 84 39.44 N 43.01 E
Güzelbahçe 130 38.21 N 26.54 E
Güzelsu 130 36.54 N 31.53 E
Güzelyurt, Kıbrıs 130 35.12 N 32.59 E
Güzelyurt, Tür. 130 38.17 N 34.23 E
Güzelyurt Körfezi ⊂ 130 35.10 N 32.50 E
Guzhang 102 28.31 N 109.57 E
Guzhen, Zhg. 100 33.19 N 117.21 E
Guzhen, Zhg. 100 22.37 N 113.11 E
Guzhu 100 26.58 N 116.16 E
Guzmán, Méx. 232 31.13 N 107.27 W
Guzmán → Ciudad Guzmán, Méx. 234 19.41 N 103.29 W
Guzmán, Laguna de ⊜ 200 31.20 N 107.30 W
Gvardejsk 76 54.39 N 21.05 E
Gvazda 78 50.44 N 40.30 E
Gwa 110 17.36 N 94.35 E
Gwabegar 166 30.36 S 148.58 E
Gwadabawa 150 13.20 N 5.15 E
Gwādar 128 25.07 N 62.19 E
Gwagwada 150 10.14 N 7.14 E
Gwai 154 19.15 S 27.42 E
Gwai ≃ 154 17.59 S 26.52 E
Gwalangu 152 2.19 N 18.11 E
Gwalchmai 44 53.15 N 4.25 W
Gwāl Haidarzai 120 30.44 N 68.48 E
Gwalia 162 28.55 S 121.20 E
Gwalior 124 26.13 N 78.10 E
Gwambygine 168a 31.59 S 116.48 E
Gwanda 154 20.57 S 29.01 E
Gwandu 150 12.30 N 4.41 E
Gwane 154 4.43 N 25.50 E
Gwangjang Bridge ✦⁵ 271b 37.33 N 127.05 E
Gwangju → Kwangju 98 35.09 N 126.54 E
Gwarzo 150 11.56 N 7.56 E
Gwasero 150 9.29 N 3.30 E
Gwash ≃ 42 52.39 N 0.27 W
Gwātar Bay ⊂ 128 25.04 N 61.36 E
Gwatt 58 46.43 N 7.38 E
Gwaun ≃ 42 52.00 N 4.58 W
Gwda ≃ 30 53.04 N 16.44 E
Gweebarra ≃ 48 54.50 N 8.20 W
Gweebarra Bay ⊂ 48 54.52 N 8.20 W
Gweedore 48 55.03 N 8.14 W
Gweesalia 48 54.07 N 9.54 W
Gwelo ≃ 154 18.45 S 28.36 E
Gwembe 154 16.30 S 27.35 E
Gwendraeth Fâch ≃ 42 51.44 N 4.18 W
Gwendraeth Fawr ≃ 42 51.43 N 4.18 W
Gwent □⁶ 42 51.43 N 2.57 W
Gweru 154 19.27 S 29.49 E
Gweta 156 20.10 S 25.18 E
Gwinhurst 285 39.47 N 75.29 W
Gwinn 190 46.16 N 87.26 W
Gwinner 198 46.13 N 97.39 W
Gwobu 154 2.37 N 26.13 E
Gwongorella National Park ♦ 171a 28.10 S 153.17 E
Gwydir ≃ 166 29.27 S 149.48 E
Gwynedd 285 40.12 N 75.15 W
Gwynedd □⁶ 28 53.00 N 4.00 W
Gwynedd Square 285 40.13 N 75.18 W
Gwynedd Valley 285 40.11 N 75.15 W
Gwynn 208 37.30 N 76.17 W
Gwynneville 218 39.39 N 85.38 W
Gwynn Island I 208 37.30 N 76.17 W
Gwynns Falls ≃ 284b 39.16 N 76.37 W
Gwynns Falls Park ♦ 284b 39.18 N 76.41 W
Gy 58 47.24 N 5.49 E
Gyál 264c 47.23 N 19.14 E
Gya La)(124 28.44 N 84.40 E
Gyáli-patak ≃ 264c 47.24 N 19.07 E
Gyangtse → Gyangzê 120 28.57 N 89.35 E
Gyangzê 120 28.57 N 89.35 E
Gyaring Co ⊜ 120 31.10 N 88.15 E
Gyaring Hu ⊜ 102 34.53 N 97.58 E
Gybdan 80 56.33 N 51.39 E
Gyda 74 70.52 N 78.30 E
Gydanskaja guba ⊂ 74 71.20 N 76.30 E
Gydanskij poluostrov ≻¹ 74 70.50 N 79.00 E
Gyebu 164 3.03 S 133.51 E
Gyemo Chen ∧ 124 27.20 N 88.52 E
Gyeongbog Palace ⚲ 271b 37.36 N 126.57 E
Gyeongju → Kyŏngju 98 35.51 N 129.14 E
Gyirong, Zhg. 120 28.29 N 85.20 E
Gyirong, Zhg. 120 28.57 N 85.15 E
Gyldenløves Fjord ⊂² 176 64.30 N 41.30 W
Gyldenløveshøj ∧² 41 55.33 N 11.52 E
Gylling 41 55.53 N 10.11 E
Gymea Bay 274a 34.02 S 151.05 E
Gym Peak ∧ 200 32.04 N 107.35 W
Gympie 166 26.11 S 152.40 E
Gyobingauk 110 18.13 N 95.39 E
Gyōda 94 36.08 N 139.28 E
Gyoma 30 46.56 N 20.50 E
Gyöngyös 30 47.47 N 19.56 E
Gyöngyös ≃ 61 47.14 N 16.55 E
Győr 30 47.42 N 17.38 E
Győr-Moson-Sopron □⁶ 30 47.35 N 17.15 E
Gypsey Race ≃ 44 54.05 N 0.12 W
Gypsum, Co., U.S. 200 39.38 N 106.57 W
Gypsum, Ks., U.S. 198 38.42 N 97.25 W
Gypsum, Oh., U.S. 214 41.29 N 82.52 W
Gypsum Creek ≃, U.S. 200 37.09 N 109.52 W
Gypsum Creek ≃, Ks., U.S. 198 38.51 N 97.25 W
Gypsum Hills ✧² 196 36.25 N 99.20 W
Gypsum Point ≻ 176 61.53 N 114.35 W
Gypsumville 184 51.45 N 98.35 W
Gysinge 40 60.17 N 16.53 E
Gyttorp 40 59.31 N 14.58 E
Gyula 30 46.39 N 21.17 E
Gyulafehérvár → Alba Iulia 38 46.04 N 23.35 E
Gžat' ≃ 76 55.56 N 34.33 E
Gžatsk 86 55.42 N 78.11 E
Gžel' 82 55.36 N 38.24 E
Gzhatsk → Gagarin 76 55.33 N 35.00 E

H

Haag → 's-Gravenhage, Ned. 52 52.06 N 4.18 E
Haag, Öst. 61 48.07 N 14.34 E
Haag am Hausruck 60 48.11 N 13.38 E
Haagen 58 47.38 N 7.40 E
Haag in Oberbayern 60 48.10 N 12.11 E
Haaksbergen 52 52.09 N 6.44 E
Haalenberg 156 26.52 S 15.30 E
Haaltert 50 50.54 N 4.00 E
Haamstede 52 51.43 N 3.45 E
Haan 56 51.11 N 7.00 E
Haapajärvi 26 63.45 N 25.20 E
Haapajärvi ⊜ 26 63.33 N 27.00 E
Haapamäki 26 62.15 N 24.28 E
Haapavesi 26 64.08 N 25.22 E
Haapiti 174s 17.34 S 149.52 W
Haapsalu 76 58.56 N 23.33 E
Haar 60 48.06 N 11.44 E
Haar ✦⁸ 263 51.26 N 7.13 E
Ha'Arava (Wādī al-'Arabah) V, Asia 132 30.10 N 35.10 E
Ha'Arava (Wādī al-Jayb) V, Asia 132 30.58 N 35.24 E
Haardt ✧ 56 49.15 N 8.00 E
Haaren, Dtsch. 52 51.34 N 8.44 E
Haaren, Ned. 52 51.36 N 5.12 E
Haarlem, Ned. 52 52.23 N 4.38 E
Haarlem, S. Afr. 158 33.44 S 23.20 E
Haarlemmermeer ✦¹ 52 52.15 N 4.38 E
Haarstrang ∧ 52 51.35 N 8.10 E
Haarzopf ✦⁸ 263 51.25 N 6.58 E
Haast 172 43.53 S 169.03 E
Haast ≃ 172 43.50 S 169.02 E
Haast Bluff 162 23.30 S 131.50 E
Haast Pass)(172 44.06 S 169.21 E
Haasts Bluff Reserve ✦⁴ 162 23.30 S 130.30 E
Haatinao, Pointe ≻ 174x 9.47 S 138.51 W
Haava, Canal ⊻ 174x 9.53 S 139.04 W
Hab ≃ 120 24.53 N 66.41 E
Habahe 86 47.53 N 86.12 E
Habana, Bahía de la ⊂ 286b 23.08 N 82.20 W
Habaqi, Zhg. 104 42.36 N 122.52 E
Habaqi, Zhg. 104 42.38 N 122.02 E
Habaqila 102 42.01 N 106.02 E
Habartov 54 50.08 N 12.33 E
Habashīyah, Jabal ✧ 144 16.40 N 49.40 E
Habaswein 154 1.01 N 39.29 E
Habawnah, Wādī V 144 17.51 N 44.59 E
Habay-la-Neuve 56 49.44 N 5.39 E
Habbān 144 14.21 N 47.05 E
Habbānīyah, Hawr al- ⊜ 128 33.17 N 43.29 E
Habbūsh 132 33.24 N 35.29 E
Hab Chauki 120 25.01 N 66.53 E
Habère-Poche 58 46.15 N 6.29 E
Haberfield 274a 33.53 S 151.08 E
Haberli 130 37.19 N 41.38 E
Habermehl Peak ∧ 9 71.49 S 6.38 E
Habīb, Wādī V 142 27.20 N 31.30 E
Habiganj 120 24.23 N 91.25 E
Habikino 96 34.33 N 135.37 E
Habīlah 140 12.41 N 22.33 E
Habinghorst 263 51.35 N 7.18 E
Habo 26 57.55 N 14.04 E
Habob, Wādī V 140 18.07 N 35.01 E
Habomai-shotō → Malaja Kuril'skaja Gr'ada II 92a 43.30 N 146.10 E
Haboro 92a 44.22 N 141.42 E
Hābra 126 22.50 N 88.38 E
Habsburg ⊥ 58 47.28 N 8.13 E
Habsheim 58 47.44 N 7.25 E
Habu 270 34.27 N 135.24 E
Habur (Nahr al-Khābūr) ≃ 130 35.08 N 40.26 E
Habutaki 270 34.25 N 135.26 E
Hache, Lac la ⊜ 182 51.50 N 121.30 W
Hachen 56 51.22 N 7.59 E
Hachenburg 56 50.39 N 7.50 E
Hachi 120 27.46 N 94.01 E
Hachijō 270 34.37 N 135.48 E
Hachijō-jima I 90 33.05 N 139.48 E
Hachiman, Nihon 94 35.45 N 136.57 E
Hachiman → Ōmi-hachiman, Nihon 94 35.08 N 136.06 E
Hachiman-misaki ≻ 94 35.08 N 140.19 E
Hachinohe 92 40.30 N 141.29 E
Hachiōji 94 35.39 N 139.20 E
Hachmühlen 52 52.10 N 9.28 E
Hacıbektaş 130 38.57 N 34.35 E
Hacienda Heights 228 34.00 N 117.57 W
Hacienda Miravalles 236 10.41 N 85.14 W
Hacienda Murciélago 236 10.55 N 85.44 W
Hacıhamza 130 41.05 N 34.28 E
Hacıkänd 84 40.31 N 46.21 E
Hacılar 130 38.39 N 35.27 E
Hacı Zeynalabdin 84 40.37 N 49.34 E
Hack, Mount ∧ 166 30.46 S 138.48 E
Hackås 26 62.55 N 14.31 E
Hackberry, Az., U.S. 200 35.22 N 113.43 W
Hackberry, La., U.S. 194 29.59 N 93.20 W
Hackberry Creek ≃, Ks., U.S. 198 38.48 N 100.03 W
Hackberry Creek ≃, Tx., U.S. 222 31.53 N 97.12 W
Hackensack 210 40.53 N 74.02 W
Hackensack ≃ 276 40.43 N 74.06 W
Hacketstown 48 52.52 N 6.33 W
Hackett, Ar., U.S. 194 35.11 N 94.24 W
Hackett, Pa., U.S. 279b 40.15 N 80.01 W
Hacketts 260 51.45 N 0.05 W
Hackettstown 210 40.52 N 74.48 W
Hacking ≃ 274a 34.04 S 151.06 E
Hacking, Port ⊂ 274a 34.05 S 151.09 E
Hackleburg 194 34.16 N 87.49 W
Hackney ✦⁸ 260 51.33 N 0.03 W
Hack Point 208 39.27 N 75.52 W
Håckren ⊜ 26 63.11 N 13.35 E
Haco 152 10.12 S 15.44 E
Hacreş Dağları ✧ 130 38.38 N 41.37 E
Hadāli 123 32.18 N 72.12 E
Hadalīya 140 16.10 N 36.06 E
Hadamar 56 50.27 N 8.02 E
Hadan, Harrat ⩪⁹ 144 21.30 N 41.23 E
Hadano 94 35.22 N 139.14 E
Hadāribah, Ra's al- ≻ 140 22.04 N 36.54 E
HaDarom □⁵ 132 30.40 N 34.50 E
Hadat 89 49.40 N 119.40 E
Hadayingzi 104 42.22 N 121.40 E
Hadd, Ra's al- ≻ 118 22.32 N 59.48 E
Haddad, Ouadi V 146 14.40 N 18.46 E
Haddādīn, Qārat al- ∧² 142 30.04 N 30.58 E
Haddam, Ct., U.S. 207 41.28 N 72.30 W
Haddam, Ks., U.S. 198 39.51 N 97.18 W
Haddenham, Eng., U.K. 42 51.46 N 0.56 W
Haddenham, Eng., U.K. 42 52.22 N 0.09 E
Haddington 46 55.58 N 2.47 W
Haddock 192 33.01 N 83.25 W
Haddon Downs 166 26.21 S 140.50 E
Haddonfield 208 39.53 N 75.02 W
Haddon Heights 208 39.52 N 75.03 W
Haddon Hills 285 39.54 N 75.03 W
Hadejia 150 12.30 N 9.59 E
Hadejia ≃ 134 12.50 N 10.51 E
Hadeln, Land ✦¹ 52 53.45 N 8.45 E
Haden 171a 27.14 S 151.53 E
Hadera 132 32.26 N 34.55 E
Hadera ≃ 132 32.27 N 34.53 E
Hadersdorf ✦⁸ 264b 48.13 N 16.14 E
Hadersfeld 264b 48.20 N 16.15 E
Haderslev 41 55.15 N 9.30 E
Haderslev Fjord ⊂ 41 55.17 N 9.40 E
Hadfield, Austl. 274b 37.42 S 144.56 E
Hadfield, Eng., U.K. 262 53.28 N 1.58 W
Hadībū 118 12.38 N 54.02 E
Hadīd, Jabal ∧² 142 30.20 N 30.06 E
Hadīd, Jabal al- ∧² 142 28.47 N 31.04 E
Hadım 130 36.59 N 32.28 E
Hadjout 34 36.31 N 2.25 E
Hadleigh, Eng., U.K. 42 52.03 N 0.58 E
Hadleigh, Eng., U.K. 260 51.33 N 0.37 E
Hadleigh Castle ⊥ 260 51.33 N 0.36 E
Hadley, Eng., U.K. 42 52.42 N 2.29 W
Hadley, Ma., U.S. 207 42.20 N 72.35 W
Hadley, Mi., U.S. 216 42.57 N 83.24 W
Hadley, N.Y., U.S. 210 43.19 N 73.50 W
Hadley, Pa., U.S. 214 41.25 N 80.14 W
Hadley Bay ⊂ 176 72.30 N 107.45 W
Hadley Creek ≃ 219 39.37 N 91.12 W
Hadlock 224 48.01 N 122.45 W
Hadlow 42 51.14 N 0.20 E
Hadlyme 207 41.25 N 72.24 W
Hadmersleben 54 51.59 N 11.18 E
Hadong, Taehan 98 35.05 N 127.44 E
Ha Dong, Viet 110 20.58 N 105.46 E
Hadramawt ✦¹ 144 15.00 N 50.00 E
Hadrian's Wall ⊥ 44 54.59 N 2.26 W
Hadrut 84 39.32 N 47.02 E
Hadsten 41 56.20 N 10.03 E
Hadsund 26 56.43 N 10.07 E
Hadyach 78 50.22 N 34.00 E
Hadyai → Hat Yai 110 7.01 N 100.28 E
Haeju 98 38.02 N 125.42 E
Haemgon-ni ✦⁸ 271b 37.35 N 126.49 E
Haena 229b 22.14 N 159.34 W
Haenam 98 34.34 N 126.35 E
Haena Point ≻ 229b 22.14 N 159.34 W
Haenertsburg 156 24.00 S 29.50 E
Haengyŏng-ni 98 42.33 N 129.56 E
Haernao 104 41.46 N 120.28 E
Hafeïra, Oued el V 148 25.18 N 10.48 W
Hafelekarspitze ∧ 64 47.19 N 11.23 E
Haffen-Mehr 52 51.44 N 6.28 E
Hafford 184 52.43 N 107.21 W
Haffouz 36 35.38 N 9.41 E
Hafik 130 39.52 N 37.24 E
Hafīra, Qā' al- ⩪ 132 31.06 N 36.14 E
Hafīrat al-'Ayda 128 26.26 N 39.10 E
Hafīt, Jabal ∧ 128 24.03 N 55.46 E
Hāfiz, Bi'r ⩪⁴ 142 30.51 N 29.40 E
Hāfizābād 123 32.04 N 73.41 E
Hāflong 120 25.11 N 93.02 E
Hafnarfjörður 24a 64.03 N 21.56 W
Haft Gel 128 31.27 N 49.27 E
Hafun, Ras ≻ 144 10.27 N 51.24 E
Haga, Nihon 94 36.32 N 140.04 E
Haga, Nihon 96 35.09 N 134.33 E
Hagachi-zaki ≻ 94 34.41 N 138.45 E
HaGadol, HaMakhtésh ⩪⁷ 132 30.56 N 34.59 E
Haga-Haga 158 32.46 S 28.14 E
Hagal 98 40.23 N 127.15 E
HaGalil (Galilee) □⁹ 132 32.54 N 35.20 E
Hagaman 210 42.59 N 74.09 W
Hagan 192 32.09 N 81.56 W
Hagari ≃ 122 15.45 N 76.56 E
Hagar Shores 216 42.13 N 86.22 W
Hagarstown 219 38.57 N 89.10 W
Hage 52 53.36 N 7.17 E
Hagelberg ∧² 54 52.08 N 12.32 E
Hagemeister Island I 180 58.40 N 161.00 W
Hagen, Dtsch. 52 52.34 N 9.26 E
Hagen, Dtsch. 52 52.12 N 7.59 E
Hagen, Dtsch. 56 51.22 N 7.28 E
Hagenbrunn 264b 48.20 N 16.25 E
Hagengebirge ✧ 64 47.32 N 13.07 E
Hagenow 54 53.26 N 11.11 E
Hagensborg 182 52.23 N 126.33 W
Hagenwerder 54 51.04 N 14.58 E
Hagere Hiywet 144 8.59 N 37.51 E
Hagere Selam 144 6.29 N 38.31 E
Hagerman, Id., U.S. 202 42.48 N 114.53 W
Hagerman, N.M., U.S. 196 33.06 N 104.19 W
Hagerman Corners 275b 43.50 N 79.18 W
Hagerstown, In., U.S. 218 39.54 N 85.09 W
Hagerstown, Md., U.S. 188 39.38 N 77.43 W
Hagersville 212 42.58 N 80.03 W
Hagetmau 32 43.40 N 0.35 W
Hagfors 40 60.02 N 13.42 E
Haggen ⊜ 40 60.06 N 15.13 E
Haggetts Pond ⊜ 283 42.39 N 71.12 W
Haggin, Mount ∧ 202 46.05 N 113.05 W
Hagi 96 34.24 N 131.25 E
Ha Giang 110 22.50 N 104.59 E
Hagitani 270 34.54 N 135.35 E
Hagiwara 94 35.52 N 137.12 E
Hagley 42 52.26 N 2.08 W
Hagley Museum ⚲ 285 39.46 N 75.35 W
Hagondange 56 49.15 N 6.10 E
HaGosherim 132 33.13 N 35.37 E
Hags Head ≻ 48 52.57 N 9.30 W
Hague, Sk., Can. 184 52.30 N 106.25 W
Hague, N.D., U.S. 198 46.01 N 99.59 W
Hague, Cap de la ≻ 32 49.43 N 1.57 W
Haguenau 56 48.49 N 7.47 E
Hagues Peak ∧ 200 40.29 N 105.38 W
Hahaïa 157a 11.33 S 43.17 E
Hahajima-rettō II 14 26.37 N 142.10 E
Haharro, Uebi ≃ 144 1.37 N 44.13 E
Hāhipur 272b 22.47 N 88.10 E
Hahira 192 30.59 N 83.22 W
Hahlen 52 52.18 N 8.50 E
Hahn am See 56 50.31 N 7.53 E
Hahnbach 60 49.32 N 11.48 E
Hahndorf 168b 35.03 S 138.49 E
Hahnenberg 263 51.12 N 7.24 E
Hahnenkamm ∧ 64 47.25 N 12.22 E
Hahnenklee-Bockswiese 52 51.51 N 10.20 E
Hahnerberg ✦⁸ 263 51.13 N 7.09 E
Hahnstätten 56 50.18 N 8.04 E
Hahntown 279b 40.19 N 79.44 W
Haho ≃ 150 6.17 N 1.23 E
Hahyŏn-ni 98 38.33 N 127.57 E
Hai ≃ 105 39.00 N 117.43 E
Hai'an 100 32.34 N 120.28 E
Haian Shanmo ✧ 100 23.25 N 121.25 E
Haibara, Nihon 94 34.32 N 135.57 E
Haibara, Nihon 94 34.44 N 138.13 E
Haibatpur 272a 28.37 N 77.26 E
Haibei 89 47.39 N 126.51 E
Haicheng, Zhg. 100 24.25 N 117.51 E
Haicheng, Zhg. 104 40.52 N 122.45 E
Haicheng ≃ 104 40.56 N 122.21 E
Haidargarh 124 26.37 N 81.22 E
Haidārpur ✦⁸ 272a 28.43 N 77.09 E
Haidenaab ≃ 60 49.36 N 12.08 E
Haiderabad → Hyderābād, India 122 17.23 N 78.29 E
Haiderabad → Hyderābād, Pāk. 120 25.22 N 68.22 E
Haidershofen 61 48.05 N 14.28 E
Haidian 105 39.59 N 116.18 E
Haiding 60 48.13 N 13.58 E
Haidmühle 60 48.50 N 13.46 E
Haïdra 36 35.34 N 8.27 E
Haidstein ∧ 60 49.13 N 12.48 E
Haidun 100 29.36 N 121.49 E
Hai Duong 110 20.56 N 106.19 E
Haifa → Hefa 132 32.50 N 35.00 E
Haifa, Bay of → Hefa, Mifraz ⊂ 132 32.52 N 35.03 E
Haifeng 100 22.59 N 115.21 E
Haifengzheng 106 31.53 N 121.46 E
Haifuzhen 106 31.59 N 121.42 E
Haig 162 31.01 S 126.05 E
Haig, Mount ∧ 182 49.17 N 114.29 W
Haiger 56 50.44 N 8.13 E
Haigerloch 58 48.22 N 8.48 E
Haigh 262 53.35 N 2.36 W
Haigler 198 40.00 N 101.56 W
Haihezhen 100 33.44 N 120.02 E
Haijima 268 35.42 N 139.21 E
Haikang 102 20.56 N 110.04 E
Haikou, Zhg. 100 28.20 N 120.06 E
Haikou, Zhg. 100 25.43 N 119.28 E
Haikou, Zhg. 100 29.04 N 117.46 E
Haikou, Zhg. 102 20.03 N 110.19 E
Haiku 229a 20.55 N 156.19 W
Hā'il 128 27.33 N 41.42 E
Hailākāndi 120 24.41 N 92.34 E
Hailar 89 49.12 N 119.42 E
Hailar ≃ 90 49.35 N 117.55 E
Hailasen 89 46.13 N 121.00 E
Hailesboro 212 44.18 N 75.27 W
Hailey, Eng., U.K. 260 51.46 N 0.01 W
Hailey, Id., U.S. 202 43.31 N 114.18 W
Haileybury 190 47.27 N 79.38 W
Haileyville 196 34.51 N 95.34 W
Hailin 89 44.35 N 129.22 E
Hailing Dao I 102 21.37 N 111.55 E
Haillicourt 50 50.28 N 2.35 E
Hailong (Meihekou) 98 42.32 N 125.38 E
Hailsham 42 50.52 N 0.16 E
Hailun 89 47.28 N 126.58 E
Hailuoto 26 65.00 N 24.43 E
Hailuoto I 26 65.02 N 24.42 E
Haiman Tepesi ∧² 267b 41.12 N 29.15 E
Haimen, Zhg. 100 28.41 N 121.27 E
Haimen, Zhg. 100 23.14 N 116.38 E
Haimen, Zhg. 106 31.55 N 121.10 E
Haimen Wan ⊂ 100 23.09 N 116.34 E
Haimhausen 60 48.19 N 11.34 E
Haimiao 98 37.13 N 119.51 E
Haiming 64 47.15 N 10.53 E
Haina 56 51.02 N 8.58 E
Hainan □⁴ 110 19.00 N 109.30 E
Hainan → Hainan Dao I 110 19.00 N 109.30 E
Hainan Dao I 110 19.00 N 109.30 E
Hainault ✦⁸ 260 51.36 N 0.06 E
Hainaut □⁴ 50 50.30 N 3.50 E
Hainaut □⁹ 50 50.15 N 3.45 E
Hainburg an der Donau 61 48.09 N 16.57 E
Hainchen 56 50.51 N 8.12 E
Haines, Ak., U.S. 180 59.14 N 135.27 W
Haines, Or., U.S. 202 44.54 N 117.56 W
Haines City 220 28.06 N 81.37 W
Haines Falls 210 42.11 N 74.05 W
Haines Junction 180 60.45 N 137.30 W
Hainesport 208 39.59 N 74.49 W
Hainesville 278 42.21 N 88.04 W
Hainewalde 54 50.54 N 14.41 E
Hainfeld 61 48.02 N 15.46 E
Hainich ✧ 54 51.05 N 10.27 E
Hainichen 54 50.58 N 13.07 E
Haining (Xiashi) 106 30.32 N 120.41 E
Hainleite ✧ 54 51.20 N 10.48 E
Hainsberg 54 50.59 N 13.38 E
Hainzenberg 64 47.13 N 11.54 E
Hai Phong 110 20.52 N 106.41 E
Haiqiao 106 31.47 N 121.19 E
Haiqing 89 47.53 N 134.40 E
Haitangxi 107 29.33 N 106.35 E
Haitan Xia ⊻ 100 25.27 N 119.38 E
Haiti (Haïti) □¹, N.A. 230 19.00 N 72.25 W
Haiti (Haïti) □¹, N.A. 238 19.00 N 72.25 W
Haitou, Zhg. 98 34.56 N 119.10 E
Haitou, Zhg. 110 19.34 N 108.58 E
Haitouji 98 35.23 N 115.19 E
Haitun 102 38.50 N 96.41 E
Haiwee Reservoirs ⊜¹ 204 36.10 N 117.57 W
Haiyan, Zhg. 102 36.54 N 101.12 E
Haiyan, Zhg. 106 30.31 N 120.57 E
Haiyang (Dongcun) 98 36.46 N 121.10 E
Haiyang Dao I 98 39.02 N 123.14 E
Haiyuan 102 36.35 N 105.40 E
Haizhou, Zhg. 98 34.34 N 119.11 E
Haizhou, Zhg. 100 22.40 N 113.10 E
Haizhoumiao 104 42.00 N 121.39 E
Haizhou Wan ⊂ 98 35.00 N 119.30 E
Haizhouyingzi 104 42.07 N 121.46 E
Hajar, Tall al- ∧² 132 33.21 N 37.03 E
Hajar Banga 140 11.30 N 23.00 E
Hajdú-Bihar □⁶ 30 47.25 N 21.30 E
Hajdúböszörmény 30 47.41 N 21.30 E
Hajdúnánás 30 47.51 N 21.26 E
Hajdúszoboszló 30 47.27 N 21.24 E
Hajeb el Ayoun 36 35.24 N 9.33 E
Hajiadian 98 41.32 N 117.10 E
Hājīganj 126 23.15 N 90.50 E
Hajiki-saki ≻ 92 38.19 N 138.31 E
Haji Langar 120 35.52 N 79.21 E
Hājīpur, India 124 25.41 N 85.13 E
Hājīpur, India 126 22.49 N 87.38 E
Hajipur, India 272b 22.57 N 88.19 E
Hājj, Wādī al- V 142 30.03 N 32.45 E
Hajnówka 30 52.45 N 23.36 E
Hajo-do I 98 34.17 N 126.03 E
Hajr, Wādī V 144 14.04 N 48.40 E
Hajūl, Wādī V 142 29.42 N 32.22 E
Häkäri ≃ 84 39.09 N 46.51 E
Hakata 96 34.12 N 133.07 E
Hakata-jima I 96 34.13 N 133.05 E
Hakataramea ≃ 172 44.44 S 170.29 E
Hakendover 56 50.48 N 4.59 E
Hakha 110 22.39 N 93.37 E
Haki 96 33.20 N 130.50 E
Hakīm, Abyār al- ⩪⁴ 146 31.36 N 23.29 E
Hakkâri 128 37.34 N 43.45 E
Hakkâri □⁴ 128 37.20 N 43.45 E
Hakken-san ∧ 92 34.10 N 135.54 E
Hakkōda-san ∧ 92 40.40 N 140.53 E
Hako-dake ∧ 92a 44.40 N 142.25 E
Hakodate 92a 41.45 N 140.43 E
Hakone 94 35.12 N 139.06 E

Symbol	English	Deutsch	Español	Français	Português
≃	River	Fluß	Río	Rivière	Rio
⩧	Canal	Kanal	Canal	Canal	Canal
⌞	Waterfall, Rapids	Wasserfall, Stromschnellen	Cascada, Rápidos	Chute d'eau, Rapides	Cascata, Rápidos
⊻	Strait	Meeresstraße	Estrecho	Détroit	Estreito
⊂	Bay, Gulf	Bucht, Golf	Bahía, Golfo	Baie, Golfe	Baía, Golfo
⊜	Lake, Lakes	See, Seen	Lago, Lagos	Lac, Lacs	Lago, Lagos
⩨	Swamp	Sumpf	Pantano	Marais	Pântano
⊡	Ice Features, Glacier	Eis- und Gletscherformen	Accidentes Glaciales	Formes glaciaires	Acidentes glaciares
⩪	Other Hydrographic Features	Andere Hydrographische Objekte	Otros Elementos Hidrográficos	Autres données hydrographiques	Outros acidentes hidrográficos
✧	Submarine Features	Untermeerische Objekte	Accidentes Submarinos	Formes de relief sous-marin	Acidentes submarinos
□	Political Unit	Politische Einheit	Unidad Politica	Entité politique	Unidade política
⚲	Cultural Institution	Kulturelle Institution	Institución Cultural	Institution culturelle	Instituição cultural
⊥	Historical Site	Historische Stätte	Sitio Histórico	Site historique	Sitio histórico
♦	Recreational Site	Erholungs- und Ferienort	Sitio de Recreo	Centre de loisirs	Area de Lazer
⊠	Airport	Flughafen	Aeropuerto	Aéroport	Aeroporto
■	Military Installation	Militäranlage	Instalación Militar	Installation militaire	Instalação militar
✦	Miscellaneous	Verschiedenes	Misceláneo	Divers	Diversos

Name (ENGLISH) / Name (DEUTSCH)	Page / Seite	Lat.°′ / Breite°′	Long.°′ / Länge°′ E = Ost
Hakone-no-seki-ato ⊥	94	35.10 N	139.02 E
Hakone-tōge)(	94	35.11 N	139.01 E
Hakone-yama ∧	94	35.14 N	139.02 E
Håksberg	40	60.11 N	15.12 E
Hakskeenpan ≚	158	26.48 S	20.12 E
Haktanır	130	36.51 N	38.50 E
Hakuba	94	36.42 N	137.52 E
Hakui	94	36.53 N	136.47 E
Hakupu	174v	19.06 S	169.50 W
Hakusan	94	34.38 N	136.21 E
Haku-san ∧	94	36.09 N	136.46 E
Haku-san-kokuritsu-kōen ◆	94	36.12 N	136.47 E
Hakushū	94	35.48 N	138.20 E
Hakuta	96	35.21 N	133.17 E
Hakuta ≃	96	35.26 N	133.15 E
Hāla	120	25.49 N	68.25 E
Halaaobao	102	42.11 N	107.20 E
Ḥalab (Aleppo)	130	36.12 N	37.10 E
Ḥalab □[8]	130	36.00 N	37.30 E
Ḥalabjah	128	35.10 N	45.59 E
Halachó	232	20.29 N	90.05 W
Halaerjige	104	42.24 N	122.11 E
Halagetu	104	42.34 N	122.40 E
Halahai	89	44.39 N	125.07 E
Halahushao	104	42.11 N	121.44 E
Ḥalā'ib	140	22.13 N	36.38 E
Halalii Lake ⊜	229b	21.52 N	160.11 W
Halamutai	86	46.10 N	84.52 E
Halangingie Point >	174v	19.03 S	169.57 W
Halasa	140	14.26 N	30.39 E
Halas-patak ≃	264c	47.24 N	19.20 E
Halataojie	104	42.30 N	122.06 E
Halatieke Shan ⋏	85	40.30 N	77.05 E
Halaula	229d	20.14 N	155.48 W
Hålaveden ⋏[2]	26	58.05 N	14.45 E
Halawa, Cape >	229a	21.10 N	156.43 W
Halawa Bay c	229a	21.10 N	156.44 W
Halawa Heights	229c	21.22 N	157.55 W
Halawotelake	120	37.17 N	90.20 E
Halbach -●-[8]	263	51.12 N	7.12 E
Halba Deset I	144	12.56 N	42.55 E
Halbe	54	52.06 N	13.42 E
Halberstadt	54	51.54 N	11.02 E
Halbert, Lake ⊜[1]	222	32.04 N	96.25 W
Halberton	42	50.55 N	3.25 W
Halbrite	184	49.30 N	103.33 W
Ḥalbūn	132	33.40 N	36.15 E
Halbury	168b	34.05 S	138.31 E
Halcombe	172	40.09 S	175.30 E
Halcon, Mount ∧	116	13.16 N	121.00 E
Halcottsville	210	42.12 N	74.36 W
Haldeman	218	38.15 N	83.19 W
Halden	26	59.09 N	11.23 E
Halden -●-[8]	263	51.23 N	7.31 E
Haldensleben	54	52.18 N	11.26 E
Haldern	52	51.46 N	6.27 E
Haldī	126	22.03 N	88.05 E
Haldī ≃	126	22.01 N	88.03 E
Haldībāri	124	26.20 N	88.46 E
Haldībunia	126	22.26 N	89.38 E
Haldimand	212	42.56 N	79.51 W
Haldimand-Norfolk □[6]	212	42.48 N	80.10 W
Haldwāni	124	29.13 N	79.31 E
Hale, Eng., U.K.	44	53.23 N	2.21 W
Hale, Eng., U.K.	262	53.20 N	2.48 W
Hale, Mo., U.S.	194	39.36 N	93.20 W
Hale ≃	162	24.56 S	135.53 E
Haleakala Crater ▲[6]	229a	20.43 N	156.13 W
Haleakala National Park ◆	229a	20.44 N	156.13 W
Haleb → Ḥalab	130	36.12 N	37.10 E
Halebarns	262	53.22 N	2.19 W
Hale Center	196	34.03 N	101.50 W
Hale Creek ≃	282	37.23 N	122.06 W
Haledon	276	40.56 N	74.11 W
Haledon Reservoir ⊜[1]	276	40.59 N	74.12 W
Hale Eddy	210	42.00 N	75.23 W
Hale Head >	262	53.19 N	2.48 W
Haleiwa	229c	21.35 N	158.06 W
Halekii-Pihana Heiaus State Monument ⊥	229a	20.54 N	156.29 W
Halenkov	30	49.19 N	18.08 E
Hales Corners	216	42.56 N	88.02 W
Halesite	207	40.52 N	73.25 W
Halesowen	42	52.26 N	2.05 W
Hale Street	260	51.13 N	0.24 E
Halesworth	42	52.21 N	1.30 E
Halewood	262	53.22 N	2.49 W
Haleyville	194	34.13 N	87.37 W
Half Assini	150	5.03 N	2.53 W
Ḥalfāyah, Naqb al- (Halfaya Pass))(	140	31.30 N	25.11 E
Halfaya Pass → Ḥalfāyah, Naqb al-)(	140	31.30 N	25.11 E
Half Day	278	42.12 N	87.56 W
Halfeti	130	37.15 N	37.52 E
Half Hollow Hills	276	40.48 N	73.21 W
Halfing	64	47.57 N	12.16 E
Halfmoon Bay, B.C., Can.	182	49.31 N	123.54 W
Halfmoon Bay, N.Z.	172	46.54 S	168.08 E
Half Moon Bay, Ca., U.S.	226	37.27 N	122.25 W
Halfmoon Bay c, Austl.	274b	37.58 S	145.00 E
Half Moon Bay c, Ca., U.S.	282	37.29 N	122.28 W
Half Moon Bay Airport ⊠	282	37.31 N	122.30 W
Half Moon Bay State Beach ◆	282	37.29 N	122.27 W
Halfway, Md., U.S.	188	39.37 N	77.45 W
Halfway, Or., U.S.	202	44.52 N	117.06 W
Halfway ≃	176	56.10 N	121.35 W
Halfway Lake ⊜	184	55.03 N	98.24 W
Halgån ≃	40	60.16 N	13.27 E
Ḥalḥūl	132	31.35 N	35.07 E
Ḥalī ⊤[4]	144	18.42 N	41.20 E
Haliburton	212	45.03 N	78.31 W
Haliburton □[6]	212	44.10 N	78.30 W
Haliburton Lake ⊜	212	45.12 N	78.24 W
Halibut Point >	283	42.42 N	70.38 W
Haliç (Golden Horn) c	267b	41.02 N	28.58 E
Halicarnassus ⊥	130	37.03 N	27.23 E
Halifax, Austl.	166	18.35 S	146.18 E
Halifax, N.S., Can.	186	44.39 N	63.36 W
Halifax, Eng., U.K.	44	53.44 N	1.52 W
Halifax, Ma., U.S.	207	41.59 N	70.51 W
Halifax, N.C., U.S.	192	36.19 N	77.35 W
Halifax, Pa., U.S.	208	40.28 N	76.55 W
Halifax, Va., U.S.	192	36.45 N	78.55 W
Halifax, Canadian Forces Base ■	186	44.43 N	63.38 W
Halifax Bay c	166	18.50 S	146.30 E
Halifax Citadel National Historic Park ◆	186	44.36 N	63.39 W
Halifax Harbour c	186	44.35 N	63.31 W
Haliimaile	229a	20.52 N	156.20 W
Halīl ≃	128	27.28 N	58.44 E
Halimatazi	104	42.37 N	122.35 E
Halim Perdanakusuma Airport ■	269e	6.16 S	106.54 E
Halimun, Gunung ∧	115a	6.42 S	106.26 E
Halingen	263	51.27 N	7.44 E
Hālisahar	126	22.56 N	88.25 E
Haliyāl	122	15.20 N	74.46 E
Haljala	76	59.26 N	26.16 E
Halkalı -●-[8]	267b	41.02 N	28.47 E
Halkapınar	130	37.25 N	34.13 E
Halkett, Cape >	180	70.49 N	152.12 W
Halkirk	46	58.30 N	3.30 W
Halkyn	262	53.14 N	3.11 W
Halkyn Mountain ∧	262	53.14 N	3.13 W
Hall, Austl.	171b	35.10 S	149.04 E
Hall, In., U.S.	218	39.33 N	86.32 W
Hall, N.Y., U.S.	210	42.48 N	77.04 W
Hällabrottet	40	59.07 N	15.12 E
Halladale ≃	46	58.33 N	3.55 W
Hallam	274b	38.01 S	145.06 E
Hallam Peak ∧	182	52.11 N	118.46 W
Halland □[9]	26	57.00 N	12.40 E
Hallandale	220	25.58 N	80.08 W
Hallands Län □[6]	26	56.45 N	13.00 E
Hallands Väderö I	26	56.26 N	12.33 E
Halla-san ∧	90	33.22 N	126.32 E
Hallau	58	47.42 N	8.27 E
Hällberga	40	59.19 N	16.36 E
Hällbybrunn	40	59.24 N	16.25 E
Hällbymagasinet ⊜[1]	26	63.56 N	17.13 E
Halle, Bel.	50	50.44 N	4.13 E
Halle, Dtsch.	52	52.04 N	8.22 E
Halle, Dtsch.	52	51.59 N	9.33 E
Halle, Dtsch.	54	51.29 N	11.58 E
Halleberg ∧[2]	26	58.23 N	12.27 E
Hällefors	40	59.47 N	14.30 E
Hälleforsnäs	40	59.10 N	16.30 E
Hallein	64	47.41 N	13.06 E
Hällekis	26	58.38 N	13.25 E
Hallen	26	63.11 N	14.05 E
Hallenberg	56	51.06 N	8.37 E
Hallencourt	50	49.59 N	1.53 E
Halle-Neustadt	54	51.29 N	11.56 E
Hallertau -●-[1]	60	48.35 N	11.45 E
Hällestad	40	58.44 N	15.34 E
Hallett, Cape >	9	72.19 S	170.18 E
Hallettsville	222	29.26 N	96.56 W
Halley ʋ[3]	9	75.36 S	26.46 W
Halliday	198	47.21 N	102.20 W
Halligen II	30	54.35 N	8.35 E
Halling	260	51.21 N	0.27 E
Hallingdalselvi ≃	26	60.24 N	9.35 E
Hällingsåfallet ⌊	26	64.20 N	14.20 E
Hall in Tirol	64	47.17 N	11.31 E
Hall Island I	180	60.40 N	173.05 W
Hall Islands II	14	8.37 N	152.00 E
Halliste ≃	76	58.31 N	25.03 E
Hall-i'-th'-Wood ◆	262	53.36 N	2.26 W
Hall Lake ⊜	176	68.41 N	82.17 W
Hall Meadow Brook Reservoir ⊜[1]	207	41.52 N	73.10 W
Hall Mountain ∧	202	48.49 N	117.15 W
Hällnäs	26	64.19 N	19.38 E
Hallock	198	48.46 N	96.56 W
Hallowell	188	44.17 N	69.47 W
Hall Peninsula >[1]	176	63.30 N	66.00 W
Halls	194	35.52 N	89.23 W
Halls Bayou ≃	222	29.12 N	95.07 W
Hallsberg	40	59.04 N	15.07 E
Halls Brook ≃	283	42.00 N	70.43 W
Halls Creek	162	18.16 S	127.46 E
Halls Creek ≃	200	37.18 N	110.45 W
Halls Gap	166	37.08 S	142.31 E
Halls Lake ⊜	212	45.07 N	78.45 W
Halls Stream ≃	206	45.01 N	71.30 W
Hållsta	40	59.18 N	16.27 E
Hallstadt	56	49.55 N	10.52 E
Hallstahammar	40	59.37 N	16.13 E
Hallstatt	64	47.33 N	13.39 E
Hallstätter See ⊜	64	47.35 N	13.39 E
Hallstavik	40	60.03 N	18.36 E
Hallstead	210	41.57 N	75.44 W
Hallsville, Mo., U.S.	219	39.07 N	92.13 W
Hallsville, Tx., U.S.	222	32.30 N	94.34 W
Halluin	50	50.47 N	3.08 E
Hallwiler See ⊜	58	47.18 N	8.13 E
Hallwood	208	37.52 N	75.35 W
Halma	56	50.05 N	5.08 E
Halmahera I	108	1.00 N	128.00 E
Halmahera, Laut (Halmahera Sea) ⊤[2]	108	1.00 S	129.00 E
Halmstad	26	56.39 N	12.50 E
Halpine Village	284c	39.04 N	77.07 W
Hals	26	57.00 N	10.19 E
Halsafjorden c[2]	26	63.03 N	8.11 E
Halsall	262	53.35 N	2.57 W
Halsbrücke	54	50.57 N	13.21 E
Halsey, Ne., U.S.	198	41.54 N	100.16 W
Halsey, Or., U.S.	202	44.23 N	123.06 W
Halsey Harbor c	116	11.45 N	119.56 E
Halsey Valley	210	42.08 N	76.27 W
Hälsingborg → Helsingborg	41	56.03 N	12.42 E
Hälsingland □[9]	26	61.30 N	17.00 E
Halstad	198	47.21 N	96.49 W
Halstead, Eng., U.K.	42	51.57 N	0.38 E
Halstead, Eng., U.K.	260	51.20 N	0.08 E
Halstead, Ks., U.S.	198	38.00 N	97.30 W
Halstenbek	52	53.38 N	9.50 E
Halsteren	52	51.32 N	4.16 E
Halstow Marshes ≋	260	51.29 N	0.33 E
Haltang ≃	102	39.00 N	94.40 E
Haltern	52	51.46 N	7.10 E
Haltiatunturi ∧	24	69.18 N	21.16 E
Haltom City	222	32.47 N	97.16 W
Halton, Eng., U.K.	44	54.05 N	2.46 W
Halton, Eng., U.K.	262	53.20 N	2.42 W
Halton □[6]	212	43.30 N	79.53 W
Halton □[8]	262	53.20 N	2.44 W
Halton Hills	212	43.39 N	79.55 W
Haltwhistle	44	54.58 N	2.27 W
Halura, Pulau I	115b	10.19 S	120.11 E
Ḥaluẕa, Ḥolot ▲[8]	132	31.05 N	34.28 E
Halūzonī, Wādī al- V	273c	30.05 N	31.24 E
Halvarsgårdarna	40	60.24 N	15.23 E
Halvarsnoren ⊜	40	59.35 N	14.36 E
Halver	56	51.11 N	7.30 E
Halvorson, Mount ∧	182	53.15 N	120.33 W
Halwell	42	50.22 N	3.43 W
Halych	78	49.08 N	24.43 E
Ham, Fr.	50	49.45 N	3.04 E
Ham, Tchad	146	10.00 N	15.41 E
Ham -●-[8]	260	51.26 N	0.19 W
Ham ≃	158	28.32 S	19.34 E
Ham, Oued el ≃	34	35.42 N	4.52 E
Ḥamad	140	15.19 N	33.43 E
Hamada	96	34.53 N	132.05 E
Hamadān	128	34.48 N	48.30 E
Hamadān □[4]	128	35.00 N	48.40 E
Ḥamāh	130	35.08 N	36.45 E
Ḥamāh □[8]	130	35.10 N	37.00 E
Hamahika-jima I	174m	26.19 N	127.57 E
Hamakeza	89	47.05 N	120.52 E
Hamakita	94	34.48 N	137.47 E
Hamale	150	10.59 N	2.44 W
Hamamatsu	94	34.42 N	137.44 E
Hamamatsukita-kichi, Kōkū-jieitai- ■	94	34.45 N	137.42 E
Hamamözü	130	40.48 N	35.02 E
Haman	98	35.15 N	128.24 E
Hamanaka	92a	43.05 N	145.10 E
Hamana-ko ⊜	94	34.45 N	137.34 E
Hamano	268	35.33 N	140.08 E
Hamaoka	94	34.39 N	138.08 E
Hamar	26	60.48 N	11.06 E
Hamasaka	96	35.37 N	134.27 E
Ḥamāṭah, Jabal ∧	140	24.12 N	35.00 E
Hamatang	98	40.12 N	124.20 E
Hama-tombetsu	92a	45.07 N	142.23 E
Hambach	56	49.04 N	7.02 E
Hambaek-san ∧	98	37.09 N	128.55 E
Hambantota	122	6.07 N	81.07 E
Hambergen	52	53.18 N	8.49 E
Hamber Provincial Park ◆	182	52.25 N	117.40 W
Hamble	42	50.52 N	1.19 W
Hambledon	42	50.56 N	1.04 W
Hambleton	44	53.52 N	2.57 W
Hambleton Hills ⋏[2]	44	54.16 N	1.12 W
Hamborn -●-[8]	263	51.29 N	6.46 E
Hambourg → Hamburg	52	53.33 N	9.59 E
Hamburg, Dtsch.	52	53.33 N	9.59 E
Hamburg, S. Afr.	158	33.17 S	27.28 E
Hamburg, Ar., U.S.	194	33.13 N	91.47 W
Hamburg, Ct., U.S.	207	41.23 N	72.21 W
Hamburg, Il., U.S.	219	39.14 N	90.43 W
Hamburg, Ia., U.S.	198	40.36 N	95.39 W
Hamburg, Mi., U.S.	216	42.27 N	83.48 W
Hamburg, N.J., U.S.	210	41.09 N	74.34 W
Hamburg, N.Y., U.S.	210	42.42 N	78.49 W
Hamburg, Pa., U.S.	208	40.33 N	75.58 W
Hamburg □[3]	52	53.35 N	10.00 E
Hamburg, Flughafen ⊠	52	53.38 N	10.00 E
Hamburg Airport ⊠	284a	42.42 N	78.55 W
Hamburg Ditch ≊	208	36.31 N	76.33 W
Hamburger Hallig >[1]	41	54.36 N	8.49 E
Hamburg Mountains ⋏	276	41.08 N	74.32 W
Hamburgo → Hamburg	52	53.33 N	9.59 E
Hamburgsund	26	58.33 N	11.16 E
Ḥamḍ, Wādī al- V	128	25.54 N	36.38 E
Ḥamḍah	144	19.02 N	43.36 E
Hamdallay Timbou	150	12.03 N	10.37 W
Hamdam Āb, Dasht-e ≚	128	34.45 N	61.30 E
Ḥamdānah	144	19.58 N	40.35 E
Hamden, Ct., U.S.	207	41.23 N	72.53 W
Hamden, N.Y., U.S.	210	42.12 N	75.00 W
Hamden, Oh., U.S.	188	39.09 N	82.31 W
Hamdibey	130	39.50 N	27.15 E
Häme -●-[1]	26	61.45 N	25.10 E
Hämeenkangas -●-[3]	26	61.45 N	22.40 E
Hämeenkylä	26	60.16 N	24.47 E
Hämeen lääni □[4]	26	61.30 N	24.30 E
Hämeenlinna	26	61.00 N	24.27 E
Hamel	168a	32.52 S	115.55 E
HaMelah, Yam → Dead Sea ⊜	132	31.30 N	35.30 E
Hämelerwald	52	52.22 N	10.05 E
Hamelin	162	26.26 S	114.11 E
Hamelin Pool c	162	26.15 S	114.05 E
Hameln	52	52.06 N	9.21 E
HaMerkaz □[5]	132	32.05 N	34.55 E
Hamer Koke	144	5.12 N	36.45 E
Hamero Hadad	144	7.34 N	42.18 E
Hamersleben	54	52.04 N	11.05 E
Hamersley Range ⋏	162	21.53 S	116.46 E
Hamersley Range National Park ◆	162	22.40 S	118.15 E
Hamersville	218	38.55 N	83.59 W
Hames Creek ≃	226	35.53 N	120.50 W
Hamgyŏng Namdo □[4]	98	40.00 N	127.30 E
Hamgyŏng Pukdo □[4]	98	41.45 N	129.50 E
Hamgyŏng-sanmaek ⋏	98	41.00 N	128.30 E
Ham House ⊥	260	51.27 N	0.19 W
Hamhŭng	98	39.54 N	127.32 E
Hami (Kumul)	102	42.48 N	93.27 E
Hamidiye	130	41.09 N	26.40 E
Hamiguitan, Mount ∧	116	6.44 N	126.11 E
Hamilton, Austl.	166	37.45 S	142.02 E
Hamilton, Ber.	240a	32.17 N	64.46 W
Hamilton, On., Can.	212	43.15 N	79.51 W
Hamilton, N.Z.	172	37.47 S	175.17 E
Hamilton, Scot., U.K.	46	55.47 N	4.03 W
Hamilton, Al., U.S.	194	34.08 N	87.59 W
Hamilton, Ak., U.S.	180	62.54 N	163.53 W
Hamilton, Ga., U.S.	192	32.45 N	84.52 W
Hamilton, Il., U.S.	190	40.23 N	91.20 W
Hamilton, In., U.S.	216	41.32 N	84.54 W
Hamilton, Ks., U.S.	198	37.58 N	96.09 W
Hamilton, Ma., U.S.	207	42.37 N	70.52 W
Hamilton, Mi., U.S.	216	42.40 N	86.00 W
Hamilton, Mo., U.S.	194	39.44 N	93.59 W
Hamilton, Mt., U.S.	202	46.14 N	114.09 W
Hamilton, N.Y., U.S.	210	42.49 N	75.32 W
Hamilton, N.C., U.S.	192	35.56 N	77.12 W
Hamilton, Oh., U.S.	218	39.23 N	84.33 W
Hamilton, R.I., U.S.	207	41.32 N	71.26 W
Hamilton, Tx., U.S.	196	31.42 N	98.07 W
Hamilton, Wa., U.S.	224	48.31 N	121.59 W
Hamilton □[6], In., U.S.	218	40.03 N	86.01 W
Hamilton □[6], N.Y., U.S.	210	43.24 N	74.25 W
Hamilton □[6], Oh., U.S.	218	39.06 N	84.31 W
Hamilton -●-[8]	284b	39.21 N	76.33 W
Hamilton ≃	166	23.30 S	139.47 E
Hamilton, Lake ⊜	220	28.03 N	81.39 W
Hamilton, Lake ⊜[1]	194	34.30 N	93.05 W
Hamilton, Mount ∧, Ak., U.S.	180	61.10 N	159.46 W
Hamilton, Mount ∧, Ca., U.S.	226	37.21 N	121.38 W
Hamilton, Mount ∧, Nv., U.S.	204	39.14 N	115.32 W
Hamilton Acres	180	64.51 N	147.40 W
Hamilton Air Force Base ■	282	38.03 N	122.31 W
Hamilton City	204	39.44 N	122.00 W
Hamilton Creek ≃	162	26.40 S	135.19 E
Hamilton Creek Indian Reserve -●-[4]	182	50.11 N	120.30 W
Hamilton Dome	200	43.46 N	108.34 W
Hamilton Harbour c	212	43.17 N	79.50 W
Hamilton Hill	168a	32.05 S	115.46 E
Hamilton Hotel	166	22.50 S	140.35 E
Hamilton Inlet c	176	54.00 N	57.30 W
Hamilton Lake ⊜	216	41.33 N	84.55 W
Hamilton Mountain ∧	188	43.25 N	74.22 W
Hamilton Park, In., U.S.	216	40.17 N	85.19 W
Hamilton Park, Pa., U.S.	208	40.02 N	76.20 W
Hamilton Sound ⊔	186	49.30 N	54.30 W
Hamilton Square	285	40.13 N	74.39 W
Hamilton-Wentworth □[6]	212	43.15 N	80.00 W
Ḥamīm, Wādī al- V	146	30.10 N	21.32 E
Hamina	26	60.34 N	27.12 E
Hamiota	184	50.11 N	100.36 W
Ḥāmir, Wādī V	128	31.37 N	42.12 E
Hamīrpur, India	123	31.41 N	76.31 E
Hamīrpur, India	124	25.57 N	80.09 E
Hamjong-ni	98	38.59 N	125.17 E
Hamler	216	41.13 N	84.02 W
Hamlet, In., U.S.	216	41.32 N	86.34 W
Hamlet, N.C., U.S.	192	34.53 N	79.41 W
Hamlet, Oh., U.S.	218	39.01 N	84.12 W
Hamlet, Mount ∧	180	68.47 N	165.57 W
Hamley Bridge	168b	34.21 S	138.41 E
Hamlin, N.Y., U.S.	210	43.18 N	77.55 W
Hamlin, Pa., U.S.	210	41.24 N	75.24 W
Hamlin, Tx., U.S.	196	32.53 N	100.08 W
Hamlin, W.V., U.S.	188	38.16 N	82.06 W
Hamlin Beach State Park ◆	210	43.22 N	77.58 W
Hamlin Lake ⊜	190	44.03 N	86.27 W
Hamlin Valley Wash V	200	38.53 N	114.01 W
Hamm	52	51.41 N	7.49 E
Hamm -●-[8], Dtsch.	263	51.12 N	6.44 E
Hamm -●-[8], Dtsch.	263	51.23 N	7.03 E
Ḥammād, Wādī V	142	29.45 N	32.24 E
Hamma Hamma ≃	224	47.33 N	123.03 W
Håmmålfjell ∧	26	62.27 N	11.17 E
Ḥammām at-Turkumān	130	36.32 N	39.03 E
Hammamet, Alg.	36	35.27 N	7.58 E
Hammamet, Tun.	148	36.24 N	10.37 E
Hammamet, Golfe de c	36	36.05 N	10.40 E
Hammam Lif	148	36.44 N	10.20 E
Ḥammānā	132	33.49 N	35.44 E
Hammar	40	58.49 N	14.57 E
Ḥammār, Hawr al- ⊜	128	30.50 N	47.10 E
Hammarby	40	60.33 N	16.34 E
Hammarn	40	59.45 N	14.30 E
Hammarö	40	59.20 N	13.31 E
Hammarön I	40	59.19 N	13.31 E
Hammarstrand	26	63.06 N	16.21 E
Hamme	50	51.06 N	4.08 E
Hamme ≃	52	53.10 N	8.44 E
Hammel	52	56.15 N	9.52 E
Hammelburg	56	50.07 N	9.53 E
Hamme-Mille	56	50.47 N	4.43 E
Hammerdal	26	63.36 N	15.21 E
Hammerfest	24	70.40 N	23.42 E
Hämmern	263	51.08 N	7.21 E
Hammershus ⊥	26	55.16 N	14.45 E
Hammersley Inlet c	224	47.12 N	123.00 W
Hammersmith -●-[8]	260	51.30 N	0.14 W
Hammerum	41	56.08 N	9.04 E
Hamminkeln	52	51.44 N	6.35 E
Hammon	196	35.37 N	99.22 W
Hammonasset ≃	207	41.16 N	72.33 W
Hammond, In., U.S.	216	41.35 N	87.30 W
Hammond, La., U.S.	194	30.30 N	90.27 W
Hammond, N.Y., U.S.	212	44.26 N	75.41 W
Hammond, Or., U.S.	224	46.12 N	123.57 W
Hammond, Wi., U.S.	190	44.58 N	92.26 W
Hammond Island I, Austl.	164	10.35 S	142.13 E
Hammond Island I, Ca., U.S.	282	38.06 N	121.57 W
Hammond Pond Park ◆	283	42.19 N	71.11 W
Hammondsport	210	42.24 N	77.13 W
Hammondsville	214	40.33 N	80.43 W
Hammondville	274a	33.57 S	150.57 E
Hammonia	158	28.43 S	27.49 E
Hammonton	208	39.38 N	74.48 W
Hamningberg	24	70.31 N	30.37 E
Ham-Nord	206	45.54 N	71.39 W
Hamoir	56	50.26 N	5.32 E
Hamont	56	51.15 N	5.33 E
HaMore, Giv'at ∧	132	32.37 N	35.21 E
Hamorton	285	39.52 N	75.39 W
Hamoyet, Jabal ∧	144	17.33 N	38.02 E
Hampden, Austl.	168b	34.09 S	139.03 E
Hampden, Nf., Can.	186	49.33 N	56.51 W
Hampden, N.Z.	172	45.19 S	170.49 E
Hampden, Me., U.S.	188	44.44 N	68.50 W
Hampden, Ma., U.S.	207	42.03 N	72.24 W
Hampden, N.D., U.S.	198	48.32 N	98.39 W
Hampden □[6]	207	42.07 N	72.36 W
Hampden Sydney	192	37.15 N	78.29 W
Hampetorp	40	59.09 N	15.40 E
Hampi	122	15.24 N	76.37 E
Hampshire	216	42.05 N	88.31 W
Hampshire □[6], Eng., U.K.	42	51.05 N	1.15 W
Hampshire □[6], Ma., U.S.	207	42.19 N	72.38 W
Hampshire Downs ⋏[1]	42	51.15 N	1.17 W
Hampshire Heights	279b	40.20 N	79.33 W
Hampstead, P.Q., Can.	275a	45.29 N	73.38 W
Hampstead, Md., U.S.	208	39.36 N	76.51 W
Hampstead, N.C., U.S.	192	34.22 N	77.42 W
Hampstead -●-[8]	260	51.33 N	0.11 W
Hampstead Heath ◆	260	51.34 N	0.10 W
Hampton, Austl.	274b	37.56 S	145.00 E
Hampton, N.B., Can.	186	45.32 N	65.51 W
Hampton, On., Can.	212	43.58 N	78.45 W
Hampton, Ar., U.S.	194	33.32 N	92.28 W
Hampton, Ct., U.S.	207	41.47 N	72.03 W
Hampton, Fl., U.S.	192	29.51 N	82.07 W
Hampton, Ga., U.S.	192	33.23 N	84.16 W
Hampton, Ia., U.S.	190	42.44 N	93.12 W
Hampton, Ne., U.S.	198	40.52 N	97.53 W
Hampton, N.H., U.S.	188	42.56 N	70.50 W
Hampton, N.J., U.S.	210	40.42 N	74.57 W
Hampton, Pa., U.S.	208	39.56 N	77.04 W
Hampton, S.C., U.S.	192	32.52 N	81.06 W
Hampton, Tn., U.S.	192	36.17 N	82.10 W
Hampton, Va., U.S.	208	37.01 N	76.20 W
Hampton -●-[8]	260	51.25 N	0.22 W
Hampton, Mount ∧	9	76.29 S	125.48 W
Hampton Bays	207	40.52 N	72.31 W
Hampton Butte ∧	202	43.46 N	120.17 W
Hampton Court Palace ʋ	42	51.24 N	0.20 W
Hampton Harbour c	162	20.40 S	116.30 E
Hampton National Historic Site ⊥	284b	39.25 N	76.35 W
Hampton Park	274b	38.02 S	145.15 E
Hampton Roads ⊤[3]	208	36.58 N	76.20 W
Hampton Roads Bridge-Tunnel -●-[5]	208	37.00 N	76.18 W
Hampton Tableland ⋏[1]	162	32.10 S	126.10 E
Hamp'yŏng	98	35.05 N	126.30 E
Hamr	54	50.35 N	13.35 E
Hamra	26	61.39 N	15.00 E
Ḥamrā', Al-Ḥamādah al- -●-[2]	146	30.00 N	12.00 E
Hamra, As Saquia al V	148	27.15 N	13.21 W
Hamra, Ouadi V	146	12.52 N	21.15 E
Ḥamrah, Jabal al- ∧	132	29.39 N	34.47 E
Ḥamran, Har ∧	132	30.41 N	34.34 E
Hamra Nationalpark ◆	26	61.45 N	14.55 E
Ḥamrat ash-Shaykh	140	14.35 N	27.58 E
Hams Bluff ▲[4]	241n	17.46 N	64.52 W
Hams Fork ≃	200	41.35 N	109.59 W
Hamstreet	42	51.04 N	0.51 E
Ham-Sud	206	45.46 N	71.36 W
Ham Tan	110	10.40 N	107.46 E
Hamtramck	216	42.23 N	83.02 W
Hāmūn, Daryācheh-ye ⊜	128	30.50 N	61.07 E
Hamur	84	39.36 N	42.59 E
Hamura	94	35.45 N	139.19 E
Hamyang	98	35.32 N	127.42 E
Hamzalı	130	38.19 N	41.09 E
Han	150	10.41 N	2.27 W
Han ≃, Zhg.	100	23.41 N	116.38 E
Han ≃, Zhg.	102	30.35 N	114.17 E
Han, Grottes de ▲[5]	56	50.08 N	5.15 E
Han, Nong ⊜	110	17.12 N	104.11 E
Hana	229a	20.45 N	155.59 W
Hanábana ≃	240p	22.23 N	80.58 W
Hanahan	192	32.55 N	80.01 W
Hanailike	85	39.16 N	76.26 E
Ḥanak	128	25.33 N	36.56 E
Hanakaoo Point >	229a	20.55 N	156.42 W
Hanalei	229b	22.12 N	159.30 W
Hanalei Bay c	229b	22.13 N	159.31 W
Hanamaki	92	39.23 N	141.07 E
Hanamaulu	229b	21.59 N	159.21 W
Hanamenu, Baie c	174x	9.46 S	139.08 W
Hanam-ni	98	38.23 N	126.43 E
Hanang ∧	154	4.26 S	35.24 E
Hanapepe	229b	21.54 N	159.35 W
Hānār Char	126	23.08 N	90.38 E
Hanataka-sen ∧	96	35.24 N	132.45 E
Hanateio	174x	9.59 S	139.06 W
Hanatetena	174x	9.58 S	139.04 W
Hanau	56	50.08 N	8.55 E
Hanaui	174x	9.45 S	139.05 W
Hanawa, Nihon	94	36.57 N	140.25 E
Hanawa, Nihon	268	35.13 N	139.53 E
Hanbury ≃	176	63.37 N	104.33 W
Hâncești	38	46.49 N	28.34 E
Hanceville, B.C., Can.	182	51.55 N	123.03 W
Hanceville, Al., U.S.	194	34.03 N	86.46 W
Hanchang	107	30.26 N	103.43 E
Hancheng, Zhg.	102	35.28 N	110.29 E
Hancheng, Zhg.	105	39.39 N	118.02 E
Hanches	261	48.36 N	1.39 E
Hanchō	270	34.49 N	135.27 E
Han-ch'ŏn ≃	271b	37.33 N	127.02 E
Hanchuan	100	30.39 N	113.48 E
Hanchung → Hanzhong	102	33.08 N	107.02 E
Hancock, Md., U.S.	188	39.41 N	78.10 W
Hancock, Mi., U.S.	190	47.07 N	88.34 W
Hancock, Mn., U.S.	198	45.29 N	95.47 W
Hancock, N.Y., U.S.	210	41.57 N	75.17 W
Hancock, Wi., U.S.	190	44.08 N	89.31 W
Hancock □[6], Il., U.S.	219	40.13 N	91.15 W
Hancock □[6], In., U.S.	218	39.47 N	85.46 W
Hancock □[6], Oh., U.S.	216	41.02 N	83.39 W
Hancock □[6], W.V., U.S.	214	40.30 N	80.33 W
Hancock, Lake ⊜	220	27.58 N	81.50 W
Hancocks Bridge	208	39.30 N	75.27 W
Hancun	105	39.24 N	116.36 E
Handa, Nihon	94	34.53 N	136.56 E
Handa, Nihon	96	34.02 N	134.02 E
Handa, Som.	144	10.40 N	51.07 E
Handa I	46	58.22 N	5.12 W
Handan	98	36.37 N	114.29 E
Handaokou	98	34.16 N	116.24 E
Handawor	123	34.24 N	74.17 E
Handen	40	59.10 N	18.08 E
Handeni	154	5.26 S	38.01 E
Handforth	262	53.21 N	2.13 W
Handlová	30	48.44 N	18.46 E
Handöl	26	63.16 N	12.26 E
Handorf	52	51.59 N	7.41 E
Handsworth	184	49.48 N	103.00 W
Handub	140	19.14 N	37.16 E
Handzame	50	51.02 N	3.00 E
Haneda Airport ⊠	268	35.33 N	139.46 E
HaNegev (Negev Desert) -●-[1]	132	30.30 N	34.55 E
Haney	224	49.13 N	122.36 W
Hane-yama ∧	96	33.14 N	131.08 E
Hane-zaki >	96	33.22 N	134.02 E
Hanford	226	36.19 N	119.38 W
Hanford Site ʋ[3]	202	46.35 N	119.30 W
Han'gang	98	34.39 N	114.38 E
Han-gang ≃	98	37.45 N	126.11 E
Hanga Roa	174z	27.09 S	109.26 W
Hangatiki	172	38.15 S	175.10 E
Hangbu	100	28.53 N	118.49 E
Hangchow → Hangzhou	106	30.15 N	120.10 E
Hangchow Bay → Hangzhou Wan c	100	30.25 N	121.00 E
Hanger ≃	144	9.35 N	36.02 E
Hanggai	106	30.35 N	119.23 E
Hanggin Houqi	102	40.55 N	107.15 E
Hanggin Qi	102	39.56 N	108.54 E
Hang Hau Town	271d	22.19 N	114.16 E
Hanging Gardens ◆	272c	18.58 N	72.48 E
Hanging Rock State Park ◆	192	36.25 N	80.15 W
Hangingstone Hill ∧[2]	42	50.39 N	3.57 W
Hanging Woman Creek ≃	202	45.19 N	106.31 W
Hangklip, Kaap >	158	34.26 S	18.48 E
Hangkou	100	29.03 N	114.27 E
Hangman Creek ≃	202	47.38 N	117.27 W
Hangö (Hanko)	26	59.50 N	22.57 E
Hangou	105	39.18 N	117.07 E
Hang-Tcheou → Hangzhou	106	30.15 N	120.10 E
Hangtou	106	31.01 N	121.35 E
Hangtschou → Hangzhou	106	30.15 N	120.10 E
Hangu, Pāk.	123	33.32 N	71.04 E
Hangu, Zhg.	105	39.15 N	117.47 E
Hangu, Zhg.	107	28.58 N	104.30 E
Hanguang	100	24.16 N	113.08 E
Hanguchang	107	29.32 N	106.21 E
Hangugang	105	39.15 N	116.56 E
Hangzhou (Hangchow)	106	30.15 N	120.10 E
Hangzhou Wan (Hangchow Bay) c	100	30.25 N	121.00 E
Hani	130	38.24 N	40.24 E
Hänigsen	52	52.29 N	10.05 E
Hanimadu I	122	6.45 N	73.09 E
Ḥanīsh II	144	13.45 N	42.45 E
Ḥanīsh al-Kabīr, Jazīrat al- I	144	13.43 N	42.45 E
Ḥanita	132	33.05 N	35.10 E
Hanjalipan	112	2.15 S	112.47 E
Hanjiagou	104	40.42 N	120.47 E
Hanjiang	100	25.30 N	119.06 E
Hanjiapuzi	104	40.48 N	123.14 E
Hanjiashu	105	39.11 N	117.04 E
Hanjiawa	106	31.16 N	119.18 E
Hankamer	222	29.51 N	94.38 W
Hankasalmi	26	62.23 N	26.26 E
Hanke	26	59.12 N	10.47 E
Hankendi	130	38.35 N	39.04 E
Hankensbüttel	54	52.44 N	10.36 E
Hankey	158	33.50 S	24.53 E
Hankins	210	41.49 N	75.05 W
Hankinson	198	46.04 N	96.54 W
Hanko → Hangö	26	59.50 N	22.57 E
Hankow → Wuhan	100	30.36 N	114.17 E
Hanks Pond ⊜	276	41.05 N	74.26 W
Hanku → Hangu	105	39.15 N	117.47 E
Hānle	120	32.48 N	79.00 E
Hanley	184	51.37 N	106.27 W
Hanmer	190	46.39 N	80.56 W
Hanmer Springs	172	42.31 S	172.49 E
Hanmiao	89	44.33 N	119.59 E
Hann ≃	164	17.10 S	126.10 E
Hann, Mount ∧	164	15.51 S	125.48 E
Hanna, Ab., Can.	182	51.38 N	111.54 W
Hanna, In., U.S.	216	41.24 N	86.46 W
Hanna, Ok., U.S.	196	35.12 N	95.53 W
Hanna, Wy., U.S.	200	41.52 N	106.33 W
Hanna City	190	40.41 N	89.47 W
Hannaford	198	47.18 N	98.11 W
Hannah	198	48.58 N	98.41 W
Hannah Bay c	176	51.05 N	79.45 W
Hannastown	214	40.21 N	79.30 W
Hannibal, Mo., U.S.	219	39.42 N	91.21 W
Hannibal, N.Y., U.S.	210	43.19 N	76.34 W
Hanningfield Reservoir ⊜[1]	260	51.39 N	0.31 E
Hannō	94	35.51 N	139.19 E
Hannover	52	52.24 N	9.44 E
Hannover □[5]	52	52.30 N	9.15 E
Hannover, Flughafen ⊠	52	52.27 N	9.42 E
Hannut	56	50.40 N	5.05 E
Hanö I	26	56.00 N	14.50 E
Hanobası	130	38.35 N	33.50 E
Hanöbukten c	26	55.45 N	14.30 E
Ha Noi	110	21.02 N	105.51 E
Hanönü	130	41.38 N	34.28 E
Hanoura	96	33.57 N	134.38 E
Hanover, On., Can.	212	44.09 N	81.02 W
Hanover → Hannover, Dtsch.	52	52.24 N	9.44 E
Hanover, S. Afr.	158	31.04 S	24.29 E
Hanover, Ct., U.S.	207	41.38 N	72.03 W
Hanover, Il., U.S.	190	42.15 N	90.16 W
Hanover, In., U.S.	218	38.42 N	85.28 W
Hanover, Ks., U.S.	198	39.53 N	96.52 W
Hanover, Ma., U.S.	207	42.06 N	70.48 W
Hanover, Mi., U.S.	216	42.06 N	84.33 W
Hanover, N.H., U.S.	188	43.42 N	72.17 W
Hanover, N.M., U.S.	200	32.48 N	108.05 W
Hanover, Oh., U.S.	214	40.04 N	82.15 W
Hanover, Pa., U.S.	208	39.48 N	76.59 W
Hanover, Va., U.S.	208	37.45 N	77.22 W
Hanover, Wi., U.S.	216	42.38 N	89.10 W
Hanover □[6]	208	37.42 N	77.20 W
Hanover, Isla I	254	51.00 S	74.40 W
Hanover Airport ⊠	276	40.50 N	74.21 W
Hanover Center	283	42.07 N	70.50 W
Hanover Park	216	42.00 N	88.09 W
Hanover Road	158	30.58 S	24.33 E
Hanoverton	214	40.45 N	80.56 W
Hanovre → Hannover	52	52.24 N	9.44 E
Hanpan, Cape >	175e	5.01 S	154.37 E
Hanryeosudo Kukrip Kongwŏn ◆	98	34.46 N	128.30 E
Hansanjiazi	104	41.44 N	122.57 E
Hansard	182	54.05 N	121.52 W
Hanscom Air Force Base ■	207	42.28 N	71.17 W
Hans Creek ≃	210	43.06 N	74.08 W
Hansdiha	124	24.36 N	87.05 E
Hansen Dam -●-[6]	280	34.16 N	118.23 W
Hansen Flood Control Basin ≚[1]	228	34.16 N	118.23 W
Hanshan	100	31.44 N	118.08 E
Hansharo ⊥	94	35.02 N	138.56 E
Hansi, India	120	32.27 N	77.50 E
Hānsi, India	123	29.06 N	75.58 E
Hansia	272b	22.48 N	88.24 E
Hanska	198	44.08 N	94.29 W
Hānskhāli	126	23.21 N	88.37 E
Hans Lollik Island I	240m	18.24 N	64.55 W
Hanslope	42	52.06 N	0.49 W
Hans Meyer Range ⋏	164	4.20 S	152.55 E
Hanson	207	42.04 N	70.52 W
Hanson ≃	162	20.15 S	133.25 E
Hanson Lake ⊜	184	54.42 N	102.49 W
Hanstholm	26	57.07 N	8.38 E
Han-sur-Lesse	56	50.08 N	5.11 E
Han-sur-Nied	56	48.59 N	6.26 E
Hansville	224	47.55 N	122.33 W
Hansweert	52	51.26 N	4.00 E
Hantaj	88	49.31 N	103.13 E
Hāntālbunia	126	22.44 N	89.31 E
Hantamsberg ⋏	158	31.22 S	19.45 E
Hantan → Handan	98	36.37 N	114.29 E
Hantes ≃	50	50.19 N	4.11 E
Hant's Harbour	186	48.01 N	53.16 W
Hantsport	186	45.04 N	64.11 W
Hantu, Pulau I	271c	1.14 N	103.45 E
Hantu, Tanjong >	114	4.18 N	100.34 E
Hantzsch ≃	176	67.32 N	72.25 W
Hanumangarh	123	29.35 N	74.19 E
Hanumān Nagar	124	26.30 N	86.51 E
Hanušovce nad Topľou	30	49.02 N	21.30 E
Hanušovice	30	50.05 N	16.55 E
Hanveden ⋏[2]	40	59.07 N	18.00 E
Hanwood	166	34.20 S	146.03 E
Hanworth -●-[8]	260	51.26 N	0.23 W
Hanxinzhuang	105	40.16 N	116.44 E
Hanyang	107	29.44 N	103.44 E
Hanyangping	102	32.41 N	108.34 E
Hanyin	102	32.42 N	108.50 E
Hanyū	94	36.10 N	139.32 E
Hanyuan	102	29.22 N	102.38 E
Hanyuangai	102	29.30 N	102.31 E
Hanzan	96	34.16 N	133.51 E
Hanzhong	102	33.08 N	107.02 E
Hanzhuang	98	34.38 N	117.24 E
Hao I[1]	14	18.15 S	140.54 W
Hao ≃	100	28.27 N	119.56 E
Haohekou	100	28.38 N	112.49 E
Haojiadian	100	31.47 N	113.44 E
Haoli → Hegang	89	47.24 N	130.17 E
Haoluqi	106	30.38 N	119.34 E
HaOn	132	32.43 N	35.38 E
Hāora	126	22.35 N	88.20 E
Hāora Bridge -●-[5]	272b	22.35 N	88.21 E
Hāora Railroad Station -●-[5]	272b	22.35 N	88.21 E
Haouach, Ouadi V	146	16.45 N	19.35 E
Haoxue	102	30.00 N	112.20 E
Haozhikou	107	29.36 N	105.02 E
Haparanda	26	65.50 N	24.10 E
Hapatoni, Baie c	174x	9.58 S	139.07 W
Hapert	52	51.23 N	5.15 E
Hapeville	192	33.39 N	84.24 W
Happ'o-ri	98	40.40 N	127.49 E
Happy	196	34.45 N	101.52 W
Happy Camp	204	41.47 N	123.22 W
Happy Jack	200	34.45 N	111.11 W
Happy Valley-Goose Bay	176	53.20 N	60.25 W
Happy Valley Race Course ◆	271d	22.16 N	114.10 E
Hapsford	262	53.16 N	2.48 W
Hapsu	98	41.13 N	128.51 E
Hapton	262	53.47 N	2.19 W
Hāpur	124	28.43 N	77.47 E
Ḥaql	128	29.18 N	34.57 E
Haquira	248	14.13 S	72.11 W
Har	164	5.20 S	133.10 E
Har, Laga ≃	154	1.40 N	39.36 E
Hara, Nihon	94	35.58 N	138.14 E
Hara, Nihon	268	35.50 N	139.46 E
Ḥaraḍ, Ar. Su.	128	24.08 N	49.05 E
Härad, Sve.	40	59.23 N	16.55 E
Ḥaraḍ, Yaman	144	16.28 N	43.04 E
Ḥarad, Jabal al- ∧	132	29.40 N	35.49 E
Haraiki I[1]	14	17.28 S	143.27 W
Harajuku	268	35.54 N	139.21 E
Haraldsted	41	55.30 N	11.47 E
Haramachi	92	37.38 N	140.58 E
Haramachida	268	35.33 N	139.27 E
Haramosh ∧	123	35.50 N	74.54 E
Haramosh Range ⋏	123	35.40 N	75.22 E
Harappa	123	30.38 N	72.52 E
Harappa Road	123	30.36 N	72.55 E
Harar → Harer	144	9.18 N	42.08 E
Harare (Salisbury)	154	17.50 S	31.03 E
Ḥarash, Bi'r al- ⊤[4]	146	25.30 N	22.12 E
Ḥarastā al-Baṣal	132	33.34 N	36.22 E
Hārāt	272b	22.53 N	88.11 E
Haraz-Djombo	146	13.57 N	19.26 E
Haraze-Mangueigne	146	9.55 N	20.48 E
Harbāti	272b	22.55 N	88.33 E
Harbert	216	41.52 N	86.38 W
Harbeson	208	38.43 N	75.17 W
Harbin	89	45.45 N	126.41 E
Harbiye	130	36.11 N	36.05 E
Harbke	54	52.12 N	11.03 E
Harbo	40	60.06 N	17.12 E
Harbonnières	50	49.51 N	2.40 E
Harboør	26	56.37 N	8.12 E
Harbor	202	42.03 N	124.15 W
Harbor Beach	190	43.50 N	82.39 W
Harbor City -●-[8]	280	33.48 N	118.17 W
Harborcreek	214	42.10 N	79.57 W
Harbord	170	33.47 S	151.17 E
Harbor Isle	276	40.36 N	73.40 W
Harbor Side	228	32.37 N	117.05 W
Harbor Springs	190	45.25 N	84.59 W
Harborton	208	37.39 N	75.49 W
Harbor Tunnel -●-[5]	284b	39.15 N	76.34 W
Harbor View	214	41.42 N	83.27 W
Harbour Breton	186	47.29 N	55.48 W
Harbour Buffett	186	47.31 N	54.05 W
Harbour Deep	186	50.22 N	56.31 W
Harbour Grace	186	47.42 N	53.13 W
Harbours, Bay of c	254	52.15 S	59.15 W
Harbourville	186	45.09 N	64.49 W
Harburg	56	48.47 N	10.41 E
Harburg -●-[8]	52	53.28 N	9.59 E
Hårby	41	55.13 N	10.07 E
Harchies	50	50.29 N	3.41 E
Harcourt, Austl.	169	37.00 S	144.15 E
Harcourt, Fr.	50	49.10 N	0.48 E
Harcuvar Mountains ⋏	200	34.00 N	113.30 W
Hard	58	47.29 N	9.41 E
Harda	124	22.20 N	77.06 E
Hardangerfjorden c[2]	26	60.10 N	6.00 E
Hardangerjøkulen ⍓	26	60.33 N	7.26 E
Hardangervidda ⋏[1]	26	60.20 N	7.30 E
Hardangervidda Nasjonalpark ◆	26	60.15 N	7.05 E
Hardapdam ⊜[1]	156	24.28 S	17.48 E
Hardee □[6]	220	27.29 N	81.48 W
Hardeeville	192	32.17 N	81.04 W
Hardegarijp	52	53.13 N	5.56 E
Hardegsen	52	51.39 N	9.49 E
Hardelot-Plage	50	50.38 N	1.35 E

Symbols in the index entries represent the broad categories identified in the key at the right. Symbols with superior numbers (⋏[1]) identify subcategories (see complete key on page *I · 1*).

Symbole im Register stellen die rechts im Schlüssel erklärten Kategorien dar. Symbole mit hochgestellten Ziffern (⋏[1]) bezeichnen Unterabteilungen einer Kategorie (vgl. vollständiger Schlüssel auf Seite *I · 1*).

Los símbolos incluídos en el texto del índice representan las grandes categorías identificadas con la clave a la derecha. Los símbolos con numeros en su parte superior (⋏[1]) identifican las subcategorías (véase la clave completa en la página *I · 1*).

Les symboles de l'index représentent les catégories indiquées dans la légende à droite. Les symboles suivis d'un indice (⋏[1]) représentent des sous-catégories (voir légende complète à la page *I · 1*).

Os símbolos incluídos no texto do índice representam as grandes categorias identificadas com a chave à direita. Os símbolos com números em sua parte superior (⋏[1]) identificam as subcategorias (veja-se a chave completa à página *I · 1*).

∧	Mountain	Berg	Montaña	Montagne	Montanha
⋏	Mountains	Gebirge	Montañas	Montagnes	Montanhas
)(	Pass	Paß	Paso	Col	Passo
V	Valley, Canyon	Tal, Cañon	Valle, Cañón	Vallée, Canyon	Vale, Canhão
≚	Plain	Ebene	Llano	Plaine	Planície
>	Cape	Kap	Cabo	Cap	Cabo
I	Island	Insel	Isla	Île	Ilha
II	Islands	Inseln	Islas	Îles	Ilhas
⊥	Other Topographic Features	Andere Topographische Objekte	Otros Elementos Topográficos	Autres données topographiques	Outros acidentes topográficos

ESPAÑOL — Nombre · Página · Lat.°′ · Long.°′ W = Oeste
FRANÇAIS — Nom · Page · Lat.°′ · Long.°′ W = Ouest
PORTUGUÊS — Nome · Página · Lat.°′ · Long.°′ W = Oeste

Nombre	Página	Lat.°′	Long.°′ W = Oeste
Hardenberg	52	52.34 N	6.37 E
Harderwijk	52	52.21 N	5.36 E
Hardesty	196	36.36 N	101.11 W
Hardey ≃	162	22.45 S	116.07 E
Hardgrave, Mount ∧ [2]	171a	27.30 S	153.29 E
Hardheim	56	49.36 N	9.28 E
Hardin, Il., U.S.	219	39.09 N	90.37 W
Hardin, Mt., U.S.	202	45.43 N	107.36 W
Hardin, Tx., U.S.	222	30.09 N	94.44 W
Hardin □ [6], Oh., U.S.	216	40.39 N	83.36 W
Hardin □ [6], Tx., U.S.	222	30.20 N	94.35 W
Harding, S. Afr.	158	30.34 S	29.58 E
Harding, Il., U.S.	216	41.31 N	88.51 W
Harding, Ma., U.S.	283	42.12 N	71.27 W
Harding, Lake ⊜ [1]	192	32.40 N	85.06 W
Harding Lake ⊜	184	56.13 N	98.23 W
Harding Lakes	208	39.27 N	74.45 W
Hardinsburg, In., U.S.	218	38.27 N	86.16 W
Hardinsburg, Ky., U.S.	194	37.46 N	86.27 W
Hardisty	182	52.40 N	111.18 W
Hardisty Lake ⊜	176	64.30 N	117.45 W
Hardoi	124	27.25 N	80.07 E
Hardoi Branch ≅	124	28.41 N	80.08 E
Hardricourt	261	49.01 N	1.54 E
Hardscrabble Wash V	200	34.39 N	109.28 W
Hardt	263	51.07 N	6.58 E
Hardtner	198	37.00 N	98.38 W
Hardwick, Ga., U.S.	192	33.04 N	83.13 W
Hardwick, Ma., U.S.	207	42.21 N	72.12 W
Hardwick, Vt., U.S.	188	44.30 N	72.22 W
Hardwood	194	30.49 N	91.23 W
Hardwood Ridge ∧	210	41.15 N	75.23 W
Hardy, Ar., U.S.	194	36.18 N	91.28 W
Hardy, Ne., U.S.	198	40.00 N	97.55 W
Hardy, Península ≻ [1]	254	55.25 S	68.30 W
Hardy Bay ⊂	176	75.02 N	115.16 W
Hardy Creek ≃	214	42.52 N	81.52 W
Hardy Lake ⊜ [1]	218	38.47 N	85.42 W
Hardy Lake State Recreation Area ♠	218	38.44 N	86.26 W
Hardys Pond ⊜	283	42.25 N	71.15 W
Hare, Mount ∧	180	66.38 N	136.12 W
Hare Bay	186	48.51 N	54.01 W
Hare Bay ⊂	186	51.18 N	55.50 W
Harefield ⧫ [8]	260	51.36 N	0.29 W
Hareid	26	62.22 N	6.02 E
Hare Indian ≃	180	66.18 N	128.38 W
Harelbeke	50	50.51 N	3.18 E
Haren, Dtsch.	52	52.47 N	7.14 E
Haren, Ned.	52	53.10 N	6.35 E
Hareøen I	176	70.25 N	54.50 W
Harer	144	9.18 N	42.08 E
Harerge □ [4]	144	8.00 N	43.00 E
Hareskov	41	55.46 N	12.25 E
Hareto	144	9.20 N	37.06 E
Harewa	144	9.55 N	41.59 E
Harewood	172	43.29 S	172.35 E
Harewood Park	284b	39.23 N	76.22 W
Harfaz	130	38.01 N	41.19 E
Harfleur	50	49.30 N	0.12 E
Harford, N.Y., U.S.	210	42.26 N	76.14 W
Harford, Pa., U.S.	210	41.47 N	75.42 W
Harford □ [6]	208	39.32 N	76.21 W
Harford Heights	279b	40.22 N	79.46 W
Harford Mills	210	42.25 N	76.12 W
Harg, Sve.	40	59.49 N	18.57 E
Harg, Sve.	40	60.11 N	18.24 E
Hargele	144	5.20 N	42.05 E
Hargeville	261	48.53 N	1.45 E
Hargeysa	144	9.35 N	44.04 E
Harghita □ [6]	38	46.35 N	25.30 E
Harghita, Munții ⩘	38	46.15 N	25.45 E
Hargrave ≃	184	54.24 N	98.48 W
Hargrave Lake ⊜	184	54.29 N	99.40 W
Hargshamn	40	60.10 N	18.28 E
Har Hu (Heihai) ⊜	102	38.15 N	97.40 E
Hāriabhānga ≃ [1]	126	21.43 N	89.05 E
Hariāna	123	31.38 N	75.51 E
Hariarapitu	114	2.33 N	98.35 E
Ḥarīb	144	14.57 N	45.30 E
Haribes	156	24.20 S	17.40 E
Ḥaricha, Ḥamâda el ⧫ [2]	148	22.36 N	3.31 W
Haridwār	124	29.58 N	78.10 E
Harigabessho	270	34.37 N	135.58 E
Harihar	122	14.31 N	75.48 E
Harihari	172	43.09 S	170.33 E
Hariharpāra	126	24.02 N	88.27 E
Harīke	123	31.10 N	74.57 E
Ḥārim	130	36.12 N	36.31 E
Ḥarim, Jabal al- ∧	128	25.58 N	56.14 E
Harima	96	34.42 N	134.53 E
Harima-nada ⫪ [2]	96	34.29 N	134.35 E
Harinagar	124	27.09 N	84.19 E
Harinākunda	126	23.39 N	89.03 E
Haringey ⧫ [8]	42	51.35 N	0.07 W
Hāringhāta ≃ [1]	126	21.54 N	89.57 E
Haringvliet ʉ	52	51.47 N	4.10 E
Haringvlietbrug ⧫ [5]	52	51.43 N	4.20 E
Haringvlietdam ⧫ [5]	52	51.50 N	4.03 E
Haripāl	272b	22.49 N	88.07 E
Haripur, India	126	24.18 N	87.05 E
Haripur, India	272b	22.56 N	88.14 E
Harīpur, Pāk.	123	33.59 N	72.56 E
Harirāmpur	126	23.42 N	89.57 E
Harīrūd (Tedžen) ≃	128	37.24 N	60.38 E
Harischandra Range ⩘	122	19.15 N	74.05 E
Ḥārithān	130	36.16 N	37.05 E
Hariyo	144	5.00 N	47.23 E
Harjavalta	26	61.19 N	22.08 E
Härjedalen □ [9]	26	62.20 N	13.00 E
Harkaway	274b	38.00 S	145.21 E
Härkeberga	40	59.42 N	17.11 E
Harkema-Opeinde	52	53.11 N	6.08 E
Harker Heights	222	31.05 N	97.40 W
Harkers Island	192	34.41 N	76.33 W
Harker Village	285	39.51 N	75.09 W
Harkness Memorial State Park ♠	207	41.18 N	72.07 W
Harkortsee ⊜	263	51.24 N	7.25 E
Harlaching ⧫ [8]	60	48.06 N	11.33 E
Harlan, In., U.S.	216	41.11 N	84.55 W
Harlan, Ia., U.S.	198	41.39 N	95.19 W
Harlan, Ky., U.S.	192	36.50 N	83.19 W
Harlan County Lake ⊜ [1]	198	40.04 N	99.16 W
Hârlău	38	47.25 N	26.54 E
Harlech	42	52.52 N	4.07 W
Harlem, Fl., U.S.	220	26.44 N	80.57 W
Harlem, Ga., U.S.	192	33.24 N	82.18 W
Harlem, Mt., U.S.	202	48.32 N	108.47 W
Harlem ⧫ [8]	276	40.49 N	73.56 W
Harlem River ʉ	276	40.48 N	73.54 W
Harlem Springs	214	40.31 N	81.02 W
Harlesden ⧫ [8]	260	51.32 N	0.15 W
Harlesiel	52	53.43 N	7.49 E
Harleston	42	52.24 N	1.18 E
Harleton	222	32.41 N	94.35 W
Hårlev	41	55.21 N	12.15 E
Harleysville	208	40.17 N	75.23 W
Harlin	171a	26.59 S	152.22 E
Harlingen, Ned.	52	53.10 N	5.24 E
Harlingen, Tx., U.S.	196	26.11 N	97.41 W
Harlinger Land ⧫ [1]	52	53.40 N	7.30 E
Harlingerode	54	51.54 N	10.31 E
Harlington ⧫ [8]	260	51.29 N	0.26 W
Harlösa	41	55.43 N	13.32 E
Harlow	42	51.47 N	0.08 E
Harlow □ [8]	260	51.44 N	0.07 E
Harlowton	202	46.26 N	109.50 W
Harlpur	272b	22.42 N	88.10 E
Harman	188	38.55 N	79.31 W
Harmancık	130	39.41 N	29.10 E
Harmånger	26	61.56 N	17.13 E
Harmanli, Blg.	38	41.56 N	25.54 E
Harmanlı, Tür.	130	37.51 N	37.45 E
Harmanschlag	61	48.39 N	14.47 E
Harmar Heights	279b	40.33 N	79.49 W
Harmarville	279b	40.32 N	79.51 W
Hármashatár-hegy ∧	264c	47.33 N	19.00 E
Harmelen	52	52.05 N	4.58 E
Harmil I	144	16.31 N	40.09 E
Harmonsburg	214	41.40 N	80.19 W
Harmonville	285	40.06 N	75.17 W
Harmony, Ca., U.S.	226	35.35 N	121.01 W
Harmony, In., U.S.	194	39.32 N	87.06 W
Harmony, Mn., U.S.	190	43.33 N	92.00 W
Harmony, N.J., U.S.	210	40.44 N	75.08 W
Harmony, Pa., U.S.	214	40.48 N	80.07 W
Harmony, R.I., U.S.	207	41.53 N	71.35 W
Harmony Brook ≃	276	40.48 N	74.34 W
Harmony Heights	220	27.29 N	80.21 W
Harmony Hills	285	39.42 N	75.41 W
Harmonyville	285	40.11 N	75.43 W
Harnai, India	122	17.48 N	73.06 E
Harnai, Pāk.	120	30.06 N	67.56 E
Harnäs	40	60.39 N	17.22 E
Harnātānr	124	27.19 N	84.01 E
Harndrup	41	55.28 N	10.02 E
Harnes	50	50.27 N	2.54 E
Härnevi	40	59.44 N	17.05 E
Harney ≃	220	25.25 N	81.10 W
Harney, Lake ⊜	220	28.45 N	81.03 W
Harney Basin ⩩ [1]	202	43.15 N	119.00 W
Harney Lake ⊜	202	43.14 N	119.07 W
Harney Peak ∧	198	43.51 N	103.31 W
Harney Pond Canal ≅	220	27.00 N	81.04 W
Härnösand	26	62.38 N	17.56 E
Haro, Esp.	34	42.35 N	2.51 W
Haro, Ityo.	144	8.28 N	38.37 E
Haro, Cabo ≻	232	27.52 N	110.54 W
Ḥarod ≃	132	32.31 N	35.33 E
Harola	272a	28.36 N	77.19 E
Harold Hill ⧫ [8]	260	51.36 N	0.13 E
Harold Parker State Forest ♠	283	42.37 N	71.05 W
Haroldswick	46a	60.41 N	0.50 W
Harold Wood ⧫ [8]	260	51.36 N	0.14 E
Haro Strait ʉ	224	48.30 N	123.15 W
Haroué	58	48.28 N	6.11 E
Harpālpur	124	25.17 N	79.20 E
Harpanahalli	122	14.48 N	75.59 E
Harpen ⧫ [8]	263	51.29 N	7.16 E
Harpenden	42	51.49 N	0.22 W
Harper, Liber.	150	4.25 N	7.43 W
Harper, Ks., U.S.	198	37.17 N	98.01 W
Harper, Tx., U.S.	196	30.18 N	99.15 W
Harper, Wa., U.S.	224	47.31 N	122.31 W
Harper, Mount ∧	180	64.14 N	143.50 W
Harper Lake ⊜	228	35.02 N	117.17 W
Harpers Ferry National Historical Park ♠	188	39.13 N	77.45 W
Harpersfield	210	42.26 N	74.41 W
Harper Town	44	54.55 N	2.31 W
Harper Woods	214	42.25 N	82.55 W
Harpille ∧	62	43.50 N	6.48 E
Harpstedt	52	52.54 N	8.35 E
Harpster	214	40.44 N	83.15 W
Harpsund ⊽	40	59.06 N	16.29 E
Harpurhey ⧫ [8]	262	53.31 N	2.13 W
Harpur Hill	262	53.14 N	1.54 W
Harpursville	210	42.11 N	75.38 W
Harqin	98	41.08 N	119.38 E
Harqin Qi (Jinshan)	98	41.56 N	118.36 E
Harquahala Mountain ∧	200	33.49 N	113.21 W
Ḥarrah	144	14.57 N	50.19 E
Ḥārrah, Jabal al- ∧	132	33.04 N	35.59 E
Harrai	124	22.37 N	79.13 E
Harran	130	36.51 N	39.00 E
Ḥarrān al-ʿAwāmīd	132	33.27 N	36.34 E
Harray, Loch of ⊜	46	59.01 N	3.13 W
Harrell	194	33.30 N	92.23 W
Harricana ≃	176	51.15 N	79.45 W
Harrietfield	46	56.25 N	3.39 W
Harrietsham	42	51.15 N	0.41 E
Harriman, N.Y., U.S.	210	41.18 N	74.09 W
Harriman, Tn., U.S.	192	35.56 N	84.33 W
Harriman Reservoir ⊜ [1]	207	42.50 N	72.53 W
Harriman State Park ♠	210	41.14 N	74.09 W
Harrington, Eng., U.K.	44	54.37 N	3.34 W
Harrington, De., U.S.	208	38.55 N	75.34 W
Harrington, Me., U.S.	188	44.37 N	67.48 W
Harrington, Wa., U.S.	202	47.28 N	118.15 W
Harrington Creek ≃	282	37.19 N	122.18 W
Harrington Drain ≅	281	42.36 N	82.54 W
Harrington Park	276	40.59 N	73.58 W
Harris, Sk., Can.	184	51.44 N	107.35 W
Harris, Scot., U.K.	46	56.59 N	6.20 W
Harris, Mn., U.S.	190	45.35 N	92.58 W
Harris, N.Y., U.S.	210	41.43 N	74.44 W
Harris, R.I., U.S.	207	41.43 N	71.31 W
Harris □ [6]	222	29.50 N	95.22 W
Harris ≃	168a	33.18 S	116.09 E
Harris ⧫ [1]	46	57.55 N	6.50 W
Harris, Lake ⊜, Austl.	162	31.08 S	135.14 E
Harris, Lake ⊜, Fl., U.S.	220	28.46 N	81.49 W
Harris, Sound of ʉ	46	57.45 N	7.10 W
Harris Bay ⊂	212	45.23 N	77.50 W
Harris Brook ≃	283	42.44 N	71.13 W
Harrisburg, Ar., U.S.	194	35.33 N	90.43 W
Harrisburg, Il., U.S.	194	37.44 N	88.32 W
Harrisburg, In., U.S.	218	39.41 N	85.11 W
Harrisburg, Ne., U.S.	198	41.33 N	103.44 W
Harrisburg, Oh., U.S.	214	40.53 N	81.13 W
Harrisburg, Or., U.S.	202	44.16 N	123.10 W
Harrisburg, Pa., U.S.	208	40.16 N	76.53 W
Harrisburg International Airport ⊠	208	40.12 N	76.45 W
Harris Creek ⊂	208	38.45 N	76.18 W
Harris Creek ≃, Austl.	274a	33.57 S	150.57 E
Harris Creek ≃, Tx., U.S.	222	32.33 N	95.08 W
Harrisfield	274b	37.57 S	145.11 E
Harris Hill	210	42.58 N	78.40 W
Harrislee	41	54.48 N	9.22 E
Harrismith, Austl.	162	32.56 S	117.52 E
Harrismith, S. Afr.	158	28.18 S	29.03 E
Harrison, Ar., U.S.	194	36.13 N	93.06 W
Harrison, Id., U.S.	202	47.27 N	116.47 W
Harrison, Il., U.S.	216	42.25 N	89.11 W
Harrison, Mi., U.S.	190	44.01 N	84.47 W
Harrison, Ne., U.S.	198	42.41 N	103.53 W
Harrison, N.J., U.S.	276	40.44 N	74.09 W
Harrison, N.Y., U.S.	210	40.58 N	73.43 W
Harrison, Oh., U.S.	218	39.15 N	84.49 W
Harrison □ [6], In., U.S.	218	38.17 N	86.07 W
Harrison □ [6], Ky., U.S.	218	38.25 N	84.19 W
Harrison □ [6], Oh., U.S.	214	40.16 N	81.05 W
Harrison □ [6], Tx., U.S.	222	32.35 N	94.35 W
Harrison ≃	224	49.14 N	121.57 W
Harrison, Cape ≻	176	54.55 N	57.55 W
Harrison Bay ⊂	180	70.30 N	151.30 W
Harrisonburg, La., U.S.	194	31.46 N	91.49 W
Harrisonburg, Va., U.S.	188	38.26 N	78.52 W
Harrison City	279b	40.21 N	79.39 W
Harrison Hot Springs	224	49.18 N	121.47 W
Harrison Islands II	176	69.13 N	90.30 W
Harrison Lake ⊜	182	49.30 N	121.50 W
Harrison Mills	224	49.14 N	121.57 W
Harrisons Brook ≃	276	40.38 N	74.34 W
Harrison Tomb State Memorial ⊥	218	39.09 N	84.46 W
Harrison Valley	214	41.57 N	77.39 W
Harrisonville, Md., U.S.	284b	39.23 N	77.50 W
Harrisonville, Mo., U.S.	194	38.39 N	94.20 W
Harrisonville, N.J., U.S.	285	39.41 N	75.15 W
Harris Park	274a	33.49 S	151.01 E
Harris Pond ⊜	283	42.45 N	71.16 W
Harris Reservoir ⊜ [1]	222	29.14 N	95.33 W
Harriston, On., Can.	212	43.54 N	80.53 W
Harriston, Ms., U.S.	194	31.43 N	91.01 W
Harristown	219	39.51 N	89.05 W
Harrisville, Austl.	171a	27.49 S	152.40 E
Harrisville, Mi., U.S.	190	44.39 N	83.17 W
Harrisville, N.Y., U.S.	212	44.09 N	75.19 W
Harrisville, Oh., U.S.	214	40.11 N	80.53 W
Harrisville, Pa., U.S.	214	41.08 N	80.00 W
Harrisville, R.I., U.S.	207	41.57 N	71.40 W
Harrisville, W.V., U.S.	188	39.12 N	81.03 W
Harrod	216	40.42 N	83.55 W
Harrodsburg	194	37.45 N	84.50 W
Harrods Creek ≃	218	38.20 N	85.38 W
Harrogate	44	54.00 N	1.33 W
Harrold	196	34.05 N	99.02 W
Harrop Lake ⊜	184	52.38 N	95.58 W
Harrow	214	42.02 N	82.55 W
Harrow ⧫ [8]	42	51.35 N	0.21 W
Harrow on the Hill ⧫ [8]	260	51.34 N	0.20 W
Harrow School ⊽ [2]	260	51.34 N	0.20 W
Harrowsmith	212	44.24 N	76.40 W
Harry S. Truman Airport ⊠	240m	18.21 N	64.59 W
Harry S. Truman Reservoir ⊜ [1]	194	38.10 N	93.45 W
Har Sai Shan ∧	102	35.28 N	97.55 E
Harsefeld	52	53.27 N	9.30 E
Harsens Island	214	42.34 N	82.34 W
Harsens Island I	281	42.35 N	82.38 W
Harsewinkel	52	51.58 N	8.13 E
Harsīn	128	34.16 N	47.35 E
Harşit ≃	130	41.01 N	38.52 E
Harskamp	52	52.07 N	5.45 E
Harsleben	54	51.52 N	11.05 E
Hârşova	38	44.41 N	27.57 E
Harstad	24	68.46 N	16.30 E
Harstena	26	58.16 N	17.01 E
Har Su	89	48.09 N	122.25 E
Harsūd	124	22.06 N	76.44 E
Harsum	52	52.12 N	9.57 E
Hart, Mi., U.S.	190	43.41 N	86.21 W
Hart, Tx., U.S.	196	34.23 N	102.07 W
Hart ≃	180	65.51 N	136.22 W
Hart, Lake ⊜, Austl.	166	31.08 S	136.24 E
Hart, Lake ⊜, Fl., U.S.	220	28.22 N	81.13 W
Ḥartā	132	32.42 N	35.51 E
Hartbees ≃	158	28.45 S	20.32 E
Hartbeesfontein	158	26.42 S	26.26 E
Hartbeespoort	158	25.44 S	27.52 E
Hartberg	61	47.17 N	15.59 E
Hartenholm	52	53.54 N	10.03 E
Hartenstein	54	50.39 N	12.40 E
Hart Fell ∧	44	55.25 N	3.25 W
Hartfield	208	37.34 N	76.30 W
Hartford, Eng., U.K.	262	53.15 N	2.33 W
Hartford, Al., U.S.	194	31.06 N	85.41 W
Hartford, Ar., U.S.	194	35.01 N	94.22 W
Hartford, Ct., U.S.	207	41.46 N	72.41 W
Hartford, Il., U.S.	219	38.50 N	90.05 W
Hartford, In., U.S.	218	38.59 N	84.57 W
Hartford, Ks., U.S.	198	38.18 N	95.57 W
Hartford, Ky., U.S.	194	37.27 N	86.54 W
Hartford, Mi., U.S.	216	42.12 N	86.10 W
Hartford, N.J., U.S.	285	39.58 N	74.53 W
Hartford, N.Y., U.S.	210	43.21 N	73.22 W
Hartford, Oh., U.S.	214	41.19 N	80.34 W
Hartford, S.D., U.S.	198	43.37 N	96.56 W
Hartford, Wi., U.S.	190	43.19 N	88.22 W
Hartford □ [6]	207	41.46 N	72.41 W
Hartford City	216	40.27 N	85.22 W
Hartha	54	51.05 N	12.58 E
Hartington	198	42.37 N	97.15 W
Hart Island I	276	40.51 N	73.46 W
Hart Lake ⊜	202	42.24 N	119.51 W
Hartland, N.B., Can.	186	46.18 N	67.32 W
Hartland, Eng., U.K.	42	50.59 N	4.29 W
Hartland, Il., U.S.	216	42.22 N	88.31 W
Hartland, Me., U.S.	188	44.53 N	69.26 W
Hartland, Mi., U.S.	216	42.39 N	83.45 W
Hartland, N.Y., U.S.	210	43.14 N	78.35 W
Hartland, Wi., U.S.	216	43.06 N	88.20 W
Hartland Point ≻	42	51.02 N	4.31 W
Hartlepool	44	54.42 N	1.11 W
Hartleton	210	40.54 N	77.10 W
Hartley, Austl.	170	33.33 S	150.11 E
Hartley, Eng., U.K.	260	51.23 N	0.19 E
Hartley, Ia., U.S.	198	43.10 N	95.28 W
Hartley, Tx., U.S.	196	35.53 N	102.24 W
Hartley Bay	182	53.25 N	129.15 W
Hartlip	260	51.21 N	0.39 E
Hart Lot	210	43.01 N	76.28 W
Hartly	208	39.10 N	75.42 W
Hartmannsdorf	54	50.53 N	12.48 E
Hartmannshain	56	50.28 N	9.16 E
Hart-Miller Island I	208	39.15 N	76.23 W
Hart Mountain ∧	184	52.29 N	101.25 W
Hartney	184	49.28 N	100.30 W
Hartola	26	61.35 N	26.01 E
Harts ≃	158	28.24 S	24.17 E
Hartsburg	219	38.41 N	92.18 W
Hartsdale	210	41.01 N	73.47 W
Hartselle	194	34.26 N	86.56 W
Härtsfeld ⧫ [1]	56	48.50 N	10.15 E
Hartshill	42	52.32 N	1.32 W
Hartshorne	196	34.50 N	95.33 W
Harts Range	162	23.00 S	134.55 E
Hartstene Island I	224	47.14 N	122.53 W
Hartstown	214	41.33 N	80.23 W
Hartsville, In., U.S.	218	39.16 N	85.41 W
Hartsville, Pa., U.S.	285	40.14 N	75.05 W
Hartsville, S.C., U.S.	192	34.22 N	80.04 W
Hartsville, Tn., U.S.	194	36.23 N	86.10 W
Hartswater	158	27.34 S	24.43 E
Hartville, Mo., U.S.	194	37.15 N	92.30 W
Hartville, Oh., U.S.	214	40.57 N	81.19 W
Hartwell	192	34.21 N	82.55 W
Hartwell Lake ⊜ [1]	192	34.30 N	82.55 W
Hartwick	210	42.39 N	75.02 W
Hartwick Pines State Park ♠	190	44.47 N	84.41 W
Hartz Mountains National Park ♠	166	43.15 S	146.50 E
Harue	94	36.08 N	136.14 E
Haruki	270	34.29 N	135.23 E
Haruku, Pulau I	164	3.34 S	128.29 E
Hārūn	140	11.20 N	25.43 E
Haruna	94	36.23 N	138.53 E
Hārūnābād	123	29.37 N	73.08 E
Haruna-san ∧	94	36.28 N	138.52 E
Haruniye	130	37.17 N	36.27 E
Haruno, Nihon	94	34.57 N	137.53 E
Haruno, Nihon	96	33.30 N	133.30 E
Harūr	122	12.04 N	78.30 E
Hārūt ≃	128	31.35 N	61.18 E
Harvard, Il., U.S.	216	42.25 N	88.36 W
Harvard, Ma., U.S.	207	42.30 N	71.35 W
Harvard, Ne., U.S.	198	40.37 N	98.05 W
Harvard University ⊽ [2]	283	42.22 N	71.07 W
Harvel, Eng., U.K.	260	51.21 N	0.22 E
Harvel, Il., U.S.	219	39.21 N	89.32 W
Harvest, Mount ∧ [2]	162	25.54 S	126.28 E
Harvey, Austl.	168a	33.05 S	115.54 E
Harvey, N.B., Can.	186	45.43 N	64.43 W
Harvey, Il., U.S.	216	41.36 N	87.38 W
Harvey, N.D., U.S.	198	47.46 N	99.56 W
Harvey ≃	168a	32.46 S	115.43 E
Harvey Estuary ⊂ [1]	168a	32.43 S	115.42 E
Harvey Mountain ∧	207	42.18 N	73.25 W
Harvey Reservoir ⊜ [1]	168a	33.05 S	115.58 E
Harveysburg	218	39.30 N	84.00 W
Harveys Lake	210	41.23 N	76.02 W
Harwell	42	51.37 N	1.18 W
Harwich, Eng., U.K.	42	51.57 N	1.17 E
Harwich, Ma., U.S.	207	41.41 N	70.04 W
Harwich Port	207	41.40 N	70.04 W
Harwick	279b	40.34 N	79.48 W
Harwinton	207	41.46 N	73.03 W
Harwood, Eng., U.K.	262	53.35 N	2.23 W
Harwood, Tx., U.S.	222	29.40 N	97.30 W
Harwood Heights	278	41.58 N	87.48 W
Harwood Mines	210	40.57 N	76.01 W
Harwood Park	284b	39.12 N	76.44 W
Haryāna □ [3]	120	29.20 N	76.20 E
Harz ⩘	54	51.45 N	10.30 E
Harzgerode	54	51.38 N	11.08 E
Ḥaṣā, Bi'r al- ⫪ [4]	140	22.58 N	35.40 E
Ḥasā, Wādī al- V	132	31.05 N	35.27 E
Hasafen	86	45.14 N	90.20 E
Ḥaṣāh, Wādī al- V	132	30.38 N	37.09 E
Hasaki	94	35.44 N	140.50 E
Hasalbag	120	37.54 N	76.44 E
Ḥasanābād	267d	35.44 N	51.19 E
Ḥasanābād-e Khāleṣeh	267d	35.37 N	51.12 E
Hasan Abdāl	123	33.49 N	72.41 E
Hasançelebi	130	38.58 N	37.54 E
Hasan Dağı ∧	130	38.08 N	34.12 E
Hasankale → Pasinler	130	39.59 N	41.41 E
Hasankeyf	130	37.43 N	41.25 E
Ḥasan Kīādeh	128	37.24 N	49.58 E
Hasanpur	124	28.43 N	78.17 E
Hasayaz	130	40.15 N	33.20 E
Ḥāṣbānī, Nahr al- ≃	132	33.11 N	35.37 E
Ḥāṣbayyā	132	33.24 N	35.41 E
Hasbek	130	39.33 N	35.33 E
Hasbergen, Dtsch.	52	52.14 N	7.57 E
Hasbergen, Dtsch.	52	53.05 N	8.40 E
Hasbrouck Heights	276	40.51 N	74.04 W
Hascosay I	46a	60.37 N	0.59 W
Hasdo ≃	120	21.44 N	82.44 E
Hasdo-Rāmpur Basin ⩩ [1]	124	22.50 N	82.35 E
Hase, Nihon	94	35.47 N	138.06 E
Hase, Nihon	270	34.32 N	135.54 E
Hase ≃, Dtsch.	52	52.41 N	7.18 E
Hase ≃, Nihon	270	34.34 N	135.38 E
Hasel ≃	54	50.32 N	10.27 E
Häselgehr	58	47.19 N	10.30 E
Haselhorst ⧫ [8]	264a	52.33 N	13.15 E
Haselünne	52	52.40 N	7.29 E
Hasenkamp	252	31.31 S	59.51 W
Ḥashā', Jabal al- ∧	144	13.45 N	44.30 E
HaShefela ⧫ [1]	132	31.40 N	34.55 E
Hashima	94	35.19 N	136.42 E
Hashimoto, Nihon	96	34.19 N	135.37 E
Hashimoto, Nihon	270	34.26 N	135.23 E
Hashira-jima I	96	34.01 N	132.25 E
Hashiri-jima I	96	34.21 N	133.27 E
Hashitai	89	49.24 N	125.18 E
Hasht Sāl ⧫ [8]	272a	28.38 N	77.03 E
Hasil, Pulau I	164	1.06 S	128.24 E
Hāsilpur	123	29.43 N	72.33 E
Ḥāsīn-e Bozorg	84	39.23 N	44.42 E
Haskayne	262	53.34 N	2.58 W
Haskeir Islands II	46	57.42 N	7.41 W
Haskell, Ok., U.S.	196	35.49 N	95.40 W
Haskell, Tx., U.S.	196	33.09 N	99.44 W
Haskell Pond ⊜	283	42.37 N	70.44 W
Hasketh Bank	262	53.43 N	2.51 W
Haskins	216	41.27 N	83.42 W
Haskovo	38	41.56 N	25.33 E
Haskovo □ [4], Blg.	38	42.02 N	25.50 E
Haskovo □ [4], Blg.	130	41.50 N	25.50 E
Hasköy, Tür.	130	40.59 N	42.52 E
Hasköy, Tür.	130	41.38 N	26.41 E
Hasköy ⧫ [8]	267b	41.02 N	28.58 E
Haslach im Kinzigtal	58	48.16 N	8.06 E
Hasle, Dan.	41	55.10 N	10.10 E
Hasle, Schw.	58	47.01 N	7.39 E
Haslemere	42	51.06 N	0.43 W
Haslett	216	42.44 N	84.24 W
Haslev	41	55.20 N	11.58 E
Haslingden	44	53.43 N	2.18 W
Haslingden Grane	262	53.42 N	2.21 W
Haslington	44	53.06 N	2.24 W
Haslital V	58	46.42 N	8.10 E
Haslum	26	59.50 N	10.22 E
Hasmark	41	55.33 N	10.28 E
Ḥasmat ʿUmar, Bi'r ⫪ [4]	140	21.46 N	34.00 E
Hāsnābād	126	22.35 N	88.55 E
Hasnācha	272b	22.26 N	88.09 E
Haspe ⧫ [8]	263	51.21 N	7.26 E
Hasperos Canyon V	200	33.50 N	105.02 W
Hasper-Stausee ⊜ [1]	263	51.18 N	7.25 E
Haspra	78	44.27 N	34.07 E
Haspres	50	50.15 N	3.25 E
Ḥaṣṣ, Jabal al- ∧ [2]	130	35.52 N	37.22 E
Hassa	130	36.50 N	36.29 E
Hassan	122	13.00 N	76.05 E
Hassard	219	39.39 N	91.40 W
Hassayampa ≃	200	33.20 N	112.43 W
Hassberge ⩘ [2]	56	50.12 N	10.29 E
Hassbergen	52	52.44 N	9.13 E
Hassel, Dtsch.	52	52.48 N	9.11 E
Hassel, Dtsch.	263	51.39 N	7.30 E
Hassel ⧫ [8]	263	51.36 N	7.03 E
Hasselbeck-Schwarzbach	263	51.16 N	6.53 E
Hasselfelde	54	51.41 N	10.51 E
Hasselfors	40	59.05 N	14.39 E
Hassels ⧫ [8]	263	51.10 N	6.53 E
Hasselt, Bel.	56	50.56 N	5.20 E
Hasselt, Ned.	52	52.35 N	6.05 E
Hassfurt	56	50.02 N	10.31 E
Hassi Bel Guebbour	148	28.46 N	6.27 E
Hassi el Ghella	34	35.28 N	1.03 W
Hassi Mameche	34	35.52 N	0.04 E
Hassi Messaoud	148	31.43 N	5.59 E
Hassi Zehana	34	35.01 N	0.53 W
Hassleben	54	53.13 N	13.41 E
Hässleholm	41	56.09 N	13.46 E
Hasslinghausen	56	51.20 N	7.17 E
Hassloch	56	49.22 N	8.16 E
Hasson Heights	214	41.26 N	79.41 W
Hästbo	40	60.27 N	16.27 E
Hasten ⧫ [8], Dtsch.	263	51.12 N	7.09 E
Hästen ⧫ [8], Dtsch.	263	51.09 N	7.06 E
Hastière-Lavaux	56	50.13 N	4.50 E
Hastings, Austl.	169	38.18 S	145.11 E
Hastings, Barb.	241g	13.04 N	59.35 W
Hastings, On., Can.	212	44.18 N	77.57 W
Hastings, N.Z.	172	39.38 S	176.51 E
Hastings, Eng., U.K.	42	50.51 N	0.36 E
Hastings, Fl., U.S.	192	29.43 N	81.30 W
Hastings, Il., U.S.	278	41.41 N	87.58 W
Hastings, Mi., U.S.	216	42.39 N	85.17 W
Hastings, Mn., U.S.	190	44.44 N	92.51 W
Hastings, Ne., U.S.	198	40.35 N	98.23 W
Hastings, N.Y., U.S.	210	43.22 N	76.09 W
Hastings, Pa., U.S.	214	40.39 N	78.42 W
Hastings □ [6]	212	44.45 N	77.40 W
Hastings Battlesite ⊥	42	50.53 N	0.31 E
Hastings-on-Hudson	276	40.59 N	73.52 W
Hastingwood	260	51.45 N	0.09 E
Hastrup	41	55.26 N	12.11 E
Hasty	198	38.06 N	102.57 W
Hasuda	94	35.59 N	139.40 E
Hasumi	96	34.52 N	132.37 E
Haswell	198	38.27 N	103.09 W
Hata	94	36.11 N	137.51 E
Hat'ae-do I	98	34.32 N	126.03 E
Ha Tan	110	18.30 N	105.20 E
Hatanagi-dam ⧫ [6]	94	35.18 N	138.12 E
Hatashō	94	35.10 N	136.15 E
Hatay (Antioch)	130	36.14 N	36.07 E
Hatay □ [4]	130	36.30 N	36.15 E
Hatboro	208	40.10 N	75.06 W
Hatch, N.M., U.S.	200	32.39 N	107.09 W
Hatch, Ut,. U.S.	200	37.38 N	112.26 W
Hat Chao Mai National Park ♠	110	7.40 N	99.35 E
Hatches Creek	162	20.56 S	135.12 E
Hatchet Creek ≃	194	32.52 N	86.20 W
Hatchet Lake	186	44.35 N	63.40 W
Hatchie ≃	194	35.35 N	89.53 W
Hatchineha, Lake ⊜	220	28.02 N	81.25 W
Hatchlands ⊥	260	51.15 N	0.28 W
Hatchmere	262	53.15 N	2.40 W
Hatchville	207	41.37 N	70.33 W
Hatch Wash V	200	38.32 N	109.36 W
Hat Creek ≃, U.S.	198	43.16 N	103.36 W
Hat Creek ≃, Ca., U.S.	204	40.59 N	121.33 W
Haţeg	38	45.37 N	22.57 E
Hateruma-shima I	175d	24.03 N	123.47 E
Hatfield, Austl.	166	33.52 S	143.45 E
Hatfield, Eng., U.K.	42	51.46 N	0.13 W
Hatfield, Eng., U.K.	44	53.34 N	1.00 W
Hatfield, Ar., U.S.	194	34.29 N	94.22 W
Hatfield, Ma., U.S.	207	42.22 N	72.35 W
Hatfield Aerodrome ⊠	260	51.46 N	0.16 W
Hatfield House ⊥	260	51.46 N	0.13 W
Hatfield Peverel	42	51.47 N	0.35 E
Hatfield Swamp ⩩	276	40.50 N	74.20 W
Hathāla	123	32.03 N	70.34 E
Hathaway Pines	226	38.07 N	120.28 W
Hatherleigh	42	50.49 N	4.04 W
Hathersage	44	53.19 N	1.38 W
Hāthras	124	27.36 N	78.03 E
Hātia ʉ	124	22.30 N	91.15 E
Ḥāṭibah, Ra's ≻	144	21.55 N	38.58 E
Ha Tien	110	10.23 N	104.29 E
Hatillo	240m	18.29 N	66.49 W
Ha Tinh	110	18.20 N	105.54 E
Hatinoe → Hachinohe	92	40.30 N	141.29 E
Hatiozi → Hachiōji	94	35.39 N	139.20 E
Hatip	130	37.46 N	32.25 E
Hātisāla	272b	22.33 N	88.32 E
Hato, Bocht van ⊂	241s	12.13 N	68.58 W
Hatogaya	94	35.50 N	139.44 E
Hato Mayor [del Rey]	238	18.46 N	69.15 W
Hato Rey	240m	18.25 N	66.03 W
Hatoyama	94	35.59 N	139.20 E
Hāt Pīplia	124	22.46 N	76.18 E
Hatsukaichi	96	34.21 N	132.20 E
Hatsu-shima I	94	35.02 N	139.10 E
Hatsutomi	268	35.46 N	140.01 E
Hatta	124	24.07 N	79.36 E
Hattab, Oued el V	36	35.23 N	9.32 E
Hattah-Kulkyne National Park ♠	166	34.40 S	142.30 E
Hattem	52	52.28 N	6.04 E
Hatten, Dtsch.	52	53.02 N	8.22 E
Hatten, Fr.	56	48.54 N	7.59 E
Hattenhofen	60	48.13 N	11.07 E
Hatteras	192	35.13 N	75.41 W
Hatteras, Cape ≻	192	35.13 N	75.32 W
Hatteras Island I	192	35.25 N	75.30 W
Hattiesburg	194	31.19 N	89.17 W
Hatting	41	55.51 N	9.46 E
Hattingen	56	51.23 N	7.10 E
Hattingspruit	158	28.09 S	30.11 E
Hatton, Eng., U.K.	262	53.20 N	2.36 W
Hatton, Scot., U.K.	46	57.25 N	1.54 W
Hatton, Al., U.S.	194	34.33 N	87.24 W
Hatton, N.D., U.S.	198	47.38 N	97.27 W
Hatton ⧫ [8]	260	51.28 N	0.25 W
Hatton Fields	226	36.33 N	121.54 W
Hattorf [am Harz]	52	51.39 N	10.14 E
Hattori, Nihon	270	34.46 N	135.27 E
Hattori, Nihon	270	34.52 N	135.36 E
Hattstatt	58	48.01 N	7.17 E
Hattstedt	41	54.31 N	9.01 E
Hatunsaray	130	37.35 N	32.21 E
Hatvan	30	47.40 N	19.41 E
Hat Yai	110	7.01 N	100.28 E
Hatzfeld ⧫ [8]	263	51.17 N	7.11 E
Hatzic	224	49.09 N	122.15 W
Hatzic Lake ⊜	224	49.10 N	122.14 W
Haubstadt	194	38.12 N	87.34 W
Hāudullāpur	272b	22.25 N	88.33 E
Hauge	26	58.18 N	6.15 E
Haugesund	26	59.25 N	5.18 E
Haugh of Urr	44	54.58 N	3.52 W
Haughton Green	262	53.27 N	2.06 W
Haugsdorf	61	48.42 N	16.05 E
Hau Hoi Wan ⊂	100	22.28 N	113.56 E
Hauhungaroa Range ⩘	172	38.50 S	175.34 E
Haukeligrend	26	59.45 N	7.31 E
Haukipudas	26	65.11 N	25.21 E
Haukivesi ⊜	26	62.06 N	28.28 E
Haukivuori	26	62.01 N	27.13 E
Hauldres, Ru des ≃	261	48.37 N	2.28 E
Haulerwijk	52	53.04 N	6.20 E
Haultain ≃	184	55.51 N	106.46 W
Haune ≃	56	50.52 N	9.43 E
Haunersdorf	60	48.36 N	12.43 E
Haunstetten	58	48.18 N	10.54 E
Haunts Creek ʉ	276	40.37 N	73.31 W
Hauppauge	210	40.49 N	73.12 W
Hauptsrus	158	26.33 S	26.18 E
Hauraki Gulf ⊂	172	36.20 S	175.05 E
Hauroko, Lake ⊜	172	46.00 S	167.20 E
Hauru, Pointe ≻	174s	17.29 S	149.55 W
Haus	64	47.25 N	13.49 E
Hausa	273a	6.37 N	3.21 E
Hausach	58	48.17 N	8.10 E
Hausham	64	47.45 N	11.50 E
Hausruck ⩘	60	48.07 N	13.35 E
Haussee ⊜	264a	52.38 N	13.41 E
Haussömmern	54	51.11 N	10.49 E
Haut, Isle au I	188	44.03 N	68.38 W
Haut Atlas ⩘	148	31.30 N	6.00 W
Haut-Bout	261	48.32 N	1.55 E
Haute Colme, Canal de la ≅	50	50.50 N	2.12 E
Hautecombe, Abbaye de ⊽ [1]	62	45.45 N	5.50 E
Haute-Corse □ [5]	36	42.30 N	9.00 E
Haute-Garonne □ [5]	32	43.25 N	1.30 E
Haute-Kotto □ [5]	152	7.00 N	23.00 E
Haute-Loire □ [5]	32	45.05 N	3.50 E
Hauteluce	62	45.45 N	6.35 E
Haute-Marne □ [5]	58	48.05 N	5.10 E
Hauterive	186	49.12 N	68.16 W
Hauterives	62	45.15 N	5.02 E
Hautes-Alpes □ [5]	62	44.40 N	6.30 E
Haute-Sangha □ [5]	152	4.30 N	16.00 E
Haute-Saône □ [5]	58	47.40 N	6.10 E
Haute-Savoie □ [5]	32	46.00 N	6.20 E
Haute Seine, Canal de la ≅	50	48.34 N	3.43 E
Hautes Fagnes ⩘	56	50.30 N	6.05 E
Hautes-Pyrénées □ [5]	32	43.00 N	0.10 E
Haute Sûre, Lac de la ⊜ [1]	56	49.52 N	5.52 E
Haute-Vienne □ [5]	32	45.50 N	1.15 E
Hauteville-Lompnes	58	45.58 N	5.36 E
Haute Volta → Burkina Faso □ [1]	150	13.00 N	1.30 W
Haut-Folin ∧	32	47.00 N	4.02 E
Haut-Kœnigsbourg, Château du ⊥	58	48.14 N	7.22 E
Haut-Mbomou □ [5]	140	6.00 N	26.00 E
Hautmont	50	50.15 N	3.56 E
Haut-Ogooué □ [4]	152	1.00 S	13.50 E
Haut-Rhin □ [5]	58	47.53 N	7.13 E
Hauts-de-Seine □ [5]	261	48.50 N	2.11 E
Hautvillers	50	49.05 N	3.57 E
Haut-Zaïre □ [4]	154	2.20 N	27.00 E
Hauula	229c	21.36 N	157.54 W
Hauzenberg	60	48.39 N	13.38 E
Hauz Rāni ⧫ [8]	272a	28.32 N	77.13 E
Havana → La Habana, Cuba	240p	23.08 N	82.22 W
Havana, Ar., U.S.	194	35.06 N	93.31 W
Havana, Fl., U.S.	192	30.37 N	84.24 W
Havana, Il., U.S.	194	40.18 N	90.03 W
Havana, N.D., U.S.	198	45.57 N	97.37 W
Havane, La → La Habana	240p	23.08 N	82.22 W
Havannah, Canal de la ʉ	175f	22.22 S	167.01 E
Havant	42	50.51 N	0.59 W
Havasu, Lake ⊜ [1]	200	34.30 N	114.20 W
Havasu Creek ≃	200	36.19 N	112.46 W
Havasupai Indian Reservation ⧫ [4]	200	36.13 N	112.40 W
Havdrup	41	55.32 N	12.08 E
Havel ≃	54	52.53 N	11.58 E
Havelange	56	50.23 N	5.14 E
Havelberg	54	52.50 N	12.04 E
Havelberg ∧ [2]	264a	52.28 N	13.12 E
Haveli	123	30.27 N	73.42 E
Haveliān	123	34.03 N	73.10 E
Havel-Kanal ≅	264a	52.36 N	13.12 E
Havelland ⧫ [1]	54	52.25 N	12.45 E
Havelländischer Grosser Hauptkanal ≅	264a	52.37 N	13.03 E
Havelländisches Luch ⩩	54	52.40 N	12.40 E
Havelock, On., Can.	212	44.26 N	77.53 W
Havelock, N.Z.	172	41.17 S	173.46 E
Havelock, N.C., U.S.	192	34.52 N	76.54 W
Havelock Island I	110	11.58 N	93.00 E
Havelock North	172	39.40 S	176.53 E
Haven	198	37.53 N	97.46 W
Haverford	285	40.00 N	75.17 W
Haverford College ⊽ [2]	285	40.00 N	75.18 W
Haverfordwest	42	51.49 N	4.58 W
Haverhill, Eng., U.K.	42	52.05 N	0.26 E
Haverhill, Ma., U.S.	207	42.46 N	71.04 W
Haverhill Airport ⊠	283	42.48 N	71.04 W
Haverhill-Riverside Airport ⊠	283	42.46 N	71.02 W
Hāveri	122	14.48 N	75.24 E
Haverigg	44	54.11 N	3.17 W
Havering ⧫ [8]	42	51.34 N	0.14 E
Havering-atte-Bower ⧫ [8]	260	51.37 N	0.11 E
Havering's Grove	260	51.38 N	0.23 E
Havern ⊜	26	62.17 N	15.07 E
Haverö	26	62.24 N	15.05 E
Haverstraw	210	41.11 N	73.57 W
Havertown	208	39.58 N	75.18 W
Haviland, Ks., U.S.	198	37.37 N	99.06 W
Haviland, Oh., U.S.	216	41.01 N	84.35 W
Haviland Brook ≃	276	41.07 N	73.33 W
Ḥavīq	128	38.10 N	48.54 E
Havířov	30	49.47 N	18.27 E
Havixbeck	52	51.58 N	7.25 E
Hävla	40	58.55 N	15.52 E
Havlíčkův Brod	30	49.36 N	15.35 E
Havnbjerg	41	55.02 N	9.48 E
Havnsø	41	55.45 N	11.20 E
Havran	130	39.33 N	27.06 E
Havré, Bel.	50	50.28 N	4.02 E
Havre → Le Havre, Fr.	50	49.30 N	0.08 E
Havre, Mt., U.S.	202	48.32 N	109.40 W
Havre-Aubert	186	47.14 N	61.51 W
Havre Aubert, Île du I	186	47.14 N	61.57 W
Havre aux Maisons, Île du I	186	47.25 N	61.47 W
Havre de Grace	208	39.32 N	76.05 W
Havre de Grace Heights	208	39.35 N	76.07 W
Havre North	202	48.36 N	109.41 W
Havre-Saint-Pierre	186	50.14 N	63.36 W
Havsa	130	41.33 N	26.49 E
Havza	130	40.58 N	35.41 E
Haw ≃	192	35.36 N	79.03 W
Hawaii □ [3]	229d	20.00 N	157.45 W
Hawaii I	229d	19.30 N	155.30 W
Hawaiian Gardens	280	33.49 N	118.04 W
Hawaiian Islands II	229d	20.30 N	157.30 W
Hawaiian Ridge ✦ [3]	14	24.00 N	165.00 W
Hawaii Volcanoes National Park ♠	229d	19.23 N	155.17 W
Hawal ≃	146	10.00 N	12.05 E
Hawarden, Sk., Can.	184	51.23 N	106.36 W
Hawarden, N.Z.	172	42.56 S	172.38 E
Hawarden, Wales, U.K.	44	53.11 N	3.02 W
Hawarden, Ia., U.S.	198	42.59 N	96.29 W
Ḥawashīyah, Wādī V	140	28.31 N	32.58 E
Haw Creek ≃	218	39.11 N	85.55 W
Hawea, Lake ⊜	172	44.30 S	169.17 E
Hawera	172	39.35 S	174.17 E
Hawes	44	54.18 N	2.12 W
Hawesville	194	37.54 N	86.45 W
Haweswater Reservoir ⊜	44	54.32 N	2.48 W
Ḥawf, Jabal ⩘ [2]	273c	29.55 N	31.21 E
Ḥawf, Wādī V	142	29.53 N	31.18 E
Hawi	229d	20.14 N	155.50 W
Hawick	44	55.25 N	2.47 W
Hawk Creek ≃	198	44.44 N	95.25 W
Hawkdun Range ⩘	172	44.46 S	170.00 E
Hawke, Cape ≻	166	32.13 S	152.34 E
Hawke Bay ⊂	172	39.20 S	177.30 E
Hawker	166	31.53 S	138.25 E
Hawkes, Mount ∧	9	83.56 S	55.45 W
Hawkes Brook ≃	283	42.45 N	71.08 W
Hawkesbury	206	45.36 N	74.37 W
Hawkesbury ≃	170	33.30 S	151.10 E
Hawkesbury Island I	182	53.38 N	129.00 W
Hawkes Pond ⊜	283	42.30 N	71.02 W
Hawkeye	190	42.56 N	91.57 W
Hawkhurst	42	51.02 N	0.30 E
Hawking	42	51.06 N	1.10 E
Hawkins, Tx., U.S.	222	32.35 N	95.12 W
Hawkins, Wi., U.S.	190	45.30 N	90.43 W
Hawkins, Lake ⊜ [1]	222	32.38 N	95.15 W
Hawkins Island I	180	60.30 N	146.00 W
Hawkinsville	192	32.17 N	83.28 W
Hawk Junction	190	48.05 N	84.34 W
Hawk Lake	184	49.48 N	93.59 W
Haw Knob ∧	192	35.19 N	84.02 W
Hawk Point	219	38.58 N	91.07 W
Hawk Run	214	40.55 N	78.12 W
Hawksbill ∧	188	38.33 N	78.23 W
Hawksbill Creek ⊂	192	26.32 N	78.43 W
Hawks Nest Point ≻	238	24.09 N	75.32 W
Hawkwell	260	51.36 N	0.40 E
Hawkwood	166	25.47 S	150.50 E
Hawley, Eng., U.K.	260	51.25 N	0.14 E
Hawley, Mn., U.S.	198	46.52 N	96.18 W
Hawley. Pa., U.S.	210	41.28 N	75.10 W
Hawleyton	210	42.01 N	75.55 W
Hawleyville	207	41.25 N	73.21 W
Haworth, Eng., U.K.	44	53.49 N	1.57 W
Haworth, N.J., U.S.	276	40.57 N	73.59 W
Haw Par Villa ⊽	271c	1.16 N	103.47 E
Hawr	142	27.52 N	30.44 E
Ḥawrān, Wādī V	128	33.58 N	42.34 E
Ḥawsh ʿĪsā	142	30.55 N	30.17 E
Hawthorn, Austl.	274b	37.49 S	145.02 E
Hawthorn, Pa., U.S.	214	41.01 N	79.17 W
Hawthorne, Ca., U.S.	228	33.54 N	118.21 W
Hawthorne, Fl., U.S.	192	29.35 N	82.05 W
Hawthorne, Nv., U.S.	204	38.31 N	118.37 W
Hawthorne, N.J., U.S.	210	40.56 N	74.09 W
Hawthorne, N.Y., U.S.	210	41.06 N	73.47 W
Hawthorne Lake ⊜	276	41.03 N	74.35 W
Hawthorne Municipal Airport ⊠	280	33.55 N	118.20 W
Hawthorne Race Course ♠	278	41.50 N	87.45 W
Hawthorn Woods	278	42.13 N	88.03 W
Ḥawwārah	132	32.32 N	35.54 E
Ḥawwārat ʿAdlān	142	29.12 N	30.58 E

≃	River	Fluß	Río	Rivière	Rio
≅	Canal	Kanal	Canal	Canal	Canal
⌊	Waterfall, Rapids	Wasserfall, Stromschnellen	Cascada, Rápidos	Chute d'eau, Rapides	Cascata, Rápidos
ʉ	Strait	Meeresstraße	Estrecho	Détroit	Estreito
⊂	Bay, Gulf	Bucht, Golf	Bahía, Golfo	Baie, Golfe	Baía, Golfo
⊜	Lake, Lakes	See, Seen	Lago, Lagos	Lac, Lacs	Lago, Lagos
⩩	Swamp	Sumpf	Pantano	Marais	Pântano
⊓	Ice Features, Glacier	Eis- und Gletscherformen	Accidentes Glaciales	Formes glaciaires	Acidentes glaciares
⫪	Other Hydrographic Features	Andere Hydrographische Objekte	Otros Elementos Hidrográficos	Autres données hydrographiques	Outros acidentes hidrográficos

✦	Submarine Features	Untermeerische Objekte	Accidentes Submarinos	Formes de relief sous-marin	Acidentes submarinos
□	Political Unit	Politische Einheit	Unidad Politica	Entité politique	Unidade política
⊽	Cultural Institution	Kulturelle Institution	Institución Cultural	Institution culturelle	Instituição cultural
⊥	Historical Site	Historische Stätte	Sitio Histórico	Site historique	Sitio histórico
♠	Recreational Site	Erholungs- und Ferienort	Sitio de Recreo	Centre de loisirs	Area de Lazer
⊠	Airport	Flughafen	Aeropuerto	Aéroport	Aeroporto
■	Military Installation	Militäranlage	Instalación Militar	Installation militaire	Instalação militar
⧫	Miscellaneous	Verschiedenes	Misceláneo	Divers	Diversos

Name	Page	Lat.°′	Long.°′
Hawwārat al-Maqṭaʿ	142	29.15 N	30.54 E
Hawza	148	27.06 N	10.55 W
Hawzen	144	13.56 N	39.28 E
Haxby	44	54.01 N	1.04 W
Haxey	44	53.29 N	0.50 W
Haxtun	198	40.38 N	102.37 W
Hay	166	34.30 S	144.51 E
Hay ≃, Austl.	166	25.14 S	138.00 E
Hay ≃, Can.	176	60.52 N	115.44 W
Hay ≃, Wi., U.S.	190	44.59 N	91.51 W
Hay, Cape ›	176	74.25 N	113.00 W
Hay, Mount ∧, Austl.	162	23.28 S	133.05 E
Hay, Mount ∧, Austl.	170	33.37 S	150.26 E
Hay, Mount ∧, N.A.	180	59.15 N	137.37 W
Hay, South Fork ≃	190	45.03 N	91.57 W
Haya	164	3.27 S	129.33 E
Haya ≃, Nihon	94	35.14 N	139.09 E
Haya ≃, Nihon	94	35.25 N	138.27 E
Hayachine-san ∧	92	39.34 N	141.29 E
Hayakawa	94	35.25 N	138.22 E
Hayama, Nihon	94	35.16 N	139.35 E
Hayama, Nihon	96	33.26 N	133.13 E
Hayang	98	35.55 N	128.47 E
Hayange	56	49.20 N	6.03 E
HaYarden → Jordan ≃	132	31.46 N	35.33 E
Hayashima	96	34.36 N	133.50 E
Hayastan → Armenia □[1]	22	40.00 N	45.00 E
Hayasui-seto ʯ	96	33.18 N	131.59 E
Haybān	140	11.13 N	30.31 E
Haybān, Jabal ∧	140	11.15 N	30.31 E
Hay Bay c	212	44.10 N	76.55 W
Haybes	56	50.00 N	4.43 E
Haychur ≃	78	47.57 N	36.11 E
Haydān, Wādī al- V	132	31.27 N	35.36 E
Haydarlı	130	38.16 N	30.23 E
Hayden, Az., U.S.	200	33.00 N	110.47 W
Hayden, Co., U.S.	200	40.29 N	107.15 W
Hayden, In., U.S.	218	38.58 N	85.44 W
Hayden Peak ∧	202	42.59 N	116.39 W
Haydenville, Ma., U.S.	207	42.22 N	72.42 W
Haydenville, Oh., U.S.	188	39.28 N	82.19 W
Haydock	44	53.28 N	2.39 W
Haydock Park Race Course ♦	262	53.29 N	2.37 W
Haydon Bridge	44	54.58 N	2.14 W
Haye, La → 's-Gravenhage	52	52.06 N	4.18 E
Hayes	194	30.06 N	92.55 W
Hayes ⊸[8], Eng., U.K.	260	51.31 N	0.25 W
Hayes ⊸[8], Eng., U.K.	260	51.23 N	0.01 E
Hayes ≃, Mb., Can.	184	57.03 N	92.09 W
Hayes ≃, N.T., Can.	176	67.18 N	95.02 W
Hayes, Mount ∧	180	63.37 N	146.43 W
Hayes Center	198	40.30 N	101.01 W
Hayes State Memorial ⊥	214	41.21 N	83.08 W
Hayesville, N.C., U.S.	192	35.02 N	83.49 W
Hayesville, Oh., U.S.	214	40.46 N	82.15 W
Hayesville, Or., U.S.	224	44.59 N	122.58 W
Hayfield, Eng., U.K.	262	53.23 N	1.57 W
Hayfield, Mn., U.S.	190	43.53 N	92.50 W
Hayford Peak ∧	204	36.40 N	115.11 W
Hayfork	204	40.33 N	123.10 W
Hayfork Bally ∧	204	40.39 N	123.13 W
Hayfork Creek ≃	204	40.37 N	123.26 W
Hay Island I	212	44.53 N	80.58 W
Hayk, Lake ⊜	144	11.21 N	39.43 E
Haykota	144	15.10 N	37.03 E
Hay Lake ⊜	212	45.23 N	78.11 W
Hay Lakes	182	53.13 N	113.03 W
Hayle	42	50.11 N	5.23 W
Haymakers Run ≃	279b	40.25 N	79.43 W
Haymana	130	39.27 N	32.30 E
Haynes	194	34.53 N	90.47 W
Haynes Creek ≃	285	39.53 N	74.50 W
Haynesville, La., U.S.	194	32.57 N	93.08 W
Haynesville, Va., U.S.	208	37.57 N	76.40 W
Hayneville	194	32.11 N	86.34 W
Haynin	144	15.50 N	48.19 E
Hay-on-Wye	42	52.04 N	3.07 W
Hay Point ›	166	21.17 S	149.18 E
Hayrabolu	130	41.12 N	27.06 E
Hay River	176	60.51 N	115.40 W
Hays, Ab., Can.	182	50.06 N	111.48 W
Hays, Ks., U.S.	198	38.52 N	99.19 W
Hays, Mt., U.S.	202	47.59 N	108.41 W
Hays □[6]	222	30.02 N	97.45 W
Hays ⊸[8]	279b	40.23 N	79.56 W
Hayshah, Sabkhat al- ⠿	146	31.45 N	15.20 E
Hays Mill Creek ≃	285	39.44 N	74.50 W
Hay Springs	198	42.41 N	102.41 W
Haystack Mountain ∧	204	41.39 N	115.38 W
Haysville, Ks., U.S.	198	37.33 N	97.21 W
Haysville, Pa., U.S.	279b	40.32 N	80.09 W
Haysyn	78	48.48 N	29.24 E
Hayti, Mo., U.S.	194	36.14 N	89.44 W
Hayti, Pa., U.S.	208	39.59 N	75.51 W
Hayti, S.D., U.S.	198	44.39 N	97.12 W
Hayvoron	78	48.22 N	29.52 E
Hayward, Ca., U.S.	226	37.40 N	122.04 W
Hayward, Wi., U.S.	190	46.00 N	91.29 W
Hayward Brook ≃	283	42.22 N	71.20 W
Hayward Municipal Airport ⊠	282	37.40 N	122.08 W
Haywards Heath	42	51.00 N	0.06 W
Haywood	184	49.40 N	98.12 W
Ḥayy, Jabal al- ∧	142	29.43 N	31.35 E
HaẒafon □[5]	132	32.50 N	35.20 E
Hazār, Kūh-e ∧	128	29.30 N	57.18 E
Hazard	192	37.14 N	83.11 W
Hazardville	207	41.59 N	72.32 W
Hazar Gölü ⊜	130	38.30 N	39.25 E
Hazārībāg	124	23.59 N	85.21 E
Hazārībāg Plateau ⋏[1]	124	24.00 N	85.10 E
Haze, Cape ›	220	26.46 N	82.10 W
Hazebrouck	50	50.43 N	2.32 E
Hazel ≃	188	38.33 N	77.51 W
Hazelbrook	170	33.44 S	150.27 E
Hazel Crest	278	41.34 N	87.41 W
Hazel Dell	224	45.40 N	122.39 W
Hazel Green	190	42.31 N	90.26 W
Hazelgrove, Austl.	170	33.40 S	149.52 E
Hazel Grove, Eng., U.K.	44	53.23 N	2.08 W
Hazel Hurst	214	41.42 N	78.35 W
Hazel Kirk	279b	40.11 N	79.57 W
Hazel Park	216	42.27 N	83.06 W
Hazel Park Raceway ♦	281	42.29 N	83.05 W
Hazelton, B.C., Can.	182	55.15 N	127.40 W
Hazelton, Id., U.S.	202	42.35 N	114.08 W
Hazelton, N.D., U.S.	198	46.29 N	100.16 W
Hazelton Mountains ⋏	182	54.30 N	128.20 W
Hazelton Peak ∧	202	44.06 N	107.03 W
Hazelwood, Mo., U.S.	219	38.46 N	90.22 W
Hazelwood, N.C., U.S.	192	35.28 N	83.00 W
Hazelwood ⊸[8]	279b	40.25 N	79.56 W
Hazen, Ar., U.S.	194	34.46 N	91.34 W
Hazen, Nv., U.S.	226	39.33 N	119.02 W
Hazen, N.D., U.S.	198	47.17 N	101.37 W
Hazen, Pa., U.S.	214	41.12 N	78.58 W
Hazen Bay c	180	61.00 N	165.10 W
Ḥazerim	132	31.14 N	34.43 E
Hazlehurst, Ga., U.S.	192	31.52 N	82.35 W
Hazlehurst, Ms., U.S.	194	31.51 N	90.23 W
Hazlet, Sk., Can.	184	50.25 N	108.36 W
Hazlet, N.J., U.S.	208	40.26 N	74.13 W
Hazleton, Ia., U.S.	190	42.37 N	91.54 W
Hazleton, Pa., U.S.	210	40.57 N	75.58 W
Hazlett, Lake ⊜	162	21.30 S	128.48 E
Ḥaẓor HaGelilit	132	32.59 N	35.33 E
Hazro, Pāk.	123	33.54 N	72.29 E
Hazro, Tür.	130	38.15 N	40.47 E
Hazu	94	34.47 N	137.08 E
He ≃, Zhg.	100	27.05 N	114.59 E
He ≃, Zhg.	102	23.26 N	111.30 E
Heacham	42	52.55 N	0.30 E
Head ≃	212	44.44 N	79.15 W
Head Bay d'Espoir	186	47.56 N	55.45 W
Headcorn	42	51.11 N	0.37 E
Headford	48	53.28 N	9.05 W
Head Lake ⊜	212	44.45 N	78.55 W
Headland	194	31.21 N	85.20 W
Headlands	154	18.14 S	32.03 E
Headley, Eng., U.K.	42	51.07 N	0.50 W
Headley, Eng., U.K.	260	51.17 N	0.16 W
Headley, Mount ∧	202	47.44 N	115.15 W
Head of the Harbor	276	40.54 N	73.10 W
Heald Green	262	53.22 N	2.14 W
Heald Moor ⊸[3]	262	53.44 N	2.10 W
Healdsburg	204	38.36 N	122.52 W
Healdton	196	34.13 N	97.29 W
Healesville	169	37.40 S	145.31 E
Healing	44	53.34 N	0.10 W
Healy, Ak., U.S.	180	63.52 N	148.58 W
Healy, Ks., U.S.	198	38.36 N	100.37 W
Healy, Mount ∧	180	63.46 N	149.01 W
Healy Lake ⊜	212	45.10 N	79.55 W
Heani, Mont ∧	174x	9.47 S	139.04 W
Heanna	174m	26.19 N	127.54 E
Heanor	44	53.01 N	1.22 W
Heany Junction	154	20.06 S	28.54 E
Heard Island I	6	53.06 S	73.30 E
Heard Pond ⊜	283	42.21 N	71.22 W
Hearne	222	30.52 N	96.35 W
Hearst	176	49.41 N	83.40 W
Hearst Island I	9	69.25 S	62.10 W
Hearst San Simeon State Historical Park ♦	226	35.42 N	121.10 W
Heart ≃, Ab., Can.	182	56.14 N	117.17 W
Heart ≃, N.D., U.S.	198	46.47 N	100.51 W
Heart Lake ⊜, Ab., Can.	182	55.02 N	111.30 W
Heart Lake ⊜, On., Can.	275b	43.44 N	79.48 W
Heart Lake Indian Reserve ⊸[4]	182	55.02 N	111.30 W
Heart Pond ⊜	283	42.34 N	71.23 W
Heart's Content	186	47.53 N	53.22 W
Heath, Ma., U.S.	207	42.40 N	72.49 W
Heath, Oh., U.S.	214	40.02 N	82.28 W
Heath, Tx., U.S.	222	32.50 N	96.29 W
Heath ≃	248	12.31 S	68.38 W
Heath, Pointe ›	186	49.05 N	61.42 W
Heathcote, Austl.	169	36.55 S	144.42 E
Heathcote, Austl.	274a	34.05 S	151.01 E
Heathcote Brook ≃	276	40.23 N	74.37 W
Heath End	42	51.22 N	1.09 W
Heatherton	274b	37.58 S	145.06 E
Heathfield	42	50.59 N	0.17 E
Heathmont	274b	37.49 S	145.15 E
Heath Springs	192	34.35 N	80.40 W
Heathsville	208	37.55 N	76.28 W
Heatley	262	53.24 N	2.27 W
Heaton Hall ⊥	262	53.32 N	2.15 W
Heaton Moor	262	53.25 N	2.11 W
Heaven, Temple of ✝[1]	271a	39.53 N	116.25 E
Heavener	194	34.53 N	94.36 W
Heaverham	260	51.18 N	0.15 E
Heaviley	262	53.24 N	2.09 W
Hebaochang	107	29.33 N	105.32 E
Hebao Dao I	100	21.52 N	113.09 E
Hebbronville	196	27.18 N	98.40 W
Hebburn	44	54.59 N	1.30 W
Hebbville	284b	39.20 N	77.46 W
Hebden Bridge	44	53.45 N	2.00 W
Hebden Water ≃	262	53.44 N	2.00 W
Hebei, Zhg.	104	40.43 N	122.12 E
Hebei, Zhg.	104	41.01 N	123.51 E
Hebei (Hopeh) □[4]	98	38.00 N	116.00 E
Hebeitun	105	39.35 N	117.07 E
Hebel	166	28.59 S	147.48 E
Heber, Az., U.S.	200	34.25 N	110.35 W
Heber, Ca., U.S.	204	32.44 N	115.32 W
Heber City	200	40.30 N	111.24 W
Heber Springs	194	35.29 N	92.01 W
Hebgen Lake ⊜[1]	202	44.47 N	111.14 W
Hebi	98	35.59 N	114.11 E
Hebian	107	30.29 N	105.08 E
Hebo, Or., U.S.	224	45.13 N	123.51 W
Hebo, Zhg.	102	31.29 N	98.58 E
Hebo, Mount ∧	224	45.12 N	123.45 W
Hébridas, Islas → Hebrides II	46	57.00 N	6.30 W
Hebrides II	22	57.00 N	6.30 W
Hebrides, Sea of the ∓[2]	46	57.07 N	6.55 W
Hebron, Nf., Can.	176	58.12 N	62.38 W
Hebron, Ct., U.S.	207	41.39 N	72.21 W
Hebron, Il., U.S.	216	42.28 N	88.25 W
Hebron, In., U.S.	216	41.19 N	87.12 W
Hebron, Ky., U.S.	218	39.03 N	84.42 W
Hebron, Md., U.S.	208	38.25 N	75.41 W
Hebron, Ne., U.S.	198	40.09 N	97.35 W
Hebron, N.D., U.S.	198	46.54 N	102.02 W
Hebron, Pa., U.S.	208	40.21 N	76.24 W
Hebron, Tx., U.S.	222	33.01 N	96.52 W
Hebron, Wi., U.S.	216	42.56 N	88.42 W
Hebron → Al-Khalīl, W.B.	132	31.32 N	35.06 E
Hebu	100	27.50 N	115.22 E
Hebutu	104	42.19 N	122.20 E
Heby	40	59.56 N	16.53 E
Hecao	105	40.21 N	116.47 E
Hecate Strait ʯ	182	53.00 N	131.00 W
Hecelchakán	232	20.10 N	90.08 W
Heceta Island I	180	55.45 N	133.35 W
Hechi	102	24.42 N	108.02 E
Hechiceros	196	28.33 N	103.38 W
Hechingen	58	48.21 N	8.58 E
Hechtel	56	51.08 N	5.21 E
Hechthausen	52	53.38 N	9.14 E
Hechuan	107	30.00 N	106.16 E
Heckelberg	54	52.44 N	13.50 E
Hecker	219	38.18 N	90.00 W
Heckington	42	52.59 N	0.18 W
Hecklingen	54	51.51 N	11.32 E
Heckscher State Park ♦	210	40.43 N	73.10 W
Hecla, Mb., Can.	184	51.08 N	96.40 W
Hecla, S.D., U.S.	198	45.52 N	98.09 W
Hecla Island I	184	51.08 N	96.45 W
Hecla Provincial Park ♦	184	51.12 N	96.35 W
Hectanooga	186	44.06 N	66.02 W
Hector, N.Z.	172	41.36 S	171.53 E
Hector, Mn., U.S.	198	44.44 N	94.42 W
Hector, Mount ∧	172	40.57 S	175.17 E
Heda	94	34.58 N	138.46 E
Hedal	26	60.37 N	9.42 E
Hedaru	154	4.30 S	37.54 E
Heddal ✝[1]	26	59.35 N	9.11 E
Hedding	285	40.06 N	74.44 W
Hédé, Fr.	32	48.18 N	1.48 W
Hede, Sve.	26	62.25 N	13.30 E
Hedehusene	41	55.39 N	12.12 E
Hedel	52	51.45 N	5.15 E
Hedemora	40	60.17 N	15.59 E
Hedemünden	56	51.23 N	9.46 E
Hedensted	41	55.46 N	9.42 E
Hedersleben	54	51.51 N	11.15 E
Hedesunda	40	60.24 N	16.59 E
Hedesundafjärdarna ⊜	40	60.20 N	17.00 E
He Devil ∧	202	45.21 N	116.33 W
Hedge End	42	50.54 N	1.18 W
Hedgerley	260	51.35 N	0.36 W
Hedian	100	32.45 N	114.18 E
Hedley, B.C., Can.	182	49.21 N	120.04 W
Hedley, Tx., U.S.	196	34.52 N	100.39 W
Hedmark □[6]	26	61.30 N	11.45 E
Hednesford	42	52.43 N	2.00 W
Hedo	174m	26.51 N	128.16 E
Hedo-misaki ›	174m	26.52 N	128.16 E
Hedon	44	53.44 N	0.12 W
Hedrick	190	41.10 N	92.18 W
Hedströmmen ≃	40	59.28 N	16.04 E
Hedutne	272c	19.10 N	73.06 E
Hedwig Village	222	29.47 N	95.27 W
Heek	52	52.07 N	7.06 E
Heel	52	51.11 N	5.53 E
Heel Point ›	174a	19.19 N	166.37 E
Heemskerk	52	52.31 N	4.40 E
Heemstede	52	52.21 N	4.37 E
Heepen	52	52.01 N	8.35 E
Heer, Bel.	56	50.10 N	4.50 E
Heer, Ned.	56	50.50 N	5.44 E
Heerde	52	52.23 N	6.03 E
Heerdt ⊸[8]	263	51.13 N	6.43 E
Heerenveen	52	52.57 N	5.55 E
Heeren-Werve	52	51.35 N	7.43 E
Heerhugowaard	52	52.40 N	4.50 E
Heerkan	107	29.32 N	103.56 E
Heerlen	56	50.54 N	5.59 E
Heesch	52	51.44 N	5.32 E
Heeslingen	52	53.19 N	9.20 E
Heessen	52	51.42 N	7.50 E
Heeze	52	51.24 N	5.35 E
Ḥefa (Haifa)	132	32.50 N	35.00 E
Ḥefa □[5]	132	32.35 N	35.00 E
Ḥefa, Mifraẓ c	132	32.52 N	35.03 E
Ḥefa, Sede-Teʿufa ⊠	132	32.49 N	35.02 E
Hefei	100	31.51 N	117.17 E
Hefengchang	107	30.26 N	104.43 E
Heffron Park ♦	274a	33.57 S	151.15 E
Heflin	194	33.38 N	85.35 W
Hegang	89	47.24 N	130.22 E
Hegau ⊸[1]	58	47.50 N	8.45 E
Hégenheim	58	47.34 N	7.32 E
Hegewisch ⊸[8]	278	41.40 N	87.33 W
Hegins	208	40.39 N	76.29 W
Hegra	26	63.28 N	11.07 E
Hegura-jima I	92	37.51 N	136.55 E
Heguri	270	34.38 N	135.42 E
Hegyeshalom	61	47.55 N	17.10 E
Hehlen	52	51.59 N	9.28 E
Heho	110	20.43 N	96.49 E
Hehou	100	28.40 N	114.28 E
Hei ≃, Zhg.	102	40.18 N	99.26 E
Hei ≃, Zhg.	105	40.44 N	116.27 E
Heicheng (Karakhoto) ⊥	102	41.47 N	101.03 E
Heichengzhen	102	36.16 N	106.06 E
Heichengzi	104	42.10 N	121.01 E
Heidayingzi	98	40.52 N	116.12 E
Heidberg ∧[2]	263	51.15 N	7.21 E
Heide	30	54.12 N	9.06 E
Heide ⊸[8], Dtsch.	263	51.26 N	7.01 E
Heide ⊸[8], Dtsch.	263	51.31 N	6.52 E
Heideck	60	49.08 N	11.07 E
Heidelberg, Austl.	169	37.45 S	145.04 E
Heidelberg, On., Can.	212	43.31 N	80.37 W
Heidelberg, Dtsch.	56	49.25 N	8.43 E
Heidelberg, S. Afr.	158	34.06 S	20.59 E
Heidelberg, S. Afr.	158	26.32 S	28.18 E
Heidelberg, Ms., U.S.	194	31.53 N	88.59 W
Heidelberg, Pa., U.S.	279b	40.23 N	80.05 W
Heidelberg □[5]	273d	26.19 S	28.16 E
Heidelberg, Schloss ⊥	56	49.24 N	8.42 E
Heidelsheim	56	49.06 N	8.38 E
Heiden, Dtsch.	52	51.59 N	8.50 E
Heiden, Schw.	58	47.27 N	9.33 E
Heiden, Port c	180	56.55 N	158.45 W
Heidenau, Dtsch.	52	53.19 N	9.39 E
Heidenau, Dtsch.	54	50.59 N	13.52 E
Heidenheim	56	49.01 N	10.44 E
Heidenheim an der Brenz	56	48.40 N	10.08 E
Heidenheimer	222	31.01 N	97.18 W
Heidenoldendorf	52	51.57 N	8.50 E
Heidenreichstein	61	48.52 N	15.07 E
Heider Ditch ≍	279a	41.31 N	82.01 W
Heiderscheid	56	49.53 N	5.54 E
Heidhausen ⊸[8]	263	51.23 N	7.01 E
Heidhof ⊸[8]	263	51.11 N	7.11 E
Heidlersburg	208	39.57 N	77.09 W
Heidouwo	105	39.42 N	117.15 E
Heigenbrücken	56	50.02 N	9.23 E
Heigoutaicun	104	41.30 N	123.01 E
Heigun-tō I	96	33.47 N	132.14 E
Heihai → Har Hu ⊜	102	38.15 N	97.40 E
Heihe → Aihui	89	50.16 N	127.28 E
Heijō → P'yŏngyang	98	39.01 N	125.45 E
Heikega-dake ∧	96	34.19 N	131.54 E
Heikendorf	54	54.22 N	10.12 E
Heil	263	51.38 N	7.35 E
Heilangkou	105	39.37 N	117.24 E
Heilbron	158	27.21 S	27.58 E
Heilbronn	56	49.08 N	9.13 E
Heilenbecker-Stausee ⊜[1]	263	51.15 N	7.22 E
Heiligenberg	58	47.49 N	9.19 E
Heiligenblut	64	47.02 N	12.50 E
Heiligendamm	54	54.08 N	11.50 E
Heiligenhafen	54	54.22 N	10.58 E
Heiligenhaus	56	51.19 N	6.59 E
Heiligensee ⊸[8]	264a	52.36 N	13.13 E
Heiligenstadt, Dtsch.	56	51.23 N	10.09 E
Heiligenstadt, Dtsch.	60	49.51 N	11.10 E
Heilin	98	35.01 N	118.58 E
Hei Ling Chau I	271d	22.15 N	114.02 E
Heilong (Amur) ≃	89	52.56 N	141.10 E
Heilongguan	102	36.19 N	111.11 E
Heilongjiang □[4]	89	48.00 N	128.00 E
Heilongtan, Zhg.	105	40.44 N	116.31 E
Heilongtan, Zhg.	105	40.02 N	116.11 E
Heilongtan Shuiku ⊜[1]	107	30.03 N	104.02 E
Heiloo	52	52.36 N	4.43 E
Heilsbronn	56	49.20 N	10.47 E
Heiltz-le-Maurupt	56	48.48 N	4.49 E
Heilungkiang → Heilongjiang □[4]	89	48.00 N	128.00 E
Heilwood	214	40.37 N	78.54 W
Heimaey I	24a	63.26 N	20.17 W
Heimbach	56	50.38 N	6.28 E
Heimbuchenthal	56	49.53 N	9.17 E
Heimburg	54	51.49 N	10.54 E
Heimdal	26	63.21 N	10.22 E
Heimenkirch	58	47.37 N	9.53 E
Heimsheim	56	48.48 N	8.51 E
Heinävesi	26	62.26 N	28.36 E
Heinersdorf, Dtsch.	54	52.27 N	14.13 E
Heinersdorf, Dtsch.	264a	52.23 N	13.20 E
Heinersdorf ⊸[8]	264a	52.34 N	13.27 E
Heiniuyingzi	98	41.07 N	120.19 E
Heino	52	52.26 N	6.14 E
Heinola	26	61.13 N	26.02 E
Heinrichshorst	54	52.20 N	11.42 E
Heinsberg	56	51.03 N	6.05 E
Heiquan	102	39.32 N	99.42 E
Heirnkut	110	25.14 N	94.45 E
Heisfelde	52	53.15 N	7.26 E
Heishan	104	41.41 N	122.07 E
Heishanguan	98	38.33 N	113.41 E
Heishantou, Zhg.	89	50.13 N	119.28 E
Heishantou, Zhg.	98	42.28 N	125.33 E
Heishui	98	42.09 N	119.28 E
Heishuisi	102	36.08 N	108.42 E
Heisingen ⊸[8]	263	51.25 N	7.04 E
Heisler	182	52.41 N	112.13 W
Heislerville	208	39.13 N	74.59 W
Heissen ⊸[8]	263	51.26 N	6.56 E
Heist-aan-Zee	50	51.21 N	3.15 E
Heist-op-den-Berg	56	51.05 N	4.43 E
Heitang	102	26.29 N	105.09 E
Heitersheim	58	47.53 N	7.40 E
Heiwa	94	35.12 N	136.44 E
Heiyanghebao	105	39.07 N	118.15 E
Heiyantang	102	27.28 N	101.11 E
Heiyanzi	105	39.13 N	118.08 E
Hejaz → Al-Ḥijāz ⊸[1]	118	24.30 N	38.30 E
Hejiachang	107	29.24 N	104.56 E
Hejian, Zhg.	98	38.26 N	116.05 E
Hejian, Zhg.	105	39.25 N	116.25 E
Hejiang	107	28.49 N	105.50 E
Hejiangzhen	107	29.16 N	104.16 E
Hejiaqiao	100	27.24 N	113.21 E
Hejiawopeng	104	41.32 N	122.07 E
Hejiaying	105	39.55 N	118.19 E
Hejiazhen	107	29.52 N	104.26 E
Hejin	102	35.39 N	110.40 E
Hejlsminde	41	55.22 N	9.37 E
Hejnsvig	41	55.41 N	8.59 E
Hekelgem	50	50.54 N	4.06 E
Hekili Point ›	229a	20.48 N	156.37 W
Hekimhan	130	38.49 N	37.56 E
Hekinan	94	34.51 N	136.58 E
Hekla ∧[1]	24a	64.00 N	19.39 W
Hekou, Zhg.	100	31.22 N	114.26 E
Hekou, Zhg.	102	36.09 N	103.22 E
Hekou, Zhg.	102	28.22 N	108.14 E
Hekou, Zhg.	102	29.57 N	111.04 E
Hekou, Zhg.	102	22.38 N	103.56 E
Hekouchang	107	29.21 N	104.21 E
Hekouji	100	32.09 N	116.04 E
Hekoujie	102	26.31 N	100.39 E
Hekpoort	158	25.55 S	27.38 E
Hel	30	54.37 N	18.48 E
Helagsfjället ∧	26	62.55 N	12.27 E
Helaluo	102	33.56 N	102.10 E
Helangou	104	41.00 N	123.25 E
Helan Shan ⋏	102	38.40 N	105.57 E
Helbe ≃	54	51.13 N	11.06 E
Helbra	54	51.33 N	11.29 E
Helchteren	56	51.03 N	5.22 E
Heldburg	54	50.17 N	10.44 E
Helden	56	51.07 N	7.56 E
Heldra	56	51.07 N	10.11 E
Heldrungen	54	51.18 N	11.13 E
Helechos, Cañada de los ≃	286a	19.22 N	99.12 W
Helemano Stream ≃	229c	21.35 N	158.06 W
Helen, Mount ∧	166	21.34 S	141.13 E
Helena, Ar., U.S.	194	34.31 N	90.35 W
Helena, Mt., U.S.	202	46.35 N	112.02 W
Helena, N.Y., U.S.	206	44.55 N	74.44 W
Helena, Oh., U.S.	214	41.21 N	83.18 W
Helena, Ok., U.S.	196	36.32 N	98.16 W
Helena ≃	168a	31.54 S	116.00 E
Helena River Reservoir ⊜[1]	168a	31.59 S	116.13 E
Helendale	228	34.45 N	117.18 W
Helenenberg	56	49.51 N	6.32 E
Helenental V	264b	48.01 N	16.11 E
Helen Island I	108	2.58 N	131.49 E
Helensburgh, Austl.	170	34.11 S	150.59 E
Helensburgh, Scot., U.K.	46	56.01 N	4.44 W
Helen Springs	162	18.26 S	133.52 E
Helensville	172	36.40 S	174.28 E
Helenville	216	43.01 N	88.41 W
Helenwood	192	36.25 N	84.32 W
Ḥeleẓ	132	31.35 N	34.40 E
Helfenberg	61	48.32 N	14.08 E
Helfenstein	208	40.45 N	76.27 W
Helfta	54	51.30 N	11.34 E
Helgaå ≃	26	55.53 N	14.08 E
Helgenæs ›[1]	41	56.08 N	10.32 E
Helgoland I	30	54.12 N	7.53 E
Helgoländer Bucht c	30	54.10 N	8.04 E
Heli	89	47.05 N	130.16 E
Helicoide ⊸[9]	286c	10.29 N	66.55 W
Helidon	171a	27.33 S	152.08 E
Heliodora	256	22.04 S	45.32 W
Heliópolis	287a	22.45 S	43.25 W
Heliopolis → Miṣr al-Jadīdah ⊸[8]	273c	30.06 N	31.20 E
Heliopolis ⊥	142	30.08 N	31.17 E
Heliopolis Aerodrome ⊠	273c	30.04 N	31.19 E
Heliopolis Racing Club ♦	273c	30.06 N	31.19 E
Heliuji	100	33.02 N	116.57 E
Helixi	106	30.40 N	118.59 E
Hell	26	63.26 N	10.54 E
Hellam	208	40.00 N	76.36 W
Hellberge ∧[2]	54	52.34 N	11.17 E
Hellbrunn, Schloss ⊥	64	47.46 N	13.04 E
Hellebæk	41	56.04 N	12.34 E
Ḥelleh ≃	128	29.10 N	50.40 E
Hellen Blazes, Lake ⊜	220	28.01 N	80.47 W
Hellendoorn	52	52.24 N	6.26 E
Hellenthal	56	50.29 N	6.26 E
Hellerau ⊸[8]	54	51.07 N	13.44 E
Hellern	52	52.15 N	7.58 E
Hellersen	263	51.12 N	7.39 E
Hellertown	208	40.34 N	75.20 W
Hellesylt	26	62.05 N	6.54 E
Hellevad	41	55.05 N	9.13 E
Hellevoetsluis	52	51.49 N	4.08 E
Hell Gate ʯ	276	40.47 N	73.56 W
Hell Hole Reservoir ⊜[1]	226	39.04 N	120.22 W
Hellifield	44	54.01 N	2.12 W
Hellín	34	38.31 N	1.41 W
Helli Ness ›	46a	60.02 N	1.10 W
Hellmonsödt	61	48.26 N	14.18 E
Hell Point ›	186	44.16 N	64.15 W
Hells Canyon V	202	45.20 N	116.45 W
Hellsee ⊜	264a	52.45 N	13.35 E
Hells Gate V	182	49.47 N	121.27 W
Hell-Ville	157b	13.25 S	48.16 E
Hellweg ⊸[1]	52	51.36 N	8.32 E
Helm	226	36.31 N	120.05 W
Helmand □[4]	128	31.00 N	64.00 E
Helmand ≃	128	31.12 N	61.34 E
Helmbrechts	54	50.14 N	11.43 E
Helmcken Falls ∟	182	51.57 N	120.11 W
Helme ≃	54	51.20 N	11.20 E
Helmeringhausen	156	25.54 S	16.57 E
Helmetta	276	40.22 N	74.25 W
Helmetta Pond ⊜	276	40.23 N	74.26 W
Helmond	52	51.29 N	5.40 E
Helmsburg	218	39.16 N	86.18 W
Helmsdale	46	58.07 N	3.40 W
Helmsdale ≃	46	58.07 N	3.40 W
Helmshore	262	53.41 N	2.20 W
Helmsley	44	54.14 N	1.04 W
Helmstedt	54	52.13 N	11.00 E
Hel'myaziv	78	49.49 N	31.49 E
Helnæs I	41	55.08 N	10.02 E
Helong	98	42.32 N	128.59 E
Helper	200	39.41 N	110.51 W
Helpmekaar	158	28.29 S	30.29 E
Helpter Berg ∧[2]	54	53.30 N	13.36 E
Helsby	44	53.16 N	2.46 W
Helsby Hill ∧[2]	262	53.16 N	2.46 W
Helsingborg	41	56.03 N	12.42 E
Helsinge	41	56.01 N	12.12 E
Helsingfors → Helsinki	26	60.10 N	24.58 E
Helsingør (Elsinore)	41	56.02 N	12.37 E
Helsinki (Helsingfors)	26	60.10 N	24.58 E
Helska, Mierzeja ›[2]	30	54.45 N	18.39 E
Helston	42	50.05 N	5.16 W
Heltonville	218	38.55 N	86.22 W
Helvecia	252	31.06 S	60.05 W
Helvellyn ∧	44	54.31 N	3.01 W
Helvick Head ›	48	52.03 N	7.33 W
Helvoirt	52	51.38 N	5.13 E
Hem ≃	50	50.51 N	2.06 E
Ḥemar, Naḥal V	132	31.08 N	35.22 E
Hemau	60	49.03 N	11.47 E
Hemāvati ≃	122	12.31 N	76.27 E
Hembe	152	1.54 N	22.42 E
Hemel Hempstead	42	51.46 N	0.28 W
Hemelingen ⊸[8]	52	53.03 N	8.53 E

ENGLISH

Name	Page	Lat.°′	Long.°′
Hemeln	52	51.30 N	9.36 E
Hemer	56	51.23 N	7.46 E
Hemet	228	33.44 N	116.58 W
Hemfjärden c	40	59.17 N	15.20 E
Hemford	186	44.30 N	64.47 W
Hemfurth-Edersee	56	51.10 N	9.02 E
Hemiksem	50	51.09 N	4.21 E
Héming	58	48.42 N	6.57 E
Hemingford	198	42.19 N	103.04 W
Hemingway	192	33.45 N	79.26 W
Hemlock, In., U.S.	216	40.25 N	86.03 W
Hemlock, N.Y., U.S.	210	42.47 N	77.36 W
Hemlock Lake ⊜	210	42.43 N	77.37 W
Hemmerde	52	51.33 N	7.48 E
Hemmerden	263	51.07 N	6.36 E
Hemmingen-Westerfeld	52	52.19 N	9.45 E
Hemmoor	52	53.41 N	9.08 E
Hemphill	194	31.20 N	93.50 W
Hempnall	42	52.30 N	1.19 E
Hempstead, N.Y., U.S.	210	40.42 N	73.37 W
Hempstead, Tx., U.S.	222	30.05 N	96.04 W
Hempstead Harbor c	276	40.50 N	73.39 W
Hempstead Lake ⊜	276	40.41 N	73.38 W
Hempstead Lake State Park ♦	276	40.41 N	73.38 W
Hemsby	42	52.41 N	1.42 E
Hemse	26	57.14 N	18.22 E
Hemsedal	26	60.52 N	8.34 E
Hemsön I	26	62.43 N	18.05 E
Hemstreet Park	210	42.54 N	73.41 W
Hemsworth	44	53.38 N	1.21 W
Hemujing	98	37.54 N	115.22 E
Henan	102	34.35 N	101.34 E
Henan (Honan) □[4]	90	34.00 N	114.00 E
Hen and Chickens II	172	35.55 S	174.45 E
Henares ≃	34	40.24 N	3.30 W
Henbury, Austl.	162	24.35 S	133.15 E
Henbury, Eng., U.K.	262	53.15 N	2.11 W
Hendek	130	40.48 N	30.45 E
Henderson, Arg.	252	36.18 S	61.43 W
Henderson, In., U.S.	218	39.40 N	85.31 W
Henderson, Ky., U.S.	194	37.50 N	87.35 W
Henderson, Mn., U.S.	190	44.31 N	93.54 W
Henderson, Ne., U.S.	198	40.46 N	97.48 W
Henderson, Nv., U.S.	204	36.02 N	114.58 W
Henderson, N.Y., U.S.	212	43.51 N	76.11 W
Henderson, N.C., U.S.	192	36.19 N	78.23 W
Henderson, Tn., U.S.	194	35.26 N	88.38 W
Henderson, Tx., U.S.	222	32.09 N	94.47 W
Henderson □[6]	222	32.13 N	95.50 W
Henderson Bay c, N.Y., U.S.	212	43.54 N	76.10 W
Henderson Bay c, Wa., U.S.	224	47.18 N	122.42 W
Henderson Creek ≃	190	40.52 N	91.02 W
Henderson Island I	6	24.22 S	128.19 W
Hendersonville, N.C., U.S.	192	35.19 N	82.27 W
Hendersonville, Pa., U.S.	214	40.18 N	80.09 W
Hendersonville, Tn., U.S.	194	36.18 N	86.37 W
Hendījān	128	30.14 N	49.43 E
Hendon ⊸[8]	260	51.35 N	0.14 W
Hendorābī, Jazīreh-ye I	128	26.40 N	53.37 E
Hendricks, Mn., U.S.	198	44.30 N	96.25 W
Hendricks, W.V., U.S.	188	39.04 N	79.37 W
Hendricks □[6]	218	39.46 N	86.26 W
Hendrik Verwoerddam ⊜[1]	158	30.40 S	25.40 E
Hendrina	158	26.11 S	29.45 E
Hendry □[6]	220	26.36 N	81.13 W
Hendrysburg	214	40.04 N	81.10 W
Hendy	42	51.43 N	4.04 W
Henefer	200	41.01 N	111.29 W
Henfield	42	50.56 N	0.17 W
Heng ≃, Zhg.	102	28.40 N	104.25 E
Heng ≃, Zhg.	107	28.57 N	105.22 E
Hengām, Jazīreh-ye I	128	26.39 N	55.53 E
Henganofi	164	6.15 S	145.35 E
Hengchow → Hengyang	102	26.54 N	112.36 E
Hengdaochuan	98	41.15 N	125.31 E
Hengdaohe	104	42.02 N	123.51 E
Hengdaohezi	89	43.13 N	126.44 E
Hengdaozi	89	43.18 N	127.18 E
Hengdong	100	27.03 N	112.57 E
Hengelo	52	52.15 N	6.45 E
Hengersberg	60	48.47 N	13.03 E
Hengfan	106	30.20 N	119.45 E
Hengfeng	100	28.24 N	117.34 E
Henggang	100	29.32 N	115.27 E
Henggouzi	89	43.12 N	124.47 E
Henghutou	104	42.05 N	124.00 E
Hengjie	106	31.13 N	119.30 E
Hengjing	106	31.11 N	120.32 E
Hengjinghong	106	30.34 N	120.59 E
Hengli	100	23.12 N	114.37 E
Henglin	106	31.42 N	120.06 E
Henglu	98	41.26 N	126.04 E
Henglutou	106	30.19 N	119.19 E
Hengmian	106	31.09 N	121.38 E
Hengoed	42	51.39 N	3.10 W
Hengsen	263	51.29 N	7.38 E
Heng Sha I	106	31.20 N	121.50 E
Hengshan, Zhg.	100	27.15 N	112.51 E
Hengshan, Zhg.	102	37.56 N	108.53 E
Hengshan, Zhg.	106	31.01 N	120.32 E
Heng Shan ∧	100	27.16 N	112.35 E
Heng Shan ⋏	102	39.30 N	113.45 E
Hengshanchang	107	30.33 N	105.24 E
Hengshanqiao	106	31.46 N	120.07 E
Hengshanxia	106	30.18 N	118.44 E
Hengshi, Zhg.	100	26.05 N	114.38 E
Hengshi, Zhg.	100	23.52 N	113.15 E
Hengshi, Zhg.	100	29.32 N	114.41 E
Hengshui	98	37.43 N	115.40 E
Hengsteysee ⊜[1]	263	51.25 N	7.28 E
Hengtangshi	106	31.41 N	121.02 E
Hengtianchi	107	29.07 N	105.01 E
Hengtianxi	107	29.05 N	105.03 E
Hengxi, Zhg.	100	29.42 N	121.35 E
Hengxi, Zhg.	100	28.46 N	120.29 E
Hengxi, Zhg.	106	31.43 N	118.46 E
Hengxian	102	22.42 N	109.13 E
Hengxiang	106	32.12 N	120.15 E
Hengxikou	100	29.26 N	121.26 E
Hengyang	102	26.54 N	112.36 E
Heniches'k	78	46.11 N	34.48 E
Hénin-Beaumont	50	50.25 N	2.56 E
Henley Beach	168b	34.55 S	138.30 E
Henley-in-Arden	42	52.17 N	1.46 W
Henley-on-Thames	42	51.32 N	0.56 W
Henlopen, Cape ›	208	38.48 N	75.05 W
Henlow	42	52.02 N	0.18 W
Hennan ⊜	26	62.06 N	15.46 E
Hennaya	34	34.58 N	1.22 W
Henneberg	54	50.29 N	10.21 E
Hennebont	32	47.48 N	3.17 W
Hennef	56	50.46 N	7.16 E
Hennen	56	51.27 N	7.39 E
Hennenman	158	27.59 S	27.01 E
Hennepin	190	41.15 N	89.21 W
Hennepin, Point ›	281	42.12 N	83.09 W
Hennersdorf	264b	48.07 N	16.22 E
Hennessey	196	36.06 N	97.53 W
Hennessey, Lake ⊜[1]	226	38.29 N	122.22 W
Hennickendorf	54	52.30 N	13.51 E
Henniez	58	46.44 N	6.54 E
Hennigsdorf	54	52.38 N	13.12 E
Henniker	188	43.10 N	71.49 W
Henning, Il., U.S.	216	40.18 N	87.42 W
Henning, Mn., U.S.	198	46.19 N	95.26 W
Henning, Tn., U.S.	194	35.40 N	89.34 W
Henri ≃	206	46.30 N	71.47 W
Henri, Cap ›	186	49.48 N	64.23 W

DEUTSCH

Name	Seite	Breite°′	Länge°′ E = Ost
Henri-Chapelle	56	50.40 N	5.56 E
Henrichemont	50	47.18 N	2.32 E
Henrichenburg	263	51.35 N	7.19 E
Henrico □[6]	208	37.30 N	77.20 W
Henrietta, N.Y., U.S.	210	43.03 N	77.36 W
Henrietta, N.C., U.S.	192	35.15 N	81.47 W
Henrietta, Tx., U.S.	196	33.49 N	98.11 W
Henrietta Maria, Cape ›	176	55.09 N	82.20 W
Henri Pittier, Parque Nacional ♦	246	10.25 N	67.43 W
Henry, Il., U.S.	190	41.06 N	89.21 W
Henry, S.D., U.S.	198	44.52 N	97.27 W
Henry □[6], In., U.S.	218	39.55 N	85.22 W
Henry □[6], Ky., U.S.	218	38.26 N	85.09 W
Henry □[6], Oh., U.S.	216	41.20 N	84.04 W
Henry ≃	162	22.40 S	115.40 E
Henry, Cape ›	208	36.55 N	76.01 W
Henry, Mount ∧	202	48.53 N	115.31 W
Henry, Mount ∧[2]	274a	33.50 S	150.38 E
Henry, Point ›	162	34.29 S	119.23 E
Henry Cowell Redwoods State Park ♦	226	37.02 N	122.03 W
Henryetta	196	35.26 N	95.58 W
Henry Island I	224	48.35 N	123.11 W
Henry Kater, Cape ›	176	69.05 N	66.44 W
Henry Mountains ⋏	200	38.00 N	110.50 W
Henrys Bend	214	41.28 N	79.37 W
Henrys Fork ≃, U.S.	200	41.00 N	109.39 W
Henrys Fork ≃, Id., U.S.	202	43.45 N	111.56 W
Henryville, P.Q., Can.	206	45.08 N	73.11 W
Henryville, In., U.S.	218	38.32 N	85.46 W
Henry W. Coe State Park ♦	226	37.12 N	121.30 W
Hensall	190	43.26 N	81.30 W
Henshaw, Lake ⊜[1]	204	33.15 N	116.45 W
Hensley	194	34.30 N	92.12 W
Hensley Lake ⊜[1]	226	37.07 N	119.53 W
Henslow, Cape ›	175e	9.56 S	160.38 E
Henson Creek ≃	284b	38.46 N	77.00 W
Hensonville	210	42.17 N	74.13 W
Henstedt-Ulzburg	52	53.47 N	9.58 E
Henstridge	42	50.59 N	2.24 W
Hentiesbaai	156	22.08 S	14.18 E
Henty	166	35.31 S	147.02 E
Henzada	110	17.38 N	95.28 E
Heorhiyivka	83	48.26 N	39.17 E
Hepburn	184	52.31 N	106.43 W
Hepburn Springs	169	37.19 S	144.09 E
Hephzibah	192	33.18 N	82.05 W
Heping, Zhg.	100	27.10 N	117.18 E
Heping, Zhg.	100	22.01 N	112.59 E
Heping, Zhg.	100	23.17 N	116.29 E
Heping, Zhg.	100	24.28 N	114.58 E
Heping, Zhg.	106	30.50 N	119.54 E
Heppenheim	56	49.39 N	8.38 E
Heppner	202	45.21 N	119.33 W
Heptonstall	262	53.45 N	2.01 W
Heptonstall Moor ≃	262	53.46 N	2.05 W
Hepu (Lianzhou)	102	21.39 N	109.11 E
Hepworth	212	44.37 N	81.09 W
Heqiao, Zhg.	100	32.55 N	118.22 E
Heqiao, Zhg.	106	31.30 N	119.53 E
Heqing	102	26.34 N	100.12 E
Hequ	102	39.26 N	111.08 E
Héraðsflói c	24a	65.45 N	14.10 W
Hera Lacinia, Tempio di ⊥	68	39.01 N	17.13 E
Herāt	128	34.20 N	62.12 E
Herāt □[4]	128	34.30 N	62.00 E
Hérault □[5]	32	43.40 N	3.30 E
Hérault ≃	32	43.17 N	3.26 E
Herbasse ≃	62	45.02 N	4.57 E
Herbault	50	47.36 N	1.08 E
Herbede	56	51.25 N	7.16 E
Herbern	52	51.44 N	7.39 E
Herbert, Sk., Can.	184	50.26 N	107.12 W
Herbert, N.Z.	172	45.14 S	170.47 E
Herbert ≃	166	18.32 S	146.17 E
Herbert, Mount ∧	172	43.41 S	172.44 E
Herbertabad	110	11.43 N	92.37 E
Herbert Hoover National Historic Site ⊥	190	41.38 N	91.23 W
Herbertingen	58	48.04 N	9.26 E
Herbert Island I	180	52.45 N	170.10 W
Herberton	166	17.23 S	145.23 E
Herbertsdale	158	34.01 S	21.46 E
Herbeumont	56	49.47 N	5.14 E
Herbignac	32	47.27 N	2.19 W
Herb Lake	184	54.47 N	99.47 W
Herblay	50	49.00 N	2.10 E
Herblet Lake ⊜	184	54.56 N	99.54 W
Herbolzheim	58	48.13 N	7.47 E
Herborn	56	50.40 N	8.17 E
Herbrechtingen	56	48.37 N	10.10 E
Herbringhauser-Stausee ⊜[1]	263	51.14 N	7.16 E
Herbsleben	54	51.07 N	10.50 E
Herbstein	56	50.34 N	9.20 E
Herceg-Novi	38	42.27 N	18.32 E
Herculaneum	219	38.16 N	90.22 W
Hércules, Méx.	232	28.02 N	103.48 W
Hercules, Ca., U.S.	282	38.01 N	122.17 W
Herdecke	56	51.24 N	7.26 E
Herdorf	56	50.46 N	7.56 E
Herdringen	52	51.25 N	7.58 E
Herðubreið ∧	24a	65.13 N	16.18 W
Heredia	236	10.00 N	84.07 W
Heredia □[4]	236	10.30 N	84.00 W
Hereford, Eng., U.K.	42	52.04 N	2.43 W
Hereford, Az., U.S.	200	31.26 N	110.05 W
Hereford, Md., U.S.	208	39.35 N	76.39 W
Hereford, Tx., U.S.	196	34.48 N	102.23 W
Hereford and Worcester □[6]	42	52.10 N	2.30 W
Hereford Cathedral ✝[1]	42	52.04 N	2.43 W
Hereford Mountain ∧	206	45.05 N	71.36 W
Hereke	130	40.48 N	29.39 E
Herekino	172	35.15 S	173.13 E
Herencia	34	39.21 N	3.22 W
Herent	56	50.54 N	4.40 E
Herentals	56	51.11 N	4.50 E
Hereroland Oos □[5]	156	21.00 S	20.00 E
Hereroland Wes □[5]	156	20.30 S	18.15 E
Herfølge	41	55.25 N	12.10 E
Herford	52	52.06 N	8.40 E
Hergatz	58	47.39 N	9.50 E
Hergisdorf	54	51.32 N	11.28 E
Hergla	36	36.02 N	10.31 E
Herhahn	56	50.33 N	6.26 E
Héricourt	58	47.35 N	6.45 E
Hérimoncourt	58	47.26 N	6.53 E
Heringen	54	51.27 N	10.52 E
Heringsdorf	54	54.18 N	11.00 E
Herington	198	38.40 N	96.56 W
Heriot	172	45.50 S	169.16 E
Herisau	58	47.23 N	9.17 E
Heritage Range ⋏	9	79.30 S	84.00 W
Herk ≃	56	50.58 N	5.07 E
Herk-de-Stad	56	50.56 N	5.10 E
Herkimer	210	43.01 N	74.59 W
Herkimer □[6]	210	43.02 N	74.59 W
Herlen → Kerulen ≃	90	48.48 N	117.00 E
Herleshausen	56	51.00 N	10.09 E
Herlev	41	55.43 N	12.27 E
Herlong	204	40.09 N	120.08 W
Herlufmagle	41	55.19 N	11.46 E
Herlufsholm	41	55.15 N	11.46 E
Hermagor	64	46.37 N	13.22 E
Herman, Mn., U.S.	198	45.48 N	96.08 W
Herman, Ne., U.S.	198	41.40 N	96.12 W
Herman, Pa., U.S.	214	40.50 N	79.49 W
Herman, Lake ⊜	282	38.05 N	122.09 W
Hermana Mayor Island I	116	15.48 N	119.48 E
Hermanas	196	27.13 N	101.14 W

Symbols in the index entries represent the broad categories identified in the key at the right. Symbols with superior numbers (⋏[1]) identify subcategories (see complete key on page *I · 1).*

Symbole im Register stellen die rechts im Schlüssel erklärten Kategorien dar. Symbole mit hochgestellten Ziffern (⋏[1]) bezeichnen Unterabteilungen einer Kategorie (vgl. vollständiger Schlüssel auf Seite *I · 1).*

Los símbolos incluídos en el texto del índice representan las grandes categorías identificadas con la clave a la derecha. Los símbolos con numeros en su parte superior (⋏[1]) identifican las subcategorías (véase la clave completa en la página *I · 1).*

Les symboles de l'index représentent les catégories indiquées dans la légende à droite. Les symboles suivis d'un indice (⋏[1]) représentent des sous-catégories (voir légende complète à la page *I · 1).*

Os símbolos incluídos no texto do índice representam as grandes categorias identificadas com a chave à direita. Os símbolos com números em sua parte superior (⋏[1]) identificam as subcategorias (veja-se a chave completa à página *I · 1).*

	English	Deutsch	Español	Français	Português
∧	Mountain	Berg	Montaña	Montagne	Montanha
⋏	Mountains	Gebirge	Montañas	Montagnes	Montanhas
)(	Pass	Paß	Paso	Col	Passo
V	Valley, Canyon	Tal, Cañon	Valle, Cañón	Vallée, Canyon	Vale, Canhão
≃	Plain	Ebene	Llano	Plaine	Planície
›	Cape	Kap	Cabo	Cap	Cabo
I	Island	Insel	Isla	Île	Ilha
II	Islands	Inseln	Islas	Îles	Ilhas
⊥	Other Topographic Features	Andere Topographische Objekte	Otros Elementos Topográficos	Autres données topographiques	Outros acidentes topográficos

ESPAÑOL

Nombre	Página	Lat.°′	Long.°′ W = Oeste
Herman Eksteen Park ♠	273d	26.10 S	28.02 E
Herma Ness ›	46a	60.50 N	0.55 W
Hermann	219	38.42 N	91.26 W
Hermannsburg, Austl.	162	23.57 S	132.45 E
Hermannsburg, Dtsch.	52	52.50 N	10.05 E
Hermannsburg Aboriginal Reserve ◆4	162	24.00 S	132.45 E
Hermanns-Denkmal ⊥	52	51.55 N	8.50 E
Hermannskogel ∧	264b	48.16 N	16.18 E
Hermannstadt → Sibiu	38	45.48 N	24.09 E
Hermano Peak ∧	200	37.13 N	108.48 W
Hermansverk	26	61.11 N	6.51 E
Hermansville	190	45.42 N	87.36 W
Hermanus	158	34.25 S	19.16 E
Hermanville	194	31.57 N	90.50 W
Hermeray	261	48.38 N	1.41 E
Hermes	50	49.22 N	2.15 E
Hermeskeil	56	49.39 N	6.56 E
Hermidale	166	31.33 S	146.43 E
Hermies	50	50.07 N	3.02 E
Herminie	214	40.15 N	79.43 W
Hermiston	202	45.50 N	119.17 W
Hermitage, Nf., Can.	186	47.33 N	55.56 W
Hermitage, Eng., U.K.	42	51.27 N	1.16 W
Hermitage, Ar., U.S.	194	33.26 N	92.10 W
Hermitage, Mo., U.S.	194	37.56 N	93.18 W
Hermitage Bay ⊂	186	47.35 N	56.05 W
Hermitage Park	284c	39.05 N	77.04 W
Hermite, Isla I	254	55.52 S	67.20 W
Hermit Islands II	164	1.30 S	145.05 E
Hermleigh	196	32.38 N	100.46 W
Hermon, S. Afr.	158	33.27 S	18.59 E
Hermon, N.Y., U.S.	212	44.28 N	75.13 W
Hermon, Mount → Shaykh, Jabal ash- ∧	132	33.26 N	35.51 E
Hermosa Beach	280	33.51 N	118.23 W
Hermosillo, Méx.	200	32.30 N	114.59 W
Hermosillo, Méx.	232	29.04 N	110.58 W
Hermoso, Cerro ∧	246	1.10 S	78.12 W
Hermsdorf	54	50.54 N	11.52 E
Hermsdorf ◆8	54	52.37 N	13.18 E
Hermyingyi	110	14.15 N	98.21 E
Hernád ≃	30	47.56 N	21.08 E
Hernals ◆8	264b	48.13 N	16.20 E
Hernandarias	252	25.22 S	54.45 W
Hernández	234	23.01 N	102.01 W
Hernandez Reservoir ◎1	226	36.22 N	120.49 W
Hernando, Arg.	252	32.25 S	63.44 W
Hernando, Fl., U.S.	220	28.54 N	82.22 W
Hernando, Ms., U.S.	194	34.49 N	89.59 W
Hernando □6	220	28.34 N	82.22 W
Hernando de Magallanes, Parque Nacional ♠	254	54.15 S	72.00 W
Hernani	116	11.20 N	125.37 E
Herndon, Ca., U.S.	226	36.49 N	119.54 W
Herndon, Ks., U.S.	198	39.54 N	100.47 W
Herndon, Pa., U.S.	210	40.42 N	76.50 W
Herndon, Va., U.S.	208	38.58 N	77.23 W
Herndon Canal ≍	226	36.46 N	119.46 W
Herne	52	51.32 N	7.13 E
Herne Bay	42	51.23 N	1.08 E
Herne Hill	168a	31.50 S	116.01 E
Herning	41	56.08 N	8.59 E
Hernwood Heights	284b	39.22 N	77.50 W
Heroica Zitácuaro	234	19.24 N	100.22 W
Herongate	260	51.36 N	0.21 E
Herongen	56	51.24 N	6.15 E
Heron Island I	166	23.26 S	151.55 E
Heron Lake	198	43.47 N	95.19 W
Hérons, Île aux I	275a	45.25 N	73.35 W
Heronsgate	260	51.38 N	0.31 W
Hérouville	261	49.06 N	2.08 E
Hérouville-Saint-Clair	32	49.12 N	0.21 W
Herpf	54	50.34 N	10.20 E
Herradura	252	26.29 S	58.18 W
Herräng	40	60.08 N	18.39 E
Herreid	198	45.50 N	100.04 W
Herrenalb	56	48.48 N	8.26 E
Herrenberg	56	48.35 N	8.52 E
Herrenchiemsee, Schloss ⊥	64	47.52 N	12.23 E
Herrera	252	28.29 S	63.04 W
Herrera □4	236	7.54 N	80.38 W
Herrera del Duque	34	39.10 N	5.03 W
Herrera de Pisuerga	34	42.36 N	4.20 W
Herrick, Austl.	166	41.06 S	147.52 E
Herrick, Il., U.S.	219	39.13 N	88.59 W
Herrick Creek ≃	182	54.20 N	121.30 W
Herrick Grove	212	44.04 N	76.12 W
Herricks	276	40.45 N	73.40 W
Herrieden	56	49.14 N	10.30 E
Herrin	194	37.48 N	89.01 W
Herring Bay ⊂	208	38.44 N	76.33 W
Herring Brook ≃	283	42.10 N	70.44 W
Herring Cove, N.S., Can.	186	44.34 N	63.34 W
Herring Cove, Ak., U.S.	182	55.21 N	131.41 W
Herring Creek ≃	208	37.49 N	77.07 W
Herringen	52	51.40 N	7.44 E
Herring Run ≃	284b	39.18 N	76.31 W
Herring Run Park ♠	284b	39.19 N	76.33 W
Herritslev	41	54.42 N	11.41 E
Herrljunga	26	58.05 N	13.02 E
Herrnburg	54	53.47 N	10.45 E
Herrnhut	54	51.01 N	14.44 E
Herrsching am Ammersee	60	48.00 N	11.10 E
Herrs Island I	279b	40.28 N	79.58 W
Herrskogen	40	59.32 N	16.15 E
Herry	50	47.13 N	2.57 E
Hersbruck	60	49.30 N	11.26 E
Herschbach	56	50.34 N	7.44 E
Herscheid	56	51.10 N	7.44 E
Herschel, Sk., Can.	184	51.38 N	108.21 W
Herschel, S. Afr.	158	30.37 S	27.12 E
Herschel Island I	180	69.35 N	139.05 W
Herscher	216	41.03 N	88.06 W
Herselt	56	51.03 N	4.53 E
Herserange	56	49.31 N	5.47 E
Hersham	260	51.22 N	0.23 W
Hershey, Ne., U.S.	198	41.09 N	101.00 W
Hershey, Pa., U.S.	208	40.17 N	76.39 W
Hersman	219	39.57 N	90.44 W
Herstadberg	40	58.38 N	16.10 E
Herstal	56	50.40 N	5.38 E
Herstmonceux	42	50.53 N	0.20 E
Herten	52	51.35 N	7.07 E
Hertford, Eng., U.K.	42	51.48 N	0.05 W
Hertford, N.C., U.S.	192	36.11 N	76.27 W
Hertford □6	208	36.28 N	77.01 W
Hertfordshire □6	42	51.50 N	0.10 W
Hertingfordbury	260	51.48 N	0.06 W
Hertsa	78	48.09 N	26.16 E
Hertsmere □8	260	51.41 N	0.17 W
Hertzogville	158	28.08 S	25.33 E
Heruncun	104	40.58 N	123.27 E
Hervás	34	40.16 N	5.51 W
Herve	56	50.38 N	5.48 E
Hervest	263	51.40 N	7.01 E
Hervey Bay ⊂	166	25.00 S	153.00 E
Herxheim	56	49.09 N	8.13 E
Héry, Fr.	50	47.54 N	3.38 E
Héry, Fr.	62	45.46 N	6.28 E
Herzberg, Dtsch.	54	52.54 N	12.58 E
Herzberg, Dtsch.	54	51.41 N	13.14 E
Herzberg am Harz	52	51.39 N	10.20 E
Herzebrock	52	51.53 N	8.14 E
Herzfelde	54	52.29 N	13.50 E
Herzhausen	56	51.11 N	8.53 E
Herzliyya	132	32.10 N	34.51 E
Herznach	58	47.28 N	8.03 E
Herzogenaurach	56	49.34 N	10.53 E

FRANÇAIS

Nom	Page	Lat.°′	Long.°′ W = Ouest
Herzogenbuchsee	58	47.12 N	7.41 E
Herzogenburg	61	48.17 N	15.42 E
Herzogenrath	56	50.52 N	6.06 E
Herzsprung	54	53.04 N	12.28 E
Heṣār, Kūh-e ⋀	120	34.50 N	66.30 E
Hesarak	267d	35.47 N	51.19 E
Hesdin	50	50.22 N	2.02 E
Hesel	52	53.18 N	7.35 E
Hesepe	52	52.26 N	7.58 E
Heshachang	107	30.37 N	105.40 E
Heshan	110	23.52 N	108.52 E
Heshangqiao	100	34.15 N	113.47 E
Heshengqiao	100	30.00 N	114.22 E
Heshi, Zhg.	100	25.04 N	118.37 E
Heshi, Zhg.	107	29.10 N	104.22 E
Heshui, Zhg.	100	24.24 N	114.56 E
Heshui, Zhg.	102	22.48 N	112.29 E
Heshuijian	100	30.33 N	116.05 E
Heshun, Zhg.	100	27.30 N	117.24 E
Heshun, Zhg.	102	37.21 N	113.35 E
Heshuo	86	42.15 N	86.53 E
Hesketh Bank	262	53.42 N	2.51 W
Hesketh Out Marsh ≋	262	53.43 N	2.55 W
Heskin Green	262	53.38 N	2.42 W
Hesler	218	38.28 N	84.47 W
Hesperange	56	49.34 N	6.09 E
Hesperia, Ca., U.S.	228	34.25 N	117.18 W
Hesperia, Mi., U.S.	190	43.34 N	86.02 W
Hesperus Mountain ∧	200	37.27 N	108.05 W
Hess ≃	180	63.34 N	133.57 W
Hesselager	41	55.10 N	10.45 E
Hesselberg ∧	56	49.04 N	10.32 E
Hesselø I	41	56.12 N	11.43 E
Hesselte	52	52.25 N	7.22 E
Hessen	54	52.01 N	10.47 E
Hessen □3	30	50.30 N	9.15 E
Hessen Cassal	216	41.00 N	85.05 W
Hessenthal	56	49.55 N	9.17 E
Hessisch Lichtenau	56	51.12 N	9.43 E
Hessisch Oldendorf	52	52.10 N	9.15 E
Hessle	44	53.44 N	0.26 W
Hesso	166	32.08 S	137.27 E
Hess Tablemount ✦3	14	17.50 N	174.15 W
Hesston, Ks., U.S.	198	38.08 N	97.25 W
Hesston, Pa., U.S.	214	40.26 N	78.07 W
Heston ◆8	260	51.29 N	0.22 W
Heswall	44	53.20 N	3.06 W
Het ≃	110	20.49 N	104.01 E
Hetai	102	23.22 N	112.19 E
Hetanbu	100	28.21 N	117.11 E
Hetang, Zhg.	100	26.40 N	119.09 E
Hetang, Zhg.	106	31.43 N	120.27 E
Hetang, Zhg.	107	28.58 N	106.03 E
Hetaundā	124	27.26 N	85.02 E
Hetch Hetchy Aqueduct ≍1	226	37.29 N	122.19 W
Hetch Hetchy Reservoir ◎1	226	37.57 N	119.43 W
Hethersett	42	52.36 N	1.11 E
Hetian, Zhg.	100	25.41 N	116.26 E
Hetian, Zhg.	100	23.19 N	115.38 E
Het Loo, Paleis ʋ	52	52.14 N	5.56 E
Hetou	100	24.18 N	113.29 E
Hetoudian	98	37.02 N	120.35 E
Hettange-Grande	56	49.24 N	6.09 E
Hettenleidelheim	56	49.32 N	8.04 E
Hettick	219	39.21 N	90.02 W
Hettingen	58	48.13 N	9.14 E
Hettinger	198	46.00 N	102.38 W
Hetton-le-Hole	44	54.50 N	1.27 W
Hettstedt	54	51.38 N	11.30 E
Hetupu	100	30.50 N	116.03 E
Hetzendorf ◆8	264b	48.10 N	16.18 E
Hetzerath	56	49.52 N	6.49 E
Het Zoute	50	51.21 N	3.18 E
Heuchin	50	50.28 N	2.16 E
Heudeber	54	51.54 N	10.50 E
Heule	50	50.50 N	3.14 E
Heuningspruit	158	27.26 S	27.28 E
Heusden, Bel.	50	51.02 N	3.48 E
Heusden, Bel.	56	51.02 N	5.16 E
Heustreu	56	50.21 N	10.15 E
Heusweiler	56	49.20 N	6.55 E
Heuvelton	212	44.37 N	75.24 W
Hève, Cap de la ›	50	49.31 N	0.04 E
Heven	263	51.26 N	7.17 E
Heverlee	56	50.52 N	4.42 E
Heves	30	47.36 N	20.17 E
Heves □6	30	47.50 N	20.15 E
Hevlín	61	48.45 N	16.23 E
Ḥevron, Naḥal V	132	31.15 N	34.50 E
Hewanorra International Airport ✈	241f	13.45 N	60.56 W
Hewitt, N.J., U.S.	210	41.08 N	74.18 W
Hewitt, Tx., U.S.	222	31.27 N	97.11 W
Hewittsville	219	39.32 N	89.19 W
Hewlett, N.Y., U.S.	276	40.38 N	73.41 W
Hewlett, Va., U.S.	208	37.55 N	77.35 W
Hewlett Bay Park	276	40.38 N	73.42 W
Hewlett Harbor	276	40.38 N	73.41 W
Hewlett Neck	276	40.37 N	73.42 W
Hewlett Point ›	276	40.50 N	73.45 W
Hewopu	104	41.14 N	122.24 E
Hewu	100	26.41 N	113.40 E
Hexen Kopf ∧	58	47.01 N	10.28 E
Hexham	44	54.58 N	2.06 W
Hexi, Zhg.	100	24.52 N	117.15 E
Hexi, Zhg.	102	24.09 N	102.39 E
Hexi, Zhg.	106	31.03 N	119.49 E
Hexian, Zhg.	100	31.43 N	118.22 E
Hexian, Zhg.	102	24.15 N	111.43 E
Hexibao	102	38.34 N	102.11 E
Hexingchang	107	30.05 N	104.35 E
Hexingjie	106	31.55 N	120.36 E
Hexiwu	105	39.38 N	116.58 E
Hex Rivierberge ⋀	158	33.25 S	19.37 E
Hextable	260	51.25 N	0.11 E
Hexton	172	38.37 S	177.58 E
Heyan	104	42.30 N	120.29 E
Heyang, Zhg.	98	35.27 N	118.33 E
Heyang, Zhg.	102	35.15 N	110.06 E
Heybeli ◆8	267b	40.53 N	29.05 E
Heybeli Ada I	267b	40.53 N	29.05 E
Heybridge, Eng., U.K.	260	51.44 N	0.41 E
Heybridge, Eng., U.K.	260	51.40 N	0.22 E
Heyburn	202	42.33 N	113.45 W
Heyerode	54	51.10 N	10.25 E
Heyrieux	62	45.38 N	5.03 E
Heysham	44	54.02 N	2.54 W
Heyuan	100	23.44 N	114.41 E
Heywood, Austl.	166	38.08 S	141.38 E
Heywood, Eng., U.K.	44	53.36 N	2.13 W
Heyworth	216	40.18 N	88.58 W
Heze (Caozhou)	98	35.17 N	115.27 E
Hezhang	102	27.00 N	104.37 E
Hezhao	98	37.08 N	115.17 E
Hezhen	100	29.56 N	120.10 E
Hezheng	102	35.25 N	103.10 E
Hezijian	105	40.13 N	116.03 E
Hezixu	100	24.54 N	115.14 E
Hezuo	102	34.58 N	102.57 E
Hiale	110	15.55 N	107.34 E
Hialeah	220	25.51 N	80.16 W
Hialeah Park Race Track ♠	220	25.51 N	80.17 W
Hiaohexi	100	31.21 N	114.02 E
Hiawassee	192	34.56 N	83.45 W
Hiawatha, Ks., U.S.	198	39.51 N	95.32 W
Hiawatha, Ut,. U.S.	200	39.29 N	111.00 W
Hiba-Dōgo-Taishaku-kokutei-kōen ♠	96	35.07 N	133.08 E
Hibaldstow	44	53.31 N	0.32 W
Hibbing	190	47.25 N	92.56 W
Hibbs, Point ›	166	42.38 S	145.15 E
Hibernia	276	40.57 N	74.30 W
Hibernia Reef ✦2	160	12.00 S	123.23 E
Hibiki-nada ⊤2	96	34.00 N	130.30 E
Hiburi-shima I	96	33.10 N	132.17 E
Hibuson Island I	116	10.27 N	125.29 E

PORTUGUÊS

Nome	Página	Lat.°′	Long.°′ W = Oeste
Hickam Air Force Base ■	229c	21.20 N	157.57 W
Hickey, Mount ∧	169	37.22 S	145.19 E
Hickman, Ca., U.S.	226	37.37 N	120.45 W
Hickman, Ky., U.S.	194	36.34 N	89.11 W
Hickman, Ne., U.S.	198	40.37 N	96.37 W
Hickman, Pa., U.S.	279b	40.23 N	80.09 W
Hickman's Harbour	186	48.06 N	53.44 W
Hickory, Ms., U.S.	194	32.19 N	89.01 W
Hickory, N.C., U.S.	192	35.43 N	81.20 W
Hickory, Pa., U.S.	214	40.18 N	80.18 W
Hickory Corners	216	42.26 N	85.22 W
Hickory Creek ≃, Il., U.S.	278	41.30 N	88.06 W
Hickory Creek ≃, Mi., U.S.	216	42.05 N	86.29 W
Hickory Creek ≃, Tx., U.S.	222	31.29 N	95.07 W
Hickory Flat	194	34.36 N	89.11 W
Hickory Hills	216	41.43 N	87.49 W
Hickory Run State Park ♠	210	41.02 N	75.41 W
Hickory Township	214	41.15 N	80.27 W
Hicks, Point ›	166	37.48 S	149.17 E
Hicks Bay	172	37.36 S	178.18 E
Hickson Lake ◎	184	56.17 N	104.25 W
Hicksville, N.Y., U.S.	210	40.46 N	73.31 W
Hicksville, Oh., U.S.	216	41.17 N	84.45 W
Hico	196	31.58 N	98.02 W
Hicpochee, Lake ◎	220	26.50 N	81.10 W
Hida → Hita	96	33.19 N	130.56 E
Hida ≃	94	35.26 N	137.03 E
Hidaka, Nihon	94	35.54 N	139.21 E
Hidaka, Nihon	96	33.55 N	135.09 E
Hidaka, Nihon	96	35.28 N	134.47 E
Hidaka ≃	96	33.52 N	135.09 E
Hidaka-sammyaku ⋀	92a	42.35 N	142.45 E
Hida-Kiso-gawa-kokutei-kōen ♠	94	35.37 N	137.15 E
Hida-kōchi ⋀1	94	36.16 N	137.05 E
Hidalgo, Méx.	232	27.47 N	99.52 W
Hidalgo, Méx.	232	25.59 N	100.27 W
Hidalgo, Méx.	232	24.15 N	99.26 W
Hidalgo □3	234	20.30 N	99.00 W
Hidalgo del Parral	232	26.56 N	105.40 W
Hida-sammyaku ⋀	94	36.25 N	137.40 E
Hiddenhausen	52	52.08 N	8.38 E
Hidden Hills	228	34.09 N	118.43 W
Hiddensee I	54	54.33 N	13.07 E
Hidden Valley, Ca., U.S.	226	38.46 N	121.09 W
Hidden Valley, Tx., U.S.	222	29.54 N	95.25 W
Hiddesen	52	51.55 N	8.50 E
Hiddinghausen	263	51.22 N	7.17 E
Hıdırbaba	130	38.47 N	39.00 E
Hidrolândia	255	16.58 S	49.14 W
Hidrolina	255	14.37 S	49.25 W
Hieflau	61	47.36 N	14.44 E
Hienghène	175f	20.41 S	164.56 E
Hierapolis → Pamukkale ⊥	130	37.58 N	29.19 E
Hierges	56	50.06 N	4.44 E
Hierro (Ferro) I	148	27.45 N	18.00 W
Hiesfeld	263	51.33 N	6.46 E
Hietzing ◆8	264b	48.11 N	16.18 E
Higashi	174m	26.38 N	128.09 E
Higashi ◆8	270	34.41 N	135.31 E
Higashibetsuin	270	34.56 N	135.34 E
Higashifuji-enshūjō ■	94	35.17 N	138.51 E
Higashihiroshima	96	34.26 N	132.42 E
Higashiichiki	92	31.40 N	130.20 E
Higashiiyayama	96	33.52 N	133.54 E
Higashiizu	94	34.48 N	139.04 E
Higashi-jima I	174f	24.47 N	141.23 E
Higashikurume	268	35.45 N	139.32 E
Higashimatsuyama	94	36.02 N	139.24 E
Higashimonzen	268	35.56 N	139.40 E
Higashimurayama	94	35.46 N	139.29 E
Higashinada ◆8	270	34.43 N	135.16 E
Higashinakano	268	35.38 N	139.25 E
Higashinari ◆8	270	34.40 N	135.33 E
Higashine	92	38.26 N	140.24 E
Higashinose	270	34.55 N	135.30 E
Higashiōizumi ◆8	268	35.45 N	139.36 E
Higashiōsaka	96	34.39 N	135.35 E
Higashishirakawa	94	35.39 N	137.19 E
Higashisumiyoshi ◆8	270	34.37 N	135.32 E
Higashitokonoo-san ∧	96	35.25 N	134.55 E
Higashitsuno	96	33.23 N	133.02 E
Higashiura, Nihon	94	34.59 N	136.58 E
Higashiura, Nihon	270	34.33 N	135.00 E
Higashiyama ◆8	270	35.00 N	135.48 E
Higashiyamato	268	35.44 N	139.26 E
Higashiyodogawa ◆8	270	34.44 N	135.31 E
Higashiyoshino	94	34.24 N	135.58 E
Higbee	194	39.18 N	92.30 W
Higganum	207	41.29 N	72.33 W
Higgins	196	36.07 N	100.02 W
Higgins, Mount ∧	224	48.19 N	121.45 W
Higgins Lake ◎	190	44.30 N	84.45 W
Higginsport	218	38.47 N	83.58 W
Higginsville, Austl.	162	31.45 S	121.43 E
Higginsville, Mo., U.S.	194	39.04 N	93.43 W
Higgs' Hope	158	29.19 S	23.16 E
Higham Ferrers	42	52.18 N	0.36 W
Higham Upshire	260	51.26 N	0.28 E
Highbank	222	31.10 N	96.50 W
High Bank Creek ≃	216	42.37 N	85.11 W
High Bar Indian Reserve ◆4	182	51.06 N	122.00 W
High Beach	260	51.39 N	0.02 E
High Bentham	44	54.08 N	2.30 W
High Bluff Island I	212	43.58 N	77.45 W
Highbridge, Eng., U.K.	42	51.13 N	2.49 W
High Bridge, N.J., U.S.	210	40.40 N	74.53 W
Highbury	164	16.25 S	143.09 E
Highcliff	279b	40.32 N	80.03 W
Higher Ballam	262	53.46 N	2.59 W
Higher Broughton ◆8	262	53.30 N	2.15 W
Higher Hogshead ∧2	262	53.42 N	2.09 W
Higher Penwortham	262	53.45 N	2.44 W
Higher Walton, Eng., U.K.	44	53.44 N	2.39 W
Higher Walton, Eng., U.K.	262	53.22 N	2.37 W
Higher Whitley	262	53.19 N	2.35 W
Highett	274b	37.57 S	145.03 E
High Falls	210	41.50 N	74.08 W
High Falls ⌞	212	43.56 N	75.23 W
High Force ⌞	44	54.38 N	2.13 W
Highgate	214	42.30 N	81.49 W
Highgate Center	206	44.56 N	73.02 W
Highgate Springs	206	44.58 N	73.06 W
Highgrove	228	34.01 N	117.20 W
High Halstow	260	51.27 N	0.34 E
High Hesket	44	54.48 N	2.48 W
High Hill	219	38.52 N	91.23 W
High Hill ∧2	276	40.49 N	73.25 W
High Hill ≃, Can.	184	56.45 N	110.30 W
High Hill ≃, Mb., Can.	184	55.52 N	94.42 W
High Hill Lake ◎	184	55.34 N	95.40 W
High Island I, H.K.	271d	22.22 N	114.21 E
High Island I, Mi., U.S.	190	45.42 N	85.40 W
High Island Creek ≃	190	44.35 N	93.54 W
High Island Reservoir ◎1	271d	22.23 N	114.21 W
Highland, Ca., U.S.	228	34.07 N	117.12 W
Highland, Il., U.S.	219	38.44 N	89.40 W
Highland, In., U.S.	216	41.33 N	87.27 W
Highland, Ks., U.S.	198	39.51 N	95.16 W
Highland, Md., U.S.	208	39.11 N	76.57 W
Highland, Mi., U.S.	281	42.38 N	83.37 W

Highland, N.Y., U.S.	210	41.43 N	73.57 W
Highland, Oh., U.S.	218	39.21 N	83.36 W
Highland, Pa., U.S.	279b	40.33 N	80.04 W
Highland □4	46	57.40 N	5.00 W
Highland □6	218	39.12 N	83.37 W
Highland Beach	220	26.25 N	80.04 W
Highland City	220	27.58 N	81.53 W
Highland Creek ≃, On., Can.	275b	43.46 N	79.08 W
Highland Creek ≃, Ca., U.S.	226	38.24 N	121.14 W
Highland Falls	210	41.22 N	73.58 W
Highland Heights, Ky., U.S.	218	39.04 N	84.27 W
Highland Heights, Oh., U.S.	214	41.33 N	81.28 W
Highland Hills	278	41.52 N	88.01 W
Highland Home	194	31.57 N	86.18 W
Highland Lake, Il., U.S.	278	42.21 N	88.04 W
Highland Lake, Ma., U.S.	283	42.41 N	72.37 W
Highland Lake, N.Y., U.S.	210	41.32 N	74.51 W
Highland Lake ◎, Ct., U.S.	207	41.54 N	73.06 W
Highland Lake ◎, Il., U.S.	278	42.22 N	88.04 W
Highland Lake ◎, N.J., U.S.	276	41.10 N	74.28 W
Highland Lakes	210	41.10 N	74.28 W
Highland-on-the-Lake	284a	42.42 N	79.59 W
Highland Park, Il., U.S.	216	42.10 N	87.48 W
Highland Park, Md., U.S.	284c	38.54 N	76.54 W
Highland Park, Mi., U.S.	216	42.24 N	83.05 W
Highland Park, N.J., U.S.	210	40.29 N	74.25 W
Highland Park, Pa., U.S.	210	40.38 N	77.35 W
Highland Park, Tx., U.S.	222	32.50 N	96.48 W
Highland Park ◆8	280	34.07 N	118.13 W
Highland Park ♠, Ma., U.S.	283	42.30 N	70.55 W
Highland Park ♠, Pa., U.S.	279b	40.29 N	79.55 W
Highland Peak ∧	226	38.33 N	119.45 W
Highland Point ›	220	25.30 N	81.12 W
Highlands, N.J., U.S.	208	40.24 N	73.59 W
Highlands, N.C., U.S.	192	35.03 N	83.11 W
Highlands, Tx., U.S.	222	29.49 N	95.03 W
Highlands □6	220	27.20 N	81.16 W
Highlands Hammock State Park ♠	220	27.28 N	81.33 W
Highland Silver Lake ◎1	219	38.47 N	89.39 W
Highlands North ◆8	273d	26.09 S	28.05 E
Highland Springs	208	37.32 N	77.19 W
Highlands Reservoir ◎1	222	29.50 N	95.02 W
Highland State Recreation Area ♠	216	42.39 N	83.33 W
Highlandtown ◆8	284b	39.17 N	76.33 W
High Laver	260	51.45 N	0.13 E
High Legh	262	53.21 N	2.27 W
Highley	42	52.27 N	2.23 W
Highmore	198	44.31 N	99.26 W
High Ongar	260	51.43 N	0.16 E
High Park ♠	275b	43.39 N	79.28 W
High Peak □8	262	53.23 N	1.55 W
High Peak ∧, Pil.	116	15.29 N	120.07 E
High Peak ∧, N.Y., U.S.	210	42.09 N	74.05 W
High Peak ◆1	44	53.22 N	1.50 W
High Point, Fl., U.S.	220	27.55 N	82.42 W
High Point, N.C., U.S.	192	35.57 N	80.00 W
Highpoint, Oh., U.S.	218	39.14 N	84.24 W
High Point ∧, N.J., U.S.	210	41.19 N	74.40 W
High Point ∧, Wy., U.S.	202	41.37 N	107.47 W
High Point State Park ♠	210	41.18 N	74.41 W
High Prairie	182	55.26 N	116.29 W
High Ridge	219	38.27 N	90.32 W
High River	182	50.35 N	113.52 W
High Rock	192	26.36 N	76.18 W
High Rock ∧	188	39.33 N	79.06 W
Highrock Indian Reserve ◆4	184	55.54 N	100.30 W
Highrock Lake ◎, Mb., Can.	184	55.45 N	100.30 W
Highrock Lake ◎, Sk., Can.	184	57.04 N	105.30 W
High Rock Lake ◎1	192	35.40 N	80.17 W
High Seat ∧	44	54.24 N	2.18 W
High Spire	208	40.12 N	76.47 W
High Springs	192	29.49 N	82.35 W
High Street ∧	44	54.29 N	2.52 W
Hightown	44	53.31 N	3.03 W
Hightstown	208	40.16 N	74.31 W
High View	210	41.33 N	74.27 W
Highwater	206	45.01 N	72.26 W
Highway City	226	36.49 N	119.54 W
High Willhays ∧	42	50.41 N	3.59 W
Highwood, Il., U.S.	216	42.11 N	87.48 W
Highwood, Mt., U.S.	202	47.35 N	110.47 W
Highwood ≃	182	50.49 N	113.47 W
Highwood Baldy ∧	202	47.27 N	110.37 W
Highwood Creek ≃	202	47.40 N	111.00 W
Highwood Mountains ⋀	202	47.25 N	110.30 W
Highworth	42	51.38 N	1.43 W
High Wycombe	42	51.38 N	0.46 W
Higlet	154	1.04 S	40.19 E
Higuera Blanca	234	19.42 N	105.10 W
Higuera de Abuya	232	24.16 N	107.04 W
Higuera de Zaragoza	232	25.59 N	109.16 W
Higueras	196	25.58 N	100.01 W
Higüero, Punta ›	240m	18.22 N	67.16 W
Higüey	238	18.37 N	68.42 W
Higuito ≃	236	14.43 N	88.40 W
Hihétro	150	7.32 N	1.06 E
Hihyā	142	30.40 N	31.36 E
Hii ≃	96	35.26 N	132.54 E
Hiidenportin kansallispuisto ♠	26	63.50 N	28.59 E
Hiiraan □4	144	4.00 N	45.30 E
Hiiumaa I	76	58.52 N	22.40 E
Hījānah, Buḥayrat al- ◎	132	33.18 N	36.36 E
Híjar	34	41.10 N	0.27 W
Hiji	96	33.22 N	131.32 E
Hiji ≃	96	33.36 N	132.29 E
Hijikawa	96	33.27 N	132.41 E
Hijiri-dake ∧	94	35.26 N	138.10 E
Hikami	96	35.10 N	135.02 E
Hikari, Nihon	94	35.39 N	140.30 E
Hikari, Nihon	96	33.58 N	131.56 E
Hikarigaoka	268	35.50 N	139.58 E
Hikawa	96	35.25 N	132.50 E
Hikawa Shrine ʋ1	268	35.54 N	139.38 E
Hiketa	96	34.13 N	134.24 E
Hiki ≃	96	33.33 N	135.27 E
Hikigawa	96	33.34 N	135.27 E
Hikimi	96	34.34 N	132.01 E
Hikimi ≃	96	34.37 N	131.48 E
Hikiura	270	34.33 N	134.58 E
Hikone	94	35.15 N	136.15 E
Hikone-jō ⊥	94	35.15 N	136.14 E
Hiko-san ∧	96	33.27 N	130.54 E
Hikueru I1	14	17.36 S	142.37 W
Hikurangi	172	35.36 S	174.18 E
Hikurangi ∧	172	37.55 S	178.04 E
Hikutaia	172	37.17 S	175.39 E
Hikutivake	174v	18.56 S	169.53 W
Hila	112	7.35 S	127.24 E

Hilaban Island I	116	12.03 N	125.34 E
Hilāl, Jabal ⋀	132	30.40 N	34.00 E
Hilāl, Ra's al- ›	146	32.57 N	22.10 E
Hilbersdorf	54	50.55 N	13.23 E
Hilbert	190	44.08 N	88.09 W
Hilbre Islands II	262	53.23 N	3.13 W
Hilbre Point ›	262	53.23 N	3.12 W
Hilchenbach	56	51.00 N	8.06 E
Hilda	184	50.28 N	110.03 W
Hildburghausen	54	50.25 N	10.44 E
Hilden	56	51.10 N	6.56 E
Hildenborough	260	51.13 N	0.15 E
Hilders	56	50.34 N	10.00 E
Hildesheim	52	52.09 N	9.57 E
Hildreth	198	40.20 N	99.02 W
Hilgen	263	51.06 N	7.09 E
Hilialawa	114	0.41 N	97.53 E
Hiligeo	114	1.22 N	97.10 E
Hiliotaluwa	114	0.44 N	97.53 E
Hill □6	222	32.02 N	97.10 W
Hillaby, Mount ∧	241g	13.12 N	59.35 W
Hill Air Force Base ■	202	41.05 N	111.58 W
Hillandale, S. Afr.	158	33.06 S	20.36 E
Hillandale, Md., U.S.	284c	39.01 N	76.58 W
Hillandale Heights	284c	39.01 N	76.59 W
Hill Bank	232	17.35 N	88.42 W
Hillburn	210	41.08 N	74.10 W
Hill City, Ks., U.S.	198	39.21 N	99.50 W
Hill City, Mn., U.S.	190	46.59 N	93.35 W
Hill City, S.D., U.S.	198	43.55 N	103.34 W
Hill Creek ≃	200	39.55 N	109.40 W
Hillcrest, Il., U.S.	216	41.57 N	89.04 W
Hillcrest, N.Y., U.S.	210	41.07 N	74.02 W
Hillcrest, N.Y., U.S.	210	42.09 N	75.53 W
Hillcrest Center	228	35.23 N	118.57 W
Hillcrest Heights	284c	38.49 N	76.57 W
Hillcrest Mines	182	49.34 N	114.23 W
Hillcrest Orchard	216	41.51 N	83.29 W
Hillcrest Park	226	38.07 N	122.16 W
Hill Cumorah ⊥	210	43.01 N	77.15 W
Hille, Dtsch.	52	52.20 N	8.44 E
Hille, Sve.	40	60.44 N	17.11 E
Hillegom	52	52.18 N	4.35 E
Hillegossen	52	51.59 N	8.37 E
Hillerød	41	55.56 N	12.19 E
Hillers Creek ≃	219	38.38 N	91.54 W
Hillesheim	56	50.18 N	6.38 E
Hilli	124	25.17 N	89.01 E
Hilliard, Fl., U.S.	192	30.41 N	81.55 W
Hilliard, Oh., U.S.	218	40.02 N	83.09 W
Hilliards	214	41.05 N	79.50 W
Hillingdon ◆8	42	51.32 N	0.27 W
Hillisburg	216	40.17 N	86.20 W
Hill Island Lake ◎	176	60.29 N	109.50 W
Hillister	194	30.40 N	94.23 W
Hillman	190	45.03 N	83.54 W
Hillman ≃	168a	33.26 S	116.48 E
Hillmersdorf	54	51.42 N	13.29 E
Hill of Fearn	46	57.45 N	3.56 W
Hills	198	43.31 N	96.21 W
Hills and Dales	214	39.42 N	84.13 W
Hillsboro, Il., U.S.	219	39.09 N	89.29 W
Hillsboro, Ks., U.S.	198	38.21 N	97.12 W
Hillsboro, Ky., U.S.	218	38.18 N	83.40 W
Hillsboro, Md., U.S.	208	38.55 N	75.56 W
Hillsboro, Mo., U.S.	219	38.13 N	90.33 W
Hillsboro, N.H., U.S.	188	43.06 N	71.53 W
Hillsboro, N.M., U.S.	200	32.55 N	107.33 W
Hillsboro, N.D., U.S.	198	47.24 N	97.03 W
Hillsboro, Oh., U.S.	218	39.12 N	83.36 W
Hillsboro, Or., U.S.	224	45.31 N	122.59 W
Hillsboro, Tx., U.S.	222	32.00 N	97.07 W
Hillsboro, Wi., U.S.	190	43.39 N	90.20 W
Hillsboro Beach	220	26.18 N	80.05 W
Hillsboro Canal ≍	220	26.19 N	80.05 W
Hillsborough, N.B., Can.	186	45.56 N	64.39 W
Hillsborough, N. Ire., U.K.	48	54.28 N	6.05 W
Hillsborough, Ca., U.S.	226	37.34 N	122.22 W
Hillsborough, N.C., U.S.	192	36.04 N	79.06 W
Hillsborough □6, Fl., U.S.	220	27.55 N	82.15 W
Hillsborough □6, N.H., U.S.	207	42.49 N	71.41 W
Hillsborough ≃	220	27.56 N	82.27 W
Hillsborough, Cape ›	166	20.54 S	149.03 E
Hillsborough Bay ⊂, P.E., Can.	186	46.10 N	63.05 W
Hillsborough Bay ⊂, Fl., U.S.	220	27.52 N	82.27 W
Hillsborough River State Park ♠	220	28.09 N	82.14 W
Hillsburgh	212	43.47 N	80.09 W
Hills Creek Lake ◎1	202	43.40 N	122.26 W
Hillsdale, Mi., U.S.	216	41.55 N	84.37 W
Hillsdale, N.J., U.S.	276	41.00 N	74.02 W
Hillsdale, N.Y., U.S.	210	42.10 N	73.31 W
Hillsdale, Pa., U.S.	214	40.45 N	78.53 W
Hillsdale □6	216	41.53 N	84.36 W
Hillsdale ◆9	282	37.32 N	122.18 W
Hillsdale Lake ◎1	198	38.40 N	94.55 W
Hills Flat	226	39.14 N	121.03 W
Hillsgrove	210	41.27 N	76.42 W
Hillside, Austl.	162	21.44 S	119.23 E
Hillside, Scot., U.K.	46	56.44 N	2.29 W
Hillside, Il., U.S.	278	41.52 N	87.54 W
Hillside, N.J., U.S.	276	40.42 N	74.13 W
Hillside ◆8	276	40.42 N	73.47 W
Hillside Gardens	216	42.16 N	84.27 W
Hillside Heights	285	39.41 N	75.41 W
Hillside Lake	210	41.36 N	73.50 W
Hillston	166	33.29 S	145.32 E
Hillsville, Pa., U.S.	214	41.00 N	80.29 W
Hillsville, Va., U.S.	192	36.45 N	80.44 W
Hillswick	46a	60.28 N	1.30 W
Hilltop	208	39.49 N	75.04 W
Hilltop Center ◆9	282	37.59 N	122.19 W
Hilltown, N. Ire., U.K.	48	54.12 N	6.09 W
Hilltown, Pa., U.S.	208	40.20 N	75.14 W
Hillview	219	39.27 N	90.33 W
Hillview Reservoir ◎1	276	40.55 N	73.52 W
Hillwood	284c	38.52 N	77.10 W
Hilmar	226	37.25 N	120.51 W
Hilo	229d	19.43 N	155.05 W
Hilo Bay ⊂	229d	19.44 N	155.05 W
Hilonghilong, Mount ∧	116	9.06 N	125.44 E
Hilongos	116	10.23 N	124.45 E
Hilpotstein	60	49.12 N	11.12 E
Hilpsford Point ›	44	54.03 N	3.12 W
Hils ∧	52	51.55 N	9.40 E
Hilshire Village	222	29.49 N	95.26 W
Hiltaba, Mount ∧	162	32.09 S	135.03 E
Hilter	52	52.08 N	8.08 E
Hilton, N.Y., U.S.	210	43.17 N	77.47 W
Hilton, Pa., U.S.	208	40.00 N	76.49 W
Hilton Head Island I	192	32.12 N	80.45 W
Hiltpoltstein	60	49.40 N	11.19 E
Hiltrop ◆8	263	51.30 N	7.15 E
Hiltrup	52	51.54 N	7.38 E
Hilvan	130	37.35 N	38.57 E
Hilvarenbeek	52	51.29 N	5.09 E
Hilversum	52	52.14 N	5.10 E
Hima	192	37.07 N	83.46 W
Himāchal Pradesh □3	120	32.00 N	77.00 E
Himalayas ⋀	120	28.00 N	84.00 E
Himāl Chulī ∧	124	28.25 N	84.39 E
Himamaylan	116	10.06 N	122.52 E
Himanka	26	64.04 N	23.39 E
Himarë	38	40.07 N	19.44 E
Himatnagar	120	23.36 N	72.57 E
Himberg	61	48.05 N	16.26 E
Hime ≃	94	37.02 N	137.49 E
Himeji	96	34.49 N	134.42 E
Hime-shima I	96	33.43 N	131.40 E
Himeville	158	29.44 S	29.31 E
Himi	94	36.51 N	136.59 E

Himmelbjerget ∧2	41	56.06 N	9.42 E
Himmelgeist ◆8	263	51.10 N	6.49 E
Himmelpforten	52	53.36 N	9.18 E
Himmelsthür	52	52.09 N	9.55 E
Himmerfjärden ⊂2	40	59.00 N	17.43 E
Himmerland ◆1	26	56.50 N	9.45 E
Himmetdede	130	38.55 N	35.07 E
Himrod	210	42.35 N	76.57 W
Ḥimṣ (Homs)	130	34.44 N	36.43 E
Ḥimṣ □8	130	34.15 N	38.00 E
Hinabangan	116	11.42 N	125.04 E
Ḥīnah	132	33.21 N	35.56 E
Hinako, Kepulauan II	114	0.52 N	97.21 E
Hinase	96	34.44 N	134.16 E
Hinatuan	116	8.23 N	126.20 E
Hinatuan Island I	116	9.47 N	125.43 E
Hinatuan Passage ʯ	116	9.45 N	125.47 E
Hinche	238	19.09 N	72.01 W
Hinchinbrook Entrance ʯ	180	60.25 N	146.50 W
Hinchinbrook Island I, Austl.	166	18.23 S	146.17 E
Hinchinbrook Island I, Ak., U.S.	180	60.22 N	146.30 W
Hinchinbrook Island National Park ♠	166	18.20 S	146.20 E
Hinckley, Eng., U.K.	42	52.33 N	1.21 W
Hinckley, Il., U.S.	216	41.46 N	88.38 W
Hinckley, Mn., U.S.	190	46.00 N	92.56 W
Hinckley, Oh., U.S.	214	41.14 N	81.45 W
Hinckley, Ut,. U.S.	200	39.19 N	112.40 W
Hinckley Reservoir ◎1	210	43.20 N	75.05 W
Hindan ≃	272a	28.30 N	77.27 E
Hindang	116	10.26 N	124.44 E
Hindaun	124	26.43 N	77.01 E
Hindelang	58	47.30 N	10.22 E
Hindelbank	58	47.03 N	7.32 E
Hindeloopen	52	52.56 N	5.24 E
Hindenburg → Zabrze	30	50.18 N	18.46 E
Hindhead	42	51.07 N	0.44 W
Hindley	44	53.32 N	2.35 W
Hindley Green	262	53.31 N	2.32 W
Hindman	192	37.20 N	82.58 W
Hindmarsh, Lake ◎	166	36.03 S	141.55 E
Hindmarsh Island I	168b	35.32 S	138.52 E
Hindmarsh Valley	168b	35.30 S	138.38 E
Hindon	42	51.06 N	2.08 W
Hinds	172	44.00 S	171.34 E
Hindsholm ›1	41	55.33 N	10.40 E
Hinds Lake ◎	186	48.57 N	57.00 W
Hindu Kush ⋀	120	36.00 N	71.30 E
Hindūmalkot	123	30.09 N	73.55 E
Hindupur	122	13.49 N	77.29 E
Hi-Nella	285	39.50 N	75.01 W
Hines	202	43.33 N	119.04 W
Hines Creek	182	56.15 N	118.36 W
Hines Creek ≃	182	55.54 N	118.37 W
Hines Peak ∧	228	34.31 N	119.05 W
Hinesville	192	31.50 N	81.35 W
Hinganghāt	122	20.34 N	78.50 E
Hingatungan	116	10.35 N	125.11 E
Hingham, Eng., U.K.	42	52.35 N	0.59 E
Hingham, Ma., U.S.	207	42.14 N	70.53 W
Hingham Bay ⊂	207	42.17 N	70.55 W
Hingham Harbor ⊂	283	42.15 N	70.53 W
Hingol ≃	128	25.23 N	65.28 E
Hingoli	122	19.43 N	77.09 E
Hinigaran	116	10.17 N	122.51 E
Hınıs	130	39.22 N	41.44 E
Hınıs ≃	130	39.18 N	42.12 E
Hinkley	228	34.56 N	117.11 W
Hinkson Creek ≃	219	38.56 N	92.23 W
Hinkston Creek ≃	188	38.18 N	84.14 W
Hinnerjoki	26	61.00 N	22.00 E
Hinnerup	41	56.16 N	10.04 E
Hinnøya I	24	68.30 N	16.00 E
Hino, Nihon	94	35.00 N	136.15 E
Hino, Nihon	94	35.41 N	139.24 E
Hino, Nihon	96	35.14 N	133.27 E
Hino ≃, Nihon	94	35.09 N	136.02 E
Hino ≃, Nihon	94	36.04 N	136.11 E
Hino ≃, Nihon	96	35.27 N	133.23 E
Hinoba-an	116	9.35 N	122.28 E
Hinode	94	35.45 N	139.14 E
Hinoemata	94	37.01 N	139.23 E
Hinohara	94	35.43 N	139.09 E
Hinojosa del Duque	34	38.30 N	5.09 W
Hinokage	92	32.39 N	131.24 E
Hinomi-saki ›, Nihon	96	33.53 N	135.04 E
Hinomi-saki ›, Nihon	96	35.26 N	132.38 E
Hinsbeck	56	51.21 N	6.17 E
Hinsdale, Il., U.S.	216	41.48 N	87.56 W
Hinsdale, Ma., U.S.	207	42.26 N	73.07 W
Hinsdale, Mt., U.S.	202	48.23 N	107.05 W
Hinsdale, N.H., U.S.	207	42.47 N	72.29 W
Hinsdale, N.Y., U.S.	210	42.10 N	78.23 W
Hinsel ◆8	263	51.26 N	7.05 E
Hinsen ◎	40	60.39 N	16.05 E
Hinte	52	53.25 N	7.11 E
Hinterbichl	64	47.01 N	12.20 E
Hinterbrühl	61	48.05 N	16.15 E
Hinterhermsdorf	54	50.55 N	14.22 E
Hinterrhein	58	46.32 N	9.12 E
Hinterrhein ≃	58	46.49 N	9.25 E
Hintersdorf	264b	48.18 N	16.13 E
Hintersee	54	53.37 N	14.16 E
Hinterstoder	61	47.41 N	14.09 E
Hintertux	64	47.07 N	11.41 E
Hinterweidenthal	56	49.12 N	7.45 E
Hinterzarten	58	47.54 N	8.06 E
Hinton, Ab., Can.	182	53.25 N	117.34 W
Hinton, Mo., U.S.	219	39.03 N	92.21 W
Hinton, Ok., U.S.	196	35.28 N	98.21 W
Hinton, W.V., U.S.	192	37.40 N	80.53 W
Hi-numa ◎	94	36.16 N	140.30 E
Hinuma ≃	94	36.16 N	140.28 E
Hinundayan	116	10.21 N	125.15 E
Hinwil	58	47.18 N	8.51 E
Hinzik	84	40.08 N	40.58 E
Hípico, Club ♠	286e	33.28 S	70.41 W
Hipólito	232	25.41 N	101.26 W
Hipólito Yrigoyen	252	32.55 S	66.20 W
Hippolytushoef	52	52.54 N	4.57 E
Hirado	92	33.22 N	129.33 E
Hirado-shima I	92	33.20 N	129.30 E
Hiraiwa-hana ›	174f	24.48 N	141.18 E
Hiraizumi	92	38.59 N	141.07 E
Hirakata, Nihon	96	34.48 N	135.38 E
Hirakata, Nihon	268	35.56 N	139.33 E
Hirakawa	270	34.52 N	135.47 E
Hīrākud	122	21.31 N	83.57 E
Hīrākud Reservoir ◎1	120	21.35 N	83.50 E
Hiram, Me., U.S.	188	43.52 N	70.48 W
Hiram, Oh., U.S.	214	41.18 N	81.08 W
Hiraman ≃	154	1.07 S	39.55 E
Hirano	175d	24.35 N	124.19 E
Hirano ◆8	270	34.36 N	135.34 E
Hirao	96	33.56 N	132.04 E
Hirao-dai ♠	96	33.45 N	130.52 E
Hiraoka → Higashiōsaka	96	34.39 N	135.35 E
Hīrāpur	124	24.22 N	79.13 E
Hirara	175d	24.48 N	125.17 E
Hirata, Nihon	94	35.15 N	136.38 E
Hirata, Nihon	96	35.26 N	132.49 E
Hiratsuka	94	35.19 N	139.21 E
Hiraya	94	35.19 N	137.37 E
Hirfanlı Barajı ◎1	130	39.10 N	33.35 E
Hirhafok	148	23.49 N	5.45 E
Hiriyūr	122	13.58 N	76.36 E
Ḥirjillah	132	33.22 N	36.18 E
Hirnyk, Ukr.	78	50.20 N	24.10 E
Hirnyk, Ukr.	83	48.04 N	37.24 E
Hirnyts'ke	78	47.42 N	34.08 E
Hirokawa, Nihon	96	33.15 N	130.32 E
Hirokawa, Nihon	96	34.01 N	135.11 E
Hirok Sāmi	128	26.02 N	63.25 E
Hiromi	96	33.15 N	132.41 E

≃ River	Fluß	Río	Rivière	Rio
≍ Canal	Kanal	Canal	Canal	Canal
⌞ Waterfall, Rapids	Wasserfall, Stromschnellen	Cascada, Rápidos	Chute d'eau, Rapides	Cascata, Rápidos
ʯ Strait	Meeresstraße	Estrecho	Détroit	Estreito
⊂ Bay, Gulf	Bucht, Golf	Bahía, Golfo	Baie, Golfe	Baía, Golfo
◎ Lake, Lakes	See, Seen	Lago, Lagos	Lac, Lacs	Lago, Lagos
≋ Swamp	Sumpf	Pantano	Marais	Pântano
✱ Ice Features, Glacier	Eis- und Gletscherformen	Accidentes Glaciales	Formes glaciaires	Acidentes glaciares
⊤ Other Hydrographic Features	Andere Hydrographische Objekte	Otros Elementos Hidrográficos	Autres données hydrographiques	Outros acidentes hidrográficos

✦ Submarine Features	Untermeerische Objekte	Accidentes Submarinos	Formes de relief sous-marin	Acidentes submarinos
□ Political Unit	Politische Einheit	Unidad Política	Entité politique	Unidade política
ʋ Cultural Institution	Kulturelle Institution	Institución Cultural	Institution culturelle	Instituição cultural
⊥ Historical Site	Historische Stätte	Sitio Histórico	Site historique	Sítio histórico
♠ Recreational Site	Erholungs- und Ferienort	Sitio de Recreo	Centre de loisirs	Área de Lazer
✈ Airport	Flughafen	Aeropuerto	Aéroport	Aeroporto
■ Military Installation	Militäranlage	Instalación Militar	Installation militaire	Instalação militar
◆ Miscellaneous	Verschiedenes	Misceláneo	Divers	Diversos

ENGLISH — Name Page Lat.°′ Long.°′
DEUTSCH — Name Seite Breite°′ Länge°′ E = Ost

Hiroo 92a 42.17 N 143.19 E
Hirooka 268 35.15 N 140.04 E
Hirosaki 92 40.35 N 140.28 E
Hiroschima
→ Hiroshima 96 34.24 N 132.27 E
Hirose 96 35.22 N 133.10 E
Hiroshima 96 34.24 N 132.27 E
Hiroshima □[5] 96 34.30 N 133.00 E
Hiro-shima I 96 34.22 N 133.43 E
Hiroshima-wan ⊂ 96 34.06 N 132.20 E
Hirosima
→ Hiroshima 96 34.24 N 132.27 E
Hirota 270 34.45 N 135.21 E
Hirsau 56 48.44 N 8.44 E
Hirschaid 56 49.49 N 10.59 E
Hirschau 60 49.33 N 11.57 E
Hirschbach 54 50.33 N 10.44 E
Hirschberg, Dtsch. 54 50.24 N 11.49 E
Hirschberg
→ Jelenia Góra, Pol. 30 50.55 N 15.46 E
Hirschfeld 54 51.23 N 13.37 E
Hirschfelde, Dtsch. 54 50.57 N 14.53 E
Hirschfelde, Dtsch. 264a 52.38 N 13.48 E
Hirschhorn 56 49.27 N 8.53 E
Hirschstetten -•-[8] 264b 48.14 N 16.29 E
Hirshfeld Brook ≃ 276 40.57 N 74.02 W
Hirsingue 58 47.35 N 7.15 E
Hirs'ke 83 48.46 N 38.30 E
Hirs'kyy Tikych ≃ 78 48.47 N 30.53 E
Hirson 50 49.55 N 4.05 E
Hirsts Hill ∧ 171a 27.13 S 152.06 E
Hirtshals 26 57.35 N 9.58 E
Hirtzfelden 58 47.55 N 7.27 E
Hirukawa 94 35.31 N 137.23 E
Hiru-zen ∧ 96 35.19 N 133.40 E
Hirwaun 42 51.45 N 3.30 W
Hisābpur 272b 22.51 N 88.32 E
Hisai, Nihon 94 34.40 N 136.28 E
Hisai, Nihon 270 34.25 N 135.28 E
Hisār 123 29.10 N 75.43 E
Hisarönü 130 41.33 N 32.02 E
Ḥisbān 132 31.48 N 35.48 E
Hisiu 164 9.05 S 146.45 E
Hisn al-ʻAbr 144 16.05 N 47.22 E
Ḥiṣn al-Qarn 144 15.11 N 49.05 E
Hispaniola I 238 19.00 N 71.00 W
Hispar Glacier ⊓ 123 36.05 N 75.20 E
Histon 42 52.15 N 0.06 E
Hisua 124 24.50 N 85.25 E
Ḥisyah 130 34.24 N 36.45 E
Hīt 128 33.38 N 42.49 E
Hita 96 33.19 N 130.56 E
Hitachi 94 36.36 N 140.39 E
Hitachi-ōta 94 36.32 N 140.31 E
Hitati
→ Hitachi 94 36.36 N 140.39 E
Hitchcock 222 29.20 N 95.00 W
Hitchin 42 51.57 N 0.17 W
Hitchins 218 38.16 N 82.55 W
Hither Green -•-[8] 260 51.27 N 0.01 W
Hither Hills State Park ♦ 207 41.01 N 72.01 W
Hitiaa 174s 17.36 S 149.18 W
Hitokura 270 34.55 N 135.25 E
Hitotsubashi University ⊛[2] 268 35.42 N 139.27 E
Hitoyoshi 92 32.13 N 130.45 E
Hitra I 26 63.33 N 8.45 E
Hittarp 41 56.06 N 12.38 E
Hittisau 58 47.27 N 9.57 E
Hitzacker 54 53.09 N 11.02 E
Hitze-Berge ∧[2] 264a 52.35 N 13.07 E
Hiu I 175f 13.10 S 166.35 E
Hiuchiga-take ∧ 94 36.57 N 139.17 E
Hiuchi-nada ⊤[2] 96 34.05 N 133.20 E
Hiūnchuli Pātan ∧ 124 28.50 N 82.37 E
Hiva Oa I 174x 9.45 S 139.00 W
Hi Vista 228 34.44 N 117.47 W
Hiwa 96 34.59 N 132.59 E
Hiwannee 194 31.48 N 88.41 W
Hiwasa 96 33.44 N 134.32 E
Hiwassee ≃ 192 35.19 N 84.47 W
Hiwassee Lake ⊜[1] 192 35.10 N 84.05 W
Hixon 182 53.27 N 122.36 W
Hixson 192 35.09 N 85.14 W
Hiyoshi, Nihon 94 35.53 N 137.45 E
Hiyoshi, Nihon 96 33.20 N 132.48 E
Hiyoshi, Nihon 96 35.09 N 135.31 E
Hiyoshi -•-[8] 268 35.33 N 139.39 E
Ḥiyyon, Naḥal V 132 30.12 N 35.07 E
Hizaonna 174m 26.24 N 127.50 E
Hjälmare kanal ≊ 40 59.24 N 15.56 E
Hjälmaren ⊜ 40 59.15 N 15.45 E
Hjälmaresund ⊔ 40 59.15 N 16.06 E
Hjarnø I 41 55.50 N 10.05 E
Hjelm I 41 56.08 N 10.48 E
Hjelmelandsvågen 26 59.14 N 6.11 E
Hjeltefjorden ⊂[2] 26 60.40 N 4.55 E
Hjembæk 41 55.42 N 11.25 E
Hjo 26 58.18 N 14.17 E
Hjøllund 41 56.05 N 9.25 E
Hjordkær 41 55.01 N 9.19 E
Hjørring 26 57.28 N 9.59 E
Hjortkvarn 40 58.53 N 15.25 E
Hjørundfjorden ⊂[2] 26 62.21 N 6.23 E
Hkakabo Razi ∧ 102 28.20 N 97.32 E
Hkok (Kok) ≃ 110 20.14 N 100.09 E
Hlabisa 158 28.08 S 31.52 E
Hladkivka 78 46.23 N 32.36 E
Hlaingbwe 110 17.08 N 97.50 E
Hlatikulu 158 27.00 S 31.25 E
Hlegu 110 17.06 N 96.14 E
Hlinsko 30 49.45 N 15.55 E
Hlobane 158 27.42 S 31.00 E
Hlobyne 78 49.23 N 33.17 E
Hlohovec 30 48.25 N 17.47 E
Hluboká ⊥ 61 49.05 N 14.25 E
Hluboká nad Vltavou 61 49.03 N 14.27 E
Hluboš 60 49.45 N 14.02 E
Hlučín 30 49.54 N 18.12 E
Hluhluwe 158 28.01 S 32.15 E
Hluhluwe Game Reserve -•-[4] 158 28.05 S 32.04 E
Hlukhiv 78 51.41 N 33.53 E
Hluti 158 27.13 S 31.35 E
Hlyboka 78 48.07 N 25.56 E
Hlynyany 78 49.49 N 24.30 E
Hmawbi 110 17.06 N 96.02 E
H. Neely Henry Lake ⊜[1] 194 33.55 N 86.05 W
Hnivan' 78 49.06 N 28.20 E
Hnyla Lypa ≃ 78 49.07 N 24.44 E
Hnylyy Tikych ≃ 78 48.47 N 30.53 E
Hnylyy Yalanets' ≃ 78 47.20 N 31.44 E
Ho 150 6.35 N 0.30 E
Hoa Binh 110 20.50 N 105.20 E
Hoa Da 110 11.11 N 108.33 E
Hoagland 216 40.56 N 84.59 W
Hoagland Ditch ≊ 216 40.48 N 86.48 W
Hoanib ≃ 156 19.27 S 12.46 E
Hoare Bay ⊂ 176 65.20 N 62.30 W
Hoarusib ≃ 156 19.03 S 12.36 E
Hoa Thoi 269c 10.44 N 106.35 E
Hoback ≃ 202 43.19 N 110.44 W
Hobart, Austl. 166 42.53 S 147.19 E
Hobart, In., U.S. 216 41.31 N 87.15 W
Hobart, N.Y., U.S. 210 42.22 N 74.40 W
Hobart, Ok., U.S. 196 35.01 N 99.05 W
Hobart, Wa., U.S. 224 47.25 N 121.58 W
Hobbs, In., U.S. 216 40.17 N 85.57 W
Hobbs, N.M., U.S. 196 32.42 N 103.08 W
Hobbs Coast ⊥[2] 9 74.45 S 131.00 W
Hobe Sound 220 27.03 N 80.08 W
Hobgood 192 36.01 N 77.23 W
Hobhole Drain ≊ 44 52.59 N 0.02 E
Hobhouse 158 29.31 S 27.08 E
Hobo 246 2.35 N 75.27 W
Hoboken, Bel. 50 51.10 N 4.21 E
Hoboken, N.J., U.S. 210 40.44 N 74.01 W
Hoboksar 86 46.47 N 85.43 E
Hobq Shamo -•-[2] 102 40.30 N 107.55 E
Hobro 26 56.38 N 9.48 E
Hobson 202 47.00 N 109.52 W
Hobson Lake ⊜ 182 52.30 N 120.20 W
Hobsons Bay ⊂ 274b 37.51 S 144.56 E
Hoburgen › 26 56.55 N 18.07 E
Hobyo 144 5.21 N 48.32 E
Hocaköy 130 41.03 N 30.17 E
Hocalar 130 38.34 N 30.00 E
Hocalı 130 38.41 N 27.41 E
Hochalmspitze ∧ 64 47.01 N 13.19 E
Hochandochtla Mountain ∧ 180 65.32 N 154.50 W
Höchberg 56 49.49 N 9.51 E
Hochburg 60 48.07 N 12.52 E
Hochdahl 56 51.13 N 6.56 E
Hochdorf 58 47.10 N 8.17 E
Höchenschwand 58 47.44 N 8.10 E
Hochfeiler (Gran Pilastro) ∧ 64 46.58 N 11.44 E
Hochfeld 156 21.28 S 17.58 E
Hochfeld -•-[8] 263 51.25 N 6.46 E
Hochfelden 56 48.45 N 7.34 E
Hochfilzen 64 47.28 N 12.37 E
Hochfinstermünz 58 46.56 N 10.29 E
Hochgern ∧ 64 47.45 N 12.30 E
Hochgolling ∧ 64 47.16 N 13.45 E
Hochheide -•-[8] 263 51.27 N 6.41 E
Hochheim, Dtsch. 56 50.01 N 8.20 E
Hochheim, Tx., U.S. 222 29.19 N 97.17 W
Ho Chi Minh City
→ Thanh Pho Ho Chi Minh 110 10.45 N 106.40 E
Hochiss ∧ 64 47.27 N 11.46 E
Hochkirch 54 51.09 N 14.34 E
Hochkönig ∧ 64 47.25 N 13.04 E
Hochkreuz ∧ 64 46.49 N 13.04 E
Hochlantsch ∧ 61 47.21 N 15.25 E
Hochlar 263 51.36 N 7.10 E
Hochneukirch 56 51.06 N 6.26 E
Hochobir ∧ 61 46.30 N 14.29 E
Hochreichhart ∧ 61 47.22 N 14.41 E
Hochries ∧ 64 47.45 N 12.14 E
Hochschwab ∧ 61 47.37 N 15.09 E
Hochschwab ⋏ 61 47.36 N 15.05 E
Hochsimmer ∧ 56 50.21 N 7.12 E
Hochspeyer 56 49.26 N 7.54 E
Höchst, Dtsch. 56 49.48 N 8.59 E
Höchst, Öst. 58 47.28 N 9.38 E
Höchst -•-[8] 56 50.07 N 8.33 E
Höchstadt an der Aisch 56 49.42 N 10.44 E
Höchstädt an der Donau 56 48.36 N 10.34 E
Höchsten -•-[8] 263 51.27 N 7.29 E
Höchstenbach 56 50.38 N 7.44 E
Hochstuhl (Veliki Stol) ∧ 61 46.26 N 14.10 E
Hochtor)(64 47.05 N 12.51 E
Hoch'uan
→ Hechuan 107 30.00 N 106.16 E
Ho Chung 271d 22.22 N 114.14 E
Hochvogel ∧ 58 47.23 N 10.26 E
Hochwildstelle ∧ 64 47.20 N 13.50 E
Hockenheim 56 49.19 N 8.33 E
Hockeroda 54 50.35 N 11.26 E
Hockessin 285 39.47 N 75.41 W
Hocking ≃ 188 39.12 N 81.45 W
Hocking Hills State Park ♦ 188 39.30 N 82.32 W
Hockley, Eng., U.K. 42 51.37 N 0.40 E
Hockley, Tx., U.S. 222 30.02 N 95.51 W
Hockomock Swamp ≡ 283 41.59 N 71.05 W
Hôḍ -•-[1] 150 16.10 N 8.40 W
Hodal 124 27.54 N 77.22 E
Hōdatsu-zan ∧ 94 36.47 N 136.49 E
Hodder ≃ 44 53.50 N 2.25 W
Hoddesdon 42 51.46 N 0.01 W
Hoddlesden 262 53.42 N 2.26 W
Hodeida
→ Al-Ḥudaydah 144 14.48 N 42.57 E
Hodenhagen 52 52.46 N 9.35 E
Hodge 194 32.16 N 92.43 W
Hodgenville 194 37.34 N 85.44 W
Hodges, Lake ⊜[1] 228 33.03 N 117.05 W
Hodges Brook ≃ 283 41.58 N 71.14 W
Hodges Hill ∧[2] 186 49.04 N 55.53 W
Hodgeville 184 50.08 N 106.58 W
Hodgkins 278 41.46 N 87.51 W
Hodgson 184 51.13 N 97.34 W
Hodgson ≃ 164 14.48 S 134.35 E
Hodgson, Mount ∧[2] 162 22.26 S 121.10 E
Hod HaSharon 132 32.09 N 34.53 E
Hodh ech Chargui □[4] 150 18.10 N 7.15 W
Hodh el Gharbi □[4] 150 16.30 N 10.00 W
Hódmezővásárhely 30 46.25 N 20.20 E
Hodmo V 144 10.41 N 46.13 E
Hodna, Chott el ⊜ 148 35.25 N 4.45 E
Hodna, Monts du ⋏ 34 35.50 N 4.50 E
Hodna, Plaine du ≚ 34 35.38 N 4.30 E
Hodnet 42 52.51 N 2.35 W
Hodogaya -•-[8] 268 35.27 N 139.36 E
Hodogaya Baseball Ground ♦ 268 35.27 N 139.35 E
Hodonín 30 48.51 N 17.08 E
Hodoš 61 46.50 N 16.20 E
Hodzana ≃ 180 66.15 N 147.48 W
Hoed 41 56.19 N 10.49 E
Hoedekenskerke 52 51.25 N 3.55 E
Hoehne 198 37.16 N 104.22 W
Hoeksche Waard I 52 51.45 N 4.30 E
Hoek van Holland 52 51.59 N 4.09 E
Hoeningen 263 51.05 N 6.41 E
Hoensbroek 56 50.55 N 5.55 E
Hœrdt 58 48.42 N 7.47 E
Hoerstgen 263 51.30 N 6.27 E
Hoeryŏng 98 42.27 N 129.44 E
Hoeyang 98 38.43 N 127.36 E
Hof, Dtsch. 54 50.18 N 11.55 E
Hof, Ísland 24a 64.34 N 14.39 W
Hofburg ⊛ 264b 48.12 N 16.22 E
Höfðakaupstaður 24a 65.50 N 20.19 W
Hofei
→ Hefei 100 31.51 N 117.17 E
Höfen, Dtsch. 56 50.32 N 6.15 E
Höfen, Dtsch. 60 49.08 N 11.21 E
Hoffman, Il., U.S. 219 38.32 N 89.16 W
Hoffman, Mn., U.S. 198 45.49 N 95.47 W
Hoffman Estates 216 42.02 N 88.04 W
Hoffman Island I 276 40.35 N 74.03 W
Hoffmans 210 42.54 N 74.05 W
Hoffman Station 284a 43.04 N 78.50 W
Hoffnung 263 51.07 N 7.13 E
Hofgeismar 52 51.30 N 9.22 E
Hofheim 56 50.07 N 8.26 E
Hofheim in Unterfranken 56 50.08 N 10.31 E
Hofkirchen an der Trattnach 60 48.13 N 13.44 E
Höflein an der Donau 264b 48.21 N 16.17 E
Hofmeyr 158 31.39 S 25.50 E
Höfn 24a 64.17 N 15.10 W
Hofors 40 60.33 N 16.17 E
Hofsjökull ⊓ 24a 64.48 N 18.50 W
Hofstade 50 50.58 N 4.02 E
Hofstede -•-[8] 263 51.30 N 7.12 E
Hofstra University ⊛[2] 276 40.43 N 73.36 W
Hōfu 96 34.03 N 131.34 E
Hofuf
→ Al-Hufūf 128 25.22 N 49.34 E
Hofweier 58 48.25 N 7.55 E
Hog, Tanjong › 116 5.18 N 119.16 E
Hogalbāria 126 23.53 N 88.51 E
Höganäs 41 56.12 N 12.33 E
Hogan Lake ⊜ 190 45.52 N 78.30 W
Hogansburg 206 44.58 N 74.39 W
Hogansville 192 33.10 N 84.54 W
Hogatza ≃ 180 66.00 N 155.29 W
Hogback Mountain ∧, U.S. 207 42.43 N 72.25 W
Hogback Mountain ∧, Mt., U.S. 202 44.54 N 112.07 W
Hogback Mountain ∧, Ne., U.S. 198 41.40 N 103.44 W
Hogback Mountain ∧, S.C., U.S. 192 35.10 N 82.17 W
Högbo 40 60.40 N 16.48 E
Hog Canyon V 226 35.42 N 120.35 W
Hog Creek ≃ 222 31.32 N 97.18 W
Hoge Veluwe, Nationale Park de ♦ 52 52.02 N 5.55 E
Högfors 40 59.59 N 15.01 E
Hoggar
→ Ahaggar ⋏ 148 23.00 N 6.30 E
Hoghton 262 53.44 N 2.35 W
Hoghton Tower ⊥ 262 53.44 N 2.34 W
Hog Island I, Ma., U.S. 283 42.40 N 70.46 W
Hog Island I, Mi., U.S. 190 45.48 N 85.22 W
Hog Island I, Vt., U.S. 206 44.57 N 73.13 W
Hog Island I, Va., U.S. 208 37.25 N 75.41 W
Hog Island Bay ⊂ 208 37.27 N 75.46 W
Hogoro 154 5.57 S 36.27 E
Hog Point › 208 37.12 N 76.41 W
Hogs Back ⊥[4] 42 51.13 N 0.40 W
Högsby 26 57.10 N 16.02 E
Högsjö 40 59.02 N 15.41 E
Hoh ≃ 224 47.45 N 124.29 W
Hoh, South Fork ≃ 224 47.46 N 124.01 W
Hohe Acht ∧ 56 50.23 N 7.00 E
Hohebach 56 49.22 N 9.44 E
Hohe Eifel ⋏ 56 50.15 N 6.45 E
Hohegeiss 54 51.40 N 10.40 E
Hohenau 252 27.05 S 55.45 W
Hohenau an der March 61 48.36 N 16.55 E
Höhenberg 61 48.46 N 14.53 E
Hohenbrunn 60 48.03 N 11.42 E
Hohenbucko 54 51.46 N 13.28 E
Hohenbudberg -•-[8] 263 51.23 N 6.40 E
Hohenburg 60 49.18 N 11.48 E
Hohendorf 54 54.01 N 13.44 E
Hohenebra 54 51.18 N 10.49 E
Hohenems 58 47.22 N 9.41 E
Hohenfels 60 49.12 N 11.51 E
Hohenfurch 58 47.51 N 10.54 E
Hohengüstow 54 53.14 N 13.59 E
Hohenhameln 52 52.15 N 10.03 E
Hohenheide 263 51.29 N 7.47 E
Hohenkammer 60 48.25 N 11.32 E
Hohenkirchen, Dtsch. 52 53.39 N 7.55 E
Hohenkirchen, Dtsch. 54 50.51 N 10.41 E
Hohenkirchen, Dtsch. 54 53.51 N 11.17 E
Hohenkirchen, Dtsch. 56 51.23 N 9.29 E
Hohenleipisch 54 51.30 N 13.34 E
Hohenleuben 54 50.43 N 12.03 E
Hohenlimburg 56 51.21 N 7.35 E
Hohenlimburg, Schloss ⊥ 263 51.21 N 7.34 E
Hohenlinden 60 48.09 N 12.00 E
Hohenmölsen 54 51.09 N 12.06 E
Hohen Neuendorf 54 52.40 N 13.16 E
Hohenpolding 60 48.23 N 12.08 E
Hohensalza
→ Inowrocław 30 52.48 N 18.15 E
Hohenschönhausen -•-[8] 264a 52.33 N 13.30 E
Hohenseeden 54 52.19 N 12.01 E
Hohenseefeld 54 51.53 N 13.18 E
Hohenstaufen 56 48.44 N 9.43 E
Hohenstein-Ernstthal 54 50.48 N 12.42 E
Hohensyburg ⊥ 56 51.25 N 7.29 E
Hohentauern 61 47.26 N 14.29 E
Hohenthurm 54 51.31 N 12.05 E
Hohenthurn 64 46.33 N 13.40 E
Hohentwiel ∧ 58 47.46 N 8.49 E
Hohenwald 194 35.32 N 87.33 W
Hohenwart 60 48.36 N 11.23 E
Hohenwarte-Stausee ⊜[1] 54 50.32 N 11.30 E
Hohenwarthe 54 52.13 N 11.42 E
Hohenwutzen 54 52.51 N 14.07 E
Hohenzethen 54 53.03 N 10.49 E
Hohenzollern, Burg ⊥ 58 48.19 N 8.58 E
Hohenzollernkanal ≊ 264a 52.32 N 13.20 E
Hoher Bogen ∧ 60 49.15 N 12.55 E
Hoher Dachstein ∧ 64 47.28 N 13.35 E
Hoher Freschen ∧ 58 47.18 N 9.46 E
Hohe Rhön ⋏ 56 50.30 N 10.00 E
Hoher Ifen ∧ 58 47.21 N 10.05 E
Hoherlehme 264a 52.19 N 13.37 E
Hoher Mechtin ∧[2] 54 53.03 N 10.55 E
Hoher Riffler ∧ 58 47.07 N 10.22 E
Hoher Sonnblick ∧ 64 47.03 N 12.57 E
Hoher Zinken ∧ 64 47.40 N 13.20 E
Hohe Tauern ⋏ 64 47.10 N 12.45 E
Hohe Warte (Monte Coglians) ∧ 64 46.37 N 12.53 E
Hoh Head › 224 47.46 N 124.29 W
Hohhot 102 40.51 N 111.40 E
Höhn 56 50.37 N 8.00 E
Hohndorf 54 50.45 N 12.40 E
Hohne 52 52.35 N 10.22 E
Hohneck, Le ∧ 58 48.02 N 7.01 E
Hohnstein 54 50.59 N 14.10 E
Hohoe 150 7.09 N 0.28 E
Hōhoku 96 34.17 N 130.57 E
Ho-Ho-Kus 276 40.59 N 74.06 W
Hohokus Brook ≃ 276 40.57 N 74.06 W
Hoholeve 78 49.56 N 33.48 E
Hoholitna ≃ 180 61.31 N 157.00 W
Hoh Sai Hu ⊜ 120 35.43 N 92.45 E
Höhscheid -•-[8] 263 51.09 N 7.04 E
Hohultslätt 26 56.58 N 15.39 E
Hohwacht 54 54.19 N 10.41 E
Hohwachter Bucht ⊂ 54 54.20 N 10.45 E
Hoh Xil Hu ⊜ 120 35.35 N 91.06 E
Hoh Xil Shan ⋏ 120 35.20 N 90.00 E
Hoi An 110 15.52 N 108.19 E
Hoihow
→ Haikou 102 20.03 N 110.19 E
Hoima 154 1.26 N 31.21 E
Hoisdorf 52 53.39 N 10.20 E
Hoisington 198 38.31 N 98.46 W
Hoisten 263 51.08 N 6.42 E
Hoi Xuan 110 20.22 N 105.07 E
Hojāi 120 26.00 N 92.51 E
Højby, Dan. 41 55.55 N 11.37 E
Højby, Dan. 41 55.20 N 10.27 E
Höje 40 59.54 N 13.33 E
Højer 26 54.58 N 8.43 E
Højerup 41 55.17 N 12.27 E
Hōjō
→ Kasai, Nihon 96 34.56 N 134.50 E
Hōjō, Nihon 96 34.54 N 134.56 E
Hōjō, Nihon 96 33.58 N 132.46 E
Hokah 190 43.45 N 91.20 W
Hokang
→ Hegang 89 47.24 N 130.17 E
Hökåsen 40 59.40 N 16.35 E
Hokendauqua 208 40.39 N 75.29 W
Hökensås ⋏[2] 26 58.11 N 14.08 E
Hokes Bluff 194 33.59 N 85.51 W
Hōki ≃ 94 36.47 N 140.08 E
Hokianga Harbour ⊂ 172 35.32 S 173.22 E
Hokitika 172 42.43 S 170.58 E
Hokkaidō □[5] 92a 44.00 N 143.00 E
Hokkaidō I 92a 44.00 N 143.00 E
Hokksund 26 59.47 N 9.59 E
Hoko ≃ 224 48.17 N 124.22 W
Hōkōji 270 34.52 N 135.07 E
Hököpinge 41 55.30 N 13.00 E
Hokota 94 36.09 N 140.31 E
Hok So Wan 271d 22.13 N 114.14 E
Hokubo 96 34.57 N 133.38 E
Hokudan 96 34.32 N 134.56 E
Hokura ≃ 94 37.10 N 138.16 E
Hokuriku-tunnel -•-[5] 94 35.42 N 136.10 E
Hokusei 94 35.09 N 136.31 E
Hola 154 1.29 S 40.02 E
Holalkere 122 14.02 N 76.11 E
Holanda
→ Netherlands □[1] 30 52.15 N 5.30 E
Hola Prystan' 78 46.31 N 32.31 E
Holbæk 41 55.43 N 11.43 E
Holbeach 42 52.49 N 0.01 E
Holbeach Marsh ≡ 42 52.52 N 0.05 E
Holberg 182 50.39 N 128.00 W
Holborn -•-[8] 260 51.31 N 0.07 W
Holbrook, Austl. 171b 35.44 S 147.19 E
Holbrook, Az., U.S. 200 34.54 N 110.09 W
Holbrook, Il., U.S. 278 41.32 N 87.38 W
Holbrook, Md., U.S. 284b 39.24 N 76.51 W
Holbrook, Ma., U.S. 207 42.09 N 71.00 W
Holbrook, Ne., U.S. 198 40.18 N 100.00 W
Holbrook, N.Y., U.S. 210 40.48 N 73.04 W
Holbrook, Lake ⊜[1] 222 32.42 N 95.33 W
Holbrook Mountain ∧[2] 212 44.25 N 77.51 W
Holckenhavn 41 55.17 N 10.47 E
Holcomb, Il., U.S. 216 42.04 N 89.06 W
Holcomb, N.Y., U.S. 210 42.54 N 77.25 W
Holcomb Creek ≃ 228 34.17 N 117.08 W
Holden, Ab., Can. 182 53.14 N 112.14 W
Holden, Ma., U.S. 207 42.21 N 71.51 W
Holden, Mo., U.S. 194 38.42 N 93.59 W
Holden, Ut,. U.S. 200 39.05 N 112.16 W
Holden, W.V., U.S. 188 37.49 N 82.03 W
Holden, Mount ∧[2] 216 41.40 N 87.03 W
Holdenstedt 52 52.55 N 10.31 E
Holden Village 224 48.12 N 120.47 W
Holdenville 196 35.04 N 96.23 W
Holder 220 28.58 N 82.25 W
Holderness ›[1] 44 53.47 N 0.10 W
Holdfast 184 50.58 N 105.25 W
Holdich 254 45.57 S 68.13 W
Holdingford 190 45.43 N 94.28 W
Holdorf 52 52.35 N 8.07 E
Holdrege 198 40.26 N 99.22 W
Holeby 41 54.43 N 11.28 E
Hole in the Mountain Peak ∧ 204 40.55 N 115.05 W
Hole Narsipur 122 12.47 N 76.15 E
Holešov 30 49.20 N 17.35 E
Holetown 241g 13.11 N 59.39 W
Holgate, S. Afr. 158 33.59 S 22.21 E
Holgate, Oh., U.S. 216 41.14 N 84.07 W
Holguín 240p 20.53 N 76.15 W
Holguín □[4] 240p 20.55 N 75.50 W
Hol-Hol 144 11.19 N 42.57 E
Holíč 30 48.49 N 17.10 E
Holiday Beach Provincial Park ♦ 214 42.02 N 83.05 W
Holiday Hills 216 42.18 N 88.13 W
Holiday Lake Amusement Park ♦ 285 40.02 N 74.56 W
Holiday Shores 219 38.55 N 89.56 W
Holitna ≃ 180 61.40 N 157.12 W
Höljes 26 60.54 N 12.36 E
Hollabrunn 61 48.34 N 16.05 E
Holladay 200 40.40 N 111.49 W
Holland, Mb., Can. 184 49.36 N 98.53 W
Holland, Mi., U.S. 216 42.47 N 86.06 W
Holland, N.Y., U.S. 210 42.38 N 78.32 W
Holland, Oh., U.S. 216 41.37 N 83.42 W
Holland, Pa., U.S. 285 40.10 N 74.59 W
Holland, Tx., U.S. 222 30.53 N 97.24 W
Holland, Va., U.S. 208 36.41 N 76.47 W
Holland □[9] 52 52.20 N 4.45 E
Holland
→ Netherlands □[1] 30 52.15 N 5.30 E
Holland ≃ 212 44.12 N 79.31 W
Holland, Mount ∧[2] 162 32.12 S 119.44 E
Hollandale 194 33.10 N 90.51 W
Holland Creek ≃ 169 36.43 S 146.06 E
Hollande, Étangs de ⊜ 261 48.44 N 1.48 E
Holland Fen ≡ 44 53.00 N 0.10 W
Hollandia
→ Jayapura 164 2.32 S 140.42 E
Holland Landing 212 44.06 N 79.29 W
Holland Park 171a 27.31 S 153.03 E
Holland Patent 210 43.14 N 75.15 W
Holland Point › 208 38.43 N 76.32 W
Holland Pond State Park ♦ 207 42.04 N 72.09 W
Hollandsbird Island I 156 24.45 S 14.34 E
Hollandsch Diep ⊔ 52 51.42 N 4.30 E
Hollandstoun 46 59.21 N 2.26 W
Holland Straits ⊔ 208 38.08 N 76.02 W
Holland Tunnel -•-[5] 276 40.44 N 74.02 W
Hollansburg 218 39.59 N 84.47 W
Holleben 54 51.26 N 11.53 E
Hollenfels, Château ⊥ 56 49.43 N 6.03 E
Höllengebirge ⋏ 64 47.48 N 13.39 E
Hollenstedt 52 53.22 N 9.43 E
Hollenstein an der Ybbs 61 47.48 N 14.46 E
Höllensteinberg ∧ 264b 48.06 N 16.11 E
Höllental V 61 47.45 N 15.47 E
Hollern 52 53.36 N 9.32 E
Holleton 162 31.57 S 119.02 E
Holley 210 43.13 N 78.01 W
Hollfeld 60 49.56 N 11.18 E
Hollick-Kenyon Plateau ⋏[1] 9 79.00 S 97.00 W
Holliday, Mo., U.S. 219 39.29 N 92.07 W
Holliday, Tx., U.S. 196 33.49 N 98.42 W
Holliday Creek ≃ 196 33.55 N 98.28 W
Holliday Park ♦ 281 42.21 N 83.24 W
Hollidaysburg 214 40.25 N 78.23 W
Hollingbourne 260 51.16 N 0.38 E
Hollingstedt 41 54.27 N 9.19 E
Hollingworth 262 53.28 N 1.59 W
Hollingworth Lake ⊜ 262 53.38 N 2.06 W
Hollins, Eng., U.K. 262 53.34 N 2.17 W
Hollins, Va., U.S. 192 37.20 N 79.56 W
Hollins Green 262 53.25 N 2.27 W
Hollinswood 284c 38.55 N 77.13 W
Hollis, N.H., U.S. 207 42.44 N 71.35 W
Hollis, Ok., U.S. 196 34.41 N 99.54 W
Hollis -•-[8] 276 40.43 N 73.46 W
Hollister 226 36.51 N 121.24 W
Hollister, Mount ∧[2] 162 22.08 S 114.01 E
Holliston 207 42.12 N 71.25 W
Hollman, Cape › 164 4.59 S 150.06 E
Holloman Air Force Base ■ 200 32.51 N 106.05 W
Holloway 214 40.10 N 81.08 W
Holloway Terrace 285 39.42 N 75.32 W
Hollow Rock 194 36.02 N 88.16 W
Hollowville 210 42.12 N 73.42 W
Hollsopple 214 40.13 N 78.56 W
Hollum 52 53.26 N 5.37 E
Höllviken ⊂ 41 55.26 N 12.54 E
Höllviksnäs 41 55.25 N 12.57 E
Holly, Co., U.S. 198 38.03 N 102.07 W
Holly, Mi., U.S. 216 42.47 N 83.37 W
Holly, Wa., U.S. 224 47.34 N 122.58 W
Holly, Mount ∧[2] 285 40.00 N 74.47 W
Holly Brook 285 39.59 N 74.48 W
Holly Grove 194 34.35 N 91.11 W
Holly Hill, Fl., U.S. 192 29.14 N 81.02 W
Holly Hill, S.C., U.S. 192 33.19 N 80.24 W
Holly Park, N.J., U.S. 208 39.53 N 74.10 W
Holly Park, Va., U.S. 284c 38.50 N 77.17 W
Holly Pond ⊜ 276 41.03 N 73.30 W
Holly River State Park ♦ 188 38.40 N 80.21 W
Holly Run ≃ 285 39.47 N 75.03 W
Holly Springs 194 34.46 N 89.26 W
Holly State Recreation Area ♦ 216 42.49 N 83.32 W
Hollywood, Ire. 48 53.06 N 6.35 W
Hollywood, Fl., U.S. 220 26.00 N 80.08 W
Hollywood, Md., U.S. 208 38.20 N 76.34 W
Hollywood, Pa., U.S. 285 40.05 N 75.06 W
Hollywood -•-[8] 228 34.06 N 118.21 W
Hollywood, Mount ∧ 280 34.08 N 118.18 W
Hollywood Bowl ♦ 280 34.07 N 118.20 W
Hollywood-Burbank Airport ⊠ 228 34.12 N 118.21 W
Hollywood Heights 219 38.39 N 89.59 W
Hollywood Indian Reservation -•-[4] 220 26.02 N 80.13 W
Hollywood Park Race Track ♦ 280 33.57 N 118.20 W
Hollywood Reservoir ⊜[1] 280 34.07 N 118.20 W
Holman 176 70.43 N 117.43 W
Hólmavík 24a 65.43 N 21.43 W
Holmdel 208 40.20 N 74.11 W
Holme, Dan. 41 56.07 N 10.11 E
Holme, Eng., U.K. 262 53.33 N 1.50 W
Holme ≃ 44 53.41 N 1.43 W
Holme Chapel 262 53.45 N 2.11 W
Holmen, Nor. 26 60.40 N 10.22 E
Holmen, Wi., U.S. 190 43.57 N 91.15 W
Holme-on-Spaulding-Moor 44 53.50 N 0.46 W
Holmes, N.Y., U.S. 210 41.31 N 73.39 W
Holmes, Pa., U.S. 285 39.54 N 75.19 W
Holmes □[6] 214 40.33 N 81.55 W
Holmes, Mount ∧ 202 44.49 N 110.51 W
Holmes Beach 220 27.31 N 82.43 W
Holmesburg -•-[8] 285 40.02 N 75.03 W
Holmes Chapel 44 53.12 N 2.22 W
Holmes Creek ≃ 194 30.30 N 85.47 W
Holmesglen 274b 37.53 S 145.06 E
Holmes Harbor ⊂ 224 48.04 N 122.32 W
Holmes Lake ⊜ 184 57.05 N 96.45 W
Holmes Reef ✦[2] 164 16.27 S 148.00 E
Holmes Run ≃ 284c 38.48 N 77.07 W
Holmes Run Acres 284c 38.51 N 77.13 W
Holmestrand 26 59.29 N 10.18 E
Holmesville, N.Y., U.S. 210 42.31 N 75.24 W
Holmesville, Oh., U.S. 214 40.37 N 81.55 W
Holmeswood 262 53.39 N 2.52 W
Holmfirth 44 53.35 N 1.46 W
Holmia 246 4.58 N 59.35 W
Holmivs'kyy 83 48.25 N 38.05 E
Holmön I 26 63.47 N 20.53 E
Holmsbu 26 59.33 N 10.27 E
Holmsjön ⊜, Sve. 26 62.41 N 16.33 E
Holmsjön ⊜, Sve. 26 62.25 N 15.20 E
Holmsund 26 63.42 N 20.21 E
Hölö 40 59.01 N 17.35 E
Holoby 78 51.06 N 24.59 E
Holod 38 46.47 N 22.08 E
Holohory ⋏ 78 49.45 N 24.35 E
Holoit, Punta › 232 21.37 N 88.08 W
Ḥolon 132 32.01 N 34.46 E
Holoog 156 27.22 S 17.55 E
Holopaw 220 28.08 N 81.04 W
Holovanivs'k 78 48.23 N 30.28 E
Holovne 78 51.21 N 24.04 E
Holroyd 274a 33.50 S 150.58 E
Holroyd ≃ 164 14.10 S 141.36 E
Holsloot 52 52.44 N 6.48 E
Holstebro 26 56.21 N 8.38 E
Holsted 41 55.30 N 8.55 E
Holstein 198 42.29 N 95.32 W
Holsteinborg ⊥ 41 55.13 N 11.28 E
Holsteinische Schweiz -•-[1] 54 54.11 N 10.36 E
Holsteinsborg (Sisimiut) 176 66.55 N 53.40 W
Holsterhausen 263 51.41 N 6.57 E
Holston ≃ 192 35.57 N 83.51 W
Holston, North Fork ≃ 192 36.33 N 82.36 W
Holston High Knob ∧ 192 36.27 N 82.05 W
Holsworthy 42 50.49 N 4.21 W
Holt, Eng., U.K. 42 52.55 N 1.05 E
Holt, Wales, U.K. 44 53.05 N 2.53 W
Holt, Al., U.S. 194 33.14 N 87.29 W
Holt, Ca., U.S. 226 37.56 N 121.26 W
Holt, Fl., U.S. 194 30.42 N 86.44 W
Holt, Mi., U.S. 216 42.38 N 84.30 W
Holt Creek ≃ 198 42.28 N 98.50 W
Holte 41 55.49 N 12.28 E
Holtemme ≃ 54 51.57 N 11.10 E
Holten 52 52.17 N 6.25 E
Holten -•-[8] 263 51.31 N 6.48 E
Holtenau -•-[8] 54 54.22 N 10.08 E
Holter Lake ⊜[1] 202 46.55 N 111.57 W
Holthausen, Dtsch. 52 52.33 N 7.17 E
Holthausen, Dtsch. 263 51.23 N 7.13 E
Holthausen, Dtsch. 263 51.12 N 7.01 E
Holthausen -•-[8] 263 51.34 N 7.26 E
Holthusen 52 53.08 N 7.18 E
Holton, In., U.S. 218 39.04 N 85.23 W
Holton, Ks., U.S. 198 39.27 N 95.44 W
Holtorf 52 52.40 N 9.13 E
Holts Summit 219 38.39 N 92.07 W
Holtsville 210 40.49 N 73.02 W
Holtug 41 55.21 N 12.25 E
Holtville 204 32.48 N 115.22 W
Holtwick 52 52.00 N 7.05 E
Holtwood 208 39.50 N 76.19 W
Holubivka 78 48.53 N 35.19 E
Holwerd 52 53.22 N 5.54 E
Holycross, Ire. 48 52.38 N 7.52 W
Holy Cross, Ak., U.S. 180 62.12 N 159.47 W
Holy Cross Mountain ∧ 182 53.47 N 120.47 W
Holyhead 44 53.19 N 4.38 W
Holyhead Bay ⊂ 44 53.23 N 4.37 W
Holy Island I, Eng., U.K. 44 55.41 N 1.48 W
Holy Island I, Scot., U.K. 46 55.32 N 5.04 W
Holy Island I, Wales, U.K. 44 53.18 N 4.37 W
Holy Island I, Ma., U.S. 283 42.43 N 70.50 W
Holyoke, Co., U.S. 198 40.35 N 102.18 W
Holyoke, Ma., U.S. 207 42.12 N 72.37 W
Holyrood 198 38.35 N 98.24 W
Holyrood Palace ⊛ 46 55.56 N 3.12 W
Holýšov 60 49.36 N 13.05 E
Holywell 44 53.17 N 3.13 W
Holywell Green 262 53.41 N 1.52 W
Holywood 48 54.38 N 5.50 W
Holzbüttgen 263 51.12 N 6.37 E
Holzen 56 51.26 N 7.31 E
Holzgau 58 47.16 N 10.21 E
Holzgerlingen 56 48.38 N 9.00 E
Holzhausen, Dtsch. 52 52.17 N 8.32 E
Holzhausen, Dtsch. 52 52.13 N 8.01 E
Holzhausen, Dtsch. 52 52.01 N 8.44 E
Holzhausen, Dtsch. 54 51.18 N 12.28 E
Holzhausen an der Haide 56 50.13 N 7.55 E
Holzheim 56 51.09 N 6.39 E
Holzkirchen 64 47.52 N 11.42 E
Holzminden 52 51.50 N 9.27 E
Holzweissig 54 51.36 N 12.18 E
Holzwickede 52 51.30 N 7.36 E
Hom ≃ 158 28.51 S 18.37 E
Homa Bay 154 0.31 S 34.27 E
Homalin 110 24.52 N 94.55 E
Homathko ≃ 182 50.55 N 124.50 W
Homathko Icefield ⊓ 182 51.05 N 124.30 W
Homberg, Dtsch. 56 50.43 N 8.59 E
Homberg, Dtsch. 56 51.02 N 9.24 E
Homberg, Dtsch. 56 51.28 N 6.43 E
Homberg, Dtsch. 263 51.18 N 6.56 E
Hombori 150 15.17 N 1.42 W
Hombori Tondo ∧ 150 15.16 N 1.40 W
Hombourg-Haut 56 49.08 N 6.46 E
Hombre Muerto, Salar del ≚ 252 25.23 S 67.06 W
Hombruch -•-[8] 263 51.29 N 7.26 E
Homburg, Dtsch. 56 49.19 N 7.20 E
Homburg
→ Bad Homburg vor der Höhe, Dtsch. 56 50.13 N 8.37 E
Home, Pa., U.S. 214 40.44 N 79.06 W
Home, Wa., U.S. 224 47.17 N 122.46 W
Homeacre 214 40.51 N 79.55 W
Home Bay ⊂, N.T., Can. 176 68.45 N 67.10 W
Home Bay ⊂, Kiribati 174d 0.53 S 169.35 E
Homebush Bay ⊂ 274a 33.50 S 151.05 E
Home Corner 216 40.31 N 85.38 W
Homécourt 56 49.14 N 5.59 E
Home Creek ≃ 196 31.29 N 99.14 W
Homedale, Id., U.S. 202 43.37 N 116.55 W
Homedale, Oh., U.S. 214 40.04 N 83.02 W
Home Gardens 228 33.52 N 117.31 W
Home Hill 166 19.40 S 147.25 E
Homeland, Ca., U.S. 228 33.44 N 117.07 W
Homeland, Fl., U.S. 220 27.49 N 81.49 W
Homeland Canal ≊ 226 35.57 N 119.27 W
Homeland Park 192 34.27 N 82.41 W
Home Place 218 39.56 N 86.08 W
Homer, Ak., U.S. 180 59.39 N 151.33 W
Homer, Ga., U.S. 192 34.20 N 83.29 W
Homer, La., U.S. 194 32.47 N 93.03 W
Homer, Mi., U.S. 216 42.08 N 84.48 W
Homer, Ne., U.S. 198 42.19 N 96.29 W
Homer, N.Y., U.S. 210 42.38 N 76.10 W
Homer, Oh., U.S. 214 40.15 N 82.31 W
Homer, Tx., U.S. 222 31.18 N 94.36 W
Homer City 214 40.32 N 79.09 W
Homert ∧[2] 263 51.11 N 7.39 E
Homer Tunnel -•-[5] 172 44.45 S 168.00 E
Homerville, Ga., U.S. 192 31.02 N 82.44 W
Homerville, Oh., U.S. 214 41.02 N 82.08 W
Homer Wash V 204 34.20 N 115.02 W
Homer Youngs Peak ∧ 202 45.19 N 113.41 W
Home Seamount ✦[3] 14 12.55 S 175.37 W
Homestead, Austl. 166 20.22 S 145.39 E
Homestead, Fl., U.S. 220 25.28 N 80.28 W
Homestead, Pa., U.S. 279b 40.24 N 79.54 W
Homestead Air Force Base ■ 220 25.29 N 80.23 W
Homestead National Monument of America ♦ 198 40.14 N 96.54 W
Homestead Valley 282 37.54 N 122.32 W
Hometown, Il., U.S. 278 41.44 N 87.43 W
Hometown, Pa., U.S. 210 40.49 N 75.59 W
Homewood, Al., U.S. 194 33.28 N 86.48 W
Homewood, Ca., U.S. 226 39.05 N 120.09 W
Homewood, Il., U.S. 216 41.33 N 87.39 W
Homewood, Oh., U.S. 218 39.23 N 84.33 W
Homewood -•-[8] 279b 40.27 N 79.54 W
Homewood Acres 278 41.34 N 87.43 W
Homeworth 214 40.50 N 81.03 W
Hominy 196 36.24 N 96.23 W
Hominy Creek ≃ 196 36.20 N 96.00 W
Hommersåk 26 58.58 N 5.42 E
Hommura 92 34.22 N 139.15 E
Homnābād 122 17.46 N 77.08 E
Homochitto ≃ 194 31.09 N 91.31 W
Homoíne 156 23.52 S 35.09 E
Homonhon Island I 116 10.44 N 125.43 E
Homosassa 220 28.46 N 82.36 W
Homosassa Bay ⊂ 220 28.45 N 82.43 W
Homosassa Springs 220 28.48 N 82.35 W
Homs
→ Al-Khums, Lībiyā 146 32.39 N 14.16 E
Homs
→ Ḥimṣ, Sūrīy. 130 34.44 N 36.43 E
Honai 96 33.30 N 132.25 E
Honaker 192 37.00 N 81.58 W
Honami 96 33.36 N 130.42 E
Honan
→ Luoyang 102 34.41 N 112.28 E
Honan
→ Henan □[4] 90 34.00 N 114.00 E
Honāvar 122 14.17 N 74.27 E
Honaz 130 37.45 N 29.17 E
Honbetsu 92a 43.07 N 143.37 E
Hon Chong 110 10.10 N 104.37 E
Honda 246 5.12 N 74.45 W
Honda, Bahía ⊂, Col. 246 12.21 N 71.47 W
Honda, Bahía ⊂, Cuba 240p 22.57 N 83.10 W
Honda, Cañada ≃ 258 33.57 S 59.21 W
Honda Bay ⊂ 116 9.53 N 118.49 E
Honddu ≃, U.K. 42 51.54 N 2.58 W
Honddu ≃, Wales, U.K. 42 51.57 N 3.23 W
Hondeklipbaai 156 30.20 S 17.18 E
Honderfontein 158 32.12 S 21.22 E
Hon Dien, Nui ∧ 110 11.33 N 108.38 E
Hondo, Ab., Can. 182 55.04 N 114.02 W
Hondo, Nihon 92 32.27 N 130.12 E
Hondo, N.M., U.S. 200 33.23 N 105.16 W
Hondo, Tx., U.S. 196 29.20 N 99.08 W
Hondo ≃, Méx. 286a 19.26 N 99.15 W
Hondo ≃, N.A. 232 18.29 N 88.19 W
Hondo, Arroyo ≃ 226 37.28 N 121.47 W
Hondo, Rio ≃, Ca., U.S. 280 33.55 N 118.10 W
Hondo, Rio ≃, N.M., U.S. 196 33.22 N 104.24 W
Hondo Creek ≃ 196 28.45 N 99.11 W
Hondoji Temple ⊛[1] 268 35.51 N 139.56 E
Hondschoote 50 50.59 N 2.35 E
Hondsrug ⋏[2] 52 52.55 N 6.50 E
Honduras □[1], N.A. 230 15.00 N 86.30 W
Honduras □[1], N.A. 236 15.00 N 86.30 W
Honduras, Cabo de › 236 16.01 N 86.02 W
Honduras, Gulf of ⊂ 230 16.10 N 87.50 W
Honduras, Port ⊂ 236 16.13 N 88.41 W
Honea Path 192 34.26 N 82.23 W
Hönebach 56 50.56 N 9.56 E
Hønefoss 26 60.10 N 10.18 E
Honeoye 210 42.47 N 77.31 W
Honeoye Creek ≃ 210 42.58 N 77.43 W
Honeoye Falls 210 42.57 N 77.35 W
Honeoye Lake ⊜ 210 42.45 N 77.31 W
Honesdale 210 41.34 N 75.15 W
Honey Brook 208 40.05 N 75.54 W
Honey Creek 216 42.44 N 88.18 W
Honey Creek ≃, Ia., U.S. 190 42.09 N 93.03 W
Honey Creek ≃, Mo., U.S. 194 39.53 N 93.34 W
Honey Creek ≃, Oh., U.S. 214 41.05 N 83.12 W
Honey Creek ≃, Pa., U.S. 208 40.36 N 77.35 W
Honey Creek ≃, Wi., U.S. 216 42.41 N 88.17 W
Honeydew 273d 26.05 S 27.55 E
Honeygo Run ≃ 284b 39.22 N 76.25 W
Honey Grove 196 33.35 N 95.54 W
Honey Lake ⊜ 204 40.16 N 120.19 W
Honeymoon Bay 224 48.49 N 124.10 W
Honeyville 200 41.38 N 112.04 W
Honfleur 50 49.25 N 0.14 E
Høng 41 55.31 N 11.18 E
Hong
→ Red ≃, Asia 110 20.17 N 106.34 E
Hong ≃, Zhg. 100 32.25 N 115.35 E
Honga 152 15.09 S 15.12 E
Hon Gai 110 20.57 N 107.05 E
Hong'an 100 31.18 N 114.37 E
Honga River ⊂ 208 38.19 N 76.10 W
Hongawa 96 33.43 N 133.19 E
Hongchang 100 34.05 N 113.20 E
Hongch'ŏn 98 37.42 N 127.52 E
Hongchoudai 100 29.03 N 121.11 E
Hongcun, Zhg. 100 27.10 N 116.48 E
Hongcun, Zhg. 106 31.01 N 119.15 E
Höngen 56 51.02 N 5.56 E

Symbols in the index entries represent the broad categories identified in the key at the right. Symbols with superior numbers (⋏[1]) identify subcategories (see complete key on page *I* · *1*).

Symbole im Register stellen die rechts im Schlüssel erklärten Kategorien dar. Symbole mit hochgestellten Ziffern (⋏[1]) bezeichnen Unterabteilungen einer Kategorie (vgl. vollständiger Schlüssel auf Seite *I* · *1*).

Los símbolos incluídos en el texto del índice representan las grandes categorías identificadas con la clave a la derecha. Los símbolos con numeros en su parte superior (⋏[1]) identifican las subcategorías (véase la clave completa en la página *I* · *1*).

Les symboles de l'index représentent les catégories indiquées dans la légende à droite. Les symboles suivis d'un indice (⋏[1]) représentent des sous-catégories (voir légende complète à la page *I* · *1*).

Os símbolos incluídos no texto do índice representam as grandes categorias identificadas com a chave à direita. Os símbolos com números em sua parte superior (⋏[1]) identificam as subcategorias (veja-se a chave completa à página *I* · *1*).

∧ Mountain	Berg	Montaña	Montagne	Montanha
⋏ Mountains	Gebirge	Montañas	Montagnes	Montanhas
)(Pass	Paß	Paso	Col	Passo
V Valley, Canyon	Tal, Cañon	Valle, Cañón	Vallée, Canyon	Vale, Canhão
≚ Plain	Ebene	Llano	Plaine	Planície
› Cape	Kap	Cabo	Cap	Cabo
I Island	Insel	Isla	Île	Ilha
II Islands	Inseln	Islas	Îles	Ilhas
⊥ Other Topographic Features	Andere Topographische Objekte	Otros Elementos Topográficos	Autres données topographiques	Outros acidentes topográficos

ESPAÑOL Nombre / FRANÇAIS Nom / PORTUGUÊS Nome	Página / Page / Página	Lat.°′	Long.°′ W = Oeste / W = Ouest / W = Oeste
Honggun	98	40.46 N	128.27 E
Honghai Wan ⊂	100	22.40 N	115.10 E
Honghe	102	23.23 N	102.35 E
Honghu	100	29.48 N	113.27 E
Hong Hu ⊜	100	29.52 N	113.23 E
Honghuaerji	89	48.15 N	120.01 E
Honghuaji	100	33.52 N	114.26 E
Honghualiangzi	89	48.06 N	123.12 E
Honghuamu	89	48.33 N	125.39 E
Hongjiang, Zhg.	100	26.49 N	120.03 E
Hongjiang, Zhg.	102	27.07 N	109.56 E
Hong Kong → Victoria	271d	22.17 N	114.09 E
Hong Kong □2, Asia	90	22.15 N	114.10 E
Hong Kong □2, Asia	100	22.15 N	114.10 E
Hong Kong I	271d	22.15 N	114.11 E
Hong Kong, University of ʊ2	271d	22.17 N	114.08 E
Hongkou Park ♠	269b	31.16 N	121.28 E
Honglai	100	25.08 N	118.32 E
Honglanbu	106	31.37 N	118.57 E
Honglinqiao	106	30.59 N	118.59 E
Hongliutai	85	39.48 N	77.26 E
Hongliuyuan	102	41.04 N	95.26 E
Honglongdian	106	30.30 N	119.00 E
Honglongtang	105	40.41 N	117.37 E
Honglu	100	25.44 N	119.20 E
Hongluan	100	28.31 N	117.01 E
Hongluo Shan ∧	104	40.56 N	120.42 E
Hongluoxian	104	41.01 N	120.53 E
Hongmeichang	105	39.50 N	115.51 E
Hongmendu	102	26.10 N	102.37 E
Hongmenkou	102	27.22 N	100.30 E
Hongmenpu	107	30.37 N	104.08 E
Hongmiaozi	107	28.47 N	104.02 E
Hong Ngu	110	10.48 N	105.21 E
Hongō, Nihon	96	34.24 N	132.59 E
Hongō, Nihon	96	34.17 N	132.02 E
Hongō ◆8	268	35.42 N	139.47 E
Hongpailou	107	30.38 N	104.01 E
Hongqi	89	44.23 N	126.32 E
Hongqiao, Zhg.	100	28.14 N	121.01 E
Hongqiao, Zhg.	105	39.50 N	117.44 E
Hongqiao, Zhg.	106	31.29 N	121.49 E
Hongqiao, Zhg.	269b	31.12 N	121.22 E
Hongqiao Ji Chang ⊠	106	31.12 N	121.20 E
Hongrie → Hungary □1	30	47.00 N	20.00 E
Hongshan, Zhg.	89	48.02 N	129.00 E
Hongshan, Zhg.	98	36.37 N	118.00 E
Hongshanzi	98	42.34 N	117.14 E
Hongshi, Zhg.	89	43.00 N	127.04 E
Hongshi, Zhg.	98	41.21 N	119.32 E
Hongshidou	104	41.52 N	122.11 E
Hongshili	98	40.41 N	125.03 E
Hongshui	102	37.24 N	104.00 E
Hongshui ≃	102	23.45 N	109.30 E
Hongshuichuan	105	40.06 N	117.55 E
Hongshuyangzi	105	40.36 N	116.36 E
Hongsŏng	98	36.36 N	126.39 E
Hongtang	100	26.06 N	119.14 E
Hongtian	100	25.52 N	117.15 E
Hongtong	102	36.19 N	111.39 E
Hongtuwan	98	41.03 N	113.39 E
Hongtu Zhang ∧	100	23.46 N	115.56 E
Honguedo, Détroit d' Ʉ	186	49.15 N	64.00 W
Hongwŏn	98	40.02 N	127.57 E
Hongxin	100	32.43 N	117.47 E
Hongxing	105	39.48 N	116.27 E
Hongxingqiao	106	30.55 N	119.52 E
Hongyang, Zhg.	100	26.32 N	119.27 E
Hongyang, Zhg.	100	23.28 N	116.13 E
Hongyanzi	104	40.38 N	120.31 E
Hongyōtoku	268	35.41 N	139.55 E
Hongze	100	33.19 N	118.53 E
Hongze Hu ⊜	100	33.16 N	118.34 E
Honiara	175e	9.26 S	159.57 E
Honiton	42	50.48 N	3.13 W
Hon-jima I	96	34.23 N	133.47 E
Honjō, Nihon	92	39.23 N	140.03 E
Honjō, Nihon	94	36.24 N	138.01 E
Honjō, Nihon	94	36.14 N	139.11 E
Honkamäki ∧2	26	62.58 N	27.05 E
Hon-kawane	94	35.07 N	138.09 E
Honker Bay ⊂	282	38.04 N	121.56 W
Hönne ≃	263	51.28 N	7.46 E
Honnecourt-sur-Escaut	50	50.02 N	3.12 E
Honningsvåg	24	70.59 N	25.59 E
Hönö	26	57.42 N	11.39 E
Honokaa	229d	20.04 N	155.28 W
Honokahua	229a	21.00 N	156.39 W
Honokawai	229a	20.57 N	156.41 W
Honolulu	229c	21.18 N	157.51 W
Honolulu □6	229c	21.19 N	157.52 W
Honolulu International Airport ⊠	229c	21.20 N	157.55 W
Honomu	229d	19.52 N	155.07 W
Honouliuli	229c	21.22 N	158.02 W
Hönow	54	52.32 N	13.38 E
Hon Quan	110	11.39 N	106.36 E
Honshū I	92	36.00 N	138.00 E
Hontoon Island State Park ♠	220	28.59 N	81.22 W
Höntrop ◆8	263	51.27 N	7.08 E
Honuapo Bay ⊂	229d	19.05 N	155.33 W
Hoo	260	51.25 N	0.34 E
Hood	226	38.22 N	121.31 W
Hood □6	222	32.25 N	97.45 W
Hood ≃, N.T., Can.	176	67.26 N	108.53 W
Hood ≃, Or., U.S.	224	45.42 N	121.30 W
Hood, East Fork ≃	224	45.36 N	121.38 W
Hood, Mount ∧	224	45.23 N	121.41 W
Hood, West Fork ≃	224	45.36 N	121.38 W
Hood Canal ⊂	224	47.35 N	123.00 W
Hood Canal Floating Bridge ◆5	224	47.52 N	122.38 W
Hoodoo Peak ∧	202	48.15 N	120.19 W
Hood Point >, Austl.	162	34.23 S	119.34 E
Hood Point >, Pap. N. Gui.	164	10.05 S	147.45 E
Hood Pond ⊜	283	42.40 N	70.57 W
Hood River	224	45.42 N	121.31 W
Hoodsport	224	47.24 N	123.08 W
Hoods Range ϰ	166	28.35 S	144.30 E
Hoof	56	51.17 N	9.20 E
Hoogerheide	52	51.25 N	4.20 E
Hoogeveen	52	52.43 N	6.29 E
Hoogeveense Vaart ≅	52	52.42 N	6.11 E
Hoogezand-Sappemeer	52	53.09 N	6.47 E
Hoogkerk	52	53.13 N	6.30 E
Hooglede	50	50.59 N	3.05 E
Hoogstede	52	52.34 N	6.56 E
Hoogstraten	56	51.24 N	4.46 E
Hoogte	158	27.28 S	28.03 E
Hoogvliet	52	51.52 N	4.21 E
Hook	42	51.17 N	0.58 W
Hook ◆8	260	51.22 N	0.18 W
Hooker	196	36.51 N	101.12 W
Hooker, Bi'r ╤4	142	30.23 N	30.20 E
Hooker Creek	162	18.20 S	130.40 E
Hooker Creek Aboriginal Reserve ◆4	162	18.10 S	130.25 E
Hook Head >	48	52.07 N	6.55 W
Hookina	166	31.45 S	138.20 E
Hook Island I	166	20.08 S	148.55 E
Hook Mountain State Park ♠	276	41.09 N	73.55 W
Hook Norton	42	51.59 N	1.29 W
Hook Point >	166	25.48 S	153.05 E
Hooks	194	33.28 N	94.15 W
Hooksiel	52	53.38 N	8.01 E
Hoolehua	229a	21.10 N	157.04 W
Hoonah	180	58.07 N	135.26 W
Hoopa	204	41.03 N	123.40 W
Hoopa Valley Indian Reservation ◆4	204	41.08 N	123.40 W
Hooper	198	41.36 N	96.32 W
Hooper Bay	180	61.31 N	166.06 W
Hooper Islands II	208	38.20 N	76.13 W
Hooper Strait Ʉ	208	38.12 N	76.03 W
Hoopersville	208	38.15 N	76.10 W
Hoopes Reservoir ⊜1	285	39.47 N	75.37 W
Hoopeston	216	40.28 N	87.40 W
Hooping Harbour	186	50.37 N	56.17 W
Hoople	198	48.32 N	97.38 W
Hoopstad	158	27.54 S	25.58 E
Hoopstick Brook ≃	276	40.39 N	74.41 W
Höör	41	55.56 N	13.32 E
Hoorn	52	52.38 N	5.04 E
Hoorn, Kap → Hornos, Cabo de >	254	55.59 S	67.16 W
Hoosac Range ϰ	207	42.45 N	73.02 W
Hoosac Tunnel ◆5	207	42.41 N	73.03 W
Hoosic ≃	210	42.54 N	73.39 W
Hoosick	210	42.52 N	73.20 W
Hoosick Falls	210	42.54 N	73.21 W
Hooton	262	53.18 N	2.57 W
Hoot Owl Estates	285	39.53 N	74.50 W
Hoover Dam ◆6	200	36.00 N	114.27 W
Hoover Reservoir ⊜1	214	40.08 N	82.53 W
Hooversville	214	40.08 N	78.54 W
Hopa	130	41.25 N	41.24 E
Hopatcong	210	40.55 N	74.39 W
Hopatcong, Lake ⊜	210	40.57 N	74.38 W
Hopatcong State Park ♠	276	40.55 N	74.40 W
Hop Bottom	210	41.42 N	75.46 W
Hop Brook ≃	276	40.19 N	74.08 W
Hope, B.C., Can.	182	49.23 N	121.26 W
Hope, Ak., U.S.	180	60.55 N	149.38 W
Hope, Ar., U.S.	194	33.40 N	93.35 W
Hope, In., U.S.	218	39.18 N	85.46 W
Hope, N.J., U.S.	210	40.54 N	74.58 W
Hope, N.D., U.S.	198	47.19 N	97.43 W
Hope, R.I., U.S.	207	41.44 N	71.33 W
Hope, Ben ∧	46	58.24 N	4.37 W
Hope, Loch ⊜	46	58.27 N	4.39 W
Hope, Point >	180	68.21 N	166.50 W
Hope Bay ⊂	212	44.55 N	81.08 W
Hopedale, Nf., Can.	176	55.28 N	60.13 W
Hopedale, Il., U.S.	194	40.25 N	89.24 W
Hopedale, La., U.S.	194	29.49 N	89.39 W
Hopedale, Ma., U.S.	207	42.07 N	71.32 W
Hopedale, Oh., U.S.	214	40.19 N	80.54 W
Hope Farm	210	41.44 N	73.40 W
Hopefield	158	33.04 S	18.22 E
Hopeh → Hebei □4	98	38.00 N	116.00 E
Hope Island I, B.C., Can.	182	50.55 N	127.53 W
Hope Island I, On., Can.	212	44.55 N	80.12 W
Hopeland	208	40.14 N	76.16 W
Hopelawn	276	40.31 N	74.17 W
Hopelchén	232	19.46 N	89.51 W
Hopeman	46	57.42 N	3.25 W
Hope Mills	192	34.58 N	78.56 W
Hopes Advance, Cap >	176	61.04 N	69.34 W
Hopetoun, Austl.	162	33.57 S	120.07 E
Hopetoun, Austl.	166	35.44 S	142.22 E
Hopetown	158	29.34 S	24.03 E
Hope Vale Aboriginal Reserve ◆4	164	15.10 S	145.15 E
Hope Valley, Austl.	168b	34.50 S	138.44 E
Hope Valley, R.I., U.S.	207	41.30 N	71.43 W
Hopewell, N.J., U.S.	208	40.23 N	74.45 W
Hopewell, Pa., U.S.	214	40.08 N	78.16 W
Hopewell, Va., U.S.	208	37.18 N	77.17 W
Hopewell Islands II	176	58.25 N	78.00 W
Hopewell Junction	210	41.35 N	73.48 W
Hopewell Village National Historic Site ⊥	208	40.12 N	75.46 W
Hopfgarten	64	47.27 N	12.10 E
Hopfgarten in Defereggen	64	46.55 N	12.31 E
Hopi → Hebi	98	35.59 N	114.11 E
Hopi Buttes ∧	200	35.20 N	110.15 W
Hopi Indian Reservation ◆4	200	35.45 N	110.35 W
Hopkins, Mi., U.S.	216	42.37 N	85.45 W
Hopkins, Mo., U.S.	194	40.33 N	94.49 W
Hopkins □6	222	33.07 N	95.35 W
Hopkins ≃	166	38.24 S	142.31 E
Hopkins, Lake ⊜	162	24.15 S	128.50 E
Hopkins Creek ≃	284a	43.17 N	78.46 W
Hopkinsville	194	36.51 N	87.29 W
Hopkinton, Ia., U.S.	190	42.20 N	91.14 W
Hopkinton, Ma., U.S.	207	42.13 N	71.31 W
Hopkinton, R.I., U.S.	207	41.27 N	71.46 W
Hopland	204	38.58 N	123.06 W
Hopólito Bouchard	252	34.43 S	63.31 W
Hoppegarten	264a	52.31 N	13.40 E
Hoppenrade	264a	52.32 N	12.56 E
Hoppo → Hepu	102	21.39 N	109.11 E
Hopsten	52	52.23 N	7.36 E
Hoptrup	41	55.11 N	9.28 E
Ho Pui	271d	22.25 N	114.03 E
Hopwood, Mount ∧	166	21.49 S	144.26 E
Hoque	152	14.39 S	13.54 E
Hoquiam	224	46.58 N	123.53 W
Hoquiam, East Fork ≃	224	46.58 N	123.54 W
Hora Califo	144	8.49 N	43.07 E
Horace Mountain ∧	180	67.40 N	149.06 W
Horadiz	84	39.27 N	47.20 E
Horado	94	35.36 N	136.50 E
Hōrai	94	34.56 N	137.34 E
Horancia	144	6.31 N	38.44 E
Horasan	130	40.03 N	42.11 E
Horatio	194	33.56 N	94.21 W
Horatio Gardens	278	42.10 N	87.57 W
Horažďovice	60	49.20 N	13.43 E
Horbachevo-Mykhaylivka	83	47.50 N	38.00 E
Horb am Neckar	58	48.26 N	8.41 E
Horbelev	41	54.49 N	12.04 E
Horbourg	58	48.05 N	7.23 E
Hörby	41	55.51 N	13.39 E
Horconcitos	236	8.19 N	82.10 W
Hordaland □6	26	60.15 N	6.30 E
Hörde ◆8	263	51.29 N	7.30 E
Horden	44	54.46 N	1.18 W
Horden ≃	164	3.50 S	141.25 E
Horezu	38	45.08 N	23.59 E
Horgen	58	47.15 N	8.36 E
Horhany ϰ	78	48.30 N	24.00 E
Hořice	30	50.22 N	15.38 E
Horicon	190	43.27 N	88.37 W
Horigane	268	35.50 N	139.27 E
Horine	219	38.16 N	90.25 W
Horinger	102	40.23 N	111.53 E
Horinouchi	94	37.14 N	138.56 E
Horinouchi ◆8	268	35.41 N	139.40 E
Horizon Tablemount ✣3	14	19.40 N	168.30 W
Horizontina	252	27.37 S	54.19 W
Horka	54	51.16 N	14.56 E
Hörken	40	60.02 N	14.56 E
Horley	42	51.11 N	0.11 W
Horlick Mountains ϰ	9	85.23 S	121.00 W
Horlivka	83	48.18 N	38.03 E
Horloff ≃	56	50.20 N	8.52 E
Hormigueros	240m	18.09 N	67.08 W
Hormoz, Jazīreh-ye I	128	27.04 N	56.28 E
Hormozgān □4	128	27.50 N	56.00 E
Hormuz, Strait of Ʉ	128	26.34 N	56.15 E
Horn, Dtsch.	52	51.52 N	8.56 E
Horn, Öst.	61	48.40 N	15.40 E
Horn ◆8	52	53.38 N	10.05 E
Horn >	24a	66.28 N	22.28 W
Horn ≃, N.T., Can.	176	61.30 N	118.01 W
Horn ≃, Europe	56	49.15 N	7.20 E
Horn, Ben ∧2	46	58.01 N	4.02 W
Horn, Cape → Hornos, Cabo de >	254	55.59 S	67.16 W
Hornaday ≃	180	69.22 N	123.50 W
Hornafjörður ⊂	24a	64.17 N	15.16 W
Hornavan ⊜	24	66.10 N	17.30 E
Hornbach	56	49.11 N	7.22 E
Hornbæk	41	56.05 N	12.28 E
Hornbeak	194	36.19 N	89.17 W
Hornbeck	194	31.19 N	93.23 W
Hornberg	58	48.13 N	8.13 E
Hornbrook	204	41.55 N	122.33 W
Hornburg	54	52.01 N	10.36 E
Hornby, On., Can.	275b	43.34 N	79.50 W
Hornby, N.Z.	172	43.33 S	172.32 E
Hornby Bay ⊂	176	66.35 N	117.50 W
Horncastle	44	53.13 N	0.07 W
Hornchurch ◆8	260	51.34 N	0.12 E
Horndal	40	60.18 N	16.25 E
Horndean	42	50.55 N	1.00 W
Horndon on the Hill	260	51.31 N	0.25 E
Horne	41	55.06 N	10.11 E
Hornebach ≃	263	51.39 N	7.38 E
Horneburg, Dtsch.	52	53.30 N	9.34 E
Horneburg, Dtsch.	263	51.38 N	7.18 E
Hörnefors	26	63.38 N	19.54 E
Hornell	210	42.19 N	77.39 W
Hornepayne	176	49.13 N	84.47 W
Hornerstown	208	40.06 N	74.30 W
Hornhausen	54	52.02 N	11.10 E
Horn Head >	48	55.14 N	7.59 W
Horn Hill	260	51.37 N	0.32 W
Horní Jiřetín	54	50.35 N	13.32 E
Hornindal	26	61.58 N	6.31 E
Hornindalsvatnet ⊜	26	61.56 N	6.22 E
Hørning	41	56.05 N	10.03 E
Hörningsholm	40	59.03 N	17.40 E
Horní Počernice	54	50.06 N	14.38 E
Hornisgrinde ∧	56	48.36 N	8.12 E
Horn Island I, Austl.	164	10.37 S	142.17 E
Horn Island I, Ms., U.S.	194	30.13 N	88.38 W
Horní Slavkov	54	50.07 N	12.46 E
Horní Stropnice	61	48.46 N	14.44 E
Hornito, Cerro ∧	236	8.39 N	82.09 W
Hornitos	226	37.30 N	120.14 W
Horní Vltavice	60	48.57 N	13.46 E
Horn Lake	194	34.58 N	90.02 W
Horn Lake ⊜	212	45.24 N	79.36 W
Hornos, Cabo de (Cape Horn) >	254	55.59 S	67.16 W
Hornos, Isla I	254	55.57 S	67.17 W
Hornos, Islas de II	288	34.25 S	57.55 W
Hornostayivka	78	47.01 N	33.44 E
Hornow	54	51.38 N	14.31 E
Hornoy	50	49.51 N	1.54 E
Horn Plateau ϰ1	176	62.15 N	119.15 W
Horn Pond ⊜	283	42.28 N	71.09 W
Hornsby, Austl.	170	33.42 S	151.06 E
Hornsby, Il., U.S.	219	39.10 N	89.45 W
Hornsbyville	208	37.11 N	76.28 W
Hornsea	44	53.55 N	0.10 W
Hornsey ◆8	260	51.35 N	0.07 W
Hornslet	41	56.19 N	10.20 E
Hornstorf	54	53.54 N	11.32 E
Hornsyld	41	55.45 N	9.51 E
Horntown	208	37.58 N	75.28 W
Hornu	50	50.26 N	3.49 E
Horodenka, Ukr.	38	48.41 N	25.29 E
Horodenka, Ukr.	78	48.41 N	25.29 E
Horodets'	78	51.17 N	26.19 E
Horodkivka	78	48.23 N	28.42 E
Horodne	78	45.53 N	28.50 E
Horodnya	78	51.53 N	31.36 E
Horodnytsya	78	50.48 N	27.20 E
Horodok, Ukr.	78	49.10 N	26.34 E
Horodok, Ukr.	78	49.47 N	23.39 E
Horodyshche, Ukr.	78	49.17 N	31.27 E
Horodyshche, Ukr.	83	48.19 N	38.39 E
Horodyshche, Ukr.	83	49.03 N	39.38 E
Horokhiv	78	50.30 N	24.45 E
Horokhuvatka	83	49.21 N	37.31 E
Horoshiri-dake ∧	92a	42.43 N	142.41 E
Horotiu	172	37.43 S	175.12 E
Hořovice	60	49.50 N	13.54 E
Horqin Youyi Qianqi (Ulan Hot)	89	46.05 N	122.05 E
Horqin Youyi Zhongqi	89	45.09 N	121.24 E
Horqin Zuoyi Houqi	89	42.58 N	122.20 E
Horqin Zuoyi Zhongqi	89	44.07 N	123.18 E
Horqueta	252	23.24 S	56.53 W
Horrabridge	42	50.31 N	4.05 W
Horrelville	172	43.20 S	172.20 E
Horrem	263	51.06 N	6.48 E
Hörsching	61	48.14 N	14.11 E
Horse ≃	184	56.43 N	111.23 W
Horseback Knob ∧2	218	39.14 N	83.06 W
Horse Cave	194	37.10 N	85.54 W
Horse Creek	200	41.25 N	105.11 W
Horse Creek ≃, U.S.	198	41.57 N	103.58 W
Horse Creek ≃, Co., U.S.	198	38.05 N	103.19 W
Horse Creek ≃, Fl., U.S.	220	27.06 N	81.58 W
Horse Creek ≃, Il., U.S.	219	39.45 N	89.34 W
Horse Creek ≃, Mo., U.S.	194	37.46 N	93.53 W
Horsefly	182	52.20 N	121.24 W
Horsefly Lake ⊜	182	52.25 N	121.00 W
Horsehead Creek ≃	198	43.17 N	103.22 W
Horsehead Lake ⊜	198	47.02 N	99.47 W
Horseheads	210	42.10 N	76.49 W
Horse Islands II	186	50.13 N	55.45 W
Horsell	260	51.19 N	0.34 W
Horseneck Brook ≃	276	41.01 N	73.38 W
Horsens	41	55.52 N	9.52 E
Horsens Fjord ⊂	41	55.50 N	10.05 E
Horseshoe Bend, Ar., U.S.	194	36.15 N	91.43 W
Horseshoe Bend, Id., U.S.	202	43.55 N	116.12 W
Horseshoe Bend National Military Park ♠	194	33.00 N	85.46 W
Horseshoe Cove ⊂	276	40.27 N	74.00 W
Horseshoe Creek ≃	198	42.27 N	104.58 W
Horseshoe Falls ʟ	284a	43.05 N	79.04 W
Horseshoe Lake ⊜, Mb., Can.	184	52.12 N	95.50 W
Horseshoe Lake ⊜, Mi., U.S.	281	42.24 N	83.45 W
Horseshoe Lake ⊜, N.J., U.S.	276	40.52 N	74.38 W
Horse Shoe Reef ✣2	240m	18.40 N	64.12 W
Horsfjärden ⊂	40	59.04 N	18.09 E
Horsford	42	52.41 N	1.15 E
Horsforth	44	53.51 N	1.39 W
Horsham, Austl.	166	36.43 S	142.13 E
Horsham, Eng., U.K.	42	51.04 N	0.21 W
Horsham, Pa., U.S.	208	40.10 N	75.07 W
Hørsholm	41	55.53 N	12.30 E
Hörsingen	54	52.16 N	11.09 E
Horsley	274a	33.51 S	150.51 E
Horslunde	41	54.54 N	11.14 E
Horšovský Týn	60	49.32 N	12.56 E
Horst, Dtsch.	52	53.48 N	9.37 E
Horst, Dtsch.	54	53.22 N	10.37 E
Horst, Ned.	52	51.27 N	6.04 E
Horst ◆8	263	51.32 N	7.02 E
Horsted Keynes	42	51.02 N	0.01 W
Hörstel	52	52.18 N	7.35 E
Horstmar, Dtsch.	52	52.05 N	7.17 E
Horstmar, Dtsch.	263	51.36 N	7.33 E
Horsunlu	130	37.55 N	28.36 E
Horta	148a	38.32 N	28.38 W
Horta □5	148a	38.30 N	29.00 W
Horta ◆8	266d	41.26 N	2.00 E
Hortaleza ◆8	266a	40.28 N	3.39 W
Horten	26	59.25 N	10.30 E
Hortobágy ◆1	30	47.35 N	21.00 E
Hortobágyi Nemzeti Park ♠	30	47.30 N	21.10 E
Horton, Eng., U.K.	260	51.28 N	0.32 W
Horton, In., U.S.	218	40.05 N	86.09 W
Horton, Ks., U.S.	198	39.39 N	95.31 W
Horton, Mi., U.S.	216	42.09 N	84.31 W
Horton ≃	180	70.00 N	126.53 W
Horton in Ribblesdale	44	54.09 N	2.17 W
Horton Kirby	260	51.23 N	0.15 E
Horton Lake ⊜	180	67.29 N	122.31 W
Hortonville, N.Y., U.S.	210	41.46 N	75.02 W
Hortonville, Wi., U.S.	190	44.20 N	88.38 W
Horumersiel	52	53.41 N	8.00 E
Hørup	41	54.56 N	9.55 E
Hørve	41	55.45 N	11.28 E
Horw	58	47.01 N	8.18 E
Horwich	44	53.37 N	2.33 W
Horwood Lake ⊜	190	48.03 N	82.20 W
Hory Matky Boží	60	49.16 N	13.27 E
Horynn' (Goryn') ≃	78	52.08 N	27.17 E
Hōryūji Temple ʊ1	270	34.36 N	135.44 E
Hosaina	144	7.38 N	37.52 E
Hösbach	56	50.00 N	9.12 E
Hosei University ʊ2	268	35.42 N	139.44 E
Hösel	56	51.19 N	6.54 E
Hosena	54	51.27 N	14.01 E
Hoséré Vokré ∧	146	8.20 N	13.15 E
Hoseynābād	128	35.33 N	47.08 E
Hoseynīyeh-ye Khodā-Dād	128	32.42 N	48.14 E
Hosford	192	30.23 N	84.47 W
Hoshāb	128	26.01 N	63.56 E
Hoshangābād	124	22.45 N	77.43 E
Hoshangābād Plain ≚	124	22.35 N	77.25 E
Hoshcha	78	50.36 N	26.41 E
Hoshiārpur, India	123	31.32 N	75.54 E
Hoshiarpur, India	272a	28.35 N	77.22 E
Hoshigajō ∧	96	34.31 N	134.19 E
Hosingen	56	50.01 N	6.05 E
Hosjö	40	60.35 N	15.46 E
Hoskins	164	5.27 S	150.30 E
Hosmer, B.C., Can.	182	49.35 N	114.57 W
Hosmer, S.D., U.S.	198	45.34 N	99.28 W
Hosoe	94	34.49 N	137.39 E
Hospental	58	46.37 N	8.34 E
Hospers	198	43.04 N	95.54 W
Hospet	122	15.16 N	76.24 E
Hospital	48	52.29 N	8.25 W
Hospital de Orbigo	34	42.28 N	5.53 W
Hossegor	32	43.40 N	1.27 W
Hosston	194	32.53 N	93.52 W
Hosta Butte ∧	200	35.35 N	108.12 W
Hoste, Isla I	254	55.15 S	69.00 W
Hostěradice	61	48.57 N	16.15 E
Hostetter	214	40.16 N	79.24 W
Hostigrām	272b	22.26 N	88.31 E
Hostivař ◆8	54	50.01 N	14.32 E
Hostivice	54	50.04 N	14.15 E
Hošt'ka	54	50.30 N	14.20 E
Hostomice	54	50.35 N	13.46 E
Hostotipaquillo	234	21.04 N	104.04 W
Hostouň	60	49.34 N	12.46 E
Hosūr	122	12.43 N	77.49 E
Hot	110	18.06 N	98.36 E
Hota	268	35.08 N	139.51 E
Hotagen	26	63.59 N	14.15 E
Hotagen ⊜	26	63.53 N	14.29 E
Hotagsfjällen ∧	26	64.20 N	14.30 E
Hotaka	94	36.20 N	137.53 E
Hotaka-dake ∧	94	36.17 N	137.39 E
Hotamış	130	37.36 N	33.13 E
Hotan	120	37.08 N	79.54 E
Hotan ≃	90	40.30 N	80.45 E
Hotarele	38	44.10 N	26.22 E
Hotazel	158	27.15 S	23.00 E
Hotchkiss	200	38.47 N	107.43 W
Hotchkissville	207	41.34 N	73.13 W
Hot Creek Range ϰ	204	38.30 N	116.25 W
Hötensleben	54	52.08 N	11.01 E
Hotevilla	200	35.55 N	110.40 W
Hotham ≃	168a	32.58 S	116.22 E
Hotham Inlet ⊂	180	66.45 N	162.00 W
Hotham Peak ∧	180	66.48 N	160.42 W
Hoting	26	64.07 N	16.10 E
Hot Springs, Mt., U.S.	202	47.36 N	114.40 W
Hot Springs → Truth or Consequences, N.M., U.S.	200	33.08 N	107.15 W
Hot Springs, N.C., U.S.	192	35.53 N	82.49 W
Hot Springs, S.D., U.S.	198	43.25 N	103.28 W
Hot Springs, Va., U.S.	192	37.59 N	79.49 W
Hot Springs National Park	194	34.30 N	93.04 W
Hot Springs Peak ∧, Ca., U.S.	204	40.22 N	120.07 W
Hot Springs Peak ∧, Nv., U.S.	204	41.22 N	117.26 W
Hot Springs State Park ♠	202	43.40 N	108.10 W
Hot Sulphur Springs	200	40.04 N	106.06 W
Hottah Lake ⊜	176	65.04 N	118.29 W
Hottentotbaai ⊂	156	26.05 S	14.58 E
Hottentotskloof	158	33.15 S	19.40 E
Hotton	56	50.16 N	5.27 E
Hötzum	54	52.13 N	10.37 E
Houaïlou	175f	21.17 S	165.38 E
Houamuang	110	20.09 N	103.38 E
Houbaishu	106	31.49 N	119.10 E
Houbao	98	41.54 N	125.14 E
Houcheng	106	31.55 N	120.26 E
Houdahepao	104	41.49 N	123.01 E
Houdain	50	50.27 N	2.32 E
Houdan	50	48.47 N	1.36 E
Houdelaincourt	58	48.33 N	5.28 E
Houdeng-Aimeries	50	50.29 N	4.08 E
Houeillès	32	44.12 N	0.02 E
Houffalize	56	50.08 N	5.47 E
Hougang	271c	1.22 N	103.54 E
Hough Green	262	53.23 N	2.47 W
Houghton, Mi., U.S.	190	47.07 N	88.34 W
Houghton, N.Y., U.S.	210	42.25 N	78.09 W
Houghton, Wa., U.S.	224	47.40 N	122.12 W
Houghton Estates ◆8	273d	26.10 S	28.04 E
Houghton Green	262	53.25 N	2.34 W
Houghton Lake	190	44.18 N	84.45 W
Houghton Lake ⊜, Sk., Can.	184	52.23 N	105.08 W
Houghton Lake ⊜, Mi., U.S.	190	44.20 N	84.45 W
Houghton-le-Spring	44	54.51 N	1.28 W
Houghton Regis	42	51.55 N	0.31 W
Houguangzhengtai	104	41.13 N	122.07 E
Hougujiazi	104	42.21 N	123.22 E
Houhuangtukan	104	41.02 N	122.29 E
Houille ≃	56	50.08 N	4.49 E
Houillères de la Sarre, Canal des ≅	56	48.42 N	6.55 E
Houilles	261	48.56 N	2.11 E
Houjiangfushan	105	40.03 N	117.09 E
Houjiaping	107	30.02 N	104.38 E
Houjiaying	105	39.51 N	117.15 E
Houjie	100	22.58 N	113.39 E
Houjiumen	104	42.38 N	123.18 E
Houkou	98	37.34 N	115.09 E
Houliujia	104	40.47 N	122.19 E
Houlka	194	34.02 N	89.01 W
Houlton	188	46.07 N	67.50 W
Houluan	105	39.13 N	116.32 E
Houma, Tonga	174w	21.09 S	175.19 W
Houma, La., U.S.	194	29.35 N	90.43 W
Houma, Zhg.	102	35.36 N	111.21 E
Houmanzhoutun	104	42.29 N	123.14 E
Houmen	100	22.51 N	115.09 E
Houmet Essouq	148	33.59 N	10.51 E
Houmont Park	222	29.50 N	95.13 W
Hound Creek ≃	202	47.13 N	111.23 W
Houndé	150	11.30 N	3.31 W
Hounslow ◆8	42	51.29 N	0.22 W
Houplines	50	50.42 N	2.55 E
Houqianjiayu	104	40.50 N	120.41 E
Houqiao	105	40.04 N	116.39 E
Hourn, Loch ⊂	46	57.08 N	5.36 W
Housatonic	207	42.15 N	73.22 W
Housatonic ≃	207	41.10 N	73.07 W
House	196	34.38 N	103.54 W
House ≃	184	56.13 N	112.31 W
House of Seven Gables ⊥	283	42.32 N	70.53 W
Houserville	214	40.50 N	77.50 W
House Springs	219	38.24 N	90.34 W
Houshan	106	31.03 N	120.21 E
Houston, B.C., Can.	182	54.24 N	126.38 W
Houston, De., U.S.	208	38.55 N	75.30 W
Houston, Mn., U.S.	190	43.45 N	91.34 W
Houston, Ms., U.S.	194	33.53 N	88.59 W
Houston, Mo., U.S.	194	37.19 N	91.57 W
Houston, Oh., U.S.	216	40.15 N	84.20 W
Houston, Pa., U.S.	214	40.14 N	80.12 W
Houston, Tx., U.S.	222	29.45 N	95.21 W
Houston □6	222	31.20 N	95.20 W
Houston ≃	194	30.16 N	93.13 W
Houston, Lake ⊜1	222	29.58 N	95.07 W
Houston County Lake ⊜1	222	31.25 N	95.35 W
Houston Creek ≃	218	38.13 N	84.15 W
Houston Intercontinental Airport ⊠	222	29.59 N	95.27 W
Houston Ship Channel ≅	222	29.21 N	94.47 W
Hout ≃	156	23.04 S	29.36 E
Houtbaai	158	34.03 S	18.21 E
Houthalen	56	51.02 N	5.22 E
Houthulst	50	50.59 N	2.57 E
Houtkop	158	26.36 S	27.52 E
Houtkraal	158	30.23 S	24.05 E
Houtman Abrolhos II	162	28.43 S	113.48 E
Houtskär I	26	60.12 N	21.22 E
Houtzdale	214	40.49 N	78.21 W
Houwuliangdian	104	41.31 N	121.55 E
Houwutaigou	104	41.46 N	121.42 E
Houx	261	48.34 N	1.37 E
Houxijie	100	28.46 N	118.49 E
Houxinlitun	104	41.05 N	122.33 E
Houxinqiu	104	42.34 N	122.43 E
Houyatai	104	41.26 N	121.49 E
Houying	105	39.42 N	118.18 E
Houyingzi	98	40.24 N	123.50 E
Houzhangcun	105	40.08 N	116.11 E
Houzhou	106	31.35 N	119.22 E
Houzitun	104	41.04 N	121.18 E
Hov	41	55.55 N	10.16 E
Hova	40	58.52 N	14.13 E
Hovborg	41	55.36 N	8.57 E
Høve, Dan.	41	55.50 N	11.30 E
Hove, Eng., U.K.	42	50.49 N	0.10 W
Hovedgård	41	55.57 N	9.58 E
Hövelhof	52	51.49 N	8.40 E
Hoven, Dan.	41	55.51 N	8.46 E
Hoven, S.D., U.S.	198	45.14 N	99.46 W
Hovenweep National Monument ♠	200	37.25 N	109.04 W
Hoverla, hora ∧	78	48.10 N	24.32 E
Hovmantorp	26	56.47 N	15.08 E
Hovran ⊜	40	60.16 N	16.03 E
Hovsta	40	59.21 N	15.13 E
Howa, Ouadi (Wādī Howar) V	140	17.30 N	27.08 E
Howakil I	144	15.10 N	40.16 E
Howar, Wādī (Ouadi Howa) V	140	17.30 N	27.08 E
Howard, Austl.	166	25.19 S	152.34 E
Howard, Ks., U.S.	198	37.28 N	96.15 W
Howard, Oh., U.S.	214	40.24 N	82.19 W
Howard, Pa., U.S.	214	41.00 N	77.39 W
Howard, S.D., U.S.	198	44.00 N	97.31 W
Howard, Wi., U.S.	190	44.32 N	88.05 W
Howard □6, In., U.S.	216	40.29 N	86.08 W
Howard □6, Md., U.S.	208	39.16 N	76.48 W
Howard Beach ◆8	276	40.40 N	73.51 W
Howard City	190	43.23 N	85.28 W
Howard Draw V	196	30.08 N	101.35 W
Howard Hanson Reservoir ⊜1	224	47.15 N	121.45 W
Howard Heights	284b	39.17 N	76.50 W
Howardian Hills ϰ2	44	54.07 N	1.00 W
Howard Island I	164	12.10 S	135.24 E
Howard Lake	190	45.03 N	94.04 W
Howard Prairie Lake ⊜1	202	42.15 N	122.20 W
Howard University ʊ2	284c	38.55 N	77.01 W
Howden	44	53.45 N	0.52 W
Howe, In., U.S.	216	41.43 N	85.25 W
Howe, Tx., U.S.	196	33.30 N	96.37 W
Howe, Cape >	166	37.31 S	149.59 E
Howe Caverns •5	210	42.42 N	74.25 W
Howe Green	260	51.42 N	0.32 E
Howe Island I	212	44.17 N	76.15 W
Howeke	150	4.50 N	7.45 W
Howell	216	42.36 N	83.55 W
Howell Airport ⊠	278	41.39 N	87.45 W
Howell Island I	219	38.40 N	90.42 W
Howells	198	41.43 N	97.00 W
Howells Pond ⊜	276	41.03 N	74.42 W
Howes Cave	210	42.41 N	74.23 W
Howe Sound Ʉ	182	49.22 N	123.18 W
Howe's Range ϰ	170	33.08 S	150.47 E
Howes Valley	170	32.50 S	150.51 E
Howey In The Hills	220	28.43 N	81.47 W
Howick, P.Q., Can.	206	45.11 N	73.51 W
Howick, S. Afr.	158	29.28 S	30.14 E
Howitt, Mount ∧	166	37.10 S	146.40 E
Howland	188	45.14 N	68.39 W
Howland Island I	14	0.48 N	176.38 W
Howley	186	49.10 N	57.07 W
Howley, Mount ∧	186	48.17 N	58.26 W
Howmore	46	57.18 N	7.23 W
Howqua ≃	169	37.14 S	146.08 E
Howrah → Hāora	126	22.35 N	88.20 E
Howse Peak ∧	182	51.49 N	116.41 W
Howser	182	50.18 N	116.57 W
Howson Peak ∧	182	54.25 N	127.44 W
Howth	48	53.23 N	6.04 W
Howth Head >	48	53.22 N	6.03 W
Ho Xa	110	17.04 N	107.02 E
Hoxie, Ar., U.S.	194	36.03 N	90.58 W
Hoxie, Ks., U.S.	198	39.21 N	100.26 W
Höxter	52	51.46 N	9.23 E
Hoxtolgay	86	46.35 N	86.01 E
Hoxton Park	274a	33.55 S	150.51 E
Hoxton Park Aerodrome ⊠	274a	33.54 S	150.50 E
Hoy I	46	58.51 N	3.18 W
Hoya, Dtsch.	52	52.48 N	9.08 E
Hōya, Nihon	94	35.43 N	139.34 E
Høyanger	26	61.13 N	6.05 E
Hoyerswerda	54	51.26 N	14.14 E
Hoylake	44	53.23 N	3.11 W
Hoyleton, Austl.	168b	34.01 S	138.33 E
Hoyleton, Il., U.S.	219	38.27 N	89.16 W
Hoym	54	51.47 N	11.19 E
Hoyos	34	40.10 N	6.43 W
Hōyo-shotō II	96	33.52 N	132.18 E
Höytiäinen ⊜	26	62.48 N	29.39 E
Hoyt Lakes	190	47.31 N	92.08 W
Hoytville, Mi., U.S.	216	42.45 N	84.53 W
Hoytville, Oh., U.S.	216	41.11 N	83.47 W
Hozain ≃	50	48.16 N	4.06 E
Hozat	130	39.07 N	39.14 E
Hozumi	94	35.24 N	136.41 E
Hpru-so	110	19.25 N	97.08 E
Hracholusky, údolní nádrž ⊜1	60	49.47 N	13.07 E
Hradec Králové	30	50.12 N	15.50 E
Hrádek	61	48.46 N	16.16 E
Hrádek nad Nisou	54	50.48 N	14.51 E
Hradiště ∧	54	50.13 N	13.08 E
Hradyz'k	78	49.13 N	33.07 E
Hranice, Česká Rep.	30	49.33 N	17.44 E
Hranice, Česká Rep.	54	50.15 N	12.10 E
Hranitne	83	47.27 N	37.52 E
Hraniv	78	48.52 N	29.34 E
Hrdlovka	54	50.36 N	13.40 E
Hrebinka	78	50.07 N	32.25 E
Hrebinky	78	49.57 N	30.12 E
Hrechyshkyne	83	48.52 N	38.54 E
Hřensko	54	50.50 N	14.14 E
Hriňová	30	48.36 N	19.31 E
Hrob	54	50.39 N	13.44 E
Hrodivka	83	48.15 N	37.23 E
Hromivka	78	46.19 N	34.06 E
Hromokliya ≃	78	47.21 N	32.14 E
Hron ≃	30	47.49 N	18.45 E
Hronov	30	50.29 N	16.12 E
Hrotovice	61	49.06 N	16.07 E
Hrubieszów	30	50.49 N	23.55 E
Hrubý Jeseník ϰ	30	50.00 N	17.20 E
Hrun'	78	50.16 N	34.36 E
Hrušovany	61	48.50 N	16.23 E
Hruzs'kyy Yalanchyk ≃	83	47.07 N	38.04 E
Hrvatska → Croatia □1	36	45.10 N	15.30 E
Hrybova Balka, lis ♠	83	48.09 N	38.37 E
Hryhorivka, Ukr.	78	46.17 N	33.44 E
Hryhorivka, Ukr.	78	51.03 N	32.51 E
Hryhorivka, Ukr.	78	50.05 N	30.39 E
Hrymayliv	78	49.20 N	26.01 E
Hrynyava	78	47.59 N	24.49 E
Hryshkivtsi	78	49.56 N	28.36 E
Hrytsiv	78	49.58 N	27.14 E
Hsenwi	110	23.18 N	97.58 E
Hsiakuan → Xiaguan	102	25.34 N	100.14 E
Hsiamen → Xiamen	100	24.28 N	118.07 E
Hsian → Xi'an	102	34.15 N	108.52 E
Hsiangt'an → Xiangtan	100	27.51 N	112.54 E
Hsiangyang → Xiangfan	102	32.03 N	112.01 E
Hsiaohungt'ou Yü I	100	21.57 N	121.36 E
Hsichih	269d	25.04 N	121.39 E
Hsichi Yü I	100	23.15 N	119.37 E
Hsich'üan Tao I	100	25.59 N	119.56 E
Hsientung	269d	25.09 N	121.44 E
Hsienyang → Xianyang	102	34.22 N	108.42 E
Hsi-hseng	110	20.09 N	97.15 E
Hsihu	100	23.58 N	120.28 E
Hsilo	100	23.48 N	120.27 E
Hsilo ≃	100	23.50 N	120.15 E
Hsim ≃	110	20.48 N	98.31 E
Hsinch'eng	100	24.08 N	121.39 E
Hsinchu	100	24.48 N	120.58 E
Hsinchuang	100	25.02 N	121.27 E
Hsinghua → Xinghua	100	32.57 N	119.50 E
Hsingt'ai → Xingtai	98	37.04 N	114.29 E
Hsinhailien → Lianyungang	98	34.39 N	119.16 E
Hsinhsiang → Xinxiang	98	35.20 N	113.51 E
Hsinhua	100	23.02 N	120.18 E
Hsining → Xining	102	36.38 N	101.55 E
Hsinking → Changchun	89	43.53 N	125.19 E
Hsinpeit'ou ◆8	269d	25.09 N	121.30 E
Hsinp'u → Lianyungang	98	34.39 N	119.16 E
Hsinshih	100	23.05 N	120.17 E
Hsintien	100	24.57 N	121.32 E
Hsintien ≃	269d	25.02 N	121.29 E
Hsinyang → Xinyang	100	32.08 N	114.04 E
Hsipaw	110	22.37 N	97.18 E
Hsiukuluan ≃	100	23.28 N	121.30 E
Hsiyü	100	23.36 N	119.30 E
Hsüanhua → Xuanhua	105	40.37 N	115.03 E
Hsüch'ang → Xuchang	100	34.03 N	113.49 E
Hsüchou → Xuzhou	98	34.16 N	117.11 E
Hsüehchia	100	23.14 N	120.10 E
Hsüeh Shan ∧	100	24.23 N	121.13 E
Hsuphāng	110	20.18 N	98.42 E
Hua'an	100	25.02 N	117.34 E
Huab ≃	156	20.52 S	13.25 E
Huabu	100	29.00 N	118.20 E
Huacaña	248	14.02 S	74.02 W
Huacao	269b	31.14 N	121.19 E
Huacaraje	248	13.33 S	63.45 W
Huachacalla	248	18.45 S	68.17 W
Huacheng	100	24.04 N	115.38 E
Huachi	102	36.43 N	107.52 E
Huachi, Laguna ⊜	248	14.11 S	63.30 W
Huachipa	286d	12.00 S	76.56 W
Huacho	248	11.07 S	77.37 W
Huachón	248	10.40 S	75.57 W
Huachos	248	13.12 S	75.31 W
Huachuca City	200	31.37 N	110.20 W
Huaco	252	30.09 S	68.31 W
Huacrachuco	248	8.39 S	77.05 W
Huade	98	41.46 N	114.16 E
Huadian	89	42.58 N	126.43 E
Huading Shan ∧	100	29.15 N	121.05 E
Huafeng	106	32.14 N	121.16 E
Huagutang	106	30.55 N	119.18 E
Hua Hin	110	12.34 N	99.58 E
Huai ≃, Zhg.	98	37.28 N	114.55 E
Huai ≃, Zhg.	100	32.58 N	118.17 E
Huaiá-Miçu ≃	250	10.52 S	53.15 W
Huai'an (Chaigoubu), Zhg.	98	40.39 N	114.27 E
Huai'an, Zhg.	100	33.32 N	119.10 E
Huaibin	100	32.28 N	115.24 E
Huaide	89	43.32 N	124.50 E
Huaidezhen, Zhg.	89	43.54 N	124.47 E
Huaidezhen, Zhg.	107	28.59 N	105.15 E
Huaihuazhenshi	106	31.05 N	119.41 E
Huaiji	102	24.01 N	112.18 E
Huailai (Shacheng)	105	40.23 N	115.33 E
Huailin	100	31.26 N	117.36 E
Huaillati	248	14.05 S	72.31 W
Huainan	100	32.40 N	117.00 E
Huaining	100	30.25 N	116.38 E
Huairou	105	40.19 N	116.37 E
Huaite → Huaide	89	43.32 N	124.50 E
Huaitunas, Lagunas ⊜	248	13.06 S	66.00 W
Huaiyang	100	33.44 N	114.53 E
Huai Yot	110	7.45 N	99.37 E
Huaiyuan	100	32.57 N	117.12 E
Huaiyu Shan ϰ	100	28.50 N	117.50 E
Huaji	100	32.46 N	115.20 E
Huajiang	102	25.50 N	110.21 E
Huajianzi	104	40.48 N	122.12 E
Huajiapuzi	104	40.52 N	123.14 E
Huajiayingzi	104	42.20 N	121.00 E
Huajimic	234	21.42 N	104.20 W
Huajintepec	234	16.36 N	98.14 W
Huajuapan de León	234	17.48 N	97.46 W

Symbol	English	Deutsch	Español	Français	Português
≃	River	Fluß	Río	Rivière	Rio
≅	Canal	Kanal	Canal	Canal	Canal
ʟ	Waterfall, Rapids	Wasserfall, Stromschnellen	Cascada, Rápidos	Chute d'eau, Rapides	Cascata, Rápidos
Ʉ	Strait	Meeresstraße	Estrecho	Détroit	Estreito
⊂	Bay, Gulf	Bucht, Golf	Bahía, Golfo	Baie, Golfe	Baía, Golfo
⊜	Lake, Lakes	See, Seen	Lago, Lagos	Lac, Lacs	Lago, Lagos
⌸	Swamp	Sumpf	Pantano	Marais	Pântano
✲	Ice Features, Glacier	Eis- und Gletscherformen	Accidentes Glaciales	Formes glaciaires	Acidentes glaciares
╤	Other Hydrographic Features	Andere Hydrographische Objekte	Otros Elementos Hidrográficos	Autres données hydrographiques	Outros acidentes hidrográficos

Symbol	English	Deutsch	Español	Français	Português
✣	Submarine Features	Untermeerische Objekte	Accidentes Submarinos	Formes de relief sous-marin	Acidentes submarinos
□	Political Unit	Politische Einheit	Unidad Politica	Entité politique	Unidade política
ʊ	Cultural Institution	Kulturelle Institution	Institución Cultural	Institution culturelle	Instituição cultural
⊥	Historical Site	Historische Stätte	Sitio Histórico	Site historique	Sitio histórico
♠	Recreational Site	Erholungs- und Ferienort	Sitio de Recreo	Centre de loisirs	Area de Lazer
⊠	Airport	Flughafen	Aeropuerto	Aéroport	Aeroporto
■	Military Installation	Militäranlage	Instalación Militar	Installation militaire	Instalação militar
◆	Miscellaneous	Verschiedenes	Misceláneo	Divers	Diversos

ENGLISH / DEUTSCH

Name	Page / Seite	Lat.°′ / Breite°′	Long.°′ / Länge°′ E = Ost
Huakou	100	25.13 N	117.35 E
Hualahuises	232	24.53 N	99.41 W
Hualalai ∧ 1	229d	19.42 N	155.52 W
Hualañé	252	34.59 S	71.49 W
Hualapai Indian Reservation ⊶ 4	200	35.38 N	113.30 W
Hualapai Mountains ⩘	200	34.50 N	113.55 W
Hualapai Peak ∧	200	35.04 N	113.54 W
Hualfín	252	27.14 S	66.50 W
Hualgayoc	248	6.46 S	78.37 W
Hualien	100	23.59 N	121.36 E
Hualien ≃	100	23.57 N	121.36 E
Hualingpuzi	104	41.31 N	123.54 E
Huallaga ≃	248	5.10 S	75.32 W
Huallamarca, Museo ☉	286d	12.05 S	77.02 W
Huallanca, Perú	248	8.49 S	77.52 W
Huallanca, Perú	248	9.51 S	76.56 W
Huallayabamba ≃	248	7.04 S	77.10 W
Hualmay	248	11.06 S	77.38 W
Hualong	102	36.05 N	102.36 E
Huamanquiquia	248	13.44 S	74.15 W
Huamantla	234	19.19 N	97.56 W
Huambo (Nova Lisboa)	152	12.44 S	15.47 E
Huambo □ 5	152	12.30 S	15.40 E
Huambos	248	6.28 S	78.58 W
Huameiao	100	26.32 N	115.47 E
Huamei Shan ∧	100	25.28 N	113.58 E
Huamuxtitlán	234	17.49 N	98.34 W
Huan ≃	100	30.40 N	114.05 E
Huanan	89	46.13 N	130.32 E
Huancabamba, Perú	248	10.21 S	75.32 W
Huancabamba, Perú	248	5.14 S	79.28 W
Huancané	248	15.12 S	69.46 W
Huancapi	248	13.41 S	74.04 W
Huancarama	248	13.39 S	73.05 W
Huancarqui	248	16.06 S	72.29 W
Huancavelica	248	12.46 S	75.02 W
Huancavelica □ 5	248	13.00 S	75.00 W
Huancaybamba	248	9.05 S	76.50 W
Huancayo	248	12.04 S	75.14 W
Huanchaca	248	20.20 S	66.39 W
Huanchaca, Serranía de ⩘	248	14.30 S	60.39 W
Huandacareo	234	19.59 N	101.17 W
Huando	248	12.29 S	74.58 W
Huang ≃, Asia	110	17.49 N	101.33 E
Huang ≃, T'aiwan	269d	25.14 N	121.37 E
Huang (Yellow) ≃, Zhg.	90	37.32 N	118.19 E
Huang'aicun	106	31.43 N	118.40 E
Huang'an	98	35.28 N	115.42 E
Huang'anshi	100	29.06 N	113.34 E
Huangbai	98	41.17 N	126.21 E
Huangbaozi	102	39.54 N	99.26 E
Huangbeipu	104	42.21 N	123.25 E
Huangcaoping	100	25.42 N	113.27 E
Huangchong	100	22.18 N	113.03 E
Huangchuan	100	32.09 N	115.03 E
Huangcun	105	39.56 N	116.11 E
Huangdaizhen	106	31.26 N	120.33 E
Huangdan	107	29.10 N	103.44 E
Huangda Yang ⊔	100	30.03 N	122.26 E
Huangdi, Zhg.	98	40.14 N	120.15 E
Huangdi, Zhg.	105	40.57 N	118.24 E
Huangdu, Zhg.	106	30.47 N	118.51 E
Huangdu, Zhg.	106	31.16 N	121.13 E
Huangduqiao	100	29.18 N	120.55 E
Huanggai Hu ⊜	100	29.44 N	113.23 E
Huanggang	100	30.27 N	114.52 E
Huanggangji	98	34.39 N	116.03 E
Huanggangkou	100	28.32 N	114.33 E
Huanggang Shan ∧	100	27.50 N	117.45 E
Huanggangshi	100	33.09 N	115.55 E
Huangguayingzi	104	41.46 N	120.46 E
Huangguoshu	102	26.02 N	105.32 E
Huang Hai → Yellow Sea ⊤ 2	90	36.00 N	123.00 E
Huanghe Kou ≃ 1	98	37.54 N	118.48 E
Huangho → Huang ≃	90	37.32 N	118.19 E
Huanghu	106	30.27 N	119.48 E
Huanghua	98	38.22 N	117.21 E
Huanghuadianzi	104	41.44 N	122.48 E
Huanghuashi	100	28.14 N	113.14 E
Huangjialing	104	42.12 N	122.55 E
Huangjialu	106	31.00 N	121.45 E
Huangjiatun	104	41.11 N	122.54 E
Huangjiazhai	106	32.01 N	121.36 E
Huangjinbu	100	28.27 N	116.47 E
Huangjing	106	31.39 N	121.06 E
Huangjinggou	107	29.37 N	104.35 E
Huangjinjing	107	29.44 N	104.38 E
Huangjinzi	89	50.02 N	127.20 E
Huangjuezhen	107	29.50 N	106.27 E
Huangkan	105	40.22 N	116.28 E
Huangkeng	100	27.35 N	117.39 E
Huangkou	102	42.46 N	93.58 E
Huanglaomen	100	29.30 N	115.49 E
Huangli	106	31.39 N	119.42 E
Huanglian	107	29.17 N	106.18 E
Huangling	102	35.41 N	109.09 E
Huanglingji	100	30.25 N	114.03 E
Huanglong, Zhg.	100	31.58 N	112.28 E
Huanglong, Zhg.	102	35.45 N	109.42 E
Huanglongxi	107	30.19 N	103.58 E
Huangmao	100	28.07 N	114.04 E
Huangmapi	100	23.30 N	114.33 E
Huangmei	100	30.04 N	115.56 E
Huangnihe, Zhg.	89	43.32 N	127.59 E
Huangnihe, Zhg.	100	31.06 N	117.22 E
Huangpi, Zhg.	100	30.53 N	114.22 E
Huangpi, Zhg.	100	26.39 N	115.51 E
Huangpu ≃	106	31.24 N	121.31 E
Huangqi	100	26.21 N	119.54 E
Huangqiao	106	32.15 N	120.13 E
Huangqiao ≃	106	32.00 N	120.20 E
Huangshahe	102	26.03 N	110.58 E
Huangshajie	100	29.03 N	113.08 E
Huangshan	98	36.57 N	122.18 E
Huangshanguan	98	37.32 N	120.16 E
Huangshapu, Zhg.	100	26.50 N	113.26 E
Huangshapu, Zhg.	100	25.08 N	112.44 E
Huangshaqiao	100	28.56 N	114.40 E
Huangshatuo	104	41.12 N	122.31 E
Huangshi, Zhg.	100	25.23 N	119.04 E
Huangshi, Zhg.	100	30.13 N	115.05 E
Huangshi, Zhg.	102	29.00 N	111.02 E
Huangshidu	100	27.44 N	116.44 E
Huangshiguan	100	26.15 N	115.54 E
Huangshui	107	30.32 N	103.55 E
Huangtan, Zhg.	100	27.44 N	119.58 E
Huangtan, Zhg.	100	26.41 N	117.17 E
Huangtan ≃	100	24.48 N	116.31 E
Huangtang, Zhg.	100	23.44 N	114.58 E
Huangtang, Zhg.	106	31.46 N	120.21 E
Huangtang, Zhg.	106	31.47 N	119.40 E
Huangtang Hu ⊜	100	30.00 N	114.12 E
Huangtankou	100	28.50 N	118.53 E
Huangtantuan	100	30.53 N	113.33 E
Huangtian	100	23.52 N	114.58 E
Huangtianfan	100	29.10 N	120.08 E
Huangtu, Zhg.	100	27.36 N	118.00 E
Huangtu, Zhg.	106	31.52 N	120.03 E
Huangtuchang	107	30.41 N	104.18 E
Huangtugang	100	31.25 N	115.05 E
Huangtukan	104	41.21 N	122.45 E
Huangtuliangzi	98	41.14 N	118.39 E
Huangtuling	100	27.18 N	113.30 E
Huangtupo	105	39.47 N	116.16 E
Huanguelén	252	37.02 S	61.57 W
Huangwan	106	30.22 N	120.48 E
Huangxian	98	37.38 N	120.29 E
Huangxu	106	32.06 N	119.37 E
Huangyaguan	105	40.14 N	117.26 E
Huangyan	100	28.39 N	121.15 E
Huangyang Shan ⩘	105	40.20 N	115.00 E
Huangyanzhuang	105	40.01 N	118.21 E
Huangyuan	102	36.40 N	101.12 E
Huangyuzeng	104	42.05 N	124.11 E
Huangze	100	29.35 N	120.55 E
Huangze Yang ⊔	100	30.36 N	122.28 E
Huangzhai	100	29.27 N	120.00 E
Huangzhong	102	36.31 N	101.40 E
Huangzhu	110	19.29 N	110.24 E
Huangzhuang, Zhg.	100	34.05 N	112.15 E
Huangzhuang, Zhg.	105	39.29 N	117.31 E
Huangzhuang, Zhg.	105	39.53 N	117.05 E
Huangzhuang Wa ⊜	105	39.33 N	117.33 E
Huaning	102	24.14 N	102.56 E
Huaniugouzi	104	41.34 N	122.35 E
Huaniupuzi	104	41.23 N	123.31 E
Huanjiang	102	24.54 N	108.21 E
Huanren	98	41.14 N	125.21 E
Huanta	248	12.56 S	74.15 W
Huantai (Suozhen)	98	36.59 N	118.06 E
Huantan	100	31.49 N	113.04 E
Huántar	248	9.26 S	77.15 W
Huánuco	248	9.55 S	76.14 W
Huánuco □ 5	248	9.30 S	75.50 W
Huanuni	248	18.16 S	66.51 W
Huanxi	100	26.34 N	113.36 E
Huanxian	102	36.39 N	107.18 E
Huanxiang ≃	105	39.34 N	117.45 E
Huanxiling	104	41.17 N	123.54 E
Huanzo, Cordillera de ⩘	248	14.30 S	73.20 W
Huapango, Presa ⊜ 1	234	20.00 N	99.40 W
Huapí, Serranías ⩘	236	12.30 N	85.00 W
Huap'ing Yü I	100	25.26 N	121.56 E
Huaqiao, Zhg.	100	28.56 N	121.27 E
Huaqiao, Zhg.	100	29.32 N	117.11 E
Huaqiao, Zhg.	102	27.28 N	110.02 E
Huaqiao, Zhg.	107	30.28 N	103.52 E
Huaqiaozhen	107	30.47 N	106.41 E
Huaqiying	106	32.10 N	118.38 E
Huara	248	19.59 S	69.47 W
Huaral	248	11.30 S	77.12 W
Huaráz	248	9.32 S	77.32 W
Huari	248	9.20 S	77.14 W
Huariaca	248	10.27 S	76.07 W
Huaribamba	248	12.16 S	74.57 W
Huarina	248	16.12 S	68.38 W
Huarmey	248	10.04 S	78.10 W
Huarochirí	248	12.09 S	76.14 W
Huarocondo	248	13.25 S	72.13 W
Huarong	100	29.30 N	112.34 E
Huasaga ≃	246	3.42 S	76.26 W
Hua Sai	110	8.02 N	100.18 E
Huascarán, Nevado ∧	248	9.07 S	77.37 W
Huasco	252	28.28 S	71.14 W
Huasco ≃	252	28.27 S	71.13 W
Huashan	98	34.39 N	116.44 E
Huashaoying	98	40.12 N	114.36 E
Huashi	106	31.50 N	120.28 E
Huatabampo	232	26.50 N	109.38 W
Huatangpu	100	25.48 N	112.52 E
Huating	102	35.09 N	106.38 E
Huatong, Zhg.	98	40.03 N	121.56 E
Huatong, Zhg.	102	23.01 N	106.36 E
Huatusco	234	19.09 N	96.57 W
Huauchinango	234	20.11 N	98.03 W
Huaura	248	11.04 S	77.36 W
Huaura ≃	248	11.06 S	77.39 W
Huautla, Méx.	234	21.02 N	98.17 W
Huautla, Méx.	234	18.08 N	96.51 W
Huaxian (Daokou), Zhg.	98	35.37 N	114.32 E
Huaxian, Zhg.	100	23.22 N	113.12 E
Huaxian, Zhg.	102	34.30 N	109.40 E
Huayan	107	30.01 N	105.02 E
Huayang	107	30.32 N	104.04 E
Huayangzhen	102	33.25 N	107.44 E
Huaying Shan ∧	107	30.10 N	106.42 E
Huayingtai	104	40.43 N	122.19 E
Huayllay	248	11.01 S	76.21 W
Huayna Potosí, Nevado ∧	248	16.16 S	68.11 W
Huaytará	248	13.36 S	75.22 W
Hua Yü I	100	23.24 N	119.19 E
Huayuan, Zhg.	98	42.17 N	127.07 E
Huayuan, Zhg.	100	31.16 N	113.58 E
Huayuan, Zhg.	102	28.34 N	109.13 E
Huayuanzui	100	33.00 N	118.16 E
Huayunca, Nevado ∧	248	14.39 S	72.28 W
Huayuri, Pampa de ≚	248	14.30 S	75.30 W
Huazhou	102	21.40 N	110.33 E
Huazi	104	41.25 N	123.29 E
Huazigou	104	41.50 N	121.01 E
Huazikou	106	32.13 N	118.57 E
Ḥubārah, Wādī V	142	27.21 N	31.39 E
Ḥubayṭah, Bi'r ⊤ 4	142	30.27 N	32.27 E
Hubbard, Ia., U.S.	190	42.18 N	93.18 W
Hubbard, Oh., U.S.	214	41.09 N	80.34 W
Hubbard, Or., U.S.	224	45.10 N	122.48 W
Hubbard, Tx., U.S.	222	31.50 N	96.47 W
Hubbard Creek ≃	196	32.54 N	98.53 W
Hubbard Creek Reservoir ⊜ 1	196	32.45 N	99.00 W
Hubbard Lake ⊜	190	44.49 N	83.34 W
Hubbards	186	44.38 N	64.04 W
Hubbardston	207	42.28 N	72.00 W
Hubbell	190	47.10 N	88.25 W
Hubbell Trading Post National Historic Site ⊥	200	35.43 N	109.33 W
Hubbelrath ⊶ 8	263	51.16 N	6.55 E
Hubei (Hupeh) □ 4	90	31.00 N	112.00 E
Huben, Öst.	64	47.03 N	10.58 E
Huben, Öst.	64	46.56 N	12.34 E
Huberdeau	206	45.58 N	74.38 W
Huber Heights	218	39.50 N	84.07 W
Hublersburg	210	40.58 N	77.37 W
Hubli-Dhārwār	122	15.21 N	75.10 E
Hubuleng	102	41.19 N	111.08 E
Hubynykha	78	48.48 N	35.15 E
Hucaogang	106	32.00 N	120.29 E
Hucclecote	42	51.51 N	2.11 W
Huch'ang	98	41.25 N	127.03 E
Hucheng	100	25.26 N	118.27 E
Huchi	100	31.08 N	117.40 E
Huchow → Huzhou	106	30.52 N	120.06 E
Huckarde ⊶ 8	263	51.32 N	7.24 E
Hückelhoven	56	51.03 N	6.13 E
Hückeswagen	56	51.08 N	7.20 E
Hucking	260	51.18 N	0.39 E
Huckingen ⊶ 8	263	51.22 N	6.43 E
Huckitta Creek ≃	162	22.38 S	135.30 E
Huckleberry Island I	276	40.53 N	73.45 W
Huckleberry Mountain ∧	202	43.51 N	122.19 W
Huckleberry Mountain ∧ 2	212	44.28 N	75.28 W
Hucknall	42	53.02 N	1.11 W
Hucqueliers	50	50.34 N	1.54 E
Hucun	105	39.02 N	115.56 E
Hudangtou	106	30.48 N	121.22 E
Huddart Park ♦	282	37.26 N	122.19 W
Hudderfield Narrow Canal ≋	262	53.29 N	2.06 W
Huddersfield	44	53.39 N	1.47 W
Huddinge	40	59.14 N	17.59 E
Huddle Park Municipal Golf Course ♦	273d	26.09 S	28.07 E
Huddunge	40	60.03 N	16.59 E
Hude	52	53.07 N	8.27 E
Huder	89	50.00 N	121.37 E
Hudgin Creek ≃	194	33.40 N	91.59 W
Hūdī	140	17.42 N	34.17 E
Hudiksvall	26	61.44 N	17.07 E
Hudong	100	22.51 N	115.56 E
Hudson, P.Q., Can.	206	45.27 N	74.09 W
Hudson, Il., U.S.	216	40.36 N	88.59 W
Hudson, In., U.S.	216	41.31 N	85.04 W
Hudson, Ia., U.S.	190	42.24 N	92.27 W
Hudson, Md., U.S.	208	38.35 N	76.15 W
Hudson, Ma., U.S.	207	42.23 N	71.34 W
Hudson, Mi., U.S.	216	41.51 N	84.21 W
Hudson, N.H., U.S.	207	42.45 N	71.26 W
Hudson, N.Y., U.S.	210	42.15 N	73.47 W
Hudson, N.C., U.S.	192	35.50 N	81.29 W
Hudson, Oh., U.S.	214	41.14 N	81.26 W
Hudson, S.D., U.S.	198	43.07 N	96.27 W
Hudson, Tx., U.S.	222	31.19 N	94.50 W
Hudson, Wi., U.S.	190	44.58 N	92.45 W
Hudson, Wy., U.S.	200	42.54 N	108.34 W
Hudson □ 6	276	40.44 N	74.02 W
Hudson ≃, U.S.	188	40.42 N	74.02 W
Hudson ≃, Ga., U.S.	192	34.14 N	83.10 W
Hudson, Cerro ∧	254	46.04 S	73.10 W
Hudson, Lake ⊜ 1	194	36.20 N	95.05 W
Hudson Bay	184	52.52 N	102.25 W
Hudson Bay ⊂	176	60.00 N	86.00 W
Hudson-Bayonet Point	220	28.21 N	82.41 W
Hudson Falls	210	43.18 N	73.35 W
Hudson Highlands State Park ♦	210	41.26 N	73.58 W
Hudson Hope	182	56.02 N	121.55 W
Hudson Lake	216	41.42 N	86.32 W
Hudson Mountains ⩘	9	74.32 S	99.20 W
Hudsons Peak ∧	171b	36.26 S	149.10 E
Hudson Strait ⊔	176	62.30 N	72.00 W
Hudsonville	216	42.52 N	85.51 W
Hudwin Lake ⊜	184	53.12 N	95.42 W
Hue	110	16.28 N	107.36 E
Huebra ≃	34	41.02 N	6.48 W
Huechucuicui, Punta >	254	41.47 S	74.02 W
Huechulafquen, Lago ⊜	254	39.46 S	71.28 W
Huechuraba	286e	33.21 S	70.40 W
Huedin	38	46.52 N	23.02 E
Huehuetán	236	15.01 N	92.22 W
Huehuetenango	236	15.20 N	91.28 W
Huehuetenango □ 5	236	15.40 N	91.35 W
Huehuetlán El Chico	234	18.21 N	98.42 W
Huejúcar	234	22.21 N	103.13 W
Huejuquilla El Alto	234	22.36 N	103.52 W
Huejutla de Reyes	234	21.08 N	98.25 W
Huelgoat	32	48.22 N	3.45 W
Huelma	34	37.39 N	3.27 W
Huelva	34	37.16 N	6.57 W
Huelva □ 4	34	37.30 N	6.55 W
Huelva, Río de ≃	34	37.27 N	6.00 W
Huenque ≃	248	16.12 S	69.44 W
Huentelauquén	252	31.35 S	71.32 W
Huércal-Overa	34	37.23 N	1.57 W
Huerfano ≃	198	38.14 N	104.15 W
Huerfano Mountain ∧	200	36.26 N	107.51 W
Huerhuero Creek ≃	226	35.40 N	120.42 W
Huerlumada	120	32.45 N	90.00 E
Huerva ≃	34	41.39 N	0.52 W
Huesca	34	42.08 N	0.25 W
Huesca □ 4	34	42.05 N	0.10 W
Huéscar	34	37.49 N	2.32 W
Hueston Woods State Park ♦	218	39.34 N	84.44 W
Huetamo de Núñez	234	18.35 N	100.53 W
Huete	34	40.08 N	2.41 W
Huey	219	38.36 N	89.17 W
Hueyapan de Ocampo	234	18.07 N	95.09 W
Hueytown	194	33.27 N	86.59 W
Hufengzhen	107	29.43 N	106.07 E
Hüffenhardt	56	49.18 N	9.04 E
Huffman	222	30.01 N	95.05 W
Huffman Dam ⊶ 6	218	39.48 N	84.05 W
Hüfingen	58	47.55 N	8.29 E
Ḥufrat an-Naḥās	140	9.45 N	24.19 E
Hufu	106	31.16 N	119.47 E
Hügel, Villa ☉	263	51.25 N	7.01 E
Huggins, Mount ∧	9	78.17 S	162.28 E
Hugh ≃	162	25.01 S	134.01 E
Hugh Butler Lake ⊜ 1	198	40.22 N	100.42 W
Hughenden	166	20.51 S	144.12 E
Hughes, Austl.	162	30.42 S	129.31 E
Hughes, Ak., U.S.	180	66.03 N	154.16 W
Hughes, Ar., U.S.	194	34.56 N	90.28 W
Hughes ≃	184	56.46 N	100.01 W
Hughes, South Fork ≃	188	39.08 N	81.20 W
Hughes Airport ⊠	280	33.58 N	118.25 W
Hughes Creek ≃	169	36.53 S	145.08 E
Hughes Springs	222	33.05 N	94.38 W
Hughesville, Md., U.S.	208	38.31 N	76.47 W
Hughesville, Pa., U.S.	210	41.14 N	76.43 W
Hugh Keenleyside Dam ⊶ 6	182	49.20 N	117.49 W
Hughson	226	37.36 N	120.52 W
Hughsonville	210	41.35 N	73.56 W
Hugh Town	42a	49.55 N	6.17 W
Hugli ≃	126	21.55 N	88.05 E
Hugli-Chinsurah	126	22.54 N	88.24 E
Hugo, Co., U.S.	198	39.08 N	103.28 W
Hugo, Ok., U.S.	196	34.00 N	95.30 W
Hugo Lake ⊜ 1	196	34.05 N	95.25 W
Hugoton	198	37.10 N	101.20 W
Hugou	100	33.23 N	117.08 E
Huguenot	210	41.25 N	74.38 W
Huguenot Lake ⊜	276	40.56 N	73.47 W
Huhehot → Hohhot	102	40.51 N	111.40 E
Huhsi	100	23.35 N	119.39 E
Hui'an, Zhg.	100	25.04 N	118.47 E
Huian, Zhg.	106	31.47 N	121.45 E
Huiarau Range ⩘	172	38.45 S	177.00 E
Huib-Hoch Plateau ⩘ 1	156	27.00 S	16.45 E
Huibie Yang ⊔	100	30.08 N	121.44 E
Huibu	100	28.18 N	115.15 E
Huichang, Zhg.	100	25.34 N	115.49 E
Huichang, Zhg.	105	39.04 N	115.04 E
Huichapan	234	20.23 N	99.39 W
Hŭich'ŏn	98	40.10 N	126.17 E
Huichou → Huizhou	100	23.05 N	114.24 E
Huichuan	102	35.11 N	104.02 E
Huicungo	248	7.17 S	76.48 W
Huidong	102	26.41 N	102.36 E
Huidui	105	39.04 N	117.16 E
Huihe, Zhg.	89	48.12 N	119.17 E
Huihe, Zhg.	106	31.45 N	121.43 E
Huiji ≃	100	33.53 N	115.36 E
Huíla	152	15.04 S	13.32 E
Huíla □ 5, Ang.	152	15.00 S	15.00 E
Huila □ 5, Col.	246	2.30 N	75.45 W
Huila, Nevado del ∧	246	3.00 N	76.00 W
Huilai	100	23.04 N	116.18 E
Huili	102	26.43 N	102.10 E
Huiliuji	100	32.50 N	115.58 E
Huillapima	252	28.44 S	65.59 W
Huilong, Zhg.	100	27.30 N	118.24 E
Huilong, Zhg.	100	25.22 N	116.24 E
Huilong, Zhg.	100	24.09 N	113.58 E
Huilong, Zhg.	107	30.28 N	105.26 E
Huilong, Zhg.	107	30.35 N	105.49 E
Huilongchang, Zhg.	107	29.41 N	104.17 E
Huilongchang, Zhg.	107	30.18 N	103.39 E
Huilongchang, Zhg.	107	30.41 N	106.34 E
Huilongchang, Zhg.	107	29.17 N	105.01 E
Huimanguillo	234	17.51 N	93.23 W
Huimin	98	37.29 N	117.29 E
Huinan (Chaoyang)	98	42.40 N	126.00 E
Huínaymarca, Lago ⊜	248	16.20 S	68.50 W
Huinca Renancó	252	34.50 S	64.23 W
Hüinghausen	263	51.11 N	7.48 E
Huining	102	35.41 N	105.08 E
Huisachal	196	26.47 N	101.07 W
Huisduinen	52	52.56 N	4.44 E
Huishan	106	31.35 N	120.16 E
Huishui	102	26.07 N	106.24 E
Huismes	50	47.14 N	0.15 E
Huisne ≃	50	47.59 N	0.11 E
Huissen	52	51.57 N	5.56 E
Huistepec	234	16.39 N	98.20 W
Huiten Nur ⊜	120	35.30 N	92.00 E
Huiting	98	34.05 N	116.04 E
Huitiupan	234	17.13 N	92.39 W
Huitong	102	26.54 N	109.31 E
Huitongqiao	102	24.43 N	98.56 E
Huittinen (Lauttakylä)	26	61.11 N	22.42 E
Huitzilán	234	19.58 N	97.41 W
Huitzo	234	17.15 N	96.52 W
Huitzuco de los Figueroa	234	18.18 N	99.21 W
Huixian	102	33.47 N	106.16 E
Huixtla	232	15.09 N	92.28 W
Huiyang → Huizhou	100	23.05 N	114.24 E
Huiyao	100	27.16 N	118.05 E
Huize	102	26.27 N	103.09 E
Huizen	52	52.17 N	5.14 E
Huizhou	100	23.05 N	114.24 E
Hujia, Zhg.	104	41.20 N	121.52 E
Hujia, Zhg.	106	31.25 N	121.37 E
Hujiadian	107	29.41 N	104.07 E
Hujiajie	104	41.06 N	122.10 E
Hujiasi	107	29.16 N	105.13 E
Hujiawopu	104	42.34 N	122.11 E
Hujiayu	105	39.28 N	115.27 E
Hujiazhuang, Zhg.	105	39.51 N	117.07 E
Hujiazhuang, Zhg.	269b	31.21 N	121.25 E
Hujie	102	24.56 N	100.32 E
Hukeng	100	27.29 N	114.18 E
Hukou	100	29.45 N	116.13 E
Hŭksan-chedo II	98	34.30 N	125.20 E
Hukui → Fukui	94	36.04 N	136.13 E
Ḥukūmah	140	13.52 N	36.07 E
Hukuntsi	156	24.02 S	21.48 E
Hukuoka → Fukuoka	96	33.35 N	130.24 E
Hukusima → Fukushima	92	37.45 N	140.28 E
Hukuyama → Fukuyama	96	34.29 N	133.22 E
Ḥula, ʿÉmeq ≚ 1	132	33.08 N	35.37 E
Hulahula ≃	180	70.00 N	144.01 W
Hulan	89	46.00 N	126.38 E
Hulan ≃	89	45.55 N	126.41 E
Hulan Ergi	89	47.13 N	123.39 E
Hulbert, Mi., U.S.	190	46.21 N	85.09 W
Hulbert, Ok., U.S.	194	35.55 N	95.08 W
Hulberton	210	43.15 N	78.04 W
Ḥulda	132	31.50 N	34.53 E
Huldrefossen ∟	26	61.28 N	5.58 E
Hulei	100	24.50 N	116.48 E
Huleia Stream ≃	229b	21.57 N	159.22 W
Hulett	198	44.40 N	104.36 W
Hulín, Česká Rep.	30	49.19 N	17.28 E
Hulin, Zhg.	89	45.46 N	132.59 E
Hulin ≃, Zhg.	89	44.55 N	122.35 E
Hulin ≃, Zhg.	89	45.19 N	124.06 E
Huliu ≃	98	40.10 N	114.33 E
Hull, P.Q., Can.	212	45.26 N	75.43 W
Hull → Kingston upon Hull, Eng., U.K.	44	53.45 N	0.20 W
Hull, Il., U.S.	219	39.43 N	91.13 W
Hull, Ia., U.S.	198	43.11 N	96.08 W
Hull, Ma., U.S.	207	42.18 N	70.54 W
Hull, Tx., U.S.	222	30.09 N	94.39 W
Hull □ 6	212	45.40 N	75.35 W
Hull ≃	44	53.44 N	0.19 W
Hullavington	42	51.33 N	2.09 W
Hull Bay ⊂	283	42.18 N	70.53 W
Hullbridge	42	51.37 N	0.38 E
Hullo	76	59.00 N	23.14 E
Hulmeville	285	40.08 N	74.55 W
Hüls, Dtsch.	56	51.22 N	6.30 E
Hüls, Dtsch.	263	51.40 N	7.08 E
Hülscheid	56	51.16 N	7.34 E
Hülser Berg ⊶ 8	263	51.24 N	6.31 E
Hülser Berg ∧ 2	263	51.23 N	6.33 E
Hulst	52	51.17 N	4.03 E
Hult	40	58.40 N	16.07 E
Hultsfred	26	57.29 N	15.50 E
Huludao	104	40.43 N	121.00 E
Hulufa	105	39.42 N	116.12 E
Hulun → Hailar	89	49.12 N	119.42 E
Hulun Nur ⊜	88	49.01 N	117.32 E
Huluyu	105	40.14 N	116.53 E
Ḥulwān	142	29.51 N	31.20 E
Ḥulwān Observatory ☉ 3	142	29.52 N	31.21 E
Hulyaypole	78	47.38 N	36.16 E
Huma, Tonga	174w	21.19 S	174.57 E
Huma, Zhg.	89	51.43 N	126.38 E
Huma ≃	89	51.40 N	126.44 E
Humacao	240m	18.09 N	65.50 W
Humahuaca	252	23.12 S	65.21 W
Humaitá, Bra.	248	7.31 S	63.02 W
Humaitá, Para.	252	27.03 S	58.33 W
Humaitá ≃	248	8.16 S	72.44 W
Humansdorp	158	34.02 S	24.46 E
Humansville	194	37.47 N	93.34 W
Humara, Jabal al- ∧	140	16.16 N	30.59 E
Humarock	283	42.08 N	70.41 W
Ḥumaydah	140	14.22 N	22.31 E
Humayingzi	98	41.06 N	116.48 E
Humayun's Tomb ⊥	272a	28.36 N	77.15 E
Humbe	152	16.40 S	14.55 E
Humbe, Serra do ⩘	152	12.13 S	15.25 E
Humbeek	50	50.58 N	4.23 E
Humber ≃, On., Can.	212	43.38 N	79.28 W
Humber ≃, Eng., U.K.	44	53.40 N	0.10 W
Humber, Mouth of the ≃ 1	44	53.32 N	0.08 E
Humber Bay ⊂	275b	43.38 N	79.29 W
Humber Bridge ⊶ 5	44	53.42 N	0.27 W
Humberside □ 6	44	53.55 N	0.40 W
Humberston	44	53.32 N	0.02 W
Humberto de Campos	250	2.37 S	43.27 W
Humber Valley Park ♦	275b	43.39 N	79.30 W
Humbird	190	44.31 N	90.53 W
Humble, Dan.	41	54.50 N	10.42 E
Humble, Tx., U.S.	222	29.59 N	95.15 W
Humboldt, Sk., Can.	184	52.12 N	105.07 W
Humboldt, Az., U.S.	200	34.30 N	112.14 W
Humboldt, Il., U.S.	194	39.36 N	88.19 W
Humboldt, Ia., U.S.	198	42.43 N	94.12 W
Humboldt, Ks., U.S.	198	37.48 N	95.26 W
Humboldt, Ne., U.S.	198	40.09 N	95.56 W
Humboldt, S.D., U.S.	198	43.38 N	97.04 W
Humboldt, Tn., U.S.	194	35.49 N	88.54 W
Humboldt ∧	175f	21.53 S	166.25 E
Humboldt ≃	204	40.02 N	118.31 W
Humboldt, North Fork ≃	204	40.56 N	115.32 W
Humboldt, Planetario ☉	286c	10.30 N	66.50 W
Humboldt, South Fork ≃	204	40.47 N	115.53 W
Humboldt Bay ⊂	204	40.47 N	124.11 W
Humboldt Lake ⊜	204	39.58 N	118.38 W
Humboldt Mountains ⩘	9	71.45 S	11.30 E
Humboldt Park ♦	278	41.54 N	87.42 W
Humboldt Redwoods State Park ♦	204	40.19 N	124.00 W
Humboldt Salt Marsh ≡	204	39.50 N	117.55 W
Hume, Ca., U.S.	204	36.47 N	118.55 W
Hume, N.Y., U.S.	210	42.29 N	78.08 W
Hume, Lake ⊜ 1	166	36.06 S	147.05 E
Hume and Hovell Lookout ♦	169	37.15 S	144.59 E
Humeburn	166	27.24 S	145.14 E
Hūmedān	128	25.24 N	59.39 E
Hu Men ⊂ 1	100	22.44 N	113.40 E
Humenné	30	48.56 N	21.55 E
Húmera	266a	40.26 N	3.47 W
Humeston	190	40.51 N	93.29 W
Humlā Karnālī ≃	124	29.38 N	81.52 E
Humlebæk	41	55.58 N	12.33 E
Hummelo	52	52.00 N	6.14 E
Hummelstown	208	40.16 N	76.43 W
Hummels Wharf	210	40.49 N	76.50 W
Hümmling ⩘	52	52.52 N	7.31 E
Humos, Isla I	254	45.38 S	73.59 W
Humpata	152	15.02 S	13.24 E
Hümpfershausen	56	50.40 N	10.13 E
Humphrey, Ar., U.S.	194	34.25 N	91.42 W
Humphrey, Ne., U.S.	198	41.41 N	97.29 W
Humphreys, Mount ∧	204	37.17 N	118.40 W
Humphreys Peak ∧	200	35.20 N	111.40 W
Humpolec	30	49.32 N	15.22 E
Humppila	26	60.56 N	23.22 E
Humptulips	224	47.13 N	123.57 W
Humptulips ≃	224	47.03 N	124.03 W
Humptulips, East Fork ≃	224	47.15 N	123.54 W
Humptulips, West Fork ≃	224	47.15 N	123.54 W
Humptulips Ridge ∧	224	47.20 N	123.45 W
Humpty Doo	164	12.38 S	131.15 E
Humula	171b	35.29 S	147.45 E
Humuya ≃	236	15.01 N	87.44 W
Hūn	146	29.07 N	15.56 E
Hun ≃, Zhg.	98	41.01 N	122.27 E
Hun ≃, Zhg.	98	40.52 N	125.42 E
Hunabasi → Funabashi	94	35.42 N	139.59 E
Húnaflói ⊂	24a	65.50 N	20.50 W
Hunan □ 4	102	28.00 N	111.00 E
Ḥunayshāt, Ghurd al- ⊥ 8	142	30.07 N	29.47 E
Hunchun	98	42.54 N	130.22 E
Huncoat	262	53.46 N	2.20 W
Hundeluft	54	51.58 N	12.20 E
Hundested	41	55.58 N	11.52 E
Hundewāli	123	31.55 N	72.38 E
Hundorp	26	61.33 N	9.54 E
Hundred	188	39.41 N	80.27 W
Hundred End	262	53.42 N	2.53 W
Hundslund	41	55.55 N	10.04 E
Hundstein ∧	64	47.20 N	12.54 E
Hundwil	58	47.22 N	9.19 E
Hunedoara	38	45.45 N	22.54 E
Hunedoara □ 6	38	45.45 N	23.00 E
Hünfeld	56	50.40 N	9.46 E
Hungary (Magyarország) □ 1, Europe	22	47.00 N	20.00 E
Hungary (Magyarország) □ 1, Europe	30	47.00 N	20.00 E
Hungchiang → Hongjiang	102	27.07 N	109.56 E
Hungen	56	50.28 N	8.54 E
Hungerford, Austl.	166	29.00 S	144.25 E
Hungerford, Eng., U.K.	42	51.26 N	1.30 W
Hungerford, Tx., U.S.	222	29.24 N	96.05 W
Hŭngho-ri	98	37.14 N	127.44 E
Hŭngin-ni	98	39.03 N	126.26 E
Hung Long	269c	10.40 N	106.39 E
Hungmao	100	24.55 N	120.58 E
Hŭngnam	98	39.50 N	127.38 E
Hungría → Hungary □ 1	30	47.00 N	20.00 E
Hungry Hill ∧	48	51.41 N	9.48 W
Hungry Horse	202	48.23 N	114.03 W
Hungry Horse Dam ⊶ 6	202	48.14 N	114.04 W
Hungry Horse Reservoir ⊜ 1	202	48.15 N	113.50 W
Hungry Lake ⊜	212	44.48 N	76.53 W
Hungry Law ∧ 2	44	55.21 N	2.24 W
Hung Yen	110	20.39 N	106.04 E
Hunhe	104	41.43 N	123.22 E
Huningue	58	47.36 N	7.35 E
Hunish, Rubha >	46	57.41 N	6.21 W
Huni Valley	150	5.28 N	1.55 W
Hunjiang (Badaojiang)	98	41.56 N	126.29 E
Hunker	279b	40.12 N	79.38 W
Ḥunkurāb, Ra's >	140	24.34 N	35.10 E
Hunlen Falls ∟	182	52.17 N	125.47 W
Hunmanby	44	54.10 N	0.19 W
Hunn ⊜	40	58.51 N	15.57 E
Hunneberg ∧ 2	26	58.20 N	12.27 E
Hunnebostrand	26	58.27 N	11.18 E
Hunnewell	219	39.40 N	91.51 W
Hunnewell Lake ⊜	219	39.42 N	91.52 W
Hunsberge ⩘	156	27.45 S	17.12 E
Hunseby	41	54.48 N	11.32 E
Hunspach	56	48.57 N	7.57 E
Hunsrück ⩘	56	49.50 N	6.40 E
Hunstanton	42	52.57 N	0.30 E
Hunstein Range ⩘	164	4.30 S	142.40 E
Hunsūr	122	12.18 N	76.17 E
Hunswinkel	263	51.05 N	7.48 E
Hunt □ 6	222	33.03 N	96.05 W
Hunte ≃	52	53.15 N	8.29 E
Hunter, N.Y., U.S.	210	42.13 N	74.13 W
Hunter, N.D., U.S.	198	47.11 N	97.13 W
Hunter ≃, Austl.	170	32.50 S	151.42 E
Hunter ≃, N.Z.	172	44.22 S	169.25 E
Hunter, Île I	14	22.24 S	172.03 E
Hunter, Mount ∧	180	62.57 N	151.05 W
Hunter, Port ⊂	170	32.55 S	151.48 E
Hunterdon □ 6	208	40.31 N	74.52 W
Hunter Island I, Austl.	166	40.32 S	144.45 E
Hunter Island I, B.C., Can.	182	51.55 N	128.05 W
Hunter Island I, N.Y., U.S.	276	40.53 N	73.47 W
Hunter Mountain ∧	210	42.10 N	74.14 W
Hunter Mountains ⩘	172	45.42 S	167.25 E
Hunter Range ⩘	170	32.50 S	150.50 E
Hunter Ridge ✦ 3	14	21.30 S	174.30 E
Hunter River	186	46.21 N	63.21 W
Hunters	182	48.07 N	118.12 W
Hunters Bay ⊂	110	19.57 N	93.19 E
Hunters Creek Village	222	29.46 N	95.24 W
Huntersfield Mountain ∧	210	42.21 N	74.21 W
Hunters Hill	274a	33.50 S	151.09 E
Hunters Point >	282	37.43 N	122.22 W
Hunter's Quay	46	55.58 N	4.55 W
Hunters Road	154	19.09 S	29.48 E
Hunters Run	208	40.05 N	77.11 W
Huntersville	192	35.25 N	80.50 W
Huntertown	216	41.13 N	85.10 W
Hunterville	172	39.56 S	175.34 E
Hunter Wash V	200	36.17 N	108.34 W
Huntingburg	194	38.17 N	86.57 W
Huntingdon, B.C., Can.	224	49.00 N	122.16 W
Huntingdon, P.Q., Can.	206	45.05 N	74.10 W
Huntingdon, Eng., U.K.	42	52.20 N	0.12 W
Huntingdon, Pa., U.S.	214	40.29 N	78.00 W
Huntingdon, Tn., U.S.	194	36.00 N	88.25 W
Huntingdon □ 6, P.Q., Can.	206	45.05 N	74.00 W
Huntingdon □ 6, Pa., U.S.	214	40.29 N	78.01 W
Huntingdon Valley	285	40.07 N	75.03 W
Huntingdon Valley Creek ≃	285	40.07 N	75.04 W
Hunting Island State Park ♦	192	32.20 N	80.30 W
Hunting Ridge	284c	38.55 N	77.12 W
Huntington, Eng., U.K.	44	54.01 N	1.04 W
Huntington, In., U.S.	216	40.52 N	85.29 W
Huntington, Ma., U.S.	207	42.14 N	72.52 W
Huntington, N.Y., U.S.	210	40.51 N	73.25 W
Huntington, Or., U.S.	202	44.21 N	117.15 W
Huntington, Tx., U.S.	222	31.16 N	94.34 W
Huntington, Ut,. U.S.	200	39.19 N	110.57 W
Huntington, Va., U.S.	284c	38.48 N	77.15 W
Huntington, W.V., U.S.	188	38.25 N	82.26 W
Huntington □ 6	216	40.53 N	85.30 W
Huntington Bay	276	40.53 N	73.24 W
Huntington Bay ⊂	276	40.55 N	73.25 W
Huntington Beach, Ca., U.S.	228	33.39 N	117.59 W
Huntington Beach, N.Y., U.S.	276	40.54 N	73.23 W
Huntington Creek ≃, Nv., U.S.	204	40.37 N	115.43 W
Huntington Creek ≃, Pa., U.S.	210	41.06 N	76.22 W
Huntington Creek ≃, Ut,. U.S.	200	39.09 N	110.55 W
Huntington Harbor ⊂	276	40.54 N	73.26 W
Huntington Lake	226	37.15 N	119.14 W
Huntington Lake ⊜ 1, Ca., U.S.	226	37.14 N	119.12 W
Huntington Lake ⊜ 1, In., U.S.	216	40.50 N	85.25 W
Huntington Library ☉ 3	280	34.08 N	118.07 W
Huntington Mills	210	41.11 N	76.14 W
Huntington Park	228	33.58 N	118.13 W
Huntington Park ♦	279a	41.29 N	81.56 W
Huntington Station	210	40.51 N	73.24 W
Huntington Woods	281	42.28 N	83.10 W
Huntingtown	208	38.36 N	76.36 W
Hunting Valley	279a	41.31 N	81.23 W
Huntingville	206	45.20 N	71.51 W
Huntland	194	35.03 N	86.16 W
Huntley, Il., U.S.	216	42.10 N	88.25 W
Huntley, Mt., U.S.	202	45.53 N	108.18 W
Huntly, N.Z.	172	37.33 S	175.10 E
Huntly, Scot., U.K.	46	57.27 N	2.47 W
Hunt Mountain ∧	202	44.44 N	107.45 W
Hunton	260	51.13 N	0.28 E
Huntsburg	214	41.32 N	81.03 W
Hunt's Cross ⊶ 8	262	53.21 N	2.51 W
Hunts Point	224	47.39 N	122.14 W
Huntsville, On., Can.	212	45.20 N	79.13 W
Huntsville, Al., U.S.	194	34.43 N	86.35 W
Huntsville, Ar., U.S.	194	36.05 N	93.44 W
Huntsville, Il., U.S.	219	40.11 N	90.52 W
Huntsville, In., U.S.	218	40.00 N	85.43 W
Huntsville, Mo., U.S.	194	39.26 N	92.33 W
Huntsville, Oh., U.S.	216	40.26 N	83.49 W
Huntsville, Tn., U.S.	192	36.24 N	84.29 W
Huntsville, Tx., U.S.	222	30.43 N	95.33 W
Huntsville, Ut,. U.S.	200	41.15 N	111.46 W
Huntsville State Park ♦	222	30.37 N	95.32 W
Hunū, Kathīb al- ⊥ 8	142	30.37 N	32.49 E
Hunucmá	232	21.01 N	89.52 W
Hunut	130	40.39 N	41.09 E
Hünxe	52	51.38 N	6.46 E
Hünxerwald ♦	263	51.40 N	6.50 E
Hunyani ≃	154	15.37 S	30.39 E
Hunyuan	98	39.48 N	113.41 E
Hun-yung	98	42.53 N	130.12 E
Hunza □ 9	123	36.30 N	75.00 E
Hunza ≃	123	35.55 N	74.22 E
Huocheng	86	44.12 N	80.26 E
Huoergeluo	89	45.35 N	120.56 E
Huokou	100	26.28 N	119.16 E
Huolong	106	32.04 N	121.17 E
Huolongmen	89	49.48 N	125.47 E
Huolu	98	38.05 N	114.18 E
Huong Hoa	110	16.37 N	106.45 E
Huong Khe	110	18.13 N	105.41 E
Huong Thuy	110	16.25 N	107.40 E
Huon Gulf ⊂	164	7.10 S	147.25 E
Huon Peninsula > 1	164	6.25 S	147.25 E
Huonville	166	43.01 S	147.02 E
Huoqiu	100	32.20 N	116.16 E
Huorili	89	49.00 N	124.41 E
Huoshan	100	31.25 N	116.20 E
Huo Shan ∧	100	31.06 N	116.12 E
Huoshaoliao	100	25.00 N	121.45 E
Huotong	100	26.53 N	119.25 E
Huotong ≃	100	26.50 N	119.32 E
Huotuolaihuduke	102	40.19 N	104.18 E
Huoxian, Zhg.	102	36.37 N	111.40 E
Huoxian, Zhg.	105	39.46 N	116.46 E
Huoyan	100	33.42 N	113.40 E
Hupeh → Hubei □ 4	90	31.00 N	112.00 E
Huqiao	106	31.25 N	119.24 E
Hura	126	23.18 N	86.39 E
Hūrand	84	38.51 N	47.22 E
Hurāsāgar ≃	126	24.04 N	89.40 E
Ḥuraydīn, Wādī V	132	30.59 N	33.53 E
Ḥuraymilā	128	25.08 N	46.08 E
Hūrayn	142	30.39 N	31.08 E
Hurd, Cape >	190	45.13 N	81.44 W
Hurdalssjøen ⊜	26	60.20 N	11.05 E
Hurdiyo	144	10.33 N	51.08 E
Hurdland	219	40.09 N	92.18 W
Hurdsfield	262	53.16 N	2.06 W
Hurepoix ⊶ 1	261	48.37 N	2.07 E
Hure Qi	98	42.44 N	121.40 E
Hurffville	285	39.46 N	75.07 W
Huri ∧ 2	154	3.41 N	37.51 E
Huriel	32	46.23 N	2.29 E
Hurleg Hu ⊜	102	37.20 N	96.54 E
Hurley, Ms., U.S.	194	30.39 N	88.29 W
Hurley, N.M., U.S.	200	32.41 N	108.07 W
Hurley, N.Y., U.S.	210	41.55 N	74.03 W
Hurley, S.D., U.S.	198	43.16 N	97.05 W
Hurley, Wi., U.S.	190	46.26 N	90.11 W
Hurleyville	210	41.44 N	74.40 W
Hurlford	46	55.36 N	4.28 W
Hurliness	46	58.47 N	3.15 W
Hurlingham	258	34.36 S	58.38 W
Hurlock	208	38.37 N	75.51 W
Hurmāgai	128	28.18 N	64.26 E
Huron, Ca., U.S.	226	36.12 N	120.06 W
Huron, Oh., U.S.	214	41.22 N	82.33 W
Huron, S.D., U.S.	198	44.21 N	98.12 W
Huron □ 6, On., Can.	212	43.45 N	81.10 W
Huron □ 6, Oh., U.S.	214	41.15 N	82.37 W
Huron ≃, Mi., U.S.	216	42.03 N	83.14 W
Huron ≃, Oh., U.S.	214	41.23 N	82.33 W
Huron, East Branch ≃	214	41.17 N	82.38 W
Huron, Lake ⊜	190	44.30 N	82.15 W
Huron, Point >	214	42.34 N	82.47 W
Huron, West Branch ≃	214	41.17 N	82.38 W
Huron Gardens	216	42.38 N	83.20 W
Huron Mountains ⩘ 2	190	46.50 N	87.55 W
Hurons, Rivière des ≃	206	45.28 N	73.16 W
Hurricane, Ak., U.S.	180	62.59 N	149.38 W
Hurricane, Ut,. U.S.	200	37.10 N	113.17 W
Hurricane, W.V., U.S.	188	38.25 N	82.01 W
Hurricane Bayou ≃	222	31.21 N	95.35 W
Hurricane Cliffs ⊥ 4	200	37.20 N	113.10 W
Hurricane Creek ≃, Ar., U.S.	194	34.05 N	92.23 W
Hurricane Creek ≃, Ga., U.S.	192	31.23 N	82.19 W
Hurricane Creek ≃, Il., U.S.	219	38.53 N	89.13 W
Hurricane Lake ⊜	198	48.25 N	99.30 W
Hurricane Wash V	200	37.00 N	113.23 W
Hurshi	126	24.17 N	88.28 E
Hursley	42	51.02 N	1.24 W
Hurso	144	9.38 N	41.38 E
Hurst	222	32.49 N	97.10 W
Hurstbourne Tarrant	42	51.17 N	1.23 W
Hurstbridge	169	37.38 S	145.12 E
Hurst Green	260	51.15 N	0.01 E
Hurstpierpoint	42	50.56 N	0.11 W
Hurstville	170	33.58 S	151.06 E
Hurstwood Reservoir ⊜ 1	262	53.47 N	2.10 W
Hurt	192	37.05 N	79.17 W
Hurtado ≃	252	30.35 S	71.11 W
Hurtaut ≃	50	49.42 N	4.01 E
Hürth	56	50.52 N	6.51 E
Hurtsboro	194	32.14 N	85.24 W
Hurunui ≃	172	42.55 S	173.17 E

Symbols in the index entries represent the broad categories identified in the key at the right. Symbols with superior numbers (⩘ 1) identify subcategories (see complete key on page *I · 1*).

Symbole im Register stellen die rechts im Schlüssel erklärten Kategorien dar. Symbole mit hochgestellten Ziffern (⩘ 1) bezeichnen Unterabteilungen einer Kategorie (vgl. vollständiger Schlüssel auf Seite *I · 1*).

Los símbolos incluídos en el texto del índice representan las grandes categorías identificadas con la clave a la derecha. Los símbolos con numeros en su parte superior (⩘ 1) identifican las subcategorías (véase la clave completa en la página *I · 1*).

Les symboles de l'index représentent les catégories indiquées dans la légende à droite. Les symboles suivis d'un indice (⩘ 1) représentent des sous-catégories (voir légende complète à la page *I · 1*).

Os símbolos incluídos no texto do índice representam as grandes categorias identificadas com a chave à direita. Os símbolos com números em sua parte superior (⩘ 1) identificam as subcategorias (veja-se a chave completa à página *I · 1*).

∧ Mountain	Berg	Montaña	Montagne	Montanha
⩘ Mountains	Gebirge	Montañas	Montagnes	Montanhas
)(Pass	Paß	Paso	Col	Passo
V Valley, Canyon	Tal, Cañon	Valle, Cañón	Vallée, Canyon	Vale, Canhão
≚ Plain	Ebene	Llano	Plaine	Planície
> Cape	Kap	Cabo	Cap	Cabo
I Island	Insel	Isla	Île	Ilha
II Islands	Inseln	Islas	Îles	Ilhas
⊥ Other Topographic Features	Andere Topographische Objekte	Otros Elementos Topográficos	Autres données topographiques	Outros acidentes topográficos

ESPAÑOL / FRANÇAIS / PORTUGUÊS

Nombre / Nom / Nome	Página / Page	Lat.°′	Long.°′ W = Oeste / W = Ouest
Hurup	26	56.45 N	8.25 E
Hurworth-on-Tees	44	54.29 N	1.31 W
Hurzuf	78	44.33 N	34.17 E
Husainābād	124	24.32 N	84.01 E
Husainīwāla	123	30.59 N	74.34 E
Husainpur	124	24.25 N	90.40 E
Husarka	78	47.23 N	36.31 E
Húsavík	24a	66.04 N	17.18 W
Husby-Långhundra	40	59.45 N	18.01 E
Huse → Higashiōsaka	96	34.39 N	135.35 E
Husen ◆[8]	263	51.33 N	7.36 E
Hushan, Zhg.	89	45.35 N	130.35 E
Hushan, Zhg.	100	28.36 N	118.59 E
Hushan, Zhg.	100	22.09 N	113.10 E
Husheib	140	14.54 N	35.07 E
Hushi	107	28.57 N	105.22 E
Hushiha	98	40.52 N	116.59 E
Hushitai	104	41.57 N	123.30 E
Hushu, Zhg.	106	31.52 N	118.59 E
Hushu, Zhg.	106	30.18 N	120.08 E
Huși	38	46.40 N	28.04 E
Husinec	60	49.03 N	13.58 E
Huskisson	170	35.02 S	150.40 E
Huskvarna	26	57.48 N	14.16 E
Huslia	180	65.42 N	156.25 W
Hussar	182	51.03 N	112.41 W
Hussigny-Godbrange	56	49.29 N	5.52 E
Hustisford	190	43.21 N	88.36 W
Huston ≃	220	25.42 N	81.17 W
Hustontown	214	40.03 N	78.02 W
Hustopeče	61	48.57 N	16.44 E
Husum, Dtsch.	41	54.28 N	9.03 E
Husum, Sve.	26	63.20 N	19.10 E
Husum, Wa., U.S.	224	45.47 N	121.29 W
Husyatyn	78	49.05 N	26.11 E
Hutaimbaru	114	1.34 N	99.44 E
Hutangqiao	106	31.46 N	119.57 E
Hutan Melintang	114	3.53 N	100.56 E
Hutanopan	114	0.41 N	99.42 E
Hutaym, Harrat ⚊[9]	128	26.15 N	40.20 E
Hutberg ∧[2]	54	52.09 N	14.33 E
Hutchins	222	32.39 N	96.43 W
Hutchinson, S. Afr.	158	31.30 S	23.09 E
Hutchinson, Ks., U.S.	198	38.03 N	97.55 W
Hutchinson, Mn., U.S.	190	44.53 N	94.22 W
Hutchinson, Pa., U.S.	214	40.13 N	79.44 W
Hutchinson ≃	276	40.52 N	73.50 W
Hutchinson Island I	220	27.25 N	80.17 W
Hutch Mountain ∧	200	34.47 N	111.22 W
Hutou, Zhg.	100	25.15 N	118.03 E
Hutou, Zhg.	100	26.04 N	118.46 E
Hutou, Zhg.	106	31.37 N	119.37 E
Hutou, Zhg.	106	32.14 N	120.17 E
Hutouya	98	37.13 N	119.46 E
Hutsonville	194	39.06 N	87.39 W
Hüttau	64	47.25 N	13.18 E
Hütteldorf ◆[8]	264b	48.12 N	16.16 E
Hüttener Berge ⋏[2]	41	54.26 N	9.40 E
Hüttenheim ◆[8]	263	51.22 N	6.43 E
Hüttental	56	50.54 N	8.02 E
Hutte Sauvage, Lac de la ⊜	176	56.15 N	64.45 W
Huttig	194	33.02 N	92.10 W
Hütting	60	48.48 N	11.07 E
Hutto	222	30.33 N	97.33 W
Hutton, Eng., U.K.	260	51.38 N	0.22 E
Hutton, Eng., U.K.	262	53.44 N	2.46 W
Hutton, Mount ∧	166	25.51 S	148.20 E
Hutton Rudby	44	54.27 N	1.17 W
Huttonsville	212	43.38 N	79.48 W
Huttrop ◆[8]	263	51.27 N	7.03 E
Hüttschlag	64	47.10 N	13.14 E
Huttwil	58	47.07 N	7.51 E
Hutubi	86	44.07 N	86.57 E
Hutuo ≃	98	38.14 N	116.05 E
Hutwisch ∧	61	47.28 N	16.13 E
Huty	78	50.08 N	35.21 E
Huu	115b	8.48 S	118.25 E
Huvalu Forest ◆[3]	174v	19.03 S	169.51 W
Huveaune ≃	62	43.15 N	5.23 E
Huvudskär I	40	58.57 N	18.34 E
Huwan	100	31.41 N	114.53 E
Huwei	100	23.43 N	120.26 E
Huwun	144	4.23 N	40.08 E
Ḥuwwārah	132	32.09 N	35.15 E
Huxford	194	31.13 N	87.28 W
Huxi	100	26.12 N	114.44 E
Huxian	102	34.09 N	108.32 E
Huxley	182	51.56 N	113.14 W
Huy	56	50.31 N	5.14 E
Huy ∧	54	51.57 N	10.57 E
Huyangzhen	100	32.25 N	112.45 E
Huyton-with-Roby	262	53.25 N	2.52 W
Huyuesi	106	30.23 N	118.45 E
Hüyük	130	37.57 N	31.37 E
Huyutou	100	26.44 N	119.49 E
Hūzgān	128	31.27 N	48.04 E
Huzhen	100	28.50 N	120.15 E
Huzhou	106	30.52 N	120.06 E
Huzhu	102	37.00 N	102.00 E
Huzhuangtun	104	40.43 N	122.33 E
Huzi	100	30.56 N	113.42 E
Huzisawa → Fujisawa	94	35.21 N	139.29 E
Hvalsø	41	55.36 N	11.50 E
Hvannadalshnúkur ∧	24a	64.01 N	16.41 W
Hvar	36	43.10 N	16.27 E
Hvar, Otok I	36	43.09 N	16.45 E
Hvardiys'ke, Ukr.	78	48.44 N	35.19 E
Hvardiys'ke, Ukr.	78	49.20 N	26.42 E
Hvardiys'ke, Ukr.	78	45.07 N	34.01 E
Hvarski Kanal ꭒ	36	43.15 N	16.37 E
Hveragerđi	24a	64.03 N	21.10 W
Hvide Sande	26	55.59 N	8.08 E
Hvidovre	41	55.39 N	12.29 E
Hvittingfoss	26	59.29 N	10.01 E
Hvizdets'	78	48.34 N	25.17 E
Hvolsvöllur	24a	63.45 N	20.10 W
Hwach'ŏn	98	38.06 N	127.41 E
Hwach'ŏn-chŏsuji ⊜[1]	98	38.07 N	127.52 E
Hwach'ŏn-ni	98	39.01 N	126.02 E
Hwainan → Huainan	100	32.40 N	117.00 E
Hwaining → Anqing	100	30.31 N	117.02 E
Hwange	154	18.22 S	26.29 E
Hwange National Park ♠	154	19.00 S	26.35 E
Hwanggong-ni	98	40.03 N	129.27 E
Hwanghae Namdo □[4]	98	38.15 N	125.30 E
Hwanghae Pukdo □[4]	98	38.30 N	126.25 E
Hwang Ho → Huang ≃	90	37.32 N	118.19 E
Hwangju	98	38.42 N	125.46 E
Hwangshih → Huangshi	100	30.13 N	115.05 E
Hyak	224	47.23 N	121.23 W
Hyakuna	174m	26.08 N	127.48 E
Hyakuri-ga-dake ∧	94	35.23 N	135.49 E
Hyakuri-kichi, Kōkū-jieitai- ■	94	36.11 N	140.25 E
Hyannis, Ma., U.S.	207	41.39 N	70.17 W
Hyannis, Ne., U.S.	198	42.00 N	101.45 W
Hyannis Port	207	41.38 N	70.18 W
Hyattsville	208	38.57 N	76.56 W
Hyattville	202	44.14 N	107.36 W
Hybla Valley	208	38.44 N	77.05 W
Hyco ≃	192	36.40 N	78.45 W
Hyco Lake ⊜[1]	192	36.30 N	79.05 W
Hydaburg	182	55.12 N	132.49 W
Hyde, N.Z.	172	45.18 S	170.15 E
Hyde, Eng., U.K.	44	53.27 N	2.04 W
Hyde, Pa., U.S.	214	41.00 N	78.28 W
Hyden, Austl.	162	32.27 S	118.53 E
Hyden, Ky., U.S.	192	37.10 N	83.22 W
Hyde Park, Guy.	246	6.30 N	58.16 W
Hyde Park, N.Y., U.S.	210	41.47 N	73.56 W
Hyde Park, Vt., U.S.	188	44.35 N	72.37 W
Hyde Park ◆[8], Il., U.S.	278	41.48 N	87.36 W
Hyde Park ◆[8], Ma., U.S.	283	42.15 N	71.08 W
Hyde Park ♠, Austl.	274a	33.53 S	151.13 E
Hyde Park ♠, Eng., U.K.	260	51.30 N	0.10 W
Hyde Park ♠, N.Y., U.S.	284a	43.06 N	79.01 W
Hyder	182	55.55 N	130.01 W
Hyderābād, India	122	17.23 N	78.29 E
Hyderābād, Pāk.	120	25.22 N	68.22 E
Hydetown	214	41.40 N	79.44 W
Hydra → Ídhra I	38	37.20 N	23.32 E
Hydraulic	182	52.36 N	121.42 W
Hydro	196	35.21 N	98.22 W
Hydrographers Passage ꭒ	166	20.45 S	150.15 E
Hyen ⊜	40	60.36 N	16.12 E
Hyères	62	43.07 N	6.07 E
Hyères, Îles d' II	62	43.00 N	6.20 E
Hyères-Plage	62	43.06 N	6.10 E
Hyesan	98	41.23 N	128.12 E
Hyland ≃	180	59.50 N	128.10 W
Hylestad	26	59.05 N	7.32 E
Hyllekrog I	41	54.36 N	11.30 E
Hyllinge, Dan.	41	55.16 N	11.37 E
Hyllinge, Sve.	41	56.06 N	12.51 E
Hyllstofta	41	56.08 N	13.16 E
Hyltebruk	26	57.00 N	13.14 E
Hymaya ≃	232	24.31 N	107.41 W
Hymera	194	39.11 N	87.18 W
Hyndburn □[8]	262	53.45 N	2.23 W
Hyndman	188	39.49 N	78.43 W
Hyndman Peak ∧	202	43.45 N	114.08 W
Hynish Bay ⊂	46	56.28 N	6.50 W
Hyōgo □[5]	96	35.00 N	135.00 E
Hyōgo ◆[8]	270	34.39 N	135.10 E
Hyŏn-ni	98	37.57 N	128.20 E
Hyōno-sen ∧	96	35.21 N	134.31 E
Hyōnosen-Ushiroyama-Nagisan-kokutei-kōen ♠	96	35.15 N	134.30 E
Hyŏpch'ŏn	98	35.35 N	128.08 E
Hyrum	200	41.38 N	111.51 W
Hyrynsalmi	26	64.40 N	28.32 E
Hysham	202	46.17 N	107.14 W
Hythe, Ab., Can.	182	55.20 N	119.33 W
Hythe, Eng., U.K.	42	51.05 N	1.05 E
Hythe, Eng., U.K.	42	50.51 N	1.24 W
Hythe End	260	51.27 N	0.32 W
Hyūga	92	32.25 N	131.38 E
Hyūga-nada ⊤[2]	92	32.00 N	131.35 E
Hyvinge → Hyvinkää	26	60.38 N	24.52 E
Hyvinkää	26	60.38 N	24.52 E

I

Nombre / Nom / Nome	Página / Page	Lat.°′	Long.°′ W = Oeste / W = Ouest
Iacanga	255	21.54 S	49.01 W
Iaciara	255	14.09 S	46.40 W
Iaco (Yaco) ≃	248	9.03 S	68.34 W
Iaçu	255	12.45 S	40.13 W
Iaeger	192	37.27 N	81.48 W
Iago	222	29.17 N	95.58 W
Iakora	157b	23.06 S	46.40 E
Ialomița □[6]	38	44.40 N	27.20 E
Ialomița ≃	38	44.42 N	27.51 E
Ialomiței, Balta ≛	38	44.30 N	28.00 E
Ialpug ≃	78	45.41 N	28.35 E
Iamonia, Lake ⊜	192	30.38 N	84.14 W
Ianaivo ≃	157b	22.56 S	46.54 E
Ianakafy	157b	23.21 S	45.28 E
Ianga	146	9.07 N	18.11 E
Iango	152	9.11 S	17.39 E
Iano, Monte ∧	267a	41.46 N	12.44 E
Iapó ≃	252	24.30 S	50.24 W
Iapu	255	19.26 S	42.13 W
Iargara	38	46.27 N	28.27 E
Iași	38	47.10 N	27.35 E
Iași □[6]	38	47.15 N	27.15 E
Iato	70	37.58 N	13.07 E
Iato ≃	70	38.04 N	13.02 E
Iatt, Lake ⊜[1]	194	31.35 N	92.40 W
Iauaretê	246	0.36 N	69.12 W
Iazu	38	44.44 N	27.25 E
Ib ≃	120	21.34 N	83.48 E
Iba, Pil.	116	15.20 N	119.58 E
Iba, Zaïre	152	3.05 S	17.38 E
'Ibādah, Wādī V	142	27.49 N	30.54 E
Ibadan	150	7.17 N	3.30 E
Ibagué	246	4.27 N	75.14 W
Ibaiti	255	23.50 S	50.10 W
Ibajay	116	11.49 N	122.10 E
Ibajay ≃	116	11.49 N	122.10 E
Ibaka	152	4.16 S	23.12 E
Ibambi	154	2.22 N	27.37 E
Ibanda	154	0.08 S	30.29 E
Ibănești	38	48.04 N	26.22 E
Ibans, Laguna de ⊂	236	15.53 N	84.52 W
Ibanshe	152	4.58 S	21.30 E
Ibapah Peak ∧	200	39.50 N	113.55 W
Ibar ≃	38	43.44 N	20.45 E
Ibara	96	34.36 N	133.28 E
Ibaraki, Nihon	94	36.17 N	140.26 E
Ibaraki, Nihon	96	34.49 N	135.34 E
Ibaraki □[5]	94	36.30 N	140.30 E
Ibarra	246	0.21 N	78.07 W
Ibarreta	252	25.13 S	59.51 W
Ibb	144	14.01 N	44.10 E
Ibba	154	4.48 N	29.06 E
Ibba ≃	140	7.09 N	28.41 E
Ibbenbüren	52	52.16 N	7.43 E
Ibeke Gembo	152	1.24 S	18.51 E
Ibembo	152	2.38 N	23.37 E
Ibenga ≃	152	2.20 N	18.08 E
Iberá, Esteros del ≛	252	28.05 S	57.05 W
Iberia, Mo., U.S.	194	38.05 N	92.17 W
Iberia, Oh., U.S.	214	40.40 N	82.51 W
Ibérica, Península >[1]	10	40.00 N	5.00 W
Ibérico, Sistema ⋏	34	41.00 N	2.30 W
Ibertioga	256	21.25 S	43.58 W
Iberville	206	45.18 N	73.14 W
Iberville □[6]	206	45.15 N	73.10 W
Iberville, Mont d' (Mount Caubvick) ∧	176	58.53 N	63.43 W
Ibese	273a	6.33 N	3.29 E
Ibeto	150	10.29 N	5.09 E
Ibi	150	8.12 N	9.45 E
Ibi ≃	94	35.03 N	136.42 E
Ibiá	255	19.29 S	46.32 W
Ibiapina	250	3.55 S	40.54 W
Ibicaraí	255	14.51 S	39.36 W
Ibicuí	255	14.51 S	39.59 W
Ibicuí ≃	252	29.25 S	56.47 W
Ibicuicito, Arroyo ≃	258	33.49 S	58.49 W
Ibicuy	258	33.44 S	59.10 W
Ibicuy ≃[1]	258	33.48 S	59.10 W
Ibigawa	94	35.29 N	136.34 E
Ibipira	250	6.31 S	44.38 W
Ibiquera	255	12.38 S	40.57 W
Ibiraci	255	20.28 S	47.08 W
Ibiraçu	255	19.50 S	40.22 W
Ibirama	252	27.04 S	49.31 W
Ibirapuã	255	17.39 S	40.07 W
Ibirapuera ◆[8]	287b	23.37 S	46.40 W
Ibirapuera, Parque ♠	287b	23.35 S	46.39 W
Ibirapuitã ≃	252	29.22 S	55.57 W
Ibirataia	255	14.04 S	39.38 W
Ibiri	154	4.56 S	32.33 E
Ibirubá	252	28.38 S	53.06 W
Ibitiara	255	12.39 S	42.13 W
Ibitinga	255	21.45 S	48.49 W
Ibitiúra De Minas	256	22.04 S	46.26 W
Ibiúna	256	23.39 S	47.13 W
Ibiza → Eivissa I	34	39.00 N	1.25 E
Iblei, Monti ⋏	70	37.10 N	14.50 E
Ibnahs	142	30.34 N	31.07 E
Ibn Hāni', Ra's >	130	35.35 N	35.43 E
Ibn Sarrār, Bi'r ⊤[4]	144	19.30 N	42.41 E
Ibo	154	12.20 S	40.35 E
Ibo ≃	96	34.46 N	134.35 E
Ibondo	154	2.38 S	32.40 E
Ibonma	164	3.28 S	133.28 E
Ibor ≃	34	39.49 N	5.33 W
Ibotirama	255	12.11 S	43.13 W
Iboundji, Mont ∧	152	1.08 S	11.48 E
Ibrah, Wādī V	140	10.36 N	24.58 E
Ibrāhīmīyah, Qārah al- ≅	142	29.10 N	31.10 E
Ibresi	80	55.18 N	47.03 E
'Ibrī	128	23.14 N	56.30 E
İbriktepe	130	41.00 N	26.30 E
Ibshān	142	31.10 N	31.10 E
Ibshawāy	142	29.22 N	30.41 E
Ibstock	42	52.42 N	1.23 W
Ibta'	132	32.47 N	36.09 E
Ibu	174m	26.45 N	128.19 E
Ibuki	94	35.24 N	136.23 E
Ibuki-jima I	96	34.08 N	133.32 E
Ibuki-sanchi ⋏	94	35.35 N	136.18 E
Ibuki-yama ∧	94	35.25 N	136.24 E
Iburg	52	52.09 N	8.02 E
Ibusuki	92	31.16 N	130.39 E
Ibwe Munyama	154	16.09 S	28.34 E
Ibychen, gora ∧	88	51.36 N	109.45 E
Ica	248	14.04 S	75.42 W
Ica □[5]	248	14.20 S	75.30 W
Ičа ≃, Lat.	76	56.52 N	26.59 E
Ica ≃, Perú	248	14.54 S	75.34 W
Iča ≃, Ross.	86	55.30 N	77.13 E
Içá (Putumayo) ≃, S.A.	246	3.07 S	67.58 W
Icabarú ≃	246	4.45 N	62.15 W
Icacos Point >	241r	10.03 N	61.56 W
Icadambanauan Island I	116	10.49 N	119.38 E
Icamaquã ≃	252	28.34 S	56.00 W
Icamole	196	25.55 N	100.43 W
Içana	246	0.21 N	67.19 W
Içana (Isana) ≃	246	0.26 N	67.19 W
Icaño, Arg.	252	28.54 S	65.19 W
Icaño, Arg.	252	28.41 S	62.54 W
Icatu	250	2.46 S	44.04 W
Iceberg Pass)(	200	40.25 N	105.45 W
Ice House Reservoir ⊜[1]	226	38.49 N	120.23 W
İçel (Mersin)	130	36.48 N	34.38 E
İçel □[4]	130	36.45 N	34.00 E
Iceland (Ísland) □[1], Europe	22	65.00 N	18.00 W
Iceland (Ísland) □[1], Europe	24a	65.00 N	18.00 W
Iceland Basin ✧[1]	10	59.00 N	23.00 W
Icém	255	20.21 S	49.12 W
Ice Mountain ∧	182	54.25 N	121.08 W
Ičera	88	58.32 N	109.47 E
Ichaikaronji	122	16.42 N	74.28 E
Ichāmati ≃, Asia	126	22.35 N	88.57 E
Ichāmati ≃, Bngl.	126	24.00 N	89.15 E
Ichang → Yichang	102	30.42 N	111.17 E
Ichawaynochaway Creek ≃	192	31.10 N	84.28 W
Ich Bajan Ajrag uul ∧	88	47.55 N	95.02 E
Ichbulag	102	45.21 N	113.10 E
Ich Buural uul ∧	88	48.00 N	94.30 E
Ichchāpuram	122	19.07 N	84.42 E
Ichdžargalan	102	45.31 N	108.48 E
Ichenhausen	58	48.22 N	10.18 E
Ichenheim	58	48.26 N	7.49 E
Ichhapur	126	22.50 N	88.24 E
Ichhāwar	124	23.01 N	77.01 E
Ichi ≃	96	34.46 N	134.41 E
Ichiba	96	34.05 N	134.17 E
Ichihara	94	35.31 N	140.05 E
Ichikai	94	36.32 N	140.06 E
Ichikawa, Nihon	94	35.44 N	139.55 E
Ichikawa, Nihon	96	34.59 N	134.46 E
Ichikawa-daimon	94	35.34 N	138.30 E
Ichilo ≃	248	15.57 S	64.42 W
Ichinohe	92	40.13 N	141.17 E
Ichinomiya, Nihon	94	35.18 N	136.48 E
Ichinomiya, Nihon	94	35.22 N	140.22 E
Ichinomiya, Nihon	94	35.39 N	138.41 E
Ichinomiya, Nihon	94	34.41 N	137.26 E
Ichinomiya, Nihon	96	34.28 N	134.51 E
Ichinomiya, Nihon	96	32.57 N	131.07 E
Ichinomiya, Nihon	96	35.07 N	134.34 E
Ichinomoto	270	34.37 N	135.50 E
Ichinose	270	34.53 N	135.10 E
Ichinoseki	92	38.55 N	141.08 E
Ichino-tani ⊥	96	34.39 N	135.07 E
Ichiu	96	33.57 N	134.04 E
Ichkeul, Lac ⊜	36	37.10 N	9.40 E
Ichnya	78	50.52 N	32.24 E
Ichoa ≃	248	15.44 S	65.15 W
Ichoca	248	17.12 S	67.17 W
Ich'on, C.M.I.K.	98	38.30 N	126.50 E
Ich'ŏn, Taehan	98	37.17 N	127.27 E
Ich Ovoo uul ∧	90	44.40 N	95.08 E
Ichtamir	88	47.30 N	100.52 E
Ichtegem	50	51.06 N	3.00 E
Ichtershausen	54	50.52 N	10.58 E
Ich'un → Yichun	90	47.42 N	128.55 E
Ich Uul, Mong.	88	48.33 N	98.40 E
Ich Uul, Mong.	88	49.27 N	101.27 E
Icicle Creek ≃	224	47.34 N	120.40 W
Ičinskaja Sopka, vulkan ∧[1]	74	55.42 N	157.35 E
Ička, gora ∧[2]	80	51.13 N	50.15 E
Ickenham ◆[8]	260	51.34 N	0.27 W
Ickern	263	51.36 N	7.21 E
Ickesburg	208	40.27 N	77.21 W
Icking	64	47.57 N	11.25 E
İçme	130	38.37 N	39.34 E
Icó	250	6.24 S	38.51 W
Icoca	152	6.11 S	16.19 E
Iconha	255	20.48 S	40.48 W
Icy Bay ⊂	180	60.00 N	141.15 W
Icy Cape >	180	70.20 N	161.52 W
Icy Strait ꭒ	180	58.18 N	135.30 W
Ida	216	41.54 N	83.34 W
Ida, Mount ∧, Austl.	162	29.14 S	120.25 E
Ida, Mount ∧, Jam.	241q	17.58 N	77.43 W
Idabel	194	33.53 N	94.49 W
Idaga Hamus	144	14.12 N	39.48 E
Ida Grove	198	42.20 N	95.28 W
Idah	150	7.07 N	6.43 E
Idaho □[3], U.S.	178	45.00 N	115.00 W
Idaho □[3], U.S.	202	45.00 N	115.00 W
Idaho City	202	43.49 N	115.50 W
Idaho Falls	202	43.28 N	112.02 W
Idaho National Engineering Laboratory ʊ[3]	202	43.40 N	112.45 W
Idaho Springs	200	39.44 N	105.00 W
Idalou	196	33.39 N	101.40 W
Idanha-a-Nova	34	39.55 N	7.14 W
Idāppādi	122	11.35 N	77.51 E
Idar	120	23.50 N	73.00 E
Idarkopf ∧	56	49.51 N	7.16 E
Idar-Oberstein	56	49.42 N	7.19 E
Idarwald ◆[3]	56	49.49 N	7.12 E
Idaville, In., U.S.	216	40.45 N	86.38 W
Idaville, Or., U.S.	224	45.30 N	123.51 W
Iddo ◆[8]	273a	6.28 N	3.23 E
Ide	96	34.47 N	135.49 E
Idel'	24	64.08 N	34.14 E
Idelès	148	23.58 N	5.53 E
Idemba	152	2.38 S	11.38 E
Iden	54	52.46 N	11.55 E
Ider	88	48.13 N	97.23 E
Iderijn ≃	88	49.16 N	100.41 E
Idermeg	88	47.40 N	111.05 E
Idfīnā	142	31.18 N	30.31 E
Idfū	140	24.58 N	32.52 E
Ídhi Óros ∧	38	35.18 N	24.43 E
Ídhra	38	37.20 N	23.29 E
Ídhra (Hydra) I	38	37.20 N	23.32 E
Idi	114	4.57 N	97.46 E
Idice ≃	64	44.35 N	11.49 E
Idi-cut	114	4.59 N	97.42 E
Ididole	144	5.53 N	43.36 E
Idifina Barrage ◆[6]	142	31.17 N	30.31 E
İdil	130	37.21 N	41.54 E
Idimu	273a	6.35 N	3.17 E
Idio	116	11.37 N	122.06 E
Idiofa	152	5.02 S	19.36 E
Iditarod ≃	180	63.02 N	158.58 W
Idjwi, Île I	154	2.09 S	29.04 E
Idkerberget	40	60.23 N	15.14 E
Idkū	142	31.18 N	30.18 E
Idkū, Buḥayrat ⊜	142	31.16 N	30.17 E
Idle ≃	44	53.27 N	0.49 W
Idle Hill	260	51.15 N	0.08 E
Idlib	130	35.55 N	36.38 E
Idlib □[8]	130	35.50 N	36.40 E
Idmū	142	28.09 N	30.41 E
Idnah	132	31.34 N	34.59 E
Idodi	154	7.47 S	35.11 E
Idomogu	273a	6.43 N	3.30 E
Idracowra	162	25.00 S	133.47 E
Idre	26	61.52 N	12.43 E
Idria	226	36.25 N	120.40 W
Idrica	76	56.21 N	28.53 E
Idrigill Point >	46	57.20 N	6.35 W
Idrija	36	46.00 N	14.01 E
Idrijca ≃	64	46.09 N	13.45 E
Idrinskoje	86	54.21 N	92.07 E
Idro	64	45.44 N	10.29 E
Idro, Lago d' ⊜	64	45.47 N	10.30 E
Idroscalo ⊜	266b	45.28 N	9.18 E
Idstedt	41	54.35 N	9.31 E
Idstein	56	50.13 N	8.16 E
Idutywa	158	32.02 S	28.16 E
Idyllwild	204	33.45 N	116.43 W
Idylside	216	41.31 N	88.07 W
Idylwood	284c	38.54 N	77.12 W
Idževan	84	40.53 N	45.07 E
Ie	174m	26.42 N	127.48 E
Iecava	76	56.36 N	24.12 E
Iecava ≃	76	56.41 N	23.42 E
Ielsi	66	41.30 N	14.48 E
Ienne	66	41.53 N	13.10 E
Iepê	255	22.40 S	51.05 W
Ieper (Ypres)	50	50.51 N	2.53 E
Ierápetra	38	35.00 N	25.45 E
Ierisós	38	40.24 N	23.52 E
Ierzu	71	39.47 N	9.31 E
Ieshima	96	34.40 N	134.32 E
Ie-shima I	174m	26.43 N	127.47 E
Ieshima-shotō II	96	34.40 N	134.32 E
Iesolo	64	45.32 N	12.38 E
Ie-suidō ꭒ	174m	26.42 N	127.51 E
If, Château d' ⊥	62	43.17 N	5.19 E
Ifakara	154	8.08 S	36.41 E
Ifako	273a	6.39 N	3.20 E
Ifalik I[1]	108	7.15 N	144.27 E
Ifanadiana	157b	21.19 S	47.39 E
Ife	150	7.30 N	4.30 E
Iferouâne	150	19.04 N	8.24 E
Iferten → Yverdon	58	46.47 N	6.39 E
Iffezheim	56	48.49 N	8.08 E
Ifni □[9]	148	29.15 N	10.08 W
Ifôghas, Adrar des ⋏	150	20.00 N	2.00 E
Ifon	150	6.58 N	5.45 E
Ifould Lake ⊜	162	30.53 S	132.09 E
Ifrane	148	33.32 N	5.06 W
Ifrane □[4]	148	33.15 N	5.05 W
Ifta	56	51.04 N	10.11 E
Ifugao □[4]	116	16.45 N	121.15 E
Iga	94	34.49 N	136.13 E
Iga ≃	94	34.45 N	136.01 E
Igal	30	46.31 N	17.55 E
Igalula, Tan.	154	5.14 S	33.00 E
Igalula, Tan.	154	5.38 S	32.38 E
Igan	112	2.49 N	111.43 E
Igan ≃	112	2.51 N	111.39 E
Iganga	154	0.37 N	33.29 E
Iganmu ◆[8]	273a	6.29 N	3.22 E
Iganna	150	7.59 N	3.14 E
Igaporã	255	13.46 S	42.43 W
Igara	250	10.24 S	40.07 W
Igaraí	256	21.25 S	46.49 W
Igara Paraná ≃	246	2.09 S	71.47 W
Igarapé-Açu	250	1.07 S	47.37 W
Igarapé Grande	250	4.41 S	44.58 W
Igarapé-Miri	250	1.59 S	48.58 W
Igaratá	256	23.12 S	46.07 W
Igarka	74	67.28 N	86.35 E
Igarra	150	7.18 N	6.07 E
Igarukiro	154	3.08 S	33.31 E
Igatpuri	122	19.42 N	73.33 E
Igaun	273a	6.42 N	3.23 E
Igawa	154	8.35 S	34.28 E
Igbaja	150	8.23 N	4.52 E
Igbobi	273a	6.32 N	3.22 E
Igboho	150	8.51 N	3.45 E
Igbologun	273a	6.25 N	3.20 E
Igbo-Ora	150	7.26 N	3.17 E
Igbor	150	7.27 N	8.34 E
Igdir, Īrān	84	39.20 N	47.30 E
Iğdır, Tür.	84	39.55 N	44.02 E
Iğdır, Tür.	130	41.14 N	33.07 E
Iğdır, Tür.	130	40.16 N	35.38 E
Igdy	128	39.54 N	56.54 E
Igea Marina	66	44.08 N	12.29 E
Igel	56	49.42 N	6.32 E
Igelfors	40	58.51 N	15.41 E
Igelsberg	58	48.32 N	8.26 E
Igel'vejem ≃	180	65.40 N	172.50 W
Igersheim	56	49.29 N	9.49 E
Iggensbach	60	48.44 N	13.08 E
Iggesund	26	61.38 N	17.04 E
Igharghar, Oued V, Afr.	148	20.25 N	6.10 E
Igharghar, Oued V, Alg.	148	28.03 N	6.15 E
Ightham	260	51.17 N	0.17 E
Ightham Mote ⊥	260	51.15 N	0.16 E
Igikpak, Mount ∧	180	67.25 N	154.58 W
Igirma	88	56.59 N	103.37 E
Igiugig	180	59.20 N	155.55 W
Iglau → Jihlava	30	49.24 N	15.36 E
Iglesia	252	30.24 S	69.13 W
Iglesias	71	39.19 N	8.32 E
Iglesiente ◆[1]	71	39.18 N	8.40 E
Igli	148	30.25 N	2.12 W
Iglino	86	54.50 N	56.26 E
Igloolik	176	69.24 N	81.49 W
Iglovo	82	55.47 N	36.40 E
Igls	64	47.14 N	11.25 E
Ignacio, Ca., U.S.	226	38.05 N	122.32 W
Ignacio, Co., U.S.	200	37.06 N	107.37 W
Ignacio de la Llave	234	18.43 N	95.59 W
Ignacio Zaragoza, Méx.	232	29.35 N	107.30 W
Ignacio Zaragoza, Méx.	234	23.15 N	98.50 W
Ignacio Zaragoza, Méx.	234	23.55 N	103.42 W
Ignalina	76	55.21 N	26.10 E
Ignatei	38	47.41 N	28.40 E
Ignatjevcy	80	57.32 N	51.39 E
Ignatovka	80	53.57 N	47.38 E
Ignatovo	82	56.10 N	37.32 E
İğneada	130	41.52 N	27.58 E
İğneada Burnu >	130	41.54 N	28.03 E
Igney	58	48.17 N	6.24 E
Ignon ≃	58	47.31 N	5.10 E
Igny	261	48.45 N	2.14 E
Igodovo	80	58.01 N	42.21 E
Igombe ≃	154	4.38 S	31.40 E
Igoumenítsa	38	39.30 N	20.16 E
Igra	80	57.33 N	53.04 E
Igreja Nova	250	10.07 S	36.39 W
Iguaçu ≃, Bra.	256	22.45 S	43.14 W
Iguaçu ≃, S.A.	252	25.36 S	54.36 W
Iguaçu, Cataratas do (Iguassu Falls) ∟	252	25.41 S	54.26 W
Iguaçu, Parque Nacional do ♠	252	25.30 S	53.50 W
Iguaí	255	14.45 S	40.04 W
Iguala	234	18.21 N	99.32 W
Igualada	34	41.35 N	1.38 E
Iguana ≃	246	7.54 N	65.46 W
Iguape	252	24.43 S	47.33 W
Iguará ≃	250	3.28 S	43.55 W
Iguassu Falls → Iguaçu, Cataratas 99do ∟	252	25.41 S	54.26 W
Iguatemi	255	23.40 S	54.34 W
Iguatemi ≃	255	23.55 S	54.10 W
Iguatu	250	6.22 S	39.18 W
Iguazú, Parque Nacional ♠	252	25.35 S	54.20 W
Iguéla	152	1.55 S	9.19 E
Iguéla, Lagune ⊂	152	1.55 S	9.25 E
Iguetti, Sebkhet ≚	148	25.05 N	9.50 W
Iguîdi, 'Erg ⚊[8]	148	26.35 N	5.40 W
Iguig	116	17.45 N	121.44 E
Igumale	150	6.49 N	7.59 E
Igumnovo	82	55.37 N	38.18 E
Igvak, Cape >	180	57.26 N	156.00 W
Igžej	88	53.59 N	103.10 E
Ihavandiffulu Atoll I[1]	122	7.00 N	72.55 E
Iheya-shima I	93b	27.04 N	127.58 E
Ihiala	150	5.51 N	6.51 E
Ihirène, Oued V	148	20.25 N	4.35 E
Ihle ≃	54	52.17 N	11.52 E
Ihlienworth	52	53.44 N	8.55 E
Ihlow	52	53.25 N	7.27 E
Ihmert	56	51.20 N	7.44 E
Ihnāsiyat al-Madīnah	142	29.05 N	30.56 E
Ihorombe	157b	23.00 S	47.33 E
Ihosy	157b	22.24 S	46.08 E
Ihosy ≃	157b	21.44 S	45.53 E
Ihotry, Lac ⊜	157b	21.56 S	43.41 E
Ihringen	58	48.02 N	7.39 E
Ihringshausen	52	51.21 N	9.31 E
Ihrlerstein	60	48.56 N	11.52 E
İhsangazi	130	41.11 N	33.33 E
Ih Tal	89	43.13 N	122.15 E
Ihtiman	38	42.26 N	23.49 E
Ihu	164	7.55 S	145.25 E
Ihugh	150	7.02 N	9.00 E
Ihwah	142	29.03 N	31.00 E
Iida	94	35.31 N	137.50 E
Iidaan	144	6.06 N	48.59 E
Iijima	94	35.40 N	137.56 E
Iijoki ≃	24	65.20 N	25.17 E
Iiktu, gora ∧	86	49.51 N	87.40 E
Iinan	94	34.27 N	136.24 E
Iinashi ≃	96	35.27 N	133.13 E
Iioka	94	35.42 N	140.43 E
Iisaku	76	59.06 N	27.19 E
Iisalmi	26	63.34 N	27.11 E
Iisvesi	26	62.40 N	27.02 E
Iitaka	94	34.26 N	136.21 E
Iittala	26	61.04 N	24.10 E
Iiyama	94	36.51 N	138.22 E
Iizuka	96	33.38 N	130.41 E
Ij ≃	88	52.34 N	96.10 E
Ija ≃	88	55.05 N	101.05 E
Ijâfene ◆[2]	134	20.30 N	8.00 W
Ijaiye	273a	6.40 N	3.18 E
Ijaji	144	8.59 N	37.13 E
Ijara	154	1.36 S	40.31 E
Ijebu-Igbo	150	6.56 N	4.01 E
Ijebu-Ode	150	6.50 N	3.56 E
Ijesa-Tedo	273a	6.30 N	3.19 E
Ijin	98	42.05 N	130.08 E
Ijira	94	35.31 N	136.44 E
IJmuiden	52	52.27 N	4.36 E
IJssel ≃	52	52.35 N	5.50 E
IJsselmeer (Zuiderzee) ⊤[2]	52	52.45 N	5.25 E
IJsselmuiden	52	52.34 N	5.56 E
IJsselstein	52	52.02 N	5.03 E
Ijuí	252	28.23 S	53.55 W
Ijuí ≃	252	27.58 S	55.20 W
Iju Junction	273a	6.40 N	3.19 E
Ijuw	174b	0.30 S	166.57 E
Iju Water Works ʊ[3]	273a	6.40 N	3.20 E
IJzendijke	52	51.19 N	3.38 E
IJzer (Yser) ≃	50	51.09 N	2.43 E
Ik ≃	80	55.55 N	52.36 E
Ika	88	59.18 N	106.12 E
Ikaalinen	26	61.46 N	23.03 E
Ikaho	94	36.30 N	138.55 E
Ikalamavony	157b	21.09 S	46.35 E
Ikali	152	2.02 S	21.02 E
Ikalou	152	4.03 S	11.48 E
Ikamatua	172	42.16 S	171.41 E
Ikamba	273b	4.22 S	15.16 E
Ikang	150	4.50 N	8.32 E
Ikara	150	11.12 N	8.15 E
Ikare	150	7.32 N	5.45 E
Ikaría I	38	37.41 N	26.20 E
Ikari-dam ◆[6]	94	36.52 N	139.42 E
Ikari-ko ⊜	94	36.56 N	139.41 E
Ikaruga	96	34.36 N	135.44 E
Ikast	41	56.08 N	9.10 E
Ikatan	180	54.45 N	163.19 W
Ikatskij chrebet ⋏	88	54.00 N	111.00 E
Ikawa	94	35.13 N	138.15 E
Ikawa-dam ◆[6]	94	35.12 N	138.13 E
Ikawhenua Range ⋏	172	38.20 S	176.56 E
Ikazaki	96	33.32 N	132.39 E
Ikeda, Nihon	92a	42.55 N	143.27 E
Ikeda, Nihon	94	35.53 N	136.21 E
Ikeda, Nihon	94	35.26 N	136.34 E
Ikeda, Nihon	94	36.25 N	137.53 E
Ikeda, Nihon	96	34.49 N	135.25 E
Ikeda, Nihon	96	34.01 N	133.48 E
Ikegawa	96	33.36 N	133.11 E
Ikej	88	54.12 N	100.04 E
Ikeja	150	6.36 N	3.21 E
Ikeja □[8]	273a	6.30 N	3.25 E
Ikela	152	1.11 S	23.16 E
Ikélemba	152	1.14 N	16.31 E
Ikelemba ≃	152	0.07 N	18.17 E
Ikema-jima I	175d	24.56 N	125.16 E
Ikerre	150	7.31 N	5.14 E
Ike-shima I	174m	26.23 N	128.00 E
Ikeura	270	34.30 N	135.25 E
Iki I	92	33.47 N	129.43 E
Iki-Burul	80	45.49 N	44.39 E
Ikimba, Lake ⊜	154	1.28 S	31.30 E
Īkinjī Maryūt	142	31.00 N	29.45 E
Ikire	150	7.23 N	4.12 E
Ikirun	150	7.55 N	4.41 E
İkizce	130	39.36 N	32.40 E
İkizdere	130	40.47 N	40.33 E
Iko	152	0.35 S	16.01 E
Ikole	150	7.49 N	5.30 E
Ikolik, Cape >	180	57.17 N	154.48 W
Ikom	150	5.58 N	8.42 E
Ikoma, Nihon	96	34.41 N	135.42 E
Ikoma, Tan.	154	2.04 S	34.37 E
Ikoma-sanchi ⋏	270	34.40 N	135.40 E
Ikoma-tunnel ◆[5]	270	34.41 N	135.41 E
Ikoma-yama ∧	270	34.40 N	135.41 E
Ikon-Chal'	84	44.18 N	41.55 E
Ikopa ≃	157b	17.01 S	46.45 E
Ikorec ≃	78	50.58 N	39.45 E
Ikorodu	150	6.37 N	3.31 E
Ikot Ekpene	150	5.12 N	7.40 E
Ikoy ≃	152	0.53 S	10.36 E
Ikoyi ◆[8]	273a	6.27 N	3.26 E
Ikoyi Island I	273a	6.27 N	3.26 E
Ikoyi Prison ʊ	273a	6.25 N	3.25 E
Ikozi	154	2.32 S	27.37 E
Ikpikpuk ≃	180	70.50 N	154.25 W
Ikra	126	23.42 N	87.07 E
Ikr'anoje	80	46.06 N	47.45 E
Ikrāsh	142	30.45 N	31.30 E
Ikša	82	56.10 N	37.31 E
Iksa ≃	86	57.48 N	82.36 E
Ikti, Cape >	180	56.00 N	158.30 W
Ikuata	273a	6.25 N	3.22 E
Ikuchi-shima I	96	34.17 N	133.07 E
Ikuji-hana >	94	36.54 N	137.25 E
Ikuktlitlig Mountain ∧	180	59.16 N	161.27 W
Ikungu	154	1.34 S	33.40 E
Ikuno	96	35.10 N	134.48 E
Ikuno ◆[8]	270	34.39 N	135.34 E
Ikurangi, Mount ∧[2]	174k	21.13 S	159.45 W
Ikusaka	94	36.25 N	137.56 E
Ikusu ≃	273b	4.24 S	15.14 E
Ikuta	268	35.36 N	139.32 E
Ikva ≃, Magy.	61	47.42 N	16.58 E
Ikva ≃, Ukr.	78	50.33 N	25.24 E
Ikwah	142	30.41 N	31.28 E
Ila, Nig.	150	8.01 N	4.55 E
Ila, Zaïre	152	2.53 S	21.05 E
Ilabaya	248	17.25 S	70.31 W
Ilacaon Point >	116	11.00 N	123.12 E
Ilagala	154	5.12 S	29.50 E
Ilagan	116	17.10 N	121.54 E
Ilagan ≃	116	17.09 N	121.54 E
Ilaiyānkudi	122	9.38 N	78.38 E
Ilaka, Madag.	157b	19.33 S	48.52 E
Ilaka, Madag.	157b	20.20 S	47.09 E
Īlām, Īrān	128	33.38 N	46.26 E
Ilām, Nepāl	124	26.55 N	87.56 E
Īlām □[4]	128	33.15 N	46.45 E
Ilam → Sri Lanka □[1]	122	7.00 N	81.00 E
Ilām Bāzār	126	23.38 N	87.32 E
Ilan	100	24.46 N	121.45 E
Ilan ≃	100	24.43 N	121.49 E
Ilanskij	88	56.14 N	96.03 E
Ilanz	58	46.46 N	9.12 E
Ilara	273a	6.42 N	3.27 E
Ilarionove	78	48.25 N	35.16 E
Ilaro	150	6.53 N	3.03 E
Ilasco	219	39.40 N	91.18 W
Ilave	248	16.06 S	69.41 W
Iława	30	53.37 N	19.33 E
Ilawe-Ekiti	150	7.37 N	5.06 E
Ilay	58	46.37 N	5.53 E
Ilbenge	74	62.49 N	124.24 E
Ilberstedt	54	51.48 N	11.40 E
Il Catalano I	71	39.53 N	8.17 E
Ilchester, Eng., U.K.	42	51.01 N	2.41 W
Ilchester, Md., U.S.	284b	39.15 N	76.45 W
Ildefonso, Islas II	254	55.44 S	69.26 W
Île-à-la-Crosse	184	55.27 N	107.53 W
Île-à-la-Crosse, Lac ⊜	184	55.40 N	107.45 W
Ilebo (Port-Francqui)	152	4.19 S	20.35 E
Île-Cadieux	275a	45.25 N	74.01 W
Île-de-France □[9]	50	49.00 N	2.20 E
Île-de-Montréal □[6]	206	45.30 N	73.40 W
Île-Jésus □[6]	206	45.35 N	73.45 W
Ilek	80	51.30 N	53.22 E
Ilek ≃	72	51.30 N	53.20 E
Ilen ≃	48	51.33 N	9.19 W
Île-Perrot	206	45.23 N	73.57 W
Ileret	154	4.19 N	36.13 E
Îles, Grand lac des ⊜	206	46.43 N	73.30 W
Îles, Lac des ⊜, P.Q., Can.	206	46.06 N	74.02 W
Îles, Lac des ⊜, Sk., Can.	184	54.26 N	109.25 W
Ilesha	150	7.38 N	4.45 E
Ilesha Ibarida	150	8.56 N	3.25 E
Ilet' ≃	80	55.56 N	48.14 E
Ilevskij Pogost	24	60.41 N	43.46 E
Ileza	24	60.43 N	43.54 E
Ilfeld	54	51.34 N	10.47 E
Ilford, Austl.	170	32.58 S	149.51 E
Ilford, Mb., Can.	184	56.04 N	95.35 W
Ilford ◆[8]	260	51.33 N	0.05 E
Ilfracombe, Austl.	166	23.30 S	144.30 E
Ilfracombe, Eng., U.K.	42	51.13 N	4.08 W
Il Fuorn	58	46.40 N	10.12 E
Ilga ≃	88	55.00 N	105.04 E
Ilgaz	130	40.56 N	33.38 E
Ilgaz Dağları ⋏	130	41.00 N	33.35 E
Ilgın	130	38.17 N	31.55 E
Ilha ◆[8]	256	23.00 S	43.33 W
Ilhabela	256	23.47 S	45.21 W
Ilha das Flores	250	10.27 S	36.33 W
Ilha Grande, Baía da ⊂	256	23.09 S	44.30 W
Ilhas, Cachoeira das ∟	250	1.03 S	57.33 W
Ilha Solteira, Reprêsa de ⊜[1]	255	20.20 S	51.20 W
Ilhavo	34	40.36 N	8.40 W
Ilhea Point >	156	23.25 S	14.27 E
Ilhéos → Ilhéus	255	14.49 S	39.02 W
Ilhéus	255	14.49 S	39.02 W
Ili ≃	86	45.24 N	74.02 E
Ilia	38	45.56 N	22.39 E
Iliamna	180	59.45 N	154.54 W
Iliamna Lake ⊜	180	59.30 N	155.00 W
Ilian, Mount ∧	116	10.26 N	119.33 E
Iliatenco	234	16.58 N	98.40 W
İliç	130	39.28 N	38.34 E
Ilıca, Tür.	130	39.52 N	27.46 E
Ilıca, Tür.	130	39.57 N	41.07 E
Ilicínia	255	20.56 S	45.50 W
Iliff	198	40.45 N	103.03 W
Iliff, Lake ⊜	276	41.02 N	74.43 W
Iligan	116	8.14 N	124.14 E
Iligan Bay ⊂	116	8.25 N	124.05 E
Ilijan	116	13.38 N	121.04 E
Ilijsk	85	43.53 N	77.10 E
Ilim ≃	88	57.38 N	102.34 E
Ilimsk	88	56.46 N	103.52 E
Ilin	116	12.15 N	121.02 E
Ilinge	158	31.59 S	27.02 E
Ilin Island I	116	12.14 N	121.05 E
Ilinka	82	54.04 N	38.12 E
Ilinza ∧	246	0.40 S	78.42 W
Ilion	210	43.00 N	75.02 W
Ilio Point >	229a	21.13 N	157.15 W
Ilioúpolis	267c	37.56 N	23.45 E
Ilir	88	55.13 N	100.40 E
Ilirska Bistrica	36	45.34 N	14.15 E
Ilisós ≃	267c	37.57 N	23.41 E
Ilizi	148	26.29 N	8.28 E
Ilja	76	54.25 N	27.18 E
Iljak	86	60.11 N	77.59 E
Iljič	85	40.50 N	68.27 E
Iljinka	80	48.32 N	41.05 E
Iljino	76	55.57 N	31.40 E
Iljinskij, Ross.	24	61.02 N	32.41 E
Iljinskij, Ross.	86	58.35 N	55.41 E
Iljinskij, Ross.	88	52.05 N	114.10 E
Iljinskij, Ross.	89	47.58 N	142.12 E
Iljinskij, Ross.	265b	55.37 N	38.06 E
Iljinskij Pogost	82	55.28 N	38.54 E
Iljinskoje, Ross.	76	56.58 N	37.11 E
Iljinskoje, Ross.	76	58.47 N	44.36 E
Iljinskoje, Ross.	76	53.14 N	35.26 E
Iljinskoje, Ross.	76	57.19 N	38.32 E
Iljinskoje, Ross.	80	56.29 N	52.49 E
Iljinskoje, Ross.	82	54.59 N	36.11 E
Iljinskoje, Ross.	82	56.34 N	35.57 E
Iljinskoje, Ross.	265b	55.46 N	37.15 E
Iljinskoje-Chovanskoje	80	56.58 N	39.46 E
Iljinsko-Podomskoje	24	61.08 N	47.56 E

Symbol	English	Deutsch	Español	Français	Português
≃	River	Fluß	Río	Rivière	Rio
≅	Canal	Kanal	Canal	Canal	Canal
∟	Waterfall, Rapids	Wasserfall, Stromschnellen	Cascada, Rápidos	Chute d'eau, Rapides	Cascata, Rápidos
ꭒ	Strait	Meeresstraße	Estrecho	Détroit	Estreito
⊂	Bay, Gulf	Bucht, Golf	Bahía, Golfo	Baie, Golfe	Baía, Golfo
⊜	Lake, Lakes	See, Seen	Lago, Lagos	Lac, Lacs	Lago, Lagos
≛	Swamp	Sumpf	Pantano	Marais	Pântano
≚	Ice Features, Glacier	Eis- und Gletscherformen	Accidentes Glaciales	Formes glaciaires	Acidentes glaciares
⊤	Other Hydrographic Features	Andere Hydrographische Objekte	Otros Elementos Hidrográficos	Autres données hydrographiques	Outros acidentes hidrográficos
✧	Submarine Features	Untermeerische Objekte	Accidentes Submarinos	Formes de relief sous-marin	Acidentes submarinos
□	Political Unit	Politische Einheit	Unidad Politica	Entité politique	Unidade política
ʊ	Cultural Institution	Kulturelle Institution	Institución Cultural	Institution culturelle	Instituição cultural
⊥	Historical Site	Historische Stätte	Sitio Histórico	Site historique	Sitio histórico
♠	Recreational Site	Erholungs- und Ferienort	Sitio de Recreo	Centre de loisirs	Area de Lazer
⊠	Airport	Flughafen	Aeropuerto	Aéroport	Aeroporto
■	Military Installation	Militäranlage	Instalación Militar	Installation militaire	Instalação militar
◆	Miscellaneous	Verschiedenes	Misceláneo	Divers	Diversos

ENGLISH

DEUTSCH

Name / Name	Page / Seite	Lat.°′ / Breite°′	Long.°′ / Länge°′ E = Ost
Iljinsko-Zaborskoje	80	57.16 N	44.23 E
Iljiny gory ⋏[2]	76	56.34 N	34.12 E
Il'ka	88	51.43 N	108.32 E
Ilkal	122	15.58 N	76.08 E
Ilkeston	42	52.59 N	1.18 W
Il'kino	80	55.13 N	41.36 E
Ilkley	44	53.55 N	1.50 W
Ill ≃, Fr.	58	48.40 N	7.53 E
Ill ≃, Öst.	58	47.17 N	9.33 E
Illabot Creek ≃	224	48.29 N	121.30 W
Illampu, Nevado ∧	248	15.50 S	68.34 W
Illana Bay ⊂	116	7.25 N	123.45 E
Illapel	252	31.38 S	71.10 W
Illasi	64	45.28 N	11.10 E
Illawarra, Lake ⊂	170	34.32 S	150.50 E
Illbillee, Mount ∧	162	27.02 S	132.30 E
Ille-et-Vilaine □[5]	32	48.10 N	1.30 W
Illéla	150	14.28 N	5.15 E
Iller ≃	58	48.23 N	9.58 E
Illertissen	58	48.13 N	10.06 E
Illescas, Esp.	34	40.07 N	3.50 W
Illescas, Méx.	234	23.13 N	102.07 W
Illfurth	58	47.40 N	7.16 E
Illhaeusern	58	48.11 N	7.26 E
Illi, Ba ≃	146	10.44 N	15.21 E
Illichivs'k	78	46.18 N	30.39 E
Illiers	50	48.18 N	1.15 E
Illimani, Nevado ∧	248	16.50 S	67.54 W
Illimo	248	6.28 S	79.51 W
Illingen	56	48.57 N	8.55 E
Illingworth	262	53.45 N	1.54 W
Illinois □[3], U.S.	178	40.00 N	89.00 W
Illinois □[3], U.S.	194	40.00 N	89.00 W
Illinois ≃, U.S.	194	35.30 N	95.06 W
Illinois ≃, Co., U.S.	200	40.45 N	106.18 W
Illinois ≃, Il., U.S.	194	38.58 N	90.27 W
Illinois ≃, Or., U.S.	202	42.33 N	124.03 W
Illinois and Michigan Canal ≋	278	41.32 N	88.05 W
Illinois at Chicago, University of ⚑[2]	278	41.52 N	87.39 W
Illinois Beach State Park ♦	216	42.26 N	87.48 W
Illinois Institute of Technology ⚑[2]	278	41.50 N	87.38 W
Illinois Peak ∧	202	47.02 N	115.04 W
Illintsi	78	49.07 N	29.12 E
Illiopolis	219	39.51 N	89.14 W
Illkirch-Graffenstaden	58	48.32 N	7.43 E
Illminster	42	50.56 N	2.55 W
Illo	150	11.33 N	3.42 E
Illovo, S. Afr.	158	30.05 S	30.50 E
Illovo, S. Afr.	273d	26.08 S	28.03 E
Illzach	58	47.47 N	7.20 E
Ilm ≃, Dtsch.	54	51.07 N	11.40 E
Ilm ≃, Dtsch.	60	48.49 N	11.45 E
Ilmajoki	26	62.44 N	22.34 E
Il'men', ozero ⊜	76	58.17 N	31.20 E
Ilmenau	54	50.41 N	10.55 E
Ilmenau ≃	54	53.23 N	10.10 E
Il'menskij zapovednik ♦	86	55.16 N	60.17 E
Il'mino	80	53.47 N	45.40 E
Ilo	248	17.38 S	71.20 W
Ilobasco	236	13.51 N	88.51 W
Ilobu	150	7.51 N	4.30 E
Iloc Island I	116	11.18 N	119.41 E
Ilocos Norte □[4]	116	18.10 N	120.45 E
Ilocos Sur □[4]	116	17.05 N	120.35 E
Iloilo	116	10.42 N	122.34 E
Iloilo □[4]	116	11.00 N	122.35 E
Iloilo Strait ⋓	116	10.43 N	122.36 E
Ilomantsi	24	62.40 N	30.55 E
Ilondola Mission	154	10.42 S	31.47 E
Ilongero	154	4.40 S	34.52 E
Ilop	164	2.54 S	141.13 E
Ilopango, Lago de ⊜	236	13.40 N	89.03 W
Ilora	150	7.45 N	3.50 E
Ilorin	150	8.30 N	4.32 E
Ilovatka	80	50.31 N	45.55 E
Ilovays'k	83	47.56 N	38.13 E
Ilovka	78	50.43 N	38.38 E
Ilovl'a	80	49.18 N	43.59 E
Ilovl'a ≃	80	49.14 N	43.54 E
Iłowa	30	51.30 N	15.12 E
Il Palone ∧	64	46.02 N	11.04 E
Il'pyrskij	74	59.56 N	164.10 E
Ilsan-ni	271b	37.41 N	126.46 E
Ilse ≃	54	52.06 N	10.35 E
Ilshofen	56	49.10 N	9.55 E
Il'skij	78	44.51 N	38.35 E
Ilskov	41	56.14 N	9.06 E
Il Telegrafo ∧	66	42.22 N	11.10 E
Ilten	52	52.21 N	9.55 E
Ilu	152	4.12 N	23.02 E
Ilubabor □[4]	144	7.50 N	35.00 E
Iluhār	126	22.48 N	90.06 E
Ilūkste	76	55.58 N	26.18 E
Ilverich	263	51.17 N	6.42 E
Ilwaco	224	46.19 N	124.03 W
Ilwaki	112	7.56 S	126.26 E
Ilwŏl-san ∧	98	36.50 N	129.06 E
İlyasbey	130	40.13 N	29.52 E
Ilz	61	47.05 N	15.55 E
Ilz ≃	60	48.35 N	13.29 E
Iłża	30	51.11 N	21.14 E
Ima	88	55.13 N	115.55 E
Ima ≃	96	33.45 N	131.01 E
Imabari	96	34.03 N	133.00 E
Imabu ≃	250	0.44 S	57.22 W
Imadomi	268	35.28 N	140.06 E
Imaichi	94	36.43 N	139.41 E
Imajō	94	35.46 N	136.12 E
Imajuku	268	35.58 N	139.21 E
Imajuku ◂[8]	268	35.29 N	139.32 E
Imaki	270	34.24 N	135.46 E
Imaloto ≃	157b	23.27 S	45.13 E
Imambara ⚑[1]	272b	22.54 N	88.25 E
Imanbaj ⊥	86	43.13 N	60.25 E
Imandan-Makit, gora ∧	88	54.07 N	117.43 E
Imandra, ozero ⊜	24	67.30 N	33.00 E
Imanombo	157b	24.26 S	45.49 E
Imantau	86	52.58 N	68.22 E
Imari	92	33.16 N	129.53 E
Imaruí	252	28.21 S	48.49 W
Imaruí, Lagoa do ⊂	252	28.21 S	48.52 W
Imasa	140	18.01 N	36.12 E
Imatra	26	61.10 N	28.46 E
Imavere	76	58.44 N	25.48 E
Imazu	94	35.24 N	136.02 E
Imbābah ◂[8]	142	30.04 N	31.13 E
Imbabura □[4]	246	0.22 N	78.25 W
Imba-numa ⊜	94	35.45 N	140.12 E
Imbariê	256	22.39 S	43.13 W
Imbituba	252	28.14 S	48.40 W
Imbituva	252	25.12 S	50.35 W
Imboaçu, Canal ≋	287a	22.48 S	43.04 W
Imboden	194	36.12 N	91.10 W
Imbonga	152	0.43 S	19.46 E
Imbundi	152	5.44 S	16.16 E
Ime, Beinn ∧	46	56.14 N	4.49 W
Imeni Abaja	86	50.44 N	69.30 E
Imeni Babuškina	76	59.45 N	43.07 E
Imeni Čapajeva	85	43.28 N	76.50 E
Imeni C'urupy	82	55.30 N	38.39 E
Imeni Džambula, Kaz.	86	45.26 N	74.24 E
Imeni Džambula, Kaz.	86	47.43 N	74.09 E
Imeni Frunze	86	46.23 N	77.20 E
Imeni Il-Go Okt'abr'a	88	55.54 N	119.36 E
Imeni Kalinina, Kaz.	85	43.16 N	74.03 E
Imeni Kalinina, Kyrg.	85	41.28 N	76.22 E
Imeni Kalinina, Ross.	80	51.51 N	52.43 E
Imeni Kalinina, Uzb.	86	43.40 N	59.07 E
Imeni Karla Libknechta	78	51.37 N	35.27 E
Imeni Kirova, Kaz.	86	46.27 N	77.13 E
Imeni Kirova, Ross.	74	59.42 N	128.12 E
Imeni Leninskogo Komsomola	86	50.45 N	66.44 E
Imeni Marta	86	46.57 N	58.58 E
Imeni Michajla Ivanoviča Kalinina	80	57.59 N	45.07 E
Imeni Molodogvardejcev	86	54.03 N	70.44 E
Imeni Panfilova	85	43.23 N	77.07 E
Imeni Poliny Osipenko	89	52.25 N	136.28 E
Imeni Sardarova Karachana	85	38.26 N	68.46 E
Imeni Ṣeredy	83	46.52 N	40.03 E
Imeni Ševčenko	86	45.58 N	61.04 E
Imeni Stepana Razina	80	54.54 N	44.18 E
Imeni Tel'mana	89	48.36 N	134.59 E
Imeni Timir'azeva	86	53.39 N	65.31 E
Imeni Vladimira Iljiča Lenina	80	53.36 N	46.58 E
Imeni Vorovskogo, Ross.	80	55.43 N	41.06 E
Imeni Vorovskogo, Ross.	82	55.43 N	38.20 E
Imeni XXI Partsjezda	86	50.43 N	67.50 E
Imeni Žel'abova	76	58.57 N	36.36 E
Imera ⊥	70	37.59 N	13.49 E
Imerimandroso	157b	17.23 S	48.38 E
Imese	152	2.07 N	18.06 E
Imgenbroich	56	50.34 N	6.16 E
Imi	144	6.28 N	42.18 E
Imías	240p	20.04 N	74.38 W
Imilac	252	24.14 S	68.53 W
Imilili ⍑[4]	148	23.18 N	15.54 W
Imi-n'Tanout	148	31.10 N	8.50 W
İmişli	84	39.52 N	48.04 E
Imittós	267c	37.57 N	23.45 E
Imittós Óros ⋏	267c	37.55 N	23.47 E
Imja-do I	98	35.05 N	126.05 E
Imjin-gang ≃	98	37.47 N	126.40 E
Imlay	204	40.39 N	118.08 W
Imlay City	190	43.01 N	83.04 W
Imlaystown	208	40.10 N	74.31 W
Imler	214	40.12 N	78.31 W
Immarna	162	30.30 S	132.09 E
Immendingen	58	47.56 N	8.44 E
Immenhausen	56	51.25 N	9.28 E
Immensen	52	52.23 N	10.04 E
Immenstaad	58	47.40 N	9.22 E
Immenstadt	58	47.33 N	10.13 E
Immigrath	263	51.06 N	6.57 E
Immingham	44	53.36 N	0.13 W
Immokalee	220	26.25 N	81.25 W
Imnaha ≃	202	45.49 N	116.46 W
Imo □[3]	150	5.30 N	7.25 E
Imo ≃	150	4.36 N	7.35 E
Imogiri	115a	7.55 S	110.23 E
Imokt'an	98	38.50 N	126.41 E
Imola	66	44.21 N	11.42 E
Imonda	164	3.20 S	141.10 E
Imore	273a	6.26 N	3.17 E
Imoro	273a	6.43 N	3.30 E
Im Ostholz ◂[8]	263	51.26 N	7.12 E
Imotski	36	43.27 N	17.13 E
Imp'a	98	35.59 N	126.49 E
Impasugong	116	8.19 N	125.00 E
Impe	152	2.44 S	15.17 E
Impendle	158	29.37 S	29.55 E
Imperatore, Campo ≚	66	42.25 N	13.40 E
Imperatriz	250	5.32 S	47.29 W
Imperia	62	43.53 N	8.03 E
Imperia □[4]	62	43.58 N	7.47 E
Imperial, Sk., Can.	184	51.22 N	105.27 W
Imperial, Perú	248	13.04 S	76.21 W
Imperial, Ca., U.S.	204	32.50 N	115.34 W
Imperial, Mo., U.S.	219	38.22 N	90.22 W
Imperial, Ne., U.S.	198	40.31 N	101.38 W
Imperial, Pa., U.S.	214	40.26 N	80.14 W
Imperial, Tx., U.S.	196	31.16 N	102.41 W
Imperial ≃	254	38.48 S	73.24 W
Imperial Beach	228	32.35 N	117.06 W
Imperial Dam ◂[6]	204	32.55 N	114.30 W
Imperial de Aragón, Canal ≋	34	42.02 N	1.33 W
Imperiale	68	40.07 N	16.35 E
Imperial Mills	182	55.00 N	111.44 W
Imperial Palace ⚑	268	35.41 N	139.45 E
Imperial Valley V	204	32.50 N	115.30 W
Impflingen	56	49.10 N	8.07 E
Impfondo	152	1.37 N	18.04 E
Imphāl	120	24.49 N	93.57 E
Impilachti	24	61.40 N	31.04 E
Impruneta	66	43.41 N	11.15 E
Impulo	152	13.53 S	13.39 E
İmralı Adası I	130	40.32 N	28.32 E
İmranlı	130	39.54 N	38.07 E
Imroz	130	40.11 N	25.55 E
Imsil	98	35.37 N	127.15 E
Imst	64	47.14 N	10.44 E
Imtān	132	32.24 N	36.49 E
Imuris	232	30.47 N	110.52 W
Imuruan Bay ⊂	116	10.40 N	119.16 E
Imuruk Basin ⊜	180	65.06 N	165.36 W
Imuruk Lake ⊜	180	65.36 N	163.10 W
Imute	273a	6.42 N	3.29 E
Imwŏn-ni	98	37.15 N	129.20 E
Ina, Nihon	94	37.10 N	139.32 E
Ina, Nihon	94	35.59 N	140.03 E
Ina, Nihon	94	35.50 N	137.57 E
Ina, Nihon	268	35.59 N	139.38 E
In'a, Ross.	74	59.24 N	144.48 E
In'a, Ross.	86	53.31 N	82.40 E
In'a, Ross.	86	50.48 N	86.37 E
Ina, Il., U.S.	194	38.09 N	88.54 W
Ina ≃, Nihon	94	37.16 N	139.33 E
Ina ≃, Nihon	96	34.43 N	135.28 E
Ina ≃, Pol.	54	53.32 N	14.38 E
In'a ≃, Ross.	74	59.23 N	144.54 E
In'a ≃, Ross.	86	54.59 N	82.59 E
Inaba	270	34.26 N	135.27 E
Inabe	94	35.07 N	136.33 E
Ina-bonchi ≚[1]	94	35.45 N	137.57 E
Inabu	94	35.13 N	137.30 E
Inaccessible Island I	10	37.17 S	12.45 W
Inada	270	34.54 N	135.08 E
Inagawa	96	34.53 N	135.22 E
Inagawan	116	9.33 N	118.39 E
Inage	268	35.38 N	140.05 E
Inagi	94	35.38 N	139.30 E
Inajá	250	8.54 S	37.49 W
Inajá ≃	250	8.53 S	49.44 W
In'akino	80	54.26 N	41.07 E
Inakona	175e	9.49 S	160.02 E
Inala	171a	27.35 S	152.58 E
Inamangando ≃	152	14.03 S	12.23 E
Inambari ≃	248	12.41 S	69.44 W
In Amguel	148	23.40 N	5.10 E
Inami, Nihon	94	36.33 N	136.58 E
Inami, Nihon	96	33.48 N	135.13 E
Inami, Nihon	96	34.45 N	134.54 E
In Amnas	148	28.05 N	9.30 E
Inampulugan Island I	116	10.28 N	122.42 E
Inamuragasaki Point ⊥	268	35.18 N	139.32 E
Inanda	273d	26.07 S	28.03 E
Inangahua Junction	172	41.51 S	171.57 E
Inanwatan	164	2.08 S	132.10 E
Iñapari	248	10.57 S	69.35 W
Inaporok	164	8.15 S	141.55 E
In'aptuk, gora ∧	88	56.22 N	110.11 E
Inari	24	68.54 N	27.01 E
Inarigda	74	63.14 N	107.27 E
Inarijärvi ⊜	24	69.00 N	28.00 E
Inas, Gunong ∧	114	5.15 N	100.56 E
Inasa	94	34.50 N	137.40 E
Inatsuki	96	33.36 N	130.43 E
Inauini ≃	248	8.30 S	67.24 W
Inawaia	164	8.40 S	146.35 E
Inawashiro-ko ⊜	92	37.29 N	140.06 E
I-n-Azaoua ⍑[4]	148	20.49 N	7.30 E
Inazawa	94	35.15 N	136.47 E
Inba	94	35.46 N	140.14 E
Inba-numa ⊜	94	35.46 N	140.12 E
In Belbel	148	27.54 N	1.10 E
Inca	34	39.43 N	2.54 E
Inca de Oro	252	26.45 S	69.54 W
Incaguasi	252	29.13 S	71.03 W
Incahuasi, Nevado de ∧	252	27.02 S	68.18 W
Ince	262	53.17 N	2.49 W
Ince Blundell	262	53.31 N	3.02 W
İnce Burun ›	130	42.06 N	34.56 E
Ince-in-Makerfield	262	53.32 N	2.37 W
İncekum Burnu ›	130	36.13 N	33.58 E
İncesu	130	38.38 N	35.11 E
Inch	48	52.08 N	9.59 W
I-n-Chaouag ≃	150	16.23 N	0.10 E
Inchard, Loch ⊂	46	58.27 N	5.04 W
Inchas Military Base ■	142	30.20 N	31.27 E
Inchbare	46	56.47 N	2.38 W
Inchcape I[2]	46	56.26 N	2.23 W
Inchelium	182	48.17 N	118.11 W
Inchiri □[4]	150	19.50 N	15.00 W
Inchmarnock I	46	55.47 N	5.09 W
Inchnadamph	46	58.09 N	4.59 W
Inch'ŏn	98	37.28 N	126.38 E
Inch'ŏn □[4]	98	37.28 N	126.38 E
Inchture	46	56.26 N	3.10 W
Inchwagh Lake ⊜	281	42.27 N	83.41 W
İncirliova	130	37.50 N	27.43 E
Incisa in Val d'Arno	66	43.40 N	11.27 E
Incline Village	226	39.16 N	119.56 W
Incomáti (Komati) ≃	156	25.46 S	32.43 E
Inconfidência	256	22.16 S	43.13 W
Inconfidentes	256	22.20 S	46.20 W
Inčoun	180	66.18 N	170.17 W
Incudine	64	46.14 N	10.22 E
Incudine, Monte ∧	36	41.51 N	9.12 E
Incy	24	65.48 N	40.26 E
Indaal, Loch ⊂	46	55.45 N	6.21 W
Indaiá ≃	255	18.27 S	45.22 W
Indaiatuba	256	23.05 S	47.14 W
Indalsälven ≃	26	62.31 N	17.27 E
Indanan	116	5.58 N	120.59 E
Indaparapeo	234	19.47 N	100.58 W
Inda Silase	144	14.05 N	38.20 E
Indaw	110	23.40 N	94.46 E
Indawgyi Lake ⊜	110	25.10 N	96.19 E
Indé	232	25.54 N	105.13 W
Inde → India □[1]	118	20.00 N	77.00 E
Inde ≃	56	50.54 N	6.21 E
Indemini	58	46.06 N	8.50 E
Independence, Ca., U.S.	204	36.48 N	118.11 W
Independence, In., U.S.	216	40.20 N	87.10 W
Independence, Ia., U.S.	190	42.28 N	91.53 W
Independence, Ks., U.S.	198	37.13 N	95.42 W
Independence, Ky., U.S.	218	38.56 N	84.32 W
Independence, La., U.S.	194	30.38 N	90.30 W
Independence, Mo., U.S.	194	39.05 N	94.24 W
Independence, Oh., U.S.	279a	41.23 N	81.38 W
Independence, Or., U.S.	202	44.51 N	123.11 W
Independence, Pa., U.S.	214	40.15 N	80.31 W
Independence, Tx., U.S.	222	30.19 N	96.21 W
Independence, Va., U.S.	192	36.37 N	81.09 W
Independence, Wi., U.S.	190	44.21 N	91.25 W
Independence ≃	188	43.45 N	75.20 W
Independence Creek ≃	196	30.27 N	101.44 W
Independence Hall ⊥	285	39.57 N	75.09 W
Independence Lake ⊜[1]	226	39.26 N	120.18 W
Independence Mountains ⋏	204	41.15 N	115.55 W
Independencia, Bol.	248	17.07 S	66.53 W
Independência, Bra.	250	5.23 S	40.19 W
Independencia, Chile	286e	33.23 S	70.40 W
Independencia, Perú	286d	11.59 S	77.02 W
Independencia, Isla I	248	14.15 S	76.12 W
Independența	38	43.58 N	28.05 E
Inder, ozero ⊜	80	48.27 N	51.54 E
Inderborskij	80	48.33 N	51.44 E
In der Bredde	263	51.20 N	7.23 E
İnderesi	130	37.50 N	35.40 E
Index	224	47.49 N	121.33 W
Index, Mount ∧	224	47.46 N	121.35 W
Indi	122	17.10 N	75.58 E
India (Bhārat) □[1]	118	20.00 N	77.00 E
India Brook ≃	276	40.47 N	74.37 W
India Gate ⊥	272a	28.37 N	77.18 E
Indialantic	220	28.05 N	80.34 W
Indian ≃, On., Can.	212	45.16 N	76.14 W
Indian ≃, On., Can.	212	44.13 N	78.08 W
Indian ≃, De., U.S.	208	38.36 N	75.10 W
Indian ≃, Ma., U.S.	283	42.47 N	70.58 W
Indian ≃, Mi., U.S.	190	45.59 N	86.15 W
Indian ≃, N.Y., U.S.	212	44.24 N	75.39 W
Indiana	214	40.37 N	79.09 W
Indiana □[6]	214	40.37 N	79.09 W
Indiana □[3], U.S.	178	40.00 N	86.15 W
Indiana □[3], U.S.	194	40.00 N	86.15 W
Indiana Dunes National Lakeshore ♦	216	41.40 N	87.00 W
Indiana Dunes State Park ♦	216	41.40 N	87.02 W
Indian Agricultural Research Institute ⚑[3]	272a	28.38 N	77.10 E
Indiana Harbor ⊂	278	41.40 N	87.27 W
Indiana Harbor Canal ≋	278	41.40 N	87.27 W
Indianapolis	218	39.46 N	86.09 W
Indianapolis International Airport ⊠	218	39.43 N	86.16 W
Indianapolis Motor Speedway ♦	218	39.48 N	86.14 W
Indian Bayou ≃	194	34.14 N	91.52 W
Indian Brook	186	46.23 N	60.32 W
Indian Caverns ⫠[5]	214	40.38 N	78.05 W
Indian Church	232	17.45 N	88.40 W
Indian Creek	278	42.14 N	87.59 W
Indian Creek ≃, U.S.	218	39.19 N	84.38 W
Indian Creek ≃, Ca., U.S.	228	35.18 N	118.26 W
Indian Creek ≃, Il., U.S.	216	41.26 N	88.46 W
Indian Creek ≃, Il., U.S.	219	39.56 N	90.32 W
Indian Creek ≃, Il., U.S.	278	42.11 N	87.55 W
Indian Creek ≃, In., U.S.	216	40.55 N	86.42 W
Indian Creek ≃, In., U.S.	218	38.10 N	86.14 W
Indian Creek ≃, In., U.S.	218	38.43 N	85.06 W
Indian Creek ≃, In., U.S.	218	39.23 N	86.29 W
Indian Creek ≃, Md., U.S.	284c	38.59 N	76.55 W
Indian Creek ≃, Mo., U.S.	194	36.33 N	94.29 W
Indian Creek ≃, Mo., U.S.	219	39.10 N	91.11 W
Indian Creek ≃, N.M., U.S.	200	36.11 N	108.23 W
Indian Creek ≃, N.Y., U.S.	276	40.43 N	73.06 W
Indian Creek ≃, Oh., U.S.	218	39.19 N	84.38 W
Indian Creek ≃, Oh., U.S.	279a	41.17 N	81.31 W
Indian Creek ≃, S.D., U.S.	198	44.39 N	103.19 W
Indian Creek ≃, Tn., U.S.	194	35.13 N	88.08 W
Indian Creek Lake ⊜[1]	222	31.44 N	95.58 W
Indianford	216	42.49 N	88.35 W
Indian Grave Mountain ∧[2]	192	32.59 N	84.21 W
Indian Harbor Beach	220	28.08 N	80.35 W
Indian Head, Sk., Can.	184	50.32 N	103.40 W
Indian Head, Md., U.S.	208	38.36 N	77.09 W
Indian Head ≃	283	42.04 N	70.52 W
Indian Head Park	278	41.47 N	87.54 W
Indian Head Pond ⊜	283	42.03 N	70.51 W
Indian Heights	216	40.25 N	86.07 W
Indian Island I	224	48.04 N	122.43 W
Indian Kentuck Creek ≃	218	38.43 N	85.16 W
Indian Lake, Mi., U.S.	216	41.59 N	86.12 W
Indian Lake, N.Y., U.S.	188	43.46 N	74.16 W
Indian Lake ⊜, On., Can.	190	47.08 N	82.08 W
Indian Lake ⊜, Mi., U.S.	190	45.59 N	86.20 W
Indian Lake ⊜, Mi., U.S.	216	42.09 N	85.29 W
Indian Lake ⊜, Mi., U.S.	216	42.00 N	86.13 W
Indian Lake ⊜, N.J., U.S.	276	40.53 N	74.29 W
Indian Lake ⊜, Oh., U.S.	216	40.29 N	83.53 W
Indian Lake Estates	220	27.48 N	81.19 W
Indian Lakes ⊜	216	41.33 N	85.25 W
Indian Lake State Park ♦	216	40.29 N	83.52 W
Indian Mills Brook ≃	285	39.47 N	74.44 W
Indian Mills Lake ⊜	285	39.48 N	74.44 W
Indian Neck	207	41.15 N	72.48 W
Indian Ocean ⍑[1]	4	10.00 S	70.00 E
Indian Ocean ⍑[1]	6	10.00 S	70.00 E
Indianola, Ia., U.S.	190	41.21 N	93.33 W
Indianola, Ms., U.S.	194	33.27 N	90.39 W
Indianola, Ne., U.S.	198	40.14 N	100.25 W
Indianola, Pa., U.S.	279b	40.34 N	79.51 W
Indianola, Wa., U.S.	224	47.45 N	122.31 W
Indianópolis	255	19.02 S	47.55 W
Indianópolis ◂[8]	287b	23.36 S	46.38 W
Indian Peak ∧, Ut., U.S.	200	38.16 N	113.53 W
Indian Peak ∧, Wy., U.S.	202	44.47 N	109.51 W
Indian Point ›	212	44.37 N	78.49 W
Indian Prairie Canal ≋	220	27.02 N	80.57 W
Indian Queen Estates	284c	38.46 N	77.02 W
Indian River	190	45.24 N	84.36 W
Indian River □[6]	220	27.43 N	80.36 W
Indian River ⊂	220	28.00 N	80.30 W
Indian River Bay ⊂	208	38.36 N	75.05 W
Indian River Inlet ⊂	208	38.37 N	75.03 W
Indian Rock ∧	224	45.59 N	120.49 W
Indian Rock Dam ◂[6]	208	39.57 N	76.45 W
Indian Rock Paintings ⊥	224	46.38 N	120.31 W
Indian Rocks Beach	220	27.52 N	82.51 W
Indian Springs, Nv., U.S.	204	36.34 N	115.40 W
Indian Springs, Va., U.S.	284c	38.49 N	77.10 W
Indian Stream ≃	206	45.03 N	71.26 W
Indiantown	220	27.01 N	80.29 W
Indian Town Point ›	240c	17.06 N	61.40 W
Indian Valley Reservoir ⊜[1]	226	39.07 N	122.32 W
Indian Village, In., U.S.	218	40.10 N	85.22 W
Indian Village, N.Y., U.S.	210	42.57 N	76.10 W
Indiaporã	255	19.57 S	50.17 W
Indiaroba	250	11.32 S	37.31 W
Indibir	144	8.05 N	37.58 E
Indico, Océano → Indian Ocean ⍑[1]	6	10.00 S	70.00 E
Indien → India □[1]	118	20.00 N	77.00 E
Indien, Océan → Indian Ocean ⍑[1]	6	10.00 S	70.00 E
Indien, territoires britanniques de l'Ocean → British Indian Ocean Territory □[2]	12	7.00 S	72.00 E
Indiera Alta	240m	18.09 N	66.53 W
Indiga	24	67.41 N	49.00 E
Indigirka ≃	74	70.48 N	148.54 E
Inđija	38	45.03 N	20.05 E
Indin	120	20.16 N	92.57 E
Indio	204	33.43 N	116.12 W
Indio ≃, Nic.	236	10.57 N	83.44 W
Indio ≃, Pan.	236	9.12 N	80.11 W
Indio, Punta ›	258	35.16 S	57.13 W
Indios, Canal de los ⋓	240p	21.56 N	83.16 W
Indira Gandhi Canal ≋	120	31.10 N	75.00 E
Indira Gandhi International Airport ⊠	272a	28.35 N	77.07 E
Indischer Ozean → Indian Ocean ⍑[1]	6	10.00 S	70.00 E
Indispensable Reefs ✤[2]	160	12.40 S	160.25 E
Indispensable Strait ⋓	175e	9.00 S	160.30 E
Indo → Indus ≃	120	24.20 N	67.47 E
Indochina ◂[1]	108	16.00 N	107.00 E
Indom	24	64.36 N	55.22 E
Indonesia □[1]	108	5.00 S	120.00 E
Indonesia, University of ⚑[2]	269e	6.12 S	106.51 E
Indonesia in Miniature ♦	269e	6.08 S	106.49 E
Indonesian Culture, Museum of ⚑[3]	269e	6.09 N	106.49 E
Indonésie → Indonesia □[1]	108	5.00 S	120.00 E
Indonesien → Indonesia □[1]	108	5.00 S	120.00 E
Indooroopilly	171a	27.30 S	152.58 E
Indore	120	22.43 N	75.50 E
Indpur	126	23.10 N	86.56 E
Indragiri ≃	112	0.22 S	103.26 E
Indramayu	115a	6.20 S	108.19 E
Indramayu, Ujung ›	115a	6.14 S	108.17 E
Indrapuri	114	5.26 N	95.27 E
Indrāvati ≃	122	18.44 N	80.16 E
Indre □[5]	32	46.45 N	1.30 E
Indre ≃	32	47.16 N	0.19 E
Indre-et-Loire □[5]	32	47.15 N	0.45 E
Indrois ≃	50	47.13 N	0.56 E
Indungo	152	14.48 S	16.17 E
Induno Olona	62	45.52 N	8.51 E
Indur → Indore	120	22.43 N	75.50 E
Indura	76	53.27 N	23.53 E
Indus ≃	120	24.20 N	67.47 E
Industry, Il., U.S.	194	40.20 N	90.36 W
Industry, Pa., U.S.	214	40.39 N	80.25 W
Industry, Tx., U.S.	222	29.58 N	96.30 W
Indwe	158	31.27 S	27.23 E
Indwe ≃	158	32.01 S	27.21 E
Ine	96	35.39 N	135.17 E
İnebolu	130	41.58 N	33.46 E
İnece	130	41.41 N	27.04 E
İnecik	130	40.56 N	27.16 E
In Ecker	148	24.09 N	5.03 E
İnegöl	130	40.05 N	29.31 E
Inerie, Gunung ∧	115b	8.52 S	120.56 E
Inés, Monte ∧	254	48.29 S	69.40 W
Ineu	38	46.26 N	21.49 E
Inez, Ky., U.S.	192	37.51 N	82.32 W
Inez, Tx., U.S.	222	28.54 N	96.47 W
Inez, Lake ⊜	276	41.01 N	74.17 W
Infanta, Pil.	116	15.50 N	119.55 E
Infanta, Pil.	116	14.45 N	121.39 E
Infante, Kaap ›	158	34.29 S	20.51 E
Inferior, Laguna ⊂	234	16.20 N	94.40 W
Inferno, Cachoeira do ∟	250	1.00 S	56.04 W
Infiernillo, Presa del ⊜[1]	234	18.35 N	101.45 W
Infiesto	34	43.21 N	5.22 W
Infreschi, Ponta degli ›	68	39.59 N	15.25 E
Ing ≃	110	20.13 N	100.27 E
Ingá	250	7.17 S	35.36 W
Ingabu	110	17.49 N	95.16 E
Ingaí	256	21.24 S	44.55 W
Ingaí ≃	256	21.23 S	44.52 W
Ingal	150	16.47 N	6.56 E
Ingalls	218	39.57 N	85.48 W
Ingalls Creek ≃	224	47.28 N	120.39 W
Ingalls Park	216	41.32 N	88.03 W
Inganda	152	0.05 S	20.57 E
Inganno ≃	70	38.04 N	14.37 E
Ingarö I	40	59.16 N	18.28 E
Ingatestone	42	51.41 N	0.22 E
Ingatestone Hall ⊥	260	51.39 N	0.23 E
Ingelfingen	56	49.18 N	9.39 E
Ingelheim	56	49.59 N	8.05 E
Ingelmunster	50	50.55 N	3.15 E
Ingelstad	26	56.45 N	14.55 E
Ingende	152	0.15 S	18.57 E
Ingeniería, Universidad Nacional de ⚑[2]	286d	12.02 S	77.02 W
Ingeniero Budge ◂[8]	288	34.43 S	58.28 W
Ingeniero Jacobacci	254	41.18 S	69.35 W
Ingeniero Juan Allan	258	34.53 S	58.11 W
Ingeniero Luiggi	252	35.25 S	64.29 W
Ingeniero Luis A. Huergo	252	39.05 S	67.14 W
Ingeniero Maschwitz	258	34.23 S	58.44 W
Ingeniero Romulo Otamendi	258	34.13 S	58.54 W
Ingeniero White	252	38.47 S	62.16 W
Ingeniero Williams	258	34.54 S	59.22 W
Ingenio La Esperanza	252	24.13 S	64.51 W
Ingenio Santa Ana	252	27.28 S	65.41 W
Ingeringbach ≃	61	47.12 N	14.49 E
Ingersheim	58	48.06 N	7.18 E
Ingersoll	212	43.02 N	80.53 W
Ingham	166	18.39 S	146.10 E
Ingham □[6]	216	42.37 N	84.22 W
Ingička	85	39.52 N	67.20 E
Ingleborough ∧	44	54.11 N	2.23 W
Ingleburn	170	34.00 S	150.52 E
Inglesa, Costa → English Coast ⫠[2]	9	73.45 S	73.00 W
Ingleside, Austl.	274a	33.41 S	151.13 E
Ingleside, On., Can.	206	45.00 N	75.00 W
Ingleside, Il., U.S.	216	42.23 N	88.09 W
Ingleside, Tx., U.S.	196	27.52 N	97.12 W
Ingleside ◂[8]	282	37.43 N	122.28 W
Ingleton	44	54.10 N	2.27 W
Inglewood, Austl.	166	28.25 S	151.05 E
Inglewood, Austl.	166	36.34 S	143.52 E
Inglewood, On., Can.	212	43.47 N	79.56 W
Inglewood, N.Z.	172	39.09 S	174.12 E
Inglewood, Ca., U.S.	228	33.57 N	118.21 W
Inglewood, Wa., U.S.	224	47.44 N	122.15 W
Inglewood Forest ◂[3]	44	54.45 N	2.50 W
Inglis, Mb., Can.	184	50.57 N	101.15 W
Inglis, Fl., U.S.	220	29.02 N	82.40 W
Inglis Lock ◂[5]	220	29.02 N	82.37 W
Ingoda ≃	88	51.42 N	115.48 E
Ingogo	158	27.32 S	29.56 E
Ingoldmells	44	53.11 N	0.20 E
Ingolstadt	60	48.46 N	11.27 E
Ingomar	279b	40.35 N	80.05 W
Ingonish	186	46.42 N	60.22 W
Ingornachoix Bay ⊂	186	50.38 N	57.20 W
Ingraham, Lake ⊜	220	25.09 N	81.08 W
Ingrāj Bāzār	124	25.00 N	88.09 E
Ingram, Pa., U.S.	279b	40.26 N	80.04 W
Ingram, Tx., U.S.	196	30.04 N	99.14 W
Ingram Bay ⊂	208	37.48 N	76.17 W
Ingrave	260	51.36 N	0.21 E
Ingrid Christensen Coast ⫠[2]	9	69.30 S	76.00 E
In Guezzam	150	19.32 N	5.42 E
Inguri ≃	84	42.24 N	41.33 E
Ingushetia → Čečnja-Ingušetija □[3]	84	43.15 N	45.40 E
Inguzet	86	58.50 N	83.52 E
Ingvallsbenning	40	60.15 N	15.53 E
Ingwavuma	158	27.09 S	32.00 E
Ingwe	154	13.02 S	26.25 E
Ingwiller	56	48.52 N	7.29 E
Inhaca, Ilha da I	158	26.03 S	32.57 E
Inhafenga	156	20.35 S	33.53 E
Inhambane	156	23.51 S	35.29 E
Inhambane □[5]	156	23.00 S	34.30 E
Inhambane, Baía de ⊂	156	23.58 S	35.51 E
Inhambupe	255	11.47 S	38.21 W
Inhaminga	156	18.24 S	35.00 E
Inhanduí ≃	255	21.37 S	52.59 W
Inhapim	255	19.33 S	42.07 W
Inharrime	156	24.29 S	35.01 E
Inharrime ≃	156	24.29 S	35.01 E
Inhassoro	156	21.33 S	35.11 E
Inhaúma	255	19.29 S	44.22 W
Inhaúma ◂[8]	287a	22.52 S	43.17 W
İnhisar	130	40.03 N	30.23 E
Inhoaíba ◂[8]	256	22.54 S	43.36 W
Inhomirim	256	22.35 S	43.10 W
Inhomirim ≃	287a	22.41 S	43.13 W
Inhul ≃	78	47.00 N	31.59 E
Inhulets'	78	47.43 N	33.14 E
Inhulets' ≃	78	46.41 N	32.48 E
Inhulo-Kam'yanka	78	48.17 N	32.30 E
Inhuma	250	6.40 S	41.42 W
Inhumas	255	16.22 S	49.30 W
Ini ≃	146	9.30 N	12.20 E
Iniesta	34	39.26 N	1.45 W
Inimutaba	255	18.45 S	44.22 W
Ining → Yining	86	43.54 N	81.21 E
Inírida ≃	246	3.55 N	67.52 W
Inisa	150	7.52 N	4.20 E
Inishbofin I, Ire.	48	53.37 N	10.15 W
Inishbofin I, Ire.	48	55.09 N	8.11 W
Inishcrone	48	54.12 N	9.06 W
Inisheer I	48	53.02 N	9.26 W
Inishkea North I	48	54.08 N	10.12 W
Inishkea South I	48	54.07 N	10.13 W
Inishmaan I	48	53.05 N	9.32 W
Inishmore I	48	53.07 N	9.45 W
Inishmurray I	48	54.26 N	8.40 W
Inishowen ›[1]	48	55.12 N	7.20 W
Inishowen Head ›	48	55.14 N	6.56 W
Inishshark I	48	53.37 N	10.18 W
Inishtrahull I	48	55.26 N	7.14 W
Inishturk I	48	53.43 N	10.08 W
Inistioge	48	52.29 N	7.04 W
Initao	116	8.30 N	124.18 E
Inje	98	38.05 N	128.09 E
Injibara	144	11.00 N	36.59 E
Injune	166	25.51 S	148.34 E
Inkeroinen	26	60.42 N	26.51 E
Inketete	152	2.37 S	21.53 E
Inkisi (Zadi) ≃	152	4.46 S	14.52 E
Inkom	202	42.47 N	112.15 W
Inkster, Mi., U.S.	216	42.17 N	83.18 W
Inkster, N.D., U.S.	198	48.09 N	97.38 W
Inland Kaikoura Range ⋏	172	42.00 S	173.40 E
Inland Lake ⊜, Mb., Can.	184	52.17 N	99.42 W
Inland Lake ⊜, Ak., U.S.	180	66.27 N	159.47 W
Inland Sea → Seto-naikai ⍑[2]	96	34.20 N	133.30 E
Inle Lake ⊜	110	20.32 N	96.55 E
Inman, Ks., U.S.	198	38.13 N	97.46 W
Inman, S.C., U.S.	192	35.02 N	82.05 W
Inman Mills	192	35.02 N	82.06 W
Inman Valley	168b	35.30 S	138.28 E
Inn (En) ≃	32	48.35 N	13.28 E
Innamincka	166	27.45 S	140.44 E
Innbach ≃	61	48.18 N	14.07 E
Innellan	46	55.54 N	4.57 W
Inner Bay ⊂	214	42.37 N	80.24 W
Innerbraz	58	47.09 N	9.55 E
Inner Channel ⋓	232	16.35 N	88.17 W
Innerferrera	58	46.31 N	9.28 E
Innerfragant	64	46.58 N	13.04 E
Inner Harbor ⊂	276	40.52 N	73.28 W
Inner Hebrides II	46	56.30 N	6.00 W
Innerkip	212	43.13 N	80.42 W
Innerleithen	46	55.38 N	3.05 W
Inner Mongolia → Nei Monggol Zizhiqu □[4]	90	43.00 N	115.00 E
Inner Sister Island I	166	39.42 S	147.55 E
Inner Sound ⋓	46	57.25 N	5.56 W
Innerste ≃	52	52.15 N	9.50 E
Innerstetalsperre ◂[6]	52	51.55 N	10.17 E
Innerthal	58	47.06 N	8.56 E
Innertkirchen	58	46.42 N	8.14 E
Innervillgraten	64	46.48 N	12.23 E
Innichen → San Candido	64	46.44 N	12.17 E
Inning	60	48.05 N	11.09 E
Innisfail, Austl.	166	17.32 S	146.02 E
Innisfail, Ab., Can.	182	52.02 N	113.57 W
Innisfil Creek ≃	212	44.08 N	79.49 W
Innisfree	182	53.22 N	111.32 W
Innisplain	171a	28.10 S	152.55 E
Innokentjevka	89	49.42 N	136.57 E
Innokentjevskij	89	48.37 N	140.10 E
Innoko ≃	180	62.14 N	159.45 W
Innolovo	265a	59.47 N	29.59 E
Innoshima	96	34.17 N	133.11 E
Inno-shima I	96	34.19 N	133.10 E
Innsbruck	64	47.16 N	11.24 E
Innviertel ◂[1]	60	48.10 N	13.15 E
Inny ≃, Ire.	48	53.33 N	7.48 W
Inny ≃, Eng., U.K.	42	50.35 N	4.17 W
Ino, Nihon	96	33.33 N	133.26 E
Ino, Va., U.S.	208	37.46 N	76.48 W
Inoã	256	22.55 S	42.57 W
Inobonto	112	0.52 N	123.57 E
Inocência	255	19.47 S	51.48 W
Inokashira Park ♦	268	35.42 N	139.34 E
Inokovka	80	52.33 N	42.34 E
Inola	196	36.09 N	95.30 W
Ino-misaki ›	96	33.01 N	133.06 E
Inongo	152	1.57 S	18.16 E
Inoni	152	3.04 S	15.39 E
İnönü	130	39.48 N	30.09 E
Inoue	270	34.48 N	135.03 E
Inowrocław	30	52.48 N	18.15 E
Inozemcevo	84	44.06 N	43.06 E
Inp'ung-dong	98	41.25 N	126.34 E
Inrath ◂[8]	263	51.21 N	6.32 E
In Rhar	148	27.10 N	1.59 E
Ins	58	47.00 N	7.06 E
In Salah	148	27.12 N	2.28 E
Insan-ni	98	41.01 N	127.21 E
Insar	80	53.52 N	44.21 E
Insar ≃	80	54.43 N	45.18 E
Insch	46	57.21 N	2.37 W
Inscription, Cape ›	162	25.29 S	112.59 E
Inscription Point ›	274a	34.00 S	151.13 E
Insel Man → Isle of Man □[2]	44	54.15 N	4.30 W
Inshar	150	8.49 N	9.40 E
Inshāṣ ar-Raml	142	30.23 N	31.27 E
Insjön	26	60.41 N	15.05 E
Ińsko	30	53.27 N	15.33 E
In Sokki, Oued V	148	29.37 N	4.13 E
Inspiration	200	33.24 N	110.52 W
Insterburg → Čern'achovsk	76	54.38 N	21.49 E
Instow	184	49.44 N	108.16 W
Insurgente José María Morelos, Parque Nacional ♦	234	19.35 N	100.55 W
Inta	24	66.02 N	60.08 E
Intendente Alvear	252	35.14 S	63.35 W
İntepe	130	40.00 N	26.20 E
Intercession City	220	28.15 N	81.30 W
Intercourse	208	40.02 N	76.06 W
Interlagos ◂[8]	287b	23.42 S	46.42 W
Interlaken, Schw.	58	46.41 N	7.51 E
Interlaken, Ma., U.S.	210	42.18 N	73.19 W
Interlaken, N.J., U.S.	208	40.14 N	74.01 W
Interlaken, N.Y., U.S.	210	42.37 N	76.43 W
Interlândia	255	16.12 S	49.02 W
Internacional (Guarulhos), Aeroporto ⊠	287b	23.29 S	46.28 W
International Amphitheatre ⚑	278	41.49 N	87.39 W
International Falls	190	48.36 N	93.24 W
International Peace Garden ♦	198	49.00 N	100.04 W
International Trade Fair ♦	267d	35.47 N	51.24 E
Interstate State Park ♦	190	45.23 N	92.40 W
Inthanon, Doi ∧	110	18.35 N	98.29 E
Intibucá	236	14.16 N	88.10 W
Intibucá □[5]	236	14.20 N	88.15 W
Intipucá	236	13.12 N	88.04 W
Intiyaco	252	28.39 S	60.05 W
Intracoastal Waterway ≋, U.S.	192	24.33 N	81.46 W
Intracoastal Waterway ≋, U.S.	196	26.04 N	97.12 W
Intragna	58	46.10 N	8.42 E
Intrånget	40	60.20 N	16.09 E
Introbio	58	45.57 N	9.27 E
Introdacqua	66	42.00 N	13.54 E
Intschön → Inch'ŏn	98	37.28 N	126.38 E
Intu	112	0.15 S	115.21 E
Intuto	246	3.39 S	74.44 W
Inubō-saki ›	94	35.42 N	140.53 E
Inukai	96	33.04 N	131.38 E
Inukjuak	176	58.27 N	78.06 W
Inútil, Bahía ⊂	254	53.30 S	69.50 W
Inuvik	180	68.25 N	133.30 W
Inuya ≃	248	10.41 S	73.30 W
Inuyama	94	35.23 N	136.56 E
In'va ≃	86	58.59 N	55.40 E
Inver	46	57.49 N	3.55 W
Inverallochy	46	57.40 N	1.55 W
Inveralochy	170	34.57 S	149.39 E
Inveraray	46	56.13 N	5.05 W
Inverarish	46	57.21 N	6.04 W
Inverarity	46	56.35 N	2.53 W
Inverbervie	46	56.51 N	2.17 W
Invercargill	172	46.24 S	168.21 E
Inverdruie	46	57.10 N	3.48 W
Inverell	166	29.47 S	151.07 E
Invergarry	46	57.02 N	4.47 W
Invergordon	46	57.42 N	4.10 W
Inverkeilor	46	56.38 N	2.32 W
Inverkeithing	46	56.02 N	3.25 W
Inverkeithny	46	57.30 N	2.37 W

Symbols in the index entries represent the broad categories identified in the key at the right. Symbols with superior numbers (⋏[1]) identify subcategories (see complete key on page *I · 1*).

Symbole im Register stellen die rechts im Schlüssel erklärten Kategorien dar. Symbole mit hochgestellten Ziffern (⋏[1]) bezeichnen Unterabteilungen einer Kategorie (vgl. vollständiger Schlüssel auf Seite *I · 1*).

Los símbolos incluídos en el texto del índice representan las grandes categorías identificadas con la clave a la derecha. Los símbolos con numeros en su parte superior (⋏[1]) identifican las subcategorías (véase la clave completa en la página *I · 1*).

Les symboles de l'index représentent les catégories indiquées dans la légende à droite. Les symboles suivis d'un indice (⋏[1]) représentent des sous-catégories (voir légende complète à la page *I · 1*).

Os símbolos incluídos no texto do índice representam as grandes categorias identificadas com a chave à direita. Os símbolos com números em sua parte superior (⋏[1]) identificam as subcategorias (veja-se a chave completa à página *I · 1*).

	English	Deutsch	Español	Français	Português
∧	Mountain	Berg	Montaña	Montagne	Montanha
⋏	Mountains	Gebirge	Montañas	Montagnes	Montanhas
)(	Pass	Paß	Paso	Col	Passo
V	Valley, Canyon	Tal, Cañon	Valle, Cañón	Vallée, Canyon	Vale, Canhão
≚	Plain	Ebene	Llano	Plaine	Planície
›	Cape	Kap	Cabo	Cap	Cabo
I	Island	Insel	Isla	Île	Ilha
II	Islands	Inseln	Islas	Îles	Ilhas
⫠	Other Topographic Features	Andere Topographische Objekte	Otros Elementos Topográficos	Autres données topographiques	Outros acidentes topográficos

ESPAÑOL · FRANÇAIS · PORTUGUÊS

Nombre / Nom / Nome	Página / Page	Lat.°′	Long.°′ W = Oeste / W = Ouest
Inverleigh	169	38.06 S	144.03 E
Inverloch	169	38.38 S	145.43 E
Invermay	184	51.48 N	103.09 W
Invermere	182	50.30 N	116.02 W
Invermoriston	46	57.13 N	4.38 W
Inverness, N.S., Can.	186	46.14 N	61.18 W
Inverness, P.Q., Can.	206	46.15 N	71.31 W
Inverness, Scot., U.K.	46	57.27 N	4.15 W
Inverness, Ca., U.S.	204	38.06 N	122.51 W
Inverness, Fl., U.S.	220	28.50 N	82.19 W
Inverness, Il., U.S.	216	42.07 N	88.05 W
Inverness, Ms., U.S.	194	33.21 N	90.35 W
Inveruglas	46	56.15 N	4.43 W
Inveruno	62	45.31 N	8.51 E
Inverurie	46	57.17 N	2.23 W
Inverway	162	17.50 S	129.38 E
Investigator Group II	162	33.45 S	134.30 E
Investigator Shoal ✢[2]	108	8.09 N	114.44 E
Investigator Strait ʊ	166	35.25 S	137.10 E
Inwood, Mb., Can.	184	50.30 N	97.30 W
Inwood, On., Can.	214	42.49 N	81.59 W
Inwood, Fl., U.S.	220	28.02 N	81.45 W
Inwood, In., U.S.	216	41.19 N	86.12 W
Inwood, Ia., U.S.	198	43.18 N	96.25 W
Inwood, N.Y., U.S.	276	40.37 N	73.44 W
Inwood Hill Park ♠	276	40.52 N	73.56 W
Inyanga	154	18.13 S	32.46 E
Inyanga Mountains ⋏	154	18.00 S	33.00 E
Inyangani ∧	154	18.20 S	32.50 E
Inyan Kara Mountain ∧	198	44.13 N	104.21 W
Inyantue	154	18.32 S	26.41 E
Inyati	154	19.39 S	28.54 E
Inyo, Mount ∧	204	36.44 N	117.59 W
Inyokern	204	35.38 N	117.48 W
Inyo Mountains ⋏	204	36.40 N	118.10 W
Inyonga	154	6.43 S	32.04 E
Inywa	110	23.56 N	96.17 E
Inza	80	53.51 N	46.21 E
Inza ≃	80	53.54 N	45.44 E
Inzago	62	45.32 N	9.29 E
Inzai	94	35.50 N	140.09 E
Inzana Lake ⊜	182	54.58 N	124.40 W
Inžavino	80	52.19 N	42.30 E
Inzell	64	47.46 N	12.44 E
Inzer	86	54.14 N	57.34 E
Inzer ≃	86	54.30 N	56.28 E
Inzersdorf ◆[8]	264b	48.09 N	16.21 E
Inzia ≃	152	3.45 S	17.57 E
Ioanna, gora ∧	180	64.50 N	178.08 E
Ioánnina	38	39.40 N	20.50 E
Ioco	224	49.18 N	122.52 W
Iō-jima (Iwo Jima) I	174f	24.47 N	141.20 E
Iokanga ≃	24	68.00 N	39.43 E
Iola, Ks., U.S.	198	37.55 N	95.23 W
Iola, Pa., U.S.	210	45.08 N	76.32 W
Iola, Tx., U.S.	222	30.46 N	96.05 W
Iola, Wi., U.S.	190	44.30 N	89.07 W
Iolgo, chrebet ⋏	86	51.30 N	86.25 E
Iolotan'	72	37.18 N	62.21 E
Ioma	164	8.20 S	147.50 E
Iôna, Ang.	152	16.50 S	12.20 E
Iona, N.S., Can.	186	45.58 N	60.48 W
Iona, Id., U.S.	202	43.31 N	111.55 W
Iona I	46	56.19 N	6.25 W
Iôna, Parque Nacional do ♠	152	16.30 S	12.00 E
Iona, Sound of ʊ	46	56.19 N	6.24 W
Iona College ʋ[2]	276	40.56 N	73.47 W
Ione, Ca., U.S.	226	38.21 N	120.55 W
Ione, Or., U.S.	202	45.30 N	119.50 W
Ione, Wa., U.S.	202	48.44 N	117.24 W
Ionia, Mi., U.S.	216	42.59 N	85.04 W
Ionia, N.Y., U.S.	210	42.56 N	77.30 W
Ionia □[6]	216	42.56 N	85.04 W
Ionian Islands → Iónioi Nísoi II	38	38.30 N	20.30 E
Ionian Sea ⊽[2]	22	39.00 N	19.00 E
Ionia State Recreation Area ♠	216	42.58 N	85.36 W
Ionico, Mare → Ionian Sea ⊽[2]	22	39.00 N	19.00 E
Ionienne, Mer → Ionian Sea ⊽[2]	22	39.00 N	19.00 E
Iónioi Nísoi □[4]	38	38.15 N	20.30 E
Iónioi Nísoi II	38	38.30 N	20.30 E
Ionische Inseln → Iónioi Nísoi II	38	38.30 N	20.30 E
Ionisches Meer → Ionian Sea ⊽[2]	22	39.00 N	19.00 E
Ionivejem ≃	180	66.12 N	174.00 W
Iony, ostrov I	74	56.26 N	143.25 E
Ioppolo	68	38.35 N	15.53 E
Ioppolo Giancaxio	70	37.23 N	13.33 E
Iordan	85	39.58 N	71.46 E
Iori (Qabırrı) ≃	84	41.03 N	46.17 E
Iorskoje ploskogorje ⋏[1]	84	41.20 N	46.00 E
Iory	85	39.30 N	67.53 E
Íos	38	36.44 N	25.17 E
Íos I	38	36.42 N	25.24 E
Ioscoe, Lake ⊜	276	41.02 N	74.19 W
Iosegun ≃	182	54.44 N	117.11 W
Iosegun Lake	182	54.29 N	116.50 W
Iō-shima I	93b	30.48 N	130.18 E
Iota	194	30.19 N	92.29 W
Iovlevo	82	56.10 N	38.20 E
Iowa	194	30.14 N	93.00 W
Iowa □[3]	178	42.15 N	93.15 W
Iowa ≃	190	41.10 N	91.02 W
Iowa, South Fork ≃	190	42.18 N	93.04 W
Iowa City	190	41.39 N	91.31 W
Iowa Falls	190	42.31 N	93.15 W
Iowa Park	196	33.57 N	98.40 W
Iō-zen ∧	94	36.31 N	136.48 E
Ipa ≃	76	52.13 N	29.08 E
Ipala	154	4.30 S	32.53 E
Ipameri	255	17.43 S	48.09 W
Ipanema ◆[8]	256	22.59 S	43.12 W
Ipanema ≃	250	9.53 S	37.15 W
Ipanguaçu	250	5.30 S	36.52 W
Ipat	24	66.13 N	56.33 E
Ipatinga	255	19.30 S	42.32 W
Ipatovo	80	45.43 N	42.53 E
Ipaumirim	250	6.47 S	38.43 W
Ipava	194	40.21 N	90.19 W
Ípeiros □[9]	38	39.40 N	20.50 E
Ipel' (Ipoly) ≃	30	47.49 N	18.52 E
Iperu	150	6.52 N	3.38 E
Iphigenia Bay ⊂	180	55.40 N	133.55 W
Iphofen	56	49.42 N	10.15 E
Ipiabas	256	22.23 S	43.53 W
Ipiales	246	0.50 N	77.37 W
Ipiaú	255	14.08 S	39.44 W
Ipiíba	256	22.52 S	42.57 W
Ipil	116	7.47 N	122.35 E
Ipin → Yibin	107	28.47 N	104.38 E
Ipirá	255	12.10 S	39.44 W
Ipiranga, Bra.	252	25.01 S	50.35 W
Ipiranga, Bra.	287a	22.43 S	43.12 W
Ipiranga ◆[8]	287b	23.36 S	46.35 W
Ipiranga ≃, Bra.	256	23.21 S	45.10 W
Ipiranga ≃, Bra.	287a	22.48 S	43.37 W
Ipiranga, Canal ≊	287a	22.46 S	43.37 W
Ipiranga, Museu do ʋ	287b	23.35 S	46.36 W
Ípiros □[4]	38	39.30 N	20.30 E
Ipita	248	19.20 S	63.32 W
Ipitinga ≃	250	0.02 N	53.01 W
Ipixuna	250	4.22 S	44.34 W
Ipixuna ≃, Bra.	248	7.11 S	71.51 W
Ipixuna ≃, Bra.	248	5.45 S	63.02 W
Ipixuna ≃, Bra.	248	6.16 S	61.52 W
Ipixuna, Igarapé ≃	250	4.32 S	52.40 W
Ipoh	114	4.35 N	101.05 E
Ipojuca ≃	250	8.25 S	34.58 W
Ipokera	154	8.03 S	35.41 E
Ipole	154	5.47 S	32.44 E
Ipoly (Ipel') ≃	30	47.49 N	18.52 E
Iporá, Bra.	255	16.28 S	51.07 W
Iporã, Bra.	255	23.59 S	53.37 W
Ipota	175f	18.48 S	169.16 E
Ippari ≃	70	36.52 N	14.26 E
Ippinghausen	56	51.17 N	9.08 E
Ipplepen	42	50.29 N	3.38 W
Ippy	152	6.15 N	21.12 E
İpsala	130	40.55 N	26.23 E
Ipswich, Austl.	171a	27.36 S	152.46 E
Ipswich, Eng., U.K.	42	52.04 N	1.10 E
Ipswich, Ma., U.S.	207	42.40 N	70.50 W
Ipswich, S.D., U.S.	198	45.26 N	99.01 W
Ipswich ≃	207	42.42 N	70.48 W
Ipswich Bay ⊂	207	42.41 N	70.42 W
Ipu	250	4.20 S	40.42 W
Ipubi	250	7.39 S	40.07 W
Ipueiras	250	4.33 S	40.43 W
Ipuh	112	3.00 S	101.30 E
Ipuiúna	256	22.06 S	46.11 W
Ipun, Isla I	254	44.37 S	74.46 W
Ipupiara	255	11.49 S	42.37 W
Iput' ≃	76	52.26 N	31.02 E
Iqaluit	176	63.44 N	68.28 W
Iqe ≃	102	38.14 N	94.18 E
Iqfahș	142	28.47 N	30.49 E
Iquique	248	20.13 S	70.10 W
Iquitos	246	3.46 S	73.15 W
Ira	196	32.35 N	101.00 W
Iraan, Pil.	116	9.04 N	117.42 E
Iraan, Tx., U.S.	196	30.54 N	101.53 W
Ira Banda	152	5.57 N	22.04 E
Irabu	175d	24.50 N	125.09 E
Irabu-jima I	175d	24.50 N	125.10 E
Iracajá, Cachoeira do ∟	248	10.29 S	64.05 W
Iracema	250	5.48 S	38.18 W
Iracoubo	250	5.29 N	53.13 W
Irago-misaki ≻	94	34.35 N	137.01 E
Irago-suidō ʊ	94	34.35 N	137.00 E
Iraí	252	27.11 S	53.15 W
Irajá ◆[8]	287a	22.51 S	43.19 W
Irajá ≃	287a	22.49 S	43.17 W
Irajol'	24	64.27 N	55.08 E
Irak → Iraq □[1]	128	33.00 N	44.00 E
Iráklia I	38	36.50 N	25.26 E
Iráklion, Ellás	38	35.20 N	25.09 E
Iráklion, Ellás	267c	38.04 N	23.46 E
Iran (Īrān) □[1], Asia	118	32.00 N	53.00 E
Iran (Īrān) □[1], Asia	128	32.00 N	53.00 E
Iran, Pegunungan ⋏	112	2.05 N	114.55 E
Iran National Arts Museum ʋ	267d	35.41 N	51.27 E
Īrānshahr	128	27.13 N	60.41 E
Irapa	246	10.34 N	62.35 W
Irapuato	234	20.41 N	101.21 W
Iraq (Al-ʿIrāq) □[1], Asia	118	33.00 N	44.00 E
Iraq (Al-ʿIrāq) □[1], Asia	128	33.00 N	44.00 E
Irará	255	12.02 S	38.46 W
Iratapuru ≃	250	0.36 S	52.35 W
Irati	252	25.27 S	50.39 W
Irati ≃	34	42.35 N	1.16 W
Irauçuba	250	3.45 S	39.47 W
Irazú, Volcán ∧[1]	236	9.58 N	83.53 W
Irba	88	58.07 N	99.00 E
Irbejskoje	88	55.39 N	95.28 E
Irbeni väin (Irbes jūras šaurums) ʊ	76	57.48 N	22.05 E
Irbes jūras šaurums (Irbeni väin) ʊ	76	57.48 N	22.05 E
Irbid	132	32.33 N	35.51 E
Irbid □[8]	132	32.30 N	35.45 E
Irbīl	128	36.11 N	44.01 E
Irbīl □[4]	128	36.10 N	44.00 E
Irbit	86	57.41 N	63.03 E
Irby	262	53.21 N	3.07 W
Irchester	42	52.16 N	0.38 W
Irdning	61	47.33 N	14.01 E
Irdyn'	78	49.23 N	31.44 E
Ire, Mount ∧	175e	9.10 S	161.05 E
Irebu	152	0.37 S	17.45 E
Irecê	250	11.18 S	41.52 W
Iregua ≃	34	42.27 N	2.24 W
Ireland (Éire) □[1], Europe	22	53.00 N	8.00 W
Ireland (Éire) □[1], Europe	48	53.00 N	8.00 W
Ireland Brook ≃	276	40.25 N	74.29 W
Iren' ≃	86	57.27 N	56.56 E
Irene, S. Afr.	158	25.53 S	28.13 E
Irene, S.D., U.S.	198	43.05 N	97.10 W
Irene, Tx., U.S.	222	31.59 N	96.52 W
Irene, Mount ∧	172	45.10 S	167.22 E
Ireng (Maú) ≃	246	3.33 N	59.51 W
Iresick Brook ≃	276	40.24 N	74.22 W
Ireton	198	42.58 N	96.19 W
Irfon ≃	42	52.09 N	3.24 W
Irgakly	84	44.22 N	44.45 E
Irgiz	86	48.37 N	61.16 E
Irgiz ≃	86	48.13 N	62.08 E
Iri	98	35.56 N	126.57 E
Irian Jaya □[4]	164	5.00 S	138.00 E
Iriba	146	15.07 N	22.15 E
Irié	150	8.17 N	9.11 W
Iriga	116	13.25 N	123.25 E
Irigny	62	45.40 N	4.49 E
Irîgui ◆[1]	150	16.43 N	5.30 W
Iriklinskij	86	51.39 N	58.38 E
Iringa	154	7.46 S	35.42 E
Iringa □[4]	154	9.00 S	35.00 E
Irinjālakuda	122	10.20 N	76.14 E
Iriomote-jima I	175d	24.20 N	123.50 E
Iriona	236	15.57 N	85.11 W
Iriri ≃, Bra.	250	3.52 S	52.37 W
Iriri ≃, Bra.	287a	22.41 S	43.05 W
Iriri Novo ≃	250	8.46 S	53.22 W
Irische See → Irish Sea ⊽[2]	28	53.30 N	5.20 W
Irish, Mount ∧	204	37.38 N	115.24 W
Irish Sea ⊽[2]	28	53.30 N	5.20 W
Irishtown	166	40.55 S	145.08 E
Irituia	250	1.46 S	47.26 W
Iriyamazu	268	35.16 N	139.39 E
Irkās, Wādī ⋁	142	28.57 N	32.00 E
Irkeštam	85	39.41 N	73.55 E
Irkinejeva ≃	88	58.30 N	96.48 E
Irkinejevo	88	58.30 N	96.49 E
Irklijevskaja	78	45.51 N	39.39 E
Irkliyiv	78	49.32 N	32.18 E
Irkoutsk → Irkutsk	88	52.16 N	104.20 E
Irkut ≃	88	52.18 N	104.15 E
Irkutsk	88	52.16 N	104.20 E
Irkutsk Oblast' □[4]	88	56.00 N	106.00 E
Irlam	44	53.28 N	2.25 W
Irland → Ireland □[1]	48	53.00 N	8.00 W
Irlanda, Mar de → Irish Sea ⊽[2]	28	53.30 N	5.20 W
Irlande → Ireland □[1]	48	53.00 N	8.00 W
Irlande, Mer d' → Irish Sea ⊽[2]	28	53.30 N	5.20 W
Irma	182	52.55 N	111.14 W
Irmauw	164	7.25 S	131.42 E
Irminger Basin ✢[1]	10	61.00 N	35.00 W
Irminio ≃	70	36.46 N	14.36 E
Irnijärvi ⊜	26	65.36 N	29.05 E
Irnsum	52	53.05 N	5.47 E
Iro, Lac ⊜	146	10.06 N	19.25 E
Iroise ⊂	32	48.15 N	4.55 W
Iron Baron	166	32.59 S	137.09 E
Iron Belt	190	46.24 N	90.19 W
Iron Bottom Sound ʊ	175e	9.15 S	160.00 E
Iron Bridge, On., Can.	190	46.17 N	83.14 W
Iron Bridge, Eng., U.K.	42	52.38 N	2.29 W
Iron Bridge Dam ◆[6]	222	32.50 N	95.54 W
Iron City	194	35.01 N	87.34 W
Iron Cove ⊂	274a	33.52 S	151.10 E
Iron Creek ≃	182	52.43 N	111.14 W
Irondale, Al., U.S.	194	33.32 N	86.42 W
Irondale, Mo., U.S.	194	37.49 N	90.40 W
Irondale, Oh., U.S.	214	40.34 N	80.43 W
Irondale ≃	212	44.49 N	78.37 W
Irondequoit	210	43.12 N	77.36 W
Irondequoit Bay ⊂	210	43.12 N	77.32 W
Iron Gate ⋁	38	44.41 N	22.31 E
Iron Gate Reservoir ⊜[1]	38	44.30 N	22.00 E
Ironia	276	40.49 N	74.37 W
Iron Knob	166	32.44 S	137.08 E
Iron Mountain	190	45.49 N	88.03 W
Iron Mountain ∧, Az., U.S.	200	33.27 N	111.10 W
Iron Mountain ∧, Ca., U.S.	280	34.17 N	117.43 W
Iron Mountains ⋏	192	36.30 N	81.50 W
Iron Range	164	12.42 S	143.18 E
Iron Range National Park ♠	164	12.44 S	143.16 E
Iron River, Mi., U.S.	190	46.05 N	88.38 W
Iron River, Wi., U.S.	190	46.33 N	91.24 W
Iron Springs	208	39.46 N	77.25 W
Ironton, Mn., U.S.	190	46.28 N	93.58 W
Ironton, Mo., U.S.	194	37.35 N	90.37 W
Ironton, Oh., U.S.	188	38.32 N	82.40 W
Ironwood	190	46.27 N	90.10 W
Ironworks Creek ≃	285	40.10 N	74.59 W
Iroquois, On., Can.	212	44.51 N	75.19 W
Iroquois, Il., U.S.	216	40.50 N	87.35 W
Iroquois, S.D., U.S.	198	44.22 N	97.51 W
Iroquois □[6]	216	40.47 N	87.44 W
Iroquois ≃	216	41.05 N	87.49 W
Iroquois Falls	190	48.46 N	80.41 W
Iroquois Lock and Dam ◆[5]	212	44.45 N	75.23 W
Irosin	116	12.42 N	124.02 E
Írottkő (Geschriebenstein) ∧	61	47.21 N	16.26 E
Irō-zaki ≻	94	34.36 N	138.51 E
Irpin'	78	50.31 N	30.15 E
Irpin' ≃	78	50.34 N	30.16 E
Irrawaddy → Ayeyarwady ≃	110	20.32 N	96.55 E
Irrawaddy, Mouths of the ≃[1]	110	15.45 N	94.50 E
Irregully Creek ≃	162	23.06 S	116.21 E
Irrel	56	49.51 N	6.28 E
Irricana	182	51.19 N	113.37 W
Irrigon	202	45.53 N	119.29 W
Irschenberg	64	47.50 N	11.55 E
Irsee	58	47.54 N	10.34 E
Irsha ≃	78	50.45 N	29.30 E
Irshava	78	48.20 N	23.03 E
Irsina	68	40.45 N	16.15 E
Irt ≃	44	54.22 N	3.26 W
Irtek ≃	80	51.28 N	52.39 E
Irthing ≃	44	54.55 N	2.50 W
Irthlingborough	42	52.20 N	0.37 W
Irtyš	86	54.29 N	74.22 E
Irtyš (Ertix) ≃	74	61.04 N	68.52 E
Irtysch → Irtyš ≃	72	61.04 N	68.52 E
Irtysh → Irtyš ≃	72	61.04 N	68.52 E
Irtyšsk	86	53.21 N	75.27 E
Irubaj	80	50.11 N	51.21 E
Iruma	94	35.50 N	139.24 E
Iruma ≃	94	35.57 N	139.30 E
Iruma Air Base ■	268	35.50 N	139.24 E
Iruma-kichi, Kaijō-jieitai- ■	94	35.50 N	139.24 E
Irumu	154	1.27 N	29.52 E
Irún	34	43.21 N	1.47 W
Irupana	248	16.28 S	67.28 W
Irurzun	34	42.55 N	1.50 W
Irú Tepuy ∧	246	5.25 N	61.02 W
Irvine, Ab., Can.	184	49.57 N	110.16 W
Irvine, Scot., U.K.	46	55.37 N	4.40 W
Irvine, Ca., U.S.	228	33.40 N	117.49 W
Irvine, Ky., U.S.	192	37.42 N	83.58 W
Irvine, Pa., U.S.	214	41.50 N	79.17 W
Irvine ≃	46	55.37 N	4.41 W
Irvine, Mount ∧	210	42.03 N	78.40 W
Irvine Creek ≃	212	43.41 N	80.25 W
Irvine Park ♠	280	33.48 N	117.45 W
Irvines Landing	182	49.38 N	124.03 W
Irvinestown	48	54.28 N	7.38 W
Irving, Il., U.S.	219	39.12 N	89.24 W
Irving, N.Y., U.S.	214	42.34 N	79.07 W
Irving, Tx., U.S.	222	32.48 N	96.56 W
Irving Park ◆[8]	278	41.57 N	87.43 W
Irvington, Il., U.S.	219	38.26 N	89.10 W
Irvington, Ky., U.S.	194	37.52 N	86.17 W
Irvington, N.J., U.S.	210	40.43 N	74.13 W
Irvington, N.Y., U.S.	210	41.02 N	73.51 W
Irvington, Oh., U.S.	218	39.51 N	84.15 W
Irvington, Va., U.S.	208	37.39 N	76.25 W
Irvington ◆[8]	284b	39.17 N	76.41 W
Irvona	214	40.46 N	78.33 W
Irwell ≃	44	53.27 N	2.17 W
Irwin, Austl.	162	29.12 S	115.04 E
Irwin, Oh., U.S.	218	40.07 N	83.29 W
Irwin, Pa., U.S.	279b	40.19 N	79.42 W
Irwin ≃	162	29.15 S	114.56 E
Irwin, Point ≻	162	35.04 S	116.56 E
Irwindale	280	34.06 N	117.56 W
Irwinton	192	32.48 N	83.10 W
Is	86	58.48 N	59.43 E
Is, Jabal ∧	140	21.49 N	35.39 E
Isa	150	13.14 N	6.24 E
ʿĪsā, Ra's ≻	144	15.11 N	42.39 E
Isaac ≃	166	22.52 S	149.20 E
Isaac Lake ⊜, B.C., Can.	182	53.10 N	120.50 W
Isaac Lake ⊜, On., Can.	212	44.47 N	81.14 W
Isaba	34	42.52 N	0.55 W
Isabel, Pil.	116	10.56 N	124.26 E
Isabel, S.D., U.S.	198	45.23 N	101.25 W
Isabel □[4]	175e	7.55 S	159.10 E
Isabela, Pil.	116	10.12 N	122.59 E
Isabela (Basilan), Pil.	116	6.42 N	121.58 E
Isabela, P.R.	240m	18.30 N	67.01 W
Isabela □[4]	116	17.00 N	122.00 E
Isabela, Cabo ≻	238	19.56 N	71.01 W
Isabela, Canal ʊ	246a	0.20 S	90.55 W
Isabela, Isla I, Ec.	246a	0.30 S	91.06 W
Isabela, Isla I, Méx.	234	21.51 N	105.55 W
Isabela de Sagua	240p	22.57 N	80.01 W
Isabelia, Cordillera ⋏	236	13.45 N	85.15 W
Isabella Indian Reservation ◆[4]	190	43.41 N	84.48 W
Isabella Lake ⊜	212	45.24 N	79.49 W
Isabella Lake ⊜[1]	204	35.40 N	118.26 W
Isabelle ≃	190	47.50 N	91.41 W
Isábena ≃	34	42.11 N	0.21 E
Isaccea	38	45.16 N	28.28 E
Ísafjarðardjúp ⊂[2]	24a	66.10 N	23.00 W
Ísafjörður	24a	66.08 N	23.13 W
Isāgarh	124	24.50 N	77.53 E
Isagatedo	273a	6.32 N	3.20 E
Isahaya	92	32.50 N	130.03 E
Isak	114	4.28 N	96.55 E
Isaka, Tan.	154	3.54 S	32.56 E
Isaka, Zaïre	152	2.35 S	18.48 E
Isaka-Buku	152	3.55 S	22.03 E
Īsa Khel	123	32.41 N	71.17 E
Isakly	80	54.08 N	51.32 E
Isakovka	86	55.45 N	74.24 E
Isakovo, Ross.	76	55.11 N	34.40 E
Isakovo, Ross.	76	60.30 N	41.13 E
Isakovo, Ross.	82	54.36 N	37.02 E
Isakovo, Ross.	265b	55.59 N	37.23 E
Ișalnița	38	44.24 N	23.44 E
Isalo, Massif de l' ⋏	157b	22.45 S	45.15 E
Isalo, Parc National de l' ♠	157b	22.45 S	45.15 E
Isana (Içana) ≃	246	0.26 N	67.19 W
Īsānagar	124	27.54 N	81.13 E
Isandhlwana ⊥	158	28.21 S	30.39 E
Isandja Etat	152	2.59 S	22.00 E
Isando	273d	26.09 S	28.12 E
Isanga	152	1.26 S	22.18 E
Isangano National Park ♠	154	11.10 S	30.40 E
Isangel	175f	19.32 S	169.16 E
Isangi	152	0.46 N	24.15 E
Is'angulovo	86	52.12 N	56.36 E
Isanlu Makutu	150	8.17 N	5.46 E
Isan-ni	98	40.46 N	128.55 E
Isanti	190	45.29 N	93.14 W
Isar ≃	60	48.49 N	12.58 E
Isara	150	6.59 N	3.41 E
Isarco (Eisack) ≃	64	46.27 N	11.18 E
Isarco, Valle ⋁	64	46.45 N	11.37 E
Isarog, Mount ∧	116	13.39 N	123.23 E
Isasi	273a	6.40 N	3.23 E
Isawa	94	35.39 N	138.38 E
Isbergues	50	50.37 N	2.27 E
Isbister	46a	60.36 N	1.19 W
İscehisar	130	38.51 N	30.45 E
Iščeino	76	52.57 N	38.50 E
Iščerskaja	84	43.43 N	45.08 E
Ischgl	58	47.01 N	10.17 E
Ischia	68	40.44 N	13.57 E
Ischia, Isola d' I	68	40.43 N	13.54 E
Ischia di Castro	66	42.33 N	11.45 E
Ischim → Išim ≃	86	57.45 N	71.12 E
Ischitella	68	41.54 N	15.54 E
Ischma → Ižma ≃	24	65.19 N	52.54 E
Ischodnaja, gora ∧	180	64.50 N	173.26 W
Ischua	210	42.15 N	78.24 W
Ischua Creek ≃	210	42.10 N	78.23 W
Iscuandé ≃	246	2.38 N	78.04 W
Isdell ≃	162	16.27 S	124.51 E
Isdes	50	47.40 N	2.15 E
Ise (Uji-yamada)	94	34.29 N	136.42 E
Ise ≃	54	52.30 N	10.33 E
Isefjord ⊂	41	55.52 N	11.49 E
Isehara	94	35.24 N	139.18 E
Išejevka	80	54.25 N	48.16 E
Iseke	154	6.25 S	35.01 E
Isel ≃	64	46.50 N	12.47 E
Iselin, N.J., U.S.	210	40.34 N	74.19 W
Iselin, Pa., U.S.	214	40.33 N	79.23 W
Iselle	58	46.12 N	8.12 E
Iseltwald	58	46.43 N	7.58 E
Isen	60	48.13 N	12.04 E
Isen ≃	60	48.15 N	12.40 E
Isenbajevo	80	56.03 N	53.25 E
Isenbüttel	52	52.26 N	10.34 E
Isenyela	154	8.36 S	33.30 E
Iseo	64	45.39 N	10.03 E
Iseo, Lago d' ⊜	64	45.43 N	10.04 E
Iseramagazi	154	4.40 S	32.09 E
Iseran, Col de l' ⋊	62	45.25 N	7.02 E
Isère □[5]	62	45.10 N	5.50 E
Isère ≃	62	44.59 N	4.51 E
Iseri	273a	6.39 N	3.23 E
Iseri-Oke	273a	6.38 N	3.23 E
Iseri-Osun	273a	6.31 N	3.17 E
Iserlohn	56	51.22 N	7.41 E
Isernhagen	52	52.26 N	9.51 E
Isernia	66	41.36 N	14.14 E
Isernia □[4]	66	41.40 N	14.15 E
Isesaki	94	36.19 N	139.12 E
Ise-Shima-kokuritsu-kōen ♠	92	34.23 N	136.48 E
Iset' ≃	86	56.36 N	66.24 E
Isetskoje	86	56.29 N	65.21 E
Ise-wan ⊂	94	34.43 N	136.43 E
Iseyin	150	7.58 N	3.36 E
Isezaki → Isesaki	92	36.19 N	139.12 E
Isfahan → Eșfahān	128	32.40 N	51.38 E
Isfana	85	39.50 N	69.31 E
Isfana ≃	85	40.13 N	69.26 E
Isfara	85	40.07 N	70.38 E
ʿIsfiyā	132	32.43 N	35.04 E
Ishenga Oswe	152	3.46 S	22.34 E
Isheri-Olofin	273a	6.35 N	3.17 E
Isherton	246	2.19 N	59.22 W
Ishi ≃	270	34.35 N	135.38 E
Ishibashi	94	36.26 N	139.52 E
Ishibe	94	35.00 N	136.04 E
Ishigaki	175d	24.20 N	124.09 E
Ishigaki-shima I	175d	24.24 N	124.12 E
Ishige	94	36.07 N	139.58 E
Ishii	96	34.04 N	134.26 E
Ishikari ≃	92a	43.15 N	141.23 E
Ishikari-dake ∧	92a	43.33 N	143.02 E
Ishikari-heiya ≚	92a	43.15 N	141.23 E
Ishikari-sanchi ⋏	92a	43.35 N	143.00 E
Ishikari-wan ⊂	92a	43.25 N	141.01 E
Ishikawa, Nihon	94	37.09 N	140.27 E
Ishikawa, Nihon	174m	26.25 N	127.50 E
Ishikawa □[5]	94	36.45 N	136.45 E
Ishiki	94	34.48 N	137.01 E
Ishikiri	270	34.41 N	135.39 E
I-shima I	96	33.51 N	134.49 E
Ishinomaki	92	38.25 N	141.18 E
Ishinomaki-wan ⊂	92	38.18 N	141.18 E
Ishioka	94	36.11 N	140.16 E
Ishiyama	270	34.58 N	135.55 E
Ishizuchi-san ∧	96	33.46 N	133.07 E
Ishkumān	123	36.32 N	73.49 E
Ishmant	142	29.12 N	31.11 E
Ishpeming	190	46.29 N	87.40 W
Ishuizu ≃	270	34.33 N	135.27 E
Ishurdi	124	24.08 N	89.05 E
Isidro Casanova	288	34.42 S	58.35 W
Isigny	32	49.19 N	1.06 W
Işık Dağı ∧	130	38.21 N	36.32 E
Işıklı	130	38.19 N	29.51 E
Işıkli Burnu ≻	267b	41.14 N	29.15 E
Isili	71	39.44 N	9.06 E
Isil'kul'	86	54.55 N	71.16 E
Išim	86	56.09 N	69.27 E
Išim ≃	86	57.45 N	71.12 E
Išimbaj	86	53.28 N	56.02 E
Išimka	86	51.24 N	67.08 E
Išimskaja step' ≚	86	55.00 N	70.00 E
Isimu	112	0.40 N	122.51 E
Isinga	88	52.55 N	112.00 E
Isiolo	154	0.21 N	37.35 E
Isiolo Game Reserve ◆[4]	154	0.32 N	37.34 E
Isipingo	158	29.59 S	30.56 E
Isipingo Beach	158	29.59 S	30.57 E
Isiro (Paulis)	154	2.47 N	27.37 E
Isis	166	25.12 S	152.13 E
Isisford	166	24.16 S	144.26 E
Iskandar	85	41.36 N	69.43 E
Iskăr ≃	38	43.44 N	24.27 E
Iskăr, Jazovir ⊜[1]	38	42.28 N	23.35 E
Iškašim	123	36.44 N	71.37 E
Iskaten', chrebet ⋏	180	66.30 N	179.00 W
Iškejevo	80	55.51 N	50.56 E
İskele	130	35.17 N	33.52 E
İskenderun	130	36.37 N	36.07 E
İskenderun Körfezi (Gulf of Alexandretta) ⊂	130	36.30 N	35.40 E
Iske-R'az'ap	80	54.36 N	49.42 E
İskilip	130	40.45 N	34.29 E
Iski-Naukat	85	40.16 N	72.36 E
Iskininskij	80	47.13 N	52.41 E
Iskitim	86	54.38 N	83.18 E
Iskona ≃	82	55.34 N	36.05 E
Iskushuban	144	10.17 N	50.14 E
Iskut ≃	180	56.42 N	131.45 W
Isla	234	18.01 N	95.30 W
Isla ≃	46	57.30 N	2.47 W
Isla, Salar de la ≚	252	25.49 S	68.53 W
Isla Cristina	34	37.12 N	7.19 W
Isla de Maipo	252	33.45 S	70.54 W
İslâhiye	130	37.03 N	36.36 E
Islāmābād → Anantnāg, India	123	33.44 N	75.09 E
Islāmābād, Pāk.	123	33.42 N	73.10 E
Isla Mala	258	34.12 S	56.21 W
Islāmkot	120	24.42 N	70.11 E
Islamorada	220	24.55 N	80.37 W
Islāmpur, India	122	17.03 N	74.16 E
Islāmpur, India	124	25.09 N	85.12 E
Islāmpur, India	124	26.16 N	88.12 E
Islāmpur, India	126	21.43 N	87.39 E
Islāmpur, India	126	24.09 N	88.28 E
Isla Mujeres	232	21.12 N	86.43 W
Island	194	37.26 N	87.08 W
Island □[6]	224	48.07 N	122.36 W
Island → Iceland □[1]	24a	65.00 N	18.00 W
Island ≃	262	53.44 N	2.51 W
Island Bay ⊂	116	9.06 N	118.10 E
Island Beach State Park ♠	208	39.50 N	74.06 W
Island Bend	171b	36.19 S	148.29 E
Island Creek	283	42.00 N	70.43 W
Island Falls, Sk., Can.	184	55.32 N	102.21 W
Island Falls, Me., U.S.	188	46.00 N	68.16 W
Island Heights	208	39.56 N	74.09 W
Islandia → Iceland □[1]	24a	65.00 N	18.00 W
Island Lagoon ⊜	166	31.30 S	136.40 E
Island Lake, Mb., Can.	184	53.58 N	94.47 W
Island Lake, Il., U.S.	216	42.17 N	88.12 W
Island Lake, Mi., U.S.	281	42.31 N	83.44 W
Island Lake ⊜	184	53.47 N	94.25 W
Island Lake State Recreation Area ♠	216	42.30 N	83.43 W
Island Park, Id., U.S.	202	44.24 N	111.19 W
Island Park, N.Y., U.S.	276	40.36 N	73.39 W
Island Park, R.I., U.S.	207	41.37 N	71.13 W
Island Park Reservoir ⊜[1]	202	44.25 N	111.29 W
Island Point ≻	162	30.20 S	115.02 E
Island Pond	188	44.48 N	71.52 W
Island Pond ⊜	186	48.25 N	56.23 W
Islands, Bay of ⊂, Nf., Can.	186	49.10 N	58.15 W
Islands, Bay of ⊂, N.Z.	172	35.12 S	174.10 E
Island View	216	40.31 N	83.53 W
Isla Patrulla	252	32.59 S	54.35 W
Islas de la Bahía □[5]	236	16.20 N	86.30 W
Islas Malvinas → Falkland Islands □[2]	254	51.45 S	59.00 W
Isla Verde	252	33.14 S	62.24 W
Isla Vista	204	34.25 N	119.50 W
Islay I	46	55.46 N	6.10 W
Islay, Punta ≻	248	17.01 S	72.07 W
Islay, Rhinns of ≻[1]	46	55.45 N	6.25 W
Islay, Sound of ʊ	46	55.50 N	6.06 W
Isle	190	46.08 N	93.28 W
Isle ≃, Fr.	32	44.55 N	0.15 W
Isle ≃, Eng., U.K.	42	50.59 N	2.53 W
Isle-Adam, Forêt de l' ♠	261	49.05 N	2.15 E
Isle-aux-Morts	186	47.35 N	58.59 W
Isle of Hope	192	31.58 N	81.05 W
Isle of Man □[2], Europe	22	54.15 N	4.30 W
Isle of Man □[2], Europe	44	54.15 N	4.30 W
Isle of Man (Ronaldsway) Airport ⊠	44	54.06 N	4.36 W
Isle of Palms	192	32.47 N	79.48 W
Isle of Wight	208	36.54 N	76.42 W
Isle of Wight □[6], Eng., U.K.	42	50.40 N	1.20 W
Isle of Wight □[6], Va., U.S.	208	36.50 N	76.42 W
Isle of Wight Bay ⊂	208	38.22 N	75.06 W
Isle Royale National Park ♠	190	48.00 N	89.00 W
Isles, Lake of the ⊜	212	44.19 N	75.59 W
Isle Saint George	214	41.43 N	82.49 W
Islesboro Island I	188	44.20 N	68.53 W
Isleta	200	34.54 N	106.41 W
Isleta Indian Reservation ◆[4]	200	34.55 N	106.45 W
Isleton	226	38.09 N	121.36 W
Islets-Caribou	186	49.30 N	67.14 W
Isleworth ◆[8]	260	51.28 N	0.20 W
Islington	207	42.13 N	71.11 W
Islington ◆[8], On., Can.	275b	43.39 N	79.32 W
Islington ◆[8], Eng., U.K.	42	51.34 N	0.06 W
Islip, Eng., U.K.	42	51.50 N	1.14 W
Islip, N.Y., U.S.	276	40.43 N	73.12 W
Islip Terrace	276	40.44 N	73.11 W
Islivig	46	58.05 N	7.11 W
Isloč' ≃	76	53.55 N	26.13 E
Islón	252	29.54 S	71.12 W
Isluga, Volcán ∧[1]	248	19.10 S	68.51 W
Ismael Cortinas (Arroyo Grande)	258	33.58 S	57.06 W
Ismailia → Al-Ismāʿīlīyah	142	30.35 N	32.16 E
Ismāʿīlīyah ◆[8]	273c	30.03 N	31.14 E
Ismāʿīlīyah, Turʿat al- ≊	142	30.04 N	31.16 E
İsmailli	130	38.56 N	27.13 E
Ismailovo	80	55.34 N	54.39 E
Ismaning	60	48.14 N	11.41 E
İsmayıllı	84	40.47 N	48.09 E
Isnā	140	25.18 N	32.33 E
Isny	58	47.41 N	10.02 E
Isoanala	157b	23.50 S	45.44 E
Isobe	94	34.22 N	136.49 E
Isogo ◆[8]	268	35.23 N	139.37 E
Isojoki	26	62.07 N	21.58 E
Isoka	154	10.10 S	32.35 E
Isokyrö	26	63.00 N	22.19 E
Isola, Fr.	62	44.11 N	7.03 E
Isola, Ms., U.S.	194	33.15 N	90.35 W
Isola, Monte ∧	64	45.42 N	10.05 E
Isola d'Asti	62	44.50 N	8.11 E
Isola del Cantone	62	44.39 N	8.57 E
Isola del Gran Sasso d'Italia	66	42.30 N	13.40 E
Isola della Scala	64	45.16 N	11.00 E
Isola del Liri	66	41.41 N	13.34 E
Isola di Capo Rizzuto	68	38.58 N	17.06 E
Isola Dovarese	64	45.10 N	10.18 E
Isola Farnese ◆[8]	66	42.01 N	12.23 E
Isola Vicentina	64	45.38 N	11.25 E
Isoletta	66	41.30 N	13.34 E
Isolillock Peak ∧	224	49.18 N	121.27 W
Isolo	273a	6.32 N	3.19 E
Isone	58	46.08 N	8.59 E
Isonzo (Soča) ≃	64	45.47 N	13.32 E
Isorella	64	45.18 N	10.19 E
Iso-Syöte ∧[2]	26	65.37 N	27.35 E
Iso-zaki ≻	94	36.23 N	140.38 E
Ispani	68	40.08 N	15.34 E
Isparta	130	37.46 N	30.33 E
Isparta □[4]	130	38.00 N	31.00 E
Isperih	38	43.43 N	26.50 E
Ispica	70	36.47 N	14.55 E
Ispica, Cava d' ⊥[5]	70	36.51 N	14.51 E
Ispikān	128	26.14 N	62.12 E
İspir	130	40.29 N	41.00 E
Ispra	62	45.49 N	8.37 E
Ispringen	56	48.55 N	8.40 E
Israel (Yisra'el) □[1], Asia	118	31.30 N	35.00 E
Israel (Yisra'el) □[1], Asia	132	31.30 N	35.00 E
Israel ≃	188	44.29 N	71.35 W
Issa	80	53.52 N	44.51 E
Issa ≃	76	56.58 N	28.47 E
Issano	246	5.49 N	59.25 W
Issaquah	224	47.31 N	122.01 W
Issaran, Ra's ≻	142	28.48 N	32.47 E
Issel (Oude IJssel) ≃	52	52.00 N	6.10 E
Isselburg	52	51.51 N	6.28 E
Isselhorst	52	51.57 N	8.24 E
Isser, Oued ≃, Alg.	34	36.52 N	3.48 E
Isser, Oued ≃, Alg.	34	35.08 N	1.28 W
Issia	150	6.29 N	6.35 W
Issigeac	32	44.44 N	0.36 E
Issime	62	45.41 N	7.51 E
Issogne	62	45.39 N	7.41 E
Issoire	32	45.33 N	3.15 E
Issole ≃	62	43.27 N	6.12 E
Issou	261	48.59 N	1.48 E
Issoudun	32	46.57 N	2.00 E
Issum	52	51.32 N	6.25 E
Issuna	154	5.23 S	34.46 E
Is-sur-Tille	58	47.31 N	5.06 E
Issy	50	48.49 N	2.17 E
Issyk	85	43.22 N	77.28 E
Issyk-Kul' (Rybačje)	85	42.26 N	76.12 E
Issyk-Kul' □[4]	85	42.15 N	77.15 E
Issyk-Kul', ozero ⊜	85	42.25 N	77.15 E
Īstādeh-ye Moqor, Āb-e ⊜	120	32.32 N	67.57 E
Istana Presidential Palace ʋ	269e	6.10 S	106.49 E
İstanbul, Tür.	130	41.01 N	28.58 E
İstanbul, Tür.	267b	41.01 N	28.58 E
İstanbul □[4]	130	41.10 N	28.45 E
Istanbul (Yeşilköy) International Airport ⊠	267b	40.58 N	28.49 E
İstanbul Boğazı (Bosporus) ʊ	130	41.06 N	29.04 E
Istanbul University ʋ[2]	267b	41.00 N	28.58 E
Isṭanhā	142	30.28 N	31.07 E
Istead Rise	260	51.24 N	0.22 E
Isteren ⊜	26	61.58 N	11.48 E
Isthmus Bay ⊂	212	45.00 N	81.15 W
Istiaía	38	38.57 N	23.09 E
İstinye ◆[8]	267b	41.06 N	29.03 E
İstisu	84	39.57 N	45.59 E
Istmina	246	5.10 N	76.39 W
Isto, Mount ∧	180	69.12 N	143.48 W
Istobensk	80	58.25 N	48.48 E
Istobnoje, Ross.	78	51.16 N	38.39 E
Istobnoje, Ross.	78	51.08 N	37.21 E
Istok	38	42.47 N	20.29 E
Istokpoga, Lake ⊜	220	27.22 N	81.17 W
Istra	82	55.55 N	36.52 E
Istra ≻[1]	36	45.15 N	14.00 E
Istra ≃	82	55.44 N	37.08 E
Istrana	64	45.41 N	12.07 E
Istres	62	43.31 N	4.59 E
Istria → Istra ≻[1]	36	45.15 N	14.00 E
Istrinskoje vodochranilišče ⊜[1]	82	56.04 N	36.49 E
Isulan	116	6.34 N	124.37 E
Isumi	94	35.17 N	140.19 E
Isumi ≃	94	35.18 N	140.25 E
Isumrud Strait ʊ	164	4.45 S	145.50 E
Isunba	273a	6.27 N	3.17 E
Iswarīpur	126	22.19 N	89.07 E
Iswepe	158	26.50 S	30.31 E
Itá	252	25.29 S	57.21 W
Itabaiana, Bra.	250	7.20 S	35.20 W
Itabaiana, Bra.	250	10.41 S	37.26 W
Itabaiana, Bra.	250	11.16 S	37.47 W
Itabapoana	255	21.18 S	40.58 W
Itabashi ◆[8]	268	35.45 N	139.43 E
Itaberá	255	23.51 S	49.09 W
Itaberaba	255	12.32 S	40.18 W
Itaberaí	255	16.02 S	49.48 W
Itabi	250	10.08 S	37.06 W
Itabira	255	19.37 S	43.13 W
Itaboca	256	22.03 S	44.05 W
Itaboraí	256	22.45 S	42.52 W
Itaboraí □[7]	287a	22.43 S	43.00 W
Itabuna	255	14.48 S	39.16 W
Itacaiuna ≃	250	5.21 S	49.08 W
Itacajá	250	8.19 S	47.46 W
Itacambiruçu ≃	255	16.44 S	42.45 W
Itacaré	255	14.18 S	39.00 W
Itacoatiara	250	3.08 S	58.25 W
Itacoatiara, Ponta de ≻	287a	22.59 S	43.02 W
Itacurubí del Rosario	252	24.29 S	56.41 W
Itacurussá	256	22.55 S	43.55 W
Itacurussá, Ilha de I	256	22.56 S	43.53 W
Itaeté	255	12.59 S	40.58 W
Itagacaba ≃	256	22.34 S	44.56 W
Itagi	255	14.10 S	40.01 W
Itaguaçu	255	19.48 S	40.51 W
Itaguaí	256	22.52 S	43.47 W
Itaguajé	255	22.37 S	51.59 W
Itaguara	255	20.23 S	44.29 W
Itaguaré, Pico do ∧	256	22.30 S	45.10 W
Itaguari ≃	255	14.11 S	44.40 W
Itaguaru	255	15.44 S	49.37 W
Itaguatins	250	5.47 S	47.29 W
Itagüí	246	6.10 N	75.36 W
Itaí	255	23.24 S	49.06 W
Itá-Ibaté	252	27.26 S	57.20 W
Itaiçaba	250	4.40 S	37.51 W
Itaim	256	22.24 S	45.53 W
Itaim ≃, Bra.	250	7.02 S	42.02 W
Itaim ≃, Bra.	256	23.07 S	45.08 W
Itaim ≃, Bra.	256	22.19 S	45.51 W
Itainópolis	250	7.24 S	41.31 W
Itaiópolis	252	26.20 S	49.56 W
Itaipava	256	22.23 S	43.08 W
Itaipu, Bra.	256	22.58 S	43.02 W
Itaipu, Bra.	287a	22.44 S	43.26 W
Itaipu, Lagoa de ⊂	287a	22.58 S	43.02 W
Itaipu, Ponta de ≻	287a	22.59 S	43.03 W
Itaipu, Represa de ⊜[1]	252	25.00 S	54.30 W
Itäisen Suomenlahden kansallispuisto ♠	26	60.15 N	27.00 E
Itaituba	250	4.17 S	55.59 W
Itajá	255	19.07 S	51.37 W
Itajaí	252	26.53 S	48.39 W
Itajaí do Sul ≃	252	27.12 S	49.39 W
Itajipora	256	22.19 S	46.28 W
Itajubá	256	22.26 S	45.27 W
Itaju do Colônia	255	15.09 S	39.44 W
Itajuípe	255	14.41 S	39.22 W
Itaka, Ross.	88	53.53 N	118.42 E
Itaka, Tan.	154	8.52 S	32.47 E
Itaki	273a	6.43 N	3.17 E
Itako	94	35.56 N	140.33 E
Itakura, Nihon	94	36.13 N	139.36 E
Itakura, Nihon	94	37.03 N	138.18 E
Itala Game Reserve ◆[4]	158	27.31 S	31.19 E
Italia → Italy □[1]	36	42.50 N	12.50 E
Itálica ⊥	34	37.30 N	6.05 W
Italie → Italy □[1]	36	42.50 N	12.50 E
Italien → Italy □[1]	36	42.50 N	12.50 E
Italy	222	32.11 N	96.53 W
Italy (Italia) □[1], Europe	22	42.50 N	12.50 E
Italy (Italia) □[1], Europe	36	42.50 N	12.50 E
Itamaraju	255	17.05 S	39.31 W

Symbol	English	Deutsch	Español	Français	Português
≃	River	Fluß	Río	Rivière	Rio
≊	Canal	Kanal	Canal	Canal	Canal
∟	Waterfall, Rapids	Wasserfall, Stromschnellen	Cascada, Rápidos	Chute d'eau, Rapides	Cascata, Rápidos
ʊ	Strait	Meeresstraße	Estrecho	Détroit	Estreito
⊂	Bay, Gulf	Bucht, Golf	Bahía, Golfo	Baie, Golfe	Baía, Golfo
⊜	Lake, Lakes	See, Seen	Lago, Lagos	Lac, Lacs	Lago, Lagos
≚	Swamp	Sumpf	Pantano	Marais	Pântano
⊓	Ice Features, Glacier	Eis- und Gletscherformen	Accidentes Glaciales	Formes glaciaires	Acidentes glaciares
⊽	Other Hydrographic Features	Andere Hydrographische Objekte	Otros Elementos Hidrográficos	Autres données hydrographiques	Outros acidentes hidrográficos
✢	Submarine Features	Untermeerische Objekte	Accidentes Submarinos	Formes de relief sous-marin	Acidentes submarinos
□	Political Unit	Politische Einheit	Unidad Politica	Entité politique	Unidade política
ʋ	Cultural Institution	Kulturelle Institution	Institución Cultural	Institution culturelle	Instituição cultural
⊥	Historical Site	Historische Stätte	Sitio Histórico	Site historique	Sitio histórico
♠	Recreational Site	Erholungs- und Ferienort	Sitio de Recreo	Centre de loisirs	Area de Lazer
⊠	Airport	Flughafen	Aeropuerto	Aéroport	Aeroporto
■	Military Installation	Militäranlage	Instalación Militar	Installation militaire	Instalação militar
◆	Miscellaneous	Verschiedenes	Misceláneo	Divers	Diversos

ENGLISH: Name | Page | Lat.°′ | Long.°′
DEUTSCH: Name | Seite | Breite°′ | Länge°′ E = Ost

Itamarandiba 255 17.51 S 42.51 W
Itamarandiba ≏ 255 17.18 S 42.48 W
Itamarati de Minas 256 21.25 S 42.49 W
Itamari 255 13.47 S 39.37 W
Itamataré 250 2.16 S 46.24 W
Itambacuri 255 18.01 S 41.42 W
Itambé 255 15.15 S 40.37 W
Itambi 256 22.44 S 42.58 W
Itami 96 34.46 N 135.25 E
Itami, Camp ■ 270 34.47 N 135.24 E
Itamonte 256 22.17 S 44.53 W
Itampolo 157b 24.41 S 43.57 E
Itānagar 120 27.09 N 93.33 E
Itandéua, Lago ⊜ 250 2.01 S 55.10 W
Itandrano 157b 21.47 S 45.17 E
Itanhaém 255 24.11 S 46.47 W
Itanhandu 256 22.18 S 44.57 W
Itanhauã ≏ 248 4.45 S 63.48 W
Itanhém 255 17.09 S 40.20 W
Itanhomi 255 19.10 S 41.52 W
Itano 96 34.07 N 134.28 E
Itaobim 255 16.34 S 41.30 W
Itaocaia 287a 22.58 S 43.01 W
Itapaci 255 14.57 S 49.34 W
Itapagipe 255 19.54 S 49.22 W
Itapajé 250 3.41 S 39.34 W
Itapanhaú ≏ 256 23.51 S 46.10 W
Itaparaná ≏ 248 5.47 S 63.03 W
Itaparica, Ilha de I 255 13.00 S 38.42 W
Itaparica, Represa de ⊜[1] 250 8.50 S 38.40 W
Itapaya 248 17.34 S 66.21 W
Itapé 255 14.54 S 39.26 W
Itapebi 255 15.56 S 39.32 W
Itapecerica 255 20.28 S 45.07 W
Itapecerica da Serra 256 23.43 S 46.50 W
Itapecerica da Serra □[7] 287b 23.44 S 46.52 W
Itapecuru-Mirim 250 3.24 S 44.20 W
Itapemirim 255 21.01 S 40.50 W
Itapera 250 2.32 S 43.47 W
Itaperina, Pointe › 157b 24.59 S 47.06 E
Itaperuna 255 21.12 S 41.54 W
Itapetim 250 7.22 S 37.11 W
Itapetinga 255 15.15 S 40.15 W
Itapetininga 255 23.36 S 48.03 W
Itapetininga ≏ 255 23.35 S 48.27 W
Itapeva, Bra. 255 23.58 S 48.52 W
Itapeva, Bra. 256 22.46 S 46.13 W
Itapevi 256 23.33 S 46.56 W
Itapevi □[7] 287b 23.31 S 46.55 W
Itapicuru 250 11.19 S 38.15 W
Itapicuru ≏, Bra. 250 2.52 S 44.12 W
Itapicuru ≏, Bra. 250 11.47 S 37.32 W
Itapipoca 250 3.30 S 39.35 W
Itapira 256 22.26 S 46.50 W
Itapiranga, Bra. 250 2.45 S 58.01 W
Itapiranga, Bra. 252 27.08 S 53.43 W
Itapirapuã 255 15.52 S 50.36 W
Itapitanga 255 14.26 S 39.34 W
Itapiúna 250 4.33 S 38.57 W
Itápolis 255 21.35 S 48.46 W
Itaporã 255 22.01 S 54.54 W
Itaporã de Goiás 250 8.02 S 48.39 W
Itaporanga, Bra. 250 7.18 S 38.10 W
Itaporanga, Bra. 255 23.42 S 49.29 W
Itaporanga d'Ajuda 250 10.59 S 37.18 W
Itapúa □[5] 252 26.50 S 55.50 W
Itapuranga 255 15.35 S 49.59 W
Itaquaí ≏ 246 4.20 S 70.12 W
Itaquaquecetuba 256 23.29 S 46.21 W
Itaquaquecetuba □[7] 287b 23.28 S 46.20 W
Itaquara 255 13.27 S 39.57 W
Itaquari 255 20.20 S 40.22 W
Itaquaxiara 287b 23.47 S 46.51 W
Itaquaxiara, Ribeirão ≏ 287b 23.44 S 46.47 W
Itaquera ●[8] 256 23.32 S 46.27 W
Itaquera, Ribeirão ≏ 287b 23.28 S 46.26 W
Itaqui 252 29.08 S 56.33 W
Itaquyry 252 24.56 S 55.13 W
Itarantim 255 15.39 S 40.03 W
Itararé 255 24.07 S 49.20 W
Itārsi 124 22.37 N 77.45 E
Itarumã 255 18.42 S 51.25 W
Itasca, Il., U.S. 278 41.58 N 88.00 W
Itasca, Tx., U.S. 222 32.09 N 97.08 W
Itasca, Lake ⊜ 198 47.11 N 95.12 W
Itasca State Park ♦ 198 47.18 N 95.18 W
Itata ≏ 252 36.23 S 72.52 W
Itatí 252 27.16 S 58.15 W
Itatiaia 256 22.30 S 44.34 W
Itatiaia, Parque Nacional do ♦ 256 22.28 S 44.37 W
Itatiba 256 23.00 S 46.51 W
Itatinga 255 23.07 S 48.36 W
Itatira 250 4.30 S 39.37 W
Itatka 86 56.49 N 85.37 E
Itatolo 273b 4.09 S 15.15 E
Itatskij 86 56.04 N 89.05 E
Itatupã 250 0.37 S 51.12 W
Itaú 250 5.50 S 37.59 W
Itaueira 250 7.36 S 43.02 W
Itaueira ≏ 250 6.41 S 42.55 W
Itaúna 255 20.04 S 44.34 W
Itaúna, Morro do ∧[2] 287a 22.46 S 43.02 W
Itāwa 124 25.32 N 76.22 E
Itazuke-kūkō ⊠ 96 33.35 N 130.28 E
Itbayat Island I 108 20.46 N 121.50 E
Itéa 38 38.26 N 22.24 E
Itenes (Guaporé) ≏ 248 11.54 S 65.01 W
Ith ∧ 52 52.05 N 9.35 E
Ithaca, Mi., U.S. 190 43.17 N 84.36 W
Ithaca, N.Y., U.S. 210 42.26 N 76.29 W
Itháki 38 38.23 N 20.42 E
Itháki I 38 38.24 N 20.42 E
Ithan Creek ≏ 285 40.00 N 75.21 W
Ithnayn 142 30.41 N 32.21 E
Ithon ≏ 42 52.12 N 3.27 W
Itigi 154 5.42 S 34.29 E
Itikawa → Ichikawa 94 35.44 N 139.55 E
Itimādpur 124 27.15 N 78.12 E
Itimbiri ≏ 152 2.02 N 22.44 E
Itinga 255 16.36 S 41.47 W
Itinga ≏ 255 16.35 S 41.45 W
Itinomiya → Ichinomiya 94 35.18 N 136.48 E
Itipo 152 0.50 S 18.35 E
Itiquira 255 17.12 S 54.07 W
Itiquira ≏ 248 17.21 S 55.37 W
Itirapina 255 22.15 S 47.49 W
Itire 273a 6.31 N 3.21 E
Itiruçu 255 13.31 S 40.09 W
Itiúba 250 10.43 S 39.51 W
Itkillik ≏ 180 70.08 N 150.57 W
Itlar' 82 56.51 N 39.17 E
Itlīdim 142 27.52 N 30.48 E
Itmīdah 142 30.46 N 31.20 E
Itmuryn, ozero ⊜ 80 49.30 N 52.22 E
Itō 94 34.58 N 139.05 E
Itobi 256 21.44 S 46.58 W
Itobo 154 4.10 S 33.01 E
Itoculo 154 14.42 S 40.18 E
Itoigawa 94 37.02 N 137.51 E
Itoko 152 1.00 S 21.45 E
Itomamo, Lac ⊜ 186 49.11 N 70.28 W
Itoman 174m 26.08 N 127.40 E
Iton ≏ 50 49.09 N 1.12 E
Itonamas ≏ 248 12.28 S 64.24 W
Itororó 255 15.07 S 40.06 W
Itri 66 41.17 N 13.32 E
Iṭsā 142 29.15 N 30.48 E
Itsukaichi, Nihon 94 35.44 N 139.13 E
Itsukaichi, Nihon 96 34.24 N 132.22 E
Itsuki 92 32.24 N 130.50 E
Itsuku-shima I 96 34.16 N 132.19 E
Itsuwa 92 32.30 N 130.10 E
Itta Bena 194 33.29 N 90.19 W
Ittel, Oued V 148 34.19 N 6.01 E
Itter ≏ 263 51.09 N 6.52 E
Ittersum 52 52.28 N 6.07 E
Itteville 261 48.31 N 2.21 E
Ittiri 71 40.36 N 8.34 E
Itú 255 23.16 S 47.19 W
Itu ≏ 252 29.25 S 55.51 W
Ituaçu 255 13.49 S 41.18 W
Ituango 246 7.04 N 75.45 W
Ituberá 255 13.44 S 39.09 W
Itucumã ≏ 248 6.59 S 69.48 W
Itueta 255 19.23 S 41.11 W
Ituí 256 21.32 S 42.55 W
Ituí ≏ 246 4.38 S 70.19 W
Ituim ≏ 252 28.35 S 51.20 W
Ituiutaba 255 18.58 S 49.28 W
Itula 154 3.29 S 27.52 E
Itumbiara 255 18.25 S 49.13 W
Itumirim 256 21.19 S 44.53 W
Itum-Kale 84 42.43 N 45.35 E
Ituna 184 51.10 N 103.30 W
Itungi Port 154 9.35 S 33.56 E
Ituni 246 5.30 N 58.14 W
Itupararanga, Represa de ⊜[1] 256 23.37 S 47.16 W
Itupeva 256 23.09 S 47.04 W
Itupeva, Rio da ≏ 256 22.03 S 47.15 W
Itupiranga 250 5.09 S 49.20 W
Ituporanga 252 27.25 S 49.36 W
Iturama 255 19.44 S 50.11 W
Iturbe 252 26.01 S 56.30 W
Iturbide 232 19.40 N 89.37 W
Ituri ≏ 154 1.40 N 27.01 E
Iturup, ostrov (Etorofu-tō) I 92a 44.35 N 147.10 E
Itutinga 256 21.18 S 44.40 W
Ituverava 255 20.20 S 47.47 W
Ituxi ≏ 248 7.18 S 64.51 W
Ituzaingó, Arg. 252 27.36 S 56.41 W
Ituzaingó, Arg. 258 34.40 S 58.40 W
Ituzaingó, Ur. 258 34.25 S 56.26 W
Itwa 124 27.20 N 82.42 E
Ityāy al-Bārūd 142 30.53 N 30.40 E
Ityopiya → Ethiopia □[1] 144 9.00 N 39.00 E
Itz ≏ 56 49.58 N 10.52 E
Itzehoe 52 53.55 N 9.31 E
Iubundha ≏ 126 24.06 N 90.20 E
Iuka, Il., U.S. 219 38.37 N 88.47 W
Iuka, Ms., U.S. 194 34.48 N 88.11 W
Iul'tin 180 67.50 N 178.48 W
Iul'tin, gora ∧ 180 67.50 N 178.25 W
Iúna 255 20.21 S 41.32 W
Iupeba 256 23.41 S 46.22 W
Iva 192 34.18 N 82.39 W
Ivaceviči 76 52.43 N 25.21 E
Ivačovo 76 60.32 N 36.22 E
Ivahona 157b 23.27 S 46.10 E
Ivaí ≏ 255 23.18 S 53.42 W
Ivaiporã 252 24.15 S 51.45 W
Ivajlovgrad 38 41.32 N 26.08 E
Ivakoany, Massif de l' ⋀ 157b 23.50 S 46.25 E
Ivalo 24 68.42 N 27.30 E
Ivalojoki ≏ 24 68.43 N 27.36 E
Ivancevo 82 55.58 N 36.07 E
Ivančice 61 49.06 N 16.23 E
Ivancovo 82 56.39 N 35.50 E
Ivanec 36 46.13 N 16.08 E
Ivane-Puste 78 48.39 N 26.11 E
Ivangorod 76 59.24 N 28.10 E
Ivangrad 38 42.50 N 19.52 E
Ivanhoe, Austl. 166 32.54 S 144.18 E
Ivanhoe, Austl. 274b 37.46 S 145.03 E
Ivanhoe, Ca., U.S. 226 36.23 N 119.13 W
Ivanhoe, Il., U.S. 278 42.17 N 88.02 W
Ivanhoe, Mn., U.S. 198 44.27 N 96.14 W
Ivanhoe, Va., U.S. 192 36.50 N 80.58 W
Ivanhoe ≏ 190 48.40 N 82.11 W
Ivanhoe Lake ⊜ 190 48.05 N 82.38 W
Ivanić Grad 36 45.42 N 16.24 E
Ivanišči, Ross. 76 56.36 N 35.13 E
Ivanišči, Ross. 80 55.46 N 40.26 E
Ivaniv 78 49.28 N 28.21 E
Ivanivka, Ukr. 78 46.58 N 30.28 E
Ivanivka, Ukr. 78 46.43 N 34.33 E
Ivanivka, Ukr. 83 48.14 N 38.58 E
Ivanivka, Ukr. 83 47.35 N 37.19 E
Ivanjci 61 46.38 N 15.54 E
Ivanjica 38 43.35 N 20.14 E
Ivankov 78 50.56 N 29.54 E
Ivankovcy 89 49.06 N 134.28 E
Ivan'kovo 82 54.44 N 37.57 E
Ivan'kovskij 80 56.39 N 40.05 E
Ivan'kovskoje vodochranilišče ⊜[1] 82 56.37 N 36.32 E
Ivanof Bay 180 55.54 N 159.29 W
Ivano-Frankivs'k 78 48.55 N 24.43 E
Ivano-Frankivs'k □[4] 78 48.45 N 24.30 E
Ivano-Frankove 78 49.55 N 23.43 E
Ivanopil' 78 49.52 N 28.12 E
Ivano-Šamševo 83 46.52 N 39.54 E
Ivanovka, Kyrg. 85 42.54 N 75.05 E
Ivanovka, Ross. 80 52.51 N 53.48 E
Ivanovka, Ross. 80 51.54 N 43.46 E
Ivanovka, Ross. 80 52.15 N 41.35 E
Ivanovka, Ross. 89 50.22 N 128.02 E
Ivanovka, Ross. 89 43.58 N 132.30 E
Ivanovo, Bela. 76 52.09 N 25.32 E
Ivanovo, Ross. 80 57.00 N 40.59 E
Ivanovo Oblast' □[4] 76 57.00 N 41.00 E
Ivanovo-Voznesensk → Ivanovo 80 57.00 N 40.59 E
Ivanovskaja, Ross. 24 60.48 N 55.52 E
Ivanovskaja, Ross. 78 45.17 N 38.29 E
Ivanovskoje, Ross. 76 59.17 N 28.49 E
Ivanovskoje, Ross. 78 51.37 N 34.57 E
Ivanovskoje, Ross. 82 55.05 N 37.50 E
Ivanovskoje, Ross. 82 54.55 N 36.50 E
Ivanovskoje, Ross. 82 55.52 N 36.55 E
Ivanovskoje, Ross. 82 56.23 N 37.07 E
Ivanovskoje, Ross. 265a 59.46 N 30.47 E
Ivan-Ozero 82 54.04 N 38.20 E
Ivan-Ozero, ozero ⊜ 82 54.07 N 38.17 E
Ivanpah Lake ⊜ 204 35.35 N 115.25 W
Ivantejevka, Ross. 80 52.16 N 49.07 E
Ivantejevka, Ross. 82 55.58 N 37.55 E
Ivantejevo 76 57.48 N 33.09 E
Ivanychi 78 50.39 N 24.20 E
Ivanytsya 78 50.47 N 32.36 E
Ivato 157b 20.37 S 47.12 E
Ivatuba 255 23.37 S 52.13 W
Ivdel' 72 60.42 N 60.24 E
Ivel ≏ 42 52.10 N 0.18 W
Ivenec 76 53.53 N 26.45 E
Iver 260 51.31 N 0.30 W
Iver Heath 260 51.32 N 0.31 W
Iverny 261 49.00 N 2.47 E
Ivigtut 176 61.12 N 48.10 W
Ivindo ≏ 152 0.09 S 12.09 E
Ivinghoe 42 51.50 N 0.37 W
Ivinheima ≏ 255 23.14 S 53.42 W
Ivje 76 53.56 N 25.46 E
Ivn'a 78 51.04 N 36.08 E
Ivnytsya 78 50.09 N 29.03 E
Ivohibe 157b 22.29 S 46.52 E
Ivolginsk 88 51.45 N 107.14 E
Ivón ≏ 248 11.06 S 66.08 W
Ivondro 157b 24.47 S 46.52 E
Ivor 208 36.54 N 76.54 W
Ivorogbo 150 5.30 N 6.21 E
Ivory Coast → Cote d'Ivoire □[1] 150 8.00 N 5.00 W
Ivory Coast ±[2] 150 5.10 N 5.00 W
Ivoryton 207 41.20 N 72.26 W
Ivösjön ⊜ 26 56.06 N 14.27 E
Ivot, Ross. 76 53.42 N 34.12 E
Ivot, Ukr. 78 51.58 N 33.28 E
Ivotka ≏ 78 51.57 N 33.22 E
Ivrea 62 45.28 N 7.52 E
İvrindi 130 39.34 N 27.29 E
Ivry-la-Bataille 50 48.53 N 1.28 E
Ivry [-sur-Seine] 50 48.49 N 2.23 E
Ivujivik 176 62.24 N 77.55 W
Ivybridge 42 50.23 N 3.56 W
Ivy Hatch 260 51.16 N 0.16 E
Ivyland 285 40.12 N 75.04 W
Iwade 96 34.15 N 135.19 E
Iwafune, Nihon 94 36.19 N 139.40 E
Iwafune, Nihon 270 34.44 N 135.54 E
Iwagi 96 34.15 N 133.09 E
Iwai 94 36.03 N 139.54 E
Iwai-shima I 96 33.47 N 131.58 E
Iwaizumi 92 39.50 N 141.48 E
Iwaki (Taira) 94 37.03 N 140.55 E
Iwaki ≏ 92 41.01 N 140.22 E
Iwaki-san ∧ 92 40.39 N 140.18 E
Iwakuni 96 34.09 N 132.11 E
Iwakuni Marine Corps Air Station ■ 96 34.08 N 132.14 E
Iwakura 94 35.17 N 136.52 E
Iwama 94 36.18 N 140.16 E
Iwami, Nihon 96 34.53 N 132.26 E
Iwami, Nihon 96 35.35 N 134.20 E
Iwami-kōgen ⋀[1] 96 35.00 N 132.30 E
Iwami-kokubun-ji ʋ[1] 96 34.56 N 132.08 E
Iwamizawa 92a 43.12 N 141.46 E
Iwamura 94 35.22 N 137.26 E
Iwanai 92a 42.58 N 140.30 E
Iwanowo → Ivanovo 80 57.00 N 40.59 E
Iwanuma 92 38.06 N 140.52 E
Iwaoka ●[8] 270 34.44 N 134.58 E
Iwase, Nihon 94 36.21 N 140.06 E
Iwase, Nihon 268 35.17 N 139.52 E
Iwata 94 34.42 N 137.48 E
Iwataki 96 35.34 N 135.09 E
Iwate □[5] 92 39.37 N 141.22 E
Iwate-san ∧ 92 39.51 N 141.00 E
Iwatsuki 94 35.57 N 139.42 E
Iwaya → Awaji, Nihon 96 34.35 N 135.01 E
Iwaya, Nihon 270 34.35 N 135.02 E
Iwayama 270 34.52 N 135.52 E
Iwazono 270 34.45 N 135.19 E
Iwo 150 7.38 N 4.11 E
Iwo Jima → Iō-jima I 174f 24.47 N 141.20 E
Iwŏn 98 40.19 N 128.39 E
Iwuy 50 50.14 N 3.19 E
Ixcán ≏ 236 16.07 N 91.05 W
Ixchiguán 236 15.12 N 91.53 W
Ixelles 56 50.50 N 4.22 E
Ixhuatlán 234 19.04 N 96.59 W
Ixiamas 248 13.45 S 68.09 W
Iximché ⊥ 236 14.44 N 90.59 W
Ixmiquilpan 234 20.29 N 99.14 W
Ixonia 216 43.09 N 88.36 W
Ixopo 158 30.08 S 30.00 E
Ixtahuacán 236 15.25 N 91.46 W
Ixtapa 234 17.39 N 101.36 W
Ixtapa, Punta › 234 17.39 N 101.40 W
Ixtapan de la Sal 234 18.50 N 99.41 W
Ixtepec 234 16.34 N 95.06 W
Ixtlahuacán del Río 234 20.52 N 103.15 W
Ixtlán 234 20.11 N 102.24 W
Ixtlán de Juárez 234 17.20 N 96.29 W
Ixtlán del Río 234 21.02 N 104.22 W
Ixworth 42 52.18 N 0.50 E
Iya ≏ 96 33.58 N 133.47 E
'Iyādh 144 14.59 N 46.51 E
'Iyāl Bakhīt 140 13.25 N 28.41 E
Iyang, Taehan 98 34.53 N 127.01 E
Iyang → Yiyang, Zhg. 102 28.36 N 112.20 E
Iyang, Gili I 115a 6.59 S 114.10 E
Iyo 96 33.46 N 132.42 E
Iyo-mishima 96 33.58 N 133.33 E
Iyo-nada ⊤[2] 96 33.40 N 132.20 E
Iž ≏ 80 55.58 N 52.38 E
Izabal 236 15.24 N 89.08 W
Izabal □[5] 236 15.30 N 89.00 W
Izabal, Lago de ⊜ 236 15.30 N 89.10 W
'Izab al-Baṣāriṭah 142 31.23 N 31.47 E
Īzad Khvāst 128 31.31 N 52.07 E
Izalco 236 13.45 N 89.40 W
'Izam, Jabal al- ∧ 132 30.51 N 35.46 E
Izamal 232 20.56 N 89.01 W
Izapa ⊥ 232 14.55 N 92.10 W
'Izbat Abū Ṣuql 132 31.09 N 33.49 E
Izberbaš 84 42.33 N 47.52 E
Izbica, Pol. 30 50.54 N 23.09 E
Izbica, Pol. 30 54.42 N 17.26 E
Izd'oškovo 76 55.08 N 33.37 E
Izegem 50 50.55 N 3.12 E
Īzeh 128 31.50 N 49.50 E
Izena-shima I 174m 26.56 N 127.56 E
Izendy 86 45.48 N 59.28 E
Izernore 58 46.13 N 5.33 E
Iževsk 80 56.51 N 53.14 E
Iževskoje 80 54.34 N 40.53 E
Izkī 128 22.56 N 57.46 E
Ižma 24 65.02 N 53.55 E
Ižma ≏ 24 65.19 N 52.54 E
Izmajlovo 80 53.43 N 47.14 E
Izmajlovo ●[8] 265b 55.48 N 37.46 E
Izmajlovo Park ♦ 265b 55.46 N 37.47 E
Izmalkovo 76 52.41 N 37.58 E
Izmayil 78 45.21 N 28.50 E
İzmir 130 38.25 N 27.09 E
İzmir □[4] 130 38.30 N 27.15 E
İzmir Körfezi c 130 38.30 N 26.50 E
İzmit (Kocaeli) 130 40.46 N 29.55 E
İzmit Körfezi c 130 40.45 N 29.35 E
Ižmorskij 86 56.11 N 86.38 E
Iznajar, Embalse de ⊜[1] 34 37.15 N 4.30 W
Iznalloz 34 37.23 N 3.31 W
İznik 130 40.26 N 29.43 E
İznik Gölü ⊜ 130 40.26 N 29.30 E
Iznoski 76 54.59 N 35.19 E
Izola 64 45.32 N 13.40 E
Izoplit 82 56.38 N 36.12 E
Izopo, Punta › 236 15.48 N 87.23 W
Ižora ≏ 265a 59.48 N 30.36 E
Izozog, Bañados del ⸬ 248 18.48 S 62.10 W
Izra' 132 32.51 N 36.15 E
Izsák 30 46.48 N 19.22 E
Iztacalco ●[8] 286a 19.23 N 99.07 W
Iztaccíhuatl, Volcán ∧[1] 234 19.11 N 98.39 W
Iztaccíhuatl y Popocatéptl, Parques Nacionales ♦ 234 19.10 N 98.38 W
Iztapa 236 13.56 N 90.43 W
Iztapalapa ●[8] 286a 19.21 N 99.06 W
Izucar de Matamoros 234 18.36 N 98.28 W
Izu-hantō ›[1] 94 34.45 N 139.00 E
Izuhara 92 34.12 N 129.17 E
Izumi, Nihon 92 32.05 N 130.22 E
Izumi, Nihon 92 38.20 N 140.53 E
Izumi, Nihon 94 35.54 N 136.40 E
Izumi, Nihon 96 34.55 N 134.55 E
Izumi, Nihon 96 34.29 N 135.26 E
Izumi ●[8] 268 35.25 N 139.30 E
Izumi-ōtsu 96 34.30 N 135.24 E
Izumi-sano 96 34.25 N 135.19 E
Izumizaki 94 37.09 N 140.17 E
Izumo 96 35.22 N 132.46 E
Izumo ≏ 94 34.38 N 136.33 E
Izumo-kokubun-ji ʋ[1] 96 35.26 N 133.06 E
Izumrud 86 57.05 N 61.23 E
Izu-nagaoka 94 35.02 N 138.56 E
Izushi 96 35.28 N 134.52 E
Izu-shotō II 6 32.00 N 140.00 E
Izu Trench ⊕[1] 6 31.00 N 142.00 E
Izuwara 270 34.53 N 135.32 E
Izvaryne 83 48.17 N 39.52 E
Izvestij CIK, ostrova II 74 75.55 N 82.30 E
Izvestkovyj 89 48.59 N 131.33 E
Izvorul Muntelui, Lacul ⊜[1] 38 47.00 N 26.00 E
Izyaslav 78 50.07 N 26.51 E
Izynžul' 86 52.24 N 90.13 E
Izyum 83 49.12 N 37.19 E

J

Ja'ār, Birkat al- ⊜ 142 30.28 N 30.10 E
Jääsjärvi ⊜ 26 61.36 N 26.07 E
Jaba, Ityo. 144 6.17 N 35.12 E
Jaba, Pap. N. Gui. 175e 6.32 S 155.12 E
Jabā, Sūrīy. 132 33.10 N 35.56 E
Jabal, Baḥr al- → Mountain Nile ≏ 136 9.30 N 30.30 E
Jabal Abyad Plateau ⋀[1] 140 19.00 N 29.00 E
Jabal al-Awliyā' 140 15.14 N 32.30 E
Jabal al-Awliyā', Khazzān (White Nile Dam) ●[6] 140 15.14 N 32.29 E
Jabalambre ∧ 34 40.06 N 1.03 W
Jabal an-Nūr 142 28.57 N 31.02 E
Jabal Aṭ-Ṭayr 142 28.14 N 30.45 E
Jabal Dūd 140 13.25 N 33.09 E
Jabal Lubnān □[4] 132 33.50 N 35.40 E
Jabalón ≏ 34 38.53 N 4.05 W
Jabal os Sarāj 120 35.07 N 69.14 E
Jabalpur 124 23.10 N 79.57 E
Jabal Qerri 140 16.15 N 32.48 E
Jabal 'Uwaybid 142 30.09 N 32.12 E
Jabālyah 132 31.32 N 34.29 E
Jabal Zuqar, Jazīrat I 144 14.00 N 42.45 E
Jabbān, Arḍ al- ●[1] 132 32.08 N 36.35 E
Jabbeke 50 51.11 N 3.05 E
Jabbi 123 32.24 N 72.06 E
Jabbū, Qā' ≚ 132 29.35 N 36.13 E
Jabbūl, Sabkhat al- ⊜ 130 36.03 N 37.39 E
Jabel 54 53.32 N 12.32 E
Jabi 114 2.32 N 102.48 E
Jabiru 164 12.40 S 132.53 E
Jabjabah, Wādī V 140 22.37 N 33.17 E
Jablah 130 35.21 N 35.55 E
Jablanac 36 44.42 N 14.54 E
Jablanica 36 43.39 N 17.45 E
Jablanica ≏ 38 43.07 N 21.57 E
Jablaničko Jezero ⊜[1] 36 43.40 N 17.50 E
Jablines 261 48.55 N 2.46 E
Jabločnyj 89 47.10 N 142.04 E
Jablonec nad Nisou 30 50.44 N 15.10 E
Jablonica 30 48.37 N 17.25 E
Jabłonka 30 49.29 N 19.41 E
Jablonné v Podještědí 54 50.48 N 14.47 E
Jablonoj → Jablonovyj chrebet ⋀ 88 53.30 N 115.00 E
Jablonovo 88 51.51 N 112.49 E
Jablonovyj chrebet ⋀ 88 53.30 N 115.00 E
Jabłonowo 30 53.24 N 19.09 E
Jablonowy-Gebirge → Jablonovyj chrebet ⋀ 88 53.30 N 115.00 E
Jablunkov 30 49.35 N 18.47 E
Jaboatão 250 8.07 S 35.01 W
Jaboncillos Creek ≏ 196 27.23 N 97.45 W
Jabonga 116 9.20 N 125.32 E
Jaborandi 255 20.40 S 48.25 W
Jaboticabal 255 21.16 S 48.19 W
Jabrat Sa'īd ⊤[4] 140 16.06 N 31.50 E
Jabron ≏ 62 44.33 N 4.45 E
Jabron, Torrent le ≏ 62 44.09 N 5.57 E
Jabung 115a 5.29 S 105.40 E
Jabung, Tanjung › 112 1.01 S 104.22 E
Jaca 34 42.34 N 0.33 W
Jacala 234 21.01 N 99.11 W
Jacaleapa 236 14.00 N 86.40 W
Jacaltenango 236 15.40 N 91.44 W
Jacana 274b 37.42 S 144.55 E
Jacaraci 255 14.51 S 42.26 W
Jacaré ≏, Bra. 248 5.49 S 63.35 W
Jacaré ≏, Bra. 250 10.10 S 41.58 W
Jacaré ≏, Bra. 255 13.50 S 40.42 W
Jacareí 256 23.19 S 45.58 W
Jacarepaguá ●[8] 256 22.56 S 43.20 W
Jacarepaguá, Lagoa de c 256 22.59 S 43.24 W
Jacarezinho 255 23.09 S 49.59 W
Jaceel V 144 10.25 N 51.01 E
Jaceruba 256 22.35 S 43.34 W
Jáchal ≏ 252 30.44 S 68.08 W
Jachenau 64 47.36 N 11.25 E
Jachroma 82 56.17 N 37.30 E
Jachroma ≏ 82 56.31 N 37.07 E
Jáchymov 54 50.20 N 12.55 E
Jaciara 255 15.59 S 54.57 W
Jacinto 255 16.10 S 40.17 W
Jacinto Aráuz 252 38.04 S 63.26 W
Jacinto City 222 29.46 N 95.14 W
Jacinto Machado 252 29.00 S 49.46 W
Jaciparaná 248 9.15 S 64.23 W
Jaciparaná ≏ 248 9.22 S 64.22 W
Jackass Creek ≏ 226 37.22 N 119.23 W
Jack Creek ≏ 202 42.59 N 121.32 W
Jackfish Lake ⊜ 184 53.05 N 108.25 W
Jackhead Harbour 184 51.52 N 97.16 W
Jack Lake ⊜ 212 44.42 N 78.03 W
Jack London State Historical Park ♦ 226 38.21 N 122.32 W
Jackman 188 45.38 N 70.15 W
Jackman Creek ≏ 224 48.30 N 121.43 W
Jack Mountain ∧, Mt., U.S. 202 46.21 N 112.18 W
Jack Mountain ∧, Wa., U.S. 224 48.47 N 120.57 W
Jackpot 204 41.59 N 114.40 W
Jacksboro, Tn., U.S. 192 36.19 N 84.11 W
Jacksboro, Tx., U.S. 196 33.13 N 98.09 W
Jacks Creek ≏ 208 40.35 N 77.33 W
Jacks Fork ≏ 194 37.12 N 91.17 W
Jacks Island I 279b 40.37 N 79.43 W
Jacks Mountain ∧ 210 40.45 N 77.30 W
Jackson, Al., U.S. 194 31.30 N 87.53 W
Jackson, Ca., U.S. 226 38.20 N 120.46 W
Jackson, Ga., U.S. 192 33.17 N 83.57 W
Jackson, Ky., U.S. 192 37.33 N 83.23 W
Jackson, La., U.S. 194 30.50 N 91.13 W
Jackson, Mi., U.S. 216 42.14 N 84.24 W
Jackson, Mn., U.S. 198 43.37 N 94.59 W
Jackson, Ms., U.S. 194 32.17 N 90.11 W
Jackson, Mo., U.S. 194 37.22 N 89.39 W
Jackson, N.J., U.S. 208 40.08 N 74.19 W
Jackson, N.C., U.S. 192 36.23 N 77.25 W
Jackson, Oh., U.S. 188 39.03 N 82.38 W
Jackson, Pa., U.S. 210 41.50 N 75.36 W
Jackson, S.C., U.S. 192 33.19 N 81.47 W
Jackson, Tn., U.S. 194 35.36 N 88.48 W
Jackson, Wy., U.S. 200 43.28 N 110.45 W
Jackson □[6], In., U.S. 218 38.53 N 86.03 W
Jackson □[6], Mi., U.S. 216 42.15 N 84.24 W
Jackson □[6], Tx., U.S. 222 29.00 N 96.35 W
Jackson ≏ 188 37.47 N 79.46 W
Jackson, Cape › 172 41.00 S 174.18 E
Jackson, Lake ⊜, Fl., U.S. 192 30.30 N 84.17 W
Jackson, Lake ⊜, Fl., U.S. 220 27.29 N 81.28 W
Jackson, Lake ⊜, Fl., U.S. 220 27.55 N 81.10 W
Jackson, Mount ∧, Ant. 9 71.23 S 63.22 W
Jackson, Mount ∧, Austl. 162 30.15 S 119.16 E
Jackson, Port c 170 33.50 S 151.16 E
Jackson Bay c 172 43.58 S 168.42 E
Jackson Brook ≏ 276 40.53 N 74.34 W
Jackson Butte ∧ 226 38.20 N 120.43 W
Jackson Center, Oh., U.S. 216 40.27 N 84.02 W
Jackson Center, Pa., U.S. 214 41.16 N 80.09 W
Jackson Creek ≏, Can. 184 49.18 N 100.50 W
Jackson Creek ≏, Ca., U.S. 226 38.18 N 121.01 W
Jackson Creek ≏, Il., U.S. 216 41.26 N 88.10 W
Jackson Head › 172 43.58 S 168.37 E
Jackson Heights ●[8] 276 40.45 N 73.53 W
Jackson Lake ⊜ 202 43.55 N 110.40 W
Jackson Lake ⊜[1] 192 33.22 N 83.52 W
Jackson Meadows Reservoir ⊜[1] 226 39.29 N 120.32 W
Jackson Mountain ∧ 188 44.46 N 70.32 W
Jackson Park ♦, On., Can. 281 42.17 N 83.01 W
Jackson Park ♦, Il., U.S. 278 41.47 N 87.35 W
Jackson's Arm 186 49.52 N 56.47 W
Jacksons Creek ≏ 169 37.40 S 144.48 E
Jacksonville, Al., U.S. 194 33.48 N 85.45 W
Jacksonville, Ar., U.S. 194 34.51 N 92.06 W
Jacksonville, Fl., U.S. 192 30.19 N 81.39 W
Jacksonville, Il., U.S. 219 39.44 N 90.13 W
Jacksonville, N.J., U.S. 285 40.03 N 74.46 W
Jacksonville, N.Y., U.S. 210 42.31 N 76.37 W
Jacksonville, N.C., U.S. 192 34.45 N 77.25 W
Jacksonville, Or., U.S. 202 42.18 N 122.57 W
Jacksonville, Tx., U.S. 222 31.57 N 95.16 W
Jacksonville, Vt., U.S. 207 42.47 N 72.49 W
Jacksonville, Lake ⊜[1] 222 31.55 N 95.17 W
Jacksonville Beach 192 30.17 N 81.23 W
Jacksonville Naval Air Station ■ 192 30.14 N 81.41 W
Jacks Reef 210 43.06 N 76.25 W
Jacks Run ≏ 279b 40.13 N 79.35 W
Jacktown Acres 279b 40.19 N 79.45 W
Jacmel 238 18.14 N 72.32 W
Jaco 232 27.50 N 104.00 W
Jacob, Morne ∧ 240e 14.46 N 61.06 W
Jacobābād 120 28.17 N 68.26 E
Jacobina 250 11.11 S 40.31 W
Jacob Island I 212 44.28 N 78.28 W
Jacob Riis Park ♦ 276 40.34 N 73.52 W
Jacobs Creek ≏ 214 40.07 N 79.44 W
Jacobsdal 158 29.13 S 24.41 E
Jacobus 208 39.53 N 76.43 W
Jacona de Plancarte 234 19.57 N 102.16 W
Jacques, Lac à ⊜ 180 66.10 N 127.25 W
Jacques-Cartier 275a 45.31 N 73.29 W
Jacques-Cartier ≏ 206 46.40 N 71.45 W
Jacques-Cartier, Détroit de ʯ 186 50.00 N 63.30 W
Jacques-Cartier, Mont ∧ 186 48.59 N 65.57 W
Jacques-Cartier, Pont ●[5] 275a 45.31 N 73.32 W
Jacquet River 186 47.55 N 66.00 W
Jacqueville 150 5.12 N 4.25 W
Jacquinot Bay c 164 5.35 S 151.30 E
Jacu ≏, Bra. 250 6.13 S 35.09 W
Jacú ≏, Bra. 256 23.05 S 45.08 W
Jacu, Rio do ≏ 287b 23.29 S 46.27 W
Jacuba ≏ 255 18.25 S 52.28 W
Jacuecanga 256 23.01 S 44.13 W
Jacuí ≏ 252 30.02 S 51.15 W
Jacuípe ≏ 255 12.30 S 39.05 W
Jacumba 204 32.37 N 116.11 W
Jacundá 250 4.33 S 49.28 W
Jacundá ≏ 250 1.57 S 50.26 W
Jacupiranga 252 24.42 S 48.00 W
Jacuriaí ≏ 250 10.57 S 39.35 W
Jacutinga 256 22.17 S 46.37 W
Jada 146 8.46 N 12.09 E
Jada'ah, Jabal ∧[2] 142 29.58 N 30.40 E
Jādabpur 126 22.29 N 88.23 E
Jaddi, Rās › 128 25.14 N 63.31 E
Jade 52 53.20 N 8.14 E
Jade Buddha, Temple of the ʋ[1] 269b 31.14 N 121.26 E
Jadebusen c 52 53.30 N 8.10 E
Jäder 40 59.25 N 16.41 E
Jäderfors 40 60.41 N 16.40 E
Jade Run ≏ 285 39.56 N 74.45 W
Jadīdah 128 34.01 N 42.28 E
Jadito Wash V 200 35.22 N 110.50 W
J.A.D. Jensens Nunatakker ∧ 176 62.45 N 48.00 W
Jadotville → Likasi 154 10.59 S 26.44 E
Jadraque 34 40.55 N 2.55 W
Jadrin 80 55.56 N 46.12 E
Jadromino 82 55.57 N 36.36 E
Jādū 146 31.57 N 12.01 E
Jægerspris 41 55.51 N 11.59 E
Jaeger Summit ∧ 154 2.52 S 35.47 E
Jaén, Esp. 34 37.46 N 3.47 W
Jaén, Perú 248 5.42 S 78.47 W
Jaén □[4] 34 38.00 N 3.30 E
Jæren ●[1] 26 58.45 N 5.45 E
Jāfarābād, India 120 20.52 N 71.22 E
Ja'farābād, Īrān 128 35.43 N 50.43 E
Jāfarpur 126 22.29 N 89.06 E
Jāfarpur ●[8] 272a 28.40 N 77.01 E
Jaffa, Cape › 166 36.58 S 139.40 E
Jaffa, Tel Aviv- → Tel Aviv-Yafo 132 32.04 N 34.46 E
Jaffna 122 9.40 N 80.00 E
Jaffna Lagoon c 122 9.35 N 80.15 E
Jaffrey 207 42.48 N 72.01 W
Jafr, Qā' al- ±[7] 132 30.17 N 36.20 E
Jagādhri 124 30.10 N 77.18 E
Jägala ≏ 76 59.29 N 25.09 E
Jagalūr 122 14.32 N 76.21 E
Jāgan 120 28.05 N 68.30 E
Jagannāthganj Ghāt 124 24.45 N 89.49 E
Jagannāthpūr 272b 22.43 N 88.19 E
Jagati 126 23.54 N 89.06 E
Jagatnagar 272b 22.47 N 88.13 E
Jagatpur ●[8] 272a 28.44 N 77.14 E
Jagatsingpur 120 20.16 N 86.10 E
Jagdalpur 122 19.04 N 82.02 E
Jagdīspur 124 25.29 N 84.25 E
Jagel 41 54.27 N 9.32 E
Jagel'urta, gora ∧[2] 24 67.33 N 38.02 E
Jagenbach 61 48.38 N 15.02 E
Jägerndorf → Krnov 30 50.05 N 17.41 E
Jagersfontein 158 29.44 S 25.29 E
Jaggayyapeta 122 16.54 N 80.06 E
Jagged Mountain ∧ 180 58.38 N 162.02 W
Jagīn ≏ 128 25.35 N 58.18 E
Jagnob ≏ 85 39.15 N 68.35 E
Jagny-sous-Bois 261 49.05 N 2.27 E
Jagodnoje, Ross. 74 62.33 N 149.40 E
Jagodnoje, Ross. 80 53.36 N 49.04 E
Jagodnyj 86 59.44 N 65.04 E
Jagraon 123 30.47 N 75.29 E
Jagst ≏ 56 49.14 N 9.11 E
Jagsthausen 56 49.19 N 9.28 E
Jagstzell 56 49.02 N 10.05 E
Jagtiāl 122 18.48 N 78.56 E
Jaguaquara 255 13.32 S 39.58 W
Jaguarão 252 32.34 S 53.23 W
Jaguarão (Yaguarón) ≏ 252 32.39 S 53.12 W
Jaguarari 250 10.16 S 40.12 W
Jaguaretama 250 5.37 S 38.46 W
Jaguari 252 29.30 S 54.41 W
Jaguari ≏, Bra. 256 22.41 S 47.17 W
Jaguari ≏, Bra. 256 23.10 S 45.55 W
Jaguariaíva 252 24.15 S 49.42 W
Jaguaribara 250 5.40 S 38.37 W
Jaguaribe 250 5.53 S 38.37 W
Jaguaribe ≏ 250 4.25 S 37.45 W
Jaguari-Mirim ≏ 256 21.59 S 47.17 W
Jaguaripe 255 13.06 S 38.53 W
Jaguariúna 256 22.41 S 46.59 W
Jaguaruna 252 28.36 S 49.02 W
Jagüé 252 28.38 S 68.24 W
Jagüey Grande 240p 22.32 N 81.08 W
Jāguli 126 22.56 N 88.32 E
Jāgulia 272b 22.44 N 88.32 E
Jagungal, Mount ∧ 171b 36.09 S 148.23 E
Jagunovskij 86 55.17 N 85.59 E
Jahānābād, India 124 25.13 N 84.59 E
Jahānābād, Pāk. 123 32.11 N 72.29 E
Jahāngīra 123 33.58 N 72.13 E
Jahāngīrābād 124 28.25 N 78.06 E
Jahangirpur ●[8] 272a 28.44 N 77.13 E
Jahānia 123 30.02 N 71.49 E
Jahannam, Qārat ∧[2] 142 29.19 N 30.09 E
Jahdānīyah, Wādī al- V 132 30.12 N 36.22 E
Jahnsdorf 54 50.44 N 12.51 E
Jahrom 128 28.31 N 53.33 E
Jahú → Jaú 255 22.18 S 48.33 W
Jaicós 250 7.21 S 41.08 W
Jaidak 120 31.58 N 66.43 E
Jaihti ≏ 126 24.08 N 86.48 E
Jaijon 123 31.21 N 76.09 E
Jailolo 108 1.05 N 127.30 E
Jaimanitas ≏ 286b 23.05 N 82.29 W
Jainca 102 35.59 N 102.02 E
Jainti 124 26.42 N 89.36 E
Jaintiāpur 120 25.08 N 92.07 E
Jaipur 120 26.55 N 75.49 E
Jaipur Hāt 124 25.06 N 89.01 E
Jais 124 26.15 N 81.32 E
Jaisalmer 120 26.55 N 70.54 E
Jaito 123 30.28 N 74.53 E
Jaja 86 56.12 N 86.26 E
Jaja ≏ 86 56.58 N 86.23 E
Jājapur 120 20.51 N 86.20 E
Jājarkoṭ 124 28.42 N 82.12 E
Jājarm 128 36.58 N 56.27 E
Jajce 36 44.21 N 17.16 E
Jajichi 174m 26.47 N 128.13 E
Jajjha 123 28.45 N 70.34 E
Jajl'u 86 51.48 N 87.36 E
Jajpan 85 40.23 N 70.48 E
Jajsan 86 50.51 N 56.14 E
Jajva 86 59.20 N 57.15 E
Jajva ≏ 86 59.13 N 56.40 E
Ják 61 47.08 N 16.35 E
Jakarta, Indon. 115a 6.10 S 106.48 E
Jakarta, Indon. 269e 6.10 S 106.48 E
Jakarta, Teluk c 115a 6.05 S 106.48 E
Jakarta Kota Station ●[5] 269e 6.08 S 106.49 E
Jakarta Raya □[4] 115a 6.10 S 106.45 E
Jakdūl ⊜ 140 17.39 N 32.59 E
Jake Creek Mountain ∧ 204 41.13 N 116.54 W
Jakenan 115a 6.45 S 111.11 E
Jākhal 123 29.48 N 75.50 E
Jakhāu 120 23.13 N 68.43 E
Jakkonen 24 66.33 N 29.52 E
Jakobsberg 40 59.26 N 17.50 E
Jakobsdalsberget ∧[2] 40 58.41 N 16.07 E
Jakobshavn (Ilulissat) 176 69.13 N 51.06 W
Jakobstad (Pietarsaari) 26 63.40 N 22.42 E
Jakovleviči 76 54.20 N 30.31 E
Jakovlevka 89 44.26 N 133.28 E
Jakovlevo, Ross. 78 50.51 N 36.27 E
Jakovlevo, Ross. 82 54.48 N 37.26 E
Jakša 24 61.48 N 56.49 E
Jakšanga 80 58.23 N 45.56 E
Jakšur-Bodja 80 57.11 N 53.09 E
Jakupica ⋀ 38 41.43 N 21.26 E
Jakutija □[3] 74 67.00 N 125.00 E
Jakutsk 74 62.00 N 129.40 E
Jal 196 32.06 N 103.11 W
Jalacingo 234 19.48 N 97.18 W
Jalaid Qi 89 46.40 N 122.55 E
Jalājil 128 25.41 N 45.28 E
Jalālābād, Afg. 120 34.26 N 70.28 E
Jalālābād, India 123 30.37 N 74.15 E
Jalālābād, India 124 27.43 N 79.40 E
Jalālah al-Baḥrīyah, Jabal ⋀[1] 142 29.20 N 32.00 E
Jalālat al-Qiblīyah, Jabal al- ⋀ 142 28.42 N 32.22 E
Jalālpur, India 124 26.19 N 82.44 E
Jalālpur, Pāk. 123 32.38 N 74.12 E
Jalālpur Pīrwāla 123 29.30 N 71.13 E
Jalan' 86 58.21 N 91.53 E
Jalán ≏ 236 14.39 N 86.12 W
Jalan Besar Stadium ♦ 271c 1.18 N 103.52 E
Jalandhar 123 31.19 N 75.34 E
Jalangi 126 24.08 N 88.42 E
Jalangi ≏ 126 23.25 N 88.22 E
Jalan Kayu 271c 1.24 N 103.52 E
Jalapa, Guat. 236 14.38 N 89.59 W
Jalapa, Méx. 234 17.43 N 92.49 W
Jalapa, Nic. 236 13.55 N 86.08 W
Jalapa □[5] 236 14.35 N 89.55 W
Jalasjärvi 26 62.30 N 22.45 E
Jalaud ≏ 116 10.45 N 122.40 E
Jālaun 124 26.09 N 79.21 E
Jal'čiki 80 55.09 N 48.01 E
Jalcocotán 234 21.28 N 105.07 W
Jalda 126 21.56 N 87.30 E
Jaleaca de Catalán 234 17.26 N 99.51 W
Jalesar 124 27.29 N 78.19 E
Jaleshwar 126 21.49 N 87.13 E
Jaleśwar 124 26.38 N 85.48 E
Jālgaon, India 122 21.01 N 75.34 E
Jālgaon, India 122 21.03 N 76.32 E
Jal'gelevo 265a 59.44 N 29.57 E
Jalhay 56 50.34 N 5.58 E
Jalingo 146 8.53 N 11.22 E
Jalirpār 126 23.13 N 89.58 E
Jalisco □[3] 234 20.20 N 103.40 W
Jallas ≏ 34 42.54 N 9.08 W
Jālna 122 19.50 N 75.53 E
Jalón ≏ 34 41.47 N 1.04 W
Jālor 120 25.21 N 72.37 E
Jalostotitlán 234 21.12 N 102.28 W
Jalpa 234 21.38 N 102.58 W
Jalpa de Méndez 234 18.08 N 93.05 W
Jalpāiguri 124 26.31 N 88.44 E
Jalpan de Serra 234 21.14 N 99.29 W
Jaltepec ≏ 234 17.26 N 94.59 W
Jáltipan de Morelos 234 17.58 N 94.42 W
Jaluit I[1] 14 6.00 N 169.35 E
Jalūlā' 128 34.16 N 45.10 E
Jalutorovsk 86 56.40 N 66.18 E
Jam, Ross. 82 55.29 N 37.45 E
Jam, Uzb. 85 40.07 N 68.11 E
Jām ≏ 128 35.10 N 61.06 E
Jamaame (Margherita) 144 0.04 N 42.45 E
Jamaare ≏ 146 12.06 N 10.14 E
Jāmāibāti 272b 22.51 N 88.08 E
Jamaica 240p 20.12 N 75.09 W
Jamaica ●[8] 276 40.42 N 73.47 W
Jamaica □[1], N.A. 230 18.15 N 77.30 W
Jamaica □[1], N.A. 241q 18.15 N 77.30 W
Jamaica Bay c 210 40.36 N 73.51 W
Jamaica Channel ʯ 238 18.00 N 75.30 W
Jamaica Plain ●[8] 283 42.19 N 71.06 W
Jamaica Pond ⊜ 283 42.19 N 71.07 W
Jamaika → Jamaica □[1] 241q 18.15 N 77.30 W
Jamaïque → Jamaica □[1] 241q 18.15 N 77.30 W
Jamal, poluostrov ›[1] 74 70.00 N 70.00 E
Jam-Alin', chrebet ⋀ 89 53.00 N 134.36 E
Jamālīyah ●[8] 273c 30.03 N 31.16 E

Symbols in the index entries represent the broad categories identified in the key at the right. Symbols with superior numbers (⋀[1]) identify subcategories (see complete key on page *I · 1).*

Symbole im Register stellen die rechts im Schlüssel erklärten Kategorien dar. Symbole mit hochgestellten Ziffern (⋀[1]) bezeichnen Unterabteilungen einer Kategorie (vgl. vollständiger Schlüssel auf Seite *I · 1).*

Los símbolos incluídos en el texto del índice representan las grandes categorías identificadas con la clave a la derecha. Los símbolos con numeros en su parte superior (⋀[1]) identifican las subcategorías (véase la clave completa en la página *I · 1).*

Les symboles de l'index représentent les catégories indiquées dans la légende à droite. Les symboles suivis d'un indice (⋀[1]) représentent des sous-catégories (voir légende complète à la page *I · 1).*

Os símbolos incluídos no texto do índice representam as grandes categorias identificadas com a chave à direita. Os símbolos com números em sua parte superior (⋀[1]) identificam as subcategorias (veja-se a chave completa à página *I · 1).*

∧ Mountain	Berg	Montaña	Montagne	Montanha
⋀ Mountains	Gebirge	Montañas	Montagnes	Montanhas
)(Pass	Paß	Paso	Col	Passo
V Valley, Canyon	Tal, Cañon	Valle, Cañón	Vallée, Canyon	Vale, Canhão
≚ Plain	Ebene	Llano	Plaine	Planície
› Cape	Kap	Cabo	Cap	Cabo
I Island	Insel	Isla	Île	Ilha
II Islands	Inseln	Islas	Îles	Ilhas
± Other Topographic Features	Andere Topographische Objekte	Otros Elementos Topográficos	Autres données topographiques	Outros acidentes topográficos

ESPAÑOL · **FRANÇAIS** · **PORTUGUÊS**

Nombre / Nom / Nome	Página / Page	Lat.°′	Long.°′ W = Oeste / Ouest
Jamalo-Neneckij □[3]	72	67.00 N	75.00 E
Jamālpur, Bngl.	124	24.55 N	89.56 E
Jamālpur, India	124	25.18 N	86.30 E
Jamālpurganj	126	23.04 N	87.59 E
Jamanchalinka	80	47.40 N	51.35 E
Jamanota ∧[2]	241s	12.29 N	69.57 W
Jamantau, gora ∧	86	54.15 N	58.06 E
Jamanxim ≃	250	4.43 S	56.18 W
Jamapará	256	21.55 S	42.43 W
Jamari ≃	248	8.27 S	63.30 W
Jamarovka	88	50.38 N	110.16 E
Jamašurma	80	55.58 N	49.36 E
Jamay	234	20.18 N	102.43 W
Jamba	152	13.50 S	15.30 E
Jāmbād	126	22.42 N	86.35 E
Jambeiro	256	23.16 S	45.41 W
Jambeiro, Serra do ⋏[2]	256	23.13 S	45.38 W
Jambelí, Canal de ⋈	246	3.00 S	80.00 W
Jamberoo	170	34.39 S	150.47 E
Jambes	56	50.28 N	4.52 E
Jambi	112	1.36 S	103.37 E
Jambi □[4]	112	1.30 S	103.00 E
Jambin	166	24.12 S	150.22 E
Jamboaye ≃	114	5.16 N	97.29 E
Jambol	38	42.29 N	26.30 E
Jambongan, Pulau I	116	6.40 N	117.27 E
Jambuair, Tanjung >	114	5.16 N	97.30 E
Jambusar	120	22.03 N	72.48 E
James ≃, Austl.	166	20.36 S	137.41 E
James ≃, Ab., Can.	182	51.55 N	114.34 W
James ≃, U.S.	198	42.52 N	97.18 W
James ≃, Mo., U.S.	194	36.45 N	93.30 W
James ≃, Va., U.S.	192	36.57 N	76.26 W
James, Isla I	254	44.57 S	74.07 W
James, Lake ⊜	216	41.42 N	85.02 W
James, Lake ⊜[1]	192	35.45 N	81.55 W
James Bay c	176	53.30 N	80.30 W
Jamesburg	208	40.21 N	74.26 W
James Bypass ≊	226	36.41 N	120.16 W
James City, N.C., U.S.	192	35.05 N	77.02 W
James City, Pa., U.S.	214	41.37 N	78.50 W
James City □[6]	208	37.17 N	76.48 W
James Craik	252	32.09 S	63.28 W
James Creek	214	40.23 N	78.10 W
James Gardens ♦	275b	43.40 N	79.31 W
James Island, B.C., Can.	224	48.37 N	123.22 W
James Island, S.C., U.S.	192	32.44 N	79.57 W
James Island I	208	38.31 N	76.20 W
Jameson Raid Memorial ⊥	273d	26.11 S	27.49 E
James Point >	192	25.21 N	76.24 W
Jamesport	194	39.58 N	93.48 W
James Price Point >	162	17.30 S	122.08 E
James Ranges ⋏	162	24.06 S	132.30 E
James River Bridge ◂[5]	208	37.00 N	76.30 W
James Ross, Cape >	176	74.40 N	114.25 W
James Ross Island I	9	64.15 S	57.45 W
James Ross Strait ⋈	176	69.40 N	95.30 W
James Smith Indian Reserve ◂[4]	184	53.08 N	104.52 W
Jamestown, Austl.	166	33.12 S	138.36 E
Jamestown, Ire.	48	53.55 N	8.02 W
Jamestown, S. Afr.	158	31.06 S	26.45 E
Jamestown, Ca., U.S.	226	37.57 N	120.25 W
Jamestown, Ks., U.S.	198	39.35 N	97.51 W
Jamestown, Ky., U.S.	194	36.59 N	85.03 W
Jamestown, Mi., U.S.	216	42.50 N	85.51 W
Jamestown, N.Y., U.S.	214	42.05 N	79.14 W
Jamestown, N.C., U.S.	192	35.59 N	79.56 W
Jamestown, N.D., U.S.	198	46.54 N	98.42 W
Jamestown, Oh., U.S.	218	39.39 N	83.44 W
Jamestown, Pa., U.S.	214	41.29 N	80.26 W
Jamestown, R.I., U.S.	207	41.29 N	71.22 W
Jamestown, Tn., U.S.	194	36.25 N	84.55 W
Jamestown ⊥	208	37.12 N	76.46 W
Jamestown Festival Park ♦	208	37.14 N	76.48 W
Jamestown Island I	208	37.12 N	76.46 W
Jamestown Reservoir ⊜[1]	198	47.15 N	98.40 W
Jamesville, N.Y., U.S.	210	42.59 N	76.04 W
Jamesville, Va., U.S.	208	37.30 N	75.55 W
Jamet, Lac ⊜	206	46.34 N	74.30 W
Jametz	56	49.26 N	5.23 E
Jamieson ≃	169	37.18 S	146.08 E
Jaminauá ≃	248	9.20 S	70.59 W
Jaminsk	76	52.46 N	28.16 E
Jaminskij	80	50.21 N	42.14 E
Jāmira ≃	126	21.45 N	87.02 E
Jamira ≃[1]	126	21.35 N	88.28 E
Jamison	208	40.16 N	75.05 W
Jamison City	210	41.18 N	76.22 W
Jamison Town	274a	33.46 S	150.41 E
Jam-Ižora	265a	59.42 N	30.36 E
Jām Jodhpur	120	21.54 N	70.01 E
Jamkhandi	122	16.31 N	75.18 E
Jamki	86	59.33 N	66.47 E
Jamkino	82	55.55 N	38.24 E
Jamm	76	58.26 N	28.03 E
Jammalamadugu	122	14.50 N	78.24 E
Jammerbugten c	26	57.20 N	9.30 E
Jammerland Bugt c	41	55.35 N	11.05 E
Jammu	123	32.42 N	74.52 E
Jammu Airport ⊠	123	32.42 N	74.51 E
Jammu and Kashmīr □[2]	120	34.00 N	76.00 E
Jāmnagar	120	22.28 N	70.04 E
Jamoigne	56	49.42 N	5.25 E
Jamor ≃	266c	38.42 N	9.15 W
Jampang-kulon	115a	7.16 S	106.37 E
Jāmpur, India	272b	22.56 N	88.12 E
Jāmpur, Pāk.	123	29.39 N	70.36 E
Jämsä	26	61.52 N	25.12 E
Jamsah	140	27.38 N	33.35 E
Jämsänkoski	26	61.55 N	25.11 E
Jamshedpur	126	22.48 N	86.11 E
Jamsk	74	59.35 N	154.10 E
Jamskaja Sloboda	82	55.29 N	36.01 E
Jāmtāra	126	23.57 N	86.48 E
Jämtland □[9]	26	63.30 N	14.00 E
Jämtlands Län □[6]	24	63.00 N	14.40 E
Jamuāni	126	21.57 N	86.14 E
Jamuga	82	56.24 N	36.40 E
Jamūi	124	24.55 N	86.13 E
Jamuna ≃, Bngl.	124	23.51 N	89.45 E
Jamuna ≃, India	272b	22.57 N	88.35 E
Jamundí	246	3.15 N	76.32 W
Jāmuria	126	23.44 N	87.02 E
Jāmurki	126	24.09 N	90.02 E
Jana ≃	74	71.31 N	136.32 E
Janāi	272b	22.43 N	88.16 E
Janāj	142	31.00 N	30.46 E
Janajkino	80	50.43 N	51.06 E
Janakpur	124	26.39 N	85.55 E
Janakpur □[8]	124	27.15 N	86.00 E
Janas	266c	38.49 N	9.26 W
Janauacá, Lago ⊜	246	3.28 S	60.17 W
Janaúba	255	15.48 S	43.19 W
Janaucu, Ilha I	250	0.30 N	50.10 W
Janaul	86	56.16 N	54.56 E
Jand	123	33.26 N	72.01 E
Janda, Laguna de la ⊜	34	36.15 N	5.51 W
Jandaia	255	17.06 S	50.07 W
Jandaia do Sul	255	23.36 S	51.39 W
Jandaíra	250	11.34 S	37.47 W
Jandalī, Wādī al- V	142	30.05 N	31.52 E
Jandaq	128	34.02 N	54.26 E
Jandelsbrunn	60	48.44 N	13.42 E
Jandiāla	123	31.36 N	75.03 E
Jandiatuba ≃	246	3.28 S	68.42 W
Jandira	256	23.31 S	46.54 W
Jandira □[7]	287b	23.32 S	46.54 W
Jandowae	166	26.47 S	151.06 E
Jandrakinot	180	64.54 N	172.32 W
Jándula ≃	34	38.03 N	4.06 W
Jándula, Embalse de ⊜[1]	34	38.30 N	4.00 W
Janeiro, Rio de ≃	250	11.51 S	45.09 W
Jane Peak ∧	172	45.20 S	168.19 E
Janes Island I	208	38.00 N	75.52 W
Janes Island State Park ♦	208	38.00 N	75.52 W
Janesville, Ca., U.S.	204	40.17 N	120.31 W
Janesville, Mn., U.S.	190	44.06 N	93.42 W
Janesville, Wi., U.S.	216	42.40 N	89.01 W
Jangal Bādhāl	126	23.07 N	89.21 E
Jangamo	156	24.06 S	35.21 E
Jangany	157b	23.14 S	45.27 E
Jangarej	24	68.46 N	61.25 E
Jangel'skij	86	53.08 N	58.59 E
Jangeru	112	2.20 S	116.29 E
Jangiabad	85	41.08 N	70.05 E
Jangi-Bazar	85	41.40 N	70.53 E
Jangijer	85	40.17 N	68.50 E
Jangijul'	85	41.07 N	69.03 E
Jangikišlak	85	40.25 N	67.10 E
Jangikurgan, Uzb.	85	40.34 N	71.09 E
Jangikurgan, Uzb.	85	41.12 N	71.44 E
Jangipāra	126	22.45 N	88.04 E
Jangīpur	124	24.28 N	88.04 E
Jangong	114	4.23 N	96.48 E
Jangoon	122	17.43 N	79.11 E
Jangulovo	80	56.26 N	50.25 E
Janikowo	30	52.45 N	18.07 E
Janīn	132	32.28 N	35.18 E
Janina → Ioánnina	38	39.40 N	20.50 E
Janino	265a	59.56 N	30.36 E
Janisjarvi, ozero ⊜	24	61.59 N	30.57 E
Janiuay	116	10.58 N	122.30 E
Janja	38	44.40 N	19.15 E
Janjina, Hrv.	36	42.56 N	17.26 E
Janjina, Madag.	157b	20.30 S	45.50 E
Janka	126	21.52 N	87.56 E
Jankan, chrebet ⋏	88	55.45 N	118.00 E
Jankāpur	126	21.54 N	87.23 E
Jan Kempdorp (Andalusia)	158	27.55 S	24.51 E
Jan Lake ⊜	184	54.55 N	102.55 W
Janlohong	112	2.15 N	117.03 E
Jan Mayen I	12	71.00 N	8.20 W
Jan Mayen Ridge ⊹[3]	10	69.00 N	8.00 W
Jannaale	144	1.48 N	44.42 E
Jannali	274a	34.01 S	151.04 E
Jannali Park ♦	274a	34.01 S	151.03 E
Janos	232	30.54 N	108.10 W
Jánoshalma	30	46.18 N	19.20 E
Jánosháza	30	47.08 N	17.10 E
János-hegy ∧	264c	47.31 N	18.58 E
Jánossomorja	61	47.47 N	17.08 E
Janoviči	76	55.17 N	30.42 E
Janowiec Wielkopolski	30	52.46 N	17.31 E
Janów Lubelski	30	50.43 N	22.24 E
Jānsath	124	29.20 N	77.51 E
Jansen	184	51.47 N	104.43 W
Jansenville	158	32.56 S	24.40 E
Janskij	74	68.28 N	134.48 E
Janskij zaliv c	74	71.50 N	136.00 E
Jantarnyj	76	54.52 N	19.57 E
Jantetelco	234	18.42 N	98.46 W
Jantikovo	80	55.32 N	47.48 E
Jantra ≃	38	43.38 N	25.34 E
Januária	255	15.29 S	44.22 W
Januário Cicco	250	6.09 S	35.35 W
Jan Van Riebeeck Park ♦	273d	26.10 S	27.59 E
Janvarcevo	80	51.26 N	52.15 E
Janville	50	48.12 N	1.53 E
Janville-sur-Juine	261	48.31 N	2.16 E
Janvry	261	48.39 N	2.09 E
Jany-Kurgan	85	43.55 N	67.15 E
Janzé	32	47.58 N	1.30 W
Janzūr	142	30.41 N	31.02 E
Jaora	120	23.38 N	75.08 E
Japan (Nihon) □[1], Asia	90	36.00 N	138.00 E
Japan (Nihon) □[1], Asia	92	36.00 N	138.00 E
Japan, Sea of ⊽[2]	90	40.00 N	135.00 E
Japan Basin ⊹[1]	12	40.00 N	135.00 E
Japanisches Meer → Japan, Sea of ⊽[2]	90	40.00 N	135.00 E
Japan Trench ⊹[1]	6	37.00 N	143.00 E
Japaratinga	250	9.05 S	35.15 W
Japaratuba	250	10.35 S	36.57 W
Japeri	256	22.39 S	43.40 W
Japi	250	6.27 S	35.56 W
Japim	248	7.37 S	72.54 W
Japla	124	24.33 N	84.01 E
Japoatã	250	10.20 S	36.48 W
Japon → Japan □[1]	92	36.00 N	138.00 E
Japón, Mar del → Japan, Sea of ⊽[2]	90	40.00 N	135.00 E
Japtiksal'a	74	69.21 N	72.32 E
Japuíba	256	22.35 S	42.42 W
Japurá	246	1.48 S	66.30 W
Japurá (Caquetá) ≃	246	3.08 S	64.46 W
Jaqué	246	7.31 N	78.10 W
Jaqueri-mirim ≃	287b	23.31 S	46.51 W
Jaquí	248	15.30 S	74.26 W
Jar	80	58.15 N	52.06 E
Jār, Jabal ∧	128	24.34 N	38.18 E
Jarābulus	130	36.49 N	38.01 E
Jarad	144	18.59 N	41.24 E
Jaradū	142	29.18 N	30.42 E
Jaraguá	255	15.45 S	49.20 W
Jaraguá ◂[8]	287b	23.27 S	46.44 W
Jaraguá, Pico do ∧	287b	23.26 S	46.46 W
Jaraguá do Sul	252	26.29 S	49.04 W
Jaraicejo	34	39.40 N	5.49 W
Jaraiz de la Vera	34	40.04 N	5.45 W
Jaral del Progreso	234	20.22 N	101.04 W
Jarales	200	34.36 N	106.45 W
Jarama ≃	34	40.02 N	3.39 W
Jarama, Canal del ≊	266a	40.18 N	3.32 W
Jaramānah	132	33.29 N	36.21 E
Jaramillo	254	47.11 S	67.09 W
Jaramor	80	56.07 N	48.44 E
Jaran' ≃	80	57.35 N	48.14 E
Jarandilla	34	40.08 N	5.39 W
Jaraniyo	144	10.42 N	39.55 E
Jaransk	80	57.19 N	47.54 E
Jarānwāla	123	31.20 N	73.26 E
Jarash	132	32.17 N	35.54 E
Jaraucu ≃	250	1.48 S	52.22 W
Jarawī, Wādī V	142	29.47 N	31.19 E
Jarbah, Jabal al- ∧	142	30.16 N	32.03 E
Jarbah, Wāhat ⊽[4]	140	29.21 N	25.20 E
Jarbidge ≃	202	42.19 N	115.39 W
Järbo	40	60.43 N	16.36 E
Jarcevo	76	55.04 N	32.41 E
Jardas al-ʿAbīd	146	32.19 N	20.56 E
Jardim, Bra.	248	21.28 S	56.09 W
Jardim, Bra.	250	7.35 S	39.16 W
Jardim América ◂[8]	287b	23.34 S	46.41 W
Jardim de Piranhas	250	6.22 S	37.20 W
Jardim do Seridó	250	6.35 S	36.46 W
Jardim Paraiso	256	22.48 S	43.35 W
Jardim Paulista ◂[8]	287b	23.35 S	46.40 W
Jardín América	252	27.03 S	55.14 W
Jardine ≃	164	10.55 S	142.13 E
Jardine River National Park ♦	164	11.20 S	142.40 E
Jardines de la Reina, Archipiélago de los II	240p	20.50 N	78.55 W
Jardinópolis	255	21.02 S	47.46 W
Jaredi	150	12.46 N	5.05 E
Jaren'ga, Ross.	24	63.27 N	53.26 E
Jarenga, Ross.	24	62.43 N	49.30 E
Jarensk	24	62.11 N	49.02 E
Järfälla	40	59.24 N	17.50 E
Jargalang	89	43.06 N	122.54 E
Jargeau	50	47.52 N	2.07 E
Jari ≃, Bra.	248	5.07 S	62.21 W
Jari ≃, Bra.	250	1.09 S	51.54 W
Jari, Lago ⊜	246	5.00 S	62.19 W
Jāria Jhānjail	124	25.02 N	90.39 E
Jaridih	124	23.38 N	86.04 E
Jarinu	256	23.06 S	46.44 W
Jarīr, Wādī al- V	128	25.38 N	42.30 E
Jarkino	88	59.08 N	99.23 E
Jarkovo	86	57.24 N	67.05 E
Jarkul'-Mat'uškino	86	55.51 N	76.06 E
Järlåsa	40	59.53 N	17.12 E
Jarmen	54	53.55 N	13.20 E
Järna	40	59.06 N	17.34 E
Jarnac	32	45.41 N	0.10 W
Jarny	56	49.09 N	5.53 E
Jaro	116	11.11 N	124.47 E
Jarochta	88	58.58 N	98.58 E
Jarocin	30	51.59 N	17.31 E
Jaroměř	30	50.21 N	15.55 E
Jaroměřice	61	49.05 N	15.53 E
Jaropolec	82	56.08 N	35.49 E
Jaroslavl'	80	57.37 N	39.52 E
Jaroslavl' Oblast' □[4]	76	57.45 N	39.00 E
Jaroslavl' Station ◂[5]	265b	55.47 N	37.39 E
Jaroslavskaja	84	44.36 N	40.27 E
Jaroslavskij	89	44.10 N	132.13 E
Jarosław	30	50.02 N	22.42 E
Järpen	26	63.21 N	13.29 E
Jarrahdale	168a	32.21 S	116.04 E
Jarratt	208	36.48 N	77.28 W
Jarreau	194	30.39 N	91.29 W
Jarrell	222	30.49 N	97.36 W
Jarrettsville	208	39.36 N	76.28 W
Jarrīs	142	27.55 N	30.46 E
Jarrow	44	54.59 N	1.29 W
Jarry, Parc ♦	275a	45.32 N	73.38 W
Jar-Sale	74	66.50 N	70.50 E
Jarsomovy	86	60.15 N	73.38 E
Jartai Yanchi ⊜	102	39.43 N	105.41 E
Jaru	248	10.26 S	62.27 W
Jaru ≃	248	10.05 S	61.59 W
Jarud Qi	89	44.37 N	120.58 E
Jaruu	88	48.08 N	96.45 E
Järva-Jaani	76	59.02 N	25.53 E
Järvakandi	76	58.47 N	24.49 E
Järvelä	26	60.52 N	25.17 E
Järvenpää	26	60.28 N	25.06 E
Jarvie	182	54.27 N	113.59 W
Jarville-la-Malgrange	58	48.40 N	6.13 E
Jarvis	212	42.53 N	80.06 W
Jarvisburg	192	36.12 N	75.52 W
Jarvis Island I	14	0.23 S	160.02 W
Järvsö	26	61.43 N	16.10 E
Jarwa	124	27.39 N	82.31 E
Jasaan	116	8.39 N	124.45 E
Jasai	272c	18.56 N	73.01 E
Jašalta	80	46.20 N	42.17 E
Jasašnaja Tašla	80	53.55 N	48.16 E
Jaša Tomić	38	45.27 N	20.51 E
Jasdan	120	22.02 N	71.12 E
Jasel'da ≃	76	52.07 N	26.28 E
Jasenevo ◂[8]	265b	55.36 N	37.33 E
Jasenki	78	51.32 N	38.12 E
Jasenovoje	82	54.10 N	36.47 E
Jasenskaja	78	46.22 N	38.16 E
Jashpurnagar	124	22.54 N	84.09 E
Jāshpur Pāts ◂[1]	124	22.55 N	84.00 E
Jasidih	124	24.31 N	86.39 E
Jasień	30	51.46 N	15.01 E
Jasienica	54	53.37 N	14.32 E
Jasikan	150	7.24 N	0.28 E
Jašil'kul', ozero ⊜	120	37.45 N	72.55 E
Jasin	114	2.19 N	102.26 E
Jasinga	115a	6.29 S	106.27 E
Jāsk	128	25.38 N	57.46 E
Jaskhar	272c	18.54 N	72.59 E
Jaškino, Ross.	80	52.41 N	53.26 E
Jaškino, Ross.	86	55.54 N	85.26 E
Jaskino, Ross.	265b	55.40 N	37.16 E
Jaškul'	80	46.11 N	45.21 E
Jaškul' ≃	80	46.15 N	45.05 E
Jasło	30	49.45 N	21.29 E
Jasmine Estates	220	28.17 N	82.42 W
Jasmund >[1]	54	54.32 N	13.35 E
Jasnaja Pol'ana ⊥	82	54.05 N	37.32 E
Jasnogorsk	82	54.29 N	37.42 E
Jasnomorskij	89	46.45 N	141.54 E
Jasnyj, Ross.	86	51.04 N	59.58 E
Jasnyj, Ross.	89	53.17 N	127.59 E
Jason Islands II	254	51.05 S	61.00 W
Jason Peninsula >[1]	9	66.10 S	61.00 W
Jasonville	194	39.09 N	87.11 W
Jasper, Ab., Can.	182	52.53 N	118.05 W
Jasper, Al., U.S.	194	33.49 N	87.16 W
Jasper, Ar., U.S.	194	36.00 N	93.11 W
Jasper, Fl., U.S.	192	30.31 N	82.56 W
Jasper, Ga., U.S.	192	34.28 N	84.25 W
Jasper, In., U.S.	194	38.23 N	86.55 W
Jasper, Mi., U.S.	216	41.48 N	84.02 W
Jasper, Mn., U.S.	198	43.51 N	96.23 W
Jasper, Mo., U.S.	194	37.20 N	94.18 W
Jasper, N.Y., U.S.	210	42.07 N	77.30 W
Jasper, Tn., U.S.	194	35.04 N	85.37 W
Jasper, Tx., U.S.	194	30.55 N	93.59 W
Jasper □[6]	216	40.57 N	87.09 W
Jasper Lake ⊜	182	53.07 N	118.00 W
Jasper National Park ♦	182	52.53 N	118.03 W
Jaspur	124	29.17 N	78.49 E
Jasra	124	25.17 N	81.48 E
Jassans-Riottier	58	45.59 N	4.45 E
Jassar	123	32.06 N	74.57 E
Jassy → Iași	38	47.10 N	27.35 E
Jassy ≃	85	40.46 N	73.05 E
Jastarnia	30	54.43 N	18.40 E
Jastrebarsko	36	45.40 N	15.39 E
Jastrebovka, Ross.	78	51.27 N	37.32 E
Jastrebovka, Ross.	82	54.36 N	36.24 E
Jastrowie	30	53.26 N	16.49 E
Jaswantnagar	124	26.53 N	78.55 E
Jászapáti	30	47.31 N	20.09 E
Jászberény	30	47.30 N	19.55 E
Jász-Nagykun-Szolnok □[6]	30	47.12 N	20.11 E
Jataí	255	17.53 S	51.43 W
Jatapu ≃	246	2.13 S	58.17 W
Jatatė ≃	232	16.15 N	91.17 W
Jati, Bra.	250	7.41 S	39.01 W
Jāti, Pāk.	120	24.21 N	68.16 E
Jatibarang	115a	6.28 S	108.17 E
Jatibonico	240p	21.56 N	79.10 W
Jatibonico del Sur ≃	240p	21.33 N	79.09 W
Jatilawang	115a	7.32 S	109.06 E
Jatiluhur, Waduk ⊜[1]	115a	6.35 S	107.20 E
Jatinegara ◂[8]	269e	6.13 S	106.52 E
Jatiroto	115a	8.07 S	113.21 E
Jatisrono	115a	7.49 S	111.07 E
Jatiwangi	115a	6.44 S	108.15 E
Jatni	120	20.10 N	85.42 E
Jatniel	273d	26.07 S	28.19 E
Jatobá ≃	255	12.23 S	54.07 W
Jatobá, Ribeirão ≃	256	21.28 S	42.49 W
Jatoi Janūbi	123	29.31 N	70.51 E
Jātrāpur	126	22.44 N	89.45 E
Jatt (Tel Gat)	132	32.24 N	35.02 E
Jatznick	54	53.35 N	13.56 E
Jáu, Ang.	152	15.12 S	13.31 E
Jaú, Bra.	255	22.18 S	48.33 W
Jaú ≃	246	1.54 S	61.26 W
Jaú, Parque Nacional do ♦	246	2.30 S	63.00 W
Jauaperi ≃	246	1.26 S	61.35 W
Jauerling ∧	61	48.20 N	15.20 E
Jaugrām	126	23.06 N	88.05 E
Jauja	248	11.48 S	75.30 W
Jauli	272a	28.44 N	77.21 E
Jaumave	234	23.25 N	99.23 W
Jaunde → Yaoundé	152	3.52 N	11.31 E
Jaune, Mer → Yellow Sea ⊽[2]	90	36.00 N	123.00 E
Jaungulbene	76	57.04 N	26.36 E
Jaunjelgava	76	56.37 N	25.05 E
Jaunpass)(	58	46.36 N	7.20 E
Jaunpiebalga	76	57.11 N	26.03 E
Jaunpils	76	56.44 N	23.01 E
Jaunpur	124	25.44 N	82.41 E
Jaupaci	255	16.18 S	50.54 W
Jauquara ≃	248	15.06 S	57.06 W
Jáuregui	258	34.36 S	59.10 W
Jauru	250	11.06 S	57.30 W
Jauru ≃, Bra.	248	16.22 S	57.46 W
Jauru ≃, Bra.	255	18.40 S	54.36 W
Jausiers	62	44.25 N	6.44 E
Jauza ≃, Ross.	82	56.25 N	36.05 E
Jauza ≃, Ross.	265b	55.45 N	37.38 E
Java	198	45.30 N	99.53 W
Java → Jawa I	115a	7.30 S	110.00 E
Java Center	210	42.39 N	78.23 W
Javādi Hills ⋏[2]	122	12.35 N	78.50 E
Javan	85	38.19 N	69.02 E
Javari (Yavarí) ≃	242	4.21 S	70.02 W
Javas	80	54.26 N	42.51 E
Java Sea → Jawa, Laut ⊽[2]	112	5.00 S	110.00 E
Java Trench ⊹[1]	12	10.30 S	110.00 E
Java Village	210	42.40 N	78.26 W
Jävenitz	54	52.31 N	11.30 E
Javier, Isla I	254	47.06 S	74.24 W
Javlenka	86	54.21 N	68.27 E
Javor ⋏	38	44.05 N	18.55 E
Javořice ∧	61	49.14 N	15.20 E
Javorie ∧	30	48.27 N	19.18 E
Javorná	60	49.13 N	13.18 E
Javorník	30	50.23 N	17.00 E
Javorová skála ∧	30	49.31 N	14.30 E
Javr ≃	24	68.09 N	30.06 E
Jävre	26	65.09 N	21.59 E
Jawa (Java) I	115a	7.30 S	110.00 E
Jawa, Laut (Java Sea) ⊽[2]	112	5.00 S	110.00 E
Jawa Barat □[4]	115a	7.00 S	107.00 E
Jawʿāliyāt, Jabal al- ∧	132	31.26 N	36.26 E
Jawāla Mukhi	123	31.53 N	76.19 E
Jawa Tengah □[4]	115a	7.30 S	110.00 E
Jawa Timur □[4]	115a	8.00 S	113.00 E
Jawbar	132	33.31 N	36.19 E
Jawf, Wādī V	144	15.50 N	45.30 E
Jawi	112	0.48 S	109.16 E
Jawor	30	51.03 N	16.11 E
Jaworzno	30	50.13 N	19.15 E
Jay, Fl., U.S.	194	30.57 N	87.09 W
Jay, Ok., U.S.	196	36.25 N	94.47 W
Jay □[6]	216	40.26 N	84.59 W
Jaya, Puncak ∧	164	4.05 S	137.11 E
Jayanca	248	6.24 S	79.50 W
Jayapura (Sukarnapura)	164	2.32 S	140.42 E
Jayb, Wādī al- (Haʿ Arava) V	132	30.58 N	35.24 E
Jay Cooke State Park ♦	190	46.41 N	92.23 W
Jay Creek Aboriginal Reserve ◂[4]	162	23.45 S	133.35 E
Jaydebpur	124	24.00 N	90.26 E
Jaynagar	126	22.36 N	90.42 E
Jaynagar Majilpur	126	22.11 N	88.25 E
Jaynes	200	32.16 N	111.01 W
Jay Peak ∧	188	44.55 N	72.32 W
Jaypur, India	122	18.51 N	82.35 E
Jaypur, India	126	23.03 N	87.27 E
Jayrūd	130	33.49 N	36.44 E
Jayton	196	33.15 N	100.34 W
Jayuya	240m	18.13 N	66.36 W
Jaywick	42	51.47 N	1.08 E
Jaz	80	54.54 N	45.13 E
Jažełbicy	76	58.02 N	32.58 E
Jazevec	24	65.43 N	46.30 E
Jazgulem ≃	85	38.12 N	71.21 E
Jazīrat Muḥammad	273c	30.07 N	31.12 E
Jazjavan	85	40.39 N	71.44 E
Jažma	24	66.56 N	44.29 E
Jaz Mūrīān, Hāmūn-e ⊜	128	27.20 N	58.55 E
Jazovaja	86	49.27 N	85.20 E
Jazykovo	80	54.18 N	47.24 E
Jazzīn	132	33.32 N	35.34 E
Jbāʿ	132	33.29 N	35.31 E
J.B. Thomas, Lake ⊜[1]	196	32.35 N	101.10 W
J. C. Murphey Lake ⊜	216	40.58 N	87.30 W
Jdiouia	34	35.57 N	0.50 E
Jeanerette	194	29.54 N	91.39 W
Jeanesville	210	40.56 N	75.58 W
Jeannette	214	40.19 N	79.36 W
Jebba	150	9.08 N	4.50 E
Jebel	38	45.33 N	21.14 E
Jebeniana	148	35.02 N	10.55 E
Jeber-Bergfrieden	54	51.59 N	12.20 E
Jeberos	248	5.17 S	76.13 W
Jebri	120	27.18 N	65.44 E
Jebus	112	1.44 S	105.29 E
Jechegnadzor	84	39.46 N	45.21 E
Jéci, Serra ∧	154	12.48 S	35.12 E
Jedane, Oued ti-n- V	148	24.55 N	6.30 E
Jedarma	88	58.44 N	102.36 E
Jedburgh	44	55.29 N	2.34 W
Jedburgh Abbey ⊍[1]	44	55.27 N	2.34 W
Jeddah → Jiddah	144	21.30 N	39.12 E
Jeddore Lake ⊜[1]	186	48.03 N	55.55 W
Jedelevo	80	53.24 N	47.45 E
Jedepo	150	5.16 N	8.20 W
Jedisa	84	42.31 N	44.16 E
Jedlesee ◂[8]	264b	48.16 N	16.23 E
Jednevo	82	56.06 N	36.14 E
Jedogon	88	54.15 N	100.15 E
Jedrovo	76	57.55 N	33.38 E
Jędrzejów	30	50.39 N	20.18 E
Jedwabne	30	53.17 N	22.19 E
Jed Water ≃	46	55.32 N	2.33 W
Jeetzel (Jeetze) ≃	54	53.09 N	11.04 E
Jefawa	140	10.57 N	23.48 E
Jeffara (Al-Jifārah) ≡	146	32.30 N	11.45 E
Jeffers	198	44.03 N	95.11 W
Jefferson, Ga., U.S.	192	34.07 N	83.34 W
Jefferson, In., U.S.	216	40.17 N	86.36 W
Jefferson, Ia., U.S.	198	42.00 N	94.22 W
Jefferson, Md., U.S.	208	39.21 N	77.31 W
Jefferson, Ma., U.S.	207	42.21 N	71.52 W
Jefferson, N.J., U.S.	285	39.45 N	75.13 W
Jefferson, N.Y., U.S.	210	42.14 N	73.54 W
Jefferson, N.Y., U.S.	210	42.29 N	74.37 W
Jefferson, N.C., U.S.	192	36.25 N	81.28 W
Jefferson, Oh., U.S.	214	41.44 N	80.46 W
Jefferson, Or., U.S.	202	44.43 N	123.00 W
Jefferson, Pa., U.S.	279b	40.18 N	80.03 W
Jefferson, S.C., U.S.	192	34.39 N	80.23 W
Jefferson, S.D., U.S.	198	42.36 N	96.33 W
Jefferson, Tx., U.S.	194	32.45 N	94.20 W
Jefferson, Wi., U.S.	216	43.00 N	88.48 W
Jefferson □[6], Il., U.S.	219	38.19 N	88.55 W
Jefferson □[6], In., U.S.	218	38.44 N	85.23 W
Jefferson □[6], Ky., U.S.	218	38.14 N	85.10 W
Jefferson □[6], Mo., U.S.	219	38.20 N	90.34 W
Jefferson □[6], N.Y., U.S.	212	43.59 N	75.55 W
Jefferson □[6], Oh., U.S.	214	40.22 N	80.37 W
Jefferson □[6], Pa., U.S.	214	41.09 N	79.05 W
Jefferson □[6], Wa., U.S.	224	47.50 N	122.36 W
Jefferson □[6], Wi., U.S.	216	43.02 N	88.46 W
Jefferson ≃	202	45.56 N	111.30 W
Jefferson, Mount ∧, U.S.	202	44.34 N	111.30 W
Jefferson, Mount ∧, Nv., U.S.	204	38.46 N	116.55 W
Jefferson, Mount ∧, Or., U.S.	202	44.40 N	121.47 W
Jefferson City, Mo., U.S.	219	38.34 N	92.10 W
Jefferson City, Tn., U.S.	192	36.07 N	83.29 W
Jefferson Farms	285	39.40 N	75.34 W
Jefferson Manor	284c	38.47 N	77.04 W
Jefferson Park ◂[8]	278	41.59 N	87.46 W
Jefferson Proving Ground ■	218	38.50 N	85.25 W
Jeffersonton	188	38.38 N	77.55 W
Jeffersontown	218	38.11 N	85.33 W
Jefferson Village	284c	38.52 N	77.10 W
Jeffersonville, Ga., U.S.	192	32.41 N	83.20 W
Jeffersonville, In., U.S.	218	38.16 N	85.44 W
Jeffersonville, N.Y., U.S.	210	41.46 N	74.56 W
Jeffersonville, Oh., U.S.	218	39.39 N	83.33 W
Jeffrey City	200	42.29 N	107.49 W
Jeffreys Bay	158	34.02 S	24.54 E
Jeffries Creek ≃	192	34.05 N	79.32 W
Jefimovka	80	52.13 N	52.03 E
Jefimovskij	76	59.30 N	34.40 E
Jefremov	76	53.09 N	38.07 E
Jefremova	82	56.13 N	38.59 E
Jefremovka	83	47.19 N	38.29 E
Jefremovo-Stepanovka	78	48.43 N	40.50 E
Jefremovskaja	82	55.25 N	38.59 E
Jega	150	12.15 N	4.23 E
Jegenstorf	58	47.03 N	7.30 E
Jegindybulak, Kaz.	86	49.45 N	76.23 E
Jegindybulak, Kaz.	86	48.42 N	81.48 E
Jegizkara, gora ∧	86	46.24 N	64.09 E
Jegorjevka	89	50.42 N	127.42 E
Jegorjevsk	82	55.23 N	39.02 E
Jegorlyk ≃	80	46.33 N	41.52 E
Jehol → Chengde	105	40.58 N	117.53 E
Jeja ≃	78	46.41 N	38.36 E
Jejsk	78	46.42 N	38.16 E
Jejskij liman c	78	46.42 N	38.25 E
Jeju → Cheju	90	33.31 N	126.32 E
Jejur	272b	22.53 N	88.08 E
Jēkabpils	76	56.29 N	25.51 E
Jekaterinburg (Sverdlovsk)	86	56.51 N	60.36 E
Jekaterinburg Oblast' □[4]	86	58.00 N	62.00 E
Jekaterinino	76	55.49 N	33.58 E
Jekaterininskoje	86	56.53 N	74.34 E
Jekaterinoslav → Dnipropetrovs'k	78	48.27 N	34.59 E
Jekaterinoslavka	89	50.23 N	129.08 E
Jekaterinovka, Kaz.	86	54.36 N	70.58 E
Jekaterinovka, Ross.	78	46.42 N	38.46 E
Jekaterinovka, Ross.	80	53.04 N	49.28 E
Jekaterinovka, Ross.	80	46.32 N	41.42 E
Jekaterinovka, Ross.	80	52.03 N	44.21 E
Jekaterinovka, Ross.	83	47.33 N	38.23 E
Jekaterinovka ◂[8]	265b	55.46 N	37.23 E
Jekaterinovskaja	78	46.20 N	39.58 E
Jekateriny, proliv ⋈, Ross.	74	44.30 N	146.45 E
Jekateriny, proliv ⋈, Ross.	92a	44.25 N	146.40 E
Jekimoviči	76	54.07 N	33.18 E
Jekpindykurylys	80	47.49 N	47.17 E
Jekyll Island I	192	31.04 N	81.25 W
Jekyll Island State Park ♦	192	31.02 N	81.25 W
Jelabuga	80	55.47 N	52.04 E
Jelai ≃, Indon.	112	2.59 S	110.45 E
Jelai ≃, Malay.	114	4.04 N	102.20 E
Jelan', Ross.	80	52.13 N	44.11 E
Jelan', Ross.	80	50.57 N	43.44 E
Jelan', Ross.	83	48.41 N	39.47 E
Jelan', Ross.	86	57.39 N	63.42 E
Jelan' ≃, Ross.	78	51.07 N	41.25 E
Jelan' ≃, Ross.	80	50.57 N	43.44 E
Jelan' ≃, Ross.	80	51.07 N	41.26 E
Jelancy	88	52.49 N	106.25 E
Jelanka	86	55.37 N	75.18 E
Jelan'-Koleno	78	51.09 N	41.14 E
Jelan'-Kolenovskij	78	51.10 N	41.10 E
Jelat'ma	80	54.58 N	41.45 E
Jelaur, Ross.	80	54.34 N	50.21 E
Jelaur, Ross.	80	53.50 N	48.48 E
Jelchovka	80	53.51 N	50.18 E
Jel'covka	86	53.15 N	86.15 E
Jel'cy, Ross.	76	56.40 N	33.51 E
Jel'cy, Ross.	82	56.11 N	38.46 E
Jelec	76	52.37 N	38.30 E
Jeleckij	24	67.03 N	64.10 E
Jelenia Góra (Hirschberg)	30	50.55 N	15.46 E
Jelenia Góra □[4]	30	51.10 N	15.30 E
Jelenskij	76	53.29 N	35.23 E
Jelep La Pass)(	124	27.23 N	88.51 E
Jelgava	76	56.39 N	23.42 E
Jelgavkrasti	76	57.28 N	24.26 E
Jelizarovo	80	58.33 N	44.50 E
Jelizavetinka	86	51.28 N	71.12 E
Jelizavetopol'skoje	86	52.51 N	60.36 E
Jelizavetovka	78	46.39 N	38.53 E
Jelizavety, mys >	89	54.26 N	142.42 E
Jelizovo	76	53.24 N	29.01 E
Jelli	154	5.22 N	31.48 E
Jellico	192	36.35 N	84.07 W
Jelling	41	55.45 N	9.26 E
Jelloway	214	40.33 N	82.18 W
Jelm Mountain ∧	200	41.06 N	105.58 W
Jel'n'a	76	54.35 N	33.11 E
Jelnat'	80	57.20 N	42.49 E
Jel'niki	80	54.37 N	43.53 E
Jeloguj ≃	74	63.13 N	87.45 E
Jelošnoje	86	55.27 N	66.44 E
Jelovo	80	57.03 N	54.54 E
Jels	41	55.21 N	9.12 E
Jelšanka, Ross.	80	51.49 N	46.23 E
Jelšanka, Ross.	80	52.35 N	47.59 E
Jelšanka Pervaja	80	52.53 N	52.02 E
Jelšava	30	48.39 N	20.14 E
Jel'sk	78	51.48 N	29.09 E
Jema ≃	144	10.09 N	38.20 E
Jemaa	150	9.27 N	8.23 E
Jemaja, Pulau I	112	2.55 N	105.45 E
Jemaluang	114	2.17 N	103.52 E
Jemantajevo	80	53.34 N	53.50 E
Jemanželinsk	86	54.45 N	61.20 E
Jember	115a	8.10 S	113.42 E
Jemca	24	63.04 N	40.20 E
Jemca ≃	24	63.15 N	41.20 E
Jemeljanovo	86	56.11 N	92.40 E
Jemel'stan	24	61.13 N	52.29 E
Jemen → Yemen □[1]	144	15.00 N	47.00 E
Jemen, Volksrepublik → Yemen □[1]	144	15.00 N	47.00 E
Jemez ≃	200	35.22 N	106.31 W
Jemez Canyon Reservoir ⊜[1]	200	35.28 N	106.39 W
Jemez Indian Reservation ◂[4]	200	35.35 N	106.45 W
Jemez Springs	200	35.46 N	106.41 W
Jemgum	52	53.16 N	7.23 E
Jeminary	86	47.32 N	85.38 E
Jemmal	148	35.38 N	10.46 E
Jemnice	61	49.01 N	15.35 E
Jempang, Kenohan ⊜	112	0.26 S	116.12 E
Jena, Dtsch.	54	50.56 N	11.35 E
Jena, La., U.S.	194	31.40 N	92.08 W
Jenašimskij Polkan, gora ∧	74	59.50 N	92.52 E
Jenaz	58	46.55 N	9.45 E
Jenbach	64	47.24 N	11.47 E
Jenbek	86	48.53 N	77.12 E
Jendarata	114	3.55 N	100.57 E
Jendongin	88	53.27 N	113.01 E
Jendouba (Souk el Arba)	148	36.30 N	8.47 E
Jendouba □[8]	148	36.30 N	8.45 E
Jeneponto	112	5.41 S	119.42 E
Jenera	216	40.54 N	83.44 W
Jeniang	114	5.49 N	100.38 E
Jenisej (Yenisey) ≃	72	71.50 N	82.40 E
Jenisejsk	86	58.27 N	92.10 E
Jenisejskij kr'až ⋏	74	59.00 N	93.00 E
Jenisejskij zaliv c	74	72.30 N	80.00 E
Jenison	216	42.54 N	85.47 W
Jenkins, Ky., U.S.	192	37.10 N	82.37 W
Jenkins, Tx., U.S.	222	32.59 N	94.44 W
Jenkins, Mount ∧	162	25.36 S	129.41 E
Jenkinson Lake ⊜[1]	226	38.44 N	120.33 W
Jenkinsville	192	34.16 N	81.17 W
Jenkintown	208	40.05 N	75.07 W
Jenks	196	36.01 N	95.58 W
Jenli	100	23.15 N	120.08 E
Jenners	214	40.08 N	79.02 W
Jennersdorf	61	46.57 N	16.08 E
Jennerstown	214	40.10 N	79.04 W
Jennifer Branch ≃	284b	39.25 N	76.30 W
Jennings, Fl., U.S.	192	30.36 N	83.05 W
Jennings, La., U.S.	194	30.13 N	92.39 W
Jennings, Mo., U.S.	219	38.43 N	90.15 W
Jennings □[6]	218	38.59 N	85.36 W
Jennings Creek ≃	216	40.53 N	84.17 W
Jennings Lodge	224	45.23 N	122.36 W
Jenotajevka	80	47.15 N	47.03 E
Jenpeg Dam ◂[6]	184	54.33 N	98.02 W
Jensen	200	40.22 N	109.20 W
Jensen Beach	220	27.15 N	80.13 W
Jens Munk Island I	176	69.42 N	79.30 W
Jens Munks Ø I	176	64.40 N	40.30 W
Jenu	112	0.36 S	109.52 E
Jen'uka	88	57.58 N	121.42 E
Jeonju → Chŏnju	98	35.49 N	127.08 E
Jepač	24	66.58 N	61.22 E
Jepara	115a	6.35 S	110.39 E
Jeparit	166	36.09 S	141.59 E
Jepelacio	248	6.07 S	76.57 W
Jepichin	80	48.16 N	45.14 E
Jepifan'	76	53.49 N	38.33 E
Jeppener	258	35.17 S	58.12 W
Jeptha Knob ∧[2]	218	38.11 N	85.07 W
Jepua (Jeppo)	26	63.24 N	22.37 E
Jequeri	255	20.27 S	42.40 W
Jequetepeque ≃	248	7.21 S	79.36 W
Jequié	255	13.51 S	40.05 W
Jequitaí	255	17.15 S	44.28 W
Jequitinhonha	255	16.26 S	41.00 W
Jequitinhonha ≃	255	15.51 S	38.53 W
Jerachtur	80	54.43 N	41.09 E
Jerada	148	34.17 N	2.13 W
Jeradou	36	36.15 N	10.23 E
Jerangle	171b	35.52 S	149.22 E
Jeransang	114	3.52 N	102.22 E
Jerantut	114	3.56 N	102.22 E
Jerba, Île de I	148	33.48 N	10.54 E
Jerbar	140	5.39 N	31.05 E
Jerbent	128	39.19 N	58.36 E
Jerbogačon	74	61.16 N	108.00 E
Jercevo	24	60.48 N	40.05 E
Jerdenevo	82	54.55 N	36.27 E
Jerécuaro	234	20.09 N	100.31 W
Jeremejevka	83	46.58 N	39.33 E
Jeremejevo	82	55.57 N	37.01 E
Jérémie	238	18.39 N	74.07 W
Jeremino	82	56.27 N	37.58 E
Jeremoabo	250	10.04 S	38.21 W
Jeremy Hill ∧[2]	207	42.45 N	71.21 W
Jeremy Point >	207	41.53 N	70.04 W
Jerevan	84	40.11 N	44.30 E
Jerez ≃	234	22.15 N	103.11 W
Jerez de García Salinas	234	22.39 N	103.00 W
Jerez de la Frontera	34	36.41 N	6.08 W
Jerez de los Caballeros	34	38.19 N	6.46 W
Jergač	86	57.28 N	56.39 E
Jergeni ⋏[2]	80	47.00 N	44.00 E
Jergeninskij	80	47.07 N	44.28 E
Jericho, Austl.	166	23.36 S	146.08 E
Jericho, N.J., U.S.	285	39.48 N	75.09 W
Jericho, N.Y., U.S.	210	40.47 N	73.32 W
Jericho → Arīḥā, W.B.	132	31.52 N	35.27 E
Jericho Dam ⊜[1]	158	26.39 S	30.28 E
Jerichow	54	52.30 N	12.01 E
Jericó, Bra.	250	6.33 S	37.48 W
Jericó, Col.	246	5.47 N	75.47 W
Jericoacoara, Ponta de >	250	2.48 S	40.29 W
Jerid, Chott ≡	148	33.42 N	8.26 E
Jerilderie	166	35.22 S	145.44 E
Jerimoth Hill ∧[2]	207	41.52 N	71.47 W
Jermak	86	52.02 N	76.55 E
Jermakovo	80	53.11 N	49.38 E
Jermakovskaja	80	48.03 N	41.17 E
Jermakovskoje	86	53.16 N	92.24 E
Jermekejevo	80	54.05 N	53.40 E
Jermentau	86	51.38 N	73.10 E
Jermentau ⋏	86	51.10 N	73.10 E
Jermica	24	66.56 N	52.15 E
Jermilovka	86	57.40 N	72.55 E
Jermiš'	80	54.46 N	42.16 E
Jermolajevo, Ross.	86	55.13 N	92.10 E
Jermolajevo, Ross.	86	52.46 N	55.47 E
Jermolino, Ross.	82	55.12 N	36.36 E
Jermolino, Ross.	82	55.57 N	36.54 E
Jermolino, Ross.	82	56.48 N	37.49 E
Jermolino, Ross.	86	57.20 N	64.43 E
Jermyn	210	41.31 N	75.32 W
Jernhatten ∧[2]	41	56.15 N	10.48 E
Jernih	114	4.25 N	97.43 E
Jeroaquara	255	15.23 S	50.25 W
Jerofej Pavlovič	89	53.58 N	122.01 E
Jerome, Az., U.S.	200	34.44 N	112.06 W
Jerome, Id., U.S.	202	42.43 N	114.31 W
Jerome, Il., U.S.	219	39.46 N	89.41 W
Jerome, Mi., U.S.	216	42.01 N	84.28 W
Jerome, Pa., U.S.	214	40.12 N	78.59 W
Jeromesville	214	40.48 N	82.11 W
Jer'omino	86	58.35 N	79.25 E
Jerónimos, Mosteiro dos ⊍[1]	266c	38.42 N	9.12 W
Jeröö	88	49.45 N	106.40 E
Jeröö ≃	88	49.54 N	106.08 E
Jeropol	74	65.15 N	168.40 E
Jerpoint Abbey ⊥	48	52.29 N	7.08 W
Jerry City	216	41.15 N	83.36 W
Jerry Slough ≃	226	35.33 N	119.31 W
Jersey	214	40.03 N	82.46 W
Jersey □[6]	219	39.07 N	90.20 W

≃ River	Fluß	Río	Rivière	Rio
≊ Canal	Kanal	Canal	Canal	Canal
∟ Waterfall, Rapids	Wasserfall, Stromschnellen	Cascada, Rápidos	Chute d'eau, Rapides	Cascata, Rápidos
⋈ Strait	Meeresstraße	Estrecho	Détroit	Estreito
c Bay, Gulf	Bucht, Golf	Bahía, Golfo	Baie, Golfe	Baía, Golfo
⊜ Lake, Lakes	See, Seen	Lago, Lagos	Lac, Lacs	Lago, Lagos
≡ Swamp	Sumpf	Pantano	Marais	Pântano
⊓ Ice Features, Glacier	Eis- und Gletscherformen	Accidentes Glaciales	Formes glaciaires	Acidentes glaciares
⊽ Other Hydrographic Features	Andere Hydrographische Objekte	Otros Elementos Hidrográficos	Autres données hydrographiques	Outros acidentes hidrográficos

⊹ Submarine Features	Untermeerische Objekte	Accidentes Submarinos	Formes de relief sous-marin	Acidentes submarinos
□ Political Unit	Politische Einheit	Unidad Politica	Entité politique	Unidade política
⊍ Cultural Institution	Kulturelle Institution	Institución Cultural	Institution culturelle	Institução cultural
⊥ Historical Site	Historische Stätte	Sitio Histórico	Site historique	Sitio histórico
♦ Recreational Site	Erholungs- und Ferienort	Sitio de Recreo	Centre de loisirs	Area de Lazer
⊠ Airport	Flughafen	Aeropuerto	Aéroport	Aeroporto
■ Military Installation	Militäranlage	Instalación Militar	Installation militaire	Instalação militar
◂ Miscellaneous	Verschiedenes	Misceláneo	Divers	Diversos

ENGLISH — Name, Page, Lat.°′, Long.°′
DEUTSCH — Name, Seite, Breite°′, Länge°′ E = Ost

Name	Page	Lat.°′	Long.°′
Jersey □[2], Europe	22	49.15 N	2.10 W
Jersey □[2], Europe	43b	49.15 N	2.10 W
Jersey City	210	40.43 N	74.04 W
Jersey City State College ✪[2]	276	40.43 N	74.05 W
Jersey Mountain ∧	202	45.29 N	115.34 W
Jersey Shore	210	41.12 N	77.16 W
Jersey Village	222	29.52 N	95.35 W
Jerseyville	219	39.07 N	90.19 W
Jerši	76	54.24 N	34.12 E
Jeršiči	76	53.40 N	32.44 E
Jeršov	80	51.20 N	48.17 E
Jeršovka	86	54.07 N	64.59 E
Jeršovo	82	55.46 N	36.52 E
Jeršovskij	86	52.29 N	59.08 E
Jertarskij	86	56.47 N	64.18 E
Jerte ≃	34	39.58 N	6.17 W
Jerteh	114	5.45 N	102.30 E
Jertoma	24	63.32 N	47.48 E
Jerumenha	250	7.05 S	43.30 W
Jerusalem → Yerushalayim	132	31.46 N	35.14 E
Jerusalem Airport ⊠	132	31.52 N	35.12 E
Jerusalim (Talusan)	116	7.26 N	122.49 E
Jeruslan ≃	80	50.15 N	45.42 E
Jervaulx Abbey ✪[1]	44	54.16 N	1.43 W
Jervis, Cape ➤	168b	35.38 S	138.06 E
Jervis Bay	170	35.08 S	150.42 E
Jervis Bay ⊂	170	35.05 S	150.44 E
Jervis Inlet ⊂	182	49.46 N	124.10 W
Jervois Range ⋏	162	22.38 S	136.05 E
Jerxheim	54	52.05 N	10.54 E
Jerykly	80	55.11 N	51.26 E
Jerzens	58	47.10 N	10.45 E
Jesenankaty ≃	80	50.32 N	51.47 E
Jesenice, Česká Rep.	54	50.04 N	13.29 E
Jesenice, Slvn.	61	46.27 N	14.04 E
Jesenice, údolní nádrž ⊜[1]	60	50.04 N	12.27 E
Jeseník	30	50.14 N	17.13 E
Jesenoviči	76	57.17 N	34.14 E
Jesensaj	80	49.54 N	51.28 E
Ješera	84	43.04 N	40.55 E
Jeserig bei Wiesenburg	54	52.05 N	12.27 E
Jesi	66	43.31 N	13.14 E
Jesil'	86	51.58 N	66.24 E
Jes'ki	76	57.56 N	36.23 E
Jesönbulag → Altaj	90	46.20 N	96.18 E
Jessej	74	68.29 N	102.10 E
Jesselton → Kota Kinabalu	112	5.59 N	116.04 E
Jessen	54	51.47 N	12.58 E
Jessentuki	84	44.03 N	42.51 E
Jesser Point ➤	158	27.32 S	32.40 E
Jessheim	26	60.09 N	11.11 E
Jessnitz	54	51.41 N	12.17 E
Jessore	124	23.10 N	89.13 E
Jessup, Md., U.S.	208	39.08 N	76.46 W
Jessup, Pa., U.S.	210	41.28 N	75.33 W
Jessup Park ♦	280	34.15 N	118.24 W
Jestetten	58	47.39 N	8.34 E
Jestřebí	54	50.38 N	14.36 E
Jésuite, Lac du ⊜	206	46.53 N	72.36 W
Jesup, Ga., U.S.	192	31.36 N	81.53 W
Jesup, Ia., U.S.	190	42.28 N	92.03 W
Jesup, Lake ⊜	220	28.43 N	81.14 W
Jesús	252	27.03 S	55.47 W
Jésus, Île I	206	45.35 N	73.45 W
Jesús Carranza	234	17.26 N	95.02 W
Jesús de Otoro	236	14.26 N	87.59 W
Jesús María, Arg.	252	30.59 S	64.06 W
Jesús María, Méx.	232	25.06 N	107.28 W
Jesús María, Méx.	234	21.58 N	102.21 W
Jesús María, Perú	286d	12.04 S	77.04 W
Jesús María ≃	234	21.51 N	104.42 W
Jesús María, Punta ➤	258	34.39 S	56.55 W
Jesús Menéndez	240p	21.10 N	76.29 W
Jet	196	36.39 N	98.10 W
Jeta, Ilha de I	150	11.53 N	16.15 W
Jetafe	116	10.09 N	124.09 E
Jetmore	198	38.05 N	99.53 W
Jet Propulsion Laboratory ✪[3]	280	34.12 N	118.11 W
Jetpur	120	21.44 N	70.37 E
Jetřichovice	54	50.49 N	14.25 E
Jett	218	38.11 N	84.49 W
Jette	50	50.52 N	4.20 E
Jettingen	58	48.23 N	10.26 E
Jeumont	50	50.18 N	4.06 E
Jeune Landing	182	50.27 N	127.30 W
Jeunieb	114	5.10 N	96.29 E
Jeuram	114	4.14 N	96.18 E
Jever	52	53.34 N	7.54 E
Jeverland ◆[1]	52	53.35 N	8.00 E
Jevgaščino	86	56.26 N	74.41 E
Jevgenjevka	85	43.31 N	77.40 E
Jevíčko	30	49.38 N	16.43 E
Jevišovice	61	48.59 N	16.00 E
Jevišovka ≃	61	48.49 N	16.28 E
Jevlaš'ovo	80	53.07 N	46.51 E
Jevnaker	26	60.15 N	10.28 E
Jevra	86	59.56 N	64.27 E
Jevrej □[3]	89	48.30 N	132.00 E
Jewel Cave National Monument ♦	198	43.42 N	103.50 W
Jewell, Ia., U.S.	190	42.18 N	93.38 W
Jewell, Ks., U.S.	198	39.40 N	98.09 W
Jewell, N.Y., U.S.	210	43.13 N	75.48 W
Jewell, Oh., U.S.	216	41.20 N	84.17 W
Jewell, Or., U.S.	224	45.56 N	123.30 W
Jewell Ridge	192	37.11 N	81.47 W
Jewell Village	218	39.10 N	85.51 W
Jewett, Il., U.S.	194	39.13 N	88.15 W
Jewett, Oh., U.S.	214	40.22 N	81.00 W
Jewett, Tx., U.S.	222	31.22 N	96.09 W
Jewett City	207	41.36 N	71.58 W
Jewett Creek ≃	212	44.22 N	75.45 W
Jewett Lake ⊜	184	56.09 N	104.40 W
Jewettville	284a	42.43 N	78.52 W
Jey ◆[8]	267d	35.41 N	51.21 E
Jeyretān	120	37.10 N	67.20 E
Jezerce ∧	38	42.26 N	19.49 E
Jezeršče	76	55.50 N	29.59 E
Jezerní hora ∧	60	49.10 N	13.11 E
Ježicha	80	58.06 N	47.40 E
Jeziorany	30	53.58 N	20.46 E
Ježovo	80	58.02 N	52.14 E
Jezreel, Valley of → Yizre'el, 'Émeq ≚	132	32.36 N	35.14 E
J. G. Strijdomdam ⊜[1]	158	27.25 S	32.05 E
Jhābua	120	22.46 N	74.36 E
Jhāhtipahāri	126	23.22 N	86.54 E
Jha Jha	124	24.46 N	86.22 E
Jhajjar	124	28.37 N	76.39 E
Jhal	120	28.17 N	67.27 E
Jhālakāti	124	22.39 N	90.12 E
Jhālārāpātan	124	24.33 N	76.10 E
Jhālāwār	124	24.36 N	76.09 E
Jhalida	124	23.22 N	85.58 E
Jhal Jhao	120	26.18 N	65.35 E
Jhālod	120	23.06 N	74.09 E
Jhang Sadar	123	31.16 N	72.19 E
Jhānsi	124	25.26 N	78.35 E
Jhānsi Post	123	33.52 N	71.24 E
Jhāpā	124	26.29 N	87.51 E
Jhārgrām	126	22.27 N	86.59 E
Jharia	126	23.45 N	86.24 E
Jhārpokhariā	126	22.10 N	86.38 E
Jhārsuguda	120	21.51 N	84.02 E
Jhawāriān	123	32.22 N	72.38 E
Jhelum	123	32.56 N	73.44 E
Jhelum ≃	123	31.12 N	72.08 E
Jhenida	124	23.33 N	89.10 E
Jhenkāri	272b	22.46 N	88.18 E
Jhikergacha	126	23.07 N	89.07 E
Jhikra	126	22.37 N	87.55 E
Jhilimili	126	22.49 N	86.37 E
Jhil Kuranga ◆[8]	272a	28.40 N	77.17 E
Jhilla ≃[1]	126	21.58 N	88.56 E
Jhinkpāni	124	22.25 N	85.47 E
Jhok Rind	120	31.27 N	70.26 E
Jhumra	123	31.34 N	73.11 E
Jhunjhunūn	120	28.08 N	75.24 E
Jiaban, Zhg.	102	25.10 N	107.03 E
Jiaban, Zhg.	102	25.38 N	107.07 E
Jiabong	116	11.46 N	124.57 E
Jiacha	120	29.11 N	92.44 E
Jiading	106	31.23 N	121.15 E
Jiāganj	126	24.14 N	88.16 E
Jiagedan	89	51.35 N	120.55 E
Jiahashitai	89	46.25 N	122.17 E
Jiahe	102	25.43 N	112.05 E
Jiajiachang, Zhg.	107	29.44 N	105.06 E
Jiajiachang, Zhg.	107	30.26 N	104.21 E
Jiajiagou, Zhg.	104	41.44 N	120.58 E
Jiajiagou, Zhg.	104	42.20 N	121.46 E
Jiajiang	107	29.45 N	103.34 E
Jiajiayuan	106	32.18 N	120.55 E
Jiakou	100	30.10 N	119.03 E
Jiakou Wa ≡	105	38.58 N	116.50 E
Jiali	120	30.47 N	93.24 E
Jialing ≃	102	29.34 N	106.35 E
Jialou	100	32.54 N	113.26 E
Jialu	106	30.26 N	118.50 E
Jialu ≃	100	33.38 N	114.36 E
Jiamingzhen	107	29.16 N	105.20 E
Jiamusi (Kiamusze)	89	46.50 N	130.21 E
Jiamuyingzi	104	41.56 N	121.43 E
Ji'an, Zhg.	98	41.06 N	126.08 E
Ji'an, Zhg.	100	27.07 N	114.58 E
Jian ≃, Zhg.	100	26.38 N	118.12 E
Jian ≃, Zhg.	104	40.59 N	121.51 E
Jian'an	89	43.04 N	125.03 E
Jianba	106	31.59 N	120.35 E
Jianbi	106	32.11 N	119.35 E
Jianchang, Zhg.	98	40.51 N	119.46 E
Jianchang, Zhg.	98	39.58 N	122.35 E
Jianchang, Zhg.	98	41.16 N	124.29 E
Ji'anchang, Zhg.	107	30.31 N	106.02 E
Jianchangying	98	40.06 N	118.49 E
Jianchapu	105	39.06 N	116.31 E
Jianchaxi, Zhg.	102	28.08 N	108.04 E
Jianchaxi, Zhg.	107	30.22 N	104.03 E
Jianchuan	102	26.34 N	99.53 E
Jiande	100	29.29 N	119.16 E
Jiang'an	107	28.44 N	105.05 E
Jiangba	100	33.08 N	118.45 E
Jiangbei (Lianglukou)	107	29.44 N	106.38 E
Jiangbeixu	100	26.20 N	115.26 E
Jiangbian	102	24.03 N	103.37 E
Jiangbianzhai	102	23.49 N	100.11 E
Jiangcheng, Zhg.	102	22.40 N	101.48 E
Jiangcheng, Zhg.	105	38.52 N	115.22 E
Jiangcun	100	28.17 N	117.49 E
Jiangdi	102	25.08 N	104.45 E
Jiangdihe	102	25.55 N	101.31 E
Jiangdu	100	32.26 N	119.34 E
Jiangduo	100	32.22 N	120.15 E
Jiange	102	32.06 N	105.29 E
Jianggezhuang	98	39.27 N	119.09 E
Jianghua (Shuikou)	102	24.58 N	111.38 E
Jianghuaqiao	106	32.05 N	120.00 E
Jiangji	100	32.19 N	115.44 E
Jiangjia, Zhg.	106	31.40 N	121.09 E
Jiangjia, Zhg.	106	31.58 N	121.28 E
Jiangjiadian	104	41.41 N	121.03 E
Jiangjiagou	104	41.44 N	121.44 E
Jiangjiaji	100	31.59 N	115.16 E
Jiangjiatun, Zhg.	104	41.42 N	122.02 E
Jiangjiatun, Zhg.	104	41.42 N	122.25 E
Jiangjin	107	29.17 N	106.15 E
Jiangjing	100	25.34 N	119.25 E
Jiangjunmiao	86	44.43 N	90.05 E
Jiangjunqiao	102	31.18 N	100.55 E
Jiangkou, Zhg.	100	27.44 N	114.49 E
Jiangkou, Zhg.	100	29.43 N	121.25 E
Jiangkou, Zhg.	100	27.27 N	118.03 E
Jiangkou, Zhg.	100	25.29 N	119.12 E
Jiangkou, Zhg.	100	27.21 N	115.31 E
Jiangkou, Zhg.	102	23.31 N	110.17 E
Jiangkou, Zhg.	102	27.37 N	108.48 E
Jiangkou, Zhg.	102	30.26 N	111.42 E
Jiangkou, Zhg.	102	33.39 N	107.12 E
Jiangkou, Zhg.	102	29.38 N	110.20 E
Jiangkou, Zhg.	107	30.14 N	103.55 E
Jiangkouji	100	32.50 N	116.16 E
Jiangkoutang	100	27.30 N	112.44 E
Jiangle	100	26.42 N	117.25 E
Jiangliadian	98	42.33 N	117.27 E
Jiangling	102	30.20 N	112.06 E
Jianglingxi	102	31.28 N	107.13 E
Jiangmen	100	22.35 N	113.05 E
Jiangmifeng	89	43.58 N	126.45 E
Jiangning	106	31.58 N	118.50 E
Jiangpu	100	32.04 N	118.37 E
Jiangqiao	89	46.48 N	123.45 E
Jiangqiaotou	106	30.37 N	120.38 E
Jiangshan	100	28.45 N	118.37 E
Jiangshan ≃	100	28.57 N	118.50 E
Jiangshe	106	31.34 N	120.08 E
Jiangshui	98	37.13 N	113.59 E
Jiangsu (Kiangsu) □[4]	90	33.00 N	120.00 E
Jiangtian	100	25.52 N	119.34 E
Jiangtun, Zhg.	102	23.41 N	112.37 E
Jiangtun, Zhg.	104	41.37 N	122.22 E
Jiangwakou	105	39.31 N	117.42 E
Jiangwan, Zhg.	100	29.25 N	118.02 E
Jiangwan, Zhg.	106	31.18 N	121.29 E
Jiangwan Airport ⊠	269b	31.20 N	121.30 E
Jiangxi	102	22.51 N	101.50 E
Jiangxi (Kiangsi) □[4]	100	28.00 N	116.00 E
Jiangxiacun	106	31.44 N	121.50 E
Jiangxiang	100	32.16 N	117.37 E
Jiangxikou	100	27.36 N	118.23 E
Jiangya	102	29.17 N	110.39 E
Jiangyi	100	29.12 N	115.46 E
Jiangyin	106	31.55 N	120.16 E
Jiangyou	102	31.47 N	104.45 E
Jiangyu, Zhg.	98	36.16 N	118.40 E
Jiangyu, Zhg.	100	27.50 N	112.46 E
Jiangyuanzhen	107	30.35 N	103.48 E
Jiangzaogang	106	32.01 N	121.03 E
Jiangzhasiji	120	30.28 N	88.55 E
Jiangzhong	120	29.10 N	93.32 E
Jianhe, Zhg.	102	26.27 N	108.33 E
Jianhe, Zhg.	105	39.14 N	118.03 E
Jianhu	100	33.28 N	119.50 E
Jianli	100	29.49 N	112.53 E
Jianling	100	32.45 N	113.12 E
Jianning	100	26.50 N	116.49 E
Jian'ou	100	27.03 N	118.19 E
Jianping (Yebaishou)	98	41.24 N	119.37 E
Jianqiao	106	30.20 N	120.12 E
Jianqigou	104	40.54 N	123.17 E
Jianshan, Zhg.	100	29.14 N	120.44 E
Jianshan, Zhg.	100	29.58 N	120.16 E
Jian Shan ∧	104	41.49 N	121.44 E
Jianshi	102	30.36 N	109.38 E
Jianshui	102	23.38 N	102.49 E
Jiantiao	100	29.04 N	121.36 E
Jiantou	105	39.26 N	115.41 E
Jiantouji	98	34.35 N	117.34 E
Jianyang, Zhg.	100	27.22 N	118.04 E
Jianyang, Zhg.	100	33.27 N	119.40 E
Jianyang, Zhg.	107	30.24 N	104.32 E
Jiao ≃	100	26.48 N	119.42 E
Jiaocheng	102	37.33 N	112.02 E
Jiaodao	105	39.39 N	116.06 E
Jiaodianzi	104	41.32 N	121.49 E
Jiaodonggou	104	40.50 N	123.58 E
Jiaohe, Zhg.	89	43.42 N	127.19 E
Jiaohe, Zhg.	98	38.01 N	116.17 E
Jiaojiapuzi	104	40.47 N	123.48 E
Jiaolai ≃, Zhg.	89	43.43 N	123.05 E
Jiaolai ≃, Zhg.	98	37.07 N	119.35 E
Jiaolai ≃, Zhg.	98	42.47 N	120.44 E
Jiaoling	100	24.41 N	116.10 E
Jiaomei	100	24.32 N	117.54 E
Jiaonan (Wanggezhuang)	98	35.51 N	119.59 E
Jiao Shan I	106	31.21 N	120.06 E
Jiaoshanhe	100	29.38 N	112.33 E
Jiaoxi	106	31.49 N	120.10 E
Jiaoxian	98	36.18 N	119.58 E
Jiaoyang	100	27.56 N	119.16 E
Jiaozhou Wan ⊂	98	36.10 N	120.15 E
Jiaozhuang	100	33.14 N	114.02 E
Jiaozuo	102	35.15 N	113.13 E
Jiapu	106	31.06 N	119.56 E
Jiashan, Zhg.	100	32.47 N	118.00 E
Jiashan, Zhg.	106	30.51 N	120.54 E
Jiashi	85	39.28 N	76.45 E
Jiashun Hu ⊜	120	34.35 N	86.05 E
Jiasi	107	29.06 N	106.24 E
Jiatan	107	30.12 N	106.29 E
Jiatanchang	107	29.09 N	106.16 E
Jiawang	98	34.27 N	117.27 E
Jiaxian, Zhg.	100	33.58 N	113.13 E
Jiaxian, Zhg.	102	38.01 N	110.31 E
Jiaxiang	98	35.25 N	116.21 E
Jiaxing	106	30.46 N	120.45 E
Jiayin	89	48.53 N	130.24 E
Jiayu	100	29.58 N	113.55 E
Jiayun Hu ⊜	120	35.02 N	85.40 E
Jiaze	106	31.42 N	119.47 E
Jiazhai	98	34.33 N	115.48 E
Jiazhuang	105	39.19 N	117.22 E
Jiazi	100	22.55 N	116.04 E
Jiazier	85	38.40 N	76.33 E
Jibacoa ≃	240p	20.15 N	77.12 W
Jibagalle	144	8.04 N	48.39 E
Jibalei	144	10.09 N	50.53 E
Jibannagar	126	23.25 N	88.50 E
Jíbaro ≃	286b	23.03 N	82.23 W
Jibat ∧	144	8.45 N	37.29 E
Jibiya	150	13.05 N	7.12 E
Jiboa ≃	236	13.22 N	89.04 W
Jibóia, Ilha da I	256	23.03 S	44.22 W
Jibuti → Djibouti	144	11.36 N	43.09 E
Jicamarca, Quebrada V	286d	12.02 S	76.57 W
Jicarilla Apache Indian Reservation ◆[4]	200	36.40 N	107.00 W
Jicarón, Isla I	246	7.16 N	81.47 W
Jicatuyo ≃	236	14.59 N	88.16 W
Jicheng	105	39.23 N	116.17 E
Jičín	30	50.26 N	15.21 E
Jicotea ≃	286b	23.01 N	82.14 W
Jidād	140	11.05 N	24.44 E
Jiddah (Jeddah)	144	21.30 N	39.12 E
Jidingxilin	120	32.52 N	92.21 E
Jidy, Wādī al- V	142	30.13 N	32.46 E
Jiebu	100	28.15 N	115.02 E
Jiedong	100	26.02 N	113.00 E
Jiegou	100	33.21 N	117.55 E
Jiehe	98	35.16 N	117.04 E
Jieji	100	33.33 N	118.24 E
Jiejiang	106	31.58 N	120.43 E
Jiejinkou	89	47.57 N	132.50 E
Jielingkou	98	40.09 N	119.15 E
Jielongchang	107	29.13 N	106.32 E
Jiemian	100	25.56 N	118.02 E
Jiepai, Zhg.	100	26.41 N	112.46 E
Jiepai, Zhg.	100	29.34 N	115.06 E
Jiepai, Zhg.	106	30.55 N	119.32 E
Jiepai, Zhg.	107	29.28 N	104.43 E
Jiepaiji	100	32.15 N	117.50 E
Jiesheng	100	22.45 N	115.25 E
Jieshi, Zhg.	100	22.51 N	115.49 E
Jieshi, Zhg.	107	29.27 N	105.17 E
Jieshi Wan ⊂	100	22.46 N	115.40 E
Jieshou, Zhg.	100	33.18 N	115.20 E
Jieshou, Zhg.	100	27.22 N	117.40 E
Jieshou, Zhg.	100	33.00 N	119.27 E
Jiexi	100	23.28 N	115.56 E
Jiexiu	102	37.05 N	111.51 E
Jieyang	100	23.35 N	116.21 E
Jiezhongdian	100	32.41 N	112.29 E
Jieznas	76	54.36 N	24.10 E
Jifjāfah, Bi'r ▾[4]	140	30.27 N	33.11 E
Jiftūn, Jazā'ir II	140	27.13 N	33.56 E
Jiggalong	162	23.25 S	120.47 E
Jiggalong Creek ≃	162	22.53 S	120.14 E
Jigongying	102	26.18 N	104.48 E
Jigongzhen	98	34.02 N	115.32 E
Jiguaní	240p	20.22 N	76.26 W
Jiguanshan, Zhg.	98	40.32 N	123.55 E
Jiguanshan, Zhg.	104	42.08 N	124.15 E
Jiguanshan, Zhg.	104	41.18 N	123.36 E
Jigüey, Bahía de ⊂	240p	22.08 N	78.05 W
Jigzhi	102	33.28 N	101.29 E
Jihe	100	32.15 N	112.48 E
Jiheier	85	38.11 N	75.46 E
Jihlava	30	49.24 N	15.36 E
Jihlava ≃	61	48.55 N	16.37 E
Jihočeský Kraj □[4]	30	49.05 N	14.30 E
Jihomoravský Kraj □[4]	30	49.10 N	16.40 E
Jiiqley	144	4.25 N	45.22 E
Jijel	148	36.48 N	5.46 E
Jijel □[5]	148	36.45 N	6.00 E
Jijia ≃	38	46.54 N	28.05 E
Jijiadianzi	98	35.31 N	118.59 E
Jijiamiao	107	29.18 N	104.06 E
Jijiapuzi	104	41.16 N	124.12 E
Jijiashi	106	32.08 N	120.18 E
Jijiaying	105	40.20 N	115.24 E
Jijiga	144	9.22 N	42.47 E
Jikawo	144	8.22 N	33.46 E
Jikawo ≃	144	8.22 N	33.47 E
Jike	102	31.00 N	99.41 E
Jilalin	89	51.19 N	119.55 E
Jilantai	102	39.47 N	105.45 E
Jilbānah, Bi'r al- ▾[4]	142	30.55 N	32.29 E
Jilemutu	89	52.14 N	120.47 E
Jilib	144	0.29 N	42.46 E
Jilibulake	120	33.05 N	93.10 E
Jili Hu ⊜	86	46.57 N	87.27 E
Jilin (Kirin)	89	43.51 N	126.33 E
Jilin (Kirin) □[4]	90	44.00 N	126.00 E
Jiliu ≃	89	52.04 N	120.48 E
Jill, Kediet ej ∧	148	22.38 N	12.33 W
Jill, Sebkhet ej ⊜	148	22.47 N	12.53 W
Jiloca ≃	34	41.21 N	1.39 W
Jilotepec de Abasolo	234	19.58 N	99.32 W
Jilotlán de los Dolores	234	19.14 N	102.59 W
Jílové	54	50.46 N	14.07 E
Jima	144	7.36 N	36.50 E
Jimbaran	115b	8.46 S	115.11 E
Jimbolia	38	45.47 N	20.43 E
Jimboomba	171a	27.50 S	153.02 E
Jimei	100	24.37 N	118.07 E
Jimena de la Frontera	34	36.26 N	5.27 W
Jiménez, Méx.	232	29.02 N	100.41 W
Jiménez, Méx.	232	27.08 N	104.55 W
Jimenez, Pil.	116	8.20 N	123.50 E
Jiménez, Arroyo ≃	288	34.44 S	58.13 W
Jiménez, Laguna de ⊜	258	35.26 S	59.01 W
Jiménez del Téul	234	23.10 N	104.05 W
Jimeta	146	9.16 N	12.27 E
Jimi ≃	164	5.20 S	144.20 E
Jimingcun	105	39.19 N	116.09 E
Jiminghe	100	30.36 N	115.32 E
Jim Ned Creek ≃	196	31.50 N	99.07 W
Jimo	98	36.23 N	120.27 E
Jimsar	86	44.00 N	89.04 E
Jim Thorpe	210	40.52 N	75.43 W
Jimuganayaji	85	38.36 N	75.39 E
Jin (Gam) ≃, Asia	110	21.55 N	105.12 E
Jin ≃, Zhg.	100	26.51 N	117.46 E
Jin ≃, Zhg.	100	24.54 N	118.35 E
Jin ≃, Zhg.	100	28.24 N	115.49 E
Jināḥ	140	25.20 N	30.31 E
Jinan (Tsinan), Zhg.	98	36.40 N	116.57 E
Jin'an, Zhg.	100	28.38 N	119.18 E
Jinbang	100	25.01 N	118.01 E
Jinbo ≃	107	28.54 N	103.40 E
Jincang	89	43.20 N	130.30 E
Jince	60	49.47 N	13.59 E
Jinchanggouliang	98	41.56 N	120.19 E
Jincheng, Zhg.	102	35.30 N	112.50 E
Jincheng, Zhg.	104	41.12 N	121.25 E
Jinchengshai	102	26.43 N	111.00 E
Jincheng Shan ∧	107	30.47 N	106.32 E
Jinchuan	102	31.25 N	102.08 E
Jinchuanqiao	102	27.18 N	101.48 E
Jincun	106	31.08 N	119.49 E
Jīnd	123	29.19 N	76.19 E
Jindabyne	171b	36.25 S	148.38 E
Jindabyne, Lake ⊜[1]	171b	36.22 S	148.37 E
Jindaichang	107	29.43 N	104.49 E
Jindālī, Bi'r ▾[4]	142	29.55 N	31.40 E
Jindřichovice	54	50.15 N	12.37 E
Jindřichův Hradec	30	49.09 N	15.00 E
Jinfeng	100	26.01 N	119.36 E
Jinfosi	102	39.29 N	99.00 E
Jing ≃, Zhg.	86	44.52 N	82.50 E
Jing ≃, Zhg.	102	34.28 N	109.00 E
Jing'an	100	28.52 N	115.20 E
Jin'gangpo	107	29.38 N	106.25 E
Jingangtou	100	27.54 N	113.40 E
Jingangtuo	107	29.10 N	106.07 E
Jing'anji	98	34.30 N	116.55 E
Jingbian	102	37.25 N	108.21 E
Jingbohu ⊜	89	43.54 N	128.54 E
Jingcheng	100	24.36 N	117.30 E
Jingde	100	30.19 N	118.31 E
Jingdezhen (Kingtechen)	100	29.16 N	117.11 E
Jingdong	102	24.28 N	100.52 E
Jingellic	171b	35.56 S	147.42 E
Jingeryu	105	39.43 N	115.36 E
Jinggang	100	28.28 N	112.46 E
Jinggangshan (Ciping)	100	26.36 N	114.05 E
Jinggongqiao	100	29.45 N	117.11 E
Jinggu	102	23.32 N	100.41 E
Jingguanzhen	107	29.55 N	106.33 E
Jinghai, Zhg.	100	23.03 N	116.31 E
Jinghai, Zhg.	105	38.56 N	116.55 E
Jinghaiwei	98	36.52 N	122.13 E
Jinghe	86	44.39 N	82.50 E
Jinghong	102	22.01 N	100.49 E
Jinghuiling	105	40.22 N	117.27 E
Jingjiang, Zhg.	102	26.19 N	100.33 E
Jingjiang, Zhg.	106	32.01 N	120.15 E
Jingjiayu	104	41.40 N	123.51 E
Jingle	102	38.24 N	111.54 E
Jinglou	100	32.39 N	112.56 E
Jingmen	102	31.00 N	112.09 E
Jingning, Zhg.	100	27.59 N	119.38 E
Jingning, Zhg.	102	35.25 N	105.56 E
Jingou	104	41.38 N	120.35 E
Jingoutun	98	41.03 N	117.27 E
Jingshan	100	31.02 N	113.05 E
Jingtai	102	37.17 N	104.09 E
Jingu	100	25.13 N	118.07 E
Jingxi	102	23.08 N	106.29 E
Jingxian, Zhg.	98	37.42 N	116.16 E
Jingxian, Zhg.	100	30.42 N	118.24 E
Jingxian, Zhg.	102	26.40 N	109.25 E
Jingxin	100	24.14 N	115.56 E
Jingxing, Zhg.	89	47.04 N	123.01 E
Jingxing, Zhg.	98	38.02 N	114.08 E
Jingyan	107	29.40 N	104.04 E
Jingyu	98	42.22 N	126.50 E
Jingyuan, Zhg.	102	36.38 N	104.37 E
Jingyuan, Zhg.	102	35.30 N	106.48 E
Jingzhi	98	36.19 N	119.23 E
Jingzichang	107	29.00 N	104.41 E
Jinhae → Chinhae	98	35.09 N	128.40 E
Jinhu	100	33.00 N	119.02 E
Jinhua	100	29.07 N	119.39 E
Jinhua ≃	100	29.06 N	119.39 E
Jinhui	106	30.59 N	121.29 E
Jining, Zhg.	98	35.25 N	116.36 E
Jining, Zhg.	102	40.57 N	113.02 E
Jinja	154	0.26 N	33.12 E
Jinjiadian	98	41.39 N	118.18 E
Jinjiang, Zhg.	100	24.50 N	118.35 E
Jinjiang, Zhg.	110	26.19 N	100.33 E
Jinjiawopeng	104	41.38 N	122.16 E
Jinjiawopu	104	42.32 N	122.10 E
Jinjiazhen	89	42.49 N	123.40 E
Jinjing, Zhg.	100	24.37 N	118.36 E
Jinjing, Zhg.	100	28.31 N	113.25 E
Jinjini	150	7.26 N	2.39 W
Jinju → Chinju	98	35.11 N	128.05 E
Jinkeng	100	27.15 N	117.14 E
Jinkichi-mori ∧	96	33.41 N	134.07 E
Jinkou, Zhg.	98	36.35 N	120.46 E
Jinkou, Zhg.	100	30.22 N	114.10 E
Jinkou, Zhg.	100	29.18 N	115.15 E
Jinkuang	102	28.20 N	101.54 E
Jinlijing	107	29.48 N	104.45 E
Jinlingsi	104	41.42 N	120.49 E
Jinlingyu	105	40.06 N	117.32 E
Jinlingzhen	98	36.49 N	118.11 E
Jinlonggou	89	51.45 N	125.51 E
Jinmachi-chūtonchi, Rikujō-jieitai- ■	92	38.25 N	140.27 E
Jinmu Jiao ➤	110	18.09 N	109.34 E
Jinnah Barrage ◆[6]	123	32.57 N	71.30 E
Jinning	102	24.41 N	102.35 E
Jinniu, Zhg.	100	31.24 N	117.12 E
Jinniu, Zhg.	100	29.59 N	114.38 E
Jinotega	236	13.06 N	86.00 W
Jinotega □[5]	236	14.00 N	85.25 W
Jinotepe	236	11.51 N	86.12 W
Jinping, Zhg.	102	26.38 N	109.03 E
Jinping, Zhg.	102	22.50 N	103.10 E
Jinpingchang	107	28.54 N	104.43 E
Jinpo	105	39.18 N	115.15 E
Jinqian ≃	102	32.52 N	110.01 E
Jinqiao	100	31.46 N	116.50 E
Jinrui	100	27.57 N	114.12 E
Jinseki	96	34.48 N	133.11 E
Jinsen → Inch'ŏn	98	37.28 N	126.38 E
Jinsha, Zhg.	100	26.12 N	118.39 E
Jinsha, Zhg.	102	27.18 N	106.10 E
Jinsha, Zhg.	106	32.06 N	121.05 E
Jinsha (Yangtze) ≃	102	28.50 N	104.36 E
Jinshan, Zhg.	89	51.51 N	126.30 E
Jinshan, Zhg.	106	30.54 N	121.09 E
Jinshanwei	106	30.44 N	121.19 E
Jinshanxiang	107	30.35 N	104.52 E
Jinshanzui	106	30.44 N	121.22 E
Jinshi	102	29.39 N	111.52 E
Jinshijing	107	29.23 N	104.08 E
Jinshuzhen	106	31.23 N	120.24 E
Jinsiniangqiao	106	30.43 N	121.15 E
Jinta	102	40.03 N	98.53 E
Jintan	106	31.45 N	119.34 E
Jintang, Zhg.	102	30.54 N	104.19 E
Jintang, Zhg.	102	30.19 N	102.19 E
Jintian	100	27.10 N	114.27 E
Jintotolo Channel ⋓	116	11.48 N	123.05 E
Jintotolo Island I	116	11.51 N	123.08 E
Jinxi, Zhg.	100	27.54 N	116.43 E
Jinxi, Zhg.	104	40.45 N	120.50 E
Jinxian, Zhg.	98	38.02 N	115.02 E
Jinxian, Zhg.	98	39.04 N	121.40 E
Jinxian, Zhg.	100	28.22 N	116.14 E
Jinxian (Dalinghe), Zhg.	104	41.11 N	121.22 E
Jinxiang, Zhg.	98	35.05 N	116.18 E
Jinxiang, Zhg.	100	27.26 N	120.35 E
Jin-ya ⊥	94	36.06 N	137.15 E
Jinyun	100	28.40 N	120.03 E
Jinz, Qā' al- ≚	132	30.45 N	36.04 E
Jinze	106	31.02 N	120.56 E
Jinzhai	100	31.44 N	115.54 E
Jinzhaizhen	100	31.32 N	115.46 E
Jinzhen	100	33.39 N	118.17 E
Jinzhong ≃	105	39.08 N	117.42 E
Jinzhou (Chinchou)	104	41.07 N	121.08 E
Jinzisi	107	29.09 N	106.22 E
Jinzū ≃	94	36.46 N	137.13 E
Jiō	270	34.58 N	135.28 E
Ji-Paraná	248	10.52 S	61.57 W
Jipijapa	246	1.20 S	80.35 W
Jipioca, Ilha I	250	1.53 N	50.12 W
Jiquí ≃	240p	21.22 N	78.32 W
Jiquilisco	236	13.19 N	88.35 W
Jiquilisco, Bahía de ⊂	236	13.10 N	88.28 W
Jiquilpan de Juárez	234	19.59 N	102.43 W
Jiquipilas	234	16.40 N	93.39 W
Jiquipilco	234	19.32 N	99.36 W
Jiquiriçá ≃	255	13.12 S	38.57 W
Jirāfī, Wādī al- (Naḥal Paran) V	132	30.24 N	35.10 E
Jirbān	140	11.03 N	30.36 E
Jiřetín	54	50.50 N	14.35 E
Jiri ≃	120	24.42 N	93.06 E
Jiříkov	54	50.59 N	14.35 E
Jirjā	140	26.20 N	31.53 E
Jirkov	54	50.30 N	13.27 E
Jīroft	128	28.40 N	57.46 E
Jīsh (Gush Ḥalav)	132	33.02 N	35.27 E
Jishou	102	28.17 N	109.29 E
Jishui, Zhg.	100	27.14 N	115.06 E
Jishui, Zhg.	100	33.46 N	115.24 E
Jisr ash-Shughūr	130	35.48 N	36.19 E
Jitan	100	24.56 N	115.43 E
Jitarning	162	32.48 S	117.59 E
Jitaúna	255	14.01 S	39.57 W
Jitianzhen	107	30.19 N	104.01 E
Jitotol	234	17.02 N	92.52 W
Jitra	114	6.16 N	100.25 E
Jituo	120	34.15 N	82.05 E
Jiu ≃	38	43.47 N	23.48 E
Jiubao	100	25.57 N	115.48 E
Jiubingtai	104	41.39 N	124.07 E
Jiucheng, Zhg.	98	38.12 N	117.18 E
Jiucheng, Zhg.	105	39.23 N	116.44 E
Jiuchuchang	107	29.55 N	104.38 E
Jiudaoliang	102	31.35 N	110.12 E
Jiudhara	126	22.24 N	89.44 E
Jiudian	106	32.10 N	120.57 E
Jiudongle	102	38.49 N	101.05 E
Jiudu	106	30.31 N	119.53 E
Jiufanxian	98	35.51 N	115.41 E
Jiufeng, Zhg.	100	24.20 N	117.02 E
Jiufeng, Zhg.	100	25.33 N	119.08 E
Jiugang	105	39.03 N	116.12 E
Jiugongan	102	29.52 N	112.00 E
Jiugongkou	105	39.50 N	114.43 E
Jiugong Shan ∧	100	29.26 N	114.42 E
Jiuguan, Zhg.	98	37.26 N	121.53 E
Jiuguan, Zhg.	106	30.51 N	120.16 E
Jiuguantao	98	36.40 N	115.25 E
Jiuhe	100	23.32 N	115.04 E
Jiuhongshui	102	37.14 N	103.57 E
Jiuhu	98	37.03 N	117.36 E
Jiuhuai'an	98	40.24 N	114.31 E
Jiuhuajie	100	30.25 N	117.51 E
Jiuhuaxian	100	23.30 N	113.16 E
Jiuhuinan	98	42.37 N	126.14 E
Jiujiang, Zhg.	100	29.36 N	115.52 E
Jiujiang, Zhg.	100	29.44 N	115.59 E
Jiujiang, Zhg.	100	22.51 N	113.02 E
Jiujiawopeng	104	40.59 N	121.22 E
Jiujiji	98	35.09 N	114.48 E
Jiujing	107	29.05 N	103.54 E
Jiukou	100	30.52 N	112.38 E
Jiuli	107	29.32 N	103.32 E
Jiulian Shan ⋏	100	24.40 N	114.46 E
Jiuliguan	100	31.50 N	114.14 E
Jiuling Shan ⋏	100	28.46 N	114.45 E
Jiulong → Kowloon, H.K.	271d	22.18 N	114.10 E
Jiulong, Zhg.	100	24.08 N	112.55 E
Jiulong, Zhg.	102	29.00 N	101.50 E
Jiulong ≃, Zhg.	100	25.59 N	117.18 E
Jiulong ≃, Zhg.	100	24.28 N	117.48 E
Jiulongchang	107	29.32 N	106.05 E
Jiulonggang	100	32.38 N	117.03 E
Jiulongpo	107	29.29 N	106.32 E
Jiulongzhen	106	31.54 N	121.34 E
Jiumen	98	40.42 N	120.27 E
Jiumianyang	100	30.16 N	113.13 E
Jiumiao	104	42.24 N	121.36 E
Jiumu	100	28.11 N	118.27 E
Jiuninghe	105	39.28 N	117.46 E
Jiuningyang	100	25.38 N	117.21 E
Jiupu, Zhg.	100	32.50 N	118.45 E
Jiupu, Zhg.	105	40.21 N	115.18 E
Jiuquan (Suzhou)	102	39.45 N	98.34 E
Jiurongcheng	98	37.21 N	122.32 E
Jiushangshui	100	33.32 N	114.32 E
Jiushan Liedao II	100	29.26 N	122.12 E
Jiushenqiu	100	33.11 N	115.08 E
Jiusiyang	100	33.41 N	118.39 E
Jiusongyu	105	40.27 N	116.58 E
Jiutai	89	44.08 N	125.50 E
Jiuwuqing	105	39.31 N	116.52 E
Jiuxian, Zhg.	98	37.53 N	117.06 E
Jiuxian, Zhg.	100	31.11 N	118.04 E
Jiuxian, Zhg.	100	33.15 N	115.35 E
Jiuxian, Zhg.	100	25.14 N	116.31 E
Jiuxian, Zhg.	100	33.32 N	113.17 E
Jiuxian, Zhg.	100	25.54 N	113.22 E
Jiuxian, Zhg.	107	30.27 N	103.51 E
Jiuxian, Zhg.	107	29.51 N	106.13 E
Jiuxian ≃	100	25.07 N	116.24 E
Jiuxiangcheng	100	33.13 N	114.49 E
Jiuyingkou	105	39.42 N	114.44 E
Jiuyingzi	104	42.03 N	121.38 E
Jiuyuanqu	102	35.09 N	111.51 E
Jiuyuhang	106	30.17 N	119.56 E
Jiuyunjie	86	44.12 N	88.05 E
Jiuzhan	89	43.57 N	126.29 E
Jiuzhen	100	24.05 N	117.42 E
Jiuzhou	105	39.30 N	116.33 E
Jiuzhuangwo	105	40.11 N	115.36 E
Jiwangmiao	269b	31.14 N	121.17 E
Jiwangtun	104	41.02 N	122.58 E
Jīwani	128	25.03 N	61.45 E
Jiwen	89	50.32 N	123.15 E
Jixi, Zhg.	89	45.17 N	130.59 E
Jixi, Zhg.	100	30.06 N	118.35 E
Jixian, Zhg.	98	35.26 N	114.05 E
Jixian, Zhg.	98	37.36 N	115.31 E
Jixian, Zhg.	105	40.03 N	117.24 E
Jixiangsi	107	30.39 N	105.32 E
Jixiashi	100	28.22 N	118.44 E
Jixingji	100	32.55 N	116.46 E
Jiyang, Zhg.	98	36.59 N	117.11 E
Jiyang, Zhg.	100	27.10 N	118.07 E
Jiyang, Zhg.	105	39.38 N	115.59 E
Jiyi	102	35.50 N	110.23 E
Jiyuan	102	35.08 N	112.35 E
Jiyun ≃	105	39.07 N	117.43 E
Jiz', Wādī al- V	144	16.19 N	52.00 E
Jīzah, Ahrāmāt al- (Pyramids of Giza) ⊥	142	29.59 N	31.08 E
Jīzah, Tur'at al- ⊼	273c	29.50 N	31.16 E
Jīzān	144	16.54 N	42.29 E
Jizayy	142	30.28 N	30.51 E
Jize	98	36.54 N	114.52 E
Jizera ≃	54	50.10 N	14.43 E
Jizl, Wādī al- V	128	25.38 N	38.21 E
Jizō-dake ∧	94	36.36 N	139.28 E
Jizō-zaki ➤	96	35.34 N	133.20 E
Joaçaba	252	27.10 S	51.30 W
Joachimsthal → Jáchymov, Česká Rep.	54	50.20 N	12.55 E
Joachimsthal, Dtsch.	54	52.58 N	13.44 E
Joaíma	255	16.39 S	41.02 W
Joal Fadiout	150	14.10 N	16.51 W
Joana Coeli	250	1.58 S	49.23 W
Joana Peres	250	3.18 S	49.42 W
Joanes	250	0.51 S	48.31 W
Joanicó	258	34.36 S	56.15 W
Joanna	192	34.24 N	81.48 W
Joanópolis	256	22.56 S	46.17 W
João Câmara	250	5.32 S	35.48 W
João Mendes ≃	287a	22.57 S	43.03 W
João Neiva	255	19.45 S	40.24 W
João Pessoa	250	7.07 S	34.52 W
João Pinheiro	255	17.45 S	46.10 W
Joaquim Egídio	256	22.53 S	46.59 W
Joaquim Távora	255	23.30 S	49.58 W
Joaquin	194	31.58 N	94.03 W
Joaquin Miller Park ♦	282	37.49 N	122.11 W
Joaquín Suárez	258	34.44 S	56.02 W
Joaquín V. González	252	25.05 S	64.11 W
Job	62	45.37 N	3.45 E
Jobabo	240p	20.54 N	77.17 W
Jobat	120	22.25 N	74.34 E
Jobo Point ➤	116	8.42 N	126.15 E
Jobos	240m	17.58 N	66.10 W
Jobos, Bahía de ⊂	240m	17.56 N	66.13 W
Job Peak ∧	204	39.35 N	118.14 W
Jobstown	285	40.02 N	74.41 W
Jochberg	64	47.23 N	12.24 E
Jock ≃	212	45.16 N	75.43 W
Jocketa	54	50.33 N	12.10 E
Jockgrim	56	49.06 N	8.17 E
Jocko ≃	202	47.20 N	114.17 W
Jocolí	252	32.35 S	68.41 W
Jo Co Marsh ≡	276	40.37 N	73.47 W
Jocón	236	15.17 N	86.58 W
Jocoro	236	13.37 N	88.01 W
Jocotán	236	14.49 N	89.23 W
Jocotepec	234	20.18 N	103.26 W
Jocotitlán	234	19.42 N	99.48 W
Jódar	34	37.50 N	3.21 W
Jodhpur	120	26.17 N	73.02 E
Jodiya	120	22.42 N	70.18 E
Jodoigne	56	50.43 N	4.52 E
Jodrell Bank Radio Telescope ✪[3]	262	53.14 N	2.18 W
Joe ≃	220	25.17 N	81.05 W
Joe Batt's Arm	186	49.44 N	54.10 W
Joel	158	28.42 S	28.21 E
Joensuu	26	62.36 N	29.46 E
Joetsu	94	37.06 N	138.15 E
Jœuf	56	49.14 N	6.01 E
Jofane	156	21.17 S	34.16 E
Joffre, Mount ∧	182	50.32 N	115.13 W
Jōganzi ≃	94	36.46 N	137.18 E
Jōga-shima I	94	35.08 N	139.37 E
Jōgawara	268	35.42 N	139.22 E
Jōge	96	34.42 N	133.07 E
Jogeshvari ◆[8]	272c	19.08 N	72.51 E
Jogeshvari Cave ⏏[5]	272c	19.08 N	72.51 E
Jõgeva	76	58.45 N	26.24 E
Jog Falls ∟	122	14.13 N	74.45 E
Joggins	186	45.42 N	64.27 W
Joghatāy	128	36.36 N	57.01 E
Jogindarnagar	123	31.59 N	76.46 E
Jogjakarta → Yogyakarta	115a	7.48 S	110.22 E
Jogui ≃	255	23.45 S	54.40 W
Jōhana	94	36.31 N	136.54 E
Johannesburg, S. Afr.	158	26.12 S	28.05 E
Johannesburg, S. Afr.	273d	26.12 S	28.05 E
Johannesburg, Ca., U.S.	228	35.22 N	117.38 W
Johannesburg □[5]	273d	26.13 S	28.02 E
Johannesburg (Jan Smuts) Airport ⊠	273d	26.08 S	28.14 E
Johanngeorgenstadt	54	50.26 N	12.43 E
Johanniskreuz	56	49.20 N	7.49 E
Johannisthal ◆[8]	264a	52.26 N	13.30 E
Jōhen	92	32.57 N	132.35 E
Johi	120	26.41 N	67.37 E
Johilla ≃	124	23.37 N	81.14 E
John ≃	180	66.55 N	151.35 W
John Boyd Thacher State Park ♦	210	42.38 N	74.01 W
John Carroll University ✪[2]	279a	41.29 N	81.32 W
John Day	202	44.24 N	118.57 W
John Day ≃	202	45.44 N	120.39 W
John Day, Middle Fork ≃	202	44.55 N	119.18 W
John Day, North Fork ≃	202	44.45 N	119.38 W
John Day, South Fork ≃	202	44.28 N	119.31 W
John Day Dam ◆[6]	224	45.43 N	120.41 W
John Day Fossil Beds National Monument ♦	202	44.34 N	119.39 W
John F. Kennedy International Airport ⊠	210	40.38 N	73.47 W
John F. Kennedy National Historic Site ⊥	283	42.21 N	71.08 W
John F. Kennedy Space Center ✪[3]	220	28.40 N	80.40 W
John Forrest National Park ♦	168a	31.53 S	116.06 E
John Hancock Center ✪	278	41.55 N	87.37 W
John H. Kerr Reservoir ⊜[1]	192	36.35 N	78.35 W
John J. Duffy Preserve ♦	278	41.39 N	87.55 W
John Martin Reservoir ⊜[1]	198	38.05 N	103.02 W
John McLaren Park ♦	282	37.43 N	122.25 W
John Muir National Historic Site ⊥	282	37.59 N	122.08 W
Johnny Run ≃	216	41.17 N	88.21 W
John o' Groats	46	58.38 N	3.05 W
John Pennekamp Coral Reef State Park ♦	220	25.11 N	80.15 W
John Redmond Reservoir ⊜[1]	198	38.18 N	95.55 W
Johns ≃	224	46.54 N	124.01 W
Johns Creek ≃	192	37.30 N	80.06 W
Johnshaven	46	56.47 N	2.20 W
Johns Hopkins University ✪[2]	284b	39.20 N	76.37 W
Johns Island I	192	32.40 N	80.05 W
Johnson, Ar., U.S.	194	36.07 N	94.09 W
Johnson, Ks., U.S.	198	37.34 N	101.45 W
Johnson, Ne., U.S.	198	40.24 N	95.59 W
Johnson, N.Y., U.S.	210	41.22 N	74.30 W
Johnson, Vt., U.S.	188	44.38 N	72.40 W
Johnson □[6], In., U.S.	218	39.29 N	86.03 W
Johnson □[6], Tx., U.S.	222	32.20 N	97.20 W
Johnson, Mount ∧	226	36.37 N	121.19 W
Johnson Bay ⊂	208	38.03 N	75.20 W
Johnsonburg, N.J., U.S.	210	40.58 N	74.53 W
Johnsonburg, N.Y., U.S.	210	42.44 N	78.18 W
Johnsonburg, Pa., U.S.	214	41.29 N	78.40 W
Johnson City, N.Y., U.S.	210	42.06 N	75.57 W
Johnson City, Tn., U.S.	192	36.18 N	82.21 W
Johnson City, Tx., U.S.	196	30.16 N	98.24 W
Johnson Creek, N.Y., U.S.	210	43.15 N	78.31 W
Johnson Creek, Wi., U.S.	216	43.04 N	88.46 W
Johnson Creek ≃, Id., U.S.	202	44.58 N	115.30 W
Johnson Creek ≃, Ky., U.S.	218	38.27 N	84.04 W
Johnson Creek ≃, N.Y., U.S.	210	43.22 N	78.16 W

Symbols in the index entries represent the broad categories identified in the key at the right. Symbols with superior numbers (⋏[1]) identify subcategories (see complete key on page *I · 1).*

Symbole im Register stellen die rechts im Schlüssel erklärten Kategorien dar. Symbole mit hochgestellten Ziffern (⋏[1]) bezeichnen Unterabteilungen einer Kategorie (vgl. vollständiger Schlüssel auf Seite *I · 1).*

Los símbolos incluídos en el texto del índice representan las grandes categorías identificadas con la clave a la derecha. Los símbolos con numeros en su parte superior (⋏[1]) identifican las subcategorías (véase la clave completa en la página *I · 1).*

Les symboles de l'index représentent les catégories indiquées dans la légende à droite. Les symboles suivis d'un indice (⋏[1]) représentent des sous-catégories (voir légende complète à la page *I · 1).*

Os símbolos incluídos no texto do índice representam as grandes categorias identificadas com a chave à direita. Os símbolos com números em sua parte superior (⋏[1]) identificam as subcategorias (veja-se a chave completa à página *I · 1).*

Symbol	English	Deutsch	Español	Français	Português
∧	Mountain	Berg	Montaña	Montagne	Montanha
⋏	Mountains	Gebirge	Montañas	Montagnes	Montanhas
)(	Pass	Paß	Paso	Col	Passo
V	Valley, Canyon	Tal, Cañon	Valle, Cañón	Vallée, Canyon	Vale, Canhão
≚	Plain	Ebene	Llano	Plaine	Planície
➤	Cape	Kap	Cabo	Cap	Cabo
I	Island	Insel	Isla	Île	Ilha
II	Islands	Inseln	Islas	Îles	Ilhas
⏏	Other Topographic Features	Andere Topographische Objekte	Otros Elementos Topográficos	Autres données topographiques	Outros acidentes topográficos

ESPAÑOL Nombre	Página	Lat.°′	Long.°′ W = Oeste
FRANÇAIS Nom	Page	Lat.°′	Long.°′ W = Ouest
PORTUGUÊS Nome	Página	Lat.°′	Long.°′ W = Oeste

Name	Page	Lat.°′	Long.°′
Johnson Creek ≃, Tx., U.S.	222	32.02 N	94.59 W
Johnson Creek ≃, Wa., U.S.	224	46.35 N	121.42 W
Johnsondale	204	35.58 N	118.32 W
Johnson Drain ≅	281	42.26 N	83.28 W
Johnson Draw V, Tx., U.S.	196	31.58 N	101.41 W
Johnson Draw V, Tx., U.S.	196	30.08 N	101.07 W
Johnson Hall State Historic Site ⊥	210	43.01 N	74.23 W
Johnson Park ♠	276	40.30 N	74.27 W
Johnson Point >	241h	13.07 N	61.12 W
Johnsons Crossing	180	60.29 N	133.16 W
Johnsons Point >	240c	17.02 N	61.53 W
Johnsons Pond ⊜	283	42.44 N	71.03 W
Johnsons Station	222	32.42 N	97.08 W
Johnsonville, N.Z.	172	41.14 S	174.47 E
Johnsonville, N.Y., U.S.	210	42.55 N	73.31 W
Johnsonville, S.C., U.S.	192	33.49 N	79.26 W
Johnston, Wales, U.K.	42	51.46 N	5.00 W
Johnston, Ia., U.S.	190	41.40 N	93.41 W
Johnston, R.I., U.S.	207	41.46 N	71.21 W
Johnston, S.C., U.S.	192	33.49 N	81.48 W
Johnston, Lake ⊜	162	32.25 S	120.30 E
Johnston Atoll I[1]	14	16.45 N	169.32 W
Johnston City	194	37.49 N	88.55 W
Johnstone	46	55.50 N	4.31 W
Johnstone Peak ∧	280	34.10 N	117.48 W
Johnstone Strait ʊ	182	50.25 N	126.00 W
Johnston Falls ∟	154	10.35 S	28.40 E
Johnstown, Co., U.S.	200	40.20 N	104.54 W
Johnstown, N.Y., U.S.	210	43.00 N	74.22 W
Johnstown, Oh., U.S.	214	40.09 N	82.41 W
Johnstown, Pa., U.S.	214	40.19 N	78.55 W
Johnstown Center	216	42.42 N	88.50 W
Johnstown Flood National Memorial ⊥	214	40.21 N	78.47 W
John Tyler Arboretum ♠	285	39.56 N	75.26 W
Jōhoku	94	36.28 N	140.22 E
Johol	114	2.36 N	102.16 E
Johor □[3]	114	2.00 N	103.30 E
Johor ≃	114	1.27 N	104.02 E
Johor, Selat ʊ	271c	1.28 N	103.48 E
Johor Baharu	114	1.28 N	103.45 E
Jöhstadt	54	50.30 N	13.05 E
Joice Island I	282	38.08 N	122.02 W
Joigny	50	47.59 N	3.24 E
Joiner	194	35.30 N	90.08 W
Joinerville	222	32.11 N	94.55 W
Joinvile	252	26.18 S	48.50 W
Joinville	58	48.27 N	5.08 E
Joinville, Lac ⊜	206	46.18 N	75.12 W
Joinville Island I	9	63.15 S	55.45 W
Joinville-le-Pont	261	48.49 N	2.28 E
Jōjima	96	33.15 N	130.26 E
Jojogan	115a	6.58 S	111.46 E
Jojutla	234	18.37 N	99.11 W
Joka	272b	22.27 N	88.18 E
Jokau	140	8.24 N	33.49 E
Jokioinen	26	60.49 N	23.28 E
Jokkmokk	24	66.37 N	19.50 E
Jökulsá á Brú ≃	24a	65.41 N	14.13 W
Jökulsárgljúfur National Park ♠	24a	66.00 N	16.20 W
Jolārpettai	122	12.34 N	78.35 E
Jolfā	128	38.57 N	45.38 E
Joliet, Il., U.S.	216	41.31 N	88.04 W
Joliet, Mt., U.S.	202	45.29 N	108.58 W
Joliet Correctional Center ♥	278	41.33 N	88.04 W
Joliett	208	40.37 N	76.27 W
Joliette	206	46.01 N	73.27 W
Joliette □[6]	206	46.25 N	74.00 W
Jolietville	218	40.03 N	86.15 W
Jollyville	222	30.27 N	97.47 W
Jolo	116	6.03 N	121.00 E
Jolo Group II	116	6.00 N	121.09 E
Jolo Island I	116	5.58 N	121.06 E
Jølstravatnet ⊜	26	61.32 N	6.13 E
Jomalig Island I	116	14.42 N	122.22 E
Jomba	102	31.27 N	98.15 E
Jombang	115a	7.33 S	112.14 E
Jombo ≃	152	10.36 S	17.32 E
Jona	58	47.14 N	8.52 E
Jonacatepec	234	18.41 N	98.48 W
Jonah	222	30.38 N	97.32 W
Jönåker	40	58.44 N	16.40 E
Jonathan Dickinson State Park ♠	220	27.01 N	80.08 W
Jonava	76	55.05 N	24.17 E
Jones, Pil.	116	16.33 N	121.42 E
Jones, Mi., U.S.	216	41.54 N	85.48 W
Jones, Ok., U.S.	196	35.33 N	97.17 W
Jones ≃	283	42.00 N	70.42 W
Jones and Laughlin Steel Corporation ♥[3], Pa., U.S.	279b	40.26 N	79.58 W
Jones and Laughlin Steel Corporation ♥[3], Pa., U.S.	279b	40.37 N	80.14 W
Jones Beach State Park ♠	210	40.35 N	73.31 W
Jonesboro, Ar., U.S.	194	35.50 N	90.42 W
Jonesboro, Ga., U.S.	192	33.31 N	84.21 W
Jonesboro, Il., U.S.	194	37.27 N	89.16 W
Jonesboro, In., U.S.	216	40.28 N	85.37 W
Jonesboro, La., U.S.	194	32.14 N	92.42 W
Jonesboro, Tn., U.S.	192	36.17 N	82.28 W
Jonesburg	219	38.51 N	91.18 W
Jones Creek	222	28.58 N	95.27 W
Jones Creek ≃, On., Can.	212	44.30 N	75.49 W
Jones Creek ≃, Tx., U.S.	222	29.08 N	96.03 W
Jones Falls ≃	284b	39.18 N	76.37 W
Jones Falls, North Branch ≃	284b	39.25 N	76.42 W
Jones Inlet c	210	40.35 N	73.34 W
Jones Mill	194	34.27 N	92.50 W
Jones Mountains ⋏	9	73.32 S	94.00 W
Jonesport	188	44.31 N	67.35 W
Jones Sound ʊ	176	76.00 N	85.09 W
Jonestown	194	34.19 N	90.27 W
Jonesville, In., U.S.	218	39.04 N	85.53 W
Jonesville, La., U.S.	194	31.37 N	91.49 W
Jonesville, Mi., U.S.	216	41.59 N	84.40 W
Jonesville, N.Y., U.S.	210	42.55 N	73.49 W
Jonesville, N.C., U.S.	192	36.14 N	80.50 W
Jonesville, S.C., U.S.	192	34.50 N	81.40 W
Jonesville, Va., U.S.	192	36.41 N	83.06 W
Jong ≃	150	7.32 N	12.23 W
Jonglei Canal ≅	136	9.21 N	31.32 E
Jongunjärvi ⊜	26	65.17 N	27.15 E
Jónico, Mar → Ionian Sea ⊤[2]	22	39.00 N	19.00 E
Joniškėlis	76	56.02 N	24.10 E
Joniškis	76	56.14 N	23.37 E
Jonkersberg	158	33.55 S	22.15 E
Jönköping	26	57.47 N	14.11 E
Jönköpings Län □[6]	26	57.30 N	14.30 E
Jonquière	186	48.24 N	71.15 W
Jonquières	62	44.07 N	4.54 E
Jonsdorf	54	50.51 N	14.43 E
Jonstorp	41	56.14 N	12.40 E
Jonuta	232	18.05 N	92.08 W
Jonvilliers	261	48.34 N	1.42 E
Jonzac	32	45.27 N	0.26 W
Joondalup, Lake ⊜	168a	31.45 S	115.47 E
Joplin, Mo., U.S.	194	37.05 N	94.30 W
Joplin, Mt., U.S.	202	48.33 N	110.46 W
Joppa, Il., U.S.	194	37.12 N	88.50 W
Joppa, Md., U.S.	208	39.26 N	76.21 W
Jóquei Clube ♠	287b	23.35 S	46.41 W
Joquicingo	234	19.03 N	99.33 W
Jora	124	26.20 N	77.49 E
Jordan, Pil.	116	10.40 N	122.35 E
Jordan, Mn., U.S.	190	44.40 N	93.37 W
Jordan, Mt., U.S.	202	47.19 N	106.54 W
Jordan, N.Y., U.S.	210	43.03 N	76.28 W
Jordan (Al-Urdun) □[1], Asia	118	31.00 N	36.00 E
Jordan (Al-Urdun) □[1], Asia	128	31.00 N	36.00 E
Jordan (Nahr al-Urdunn) (HaYarden) ≃, Asia	132	31.46 N	35.33 E
Jordan ≃, B.C., Can.	224	48.26 N	124.08 W
Jordan ≃, Ut,. U.S.	200	40.49 N	112.08 W
Jordan Creek ≃	202	42.52 N	117.38 W
Jordânia	255	15.54 S	40.11 W
Jordania → Jordan □[1]	128	31.00 N	36.00 E
Jordanie → Jordan □[1]	128	31.00 N	36.00 E
Jordanien → Jordan □[1]	128	31.00 N	36.00 E
Jordan Lake ⊜	216	42.46 N	85.09 W
Jordanów	30	49.40 N	19.50 E
Jordans	260	51.37 N	0.36 W
Jordan Valley	202	42.58 N	117.03 W
Jordanville	210	42.55 N	74.57 W
Jordão ≃	252	25.46 S	52.07 W
Jordbro	40	59.09 N	18.07 E
Jördenstorf	54	53.52 N	12.37 E
Jordet	26	61.25 N	12.09 E
Jorge Chávez, Aeropuerto Internacional ⊠	286d	12.02 S	77.07 W
Jorge Grego, Ilha I	256	23.13 S	44.09 W
Jorge Montt, Isla I	254	51.20 S	74.45 W
Jorge V, Costade → George V Coast ⊐[2]	9	68.30 S	147.30 E
Jorge VI, Estrecho de → George VI Sound ʊ	9	71.00 S	68.00 W
Jorhāt	120	26.46 N	94.13 E
Jork	52	53.32 N	9.41 E
Jorm	120	36.52 N	70.51 E
Jörn	26	65.04 N	20.02 E
Jornado del Muerto ◆[2]	200	33.20 N	106.50 W
Joroinen	26	62.11 N	27.50 E
Jorong	112	3.58 S	114.56 E
Jørpeland	26	59.01 N	6.03 E
J'orzovka	80	48.56 N	44.38 E
Jos	150	9.55 N	8.53 E
Jose Abad Santos	116	5.38 N	125.27 E
José Batlle y Ordóñez	252	33.28 S	55.07 W
José Bonifácio	255	21.03 S	49.41 W
José Cardel	234	19.22 N	96.22 W
José C. Paz	258	34.30 S	58.45 W
José de Freitas	250	4.45 S	42.35 W
José de San Martín	254	44.02 S	70.29 W
José Enrique Rodó (Drabble)	258	33.41 S	57.34 W
José Francisco Vergara	252	22.28 S	69.38 W
Joselândia	248	16.32 S	56.12 W
José Martí, Aeropuerto Internacional ⊠	286b	23.00 N	82.24 W
Jose Panganiban	116	14.17 N	122.41 E
José Pedro Varela	252	33.27 S	54.32 W
Joseph	202	45.21 N	117.13 W
Joseph, Lac ⊜	176	52.45 N	65.15 W
Joseph, Lake ⊜	212	45.10 N	79.44 W
Joseph Bonaparte Gulf c	164	14.15 S	128.30 E
Joseph City	200	34.57 N	110.20 W
Joseph Creek ≃	202	46.03 N	117.01 W
Joseph Davis State Park ♠	284a	43.13 N	79.03 W
Josephine, Pa., U.S.	214	40.29 N	79.11 W
Josephine, Tx., U.S.	222	33.04 N	96.19 W
Josephine, Lake ⊜	220	27.24 N	81.26 W
Josephine Peak ∧	280	34.17 N	118.09 W
Josephstaal	164	4.44 S	145.01 E
José Santos Arévalo	258	35.10 S	59.14 W
Joshīmath	120	30.34 N	79.34 E
Jōshin-Etsu-kōgen-kokuritsu-kōen ♠	94	36.46 N	138.40 E
Joshua	222	32.28 N	97.23 W
Joshuas Creek ≃	275b	43.29 N	79.37 W
Joshua Tree	204	34.08 N	116.18 W
Joshua Tree National Monument ♠	204	33.55 N	116.00 W
Joshua Trees State Park ♠	228	34.41 N	117.47 W
Joškar-Ola	80	56.38 N	47.52 E
Jos Plateau ⋏[1]	150	9.30 N	9.00 E
Jossa	56	50.14 N	9.35 E
Josselin	32	47.57 N	2.33 W
Jossigny	50	48.50 N	2.45 E
Jostedalsbreen ⊐	26	61.40 N	7.00 E
Jost Van Dyke I	240m	18.28 N	64.45 W
Jōtō ◆[8]	270	34.42 N	135.34 E
Jotunheimen ⋏	26	61.38 N	8.18 E
Jotunheimen Nasjonalpark ♠	26	61.35 N	8.30 E
Jouarre	50	48.56 N	3.08 E
Jouars-Pontchartrain	261	48.47 N	1.54 E
Joubertina	158	33.50 S	23.51 E
Joué-lès-Tours	50	47.21 N	0.40 E
Jougne	58	46.46 N	6.24 E
Jouques	62	43.38 N	5.38 E
Jourdanton	196	28.55 N	98.32 W
Joure	52	52.57 N	5.47 E
Joutsa	26	61.44 N	26.07 E
Joutseno	26	61.06 N	28.30 E
Joutsijärvi	24	66.40 N	28.00 E
Joux, Lac de ⊜	58	46.38 N	6.18 E
Joux, Vallée de V	58	46.35 N	6.15 E
Jouy	50	48.31 N	1.33 E
Jouy-en-Josas	261	48.46 N	2.10 E
Jouy-le-Moutier	261	49.01 N	2.03 E
Jouy-le-Potier	50	47.45 N	1.49 E
Jovellanos	240p	22.48 N	81.12 W
Jovellar	116	13.04 N	123.36 E
Jovet, Mont ∧	62	45.30 N	6.39 E
Joveyn ≃	128	36.48 N	56.28 E
Joviânia	255	17.49 S	49.30 W
Jowai	120	25.27 N	92.12 E
Jowhar	144	2.46 N	45.31 E
Jowlaenga, Mount ∧	162	17.21 S	122.56 E
Jowzjān □[4]	120	36.30 N	66.00 E
Joy	190	41.12 N	90.55 W
Joy, Mount ∧	180	63.46 N	132.55 W
Joyce	194	31.56 N	92.35 W
Joyeuse	62	44.29 N	4.14 E
Jōyō	96	34.51 N	135.47 E
Joyous Pavilion Park ♠	271a	39.52 N	116.22 E
Joyuda	240m	18.07 N	67.11 W
Józefów	30	52.09 N	21.12 E
J. Percy Priest Lake ⊜[1]	194	36.05 N	86.30 W
Ju ≃, Zhg.	100	30.38 N	114.51 E
Ju ≃, Zhg.	105	39.45 N	117.35 E
Juaba	250	2.23 S	49.33 W
Juagdan	116	10.00 N	124.35 E
Juami ≃	246	1.45 S	67.30 W
Juanacatlán	234	20.31 N	103.10 W
Juana Díaz	240m	18.03 N	66.31 W
Juan Aldama	232	24.19 N	103.21 W
Juan Anchorena ◆[8]	288	34.29 S	58.30 W
Juan Atucha	258	35.32 S	59.21 W
Juan B. Arruabarrena	252	30.20 S	58.19 W
Juan Bautista Alberdi	252	27.35 S	65.37 W
Juan Blanco, Arroyo ≃	258	35.05 S	57.26 W
Juancheng	98	35.35 N	115.29 E
Juan de Fuca, Strait of ʊ	224	48.18 N	124.00 W
Juan de Garay	254	38.52 S	64.34 W
Juan de Mena	252	24.55 S	56.44 W
Juan de Nova, Île I	138	17.03 S	42.45 E
Juan Díaz Covarrubias	234	18.07 N	95.09 W
Juan E. Barra	252	37.48 S	60.29 W
Juan Eugenio	232	25.10 N	103.20 W
Juan Fernández, Archipiélago II	244	33.00 S	80.00 W
Juan González Grande, Arroyo ≃	258	34.00 S	58.14 W
Juan González Romero ◆[8]	286a	19.30 N	99.04 W
Juangriego	246	11.05 N	63.57 W
Juan Gualberto Gómez	240p	22.52 N	81.33 W
Juan Guerra	248	6.35 S	76.21 W
Juanita	224	47.42 N	122.13 W
Juan Jorba	252	33.37 S	65.16 W
Juan José Castelli	252	25.57 S	60.37 W
Juán José Perez	248	15.14 S	68.58 W
Juanjuí	248	7.11 S	76.45 W
Juankoski	26	63.04 N	28.21 E
Juan-les-Pins	62	43.34 N	7.06 E
Juan L. Lacaze	258	34.26 S	57.27 W
Juan N. Fernández	252	38.00 S	59.16 W
Juan Perez Sound ʊ	182	52.30 N	131.18 W
Juan Ramírez, Isla I	234	21.50 N	97.40 W
Juan Rodríguez Clara	234	18.00 N	95.25 W
Juan Tronconi	258	35.30 S	59.15 W
Juan Viñas	236	9.54 N	83.45 W
Juárez, Méx.	232	27.37 N	100.44 W
Juárez → Ciudad Juárez, Méx.	232	31.44 N	106.29 W
Juárez, Méx.	232	30.19 N	108.05 W
Juárez, Méx.	234	17.39 N	93.10 W
Juárez, Cerro ∧	234	20.37 N	99.17 W
Juárez, Sierra ⋏	234	17.30 N	96.30 W
Juárez, Sierra de ⋏	232	32.00 N	115.50 W
Juarzon	150	5.20 N	8.52 W
Juatinga, Ponta de >	256	23.17 S	44.30 W
Juazeirinho	250	7.04 S	36.35 W
Juàzeiro	250	9.25 S	40.30 W
Juazeiro do Norte	250	7.12 S	39.20 W
Jūbā	154	4.51 N	31.37 E
Juba ≃	248	14.59 S	57.44 W
Jubachstausee ⊜[1]	263	51.10 N	7.37 E
Jūbāl, Maḍīq ʊ	140	27.40 N	33.55 E
Jubal, Strait of → Jūbāl, Maḍīq ʊ	140	27.40 N	33.55 E
Jubayl (Byblos)	130	34.07 N	35.39 E
Jubaysho	144	5.48 N	37.22 E
Jubayt	140	18.57 N	36.50 E
Jubba (Genale) ≃	144	0.15 S	42.38 E
Jubbada Dhexe □[4]	144	1.00 N	43.00 E
Jubbada Hoose □[4]	144	0.00	42.00 E
Jubbah	128	28.02 N	40.56 E
Jubb al-Jarrāḥ	130	34.49 N	37.19 E
Jubbātā al-Khashab	132	33.13 N	35.49 E
Jubb Jannīn	132	33.37 N	35.47 E
Jubbulpore → Jabalpur	124	23.10 N	79.57 E
Jubilee Downs	162	18.22 S	125.17 E
Jubilee Lake ⊜, Austl.	162	29.12 S	126.38 E
Jubilee Lake ⊜, Nf., Can.	186	48.04 N	55.11 W
Jubones ≃	246	3.13 S	79.57 W
Jūbu-san ∧	270	34.50 N	135.55 E
Juby, Cap >	148	27.58 N	12.55 W
Júcar (Xúquer) ≃	34	39.09 N	0.14 W
Juçara	255	15.53 S	50.51 W
Júcaro	240p	21.37 N	78.51 W
Jucás	250	6.32 S	39.32 W
Jüchen	56	51.06 N	6.30 E
Juchhöh	54	50.24 N	11.52 E
Juchipila	234	21.25 N	103.07 W
Juchipila ≃	234	21.03 N	103.25 W
Juchitán de Zaragoza	234	16.26 N	95.01 W
Juchitepec	234	19.06 N	98.53 W
Juchitlán	234	20.05 N	104.07 W
Juchnov	76	54.45 N	35.14 E
Juchoviči	76	56.02 N	28.39 E
Jucuapa	236	13.31 N	88.24 W
Jucurucu ≃	255	17.21 S	39.13 W
Jucurutu	250	6.02 S	37.01 W
Judaea □[9]	132	31.35 N	35.00 E
Judas, Punta >	236	9.31 N	84.32 W
Judaydat al-Khās	132	33.24 N	36.33 E
Judaydat ʿArṭūz	132	33.26 N	36.10 E
Juddah → Jiddah	144	21.30 N	39.12 E
Jude Island I	186	47.15 N	54.49 W
Judenau	61	48.17 N	16.00 E
Judenburg	61	47.10 N	14.40 E
Judges Hill ∧[2]	283	42.12 N	70.49 W
Judian	102	27.20 N	99.36 E
Judinki, Ross.	82	54.37 N	37.17 E
Judinki, Ross.	82	55.27 N	35.48 E
Judino, Ross.	76	58.43 N	39.17 E
Judino, Ross.	80	55.51 N	48.55 E
Judino, Ross.	82	54.09 N	38.19 E
Judino, Ross.	265b	55.40 N	37.12 E
Judío, Rambla del ≃	34	38.15 N	1.27 W
Judique	186	45.52 N	61.30 W
Judith ≃	202	47.44 N	109.38 W
Judith, Point >	207	41.22 N	71.29 W
Judith Gap	202	46.40 N	109.45 W
Judith Mountains ⋏	202	47.12 N	109.15 W
Judith Peak ∧	202	47.13 N	109.13 W
Judoma ≃	74	59.08 N	135.06 E
Judson, S.C., U.S.	192	34.50 N	82.27 W
Judson, Tx., U.S.	222	32.35 N	94.45 W
Judsonia	194	35.16 N	91.38 W
Jue ≃	100	31.42 N	113.20 E
Juehedian	105	39.26 N	117.06 E
Juelsminde	41	55.43 N	10.01 E
Juexi	100	29.27 N	121.57 E
Juexizhen	107	28.55 N	104.16 E
Jufari ≃	246	1.13 S	62.00 W
Jufayr, Bi'r al- ⊤[4]	142	30.49 N	32.40 E
Jufrah, Wādī al- V	142	30.24 N	31.35 E
Jug	86	57.43 N	56.10 E
Jug ≃	24	60.45 N	46.20 E
Jughna	140	12.24 N	25.06 E
Jugo-Kamskij	86	57.42 N	55.35 E
Jugon	32	48.25 N	2.20 W
Jugo-Osetija (South Ossetia) □[9]	84	42.20 N	44.00 E
Jugoslavija → Yugoslavia □[1]	22	44.00 N	21.00 E
Jugoslawien → Yugoslavia □[1]	22	44.00 N	21.00 E
Jugo-Zapad ◆[8]	265b	55.40 N	37.32 E
Juḥā	144	16.41 N	42.54 E
Jühnsdorf	264a	52.18 N	13.23 E
Jühnsdorfer Heide ◆[3]	264a	52.19 N	13.24 E
Juhu ◆[8]	272c	19.07 N	72.49 E
Juhua Dao I	98	40.29 N	120.47 E
Juhu Airport ⊠	272c	19.06 N	72.50 E
Jui	272c	19.01 N	73.05 E
Juidongshan	100	23.46 N	117.31 E
Juigalpa	236	12.05 N	85.24 W
Juillac	32	45.19 N	1.19 E
Juilly	261	49.01 N	2.42 E
Juína ≃	248	12.36 S	58.57 W
Juine ≃	50	48.32 N	2.23 E
Juist	52	53.40 N	6.59 E
Juist I	52	53.40 N	7.00 E
Juisui	100	23.30 N	121.21 E
Juiz de Fora	256	21.45 S	43.20 W
Jūjō Base ■	268	35.45 N	139.43 E
Jujurieux	58	46.02 N	5.25 E
Jujuy → San Salvador de Jujuy	252	24.11 S	65.18 W
Jujuy □[4]	252	23.00 S	66.00 W
Jukagirskoje ploskogorje ⋏[1]	74	66.00 N	155.00 E
Jukamenskoje	80	57.53 N	52.15 E
Jukonda ≃	86	59.38 N	67.26 E
Juksa	86	56.55 N	85.10 E
Juksejevo	24	59.52 N	54.19 E
Jukskei ≃	273d	26.06 S	28.06 E
Jukta	74	63.23 N	105.41 E
Jula ≃	24	63.49 N	44.44 E
Julāna	124	29.08 N	76.25 E
Julayfah, Bi'r al- ⊤[4]	142	30.43 N	29.35 E
Julbach	60	48.40 N	13.52 E
Juldybajevo	86	52.20 N	57.52 E
Julebu	98	40.09 N	113.36 E
Julesburg	198	40.59 N	102.15 W
Juli	248	16.13 S	69.27 W
Juliaca	248	15.30 S	70.08 W
Julia Creek	166	20.39 S	141.45 E
Julia Creek ≃	166	20.00 S	141.11 E
Julian	214	40.52 N	77.56 W
Juliana, Lake ⊜	220	28.07 N	81.48 W
Julianakanaal ≅	56	51.05 N	5.50 E
Julian Alps ⋏	36	46.00 N	14.00 E
Juliana Top ∧	250	3.41 N	56.32 W
Julianehåb (Qaqortoq)	176	60.43 N	46.01 W
Julia Pfeiffer Burns State Park ♠	226	36.10 N	120.40 W
Jülich	56	50.55 N	6.21 E
Juliénas	58	46.14 N	4.43 E
Juliette, Lake ⊜[1]	192	33.05 N	83.50 W
Julijske Alpe → Julian Alps ⋏	36	46.00 N	14.00 E
Julimes	232	28.25 N	105.27 W
Júlio de Castilhos	252	29.14 S	53.41 W
Julio Prestes, Estação ◆[5]	287b	23.32 S	46.38 W
Julita ♥	40	59.09 N	16.02 E
Juliuhe	104	42.03 N	122.55 E
Juliustown	285	40.00 N	74.40 W
Julu	98	37.13 N	115.01 E
Juma	24	65.07 N	33.16 E
Juma ≃	98	39.34 N	115.42 E
Jumaguzino	86	52.54 N	56.23 E
Jumapolo	115a	7.42 S	111.00 E
Jumaševo	80	54.59 N	54.25 E
Jumay, Volcán ∧[1]	236	14.41 N	89.59 W
Jumbilla	248	5.54 S	77.45 W
Jumbo	154	17.28 S	30.55 E
Jumbo, Raas >	144	1.39 S	41.36 E
Jumboo	144	0.15 S	42.38 E
Jumbo Peak ∧	204	36.12 N	114.11 W
Jumeauville	261	48.55 N	1.47 E
Jumentos Cays II	238	22.42 N	75.55 W
Jumet	50	50.26 N	4.25 E
Jumièges	50	49.26 N	0.49 E
Jumilla	34	38.29 N	1.17 W
Jumlā	124	29.17 N	82.10 E
Jummayzat Banī ʿAmr	142	30.48 N	31.32 E
Jump ≃	190	45.17 N	91.05 W
Jump, North Fork ≃	190	45.25 N	90.40 W
Jump, South Fork ≃	190	45.25 N	90.40 W
Jumt uul ∧	102	44.29 N	97.10 E
Jūn	132	33.35 N	35.27 E
Jun ≃	100	25.57 N	118.03 E
Jūnāgadh	120	21.31 N	70.28 E
Junan (Shizilu)	98	35.11 N	118.51 E
Junayfah	142	30.12 N	32.25 E
Junaynah, Ra's al- ∧	140	29.01 N	33.58 E
Juncal, Isla I	258	33.58 S	58.24 W
Juncal do Norte ≡	266c	38.52 N	8.59 W
Juncal do Sul ≡	266c	38.51 N	8.58 W
Juncheng	98	38.57 N	114.41 E
Juncos	240m	18.14 N	65.55 W
Junction, Tx., U.S.	196	30.29 N	99.46 W
Junction, Ut,. U.S.	200	38.14 N	112.13 W
Junction City, Ar., U.S.	194	33.00 N	92.43 W
Junction City, Il., U.S.	219	38.34 N	89.07 W
Junction City, Ks., U.S.	198	39.01 N	96.49 W
Junction City, Ky., U.S.	194	37.35 N	84.47 W
Junction City, Or., U.S.	202	44.13 N	123.12 W
Junction City, Wa., U.S.	224	46.58 N	123.46 W
Jundah	166	24.50 S	143.04 E
Jundiaí	256	23.11 S	46.52 W
Jundiaí ≃, Bra.	256	23.32 S	46.15 W
Jundiaí ≃, Bra.	256	23.11 S	47.16 W
Jundiaí do Sul	255	23.27 S	50.17 W
Jundiaí-mirim ≃	256	23.10 S	46.56 W
Jundiapeba	256	23.33 S	46.15 W
Jundu Shan ⋏	105	40.30 N	116.05 E
Juneau, Ak., U.S.	180	58.20 N	134.27 W
Juneau, Wi., U.S.	190	43.24 N	88.42 W
Junee	166	34.52 S	147.35 E
June in Winter, Lake ⊜	220	27.18 N	81.24 W
June Lake	226	37.46 N	119.04 W
June Park	220	28.04 N	80.41 W
Jungapeo de Juárez	234	19.27 N	100.29 W
Jungar Qi	102	39.49 N	111.10 E
Jungbluth Ditch ≅	279a	41.27 N	82.07 W
Jungfernheide ◆[3]	264a	52.34 N	13.17 E
Jungfernheide, Volkspark ♠	264a	52.33 N	13.16 E
Jungfern-Inseln → Virgin Islands □[2]	240m	18.20 N	64.50 W
Jungfern-See ⊜	264a	52.25 N	13.05 E
Jungfrau ∧	58	46.32 N	7.58 E
Jungfraujoch ◆	58	46.33 N	7.58 E
Junggar Pendi (Dzungarian Basin) ≚[1]	86	45.00 N	88.00 E
Jungle Habitat ♠	276	41.08 N	74.21 W
Junglinster	56	49.43 N	6.15 E
Jungshāhi	120	24.51 N	67.46 E
Juniata	198	40.35 N	98.30 W
Juniata □[6]	208	40.34 N	77.24 W
Juniata ◆[8]	285	40.01 N	75.07 W
Juniata ≃	188	40.24 N	77.01 W
Juniata, Frankstown Branch ≃	214	40.34 N	78.03 W
Juniata, Raystown Branch ≃	214	40.25 N	77.58 W
Juniata Gap	214	40.33 N	78.26 W
Juniata Terrace	208	40.35 N	77.34 W
Junín, Arg.	252	34.35 S	60.57 W
Junín, Ec.	246	0.56 S	80.13 W
Junín, Perú	248	11.10 S	76.00 W
Junín □[5]	248	11.30 S	75.00 W
Junín, Lago de ⊜	248	11.02 S	76.06 W
Junín de los Andes	254	39.56 S	71.05 W
Junior	188	38.59 N	79.57 W
Juniper	186	46.33 N	67.13 W
Junipero Serra Peak ∧	226	36.08 N	121.25 W
Juniville	50	49.24 N	4.23 E
Jūniyah	130	33.59 N	35.38 E
Junk Bay c	271d	22.17 N	114.15 E
Jun Kharchanai	123	36.52 N	75.01 E
Junk Island I	271d	22.17 N	114.16 E
Junkou	100	26.42 N	116.49 E
Junlian	102	28.08 N	104.35 E
Junliangcheng	105	39.04 N	117.27 E
Junling	100	28.17 N	116.28 E
Junnar	122	19.12 N	73.53 E
Juno Beach	220	26.52 N	80.04 W
Junqalī □[4]	140	7.30 N	32.20 E
Junqueiro	250	9.56 S	36.29 W
Junqueirópolis	255	21.32 S	51.26 W
Junsele	26	63.41 N	16.54 E
Juntas	236	10.16 N	85.00 W
Jun Ul Shan ⋏	102	37.30 N	97.00 E
Junxian	102	32.31 N	111.30 E
Jūō	94	36.40 N	140.41 E
Juodkrantė	76	55.33 N	21.08 E
Juodupė	76	56.05 N	25.37 E
Juojärvi ⊜	26	62.43 N	28.33 E
Juozapinės kalnas ∧[2]	76	54.32 N	25.37 E
Juparanã, Lagoa ⊜	255	19.35 S	40.18 W
Jupilingo ≃	236	14.48 N	89.14 W
Jupille	56	50.39 N	5.38 E
Jupiter	220	26.56 N	80.05 W
Jupiter ≃	186	49.29 N	63.37 W
Jupiter Inlet c	220	26.57 N	80.04 W
Jupiter Island I	220	27.04 N	80.07 W
Juqueri ≃	256	23.24 S	46.52 W
Juqueri, Reservatório do ⊜[1]	256	23.20 S	46.38 W
Juqueriquerê, Serra do ⋏	256	23.43 S	45.37 W
Juquiá	252	24.19 S	47.38 W
Juquiá ≃	256	23.56 S	47.09 W
Juquiá, Ponta do >	252	24.25 S	47.00 W
Juquiá-guaçu ≃	256	24.00 S	47.16 W
Juquitiba	256	23.57 S	47.03 W
Jur	74	59.52 N	137.39 E
Jur ≃	140	8.39 N	29.18 E
Jura	38	47.31 N	29.04 E
Jura □[3]	58	47.20 N	7.15 E
Jura □[5]	58	46.50 N	5.50 E
Jura ⋏	58	46.45 N	6.30 E
Jura I	46	56.00 N	5.50 W
Jūra ≃	76	55.03 N	22.09 E
Jura, Sound of ʊ	46	55.57 N	5.48 W
Juramento	255	16.50 S	43.35 W
Juratiški	76	54.02 N	25.54 E
Jurayrah, Jabal al- ∧	128	24.06 N	39.16 E
Jurays wa ʿIzbatuhā	142	30.19 N	30.55 E
Jurbarkas	76	55.05 N	22.48 E
Jurcevo	76	60.02 N	32.36 E
Juréia	256	21.17 S	46.22 W
Jurenino	76	59.24 N	42.47 E
Jurevići	78	51.57 N	29.32 E
Jurf ad-Darāwīsh	132	30.42 N	35.52 E
Jurga	86	55.42 N	84.51 E
Jurgamyš	86	55.21 N	64.28 E
Jurgenson Woods ♠	278	41.34 N	87.36 W
Jurien	162	30.19 S	115.02 E
Juriesfontein	158	31.40 S	22.08 E
Juring	164	6.26 S	134.20 E
Jurino	80	56.18 N	46.18 E
Jurja	24	59.03 N	49.14 E
Jurjev → Tartu	76	58.23 N	26.43 E
Jurjevec	80	57.18 N	43.06 E
Jurjev-Pol'skij	80	56.30 N	39.41 E
Jurjevskoje	82	55.05 N	36.13 E
Jurla	86	59.17 N	54.19 E
Jurlovo, Ross.	82	55.54 N	37.16 E
Jurlovo, Ross.	82	55.19 N	35.52 E
Jūrmala	76	56.58 N	23.42 E
Jurong, Sing.	271c	1.19 N	103.43 E
Jurong, Zhg.	106	31.57 N	119.10 E
Jurong ≃	271c	1.18 N	103.44 E
Jurong, Selat ʊ	271c	1.18 N	103.42 E
Jurovo, Ross.	80	57.30 N	43.50 E
Jurovo, Ross.	82	55.30 N	38.22 E
Jurovskoje	86	59.29 N	69.02 E
Jursla	40	58.40 N	16.11 E
Jurty	88	56.03 N	97.37 E
Juruá	246	3.27 S	66.03 W
Juruá ≃	242	2.37 S	65.44 W
Juruaia	256	21.15 S	46.35 W
Juruá-mirim ≃	248	8.08 S	72.48 W
Juruena ≃	248	7.20 S	58.03 W
Jurujuba, Enseada de c	287a	22.56 S	43.07 W
Jurumirim, Represa ⊜[1]	255	23.20 S	49.15 W
Jurumkuvejem ≃	180	66.14 N	173.35 E
Jurupari ≃	248	7.45 S	70.10 W
Jurupari, Arquipélago II	250	0.07 N	50.30 W
Jurupari, Ilha de I	250	0.20 N	50.07 W
Juruti	250	2.09 S	56.04 W
Jur'uzan'	86	54.52 N	58.26 E
Jur'uzan' ≃	86	55.42 N	57.00 E
Jurva	26	62.41 N	21.59 E
Jušala	86	57.04 N	64.17 E
Juscelândia	255	15.20 S	51.19 W
Jusepín	246	9.45 N	63.31 W
Jushiguan	102	24.47 N	97.38 E
Jūshiyama	94	35.06 N	136.46 E
Juskatla	182	53.37 N	132.18 W
Jus'ki	80	56.39 N	53.05 E
Juškovo	76	59.46 N	45.11 E
Juškozero	24	64.44 N	32.06 E
Jūsō ◆[8]	270	34.43 N	135.28 E
Jussey	58	47.49 N	5.54 E
Justa	80	47.07 N	46.18 E
Justice	278	41.44 N	87.50 W
Justin	222	33.05 N	97.18 W
Justineberg ∧[2]	40	58.43 N	15.04 E
Justiniano Posse	252	32.53 S	62.40 W
Justo Daract	252	33.52 S	65.11 W
Justus	214	40.42 N	81.35 W
Jušut ≃	80	56.12 N	48.23 E
Jus'va	24	58.56 N	54.57 E
Jutaí	248	5.11 S	68.54 W
Jutaí ≃	242	2.43 S	66.57 W
Jutaza	80	54.35 N	53.16 E
Jütchendorf	264a	52.16 N	13.10 E
Jüterbog	54	51.59 N	13.04 E
Juththah, Jabal al- ∧	132	30.12 N	35.36 E
Juti	255	22.52 S	54.37 W
Jutiapa	236	14.17 N	89.54 W
Jutiapa □[5]	236	14.10 N	89.50 W
Juticalpa	236	14.42 N	86.15 W
Jutiquile	236	14.45 N	86.08 W
Jutland → Jylland ◆[1]	26	56.00 N	9.15 E
Jutogh	123	31.06 N	77.07 E
Jutrosin	30	51.40 N	17.10 E
Juupajoki	26	61.47 N	24.27 E
Juuru	76	59.04 N	24.59 E
Juva	26	61.54 N	27.51 E
Juventud, Isla de la (Isla de Pinos) I	240p	21.40 N	82.50 W
Juvisy-sur-Orge	50	48.41 N	2.23 E
Juvuln ⊜	26	63.43 N	13.09 E
Juwana	115a	6.42 S	111.09 E
Juwangi	115a	7.10 S	110.45 E
Juxi	100	27.30 N	119.08 E
Juxian	98	35.37 N	118.54 E
Juxing	106	31.56 N	121.33 E
Juyanhai → Gaxun Nur ⊜	102	42.22 N	100.34 E
Juye	98	35.23 N	116.06 E
Jūyom	128	28.34 N	53.56 E
Juyongguan	105	40.18 N	116.04 E
Juža	80	56.35 N	42.01 E
Juzennecourt	58	48.11 N	4.59 E
Juzi ≃	98	40.18 N	123.35 E
Juziers	261	49.00 N	1.51 E
Južna Morava ≃	38	43.41 N	21.24 E
Južno-Aleksandrovka	88	55.51 N	96.10 E
Južno-Aličurskij chrebet ⋏	120	37.30 N	73.20 E
Južno-Golodnostepskij kanal ≅	85	40.15 N	69.08 E
Južno-Jenisejskij	86	58.48 N	94.39 E
Južno-Mujskij chrebet ⋏	88	55.40 N	114.00 E
Južno-Sachalinsk	89	46.58 N	142.42 E
Južno-Suchokumsk	84	44.37 N	45.34 E
Južno-Ural'sk	86	54.26 N	61.15 E
Južnyj, Kaz.	86	49.21 N	73.01 E
Južnyj, Ross.	80	56.08 N	44.09 E
Južnyj, Ross.	80	47.20 N	41.51 E
Južnyj, Ross.	86	53.14 N	83.42 E
Južnyj, Ross.	86	53.33 N	60.02 E
Južnyj, mys >	74	57.45 N	156.45 E
Južnyj-Alamyšik	85	40.46 N	72.38 E
Južnyj Prijut	84	43.12 N	41.55 E
Južnyj Ural ⋏	86	54.00 N	58.30 E
Juzovka → Donets'k	83	48.00 N	37.48 E
Jwālahari ◆[8]	272a	28.40 N	77.06 E
Jwayyā	132	33.14 N	35.19 E
Jyderup	41	55.40 N	11.26 E
Jylland (Jutland) ◆[1]	26	56.00 N	9.15 E
Jyllinge	41	55.45 N	12.07 E
Jyväskylä	26	62.14 N	25.44 E
K			
K2 (Qogir Feng) ∧	123	35.53 N	76.30 E
Ka ≃	150	11.40 N	4.10 E
Kaaawa	229c	21.33 N	157.51 W
Kaabong	154	3.31 N	34.08 E
Kaachka	128	37.21 N	59.36 E
Kaala ∧	229c	21.31 N	158.09 W
Kaalaea	229c	21.28 N	157.51 W
Kaala-Gomén	175f	20.40 S	164.25 E
Kaalspruit	158	29.15 S	26.10 E
Kaapahu Bay c	229a	20.39 N	156.05 W
Kaapmuiden	156	25.33 S	31.20 E
Kaappunt >	158	34.21 S	18.30 E
Kaapstad → Cape Town	158	33.55 S	18.22 E
Kaarli	76	59.24 N	26.27 E
Kaarssen	54	53.12 N	11.02 E
Kaarst	56	51.14 N	6.37 E
Kaaterskill Creek ≃	210	42.13 N	73.53 W
Kaatoan, Mount ∧	116	8.07 N	124.55 E
Kaatsheuvel	52	51.40 N	5.02 E
Kaavi	26	62.59 N	28.30 E
Kaba	150	10.09 N	11.40 W
Kaba ≃	86	47.53 N	86.12 E
Kaba, Goulbin V	150	13.42 N	6.19 E
Kabacan	116	7.08 N	124.49 E
Kabacan ≃	116	7.08 N	124.50 E
Kabadak	126	22.13 N	89.19 E
Kabadak ≃[1]	126	22.13 N	89.18 E
Kabadüz	130	40.53 N	37.56 E
Kabaena, Pulau I	112	5.15 S	121.55 E
Kabaena, Selat ʊ	112	5.00 S	122.00 E
Kabah ⊥	232	20.07 N	89.29 W
Kabala	150	9.35 N	11.33 W
Kabale	154	1.15 S	29.59 E
Kabalebo ≃	250	5.02 N	57.21 W
Kabalega Falls ∟	154	2.17 N	31.41 E
Kabalega Falls National Park ♠	154	2.15 N	31.50 E
Kabali, Indon.	112	1.42 S	121.54 E
Kabalı, Tür.	130	41.52 N	35.05 E
Kabalo	154	6.03 S	26.55 E
Kabambare	154	4.42 S	27.43 E
Kaban'	86	54.39 N	66.28 E
Kabangu Kuta	154	14.00 S	24.03 E
Kabanjahe	114	3.06 N	98.30 E
Kabankalan	116	9.59 N	122.49 E
Kabanovka	80	53.39 N	51.18 E
Kabanovo	86	55.20 N	70.52 E
Kabansk	88	52.03 N	106.39 E
Kabardinka	78	44.39 N	37.57 E
Kabardino-Balkarija □[3]	84	43.30 N	43.30 E
Kabasalan	116	7.48 N	122.45 E
Kabayan	116	16.37 N	120.51 E
Kabba	150	7.50 N	6.03 E
Kabbani ≃	122	12.13 N	76.54 E
Kåbdalis	24	66.10 N	20.00 E
Kabd aṣ-Ṣārim ◆[1]	130	34.34 N	39.33 E
Kabd Warqah ◆[1]	130	34.20 N	39.37 E
Kabel ◆[8]	263	51.24 N	7.29 E
Kabenung Lake ⊜	190	48.16 N	85.00 W
Kabetogama Lake ⊜	190	48.28 N	92.59 W
Kabeya	154	5.40 S	27.58 E
Kab-hegy ∧	30	47.03 N	17.39 E
Kabia ≃	146	9.54 N	15.10 E
Kabid, Wādī V	132	30.08 N	36.31 E
Kabinakagami Lake ⊜	190	48.54 N	84.25 W
Kabin Buri	110	13.59 N	101.43 E
Kabinda	152	6.08 S	24.29 E
Kabinu	112	4.00 N	116.05 E
Kabir	112	8.17 S	124.13 E
Kabira	175d	24.27 N	124.08 E
Kabīr Kili	123	33.11 N	71.19 E
Kabīr Kūh ⋏	128	33.25 N	46.45 E
Kabīrwāla	123	30.24 N	71.52 E
Kabkābīyah	140	13.39 N	24.05 E
Kablow	264a	52.18 N	13.44 E
Kablower Ziegelei	264a	52.19 N	13.43 E
Kablukovo, Ross.	82	56.50 N	36.12 E
Kablukovo, Ross.	82	56.02 N	38.10 E
Kablumgu, Cape >	164	6.20 S	150.00 E
Kabna	140	19.10 N	32.41 E
Kabo	152	7.39 N	18.37 E
Kabobo	154	5.07 S	29.03 E
Kaboe ≃	158	28.55 S	19.17 E
Kābol	120	34.31 N	69.12 E
Kābol □[4]	120	34.30 N	69.15 E
Kābol ≃	120	33.55 N	72.14 E
Kabompo	154	13.36 S	24.12 E
Kabompo ≃	138	14.10 S	23.11 E
Kabondo-Dianda	154	8.53 S	25.40 E
Kabongo, Zaïre	154	7.19 S	25.35 E
Kabongo, Zaïre	154	8.43 S	28.11 E
Kabongo-Lunda, Chutes ∟	152	7.34 S	17.17 E
Kaboro	152	6.59 N	17.33 E
Kabot	150	10.48 N	14.57 W
Kabotshome	154	3.46 S	26.54 E
Kabou, Centraf.	152	5.20 N	21.43 E
Kabou, Togo	150	9.27 N	0.49 E
Kaboudia, Rass >	148	35.14 N	11.10 E
Kaboul → Kābol	120	34.31 N	69.12 E
Kabr	140	10.54 N	26.50 E
Kabri	132	33.01 N	35.09 E
Kabūdarāhang	128	35.12 N	48.44 E
Kabūd Gonbad	128	37.00 N	59.45 E
Kābul → Kābol	120	34.30 N	69.11 E
Kabunda	154	12.25 S	29.22 E
Kabunga	154	1.42 S	28.08 E
Kabura ≃	94	36.17 N	139.04 E
Kaburuang, Pulau I	108	3.48 N	126.48 E
Kabūshīyah	140	16.53 N	33.42 E
Kabwanga	152	7.01 S	22.37 E
Kabwe (Broken Hill)	154	14.27 S	28.27 E
Kabwe-Katanda	152	7.59 S	24.29 E
Kabychivka	83	49.28 N	39.45 E
Kabylie ◆[1]	34	36.30 N	4.30 E
Kačalinskaja	80	49.07 N	44.03 E
Kačanik	38	42.13 N	21.14 E
Kačanovo	76	57.28 N	27.46 E
Kacbachskij	86	52.58 N	59.40 E
Kačerginė	76	54.56 N	23.44 E
Kacha	78	44.47 N	33.32 E
Kacha ≃[1]	126	22.23 N	89.54 E
Kachagalau ∧	154	2.19 N	35.03 E
Kach'ang-ni	98	38.24 N	126.11 E
Kachati	84	42.30 N	41.46 E
Kachchh, Gulf of c	120	22.36 N	69.30 E
Kachemak Bay c	180	59.35 N	151.30 W
Kachess Lake ⊜[1]	224	47.20 N	121.14 W
Kachhwa	124	25.13 N	82.43 E
Kachi	84	41.26 N	46.56 E
Kachia	150	9.53 N	7.58 E
Kachib	84	42.25 N	46.36 E
Kachin □[3]	102	26.00 N	97.30 E
Kach'i-ri	98	34.27 N	126.08 E
Kachisi	144	9.39 N	37.50 E
Kachkarivka	78	47.06 N	33.44 E

Symbol	English	Deutsch	Español	Français	Português
≃	River	Fluß	Río	Rivière	Rio
≅	Canal	Kanal	Canal	Canal	Canal
∟	Waterfall, Rapids	Wasserfall, Stromschnellen	Cascada, Rápidos	Chute d'eau, Rapides	Cascata, Rápidos
ʊ	Strait	Meeresstraße	Estrecho	Détroit	Estreito
c	Bay, Gulf	Bucht, Golf	Bahía, Golfo	Baie, Golfe	Baía, Golfo
⊜	Lake, Lakes	See, Seen	Lago, Lagos	Lac, Lacs	Lago, Lagos
≡	Swamp	Sumpf	Pantano	Marais	Pântano
⊐	Ice Features, Glacier	Eis- und Gletscherformen	Accidentes Glaciales	Formes glaciaires	Acidentes glaciares
⊤	Other Hydrographic Features	Andere Hydrographische Objekte	Otros Elementos Hidrográficos	Autres données hydrographiques	Outros acidentes hidrográficos
✦	Submarine Features	Untermeerische Objekte	Accidentes Submarinos	Formes de relief sous-marin	Acidentes submarinos
□	Political Unit	Politische Einheit	Unidad Politica	Entité politique	Unidade política
♥	Cultural Institution	Kulturelle Institution	Institución Cultural	Institution culturelle	Institução cultural
⊥	Historical Site	Historische Stätte	Sitio Histórico	Site historique	Sitio histórico
♠	Recreational Site	Erholungs- und Ferienort	Sitio de Recreo	Centre de loisirs	Area de Lazer
⊠	Airport	Flughafen	Aeropuerto	Aéroport	Aeroporto
■	Military Installation	Militäranlage	Instalación Militar	Installation militaire	Instalação militar
◆	Miscellaneous	Verschiedenes	Misceláneo	Divers	Diversos

Name	Page	Lat.°′	Long.°′
Kachowka-Stausee → Kakhovs'ke vodoskhovyshche ⊜[1]	78	47.25 N	34.10 E
K'achta	88	50.26 N	106.25 E
Kachua, Bngl.	126	22.39 N	89.53 E
Kachua, Bngl.	126	23.21 N	90.54 E
Kačiry	86	53.05 N	76.07 E
Kačkanar	86	58.42 N	59.38 E
Kačkanar, gora ʌ	86	58.47 N	59.23 E
Kaçkar Dağı ʌ	130	40.50 N	41.10 E
Kačug	88	53.58 N	105.52 E
Kada ≃	88	55.03 N	102.04 E
Kadada ≃	80	53.09 N	46.01 E
Kadaingti	110	17.37 N	97.32 E
Kadaiyanallūr	122	9.05 N	77.21 E
Kadamatt Island I	122	11.14 N	72.47 E
Kadaň	54	50.20 N	13.15 E
Kadanai (Kadaney) ≃	120	31.02 N	66.09 E
Kadaney (Kadanai) ≃	120	31.02 N	66.09 E
Kadan Kyun I	110	12.30 N	98.22 E
Kadapongan, Pulau I	112	4.43 S	115.44 E
Kadassa ≃	115b	9.24 S	120.02 E
Kaddam ⊜[1]	122	19.07 N	78.46 E
Kade	150	6.05 N	0.50 W
Kadéï ≃	152	3.31 N	16.05 E
Kadena	174m	26.22 N	127.45 E
Kadena Airfield ⊠	174m	26.22 N	127.45 E
Kadeshiki	80	58.08 N	49.11 E
Kadetrenden (Kadet Rinne) ʮ	41	54.30 N	12.15 E
Kadet Rinne (Kadetrenden) ʮ	41	54.30 N	12.15 E
Kadgo, Lake ⊜	162	26.42 S	127.18 E
Kadi	120	23.18 N	72.20 E
Kadiana	150	10.45 N	6.30 W
Kadıköy	130	40.46 N	26.46 E
Kadina	168b	33.58 S	137.43 E
Kading ≃	110	18.19 N	104.00 E
Kadınhanı	130	38.15 N	32.14 E
Kadiolo	150	10.33 N	5.46 W
Kadipaten	115a	6.46 S	108.10 E
Kādīpur	124	26.10 N	82.23 E
Kadiri	122	14.07 N	78.10 E
Kadirli	130	37.23 N	36.05 E
Kadışehri	130	40.00 N	35.49 E
Kadiyevka → Stakhanov	83	48.34 N	38.40 E
Kadja, Ouadi (Wādī Kaja) V	146	12.02 N	22.28 E
Kadkan	128	35.35 N	58.50 E
Kadnikov	76	59.30 N	40.20 E
Kadnikovskij	76	60.19 N	40.15 E
Kado	150	7.39 N	9.44 E
Ka-do I	98	39.33 N	124.40 E
Kadodo	140	11.04 N	29.31 E
Kadogawa	92	32.28 N	131.39 E
Kadoka	198	43.50 N	101.30 W
Kadom	80	54.34 N	42.30 E
Kadoma, Nihon	270	34.44 N	135.35 E
Kadoma, Zimb.	154	18.21 S	29.55 E
Kadoškino	80	54.01 N	44.25 E
Kadov	60	49.24 N	13.47 E
Kaduj	76	59.12 N	37.09 E
Kadumbul ≃	115b	9.42 S	120.32 E
Kaduna	150	10.33 N	7.27 E
Kaduna □[3]	150	10.30 N	7.45 E
Kaduna ≃	150	8.45 N	5.45 E
Kāduqlī	140	11.01 N	29.43 E
Kadūr	122	13.34 N	76.01 E
Kadyj	80	57.47 N	43.11 E
Kadykčan	74	63.02 N	146.50 E
Kadyšovo	80	54.20 N	46.45 E
Kadžerom	24	64.41 N	55.54 E
Kadži-Saj	85	42.08 N	77.10 E
Kaech'ŏn	98	39.42 N	125.53 E
Kaédi	150	16.09 N	13.30 W
Kaedo-ri	98	34.35 N	127.39 E
Kaegudeck Lake ⊜	186	48.07 N	55.11 W
Kaélé	146	10.07 N	14.27 E
Kaena Point ›	229c	21.35 N	158.17 W
Kaeo	172	35.06 S	173.47 E
Kaesŏng	98	37.59 N	126.33 E
Kāf	128	31.24 N	37.24 E
Kafakumba	152	9.41 S	23.44 E
Kafan	84	39.13 N	46.24 E
Kafanchan	150	9.36 N	8.17 E
Kaffraria □[9]	158	31.30 S	28.30 E
Kaffrine	150	14.06 N	15.33 W
Kafia Kingi	140	9.16 N	24.25 E
Kafin	150	9.30 N	7.04 E
Kafinda	154	12.39 S	30.20 E
Kafin Madaki	150	10.41 N	9.46 E
Kafirévs, Ákra ›	38	38.09 N	24.36 E
Kafirnigan ≃	120	36.58 N	68.02 E
Kafo ≃	154	1.08 N	31.05 E
Kafr ad-Dawwār	142	31.08 N	30.07 E
Kafr ad-Difrāwī	142	31.03 N	30.40 E
Kafr al-ʿĀ'id	142	30.27 N	31.35 E
Kafr al-Baṭṭīkh	142	31.24 N	31.44 E
Kafr al-Jarā'idah	142	31.13 N	31.16 E
Kafr ash-Shaykh	142	31.07 N	30.56 E
Kafr ash-Shaykh □[4]	142	31.15 N	30.50 E
Kafrat Ṭā'il Mūsā	142	30.53 N	29.44 E
Kafr at-Tamīmī	142	30.37 N	31.21 E
Kafr az-Zayyāt	142	30.49 N	30.49 E
Kafr Diyamā	142	30.48 N	30.52 E
Kafr el-Zaiyat → Kafr az-Zayyāt	142	30.49 N	30.49 E
Kafr Ḥakīm	273c	30.05 N	31.07 E
Kafr Ḥūnah	132	33.29 N	35.35 E
Kafr Kanna	132	32.45 N	35.20 E
Kafr Kilā al-Bāb	142	30.41 N	31.09 E
Kafr Nabrakh	132	33.42 N	35.38 E
Kafr Naffākh	132	33.04 N	35.44 E
Kafr Nāsij	132	33.09 N	36.03 E
Kafr Rabīʿ	142	30.42 N	30.50 E
Kafr Saʿd	142	31.19 N	31.39 E
Kafr Salīm	142	31.09 N	30.06 E
Kafr Ṣaqr	142	30.48 N	31.37 E
Kafr Shanawān	142	30.30 N	31.01 E
Kafr Shibīn	142	30.18 N	31.18 E
Kafr Shīmā	132	33.49 N	35.32 E
Kafr Shukr	142	30.33 N	31.16 E
Kafr Sūsah	132	33.29 N	36.16 E
Kafr Takhārīm	130	36.07 N	36.31 E
Kafr Ṭarkhān al-Gharbī	142	29.29 N	31.13 E
Kafr Yasif	132	32.57 N	35.10 E
Kafue	154	15.47 S	28.11 E
Kafue ≃	154	15.56 S	28.55 E
Kafue Flats ≚	154	15.40 S	27.25 E
Kafue Gorge V	154	15.54 S	28.34 E
Kafue National Park ♦	154	15.00 S	25.45 E
Kafulwe Mission	154	9.00 S	29.02 E
Kafumba	152	5.23 S	18.55 E
Kafwira	154	12.10 S	27.33 E
Kaga	94	36.18 N	136.18 E
Kaga Bandoro	152	6.59 N	19.11 E
Kagalaska Island I	180	51.47 N	176.23 W
Kagal'nickaja	83	46.53 N	40.09 E
Kagal'nik	83	47.05 N	39.19 E
Kagal'nik ≃	83	47.04 N	39.18 E
Kagami	96	33.37 N	133.26 E
Kagamigahara	94	35.24 N	136.54 E
Kagamil Island I	180	53.00 N	169.43 W
Kagamino	96	35.05 N	133.56 E
Kāgān, Pāk.	123	34.47 N	73.32 E
Kagan, Uzb.	128	39.43 N	64.33 E
Kagan Valley V	123	34.25 N	73.17 E
Kagarko	150	9.29 N	7.41 E
Kagawa	96	34.15 N	134.02 E
Kagawa □[5]	96	34.15 N	134.00 E
Kagawong, Lake ⊜	190	45.49 N	82.18 W
Kagaznagar	122	19.18 N	79.50 E
Kåge	26	64.50 N	20.59 E
Kagelike	120	37.20 N	87.02 E
Kagera (Akagera) ≃	154	0.57 S	31.47 E
Kågeröd	41	56.01 N	13.06 E
Kâgheṭ ⊕[1]	148	24.00 N	7.30 W
Kâğıthane ⊕[8]	267b	41.04 N	28.58 E
Kagitumba	154	1.04 S	30.27 E
Kağızman	84	40.09 N	43.08 E
Käglan ⋏[2]	40	59.23 N	15.31 E
Kagmar	140	14.24 N	30.25 E
Kagopal	146	8.17 N	16.27 E
Kagoshima	92	31.36 N	130.33 E
Kagoshima □[5]	93b	29.00 N	129.30 E
Kagoshima-wan C	92	31.25 N	130.38 E
Kagran ⊕[8]	264b	48.15 N	16.27 E
Kagulu	154	1.15 N	33.18 E
Kagyo-ri	98	34.25 N	126.48 E
Kahalīya, Jabal ʌ	142	29.55 N	32.09 E
Kahaluu	229c	21.27 N	157.50 W
Kahama	154	3.50 S	32.36 E
Kahana Bay C	229c	21.34 N	157.52 W
Kaharlyk	78	49.51 N	30.50 E
Kahayan ≃	112	3.20 S	114.04 E
Kahe	154	3.30 S	37.26 E
Kahemba	152	7.17 S	19.00 E
Kahia	154	6.21 S	28.24 E
Kahiu Point ›	229a	21.13 N	156.58 W
Kaḥk	142	29.25 N	30.38 E
Kahl ≃	56	50.04 N	9.00 E
Kahla	54	50.48 N	11.35 E
Kahl am Main	56	50.04 N	9.00 E
Kahlenberg ʌ[2]	264b	48.16 N	16.21 E
Kahler Asten ʌ	56	51.11 N	8.29 E
Kahlersberg ʌ	64	47.32 N	13.02 E
Kāhna	123	31.22 N	74.22 E
Kahnūj	128	27.58 N	57.45 E
Kahoka	194	40.25 N	91.43 W
Kahoku, Nihon	96	33.39 N	133.47 E
Kahoku, Nihon	96	33.06 N	130.41 E
Kahoku-gata ⊜	94	36.40 N	136.41 E
Kahoolawe I	229a	20.33 N	156.37 W
Kahouanne, Îlet à I	241o	16.22 N	61.47 W
Kahoué, Mont ʌ	150	7.06 N	7.15 W
Kahramanmaraş	130	37.36 N	36.55 E
Kahraman Maraş □[4]	130	38.00 N	37.05 E
Kahror Pakka	123	29.37 N	71.55 E
Kahshe Lake ⊜	212	44.52 N	79.16 W
Kâhta	130	37.46 N	38.36 E
Kahuku	229c	21.40 N	157.57 W
Kahuku Point ›	229c	21.43 N	157.59 W
Kahului	229a	20.54 N	156.28 W
Kahului Airport ⊠	229a	20.54 N	156.26 W
Kahului Bay C	229a	20.54 N	156.28 W
Kahurangi Point ›	172	40.47 S	172.13 E
Kahūta	123	33.35 N	73.23 E
Kahuzi-Biega, Parc National de ♦	154	1.50 N	28.40 E
Kahyŏn-bong ʌ	271b	37.38 N	126.39 E
Kahyŏn-ni	271b	37.32 N	126.44 E
Kai	164	2.15 S	136.32 E
Kai, Kepulauan II	164	5.35 S	132.45 E
Kai, Tanjung ›	112	2.52 S	118.45 E
Kaia, Wādī V	140	11.31 N	24.15 E
Kaiai, Jabal ʌ	140	19.54 N	36.48 E
Kaiama	150	9.37 N	3.58 E
Kaiapit	164	6.15 S	146.15 E
Kaiapoi	172	43.23 S	172.40 E
Kaibab Indian Reservation ⊕[4]	200	36.55 N	112.40 W
Kaibab Plateau ⋏[1]	200	36.30 N	112.15 W
Kaibara	96	35.08 N	135.05 E
Kai Beab	164	7.29 S	139.40 E
Kaibing	61	47.12 N	15.50 E
Kaibito Plateau ⋏[1]	200	36.40 N	111.20 W
Kaichengqiao	100	31.18 N	117.44 E
Kaida	94	35.56 N	137.36 E
Kaidori	268	35.37 N	139.27 E
Kaidu ≃	90	41.55 N	86.38 E
Kaiedin	140	9.45 N	32.11 E
Kaieteur Fall ∟	246	5.10 N	59.28 W
Kaieteur National Park ♦	246	5.10 N	59.45 W
Kaifeng	98	34.51 N	114.21 E
Kaifu	96	33.35 N	134.21 E
Kaifu ≃	96	33.35 N	134.22 E
Kaihe	98	35.42 N	116.20 E
Kaihu	172	35.46 S	173.42 E
Kaihua	100	29.09 N	118.23 E
Kai Iwi	172	39.51 S	174.56 E
Kaijian	102	23.42 N	111.48 E
Kaijiang	102	31.05 N	107.55 E
Kaijo → Kaesŏng	98	37.59 N	126.33 E
Kai Kecil I	164	5.45 S	132.40 E
Kaikohe	172	35.25 S	173.48 E
Kaikoura	172	42.25 S	173.41 E
Kaikoura Peninsula ›[1]	172	42.26 S	173.42 E
Kaikukang	89	53.07 N	124.46 E
Kailahun	150	8.17 N	10.34 W
Kailas → Kangrinboqê Feng ʌ	120	31.04 N	81.18 E
Kailāshahar	120	24.20 N	92.01 E
Kaili	102	26.35 N	107.55 E
Kailu	89	43.36 N	121.14 E
Kailua	229c	21.24 N	157.44 W
Kailua Bay C	229c	21.25 N	157.44 W
Kailua Kona	229d	19.22 N	155.59 W
Kaim ≃	164	6.40 S	141.45 E
Kaimai Range ⋏	172	37.45 S	175.55 E
Kaïmaktsalán ʌ	38	40.58 N	21.48 E
Kaimana	164	3.39 S	133.45 E
Kaimanawa Mountains ⋏	172	39.15 S	175.54 E
Kaiman-Inseln → Cayman Islands □[2]	238	19.30 N	80.40 W
Kaimenshan	104	41.03 N	123.08 E
Kaimganj	124	27.34 N	79.21 E
Kaimon-dake ʌ	92	31.11 N	130.32 E
Kain	50	50.38 N	3.22 E
Käina	76	58.50 N	22.45 E
Kainab ≃	158	28.31 S	19.35 E
Kainach ≃	61	46.54 N	15.31 E
Kainan, Nihon	96	33.36 N	134.22 E
Kainan, Nihon	96	34.09 N	135.12 E
Kainantu	164	6.15 S	145.55 E
Kainda	85	42.50 N	73.41 E
Kai-Ndunda	152	5.42 S	12.42 E
Kaingan ≃	115a	7.44 S	107.54 E
Kainji Lake ⊜[1]	150	10.30 N	4.35 E
Kaioba	112	5.20 S	122.37 E
Kaipara Harbour C	172	36.25 S	174.13 E
Kaiparowits Plateau ⋏[1]	200	37.20 N	111.15 W
Kaiping, Zhg.	102	22.23 N	112.35 E
Kaiping, Zhg.	105	39.41 N	118.16 E
Kaipuri, Pulau I	164	1.51 S	137.01 E
Kairābani	126	24.08 N	87.02 E
Kairaku-en ♦	94	36.22 N	140.27 E
Kairāna	124	29.24 N	77.12 E
Kairatu	164	3.21 S	128.22 E
Kairiru Island I	164	3.20 S	143.35 E
Kairo → Al-Qāhirah	142	30.03 N	31.15 E
Kairouan	148	35.41 N	10.07 E
Kairouan □[8]	148	35.30 N	9.55 E
Kairuku	164	8.50 S	146.35 E
Kaisarganj	124	27.15 N	81.33 E
Kaisariani	267c	37.58 N	23.47 E
Kaisariani Monastery ʊ[1]	267c	37.58 N	23.47 E
Kaisergebirge ⋏	64	47.36 N	12.20 E
Kaisermühlen ⊕[8]	264b	48.14 N	16.26 E
Kaiser Pass)(	226	37.17 N	119.06 W
Kaisersesch	56	50.14 N	7.08 E
Kaiserslautern	56	49.26 N	7.46 E
Kaiserstuhl ⋏[2]	58	48.06 N	7.40 E
Kaiserswerth ⊕[8]	263	51.18 N	6.44 E
Kaiser-Wilhelm-Museum ʊ	263	51.20 N	6.34 E
Kaishantun	98	42.43 N	129.43 E
Kaisheim	56	48.46 N	10.48 E
Kaišiadorys	76	54.52 N	24.27 E
Kait, Tanjung ›	112	3.14 S	106.05 E
Kaita	96	34.20 N	132.32 E
Kaitaia	172	35.07 S	173.16 E
Kaitaichi-chūtonchi, Rikujō-jieitai- ■	96	34.21 N	132.32 E
Kai Tak Airport ⊠	271d	22.20 N	114.12 E
Kaitangata	172	46.18 S	169.51 E
Kaitersberg ⋏	60	49.11 N	12.57 E
Kaithal	124	29.48 N	76.23 E
Kaituma ≃	246	8.11 N	59.41 W
Kaiwaka	172	36.10 S	174.27 E
Kaiwatu	164	8.07 S	127.49 E
Kaiwi Channel ʮ	229b	21.15 N	157.30 W
Kaixian	102	31.13 N	108.25 E
Kaiyang	102	26.58 N	106.40 E
Kaiyuan, Zhg.	102	23.44 N	103.11 E
Kaiyuan, Zhg.	104	42.32 N	124.01 E
Kaiyuancheng	98	42.37 N	124.04 E
Kaiyuh Mountains ⋏	180	64.00 N	158.00 W
Kaizhou	104	41.22 N	121.19 E
Kaizu	94	35.13 N	136.38 E
Kaizuka	96	34.27 N	135.21 E
Kaja, Wādī (Ouadi Kadja) V	146	12.02 N	22.28 E
Kajaani	26	64.14 N	27.41 E
Kajabbi	166	20.02 S	140.02 E
Kajakī, Band-e ⊜[1]	128	32.22 N	65.16 E
Kajang, Indon.	112	5.20 S	120.21 E
Kajang, Malay.	114	2.59 N	101.47 E
Kajang, Gunong ʌ	114	2.46 N	104.09 E
Kajasan	86	55.12 N	62.16 E
Kajasula	84	44.19 N	44.59 E
Kajen	115a	7.02 S	109.34 E
Kajgy	86	50.55 N	64.43 E
Kajiado	154	1.51 S	36.47 E
Kajikazawa	94	35.33 N	138.27 E
Kajiki	92	31.44 N	130.40 E
Kājlāgarh	126	22.02 N	87.47 E
Kajmanačicha	86	53.32 N	75.11 E
Kajmonovo	88	56.50 N	104.54 E
Kajmysovy	86	59.48 N	76.31 E
Kajnar	86	49.12 N	77.25 E
Kajo Kaji	154	3.53 N	31.40 E
Kajrakkum	85	40.16 N	69.49 E
Kajrakkumskoje vodochranilišče ⊜[1]	85	40.20 N	70.10 E
Kajrakty	86	48.31 N	73.14 E
Kajsackoje	80	49.44 N	46.51 E
Kājū ≃	128	25.34 N	61.13 E
Kājulia	126	23.01 N	89.57 E
Kajuru	150	10.21 N	7.40 E
Kaka, Centraf.	140	6.01 N	26.30 E
Kākā, Sūd.	140	10.36 N	32.11 E
Kaka, Lae o ›	229a	20.31 N	156.33 W
Kakabeka Falls ∟	190	48.24 N	89.37 W
Kakabia, Pulau I	112	6.54 S	122.13 E
Kakadu National Park ♦	164	13.00 S	132.45 E
Kakagi Lake ⊜	184	49.13 N	93.52 W
Kakamas	158	28.45 S	20.33 E
Kakamega	154	0.17 N	34.45 E
Kakamigahara	94	35.24 N	136.54 E
Kakana	110	9.07 N	92.49 E
Kakanui Mountains ⋏	172	45.09 S	170.26 E
Kaka Point	172	46.23 S	169.47 E
Kakaramea	172	39.43 S	174.27 E
Kakasa	164	9.20 S	148.45 E
Kakata	150	6.35 N	10.19 W
Kakatahi	172	39.41 S	175.20 E
Kākdwīp	126	21.53 N	88.11 E
Kake, Nihon	96	34.36 N	132.19 E
Kake, Ak., U.S.	180	56.58 N	133.56 W
Kakegawa	94	34.46 N	138.01 E
Kakehashi ≃	94	36.25 N	136.25 E
Kakelwe	154	4.49 S	29.00 E
Kakenge	152	4.51 S	21.55 E
Kakeya	96	35.11 N	132.49 E
Kakhonak	180	59.26 N	154.51 W
Kakhovka	78	46.47 N	33.30 E
Kakhovs'ke vodoskhovyshche ⊜[1]	78	47.25 N	34.10 E
Kakhra	126	21.38 N	87.27 E
Kākī	128	28.19 N	51.34 E
Kākināda	122	16.56 N	82.13 E
Kakino	80	55.12 N	44.53 E
Kakinoki	96	34.26 N	131.52 E
Kakisa Lake ⊜	176	60.55 N	117.40 W
Kakizaki	92	37.15 N	138.25 E
Kako ≃, Guy.	246	5.46 N	60.35 W
Kako ≃, Nihon	96	34.44 N	134.49 E
Kakoaka	156	18.40 S	24.22 E
Kakogawa	96	34.46 N	134.51 E
Kakrāla	272a	28.33 N	77.25 E
Kāksa	126	23.28 N	87.28 E
Kaktovik	180	70.08 N	143.37 W
Kakuda	92	37.58 N	140.47 E
Kakui-shima I	96	34.43 N	134.19 E
Kakuma	154	3.43 N	34.52 E
Kakunodate	92	39.35 N	140.34 E
Kakus ≃	112	2.46 N	113.01 E
Kakwa ≃	182	54.36 N	118.28 W
Kala	146	12.05 N	14.27 E
Kala ≃	122	8.18 N	79.50 E
Kalaa Kebira	148	35.52 N	10.32 E
Kalaallit Nunaat → Greenland □[2]	16	70.00 N	40.00 W
Kalaa Sghira	36	35.49 N	10.33 E
Kālābāgh	123	32.58 N	71.34 E
Kalabahi	112	8.13 S	124.31 E
Kalabáka	38	39.42 N	21.43 E
Kalabakan	112	4.25 N	117.29 E
Kalabo	152	14.57 S	22.40 E
Kalabula	86	43.24 N	83.06 E
Kalač	78	50.25 N	41.01 E
Kalačinsk	86	55.03 N	74.34 E
Kalač-Kurtlak	80	49.00 N	42.26 E
Kalač-na-Donu	80	48.43 N	43.31 E
Kalačskaja vozvyšennost' ⋏[1]	80	50.30 N	41.30 E
Kaladan ≃	110	20.09 N	92.57 E
Kaladar	212	44.39 N	77.07 W
Kalae	229a	21.10 N	157.00 W
Ka Lae ›	229d	18.55 N	155.41 W
Kalaena ≃	112	2.40 S	120.53 E
Kalagan	89	50.30 N	119.55 E
Kalagwe	110	22.31 N	96.31 E
Kalahari Desert ⊕[2]	156	24.00 S	21.30 E
Kalahari Gemsbok National Park ♦	156	25.30 S	20.30 E
Kalaheo	229b	21.55 N	159.31 W
Kālaia	126	22.23 N	90.36 E
Kalai-Chumb	85	38.28 N	70.46 E
Kalai-Mor	128	35.39 N	62.33 E
Kalais	80	52.38 N	42.38 E
Kalaiyā	124	27.02 N	85.00 E
Kalajka	88	58.28 N	111.46 E
Kalajoki	26	64.15 N	23.57 E
Kalajoki ≃	26	64.17 N	23.55 E
Kalakamate	156	20.39 S	27.21 E
Kalakan	88	55.08 N	116.45 E
Kalakan ≃	88	55.07 N	116.46 E
Kalakepen	114	2.45 N	97.50 E
Kalām	123	35.32 N	72.35 E
Kalama, Wa., U.S.	224	46.00 N	122.50 W
Kalama, Zaïre	154	2.55 S	28.33 E
Kalama ≃	224	46.02 N	122.52 W
Kalama, Pulau I	112	3.15 N	125.28 E
Kalámai	38	37.04 N	22.07 E
Kalamákion	267c	37.55 N	23.43 E
Kalamalka Lake ⊜	182	50.09 N	119.22 W
Kalamariá	0	40.35 N	22.58 E
Kalamazoo	216	42.17 N	85.35 W
Kalamazoo □[6]	216	42.14 N	85.32 W
Kalamazoo ≃	216	42.40 N	86.10 W
Kalamazoo, North Branch ≃	216	42.14 N	84.44 W
Kalamazoo, South Branch ≃	216	42.14 N	84.44 W
Kalamazoo Lake C	216	42.39 N	86.13 W
Kalamb	122	19.03 N	73.57 E
Kalamba	152	0.26 S	18.17 E
Kalambau, Pulau I	112	4.55 S	115.39 E
Kalambo Falls ∟	154	8.36 S	31.14 E
Kalamboli	272c	19.01 N	73.06 E
Kalamits'ka zatoka C	78	45.05 N	33.23 E
Kalamo	216	42.32 N	85.01 W
Kalampising	112	3.44 N	116.42 E
Kalamunda	168a	31.57 S	116.03 E
Kalamunda National Park ♦	168a	31.59 S	116.04 E
Kalana	150	10.47 N	8.12 W
Kalanchak	78	46.16 N	33.17 E
Kalandula	152	9.06 S	15.57 E
Kalange-Bushimaie ≃	152	7.55 S	23.11 E
Kalanguj	88	51.01 N	116.31 E
Kalankalan	150	10.07 N	8.54 W
Kalannie	162	30.21 S	117.04 E
Kalanshiyū ar-Ramlī al-Kabīr, Sarīr ⊥[8]	146	28.00 N	23.00 E
Kālānwāli	123	29.51 N	74.57 E
Kalao, Pulau I	112	7.18 S	120.58 E
Kalaong	116	6.04 N	124.28 E
Kalaotoa, Pulau I	112	7.22 S	121.47 E
Kalapana	229d	19.21 N	154.58 W
Kalāpāra	126	21.59 N	90.14 E
Kalar ≃	88	55.23 N	116.18 E
Kalār, Kūh-e ʌ	128	31.50 N	50.53 E
Kälarne	26	62.59 N	16.05 E
Kālāroa	126	22.52 N	89.02 E
Kalasarv	84	39.11 N	48.03 E
Kalasi	86	48.43 N	86.59 E
Kalasin, Indon.	112	0.12 N	114.16 E
Kalasin, Thai	110	16.29 N	103.30 E
Kalašnikovo	76	57.17 N	35.13 E
Kalāt	120	29.02 N	66.35 E
Kalatungan Mountain ʌ	116	7.58 N	124.47 E
Kalaupapa	229a	21.11 N	156.59 W
Kalaupapa National Historical Park ♦	229a	21.12 N	156.58 W
Kalaupapa Peninsula ›[1]	229a	21.13 N	156.58 W
Kalauri	84	41.49 N	45.42 E
Kalaus ≃	80	45.43 N	44.07 E
Kalavárdha	38	36.20 N	27.57 E
Kalávrita	38	38.01 N	22.06 E
Kalaw	110	20.38 N	96.34 E
Kalawao □[6]	229a	21.12 N	156.58 W
Kal'azin	76	57.15 N	37.52 E
Kalb, Nahr al- ≃	132	33.57 N	35.35 E
Kalb, Ra's al- ›	144	14.02 N	48.41 E
Kalbā'	128	25.03 N	56.21 E
Kälbäcär	84	40.07 N	46.02 E
Kalbar	171a	27.56 S	152.37 E
Kalbarri	162	27.42 S	114.09 E
Kalbarri National Park ♦	162	27.45 S	114.25 E
Kalbe	54	52.40 N	11.25 E
Kalbinskij chrebet ⋏	86	49.10 N	83.00 E
Kalchās	120	29.21 N	69.42 E
Kal'chyk ≃	83	47.07 N	37.36 E
Kaldırım ≃	267b	41.10 N	29.12 E
Kaldygajty ≃	80	49.20 N	52.38 E
Kale, Tür.	130	40.23 N	39.39 E
Kale, Tür.	130	36.14 N	29.59 E
Kale, Tür.	130	37.26 N	28.51 E
Kalecik, Tür.	130	40.06 N	33.25 E
Kalecik, Tür.	130	37.17 N	39.02 E
Kaleden	182	49.23 N	119.35 W
Kaledupa, Pulau I	112	5.32 S	123.47 E
Kalegauk Island I	110	15.32 N	97.40 E
Kalehe	154	2.06 S	28.55 E
Kaleindaung ≃	110	18.50 N	94.00 E
Kalema, Tan.	154	1.12 S	31.50 E
Kalema, Zaïre	152	4.08 S	24.15 E
Kalemie (Albertville)	154	5.56 S	29.12 E
Kalemyo	120	23.12 N	94.10 E
Kalene Hill	152	11.11 S	24.10 E
Kaleščatovka	83	49.35 N	39.55 E
Kaletwa	110	21.45 N	92.48 E
Kalety	30	50.34 N	18.54 E
Kalevala	24	65.13 N	31.08 E
Kalewa	110	23.12 N	94.17 E
Kale Water ≃	46	55.32 N	2.28 W
Kaleybar	128	38.47 N	47.02 E
Kálfafell	24a	63.58 N	17.40 W
Kalga	88	50.57 N	118.48 E
Kalgačicha	24	63.20 N	36.44 E
Kalgan, Austl.	162	34.53 S	118.01 E
Kalgan → Zhangjiakou, Zhg.	105	40.50 N	114.53 E
Kalgin Island I	180	60.28 N	151.55 W
Kalgoorlie-Boulder	162	30.45 S	121.28 E
Kalhe	272c	18.52 N	73.06 E
Kali	150	12.10 N	11.29 W
Kāli ≃[1]	126	23.40 N	89.12 E
Kālia	126	23.03 N	89.38 E
Kāliāganj	124	25.38 N	88.19 E
Kāliāghaj ≃	126	22.10 N	87.50 E
Kāliākair	126	24.05 N	90.14 E
Kaliakra, nos ›	38	43.21 N	28.27 E
Kalianda	115a	5.45 S	105.38 E
Kalianget	115a	7.03 S	113.56 E
Kalibek, ozero ⊜	86	53.52 N	70.40 E
Kālībhīt Hills ⋏[2]	124	22.10 N	77.30 E
Kalibo	116	11.43 N	122.22 E
Kalida	216	40.59 N	84.12 W
Kalifornien, Golf von → California, Golfo de C	232	28.00 N	112.00 W
Kālī Gaṇḍakī ≃	124	27.42 N	84.25 E
Kāliganga ≃	126	23.43 N	90.15 E
Kālīganj, Bngl.	126	23.55 N	90.34 E
Kālīganj, Bngl.	126	23.25 N	89.08 E
Kālīganj, Bngl.	126	22.28 N	89.02 E
Kāliganj, India	126	23.44 N	88.14 E
Kalihiwai ≃	229b	22.13 N	159.26 W
Kalijati	115a	6.32 S	107.40 E
Kālikāpur, Bngl.	126	22.43 N	89.26 E
Kālikāpur, Bngl.	126	23.46 N	89.55 E
Kālikāpur, India	126	22.37 N	86.17 E
Kālikāpur, India	272b	22.29 N	88.32 E
Kalikino, Ross.	76	52.57 N	39.50 E
Kalikino, Ross.	80	52.55 N	54.05 E
Kalima, Zaïre	154	2.34 S	26.37 E
Kalima, Zhg.	104	41.32 N	122.40 E
Kalimantan → Borneo I	112	0.30 N	114.00 E
Kalimantan Barat □[4]	112	0.30 N	110.00 E
Kalimantan Selatan □[4]	112	2.30 S	115.30 E
Kalimantan Tengah □[4]	112	2.00 S	113.30 E
Kalimantan Timur □[4]	112	1.30 N	116.30 E
Kálimnos	38	36.57 N	26.59 E
Kálimnos I	38	37.00 N	27.00 E
Kālimpang	124	27.04 N	88.29 E
Kalina, Pointe de ›	273b	4.18 S	15.16 E
Kālīnadi ≃	122	14.50 N	74.08 E
Kālinagar	126	22.26 N	88.51 E
Kalinga-Apayao □[4]	116	17.50 N	121.10 E
Kalinga Bil ⊜	272b	22.33 N	88.33 E
Kalinin, Ross.	80	47.11 N	42.10 E
Kalinin → Tver', Ross.	82	56.52 N	35.55 E
Kalininabad	85	39.45 N	69.08 E
Kaliningrad (Königsberg), Ross.	76	54.43 N	20.30 E
Kaliningrad, Ross.	82	55.55 N	37.49 E
Kaliningrad Oblast' □[4]	76	54.45 N	21.15 E
Kalinino, Ross.	78	45.07 N	39.00 E
Kalinino, Ross.	80	46.21 N	48.53 E
Kalinino, Ross.	86	57.20 N	56.20 E
Kalinino, Ross.	89	49.24 N	129.20 E
Kalininsk, Kyrg.	85	42.29 N	72.06 E
Kalininsk, Ross.	80	51.30 N	44.28 E
Kalininskaja, Ross.	78	45.29 N	38.40 E
Kalininskaja, Ross.	80	47.52 N	42.15 E
Kalinins'ke	78	47.07 N	32.59 E
Kalininskoje	85	42.50 N	73.49 E
Kalinkoviči	76	52.08 N	29.21 E
Kalinku	154	11.12 S	33.12 E
Kalinovik	38	43.31 N	18.26 E
Kalinovka, Kaz.	86	49.58 N	55.22 E
Kalinovka, Ross.	78	51.54 N	34.28 E
Kalinovo	82	54.54 N	37.17 E
Kālipur	272b	22.41 N	88.17 E
Kaliro	154	0.54 N	33.30 E
Kalis	144	8.23 N	49.05 E
Kalisat	115a	8.08 S	113.48 E
Kalisch → Kalisz	30	51.46 N	18.06 E
Kāli Sindh ≃	124	25.32 N	76.17 E
Kalispell	202	48.11 N	114.18 W
Kalistraticha	86	52.59 N	83.35 E
Kalisz	30	51.46 N	18.06 E
Kalisz □[4]	30	51.40 N	17.45 E
Kalisz Pomorski	30	53.19 N	15.54 E
Kalitva ≃	78	48.10 N	40.46 E
Kaliua	154	5.04 S	31.48 E
Kaliveli Tank ⊜[1]	122	12.05 N	79.50 E
Kaliwiro	115a	7.27 S	109.51 E
Kaliwungu	115a	6.57 S	110.14 E
Kalix	26	65.51 N	23.08 E
Kalixälven ≃	24	65.50 N	23.11 E
Kālka	123	30.50 N	76.56 E
Kālkāji ⊕[8]	272a	28.33 N	77.16 E
Kalkaman	86	51.58 N	76.02 E
Kalkan	130	36.15 N	29.24 E
Kalkar	52	51.44 N	6.18 E
Kalkaska	190	44.44 N	85.10 W
Kalkfeld	156	20.53 S	16.11 E
Kalkfontein	156	22.08 S	20.53 E
Kalkfonteindam ⊜[1]	158	29.30 S	25.15 E
Kalkhorst	54	53.58 N	11.02 E
Kalkım	130	39.48 N	27.13 E
Kālkini	126	23.06 N	90.16 E
Kalkmond	158	28.40 S	20.26 E
Kalkrand	156	24.03 S	17.33 E
Kalksburg ⊕[8]	264b	48.08 N	16.15 E
Kalk-See ⊜	264a	52.26 N	13.46 E
Kalkstasie	158	30.00 S	18.55 E
Kalkum ⊕[8]	263	51.18 N	6.46 E
Kalkutta → Calcutta	126	22.32 N	88.22 E
Kalkwerf	158	28.39 S	21.43 E
Kall	56	50.32 N	6.32 E
Kallakkurichchi	122	11.44 N	78.58 E
Kallakoopah Creek ≃	166	27.29 S	138.15 E
Kållandsö I	26	58.40 N	13.09 E
Kallang ≃	271c	1.19 N	103.52 E
Kallar Kahār	123	32.47 N	72.42 E
Kallaste	76	58.39 N	27.09 E
Kallavesi ⊜	26	62.50 N	27.45 E
Kalletal	52	52.06 N	8.56 E
Källfallet	40	59.50 N	15.31 E
Kallhäll	40	59.27 N	17.48 E
Kalliecahoolie Lake ⊜	184	54.14 N	95.29 W
Kallinge	26	56.14 N	15.17 E
Kallista	274b	37.53 S	145.22 E
Kallithéa	267c	37.57 N	23.42 E
Kallmünz	60	49.09 N	11.58 E
Kallnach	58	47.01 N	7.14 E
Kallsjön ⊜	26	63.37 N	13.00 E
Kalmakkora	86	44.03 N	78.44 E
Kalmakkyrgan ≃	86	46.58 N	64.30 E
Kalmar	26	56.40 N	16.22 E
Kalmar Län □[6]	26	57.20 N	16.00 E
Kalmarsund ʮ	26	56.40 N	16.25 E
Kalmit ʌ	56	49.19 N	8.05 E
Kal'mius ≃	83	47.05 N	37.34 E
Kalmthout	50	51.23 N	4.28 E
Kalmyckije Mysy	86	51.53 N	82.16 E
Kalmykia → Kalmykija □[3]	72	46.30 N	45.30 E
Kalmykija □[3]	72	46.30 N	45.30 E
Kalmykivka, Ukr.	83	49.17 N	38.39 E
Kalmykivka, Ukr.	83	49.17 N	39.52 E
Kalmykov	80	49.01 N	42.49 E
Kalmykovo	80	49.03 N	51.47 E
Kālna	126	23.13 N	88.22 E
Kalnciems	76	56.50 N	23.37 E
Kalnibolotskaja	78	46.01 N	40.28 E
Kalničko Gorje ⋏	36	46.10 N	16.30 E
Kal'nyboloto	78	48.44 N	31.00 E
Kalo	164	10.00 S	147.45 E
Kálócfa	61	46.45 N	16.34 E
Kalocsa	30	46.32 N	18.59 E
Kalofer	38	42.37 N	24.59 E
Kalohi Channel ʮ	229a	21.00 N	156.56 W
Kaloko	154	6.47 S	25.48 E
Kalol, India	120	22.36 N	73.27 E
Kālol, India	120	23.15 N	72.29 E
Kalole	154	3.42 S	27.22 E
Kalolio	112	0.11 S	121.38 E
Kaloli Point ›	229d	19.38 N	154.57 W
Kalomo	154	17.02 S	26.30 E
Kalomo ≃	154	17.57 S	26.24 E
Kalona	190	41.28 N	91.42 W
Kalonda	152	4.48 S	17.33 E
Kalone Peak ʌ	182	52.38 N	126.37 W
Kalonga	154	9.10 S	27.25 E
Kalorama	274b	37.49 S	145.22 E
Kaloran	115a	7.15 S	110.15 E
Kalø Vig C	41	56.15 N	10.25 E
Kalpáki	38	39.53 N	20.38 E
Kalpeni Island I	122	10.05 N	73.38 E
Kālpi	124	26.07 N	79.44 E
Kāl Qalʿeh	128	32.38 N	62.32 E
Kalri	123	31.39 N	72.33 E
Kalsdorf bei Graz	61	46.57 N	15.28 E
Kalskag	180	61.30 N	160.23 W
Kalsūbai ʌ	122	19.36 N	73.43 E
Kaltag	180	64.20 N	158.44 W
Kaltan	86	53.30 N	87.17 E
Kaltbrunn	58	47.12 N	9.02 E
Kalte Herberge ʌ	56	50.03 N	7.59 E
Kalteneber	56	51.19 N	10.08 E
Kaltenhouse	56	48.48 N	7.50 E
Kaltenkirchen	52	53.50 N	9.58 E
Kaltenleutgeben	264b	48.07 N	16.12 E
Kaltennordheim	56	50.38 N	10.10 E
Kaltensundheim	56	50.36 N	10.10 E
Kalter Gang ≃	264b	48.02 N	16.25 E
Kalthof	263	51.26 N	7.40 E
Kal'tino	265a	59.58 N	30.40 E
Kaltungo	146	9.50 N	11.19 E
Kaluga	82	54.31 N	36.16 E
Kaluga Oblast' □[4]	76	54.30 N	35.30 E
Kalugino, Kaz.	80	48.22 N	51.33 E
Kalugino, Ross.	82	54.59 N	37.11 E
Kalukalukuang, Pulau I	112	5.14 S	117.38 E
Kālu Khuhar	120	25.08 N	67.46 E
Kalulushi	154	12.50 S	28.03 E
Kalumba, Mount ʌ	166	31.49 S	146.22 E
Kalumburu	164	14.18 S	126.39 E
Kalumburu Aboriginal Reserve ⊕[4]	164	14.15 S	126.50 E
Kalundborg	41	55.41 N	11.06 E
Kalundborg Fjord C	41	55.41 N	11.00 E
Kālundri	272c	18.59 N	73.08 E
Kalundu, Zaïre	154	3.26 S	29.08 E
Kalundu, Zam.	154	10.16 S	29.24 E
Kalungwishi ≃	154	9.01 S	28.57 E
Kalūr Kot	123	32.09 N	71.16 E
Kalush	78	49.03 N	24.23 E
Kałuszyn	30	52.13 N	21.49 E
Kalutara	122	6.35 N	79.58 E
Kalvåg	26	61.46 N	4.53 E
Kalvarija	76	54.21 N	23.14 E
Kälväz	84	38.39 N	48.18 E
Kalvehave	41	55.00 N	12.10 E
Kälviä	26	63.52 N	23.26 E
Kalwa	272c	19.12 N	72.59 E
Kalwang	61	47.26 N	14.46 E
Kalwaria Zebrzydowska	30	49.52 N	19.41 E
Kalyān	122	19.15 N	73.09 E
Kalyāndurg	122	14.33 N	77.06 E
Kalynivka, Ukr.	78	50.14 N	30.14 E
Kalynivka, Ukr.	78	49.27 N	28.32 E
Kalynove	83	48.34 N	38.31 E
Kam ≃	146	8.15 N	11.00 E
Kama, Mya.	110	19.02 N	95.06 E
Kama, Ross.	80	56.19 N	54.06 E
Kama, Ross.	86	60.08 N	62.10 E
Kama, Zaïre	154	3.32 S	27.07 E
Kama ≃, Ross.	72	55.45 N	52.00 E
Kama ≃, Ross.	86	55.35 N	76.54 E
Kamachumu	154	1.35 S	31.37 E
Kamado-zaki ›	96	33.04 N	132.02 E
Kamae	92	32.48 N	131.56 E
Kamagaya	94	35.45 N	140.01 E
Kamaiki Point ›	229a	20.46 N	156.50 W
Kamaishi	92	39.16 N	141.53 E
Kama-iwa I	174f	24.47 N	141.17 E
Kamajai	76	55.49 N	25.30 E
Kamakou ʌ	229a	21.07 N	156.52 W
Kamakura	94	35.19 N	139.33 E
Kamakwie	150	9.30 N	12.14 W
Kamal	115a	7.10 S	112.42 E
Kamālia	123	30.44 N	72.39 E
Kamamaung	110	17.21 N	97.40 E
Kāman, India	124	27.39 N	77.16 E
Kaman, Tür.	130	39.22 N	33.44 E
Kaman ≃	110	14.48 N	106.51 E
Kamana	154	5.59 S	24.56 E
Kamanashi ≃	94	35.33 N	138.28 E
Kamango	154	0.39 N	29.53 E
Kamaniskeg Lake ⊜	212	45.25 N	77.42 W
Kamanjab	156	19.35 S	14.51 E
Kamapanda	152	12.00 S	24.10 E
Kamara Forest ♦	264c	47.26 N	19.00 E
Kamarān I	144	15.21 N	42.35 E
Kamaran, Hadjer ʌ	146	12.41 N	21.46 E
Kamarang ≃	246	5.53 N	60.35 W
Kāmāreddi	122	18.19 N	78.21 E
Kāmārhāti	272b	22.40 N	88.22 E
Kamarik	130	39.37 N	39.18 E
Kāmārkhāli Ghāt	126	23.32 N	89.33 E
Kāmārkunda	272b	22.49 N	88.13 E
Kamas	200	40.38 N	111.16 W
Kamata ⊕[8]	268	35.33 N	139.43 E
Kamatsi Lake ⊜	184	56.10 N	102.15 W
Kamay	196	33.51 N	98.48 W
Kamba	150	11.53 N	3.36 E
Kamba Kota	152	7.10 N	17.54 E
Kambalda	162	31.12 S	121.40 E
Kambam	122	9.44 N	77.18 E
Kambang	112	1.42 S	100.42 E
Kambanga	152	13.23 S	23.03 E
Kambar	120	27.36 N	68.00 E
Kambara	94	35.07 N	138.36 E
Kambara Island I	175g	18.57 S	178.57 W
Kambara-tunnel ⊕[5]	94	35.02 N	138.31 E
Kambarka	80	56.17 N	54.12 E
Kambia	150	9.07 N	12.55 W
Kambja	76	58.14 N	26.42 E
Kambolé	150	8.45 N	1.36 E
Kambole Mission	154	8.46 S	30.46 E
Kambove	154	10.52 S	26.38 E
Kambu	115b	8.23 S	118.20 E
Kambuye	152	7.18 S	22.50 E
Kamčatka ≃	74	56.15 N	162.30 E
Kamčatka, poluostrov (Kamchatka) ›[1]	74	56.00 N	160.00 E
Kamčatskij poluostrov ›[1]	74	56.15 N	163.00 E
Kamčatskij zaliv C	74	55.35 N	162.21 E
Kamchatka → Kamčatka, poluostrov ›[1]	74	56.00 N	160.00 E
Kâmchay Méa	110	11.35 N	105.40 E
Kamčija ≃	38	43.02 N	27.53 E
Kāmdebpur, India	272b	22.47 N	88.30 E
Kāmdebpur, India	272b	22.54 N	88.20 E
Kāmdeysh	123	35.24 N	71.20 E
Kameari ⊕[8]	268	35.46 N	139.51 E
Kameda	92	37.52 N	139.07 E
Kameel	158	26.38 S	24.58 E
Kamegamori ʌ	96	33.47 N	133.12 E
Kameido ⊕[8]	268	35.42 N	139.50 E
Kamelik ≃	80	52.06 N	49.30 E
Kamen', Bela.	76	55.01 N	28.53 E
Kamen, Dtsch.	52	51.35 N	7.40 E
Kamen', gora ʌ	74	69.06 N	94.48 E
Kamenda	154	6.28 S	24.33 E
Kamenec	76	52.24 N	23.49 E
Kameng ≃	120	26.38 N	92.54 E
Kamenický Šenov	54	50.45 N	14.29 E
Kamenjak, Rt ›	36	44.46 N	13.55 E
Kamenka, Kaz.	80	51.07 N	50.19 E
Kamenka, Kaz.	85	42.55 N	72.50 E
Kamenka, Kaz.	86	52.22 N	69.04 E
Kamenka, Ross.	24	65.54 N	44.05 E
Kamenka, Ross.	78	50.43 N	39.25 E
Kamenka, Ross.	80	56.11 N	45.35 E
Kamenka, Ross.	80	57.23 N	41.49 E
Kamenka, Ross.	80	53.13 N	44.03 E
Kamenka, Ross.	80	52.04 N	41.49 E
Kamenka, Ross.	82	54.43 N	38.19 E
Kamenka, Ross.	82	56.11 N	37.18 E
Kamenka, Ross.	82	55.13 N	36.59 E
Kamenka, Ross.	86	58.33 N	95.51 E
Kamenka, Ross.	89	44.28 N	136.01 E
Kamenka, Ross.	265a	59.59 N	30.53 E
Kamenka ⊕[8]	265a	60.03 N	30.11 E
Kamenka ≃, Ross.	83	47.30 N	38.54 E
Kamenka ≃, Ross.	88	58.33 N	95.51 E
Kamenka ≃, Ross.	265a	60.01 N	30.12 E
Kamen'-na-Obi	86	53.47 N	81.20 E
Kamennogorsk	24	60.58 N	29.07 E
Kamennomostskij	84	44.18 N	40.12 E
Kamennyj Brod	83	47.26 N	39.51 E
Kamennyj Jar	80	48.27 N	45.34 E
Kamenolomni	83	47.40 N	40.13 E
Kamen'-Rybolov	89	44.46 N	132.02 E
Kamensk	88	51.58 N	106.36 E
Kamenskij	80	50.53 N	45.29 E
Kamenskoje, Ross.	74	62.30 N	166.12 E
Kamenskoje, Ross.	82	55.16 N	36.50 E
Kamensk-Šachtinskij	83	48.21 N	40.19 E
Kamensk-Ural'skij	86	56.28 N	61.54 E
Kamenz	54	51.16 N	14.06 E
Kameoka	96	35.00 N	135.35 E
Kamerik	52	52.06 N	4.54 E
Kamerun → Cameroon □[1]	134	6.00 N	12.00 E
Kamerunberg → Cameroon Mountain ʌ	152	4.12 N	9.11 E
Kames	46	55.54 N	5.15 W
Kameškovo	80	56.21 N	41.00 E
Kāmet ʌ	120	30.54 N	79.37 E
Kameur, Bahr ≃	146	9.26 N	20.50 E
Kameyama	94	34.51 N	136.27 E
Kami, Nihon	94	34.41 N	137.42 E
Kami, Nihon	96	35.05 N	134.53 E
Kamiah	202	46.13 N	116.01 W
Kamiak Butte ʌ	202	46.52 N	117.10 W
Kamiakotani	270	34.56 N	135.23 E
Kamiasō	268	35.35 N	139.30 E
Kamień Krajeński	30	53.33 N	17.32 E
Kamienna ≃	30	51.06 N	21.47 E
Kamienna Góra	30	50.47 N	16.01 E
Kamień Pomorski	30	53.58 N	14.46 E
Kamieńsk	30	51.12 N	19.30 E
Kamieskroon	156	30.09 S	17.56 E
Kamifukuoka	94	35.52 N	139.32 E
Kamigōri	96	34.52 N	134.22 E
Kamigyō ⊕[8]	270	35.02 N	135.45 E
Kamiichi	94	36.42 N	137.22 E
Kamiishihara	268	35.39 N	139.32 E
Kamiiso	92a	41.49 N	140.39 E
Kamiita	96	34.07 N	134.24 E
Kami-jima I	94	34.33 N	136.59 E
Kamikamagari-jima I	96	34.11 N	132.44 E
Kamikatsu	96	33.53 N	134.24 E
Kamikawa, Nihon	92a	43.51 N	142.46 E
Kamikawa, Nihon	94	36.13 N	139.07 E
Kamikitazawa ⊕[8]	268	35.40 N	139.38 E

Symbols in the index entries represent the broad categories identified in the key at the right. Symbols with superior numbers (⋏[1]) identify subcategories (see complete key on page *I · 1)*.

Symbole im Register stellen die rechts im Schlüssel erklärten Kategorien dar. Symbole mit hochgestellten Ziffern (⋏[1]) bezeichnen Unterabteilungen einer Kategorie (vgl. vollständiger Schlüssel auf Seite *I · 1)*.

Los símbolos incluídos en el texto del índice representan las grandes categorías identificadas con la clave a la derecha. Los símbolos con numeros en su parte superior (⋏[1]) identifican las subcategorías (véase la clave completa en la página *I · 1)*.

Les symboles de l'index représentent les catégories indiquées dans la légende à droite. Les symboles suivis d'un indice (⋏[1]) représentent des sous-catégories (voir légende complète à la page *I · 1)*.

Os símbolos incluídos no texto do índice representam as grandes categorias identificadas com a chave à direita. Os símbolos com números em sua parte superior (⋏[1]) identificam as subcategorias (veja-se a chave completa à página *I · 1)*.

English	Deutsch	Español	Français	Português
ʌ Mountain	Berg	Montaña	Montagne	Montanha
⋏ Mountains	Gebirge	Montañas	Montagnes	Montanhas
)(Pass	Paß	Paso	Col	Passo
V Valley, Canyon	Tal, Cañon	Valle, Cañón	Vallée, Canyon	Vale, Canhão
≚ Plain	Ebene	Llano	Plaine	Planície
› Cape	Kap	Cabo	Cap	Cabo
I Island	Insel	Isla	Île	Ilha
II Islands	Inseln	Islas	Îles	Ilhas
⊥ Other Topographic Features	Andere Topographische Objekte	Otros Elementos Topográficos	Autres données topographiques	Outros acidentes topográficos

ESPAÑOL: Nombre | Página | Lat.°′ | Long.°′ W = Oeste
FRANÇAIS: Nom | Page | Lat.°′ | Long.°′ W = Ouest
PORTUGUÊS: Nome | Página | Lat.°′ | Long.°′ W = Oeste

Nombre / Nom / Nome	Página / Page	Lat.°′	Long.°′
Kamikume	270	34.55 N	135.03 E
Kâmil	130	41.07 N	34.47 E
Kamilukuak Lake ⊜	176	62.22 N	101.40 W
Kamimaki	270	34.34 N	135.43 E
Kamimizo	268	35.33 N	139.22 E
Kamina	154	8.44 S	25.00 E
Kaminaka, Nihon	94	35.28 N	135.51 E
Kaminaka, Nihon	96	33.48 N	134.22 E
Kaminak Lake ⊜	176	62.10 N	95.00 W
Kaminaljuyú ⊥	236	14.38 N	90.33 W
Kaminka	83	49.38 N	39.22 E
Kamin'-Kashyrs'kyy	78	51.38 N	24.58 E
Kaminoho	94	35.37 N	137.03 E
Kaminokawa	94	36.26 N	139.55 E
Kaminokuni	92a	41.48 N	140.06 E
Kaminoseki	96	33.49 N	132.07 E
Kaminoyama	92	38.09 N	140.17 E
Kaminskij	80	57.10 N	41.28 E
Kaminuriak Lake ⊜	176	63.00 N	95.40 W
Kamioka	94	36.16 N	137.18 E
Kamiotawa	270	34.54 N	135.31 E
Kamioyamada	268	35.35 N	139.24 E
Kámiros ⊥	38	36.19 N	27.57 E
Kamisato	94	36.15 N	139.09 E
Kamishak Bay ⊂	180	59.15 N	153.45 W
Kamishii	94	36.04 N	136.24 E
Kamishinden	270	34.49 N	135.30 E
Kamisunagawa	92a	43.30 N	142.00 E
Kamitaira	94	36.24 N	136.54 E
Kamitakara	94	36.17 N	137.22 E
Kamitakino	270	34.57 N	134.59 E
Kamitomi	268	35.49 N	139.31 E
Kamitonda	96	33.43 N	135.27 E
Kamitsuruma	268	35.31 N	139.25 E
Kamitsushima	92	34.50 N	129.28 E
Kamituga	154	3.04 S	28.11 E
Kamiura	96	33.03 N	131.55 E
Kamiyahagi	94	35.18 N	137.29 E
Kamiyama	96	33.58 N	134.23 E
Kamiyamada	94	36.28 N	138.09 E
Kamiyama-jima I	174m	26.15 N	127.35 E
Kamiyugi	268	35.37 N	139.23 E
Kamīzgān	84	38.58 N	47.44 E
Kamkhat Muḥaywir ∧[2]	132	31.08 N	36.30 E
Kamku	120	27.30 N	96.30 E
Kamla (Kamlā) ≃	124	25.37 N	86.40 E
Kamlach ≃	58	48.30 N	10.22 E
Kamloops	182	50.40 N	120.20 W
Kamloops Indian Reserve ◆[4]	182	50.42 N	120.20 W
Kamloops Lake ⊜	182	50.43 N	120.33 W
Kammon-kaikyō ʊ	96	33.56 N	130.56 E
Kammon-kyō ◆[5]	96	33.56 N	130.55 E
Kammuri-yama ∧	96	34.28 N	132.05 E
Kamnik	36	46.13 N	14.37 E
Kamniokan	88	56.17 N	111.57 E
Kamo, Haya.	84	40.22 N	45.08 E
Kamo, N.Z.	172	35.41 S	174.19 E
Kamo, Nihon	92	37.39 N	139.03 E
Kamo, Nihon	94	34.50 N	138.46 E
Kamo, Nihon	96	34.45 N	135.52 E
Kamo, Nihon	96	35.10 N	134.04 E
Kamo, Nihon	96	35.20 N	132.55 E
Kamo, Nihon	270	34.55 N	135.13 E
Kamo ≃, Nihon	94	35.06 N	140.06 E
Kamo ≃, Nihon	96	33.56 N	133.09 E
Kamo ≃, Nihon	270	34.56 N	135.44 E
Kamoa Mountains ⋏	246	1.37 N	59.00 W
Kamoda-misaki ›	96	33.50 N	134.45 E
Kamogata	96	34.32 N	133.35 E
Kamogawa, Nihon	94	35.06 N	140.06 E
Kamogawa, Nihon	96	34.51 N	133.49 E
Kamohio Bay ⊂	229a	20.31 N	156.36 W
Kamojima	96	34.04 N	134.21 E
Kāmoke	123	31.58 N	74.13 E
Kamoshida ◆[8]	268	35.34 N	139.30 E
Kamoto	96	33.00 N	130.45 E
Kamp	56	50.14 N	7.37 E
Kamp ≃	61	48.23 N	15.48 E
Kāmpa	272b	22.56 N	88.28 E
Kampala	154	0.19 N	32.25 E
Kampar	114	4.18 N	101.09 E
Kampar ≃	112	0.32 N	103.08 E
Kamparkalns ∧[2]	76	57.18 N	22.47 E
Kampar Kanan ≃	112	0.16 N	101.41 E
Kampen	52	52.33 N	5.54 E
Kampene	154	3.36 S	26.40 E
Kampfe, Lake ⊜	276	41.02 N	74.21 W
Kamphaeng, Khao ∧	110	14.37 N	99.18 E
Kamphaeng Phet	110	16.28 N	99.30 E
Kampil	124	27.37 N	79.17 E
Kampinoski Park Narodowy ♦	30	52.20 N	20.35 E
Kampire Dior ∧	123	36.38 N	74.23 E
Kamp-Lintfort	52	51.30 N	6.31 E
Kamp'o	98	35.48 N	129.29 E
Kampolombo, Lake ⊜	154	11.37 S	29.42 E
Kampong Ayer Puteh	114	4.16 N	103.12 E
Kampong Baharu	114	3.43 N	103.17 E
Kampong Benta	114	3.32 N	103.22 E
Kampong Buloh	114	5.32 N	102.45 E
Kâmpóng Cham	110	12.00 N	105.27 E
Kampong Chenor	114	3.29 N	102.36 E
Kâmpóng Chhnăng	110	12.15 N	104.40 E
Kampong Dong	114	3.54 N	101.54 E
Kampong Guchil	114	5.33 N	102.14 E
Kampong Jabor	114	3.57 N	103.20 E
Kampong Jerangau	114	4.51 N	103.12 E
Kampong Kandang	114	2.11 N	102.18 E
Kâmpóng Kântuŏt	110	11.26 N	104.49 E
Kampong Kenyam	114	4.31 N	102.28 E
Kampong Kuala Kemaman	114	4.14 N	103.27 E
Kampong Lamir	114	3.36 N	103.21 E
Kampong Lawa	114	5.40 N	101.42 E
Kampong Mengkarak	114	3.19 N	102.27 E
Kampong Merang	114	5.32 N	102.57 E
Kampong Nuri	114	5.02 N	102.23 E
Kampong Penarek	114	5.37 N	102.48 E
Kampong Raja	114	5.48 N	102.35 E
Kampong Renggong	114	4.33 N	102.35 E
Kâmpóng Saôm	110	10.38 N	103.30 E
Kâmpóng Saôm, Chhâk ⊂	110	10.50 N	103.32 E
Kampong Sebuyau	112	1.31 N	110.56 E
Kampong Sekendi	114	3.43 N	100.56 E
Kampong Surau	114	5.49 N	100.54 E
Kampong Tanjong Batu	114	3.12 N	103.27 E
Kampong Tebing Runtoh	271c	1.26 N	103.40 E
Kâmpóng Thum	110	12.42 N	104.54 E
Kâmpóng Trâlach	110	11.54 N	104.47 E
Kampong Ulu	110	10.03 N	98.33 E
Kampong Ulu Chalok	114	5.26 N	102.50 E
Kâmpôt	110	10.37 N	104.11 E
Kampsville	194	39.18 N	90.37 W
Kampti	150	10.08 N	3.27 W
Kâmpŭchéa → Cambodia □[1]	110	13.00 N	105.00 E
Kampung ≃	164	5.44 S	138.24 E
Kampungbaru	112	1.12 S	102.57 E
Kampville	219	38.51 N	90.33 W
Kāmrānga	126	23.14 N	90.47 E
Kamrau, Teluk ⊂	164	3.32 S	133.37 E
Kamsack	184	51.34 N	101.54 W
Kamsdorf	54	50.38 N	11.28 E
Kamskij	24	60.04 N	53.13 E
Kamskoje Ustje	80	55.13 N	49.16 E
Kamskoje vodochranilišče ⊜[1]	86	58.52 N	56.15 E
Kamslybas, ozero ⊜	86	46.12 N	61.48 E
Kamsu-ri	98	38.03 N	125.54 E
Kamsuuma	144	0.15 N	42.47 E
Kāmthi	120	21.14 N	79.12 E
Kam Tin	271d	22.27 N	114.03 E
Kamuchawie Lake ⊜	184	56.18 N	101.59 W
Kamudilo	154	7.42 S	27.18 E
Kamuela (Waimea)	229d	20.01 N	155.48 W
Kamui-misaki ›	92a	43.20 N	140.21 E
Kámuk, Cerro ∧	236	9.17 N	83.04 W
Kamuli	154	0.57 N	33.07 E
Kamundan ≃	164	2.17 S	132.39 E
Kamutambaie ≃	152	7.17 S	23.41 E
Kamwandu	152	6.04 S	22.42 E
Kam'yane, Ukr.	78	51.31 N	27.38 E
Kam'yane, Ukr.	78	47.53 N	35.25 E
Kam'yanets'-Podil's'kyy	78	48.41 N	26.36 E
Kam'yanka, Ukr.	78	49.02 N	32.06 E
Kam'yanka, Ukr.	83	49.07 N	37.18 E
Kam'yanka ≃, Ukr.	78	49.47 N	30.01 E
Kam'yanka ≃, Ukr.	83	49.35 N	39.05 E
Kam'yanka-Buz'ka	78	50.07 N	24.20 E
Kam'yanka-Dniprovs'ka	78	47.29 N	34.25 E
Kam'yans'ke	78	45.49 N	29.16 E
Kam'yanyy Brid	78	50.25 N	27.49 E
Kamyšet	88	55.12 N	98.42 E
Kamyšev, Ross.	80	46.39 N	42.38 E
Kamyšev, Ross.	80	46.53 N	42.31 E
Kamyševatskaja	78	46.25 N	37.57 E
Kamyševskaja	80	47.37 N	41.49 E
Kamyshna (Kamyšnaja) ≃	83	48.55 N	39.55 E
Kamyšin	80	50.06 N	45.24 E
Kamyškurgon	85	40.34 N	70.24 E
Kamyšla	80	54.07 N	52.10 E
Kamyšlov	86	56.52 N	62.43 E
Kamyslybas	86	46.11 N	61.57 E
Kamyšnaja (Kamyshna) ≃	83	48.55 N	39.55 E
Kamyšnoje	86	51.58 N	61.47 E
Kamyšovyj	80	46.26 N	45.12 E
Kamyš-Samarskich Ozer, razlivy ∷	80	48.50 N	50.50 E
Kamyz'ak	80	46.07 N	48.05 E
Kamyz'ak ≃	80	46.00 N	48.06 E
Kan, Īrān	128	35.45 N	51.16 E
Kan, Sūd.	140	9.01 N	31.47 E
Kan ≃	86	56.31 N	93.47 E
Kana ≃	154	18.30 S	27.22 E
Kanaaupscow ≃	176	53.39 N	77.09 W
Kanab	200	37.02 N	112.31 W
Kanab Creek ≃	200	36.24 N	112.38 W
Kanab Plateau ⋏[1]	200	36.40 N	112.45 W
Kanada	96	33.41 N	130.47 E
Kanada → Canada □[1]	176	60.00 N	95.00 W
Kanadej	80	53.10 N	47.30 E
Kanae	94	35.30 N	137.49 E
Kanafis	140	9.48 N	25.40 E
Kanaga Island I	180	51.45 N	177.10 W
Kanaga Volcano ∧[1]	180	51.50 N	177.09 W
Kanagawa □[5]	94	35.30 N	139.30 E
Kanagawa ◆[8]	268	35.28 N	139.38 E
Kanagi	96	34.53 N	132.11 E
Kanai	268	35.35 N	139.28 E
Kānāipur	126	23.33 N	89.47 E
Kanairiktok ≃	176	55.05 N	60.20 W
Kanā'is, Ra's al- ›	140	31.15 N	27.51 E
Kanajevka, Ross.	80	53.07 N	45.35 E
Kanajevka, Ross.	80	52.12 N	49.40 E
Kanaka Creek ≃	226	39.25 N	120.57 W
Kanakapura	122	12.33 N	77.25 E
Kanakeswar	126	23.09 N	90.25 E
Kanākir	132	33.15 N	36.05 E
Kanal	64	46.05 N	13.38 E
Kanal-Inseln → Channel Islands II	28	49.20 N	2.20 W
Kanam	164	3.25 S	152.10 E
Kanamachi ◆[8]	268	35.46 N	139.53 E
Kanamori	268	35.32 N	139.28 E
Kanan	270	34.29 N	135.38 E
Kananaskis ≃	182	51.05 N	115.03 W
Kananga (Luluabourg)	152	5.54 S	22.25 E
Kananggar	115b	10.03 S	120.22 E
Kanangra-Boyd National Park ♦	170	34.00 S	150.06 E
Kananikol'skoje	86	52.47 N	57.29 E
Kanaoka	270	34.33 N	135.32 E
Kanapou Bay ⊂	229a	20.33 N	156.33 W
Kanarase-yama ∧	96	33.26 N	131.15 E
Kanarraville	200	37.32 N	113.10 W
Kanaš	80	55.31 N	47.30 E
Kanasagō	94	36.33 N	140.28 E
Kanata	212	45.19 N	75.54 W
Kanaudi	124	23.36 N	81.23 E
Kanava, Ross.	24	61.07 N	54.58 E
Kanava, Ross.	80	47.13 N	45.24 E
Kanavka	80	50.19 N	48.33 E
Kanawha	190	42.56 N	93.47 W
Kanawha ≃	188	38.50 N	82.08 W
Kanaya, Nihon	94	34.49 N	138.08 E
Kanaya, Nihon	96	34.04 N	135.15 E
Kanaya, Nihon	268	35.10 N	139.50 E
Kanayama	94	35.39 N	137.09 E
Kanazawa	94	36.34 N	136.39 E
Kanazawa ◆[8]	268	35.20 N	139.38 E
Kanazu	94	36.13 N	136.14 E
Kanbalu	110	23.12 N	95.31 E
Kanbauk	110	14.36 N	98.02 E
Kančalan ≃	180	65.08 N	176.25 E
Kanchanaburi	110	14.01 N	99.32 E
Kanchanadit	110	9.10 N	99.28 E
Kānchenjunga (Kañchanjanggā) ∧	124	27.42 N	88.08 E
Kānchipuram	122	12.50 N	79.43 E
Kanchow → Ganzhou	100	25.54 N	114.55 E
Kānchrāpāra	126	22.57 N	88.28 E
Kańczuga	30	49.59 N	22.24 E
Kanda	96	33.47 N	130.59 E
Kanda ◆[8]	268	35.42 N	139.46 E
Kandabulak	80	53.58 N	50.44 E
Kandāghāt	123	30.59 N	77.07 E
Kandahar	184	51.46 N	104.21 W
Kandāhu	120	27.33 N	69.24 E
Kanda-Kanda	152	6.56 S	23.36 E
Kandala	152	6.02 S	19.24 E
Kandalakša	24	67.09 N	32.21 E
Kandalakšskaja guba ⊂	24	66.55 N	32.45 E
Kandalakšskij zapovednik ♦	24	68.50 N	37.30 E
Kandang	114	3.03 N	97.20 E
Kandangan	112	2.47 S	115.16 E
Kandanghaur	115a	6.21 S	108.06 E
Kandat	86	57.08 N	89.02 E
Kandava	76	57.05 N	22.49 E
Kandavu Island I	175g	19.03 S	178.13 E
Kandavu Passage ʊ	175g	18.45 S	178.00 E
Kandé	150	9.57 N	1.03 E
Kandel	56	49.05 N	8.11 E
Kandel ∧	58	48.04 N	8.01 E
Kander ≃	58	46.43 N	7.38 E
Kandern	58	47.43 N	7.40 E
Kandersteg	58	46.30 N	7.40 E
Kandhkot	120	28.14 N	69.11 E
Kāndhla	124	29.19 N	77.16 E
Kandi, Bénin	150	11.08 N	2.56 E
Kandi, India	126	23.57 N	88.02 E
Kandi, Tanjung ›	112	1.19 N	121.28 E
Kandia ≃	123	35.28 N	73.18 E
Kandiāro	120	27.04 N	68.13 E
Kandik ≃	180	65.24 N	142.34 W
Kandilli ◆[8]	267b	41.04 N	29.03 E
Kandıra	130	41.04 N	30.09 E
Kandivli ◆[8]	272c	19.12 N	72.51 E
Kandla	120	23.02 N	70.14 E
Kando ≃	96	35.22 N	132.40 E
Kandor, Ouadi V	146	17.13 N	20.52 E
Kandos	170	32.52 S	149.58 E
Kāndra	126	23.44 N	87.58 E
Kandrāch	120	25.29 N	65.29 E
Kandreho	157b	17.29 S	46.06 E
Kandrian	164	6.15 S	149.35 E
Kandry	80	54.34 N	54.07 E
Kandufuri I	122	7.05 N	72.48 E
Kandute I	122	6.20 N	72.57 E
Kandy	122	7.18 N	80.38 E
Kane, Il., U.S.	219	39.11 N	90.21 W
Kane, Pa., U.S.	214	41.39 N	78.48 W
Kane □[6]	216	41.53 N	88.18 W
Kaneda	268	35.28 N	139.22 E
Kaneilio Point ›	229c	21.27 N	158.12 W
Kanektok ≃	180	59.45 N	161.55 W
Kanem □[5]	146	15.00 N	16.00 E
Kanemi	116	6.55 N	123.58 E
Kaneohe	229c	21.25 N	157.48 W
Kaneohe Bay ⊂	229c	21.28 N	157.49 W
Kaneohe Bay Marine Corps Air Station ■	229c	21.27 N	157.46 W
Kaneville	216	41.50 N	88.31 W
Kanevskaja	78	46.05 N	38.57 E
Kaneyama	94	35.28 N	137.06 E
Kanfanar	64	45.07 N	13.51 E
Kang	156	23.41 S	22.50 E
Kangaba	150	11.56 N	8.25 W
Kangal	130	39.15 N	37.24 E
Kangalassy	74	62.23 N	129.59 E
Kangān	128	27.50 N	52.03 E
Kānganheri ◆[8]	272a	28.33 N	76.59 E
Kanganpur	123	30.46 N	74.08 E
Kangar	114	6.26 N	100.12 E
Kangaré	150	11.35 N	8.10 W
Kangarilla	168b	35.09 S	138.40 E
Kangaroo ≃	170	34.46 S	150.18 E
Kangaroo Creek Reservoir ⊜[1]	168b	34.52 S	138.46 E
Kangaroo Flat	168b	34.33 S	138.40 E
Kangaroo Ground	274b	37.41 S	145.13 E
Kangaroo Island I	166	35.50 S	137.06 E
Kangaroo Valley	170	34.44 S	150.32 E
Kangasala	26	61.28 N	24.05 E
Kangasniemi	26	61.59 N	26.38 E
Kangāvar	128	34.30 N	47.58 E
Kangbao	98	41.53 N	114.40 E
Kangding	102	30.03 N	102.02 E
Kangdong	98	39.09 N	126.05 E
Kangdu	100	27.00 N	116.36 E
Kangean, Kepulauan II	112	6.55 S	115.30 E
Kangean, Pulau I	112	6.54 S	115.20 E
Kangen ≃	140	6.47 N	33.09 E
Kanggezhuang	105	40.26 N	116.44 E
Kanggup'o	98	41.07 N	127.31 E
Kanggye	98	40.58 N	126.34 E
Kanggyŏng	98	36.10 N	127.00 E
Kanghwa	98	37.45 N	126.30 E
Kanghwa-do I	98	37.40 N	126.27 E
Kanghwa-man ⊂	98	37.20 N	126.35 E
Kangil	88	52.15 N	116.20 E
Kangiqsualujjuaq	176	58.41 N	65.57 W
Kangiqsujuaq	176	61.36 N	71.58 W
Kangirsuk	176	60.01 N	70.01 W
Kangjin	98	34.39 N	126.45 E
Kangjinjing	89	46.12 N	126.48 E
Kangkar Lenggor	114	2.16 N	103.44 E
Kangkar Teberau	114	1.32 N	103.45 E
Kangley	216	41.09 N	88.53 W
Kangly	85	40.07 N	67.54 E
Kangmaer	124	30.45 N	85.34 E
Kangmar	120	28.34 N	89.51 E
Kangnam ◆[8]	271b	37.30 N	127.01 E
Kangnam-sanmaek ⋏	98	40.30 N	125.30 E
Kangnichumike	120	33.10 N	80.59 E
Kangnŭng	98	37.45 N	128.54 E
Kango	152	0.09 N	10.08 E
Kangoku-iwa I	174f	24.48 N	141.17 E
Kangombe	152	14.03 S	23.40 E
Kangongo	152	17.57 S	21.02 E
Kangowa	152	9.55 S	22.48 E
Kangping	98	42.44 N	123.21 E
Kāngpokpi	120	25.08 N	93.58 E
Kangpu	102	27.43 N	99.00 E
Kāngra	123	32.06 N	76.16 E
Kangrinboqê Feng ∧	120	31.04 N	81.18 E
Kangshan	100	22.48 N	120.17 E
Kangsŏ	98	38.58 N	125.26 E
Kangsŏ-ri	98	38.06 N	126.58 E
Kangto ∧	120	27.52 N	92.30 E
Kangtuyingzi	104	41.47 N	121.31 E
Känguruh-Insel → Kangaroo Island I	166	35.50 S	137.06 E
Kangwŏn Do □[4], C.M.I.K.	98	38.45 N	127.35 E
Kangwŏn Do □[4], Taehan	98	37.45 N	128.15 E
Kangxianzhuang	105	39.06 N	116.27 E
Kangyidaung	110	16.56 N	94.54 E
Kangzhuang	105	40.23 N	115.53 E
Kanhar ≃	124	24.28 N	83.08 E
Kanheri Caves ⊥[5]	272c	19.13 N	72.52 E
Kanholmsfjärden ʊ	40	59.20 N	18.47 E
Kanhsien → Ganzhou	100	25.54 N	114.55 E
Kani, C. Iv.	150	8.29 N	6.36 W
Kani, Mya.	110	22.26 N	94.50 E
Kani, Nihon	94	35.22 N	137.04 E
Kaniama	152	7.31 S	24.11 E
Kaniamba	154	7.27 S	26.57 E
Kanibadam	85	40.17 N	70.25 E
Kanie	94	35.08 N	136.48 E
Kaniepa	154	9.00 S	27.21 E
Kaniere	172	42.45 S	171.00 E
Kaniere, Lake ⊜	172	42.50 S	171.09 E
Kaniet Islands II	164	0.53 S	145.30 E
Kanifay	174q	9.32 N	138.06 E
Kanigiri	122	15.24 N	79.31 E
Kanihāula ◆[8]	272a	28.44 N	77.01 E
Kanin	54	52.17 N	12.50 E
Kanin, poluostrov ›[1]	24	68.00 N	45.00 E
Kanina	124	28.20 N	76.19 E
Kaningo	154	0.49 S	38.32 E
Kanin-Kamen' ∧	24	68.18 N	45.00 E
Kanin Nos	24	68.39 N	43.14 E
Kanin Nos, mys ›	24	68.39 N	43.16 E
Kaniv	78	49.44 N	31.28 E
Kaniva	166	36.23 S	141.15 E
Kanivs'ke vodoskhovyshche ⊜[1]	78	50.00 N	31.20 E
Kanjiža	38	46.04 N	20.04 E
Kānjur ◆[8]	272c	19.08 N	72.56 E
Kanjut Sār ∧	123	36.14 N	75.22 E
Kankaanpää	26	61.48 N	22.25 E
Kankakee	216	41.07 N	87.51 W
Kankakee □[6]	216	41.07 N	87.52 W
Kankakee ≃	216	41.23 N	88.16 W
Kankakee River State Park ♦	216	41.12 N	87.59 W
Kankan	150	10.23 N	9.18 W
Kankar ◆[8]	272a	28.46 N	77.06 E
Kankéla	150	10.50 N	6.40 W
Kānker	122	20.17 N	81.29 E
Kankō → Hamhŭng	98	39.54 N	127.32 E
Kankossa	150	15.56 N	11.31 W
Kankunskij	74	57.37 N	126.08 E
Kanlıavşar	130	37.13 N	38.16 E
Kanlıca ◆[8]	267b	41.06 N	29.04 E
Kanmaw Kyun I	110	11.40 N	98.28 E
Kanmen	100	28.06 N	121.16 E
Kanmuri-jima I	96	35.41 N	135.25 E
Kanmuri-yama ∧	92	34.28 N	132.05 E
Kanna ≃	94	36.17 N	139.09 E
Kannabe	96	34.32 N	133.23 E
Kannabi-san ∧[2]	270	34.48 N	135.44 E
Kannack	110	14.07 N	108.37 E
Kannad	122	20.16 N	75.08 E
Kanna-kō ⊂	174m	26.28 N	127.58 E
Kannami	94	35.05 N	138.57 E
Kannapolis	192	35.29 N	80.37 W
Kannauj	124	27.04 N	79.55 E
Kanniyākumari	122	8.05 N	77.34 E
Kannod	124	22.40 N	76.44 E
Kannonkoski	26	62.58 N	25.15 E
Kannon-zaki ›	268	35.15 N	139.45 E
Kannose ≃	96	34.54 N	132.49 E
Kannus	26	63.54 N	23.54 E
Kano, Nig.	150	12.00 N	8.30 E
Kano, Nihon	96	34.14 N	131.49 E
Kano □[3]	150	11.45 N	9.00 E
Kano ≃, Nig.	150	11.50 N	8.31 E
Kano ≃, Nihon	94	35.05 N	138.52 E
Kanona	210	42.22 N	77.22 W
Kanoneiland	158	28.39 S	21.05 E
Kanonerskij, ostrov I	265a	59.54 N	30.13 E
Kanonji	96	34.07 N	133.39 E
Kanopolis	198	38.42 N	98.09 W
Kanopolis Lake ⊜[1]	198	38.38 N	98.00 W
Kanorado	198	39.19 N	102.02 W
Kanosh	200	38.48 N	112.26 W
Kanouse Brook ≃	276	41.02 N	74.26 W
Kanouse Mountain ∧	276	41.04 N	74.25 W
Kan'ovka	24	67.08 N	39.40 E
Kanovlei	156	19.10 S	19.23 E
Kanowit	112	2.06 N	112.09 E
Kanoya	92	31.23 N	130.51 E
Kanō-zan ∧[2]	268	35.15 N	139.57 E
Kanpetlet	110	21.12 N	94.02 E
Kanpoli	272c	19.04 N	73.09 E
Kānpur	124	26.28 N	80.21 E
Kanra	94	36.13 N	138.55 E
Kansa ≃	94	34.55 N	137.34 E
Kansaj	85	40.30 N	69.41 E
Kansanshi	154	12.05 S	26.26 E
Kānsāripāra	272b	22.56 N	88.14 E
Kansas, Il., U.S.	194	39.33 N	87.56 W
Kansas, Oh., U.S.	214	41.14 N	83.17 W
Kansas □[3], U.S.	178	38.45 N	98.15 W
Kansas □[3], U.S.	198	38.45 N	98.15 W
Kansas ≃	198	39.07 N	94.36 W
Kansas City, Ks., U.S.	198	39.06 N	94.37 W
Kansas City, Mo., U.S.	194	39.05 N	94.34 W
Kansau	110	23.50 N	93.35 E
Kansei Gakuin University ⌂[2]	270	34.46 N	135.21 E
Kansei University ⌂[2]	270	34.46 N	135.31 E
Kansenia	154	10.19 S	26.02 E
Kanshan	106	30.12 N	120.25 E
Kanshi	100	24.56 N	116.54 E
Kansk	86	56.13 N	95.41 E
Kansŏng	98	38.22 N	128.29 E
Kansu	85	39.45 N	75.02 E
Kansu → Gansu □[4]	102	37.00 N	103.00 E
Kansyat	164	2.15 S	138.51 E
Kant	85	42.55 N	74.55 E
Kantabrisches Gebirge → Cantábrica, Cordillera ⋏	34	43.00 N	5.00 W
Kantalvi	272c	18.54 N	73.03 E
Kantang	110	7.25 N	99.31 E
Kāntāphor	124	22.35 N	76.34 E
Kantchari	150	12.29 N	1.31 E
Kantché	150	13.33 N	8.28 E
Kantemirovka, Kaz.	85	42.51 N	70.20 E
Kantemirovka, Ross.	83	49.41 N	39.51 E
Kānth	124	29.04 N	78.38 E
Kantharalak	110	14.39 N	104.39 E
Kānthi Coastal Plain ≚	126	21.45 N	87.45 E
Kantishna ≃	180	64.45 N	149.58 W
Kantner	214	40.06 N	78.56 W
Kantō-heiya ≚	94	36.00 N	139.30 E
Kanton → Guangzhou	100	23.06 N	113.16 E
Kanton (Canton) I	174h	2.50 S	171.40 W
Kantorp	40	59.01 N	16.28 E
Kantō-sanchi ⋏, Nihon	92	35.50 N	138.50 E
Kantō-sanchi ⋏, Nihon	94	35.59 N	138.43 E
Kantuanji	100	32.59 N	116.19 E
Kantubek	86	45.07 N	59.16 E
Kantu-long	110	19.57 N	97.36 E
Kantunilkin	232	21.06 N	87.29 W
Kanturk	48	52.10 N	8.55 W
Kanuku Mountains ⋏	246	3.12 N	59.30 W
Kanuma	94	36.33 N	139.44 E
Kanus	156	27.54 S	18.40 E
Kanuti ≃	180	66.26 N	153.02 W
Kan'utino	76	55.33 N	33.14 E
Kanye	156	24.59 S	25.19 E
Kanygtokynmangkyn, laguna ⊂	180	69.20 N	178.45 E
Kanyu	156	20.05 S	24.39 E
Kanyutkwin	110	18.21 N	96.30 E
Kanzaki ≃	270	34.42 N	135.25 E
Kanzanavolok	24	62.23 N	36.58 E
Kanzenze	154	10.31 S	25.12 E
Kanzi	98	39.34 N	122.39 E
Kaohiung → Kaohsiung	100	22.38 N	120.17 E
Kaohsiung	100	22.38 N	120.17 E
Kaohsiunghsien	100	22.38 N	120.21 E
Kaoje	150	11.14 N	4.07 E
Kaoka Bay ⊂	175e	9.42 S	160.40 E
Kaokoland □[5]	156	18.15 S	13.00 E
Kaoko Otavi	156	18.14 S	13.40 E
Kaoko Veld ⋏[1]	156	20.00 S	14.00 E
Kaolack	150	14.09 N	16.04 W
Kaolack □[4]	150	14.00 N	15.30 W
Kaolin	285	39.48 N	75.43 W
Kaolun → Kowloon	271d	22.18 N	114.10 E
Kaoma	154	14.47 S	24.48 E
Kaongweshi ≃	152	7.53 S	22.20 E
Kaoping → Changzhi	102	36.11 N	113.08 E
Kaoshanji	105	40.11 N	117.17 E
Kaoshanpu	100	30.54 N	114.32 E
Kaouadja ≃	140	6.45 N	24.15 E
Kaouar ◆[1]	146	19.00 N	12.40 E
Kao Valley V	158	28.54 S	18.06 E
Kapaa	229b	22.04 N	159.19 W
Kapadvanj	120	23.01 N	73.04 E
Kapahiang	112	3.39 S	102.34 E
Kapal	86	45.08 N	79.03 E
Kapalong	116	7.35 N	125.42 E
Kapan	112	9.44 S	124.17 E
Kapanga, Zaïre	152	8.21 S	22.35 E
Kapanga, Zaïre	152	5.04 S	16.58 E
Kapangan	116	16.35 N	120.35 E
Kapaonik ⋏	38	43.20 N	20.50 E
Kāpāsia	126	24.07 N	90.32 E
Kapatagan	116	7.52 N	123.44 E
Kapatu	154	9.43 S	30.42 E
Kapčagaj	85	43.53 N	77.12 E
Kapčagajskoje vodochranilišče ⊜[1]	86	43.50 N	78.00 E
Kapchorwa	154	1.24 N	34.27 E
Kapedo	154	1.10 N	36.06 E
Kapelle	52	51.28 N	3.58 E
Kapellen, Bel.	50	51.19 N	4.26 E
Kapellen, Dtsch.	56	51.25 N	6.35 E
Kapellen, Dtsch.	263	51.08 N	6.38 E
Kapellen, Öst.	61	47.38 N	15.37 E
Kapelle-op-den-Bos	50	51.01 N	4.22 E
Kapellerfeld	264b	48.19 N	16.30 E
Kapelln	61	48.15 N	15.45 E
Kapellskär	40	59.43 N	19.04 E
Kapema	154	10.42 S	28.24 E
Kapenguria	154	1.04 N	35.07 E
Kapfenberg	61	47.26 N	15.18 E
Kapia	152	4.17 S	19.46 E
Kapıdağ Yarımadası ›[1]	130	40.28 N	27.50 E
Kapikik Lake ⊜	184	51.32 N	91.57 W
Kapikog Lake ⊜	212	45.09 N	79.53 W
Kapilmuni	126	22.42 N	89.20 E
Kapingamarangi I[1]	14	1.04 N	154.46 E
Kapiri Mposhi	154	13.58 S	28.41 E
Kāpīsā □[4]	120	34.45 N	69.30 E
Kapiskau ≃	176	52.47 N	81.55 W
Kapit	112	2.01 N	112.56 E
Kapitanivka	78	48.54 N	31.42 E
Kapiti Island I	172	40.52 S	174.54 E
Kapiura ≃	164	5.45 S	150.35 E
Kapka, Massif du ⋏	146	15.07 N	21.45 E
Kapkataš	85	40.23 N	74.20 E
Kapkatas, chrebet ⋏	85	41.50 N	76.10 E
Kapkinka	80	48.08 N	43.51 E
Kaplan	194	29.59 N	92.17 W
Kaplice	61	48.45 N	14.30 E
Kapoe	110	9.35 N	98.40 E
Kapoeta	154	4.47 N	33.35 E
Kapona	154	7.11 S	29.09 E
Kaponga	172	39.26 S	174.09 E
Kaporskoje	265a	59.45 N	29.58 E
Kapos ≃	30	46.44 N	18.30 E
Kaposvár	30	46.22 N	17.47 E
Kaposvar Creek ≃	184	50.31 N	101.55 W
Kapotn'a ◆[8]	265b	55.38 N	37.48 E
Kapowsin	224	46.59 N	122.13 W
Kapowsin, Lake ⊜	224	46.58 N	122.13 W
Kapp	26	60.42 N	10.52 E
Kappar	128	25.19 N	62.42 E
Kappel	56	50.00 N	7.21 E
Kappeln	41	54.40 N	9.56 E
Kappelshamn	26	57.51 N	18.47 E
Kapps	156	22.22 S	17.52 E
Kapralicha	86	56.11 N	67.15 E
Kaprijke	50	51.13 N	3.36 E
Kaprun	64	47.16 N	12.46 E
Kapsabet	154	0.12 N	35.06 E
Kapsan	98	41.04 N	128.19 E
Kapstadt → Cape Town	158	33.55 S	18.22 E
Kaptai	120	22.21 N	92.17 E
Kaptipada	126	21.31 N	86.32 E
Kaptol	36	45.26 N	17.44 E
Kapuas ≃, Indon.	112	0.25 S	109.40 E
Kapuas ≃, Indon.	112	3.01 S	114.20 E
Kapuas Hulu, Pegunungan ⋏	112	1.15 N	113.30 E
Kapulo	154	8.18 S	29.15 E
Kapunda	168b	34.21 S	138.54 E
Kapūrthala	123	31.23 N	75.23 E
Kapur Utara, Pegunungan ⋏	115a	6.52 S	111.30 E
Kapuskasing	176	49.25 N	82.26 W
Kapuskasing ≃	176	49.49 N	82.00 W
Kapuskasing Lake ⊜	190	48.30 N	82.55 W
Kapustin Jar	80	48.36 N	45.45 E
Kapustyane	78	48.57 N	31.14 E
Kapuvár	30	47.36 N	17.02 E
Kap Verde → Cape Verde □[1]	150a	16.00 N	24.00 W
Kapyrevščina	76	55.15 N	32.53 E
Kara	74	69.14 N	65.00 E
Kara ≃	150	10.01 N	0.25 E
Karaali	130	39.40 N	32.57 E
Karaaul	86	48.57 N	79.15 E
Karababa Dağı ∧	130	39.31 N	36.10 E
Kara-Balta	85	42.50 N	73.52 E
Karabanovo	82	56.19 N	38.42 E
Karabaš, Ross.	80	54.42 N	52.36 E
Karabaš, Ross.	86	55.29 N	60.14 E
Karabau	80	48.26 N	52.54 E
Karabekaul	128	38.30 N	64.08 E
Karabiğa	130	40.24 N	27.18 E
Karabil', vozvyšennost' ⋏[1]	128	36.25 N	64.00 E
Kara-Bogaz-Gol, zaliv ⊂	72	41.00 N	53.15 E
Karabudachkent	84	42.41 N	47.34 E
Karabük	130	41.12 N	32.37 E
Karabula	88	58.08 N	97.23 E
Karabula ≃	88	58.22 N	97.02 E
Karabulak, Kaz.	85	42.32 N	69.46 E
Karabulak, Kaz.	86	44.54 N	78.30 E
Karabulak, Kaz.	86	47.34 N	84.41 E
Karabulak, Kyrg.	85	39.51 N	69.38 E
Karabulduk	130	40.50 N	38.34 E
Karaburun	130	38.37 N	26.31 E
Karabutak	86	49.59 N	60.10 E
Karacabey	130	40.13 N	28.21 E
Karacadağ, Tür.	130	41.57 N	27.40 E
Karacadağ, Tür.	130	37.43 N	39.37 E
Karaca Dağ ∧	130	37.40 N	39.50 E
Karačajevo-Čerkesija □[3]	84	44.00 N	42.00 E
Karačajevsk	84	43.45 N	41.54 E
Karacaköy	130	41.24 N	28.22 E
Karacaoğlan	130	41.31 N	27.07 E
Karacasu	130	37.43 N	28.37 E
Karacaviran	130	39.44 N	38.08 E
Karaçay	130	36.10 N	36.02 E
Karaçayır	130	39.55 N	37.01 E
Karačev	76	53.07 N	35.00 E
Karachay → Karačajevo-Čerkesija □[3]	84	44.00 N	42.00 E
Karāchi	120	24.52 N	67.03 E
Karachtaj	85	40.55 N	69.46 E
Karači	80	57.59 N	50.28 E
Karād	122	17.17 N	74.12 E
Kara Dağ ∧	130	40.22 N	39.05 E
Karadarja ≃	85	40.54 N	71.45 E
Karadeniz → Black Sea ∓[2]	22	43.00 N	35.00 E
Karadere	130	40.40 N	30.50 E
Karadirek	130	38.34 N	30.11 E
Karaftit	88	54.12 N	111.54 E
Karagaj, Kaz.	80	48.39 N	47.38 E
Karagaj, Ross.	80	58.16 N	54.56 E
Karagajly	86	49.20 N	75.48 E
Karaganda	86	49.50 N	73.10 E
Karaganda □[8]	86	50.00 N	74.00 E
Karagel	128	39.23 N	53.11 E
Karagičevskij	80	50.11 N	42.55 E
Karaginskij, ostrov I	74	58.50 N	164.00 E
Karaginskij zaliv ⊂	74	58.50 N	164.00 E
Karagola Road	124	25.29 N	87.23 E
Karagöl Dağı ∧	130	40.32 N	38.10 E
Kara Gölü ⊜	130	36.42 N	29.50 E
Karagoš, gora ∧	86	51.44 N	89.24 E
Karagužicha	86	50.47 N	83.00 E
Karahallı	130	38.20 N	29.32 E
Karaia	124	25.54 N	78.01 E
Karaičev	80	48.37 N	42.13 E
Karaidel'	86	55.50 N	56.53 E
Karaidel'skij	86	55.49 N	57.05 E
Kāraikāl	122	10.55 N	79.50 E
Kāraikkudi	122	10.04 N	78.47 E
Karaisalı	130	37.16 N	35.03 E
Karaitivu I	122	8.23 N	79.47 E
Karaj	128	35.48 N	50.59 E
Karaj ≃	267d	35.35 N	51.11 E
Karajantak	85	40.03 N	67.54 E
Karak	114	3.24 N	102.02 E
Karakabak	86	50.33 N	75.09 E
Karakain	85	41.26 N	74.19 E
Kara-Kala	128	38.26 N	56.18 E
Karakalpak Respublika □[3]	86	43.00 N	59.00 E
Karakaralong, Pulau II	112	4.30 N	125.30 E
Karakastek	85	43.08 N	76.06 E
Karakavak	85	39.41 N	72.43 E
Karakax ≃	120	37.00 N	79.45 E
Karakaya Barajı ⊜[1]	130	38.25 N	38.45 E
Karakeçı	130	37.26 N	39.26 E
Karakeçili	130	39.36 N	33.23 E
Karakelong, Pulau I	108	4.15 N	126.48 E
Karakemer	85	42.55 N	75.20 E
Karakendža	85	39.14 N	71.31 E
Karakitang, Pulau I	112	3.11 N	125.32 E
Karakoin, ozero ⊜	86	46.10 N	68.45 E
Karakojsu ≃	84	42.33 N	46.58 E
Karakojun ≃	85	41.10 N	75.45 E
Karakol (Prževal'sk)	85	42.29 N	78.24 E
Karakolka	85	41.32 N	77.23 E
Karakoram Pass)(	120	35.30 N	77.50 E
Karakoram Range ⋏	120	35.30 N	77.00 E
Karakoro ≃	150	14.43 N	12.03 W
Karaksar	88	51.16 N	115.58 E
Karakudžur ≃	85	41.59 N	75.42 E
Karakul', Ross.	86	57.26 N	70.51 E
Karakul', Taj.	85	39.02 N	73.33 E
Karakul', Uzb.	128	39.32 N	63.50 E
Karakul', ozero ⊜	85	39.05 N	73.25 E
Karakulak	130	39.59 N	40.01 E
Kara-Kul'dža	85	40.37 N	73.35 E
Karakul'dža ≃	85	40.39 N	73.26 E
Karakulino	80	56.01 N	53.43 E
Karakul'skoje	86	54.04 N	62.26 E
Karakum	86	46.49 N	79.33 E
Karakumskij kanal ≊	128	37.35 N	61.50 E
Karakumy ◆[2]	72	39.00 N	60.00 E
Karakuni	270	34.28 N	135.28 E
Karakurt	130	40.10 N	42.36 E
Karala ◆[8]	272a	28.44 N	77.02 E
Karalat	80	45.55 N	48.18 E
Karalon	88	57.02 N	115.52 E
Karalundi	162	26.07 S	118.41 E
Karam	88	55.09 N	107.37 E
Karama ≃	112	2.18 S	119.06 E
Karamağara	130	39.42 N	35.31 E
Karamai → Karamay	86	45.30 N	84.55 E
Karaman	130	37.11 N	33.14 E
Karaman □[4]	130	37.00 N	33.00 E
Karamanlı	130	37.22 N	29.49 E
Karamay	86	45.30 N	84.55 E
Karambu	112	3.51 S	116.04 E
Karamea	172	41.15 S	172.07 E
Karamea ≃	172	41.16 S	172.06 E
Karamea Bight ⊂[3]	172	41.30 S	171.40 E
Karamıkbataklığı ∷	130	38.25 N	30.50 E
Karamnisa Nāla ⊜[1]	124	25.42 N	83.25 E
Karamoja □[5]	154	2.50 N	34.15 E
Karamola, gora ∧	86	47.58 N	66.35 E
Karamürsel	130	40.42 N	29.36 E
Karamurt	85	42.19 N	69.58 E
Karamyš ≃	80	51.20 N	45.00 E
Karamyševo, Ross.	76	57.45 N	28.45 E
Karamyševo, Ross.	82	54.46 N	36.07 E
Karamyševo, Ross.	88	57.34 N	100.55 E
Karamzino	76	56.00 N	34.33 E
Karang, Gunung ∧	115a	6.16 S	106.03 E
Karang, Tanjung ›	112	0.38 S	119.44 E
Karangagung	112	2.22 S	104.27 E
Karangampel	115a	6.28 S	108.27 E
Karangana	150	12.13 N	5.02 W
Karangasem	115b	8.27 S	115.37 E
Karangbinangun	115a	7.01 S	112.30 E
Karangbolang, Ujung ›	115a	7.46 S	109.02 E
Karangbolong	115a	7.45 S	109.28 E
Karanggede	115a	7.22 S	110.37 E
Karangkates, Waduk ⊜[1]	115a	8.11 S	112.34 E
Karangkobar	115a	7.16 S	109.44 E
Karangnunggal	115a	7.38 S	108.06 E
Karangpandan	115a	7.37 S	111.04 E
Karangsembung	115a	6.51 S	108.39 E
Kāranja	122	20.29 N	77.29 E
Karanjia	120	21.47 N	85.58 E
Karanpura	123	29.50 N	73.27 E
Karaoba, Kaz.	86	53.17 N	65.06 E
Karaoba, Kaz.	86	47.03 N	56.20 E
Karaoğlan	130	39.14 N	39.13 E
Karaoj	86	45.54 N	74.45 E
Karaozek, Kaz.	85	43.43 N	77.23 E
Karaozek, Kaz.	86	45.03 N	65.18 E
Karaozek, Uzb.	86	43.16 N	58.40 E
Karapınar, Tür.	130	37.43 N	33.33 E
Karapınar, Tür.	130	41.30 N	32.12 E
Karapyshi	78	49.38 N	30.47 E
Karaš	80	56.54 N	39.24 E
Karas, Pulau I	164	3.27 S	132.40 E
Karasaj	85	41.34 N	77.49 E
Kara-Sal ≃	80	47.22 N	43.38 E
Karaşar	130	40.20 N	32.00 E
Karasay	120	36.47 N	83.48 E
Karasburg	156	28.00 S	18.43 E
Karasburg □[5]	156	28.00 S	18.45 E
Kara Sea → Karskoje more ∓[2]	72	76.00 N	80.00 E
Karašengel'	86	47.29 N	75.35 E
Karašjåkka ≃	24	69.26 N	25.49 E
Karasjok	24	69.27 N	25.30 E
Karaskan	85	41.03 N	71.49 E
Karasor, ozero ⊜, Kaz.	86	51.57 N	75.45 E
Karasor, ozero ⊜, Kaz.	86	49.54 N	75.32 E
Karasu, Kaz.	86	51.20 N	62.21 E
Karasu, Kaz.	86	52.40 N	65.28 E
Kara-Su, Kyrg.	85	40.44 N	72.53 E
Karasu, Kyrg.	85	43.03 N	73.57 E
Karasu, Nihon	94	34.39 N	136.32 E
Karasu, Tür.	130	41.06 N	30.41 E
Karasu ≃, Nihon	94	36.15 N	139.17 E
Karasu ≃, Tür.	130	39.07 N	38.44 E
Karasuk	86	53.44 N	78.02 E
Karasuk ≃	86	53.35 N	77.30 E
Karasuyama	94	36.39 N	140.09 E
Karata	84	42.35 N	46.21 E
Karatal, Kaz.	86	45.07 N	77.54 E
Karatal, Kaz.	86	47.36 N	85.12 E
Karatal ≃	86	46.26 N	77.10 E
Karataş, Tür.	130	38.34 N	28.17 E
Karataş, Tür.	130	36.36 N	35.21 E
Karataş Burun ›	130	36.35 N	35.22 E
Karatau	85	43.10 N	70.28 E
Karatau, chrebet ⋏, Kaz.	72	43.50 N	68.30 E
Karatau, chrebet ⋏, Taj.	85	38.10 N	69.00 E
Karateginskij chrebet ⋏	85	38.50 N	69.40 E
Karatepe Milli Parkı ♦	130	37.17 N	36.13 E
Karatia	126	24.14 N	89.58 E
Karatobe	80	49.41 N	53.31 E
Karatogaj	86	48.42 N	59.40 E
Karaton	86	46.25 N	53.30 E
Karatoya ≃	124	24.13 N	89.36 E
Karatschi → Karāchi	120	24.52 N	67.03 E
Karatsu	92	33.26 N	129.58 E
Karaturuk	85	43.33 N	77.59 E
Karatuzskoje	86	53.36 N	92.53 E
Karau	164	3.45 S	144.20 E
Karaul	74	70.06 N	83.08 E
Karauli	124	26.30 N	77.01 E
Karault'ob'o	85	40.33 N	75.57 E
Karaunk'ur ≃	85	40.54 N	72.20 E
Karaurğan	130	40.15 N	42.17 E
Karauzak	86	42.59 N	60.02 E
Karauzek	80	47.15 N	48.25 E
Karavan	85	41.30 N	71.45 E
Karavannoje, Ross.	80	45.59 N	47.08 E
Karavannoje, Ross.	80	57.47 N	47.41 E
Karave	272c	19.01 N	73.01 E
Karawa	152	3.20 N	20.18 E
Karawang	115a	6.19 S	107.17 E
Karawang, Tanjung ›	115a	5.56 S	107.00 E
Karawanken ⋏	36	46.30 N	14.25 E
Karayaka	130	40.45 N	36.37 E
Karayashnyk	83	49.22 N	39.10 E
Karayazı	130	39.41 N	42.08 E
Karaye	150	11.48 N	8.02 E
Karayün	130	39.41 N	37.19 E
Karažal	86	48.02 N	70.49 E
Karbalā'	128	32.36 N	44.02 E
Karbalā' □[4]	128	32.00 N	42.15 E
Karbenning	40	60.02 N	16.04 E

	English	Deutsch	Español	Français	Português
≃	River	Fluß	Río	Rivière	Rio
≊	Canal	Kanal	Canal	Canal	Canal
∟	Waterfall, Rapids	Wasserfall, Stromschnellen	Cascada, Rápidos	Chute d'eau, Rapides	Cascata, Rápidos
ʊ	Strait	Meeresstraße	Estrecho	Détroit	Estreito
⊂	Bay, Gulf	Bucht, Golf	Bahía, Golfo	Baie, Golfe	Baía, Golfo
⊜	Lake, Lakes	See, Seen	Lago, Lagos	Lac, Lacs	Lago, Lagos
∷	Swamp	Sumpf	Pantano	Marais	Pântano
⊽	Ice Features, Glacier	Eis- und Gletscherformen	Accidentes Glaciales	Formes glaciaires	Acidentes glaciares
∓	Other Hydrographic Features	Andere Hydrographische Objekte	Otros Elementos Hidrográficos	Autres données hydrographiques	Outros acidentes hidrográficos
✣	Submarine Features	Untermeerische Objekte	Accidentes Submarinos	Formes de relief sous-marin	Acidentes submarinos
□	Political Unit	Politische Einheit	Unidad Politica	Entité politique	Unidade política
⌂	Cultural Institution	Kulturelle Institution	Institución Cultural	Institution culturelle	Instituição cultural
⊥	Historical Site	Historische Stätte	Sitio Histórico	Site historique	Sitio histórico
♦	Recreational Site	Erholungs- und Ferienort	Sitio de Recreo	Centre de loisirs	Area de Lazer
⊠	Airport	Flughafen	Aeropuerto	Aéroport	Aeroporto
■	Military Installation	Militäranlage	Instalación Militar	Installation militaire	Instalação militar
◆	Miscellaneous	Verschiedenes	Misceláneo	Divers	Diversos

Kårberg 40 58.58 N 14.57 E
Karbeyaz 130 36.02 N 36.12 E
Kårböle 26 61.59 N 15.19 E
Karby 40 59.34 N 18.13 E
Karcag 30 47.19 N 20.56 E
Karczew 30 52.06 N 21.15 E
Kardail ≐ 80 50.43 N 42.54 E
Kardašova Řečice 61 49.11 N 14.53 E
Kardeljevo 36 43.04 N 17.26 E
Karden 56 50.11 N 7.17 E
Kardhámaina 38 36.47 N 27.09 E
Kardhámila 38 38.32 N 26.05 E
Kardhítsa 38 39.21 N 21.55 E
Kärdla 76 59.00 N 22.45 E
Kardymovo 76 54.54 N 32.26 E
Kărdžali 38 41.39 N 25.22 E
Kardžin 84 43.16 N 44.16 E
Karea 272b 22.42 N 88.33 E
Kareeberge ⋏ 158 30.53 S 21.57 E
Kareedouw 158 33.57 S 24.18 E
Kareli 84 42.01 N 43.54 E
Karelia → Karelija □[3] 24 64.00 N 32.30 E
Karelia □[9] 24 63.00 N 32.00 E
Karelija □[3] 24 64.00 N 32.30 E
Karel'skij Gorodok 76 58.04 N 36.30 E
Karema, Pap. N. Gui. 164 9.12 S 147.14 E
Karema, Tan. 154 6.49 S 30.26 E
Karen 110 12.51 N 92.53 E
Karenga ≐ 88 54.28 N 116.32 E
Karepino 24 61.02 N 57.02 E
Karera 272a 28.41 N 77.23 E
Karesuando 24 68.25 N 22.30 E
Kärevere 76 58.26 N 26.29 E
Kāreyz-e Elyās 128 35.25 N 61.20 E
Kargali 80 55.12 N 50.54 E
Kargalinskaja 84 43.44 N 46.30 E
Karganaj 180 65.21 N 175.25 E
Kargapazarı Dağları ⋏ 130 40.07 N 41.35 E
Kargapolje 86 55.57 N 64.27 E
Kargasok 86 59.07 N 80.53 E
Kargat 86 55.10 N 80.17 E
Kargat ≐ 86 54.37 N 78.12 E
Kargı 130 41.08 N 34.30 E
Kargil 123 34.34 N 76.06 E
Karginskaja 80 49.21 N 41.38 E
Karginskij ≐ 265a 59.50 N 30.01 E
Kargopol' 24 61.30 N 38.58 E
Karguéri 146 13.27 N 10.25 E
Karhal 124 27.01 N 78.57 E
Karhijärvi ⊜ 26 61.35 N 22.30 E
Karhula 26 60.31 N 26.57 E
Kari 146 11.14 N 10.34 E
Karia-ba-Mohammed 148 34.19 N 5.10 W
Kariaí 38 40.16 N 24.15 E
Karianga 157b 22.22 S 47.26 E
Kariba 154 16.30 S 28.45 E
Kariba, Lake ⊜[1] 154 17.00 S 28.00 E
Karibib 156 21.58 S 15.51 E
Karibib □[5] 156 22.20 S 16.00 E
Karibisches Meer → Caribbean Sea ≂[2] 230 15.00 N 73.00 W
Karibumba 154 0.22 N 29.22 E
Kariega ≐ 158 33.03 S 23.28 E
Karigasniemi 24 69.24 N 25.50 E
Karikari, Cape › 172 34.47 S 173.24 E
Karimata 175d 24.54 N 125.17 E
Karimata, Kepulauan II 112 1.25 S 109.05 E
Karimata, Pulau I 112 1.36 S 108.55 E
Karimata, Selat (Karimata Strait) ⊍ 112 2.05 S 108.40 E
Karīmganj 120 24.52 N 92.21 E
Karīmnagar 122 18.26 N 79.09 E
Karīmpur 126 23.58 N 88.37 E
Karimun, Pulau I 114 1.03 N 103.22 E
Karimunjawa, Kepulauan II 115a 5.50 S 110.25 E
Karimunjawa, Pulau I 115a 5.51 S 110.27 E
Karin, Som. 144 10.59 N 49.13 E
Karin, Som. 144 10.51 N 45.47 E
Karino 82 54.42 N 38.56 E
Karin Seamount ◆[3] 14 17.55 N 168.58 W
Karinskoje 82 55.42 N 36.41 E
Karintorf 80 58.33 N 50.11 E
Karis (Karjaa) 26 60.05 N 23.40 E
Karise 41 55.18 N 12.13 E
Karisimbi, Volcan ∧[1] 154 1.30 S 29.27 E
Káristos 38 38.00 N 24.24 E
Kariya 94 34.59 N 136.59 E
Kariye Museum ☩[1] 267b 41.01 N 28.55 E
Kārīz 128 34.49 N 60.47 E
Karjaa → Karis 26 60.05 N 23.40 E
Karjepolje 24 65.34 N 43.40 E
Kārkal 122 13.12 N 74.59 E
Karkalaj 80 57.00 N 52.24 E
Karkaralinsk 86 49.23 N 75.21 E
Karkar Dūmān ◆[8] 272a 28.39 N 77.18 E
Karkar Island I 164 4.40 S 146.00 E
Karkas, Kūh-e ∧ 128 33.29 N 51.50 E
Karkheh ≐ 128 31.46 N 47.55 E
Karkīndar 128 25.47 N 59.15 E
Karkinits'ka zatoka ⊂ 78 45.55 N 33.00 E
Karkkila 26 60.32 N 24.11 E
Karkku 26 61.25 N 23.01 E
Karkom, Har ∧ 132 30.17 N 34.44 E
Karkonoski Park Narodowy ♠ 30 50.45 N 15.35 E
Kärla 76 58.20 N 22.15 E
Karlholmsbruk 40 60.31 N 17.35 E
Karlik Shan ∧ 102 43.08 N 94.20 E
Karlino 30 54.03 N 15.51 E
Karlıova 130 39.18 N 41.01 E
Karlivka 78 49.27 N 35.08 E
Karl-Marx-Stadt → Chemnitz 54 50.50 N 12.55 E
Karlobag 36 44.32 N 15.05 E
Karlo-Marksove 83 48.16 N 38.09 E
Karloske ≐ 184 55.41 N 93.56 W
Karlovac 36 45.29 N 15.34 E
Karlovo 38 42.38 N 24.48 E
Karlovy Vary (Carlsbad) 54 50.11 N 12.52 E
Karlsbad → Karlovy Vary 54 50.11 N 12.52 E
Karlsborg, Sve. 26 58.32 N 14.31 E
Karlsborg, Sve. 26 65.48 N 23.17 E
Karlsburg → Alba Iulia 38 46.04 N 23.35 E
Karlsby 40 58.38 N 15.08 E
Karlsfeld 60 48.13 N 11.28 E
Karlshafen 52 51.38 N 9.27 E
Karlshamn 26 56.10 N 14.51 E
Karlshorst ◆[8] 264a 52.29 N 13.32 E
Karlshorst, Trabrennbahn ♠ 264a 52.29 N 13.31 E
Karlshuld 60 48.41 N 11.18 E
Karlskoga 40 59.20 N 14.31 E
Karlskrona 26 56.10 N 15.35 E
Karlslunde Strand 41 55.34 N 12.14 E
Karlsöarna II 26 57.17 N 17.58 E
Karlsruhe 56 49.03 N 8.24 E
Karlsruhe □[5], Dtsch. 56 49.20 N 8.45 E
Karlsruhe □[5], Dtsch. 58 48.30 N 8.30 E
Karlstad, Sve. 40 59.22 N 13.30 E
Karlstad, Mn., U.S. 198 48.34 N 96.31 W
Karlstadt 56 49.57 N 9.45 E
Karlstift 61 48.35 N 14.45 E
Karluk, Ross. 88 53.27 N 105.58 E
Karluk, Ak., U.S. 180 57.34 N 154.28 W
Karl'uk, Uzb. 85 38.12 N 67.42 E
Karma 150 13.40 N 1.49 E
Karma, Ouadi V 146 15.38 N 20.01 E
Karmah 140 19.38 N 30.25 E
Karmāla 122 18.25 N 75.12 E
Karmanovka 80 49.24 N 50.22 E
Karmanovo 76 55.52 N 34.52 E
Karmansbo 40 59.42 N 15.44 E
Karmatānr 126 24.05 N 86.42 E
Karmel, Har (Mount Carmel) ∧ 132 32.44 N 35.02 E
Karmi'el 132 32.55 N 35.18 E
Karmiyya 132 31.36 N 34.33 E
Karmøy I 26 59.15 N 5.15 E
Karnack 194 32.40 N 94.10 W
Karnak → Al-Karnak, Miṣr 140 25.43 N 32.39 E
Karnak, Il., U.S. 194 37.17 N 88.58 W
Karnāl 124 29.41 N 76.59 E
Karnāla Fort ⊥ 272c 18.53 N 73.07 E
Karṇāli □[8] 124 29.30 N 82.30 E
Karṇāli ≐ 124 28.15 N 81.05 E
Karnap ◆[8] 263 51.31 N 7.01 E
Karnaphuli Reservoir ⊜[1] 120 22.42 N 92.12 E
Karnātaka □[3] 122 14.00 N 76.00 E
Karnaukhivka 78 48.28 N 34.44 E
Karnes □[6] 222 29.00 N 97.47 W
Karnes City 196 28.53 N 97.54 W
Karni 150 10.40 N 2.37 W
Karniki 82 54.12 N 38.05 E
Karnische Alpen (Alpi Carniche) ⋏ 64 46.40 N 13.00 E
Karnobat 38 42.39 N 26.59 E
Karns City 214 41.00 N 79.44 W
Kärnten □[3] 30 46.50 N 13.50 E
Karnzow 54 52.59 N 12.26 E
Karoi 154 16.50 S 29.40 E
Karokh 128 34.28 N 62.35 E
Karoli 124 22.55 N 79.04 E
Karolinenhof ◆[8] 264a 52.23 N 13.38 E
Karomatan 116 7.46 N 123.44 E
Karompa Lompo, Pulau I 112 7.15 S 121.45 E
Karon 126 24.07 N 86.44 E
Karonga 154 9.56 S 33.56 E
Karonie 162 30.58 S 122.32 E
Karoonda 166 35.06 S 139.54 E
Karor 123 31.13 N 70.57 E
Karora 140 17.42 N 38.22 E
Karos 158 28.24 S 21.35 E
Káros I 38 36.53 N 25.39 E
Karosa 112 1.48 S 119.20 E
Karoso, Tanjung › 115b 9.33 S 118.50 E
Karotho Post 154 5.11 N 35.50 E
Karou 150 15.07 N 0.39 E
Karow, Dtsch. 54 52.20 N 12.15 E
Karow, Dtsch. 54 53.32 N 12.15 E
Karow ◆[8] 264a 52.37 N 13.29 E
Karpathen → Carpathian Mountains ⋏ 22 48.00 N 24.00 E
Kárpathos, Ellás 38 35.30 N 27.14 E
Kárpathos, Ellás 130 35.31 N 27.12 E
Kárpathos I 38 35.40 N 27.10 E
Karpats'kyy Pryrodnyy Natsional'nyy Park ♠ 78 48.25 N 24.30 E
Karpenísion 38 38.55 N 21.40 E
Karpinsk 86 59.45 N 60.01 E
Karpivka 83 49.10 N 37.43 E
Karpogory 24 64.00 N 44.24 E
Karpovo, Ross. 76 60.02 N 36.43 E
Karpovo, Ross. 82 55.35 N 38.34 E
Karpunicha 80 57.42 N 45.20 E
Karpuninskij 86 58.43 N 61.50 E
Karpuzlu 130 37.33 N 27.50 E
Karratha 162 20.44 S 116.51 E
Karrats Fjord ⊂[2] 176 71.20 N 54.00 W
Karrebæksminde 41 55.11 N 11.40 E
Karres 58 47.13 N 10.47 E
Kärrgruvan 40 60.05 N 15.56 E
Karridale 162 34.13 S 115.05 E
Kars 84 40.36 N 43.05 E
Kars □[4] 84 40.35 N 43.00 E
Kars ≐ 84 40.37 N 43.41 E
Karša 80 49.48 N 51.27 E
Karsakpaj 86 47.49 N 66.41 E
Karsakuwigamak Lake ⊜ 184 56.22 N 99.30 W
Kärsämäki 26 63.58 N 25.46 E
Karsantı 130 37.33 N 35.24 E
Kārsava 76 56.47 N 27.40 E
Karsdorf 54 51.17 N 11.39 E
Karši 128 38.53 N 65.48 E
Karsin 30 53.54 N 17.56 E
Karšinskaja step' ≚ 128 39.10 N 65.00 E
Karskije Vorota, proliv ⊍ 72 70.30 N 58.00 E
Karskoje more (Kara Sea) ≂[2] 72 76.00 N 80.00 E
Karsovaj 80 58.14 N 53.11 E
Karst → Kras ⋏[1] 64 45.48 N 14.00 E
Kårsta, Sve. 40 59.39 N 18.14 E
Kärsta, Sve. 40 59.40 N 16.49 E
Karstädt 54 53.09 N 11.44 E
Karstula 26 62.52 N 24.47 E
Karsun 80 54.11 N 46.59 E
Kartajol' 24 64.32 N 53.14 E
Kartala ∧ 157a 11.45 S 43.22 E
Kartaly 86 53.03 N 60.40 E
Kartārpur 123 31.27 N 75.30 E
Karthaus 214 41.07 N 78.07 W
Kartlijskij chrebet ⋏ 84 42.10 N 44.55 E
Kartosuro 115a 7.33 S 110.44 E
Karttula 26 62.53 N 26.58 E
Kartuzy 30 54.20 N 18.12 E
Kartzow 54 52.29 N 12.58 E
Käru 76 58.50 N 25.11 E
Karuah ≐ 170 32.39 S 151.58 E
Karufa 164 3.50 S 133.27 E
Karuizawa 94 36.21 N 138.38 E
Karukuwisa 156 18.56 S 19.40 E
Karumai 92 40.19 N 141.28 E
Karumba 166 17.29 S 140.50 E
Kārūn ≐ 128 30.26 N 48.10 E
Karungi 26 66.03 N 23.57 E
Karungu 154 0.51 S 34.09 E
Karuni 115b 9.26 S 119.19 E
Karunjie 164 16.18 S 127.12 E
Karunki 26 66.02 N 24.01 E
Karup 41 56.18 N 9.10 E
Karup ≐ 41 56.18 N 9.10 E
Karūr 122 10.57 N 78.05 E
Karuscia, Punta › 70 36.49 N 11.59 E
Karvala 265a 59.41 N 30.09 E
Karviná 30 49.50 N 18.30 E
Kārwār 122 14.48 N 74.08 E
Karwendel ⋏ 64 47.27 N 11.20 E
Karwi 124 25.12 N 80.54 E
Karym 86 60.07 N 66.41 E
Karymskoje, Ross. 88 51.37 N 114.21 E
Karymskoje, Ross. 88 54.07 N 101.49 E
Karza 86 58.35 N 80.50 E
Karzachi 84 41.15 N 43.16 E
Kas, Sūd. 140 12.30 N 24.17 E
Kaş, Tür. 130 36.12 N 29.38 E
Kas ≐ 86 59.40 N 90.00 E
Kasaan 182 55.32 N 132.24 W
Kasabi 152 14.48 S 23.42 E
Kasach ≐ 84 40.03 N 43.52 E
Kasadi ≐ 272c 19.01 N 73.03 E
Kasa-do I 98 34.28 N 126.03 E
Kasado-shima I 96 33.57 N 131.51 E
Kasagi 94 34.45 N 135.56 E
Kasagi-sanchi ⋏ 270 34.37 N 135.56 E
Kasagi-yama ∧ 94 35.31 N 137.21 E
Kasahara 94 35.17 N 137.09 E
Kasahata 268 35.54 N 139.25 E
Kasai 96 34.56 N 134.50 E
Kasai ◆[8] 268 35.39 N 139.53 E
Kasai (Cassai) ≐, Afr. 152 3.02 S 16.57 E
Kāsai ≐, India 124 22.09 N 87.50 E
Kasai-Occidental □[4] 152 5.30 S 21.40 E
Kasai-Oriental □[4] 152 4.00 S 23.30 E
Kasaji 152 10.22 S 23.27 E
Kasakake 94 36.23 N 139.17 E
Kasama, Nihon 94 36.23 N 140.16 E
Kasama, Zam. 154 10.13 S 31.12 E
Kasamatsu 94 35.22 N 136.46 E
Kasan → Kazan', Ross. 80 55.49 N 49.08 E
Kasan, Uzb. 128 39.02 N 65.35 E
Kasan-dong 98 41.18 N 126.55 E
Kasane 156 17.50 S 25.05 E
Kasanga 154 8.28 S 31.09 E
Kasangale 152 6.20 S 22.42 E
Kasangeshi ≐ 152 8.24 S 21.56 E
Kasangulu 152 4.36 S 15.10 E
Kasanka National Park ♠ 154 12.35 S 30.12 E
Kasano-misaki › 94 36.21 N 136.18 E
Kasansaj 85 41.15 N 71.32 E
Kasansaj ≐ 85 40.57 N 71.30 E
Kasaoka 96 34.30 N 133.30 E
Kāsaragod 122 12.30 N 75.00 E
Kasari ≐ 76 58.45 N 23.49 E
Kašary 78 49.03 N 41.00 E
Kasatori-yama ∧, Nihon 94 34.44 N 136.18 E
Kasatori-yama ∧, Nihon 96 33.33 N 132.55 E
Kasauli 123 30.55 N 76.57 E
Kasba 124 25.51 N 87.33 E
Kasbagoas 126 24.11 N 88.30 E
Kasba Kamarda 126 21.46 N 87.21 E
Kasba Lake ⊜ 176 60.18 N 102.07 W
Kasba Mirgoda 126 21.42 N 87.28 E
Kasba Nārāyangarh 126 22.10 N 87.23 E
Kasba Patāspur 126 22.02 N 87.32 E
Kasba-Tadla 148 32.34 N 6.18 W
Kaschau → Košice 30 48.43 N 21.15 E
Kåseberga 26 55.23 N 14.04 E
Kaseda 92 31.25 N 130.19 E
Kasempa 154 13.27 S 25.50 E
Kasenga 154 10.22 S 28.38 E
Kasenyi 154 1.24 N 30.26 E
Kasese, Ug. 154 0.10 N 30.05 E
Kasese, Zaïre 154 1.38 S 27.07 E
Kaset Sombun 110 16.17 N 101.57 E
Kasfareet Military Base ■ 142 30.15 N 32.24 E
Kāsganj 124 27.49 N 78.39 E
Kashabowie Lake ⊜ 190 48.42 N 90.25 W
Kashaf ≐ 128 35.58 N 61.07 E
Kashagawigamog Lake ⊜ 212 44.59 N 78.37 W
Kāshān 128 33.59 N 51.29 E
Kashasha 154 1.44 S 31.37 E
Kashegelok 180 60.50 N 157.50 W
Kashgar → Kashi 85 39.29 N 75.59 E
Kashi 85 39.29 N 75.59 E
Kashiba 96 34.33 N 135.42 E
Kashihara 96 34.30 N 135.46 E
Kashiji Plain ≚ 152 13.20 S 22.30 E
Kashileshi ≐ 152 9.46 S 23.05 E
Kashima, Nihon 92 33.07 N 130.06 E
Kashima, Nihon 94 35.58 N 140.38 E
Kashima, Nihon 94 36.58 N 136.55 E
Kashima, Nihon 96 35.30 N 133.01 E
Kashima-jingū ☩[1] 94 35.59 N 140.40 E
Kashima-nada ≂[2] 94 36.15 N 140.45 E
Kashima-Yariga-take ∧ 94 36.37 N 137.45 E
Kashimo 94 35.43 N 137.23 E
Kāshināthpur 126 23.58 N 89.37 E
Kashing → Jiaxing 106 30.46 N 120.45 E
Kashio ◆[8] 268 35.25 N 139.33 E
Kāshīpur, India 124 29.13 N 78.57 E
Kāshipur, India 126 23.26 N 86.40 E
Kashitu 154 13.42 S 28.40 E
Kashiwa 94 35.52 N 139.59 E
Kashiwara 96 34.35 N 135.37 E
Kashiwazaki, Nihon 92 37.22 N 138.33 E
Kashiwazaki, Nihon 268 35.56 N 139.42 E
Kashlahach ≐ 83 47.45 N 37.16 E
Kāshmar 128 35.12 N 58.27 E
Kashmir → Jammu and Kashmīr □[2] 120 34.00 N 76.00 E
Kashmir, Vale of V 123 34.00 N 75.00 E
Kashmor 120 28.26 N 69.35 E
Kashmūnḍ Ghar ⋏ 123 34.42 N 70.31 E
Kashperivka 78 49.26 N 29.41 E
Kashunuk ≐ 180 61.18 N 165.36 W
Kashwakamak Lake ⊜ 212 44.50 N 77.04 W
Kasia 124 26.45 N 83.55 E
Kāsiāni 126 23.14 N 89.45 E
Kasiāri 126 22.08 N 87.14 E
Kasidiji ≐ 152 7.57 S 23.12 E
Kasigau ∧ 154 3.50 S 38.40 E
Kasigluk 180 60.52 N 162.32 W
Kasilof 180 60.24 N 151.18 W
Kasilovo 78 50.38 N 35.37 E
Kasimbar 112 0.09 S 120.00 E
Kasimov 80 54.56 N 41.24 E
Kāsimpur, Bngl. 126 23.59 N 90.19 E
Kāsimpur, India 272b 22.46 N 88.31 E
Kašin 76 57.21 N 37.37 E
Kāsināthpur 272b 22.35 N 88.31 E
Kasinge 154 6.20 S 26.59 E
Kasinka 156 18.13 S 24.22 E
Kāsipur 272b 22.25 N 88.10 E
Kašira 82 54.51 N 38.10 E
Kaširka ≐ 82 54.52 N 38.13 E
Kasiruta, Pulau I 108 0.25 S 127.12 E
Kasiui, Pulau I 164 4.30 S 131.40 E
Kasiwa → Kashiwa 94 35.52 N 139.59 E
Kaskabulak 86 49.34 N 79.52 E
Kaškadarja □[8] 128 39.00 N 66.00 E
Kaskaden-Kette → Cascade Range ⋏ 202 45.00 N 121.30 W
Kaskana 85 40.45 N 69.36 E
Kaskaskia ≐ 194 37.59 N 89.56 W
Kaskaskia, East Fork ≐ 219 38.43 N 89.09 W
Kaskaskia, North Fork ≐ 219 38.46 N 89.09 W
Kaskattama ≐ 176 57.03 N 90.07 W
Kaskelen 85 43.12 N 76.37 E
Kaskelen ≐ 85 43.53 N 77.08 E
Kaskinen → Kaskö 26 62.23 N 21.13 E
Kaskö (Kaskinen) 26 62.23 N 21.13 E
Kaslātu ∧ 124 23.58 N 84.54 E
Kasli 86 55.53 N 60.46 E
Kaslo 182 49.55 N 116.55 W
Kasn'a 76 55.24 N 34.20 E
Kasn'a ≐ 76 55.51 N 34.25 E
Kaso ≐ 115a 7.25 S 106.40 E
Kasongo 154 4.27 S 26.40 E
Kasongo-Lunda 152 6.28 S 16.49 E
Kásos I 38 35.22 N 26.56 E
Kasota 190 44.18 N 93.57 W
Kaspi 84 41.57 N 44.25 E
Kaspijsk 84 42.52 N 47.38 E
Kaspijskij 22 45.22 N 47.24 E
Kaspijskoje more → Caspian Sea ≂[2] 72 42.00 N 50.30 E
Kaspische Senke → Prikaspijskaja nizmennost' ≚ 80 48.00 N 52.00 E
Kaspisches Meer → Caspian Sea ≂[2] 72 42.00 N 50.30 E
Kaspl'a 76 55.00 N 31.38 E
Kaspl'a ≐ 76 55.24 N 30.43 E
Kasr, Ra's › 140 18.02 N 38.35 E
Kasrik 130 38.13 N 41.54 E
Kassa → Košice 30 48.43 N 21.15 E
Kassab 130 35.56 N 35.59 E
Kassai → Cassai (Kasai) ≐ 152 3.02 S 16.57 E
Kassalā 140 15.28 N 36.24 E
Kassalā □[4] 140 15.00 N 35.00 E
Kassándra ›[1] 38 40.06 N 23.22 E
Kassándras, Kólpos ⊂ 38 40.06 N 23.30 E
Kassel 56 51.19 N 9.29 E
Kassel □[5] 56 51.10 N 9.20 E
Kasserine 148 35.11 N 8.48 E
Kasserine □[8] 148 35.00 N 8.45 E
Kasshabog Lake ⊜ 212 44.38 N 77.58 W
Kassikaityu ≐ 246 1.49 N 58.32 W
Kassinger 140 18.45 N 31.54 E
Kassîr, Sabkhat al- ⊜ 130 35.03 N 41.07 E
Kasslerfeld ◆[8] 263 51.26 N 6.45 E
Kasson 190 44.01 N 92.45 W
Kassou 150 11.35 N 2.03 W
Kassoum 150 13.05 N 3.18 W
Kastamonu 130 41.22 N 33.47 E
Kastamonu □[4] 130 41.40 N 33.45 E
Kastanéai 38 41.38 N 26.28 E
Kastelholm 26 60.14 N 20.04 E
Kastellaun 56 50.04 N 7.26 E
Kasterlee 56 51.15 N 4.57 E
Kastiyu, Puntan › 174n 14.57 N 145.40 E
Kastl, Dtsch. 60 49.50 N 11.54 E
Kastl, Dtsch. 60 49.22 N 11.42 E
Kastorf 52 53.44 N 10.34 E
Kastoría 38 40.31 N 21.15 E
Kastorías, Límni ⊜ 38 40.30 N 21.17 E
Kastornoje 78 51.50 N 38.06 E
Kastrávion, Tekhnití Límni ⊜[1] 38 38.50 N 21.20 E
Kastrup Lufthavn ⊠ 41 55.38 N 12.39 E
Kasuga, Nihon 94 35.28 N 136.29 E
Kasuga, Nihon 96 33.32 N 130.27 E
Kasuga, Nihon 96 35.10 N 135.06 E
Kasugai, Nihon 94 35.14 N 136.58 E
Kasugai, Nihon 94 35.39 N 138.39 E
Kasuga-kōkūkichi, Kaijō-jieitai- ■ 96 33.31 N 130.28 E
Kasuga Shrine ☩[1] 270 34.41 N 135.51 E
Kasuka 158 33.40 S 26.41 E
Kasukabe 94 35.58 N 139.45 E
Kasukawa 94 36.24 N 139.13 E
Kasulu 154 4.34 S 30.06 E
Kasumi 96 35.38 N 134.38 E
Kasumiga-ura ⊜ 94 36.00 N 140.25 E
Kasumkent 84 41.41 N 48.07 E
Kasungan 112 1.58 S 113.24 E
Kasungu 154 13.01 S 33.30 E
Kasungu National Park ♠ 154 12.55 S 33.15 E
Kasupe 154 15.10 S 35.15 E
Kasūr 123 31.07 N 74.27 E
Kaszuby ◆[1] 30 54.10 N 18.15 E
Kata 88 58.46 N 102.40 E
Kataba 154 16.05 S 25.10 E
Kataeregi 150 9.22 N 6.17 E
Katagum 146 12.17 N 10.21 E
Katahdin, Mount ∧ 188 45.55 N 68.55 W
Katai 272c 19.10 N 73.05 E
Katajevo 88 50.57 N 108.41 E
Katajsk 86 56.18 N 62.35 E
Katako-Kombe 152 3.24 S 24.25 E
Katakura 270 34.29 N 135.31 E
Katakwi 154 1.55 N 33.57 E
Katale 154 4.59 S 31.03 E
Katalla 180 60.12 N 144.31 W
Katanda 154 0.50 S 29.22 E
Katanga □[9] 138 10.00 S 26.00 E
Katanga ≐ 74 60.08 N 102.13 E
Katangi 124 23.27 N 79.47 E
Katanglad Mountains ⋏ 116 8.06 N 124.54 E
Katangli 89 51.42 N 143.14 E
Katanimara 126 22.17 N 87.11 E
Katanning 162 33.42 S 117.33 E
Katano 270 34.47 N 135.40 E
Katano-hana › 174f 24.49 N 141.20 E
Katanti 154 2.18 S 27.08 E
Kataoka 270 35.03 N 135.58 E
Katapakishi 152 8.15 S 22.49 E
Katar → Qatar □[1] 128 25.00 N 51.10 E
Katara, Depresión de → Qaṭṭārah, Munkhafaḍ al- ⊥[7] 140 30.00 N 27.30 E
Katârniān Ghāt 124 28.20 N 81.09 E
Katase 268 35.19 N 139.29 E
Katashina 94 36.46 N 139.14 E
Katašin 76 52.36 N 32.10 E
Katav-Ivanovsk 86 54.45 N 58.12 E
Katayama 268 35.46 N 139.34 E
Katchall Island I 110 7.57 N 93.22 E
Katchewanooka Lake ⊜ 212 44.27 N 78.16 W
Katchin-wan ⊂ 174m 26.18 N 127.53 E
Katchirga 150 14.03 N 0.06 E
Katchiungo 152 12.35 S 16.13 E
Kateel ≐ 180 65.28 N 157.35 W
Katélé 150 10.38 N 5.37 W
Katena-wan ⊂ 174m 26.50 N 128.05 E
Katepwa Beach 184 50.42 N 103.38 W
Katerbow 54 52.59 N 12.39 E
Kateríni 38 40.16 N 22.30 E
Katerloch ⊥[5] 61 47.16 N 15.32 E
Katernberg ◆[8], Dtsch. 263 51.16 N 7.06 E
Katernberg ◆[8], Dtsch. 263 51.29 N 7.04 E
Katerynopil' 78 48.56 N 30.59 E
Katesbridge 48 54.18 N 6.08 W
Kates Needle ∧ 180 57.03 N 132.03 W
Katešovo 82 54.08 N 37.00 E
Katete, Malaŵi 154 12.17 S 33.39 E
Katete, Zam. 154 14.05 S 32.07 E
Katex 84 41.39 N 46.34 E
Katghora 124 22.30 N 82.33 E
Katha 110 24.11 N 96.21 E
Kathangor, Jabal ∧ 140 5.45 N 33.59 E
Katherine 164 14.28 S 132.16 E
Katherine ≐ 164 14.39 S 131.42 E
Katherine Creek ≐ 166 23.48 S 143.42 E
Katherine Gorge National Park ♠ 164 14.10 S 132.30 E
Kāthgodām 124 29.16 N 79.32 E
Kāthiāwār Peninsula ›[1] 120 22.00 N 71.00 E
Kathīb, Ra's › 144 14.55 N 42.53 E
Kathla 123 31.59 N 76.47 E
Kathleen 220 28.07 N 82.01 W
Kathleen Valley 162 27.23 S 120.38 E
Kathlow 54 51.43 N 14.29 E
Kāṭhmāṇḍau 124 27.43 N 85.19 E
Kathmandu → Kāṭhmāṇḍau 124 27.43 N 85.19 E
Kathor 120 21.18 N 72.56 E
Kathrabbā 132 31.08 N 35.37 E
Kathua 123 32.22 N 75.31 E
Kāthuli 126 23.52 N 88.40 E
Kati 150 12.44 N 8.04 W
Kātiādi 126 24.15 N 90.48 E
Katibas ≐ 112 2.01 N 112.33 E
Katihār 124 25.32 N 87.35 E
Katikati 172 37.33 S 175.55 E
Katima Mulilo 152 17.27 S 24.14 E
Katimik Lake ⊜ 184 52.54 N 99.22 W
Katiola 150 8.08 N 5.06 W
Katipunan 116 8.31 N 123.17 E
Katiti Aboriginal Land Reserve ◆[4] 162 25.10 S 131.15 E
Kātlang 123 34.22 N 72.05 E
Katlehong 273d 26.19 S 28.09 E
Katlenburg-Duhm 52 51.41 N 10.06 E
Katmai, Mount ∧ 180 58.17 N 154.56 W
Katmai National Park ♠ 180 58.30 N 155.00 W
Kātmāndu → Kāṭhmāṇḍau 124 27.43 N 85.19 E
Katni → Murwāra, India 124 23.51 N 80.24 E
Katni, Ross. 80 57.59 N 47.46 E
Káto Akhaïa 38 38.09 N 21.32 E
Kātol 120 21.16 N 78.35 E
Katompi 154 6.11 S 26.20 E
Katonah 210 41.16 N 73.41 W
Katonga ≐ 154 0.34 N 31.50 E
Katon-Karagaj 86 49.11 N 85.37 E
Katoomba 170 33.42 S 150.18 E
Katopa 154 2.45 S 25.06 E
Katori-jingū ☩[1] 94 35.52 N 140.30 E
Katoúna 38 38.47 N 21.07 E
Katovice 60 49.16 N 13.49 E
Katowice 30 50.16 N 19.00 E
Katowice □[4] 30 50.15 N 19.00 E
Katra 123 32.59 N 74.57 E
Kātrās 126 23.48 N 86.17 E
Katričev 80 49.23 N 45.33 E
Kātrīnā, Jabal ∧ 140 28.31 N 33.57 E
Katrine, Loch ⊜ 46 56.15 N 4.31 W
Katrineholm 40 59.00 N 16.12 E
Katsch, Golf von → Kachchh, Gulf of ⊂ 120 22.36 N 69.30 E
Katschbach ≐ 61 47.08 N 14.17 E
Katschberg)(64 47.03 N 13.37 E
Katsepe 157b 15.45 S 46.15 E
Katshungu 154 2.27 S 27.23 E
Katsina 150 13.00 N 7.32 E
Katsina □[3] 150 12.20 N 7.45 E
Katsina Ala 150 7.10 N 9.17 E
Katsina Ala ≐ 152 7.48 N 8.52 E
Katsunuma 94 35.39 N 138.44 E
Katsura ◆[8] 270 34.59 N 135.42 E
Katsura ≐, Nihon 94 35.36 N 139.15 E
Katsura ≐, Nihon 94 34.53 N 135.42 E
Katsura ≐, Nihon 96 34.02 N 134.35 E
Katsura ≐, Nihon 270 34.53 N 135.42 E
Katsuragi 96 34.15 N 135.30 E
Katsuragi-san ∧ 96 34.20 N 135.27 E
Katsushika ◆[8] 268 35.43 N 139.51 E
Katsuta, Nihon 94 36.24 N 140.30 E
Katsuta, Nihon 96 35.04 N 134.11 E
Katsuura, Nihon 94 35.08 N 140.18 E
Katsuura, Nihon 96 33.56 N 134.30 E
Katsuyama, Nihon 94 36.03 N 136.30 E
Katsuyama, Nihon 96 35.05 N 133.41 E
Kattakurgan 72 39.55 N 66.15 E
Kattara-Senke → Qaṭṭārah, Munkhafaḍ al- ⊥[7] 140 30.00 N 27.30 E
Kattarp 41 56.09 N 12.46 E
Katta-Taldyk 85 40.19 N 73.12 E
Kattaviá 38 35.57 N 27.46 E
Kattegat ⊍ 26 57.00 N 11.00 E
Katternberg ◆[8] 263 51.09 N 7.02 E
Katthammarsvik 26 57.26 N 18.50 E
Kattowitz → Katowice 30 50.16 N 19.00 E
Kattrup 41 55.57 N 9.56 E
Kāttuputtūr 122 10.59 N 78.14 E
Katul, Jabal ∧ 140 14.16 N 29.23 E
Katuma 154 6.10 S 30.34 E
Katumba 154 7.45 S 25.18 E
Katun' ≐ 86 52.25 N 85.05 E
Katunino 80 58.01 N 45.39 E
Katunki 80 56.50 N 43.14 E
Kātūria 124 24.44 N 86.43 E
Katu Shan ∧ 86 45.40 N 82.55 E
Katusice 54 50.26 N 14.50 E
Kātwa 126 23.39 N 88.08 E
Katwijk aan de Rijn 52 52.11 N 4.26 E
Katwijk aan Zee 52 52.13 N 4.24 E
Katy 222 29.47 N 95.49 W
Katyn 76 54.47 N 31.44 E
Kąty Wrocławskie 30 51.02 N 16.46 E
Katzenbuckel ∧ 56 49.28 N 9.02 E
Katzenelnbogen 56 50.17 N 7.59 E
Katzenfurt 56 50.37 N 8.21 E
Katzhütte 54 50.33 N 11.03 E
Kaua ≐ 156 19.24 S 22.03 E
Kauai □[6] 229b 21.59 N 159.22 W
Kauai I 229b 22.00 N 159.30 W
Kauai Channel ⊍ 229b 21.45 N 158.50 W
Kaub 56 50.05 N 7.46 E
Kau Desert ◆[2] 229d 19.21 N 155.19 W
Kaufbeuren 58 47.53 N 10.37 E
Kaufering 58 48.05 N 10.52 E
Kaufman 222 32.35 N 96.18 W
Kaufman □[6] 222 32.38 N 96.18 W
Kaufungen 56 51.17 N 9.38 E
Kaugama 150 12.28 N 9.44 E
Kauhajoki 26 62.26 N 22.11 E
Kauhanevan-Pohjankankaan kansallispuisto ♠ 26 62.08 N 22.25 E
Kauhava 26 63.06 N 23.05 E
Kauiki Head › 229a 20.45 N 155.59 W
Kaukapakapa 172 36.37 S 174.30 E
Kaukasus → Caucasus ⋏ 84 42.30 N 45.00 E
Kaukauna 190 44.16 N 88.16 W
Kaukau Veld ⋏[1] 156 19.30 S 20.30 E
Kaukhāli 126 22.38 N 90.04 E
Kaukura I[1] 14 15.45 S 146.42 W
Kaula I 229d 21.45 N 160.30 W
Kaulakahi Channel ⊍ 229b 22.00 N 159.53 W
Kaulille 56 51.11 N 5.31 E
Kauliranta 24 66.27 N 23.41 E
Kaŭl-li 98 37.58 N 124.37 E
Kaulsdorf 54 50.37 N 11.26 E
Kaulsdorf ◆[8] 264a 52.31 N 13.33 E
Kaulsdorf-Süd ◆[8] 264a 52.29 N 13.34 E
Kaumakani 229b 21.55 N 159.37 W
Kaumalapau 229a 20.47 N 156.59 W
Kaunakakai 229a 21.05 N 157.01 W
Kaunas 76 54.54 N 23.54 E
Kauneonga Lake 210 41.41 N 74.50 W
Kauner Tal V 64 47.01 N 10.44 E
Kaunghein 110 25.40 N 95.26 E
Kauniainen → Grankulla 26 60.13 N 24.45 E
Kaunuunui › 229b 21.56 N 160.10 W
Kaup 164 3.50 S 144.00 E
Kaupanger 26 61.11 N 7.14 E
Kaura Namoda 150 12.35 N 6.35 E
Kauriyāla Ghāt 124 28.23 N 81.02 E
Kauru 150 10.33 N 8.12 E
Kausa 272c 19.10 N 73.02 E
Kau Sai Chau I 271d 22.22 N 114.18 E
Kausala 26 60.54 N 26.22 E
Kaustinen 26 63.32 N 23.42 E
Kauswagan 116 8.11 N 124.05 E
Kautokeino 24 69.00 N 23.02 E
Kauttua 26 61.06 N 22.10 E
Kau-ye Kyun I 110 11.01 N 98.32 E
Kavača 74 60.16 N 169.51 E
Kavacık 130 39.40 N 28.30 E
Kavadarci 38 41.26 N 22.00 E
Kavajë 38 41.11 N 19.33 E
Kavak, Tür. 130 38.24 N 39.26 E
Kavak, Tür. 130 41.05 N 36.03 E
Kavak, Tür. 130 39.18 N 37.30 E
Kavakbaşı 130 38.29 N 41.49 E
Kavaklıdere 130 37.26 N 28.22 E
Kavála 38 40.56 N 24.25 E
Kavalerovo 89 44.15 N 135.04 E
Kāvali 122 14.55 N 79.59 E
Kavango □[5] 156 18.30 S 20.15 E
Kavaratti 122 10.34 N 72.39 E
Kavaratti Island I 122 10.33 N 72.38 E
Kavarna 38 43.25 N 28.20 E
Kavendou, Mont ∧ 150 10.41 N 12.12 W
Kāveri ≐ 122 11.09 N 79.52 E
Kāveri Falls └ 122 12.18 N 77.17 E
Kaverino, Ross. 80 54.10 N 41.47 E
Kaverino, Ross. 82 56.11 N 36.15 E
Kavieng 164 2.35 S 150.50 E
Kavimba 156 18.02 S 24.38 E
Kavīr, Dasht-e ◆[2] 128 34.40 N 54.30 E
Kavkazskij zapovednik ♠ 84 43.55 N 40.30 E
Kävlinge 41 55.48 N 13.06 E
Kävlingeån ≐ 41 55.47 N 13.06 E
Kavungo 152 11.31 S 23.03 E
Kavuu ≐ 154 7.40 S 31.46 E
Kavykuči-Gazimurskije 88 51.22 N 118.10 E
Kaw, Guy. fr. 250 4.29 N 52.02 W
Kaw, Ok., U.S. 196 36.46 N 96.50 W
Kawa 110 17.05 N 96.28 E
Kawaba 94 36.41 N 139.07 E
Kawabe, Nihon 94 35.29 N 137.04 E
Kawabe, Nihon 96 33.55 N 135.11 E
Kawachi, Nihon 94 36.24 N 136.38 E
Kawachi, Nihon 94 36.37 N 139.56 E
Kawachi, Nihon 94 35.53 N 140.15 E
Kawachi-nagano 96 34.27 N 135.34 E
Kawagama Lake ⊜ 212 45.18 N 78.45 W
Kawage 94 34.47 N 136.33 E
Kawagoe 94 35.55 N 139.29 E
Kawaguchi 94 35.48 N 139.43 E
Kawaguchiko 94 35.30 N 138.46 E
Kawaguchi-ko ⊜ 94 35.31 N 138.45 E
Kawahara 96 35.24 N 134.12 E
Kawai, Nihon 94 36.18 N 137.07 E
Kawai, Nihon 270 34.35 N 135.45 E
Kawaihae Bay ⊂ 229d 20.02 N 155.50 W
Kawaihoa › 229b 21.47 N 160.12 W
Kawaikini ∧ 229b 22.05 N 159.29 W
Kawailoa 229c 21.36 N 158.05 W
Kawailoa Beach 229c 21.37 N 158.04 W
Kawajiri 96 34.14 N 132.42 E
Kawakami, Nihon 94 35.58 N 138.35 E
Kawakami, Nihon 96 34.44 N 133.29 E
Kawakami, Nihon 96 35.17 N 133.39 E
Kawakawa 172 35.23 S 174.04 E
Kawakubo 270 34.54 N 135.38 E
Kawali 115a 7.11 S 108.22 E
Kawama Mission 154 10.04 S 28.37 E
Kawamata 92 37.39 N 140.36 E
Kawambwa 154 9.47 S 29.05 E
Kawamoto, Nihon 94 36.09 N 139.17 E
Kawamoto, Nihon 96 34.59 N 132.30 E
Kawane 94 34.57 N 138.05 E
Kawanishi, Nihon 94 37.09 N 138.45 E
Kawanishi, Nihon 96 34.49 N 135.24 E
Kawanishi, Nihon 270 34.35 N 135.47 E
Kawanoe 96 34.01 N 133.34 E
Kawara, Nihon 96 33.40 N 130.51 E
Kawara, Nihon 270 34.59 N 135.18 E
Kawara Débé 150 12.20 N 3.26 E
Kawarai 268 35.25 N 140.05 E
Kawardha 124 22.01 N 81.15 E
Kawartha Park 212 44.32 N 78.12 W
Kawasaki, Nihon 94 35.32 N 139.43 E
Kawasaki, Nihon 96 33.35 N 130.49 E
Kawasaki-kō ⊂ 268 35.30 N 139.47 E
Kawasaki Stadium ♠ 268 35.32 N 139.43 E
Kawashima, Nihon 94 35.21 N 136.50 E
Kawashima, Nihon 94 35.59 N 139.30 E
Kawashima, Nihon 96 34.04 N 134.19 E
Kawashima ◆[8] 268 35.28 N 139.35 E
Kawashiri-misaki › 96 34.26 N 130.58 E
Kawatana 92 33.04 N 129.52 E
Kawauchi 96 33.48 N 132.55 E
Kawau Island I 172 36.25 S 174.51 E
Kawawa ◆[8] 268 35.31 N 139.33 E
Kawayan 116 11.41 N 124.21 E
Kawazu 94 34.44 N 138.59 E
Kawbein 110 16.33 N 97.52 E
Kawdut 110 15.31 N 97.47 E
Kawe 164 7.50 S 138.14 E
Kawe, Pulau I 164 0.03 S 130.07 E
Kaweenakumik Lake ⊜ 184 52.52 N 99.30 W
Kaweka ∧ 172 39.17 S 176.23 E
Kaweka Range ⋏ 172 39.15 S 176.20 E
Kawerau 172 38.03 S 176.43 E
Kawhia 172 38.04 S 174.49 E
Kawhia Harbour ⊂ 172 38.05 S 174.50 E
Kawich Peak ∧ 204 37.58 N 116.27 W
Kawich Range ⋏ 204 37.40 N 116.30 W
Kawin 164 2.45 S 150.45 E
Kawinda 115b 8.07 S 118.04 E
Kawit 269f 14.27 N 120.54 E
Kawkabān 144 15.40 N 43.52 E
Kawkareik 110 16.33 N 98.14 E
Kaw Lake ⊜[1] 196 36.55 N 96.57 W
Kawludo 110 18.29 N 97.19 E
Kawm 140 13.31 N 22.50 E
Kawm al-Farā'in (Buto) ⊥ 142 31.11 N 30.45 E
Kawm ar-Rāhib 142 28.20 N 30.37 E
Kawm Birah 273c 30.05 N 31.08 E
Kawm Dafanah (Daphnæ) ⊥ 142 30.52 N 32.11 E
Kawm Ḥamādah 142 30.46 N 30.42 E
Kawm Ishfīn 273c 30.11 N 31.15 E
Kawm Ishū 142 31.07 N 30.00 E
Kawm Ju'ayf (Naucratis) ⊥ 142 30.54 N 30.36 E
Kawm Umbū 140 24.28 N 32.57 E
Kawnglanghpu 102 27.04 N 98.21 E
Kawnipi Lake ⊜ 190 48.24 N 91.14 W
Kawthaung 110 9.59 N 98.33 E
Kax ≐ 86 43.40 N 81.45 E
Kaxgar ≐ 85 39.40 N 78.00 E
Kaya, Burkina 150 13.05 N 1.05 W
Kaya, Nihon 96 35.30 N 135.06 E
Kayaapu 112 5.26 S 102.24 E
Kayadibi, Tür. 130 39.29 N 36.43 E
Kayadibi, Tür. 130 39.55 N 34.15 E
Kayah □[3] 110 19.15 N 97.30 E
Kayak Island I 180 59.52 N 144.30 W
Kāyalpattinam 122 8.34 N 78.07 E
Kāyamba 272b 22.41 N 88.32 E
Kayambi 154 9.27 S 31.58 E
Kayan 110 16.54 N 96.34 E
Kayan ≐ 112 2.55 N 117.35 E
Kayangel Islands II 108 8.04 N 134.43 E
Kayang-san ∧[2] 271b 37.33 N 126.43 E
Kāyankulam 122 9.11 N 76.30 E
Kayapa 116 16.22 N 120.53 E
Kayapınar 130 37.34 N 41.10 E
Kayaş 130 39.56 N 32.58 E
Kaya-san ∧ 98 35.49 N 128.07 E
Kaya-san Kukrip Kongwŏn ♠ 98 35.47 N 128.06 E
Kaycee 200 43.42 N 106.38 W
Kayeli 164 3.23 S 127.06 E
Kayembe-Mukulu 152 9.03 S 23.57 E
Kayen 115a 6.54 S 110.59 E
Kayenta 200 36.43 N 110.15 W
Kayes, Congo 152 4.25 S 11.41 E
Kayes, Mali 150 14.27 N 11.26 W
Kayes □[4] 150 14.00 N 11.00 W
Kay Gardens 285 39.45 N 75.25 W
Kayima 150 8.53 N 11.10 W
Kayin □[3] 110 17.30 N 97.45 E
Kayiry 78 46.57 N 33.43 E
Kayış Dağı ∧ 267b 40.59 N 29.10 E
Kaymakçı 130 38.10 N 28.08 E
Kaymaz, Tür. 130 39.31 N 31.11 E
Kaymaz, Tür. 130 40.55 N 30.18 E
Kayna 54 50.59 N 12.14 E
Kaynar 130 38.55 N 36.28 E
Kayō, Nihon 96 34.51 N 133.42 E
Kayō, Nihon 174m 26.33 N 128.07 E
Kayoa, Pulau I 164 0.05 S 127.25 E
Kayombo 154 9.36 S 25.37 E
Kaypak 130 37.08 N 36.27 E
Kay Point › 180 69.18 N 138.22 W
Kayser Gebergte ⋏ 250 3.03 N 56.35 W
Kayseri 130 38.43 N 35.30 E
Kayseri □[4] 130 38.30 N 35.55 E
Kaysersberg 58 48.08 N 7.15 E
Kaysville 200 41.02 N 111.56 W
Kayuadi, Pulau I 112 6.49 S 120.47 E

Symbols in the index entries represent the broad categories identified in the key at the right. Symbols with superior numbers (⋏[1]) identify subcategories (see complete key on page *I · 1)*.

Symbole im Register stellen die rechts im Schlüssel erklärten Kategorien dar. Symbole mit hochgestellten Ziffern (⋏[1]) bezeichnen Unterabteilungen einer Kategorie (vgl. vollständiger Schlüssel auf Seite *I · 1)*.

Los símbolos incluídos en el texto del índice representan las grandes categorías identificadas con la clave a la derecha. Los símbolos con numeros en su parte superior (⋏[1]) identifican las subcategorías (véase la clave completa en la página *I · 1)*.

Les symboles de l'index représentent les catégories indiquées dans la légende à droite. Les symboles suivis d'un indice (⋏[1]) représentent des sous-catégories (voir légende complète à la page *I · 1)*.

Os símbolos incluídos no texto do índice representam as grandes categorias identificadas com a chave à direita. Os símbolos com números em sua parte superior (⋏[1]) identificam as subcategorias (veja-se a chave completa à página *I · 1)*.

∧	Mountain	Berg	Montaña	Montagne	Montanha
⋏	Mountains	Gebirge	Montañas	Montagnes	Montanhas
)(	Pass	Paß	Paso	Col	Passo
V	Valley, Canyon	Tal, Cañon	Valle, Cañón	Vallée, Canyon	Vale, Canhão
≚	Plain	Ebene	Llano	Plaine	Planície
›	Cape	Kap	Cabo	Cap	Cabo
I	Island	Insel	Isla	Île	Ilha
II	Islands	Inseln	Islas	Îles	Ilhas
⊥	Other Topographic Features	Andere Topographische Objekte	Otros Elementos Topográficos	Autres données topographiques	Outros acidentes topográficos

ESPAÑOL: Nombre / Página / Lat.°′ / Long.°′ W = Oeste
FRANÇAIS: Nom / Page / Lat.°′ / Long.°′ W = Ouest
PORTUGUÊS: Nome / Página / Lat.°′ / Long.°′ W = Oeste

Nombre / Nom / Nome	Página / Page	Lat.°′	Long.°′
Kayuagung	112	3.24 S	104.50 E
Kayumas	115a	7.50 S	114.08 E
Kayuta Lake ⊜	210	43.25 N	75.12 W
Kayuyu	154	3.39 S	26.21 E
Kazachskij melkosopočnik ⋀[2]	86	49.00 N	72.00 E
Kazachstan → Kazakhstan □[1]	72	48.00 N	68.00 E
Kazačij	83	46.58 N	40.03 E
Kazačinskoje, Ross.	86	57.49 N	93.17 E
Kazačinskoje, Ross.	88	56.16 N	107.36 E
Kazačje	74	70.44 N	136.13 E
Kazačka	80	51.28 N	43.56 E
Kazackij	86	49.20 N	58.31 E
Kazakdarja	86	43.27 N	59.46 E
Kazakevičevo	89	48.17 N	134.46 E
Kazakhstan □[1], Asia	72	48.00 N	68.00 E
Kazakhstan □[1], Asia	86	47.00 N	76.00 E
Kazaki	76	52.38 N	38.16 E
Kazakstan → Kazakhstan □[1]	72	48.00 N	68.00 E
Kazal'cevo	86	59.18 N	80.30 E
Kazalinsk	86	45.46 N	62.07 E
Kazan'	80	55.49 N	49.08 E
Kazan ≃	176	64.02 N	95.30 W
Kazancı	130	36.30 N	32.53 E
Kazandžik	128	39.16 N	55.32 E
Kazanka, Kaz.	86	53.20 N	67.27 E
Kazanka, Ukr.	78	47.50 N	32.49 E
Kazanka ≃	80	55.48 N	49.01 E
Kazanlăk	38	42.38 N	25.21 E
Kazan Lake ⊜	184	55.33 N	108.21 W
Kazanlı	130	36.50 N	34.45 E
Kazanovka	76	53.46 N	38.34 E
Kazan-rettō (Volcano Islands) II	14	25.00 N	141.00 E
Kazanskaja	78	49.48 N	41.09 E
Kazanskoje, Ross.	82	54.59 N	37.39 E
Kazanskoje, Ross.	86	55.38 N	69.14 E
Kazan' Station ◆[5]	265b	55.46 N	37.40 E
Kazantyp, mys ≻	78	45.28 N	35.51 E
Kazarman	85	41.24 N	74.03 E
Kazatkul'	86	55.02 N	76.03 E
Kazbegi	84	42.39 N	44.39 E
Kazbek, gora ∧	84	42.42 N	44.31 E
Kaz Dağı ∧	130	39.42 N	26.50 E
Kazembe	154	12.11 S	32.37 E
Kazenyy Torets' ≃	83	48.54 N	37.46 E
Kāzerūn	128	29.37 N	51.38 E
Kazgorodok, Kaz.	86	52.53 N	70.42 E
Kazgorodok, Kaz.	86	49.56 N	71.36 E
Kažim	24	60.20 N	51.30 E
Kazimierza Wielka	30	50.16 N	20.30 E
Kazimierz Dolny	30	51.20 N	21.58 E
Kazincbarcika	30	48.16 N	20.37 E
Kazinka, Ross.	76	52.32 N	39.42 E
Kazinka, Ross.	78	50.14 N	37.50 E
Kāzipāra	272b	22.43 N	88.31 E
Kāzīr Char	126	22.46 N	90.33 E
Kaziza	152	10.42 S	23.52 E
Kazlų Rūda	76	54.46 N	23.30 E
Kaz'minskoje	84	44.35 N	41.41 E
Kaznačejevo	82	54.31 N	37.16 E
Kazo	94	36.07 N	139.36 E
Kaztalovka	80	49.46 N	48.42 E
Kazuma Pan National Park ♠	154	18.15 S	25.33 E
Kazumba	152	6.25 S	22.02 E
Kazungula	154	17.45 S	25.20 E
Kazuno	92	40.11 N	140.47 E
Kazvin → Qazvīn	128	36.16 N	50.00 E
Kazy	128	39.13 N	57.30 E
Kazym	74	63.40 N	67.14 E
Kazym ≃	74	63.54 N	65.50 E
Kazyr ≃	86	53.47 N	92.53 E
Kbal Dâmrei	110	14.07 N	105.21 E
Kbelnice	60	49.18 N	13.59 E
Kbely ◆[8]	54	50.07 N	14.32 E
Kcynia	30	53.00 N	17.30 E
Kdyně	60	49.23 N	13.02 E
Kéa	38	37.38 N	24.21 E
Kéa I	38	37.34 N	24.22 E
Keaau	229d	19.37 N	155.02 W
Keady	48	54.15 N	6.42 W
Keahole Point ≻	229d	19.44 N	156.03 W
Keal, Loch na ⊂	46	56.28 N	6.04 W
Kealaikahiki, Lae o ≻	229a	20.32 N	156.42 W
Kealaikahiki Channel ʊ	229a	20.37 N	156.50 W
Kealakekua Bay ⊂	229d	19.28 N	155.56 W
Kealia	229b	22.06 N	159.18 W
Keams Canyon	200	35.48 N	110.11 W
Keanae	229a	20.51 N	156.09 W
Keanapapa Point ≻	229a	20.54 N	157.04 W
Kean College of New Jersey ʋ[2]	276	40.41 N	74.14 W
Keansburg	208	40.25 N	74.12 W
Kearney, Mo., U.S.	194	39.22 N	94.21 W
Kearney, Ne., U.S.	198	40.41 N	99.04 W
Kearney, Pa., U.S.	214	40.08 N	78.12 W
Kearns	200	40.39 N	111.59 W
Kearny, Az., U.S.	200	33.03 N	110.54 W
Kearny, N.J., U.S.	210	40.46 N	74.08 W
Kearsley	262	53.32 N	2.23 W
Kearsley Creek ≃	216	43.04 N	83.40 W
Keasbey	276	40.31 N	74.19 W
Keb' ≃	76	57.44 N	28.28 E
Kebajoran ◆[8]	269e	6.13 S	106.46 E
Keban	130	38.48 N	38.45 E
Keban Barajı ⊜[1]	130	38.50 N	39.20 E
Kebanyartimur	115a	7.09 S	112.52 E
Kébara	152	2.27 S	14.25 E
Kebbi	150	12.08 N	4.44 E
Kebeiti	120	36.47 N	79.29 E
Kébémer	150	15.22 N	16.27 W
Kébi, Mayo ≃	146	9.18 N	13.33 E
Kebili	148	33.42 N	8.58 E
Kebîr, Oued el ≃	34	36.50 N	6.07 E
Kebnekaise ∧	24	67.53 N	18.33 E
Kebock Head ≻	46	58.01 N	6.20 W
Kebri Dehar	144	6.47 N	44.17 E
Kebumen	115a	7.40 S	109.39 E
Keb'uty	80	45.50 N	44.14 E
Keče	85	43.14 N	71.22 E
Kecel	30	46.32 N	19.16 E
Kech ≃	128	26.00 N	62.44 E
Kechika ≃	176	59.36 N	127.05 W
Keçiborlu	130	37.57 N	30.18 E
Kecksburg	214	40.11 N	79.28 W
Kecskemét	30	46.54 N	19.42 E
Kedah □[3]	114	6.00 N	100.40 E
Kėdainiai	76	55.17 N	24.00 E
Kédange-sur-Canner	56	49.19 N	6.20 E
Kedārnāth	124	30.44 N	79.04 E
Kedārpur	126	23.18 N	90.27 E
Kedges Straits ʊ	208	38.03 N	76.02 W
Kedgwick	186	47.39 N	67.21 W
Kedgwick ≃	186	47.40 N	67.29 W
Kédhron	38	39.13 N	22.03 E
Kedian	100	31.23 N	112.51 E
Kediri	115a	7.49 S	112.01 E
Kedjebi	150	8.12 N	0.25 E
Kedon	74	64.08 N	159.14 E
Kedong	89	48.02 N	126.15 E
Kédougou	150	12.33 N	12.11 W
Kedrasju	24	64.36 N	60.24 E
Kedrikí Makedhonía □[4]	38	40.30 N	23.00 E
Kedrovka	86	55.32 N	86.03 E
Kedu	102	26.33 N	104.21 E
Kedungdung	115a	7.06 S	113.15 E
Kedungjati	115a	7.10 S	110.37 E
Kedungwuni	115a	6.58 S	109.39 E
Kedvavom	24	64.15 N	53.27 E
Kędzierzyn Kozle	30	50.20 N	18.12 E
Keecheus Lake ⊜	224	47.22 N	121.22 W
Keefer	218	38.32 N	84.38 W
Keefers	182	50.02 N	121.33 W
Keego Harbor	216	42.36 N	83.20 W
Keelby	44	53.34 N	0.15 W
Keele	42	53.00 N	2.17 W
Keele ≃	180	64.24 N	124.50 W
Keele Peak ∧	180	63.26 N	130.19 W
Keeley Lake ⊜	184	54.54 N	108.08 W
Keeling Islands → Cocos Islands □[2]	12	12.10 S	96.55 E
Keels	186	48.36 N	53.24 W
Keelung → Chilung	100	25.08 N	121.44 E
Keen, Mount ∧	46	56.58 N	2.54 W
Keene, On., Can.	212	44.15 N	78.10 W
Keene, Ca., U.S.	228	35.13 N	118.33 W
Keene, Ky., U.S.	192	37.56 N	84.38 W
Keene, N.H., U.S.	188	42.56 N	72.16 W
Keene, Oh., U.S.	214	40.21 N	81.52 W
Keene, Tx., U.S.	222	32.23 N	97.19 W
Keenesburg	200	40.06 N	104.31 W
Keeney Knob ∧	192	37.47 N	80.42 W
Keeneyville	278	41.59 N	88.07 W
Keep River National Park ♠	164	15.48 S	129.03 E
Keerbergen	56	51.00 N	4.37 E
Keer-Weer, Cape ≻	164	13.58 S	141.30 E
Keeseg ∧	64	46.58 N	12.14 E
Keeseville	188	44.30 N	73.28 W
Keesler Air Force Base ■	194	30.26 N	88.55 W
Keetmanshoop	156	26.36 S	18.08 E
Keetmanshoop □[5]	156	26.30 S	19.00 E
Keewatin, On., Can.	184	49.46 N	94.34 W
Keewatin, Mn., U.S.	190	47.23 N	93.04 W
Kefa □[4]	144	6.50 N	36.00 E
Kefallinía I	38	38.15 N	20.35 E
Kéfalos	38	36.45 N	27.00 E
Kefamenanu	112	9.27 S	124.29 E
Kefar 'Azza	132	31.29 N	34.32 E
Kefar Blum	132	33.10 N	35.36 E
Kefar 'Ezyon	132	31.39 N	35.08 E
Kefar Naḥum (Capernaum) ⊥	132	32.53 N	35.34 E
Kefar Sava	132	32.10 N	34.54 E
Kefar Shammay	132	32.57 N	35.27 E
Kefar Szold	132	33.11 N	35.39 E
Kefar Vitkin	132	32.23 N	34.53 E
Kefar Warburg	132	31.43 N	34.44 E
Kefar Yona	132	32.19 N	34.55 E
Kefermarkt	61	48.26 N	14.32 E
Keffi	150	8.51 N	7.52 E
Keffin Hausa	150	12.15 N	9.58 E
Keflavík	24a	64.02 N	22.36 W
Keftya	144	13.54 N	37.07 E
Kega	24	65.10 N	36.54 E
Ke Ga, Mui ≻, Viet	110	10.42 N	107.58 E
Ke Ga, Mui ≻, Viet	110	12.53 N	109.28 E
Kegalla	122	7.15 N	80.21 E
Kégashka	186	50.12 N	61.17 W
Kégashka, Lac ⊜	186	50.20 N	61.25 W
Kegejli	86	42.45 N	59.35 E
Kegnæs ≻[1]	41	54.52 N	9.59 E
Kegon-no-taki ⌞	94	36.44 N	139.31 E
Kegonsa, Lake ⊜	216	42.58 N	89.15 W
Kegonzhake	120	33.00 N	87.53 E
Keg River	176	57.48 N	117.52 W
Kegums	76	56.46 N	24.45 E
Kegworth	42	52.50 N	1.16 W
Kehdingen, Land ◆[1]	52	53.45 N	9.15 E
Kehiwin Indian Reserve ◆[4]	182	54.07 N	110.48 W
Kehl	56	48.35 N	7.50 E
Kehlen	58	47.41 N	9.33 E
Kehoe	218	38.28 N	83.03 W
Kehra	76	59.20 N	25.20 E
Kehrigk	54	52.09 N	13.55 E
Ke-hsi Mānsām	110	21.56 N	97.50 E
Kehychivka	78	49.17 N	35.46 E
Keig	46	57.15 N	2.39 W
Keighley	44	53.52 N	1.54 W
Keihoku	96	35.09 N	135.38 E
Keijō → Sŏul	98	37.33 N	126.58 E
Keila	76	59.18 N	24.25 E
Keilor	169	37.43 S	144.50 E
Keimoes	158	28.41 S	21.00 E
Kei Mouth	158	32.41 S	28.22 E
Keio University ʋ[2]	268	35.38 N	139.45 E
Kei Road	158	32.42 S	27.32 E
Keiser	194	35.40 N	90.05 W
Keiskammahoek	158	32.41 S	27.09 E
Keiskammapunt ≻	158	32.40 S	27.10 E
Keïta	150	14.46 N	5.46 E
Kéita, Bahr ≃	146	9.14 N	18.21 E
Keitele	26	63.11 N	26.22 E
Keitele ⊜	26	62.55 N	26.00 E
Keith, Austl.	166	36.06 S	140.21 E
Keith, Scot., U.K.	46	57.32 N	2.57 W
Keith Arm ⊂	176	65.20 N	122.15 W
Keithley Creek	182	52.45 N	121.24 W
Keithsburg	190	41.05 N	90.56 W
Keiyasi	175g	17.54 S	177.45 E
Keizer	224	44.59 N	123.01 W
Kejaman	112	2.39 N	113.45 E
Kejimkujik National Park ♠	186	44.21 N	65.18 W
Kejngypil'gyn, laguna ⊂	180	63.30 N	178.50 E
Kejni, gora ∧	180	64.30 N	174.54 W
Kejvy ⋀	24	67.35 N	38.00 E
Kekaha	229b	21.58 N	159.42 W
Kekek ≃	190	48.24 N	75.48 W
Kekerengu	172	42.00 S	174.01 E
Kékes ∧	30	47.55 N	20.02 E
Kekeyaer	85	38.02 N	75.05 E
Kek Lok Si ʋ[1]	114	5.23 N	100.14 E
Kekpāra	126	22.27 N	86.35 E
Kekri	120	25.58 N	75.09 E
Kekurnoi, Cape ≻	180	57.44 N	155.15 W
Kelafo	144	5.40 N	44.20 E
Kelai ≃	112	2.10 N	117.29 E
Kelan	102	38.43 N	111.32 E
Kelanang	114	2.48 N	101.26 E
Kelang	114	3.02 N	101.27 E
Kelang, Pulau I, Indon.	164	3.12 S	127.44 E
Kelang, Pulau I, Malay.	114	3.00 N	101.18 E
Kelani ≃	122	6.58 N	79.52 E
Kelantan	114	0.51 N	101.40 E
Kelantan □[3]	114	5.20 N	102.00 E
Kelantan ≃	114	6.11 N	102.15 E
Kelapa	112	1.52 S	105.42 E
Kelasuri	84	43.08 N	41.13 E
Kelat	218	38.32 N	84.19 W
Kelayres	210	40.54 N	76.00 W
Kelb, Ouadi ∨	146	15.19 N	18.51 E
Kelberg	56	50.17 N	6.55 E
Kelbia, Sebkhet ⊜	36	35.51 N	10.16 E
Kelbra	54	51.26 N	11.02 E
Keld Ula ∧	86	43.20 N	85.25 E
Kel'd'ušovo	80	55.01 N	44.59 E
Keleft	128	37.21 N	66.15 E
Kelegou	98	41.57 N	118.11 E
Kélékélé	273b	4.20 S	15.08 E
Kelem	144	4.48 N	35.58 E
Kelenföld ◆[8]	264c	47.28 N	19.03 E
Kelenken, gora ∧	180	66.07 N	170.52 W
Keles, Tür.	130	39.55 N	29.14 E
Keles, Uzb.	85	41.24 N	69.12 E
Keles ≃	85	41.02 N	68.37 E
Keleti-főcsatorna ≋	30	48.01 N	21.20 E
Keleti Pályaudvar ◆[5]	264c	47.30 N	19.06 E
Kelheim	60	48.55 N	11.52 E
Kelibia	148	36.51 N	11.06 E
Kelkheim	56	50.08 N	8.26 E
Kelkit	130	40.08 N	39.27 E
Kelkit ≃	130	40.46 N	36.32 E
Kell	219	38.30 N	88.54 W
Kellé	152	0.06 S	14.33 E
Kellen	52	51.48 N	6.10 E
Kellenhusen	54	54.11 N	11.03 E
Keller, Tx., U.S.	222	32.56 N	97.15 W
Keller, Va., U.S.	208	37.37 N	75.45 W
Keller, Wa., U.S.	182	48.04 N	118.41 W
Kellerberg	64	46.40 N	13.42 E
Kellerberrin	162	31.38 S	117.43 E
Kellerjoch ∧	64	47.19 N	11.46 E
Keller Lake ⊜, N.T., Can.	176	64.00 N	121.30 W
Keller Lake ⊜, Sk., Can.	184	56.04 N	106.46 W
Kellerovka	86	53.50 N	69.17 E
Keller Peak ∧	228	34.12 N	117.03 W
Kellett, Cape ≻	176	71.59 N	125.34 W
Kellettville	214	41.33 N	79.16 W
Kelleys Island	214	41.36 N	82.42 W
Kelleys Island I	214	41.36 N	82.42 W
Kelliher	184	51.15 N	103.44 W
Kellinghusen	52	53.57 N	9.43 E
Kellmünz	58	48.07 N	10.08 E
Kelloe	44	54.43 N	1.28 W
Kellogg, Id., U.S.	202	47.32 N	116.07 W
Kellogg, Ia., U.S.	190	41.43 N	92.54 W
Kellogg, Mn., U.S.	190	44.18 N	91.59 W
Kellogg Marsh	224	48.05 N	122.07 W
Kelloggsville	214	41.52 N	80.36 W
Kellojärvi ⊜	26	64.16 N	29.03 E
Kelloselkä	24	66.56 N	28.50 E
Kells → Ceanannus Mór, Ire.	48	53.44 N	6.53 W
Kells, N. Ire., U.K.	48	54.48 N	6.13 W
Kelly Air Force Base ■	196	29.24 N	98.35 W
Kelly Lake ⊜	180	65.30 N	126.10 W
Kelly Run ≃, Pa., U.S.	279b	40.15 N	79.55 W
Kelly Run ≃, Pa., U.S.	279b	40.13 N	79.45 W
Kellyville, Austl.	274a	33.43 S	150.57 E
Kellyville, Ok., U.S.	196	35.56 N	96.12 W
Kelmė	76	55.38 N	22.56 E
Kel'mentsi	78	48.27 N	26.50 E
Kelmet	144	16.04 N	38.55 E
Kelmscott	168a	32.07 S	116.01 E
Kelo	146	9.19 N	15.48 E
Kelolokan	112	1.08 N	117.54 E
Kelottijärvi	24	68.31 N	22.04 E
Kelowna	182	49.53 N	119.29 W
Kelsall	44	53.13 N	2.43 W
Kelsey Bay	182	50.24 N	125.57 W
Kelsey Head ≻	42	50.24 N	5.08 W
Kelsey Lake ⊜	184	53.37 N	101.02 W
Kelseyville	204	38.58 N	122.50 W
Kelso, Scot., U.K.	46	55.36 N	2.25 W
Kelso, Wa., U.S.	224	46.08 N	122.54 W
Kelsterbach	56	50.04 N	8.32 E
Kel'temašat	85	42.30 N	70.17 E
Kelty	46	56.08 N	3.23 W
Keluang	114	2.02 N	103.19 E
Keluang, Tanjung ≻	112	3.02 S	110.39 E
Kelud, Gunung ∧	115a	7.56 S	112.18 E
Keluo ≃	89	49.22 N	125.15 E
Keluotun	89	49.16 N	125.44 E
Kelvedon	42	51.51 N	0.42 E
Kelvedon Hatch	260	51.40 N	0.16 E
Kelvington	184	52.10 N	103.30 W
Kelvin Seamount ✢[3]	16	38.50 N	64.00 W
Kelyexeed	144	8.46 N	49.12 E
Kelzenberg	263	51.07 N	6.30 E
Kem'	24	64.57 N	34.36 E
Kem' ≃, Ross.	24	64.57 N	34.41 E
Kem' ≃, Ross.	86	58.31 N	92.04 E
Kema	112	1.23 N	125.04 E
Kema ≃, Ross.	76	60.16 N	37.20 E
Kema ≃, Ross.	76	59.21 N	44.29 E
Ké Macina	150	13.58 N	5.22 W
Kémah, Congo	273b	4.11 S	15.13 E
Kemah, Tür.	130	39.36 N	39.02 E
Kemah, Tx., U.S.	222	29.32 N	95.01 W
Kemaliye	130	39.16 N	38.29 E
Kemalpaşa, Tür.	130	41.30 N	41.30 E
Kemalpaşa, Tür.	130	38.25 N	27.26 E
Kemano	182	53.34 N	127.56 W
Kemasik	114	4.25 N	103.27 E
Kemayan	114	3.08 N	102.22 E
Kemayoran Airport ⊠	269e	6.09 S	106.51 E
Kembani	112	1.34 S	122.54 E
Kembé	152	4.36 N	21.54 E
Kemberg	54	51.46 N	12.38 E
Kemblesville	208	39.45 N	75.50 W
Kembolcha	144	11.02 N	39.43 E
Kembs	58	47.41 N	7.30 E
Kembul	164	5.55 S	150.40 E
Kemčug ≃	86	57.14 N	90.31 E
Kemena ≃	112	3.10 N	113.03 E
Kemeneshát ⋀[2]	61	46.58 N	16.40 E
Kemer, Tür.	130	36.38 N	29.21 E
Kemer, Tür.	130	36.36 N	30.34 E
Kemer, Tür.	130	37.21 N	30.04 E
Kemer ≃	267b	41.04 N	29.07 E
Kemer Barajı ⊜[1]	130	37.34 N	28.31 E
Kemerburgaz ◆[8]	267b	41.09 N	28.54 E
Kemerhisar	130	37.49 N	34.36 E
Kemerovo	86	55.20 N	86.05 E
Kemerovo Oblast' □[4]	86	55.00 N	87.00 E
Kemi	26	65.49 N	24.32 E
Kemie	26	62.14 N	30.20 E
Kemijärvi	24	66.40 N	27.25 E
Kemijärvi ⊜	24	66.36 N	27.24 E
Kemijoki ≃	24	65.47 N	24.30 E
Kemiö → Kimito	26	60.10 N	22.45 E
Keml'a	80	54.42 N	45.15 E
Kemmel	50	50.47 N	2.49 E
Kemmelberg ∧[2]	50	50.47 N	2.50 E
Kemmerer	200	41.47 N	110.32 W
Kemminghausen ◆[8]	263	51.34 N	7.29 E
Kemmuna (Comino) I	36	36.00 N	14.20 E
Kemnader See ⊜	263	51.25 N	7.15 E
Kemnath	60	49.52 N	11.54 E
Kemnay	46	57.14 N	2.27 W
Kemnitz	54	54.04 N	13.31 E
Kémo-Gribingui □[5]	152	6.00 N	19.00 E
Kemp	222	32.26 N	96.13 W
Kemp, Lake ⊜[1]	196	33.45 N	99.13 W
Kemparana	150	12.50 N	4.56 W
Kemp Coast ⍓[2]	9	67.10 S	58.00 E
Kempele	26	64.55 N	25.30 E
Kempen	56	51.22 N	6.25 E
Kempen ◆[1]	56	51.10 N	5.20 E
Kempener Land ◆[1]	263	51.19 N	6.29 E
Kempenfelt Bay ⊂	212	44.23 N	79.36 W
Kempenich	56	50.25 N	7.07 E
Kemper → Quimper	32	48.00 N	4.06 W
Kempisch Kanaal ≋	56	51.10 N	4.49 E
Kemp Mill	284c	39.02 N	77.01 W
Kempner	196	31.05 N	98.00 W
Kemp Peninsula ≻[1]	9	73.08 S	60.15 W
Kemps Bay	238	24.02 N	77.33 W
Kemps Creek ≃	274a	33.51 S	150.46 E
Kempsey, Austl.	166	31.05 S	152.50 E
Kempsey, Eng., U.K.	42	52.08 N	2.12 W
Kempston	42	52.07 N	0.30 W
Kempt, Lac ⊜	176	47.25 N	74.22 W
Kempten (Allgäu)	58	47.43 N	10.19 E
Kempton, Il., U.S.	216	40.56 N	88.14 W
Kempton, In., U.S.	216	40.17 N	86.13 W
Kempton Park	158	26.06 S	28.14 E
Kempton Park □[5]	273d	26.06 S	28.14 E
Kempton Park Race Course ♠	260	51.25 N	0.23 W
Kemptville	212	45.01 N	75.38 W
Kemptville Creek ≃	212	45.03 N	75.39 W
Kemsing	260	51.18 N	0.14 E
Kemubu	114	5.18 N	102.01 E
Kemujan, Pulau I	115a	5.48 S	110.28 E
Kemul, Kong ∧	112	1.52 N	116.11 E
Ken ≃	124	25.46 N	80.31 E
Ken, Loch ⊜	44	55.02 N	4.02 W
Ken, Water of ≃	44	55.04 N	4.08 W
Kena ≃	24	62.05 N	39.06 E
Kenai	180	60.33 N	151.15 W
Kenai Fjords National Park ♠	180	59.45 N	150.00 W
Kenai Mountains ⋀	180	60.00 N	150.00 W
Kenai Peninsula ≻[1]	180	60.10 N	150.00 W
Kenamuke Swamp ⩸	140	6.15 N	33.48 E
Kenansville, Fl., U.S.	220	27.52 N	80.59 W
Kenansville, N.C., U.S.	192	34.57 N	77.57 W
Kenaral	85	42.32 N	72.08 E
Kenašči	80	50.32 N	53.20 E
Kenashiga-sen ∧	96	35.14 N	133.31 E
Kenaston	184	51.30 N	106.18 W
Kenberma	283	42.17 N	70.52 W
Kenbridge	192	36.57 N	78.07 W
Kenda	126	23.12 N	86.32 E
Kendai	124	22.45 N	82.37 E
Kendal, Sk., Can.	184	50.15 N	103.37 W
Kendal, Indon.	115a	6.55 S	110.12 E
Kendal, S. Afr.	158	26.04 S	28.58 E
Kendal, Eng., U.K.	44	54.20 N	2.45 W
Kendall, Austl.	166	31.38 S	152.43 E
Kendall, Fl., U.S.	220	25.40 N	80.19 W
Kendall, Mi., U.S.	216	42.22 N	85.49 W
Kendall, N.Y., U.S.	210	43.20 N	78.02 W
Kendall, Wi., U.S.	190	43.47 N	90.22 W
Kendall □[6]	216	41.38 N	88.27 W
Kendall, Cape ≻	176	63.36 N	87.09 W
Kendall, Mount ∧	172	41.22 S	172.24 E
Kendall Park	208	40.31 N	74.24 W
Kendallville	216	41.26 N	85.15 W
Kendari	112	3.57 S	122.35 E
Kendari, Teluk ⊂	112	3.57 S	122.38 E
Kendawangan	112	2.32 S	110.12 E
Kende	150	11.30 N	4.12 E
Kendenup	162	34.29 S	117.39 E
Kendghāta	126	24.05 N	87.10 E
Kendikolu I	122	5.57 N	73.24 E
Kendiktas ⋀	85	43.35 N	74.45 E
Kendleton	222	29.27 N	96.00 W
Kendrāparha	120	20.30 N	86.25 E
Kendrew	158	32.31 S	24.30 E
Kendrick, Fl., U.S.	192	29.22 N	82.12 W
Kendrick, Id., U.S.	202	46.36 N	116.38 W
Kendrick Creek ≃	226	38.00 N	119.50 W
Kendua	272b	22.34 N	88.10 E
Kendu Bay	154	0.22 S	34.39 E
Kendujhargarh	120	21.38 N	85.35 E
Kendyrlik	86	47.30 N	85.12 E
Kenedy	196	28.49 N	97.50 W
Kenefick	222	30.07 N	94.51 W
Kenema	150	7.52 N	11.12 W
Kenes, Kaz.	85	43.41 N	67.49 E
Kenes, Kaz.	85	43.59 N	73.35 E
Kenesaw	198	40.37 N	98.39 W
Kenga	86	57.27 N	80.57 E
Kenga ≃	86	58.05 N	80.37 E
Kenge	152	4.52 S	16.59 E
Kengeja	154	5.25 S	39.44 E
Kēng Hkam, Mya.	110	21.01 N	98.29 E
Keng Hkam, Mya.	110	21.27 N	97.03 E
Kengkou, Zhg.	100	29.48 N	117.22 E
Kengkou, Zhg.	100	28.27 N	120.26 E
Kengtian	100	25.54 N	119.26 E
Kēng Tung	110	21.17 N	99.36 E
Kengun-chūtonchi, Rikujō-jieitai- ■	92	32.46 N	130.45 E
Kenhardt	158	29.19 S	21.12 E
Kenhorst	208	40.18 N	75.57 W
Kenia	152	2.43 S	17.04 E
Kenia → Kenya □[1]	154	1.00 N	38.00 E
Kenia → Kirinyaga ∧	154	0.10 S	37.20 E
Kéniéba	150	12.50 N	11.14 W
Kenilworth, Eng., U.K.	42	52.21 N	1.34 W
Kenilworth, Il., U.S.	278	42.05 N	87.43 W
Kenilworth, N.J., U.S.	276	40.40 N	74.17 W
Kenilworth, Pa., U.S.	208	40.14 N	75.38 W
Kenilworth, Ut,. U.S.	200	39.41 N	110.48 W
Kenilworth Castle ⊥	42	52.21 N	1.34 W
Keningau	112	5.20 N	116.10 E
Kenitra	148	34.16 N	6.40 W
Kenitra □[4]	148	34.30 N	6.00 W
Kenley ◆[8]	260	51.19 N	0.06 W
Kenli (Xishuanghe)	98	37.40 N	118.35 E
Kenly	192	35.35 N	78.07 W
Kenmare, Ire.	48	51.53 N	9.35 W
Kenmare, N.D., U.S.	198	48.40 N	102.04 W
Kenmare River ≃	48	51.45 N	10.00 W
Kenmawr	279b	40.28 N	80.06 W
Kenmore, Scot., U.K.	46	56.34 N	3.59 W
Kenmore, N.Y., U.S.	210	42.57 N	78.52 W
Kenmore, Wa., U.S.	224	47.45 N	122.14 W
Kennard, In., U.S.	218	39.54 N	85.31 W
Kennard, Pa., U.S.	214	41.28 N	80.20 W
Kennard, Tx., U.S.	222	31.22 N	95.11 W
Kennebec	198	43.54 N	99.51 W
Kennebec ≃	188	44.00 N	69.50 W
Kennebecasis Bay ⊂	186	45.25 N	66.00 W
Kennebec Lake ⊜	212	44.43 N	77.00 W
Kennebunk	188	43.23 N	70.32 W
Kennedale	222	32.38 N	97.13 W
Kennedy, Al., U.S.	194	33.35 N	87.59 W
Kennedy, N.Y., U.S.	214	42.09 N	79.06 W
Kennedy, Zimb.	154	18.52 S	27.10 E
Kennedy, Cape → Canaveral, Cape ≻	220	28.27 N	80.32 W
Kennedy, Mount ∧, B.C., Can.	182	50.49 N	125.33 W
Kennedy, Mount ∧, Yk., Can.	180	60.30 N	139.00 W
Kennedy Entrance ʊ	180	59.00 N	152.00 W
Kennedy Lake ⊜	182	49.05 N	125.40 W
Kennedy Peak ∧	110	23.19 N	93.45 E
Kennedy Range ⋀	162	24.30 S	115.00 E
Kennedyville	208	39.18 N	75.59 W
Kennemerduinen, Nationale Park de ♠	52	52.25 N	4.35 E
Kenner	194	29.59 N	90.14 W
Kennerdell	214	41.16 N	79.51 W
Kennet ≃	42	51.28 N	0.57 W
Kennetcook	186	45.11 N	63.44 W
Kenneth City	220	27.49 N	82.44 W
Kennett	194	36.14 N	90.03 W
Kennett ≃	42	52.26 N	0.28 E
Kennett Square	208	39.50 N	75.42 W
Kennewick	202	46.12 N	119.08 W
Kenney	219	40.06 N	89.05 W
Kenney Dam ◆[6]	182	53.37 N	124.58 W
Kennington, Eng., U.K.	42	51.10 N	0.54 E
Kennington, Eng., U.K.	42	51.43 N	1.15 W
Kennisis Lake ⊜	212	45.13 N	78.39 W
Kenn Reef ✢[2]	160	21.12 S	155.46 E
Kenny	222	30.03 N	96.20 W
Kennydale	224	47.31 N	122.12 W
Kennywood Park ♠	279b	40.23 N	79.52 W
Kénogami	186	48.26 N	71.14 W
Kenogami ≃	176	51.06 N	84.28 W
Kénogami, Lac ⊜	186	48.20 N	71.23 W
Kenogamissi Lake ⊜	190	48.15 N	81.31 W
Keno Hill	180	63.55 N	135.18 W
Kenora	184	49.47 N	94.29 W
Kenosha	216	42.35 N	87.49 W
Kenosha □[6]	216	42.35 N	88.03 W
Kenova	188	38.23 N	82.34 W
Kenoza Lake	210	41.44 N	74.57 W
Kenoza Lake ⊜	283	42.47 N	71.03 W
Kenozero, ozero ⊜	24	62.03 N	38.14 E
Ken Rock	216	42.15 N	89.03 W
Kensal	198	47.18 N	98.43 W
Kense	86	46.49 N	68.20 E
Kensett	194	35.13 N	91.40 W
Kensico Lake ⊜	276	41.07 N	73.45 W
Kensico Reservoir ⊜[1]	210	41.05 N	73.46 W
Kensington, Austl.	274a	33.55 S	151.14 E
Kensington, P.E., Can.	186	46.26 N	63.38 W
Kensington, Ca., U.S.	226	37.54 N	122.16 W
Kensington, Ct., U.S.	207	41.38 N	72.46 W
Kensington, Ks., U.S.	198	39.46 N	99.01 W
Kensington, Md., U.S.	284c	39.01 N	77.04 W
Kensington, Oh., U.S.	214	40.44 N	80.57 W
Kensington ◆[8], S. Afr.	273d	26.12 S	28.06 E
Kensington ◆[8], N.Y., U.S.	276	40.39 N	73.58 W
Kensington ◆[8], Pa., U.S.	285	39.58 N	75.08 W
Kensington and Chelsea ◆[8]	260	51.29 N	0.11 W
Kensington Estates	284c	39.02 N	77.05 W
Kensington Metropolitan Park ♠	281	42.32 N	83.39 W
Kensington Park	220	27.22 N	82.31 W
Kent, S.L.	150	8.10 N	13.10 W
Kent, Ct., U.S.	207	41.43 N	73.28 W
Kent, N.Y., U.S.	210	43.20 N	78.08 W
Kent, Oh., U.S.	214	41.09 N	81.21 W
Kent, Or., U.S.	224	45.11 N	120.41 W
Kent, Wa., U.S.	224	47.22 N	122.14 W
Kent □[6], On., Can.	214	42.25 N	82.10 W
Kent □[6], Eng., U.K.	42	51.15 N	0.40 E
Kent □[6], De., U.S.	208	39.10 N	75.32 W
Kent □[6], Md., U.S.	208	39.13 N	76.04 W
Kent □[6], Mi., U.S.	216	42.56 N	85.33 W
Kent □[6], R.I., U.S.	207	41.40 N	71.38 W
Kent ≃	44	54.15 N	2.48 W
Kent, Vale of ∨	42	51.10 N	0.30 E
Kent Acres	208	39.07 N	75.31 W
Kentallen	46	56.39 N	5.15 W
Kentani	158	32.31 S	28.19 E
Kentau	85	43.36 N	68.36 E
Kent Bridge	214	42.31 N	82.04 W
Kent County Airport ⊠	216	42.54 N	85.39 W
Kentfield	282	37.57 N	122.33 W
Kent Group II	166	39.27 S	147.20 E
Kenthurst	274a	33.40 S	151.00 E
Kent Island I	208	38.55 N	76.20 W
Kent Lake ⊜	216	42.32 N	83.40 W
Kentland, In., U.S.	216	40.46 N	87.26 W
Kentland, Md., U.S.	284c	38.55 N	76.53 W
Kenton, Eng., U.K.	42	50.38 N	3.28 W
Kenton, De., U.S.	208	39.13 N	75.39 W
Kenton, Mi., U.S.	190	46.29 N	88.53 W
Kenton, Oh., U.S.	216	40.38 N	83.36 W
Kenton, Tn., U.S.	194	36.12 N	89.00 W
Kenton □[6]	218	38.56 N	84.33 W
Kent Park	283	42.06 N	70.41 W
Kent Park ♠	273d	26.08 S	28.04 E
Kent Peninsula ≻[1]	176	68.30 N	107.00 W
Kent Point ≻	208	38.50 N	76.22 W
Kentucky □[3]	178	37.30 N	85.15 W
Kentucky ≃	218	38.41 N	85.11 W
Kentucky, Middle Fork ≃	192	37.35 N	83.40 W
Kentucky, North Fork ≃	192	37.34 N	83.42 W
Kentucky, South Fork ≃	192	37.34 N	83.42 W
Kentucky Horse Park ♠	218	38.08 N	84.31 W
Kentucky Lake ⊜[1]	194	36.25 N	88.05 W
Kent Village	284c	38.55 N	76.53 W
Kentville	186	45.05 N	64.30 W
Kentwood, La., U.S.	194	30.56 N	90.30 W
Kentwood, Mi., U.S.	216	42.52 N	85.38 W
Kent Woodlands	282	37.57 N	122.34 W
Kenvil	276	40.52 N	74.37 W
Kenwick	168a	32.02 S	115.58 E
Kenwood, Ca., U.S.	226	38.25 N	122.33 W
Kenwood, Md., U.S.	284b	39.21 N	76.31 W
Kenwood, Oh., U.S.	218	39.12 N	84.22 W
Kenwood ◆[8]	278	41.49 N	87.36 W
Kenwood ⊥	260	51.34 N	0.10 W
Kenya □[1]	154	1.00 N	38.00 E
Kenya, Mount → Kirinyaga ∧	154	0.10 S	37.20 E
Kenyon, Eng., U.K.	262	53.27 N	2.34 W
Kenyon, Mn., U.S.	190	44.16 N	92.59 W
Kenyon, R.I., U.S.	207	41.26 N	71.37 W
Ken-zaki ≻	268	35.08 N	139.41 E
Kenzingen	58	48.11 N	7.46 E
Kenzou	152	4.10 N	15.02 E
Keokea	229a	20.42 N	156.21 W
Keokuk	190	40.23 N	91.23 W
Keoladeo National Park ♠	124	27.10 N	77.20 E
Keonchi	124	22.38 N	81.47 E
Keo Neua, Col de)(	110	18.23 N	105.09 E
Keon Park	274b	37.42 S	145.01 E
Keosauqua	190	40.43 N	91.57 W
Keota, Ia., U.S.	190	41.21 N	91.57 W
Keota, Ok., U.S.	196	35.15 N	94.55 W
Keowee, Lake ⊜[1]	192	34.45 N	82.55 W
Kepa (Mittagskogel) ∧	61	46.31 N	13.57 E
Kepala Batas	114	5.31 N	100.26 E
Kepanjen	115a	8.07 S	112.34 E
Kepi	164	6.32 S	139.19 E
Kępice	30	54.15 N	16.52 E
Kepina	24	65.24 N	41.50 E
Keping Shan ⋀	85	40.00 N	77.10 E
Kępno	30	51.17 N	17.59 E
Kepo	112	2.56 S	106.33 E
Keppel Bay ⊂	166	23.21 S	150.55 E
Keppel Harbour ⊂	271c	1.16 N	103.50 E
Kepsut	130	39.41 N	28.09 E
Keptown	219	39.05 N	88.40 W
Kequan	98	36.04 N	114.00 E
Kerala □[3]	122	10.00 N	76.30 E
Keram ≃	164	4.07 S	144.07 E
Keramian, Pulau I	112	5.04 S	114.36 E
Kerandin	112	0.12 S	104.46 E
Kerang	166	35.44 S	143.55 E
Keranyo	144	5.04 N	38.18 E
Keratéa	38	37.48 N	23.59 E
Keratsínion	267c	37.58 N	23.37 E
Keraudren, Cape ≻	162	19.57 S	119.45 E
Kerava	26	60.24 N	25.07 E
Keravat	164	4.19 S	152.01 E
Kerbat ≃	114	5.01 N	102.51 E
Kerbela → Karbalā'	128	32.36 N	44.02 E
Kerbi ≃	89	52.28 N	136.25 E
Kerby	202	42.11 N	123.39 W
Kerčel'	86	59.18 N	64.46 E
Kerčemja	24	61.28 N	53.50 E
Kerčenskij proliv (Kerchens'ka protoka) ʊ	78	45.22 N	36.38 E
Kerčevskij	24	59.55 N	56.17 E
Kerch	78	45.22 N	36.27 E
Kerchens'ka protoka (Kerčenskij proliv) ʊ	78	45.22 N	36.38 E
Kerchens'kyy pivostriv ≻[1]	78	45.15 N	36.00 E
Kerckhoff Lake ⊜[1]	226	37.09 N	119.31 W
Kéré	154	5.16 N	26.11 E
Kéré ≃	140	5.19 N	25.40 E
Kerec, mys ≻	24	65.20 N	39.40 E
Kerej, ozero ⊜	86	50.08 N	68.45 E
Kerema	164	8.00 S	145.45 E
Keremeos	182	49.12 N	119.50 W
Kerem Maharal	132	32.39 N	34.59 E
Kerempe Burnu ≻	130	42.01 N	33.21 E
Keren	144	15.46 N	38.28 E
Kerend	128	34.16 N	46.15 E
Kerens	222	32.07 N	96.13 W
Kerepes	264c	47.34 N	19.18 E
Keret'	24	66.16 N	33.34 E
Keret', ozero ⊜	24	65.55 N	32.56 E
Kerewan	150	13.29 N	16.10 W
Kerga	24	62.39 N	46.00 E
Kerguélen, Îles II	6	49.15 S	69.10 E
Kerguelen Plateau ✢[3]	6	55.00 S	75.00 E
Kerhonkson	210	41.46 N	74.17 W
Kerian ≃	114	5.10 N	100.26 E
Kericho	154	0.22 S	35.17 E
Keri Kera	140	12.21 N	32.46 E
Kerikeri	172	35.13 S	173.58 E
Kerimäki	26	61.55 N	29.17 E
Kerinci, Gunung ∧	112	1.42 S	101.16 E
Kerio ≃	154	2.59 N	36.07 E
Keríon	38	37.40 N	20.48 E
Keritang	112	0.51 S	102.39 E
Keriya ≃	120	38.30 N	82.10 E
Kerka ≃	61	46.28 N	16.36 E
Kerkafalva	61	46.46 N	16.30 E
Kerkdriel	52	51.46 N	5.20 E
Kerkebet	144	16.18 N	37.24 E
Kerken	56	51.27 N	6.22 E
Kerkenna, Îles II	148	34.44 N	11.12 E
Kerkhove	50	50.48 N	3.30 E
Kerkhoven	198	45.11 N	95.19 W
Kerki, Ross.	24	63.43 N	54.05 E
Kerki, Turk.	128	37.50 N	65.12 E
Kérkira (Corfu)	38	39.36 N	19.56 E
Kérkira (Corfu) I	38	39.40 N	19.45 E
Kerkrade [-Holz]	56	50.52 N	6.04 E
Kerling	114	3.35 N	101.36 E
Kermadec Islands II	14	29.16 S	177.55 W
Kermadec Ridge ✢[3]	14	30.30 S	178.30 W
Kermadec Trench ✢[1]	14	30.00 S	177.00 W
Kermajärvi ⊜	26	62.28 N	28.40 E
Kermān, Īrān	128	30.17 N	57.05 E
Kerman, Ca., U.S.	226	36.43 N	120.04 W
Kermān □[4]	128	29.00 N	57.30 E
Kermit	196	31.51 N	103.05 W
Kermit Roosevelt Seamount ✢[3]	16	39.35 N	146.00 W
Kermode, Mount ∧	182	52.57 N	131.51 W
Kern □[6]	228	35.20 N	118.55 W
Kern ≃	204	35.13 N	119.17 W
Kern, South Fork ≃	204	35.40 N	118.27 W
Kern City	228	35.18 N	119.05 W
Kernersville	192	36.07 N	80.04 W
Kernforschungszentrum ʋ[3]	56	49.07 N	8.26 E
Kernhof	61	47.49 N	15.32 E
Kern Island Canal ≋	228	35.22 N	119.01 W
Kern Lake Bed ⊜	228	35.10 N	119.05 W
Kern River Channel ≃[1]	226	35.49 N	119.40 W
Kernville	204	35.45 N	118.25 W
Keroh	114	5.43 N	101.00 E
Keros	24	60.44 N	52.50 E
Kérou	150	10.50 N	2.06 E
Kérouané	150	9.16 N	9.01 W
Kerowagi	164	5.50 S	144.50 E
Kerpen	56	50.52 N	6.41 E
Kerr	214	41.03 N	78.25 W
Kerrera I	46	56.23 N	5.34 W
Kerridge	262	53.17 N	2.06 W
Kerridge Hill ∧[2]	262	53.17 N	2.06 W
Kerrobert	184	51.55 N	109.08 W
Kerrtown	214	41.38 N	80.10 W
Kerruish Park ♠	279a	41.26 N	81.34 W
Kerrville	196	30.02 N	99.08 W
Kerry	42	52.30 N	3.16 W
Kerry □[6]	48	52.10 N	9.30 W
Kerry Head ≻	48	52.25 N	9.57 W
Kersa	144	9.28 N	41.53 E
Kersbrook	168b	34.47 S	138.51 E
Kersey	214	41.21 N	78.35 W
Kershaw	192	34.33 N	80.35 W
Kersinyane	150	15.24 N	10.10 W
Kersley	182	52.49 N	122.25 W
Kerspestausee ⊜[1]	263	51.08 N	7.30 E
Kerstenhausen	56	51.04 N	9.13 E
Kert, Oued ≃	34	35.15 N	3.15 W
Kertamulia	112	0.23 S	109.09 E
Kerteh	114	4.31 N	103.27 E
Kerteminde	41	55.27 N	10.40 E
Kertosono	115a	7.35 S	112.06 E
Kerulen (Cherlen) (Herlen) ≃	90	48.48 N	117.00 E
Kerva	80	55.37 N	39.35 E
Kerzaz	148	29.30 N	1.37 W
Kerzendorf	264a	52.16 N	13.17 E
Kerženec	80	56.28 N	44.26 E
Kerženec ≃	80	56.05 N	45.03 E
Kerzers	58	46.58 N	7.12 E
Kesabpur	126	22.55 N	89.13 E
Ke Sach	110	9.46 N	105.59 E
Kesagami Lake ⊜	176	50.23 N	80.15 W
Kesälahti	26	61.54 N	29.50 E
Keşan	130	40.51 N	26.37 E
Keşap	130	40.55 N	38.31 E
Kesbern	263	51.20 N	7.42 E
Kesch, Piz ∧	58	46.38 N	9.52 E
Kesem ≃	144	9.14 N	40.06 E
Kesennuma	92	38.54 N	141.35 E
Kesh	48	54.32 N	7.43 W
Keshan	89	48.02 N	125.51 E
Keshena	190	44.53 N	88.38 W
Keshendeh	120	36.05 N	66.51 E
Keshequa Creek ≃	210	42.43 N	77.50 W
Keshod	120	21.18 N	70.15 E
Keşiş Dağları ⋀	130	39.50 N	39.45 E
Keskastel	56	48.58 N	7.02 E
Keskin	130	39.41 N	33.37 E
Keski-Suomen lääni □[4]	26	62.30 N	25.30 E
Keskozero	24	61.24 N	33.12 E
Keskuvejem, gora ∧	180	66.12 N	177.40 W
Kes'ma	76	58.27 N	37.04 E
Kesova Gora	76	57.35 N	37.17 E
Kespur	126	22.35 N	87.29 E
Kesra	36	35.49 N	9.22 E
Kessebüren	263	51.31 N	7.43 E
Kessel	56	51.08 N	4.37 E
Kesselsdorf	54	51.02 N	13.35 E
Kessingland	42	52.25 N	1.42 E
Kesswil	58	47.36 N	9.20 E
Kestel Gölü ⊜	130	37.24 N	30.28 E
Kestell	158	28.19 S	28.38 E
Kesten'ga	24	65.55 N	31.47 E
Kestilä	26	64.21 N	26.17 E
Keston ◆[8]	260	51.22 N	0.02 E
Keswick, On., Can.	212	44.15 N	79.28 W
Keswick, Eng., U.K.	44	54.37 N	3.08 W
Keszthely	30	46.46 N	17.15 E
Ket' ≃	86	58.55 N	81.32 E
Keta	150	5.55 N	1.00 E
Keta ≃	94	34.56 N	137.50 E
Keta, ozero ⊜	74	68.44 N	90.00 E
Ketaka	96	35.30 N	134.03 E
Keta Lagoon ⊂	150	5.54 N	0.56 E
Ketam, Pulau I	271c	1.24 N	103.57 E
Ketama	34	34.50 N	4.37 W
Ketang	100	22.58 N	115.28 E
Ketapang, Indon.	112	1.52 S	109.59 E
Ketapang, Indon.	115a	6.54 S	113.17 E
Ketapang, Indon.	115a	5.44 S	105.48 E
Ketaun	112	3.23 S	101.49 E
Ketčenery	80	47.18 N	44.31 E
Ketchikan	182	55.21 N	131.35 W
Ketchum	202	43.40 N	114.21 W
Kete Krachi	150	7.46 N	0.03 W
Ketelmeer ⊜	52	52.35 N	5.45 E
Keti Bandar	120	24.08 N	67.27 E
Ketingwan ∧	154	0.40 N	35.50 E
Ketoj, ostrov I	74	47.20 N	152.28 E
Kétou	150	7.22 N	2.36 E
Ketovo	86	55.21 N	65.18 E
Kętrzyn (Rastenburg)	30	54.06 N	21.23 E

Symbol	English	Deutsch	Español	Français	Português
≃	River	Fluß	Río	Rivière	Rio
≋	Canal	Kanal	Canal	Canal	Canal
⌞	Waterfall, Rapids	Wasserfall, Stromschnellen	Cascada, Rápidos	Chute d'eau, Rapides	Cascata, Rápidos
ʊ	Strait	Meeresstraße	Estrecho	Détroit	Estreito
⊂	Bay, Gulf	Bucht, Golf	Bahía, Golfo	Baie, Golfe	Baía, Golfo
⊜	Lake, Lakes	See, Seen	Lago, Lagos	Lac, Lacs	Lago, Lagos
⩸	Swamp	Sumpf	Pantano	Marais	Pântano
⍓	Ice Features, Glacier	Eis- und Gletscherformen	Accidentes Glaciales	Formes glaciaires	Acidentes glaciares
⊤	Other Hydrographic Features	Andere Hydrographische Objekte	Otros Elementos Hidrográficos	Autres données hydrographiques	Outros acidentes hidrográficos

Symbol	English	Deutsch	Español	Français	Português
✢	Submarine Features	Untermeerische Objekte	Accidentes Submarinos	Formes de relief sous-marin	Acidentes submarinos
□	Political Unit	Politische Einheit	Unidad Politica	Entité politique	Unidade política
ʋ	Cultural Institution	Kulturelle Institution	Institución Cultural	Institution culturelle	Instituição cultural
⊥	Historical Site	Historische Stätte	Sitio Histórico	Site historique	Sitio histórico
♠	Recreational Site	Erholungs- und Ferienort	Sitio de Recreo	Centre de loisirs	Area de Lazer
⊠	Airport	Flughafen	Aeropuerto	Aéroport	Aeroporto
■	Military Installation	Militäranlage	Instalación Militar	Installation militaire	Instalação militar
◆	Miscellaneous	Verschiedenes	Misceláneo	Divers	Diversos

Ketsch 56 49.22 N 8.31 E
Ketta 152 1.28 N 15.56 E
Kettering, Eng., U.K. 42 52.24 N 0.44 W
Kettering, Md., U.S. 284c 38.53 N 76.49 W
Kettering, Oh., U.S. 218 39.41 N 84.10 W
Kettinge 41 54.42 N 11.45 E
Kettle ≐, Mb., Can. 184 56.23 N 94.34 W
Kettle ≐, N.A. 182 48.42 N 118.07 W
Kettle ≐, Mn., U.S. 190 45.52 N 92.45 W
Kettle Creek ≐, On., Can. 212 42.40 N 81.13 W
Kettle Creek ≐, Pa., U.S. 210 41.18 N 77.51 W
Kettle Creek State Park ♦ 214 41.23 N 77.56 W
Kettle Falls 202 48.36 N 118.03 W
Kettleman City 226 36.00 N 119.57 W
Kettleman Hills ⋏[2] 226 36.00 N 120.00 W
Kettle Rapids Dam ◆[6] 184 56.23 N 94.38 W
Kettlersville 216 40.22 N 84.16 W
Kettleshulme 262 53.19 N 2.01 W
Kettlewell 44 54.09 N 2.02 W
Kettwig 56 51.22 N 6.56 E
Kety 30 49.53 N 19.13 E
Ketzin 54 52.28 N 12.50 E
Keudemane 114 5.15 N 96.55 E
Keudepasi 114 4.18 N 95.56 E
Keudeteunom 114 4.27 N 95.48 E
Keudeunga 114 5.01 N 95.22 E
Keuka Lake ⊜ 210 42.27 N 77.10 W
Keuka Lake, West Branch ⊂ 210 42.33 N 77.09 W
Keuka Park 210 42.37 N 77.06 W
Keukenhof ♦ 52 52.16 N 4.33 E
Keul' 88 58.25 N 102.49 E
Keula 54 51.20 N 10.31 E
Keum ≐ 86 59.32 N 70.35 E
Keurboomsrivier 158 34.00 S 23.24 E
Keurusselkä ⊜ 26 62.10 N 24.40 E
Keuruu 26 62.16 N 24.42 E
Kevdo-Mel'sitovo 80 53.09 N 43.54 E
Kevelaer 52 51.35 N 6.15 E
Kevin 202 48.44 N 111.57 W
Kevsala 80 45.48 N 42.41 E
Kew, Austl. 169 37.49 S 145.02 E
Kew, T./C. Is. 238 21.54 N 72.02 W
Kewanee 190 41.14 N 89.55 W
Kewanna 216 41.01 N 86.25 W
Kewaunee 190 44.27 N 87.30 W
Keweenaw Bay ⊂ 190 46.56 N 88.23 W
Keweenaw Peninsula >[1] 190 47.12 N 88.25 W
Keweenaw Point > 190 47.30 N 87.50 W
Kew Gardens ♦, On., Can. 275b 43.40 N 79.18 W
Kew Gardens ♦, Eng., U.K. 260 51.28 N 0.18 W
Key, Lough ⊜ 48 54.00 N 8.15 W
Keyala 154 4.27 N 32.52 E
Keyangkeer Shan ∧ 120 31.20 N 87.13 E
Keya Paha ≐ 198 42.54 N 99.00 W
Key Biscayne 220 25.42 N 80.10 W
Keyes, Ca., U.S. 226 37.33 N 120.54 W
Keyes, Ok., U.S. 196 36.48 N 102.15 W
Keyesport 219 38.44 N 89.17 W
Keyhole Reservoir ⊜[1] 198 44.21 N 104.51 W
Keyhole State Park ♦ 198 44.19 N 104.48 W
Keyihe 89 50.40 N 122.27 E
Keyingham 44 53.42 N 0.07 W
Key Largo 220 25.04 N 80.28 W
Key Largo I 220 25.16 N 80.19 W
Keymer 42 50.55 N 0.08 W
Keynes Hill ∧[2] 168b 34.37 S 139.06 E
Keyneton 168b 34.34 S 139.08 E
Keynsham 42 51.26 N 2.30 W
Keynshamburg 154 19.15 S 29.39 E
Keyport, N.J., U.S. 276 40.25 N 74.12 W
Keyport, Wa., U.S. 224 47.42 N 122.38 W
Keyport Harbor ⊂ 276 40.26 N 74.12 W
Keysborough 274b 38.00 S 145.10 E
Keysbrook 168a 32.26 S 115.59 E
Keyser 188 39.26 N 78.58 W
Keystone, In., U.S. 216 40.36 N 85.16 W
Keystone, Ia., U.S. 190 41.59 N 92.11 W
Keystone, S.D., U.S. 198 43.53 N 103.25 W
Keystone, W.V., U.S. 192 37.24 N 81.27 W
Keystone Lake ⊜[1], Ok., U.S. 196 36.15 N 96.25 W
Keystone Lake ⊜[1], Pa., U.S. 214 40.45 N 79.15 W
Keystone Peak ∧ 200 31.53 N 111.13 W
Keystone State Park ♦ 214 40.23 N 79.24 W
Keysville, Fl., U.S. 220 27.52 N 82.06 W
Keysville, Va., U.S. 192 37.02 N 78.29 W
Keytesville 194 39.26 N 92.56 W
Key West 220 24.33 N 81.46 W
Key West Island I 220 24.33 N 81.47 W
Key West Naval Air Station ■ 220 24.34 N 81.41 W
Keyworth 42 52.52 N 1.05 W
Kez 80 57.53 N 53.43 E
Kezi 154 20.58 S 28.32 E
Kezilesu Zizhizhou □[8] 85 40.00 N 75.30 E
Kežma 88 58.59 N 101.09 E
Kežmarok 30 49.08 N 20.25 E
Kgalagadi □[5] 156 25.00 S 22.00 E
Kgatleng □[5] 156 24.28 S 26.05 E
Kgokgole ≐ 158 26.44 S 22.28 E
Kgun Lake ⊜ 180 61.32 N 163.45 W
Khaanziir, Ras > 144 10.55 N 45.47 E
Khabab 132 33.00 N 36.16 E
Khabīr, Kūh-e ∧ 128 28.48 N 56.26 E
Khābūr, Nahr al- (Habur) ≐ 130 35.08 N 40.26 E
Khadar 272a 28.33 N 77.22 E
Khadari, Wādī al- V 140 10.29 N 26.15 E
Khadaungnge Taung ∧ 110 18.57 N 94.37 E
Khadki (Kirkee) 122 18.34 N 73.52 E
Khadra 34 36.15 N 0.35 E
Khadzhybeys'kyy lyman ⊜ 78 46.39 N 30.33 E
Khafūrī, Wādī V 142 29.37 N 32.04 E
Khagaria 124 25.30 N 86.29 E
Khagdon ≐[1] 126 22.09 N 90.05 E
Khagrāmuri 272b 22.26 N 88.14 E
Khaïdhárion 267c 38.01 N 23.38 E
Khair 124 27.57 N 77.50 E
Khairābād 124 27.32 N 80.45 E
Khairāgarh 120 21.25 N 80.58 E
Khairbani 126 24.14 N 87.05 E
Khairna 272c 19.06 N 73.01 E
Khairpur, Pāk. 120 27.32 N 68.46 E
Khairpur, Pāk. 123 29.35 N 72.14 E
Khairwāra 124 23.59 N 73.35 E
Khajrāho 120 24.50 N 79.58 E
Khajuri 126 21.52 N 87.58 E
Khajuri ◆[8] 272a 28.43 N 77.16 E
Khakassia — Chakasija □[3] 86 53.00 N 90.00 E
Kha Khaeng ≐ 110 14.55 N 99.07 E
Khakhea 156 24.51 S 23.20 E
Khalándrion 267c 38.01 N 23.48 E
Khalatse 123 34.20 N 76.49 E
Khālidī, Khirbat al- ⊥ 132 29.39 N 35.14 E
Khalkhāl 128 37.37 N 48.32 E
Khalkhalah 132 33.04 N 36.32 E
Khálki I 38 36.17 N 27.35 E
Khalkidhikí □[9] 38 40.25 N 23.27 E
Khalkís 38 38.28 N 23.36 E
Khalsar 120 34.31 N 77.41 E
Khalturyne 78 49.31 N 35.17 E
Khambhāliya 120 22.12 N 69.39 E
Khambhāt 120 22.18 N 72.37 E
Khambhāt, Gulf of ⊂ 122 21.00 N 72.30 E
Khāmgaon 122 20.41 N 76.34 E
Khamir 144 16.05 N 43.55 E
Khāmis, Ash-Shallāl al- (Fifth Cataract) ∟ 140 18.23 N 33.47 E
Khamīs Mushayt 144 18.18 N 42.44 E
Khamkeut 110 18.15 N 104.43 E
Khamma 70 36.47 N 12.02 E
Khammam 122 17.15 N 80.09 E
Khamsah 142 30.25 N 32.23 E
Khan ≐, Lao 110 19.54 N 102.09 E
Khan ≐, Namibia 156 22.37 S 14.56 E
Khāna 126 23.20 N 87.44 E
Khānābād 120 36.41 N 69.07 E
Khān Abū Shāmāt 132 33.40 N 36.54 E
Khānākul 126 22.43 N 87.51 E
Khān al-Baghdādī 128 33.51 N 42.33 E
Khānaqīn 128 34.21 N 45.22 E
Khān Arnabah 132 33.11 N 35.53 E
Khancoban 171b 36.12 S 148.05 E
Khandaghosh 126 23.13 N 87.41 E
Khandela 120 27.36 N 75.30 E
Khandwa 124 21.50 N 76.20 E
Khān-e Chahār Bāgh, Afg. 120 35.58 N 69.38 E
Khān-e Chahār Bāgh, Afg. 128 37.00 N 65.14 E
Khāneh Khvodī 128 36.02 N 55.59 E
Khānewāl 123 30.18 N 71.56 E
Khāngāh Dogrān 123 31.50 N 73.37 E
Khāngarh, Pāk. 120 28.22 N 71.43 E
Khāngarh, Pāk. 123 29.55 N 71.10 E
Khangkhai 110 19.28 N 103.15 E
Khaniá 38 35.31 N 24.02 E
Khaníon, Kólpos ⊂ 38 35.34 N 23.48 E
Khānkurda 126 22.00 N 87.25 E
Khanna 123 30.42 N 76.13 E
Khanna, Qā' ≐ 132 32.04 N 36.26 E
Khānozai 120 30.37 N 67.19 E
Khānpur, India 272b 22.40 N 88.16 E
Khānpur, Pāk. 123 28.39 N 70.39 E
Khānpur ◆[8], India 272a 28.34 N 77.01 E
Khānpur ◆[8], India 272a 28.31 N 77.14 E
Khān Shaykhūn 130 35.26 N 36.38 E
Khanty-Mansiysk — Chanty-Mansijsk 74 61.00 N 69.06 E
Khān Yūnus 132 31.21 N 34.19 E
Khao Laem Reservoir ⊜[1] 110 14.50 N 98.30 E
Khao Saming 110 12.21 N 102.27 E
Khao Sok National Park ♦ 110 8.55 N 98.35 E
Khao Yoi 110 13.14 N 99.50 E
Khapalu 123 35.10 N 76.20 E
Khaptad National Park ♦ 124 29.28 N 81.10 E
Kharab, Ghoubet al ⊂ 144 11.30 N 42.35 E
Kharabā 132 32.34 N 36.27 E
Kharagdiha 124 24.25 N 86.10 E
Kharagpur, India 124 25.07 N 86.33 E
Kharagpur, India 126 22.20 N 87.20 E
Kharak 123 33.07 N 71.06 E
Kharān 120 28.35 N 65.25 E
Kharānoq 128 32.20 N 54.39 E
Kharar, India 123 30.45 N 76.39 E
Kharar, India 126 22.42 N 87.41 E
Kharāvli ∧[2] 272c 18.54 N 72.55 E
Kharāyij, Sabkhat al- ⊜ 130 35.40 N 37.20 E
Kharaz, Jabal ∧ 144 12.44 N 44.09 E
Kharbatā 132 31.57 N 35.04 E
Kharbine — Harbin 89 45.45 N 126.41 E
Khardaha 272b 22.44 N 88.22 E
Khārghar 272c 19.03 N 73.04 E
Kharg Island — Khārk, Jazīreh-ye I 128 29.15 N 50.20 E
Khargon 124 21.49 N 75.36 E
Khāriān Cantonment 123 32.49 N 73.52 E
Khariār Road 122 20.54 N 82.31 E
Khārijah, Al-Wāḥāt al- ∓[4] 140 25.20 N 30.35 E
Kharīm, Jabal ∧ 132 30.17 N 33.58 E
Kharīt, Wādī al- V 140 24.26 N 33.03 E
Khārk, Jazīreh-ye (Kharg Island) I 128 29.15 N 50.20 E
Kharkiv (Kharkov) 78 50.00 N 36.15 E
Kharkiv □[4] 78 49.30 N 36.30 E
Kharkov — Kharkiv 78 50.00 N 36.15 E
Kharmān, Kūh-e ∧ 128 29.13 N 53.35 E
Kharri 272b 22.55 N 88.14 E
Kharsāwān 124 22.48 N 85.50 E
Kharsia 124 21.58 N 83.07 E
Khartoum — Al-Kharṭūm 140 15.36 N 32.32 E
Khartoum North — Al-Kharṭūm Bahrī 140 15.38 N 32.33 E
Khartsyz'k 83 48.02 N 38.09 E
Khartum — Al-Kharṭūm 140 15.36 N 32.32 E
Kharumwa 154 3.12 S 32.39 E
Khāsbāti 272b 22.55 N 88.25 E
Khasebake 156 20.41 S 24.29 E
Khāsh, Afg. 128 31.31 N 62.52 E
Khāsh, Īrān 128 28.14 N 61.14 E
Khāsh ≐ 128 31.11 N 62.05 E
Khāsh, Dasht-e ◆[2] 128 31.50 N 62.30 E
Khashab, Jabal al- ∧[2] 142 29.56 N 31.01 E
Khashm al-Qirbah 140 14.58 N 35.55 E
Khashm al-Qirbah, Khazzān ⊜[1] 140 14.40 N 35.55 E
Khashshab, Tur'at al- ≐ 273c 29.53 N 31.17 E
Khashum 144 12.27 N 28.02 E
Khāṣṣ Konar 120 34.39 N 70.54 E
Khaskovo — Haskovo 38 41.56 N 25.33 E
Khatauli 124 29.17 N 77.43 E
Khātegaon 124 22.36 N 76.55 E
Khātra 126 22.59 N 86.51 E
Khatt, Oued al V 148 26.45 N 13.03 W
Khaur 123 33.16 N 72.28 E
Khāvda 120 23.51 N 69.43 E
Khawrah 144 14.26 N 46.09 E
Khawsa 110 15.03 N 97.50 E
Khayālā ◆[8] 272a 28.40 N 77.06 E
Khaybar, Harrat ⊥[9] 144 25.30 N 39.45 E
Khayelitsha 158 34.05 S 18.40 E
Khayerpur 272b 22.35 N 88.26 E
Khayl, Kathīb al- ⊥[8] 142 30.33 N 32.28 E
Khayra Bil ⊜ 272b 22.52 N 88.45 E
Khayrasole 126 23.48 N 87.16 E
Khayung ≐ 110 15.07 N 104.42 E
Kheardaha 272b 22.29 N 88.28 E
Khe Bo 110 19.10 N 104.40 E
Khed 122 17.43 N 73.23 E
Khefapur 272a 28.30 N 77.05 E
Khejurdaha 272b 22.59 N 88.10 E
Khemis 148 36.16 N 2.13 E
Khemis el Khechna 34 36.39 N 3.20 E
Khemisset 148 33.50 N 6.03 W
Khemisset □[4] 148 33.50 N 6.03 W
Khem Karan 123 31.09 N 74.34 E
Khemmarat 110 16.03 N 105.13 E
Khenchla 148 35.28 N 7.11 E
Khenifra 148 33.00 N 5.40 W
Khenifra □[4] 148 32.35 N 5.10 W
Khenjān 120 35.36 N 68.55 E
Khepuriya 272b 22.59 N 88.19 E
Khera ◆[8] 272a 28.46 N 77.08 E
Kheri 124 27.54 N 80.48 E
Kheri Branch ≋ 124 28.11 N 80.25 E
Kherli 124 27.12 N 77.02 E
Kherrata 34 36.31 N 5.26 E
Khersān ≐ 128 31.33 N 50.22 E
Kherson 78 46.38 N 32.35 E
Kherson □[4] 78 46.45 N 33.30 E
Khersones, mys > 78 44.35 N 33.23 E
Khetia 120 21.40 N 74.35 E
Khevāj 120 38.13 N 71.02 E
Khewāri 120 26.36 N 68.52 E
Khewra 123 32.39 N 73.01 E
Kheyr Khāneh 128 34.57 N 63.37 E
Khichīwāra Plateau ⋏[1] 124 24.25 N 77.30 E
Khichripur ◆[8] 272a 28.37 N 77.19 E
Khilchipur 124 24.02 N 76.34 E
Khilkāpur 272b 22.46 N 88.29 E
Khimki — Chimki 82 55.54 N 37.26 E
Khíos 38 38.22 N 26.08 E
Khíos (Chios) I 38 38.22 N 26.00 E
Khipro 120 25.50 N 69.22 E
Khirbat al-Ghazālah 132 32.44 N 36.12 E
Khirbat 'Awwād 132 32.19 N 36.43 E
Khirbat Qanāfār 132 33.38 N 35.43 E
Khirbat Umm as-Surab 132 32.26 N 36.19 E
Khirbitā 142 30.45 N 30.40 E
Khiri Mat 110 16.50 N 99.48 E
Khirpai 126 22.42 N 87.37 E
Khirr, Wādī al- V 128 31.51 N 44.29 E
Khisfīn 132 32.51 N 35.49 E
Khiuri Khala ∧ 124 29.58 N 81.18 E
Khiva — Chiva 72 41.24 N 60.22 E
Khlibodarivka 83 47.29 N 37.23 E
Khlong Khlung 110 16.12 N 99.43 E
Khlong Thom 110 7.56 N 99.09 E
Khlong Yai 110 11.46 N 102.54 E
Khlung 110 12.27 N 102.14 E
Khmel'nyts'kyy 78 49.25 N 27.00 E
Khmel'nyts'kyy □[4] 78 49.30 N 27.00 E
Khmel'ove 78 48.34 N 31.24 E
Khmil'nyk 78 49.33 N 27.57 E
Khoai, Hon I 110 8.26 N 104.50 E
Khodoriv 78 49.24 N 24.17 E
Khogali 140 6.08 N 27.47 E
Khojāng ∧ 124 28.41 N 85.09 E
Khok Kloi 110 8.17 N 98.19 E
Khok Pho 110 6.43 N 101.06 E
Khoksa 126 23.48 N 89.17 E
Khok Samrong 110 15.04 N 100.44 E
Kholargós 267c 38.00 N 23.48 E
Kholm 120 36.42 N 67.41 E
Kholmy 78 51.52 N 32.36 E
Kholombidzo Falls ∟ 154 15.54 S 34.44 E
Khomām 128 37.22 N 49.40 E
Khomas Hochland ⋏[1] 156 22.30 S 16.30 E
Khomeyn 128 33.38 N 50.04 E
Khomeynīshahr 128 32.41 N 51.31 E
Khomodimo 156 22.46 S 23.52 E
Khomutets' 78 50.06 N 33.44 E
Khondmāl Hills ⋏[2] 122 20.20 N 84.00 E
Khong — Mekong ≐ 12 10.33 N 105.24 E
Khoni 272c 19.10 N 73.07 E
Khon Kaen 110 16.26 N 102.50 E
Khóra 38 37.04 N 21.43 E
Khorāsān □[4] 128 35.00 N 58.00 E
Khóra Sfakíon 38 35.12 N 24.09 E
Khordha 120 20.11 N 85.37 E
Khorel 272b 22.42 N 88.19 E
Khorol 78 49.47 N 33.17 E
Khorol ≐ 78 49.28 N 33.47 E
Khorostkiv 78 49.13 N 25.55 E
Khorramābād 128 33.30 N 48.20 E
Khorram Daraq 128 36.26 N 48.36 E
Khorramshahr 128 30.25 N 48.11 E
Khoru 272b 22.51 N 88.31 E
Khoryna ≐ 83 49.23 N 38.13 E
Khossanto 150 13.08 N 11.58 W
Khoteshiv 78 51.43 N 24.47 E
Khotin' 78 51.07 N 34.46 E
Khotyn 78 48.29 N 26.30 E
Khouribga 148 32.54 N 6.57 W
Khouribga □[4] 148 32.50 N 6.30 W
Khowai 120 24.06 N 91.38 E
Khowāng 120 27.16 N 94.53 E
Khowst 120 33.22 N 69.57 E
Khrestyshche 83 48.55 N 37.30 E
Khrisokhoús, Kólpos ⊂ 130 35.06 N 32.25 E
Khrisoúpolis 38 40.58 N 24.42 E
Khrystoforivka 78 47.59 N 33.05 E
Khrystynivka 78 48.49 N 29.58 E
Khudiān 123 30.59 N 74.17 E
Khuff 128 24.57 N 44.42 E
Khugaung 110 26.07 N 98.18 E
Khūgīānī Šānī 120 31.31 N 66.12 E
Khuis 156 26.37 S 21.45 E
Khuīyāla 120 27.14 N 70.30 E
Khu Khan 110 14.42 N 104.12 E
Khukhra 78 50.13 N 34.49 E
Khulna 124 22.48 N 89.33 E
Khulna □[5] 126 22.45 N 89.30 E
Khūm Bathéay 110 11.59 N 104.57 E
Khumbur Khūlē Ghar ∧ 120 32.49 N 68.47 E
Khungdugang ∧ 124 27.31 N 89.02 E
Khūnjerāb Pass)(123 36.52 N 75.27 E
Khun Tan, Doi ∧ 110 18.30 N 99.20 E
Khunti 124 23.05 N 85.17 E
Khūr 128 32.57 N 58.26 E
Khurai 124 24.03 N 78.19 E
Khuralji Khās ◆[8] 272a 28.39 N 77.17 E
Khuria Tank ⊜[1] 124 22.25 N 81.36 E
Khurigāchi 272b 22.49 N 88.20 E
Khurīyā Murīyā, Jazā'ir II 118 17.30 N 56.00 E
Khurja 124 28.15 N 77.51 E
Khurli 120 28.59 N 65.52 E
Khurramshahr — Khorramshahr 128 30.25 N 48.11 E
Khūsf 128 32.46 N 58.53 E
Khushāb 123 32.18 N 72.21 E
Khushālgarh 123 33.30 N 71.54 E
Khushk Khurd ◆[8] 272a 28.46 N 77.10 E
Khust 78 48.10 N 23.18 E
Khutubi ≐ 86 44.45 N 86.25 E
Khuwayy 140 13.05 N 29.14 E
Khuzdār 120 27.48 N 66.37 E
Khūzestān □[4] 128 31.00 N 49.00 E
Khvāf 128 34.33 N 60.08 E
Khvājeh Moḥammad, Kūh-e ⋏ 120 36.22 N 70.17 E
Khvājeh Ra'ūf 120 33.19 N 64.43 E
Khvor 128 33.47 N 55.03 E
Khvormūj 128 28.39 N 51.23 E
Khvoy 128 38.33 N 44.58 E
Khwae Noi ≐ 110 14.01 N 99.32 E
Khyber Pass)(123 34.05 N 71.10 E
Khyriv 78 49.33 N 22.49 E
Kia 175e 7.33 S 158.26 E
Kialwe 154 9.22 S 27.08 E
Kiama, Austl. 170 34.41 S 150.51 E
Kiama, Zaïre 152 7.15 S 17.44 E
Kiamba 116 5.59 N 124.37 E
Kiambi 154 7.20 S 28.01 E
Kiamboni, Kap — Jumbo, Raas > 144 1.39 S 41.36 E
Kiambu 154 1.10 S 36.50 E
Kiamesha Lake 210 41.41 N 74.40 W
Kiamichi ≐ 194 33.57 N 95.14 W
Kiamika ≐ 206 46.38 N 75.15 W
Kiamika, Barrage ◆[6] 206 46.37 N 75.08 W
Kiamika, Réservoir ⊜[1] 206 46.40 N 75.05 W
Kiamusze — Jiamusi 89 46.50 N 130.21 E
Kian — Ji'an 100 27.07 N 114.58 E
Kiana 180 66.59 N 160.25 W
Kiandra 171b 35.53 S 148.30 E
Kiangara 157b 17.58 S 47.02 E
Kiangarow, Mount ∧ 166 26.49 S 151.33 E
Kiangsi — Jiangxi □[4] 100 28.00 N 116.00 E
Kiangsu — Jiangsu □[4] 90 33.00 N 120.00 E
Kiantajärvi ⊜ 26 65.03 N 29.07 E
Kiaohsien — Jiaoxian 98 36.18 N 119.58 E
Kibæk 41 56.02 N 8.51 E
Kibaha 154 6.46 S 38.55 E
Kibali ≐ 154 3.37 N 28.34 E
Kibali-Sturi Game Reserve ◆[4] 154 2.45 N 29.33 E
Kibamba 154 4.53 S 26.33 E
Kibanga Port 154 0.11 N 32.52 E
Kibangou 152 3.27 S 12.21 E
Kibanseke 273b 4.26 S 15.23 E
Kibar 120 32.20 N 78.01 E
Kibara 154 2.09 S 33.27 E
Kibāsī 128 30.34 N 47.50 E
Kibau Iyayi 154 8.52 S 34.32 E
Kibawe 116 7.34 N 125.00 E
Kibaya 154 5.18 S 36.34 E
Kibenga 152 7.55 S 17.35 E
Kibeni 164 7.25 S 143.48 E
Kiberashi 154 5.23 S 37.26 E
Kiberege 154 7.57 S 36.52 E
Kibi 150 6.10 N 0.33 W
Kibi-kōgen ⋏[1] 96 34.45 N 133.15 E
Kibila 154 8.14 S 26.23 E
Kibiti 154 7.44 S 38.57 E
Kibler Park 273d 26.18 S 28.00 E
Kiboga 154 1.02 N 30.58 E
Kiboko 154 2.15 S 37.42 E
Kibombo 154 3.54 S 25.55 E
Kibondo 154 3.35 S 30.42 E
Kibouendé, Congo 273b 4.19 S 15.11 E
Kibouendé, Congo 273b 4.17 S 15.09 E
Kibouendé I 273b 4.11 S 15.09 E
Kibouendé II 273b 4.12 S 15.09 E
Kibre Mengist 144 5.52 N 39.00 E
Kıbrıs — Cyprus □[1] 130 35.00 N 33.00 E
Kıbrısçık 130 40.25 N 31.51 E
Kibumbu 154 3.32 S 29.45 E
Kibungo 154 2.10 S 30.32 E
Kibuye, Bdi. 154 3.40 S 29.59 E
Kibuye, Rw. 154 2.03 S 29.21 E
Kibwesa 154 6.28 S 29.57 E
Kibwezi 154 2.25 S 37.58 E
Kibworth Harcourt 42 52.32 N 0.59 W
Kičevo 38 41.31 N 20.57 E
Kichčik 74 53.24 N 156.03 E
Kichijōji 268 35.42 N 139.35 E
Kickapoo ≐ 190 43.05 N 90.53 W
Kickapoo Creek ≐, Il., U.S. 194 40.08 N 89.27 W
Kickapoo Creek ≐, Il., U.S. 219 40.08 N 89.27 W
Kickapoo Creek ≐, Tx., U.S. 196 31.31 N 99.58 W
Kickapoo Creek ≐, Tx., U.S. 222 30.47 N 95.08 W
Kickapoo Creek ≐, Tx., U.S. 222 32.16 N 95.28 W
Kicking Horse Pass)(182 51.27 N 116.18 W
Kičkino 80 47.05 N 44.02 E
Kičma 80 57.12 N 48.55 E
Kičmengskij Gorodok 24 59.59 N 45.48 E
Kičuj ≐ 80 55.13 N 51.16 E
Kidal 150 18.26 N 1.24 E
Kidapawan 116 7.01 N 125.03 E
Kidatu 154 7.42 S 36.57 E
Kidbrooke ◆[8] 260 51.28 N 0.02 E
Kidderminster 42 52.23 N 2.14 W
Kidderpore ◆[8] 272b 22.31 N 88.19 E
Kidderpore Docks ◆[5] 272b 22.33 N 88.19 E
Kidd's Beach 158 33.09 S 27.42 E
Kidepo National Park ♦ 154 3.50 N 33.40 E
Kidete, Tan. 154 6.25 S 37.16 E
Kidete, Tan. 154 6.39 S 36.42 E
Kidira 150 14.28 N 12.13 W
Kidlington 42 51.50 N 1.17 W
Kidnappers, Cape > 172 39.39 S 177.07 E
Kido 164 9.15 S 146.55 E
Kidričevo 61 46.24 N 15.47 E
Kidron 214 40.44 N 81.45 W
Kidsgrove 44 53.06 N 2.15 W
Kidston 166 18.53 S 144.10 E
Kidugallo 154 6.47 S 38.12 E
Kidul, Pegunungan ⋏ 115a 8.13 S 111.30 E
Kidwelly 42 51.45 N 4.18 W
Kiefersfelden 64 47.37 N 12.11 E
Kiekebusch 264a 52.21 N 13.33 E
Kiel, Dtsch. 41 54.20 N 10.08 E
Kiel, Wi., U.S. 190 43.54 N 88.02 W
Kiel Canal — Nord-Ostsee-Kanal ≋ 30 53.53 N 9.08 E
Kielce 30 50.52 N 20.37 E
Kielce □[4] 30 50.30 N 20.30 E
Kielder 44 55.14 N 2.35 W
Kielder Reservoir ⊜[1] 44 55.11 N 2.30 W
Kieler Bucht (Kiel Bay) ⊂ 41 54.35 N 10.35 E
Kieler Förde ⊂ 41 54.24 N 10.12 E
Kiembara 150 13.15 N 2.44 W
Kienberg 264a 52.40 N 12.54 E
Kienge 154 10.34 S 27.33 E
Kienitz 54 52.40 N 14.26 E
Kiens — Chienes 64 46.48 N 11.50 E
Kiental 58 46.35 N 7.43 E
Kierling 264b 48.19 N 16.17 E
Kierspe 56 51.08 N 7.35 E
Kierspe-Bahnhof 263 51.08 N 7.37 E
Kiester 190 43.32 N 93.42 W
Kieta 175e 6.13 S 155.38 E
Kietrz 30 50.05 N 18.01 E
Kietz 54 52.34 N 14.36 E
Kiev — Kyyiv 78 50.26 N 30.31 E
Kiev Station ◆[5] 265b 55.45 N 37.34 E
Kiew — Kyyiv 78 50.26 N 30.31 E
Kifaya 150 12.10 N 13.04 W
Kiffa 150 16.37 N 11.24 W
Kifisiá 38 38.04 N 23.48 E
Kifisós ≐, Ellás 38 38.26 N 23.15 E
Kifisós ≐, Ellás 267c 37.57 N 23.40 E
Kifrī 128 34.42 N 44.58 E
Kifrī, Jabal ∧ 142 27.48 N 32.50 E
Kigač ≐ 80 46.28 N 49.12 E
Kigali 154 1.57 S 30.04 E
Kiği 130 39.19 N 40.21 E
Kigille 140 8.40 N 34.02 E
Kigoma 154 4.52 S 29.38 E
Kigoma □[4] 154 4.30 S 30.30 E
Kigun, Cape > 180 52.00 N 175.21 W
Kigwa 154 5.10 S 33.08 E
Kihei 229a 20.47 N 156.27 W
Kihikihi 172 38.02 S 175.21 E
Kihniö 26 62.12 N 23.11 E
Kihnu I 76 58.08 N 24.00 E
Kiholo Bay ⊂ 229d 19.52 N 155.56 W
Kihundo 154 9.25 S 38.59 E
Kihurio 154 4.28 S 38.04 E
Kii-hantō >[1] 92 34.00 N 135.45 E
Kiik 86 47.31 N 72.55 E
Kiikkaškan 86 49.28 N 77.04 E
Kiiminginjoki ≐ 26 65.12 N 25.18 E
Kii-nagashima 92 34.12 N 136.20 E
Kiirun — Chilung 100 25.08 N 121.44 E
Kii-sanchi ⋏ 92 34.00 N 135.50 E
Kii-suidō ʊ 96 33.55 N 134.55 E
Kija ≐ 86 56.52 N 86.39 E
Kijabe 154 0.56 S 36.34 E
Kijakty, ozero ⊜ 86 50.00 N 69.15 E
Kijal 114 4.21 N 103.29 E
Kijaly 86 54.17 N 69.41 E
Kijasovo 80 56.21 N 53.07 E
Kijevka, Kaz. 86 50.16 N 71.34 E
Kijevka, Ross. 80 46.05 N 42.57 E
Kijevka, Ross. 80 50.46 N 48.28 E

ENGLISH Name	Page	Lat.°′	Long.°′

Kijevskoje 78 45.03 N 37.52 E
Kijima-chosuichi ⊜ 96 35.04 N 132.44 E
Kijimadaira 94 36.51 N 138.24 E
Kijima-dam ◆[6] 96 35.05 N 132.44 E
Kijma 86 51.35 N 67.34 E
Kijoka 174m 26.42 N 128.09 E
Kikagati 154 1.02 S 30.40 E
Kikai-shima I 93b 28.19 N 129.59 E
Kikale 154 7.50 S 39.12 E
Kikati ≐ 152 14.48 S 12.28 E
Kikenka ≐ 265a 59.52 N 30.04 E
Kikerino 76 59.28 N 29.35 E
Kikerk Lake ⊜ 176 67.20 N 113.20 W
Kikimi 273b 4.26 S 15.25 E
Kikimorka 80 58.10 N 49.27 E
Kikinda 38 45.50 N 20.28 E
Kikládhes (Cyclades) II 38 37.30 N 25.00 E
Kiklah 146 32.05 N 12.41 E
Kiknur 80 57.19 N 47.14 E
Kikombo, Zaïre 152 5.59 S 18.09 E
Kikombo, Zaïre 152 5.40 S 18.48 E
Kikongo 152 4.16 S 17.11 E
Kikori 164 7.25 S 144.15 E
Kikori ≐ 164 7.10 S 144.05 E
Kikorze 54 53.39 N 15.01 E
Kiku ≐ 94 34.39 N 138.04 E
Kikuchi 96 32.59 N 130.49 E
Kikuchi ≐ 96 32.56 N 130.35 E
Kikugawa, Nihon 94 34.45 N 138.05 E
Kikugawa, Nihon 96 34.07 N 131.02 E
Kikuka 96 33.02 N 130.46 E
Kikuma 96 34.03 N 132.53 E
Kikuna 268 35.10 N 139.40 E
Kikusui 96 32.58 N 130.36 E
Kikvidze, Ross. 80 50.53 N 42.46 E
Kikvidze, Ross. 80 50.44 N 43.03 E
Kikvorsberg ⋏ 158 31.17 S 25.20 E
Kikwit 152 5.02 S 18.49 E
Kil 26 59.30 N 13.19 E
Kilaån ≐ 40 58.44 N 17.01 E
Kilafors 26 61.14 N 16.34 E
Kila Kila 164 9.30 S 147.10 E
Kīlakkarai 122 9.14 N 78.47 E
Kilambé, Cerro ∧ 236 13.34 N 85.42 W
Kilauea 229b 22.12 N 159.24 W
Kilauea Crater ⊥[6] 229d 19.25 N 155.17 W
Kilauea Point > 229b 22.14 N 159.24 W
Kilb 61 48.06 N 15.24 E
Kilbaha 48 52.33 N 9.52 W
Kilbarchan 46 55.50 N 4.33 W
Kılbasan 130 37.20 N 33.12 E
Kilbeggan 48 53.22 N 7.29 W
Kilbirnie 46 55.46 N 4.41 W
Kilbourne, Il., U.S. 219 40.09 N 90.01 W
Kilbourne, Oh., U.S. 214 40.20 N 82.58 W
Kilbrannan Sound ʊ 46 55.40 N 5.25 W
Kilbride 46 57.05 N 7.27 W
Kilbuck Mountains ⋏ 180 60.50 N 159.45 W
Kilbuck Run ≐ 279b 40.31 N 80.08 W
Kilcar 48 54.38 N 8.35 W
Kilchberg 58 47.19 N 8.33 E
Kilchis ≐ 224 45.30 N 123.52 W
Kilchoan 46 56.42 N 6.06 W
Kilchreest 48 53.10 N 8.38 W
Kilchrenan 46 56.21 N 5.11 W
Kilchu 98 40.58 N 129.20 E
Kilcock 48 53.24 N 6.40 W
Kilcolgan 48 53.13 N 8.52 W
Kilconnell 48 53.20 N 8.25 W
Kilcoole 48 53.06 N 6.04 W
Kilcormac 48 53.10 N 7.43 W
Kilcoy 171a 26.57 S 152.33 E
Kilcreggan 46 55.59 N 4.50 W
Kilcullen 48 53.08 N 6.45 W
Kildare (Saint-Ambroise-de-Kildare), P.Q., Can. 206 46.05 N 73.32 W
Kildare, Ire. 48 53.10 N 6.55 W
Kildare □[6] 48 53.15 N 6.45 W
Kildare, Cape > 186 46.52 N 63.58 W
Kildeer 278 42.10 N 88.03 W
Kil'din, ostrov I 24 69.22 N 34.12 E
Kil'dinstroj 24 68.48 N 33.06 E
Kildonan, B.C., Can. 182 49.00 N 125.00 W
Kildonan, Scot., U.K. 46 58.10 N 3.51 W
Kildonan, Zimb. 154 17.21 S 30.37 E
Kildonan, Strath of V 46 58.09 N 3.51 W
Kildorrery 48 52.14 N 8.26 W
Kildrummy Castle ⊥ 46 57.14 N 2.52 W
Kildurk 164 16.26 S 129.37 E
Kilemary 80 56.47 N 46.52 E
Kilembe, Ug. 154 0.12 N 30.00 E
Kilembe, Zaïre 152 5.42 S 19.55 E
Kilfenora 48 52.59 N 9.13 W
Kilfinnane 48 52.21 N 8.28 W
Kilgard 224 49.03 N 122.12 W
Kilgarvan 48 51.54 N 9.27 W
Kilgore, Oh., U.S. 214 40.28 N 81.00 W
Kilgore, Tx., U.S. 222 32.23 N 94.52 W
Kilham 44 54.04 N 0.23 W
Kili I 14 5.39 N 169.04 E
Kilian Island I 176 73.35 N 107.53 W
Kilibo 150 8.34 N 2.36 E
Kılıç 130 40.38 N 29.23 E
Kilifi 154 3.38 S 39.51 E
Kilikollūr 122 8.54 N 76.39 E
Kilima 154 0.59 S 29.12 E
Kilimanjaro □[4] 154 3.45 S 37.45 E
Kilimanjaro ∧ 154 3.04 S 37.22 E
Kilimanjaro Game Reserve ◆[4] 154 3.05 S 37.20 E
Kilimatinde 154 5.51 S 34.57 E
Kilimavony 157b 23.48 S 43.41 E
Kilimli 130 41.28 N 31.50 E
Kilindoni 154 7.55 S 39.39 E
Kilingi-Nõmme 76 58.09 N 24.58 E
Kilis 130 36.44 N 37.05 E
Kiliya 78 45.27 N 29.16 E
Kilkare Woods 282 37.38 N 121.55 W
Kilkee 48 52.41 N 9.38 W
Kilkeel 48 54.04 N 6.00 W
Kilkelly 48 53.53 N 8.51 W
Kilkenny (Cill Chainnigh) 48 52.39 N 7.15 W
Kilkenny □[6] 48 52.40 N 7.20 W
Kilkerrin 48 53.33 N 8.34 W
Kilkhampton 42 50.53 N 4.29 W
Kilkieran 48 53.19 N 9.43 W
Kilkieran Bay ⊂ 48 53.15 N 9.45 W
Kilkís 38 41.00 N 22.53 E
Killadoon 48 53.42 N 9.56 W
Killadysert 48 52.41 N 9.06 W
Killala 48 54.13 N 9.13 W
Killala Bay ⊂ 48 54.15 N 9.10 W
Killaloe 48 52.48 N 8.27 W
Killaloe Station 190 45.33 N 77.25 W
Killam 182 52.47 N 111.51 W
Killara 274a 33.46 S 151.09 E
Killarney, Austl. 166 28.20 S 152.18 E
Killarney, Mb., Can. 184 49.12 N 99.42 W
Killarney, On., Can. 190 45.58 N 81.31 W
Killarney, Ire. 48 52.03 N 9.30 W
Killarney, Lake ⊜ 240b 25.03 N 77.27 W
Killarney, Lakes of ⊜ 48 52.01 N 9.30 W
Killarney Heights 274a 33.46 S 151.13 E
Killarney Provincial Park ♦ 190 46.05 N 81.30 W
Killashandra 48 54.00 N 7.32 W
Killavally 48 53.45 N 9.23 W
Killawog 210 42.24 N 76.01 W
Killbear Provincial Park ♦ 212 45.21 N 80.12 W
Kill Buck, N.Y., U.S. 210 42.10 N 78.41 W
Killbuck, Oh., U.S. 214 40.29 N 81.59 W
Killbuck Creek ≐, Il., U.S. 216 42.10 N 89.06 W
Killbuck Creek ≐, In., U.S. 218 40.07 N 85.41 W
Killbuck Creek ≐, Oh., U.S. 214 40.20 N 81.57 W

DEUTSCH Name	Seite	Breite°′	Länge°′ E = Ost

Killdeer 198 47.22 N 102.45 W
Killean 46 55.39 N 5.40 W
Killearn 46 56.03 N 4.22 W
Killeen 222 31.07 N 97.43 W
Killen 194 34.51 N 87.32 W
Killenaule 48 52.34 N 7.40 W
Killeter 48 54.40 N 7.41 W
Kıllıdağ ∧ 130 40.21 N 42.10 E
Killik ≐ 180 69.00 N 153.58 W
Killilan 46 57.19 N 5.25 W
Killimor 48 53.10 N 8.17 W
Killin 46 56.28 N 4.19 W
Killington Peak ∧ 188 43.36 N 72.49 W
Killingworth 207 41.21 N 72.33 W
Killíni 38 37.55 N 21.09 E
Killíni ∧ 38 37.57 N 22.23 E
Killiniq Island I 176 60.24 N 64.40 W
Killinkoski 26 62.24 N 23.52 E
Killorglin 48 52.06 N 9.47 W
Killough 48 54.16 N 5.39 W
Killpecker Creek ≐ 202 41.35 N 109.14 W
Killucan 48 53.31 N 7.07 W
Kill Van Kull ʊ 276 40.39 N 74.05 W
Killybegs 48 54.38 N 8.27 W
Killyleagh 48 54.24 N 5.39 W
Kilmacolm 46 55.54 N 4.38 W
Kilmacthomas 48 52.12 N 7.25 W
Kilmaine 48 53.34 N 9.09 W
Kilmallock 48 52.23 N 8.34 W
Kilmaluag 46 57.41 N 6.17 W
Kilmarnock, Scot., U.K. 46 55.36 N 4.30 W
Kilmarnock, Va., U.S. 208 37.42 N 76.22 W
Kilmartin 46 56.07 N 5.29 W
Kilmar Tor ∧[2] 42 50.33 N 4.28 W
Kilmaurs 46 55.39 N 4.32 W
Kilmelford 46 56.16 N 5.29 W
Kil'mez', Ross. 80 56.57 N 51.04 E
Kil'mez', Ross. 80 57.04 N 51.21 E
Kil'mez' ≐ 80 56.58 N 50.28 E
Kilmichael 194 33.26 N 89.34 W
Kilmichael Point > 48 52.44 N 6.10 W
Kilmore 169 37.18 S 144.57 E
Kilmore Creek ≐ 216 40.20 N 86.38 W
Kilmory 46 57.03 N 6.22 W
Kilnaleck 48 53.52 N 7.19 W
Kilninver 46 56.20 N 5.31 W
Kilo 115b 8.21 S 118.24 E
Kilokri ◆[8] 272a 28.35 N 77.16 E
Kiloli 154 6.50 S 33.23 E
Kilombero ≐ 154 8.31 S 37.22 E
Kilomines 154 1.48 N 30.14 E
Kilondo 154 9.46 S 34.21 E
Kilosa 154 6.50 S 36.59 E
Kilpisjärvi 24 69.03 N 20.48 E
Kilrea 48 54.58 N 6.35 W
Kilrenny 46 56.14 N 2.41 W
Kilrush 48 52.39 N 9.30 W
Kilsbergen ⋏[2] 40 59.20 N 14.47 E
Kilsmo 40 59.04 N 15.31 E
Kilsyth, Austl. 274b 37.48 S 145.19 E
Kilsyth, Scot., U.K. 46 55.59 N 4.04 W
Kiltealy 48 52.34 N 6.45 W
Kiltimagh 48 53.51 N 9.01 W
Kiltoom 48 53.28 N 8.01 W
Kilttān Island I 122 11.29 N 73.00 E
Kiltu-ri 98 34.35 N 127.20 E
Kilwa 154 9.18 S 28.25 E
Kilwa Island I 154 9.20 S 28.33 E
Kilwa Kivinje 154 8.45 S 39.24 E
Kilwa Masoko 154 8.56 S 39.31 E
Kilwinning 46 55.40 N 4.42 W
Kim 198 37.14 N 103.21 W
Kim ≐ 152 5.28 N 11.07 E
Kima 154 1.26 S 26.43 E
Kimaam 164 7.58 S 138.53 E
Kimamba 154 6.47 S 37.08 E
Kimande 154 7.22 S 35.30 E
Kīmān Fāris (Crocodilopolis) (Arsinoe) ⊥ 142 29.19 N 30.50 E
Kimba 166 33.09 S 136.25 E
Kimball, Mn., U.S. 190 45.19 N 94.18 W
Kimball, Ne., U.S. 198 41.14 N 103.39 W
Kimball, S.D., U.S. 198 43.44 N 98.57 W
Kimball, Mount ∧ 180 63.14 N 144.39 W
Kimbanda 152 4.07 S 17.59 E
Kimbe 164 5.31 S 150.10 E
Kimbe Bay ⊂ 164 5.30 S 150.30 E
Kimberley, B.C., Can. 182 49.41 N 115.59 W
Kimberley, S. Afr. 158 28.43 S 24.46 E
Kimberley, Eng., U.K. 44 52.59 N 1.16 W
Kimberley Downs 162 17.24 S 124.22 E
Kimberley Plateau ⋏[1] 160 17.00 S 127.00 E
Kimberling City 194 36.38 N 93.28 W
Kimberly, Id., U.S. 202 42.32 N 114.21 W
Kimberly, Wi., U.S. 190 44.16 N 88.20 W
Kimberton 208 40.08 N 75.34 W
Kimbolton, N.Z. 172 40.03 S 175.47 E
Kimbolton, Eng., U.K. 42 52.18 N 0.24 W
Kimbolton, Oh., U.S. 214 40.09 N 81.34 W
Kimbongo 152 6.08 S 18.01 E
Kimbwala 273b 4.22 S 15.12 E
Kimch'aek (Sŏngjin) 98 40.41 N 129.12 E
Kimch'ŏn 98 36.07 N 128.05 E
Kimerka ≐ 82 56.52 N 37.22 E
Kimhae 98 35.14 N 128.52 E
Kimhwa 98 38.26 N 127.36 E
Kími 38 38.37 N 24.06 E
Kimil'tej 88 54.08 N 101.59 E
Kimito (Kemiö) 26 60.10 N 22.45 E
Kimito I 26 60.07 N 22.40 E
Kimi-tōge ∧[2] 270 34.43 N 135.06 E
Kimi-tōge)(96 34.23 N 135.37 E
Kimitsu 94 35.20 N 139.54 E
Kimiwan Lake ⊜ 182 55.45 N 116.54 W
Kimje 98 35.48 N 126.52 E
Kim Kim ≐ 271c 1.26 N 103.58 E
Kimmell 216 41.23 N 85.32 W
Kim-me-ni-oli Wash V 200 36.07 N 108.11 W
Kímolos I 38 36.48 N 24.34 E
Kimongo 152 4.29 S 12.58 E
Kimovsk 76 53.58 N 38.32 E
Kimpangu 152 5.51 S 15.01 E
Kim Plan 279b 40.20 N 79.44 W
Kimp'o 271b 37.37 N 126.43 E
Kimp'o Airport ⊠ 271b 37.33 N 126.48 E
Kimpombo 273b 4.17 S 15.10 E
Kimpō-zan ∧ 94 35.53 N 138.38 E
Kimry 82 56.52 N 37.21 E
Kimsquit 182 52.49 N 126.58 W
Kimstad 40 58.32 N 15.58 E
Kimu ≐ 268 35.56 N 139.57 E
Kimuenza 273b 4.27 S 15.17 E
Kimvula 152 5.44 S 15.58 E
Kimwanga 154 7.08 S 28.42 E
Kin 174m 26.26 N 127.55 E
Kinabalian, Mount ∧ 116 8.14 N 125.25 E
Kinabalu, Gunong ∧ 112 6.05 N 116.33 E
Kinabalu National Park ♦ 112 6.05 N 116.33 E
Kinabatangan ≐ 112 5.42 N 118.23 E
Kınalı ◆[8] 267b 40.55 N 29.03 E
Kınalı Ada I 267b 40.55 N 29.03 E
Kinangaly ∧ 157b 19.12 S 45.40 E
Kinango 154 4.08 S 39.19 E
Kinapusan Island I 116 5.13 N 120.40 E
Kinara 164 2.16 S 132.44 E
Kinasa 94 36.42 N 138.01 E
Kinaūni 272a 28.39 N 77.23 E
Kinbasket Lake ⊜[1] 182 51.58 N 118.03 W
Kinbrace 46 58.15 N 3.56 W
Kinbuck 46 56.13 N 3.57 W
Kincaid, Sk., Can. 184 49.39 N 107.00 W
Kincaid, Il., U.S. 219 39.35 N 89.24 W
Kincardine, On., Can. 190 44.11 N 81.38 W
Kincardine, Scot., U.K. 46 56.04 N 3.44 W
Kinchafoonee Creek ≐ 192 31.38 N 84.10 W

Symbols in the index entries represent the broad categories identified in the key at the right. Symbols with superior numbers (⋏[1]) identify subcategories (see complete key on page *I · 1*).

Symbole im Register stellen die rechts im Schlüssel erklärten Kategorien dar. Symbole mit hochgestellten Ziffern (⋏[1]) bezeichnen Unterabteilungen einer Kategorie (vgl. vollständiger Schlüssel auf Seite *I · 1*).

Los símbolos incluídos en el texto del índice representan las grandes categorías identificadas con la clave a la derecha. Los símbolos con numeros en su parte superior (⋏[1]) identifican las subcategorías (véase la clave completa en la página *I · 1*).

Les symboles de l'index représentent les catégories indiquées dans la légende à droite. Les symboles suivis d'un indice (⋏[1]) représentent des sous-catégories (voir légende complète à la page *I · 1*).

Os símbolos incluídos no texto do índice representam as grandes categorias identificadas com a chave à direita. Os símbolos com números em sua parte superior (⋏[1]) identificam as subcategorias (veja-se a chave completa à página *I · 1*).

∧ Mountain	Berg	Montaña	Montagne	Montanha
⋏ Mountains	Gebirge	Montañas	Montagnes	Montanhas
)(Pass	Paß	Paso	Col	Passo
V Valley, Canyon	Tal, Cañon	Valle, Cañón	Vallée, Canyon	Vale, Canhão
≡ Plain	Ebene	Llano	Plaine	Planície
> Cape	Kap	Cabo	Cap	Cabo
I Island	Insel	Isla	Île	Ilha
II Islands	Inseln	Islas	Îles	Ilhas
⊥ Other Topographic Features	Andere Topographische Objekte	Otros Elementos Topográficos	Autres données topographiques	Outros acidentes topográficos

ESPAÑOL

Nombre	Página	Lat.°′	Long.°′ W = Oeste
Kinchang	110	26.32 N	98.02 E
Kinchara	272b	22.53 N	88.32 E
Kinchega National Park ♦	166	32.30 S	142.20 E
Kincheloe Air Force Base ■	190	46.15 N	84.28 W
Kincolith	182	55.00 N	129.57 W
Kincraig	46	57.08 N	3.55 W
Kinda, Zaïre	152	4.47 S	21.48 E
Kinda, Zaïre	154	9.18 S	25.04 E
Kindadal	112	1.35 S	123.11 E
Kindanba	152	3.44 S	14.31 E
Kindarun Mountain ∧	170	32.49 S	150.41 E
Kindberg	61	47.31 N	15.27 E
Kinde	190	43.56 N	82.59 W
Kindeje	152	7.07 S	13.44 E
Kindel'a	80	51.36 N	52.58 E
Kindel'a ≃	80	51.30 N	52.45 E
Kindelbrück	54	51.16 N	11.05 E
Kindele	152	8.39 S	24.11 E
Kinder	194	30.29 N	92.51 W
Kinderhook, Il., U.S.	219	39.42 N	91.09 W
Kinderhook, Mi., U.S.	216	41.48 N	85.00 W
Kinderhook, N.Y., U.S.	210	42.23 N	73.41 W
Kinderhook Creek ≃	210	42.19 N	73.45 W
Kinder Reservoir ⊜[1]	262	53.23 N	1.55 W
Kinder Scout ∧	44	53.23 N	1.52 W
Kindersley	184	51.27 N	109.10 W
Kindia	150	10.04 N	12.51 W
Kindikan	88	56.02 N	115.15 E
Kinding	60	49.00 N	11.23 E
Kindley Field ⊠	240a	32.22 N	64.40 W
Kindred	198	46.38 N	97.01 W
Kindu	154	2.57 S	25.56 E
Kindykty, ozero ⊜	86	51.15 N	62.14 E
Kinel'	80	53.14 N	50.39 E
Kinel'-Čerkasy	80	53.29 N	51.29 E
Kinel'skije jary ⩚[1]	80	53.42 N	52.00 E
Kineo, Mount ∧	188	45.42 N	69.44 W
Kinesi	154	1.28 S	33.52 E
Kinešma	80	57.26 N	42.09 E
Kineton	42	52.10 N	1.30 W
Kinfauns	46	56.22 N	3.21 W
King	192	36.16 N	80.21 W
King □[6]	224	47.26 N	121.48 W
King ≃, Austl.	164	14.41 S	131.59 E
King ≃, Austl.	169	36.41 S	146.25 E
King, Lake ⊜	162	25.38 S	120.06 E
King, Mont ∧	212	45.29 N	75.52 W
King, Mount ∧	166	25.10 S	147.31 E
Kingabwa ◄[8]	273b	4.19 S	15.20 E
King and Queen □[6]	208	37.42 N	76.50 W
King and Queen Court House	208	37.40 N	76.52 W
Kingaroy	166	26.33 S	151.50 E
Kingarth	46	55.46 N	5.03 W
King City, On., Can.	212	43.56 N	79.32 W
King City, Ca., U.S.	226	36.12 N	121.07 W
King City, Mo., U.S.	194	40.03 N	94.31 W
King Cove	180	55.04 N	162.19 W
Kingdom City	219	38.58 N	91.56 W
King Edward ≃	164	14.14 S	126.35 E
Kingersheim	58	47.48 N	7.20 E
King Ferry	210	42.39 N	76.37 W
Kingfield	188	44.57 N	70.09 W
Kingfisher	196	35.51 N	97.55 W
King George	208	38.16 N	77.11 W
King George □[6]	208	38.15 N	77.10 W
King George, Mount ∧	182	50.35 N	115.24 W
King George Bay c	254	51.33 S	60.37 W
King George Island I	9	62.00 S	58.15 W
King George Islands II	176	57.20 N	78.25 W
King George's Dock ◄[5]	272b	22.32 N	88.18 E
King George Sound ⋓	162	35.03 S	117.57 E
King George's Reservoir ⊜[1]	260	51.39 N	0.01 W
King George VI Reservoir ⊜[1]	260	51.27 N	0.32 W
King Hill	202	43.00 N	115.12 W
Kinghorn	46	56.04 N	3.10 W
Kingie ≃	46	57.04 N	5.08 W
Kingisepp	76	59.22 N	28.36 E
King Island I, Austl.	166	39.50 S	144.00 E
King Island I, B.C., Can.	182	52.12 N	127.42 W
King Island I, Ak., U.S.	180	64.58 N	168.05 W
Kinglake National Park ♦	169	37.35 S	145.25 E
King Lear Peak ∧	204	41.12 N	118.34 W
King Leopold Ranges ⩚	160	17.30 S	125.45 E
Kingman, Az., U.S.	200	35.11 N	114.03 W
Kingman, Ks., U.S.	198	37.38 N	98.06 W
Kingman Reef ✦[2]	14	6.24 N	162.22 W
King Mountain ∧, B.C., Can.	180	58.17 N	128.54 W
King Mountain ∧, Ok., U.S.	196	34.52 N	99.17 W
King Mountain ∧, Or., U.S.	202	42.42 N	123.14 W
King Mountain ∧, Or., U.S.	202	43.49 N	118.52 W
King of Prussia	208	40.05 N	75.23 W
King of Prussia Plaza ◄[9]	285	40.05 N	75.25 W
Kingoma	152	5.11 S	13.34 E
Kingoma-Ngoma	152	5.50 S	16.49 E
Kingombe, Zaïre	154	3.56 S	26.35 E
Kingombe, Zaïre	154	7.24 S	26.11 E
Kingoonya	162	30.54 S	135.18 E
Kingoué	152	3.43 S	14.09 E
King Peak ∧	204	40.10 N	124.08 W
King Peninsula ≻[1]	9	73.12 S	101.00 W
Kingri	120	30.27 N	69.49 E
Kings, Il., U.S.	216	42.00 N	89.06 W
Kings, Ms., U.S.	194	32.23 N	90.51 W
Kings □[6], Ca., U.S.	226	36.20 N	119.39 W
Kings □[6], N.Y., U.S.	210	40.42 N	74.00 W
Kings ≃, Ar., U.S.	194	36.29 N	93.35 W
Kings ≃, Ca., U.S.	226	36.03 N	119.49 W
Kings ≃, Nv., U.S.	204	41.31 N	118.08 W
Kings, Middle Fork ≃	204	36.50 N	118.52 W
Kings, North Fork ≃, Ca., U.S.	204	36.52 N	119.08 W
Kings, North Fork ≃, Ca., U.S.	226	36.18 N	119.52 W
Kings, South Fork ≃	226	36.18 N	119.52 W
King Salmon	180	58.41 N	156.39 W
King Salmon ≃	180	58.15 N	157.30 W
Kingsbarns	46	56.18 N	2.39 W
Kings Beach	226	39.14 N	120.01 W
Kingsbridge	42	50.17 N	3.46 W
Kingsburg	226	36.30 N	119.33 W
Kingsbury, Eng., U.K.	42	52.35 N	1.40 W
Kingsbury, In., U.S.	216	41.31 N	86.42 W
Kingsbury ◄[8]	260	51.35 N	0.17 W
Kings Canyon National Park ♦	204	36.48 N	118.30 W
Kingsclere	42	51.20 N	1.14 W
Kingscote	168b	35.40 S	137.38 E
Kingscourt	48	53.53 N	6.48 W
Kings Creek	218	40.10 N	83.44 W
Kings Creek ≃, Austl.	171a	27.57 S	151.42 E
Kings Creek ≃, Tx., U.S.	222	32.25 N	96.15 W
King's Cross Station ◄[5]	260	51.32 N	0.07 W
Kings Dominion ♦	208	37.51 N	77.27 W
Kingsdown, Eng., U.K.	42	51.11 N	1.25 E
Kingsdown, Eng., U.K.	260	51.21 N	0.17 E
Kings Falls ∟	212	43.55 N	75.38 W

FRANÇAIS

Nom	Page	Lat.°′	Long.°′ W = Ouest
Kingsford, Austl.	274a	33.56 S	151.14 E
Kingsford, Mi., U.S.	190	45.47 N	88.04 W
Kingsford Heights	216	41.29 N	86.42 W
Kingsford Smith Airport ⊠	170	33.57 S	151.11 E
Kingsgate	182	49.00 N	116.11 W
Kingsgrove	274a	33.57 S	151.06 E
Kingshill	241n	17.44 N	64.48 W
Kingshouse	46	56.21 N	4.19 W
Kings Island ♦	218	39.21 N	84.16 W
Kingskerswell	42	50.30 N	3.33 W
Kingsland, Eng., U.K.	42	52.15 N	2.47 W
Kingsland, Ar., U.S.	194	33.51 N	92.17 W
Kingsland, Ga., U.S.	192	30.47 N	81.41 W
Kingsland, Tx., U.S.	196	30.40 N	98.26 W
Kingsland, Va., U.S.	208	37.24 N	77.26 W
Kings Langley	42	51.43 N	0.28 W
Kingsley, S. Afr.	158	27.55 S	30.33 E
Kingsley, Eng., U.K.	42	53.01 N	1.59 W
Kingsley, Eng., U.K.	262	53.16 N	2.40 W
Kingsley, Ia., U.S.	198	42.35 N	95.58 W
Kingsley, Mi., U.S.	190	44.35 N	85.32 W
Kingsley, Pa., U.S.	210	41.46 N	75.45 W
Kingsley Dam ◄[6]	198	41.11 N	101.39 W
King's Lynn	42	52.45 N	0.24 E
Kings Manor	285	40.05 N	75.21 W
Kingsmere Lake ⊜	184	54.06 N	106.27 W
Kings Mills	218	39.21 N	84.14 W
Kings Mountain	192	35.14 N	81.20 W
Kings Mountain National Military Park ♦	192	35.07 N	81.33 W
King Solomon's Mines → Mikhrot Shelomo Hamelekh ⊥	132	29.45 N	34.56 E
King Sound ⋓	162	17.00 S	123.30 E
Kings Park, N.Y., U.S.	210	40.53 N	73.16 W
Kings Park, Va., U.S.	284c	38.48 N	77.14 W
Kings Park ♦	168a	31.57 S	115.49 E
Kings Peak ∧	200	40.46 N	110.22 W
Kings Plaza ◄[9]	276	40.37 N	73.55 W
King's Point, Nf., Can.	186	49.35 N	56.11 W
Kings Point, N.Y., U.S.	210	40.49 N	73.44 W
Kingsport	192	36.32 N	82.33 W
King's Sutton	42	52.01 N	1.16 W
Kingsteignton	42	50.33 N	3.35 W
King Sterndale	262	53.15 N	1.52 W
Kingsthorpe	171a	27.29 S	151.49 E
Kingston, Austl.	171a	27.40 S	153.07 E
Kingston, N.S., Can.	186	44.59 N	64.57 W
Kingston, On., Can.	212	44.14 N	76.30 W
Kingston, Jam.	241q	18.00 N	76.48 W
Kingston, N.Z.	172	45.20 S	168.42 E
Kingston, Norf. I.	174c	29.03 S	167.58 E
Kingston, Ga., U.S.	192	34.14 N	84.56 W
Kingston, Il., U.S.	216	42.06 N	88.46 W
Kingston, Ma., U.S.	207	41.59 N	70.43 W
Kingston, Mo., U.S.	194	39.38 N	94.02 W
Kingston, N.J., U.S.	276	40.22 N	74.36 W
Kingston, N.Y., U.S.	210	41.55 N	73.59 W
Kingston, Oh., U.S.	218	39.28 N	82.54 W
Kingston, Ok., U.S.	196	33.59 N	96.43 W
Kingston, Pa., U.S.	210	41.15 N	75.53 W
Kingston, R.I., U.S.	207	41.29 N	71.31 W
Kingston, Tn., U.S.	192	35.52 N	84.30 W
Kingston, Wa., U.S.	224	47.48 N	122.30 W
Kingston Bay c	283	42.00 N	70.42 W
Kingston Mills	212	44.17 N	76.27 W
Kingston Southeast	166	36.50 S	139.51 E
Kingston upon Hull	44	53.45 N	0.20 W
Kingston [upon Thames]	28	51.25 N	0.19 W
Kingston [upon Thames] ◄[8]	42	51.25 N	0.19 W
Kingstown → Dún Laoghaire, Ire.	48	53.17 N	6.08 W
Kingstown, St. Vin.	241h	13.09 N	61.14 W
Kingstree	192	33.40 N	79.49 W
Kingsville, Austl.	274b	37.49 S	144.52 E
Kingsville, On., Can.	214	42.02 N	82.45 W
Kingsville, Md., U.S.	284b	39.26 N	76.25 W
Kingsville, Oh., U.S.	214	41.53 N	80.41 W
Kingsville, Tx., U.S.	196	27.30 N	97.51 W
Kingsville Naval Air Station ■	196	27.31 N	97.47 W
Kingswear	42	50.21 N	3.34 W
Kingswinford	42	52.29 N	2.10 W
Kingswood, Austl.	274a	33.46 S	150.43 E
Kingswood, S. Afr.	158	27.29 S	25.46 E
Kingswood, Eng., U.K.	42	51.27 N	2.22 W
Kingswood, Eng., U.K.	260	51.17 N	0.13 W
Kingswood Park	285	40.07 N	74.51 W
King's Worthy	42	51.06 N	1.18 W
Kingtechen → Jingdezhen	100	29.16 N	117.11 E
Kington	42	52.12 N	3.01 W
Kingunda	152	6.34 S	16.58 E
Kingungi	152	5.24 S	17.56 E
Kingussie	46	57.05 N	4.03 W
King William	208	37.41 N	77.00 W
King William □[6]	208	37.42 N	77.05 W
King William Island I	176	69.00 N	97.30 W
King William's Town	158	32.51 S	27.22 E
Kingwood, Tx., U.S.	222	29.54 N	95.18 W
Kingwood, W.V., U.S.	188	39.28 N	79.41 W
Kinh Duc	110	11.49 N	107.58 E
Kinhwa → Jinhua	100	29.07 N	119.39 E
Kınık	130	39.05 N	27.23 E
Kinira ≃	158	31.12 S	29.17 E
Kinistino	184	52.57 N	105.00 W
Kinjar Khās	123	29.55 N	70.58 E
Kinkala	152	4.22 S	14.46 E
Kinker Creek ≃	282	38.02 N	121.52 W
Kinkony, Lac ⊜	157b	16.08 S	45.50 E
Kinkora	285	40.07 N	74.45 W
Kinleith	172	38.16 S	175.54 E
Kinloch	46	57.01 N	6.17 W
Kinlochbervie	46	58.28 N	5.03 W
Kinlocheil	46	56.51 N	5.20 W
Kinlochewe	46	57.36 N	5.20 W
Kinloch Hourn	46	57.06 N	5.22 W
Kinlochleven	46	56.42 N	4.58 W
Kinloch Rannoch	46	56.42 N	4.11 W
Kinloss	46	57.37 N	3.34 W
Kinmount	212	44.47 N	78.39 W
Kinmundy	219	38.46 N	88.50 W
Kinn	26	61.36 N	4.45 E
Kinna	26	57.30 N	12.41 E
Kinnaird	182	49.17 N	117.39 W
Kinnaird Head ≻	46	57.42 N	2.00 W
Kinnegad	48	53.26 N	7.05 W
Kinnekulle ∧[2]	26	58.35 N	13.23 E
Kinnelon	210	40.59 N	74.23 W
Kinnel Water ≃	44	55.08 N	3.25 W
Kinneret	132	32.43 N	35.33 E
Kinneret, Yam (Sea of Galilee) ⊜	132	32.48 N	35.35 E
Kinneret-Negev Conduit ≅[1]	132	32.52 N	35.32 E
Kinnerley	42	52.47 N	2.59 W
Kinniconick Creek ≃	218	38.37 N	83.09 W
Kinnula	26	63.22 N	24.58 E
Kino ≃	96	34.13 N	135.09 E
Kinoe	96	34.14 N	132.55 E
Kinogitan	116	9.00 N	124.48 E
Kinojévis ≃	190	48.23 N	78.21 W
Kinomoto	94	35.30 N	136.13 E
Kinonge ≃	206	45.39 N	74.55 W
Kinoni	154	0.39 S	30.27 E
Kinosaki	96	35.37 N	134.49 E
Kinpoku-san ∧	92	38.05 N	138.22 E

PORTUGUÊS

Nome	Página	Lat.°′	Long.°′ W = Oeste
Kinrola	166	23.46 S	148.45 E
Kinross, S. Afr.	158	26.22 S	29.03 E
Kinross, Scot., U.K.	46	56.13 N	3.27 W
Kin-saki ≻	174m	26.26 N	127.57 E
Kinsale, Ire.	48	51.42 N	8.32 W
Kinsale, Va., U.S.	208	38.01 N	76.34 W
Kinsale, Old Head of ≻	48	51.36 N	8.32 W
Kinsale Harbour c	48	51.41 N	8.30 W
Kinsarvik	26	60.23 N	6.43 E
Kinschasa → Kinshasa	152	4.18 S	15.18 E
Kinshasa (Léopoldville), Zaïre	152	4.18 S	15.18 E
Kinshasa (Léopoldville), Zaïre	273b	4.18 S	15.18 E
Kinshasa □[4]	152	4.18 S	15.18 E
Kinshasa (Ndjili) Airport ⊠, Zaïre	273b	4.23 S	15.27 E
Kinshasa (Ndolo) Airport ⊠, Zaïre	273b	4.20 S	15.19 E
Kinshasa-Est ◄[8]	273b	4.18 S	15.18 E
Kinshasa-Ouest ◄[8]	273b	4.20 S	15.15 E
Kins'ka ≃	78	47.40 N	35.22 E
Kinsley	198	37.55 N	99.24 W
Kinsman, Il., U.S.	216	41.11 N	88.34 W
Kinsman, Oh., U.S.	214	41.27 N	80.36 W
Kinston, Al., U.S.	194	31.12 N	86.10 W
Kinston, N.C., U.S.	192	35.15 N	77.34 W
Kintamani	115b	8.14 S	115.19 E
Kintamo, Rapides de ∟	273b	4.19 S	15.15 E
Kintampo	150	8.03 N	1.43 W
Kintap	112	3.51 S	115.13 E
Kintari, Mont ∧[2]	273b	4.08 S	15.23 E
Kintélé	273b	4.09 S	15.21 E
Kintinian	150	11.36 N	9.23 W
Kintinku	154	5.53 S	35.14 E
Kintobongo-Bunge	154	8.54 S	26.23 E
Kintore	46	57.13 N	2.21 W
Kintore, Mount ∧	162	26.34 S	130.30 E
Kintore Range ⩚	162	23.25 S	129.20 E
Kintsana	273b	4.19 S	15.10 E
Kintus	86	60.09 N	71.25 E
Kintyre ≻[1]	46	55.32 N	5.35 W
Kintyre, Mull of ≻	46	55.17 N	5.55 W
Kinu ≃	94	35.56 N	139.57 E
Kinuseo Falls ∟	182	54.47 N	121.12 W
Kinuso	182	55.20 N	115.25 W
Kinvarra	48	53.08 N	8.55 W
Kinver	42	52.27 N	2.14 W
Kin-wan c	174m	26.25 N	127.54 E
Kinwood	222	29.56 N	95.23 W
Kinyangiri	154	4.27 S	34.37 E
Kinyeti ∧	154	3.57 N	32.54 E
Kinzia	152	3.36 S	18.26 E
Kinzig ≃, Dtsch.	56	50.08 N	8.54 E
Kinzig ≃, Dtsch.	58	48.37 N	7.49 E
Kinzua	202	44.59 N	120.03 W
Kinzua Creek ≃	214	41.47 N	78.50 W
Kinzua Dam ◄[6]	214	41.50 N	79.01 W
Kioga-See → Kyoga, Lake ⊜	154	1.30 N	33.00 E
Kioshkokwi Lake ⊜	190	46.05 N	78.52 W
Kioto → Kyōto	94	35.00 N	135.45 E
Kiowa, Co., U.S.	198	39.20 N	104.27 W
Kiowa, Ks., U.S.	198	37.01 N	98.29 W
Kiowa, Ok., U.S.	196	34.43 N	95.53 W
Kiowa Creek ≃, U.S.	196	36.46 N	99.55 W
Kiowa Creek ≃, Co., U.S.	198	40.20 N	104.05 W
Kipahigan Lake ⊜	184	55.20 N	101.55 W
Kipandi	152	5.19 S	16.46 E
Kipanga	154	6.14 S	35.21 E
Kiparissía	38	37.14 N	21.40 E
Kiparissiakós Kólpos c	38	37.37 N	21.24 E
Kipatimu	154	8.29 S	38.56 E
Kipawa ≃	190	47.03 N	79.23 W
Kipawa, Lac ⊜	190	46.55 N	79.00 W
Kipawa, Réserve ♦	190	47.15 N	78.15 W
Kipembawe	154	7.39 S	33.24 E
Kipengere Range ⩚	154	9.10 S	34.15 E
Kipijevo	24	65.40 N	54.30 E
Kipili	154	7.26 S	30.36 E
Kipini	154	2.32 S	40.31 E
Kipling	184	50.10 N	102.38 W
Kipnuk	180	59.56 N	164.03 W
Kippax	44	53.46 N	1.22 W
Kippen	46	56.08 N	4.11 W
Kippenheim	58	48.17 N	7.49 E
Kippure ∧	48	53.10 N	6.20 W
Kípros → Cyprus □[1]	130	35.00 N	33.00 E
Kipsdorf	54	50.47 N	13.32 E
Kipton	214	41.16 N	82.18 W
Kipushi	154	11.46 S	27.14 E
Kipushia, Zaïre	154	6.10 S	25.12 E
Kipushia, Zaïre	154	12.58 S	29.30 E
Kira, Nihon	94	34.49 N	137.05 E
Kir'a, Ross.	80	55.04 N	46.53 E
Kirakira	175e	10.27 S	161.55 E
Kirandul	122	18.40 N	81.16 E
Kirane	150	15.25 N	10.14 W
Kiranlık	130	39.07 N	41.41 E
Kiranomena	157b	18.17 S	46.03 E
Kīratpur	124	29.31 N	78.12 E
Kiraz	130	38.13 N	28.13 E
Kirazlı	130	40.02 N	26.41 E
Kırbaçbayırı ∧	267b	40.56 N	29.10 E
Kırbaşı	130	40.01 N	31.50 E
Kirbla	76	58.44 N	23.57 E
Kirby Muxloe	42	52.38 N	1.13 W
Kirbys Creek ≃	208	36.28 N	77.06 W
Kirbyville	194	30.39 N	93.53 W
Kırçal	130	41.39 N	35.16 E
Kırcasalih	130	41.23 N	26.48 E
Kirchardt	56	49.12 N	8.59 E
Kirchbach in Steiermark	61	46.54 N	15.44 E
Kirchberg, Dtsch.	54	50.37 N	12.32 E
Kirchberg, Dtsch.	56	49.12 N	9.58 E
Kirchberg, Dtsch.	56	49.56 N	7.24 E
Kirchberg, Dtsch.	60	48.54 N	13.11 E
Kirchberg, Schw.	58	47.05 N	7.35 E
Kirchberg, Schw.	58	47.25 N	9.03 E
Kirch-Berg ∧[2]	264a	52.27 N	13.02 E
Kirchberg am Wagram	61	48.26 N	15.53 E
Kirchberg an der Pielach	61	48.02 N	15.26 E
Kirchberg in Tirol	64	47.27 N	12.19 E
Kirchbichl	64	47.31 N	12.05 E
Kirchderne ◄[8]	263	51.33 N	7.30 E
Kirchdorf, Dtsch.	52	52.36 N	8.49 E
Kirchdorf, Dtsch.	54	54.00 N	11.26 E
Kirchdorf an der Krems	61	47.56 N	14.07 E
Kirchdorf im Wald	60	48.55 N	13.16 E
Kirchen	56	50.48 N	7.53 E
Kirchende	263	51.25 N	7.26 E
Kirchenlaibach	60	49.53 N	11.46 E
Kirchenlamitz	54	50.09 N	11.56 E
Kirchenthumbach	60	49.45 N	11.43 E
Kirchhain	56	50.49 N	8.55 E
Kirchham	60	48.21 N	13.16 E
Kirchheiligen	54	51.11 N	10.42 E
Kirchheimbolanden	56	49.40 N	8.00 E
Kirchheim in Schwaben	58	48.10 N	10.30 E
Kirchheim unter Teck	56	48.39 N	9.27 E
Kirchhellen	52	51.36 N	6.55 E
Kirchhellen Heide ◄[3]	263	51.36 N	6.53 E
Kirchhofen	264a	52.22 N	13.53 E
Kirchhörde ◄[8]	263	51.27 N	7.27 E
Kirchhundem	56	51.05 N	8.05 E
Kirchlengern	52	52.12 N	8.35 E
Kirchlinde ◄[8]	263	51.32 N	7.22 E
Kirchlinteln	52	52.56 N	9.19 E
Kirchmöser	54	52.22 N	12.25 E
Kirchroth	60	48.57 N	12.33 E
Kirchschlag in der Buckligen Welt	61	47.31 N	16.18 E
Kirchveischede	56	51.05 N	7.59 E
Kirchwalsede	52	53.01 N	9.23 E
Kirchwerder ◄[8]	52	53.25 N	10.11 E
Kirchzarten	58	47.58 N	7.56 E
Kircubbin	48	54.29 N	5.32 W
Kirda	85	41.06 N	69.00 E
Kirdāsah	142	30.02 N	31.07 E
Kireç	130	39.33 N	28.22 E
Kirej ≃	88	54.12 N	100.40 E
Kirejevo	80	50.01 N	44.29 E
Kirejevsk	76	53.56 N	37.56 E
Kirejkovo	76	53.38 N	35.49 E
Kirenga ≃	88	57.47 N	108.07 E
Kirensk	88	57.46 N	108.08 E
Kirghizia → Kyrgyzstan □[1]	72	41.30 N	75.00 E
Kirgili	85	40.24 N	71.43 E
Kirgizija → Kyrgyzstan □[1]	72	41.30 N	75.00 E
Kirgiziya → Kyrgyzstan □[1]	72	41.30 N	75.00 E
Kirgiz-Mijaki	86	53.38 N	54.47 E
Kirgizskij chrebet ⩚	85	42.30 N	74.00 E
Kiri	152	1.27 S	19.00 E
Kiribati □[1]	14	5.00 S	170.00 W
Kiribati II	14	0.30 S	174.00 E
Kiries West	158	26.34 S	19.00 E
Kiriga-mine ∧	94	36.06 N	138.12 E
Kırıkhan, Tür.	130	39.32 N	41.20 E
Kırıkhan, Tür.	130	36.32 N	36.19 E
Kirikiri Prisons ᵾ	273a	6.27 N	3.19 E
Kırıkkale	130	39.50 N	33.31 E
Kırıkkale □[4]	130	40.00 N	33.45 E
Kirillov	76	59.52 N	38.23 E
Kirillovka	265b	55.57 N	37.20 E
Kirillovo, Ross.	80	57.07 N	45.27 E
Kirillovo, Ross.	80	53.47 N	42.40 E
Kirillovskoje	76	60.28 N	29.17 E
Kirin → Jilin	89	43.51 N	126.33 E
Kirin → Jilin □[4]	90	44.00 N	126.00 E
Kirinyaga (Mount Kenya) ∧	154	0.10 S	37.20 E
Kirishima-Yaku-kokuritsu-kōen ♦	92	31.55 N	130.51 E
Kirishima-yama ∧	92	31.56 N	130.52 E
Kiriši	76	59.27 N	32.02 E
Kiritimati (Christmas Island) I[1]	174o	1.52 N	157.20 W
Kiriwina Island I	164	8.35 S	151.05 E
Kiriwina Islands II	164	8.35 S	151.05 E
Kirizume-tōge ∧[2]	270	34.56 N	135.16 E
Kirjanovskaja Kontora	88	58.18 N	104.13 E
Kirka	130	39.17 N	30.33 E
Kirkabister	46a	60.07 N	1.08 W
Kırkağaç	130	39.06 N	27.40 E
Kirkbride	44	54.54 N	3.12 W
Kirkburton	44	53.37 N	1.42 W
Kirkby	44	53.29 N	2.54 W
Kirkby in Ashfield	44	53.06 N	1.15 W
Kirkby Lonsdale	44	54.13 N	2.36 W
Kirkby Malzeard	44	54.11 N	1.38 W
Kirkbymoorside	44	54.16 N	0.55 W
Kirkby Stephen	44	54.28 N	2.20 W
Kirkcaldy	46	56.07 N	3.10 W
Kirkcolm	44	54.58 N	5.05 W
Kirkconnel	44	55.23 N	4.00 W
Kirkcudbright	44	54.50 N	4.03 W
Kirkcudbright Bay c	44	54.48 N	4.04 W
Kirkdale ◄[8]	262	53.26 N	2.59 W
Kirkeby	41	56.09 N	9.27 E
Kirkee → Khadki	122	18.34 N	73.52 E
Kirkenær	26	60.28 N	12.03 E
Kirkenes	24	69.40 N	30.03 E
Kirke Stillinge	41	55.26 N	11.15 E
Kirkham	44	53.47 N	2.53 W
Kirkhill	46	57.28 N	4.26 W
Kirkintilloch	46	55.57 N	4.10 W
Kirkjubæjarklaustur	24a	63.47 N	18.04 W
Kirkkonummi → Kyrkslätt	26	60.07 N	24.26 E
Kirkland, P.Q., Can.	275a	45.27 N	73.52 W
Kirkland, Il., U.S.	216	42.05 N	88.51 W
Kirkland, Tx., U.S.	196	34.23 N	100.04 W
Kirkland, Wa., U.S.	224	47.40 N	122.12 W
Kirkland Creek ≃	200	34.32 N	113.00 W
Kirkland Lake	190	48.09 N	80.02 W
Kırklar Dağı ∧	130	40.32 N	40.35 E
Kırklareli	130	41.44 N	27.12 E
Kırklareli □[4]	130	41.40 N	27.30 E
Kirklees □[8]	262	53.36 N	1.52 W
Kirkleyditch	262	53.18 N	2.12 W
Kirklin	194	40.11 N	86.21 W
Kirkliston	46	55.58 N	3.25 W
Kirk Michael, I. of Man	44	54.17 N	4.35 W
Kirkmichael, Scot., U.K.	46	56.43 N	3.29 W
Kirkmuirhill	46	55.40 N	3.55 W
Kirkness Lake ⊜	184	51.32 N	93.56 W
Kirkpatrick, Mount ∧	9	84.20 S	166.19 E
Kirkpatrick Lake ⊜	182	51.52 N	111.18 W
Kirk Sandall	44	53.33 N	1.04 W
Kirksville, Il., U.S.	219	39.34 N	88.40 W
Kirksville, Mo., U.S.	194	40.11 N	92.34 W
Kirkton	46	56.13 N	2.55 W
Kirkton of Culsalmond	46	57.23 N	2.34 W
Kirkton of Glenisla	46	56.44 N	3.17 W
Kirktown of Auchterless	46	57.27 N	2.28 W
Kirkūk	128	35.28 N	44.28 E
Kirkville	210	43.05 N	75.57 W
Kirkwall	46	58.59 N	2.58 W
Kirkwood, S. Afr.	158	33.24 S	25.26 E
Kirkwood, De., U.S.	208	39.34 N	75.41 W
Kirkwood, Il., U.S.	190	40.51 N	90.44 W
Kirkwood, Mo., U.S.	219	38.35 N	90.24 W
Kirkwood, N.J., U.S.	285	39.50 N	75.01 W
Kirkwood, N.Y., U.S.	210	42.02 N	75.48 W
Kirmir ≃	130	40.07 N	31.43 E
Kirn	56	49.47 N	7.28 E
Kirnāhar	126	23.45 N	87.52 E
Kirotshe	154	1.37 S	29.02 E
Kirov, Ross.	76	54.05 N	34.20 E
Kirov, Ross.	80	58.38 N	49.42 E
Kirovabad → Gäncä	84	40.40 N	46.22 E
Kirovakan	84	40.48 N	44.30 E
Kirove, Ukr.	78	47.41 N	35.46 E
Kirove, Ukr.	83	48.23 N	37.55 E
Kirovgrad	86	57.26 N	60.04 E
Kirovka	86	47.07 N	82.00 E
Kirovo, Bela.	78	51.29 N	29.24 E
Kirovo, Ross.	86	55.33 N	63.46 E
Kirovo, Uzb.	85	40.26 N	70.34 E
Kirov Oblast' □[4]	24	59.00 N	50.00 E
Kirovo-Čepeck	80	58.33 N	50.01 E
Kirovohrad	78	48.30 N	32.18 E
Kirovohrad □[4]	78	48.30 N	32.00 E
Kirovsk, Bela.	76	53.16 N	29.29 E
Kirovsk, Ross.	24	67.37 N	33.35 E
Kirovsk, Ross.	265a	59.52 N	31.00 E
Kirovsk, Turk.	128	37.42 N	60.23 E
Kirovs'k, Ukr.	83	49.01 N	37.56 E
Kirovs'k, Ukr.	83	48.38 N	38.39 E
Kirovs'ke, Ukr.	78	48.33 N	34.53 E
Kirovs'ke, Ukr.	78	45.14 N	35.13 E
Kirovs'ke, Ukr.	83	48.09 N	38.21 E
Kirovskij, Kaz.	86	44.52 N	78.12 E
Kirovskij, Ross.	74	54.18 N	155.47 E
Kirovskij, Ross.	80	45.51 N	48.07 E
Kirovskij, Ross.	89	54.26 N	126.55 E
Kirovskij, Ross.	89	45.07 N	133.30 E
Kirovskije ostrova II	265a	59.58 N	30.15 E
Kirovskoje	85	42.39 N	71.35 E
Kirov Stadium ♦	265a	59.58 N	30.14 E
Kirov Theatre ᵾ	265a	59.55 N	30.18 E
Kirpičnyj Zavod	265a	60.01 N	30.48 E
Kirpil'skaja	78	45.23 N	39.43 E
Kirriemuir	46	56.41 N	3.01 W
Kirs	86	59.21 N	52.14 E
Kirsanov	80	52.38 N	42.43 E
Kirsanovka	80	52.30 N	52.53 E
Kirschau	54	51.04 N	14.27 E
Kırşehir	130	39.09 N	34.10 E
Kırşehir □[4]	130	39.20 N	34.10 E
Kīrthar National Park ♦	120	25.50 N	67.40 E
Kīrthar Range ⩚	120	27.00 N	67.10 E
Kirtland, N.M., U.S.	200	36.44 N	108.21 W
Kirtland, Oh., U.S.	214	41.37 N	81.21 W
Kirtland Air Force Base ■	200	35.02 N	106.37 W
Kirtland Hills	214	41.37 N	81.24 W
Kirtle Water ≃	44	54.58 N	3.05 W
Kirton	42	52.56 N	0.04 W
Kirton in Lindsey	44	53.28 N	0.36 W
Kirtorf	56	50.46 N	9.06 E
Kiruna	24	67.51 N	20.16 E
Kirundu	154	0.44 S	25.32 E
Kirurumo	154	5.53 S	34.11 E
Kirvin	222	31.46 N	96.20 W
Kirwan Heights	279b	40.22 N	80.06 W
Kirwee	172	43.30 S	172.13 E
Kirwin	198	39.40 N	99.07 W
Kirwin Reservoir ⊜[1]	198	39.39 N	99.10 W
Kiryandongo	154	1.53 N	32.03 E
Kiryū	94	36.24 N	139.20 E
Kirza	86	54.14 N	81.40 E
Kiržač	82	56.09 N	38.52 E
Kiržač ≃	82	55.52 N	39.04 E
Kisa, Nihon	96	34.43 N	132.59 E
Kisa, Sve.	26	57.59 N	15.37 E
Kisai	94	36.06 N	139.35 E
Kisaichi	270	34.46 N	135.42 E
Kisakata	92	39.13 N	139.54 E
Kisaki	154	7.28 S	37.36 E
Kis Alföld ⩸	61	47.35 N	17.00 E
Kišaly	76	54.23 N	43.12 E
Kisambo	152	6.25 S	18.14 E
Kisanga	154	2.29 N	26.35 E
Kisangani (Stanleyville)	154	0.30 S	25.12 E
Kisantu	152	5.07 S	15.05 E
Kisar, Pulau I	112	8.05 S	127.10 E
Kisaralik ≃	180	60.51 N	161.16 W
Kisaran	114	2.59 N	99.37 E
Kisarawe	154	6.54 S	39.04 E
Kisarazu	94	35.23 N	139.55 E
Kisarazu-Kichi, Kōkū-jieitai ■	94	35.24 N	139.55 E
Kisawa	96	33.49 N	134.18 E
K.I. Sawyer Air Force Base ■	190	46.21 N	87.25 W
Kisbér	30	47.30 N	18.02 E
Kisbey	184	49.38 N	102.41 W
Kise ≃	94	35.06 N	138.53 E
Kiselevsk → Kisel'ovsk	86	54.00 N	86.39 E
Kisel'ovka	80	47.18 N	44.07 E
Kisel'ovsk	86	54.00 N	86.39 E
Kisengwa	154	6.00 S	25.50 E
Kisen-yama ∧[2]	270	34.54 N	135.51 E
Kiser Lake ⊜	218	40.11 N	83.58 W
Kīsh, Jazīreh-ye I	128	26.32 N	53.56 E
Kishanda	154	1.42 S	31.34 E
Kishanganga ≃	123	34.22 N	73.30 E
Kishanganj	124	26.07 N	87.56 E
Kishangarh	120	27.52 N	70.34 E
Kishangarh ◄[8]	272a	28.31 N	77.08 E
Kishangarh Bās	120	26.34 N	74.52 E
Kishb, Ḥarrat al- •[9]	144	23.00 N	41.25 E
Kishi, Nig.	150	9.05 N	3.52 E
Kishi, Zaïre	154	10.04 S	26.26 E
Kishida ≃	96	35.38 N	134.27 E
Kishigawa	96	34.13 N	135.20 E
Kishikas ≃	184	52.45 N	91.43 W
Kishimoto	96	35.23 N	133.25 E
Kishinev → Chişinău	38	47.00 N	28.50 E
Kishiwada	96	34.28 N	135.22 E
Kishorganj	124	24.26 N	90.46 E
Kishorn, Loch c	46	57.21 N	5.41 W
Kishtwār	123	33.19 N	75.46 E
Kishwaukee ≃	216	42.11 N	89.08 W
Kishwaukee, South Branch ≃	216	42.12 N	88.59 W
Kisia	152	4.35 S	18.22 E
Kisigo ≃	154	7.03 S	35.50 E
Kisii	154	0.41 S	34.46 E
Kisiju	154	7.24 S	39.20 E
Kiši-Karoj, ozero ⊜	86	54.03 N	71.20 E
Kisika-zaki ≻	93b	30.50 N	131.04 E
Kısıklı ◄[8]	267b	41.01 N	29.03 E
Kısır Dağı ∧	84	40.58 N	43.04 E
Kısırkaya ◄[8]	267b	41.14 N	28.58 E
Kısırmandıra ◄[8]	267b	41.14 N	28.49 E
Kisiwada → Kishiwada	96	34.28 N	135.22 E
Kisiwani	154	4.08 S	37.57 E
Kisizi	154	1.00 S	29.56 E
Kiska Island I	181a	52.00 N	177.30 E
Kiskatinaw ≃	182	56.06 N	120.08 W
Kiska Volcano ∧[1]	181a	52.07 N	177.36 E
Kis-Kevély ∧[2]	264c	47.38 N	18.59 E
Kiski Lake ⊜	184	54.46 N	98.55 W
Kiskimere	279b	40.37 N	79.35 W
Kiskiminetas ≃	214	40.41 N	79.40 W
Kiskittogisu Lake ⊜	184	54.13 N	98.20 W
Kiskitto Lake ⊜	184	54.16 N	98.34 W
Kiskörei-viztároló ⊜[1]	30	47.35 N	20.40 E
Kiskőrös	30	46.38 N	19.17 E
Kiskunfélegyháza	30	46.43 N	19.52 E
Kiskunhalas	30	46.26 N	19.30 E
Kiskunmajsa	30	46.30 N	19.45 E
Kiskunsági Nemzeti Park ♦	30	46.40 N	19.25 E
Kisl'akovskaja	78	46.27 N	39.40 E
Kislovo	80	49.54 N	45.25 E
Kislovodsk	84	43.55 N	42.44 E
Kismaayo	144	0.22 S	42.32 E
Kismet	276	40.38 N	73.12 W
Kisnema	76	60.20 N	37.39 E
Kiso, Nihon	94	35.56 N	137.47 E
Kiso, Nihon	268	35.34 N	139.26 E
Kiso ≃	94	35.02 N	136.45 E
Kisofukushima	94	35.51 N	137.42 E
Kisogawa	94	35.20 N	136.47 E
Kisoripur	126	22.05 N	88.34 E
Kisoro	154	1.17 S	29.41 E
Kiso-sammyaku ⩚	94	35.43 N	137.50 E
Kisozaki	94	35.04 N	136.44 E
Kispest ◄[8]	264c	47.27 N	19.08 E
Kispiox	182	55.21 N	127.41 W
Kispiox ≃	182	55.16 N	127.41 W
Kispiox Mountain ∧	182	55.25 N	127.57 W
Kissamos	38	35.30 N	23.38 E
Kissena Park ♦	276	40.45 N	73.49 W
Kisseynew Lake ⊜	184	54.58 N	101.35 W
Kissidougou	150	9.11 N	10.06 W
Kissimmee	220	28.17 N	81.24 W
Kissimmee ≃	220	27.10 N	80.53 W
Kissimmee, Lake ⊜	220	27.55 N	81.16 W
Kissing	60	48.18 N	10.59 E
Kississing	184	55.07 N	101.07 W
Kississing Lake ⊜	184	55.10 N	101.20 W
Kisslegg	58	47.47 N	9.53 E
Kissū, Jabal ∧	140	21.35 N	25.09 E
Kista	80	46.05 N	43.06 E
Kistanje	36	43.59 N	15.58 E
Kistarcsa	264c	47.33 N	19.16 E
Kistendej	80	52.08 N	43.39 E
Kistigan Lake ⊜	184	54.38 N	92.37 W
Kistler	214	40.22 N	77.51 W
Kisújszállás	30	47.13 N	20.46 E
Kisuki	96	35.17 N	132.54 E
Kisumu	154	0.06 S	34.45 E
Kisvárda	30	48.13 N	22.05 E
Kiswere	154	9.26 S	39.33 E
Kita	150	13.03 N	9.29 W
Kita ◄[8], Nihon	268	35.45 N	139.44 E
Kita ◄[8], Nihon	270	34.45 N	135.08 E
Kita ◄[8], Nihon	270	35.03 N	135.45 E
Kita ◄[8], Nihon	270	34.42 N	135.30 E
Kitaaiki	94	36.04 N	138.34 E
Kita-Daitō-jima I	90	25.57 N	131.18 E
Kitafuji-enshūjō ■	94	35.25 N	138.48 E
Kitagata	94	35.26 N	136.41 E
Kitagawa	96	33.27 N	134.03 E
Kitagi-shima I	96	34.23 N	133.32 E
Kitaibaraki	94	36.48 N	140.45 E
Kitain Temple ᵾ[1]	268	35.54 N	139.30 E
Kita-Iō-jima I	14	25.26 N	141.17 E
Kitairiso	268	35.50 N	139.26 E
Kitajima	96	34.05 N	134.35 E
Kitakami	92	39.18 N	141.07 E
Kitakami ≃	92	38.25 N	141.19 E
Kitakami-kōchi ⩚	92	39.30 N	141.30 E
Kitakata	92	37.39 N	139.52 E
Kitakyuschu → Kitakyūshū	96	33.53 N	130.50 E
Kitakyūshū	96	33.53 N	130.50 E
Kitakyushu-kokutei-kōen ♦	96	33.45 N	130.50 E
Kitale	154	1.01 N	35.00 E
Kitamachi ◄[8]	268	35.46 N	139.39 E
Kitamba ◄[8]	273b	4.19 S	15.14 E
Kitami	92a	43.48 N	143.54 E
Kitami-sanchi ⩚	92a	44.22 N	142.43 E
Kitamoto	94	36.02 N	139.32 E
Kita-Nagato-kaigan-kokutei-kōen ♦	96	34.24 N	131.16 E
Kitanakagusuku	174m	26.21 N	127.51 E
Kitanda, Zaïre	154	6.36 S	26.27 E
Kitanda, Zaïre	154	9.59 S	27.28 E
Kitangari	154	10.39 S	39.20 E
Kitangiri, Lake ⊜	154	4.05 S	34.19 E
Kitangua	152	6.17 S	20.22 E
Kitano, Nihon	96	33.20 N	130.35 E
Kitano, Nihon	268	35.47 N	139.26 E
Kitanoshinden	268	35.48 N	139.26 E
Kitatachibana	94	36.29 N	139.03 E
Kitatajima	268	35.56 N	139.30 E
Kitatawara	270	34.44 N	135.42 E
Kitaura	94	36.04 N	140.32 E
Kita-ura ⊜	94	36.00 N	140.34 E
Kitava Island I	164	8.40 S	151.20 E
Kitaya	154	10.39 S	40.10 E
Kit Carson, Ca., U.S.	226	38.41 N	120.07 W
Kit Carson, Co., U.S.	198	38.45 N	102.47 W
Kitchener, Austl.	162	31.02 S	124.11 E
Kitchener, On., Can.	212	43.27 N	80.29 W
Kitee	26	62.06 N	30.09 E
Kitega → Gitega	154	3.26 S	29.56 E
Kiteiyab	140	17.12 N	33.43 E
Kitenda	152	6.53 S	17.21 E
Kitenevo	82	56.21 N	36.13 E
Kitengo	152	7.26 S	24.08 E
Kitéssa	154	5.20 N	25.20 E
Kitgum	154	3.18 N	32.53 E
Kíthira	38	36.09 N	23.00 E
Kíthira I	38	36.20 N	22.58 E
Kíthnos	38	37.26 N	24.26 E
Kíthnos I	38	37.25 N	24.28 E
Kitimat	182	54.03 N	128.33 W
Kitimat ≃	182	54.06 N	128.38 W
Kitimat Ranges ⩚	182	53.30 N	128.50 W
Kitinen ≃	24	67.08 N	27.29 E
Kitíou, Akrotírion ≻	130	34.48 N	33.36 E
Kitlope ≃	182	53.10 N	127.45 W
Kitlope Lake ⊜	182	53.07 N	127.47 W
Kitō, Nihon	94	34.42 N	138.03 E
Kitō, Nihon	96	33.46 N	134.12 E
Kitoj ≃	88	52.39 N	103.56 E
Kitridge Point ≻	241g	13.09 N	59.25 W
Kitsap □[6]	224	47.41 N	122.44 W
Kitscoty	184	53.20 N	110.20 W
Kit's Coty House ᵾ	260	51.19 N	0.30 E
Kitshua-Nseke	152	4.26 S	19.36 E
Kitsman'	78	48.27 N	25.44 E
Kitsuki	92	33.25 N	131.37 E
Kitsuregawa	94	36.43 N	140.01 E
Kittanning	214	40.48 N	79.31 W
Kittatinny Mountain ∧	210	41.10 N	74.55 W
Kittatinny Tunnel ◄[5]	214	40.09 N	77.41 W
Kittendorf	54	53.37 N	12.54 E
Kittery	188	43.05 N	70.44 W
Kitt Green	262	53.33 N	2.41 W
Kittilä	24	67.40 N	24.54 E
Kittitas	202	46.59 N	120.24 W
Kittitas □[6]	224	47.13 N	121.01 W
Kitt Peak National Observatory ᵾ[3]	200	31.58 N	111.36 W
Kittsee	61	48.05 N	17.04 E
Kitu	154	7.38 S	27.42 E
Kitui	154	1.22 S	38.01 E
Kitumbeine ∧[1]	154	2.44 S	36.16 E
Kitunda	154	6.48 S	33.13 E
Kitutu	154	3.17 S	28.05 E
Kitwanga	182	55.06 N	128.03 W
Kitwangar Indian Reserve ◄[4]	182	55.06 N	128.04 W
Kitwe	154	12.49 S	28.13 E
Kitwitwi	156	17.25 S	18.25 E
Kityang → Jieyang	100	23.35 N	116.21 E
Kitzbühel	64	47.27 N	12.23 E
Kitzbüheler Alpen ⩚	64	47.20 N	12.20 E
Kitzingen	56	49.44 N	10.09 E
Kitzscher	54	51.09 N	12.33 E
Kiukiang → Jiujiang	100	29.44 N	115.59 E
Kiukiu, Pointe ≻	174x	9.47 S	139.09 W
Kiul	124	25.09 N	86.06 E
Kiunga, Kenya	154	1.45 S	41.29 E
Kiunga, Pap. N. Gui.	164	6.10 S	141.15 E
Kiuruvesi	26	63.39 N	26.37 E
Kiuschu → Kyūshū I	92	33.00 N	131.00 E
Kivak	180	64.16 N	172.57 W
Kivalina	180	67.44 N	164.33 W
Kiveriči	76	57.22 N	36.36 E
Kivertsi	78	50.50 N	25.27 E
Kivijärvi	26	63.04 N	25.03 E
Kivijärvi ⊜	26	63.10 N	25.09 E
Kivik	26	55.41 N	14.15 E
Kiviõli	76	59.21 N	26.57 E
Kivshyvata	78	49.29 N	30.38 E
Kivu □[4]	154	2.30 S	27.00 E
Kivu, Lac ⊜	154	2.00 S	29.10 E
Kiwaba N'zogi	152	8.57 S	16.32 E
Kiwai Island I	164	8.30 S	143.25 E
Kiwalik	180	66.02 N	161.50 W
Kiwanis Lake	214	41.28 N	81.09 W
Kiyama	96	33.25 N	130.32 E
Kīyāmakī Dāgh ∧	84	38.47 N	45.51 E
Kiyan	174m	26.05 N	127.40 E
Kiyan-zaki ≻	174m	26.05 N	127.39 E
Kıyıköy	130	41.38 N	28.05 E
Kiyiu Lake ⊜	184	51.38 N	108.55 W
Kiyl ≃	86	49.25 N	54.50 E
Kiyokawa	94	35.29 N	139.17 E
Kiyomi	94	36.07 N	137.11 E
Kiyosawa	94	35.03 N	138.15 E
Kiyose	94	35.47 N	139.32 E
Kiyosu	94	35.13 N	136.50 E
Kiyosumi-yama ∧	94	35.09 N	140.09 E
Kiyotani	270	34.52 N	134.59 E
Kiyotsu ≃	94	37.03 N	138.41 E
Kizel	86	59.03 N	57.40 E
Kizevatovo	80	53.13 N	45.18 E
Kızıl ≃	130	41.44 N	35.58 E

Symbol	English	Deutsch	Español	Français	Português
≃	River	Fluß	Río	Rivière	Rio
≅	Canal	Kanal	Canal	Canal	Canal
∟	Waterfall, Rapids	Wasserfall, Stromschnellen	Cascada, Rápidos	Chute d'eau, Rapides	Cascata, Rápidos
⋓	Strait	Meeresstraße	Estrecho	Détroit	Estreito
c	Bay, Gulf	Bucht, Golf	Bahía, Golfo	Baie, Golfe	Baía, Golfo
⊜	Lake, Lakes	See, Seen	Lago, Lagos	Lac, Lacs	Lago, Lagos
⩸	Swamp	Sumpf	Pantano	Marais	Pântano
⌂	Ice Features, Glacier	Eis- und Gletscherformen	Accidentes Glaciales	Formes glaciaires	Acidentes glaciares
⊤	Other Hydrographic Features	Andere Hydrographische Objekte	Otros Elementos Hidrográficos	Autres données hydrographiques	Outros acidentes hidrográficos
✦	Submarine Features	Untermeerische Objekte	Accidentes Submarinos	Formes de relief sous-marin	Acidentes submarinos
□	Political Unit	Politische Einheit	Unidad Politica	Entité politique	Unidade política
ᵾ	Cultural Institution	Kulturelle Institution	Institución Cultural	Institution culturelle	Institução cultural
⊥	Historical Site	Historische Stätte	Sitio Histórico	Site historique	Sitio histórico
♦	Recreational Site	Erholungs- und Ferienort	Sitio de Recreo	Centre de loisirs	Area de Lazer
⊠	Airport	Flughafen	Aeropuerto	Aéroport	Aeroporto
■	Military Installation	Militäranlage	Instalación Militar	Installation militaire	Instalação militar
◄	Miscellaneous	Verschiedenes	Misceláneo	Divers	Diversos

Name	Page	Lat.°′	Long.°′
Kızıl Adalar II	130	40.52 N	29.05 E
Kızılcabölük	130	37.37 N	29.01 E
Kızılcadağ	130	37.01 N	29.58 E
Kızılcahamam	130	40.28 N	32.39 E
Kızılçakçak	84	40.46 N	43.37 E
Kızıldağ Milli Parkı ♦	130	37.58 N	31.28 E
Kızıldikme	130	39.05 N	37.01 E
Kızılhisar	130	37.33 N	29.18 E
Kızılırmak	130	40.21 N	33.59 E
Kızılören	130	37.52 N	32.07 E
Kizil'skoje	86	52.44 N	58.54 E
Kızılsu	130	37.28 N	42.13 E
Kiziltašskij liman ⊂	78	45.07 N	37.05 E
Kızıltepe	130	37.12 N	40.36 E
Kızıltoprak ⊸ 8	267b	40.58 N	29.03 E
Kizil'urt	84	43.12 N	46.53 E
Kızılyaka	130	37.09 N	32.54 E
Kižimiz, gora ∧	24	63.12 N	58.48 E
Kizimkazi	154	6.27 S	39.28 E
Kižinga	88	51.51 N	109.55 E
Kizir ≃	86	53.51 N	93.06 E
Kızkalesi ⊥	130	36.28 N	34.04 E
Kızkulesi ⊸ 5	267b	41.01 N	29.00 E
Kizl'ar	84	43.50 N	46.40 E
Kizl'arskij zaliv ⊂	84	44.33 N	46.55 E
Kizner	80	56.17 N	51.31 E
Kiz'oma	24	61.08 N	44.50 E
Kizu	96	34.44 N	135.49 E
Kizu ≃	94	34.53 N	135.42 E
Kizuki	268	35.34 N	139.40 E
Kizuri	270	34.39 N	135.34 E
Kizyl-Ajak	128	37.40 N	65.23 E
Kizyl-Arvat	128	38.58 N	56.15 E
Kizyl-Atrek	128	37.36 N	54.46 E
Kizyl-Su	128	39.48 N	53.01 E
Kjellerup	41	56.17 N	9.26 E
Kjøbenhavn → København	41	55.40 N	12.35 E
Kjustendil	38	42.17 N	22.41 E
Klaarstroom	158	33.20 S	22.32 E
Klaaswaal	52	51.46 N	4.26 E
Klabat, Gunung ∧	112	1.28 N	125.02 E
Kladanj	38	44.13 N	18.41 E
Kladbišči	80	55.32 N	45.33 E
Kläden	54	52.38 N	11.39 E
Kladkovo	82	55.24 N	38.51 E
Kladno	54	50.08 N	14.05 E
Kladovo	38	44.37 N	22.37 E
Kladow ⊸ 8	54	52.27 N	13.09 E
Kladruby	60	49.43 N	12.59 E
Klaeng	110	12.47 N	101.39 E
Klagan	112	5.58 N	117.27 E
Klagenfurt	61	46.37 N	14.18 E
Klågerup	41	55.36 N	13.15 E
Klagshamn	41	55.32 N	12.55 E
Klagstorp	41	55.24 N	13.22 E
Klahoose Indian Reserve ⊸ 4	182	50.31 N	124.19 W
Klaipėda (Memel)	76	55.43 N	21.07 E
Klakah	115a	7.59 S	113.15 E
Klamath	204	41.31 N	124.02 W
Klamath ≃	204	41.33 N	124.04 W
Klamath Falls	202	42.13 N	121.46 W
Klamath Marsh ≋	202	42.54 N	121.44 W
Klamath Mountains ⋀	204	41.40 N	123.20 W
K. Lamido	146	9.21 N	11.12 E
Klämmingen ⊜	40	59.07 N	17.15 E
Klammpass)(	64	47.17 N	13.05 E
Klamono	164	1.08 S	131.30 E
Klang → Kelang	114	3.02 N	101.27 E
Klangenan	115a	6.42 S	108.26 E
Klangpi	110	22.59 N	93.20 E
Klarälven (Trysilelva) ≃	26	59.23 N	13.32 E
Kl'as'ma	265b	55.59 N	37.50 E
Klášterec	54	50.24 N	13.10 E
Kl'asticy	76	55.53 N	28.36 E
Klaten	115a	7.42 S	110.35 E
Klatovy	60	49.24 N	13.18 E
Klausdorf, Dtsch.	54	54.20 N	13.01 E
Klausdorf, Dtsch.	54	54.18 N	10.15 E
Klausenburg → Cluj-Napoca	38	46.47 N	23.36 E
Klausenpass)(	58	46.52 N	8.51 E
Kl'avlino	80	54.17 N	52.01 E
Klawer	158	31.44 S	18.36 E
Klawock	182	55.33 N	133.06 W
Klazienaveen	52	52.44 N	7.00 E
Kl'az'ma	82	55.58 N	37.27 E
Kl'az'ma ≃	80	56.10 N	42.58 E
Kl'az'minskoje vodochranilišče ⊜ 1	265b	55.59 N	37.35 E
Kleberg	222	32.40 N	96.37 W
Kleck	76	53.04 N	26.38 E
Kłecko	30	52.38 N	17.26 E
Kleczew	30	52.23 N	18.10 E
Kledering ⊸ 8	264b	48.08 N	16.26 E
Kleef	263	51.11 N	6.56 E
Kleena Kleene	182	51.57 N	124.50 W
Kleinasien → Asia Minor □ 9	22	39.00 N	32.00 E
Kleinbegin	158	28.50 S	21.36 E
Klein-Blesbokspruit ≃	273d	26.16 S	28.29 E
Kleinbodungen	54	51.28 N	10.32 E
Klein Bonaire I	241s	12.10 N	68.18 W
Klein Bünzow	54	53.53 N	13.48 E
Kleinburg	275b	43.50 N	79.38 W
Klein Curaçao I	241s	12.00 N	68.40 W
Kleine Elster ≃	54	51.32 N	13.23 E
Kleine Emme ≃	58	47.04 N	8.17 E
Kleine Emscher ≃	263	51.31 N	6.43 E
Kleine Erlauf ≃	61	48.07 N	15.08 E
Kleineichen	263	51.08 N	7.21 E
Kleine Laber ≃	60	48.55 N	12.31 E
Kleinenberg	52	51.35 N	8.58 E
Kleinenbroich	263	51.12 N	6.35 E
Kleinengstingen	58	48.23 N	9.18 E
Kleiner Jasmunder Bodden ⊂	54	54.28 N	13.32 E
Kleiner Ravens-Berg ∧ 2	264a	52.22 N	13.04 E
Kleiner Wannsee ⊜	264a	52.25 N	13.10 E
Kleiner Zern-See ⊜	264a	52.26 N	12.55 E
Kleine Spree ≃	54	51.31 N	14.24 E
Kleines Walsertal V	64	47.23 N	10.12 E
Kleinfeltersville	208	40.18 N	76.15 W
Kleinglödnitz	61	46.51 N	14.08 E
Kleinhammer	263	51.14 N	7.46 E
Klein-Jukskei ≃	273d	26.08 S	27.56 E
Klein-Karas	156	27.32 S	18.06 E
Klein Karroo → Little Karroo ⋀ 1	158	33.45 S	21.30 E
Klein Kienitz	264a	52.18 N	13.29 E
Kleinlützel	58	47.26 N	7.25 E
Kleinmachnow	54	52.24 N	13.15 E
Klein Marzehns	54	52.01 N	12.37 E
Kleinmond	158	34.21 S	19.03 E
Klein-Olifants ≃	158	25.41 S	29.19 E
Kleinschönebeck	264a	52.29 N	13.43 E
Klein-Soutpan	158	30.26 S	22.26 E
Klein-Vis ≃	158	33.05 S	26.00 E
Klein Wanzleben	54	52.04 N	11.21 E
Klein Ziethen	264a	52.23 N	13.27 E
Klein Ziethener-Berge ∧ 2	264a	52.22 N	13.26 E
Klekovača ∧	36	44.26 N	16.31 E
Klementjevka	86	50.16 N	80.56 E
Klementjevo	82	55.38 N	36.01 E
Klemme	190	43.00 N	93.36 W
Klemtu	182	52.36 N	128.31 W
Klenovka	80	57.45 N	54.19 E
Klenovo	82	55.19 N	37.21 E
Klerksdorp	158	26.58 S	26.39 E
Klerkskraal	158	26.15 S	27.10 E
Klesiv	78	51.19 N	26.54 E
Klésso	150	10.57 N	3.59 W
Klet' ∧	61	48.52 N	14.17 E
Kletn'a	76	53.23 N	33.12 E
Kletskij	80	49.19 N	43.04 E
Kletsko-Počtovskij	80	49.36 N	43.03 E
Klettgau ⊸ 1	58	47.40 N	8.25 E
Klettwitz	54	51.32 N	13.53 E
Klevan'	78	50.44 N	26.02 E
Kleve	52	51.48 N	6.09 E
Klevenka	80	52.07 N	49.33 E
Kley ⊸ 8	263	51.30 N	7.22 E
Klibreck, Ben ∧	46	58.14 N	4.22 W
Kličev	76	53.29 N	29.21 E
Klička	88	50.26 N	118.00 E
Klickitat	224	45.49 N	121.09 W
Klickitat □ 6	224	45.50 N	121.07 W
Klickitat ≃	224	45.42 N	121.17 W
Kliedbruch ⊸ 1	263	51.22 N	6.33 E
Klietz	54	52.40 N	12.04 E
Klimino	88	58.39 N	98.42 E
Klimoviči	76	53.37 N	31.58 E
Klimovo, Ross.	76	52.23 N	32.11 E
Klimovo, Ross.	82	55.22 N	38.52 E
Klimovsk	82	55.22 N	37.32 E
Klimovskoje	82	54.42 N	37.48 E
Klimov Zavod	76	54.50 N	34.55 E
Klimpfjäll	24	65.04 N	14.52 E
Klin, Ross.	82	56.20 N	36.44 E
Klin, Ross.	82	55.19 N	36.20 E
Klinaklini ≃	182	51.05 N	125.36 W
Klin-Bel'din	82	54.45 N	39.13 E
Klincovka	80	51.41 N	49.11 E
Klincy	76	52.47 N	32.14 E
Kline Ditch ≚	279a	41.28 N	82.04 W
Kling	116	5.58 N	124.42 E
Klingbach ≃	56	49.10 N	8.20 E
Klingenberg	54	50.55 N	13.31 E
Klingenberg am Main	56	49.47 N	9.11 E
Klingenmünster	56	49.08 N	8.01 E
Klingenthal	54	50.21 N	12.28 E
Klinger Lake ⊜	216	41.47 N	85.33 W
Klingerstown	208	40.40 N	76.41 W
Klinghardtberge ∧	156	27.18 S	15.48 E
Klingnau	58	47.35 N	8.15 E
Klink	54	53.29 N	12.37 E
Klínovec ∧	54	50.24 N	12.58 E
Klinsko-Dmitrovskaja gr'ada ∧	82	56.15 N	37.30 E
Klintehamn	26	57.24 N	18.12 E
Klintsy → Klincy	76	52.47 N	32.14 E
Klip ≃, S. Afr.	158	27.03 S	29.03 E
Klip ≃, S. Afr.	273d	26.19 S	27.53 E
Klipbakken	158	28.50 S	21.21 E
Klipdale	158	34.19 S	19.57 E
Klipdam	158	27.35 S	19.56 E
Kliplev	41	54.56 N	9.25 E
Klippan	41	56.08 N	13.06 E
Klipplaat	158	33.02 S	24.21 E
Klippoortjie	273d	26.13 S	28.10 E
Klipriviersberg ⋀	273d	26.17 S	28.02 E
Kliptown	273d	26.17 S	27.53 E
Klipwerf	158	31.09 S	19.52 E
Klishkivtsi	78	48.26 N	26.15 E
Klisura	38	42.42 N	24.27 E
Klitmøller	26	57.02 N	8.31 E
Klitten	54	51.20 N	14.36 E
Klixbüll	41	54.48 N	8.53 E
Ključ	36	44.32 N	16.47 E
Klobbicke	264a	52.46 N	13.48 E
Klobouky	61	49.00 N	16.52 E
Kłobuck	30	50.55 N	18.57 E
Klobuticy	76	58.35 N	29.35 E
Kłodawa	30	52.16 N	18.55 E
Kłodzko	30	50.27 N	16.39 E
Kløfta	26	60.04 N	11.09 E
Kłomnice	30	50.56 N	19.21 E
Klondike	216	40.28 N	86.57 W
Klondike □ 9	180	63.30 N	139.00 W
Klondike ≃	180	64.05 N	139.26 W
Klöntaler See ⊜	58	47.02 N	8.58 E
Klooga	76	59.19 N	24.16 E
Kloosterveen	52	52.59 N	6.33 E
Kloosterzande	52	51.22 N	4.02 E
Kloster	54	54.35 N	13.06 E
Klosterfelde	54	52.48 N	13.28 E
Klosterhardt ⊸ 8	263	51.31 N	6.53 E
Klösterle	58	47.08 N	10.05 E
Klostermansfeld	54	51.35 N	11.29 E
Klosterneuburg	61	48.18 N	16.20 E
Kloster Oesede	52	52.12 N	8.07 E
Klosters	58	46.54 N	9.53 E
Klostertal V	58	47.08 N	9.59 E
Kloster Zinna	54	52.01 N	13.07 E
Kloten, Schw.	58	47.27 N	8.35 E
Kloten, Sve.	40	59.54 N	15.17 E
Klotz, Lac ⊜	176	60.32 N	73.40 W
Klötze	54	52.38 N	11.10 E
Kloulklubed	175b	7.02 N	134.15 E
Klouto	150	6.57 N	0.34 E
Kluane ≃	180	61.53 N	139.43 W
Kluane Lake ⊜	180	61.15 N	138.40 W
Kluane National Park ♦	180	60.45 N	139.30 W
Kluang	112	2.41 S	103.54 E
Kl'učevaja	24	65.16 N	41.32 E
Kl'učevskaja Sopka, vulkan ∧ 1	74	56.04 N	160.38 E
Kl'učevskij	88	53.33 N	119.26 E
Kluchorskij, pereval)(	84	43.15 N	41.54 E
Kl'uči, Ross.	74	56.18 N	160.51 E
Kl'uči, Ross.	80	51.59 N	46.31 E
Kl'uči, Ross.	80	51.26 N	45.11 E
Kl'uči, Ross.	86	52.16 N	79.10 E
Kl'učovka, Kyrg.	85	42.34 N	71.48 E
Kl'učovka, Ross.	86	51.22 N	55.48 E
Kluczbork	30	50.59 N	18.13 E
Kluess	54	53.46 N	12.14 E
Kluet ≃	114	3.04 N	97.20 E
Kl'ukvenka	86	58.34 N	85.55 E
Klukwan	180	59.24 N	135.54 W
Klundert	52	51.40 N	4.32 E
Klungkung	115b	8.32 S	115.24 E
Klüppelberg	56	51.06 N	7.28 E
Klüterthöhle ⫠ 5	52	51.18 N	7.21 E
Klutina Lake ⊜	180	61.37 N	146.55 W
Klütz	54	53.58 N	11.10 E
Klynkyne	83	47.17 N	38.15 E
Knaben gruver	26	58.39 N	7.04 E
Knaddah	130	35.45 N	36.12 E
Kn'aginino	80	55.49 N	45.03 E
Knaik ≃	46	56.14 N	3.52 W
Knapdaar	158	30.43 S	26.09 E
Knapdale ⊸ 1	46	55.55 N	5.30 W
Knaphill	260	51.19 N	0.37 W
Knapp	190	44.57 N	92.04 W
Knapp Creek	210	42.00 N	78.30 W
Knappenberg	61	46.56 N	14.35 E
Knäred	26	56.32 N	13.19 E
Knaresborough	44	54.00 N	1.27 W
Knargram	126	24.01 N	87.59 E
Knauertown	285	40.10 N	75.44 W
Knauthain ⊸ 8	54	51.16 N	12.18 E
Kn'ažaja Bajgora	76	52.23 N	40.02 E
Kn'azevka	86	57.35 N	74.10 E
Kn'ažji Gory	76	56.05 N	35.14 E
Kn'ažovo	76	59.40 N	43.54 E
Knebel	41	56.13 N	10.30 E
Knebworth	42	51.52 N	0.12 W
Kneehills Creek ≃	182	51.30 N	112.50 W
Knee Lake ⊜, Mb., Can.	184	55.03 N	94.40 W
Knee Lake ⊜, Sk., Can.	184	55.51 N	107.00 W
Knesebeck	54	52.41 N	10.42 E
Knesselare	50	51.08 N	3.25 E
Knetzgau	56	50.00 N	10.33 E
Knevicy	76	57.56 N	32.14 E
Kneža	38	43.30 N	24.05 E
Knić	38	43.55 N	20.43 E
Knickerbocker	196	31.16 N	100.38 W
Kniebis	58	48.28 N	8.17 E
Knife ≃	198	47.20 N	101.23 W
Knife Lake ⊜	184	53.47 N	91.20 W
Knife River Indian Villages National Historic Site ⊥	198	47.21 N	101.23 W
Knight Inlet ⊂	182	50.41 N	125.40 W
Knight Island I	180	60.20 N	147.45 W
Knighton	42	52.21 N	3.03 W
Knightsen	226	37.58 N	121.40 W
Knights Landing	226	38.47 N	121.43 W
Knightstown	218	39.47 N	85.31 W
Knightville Dam ⊸ 6	207	42.17 N	72.52 W
Knik Arm ⊂	180	61.25 N	149.45 W
Knin	36	44.02 N	16.12 E
Knippa	196	29.18 N	99.38 W
Knislinge	26	56.11 N	14.05 E
Knittelfeld	61	47.14 N	14.50 E
Knittlingen	56	49.01 N	8.45 E
Knivsbjerg ∧ 2	41	55.08 N	9.27 E
Knivsta	40	59.43 N	17.48 E
Knjaževac	38	43.34 N	22.16 E
Knob, Cape ≻	162	34.32 S	119.16 E
Knobby Head ≻	162	29.40 S	114.58 E
Knob Noster	194	38.45 N	93.33 W
Knob Peak ∧	116	12.28 N	121.21 E
Knoc	48	52.38 N	9.20 W
Knock	46	57.33 N	2.45 W
Knockholt	260	51.18 N	0.06 E
Knockholt Pound	260	51.19 N	0.08 E
Knocklayd ∧	48	55.09 N	6.15 W
Knocklong	48	52.26 N	8.24 W
Knockmealdown Mountains ⋀	48	52.10 N	8.00 W
Knokke	50	51.21 N	3.17 E
Knole ⊥	260	51.16 N	0.12 E
Knolls Green	262	53.19 N	2.18 W
Knollwood, Ct., U.S.	207	41.16 N	72.23 W
Knollwood, Il., U.S.	278	42.17 N	87.53 W
Knollwood, Md., U.S.	284c	39.02 N	76.58 W
Knollwood Park	216	42.14 N	84.22 W
Knon ⊜	40	60.12 N	13.40 E
Knossós ⊥	38	35.20 N	25.10 E
Knottingley	44	53.43 N	1.14 W
Knott's Berry Farm ♦	280	33.50 N	118.00 W
Knotts Island	208	36.31 N	75.56 W
Knotty Ash ⊸ 8	262	53.25 N	2.54 W
Knotty Green	260	51.37 N	0.39 W
Knowland State Arboretum and Park ♦	282	37.45 N	122.09 W
Knowle	42	52.23 N	1.43 W
Knowlesville	210	43.14 N	78.19 W
Knowlton Lake ⊜	212	44.28 N	76.41 W
Knowltonwood	285	39.53 N	75.24 W
Knowsley	262	53.27 N	2.51 W
Knowsley □ 8	262	53.27 N	2.50 W
Knowsley Hall ʊ	262	53.26 N	2.50 W
Knowsley Park ♦	262	53.27 N	2.49 W
Knox, In., U.S.	216	41.17 N	86.37 W
Knox, N.Y., U.S.	210	42.40 N	74.07 W
Knox, Pa., U.S.	214	41.14 N	79.32 W
Knox □ 6, Mo., U.S.	219	40.08 N	92.09 W
Knox □ 6, Oh., U.S.	214	40.23 N	82.29 W
Knox, Cape ≻	182	54.11 N	133.04 W
Knoxboro	210	42.58 N	75.36 W
Knox City, Mo., U.S.	219	40.08 N	92.00 W
Knox City, Tx., U.S.	196	33.25 N	99.49 W
Knox Coast ⫠ 2	9	66.30 S	105.00 E
Knox Dale	214	41.05 N	79.02 W
Knoxfield	274b	37.53 S	145.15 E
Knox Lake ⊜ 1	214	40.31 N	82.30 W
Knoxville, Ga., U.S.	192	32.43 N	83.59 W
Knoxville, Il., U.S.	190	40.54 N	90.17 W
Knoxville, Ia., U.S.	190	41.19 N	93.06 W
Knoxville, Pa., U.S.	210	41.57 N	77.26 W
Knoxville, Tn., U.S.	192	35.57 N	83.55 W
Knuckles ∧	122	7.24 N	80.48 E
Knudshoved Odde ≻ 1	41	55.03 N	11.45 E
Knüll ∧	56	50.53 N	9.24 E
Knutby	40	59.55 N	18.15 E
Knuthenborg	41	54.50 N	11.30 E
Knutsford	44	53.19 N	2.22 W
Knysna	158	34.02 S	23.02 E
Knyszyn	30	53.19 N	22.55 E
Koala Sanctuary ⊸ 4	274a	33.40 S	151.10 E
Koani	154	6.08 S	39.17 E
Kob'	88	55.25 N	101.24 E
Koba	112	2.29 S	106.24 E
Kob'aj	74	63.34 N	126.30 E
Kőbánya ⊸ 8	264c	47.29 N	19.10 E
Kobarid	36	46.15 N	13.35 E
Kobar Sink ⫠ 7	144	13.35 N	40.50 E
Kobayashi	92	31.59 N	130.59 E
Kōbe, Nihon	96	34.41 N	135.10 E
Kōbe, Nihon	270	34.41 N	135.10 E
Kōbe-kō ⊂	270	34.40 N	135.12 E
Kobelyaky	78	49.09 N	34.12 E
København (Copenhagen)	41	55.40 N	12.35 E
København □ 6	41	55.45 N	12.25 E
Kōbe University ʊ 2	270	34.43 N	135.14 E
Kobi	84	42.33 N	44.32 E
Koblenz, Dtsch.	56	50.21 N	7.35 E
Koblenz, Schw.	58	47.37 N	8.14 E
Koblenz □ 5	56	50.10 N	7.30 E
Kobo, Ityo.	144	12.11 N	39.33 E
Kobo, Zaïre	152	4.54 S	17.09 E
Ko-boke ♦	96	33.50 N	133.46 E
Koboko	154	3.25 N	30.58 E
Koboldo	89	52.58 N	132.42 E
Kobona	76	60.01 N	31.36 E
Kobou ≃	152	6.13 N	23.19 E
Kobowen Swamp ≋	144	5.38 N	33.54 E
Koboža	76	58.49 N	35.01 E
Koboža ≃	76	58.52 N	36.17 E
Kobra	24	60.03 N	50.44 E
Kobrin	76	52.13 N	24.21 E
Kobrinskoje	76	59.25 N	30.07 E
Kobroor, Pulau I	164	6.12 S	134.32 E
Kobuchizawa	94	35.52 N	138.19 E
Kobuga-hara ♦	94	36.40 N	139.35 E
Kobuk	180	66.54 N	156.52 W
Kobuk ≃	180	66.45 N	161.00 W
Kobuk Valley National Park ♦	180	67.20 N	159.00 W
Kobuleti	84	41.50 N	41.47 E
Kobushiga-take ∧	94	35.54 N	138.44 E
Kobylanka	54	53.19 N	14.50 E
Kobylin	30	51.43 N	17.13 E
Kobyl'nik	76	54.56 N	26.41 E
Kobyzhcha	78	50.49 N	31.30 E
Kocaali	130	41.03 N	30.52 E
Kocaaliler	130	37.19 N	30.44 E
Kocaavşar ≃	130	40.08 N	27.57 E
Kocaeli → İzmit	130	40.46 N	29.55 E
Kocaeli □ 4	130	40.55 N	29.55 E
Koçali	130	37.55 N	38.15 E
Kočani	38	41.55 N	22.25 E
Koçarlı	130	37.45 N	27.42 E
Kocasinan ⊸ 8	267b	41.01 N	28.50 E
Koçbaşı Tepe ∧	84	39.25 N	43.21 E
Kočečum ≃	74	64.17 N	101.10 E
Kočelajevo	80	54.01 N	44.02 E
Kočemary	80	54.50 N	40.58 E
Kočen'ajevka	80	53.52 N	46.59 E
Kočen'ga, Ross.	76	60.09 N	43.33 E
Kočenga, Ross.	88	55.55 N	104.06 E
Kočenga ≃	88	55.55 N	104.06 E
Kočerdyk	86	54.35 N	62.58 E
Kočerga	88	55.15 N	103.46 E
Kočetovka, Ross.	80	55.16 N	46.07 E
Kočetovka, Ross.	80	52.58 N	40.29 E
Kočevar	76	60.26 N	42.11 E
Kočevje	36	45.38 N	14.52 E
Kočevo	86	59.36 N	54.18 E
Koch'am-ni	98	41.06 N	129.23 E
Kŏch'ang, Taehan	98	35.26 N	126.42 E
Kŏch'ang, Taehan	98	35.41 N	127.55 E
Kochanoviči	76	55.52 N	28.08 E
Kochanovo	76	54.28 N	30.01 E
Koch Bihār	124	26.19 N	89.26 E
Kochel	64	47.39 N	11.22 E
Kochelsee ⊜	64	47.38 N	11.20 E
Kochena	158	27.00 S	18.50 E
Kocher ≃	56	49.14 N	9.12 E
Kocheriv	78	50.21 N	29.21 E
Kōchi, Nihon	96	33.33 N	133.33 E
Kōchi, Nihon	96	34.28 N	132.53 E
Kōchi □ 5	96	33.40 N	133.30 E
Kōchi-dani ♦	94	34.34 N	136.10 E
Kochinda	174m	26.08 N	127.43 E
Koch Island I	176	69.38 N	78.15 W
Kochiu → Gejiu	90	23.22 N	103.06 E
Kochma	80	56.56 N	41.06 E
Koch Peak ∧	202	45.02 N	111.28 W
Kochugaon	124	26.34 N	90.04 E
Kock	30	51.39 N	22.27 E
Kočki, Ross.	86	52.24 N	80.40 E
Kočki, Ross.	86	54.20 N	80.29 E
Kočkor-Ata	85	41.04 N	72.29 E
Kočkorka	85	42.14 N	75.45 E
Kocksoord	273d	26.13 S	27.39 E
Kočkurovo	80	54.02 N	45.26 E
Kočmes	24	66.12 N	60.44 E
Kočon'ovo	86	55.02 N	82.12 E
Kočov	60	49.49 N	12.44 E
Kočubej	84	44.24 N	46.33 E
Kočubejevskoje	84	44.41 N	41.41 E
Kōda, Nihon	94	34.52 N	137.10 E
Kōda, Nihon	96	34.42 N	132.45 E
Kodačdikost	24	63.11 N	55.49 E
Kodaikānal	122	10.14 N	77.29 E
Kodaira	94	35.44 N	139.29 E
Kodama	94	36.11 N	139.08 E
Kodar, chrebet ⋀	88	57.15 N	118.10 E
Kodāri	124	27.56 N	85.56 E
Kodarma	124	24.28 N	85.36 E
Kodera ⊸ 8	270	34.41 N	135.04 E
Kodersdorf	54	51.15 N	14.53 E
Kodi	152	3.34 S	22.12 E
Kodiak	180	57.48 N	152.23 W
Kodiak Island I	180	57.30 N	153.30 W
Kodiang	114	6.24 N	100.18 E
Kodinār	120	20.47 N	70.42 E
Kodino	24	63.43 N	39.41 E
Kodo ≃	152	7.05 N	19.10 E
Kodo, Jabal ∧	140	12.26 N	23.38 E
Kodok	140	9.53 N	32.07 E
Kodori ≃	84	42.47 N	41.10 E
Kodorskij chrebet ⋀	84	43.00 N	42.00 E
Kodra	78	50.36 N	29.34 E
Kodyma	78	48.07 N	29.07 E
Kodyma ≃	78	48.01 N	30.48 E
Kodžori	84	41.40 N	44.41 E
Koegas	158	29.16 S	22.20 E
Koehn Lake ⊜	228	35.20 N	117.53 W
Koekelare	50	51.05 N	2.58 E
Koekenaap	158	31.30 S	18.18 E
Koeltztown	219	38.19 N	92.03 W
Koenigsmacker	56	49.24 N	6.17 E
Koersel	56	51.04 N	5.16 E
Koes	156	25.59 S	19.08 E
Kofa Mountains ⋀	200	33.20 N	114.00 W
Kofçaz	130	41.58 N	27.12 E
Kofeld	58	47.44 N	9.41 E
Köfering	60	48.56 N	12.12 E
Koffiefontein	158	29.30 S	25.00 E
Kofiau, Pulau I	164	1.11 S	129.50 E
Köflach	61	47.04 N	15.05 E
Koforidua	150	6.03 N	0.17 W
Kōfu, Nihon	94	35.39 N	138.35 E
Kōfu, Nihon	96	35.17 N	133.30 E
Koga, Nihon	94	36.11 N	139.43 E
Koga, Nihon	96	33.40 N	130.30 E
Koga, Tan.	154	6.14 S	32.25 E
Kogaluc ≃	176	59.40 N	77.35 W
Kogaluc, Baie ⊂	176	59.20 N	77.50 W
Kogaluk ≃	176	56.12 N	61.44 W
Kogan	166	27.03 S	150.46 E
Kogane	268	35.50 N	139.56 E
Koganei	94	35.42 N	139.32 E
Kogarah	274a	33.58 S	151.08 E
Kogarah Bay ⊂	274a	33.59 S	151.07 E
Køge, Dan.	41	55.27 N	12.11 E
Kōge, Nihon	96	35.24 N	134.15 E
Køge Bugt ⊂, Dan.	41	55.30 N	12.20 E
Køge Bugt ⊂, Kal. Nun.	176	65.00 N	40.30 W
Kogin Baba	146	7.55 N	11.30 E
Koglhof	61	47.19 N	15.40 E
Kogon ≃	150	11.09 N	14.42 W
Kogoni	150	14.44 N	6.02 W
Kŏgŭm-do I	98	34.27 N	127.11 E
Kohak	128	25.44 N	62.33 E
Kohala Mountains ⋀	229d	20.05 N	155.45 W
Kohama-shima I	175d	24.19 N	123.59 E
Kohāt	123	33.35 N	71.26 E
Kohāt ≃	123	33.24 N	71.48 E
Kohatk Wash V	200	32.38 N	111.55 W
Kohila	76	59.10 N	24.45 E
Kohīma	120	25.40 N	94.07 E
Kohistān □ 9	123	35.03 N	72.52 W
Kohlberg ∧ 2	263	51.18 N	7.46 E
Kohler	190	43.44 N	87.46 W
Kohlstädt	52	51.50 N	8.52 E
Kohoku	94	35.26 N	136.15 E
Kōhoku ⊸ 8	268	35.31 N	139.38 E
Kohren-Sahlis	54	51.01 N	12.36 E
Kohsān	128	34.39 N	61.12 E
Kohtla-Järve	76	59.24 N	27.15 E
Kohu → Kōfu	94	35.39 N	138.35 E
Kohukohu	172	35.21 S	173.32 E
Kohŭng	98	34.37 N	127.16 E
Kohunlich ⊥	232	18.27 N	89.01 W
Kohuratahi	172	39.06 S	174.46 E
Kohyl'nyk (Cogâlnic) ≃	78	45.51 N	29.38 E
Koide	94	37.13 N	138.57 E
Koidern	180	61.58 N	140.25 W
Koidu	150	8.38 N	10.59 W
Koigi	76	58.50 N	25.45 E
Koihoa	110	8.12 N	93.29 E
Koil-Aligarh → Alīgarh	124	27.53 N	78.05 E
Koimbani	157a	11.37 S	43.23 E
Koindu	150	8.26 N	10.19 W
Koin-ni	98	40.28 N	126.22 E
Koito ≃	94	35.21 N	139.52 E
Kojandy	86	49.51 N	75.40 E
Kojda	24	66.23 N	42.31 E
Kŏje-do I	98	34.52 N	128.37 E
Kojetín	30	49.21 N	17.18 E
Kojgorodok	24	60.26 N	50.58 E
Ko-jima I	92a	41.22 N	139.48 E
Kojima-ko ⊜ 1	96	34.37 N	134.00 E
Kojŏ	98	38.57 N	127.51 E
Kojonup	162	33.50 S	117.09 E
Kojsary	85	42.33 N	78.10 E
Kojsug	83	47.07 N	39.41 E
Kojtas, Kaz.	86	51.32 N	76.15 E
Kojtaš, Uzb.	85	40.11 N	67.19 E
Kok (Hkok) ≃	110	20.14 N	100.09 E
Kōka	94	34.54 N	136.13 E
Koka, Lake ⊜ 1	144	8.23 N	39.05 E
Kokai ≃	94	35.52 N	140.08 E
K'okajgyr	85	40.43 N	75.37 E
Kokalaat	86	49.47 N	64.15 E
Kokand	85	40.33 N	70.57 E
Kokanee Glacier Provincial Park ♦	182	49.47 N	117.10 W
Kokankišlak	85	40.56 N	72.30 E
Kökar I	26	59.56 N	20.55 E
Kokas	164	2.42 S	132.26 E
Kokašice	60	49.53 N	12.57 E
Kokava nad Rimavicou	30	48.34 N	19.50 E
Kokawa	96	34.16 N	135.24 E
K'okbel'	85	40.17 N	72.55 E
Kokčetav	86	53.17 N	69.25 E
Kokčetav □ 8	86	53.30 N	70.00 E
Kokčetavskaja vozvyšennost' ⋀ 1	86	52.50 N	69.00 E
Kokee State Park ♦	229b	22.08 N	159.40 W
Kokemäenjoki ≃	26	61.33 N	21.42 E
Kokemäki	26	61.15 N	22.21 E
Kokenau	164	4.43 S	136.26 E
Ko Kha	110	18.11 N	99.24 E
Kokhav HaYarden (Belvoir) ⊥	132	32.36 N	35.31 E
Kókhi, Ákra ≻	267c	37.53 N	23.27 E
Koki	150	15.30 N	15.59 W
Kokinu	268	35.59 N	139.59 E
Kokiu → Gejiu	102	23.22 N	103.06 E
Kok-Jangak	85	41.02 N	73.12 E
Kokka	140	20.00 N	30.35 E
Kokkilai Lagoon ⊂	122	9.00 N	80.56 E
Kokkola (Karleby)	26	63.50 N	23.07 E
Kokku	98	40.22 N	128.44 E
Koknese	76	56.39 N	25.29 E
Koko	150	11.26 N	4.32 E
Kokoda	164	8.52 S	147.45 E
Koko Head ≻	229c	21.16 N	157.42 W
Kokola	154	0.47 N	29.36 E
Kokole Point ≻	229b	21.59 N	159.46 W
Kokolik ≃	180	69.46 N	163.00 W
Kokolopozo	150	5.08 N	6.05 W
K'ok'omeren ≃	85	41.43 N	73.54 E
Kokomo, Hi., U.S.	229a	20.52 N	156.18 W
Kokomo, In., U.S.	216	40.29 N	86.08 W
Kokomo, Ms., U.S.	194	31.11 N	90.00 W
Kokong	156	24.27 S	23.03 E
Kokonoe	96	33.10 N	131.10 E
Koko Nor → Qinghai Hu ⊜	102	36.50 N	100.20 E
Kokopo	164	4.20 S	152.15 E
Kokorevka	76	52.35 N	34.16 E
Kokosing ≃	214	40.22 N	82.12 W
Kokos-Inseln → Cocos (Keeling) Islands □ 2	14	12.10 S	96.55 E
Kokoškino	265b	55.38 N	37.11 E
Kokpāra Narsinghgarh	126	22.31 N	86.33 E
Kokpaš	86	51.12 N	87.45 E
Kokpekty	86	48.45 N	82.24 E
Kokrājhār	124	26.24 N	90.16 E
Kokrines	180	64.56 N	154.42 W
Kokrines Hills ⋀ 2	180	65.15 N	154.00 W
Koksa ≃	86	50.16 N	85.36 E
Kokšaalatau, chrebet ⋀	72	41.00 N	78.00 E
Koksan	98	38.46 N	126.40 E
Koksaraj	85	42.40 N	68.08 E
Kokšekol', ozero ⊜	86	46.05 N	62.00 E
Koksijde	50	51.07 N	2.38 E
Koksilah	224	48.40 N	123.38 W
Koksilah ≃	224	48.45 N	123.39 W
Koksoak ≃	176	58.32 N	68.10 W
Koksŏng	98	35.17 N	127.17 E
Koksovyj	78	48.12 N	40.39 E
Kokstad	158	30.32 S	29.29 E
Koksu, Kaz.	85	41.27 N	68.01 E
Koksu, Kaz.	86	44.59 N	77.56 E
Koktal	86	44.09 N	79.48 E
Koktas, Kaz.	86	47.33 N	70.55 E
Koktas, Kaz.	86	45.59 N	73.32 E
Kok-Taš, Kyrg.	85	41.12 N	72.25 E
Kokterek	80	49.25 N	49.15 E
Koktubek	86	48.07 N	56.51 E
Kokubu, Nihon	92	31.44 N	130.46 E
Kokubu, Nihon	96	34.56 N	132.07 E
Kokubunji, Nihon	94	36.22 N	139.51 E
Kokubunji, Nihon	96	34.18 N	133.58 E
Kokubunji, Nihon	268	35.42 N	139.29 E
Kokubunji Temple ʊ 1	268	35.44 N	139.55 E
Kokufu	96	35.28 N	134.16 E
Kokuj	88	52.13 N	117.33 E
Kokujbel' ≃	85	38.21 N	72.46 E
Kokžar	86	49.01 N	60.10 E
Kol ≃	128	26.59 N	55.47 E
Kola, Indon.	164	5.26 S	134.29 E
Kola, Ross.	24	68.53 N	33.01 E
Kola ≃	24	68.53 N	33.02 E
Kolachel	122	8.10 N	77.15 E
Kolāchi ≃	120	27.08 N	67.02 E
Kolageran	84	40.58 N	44.37 E
Kolahun	150	8.24 N	10.02 W
Kolaka	112	4.03 S	121.36 E
Kolambo	152	7.34 S	21.58 E
Kolambugan	116	8.07 N	123.55 E
Kolangār	120	34.02 N	69.01 E
Kola Peninsula → Kol'skij poluostrov ≻ 1	24	67.30 N	37.00 E
Kolār	122	13.08 N	78.08 E
Kolāras	124	25.14 N	77.36 E
Kolār Gold Fields	122	12.55 N	78.17 E
Kolari	24	67.20 N	23.48 E
Kolarovgrad → Šumen	38	43.16 N	26.55 E
Kolárovo	30	47.52 N	18.02 E
Kolašin	38	42.49 N	19.31 E
Kolāyat	120	27.50 N	72.57 E
Kolbači	89	54.22 N	123.02 E
Kolbäck	40	59.34 N	16.15 E
Kolbäcksån ≃	40	59.32 N	16.16 E
Kol'baj, gora ∧ 2	86	43.43 N	53.57 E
Kolbano	112	10.02 S	124.31 E
Kolbča	76	53.39 N	29.14 E
Kolberg → Kołobrzeg	30	54.12 N	15.33 E
Kolbermoor	64	47.51 N	12.04 E
Kolbio	144	1.10 S	41.15 E
Kolbnitz	64	46.52 N	13.19 E
Kolbotn	26	59.49 N	10.48 E
Kolbuszowa	30	50.15 N	21.47 E
Kolby Kås	41	55.48 N	10.33 E
Kolchida ≚	84	42.15 N	42.00 E
Kolchozabad	120	37.27 N	68.31 E
Kol'covo	82	54.27 N	36.40 E
Kol'čuga	82	55.43 N	37.12 E
Kol'čugino	80	56.18 N	39.23 E
Kołczewo	54	53.58 N	14.38 E
Kolda	150	12.53 N	14.57 W
Kolda □ 4	150	12.50 N	14.50 W
Kolding	41	55.31 N	9.29 E
Kolding Fjord ⊂	41	55.30 N	9.35 E
Kole, Zaïre	152	3.27 S	22.29 E
Kole, Zaïre	154	2.07 N	25.26 E
Kolea	34	36.38 N	2.46 E
Kolebīra	124	22.43 N	84.42 E
Kole Kalyan ⊸ 8	272c	19.06 N	72.51 E
Kolenfeld	52	52.24 N	9.27 E
Koleno	80	51.52 N	44.07 E
Kolenté	150	10.06 N	12.37 W
Kolenté (Great Scarcies) ≃	150	8.55 N	13.08 W
Kolga	76	59.32 N	25.42 E
Kolgujev, ostrov I	24	69.05 N	49.15 E
Kolhāpur, India	122	16.06 N	78.16 E
Kolhāpur, India	122	16.42 N	74.13 E
Kolho	26	62.08 N	24.31 E
Koli	76	59.30 N	34.30 E
Koli ∧ 2	26	63.06 N	29.48 E
Koli, Jabal ∧	140	14.05 N	25.31 E
Kolia	150	9.46 N	6.28 W
Koliba (Corubal) ≃	150	11.57 N	15.06 W
Koliganek	180	59.48 N	157.25 W
Kolima ⊜	26	63.16 N	25.50 E
Kolimbine ≃	150	14.26 N	11.23 W
Kolín	30	50.01 N	15.13 E
Kolisne	78	46.02 N	29.56 E
Kolka	76	57.45 N	22.35 E
Kølkær	41	56.04 N	9.06 E
Kolkasrags ≻	76	57.47 N	22.36 E
Kolkwitz	54	51.45 N	14.15 E
Kolky, Ukr.	78	51.07 N	25.41 E
Kolky, Ukr.	78	51.37 N	26.37 E
Kollbach ≃	60	48.36 N	12.58 E
Kölleda	54	51.11 N	11.15 E
Kollegāl	122	12.09 N	77.07 E
Kolleru Lake ⊜	122	16.39 N	81.13 E
Kollum	52	53.16 N	6.09 E
Kollund	41	54.51 N	9.27 E
Kolmanskop	156	26.40 S	15.12 E
Kolmården	40	58.40 N	16.23 E
Kolmården ⋀ 2	40	58.41 N	16.35 E
Kolmårdens Djurpark ♦	40	58.40 N	16.29 E
Kolmogorovo	86	59.15 N	91.20 E
Köln (Cologne)	56	50.56 N	6.59 E
Köln □ 5	56	50.55 N	6.40 E
Köln-Bonn, Flughafen ⊠	56	50.50 N	7.10 E
Kolno	30	53.25 N	21.56 E
Kolo, Niger	150	13.14 N	2.20 E
Koło, Pol.	30	52.12 N	18.38 E
Kolo, Tan.	154	4.44 S	35.50 E
Koloa	229b	21.54 N	159.28 W
Kolobovo	80	56.42 N	41.21 E
Kołobrzeg	30	54.12 N	15.33 E
Koloč' ≃	82	55.34 N	35.52 E
Kolochau	54	51.44 N	13.16 E
Kolodn'a	76	54.48 N	32.09 E
Kologriv	76	58.51 N	44.17 E
Kologrivovka	80	51.44 N	45.20 E
Kolojar	80	52.34 N	46.58 E
Kolok (Golok) ≃	114	6.15 N	102.05 E
Kolokani	150	13.35 N	8.02 W
Koloko	150	11.05 N	5.19 W
Kolokol'covka, Ross.	80	52.36 N	49.48 E
Kolokol'covka, Ross.	80	51.12 N	44.36 E
Kololo	144	7.29 N	41.58 E
Kolom'agi ⊸ 8	265a	60.00 N	30.17 E
Kolom'agi Airport ⊠	265a	60.01 N	30.17 E
Kolomak	78	49.50 N	35.18 E
Kolombangara Island I	175e	8.00 S	157.05 E
Kolomea → Kolomyya	78	48.32 N	25.04 E
Kolomenka ≃	82	55.06 N	38.46 E
Kolomenskaja Sloboda	82	54.22 N	38.15 E
Kolomenskoje ⊸ 8	265b	55.40 N	37.41 E
Kolomna	82	55.05 N	38.49 E
Kolomyya	78	48.32 N	25.04 E
Kolondiéba	150	11.05 N	6.54 W
Kolonga	174w	21.08 S	175.04 W
Kolonia	174r	6.58 N	158.13 E
Kolonie Stolp	264a	52.28 N	13.46 E
Kolono	112	4.18 S	122.41 E
Kolonodale	112	2.00 S	121.19 E
Kolora	272b	22.55 N	88.22 E
Kolosib	120	24.14 N	92.42 E
Kolosovka	86	56.28 N	73.36 E
Kolovai	174w	21.06 S	175.20 W
Kolovertnoje	80	50.36 N	51.06 E
Kolowana Watobo, Teluk ⊂	112	5.00 S	123.06 E
Kolozsvár → Cluj-Napoca	38	46.47 N	23.36 E
Kolp' ≃	76	59.20 N	36.49 E
Kolpaševo	86	58.20 N	82.50 E
Kolpino	76	59.45 N	30.36 E
Kölpinsee ⊜	54	53.30 N	12.34 E
Kolpny	76	52.15 N	37.02 E
Kölsa	54	51.28 N	12.13 E
Kol'skij poluostrov (Kola Peninsula) ≻ 1	24	67.30 N	37.00 E
Kolsnaren ⊜	40	59.02 N	16.01 E
Kolsva	40	59.36 N	15.50 E
Kol'togan	85	43.51 N	67.25 E
Koltovskaja	80	52.47 N	44.16 E
Koltubanovskij	80	52.57 N	52.02 E
Koltuši	265a	59.56 N	30.40 E
Kol'ubakino	82	55.40 N	36.32 E
Kolubara ≃	38	44.40 N	20.15 E
Kol'učinskaja guba ⊂	180	66.40 N	174.30 W
Koluel Kayke	254	46.43 S	68.14 W
Kolumbien → Colombia □ 1	246	4.00 N	72.00 W
Kol'upanovo	82	54.26 N	36.14 E
Koluškino	78	48.39 N	40.56 E
Koluszki	30	51.44 N	19.49 E
Koluton	86	51.43 N	69.25 E
Koluton ≃	86	51.42 N	69.10 E
Kolva ≃	24	65.55 N	57.15 E
Kolvereid	24	64.51 N	11.32 E
Kølvrå	41	56.18 N	9.08 E
Kolwezi	154	10.43 S	25.28 E
Kolyadivka	83	49.05 N	39.12 E
Kolyberovo	82	55.16 N	38.44 E
Kolyčevo	82	55.30 N	37.52 E
Kolyma ≃	74	69.30 N	161.00 E
Kolymskaja	74	68.44 N	158.44 E
Kolymskaja nizmennost' ≚	74	68.30 N	154.00 E
Kolyšlej	80	52.42 N	44.32 E
Kolyšovo	82	54.54 N	36.57 E
Kolyvan', Ross.	86	51.18 N	82.34 E
Kolyvan', Ross.	86	55.18 N	82.45 E
Kom → Qom	128	34.39 N	50.54 E
Kom ∧	38	43.10 N	23.03 E
Kom ≃	152	2.18 N	11.40 E
Koma, Ityo.	144	8.27 N	36.52 E
Koma, Mya.	110	15.39 N	98.12 E
Koma, Ross.	86	55.02 N	91.19 E
Koma ≃	94	35.59 N	139.26 E
Komadougou Yobé (Komadugu Yobe) ≃	146	13.43 N	13.20 E
Komadugu Gana ≃	146	13.05 N	12.24 E
Komadugu Yobe (Komadougou Yobé) ≃	146	13.43 N	13.20 E
Komae	94	35.38 N	139.35 E
Komagane	94	35.43 N	137.55 E
Komaga-take ∧, Nihon	92a	42.04 N	140.41 E
Komaga-take ∧, Nihon	94	35.45 N	138.14 E
Komaga-take ∧, Nihon	94	35.47 N	137.48 E
Komagome ⊸ 8	268	35.44 N	139.45 E
Komaki	94	35.17 N	136.55 E
Komandorskije ostrova II	74	55.00 N	167.00 E
Komandorski Village	226	37.43 N	121.54 W
Komariči	76	52.27 N	34.47 E
Komarin	78	51.26 N	30.31 E
Komarivka	78	51.14 N	32.07 E
Komárno, Slvk.	30	47.45 N	18.09 E
Komarno, Ukr.	78	49.38 N	23.42 E
Komarnyky	78	49.00 N	23.04 E
Komárom	30	47.44 N	18.08 E
Komárom-Esztergom □ 6	30	47.40 N	18.15 E
Komarovo	76	58.39 N	33.26 E
Komarovy	86	60.26 N	75.50 E
Komati (Incomáti) ≃	156	25.46 S	32.43 E
Komatipoort	156	25.25 S	31.55 E
Komatsu, Nihon	94	36.24 N	136.27 E
Komatsu, Nihon	96	33.53 N	133.07 E
Komatsu-kūkō ⊠	94	36.24 N	136.26 E
Komatsushima	96	34.00 N	134.35 E
Kombissiri	150	12.04 N	1.20 W
Kombone	152	4.37 N	9.19 E
Komdhārā	272b	22.53 N	88.14 E
Kome Island I	154	0.06 S	32.45 E
Komen	64	45.49 N	13.44 E
Komenda	150	5.03 N	1.29 W
Komenoi	268	35.55 N	140.01 E
Komering ≃	112	2.59 S	104.50 E
Komeshia	154	8.01 S	27.07 E
Komfane	164	5.39 S	134.44 E
Komga	158	32.35 S	27.55 E
Komi □ 3	72	64.00 N	54.00 E
Kominato → Amatsu-kominato	94	35.07 N	140.10 E

Symbols in the index entries represent the broad categories identified in the key at the right. Symbols with superior numbers (⋀ 1) identify subcategories (see complete key on page *I · 1*).

Symbole im Register stellen die rechts im Schlüssel erklärten Kategorien dar. Symbole mit hochgestellten Ziffern (⋀ 1) bezeichnen Unterabteilungen einer Kategorie (vgl. vollständiger Schlüssel auf Seite *I · 1*).

Los símbolos incluídos en el texto del índice representan las grandes categorías identificadas con la clave a la derecha. Los símbolos con numeros en su parte superior (⋀ 1) identifican las subcategorías (véase la clave completa en la página *I · 1*).

Les symboles de l'index représentent les catégories indiquées dans la légende à droite. Les symboles suivis d'un indice (⋀ 1) représentent des sous-catégories (voir légende complète à la page *I · 1*).

Os símbolos incluídos no texto do índice representam as grandes categorias identificadas com a chave à direita. Os símbolos com números em sua parte superior (⋀ 1) identificam as subcategorias (veja-se a chave completa à página *I · 1*).

∧ Mountain	Berg	Montaña	Montagne	Montanha
⋀ Mountains	Gebirge	Montañas	Montagnes	Montanhas
)(Pass	Paß	Paso	Col	Passo
V Valley, Canyon	Tal, Cañon	Valle, Cañón	Vallée, Canyon	Vale, Canhão
≚ Plain	Ebene	Llano	Plaine	Planície
≻ Cape	Kap	Cabo	Cap	Cabo
I Island	Insel	Isla	Île	Ilha
II Islands	Inseln	Islas	Îles	Ilhas
⫠ Other Topographic Features	Andere Topographische Objekte	Otros Elementos Topográficos	Autres données topographiques	Outros acidentes topográficos

ESPAÑOL Nombre / FRANÇAIS Nom / PORTUGUÊS Nome	Página / Page	Lat.°′	Long.°′ W = Oeste / W = Ouest
Kominternivs'ke	78	46.49 N	30.56 E
Komin Yanga	150	11.42 N	0.08 E
Komi-Perm'ackij Avtonomnyj Okrug ◻[8]	24	60.00 N	54.30 E
Komissarovka	83	48.07 N	40.09 E
Komissarovo	89	44.59 N	131.46 E
Komissarovskij	80	47.29 N	42.59 E
Komkans	158	31.16 S	18.09 E
Komló	30	46.12 N	18.16 E
Kommadagga	158	33.09 S	25.55 E
Kommandodrif	158	27.30 S	26.14 E
Kommandokraal	158	33.06 S	22.51 E
Kommetjie	158	34.08 S	18.21 E
Kommunal'naja	88	52.03 N	115.06 E
Kommunar, Ross.	80	58.10 N	43.33 E
Kommunar, Ross.	86	54.20 N	89.18 E
Kommunarka	265b	55.34 N	37.29 E
Kommunary	26	60.54 N	29.47 E
Kommunizma, pik ∧	85	38.57 N	72.01 E
Komo ≃	152	0.09 N	9.50 E
Komodo	115b	8.35 S	119.30 E
Komodo, Pulau I	115b	8.36 S	119.30 E
Komoé ≃	150	5.12 N	3.44 W
Komoé, Parc National de la ♠	150	9.00 N	3.30 W
Komoka	214	42.57 N	81.26 W
Komono, Congo	152	3.15 S	13.14 E
Komono, Nihon	94	35.00 N	136.31 E
Komoran, Pulau I	164	8.18 S	138.45 E
Komoren → Comoros ◻[1]	157a	12.10 S	44.10 E
Komorin, Kap → Comorin, Cape ›	122	8.04 N	77.34 E
Komorn → Komárno	30	47.45 N	18.09 E
Komoro	94	36.19 N	138.26 E
Komotau → Chomutov	54	50.28 N	13.26 E
Komotiní	38	41.08 N	25.25 E
Kompaniyivka	78	48.15 N	32.12 E
Kompasberg ∧	158	31.45 S	24.32 E
Kompiam	164	5.20 S	143.55 E
Kompot	112	0.24 N	124.10 E
Komsomolabad	85	38.52 N	69.57 E
Komsomolec	86	53.45 N	62.02 E
Komsomolec, ostrov I	74	80.30 N	95.00 E
Komsomolec, zaliv ⊂	72	45.30 N	52.45 E
Komsomol'sk, Ross.	80	57.02 N	40.21 E
Komsomol'sk, Ross.	86	55.38 N	88.11 E
Komsomol'sk, Ross.	86	57.27 N	86.02 E
Komsomol'sk, Turk.	128	39.02 N	63.36 E
Komsomol's'ke, Ukr.	78	49.35 N	36.30 E
Komsomol's'ke, Ukr.	78	49.43 N	28.40 E
Komsomol's'ke, Ukr.	83	47.40 N	38.05 E
Komsomol'skij, Kaz.	86	51.40 N	66.39 E
Komsomol'skij, Kaz.	86	47.20 N	53.42 E
Komsomol'skij, Ross.	80	54.27 N	45.49 E
Komsomol'skij, Ross.	89	50.22 N	142.10 E
Komsomol'sk-na-Amure	89	50.35 N	137.02 E
Komsomol'sk-na-Ust'urte	86	44.03 N	58.20 E
Komsomol'skoje, Ross.	80	55.16 N	47.33 E
Komsomol'skoje, Ross.	80	50.46 N	47.03 E
Komsomol'skoje, Ross.	88	52.29 N	111.06 E
Komsomol'skoj Pravdy, ostrova II	74	77.20 N	107.40 E
Komsomol's'kyy	83	47.40 N	37.26 E
Kŏmun-do I	98	34.02 N	127.19 E
Kömürcüpinar ◆[8]	267b	41.15 N	28.51 E
Komusan	98	42.08 N	129.41 E
Kom'yanka ≃	78	47.39 N	34.02 E
Komyshnya	78	50.12 N	33.41 E
Komyshuvakha, Ukr.	78	47.43 N	35.32 E
Komyshuvakha, Ukr.	83	48.42 N	38.23 E
Kona, India	272b	22.37 N	88.18 E
Kona, Mali	150	14.57 N	3.53 W
Kona Coast ⊻[2]	229d	19.25 N	155.55 W
Konakovo	82	56.42 N	36.46 E
Konakpınar, Tür.	130	38.53 N	37.22 E
Konakpınar, Tür.	130	39.26 N	27.53 E
Konan → Hŭngnam, C.M.I.K.	98	39.50 N	127.38 E
Konan, C. Iv.	150	8.21 N	8.00 W
Kōnan, Nihon	94	35.20 N	136.53 E
Kōnan, Nihon	94	34.56 N	136.11 E
Kōnan ◆[8]	268	35.22 N	139.35 E
Konar (Kunar) ≃	123	34.25 N	70.32 E
Konārak	120	19.54 N	86.07 E
Konār Dam ◆[6]	124	23.58 N	85.45 E
Konarhā ◻[4]	120	35.15 N	71.00 E
Konawa	196	34.57 N	96.45 W
Končanskoje-Suvorovskoje	76	58.39 N	34.04 E
Konch	124	25.59 N	79.09 E
Konda	74	61.20 N	63.58 E
Konda ≃, Ross.	86	60.40 N	69.46 E
Konda ≃, Ross.	88	53.30 N	113.32 E
Kondagaon	122	19.36 N	81.40 E
Konde	154	4.57 S	39.45 E
Kondega	76	60.14 N	33.30 E
Kondiaronk, Lac ⊜	190	46.56 N	76.45 W
Kondinin	162	32.30 S	118.16 E
Kondinskoje	86	59.40 N	67.22 E
Kondli ◆[8]	272a	28.37 N	77.19 E
Kondoa	154	4.54 S	35.47 E
Kondol'	80	52.49 N	45.03 E
Kondolole	154	1.20 N	25.58 E
Kondopoga	24	62.12 N	34.17 E
Kondorfa	61	46.54 N	16.24 E
Kondratjevo, Ross.	76	60.38 N	28.08 E
Kondratjevo, Ross.	88	57.21 N	98.11 E
Kondrovka	80	54.36 N	43.17 E
Kondrovo	82	54.48 N	35.56 E
Konduga	146	11.39 N	13.24 E
Kondukūr	122	15.13 N	79.55 E
Kondurča ≃	80	53.31 N	50.24 E
Kondūz	120	37.45 N	68.51 E
Kondūz ◻[4]	120	36.45 N	68.30 E
Koné	175f	21.04 S	164.52 E
Koné, Passe de ⊔	175f	21.08 S	164.41 E
Konecbor	24	64.52 N	57.44 E
Konergino	180	65.54 N	178.50 W
Konfara	150	11.55 N	8.50 W
Kong, C. Iv.	150	9.09 N	4.37 W
Køng, Dan.	41	55.07 N	11.50 E
Kông ≃	110	13.32 N	105.58 E
Kŏng, Kaôh I	110	11.20 N	103.00 E
Kongakut ≃	180	69.48 N	141.50 W
Kongbo	152	4.44 N	21.23 E
Kongcheng	100	31.02 N	117.05 E
Kongeå ≃	41	55.23 N	8.40 E
Kongens Lyngby	41	55.46 N	12.31 E
Kongfang	100	27.58 N	116.53 E
Kongiganak	180	59.58 N	162.45 W
Konginkangas	26	62.46 N	25.48 E
Kongjiamatou	105	39.07 N	116.10 E
Kongjiatun	104	40.42 N	124.04 E
Kongjiawopeng	89	43.58 N	122.41 E
Kongjiazhuang	105	40.47 N	114.48 E
Kongju	98	36.27 N	127.07 E
Konglong	100	29.56 N	115.54 E
Konglongshan	105	40.33 N	117.17 E
Konglu	102	27.16 N	97.56 E
Kongmoon → Jiangmen	100	22.35 N	113.05 E
Kongo → Congo ≃	138	6.04 S	12.24 E
Kongo, Republik → Zaire ◻[1]	138	4.00 S	25.00 E
Kongō-Ikoma-kokutei-kōen ♠	96	34.28 N	135.40 E
Kongolo, Zaïre	154	5.26 S	24.49 E
Kongolo, Zaïre	154	5.23 S	27.00 E
Kongor	140	7.10 N	31.21 E
Kongō-sanchi ⋏	270	34.27 N	135.41 E
Kongoussi	150	13.19 N	1.32 W
Kongō-zan ∧	96	34.25 N	135.41 E
Kongsberg	26	59.39 N	9.39 E
Kongsvinger	26	60.12 N	12.00 E
Kongsvoll	26	62.18 N	9.37 E
Kongtan	107	29.10 N	104.42 E
Kongur Shan ∧	85	38.37 N	75.20 E
Kongwa	154	6.12 S	36.25 E
Kongyangcun	106	31.23 N	118.54 E
Kongzhen	106	31.29 N	119.00 E
Koni	154	10.42 S	27.15 E
Koni ≃	150	13.05 N	5.37 W
Koniakari	150	14.34 N	10.54 W
Konice	30	49.35 N	16.53 E
Koniecpol	30	50.48 N	19.41 E
Königgrätz → Hradec Králové	30	50.12 N	15.50 E
Königheim	56	49.37 N	9.35 E
Königin Alexandra-Kette → Queen Alexandra Range ⋏	9	84.00 S	168.00 E
Königin Fabiola-Gebirge → Queen Fabiola Mountains ⋏	9	71.30 S	35.40 E
Königin Mary-Küste → Queen Mary Coast ⊻[2]	9	67.00 S	96.00 E
Königin Maud-Land → Queen Maud Land ◆[1]	9	72.30 S	12.00 E
König-Otto-Höhle ⊻[5]	60	49.15 N	11.42 E
Königsbach	56	48.58 N	8.36 E
Königsberg, Dtsch.	56	50.05 N	10.34 E
Königsberg → Kaliningrad, Ross.	76	54.43 N	20.30 E
Königsborn	263	51.33 N	7.41 E
Königsbrück	54	51.16 N	13.54 E
Königsbrunn, Dtsch.	58	48.16 N	10.53 E
Königsbrunn, Öst.	264b	48.21 N	16.25 E
Königsdorf	64	47.49 N	11.28 E
Königsee	54	50.39 N	11.05 E
Königsfelden ⚑[1]	58	47.29 N	8.14 E
Königsfeld im Schwarzwald	58	48.08 N	8.25 E
Königshain	54	51.11 N	14.52 E
Königshardt ◆[8]	263	51.33 N	6.51 E
Königsheim	58	48.06 N	8.51 E
Königshofen im Grabfeld	54	50.18 N	10.29 E
Königslutter	54	52.15 N	10.49 E
Königsmoor ◆[3]	52	53.15 N	9.40 E
Königssee	64	47.33 N	12.58 E
Königssee ⊜	64	47.36 N	12.59 E
Königsstuhl ⊻[4]	54	54.34 N	13.40 E
Königstein, Dtsch.	54	50.55 N	14.04 E
Königstein, Dtsch.	56	50.11 N	8.29 E
Königstein, Dtsch.	60	49.37 N	11.38 E
Königstetten	264b	48.18 N	16.09 E
Königswalde	54	50.33 N	13.02 E
Königswartha	54	51.18 N	14.20 E
Königswiesen	61	48.24 N	14.50 E
Königswinter	56	50.40 N	7.11 E
Königs Wusterhausen	54	52.18 N	13.37 E
Konin	30	52.13 N	18.16 E
Konin ◻[4]	30	52.20 N	18.20 E
Konispol	38	39.39 N	20.10 E
Kónitsa	38	40.02 N	20.45 E
Köniz	58	46.56 N	7.25 E
Konjic	38	43.39 N	17.57 E
Könkämäälven ≃	24	68.29 N	22.17 E
Konkapot ≃	210	42.03 N	73.20 W
Konkiep ≃	156	28.03 S	17.21 E
Konkō	96	34.32 N	133.37 E
Kon'-Kolodez'	76	52.08 N	39.11 E
Konkouré ≃	150	9.58 N	13.42 W
Kon'kove	83	47.20 N	38.10 E
Konkudera	88	57.33 N	112.30 E
Konkug University ⚑[2]	271b	37.32 N	127.05 E
Konnagar	126	22.42 N	88.22 E
Könnern	54	51.40 N	11.46 E
Konnevesi ⊜	26	62.40 N	26.35 E
Konnur	122	16.12 N	74.45 E
Kōno	94	35.49 N	136.04 E
Konobejevo	82	55.24 N	38.40 E
Konohana ◆[8]	270	34.41 N	135.26 E
Kōnoike	270	34.42 N	135.37 E
Konolfingen	58	46.53 N	7.38 E
Konongo	150	6.37 N	1.11 W
Konoša	24	60.58 N	40.15 E
Kōno-shima I	96	34.28 N	133.31 E
Kōnosu	94	36.03 N	139.31 E
Konotop	78	51.14 N	33.12 E
Konovalovka	80	53.06 N	51.34 E
Kon'ovo, Ross.	24	62.08 N	39.16 E
Kon'ovo, Ross.	86	56.18 N	70.43 E
Konqi ≃	90	40.40 N	90.10 E
Konradshöhe ◆[8]	264a	52.35 N	13.14 E
Konradsreuth	54	50.16 N	11.50 E
Konsankoro	150	9.02 N	9.00 W
Konsen-daichi ⋏[1]	92a	43.25 N	144.52 E
Końskie	30	51.12 N	20.26 E
Konsomol's'kyy	83	48.07 N	39.39 E
Konstabel	158	33.16 S	20.17 E
Konstantinopel → İstanbul	130	41.01 N	28.58 E
Konstantinovka, Ross.	80	56.41 N	50.53 E
Konstantinovka, Ross.	265a	59.47 N	30.08 E
Konstantinovka, Ukr.	83	47.52 N	37.24 E
Konstantinovo	82	56.33 N	38.02 E
Konstantinovsk	80	47.35 N	41.06 E
Konstantinovskij	76	57.50 N	39.36 E
Konstantinovskije Porogi	76	60.34 N	37.04 E
Konstantynów Łódzki	30	51.45 N	19.20 E
Konstanz	58	47.40 N	9.10 E
Kontagora	150	10.24 N	5.28 E
Kontcha	152	7.58 N	12.14 E
Kontejevo	80	58.26 N	41.21 E
Kontha	110	19.30 N	96.03 E
Kontich	50	51.08 N	4.27 E
Kontiolahti	26	62.46 N	29.51 E
Kontiomäki	26	64.21 N	28.09 E
Kontseba	78	48.07 N	29.56 E
Kon Tum	110	14.21 N	108.00 E
Kontum, Plateau du ⋏[1]	110	13.55 N	108.05 E
Kōnu	96	34.42 N	133.05 E
Kon'uchovo	86	55.08 N	70.38 E
Konus, gora ∧	180	67.34 N	178.10 E
Konya	130	37.52 N	32.31 E
Konya ◻[4]	130	38.00 N	33.00 E
Konyr	80	50.25 N	53.25 E
Konyrat	80	49.36 N	47.01 E
Konyrolen	86	44.16 N	79.19 E
Konyševka	78	51.51 N	35.18 E
Konystanu	80	48.51 N	53.20 E
Konz	56	49.42 N	6.34 E
Konza	154	1.45 S	37.07 E
Konžakovskij Kamen', gora ∧	86	59.38 N	59.08 E
Konzell	60	49.04 N	12.43 E
Koocanusa, Lake ⊜[1]	202	49.00 N	115.10 W
Koog [aan de Zaan]	52	52.27 N	4.49 E
Kookynie	162	29.20 S	121.29 E
Koolamarra	166	20.12 S	140.14 E
Koolatah	164	15.53 S	142.27 E
Koolau Range ⋏	229c	21.35 N	158.00 W
Kooloonong	166	34.53 S	143.09 E
Koolskamp	50	51.00 N	3.12 E
Koolyanobbing	162	30.50 S	119.35 E
Koolywurtie	168b	34.38 S	137.37 E
Koombana Bay ⊂	168a	33.18 S	115.36 E
Koonap ≃	158	33.03 S	26.39 E
Koondrook	166	35.39 S	144.08 E
Koonga	76	58.35 N	24.12 E
Koonibba	162	31.58 S	133.27 E
Koontz Lake	216	41.25 N	86.29 W
Koontz Lake ⊜	216	41.25 N	86.28 W
Koopan-Noord	158	26.53 S	20.41 E
Koopan-Suid	158	27.15 S	20.22 E
Koopmansfontein	158	28.14 S	24.01 E
Koorawatha	166	34.02 S	148.33 E
Koorda	162	30.50 S	117.29 E
Koosa	76	58.33 N	27.07 E
Koosfontein	158	27.22 S	25.27 E
Koosharem	200	38.30 N	111.52 W
Kooskia	202	46.08 N	115.58 W
Koossa	150	9.32 N	8.32 W
Kootenai (Kootenay) ≃	182	49.15 N	117.39 W
Kootenay (Kootenai) ≃	182	49.15 N	117.39 W
Kootenay Indian Reserve ◆[4]	182	49.37 N	115.45 W
Kootenay Lake ⊜	182	49.35 N	116.50 W
Kootenay National Park ♠	182	51.00 N	116.00 W
Kootjieskolk	158	31.15 S	20.21 E
Kootwijk	52	52.12 N	5.45 E
Koo-wee-rup	169	38.12 S	145.30 E
Kopa	85	43.32 N	75.50 E
Kopa ≃	85	43.40 N	76.15 E
Kopāganj	124	26.01 N	83.34 E
Kopāi ≃	126	23.48 N	87.47 E
Kopanbulak	86	48.56 N	80.52 E
Kopang	115b	8.39 S	116.21 E
Kopanovka	80	47.27 N	46.48 E
Kopanskaja	78	46.17 N	38.29 E
Kopapan	80	50.20 N	50.26 E
Kopargaon	122	19.53 N	74.29 E
Koparkhairna	272c	19.06 N	72.59 E
Koparpāda	272c	19.02 N	73.04 E
Kópasker	24a	66.20 N	16.24 W
Kopatkeviči	76	52.19 N	28.49 E
Kópavogur	24a	64.06 N	21.50 W
Kopayhorod	78	48.51 N	27.48 E
Kopceviči	76	52.14 N	28.19 E
Kopé, Mont ∧[2]	150	4.59 N	7.27 W
Kopejsk	86	55.07 N	61.37 E
Kopenhagen → København	41	55.40 N	12.35 E
Köpenick ◆[8]	54	52.27 N	13.34 E
Köpenick, Schloss ⚑	264a	52.27 N	13.34 E
Koper	36	45.33 N	13.44 E
Köpernitz	54	53.04 N	12.56 E
Kopervik	26	59.17 N	5.18 E
Kopetdag, chrebet ⋏	128	37.50 N	58.00 E
Kopeysk → Kopejsk	86	55.07 N	61.37 E
Kop Geçidi)(	130	40.03 N	40.33 E
Kopice	54	53.44 N	14.32 E
Köping	40	59.31 N	16.00 E
Kopisty	54	50.34 N	13.35 E
Kopjevo	86	55.03 N	89.50 E
Koplik	38	42.13 N	19.26 E
Köpmanholmen	26	63.10 N	18.34 E
Kopnino	82	56.53 N	38.29 E
Kopondei, Tanjung ›	115b	8.04 S	122.52 E
Koporje	76	59.44 N	29.01 E
Koporskaja guba ⊂	76	59.52 N	28.55 E
Koppal	122	15.21 N	76.09 E
Koppang	26	61.34 N	11.04 E
Koppány ≃	30	46.35 N	18.26 E
Kopparberg	40	59.52 N	14.59 E
Kopparbergs Län ◻[6]	26	61.00 N	14.30 E
Koppel	214	40.50 N	80.19 W
Kopperå	26	63.24 N	11.51 E
Kopperby	41	54.38 N	9.56 E
Kopperl	222	32.04 N	97.30 W
Koppi	89	48.32 N	140.07 E
Koppi ≃	89	48.33 N	140.08 E
Koppies	158	27.20 S	27.30 E
Koppom	26	59.43 N	12.09 E
Kopri	272c	19.11 N	72.58 E
Koprivnica	36	46.10 N	16.50 E
Köprü ≃	130	36.50 N	31.10 E
Köprülü Kanyon Milli Parkı ♠	130	37.20 N	31.18 E
Köprüören	130	39.30 N	29.47 E
Kopt'ovo	80	56.43 N	40.31 E
Kopychyntsi	78	49.06 N	25.55 E
Kopyl'	76	53.09 N	27.05 E
Kopylovka	86	58.40 N	82.22 E
Kopylovo, Ross.	24	60.35 N	45.02 E
Kopylovo, Ross.	82	56.26 N	36.25 E
Kopys'	76	54.19 N	30.18 E
Kor ≃	128	29.36 N	53.18 E
Kōra	94	35.12 N	136.15 E
Koraa Shiir	144	3.18 N	46.16 E
Korab (Maja e Korabit) ∧	38	41.47 N	20.34 E
Kor Aban	144	3.58 N	42.44 E
Korabit, Maja e (Korab) ∧	38	41.47 N	20.34 E
Korablino	80	53.55 N	40.01 E
Korahe	144	6.35 N	44.23 E
Kor'akovka	86	52.24 N	77.08 E
Kor'akskaja Sopka, vulkan ∧[1]	74	53.20 N	158.43 E
Kor'akskoje nagorje ⋏	74	62.30 N	172.00 E
Kōrakuen ♠	96	34.38 N	133.53 E
Korakuen Stadium ♠	268	35.43 N	139.45 E
Korallenmeer → Coral Sea ⊤[2]	14	20.00 S	158.00 E
Koralpe ⋏	61	46.50 N	14.58 E
Korannaberg ⋏	158	27.25 S	22.32 E
Korapun	164	5.25 S	152.00 E
Korāput	122	18.49 N	82.43 E
Korarou, Lac ⊜	150	15.15 N	3.16 W
Korat → Nakhon Ratchasima	110	14.58 N	102.07 E
Koratla	122	18.49 N	78.43 E
Kor'ažma	24	61.18 N	47.06 E
Korba, India	124	22.21 N	82.41 E
Korba, Tun.	36	36.35 N	10.52 E
Korbach	56	51.16 N	8.52 E
Korbeta	144	13.03 N	39.43 E
Korbol	146	10.01 N	17.43 E
Korbous	36	36.49 N	10.35 E
Korbu, Gunong ∧	114	4.43 N	101.17 E
Korçë	38	40.37 N	20.46 E
Korcovo	76	58.52 N	42.13 E
Korčula	36	42.58 N	17.08 E
Korčula, Otok I	36	42.57 N	16.50 E
Korčulanski Kanal ⊔	36	43.03 N	16.40 E
Kordestān ◻[4]	128	35.30 N	47.00 E
Kord Kūy	128	36.48 N	54.07 E
Kordovo	86	54.06 N	93.17 E
Korea, North ◻[1], Asia	90	40.00 N	127.00 E
Korea, North ◻[1], Asia	98	40.00 N	127.00 E
Korea, South ◻[1], Asia	90	36.30 N	128.00 E
Korea, South ◻[1], Asia	98	36.30 N	128.00 E
Korea Bay ⊂	98	39.00 N	124.00 E
Korea Strait ⊔	90	34.00 N	129.00 E
Korea University ⚑[2]	271b	37.36 N	127.02 E
Korekozevo	82	54.20 N	36.11 E
Korelakša	24	65.33 N	32.22 E
Koreliči	76	53.34 N	26.08 E
Korem	144	12.30 N	39.30 E
Koré Mayroua	150	13.18 N	3.55 E
Koren (Die Wurzen))(	64	46.31 N	13.45 E
Korenkovo	78	45.07 N	36.24 E
Koren'ovo, Ross.	78	51.25 N	34.55 E
Koren'ovo, Ross.	265b	55.40 N	38.00 E
Korenovsk	78	45.29 N	39.28 E
Korets', Ukr.	78	50.37 N	27.09 E
Korets', Ukr.	78	50.35 N	27.01 E
Korf	74	60.19 N	165.50 E
Korfovskij	89	48.13 N	135.03 E
Korga	158	30.12 S	20.28 E
Korgan	130	40.44 N	37.13 E
Korgašino	82	54.45 N	37.41 E
Kõrgessaare	76	58.59 N	22.28 E
Korgonskij chrebet ⋏	86	50.45 N	84.30 E
Korgöz	84	40.18 N	49.38 E
Korgus	140	19.13 N	33.29 E
Korhogo	150	9.27 N	5.38 W
Kōri	270	34.47 N	135.39 E
Koridhallós	267c	37.59 N	23.39 E
Korido	164	0.50 S	135.35 E
Koriella	169	37.10 S	145.39 E
Korienzé	150	15.24 N	3.47 W
Korim	164	0.54 S	136.02 E
Korima, Oued el ᐯ	148	33.51 N	0.23 W
Koringberg	158	33.01 S	18.40 E
Koringplaas	158	32.48 S	20.58 E
Korinth	41	55.08 N	10.21 E
Korinthiakós Kólpos (Gulf of Corinth) ⊂	38	38.19 N	22.04 E
Kórinthos (Corinth)	38	37.56 N	22.56 E
Korínthou, Dhiórix ≊	38	37.57 N	22.56 E
Kőris-hegy ∧	30	47.18 N	17.45 E
Koritsa → Korçë	38	40.37 N	20.46 E
Köritz	54	52.51 N	12.27 E
Kōriyama, Nihon	92	37.24 N	140.23 E
Kōriyama → Yamato-kōriyama, Nihon	96	34.38 N	135.47 E
Korizo, Passe de)(	146	22.28 N	15.27 E
Korkino, Ross.	86	54.54 N	61.23 E
Korkino, Ross.	88	54.23 N	105.14 E
Korkinskoje, ozero ⊜	265a	59.55 N	30.44 E
Korkuteli	130	37.04 N	30.13 E
Korla	90	41.44 N	86.09 E
Korl'aki	80	57.06 N	46.57 E
Korliki	74	61.31 N	82.22 E
Korma, Bela.	76	53.08 N	30.48 E
Korma, Bela.	76	52.21 N	31.31 E
Körmend	30	47.01 N	16.37 E
Kormilovka	86	55.00 N	74.06 E
Kormovoje	80	46.17 N	43.30 E
Kornat, Otok I	36	43.50 N	15.16 E
Körnebach ≃	263	51.35 N	7.38 E
Kornejevka, Kaz.	86	54.01 N	68.27 E
Kornejevka, Kaz.	86	50.12 N	74.19 E
Kornejevka, Ross.	80	51.45 N	48.46 E
Kornelimünster	56	50.43 N	6.11 E
Körner, Dtsch.	54	51.13 N	10.35 E
Korner, Mt., U.S.	182	48.59 N	112.15 W
Korneuburg	61	48.21 N	16.20 E
Kórnik	30	52.17 N	17.04 E
Kornilovo	86	53.32 N	81.05 E
Kornouchovo	80	55.33 N	49.53 E
Korn'ovo	265a	60.03 N	30.45 E
Kornsjø	26	58.57 N	11.39 E
Kornwestheim	56	48.52 N	9.11 E
Kornyn	78	50.06 N	29.32 E
Koro, C. Iv.	150	8.34 N	7.28 W
Koro, Mali	150	14.04 N	3.05 W
Koro I	175g	17.19 S	179.23 E
Koroba	164	5.40 S	142.45 E
Koroča	78	50.48 N	37.11 E
Korodougou Markala	150	12.26 N	6.17 W
Köroğlu Tepesi ∧	130	40.31 N	31.53 E
Korogwe	154	5.09 S	38.29 E
Koroit	166	38.17 S	142.22 E
Korolenko, gora ∧	88	58.15 N	115.01 E
Koroleve	78	48.09 N	23.08 E
Korolevskij Belok, gora ∧	86	51.00 N	83.43 E
Korol'ovščina	76	55.49 N	31.45 E
Korom, Bahr ≃	146	10.35 N	19.45 E
Koromba ∧	175g	17.53 S	177.34 E
Koromiri I	174k	21.15 S	159.43 W
Koromo → Toyota	94	35.05 N	137.09 E
Koronadal	116	6.30 N	124.51 E
Koróni	38	36.48 N	21.56 E
Korónia, Límni ⊜	38	40.41 N	23.05 E
Koronowo	30	53.19 N	17.57 E
Korop	78	51.34 N	32.56 E
Koropélé	152	4.44 N	17.11 E
Koropíon	38	37.54 N	23.53 E
Koror	175b	7.20 N	134.29 E
Koror I	175b	7.20 N	134.30 E
Kororoit Creek ≃	274b	37.52 S	144.52 E
Körös ≃	30	46.43 N	20.12 E
Koro Sea ⊤[2]	175g	18.00 S	179.50 E
Korosten'	78	50.57 N	28.39 E
Korostyshiv	78	50.19 N	29.03 E
Korotkova	88	56.43 N	107.55 E
Korotojak	78	50.59 N	39.10 E
Koro Toro	146	16.05 N	18.30 E
Korotovo	76	58.57 N	37.28 E
Korotyš	76	52.22 N	37.27 E
Korovin Island I	180	55.25 N	160.15 W
Korovino, Ross.	78	51.25 N	36.45 E
Korovino, Ross.	80	53.49 N	53.03 E
Korovin Volcano ∧[1]	180	52.22 N	174.10 W
Korovou	175g	17.57 S	178.21 E
Korovyntsi	78	50.48 N	33.45 E
Koroyanitu ∧	175g	17.40 S	177.35 E
Korožečna ≃	76	57.32 N	38.18 E
Korpilahti	26	62.01 N	25.33 E
Korpo (Korppoo)	26	60.10 N	21.34 E
Korså	40	60.38 N	16.08 E
Korsakov	89	46.38 N	142.46 E
Korsakovo	76	53.16 N	37.21 E
Korschenbroich	56	51.11 N	6.31 E
Korselbränna	26	64.27 N	15.35 E
Korševo	78	51.11 N	40.07 E
Korsika → Corse I	36	42.00 N	9.00 E
Korsnäs, Suomi	26	62.47 N	21.12 E
Korsnäs, Sve.	40	60.35 N	15.43 E
Korsør	41	55.20 N	11.09 E
Korsør Nor ⊂	41	55.20 N	11.11 E
Koršunovo	88	58.37 N	110.10 E
Korsun'-Shevchenkivs'kyy	78	49.26 N	31.16 E
Korsze	30	54.10 N	21.09 E
Kortelisy	78	51.51 N	24.25 E
Kortgene	52	51.34 N	3.48 E
Kortkeros	24	61.49 N	51.28 E
Kortrijk (Courtrai)	50	50.50 N	3.16 E
Kortuz, gora ∧	86	54.33 N	91.56 E
Koruçam Burnu ›	130	35.24 N	32.56 E
Korucu	130	39.28 N	27.22 E
Korumburra	169	38.26 S	145.49 E
Korwai	124	24.08 N	78.03 E
Kōryō	96	34.33 N	135.45 E
Koryŏng	98	35.44 N	128.15 E
Koryta	60	49.24 N	13.13 E
Koryukivka	78	51.46 N	32.14 E
Korženevskoj, pik ∧	85	39.04 N	72.00 E
Korževka	80	54.12 N	46.22 E
Kos	38	36.53 N	27.18 E
Kos (Cos) I	38	36.50 N	27.10 E
Kosa, Ityo.	144	7.51 N	36.51 E
Kosa, Ross.	24	59.56 N	54.55 E
Kosa, Ross.	88	54.47 N	108.52 E
Kosa ≃, Ross.	24	60.11 N	55.10 E
Kosa ≃, Ross.	80	58.26 N	51.15 E
Kosa ⊥	150	15.50 N	7.00 W
Kosa Arabats'ka strilka ›[2]	78	45.40 N	35.00 E
Koš-Agač	86	50.00 N	88.40 E
Kosai	94	34.43 N	137.33 E
Kosaja, šivera ∟	88	58.24 N	97.48 E
Kosaja Gora	82	54.07 N	37.33 E
Kosaka	92	40.19 N	140.44 E
Kosan	98	38.52 N	127.24 E
Košankol'	80	49.56 N	48.11 E
Koščagyl	86	46.51 N	53.48 E
Kösching	60	48.49 N	11.30 E
Kościan	30	52.06 N	16.38 E
Kościerzyna	30	54.08 N	18.00 E
Kosciusko	194	33.03 N	89.35 W
Kosciusko ◻[6]	216	41.14 N	85.51 W
Kosciusko, Mount ∧	171b	36.27 S	148.16 E
Kosciusko National Park ♠	166	36.10 S	148.15 E
Kös Dağı ∧	130	40.59 N	34.25 E
Kosdaulet, peski ◆[2]	80	47.45 N	49.30 E
Kose, Eesti	76	59.11 N	25.10 E
Kose, Nihon	270	34.25 N	135.46 E
Köse, Tür.	130	40.13 N	39.39 E
Kösedağı ∧	130	39.54 N	42.39 E
Kösefakılı	130	39.36 N	34.09 E
Košelevka	82	55.09 N	38.05 E
Košelicha	80	55.02 N	43.33 E
Košerovo	82	55.38 N	38.22 E
Koserow	54	54.03 N	13.59 E
Kosha	140	20.49 N	30.32 E
Koshien Stadium ♠	270	34.42 N	135.22 E
Koshigaya	94	35.54 N	139.48 E
Koshigoe	268	35.18 N	139.30 E
Koshikijima-rettō II	92	31.45 N	129.49 E
Koshino	94	36.02 N	136.01 E
Koshk-e Kohneh	128	34.52 N	62.31 E
Koshkonong	194	36.35 N	91.38 W
Koshkonong, Lake ⊜	216	42.52 N	88.58 W
Koshkonong Creek ≃	216	42.53 N	88.59 W
Koshlong Lake ⊜	212	44.58 N	78.29 W
Kōshoku	94	36.32 N	138.06 E
Koshu → Kwangju	98	35.09 N	126.54 E
Kosī ◻[8]	124	27.15 N	87.15 E
Kosi ≃	124	25.26 N	87.22 E
Košice	30	48.43 N	21.15 E
Kosigi	122	15.51 N	77.16 E
Kosi Kalan	124	27.48 N	77.26 E
Kosikovo	76	59.52 N	43.23 E
Kosimeer ⊜	158	26.55 S	32.52 E
Kosino, Ross.	80	58.23 N	51.17 E
Kosino, Ross.	82	55.43 N	37.52 E
Kosiv	78	48.19 N	25.05 E
Kosju	24	65.38 N	59.03 E
Kosju ≃	24	66.18 N	59.53 E
Kosjuvom	24	66.17 N	59.50 E
Köşk	130	37.51 N	28.03 E
Koskaecodde Lake ⊜	186	48.00 N	55.20 W
Koškar	80	47.27 N	53.29 E
Koški, Ross.	80	54.12 N	50.28 E
Koski, Suomi	26	60.39 N	23.09 E
Koškino	80	56.20 N	50.49 E
Koskol'	86	49.31 N	67.05 E
Koskuduk	86	44.06 N	77.22 E
Koskullskulle	24	67.12 N	20.50 E
Koslan	24	63.28 N	48.52 E
Köslin → Koszalin	30	54.12 N	16.09 E
Kosmonosy	54	50.26 N	15.00 E
Kosmynino	80	57.35 N	40.46 E
Kosoba, gora ∧	86	48.15 N	79.40 E
Kosogor	80	57.07 N	47.34 E
Kosoj, porog ∟, Ross.	86	57.30 N	95.30 E
Kosoj, porog ∟, Ross.	88	57.44 N	96.20 E
Kosolapovo	80	56.57 N	49.37 E
Kosŏng, C.M.I.K.	98	38.40 N	128.19 E
Kosŏng, Taehan	98	34.58 N	128.18 E
Kosovo-Metohija ◻[4]	38	42.35 N	21.00 E
Kosovska Mitrovica	38	42.53 N	20.52 E
Kosový potok ≃	60	49.46 N	12.48 E
Kosrae I	14	5.19 N	162.59 E
Kösreli	130	37.11 N	35.59 E
Kossdorf	54	51.29 N	13.14 E
Kosse	222	31.18 N	96.38 W
Kössen	64	47.40 N	12.24 E
Kossindi	152	3.51 N	16.19 E
Kösslarn	60	48.22 N	13.07 E
Kossol Passage ⊔	175b	7.52 N	134.36 E
Kossol Reef ✦[2]	175b	7.57 N	134.41 E
Kossou, Lac de ⊜[1]	150	7.25 N	5.45 W
Kossovo	76	52.45 N	25.09 E
Kossuth	214	41.17 N	79.35 W
Kosta	26	56.51 N	15.23 E
Kostajnica	36	45.14 N	16.33 E
Košt'any	54	50.39 N	13.45 E
Koš-Tegirmen	85	42.47 N	73.53 E
Kostelec nad Labem	54	50.11 N	14.35 E
Kostenec	38	42.16 N	23.49 E
Koster	158	25.57 S	26.42 E
Kosterevo	80	55.56 N	39.37 E
Kosteröarna I	26	58.54 N	11.02 E
Koštice	54	50.24 N	13.55 E
Kostino, Ross.	80	52.11 N	51.20 E
Kostino, Ross.	80	52.24 N	51.39 E
Kostino, Ross.	82	56.18 N	37.43 E
Kostino, Ross.	265b	55.55 N	37.51 E
Kostino-Otdelec	78	51.33 N	41.26 E
Kost'kovo	76	60.02 N	33.14 E
Košt'ob'o	85	41.06 N	74.15 E
Kostomukša	24	64.41 N	30.49 E
Kostonjärvi ⊜	26	65.47 N	28.27 E
Kostopil'	78	50.53 N	26.26 E
Kostroma	76	57.46 N	40.55 E
Kostroma ≃	24	57.47 N	40.55 E
Kostroma Oblast' ◻[4]	24	58.30 N	44.00 E
Kostrovo	82	55.53 N	36.42 E
Kostryzhivka	78	48.38 N	25.41 E
Kostrzyn	30	52.37 N	14.39 E
Kost'ukoviči	76	53.20 N	32.03 E
Kost'ukovka	76	52.32 N	30.56 E
Kostyantynivka, Ukr.	78	49.57 N	35.07 E
Kostyantynivka, Ukr.	78	47.51 N	31.09 E
Kostyantynivka, Ukr.	83	48.32 N	37.43 E
Kosugaya ◆[8]	268	35.22 N	139.33 E
Kosuge	94	35.45 N	138.57 E
Kosugi	94	36.43 N	137.06 E
Kosum Phisai	110	16.13 N	103.01 E
Koszalin (Köslin)	30	54.12 N	16.09 E
Koszalin ◻[4]	30	54.00 N	16.00 E
Kőszeg	30	47.23 N	16.33 E
Koszyce	30	50.11 N	20.35 E
Kota, India	120	25.11 N	75.50 E
Kota, India	124	22.18 N	82.02 E
Kota, Malay.	114	5.35 N	100.23 E
Kota, Malay.	114	2.31 N	102.10 E
Kotaagung	112	5.30 S	104.38 E
Kotabaharu, Indon.	112	0.48 S	111.33 E
Kota Baharu, Malay.	114	6.08 N	102.15 E
Kotabangun	112	0.16 S	116.35 E
Kotabaru, Indon.	112	3.14 S	116.13 E
Kotabaru, Indon.	112	1.08 S	101.43 E
Kotabaru → Jayapura, Indon.	164	2.32 S	140.42 E
Kota Belud	112	6.25 N	116.31 E
Kotabumi	112	4.50 S	104.54 E
Kotabunan	112	0.49 N	124.38 E
Kotadabok	112	0.30 S	104.33 E
Kot Addu	123	30.28 N	70.58 E
Kotagiri	122	11.26 N	76.53 E
Kot'ajevka	80	46.33 N	48.46 E
Kotake	96	33.41 N	130.43 E
Kota Kinabalu (Jesselton)	112	5.59 N	116.04 E
Kota Kota → Nkhotakota	154	12.57 S	34.17 E
Kotālpur	126	23.02 N	87.36 E
Kotamobagu	112	0.46 N	124.19 E
Kotanemel', gora ∧	86	47.43 N	77.18 E
Kotapinang	114	1.53 N	100.05 E
Kotari ⋏	36	44.05 N	15.30 E
Kotaringin	114	0.53 N	102.03 E
Kota Sarang Semut	114	5.59 N	100.24 E
Kotatengah	114	1.05 N	100.33 E
Kota Tinggi	114	1.44 N	103.54 E
Kotawaringin	112	2.29 S	111.25 E
Kotchāndpur	124	23.24 N	89.01 E
Kotcho Lake ⊜	176	59.05 N	121.10 W
Kot Chutta	123	29.53 N	70.39 E
Kotdwāra	124	29.45 N	78.32 E
Kotel	38	42.53 N	26.27 E
Kotel'nič	80	58.18 N	48.20 E
Kotel'niki	82	55.39 N	37.52 E
Kotel'nikovo	80	47.38 N	43.09 E
Kotel'nyj, ostrov I	74	75.45 N	138.44 E
Kotel'va	78	50.05 N	34.45 E
Kot Fateh	123	30.07 N	75.05 E
Köthen	54	51.45 N	11.58 E
Koti → Kōchi	96	33.33 N	133.33 E
Kotido	154	3.00 N	34.06 E
Kotikovo	89	49.08 N	144.13 E
Kotivka	78	49.08 N	34.57 E
Kotka	26	60.28 N	26.55 E
Kot Kapūra	123	30.35 N	74.54 E
Kotkino	24	67.02 N	51.03 E
Kotla	123	32.15 N	76.02 E
Kotl'akovo	82	56.17 N	35.49 E
Kotlas	24	61.16 N	46.35 E
Kotli	123	33.31 N	73.55 E
Kotlik	180	63.02 N	163.33 W
Kotlin, ostrov I	76	60.00 N	29.46 E
Kotly	76	59.36 N	28.45 E
Kot Mūmin	123	32.11 N	73.02 E
Kotō	94	35.08 N	136.14 E
Kōtō ◆[8]	268	35.41 N	139.48 E
Kotō ≃, Nihon	96	34.21 N	134.02 E
Koto ≃, Nihon	96	33.58 N	131.13 E
Kotobiki-san ∧	96	35.03 N	132.47 E
Kotohira	96	34.11 N	133.49 E
Kotohira-gu ⚑[1]	96	34.11 N	133.49 E
Kotohira-yama ∧	96	34.11 N	133.48 E
Kotonami	96	34.10 N	133.56 E
Koton-Karifi	150	8.08 N	6.48 E
Kotonkoro	150	11.02 N	5.58 E
Kotor	38	42.25 N	18.46 E
Kotoriba	36	46.21 N	16.49 E
Kotorovo	80	54.54 N	41.35 E
Kotor Varoš	36	44.37 N	17.23 E
Kotouba	150	8.41 N	3.12 W
Kotovo	80	50.18 N	44.50 E
Kotovsk, Ross.	80	52.36 N	41.32 E
Kotovs'k, Ukr.	78	47.45 N	29.33 E
Kot Pūtli	124	27.43 N	76.12 E
Kotra, India	120	24.22 N	73.10 E
Kotra, India	272b	22.46 N	88.34 E
Kot Rādha Kishan	123	31.10 N	74.06 E
Kotri	120	25.22 N	68.18 E
Kotri Allāhrakhio	120	24.24 N	67.50 E
Kotrung → Uttarpara-Kotrung	272b	22.40 N	88.21 E
Kötschach [-Mauthen]	64	46.40 N	13.00 E
Kot Sultān	123	30.46 N	70.56 E
Kōtsu-zan ∧	96	34.01 N	134.12 E
Kottagūdem	122	17.33 N	80.38 E
Kottas Mountains ⋏	9	74.20 S	12.00 W
Kottayam	122	9.35 N	76.31 E
Kotte → Sri Jayawardenepura	122	6.54 N	79.54 E
Kottingbrunn	61	47.57 N	16.14 E
Kotto ≃	136	4.14 N	22.02 E
Kotton	144	9.35 N	50.28 E
Kottūru	122	14.49 N	76.13 E
Kotuj ≃	74	71.55 N	102.05 E
Kotwālīpāra	126	22.59 N	89.59 E
Kotzebue	180	66.53 N	162.39 W
Kotzebue Sound ⊔	180	66.20 N	163.00 W
Kötzting	60	49.11 N	12.52 E
Koualé	150	11.24 N	7.01 W
Kou'an	106	32.19 N	119.52 E
Kouandé	150	10.20 N	1.42 E
Kouango	152	4.58 N	19.59 E
Kouassi-Datékro	150	7.49 N	3.31 W
Koubansaki	273b	4.22 S	15.09 E
Koubia	150	11.35 N	11.54 W
Kouchibouguac National Park ♠	186	46.50 N	65.00 W
Koudougou	150	12.15 N	2.22 W
Kouéré	150	10.27 N	3.59 W
Kouffo ≃	150	6.35 N	1.59 E
Kouga	146	9.56 N	21.03 E
Kouga ≃	158	33.37 S	22.14 E
Kougaberge ⋏	158	33.40 S	23.50 E
Kougarok Mountain ∧	180	65.41 N	165.13 W
K'ouhu	100	23.35 N	120.11 E
Kouilou ◻[5]	152	4.30 S	12.00 E
Kouilou ≃	152	4.28 S	11.41 E
Koukdjuak ≃	176	66.45 N	73.09 W
Kouki	152	7.10 N	17.18 E
Koúklia	130	34.42 N	32.34 E
Koukourou ≃	152	7.32 N	19.42 E
Koukourou-Bamingui, Réserve de Faune du ◆[4]	152	7.20 N	20.00 E
Koula ≃	229b	21.54 N	159.36 W
Koulamoutou	152	1.08 S	12.29 E
Koulikoro	150	12.53 N	7.33 W
Koulikoro ◻[4]	150	13.00 N	8.00 W
Koulouguidi	150	13.27 N	11.03 W
Koulountou ≃	150	13.15 N	13.37 W
Koumac	175f	20.33 S	164.17 E
Koumac, Grand Récif de ✦[2]	175f	20.32 S	164.04 E
Koumala	166	21.37 S	149.15 E
Koumaméyong	152	0.11 N	11.51 E
Koumankou	150	12.06 N	6.08 W
Koumbakara	150	12.42 N	14.29 W
Koumbal	146	9.26 N	22.39 E
Koumbala ≃	146	9.14 N	20.42 E
Koumbia, Burkina	150	11.14 N	3.42 W
Koumbia, Guinée	150	11.48 N	13.30 W
Koumbisaleh ⊥	150	15.46 N	7.59 W
Koumbouma	150	10.24 N	12.56 W
Koumi	94	36.05 N	138.29 E
Koumpentoum	150	13.59 N	14.34 W
Koumra	146	8.55 N	17.33 E
Koundara	150	12.29 N	13.18 W
Koundé	152	6.07 N	14.38 E
Koundian ⊥	150	13.10 N	10.41 W
Koundougou	150	11.44 N	4.31 W
Koun-Fao	150	7.29 N	3.15 W
Koungheul	150	13.59 N	14.48 W
Koungoulou	152	3.32 S	13.20 E
Kouniohou	150	7.40 N	0.48 E
Kounradskij	86	46.59 N	75.00 E
Kountze	194	30.22 N	94.18 W
Koupé, Mont ∧	152	4.47 N	9.43 E
Koupéla	150	12.11 N	0.21 W
Kouragué	150	12.18 N	10.02 W
Kourak	86	54.50 N	84.40 E
Kouriles, Détroit des → Pervyj Kuril'skij proliv ⊔	74	50.50 N	156.36 E
Kouri-shima I	174m	26.42 N	128.01 E
Kourou	250	5.09 N	52.39 W
Kouroukoto	150	12.35 N	10.05 W
Kourouma	150	11.37 N	4.48 W
Kourouninkoto	150	13.52 N	9.35 W
Kouroussa	150	10.39 N	9.53 W
Koury	150	12.11 N	4.48 W
Koussanar	150	13.52 N	14.05 W
Koussané, Mali	150	14.53 N	11.14 W
Koussane, Sén.	150	14.08 N	12.26 W
Kousser, Massif de ∧	148	32.02 N	5.59 W
Koussi, Emi ∧	146	19.50 N	18.30 E
Koussili	150	13.30 N	11.38 W
Koutia Ba	150	14.11 N	14.28 W
Koutiala	150	12.23 N	5.28 W
Kouto	150	9.53 N	6.25 W
Koutou	98	38.35 N	114.24 E
Koutoumo, Île I	175f	22.40 S	167.33 E
Kouts	216	41.19 N	87.01 W
Kouvola	26	60.52 N	26.42 E
Kouya ≃	150	10.09 N	9.45 W
Kouyou ≃	152	0.45 S	16.38 E
Kova	88	58.18 N	100.21 E
Kova ≃	88	58.18 N	100.18 E
Kovada Milli Parkı ♠	130	37.32 N	30.53 E

≃ River	Fluß	Río	Rivière	Rio
≊ Canal	Kanal	Canal	Canal	Canal
∟ Waterfall, Rapids	Wasserfall, Stromschnellen	Cascada, Rápidos	Chute d'eau, Rapides	Cascata, Rápidos
⊔ Strait	Meeresstraße	Estrecho	Détroit	Estreito
⊂ Bay, Gulf	Bucht, Golf	Bahía, Golfo	Baie, Golfe	Baía, Golfo
⊜ Lake, Lakes	See, Seen	Lago, Lagos	Lac, Lacs	Lago, Lagos
≡ Swamp	Sumpf	Pantano	Marais	Pântano
⌂ Ice Features, Glacier	Eis- und Gletscherformen	Accidentes Glaciales	Formes glaciaires	Acidentes glaciares
⊤ Other Hydrographic Features	Andere Hydrographische Objekte	Otros Elementos Hidrográficos	Autres données hydrographiques	Outros acidentes hidrográficos

✦ Submarine Features	Untermeerische Objekte	Accidentes Submarinos	Formes de relief sous-marin	Acidentes submarinos
◻ Political Unit	Politische Einheit	Unidad Politica	Entité politique	Unidade política
⚑ Cultural Institution	Kulturelle Institution	Institución Cultural	Institution culturelle	Instituição cultural
⊥ Historical Site	Historische Stätte	Sitio Histórico	Site historique	Sitio histórico
♠ Recreational Site	Erholungs- und Ferienort	Sitio de Recreo	Centre de loisirs	Area de Lazer
⊠ Airport	Flughafen	Aeropuerto	Aéroport	Aeroporto
■ Military Installation	Militäranlage	Instalación Militar	Installation militaire	Instalação militar
◆ Miscellaneous	Verschiedenes	Misceláneo	Divers	Diversos

Kovaksa 80 55.31 N 43.30 E
Kovalivka 78 47.16 N 31.43 E
Kovarskas 76 55.26 N 24.55 E
Kovarzino 76 60.09 N 38.33 E
Kovdor 24 67.34 N 30.22 E
Kovdozero, ozero @ 24 66.47 N 32.00 E
Kovel' 78 51.14 N 24.41 E
Kovernino 80 57.07 N 43.49 E
Kovilpatti 122 9.10 N 77.52 E
Kovin 38 44.45 N 20.59 E
Kovno
— Kaunas 76 54.54 N 23.54 E
Kovrina Vtoraja 80 47.01 N 41.44 E
Kovrov 80 56.22 N 41.18 E
Kovsuh ≃ 83 48.48 N 39.17 E
Kovūr 122 14.29 N 79.59 E
Kovvur 122 17.01 N 81.44 E
Kovylkin 80 48.16 N 41.28 E
Kovylkino 80 54.02 N 43.56 E
Kovža 24 61.09 N 38.58 E
Kovžinskij Zavod 76 60.24 N 37.04 E
Kowal 30 52.32 N 19.09 E
Kowalewo Pomorskie 30 53.10 N 18.53 E
Kowangge 115b 8.16 S 118.32 E
Kowanyama 164 15.28 S 141.44 E
Kowanyama Aboriginal Reserve ◆[4] 164 15.15 S 141.45 E
Kowār 126 24.13 N 86.11 E
Koweït
— Kuwait □[1] 128 29.30 N 47.45 E
Kowel
— Kovel' 78 51.14 N 24.41 E
Kowghān ≃ 128 34.15 N 62.57 E
Kowhitirangi 172 42.52 S 171.01 E
Kowie
— Port Alfred 158 33.36 S 26.55 E
Kowkcheh ≃ 120 37.10 N 69.23 E
Kowloon City 271d 22.19 N 114.11 E
Kowloon Peak ∧ 271d 22.21 N 114.13 E
Kowmung ≃ 170 33.52 S 150.16 E
Kowŏn 98 39.26 N 127.14 E
Kowt-e 'Ashrow 120 34.27 N 68.48 E
Koxtag 120 37.23 N 78.05 E
Kōya 96 34.12 N 135.35 E
Koyadaira 96 33.56 N 134.13 E
Kōyaguchi 96 34.18 N 135.33 E
Koyama ◆[8] 268 35.37 N 139.43 E
Kōyama-ike @ 96 35.30 N 134.09 E
Kōyama-misaki > 96 34.40 N 131.36 E
Koyambattur
— Coimbatore 122 11.00 N 76.58 E
Koyang-ni 98 37.42 N 126.56 E
Kōya-Ryūjin-kokutei-kōen ◆ 96 34.10 N 135.35 E
Köyceğiz 130 36.57 N 28.41 E
Köyceğiz Gölü @ 130 36.55 N 28.40 E
Koyna Reservoir @[1] 122 17.25 N 73.45 E
Koyra ≃[1] 126 22.27 N 89.16 E
Koyuk 180 64.56 N 161.08 W
Koyuk ≃ 180 64.55 N 161.12 W
Koyukuk 180 64.53 N 157.43 W
Koyukuk ≃ 180 64.56 N 157.30 W
Koyukuk, Middle Fork ≃ 180 67.03 N 151.04 W
Koyukuk, North Fork ≃ 180 67.03 N 151.04 W
Koyukuk, South Fork ≃ 180 66.35 N 151.57 W
Koyulhisar 130 40.18 N 37.51 E
Koža 80 57.47 N 48.57 E
Kozacha Lopan' 78 50.21 N 36.11 E
Kozachi Laheri 78 46.42 N 32.59 E
Kozakai 94 34.48 N 137.22 E
Kōzaki 94 35.54 N 140.24 E
Kō-zaki > 92 34.05 N 129.13 E
Kozaklı 130 39.14 N 34.49 E
Kōzan, Nihon 96 34.35 N 133.03 E
Kozan, Tür. 130 37.27 N 35.49 E
Kozáni 38 40.18 N 21.47 E
Koz'any, Bela. 76 55.18 N 26.52 E
Kožany, Ross. 76 52.48 N 31.44 E
Kozara ∧ 36 45.00 N 16.50 E
Kozarac 36 44.58 N 16.51 E
Kozats'ke 78 51.18 N 33.29 E
Kozdinga 24 63.43 N 47.32 E
Kozelets' 78 50.55 N 31.08 E
Kozel'shchyna 78 49.13 N 33.51 E
Kozel'sk 82 54.02 N 35.48 E
Koževnikovo 86 56.16 N 84.00 E
Kozhanka 78 49.58 N 29.46 E
Kozhikode
— Calicut 122 11.15 N 75.46 E
Koziegłowy 30 50.36 N 19.09 E
Kozienice 30 51.35 N 21.33 E
Kožim 24 65.48 N 59.28 E
Kozino 265b 55.54 N 37.11 E
Kozjak (Possruck) ∧ 61 46.37 N 15.28 E
Kozliv 78 49.33 N 25.20 E
Kozlov Bereg 76 58.57 N 27.44 E
Kozlovka, Ross. 78 51.39 N 41.16 E
Kozlovka, Ross. 78 50.52 N 40.27 E
Kozlovka, Ross. 80 55.52 N 48.14 E
Kozlovka, Ross. 80 52.33 N 45.41 E
Kozlovo, Ross. 76 57.34 N 35.29 E
Kozlovo, Ross. 82 56.31 N 36.16 E
Kozlovščina 76 53.19 N 25.18 E
Kozlu, Tür. 130 41.26 N 31.46 E
Kozlu, Tür. 130 40.37 N 36.30 E
Kozluk 130 38.11 N 41.29 E
Kožmin 30 51.50 N 17.28 E
Koz'mino 24 61.56 N 48.19 E
Koz'modemjansk 80 56.20 N 46.36 E
Koz'mogorodskoje 24 65.32 N 44.55 E
Kozova 78 49.26 N 25.09 E
Kožpos'olok 24 63.10 N 38.06 E
Kožuchovo 265b 55.43 N 37.54 E
Kożuchów 30 51.45 N 15.35 E
Kozuka 268 35.09 N 139.57 E
Kōzuki 96 34.59 N 134.20 E
Kozukue ◆[8] 268 35.30 N 139.36 E
Kozul'ka 86 56.10 N 91.24 E
Kožurla 86 55.21 N 79.02 E
Kōzu-shima I 92 34.13 N 139.10 E
Kozuya 270 34.52 N 135.45 E
Kozyatyn 78 49.43 N 28.50 E
Kozyn 78 50.14 N 30.39 E
Kpandae 150 8.28 N 0.01 W
Kpandu 150 7.00 N 0.18 E
Kpong 150 6.09 N 0.04 E
Kpo Range ∧ 150 7.15 N 10.15 W
Kra, Isthmus of ⊥[3] 110 10.20 N 99.00 E
Kraai ≃ 158 30.40 S 26.45 E
Kraaifontein 158 33.50 S 18.43 E
Kraal 158 26.34 S 28.26 E
Kraankuil 158 29.52 S 24.10 E
Krabbendijke 52 51.26 N 4.07 E
Krabi 110 8.04 N 98.55 E
Krâchéh 110 12.29 N 106.01 E
Krackow 54 53.20 N 14.16 E
Kraftsdorf 54 50.52 N 11.55 E
Kragan 115a 6.42 S 111.37 E
Kragenæs 41 54.55 N 11.22 E
Kragerø 26 58.52 N 9.25 E
Kraghave 41 54.48 N 11.53 E
Kragujevac 38 44.01 N 20.55 E
Krahenhöhe ◆[1] 263 51.10 N 7.06 E
Kraiburg 60 48.10 N 12.26 E
Kraichgau ◆[1] 56 49.10 N 8.50 E
Krainburg
— Kranj 36 46.15 N 14.21 E
Krainka 82 54.07 N 36.21 E
Krai-Russkije 80 57.23 N 46.50 E
Krajčikovo 86 56.16 N 73.20 E
Krajenka 30 53.19 N 17.00 E
Krajeva 89 44.54 N 131.08 E
Krajneje 80 47.29 N 46.01 E
Krajnik Dolny 54 53.05 N 14.25 E
Krajnovka 84 43.57 N 47.24 E
Krakatau ∧[1] 115a 6.07 S 105.24 E
Krakatoa
— Krakatau ∧[1] 115a 6.07 S 105.24 E
Krakau
— Kraków 30 50.03 N 19.58 E
Krâkôr 110 12.32 N 104.12 E
Krakovets' 78 49.57 N 23.07 E
Krakovo 80 53.36 N 50.51 E
Krakow, Dtsch. 54 53.39 N 12.16 E
Kraków, Pol. 30 50.03 N 19.58 E
Kraków □[4] 30 49.50 N 20.00 E
Krakower See @ 54 53.37 N 12.17 E
Kraksaan 115a 7.46 S 113.25 E
Kraksdorf 54 54.18 N 11.04 E
Kralendijk 241s 12.10 N 68.17 W
Kralice 61 49.11 N 16.12 E
Kraljevica 36 45.16 N 14.34 E
Kraljevo 38 43.43 N 20.41 E
Kralovice 60 49.59 N 13.29 E
Královské Vinohrady ◆[8] 54 50.01 N 14.29 E
Kralupy nad Vltavou 54 50.11 N 14.18 E
Kralupy u Chomutova 54 50.25 N 13.20 E
Králův Dvůr 60 49.56 N 14.02 E
Kramators'k 83 48.43 N 37.32 E
Kramer 216 40.20 N 87.17 W
Kramfors 26 62.56 N 17.47 E
Krammer Ц 52 51.38 N 4.15 E
Kramolin 61 47.40 N 15.32 E
Krampen 264a 52.28 N 13.04 E
Krampnitz 264a 52.27 N 13.03 E
Krampnitzsee @ 64 47.27 N 11.52 E
Kramsach
Kranebitten, Flughafen ⊠ 64 47.16 N 11.20 E
Kranenburg 52 51.47 N 6.03 E
Krångede 26 63.09 N 16.05 E
Kranichfeld 54 50.51 N 11.12 E
Kraniídhion 38 37.22 N 23.10 E
Kranj 36 46.15 N 14.21 E
Kranji, Sing. 271c 1.26 N 103.46 E
Kranji, Sing. 271c 1.26 N 103.45 E
Kranji ≃ 271c 1.26 N 103.45 E
Kranji Reservoir @[1] 271c 1.26 N 103.45 E
Kranji War Memorial ⊥ 271c 1.26 N 103.45 E
Kranjska Gora 64 46.29 N 13.47 E
Krasnaja Pol'ana 84 43.41 N 40.13 E
Kranskop 158 29.00 S 30.47 E
Kranskop ∧ 158 27.43 S 29.41 E
Kranzberg 156 21.55 S 15.43 E
Krapina 36 46.10 N 15.52 E
Krapivinskij 86 55.00 N 86.49 E
Krapivna 76 53.38 N 35.31 E
Krapkowice 30 50.29 N 17.56 E
Krapperup 41 56.16 N 12.31 E
Krapuh 114 3.39 N 98.10 E
Kras (Karst) ∧[1] 64 45.48 N 14.00 E
Krasavino 24 60.58 N 46.26 E
Krasavka 80 51.11 N 43.24 E
Krasieo ≃ 110 14.49 N 100.05 E
Krasino 72 70.45 N 54.27 E
Krasivaja Meča ≃ 76 52.55 N 39.03 E
Krasivka 80 52.16 N 42.31 E
Krasivoje 86 51.54 N 66.46 E
Kraskino 89 42.44 N 130.48 E
Kraskovo 265b 55.39 N 37.59 E
Krāslava 76 55.54 N 27.10 E
Kraslice 54 50.18 N 12.31 E
Krasna ≃ 83 49.01 N 38.15 E
Krásný Dvůr 54 50.15 N 13.22 E
Krasnaja Gora, Ross. 76 54.34 N 31.26 E
Krasnaja Gora, Ross. 76 53.01 N 31.37 E
Krasnaja Gora, Ross. 80 60.16 N 35.42 E
Krasnaja Gorbatka 80 55.52 N 41.46 E
Krasnaja Gorka 80 56.12 N 43.04 E
Krasnaja Jaranga 180 65.40 N 172.50 W
Krasnaja Jaruga 78 50.48 N 35.39 E
Krasnaja Pachra 82 55.27 N 37.17 E
Krasnaja Pol'ana, Ross. 80 56.15 N 51.09 E
Krasnaja Pol'ana, Ross. 80 52.13 N 53.38 E
Krasnaja Pol'ana, Ross. 80 46.06 N 41.30 E
Krasnaja Sloboda, Azer. 84 41.24 N 48.31 E
Krasnaja Sloboda, Bela. 76 52.51 N 27.10 E
Krasnaja Vol'a 76 52.23 N 27.04 E
Krasnaja Zar'a 76 52.47 N 37.41 E
Krásná Lípa 54 50.54 N 14.31 E
Krasn'anka 80 51.04 N 47.56 E
Krasna Polyana 78 47.33 N 37.43 E
Krasne 83 48.23 N 39.31 E
Krasneno 180 64.38 N 174.48 E
Kraśnik 30 50.56 N 22.13 E
Krasni Okny 78 47.32 N 29.27 E
Krasnivka 83 47.24 N 37.26 E
Krasnoarmejsk, Kaz. 86 53.50 N 69.42 E
Krasnoarmejsk, Ross. 80 51.02 N 45.42 E
Krasnoarmejsk, Ross. 82 56.08 N 38.08 E
Krasnoarmejskaja 78 45.23 N 38.12 E
Krasnoarmejskij, Ross. 74 69.35 N 172.00 E
Krasnoarmejskij, Ross. 80 47.01 N 42.12 E
Krasnoarmejskoje, Ross. 80 55.46 N 47.11 E
Krasnoarmejskoje, Ross. 80 52.44 N 50.02 E
Krasnoarmiys'k 83 48.17 N 37.11 E
Krasnoarmiys'ke 78 46.44 N 33.52 E
Krasnoborsk, Ross. 24 61.34 N 45.53 E
Krasnoborsk, Ross. 80 53.46 N 48.04 E
Krasnobród 30 50.33 N 23.13 E
Krasnobrodskij 86 54.10 N 86.28 E
Krasnodar 84 45.02 N 39.00 E
Krasnodar Kraj □[8] 78 45.30 N 39.00 E
Krasnodarskoje vodochranilišče @[1] 78 45.06 N 39.31 E
Krasnodon, Ross. 80 48.17 N 39.48 E
Krasnodon, Ukr. 83 48.18 N 39.37 E
Krasnofarforny 76 59.08 N 31.51 E
Krasnoflotskoje 80 50.04 N 41.14 E
Krasnogorka 83 43.15 N 75.10 E
Krasnogorodskoje 76 56.50 N 28.17 E
Krasnogorsk, Ross. 82 55.50 N 37.20 E
Krasnogorsk, Ross. 89 48.24 N 142.06 E
Krasnogorskij, Ross. 80 56.09 N 48.20 E
Krasnogorskij, Ross. 86 54.36 N 61.15 E
Krasnogorskij, Uzb. 85 41.09 N 69.39 E
Krasnogorskoje, Ross. 80 57.42 N 52.30 E
Krasnogvardejsk, Ross. 86 52.18 N 86.12 E
Krasnogvardejskij 80 57.22 N 62.20 E
Krasnogvardejskij 85 39.46 N 67.16 E
Krasnogvardejsk 82 54.04 N 37.46 E
Krasnogvardejskoje, Kaz. 86 51.24 N 69.18 E
Krasnogvardejskoje, Ross. 78 50.39 N 38.24 E
Krasnogvardejskoje, Ross. 80 45.51 N 41.31 E
Krasnohorivka 83 48.00 N 37.31 E
Krasnohrad 78 49.22 N 35.27 E
Krasnohvardiys'ke 78 45.29 N 34.17 E
Krasnojar 80 48.54 N 51.56 E
Krasnojarka, Ross. 86 55.20 N 72.49 E
Krasnojarka, Ross. 86 59.26 N 60.30 E
Krasnojarsk, Armii, proliv Ц 74 80.00 N 94.35 E
Krasnojarovo 89 51.27 N 128.28 E
Krasnojarsk 86 56.01 N 92.50 E
Krasnojarskij 86 51.58 N 59.55 E
Krasnojarskij Kraj □[8] 86 56.00 N 92.22 E
Krasnojarskoje vodochranilišče @[1] 86 55.00 N 92.00 E
Krasnoje, Bela. 76 54.14 N 27.05 E
Krasnoje, Ross. 24 59.12 N 47.49 E
Krasnoje, Ross. 76 53.06 N 33.55 E
Krasnoje, Ross. 76 52.51 N 38.47 E
Krasnoje, Ross. 78 50.56 N 38.41 E
Krasnoje, Ross. 78 50.21 N 38.50 E
Krasnoje, Ross. 78 46.44 N 39.34 E
Krasnoje, Ross. 82 54.26 N 38.38 E
Krasnoje, Ross. 86 54.37 N 85.23 E
Krasnoje, ozero @ 74 64.30 N 174.24 E
Krasnoje Echo 80 55.48 N 40.42 E
Krasnoje Gorodišče 82 54.04 N 38.44 E
Krasnoje-na-Volge 80 57.31 N 41.14 E
Krasnoje Selo, Ross. 80 48.02 N 45.13 E
Krasnoje Selo, Ross. 80 48.46 N 42.20 E
Krasnoje Selo, Ross. 265a 59.44 N 30.05 E
Krasnoje Znam'a, Ross. 76 57.26 N 35.13 E
Krasnoje Znam'a, Turk. 128 36.58 N 62.30 E
Krasnokamsk 86 58.04 N 55.48 E
Krasnokutsk, Kaz. 86 53.01 N 75.59 E
Krasnokuts'k, Ukr. 78 50.06 N 35.09 E
Krasnolesje 76 54.24 N 22.23 E
Krasnolesnyj 78 51.53 N 39.35 E
Krasnoluki 76 54.37 N 28.50 E
Krasnomajskij 76 57.37 N 34.22 E
Krasnookt'abr'skij, Kyrg. 85 42.50 N 74.18 E
Krasnookt'abr'skij, Ross. 80 56.40 N 47.45 E
Krasnookt'abr'skij, Ross. 80 48.53 N 44.45 E
Krasnoostrovskij 76 60.18 N 28.40 E
Krasnopavlivka 78 49.08 N 36.19 E
Krasnoperekops'k 78 45.57 N 33.47 E
Krasnopillya 78 50.46 N 35.16 E
Krasnopolje 76 53.20 N 31.24 E
Krasnorečenskij 89 44.41 N 135.14 E
Krasnorichens'ke 83 49.11 N 38.24 E
Krasnoščel'je 24 67.21 N 37.02 E
Krasnoščekovo 86 51.40 N 82.45 E
Krasnosel'kup 74 65.41 N 82.28 E
Krasnosel'skij 30 53.03 N 21.10 E
Krasnosil's'ke 78 45.25 N 32.42 E
Krasnoslobodsk, Ross. 80 54.26 N 43.48 E
Krasnoslobodsk, Ross. 80 48.42 N 44.34 E
Krasnotorka 83 48.41 N 37.31 E
Krasnoturansk 86 54.16 N 91.29 E
Krasnoturjinsk 86 59.46 N 60.12 E
Krasnoufimsk 86 56.37 N 57.46 E
Krasnoural'sk 86 58.21 N 60.03 E
Krasnousol'skij 86 53.54 N 56.27 E
Krasnovidovo 80 55.21 N 40.24 E
Krasnovišersk 24 60.23 N 56.59 E
Krasnovka 83 48.47 N 40.07 E
Krasnovodsk 128 40.00 N 53.00 E
Krasnovodsk poluostrov >[1] 128 40.30 N 53.15 E
Krasnovodskij zaliv C 128 39.55 N 53.15 E
Krasnoyarsk
— Krasnojarsk 86 56.01 N 92.50 E
Krasnoyil's'k 78 48.01 N 25.34 E
Krasnozatonskij 24 61.41 N 50.58 E
Krasnozavodsk 82 56.27 N 38.13 E
Krasnoznamensk 76 54.57 N 22.30 E
Krasnoznamenskij 86 51.03 N 69.30 E
Krasnoz'orskoje 86 53.59 N 79.14 E
Krasnye Baki 80 57.08 N 45.10 E
Krasnyje Barrikady 80 46.14 N 47.53 E
Krasnyje Četai 80 55.41 N 46.58 E
Krasnyje Gory 76 58.57 N 29.29 E
Krasnyje Tkači 80 57.30 N 39.45 E
Krasnyj Gorodok 76 57.11 N 33.44 E
Krasnyj Gul'aj 80 54.01 N 48.22 E
Krasnyj Jar, Kaz. 86 53.20 N 69.14 E
Krasnyj Jar, Ross. 80 46.33 N 48.21 E
Krasnyj Jar, Ross. 80 53.30 N 50.22 E
Krasnyj Jar, Ross. 80 51.38 N 46.25 E
Krasnyj Jar, Ross. 80 50.37 N 44.52 E
Krasnyj Jar, Ross. 80 50.42 N 44.46 E
Krasnyj Jar, Ross. 86 55.54 N 86.57 E
Krasnyj Jar, Ross. 86 55.14 N 72.56 E
Krasnyj Jar, Ross. 86 57.07 N 84.33 E
Krasnyj Jar, Ross. 86 55.26 N 56.12 E
Krasnyj Kl'uč 86 50.57 N 46.58 E
Krasnyj Kut 80 50.57 N 46.58 E
Krasnyj Liman 78 51.32 N 39.50 E
Krasnyj Log 78 51.23 N 39.46 E
Krasnyj Luč 76 57.04 N 30.05 E
Krasnyj Majak 80 56.03 N 41.23 E
Krasnyj Manyč, Ross. 80 46.33 N 42.10 E
Krasnyj Manyč, Ross. 80 45.31 N 44.42 E
Krasnyj Manyč, Ross. 80 46.59 N 41.07 E
Krasnyj Meliorator 80 50.02 N 46.06 E
Krasnyj Okt'abr', Kaz. 86 46.50 N 75.59 E
Krasnyj Okt'abr', Ross. 80 51.33 N 45.34 E
Krasnyj Okt'abr', Ross. 80 56.06 N 41.23 E
Krasnyj Okt'abr', Ross. 82 56.07 N 38.53 E
Krasnyj Okt'abr', Ross. 82 55.37 N 36.30 E
Krasnyj Okt'abr', Ross. 86 55.37 N 64.48 E
Krasnyj Partizan 80 46.20 N 43.10 E
Krasnyj Profintern 80 57.45 N 40.27 E
Krasnyj Rog 76 52.57 N 33.45 E
Krasnyj Steklovar 80 56.13 N 48.47 E
Krasnyj Stroitel' ◆[8] 265b 55.35 N 37.37 E
Krasnyj Sulin 83 47.54 N 40.04 E
Krasnyj Tekstil'ščik 80 51.23 N 45.50 E
Krasnyj Tkač 82 55.28 N 39.05 E
Krasnystaw 30 50.59 N 23.10 E
Krasnyy Kut 83 48.12 N 38.48 E
Krasnyy Luch 83 48.08 N 38.56 E
Krasnyy Lyman 83 48.59 N 37.49 E
Krasnyy Perekop 78 46.41 N 33.42 E
Krasnyye Okny 78 47.32 N 29.27 E
Krasucha 76 57.23 N 33.12 E
Kras'ukovskaja 83 47.31 N 40.03 E
Krasyliv 78 49.39 N 26.59 E
Krasza (Crasna) ≃ 38 47.50 N 22.41 E
Kratovo 38 42.05 N 22.11 E
Krauchenwies 58 48.01 N 9.14 E
Kraul Mountains ∧ 9 73.10 S 14.10 W
Krauschwitz 54 51.31 N 14.41 E
Krauterin ∧ 61 47.41 N 15.05 E
Krautheim 56 49.23 N 9.38 E
Kravaře, Česká Rep. 30 49.56 N 18.01 E
Kravaře, Česká Rep. 54 50.38 N 14.24 E
Kray ◆[8] 263 51.28 N 7.05 E
Kražiai 76 55.36 N 22.41 E
Krbava ◆[1] 36 44.40 N 15.35 E
Kreamer Island I 220 26.46 N 80.44 W
Kreba 54 51.20 N 14.40 E
Krebs 196 34.55 N 95.42 W
Krečetovo 24 60.56 N 37.52 E
Krečevicy 76 58.37 N 31.21 E
Krefeld 56 51.20 N 6.34 E
Kregme 41 55.57 N 12.04 E
Kreiensen 52 51.51 N 9.58 E
Kreischa 54 50.56 N 13.45 E
Kremastón, Tekhnití Límni @[1] 38 38.55 N 21.30 E
Kremenchuk 78 49.04 N 33.25 E
Kremenchuts'ke vodoskhovyshche @[1] 78 49.20 N 32.30 E
Kremenets' 78 50.07 N 25.45 E
Kremenivka 83 47.20 N 37.29 E
Kremenskoj 80 47.49 N 41.08 E
Kremenskoje 82 55.06 N 35.57 E
Kreminna 83 49.03 N 38.14 E
Kremlin ◆ 265b 55.45 N 37.37 E
Kremmen 54 52.45 N 13.01 E
Kremmling 200 40.03 N 106.23 W
Kremnica 30 48.43 N 18.54 E
Krempe 52 53.50 N 9.29 E
Krems ≃, Öst. 61 48.14 N 14.19 E
Krems ≃, Öst. 61 48.25 N 15.36 E
Krems an der Donau 61 48.25 N 15.36 E
Kremsbrücke 64 46.57 N 13.37 E
Kremsmünster 61 48.03 N 14.08 E
Krenitzin Islands II 180 54.08 N 166.00 W
Krensitz 54 51.29 N 12.27 E
Krepkaja ≃ 83 47.35 N 39.23 E
Krepoljin 38 44.16 N 21.37 E
Kreščhonka 86 55.52 N 80.06 E
Kresgeville 210 40.54 N 75.30 W
Kress 196 34.22 N 101.45 W
Kressbronn 58 47.35 N 9.36 E
Kressey Lake @ 285 39.44 N 75.07 W
Kresta, zaliv C 180 66.00 N 179.15 W
Krestcy, Ross. 76 58.15 N 32.31 E
Krestcy, Ross. 76 58.23 N 39.00 E
Krestjanskij 80 40.32 N 69.02 E
Krestjanskoje 85 45.34 N 42.56 E
Krest-Major 74 67.37 N 144.45 E
Krestovaja Guba 72 74.07 N 55.33 E
Krestovo-Gorodišče 80 54.10 N 48.36 E
Krestovyj, pereval)(84 42.32 N 44.28 E
Kresty 82 55.16 N 37.06 E
Kreta
— Kríti I 38 35.15 N 25.00 E
Kretek 115a 7.59 S 110.19 E
Kretinga 76 55.53 N 21.13 E
Kreuth 64 47.38 N 11.44 E
Kreuzau 56 50.45 N 6.29 E
Kreuzberg 263 51.09 N 7.27 E
Kreuzberg ◆[8] 264a 52.30 N 13.23 E
Kreuzberg ∧ 56 50.22 N 9.58 E
Kreuzeck-Gruppe ∧ 64 46.51 N 13.06 E
Kreuzen 64 46.40 N 13.35 E
Kreuzlingen 58 47.39 N 9.11 E
Kreuznach
— Bad Kreuznach 56 49.52 N 7.51 E
Kreuztal 56 50.58 N 7.59 E
Krevo 76 54.19 N 26.17 E
Kreyenhagen 56 52.55 N 10.42 E
Krian 115a 7.24 S 112.35 E
Kría Vrísi 38 40.41 N 22.18 E
Kribi 152 2.57 N 9.55 E
Kričov 76 53.42 N 31.43 E
Kriebstein, Burg ⊥ 54 51.02 N 13.00 E
Krieglach 61 47.33 N 15.34 E
Kriel 112 5.11 S 103.56 E
Kriens 58 47.02 N 8.17 E
Krigugjun, mys > 180 65.30 N 171.05 W
Krilfon, mys > 89 45.53 N 142.05 E
Krim
— Kryms'kyy pivostriv >[1] 78 45.00 N 34.00 E
Krimice 60 49.46 N 13.15 E
Krim-Krim 146 8.58 N 15.48 E
Krimmler Wasserfälle L 64 47.12 N 12.10 E
Krimnicksee @ 264a 52.18 N 13.39 E
Krimpen aan de IJssel 52 51.54 N 4.35 E
Krimskij 80 47.39 N 40.44 E
Kriničnо-Lugskoje 83 47.45 N 39.12 E
Kripens'kyy 83 48.06 N 39.03 E
Krishna ≃ 122 15.57 N 80.59 E
Krishna, Mouths of the ≃[1] 122 15.43 N 80.55 E
Krishnachaadrapur 126 21.50 N 86.49 E
Krishnagiri 122 12.32 N 78.14 E
Krishnamāti 272b 22.40 N 88.32 E
Krishnanagar, India 126 23.24 N 88.30 E
Krishnanagar, India 126 23.13 N 87.33 E
Krishnapur, Bngl. 126 23.30 N 89.56 E
Krishnapur, India 272b 22.36 N 88.26 E
Krishnarāja Sāgara @[1] 122 12.30 N 76.26 E
Krishnarājpet 122 12.40 N 76.30 E
Krishnarāmpur 126 22.43 N 88.14 E
Kristdala 26 57.24 N 16.11 E
Kristiania
— Oslo 26 59.55 N 10.45 E
Kristianopel 26 56.15 N 16.02 E
Kristiansand 26 58.10 N 8.00 E
Kristianstad 26 56.02 N 14.08 E
Kristianstads Län □[6] 26 56.15 N 14.00 E
Kristiansund 26 63.07 N 7.45 E
Kristiinankaupunki
— Kristinestad 26 62.17 N 21.23 E
Kristineberg 26 65.04 N 18.35 E
Kristinehamn 40 59.20 N 14.07 E
Kristinestad (Kristiinankaupunki) 26 62.17 N 21.23 E
Kríti □[4] 38 35.15 N 25.00 E
Kríti (Crete) I 38 35.29 N 24.42 E
Kritikón Pélagos (Sea of Crete) ⊤[2] 38 35.46 N 23.54 E
Kritzendorf 264b 48.20 N 16.18 E
Kriuša 82 54.28 N 36.24 E
Kriv'ačka 80 58.40 N 45.24 E
Krivaja ≃ 38 44.27 N 18.09 E
Kriv'anskaja 83 47.24 N 40.10 E
Kriva Palanka 38 42.12 N 22.20 E
Krivići 82 55.28 N 38.12 E
Krivinka 76 55.08 N 30.18 E
Krivodol 38 43.23 N 23.29 E
Krivoj Buzan 80 46.31 N 48.33 E
Křivoklát 60 50.02 N 13.54 E
Krivonosovo 78 49.55 N 39.16 E
Krivorožje 78 48.51 N 40.45 E
Krivošeino 86 57.20 N 83.56 E
Krivošin 76 52.52 N 26.08 E
Krivoy Rog
— Kryvyy Rih 78 47.55 N 33.21 E
Kriwoi-Rog
— Kryvyy Rih 78 47.55 N 33.21 E
Križevci 36 46.02 N 16.33 E
Krk, Otok I 36 45.05 N 14.35 E
Krkonošský národní park ◆ 54 50.45 N 15.35 E
Krn ∧ 64 46.16 N 13.40 E
Krnov 30 50.05 N 17.41 E
Krobia 30 51.47 N 16.58 E
Krøderen @ 26 60.15 N 9.38 E
Krogager 41 56.20 N 8.48 E
Krögis 54 51.07 N 13.22 E
Krokek 40 58.40 N 16.24 E
Kroken 24 65.22 N 14.20 E
Krokodil ≃, S. Afr. 156 25.26 S 31.58 E
Krokodil ≃, S. Afr. 156 24.12 S 26.52 E
Krokom 26 63.19 N 14.30 E
Krokowa 30 54.48 N 18.11 E
Krolevets' 78 51.33 N 33.23 E
Kröller-Müller, Rijksmuseum ✻ 52 52.05 N 5.50 E
Krölpa 54 50.41 N 11.32 E
Krom ≃ 158 33.53 S 19.01 E
Krombi Pits 156 19.30 S 25.02 E
Kroměříž 30 49.18 N 17.24 E
Krommenie 52 52.30 N 4.46 E
Krompachy 30 48.56 N 20.52 E
Kromy 76 52.43 N 35.48 E
Kronach 54 50.14 N 11.20 E
Kronberg 56 50.10 N 8.30 E
Kronborg ⊥ 41 56.02 N 12.38 E
Krone 263 51.27 N 7.20 E
Krong Kaôh Kŏng 110 11.37 N 102.59 E
Krŏng Kêb 110 10.29 N 104.19 E
Kronobergs Län □[6] 26 56.40 N 14.40 E
Kronoby (Kruunupyy) 26 63.43 N 23.02 E
Kronockaja Sopka, vulkan ∧[1] 74 54.44 N 160.31 E
Kronockij zaliv C 74 54.12 N 160.36 E
Kronoki 74 54.36 N 161.10 E
Kronshagen 41 54.20 N 10.05 E
Kronstadt
— Brașov, Rom. 38 45.39 N 25.37 E
Kronštadt, Ross. 76 59.59 N 29.45 E
Kronwa 110 15.25 N 98.26 E
Kroondal 158 25.45 S 27.19 E
Kroonstad 158 27.46 S 27.12 E
Kröpelin 54 54.04 N 11.48 E
Kropotkin, Ross. 72 45.26 N 40.34 E
Kropotkin, Ross. 88 58.30 N 115.17 E
Kropotkina, gora ∧ 88 53.43 N 117.32 E
Kropp 41 54.24 N 9.31 E
Kroppefjäll ∧[2] 26 58.40 N 12.13 E
Kroppenstedt 54 51.56 N 11.18 E
Kropstädt 54 51.58 N 12.44 E
Kropufino 76 60.23 N 39.10 E
Krościenko 30 49.27 N 20.26 E
Kroshna 78 50.18 N 28.39 E
Krošlin 54 54.07 N 13.45 E
Krośniewice 30 52.16 N 19.10 E
Krosno 30 49.42 N 21.46 E
Krosno □[4] 30 49.30 N 22.00 E
Krosno Odrzańskie 30 52.04 N 15.05 E
Krossen 54 50.58 N 11.59 E
Krostitz 54 51.28 N 12.27 E
Krotoszyn 30 51.42 N 17.26 E
Krotovka 80 53.18 N 51.12 E
Krotovo 86 56.57 N 69.20 E
Krotz Springs 194 30.32 N 91.45 W
Kröv 56 49.59 N 7.05 E
Kroya 115a 7.38 S 109.14 E
Krško 36 45.58 N 15.29 E
Krsy 60 49.54 N 13.03 E
Kr'učkov 80 48.01 N 43.09 E
Kr'učkovo 76 57.03 N 35.34 E
Kruckow 54 53.54 N 13.14 E
Krudenburg 263 51.39 N 6.45 E
Kruenggeukueh 114 5.15 N 97.02 E
Kruengluak 114 2.50 N 97.45 E
Kruft 56 50.23 N 7.20 E
Kruger National Park ◆ 156 24.00 S 31.40 E
Krugersdorp 158 26.05 S 27.35 E
Krugersdorp □[5] 273d 26.05 S 27.35 E
Krugersdorp Race Course ◆ 273d 26.08 S 27.45 E
Krugersdorp West 273d 26.06 S 27.45 E
Krugloje, Bela. 76 54.15 N 29.48 E
Krugloje, Ross. 83 47.01 N 39.15 E
Kruglooz'ornoje 86 55.13 N 79.01 E
Kruglooz'ornyj 80 51.06 N 51.17 E
Kruglyži 80 58.31 N 47.42 E
Krugzell 58 47.47 N 10.15 E
Krui 112 5.11 S 103.56 E
Kruidfontein 158 32.51 S 21.57 E
Kruiningen 52 51.27 N 4.02 E
Kruis, Kaap > 156 21.49 S 13.57 E
Kruisfontein 158 34.00 S 24.43 E
Kruishoutem 50 50.54 N 3.31 E
Kruisland 52 51.34 N 4.24 E
Kruisrivier 158 33.26 S 21.55 E
Kruisvallei 158 33.53 S 23.10 E
Krujë 38 41.30 N 19.48 E
Krukira, Laguna de C 236 13.56 N 83.30 W
Kr'ukov 80 47.24 N 42.28 E
Kr'ukovo, Ross. 74 66.30 N 159.31 E
Kr'ukovo, Ross. 82 55.59 N 37.11 E
Kr'ukovo, Ross. 82 55.28 N 36.32 E
Kr'ukovo, Ross. 83 47.40 N 39.13 E
Krukut, Kali ≃ 269e 6.12 S 106.48 E
Krulevščina 76 55.02 N 27.45 E
Krumasye 164 1.40 S 133.09 E
Krumbach, Dtsch. 58 47.58 N 9.02 E
Krumbach, Dtsch. 58 48.14 N 10.22 E
Krumme Lanke @ 264a 52.27 N 13.14 E
Krummendammer Heide ◆[3] 264a 52.28 N 13.39 E
Krummensee 264a 52.36 N 13.42 E
Krumme Steyrling ≃ 61 47.54 N 14.14 E
Krummhörn 52 53.26 N 7.06 E
Krummhörn ◆[1] 52 53.25 N 7.10 E
Krumovgrad 38 41.28 N 25.39 E
Krumroy 214 39.58 N 81.24 W
Krün 64 47.30 N 11.16 E
Krung Thep (Bangkok), Thai 110 13.45 N 100.31 E
Krung Thep (Bangkok), Thai 269a 13.45 N 100.31 E
Krung Thep Mahanakhon □[4] 269a 13.47 N 100.43 E
Krung Thon Bridge ◆[5] 269a 13.47 N 100.30 E
Krupá 54 50.08 N 13.41 E
Krupec 78 51.38 N 34.21 E
Krüpel-See @ 264a 52.18 N 13.42 E
Krupina 30 48.21 N 19.04 E
Krupki 76 54.19 N 29.08 E
Kruså 41 54.50 N 9.25 E
Kruščica jezero @[1] 36 44.39 N 15.19 E
Krusenstern, Cape > 180 67.07 N 163.43 W
Kruševac 38 43.35 N 21.20 E
Kruševo 38 41.22 N 21.14 E
Krušinovka 76 53.14 N 29.50 E
Krušné hory (Erzgebirge) ∧ 54 50.30 N 13.15 E
Kruszwica 30 52.41 N 18.19 E
Krutaja, Ross. 24 63.02 N 54.38 E
Krutaja, Ross. 86 57.24 N 76.27 E
Krutaja Gorka 86 55.25 N 73.15 E
Krutec, Ross. 76 57.15 N 29.23 E
Krutec, Ross. 76 60.17 N 39.25 E
Krutec, Ross. 82 56.10 N 38.33 E
Krutica, Ross. 86 53.58 N 81.14 E
Krutica, Ross. 86 56.49 N 77.10 E
Krutinka 86 56.01 N 71.31 E
Krutoje 76 52.26 N 37.28 E
Krutoj Log 86 53.37 N 80.45 E
Krutoj Majdan 80 55.35 N 44.04 E
Krutyje Verchi 82 54.19 N 36.26 E
Kruunupyy
— Kronoby 26 63.43 N 23.02 E
Kružensterna, proliv Ц 74 48.30 N 153.50 E
Kruzof Island I 180 57.10 N 135.40 W
Krydor 184 52.47 N 107.03 W
Krylatskoje ◆[8] 265b 55.45 N 37.26 E
Krylbo 40 60.08 N 16.13 E
Krylovskaja 78 46.07 N 39.19 E
Krym 83 47.19 N 39.31 E
Krym, Respublika □[3] 78 45.00 N 34.00 E
Krymsk 84 44.56 N 38.00 E
Kryms'ke 83 48.48 N 38.48 E
Kryms'ki hory ∧ 78 44.45 N 34.25 E
Krymskij 78 47.40 N 41.03 E
Kryms'kyy pivostriv (Crimean Peninsula) >[1] 78 45.00 N 34.00 E
Krynica 30 49.25 N 20.56 E
Krynki 30 53.16 N 23.47 E
Krynychky 78 48.22 N 34.27 E
Krynychne 78 45.40 N 28.45 E
Kryva kosa >[2] 83 47.02 N 38.06 E
Kryva Ruda 78 49.31 N 33.24 E
Kryve Ozero 78 47.56 N 30.21 E
Kryvyy Rih 78 47.55 N 33.21 E
Kryvyy Torets' ≃ 83 48.40 N 37.46 E
Kryzhopil' 78 48.23 N 28.52 E
Kryžina, chrebet ∧ 88 54.00 N 95.00 E
Kryzs'ke 83 49.28 N 39.38 E
Krzepice 30 50.58 N 18.44 E
Krzeszowice 30 50.09 N 19.39 E
Krzeszyce 54 52.36 N 15.01 E
Krzna ≃ 30 52.08 N 23.31 E
Krzywiń 30 51.58 N 16.49 E
Krzyż 30 52.54 N 16.01 E
Ksar Chellala 148 35.13 N 2.18 E
Ksar el Barka 150 18.24 N 12.13 W
Ksar-el-Kebir 148 35.01 N 5.54 W
Ksar-el-Seghir 34 35.50 N 5.32 W
Ksar Hellal 36 35.39 N 10.54 E
Ksaverivka 78 50.03 N 30.12 E
Ksel, Djebel ∧ 148 33.44 N 1.10 E
Kšen' ≃ 76 52.23 N 37.44 E
Ksenjevka 88 53.34 N 118.44 E
Ksenofontova 24 60.58 N 56.12 E
Kšenskij 78 51.52 N 37.43 E
Książ Wielkopolski 30 52.05 N 17.14 E
Ksob, Oued ≃ 36 35.46 N 4.34 E
Ksour, Monts des ∧ 148 32.45 N 0.30 W
Ksour Essaf 148 35.25 N 11.00 E
Kstovo 80 56.11 N 44.11 E
Kū', Wādī al- V 140 13.37 N 25.15 E
Kuah 114 6.19 N 99.51 E
Kuai ≃ 100 33.09 N 117.32 E
Kuala, Indon. 112 2.55 N 105.48 E
Kuala, Indon. 114 3.32 N 98.24 E
Kualabee 114 4.24 N 96.03 E
Kuala Berang 114 5.04 N 103.01 E
Kualabiu 112 0.28 S 102.40 E
Kuala Kangsar 114 4.46 N 100.56 E
Kualakapuas 112 3.01 S 114.21 E
Kuala Kedah 114 6.06 N 100.18 E
Kuala Kelawang 114 2.56 N 102.05 E
Kuala Kerai 114 5.32 N 102.12 E
Kuala Kerau 114 3.43 N 102.22 E
Kualakeriau 112 0.50 N 113.20 E
Kuala Ketil 114 5.36 N 100.39 E
Kuala Kubu Baharu 114 3.34 N 101.39 E
Kuala Kurau 114 5.01 N 100.26 E
Kualakurun 112 1.07 S 113.53 E
Kualalangsa 114 4.32 N 98.01 E
Kuala Lipis 114 4.11 N 102.03 E
Kuala Lumpur 114 3.10 N 101.42 E
Kuala Lumpur □[3] 114 3.10 N 101.42 E
Kualamanjual 112 1.25 S 112.00 E
Kuala Nerang 114 6.15 N 100.36 E
Kualapesaguan 112 2.01 S 110.08 E
Kuala Pilah 114 2.44 N 102.15 E
Kualapuu 229a 21.09 N 157.02 W
Kuala Selangor 114 3.21 N 101.15 E
Kualasimpang 114 4.17 N 98.03 E
Kuala Terengganu 114 5.20 N 103.08 E
Kualu ≃ 114 2.45 N 100.00 E
Kuamut 112 5.13 N 117.30 E
Kuamut ≃ 112 5.13 N 117.32 E
Kuanbang 98 40.29 N 120.04 E
Kuancheng, Zhg. 98 40.37 N 118.31 E
Kuancheng, Zhg. 105 40.38 N 118.27 E
Kuandang 112 0.52 N 122.55 E
Kuandian 98 40.43 N 124.44 E
Kuando
— Cuando ≃ 152 18.27 S 23.32 E
Kuanhsi 100 24.48 N 121.10 E
Kuanmiao 100 22.58 N 120.19 E
Kuanshan 100 23.03 N 121.09 E
Kuan Shan ∧ 100 23.14 N 120.54 E
Kuantan 114 3.48 N 103.20 E
Kuantan ≃ 114 3.50 N 103.17 E
Kuanyin 100 25.02 N 121.04 E
Kuanyün
— Guanyun 98 34.20 N 119.17 E
Kuanza
— Cuanza ≃ 152 9.19 S 13.08 E
Kuba
— Cuba □[1] 240p 21.30 N 80.00 W
Kuban' ≃ 72 45.20 N 37.30 E
Kubbī 140 11.08 N 25.14 E
Kubbum 140 11.47 N 23.47 E
Kubena ≃ 76 59.36 N 39.39 E
Kubenskoje 76 59.26 N 39.40 E
Kubenskoje, ozero @ 76 59.40 N 39.25 E
Kubiki 94 37.11 N 138.20 E
Kubinka 82 55.35 N 36.43 E
Kubitzer Bodden C 54 54.24 N 13.12 E
Küblis 58 46.55 N 9.47 E
Kubn'a ≃ 80 55.31 N 48.27 E
Kubokawa 96 33.12 N 133.08 E
Kubor, Mount ∧ 164 6.05 S 144.45 E
Kubr' ≃ 82 56.52 N 38.17 E
Kubrat 38 43.48 N 26.30 E
Kubu 115b 8.16 S 115.35 E
Kubuchaj 88 50.30 N 114.48 E
Kubu Gajah 114 4.10 N 100.41 E
Kubumesaai 112 1.31 N 115.06 E
Kubutambahan 115b 8.05 S 115.10 E
Kučema 24 65.37 N 42.28 E
Kučen'ajevo 80 54.44 N 46.24 E
Kučevo 38 44.27 N 21.44 E
Kuchaiburi 126 22.16 N 86.10 E
Kuchaman 120 27.09 N 74.52 E
Kuch'ang-ni 98 40.09 N 124.46 E
Kuchelebai 154 1.29 N 35.01 E
Kuchen Spitze ∧ 64 47.03 N 10.14 E
Kuchinarai 110 16.32 N 104.04 E
Kuching 112 1.33 N 110.20 E
Kuchinoerabu-jima I 93b 30.28 N 130.12 E
Kuchino-shima I 93b 29.57 N 129.57 E
Kuchiwa 96 34.53 N 132.55 E
Kuchl 64 47.37 N 13.09 E
Kūchnay Darweyshān 128 30.59 N 64.11 E
Kuchterin Lug 89 52.25 N 128.05 E
Kuchtinka 82 54.29 N 38.10 E
Kuchurhan ≃ 78 46.43 N 29.53 E
Kučino 265b 55.45 N 37.58 E
Kučkak 85 40.15 N 70.20 E
Kučki 80 53.01 N 44.29 E
Kučové 38 40.48 N 19.54 E
Küçük Ağrı Dağı ∧ 84 39.40 N 44.25 E
Küçükbahçe 130 38.33 N 26.24 E
Küçükbakkal ◆[8] 267b 40.58 N 29.06 E
Küçükçekmece ◆[8] 267b 40.59 N 28.46 E
Küçükçekmece Gölü @ 267b 41.00 N 28.46 E
Küçükköy ◆[8] 267b 41.04 N 28.54 E
Küçükkuyu 130 39.32 N 26.36 E
Küçüksu ◆[1] 267b 41.04 N 29.05 E
Kučukskoje, ozero @ 86 52.42 N 79.46 E
Kucur, Tanjung > 115a 8.39 S 114.34 E
Kūd 123 33.05 N 75.17 E
Kuda 82 52.25 N 104.08 E
Kudaka-jima I 174m 26.09 N 127.54 E
Kudamatsu 96 34.00 N 131.52 E
Kudanggou 104 41.06 N 124.00 E
Kudap 114 1.17 N 102.26 E
Kudara, Ross. 88 52.13 N 106.39 E
Kudara, Taj. 85 38.25 N 72.41 E
Kudara 88 38.19 N 72.28 E
Kudara-Somon 88 50.10 N 107.25 E
Kudat 112 6.53 N 116.50 E
Kudejevskij 86 54.52 N 56.46 E
Kudene 164 6.14 S 138.29 E
Kudever' 76 56.47 N 29.23 E
Kudirkos Naumiestis 76 54.46 N 22.53 E
Kudongho 98 35.31 N 126.29 E
Kudoyama 96 34.17 N 135.34 E
Kudremukh ∧ 122 13.08 N 75.16 E
Kudrovo 265a 59.54 N 30.31 E
Kudus 115a 6.48 S 110.50 E
Kudyat al-Islām 132 27.30 N 30.45 E
Kudymkar 86 59.01 N 54.39 E
Kuee Ruins ⊥ 229d 19.21 N 155.23 W
Kueishan Tao I 100 24.51 N 121.57 E
Kueisui
— Hohhot 102 40.51 N 111.40 E
Kueiyang
— Guiyang 102 26.35 N 106.43 E
Kuekvun' ≃ 180 69.14 N 179.25 E
Kuēnlun
— Kunlun Shan ∧ 120 36.30 N 88.00 E
Kuerbin 89 49.25 N 128.59 E
K'uerhlo
— Korla 90 41.44 N 86.09 E
Kufayr az-Zayt 132 33.26 N 35.44 E
Kufayr Yābūs 132 33.42 N 36.01 E
Kufrinjah 132 32.18 N 35.42 E

Symbols in the index entries represent the broad categories identified in the key at the right. Symbols with superior numbers (∧[1]) identify subcategories (see complete key on page I · 1).

Symbole im Register stellen die rechts im Schlüssel erklärten Kategorien dar. Symbole mit hochgestellten Ziffern (∧[1]) bezeichnen Unterabteilungen einer Kategorie (vgl. vollständiger Schlüssel auf Seite *I · 1*).

Los símbolos incluídos en el texto del índice representan las grandes categorías identificadas con la clave a la derecha. Los símbolos con numeros en su parte superior (∧[1]) identifican las subcategorías (véase la clave completa en la página *I · 1*).

Les symboles de l'index représentent les catégories indiquées dans la légende à droite. Les symboles suivis d'un indice (∧[1]) représentent des sous-catégories (voir légende complète à la page *I · 1*).

Os símbolos incluídos no texto do índice representam as grandes categorias identificadas com a chave à direita. Os símbolos com números em sua parte superior (∧[1]) identificam as subcategorias (veja-se a chave completa à página *I · 1*).

ENGLISH	DEUTSCH	ESPAÑOL	FRANÇAIS	PORTUGUÊS
∧ Mountain	Berg	Montaña	Montagne	Montanha
∧ Mountains	Gebirge	Montañas	Montagnes	Montanhas
)(Pass	Paß	Paso	Col	Passo
V Valley, Canyon	Tal, Cañon	Valle, Cañón	Vallée, Canyon	Vale, Canhão
≃ Plain	Ebene	Llano	Plaine	Planície
> Cape	Kap	Cabo	Cap	Cabo
I Island	Insel	Isla	Île	Ilha
II Islands	Inseln	Islas	Îles	Ilhas
◆ Other Topographic Features	Andere Topographische Objekte	Otros Elementos Topográficos	Autres données topographiques	Outros acidentes topográficos

ESPAÑOL Nombre	Página	Lat.°′	Long.°′ W = Oeste
Kufstein	64	47.35 N	12.10 E
Kufūr Bilshāy	142	30.51 N	30.48 E
Kufūr Najm	142	30.44 N	31.35 E
Kuga, Nihon	96	34.05 N	132.05 E
Kuga, Nihon	96	33.56 N	132.16 E
Kugaluk ≃	180	69.10 N	131.00 W
Kugaly	86	44.29 N	78.40 E
Kugarčino	80	55.33 N	50.29 E
Kugart ≃	85	40.52 N	72.53 E
Kugas	85	38.21 N	70.48 E
Kugej	83	46.53 N	39.19 E
Kugesi	80	56.02 N	47.18 E
Kugmallit Bay ⊂	180	69.33 N	133.25 W
Kugojeja ≃	78	46.34 N	39.38 E
Kuguno	94	36.03 N	137.16 E
Kuḥaylī	140	19.25 N	32.50 E
Kühbach	60	48.29 N	11.11 E
Kūhdasht	128	33.32 N	47.36 E
Kūh Lab, Ra's-e >	128	25.17 N	60.28 E
Kuḥlīyah, Wādī V	142	30.05 N	31.58 E
Kühlungsborn	54	54.09 N	11.43 E
Kuhmo	26	64.08 N	29.31 E
Kuhmoinen	26	61.34 N	25.11 E
Kühnhausen	54	51.02 N	10.58 E
Kühnsdorf	61	46.37 N	14.37 E
Kūhpāyeh	128	32.43 N	52.26 E
Kühren	54	51.20 N	12.50 E
Kuhstedt	52	53.23 N	8.58 E
Kui	164	7.30 S	147.15 E
Kuibyschew → Samara	80	53.12 N	50.09 E
Kuidesu	98	41.46 N	119.29 E
Kuidou	100	25.10 N	118.11 E
Kuikkol', ozero ⊜	86	50.57 N	64.30 E
Kuikui, Lae o >	229a	20.36 N	156.35 W
Kuilāpāl	126	22.50 N	86.38 E
Kuinre	52	52.47 N	5.50 E
Kuiseb ≃	156	22.59 S	14.31 E
Kuishi-yama ∧, Nihon	96	33.51 N	133.35 E
Kuishi-yama ∧, Nihon	96	33.40 N	133.31 E
Kuitan	100	23.05 N	115.58 E
Kuiten Uul ∧	86	49.08 N	87.49 E
Kuito	152	12.22 S	16.56 E
Kuiu Island I	180	56.45 N	134.10 W
Kuivaniemi	26	65.35 N	25.11 E
Kuivastu	76	58.35 N	23.22 E
Kuja, Ross.	24	67.46 N	53.10 E
Kuja, Ross.	24	65.05 N	40.06 E
Kujang	98	39.52 N	126.01 E
Kujani Game Reserve ◆[4]	150	7.10 N	0.50 W
Kujawy ◆[1]	30	52.45 N	18.30 E
Kujbyšev → Samara, Ross.	80	53.12 N	50.09 E
Kujbyšev, Ross.	86	55.27 N	78.19 E
Kujbyševo, Ross.	83	47.49 N	38.55 E
Kujbyševo, Uzb.	85	40.22 N	71.17 E
Kujbyševskij, Kaz.	86	53.15 N	66.51 E
Kujbyševskij, Uzb.	72	37.52 N	68.44 E
Kujbyševskij Zaton	80	55.09 N	49.12 E
Kujbyševskoje vodochranilišče ⊜[1]	80	54.30 N	48.30 E
Kujeda	86	56.26 N	55.35 E
Kujgan	86	45.25 N	74.10 E
Kujgenkol'	80	49.17 N	47.59 E
Kuji	92	40.11 N	141.46 E
Kuji ≃	94	36.29 N	140.37 E
Kujirai	268	35.56 N	139.27 E
Kujl'uk	85	41.15 N	69.20 E
Kujman'	76	52.52 N	39.16 E
Kujŏng-ni	98	37.53 N	125.54 E
Kujtun	88	54.21 N	101.29 E
Kujū	96	33.01 N	131.18 E
Kujūkuri	94	35.32 N	140.25 E
Kujūkuri-hama △[2]	94	35.35 N	140.30 E
Kujū-san ∧	96	33.05 N	131.15 E
Kuk ∧	64	46.16 N	13.45 E
Kuk ≃	180	70.36 N	160.00 W
Kukaklek Lake ⊜	180	59.09 N	155.20 W
Kukalaya ≃	236	13.39 N	83.37 W
Kukan	89	49.12 N	133.28 E
Kukarino	82	55.31 N	35.59 E
Kukawa	146	12.56 N	13.35 E
Kukerin	162	33.11 S	118.05 E
Kukës	38	42.05 N	20.24 E
Kuke Shan ∧∧	85	40.00 N	75.00 E
Kuki	94	36.04 N	139.40 E
Kukipi	164	8.10 S	146.05 E
Kukkola	26	65.59 N	24.04 E
Kukmirn	61	47.04 N	16.13 E
Kukmor	80	56.13 N	50.54 E
Kukoboj	76	58.42 N	39.54 E
Kukol'	76	59.52 N	32.35 E
Kükong → Shaoguan	100	24.50 N	113.37 E
Kukpowruk ≃	180	69.35 N	163.00 W
Kukpuk ≃	180	68.23 N	166.20 W
Kukshi	120	22.12 N	74.45 E
Kukuj	76	59.21 N	32.33 E
Kuku-Nor → Qinghai Hu ⊜	102	36.50 N	100.20 E
Kukup	114	1.19 N	103.27 E
Kuku Point >	174a	19.18 N	166.34 E
Kukuri Mukuri Char I	126	21.56 N	90.39 E
Kukuštan	86	57.38 N	56.30 E
Kula, Blg.	38	43.53 N	22.31 E
Kula, Jugo.	38	45.36 N	19.32 E
Kula, Tür.	130	38.32 N	28.40 E
Kula, Hi., U.S.	229a	20.52 N	156.40 W
Kul'ab	120	37.55 N	69.46 E
Kul'ab □[4]	85	38.15 N	69.45 E
Kulāchi	123	31.56 N	70.27 E
Kulagi	76	52.56 N	32.24 E
Kula Gulf ʯ	175e	8.05 S	157.18 E
Kulai	114	1.40 N	103.36 E
Kulaj	86	57.42 N	75.15 E
Kula Kangri ∧	124	28.03 N	90.27 E
Kulākh	144	21.18 N	40.41 E
Kulakovo, Ross.	82	55.06 N	37.28 E
Kulakovo, Ross.	86	58.06 N	93.57 E
Kulakši	86	47.12 N	55.24 E
Kulal, Mount ∧	154	2.43 N	36.56 E
Kulanak	85	41.22 N	75.31 E
Kulandy	86	46.08 N	59.31 E
Kulanutpes ≃	86	50.21 N	69.08 E
Kular	74	70.41 N	134.22 E
Kulassein Island I	116	6.25 N	120.41 E
Kulaura	120	24.32 N	92.03 E
Kulautuva	76	54.58 N	23.38 E
Kulaykilī	140	11.21 N	25.36 E
Kul'či	89	53.33 N	139.36 E
Kuldīga	76	56.58 N	21.59 E
Kuldja → Yining	86	43.54 N	81.21 E
Kul'dur	89	49.13 N	131.38 E
Kule	156	23.05 S	20.05 E
Kulebaki	80	55.24 N	42.32 E
Kulejevo	86	59.40 N	80.59 E
Kulen Vakuf	36	44.34 N	16.06 E
Kulešovka	83	47.05 N	39.33 E
Kulevčinskij	86	53.12 N	61.26 E
Kulgām	123	33.39 N	75.01 E
Kulgera	162	25.50 S	133.18 E
Kulgunino	86	53.35 N	56.56 E
Kuligi	80	58.11 N	53.46 E
Kulikovka	80	52.14 N	47.36 E
Kulikovo	76	52.14 N	39.35 E
Kulikovskij	80	50.51 N	42.34 E
Kulim	114	5.22 N	100.34 E
Kulin	162	32.40 S	118.10 E
Kuliushucun	105	40.07 N	116.34 E
Kulju	26	61.23 N	23.46 E
Kulkyne Creek ≃	166	30.16 S	144.12 E
Kullaberg ∧∧[2]	41	56.18 N	12.30 E
Kullamaa	76	58.53 N	24.05 E
Küllenhahn ◆[8]	263	51.14 N	7.08 E
Küllstedt	56	51.16 N	10.17 E
Kullu	123	31.58 N	77.06 E
Kulm	198	46.18 N	98.57 W
Kulmbach	54	50.06 N	11.27 E

FRANÇAIS Nom	Page	Lat.°′	Long.°′ W = Ouest
Kulnura	170	33.14 S	151.13 E
Kuloj, Ross.	24	64.58 N	43.28 E
Kuloj, Ross.	24	61.02 N	42.29 E
Kuloj ≃, Ross.	24	66.03 N	43.22 E
Kuloj ≃, Ross.	76	60.25 N	42.30 E
Kuloli	85	39.22 N	68.03 E
Kulongshan	98	41.43 N	116.54 E
Kulongshanpuzi	104	41.16 N	123.59 E
Kulotino	76	58.27 N	33.21 E
Kulp	130	38.30 N	41.02 E
Kulpahar	124	25.19 N	79.39 E
Kulpara	168b	34.04 S	138.02 E
Kulpawn ≃	150	10.21 N	1.05 W
Kulpi	126	22.06 N	88.15 E
Kul'pino	82	56.18 N	37.09 E
Kulpmont	208	40.47 N	76.28 W
Kulpsville	285	40.15 N	75.20 W
Kul'sary	86	46.59 N	54.01 E
Kulsbjerge ∧∧[2]	41	55.01 N	12.01 E
Külsheim	56	49.40 N	9.31 E
Kültepe ⊥	130	38.44 N	35.34 E
Kulti	126	23.44 N	86.51 E
Kultikri	126	22.10 N	87.09 E
Kultuk	88	51.44 N	103.42 E
Kulu	130	39.06 N	33.05 E
Kuluha, Jabal ∧	140	15.31 N	23.25 E
Kulumadau	164	9.03 S	152.43 E
Kulunda	86	52.35 N	78.57 E
Kulunda ≃	86	52.59 N	79.48 E
Kulundinskaja step' ⩡	86	53.00 N	79.00 E
Kulundinskoje, ozero ⊜	86	53.00 N	79.36 E
Kuluqi	89	50.23 N	124.13 E
Kulwin	166	35.02 S	142.33 E
Kulykiv	78	49.58 N	24.04 E
Kulykivka	78	51.23 N	31.37 E
Kum ≃	130	38.38 N	27.32 E
Kuma	96	33.39 N	132.54 E
Kuma ≃, Nihon	92	32.30 N	130.34 E
Kuma ≃, Ross.	72	44.56 N	47.00 E
Kuma ≃, Ross.	86	59.32 N	66.45 E
Kumagaya	94	36.08 N	139.23 E
Kumai, Indon.	112	3.23 S	112.33 E
Kumai, Indon.	112	2.44 S	111.43 E
Kumai, Teluk ⊂	112	3.00 S	111.43 E
Kumaishi	92a	42.08 N	139.59 E
Kumajri	84	40.48 N	43.50 E
Kumakanda	88	52.44 N	116.55 E
Kumalarang	116	7.44 N	123.08 E
Kumamba, Kepulauan II	164	1.36 S	138.45 E
Kumamoto	92	32.48 N	130.43 E
Kumamoto □[5]	96	32.58 N	130.55 E
Kumano, Nihon	92	33.54 N	136.05 E
Kumano, Nihon	96	34.20 N	132.34 E
Kumano ≃	92	33.44 N	136.01 E
Kumano-nada ⊤[2]	92	33.47 N	136.20 E
Kumanovo	38	42.08 N	21.43 E
Kumār ≃[1], Bngl.	126	23.31 N	89.28 E
Kumār ≃[1], Bngl.	126	23.11 N	90.10 E
Kumara, N.Z.	172	42.38 S	171.11 E
Kumara, Ross.	89	51.37 N	126.47 E
Kumārapālaiyam	122	11.28 N	77.43 E
Kumardhubi	126	23.48 N	86.43 E
Kumarganj	126	22.59 N	87.44 E
Kumārghāt	120	24.04 N	92.04 E
Kumārgrām	124	26.37 N	89.50 E
Kumāri ≃	126	22.57 N	86.48 E
Kumārkhāli	124	23.51 N	89.15 E
Kumarl	162	32.47 S	121.33 E
Kumasi	150	6.41 N	1.35 W
Kumatori	270	34.24 N	135.22 E
Kumawa, Pegunungan ∧∧	164	3.50 S	132.50 E
Kumba	152	4.38 N	9.25 E
Kumbakonam	122	10.58 N	79.23 E
Kumba Pits	156	18.45 S	24.45 E
Kumbar	140	12.03 N	30.16 E
Kumbarilla	166	27.19 S	150.53 E
Kumbe	164	8.21 S	140.13 E
Kumbel'	85	42.30 N	73.11 E
Kŭmch'ŏn	98	38.10 N	126.29 E
Kum-Dag	128	39.16 N	54.35 E
Kumdah ⊤[4]	144	20.23 N	45.05 E
Kumdan ∧	123	35.09 N	77.35 E
Kumdanlı	130	38.19 N	30.59 E
Kume	96	35.03 N	133.54 E
Kume-jima I	93b	26.20 N	126.47 E
Kumenan	96	34.56 N	133.58 E
Kumeny	80	58.07 N	49.56 E
Kŭm-gang ≃	98	36.00 N	126.40 E
Kŭmgang-san ∧	98	38.35 N	128.10 E
Kŭmhwa	98	38.17 N	127.28 E
Kumi	154	1.29 N	33.56 E
Kumihama	96	35.36 N	134.55 E
Kuminovskoje	86	57.48 N	64.07 E
Kuminskij	86	58.40 N	66.04 E
Kumiyama	270	34.53 N	135.45 E
Kumizawa ◆[8]	268	35.23 N	139.31 E
Kumköy ◆[8]	267b	41.15 N	29.02 E
Kumla	40	59.08 N	15.08 E
Kumli	84	43.58 N	46.04 E
Kumlinge I	26	60.16 N	20.47 E
Kumluca, Tür.	130	36.22 N	30.18 E
Kumluca, Tür.	130	41.27 N	32.28 E
Kummelnäs	40	59.21 N	18.17 E
Kummerow	54	54.17 N	12.53 E
Kummerower See ⊜	54	53.49 N	12.52 E
Kümmersbruck	60	49.25 N	11.53 E
Kumo	146	10.03 N	11.13 E
Kŭmŏ-do I	98	34.31 N	127.45 E
Kumon Range ∧∧	102	26.30 N	97.15 E
Kumora	88	55.53 N	111.13 E
Kumosō-yama ∧	96	33.54 N	134.18 E
Kumotori-yama ∧	94	35.51 N	138.57 E
Kumphawapi	110	17.07 N	103.01 E
Kumrābād	126	24.10 N	87.16 E
Kumru	130	40.53 N	37.17 E
Kŭmsan	98	36.07 N	127.30 E
Kŭmsan-ni	98	37.55 N	125.41 E
Kumsenga	154	3.47 S	30.25 E
Kumta	122	14.25 N	74.24 E
Kumu	154	3.04 N	25.09 E
Kumu ≃	114	1.24 N	100.43 E
Kumuch	84	42.11 N	47.07 E
Kumukahi, Cape >	229d	19.31 N	154.49 W
Kumukuli	120	37.33 N	88.50 E
Kumusi ≃	164	8.35 S	148.00 E
Kümüx	86	42.14 N	88.11 E
Kumzār	128	26.20 N	56.25 E
Kuna	202	43.29 N	116.25 W
Kunar (Konar) ≃	123	34.25 N	70.32 E
Kunašak	86	55.43 N	61.36 E
Kunashiri-tō → Kunašir, ostrov I	92a	44.10 N	146.00 E
Kunašir, ostrov (Kunashiri-tō) I	92a	44.10 N	146.00 E
Kun'batar	84	44.17 N	45.34 E
Kuncheng Hu ⊜	106	31.35 N	120.45 E
Kunchhā	124	28.08 N	84.20 E
Kunc'ovo ◆[8]	265b	55.44 N	37.26 E
Kunda, Eesti	76	59.29 N	26.32 E
Kunda, Zaïre	154	3.57 S	26.35 E
Kunda Hills ∧∧[2]	122	11.10 N	76.30 E
Kundahit	126	23.58 N	87.10 E
Kundam	124	23.13 N	80.21 E
Kundāpura	122	13.38 N	74.42 E
Kundar ≃	120	31.56 N	69.19 E
Kundat	86	55.14 N	87.51 E
Kundelungu, Parc National de ♠	154	10.30 S	27.45 E
Kunderu ≃	122	14.38 N	78.42 E
Kundi	154	1.08 S	40.41 E
Kundiān	123	32.27 N	71.28 E
Kundiawa	164	6.00 S	145.00 E
Kundima	164	4.14 S	143.52 E
Kundl	64	47.28 N	11.59 E
Kundla	120	21.20 N	71.18 E
Kundr'učje ≃	83	47.52 N	40.15 E

PORTUGUÊS Nome	Página	Lat.°′	Long.°′ W = Oeste
Kundur, Pulau I	112	0.45 N	103.26 E
Kunene (Cunene) ≃	152	17.20 S	11.50 E
Kunersdorf, Forst ◆[3]	264a	52.17 N	12.59 E
Kunes	24	70.21 N	26.31 E
Künes ≃	86	43.55 N	80.55 E
Kunga ≃[1]	126	21.45 N	89.30 E
Kungälv	26	57.52 N	11.58 E
Kungana	146	7.50 N	10.42 E
Kungchuling → Huaide	89	43.32 N	124.50 E
Kungej-Alatau, chrebet ∧∧	85	42.50 N	77.00 E
Kunggyü Yumco ⊜	124	30.35 N	82.09 E
Kunghit Island I	182	52.06 N	131.04 W
Kunghsi	100	24.37 N	121.16 E
Kung-pei-tien	269d	25.06 N	121.38 E
Kungrad	86	43.06 N	58.54 E
Kungsängen	40	59.29 N	17.45 E
Kungsängen flygplats ⊠	40	58.36 N	16.15 E
Kungsbacka	26	57.29 N	12.04 E
Kungsgården	40	60.36 N	16.37 E
Kungshamn	26	58.22 N	11.15 E
Kungsör	40	59.25 N	16.05 E
Kungu	152	2.47 N	19.12 E
Kungur	86	57.25 N	56.57 E
Kunhār ≃	123	34.17 N	73.29 E
Kunhegyes	30	47.22 N	20.38 E
Kunhing	110	21.18 N	98.26 E
Kuni	94	36.35 N	138.38 E
Kunia	229c	21.29 N	158.07 W
Kunigami	174m	26.45 N	128.10 E
Kunimi	96	33.41 N	131.36 E
Kuningan	115a	6.59 S	108.29 E
Kunisaki	96	33.33 N	131.45 E
Kunisaki-hantō >[1]	96	33.30 N	131.40 E
Kunitachi	268	35.41 N	139.26 E
Kuni Vyselki	82	54.18 N	38.41 E
Kunja	76	56.18 N	30.59 E
Kunja ≃, Ross.	76	57.09 N	31.10 E
Kunja ≃, Ross.	82	56.31 N	38.12 E
Kunjāh	123	32.32 N	73.59 E
Kunkle	216	41.38 N	84.30 W
Kunkletown	210	40.51 N	75.27 W
Kunkuri	124	22.45 N	83.57 E
Kunlong	110	23.25 N	98.39 E
Kunlun Shan ∧∧	120	36.30 N	88.00 E
Kunming	102	25.05 N	102.40 E
Kunming Hu ⊜	271a	39.59 N	116.15 E
Kunmunya Aboriginal Reserve ◆[4]	164	15.45 S	124.45 E
Kunnamkulam	122	10.39 N	76.05 E
Kunost'	76	60.01 N	37.38 E
Kunovice	30	49.03 N	17.29 E
Kunow	54	53.00 N	12.07 E
Kunowice	54	52.20 N	14.50 E
Kunrau	54	52.35 N	11.01 E
Kunsan	98	35.58 N	126.41 E
Kunshan	106	31.23 N	120.57 E
Kunszentmárton	30	46.51 N	20.18 E
Kuntair	150	13.32 N	16.13 W
Kuntaur	150	13.40 N	14.48 W
Kuntiki	86	58.29 N	76.24 E
Kunting	100	29.48 N	121.56 E
Kuntshankoie	152	3.20 S	23.34 E
Kuntuolun	102	45.13 N	115.21 E
Kununurra	164	15.47 S	128.44 E
Kunwi	98	36.15 N	128.34 E
Kunya	150	12.14 N	8.34 E
Kun'ye	83	49.23 N	37.15 E
Kunyo	144	6.17 N	42.33 E
Kunžak	61	49.07 N	15.11 E
Künzell	56	50.33 N	9.42 E
Künzelsau	56	49.16 N	9.41 E
Künzing	60	48.40 N	13.05 E
Kunzulu	152	3.29 S	16.09 E
Kuocang Shan ∧∧	100	28.36 N	120.30 E
Kuohsing	100	24.02 N	120.51 E
Kuokegan	120	37.30 N	89.55 E
Kuolajarvi	24	66.58 N	29.12 E
Kuop I[1]	175c	7.03 N	151.56 E
Kuopio	26	62.54 N	27.41 E
Kuopion lääni □[4]	26	63.00 N	27.30 E
Kuortane	26	62.48 N	23.30 E
Kupa ≃	36	45.28 N	16.24 E
Kup'abal	271b	37.37 N	126.54 E
Kupang	112	10.10 S	123.35 E
Kupang, Teluk ⊂	112	10.04 S	123.40 E
Kupanskoje	82	56.51 N	38.43 E
Kuparuk ≃	180	70.25 N	148.55 W
Kupava	80	51.07 N	42.57 E
Kupavna	265b	55.45 N	38.08 E
Kuper Island I	224	48.58 N	123.39 W
Kupferberg	263	51.09 N	7.27 E
Kupferdreh ◆[8]	263	51.23 N	7.05 E
Kupfermühle	41	54.50 N	9.24 E
Kupferzell	56	49.14 N	9.41 E
Kupiano	164	10.05 S	148.11 E
Kupino	86	54.22 N	77.18 E
Kupiškis	76	55.50 N	24.58 E
Küplü, Tür.	130	41.07 N	26.21 E
Küplü, Tür.	130	40.06 N	30.00 E
Kupol, gora ∧	180	68.38 N	174.45 E
Kuppenheim	56	48.49 N	8.15 E
Kupper Airport ⊠	276	40.31 N	74.36 W
Kupreanof	180	56.49 N	132.57 W
Kupreanof Island I	180	56.50 N	133.30 W
Kupreanof Point >	180	55.34 N	159.35 W
Kupres	36	44.00 N	17.17 E
Küps	54	50.11 N	11.16 E
Kupuri	89	54.44 N	130.30 E
Kup'yans'k	83	49.42 N	37.38 E
Kup'yans'k-Vuzlovyy	83	49.39 N	37.39 E
Kupychiv	78	51.00 N	24.44 E
Kuqa	90	41.43 N	82.54 E
Kür (Kura) ≃, Asia	84	39.24 N	49.19 E
Kur ≃, Ross.	89	48.44 N	134.14 E
Kur, Pulau I	164	5.20 S	132.00 E
Kura (Kür) ≃, Asia	84	39.24 N	49.19 E
Kura ≃, Ross.	84	44.06 N	44.57 E
Kurabuchi	94	36.25 N	138.48 E
Kurach	84	41.36 N	47.46 E
Kurach ≃	84	41.40 N	48.11 E
Kuragaty	85	43.06 N	72.59 E
Kuragaty ≃	85	43.57 N	73.34 E
Kuragino	86	53.53 N	92.40 E
Kurahashi	96	34.06 N	132.30 E
Kurahashi-jima I	96	34.08 N	132.31 E
Kuraj	86	56.42 N	95.29 E
Kurajlysaj	80	50.07 N	51.51 E
Kurakaki	270	34.59 N	135.28 E
Kurakhivka	83	48.02 N	37.23 E
Kurakhove	83	47.59 N	37.16 E
Kurakino, Ross.	80	52.33 N	44.03 E
Kurakino, Ross.	82	54.30 N	35.48 E
Kurakovo	82	54.05 N	37.14 E
Kūrāli	123	30.50 N	76.35 E
Kuram	85	43.33 N	78.08 E
Kuramā', Ḥarrat △[9]	128	24.30 N	40.15 E
Kurama-yama ∧	96	35.07 N	135.46 E
Kuraminskij chrebet ∧∧	85	40.45 N	70.10 E
Kuramo Waters ⊂	273a	6.26 N	3.26 E
Kuranami	268	35.27 N	140.00 E
Kuraon	124	24.59 N	82.05 E
Kurar ◆[8]	272c	19.11 N	72.52 E
Kurašasaj	86	50.18 N	56.55 E
Kurashiki	96	34.35 N	133.46 E
Kurasiki → Kurashiki	96	34.35 N	133.46 E
Kurate	96	33.47 N	130.41 E
Kurauli	124	27.24 N	78.59 E
Kuraymah	140	18.33 N	31.51 E
Kurayoshi	96	35.26 N	133.49 E
Kurayyimah	132	32.16 N	35.36 E
Kurba	80	57.34 N	39.32 E
Kurba ≃	88	52.02 N	108.30 E
Kurbağa Gölü ⊜	130	38.21 N	35.17 E
Kurbağalı ≃	267b	40.59 N	29.02 E
Kurbatovo	86	55.34 N	91.10 E
Kurbulik	88	53.45 N	108.57 E
Kurčaloj	84	43.12 N	46.05 E
Kurchatov	78	51.39 N	35.36 E
Kur-Čilik ≃	85	43.50 N	78.06 E
Kurčum	86	48.37 N	83.40 E
Kurdaj	85	43.21 N	74.59 E
Kürdämir	84	40.21 N	48.08 E
Kurdgelauri	84	41.58 N	45.32 E
Kür dili >[2]	84	39.03 N	49.13 E
Kurdistan □[9]	128	37.00 N	45.00 E
Kurdufān al-Janūbīyah □[4]	140	11.00 N	30.00 E
Kurdufān ash-Shamālīyah □[4]	140	14.00 N	29.45 E
Kurduvādi	122	18.05 N	75.26 E
Kurdyumivka	83	48.28 N	37.59 E
Kure, Austl.	164	15.27 S	124.33 E
Kure, Nihon	96	34.14 N	132.34 E
Küre, Tür.	130	41.48 N	33.43 E
Kure Atoll I[1]	14	28.25 N	178.25 W
Küre Dağları ∧∧	130	41.45 N	34.00 E
Kurejka ≃	74	66.30 N	87.12 E
Kurejskaja	88	58.56 N	111.20 E
Kurenalus	26	65.21 N	26.59 E
Kurenec	76	54.33 N	26.57 E
Kuresaare	76	58.15 N	22.28 E
Kurgal'džinskij	86	50.36 N	70.01 E
Kurgan	86	55.26 N	65.18 E
Kurgan Oblast' □[4]	86	55.30 N	64.30 E
Kurgan-T'ube	120	37.50 N	68.48 E
Kurgan T'ube □[4]	85	38.15 N	68.50 E
Kurgasyn	86	49.15 N	66.43 E
Kurgatej	88	54.23 N	99.27 E
Kurgolovo	76	59.46 N	28.06 E
Kurhan-Mechetnyy, hora ∧[2]	83	48.06 N	39.21 E
Kuria I	14	0.14 N	173.25 E
Kuria Muria Islands → Khurīyā Murīyā, Jazā'ir II	118	17.30 N	56.00 E
Kuriasol	126	22.06 N	86.39 E
Kuridala	166	21.17 S	140.30 E
Kurīgrām	124	25.49 N	89.39 E
Kurihama	268	35.13 N	139.43 E
Kurihashi	94	36.08 N	139.42 E
Kurikka	26	62.37 N	22.25 E
Kurilen → Kuril'skije ostrova II	74	46.10 N	152.00 E
Kurilen-Strasse → Pervyj Kuril'skij proliv ʯ	74	50.50 N	156.36 E
Kuriles, Islas → Kuril'skije ostrova II	74	46.10 N	152.00 E
Kuril Islands → Kuril'skije ostrova II	74	46.10 N	152.00 E
Kurilovka	80	50.44 N	48.02 E
Kuril'sk	74	45.14 N	147.53 E
Kuril'skije ostrova (Kuril Islands) II	74	46.10 N	152.00 E
Kuril Strait → Pervyj Kuril'skij proliv ʯ	74	50.50 N	156.36 E
Kuril Trench ✢[1]	6	47.00 N	155.00 E
Kuřim	30	49.18 N	16.32 E
Kurimoto	94	35.49 N	140.30 E
Kurin'	78	51.09 N	32.44 E
Ku-Ring-Gai Chase National Park ♠	170	33.38 S	151.15 E
Kurinjippadi	122	11.34 N	79.36 E
Kurinwás ≃	236	12.49 N	83.41 W
Kuripapango	172	39.23 S	176.21 E
Kuriyama, Nihon	92a	43.03 N	141.47 E
Kuriyama, Nihon	94	36.52 N	139.37 E
Kurja, Ross.	24	61.42 N	57.09 E
Kurja, Ross.	86	51.36 N	82.19 E
Kurjanovskaja	76	60.19 N	41.33 E
Kurkijoki	26	61.18 N	29.54 E
Kurkino, Ross.	76	53.26 N	38.40 E
Kurkino, Ross.	265b	55.53 N	37.23 E
Kurkliai	76	55.25 N	25.03 E
Kurl ◆[8]	263	51.35 N	7.35 E
Kurla ◆[8]	272c	19.05 N	72.53 E
Kurlackoje	83	47.21 N	39.03 E
Kurleja	88	52.11 N	119.11 E
Kurlin	80	51.48 N	51.00 E
Kurlovskij	80	55.27 N	40.36 E
Kurmanajevka	80	52.31 N	52.06 E
Kurmani	126	22.47 N	89.53 E
Kurmankol'	80	49.09 N	48.27 E
Kurmenty	85	42.48 N	78.15 E
Kurmuk	140	10.33 N	34.17 E
Kurnell	274a	34.01 S	151.13 E
Kurnell Peninsula >[1]	274a	34.02 S	15.11 E
Kurnool	122	15.50 N	78.03 E
Kurobane	94	36.51 N	140.07 E
Kurobe	94	36.51 N	137.26 E
Kurobe ≃	94	36.55 N	137.25 E
Kurobe-dam ◆[6]	94	36.36 N	137.38 E
Kurodashō	96	35.01 N	135.00 E
Kurogi	96	33.12 N	130.40 E
Kurohone	94	36.30 N	139.17 E
Kuroishi	92	40.38 N	140.36 E
Kuroiso	94	36.58 N	140.03 E
Kuroo-tōge)(	96	35.11 N	134.12 E
Kuropatkino, Ross.	80	46.32 N	45.20 E
Kuropatkino, Uzb.	85	39.57 N	67.27 E
Kurort-Darasun	88	51.12 N	113.44 E
Kurose	96	34.19 N	132.40 E
Kurose ≃	96	34.13 N	132.36 E
Kuro-shima I, Nihon	93b	30.50 N	129.57 E
Kuro-shima I, Nihon	175d	24.19 N	124.05 E
Kurosu	268	35.51 N	139.23 E
Kurovo	82	55.49 N	36.00 E
Kurovskoje	82	55.34 N	38.55 E
Kurow	172	44.44 S	170.28 E
Kuroya	268	35.55 N	139.44 E
Kurrajong	170	33.33 S	150.40 E
Kurram	120	30.06 N	66.31 E
Kurram ≃	123	32.36 N	71.20 E
Kurri Kurri	170	32.49 S	151.29 E
Kuršab ≃	85	40.46 N	73.06 E
Kursavka	84	44.28 N	42.31 E
Kursela	124	25.27 N	87.15 E
Kuršėnai	76	56.00 N	22.56 E
Kurseong	120	26.53 N	88.17 E
Kursk	78	51.42 N	36.12 E
Kurskaja	84	44.03 N	44.27 E
Kurskaja kosa >[2]	76	55.18 N	21.00 E
Kurskij zaliv ⊂	76	55.00 N	21.00 E
Kursk Oblast' □[4]	78	51.40 N	36.00 E
Kursk Station ◆[5]	265b	55.46 N	37.40 E
Kuršumlija	38	43.08 N	21.17 E
Kurşunlu, Tür.	130	40.51 N	33.16 E
Kurşunlu, Tür.	130	38.40 N	37.51 E
Kurtalan	130	37.57 N	41.42 E
Kurtamyš	86	54.55 N	64.27 E
Kurtatsch → Cortaccia	64	46.19 N	11.13 E
Kürten, Dtsch.	56	51.03 N	7.16 E
Kurten, Tx., U.S.	222	30.47 N	96.16 W
Kurthasanlı	130	38.20 N	32.11 E
Kurth Lake ⊜	222	31.26 N	94.42 W
Kūrtī	140	18.07 N	31.33 E
Kurtino	82	54.59 N	38.17 E
Kurtinskoje vodochranilišče ⊜[1]	85	43.50 N	76.20 E
Kurtistown	229d	19.36 N	155.03 W
Kurtoğlu Burnu >	130	36.35 N	28.50 E
Kurtušibinskij chrebet ∧∧	88	52.10 N	93.30 E
Kurty ≃	85	44.05 N	76.20 E
Kurtz	218	38.58 N	86.12 W
Kuru, Sūd.	140	7.43 N	26.31 E
Kuru, Suomi	26	61.52 N	23.44 E
Kuru ≃	140	9.08 N	26.57 E
Kurucaşile	130	41.50 N	32.43 E
Kuruçay	130	39.39 N	38.29 E
Kuruçeşme ◆[8]	267b	41.03 N	29.02 E
Kuruktag ∧∧	90	41.30 N	90.00 E
Kurum	164	4.45 S	145.55 E
Kuruman	158	27.28 S	23.28 E
Kuruman ≃	158	26.56 S	20.39 E
Kurumanheuwels ∧∧[2]	158	27.40 S	23.25 E
Kurumdy, gora ∧	85	39.28 N	73.32 E
Kurume	96	33.19 N	130.31 E
Kurumkan	88	54.18 N	110.18 E
Kurun ≃	144	5.30 N	34.17 E
Kurunegala	122	7.29 N	80.22 E
Kurungbaja, Tanjung >	115b	8.15 S	120.35 E
Kurung Tank ⊜[1]	124	22.19 N	82.14 E
Kurunzulaj	88	51.00 N	117.10 E
Kuruqi	89	48.58 N	123.50 E
Kurur, Jabal ∧	140	20.31 N	31.32 E
Kurusaj	85	40.35 N	69.24 E
Kurushima-kaikyo ʯ	96	34.07 N	133.00 E
Kuruson-zan ∧	96	34.12 N	130.58 E
Kuryachivka, Ukr.	83	49.39 N	38.42 E
Kuryachivka, Ukr.	83	49.22 N	39.36 E
Kurylys	86	48.38 N	60.47 E
Kuryongp'o	98	35.59 N	129.32 E
Kurzeme □[9]	76	56.50 N	22.30 E
Kusa	86	55.20 N	59.29 E
Kusabe	270	34.31 N	135.29 E
Kuşadası	130	37.51 N	27.15 E
Kuşadası Körfezi ⊂	130	37.50 N	27.08 E
Kusak ≃	86	47.50 N	75.45 E
Kušalino	76	57.07 N	36.05 E
Kusan-ni, Taehan	98	37.43 N	128.49 E
Kusan-ni, Taehan	271b	37.29 N	126.45 E
Kusatsu, Nihon	94	36.37 N	138.36 E
Kusatsu, Nihon	94	35.00 N	135.57 E
Kusawa Lake ⊜	180	60.20 N	136.15 W
Kusaybah, Bi'r ⊤[4]	140	22.41 N	29.55 E
Kuščovskaja	78	46.33 N	39.37 E
Kuse	96	35.04 N	133.45 E
Kusel	56	49.32 N	7.24 E
Kusey	54	52.36 N	11.05 E
Kuş Gölü ⊜	130	40.10 N	27.57 E
Kuş Gölü Milli Parkı ♠	130	40.15 N	27.55 E
Kushaka	150	10.32 N	6.48 E
Kushālgarh	120	23.10 N	74.27 E
Kusheriki	150	10.33 N	6.28 E
Kushi	174m	26.33 N	128.06 E
Kushida ≃	94	34.36 N	136.34 E
Kushigata	94	35.36 N	138.28 E
Kushihiki	268	35.55 N	139.36 E
Kushikino	92	31.44 N	130.16 E
Kushima	92	31.29 N	131.14 E
Kushimoto	92	33.28 N	135.47 E
Kushira	270	34.28 N	135.43 E
Kushiro	92a	42.58 N	144.23 E
Kushnytsya	78	48.27 N	23.14 E
Kushog Lake ⊜	212	45.05 N	78.48 W
Kushtia	124	23.55 N	89.07 E
Kushuhum	78	47.42 N	35.14 E
Kushui	102	42.11 N	94.25 E
Kusiro → Kushiro	92a	42.58 N	144.23 E
Kusiyāra ≃	120	24.36 N	91.44 E
Kuška	128	35.16 N	62.20 E
Kuška ≃	128	36.00 N	62.40 E
Kuskokwim ≃	180	60.17 N	162.27 W
Kuskokwim, North Fork ≃	180	63.06 N	154.37 W
Kuskokwim, South Fork ≃	180	63.06 N	154.37 W
Kuskokwim Bay ⊂	180	59.45 N	162.25 W
Kuskokwim Mountains ∧∧	180	62.30 N	156.00 W
Kuskovo ◆[8]	265b	55.44 N	37.49 E
Kuškušara	24	64.58 N	40.21 E
Kuśmā	124	28.14 N	83.41 E
Kušmurun	86	52.27 N	64.36 E
Kušmurun, ozero ⊜	86	52.40 N	64.48 E
Küsnacht	58	47.19 N	8.35 E
Kušnarenkovo	86	55.06 N	55.22 E
Kusŏng	98	39.59 N	125.15 E
Kusria	272b	22.58 N	88.14 E
Kussharo-ko ⊜	92a	43.38 N	144.21 E
Küssnacht am Rigi	58	47.05 N	8.27 E
Kustanaj	86	53.10 N	63.35 E
Kustanaj □[8]	86	53.00 N	63.00 E
Kustar'ovka	80	54.16 N	42.16 E
Küsten-Gebirge → Coast Mountains ∧∧	176	55.00 N	129.00 W
Küstenkanal ≅	52	52.57 N	7.18 E
Küsten-Ketten → Coast Ranges ∧∧	178	41.00 N	123.30 W
Kusthalia	126	23.29 N	87.03 E
Kūstī	140	13.10 N	32.40 E
Kusu, Nihon	94	34.55 N	136.38 E
Kusu, Nihon	96	33.16 N	131.09 E
Kušum ≃	80	48.54 N	50.32 E
Kusumba	272b	22.27 N	88.24 E
Kusumbāni ∧	126	21.57 N	86.26 E
Kušumskij	80	51.38 N	48.21 E
Kusung	98	36.18 N	128.55 E
Kusunoki	96	34.03 N	131.15 E
K'us'ur	74	70.39 N	127.15 E
Kušva	86	58.18 N	59.45 E
Kut, Ko I	110	11.40 N	102.35 E
Kuta	150	9.52 N	6.43 E
Kuta ≃	88	56.46 N	105.40 E
Kutabaru	112	0.44 S	102.56 E
Kutabuloh	114	3.28 N	97.04 E
Kutacane	114	3.30 N	97.48 E
Kütahya	130	39.25 N	29.59 E
Kütahya □[4]	130	39.20 N	29.30 E
Kutais	78	44.32 N	39.18 E
Kutaisi	84	42.15 N	42.40 E
Kutāmat al-Ghābah	142	30.55 N	30.54 E
Kutanibong	114	3.53 N	96.22 E
Kutaradja → Banda Aceh	114	5.34 N	95.20 E
Kutarere	172	38.03 S	177.09 E
Kutasawang	114	5.08 N	96.54 E
Kutch, Rann of (Rann of Kachchh) ◆[1]	120	24.05 N	70.10 E
Kutchan	92a	42.54 N	140.45 E
Kutcharo-ko ⊜	92a	45.09 N	142.19 E
Kutejnikovo	83	47.34 N	39.46 E
Kutenholz	52	53.29 N	9.19 E
Kuteynykove	83	47.49 N	38.18 E
Kutima	88	57.10 N	108.16 E
Kutima ≃	88	57.08 N	108.14 E
Kutina	36	45.29 N	16.46 E
Kutiyāna	120	21.38 N	69.59 E
Kutkai	110	23.27 N	97.56 E
Kutluškino	80	55.14 N	50.24 E
Kutná Hora	30	49.57 N	15.16 E
Kutno	30	52.15 N	19.23 E
Kutoarjo	115a	7.43 S	109.54 E
Kutomara	88	51.06 N	118.49 E
Kutse Game Reserve ◆[4]	156	23.30 S	24.05 E
Kutsuki	94	35.21 N	135.55 E
Küttigen	58	47.25 N	8.03 E
Kuttura	24	68.24 N	26.28 E
Kuttusoja	24	67.46 N	28.50 E
Kuttuzi	265a	59.45 N	30.04 E
Kutu	152	2.44 S	18.09 E
Kutubdia Island I	120	21.50 N	91.52 E
Kutubu, Lake ⊜	164	6.23 S	143.18 E
Kutukovo	80	54.26 N	40.31 E
Kutulik	88	53.21 N	102.48 E
Kutulo, Lagh ≃	154	2.08 N	40.56 E
Kutuluk ≃	80	53.19 N	51.09 E
Kutum	140	14.12 N	24.40 E
Kutu-Moke	152	3.12 S	17.21 E
Kúty, Slvk.	30	48.40 N	17.03 E
Kuty, Ukr.	78	48.16 N	25.10 E
Kutztown	210	40.31 N	75.46 W
Kuujjuaq	176	58.06 N	68.25 W
Kuuli-Majak	128	40.14 N	52.42 E
Kuurne	50	50.51 N	3.17 E
Kuusamo	26	65.58 N	29.11 E
Kuusankoski	26	60.54 N	26.38 E
Kuva	85	40.32 N	72.05 E
Kuvak-Nikol'skoje	80	53.37 N	43.30 E
Kuvandyk	86	51.28 N	57.21 E
Kuvango	152	14.28 S	16.20 E
Kuvasaj	85	40.18 N	71.58 E
Kuvet ≃	180	69.14 N	175.00 E
Kuvšinovo	76	57.02 N	34.10 E
Kuwabara	270	34.53 N	135.15 E
Kuwait → Al-Kuwayt	128	29.20 N	47.59 E
Kuwait (Al-Kuwayt) □[1], Asia	118	29.30 N	47.45 E
Kuwait (Al-Kuwayt) □[1], Asia	128	29.30 N	47.45 E
Kuwait Bay → Kuwayt, Jūn al- ⊂	128	29.30 N	48.00 E
Kuwana	94	35.04 N	136.42 E
Kuwayt, Jūn al- (Kuwait Bay) ⊂	128	29.30 N	48.00 E
Kuyāli	126	22.31 N	86.11 E
Kuyal'nyts'kyy lyman ⊜	78	46.40 N	30.42 E
Kuybyshev → Samara	80	53.12 N	50.09 E
Kuybysheve, Ukr.	78	47.22 N	36.39 E
Kuybysheve, Ukr.	78	44.38 N	33.52 E
Kuybyshevka	78	47.37 N	31.42 E
Kuye ≃	102	38.30 N	110.44 E
Kūysanjaq	128	36.05 N	44.38 E
Kuyucak, Tür.	130	37.51 N	38.21 E
Kuyucak, Tür.	130	37.55 N	28.28 E
Kuyuwini ≃	246	2.16 N	58.16 W
Kuyuyukak, Cape >	180	56.54 N	156.50 W
Kuzaranda	24	62.22 N	35.37 E
Kuze	94	35.33 N	136.30 E
Kuze ◆[8]	270	34.57 N	135.43 E
Kuzedejevo	86	53.20 N	87.10 E
Kuzemivka	83	49.31 N	37.59 E
Kuzemyn	78	50.09 N	34.39 E
Kužener	80	56.48 N	48.56 E
Kuženkino	76	57.44 N	33.59 E
Kuzitrin ≃	180	65.10 N	165.28 W
Kuzkejevo	80	55.46 N	52.48 E
Kuz'miniči	76	54.16 N	33.42 E
Kuz'minka ≃	265a	59.48 N	30.31 E
Kuz'minki ◆[8]	265b	55.42 N	37.48 E
Kuz'mino, Ross.	82	55.09 N	37.53 E
Kuz'mino, Ross.	82	56.36 N	37.55 E
Kuzmiščevo	82	54.46 N	37.12 E
Kuz'movka	74	62.19 N	92.02 E
Kuznečicha	80	54.43 N	49.38 E
Kuznečikovo	82	56.13 N	36.35 E
Kuzneck, Ross.	80	53.07 N	46.36 E
Kuzneck → Novokuzneck, Ross.	86	53.45 N	87.06 E
Kuzneckij Alatau ∧∧	86	54.45 N	88.00 E
Kuznečnoje	26	61.09 N	29.52 E
Kuznecova	89	46.16 N	138.03 E
Kuznecovka	76	56.18 N	28.33 E
Kuznecovo, Ross.	82	55.30 N	38.21 E
Kuznecovo, Ross.	82	55.27 N	36.57 E
Kuznecovo, Ross.	86	59.15 N	63.28 E
Kuznecovskij	80	47.25 N	40.57 E
Kuznecy	82	55.51 N	38.40 E
Kuznetsk → Kuzneck	80	53.07 N	46.36 E
Kuznetsovo-Mykhaylivka	83	47.27 N	38.13 E
Kuznetsovs'k	78	51.22 N	25.53 E
Kuzomen', Ross.	24	64.17 N	42.53 E
Kuzomen', Ross.	24	66.17 N	36.54 E
Kuzovatovo	80	53.33 N	47.41 E
Kuzucubelen	130	36.51 N	34.27 E
Kuzuha	270	34.52 N	135.41 E
Kuzuryū ≃	94	36.13 N	136.08 E
Kuzuu	94	36.24 N	139.37 E
Kuzyaka	130	41.14 N	33.44 E
Kvænangen ⊂[2]	24	70.05 N	21.13 E
Kværndrup	41	55.10 N	10.32 E
Kvaisi	84	42.31 N	43.40 E
Kvaløy I	24	69.40 N	18.30 E
Kvaløya I	24	70.37 N	23.52 E
Kvam	26	61.40 N	9.42 E
Kvanløse	41	55.39 N	11.41 E
Kvanndal	26	60.29 N	6.36 E
Kvareli	84	41.56 N	45.54 E
Kvarner ⊂	36	44.45 N	14.15 E
Kvarnerić ʯ	36	44.45 N	14.35 E
Kvarnsveden	40	60.31 N	15.24 E
Kvarntorp	40	59.08 N	15.15 E
Kvarsa	80	56.58 N	53.57 E
Kvarsebo	40	58.39 N	16.39 E
Kvašenki	82	56.48 N	37.33 E
Kvenna ≃	26	60.01 N	7.56 E
Kverkfjöll ∧	24a	64.43 N	16.38 W
Kvichak Bay ⊂	180	58.48 N	157.30 W
Kvicksund	40	59.27 N	16.19 E
Kvidinge	41	56.08 N	13.04 E
Kvien ⊜	40	60.24 N	13.48 E
Kvikkjokk	24	66.55 N	17.50 E
Kvilda	60	49.01 N	13.35 E
Kvina ≃	26	58.17 N	6.56 E
Kvismare kanal ≅	40	59.12 N	15.11 E
Kvissleby	26	62.17 N	17.21 E
Kvistbro	40	59.09 N	14.49 E
Kvistgård	41	55.59 N	12.30 E
Kvitok	88	56.03 N	98.30 E
Kwa ≃	152	3.10 S	16.11 E
Kwachaga	154	5.38 S	38.08 E
Kwada	164	6.09 S	141.53 E
Kwahae-ri ◆[8]	271b	37.33 N	126.50 E
Kwahu Plateau ∧∧[1]	150	6.30 N	0.30 W
Kwai → Khwae Noi ≃	110	14.00 N	99.33 E
Kwajalein I[1]	14	9.05 N	167.20 E
Kwajok	140	8.19 N	28.00 E
Kwakoegron	250	5.15 N	55.20 W
Kwale, Kenya	154	4.11 S	39.27 E
Kwale, Nig.	150	5.46 N	6.26 E
Kwambilo ≃	273b	4.26 S	15.20 E
Kwa-Mbonambi	158	28.36 S	32.05 E
Kwamisa ∧	150	7.08 N	1.53 W
Kwamouth	152	3.10 S	16.12 E
Kwa Mtoro	154	5.14 S	35.26 E
Kwanak-san ∧	271b	37.27 N	126.58 E
Kwando (Cuando) ≃	152	18.27 S	23.32 E
Kwangchow → Guangzhou	100	23.06 N	113.16 E
Kwangju	98	35.09 N	126.54 E
Kwangju □[4]	98	35.09 N	126.55 E
Kwango (Cuango) ≃	152	3.14 S	17.23 E
Kwangsi Chuang Autonomous Region → Guangxi Zhuangzu Zizhiqu □[4]	102	24.00 N	109.00 E
Kwangtung → Guangdong □[4]	90	23.00 N	113.00 E
Kwangwazi	154	7.47 S	38.15 E
Kwangyang	98	34.59 N	127.34 E
Kwania, Lake ⊜	154	1.45 N	32.45 E
Kwanmo-bong ∧	98	41.42 N	129.13 E
Kwansan-ni	271b	37.43 N	126.51 E
Kwanto Plain → Kantō-heiya ⩡	94	36.00 N	139.30 E
Kwara □[3]	150	8.45 N	5.00 E
Kware	150	13.12 N	5.14 E
Kwa-Thema	273d	26.18 S	28.23 E
Kwatisore	164	3.15 S	134.57 E
Kwazulu → Natal □[4]	158	28.40 S	30.40 E
Kweichow → Guizhou □[4]	102	27.00 N	107.00 E
Kweihwa → Hohhot	102	40.51 N	111.40 E

Symbol	English	Deutsch	Español	Français	Português
≃	River	Fluß	Río	Rivière	Rio
≅	Canal	Kanal	Canal	Canal	Canal
⌊	Waterfall, Rapids	Wasserfall, Stromschnellen	Cascada, Rápidos	Chute d'eau, Rapides	Cascata, Rápidos
ʯ	Strait	Meeresstraße	Estrecho	Détroit	Estreito
⊂	Bay, Gulf	Bucht, Golf	Bahía, Golfo	Baie, Golfe	Baía, Golfo
⊜	Lake, Lakes	See, Seen	Lago, Lagos	Lac, Lacs	Lago, Lagos
⩩	Swamp	Sumpf	Pantano	Marais	Pântano
⩐	Ice Features, Glacier	Eis- und Gletscherformen	Accidentes Glaciales	Formes glaciaires	Acidentes glaciares
⊤	Other Hydrographic Features	Andere Hydrographische Objekte	Otros Elementos Hidrográficos	Autres données hydrographiques	Outros acidentes hidrográficos

Symbol	English	Deutsch	Español	Français	Português
✢	Submarine Features	Untermeerische Objekte	Accidentes Submarinos	Formes de relief sous-marin	Acidentes submarinos
□	Political Unit	Politische Einheit	Unidad Politica	Entité politique	Unidade política
⊌	Cultural Institution	Kulturelle Institution	Institución Cultural	Institution culturelle	Instituição cultural
⊥	Historical Site	Historische Stätte	Sitio Histórico	Site historique	Sitio histórico
♠	Recreational Site	Erholungs- und Ferienort	Sitio de Recreo	Centre de loisirs	Area de Lazer
⊠	Airport	Flughafen	Aeropuerto	Aéroport	Aeroporto
■	Military Installation	Militäranlage	Instalación Militar	Installation militaire	Instalação militar
◆	Miscellaneous	Verschiedenes	Misceláneo	Divers	Diversos

ENGLISH / DEUTSCH

Name	Page / Seite	Lat.°′ / Breite°′	Long.°′ / Länge°′ E = Ost
Kweijang → Guiyang	102	26.35 N	106.43 E
Kweilin → Guilin	102	25.17 N	110.17 E
Kweisui → Hohhot	102	40.51 N	111.40 E
Kweiyang → Guiyang	102	26.35 N	106.43 E
Kwekwe	154	18.55 S	29.49 E
Kweneng □ 5	156	24.00 S	24.00 E
Kwenge (Caengo) ≃	152	4.50 S	18.42 E
Kwesimintim	150	4.54 N	1.47 W
Kwethluk	180	60.49 N	161.27 W
Kwethluk ≃	180	60.46 N	161.26 W
Kwidzyn	30	53.45 N	18.56 E
Kwigillingok	180	59.51 N	163.08 W
Kwiguk	180	62.45 N	164.28 W
Kwiha	144	13.31 N	39.32 E
Kwikila	164	9.48 S	147.41 E
Kwilu (Cuilo) ≃	152	3.22 S	17.22 E
Kwinana	168a	32.15 S	115.48 E
Kwitaro ≃	246	3.19 N	58.47 W
Kwobrup	162	33.37 S	117.46 E
Kwoka, Gunung ∧	164	0.31 S	132.27 E
Kwolla	150	9.00 N	9.15 E
Kwun Tong	271d	22.19 N	114.12 E
Kyabé	146	9.27 N	18.57 E
Kyabra	166	26.18 S	143.10 E
Kyabra Creek ≃	166	25.36 S	142.55 E
Kyabram	166	36.19 S	145.03 E
Kyaikkami	110	16.04 N	97.34 E
Kyaiklat	110	16.26 N	95.44 E
Kyaikto	110	17.18 N	97.01 E
Kya-in	110	16.02 N	98.08 E
Kyaka	154	1.16 S	31.25 E
Kyalite	166	34.57 S	143.29 E
Kyancutta	166	33.08 S	135.34 E
Ky Anh	110	18.05 N	106.18 E
Kyat-aw	110	12.29 N	98.19 E
Kyaukhnyat	110	18.15 N	97.31 E
Kyaukkyi	110	18.19 N	96.46 E
Kyaukme	110	22.32 N	97.02 E
Kyaukpa	110	13.05 N	98.59 E
Kyaukpyu, Mya.	110	19.05 N	93.52 E
Kyaukpyu, Mya.	110	19.26 N	93.33 E
Kyaukse	110	21.36 N	96.08 E
Kyauktaw	110	20.51 N	92.59 E
Kyaunggon	110	17.06 N	95.11 E
Kybartai	76	54.39 N	22.45 E
Kybean	171b	36.22 S	149.25 E
Kybeyan Range ⋏	171b	36.10 S	149.30 E
Kyburz	226	38.47 N	120.18 W
Kydra	171b	36.27 S	149.23 E
Kyeamba	171b	35.26 S	147.37 E
Kyeamba Creek ≃	171b	35.06 S	147.29 E
Kyebang-san ∧	98	37.43 N	128.29 E
Kyegegwa	154	0.29 N	31.03 E
Kyeikdon	110	16.00 N	98.24 E
Kyeintali	110	18.00 N	94.29 E
Kyenjojo	154	0.37 N	30.38 E
Kyeryong-san Kukrip Kongwŏn ♦	98	36.21 N	127.13 E
Kyes Peak ∧	224	47.57 N	121.19 W
Kyffhäuser-Denkmal ⊥	54	51.23 N	11.06 E
Kyffhäuser Gebirge ⋏	54	51.23 N	11.05 E
Kyidaunggan	110	19.53 N	96.12 E
Kyindwe	110	20.58 N	93.51 E
Kyje ⊸ 8	54	50.04 N	14.32 E
Kyjov	30	49.01 N	17.08 E
Kykladen → Kikládhes II	38	37.30 N	25.00 E
Kykotsmovi Village	200	35.52 N	110.37 W
Kykva	80	57.22 N	53.50 E
Kylās ∧	124	25.18 N	90.45 E
Kyle, Sk., Can.	184	50.50 N	108.02 W
Kyle, S.D., U.S.	198	43.25 N	102.10 W
Kyle, Tx., U.S.	196	29.59 N	97.52 W
Kyle □ 9	46	55.29 N	4.24 W
Kyle, Lake ⊜ 1	154	20.14 S	31.00 E
Kyleakin	46	57.16 N	5.44 W
Kyle of Lochalsh	46	57.17 N	5.43 W
Kylerhea	46	57.14 N	5.41 W
Kylertown	214	41.00 N	78.10 W
Kylestrome	46	58.16 N	5.02 W
Kyll ≃	56	49.48 N	6.42 E
Kyllburg	56	50.02 N	6.35 E
Kym ≃	42	52.14 N	0.17 W
Kymen lääni □ 4	26	61.00 N	28.00 E
Kymijoki ≃	26	60.30 N	26.52 E
Kyn	86	57.52 N	58.38 E
Kyndby	41	55.48 N	11.56 E
Kyneton	169	37.15 S	144.27 E
Kynnefjäll ∧ 2	26	58.42 N	11.41 E
Kynšperk nad Ohří	54	50.04 N	12.32 E
Kynuna	166	21.35 S	141.55 E
Kyodong-do I	98	37.45 N	126.16 E
Kyoga, Lake ⊜	154	1.30 N	33.00 E
Kyōga-misaki ›	96	35.46 N	135.13 E
Kyogle	166	28.37 S	153.00 E
Kyoha-ri	271b	37.46 N	126.46 E
Kyohyŏn-ni	271b	37.43 N	126.58 E
Kyom ≃	140	8.58 N	28.13 E
Kyŏmip'o → Songnim	98	38.44 N	125.38 E
Kyonan	94	35.07 N	139.50 E
Kyondo	110	16.35 N	98.03 E
Kyŏnggi Do □ 4	98	37.30 N	127.15 E
Kyŏnggi-man ⊂	98	37.25 N	126.00 E
Kyŏngju	98	35.51 N	129.14 E
Kyŏngju Kukrip Kongwŏn ♦	98	35.47 N	129.15 E
Kyŏngsan	98	35.48 N	128.43 E
Kyŏngsang Namdo □ 4	98	35.15 N	128.30 E
Kyŏngsang Pukdo □ 4	98	36.15 N	128.45 E
Kyŏngsŏng, C.M.I.K.	98	41.35 N	129.36 E
Kyŏngsŏng → Sŏul, Taehan	98	37.33 N	126.58 E
Kyŏngwŏn	98	42.48 N	130.09 E
Kyônkadun	110	16.04 N	95.38 E
Kyonmange	110	16.30 N	95.50 E
Kyonpyaw	110	17.18 N	95.12 E
Kyotera	154	0.33 S	31.19 E
Kyōto, Nihon	94	35.00 N	135.45 E
Kyōto, Nihon	270	35.00 N	135.45 E
Kyōto □ 5	94	35.05 N	135.45 E
Kyōto-bonchi ⋏	270	35.03 N	135.45 E
Kyōto Race Track ♦	270	34.54 N	135.44 E
Kyōto University ɤ 2	270	35.02 N	135.46 E
Kyōwa	94	36.19 N	140.03 E
Kyōyomi-dake ∧	96	33.31 N	131.02 E
Kypšak, ozero ⊜	86	50.09 N	68.28 E
Kyra	88	49.36 N	111.58 E
Kyra ≃	88	49.24 N	112.19 E
Kyrčany	80	57.37 N	50.10 E
Kyren	88	51.41 N	102.08 E
Kyrenia → Girne	130	35.20 N	33.19 E
Kyrgyzstan □ 1, Asia	72	41.30 N	75.00 E
Kyrgyzstan □ 1, Asia	85	41.30 N	75.00 E
Kyritz	54	52.56 N	12.23 E
Kyrkheden	40	60.10 N	13.29 E
Kyrkkazyk	85	42.30 N	72.20 E
Kyrksæterøra	26	63.17 N	9.06 E
Kyrkslätt (Kirkkonummi)	26	60.07 N	24.26 E
Kyrö	26	60.42 N	22.45 E
Kyrönjoki ≃	26	63.14 N	21.45 E
Kyrösjärvi ⊜	26	61.45 N	23.10 E
Kyröskoski	26	61.40 N	23.11 E
Kyrta	24	64.04 N	57.42 E
Kyrykivka	78	50.22 N	35.07 E
Kyrykkuduk	80	49.51 N	51.54 E
Kyshen'ky	78	48.53 N	34.08 E
Kyshyn	78	51.08 N	27.41 E
Kyslivka	83	49.38 N	37.53 E
Kyslyakivka	78	46.44 N	31.59 E
Ky Son	110	19.24 N	104.08 E
Kyštovka	86	56.33 N	76.38 E
Kyštym	86	55.42 N	60.34 E
Kysykkamys	80	49.14 N	50.19 E
Kyte ≃	190	42.00 N	89.19 W
Kytlym	86	59.30 N	59.12 E
Kytmanovo	86	53.28 N	85.28 E
Kyūhōji	270	34.38 N	135.35 E
Kyunchaung	110	15.33 N	98.15 E
Kyundon	110	20.31 N	95.44 E
Kyungyi I	110	15.04 N	97.44 E
Kyunhla	110	23.21 N	95.18 E
Kyuquot	182	50.02 N	127.23 W
Kyuquot Sound ʉ	182	50.05 N	127.15 W
Kyūroku-jima I	92	40.32 N	139.29 E
Kyū-shizudani-gakkō ⊥	96	34.45 N	134.13 E
Kyūshū I	92	33.00 N	131.00 E
Kyushu-Palau Ridge ⌖ 3	14	20.00 N	136.00 E
Kyūshū-sanchi ⋏	92	32.35 N	131.17 E
Kywebwe	110	18.42 N	96.25 E
Kywong	166	34.59 S	146.44 E
Kyyiv (Kiev)	78	50.26 N	30.31 E
Kyyiv □ 4	78	50.15 N	30.30 E
Kyyivs'ke vodoskhovyshche ⊜ 1	78	51.00 N	30.25 E
Kyyjärvi	26	63.02 N	24.34 E
Kyyvesi ⊜	26	61.58 N	27.07 E
Kyzas	86	52.20 N	89.20 E
Kyzyl	88	51.42 N	94.27 E
Kyzylagaš	86	45.54 N	81.37 E
Kyzylaryk	85	43.57 N	70.42 E
Kyzylbejit	85	41.30 N	72.24 E
Kyzyl-Chaja	86	50.03 N	89.54 E
Kyzyl-Chem (Šišchid) ≃	88	51.21 N	96.58 E
Kyzyl-Džar	85	41.17 N	72.02 E
Kyzylemgek	85	41.57 N	74.56 E
Kyzylespe	86	47.27 N	73.53 E
Kyzylkak, ozero ⊜	86	53.25 N	73.48 E
Kyzyl-Kija	85	40.16 N	72.08 E
Kyzyl-Kommuna	86	48.44 N	67.32 E
Kyzylkum ⊸ 2	72	42.00 N	64.00 E
Kyzylkup	128	40.38 N	53.58 E
Kyzyl-Mažalyk	86	51.10 N	90.32 E
Kyzylmazar	85	39.39 N	68.25 E
Kyzyloba	80	49.37 N	50.38 E
Kyzylsu ≃	85	39.17 N	71.23 E
Kyzyltas, gory ⋏	86	48.30 N	74.50 E
Kyzyltau	86	47.53 N	72.05 E
Kyzylt'ob'o	85	42.13 N	75.16 E
Kyzyltu, Kaz.	86	47.46 N	59.08 E
Kyzyltu, Kaz.	86	47.43 N	75.42 E
Kyzyltu, Kyrg.	85	42.11 N	76.40 E
Kyzyluj	86	48.07 N	65.28 E
Kyzylžar	86	48.17 N	69.39 E
Kzyl-Kuga	80	48.28 N	53.01 E
Kzyl-Orda	86	44.48 N	65.28 E
Kzyl-Orda □ 8	86	45.00 N	64.00 E
Kzyltu	86	53.38 N	72.20 E
L			
La'a	102	29.44 N	101.26 E
Laa an der Thaya	61	48.43 N	16.23 E
Laaben	61	48.06 N	15.52 E
Laaber	60	49.04 N	11.53 E
Laaberberg	60	48.46 N	12.01 E
Laab im Walde	264b	48.09 N	16.11 E
Laacher See ⊜	56	50.25 N	7.16 E
Laaerberg ∧ 2	264b	48.09 N	16.24 E
Laage	54	53.56 N	12.20 E
La Aguja, Cabo de ›	246	11.18 N	74.12 W
Laakajärvi ⊜	26	63.50 N	27.55 E
Laakirchen	64	47.58 N	13.49 E
La Albuera	34	38.43 N	6.49 W
La Alcarria ⊸ 1	34	40.45 N	2.45 W
La Aldea	234	20.54 N	101.29 W
La Aldehuela	266a	40.18 N	3.36 W
La Algaba	34	37.28 N	6.01 W
La Almarcha	34	39.41 N	2.22 W
La Almunia de Doña Godina	34	41.29 N	1.22 W
Laanecoorie Reservoir ⊜ 1	169	36.52 S	143.53 E
La Antigua, Salina ≚	252	30.00 S	66.06 W
La Antorcha, Cerro ∧	234	21.43 N	102.45 W
Laar ⊸ 8	263	51.28 N	6.43 E
La Araucanía □ 4	252	38.45 S	72.30 W
La Arena, Pan.	236	7.58 N	80.28 W
La Arena, Perú	248	5.20 S	80.44 W
Laas → Lasa	64	46.37 N	10.42 E
Laas Caanood	144	8.28 N	47.21 E
La Ascención	232	24.20 N	99.55 W
Laas Dawaco	144	10.28 N	49.05 E
Laas Dhaareed	144	10.10 N	45.59 E
Laase	54	53.04 N	11.18 E
Laas Qoray	144	11.10 N	48.13 E
La Asunción	246	11.02 N	63.53 W
La Atravesada, Loma ∧ 2	232	29.57 N	112.12 W
Laatzen	52	52.19 N	9.47 E
Laau Point ›	229a	21.06 N	157.19 W
La Aurora	286e	33.36 S	70.38 W
La Azufrosa	196	28.14 N	100.50 W
Laba ≃	78	45.11 N	39.42 E
La Babia	232	28.34 N	102.04 W
Labadie	219	38.31 N	90.51 W
Labadieville	194	29.50 N	90.57 W
La Baie	186	48.19 N	70.53 W
La Balme-de-Sillingy	58	45.58 N	6.02 E
La Balme-les-Grottes	62	45.51 N	5.20 E
Laban	208	37.24 N	76.17 W
La Banda	252	27.44 S	64.15 W
La Bandera, Cerro ∧	232	24.35 N	105.07 W
La Bañeza	34	42.18 N	5.54 W
La Barca	234	20.17 N	102.34 W
La Barceloneta ⊸ 8	266d	41.22 N	2.11 E
La Barge	200	42.15 N	110.11 W
La Barge Creek ≃	200	42.14 N	110.10 W
La Barra	236	12.54 N	83.32 W
La Barre-en-Ouche	50	48.57 N	0.40 E
La Barrita	236	14.05 N	91.03 W
La Barr Meadows	226	39.11 N	121.02 W
Labason	116	8.04 N	122.31 E
La Bassée	50	50.32 N	2.48 E
Labastide-Murat	32	44.39 N	1.34 E
La Bastide-Puylaurent	62	44.36 N	3.54 E
La Bâte	261	48.35 N	2.01 E
La Baule-Escoublac	32	47.17 N	2.24 W
La Bazoche-Gouet	50	48.08 N	0.59 E
L'Abbé	261	48.34 N	1.50 E
Labdah (Leptis Magna) ⊥	146	32.38 N	14.18 E
Labé	150	11.19 N	12.17 W
Labe (Elbe) ≃	30	53.50 N	9.00 E
Labégude	62	44.39 N	4.22 E
La Bégude-Blanche	62	43.55 N	6.08 E
La Bégude-de-Mazenc	62	44.32 N	4.56 E
Labelle, P.Q., Can.	206	46.16 N	74.44 W
La Belle, Fl., U.S.	220	26.45 N	81.26 W
La Belle, Mo., U.S.	219	40.07 N	91.54 W
Labelle □ 6	206	46.20 N	75.00 W
Labelle, Lac ⊜, P.Q., Can.	206	46.13 N	74.52 W
La Belle, Lac ⊜, Wi., U.S.	216	43.08 N	88.31 W
Labengke, Pulau I	112	3.27 S	122.25 E
La Bérarde	62	44.56 N	6.18 E
Laberge, Lake ⊜	180	61.11 N	135.12 W
La Berra ∧	58	46.41 N	7.11 E
Laberweinting	60	48.48 N	12.19 E
La Besace	56	49.34 N	4.58 E
Labette Creek ≃	198	37.03 N	95.05 W
Labi	112	4.25 N	114.22 E
La Biche ≃	182	55.01 N	112.44 W
Labico	66	41.47 N	12.53 E
Labin	36	45.05 N	14.07 E
Labinsk	84	44.38 N	40.44 E
Labis	114	2.23 N	103.02 E
La Bisbal	34	41.57 N	3.03 E
Łabiszyn	30	52.57 N	17.55 E
Lablābah, Wādī al- ∨	273c	30.02 N	31.19 E
La Blanca	286e	33.31 S	70.41 W
La Blanca Grande, Laguna ⊜	252	38.26 S	63.55 W
Labná ⊥	232	20.11 N	89.34 W
Labo	116	14.09 N	122.51 E
Labo ≃	116	14.11 N	122.56 E
Labo, Mount ∧	116	14.01 N	122.48 E
Laboe	54	54.24 N	10.15 E
La Boissière	261	48.46 N	1.59 E
La Boissière-Ecole	261	48.41 N	1.39 E
La Bollène-Vésubie	62	43.59 N	7.20 E
La Bonneville-sur-Iton	50	49.00 N	1.02 E
Laboratory	214	40.09 N	80.13 W
Laborde, Arg.	252	33.09 S	62.51 W
La Borde, Fr.	261	48.32 N	2.50 E
Laborec ≃	30	48.36 N	22.00 E
Laborie	241f	13.45 N	61.00 W
Labouchere, Mount ∧	162	25.12 S	118.18 E
Labouheyre	32	44.13 N	0.55 W
Laboulaye	252	34.07 S	63.24 W
La Bouverie	50	50.24 N	3.52 E
La Boyera, Ven.	286c	10.25 N	66.50 W
La Boyera, Ven.	286c	10.23 N	66.57 W
Lābpur	126	23.50 N	87.49 E
Labrador ⊸ 1	176	54.00 N	62.00 W
Labrador Basin ⌖ 1	16	53.00 N	48.00 W
Labrador City	176	52.57 N	66.55 W
Labrador Sea ⊤ 2	176	57.00 N	53.00 W
Lábrea, Bra.	248	7.16 S	64.47 W
La Brea, Trin.	241r	10.15 N	61.37 W
Labrède	32	44.41 N	0.31 W
La Bresse	58	48.00 N	6.53 E
La Brévine	58	46.59 N	6.36 E
Labrieville, Réserve ♦	186	49.20 N	69.40 W
La Brigue	62	44.04 N	7.37 E
La Brillanne	62	43.55 N	5.53 E
Labrit	32	44.07 N	0.33 W
La Broquerie	184	49.28 N	96.27 W
Labroye	50	50.17 N	1.59 E
Labry	56	49.10 N	5.52 E
Labuan, Pulau I	112	5.21 N	115.13 E
Labuha	164	0.37 S	127.29 E
Labuhan	115a	6.22 S	105.50 E
Labuhanbajo	115b	8.29 S	119.54 E
Labuhanbatu	114	2.12 N	100.12 E
Labuhanbilik	114	2.31 N	100.10 E
Labuhandeli	114	3.45 N	98.41 E
Labuhanhaji, Indon.	114	3.33 N	97.00 E
Labuhanhaji, Indon.	115b	8.42 S	116.34 E
Labuhanmarege	112	7.06 S	120.40 E
Labuhanmaringgai	115a	5.21 S	105.48 E
Labuhanruku	114	3.13 N	99.35 E
Labuk ≃	112	5.54 N	117.30 E
Labuk, Telukan ⊂	116	6.07 N	117.46 E
Labu Kananga	115b	8.08 S	117.47 E
Labutta	110	16.09 N	94.46 E
Labytnangi	72	66.39 N	66.21 E
Lač, Ross.	24	63.18 N	54.28 E
Laç, Shq.	38	41.38 N	19.43 E
Lac □ 5	146	13.30 N	14.15 E
Lača, ozero ⊜	24	61.20 N	38.48 E
La Cadena	196	25.53 N	104.12 W
L'Acadie	275a	45.19 N	73.21 W
L'Acadie ≃	206	45.29 N	73.16 W
La Cadière-d'Azur	62	43.12 N	5.46 E
Lacadivas, Islas → Lakshadweep II	122	10.00 N	73.00 E
Laca Jahuira ≃	248	19.21 S	67.54 W
La Cal ≃	248	17.27 S	58.15 W
Lac-à-la-Tortue	206	46.37 N	72.38 W
La Calera, Chile	252	32.47 S	71.12 W
La Calera, Perú	286d	12.12 S	76.54 W
Lac-Allard	186	50.33 N	63.25 W
Lacamas Creek ≃	224	46.20 N	122.55 W
Lacamas Lake ⊜	224	45.37 N	122.26 W
La Campana, Esp.	34	37.34 N	5.26 W
La Campana, Méx.	234	22.45 N	105.35 W
La Cañada	234	20.37 N	100.19 W
La Cañada, Cerro ∧	234	21.24 N	99.13 W
La Canada Flintridge	228	34.12 N	118.12 W
La Canada Verde Creek ≃	280	33.52 N	118.02 W
Lacanau	32	44.59 N	1.05 W
Lacanau, Lac de ⊂	32	44.58 N	1.07 W
La Candelaria, Arg.	252	26.06 S	65.06 W
La Candelaria, Méx.	200	31.07 N	106.29 W
La Cañiza	34	42.13 N	8.16 W
La Canourgue	32	44.26 N	3.13 E
Lacantún ≃	232	16.36 N	90.39 W
La Capelle-en-Thiérache	50	49.58 N	3.55 E
La Capelle-lès-Boulogne	50	50.44 N	1.42 E
Lacapelle-Marival	32	44.44 N	1.54 E
La Carlota, Arg.	252	33.26 S	63.18 W
La Carlota, Pil.	116	10.25 N	122.55 E
Lacarne	214	41.31 N	83.03 W
La Carolina	34	38.15 N	3.37 W
La Casita	234	23.43 N	104.46 W
La Castellana	116	10.20 N	123.03 E
Lacaune	32	43.43 N	2.42 E
Lac-Bellemare	206	46.34 N	72.55 W
Lac-Brome	206	45.13 N	72.31 W
Laccadive, Minicoy, and Amīndīvi → Lakshadweep □ 3	122	10.00 N	73.00 E
Laccadive Islands → Lakshadweep II	122	10.00 N	73.00 E
Lacchiarella	62	45.19 N	9.08 E
Lacco Ameno	68	40.45 N	13.54 E
Lac Courte Oreilles Indian Reservation ⊸ 4	190	45.55 N	91.19 W
Lac du Flambeau	190	45.59 N	89.51 W
Lac du Flambeau Indian Reservation ⊸ 4	190	45.59 N	89.53 W
Laceby	44	53.32 N	0.10 W
Lacedonia	68	41.03 N	15.25 E
La Ceiba, Hond.	236	15.47 N	86.50 W
La Ceiba, Ven.	246	9.28 N	71.04 W
La Celle-les-Bordes	261	48.38 N	1.57 E
La Celle-Saint-Cloud	261	48.51 N	2.08 E
La Celle-Saint-Cyr	50	47.58 N	3.18 E
La Center, Ky., U.S.	194	37.04 N	88.58 W
La Center, Wa., U.S.	224	45.52 N	122.40 W
Lacepede Bay ⊂	166	36.47 S	139.45 E
Lacerdónia	156	18.01 S	35.30 E
Laces (Latsch)	64	46.37 N	10.52 E
Lac-Etchemin	186	46.24 N	70.30 W
Lacey	224	47.02 N	122.49 W
Lacey Creek ≃	278	41.50 N	88.03 W
Laceyville	210	41.39 N	76.10 W
Lac-Frontière	186	46.42 N	70.00 W
La Chaise-Dieu	62	45.19 N	3.42 E
La Chambre	62	45.22 N	6.18 E
La Chapelle-d'Angillon	50	47.22 N	2.26 E
La Chapelle-en-Vercors	62	44.58 N	5.25 E
La Chapelle-Gauthier	261	48.33 N	2.54 E
La Chapelle-la-Reine	50	48.19 N	2.35 E
La Chapelle-Saint-Luc	50	48.20 N	4.03 E
La Chapelle-Vendômoise	50	47.40 N	1.15 E
La Charité-sur-Loire	50	47.11 N	3.01 E
La Chartre-sur-le-Loir	50	47.44 N	0.35 E
La Châtaigneraie	32	46.39 N	0.44 W
La Châtre	32	46.35 N	1.59 E
Lachaussée, Étang de ⊜	56	49.02 N	5.48 E
La Chaux-de-Fonds	58	47.06 N	6.50 E
Lachay, Punta ›	248	11.18 S	77.39 W
Lach Dennis	262	53.15 N	2.26 W
Lachdenpochja	24	61.31 N	30.08 E
Lachen	58	47.12 N	8.51 E
Lachenaie	275a	45.42 N	73.34 W
Lachendorf	52	52.37 N	10.14 E
Lachhmangarh Sīkar	120	27.49 N	75.02 E
L'achi	80	55.20 N	41.56 E
Lachine	206	45.26 N	73.40 W
Lachine, Canal de ≋	275a	45.26 N	73.40 W
Lachine, Rapides de ⌞	275a	45.25 N	73.36 W
La Chira, Punta ›	286d	12.13 S	77.03 W
La Chivera	286c	10.37 N	66.54 W
Lachkaltsap Indian Reserve ⊸ 4	182	55.03 N	129.34 W
Lachlan ≃	166	34.21 S	143.57 E
La Chorrera, Col.	246	0.44 S	73.01 W
La Chorrera, Pan.	236	8.53 N	79.47 W
L'achoviči, Bela.	76	53.02 N	26.16 E
L'achoviči, Bela.	76	52.23 N	27.55 E
L'achovskije ostrova II	74	73.30 N	141.00 E
La Choza	258	34.47 S	59.07 W
La Choza, Arroyo ≃	258	34.40 S	58.58 W
Lachta ⊸ 8	265a	60.00 N	30.09 E
Lachtinskij Razliv, ozero ⊜	265a	60.00 N	30.11 E
Lachute	206	45.38 N	74.20 W
Lachva	76	52.13 N	27.04 E
La Ciénaga	252	27.30 S	66.57 W
La Ciénega	234	16.54 N	96.46 W
Lâçin	130	40.47 N	34.54 E
La Cinta Creek ≃	196	35.24 N	104.06 W
La Ciotat	62	43.10 N	5.36 E
La Cisterna	286e	33.33 S	70.41 W
La Citadelle ⊥	238	19.35 N	72.14 W
La Ciudad	234	23.44 N	105.42 W
Lack	48	54.33 N	7.35 W
Lackawanna	210	42.49 N	78.49 W
Lackawanna □ 6	210	41.24 N	75.40 W
Lackawanna ≃	210	41.21 N	75.47 W
Lackawanna, Lake ⊜	276	40.57 N	74.42 W
Lackawanna State Park ♦	210	41.33 N	75.44 W
Lackawaxen	210	41.29 N	74.59 W
Lackawaxen ≃	210	41.29 N	74.59 W
Lackey	208	37.14 N	76.33 W
Lackland Air Force Base ■	196	29.27 N	98.37 W
Läckö	26	58.41 N	13.13 E
Lackoje	76	58.05 N	38.08 E
Lac La Belle	216	43.09 N	88.32 W
Lac la Biche	182	54.46 N	111.58 W
Lac la Hache	182	51.49 N	121.28 W
Lac la Ronge Provincial Park ♦	184	55.15 N	104.55 W
La Clayette	32	46.18 N	4.19 E
Laclede, Id., U.S.	182	48.10 N	116.45 W
La Clede, Il., U.S.	219	38.53 N	88.43 W
Laclede, Mo., U.S.	194	39.47 N	93.09 W
La Clotilde	252	27.08 S	60.40 W
La Clusaz	58	45.54 N	6.25 E
La Cluse	58	46.10 N	5.34 E
La Cluse-et-Mijoux	58	46.53 N	6.23 E
Lacmalac	171b	35.19 S	148.19 E
Lac-Masson	206	46.02 N	74.04 W
Lac-Mégantic	188	45.36 N	70.53 W
Lacob ti-duyong, Mount ∧	116	17.35 N	121.09 E
La Cocha	252	27.47 S	65.34 W
Lacolle	206	45.05 N	73.22 W
Lacolle ≃	206	45.04 N	73.20 W
La Colle-sur-Loup	62	43.41 N	7.06 E
La Colmena	286a	19.36 N	99.18 W
La Colorada	232	28.41 N	110.25 W
La Columna → Bolívar, Pico ∧	246	8.30 N	71.02 W
La Coma	232	24.28 N	98.19 W
Lacombe, Ab., Can.	182	52.28 N	113.44 W
Lacombe, La., U.S.	194	30.18 N	89.56 W
Lacon	190	41.01 N	89.24 W
Lacona, Ia., U.S.	190	41.11 N	93.22 W
Lacona, N.Y., U.S.	212	43.38 N	76.04 W
La Concepción, Pan.	236	8.31 N	82.37 W
La Concepción, Ven.	246	10.38 N	71.50 W
La Condamine-Châtelard	62	44.27 N	6.45 E
Laconi	71	39.51 N	9.03 E
Laconia	188	43.31 N	71.28 W
La Conner	224	48.23 N	122.29 W
La Consulta	252	33.44 S	69.07 W
Lacoochee	220	28.27 N	82.10 W
La Coruña	34	43.22 N	8.23 W
La Coruña □ 4	34	43.00 N	8.35 W
Lacoste, Fr.	62	43.50 N	5.18 E
La Coste, Tx., U.S.	196	29.19 N	98.49 W
La Côte-Saint-André	62	45.23 N	5.15 E
La Courneuve	261	48.56 N	2.23 E
La Couronne	62	43.20 N	5.03 E
La Courtine	32	45.42 N	2.16 E
Lac qui Parle ≃	198	45.01 N	95.53 W
Lac qui Parle, West Branch ≃	198	44.55 N	96.02 W
La Crau	62	43.09 N	6.04 E
Lacre Punt ›	241s	12.02 N	68.15 W
La Crescent	190	43.49 N	91.18 W
La Crescenta	228	34.13 N	118.14 W
La Croft	214	40.39 N	80.35 W
Lacroix-Saint-Ouen	50	49.21 N	2.47 E
La Crosse, In., U.S.	216	41.19 N	86.53 W
La Crosse, Ks., U.S.	198	38.31 N	99.18 W
La Crosse, Va., U.S.	192	36.41 N	78.05 W
Lacrosse, Wa., U.S.	202	46.49 N	117.53 W
La Crosse, Wi., U.S.	190	43.48 N	91.14 W
La Crosse ≃	190	43.49 N	91.16 W
La Cruz, Arg.	252	29.10 S	56.38 W
La Cruz, Col.	246	1.35 N	76.58 W
La Cruz, C.R.	236	11.04 N	85.39 W
La Cruz, Méx.	196	28.33 N	100.48 W
La Cruz, Ur.	258	33.56 S	56.15 W
La Cruz, Cerro ∧	234	17.55 N	101.31 W
La Cruz de Río Grande	236	13.06 N	84.10 W
Lac-Saguay	206	46.30 N	75.09 W
Lac Seul	184	50.20 N	92.16 W
Lac Seul Indian Reserve ⊸ 4	184	50.15 N	92.10 W
La Cuchilla	234	18.54 N	103.19 W
La Cuesta, C.R.	236	8.30 N	82.50 W
La Cuesta, Méx.	234	20.10 N	104.51 W
La Cuesta, P.R.	240m	18.25 N	66.49 W
La Cumbre, Arg.	252	30.58 S	64.30 W
La Cumbre, Ven.	286c	10.32 N	66.57 W
La Cumbre, Volcán ∧ 1	246a	0.20 S	91.30 W
La Cure	58	46.28 N	6.05 E
Lacy Fork ≃	222	32.24 N	96.08 W
La Cygne	198	38.21 N	94.45 W
Lacy-Lakeview	222	31.37 N	97.06 W
Lada, Teluk ⊂	115a	6.29 S	105.44 E
Ladainha	255	17.39 S	41.44 W
Ladākh □ 9	120	35.10 N	76.10 E
Ladākh Range ⋏	120	34.00 N	78.00 E
Ladan	78	50.31 N	32.35 E
La Dang, Ko I	114	6.33 N	99.18 E
Ladang Jagor	114	4.42 N	101.35 E
Ladara	114	1.28 N	97.28 E
Ladário	248	19.01 S	57.35 W
Ladbergen	52	52.08 N	7.44 E
Ladby	41	55.26 N	10.38 E
Ladd	190	41.22 N	89.13 W
Låddenhøj ∧ 2	41	56.13 N	9.48 E
Ladder Creek ≃	198	38.48 N	100.52 W
Laddingford	260	51.12 N	0.25 E
Laddonia	219	39.14 N	91.38 W
Ladeburg	264a	52.42 N	13.35 E
La Défense ɤ	261	48.53 N	2.15 E
La Dehesa	286e	33.22 S	70.33 W
La Dent d'Oche ∧	58	46.21 N	6.44 E
Ladera Heights	280	33.59 N	118.22 W
La Désirade I	241o	16.19 N	61.03 W
Ládhi	38	41.27 N	26.17 E
Ladhurka	126	23.22 N	86.32 E
La Digue I	138	4.21 S	55.50 E
Lâdik	130	40.55 N	35.55 E
Ladinger Spitze ∧	61	46.51 N	14.39 E
L'adiny	24	61.33 N	38.20 E
Ladismith	158	33.30 S	21.16 E
Ladispoli	66	41.56 N	12.05 E
Lādīz	128	28.56 N	61.19 E
Ladner	224	49.05 N	123.05 W
Lādnūn	120	27.39 N	74.23 E
Ladoga	194	39.54 N	86.48 W
Ladoga, Lake → Ladožskoje ozero ⊜	24	61.00 N	31.30 E
La Dolorita	286c	10.29 N	66.47 W
Ladon	50	48.00 N	2.32 E
Ladonia	196	33.25 N	95.56 W
La Dorada	246	5.27 N	74.40 W
La Dormida	252	33.21 S	67.55 W
Lado Sarāi ⊸ 8	272a	28.32 N	77.12 E
Ladovskaja Balka	80	45.38 N	41.25 E
Ladožskaja	78	45.19 N	39.54 E
Ladožskoje Ozero	76	60.08 N	31.04 E
Ladožskoje ozero (Lake Ladoga) ⊜	24	61.00 N	31.30 E
Lādpur ⊸ 8	272a	28.44 N	76.59 E
Ladrillero, Golfo ⊂	254	49.20 S	75.37 W
Ladson	192	32.59 N	80.06 W
Ladue	219	38.38 N	90.23 W
Ladue ≃	180	63.09 N	140.25 W
Laduozong	102	31.27 N	97.19 E
Laduškin	76	54.36 N	20.11 E
Ladva	24	61.21 N	34.34 E
Ladva-Vetka	24	61.21 N	34.27 E
Lādwa	124	29.59 N	77.03 E
L'ady, Bela.	76	54.36 N	31.10 E
Lady, Fr.	261	48.35 N	2.54 E
L'ady, Ross.	76	58.38 N	28.47 E
Lady Ann Strait ʉ	176	75.40 N	79.50 W
Ladybank	46	56.16 N	3.08 W
Lady Barron	166	40.12 S	148.14 E
Ladybower Reservoir ⊜ 1	44	53.20 N	1.45 W
Ladybrand	158	29.19 S	27.25 E
Lady Elliot Island I	166	24.07 S	152.42 E
Lady Evelyn Lake ⊜	190	47.20 N	80.10 W
Lady Frere	158	31.44 S	27.16 E
Lady Grey	158	30.45 S	27.13 E
Lady Lake	220	28.55 N	81.55 W
Ladysmith, Austl.	171b	35.12 S	147.31 E
Ladysmith, B.C., Can.	182	48.58 N	123.49 W
Ladysmith, S. Afr.	158	28.34 S	29.45 E
Ladysmith, Wi., U.S.	190	45.27 N	91.06 W
Ladyženka	86	51.00 N	68.42 E
Ladyzhyn	78	48.41 N	29.15 E
Ladžanurges	84	42.37 N	42.50 E
Lae	164	6.45 S	147.00 E
Lae I 1	14	8.56 N	166.14 E
Laem, Khao ∧	110	14.27 N	101.30 E
Laem Ngop	110	12.10 N	102.26 E
La Encantada	232	25.17 N	101.04 W
La Encarnacion	234	23.23 N	98.01 W
Laer	52	52.03 N	7.21 E
Laer ⊸ 8	263	51.28 N	7.16 E
Lærdalsøyri	26	61.06 N	7.29 E
La Escondida	196	26.17 N	99.46 W
La Esmeralda, Méx.	232	27.17 N	103.39 W
La Esmeralda, Para.	252	22.13 S	62.38 W
La Esmeralda, Ven.	246	3.10 N	65.33 W
Læsø I	26	57.16 N	11.01 E
La Esperanza, Cuba	240p	22.46 N	83.44 W
La Esperanza, Hond.	236	14.20 N	88.10 W
La Esperanza, Méx.	196	26.46 N	104.00 W
La Esperanza, Méx.	200	32.06 N	114.47 W
La Esperanza, Perú	248	8.05 S	79.04 W
La Esperanza, P.R.	240m	18.22 N	66.07 W
La Estación ⊸ 8	266a	40.27 N	3.48 W
La Estrada	34	42.41 N	8.29 W
La Estrella, Bol.	248	16.30 S	63.45 W
La Estrella, Ven.	286c	10.25 N	66.48 W
La Estrella, Cerro ∧	286a	19.20 N	99.05 W
Lafa	89	43.50 N	127.19 E
La Falda	252	31.05 S	64.30 W
La Farge	190	43.34 N	90.38 W
LaFargeville	212	44.11 N	75.57 W
Lafayette, Fr.	62	45.35 N	5.04 E
Lafayette, Al., U.S.	194	32.53 N	85.24 W
Lafayette, Ca., U.S.	226	37.53 N	122.07 W
Lafayette, Co., U.S.	198	39.59 N	105.05 W
Lafayette, Ga., U.S.	192	34.42 N	85.16 W
Lafayette, In., U.S.	216	40.25 N	86.52 W
Lafayette, La., U.S.	194	30.13 N	92.01 W
Lafayette, Mn., U.S.	190	44.26 N	94.23 W
Lafayette, N.J., U.S.	210	41.05 N	74.41 W
La Fayette, N.Y., U.S.	210	42.54 N	76.06 W
Lafayette, Oh., U.S.	216	40.46 N	83.57 W
Lafayette, Or., U.S.	224	45.14 N	123.06 W
La Fayette, R.I., U.S.	207	41.34 N	71.28 W
Lafayette, Tn., U.S.	194	36.31 N	86.01 W
La Fayette, Tx., U.S.	222	32.54 N	94.51 W
Lafayette, Mount ∧	188	44.10 N	71.38 W
Lafayette Hill	285	40.05 N	75.15 W
Lafayette Reservoir ⊜ 1	282	37.53 N	122.08 W
Lafayette Water Tunnel ⊸ 5	282	37.54 N	122.12 W
La Fé	240p	21.45 N	82.45 W
La Fère	50	49.40 N	3.22 E
La Feria	196	26.09 N	97.49 W
Laferrere	288	34.45 S	58.35 W
La Ferrière-sur-Risle	50	48.59 N	0.48 E
La Ferté-Alais	50	48.29 N	2.21 E
La Ferté-Bernard	50	48.11 N	0.40 E
La Ferté-Frênel	50	48.50 N	0.30 E
La Ferté-Gaucher	50	48.47 N	3.18 E
La Ferté-Imbault	50	47.23 N	1.58 E
La Ferté-Macé	32	48.36 N	0.22 W
La Ferté-Milon	50	49.10 N	3.07 E
La Ferté-Saint-Aubin	50	47.43 N	1.56 E
La Ferté-sous-Jouarre	50	48.57 N	3.08 E
Laferté-sur-Amance	58	47.50 N	5.42 E
La Ferté-Vidame	50	48.37 N	0.55 E
La Ferté-Villeneuil	50	47.59 N	1.21 E
Lafferty	214	40.06 N	81.01 W
Laffrey	62	45.02 N	5.46 E
Lafia	150	8.30 N	8.30 E
Lafiagi	150	8.52 N	5.25 E
Laflamme ≃	190	48.56 N	77.18 W
Laflèche, P.Q., Can.	275a	45.30 N	73.28 W
Lafleche, Sk., Can.	184	49.43 N	106.35 W
La Flèche, Fr.	32	47.42 N	0.05 W
La Floresta	266d	41.27 N	2.04 E
La Florida, Chile	286e	33.33 S	70.34 W
La Florida, Esp.	266d	41.31 N	2.12 E
La Florida, Guat.	232	16.33 N	90.27 W
Lafnitz ≃	61	46.57 N	16.16 E
La Foa	175f	21.43 S	165.50 E
La Foce	62	44.08 N	9.47 E
La Follette	192	36.22 N	84.07 W
Lafon	154	5.02 N	32.27 E
Lafontaine, P.Q., Can.	206	45.48 N	74.01 W
La Fontaine, In., U.S.	216	40.40 N	85.43 W
Lafontaine, Parc ♦	275a	45.32 N	73.34 W
Lafourche, Bayou ≃	194	29.05 N	90.14 W
La Foux, Fr.	62	43.16 N	6.35 E
La Foux, Fr.	62	44.17 N	6.34 E
La Fragua	252	26.05 S	64.20 W
La Francia	252	31.24 S	62.38 W
La Fregeneda	34	40.59 N	6.52 W
La Frette-sur-Seine	261	48.58 N	2.11 E
La Fría	246	8.13 N	72.15 W
Lafrimbolle	58	48.36 N	7.01 E
La Fuente de San Esteban	34	40.48 N	6.15 W
Laga, Monti della ⋏	66	42.37 N	13.24 E
La Gacilly	28	47.46 N	2.09 W
Lagaip ≃	164	5.05 S	142.40 E
La Galite I	36	37.32 N	8.56 E
La Gallareta	252	29.34 S	60.23 W
La Gallega	34	41.54 N	3.16 W
Lagan	26	56.55 N	13.59 E
Lagan ≃, Sve.	26	56.33 N	12.56 E
Lagan ≃, N. Ire., U.K.	48	54.37 N	5.53 W
Lagangzong	120	28.05 N	91.04 E
Lagantu	102	42.20 N	108.22 E
La Garde	62	43.07 N	6.01 E
La Garde-Freinet	62	43.19 N	6.28 E
La Garenne-Colombes	261	48.55 N	2.15 E
Lagarina, Val ∨	64	45.45 N	11.00 E
Lagarto, Bra.	250	10.54 S	37.41 W
Lagarto, C.R.	236	10.07 N	84.56 W
Lagarto Creek ≃	196	28.08 N	97.56 W
Lagawe	116	16.49 N	121.06 E
Lagay	116	14.06 N	122.12 E
Lagayan	116	17.43 N	120.42 E
Lage, Dtsch.	52	51.59 N	8.48 E
Lage, Esp.	34	43.13 N	9.00 W
Lage, Zhg.	120	29.26 N	85.51 E
Lagedu	102	26.24 N	101.11 E
Lågen ≃, Nor.	26	59.03 N	10.05 E
Lågen ≃, Nor.	26	61.08 N	10.25 E
Lägerdorf	52	53.53 N	9.34 E
Lages	252	27.48 S	50.19 W
Lageuen	114	4.44 N	95.31 E
Lage Zwaluwe	52	51.43 N	4.41 E
Laggan	46	57.02 N	4.16 W
Laggan, Loch ⊜ 1	46	56.57 N	4.28 W
Laggan Bay ⊂	46	55.41 N	6.19 W
Lagginhorn ∧	58	46.11 N	8.01 E
Laghmān □ 4	120	35.00 N	70.15 E
Laghouat	148	33.50 N	2.59 E
Laghouat □ 5	148	32.00 N	3.30 E
Laghy	48	54.37 N	8.05 W
La Giettaz	62	45.52 N	6.30 E
La Giganta, Cerro ∧	234	21.08 N	101.19 W
La Giustiniana ⊸ 8	267a	41.59 N	12.24 E
La Gleize	56	50.25 N	5.51 E
La Gloria	246	8.37 N	73.48 W
Lagnieu	58	45.54 N	5.21 E
Lagny	50	48.52 N	2.43 E
Lagny-le-Sac	261	49.05 N	2.45 E
Lago	68	39.10 N	16.09 E
Lago, Mount ∧	224	48.51 N	120.32 W
Lagoa Branca	256	21.54 S	47.02 W
Lagoa da Prata	255	20.01 S	45.33 W
Lagoa Formosa	255	18.47 S	46.24 W
Lago Argentino → Calafate	254	50.20 S	72.18 W
Lagoa Santa	255	19.38 S	43.53 W
Lagoa Vermelha	252	28.13 S	51.32 W
Lago Blanco	254	45.55 S	71.15 W
Lago da Pedra	250	4.20 S	45.10 W
Lagodechi	84	41.49 N	46.18 E
Lagodechskij zapovednik ♦	84	41.53 N	46.22 E
Lagoinha	256	23.06 S	45.11 W
Lagolândia	255	15.37 S	49.02 W
Lagolovo	265a	59.42 N	30.00 E
Lagonegro	68	40.07 N	15.46 E
Lagonglong	116	8.48 N	124.47 E
Lagonoy	116	13.44 N	123.31 E
Lagonoy Gulf ⊂	116	13.35 N	123.45 E
Lagopesole, Castel di ⊥	68	40.48 N	15.45 E
Lago Posadas	254	47.32 S	71.45 W
Lagorai, Catena del ⋏	64	46.18 N	11.35 E
Lago Ranco	254	40.20 S	72.38 W
La Gorgue	50	50.38 N	2.42 E
Lagos, Ang.	152	16.04 S	17.03 E
Lagos, Nig.	150	6.27 N	3.24 E
Lagos, Nig.	273a	6.27 N	3.24 E
Lagos, Port.	34	37.06 N	8.40 W
Lagos □ 3	150	6.30 N	3.30 E
Lagos (Ikeja) Airport ⊠	273a	6.35 N	3.20 E
Lagos, University of ɤ 2	273a	6.32 N	3.24 E
Lagosanto	66	44.46 N	12.08 E
Lagos de Moreno	234	21.21 N	101.55 W
Lagos Harbour ⊂	273a	6.26 N	3.24 E
Lagos Island I	273a	6.27 N	3.26 E
Lagos Lagoon ⊂	273a	6.30 N	3.26 E
Lagos Terminus ⊸ 5	273a	6.28 N	3.23 E
La Gouèra	148	20.48 N	17.08 W
La Goulette	148	36.49 N	10.18 E
Lago Viedma	254	49.48 S	72.07 W
La Granadella	34	41.21 N	0.40 E
La Grand'Combe	62	44.13 N	4.02 E
La Grande	202	45.19 N	118.05 W
La Grande Deux, Réservoir ⊜ 1	176	53.40 N	76.55 W
La Grande Moucherolle ∧	62	45.00 N	5.34 E
La Grande Quatre, Réservoir ⊜ 1	176	54.00 N	73.15 W
La Grange, Austl.	162	18.41 S	121.45 E
LaGrange, Ca., U.S.	226	37.40 N	120.28 W
La Grange, Ga., U.S.	192	33.02 N	85.01 W
La Grange, Il., U.S.	216	41.48 N	87.52 W
Lagrange, In., U.S.	216	41.39 N	85.25 W
La Grange, Ky., U.S.	218	38.24 N	85.22 W
La Grange, Mo., U.S.	219	40.02 N	91.29 W
La Grange, N.C., U.S.	192	35.18 N	77.47 W
Lagrange, Oh., U.S.	214	41.14 N	82.07 W
La Grange, Tx., U.S.	222	29.54 N	96.52 W
Lagrange, Wy., U.S.	198	41.38 N	104.10 W
Lagrange □ 6	216	41.39 N	85.25 W
Lagrange Bay ⊂	162	18.38 S	121.42 E
La Grange Highlands	278	41.50 N	87.51 W
La Grange Lock and Dam ⊸ 5	219	39.57 N	90.32 W
La Grange Park	278	41.50 N	87.51 W
Lagrangeville	210	41.39 N	73.46 W
La Granja	286e	33.32 S	70.39 W
La Gran Piedra ∧	240p	20.01 N	75.38 W
La Gran Sabana ≚	246	5.30 N	61.30 W
La Grave	62	45.03 N	6.18 E
La Grita	246	8.08 N	71.59 W
Lagro	216	40.50 N	85.43 W
La Groise	50	50.05 N	3.41 E
La Grue Bayou ≃	194	34.05 N	91.10 W
Lagu	102	26.26 N	101.30 E
La Guadeloupe (Saint-Évariste)	188	45.57 N	70.56 W
La Guajira □ 5	246	11.30 N	72.30 W
La Guajira, Península de › 1	246	12.00 N	71.40 W
La Guardia, Arg.	252	29.33 S	65.27 W
La Guardia, Bol.	248	17.54 S	63.20 W
Laguardia, Esp.	34	42.33 N	2.35 W
La Guardia, Esp.	34	41.54 N	8.53 W
La Guardia Airport ⊠	210	40.46 N	73.53 W
La Gudiña	34	42.04 N	7.08 W
La Guêpière	261	48.35 N	1.50 E
La Guerche-de-Bretagne	32	47.56 N	1.14 W
La Guerche-sur-l'Aubois	32	46.57 N	2.57 E
Laguiole	32	44.41 N	2.51 E
Laguna, Bra.	252	28.29 S	48.47 W
Laguna, N.M., U.S.	200	35.02 N	107.22 W
Laguna □ 4	116	14.10 N	121.20 E
Laguna ≃	226	38.16 N	121.23 W
Laguna, Arroyo de la ≃	282	37.35 N	121.53 W
Laguna, Ilha da I	250	1.40 S	51.00 W
Laguna Beach	228	33.32 N	117.46 W
Laguna Blanca	240p	20.27 N	76.07 W
Laguna Blanca, Parque Nacional ♦	254	39.00 S	70.18 W
Laguna Creek ≃	200	36.54 N	109.45 W
Laguna Dam ⊸ 6	200	32.50 N	114.31 W

Symbols in the index entries represent the broad categories identified in the key at the right. Symbols with superior numbers (⋏ 1) identify subcategories (see complete key on page *I · 1).*

Symbole im Register stellen die rechts im Schlüssel erklärten Kategorien dar. Symbole mit hochgestellten Ziffern (⋏ 1) bezeichnen Unterabteilungen einer Kategorie (vgl. vollständiger Schlüssel auf Seite *I · 1).*

Los símbolos incluídos en el texto del índice representan las grandes categorías identificadas con la clave a la derecha. Los símbolos con numeros en su parte superior (⋏ 1) identifican las subcategorías (véase la clave completa en la página *I · 1).*

Les symboles de l'index représentent les catégories indiquées dans la légende à droite. Les symboles suivis d'un indice (⋏ 1) représentent des sous-catégories (voir légende complète à la page *I · 1).*

Os símbolos incluídos no texto do índice representam as grandes categorias identificadas com a chave à direita. Os símbolos com números em sua parte superior (⋏ 1) identificam as subcategorias (veja-se a chave completa à página *I · 1).*

∧ Mountain	Berg	Montaña	Montagne	Montanha
⋏ Mountains	Gebirge	Montañas	Montagnes	Montanhas
)(Pass	Paß	Paso	Col	Passo
∨ Valley, Canyon	Tal, Cañon	Valle, Cañón	Vallée, Canyon	Vale, Canhão
≚ Plain	Ebene	Llano	Plaine	Planície
› Cape	Kap	Cabo	Cap	Cabo
I Island	Insel	Isla	Île	Ilha
II Islands	Inseln	Islas	Îles	Ilhas
⏏ Other Topographic Features	Andere Topographische Objekte	Otros Elementos Topográficos	Autres données topographiques	Outros acidentes topográficos

ESPAÑOL

Nombre	Página	Lat.°′	Long.°′ W = Oeste
Laguna de Pozuelos, Monumento Natural ♦, Arg.	248	22.20 S	66.00 W
Laguna de Pozuelos, Monumento Natural ♦, Arg.	252	22.20 S	66.00 W
Laguna Hills	228	33.36 N	117.42 W
Laguna Indian Reservation ◂•[4]	200	35.00 N	107.20 W
Laguna Lake ⊜	226	35.16 S	120.42 W
Laguna Larga	252	31.46 S	63.48 W
Laguna Limpia	252	26.29 S	59.41 W
Laguna Niguel	228	33.31 N	117.43 W
Laguna Paiva	252	31.19 S	60.39 W
Laguna Park	222	31.52 N	97.23 W
Lagunas	248	5.14 S	75.38 W
Laguna San Rafael, Parque Nacional ♦	254	47.00 S	73.30 W
Lagunas de Chacagua, Parque Nacional ♦	234	16.00 N	97.00 W
Lagunas de Montebello, Parque Nacional ♦	236	16.05 N	91.45 W
Lagunas de Zempoala, Parque Nacional ♦	234	19.08 N	99.20 W
Lagundo	64	46.41 N	11.08 E
Lagunillas, Bol.	248	19.38 S	63.43 W
Lagunillas, Méx.	234	21.34 N	99.35 W
Lagunillas → Ciudad Ojeda, Ven.	246	10.12 N	71.19 W
Lagunillas, Ven.	246	8.31 N	71.24 W
Lagunillás, Laguna ⊜	248	15.44 S	70.43 W
Laguntara c	236	15.35 N	84.05 W
L'agušje	86	54.24 N	77.59 E
Laguyu	104	41.43 N	123.49 E
Laha	89	48.10 N	124.39 E
La Habana (Havana), Cuba	240p	23.08 N	82.22 W
La Habana (Havana), Cuba	286b	23.08 N	82.22 W
La Habana □[4]	240p	22.45 N	82.10 W
La Habana, Universidad de ◒[2]	286b	23.08 N	82.22 W
La Habra	228	33.55 N	117.56 W
La Habra Heights	280	33.57 N	117.57 W
Lahad Datu	112	5.02 N	118.19 E
Lahad Datu, Telukan c	112	4.50 N	118.30 E
Lahaina	229a	20.52 N	156.40 W
Laham	112	0.22 N	115.24 E
Lahār	124	26.12 N	78.57 E
La Harpe, Il., U.S.	190	40.35 N	90.58 W
La Harpe, Ks., U.S.	198	37.55 N	95.17 W
Lāharpur	124	27.43 N	80.54 E
Lahaska	208	40.21 N	75.02 W
Lahat, Indon.	112	3.48 S	103.32 E
Lahat, Malay.	114	4.33 N	101.02 E
La Hauteville	261	48.42 N	1.37 E
La Havane → La Habana	240p	23.08 N	82.22 W
LaHave ≃	186	44.14 N	64.20 W
La Haye → 's-Gravenhage	52	52.06 N	4.18 E
La Haye-du-Puits	32	49.18 N	1.33 W
La Häy-les-Rosas	261	48.47 N	2.21 E
Lähden	52	52.45 N	7.34 E
Lāhe	110	26.20 N	95.26 E
Laheria Sarai	124	26.07 N	85.54 E
Lahewa	114	1.24 N	97.11 E
Lahfān, Bi'r ⊤[4]	132	31.01 N	33.52 E
Lahi, Ava ⋓	174w	21.02 S	175.11 W
Lahıç	84	40.51 N	48.24 E
La Higuera	252	29.30 S	71.17 W
Laḥij	144	13.02 N	44.54 E
Lāhījān	128	37.12 N	50.01 E
Lāhithah	132	32.59 N	36.35 E
Lahn ≃	56	50.18 N	7.37 E
Lahnstein	56	50.19 N	7.36 E
Laholm	26	56.31 N	13.02 E
Laholmsbukten c	26	56.35 N	12.50 E
La Honda	226	37.19 N	122.16 W
La Honda Creek ≃	282	37.18 N	122.16 W
Lahontan Reservoir ⊜[1]	226	39.23 N	119.09 W
Lahontan State Recreation Area ♦	226	39.28 N	119.03 W
Lahor → Lahore, Pāk.	123	31.35 N	74.18 E
Lāhor, Pāk.	123	34.03 N	72.22 E
Lahore	123	31.35 N	74.18 E
La Horqueta	246	3.06 N	72.50 W
La Horqueta, Arroyo ≃	288	34.41 S	58.51 W
La Houssaye-en-Brie	261	48.45 N	2.53 E
Lahr	58	48.20 N	7.52 E
Lahri	120	29.11 N	68.13 E
Lāhrūd	128	38.30 N	47.49 E
Laḥṭah, Wādī V	142	29.44 N	32.45 E
Lahti	26	60.58 N	25.40 E
La Huaca	248	4.54 S	80.57 W
La Huacana	234	18.58 N	101.49 W
La Huerta, Méx.	234	19.28 N	104.39 W
La Huerta, N.M., U.S.	196	32.27 N	104.13 W
La Hunière	261	48.36 N	1.52 E
Lahuy Island I	116	13.56 N	123.50 E
Laï	146	9.24 N	16.18 E
Laiagam	164	5.30 S	143.20 E
Lai'an	100	32.27 N	118.25 E
Laibach → Ljubljana	36	46.03 N	14.31 E
Laibin	102	23.42 N	109.22 E
Lai Chau	110	22.02 N	103.10 E
Laichingen	58	48.29 N	9.41 E
Laichow Bay → Laizhou Wan c	98	37.36 N	119.30 E
Laide	46	57.52 N	5.32 W
Laidley	171a	27.38 S	152.24 E
Laidley Creek ≃	171a	27.31 S	152.24 E
Laidon, Loch ⊜	46	56.39 N	4.40 W
Laie	229c	21.39 N	157.55 W
Laifang	100	25.56 N	116.54 E
Laifeng, Zhg.	102	29.31 N	109.15 E
Laifeng, Zhg.	107	30.14 N	105.17 E
Laifengzhen	107	29.26 N	106.13 E
L'Aigle	50	48.45 N	0.38 E
L'Aigle Creek ≃	194	33.12 N	92.08 W
Laignes	50	47.50 N	4.22 E
Laigou	100	33.56 N	117.06 E
Laigueglia	62	43.58 N	8.09 E
Laihia	26	62.58 N	22.01 E
Lai-hka	110	21.16 N	97.40 E
Lailly-en-Val	50	47.46 N	1.41 E
Laïmbélé, Mont ∧	175f	16.20 S	167.31 E
Lainate	266b	45.34 N	9.02 E
Lainbach	61	47.38 N	14.46 E
La Independencia, Bahía de c	248	14.15 S	76.10 W
Laingsburg, S. Afr.	158	33.11 S	20.51 E
Laingsburg, Mi., U.S.	216	42.53 N	84.21 W
Lainioälven ≃	24	67.22 N	23.39 E
La Inmaculada	232	29.55 N	111.48 W
Laino Borgo	68	39.57 N	15.59 E
Lainsitz (Lužnice) ≃	61	49.13 N	14.42 E
Lainville	261	49.04 N	1.49 E
Lainz ◂•[8]	264b	48.11 N	16.17 E
Lainzer Tiergarten ♦	264b	48.10 N	16.14 E
Lair, Scot., U.K.	46	57.29 N	5.20 W
Lair, Ky., U.S.	218	38.20 N	84.18 W
Laird Hill	222	32.21 N	94.54 W
Lairdsville	210	41.14 N	76.37 W
Lairg	46	58.01 N	4.25 W
Laïri	146	10.49 N	17.06 E
Laïri, Batha de ≃	146	12.28 N	16.45 E
Laïriri, Pic ∧	175f	15.27 S	166.48 E
Lais, Indon.	112	0.47 N	120.27 E
Lais, Indon.	112	3.32 S	102.03 E
Lais, Pil.	116	6.20 N	125.39 E

FRANÇAIS

Nom	Page	Lat.°′	Long.°′ W = Ouest
Laisamis	154	1.36 N	37.48 E
Laiševo	80	55.24 N	49.32 E
Laishan	98	37.24 N	121.23 E
Laishui	105	39.23 N	115.42 E
Laissac	32	44.23 N	2.49 E
Laissey	58	47.18 N	6.14 E
Laisu	107	29.16 N	105.47 E
Laisvall	24	66.05 N	17.10 E
Laitan	107	29.06 N	106.10 E
Laitila	26	60.53 N	21.41 E
Laives (Leifers)	64	46.26 N	11.20 E
Laiwu	98	36.12 N	117.38 E
Laiwui	164	1.22 S	127.40 E
Laixi (Shuiji)	98	36.51 N	120.29 E
Laiya	116	13.40 N	121.24 E
Laiyang	98	36.58 N	120.44 E
Laiyuan, Zhg.	98	39.18 N	114.44 E
Laiyuan, Zhg.	100	25.36 N	117.01 E
Laizhou Wan (Laichow Bay) c	98	37.36 N	119.30 E
Laja ≃, Chile	252	37.16 S	72.43 W
Laja ≃, Méx.	234	20.30 N	100.46 W
Laja ≃, Ross.	24	66.20 N	56.16 E
Laja, Laguna de la ⊜	252	37.21 S	71.19 W
Laja, Salto del ∟	252	37.22 S	71.25 W
Lajajalpan ≃	234	20.17 N	97.32 W
La Jalca	248	6.29 S	77.43 W
La Jara	200	37.16 N	105.57 W
La Jara ◂•[1]	34	39.42 N	4.54 W
La Jara Canyon V	200	36.50 N	107.30 W
La Jara Creek ≃	200	37.22 N	105.46 W
La Jarrie	32	46.08 N	1.00 W
Lajas, Cuba	240p	22.25 N	80.18 W
Lajas, P.R.	240m	18.03 N	67.04 W
La Javie	62	44.10 N	6.21 E
Laje	255	13.10 S	39.25 W
Laje, Ilha da I	287a	22.57 S	43.09 W
Laje, Ponta da ›	266c	38.40 N	9.19 W
Laje, Ribeira de ≃	266c	38.41 N	9.19 W
Lajeado	252	29.27 S	51.58 W
Lajeado Velho ◂•[8]	287b	23.32 S	46.23 W
Lajedo	250	8.40 S	36.19 W
Lajes	250	5.41 S	36.14 W
Lajes, Ribeirão das ≃	256	22.38 S	43.42 W
Lajinha	255	20.09 S	41.37 W
Laji Shan ⟑	102	36.13 N	102.15 E
Lajkovo	265b	55.42 N	37.13 E
La Jolla, Ca., U.S.	204	32.51 N	117.16 W
La Jolla, Ca., U.S.	228	32.51 N	117.16 W
La Jolla, Point ›	228	32.51 N	117.17 W
Lajord	184	50.14 N	104.09 W
La Jose	214	40.50 N	78.41 W
Lajosmizse	30	47.02 N	19.34 E
La Joya, Méx.	196	26.26 N	101.08 W
La Joya, Perú	248	16.44 S	71.51 W
La Joya, Cerro ∧	234	20.06 N	101.38 W
La Joya, Laguna c	234	15.55 N	93.40 W
La Joya de Atotonilco	234	23.35 N	104.20 W
Lajta (Leitha) ≃	61	47.54 N	17.17 E
Lajtamak	86	58.25 N	67.25 E
Lajturi	84	41.55 N	41.55 E
La Junta	198	37.59 N	103.32 W
Lakaband	120	31.00 N	69.30 E
Lakahia, Teluk c	164	4.00 S	134.38 E
Lakamané	150	14.31 N	9.55 W
Lakar Kūh ∧	128	31.02 N	57.06 E
Lakatoro	175f	16.07 S	167.25 E
Lake	194	32.20 N	89.19 W
Lake □[6], Ca., U.S.	226	39.01 N	122.33 W
Lake □[6], Fl., U.S.	220	28.42 N	81.39 W
Lake □[6], Il., U.S.	216	42.22 N	87.50 W
Lake □[6], In., U.S.	216	41.25 N	87.22 W
Lake □[6], Oh., U.S.	214	41.43 N	81.15 W
Lake Accotink Park ♦	284c	38.48 N	77.14 W
Lake Albert	171b	35.10 S	147.23 E
Lake Alfred	220	28.05 N	81.43 W
Lake Alpine	226	38.28 N	120.00 W
Lake Andes	198	43.09 N	98.32 W
Lake Angelus	281	42.42 N	83.19 W
Lake Ariel	210	41.27 N	75.23 W
Lake Arrowhead	228	34.14 N	117.11 W
Lake Arthur, La., U.S.	194	30.04 N	92.40 W
Lake Arthur, N.M., U.S.	196	32.59 N	104.21 W
Lake Barcroft	284c	38.51 N	77.09 W
Lake Bathurst	170	35.01 S	149.36 E
Lake Benton	198	44.15 N	96.17 W
Lake Beseck	207	41.31 N	72.44 W
Lake Bluff	216	42.16 N	87.50 W
Lake Brownwood	196	31.49 N	99.02 W
Lake Buena Vista	220	28.23 N	81.31 W
Lake Butler	192	30.01 N	82.20 W
Lake Cable	214	40.52 N	81.27 W
Lake Camm	162	32.59 S	119.35 E
Lake Cargelligo	166	33.18 S	146.23 E
Lake Carmel	210	41.27 N	73.40 W
Lake Charles	194	30.13 N	93.13 W
Lake Chelan National Recreation Area ♦	224	48.20 N	120.40 W
Lake City, Ar., U.S.	194	35.48 N	90.26 W
Lake City, Co., U.S.	200	38.01 N	107.18 W
Lake City, Fl., U.S.	192	30.11 N	82.38 W
Lake City, Il., U.S.	219	39.45 N	88.43 W
Lake City, Ia., U.S.	198	42.16 N	94.44 W
Lake City, Mi., U.S.	190	44.20 N	85.12 W
Lake City, Mn., U.S.	190	44.26 N	92.16 W
Lake City, Pa., U.S.	214	42.00 N	80.20 W
Lake City, S.C., U.S.	192	33.52 N	79.45 W
Lake City, Tn., U.S.	192	36.13 N	84.09 W
Lake Clarke Shores	220	26.39 N	80.04 W
Lake Clark National Park ♦	180	60.30 N	153.15 W
Lake Coleridge	172	43.22 S	171.32 E
Lake Como, N.Y., U.S.	210	42.41 N	76.18 W
Lake Como, Pa., U.S.	210	41.51 N	75.20 W
Lake Corpus Christi State Park ♦	196	28.05 N	97.52 W
Lake Cowichan	224	48.50 N	124.03 W
Lake Creek ≃	222	30.16 N	95.29 W
Lake Crescent	224	48.06 N	123.50 W
Lake Crystal	190	44.06 N	94.13 W
Lake Dalecarlia	216	41.20 N	87.24 W
Lake Dallas	222	33.07 N	97.02 W
Lake Delta	210	43.17 N	75.28 W
Lake Delton	190	43.36 N	89.47 W
Lakedemonovka	83	47.12 N	38.33 E
Lake Dennison State Park ♦	207	42.38 N	72.05 W
Lake District ◂•[1]	44	54.30 N	3.10 W
Lake District National Park ♦	44	54.30 N	3.05 W
Lake Eliza	216	41.26 N	87.10 W
Lake Elsinore	228	33.38 N	117.20 W
Lake Elsinore State Recreation Area ♦	228	33.41 N	117.22 W
Lake Entrance ⋓	170	33.05 S	151.39 E
Lake Errock	224	49.13 N	122.02 W
Lake Eyre National Park ♦	166	28.30 S	137.30 E
Lake Fairfax County Park ♦	284c	38.58 N	77.19 W
Lake Fenton	216	42.52 N	83.43 W
Lakefield, On., Can.	212	44.26 N	78.16 W
Lakefield, S. Afr.	273d	26.11 S	28.18 E
Lakefield, Mn., U.S.	198	43.40 N	95.10 W
Lakefield National Park ♦	164	15.00 S	144.05 E
Lake Forest, Fl., U.S.	192	25.58 N	80.11 W
Lake Forest, Il., U.S.	216	42.12 N	87.53 W
Lake Forest, N.J., U.S.	276	40.58 N	74.36 W
Lake Forest Park	224	47.45 N	122.17 W
Lake Fork	219	39.58 N	89.21 W
Lake Fork ≃, Il., U.S.	219	40.05 N	89.25 W
Lake Fork ≃, Ut., U.S.	200	40.13 N	110.07 W

PORTUGUÊS

Nome	Página	Lat.°′	Long.°′ W = Oeste
Lake Fork, North Fork ≃	219	39.56 N	89.14 W
Lake Fork Creek ≃	222	32.36 N	95.21 W
Lake Fork Reservoir ⊜[1]	222	32.50 N	95.35 W
Lake Geneva	216	42.36 N	88.26 W
Lake George	188	43.25 N	73.42 W
Lake Grace	162	33.06 S	118.28 E
Lake Grinnell	276	41.06 N	74.38 W
Lake Grove	276	40.51 N	73.06 W
Lake Hamilton	220	28.07 N	81.42 W
Lake Harbor	220	26.42 N	80.48 W
Lake Harbour	176	62.51 N	69.53 W
Lake Harmony	210	41.04 N	75.36 W
Lake Havasu City	200	34.29 N	114.19 W
Lake Havasu State Park ♦	200	34.29 N	114.21 W
Lake Helen	220	28.58 N	81.14 W
Lake Hiawatha	210	40.52 N	74.22 W
Lake Hill	210	42.04 N	74.11 W
Lake Hills, In., U.S.	216	41.28 N	87.27 W
Lake Hills, Wa., U.S.	224	47.36 N	122.08 W
Lake Hopatcong	210	40.55 N	74.39 W
Lake Hughes	228	34.40 N	118.26 W
Lake Huntington	210	41.41 N	75.00 W
Lakehurst	208	40.00 N	74.18 W
Lakehurst Naval Air Station ■	208	40.01 N	74.18 W
Lake Illawarra	170	34.33 S	150.52 E
Lake Intervale	276	40.53 N	74.25 W
Lake in the Hills	216	42.10 N	88.19 W
Lake Isabella	204	35.39 N	118.28 W
Lake Jackson	222	29.02 N	95.26 W
Lake Jem	220	28.45 N	81.40 W
Lakekamu ≃	164	8.10 S	146.15 E
Lake Katrine	210	41.59 N	73.59 W
Lake King	162	33.05 S	119.40 E
Lake Lackawanna	210	40.57 N	74.42 W
Lakeland, Fl., U.S.	220	28.03 N	81.57 W
Lakeland, Ga., U.S.	192	31.02 N	83.04 W
Lakeland, Mi., U.S.	216	42.28 N	83.51 W
Lakeland, N.Y., U.S.	210	43.06 N	76.15 W
Lakeland Park	216	42.21 N	88.17 W
Lakeland Village	228	33.39 N	117.22 W
Lake Lenape	210	41.01 N	74.44 W
Lake Linden	190	47.11 N	88.26 W
Lake Lookover	276	41.09 N	74.24 W
Lake Loramie State Park ♦	216	40.23 N	84.20 W
Lake Louise, Ab., Can.	182	51.26 N	116.11 W
Lake Louise, Wa., U.S.	224	47.05 N	122.36 W
Lake Lucerne	214	41.24 N	81.21 W
Lake Luzerne	210	43.18 N	73.50 W
Lake Mackay Reserve ◂•[4]	162	22.00 S	129.45 E
Lake Magdalene	220	28.05 N	82.28 W
Lake Malawi National Park ♦	154	14.00 S	34.55 E
Lake Manyara National Park ♦	154	3.30 S	36.25 E
Lake Mary	220	28.45 N	81.19 W
Lakemba	274a	33.55 S	151.05 E
Lakemba Island I	175g	18.13 S	178.47 W
Lakemba Passage ⋓	175g	17.53 S	178.32 W
Lake Mead National Recreation Area ♦	200	36.00 N	114.30 W
Lake Meredith National Recreation Area ♦	196	35.40 N	101.40 W
Lake Mills, Ia., U.S.	190	43.25 N	93.31 W
Lake Mills, Wi., U.S.	216	43.04 N	88.54 W
Lake Milton	214	41.06 N	80.58 W
Lake Minchumina	180	63.53 N	152.19 W
Lake Monroe	220	28.50 N	81.19 W
Lakemont, N.Y., U.S.	210	42.31 N	76.56 W
Lakemont, Pa., U.S.	214	40.28 N	78.23 W
Lakemoor	216	42.20 N	88.12 W
Lakemore	214	41.01 N	81.25 W
Lake Mountain ∧	169	37.31 S	145.54 E
Lake Murray	164	7.00 S	141.29 E
Lake Murray State Park ♦	196	34.01 N	97.00 W
Laken ◂•[8]	50	50.52 N	4.25 E
Lake Nakuru National Park ♦	154	0.20 S	36.05 E
Lake Nash	166	21.00 S	137.55 E
Lake Nepessing	216	43.02 N	83.22 W
Lakenheath	42	52.25 N	0.31 E
Lake Norden	198	44.34 N	97.12 W
Lake Normandy Estates	284c	39.03 N	77.11 W
Lake Odessa	216	42.47 N	85.08 W
Lake of the Ozarks State Park ♦	194	38.08 N	92.40 W
Lake of the Woods	216	41.26 N	86.14 W
Lake on the Mountain Provincial Park ♦	212	44.02 N	77.05 W
Lake Orion	216	42.47 N	83.14 W
Lake Orion Heights	216	42.46 N	83.18 W
Lake Oroville State Recreational Area ♦	226	39.32 N	121.27 W
Lake Oswego	224	45.25 N	122.39 W
Lake Ozark	194	38.11 N	92.38 W
Lakepa	174v	18.59 S	169.48 W
Lake Panasoffkee	220	28.46 N	82.07 W
Lake Paringa	172	43.43 S	169.29 E
Lake Park, Fl., U.S.	220	26.48 N	80.04 W
Lake Park, Ia., U.S.	198	43.27 N	95.19 W
Lake Park, Mn., U.S.	198	46.53 N	96.05 W
Lake Pine	208	39.52 N	74.51 W
Lake Placid, Fl., U.S.	220	27.17 N	81.21 W
Lake Placid, N.Y., U.S.	188	44.16 N	73.58 W
Lake Pleasant	188	43.28 N	74.25 W
Lakeport, Ca., U.S.	204	39.02 N	122.54 W
Lakeport, Mi., U.S.	190	43.07 N	82.30 W
Lakeport, N.Y., U.S.	210	43.09 N	75.52 W
Lake Preston	198	44.21 N	97.22 W
Lake Providence	194	32.48 N	91.10 W
Lake Pukaki	172	44.11 S	170.09 E
Lakeridge, Nv., U.S.	226	39.02 N	119.56 W
Lake Ridge, N.J., U.S.	276	40.24 N	74.15 W
Lake Riviera	208	40.03 N	74.10 W
Lake Ronkonkoma	276	40.50 N	73.07 W
Lake Saint Louis	219	38.48 N	90.45 W
Lake Sammamish State Park ♦	224	47.33 N	122.03 W
Lake San Marcos	228	33.09 N	117.12 W
Lake Sawyer	224	47.20 N	122.03 W
Lakes Bay c	208	39.22 N	74.30 W
Lakes District	224	47.10 N	122.31 W
Lakes Entrance	166	37.53 S	147.59 E
Lake Shawnee	276	40.59 N	74.36 W
Lakeshore, Ca., U.S.	226	37.15 N	119.12 W
Lake Shore, Md., U.S.	208	39.06 N	76.29 W
Lake Shore, Mi., U.S.	216	42.38 N	86.14 W
Lakeshore, Ms., U.S.	194	30.14 N	89.26 W
Lake Shore, Wa., U.S.	224	45.42 N	122.42 W
Lakeside, N.S., Can.	186	44.38 N	63.41 W
Lakeside, S. Afr.	273d	26.06 S	28.09 E
Lakeside, Az., U.S.	200	34.09 N	109.58 W
Lakeside, Ca., U.S.	228	32.51 N	116.55 W
Lakeside, Ct., U.S.	207	41.25 N	73.13 W
Lakeside, Ct., U.S.	207	41.40 N	73.14 W
Lakeside, Mi., U.S.	216	41.51 N	86.40 W
Lakeside, Mt., U.S.	202	48.01 N	114.13 W
Lakeside, Oh., U.S.	214	41.32 N	82.44 W
Lakeside, Or., U.S.	202	43.34 N	124.10 W
Lakeside, Va., U.S.	208	37.36 N	77.28 W
Lakeside ◂•[9]	281	42.37 N	83.00 W
Lakeside Village	222	32.02 N	97.30 W
Lake Station	216	41.34 N	87.14 W
Lake Stevens	224	48.01 N	122.04 W

Lake Stockholm	276	41.04 N	74.31 W
Lake Success	276	40.46 N	73.43 W
Lake Superior Provincial Park ♦	190	47.32 N	84.50 W
Lake Swannanoa	276	41.01 N	74.31 W
Lake Taghkanic State Park ♦	210	42.06 N	73.43 W
Lake Tahoe Airport ⊠	226	38.54 N	120.00 W
Lake Tahoe-Nevada State Park ♦	226	39.13 N	119.55 W
Lake Tamarack	210	41.06 N	74.32 W
Lake Tekapo	172	44.01 S	170.30 E
Lake Telemark	276	40.57 N	74.30 W
Lake Temescal Regional Park ♦	282	37.51 N	122.14 W
Laketon	216	40.58 N	85.50 W
Laketown	200	41.49 N	111.19 W
Lake Varley	162	32.46 S	119.27 E
Lake View, Ar., U.S.	194	34.24 N	90.50 W
Lakeview, Ca., U.S.	228	33.50 N	117.07 W
Lakeview, Ga., U.S.	192	34.58 N	85.15 W
Lake View, Ia., U.S.	198	42.18 N	95.03 W
Lakeview, Mi., U.S.	190	43.26 N	85.16 W
Lake View, N.Y., U.S.	210	42.42 N	78.56 W
Lakeview, Oh., U.S.	216	40.29 N	83.56 W
Lakeview, Or., U.S.	202	42.11 N	120.20 W
Lake View, S.C., U.S.	192	34.20 N	79.09 W
Lakeview, Tx., U.S.	194	29.55 N	93.54 W
Lakeview, Tx., U.S.	196	34.40 N	100.42 W
Lakeview, Wa., U.S.	224	47.10 N	122.30 W
Lakeview ◂•[8]	278	41.57 N	87.39 W
Lakeview Mountain ∧, B.C., Can.	182	49.03 N	120.09 W
Lakeview Mountain ∧, Wa., U.S.	224	46.22 N	121.24 W
Lakeview Park ♦	285	40.12 N	75.32 W
Lake Village, Ar., U.S.	194	33.19 N	91.16 W
Lake Village, In., U.S.	216	41.08 N	87.27 W
Lakeville, Ct., U.S.	207	41.57 N	73.26 W
Lakeville, In., U.S.	216	41.31 N	86.16 W
Lakeville, Mi., U.S.	214	42.49 N	83.09 W
Lakeville, Mn., U.S.	190	44.38 N	93.14 W
Lakeville, N.Y., U.S.	210	42.50 N	77.42 W
Lakeville, Oh., U.S.	214	40.40 N	82.07 W
Lakeville Lake ⊜	214	42.50 N	83.09 W
Lake Wales	220	27.54 N	81.35 W
Lake Whitney State Park ♦	222	31.55 N	97.22 W
Lake Wilson	198	43.59 N	95.57 W
Lake Winola	210	41.30 N	75.50 W
Lakewood, Ca., U.S.	228	33.51 N	118.07 W
Lakewood, Co., U.S.	200	39.42 N	105.04 W
Lakewood, Il., U.S.	216	39.19 N	88.54 W
Lakewood, Mi., U.S.	216	42.18 N	85.31 W
Lakewood, N.J., U.S.	208	40.05 N	74.13 W
Lakewood, N.Y., U.S.	214	42.06 N	79.20 W
Lakewood, Oh., U.S.	214	41.28 N	81.47 W
Lakewood, Pa., U.S.	210	41.51 N	75.22 W
Lakewood, Wa., U.S.	224	48.09 N	122.12 W
Lakewood, Wi., U.S.	190	45.18 N	88.31 W
Lakewood Center ◂•[9]	280	33.51 N	118.09 W
Lakewood Park	198	48.04 N	98.56 W
Lakewood Park ♦	279a	41.29 N	81.47 W
Lakewood Shores	216	41.17 N	88.10 W
Lake Worth, Fl., U.S.	220	26.36 N	80.03 W
Lake Worth, Tx., U.S.	222	32.49 N	97.27 W
Lake Zurich	216	42.11 N	88.05 W
Lakhdaria	34	36.34 N	3.35 E
Lākheri	124	25.40 N	76.10 E
Lakhīmpur	124	27.57 N	80.46 E
Lakhipur, India	120	24.48 N	93.01 E
Lakhipur, India	124	26.02 N	90.18 E
Lakhish	132	31.34 N	34.51 E
Lakhish V	132	31.49 N	34.38 E
Lakhnādon	124	22.36 N	79.36 E
Lakhya ≃	126	23.35 N	90.31 E
Läki	84	40.34 N	47.26 E
Laki ≃	115a	7.30 S	107.25 E
Lakin	198	37.56 N	101.15 W
Lakinsk	80	56.01 N	39.57 E
Lakkadiven → Lakshadweep II	122	10.00 N	73.00 E
Lakki	123	32.36 N	70.55 E
Laknau → Lucknow	124	26.51 N	80.55 E
Lakonikós Kólpos c	38	36.25 N	22.37 E
Lakor, Pulau I	164	8.14 S	128.10 E
Lakota, C. Iv.	150	5.51 N	5.41 W
Lakota, Ia., U.S.	190	43.22 N	94.05 W
Lakota, N.D., U.S.	198	48.02 N	98.20 W
Laksefjorden c[2]	24	70.58 N	27.00 E
Lakselv	24	70.04 N	24.56 E
Lakshadweep □[8]	122	10.00 N	73.00 E
Lakshadweep II	122	10.00 N	73.00 E
Lakshadweep Sea ⊤[2]	12	7.00 N	76.00 E
Lākshām	124	23.14 N	91.08 E
Lakshamannāth	126	21.51 N	87.13 E
Lakshmanpur	272b	22.38 N	88.16 E
Lakshmeshwar	122	15.08 N	75.28 E
Lakshmi, Char I	126	21.57 N	90.33 E
Lakshmikantapur	126	22.07 N	88.20 E
Lakshmi Narayan Temple ◒[1]	272a	28.38 N	77.12 E
Lakshmīpur	126	22.57 N	90.50 E
Lakshmisāgar	126	22.55 N	87.01 E
Lala	116	7.59 N	123.46 E
Lalafuta ≃	154	13.57 S	24.41 E
La Laguna → San Cristóbal de la Laguna	148	28.29 N	16.19 W
La Lagunita	234	23.41 N	105.44 W
La Laja	252	37.16 S	72.42 W
La Lajilla	232	26.47 N	99.37 W
Lāla Mūsa	123	32.42 N	73.58 E
Lalana ≃	234	17.49 N	95.09 W
Lalapansi	154	19.16 S	30.15 E
Lâlapaşa	130	41.50 N	26.44 E
Lalatuncun	104	41.44 N	122.00 E
La Lava	248	19.55 S	65.38 W
Lalbenque	32	44.20 N	1.33 E
L'Albufera ⊜	34	39.20 N	0.22 W
Laleham, Austl.	166	23.58 S	148.46 E
Laleham, Eng., U.K.	260	51.25 N	0.30 W
Lāleh Zār, Kūh-e ∧	128	29.24 N	56.45 E
La Leona	196	25.52 N	101.05 W
La Leonesa	252	27.03 S	58.43 W
Lalera	152	0.22 N	11.28 E
Lalevade-d'Ardèche	62	44.39 N	4.19 E
Lālganj	124	25.52 N	85.11 E
Lālgarh	126	22.35 N	87.03 E
Lāliān	123	31.49 N	72.48 E
Lalibela	144	12.02 N	39.02 E
La Libertad, El Sal.	236	13.29 N	89.19 W
La Libertad, Guat.	232	16.47 N	90.07 W
La Libertad, Hond.	236	14.43 N	87.36 W
La Libertad, Nic.	236	12.13 N	85.10 W
La Libertad □[5]	248	8.00 S	78.30 W
La Ligua	252	32.27 S	71.14 W
La Lima, Hond.	236	15.24 N	87.56 W
La Lima, It.	66	44.04 N	10.46 E
La Limpia, Laguna ⊜	258	35.37 S	57.49 W
Lalín	34	42.39 N	8.07 W
Lalin ≃	89	45.29 N	125.26 E
Lalinde	32	44.51 N	0.44 E
Lalindi	115b	10.12 S	120.10 E
Lalindu ≃	112	3.28 S	122.05 E
La Línea	34	36.10 N	5.19 W
L'alino	82	54.29 N	39.06 E
Lalitpur	124	24.41 N	78.25 E
La Llagosta	266d	41.31 N	2.12 E
Lalla Khedidja, Tamgout de ∧	34	36.27 N	4.15 E
Lal Lal Reservoir ⊜[1]	169	37.40 S	144.04 E
Lālmanir Hāt	124	25.54 N	89.27 E

Lālmohan	126	22.13 N	90.42 E
Laloa	112	4.50 S	121.54 E
La Loche	184	56.29 N	109.27 W
La Loche ≃	184	56.09 N	109.08 W
La Loche, Lac ⊜	184	56.25 N	109.30 W
Laloki	164	9.25 S	147.15 E
La Londe	62	43.08 N	6.14 E
La Lora ⟑[1]	34	42.45 N	4.00 W
Lalor Park	274a	33.45 S	150.56 E
La Loupe	50	48.28 N	1.01 E
Lalouvesc	62	45.07 N	4.32 E
La Louvière	50	50.28 N	4.11 E
L'Alpe-d'Huez	62	45.06 N	6.04 E
Lālpur, Bngl.	126	24.11 N	88.58 E
Lālpur, India	120	22.12 N	69.58 E
Lal'sk	24	60.44 N	47.34 E
Lālsot	124	26.34 N	76.20 E
Lālua	126	21.57 N	90.18 E
La Luz, Méx.	196	25.52 N	97.37 W
La Luz, Méx.	232	24.12 N	97.52 W
La Luz, Nic.	236	13.44 N	84.47 W
La Luz, N.M., U.S.	200	32.58 N	105.56 W
Lam	60	49.12 N	13.03 E
Lama ≃, Ross.	82	56.29 N	36.10 E
Lama ≃, Zhg.	104	42.11 N	123.29 E
Lama, ozero ⊜	74	69.30 N	90.30 E
L'Amable Lake ⊜	212	45.01 N	77.49 W
La Macarena, Parque Nacional ♦	246	2.40 N	73.45 W
La Macarena, Serranía de ⟑	246	2.45 N	73.55 W
La Maddalena	71	41.13 N	9.24 E
Lama dei Peligni	66	42.02 N	14.11 E
La Madeleine	50	50.39 N	3.04 E
Lamadong	98	40.39 N	119.39 E
La Madrague	62	43.14 N	5.22 E
La Madrid, Arg.	252	27.38 S	65.15 W
Lamadrid, Méx.	196	27.05 N	101.50 W
Lamag	112	5.29 N	117.49 E
La Magdalena, Río de ≃	286a	19.21 N	99.11 W
Lamagoumen	105	40.52 N	116.39 E
Lamahuang	104	42.27 N	121.33 E
La Mailleraye-sur-Seine	50	49.29 N	0.46 E
Lamainong	114	3.49 N	96.46 E
La Majada	286c	10.27 N	67.01 W
Lama-Kara	150	9.33 N	1.12 E
La Malbaie	186	47.39 N	70.10 W
La Malinche, Parque Nacional ♦	234	19.15 N	98.05 W
Lamaline	186	46.52 N	55.49 W
La Malmaison ⊥	261	48.52 N	2.10 E
Lamaload Reservoir ⊜[1]	262	53.16 N	2.02 W
Lama Mocogno	64	44.18 N	10.45 E
La Mancha ◂•[1]	34	38.50 N	3.00 W
La Mancha, Canal de → English Channel ⋓	28	50.20 N	1.00 W
Lamandau ≃	112	2.42 S	111.34 E
Lamap	175f	16.26 S	167.43 E
Lamar, Co., U.S.	198	38.05 N	102.37 W
Lamar, Mo., U.S.	194	37.29 N	94.16 W
Lamar, Pa., U.S.	210	41.01 N	77.32 W
Lamar, S.C., U.S.	192	34.10 N	80.03 W
Lamar ≃	202	44.56 N	110.24 W
La Marañosa	266a	40.17 N	3.35 W
Lamarche	58	48.04 N	5.47 E
Lamarche-sur-Saône	58	47.16 N	5.23 E
Lamari ≃	164	6.54 S	145.25 E
La Mariposa, Embalse ⊜[1]	286c	10.24 N	66.56 W
La Mariscala	252	34.03 S	54.47 W
La Marmora, Punta ∧	71	39.59 N	9.20 E
La Marolle-en-Sologne	50	47.35 N	1.47 E
La Maroma	196	28.34 N	100.45 W
Lamarque, Arg.	252	39.24 S	65.42 W
La Marque, Tx., U.S.	222	29.22 N	94.58 W
La Marsa	36	36.53 N	10.20 E
La Martre	62	43.46 N	6.36 E
Lamas	248	6.25 S	76.35 W
La Masica	236	15.37 N	87.07 W
Lamastre	62	44.59 N	4.35 E
La Matanza → San Justo	258	34.40 S	58.33 W
La Matanza □[5]	288	34.46 S	58.37 W
Lama Temple ◒[1]	271a	39.56 N	116.25 E
La Mauricie, Parc National de (La Mauricie National Park) ♦	206	46.50 N	73.00 W
La Maya, Cuba	240p	20.10 N	75.39 W
Lamaya, Zhg.	102	29.50 N	99.53 E
Lamayingzi	104	42.09 N	121.50 E
Lambach	60	48.05 N	13.53 E
Lamballe	32	48.28 N	2.31 W
Lambaréné	152	0.42 S	10.13 E
Lambari	256	21.58 S	45.21 W
Lambari ≃, Bra.	255	19.30 S	45.00 W
Lambari ≃, Bra.	256	21.47 S	45.13 W
Lambasa	175g	16.26 S	179.24 E
Lambayeque	248	6.42 S	79.55 W
Lambayeque □[5]	248	6.20 S	80.00 W
Lambayeque ≃	248	6.43 S	79.54 W
Lambay Island I	48	53.29 N	6.01 W
Lambe	273a	6.42 N	3.21 E
Lambersart	50	50.39 N	3.02 E
Lambert, Ms., U.S.	194	34.12 N	90.17 W
Lambert, Mt., U.S.	198	47.41 N	104.37 W
Lambert, Cape ›, Austl.	162	20.35 S	117.10 E
Lambert, Cape ›, Pap. N. Gui.	164	4.12 S	151.32 E
Lambert Glacier ⍓	9	71.00 S	70.00 E
Lamberton	198	44.13 N	95.15 W
Lambert-Saint Louis International Airport ⊠	219	38.45 N	90.22 W
Lambertsbaai → Lambert's Bay	158	32.05 S	18.17 E
Lambert's Bay	158	32.05 S	18.17 E
Lambertville, Mi., U.S.	216	41.45 N	83.37 W
Lambertville, N.J., U.S.	208	40.21 N	74.56 W
Lambesc	62	43.39 N	5.16 E
Lambeth	214	42.54 N	81.18 W
Lambeth ◂•[8]	42	51.30 N	0.07 W
L'ambir'	80	54.17 N	45.07 E
Lambo Katenga	154	5.02 S	28.48 E
Lambomakondro	157b	22.41 S	44.44 E
Lambourn	42	51.31 N	1.31 W
Lambourne ≃	42	51.24 N	1.18 W
Lambourne End	260	51.38 N	0.08 E
Lambrama	248	13.52 S	72.46 W
Lambrate ◂•[8]	266b	45.29 N	9.15 E
Lambrecht	56	49.22 N	8.04 E
Lambrechten	60	48.19 N	13.31 E
Lambrechts Drift	158	28.31 S	21.43 E
Lambro ≃	62	45.08 N	9.32 E
Lambro, Parco ♦	266b	45.30 N	9.15 E
Lambs Creek	210	41.51 N	77.06 W
Lambs Terrace	285	39.46 N	75.02 W
Lambton	273d	26.15 S	28.10 E
Lambton □[6]	214	42.45 N	82.15 W
Lambton, Cape ›	176	71.05 N	123.10 W
Lambu	164	3.09 S	151.41 E
Lambunao	116	11.03 N	122.29 E
L'amca	24	64.27 N	37.04 E
Lamdessar	164	7.12 S	131.58 E
Lame, Nig.	150	10.23 N	9.13 E
Lamé, Tchad	146	9.15 N	14.32 E
La Meca → Makkah	144	21.27 N	39.49 E
La Mecque → Makkah	144	21.27 N	39.49 E
Lame Deer	202	45.37 N	106.39 W

La Media Luna, Arrecifes de ⟡[2]	236	15.13 N	82.36 W
La Méditerranée → Mediterranean Sea ⊤[2]	10	35.00 N	20.00 E
Lamego	34	41.06 N	7.49 W
La Meije ∧	62	45.00 N	6.18 E
Lameirão, Morro do ∧[2]	287a	22.54 S	43.31 W
La Membrolle-sur-Choisille	50	47.26 N	0.38 E
La Mendieta	252	24.19 S	64.58 W
L'amen'ga	76	59.51 N	44.31 E
Lamentin	241o	16.16 N	61.38 W
Lamèque	186	47.47 N	64.38 W
Lamèque, Île I	186	47.48 N	64.36 W
La Merced, Arg.	252	28.10 S	65.41 W
La Merced, Arg.	252	24.58 S	65.29 W
La Merced, Perú	248	11.03 S	75.19 W
Lameroo	166	35.20 S	140.31 E
La Mesa, Pan.	236	8.09 N	81.11 W
La Mesa, Ca., U.S.	228	32.46 N	117.01 W
La Mesa, N.M., U.S.	200	32.07 N	106.42 W
Lamesa, Tx., U.S.	196	32.44 N	101.57 W
La Mesa Dam ◂•[6]	269f	14.43 N	121.04 E
La Meta ∧	66	41.41 N	13.56 E
Lamía	38	38.54 N	22.26 E
L'amin ≃	74	61.18 N	71.48 E
Lamine ≃	194	38.59 N	92.51 W
La Minerve	206	46.15 N	74.56 W
Laming ≃	61	47.25 N	15.16 E
Lamington ≃	210	40.38 N	74.41 W
Lamington, Mount ∧[1]	164	8.56 S	148.10 E
Lamington National Park ♦	166	28.15 S	153.12 E
La Mira	234	18.02 N	102.19 W
La Mirada	228	33.55 N	118.00 W
La Mirada Creek ≃	280	33.53 N	118.01 W
La Misión	204	32.05 N	116.50 W
Lamitan	116	6.39 N	122.08 E
Lamlam, Mount ∧[2]	174p	13.20 N	144.40 E
Lamlash	46	55.32 N	5.08 W
Lamma Island I	271d	22.12 N	114.07 E
Lammefjord c	41	55.48 N	11.43 E
Lammerlaw Top ∧	172	45.40 S	169.38 E
Lammermuir ◂•[1]	46	55.50 N	2.25 W
Lammermuir Hills ⟑[2]	46	55.50 N	2.44 W
Lammeulo	114	5.15 N	95.56 E
Lammhult	26	57.10 N	14.35 E
Lammi	26	61.05 N	25.01 E
Lamming Mills	182	53.22 N	120.18 W
Lamogai	164	5.50 S	149.20 E
La Moille, Il., U.S.	190	41.31 N	89.16 W
Lamoille, Nv., U.S.	204	40.43 N	115.28 W
Lamoille ≃	188	44.35 N	73.10 W
La Moine ≃	194	39.59 N	90.31 W
La Moine, East Fork ≃	194	40.24 N	90.56 W
Lamoka Lake ⊜	210	42.24 N	77.05 W
La Molina	286d	12.05 S	76.57 W
Lamon Bay c	116	14.25 N	122.00 E
Lamone ≃	66	44.31 N	12.15 E
Lamongan	115a	7.07 S	112.25 E
Lamongan, Gunung ∧	115a	7.58 S	113.20 E
Lamoni	190	40.37 N	93.56 W
Lamont, Ab., Can.	182	53.46 N	112.48 W
Lamont, Ca., U.S.	228	35.15 N	118.54 W
Lamont, Ia., U.S.	190	42.35 N	91.38 W
Lamont, Mi., U.S.	216	43.01 N	86.09 W
Lamont, Ok., U.S.	196	36.41 N	97.33 W
La Monte	194	38.46 N	93.25 W
La Mosquitia □[9]	236	15.00 N	83.45 W
La Mothe, Lac ⊜[1]	186	48.46 N	71.09 W
La Mothe-Achard	32	46.37 N	1.40 W
Lamotrek I[1]	14	7.30 N	146.20 E
La Mott	285	40.04 N	75.08 W
La Motte, Lac ⊜	190	48.24 N	78.03 W
Lamotte-Beuvron	50	47.36 N	2.01 E
La Motte-Chalançon	62	44.29 N	5.23 E
La Motte-du-Caire	62	44.21 N	6.02 E
Lamoura	58	46.24 N	5.58 E
La Moure	198	46.21 N	98.17 W
La Moustique ≃	241o	16.11 N	61.35 W
Lampa	248	15.21 S	70.22 W
Lampang	110	18.18 N	99.31 E
Lampasas	196	31.03 N	98.10 W
Lampasas ≃	196	30.59 N	97.24 W
Lampazos de Naranjo	232	27.01 N	100.31 W
Lampedusa	70a	35.30 N	12.36 E
Lampedusa, Isola di I	70a	35.31 N	12.35 E
Lampertheim	56	49.35 N	8.28 E
Lampeter, Wales, U.K.	42	52.07 N	4.05 W
Lampeter, Pa., U.S.	208	39.58 N	76.14 W
Lamphun	110	18.35 N	99.01 E
Lampinsaari	26	64.25 N	25.09 E
Lampione, Isolotto di I	70a	35.34 N	12.19 E
Lampman	184	49.23 N	102.45 W
Lamprechtshausen	64	47.59 N	12.57 E
Lampung □[4]	112	5.00 S	105.00 E
Lampung, Teluk c	115a	5.40 S	105.20 E
Lamskoje	76	52.57 N	38.02 E
Lamspringe	52	51.58 N	10.00 E
Lamstedt	52	53.38 N	9.05 E
Lāmta	124	22.08 N	80.07 E
Lam Tong Hoi Hap ⋓	271d	22.15 N	114.15 E
Lamu, Kenya	154	2.16 S	40.54 E
Lāmu, Mya.	110	19.14 N	94.10 E
Lamud	248	6.09 S	77.55 W
La Muerte, Cerro ∧	236	9.33 N	83.44 W
Lam Uk Wei	271d	22.26 N	114.22 E
La Mure	62	44.54 N	5.47 E
Lamure-sur-Azergues	58	46.04 N	4.30 E
La Mutua	234	22.23 N	99.18 W
Lan' ≃, Bela.	76	52.09 N	27.18 E
Lan ≃, Zhg.	104	41.14 N	123.32 E
Lan, Loi ∧	110	19.40 N	97.55 E
Lana	64	46.37 N	11.09 E
Lanai I	229a	20.50 N	156.55 W
Lanai City	229a	20.49 N	156.55 W
Lanaihale ∧	229a	20.49 N	156.52 W
Lanaken	56	50.53 N	5.39 E
Lanalhue, Lago ⊜	252	37.55 S	73.18 W
La Nana, Bayou ≃	222	31.27 N	94.43 W
Lanao del Norte □[4]	116	8.10 N	124.00 E
Lanao del Sur □[4]	116	7.50 N	124.25 E
La Napoule	62	43.31 N	6.56 E
Lanarce	62	44.44 N	4.00 E
Lanark, On., Can.	212	45.01 N	76.22 W
Lanark, Scot., U.K.	46	55.41 N	3.46 W
Lanark, Il., U.S.	190	42.06 N	89.50 W
Lanark, Pa., U.S.	208	40.33 N	75.26 W
Lanark □[6]	212	45.05 N	76.20 W
La Nartelle	62	43.19 N	6.39 E
Lanas	112	5.20 N	116.30 E
La Nava de Ricomalillo	34	39.39 N	4.59 W
Lanbi Kyun I	110	10.50 N	98.15 E
Lanboyan Point ›	116	8.18 N	122.56 E
Lancang	102	23.00 N	100.02 E
Lancang → Mekong ≃	12	10.33 N	105.24 E
Lancashire	285	39.49 N	75.29 W
Lancashire □[6]	44	53.45 N	2.40 W
Lancashire Plain ≚	44	53.40 N	2.45 W
Lancaster, On., Can.	206	45.08 N	74.30 W
Lancaster, Eng., U.K.	44	54.03 N	2.48 W
Lancaster, Ca., U.S.	228	34.41 N	118.08 W
Lancaster, Ky., U.S.	192	37.37 N	84.34 W
Lancaster, Ma., U.S.	207	42.27 N	71.40 W
Lancaster, Mn., U.S.	198	48.51 N	96.48 W
Lancaster, Mo., U.S.	194	40.31 N	92.31 W
Lancaster, N.H., U.S.	188	44.29 N	71.34 W
Lancaster, N.Y., U.S.	210	42.54 N	78.40 W
Lancaster, Oh., U.S.	188	39.43 N	82.36 W
Lancaster, Pa., U.S.	208	40.02 N	76.18 W
Lancaster, S.C., U.S.	192	34.43 N	80.46 W

≃	River	Fluß	Río	Rivière	Rio
⩧	Canal	Kanal	Canal	Canal	Canal
∟	Waterfall, Rapids	Wasserfall, Stromschnellen	Cascada, Rápidos	Chute d'eau, Rapides	Cascata, Rápidos
⋓	Strait	Meeresstraße	Estrecho	Détroit	Estreito
c	Bay, Gulf	Bucht, Golf	Bahía, Golfo	Baie, Golfe	Baía, Golfo
⊜	Lake, Lakes	See, Seen	Lago, Lagos	Lac, Lacs	Lago, Lagos
⩩	Swamp	Sumpf	Pantano	Marais	Pântano
⍓	Ice Features, Glacier	Eis- und Gletscherformen	Accidentes Glaciales	Formes glaciaires	Acidentes glaciares
⊤	Other Hydrographic Features	Andere Hydrographische Objekte	Otros Elementos Hidrográficos	Autres données hydrographiques	Outros acidentes hidrográficos

⟡	Submarine Features	Untermeerische Objekte	Accidentes Submarinos	Formes de relief sous-marin	Acidentes submarinos
□	Political Unit	Politische Einheit	Unidad Politica	Entité politique	Unidade política
◒	Cultural Institution	Kulturelle Institution	Institución Cultural	Institution culturelle	Instituição cultural
⊥	Historical Site	Historische Stätte	Sitio Histórico	Site historique	Sitio histórico
♦	Recreational Site	Erholungs- und Ferienort	Sitio de Recreo	Centre de loisirs	Area de Lazer
⊠	Airport	Flughafen	Aeropuerto	Aéroport	Aeroporto
■	Military Installation	Militäranlage	Instalación Militar	Installation militaire	Instalação militar
◂•	Miscellaneous	Verschiedenes	Misceláneo	Divers	Diversos

Lancaster, Tx., U.S. 222 32.38 N 96.47 W
Lancaster, Va., U.S. 208 37.46 N 76.28 W
Lancaster, Wi., U.S. 190 42.50 N 90.42 W
Lancaster □6, Pa., U.S. 208 40.02 N 76.19 W
Lancaster □6, Va., U.S. 208 37.45 N 76.30 W
Lancaster Canal ≋ 262 53.46 N 2.43 W
Lancaster Sound ⊻ 176 74.13 N 84.00 W
Lancaster Village 285 39.45 N 75.35 W
Lančchuti 84 42.06 N 42.01 E
Lance Creek 200 43.01 N 104.38 W
Lance Creek ≃ 198 43.22 N 104.16 W
Lancefield 169 37.17 S 144.44 E
Lancelin 162 31.02 S 115.20 E
Lancelot, Mount ∧ 162 26.13 S 123.12 E
Lancey 62 45.14 N 5.53 E
Lanchang 114 3.30 N 102.11 E
Lanchester 44 54.49 N 1.44 W
Lanchow — Lanzhou 102 36.03 N 103.41 E
Lanchyn 78 48.34 N 24.45 E
Lanciano 66 42.14 N 14.23 E
Lancin 62 45.43 N 5.24 E
Lancing 42 50.50 N 0.19 W
Lanco 254 39.24 S 72.46 W
Lancones 246 4.35 S 80.30 W
Lancun 98 36.24 N 120.10 E
Łańcut 30 50.05 N 22.13 E
Lancy 58 46.11 N 6.07 E
Landana 152 5.13 S 12.08 E
Landang Gua 116 6.58 N 122.15 E
Landau 56 49.12 N 8.07 E
Landau an der Isar 60 48.40 N 12.43 E
Landay 128 30.31 N 63.47 E
Land Between the Lakes ◆ 194 36.55 N 88.05 W
Landeck 58 47.08 N 10.34 E
Landen 56 50.45 N 5.05 E
Landenberg 208 39.47 N 75.46 W
Landenhausen 56 50.36 N 9.28 E
Lander 200 42.49 N 108.43 W
Lander ≃ 162 20.25 S 132.00 E
Landerneau 32 48.27 N 4.15 W
Landes □5 32 44.20 N 1.00 W
Landes ✈1 32 44.15 N 1.00 W
Landesbergen 52 52.33 N 9.07 E
Landeskrone ∧2 54 51.08 N 14.56 E
Landess 216 40.37 N 85.34 W
Landete 34 39.54 N 1.22 W
Landham Brook ≃ 283 42.22 N 71.25 W
Landhausen 263 51.24 N 7.45 E
Landi 98 36.35 N 119.59 E
Landi Kotal 123 34.06 N 71.09 E
Landina 86 59.12 N 67.02 E
Landing 210 40.54 N 74.40 W
Landing Lake ⊜ 184 55.17 N 97.26 W
Landis, Sk., Can. 184 52.12 N 108.28 W
Landis, N.C., U.S. 192 35.32 N 80.36 W
Landisburg 208 40.20 N 77.18 W
Landisville 208 40.06 N 76.25 W
Landivisiau 32 48.31 N 4.04 W
Landkey 42 51.04 N 4.00 W
Landkirchen 54 54.27 N 11.08 E
Lando 192 34.46 N 81.00 W
Land O'Lakes, Fl., U.S. 220 28.11 N 82.34 W
Land O'Lakes, Wi., U.S. 190 46.10 N 89.13 W
Landor 162 25.09 S 116.54 E
Landos 62 44.51 N 3.50 E
Landösjön ⊜ 26 63.35 N 14.04 E
Landover Estates 284c 38.56 N 76.54 W
Landover Hills 284c 38.57 N 76.53 W
Landover Mall ✈9 284c 38.55 N 76.51 W
Landquart 58 46.58 N 9.33 E
Landquart ≃ 58 46.58 N 9.32 E
Landrecies 50 50.08 N 3.42 E
Landres 56 49.19 N 5.48 E
Landreth Draw V 196 31.14 N 102.29 W
Landriano 62 45.19 N 9.15 E
Landri Sales 250 7.16 S 43.55 W
Landro (Höhlenstein) 64 46.39 N 12.14 E
Landrum 192 35.10 N 82.11 W
Landry 62 45.34 N 6.45 E
Landsberg 54 51.31 N 12.10 E
Landsberg am Lech 58 48.05 N 10.55 E
Landsberg an der Warthe — Gorzów Wielkopolski 30 52.44 N 15.15 E
Landsborough 166 26.49 S 152.58 E
Landsborough Creek ≃ 166 22.30 S 144.33 E
Landsbro 26 57.22 N 14.54 E
Land's End >, Eng., U.K. 42 50.03 N 5.44 W
Lands End >, Ca., U.S. 228 33.28 N 118.36 W
Lands End >, R.I., U.S. 207 41.27 N 71.19 W
Landshut 60 48.33 N 12.09 E
Landskrona 41 55.52 N 12.50 E
Landsman Creek ≃ 198 39.35 N 102.19 W
Landsmeer 52 52.26 N 4.52 E
Landštejn 61 49.00 N 15.13 E
Landstuhl 56 49.25 N 7.34 E
Landweg 263 51.29 N 7.37 E
Landwehrbach ≃ 263 51.26 N 6.26 E
Lane 219 40.07 N 88.51 W
Lane ≃ 50 47.17 N 0.05 E
Lane City 222 29.13 N 96.02 W
Lane Cove 274a 33.49 S 151.10 E
Lane Cove ≃ 274a 33.48 S 151.09 E
Lane Cove River Park ◆ 274a 33.47 S 151.09 E
La Negra 252 23.45 S 70.19 W
Lane Mountain ∧ 228 35.05 N 116.56 W
Lanersbach 64 47.09 N 11.44 E
Lanesboro, Ma., U.S. 207 42.31 N 73.14 W
Lanesboro, Mn., U.S. 190 43.43 N 91.58 W
Lanesboro, Pa., U.S. 210 41.57 N 75.35 W
Lanester 32 47.46 N 3.21 W
Lanesville, In., U.S. 218 38.14 N 85.59 W
Lanesville, N.Y., U.S. 210 42.08 N 74.16 W
Lanesville, Va., U.S. 208 37.37 N 76.59 W
Lanett 194 32.52 N 85.11 W
La Neuveville 58 47.04 N 7.06 E
Laneville 222 31.58 N 94.49 W
Lanexa 208 37.24 N 76.55 W
Lanezi Lake ⊜ 182 53.03 N 120.56 W
Lang 184 49.56 N 104.23 W
La'nga Co ⊜ 124 30.42 N 81.16 E
Langadhás 38 40.45 N 23.04 E
Langádhia 38 37.41 N 22.02 E
Langa-Langa 152 3.54 S 15.56 E
Langan Creek ≃ 216 40.57 N 87.49 W
Langano, Lake ⊜ 144 7.35 N 38.48 E
Langao 102 32.13 N 109.02 E
Langar, Afg. 120 37.02 N 73.47 E
L'angar, Kyrg. 85 40.25 N 73.07 E
L'angar, Taj. 123 37.02 N 72.42 E
Langara 112 4.02 S 123.00 E
Langara Island I 182 54.14 N 133.00 W
Langarūd 128 37.11 N 50.10 E
L'angasovo 80 58.32 N 49.30 E
Langat ≃ 114 2.54 N 101.22 E
Langau 61 48.49 N 15.42 E
Langavat, Loch ⊜ 46 58.04 N 6.48 W
Långban 40 59.51 N 14.15 E
Langbank 184 50.05 N 102.20 W
Lang Bay 182 49.47 N 124.21 W
Langberg ∧ 158 28.20 S 22.35 E
Langburkersdorf 54 51.02 N 14.14 E
Langda 102 31.12 N 96.59 E
Langdai 102 26.06 N 105.20 E
Langdon 198 48.45 N 98.22 W
Langdondale 214 40.08 N 78.15 W
Langdon Hills 260 51.34 N 0.25 E
Langeac 32 45.06 N 3.30 E
Langeais 50 47.20 N 0.24 E
Langebaan 158 33.06 S 18.02 E
Langeberg ∧ 158 33.55 S 20.30 E
Lange Berge ∧2 56 50.20 N 10.55 E
Langebrück 54 51.07 N 13.50 E
Langeland I 41 55.00 N 10.50 E
Langelandsbælt ⊻ 41 54.50 N 10.55 E
Längelmävesi ⊜ 26 61.32 N 24.22 E
Langeloth 214 40.21 N 80.24 W
Langelsheim 52 51.56 N 10.19 E
Langemark 50 50.55 N 2.55 E
Langen, Dtsch. 52 53.36 N 8.35 E
Langen, Dtsch. 56 49.59 N 8.41 E
Langenargen 58 47.35 N 9.32 E
Langenau, Dtsch. 54 50.50 N 13.18 E
Langenau, Dtsch. 58 48.30 N 10.07 E
Langenberg, Dtsch. 52 51.46 N 8.19 E
Langenberg, Dtsch. 56 51.21 N 7.09 E
Langenbernsdorf 54 50.45 N 12.19 E
Langenbielau — Bielawa 30 50.41 N 16.38 E
Langenbochum 263 51.37 N 7.07 E
Langenbruck 58 47.21 N 7.46 E
Langenburg, Sk., Can. 184 50.50 N 101.43 W
Langenburg, Dtsch. 56 49.15 N 9.50 E
Langendorf 54 51.11 N 11.58 E
Langendreer ✈8 263 51.28 N 7.19 E
Langeneichstädt 54 51.20 N 11.41 E
Langenfeld, Dtsch. 56 51.07 N 6.56 E
Längenfeld, Öst. 64 47.04 N 10.58 E
Langenhagen 52 52.27 N 9.44 E
Langenhessen 54 50.45 N 12.22 E
Langenhorn 41 54.41 N 8.53 E
Langenhorst 263 51.22 N 7.02 E
Langenlois 61 48.28 N 15.40 E
Langennaundorf 54 51.36 N 13.20 E
Langenneufnach 58 48.16 N 10.36 E
Langenselbold 56 50.10 N 9.02 E
Langensteinach 56 49.30 N 10.10 E
Langenthal 58 47.13 N 7.47 E
Langenwang 61 47.34 N 15.37 E
Langenweddingen 54 52.02 N 11.31 E
Langenwetzendorf 54 50.41 N 12.05 E
Langenzenn 56 49.30 N 10.48 E
Langenzersdorf 61 48.18 N 16.22 E
Langeoog 52 53.45 N 7.29 E
Langeoog I 52 53.46 N 7.32 E
Langerfeld ✈8 263 51.16 N 7.15 E
Langer See ⊜ 264a 52.25 N 13.38 E
Langerwehe 56 50.49 N 6.22 E
Langeskov 41 55.22 N 10.36 E
Langesund 26 59.00 N 9.45 E
Langevåg 26 62.27 N 6.12 E
Langewiesen 54 50.40 N 10.58 E
Langfang — Anci 105 39.31 N 116.41 E
Langfjorden c2 26 62.43 N 7.30 E
Langford, B.C., Can. 224 48.27 N 123.30 W
Langford, Eng., U.K. 260 51.45 N 0.40 E
Langford, N.Y., U.S. 210 42.35 N 78.51 W
Langford, S.D., U.S. 198 45.36 N 97.49 W
Langförden 52 52.47 N 8.14 E
Langgam 112 0.15 N 101.43 E
Langgapayung 114 1.43 N 99.59 E
Langgöns 56 50.30 N 8.40 E
Langhalsen ⊜ 40 58.56 N 16.41 E
Langham 184 52.22 N 106.57 W
Langhe □9 62 44.30 N 8.00 E
Langhirano 64 44.37 N 10.16 E
Langho 262 53.48 N 2.27 W
Langholm 44 55.09 N 3.00 W
Langhorne 208 40.10 N 74.55 W
Langhorne Acres 285 40.11 N 74.55 W
Langhorne Creek 168b 35.18 S 139.02 E
Langhorne Gardens 285 40.11 N 74.53 W
Langhorne Manor 285 40.10 N 74.55 W
Langhorne Terrace 285 40.10 N 74.57 W
Langji Shan I 100 28.32 N 121.36 E
Langjökull ⊼ 24a 64.42 N 20.12 W
Langka 100 27.52 N 113.30 E
Lang Ka, Doi ∧ 110 19.00 N 99.24 E
Langkawi, Pulau I 114 6.22 N 99.50 E
Langkesi, Kepulauan II 112 5.18 S 124.20 E
Langklip 158 28.12 S 20.20 E
Langkrans 158 27.47 S 31.03 E
Langlade I 186 46.50 N 56.20 W
Lang Lang ≃ 169 38.17 S 145.31 E
Langley, B.C., Can. 224 49.06 N 122.39 W
Langley, Eng., U.K. 260 51.30 N 0.33 W
Langley, Eng., U.K. 260 51.14 N 0.35 E
Langley, Eng., U.K. 262 53.15 N 2.05 W
Langley, Ok., U.S. 196 36.27 N 95.02 W
Langley, S.C., U.S. 192 33.31 N 81.50 W
Langley, Wa., U.S. 224 48.02 N 122.24 W
Langley Air Force Base ■ 208 37.05 N 76.21 W
Langley Forest 284c 38.57 N 77.10 W
Langley Hill ∧2 287 37.20 N 122.14 W
Langley Park 284c 38.59 N 76.58 W
Langleyville 219 39.34 N 89.21 W
Langlo ≃ 166 26.26 S 146.05 E
Langlois 202 42.55 N 124.26 W
Langmazong 120 30.52 N 89.58 E
Lang Mo 110 17.14 N 106.27 E
Långnäs 26 60.06 N 20.17 E
Langnau 58 46.57 N 7.47 E
Langogne 62 44.43 N 3.51 E
Langon 32 44.33 N 0.15 W
Langøya I 24 68.44 N 14.50 E
Langping 102 30.38 N 110.21 E
Langport 42 51.02 N 2.50 W
Langqiao 100 30.30 N 118.24 E
Langquaid 60 48.49 N 12.03 E
Langreo — Sama [de Langreo] 34 43.18 N 5.41 W
Langres 58 47.52 N 5.20 E
Langres, Plateau de ∧1 58 47.41 N 5.03 E
Langruth 184 50.24 N 98.38 W
Langruzong 120 31.50 N 91.25 E
Langsa 114 4.28 N 97.58 E
Langsa, Teluk c 114 4.35 N 98.00 E
Langschede 263 51.29 N 7.43 E
Långsele 26 63.11 N 17.04 E
Langshan, Zhg. 102 41.12 N 107.22 E
Langshan, Zhg. 105 40.22 N 115.41 E
Langsheim 60 48.27 N 10.01 E
Långsjön ⊜ 40 59.00 N 17.27 E
Langsnek ⊥ 158 27.28 S 29.55 E
Lang Son 110 21.50 N 106.44 E
Langstaff 275b 43.50 N 79.25 W
Langst-Kierst 263 51.18 N 6.43 E
Lang Suan 110 9.57 N 99.04 E
Långsvan ⊜ 40 59.43 N 15.49 E
Langtang National Park ◆ 124 28.10 N 85.30 E
Langtian 100 25.11 N 113.28 E
Langting 120 25.30 N 93.07 E
Langton 212 42.45 N 80.35 W
Langtoutun 89 46.51 N 121.54 E
Langtuozi 104 41.01 N 121.43 E
Langu 110 6.53 N 99.47 E
Langue 236 13.37 N 87.39 W
Languedoc □9 32 44.00 N 4.00 E
Langui Layo, Laguna de ⊜ 248 14.29 S 71.13 W
L'Anguille ≃ 194 34.44 N 90.40 W
Langula 54 51.09 N 10.25 E
Langundu, Tanjung > 115b 8.49 S 118.58 E
Langwarden 52 53.36 N 8.19 E
Langwedel 52 52.59 N 9.12 E
Langweer 52 52.57 N 5.43 E
Langweid 58 48.29 N 10.51 E
Langweiler 56 49.40 N 7.31 E
Langwies 58 46.49 N 9.43 E
Langwo 104 41.13 N 121.44 E
Langwozhuang 105 39.05 N 115.37 E
Langxi 106 31.08 N 119.10 E
Langxi ≃ 106 31.10 N 118.59 E
Langzhong 102 31.35 N 105.59 E
Langzishan 104 41.02 N 123.23 E
Lanham 284c 38.58 N 76.51 W
Lanhil Island I 116 6.46 N 122.22 E
Lanibga, Mount ∧ 116 10.27 N 123.56 E
Lanigan 184 51.52 N 105.02 W
Lanigan Creek ≃ 184 51.23 N 105.13 W
Lanín, Parque Nacional ◆ 254 39.36 S 71.24 W
Lanín, Volcán ∧1 254 39.38 S 71.30 W
Lanivtsi 78 49.52 N 26.05 E
Lanjiang 107 30.24 N 105.11 E
Lankao (Lanfeng) 98 34.50 N 114.49 E
Länkäran 84 38.45 N 48.50 E
Lanker See ⊜ 54 54.12 N 10.17 E
Lankeys Creek 171b 35.49 S 147.39 E
Länkipohja 26 61.44 N 24.48 E
Lanklaar 56 51.01 N 5.44 E
Lank-Latum 263 51.18 N 6.41 E
Lankou 100 23.59 N 115.05 E
Lankoviri 146 9.00 N 11.25 E
Lankwitz ✈8 264a 52.26 N 13.21 E
Lanling 89 45.15 N 126.12 E
Lannabruk 40 59.14 N 14.56 E
Lannach 61 46.56 N 15.19 E
Lännaholm 40 59.53 N 17.57 E
Lannemezan 32 43.08 N 0.23 E
Lannilis 32 48.34 N 4.31 W
Lannion 32 48.44 N 3.28 W
Lannon 216 43.08 N 88.09 W
L'Annonciation 206 46.25 N 74.52 W
Lanoka Harbor 208 39.52 N 74.10 W
Lanoraie 206 45.58 N 73.13 W
La Noria 258 35.10 S 58.48 W
Lanping 102 26.29 N 99.23 E
Lanqibao 104 40.56 N 122.05 E
Lanqikoucun 104 40.52 N 122.26 E
Lanqipuzi 104 42.12 N 123.15 E
Lanquín 236 15.34 N 89.58 W
Lans, Montagnes de ∧ 62 44.52 N 5.29 E
Lansdale 208 40.14 N 75.17 W
Lansdowne, Austl. 162 17.53 S 126.39 E
Lansdowne, Austl. 274a 33.54 S 150.59 E
Lansdowne, On., Can. 212 44.24 N 76.01 W
Lansdowne, India 124 29.50 N 78.41 E
Lansdowne, Md., U.S. 284b 39.14 N 76.39 W
Lansdowne, Pa., U.S. 285 39.56 N 75.16 W
L'Anse, Mi., U.S. 190 46.45 N 88.27 W
Lanse, Pa., U.S. 214 40.59 N 78.08 W
L'Anse-aux-Meadows National Historic Park ◆ 186 51.36 N 55.32 W
L'anse Creuse Bay c 214 42.34 N 82.49 W
L'Anse Indian Reservation ✈4 190 46.48 N 88.22 W
Lans-en-Vercors 62 45.07 N 5.35 E
Lansford, N.D., U.S. 198 48.37 N 101.22 W
Lansford, Pa., U.S. 210 40.49 N 75.52 W
Lanshan 102 25.18 N 111.52 E
Lanshantou 98 35.07 N 119.21 E
Lansing, Il., U.S. 216 41.33 N 87.32 W
Lansing, Ia., U.S. 190 43.21 N 91.12 W
Lansing, Ks., U.S. 198 39.14 N 94.54 W
Lansing, Mi., U.S. 216 42.43 N 84.33 W
Lansing, N.Y., U.S. 210 42.32 N 76.30 W
Lansing, Oh., U.S. 214 40.04 N 80.47 W
Lansing ✈8 275b 43.45 N 79.25 W
Lansing ≃ 216 42.46 N 84.25 W
Lansing Municipal Airport ✈ 278 41.32 N 87.32 W
Lanškroun 30 49.55 N 16.37 E
Lanslebourg 62 45.17 N 6.52 E
Lanslevillard 62 45.17 N 6.55 E
Lanstrop ✈8 263 51.34 N 7.34 E
Lantana 220 26.35 N 80.03 W
Lantang 100 23.25 N 114.56 E
Lantau Island I 100 22.17 N 113.59 E
Lanta Yai, Ko I 110 7.35 N 99.05 E
Lanterne ≃ 58 47.44 N 6.03 E
Lantewa 146 12.16 N 11.44 E
Lantian 102 34.03 N 109.12 E
Lantianba 107 28.52 N 105.26 E
Lantianchang 271a 39.58 N 116.17 E
Lantsch 58 46.41 N 9.34 E
Lantschou — Lanzhou 102 36.03 N 103.41 E
Lantzville 224 49.15 N 124.05 W
La Nurra ✈1 71 40.45 N 8.15 E
Lanús 258 34.43 S 58.24 W
Lanús □5 288 34.42 S 58.28 W
Lanusei 71 39.53 N 9.32 E
Lanuvio 66 41.40 N 12.42 E
Lanuza 116 9.14 N 126.04 E
Lanuza Bay c 116 9.17 N 126.04 E
Lanxi, Zhg. 89 46.15 N 126.15 E
Lanxi, Zhg. 100 29.12 N 119.28 E
Lanxian 102 38.22 N 111.46 E
Lány 61 50.06 N 13.57 E
Lan Yü I 100 22.03 N 121.32 E
Lanzada 64 46.15 N 9.51 E
Lanzarote I 148 29.00 N 13.40 W
Lanzendorf 264b 48.06 N 16.26 E
Lanzhou (Lanchow) 102 36.03 N 103.41 E
Lanzo Torinese 62 45.16 N 7.28 E
Lao — Laos □1 110 18.00 N 105.00 E
Lao ≃, It. 68 39.47 N 15.48 E
Lao ≃, Thai 110 19.55 N 99.54 E
Lao ≃, Zhg. 100 29.11 N 116.00 E
Laoag 116 18.12 N 120.36 E
Laoag ≃ 116 18.12 N 120.31 E
Laoang 116 12.34 N 125.00 E
Laoang Island I 116 12.35 N 125.01 E
Lao Bao 110 16.37 N 106.36 E
Laobian, Zhg. 104 41.58 N 123.10 E
Laobian, Zhg. 104 40.42 N 122.21 E
Lao Cai 110 22.30 N 103.57 E
Laochang, Zhg. 102 24.34 N 104.11 E
Laochang, Zhg. 107 29.30 N 106.36 E
Laocheng 104 42.37 N 124.24 E
Laodafang 104 41.40 N 122.40 E
Laodao ≃ 100 28.16 N 112.58 E
Laodaodian 89 51.16 N 126.40 E
Laofengkou 86 46.11 N 83.38 E
Laofu 98 42.13 N 118.17 E
Laogang 106 31.01 N 121.49 E
Laoge 100 32.49 N 119.52 E
Laoguan 100 27.38 N 113.36 E
Laoguanpu 104 40.52 N 120.51 E
Laoha ≃ 90 43.24 N 120.39 E
Laohaotuo 104 41.25 N 122.46 E
Laoheba 107 28.51 N 103.49 E
Laoheishan 89 43.45 N 130.52 E
Laoheshangtai 104 40.43 N 120.49 E
Laohokow — Guanghua 102 32.25 N 111.36 E
Laohuk'ou 100 24.53 N 121.03 E
Laohumiao 271a 39.58 N 116.20 E
Laohutuozi 104 42.05 N 122.34 E
Laois □6 48 53.00 N 7.24 W
Laojiezi 105 40.22 N 114.47 E
Laojunmiao — Yumen 102 39.56 N 97.51 E
Laoka 89 52.47 N 125.52 E
Laolao, Bahía c 174n 15.08 N 145.46 E
Lao Ling ∧ 89 43.27 N 130.11 E
Laolong ≃ 106 32.11 N 120.00 E
Laolongtan 107 30.01 N 104.48 E
Laomencun 106 30.51 N 119.11 E
Laon 50 49.34 N 3.40 E
Laona, N.Y., U.S. 214 42.25 N 79.19 W
Laona, Wi., U.S. 190 45.33 N 88.40 W
La Orchila, Isla I 246 11.48 N 66.09 W
La Orotava 148 28.23 N 16.31 W
La Oroya 248 11.32 S 75.54 W
Laos (Lao) □1, Asia 108 18.00 N 105.00 E
Laos (Lao) □1, Asia 110 18.00 N 105.00 E
Laoshan (Licun) 98 36.10 N 120.25 E
Laoshan Wan c 98 36.24 N 120.45 E
Laosolu 114 3.11 N 98.02 E
Laotto 216 41.17 N 85.12 W
Laou, Oued ≃ 34 35.29 N 5.04 W
Laowushi 106 31.43 N 121.00 E
Laoxinkou 100 30.12 N 112.50 E
Laoyemiao 98 41.03 N 119.53 E
Laoyezhuang 106 32.16 N 120.04 E
Laoyingpan 100 26.34 N 115.10 E
Laozha 106 31.35 N 121.07 E
Laozhen 100 31.34 N 118.19 E
Laozhong 98 33.56 N 114.51 E
Laozhuangzi 105 39.44 N 118.05 E
Laozishan 100 33.11 N 118.36 E
Lapa 252 25.45 S 49.42 W
Lapa ✈8, Bra. 287a 22.55 S 43.11 W
Lapa ✈8, Bra. 287b 23.32 S 46.42 W
Lapac Island I 116 5.32 N 120.47 E
Lapai 150 9.06 N 6.45 E
Lapaich, Sgurr na ∧ 46 57.21 N 5.04 W
Lapalisse 32 46.15 N 3.38 E
La Palma, Col. 246 5.22 N 74.24 W
La Palma, Cuba 240p 22.45 N 83.33 W
La Palma, El Sal. 236 14.19 N 89.11 W
La Palma, Méx. 234 17.05 N 99.29 W
La Palma, Méx. 234 20.09 N 102.46 W
La Palma, Pan. 246 8.25 N 78.09 W
La Palma, Pan. 246 7.42 N 80.12 W
La Palma, Ca., U.S. 280 33.50 N 118.02 W
La Palma I 148 28.40 N 17.52 W
La Palma ≃ 240p 23.03 N 80.54 W
La Palma de Cervelló 266d 41.25 N 1.58 E
La Palma del Condado 34 37.23 N 6.33 W
La Palmita 196 25.57 N 99.18 W
La Paloma 252 34.40 S 54.10 W
La Palud 62 43.47 N 6.20 E
La Pampa □4 252 37.00 S 66.00 W
La Panza Range ∧ 226 35.18 N 120.18 W
Lapão 250 11.24 S 41.50 W
La Paragua 246 6.50 N 63.20 W
Laparan Island I 116 5.54 N 119.59 E
La Parota 234 18.20 N 101.08 W
La Pasión, Laguna c 234 15.59 N 97.40 W
La Pasión, Río de ≃ 232 16.28 N 90.33 W
La Patrie 206 45.24 N 71.15 W
La Paz, Arg. 252 30.45 S 59.39 W
La Paz, Arg. 252 33.28 S 67.33 W
La Paz, Bol. 248 16.30 S 68.09 W
La Paz, Col. 246 10.23 N 73.10 W
La Paz, Hond. 236 14.16 N 87.40 W
La Paz, Méx. 232 24.10 N 110.18 W
La Paz, Méx. 234 23.41 N 100.43 W
La Paz, Pil. 116 8.19 N 125.43 E
Lapaz, In., U.S. 216 41.28 N 86.18 W
La Paz, Ur. 258 34.21 S 57.18 W
La Paz, Ur. 258 34.46 S 56.15 W
La Paz □5, Bol. 248 15.30 S 68.00 W
La Paz □5, Hond. 236 14.15 N 87.50 W
La Paz, Bahía c 232 24.09 N 110.25 W
La Paz, Río de ≃ 248 16.27 S 67.19 W
La Paz Centro 236 12.20 N 86.41 W
Lape 115b 8.39 S 117.27 E
La Pedrera 246 1.18 S 69.43 W
Lapeer 216 43.03 N 83.19 W
Lapeer □6 216 43.00 N 83.20 W
Lapel 218 40.04 N 85.50 W
La Penne-sur-Huveaune 62 43.17 N 5.31 E
La Perla, Méx. 196 28.18 N 104.33 W
La Perla, Méx. 232 28.18 N 104.38 W
La Perla, Perú 286d 12.05 S 77.08 W
La Perouse 170 33.59 S 151.14 E
La Perouse, Bahía c 174z 27.04 S 109.18 W
La Perouse Bay c 229a 20.36 N 156.25 W
La Perouse Strait ⊻ 89 45.45 N 142.00 E
La Pesca 234 23.46 N 97.47 W
La Pesse 58 46.18 N 5.51 E
La Petite-Pierre 56 48.52 N 7.19 E
Lapford 42 50.55 N 3.47 W
Lapham Hill ∧2 216 43.02 N 88.24 W
L'apičev 80 48.30 N 43.32 E
La Piedad de Cabadas 234 20.21 N 102.00 W
La Pimienta 234 21.28 N 99.01 W
La Pine 202 43.40 N 121.30 W
Lapinig Island I 116 10.06 N 124.34 E
Lapinjärvi (Lappträsk) 26 60.38 N 26.13 E
Lapin lääni □4 24 68.00 N 27.00 E
Lapinlahti 26 63.22 N 27.24 E
Lapino 82 54.57 N 37.49 E
La Pintada 236 8.36 N 80.27 W
La Pintana 286e 33.35 S 70.38 W
La Pizzuta ∧ 70 38.00 N 13.16 E
La Place, Il., U.S. 219 39.48 N 88.43 W
La Place, La., U.S. 194 30.03 N 90.28 W
Lap Lae 110 17.39 N 100.02 E
La Plaine 240d 15.20 N 61.15 W
Lapland □9 24 68.00 N 25.00 E
Laplandija 24 68.16 N 33.19 E
Laplandskij zapovednik ✈4 24 67.50 N 32.10 E
La Plata, Arg. 258 34.55 S 57.57 W
La Plata, Col. 246 2.23 N 75.53 W
La Plata, Md., U.S. 208 38.31 N 76.58 W
La Plata, Mo., U.S. 194 40.01 N 92.29 W
La Plata □5 288 34.55 S 58.04 W
La Plata ≃ 200 36.54 N 108.14 W
La Plata, Lago ⊜ 254 44.53 S 71.50 W
La Plata, Río de c1 240m 18.20 N 66.14 W
La Plata, Universidad Nacional de ⊻2 288 35.55 S 57.57 W
La Plata Peak ∧ 200 39.02 N 106.28 W
La Playa ✈8 286b 23.06 N 82.27 W
La Playa Corrida de San Juan, Punta > 234 18.36 N 103.42 W
La Plonge Indian Reserve ✈4 184 55.15 N 107.36 W
La Plume 210 41.34 N 75.45 W
La Pobla de Segur 34 42.14 N 0.59 E
La Pocatière 186 47.22 N 70.02 W
La Poile 186 47.41 N 58.24 W
La Poile Bay c 186 47.38 N 58.20 W
Lapominka 24 64.48 N 40.28 E
La Pomme 62 43.25 N 5.35 E
Laponie — Lapland □9 24 68.00 N 25.00 E
Laporte, Co., U.S. 200 40.38 N 105.08 W
La Porte, In., U.S. 216 41.36 N 86.43 W
La Porte, Oh., U.S. 279a 41.19 N 82.05 W
Laporte, Pa., U.S. 210 41.25 N 76.30 W
La Porte, Tx., U.S. 222 29.39 N 95.01 W
La Porte □6 216 41.36 N 86.43 W
La Porte City 190 42.18 N 92.11 W
Laposo, Bulu ∧ 112 4.29 S 119.47 E
La Potherie, Lac ⊜ 176 58.50 N 72.35 W
Lapoutroie 58 48.09 N 7.10 E
La Poveda 266a 40.19 N 3.29 W
La Poza Grande 232 25.50 N 112.05 W
Lappago (Lappach) 64 46.55 N 11.48 E
Lappajärvi 26 63.12 N 23.38 E
Lappajärvi ⊜ 26 63.08 N 23.40 E
Lappeenranta 26 61.04 N 28.11 E
Lappfjärd (Lapväärtti) 26 62.15 N 21.32 E
Lappi 26 61.06 N 21.50 E
Lappland — Lapland □9 24 68.00 N 25.00 E
Lappträsk — Lapinjärvi 26 60.38 N 26.13 E
La Prairie 206 45.25 N 73.30 W
Laprairie □6 206 45.20 N 73.35 W
La Prele Creek ≃ 200 42.50 N 105.30 W
La Presa 232 24.25 N 111.34 W
Laprida, Arg. 252 37.33 S 60.49 W
Laprida, Arg. 252 28.23 S 64.33 W
La Pryor 196 28.57 N 99.51 W
Lapšanga 80 57.27 N 45.03 E
Lapseki 130 40.20 N 26.41 E
Lapta 130 35.20 N 33.10 E
Laptev Sea — Laptevych, more ⊤2 74 76.00 N 126.00 E
Laptevych, more (Laptev Sea) ⊤2 74 76.00 N 126.00 E
Lapua 26 62.57 N 23.00 E
Lapuanjoki ≃ 26 63.34 N 22.30 E
La Puebla de Cazalla 34 37.14 N 5.19 W
La Puebla de Montalbán 34 39.52 N 4.21 W
La Puente 228 34.01 N 117.56 W
La Puerta 252 28.10 S 65.48 W
Lapu-Lapu (Opon) 116 10.19 N 123.57 E
La Punt 58 46.35 N 9.55 E
La Punta 286d 12.05 S 77.11 W
La Purísima, Chile 286e 33.34 S 70.39 W
La Purísima, Méx. 232 26.10 N 112.04 W
Lăpuş 38 47.30 N 24.01 E
La Push 224 47.54 N 124.38 W
Lapuyan 116 7.36 N 123.12 E
Lapväärtti — Lappfjärd 26 62.15 N 21.32 E
Lapwai 202 46.24 N 116.48 W
Łapy 30 53.00 N 22.53 E
La Queue-en-Brie 261 48.47 N 2.35 E
La Queue-lès-Yvelines 261 48.48 N 1.46 E
La Quiaca 252 22.06 S 65.37 W
L'Aquila 66 42.22 N 13.22 E
L'Aquila □4 66 42.05 N 13.40 E
Lār 128 27.41 N 54.17 E
Lara 169 38.01 S 144.24 E
Lara □3 246 10.10 N 69.50 W
Larabanga 150 9.13 N 1.51 W
Laracha 34 43.15 N 8.35 W
Larache 148 35.12 N 6.10 W
Laragne-Montéglin 62 44.19 N 5.49 E
Lārak, Jazīreh-ye I 128 26.52 N 56.22 E
Laramate 248 14.15 S 74.52 W
La Rambla 34 37.36 N 4.44 W
Laramie 200 41.18 N 105.35 W
Laramie ≃ 200 42.12 N 104.32 W
Laramie Mountains ∧ 200 42.00 N 105.40 W
Laramie Peak ∧ 200 42.17 N 105.27 W
Laranjaí ≃ 255 23.12 S 53.45 W
Laranjal 255 21.22 S 42.28 W
Laranjeiras 250 10.48 S 37.10 W
Laranjeiras ✈8 287a 22.56 S 43.11 W
Laranjeiras do Sul 252 25.25 S 52.25 W
Larantuka 115b 8.21 S 122.59 E
Laraos 248 12.17 S 75.50 W
Larap 116 14.18 N 122.39 E
Larat 164 7.09 S 131.45 E
Larat, Pulau I 164 7.10 S 131.50 E
Laravale 171a 28.05 S 152.56 E
La Raya, Abra)(248 14.35 S 70.59 W
L'Arbaa Naït Irathen 34 36.38 N 4.12 E
Larb Creek ≃ 202 48.25 N 107.16 W
L'Arbresle 62 45.50 N 4.37 E
Lärbro 26 57.47 N 18.47 E
Larbut, Jazīrat I 140 18.47 N 37.33 E
Larche, Col de (Colle della Maddalena))(62 44.25 N 6.53 E
Larchmont 210 40.55 N 73.45 W
Larchmont Harbor c 276 40.55 N 73.45 W
Larchwood 198 43.27 N 96.26 W
Lardaro 64 45.58 N 10.39 E
Larde 154 16.28 S 39.43 E
Lardeau 182 50.09 N 116.57 W
Larderello 66 43.14 N 10.53 E
Larder Lake ⊜ 190 48.05 N 79.36 W
Lardier, Cap > 62 43.09 N 6.37 E
L'Ardoise 186 45.37 N 60.45 W
Lardy 261 48.31 N 2.16 E
Lare 154 0.20 N 37.56 E
Laredo, Esp. 34 43.24 N 3.25 W
Laredo, Tx., U.S. 196 27.30 N 99.30 W
Laredo Sound ⊻ 182 52.30 N 128.53 W
La Reforma, Méx. 232 25.06 N 108.05 W
La Reforma, Méx. 236 16.34 N 97.51 W
La Reina 286e 33.27 S 70.33 W
Laren 52 52.15 N 5.14 E
Larena 116 9.15 N 123.35 E
La Réole 32 44.35 N 0.02 W
Lares, Perú 248 13.04 S 72.05 W
Lares, P.R. 240m 18.18 N 66.53 W
Larga 38 48.23 N 26.50 E
Larga, Laguna ⊜ 196 27.30 N 97.30 W
Large, Île du I 275a 45.19 N 73.52 W
Largentière 62 44.32 N 4.18 E
L'Argentière-la-Bessée 62 44.47 N 6.33 E
Lar Gerd 120 35.29 N 66.40 E
Largo 220 27.54 N 82.47 W
Largo, Cañon V 200 36.44 N 107.44 W
Largo, Cayo I 240p 21.38 N 81.28 W
Largo Creek ≃ 200 34.29 N 108.51 W
Largoward 46 56.15 N 2.51 W
Largs 46 55.48 N 4.52 W
Largue ≃ 62 43.51 N 5.52 E
Lari, It. 66 43.34 N 10.35 E
Lari, Perú 248 15.37 S 71.46 W
Lariang 112 1.26 S 119.17 E
Lariang ≃ 112 1.25 S 119.17 E
La Ricamarie 62 45.24 N 4.22 E
Larimer 214 40.21 N 79.44 W
Larimore 198 47.54 N 97.37 W
Larino 66 41.48 N 14.54 E
La Rioja 252 29.26 S 66.51 W
La Rioja □4, Arg. 252 30.00 S 67.30 W
La Rioja □4, Esp. 34 42.15 N 2.30 W
Lárisa 38 39.38 N 22.25 E
Larisa Station ✈5 267c 37.59 N 23.43 E
Larjak 74 61.16 N 80.15 E
Larjan 76 59.30 N 33.47 E
Larjegan ≃ 86 60.30 N 77.44 E
Lārkāna 120 27.33 N 68.13 E
Larkhall 46 55.45 N 3.59 W
Lark Harbour 186 49.06 N 58.23 W
Larkhill 42 51.12 N 1.50 W
Larkspur 226 37.56 N 122.30 W
Larksville 210 41.14 N 75.55 W
Larnaca — Lárnax 130 34.55 N 33.38 E
Lárnakos, Kólpos c 130 34.55 N 33.45 E
Lárnax (Larnaca) 130 34.55 N 33.38 E
Larne 48 54.51 N 5.49 W
Larned 198 38.10 N 99.05 W
Larne Lough c 48 54.47 N 5.45 W
Laro 146 8.11 N 12.18 E
La Robla 34 42.48 N 5.37 W
La Roca de la Sierra 34 39.07 N 6.41 W
La Roche 58 46.42 N 7.08 E
La Roche-Bernard 32 47.31 N 2.18 W
La Roche-de-Rame 62 44.45 N 6.35 E
La Roche-Derrien 32 48.45 N 3.16 W
La Roche-des-Arnauds 62 44.34 N 5.57 E
La Roche-en-Ardenne 56 50.11 N 5.35 E
La Roche-en-Brenil 50 47.22 N 4.10 E
La Rochefoucauld 32 45.45 N 0.23 E
La Roche-Guyon 50 49.05 N 1.38 E
La Rochelle 32 46.10 N 1.10 W
Laroche-Saint-Cydroine 50 47.58 N 3.31 E
La Roche-sur-Foron 58 46.04 N 6.19 E
La Roche-sur-Yon 32 46.40 N 1.26 W
La Rochette, Fr. 62 45.28 N 6.07 E
La Rochette, Fr. 261 48.30 N 2.40 E
Larochette, Lux. 56 49.47 N 6.15 E
La Roda 34 39.13 N 2.09 W
La Romaine 186 50.13 N 60.40 W
La Romana 238 18.25 N 68.58 W
Larona 112 2.45 S 121.20 E
La Ronge 184 55.06 N 105.17 W
Laroquebrou 32 44.58 N 2.11 E
La Roquebrussanne 62 43.20 N 5.59 E
Larose 194 29.34 N 90.22 W
La Rosita 234 13.53 N 84.24 W
La Route 261 48.48 N 2.47 E
Larrabee State Park ◆ 224 48.41 N 122.29 W
Larreynaga 236 12.40 N 86.34 W
Larrey Point > 162 19.58 S 119.07 E
Larrimah 164 15.35 S 133.12 E
Larringes 58 46.22 N 6.35 E
Larrison Creek ≃ 222 31.27 N 95.03 W
Larroque 252 33.02 S 59.01 W
Larrys Creek ≃ 210 41.13 N 77.13 W
Larrys River 186 45.13 N 61.23 W
Larsen Air Park ✈ 281 42.11 N 83.33 W
Larsen Bay 180 57.33 N 154.00 W
Larsen Ice Shelf ⊼ 9 68.30 S 62.30 W
Larteh Aheneasi 150 5.56 N 0.04 E
La Rubia 252 30.06 S 61.48 W
La Rue, Oh., U.S. 214 40.35 N 83.23 W
Larue, Tx., U.S. 222 32.07 N 95.41 W
La Rumorosa 204 32.34 N 116.06 W
Laruns 32 42.59 N 0.25 W
Larus Lake ⊜ 184 51.17 N 94.40 W
Larvik 26 59.04 N 10.00 E
Larwill 216 41.10 N 85.37 W
Laryne 78 47.53 N 37.56 E
Larzac, Causse du ∧1 32 43.50 N 3.25 E
Lasa (Laas) 64 46.37 N 10.42 E
La Sabana 252 27.52 S 59.57 W
Las Adjuntas 286c 10.26 N 67.01 W
La Sagne 58 47.03 N 6.48 E
La Sal 200 38.18 N 109.14 W
La Salada, Laguna ⊜ 234 22.28 N 98.20 W
La Salette-Fallavaux 62 44.51 N 5.59 E
La Salle, On., Can. 214 42.14 N 83.06 W
La Salle, P.Q., Can. 206 45.26 N 73.38 W
Lasalle, Fr. 62 44.03 N 3.51 E
La Salle, It. 62 45.45 N 7.04 E
La Salle, Co., U.S. 200 40.20 N 104.42 W
La Salle, Il., U.S. 216 41.20 N 89.06 W
La Salle □6 216 41.21 N 88.51 W
La Salle ≃ 184 49.45 N 97.08 W
Lasalle, Parc ◆ 275a 45.26 N 73.40 W
La Salle College ⊻2 285 40.02 N 75.09 W
La Salle Gardens 216 42.39 N 83.21 W
Las Almejas, Bahía c 232 24.29 N 111.44 W
La Sal Mountains ∧ 200 38.30 N 109.14 W
Lasan 112 1.14 N 115.13 E
Lasanga Island I 164 7.25 S 147.16 E
Las Animas 198 38.04 N 103.13 W
La Santa, Cerro ∧ 240m 18.07 N 66.03 W
Las Arenas 240m 18.02 N 67.09 W
La Sarraz 58 46.40 N 6.31 E
La Sarre 190 48.48 N 79.12 W
La Sarre ≃ 190 48.43 N 79.16 W
Las Arrias 252 30.21 S 63.35 W
La Sauceda 196 28.26 N 100.38 W
La Saulce 62 44.25 N 6.01 E
Las Auras 196 26.25 N 99.20 W
Las Aves, Isla I 238 15.42 N 63.38 W
Las Aves, Islas II 246 12.00 N 67.30 W
Las Ballenas, Canal de ⊻ 232 29.10 N 113.29 W
Lasberg 61 48.28 N 14.32 E
Las Blancas 196 25.42 N 97.35 W
Las Bonitas 246 7.52 N 65.40 W
Las Breñas 252 27.05 S 61.05 W
Låsby 41 56.09 N 9.49 E
Las Cabezas de San Juan 34 36.59 N 5.56 W
Las Cabras 252 34.18 S 71.19 W
Las Cañas ≃ 234 22.29 N 105.36 W
Lascano 252 33.40 S 54.12 W
Lascar, Volcán ∧1 252 23.23 S 67.45 W
Lascari 70 38.00 N 13.56 E
Las Casas — San Cristóbal de las Casas 234 16.45 N 92.38 W
Las Catitas 252 33.18 S 68.02 W
Las Catonas, Arroyo ≃ 288 34.37 S 58.43 W
Lascaux, Grotte de ⊥5 32 45.01 N 1.08 E
Las Cejas 252 26.53 S 64.44 W
L'Ascension 206 46.33 N 74.50 W
Las Chacras 258 35.05 S 59.10 W
Las Choapas 234 17.55 N 94.05 W
La Scie 186 49.57 N 55.36 W
Las Coloradas 254 39.33 S 70.35 W
Las Condes 286e 33.22 S 70.31 W
Lascone, Monte ∧2 267a 41.59 N 12.23 E
Las Cruces 200 32.18 N 106.46 W
Las Cuevas 232 29.38 N 101.19 W
Las Delicias 232 15.58 N 91.50 W
La Selle, Morne ∧ 238 18.22 N 71.59 W
La Selva Beach 226 36.55 N 121.51 W
Lasem 115a 6.42 S 111.26 E
La Serena 252 29.54 S 71.16 W
La Serena ✈1 34 38.45 N 5.30 W
La Seyne-sur-Mer 62 43.06 N 5.53 E
Las Flores, Arg. 252 36.03 S 59.07 W
Las Flores, Arg. 252 30.19 S 69.12 W
Las Flores, Méx. 234 18.22 N 93.10 W
Las Flores, P.R. 240m 18.03 N 66.22 W
Las Flores, Ven. 286c 10.34 N 66.56 W
Las Flores, Arroyo ≃ 252 35.36 S 59.01 W
Las Flores, Cerro ∧ 234 16.43 N 95.30 W
Las Flores Canyon V 280 34.03 N 118.38 W
Las Flores Chica, Laguna ⊜ 258 35.30 S 59.01 W
Las Flores Grande, Laguna ⊜ 258 35.34 S 59.02 W
Las Garcitas 252 26.35 S 59.48 W
Las Guacamayas 234 18.02 N 102.12 W
Las Guayabas 232 24.00 N 97.45 W
Lasham 42 51.11 N 1.03 W
Las Harquetas, Arroyo ≃ 288 34.29 S 58.38 W
Lashburn 184 53.08 N 109.36 W
Lāsh-e Joveyn 128 31.43 N 61.37 E
Las Heras, Arg. 252 32.51 S 68.49 W
Las Heras, Arg. 254 46.33 S 68.57 W
Lashio 110 22.56 N 97.45 E
Lashkar — Gwalior 124 26.13 N 78.10 E
Lashkar Gāh 128 31.35 N 64.21 E
Las Hormigas 232 25.30 N 98.44 W
Lasht 123 36.48 N 73.01 E
Lasia, Pulau I 114 2.10 N 96.39 E
La Sierra, Montaña ∧ 236 14.04 N 87.54 W
Las Iglesias 196 27.35 N 101.21 W
Las Iglesias, Cerro ∧ 232 26.16 N 106.38 W
La Sila ∧ 68 39.15 N 16.30 E
La Silgata 66 43.58 N 11.38 E
La Silla de Caracas ∧ 286c 10.33 N 66.51 W
Łasin 30 53.32 N 19.05 E
Lašino 80 58.16 N 49.59 E
Lasjerd 128 35.24 N 53.04 E
Łask 30 51.36 N 19.07 E
Łaskarzew 30 51.48 N 21.35 E
L'askel'a 24 61.45 N 30.43 E
Laško 36 46.09 N 15.14 E
L'askoviči 78 52.07 N 28.09 E
Las Lajas, Arg. 252 38.31 S 70.22 W
Las Lajas, Pan. 236 8.15 N 81.52 W
Las Lajitas 252 24.41 S 64.15 W
Las Lomas 246 4.40 S 80.15 W
Las Lomitas 252 24.42 S 60.36 W
Lašma 80 54.56 N 41.09 E
Las Malvinas 252 34.50 S 68.15 W
Lašmanka 80 54.44 N 51.28 E
Las Mareas 240m 17.56 N 66.09 W
Las Margaritas 232 16.19 N 91.59 W
Las Margaritas, Laguna ⊜ 258 35.32 S 57.56 W
Las Marianas 258 35.04 S 59.31 W
Las Marías 240m 18.15 N 67.00 W
Las Marismas ≋ 34 37.00 N 6.15 W
Las Mayas 286c 10.26 N 66.56 W
Las Mercedes 246 9.07 N 66.24 W
Las Mesas de San Isidro 234 21.55 N 100.15 W
Las Minas 286c 10.27 N 66.52 W

Symbols in the index entries represent the broad categories identified in the key at the right. Symbols with superior numbers (∧1) identify subcategories (see complete key on page *I · 1*).

Symbole im Register stellen die rechts im Schlüssel erklärten Kategorien dar. Symbole mit hochgestellten Ziffern (∧1) bezeichnen Unterabteilungen einer Kategorie (vgl. vollständiger Schlüssel auf Seite *I · 1*).

Los símbolos incluidos en el texto del índice representan las grandes categorías identificadas con la clave a la derecha. Los símbolos con numeros en su parte superior (∧1) identifican las subcategorías (véase la clave completa en la página *I · 1*).

Les symboles de l'index représentent les catégories indiquées dans la légende à droite. Les symboles suivis d'un indice (∧1) représentent des sous-catégories (voir légende complète à la page *I · 1*).

Os símbolos incluídos no texto do índice representam as grandes categorias identificadas com a chave à direita. Os símbolos com números em sua parte superior (∧1) identificam as subcategorias (veja-se a chave completa à página *I · 1*).

∧ Mountain	Berg	Montaña	Montagne	Montanha
∧ Mountains	Gebirge	Montañas	Montagnes	Montanhas
)(Pass	Paß	Paso	Col	Passo
V Valley, Canyon	Tal, Cañon	Valle, Cañón	Vallée, Canyon	Vale, Canhão
≍ Plain	Ebene	Llano	Plaine	Planície
> Cape	Kap	Cabo	Cap	Cabo
I Island	Insel	Isla	Île	Ilha
II Islands	Inseln	Islas	Îles	Ilhas
⊥ Other Topographic Features	Andere Topographische Objekte	Otros Elementos Topográficos	Autres données topographiques	Outros acidentes topográficos

ESPAÑOL

Nombre	Página	Lat.°′	Long.°′ W = Oeste
Las Minas, Cerro ∧	236	14.33 N	88.39 W
Las Minillas, Cerro ∧	286e	33.31 S	70.29 W
Las Moras Creek ≃	196	29.00 N	100.39 W
Las Mulas, Laguna ⊜	258	35.32 S	57.54 W
Las Navas	116	12.21 N	125.02 E
Las Nieves	232	26.24 N	105.22 W
Las Nopaleras, Cerro ∧	232	25.08 N	103.14 W
La Solana	34	38.56 N	3.14 W
La Soledad, Cerro ∧	232	26.32 N	107.17 W
Lasolo	112	3.29 S	122.04 E
Lasolo ≃	112	3.28 S	122.06 E
Las Ortegas, Arroyo ≃	288	34.45 S	58.32 W
Las Ovejas	252	37.01 S	70.45 W
Las Palmas, Arg.	252	27.04 S	58.42 W
Las Palmas, Arg.	258	34.05 S	59.10 W
Las Palmas, Pan.	236	8.08 N	81.27 W
Las Palmas, P.R.	240m	17.59 N	66.02 W
Las Palmas □[4]	148	28.25 N	14.15 W
Las Palmas de Gran Canaria	148	28.06 N	15.24 W
Las Palomas	200	31.44 N	107.37 W
Las Perdices, Canal ≍	286e	33.31 S	70.33 W
La Spezia	62	44.07 N	9.50 E
La Spezia □[4]	62	44.15 N	9.42 E
Las Piedras, P.R.	240m	18.11 N	65.52 W
Las Piedras, Ur.	258	34.44 S	56.13 W
Las Piedras, Río de ≃	248	12.30 S	69.14 W
Las Piñas, Pil.	269f	14.29 N	120.59 E
Las Piñas, P.R.	240m	18.15 N	65.55 W
Las Plumas	254	43.43 S	67.15 W
Lasqueti Island I	182	49.29 N	124.17 W
Las Raices Creek ≃	196	28.09 N	99.02 W
Las Ratas, Cerro ∧	234	18.37 N	103.37 W
Las Rejas	286e	33.28 S	70.44 W
Las Rosas, Arg.	252	32.28 S	61.34 W
Las Rosas, Chile	286e	33.35 S	70.37 W
Las Rosas, Méx.	232	16.24 N	92.23 W
Las Rozas de Madrid	266a	40.29 N	3.52 W
Las Sales, Canal ≍	286a	19.26 N	99.03 W
Lassan	54	53.57 N	13.50 E
Lassance	255	17.54 S	44.34 W
Lassater	222	32.49 N	94.30 W
Lassay	32	48.26 N	0.30 W
Lassee	61	48.13 N	16.49 E
Lassellsville	210	43.03 N	74.36 W
Lassen Peak ∧[1]	204	40.29 N	121.31 W
Lassen Volcanic National Park ♠	204	40.30 N	121.19 W
Lassigny	50	49.35 N	2.51 E
Lassnitz ≃	61	46.46 N	15.32 E
Lassnitzhöhe	61	47.05 N	15.35 E
Lasso ∧[2]	174n	15.02 N	145.38 E
L'Assomption	206	45.50 N	73.25 W
L'Assomption □[6]	206	45.48 N	73.35 W
L'Assomption ≃	206	45.43 N	73.29 W
Lasswade	46	55.53 N	3.08 W
Lassy	261	49.06 N	2.27 E
Las Tablas	246	7.46 N	80.17 W
Lastarrio, Parque Nacional ♠	254	44.50 S	72.05 W
Las Tinajas	252	27.27 S	62.55 W
Last Mountain ∧	184	51.07 N	104.54 W
Last Mountain Lake ⊜	184	51.05 N	105.10 W
Las Toscas	252	28.21 S	59.17 W
Lastoursville	152	0.49 S	12.42 E
Lastovo, Otok I	36	42.45 N	16.53 E
Lastovski Kanal ʯ	36	42.50 N	16.59 E
Lastra a Signa	66	43.46 N	11.06 E
Las Trampas Creek ≃	282	37.53 N	122.03 W
Las Trampas Peak ∧	282	37.50 N	122.03 W
Las Trampas Regional Park ♠	282	37.50 N	122.03 W
Las Trampas Ridge ∧	282	37.49 N	122.02 W
Lästringe	40	58.54 N	17.18 E
Las Truchas	234	17.55 N	102.12 W
Lastrup	52	52.48 N	7.52 E
Las Tunas	240p	20.58 N	76.57 W
Las Tunas □[4]	240p	21.00 N	77.00 W
Las Tunas, Arroyo ≃	288	34.27 S	58.41 W
Las Tunas, Punta ›	240m	18.30 N	66.38 W
Las Tunas Beach ♠	280	34.02 N	118.36 W
Las Tunas Grandes, Laguna ⊜	252	35.58 S	62.25 W
La Suze	32	47.54 N	0.02 E
Las Varas, Méx.	232	29.29 N	108.01 W
Las Varas, Méx.	234	21.10 N	105.10 W
Las Varillas	252	31.52 S	62.43 W
Las Vegas, P.R.	240m	18.11 N	67.02 W
Las Vegas, Nv., U.S.	204	36.10 N	115.08 W
Las Vegas, N.M., U.S.	200	35.36 N	105.13 W
Las Vegas, Ven.	246	9.35 N	68.37 W
Las Vigas de Ramirez	234	19.38 N	97.05 W
La Tabatière	186	50.50 N	58.58 W
Latacunga	246	0.56 S	78.37 W
Latady Island I	9	70.45 S	74.35 W
La Tagua	246	0.03 S	74.40 W
Latakia → Al-Lādhiqīyah	130	35.31 N	35.47 E
Latakia □[9]	130	35.20 N	36.00 E
Latambar	123	33.07 N	70.52 E
Lata Mountain ∧	174y	14.14 S	169.29 W
La Tapona	234	22.48 N	100.38 W
Låtefossen ∟	26	59.57 N	6.37 E
Latehar	124	23.45 N	84.30 E
Lately Common	262	53.29 N	2.30 W
Latera	66	42.38 N	11.50 E
Laterina	66	43.31 N	11.43 E
Laterns	58	47.16 N	9.43 E
Laterrière	186	48.18 N	71.06 W
Laterza	68	40.37 N	16.48 E
La Teste-de-Buch	32	44.38 N	1.09 W
La Tetilla, Cerro ∧	234	20.21 N	104.59 W
Latexo	222	31.24 N	95.29 W
Latgale □[9]	76	56.20 N	27.10 E
Latham, Austl.	162	29.45 S	116.26 E
Latham, Il., U.S.	219	39.58 N	89.10 W
Latham, N.Y., U.S.	210	42.44 N	73.45 W
Latham, Oh., U.S.	218	39.06 N	83.15 W
Lathan ≃	50	47.27 N	0.08 E
Lathen	52	52.52 N	7.19 E
Latheron	46	58.17 N	3.23 W
Lāthi	120	21.43 N	71.23 E
Lathrop, Ca., U.S.	226	37.49 N	121.16 W
Lathrop, Mo., U.S.	194	39.32 N	94.19 W
Lathrup Village	281	42.29 N	83.14 W
La Thuile	62	45.43 N	6.57 E
La Tiama	286c	10.26 N	66.46 W
Latian, Mount ∧	116	6.13 N	125.30 E
Latiano	68	40.33 N	17.43 E
Latimer, Eng., U.K.	260	51.41 N	0.33 W
Latimer, Ia., U.S.	190	42.45 N	93.22 W
Latina	66	41.28 N	12.52 E
Latina □[4]	66	41.27 N	13.06 E
Latiri	140	9.10 N	25.43 E
Latisana	64	45.47 N	13.00 E
Latjuga	24	64.16 N	48.46 E
Latnaja	78	51.43 N	38.55 E
La Toma	252	33.03 S	65.37 W
Laton	226	36.26 N	119.41 W
Latonovo	83	47.29 N	38.38 E
Latornell ≃	182	54.58 N	118.00 W
La Torrecilla ∧	240m	18.12 N	66.20 W
La Tortuga, Isla I	246	10.56 N	65.20 W
Latorytsya ≃	30	48.28 N	21.50 E
Latouche Island I	180	60.00 N	147.55 W
Latouche Treville, Cape ›	162	18.27 S	121.49 E
La Tour	62	43.57 N	7.11 E
La Tour-d'Aigues	62	43.44 N	5.33 E
La Tour-d'Auvergne	32	45.32 N	2.41 E
La Tour-de-Peilz	58	46.27 N	6.49 E
La Tour-du-Pin	62	45.34 N	5.27 E

FRANÇAIS

Nom	Page	Lat.°′	Long.°′ W = Ouest
La Tourette Park ♠	276	40.35 N	74.08 W
Latowicz	30	52.02 N	21.48 E
Lat Phrao, Khlong ≍	269a	13.48 N	100.35 E
La Tremblade	32	45.46 N	1.08 W
La Trimouille	32	46.28 N	1.02 E
La Trinidad, Arg.	252	27.24 S	65.31 W
La Trinidad, Nic.	236	12.58 N	86.14 W
La Trinidad, Pil.	116	16.28 N	120.35 E
La Trinidad, Ven.	286c	10.27 N	66.52 W
La Trinidad de Orichuna	246	7.07 N	69.45 W
La Trinitaria	232	16.07 N	92.03 W
La Trinité	240e	14.44 N	60.58 W
Latrobe, Austl.	166	41.14 S	146.24 E
Latrobe, Pa., U.S.	214	40.19 N	79.22 W
La Trobe ≃	169	38.10 S	146.32 E
Latrobe University ⚘[2]	274b	37.43 S	145.03 E
La Tronche	62	45.12 N	5.44 E
Latronico	68	40.05 N	16.01 E
Latsch → Laces	64	46.37 N	10.52 E
Latta	192	34.20 N	79.25 W
Lattarico	68	39.28 N	16.08 E
Lattasburg	214	40.53 N	82.06 W
Latterbach	58	46.40 N	7.35 E
Lattingtown	276	40.54 N	73.36 W
Latty	216	41.05 N	84.35 W
La Tuilerie	261	48.34 N	2.08 E
La Tuilière	62	44.11 N	5.32 E
Latuna	112	8.23 S	124.06 E
La Tuque	176	47.26 N	72.47 W
Lātūr	122	18.24 N	76.35 E
La Turbie	62	43.45 N	7.24 E
Latvia (Latvija) □[1], Europe	22	57.00 N	25.00 E
Latvia (Latvija) □[1], Europe	76	57.00 N	25.00 E
Lau, Nig.	146	9.13 N	11.17 E
Lau, Pap. N. Gui.	164	5.50 S	151.20 E
Laubach	56	50.33 N	8.59 E
Lau Basin ✢[1]	14	20.00 S	177.00 W
Laubusch	54	51.28 N	14.10 E
Laubuseschbach	56	50.24 N	8.20 E
Lauca ≃	248	19.10 S	68.10 W
Lauca, Parque Nacional ♠	248	18.20 S	69.15 W
Laucha	54	51.13 N	11.41 E
Lauchhammer	54	51.30 N	13.47 E
Lauchheim	56	48.52 N	10.14 E
Lauda-Königshofen	56	49.34 N	9.41 E
Lauder	46	55.43 N	2.45 W
Lauderdale	194	32.31 N	88.30 W
Lauderdale V	46	55.43 N	2.42 W
Lauderdale-by-the-Sea	220	26.12 N	80.07 W
Lauderdale Lakes	220	26.09 N	80.12 W
Lauderhill	220	26.08 N	80.12 W
Laudun	62	44.06 N	4.40 E
Lauenbrück	52	53.12 N	9.33 E
Lauenburg, Dtsch.	52	53.22 N	10.33 E
Lauenburg → Lębork, Pol.	30	54.33 N	17.44 E
Lauenförde	52	51.39 N	9.23 E
Lauenstein, Dtsch.	52	52.04 N	9.33 E
Lauenstein, Dtsch.	54	50.31 N	11.20 E
Lauenstein, Dtsch.	54	50.47 N	13.49 E
Lauer ≃	56	50.18 N	10.10 E
Lauerzer See ⊜	58	47.02 N	8.36 E
Lauf an der Pegnitz	60	49.30 N	11.17 E
Läufelfingen	58	47.24 N	7.51 E
Laufen, Dtsch.	64	47.57 N	12.56 E
Laufen, Schw.	58	47.25 N	7.30 E
Laufenburg (Baden), Dtsch.	58	47.35 N	8.04 E
Laufenburg (Baden), Schw.	58	47.33 N	8.04 E
Laufersfort, Schloss ⊥	263	51.25 N	6.37 E
Lauffen am Neckar	56	49.05 N	9.10 E
Laugharne	42	51.47 N	4.28 W
Laughery Creek ≃	218	39.02 N	84.53 W
Laughlen, Mount ∧	162	23.23 S	134.23 E
Laughlin Air Force Base ■	196	29.22 N	100.47 W
Laughlin Peak ∧	196	36.38 N	104.12 W
Laughlintown	214	40.13 N	79.12 W
Lau Group II	175g	18.20 S	178.30 W
Lauingen	56	48.34 N	10.25 E
Lauis → Lugano	58	46.01 N	8.58 E
Laukaa	26	62.25 N	25.57 E
Laukuva	76	55.37 N	22.14 E
Laul'u	89	45.46 N	135.16 E
Laun	110	10.07 N	98.46 E
Launceston, Austl.	166	41.26 S	147.08 E
Launceston, Eng., U.K.	42	50.38 N	4.21 W
Laundi, Tanjung ›	115b	9.28 S	120.12 E
Laune ≃	48	52.07 N	9.48 W
Launglon	110	13.58 N	98.07 E
Laungowāl	123	30.13 N	75.41 E
La Unión, Chile	254	40.17 S	73.05 W
La Unión, Col.	246	1.36 N	77.09 W
La Unión, El Sal.	236	13.20 N	87.51 W
La Unión, Esp.	34	37.37 N	0.52 W
La Unión, Méx.	234	17.58 N	101.49 W
La Unión, Perú	248	9.46 S	76.48 W
La Unión, Perú	248	5.24 S	80.45 W
La Union, Pil.	116	6.42 N	126.05 E
La Union, N.M., U.S.	200	31.57 N	106.39 W
La Unión, Ven.	246	8.13 N	67.46 W
La Unión, Ven.	286c	10.25 N	66.48 W
La Union □[4]	116	16.35 N	120.25 E
Launois-sur-Vence	56	49.39 N	4.32 E
Launsdorf	61	46.46 N	14.27 E
Laupen	58	46.54 N	7.14 E
Laupendahl ◆[8]	263	51.21 N	6.56 E
Laupheim	58	48.14 N	9.52 E
Laur	116	15.35 N	121.11 E
Laura, Austl.	164	15.34 S	144.28 E
Laura, Oh., U.S.	218	39.59 N	84.24 W
La Urbana	246	7.08 N	66.56 W
Laureana di Borrello	68	38.30 N	16.05 E
Laurel, De., U.S.	208	38.33 N	75.34 W
Laurel, Fl., U.S.	220	27.07 N	82.27 W
Laurel, In., U.S.	218	39.30 N	85.11 W
Laurel, Md., U.S.	208	39.05 N	76.50 W
Laurel, Ms., U.S.	194	31.41 N	89.07 W
Laurel, Mt., U.S.	202	45.40 N	108.46 W
Laurel, Ne., U.S.	198	42.25 N	97.05 W
Laurel, Va., U.S.	208	37.38 N	77.30 W
Laurel, Wa., U.S.	224	45.57 N	121.23 W
Laurel ≃	192	36.57 N	84.18 W
Laurel, Mount ∧[2]	285	39.56 N	74.53 W
Laurel Bay	192	32.33 N	80.44 W
Laureldale, N.J., U.S.	208	39.29 N	74.41 W
Laureldale, Pa., U.S.	208	40.23 N	75.55 W
Laureles	252	31.22 S	55.51 W
Laureles, Isla de los I	258	33.45 S	59.23 W
Laurel Gardens	279b	40.31 N	80.01 W
Laurel Hill, Austl.	171b	35.37 S	148.05 E
Laurel Hill, N.C., U.S.	192	34.48 N	79.32 W
Laurel Hill ∧	214	40.15 N	79.05 W
Laurel Hollow	276	40.52 N	73.28 W
Laurel Reservoir ⊜[1]	276	41.10 N	73.33 W
Laurel Ridge State Park ♠	188	39.58 N	79.23 W
Laurel River Lake ⊜[1]	192	36.55 N	84.15 W
Laurel Run	210	41.13 N	75.51 W
Laurel Run ≃	208	40.20 N	77.20 W
Laurel Springs	285	39.49 N	75.00 W
Laurelton	210	40.52 N	77.11 W
Laurelville, Oh., U.S.	188	39.28 N	82.44 W
Laurelville, Pa., U.S.	214	40.09 N	79.29 W
Laurenburg	56	50.20 N	7.54 E
Laurence Harbor	276	40.27 N	74.14 W
Laurencekirk	46	56.50 N	2.29 W
Laurens, Ia., U.S.	198	42.50 N	94.51 W
Laurens, N.Y., U.S.	210	42.32 N	75.06 W
Laurens, S.C., U.S.	192	34.29 N	82.00 W

PORTUGUÊS

Nome	Página	Lat.°′	Long.°′ W = Oeste
Laurentides	206	45.51 N	73.46 W
Laurentides, Les ⩕[1]	176	48.00 N	71.00 W
Laurentides, Parc Provincial des ♠	186	47.40 N	71.30 W
Laurenzana	68	40.28 N	15.58 E
Lauria	68	40.02 N	15.50 E
Lau Ridge ✢[3]	14	21.00 S	178.30 W
Laurie Island I	9	60.45 S	44.35 W
Laurie Lake ⊜	184	56.34 N	101.54 W
Laurier, Mb., Can.	184	50.54 N	99.33 W
Laurier, P.Q., Can.	206	46.32 N	71.38 W
Laurière	32	46.05 N	1.28 E
Laurierville	206	46.18 N	71.39 W
Laurinburg	192	34.46 N	79.27 W
Laurino	68	40.20 N	15.20 E
Laurito	68	40.10 N	15.24 E
Lauritsala	26	61.04 N	28.16 E
Lauritzen Bay ⊂	9	69.05 S	156.50 E
Laurium	190	47.14 N	88.26 W
Lauriya Nandangarh	124	26.59 N	84.24 E
Lauro, Monte ∧	70	37.07 N	14.49 E
Laurys Station	208	40.43 N	75.32 W
Lausanne	58	46.31 N	6.38 E
Lauscha	54	50.28 N	11.10 E
Laut	86	59.18 N	66.02 E
Laut, Pulau I, Indon.	112	3.40 S	116.10 E
Laut, Pulau I, Indon.	112	4.43 N	107.59 E
Laut, Selat ʯ	112	3.25 S	116.03 E
Lauta	54	51.27 N	14.04 E
Lautaro	252	38.31 S	72.27 W
Lautaro, Volcán ∧[1]	254	49.00 S	73.32 W
Lautem	112	8.22 S	126.54 E
Lautenbach	58	47.57 N	7.09 E
Lautenthal	52	51.52 N	10.17 E
Lauter ≃, Dtsch.	56	49.39 N	7.35 E
Lauter ≃, Europe	56	48.58 N	8.11 E
Lauterach	58	47.29 N	9.44 E
Lauterbach, Dtsch.	56	50.38 N	9.24 E
Lauterbach, Dtsch.	58	48.14 N	8.20 E
Lauterbourg	56	48.59 N	8.11 E
Lauterbrunnen	58	46.36 N	7.55 E
Lauterecken	56	49.39 N	7.35 E
Lauterhofen	60	49.22 N	11.37 E
Lauter [Sachsen]	54	50.33 N	12.44 E
Laut Kecil, Kepulauan II	112	4.50 S	115.45 E
Lautoka	175g	17.37 S	177.27 E
Lauttakylä → Huittinen	26	61.11 N	22.42 E
Laut Tawar, Danau ⊜	114	4.38 N	96.54 E
Lauwe	50	50.48 N	3.11 E
Lauwerszee ⊂	52	53.20 N	6.12 E
Lauzerte	32	44.15 N	1.08 E
Lauzon	206	46.50 N	71.10 W
Lauzun	32	44.38 N	0.28 E
Lava (Łyna) ≃	76	54.37 N	21.14 E
Lava, Nosy I	157b	14.33 S	47.36 E
Lava Beds National Monument ♠	204	41.42 N	121.30 W
Lavaca □[6]	222	29.22 N	96.55 W
Lavaca ≃	196	28.50 N	96.36 W
Lavaca Bay ⊂	196	28.35 N	96.35 W
La Vacherie	62	44.53 N	5.11 E
Lavagh More ∧	48	54.45 N	8.05 W
Lavagna	62	44.18 N	9.20 E
Lavagna ≃	62	44.21 N	9.20 E
Lava Hot Springs	202	42.37 N	112.00 W
Lavaisse	252	33.49 S	65.25 W
Laval, P.Q., Can.	206	45.35 N	73.45 W
Laval, Fr.	32	48.04 N	0.46 W
Laval-des-Rapides ◆[8]	275a	45.33 N	73.42 W
La Valette → Valletta	36	35.54 N	14.31 E
La Valette-du-Var	62	43.08 N	5.59 E
La Vall d'Uixo	34	39.49 N	0.14 W
Lavalle, Arg.	252	29.01 S	59.11 W
Lavalle, Arg.	252	28.12 S	65.08 W
Lavalleja → Minas	252	34.23 S	55.14 W
Lavallette	208	39.58 N	74.04 W
La Valley	200	37.06 N	105.20 W
Laval-Ouest ◆[8]	275a	45.33 N	73.52 W
Lavaltrie	206	45.53 N	73.17 W
Lavamünd	61	46.39 N	14.56 E
Lāvān, Jazīreh-ye I	128	26.48 N	53.15 E
Lavan, Naḥal V	132	30.57 N	34.21 E
Lavanono	157b	25.24 S	44.55 E
Lavant ≃	61	46.38 N	14.57 E
Lavapié, Punta ›	252	37.09 S	73.35 W
Lávara	38	41.16 N	26.22 E
Lavaraty	157b	23.16 S	46.59 E
Lavardac	32	44.11 N	0.18 E
Lavarone	64	45.56 N	11.15 E
Lavassaare	76	58.31 N	24.22 E
Lava-Tudo ≃	252	28.26 S	50.25 W
Laveaga Peak ∧	226	36.53 N	121.11 W
La Vecilla de Curueño	34	42.51 N	5.24 W
La Vega	238	19.13 N	70.31 W
La Vega ◆[8]	286c	10.28 N	66.57 W
Lavela	24	63.38 N	45.31 E
La Vela, Cabo de ›	246	12.15 N	72.11 W
La Vela de Coro	246	11.27 N	69.34 W
Lavelanet	32	42.56 N	1.51 E
Lavelle	208	40.46 N	76.22 W
Lavello	68	41.03 N	15.48 E
Laven	41	56.07 N	9.43 E
La Venada	196	25.50 N	97.30 W
Lavendon	42	52.11 N	0.40 W
Lavenham	42	52.06 N	0.47 E
Laveno	58	45.55 N	8.37 E
Lavenone	64	45.44 N	10.26 E
La Venta ≃	234	16.59 N	93.46 W
La Venta ⊥	234	18.08 N	94.03 W
Laventie	50	50.38 N	2.46 E
La Ventura	232	24.38 N	100.54 W
Laver ≃	44	54.08 N	1.30 W
Lavéra	62	43.23 N	5.02 E
La Vera ◆[1]	34	40.20 N	5.30 W
La Verde, Arg.	252	27.08 S	59.23 W
La Verde, Arg.	258	34.44 S	59.16 W
Laverdière, Lac ⊜	206	46.50 N	74.28 W
L'Averdy, Cape ›	175e	5.33 S	155.04 E
La Vérendrye, Réserve ♠	190	47.30 N	77.30 W
La Vergne	194	36.00 N	86.34 W
La Verna ⚘[1]	66	43.42 N	11.54 E
La Verne, Ca., U.S.	280	34.06 N	117.46 W
Laverne, Ok., U.S.	196	36.42 N	99.53 W
La Vernia	196	29.21 N	98.07 W
Laverock	285	40.05 N	75.11 W
La Verpillière	62	45.38 N	5.09 E
La Verrière	261	48.45 N	1.57 E
Lavers Hill	169	38.40 S	143.24 E
Laverton, Austl.	162	28.38 S	122.25 E
Laverton, Austl.	169	37.52 S	144.45 E
Laverton Royal Australian Air Force Base ■	169	37.52 S	144.43 E
La Veta	200	37.30 N	105.00 W
Lavezares	116	12.32 N	124.20 E
Lavezzi, Îles II	71	41.20 N	9.15 E
Lavezzola	66	44.34 N	11.52 E
Lavia	26	61.36 N	22.36 E
Laviano	68	40.47 N	15.18 E
Lavic Lake ⊜	204	34.40 N	116.21 W
La Victoria, Perú	286d	12.04 S	77.02 W
La Victoria, Ven.	246	10.14 N	67.20 W
Lavieille, Lake ⊜	190	45.51 N	78.14 W
Lavik	26	61.06 N	5.30 E
La Vila Joiosa	34	38.30 N	0.14 W
La Villa	64	46.36 N	11.54 E
La Villa ≃	236	7.59 N	80.23 W
La Ville-du-Bois	261	48.40 N	2.16 E
La Villeneuve-Saint-Martin	261	49.04 N	1.58 E
Lavillette	186	47.16 N	65.18 W
Lavin	58	46.46 N	10.06 E
La Viña, Arg.	252	25.27 S	65.35 W
Lavina, Mt., U.S.	202	46.17 N	108.56 W
Lavinio Lido di Enea	66	41.30 N	12.05 E
Laviolette, Lac ⊜	206	46.51 N	73.58 W
La Virginia	246	4.54 N	75.53 W
Lavis	64	46.08 N	11.07 E
La Vista	198	41.11 N	96.01 W
Lavon	222	33.02 N	96.26 W
Lavonia	192	34.26 N	83.06 W
Lavon Lake ⊜[1]	222	33.05 N	96.28 W
Lavougba	152	5.46 N	23.21 E
La Voulte-sur-Rhône	62	44.48 N	4.47 E
Lavoûte-sur-Loire	62	45.07 N	3.54 E
Lavoutte, Anse ⊂	241f	14.06 N	60.56 W
Lavradia	266c	38.40 N	9.03 W
Lavras	256	21.14 S	45.00 W
Lavras ≃	287a	23.00 S	43.33 W
Lavras da Mangabeira	250	6.45 S	38.57 W
Lavras do Sul	252	30.49 S	53.55 W
Lavrentija	180	65.35 N	171.00 W
Lavrentija, zaliv ⊂	180	65.40 N	171.15 W
Lavrinhas	256	22.35 S	44.54 W
Lávrion	38	37.44 N	24.04 E
Lavumisa	158	27.19 S	31.54 E
Lavushi Manda National Park ♠	154	12.20 S	30.50 E
Lawa	116	6.12 N	125.41 E
Lawai	229b	21.55 N	159.30 W
Lawang	115a	7.49 S	112.42 E
La Wantzenau	58	48.40 N	7.50 E
La Ward	222	28.51 N	96.28 W
Lawas	112	4.51 N	115.24 E
Lawatu	112	2.53 S	120.18 E
Lawdar	144	13.53 N	45.52 E
Lawele	112	5.13 S	122.57 E
Lawers, Ben ∧	46	56.34 N	4.13 W
Laweueng	114	5.31 N	95.52 E
Lawford Lake ⊜	184	54.30 N	96.43 W
Lawgi	166	24.34 S	150.39 E
Lawin	114	5.18 N	101.04 E
Lawin, Pulau I	164	1.31 S	128.44 E
Lawit, Gunong ∧	114	5.25 N	102.35 E
Lawksawk	110	21.15 N	96.52 E
Lawler	190	43.04 N	92.09 W
Lawlor, Mount ∧	280	34.16 N	118.06 W
Lawn, Nf., Can.	186	46.57 N	55.32 W
Lawn, Pa., U.S.	208	40.13 N	76.32 W
Lawn, Tx., U.S.	196	32.08 N	99.49 W
Lawn Bay ⊂	186	46.53 N	55.35 W
Lawndale, Ca., U.S.	228	33.53 N	118.21 W
Lawndale, Il., U.S.	219	40.13 N	89.17 W
Lawndale, N.C., U.S.	192	35.24 N	81.33 W
Lawndale ◆[8], Il., U.S.	278	41.51 N	87.43 W
Lawndale ◆[8], Pa., U.S.	285	40.03 N	75.05 W
Lawnes Creek ≃	208	37.08 N	76.40 W
Lawn Hill	166	18.35 S	138.35 E
Lawn Hill Creek ≃	166	18.03 S	139.09 E
Lawn Hill National Park ♠	166	18.45 S	138.27 E
Lawnside	285	39.51 N	75.01 W
Lawowa	112	4.26 S	122.56 E
Lawqah	128	29.49 N	42.45 E
Lawra	150	10.39 N	2.52 W
Lawrence, N.Z.	172	45.55 S	169.41 E
Lawrence, In., U.S.	218	39.50 N	86.01 W
Lawrence, Ks., U.S.	198	38.58 N	95.14 W
Lawrence, Ma., U.S.	207	42.42 N	71.09 W
Lawrence, Mi., U.S.	216	42.13 N	86.03 W
Lawrence, Ne., U.S.	198	40.17 N	98.15 W
Lawrence, N.Y., U.S.	276	40.36 N	73.43 W
Lawrence, Pa., U.S.	279b	40.18 N	80.09 W
Lawrence, Tx., U.S.	222	32.45 N	96.21 W
Lawrence □[6], In., U.S.	218	38.52 N	86.29 W
Lawrence □[6], Pa., U.S.	214	41.00 N	80.20 W
Lawrence, Lake ⊜	224	46.51 N	122.34 W
Lawrence Brook ≃	276	40.29 N	74.24 W
Lawrenceburg, In., U.S.	218	39.05 N	84.51 W
Lawrenceburg, Ky., U.S.	218	38.02 N	84.54 W
Lawrenceburg, Tn., U.S.	194	35.14 N	87.20 W
Lawrence Fork ≃	198	41.36 N	103.14 W
Lawrence Institute of Technology ⚘[2]	281	42.28 N	83.15 W
Lawrence Marsh ⩸	276	40.36 N	73.42 W
Lawrence Municipal Airport ⊠	283	42.43 N	71.07 W
Lawrence Park	214	42.09 N	80.01 W
Lawrencepur	123	33.50 N	72.30 E
Lawrenceville, Il., U.S.	194	38.43 N	87.40 W
Lawrenceville, N.J., U.S.	208	40.17 N	74.43 W
Lawrenceville, Pa., U.S.	210	42.00 N	77.08 W
Lawrenceville, Va., U.S.	192	36.45 N	77.50 W
Lawrenceville ◆[8]	279b	40.28 N	79.57 W
Lawson, Austl.	170	33.43 S	150.26 E
Lawson, Mo., U.S.	194	39.26 N	94.12 W
Lawson Heights	214	40.18 N	79.23 W
Lawsonia	208	37.58 N	75.50 W
Lawsons Creek ≃	170	32.35 S	149.43 E
Lawtey	192	30.02 N	82.04 W
Lawton, Ky., U.S.	218	38.16 N	83.13 W
Lawton, Mi., U.S.	216	42.10 N	85.50 W
Lawton, N.D., U.S.	198	48.18 N	98.22 W
Lawton, Ok., U.S.	196	34.36 N	98.23 W
Lawton ◆[8]	286b	23.06 N	82.21 W
Lawu, Gunung ∧	115a	7.38 S	111.11 E
Lawyer Creek ≃	202	46.14 N	116.01 W
Lawyersville	210	42.42 N	74.30 W
Lawz, Jabal al- ∧	128	28.40 N	35.18 E
Laxå	40	58.59 N	14.37 E
Laxay	46	58.09 N	6.35 W
Laxenburg	264b	48.04 N	16.21 E
Laxenburger Park ♠	264b	48.04 N	16.22 E
Laxey	44	54.14 N	4.23 W
Laxford, Loch ⊂	46	58.23 N	5.06 W
Lax Kw'alaams	182	54.33 N	130.25 W
Laxou	58	48.41 N	6.09 E
Layang Layang	114	1.49 N	103.29 E
Laye ≃	62	43.54 N	5.48 E
La Yesca	234	21.19 N	104.02 W
Layhill	208	39.05 N	77.03 W
Laylā	144	22.17 N	46.45 E
Lay Lake ⊜[1]	194	33.10 N	86.35 W
Layou	241h	13.12 N	61.17 W
Layou ≃	240d	15.23 N	61.26 W
La'youn □[4]	148	27.55 N	12.15 W
Lay-Saint-Christophe	56	48.45 N	6.12 E
Laysan Island I	14	25.50 N	171.50 W
Layton, N.J., U.S.	210	41.13 N	74.50 W
Layton, Ut,. U.S.	200	41.03 N	111.58 W
Laytons Lake ⊜	285	39.42 N	75.26 W
Laytonville	204	39.41 N	123.28 W
Laytown	48	53.40 N	6.14 W
Laž	80	57.11 N	49.14 E
La Zarca	232	25.50 N	104.44 W
Lazarev	89	52.13 N	141.32 E
Lazarevo	80	56.49 N	50.15 E
Lazarevskoje	84	43.55 N	39.20 E
Lazarivo	157b	23.54 S	44.59 E
Lazaro Cárdenas, Méx.	196	25.23 N	103.10 W
Lázaro Cárdenas, Méx.	232	30.33 N	115.56 W
Lázaro Cárdenas, Méx.	234	17.57 N	102.12 W
Lázaro Cárdenas, Presa ⊜[1]	232	25.35 N	105.02 W
Lazdijai	76	54.14 N	23.31 E
Lazha	102	26.26 N	101.50 E
Lazhulong	120	35.08 N	81.33 E
Lazi	116	9.08 N	123.38 E
Lazio □[4]	66	42.00 N	12.30 E
Lazirky	78	50.06 N	32.39 E
Lazise	64	45.30 N	10.44 E
Lazo	89	43.25 N	133.55 E
La Zorra, Quebrada ≃	286c	10.36 N	67.03 W
Lazovskij zapovednik ♠	89	43.00 N	133.55 E
Lazzaro	68	37.58 N	15.40 E
Lazzate	266b	45.40 N	9.05 E
Lea ≃	42	51.30 N	0.01 E
Léach	110	12.21 N	103.46 E
Leach ≃	42	51.41 N	1.39 W
Leach Pond ⊜	283	42.04 N	71.09 W
Leachville	194	35.56 N	90.15 W
Leacock	208	40.05 N	76.12 W
Lead	198	44.21 N	103.45 W
Leadbetter Point ›	224	46.38 N	124.03 W
Leadburn	46	55.47 N	3.14 W
Leadenham	44	53.05 N	0.34 W
Leaden Roding	260	51.48 N	0.19 E
Leader	184	50.53 N	109.31 W
Leader Water ≃	46	55.36 N	2.41 W
Leadgate	44	54.52 N	1.48 W
Lead Hill ∧[2]	194	37.06 N	92.38 W
Leadhills	44	55.25 N	3.47 W
Leadon ≃	42	51.53 N	2.16 W
Leadore	202	44.40 N	113.21 W
Leadville	200	39.15 N	106.17 W
Leaf ≃, Mn., U.S.	198	46.29 N	94.53 W
Leaf ≃, Ms., U.S.	194	31.00 N	88.45 W
Leaf Lake ⊜	184	53.02 N	102.07 W
Leaghur, Lake ⊜	166	33.35 S	143.04 E
League, Slieve ∧	48	54.39 N	8.44 W
League City	222	29.30 N	95.05 W
Leakesville	194	31.09 N	88.33 W
Leakey	196	29.43 N	99.45 W
Leakin Park ♠	284b	39.18 N	76.42 W
Leak Run ≃	279b	40.27 N	79.47 W
Leaksville	192	36.29 N	79.53 W
Lealman	220	27.49 N	82.40 W
Lealui	152	15.10 S	23.02 E
Leam ≃	42	52.17 N	1.14 W
Leamington	214	42.03 N	82.36 W
Leamington Spa → Royal Leamington Spa	42	52.18 N	1.31 W
Le'an	100	27.24 N	115.48 E
Leán ≃	236	15.47 N	87.20 W
Leander Point ›	162	29.16 S	114.56 E
Leandro	250	5.59 S	44.55 W
Leandro N. Alem	252	27.36 S	55.19 W
Leane, Lough ⊜	48	52.05 N	9.35 W
Leannan ≃	48	55.02 N	7.38 W
Leano, Monte ∧	66	41.20 N	13.13 E
Learmonth	162	22.15 S	114.05 E
Leary	192	31.29 N	84.30 W
Leaside □[8]	275b	43.42 N	79.22 W
Leask	184	53.00 N	106.45 W
Leatherhead	42	51.18 N	0.20 W
Leatherman Peak ∧	202	44.05 N	113.44 W
Leatherwood Creek ≃	218	38.49 N	86.30 W
Lea Town	262	53.46 N	2.48 W
Leavenworth, Ks., U.S.	198	39.18 N	94.55 W
Leavenworth, Wa., U.S.	224	47.35 N	120.39 W
Leavesden Aerodrome ⊠	260	51.42 N	0.27 W
Leavittsburg	214	41.14 N	80.52 W
Leawood	194	37.03 N	94.31 W
Łeba	30	54.47 N	17.33 E
Łeba ≃	30	54.47 N	17.33 E
Lebach	56	49.24 N	6.54 E
Lebak	116	6.32 N	124.03 E
Lebam	224	46.33 N	123.32 W
Lébamba	152	2.12 S	11.30 E
Lebango	152	0.22 N	14.49 E
Lebanon, Ct., U.S.	207	41.38 N	72.13 W
Lebanon, Il., U.S.	219	38.36 N	89.48 W
Lebanon, In., U.S.	218	40.02 N	86.28 W
Lebanon, Ks., U.S.	198	39.48 N	98.33 W
Lebanon, Ky., U.S.	194	37.34 N	85.15 W
Lebanon, Mo., U.S.	194	37.40 N	92.39 W
Lebanon, N.H., U.S.	188	43.38 N	72.15 W
Lebanon, N.J., U.S.	210	40.38 N	74.50 W
Lebanon, N.Y., U.S.	210	42.47 N	75.39 W
Lebanon, Oh., U.S.	218	39.26 N	84.12 W
Lebanon, Or., U.S.	202	44.32 N	122.54 W
Lebanon, Pa., U.S.	208	40.20 N	76.24 W
Lebanon, S.D., U.S.	198	45.04 N	99.46 W
Lebanon, Tn., U.S.	194	36.12 N	86.17 W
Lebanon, Va., U.S.	192	36.54 N	82.04 W
Lebanon □[6]	208	40.20 N	76.25 W
Lebanon (Lubnān) □[1], Asia	118	34.00 N	36.00 E
Lebanon (Lubnān) □[1], Asia	128	34.00 N	36.00 E
Lebanon Junction	194	37.50 N	85.43 W
Lebanon Mountains → Lubnān, Jabal ⩕	132	34.00 N	36.00 E
Lebanon Springs	210	42.29 N	73.23 W
Le Bar-sur-le-Loup	62	43.42 N	6.59 E
Leb'ažje, Kaz.	86	51.28 N	77.46 E
Leb'ažje, Ross.	80	57.25 N	49.32 E
Leb'ažje, Ross.	86	55.16 N	66.29 E
Lebbeke	50	51.00 N	4.08 E
Le Béage	62	44.51 N	4.07 E
Le Beausset	62	43.12 N	5.48 E
Lebec	228	34.50 N	118.51 W
Lebed'an'	76	53.01 N	39.09 E
Lebedevka, Kaz.	86	50.09 N	54.07 E
Lebedevka, Ross.	80	51.06 N	47.09 E
Lebedevka, Ross.	86	56.48 N	66.57 E
Lebedi	78	51.17 N	37.38 E
Lebedino	80	55.14 N	49.50 E
Lebedyn, Ukr.	78	48.59 N	31.31 E
Lebedyn, Ukr.	78	50.36 N	34.30 E
Leben, Oued el V	148	34.37 N	10.01 E
Lebesby	24	70.34 N	26.59 E
Le Bessat	62	45.22 N	4.31 E
Le Bihan Falls ∟	158	29.51 S	28.03 E
Le Biot	58	46.16 N	6.38 E
Lebir ≃	114	5.33 N	102.12 E
Le Blanc	32	46.38 N	1.04 E
Le Blanc-Mesnil	261	48.56 N	2.28 E
Le Bleymard	62	44.29 N	3.44 E
Leblon ◆[8]	287a	22.59 S	43.13 W
Lebo, Ks., U.S.	198	38.25 N	95.51 W
Lebo, Zaïre	152	4.29 N	23.57 E
Le Bois-de-Cise	50	50.05 N	1.26 E
Le Bois-Dieu	261	48.39 N	1.43 E
Le Bois-d'Oingt	58	45.55 N	4.35 E
Lebombo Mountains ⩕[2]	156	25.15 S	32.00 E
Lebongtandai	112	3.01 S	101.54 E
Le Boréon	62	44.07 N	7.17 E
Lębork	30	54.33 N	17.44 E
Le Boulay	261	48.47 N	1.40 E
Le Bourg-d'Oisans	62	45.03 N	6.02 E
Le Bourget	261	48.56 N	2.26 E
Le Bourget-du-Lac	62	45.39 N	5.52 E
Le Brassus	58	46.35 N	6.13 E
Lebrija	34	36.55 N	6.04 W
Lebrija ≃	246	8.08 N	73.47 W
Le Broc	62	43.49 N	7.10 E
Le Brugeron	62	45.43 N	3.43 E
Łebsko, Jezioro ⊂	30	54.44 N	17.24 E
Lebu	252	37.37 S	73.39 W
Le Bugue	32	44.55 N	0.56 E
Le Buisson de Massoury ⩸	261	48.30 N	2.43 E
Lebus	54	52.25 N	14.32 E
Le Caire → Al-Qāhirah	142	30.03 N	31.15 E
Le Camp-du-Castellet	62	43.15 N	5.45 E
Le Cannet	62	43.34 N	7.01 E
Lecanto	220	28.51 N	82.29 W
Le Cap → Cap-Haïtien, Haï.	238	19.45 N	72.12 W
Le Cap → Cape Town, S. Afr.	158	33.55 S	18.22 E
Le Carbet	240e	14.43 N	61.11 W
Le Cateau	50	50.06 N	3.33 E
Le Catelet	50	50.00 N	3.15 E
Lecce	68	40.23 N	18.11 E
Lecce □[4]	68	40.13 N	18.10 E
Lecce, Tavoliere di ≍	68	40.30 N	17.35 E
Lecce nei Marsi	66	41.56 N	13.41 E
Lečchumskij chrebet ⩕	84	42.45 N	43.05 E
Lecco	62	45.51 N	9.23 E
Lecco, Lago di ⊜	58	45.55 N	9.19 E
Le Center	190	44.23 N	93.43 W
Lech	58	47.12 N	10.09 E
Lech ≃	30	48.44 N	10.56 E
Le Châble, Fr.	58	46.06 N	6.06 E
Le Châble, Schw.	58	46.05 N	7.12 E
L'Échalp	62	44.45 N	7.00 E
Le Chambon-Feugerolles	62	45.24 N	4.19 E
Le Chambon-sur-Lignon	62	45.03 N	4.18 E
Le Champ-Renault	261	49.06 N	2.31 E
Lechang	100	25.09 N	113.21 E
Le Chasseral ∧	58	47.08 N	7.03 E
Le-Château-d'Oléron	32	45.53 N	1.11 W
Le Châtelard, Fr.	62	45.41 N	6.08 E
Le Châtelard, Schw.	58	46.04 N	6.58 E
Le Châtelet	32	46.39 N	2.17 E
Le Châtelet-en-Brie	50	48.30 N	2.48 E
Lechbruck	58	47.42 N	10.47 E
Leche, Laguna de la ⊂	240p	22.13 N	78.38 W
Le Chêne-Rogneux	261	48.46 N	1.46 E
Le Chesnay	261	48.50 N	2.07 E
Le Chesne	56	49.31 N	4.46 E
Le Cheylard	62	44.54 N	4.25 E
Lechfeld ≍	58	48.10 N	10.50 E
Lechiguanas, Islas de las II	252	33.26 S	59.42 W
Lechlade	42	51.43 N	1.41 W
Lechleiten	58	47.16 N	10.12 E
Lechta	24	60.49 N	48.28 E
Lechtaler Alpen ⩕	64	47.15 N	10.30 E
Lechuga, Arroyo ≃	286b	23.01 N	82.16 W
Lechuguilla, Cerro ∧	234	22.19 N	104.15 W
Lecinone, Monte ∧	267a	41.59 N	12.48 E
Leck	41	54.46 N	8.58 E
Le Claire	190	41.36 N	90.21 W
Lecompte	194	31.05 N	92.24 W
Leconfield	44	53.52 N	0.27 W
Léconi	152	1.35 S	14.14 E
Lecontes Mills	214	41.05 N	78.17 W
Le Cornate ∧	66	43.10 N	10.57 E
Le Coudray-Montceaux	261	48.34 N	2.31 E
Le Coudray-Saint-Germer	50	49.25 N	1.50 E
Le Creusot	58	46.48 N	4.26 E
Le Croci di Acerno)(	68	40.47 N	15.02 E
Le Croisic	32	47.18 N	2.31 W
Le Crotoy	50	50.13 N	1.37 E
Łęczna	30	51.19 N	22.52 E
Łęczyca	30	52.04 N	19.13 E
Leda ≃	52	53.12 N	7.26 E
Ledaig	46	56.30 N	5.23 W
Led'anaja, gora ∧	74	61.53 N	171.09 E
Ledang, Gunong ∧	114	2.22 N	102.37 E
Ledava ≃	61	46.29 N	16.35 E
Ledbetter	222	30.09 N	96.48 W
Ledbury	42	52.02 N	2.25 W
Lede	50	50.58 N	3.58 E
Ledenice	61	48.57 N	14.37 E
Lederach	285	40.16 N	75.24 W
Le Deschaux	58	46.57 N	5.30 E
Ledesma	34	41.05 N	6.00 W
Ledgewood	276	40.52 N	74.39 W
Ledi, Ben ∧	46	56.15 N	4.19 W
Le Diamant	240e	14.29 N	61.02 W
Lediba	152	3.03 S	16.32 E
Lédignan	62	43.59 N	4.06 E
Ledkovo	24	67.14 N	50.30 E
Lednice	61	48.48 N	16.48 E
Ledo, India	120	27.18 N	95.44 E
Ledo, Indon.	112	1.02 N	109.36 E
Lêdo, Cabo ›	152	9.41 S	13.12 E
Ledong	110	18.45 N	109.12 E
Le Donjon	32	46.21 N	3.48 E
Le Dorat	32	46.13 N	1.05 E
Le Doré, Lac ⊜	186	51.17 N	61.23 W
Ledra ≃	64	46.13 N	13.02 E
Ledsham	262	53.16 N	2.58 W
Ledu	102	36.32 N	102.25 E
Leduc	182	53.16 N	113.33 W
Ledung	114	2.45 N	99.59 E
Ledyard Bay ⊂	180	69.30 N	164.30 W
Lędyczek	30	53.33 N	16.58 E
Lee, Il., U.S.	216	41.48 N	88.56 W
Lee, Ma., U.S.	207	42.18 N	73.14 W
Lee □[6], Fl., U.S.	220	26.34 N	81.55 W
Lee □[6], Il., U.S.	216	41.50 N	89.29 W
Lee □[6], Tx., U.S.	222	30.20 N	96.55 W
Lee ≃	48	51.54 N	8.22 W
Lee Boulevard Heights	284c	38.52 N	77.09 W
Lee Center	210	43.18 N	75.31 W
Leechburg	214	40.37 N	79.36 W
Leechburg Airport ⊠	279b	40.37 N	79.34 W
Leech Lake ⊜, Sk., Can.	184	51.04 N	102.30 W
Leech Lake ⊜, Mn., U.S.	190	47.09 N	94.23 W
Leech Lake Indian Reservation ◆[4]	190	47.30 N	94.27 W
Leechtown	224	48.30 N	123.42 W
Leedey	196	35.52 N	99.20 W
Leedom Estates	285	39.41 N	75.35 W
Leeds, Eng., U.K.	44	53.50 N	1.35 W
Leeds, Al., U.S.	194	33.32 N	86.32 W
Leeds, N.Y., U.S.	210	42.15 N	73.54 W
Leeds, N.D., U.S.	198	48.17 N	99.26 W
Leeds and Bradford (Yeadon) Airport ⊠	44	53.52 N	1.38 W
Leeds and Grenville □[6]	212	44.45 N	75.50 W
Leeds and Liverpool Canal ≍	262	53.25 N	2.59 W
Leeds Point	208	39.29 N	74.25 W
Leedstown	42	50.10 N	5.22 W
Leegebruch	54	52.43 N	13.11 E
Leek, Ned.	52	53.09 N	6.24 E
Leek, Eng., U.K.	44	53.06 N	2.01 W
Leelanau, Lake ⊜	190	44.55 N	85.43 W
Leelanau Peninsula ›[1]	190	45.10 N	85.35 W
Leeming	44	54.17 N	1.32 W
Leenaun	48	53.36 N	9.45 W
Leende	52	51.21 N	5.33 E
Lee-on-the-Solent	42	50.47 N	1.12 W
Lee Park	210	41.14 N	75.55 W
Leeper	214	41.22 N	79.18 W
Leer	52	53.14 N	7.26 E
Leerdam	52	51.54 N	5.05 E
Leerhafe	52	53.32 N	7.47 E
Leersum	52	52.01 N	5.26 E
Lees	262	53.32 N	2.04 W
Leesburg, Fl., U.S.	220	28.48 N	81.52 W
Leesburg, Ga., U.S.	192	31.43 N	84.10 W
Leesburg, In., U.S.	216	41.19 N	85.51 W
Leesburg, N.J., U.S.	208	39.15 N	74.59 W
Leesburg, Oh., U.S.	218	39.20 N	83.33 W
Leesburg, Tx., U.S.	222	32.59 N	95.05 W
Leesburg, Va., U.S.	208	39.06 N	77.33 W
Lees Creek ≃	218	39.21 N	83.29 W
Leese	52	52.30 N	9.06 E

Symbol	English	Deutsch	Español	Français	Português
≃	River	Fluß	Río	Rivière	Rio
≍	Canal	Kanal	Canal	Canal	Canal
∟	Waterfall, Rapids	Wasserfall, Stromschnellen	Cascada, Rápidos	Chute d'eau, Rapides	Cascata, Rápidos
ʯ	Strait	Meeresstraße	Estrecho	Détroit	Estreito
⊂	Bay, Gulf	Bucht, Golf	Bahía, Golfo	Baie, Golfe	Baía, Golfo
⊜	Lake, Lakes	See, Seen	Lago, Lagos	Lac, Lacs	Lago, Lagos
⩸	Swamp	Sumpf	Pantano	Marais	Pântano
⍓	Ice Features, Glacier	Eis- und Gletscherformen	Accidentes Glaciales	Formes glaciaires	Acidentes glaciares
⫧	Other Hydrographic Features	Andere Hydrographische Objekte	Otros Elementos Hidrográficos	Autres données hydrographiques	Outros acidentes hidrográficos
✢	Submarine Features	Untermeerische Objekte	Accidentes Submarinos	Formes de relief sous-marin	Acidentes submarinos
□	Political Unit	Politische Einheit	Unidad Política	Entité politique	Unidade política
⚘	Cultural Institution	Kulturelle Institution	Institución Cultural	Institution culturelle	Instituição cultural
⊥	Historical Site	Historische Stätte	Sitio Histórico	Site historique	Sitio histórico
♠	Recreational Site	Erholungs- und Ferienort	Sitio de Recreo	Centre de loisirs	Area de Lazer
⊠	Airport	Flughafen	Aeropuerto	Aéroport	Aeroporto
■	Military Installation	Militäranlage	Instalación Militar	Installation militaire	Instalação militar
◆	Miscellaneous	Verschiedenes	Misceláneo	Divers	Diversos

Name	Page	Lat.°′	Long.°′
Leesport	208	40.27 N	75.58 W
Lees Summit	194	38.55 N	94.23 W
Leeste	52	52.59 N	8.49 E
Leeston	172	43.46 S	172.18 E
Leesville, Il., U.S.	216	41.01 N	87.33 W
Leesville, In., U.S.	218	38.51 N	86.18 W
Leesville, La., U.S.	194	31.08 N	93.15 W
Leesville, Oh., U.S.	214	40.27 N	81.13 W
Leesville, S.C., U.S.	192	33.54 N	81.30 W
Leesville, Tx., U.S.	222	29.24 N	97.45 W
Leesville Lake ⊜[1], Oh., U.S.	214	40.30 N	81.10 W
Leesville Lake ⊜[1], Va., U.S.	192	37.05 N	79.25 W
Leeton	166	34.33 S	146.24 E
Leetonia	214	40.52 N	80.45 W
Leetsdale	214	40.33 N	80.12 W
Leeudoringstad	158	27.15 S	26.10 E
Leeu-Gamka	158	32.47 S	21.59 E
Leeupan ≚	273d	26.14 S	28.19 E
Leeuwarden	52	53.12 N	5.46 E
Leeuwin, Cape ›	162	34.22 S	115.08 E
Lee Vining	226	37.57 N	119.07 W
Leeward Islands II	238	17.00 N	63.00 W
Le Faouët	28	48.02 N	3.29 W
Le Fayet	58	45.55 N	6.42 E
Lefèvre, Pointe ›	175f	20.54 S	167.01 E
Leffe	62	45.48 N	9.53 E
Lefferts, Lake ⊜	276	40.25 N	74.14 W
Léfini ≃	152	2.57 S	16.10 E
Léfini, Réserve de Chasse de la ◆[4]	152	2.58 S	15.25 E
Lefke	130	35.07 N	32.51 E
Le Focette	64	43.55 N	10.13 E
Leforest	50	50.26 N	3.04 E
Lefors	196	35.26 N	100.48 W
Le François	240e	14.37 N	60.54 W
Le Freney-d'Oisans	62	45.02 N	6.07 E
Lefroy	212	44.16 N	79.34 W
Lefroy, Lake ⊜	162	31.15 S	121.40 E
Leftrook Lake ⊜	184	56.05 N	98.36 W
Lega Hida	144	7.56 N	41.04 E
Legal	182	53.57 N	113.35 W
Leganés	34	40.19 N	3.45 W
Le Gardeur	206	45.45 N	73.28 W
Legaspi	116	13.08 N	123.44 E
Legau	58	47.51 N	10.07 E
Legden	52	52.02 N	7.07 E
Legendre ≃	206	45.44 N	71.08 W
Legendre Island I	162	20.23 S	116.54 E
Leggett, Ca., U.S.	204	39.51 N	123.42 W
Leggett, Tx., U.S.	222	30.49 N	94.52 W
Leghorn → Livorno	66	43.33 N	10.19 E
Legion Mine	154	21.23 S	28.33 E
Legion of Honor, Palace of the ʋ	282	37.47 N	122.30 W
Legionowo	30	52.25 N	20.56 E
Legnago	64	45.11 N	11.18 E
Legnano	62	45.36 N	8.54 E
Legnica (Liegnitz)	30	51.13 N	16.09 E
Legnica □[4]	30	51.25 N	16.10 E
Le Gosier	241o	16.12 N	61.30 W
Le Grand	226	37.13 N	120.14 W
LeGrand, Cape ›	162	34.01 S	122.06 E
Le Grand-Lucé	50	47.52 N	0.28 E
Le Grand-Quevilly	50	49.25 N	1.02 E
Le Grand-Serre	62	45.16 N	5.06 E
Le Grand Wintersberg ∧[2]	56	48.59 N	7.37 E
Le Grau-du-Roi	62	43.32 N	4.08 E
Le Gua	62	45.01 N	5.37 E
Le Guelta	34	36.22 N	0.50 E
Leguga	154	3.23 N	25.02 E
Legume	166	28.25 S	152.19 E
Legundi, Pulau I	115a	5.50 S	105.16 E
Leh	123	34.10 N	77.35 E
Le Havre	50	49.30 N	0.08 E
Lehčevo	38	43.32 N	23.32 E
Le Hérie-la-Viéville	50	49.49 N	3.38 E
Lehesten	54	50.29 N	11.28 E
Lehi	200	40.23 N	111.50 W
Lehigh, Ia., U.S.	190	42.21 N	94.03 W
Lehigh, Ok., U.S.	196	34.28 N	96.12 W
Lehigh □[6]	208	40.36 N	75.29 W
Lehigh ≃	210	40.41 N	75.12 W
Lehigh Acres	220	26.37 N	81.37 W
Lehighton	210	40.50 N	75.42 W
Lehinch	48	52.56 N	9.21 W
Lehnin	54	52.19 N	12.44 E
Lehnitz	54	52.44 N	13.15 E
Lehnitz See ⊜	264a	52.45 N	13.16 E
Leho	140	7.07 N	33.52 E
Le Hohwald	58	48.24 N	7.20 E
Le Houlme	50	49.31 N	1.02 E
Lehr	198	45.59 N	99.32 W
Lehra Gāga	123	29.55 N	75.49 E
Lehrbach	56	50.47 N	9.04 E
Lehrberg	56	49.21 N	10.30 E
Lehre	54	52.19 N	10.40 E
Lehrte	52	52.22 N	9.59 E
Lehstedt	52	52.14 N	10.12 E
Lehtimäki	26	62.47 N	23.55 E
Lehtrār Bāla	123	33.42 N	73.26 E
Lehtse	76	59.15 N	25.50 E
Lehua I	229b	22.01 N	160.06 W
Lehututu	156	23.58 S	21.51 E
Lei ≃	100	26.54 N	112.39 E
Leiah	123	30.58 N	70.56 E
Leião	266c	38.44 N	9.18 W
Leibnitz	61	46.47 N	15.32 E
Leibo	102	28.19 N	103.21 E
Leicester, Eng., U.K.	42	52.38 N	1.05 W
Leicester, Ma., U.S.	207	42.14 N	71.54 W
Leicester, N.Y., U.S.	210	42.46 N	77.53 W
Leicestershire □[6]	42	52.40 N	1.10 W
Leichhardt	274a	33.53 S	151.07 E
Leichhardt ≃	166	17.35 S	139.48 E
Leichhardt Falls ʟ	166	18.14 S	139.53 E
Leichhardt Range ⋏	166	20.40 S	147.25 E
Leichlingen	56	51.06 N	7.01 E
Leiden	52	52.09 N	4.30 E
Leiderdorp	52	52.09 N	4.32 E
Leidschendam	52	52.05 N	4.24 E
Leie (Lys) ≃	50	51.03 N	3.43 E
Leiferde	52	52.26 N	10.26 E
Leigh, N.Z.	172	36.17 S	174.49 E
Leigh, Eng., U.K.	44	53.30 N	2.33 W
Leigh, Eng., U.K.	260	51.12 N	0.13 E
Leigh ≃	169	38.06 S	144.03 E
Leigh Canal ≅	262	53.28 N	2.21 W
Leigh Creek	166	30.28 S	138.25 E
Leighlinbridge	48	52.44 N	6.59 W
Leigh-on-Sea	42	51.33 N	0.38 E
Leighton	194	34.42 N	87.31 W
Leighton Buzzard	42	51.55 N	0.40 W
Leikanger	26	61.10 N	6.52 E
Leiktho	110	19.13 N	96.35 E
Leimbach	54	51.36 N	11.28 E
Leimstruth	56	50.59 N	8.19 E
Lein ≃	56	48.54 N	10.01 E
Leinan	184	50.30 N	107.46 W
Leinburg	60	49.27 N	11.19 E
Leine ≃	52	52.43 N	9.36 E
Leinefelde, Dtsch.	52	51.23 N	10.20 E
Leinefelde, Dtsch.	54	51.23 N	10.20 E
Leinfelden-Echterdingen	56	48.41 N	9.08 E
Leinster	162	27.51 S	120.36 E
Leinster □[9]	48	53.05 N	7.00 W
Leinster, Mount ∧	48	52.37 N	6.44 W
Leintwardine	42	52.23 N	2.51 W
Leipalingis	76	54.05 N	23.51 E
Leipheim	58	48.27 N	10.13 E
Leipoldtville	158	32.14 S	18.30 E
Leipsic, De., U.S.	208	39.14 N	75.31 W
Leipsic, In., U.S.	218	38.40 N	86.22 W
Leipsic, Oh., U.S.	216	41.05 N	83.59 W
Leipsic ≃	208	39.15 N	75.24 W
Leipzig	54	51.19 N	12.20 E
Leiria	34	39.45 N	8.48 W
Leirvik	26	59.45 N	5.30 E
Leisach	64	46.48 N	12.45 E
Leishendian	107	28.58 N	106.40 E
Leisi	76	58.34 N	22.39 E
Leisler, Mount ∧	162	23.28 S	129.17 E
Leisnig	54	51.09 N	12.56 E
Leiston	42	52.12 N	1.34 E
Leisure City	220	25.29 N	80.25 W
Leitariegos, Puerto de)(	34	43.00 N	6.25 W
Leitchfield	194	37.28 N	86.17 W
Leiters Ford	216	41.07 N	86.23 W
Leith	46	55.59 N	3.10 W
Leith, Water of ≃	46	55.59 N	3.11 W
Leitha (Lajta) ≃	61	47.54 N	17.17 E
Leithagebirge ⋏	61	47.52 N	16.35 E
Leithe ◆[8]	263	51.29 N	7.06 E
Leith Hill ∧[2]	42	51.11 N	0.23 W
Leitre	164	2.50 S	141.40 E
Leitrim	48	54.00 N	8.04 W
Leitrim □[6]	48	54.20 N	8.20 W
Leitzkau	54	52.03 N	11.57 E
Leixi	100	27.10 N	112.52 E
Leixlip	48	53.22 N	6.29 W
Leiyang	100	26.24 N	112.51 E
Lei Yue Mun)(	271d	22.16 N	114.14 E
Leizhou Bandao ›[1]	102	21.15 N	110.09 E
Leizhuang	98	39.47 N	118.34 E
Lejasciems	76	57.17 N	26.35 E
Lek ≃	52	51.55 N	4.34 E
Lékana	152	2.19 S	14.36 E
Le Kef → El Kef	148	36.11 N	8.43 E
Lékéti ≃	152	1.36 S	14.57 E
Lekhainá	38	37.56 N	21.17 E
Lekir	114	4.07 N	100.44 E
Lekitobi	112	1.58 S	124.33 E
Lekkeroog	158	30.43 S	20.00 E
Lekkerwater	156	23.38 S	17.14 E
Lekma ≃	80	58.18 N	52.04 E
Łęknice	54	51.35 N	14.45 E
Lékoni ≃	152	1.11 S	13.16 E
Lekotero	152	0.46 S	23.51 E
Lékoumou □[5]	152	3.00 S	13.30 E
Le Kreïder	148	34.06 N	0.02 E
Le Kremlin-Bicêtre	261	48.49 N	2.21 E
Leksand	26	60.44 N	14.59 E
Leksberg	40	59.41 N	13.49 E
Leksozero, ozero ⊜	24	63.46 N	30.58 E
Leksvik	26	63.40 N	10.37 E
Lela	152	5.03 S	12.29 E
Le Lac-d'Issarlès	62	44.49 N	4.04 E
Le Lamentin	240e	14.37 N	61.01 W
Leland, Il., U.S.	216	41.37 N	88.48 W
Leland, Mi., U.S.	190	45.01 N	85.45 W
Leland, Ms., U.S.	194	33.24 N	90.53 W
Leland Grove	219	39.47 N	89.41 W
Leland Lake ⊜	224	47.53 N	122.53 W
Lelång ⊜	26	59.08 N	12.10 E
Lelant	42	50.11 N	5.26 W
Le Laus	62	44.31 N	6.09 E
Le Lauzet-Ubaye	62	44.26 N	6.26 E
Le Lavandou	62	43.08 N	6.22 E
Lel'čicy	78	51.47 N	28.19 E
Leleiwi Point ›	229d	19.44 N	155.00 W
Leleque	254	42.23 S	71.03 W
Leles	115a	7.07 S	107.53 E
Lelewau	112	3.02 S	121.05 E
Lélex	58	46.18 N	5.57 E
Le Liège	50	47.13 N	1.06 E
Le Limbé	238	19.42 N	72.24 W
Leling	98	37.45 N	117.12 E
Lelingluang	164	7.09 S	131.43 E
Lelintah	164	2.03 S	130.16 E
Le Lion-d'Angers	32	47.38 N	0.43 W
Leli Shan ∧	120	33.26 N	81.42 E
Le Locle	58	47.03 N	6.45 E
Lelogama	112	9.44 S	123.57 E
Le Lorrain	240e	14.50 N	61.04 W
Le Luc	62	43.23 N	6.19 E
Le Lude	50	47.39 N	0.09 E
Lelydorp	250	5.42 N	55.16 W
Lelystad	52	52.31 N	5.27 E
Lema	150	12.57 N	4.14 E
Lemahabang	115a	6.17 S	107.27 E
Le Maire, Estrecho de)(	254	54.50 S	65.00 W
Léman, Lac → Geneva, Lake ⊜	58	46.25 N	6.30 E
Lemankoa	175e	5.02 S	154.35 E
Le Mans	50	48.00 N	0.12 E
Le Marin	240e	14.28 N	60.53 W
Le Markstein	58	47.56 N	7.02 E
Le Mars	198	42.47 N	96.09 W
Lema Shilindi	144	4.55 N	42.02 E
Lemay	219	38.32 N	90.17 W
Lemay, Lac ⊜	186	50.35 N	68.25 W
Lembach	56	49.00 N	7.48 E
Lembach im Mühlkreis	60	48.29 N	13.53 E
Lemba-Gaba	273b	4.27 S	15.18 E
Lembak	112	0.52 N	117.32 E
Lembang	115a	6.49 S	107.36 E
Lembeck	52	51.45 N	7.00 E
Lembeek	50	50.43 N	4.13 E
Lembeh, Pulau I	112	1.26 N	125.13 E
Lembeni	154	3.47 S	37.37 E
Lemberg, Sk., Can.	184	50.44 N	103.13 W
Lemberg, Fr.	56	49.00 N	7.23 E
Lemberg → L'viv, Ukr.	78	49.50 N	24.00 E
Lemberg ∧	58	48.09 N	8.45 E
Lembruch	52	52.31 N	8.22 E
Lembu, Gunung ∧	114	4.12 N	97.24 E
Lemdiyya	148	36.12 N	2.50 E
Lemdiyya □[5]	148	35.50 N	3.00 E
Leme	255	22.12 S	47.24 W
Leme, Morro do ∧[2]	287a	22.58 S	43.10 W
Le Mée-sur-Seine	261	48.32 N	2.38 E
Lemei Rock ∧	224	46.01 N	121.46 W
Lemele	52	52.27 N	6.25 E
Le Mêle-sur-Sarthe	50	48.31 N	0.21 E
Lemene ≃	64	45.37 N	12.53 E
Lemeris, Cape ›	164	3.15 S	152.03 E
Le Merlerault	50	48.42 N	0.18 E
Lemery	116	13.53 N	120.55 E
Lemeškino	80	51.01 N	44.27 E
Le Mesle	261	48.43 N	1.41 E
Le Mesnil-Amelot	261	49.01 N	2.36 E
Le Mesnil-Aubry	261	49.03 N	2.24 E
Le Mesnil-le-Roi	261	48.56 N	2.08 E
Le Mesnil-Saint-Denis	261	48.45 N	1.58 E
Le Mesnil-sur-Oger	50	48.57 N	4.01 E
Lemesós (Limassol)	130	34.40 N	33.02 E
Lemeta	180	64.52 N	147.44 W
Lemförde	52	52.28 N	8.22 E
Lemfu	152	5.18 S	15.13 E
Lemgo	52	52.02 N	8.54 E
Lemhi ≃	202	45.12 N	113.53 W
Lemhi Pass)(	202	44.58 N	113.27 W
Lemhi Range ⋏	202	44.30 N	113.25 W
Lemie	62	45.14 N	7.17 E
Lemierzyce	54	52.35 N	14.56 E
Lemieux Islands II	176	64.30 N	64.40 W
Lemin	102	21.11 N	109.42 E
Leming	196	29.04 N	98.29 W
Lemitar	200	34.09 N	106.54 W
Lemke	52	52.39 N	9.09 E
Lemland I	26	60.03 N	20.09 E
Lemmatsi	76	58.20 N	26.37 E
Lemmenjoen kansallispuisto ♠	24	68.40 N	26.00 E
Lemmer	52	52.50 N	5.42 E
Lemmon	198	45.56 N	102.09 W
Lemmon, Mount ∧	200	32.26 N	110.47 W
Lemnos → Límnos I	38	39.54 N	25.21 E
Lemoenshoek	158	33.51 S	20.51 E
Lemoine, Lac ⊜	190	48.00 N	78.00 W
Lemon, Lake ⊜	218	39.16 N	86.25 W
Le Monastier	62	44.56 N	4.00 E
Lemoncove	204	36.23 N	119.01 W
Lemon Creek ≃	276	40.31 N	74.12 W
Le Monêtier-les-Bains	62	44.59 N	6.31 E
Lemon Grove	228	32.44 N	117.01 W
Lemon Heights	280	33.46 N	117.48 W
Lemont, Il., U.S.	216	41.40 N	88.00 W
Lemont, Pa., U.S.	214	40.49 N	77.49 W
Le Montet	32	46.25 N	3.03 E
Le Mont-Saint-Michel ʋ[1]	32	48.38 N	1.32 W
Lemoore	226	36.18 N	119.46 W
Lemoore Naval Air Station ■	226	36.15 N	119.57 W
Lemoro	112	1.25 S	121.05 E
Le Moule	241o	16.20 N	61.21 W
Le Moutier	261	48.50 N	1.42 E
LeMoyne, P.Q., Can.	275a	45.31 N	73.29 W
Lemoyne, Oh., U.S.	214	41.30 N	83.28 W
Lemoyne, Pa., U.S.	208	40.15 N	76.54 W
Lempa ≃	236	13.14 N	88.49 W
Lempäälä	26	61.19 N	23.45 E
Lempe	112	1.40 S	120.14 E
Lempira □[5]	236	14.20 N	88.40 W
Lemro ≃	110	20.25 N	93.20 E
Lemsid	148	26.32 N	13.49 W
Lemukutan, Pulau I	112	0.45 N	108.43 E
Le Murge ⋏[1]	68	40.52 N	16.42 E
Lemutan	112	3.03 N	115.49 E
Le Muy	62	43.28 N	6.33 E
Lemva ≃	24	66.30 N	61.48 E
Lemvig	26	56.32 N	8.18 E
Lemyethna	110	17.36 N	95.09 E
Len ≃	260	51.16 N	0.31 E
Lena, Il., U.S.	190	42.22 N	89.49 W
Lena, Wi., U.S.	190	44.57 N	88.02 W
Lena ≃	74	72.25 N	126.40 E
Lenangguar	115b	8.44 S	117.24 E
Lenape	285	39.55 N	75.38 W
Lenart	36	46.35 N	15.50 E
Lenasia	273d	26.17 S	27.50 E
Lenawee □[6]	216	41.53 N	84.04 W
Lencloître	32	46.49 N	0.20 E
Lençóis	255	12.34 S	41.23 W
Lençois Maranhenses, Parque Nacional dos ♠	250	2.25 S	43.15 W
Lend	64	47.18 N	13.04 E
Lenda ≃	154	1.20 N	28.01 E
Lendava	61	46.34 N	16.27 E
Lendelede	50	50.53 N	3.14 E
Lendery	24	63.26 N	31.03 E
Lendinara	64	45.05 N	11.36 E
Lendorf	64	46.50 N	13.26 E
Lendringsen	56	51.24 N	7.49 E
Le Neubourg	50	49.09 N	0.55 E
Lenga	114	2.17 N	102.49 E
Lengduqiao	106	30.27 N	119.15 E
Lengede	52	52.12 N	10.18 E
Lengefeld	54	50.43 N	13.11 E
Lengelscheid	263	51.08 N	7.40 E
Lengenfeld, Dtsch.	54	50.34 N	12.22 E
Lengenfeld, Dtsch.	56	51.13 N	10.13 E
Lenger	85	42.12 N	69.54 E
Lengerich, Dtsch.	52	52.11 N	7.50 E
Lengerich, Dtsch.	52	52.33 N	7.32 E
Lenggor ≃	114	2.25 N	103.37 E
Lenggries	64	47.41 N	11.34 E
Lenghu	90	38.30 N	93.15 E
Lengjiagou	104	41.40 N	121.37 E
Lengkong	115a	7.32 S	112.04 E
Lenglingen ⊜	26	64.14 N	13.45 E
Lengnau	58	47.11 N	7.22 E
Lengoué	152	1.13 N	15.43 E
Lengoué ≃	152	0.49 N	15.47 E
Lengshuichang	107	29.27 N	106.26 E
Lengshuikeng	100	27.55 N	117.08 E
Lengshuitan	102	26.27 N	111.35 E
Lengua de Vaca, Punta ›	252	30.14 S	71.38 W
Lengulu	154	3.15 N	26.30 E
Lengwe National Park ♠	154	16.15 S	34.45 E
Lengzipu	104	41.42 N	122.47 E
Lenham	42	51.14 N	0.43 E
Lenhartsville	208	40.34 N	75.53 W
Lenhovda	26	57.00 N	15.17 E
Lenina, gora ∧[2]	265b	55.42 N	37.31 E
Lenina, ozero ⊜	78	48.33 N	35.12 E
Lenina, pik ∧	85	39.20 N	72.55 E
Leninabad → Chudžand	85	40.17 N	69.37 E
Leninakan → Kumajri	84	40.48 N	43.50 E
Lenin Central Stadium ♠	265b	55.43 N	37.33 E
Lenin-Džol	85	41.03 N	72.38 E
Lenine	78	45.18 N	35.47 E
Leningori	84	42.07 N	44.29 E
Leningrad → Sankt-Peterburg	76	59.55 N	30.15 E
Leningrado → Sankt-Peterburg	76	59.55 N	30.15 E
Leningrad Oblast' □[4]	24	60.00 N	32.00 E
Leningradskaja	78	46.19 N	39.24 E
Leningradskaja ʋ[3]	9	69.30 S	159.23 E
Leningradskij	85	38.06 N	70.01 E
Leningradskoje	86	53.33 N	71.35 E
Lenino ◆[8]	265b	55.37 N	37.41 E
Leninogorsk, Kaz.	86	50.27 N	83.32 E
Leninogorsk, Ross.	80	54.36 N	52.30 E
Leninpol'	85	42.29 N	71.55 E
Leninsk, Kaz.	86	45.40 N	63.20 E
Leninsk, Ross.	80	46.08 N	43.46 E
Leninsk, Ross.	80	48.42 N	45.11 E
Leninsk, Ross.	86	54.55 N	59.54 E
Leninsk, Uzb.	85	40.38 N	72.15 E
Leninskaja Sloboda	80	56.05 N	44.28 E
Lenins'ke, Ukr.	78	45.16 N	35.54 E
Lenins'ke, Ukr.	78	51.27 N	33.18 E
Lenins'ke, Ukr.	83	48.05 N	39.31 E
Leninskij, Kaz.	86	52.13 N	76.47 E
Leninskij, Ross.	80	46.31 N	44.28 E
Leninskij, Ross.	80	56.34 N	45.56 E
Leninskij, Ross.	82	54.18 N	37.28 E
Leninsk-Kuzneckij	86	54.38 N	86.10 E
Leninskoje, Kaz.	80	49.03 N	49.56 E
Leninskoje, Kaz.	85	41.45 N	69.23 E
Leninskoje, Kaz.	86	50.44 N	57.53 E
Leninskoje, Kaz.	86	54.04 N	65.22 E
Leninskoje, Kyrg.	85	40.42 N	73.11 E
Leninskoje, Ross.	80	58.19 N	47.06 E
Leninskoje, Ross.	89	47.56 N	132.38 E
Lenin-Stausee → Kujbyševskoje vodochranilišče ⊜[1]	80	54.30 N	48.30 E
Leninžol	80	49.20 N	47.05 E
Lenk	58	46.28 N	7.27 E
Lenkerville	208	40.32 N	76.58 W
Len'ki	86	52.57 N	80.26 E
Lenmalu	164	1.44 S	130.13 E
Lennard, Mount ∧[2]	168a	33.21 S	115.53 E
Lenne ≃	56	51.25 N	7.30 E
Lennegebirge ⋏	52	51.15 N	8.00 E
Lennep	56	51.12 N	7.16 E
Lennep ◆[8]	52	51.12 N	7.16 E
Lennestadt	56	51.08 N	8.01 E
Lenni	285	39.54 N	75.27 W
Lennon	216	42.59 N	83.56 W
Lennonville	162	27.58 S	117.50 E
Lennox, Ca., U.S.	228	33.56 N	118.21 W
Lennox, S.D., U.S.	198	43.21 N	96.53 W
Lennox □[9]	46	56.02 N	4.15 W
Lennox, Isla I	254	55.18 S	66.50 W
Lennox and Addington □[6]	212	44.30 N	77.00 W
Lennoxtown	46	55.59 N	4.12 W
Lennoxville	206	45.22 N	71.51 W
Leno	64	45.22 N	10.13 E
Lenoir	192	35.54 N	81.32 W
Lenoir City	192	35.47 N	84.15 W
Le Noirmont	58	47.13 N	6.58 E
Lenola	66	41.24 N	13.28 E
Lenora	60	48.56 N	13.48 E
Lenore Lake ⊜	184	52.30 N	105.00 W
Le Nouvion-en-Thiérache	50	50.01 N	3.47 E
Lenox, Ga., U.S.	192	31.16 N	83.27 W
Lenox, Ia., U.S.	198	40.52 N	94.33 W
Lenox, Ma., U.S.	207	42.22 N	73.17 W
Lenox, Tn., U.S.	194	36.05 N	89.29 W
Lenox Dale	207	42.20 N	73.14 W
Lens	50	50.26 N	2.50 E
Lensahn	54	54.13 N	10.52 E
Lensk	74	61.00 N	114.50 E
Lenskoje	86	58.09 N	63.11 E
Lenswood	168b	34.55 S	138.49 E
Lentate sul Seveso	266b	45.41 N	9.07 E
Lentechi	84	42.48 N	42.44 E
Lenti	30	46.37 N	16.33 E
Lenting	60	48.48 N	11.28 E
Lentini	70	37.17 N	15.00 E
Lentner	219	39.43 N	92.09 W
Lentua ⊜	26	64.14 N	29.36 E
Lentvaris	76	54.39 N	25.03 E
Lenwood	228	34.53 N	117.07 W
Lenya	110	11.28 N	99.00 E
Lenya ≃	110	11.40 N	98.43 E
Lenz	273d	26.19 S	27.49 E
Lenzburg	58	47.23 N	8.11 E
Lenzen	54	53.05 N	11.28 E
Lenzerheide (Lai)	58	46.44 N	9.33 E
Lenzinghausen	52	52.07 N	8.28 E
Lenzkirch	58	47.52 N	8.12 E
Léo, Burkina	150	11.06 N	2.06 W
Leo, In., U.S.	216	41.13 N	85.00 W
Leoben	61	47.23 N	15.06 E
Leo Carrillo State Beach ♠	228	34.03 N	118.56 W
Léogâne	238	18.31 N	72.38 W
Leogang	64	47.26 N	12.45 E
Leola, Ar., U.S.	194	34.10 N	92.35 W
Leola, Pa., U.S.	208	40.05 N	76.11 W
Leola, S.D., U.S.	198	45.43 N	98.56 W
Leominster, Eng., U.K.	42	52.14 N	2.45 W
Leominster, Ma., U.S.	207	42.31 N	71.45 W
León, Esp.	34	42.36 N	5.34 W
Léon, Fr.	32	43.53 N	1.18 W
León, Nic.	236	12.26 N	86.53 W
Leon, Pil.	116	10.47 N	122.23 E
Leon, Ia., U.S.	190	40.44 N	93.44 W
Leon, Ks., U.S.	198	37.41 N	96.46 W
Leon, N.Y., U.S.	210	42.18 N	79.01 W
León □[4]	34	42.35 N	6.00 W
León □[5]	236	12.35 N	86.35 W
Leon □[6]	222	31.18 N	95.55 W
León □[9]	34	42.00 N	6.00 W
Leon ≃	196	30.59 N	97.24 W
Leon, Arroyo ≃	282	37.28 N	122.25 W
León, Montes de ⋏	34	42.30 N	6.18 W
Leona	222	31.09 N	95.58 W
Leona ≃	196	28.45 N	99.11 W
Leona, Punta ›	236	9.41 N	84.41 W
Leonard, Mi., U.S.	214	42.51 N	83.08 W
Leonard, Mo., U.S.	219	39.53 N	92.10 W
Leonard, N.D., U.S.	198	46.39 N	97.14 W
Leonard, Tx., U.S.	196	33.22 N	96.14 W
Leonardo	276	40.25 N	74.03 W
Leonardo da Vinci, Aeroporto Intercontinentale ⊠	66	41.48 N	12.13 E
Leonardsburg	214	40.21 N	82.59 W
Leonardsville	210	42.48 N	75.15 W
Leonardtown	208	38.17 N	76.38 W
Leonardville, Namibia	156	23.29 S	18.49 E
Leonardville, Ks., U.S.	198	39.21 N	96.51 W
Leona Vicario	200	32.10 N	115.10 W
Leonberg	56	48.48 N	9.01 E
Leonbronn	56	49.03 N	8.53 E
Leondale	273d	26.18 S	28.12 E
Leondárion	267c	37.59 N	23.51 E
León [de los Aldamas]	234	21.07 N	101.40 W
Leonding	61	48.16 N	14.15 E
Leone	174u	14.20 S	170.47 W
Leone, Golfo del → Lion, Golfe du ⊂	32	43.00 N	4.00 E
Leone, Monte ∧	58	46.15 N	8.06 E
Leones	252	32.39 S	62.18 W
Leonessa	66	42.34 N	12.58 E
Leonforte	70	37.38 N	14.23 E
Leongatha	169	38.29 S	145.57 E
León Guzmán	196	25.31 N	103.34 W
Leonia	276	40.51 N	73.59 W
Leonicha	76	59.37 N	38.51 E
Leonidas	216	42.01 N	85.21 W
Leonídhion	38	37.10 N	22.52 E
Leonidovo	89	49.17 N	142.50 E
Leon Junction	222	31.20 N	97.36 W
Leonora	162	28.53 S	121.20 E
Leonovo	82	55.26 N	38.42 E
Leontjevka	85	43.03 N	69.50 E
Leontjevo	76	58.58 N	36.37 E
Leonville	194	30.28 N	91.58 W
Leopard	285	40.01 N	75.27 W
Leopold	169	38.11 S	144.28 E
Leopold and Astrid Coast ⫠[2]	9	67.10 S	84.10 E
Leopoldau ◆[8]	264b	48.16 N	16.27 E
Leopold Downs	162	17.52 S	125.25 E
Léopold II, Lac → Mai-Ndombe, Lac ⊜	152	2.00 S	18.20 E
Leopoldina	256	21.32 S	42.38 W
Leopoldkanaal ≅	50	51.14 N	3.46 E
Leopoldo de Bulhões	255	16.37 S	48.46 W
Leopoldo y Astrid, Costa → Leopold and Astrid Coast ⫠[2]	9	67.10 S	84.10 E
Leopoldsburg	56	51.07 N	5.15 E
Leopoldsdorf	264b	48.06 N	16.24 E
Leopoldshagen	54	53.46 N	13.53 E
Leopoldstadt ◆[8]	264b	48.13 N	16.23 E
Léopoldville → Kinshasa	152	4.18 S	15.18 E
Leoti	198	38.28 N	101.21 W
Leova	38	46.29 N	28.15 E
Leoville	184	53.37 N	107.35 W
Le Pailly	58	47.48 N	5.25 E
Le Palais	32	47.21 N	3.09 W
Lepanto, C.R.	236	9.57 N	85.02 W
Lepanto → Návpaktos, Ellás	38	38.23 N	21.50 E
Lepanto, Ar., U.S.	194	35.36 N	90.19 W
Lepar, Pulau I	112	2.57 S	106.50 E
Le Parcq	50	50.23 N	2.06 E
Le Pâté	261	48.32 N	2.18 E
Lepe	34	37.15 N	7.12 W
Le Péage-de-Roussillon	62	45.22 N	4.48 E
Le Pecq	261	48.54 N	2.07 E
Lepel'	76	54.53 N	28.42 E
Le Pellerin	32	47.12 N	1.45 W
Lepembusu, Keli ∧	115b	8.40 S	121.49 E
Le Perray-en-Yuelines	261	48.42 N	1.51 E
Le Perreux-sur-Marne	261	48.51 N	2.30 E
Lepeški	82	56.05 N	38.07 E
Le Petit-Clamart ʋ	261	48.47 N	2.14 E
Le Petit-Couronne	50	49.23 N	1.01 E
Le Petit-Quevilly	50	49.26 N	1.02 E
Lephepe	156	23.20 S	25.50 E
Lépi	152	12.52 S	15.26 E
Le Piastre	66	44.00 N	10.50 E
Lepihué	254	41.37 S	73.36 W
Le Pin	261	48.55 N	2.38 E
Le Pin-au-Haras	50	48.44 N	0.09 E
L'Épine, Fr.	56	48.58 N	4.28 E
L'Épine, Fr.	261	48.32 N	2.21 E
Leping	100	28.57 N	117.05 E
Lepini, Monti ⋏	66	41.35 N	13.00 E
Lépin-le-Lac	62	45.32 N	5.47 E
L'Épiphanie	206	45.51 N	73.30 W
Le Plessis-aux-Bois	261	49.00 N	2.46 E
Le Plessis-Belleville	50	49.06 N	2.46 E
Le Plessis-Bouchard	261	49.00 N	2.14 E
Le Plessis-Pâté	261	48.37 N	2.20 E
Le Plessis-Trévise	261	48.49 N	2.34 E
Leplyavo	78	49.48 N	31.32 E
Lépo, Lagoa de ⊜	152	17.08 S	19.00 E
Le Poët	62	44.17 N	5.53 E
Le Pont	58	46.40 N	6.20 E
Le Pont-de-Beauvoisin	62	45.32 N	5.40 E
Le Pont-de-Montvert	62	44.22 N	3.45 E
Le Pontel	261	48.49 N	1.53 E
Lepontine, Alpi ⋏	58	46.25 N	8.40 E
Leporano	68	40.23 N	17.20 E
Le Port	157c	20.55 S	55.18 E
Le Portel	50	50.42 N	1.34 E
Le Port-Marly	261	48.53 N	2.06 E
Le Pouzin	62	44.45 N	4.45 E
Leppävirta	26	62.29 N	27.47 E
Lepperton	172	39.04 S	174.13 E
Leppin	54	52.53 N	11.34 E
Leppington	274a	33.58 S	150.49 E
Le Pradet	62	43.06 N	6.01 E
Lepreau, Point ›	186	45.04 N	66.27 W
Le Prêcheur	240e	14.48 N	61.14 W
Le Pré-Saint-Gervais	261	48.53 N	2.25 E
Le Prese	58	46.18 N	10.04 E
Lepsinsk	86	45.32 N	80.37 E
Lepsy, Kaz.	86	46.15 N	78.55 E
Lepsy, Kaz.	86	46.18 N	78.20 E
Le Puy	62	45.02 N	3.53 E
Le Quesnoy	50	50.15 N	3.38 E
Léraba ≃	150	9.42 N	4.35 W
Le Raincy	261	48.54 N	2.31 E
Le Rayol-Canadel-sur-Mer	62	43.10 N	6.28 E
Le Raysville	210	41.51 N	76.11 W
Lerberget	41	56.11 N	12.33 E
Lercara Friddi	70	37.45 N	13.36 E
Lerche ◆[8]	263	51.37 N	7.43 E
Lerderderg ≃	169	37.42 S	144.30 E
Lerdo → Ciudad Lerdo	196	25.32 N	103.32 W
Léré, Fr.	50	47.28 N	2.52 E
Léré, Mali	150	15.43 N	4.55 W
Lere, Nig.	150	9.43 N	9.21 E
Léré, Tchad	146	9.39 N	14.13 E
Lereh	164	3.08 S	139.54 E
Lerek ∧	114	3.47 N	102.47 E
Le Reposoir	58	46.00 N	6.33 E
Leri ≃	42	52.32 N	4.02 W
Leribe	158	28.58 S	28.00 E
Lerici	64	44.04 N	9.55 E
Lérida, Col.	246	0.10 N	70.42 W
Lérida → Lleida, Esp.	34	41.37 N	0.37 E
Lerik	84	38.46 N	48.25 E
Lérins, Îles de II	62	43.31 N	7.03 E
Lerma	34	42.02 N	3.45 W
Lerma ≃	234	20.13 N	102.46 W
Lermontovka	89	47.10 N	134.20 E
Lermoos	64	47.24 N	10.53 E
Lerno, Monte ∧	71	40.37 N	9.10 E
Le Robert	240e	14.41 N	60.57 W
Léros I, Ellás	38	37.08 N	26.52 E
Léros I, Ellás	267c	37.59 N	23.32 E
Lérouville	56	48.47 N	5.33 E
Leroux Wash V	200	34.54 N	110.12 W
Le Roy, Il., U.S.	216	40.21 N	88.45 W
Leroy, In., U.S.	216	41.22 N	87.16 W
Le Roy, Ks., U.S.	198	38.05 N	95.38 W
Le Roy, Mn., U.S.	190	43.30 N	92.30 W
Le Roy, N.Y., U.S.	210	42.58 N	77.59 W
Le Roy, Pa., U.S.	210	41.41 N	76.43 W
Leroy, Tx., U.S.	222	31.44 N	97.01 W
Lerum	26	57.46 N	12.16 E
Le Russey	58	47.10 N	6.44 E
Lerwick	46a	60.09 N	1.09 W
Léry	206	45.21 N	73.48 W
Lesa	62	45.50 N	8.34 E
Les Abrets	62	45.32 N	5.35 E
Les Abymes	241o	16.16 N	61.31 W
Lesage, Lac ⊜	206	46.19 N	75.03 W
Le Saint-Esprit	240e	14.34 N	60.57 W
Les Aix-d'Angillon	50	47.12 N	2.34 E
Les Allues	62	45.26 N	6.33 E
Les Alluets-le-Roi	261	48.55 N	1.55 E
Les Andelys	50	49.15 N	1.25 E
Les Anses-d'Arlets	240e	14.29 N	61.05 W
Le Sappy-en-Chartreuse	62	45.16 N	5.47 E
Les Arcs	62	43.27 N	6.29 E
Lesatima, Oldoinyo ∧	154	0.19 S	36.37 E
Le Sauze	62	44.22 N	6.41 E
Les Baux-en-Provence	62	43.45 N	4.48 E
Les Bézards	50	47.48 N	2.44 E
Les Bordes	261	48.39 N	1.58 E
Les Borges Blanques	34	41.31 N	0.52 E
Lesbos → Lésvos I	38	39.10 N	26.20 E
Les Bouchoux	58	46.18 N	5.49 E
Les Bréviaires	261	48.42 N	1.49 E
Lesbury	44	55.24 N	1.36 W
L'Escarène	62	43.50 N	7.21 E
Les Cayes	238	18.12 N	73.45 W
Les Chaises	261	48.39 N	1.42 E
Les Chapieux	62	45.42 N	6.44 E
Leschenault, Cape ›	162	31.18 S	115.27 E
Leschenault Estuary ⊂[1]	168a	33.15 S	115.42 E
Lesches	261	48.54 N	2.47 E
Les Clayes-sous-Bois	261	48.49 N	1.59 E
Les Contamines-Montjoie	62	45.50 N	6.44 E
Les Diablerets	58	46.21 N	7.10 E
Les Diablerets ∧	58	46.19 N	7.12 E
Lesdiboderi	146	8.28 N	12.35 E
Les Echarmeaux	58	46.10 N	4.27 E
Les Échelles	62	45.26 N	5.45 E
Les Écureuils	206	46.39 N	71.43 W
Le Semnoz ∧	62	45.48 N	6.07 E
Leseru	154	0.35 N	35.10 E
Les Essarts	32	46.46 N	1.14 W
Les Essarts-le-Roi	261	48.43 N	1.54 E
Les Estables	62	44.54 N	4.10 E
Les Étangs	56	49.09 N	6.23 E
Les Fonts	266d	41.32 N	2.02 E
Les Fourgs	58	46.50 N	6.25 E
Les Galleries d'Anjou ◆[9]	275a	45.35 N	73.34 W
Les Gâtines	261	48.48 N	1.58 E
Les Gets	58	46.09 N	6.40 E
Les Granges-le-Roi	261	48.30 N	2.01 E
Les Grésillons	261	48.56 N	2.01 E
Les Halles	62	45.43 N	4.26 E
Leshan	107	29.34 N	103.45 E
Les Haudères	58	46.05 N	7.31 E
Les Hautes-Rivières	56	49.53 N	4.50 E
Les Herbiers	32	46.52 N	1.01 W
Les Houches	62	45.53 N	6.48 E
Lesignano de'Bagni	64	44.39 N	10.18 E
Lésigny	261	48.45 N	2.37 E
Lesima, Monte ∧	62	44.41 N	9.15 E
Lesina	68	41.52 N	15.21 E
Lesina, Lago di ⊂	68	41.53 N	15.26 E
Les Islettes	56	49.06 N	5.00 E
Lesjaskog	26	62.15 N	8.22 E
Lesjöfors	40	59.59 N	14.11 E
Lesken	84	43.16 N	43.48 E
Lesko	30	49.29 N	22.21 E
Leskovac	38	42.59 N	21.57 E
Leskov Island I	18	56.40 S	28.10 W
Les'ky	78	49.19 N	32.13 E
Les Laumes	58	47.32 N	4.27 E
Les Lecques	62	43.11 N	5.40 E
Leslie, S. Afr.	158	26.27 S	28.55 E
Leslie, Scot., U.K.	46	56.12 N	3.13 W
Leslie, Ar., U.S.	194	35.49 N	92.33 W
Leslie, Ga., U.S.	192	31.57 N	84.05 W
Leslie, Mi., U.S.	216	42.27 N	84.25 W
Leslie, W.V., U.S.	188	38.02 N	80.43 W
Les Lilas	261	48.53 N	2.25 E
Les Loges	261	48.34 N	2.03 E
Les Loges-en-Josas	261	48.46 N	2.09 E
Lesmahagow	46	55.39 N	3.55 W
Les Marécottes	58	46.07 N	7.00 E
Les Mées	62	44.02 N	5.59 E
Les Mesnuls	50	48.45 N	1.50 E
Lesmo	266b	45.39 N	9.18 E
Les Molières	261	48.40 N	2.04 E
Les Monges ∧	62	44.16 N	6.12 E
Lesmont	50	48.26 N	4.25 E
Les Mosses	58	46.24 N	7.07 E
Lesmurdie Falls National Park ♠	168a	32.01 S	116.04 E
Les Mureaux	261	49.00 N	1.55 E
Leśna	30	51.02 N	15.16 E
Lesna ≃	76	52.10 N	23.33 E
Lesnaja	76	52.59 N	25.46 E
Lesneven	32	48.34 N	4.19 W
Les Neyrolles	58	46.08 N	5.38 E
Lešnica	38	44.39 N	19.19 E
Lesnoj, Ross.	24	59.48 N	52.08 E
Lesnoj, Ross.	80	54.11 N	40.27 E
Lesnoj, Ross.	86	56.57 N	67.15 E
Lesnoj ◆[8]	265a	60.00 N	30.19 E
Lesnoje	76	58.17 N	35.32 E
Lesnoje Konobejevo	80	54.02 N	41.55 E
Lesnoje Mat'unino	80	53.27 N	47.26 E
Lesnoj Gorodok	265b	55.39 N	37.13 E
Lesnoj park ♠	265a	59.59 N	30.21 E
Lesný ∧	60	50.02 N	12.37 E
Lesnyje Pol'any, Ross.	24	58.58 N	52.26 E
Lesnyje Pol'any, Ross.	265b	55.57 N	37.53 E
Lesogorsk, Ross.	80	55.06 N	43.56 E
Lesogorsk, Ross.	88	56.03 N	99.33 E
Lesogorsk, Ross.	89	49.27 N	142.08 E
Lesogorskij	24	61.02 N	28.53 E
Lesong, Gunong ∧	114	2.44 N	103.17 E
Lesopil'noje	89	46.44 N	134.20 E
Lesosibirsk	86	58.16 N	92.29 E
Lesotho □[1], Afr.	138	29.30 S	28.30 E
Lesotho □[1], Afr.	158	29.30 S	28.30 E
Lesozavodsk	89	45.28 N	133.27 E
Lesozavodskij	24	66.44 N	32.49 E
Les Pavillons-sous-Bois	261	48.55 N	2.30 E
Les Pieux	32	49.31 N	1.48 W
Les Planches-en-Montagne	58	46.40 N	6.01 E
Les Ponts-de-Martel	58	46.54 N	6.41 E
Les Posets ∧	34	42.39 N	0.25 E
Les Praz-de-Chamonix	58	45.56 N	6.52 E
Lesquin	50	50.35 N	3.07 E
Les Riceys	50	47.59 N	4.22 E
Les Roches-l'Evêque	50	47.47 N	0.53 E
Les Rousses	58	46.29 N	6.04 E
Les Ruelles	261	48.40 N	1.37 E
Les Sables-d'Olonne	32	46.30 N	1.47 W
Lessach	64	47.11 N	13.49 E
Les Saintes II	241o	15.52 N	61.37 W
Les Salles-sur-Verdon	62	43.46 N	6.12 E
Lessay	32	49.13 N	1.32 W
Les Scaffarels	62	43.57 N	6.41 E
Lesse ≃	56	50.14 N	4.54 E
Lessebo	26	56.45 N	15.16 E
Lessen → Lessines	50	50.43 N	3.50 E
Lesser Antilles II	238	15.00 N	61.00 W
Lesser Caucasus ⋏	84	41.00 N	44.35 E
Lesser Khingan Range → Xiao Hinggan Ling ⋏	89	48.45 N	127.00 E
Lesser Slave ≃	182	55.10 N	114.03 W
Lesser Slave Lake ⊜	182	55.25 N	115.30 W
Lesser Sunda Islands → Tenggara, Nusa II	108	9.00 S	120.00 E
Lessines (Lessen)	50	50.43 N	3.50 E
Lessini, Monti ⋏	64	45.41 N	11.13 E
L'Estaque	62	43.22 N	5.20 E
Leste ≃	250	6.20 S	57.46 W
Lester, Pa., U.S.	285	39.52 N	75.17 W
Lester, Wa., U.S.	224	47.12 N	121.29 W
Lester B. Pearson International Airport ⊠	212	43.41 N	79.38 W
Les Tessiers	62	44.24 N	4.16 E
Les Thilliers-en-Vexin	50	49.14 N	1.36 E
Lestijärvi	26	63.32 N	24.39 E
Lestijoki ≃	26	64.04 N	23.38 E
Lestkov	60	49.54 N	12.52 E
Lestock	184	51.18 N	104.00 W
L'Estréchure	62	44.06 N	3.47 E
Les Trois-Îlets	240e	14.32 N	61.02 W
Les Trois Lacs ⊜	206	45.48 N	71.54 W
Le Sueur	190	44.30 N	93.52 W
Le Sueur ≃	190	44.07 N	94.03 W
Lesueur, Mount ∧[2]	162	30.10 S	115.11 E
Lešukonskoje	24	64.54 N	45.40 E
Les Ulis	261	48.41 N	2.11 E
Lesung, Tanjung ›	115a	6.28 S	105.40 E
Lesunovo	80	55.40 N	43.07 E
Les Vans	62	44.24 N	4.08 E
Les Verrières	58	46.54 N	6.30 E
Lésvos (Lesbos) I	38	39.10 N	26.20 E
Leszno	30	51.51 N	16.35 E
Leszno □[4]	30	51.45 N	16.45 E
Letälven ≃	40	59.05 N	14.20 E
L'Étang-la-Ville	261	48.52 N	2.05 E
Letcher	198	43.53 N	98.08 W
Letchmore Heath	260	51.40 N	0.20 W
Letchworth	42	51.58 N	0.14 W
Letchworth State Park ♠	210	42.42 N	77.56 W
Letea, Ostrovul I	38	45.20 N	29.20 E
Le Teil	62	44.33 N	4.41 E
Le Temple	261	49.00 N	1.58 E
Letenye	30	46.26 N	16.43 E
Le Tertre-Saint-Denis	261	48.56 N	1.36 E
Lethbridge, Austl.	274a	33.44 S	150.48 E
Lethbridge, Ab., Can.	182	49.42 N	112.50 W
Lethbridge, Nf., Can.	186	48.21 N	53.52 W
Le Theil-sur-Huisne	50	48.16 N	0.42 E
Lethem	246	3.23 N	59.48 W
Le Thillay	261	49.00 N	2.28 E
Le Thillot	58	47.53 N	6.46 E
Le Tholy	58	48.05 N	6.45 E
Le Thor	62	43.56 N	5.00 E
Le Thoronet	62	43.27 N	6.18 E
Leti, Kepulauan II	164	8.13 S	127.50 E
Leti, Pulau I	112	8.12 S	127.41 E
Leticia	246	4.09 S	69.57 W
Leting	98	39.27 N	118.53 E
Letino	68	41.26 N	14.17 E
Letjiesbos	158	32.34 S	22.16 E
Letka	24	59.36 N	49.22 E
Letlhakane	156	21.27 S	25.30 E
Letlhakeng	156	24.08 S	25.02 E
Letmathe	56	51.22 N	7.37 E
Letn'aja Zolotica	24	64.57 N	36.50 E
Letnerečenskij	24	64.17 N	34.23 E
Le Touquet-Paris-Plage	50	50.31 N	1.35 E
Le Touvet	62	45.21 N	5.57 E
Letovo	265b	55.34 N	37.24 E
Letpadan	110	17.47 N	95.45 E
Le Trait	50	49.28 N	0.49 E
Le Trayas	62	43.28 N	6.55 E

ENGLISH	DEUTSCH
Name / Page / Lat.°′ / Long.°′	Name / Seite / Breite°′ / Länge°′ E = Ost

Symbols in the index entries represent the broad categories identified in the key at the right. Symbols with superior numbers (⋏[1]) identify subcategories (see complete key on page *I · 1*).

Symbole im Register stellen die rechts im Schlüssel erklärten Kategorien dar. Symbole mit hochgestellten Ziffern (⋏[1]) bezeichnen Unterabteilungen einer Kategorie (vgl. vollständiger Schlüssel auf Seite *I · 1*).

Los símbolos incluídos en el texto del índice representan las grandes categorías identificadas con la clave a la derecha. Los símbolos con numeros en su parte superior (⋏[1]) identifican las subcategorías (véase la clave completa en la página *I · 1*).

Les symboles de l'index représentent les catégories indiquées dans la légende à droite. Les symboles suivis d'un indice (⋏[1]) représentent des sous-catégories (voir légende complète à la page *I · 1*).

Os símbolos incluídos no texto do índice representam as grandes categorias identificadas com a chave à direita. Os símbolos com números em sua parte superior (⋏[1]) identificam as subcategorias (veja-se a chave completa à página *I · 1*).

∧ Mountain	Berg	Montaña	Montagne	Montanha
⋏ Mountains	Gebirge	Montañas	Montagnes	Montanhas
)(Pass	Paß	Paso	Col	Passo
V Valley, Canyon	Tal, Cañon	Valle, Cañón	Vallée, Canyon	Vale, Canhão
≚ Plain	Ebene	Llano	Plaine	Planície
› Cape	Kap	Cabo	Cap	Cabo
I Island	Insel	Isla	Île	Ilha
II Islands	Inseln	Islas	Îles	Ilhas
♠ Other Topographic Features	Andere Topographische Objekte	Otros Elementos Topográficos	Autres données topographiques	Outros acidentes topográficos

ESPAÑOL

Nombre	Página	Lat.°′	Long.°′ W = Oeste
Le Tremblay-sur-Mauldre	261	48.47 N	1.53 E
Le Tréport	50	50.04 N	1.22 E
Letschin	54	52.39 N	14.21 E
Letsôk-aw Kyun I	110	11.37 N	98.15 E
Letter	52	52.24 N	9.38 E
Letterfrack	48	53.33 N	10.00 W
Letterkenny	48	54.57 N	7.44 W
Lettermullan	48	53.13 N	9.42 W
Letterston	42	51.56 N	5.00 W
Lettonie → Latvia □[1]	72	57.00 N	25.00 E
Letts	218	39.14 N	85.35 W
Letung	112	2.58 N	105.42 E
Letychiv	78	49.23 N	27.37 E
Letzlingen	54	52.26 N	11.29 E
Leu	38	44.11 N	24.00 E
Léua	152	11.34 S	20.32 E
Leubnitz	54	50.43 N	12.21 E
Leubsdorf	54	50.48 N	13.08 E
Leuca	68	39.48 N	18.21 E
Leucadia	228	33.04 N	117.18 W
Leucate, Étang de c	32	42.51 N	3.00 E
Leuchars	46	56.23 N	2.53 W
Leuchtenberg	60	49.36 N	12.15 E
Leudeville	261	48.34 N	2.20 E
Leuenberger Forst ◆[3]	264a	52.40 N	13.53 E
Leuglay	58	47.49 N	4.48 E
Leuk	58	46.19 N	7.38 E
Leukerbad	58	46.23 N	7.38 E
Leulumoega	175a	13.49 S	171.55 W
Leumeah	274a	34.03 S	150.50 E
Leuna	54	51.19 N	12.01 E
Leupoldsgrün	54	50.17 N	11.47 E
Leura	170	33.43 S	150.20 E
Leura, Mount ∧[2]	169	38.15 S	143.09 E
Leuser, Gunung ∧	114	3.45 N	97.11 E
Leušinskij Tuman, ozero ⊜	86	59.42 N	65.35 E
Leutenberg	54	50.34 N	11.28 E
Leutersdorf	54	50.57 N	14.40 E
Leutershausen	56	49.18 N	10.24 E
Leutesdorf	56	50.27 N	7.23 E
Leutkirch	58	47.49 N	10.01 E
Leuven (Louvain)	56	50.53 N	4.42 E
Leuville-sur-Orge	261	48.37 N	2.16 E
Leuwiliang	115a	6.34 S	106.37 E
Leuze, Bel.	50	50.36 N	3.36 E
Leuze, Bel.	56	50.34 N	4.54 E
Levack	190	46.38 N	81.23 W
Levádhia	38	38.25 N	22.54 E
Levaja Mama ≃	88	57.10 N	111.54 E
Le Val-d'Ajol	58	47.55 N	6.29 E
Le Val-d'Albian	261	48.45 N	2.11 E
Levallois-Perret	261	48.54 N	2.18 E
Le Val-Saint-Germain	261	48.34 N	2.04 E
Levan	200	39.33 N	111.51 W
Levanger	26	63.45 N	11.18 E
Levanna, Monte ∧	62	45.24 N	7.12 E
Levant, Île du I	62	43.03 N	6.28 E
Levante, Riviera di ⩋[2]	62	44.15 N	9.30 E
Levanto	62	44.10 N	9.38 E
Levanzo	70	37.59 N	12.20 E
Levanzo, Isola di I	70	38.00 N	12.20 E
Levaši	84	42.27 N	47.20 E
Le Vauclin	240e	14.33 N	60.51 W
Levdym	86	60.29 N	66.19 E
Leveaux Mountain ∧[2]	190	47.37 N	90.47 W
Levél	61	47.54 N	17.12 E
Level, Isla I	254	44.29 S	74.23 W
Level Green	279b	40.24 N	79.43 W
Levelland	196	33.35 N	102.22 W
Levelock	180	59.07 N	156.52 W
Level Park	216	42.22 N	85.18 W
Leven, Eng., U.K.	44	53.53 N	0.19 W
Leven, Scot., U.K.	46	56.12 N	3.00 W
Leven ≃, Eng., U.K.	44	54.14 N	3.01 W
Leven ≃, Eng., U.K.	44	54.31 N	1.21 W
Leven, Loch ⊜, Scot., U.K.	46	56.12 N	3.22 W
Leven, Loch ⊜, Scot., U.K.	46	56.41 N	5.07 W
Leven Point ›	158	27.55 S	32.35 E
Levens	62	43.52 N	7.13 E
Levenshulme ◆[8]	262	53.27 N	2.10 W
Levent	130	38.27 N	37.52 E
Leventina, Valle V	58	46.25 N	8.52 E
Leveque, Cape ›	162	16.24 S	122.56 E
Leverano	68	40.17 N	18.00 E
Leverburgh	46	57.45 N	7.00 W
Leveretts Chapel	222	32.19 N	94.55 W
Levering	190	45.38 N	84.47 W
Leverkusen	56	51.03 N	6.59 E
Levern	52	52.22 N	8.26 E
Lever Park ♦	262	53.37 N	2.34 W
Le Vésinet	261	48.54 N	2.08 E
Le Vésuve → Vesuvio ∧[1]	68	40.49 N	14.26 E
Leviathan Peak ∧	226	38.41 N	119.37 W
Levice	30	48.13 N	18.37 E
Levicha	86	57.36 N	59.55 E
Levick, Mount ∧	9	74.08 S	163.12 E
Levico	64	46.01 N	11.18 E
Levie	36	41.42 N	9.07 E
Levier	58	46.57 N	6.08 E
Le Vigan	32	43.59 N	3.35 E
Levin	172	40.37 S	175.17 E
Levino	76	60.29 N	37.30 E
Lévis	206	46.48 N	71.11 W
Lévis □[6]	206	46.40 N	71.15 W
Levisa Fork ≃	192	38.06 N	82.36 W
Lévis-Saint Nom	261	48.43 N	1.58 E
Levítha I	38	37.00 N	26.28 E
Levittown, P.R.	240m	18.27 N	66.14 W
Levittown → Willingboro, N.J., U.S.	208	40.03 N	74.53 W
Levittown, N.Y., U.S.	210	40.43 N	73.30 W
Levittown, Pa., U.S.	208	40.09 N	74.49 W
Levittown Discount World ◆[9]	285	40.09 N	74.49 W
Lévka Óri ∧	38	35.18 N	24.01 E
Levkás	38	38.50 N	20.41 E
Levkás I	38	38.39 N	20.27 E
Levkímmi	38	39.25 N	20.04 E
Levoča	30	49.02 N	20.36 E
Levokumskoje	84	44.48 N	44.39 E
Levroux	32	46.59 N	1.37 E
Levski	38	43.22 N	25.08 E
Lev Tolstoj	76	53.13 N	39.27 E
Levuka	175g	17.41 S	178.50 E
Lėvuo ≃	76	56.04 N	24.23 E
Levyj Tuzlov ≃	83	47.35 N	39.23 E
Lewapaku	115b	9.43 S	119.55 E
Lewbeach	210	42.00 N	74.47 W
Lewe	110	19.38 N	96.07 E
Lewedorp	52	51.30 N	3.45 E
Lewellen	198	41.19 N	102.08 W
Lewer ≃	156	25.30 S	17.45 E
Lewes, Eng., U.K.	42	50.52 N	0.01 E
Lewes, De., U.S.	208	38.46 N	75.08 W
Lewin Brzeski	30	50.46 N	17.37 E
Lewis, Ia., U.S.	198	41.18 N	95.04 W
Lewis, Ks., U.S.	198	37.56 N	99.15 W
Lewis □[6], Ky., U.S.	218	38.32 N	83.21 W
Lewis □[6], Mo., U.S.	219	40.08 N	91.45 W
Lewis □[6], N.Y., U.S.	212	43.47 N	75.29 W
Lewis □[6], Wa., U.S.	224	46.35 N	122.22 W
Lewis ≃	224	45.51 N	122.48 W
Lewis, Butt of ›	46	58.31 N	6.16 W
Lewis, East Fork ≃	224	45.52 N	122.43 W
Lewis, Isle of I	46	58.10 N	6.40 W
Lewis, Mount ∧	204	40.24 N	116.51 W
Lewis and Clark ≃	224	46.10 N	123.52 W
Lewis and Clark Cavern State Park ♦	202	45.49 N	111.13 W

FRANÇAIS

Nom	Page	Lat.°′	Long.°′ W = Ouest
Lewis and Clark Lake ⊜[1]	198	42.50 N	97.45 W
Lewis and Clark Range ⋏	202	47.30 N	113.00 W
Lewisberry	208	40.08 N	76.52 W
Lewisburg, Ky., U.S.	194	36.59 N	86.56 W
Lewisburg, Oh., U.S.	218	39.50 N	84.32 W
Lewisburg, Pa., U.S.	210	40.57 N	76.53 W
Lewisburg, Tn., U.S.	194	35.26 N	86.47 W
Lewisburg, W.V., U.S.	188	37.48 N	80.26 W
Lewis Center	214	40.12 N	83.01 W
Lewis Creek ≃, Ca., U.S.	226	35.17 N	120.58 W
Lewis Creek ≃, In., U.S.	218	39.22 N	85.51 W
Lewis Creek Reservoir ⊜[1]	222	30.26 N	95.32 W
Lewisdale	284c	38.58 N	76.58 W
Lewisetta	208	38.01 N	76.28 W
Lewis Gut c	276	41.09 N	73.09 W
Lewisham	273d	26.07 S	27.49 E
Lewisham ◆[8]	42	51.27 N	0.01 E
Lewisham Location	273d	26.10 S	27.47 E
Lewis-Lockport Airport ⊠	278	41.36 N	88.05 W
Lewis Pass)(	172	42.23 S	172.24 E
Lewisport	194	37.56 N	86.54 W
Lewisporte	186	49.15 N	55.03 W
Lewis Range ⋏, Austl.	162	20.20 S	128.40 E
Lewis Range ⋏, Mt., U.S.	202	48.35 N	113.40 W
Lewis Run	214	41.52 N	78.39 W
Lewis Run ≃	279b	40.17 N	79.55 W
Lewis Smith Lake ⊜[1]	194	34.05 N	87.07 W
Lewiston, Ca., U.S.	204	40.43 N	122.48 W
Lewiston, Id., U.S.	202	46.25 N	117.01 W
Lewiston, Me., U.S.	188	44.06 N	70.12 W
Lewiston, Mi., U.S.	190	44.53 N	84.18 W
Lewiston, Mn., U.S.	190	43.59 N	91.52 W
Lewiston, N.Y., U.S.	210	43.10 N	79.02 W
Lewiston, Ut,. U.S.	200	41.58 N	111.51 W
Lewiston Orchards	202	46.23 N	116.59 W
Lewistown, Il., U.S.	194	40.23 N	90.09 W
Lewistown, Md., U.S.	208	39.32 N	77.24 W
Lewistown, Mo., U.S.	219	40.05 N	91.48 W
Lewistown, Mt., U.S.	202	47.03 N	109.25 W
Lewistown, Oh., U.S.	216	40.25 N	83.53 W
Lewistown, Pa., U.S.	208	40.35 N	77.34 W
Lewisville, N.B., Can.	186	46.06 N	64.46 W
Lewisville, Ar., U.S.	194	33.21 N	93.34 W
Lewisville, In., U.S.	218	39.48 N	85.21 W
Lewisville, Pa., U.S.	208	39.43 N	75.53 W
Lewisville, Tx., U.S.	222	33.02 N	96.59 W
Lewisville Dam ◆[6]	222	33.05 N	96.55 W
Lewisville Lake ⊜[1]	196	33.08 N	97.00 W
Lewoleba	112	8.23 S	123.24 E
Lewotobi-lakilaki, Ili ∧	115b	8.32 S	122.46 E
Lewvan	184	50.00 N	104.06 W
Lexa	194	34.35 N	90.44 W
Lexington, Ga., U.S.	192	33.52 N	83.06 W
Lexington, Il., U.S.	216	40.38 N	88.47 W
Lexington, In., U.S.	218	38.39 N	85.37 W
Lexington, Ky., U.S.	218	38.02 N	84.30 W
Lexington, Ma., U.S.	207	42.26 N	71.13 W
Lexington, Mi., U.S.	190	43.16 N	82.31 W
Lexington, Ms., U.S.	194	33.06 N	90.03 W
Lexington, Mo., U.S.	194	39.11 N	93.52 W
Lexington, Ne., U.S.	198	40.46 N	99.44 W
Lexington, N.Y., U.S.	210	42.15 N	74.22 W
Lexington, N.C., U.S.	192	35.49 N	80.15 W
Lexington, Oh., U.S.	214	40.40 N	82.34 W
Lexington, Ok., U.S.	196	35.00 N	97.20 W
Lexington, Or., U.S.	202	45.26 N	119.41 W
Lexington, S.C., U.S.	192	33.58 N	81.14 W
Lexington, Tn., U.S.	194	35.39 N	88.23 W
Lexington, Tx., U.S.	222	30.25 N	97.01 W
Lexington, Va., U.S.	192	37.47 N	79.26 W
Lexington Park	208	38.16 N	76.27 W
Lexington Reservoir ⊜[1]	226	37.12 N	121.59 W
Lexton	169	37.17 S	143.31 E
Leybourne	260	51.18 N	0.25 E
Leyburn	44	54.19 N	1.49 W
Leyden → Leiden	52	52.09 N	4.30 E
Leye	102	24.48 N	106.34 E
Leyland	44	53.42 N	2.42 W
Leyond ≃	184	51.40 N	96.32 W
Léyou ≃	152	1.07 S	13.08 E
Leyre ≃	32	44.39 N	1.01 W
Leysdown-on-Sea	42	51.24 N	0.55 E
Leysin	58	46.21 N	7.01 E
Leyte	116	11.23 N	124.29 E
Leyte □[4]	116	10.50 N	124.55 E
Leyte I	116	10.50 N	124.50 E
Leyte Gulf c	116	10.50 N	125.25 E
Leyton ◆[8]	260	51.33 N	0.01 W
Leyu	106	31.55 N	120.43 E
Lèz ≊	62	43.31 N	3.55 E
Leža	76	58.56 N	40.45 E
Leža ≃	76	59.15 N	40.10 E
Leżajsk	30	50.16 N	22.24 E
Lezama	246	9.43 N	66.24 W
Lézarde ≃	240e	14.36 N	61.01 W
Lézat	58	46.30 N	5.56 E
Lèze ≃	62	43.40 N	5.28 E
Lezhë	38	41.47 N	19.39 E
Lezhi	107	30.17 N	105.02 E
Ležn'ovo	80	56.46 N	40.53 E
Lezzeno	58	45.56 N	9.11 E
L'gov	78	51.43 N	35.17 E
Lhasa	120	29.40 N	91.09 E
Lhasa ≃	120	29.21 N	90.45 E
L'Hautil	261	49.00 N	2.01 E
Lhazê	120	29.10 N	87.42 E
L'Hillil	34	35.41 N	0.19 E
Lhokkruet	114	4.52 N	95.24 E
Lhoknga	114	5.29 N	95.15 E
Lhokseumawe	114	5.10 N	97.08 E
Lhoksukon	114	5.03 N	97.19 E
L'Hôpital-sous-Rochefort	62	45.46 N	3.56 E
Lhorong	102	30.45 N	96.09 E
L'Hospitalet de Llobregat	34	41.22 N	2.08 E
Lhotse ∧	124	27.57 N	86.56 E
Lhozhag	120	28.24 N	90.49 E
Lhuis	62	45.45 N	5.32 E
Lhuntsi Dzong	120	27.39 N	91.09 E
Lhünzê	120	28.25 N	92.31 E
Li	110	17.48 N	98.57 E
Li ≃, Thai	110	18.26 N	98.42 E
Li ≃, Zhg.	100	33.11 N	115.07 E
Li ≃, Zhg.	102	29.24 N	112.01 E
Lian ≃, Zhg.	100	25.46 N	115.38 E
Lian ≃, Zhg.	100	24.02 N	113.18 E
Lian ≃, Zhg.	102	24.02 N	113.18 E
Lian ≃, Zhg.	102	27.48 N	112.52 E
Liancheng	100	25.44 N	116.46 E
Liancourt	50	49.20 N	2.28 E
Liane ≃	50	50.43 N	1.36 E
Liang	164	3.30 S	128.19 E
Lianga	116	8.38 N	126.06 E
Lianga Bay c	116	8.37 N	126.12 E
Liang'anchang	107	30.30 N	104.56 E
Liangbao	102	34.37 N	110.45 E
Liangbingbao	89	45.48 N	128.19 E
Liangbingtai	89	43.12 N	128.47 E
Liangbuaya	112	0.05 N	116.46 E
Liangchahe	107	29.03 N	106.18 E
Liangcheng	98	35.35 N	119.35 E
Liangcun	100	26.36 N	115.34 E
Liangdang	102	33.56 N	106.12 E
Liangdawa	105	40.39 N	117.37 E
Liangfengwu	107	30.11 N	105.22 E
Lianggezhuang	105	39.21 N	115.22 E
Lianghe, Zhg.	89	45.09 N	128.45 E
Lianghe, Zhg.	102	24.51 N	98.25 E

PORTUGUÊS

Nome	Página	Lat.°′	Long.°′ W = Oeste
Liangheguan	102	32.52 N	109.19 E
Lianghekou, Zhg.	102	33.42 N	104.25 E
Lianghekou, Zhg.	102	29.14 N	108.40 E
Lianghekou, Zhg.	102	31.27 N	102.13 E
Lianghekou, Zhg.	107	28.55 N	106.03 E
Liangiu	98	35.12 N	117.47 E
Liangjia	107	29.29 N	105.33 E
Liangjiadian	98	39.10 N	121.54 E
Liangjiafang	98	41.04 N	117.18 E
Liangjianfang	105	40.45 N	117.20 E
Liangjiang	102	23.23 N	108.22 E
Liangjiangkou	98	42.38 N	128.05 E
Liangjiawazi	104	40.40 N	120.42 E
Liangjiazi	104	42.13 N	122.31 E
Liangkou	100	23.43 N	113.43 E
Lianglukou	107	29.18 N	106.15 E
Liangmen	98	35.34 N	114.54 E
Liangmentou	100	28.58 N	121.12 E
Liangmushi	106	30.46 N	119.35 E
Liangpa	102	24.10 N	106.13 E
Liangpeng	106	30.47 N	119.38 E
Liangping	102	30.41 N	107.49 E
Liang Shan ∧	102	23.45 N	99.45 E
Liangshui ≃	271a	39.49 N	116.40 E
Liangtian	100	25.37 N	113.00 E
Liangtinghe	100	30.20 N	116.12 E
Liangtoumen	100	29.31 N	120.45 E
Liangtun	98	40.14 N	122.34 E
Liangwangzhuang	105	39.01 N	116.58 E
Liangxiangzhen	105	39.44 N	116.08 E
Liangying	100	23.14 N	116.21 E
Liangyuan	100	32.00 N	117.34 E
Liangzhu	106	30.23 N	120.03 E
Liangzi Hu ⊜	100	30.16 N	114.34 E
Lianhe	98	42.36 N	125.37 E
Lian Hu ⊜	106	32.02 N	119.32 E
Lianhua	100	27.07 N	113.57 E
Lianhuachi	105	40.28 N	116.33 E
Lianhuapao	89	45.32 N	129.50 E
Lianhua Shan ⋏	100	23.40 N	116.00 E
Lianjiang, Zhg.	100	26.12 N	119.31 E
Lianjiang, Zhg.	102	21.38 N	110.15 E
Lianjiechang	107	29.41 N	104.30 E
Liannan (Sanjiang)	102	24.38 N	112.10 E
Lianozovo ◆[8]	265b	55.54 N	37.35 E
Lianping	100	24.22 N	114.31 E
Lianpu	100	26.02 N	118.38 E
Lianshanguan	104	40.58 N	123.46 E
Lianshi	106	30.42 N	120.26 E
Lianshui	100	33.47 N	119.16 E
Liansiji	98	33.58 N	114.24 E
Liantang	106	31.37 N	120.38 E
Lianxian	102	24.48 N	112.25 E
Lianyin	89	53.28 N	123.51 E
Lianyuan (Lantian)	102	27.42 N	111.19 E
Lianyungang, Zhg.	98	34.44 N	119.30 E
Lianyungang (Xinpu), Zhg.	98	34.39 N	119.16 E
Lianyun Shan ∧	100	28.32 N	113.50 E
Lianzhou → Hepu	102	21.39 N	109.11 E
Liao ≃	90	40.50 N	121.48 E
Liaobinta	104	42.08 N	123.04 E
Liaocheng	98	36.30 N	115.59 E
Liaodong Bandao (Liaotung Peninsula) ›[1]	98	40.00 N	122.20 E
Liaodong Wan (Gulf of Liaotung) c	98	40.30 N	121.30 E
Liaohe Kou c[1]	104	40.42 N	122.05 E
Liaojiangshi	100	26.05 N	113.17 E
Liaoning □[4]	90	41.00 N	123.00 E
Liaotung, Gulf of → Liaodong Wan c	98	40.30 N	121.30 E
Liaotung Peninsula → Liaodong Bandao ›[1]	98	40.00 N	122.20 E
Liaoyang	104	41.17 N	123.11 E
Liaoyangwopu	89	43.00 N	123.28 E
Liaoyuan	89	42.54 N	125.07 E
Liaozhong	104	41.31 N	122.44 E
Liapádhes	38	39.40 N	19.44 E
Liāquatpur	123	28.56 N	70.57 E
Liard ≃	176	61.52 N	121.18 W
Liāri	120	25.41 N	66.29 E
Liart	50	49.46 N	4.20 E
Liat, Pulau I	112	2.53 S	107.05 E
Liathach ∧	46	57.35 N	5.29 W
Lib I	14	8.19 N	167.25 E
Libagon	116	10.18 N	125.03 E
Liban → Lebanon □[1]	128	34.00 N	36.00 E
Libanga	152	0.19 N	18.41 E
Líbano	246	4.55 N	75.04 W
Libano → Lebanon □[1]	128	34.00 N	36.00 E
Libanon → Lebanon □[1]	128	34.00 N	36.00 E
Libau → Liepāja	76	56.31 N	21.01 E
Libby	202	48.23 N	115.33 W
Libby Dam ◆[6]	202	48.24 N	115.20 W
Libčeves	54	50.26 N	13.50 E
Libčice nad Vltavou	54	50.10 N	14.20 E
Liběchov	54	50.20 N	14.28 E
Libenge	152	3.39 N	18.38 E
Liberal, Ks., U.S.	198	37.02 N	100.55 W
Liberal, Mo., U.S.	194	37.33 N	94.31 W
Liberdade	256	22.01 S	44.19 W
Liberdade ◆[8]	287b	23.35 S	46.37 W
Liberdade ≃, Bra.	248	7.10 S	71.51 W
Liberdade ≃, Bra.	250	9.40 S	52.17 W
Liberec	30	50.46 N	15.03 E
Liberia	236	10.38 N	85.27 W
Liberia □[1], Afr.	134	6.30 N	9.30 W
Liberia □[1], Afr.	150	6.30 N	9.30 W
Liberta	240c	17.02 N	61.47 W
Libertad, Arg.	258	34.42 S	58.41 W
Libertad, Ur.	258	34.38 S	56.39 W
Libertad, Ven.	246	9.23 N	68.44 W
Libertad, Ven.	246	8.20 N	69.37 W
Libertador □[5]	286c	10.27 N	66.57 W
Libertador General Bernardo O'Higgins □[4]	252	34.30 S	71.00 W
Libertador General San Martín	252	23.48 S	64.48 W
Liberty, Il., U.S.	219	39.53 N	91.06 W
Liberty, In., U.S.	218	39.38 N	84.55 W
Liberty, Ky., U.S.	194	37.19 N	84.56 W
Liberty, Ms., U.S.	194	31.09 N	90.48 W
Liberty, Mo., U.S.	194	39.14 N	94.25 W
Liberty, Ne., U.S.	198	40.05 N	96.28 W
Liberty, N.Y., U.S.	210	41.48 N	74.44 W
Liberty, N.C., U.S.	192	35.51 N	79.34 W
Liberty, Pa., U.S.	210	41.34 N	77.06 W
Liberty, Pa., U.S.	279b	40.20 N	79.51 W
Liberty, S.C., U.S.	192	34.47 N	82.41 W
Liberty, Tx., U.S.	222	30.03 N	94.47 W
Liberty □[6]	222	30.12 N	94.50 W
Liberty Acres	280	34.04 N	118.12 W
Liberty Center, In., U.S.	216	40.41 N	85.16 W
Liberty Center, Oh., U.S.	216	41.26 N	84.00 W
Liberty City	222	32.27 N	94.57 W
Liberty Corner	276	40.39 N	74.34 W
Liberty Ditch ≊	226	36.31 N	120.02 W
Liberty Farms	226	38.19 N	121.42 W
Liberty Hill	196	30.40 N	97.55 W
Liberty Island I	276	40.41 N	74.03 W
Liberty Lake ⊜[1]	208	39.25 N	76.53 W
Liberty Manor	284b	39.21 N	76.47 W
Liberty Mills	216	41.02 N	85.44 W
Liberty Park	216	41.26 N	87.22 W
Libertytown	208	39.29 N	77.14 W
Liberty Tree Mall ◆[9]	283	42.33 N	70.57 W
Liberty Tunnel ◆[5]	279b	40.26 N	80.01 W
Libertyville	216	42.16 N	87.57 W
Líbeznice	54	50.10 N	14.30 E
Libia → Libya □[1]	146	27.00 N	17.00 E
Libibi	152	14.42 S	17.44 E
Libishan	106	30.45 N	119.20 E
Lībiyā → Libya □[1]	146	27.00 N	17.00 E
Lībīyah, Aṣ-Ṣaḥrā' al- (Libyan Desert) ◆[2]	136	24.00 N	25.00 E
Liblín	60	49.55 N	13.32 E
Libni, Jabal ∧[2]	132	30.44 N	33.50 E
Libo	102	25.28 N	107.53 E
Libobo, Tanjung ›	164	0.54 S	128.28 E
Liboc ≃	54	50.10 N	13.31 E
Libochovice	54	50.22 N	14.03 E
Libode	158	31.33 S	29.02 E
Liboi	154	0.24 N	40.57 E
Liboko	152	2.43 N	21.28 E
Libomyšl	60	49.52 N	14.00 E
Libona	116	8.20 N	124.44 E
Liboumba ≃	152	0.38 N	12.54 E
Libourne	32	44.55 N	0.14 W
Libramont	56	49.55 N	5.23 E
Library	214	40.18 N	80.02 W
Librazhd	38	41.11 N	20.19 E
Libres	234	19.28 N	97.41 W
Libreville	152	0.23 N	9.27 E
Librizzi	70	38.06 N	14.57 E
Libro Point ›	116	11.26 N	119.29 E
Libu	102	23.41 N	111.30 E
Libucan Island I	116	11.54 N	124.39 E
Libuganon ≃	116	7.27 N	125.47 E
Libunga	154	1.49 N	26.35 E
Liburung	112	3.55 S	120.09 E
Libušín	54	50.09 N	14.04 E
Libya (Lībiyā) □[1], Afr.	136	27.00 N	17.00 E
Libya (Lībiyā) □[1], Afr.	146	27.00 N	17.00 E
Libyan Desert → Lībīyah, Aṣ-Ṣaḥrā' al- ◆[2]	136	24.00 N	25.00 E
Libyan Plateau → Aḍ-Ḍiffah ⋏[1]	140	30.30 N	25.30 E
Libye → Libya □[1]	146	27.00 N	17.00 E
Libyen → Libya □[1]	146	27.00 N	17.00 E
Libysche Wüste → Lībīyah, Aṣ-Ṣaḥrā' al- ◆[2]	136	24.00 N	25.00 E
Licancábur, Volcán ∧[1]	248	22.50 S	67.50 W
Licantén	252	34.59 S	72.00 W
Licata	70	37.06 N	13.56 E
Licciana Nardi	64	44.16 N	10.02 E
Lice	130	38.28 N	40.39 E
Lich	56	50.33 N	8.50 E
Lichačova, mys ›	89	42.44 N	132.51 E
Lichaja ≃	83	48.08 N	40.15 E
Lichang	107	28.53 N	104.26 E
Licheng	102	36.30 N	113.21 E
Lichères-Près-Aigremont	50	47.43 N	3.51 E
Lichfield	42	52.42 N	1.48 W
Lichinga	154	13.18 S	35.14 E
Lichitișeni	38	46.23 N	27.17 E
Lichoborka ≃	265b	55.50 N	37.38 E
Lichoslavl'	76	57.07 N	35.28 E
Lichovskoj	83	48.07 N	40.12 E
Lichtaart	56	51.14 N	4.54 E
Lichte	54	50.31 N	11.10 E
Lichtenau	56	48.43 N	8.01 E
Lichtenberg, Dtsch.	54	50.23 N	11.40 E
Lichtenberg, Fr.	56	48.55 N	7.29 E
Lichtenberg ◆[8]	264a	52.31 N	13.29 E
Lichtenburg	158	26.08 S	26.08 E
Lichtendorf	263	51.28 N	7.37 E
Lichtenfels	56	50.09 N	11.04 E
Lichtenplatz ◆[8]	263	51.15 N	7.12 E
Lichtenrade ◆[8]	264a	52.23 N	13.25 E
Lichtensee	54	51.23 N	13.22 E
Lichtensteig	58	47.19 N	9.05 E
Lichtenstein	54	50.45 N	12.37 E
Lichtenstein, Schloss ♥	58	48.24 N	9.15 E
Lichtentanne	54	50.42 N	12.25 E
Lichtenvoorde	52	51.59 N	6.34 E
Lichterfelde ◆[8]	264a	52.26 N	13.19 E
Lichtervelde	50	51.02 N	3.09 E
Lichuan, Zhg.	100	27.18 N	116.53 E
Lichuan, Zhg.	102	30.18 N	108.51 E
Lick Creek ≃, Il., U.S.	219	39.42 N	89.41 W
Lick Creek ≃, In., U.S.	218	38.33 N	86.31 W
Lick Creek ≃, Mo., U.S.	219	39.31 N	91.39 W
Lick Creek ≃, Oh., U.S.	216	41.21 N	84.25 W
Lick Creek ≃, Tn., U.S.	192	36.11 N	83.10 W
Lickershamn	26	57.50 N	18.31 E
Licking	194	37.29 N	91.51 W
Licking □[6]	214	40.10 N	82.30 W
Licking ≃, Ky., U.S.	188	39.06 N	84.30 W
Licking ≃, Oh., U.S.	214	40.03 N	82.20 W
Licking, North Fork ≃, Ky., U.S.	218	38.35 N	84.13 W
Licking, North Fork ≃, Oh., U.S.	214	40.03 N	82.23 W
Licking, South Fork ≃	218	38.41 N	84.20 W
Lickingville	214	41.23 N	79.22 W
Lick Observatory ♥[3]	226	37.22 N	121.37 W
Ličko Polje ≡	36	44.35 N	15.25 E
Lick Run ≃, Pa., U.S.	210	41.12 N	77.32 W
Lick Run ≃, Pa., U.S.	279b	40.17 N	79.57 W
Licodia Eubea	70	37.09 N	14.42 E
Licosa, Punta ›	68	40.15 N	14.54 E
Licun	98	38.32 N	117.08 E
Licungo ≃	154	17.40 S	37.15 E
Lid'	76	59.39 N	35.05 E
Lida	76	53.53 N	25.18 E
Lidan ≃	26	58.31 N	13.09 E
Lidao	98	37.15 N	122.32 E
Lidarentuncun	104	41.32 N	123.12 E
Lidcombe	274a	33.52 S	151.03 E
Liddel Water ≃	44	55.04 N	2.57 W
Liddesdale V	44	55.12 N	2.46 W
Liddon Gulf c	176	75.03 N	113.00 W
Liden	26	62.42 N	16.48 E
Lidesi	100	33.33 N	115.53 E
Lidgerwood	198	46.04 N	97.09 W
Lidgetton	158	29.25 S	30.05 E
Lidian	107	28.57 N	103.44 E
Lídice, Bra.	256	22.51 S	44.12 W
Lídice, Pan.	236	8.45 N	79.54 W
Lidice ⊥	54	50.03 N	14.08 E
Lidingö	40	59.22 N	18.08 E
Lidköping	26	58.30 N	13.10 E
Lido	64	45.25 N	12.22 E
Lido, Litorale di ⩋[2]	64	45.23 N	12.21 E
Lido, Porto di c	64	45.26 N	12.25 E
Lido Beach	276	40.35 N	73.38 W
Lido di Camaiore	64	43.54 N	10.13 E
Lido di Castel Fusano ◆[8]	66	41.43 N	12.20 E
Lido di Iesolo	64	45.30 N	12.39 E
Lido di Metaponto	68	40.22 N	16.50 E
Lido di Ostia ◆[8]	66	41.44 N	12.14 E
Lido di Pomposa	66	44.45 N	12.14 E
Lido di Siponto	68	41.37 N	15.55 E
Lido Key I	220	27.19 N	82.35 W
Lidsjön ⊜	40	58.55 N	16.51 E
Lidu	107	30.35 N	106.04 E
Lidzbark	30	53.17 N	19.49 E
Lidzbark Warmiński	30	54.09 N	20.35 E
Liebenau, Dtsch.	52	52.36 N	9.05 E
Liebenau, Öst.	61	48.32 N	14.49 E
Liebenbergsvlei ≃	158	27.20 S	28.31 E
Liebenburg	52	52.01 N	10.26 E
Liebenwalde	54	52.52 N	13.23 E
Lieberhausen	56	51.03 N	7.40 E
Lieberose	54	51.59 N	14.17 E
Liebertwolkwitz	54	51.17 N	12.28 E
Liebig, Mount ∧	162	23.18 S	131.22 E
Liebstadt	54	50.52 N	13.51 E
Liechtenstein □[1], Europe	22	47.09 N	9.35 E
Liechtenstein □[1], Europe	58	47.09 N	9.35 E
Liechtensteinklamm V	64	47.18 N	13.12 E
Liedberg	263	51.10 N	6.32 E
Liedekerke	50	50.52 N	4.05 E
Liège (Luik)	56	50.38 N	5.34 E
Liège □[4]	56	50.30 N	5.30 E
Liège, Aéroport ⊠	56	50.39 N	5.30 E
Liegnitz → Legnica	30	51.13 N	16.09 E
Lieja → Liège	56	50.38 N	5.34 E
Lieksa	26	63.19 N	30.01 E
Lielais Liepu kalns ∧[2]	76	56.25 N	27.50 E
Lielupe ≃	76	57.01 N	23.56 E
Lielvārde	76	56.43 N	24.51 E
Liemienzhen	107	30.29 N	106.05 E
Lienart	154	3.04 N	25.31 E
Lienchou → Hepu	102	21.39 N	109.11 E
Lienen	52	52.09 N	7.58 E
Lienz	64	46.50 N	12.47 E
Liepāja	76	56.31 N	21.01 E
Liepājas ezers ⊜	76	56.27 N	21.03 E
Liepe	54	53.58 N	13.56 E
Liepna	76	57.25 N	27.25 E
Liepnitzsee ⊜	264a	52.45 N	13.30 E
Lièpvre	58	48.16 N	7.17 E
Lier (Lierre)	50	51.08 N	4.34 E
Lierenfeld ◆[8]	263	51.13 N	6.51 E
Lierna	58	45.57 N	9.18 E
Liernais	50	47.12 N	4.17 E
Lierneux	56	50.18 N	5.48 E
Liershizhai	104	41.49 N	123.43 E
Liesborn	52	51.43 N	8.15 E
Lieser ≃, Dtsch.	56	49.55 N	7.01 E
Lieser ≃, Öst.	64	46.47 N	13.39 E
Lieshout	52	51.32 N	5.35 E
Liesing ◆[8]	264b	48.08 N	16.17 E
Liesing ≃	264b	48.08 N	16.28 E
Liesingbach ≃	61	47.20 N	15.02 E
Liesjärven kansallispuisto ♦	26	60.40 N	23.54 E
Lieskau	54	51.37 N	13.48 E
Liesse	50	49.37 N	3.48 E
Liessies	50	50.07 N	4.05 E
Liestal	58	47.29 N	7.44 E
Liești	38	45.38 N	27.32 E
Lietuva → Lithuania □[1]	72	56.00 N	24.00 E
Lietzow	54	54.29 N	13.30 E
Lieurey	50	49.14 N	0.29 E
Lieusaint	261	48.38 N	2.33 E
Lieutel ≃	261	48.49 N	1.52 E
Lieutenant Robert J. Palenscar Memorial Airport ⊠	285	39.51 N	75.03 W
Liévin	50	50.25 N	2.46 E
Lièvre, Rivière du ≃	176	45.31 N	75.26 W
Lièvres, Île aux I	186	47.51 N	69.44 W
Liezen	61	47.35 N	14.15 E
Lifanga	152	0.19 N	21.57 E
Liffey ≃	48	53.21 N	6.16 W
Liffol-le-Grand	58	48.19 N	5.35 E
Lifford	48	54.50 N	7.29 W
Liffré	32	48.13 N	1.30 W
Lifjell ∧	26	59.30 N	8.52 E
Lifoku	152	0.04 S	21.18 E
Lifou I	175f	20.53 S	167.13 E
Lifoula	273b	4.06 S	15.25 E
Lifton	42	50.39 N	4.17 W
Liftwood	285	39.47 N	75.31 W
Lifune ≃	152	8.21 S	13.22 E
Ligačovo	265b	55.56 N	37.15 E
Ligang	100	30.04 N	121.52 E
Ligao, Pil.	116	13.14 N	123.32 E
Ligao, Pil.	116	6.17 N	124.09 E
Ligasa	152	0.42 N	23.45 E
Ligezhuang, Zhg.	105	39.49 N	115.56 E
Ligezhuang, Zhg.	105	39.42 N	118.12 E
Light ≃	168b	34.35 S	138.22 E
Lightfoot	208	37.20 N	76.45 W
Lighthouse Beach ⩋[2]	273a	6.24 N	3.22 E
Lighthouse Point	220	26.16 N	80.05 W
Lighthouse Point ›, On., Can.	214	41.50 N	82.38 W
Lighthouse Point ›, Fl., U.S.	192	29.54 N	84.21 W
Lighthouse Point ›, Mi., U.S.	190	45.13 N	85.32 W
Lighthouse Reef ✤[2]	232	17.20 N	87.32 W
Lightning Creek ≃, Sk., Can.	184	49.12 N	101.43 W
Lightning Creek ≃, N.A.	224	48.50 N	121.03 W
Lightning Creek ≃, Wy., U.S.	198	43.11 N	104.44 W
Lightning Ridge	166	29.26 S	147.59 E
Lightstreet	210	41.02 N	76.25 W
Lightsville	216	40.18 N	84.42 W
Ligist	61	46.59 N	15.12 E
Lignano Pineta	64	45.40 N	13.07 E
Lignano Sabbiadoro	64	45.42 N	13.09 E
Lignières	32	46.45 N	2.11 E
Lignite	198	48.52 N	102.33 W
Lignon ≃	62	45.44 N	4.08 E
Lignumvitae Key I	220	24.55 N	80.42 W
Ligny-en-Barrois	58	48.41 N	5.20 E
Ligny-en-Cambrésis	50	50.06 N	3.22 E
Ligny-le-Châtel	50	47.54 N	3.45 E
Ligny-le-Ribault	50	47.41 N	1.47 E
Ligonha ≃	154	16.54 S	39.09 E
Ligonier, In., U.S.	216	41.27 N	85.35 W
Ligonier, Pa., U.S.	214	40.14 N	79.14 W
Ligovo	76	60.13 N	31.48 E
Ligovo ◆[8]	265a	59.50 N	30.12 E
Ligovskij kanal ≊	265a	59.47 N	30.10 E
Liguantu	105	40.24 N	115.45 E
Ligueil	32	47.03 N	0.49 E
Ligui	232	25.43 N	111.16 W
Ligure, Mar → Ligurian Sea ⊤[2]	36	43.30 N	9.00 E
Liguria □[4]	36	44.30 N	8.50 E
Liguria, Mar de → Ligurian Sea ⊤[2]	36	43.30 N	9.00 E
Ligurian Sea ⊤[2]	36	43.30 N	9.00 E
Ligurisches Meer → Ligurian Sea ⊤[2]	36	43.30 N	9.00 E
Lihir Group II	164	3.05 S	152.40 E
Lihir Island I	164	3.05 S	152.35 E
Lihoi Seamount ✤[3]	14	18.56 N	155.16 W
Lihou Reef and Cays ✤[2]	166	17.25 S	151.40 E
Lihu	100	23.23 N	116.03 E
Lihue	229b	21.58 N	159.22 W
Lihue Airport ⊠	229b	21.59 N	159.21 W
Lihuel Calel, Parque Nacional ♦, Arg.	252	37.58 S	65.32 W
Lihuel Calel, Parque Nacional ♦, Arg.	254	37.58 S	65.32 W
Lihula	76	58.41 N	23.50 E
Liji, Zhg.	100	31.59 N	115.51 E
Liji, Zhg.	100	33.48 N	117.48 E
Lijia, Zhg.	98	37.49 N	118.01 E
Lijia, Zhg.	104	41.43 N	122.20 E
Lijiaba	107	29.37 N	105.33 E
Lijiadian	104	42.07 N	121.14 E
Lijiajie	107	29.49 N	105.30 E
Lijiakou	105	39.12 N	116.29 E
Lijiang	102	26.57 N	100.15 E
Lijiapuzi	104	40.59 N	123.38 E
Lijiaqiao, Zhg.	105	40.03 N	116.40 E
Lijiaqiao, Zhg.	105	39.47 N	117.47 E
Lijiaqiao, Zhg.	106	31.38 N	120.00 E
Lijiatun	104	41.19 N	121.23 E
Lijiatuo	107	29.28 N	106.33 E
Lijiawobao	104	41.00 N	122.26 E
Lijiaxiang	106	30.57 N	119.59 E
Lijiazao	105	39.17 N	118.19 E
Lijin, Zhg.	98	37.29 N	118.16 E
Lijin, Zhg.	104	41.40 N	121.20 E
Lik ≃	110	18.31 N	102.31 E
Likako	152	0.15 N	21.00 E
Likang	100	22.47 N	120.29 E
Likasi (Jadotville)	154	10.59 S	26.44 E
Likati	152	3.21 N	23.53 E
Likati ≃	152	2.53 N	24.03 E
Likely	182	52.37 N	121.34 W
Likėnai	76	56.12 N	24.37 E
Likete	152	0.43 S	21.25 E
Likhu ≃	124	27.15 N	86.12 E
Liki	112	1.36 S	101.11 E
Likimi	152	2.50 N	20.45 E
Likino	82	55.38 N	37.08 E
Likino-Dulevo	82	55.43 N	38.58 E
Liknes	26	58.19 N	6.59 E
Likoma Island I	154	12.05 S	34.45 E
Likou, Zhg.	100	29.53 N	117.28 E
Likou, Zhg.	100	33.51 N	113.20 E
Likou, Zhg.	106	31.24 N	120.37 E
Likouala □[5]	152	2.00 N	17.30 E
Likouala ≃	152	1.13 S	16.48 E
Likouala aux Herbes ≃	152	0.50 S	17.11 E
Likova ≃	265b	55.34 N	37.21 E
Likstammen ⊜	40	58.58 N	17.12 E
Liku	174v	19.02 S	169.47 W
Likupang	112	1.41 N	125.04 E
Likus ≃	236	14.14 N	83.35 W
Likuyu	154	10.20 S	36.14 E
Lilanchengzhen	105	39.12 N	116.43 E
Lilanga	152	0.34 S	23.55 E
Lilasi	124	29.22 N	84.30 E
Lilbert	222	31.44 N	94.54 W
Lilbourn	194	36.35 N	89.36 W
L'Île-Bouchard	32	47.07 N	0.25 E
Lilenga	152	0.54 N	22.06 E
L'Île-Rousse	36	42.38 N	8.56 E
Lili	106	31.00 N	120.42 E
Lilian Point ›	174d	0.53 S	169.35 E
Lilienfeld	61	48.03 N	15.36 E
Lilienthal	52	53.08 N	8.55 E
Liling	100	27.40 N	113.30 E
Lilio	116	14.08 N	121.26 E
Liljendal	40	60.08 N	14.04 E
Lilla Bharwana	123	32.34 N	72.45 E
Lilla Edet	26	58.08 N	12.08 E
Lillån	40	59.19 N	15.13 E
Lillby	26	63.28 N	23.00 E
Lille	50	50.38 N	3.04 E
Lillebælt ⊔	41	55.20 N	9.45 E
Lillebonne	50	49.31 N	0.33 E
Lillehammer	26	61.08 N	10.30 E
Lille-Lesquin, Aéroport ⊠	50	50.35 N	3.07 E
Lillerød	41	55.52 N	12.22 E
Lillers	50	50.34 N	2.29 E
Lillesand	26	58.15 N	8.24 E
Lilleshall	42	52.44 N	2.21 W
Lillestrøm	26	59.57 N	11.05 E
Lille Værløse	41	55.47 N	12.23 E
Lillhärdal	26	61.51 N	14.04 E
Lillian	222	32.30 N	97.11 W
Lillington	192	35.23 N	78.48 W
Lillinonah Lake ⊜[1]	207	41.28 N	73.21 W
Lilli Pilli	274a	34.04 S	151.07 E
Lillo	34	39.43 N	3.18 W
Lillooet	182	50.42 N	121.56 W
Lillooet ≃	182	49.45 N	122.08 W
Lillooet Lake ⊜	182	50.13 N	122.29 W
Lilly	214	40.25 N	78.37 W
Lilly Creek ≃	222	32.47 N	94.56 W
Liloan	116	10.09 N	125.07 E
Lilongwe	154	13.59 S	33.44 E
Lilo Viejo	252	26.56 S	62.58 W
Liloy	116	8.08 N	122.40 E
Liluāh	272b	22.35 N	88.23 E
Lily	192	37.01 N	84.04 W
Lily Cache Creek ≃	278	41.41 N	88.07 W
Lilydale, Austl.	166	41.15 S	147.13 E
Lilydale, Austl.	169	37.45 S	145.21 E
Lily Dale, N.Y., U.S.	214	42.21 N	79.19 W
Lilyfield	274a	33.52 S	151.10 E
Lilyvale	273d	26.06 S	28.25 E
Lim ≃, Afr.	152	7.54 N	15.46 E
Lim ≃, Europe	38	43.45 N	19.13 E
Lima, Arg.	258	34.03 S	59.12 W
Lima, Para.	252	23.54 S	56.20 W
Lima, Perú	248	12.03 S	77.03 W
Lima, Perú	286d	12.03 S	77.03 W
Lima, Sve.	26	60.56 N	13.26 E
Lima, Il., U.S.	219	40.11 N	91.23 W
Lima, Mt., U.S.	202	44.38 N	112.35 W
Lima, N.Y., U.S.	210	42.54 N	77.36 W
Lima, Oh., U.S.	216	40.44 N	84.06 W
Lima, Pa., U.S.	285	39.55 N	75.26 W
Lima □[5]	248	12.00 S	76.35 W
Lima (Limia) ≃, Europe	34	41.41 N	8.50 W
Lima ≃, It.	64	44.00 N	10.35 E
Lima, Punta ›	240m	18.11 N	65.41 W
Lima Center	216	42.47 N	88.49 W
Limache	252	33.01 S	71.16 W
Lima Duarte	256	21.51 S	43.48 W
Liman, Ross.	80	45.47 N	47.14 E
Liman, Yis.	132	33.03 N	35.06 E
Liman ≃	115a	6.29 S	105.48 E
Limanowa	30	49.43 N	20.26 E
Limão ◆[8]	287b	23.30 S	46.40 W
Limapuluh	114	3.10 N	99.26 E
Lima Reservoir ⊜[1]	202	44.38 N	112.17 W
Limarí ≃	252	30.44 S	71.43 W
Limas	112	0.14 N	104.31 E
Limasawa Island I	116	9.56 N	125.05 E
Limassa	152	4.14 N	22.02 E
Limassol → Lemesós	130	34.40 N	33.02 E
Limavady	48	55.03 N	6.57 W
Limaville	214	40.59 N	81.09 W
Limay, Fr.	50	49.00 N	1.44 E
Limay, Pil.	116	14.34 N	120.36 E
Limay ≃	254	38.59 S	68.00 W
Limay Mahuida	252	37.12 S	66.42 W
Limbach-Oberfrohna	54	50.51 N	12.45 E
Limbadi	68	38.33 N	15.58 E
Limbang	112	4.45 N	115.00 E
Limbang ≃	112	4.50 N	115.01 E
Limbani	248	14.08 S	69.42 W
Limbara, Monte ∧	71	40.51 N	9.10 E
Limbaži	76	57.31 N	24.42 E
Līmbdi	120	22.34 N	71.48 E
Limbe	154	15.49 S	35.03 E
Limbiate	62	45.36 N	9.07 E
Limboto	112	0.37 N	122.57 E
Limbourg	56	50.37 N	5.56 E
Limbrick	262	53.38 N	2.36 W
Limbueta	152	12.30 S	18.42 E
Limbunya	164	17.14 S	129.50 E
Limburg □[4], Bel.	56	51.00 N	5.30 E
Limburg □[4], Ned.	52	51.14 N	5.50 E
Limburg an der Lahn	56	50.23 N	8.04 E
Limburgerhof	56	49.25 N	8.24 E
Lim Chu Kang	271c	1.26 N	103.43 E
Limecrest	218	39.54 N	83.48 W
Limefield	262	53.37 N	2.18 W
Limeira	255	22.34 S	47.24 W
Limekiln Canyon V	280	34.18 N	118.33 W
Lime Lake	210	42.26 N	78.29 W
Limen	100	27.07 N	119.19 E
Limena	64	45.29 N	11.50 E
Limentra ≃	64	44.14 N	11.03 E

≃	River	Fluß	Río	Rivière	Rio
≊	Canal	Kanal	Canal	Canal	Canal
⌞	Waterfall, Rapids	Wasserfall, Stromschnellen	Cascada, Rápidos	Chute d'eau, Rapides	Cascata, Rápidos
⊔	Strait	Meeresstraße	Estrecho	Détroit	Estreito
c	Bay, Gulf	Bucht, Golf	Bahía, Golfo	Baie, Golfe	Baía, Golfo
⊜	Lake, Lakes	See, Seen	Lago, Lagos	Lac, Lacs	Lago, Lagos
≡	Swamp	Sumpf	Pantano	Marais	Pântano
⊼	Ice Features, Glacier	Eis- und Gletscherformen	Accidentes Glaciales	Formes glaciaires	Acidentes glaciares
⊤	Other Hydrographic Features	Andere Hydrographische Objekte	Otros Elementos Hidrográficos	Autres données hydrographiques	Outros acidentes hidrográficos

✤	Submarine Features	Untermeerische Objekte	Accidentes Submarinos	Formes de relief sous-marin	Acidentes submarinos
□	Political Unit	Politische Einheit	Unidad Politica	Entité politique	Unidade política
♥	Cultural Institution	Kulturelle Institution	Institución Cultural	Institution culturelle	Instituição cultural
⊥	Historical Site	Historische Stätte	Sitio Histórico	Site historique	Sitio histórico
♦	Recreational Site	Erholungs- und Ferienort	Sitio de Recreo	Centre de loisirs	Area de Lazer
⊠	Airport	Flughafen	Aeropuerto	Aéroport	Aeroporto
■	Military Installation	Militäranlage	Instalación Militar	Installation militaire	Instalação militar
◆	Miscellaneous	Verschiedenes	Misceláneo	Divers	Diversos

Limerick, Sk., Can. 184 49.40 N 106.15 W
Limerick (Luimneach), Ire. 48 52.40 N 8.38 W
Limerick, Pa., U.S. 285 40.14 N 75.32 W
Limerick □6 48 52.30 N 8.45 W
Limerick Lake ◎ 212 44.54 N 77.37 W
Limerock 207 41.55 N 71.28 W
Lime Springs 190 43.27 N 92.17 W
Limestone, Austl. 162 21.11 S 119.50 E
Limestone, Fl., U.S. 220 27.21 N 81.53 W
Limestone, Me., U.S. 186 46.54 N 67.49 W
Limestone, N.Y., U.S. 210 42.01 N 78.37 W
Limestone, Pa., U.S. 214 41.08 N 79.20 W
Limestone □6 222 31.35 N 96.35 W
Limestone ≃ 184 56.31 N 94.07 W
Limestone, Lake ◎1 222 31.25 N 96.20 W
Limestone Bay c 184 53.50 N 98.50 W
Limestone Canyon V 280 33.45 N 117.41 W
Limestone Creek ≃ 210 43.06 N 75.58 W
Limestone Lake ◎, Mb., Can. 184 56.35 N 96.00 W
Limestone Lake ◎, Sk., Can. 184 54.36 N 103.18 W
Limestone Point >1 184 53.50 N 98.50 W
Limestone Point Lake ◎ 184 55.07 N 100.32 W
Lime Street Station ➜5 262 53.25 N 2.59 W
Lime Village 180 61.21 N 155.28 W
Limfjorden ∪ 26 56.55 N 9.10 E
Limhamn ➜8 41 55.35 N 12.54 E
Limia (Lima) ≃ 34 41.41 N 8.50 W
Limina 70 37.56 N 15.17 E
Liminka 26 64.49 N 25.24 E
Liminzhen 98 34.31 N 115.56 E
Limit Brook ≃ 283 42.42 N 71.25 W
Limmared 26 57.32 N 13.21 E
Limmaren ◎ 40 59.44 N 18.43 E
Limmen 52 52.34 N 4.41 E
Limmen Bight c3 164 14.45 S 135.40 E
Limmen Bight ≃ 164 15.07 S 135.44 E
Límnos I 38 39.54 N 25.21 E
Limoeiro 250 7.52 S 35.27 W
Limoeiro do Norte 250 5.08 S 38.05 W
Limoges, On., Can. 212 45.20 N 75.15 W
Limoges, Fr. 32 45.50 N 1.16 E
Limoges-Fourches 261 48.38 N 2.40 E
Limogne 32 44.24 N 1.46 E
Limón, Hond. 236 15.52 N 85.33 W
Limon, Co., U.S. 198 39.15 N 103.41 W
Limón □4 236 10.00 N 83.15 W
Limonar 240p 22.57 N 81.24 W
Limone Piemonte 62 44.12 N 7.34 E
Limone sul Garda 64 45.49 N 10.47 E
Limours 50 48.39 N 2.05 E
Limousin, Plateaux du ⩘1 32 45.50 N 1.15 E
Limoux 32 43.04 N 2.14 E
Limpopo ≃ 156 25.15 S 33.30 E
Limpsfield 42 51.16 N 0.01 E
Limski kanal c 64 45.07 N 13.38 E
Limu 102 25.02 N 110.51 E
Limuru 154 1.06 S 36.39 E
Linachamari 24 69.40 N 31.20 E
Līnah 128 28.42 N 43.48 E
Lin'an 106 30.14 N 119.43 E
Linanäs 40 59.28 N 18.31 E
Linao Bay c 116 6.45 N 124.00 E
Linapacan Island I 116 11.27 N 119.49 E
Linapacan Strait ∪ 116 11.37 N 119.56 E
Linares, Chile 252 35.51 S 71.36 W
Linares, Col. 246 1.23 N 77.31 W
Linares, Esp. 34 38.05 N 3.38 W
Linares, Méx. 232 24.52 N 99.34 W
Linariá 38 38.50 N 24.32 E
Linaro, Capo > 66 42.02 N 11.50 E
Linas 261 48.38 N 2.16 E
Linas, Monte ∧ 71 39.27 N 8.37 E
Linas-Montlhéry, Domaine Militaire de ■ 261 48.37 N 2.13 E
Linate, Aeroporto di ⊠ 62 45.27 N 9.16 E
Lincai 100 33.50 N 114.56 E
Lincang 102 23.45 N 102.20 E
Lince 286d 12.06 S 77.03 W
Linch 200 43.36 N 106.11 W
Lincheng, Zhg. 98 37.27 N 114.29 E
Lincheng, Zhg. 106 30.55 N 119.47 E
Linch'ing → Linqing 98 36.53 N 115.41 E
Lincoln, Arg. 252 34.52 S 61.32 W
Lincoln, On., Can. 212 43.10 N 79.29 W
Lincoln, N.Z. 172 43.39 S 172.29 E
Lincoln, Eng., U.K. 44 53.14 N 0.33 W
Lincoln, Ar., U.S. 194 35.56 N 94.25 W
Lincoln, Ca., U.S. 226 38.53 N 121.17 W
Lincoln, De., U.S. 208 38.52 N 75.25 W
Lincoln, Il., U.S. 219 40.08 N 89.21 W
Lincoln, In., U.S. 216 40.37 N 86.12 W
Lincoln, Ks., U.S. 198 39.02 N 98.08 W
Lincoln, Me., U.S. 188 45.21 N 68.30 W
Lincoln, Ma., U.S. 207 42.25 N 71.18 W
Lincoln, Mi., U.S. 190 44.41 N 83.24 W
Lincoln, Mo., U.S. 194 38.23 N 93.20 W
Lincoln, Mt., U.S. 202 46.57 N 112.40 W
Lincoln, Ne., U.S. 198 40.48 N 96.40 W
Lincoln, N.H., U.S. 188 44.02 N 71.40 W
Lincoln, Pa., U.S. 208 40.12 N 76.12 W
Lincoln, Pa., U.S. 279b 40.18 N 79.51 W
Lincoln, R.I., U.S. 207 41.54 N 71.25 W
Lincoln, Tx., U.S. 222 30.17 N 96.52 W
Lincoln □6, Mo., U.S. 219 39.05 N 90.57 W
Lincoln □6, Or., U.S. 224 44.59 N 123.52 W
Lincoln, Mount ∧ 200 39.21 N 106.07 W
Lincoln Acres 228 32.40 N 117.04 W
Lincoln Boyhood National Memorial ⊥ 194 38.10 N 86.58 W
Lincoln Cathedral ᵛ1 44 53.14 N 0.33 W
Lincoln Center ᵛ 276 40.46 N 73.59 W
Lincoln City 224 44.57 N 124.00 W
Lincoln Creek ≃, Ne., U.S. 198 40.54 N 97.06 W
Lincoln Creek ≃, Wa., U.S. 224 46.45 N 123.02 W
Lincolndale 210 41.19 N 73.43 W
Lincoln Estates 278 41.31 N 87.49 W
Lincoln Heights, Oh., U.S. 214 40.47 N 82.30 W
Lincoln Heights, Oh., U.S. 218 39.15 N 84.28 W
Lincoln Heights, Pa., U.S. 279b 40.19 N 79.37 W
Lincoln Home National Historic Site ⊥ 219 39.47 N 89.38 W
Lincolnia Heights 284c 38.50 N 77.09 W
Lincoln Memorial ⊥ 284c 38.53 N 77.03 W
Lincoln Park, Co., U.S. 200 38.25 N 105.13 W
Lincoln Park, Ga., U.S. 192 32.52 N 84.19 W
Lincoln Park, Mi., U.S. 216 42.15 N 83.10 W
Lincoln Park, N.J., U.S. 276 40.55 N 74.18 W
Lincoln Park, N.Y., U.S. 210 41.57 N 74.00 W
Lincoln Park ♦, Ca., U.S. 282 37.46 N 122.30 W
Lincoln Park ♦, Il., U.S. 278 41.56 N 87.38 W
Lincoln Park Airport ⊠ 276 40.57 N 74.19 W
Lincoln Place ➜8 279b 40.22 N 79.55 W
Lincoln Sea ⊤2 16 83.00 N 56.00 W
Lincolnshire 216 42.11 N 87.54 W
Lincolnshire □6 28 52.55 N 0.22 W
Lincoln's New Salem State Park ♦ 219 39.58 N 89.52 W
Lincoln Tomb State Memorial ⊥ 219 39.50 N 89.39 W
Lincolnton, Ga., U.S. 192 33.47 N 82.28 W
Lincolnton, N.C., U.S. 192 35.28 N 81.15 W
Lincoln Tunnel ➜5 276 40.46 N 74.01 W
Lincoln University 208 39.48 N 75.55 W
Lincoln Village, Ca., U.S. 226 38.00 N 121.19 W
Lincoln Village, Oh., U.S. 218 39.57 N 83.08 W
Lincolnville 214 41.47 N 79.51 W
Lincolnwood 278 42.00 N 87.43 W
Lincolnwood Hills 278 41.31 N 87.54 W
Linconia 285 40.08 N 74.59 W
Lincroft 208 40.19 N 74.07 W
Lind 202 46.58 N 118.36 W
Linda, Ross. 80 56.37 N 44.07 E
Linda, Ca., U.S. 226 39.07 N 121.32 W
Linda-a-Velha 266c 38.43 N 9.14 W
Lindale, Ga., U.S. 192 34.11 N 85.10 W
Lindale, Tx., U.S. 222 32.30 N 95.24 W
Lindau, Dtsch. 41 54.36 N 9.47 E
Lindau, Dtsch. 52 51.39 N 10.07 E
Lindau, Dtsch. 54 52.02 N 12.06 E
Lindau, Dtsch. 58 47.33 N 9.41 E
Lindbergh 219 39.02 N 92.08 W
Lindbergh Field ⊠ 228 32.44 N 117.11 W
Lind Coulee V 202 47.00 N 119.10 W
Linde ≃ 74 64.57 N 124.36 E
Lindelse 41 54.52 N 10.44 E
Linden, Guy. 246 6.00 N 58.18 W
Linden, Al., U.S. 194 32.18 N 87.47 W
Linden, Ca., U.S. 226 38.01 N 121.05 W
Linden, In., U.S. 194 40.11 N 86.54 W
Linden, Mi., U.S. 216 42.48 N 83.46 W
Linden, N.J., U.S. 210 40.37 N 74.14 W
Linden, Pa., U.S. 210 41.14 N 77.08 W
Linden, Pa., U.S. 279b 40.14 N 80.08 W
Linden, Tn., U.S. 194 35.37 N 87.50 W
Linden, Tx., U.S. 194 33.00 N 94.21 W
Linden ➜8 273d 26.08 S 28.00 E
Linden Airport ⊠ 276 40.37 N 74.15 W
Lindenberg, Dtsch. 54 53.02 N 12.07 E
Lindenberg, Dtsch. 54 52.36 N 13.31 E
Lindenberg, Dtsch. 54 52.12 N 14.07 E
Lindenberg im Allgäu 58 47.36 N 9.53 E
Linden-Dahlhausen ➜8 263 51.26 N 7.09 E
Lindenfels 56 49.41 N 8.47 E
Lindenhorst ➜8 263 51.33 N 7.27 E
Lindenhurst, Il., U.S. 216 42.24 N 88.01 W
Lindenhurst, N.Y., U.S. 210 40.41 N 73.22 W
Lindenhurst, Pa., U.S. 285 40.14 N 74.54 W
Linden Park 216 40.13 N 85.23 W
Lindenthal 54 51.24 N 12.20 E
Lindenwold 208 39.49 N 74.59 W
Lindenwood, Il., U.S. 216 42.03 N 89.02 W
Lindenwood, In., U.S. 218 39.41 N 86.09 W
Linderhausen 263 51.18 N 7.17 E
Linderhof, Schloss ⊥ 64 47.34 N 10.57 E
Lindern 52 52.50 N 7.46 E
Linderöd 41 55.56 N 13.49 E
Linderödsåsen ⩘2 26 55.53 N 13.56 E
Lindesay, Mount ∧2 162 34.49 S 117.18 E
Lindesberg 40 59.35 N 15.15 E
Lindesnäs 40 60.20 N 14.32 E
Lindesnes > 26 58.00 N 7.02 E
Lindfield, Austl. 274a 33.47 S 151.10 E
Lindfield, Eng., U.K. 42 51.01 N 0.05 W
Lindfors 40 59.36 N 13.49 E
Lindholmen 40 59.35 N 18.06 E
Lindhorst 52 52.21 N 9.17 E
Líndhos 38 36.06 N 28.04 E
Líndhos ⊥ 38 36.06 N 28.05 E
Lindi 154 10.00 S 39.43 E
Lindi □4 154 9.15 S 38.45 E
Lindi ≃ 154 0.33 N 25.05 E
Lindian 89 47.11 N 124.52 E
Lindis Pass)(172 44.36 S 169.40 E
Lindkirchen 60 48.40 N 11.47 E
Lindlar 56 51.01 N 7.23 E
Lindley, S. Afr. 158 28.00 S 27.57 E
Lindley, N.Y., U.S. 210 42.02 N 77.08 W
Lind National Park ♦ 166 37.35 S 149.05 E
Lindö 40 58.37 N 16.15 E
Lindóia 256 22.31 S 46.39 W
Lindome 26 57.34 N 12.05 E
Lindon 198 39.44 N 103.24 W
Lindong, Zhg. 100 26.03 N 118.49 E
Lindong, Zhg. 105 39.51 N 117.41 E
Lindow 54 52.58 N 13.00 E
Lind Point > 240m 18.20 N 64.48 W
Lindre, Étang de ◎1 56 48.47 N 6.45 E
Lindsay, On., Can. 212 44.21 N 78.44 W
Lindsay, Ca., U.S. 204 36.12 N 119.05 W
Lindsay, Ne., U.S. 198 41.42 N 97.41 W
Lindsay, Ok., U.S. 196 34.50 N 97.36 W
Lindsborg 198 38.34 N 97.40 W
Lindsey 214 41.25 N 83.13 W
Lindved 41 55.47 N 9.35 E
Lindy Lake 276 41.05 N 74.22 W
Lineboro 208 39.43 N 76.50 W
Line Creek ≃ 194 33.34 N 88.42 W
Line Islands II 14 0.05 N 157.00 W
Line Lexington 208 40.17 N 75.16 W
Line Mountain ∧ 210 40.45 N 76.37 W
Linesville 214 41.39 N 80.25 W
Lineville, Al., U.S. 194 33.18 N 85.45 W
Lineville, Ia., U.S. 190 40.34 N 93.31 W
Línevo 86 54.05 N 83.24 E
Linfen 102 36.05 N 111.32 E
Linfield 208 40.13 N 75.34 W
Linford 260 51.29 N 0.25 E
Ling ≃ 46 57.19 N 5.27 W
Ling'an 106 30.36 N 120.30 E
Linganamakki Reservoir ◎1 122 14.04 N 74.54 E
Lingao 102 19.54 N 109.40 E
Lingayen 116 16.01 N 120.14 E
Lingayen Gulf c 116 16.15 N 120.14 E
Lingbi 100 33.33 N 117.33 E
Lingbo 26 61.03 N 16.41 E
Lingchuan, Zhg. 102 25.26 N 110.15 E
Lingchuan, Zhg. 102 35.46 N 113.26 E
Lingda 106 31.12 N 119.18 E
Lingdale 44 54.32 N 0.57 W
Lingdianzhen 106 31.51 N 121.25 E
Lingdou 100 26.22 N 118.56 E
Lingen 52 52.31 N 7.19 E
Lingesestausee ◎1 263 51.06 N 7.32 E
Lingfengwei 100 24.44 N 115.35 E
Lingfield 42 51.11 N 0.01 W
Lingga, Kepulauan II 112 0.05 S 104.35 E
Lingga, Pulau I 112 0.12 S 104.35 E
Lingham Lake ◎ 212 44.46 N 77.25 W
Linghe 98 36.23 N 119.03 E
Linghu 106 30.44 N 120.10 E
Lingig 116 8.02 N 126.24 E
Lingjiachang 107 29.28 N 104.54 E
Lingjiaqiao 106 30.09 N 120.04 E
Lingkar Dzong 124 28.45 N 90.36 E
Lingkou, Zhg. 100 29.16 N 120.38 E
Lingkou, Zhg. 106 31.57 N 119.38 E
Lingle 200 42.08 N 104.20 W
Linglestown 208 40.21 N 76.48 W
Lingling 102 26.13 N 111.37 E
Linglongta 98 40.54 N 119.59 E
Lingma 102 23.22 N 107.53 E
Lingolsheim 58 48.34 N 7.41 E
Lingomo 152 0.38 N 21.59 E
Lingqiu 98 39.24 N 114.13 E
Lingshan, Zhg. 98 36.33 N 120.27 E
Lingshan, Zhg. 102 22.28 N 109.17 E
Lingshanwei 98 35.58 N 120.13 E
Lingshi 102 36.54 N 111.43 E
Lingshou 98 38.18 N 114.24 E
Lingshui 110 18.31 N 110.01 E
Lingtangqiao 100 32.43 N 119.14 E
Linguaglossa 70 37.50 N 15.08 E
Linguère 150 15.24 N 15.07 W
Lingwala 273b 4.22 S 15.17 E
Lingwood 42 52.37 N 1.29 E
Lingwu 102 38.06 N 106.21 E
Lingxian, Zhg. 98 37.21 N 116.34 E
Lingxian, Zhg. 100 26.30 N 113.46 E
Lingxiazhu 100 29.03 N 119.46 E
Lingyuan 98 41.15 N 119.16 E
Lingzhuangzi 105 39.04 N 117.09 E
Lingzinan 105 39.29 N 115.15 E
Linh, Ngoc ∧ 110 15.04 N 107.59 E
Linhai 100 28.51 N 121.07 E
Linhares 255 19.25 S 40.04 W
Linh Cam 110 18.31 N 105.34 E
Linhe 102 40.51 N 107.30 E
Linhezhuang 105 40.04 N 117.39 E
Linhigh 284b 39.21 N 76.31 W
Linhó 266c 38.46 N 9.23 W
Linhsia → Linxia 102 35.35 N 103.13 E
Linhuaiguan 100 32.55 N 117.40 E
Linhuanji 100 33.42 N 116.33 E
Lini → Linyi 98 35.04 N 118.22 E
Linjiang, Zhg. 98 41.44 N 126.55 E
Linjiang, Zhg. 100 27.50 N 118.26 E
Linjiang, Zhg. 100 28.04 N 115.21 E
Linjiang, Zhg. 102 33.01 N 105.01 E
Linjiangchang 107 29.14 N 105.58 E
Linjianghu 100 28.41 N 117.54 E
Linjiangsi 107 30.15 N 104.37 E
Linjiatai 104 40.43 N 123.57 E
Linkenheim 56 49.07 N 8.24 E
Linköping 26 58.25 N 15.37 E
Linkou 89 45.15 N 130.16 E
Linksfield ➜8 273d 26.10 S 28.06 E
Linksmakalnis 76 54.45 N 23.55 E
Linksness 46 58.56 N 3.19 W
Linkuva 76 56.05 N 23.59 E
Linkwood 208 38.32 N 75.57 W
Linli 102 29.18 N 111.30 E
Linlithgow 46 55.59 N 3.37 W
Linmeyer 273d 26.16 S 28.04 E
Linn, Ks., U.S. 198 39.40 N 97.05 W
Linn, Mo., U.S. 219 38.29 N 91.51 W
Linn ➜8 263 51.20 N 6.38 E
Linnancang 105 39.50 N 117.37 E
Linnansaaren kansallispuisto ♦ 26 62.07 N 28.31 E
Linndale 279a 41.27 N 81.46 W
Linne 52 51.10 N 5.57 E
Linnell 226 36.21 N 119.11 W
Linnés Hammarby ⊥ 40 59.49 N 17.46 E
Linn Grove 216 40.38 N 85.01 W
Linnhe, Loch c 46 56.39 N 5.21 W
Linnich 56 50.59 N 6.16 E
Linntown 210 40.58 N 76.54 W
Linnville Bayou ≃ 222 28.57 N 95.42 W
Linosa 70a 35.51 N 12.52 E
Linosa, Isola di I 70a 35.51 N 12.52 E
Lin'ovo 80 50.53 N 44.51 E
Linow 54 53.06 N 12.49 E
Linping → Yuhang 106 30.25 N 120.18 E
Linpu 100 30.03 N 120.15 E
Linqi, Zhg. 98 35.48 N 113.53 E
Linqi, Zhg. 100 29.51 N 119.06 E
Linqing 98 36.53 N 115.41 E
Linqu 98 36.32 N 118.31 E
Linquan 100 33.06 N 115.13 E
Linru 100 34.11 N 112.49 E
Linruzhen 100 34.17 N 112.35 E
Lins 255 21.40 S 49.45 W
Linshan 100 30.09 N 120.59 E
Linshanhe 100 30.44 N 114.52 E
Linshengpu 104 41.34 N 123.20 E
Linshui 102 30.21 N 106.59 E
Linslade 42 51.55 N 0.41 W
Linstead 241q 18.08 N 77.02 W
Linta ≃ 157b 25.02 S 44.05 E
Lintan 102 34.37 N 103.40 E
Lintao 102 35.27 N 103.46 E
Linté 152 5.24 N 11.42 E
Linth ≃ 58 47.07 N 9.07 E
Linthal, Fr. 58 47.56 N 7.08 E
Linthal, Schw. 58 46.55 N 9.00 E
Linthicum Heights 284b 39.12 N 76.39 W
Linthkanal ≍ 58 47.13 N 8.57 E
Linthwaite 262 53.37 N 1.51 W
Lintingkou 105 39.39 N 117.30 E
Linton, Austl. 169 37.41 S 143.34 E
Linton, N.Z. 172 40.26 S 175.33 E
Linton, Eng., U.K. 42 52.06 N 0.17 E
Linton, Eng., U.K. 260 51.13 N 0.31 E
Linton, In., U.S. 194 39.02 N 87.09 W
Linton, N.D., U.S. 198 46.16 N 100.13 W
Lintong 102 34.21 N 109.11 E
Linton Park ♦ 260 51.13 N 0.31 E
Lintorf 52 51.20 N 6.49 E
Linum 264a 52.46 N 12.53 E
Linville, Austl. 171a 26.51 S 152.16 E
Linville, N.C., U.S. 192 36.03 N 81.52 W
Linwood, Austl. 168b 34.21 S 138.46 E
Linwood, In., U.S. 218 40.12 N 85.41 W
Linwood, Ma., U.S. 207 42.05 N 71.38 W
Linwood, N.J., U.S. 208 39.20 N 74.34 W
Linwood, Pa., U.S. 285 39.49 N 75.24 W
Linworth 214 40.06 N 83.04 W
Linwu, Zhg. 98 36.14 N 119.17 E
Linwu, Zhg. 102 25.16 N 112.20 E
Linxi, Zhg. 90 43.30 N 118.00 E
Linxi, Zhg. 98 36.52 N 115.32 E
Linxia 102 35.35 N 103.13 E
Linxian, Zhg. 98 36.04 N 113.50 E
Linxian, Zhg. 102 37.58 N 110.59 E
Linxiang 100 29.28 N 113.30 E
Linyanti 156 18.04 S 24.01 E
Linyanti ≃ 156 17.58 S 24.16 E
Linyi, Zhg. 98 35.04 N 118.22 E
Linyi, Zhg. 98 37.13 N 116.51 E
Linyi, Zhg. 102 35.15 N 110.59 E
Linying 100 33.50 N 113.57 E
Linyü → Shanhaiguan 98 40.01 N 119.44 E
Linyüan 100 22.30 N 120.23 E
Linz, Dtsch. 56 50.34 N 7.17 E
Linz, Öst. 61 48.18 N 14.18 E
Linze, Zhg. 100 33.03 N 119.38 E
Linze, Zhg. 102 39.19 N 100.17 E
Linzgau ➜1 58 47.45 N 9.16 E
Linzhai 100 24.18 N 115.03 E
Linzhang 98 36.21 N 114.36 E
Linzhi 120 29.25 N 94.22 E
Linzikou 100 28.42 N 112.46 E
Linzolo 152 4.25 S 15.07 E
Lioko, Zaïre 152 0.02 N 22.04 E
Lioko, Zaïre 152 1.25 N 23.07 E
Lio Matoh 112 3.10 N 115.14 E
Liomer 50 49.51 N 1.49 E
Lion, Golfe du c 32 43.00 N 4.00 E
Lionel Town 241q 17.48 N 77.14 W
Lioni 68 40.52 N 15.11 E
Lion Rock ∧2 271d 22.22 N 114.11 E
Lion Rock Tunnel ➜5 271d 22.21 N 114.09 E
Lions Den 154 17.16 S 30.02 E
Lion's Head 212 44.59 N 81.15 W
Lionville 208 40.03 N 75.39 W
Lioppa 112 7.40 S 126.00 E
Liouesso 152 1.02 N 15.43 E
Liozno 76 55.02 N 30.48 E
Lipa 116 13.57 N 121.10 E
Lipan 196 32.31 N 98.03 W
Lipany 30 49.10 N 20.58 E
Lipari 70 38.28 N 14.57 E
Lipari, Isola I 70 38.29 N 14.56 E
Lipatkain 112 0.01 S 101.13 E
Lipayan 104 42.13 N 123.23 E
Lipeck 76 52.37 N 39.35 E
Lipeck Oblast' □4 76 52.30 N 39.00 E
Liperi 26 62.32 N 29.22 E
Lipetsk → Lipeck 76 52.37 N 39.35 E
Lipez, Cerro ∧ 248 21.53 S 66.52 W
Liphook 42 51.05 N 0.49 W
Lipiany 30 53.00 N 14.59 E
Lipicy 76 53.22 N 37.17 E
Lipin Bor 76 60.16 N 37.57 E
Liping 102 26.17 N 109.00 E
Lipis ≃ 114 4.10 N 102.04 E
Lipiyu 104 41.09 N 123.36 E
Lipka ≃ 265b 55.45 N 37.11 E
Lipki 76 53.58 N 37.42 E
Lipník nad Bečvou 30 49.31 N 17.35 E
Lipniški 76 54.00 N 25.37 E
Lipno 30 52.51 N 19.10 E
Lipno, údolní Nádrž ◎1 61 48.43 N 14.04 E
Lipno nad Vltavou 61 48.38 N 14.14 E
Lipoa Point > 229a 21.02 N 156.38 W
Lipova 38 46.05 N 21.40 E
Lipovcy 89 44.11 N 131.44 E
Lipovka, Ross. 78 50.52 N 40.02 E
Lipovka, Ross. 80 52.26 N 46.11 E
Lipovka, Ross. 80 49.46 N 44.56 E
Lippborg 52 51.40 N 8.02 E
Lippe ≃ 52 51.39 N 6.38 E
Lipperode 52 51.41 N 8.22 E
Lippetal 52 51.40 N 8.06 E
Lippoldsberg 52 51.37 N 9.33 E
Lippstadt 52 51.40 N 8.19 E
Lipscomb 196 36.14 N 100.16 W
Lipsko 30 51.09 N 21.39 E
Lipsoí I, Ellás 38 37.20 N 26.45 E
Lipsoí I, Ellás 130 37.20 N 26.45 E
Lipton 184 50.54 N 103.50 W
Liptovská Teplička 30 48.59 N 20.06 E
Liptovský Mikuláš 30 49.06 N 19.37 E
Liptrap, Cape > 166 38.54 S 145.55 E
Lipu 102 24.25 N 110.29 E
Lipu La)(124 30.21 N 81.05 E
Liqiao 107 29.03 N 104.48 E
Lira, Ug. 154 2.15 N 32.54 E
Lira, Ven. 286c 10.26 N 66.46 W
Liranga 152 0.40 S 17.36 E
Lirangdian 105 39.14 N 116.14 E
Lircay 248 12.56 S 74.43 W
Liren 100 33.55 N 118.47 E
Lirentuncun 104 41.24 N 122.59 E
Liri ≃ 66 41.25 N 13.52 E
Liro 175f 16.27 S 168.13 E
Liro ≃ 58 46.18 N 9.23 E
Lisakovsk 86 52.36 N 62.37 E
Lisala 152 2.09 N 21.31 E
Lisavy 82 56.33 N 38.32 E
Lisboa (Lisbon), Port. 34 38.43 N 9.08 W
Lisboa (Lisbon), Port. 266c 38.43 N 9.08 W
Lisboa □5 266c 38.48 N 9.16 W
Lisbon → Lisboa, Port. 34 38.43 N 9.08 W
Lisbon, Il., U.S. 216 41.29 N 88.29 W
Lisbon, Md., U.S. 208 39.20 N 77.04 W
Lisbon, N.H., U.S. 188 44.12 N 71.54 W
Lisbon, N.D., U.S. 198 46.26 N 97.40 W
Lisbon, Oh., U.S. 214 40.46 N 80.46 W
Lisbon Falls 188 43.59 N 70.03 W
Lisbonne → Lisboa 34 38.43 N 9.08 W
Lisburn 48 54.31 N 6.03 W
Lisburne, Cape > 180 68.52 N 166.14 W
Lisburne Peninsula >1 180 68.30 N 165.15 W
Liscannor Bay c 48 52.55 N 9.25 W
Liscarney 48 53.43 N 9.35 W
Liscia ≃ 71 41.11 N 9.19 E
Liscia, Lago di ◎ 71 41.00 N 9.16 E
Lisdoonvarna 48 53.01 N 9.15 W
Liseleje 41 56.01 N 11.59 E
Lishan, Zhg. 100 31.50 N 113.16 E
Lishan, Zhg. 104 41.10 N 123.00 E
Lishangzhuang 105 39.35 N 118.11 E
Lishanke 98 40.41 N 119.53 E
Lishchynivka 78 49.16 N 34.14 E
Lishe 100 29.48 N 121.28 E
Lishe ≃ 102 24.18 N 101.32 E
Lishi, Zhg. 102 37.32 N 111.09 E
Lishi, Zhg. 106 31.14 N 120.37 E
Lishi, Zhg. 107 29.10 N 105.42 E
Lishizhen, Zhg. 107 29.04 N 106.15 E
Lishizhen, Zhg. 107 29.20 N 105.24 E
Lishu 89 43.21 N 124.37 E
Lishui, Zhg. 100 28.27 N 119.54 E
Lishui, Zhg. 106 31.39 N 119.01 E
Lishuzhen 89 45.05 N 130.41 E
Lisianski Island I 14 26.02 N 174.00 W
Lisica ≃ 86 58.34 N 85.11 E
Lisichansk → Lysychans'k 83 48.55 N 38.26 E
Lisicy 82 56.47 N 36.21 E
Lisieux, Sk., Can. 184 49.17 N 105.59 W
Lisieux, Fr. 50 49.09 N 0.14 E
Lisij Nos 265a 60.01 N 30.00 E
Líšina 60 49.37 N 13.10 E
Lisitu 154 9.39 S 34.39 E
Lisivshchyna 78 50.47 N 28.35 E
Lisizhuang 105 38.55 N 115.07 E
Lisja 80 57.15 N 54.22 E
Liska ≃ 80 48.32 N 43.08 E
Liskeard 42 50.28 N 4.28 W
Liski, Ross. 78 50.59 N 39.30 E
Liski, Ross. 78 50.56 N 39.29 E
Lískova 60 49.25 N 12.43 E
L'Isle, Schw. 58 46.37 N 6.25 E
Lisle, Il., U.S. 216 41.48 N 88.04 W
Lisle, N.Y., U.S. 210 42.21 N 76.00 W
L'Isle-Adam 50 49.07 N 2.14 E
L'Isle Jourdain 32 46.14 N 0.41 E
L'Isle-sur-la-Sorgue 62 43.55 N 5.03 E
L'Isle-sur-le-Doubs 58 47.27 N 6.35 E
L'Isle-sur-Serein 50 47.35 N 4.00 E
Lisman 194 32.10 N 88.16 W
Lismore, Austl. 166 28.48 S 153.17 E
Lismore, Austl. 169 37.58 S 143.20 E
Lismore, N.S., Can. 186 45.42 N 62.16 W
Lismore, Ire. 48 52.08 N 7.55 W
Lismore Castle ⊥ 48 52.08 N 7.52 W
Lismore Island I 46 56.29 N 5.33 W
Lisnaskea 48 54.15 N 7.27 W
Lisö >1 40 58.55 N 17.45 E
Lišov 61 49.01 N 14.37 E
Liss 42 51.03 N 0.55 W
Lissabon → Lisboa 34 38.43 N 9.08 W
Lissberg 56 50.22 N 9.05 E
Lisse 52 52.15 N 4.33 E
Lisses 261 48.36 N 2.26 E
Lissewege 50 51.18 N 3.11 E
Lissie 222 29.33 N 96.13 W
Lissingen 56 50.14 N 6.38 E
Lissone 62 45.37 N 9.14 E
Lissy 261 48.38 N 2.42 E
Lista 80 47.44 N 45.54 E
Lista >1 26 58.07 N 6.40 E
Lister ≃ 263 51.05 N 7.45 E
Lištica 36 43.23 N 17.36 E
Listowel, On., Can. 212 43.44 N 80.57 W
Listowel, Ire. 48 52.27 N 9.29 W
Listv'anka 88 51.52 N 104.51 E
Listv'anskij 86 54.27 N 83.29 E
Lisui 105 40.05 N 116.44 E
Lit 26 63.19 N 14.49 E
Lita 100 27.22 N 116.34 E
Litang, Malay. 112 5.20 N 118.31 E
Litang, Zhg. 102 23.11 N 109.05 E
Litang, Zhg. 102 30.00 N 100.16 E
Litang ≃ 102 28.04 N 101.30 E
Litani ≃ 250 3.40 N 54.00 W
Līṭānī, Nahr al- ≃ 132 33.20 N 35.14 E
Litava ≃ 61 49.02 N 16.36 E
Litcham 42 52.44 N 0.47 E
Litchfield, Ct., U.S. 207 41.44 N 73.11 W
Litchfield, Il., U.S. 219 39.10 N 89.39 W
Litchfield, Mi., U.S. 216 42.02 N 84.45 W
Litchfield, Mn., U.S. 190 45.07 N 94.31 W
Litchfield, Ne., U.S. 198 41.09 N 99.09 W

ENGLISH — Name, Page, Lat.°′, Long.°′ · DEUTSCH — Name, Seite, Breite°′, Länge°′ E = Ost

Litchfield, Oh., U.S. 214 41.10 N 82.02 W
Litchfield □6 207 41.45 N 73.11 W
Litchfield Park 200 33.29 N 112.21 W
Litchville 198 46.39 N 98.11 W
Literberry 219 39.51 N 90.12 W
Līth, Wādī al- V 144 20.40 N 40.35 E
Litherland 44 53.28 N 2.59 W
Lithgow 170 33.29 S 150.09 E
Lithia 220 27.51 N 82.10 W
Líthinon, Ákra > 38 34.55 N 24.44 E
Lithonia 192 33.42 N 84.06 W
Lithuania (Lietuva) □1, Europe 22 56.00 N 24.00 E
Lithuania (Lietuva) □1, Europe 76 56.00 N 24.00 E
Litian 100 26.58 N 114.10 E
Litija 36 46.03 N 14.50 E
Litipāra 124 24.42 N 87.37 E
Lititz 208 40.09 N 76.18 W
Litke 89 53.57 N 140.15 E
Litókhoron 38 40.06 N 22.30 E
Litoko 154 1.13 S 24.47 E
Litoměřice 54 50.35 N 14.09 E
Litomyšl 30 49.52 N 16.19 E
Litoo 154 9.54 S 38.24 E
Litouqiao 106 31.15 N 118.54 E
Litovel 30 49.42 N 17.05 E
Litovko 89 49.15 N 135.11 E
Litschau 61 48.57 N 15.03 E
Littau 58 47.03 N 8.16 E
Little ≃, Austl. 169 38.01 S 144.35 E
Little ≃, On., Can. 281 42.20 N 82.56 W
Little ≃, U.S. 194 35.32 N 90.25 W
Little ≃, U.S. 194 33.37 N 93.52 W
Little ≃, Al., U.S. 194 31.18 N 87.46 W
Little ≃, Al., U.S. 194 34.16 N 85.40 W
Little ≃, Ct., U.S. 207 41.36 N 72.03 W
Little ≃, Ga., U.S. 192 30.51 N 83.21 W
Little ≃, Ga., U.S. 192 33.39 N 82.32 W
Little ≃, Ga., U.S. 192 33.14 N 83.24 W
Little ≃, In., U.S. 216 40.53 N 85.32 W
Little ≃, Ky., U.S. 194 36.51 N 87.58 W
Little ≃, La., U.S. 194 31.38 N 91.49 W
Little ≃, Ma., U.S. 283 42.37 N 70.42 W
Little ≃, Ma., U.S. 283 42.46 N 70.51 W
Little ≃, N.Y., U.S. 210 43.18 N 75.43 W
Little ≃, N.C., U.S. 192 35.15 N 78.42 W
Little ≃, N.C., U.S. 192 35.21 N 78.02 W
Little ≃, Ok., U.S. 196 35.00 N 96.25 W
Little ≃, S.C., U.S. 192 34.10 N 81.11 W
Little ≃, S.C., U.S. 192 33.56 N 82.25 W
Little ≃, S.C., U.S. 192 34.11 N 81.45 W
Little ≃, Tn., U.S. 192 35.51 N 83.57 W
Little ≃, Tx., U.S. 222 30.51 N 96.41 W
Little ≃, Va., U.S. 192 37.05 N 80.32 W
Little ≃, Va., U.S. 208 37.49 N 77.26 W
Little, Mountain Fork ≃ 194 33.57 N 94.34 W
Little Abaco I 238 26.53 N 77.43 W
Little Alfold → Kis Alföld ≃ 61 47.30 N 17.00 E
Little Amwell 260 51.47 N 0.02 W
Little Andaman I 110 10.45 N 92.30 E
Little Arkansas ≃ 198 37.43 N 97.22 W
Little Auglaize ≃ 216 41.07 N 84.25 W
Little Averill Lake ◎ 206 44.57 N 71.44 W
Little Baddow 260 51.44 N 0.35 E
Little Barrier Island I 172 36.12 S 175.05 E
Little Bay 186 47.41 N 58.24 W
Little Bay c 276 40.48 N 73.47 W
Little Bay Islands 186 49.39 N 55.47 W
Little Bear ≃ 200 41.42 N 111.57 W
Little Bear Creek ≃ 196 37.43 N 101.43 W
Little Bear Creek Reservoir ◎1 194 34.25 N 87.57 W
Little Beaver Creek ≃, U.S. 198 46.17 N 103.56 W
Little Beaver Creek ≃, U.S. 198 39.49 N 101.03 W
Little Beaver Creek ≃, U.S. 214 40.38 N 80.31 W
Little Beaver Creek ≃, Wa., U.S. 224 48.54 N 121.06 W
Little Beaver Creek, Middle Fork ≃ 214 40.43 N 80.37 W
Little Beaver Creek, North Fork ≃ 214 40.43 N 80.33 W
Little Beaver Creek, West Fork ≃ 214 40.43 N 80.37 W
Little Belt → Lillebælt ∪ 41 55.20 N 9.45 E
Little Belt Mountains ⩘ 202 46.45 N 110.35 W
Little Berkhamsted 260 51.45 N 0.08 W
Little Bighorn ≃ 202 45.44 N 107.34 W
Little Billabong 171b 35.35 S 147.32 E
Little Bitter Lake → Murrah aṣ-Ṣughrā, Al-Buḥayrah al- ◎ 142 30.13 N 32.33 E
Little Bitterroot ≃ 202 47.30 N 114.19 W
Little Black ≃, U.S. 194 36.25 N 90.45 W
Little Black ≃, Ak., U.S. 180 66.26 N 143.49 W
Little Black Bear Indian Reserve ➜4 184 51.00 N 103.23 W
Little Blackfoot ≃ 202 46.31 N 112.48 W
Little Blue ≃, U.S. 198 39.41 N 96.40 W
Little Blue ≃, In., U.S. 218 39.32 N 85.46 W
Littleborough 44 53.39 N 2.05 W
Little Bow ≃ 182 49.53 N 112.29 W
Little Brazos ≃ 222 30.38 N 96.31 W
Little Brokenstraw Creek ≃ 214 41.50 N 79.23 W
Little Brosna ≃ 48 53.10 N 8.05 W
Little Buffalo ≃ 176 61.00 N 113.46 W
Little Bullhead 184 51.40 N 96.51 W
Little Burstead 260 51.36 N 0.24 E
Little Calumet ≃ 278 41.39 N 87.34 W
Little Catalina 186 48.33 N 53.02 W
Little Cayman I 238 19.41 N 80.03 W
Little Cedar ≃ 190 42.57 N 92.31 W
Little Chalfont 260 51.40 N 0.34 W
Little Chartiers Creek ≃ 279b 40.17 N 80.08 W
Little Choptank River c 208 38.32 N 76.13 W
Little Churchill ≃ 184 57.15 N 95.21 W
Little Chute 190 44.16 N 88.19 W
Little Coco Island I 110 14.00 N 93.13 E
Little Colorado ≃ 200 36.11 N 111.48 W
Little Compton 207 41.30 N 71.10 W
Little Cooley 214 41.44 N 79.53 W
Little Cottonwood ≃ 198 44.15 N 94.20 W
Little Creek 208 39.10 N 75.26 W
Little Creek ≃ 285 39.56 N 74.48 W
Little Creek Naval Amphibious Base ■ 208 36.55 N 76.10 W
Little Creek Reservoir ◎1 208 37.20 N 76.50 W
Little Cumbrae Island I 46 55.43 N 4.57 W
Little Current 190 45.58 N 81.56 W
Little Current ≃ 176 50.57 N 84.36 W
Little Cypress Bayou ≃ 194 32.41 N 94.15 W
Little Cypress Creek ≃ 222 32.39 N 94.42 W
Little Darby Creek ≃ 218 39.53 N 83.13 W
Little Dart ≃ 42 50.54 N 3.51 W
Little Deep Creek ≃ 198 48.35 N 100.52 W
Little Deer Creek ≃, In., U.S. 216 40.36 N 86.28 W
Little Deer Creek ≃, Pa., U.S. 279b 40.33 N 79.50 W
Little Deschutes ≃ 202 43.51 N 121.27 W
Little Desert ➜2 166 36.35 S 141.20 E
Little Desert National Park ♦ 166 36.25 S 141.25 E
Little Diomede Island I 180 65.45 N 168.57 W
Little Don ≃ 275b 43.42 N 79.20 W
Little Dry Creek ≃, Ca., U.S. 226 39.22 N 121.52 W
Little Dry Creek ≃, Mt., U.S. 202 47.21 N 106.22 W
Little Ease Run ≃ 285 39.39 N 75.04 W
Little Eau Pleine ≃ 190 44.40 N 89.41 W
Little Egg Harbor c 208 39.35 N 74.18 W
Little Elkhart ≃ 216 41.43 N 85.49 W
Little End 260 51.41 N 0.14 E
Little Etobicoke Creek ≃ 275b 43.37 N 79.34 W
Little Exuma I 238 23.27 N 75.37 W
Little Fabius ≃ 219 39.59 N 91.59 W
Little Falls, Mn., U.S. 190 45.58 N 94.21 W
Little Falls, N.J., U.S. 276 40.52 N 74.12 W
Little Falls, N.Y., U.S. 210 43.02 N 74.51 W
Little Falls ≃ 208 39.36 N 76.38 W
Little Falls Dam ➜6 284c 38.57 N 77.08 W
Little Farms 218 39.57 N 83.10 W
Little Ferry 276 40.51 N 74.02 W
Littlefield 196 33.55 N 102.19 W
Little Flatrock ≃ 218 39.26 N 85.33 W
Littlefork 190 48.23 N 93.33 W
Little Fork ≃ 190 48.31 N 93.35 W
Little Fort 182 51.25 N 120.12 W
Little Genesee 210 42.02 N 78.13 W
Little Gold ≃ 162 18.01 S 126.29 E
Little Gunpowder Falls ≃ 208 39.23 N 76.22 W
Littlehampton 42 50.48 N 0.33 W
Little Harbour Deep 186 50.15 N 56.33 W
Little Haw Creek ≃ 192 29.23 N 81.24 W
Little Hawk Lake ◎ 212 45.10 N 78.42 W
Little Hoosic ≃ 210 42.49 N 73.20 W
Little Hope 214 42.06 N 79.49 W
Little Hulton 262 53.32 N 2.25 W
Little Humboldt ≃ 204 41.00 N 117.43 W
Little Humboldt, North Fork ≃ 204 41.24 N 117.10 W
Little Humboldt, South Fork ≃ 204 41.24 N 117.10 W
Little Hurricane Creek ≃ 192 31.23 N 82.19 W
Little Inagua I 238 21.30 N 73.00 W
Little Indian Creek ≃, Il., U.S. 216 41.31 N 88.46 W
Little Indian Creek ≃, In., U.S. 218 38.12 N 86.08 W
Little Island Pond ◎ 283 42.43 N 71.17 W
Littlejohns Creek ≃ 226 37.52 N 121.14 W
Little Juniata ≃ 214 40.34 N 78.03 W
Little Juniata Creek ≃ 208 40.23 N 77.02 W
Little Kanawha ≃ 188 39.16 N 81.34 W
Little Kanawha, West Fork ≃ 188 38.57 N 81.16 W
Little Karroo (Klein Karroo) ⩘1 158 33.45 S 21.30 E
Little Kentucky ≃ 218 38.41 N 85.12 W
Little Klickitat ≃ 224 45.51 N 121.04 W
Little Koniuji Island I 180 55.01 N 159.26 W
Little Lake ◎, On., Can. 212 44.26 N 79.40 W
Little Lake ◎, La., U.S. 194 29.30 N 90.10 W
Little Laramie ≃ 200 41.28 N 105.44 W
Little Laver 260 51.46 N 0.14 E
Little Leigh 262 53.17 N 2.35 W
Little Lever 262 53.34 N 2.22 W
Little Limestone Lake ◎ 184 53.46 N 99.18 W
Little London 241q 18.15 N 78.13 W
Little Lost ≃ 202 43.46 N 112.58 W
Little Lun ≃ 116 6.02 N 125.17 E
Little Mahoning Creek ≃ 214 40.49 N 79.00 W
Little Maitland ≃ 212 43.52 N 81.18 W
Little Manatee ≃ 220 27.42 N 82.28 W
Little Manatee, South Fork ≃ 220 27.39 N 82.18 W
Little Manistee ≃ 190 44.15 N 86.19 W
Little Manitou Lake ◎ 184 51.45 N 105.30 W
Little Marco Pass c 220 26.01 N 81.46 W
Little Marsh 210 41.53 N 77.24 W
Little Meadows 210 41.59 N 76.08 W
Little Mecatina ≃ 176 50.28 N 59.35 W
Little Medicine Bow ≃ 200 41.58 N 106.18 W
Little Mexico 196 30.57 N 102.52 W
Little Miami ≃ 218 39.05 N 84.26 W
Little Miami, East Fork ≃ 218 39.09 N 84.18 W
Little Miami, North Fork ≃ 218 39.48 N 83.47 W
Littlemill 46 57.32 N 3.49 W
Little Mississippi ≃ 212 45.17 N 77.35 W
Little Missouri ≃, U.S. 198 47.30 N 102.25 W
Little Missouri ≃, Ar., U.S. 194 33.49 N 92.54 W
Little Mountain ∧ 208 40.47 N 76.40 W
Little Muddy ≃, Il., U.S. 194 37.50 N 89.11 W
Little Muddy ≃, N.D., U.S. 198 48.12 N 103.36 W
Little Mulberry Creek ≃ 194 32.26 N 86.51 W
Little Naches ≃ 224 46.58 N 121.08 W
Little Nahant 283 42.25 N 70.56 W
Little Namaqualand □9 156 29.00 S 17.00 E
Little Neck 283 42.42 N 70.48 W
Little Neck ➜8 276 40.46 N 73.44 W
Little Neck Bay c 276 40.47 N 73.46 W
Little Nemaha ≃ 198 40.19 N 95.40 W
Little Neshaminy Creek ≃ 285 40.15 N 75.02 W
Little Niangua ≃ 194 38.04 N 92.54 W
Little Nicobar I 110 7.20 N 93.40 E
Little Ohoopee ≃ 192 32.27 N 82.24 W
Little Osage ≃ 194 38.02 N 94.14 W
Little Otter Creek ≃ 212 42.44 N 80.51 W
Little Ouse ≃ 42 52.30 N 0.22 E
Little Panoche Creek ≃ 226 36.50 N 120.42 W
Little Patuxent ≃ 284b 39.11 N 76.52 W
Little Paxton 42 52.15 N 0.15 W
Little Peconic Bay c 207 40.59 N 72.24 W
Little Pee Dee ≃ 192 33.42 N 79.11 W
Little Pic ≃ 190 48.48 N 86.37 W
Little Pine and Lucky Man Indian Reserve ➜4 184 52.56 N 109.05 W
Little Pine Creek ≃, Pa., U.S. 210 41.18 N 77.22 W
Little Pine Creek ≃, Pa., U.S. 279b 40.31 N 79.57 W
Little Pine Island I 220 26.36 N 82.05 W
Little Pine Key I 220 24.44 N 81.19 W
Little Pine State Park ♦ 210 41.22 N 77.20 W
Little Pipe Creek ≃ 208 39.36 N 77.16 W
Little Platte ≃ 194 39.24 N 94.41 W
Little Plum Creek ≃ 279b 40.30 N 79.51 W
Little Popo Agie ≃ 202 42.54 N 108.35 W
Little Porcupine Creek ≃, Mt., U.S. 202 46.18 N 106.34 W
Little Porcupine Creek ≃, Mt., U.S. 202 48.02 N 106.04 W
Littleport 42 52.28 N 0.19 E
Little Portage Creek ≃ 216 42.00 N 85.27 W
Little Powder ≃ 198 45.28 N 105.20 W
Little Pucketa Creek ≃ 279b 40.33 N 79.45 W
Little Quill Lake ◎ 184 51.55 N 104.05 W
Little Rann of Kachchh ≚ 120 23.25 N 71.15 E

Symbols in the index entries represent the broad categories identified in the key at the right. Symbols with superior numbers (⩘1) identify subcategories (see complete key on page *I · 1*).

Symbole im Register stellen die rechts im Schlüssel erklärten Kategorien dar. Symbole mit hochgestellten Ziffern (⩘1) bezeichnen Unterabteilungen einer Kategorie (vgl. vollständiger Schlüssel auf Seite *I · 1*).

Los símbolos incluídos en el texto del índice representan las grandes categorías identificadas con la clave a la derecha. Los símbolos con numeros en su parte superior (⩘1) identifican las subcategorías (véase la clave completa en la página *I · 1*).

Les symboles de l'index représentent les catégories indiquées dans la légende à droite. Les symboles suivis d'un indice (⩘1) représentent des sous-catégories (voir légende complète à la page *I · 1*).

Os símbolos incluídos no texto do índice representam as grandes categorias identificadas com a chave à direita. Os símbolos com números em sua parte superior (⩘1) identificam as subcategorias (veja-se a chave completa à página *I · 1*).

∧ Mountain	Berg	Montaña	Montagne	Montanha
⩘ Mountains	Gebirge	Montañas	Montagnes	Montanhas
)(Pass	Paß	Paso	Col	Passo
V Valley, Canyon	Tal, Cañon	Valle, Cañón	Vallée, Canyon	Vale, Canhão
≚ Plain	Ebene	Llano	Plaine	Planície
> Cape	Kap	Cabo	Cap	Cabo
I Island	Insel	Isla	Île	Ilha
II Islands	Inseln	Islas	Îles	Ilhas
⩡ Other Topographic Features	Andere Topographische Objekte	Otros Elementos Topográficos	Autres données topographiques	Outros acidentes topográficos

ESPAÑOL Nombre	Página	Lat.°′	Long.°′ W = Oeste
Little Red ≏	194	35.11 N	91.27 W
Little Red, Middle Fork ≏	194	35.37 N	92.11 W
Little Red Deer ≏	182	52.04 N	114.09 W
Little Red River Indian Reserve ⬥[4]	184	53.30 N	105.58 W
Little Redstone Lake ⊜	212	45.13 N	78.34 W
Little River, Austl.	169	37.58 S	144.30 E
Little River, N.Z.	172	43.46 S	172.47 E
Little River, Ks., U.S.	198	38.23 N	98.00 W
Little River, Tx., U.S.	222	30.59 N	97.22 W
Little Rock, Ar., U.S.	194	34.44 N	92.17 W
Littlerock, Ca., U.S.	228	34.31 N	117.59 W
Little Rock, Il., U.S.	216	41.43 N	88.34 W
Little Rock, Ia., U.S.	198	43.26 N	95.52 W
Littlerock, Wa., U.S.	224	46.54 N	123.01 W
Little Rock ≏	198	43.16 N	96.15 W
Little Rock Air Force Base ■	194	34.55 N	92.10 W
Little Rock Creek ≏	228	34.28 N	118.01 W
Little Rock Wash V	228	34.42 N	118.02 W
Little Rocky Mountains ⩘	202	47.50 N	108.10 W
Little Rouge Creek ≏	212	43.48 N	79.08 W
Little Ruaha ≏	154	7.17 S	35.28 E
Little Sable Point ≻	190	43.38 N	86.32 W
Little Sac ≏	194	37.39 N	93.46 W
Little Sachigo Lake ⊜	184	54.09 N	92.11 W
Little Saint Bernard Pass → Petit-Saint-Bernard, Col du)(	62	45.41 N	6.53 E
Little Salkehatchie ≏	192	32.37 N	80.53 W
Little Salmon ≏, Id., U.S.	202	45.25 N	116.19 W
Little Salmon ≏, N.Y., U.S.	212	43.32 N	76.16 W
Little Salmon, North Branch ≏	212	43.24 N	76.09 W
Little Salmon, South Branch ≏	212	43.24 N	76.09 W
Little Salmon Lake ⊜	180	62.12 N	134.45 W
Little Salt Lake ⊜	200	37.55 N	112.53 W
Little Sandy ≏	188	38.35 N	82.51 W
Little Sandy, East Fork ≏	188	38.30 N	82.50 W
Little Sandy Creek ≏	200	42.06 N	109.27 W
Little Sandy Desert ⬥[2]	162	24.20 S	120.50 E
Little Saskatchewan ≏	184	49.52 N	100.07 W
Little Scarcies ≏	150	8.51 N	13.09 W
Little Scioto ≏, Oh., U.S.	214	40.31 N	83.12 W
Little Scioto ≏, Oh., U.S.	218	38.46 N	82.53 W
Little Sewickley Creek ≏, Pa., U.S.	279b	40.15 N	79.45 W
Little Sewickley Creek ≏, Pa., U.S.	279b	40.33 N	80.12 W
Little Silver	276	40.20 N	74.02 W
Little Sioux ≏	198	41.49 N	96.04 W
Little Sioux, West Fork ≏	198	42.04 N	96.00 W
Little Sitkin Island I	181a	51.55 N	178.30 E
Little Smoky ≏	182	55.42 N	117.38 W
Little Snake ≏	200	40.27 N	108.26 W
Little Sodus Bay ⊂	210	43.20 N	76.43 W
Little Southwest Miramichi ≏	186	46.57 N	65.50 W
Little Stanney	262	53.15 N	2.53 W
Little Stony Creek ≏	226	39.20 N	122.31 W
Little Stour ≏	42	51.19 N	1.15 E
Littlestown	208	39.44 N	77.05 W
Little Stukeley	42	52.21 N	0.13 W
Little Sugarloaf ʌ[2]	274b	37.41 S	145.19 E
Little Sur ≏	226	36.20 N	121.54 W
Little Sutton	262	53.17 N	2.57 W
Little Swatara Creek ≏	208	40.24 N	76.29 W
Little Tallapoosa ≏	192	33.18 N	85.34 W
Little Tanaga Island I	180	51.48 N	176.10 W
Little Tennessee ≏	192	35.47 N	84.15 W
Little Thurrock	260	51.28 N	0.21 E
Little Timber Creek ≏	285	39.53 N	75.08 W
Little Tinicum Island I	285	39.51 N	75.17 W
Little Tobago I, Br. Vir. Is.	240m	18.26 N	64.51 W
Little Tobago I, Trin.	241r	11.18 N	60.30 W
Little Toby Creek ≏	214	41.22 N	78.49 W
Littleton, Eng., U.K.	260	51.24 N	0.28 W
Littleton, Co., U.S.	200	39.36 N	105.00 W
Littleton, Ma., U.S.	207	42.32 N	71.30 W
Littleton, N.H., U.S.	188	44.18 N	71.46 W
Littleton, N.C., U.S.	192	36.26 N	77.54 W
Littleton, W.V., U.S.	188	39.41 N	80.31 W
Little Traverse Bay ⊂	190	45.24 N	85.03 W
Little Truckee ≏	226	39.25 N	120.05 W
Little Turtle ≏	184	48.46 N	92.36 W
Little Turtle State Recreation Area ♠	216	40.50 N	85.26 W
Little Valley	210	42.15 N	78.48 W
Little Vermilion ≏	216	41.20 N	89.05 W
Little Vermilion Lake ⊜	184	51.16 N	93.50 W
Little Vienna Estates	284c	38.54 N	77.18 W
Little Wabash ≏	194	37.54 N	88.05 W
Little Walsingham	42	52.54 N	0.51 E
Little Waltham	260	51.47 N	0.29 E
Little Warley	260	51.35 N	0.19 E
Little Washita ≏	196	34.58 N	97.51 W
Little Wellington, Isla I	254	48.30 S	74.45 W
Little White ≏	198	43.44 N	100.40 W
Little White Mountain ʌ	182	49.42 N	119.20 W
Little White Salmon ≏	224	45.43 N	121.38 W
Little Wichita ≏	196	33.54 N	97.59 W
Little Wichita, East Fork ≏	196	33.52 N	98.07 W
Little Wind ≏	202	42.57 N	108.29 W
Little Wind, North Fork ≏	202	43.01 N	108.53 W
Little Wind, South Fork ≏	202	43.01 N	108.53 W
Little Wolf ≏	190	44.23 N	88.48 W
Little Wood ≏	202	42.57 N	114.21 W
Little York, In., U.S.	218	38.42 N	85.54 W
Little York, N.Y., U.S.	210	42.42 N	76.10 W
Little Zab (Zāb-e Kūchek) (Az-Zāb aṣ-Ṣaghīr) ≏	128	35.12 N	43.25 E
Littoral □[4]	152	4.13 N	10.25 E
Litunga	152	13.17 S	16.43 E
Litvínov	54	50.37 N	13.36 E
Litvinovo	76	59.34 N	38.01 E
Litvinskoje	86	50.42 N	72.42 E
Lityn	78	49.20 N	28.05 E
Litzmannstadt → Łódź	30	51.46 N	19.30 E
Liu ≏, Zhg.	98	41.48 N	122.43 E
Liu ≏, Zhg.	98	42.45 N	126.04 E
Liu ≏, Zhg.	98	40.38 N	118.09 E
Liu ≏, Zhg.	102	23.52 N	109.45 E
Liu ≏, Zhg.	105	40.38 N	118.09 E
Liu ≏, Zhg.	106	31.31 N	121.18 E
Liuanzhuang	105	39.14 N	117.11 E
Liuba	102	33.32 N	107.07 E
Liubotong	100	31.26 N	116.00 E
Liucao	106	31.07 N	121.41 E
Liuchen	102	23.09 N	110.29 E
Liucheng, Zhg.	100	24.03 N	115.08 E
Liucheng, Zhg.	100	28.36 N	119.34 E
Liucheng, Zhg.	102	24.32 N	109.21 E
Liuchengba	102	27.27 N	102.53 E
Liuch'iu Hsü I	100	22.21 N	120.22 E
Liuchow → Liuzhou	102	24.19 N	109.24 E

FRANÇAIS Nom	Page	Lat.°′	Long.°′ W = Ouest
Liucun	106	30.44 N	119.23 E
Liucura	252	38.39 S	71.05 W
Liudaogou	98	41.34 N	127.12 E
Liudaohe	105	40.39 N	116.12 E
Liudongqiao	106	31.03 N	119.32 E
Liudu	100	26.44 N	119.33 E
Liuduo	100	34.01 N	120.17 E
Liuduzhuang	105	39.27 N	117.50 E
Liuerbao	104	41.13 N	122.55 E
Liufang	100	27.56 N	116.22 E
Liufangling	100	30.27 N	114.27 E
Liufentzu	269d	24.57 N	121.35 E
Liugezhuang, Zhg.	98	38.33 N	116.30 E
Liugezhuang, Zhg.	105	40.03 N	118.16 E
Liugou	105	40.57 N	118.18 E
Liugu ≏	98	40.22 N	120.26 E
Liuguan	100	29.56 N	113.08 E
Liuguantun	104	41.20 N	121.21 E
Liuhang	106	31.21 N	121.22 E
Liuhe, Zhg.	98	42.15 N	125.43 E
Liuhe, Zhg.	100	33.20 N	112.48 E
Liuhe, Zhg.	100	30.46 N	113.12 E
Liuhe, Zhg.	100	32.22 N	118.49 E
Liuhe, Zhg.	100	30.20 N	115.36 E
Liuhe, Zhg.	105	39.31 N	118.17 E
Liuhe, Zhg.	106	31.30 N	121.15 E
Liuhegou	104	41.56 N	122.44 E
Liuheita	104	42.09 N	123.56 E
Liuhejie	102	24.26 N	101.35 E
Liuhekou	105	40.39 N	118.09 E
Liuheng Dao I	100	29.43 N	122.08 E
Liuhuang	100	23.58 N	116.28 E
Liuhudang	104	42.31 N	122.22 E
Liujia	102	24.54 N	107.49 E
Liujiachang	107	29.46 N	103.49 E
Liujiachuan	105	40.07 N	114.47 E
Liujiadai	106	31.57 N	120.23 E
Liujiadian	89	50.07 N	124.17 E
Liujiadu	106	32.15 N	120.33 E
Liujiafen	105	39.58 N	115.47 E
Liujiagangzi	104	41.28 N	122.33 E
Liujiagou	98	37.47 N	120.53 E
Liujiahe, Zhg.	100	32.06 N	113.21 E
Liujiahe, Zhg.	104	40.40 N	123.58 E
Liujiang	98	40.04 N	119.34 E
Liujiashan	105	40.14 N	114.49 E
Liujiatun, Zhg.	104	41.52 N	122.44 E
Liujiatun, Zhg.	104	41.51 N	122.05 E
Liujiatun, Zhg.	104	42.08 N	122.44 E
Liujiawopeng	104	42.16 N	123.01 E
Liujiazhai	269b	31.21 N	121.27 E
Liujiazhen	106	32.04 N	121.30 E
Liujiazi, Zhg.	98	41.00 N	120.13 E
Liujiazi, Zhg.	104	42.36 N	122.15 E
Liujiazi, Zhg.	104	41.48 N	123.47 E
Liujingcun	105	39.27 N	115.26 E
Liujisu	105	40.01 N	117.13 E
Liukeshu	86	44.59 N	90.12 E
Liuku	102	25.48 N	98.52 E
Liuli	154	11.05 S	34.38 E
Liulicun	271a	39.56 N	116.28 E
Liulidian	106	31.31 N	119.17 E
Liuligou	104	41.24 N	121.29 E
Liulihezhen	105	39.36 N	116.01 E
Liulin	100	31.34 N	113.14 E
Liuliwei	100	24.20 N	114.03 E
Liulongtai	104	41.32 N	120.56 E
Liumachang	107	29.51 N	104.54 E
Liumaogou	89	48.12 N	127.13 E
Liupangtun	104	41.36 N	123.28 E
Liupan Shan ⩘	102	35.40 N	106.40 E
Liuqianhutun	104	42.01 N	123.41 E
Liuqiao	106	32.11 N	120.51 E
Liuquan, Zhg.	98	34.27 N	117.20 E
Liuquan, Zhg.	105	39.22 N	116.18 E
Liurenba	100	29.57 N	114.49 E
Liushi, Zhg.	98	38.33 N	115.44 E
Liushi, Zhg.	100	28.03 N	120.51 E
Liushilipu	100	32.45 N	115.58 E
Liushi Shan ʌ	120	36.15 N	82.05 E
Liushouying	98	39.48 N	119.19 E
Liushudian	98	35.54 N	119.30 E
Liushudixia	104	42.26 N	121.14 E
Liushui	89	44.17 N	124.15 E
Liushuigou	100	31.34 N	112.27 E
Liushuquan	105	39.21 N	118.06 E
Liusiqiao	100	29.47 N	116.21 E
Liusong	105	39.40 N	117.08 E
Liuta	98	35.52 N	115.18 E
Liutai	98	41.20 N	113.43 E
Liutaizi	104	41.46 N	122.39 E
Liutang	102	24.58 N	110.21 E
Liutiaozhaicun	104	41.29 N	123.12 E
Liutuan	98	36.56 N	119.22 E
Liutuhutun	104	40.44 N	120.32 E
Liuwanglou	98	34.48 N	116.28 E
Liuwa Plain ≚	152	14.30 S	22.40 E
Liuwa Plain National Park ♠	152	14.30 S	22.40 E
Liuwei	106	32.16 N	119.28 E
Liuwudian	100	24.36 N	118.13 E
Liuxi ≏	100	23.22 N	112.54 E
Liuxia	106	30.15 N	120.03 E
Liuyang	100	28.09 N	113.38 E
Liuyang ≏	100	28.13 N	112.58 E
Liuyuan	98	36.10 N	114.34 E
Liuyuankou	98	34.54 N	114.20 E
Liuzhai	102	25.15 N	107.20 E
Liuzhou	102	24.19 N	109.24 E
Liuzhuang	100	33.10 N	120.19 E
Livada	38	47.52 N	23.07 E
Livadija	89	42.50 N	132.39 E
Livanátai	38	38.42 N	23.03 E
Līvāni	76	56.22 N	26.11 E
Livanjsko Polje ≚	36	43.55 N	16.45 E
Livanovka	86	52.06 N	61.59 E
Livarot	50	49.01 N	0.09 E
Lively, On., Can.	190	46.26 N	81.09 W
Lively, Va., U.S.	208	37.47 N	76.31 W
Lively Island I	254	52.02 S	58.30 W
Livengood	180	65.32 N	148.33 W
Livenka, Ross.	78	50.26 N	38.18 E
Livenka, Ross.	78	50.44 N	40.14 E
Livenza ≏	64	45.35 N	12.51 E
Live Oak, Ca., U.S.	226	39.16 N	121.39 W
Live Oak, Fl., U.S.	192	30.17 N	82.59 W
Live Oak Creek ≏	196	30.39 N	101.42 W
Liverdun	56	48.45 N	6.03 E
Liverdy-en-Brie	261	48.42 N	2.47 E
Livergnano	66	44.19 N	11.21 E
Liveringa	162	18.03 S	124.10 E
Livermore, Ca., U.S.	226	37.40 N	121.46 W
Livermore, Ia., U.S.	190	42.52 N	94.11 W
Livermore, Ky., U.S.	194	37.29 N	87.07 W
Livermore, Mount ʌ	196	30.38 N	104.10 W
Livermore Falls	188	44.28 N	70.11 W
Liverpool, Austl.	170	33.54 S	150.56 E
Liverpool, N.S., Can.	186	44.02 N	64.43 W
Liverpool, Eng., U.K.	44	53.25 N	2.55 W
Liverpool, Eng., U.K.	262	53.25 N	2.55 W
Liverpool, In., U.S.	216	41.34 N	87.18 W
Liverpool, N.Y., U.S.	210	43.06 N	76.13 W
Liverpool, Pa., U.S.	208	40.34 N	76.59 W
Liverpool, Tx., U.S.	222	29.18 N	95.17 W
Liverpool □[8]	262	53.25 N	2.55 W
Liverpool ≏	164	12.02 S	134.13 E
Liverpool (Speke) Airport ⊠	44	53.21 N	2.52 W
Liverpool, Cape ≻	176	73.38 N	78.06 W
Liverpool, University of ⊌[2]	262	53.24 N	2.58 W
Liverpool Bay ⊂, N.T., Can.	180	69.45 N	130.00 W
Liverpool Bay ⊂, N.S., Can.	186	44.02 N	64.41 W
Liverpool Bay ⊂, Eng., U.K.	44	53.30 N	3.16 W
Liverpool Football Ground ♠	262	53.26 N	2.57 W
Liverpool Heights	210	43.07 N	76.13 W

PORTUGUÊS Nome	Página	Lat.°′	Long.°′ W = Oeste
Liverpool Range ⩘	166	31.40 S	150.30 E
Livet-et-Gavet	62	45.06 N	5.56 E
Livigno	64	46.32 N	10.04 E
Livilliers	261	49.06 N	2.06 E
Lívingston, Guat.	236	15.50 N	88.45 W
Livingston, Scot., U.K.	46	55.53 N	3.32 W
Livingston, Al., U.S.	194	32.35 N	88.11 W
Livingston, Ca., U.S.	226	37.23 N	120.43 W
Livingston, Il., U.S.	194	38.58 N	89.45 W
Livingston, Ky., U.S.	192	37.17 N	84.12 W
Livingston, La., U.S.	194	30.30 N	90.44 W
Livingston, Mt., U.S.	202	45.39 N	110.33 W
Livingston, N.J., U.S.	210	40.47 N	74.18 W
Livingston, N.Y., U.S.	210	42.09 N	73.47 W
Livingston, Tn., U.S.	194	36.23 N	85.19 W
Livingston, Tx., U.S.	222	30.42 N	94.55 W
Livingston, Wi., U.S.	190	42.54 N	90.25 W
Livingston □[6], Il., U.S.	216	40.53 N	88.38 W
Livingston □[6], Mi., U.S.	216	42.38 N	83.50 W
Livingston □[6], N.Y., U.S.	210	42.48 N	77.49 W
Livingstone	154	17.50 S	25.53 E
Livingstone, Chutes de (Livingstone Falls) ʟ	152	4.50 S	14.30 E
Livingstone, Lake ⊜[1]	222	30.50 N	95.30 W
Livingstone Falls → Livingstone, Chutes de ʟ	152	4.50 S	14.30 E
Livingstone Lake ⊜	212	45.22 N	78.43 W
Livingstonia	154	10.36 S	34.07 E
Livingston Island I	9	62.35 S	60.30 W
Livingston Mall ⬥[9]	276	40.47 N	74.21 W
Livingston Manor	210	41.54 N	74.49 W
Livno	36	43.50 N	17.01 E
Livny	76	52.25 N	37.37 E
Livojoki ≏	26	65.24 N	26.48 E
Livonia, In., U.S.	218	38.34 N	86.17 W
Livonia, La., U.S.	194	30.33 N	91.33 W
Livonia, Mi., U.S.	216	42.22 N	83.21 W
Livonia, N.Y., U.S.	210	42.49 N	77.40 W
Livonia Center	210	42.49 N	77.38 W
Livonia Mall ⬥[9]	281	42.26 N	83.20 W
Livorno (Leghorn)	66	43.33 N	10.19 E
Livorno □[4]	66	43.14 N	10.35 E
Livorno Ferraris	62	45.17 N	8.05 E
Livourne → Livorno	66	43.33 N	10.19 E
Livramento → Santana do Livramento	252	30.53 S	55.31 W
Livramento do Brumado	255	13.39 S	41.50 W
Livron-sur-Drôme	62	44.46 N	4.51 E
Livry-Gargan	261	48.56 N	2.33 E
Livry-sur-Seine	261	48.31 N	2.41 E
Liwa	112	5.04 S	104.06 E
Liwale	154	9.46 S	37.56 E
Liwale Chini	154	9.41 S	38.01 E
Liwan	154	4.54 N	35.40 E
Liwonde	154	14.52 S	35.28 E
Liwonde National Park ♠	154	14.50 S	35.20 E
Liwung ≏	115a	6.08 S	106.49 E
Lixi, Zhg.	100	29.15 N	114.46 E
Lixi, Zhg.	100	27.39 N	116.19 E
Lixian, Zhg.	98	38.29 N	115.34 E
Lixian, Zhg.	102	34.11 N	105.02 E
Lixian, Zhg.	102	29.30 N	111.37 E
Lixian, Zhg.	105	39.33 N	116.26 E
Lixian → Black ≏	110	21.15 N	105.20 E
Lixin, Zhg.	100	26.52 N	116.42 E
Lixin, Zhg.	100	33.06 N	116.08 E
Lixing	100	33.28 N	115.28 E
Lixingzhuang	105	39.25 N	117.56 E
Lixoúrion	38	38.12 N	20.26 E
Lixus ⊥	34	35.16 N	6.13 W
Liyang, Zhg.	98	37.28 N	113.37 E
Liyang, Zhg.	106	31.26 N	119.29 E
Liyuanbao	100	25.16 N	112.55 E
Liyujiang	100	25.57 N	113.15 E
Lizard	42	49.58 N	5.12 W
Lizarda	250	9.36 S	46.41 W
Lizard Head Peak ʌ	200	42.47 N	109.11 W
Lizard Island I	164	14.40 S	145.28 E
Lizard Point ≻	42	49.56 N	5.13 W
Lizard Point Indian Reserve ⬥[4]	184	50.40 N	100.57 W
Lize	107	30.08 N	106.11 E
Lizhai	106	31.34 N	121.45 E
Lizhou	102	28.08 N	102.10 E
Lizhu	100	29.56 N	120.30 E
Lizhuang, Zhg.	100	34.24 N	116.30 E
Lizhuang, Zhg.	107	28.47 N	104.46 E
Lizhuangqiao	106	31.48 N	119.37 E
Lizinovka	78	50.08 N	39.28 E
Liziwei	107	30.19 N	106.39 E
Lizy-sur-Ourcq	50	49.01 N	3.02 E
Lizzana	64	45.51 N	11.03 E
Lizzanello	68	40.18 N	18.13 E
Lizzano	68	40.23 N	17.27 E
Lizzano in Belvedere	64	44.10 N	10.53 E
Ljalovo	82	56.03 N	37.14 E
Ljan	26	59.51 N	10.48 E
Ljubelj (Loiblpass))(	61	46.26 N	14.16 E
Ljubija	36	44.56 N	16.37 E
Ljubimec	38	41.50 N	26.05 E
Ljubinje	38	42.57 N	18.05 E
Ljubljana	36	46.03 N	14.31 E
Ljubovija	38	44.11 N	19.22 E
Ljubuški	36	43.12 N	17.33 E
Ljugarn	26	57.19 N	18.42 E
Ljunga	40	58.31 N	16.21 E
Ljungan ≏	26	62.19 N	17.23 E
Ljungaverk	26	62.29 N	16.03 E
Ljungby	26	56.50 N	13.56 E
Ljungbyhed	41	56.04 N	13.12 E
Ljungbyholm	26	56.38 N	16.10 E
Ljungdalen	26	62.51 N	12.47 E
Ljungsbro	26	58.31 N	15.30 E
Ljungskile	26	58.14 N	11.55 E
Ljusdal	26	61.50 N	16.05 E
Ljusfallshammar	40	58.47 N	15.29 E
Ljusnan ≏	26	61.12 N	17.08 E
Ljusnaren ⊜	40	59.51 N	14.56 E
Ljusne	26	61.13 N	17.08 E
Ljusterö I	40	59.31 N	18.37 E
Ljutomer	36	46.31 N	16.12 E
Llagas Creek ≏	226	36.58 N	121.31 W
Llaima, Volcán ʌ[1]	252	38.43 S	71.43 W
Llamara, Salar de ≚	248	21.13 S	69.40 W
Llanaber	42	52.45 N	4.05 W
Llanaelhaearn	42	52.59 N	4.24 W
Llanarth	42	52.12 N	4.18 W
Llanarthney	42	51.52 N	4.09 W
Llanbedrog	42	52.52 N	4.29 W
Llanberis, Pass of V	44	53.06 N	4.04 W
Llanbister	42	52.21 N	3.18 W
Llanboidy	42	51.54 N	4.36 W
Llanbryde	46	57.37 N	3.13 W
Llanbrynmair	42	52.37 N	3.57 W
Llançà	34	42.22 N	3.09 E
Llancanelo, Laguna ⊜	252	35.35 S	69.09 W
Llandaff	42	51.30 N	3.14 W
Llandaff Cathedral ⊌[1]	42	51.29 N	3.15 W
Llanddewi Brefi	42	52.10 N	3.57 W
Llandeilo	42	51.52 N	3.59 W
Llandilo	274a	33.43 S	150.45 E
Llandinam	42	52.29 N	3.26 W
Llandissilio	42	51.53 N	4.44 W
Llandovery	42	51.59 N	3.48 W
Llandrindod Wells	42	52.15 N	3.23 W
Llandudno	44	53.19 N	3.49 W
Llandybie	42	51.50 N	4.00 W
Llandysul	42	52.02 N	4.19 W
Llanelli	42	51.42 N	4.10 W

Llanelltyd	42	52.45 N	3.54 W
Llanelly	169	36.44 S	143.51 E
Llanenddwyn	42	52.49 N	4.06 W
Llanerchymedd	44	53.20 N	4.22 W
Llanes	34	43.25 N	4.45 W
Llanfaethlu	44	53.21 N	4.32 W
Llanfair-Caereinion	42	52.39 N	3.20 W
Llanfairfechan	44	53.15 N	3.58 W
Llanfairpwllgwyngyll	44	53.13 N	4.12 W
Llanfrynach	42	51.56 N	3.21 W
Llanfyllin	42	52.46 N	3.17 W
Llanfynydd	42	51.56 N	4.06 W
Llanfyrnach	42	51.57 N	4.35 W
Llangadog	42	51.56 N	3.53 W
Llangefni	44	53.16 N	4.18 W
Llangennech	42	51.41 N	4.04 W
Llangollen	42	52.58 N	3.10 W
Llangollen Estates	208	39.39 N	75.37 W
Llangranog	42	52.09 N	4.29 W
Llangurig	42	52.25 N	3.36 W
Llangwyryfon	42	52.19 N	4.03 W
Llangynog	42	52.50 N	3.25 W
Llanharan	42	51.33 N	3.25 W
Llanidloes	42	52.27 N	3.32 W
Llanilar	42	52.21 N	4.01 W
Llanllyfni	44	53.03 N	4.17 W
Llano	196	30.45 N	98.40 W
Llano ≏	196	30.35 N	98.25 W
Llano Colorado	204	31.38 N	115.55 W
Llanon	42	52.17 N	4.10 W
Llanos ≚	246	5.00 N	70.00 W
Llanpumsaint	42	51.56 N	4.18 W
Llanquihue	254	41.15 S	73.01 W
Llanquihue, Lago ⊜	254	41.08 S	72.48 W
Llanrhaeadr-ym-Mochnant	42	52.51 N	3.17 W
Llanrhidian	42	51.37 N	4.11 W
Llanrhystud	42	52.18 N	4.09 W
Llanrwst	44	53.08 N	3.48 W
Llansantffraid-ym-Mechain	42	52.47 N	3.08 W
Llansawel	42	52.01 N	4.00 W
Llantrisant	42	51.33 N	3.23 W
Llantwit Major	42	51.25 N	3.30 W
Llanuwchllyn	42	52.52 N	3.41 W
Llanwenog	42	52.06 N	4.12 W
Llanwrda	42	51.58 N	3.53 W
Llanwrtyd Wells	42	52.07 N	3.38 W
Llanybydder	42	52.04 N	4.09 W
Llata	248	9.25 S	76.47 W
Llavallol ⬥[8]	288	34.48 S	58.28 W
Llay	44	53.06 N	2.59 W
Lleida	34	41.37 N	0.37 E
Lleida □[4]	34	42.00 N	1.10 E
Llentrisca, Cap ≻	34	38.51 N	1.14 E
Llera de Canales	234	23.19 N	99.01 W
Llerena	34	38.14 N	6.01 W
Lleulleu, Lago ⊜	252	38.09 S	73.20 W
Lleyn Peninsula ≻[1]	42	52.54 N	4.30 W
Llica	248	19.52 S	68.16 W
Llico	252	34.46 S	72.05 W
Lliria	34	39.38 N	0.36 W
Llivia	32	42.28 N	1.59 E
Llobregat ≏	34	41.19 N	2.09 E
Llobregat, Delta del ≚[2]	266d	41.17 N	2.08 E
Llorente	116	11.25 N	125.33 E
Llorente ≏	116	11.25 N	125.33 E
Llorona, Punta ≻	236	8.39 N	83.45 W
Lloyd	218	38.37 N	82.51 W
Lloyd Harbor	210	40.54 N	73.27 W
Lloyd Harbor ⊂	276	40.55 N	73.27 W
Lloydminster	184	53.17 N	110.00 W
Lloyd Neck ≻[1]	276	40.56 N	73.28 W
Lloyd Point ≻	210	40.57 N	73.29 W
Lloyds ≏	186	48.33 N	57.13 W
Llucena	34	40.08 N	0.17 W
Llucmajor	34	39.29 N	2.54 E
Llullaillaco, Volcán ʌ[1]	252	24.43 S	68.33 W
Llusco	248	14.21 S	72.07 W
Lluta ≏	248	18.24 S	70.19 W
Llyn Brianne Reservoir ⊜[1]	42	52.08 N	3.45 W
Llyswen	42	52.02 N	3.17 W
Llys-y-frân Reservoir ⊜[1]	42	51.53 N	4.51 W
Lnáře	60	49.28 N	13.47 E
Lo (Panlong) ≏	110	21.18 N	105.25 E
Loa	200	38.24 N	111.38 W
Loa ≏, Chile	244	21.26 S	70.04 W
Loa ≏, Congo	273b	4.20 S	15.11 E
Loami	194	39.40 N	89.51 W
Loanda → Luanda, Ang.	152	8.48 S	13.14 E
Loanda, Bra.	255	22.54 S	53.10 W
Loanda, Gabon	152	0.55 S	9.00 E
Loande ≏	152	8.41 S	17.56 E
Loange (Luangue) ≏	152	4.17 S	20.02 E
Loango Buele	152	5.10 S	12.59 E
Loanhead	46	55.53 N	3.09 W
Loanja ≏	154	17.22 S	24.48 E
Loano	62	44.08 N	8.15 E
Loantaka Brook ≏	276	40.43 N	74.28 W
Lo Aranguiz	286e	33.23 S	70.40 W
Loay	116	9.36 N	124.01 E
Lob' ≏	82	56.29 N	35.51 E
Lobamba	158	26.27 S	31.12 E
Loban	24	65.44 N	45.25 E
Loban' ≏	80	56.58 N	51.12 E
Lobanovo	76	53.04 N	38.14 E
Lobanovskije Vyselki	82	54.18 N	38.58 E
Lo Barnechea	286e	33.21 S	70.31 W
Lobaski	80	54.38 N	45.09 E
Lobatos	234	22.49 N	103.24 W
Lobatse	156	25.11 S	25.40 E
Löbau	54	51.05 N	14.40 E
Lobau ≚	264b	48.10 N	16.32 E
Lobaye □[5]	152	4.00 N	18.30 E
Lobaye ≏	152	3.41 N	18.35 E
Lobbes	50	50.21 N	4.15 E
Lobbs Run ≏	279b	40.15 N	79.55 W
Lobdell Lake ⊜	216	42.48 N	83.48 W
Löbejün	54	51.38 N	11.53 E
Lobelville	194	35.46 N	87.47 W
Lo Benitez	286e	33.34 S	70.42 W
Lobenstein	54	50.26 N	11.38 E
Lobería	252	38.09 S	58.47 W
Lo Bernales	286e	33.34 S	70.34 W
Löberöd	41	55.47 N	13.30 E
Lobethal	168b	34.54 S	138.52 E
Łobez	30	53.39 N	15.36 E
Lobito	152	12.20 S	13.34 E
Lobitos	246	4.26 S	81.17 W
Lobitos Creek ≏	282	37.22 N	122.24 W
Lobkoviči	76	53.50 N	31.45 E
Lobn'a	82	56.01 N	37.30 E
Löbnitz, Dtsch.	54	51.35 N	12.28 E
Löbnitz, Dtsch.	54	54.17 N	12.43 E
Lobo, Indon.	164	3.45 S	134.05 E
Lobo, Pil.	116	13.39 N	121.13 E
Lobo ≏	150	6.02 N	6.47 W
Loboko	152	0.45 S	16.38 E
Lobos	258	35.11 S	59.06 W
Lobos, Cay I	238	22.24 N	77.32 W
Lobos, Isla I	232	27.20 N	110.36 W
Lobos, Isla de I, Esp.	148	28.45 N	13.49 W
Lobos, Isla de I, Méx.	234	21.27 N	97.13 W
Lobos, Laguna de ⊜	258	35.17 S	59.07 W
Lobos, Point ≻	226	37.47 N	122.31 W
Lobos, Punta ≻	248	21.01 S	70.11 W
Lobos de Afuera, Islas II	248	6.57 S	80.42 W
Lobos de Tierra, Isla I	248	6.27 S	80.52 W
Lo Boza	286e	33.23 S	70.46 W
Lobskoje	24	62.45 N	35.16 E
Lobstädt	54	51.08 N	12.29 E
Löbtau ⬥[8]	54	51.03 N	13.42 E
Loburg	54	52.07 N	12.05 E
Lobva	86	59.12 N	60.30 E

Łobżenica	30	53.16 N	17.15 E
Locana	62	45.25 N	7.27 E
Locana, Val di V	62	45.25 N	7.27 E
Locarno	58	46.10 N	8.48 E
Lo Castillo, Aeropuerto ⊠	286e	33.23 S	70.36 W
Locate Triulzi	62	45.21 N	9.13 E
Loccum	52	52.27 N	9.08 E
Loceri	71	39.51 N	9.35 E
Loch	169	38.22 S	145.43 E
Lochaber ⬥[1]	46	56.57 N	5.06 W
Lochailort	46	56.53 N	5.40 W
Lochaline	46	56.32 N	5.47 W
Locharbriggs	44	55.06 N	3.35 W
Lochar Water ≏	44	54.59 N	3.27 W
Lochboisdale	46	57.09 N	7.19 W
Lochcarron	46	57.24 N	5.30 W
Lochdon	46	56.26 N	5.41 W
Lochearn	284b	39.21 N	76.43 W
Lochearnhead	46	56.23 N	4.17 W
Lochem	52	52.09 N	6.25 E
Loches	50	47.08 N	1.00 E
Lochgair	46	56.03 N	5.20 W
Loch Garman → Wexford	48	52.20 N	6.27 W
Lochgelly	46	56.08 N	3.19 W
Lochgilphead	46	56.03 N	5.26 W
Lochgoilhead	46	56.10 N	4.54 W
Lochiel	168b	33.56 S	138.10 E
Lochindorb ⊜	46	57.24 N	3.43 W
Lochino	265b	55.42 N	37.19 E
Lochinvar National Park ♠	154	15.55 S	27.15 E
Lochinver	46	58.09 N	5.15 W
Lochmaben	44	55.08 N	3.27 W
Lochmaddy	46	57.36 N	7.11 W
Lochnagar ʌ	46	56.57 N	3.16 W
Lochovice	60	49.51 N	13.59 E
Lochranza	46	55.42 N	5.18 W
Loch Raven Dam ⬥[6]	284b	39.26 N	76.33 W
Loch Raven Reservoir ⊜[1]	208	39.27 N	76.34 W
Lochristi	50	51.06 N	3.50 E
Lochsa ≏	202	46.08 N	115.36 W
Loch Sheldrake	210	41.46 N	74.39 W
Loch Sport	166	38.03 S	147.36 E
Lochwinnoch	46	55.48 N	4.39 W
Lochy, Loch ⊜	46	56.57 N	4.53 W
Lock	166	33.34 S	135.46 E
Lock and Dam No. 20 ⬥[6], U.S.	219	40.09 N	91.30 W
Lock and Dam No. 21 ⬥[6], U.S.	219	39.54 N	91.26 W
Lock and Dam No. 22 ⬥[6], U.S.	219	39.39 N	91.16 W
Lock and Dam No. 24 ⬥[6], U.S.	219	39.22 N	90.55 W
Lock and Dam No. 25 ⬥[6], U.S.	219	39.01 N	90.41 W
Locke, Ca., U.S.	226	38.15 N	121.31 W
Locke, In., U.S.	216	41.28 N	86.00 W
Locke, N.Y., U.S.	210	42.39 N	76.25 W
Lockeford	226	38.10 N	121.09 W
Lockenhaus	61	47.24 N	16.25 E
Lockeport	186	43.42 N	65.07 W
Lockerbie	44	55.07 N	3.22 W
Lockesburg	194	33.58 N	94.10 W
Lockhart, Austl.	166	35.14 S	146.43 E
Lockhart, Fl., U.S.	220	28.37 N	81.26 W
Lockhart, Tx., U.S.	222	29.53 N	97.40 W
Lockhart River Aboriginal Reserve ⬥[4]	164	13.00 S	143.15 E
Lock Haven	210	41.08 N	77.26 W
Lockheed Aircraft Corporation ⊌[3], Ca., U.S.	280	34.12 N	118.22 W
Lockheed Aircraft Corporation ⊌[3], Ca., U.S.	282	37.25 N	122.02 W
Lockington	216	40.12 N	84.13 W
Lock Mountain ʌ	214	40.25 N	78.18 W
Lockney	196	34.07 N	101.26 W
Löcknitz	54	53.27 N	14.12 E
Löcknitz ≏, Dtsch.	54	53.07 N	11.16 E
Löcknitz ≏, Dtsch.	264a	52.25 N	13.49 E
Lockport, Mb., Can.	184	50.05 N	96.56 W
Lockport, Il., U.S.	216	41.35 N	88.03 W
Lockport, La., U.S.	194	29.39 N	90.32 W
Lockport, N.Y., U.S.	210	43.10 N	78.41 W
Lockport Lock ⬥[5]	278	41.35 N	88.04 W
Locks Heath	42	50.52 N	1.15 W
Locksley Park	210	42.45 N	78.52 W
Lockvattnet ⊜	40	59.03 N	17.05 E
Lockview	279b	40.10 N	79.55 W
Lockwood, Ca., U.S.	226	35.56 N	121.05 W
Lockwood, Mo., U.S.	194	37.23 N	93.57 W
Lockwood Corners	214	41.00 N	81.34 W
Lockyer Creek ≏	171a	27.25 S	152.36 E
Locminé	28	47.53 N	2.50 W
Loc Ninh	110	11.51 N	106.36 E
Loco, Bayou ≏	222	31.28 N	94.44 W
Locon	50	50.34 N	2.40 E
Locorotondo	68	40.45 N	17.20 E
Locri	68	38.14 N	16.16 E
Locri Epizefiri ⊥	68	38.12 N	16.13 E
Locroja	248	12.41 S	74.26 W
Locsin	116	13.09 N	123.43 E
Locumba	248	17.36 S	70.46 W
Locumba ≏	248	17.54 S	70.57 W
Locust	208	40.18 N	73.59 W
Locust Creek ≏	194	39.40 N	93.17 W
Locust Fork ≏	194	33.33 N	87.11 W
Locust Grove, N.Y., U.S.	276	40.48 N	73.30 W
Locust Grove, Ok., U.S.	196	36.12 N	95.10 W
Locust Lake State Park ♠	208	40.46 N	76.08 W
Locust Point ≻	276	40.49 N	73.48 W
Locust Valley	210	40.53 N	73.36 W
Lod (Lydda)	132	31.58 N	34.54 E
Lod, Nemel-Te'ufa (Ben Gurion Airport) ⊠	132	31.59 N	34.53 E
Loda	216	40.31 N	88.04 W
Lodal Creek ≏	285	40.14 N	75.27 W
Löddeköpinge	41	55.46 N	13.01 E
Loddon	42	52.32 N	1.29 E
Loddon ≏, Austl.	166	35.32 S	143.52 E
Loddon ≏, Eng., U.K.	42	51.30 N	0.53 W
Lodè	71	40.35 N	9.32 E
Lodejnoje Pole	76	60.44 N	33.30 E
Lodenau	54	51.24 N	14.57 E
Löderburg	54	51.52 N	11.32 E
Lodève	32	43.43 N	3.19 E
Lodge Creek ≏	202	48.35 N	109.10 W
Lodge Grass	202	45.18 N	107.21 W
Lodgepole, Ab., Can.	182	53.06 N	115.19 W
Lodgepole, Ne., U.S.	198	41.08 N	102.38 W
Lodgepole Creek ≏	198	40.57 N	102.22 W
Lodhāsuli	126	22.19 N	87.03 E
Lodhrān	123	29.32 N	71.38 E
Lodi, It.	62	45.19 N	9.30 E
Lodi, Ca., U.S.	226	38.07 N	121.16 W
Lodi, N.J., U.S.	210	40.52 N	74.05 W
Lodi, N.Y., U.S.	210	42.36 N	76.49 W
Lodi, Oh., U.S.	214	41.02 N	82.00 W
Lodi, Wi., U.S.	190	43.18 N	89.31 W
Lodi Park ♠	272a	28.36 N	77.13 E
Lodi Vecchio	62	45.18 N	9.24 E
Lodja	152	3.29 S	23.26 E
Lodosa	34	42.25 N	2.05 W
Lodoyo	115a	8.10 S	112.13 E
Lodrone	64	45.50 N	10.32 E
Lods	58	47.03 N	6.15 E
Lodsch → Łódź	30	51.46 N	19.30 E
Lodwar	154	3.07 N	35.36 E
Łódź	30	51.46 N	19.30 E

Łódź □[4]	30	51.50 N	19.25 E
Loe Āgra	123	34.35 N	71.43 E
Loei	110	17.29 N	101.35 E
Loei ≏	110	17.51 N	101.37 E
Loen	26	61.52 N	6.52 E
Loenen	52	52.07 N	6.01 E
Loengo	154	4.45 S	26.27 E
Loeriesfontein	158	30.56 S	19.26 E
Lo Espejo	286e	33.32 S	70.43 W
Lo Espejo, Canal ≖	286e	33.32 S	70.43 W
Lofa ≏	150	6.36 N	11.08 W
Lofer	64	47.35 N	12.41 E
Löffingen	58	47.53 N	8.20 E
Lofoten II	24	68.30 N	15.00 E
Lofoten Basin ✢[1]	10	70.00 N	4.00 E
Lofthouse	44	53.44 N	1.29 W
Lofthus	26	60.20 N	6.40 E
Loftus, Austl.	274a	34.03 S	151.03 E
Loftus, Eng., U.K.	44	54.33 N	0.53 W
Lofty, Mount ʌ, Austl.	168b	34.59 S	138.42 E
Lofty, Mount ʌ, Austl.	274b	37.43 S	145.17 E
Log	80	49.29 N	43.52 E
Loga, Dtsch.	52	53.14 N	7.29 E
Loga, Niger	150	13.37 N	3.14 E
Logačovka	80	52.23 N	52.21 E
Logan, Ia., U.S.	198	41.38 N	95.47 W
Logan, Ks., U.S.	198	39.39 N	99.34 W
Logan, N.M., U.S.	196	35.22 N	103.25 W
Logan, Oh., U.S.	188	39.32 N	82.24 W
Logan, Ut,. U.S.	200	41.44 N	111.50 W
Logan, W.V., U.S.	188	37.50 N	81.59 W
Logan □[6], Il., U.S.	219	40.09 N	89.22 W
Logan □[6], Oh., U.S.	216	40.22 N	83.46 W
Logan ⬥[8]	285	40.02 N	75.09 W
Logan ≏, Austl.	171a	27.43 S	153.18 E
Logan ≏, Ab., Can.	182	55.09 N	111.42 W
Logan ≏, Ut,. U.S.	200	41.44 N	111.57 W
Logan, Mount ʌ, Yk., Can.	180	60.34 N	140.24 W
Logan, Mount ʌ, Wa., U.S.	224	48.32 N	120.57 W
Logan Creek ≏, Ca., U.S.	226	39.22 N	122.06 W
Logan Creek ≏, Mo., U.S.	194	37.11 N	90.49 W
Logan Creek ≏, Ne., U.S.	198	41.37 N	96.29 W
Logandale	204	36.35 N	114.29 W
Logan International Airport ⊠	283	42.22 N	71.00 W
Logan Lake ⊜	212	44.52 N	78.59 W
Logan Martin Lake ⊜[1]	194	33.40 N	86.15 W
Logan Mountains ⩘	180	61.45 N	128.38 W
Logan Pass)(	202	48.42 N	113.43 W
Logansport, In., U.S.	216	40.45 N	86.21 W
Logansport, La., U.S.	194	31.58 N	93.59 W
Logan Square ⬥[8]	278	41.56 N	87.42 W
Loganton	210	41.02 N	77.18 W
Loganville, Ga., U.S.	192	33.50 N	83.54 W
Loganville, Pa., U.S.	208	39.52 N	76.42 W
Logärden ⊜	40	60.37 N	16.00 E
Lögdeälven ≏	26	63.33 N	19.25 E
Logduz	76	60.00 N	44.41 E
Loge ≏, Ang.	152	10.12 S	17.00 E
Loge ≏, Ang.	152	7.49 S	13.06 E
Logia	164	2.55 S	151.27 E
Loginovo	82	55.42 N	38.44 E
Logirim	154	4.43 N	33.14 E
Logišin	76	52.20 N	25.59 E
Lognes	261	48.50 N	2.38 E
Lognes-Émerainville, Aérodrome de ⊠	261	48.49 N	2.37 E
Logo	154	5.20 N	30.18 E
Logojsk	76	54.12 N	27.49 E
Logone ≏	146	12.06 N	15.02 E
Logone Birni	146	11.47 N	15.06 E
Logone Gana	146	11.33 N	15.09 E
Logone-Occidental □[5]	146	8.50 N	16.00 E
Logone Occidental ≏	146	9.07 N	16.26 E
Logone-Oriental □[5]	146	8.15 N	16.20 E
Logone Oriental ≏	146	9.07 N	16.26 E
Logoualé	150	7.07 N	7.33 W
Logovskij	80	48.26 N	43.23 E
Log pod Mangartom	64	46.24 N	13.36 E
Logroño	34	42.28 N	2.27 W
Logrosán	34	39.20 N	5.29 W
Løgstør	26	56.58 N	9.15 E
Logtāk Lake ⊜	120	24.33 N	93.50 E
Løgten	41	56.17 N	10.19 E
Logudoro ⬥[1]	71	40.35 N	8.40 E
Logue Brook Dam ⬥[6]	168a	33.00 S	115.57 E
Løgumgårde	41	55.05 N	8.57 E
Løgumkloster	41	55.03 N	8.57 E
Logumukum	154	0.27 N	36.05 E
Logy Creek ≏	224	46.11 N	120.35 W
Loh I	175f	13.21 S	166.38 E
Lohāgara	126	23.11 N	89.39 E
Lohals	41	55.08 N	10.55 E
Lohārdaga	124	23.26 N	84.41 E
Lohāru	120	28.27 N	75.49 E
Lohatlha	158	28.02 S	23.04 E
Lohausen ⬥[8]	263	51.16 N	6.44 E
Lohauserholz ⬥[8]	263	51.39 N	7.48 E
Lohberg	263	51.35 N	6.46 E
Löhdorf ⬥[8]	263	51.09 N	7.01 E
Lo Hermida	286e	33.29 S	70.33 W
Lohfelden	56	51.16 N	9.32 E
Lohheide ⬥[8]	263	51.30 N	6.40 E
Lohiān	123	31.10 N	75.11 E
Lohiniva	24	67.10 N	24.58 E
Lohit ≏	120	27.48 N	95.28 E
Lohja	26	60.15 N	24.05 E
Lohjanharju ʌ	26	60.15 N	24.30 E
Lohjanjärvi ⊜	26	60.15 N	23.55 E
Löhlbach	56	51.04 N	8.58 E
Lohmar	56	50.50 N	7.13 E
Lohme, Dtsch.	54	54.35 N	13.37 E
Löhme, Dtsch.	264a	52.37 N	13.40 E
Lohmen, Dtsch.	54	50.59 N	13.59 E
Lohmen, Dtsch.	54	53.41 N	12.05 E
Lohmühle	263	51.31 N	6.40 E
Lohne, Dtsch.	52	52.42 N	8.12 E
Löhne, Dtsch.	52	52.11 N	8.41 E
Löhnen	263	51.36 N	6.39 E
Lohnsburg	60	48.09 N	13.24 E
Loho → Luohe	100	33.35 N	114.01 E
Lohr am Main	56	50.00 N	9.34 E
Lohrville	198	42.16 N	94.32 W
Lohsa	54	51.23 N	14.24 E
Loi ≏	110	21.19 N	100.44 E
Loi, Phou ʌ	110	20.16 N	103.12 E
Loiano	66	44.16 N	11.19 E
Loiblpass (Ljubelj))(	61	46.26 N	14.16 E
Loiborsoit	154	3.52 S	36.26 E
Loi-kaw	110	19.41 N	97.13 E
Loile ≏	152	0.52 S	20.12 E
Loimaa	26	60.51 N	23.03 E
Loimijoki ≏	26	61.13 N	22.38 E
Loi Mwe	110	21.11 N	99.46 E
Loing ≏	50	48.23 N	2.48 E
Loing, Canal du ≖	50	48.22 N	2.50 E
Loir ≏	32	47.33 N	0.32 W
Loira → Loire ≏	32	47.16 N	2.11 W
Loire	62	45.33 N	4.48 E
Loire □[5]	32	45.30 N	4.00 E
Loire ≏	32	47.16 N	2.11 W
Loire, Canal latéral à la ≖	50	47.37 N	2.44 E
Loire-Atlantique □[5]	32	47.20 N	1.35 W
Loiret □[5]	50	47.55 N	2.20 E
Loiret ≏	50	47.52 N	1.48 E
Loir-et-Cher □[5]	50	47.30 N	1.30 E
Loïs, Lac ⊜	190	48.34 N	78.44 W
Loisach ≏	64	47.56 N	11.27 E

Symbol	English	Deutsch	Español	Français	Português
≏	River	Fluß	Río	Rivière	Rio
≖	Canal	Kanal	Canal	Canal	Canal
ʟ	Waterfall, Rapids	Wasserfall, Stromschnellen	Cascada, Rápidos	Chute d'eau, Rapides	Cascata, Rápidos
ʊ	Strait	Meeresstraße	Estrecho	Détroit	Estreito
⊂	Bay, Gulf	Bucht, Golf	Bahía, Golfo	Baie, Golfe	Baía, Golfo
⊜	Lake, Lakes	See, Seen	Lago, Lagos	Lac, Lacs	Lago, Lagos
≚	Swamp	Sumpf	Pantano	Marais	Pântano
❄	Ice Features, Glacier	Eis- und Gletscherformen	Accidentes Glaciales	Formes glaciaires	Acidentes glaciares
✦	Other Hydrographic Features	Andere Hydrographische Objekte	Otros Elementos Hidrográficos	Autres données hydrographiques	Outros acidentes hidrográficos
✢	Submarine Features	Untermeerische Objekte	Accidentes Submarinos	Formes de relief sous-marin	Acidentes submarinos
□	Political Unit	Politische Einheit	Unidad Política	Entité politique	Unidade política
⊌	Cultural Institution	Kulturelle Institution	Institución Cultural	Institution culturelle	Instituição cultural
⊥	Historical Site	Historische Stätte	Sitio Histórico	Site historique	Sitio histórico
♠	Recreational Site	Erholungs- und Ferienort	Sitio de Recreo	Centre de loisirs	Area de Lazer
⊠	Airport	Flughafen	Aeropuerto	Aéroport	Aeroporto
■	Military Installation	Militäranlage	Instalación Militar	Installation militaire	Instalação militar
⬥	Miscellaneous	Verschiedenes	Misceláneo	Divers	Diversos

Loisdale 284c 38.46 N 77.11 W
Loisia 58 46.29 N 5.27 E
Loison ≃ 56 49.30 N 5.17 E
Loitz 54 53.58 N 13.07 E
Loíza, Lago ⊜[1] 240m 18.17 N 66.00 W
Loíza Aldea 240m 18.26 N 65.53 W
Loja, Ec. 246 4.00 S 79.13 W
Loja, Esp. 34 37.10 N 4.09 W
Loja □[4] 246 4.10 S 79.30 W
Lojang
→ Luoyang 102 34.41 N 112.28 E
Lojev 78 51.56 N 30.46 E
Lojga 24 61.05 N 44.37 E
Lojno 24 59.44 N 52.39 E
Løjt Kirkeby 41 55.05 N 9.28 E
Loka, Sūd. 154 4.16 N 31.01 E
Loka, Zaïre 152 0.20 N 17.57 E
Loka brunn 40 59.36 N 14.28 E
Lokachi 78 50.44 N 24.39 E
Lokako 152 2.14 S 21.45 E
Lokalema 152 1.59 N 22.17 E
Lokan ≃ 116 5.25 N 117.44 E
Lokandu 154 2.31 S 25.47 E
Lokan tekojärvi ⊜[1] 24 67.55 N 27.40 E
Lökbatan 84 40.20 N 49.43 E
Løken 26 59.48 N 11.29 E
Lokeren 50 51.06 N 4.00 E
Loket 54 50.09 N 12.43 E
Lokhvytsya 78 50.22 N 33.16 E
Lokichar 154 2.23 N 35.39 E
Lokichokio 154 4.12 N 34.21 E
Lokitaung 154 4.16 N 35.45 E
Lokka 24 67.49 N 27.44 E
Løkken 26 57.22 N 9.43 E
Løkken verk 26 63.08 N 9.42 E
Lokn'a 76 56.50 N 30.09 E
Loknaš ≃ 82 56.11 N 36.04 E
Loko 150 8.02 N 7.49 E
Lokofa-Bokolongo 152 0.12 N 19.22 E
Lokoja 150 7.47 N 6.45 E
Lokolama 152 2.34 S 19.53 E
Lokolenge 152 1.11 N 22.40 E
Lokolo ≃ 152 0.43 S 19.40 E
Lokomo 152 2.41 N 15.19 E
Lokoro ≃ 152 1.43 S 18.23 E
Lokossa 150 6.38 N 1.43 E
Lokosso 150 10.19 N 3.40 W
Lokot', Ross. 76 52.34 N 34.34 E
Lokot', Ross. 86 51.11 N 81.11 E
Lokoua ≃ 273b 4.06 S 15.16 E
Loksa 76 59.35 N 25.45 E
Loks Land I 176 62.26 N 64.38 W
Loktyši 76 52.50 N 26.43 E
Lokve 64 46.01 N 13.49 E
Loky 157b 12.47 S 49.39 E
Lol 140 6.26 N 29.37 E
Lol ≃ 140 9.13 N 28.59 E
Lóla, Ang. 152 14.22 S 13.42 E
Lola, Guinée 150 7.48 N 8.32 W
Lola, Mount ∧ 226 39.26 N 120.22 W
Lolengi 152 0.07 N 20.59 E
Loleta 204 40.38 N 124.13 W
Lolingo 152 0.55 N 22.38 E
Loliondo 154 2.03 S 35.37 E
Lolita 222 28.50 N 96.32 W
Lolland I 41 54.46 N 11.30 E
Lollar 56 50.39 N 8.42 E
Lolo, Mt., U.S. 202 46.45 N 114.04 W
Lolo, Zaïre 152 2.13 N 23.00 E
Lolo ≃ 152 1.07 S 12.28 E
Lolobau Island I 164 4.55 S 151.10 E
Lolo Creek ≃, Id., U.S. 202 46.26 N 116.10 W
Lolo Creek ≃, Mt., U.S. 202 46.45 N 114.03 W
Lolodorf 152 3.14 N 10.44 E
Lolo Pass)(202 46.38 N 114.35 W
Lolotique 236 13.33 N 88.21 W
Lolowai 175f 15.18 S 168.00 E
Loltong 175f 15.33 S 168.08 E
Lolvavana, Passage ɥ 175f 15.26 S 168.12 E
Lolwa 154 1.22 N 29.31 E
Lolworth Range ⋀ 166 20.20 S 145.15 E
Lom, Blg. 38 43.49 N 23.14 E
Lom, Česká Rep. 54 50.37 N 13.40 E
Lom, Nor. 26 61.50 N 8.33 E
Lom, Ross. 80 57.54 N 39.12 E
Lom ∧ 60 49.54 N 13.12 E
Lom ≃, Afr. 152 5.20 N 13.24 E
Lom ≃, Blg. 38 43.50 N 23.15 E
Loma 144 6.55 N 37.34 E
Loma, Point › 228 32.41 N 117.14 W
Loma Blanca, Chile 286e 33.30 S 70.47 W
Loma Blanca, Méx. 200 31.35 N 106.17 W
Loma Bonita 234 18.07 N 95.53 W
Loma Echegareña 234 22.53 N 105.51 W
Lomakino 85 40.05 N 68.10 E
Lomako ≃ 152 0.50 N 20.50 E
Loma Linda 228 34.02 N 117.15 W
Lomaloma 175g 17.17 S 178.59 W
Lomami ≃ 138 0.46 N 24.16 E
Loma Mountains ⋀ 150 9.10 N 11.07 W
Loma Ridge ∧ 280 33.45 N 117.43 W
Lomas, Bahía ⊂ 254 52.35 S 69.05 W
Lomas Alegres 234 17.38 N 92.36 W
Lomas Chapultepec ◆[8] 286a 19.26 N 99.13 W
Lomas del Real 234 22.30 N 97.54 W
Lomas de Monreal 200 31.17 N 110.56 W
Lomas de Zamora 258 34.46 S 58.24 W
Lomas de Zamora □[5] 288 34.45 S 58.24 W
Loma Verde 258 35.16 S 58.24 W
Lomax, Il., U.S. 190 40.41 N 91.04 W
Lomax, Tx., U.S. 222 29.41 N 95.04 W
Łomazy 30 51.55 N 23.10 E
Lomazzo 62 45.42 N 9.02 E
Lomba ≃ 152 15.36 S 21.32 E
Lombagin 112 0.55 N 124.04 E
Lombard 216 41.52 N 88.00 W
Lombardia □[4] 36 45.40 N 9.30 E
Lombardy East 273d 26.07 S 28.08 E
Lombe 152 9.27 S 16.13 E
Lomblen, Pulau I 112 8.25 S 123.30 E
Lombo do Tejo, Mouchão do I 266c 38.52 N 9.00 W
Lombok 115b 8.30 S 116.40 E
Lombok I 115b 8.45 S 116.30 E
Lombok, Selat ɥ 115b 8.30 S 115.50 E
Lombong 114 1.48 N 103.51 E
Lomé 150 6.08 N 1.13 E
Lomela 152 2.18 S 23.17 E
Lomela ≃ 152 0.14 S 20.42 E
Lomellina □[9] 62 45.15 N 8.45 E
Lometa 196 31.13 N 98.23 W
Lomi 24 67.05 N 16.09 E
Lomié 152 3.10 N 13.37 E
Lomira 190 43.35 N 88.26 W
Lo Miranda 252 34.11 S 70.54 W
Lomita 228 33.47 N 118.18 W
Lom Kao 110 16.53 N 101.14 E
Lomma 41 55.41 N 13.05 E
Lommabukten ⊂ 41 55.40 N 12.58 E
Lommatzsch 54 51.12 N 13.18 E
Lomme 50 50.39 N 2.59 E
Lomme ≃ 56 50.08 N 5.10 E
Lommel 56 51.14 N 5.18 E
Lomnice ≃ 60 49.26 N 14.04 E
Lomnice nad Popelkou 30 50.32 N 15.22 E
Lomond 182 50.21 N 112.39 W
Lomond, Loch ⊜, N.S., Can. 186 45.46 N 60.35 W
Lomond, Loch ⊜, On., Can. 190 48.15 N 89.20 W
Lomond, Loch ⊜, Scot., U.K. 46 56.08 N 4.38 W
Lomond, Loch ⊜, Il., U.S. 278 42.17 N 88.01 W
Lomonosov 265a 59.55 N 29.46 E
Lomonosov Moscow State University ʊ[2] 265b 55.43 N 37.32 E
Lomonosovskij 86 52.50 N 66.28 E
Lomovoje 24 64.01 N 40.40 E
Lompobatang, Gunung ∧ 112 5.20 S 119.55 E
Lompoc 204 34.38 N 120.27 W
Lom Sak 110 16.47 N 101.15 E
Lomuvatka 83 48.27 N 38.34 E
Lomy 88 52.17 N 117.59 E
Łomża 30 53.11 N 22.05 E
łomża □[4] 30 53.00 N 22.15 E
Lonaconing 188 39.33 N 78.58 W
Lonate Pozzolo 62 45.36 N 8.45 E
Lonato 64 45.27 N 10.29 E
Lonāvale 122 18.45 N 73.25 E
Lončakovo 89 47.05 N 134.10 E
Loncoche 254 39.22 S 72.38 W
Loncon ≃ 64 45.42 N 12.47 E
Loncopué 252 38.04 S 70.37 W
Londela-Kaye 152 4.51 S 13.24 E
Londerzeel 50 51.00 N 4.18 E
Londinières 50 49.50 N 1.24 E
Londo 154 2.03 N 25.43 E
Londoko 89 49.02 N 131.59 E
London, On., Can. 212 42.59 N 81.14 W
London, Kiribati 174o 1.58 N 157.28 W
London, Eng., U.K. 42 51.30 N 0.10 W
London, Eng., U.K. 260 51.30 N 0.10 W
London, Ar., U.S. 194 35.19 N 93.15 W
London, Ca., U.S. 226 36.30 N 119.25 W
London, Ky., U.S. 192 37.07 N 84.05 W
London, Oh., U.S. 218 39.53 N 83.26 W
London, Tx., U.S. 196 30.41 N 99.35 W
London, Wi., U.S. 216 43.03 N 89.01 W
London (Gatwick) Airport ⊠, Eng., U.K. 42 51.09 N 0.21 W
London (Heathrow) Airport ⊠, Eng., U.K. 42 51.27 N 0.28 W
London Colney 260 51.43 N 0.18 W
Londonderry, N.S., Can. 186 45.29 N 63.36 W
Londonderry (Derry), N. Ire., U.K. 48 54.59 N 7.20 W
Londonderry, N.H., U.S. 207 42.51 N 71.22 W
Londonderry, Oh., U.S. 214 39.16 N 82.47 W
Londonderry, Cape › 164 13.45 S 126.55 E
Londonderry, Isla I 254 55.03 S 70.35 W
Londontowne 208 38.59 N 76.32 W
London Zoo ✦ 260 51.32 N 0.09 W
Londres, Arg. 252 27.43 S 67.07 W
Londres
→ London, Eng., U.K. 42 51.30 N 0.10 W
Londrina 255 23.18 S 51.09 W
Lonedell 219 38.18 N 90.50 W
Lone Grove 196 34.10 N 97.15 W
Lonely Lake ⊜ 184 51.09 N 99.05 W
Lonelyville 276 40.39 N 73.11 W
Lone Mountain ∧ 204 38.02 N 117.29 W
Lone Oak, Ky., U.S. 194 37.02 N 88.39 W
Lone Oak, Tx., U.S. 222 33.01 N 95.57 W
Lone Pine 204 36.36 N 118.03 W
Lone Pine Koala Sanctuary ✦ 171a 27.32 S 152.57 E
Lone Rock 190 43.11 N 90.11 W
Lone Star 222 32.56 N 94.43 W
Lone Tree 190 41.29 N 91.25 W
Lone Tree Creek ≃, U.S. 200 40.25 N 104.35 W
Lone Tree Creek ≃, Ca., U.S. 226 37.53 N 121.14 W
Lone Wolf 196 34.59 N 99.14 W
Long 110 18.05 N 99.50 E
Long ≃, Fr. 50 47.41 N 0.28 E
Long ≃, Zhg. 100 23.26 N 114.38 E
Long ≃, Zhg. 102 24.32 N 109.15 E
Long ≃, Zhg. 105 39.23 N 116.49 E
Longa 152 14.42 S 18.32 E
Longa ≃, Ang. 152 16.25 N 19.04 E
Longa ≃, Ang. 152 10.15 S 13.30 E
Longá ≃, Bra. 250 3.09 S 41.56 W
Longa, proliv ɥ 74 70.20 N 178.00 E
Longairo 154 4.30 N 32.17 E
Long Akah 112 3.19 N 114.47 E
Long'an 102 25.03 N 109.00 E
Longana 175f 15.20 S 167.55 E
Long'anqiao 89 47.31 N 124.27 E
Longare 64 45.29 N 11.36 E
Longarone 64 46.16 N 12.18 E
Long Arroyo V 196 33.04 N 104.17 W
Longasy 24 61.58 N 35.09 E
Longaví 252 35.58 S 71.41 W
Longbangun 112 0.36 N 115.11 E
Long Bar Harbor 208 39.27 N 76.15 W
Long Barn 226 38.05 N 120.08 W
Long Bay ⊂, Austl. 274a 33.58 S 151.16 E
Long Bay ⊂, U.S. 192 33.35 N 78.45 W
Long Beach, Ca., U.S. 228 33.46 N 118.11 W
Long Beach, In., U.S. 216 41.44 N 86.51 W
Long Beach, Ms., U.S. 194 30.21 N 89.09 W
Long Beach, N.Y., U.S. 210 40.35 N 73.39 W
Long Beach, Wa., U.S. 224 46.21 N 124.03 W
Long Beach ⊥[2] 208 39.39 N 74.11 W
Long Beach Breakwater ◆[5] 280 33.43 N 118.09 W
Long Beach Middle Harbor ⊂ 280 33.45 N 118.13 W
Long Beach Municipal Airport ⊠ 280 33.49 N 118.09 W
Long Beach Naval Station ■ 280 33.45 N 118.14 W
Longbeleh 112 0.16 N 116.11 E
Long Belepai 112 2.45 N 114.04 E
Longbenton 44 55.02 N 1.35 W
Longboat Key 220 27.24 N 82.39 W
Longboat Key I 220 27.23 N 82.39 W
Long Branch, N.J., U.S. 208 40.18 N 73.59 W
Longbranch, Wa., U.S. 224 47.12 N 122.45 W
Long Branch □[8] 275b 43.35 N 79.32 W
Long Branch ≃ 219 39.23 N 91.49 W
Long Branch Lake ⊜[1] 194 39.49 N 92.31 W
Longbu 100 25.32 N 115.24 E
Long Buckby 42 52.19 N 1.04 W
Long Cane Creek ≃ 192 33.57 N 82.24 W
Long Canyon V 226 38.59 N 120.41 W
Long Cay I 238 22.37 N 74.20 W
Longchamp, Hippodrome de ✦ 261 48.51 N 2.14 E
Longchamps, Arg. 258 34.52 S 58.23 W
Longchamps, Bel. 56 50.03 N 5.42 E
Longchang, Zhg. 104 40.53 N 123.08 E
Longchang, Zhg. 107 29.21 N 105.17 E
Longchaumois 58 46.27 N 5.56 E
Longchêne 261 48.38 N 2.00 E
Longchuan, Zhg. 100 24.07 N 115.17 E
Longchuan, Zhg. 102 24.14 N 97.45 E
Longchuan (Shweli) ≃ 102 23.56 N 96.17 E
Long Creek, Il., U.S. 219 39.48 N 88.50 W
Long Creek, Or., U.S. 202 44.42 N 119.06 W
Long Creek ≃ 184 49.07 N 103.00 W
Long Crendon 42 51.47 N 1.01 W
Longcun 100 23.34 N 115.33 E
Longde 102 35.28 N 106.22 E
Longdendale V 262 53.29 N 1.56 W
Long Ditton 260 51.23 N 0.20 W
Longdongtuo 107 29.59 N 106.21 E
Longdor, gora ∧ 88 58.24 N 116.47 E
Longdou 100 27.25 N 117.24 E
Longdu 106 31.51 N 118.56 E
Long Eaton 42 52.54 N 1.15 W
Longeau 58 47.46 N 5.18 E
Long Eddy 210 41.51 N 75.08 W
Longfellow National Historic Site ⊥ 283 42.23 N 71.08 W
Longfengchang 107 30.26 N 105.38 E
Longfengkan 104 41.51 N 124.01 E
Longfengyutun 104 40.39 N 122.57 E
Longfield 260 51.24 N 0.18 E
Longford, Austl. 166 38.10 S 147.05 E
Longford, Ire. 48 53.44 N 7.47 W
Longford, Md., U.S. 284b 39.25 N 76.39 W
Longford □[6] 48 53.40 N 7.40 W
Longford Park ✦ 262 53.27 N 2.17 W
Longframlington 44 55.18 N 1.47 W
Longgang, Zhg. 100 29.38 N 114.57 E
Longgang, Zhg. 100 33.22 N 120.04 E
Longgang, Zhg. 102 24.41 N 101.09 E
Longgangzi 104 42.09 N 123.26 E
Long Green 208 39.28 N 76.31 W
Long Grove 216 42.11 N 88.00 W
Longguan 105 40.47 N 115.34 E
Longgudu 100 27.45 N 116.14 E
Longguntur 112 0.13 N 112.12 E
Long Harbour 186 47.26 N 53.48 W
Long Harbour ⊂, Nf., Can. 186 47.44 N 55.01 W
Long Harbour ⊂, H.K. 271d 22.27 N 114.20 E
Longhorn Cavern State Park ✦ 196 30.20 N 98.30 W
Longhorsley 44 55.15 N 1.46 W
Longhoughton 44 55.26 N 1.36 W
Long Hu ⊜ 100 29.58 N 116.10 E
Longhua, Zhg. 98 41.17 N 117.37 E
Longhua, Zhg. 100 22.42 N 113.59 E
Longhua, Zhg. 100 23.37 N 114.14 E
Longhua, Zhg. 106 31.09 N 121.26 E
Longhua Airport ⊠ 269b 31.10 N 121.26 E
Longhua Pagoda ʊ[1] 269b 31.11 N 121.26 E
Longhui, Zhg. 100 25.32 N 114.47 E
Longhui (Taohuaping), Zhg. 102 27.00 N 110.59 E
Longhui, Zhg. 107 29.32 N 104.48 E
Longhutang 106 31.52 N 119.59 E
Longi 70 38.01 N 14.45 E
Longido 154 2.44 S 36.41 E
Longiram 112 0.02 S 115.38 E
Long Island I, Antig. 240c 17.08 N 61.45 W
Long Island I, Austl. 166 22.09 S 149.54 E
Long Island I, Ba. 238 23.15 N 75.07 W
Long Island I, Nf., Can. 186 47.35 N 54.05 W
Long Island I, N.T., Can. 176 54.50 N 79.20 W
Long Island I, N.S., Can. 186 44.20 N 66.15 W
Long Island I, Ak., U.S. 182 54.54 N 132.45 W
Long Island I, Ma., U.S. 283 42.19 N 70.58 W
Long Island I, N.Y., U.S. 188 40.50 N 73.00 W
Long Island I, Wa., U.S. 224 46.27 N 123.58 W
Long Island City ◆[8] 276 40.45 N 73.56 W
Long Island MacArthur Airport ⊠ 210 40.48 N 73.06 W
Long Island Sound ɥ 188 41.05 N 72.58 W
Long Island University ʊ[2], N.Y., U.S. 276 40.41 N 73.59 W
Long Island University (C.W. Post Center) ʊ[2], N.Y., U.S. 276 40.49 N 73.36 W
Longitudinal, Valle V 252 36.00 S 72.00 W
Long Jetty 170 33.22 S 151.29 E
Longji 107 29.23 N 106.04 E
Longjiadian 104 42.10 N 120.47 E
Longjiang, Zhg. 89 47.19 N 123.12 E
Longjiang, Zhg. 100 22.53 N 113.04 E
Longjiang, Zhg. 100 22.59 N 116.13 E
Longjiang, Zhg. 107 29.48 N 105.03 E
Longjie 107 29.53 N 104.32 E
Longjin 100 28.37 N 116.37 E
Longjing 100 23.53 N 112.52 E
Longjohn Slough ≃ 278 41.43 N 87.53 W
Longjumeau 50 48.42 N 2.18 E
Longka 120 33.12 N 79.47 E
Longkamp 56 49.53 N 7.07 E
Longkangji 100 33.09 N 116.54 E
Long Ke 271d 22.23 N 114.22 E
Long Key I, Fl., U.S. 220 24.49 N 80.49 W
Long Key I, Fl., U.S. 220 27.44 N 82.45 W
Long King Creek ≃ 222 30.34 N 94.58 W
Longkou, Zhg. 98 37.38 N 120.18 E
Longkou, Zhg. 100 32.56 N 114.57 E
Longkou, Zhg. 100 29.57 N 113.47 E
Longkou, Zhg. 100 26.11 N 115.15 E
Longkouqiao 85 39.40 N 77.09 E
Long Lake, Il., U.S. 216 42.22 N 88.08 W
Long Lake, N.Y., U.S. 188 43.58 N 74.25 W
Long Lake, Tx., U.S. 222 31.39 N 95.47 W
Long Lake ⊜, On., Can. 212 44.41 N 76.45 W
Long Lake ⊜, Mi., U.S. 190 45.12 N 83.30 W
Long Lake ⊜, Mi., U.S. 281 42.37 N 83.44 W
Long Lake ⊜, Mi., U.S. 281 42.36 N 83.28 W
Long Lake ⊜, N.Y., U.S. 188 44.04 N 74.20 W
Long Lake ⊜, N.D., U.S. 198 46.43 N 100.07 W
Long Lake ⊜, Wa., U.S. 224 47.03 N 122.47 W
Long Lake ⊜[1] 202 47.50 N 117.40 W
Long Lake Creek ≃ 198 46.40 N 100.13 W
Long Lake Shores 281 42.35 N 83.19 W
Long Lama 112 3.46 N 114.24 E
Longlaville 56 49.32 N 5.47 E
Longleaf 194 31.00 N 92.34 W
Long Leaf Park 192 34.12 N 77.56 W
Longleat ʊ 42 51.12 N 2.17 W
Longlegged Lake ⊜ 184 50.46 N 94.08 W
Longli 102 26.26 N 106.58 E
Longlin 102 24.49 N 105.31 E
Longling 102 24.39 N 98.40 E
Longmeadow 207 42.03 N 72.35 W
Long Melford 42 52.05 N 0.43 E
Longmen, Zhg. 89 48.55 N 126.54 E
Longmen, Zhg. 100 29.53 N 119.57 E
Longmen, Zhg. 100 24.56 N 118.04 E
Longmen, Zhg. 100 25.06 N 116.58 E
Longmen, Zhg. 100 23.44 N 114.15 E
Longmen, Zhg. 107 29.27 N 104.59 E
Longmen, Zhg. 107 29.12 N 106.13 E
Longmenchang 107 30.53 N 106.10 E
Longmensuo 98 40.56 N 115.54 E
Longmenzhang 107 28.59 N 106.13 E
Longming 102 22.59 N 107.11 E
Longmire 224 46.45 N 121.49 W
Long Moc 110 18.51 N 105.01 E
Longmont 200 40.10 N 105.06 W
Longmorn 46 57.36 N 3.17 W
Long Mountain ∧ 194 36.41 N 92.26 W
Long Mountain ∧[2] 42 52.39 N 3.09 W
Longmu 100 24.16 N 115.28 E
Longnan 100 24.54 N 114.48 E
Longnawan 112 1.54 N 114.53 E
Long Neck ›[1] 276 41.03 N 73.29 W
Long Neck Point › 276 41.02 N 73.29 W
Longniddry 46 55.58 N 2.53 W
Longnüsi 107 30.23 N 106.11 E
Longny-au-Perche 50 48.32 N 0.45 E
Longobucco 68 39.27 N 16.37 E
Longperrier 261 49.03 N 2.40 E
Long Pine 198 42.32 N 99.42 W
Longping 100 29.53 N 115.41 E
Long Plains 168b 34.21 S 138.22 E
Long Point, Austl. 274a 34.01 S 150.54 E
Long Point, Il., U.S. 216 41.00 N 88.54 W
Long Point ›, Ba. 240b 25.01 N 77.20 W
Long Point ›, Nf., Can. 186 48.48 N 58.46 W
Long Point ›, N.S., Can. 186 46.51 N 60.18 W
Long Point ›, On., Can. 212 44.06 N 76.29 W
Long Point ›, On., Can. 212 44.32 N 80.18 W
Long Point ›, Pil. 116 9.39 N 118.20 E
Long Point ›, Ca., U.S. 280 33.44 N 118.23 W
Long Point ›, Vir. Is., U.S. 240m 18.18 N 64.53 W
Long Point ›[1], Mb., Can. 184 53.02 N 98.40 W
Long Point ›[1], On., Can. 214 42.34 N 80.15 W
Long Point Bay ⊂ 212 42.40 N 80.14 W
Long Point Creek ≃ 216 41.02 N 88.48 W
Long Point Provincial Park ✦ 214 42.35 N 80.35 W
Long Pond ⊜, U.S. 283 42.41 N 71.21 W
Long Pond ⊜, Ma., U.S. 207 41.43 N 70.04 W
Long Pond ⊜, Ma., U.S. 207 41.48 N 70.57 W
Longpont, Fr. 50 49.16 N 3.13 E
Longpont, Fr. 261 48.38 N 2.17 E
Longport 208 39.18 N 74.31 W
Long Prairie 198 45.58 N 94.51 W
Long Prairie ≃ 198 46.20 N 94.36 W
Longpré-les-Corps-Saints 50 50.01 N 1.59 E
Long Preston 44 54.02 N 2.15 W
Longqiantai 104 41.23 N 120.52 E
Longqu, Zhg. 98 34.16 N 114.49 E
Longqu, Zhg. 98 34.54 N 116.47 E
Longquan 100 28.04 N 119.07 E
Longquan ≃ 100 28.17 N 119.44 E
Longquanguan 98 38.55 N 113.51 E
Longquan Shan ⋀ 107 30.25 N 104.15 E
Longquanyi 107 30.34 N 104.16 E
Longquanzhen 107 30.21 N 104.39 E
Long Range Mountains ⋀ 186 49.20 N 57.30 W
Longreach 166 23.26 S 144.15 E
Long Reach ⊂ 186 45.26 N 66.09 W
Long Reach ɥ 212 44.07 N 77.04 W
Long Reef ✣[2] 164 11.11 S 151.40 E
Long Reef Point › 274a 33.45 S 151.19 E
Longridge 44 53.51 N 2.36 W
Long Run ≃, Il., U.S. 278 41.37 N 88.03 W
Long Run ≃, Pa., U.S. 279b 40.20 N 79.48 W
Long-Sault 206 45.02 N 74.53 W
Long Sault Dam ◆[6] 206 45.00 N 74.45 W
Long Sault Islands II 206 45.00 N 74.55 W
Longsegah 112 2.15 N 116.42 E
Longshan, Zhg. 100 33.36 N 116.18 E
Longshan, Zhg. 102 29.28 N 109.20 E
Longshansuo 100 30.05 N 121.33 E
Longsheng, Zhg. 102 25.48 N 110.00 E
Longsheng, Zhg. 107 30.36 N 105.21 E
Longshizhen, Zhg. 107 30.12 N 106.26 E
Longshizhen, Zhg. 107 29.23 N 105.10 E
Longshu 107 29.33 N 105.45 E
Longs Peak ∧ 200 40.15 N 105.37 W
Long Stratton 42 52.29 N 1.14 E
Long Sutton 42 52.47 N 0.08 E
Longtaichang 107 30.04 N 105.34 E
Longtan, Zhg. 100 23.40 N 113.24 E
Longtan, Zhg. 102 28.20 N 108.52 E
Longtan, Zhg. 106 32.11 N 119.04 E
Longtan, Zhg. 106 31.20 N 118.45 E
Longtansi 107 30.42 N 104.10 E
Longtanzhen 107 29.19 N 104.35 E
Long Teru 112 3.52 N 114.15 E
Long Thanh 110 10.47 N 106.57 E
Longtian 100 25.38 N 119.28 E
Longtian'an 106 31.10 N 120.49 E
Long Tom ≃ 202 44.23 N 123.15 W
Longton, Eng., U.K. 44 53.43 N 2.48 W
Longton, Eng., U.K. 262 53.43 N 2.48 W
Longton, Ks., U.S. 198 37.22 N 96.04 W
Longtou 98 38.51 N 121.18 E
Longtoupu 100 27.54 N 113.12 E
Longtouwei 100 25.14 N 115.24 E
Longtown 44 55.01 N 2.58 W
Long Truong 269c 10.49 N 106.49 E
Longué 32 47.23 N 0.06 W
Longueau 50 49.52 N 2.21 E
Longuenesse 50 50.44 N 1.24 E
Longuesse 261 49.04 N 1.56 E
Longueuil 206 45.32 N 73.30 W
Longueville, Austl. 274a 33.50 S 151.10 E
Longueville, Fr. 50 48.31 N 3.15 E
Longueville-sur-Scie 50 49.48 N 1.06 E
Longuyon 56 49.26 N 5.36 E
Long Valley 210 40.47 N 74.46 W
Long Valley Creek ≃, Ca., U.S. 226 39.03 N 122.34 W
Long Valley Creek ≃, Nv., U.S. 226 39.31 N 119.39 W
Longvic 58 47.17 N 5.04 E
Longview, Ab., Can. 182 50.32 N 114.14 W
Longview, N.C., U.S. 192 35.43 N 81.23 W
Longview, Tx., U.S. 222 32.30 N 94.44 W
Longview, Wa., U.S. 224 46.08 N 122.56 W
Longview Heights 222 32.30 N 94.41 W
Longvilliers 261 48.35 N 2.00 E
Longvilly 56 50.01 N 5.50 E
Longwai 112 0.42 N 116.39 E
Longwan 105 38.57 N 116.10 E
Longwangmiao, Zhg. 98 36.12 N 115.13 E
Longwangmiao, Zhg. 102 40.36 N 95.52 E
Longwangmiao, Zhg. 104 41.38 N 121.04 E
Longwangmiao, Zhg. 104 42.35 N 123.42 E
Longwarry 169 38.07 S 145.46 E
Longwen 100 24.36 N 116.21 E
Longwo 100 23.28 N 115.17 E
Longwokou 106 32.18 N 119.52 E
Longwood 220 28.42 N 81.20 W
Longwood Gardens ✦ 285 39.52 N 75.40 W
Longwood Lake 276 40.59 N 74.52 W
Longwood Park 192 34.55 N 79.42 W
Longworth 182 53.55 N 121.28 W
Longwy 56 49.31 N 5.46 E
Longxi
→ Zhangzhou, Zhg. 100 24.33 N 117.39 E
Longxi, Zhg. 102 34.56 N 104.47 E
Longxi, Zhg. 107 29.59 N 106.09 E
Longxian, Zhg. 102 34.51 N 106.59 E
Longxian, Zhg. 107 29.09 N 105.50 E
Long Xuyen 110 10.23 N 105.25 E
Longyan 100 25.08 N 117.02 E
Longyao 98 37.23 N 114.41 E
Longyou 100 29.02 N 119.10 E
Longyou ≃ 106 32.08 N 120.38 E
Longyuanba 100 24.56 N 114.27 E
Longzhaogou 98 40.49 N 124.36 E
Longzhen 89 48.41 N 126.42 E
Longzhou 102 22.22 N 106.52 E
Loni 272a 28.45 N 77.17 E
Lonigo 64 45.23 N 11.23 E
Löningen 52 52.44 N 7.46 E
Lonja ≃ 36 45.27 N 16.41 E
Lonkala 152 4.37 S 23.14 E
Lönnewitz 54 51.34 N 13.11 E
Lonny 56 49.49 N 4.35 E
Lonoke 194 34.47 N 91.53 W
Lonquimay, Volcán ∧[1] 252 38.22 S 71.34 W
Lönsboda 26 56.24 N 14.19 E

ENGLISH				DEUTSCH			
Name	Page	Lat.°′	Long.°′	Name	Seite	Breite°′	Länge°′ E = Ost

Lønsdal 24 66.44 N 15.28 E
Lonsdale 190 44.28 N 93.25 W
Lonsdale, Point › 169 38.17 S 144.37 E
Lons-le-Saunier 58 46.40 N 5.33 E
Lonton 110 25.06 N 96.17 E
Lontra ≃ 250 6.37 S 48.39 W
Lontra, Ribeirão da ≃ 255 21.28 S 53.37 W
Lonua ≃ 152 1.16 N 22.38 E
Lonzhen 107 30.00 N 103.59 E
Loo 84 43.43 N 39.36 E
Looc 116 12.16 N 121.59 E
Looe 42 50.21 N 4.28 W
Loogootee 194 38.40 N 86.54 W
Looking Glass ≃ 216 42.52 N 84.54 W
Lookout 210 41.47 N 75.11 W
Lookout, Cape ›, N.C., U.S. 192 34.35 N 76.32 W
Lookout, Cape ›, Or., U.S. 224 45.20 N 124.00 W
Lookout, Point ›, Austl. 171a 27.26 S 153.33 E
Lookout, Point ›, Md., U.S. 208 38.02 N 76.19 W
Lookout Mountain ∧, U.S. 194 34.25 N 85.40 W
Lookout Mountain ∧, Or., U.S. 202 44.20 N 120.22 W
Lookout Mountain ∧, Or., U.S. 224 45.21 N 121.31 W
Lookout Mountain ∧, Wa., U.S. 224 48.40 N 122.22 W
Lookout Pass)(202 47.27 N 115.42 W
Lookout Point Lake ⊜[1] 202 43.52 N 122.40 W
Lookout Ridge ⋀ 180 69.07 N 158.36 W
Loolmalassin ∧[1] 154 3.03 S 35.49 E
Loomis, Ca., U.S. 226 38.49 N 121.12 W
Loomis, Ne., U.S. 198 40.28 N 99.30 W
Loomis, Wa., U.S. 182 48.49 N 119.37 W
Loon 116 9.48 N 123.47 E
Loon ≃ 184 55.50 N 101.59 W
Loon Creek ≃ 202 44.49 N 114.49 W
Loongana 162 30.57 S 127.02 E
Loon Lake ⊜, Can. 184 55.51 N 102.00 W
Loon Lake ⊜, Mi., U.S. 281 42.41 N 83.22 W
Loon Lake ⊜[1] 226 39.00 N 120.18 W
Loon op Zand 52 51.38 N 5.04 E
Loop 196 32.55 N 102.25 W
Loop ◆[8] 278 41.53 N 87.38 W
Loop Head › 48 52.34 N 9.56 W
Loosdorf 61 48.12 N 15.24 E
Loosduinen ◆[8] 52 52.04 N 4.13 E
Loose, Dtsch. 41 54.31 N 9.53 E
Loose, Eng., U.K. 260 51.14 N 0.31 E
Loose Creek 219 38.30 N 91.57 W
Lop 120 37.02 N 80.15 E
Lop ≃ 110 13.18 N 107.37 E
Lopandino 76 52.28 N 34.49 E
Lopanka 80 46.24 N 40.59 E
Lopar'ovo 80 58.20 N 42.41 E
Lopasn'a ≃ 82 54.51 N 37.52 E
Lopatiči 76 53.34 N 30.53 E
Lopatin 84 43.53 N 47.41 E
Lopatina, gora ∧ 89 50.52 N 143.10 E
Lopatino, Ross. 80 52.37 N 45.47 E
Lopatino, Ross. 82 54.45 N 37.00 E
Lopatino, Ross. 89 48.24 N 142.15 E
Lopatinskij 82 55.21 N 38.34 E
Lopatka, mys › 74 50.52 N 156.40 E
Lopatovo 76 56.08 N 29.12 E
Lopatyn 78 50.13 N 24.50 E
Lop Buri 110 14.48 N 100.37 E
Lopé-Okanda, Réserve de Chasse de ◆[4] 152 0.30 S 11.40 E
Lopévi I 175f 16.30 S 168.21 E
López, Méx. 232 27.00 N 105.02 W
Lopez, Pa., U.S. 210 41.27 N 76.20 W
Lopez, Wa., U.S. 224 48.31 N 122.54 W
López, Arroyo de ≃ 258 35.26 S 57.35 W
Lopez, Cap › 152 0.37 S 8.43 E
Lopez Bay ⊂ 116 13.56 N 122.12 E
Lopez Island I 224 48.30 N 122.54 W
Lopez Lake ⊜[1] 226 35.12 N 120.28 W
Lopik 52 51.58 N 4.56 E
Lop Nor
→ Lop Nur ⊜ 90 40.20 N 90.15 E
Lop Nur (Lop Nor) ⊜ 90 40.20 N 90.15 E
Lopori ≃ 152 1.14 N 19.49 E
Lopotovo 82 56.04 N 36.49 E
Loppersum 52 53.19 N 6.45 E
Loppi 26 60.43 N 24.27 E
Lo Prado 286e 33.26 S 70.45 W
Lopšen'ga 24 64.58 N 37.41 E
Lopt'uga 24 63.16 N 47.56 E
Lopuchovka, Ross. 80 51.59 N 44.42 E
Lopuchovka, Ross. 80 50.37 N 44.29 E
Łopuszno 30 50.57 N 20.15 E
Lora 123 33.53 N 73.17 E
Lora ≃ 246 9.25 N 72.25 W
Lora, Hāmūn-i- ⊜ 128 29.20 N 64.50 E
Lora Creek ≃ 162 28.10 S 135.22 E
Lora del Río 34 37.39 N 5.32 W
Lorain 214 41.27 N 82.10 W
Lorain □[6] 214 41.22 N 82.06 W
Lorain County Regional Airport ⊠ 279a 41.20 N 82.11 W
Loraine, Ca., U.S. 228 35.19 N 118.25 W
Loraine, Il., U.S. 219 40.09 N 91.13 W
Loraine, Tx., U.S. 196 32.24 N 100.42 W
Loralai 120 30.22 N 68.36 E
Loramie, Lake ⊜[1] 216 40.23 N 84.18 W
Loramie Creek ≃ 216 40.11 N 84.14 W
Lorca 34 37.40 N 1.42 W
Lorch, Dtsch. 56 48.49 N 9.40 E
Lorch, Dtsch. 56 50.02 N 7.48 E
Lorchhausen 56 50.03 N 7.47 E
Lord Howe Island I 160 31.33 S 159.05 E
Lord Howe Rise ✣[3] 14 32.00 S 162.00 E
Lord Howe Seamounts ✣[3] 14 28.00 S 159.00 E
Lord Mayor Bay ⊂ 176 69.44 N 92.00 W
Lordsburg 200 32.21 N 108.42 W
Lord's Cricket Ground ✦ 260 51.32 N 0.10 W
Lordstown 214 41.09 N 80.53 W
Lords Valley 210 41.23 N 75.04 W
Loreauville 194 30.03 N 91.44 W
Loreley ✦ 56 50.08 N 7.44 E
Lorena, Bra. 256 22.44 S 45.08 W
Lorena, Tx., U.S. 222 31.23 N 97.13 W
Lorengau 164 2.00 S 147.15 E
Lorentz ≃ 164 5.23 S 138.04 E
Lorentzen 56 48.57 N 7.10 E
Lorenzago di Cadore 64 46.29 N 12.28 E
Lorenzo 196 33.40 N 101.32 W
Lorenzo Geyres (Queguay) 252 32.05 S 57.55 W
Loreo 64 45.04 N 12.11 E
Lorestān □[4] 128 33.30 N 48.30 E
Loreto, Arg. 252 27.46 S 57.17 W
Loreto, Bol. 248 15.13 S 64.40 W
Loreto, Bra. 250 7.05 S 45.09 W
Loreto, It. 66 43.26 N 13.36 E
Loreto, Méx. 232 26.01 N 111.21 W
Loreto, Méx. 234 22.16 N 101.58 W
Loreto, Para. 252 23.16 S 57.11 W
Loreto, Pil. 116 8.12 N 125.45 E
Loreto, Pil. 116 10.21 N 125.34 E
Loreto □[5] 246 3.00 S 75.00 W
Loreto Aprutino 66 42.26 N 13.59 E
Loreto Mocagua 246 3.48 S 70.15 W
Lorette, Mb., Can. 184 49.44 N 96.52 W
Lorette, Fr. 62 45.31 N 4.35 E
Loretteville 206 46.51 N 71.21 W
Loretto
→ Loreto, It. 66 43.26 N 13.36 E
Loretto, Ky., U.S. 194 37.38 N 85.24 W
Loretto, Pa., U.S. 214 40.30 N 78.37 W
Loretto, Tn., U.S. 194 35.04 N 87.26 W
Lorgues 62 43.29 N 6.22 E
Lorian Swamp ⩸ 154 0.40 N 39.35 E
Lorica 246 9.14 N 75.49 W
Lorida 220 27.26 N 81.15 W
Lorient 32 47.45 N 3.22 W
L'Orignal 206 45.37 N 74.42 W
Lorimer Park ✦ 285 40.06 N 75.05 W
Lorimor 194 41.07 N 94.03 W
Loring, Aeródromo de ⊠ 266a 40.22 N 3.47 W
Loring Air Force Base ■ 186 46.57 N 67.54 W
Lorino 180 65.30 N 171.43 W
Loriol-sur-Drôme 62 44.45 N 4.49 E
Loris 192 34.03 N 78.53 W
Lorman 194 31.49 N 91.03 W
L'Orme 261 48.39 N 1.41 E
Lormes 50 47.17 N 3.49 E
Lorn, Firth of ⊂[1] 46 56.20 N 5.45 W
Lorna Glen 162 26.14 S 121.33 E
Lorne, Austl. 169 38.33 S 143.59 E
Lorne, N.B., Can. 186 47.53 N 66.08 W
Loro Ciuffenna 66 43.35 N 11.38 E
Loronyo 154 4.39 N 32.38 E
Lorquin 58 48.40 N 7.00 E
Lörrach 58 47.37 N 7.40 E
Lorraine □[9] 32 49.00 N 6.00 E
Lorrez-le-Bocage 50 48.14 N 2.54 E
Lorris 50 47.53 N 2.31 E
Lorsch 56 49.39 N 8.34 E
Lorsica 62 44.26 N 9.16 E
Lorup 52 52.55 N 7.38 E
Lorze ≃ 58 47.15 N 8.25 E
Los 26 61.44 N 15.10 E
Los, Îles de II 150 9.30 N 13.48 W
Losa, Nuraghe ⊥ 71 40.07 N 8.46 E
Losada ≃ 246 2.12 N 73.55 W
Los Aguacates 286c 10.35 N 66.48 W
Los Alamitos 280 33.48 N 118.04 W
Los Alamitos Armed Forces Reserve Center ■ 280 33.47 N 118.03 W
Los Alamitos Race Course ✦ 280 33.48 N 118.03 W
Los Alamos, Ca., U.S. 204 34.44 N 120.16 W
Los Alamos, N.M., U.S. 200 35.53 N 106.19 W
Los Aldamas 232 26.03 N 99.11 W
Los Alerces, Parque Nacional ✦ 254 42.50 S 71.52 W
Los Altos, Méx. 196 26.14 N 98.28 W
Los Altos, Ca., U.S. 226 37.23 N 122.06 W
Los Altos Hills 226 37.22 N 122.08 W
Los Amates, Guat. 236 15.16 N 89.06 W
Los Amates, Méx. 234 18.08 N 102.15 W
Los Americanos, Barra I 232 24.50 N 97.35 W
Los Andes 252 32.50 S 70.37 W
Los Ángeles, Chile 252 37.28 S 72.21 W
Los Angeles, Ca., U.S. 228 34.03 N 118.14 W
Los Angeles, Ca., U.S. 280 34.03 N 118.14 W
Los Angeles □[6] 228 34.20 N 118.10 W
Los Angeles ≃ 228 33.46 N 118.12 W
Los Angeles Aqueduct ≚[1] 204 35.22 N 118.05 W
Los Angeles Coliseum and Sports Arena ✦ 280 34.01 N 118.17 W
Los Angeles Convention Center ʊ 280 34.03 N 118.17 W
Los Angeles County Fairgrounds ✦ 280 34.05 N 117.46 W
Los Angeles County Museum of Art ʊ 280 34.05 N 118.22 W
Los Angeles Harbor ⊂ 280 33.42 N 118.16 W
Los Angeles International Airport ⊠ 228 33.56 N 118.24 W
Los Antiguos 254 46.33 S 71.37 W
Losantville 218 40.01 N 85.10 W
Losap I[1] 14 6.54 N 152.44 E
Los Arabos 240p 22.44 N 80.43 W
Losarang 115a 6.24 S 108.10 E
Los Aros 234 22.46 N 102.57 W
Los Banos 226 37.03 N 120.50 W
Los Banos Creek ≃ 226 37.20 N 120.57 W
Los Banos Creek, North Fork ≃ 226 36.57 N 121.07 W
Los Banos Creek, South Fork ≃ 226 36.57 N 121.07 W
Los Banos Reservoir ⊜[1] 226 36.59 N 120.57 W
Los Berros 252 31.57 S 68.39 W
Los Blancos 252 23.36 S 62.36 W
Los Bolones, Cerro ∧, Méx. 232 16.50 N 92.38 W
Los Bolones, Cerro ∧, Méx. 234 16.39 N 92.34 W
Los Cardales 258 34.20 S 58.59 W
Los Cerrillos, Arg. 252 31.57 S 65.28 W
Los Cerrillos, Ur. 258 34.37 S 56.22 W
Los Cerrillos, Aeropuerto ⊠ 286e 33.30 S 70.43 W
Los Cerritos Center ◆[9] 280 33.52 N 118.05 W
Los Chacos 248 14.33 S 62.11 W
Löschenrod 56 50.30 N 9.41 E
Los Chiles 236 11.02 N 84.43 W
Los Conquistadores 252 30.36 S 58.28 W
Los Coronados, Islas II 204 32.25 N 117.15 W
Los Coyotes Indian Reservation ◆[4] 204 33.20 N 116.35 W
Los Cuatro Álamos 286e 33.32 S 70.44 W
Los Dos Caminos 286c 10.31 N 66.50 W
Los Ebanos 196 26.14 N 98.34 W
Loseley House ⊥ 260 51.13 N 0.36 W
Los Esclavos ≃ 236 13.50 N 90.20 W
Losevo 78 50.40 N 40.02 E
Los Flamencos, Laguna ⊜ 258 35.36 S 58.42 W
Los Frailes, Picacho ∧ 234 23.53 N 106.03 W
Los Frentones 252 26.25 S 61.25 W
Los Fresnos 196 26.04 N 97.29 W
Los Garzas 196 26.23 N 99.46 W
Los Gatos 226 37.13 N 121.58 W
Los Gatos Creek ≃, Ca., U.S. 226 36.13 N 120.08 W
Los Gatos Creek ≃, Ca., U.S. 226 37.20 N 121.54 W
Los Glaciares, Parque Nacional ✦ 254 49.52 S 73.05 W
Los Guerras 196 26.25 N 99.05 W
Loshan
→ Leshan 107 29.34 N 103.45 E
Losheim 56 49.30 N 6.44 E
Los Hermanos, Islas II 246 11.45 N 64.25 W
Los Herreras 196 25.55 N 99.24 W
Loshkarivka 78 47.57 N 34.12 E
Los Huacales, Cerro ∧ 234 22.19 N 101.34 W
Losi 273a 6.40 N 3.31 E
Łosice 30 52.14 N 22.43 E
Los Idolos, Parque Arquelógico de ⊥ 246 1.55 N 76.10 W
Lošinj, Otok I 36 44.36 N 14.24 E
Losinoborskaja 86 58.27 N 89.28 E
Losino-Petrovskij 82 55.52 N 38.12 E
Los Jazmines, Presa ⊜[1] 286a 19.25 N 99.16 W
Los Juríes 252 28.28 S 62.06 W
Loskopdam ⊜[1] 156 25.23 S 29.20 E

Symbols in the index entries represent the broad categories identified in the key at the right. Symbols with superior numbers (⋀[1]) identify subcategories (see complete key on page I · 1).

Symbole im Register stellen die rechts im Schlüssel erklärten Kategorien dar. Symbole mit hochgestellten Ziffern (⋀[1]) bezeichnen Unterabteilungen einer Kategorie (vgl. vollständiger Schlüssel auf Seite I · 1).

Los símbolos incluídos en el texto del índice representan las grandes categorías identificadas con la clave a la derecha. Los símbolos con numeros en su parte superior (⋀[1]) identifican las subcategorías (véase la clave completa en la página I · 1).

Les symboles de l'index représentent les catégories indiquées dans la légende à droite. Les symboles suivis d'un indice (⋀[1]) représentent des sous-catégories (voir légende complète à la page I · 1).

Os símbolos incluídos no texto do índice representam as grandes categorias identificadas com a chave à direita. Os símbolos com números em sua parte superior (⋀[1]) identificam as subcategorias (veja-se a chave completa à página I · 1).

∧ Mountain	Berg	Montaña	Montagne	Montanha
⋀ Mountains	Gebirge	Montañas	Montagnes	Montanhas
)(Pass	Paß	Paso	Col	Passo
V Valley, Canyon	Tal, Cañon	Valle, Cañón	Vallée, Canyon	Vale, Canhão
≃ Plain	Ebene	Llano	Plaine	Planície
› Cape	Kap	Cabo	Cap	Cabo
I Island	Insel	Isla	Île	Ilha
II Islands	Inseln	Islas	Îles	Ilhas
✦ Other Topographic Features	Andere Topographische Objekte	Otros Elementos Topográficos	Autres données topographiques	Outros acidentes topográficos

ESPAÑOL

Nombre	Página	Lat.°′	Long.°′ W = Oeste
Loskop Dam Game Reserve ◆[4]	156	25.23 S	29.20 E
Los Lagos	254	39.51 S	72.50 W
Los Lagos □[4]	254	41.45 S	73.00 W
Los Llanos	240m	18.03 N	66.24 W
Los Llanos [de Aridane]	148	28.39 N	17.54 W
Los López	196	26.15 N	99.05 W
Los Lunas	200	34.48 N	106.43 W
Los Manglares de Tumbes, Santuario Nacional ♠	246	2.25 S	80.20 W
Los Maribios, Cordillera ⋌	236	12.35 N	86.50 W
Los Médanos, Istmo de ±[3]	241s	11.35 N	69.45 W
Los Menucos	254	40.50 S	68.08 W
Los Micos, Laguna de c	236	15.45 N	87.36 W
Los'mino	76	55.04 N	34.24 E
Los Mochis	232	25.45 N	108.57 W
Los Molinos	204	40.01 N	122.05 W
Los Muermos	254	41.24 S	73.29 W
Los Naranjos	286c	10.27 N	66.48 W
Los Navalmorales	34	39.43 N	4.38 W
Lošnica	76	54.17 N	28.46 E
Los Nietos	280	33.58 N	118.04 W
Løsning	41	55.48 N	9.42 E
Los Nogales	196	26.16 N	99.43 W
Losolava	175f	14.11 S	167.34 E
Los Olmos Creek ≃, Tx., U.S.	196	27.20 N	97.40 W
Los Olmos Creek ≃, Tx., U.S.	196	26.21 N	98.48 W
Los Osos	226	35.19 N	120.50 W
Los Oyameles	234	19.43 N	97.32 W
Los Padillas	200	34.58 N	106.41 W
Los Palacios, Arg.	252	29.22 S	68.11 W
Los Palacios, Cuba	240p	22.35 N	83.15 W
Los Palacios y Villafranca	34	37.10 N	5.56 W
Los Perros, Arroyo ≃	288	34.37 S	58.46 W
Los Pinos ◆[8]	286b	23.04 N	82.23 W
Los Pinos ≃	200	36.56 N	107.36 W
Los Placeres del Oro	234	18.13 N	100.54 W
Los Polvorines	288	34.30 S	58.41 W
Los Quillayes	286e	33.34 S	70.37 W
Los Quirquinchos	252	33.22 S	61.43 W
Los Rábanos	240m	18.11 N	66.50 W
Los Ramones	196	25.42 N	99.37 W
Los Remedios ≃	286a	19.31 N	99.05 W
Los Reyes de Salgado	234	19.35 N	102.29 W
Los Reyes la Paz	286a	19.21 N	98.58 W
Los Ríos □[4]	246	1.30 S	79.25 W
Los Rodríguez	232	27.11 N	101.21 W
Los Roques, Islas II	246	11.50 N	66.45 W
Lossa ≃	54	51.18 N	11.10 E
Los Santos □[4]	236	7.55 N	80.25 W
Los Santos de Maimona	34	38.27 N	6.23 W
Los Sauces	252	37.58 S	72.50 W
Lossburg	58	48.25 N	8.27 E
Lössel	263	51.21 N	7.39 E
Losser	52	52.15 N	7.00 E
Los Serranos	228	33.59 N	117.42 W
Lossie ≃	46	57.43 N	3.16 W
Lossiemouth	46	57.43 N	3.18 W
Lössnitz	54	50.37 N	12.43 E
Lost ≃, U.S.	202	41.56 N	121.30 W
Lost ≃, In., U.S.	194	38.33 N	86.49 W
Lost ≃, Mn., U.S.	198	47.51 N	96.02 W
Lost ≃, W.V., U.S.	188	39.05 N	78.36 W
Lostant	216	41.09 N	89.04 W
Los Taques	246	11.50 N	70.16 W
Lost Bridge State Recreation Area ♠	216	40.45 N	85.37 W
Lost Creek ≃, Al., U.S.	194	33.38 N	87.14 W
Lost Creek ≃, Ar., U.S.	194	34.10 N	92.31 W
Lost Creek ≃, Oh., U.S.	218	39.58 N	84.09 W
Lost Creek ≃, Ut,. U.S.	200	41.04 N	111.32 W
Lost Creek ≃, Wy., U.S.	200	42.01 N	108.11 W
Lost Draw V	196	32.58 N	102.02 W
Los Telares	252	28.59 S	63.26 W
Los Teques	246	10.21 N	67.02 W
Los Testigos, Islas II	246	11.22 N	63.06 W
Lost Hills	226	35.36 N	119.41 W
Lostine ≃	202	45.33 N	117.29 W
Lost Lake ⊜, Or., U.S.	224	45.29 N	121.49 W
Lost Lake ⊜, Wa., U.S.	224	47.20 N	121.24 W
Lost Nation	190	41.57 N	90.49 W
Lostock ≃	262	53.40 N	2.48 W
Lostock Gralam	262	53.16 N	2.28 W
Los Trancos Creek ≃	282	37.25 N	122.12 W
Los Trancos Woods	282	37.21 N	122.12 W
Lost River Range ⋌	202	44.10 N	113.35 W
Lost Trail Pass)(	202	45.41 N	113.57 W
Lostwithiel	42	50.25 N	4.40 W
Losuia	164	8.32 S	151.04 E
Los Vidrios	232	31.59 N	113.28 W
Los Vilos	252	31.55 S	71.31 W
Los Yébenes	34	39.34 N	3.53 W
Losynivka	78	50.51 N	31.54 E
Lot □[5]	32	44.35 N	1.40 E
Lot ≃	32	44.18 N	0.20 E
Lota	252	37.05 S	73.10 W
Lotagipi Swamp (Lotikipi Plain) ≡	144	4.36 N	34.55 E
Lotak	112	0.11 S	115.54 E
Lotbinière □[6]	206	46.30 N	71.40 W
Lotela, Lake ⊜	220	27.34 N	81.29 W
Løten	26	60.49 N	11.19 E
Lot-et-Garonne □[5]	32	44.20 N	0.20 E
Lotfābād	128	37.32 N	59.20 E
Lothair, S. Afr.	158	26.26 S	30.27 E
Lothair, Ky., U.S.	192	37.14 N	83.10 W
Lothian □[4]	46	55.55 N	3.05 W
Lothringen → Lorraine □[9]	32	49.00 N	6.00 E
Lotikipi Plain (Lotagipi Swamp) ≡	144	4.36 N	34.55 E
Loto	152	2.49 S	22.29 E
Loto ≃	152	1.55 S	22.09 E
Lotofaga	175a	13.59 S	171.50 W
Lotoi ≃	152	1.35 S	18.30 E
Lotorp	40	58.44 N	15.50 E
Lotošino	76	56.14 N	35.38 E
Lotrului, Munții ⋌	38	45.30 N	23.52 E
Lotsane ≃	156	22.41 S	28.11 E
Lötschberg Tunnel ◆[5]	58	46.25 N	7.45 E
Lötschental V	58	46.25 N	7.50 E
Lotseninsel I	41	54.40 N	10.01 E
Lott	222	31.12 N	97.02 W
Lotta ≃	24	68.36 N	31.06 E
Lotte	52	52.17 N	7.55 E
Lottivue	214	42.40 N	82.46 W
Löttringhausen ◆[8]	263	51.27 N	7.27 E
Lottsburg	208	37.57 N	76.31 W
Lotts Creek ≃	192	32.09 N	81.47 W
Lottsford Branch ≃	284c	38.55 N	76.49 W
Lottstetten	58	47.38 N	8.34 E
Lotuke, Jabal ∧	154	4.07 N	33.48 E
Lotung	100	24.41 N	121.46 E
Lotzorai	71	39.58 N	9.39 E
Louang Namtha	110	20.57 N	101.25 E
Louangphrabang	110	19.52 N	102.08 E
L'Ouarsenis, Massif de ⋌	34	35.40 N	1.50 E
Loubaresse	62	44.36 N	4.03 E
Loube, Montagne de la ∧	62	43.22 N	5.59 E
Loubetsi	152	3.12 S	12.10 E

FRANÇAIS

Nom	Page	Lat.°′	Long.°′ W = Ouest
Louchi	24	66.04 N	33.00 E
Loučim	60	49.22 N	13.07 E
Loučná ∧	54	50.39 N	13.37 E
Loude	98	35.54 N	117.18 E
Loudéac	32	48.10 N	2.45 W
Louden Cove c	276	41.05 N	73.43 W
Loudes	62	45.05 N	3.45 E
Loudima Poste	152	4.07 S	13.04 E
Loudon	192	35.43 N	84.20 W
Loudonville, N.Y., U.S.	210	42.42 N	73.45 W
Loudonville, Oh., U.S.	214	40.38 N	82.14 W
Loudoun □[6]	208	39.05 N	77.30 W
Loudun	32	47.01 N	0.05 E
Loué	32	48.00 N	0.09 W
Loue ≃	58	47.01 N	5.27 E
Louga	150	15.37 N	16.13 W
Louga □[4]	150	15.25 N	15.30 W
Louge	252	36.57 S	61.40 W
Louge ≃	32	43.27 N	1.20 E
Lougguéré ≃	150	15.35 N	14.47 W
Loughborough	42	52.47 N	1.11 W
Loughborough Lake ⊜	212	44.23 N	76.30 W
Loughermore ∧[2]	48	54.59 N	7.05 W
Loughman	220	28.14 N	81.34 W
Loughor	42	51.40 N	4.04 W
Loughor ≃	42	51.40 N	4.04 W
Loughrea	48	53.12 N	8.34 W
Loughros More Bay c	48	54.47 N	8.35 W
Loughton	260	51.39 N	0.03 E
Louhans	58	46.38 N	5.13 E
Louin	194	32.04 N	89.15 W
Louisa, Ky., U.S.	192	38.06 N	82.36 W
Louisa, Va., U.S.	192	38.01 N	78.00 W
Louisa, Lake ⊜, On., Can.	212	45.28 N	78.30 W
Louisa, Lake ⊜, Fl., U.S.	220	28.29 N	81.44 W
Louisbourg	186	45.55 N	59.58 W
Louis Bull Indian Reserve ◆[4]	182	52.53 N	113.31 W
Louisburg, Ks., U.S.	198	38.37 N	94.40 W
Louisburg, N.C., U.S.	192	36.05 N	78.18 W
Louisburgh	48	53.46 N	9.51 W
Louisdale	186	45.36 N	61.04 W
Louise, Ms., U.S.	194	32.58 N	90.35 W
Louise, Tx., U.S.	222	29.06 N	96.25 W
Louise, Lac ⊜, P.Q., Can.	206	45.43 N	71.25 W
Louise, Lac ⊜, P.Q., Can.	206	45.46 N	74.25 W
Louise, Lake ⊜	180	62.20 N	146.30 W
Louise Island I	182	52.58 N	131.50 W
Louiseville	206	46.15 N	72.57 W
Louis Gentil → Youssoufia	148	32.16 N	8.33 W
Louisiade Archipelago II	160	11.00 S	153.00 E
Louisiana	219	39.26 N	91.03 W
Louisiana □[3], U.S.	178	31.15 N	92.15 W
Louisiana □[3], U.S.	194	31.15 N	92.15 W
Louisiana ʊ	41	55.58 N	12.33 E
Lou Island I	164	2.25 S	147.20 E
Louis Trichardt	156	23.01 S	29.43 E
Louisvale	158	28.33 S	21.12 E
Louisville, On., Can.	214	42.28 N	82.07 W
Louisville, Al., U.S.	194	31.47 N	85.33 W
Louisville, Ga., U.S.	192	33.00 N	82.24 W
Louisville, Il., U.S.	194	38.46 N	88.30 W
Louisville, Ky., U.S.	218	38.15 N	85.45 W
Louisville, Ms., U.S.	194	33.07 N	89.03 W
Louisville, Ne., U.S.	198	40.59 N	96.09 W
Louisville, Oh., U.S.	214	40.50 N	81.15 W
Louisville Ridge ✢[3]	14	31.00 S	172.30 W
Louisville Seamount ✢[3]	14	31.15 S	172.15 W
Louis-XIV, Pointe >	176	54.37 N	79.45 W
Loujiaying	98	42.04 N	116.04 E
Loukanga	273b	4.20 S	15.09 E
Loukkos, Oued ≃	34	35.12 N	6.09 W
Loukoua ≃	273b	4.09 S	15.08 E
Loulé	34	37.08 N	8.02 W
Loum	152	4.43 N	9.44 E
Loumou	273b	4.08 S	15.09 E
Lount Lake ⊜	184	50.10 N	94.20 W
Louny	54	50.19 N	13.46 E
Loup ≃, Fr.	62	43.38 N	7.09 E
Loup ≃, Ne., U.S.	198	41.24 N	97.19 W
Loup, Gorge du V	56	49.47 N	6.23 E
Loup, Rivière du ≃	206	46.13 N	72.55 W
Loup City	198	41.16 N	98.57 W
Loups Marins, Lacs des ⊜	176	56.30 N	73.45 W
Lourches	50	50.19 N	3.21 E
Lourdes, Nf., Can.	186	48.39 N	59.00 W
Lourdes, Fr.	32	43.06 N	0.03 W
Lourel de Baixo	266c	38.49 N	9.22 W
Lourenço	250	2.30 N	51.40 W
Lourenço Marques → Maputo	156	25.58 S	32.35 E
Lourenço Velho	256	22.22 S	45.19 W
Lourenço Velho ≃, Bra.	256	23.26 S	45.35 W
Lourenço Velho ≃, Bra.	256	22.22 S	45.31 W
Loures	34	38.50 N	9.10 W
Loures ≃	266c	38.50 N	9.08 W
Lourinhã	34	39.14 N	9.19 W
Lourmarin	62	43.46 N	5.22 E
Lourosa	34	40.19 N	7.56 W
Loury	50	48.00 N	2.05 E
Lousã, Port.	34	40.07 N	8.15 W
Lousa, Port.	266c	38.53 N	9.12 W
Louse Creek ≃	198	46.22 N	100.57 W
Lou Shan ∧	89	45.15 N	128.58 E
Louta	150	13.30 N	3.10 W
Loutang	106	31.26 N	121.12 E
Loutézou, Île de I	273b	4.22 S	15.10 E
Louth, Austl.	166	30.32 S	145.07 E
Louth, Ire.	44	53.57 N	6.33 W
Louth, Ire.	48	53.57 N	6.33 W
Louth, Eng., U.K.	44	53.22 N	0.01 W
Louth □[6]	48	53.55 N	6.30 W
Louth Bay c	166	34.34 S	136.02 E
Louti, Mayo ≃	146	9.38 N	13.56 E
Loutit Bay c	169	38.33 S	144.00 E
Loutrá Aidhipsoú	38	38.51 N	23.02 E
Loutre ≃	219	38.42 N	91.25 W
Loutre, Bayou de ≃	194	32.41 N	92.08 W
Loutrópirgos	267c	38.02 N	23.28 E
Louvain → Leuven	56	50.53 N	4.42 E
Louveciennes	261	48.52 N	2.07 E
Louveigné	56	50.32 N	5.42 E
Louveira	256	23.04 S	46.58 W
Louviers, Fr.	50	49.13 N	1.10 E
Louviers, Co., U.S.	200	39.28 N	105.00 W
Louvre ʊ	261	48.52 N	2.20 E
Louvres	50	49.02 N	2.30 E
Louvroil	50	50.16 N	3.58 E
Louwsburg	158	27.37 S	31.07 E
Lou Yaeger, Lake ⊜[1]	219	39.10 N	89.37 W
Lövånger	26	64.22 N	21.18 E
Lovászi	61	46.33 N	16.34 E
Lovat' ≃	76	58.14 N	31.28 E
Lovcy	82	55.00 N	39.15 E
Love	184	53.29 N	104.09 W
Loveč	38	43.08 N	24.43 E
Loveč □[4]	38	43.11 N	25.10 E
Love Clough	262	53.44 N	2.17 W
Lovedale	279b	40.17 N	79.52 W
Lovejoy	219	38.39 N	90.10 W
Lovelady	222	31.08 N	95.27 W
Loveland, Co., U.S.	200	40.23 N	105.04 W
Loveland, Oh., U.S.	218	39.16 N	84.16 W
Lovell	202	44.50 N	108.23 W
Lovell Island I	283	42.20 N	70.56 W
Lovelock	204	40.10 N	118.28 W

PORTUGUÊS

Nome	Página	Lat.°′	Long.°′ W = Oeste
Lovely	192	37.49 N	82.24 W
Love Point >	208	39.02 N	76.18 W
Lovere	64	45.49 N	10.04 E
Lovering, Lac ⊜	206	45.10 N	72.09 W
Lovero	64	46.14 N	10.14 E
Loves Green	260	51.43 N	0.24 E
Loves Park	216	42.19 N	89.03 W
Loviisa → Lovisa	26	60.27 N	26.14 E
Lovilia	190	41.08 N	92.54 W
Loving, N.M., U.S.	196	32.17 N	104.05 W
Loving, Tx., U.S.	196	33.16 N	98.31 W
Lovingston	192	37.45 N	78.52 W
Lovington, Il., U.S.	219	39.42 N	88.37 W
Lovington, N.M., U.S.	196	32.56 N	103.20 W
Lovisa (Loviisa)	26	60.27 N	26.14 E
Lövő	61	47.30 N	16.47 E
Lovö I	40	59.20 N	17.50 E
Lovoi ≃	154	8.14 S	26.39 E
Lovosice	54	50.31 N	14.03 E
Lovozero, Ross.	24	68.00 N	35.00 E
Lovozero, Ross.	24	65.00 N	29.50 E
Lovozero, ozero ⊜	24	67.54 N	35.12 E
Lovrenc	61	46.32 N	15.23 E
Lövstabruk	40	60.24 N	17.53 E
Lövstabukten c	40	60.35 N	17.45 E
Lövstad slott ⊥	40	58.33 N	16.02 E
Lóvua, Ang.	152	11.36 S	23.53 E
Lóvua, Ang.	152	7.20 S	20.16 E
Lovua (Lóvua) ≃	152	6.07 S	20.35 E
Low	188	45.48 N	75.57 W
Low, Cape >	176	63.07 N	85.18 W
Lowa	154	1.24 S	25.51 E
Lowa ≃	154	1.24 S	25.51 E
Lowāda	126	22.27 N	87.37 E
Lowat → Lovat' ≃	76	58.14 N	31.28 E
Lowber	279b	40.15 N	79.46 W
Lowden	190	41.51 N	90.55 W
Lowder Brook ≃	283	43.14 N	71.11 W
Lowell, Ar., U.S.	194	36.15 N	94.07 W
Lowell, In., U.S.	216	41.17 N	87.25 W
Lowell, Ma., U.S.	207	42.38 N	71.19 W
Lowell, Mi., U.S.	216	42.56 N	85.20 W
Lowell, Or., U.S.	202	43.55 N	122.46 W
Lowell, Lake ⊜[1]	202	43.33 N	116.40 W
Lowell, University of ʊ[2]	283	42.39 N	71.20 W
Lowell-Dracut State Forest ♠	283	42.40 N	71.22 W
Lowelli	140	5.59 N	33.45 E
Lowellville	214	41.02 N	80.32 W
Löwen → Leuven	56	50.53 N	4.42 E
Löwen ≃	158	26.51 S	18.17 E
Löwenberg	54	52.54 N	13.08 E
Löwenbruch	264a	52.18 N	13.19 E
Löwenstein	56	49.06 N	9.22 E
Lowe Pond ⊜	283	42.41 N	70.59 W
Lower Aetna Lake ⊜	285	39.51 N	74.48 W
Lower Arrow Lake ⊜	182	49.40 N	118.08 W
Lower Bay c	208	40.33 N	74.02 W
Lower Bear River Reservoir ⊜[1]	226	38.33 N	120.14 W
Lower Bershire Valley	276	40.54 N	74.37 W
Lower Beverley Lake ⊜	212	44.36 N	76.09 W
Lower Broughton ◆[8]	262	53.29 N	2.15 W
Lower Brule Indian Reservation ◆[4]	198	44.05 N	99.44 W
Lower Buckhorn Lake ⊜	212	44.33 N	78.17 W
Lower Burrell	214	40.33 N	79.45 W
Lower California → Baja California >[1]	232	28.00 N	113.30 W
Lower Chittering	168a	31.34 S	116.06 E
Lower Crystal Springs Reservoir ⊜[1]	226	37.32 N	122.22 W
Lower Darwen	262	53.43 N	2.28 W
Lower Egypt → Miṣr Baḥrī □[9]	140	31.00 N	31.00 E
Lower Eltham Park ♠	274b	37.45 S	145.09 E
Lower Elwha Indian Reservation ◆[4]	224	48.09 N	123.33 W
Lower Fort Garry National Historic Park ♠	184	50.07 N	96.55 W
Lower Ganga Canal ≊	124	26.27 N	80.17 E
Lower Gap c	212	44.10 N	76.35 W
Lower Halstow	260	51.22 N	0.40 E
Lower Hay Lake ⊜	212	45.25 N	78.13 W
Lower Higham	260	51.26 N	0.28 E
Lower Huron Metropolitan Park ♠	281	42.12 N	83.25 W
Lower Hutt	172	41.13 S	174.55 E
Lower Kalskag	180	61.31 N	160.22 W
Lower Keechi Creek ≃	222	31.08 N	95.46 W
Lower Klamath Lake ⊜	204	41.55 N	121.42 W
Lower Lake	226	38.55 N	122.36 W
Lower Lake ⊜	204	41.15 N	120.02 W
Lower Loteni	158	29.32 S	29.36 E
Lower Manitou Lake ⊜	184	49.15 N	93.00 W
Lower Matecumbe Key I	220	24.51 N	80.43 W
Lower Montville	276	40.54 N	74.22 W
Lower Mystic Lake ⊜	283	42.26 N	71.09 W
Lower Nazeing	260	51.44 N	0.01 E
Lower Otay Lake ⊜[1]	228	32.37 N	116.55 W
Lower Paia	229a	20.55 N	156.23 W
Lower Paudash Lake ⊜	212	44.58 N	78.01 W
Lower Peirce Reservoir ⊜[1]	271c	1.22 N	103.49 E
Lower Peover	262	53.16 N	2.23 W
Lower Place	262	53.36 N	2.09 W
Lower Plenty	274b	37.44 S	145.06 E
Lower Portland	170	33.27 S	150.53 E
Lower Post	176	59.55 N	128.30 W
Lower Red Lake ⊜	198	48.00 N	94.50 W
Lower River Rouge ≃	281	42.18 N	83.14 W
Lower Rouge Parkway ♠	281	42.18 N	83.20 W
Lower Saxony → Niedersachsen □[3]	30	52.40 N	9.00 E
Lower Stoke	260	51.27 N	0.38 E
Lower Trajan's Wall ⊥	38	45.40 N	28.30 E
Lower Ugashik Lake ⊜	180	57.30 N	156.56 W
Lower Van Norman Lake ⊜[1]	280	34.17 N	118.29 W
Lower West Pubnico	186	43.38 N	65.48 W
Lower Whitley	262	53.18 N	2.35 W
Lower Wood's Harbour	186	43.31 N	65.44 W
Lowery, Lake ⊜	220	28.07 N	81.41 W
Lower Zambezi International Game Park ◆[4]	154	15.30 S	29.35 E
Lowestoft	42	52.29 N	1.45 E
Lowgar □[4]	120	33.50 N	69.00 E
Lowick	44	55.38 N	2.00 W
Łowicz	30	52.07 N	19.56 E
Lowman	210	42.02 N	76.44 W
Lowmoor	192	37.47 N	79.53 W
Lowood	171a	27.28 S	152.35 E
Lowr̲ah (Pishīn Lora) ≃	120	29.09 N	64.55 E
Lowries Run ≃	279b	40.30 N	80.05 W
Low Rocky Point >	166	43.00 S	145.30 E

Lowry Air Force Base ■	198	39.43 N	104.53 W
Lowry City	194	38.08 N	93.43 W
Lowther ≃	44	54.39 N	2.44 W
Lowther Hills ⋌[2]	44	55.19 N	3.38 W
Lowton	262	53.28 N	2.35 W
Lowton Common	262	53.29 N	2.33 W
Lowville, N.Y., U.S.	212	43.47 N	75.29 W
Lowville, Pa., U.S.	214	42.01 N	79.49 W
Loxahatchee	220	26.49 N	80.13 W
Loxley	194	30.37 N	87.45 W
Loxstedt	52	53.28 N	8.38 E
Loxten	52	52.03 N	8.08 E
Loxton, Austl.	166	34.27 S	140.35 E
Loxton, S. Afr.	158	31.30 S	22.22 E
Loyal	190	44.44 N	90.29 W
Loyal, Loch ⊜	46	58.23 N	4.22 W
Loyalhanna	214	40.19 N	79.21 W
Loyalhanna Creek ≃	214	40.28 N	79.27 W
Loyalhanna Lake ⊜[1]	214	40.25 N	79.28 W
Loyalsock Creek ≃	210	41.14 N	76.56 W
Loyalton	204	39.40 N	120.14 W
Loyalty Islands → Loyauté, Îles II	175f	21.00 S	167.00 E
Loyang, Sing.	271c	1.22 N	103.58 E
Loyang → Luoyang, Zhg.	102	34.41 N	112.28 E
Loyauté, Îles (Loyalty Islands) II	175f	21.00 S	167.00 E
Loyne, Loch ⊜	46	57.06 N	5.00 W
Loyola College ʊ[2]	284b	39.21 N	76.37 W
Loyola Marymount University ʊ[2]	280	33.58 N	118.25 W
Loyola University ʊ[2]	278	42.00 N	87.39 W
Loyoro	154	3.21 N	34.16 E
Loysburg	214	40.10 N	78.23 W
Loysville	208	40.22 N	77.21 W
Lozano	258	34.51 S	59.03 W
Lozère □[5]	32	44.30 N	3.30 E
Lozère, Mont ⋌	62	44.25 N	3.46 E
Loznica	38	44.32 N	19.13 E
Ložnikovo, Ross.	86	56.54 N	73.56 E
Ložnikovo, Ross.	88	51.22 N	117.03 E
Loznoje	80	49.17 N	44.26 E
Lozno-Oleksandrivka	78	49.50 N	38.44 E
L'Ozone ◆[8]	273b	4.21 S	15.14 E
Lozova	78	48.54 N	36.20 E
Lozovaja	86	53.17 N	77.45 E
Lozove, Ukr.	78	49.18 N	27.18 E
Lozove, Ukr.	83	49.28 N	37.54 E
Lozove, Ukr.	83	49.13 N	37.36 E
Lozoyuela	34	40.55 N	3.37 W
Loz'va ≃	86	59.36 N	62.20 E
Lozzo di Cadore	64	46.29 N	12.27 E
Lu	62	45.00 N	8.29 E
Lu ≃	100	27.04 N	115.00 E
Lua ≃	152	2.46 N	18.26 E
Luabo	156	18.30 S	36.10 E
Luabu ≃	152	2.46 S	18.19 E
Luachimo ≃	152	6.33 S	20.59 E
Luaha-sibuha	110	0.31 S	98.28 E
Luala ≃	154	17.57 S	36.30 E
Lualaba ≃	154	0.26 N	25.20 E
Luali	152	5.06 S	12.29 E
Lualoje ≃	152	12.18 S	21.38 E
Luama ≃	154	4.46 S	26.53 E
Luambe National Park ♠	154	12.25 S	32.15 E
Luambimba ≃	152	15.00 S	22.48 E
Luampa	154	15.03 S	24.28 E
Luampa ≃	154	14.33 S	24.10 E
Lu'an	100	31.44 N	116.31 E
Luan ≃	98	39.20 N	119.10 E
Luana ≃	152	7.56 S	21.06 E
Luan Balu	114	2.38 N	96.13 E
Luancheng, Zhg.	98	37.53 N	114.39 E
Luancheng, Zhg.	102	22.45 N	108.51 E
Luanchuan	102	33.51 N	111.36 E
Luancundo ≃	152	16.25 S	21.27 E
Luanda	152	8.48 S	13.14 E
Luanda □[5]	152	9.00 S	13.15 E
Luando ≃	152	10.19 S	16.40 E
Luando, Réserva do ◆[4]	152	11.10 S	17.30 E
Luang, Khao ∧	110	8.31 N	99.47 E
Luang, Thale c	110	7.30 N	100.15 E
Luang Chiang Dao, Doi ∧	110	19.23 N	98.54 E
Luanginga (Luanguinga) ≃	152	15.11 S	22.56 E
Luang Prabang → Louangphrabang	110	19.52 N	102.08 E
Luang Prabang Range ⋌	110	18.30 N	101.15 E
Luangue	152	7.19 S	19.38 E
Luangue (Loange) ≃	152	4.17 S	20.02 E
Luanguinga (Luanginga) ≃	152	15.11 S	22.56 E
Luangwa (Aruângua) ≃	154	15.36 S	30.25 E
Luanhaizi	120	34.27 N	93.12 E
Luanhe	105	40.57 N	117.44 E
Luannan (Bencheng)	98	39.32 N	118.39 E
Luanping (Anjiangying)	98	40.57 N	117.20 E
Luanshishan	104	42.10 N	123.41 E
Luanshya	154	13.08 S	28.24 E
Luán Toro	252	36.12 S	65.06 W
Luanxian	98	39.45 N	118.44 E
Luanza	154	8.42 S	28.42 E
Luapula □[4]	154	10.55 S	29.00 E
Luapula ≃	154	9.26 S	28.33 E
Luar, Danau ⊜	112	0.55 N	112.15 E
Luarca	34	43.32 N	6.32 W
Luashi	152	10.56 S	23.37 E
Luashi ≃	152	10.41 S	22.55 E
Luassinga ≃	152	15.47 S	18.50 E
Luati	152	14.35 S	21.13 E
Luatira	152	12.52 S	17.14 E
Luau	152	10.42 S	22.12 E
Lua-Vindu ≃	152	3.38 N	19.16 E
Luba	152	3.27 N	8.33 E
Lubaantun ⊥	232	16.17 N	88.58 W
Lubaczów	30	50.10 N	23.07 E
Lubalo	152	9.12 S	19.16 E
Lubalo ≃	152	7.22 S	19.20 E
Lubamiti	152	2.29 S	17.47 E
L'uban', Bela.	76	52.48 N	27.59 E
L'uban', Bela.	76	52.37 N	29.08 E
Lubań, Pol.	30	51.08 N	15.18 E
L'uban', Ross.	76	59.21 N	31.13 E
Lubāna	76	56.54 N	26.43 E
Lubang	116	13.52 N	120.07 E
Lubang Island I	116	13.46 N	120.11 E
Lubang Islands II	116	13.46 N	120.15 E
Lubango	152	14.55 S	13.30 E
Lubanowo	54	53.09 N	14.36 E
Lubāns ⊜	76	56.46 N	26.53 E
Lubansenshi ≃	154	11.21 S	30.35 E
Lub'any	80	56.02 N	51.24 E
Lubao	100	23.22 N	112.55 E
Lübars, Dtsch.	54	52.39 N	12.02 E
Lübars, Dtsch.	54	52.10 N	12.09 E
Lübars ◆[8]	264a	52.37 N	13.22 E
Lubartów	30	51.28 N	22.38 E
Lubawa	30	53.30 N	19.45 E
Lubaynī, Baḥr al- ≊	273c	29.56 N	31.11 E
Lübbecke	52	52.18 N	8.36 E
Lübben	54	51.56 N	13.53 E
Lübbenau	54	51.52 N	13.57 E
Lubber Brook ≃	283	42.33 N	71.09 W
Lubbers Run ≃	276	40.56 N	74.43 W
Lübbesee ⊜	54	53.05 N	13.34 E
Lubbock	196	33.34 N	101.51 W
Lübbow	54	52.54 N	11.10 E
Lubbub Creek ≃	194	33.04 N	88.10 W
L'ubča	76	53.45 N	26.03 E
Lubec	188	44.51 N	66.59 W
Lübeck	54	53.52 N	10.40 E

Lübecker Bucht c	54	54.00 N	10.55 E
Lubefu	152	4.43 S	24.25 E
Lubefu ≃	152	4.10 S	23.00 E
Lubelska, Wyżyna ⋌[2]	30	51.00 N	23.00 E
Lubembe (Luembe) ≃	152	6.37 S	21.05 E
Lüben → Lubin	30	51.24 N	16.13 E
Lubenec	54	50.06 N	13.20 E
L'ubercy	82	55.41 N	37.53 E
Lubéron, Montagne du ⋌	62	43.48 N	5.22 E
Lubersac	32	45.27 N	1.24 E
Lübesse	54	53.29 N	11.28 E
Lubi ≃	152	4.58 S	23.26 E
Lubiana → Ljubljana	36	46.03 N	14.31 E
Lubic Island I	116	10.58 N	120.44 E
L'ubickoje	80	51.46 N	49.19 E
Lubień Kujawski	30	52.25 N	19.10 E
Lubilash ≃	152	6.02 S	23.45 E
Lubile	154	2.55 S	26.45 E
L'ubim	80	58.22 N	40.41 E
L'ubimovka, Kaz.	86	52.15 N	66.45 E
L'ubimovka, Ross.	78	51.31 N	35.37 E
Lubin, Pol.	30	51.24 N	16.13 E
Lubin, Pol.	54	53.50 N	14.25 E
L'ubino	86	57.30 N	88.47 E
L'ubinskij	86	55.09 N	72.42 E
Lubishi ≃	152	6.54 S	24.09 E
Lubja ≃	265a	59.58 N	30.30 E
Lublin	30	51.15 N	22.35 E
Lublin □[4]	30	51.30 N	22.30 E
Lubliniec	30	50.40 N	18.41 E
L'ublino ◆[8]	265b	55.41 N	37.44 E
Lubmin	54	54.08 N	13.37 E
Lubnān → Lebanon □[1]	128	34.00 N	36.00 E
Lubnān, Jabal (Lebanon Mountains) ⋌	132	34.00 N	36.00 E
L'ubnica	76	57.58 N	32.42 E
Lubny	78	50.01 N	33.00 E
L'ubochna	76	53.31 N	34.23 E
Lubok China	114	2.27 N	102.04 E
Lubomierz	30	51.01 N	15.30 E
Luboń	30	52.23 N	16.54 E
Lubondai	152	6.34 S	22.39 E
Lubondoi	154	8.02 S	26.31 E
L'ubostan'	78	51.19 N	35.44 E
Lubraniec	30	52.33 N	18.50 E
Lubsko	30	51.46 N	14.59 E
Lubsza ≃	54	51.56 N	14.43 E
Lübtheen	54	53.18 N	11.04 E
Lubu, Indon.	112	0.46 S	122.30 E
Lubu, Zhg.	102	23.09 N	112.13 E
Lubuagan	116	17.21 N	121.10 E
L'ubučany	82	55.15 N	37.33 E
Lubudi, Zaïre	152	6.51 S	21.18 E
Lubudi, Zaïre	154	9.57 S	25.58 E
Lubudi ≃, Zaïre	152	4.03 S	21.23 E
Lubudi ≃, Zaïre	154	9.13 S	25.38 E
Lubue	152	4.09 S	19.52 E
Lubue ≃	152	4.10 S	19.53 E
Lubukambacang	112	0.37 S	101.25 E
Lubukbatang	112	4.03 S	104.12 E
Lubukbertubung	112	0.02 N	102.08 E
Lubuklinggau	112	3.18 S	102.52 E
Lubukpakam	114	3.33 N	98.52 E
Lubukraya, Dolok ∧	114	1.29 N	99.13 E
Lubuksikaping	112	0.08 N	100.10 E
Lubumbaschi → Lubumbashi	154	11.40 S	27.28 E
Lubumbashi (Élisabethville)	154	11.40 S	27.28 E
Lubunda	154	5.10 S	26.40 E
Lubutu	154	0.44 S	26.35 E
Luby	54	50.12 N	12.25 E
L'ubytino	76	58.49 N	33.23 E
Lübz	54	53.27 N	12.01 E
Lučak	85	38.23 N	67.25 E
Lucala	152	9.16 S	15.15 E
Lucala ≃, Ang.	152	9.37 S	14.14 E
Lucala ≃, Ang.	152	6.38 S	12.34 E
Lucan, On., Can.	190	43.11 N	81.24 W
Lucan, Ire.	48	53.22 N	6.27 W
Lucanas	248	14.36 S	74.15 W
Lucania □[9]	68	40.30 N	16.00 E
Lucania, Mount ∧	180	61.01 N	140.28 W
Lucano	152	11.16 S	21.38 E
Lucaogou	102	42.26 N	96.55 E
Lucapa	152	8.36 S	20.54 E
Lucas, Ia., U.S.	190	41.01 N	93.27 W
Lucas, Ks., U.S.	198	39.03 N	98.32 W
Lucas, Oh., U.S.	214	40.45 N	82.30 W
Lucas, Tx., U.S.	222	33.05 N	96.35 W
Lucas □[6]	214	41.39 N	83.32 W
Lucas González	252	32.24 S	59.33 W
Lucas Heights	274a	34.02 S	150.58 E
Lucas Valley	282	38.03 N	122.35 W
Lucasville	218	38.52 N	82.59 W
Lucban	116	14.06 N	121.33 E
Lucca	66	43.50 N	10.29 E
Lucca □[4]	64	44.02 N	10.27 E
Lucca Sicula	70	37.35 N	13.18 E
Lucé	50	48.26 N	1.28 E
Luce, Water of ≃	44	54.52 N	4.48 W
Lucea	241q	18.27 N	78.10 W
Luce Bay c	44	54.47 N	4.50 W
Luce Bayou ≃	222	30.03 N	95.07 W
Lucedale	194	30.55 N	88.35 W
Lucena, Esp.	34	37.24 N	4.29 W
Lucena, Pil.	116	13.56 N	121.37 E
Lucenay-l'Évêque	32	47.05 N	4.15 E
Luc-en-Diois	62	44.37 N	5.27 E
Lučenec	30	48.20 N	19.40 E
Lucens	58	46.42 N	6.50 E
Luceque	152	14.41 S	15.04 E
Lucera	68	41.30 N	15.20 E
Lucéram	62	43.53 N	7.22 E
Lucerne → Luzern, Schw.	58	47.03 N	8.18 E
Lucerne, Ca., U.S.	204	39.05 N	122.47 W
Lucerne, In., U.S.	216	40.52 N	86.24 W
Lucerne, Lake → Vierwaldstätter See ⊜	58	47.00 N	8.28 E
Lucerne Lake ⊜	228	34.31 N	116.57 W
Lucernemines	214	40.33 N	79.09 W
Lucerne Valley	228	34.26 N	116.58 W
Lucero	200	30.49 N	106.30 W
Lucero, Lake ⊜	200	32.42 N	106.25 W
Lučesa ≃	76	55.10 N	30.11 E
Luch	80	57.01 N	42.15 E
Luch ≃	80	56.14 N	42.25 E
Luchang	102	26.23 N	102.18 E
Luchena ≃	34	37.44 N	1.50 W
Lucheng, Zhg.	102	24.21 N	106.00 E
Lücheng, Zhg.	106	31.55 N	119.44 E
Lucheng, Zhg.	106	31.47 N	120.02 E
Luché-Pringé	50	47.42 N	0.05 E
Lucheringo ≃	154	11.43 S	36.17 E
Luchibe ≃	152	12.07 S	21.13 E
Luchico (Lushiko) ≃	152	6.13 S	19.40 E
Luchou	269d	25.05 N	121.28 E
Luchovicy	82	54.59 N	39.03 E
Lüchow, Dtsch.	54	52.58 N	11.10 E
Luchow → Luzhou, Zhg.	107	28.54 N	105.27 E
Lüchtringen	52	51.47 N	9.25 E
Luchuan	102	22.19 N	110.11 E
Luci	100	29.52 N	119.47 E
Luciara	250	10.27 S	50.32 W
Lucie ≃	250	3.35 N	57.38 W
Lucikou	100	28.56 N	116.04 E
Lučin	76	53.01 N	30.01 E
Lucinda, Austl.	166	18.32 S	146.20 E
Lucinda, Pa., U.S.	214	41.19 N	79.22 W
Lucindale	166	36.59 S	140.22 E
Lucio Vázquez	234	22.47 N	99.46 W

Lucipara, Kepulauan II	164	5.30 S	127.33 E
Lucira	152	13.51 S	12.31 E
Lucito	66	41.44 N	14.41 E
Luci Yu I	100	25.07 N	119.22 E
Luck	190	45.34 N	92.28 W
Luck, Mount ∧[2]	162	28.47 S	123.33 E
Lucka	54	51.06 N	12.20 E
Luckau	54	51.51 N	13.43 E
Luckeesarai	124	25.11 N	86.05 E
Luckenwalde	54	52.05 N	13.10 E
Luckey	214	41.27 N	83.29 W
Luckhoff	158	29.44 S	24.43 E
Luckiamute ≃	202	44.45 N	123.09 W
Luck Lake ⊜	184	51.05 N	107.07 W
Lucknow, On., Can.	190	43.57 N	81.31 W
Lucknow, India	124	26.51 N	80.55 E
Lucknow, Pa., U.S.	208	40.20 N	76.54 W
Lucknow Branch ≊	124	27.57 N	80.03 E
Lucky Lake	184	51.00 N	107.10 W
Lucky Peak Lake ⊜[1]	202	43.33 N	116.00 W
Luco dei Marsi	66	41.58 N	13.28 E
Lucomagno, Passo del)(	58	46.33 N	8.49 E
Luçon, Fr.	32	46.27 N	1.10 W
Lucon, Pa., U.S.	285	40.14 N	75.25 W
Luconha ≃	152	12.54 S	21.15 E
Lucun, Zhg.	98	36.12 N	118.01 E
Lucun, Zhg.	106	30.49 N	119.26 E
Lucunga ≃	152	6.57 S	12.48 E
Lucungu ≃	152	6.41 S	14.26 E
Lucusse	152	12.32 S	20.48 E
Lucy Creek	166	22.25 S	136.20 E
Lüda → Dalian	98	38.53 N	121.35 E
Luda Kamčija ≃	38	43.03 N	27.29 E
Ludao	89	43.51 N	129.19 E
Ludbreg	36	46.15 N	16.37 E
Luddan	123	29.54 N	72.34 E
Luddenden	262	53.44 N	1.56 W
Luddenham	274a	33.53 S	150.41 E
Luddesdown	260	51.22 N	0.24 E
Lüdenscheid	56	51.13 N	7.38 E
Lüder ≃	56	50.31 N	9.27 E
Lüderitz, Dtsch.	54	52.30 N	11.44 E
Lüderitz, Namibia	156	26.38 S	15.10 E
Lüderitz □[5]	156	26.30 S	15.45 E
Lüdersdorf	54	53.47 N	10.46 E
Ludgershall	42	51.16 N	1.37 W
Ludgo	40	58.55 N	17.08 E
Ludhiāna	123	30.54 N	75.51 E
Ludian	102	27.11 N	103.33 E
Luding	102	29.55 N	102.15 E
Lüdinghausen	52	51.46 N	7.26 E
Ludington	190	43.57 N	86.27 W
Ludingtonville	210	41.29 N	73.39 W
L'udinovo	76	53.52 N	34.27 E
L'udkovo	76	54.36 N	34.43 E
Ludlam Bay c	208	39.10 N	74.42 W
Ludlow, Eng., U.K.	42	52.22 N	2.43 W
Ludlow, Il., U.S.	216	40.23 N	88.08 W
Ludlow, Ky., U.S.	218	39.05 N	84.32 W
Ludlow, Ma., U.S.	207	42.09 N	72.28 W
Ludlow, Pa., U.S.	214	41.43 N	78.56 W
Ludlow, Vt., U.S.	188	43.23 N	72.42 W
Ludlow Falls	218	40.00 N	84.20 W
Ludlowville	210	42.33 N	76.32 W
Ludogorie ◆[1]	38	43.46 N	26.56 E
Ludonghe	102	25.53 N	103.33 E
Ludoni	76	58.12 N	29.21 E
Ludowici	192	31.42 N	81.44 W
Luduș	38	46.29 N	24.05 E
Ludvika	40	60.09 N	15.11 E
Ludwigkanal ≊	60	49.05 N	11.27 E
Ludwigsburg	56	48.53 N	9.11 E
Ludwigsfelde	54	52.17 N	13.16 E
Ludwigsfelder-Heide ◆[3]	264a	52.18 N	13.14 E
Ludwigshafen	56	49.29 N	8.26 E
Ludwigshafen am Bodensee	58	47.49 N	9.03 E
Ludwigslust	54	53.19 N	11.30 E
Ludwigsort → Laduškin	76	54.36 N	20.11 E
Ludwigsstadt	54	50.30 N	11.23 E
Ludwigstein, Burg ⊥	56	51.20 N	9.55 E
Ludza	76	56.33 N	27.43 E
Lue	170	32.39 S	149.51 E
Luebo	152	5.21 S	21.25 E
Lueders	196	32.48 N	99.37 W
Lueg, Pass)(	64	47.34 N	13.12 E
Lueki	154	3.22 S	25.51 E
Luele ≃	152	7.55 S	20.09 E
Luemba	154	3.42 S	28.40 E
Luembe (Lubembe) ≃, Afr.	152	6.37 S	21.05 E
Luembé ≃, Zaïre	154	6.43 S	24.11 E
Luena, Ang.	152	11.47 S	19.52 E
Luena, Zaïre	154	9.27 S	25.47 E
Luena ≃, Ang.	152	12.31 S	22.34 E
Luena ≃, Zam.	152	14.45 S	23.25 E
Luena Flats ≡	152	14.50 S	23.20 E
Luengué ≃	152	16.54 S	21.52 E
Luenha (Ruenya) ≃	154	16.24 S	33.48 E
Lueo ≃	152	9.06 S	23.51 E
Luepa	246	5.43 N	61.31 W
Lueta	152	7.19 S	22.06 E
Lueta ≃	152	7.04 S	21.40 E
Lueyang	102	33.20 N	106.10 E
Lüfangsicun	104	41.25 N	123.22 E
Lufeng, Zhg.	100	22.57 N	115.38 E
Lufeng, Zhg.	102	25.07 N	102.07 E
Lufico	152	6.24 S	13.23 E
Lufira ≃	154	8.16 S	26.27 E
Lufkin	222	31.20 N	94.43 W
Luftekopf ∧[2]	56	50.05 N	7.37 E
Lufubu ≃	154	8.36 S	30.47 E
Lufuidje ≃	152	12.52 S	22.47 E
Lufupa	154	10.37 S	24.56 E
Lufupa ≃	154	14.37 S	26.12 E
Luga	76	58.44 N	29.52 E
Luga ≃	76	59.40 N	28.18 E
Lugagnano Val d'Arda	62	44.49 N	9.50 E
Lugang, Zhg.	100	31.17 N	118.22 E
Lugang, Zhg.	100	27.23 N	115.36 E
Luganga	154	7.31 S	35.32 E
Lugano	58	46.01 N	8.58 E
Lugano, Lago di ⊜	58	46.00 N	9.00 E
Lugansk → Luhans'k	83	48.34 N	39.20 E
Luganville	175f	15.32 S	167.10 E
Lugards Falls ʟ	154	3.03 S	38.42 E
Lugareño	240p	21.33 N	77.28 W
Lugarno	274a	33.59 S	151.03 E
Lugau	54	50.44 N	12.44 E
Lügde	52	51.57 N	9.15 E
Lugela	154	16.25 S	36.43 E
Lugenda	154	12.30 S	37.43 E
Lugenda ≃	154	11.25 S	38.33 E
Lugg ≃	42	52.02 N	2.38 W
Luggarus → Locarno	58	46.10 N	8.48 E
Luginino	76	57.43 N	35.17 E
Lugnano in Teverina	66	42.34 N	12.20 E
Lugnaquillia Mountain ∧	48	52.58 N	6.27 W
Lugnås	40	58.39 N	13.42 E
Lugny	58	46.28 N	4.49 E
Lugo, Esp.	34	43.00 N	7.34 W
Lugo, It.	66	44.25 N	11.54 E
Lugo □[4]	34	43.00 N	7.25 W
Lugoj	38	45.41 N	21.54 E
Lugongshi	106	31.38 N	121.12 E
Lugos → Lugoj	38	45.41 N	21.54 E
Lugouqiao	105	39.51 N	116.13 E
Lugovaja Subbota	86	59.52 N	69.45 E
Lugovoj, Kaz.	85	42.56 N	72.45 E
Lugovoj, Ross.	86	59.44 N	65.55 E

≃	River	Fluß	Río	Rivière	Rio
≊	Canal	Kanal	Canal	Canal	Canal
ʟ	Waterfall, Rapids	Wasserfall, Stromschnellen	Cascada, Rápidos	Chute d'eau, Rapides	Cascata, Rápidos
)(	Strait	Meeresstraße	Estrecho	Détroit	Estreito
c	Bay, Gulf	Bucht, Golf	Bahía, Golfo	Baie, Golfe	Baía, Golfo
⊜	Lake, Lakes	See, Seen	Lago, Lagos	Lac, Lacs	Lago, Lagos
≡	Swamp	Sumpf	Pantano	Marais	Pântano
⛉	Ice Features, Glacier	Eis- und Gletscherformen	Accidentes Glaciales	Formes glaciaires	Acidentes glaciares
⊤	Other Hydrographic Features	Andere Hydrographische Objekte	Otros Elementos Hidrográficos	Autres données hydrographiques	Outros acidentes hidrográficos
✢	Submarine Features	Untermeerische Objekte	Accidentes Submarinos	Formes de relief sous-marin	Acidentes submarinos
□	Political Unit	Politische Einheit	Unidad Politica	Entité politique	Unidade política
ʊ	Cultural Institution	Kulturelle Institution	Institución Cultural	Institution culturelle	Instituição cultural
⊥	Historical Site	Historische Stätte	Sitio Histórico	Site historique	Sitio histórico
♠	Recreational Site	Erholungs- und Ferienort	Sitio de Recreo	Centre de loisirs	Area de Lazer
⊠	Airport	Flughafen	Aeropuerto	Aéroport	Aeroporto
■	Military Installation	Militäranlage	Instalación Militar	Installation militaire	Instalação militar
◆	Miscellaneous	Verschiedenes	Misceláneo	Divers	Diversos

ENGLISH / DEUTSCH

Name	Page	Lat.°′	Long.°′
Lugovoje	85	42.55 N	72.43 E
Lugovskij	88	58.02 N	112.54 E
Lugovskoje	80	50.38 N	46.28 E
Lugu	102	28.21 N	102.09 E
Lugulu ≃	154	2.17 S	26.32 E
Lugunga ∧	154	6.47 S	36.19 E
Luguru	154	2.55 S	33.58 E
Lugus Island I	116	5.41 N	120.50 E
Luhan' ≃	83	48.37 N	39.27 E
Luhanchyk ≃	83	48.35 N	39.32 E
Luhanka	26	61.47 N	25.42 E
Luhans'k	83	48.34 N	39.20 E
Luhans'k □[4]	78	49.00 N	39.00 E
Luhans'ke	83	48.26 N	38.15 E
Luhe	60	49.35 N	12.09 E
Luhe ≃	52	53.18 N	10.11 E
Lühedian	100	32.33 N	114.28 E
Lühmannsdorf	54	54.00 N	13.38 E
Luhombero ≃	154	8.24 S	37.12 E
Luhsien → Luzhou	107	28.54 N	105.27 E
Luhuo	102	31.26 N	100.48 E
Luhyny	78	51.04 N	28.24 E
Lui ≃, Ang.	152	8.41 S	17.56 E
Lui ≃, Zam.	152	16.21 S	23.18 E
Lui, Beinn ∧	46	56.24 N	4.49 W
Luia	152	8.26 S	21.45 E
Luia (Ruya) ≃, Afr.	154	16.34 S	33.12 E
Luia ≃, Ang.	152	8.24 S	21.42 E
Lúia ≃, Moç.	154	15.34 S	32.58 E
Luiana	152	17.23 S	23.03 E
Luiana ≃	152	17.27 S	23.14 E
Luichart, Loch ⊜	46	57.37 N	4.46 W
Luido	156	21.31 S	34.41 E
Luie ≃	152	4.33 S	17.41 E
Luik → Liège	56	50.38 N	5.34 E
Luilaka ≃	152	0.52 S	20.12 E
Luilu ≃	152	6.22 S	23.50 E
Luimbale	152	12.15 S	15.19 E
Luimneach → Limerick	48	52.40 N	8.38 W
Luing I	46	56.13 N	5.40 W
Luino	58	46.00 N	8.44 E
Luio ≃	152	13.15 S	21.39 E
Luipaardsvlei	273d	26.16 S	27.42 E
Luiro ≃	24	67.08 N	27.29 E
Luisant	50	48.25 N	1.29 E
Luís Correia	250	2.53 S	41.40 W
Luisen-Berg ∧[2]	264a	52.27 N	13.07 E
Luisenthal	54	50.47 N	10.43 E
Luís Gomes	250	6.25 S	38.23 W
Luis Guillón	288	34.48 S	58.27 W
Luishia	154	11.10 S	27.02 E
Luis Moya, Méx.	234	22.25 N	102.15 W
Luis Moya, Méx.	234	23.05 N	103.56 W
Luis Muñoz Marin, Aeropuerto Internacional ⊠	240m	18.27 N	66.00 W
Luis Peña, Cayo de I	240m	18.18 N	65.20 W
Luis Pereira, Arroyo ≃	258	34.33 S	57.02 W
Luita	152	8.04 S	19.25 E
Luitpold Coast ⊥[2]	9	78.30 S	32.00 W
Luiza	152	7.12 S	22.25 E
Luiza ≃	152	7.35 S	22.40 E
Luizavo ≃	152	11.42 S	23.12 E
Luizi	154	6.03 S	27.28 E
Luiziânia	255	21.41 S	50.17 W
Luján, Arg.	252	33.03 S	68.52 W
Luján, Arg.	252	32.22 S	65.57 W
Luján, Arg.	258	34.34 S	59.07 W
Luján ≃	288	34.26 S	58.32 W
Lujia, Zhg.	106	31.15 N	121.37 E
Lujia, Zhg.	106	31.19 N	121.03 E
Lujia, Zhg.	269b	31.22 N	121.18 E
Lujiabang	106	31.20 N	121.01 E
Lujiachang	107	30.14 N	105.34 E
Lujiagangzi	104	42.05 N	122.59 E
Lujiang	100	31.14 N	117.17 E
Lujiao	100	29.10 N	112.52 E
Lujiaoxi	107	28.55 N	105.48 E
Lujiaqiao, Zhg.	106	31.47 N	120.27 E
Lujiaqiao, Zhg.	107	28.50 N	106.21 E
Lujiatun, Zhg.	98	40.14 N	122.11 E
Lujiatun, Zhg.	104	41.58 N	122.38 E
Lujiatun, Zhg.	104	42.18 N	124.15 E
Lujiatun, Zhg.	104	41.10 N	121.56 E
Lujiazhou	100	28.16 N	114.35 E
L'uk	80	56.55 N	52.48 E
Lukachukai Wash V	200	36.39 N	109.36 W
Lukačok	89	53.03 N	132.16 E
Lukala	152	5.31 S	14.32 E
Lukang	100	24.03 N	120.25 E
Lukanga, Zaïre	152	1.00 S	18.08 E
Lukanga, Zaïre	152	1.41 S	18.09 E
Lukanga Swamp ☷	154	14.25 S	27.45 E
Luk'anovo	82	54.52 N	37.25 E
Lukašin	84	40.12 N	44.01 E
Lukaškin Jar	86	60.20 N	78.24 E
Luke, Mount ∧	162	27.13 S	116.48 E
Luke Air Force Base ■	200	33.32 N	112.22 W
Lukenie ≃	152	2.44 S	18.09 E
Lukens, Mount ∧	280	34.16 N	118.14 W
Lukeville	200	31.52 N	112.48 W
Luki	76	53.29 N	26.15 E
Lukino, Ross.	82	55.26 N	37.04 E
Lukino, Ross.	82	55.50 N	36.49 E
Lukiv	78	51.13 N	24.19 E
Lukka	140	14.33 N	23.42 E
Luknovo	80	56.12 N	42.03 E
Lukojanov	80	55.02 N	44.30 E
Lukolela, Zaïre	152	5.23 S	24.32 E
Lukolela, Zaïre	152	1.03 S	17.12 E
Lukong	107	29.31 N	105.39 E
Lukoshi ≃	152	10.05 S	22.59 E
Lukosi	154	18.30 S	26.30 E
Lukoškino	82	55.19 N	37.16 E
Lukou, Zhg.	100	27.14 N	114.04 E
Lukou, Zhg.	106	31.48 N	118.52 E
Lukoupu	100	29.30 N	113.26 E
Lukouyu	100	28.24 N	113.18 E
Lukovit	38	43.12 N	24.10 E
Lukovskaja	80	50.35 N	41.52 E
Łuków	30	51.56 N	22.23 E
Lükqün	86	42.44 N	89.42 E
Lukuga ≃	154	5.40 S	26.55 E
Lukula	152	5.23 S	12.57 E
Lukula ≃, Afr.	152	5.08 S	12.28 E
Lukula ≃, Zaïre	152	4.13 S	17.58 E
Lukuledi ≃	154	10.05 S	39.42 E
Lukulu	152	14.25 S	23.12 E
Lukulu ≃	154	10.56 S	31.05 E
Lukumburu	154	9.45 S	35.09 E
Lukunga ≃	273b	4.25 S	15.14 E
Lukuni	152	5.52 S	17.11 E
Lukusashi ≃	154	14.38 S	30.00 E
Lukusuzi National Park ♦	154	12.50 S	32.35 E
Lula, It.	71	40.28 N	9.29 E
Lula, Ms., U.S.	194	34.27 N	90.28 W
Lula, Zaïre	152	5.22 S	16.02 E
Luleå	26	65.34 N	22.10 E
Luleälven ≃	24	65.35 N	22.03 E
Lüleburgaz	130	41.24 N	27.21 E
Lules	252	26.56 S	65.21 W
Luliang	102	25.05 N	103.36 E
Lüliang Shan ⋀⋀	102	37.25 N	111.20 E
Luliāni	123	31.15 N	74.25 E
Luliao	269d	25.07 N	121.39 E
Luling	222	29.40 N	97.38 W
Lullingstone Castle ⊥	260	51.21 N	0.12 E
Lulo ≃	152	9.25 S	18.14 E
Lulong	98	39.54 N	118.50 E
Lulonga	152	0.37 N	18.23 E
Lulonga ≃	152	0.43 N	18.23 E
Lulu ≃	152	1.18 N	23.42 E
Lulua ≃	152	5.02 S	21.07 E
Luluabourg → Kananga	152	5.54 S	22.25 E
Lulu Island I, B.C., Can.	224	49.09 N	123.05 W
Lulu Island I, Ak., U.S.	182	55.28 N	133.30 W
Luluo	98	37.06 N	113.58 E
Lulworth, Mount ∧	162	26.53 S	117.42 E
Lumai	152	13.31 S	21.21 E
Lumajang	115a	8.08 S	113.13 E
Lumajangdong Co ⊜	120	34.00 N	81.45 E
Lumaku, Gunong ∧	112	4.52 N	115.38 E
Lumaling	120	29.53 N	92.37 E
Lumb	262	53.42 N	1.58 W
Lumbala ≃	152	12.38 S	22.34 E
Lumbala Kaquengue	152	12.39 S	22.34 E
Lumbala N'guimbo	152	14.08 S	21.25 E
Lumbangaraga	114	1.53 N	99.04 E
Lumbanlobu	114	2.31 N	99.08 E
Lumbe ≃	152	16.42 S	23.42 E
Lumber ≃	192	34.12 N	79.10 W
Lumber City	192	31.55 N	82.40 W
Lumberport	188	39.22 N	80.20 W
Lumberton, Ms., U.S.	194	31.00 N	89.27 W
Lumberton, N.J., U.S.	285	39.57 N	74.48 W
Lumberton, N.C., U.S.	192	34.37 N	79.00 W
Lumberton, Tx., U.S.	194	30.16 N	94.10 W
Lumbinī □[8]	124	27.45 N	83.30 E
Lumbis	112	4.18 N	116.15 E
Lumbo	154	15.00 S	40.44 E
Lumbovka	24	67.44 N	40.30 E
Lumbrales	34	40.56 N	6.43 W
Lumbrein	58	46.41 N	9.08 E
Lumbres	50	50.42 N	2.08 E
Lumbwa	154	0.12 S	35.28 E
Lumby	182	50.15 N	118.58 W
Lumding	120	25.45 N	93.10 E
Lumege ≃	152	11.55 S	20.58 E
Lumerau ≃	116	5.21 N	118.53 E
Lumi	164	3.29 S	142.02 E
Lumiei ≃	64	46.24 N	12.51 E
Luminárias	256	21.30 S	44.54 W
Luminosa	256	22.35 S	45.38 W
Lumintao ≃	116	12.43 N	120.55 E
Lummen	56	50.59 N	5.12 E
Lummi Bay ⊂	224	48.46 N	122.41 W
Lummi Indian Reservation ◆[4]	224	48.48 N	122.38 W
Lummi Island	224	48.42 N	122.40 W
Lummi Island I	224	48.42 N	122.40 W
Lumphanan	46	57.07 N	2.41 W
Lumphăt	110	13.30 N	106.59 E
Lumphini Park ♦	269a	13.44 N	100.33 E
Lumpkin	192	32.03 N	84.47 W
Lumpun ≃	80	57.01 N	51.22 E
Lumsån ≃	40	59.59 N	15.26 E
Lumsås	41	55.57 N	11.31 E
Lumsden, Nf., Can.	186	49.19 N	53.37 W
Lumsden, Sk., Can.	184	50.34 N	104.53 W
Lumsden, N.Z.	172	45.44 S	168.27 E
Lumsden, Scot., U.K.	46	57.15 N	2.52 W
Lumsheden	40	60.43 N	16.15 E
Lums Pond State Park ♦	208	39.34 N	75.43 W
Lumu, Indon.	112	2.11 S	119.09 E
Lumu, Zhg.	106	31.22 N	120.37 E
Lumuna	154	3.46 S	26.24 E
Lumuna ≃	152	16.59 S	21.25 E
Lumut, Indon.	114	1.33 N	98.56 E
Lumut, Malay.	114	4.14 N	100.38 E
Lumut, Tanjung ›	112	3.50 S	105.57 E
Lumwana	154	11.50 S	25.10 E
Lün, Mong.	88	47.24 N	102.52 E
Lün, Mong.	88	47.52 N	105.15 E
Luna, Pil.	116	16.51 N	120.23 E
Luna, Pil.	116	18.18 N	121.21 E
Luna ≃	246	4.32 S	60.41 W
Lunada Bay ⊂	280	33.46 N	118.25 W
Lunain ≃	50	48.20 N	2.47 E
Lunamatrona	71	39.39 N	8.54 E
Lunan	102	24.49 N	103.16 E
Lunan Bay ⊂	46	56.39 N	2.28 W
Lunano	66	43.44 N	12.26 E
Luna Pier	216	41.48 N	83.26 W
Lūnāvāda	120	23.08 N	73.37 E
Luncarty	46	56.27 N	3.28 W
Lund, B.C., Can.	182	49.58 N	124.44 W
Lund, Sve.	41	55.42 N	13.11 E
Lund, Nv., U.S.	204	38.51 N	115.00 W
Lunda ≃, Ang.	152	6.07 S	13.52 E
L'unda ≃, Ross.	80	56.32 N	46.03 E
Lundåkrabukten ⊂	41	55.48 N	12.53 E
Lundale	188	37.48 N	81.44 W
Lunda Norte □[5]	152	8.45 S	19.45 E
Lundar	184	50.42 N	98.02 W
Lunda Sul □[5]	152	10.00 S	20.30 E
Lundazi	154	12.19 S	33.13 E
Lundby	41	55.07 N	11.53 E
Lunde	41	55.29 N	10.21 E
Lundeborg	41	55.08 N	10.47 E
Lunden	41	54.20 N	9.01 E
Lunderskov	41	55.29 N	9.18 E
Lundevatn ⊜	26	58.22 N	6.36 E
Lundi ≃	154	21.43 S	32.34 E
Lundsberg	40	59.30 N	14.10 E
Lundsfjärden ⊜	40	59.38 N	14.41 E
Lundy I	42	51.10 N	4.40 W
Lundys Lane	214	41.53 N	80.21 W
Lune ≃	44	54.02 N	2.50 W
Lüneburg	52	53.15 N	10.23 E
Lüneburg □[5]	52	53.15 N	10.00 E
Lüneburger Heide ◆[1]	52	53.10 N	10.20 E
Lunel	62	43.41 N	4.08 E
Lünen	52	51.36 N	7.32 E
Lunenburg, N.S., Can.	186	44.23 N	64.19 W
Lunenburg, Ma., U.S.	207	42.35 N	71.43 W
Lunenburg, Va., U.S.	192	36.57 N	78.15 W
Luneray	50	49.50 N	0.55 E
Lünern	263	51.33 N	7.46 E
Lunéville	56	48.36 N	6.30 E
Lunga I	46	56.13 N	5.42 W
Lunga ≃, Ang.	152	5.59 S	16.20 E
Lunga ≃, Zam.	154	14.34 S	26.25 E
Lungälven ≃	40	59.34 N	14.10 E
Lunga Reservoir ⊜[1]	208	38.32 N	77.28 W
Lungau ◆[1]	64	47.07 N	13.39 E
Lungavilla	62	45.02 N	9.04 E
Lungch'i → Zhangzhou	100	24.33 N	117.39 E
Lunge	152	12.12 S	16.05 E
Lunge'nake	120	31.45 N	85.55 E
Lungern	58	46.47 N	8.10 E
Lunggar	120	31.10 N	84.00 E
Lunghezza ◆[8]	267a	41.55 N	12.40 E
Lungi	150	8.38 N	13.13 W
Lunglei	120	22.53 N	92.44 E
Lungro	68	39.44 N	16.07 E
Lungsang	124	29.51 N	88.41 E
Lungt'an	100	24.52 N	121.12 E
Lungué-Bungo (Lungwebungu) ≃	152	14.19 S	23.14 E
Lunguya	154	3.23 S	32.24 E
Lungwebungu (Lungué-Bungo) ≃	152	14.19 S	23.14 E
Lūni	120	26.00 N	73.00 E
Lūni ≃	120	24.41 N	71.15 E
Luni ⊥	64	44.04 N	10.01 E
Lunia-Bubi	154	7.30 S	24.49 E
Lunigiana ◆[1]	64	44.15 N	9.50 E
Lunin	76	52.18 N	26.38 E
Luninec	76	52.15 N	26.48 E
Lunino, Ross.	80	53.35 N	45.14 E
Lunino, Ross.	82	54.09 N	38.29 E
Lunjiao	100	22.53 N	113.13 E
Lūnkaransar	120	28.29 N	73.44 E
Lunnaja, gora ∧	180	68.14 N	174.20 E
Lunndörrsfjällen ∧	26	63.00 N	13.00 E
Lunno	76	53.27 N	24.16 E
Lunongzha	106	31.59 N	120.55 E
Lunsar	150	8.41 N	12.32 W
Lunsemfwa ≃	154	14.54 S	30.12 E
Lunt	262	53.31 N	2.59 W
Lunteren	52	52.05 N	5.37 E
Lunyuk	115b	8.57 S	117.14 E
Lunz am See	61	47.51 N	15.03 E
Lunzenau	54	50.58 N	12.45 E
Lunzhen	98	36.47 N	116.34 E
Luo ≃, Zhg.	102	34.42 N	110.15 E
Luo ≃, Zhg.	102	34.48 N	113.04 E
Luoba, Zhg.	100	24.51 N	114.13 E
Luoba, Zhg.	107	29.08 N	106.11 E
Luobei (Fengxiang)	89	47.34 N	130.50 E
Luobo	102	28.22 N	101.38 E
Luobu	102	24.30 N	109.40 E
Luobumiao	102	40.19 N	107.30 E
Luochanghe	100	31.01 N	117.18 E
Luocheng, Zhg.	102	24.51 N	108.59 E
Luocheng, Zhg.	107	29.23 N	104.01 E
Luochuan	102	35.55 N	109.26 E
Luoci	102	25.19 N	102.18 E
Luodian	106	31.25 N	121.20 E
Luoding	102	22.47 N	111.31 E
Luoduzhen	107	30.22 N	106.35 E
Luofa	105	39.25 N	116.50 E
Luofang, Zhg.	100	28.40 N	115.04 E
Luofang, Zhg.	100	27.52 N	115.06 E
Luofu, Zaïre	154	0.10 S	29.14 E
Luofu, Zhg.	100	24.32 N	115.35 E
Luogang, Zhg.	100	23.11 N	113.30 E
Luogang, Zhg.	100	24.25 N	115.38 E
Luogosanto	71	41.03 N	9.13 E
Luoguhe	89	53.18 N	121.30 E
Luohan Shan ∧	100	25.51 N	119.13 E
Luohe	100	33.35 N	114.01 E
Luoheya	98	35.46 N	118.54 E
Luohua	100	26.35 N	118.43 E
Luoji	100	32.06 N	117.16 E
Luojiachang	107	30.49 N	106.32 E
Luojiang	102	31.21 N	104.28 E
Luojiatang	106	30.18 N	120.13 E
Luojiatun, Zhg.	98	40.11 N	118.34 E
Luojiatun, Zhg.	104	42.06 N	122.44 E
Luojiatun, Zhg.	104	40.55 N	122.04 E
Luojiawei	100	26.55 N	115.02 E
Luoke	100	24.07 N	114.28 E
Luokeng	100	24.32 N	113.23 E
Luokou, Zhg.	100	28.54 N	117.24 E
Luokou, Zhg.	100	25.46 N	115.39 E
Luolong	107	28.49 N	104.46 E
L'Uomo di Cagna ∧	71	41.33 N	9.04 E
Luonan	102	34.05 N	110.04 E
Luoning	102	34.25 N	111.42 E
Luoping	102	24.59 N	104.21 E
Luoqi	102	29.48 N	106.56 E
Luoqiao	100	26.28 N	119.01 E
Luoquanzhen	107	29.50 N	104.31 E
Luoshan, Zhg.	100	32.13 N	114.32 E
Luoshan, Zhg.	100	29.41 N	113.18 E
Luoshan, Zhg.	105	39.55 N	117.33 E
Luoshe, Zhg.	106	31.39 N	120.11 E
Luoshe, Zhg.	106	30.41 N	120.04 E
Luoshuihe	98	39.27 N	114.19 E
Luossa ≃	152	8.24 S	17.03 E
Luotian	100	30.48 N	115.22 E
Luotuodian	100	32.13 N	113.49 E
Luotuoqiao	100	29.56 N	121.32 E
Luotuo Shan ∧	104	42.14 N	121.42 E
Luowenba	102	31.48 N	107.48 E
Luowenyu	105	40.16 N	117.57 E
Luoxi	100	29.05 N	114.58 E
Luoxiao Shan ⋀⋀	100	26.00 N	114.00 E
Luoyang (Loyang), Zhg.	102	34.41 N	112.28 E
Luoyang, Zhg.	106	31.39 N	120.05 E
Luoyuan	100	26.31 N	119.32 E
Luoyuan Wan ⊂	100	26.25 N	119.43 E
Luoyukou	102	38.23 N	110.43 E
Luozhexi	107	29.02 N	103.54 E
Luozi	152	4.57 S	14.08 E
Lupala	156	17.50 S	19.06 E
Lupani	154	18.54 S	27.44 E
Lupao	116	15.53 N	120.54 E
Lupar ≃	112	1.30 N	111.00 E
Łupawa	30	54.26 N	17.24 E
Lupberg	60	49.09 N	11.45 E
Lupembe	154	9.15 S	35.15 E
Lupeni	38	45.22 N	23.13 E
Lupire	152	14.36 S	19.29 E
Lupiro	154	8.23 S	36.40 E
Lupon	116	6.54 N	126.00 E
Luppa	54	51.20 N	12.57 E
Luputa	152	7.10 S	23.42 E
Luqiao, Zhg.	100	32.34 N	117.14 E
Luqiao, Zhg.	100	28.35 N	121.22 E
Luqu	102	34.41 N	102.22 E
Luque	34	37.33 N	4.16 W
Luquillo	240m	18.22 N	65.43 W
Luquillo, Sierra de ⋀⋀	240m	18.17 N	65.47 W
Lūrah ≃	120	31.33 N	66.33 E
Luray	188	38.39 N	78.27 W
Lure	58	47.41 N	6.30 E
Lure, Montagne de ⋀⋀	62	44.07 N	5.47 E
Lureco ≃	154	12.28 S	37.40 E
Luremo	152	8.31 S	17.50 E
Lurgan	48	54.28 N	6.20 W
Luribay	248	17.06 S	67.39 W
Lurigancho	286d	12.02 S	77.01 W
Lurín	248	12.17 S	76.52 W
Lúrio	154	13.35 S	40.30 E
Lúrio ≃	154	13.35 S	40.32 E
Lurisia	62	44.18 N	7.42 E
Lurnea	274a	33.56 S	150.54 E
Lurö I	26	58.48 N	13.14 E
Lürrip ◆[8]	263	51.12 N	6.28 E
Lusahunga	154	2.52 S	31.15 E
Lusaka, Zaïre	154	7.10 S	29.27 E
Lusaka, Zam.	154	15.25 S	28.17 E
Lusaka □[4]	154	15.25 S	29.00 E
Lusakert	84	40.23 N	44.36 E
Lusambo	152	4.58 S	23.27 E
Lusancay Islands and Reefs II	164	8.25 S	150.20 E
Lusanga	152	4.50 S	18.44 E
Lusangaye	154	4.54 S	26.00 E
Lusangi	154	4.37 S	27.08 E
Luscar	182	53.04 N	117.24 W
Luseke	152	2.51 S	23.08 E
Luseland	184	52.05 N	109.24 W
Lusen ∧	60	48.56 N	13.31 E
Lusenga Plain National Park ♦	154	9.30 S	29.10 E
Lusengo	152	1.46 N	19.29 E
Luserna San Giovanni	62	44.48 N	7.15 E
Lush, Mount ∧	164	17.02 S	127.30 E
Lushan, Zhg.	100	33.45 N	112.53 E
Lushan, Zhg.	102	30.15 N	102.58 E
Lu Shan ∧	100	29.31 N	115.58 E
Lu Shan ⋀⋀	98	36.05 N	118.05 E
Lushanguanliju	100	29.33 N	115.58 E
Lushi	102	34.05 N	111.01 E
Lushiko (Luchico) ≃	152	6.13 S	19.40 E
Lüshikou	100	29.16 N	120.17 E
Lushnje	38	40.56 N	19.42 E
Lushoto	154	4.47 S	38.17 E
Lushui	102	26.00 N	98.51 E
Lüshun (Port Arthur)	98	38.48 N	121.16 E
Lüsi	106	32.03 N	121.36 E
Lusi ≃	115a	7.05 S	110.55 E
Lusiana	64	45.47 N	11.34 E
Lusignan	32	46.26 N	0.07 E
Lusignan, Lac ⊜	206	46.40 N	74.09 W
Lusigny-sur-Barse	50	48.15 N	4.16 E
Lusikisiki	158	31.25 S	29.30 E
L'usino	76	52.38 N	26.31 E
Lusk, Ire.	48	53.32 N	6.10 W
Lusk, Wy., U.S.	200	42.45 N	104.27 W
Lus-la-Croix-Haute	62	44.40 N	5.42 E
Lusongwa	152	12.58 S	24.16 E
Luspebryggan	24	67.01 N	19.51 E
Lussac-les-Châteaux	32	46.24 N	0.44 E
Lussan	62	44.09 N	4.22 E
Luṣṣān, Wādī V	132	30.30 N	34.18 E
Lustenau	58	47.26 N	9.39 E
Luster	26	61.26 N	7.24 E
Lustin	56	50.23 N	4.53 E
Lustrafjorden ⊂[2]	26	61.20 N	7.22 E
Lüstringen	52	52.16 N	8.08 E
Lusutfu (Maputo) (Great Usutu) ≃	158	26.11 S	32.42 E
Luswishi ≃	154	13.55 S	27.24 E
Lūt, Dasht-e ◆[2]	128	32.00 N	58.00 E
Lü-ta → Dalian	98	38.53 N	121.35 E
L'uta ≃	76	58.37 N	28.40 E
Lutago (Luttach)	64	46.57 N	11.55 E
Lutai	100	33.32 N	115.03 E
Lütan, Zhg.	98	34.07 N	114.27 E
Lütan, Zhg.	100	28.57 N	119.46 E
Lutang	100	25.39 N	112.46 E
Lutao	116	10.00 N	124.04 E
Lü Tao I	100	22.40 N	121.29 E
Lutcher	194	30.02 N	90.41 W
Lute	284c	39.04 N	77.03 W
Lutembo	152	13.26 S	21.16 E
Lutembo ≃	152	12.03 S	22.15 E
Lutesville	194	37.18 N	89.58 W
Lutéte ≃	152	9.21 S	15.14 E
Lutexu ≃	273b	4.24 S	15.12 E
Lütgendortmund ◆[8]	263	51.30 N	7.21 E
Luthe	52	52.26 N	9.28 E
Luther, Mi., U.S.	190	44.02 N	85.40 W
Luther, Ok., U.S.	196	35.39 N	97.11 W
Luther Lake ⊜	212	43.55 N	80.26 W
Luthersburg	214	41.03 N	78.43 W
Lutherville-Timonium	284b	39.25 N	76.37 W
Luthrie	46	56.21 N	3.05 W
Luti	175e	7.14 S	156.59 E
Lutian, Zhg.	100	26.33 N	114.38 E
Lütian, Zhg.	100	23.48 N	113.56 E
Lütjenburg	54	54.17 N	10.35 E
Lütjensee	52	53.39 N	10.22 E
Luton, Eng., U.K.	42	51.53 N	0.25 W
Luton, Eng., U.K.	260	51.22 N	0.32 E
Lutong	112	4.28 N	114.00 E
Lutosn'a ≃	82	56.26 N	36.52 E
Lutou	100	32.16 N	112.53 E
Lutry	58	46.30 N	6.41 E
Lutshi	154	4.09 S	26.30 E
Lutshima ≃	152	5.22 S	18.59 E
Luts'k	78	50.44 N	25.20 E
Luttach → Lutago	64	46.57 N	11.55 E
Lutter am Barenberge	52	51.59 N	10.16 E
Lutterbach	58	47.46 N	7.17 E
Lutterworth	42	52.28 N	1.10 W
Lüttich → Liège	56	50.38 N	5.34 E
Luttrell	192	36.11 N	83.44 W
Lüttringhausen ◆[8]	263	51.13 N	7.14 E
Lutuai ≃	152	12.33 S	20.16 E
Lutuhyne	83	48.24 N	39.13 E
Lutz	220	28.09 N	82.27 W
Lützel	56	50.58 N	8.10 E
Lutzelbourg	56	48.44 N	7.15 E
Lützelflüh	58	47.00 N	7.41 E
Lützen	54	51.15 N	12.08 E
Lutzerath	56	50.07 N	7.00 E
Lutz Hill	284b	39.20 N	76.32 W
Lützow	54	53.40 N	11.11 E
Lützow-Holm Bay ⊂	9	69.10 S	37.30 E
Lutzputs	158	28.03 S	20.40 E
Lützschena	54	51.23 N	12.16 E
Lutzville	158	31.33 S	18.22 E
Luud, Waadi V	144	10.17 N	50.14 E
Luuq	144	3.48 N	42.33 E
Luus	102	45.30 N	105.45 E
Luverne, Al., U.S.	194	31.42 N	86.15 W
Lu Verne, Ia., U.S.	190	42.54 N	94.04 W
Luverne, Mn., U.S.	198	43.39 N	96.12 W
Luvo	152	5.51 S	14.05 E
Luvo ≃	152	10.18 S	17.08 E
Luvua	154	8.48 S	25.19 E
Lúvua ≃, Ang.	152	11.57 S	22.30 E
Luvua ≃, Zaïre	154	6.46 S	26.58 E
Luvuvhu ≃	156	22.40 S	30.55 E
Luwegu ≃	154	8.31 S	37.23 E
Luwingu	154	10.15 S	29.55 E
Luwuk, Indon.	112	0.56 S	122.47 E
Luwuk → Banggai, Indon.	112	1.34 S	123.30 E
Luxana Bay ⊂	182	52.03 N	131.00 W
Luxapallila Creek ≃	194	33.28 N	88.26 W
Luxembourg	56	49.36 N	6.09 E
Luxembourg □[4]	56	50.00 N	5.30 E
Luxembourg □[1], Europe	22	49.45 N	6.05 E
Luxembourg □[1], Europe	56	49.45 N	6.05 E
Luxembourg, Aéroport de ⊠	56	49.37 N	6.10 E
Luxembourg, Jardin du ♦	261	48.51 N	2.19 E
Luxemburg	190	44.32 N	87.42 W
Luxemburg → Luxembourg □[1]	56	49.45 N	6.05 E
Luxemburgo → Luxembourg □[1]	56	49.45 N	6.05 E
Luxeuil-les-Bains	58	47.49 N	6.23 E
Luxi, Zhg.	102	24.32 N	103.41 E
Luxi (Mangshi), Zhg.	102	24.20 N	98.25 E
Lüxia	100	26.41 N	120.06 E
Luxian	107	28.55 N	105.29 E
Luxiang, Zhg.	106	31.32 N	120.45 E
Lüxiang, Zhg.	106	30.50 N	121.10 E
Luxi Dao I	100	27.59 N	121.11 E
Luxikou	100	29.54 N	113.42 E
Luxmanor	284c	39.02 N	77.07 W
Luxor → Al-Uqṣur, Miṣr	140	25.41 N	32.39 E
Luxor, Pa., U.S.	214	40.20 N	79.28 W
Luxora	194	35.45 N	89.55 W
Luxu	106	31.01 N	120.50 E
Lu Xun Museum ♉	269b	31.16 N	121.28 E
Lüxuqiao	106	31.50 N	119.31 E
Luy ≃	32	43.39 N	1.08 W
Luyan	106	30.25 N	120.53 E
Lüyang	104	41.23 N	121.40 E
Luyanó ≃	286b	23.07 N	82.21 W
Luyeh	100	22.55 N	121.08 E
Luyi	100	33.53 N	115.28 E
Luynes	50	47.23 N	0.33 E
Luyu	106	31.34 N	121.41 E
Luyuan, Zhg.	106	31.51 N	120.38 E
Luyuan, Zhg.	271a	39.54 N	116.27 E
Luz, Bra.	255	19.48 S	45.40 W
Luz, Bra.	287a	22.48 S	43.05 W
Luz ◆[8]	266c	38.46 N	9.10 W
Luz, Estação da ◆[5]	287b	23.32 S	46.38 W
Luz, Isla I	254	45.30 S	73.59 W
Luz, Ponta da ›	287a	22.47 S	43.05 W
Luza, Ross.	24	62.42 N	37.06 E
Luza, Ross.	24	60.39 N	47.10 E
Luža, Ross.	76	59.58 N	31.56 E
Luža ≃	82	55.03 N	36.35 E
Luzarches	50	49.07 N	2.25 E
Luzern	58	47.03 N	8.18 E
Luzern □[3]	58	47.05 N	8.05 E
Luzerne	210	41.17 N	75.54 W
Luzerne □[6]	210	41.14 N	75.53 W
Luzhai, Zhg.	102	24.31 N	109.50 E
Luzhai, Zhg.	269b	31.20 N	121.22 E
Luzhi	106	31.16 N	120.52 E
Luzhou	107	28.54 N	105.27 E
Luziânia	255	16.15 S	47.56 W
Lužické hory ⋀⋀	54	50.48 N	14.40 E
Luzilândia	250	3.28 S	42.22 W
Lužki, Bela.	76	55.21 N	27.52 E
Lužki, Ross.	82	54.51 N	37.36 E
Lužná	54	50.06 N	13.45 E
Lužnice ≃	30	49.14 N	14.23 E
Lužniki ◆[8]	265b	55.43 N	37.33 E
Luzon I	116	16.00 N	121.00 E
Luzon Strait)(	108	20.30 N	121.00 E
Lužskaja guba ⊂	76	59.45 N	28.20 E
Luzy	32	46.48 N	3.58 E
Luzzara	64	44.58 N	10.41 E
Luzzi	68	39.27 N	16.17 E
L'va ≃	78	52.00 N	27.36 E
L'va Tolstogo	82	54.37 N	36.03 E
L'viv	78	49.50 N	24.00 E
L'viv □[4]	78	49.30 N	24.00 E
Lvov → L'viv	78	49.50 N	24.00 E
L'vovskij	82	55.19 N	37.31 E
Lwów → L'viv	78	49.50 N	24.00 E
Lwówek	30	52.28 N	16.10 E
Lwówek Śląski	30	51.07 N	15.35 E
Lyadova ≃	78	48.28 N	27.37 E
Lyall, Mount ∧	172	45.17 S	167.34 E
Lyallpur → Faisalabad	123	31.25 N	73.05 E
Lyantonde	154	0.24 S	31.09 E
Lyashchivka	78	49.33 N	32.41 E
Lybster	46	58.18 N	3.18 W
Lycaonia □[9]	130	37.50 N	33.15 E
Lychen	54	53.12 N	13.19 E
Lychkove	78	49.06 N	35.12 E
Lycia □[9]	130	36.20 N	30.00 E
Lyck → Ełk	30	53.50 N	22.22 E
Lyckeby	26	56.12 N	15.39 E
Lyčkovo	76	57.55 N	32.24 E
Lycksele	26	64.36 N	18.40 E
Lycoming □[6]	210	41.14 N	77.00 W
Lycoming Creek ≃	210	41.13 N	77.02 W
Lydd	42	50.57 N	0.55 E
Lydda → Lod	132	31.58 N	34.54 E
Lydden ≃	42	50.56 N	2.22 W
Lydenburg	156	25.10 S	30.29 E
Lydenburgh County Park ♦	276	40.50 N	73.14 W
Lydford	42	50.39 N	4.06 W
Lydgate	262	53.44 N	2.07 W
Lydham	42	52.31 N	2.58 W
Lydia □[9]	130	38.40 N	27.30 E
Lydia Mills	192	34.28 N	81.55 W
Lydiate	262	53.32 N	2.57 W
Lydick	216	41.42 N	86.22 W
Lydney	42	51.44 N	2.32 W
Lye Green	260	51.43 N	0.35 W
Lyell, Mount ∧, Can.	182	51.57 N	117.06 W
Lyell, Mount ∧, Ca., U.S.	226	37.44 N	119.16 W
Lyell Brown, Mount ∧	162	23.21 S	130.24 E
Lyell Island I	182	52.40 N	131.30 W
Lyerly	192	34.24 N	85.24 W
Lyford	196	26.24 N	97.47 W
Lygnern ⊜	26	57.29 N	12.20 E
Lyhivka	78	49.08 N	36.03 E
Lykens	208	40.34 N	76.42 W
Lykhivka	78	48.41 N	33.55 E
Lykošino	76	58.07 N	33.43 E
Lyle, Mn., U.S.	190	43.30 N	92.56 W
Lyle, Wa., U.S.	224	45.41 N	121.17 W
Lyles	194	35.55 N	87.20 W
Lyman, Ukr.	78	49.36 N	36.27 E
Lyman, Ukr.	78	45.41 N	29.45 E
Lyman, Ukr.	83	49.21 N	38.57 E
Lyman, Ne., U.S.	198	41.55 N	104.02 W
Lyman, S.C., U.S.	192	34.56 N	82.07 W
Lyman, Wa., U.S.	224	48.31 N	122.03 W
Lyman, Wy., U.S.	200	41.19 N	110.17 W
Lymans'ke	78	46.38 N	30.00 E
Lymbel'karamo	86	60.15 N	83.32 E
Lyme	207	41.18 N	72.19 W
Lyme Bay ⊂	42	50.38 N	3.00 W
Lyme Hall ⊥	262	53.20 N	2.03 W
Lyme Park ♦	262	53.21 N	2.04 W
Lyme Regis	42	50.44 N	2.57 W
Lyminge	42	51.08 N	1.05 E
Lymington	42	50.46 N	1.33 W
Lymkoj	86	59.31 N	70.22 E
Lymm	262	53.23 N	2.29 W
Lympne	42	51.05 N	1.02 E
Lympstone	42	50.39 N	3.25 W
Lymyshivka	78	52.04 N	31.38 E
Lyn	212	44.35 N	75.47 W
Łyna (Lava) ≃	76	54.37 N	21.14 E
Lynæs	41	55.57 N	11.52 E
Lynbrook	276	40.39 N	73.41 W
Lynch, Ky., U.S.	192	36.57 N	82.55 W
Lynch, Ne., U.S.	198	42.49 N	98.27 W
Lynch, Lac ⊜	190	46.25 N	77.05 W
Lynchburg, Oh., U.S.	218	39.14 N	83.47 W
Lynchburg, S.C., U.S.	192	34.03 N	80.04 W
Lynchburg, Tn., U.S.	194	35.16 N	86.22 W
Lynchburg, Va., U.S.	192	37.24 N	79.08 W
Lynches ≃	192	33.50 N	79.22 W
Lynchville	214	41.26 N	78.34 W
Lynd ≃	164	16.28 S	143.18 E
Lynde Creek ≃	212	43.51 N	78.57 W
Lynden, On., Can.	212	43.14 N	80.09 W
Lynden, Wa., U.S.	224	48.56 N	122.27 W
Lyndhurst, Austl.	166	19.12 S	144.23 E
Lyndhurst, Austl.	166	30.17 S	138.21 E
Lyndhurst, Austl.	274b	38.03 S	145.15 E
Lyndhurst, Eng., U.K.	42	50.52 N	1.34 W
Lyndhurst, N.J., U.S.	276	40.48 N	74.07 W
Lyndhurst, Oh., U.S.	214	41.31 N	81.29 W
Lyndoch	168b	34.37 S	138.53 E
Lyndon, Austl.	162	23.37 S	115.15 E
Lyndon, Ks., U.S.	198	38.38 N	95.41 W
Lyndon, Ky., U.S.	218	38.15 N	85.36 W
Lyndon ≃	162	23.29 S	114.06 E
Lyndon B. Johnson, Lake ⊜[1]	196	30.35 N	98.25 W
Lyndon B. Johnson Historical Park ♦	196	30.15 N	98.38 W
Lyndon B. Johnson Space Center ♉[3]	222	29.34 N	95.05 W
Lyndonville, N.Y., U.S.	210	43.19 N	78.23 W
Lyndonville, Vt., U.S.	188	44.32 N	72.00 W
Lyndora	214	40.51 N	79.55 W
Lyne	260	51.23 N	0.33 W
Lyne ≃, Eng., U.K.	44	54.58 N	3.01 W
Lyne ≃, Eng., U.K.	44	55.12 N	1.31 W
Lyneham	42	51.31 N	1.58 W
Lynemouth	44	55.12 N	1.31 W
Lyne Water ≃	46	55.39 N	3.16 W
Lynga	80	57.17 N	53.04 E
Lyngdal	26	58.08 N	7.05 E
Lynge	41	55.51 N	12.17 E
Lyngen	24	69.34 N	20.10 E
Lyngen ⊂[2]	24	69.58 N	20.30 E
Lyngør	26	58.38 N	9.10 E
Lynher ≃	42	50.28 N	4.12 W
Lynmouth	42	51.15 N	3.50 W
Lynn, Al., U.S.	194	34.02 N	87.32 W
Lynn, In., U.S.	218	40.02 N	84.56 W
Lynn, Ma., U.S.	207	42.28 N	70.57 W
Lynn ≃	212	42.47 N	80.12 W
Lynn Canal ⊂	180	58.50 N	135.15 W
Lynndyl	200	39.31 N	112.22 W
Lynne Acres	284b	39.21 N	76.45 W
Lynnfield	207	42.32 N	71.02 W
Lynn Garden	192	36.34 N	82.34 W
Lynn Harbor ⊂	283	42.27 N	70.57 W
Lynn Haven	194	30.14 N	85.38 W
Lynn Lake	184	56.51 N	101.03 W
Lynnville	190	41.34 N	92.47 W
Lynnwood, Pa., U.S.	210	41.14 N	75.56 W
Lynnwood, Pa., U.S.	214	40.07 N	79.51 W
Lynnwood, Wa., U.S.	224	47.49 N	122.18 W
Lynn Woods ♦	283	42.29 N	70.59 W
Lynovytsya	78	50.28 N	32.22 E
Lynton	42	51.15 N	3.50 W
Lyntupy	76	55.03 N	26.19 E
Lynwood, Ca., U.S.	228	33.55 N	118.12 W
Lynwood, Il., U.S.	278	41.32 N	87.32 W
Lynx Lake ⊜	176	62.25 N	106.15 W
Lyø I	41	55.02 N	10.10 E
Lyon	62	45.45 N	4.51 E
Lyon □[6]	226	39.00 N	119.15 W
Lyon ≃	46	56.37 N	4.01 W
Lyon, Gare ◆[5]	261	48.51 N	2.23 E
Lyon, Glen V	46	56.35 N	4.20 W
Lyon, Loch ⊜	46	56.32 N	4.36 W
Lyon Inlet ⊂	176	66.32 N	83.53 W
Lyon Mountain	188	44.43 N	73.54 W
Lyon Mountain ∧	188	44.41 N	73.53 W
Lyonnais □[9]	62	45.45 N	4.30 E
Lyonnais, Monts du ⋀⋀	62	45.40 N	4.30 E
Lyons, Co., U.S.	200	40.13 N	105.16 W
Lyons, Ga., U.S.	192	32.12 N	82.19 W
Lyons, Il., U.S.	216	41.48 N	87.49 W
Lyons, In., U.S.	194	38.59 N	87.04 W
Lyons, Ks., U.S.	198	38.20 N	98.12 W
Lyons, Mi., U.S.	216	42.58 N	84.56 W
Lyons, Ne., U.S.	198	41.56 N	96.28 W
Lyons, N.Y., U.S.	210	43.03 N	76.59 W
Lyons, Oh., U.S.	216	41.41 N	84.04 W
Lyons, Tx., U.S.	222	30.23 N	96.34 W
Lyons, Wi., U.S.	216	42.39 N	88.21 W
Lyons ≃	162	25.02 S	115.09 E
Lyon-Satolas, Aéroport de ⊠	62	45.43 N	5.04 E
Lyons Creek ≃	284a	43.03 N	79.04 W
Lyons Falls	212	43.37 N	75.22 W
Lyons-la-Forêt	50	49.24 N	1.28 E
Lyons Plains	207	41.13 N	73.21 W
Lyons Run ≃	279b	40.25 N	79.43 W
Lyon Station	208	40.28 N	75.45 W
Lyonsville	276	40.57 N	74.25 W
Lypets'ke Druhe	78	47.46 N	29.41 E
Lypova Dolyna	78	50.35 N	33.48 E
Lypovets'	78	49.14 N	29.03 E
Lyptsi	78	50.13 N	36.25 E
Lyracrumpane	48	52.20 N	9.30 W
Lyrestad	40	58.48 N	14.04 E
Lys (Leie) ≃, Europe	50	51.03 N	3.43 E
Lys ≃, It.	62	45.36 N	7.47 E
Lysá ∧	60	49.29 N	12.42 E
Lysa Hora	78	48.11 N	31.06 E
Lysaker	26	59.54 N	10.36 E
Lysá pod Makytou	30	49.12 N	18.13 E
Lysefjorden ⊂[2]	26	59.00 N	6.14 E
Lysekil	26	58.16 N	11.26 E
Lysets'	78	48.52 N	24.36 E
Lyshnivka	78	51.28 N	25.25 E
Łysica ∧	30	50.54 N	20.55 E
Lysjön ⊜	40	60.07 N	14.18 E
Lyskovo	80	56.04 N	45.02 E
Lysogorka	83	47.42 N	39.12 E
Lyss	58	47.04 N	7.18 E
Lysterfield	274b	37.56 S	145.18 E
Lysterfield ∧[2]	274b	37.56 S	145.16 E
Lysterfield Reservoir ⊜[1]	274b	37.58 S	145.18 E
Lyster Station	206	46.22 N	71.37 W
Lys'va	86	58.07 N	57.47 E
Lys'va ≃	80	58.15 N	54.47 E
Lysyanka	78	49.16 N	30.50 E
Lysychans'k	83	48.55 N	38.26 E
Lysyje Gory	80	51.32 N	44.46 E
Lytham Saint Anne's	44	53.45 N	2.57 W
Lytkarino	82	55.35 N	37.54 E
Lytle	196	29.13 N	98.47 W
Lytle Creek ≃	228	34.09 N	117.23 W
Lyttelton, N.Z.	172	43.35 S	172.42 E
Lyttelton, S. Afr.	158	25.50 S	28.11 E
Lytton	182	50.14 N	121.34 W
Lytton Springs	222	30.00 N	97.37 W
Lytvynivka	83	49.18 N	39.27 E
Lyubar	78	49.55 N	27.44 E
Lyubashivka	78	47.51 N	30.15 E
Lyubech	78	51.42 N	30.39 E
Lyubertsy → L'ubercy	82	55.41 N	37.53 E
Lyubeshiv	78	51.46 N	25.31 E
Lyuboml'	78	51.14 N	24.01 E
Lyubotyn	78	49.57 N	35.57 E
Lyubymivka	78	46.47 N	33.34 E
Lyuten'ka	78	50.13 N	34.02 E
Lyzyne	83	49.33 N	38.51 E

M

Name	Page	Lat.°′	Long.°′
Ma ≃	110	19.47 N	105.56 E
Ma, Oued el V, Alg.	148	27.45 N	7.45 W
Ma, Oued el V, Maur.	148	24.03 N	9.10 W
Maadid, Djebel ∧	34	35.52 N	4.46 E
Maalaea Bay ⊂	229a	20.47 N	156.29 W
Ma'alot-Tarshiḥa	132	33.01 N	35.17 E
Maam Cross	48	53.27 N	9.31 W
Ma'ān	132	30.12 N	35.44 E
Ma'ān □[8]	132	30.20 N	36.30 E
Maaninka	26	63.09 N	27.18 E
Ma'anshan, Zhg.	100	31.42 N	118.30 E
Maanshan, Zhg.	107	29.52 N	104.59 E
Ma-ao	116	10.29 N	122.59 E
Maap I	174q	9.35 N	138.11 E
Maar	140	6.54 N	31.33 E
Maardu	76	59.28 N	25.02 E
Maarianhamina → Mariehamn	26	60.06 N	19.57 E
Ma'ārik, Qārat al- ∧[2]	142	29.59 N	30.52 E
Ma'arrat an-Nu'mān	130	35.38 N	36.40 E
Ma'arrat Miṣrīn	130	36.01 N	36.40 E
Ma'arrat Ṣaydnāyā	132	33.41 N	36.23 E
Maarssen	52	52.08 N	5.08 E
Maas	48	54.50 N	8.22 W
Maas (Meuse) ≃	30	51.49 N	5.01 E
Maasbracht	52	51.08 N	5.53 E
Maasdam	52	51.47 N	4.32 E
Maaseik	56	51.06 N	5.48 E
Maasholm	41	54.41 N	9.59 E
Maasin	116	10.08 N	124.50 E
Maasmechelen	56	50.58 N	5.42 E
Maasniel	52	51.13 N	6.01 E
Maassluis	52	51.55 N	4.15 E
Maastricht	56	50.52 N	5.43 E
Maave	156	21.03 S	34.47 E
Ma-ayon ≃	116	11.25 N	122.46 E
Maba	100	32.59 N	118.48 E
Maba, Ouadi V	146	15.10 N	21.00 E
Mababe Depression ⊥[7]	156	18.50 S	24.15 E
Mabaduan	164	9.16 S	142.44 E
Mabaho, Mount ∧	116	9.15 N	125.42 E
Mabaia	152	7.13 S	14.03 E
Mabalacat	116	15.14 N	120.34 E
Mabalane	156	23.37 S	32.31 E
Mabana	224	48.05 N	122.24 W
Mabanga	152	1.30 N	19.06 E
Mabank	222	32.21 N	96.06 W
Mabaoquan	105	40.09 N	115.53 E
Ma'barot	132	32.22 N	34.54 E
Mabaruma	246	8.12 N	59.47 W
Mabashi	268	35.49 N	139.55 E
Mabau	112	2.14 S	111.54 E
Mabay	240p	20.16 N	76.40 W
Mabber, Ras ›	144	9.28 N	50.50 E
Mabel Creek	162	29.01 S	134.17 E
Mabeleapodi	156	20.58 S	22.36 E
Mabel Lake ⊜	182	50.35 N	118.44 W
Maben	194	33.33 N	89.05 W
Mabenga-Cité	152	3.39 S	18.40 E
Mabenge	152	4.14 N	24.09 E
Maberry, Loch ⊜	44	55.02 N	4.41 W
Mabeti ≃	92	40.31 N	141.31 E
Mabeul	36	36.27 N	10.46 E
Mabi, Nihon	96	34.38 N	133.41 E
Mabi, Zhg.	100	26.21 N	119.36 E
Mabi, Zhg.	102	35.59 N	112.15 E

Symbols in the index entries represent the broad categories identified in the key at the right. Symbols with superior numbers (⋀⋀[1]) identify subcategories (see complete key on page *I* · *1*).

Symbole im Register stellen die rechts im Schlüssel erklärten Kategorien dar. Symbole mit hochgestellten Ziffern (⋀⋀[1]) bezeichnen Unterabteilungen einer Kategorie (vgl. vollständiger Schlüssel auf Seite *I* · *1*).

Los símbolos incluídos en el texto del índice representan las grandes categorías identificadas con la clave a la derecha. Los símbolos con numeros en su parte superior (⋀⋀[1]) identifican las subcategorías (véase la clave completa en la página *I* · *1*).

Les symboles de l'index représentent les catégories indiquées dans la légende à droite. Les symboles suivis d'un indice (⋀⋀[1]) représentent des sous-catégories (voir légende complète à la page *I* · *1*).

Os símbolos incluídos no texto do índice representam as grandes categorias identificadas com a chave à direita. Os símbolos com números em sua parte superior (⋀⋀[1]) identificam as subcategorias (veja-se a chave completa à página *I* · *1*).

Symbol	English	Deutsch	Español	Français	Português
∧	Mountain	Berg	Montaña	Montagne	Montanha
⋀⋀	Mountains	Gebirge	Montañas	Montagnes	Montanhas
)(	Pass	Paß	Paso	Col	Passo
V	Valley, Canyon	Tal, Cañon	Valle, Cañón	Vallée, Canyon	Vale, Canhão
≚	Plain	Ebene	Llano	Plaine	Planície
›	Cape	Kap	Cabo	Cap	Cabo
I	Island	Insel	Isla	Île	Ilha
II	Islands	Inseln	Islas	Îles	Ilhas
⊥	Other Topographic Features	Andere Topographische Objekte	Otros Elementos Topográficos	Autres données topographiques	Outros acidentes topográficos

ESPAÑOL — FRANÇAIS — PORTUGUÊS

Nombre / Nom / Nome	Página / Page	Lat.°′	Long.°′ W = Oeste / W = Ouest
Mabian	107	28.48 N	103.41 E
Mabian ≃	107	29.08 N	103.58 E
Mablethorpe	44	53.21 N	0.15 E
Mableton	192	33.49 N	84.34 W
Mabole ≃	150	9.01 N	12.44 W
Maboma	154	2.32 N	28.13 E
Mabonto	150	8.52 N	11.49 W
Mabote	156	22.03 S	34.09 E
Mabou	186	46.05 N	61.22 W
Mabrak, Jabal ∧	132	30.13 N	35.29 E
Mabrous ╤ [4]	146	21.13 N	13.38 E
Mabrūk, Lībiyā	146	29.50 N	17.10 E
Mabrūk, Sūd.	140	8.07 N	29.25 E
Mabton	202	46.12 N	119.59 W
Mabuasehube Game Reserve ✦ [4]	156	25.10 S	22.10 E
Mabuguai	100	29.49 N	112.42 E
Mabuki	154	2.59 S	33.11 E
Mabuni	174m	26.05 N	127.43 E
Mabwe	154	8.39 S	26.31 E
Mača, Ross.	74	59.54 N	117.35 E
Maca, Ven.	286c	10.28 N	66.48 W
Maca, Cerro ∧	254	45.06 S	73.12 W
Macachín	252	37.09 S	63.39 W
Macaco, Morro do ∧ [2]	287a	22.56 S	43.07 W
Macacos, Ilha dos I	250	1.20 S	50.35 W
Macacu ≃	256	22.42 S	43.02 W
Macaé	255	22.23 S	41.47 W
Macaíba	250	5.51 S	35.21 W
Macajalar Bay ⊂	116	8.37 N	124.38 E
Macajuba	255	12.09 S	40.22 W
Macalaya	116	12.53 N	123.46 E
Macalelon	116	13.45 N	122.08 E
Macalister	182	52.27 N	122.24 W
Macalister ≃	166	38.02 S	146.59 E
Macalister, Mount ∧	170	34.27 S	149.45 E
Macallum Lake ⊜	184	55.02 N	108.25 W
Macaloge	154	12.25 S	35.25 E
MacAlpine Lake ⊜	176	66.40 N	103.15 W
Macamic, Lac ⊜	190	48.48 N	78.59 W
Macan, Kepulauan II	112	7.00 S	121.00 E
Macao → Macau, Macau	100	22.14 N	113.35 E
Macão, Port.	34	39.33 N	8.00 W
Macao → Macau □ [2]	100	22.10 N	113.33 E
Macapá	250	0.02 N	51.03 W
Macará	246	4.23 S	79.57 W
Macarani	255	15.33 S	40.24 W
Macarao	286c	10.26 N	67.02 W
Macarao ≃	286c	10.26 N	67.01 W
Macareo, Caño ≃ [1]	246	9.47 N	61.37 W
Macari ≃	250	1.52 N	50.31 W
MacArthur, Pil.	116	10.50 N	125.00 E
MacArthur, Il., U.S.	278	41.39 N	87.44 W
Macas	246	2.19 S	78.07 W
Macatawa ≃	216	42.48 N	86.05 W
Macatawa, Lake ⊂	216	42.47 N	86.10 W
Macaterick, Loch ⊜	44	55.12 N	4.26 W
Macau, Bra.	250	5.07 S	36.38 W
Macau (Aomen), Macau	100	22.14 N	113.35 E
Macau □ [2], Asia	90	22.10 N	113.33 E
Macau □ [2], Asia	100	22.10 N	113.33 E
Macau, Ilha I	156	20.55 S	35.05 E
Macauã ≃	248	9.13 S	68.44 W
Macaúbas	255	13.02 S	42.42 W
Macaya, Pic ∧	238	18.25 N	74.00 W
Macaza ≃	206	46.21 N	74.47 W
Maccarese ✦ [8]	267a	41.53 N	12.13 E
Maccarese, Bonifica di ✦ [1]	267a	41.51 N	12.13 E
Macchiagodena	66	41.33 N	14.24 E
MacClenny	192	30.16 N	82.07 W
Macclesfield, Austl.	168b	35.10 S	138.50 E
Macclesfield, Eng., U.K.	44	53.16 N	2.07 W
Macclesfield □ [8]	262	53.17 N	2.15 W
Macclesfield Canal ≌	262	53.24 N	2.03 W
Macclesfield Forest ✦ [3]	262	53.15 N	2.03 W
Macdhui, Ben ∧	158	30.39 S	27.58 E
MacDill Air Force Base ■	220	27.51 N	82.29 W
Macdonald ≃	170	33.23 S	150.59 E
Macdonald, Lake ⊜	162	23.30 S	129.00 E
MacDonald Downs	162	22.27 S	135.13 E
Macdonald Lake ⊜	212	45.14 N	78.34 W
MacDonald Pass)(	202	46.34 N	112.18 W
Macdonald Range ⩘	182	49.12 N	114.46 W
MacDonnell Ranges ⩘	162	23.45 S	133.20 E
Macdonnel Peninsula ≻ [1]	168b	35.47 S	138.00 E
MacDowell Lake ⊜	184	52.15 N	92.45 W
Macduff	46	57.40 N	2.29 W
Macdui, Ben ∧	46	57.05 N	3.38 W
Mačecha	80	50.48 N	43.17 E
Maceday Lake ⊜	281	42.42 N	83.26 W
Macedo de Cavaleiros	34	41.32 N	6.58 W
Macedon, Austl.	169	37.25 S	144.34 E
Macedon, N.Y., U.S.	210	43.04 N	77.17 W
Macedonia, Ct., U.S.	207	41.47 N	73.30 W
Macedonia, Oh., U.S.	214	41.18 N	81.30 W
Macedonia □ [9]	38	41.00 N	23.00 E
Macedonia □ [1], Europe	22	41.50 N	22.00 E
Macedonia (Makedonija) □ [1], Europe	38	41.50 N	22.00 E
Macedonia Brook State Park ♠	207	41.47 N	73.29 W
Maceió	250	9.40 S	35.43 W
Maceira	266c	38.52 N	9.19 W
Macenta	150	8.33 N	9.28 W
Maceo	246	6.33 N	74.47 W
Macerata	66	43.18 N	13.27 E
Macerata □ [4]	66	43.12 N	13.10 E
Macerata Feltria	66	43.48 N	12.26 E
MacFarlane ≃	176	59.12 N	107.58 W
Macfarlane, Lake ⊜	166	31.55 S	136.42 E
Macfarlane, Mount ∧	172	43.56 S	169.23 E
Macgillycuddy's Reeks ⩘	48	51.55 N	9.45 W
MacGregor	184	49.57 N	98.49 W
Machacamarca	248	18.10 S	67.02 W
Machache ∧	158	29.21 S	27.55 E
Machachi	246	0.30 S	78.34 W
Machačkala	84	42.58 N	47.30 E
Machada, Mata Nacional da ♠	266c	38.36 N	9.02 W
Machadinho ≃	248	9.00 S	61.52 W
Machado	256	21.41 S	45.56 W
Machado ≃, Bra.	248	8.03 S	62.52 W
Machado ≃, Bra.	256	21.38 S	45.52 W
Machadodorp	156	25.40 S	30.14 E
Machagai	252	26.56 S	60.03 W
Machaila	156	22.15 S	32.55 E
Machakos	154	1.31 S	37.16 E
Machala	246	3.16 S	79.58 W
Machalí	252	34.11 S	70.40 W
Machalilla, Parque Nacional ♠	246	1.30 S	80.45 W
Machalino	80	53.05 N	46.14 E
Māchalpur	124	24.08 N	76.18 E
Machaneng	156	23.10 S	27.26 E
Machang, Malay.	114	5.46 N	102.13 E
Machang, Zhg.	98	34.06 N	119.02 E
Machang, Zhg.	98	42.05 N	119.42 E
Machanga	156	20.58 S	34.59 E
Machangcun	105	38.54 N	115.26 E
Machangfu	102	25.14 N	103.45 E
Machang Jianhe ≃	105	39.00 N	117.40 E
Machaquilá ≃	236	16.13 N	90.01 W
Machattie, Lake ⊜	166	24.50 S	139.48 E
Machault	50	49.21 N	4.30 E
Machava	156	25.54 S	32.29 E
Machaze	156	20.51 S	33.26 E
Machecoul	32	47.00 N	1.50 W
Macheke	154	18.05 S	31.51 E
Machekhy	78	49.31 N	34.26 E
Machelen	50	50.55 N	4.26 E
Macheng	100	31.13 N	115.00 E
Macherio	266b	45.38 N	9.16 E
Māčherla	122	16.29 N	79.26 E
Machern	54	51.21 N	12.37 E
Machery	261	48.36 N	2.05 E
Machesna Mountain ∧	226	35.17 N	120.14 W
Machesney Park	216	42.20 N	89.03 W
Māchhīwāra	123	30.55 N	76.12 E
Machhlīshahr	124	25.41 N	82.25 E
Machias, Me., U.S.	188	44.42 N	67.27 W
Machias, N.Y., U.S.	210	42.25 N	78.30 W
Machias ≃	188	44.43 N	67.22 W
Machias Bay ⊂	188	44.40 N	67.20 W
Machichaco, Cabo ≻	34	43.27 N	2.45 W
Machichi ≃	184	57.03 N	92.06 W
Machico	148	32.42 N	16.46 W
Machida	94	35.32 N	139.27 E
Machile ≃	154	17.26 S	25.02 E
Machilīpatnam (Bandar)	122	16.10 N	81.08 E
Machindžauri	84	41.40 N	41.43 E
Machiques	246	10.04 N	72.34 W
Machiya ≃	94	35.01 N	136.42 E
Machkund ⊜ [1]	122	18.26 N	82.35 E
Machmud-Mekteb	84	44.26 N	45.13 E
Machn'ovo	86	58.27 N	61.42 E
Macho, Arroyo del V	196	33.36 N	104.28 W
Machočen, porog ⌞	88	57.23 N	121.29 E
Machona, Laguna ⊂	234	18.20 N	93.40 W
Machrihanish	46	55.26 N	5.45 W
Machtaly	85	41.22 N	68.02 E
Machupicchu	248	13.07 S	72.34 W
Machupicchu ⊥	248	13.07 S	72.34 W
Machupo ≃	248	12.34 S	64.25 W
Machynlleth	42	52.35 N	3.51 W
Maciá, Arg.	252	32.10 S	59.23 W
Macia, Moç.	156	25.03 S	33.10 E
Maciel, Arroyo ≃, Ur.	258	33.42 S	57.59 W
Maciel, Arroyo ≃, Ur.	258	33.36 S	56.31 W
Măcin	38	45.15 N	28.08 E
Macina → Massina ✦ [1]	150	14.30 N	5.00 W
Macintyre ≃	166	28.38 N	149.41 E
Maçka	130	40.48 N	39.38 E
Mačkassy	80	52.46 N	45.34 E
Mackay, Austl.	166	21.09 S	149.11 E
Mackay, Id., U.S.	202	43.54 N	113.36 W
MacKay ≃	184	57.03 N	111.55 W
Mackay, Lake ⊜	162	22.30 S	129.00 E
MacKay Lake ⊜	176	63.55 N	110.25 W
Mackenrode	54	51.33 N	10.33 E
Mackenzie	246	6.00 N	58.17 W
Mackenzie ≃, Austl.	166	23.38 S	149.46 E
Mackenzie ≃, N.T., Can.	176	69.15 N	134.08 W
MacKenzie Bay ⊂, Ant.	9	68.20 S	71.15 E
Mackenzie Bay ⊂, Can.	180	69.00 N	136.30 W
Mackenzie Delta ≚ [2]	180	68.50 N	135.25 W
Mackenzie Mountains ⩘	180	64.00 N	130.00 W
Mackeyville	210	41.03 N	77.28 W
Mackinac, Straits of ⊔	190	45.49 N	84.42 W
Mackinac Bridge ✦ [5]	190	45.50 N	84.45 W
Mackinac Island	190	45.50 N	84.37 W
Mackinac Island I	190	45.51 N	84.38 W
Mackinac Island State Park ♠	190	45.52 N	84.40 W
Mackinaw	190	40.32 N	89.21 W
Mackinaw ≃	194	40.33 N	89.44 W
Mackinaw City	190	45.47 N	84.43 W
Mackinnon Road	154	3.44 S	39.03 E
Macklin	184	52.20 N	109.56 W
Mačkovci	61	46.47 N	16.09 E
M'ačkovo, Ross.	82	55.13 N	38.40 E
M'ačkovo, Ross.	82	56.21 N	39.03 E
Macksville, Austl.	166	30.43 S	152.55 E
Macksville, Ks., U.S.	198	38.57 N	98.58 W
Maclean	166	29.28 S	153.13 E
Macleantown	158	32.47 S	27.45 E
Maclear	158	31.02 S	28.23 E
Macleay ≃	166	30.52 S	153.01 E
Macleod	274b	37.43 S	145.04 E
Macleod, Lake ⊜	162	24.00 S	113.35 E
Maclovia Herrera	232	29.05 N	105.08 W
Macmillan ≃	180	62.52 N	135.55 W
Macocolo	152	6.47 S	16.08 E
Macolin	58	47.09 N	7.14 E
Macolla, Punta ≻	241s	12.06 N	70.13 W
Macolo	152	7.05 S	16.48 E
Macomb	190	40.27 N	90.40 W
Macomb □ [6]	214	42.40 N	82.54 W
Macomb Mall ✦ [9]	281	42.32 N	82.55 W
Macomer	71	40.16 N	8.47 E
Macomia	154	12.15 S	40.08 E
Macon, Bel.	50	50.03 N	4.13 E
Mâcon, Fr.	58	46.18 N	4.50 E
Macon, Ga., U.S.	192	32.50 N	83.37 W
Macon, Il., U.S.	219	39.42 N	88.59 W
Macon, Ms., U.S.	194	33.06 N	88.33 W
Macon, Mo., U.S.	194	39.44 N	92.28 W
Macon □ [6], Il., U.S.	219	39.51 N	89.32 W
Macon □ [6], Mo., U.S.	219	39.50 N	92.20 W
Macon, Bayou ≃	194	31.55 N	91.33 W
Macon Creek ≃	216	41.58 N	83.38 W
Macondo	152	12.35 S	23.44 E
Macondo ≃	152	13.23 S	23.03 E
Mâconnais, Monts du ⩘	58	46.18 N	4.45 E
Macorís, Cabo ≻	238	19.47 N	70.28 W
Macosquin	48	55.06 N	6.43 W
Macossa	156	17.52 S	33.56 E
Macouba, Pointe de ≻	240e	14.53 N	61.09 W
Macoun Lake ⊜	184	56.32 N	103.50 W
Macoupin □ [6]	219	39.17 N	89.53 W
Macoupin Creek ≃	219	39.11 N	90.36 W
Macovane	156	21.28 S	35.04 E
Macpherson, Mount ∧ [2]	162	21.49 S	121.35 E
Macquarie ≃, Austl.	166	41.44 S	147.08 E
Macquarie ≃, Austl.	166	30.07 S	147.24 E
Macquarie, Lake ⊜	170	33.05 S	151.35 E
Macquarie Fields	274a	33.59 S	150.53 E
Macquarie Harbour ⊂	166	42.19 S	145.23 E
Macquarie Island I	9	54.30 S	158.56 E
Macquarie Marshes ≡	166	30.50 S	147.32 E
Macquarie Pass National Park ♠	170	34.34 S	150.39 E
Macquarie Ridge ✣ [3]	9	57.00 S	159.00 E
Macquarie University ʊ [2]	274a	33.46 S	151.06 E
MacRitchie Reservoir ⊜ [1]	271c	1.21 N	103.50 E
Mac. Robertson Land ✦ [1]	9	68.10 S	65.00 E
Macrohon	116	10.05 N	124.56 E
Macroom	48	51.54 N	8.57 W
Mactan Island I	116	10.18 N	123.58 E
MacTier	212	45.08 N	79.47 W
Macuco de Minas	256	21.46 S	44.47 W
Macucuau ≃	246	0.37 S	61.24 W
Macuelizo	236	15.18 N	88.31 W
Macugnaga	58	45.58 N	7.58 E
Macujer	246	0.23 N	72.55 W
Macul	286e	33.30 S	70.34 W
Maculabo Island I	116	14.24 N	122.49 E
Macumba ≃	162	27.52 S	137.12 E
Macungie	208	40.30 N	75.33 W
Macunqiao	100	33.50 N	116.13 E
Macuro	246	10.39 N	61.56 W
Macusani	248	14.05 S	70.26 W
Macuspana	234	17.46 N	92.36 W
Macusse	152	17.51 S	20.21 E
Macuto	286c	10.37 N	66.53 W
Macuze	156	17.42 S	37.11 E
Macy	216	40.57 N	86.07 W
Mad ≃, On., Can.	212	44.25 N	79.54 W
Mad ≃, Ca., U.S.	204	40.57 N	124.07 W
Mad ≃, N.Y., U.S.	212	43.20 N	75.44 W
Mad ≃, Oh., U.S.	188	39.46 N	84.11 W
Mad ≃, Vt., U.S.	188	44.18 N	72.41 W
Mada ≃	150	7.59 N	7.55 E
Ma'dabā	132	31.43 N	35.48 E
Madagascar (Madagasikara) □ [1], Afr.	138	19.00 S	46.00 E
Madagascar (Madagasikara) □ [1], Afr.	157b	19.00 S	46.00 E
Madagascar Basin ✣ [1]	12	27.00 S	53.00 E
Madagascar Plateau ✣ [3]	10	30.00 S	45.00 E
Madagasikara → Madagascar □ [1]	157b	19.00 S	46.00 E
Madagaskar → Madagascar □ [1]	157b	19.00 S	46.00 E
Madagiz	84	40.19 N	46.44 E
Madagoi, Bohol V	144	0.44 N	42.56 E
Madā'in Ṣāliḥ	128	26.48 N	37.53 E
Madajevo	80	54.48 N	44.31 E
Madama	146	21.58 N	13.39 E
Madame, Isle I	186	45.33 N	61.02 W
Madan	38	41.30 N	24.57 E
Madanapalle	122	13.33 N	78.30 E
Madang, Pap. N. Gui.	164	5.15 S	145.50 E
Madang, Zhg.	100	29.58 N	116.40 E
Madang □ [5]	164	5.00 S	145.30 E
Madanpur	272b	22.40 N	88.32 E
Madanpur Dabās ✦ [8]	272a	28.43 N	77.02 E
Madaoua	150	14.05 N	5.58 E
Mādār Gāng ≃ [1]	126	22.12 N	89.04 E
Mādāri Hāt	124	26.42 N	89.17 E
Mādārīpur	124	23.10 N	90.12 E
Madarounfa	150	13.18 N	7.09 E
Mādārpur	272b	22.54 N	88.27 E
Madau Island I	164	8.58 S	152.28 E
Madawaska, On., Can.	212	45.30 N	77.59 W
Madawaska, Me., U.S.	186	47.21 N	68.19 W
Madawaska ≃	212	45.27 N	76.21 W
Madawaska Highlands ⩘ [1]	212	45.15 N	77.35 W
Madawaska Lake ⊜	212	45.20 N	78.23 W
Madaxmaroodi	144	2.39 N	44.36 E
Madaya, Mya.	110	22.13 N	96.07 E
Maḍāyā, Sūrīy.	132	33.41 N	36.06 E
Madbar	140	6.19 N	30.40 E
Mad Creek ≃	210	42.55 N	77.59 W
Maddalena, Colle della (Col de Larche))(	62	44.25 N	6.53 E
Maddalena, Isola I	71	41.14 N	9.25 E
Maddaloni	68	41.02 N	14.23 E
Maddela	116	16.21 N	121.41 E
Madden, Mount ∧	162	33.12 S	119.51 E
Maddington	168a	32.03 S	115.59 E
Maddock	198	47.57 N	99.31 W
Maddy, Loch ⊂	46	57.36 N	7.08 W
Made	52	51.41 N	4.46 E
Madeir	140	7.50 N	29.12 E
Madeira	218	39.11 N	84.21 W
Madeira I	148	32.44 N	17.00 W
Madeira ≃	242	3.22 S	58.45 W
Madeira, Arquipélago da II	148	32.40 N	16.45 W
Madeira Beach	220	27.48 N	82.48 W
Madeirinha ≃	248	8.31 S	60.46 W
Madeirinha, Paraná ≃ [1]	246	3.25 S	58.51 W
M'adel'	76	54.53 N	26.57 E
Mädelegabel ∧	58	47.18 N	10.18 E
Madeleine, Îles de la II	186	47.30 N	61.45 W
Madeleine, Pointe ≻	275a	45.27 N	73.57 W
Madeleine-Centre	186	49.15 N	65.21 W
Madeley, Eng., U.K.	42	52.59 N	2.20 W
Madeley, Eng., U.K.	42	52.39 N	2.28 W
Madelia	190	44.03 N	94.25 W
Madeline Island I	190	46.50 N	90.40 W
Maden, Tür.	130	38.23 N	39.40 E
Maden, Tür.	130	40.11 N	40.25 E
Madenijet	86	47.53 N	78.37 E
Madera, Méx.	232	29.12 N	108.07 W
Madera, Ca., U.S.	226	36.57 N	120.03 W
Madera, Pa., U.S.	214	40.49 N	78.26 W
Madera □ [6]	226	37.15 N	119.45 W
Madera Canal ≌	226	37.05 N	119.59 W
Madera Lake ⊜ [1]	226	37.02 N	119.59 W
Madera Peak ∧	226	37.32 N	119.23 W
Maderas, Islas → Madeira, Arquipélago da II	148	32.40 N	16.45 W
Maderas, Volcán ∧ [1]	236	11.27 N	85.31 W
Maderno	64	45.38 N	10.35 E
Madgaon (Margao)	122	15.18 N	73.57 E
Madh ✦ [8]	272c	19.08 N	72.47 E
Madhepura	124	25.55 N	86.47 E
Madhkūr, Bi'r ╤ [4]	142	30.42 N	32.32 E
Mādhopur	123	32.22 N	75.36 E
Madhubani	124	26.22 N	86.05 E
Madhudaha	272b	22.31 N	88.25 E
Madhugiri	122	13.40 N	77.12 E
Madhumati ≃ [1]	126	22.53 N	89.52 E
Madhupar	126	22.54 N	86.28 E
Madhupur	126	24.16 N	86.39 E
Madhya Bhārat Pathār ✦ [1]	124	25.00 N	77.00 E
Madhyamgrām	272b	22.42 N	88.27 E
Madhya Pradesh □ [3]	118	23.00 N	79.00 E
Madia	154	7.08 S	26.00 E
Madian	106	32.15 N	119.58 E
Madibi	152	4.18 S	18.24 E
Madibira	154	8.12 S	34.49 E
Madibogo	158	26.25 S	25.10 E
Madida	98	42.57 N	130.48 E
Madidi ≃	248	12.32 S	66.52 W
Madill	196	34.05 N	96.46 W
Madimba, Ang.	152	6.31 S	14.21 E
Madimba, Zaïre	152	4.58 S	15.08 E
Madina	150	13.24 N	8.51 W
Madina do Boé	150	11.45 N	14.13 W
Madinani	150	9.37 N	6.57 W
Madinat al-Abyār	146	32.11 N	20.36 E
Madīnat ash-Sha'b (Al-Ittihad)	144	12.50 N	44.56 E
Madīnat ath Thawrah	130	35.52 N	38.34 E
Madine, Lac de ⊜	56	48.54 N	5.42 E
Madingo	152	4.07 S	11.22 E
Madingou	152	4.09 S	13.34 E
Madingzi	104	42.08 N	120.52 E
Madi Opei	154	3.37 N	33.05 E
Madirobe	157b	16.04 S	46.15 E
Madirovalo	157b	16.26 S	46.30 E
Madison, Al., U.S.	194	34.41 N	86.44 W
Madison, Ca., U.S.	226	38.41 N	121.58 W
Madison, Ct., U.S.	207	41.16 N	72.35 W
Madison, Fl., U.S.	192	30.28 N	83.24 W
Madison, Ga., U.S.	192	33.35 N	83.28 W
Madison, Il., U.S.	219	38.40 N	90.09 W
Madison, In., U.S.	218	38.44 N	85.22 W
Madison, Ks., U.S.	198	38.08 N	96.08 W
Madison, Me., U.S.	188	44.47 N	69.52 W
Madison, Md., U.S.	208	38.30 N	76.13 W
Madison, Mn., U.S.	198	45.00 N	96.11 W
Madison, Mo., U.S.	219	39.28 N	92.12 W
Madison, Ne., U.S.	198	41.49 N	97.27 W
Madison, N.J., U.S.	210	40.45 N	74.25 W
Madison, N.Y., U.S.	210	42.53 N	75.30 W
Madison, N.C., U.S.	192	36.23 N	79.57 W
Madison, Oh., U.S.	214	41.46 N	81.03 W
Madison, Pa., U.S.	279b	40.15 N	79.41 W
Madison, S.D., U.S.	198	44.00 N	97.06 W
Madison, Va., U.S.	188	38.22 N	78.15 W
Madison, W.V., U.S.	188	38.04 N	81.49 W
Madison, Wi., U.S.	216	43.04 N	89.24 W
Madison □ [6], Il., U.S.	219	38.49 N	89.58 W
Madison □ [6], In., U.S.	218	40.10 N	85.41 W
Madison □ [6], N.Y., U.S.	210	43.05 N	75.42 W
Madison □ [6], Oh., U.S.	218	39.53 N	83.27 W
Madison □ [6], Tx., U.S.	222	30.58 N	95.55 W
Madison ≃	202	45.56 N	111.30 W
Madison, West Fork ≃	202	44.55 N	111.35 W
Madisonburg, Oh., U.S.	214	40.51 N	81.55 W
Madisonburg, Pa., U.S.	210	40.55 N	77.31 W
Madison Heights, Mi., U.S.	216	42.29 N	83.06 W
Madison Heights, Va., U.S.	192	37.25 N	79.07 W
Madison Mills	218	39.40 N	83.20 W
Madison-on-the-Lake	214	41.42 N	81.24 W
Madison Park	276	40.26 N	74.19 W
Madison Range ⩘	202	45.15 N	111.20 W
Madison Square Garden ♠	276	40.45 N	74.00 W
Madisonville, Ky., U.S.	194	37.19 N	87.29 W
Madisonville, La., U.S.	194	30.24 N	90.09 W
Madisonville, Tn., U.S.	192	35.31 N	84.21 W
Madisonville, Tx., U.S.	222	30.56 N	95.54 W
Madiun	115a	7.37 S	111.31 E
Madiun ≃	115a	7.23 S	111.27 E
Madiyi	102	28.14 N	110.30 E
Madjingo	152	1.23 N	14.06 E
Madjoari	150	11.26 N	1.15 E
Madley, Mount ∧	162	24.31 S	123.58 E
Madoc	212	44.30 N	77.28 W
Mado Gashi	154	0.44 N	39.10 E
Madoi	102	34.53 N	98.24 E
Madol	140	9.02 N	27.46 E
Madon ≃	58	48.36 N	6.06 E
Madona	76	56.51 N	26.13 E
Madonie ⩘	70	37.52 N	13.58 E
Madonna (Unserfrau)	64	46.43 N	10.52 E
Madonna della Guardia ʊ [1]	62	44.29 N	8.51 E
Madonna della Quercia ʊ [1]	66	42.25 N	12.06 E
Madonna dell'Olmo	62	44.25 N	7.32 E
Madonna del Sasso ʊ [1]	58	46.11 N	8.33 E
Madonna di Campiglio	64	46.14 N	10.49 E
Madonna di Tirano	64	46.13 N	10.09 E
Madora	76	53.09 N	30.11 E
Madougou	150	14.24 N	3.05 W
Madrakah	144	21.59 N	39.59 E
Madrakah, Ra's al- ≻	118	19.00 N	57.50 E
Madras, India	122	13.05 N	80.17 E
Madras, Or., U.S.	202	44.38 N	121.07 W
Madras → Tamil Nādu □ [3]	122	11.00 N	78.15 E
Madre, Laguna ⊂, Méx.	232	25.00 N	97.40 W
Madre, Laguna ⊂, Tx., U.S.	196	27.00 N	97.35 W
Madre, Sierra ⩘	116	16.20 N	122.00 E
Madre de Chiapas, Sierra ⩘	232	15.30 N	92.35 W
Madre de Deus de Minas	256	21.29 S	44.20 W
Madre de Dios □ [5]	248	12.00 S	70.15 W
Madre de Dios ≃	248	10.23 S	65.24 W
Madre de Dios, Isla I	254	50.15 S	75.05 W
Madre del Sur, Sierra ⩘	234	17.00 N	100.00 W
Madre Occidental, Sierra ⩘	232	25.00 N	105.00 W
Madre Oriental, Sierra ⩘	232	22.00 N	99.30 W
Madre Vieja ≃	236	14.01 N	91.26 W
Madrid, Col.	246	4.44 N	74.16 W
Madrid, Esp.	34	40.24 N	3.41 W
Madrid, Esp.	266a	40.24 N	3.41 W
Madrid, Pil.	116	9.15 N	126.00 E
Madrid, Al., U.S.	194	31.02 N	85.23 W
Madrid, Ia., U.S.	190	41.52 N	93.49 W
Madrid, Ne., U.S.	198	40.51 N	101.32 W
Madrid □ [4]	34	40.30 N	3.40 W
Madridejos, Esp.	34	39.28 N	3.32 W
Madridejos, Pil.	116	11.18 N	123.44 E
Madrigalejo	34	39.09 N	5.37 W
Madrillon	284c	38.55 N	77.14 W
Madriz □ [5]	236	13.30 N	86.30 W
Madroñera	34	39.26 N	5.46 W
Madruga	240p	22.55 N	81.51 W
Madrūsah	146	24.48 N	14.32 E
Madsen	184	50.58 N	93.55 W
Madsūs, Bi'r ╤ [4]	142	29.15 N	32.19 E
Maducang Island I	116	10.42 N	120.15 E
Maduda	152	4.55 S	13.06 E
Maduo	152	1.24 S	20.44 E
Madura, Austl.	162	31.55 S	127.00 E
Madura → Madurai, India	122	9.56 N	78.07 E
Madura I	115a	7.00 S	113.20 E
Madura, Selat ⊔	115a	7.25 S	113.25 E
Madurai	122	9.56 N	78.07 E
Madurāntakam	122	12.31 N	79.54 E
Madureira, Serra de ⩘	287a	22.49 S	43.31 W
Maduru ≃	122	7.52 N	81.31 E
Madwar al-Bighāl ∧ [2]	142	29.09 N	29.54 E
Madžalis	84	42.08 N	47.50 E
Mãe, Ilha da I	287a	22.59 S	43.04 W
Maeander Reef ✣ [2]	116	8.05 N	119.18 E
Maebaru	92	33.33 N	130.12 E
Maebashi	94	36.23 N	139.04 E
Maeda	270	34.55 N	135.08 E
Mãe dos Homens	256	22.52 S	46.37 W
Maegye-ri	98	34.45 N	126.18 E
Mae Hong Son	110	19.16 N	97.56 E
Mae Klong ≃	110	13.21 N	100.00 E
Maenclochog	42	51.54 N	4.48 W
Maengsan	98	39.40 N	126.30 E
Maeno ✦ [8]	268	35.46 N	139.42 E
Maenza	66	41.31 N	13.11 E
Mae Ramat	110	16.58 N	98.31 E
Mae Rim	110	18.54 N	98.57 E
Maerkansu	85	39.19 N	73.53 E
Ma'erna	102	31.13 N	102.02 E
Maer Shan ∧	102	26.18 N	100.20 E
Mae Sariang	110	18.10 N	97.56 E
Maeser	200	40.28 N	109.35 W
Mae Sot	110	16.43 N	98.34 E
Maesteg	42	51.37 N	3.40 W
Maestra, Sierra ⩘	240p	20.00 N	76.45 W
Maestre de Campo Island I	116	12.56 N	121.42 E
Maestu	34	42.44 N	2.27 W
Mae Tha	110	18.28 N	99.08 E
Maevarano ≃	157b	14.35 S	47.58 E
Maevatanana	157b	16.56 S	46.49 E
Maéwo I	175f	15.10 S	168.10 E
Ma'fan	146	25.55 N	14.29 E
Mafang	105	40.02 N	117.01 E
Mafangchang	107	29.24 N	106.06 E
Mafangcun	105	40.09 N	116.24 E
Ma Faro ✣ [2]	122	5.50 N	73.26 E
Mafeking	184	52.41 N	101.06 W
Mafembage	152	14.32 S	21.42 E
Mafengtun	104	40.49 N	122.54 E
Mafeteng	158	29.51 S	27.15 E
Maffliers	261	49.05 N	2.19 E
Maffra	166	37.58 S	146.59 E
Mafia Channel ⊔	154	8.10 S	39.40 E
Mafia Island I	154	7.50 S	39.50 E
Mafikeng	156	25.53 S	25.39 E
Mafou ≃	150	10.32 N	10.08 W
Mafra, Bra.	252	26.07 S	49.49 W
Mafra, Port.	34	38.56 N	9.20 W
Magadan	74	59.34 N	150.48 E
Magadi	154	1.54 S	36.17 E
Magadi, Lake ⊜	154	1.52 S	36.17 E
Magaguadavic Lake ⊜	186	45.43 N	67.12 W
Magai-butsu ʊ [1]	96	33.05 N	131.45 E
Magalhães Bastos ✦ [8]	287a	22.53 S	43.23 W
Magalhães de Almeida	250	3.24 S	42.12 W
Magaliesberg ⩘	158	25.50 S	27.30 E
Magallanes → Punta Arenas, Chile	254	53.09 S	70.55 W
Magallanes, Pil.	116	12.50 N	123.50 E
Magallanes, Estrecho de (Strait of Magellan) ⊔	254	54.00 S	71.00 W
Magallanes y de la Antártica Chilena □ [4]	254	53.00 S	72.00 W
Maganga	154	0.51 N	26.22 E
Magangué	246	9.14 N	74.45 W
Magansk	88	55.52 N	93.15 E
Maganuy ≃	116	6.55 N	124.30 E
Magara, India	126	22.34 N	87.34 E
Mağara, Tür.	130	36.43 N	33.52 E
Magaramkent	84	41.37 N	48.21 E
Magaria	150	13.00 N	8.54 E
Magat ≃	116	17.02 N	121.49 E
Magazine Mountain ∧	194	35.10 N	93.38 W
Magazzolo ≃	70	37.25 N	13.15 E
Magboro	273a	6.43 N	3.24 E
Magburaka	150	8.43 N	11.57 W
Magdagači	89	53.27 N	125.48 E
Magdalena, Arg.	258	35.04 S	57.32 W
Magdalena, Bol.	248	13.20 S	64.08 W
Magdalena, Méx.	234	20.55 N	103.57 W
Magdalena, Perú	248	6.21 S	77.49 W
Magdalena, Perú	286d	12.06 S	77.05 W
Magdalena, N.M., U.S.	200	34.07 N	107.14 W
Magdalena □ [5]	246	10.00 N	74.00 W
Magdalena ≃, Col.	246	11.06 N	74.51 W
Magdalena ≃, Méx.	232	30.48 N	112.32 W
Magdalena, Bahía ⊂	232	24.35 N	112.00 W
Magdalena, Isla I, Chile	254	44.40 S	73.10 W
Magdalena, Isla I, Méx.	232	24.55 N	112.15 W
Magdalena, Punta ≻	246	3.56 N	77.21 W
Magdalena Contreras ✦ [8]	286a	19.18 N	99.17 W
Magdalena de Kino	232	30.38 N	110.57 W
Magdalena Peñasco	234	17.14 N	97.34 W
Magdalena Teitipac	234	16.54 N	96.34 W
Magdalena Tequisistlán	234	16.22 N	95.15 W
Magdalen Laver	260	51.45 N	0.11 E
Magdeborn	54	51.14 N	12.26 E
Magdeburg	54	52.07 N	11.38 E
Magdeburger Börde ≚	54	52.00 N	11.30 E
Magdeburgo → Magdeburg	54	52.07 N	11.38 E
Magdiwang	116	12.30 N	122.31 E
Magdonskij, porog ⌞	88	57.45 N	100.55 E
Māge	110	26.33 N	98.33 E
Magé □ [7]	287a	22.41 S	43.07 W
Magee	194	31.52 N	89.44 W
Magee, Island ≻ [1]	48	54.49 N	5.42 W
Magelang	115a	7.28 S	110.13 E
Magellan, Strait of → Magallanes, Estrecho de ⊔	254	54.00 S	71.00 W
Magellan-Strasse → Magallanes, Estrecho de ⊔	254	54.00 S	71.00 W
Magén	132	31.18 N	34.26 E
Magenta	62	45.28 N	8.53 E
Magenta, Lake ⊜	162	33.26 S	119.10 E
Magerøy I	24	71.03 N	25.45 E
Magetan	115a	7.39 S	111.20 E
Magezhuang	105	40.08 N	117.59 E
Maggia	58	46.15 N	8.42 E
Maggia ≃	58	46.09 N	8.48 E
Maggia, Valle V	58	46.17 N	8.40 E
Maggie Creek ≃	204	40.43 N	116.05 W
Maggiorasca, Monte ∧	62	44.33 N	9.29 E
Maggiore ≃	267a	41.54 N	12.16 E
Maggiore, Lago ⊜	36	46.00 N	8.40 E
Maggiore, Monte ∧	68	41.14 N	14.12 E
Maghāghah	142	28.39 N	30.50 E
Maghama	150	15.31 N	12.51 W
Maghar	132	32.53 N	35.24 E
Maghdūshah	132	33.31 N	35.23 E
Maghera	48	54.51 N	6.40 W
Magherafelt	48	54.45 N	6.36 W
Maghniyya	148	34.50 N	1.50 W
Magholpur ✦ [8]	272a	28.42 N	77.06 E
Maghull	44	53.32 N	2.57 W
Magician Lake ⊜	216	42.04 N	86.10 W
Magic Mountain ♠	228	34.26 N	118.36 W
Magic Reservoir ⊜ [1]	202	43.17 N	114.23 W
Magill, Lac ⊜	206	45.35 N	71.17 W
Magill Heights	279b	40.37 N	79.52 W
Magill Lake ⊜	184	54.45 N	94.58 W
Mágina ∧	34	37.43 N	3.28 W
Maginu	268	35.35 N	139.36 E
Magione	66	43.08 N	12.12 E
Magisano	68	39.01 N	16.37 E
Magiscatzín	234	22.48 N	98.42 W
Magiss Lake ⊜	184	52.59 N	91.40 W
Maglaj	38	44.33 N	18.06 E
Magliana ✦ [8]	267a	41.50 N	12.25 E
Magliana, Fosso ≃	267a	41.49 N	12.25 E
Magliano dei Marsi	66	42.05 N	13.22 E
Magliano in Toscana	66	42.36 N	11.17 E
Magliano Sabina	66	42.22 N	12.29 E
Maglie	68	40.07 N	18.19 E
Maglód	264c	47.27 N	19.21 E
M'aglovo	265a	59.53 N	30.41 E
Magnago	266b	45.35 N	8.48 E
Magnanville	261	48.58 N	1.41 E
Magnet	184	51.19 N	99.30 W
Magnetawan ≃	190	45.46 N	80.37 W
Magnetic Island I	166	19.08 S	146.50 E
Magnetic Springs	214	40.21 N	83.16 W
Magnetischer Nordpol → North Magnetic Pole ✦	16	77.19 N	101.49 W
Magnetischer Südpol → South Magnetic Pole ✦	9	65.18 S	139.30 E
Magnières	58	48.27 N	6.34 E
Magnitka	86	55.21 N	59.43 E
Magnitogorsk	86	53.27 N	59.04 E
Magnitostroj	80	51.43 N	53.05 E
Magnolia, Ar., U.S.	194	33.16 N	93.14 W
Magnolia, De., U.S.	208	39.04 N	75.28 W
Magnolia, Ma., U.S.	283	42.35 N	70.43 W
Magnolia, Mn., U.S.	198	43.38 N	96.04 W
Magnolia, Ms., U.S.	194	31.08 N	90.27 W
Magnolia, N.J., U.S.	285	39.51 N	75.02 W
Magnolia, Oh., U.S.	214	40.39 N	81.17 W
Magnolia, Tx., U.S.	222	30.13 N	95.45 W
Magnor	26	59.57 N	12.12 E
Magny-en-Vexin	50	49.09 N	1.47 E
Magny-le-Hongre	261	48.52 N	2.49 E
Magny-les-Hameaux	261	48.44 N	2.04 E
Mago	89	53.15 N	140.13 E
Magog	206	45.16 N	72.09 W
Magog ≃	206	45.24 N	71.54 W
Magog, Lake ⊜	206	45.18 N	72.03 W
Magoito	266c	38.52 N	9.26 W
Magome ✦ [8]	268	35.35 N	139.43 E
Mago National Park ♠	144	5.30 N	36.15 E
Magonoy	116	6.54 N	124.33 E
Magoro	154	1.44 N	34.06 E
Magothy Bay ⊂	208	37.10 N	75.55 W
Magothy River ⊂	208	39.04 N	76.28 W
Magoúla	267c	38.04 N	23.32 E
Magoye	154	16.00 S	27.37 E
Magozal, Méx.	232	21.34 N	97.59 W
Magozal, Méx.	234	21.34 N	97.59 W
M'agozero	76	60.21 N	34.50 E
Magpie	186	50.19 N	64.30 W
Magpie ≃, On., Can.	190	47.56 N	84.50 W
Magpie ≃, P.Q., Can.	186	50.19 N	64.27 W
Magpie, Lac ⊜	186	51.00 N	64.41 W
Magpie Ouest ≃	186	51.02 N	64.42 W
Magra	126	22.59 N	88.22 E
Magra ≃	64	44.03 N	9.58 E
Magra Hāt	126	22.14 N	88.23 E
Magrath	182	49.25 N	112.52 W
Magrè (Margreid)	64	46.17 N	11.12 E
Magro ≃	34	39.11 N	0.25 W
Magruder Mountain ∧	204	37.25 N	117.33 W
Magsaysay (Linugos)	116	9.01 N	125.11 E
Magsingal	116	17.41 N	120.25 E
Magu ≃	250	2.56 S	41.55 W
Maguan	102	22.59 N	104.19 E
Maguanying	271a	39.52 N	116.17 E
Maguari, Cabo ≻	250	0.18 S	48.22 W
Magude	156	25.02 S	32.40 E
Magudu	158	27.31 S	31.40 E
Magueyes	196	25.44 N	97.47 W
Maguindanao □ [4]	116	6.55 N	124.20 E
Magumeri	146	12.08 N	12.50 E
Māgura	124	23.29 N	89.25 E
Maguru	150	12.28 N	6.35 E
Maguse Lake ⊜	176	61.40 N	95.10 W
Maguzhan	120	31.15 N	88.00 E
Magway, Mya.	110	20.09 N	94.55 E
Magway, Mya.	110	20.30 N	94.30 E
Magwe	154	4.08 N	32.17 E
Magwood Park ♠	275b	43.39 N	79.30 W
Magyarország → Hungary □ [1]	30	47.00 N	20.00 E
Mahābād	128	36.45 N	45.43 E
Mahābaleshwar	122	17.55 N	73.40 E
Mahabe	157b	17.05 S	45.20 E
Mahābhārat Lek ⩘	124	27.40 N	84.30 E
Mahabo, Madag.	157b	23.40 S	46.08 E
Mahabo, Madag.	157b	20.23 S	44.40 E
Mahād	122	18.05 N	73.25 E
Mahadday Weyn	144	2.58 N	45.32 E
Mahādebpur	126	23.51 N	89.53 E
Mahādeo Hills ⩘ [2]	122	22.22 N	78.34 E
Mahādeo Range ⩘	122	17.50 N	74.15 E
Mahaffey	214	40.52 N	78.43 W
Mahagi	154	2.18 N	30.59 E
Mahagi Port	154	2.09 N	31.14 E
Mahai	102	38.17 N	94.13 E
Mahaica-Berbice □ [4]	246	6.20 N	57.50 W
Mahaicony Village	246	6.36 N	57.48 W
Mahajamba ≃	157b	15.33 S	47.08 E
Mahajamba, Helodranon' i ⊂	157b	15.24 S	47.05 E
Mahājan	123	28.47 N	73.50 E
Mahajanga	157b	15.43 S	46.19 E
Mahajanga □ [4]	157b	17.00 S	46.00 E
Mahajilo ≃	157b	19.42 S	45.22 E
Maḥajjah	132	32.57 N	36.14 E
Mahākālī □ [8]	124	29.30 N	80.30 E
Mahākālī (Sārda) ≃	124	27.21 N	81.23 E
Mahakam ≃	112	0.35 S	117.17 E
Mahālandi	126	24.04 N	88.07 E
Mahalatswe	156	23.05 S	26.51 E
Mahalla el-Kubra → Al-Maḥallah al-Kubrā	142	30.58 N	31.10 E
Maḥallāt	128	33.55 N	50.27 E
Maḥallat Kayl	142	31.01 N	30.17 E
Maḥallat Marḥūm	142	30.48 N	30.57 E
Maḥallat Minūf	142	30.53 N	30.58 E
Maḥallat Zayyād	142	31.02 N	31.14 E
Maham	124	28.59 N	76.18 E
Mahamba	158	27.07 S	31.10 E
Mahānadi ≃	118	20.19 N	86.45 E
Mahānadpati	126	23.00 N	88.16 E
Mahānanda ≃	124	24.29 N	88.18 E
Mahanay Island I	116	10.12 N	124.14 E
Mahanoro	157b	19.54 S	48.48 E
Mahanoy City	208	40.48 N	76.08 W
Mahanoy Creek ≃	208	40.42 N	76.51 W
Mahantango Creek ≃	208	40.47 N	76.56 W
Mahantango Mountain ∧	208	40.40 N	76.45 W
Mahao	89	43.10 N	127.59 E
Mahape	272c	19.07 N	73.01 E
Mahārājganj, India	124	26.07 N	84.29 E
Mahārājganj, India	124	27.09 N	83.34 E
Mahārājpur, India	124	25.01 N	79.44 E
Mahārājpur, India	272a	28.39 N	77.20 E
Mahārāshtra □ [3]	122	19.00 N	76.00 E
Maḥārīq, Wādī V	142	27.48 N	31.47 E
Mahārlū, Daryācheh-ye ⊜	128	29.25 N	52.50 E
Mahāsamund	120	21.06 N	82.06 E
Maha Sarakham	110	16.11 N	103.18 E
Maha Sawat, Khlong ≌	269a	13.47 N	100.28 E
Mahasoa	157b	22.12 S	46.06 E
Mahasolo	157b	19.07 S	46.22 E
Mahates	246	10.14 N	75.12 W
Mahatsinjo	157b	21.26 S	45.51 E
Maḥaṭṭat al-Ḥafīf	132	32.12 N	37.08 E
Mahaut	240d	15.21 N	61.25 W
Mahavavy ≃, Madag.	157b	15.57 S	45.54 E
Mahavavy ≃, Madag.	157b	13.00 S	48.55 E
Mahaweli ≃	122	8.27 N	81.13 E
Mahaxai	110	17.25 N	105.12 E
Maḥbas, Wādī al- V	140	15.50 N	29.45 E
Mahbūbābād	122	17.37 N	80.01 E
Mahbūbnagar	122	16.44 N	77.59 E
Mahd adh-Dhahab	128	23.30 N	40.52 E
Mahdalynivka	78	48.55 N	34.54 E
Mahdāt, Bi'r al- ╤ [4]	142	30.44 N	32.32 E
Mahdia, Guy.	246	5.16 N	59.09 W
Mahdia, Tun.	148	35.30 N	11.04 E
Mahdia □ [8]	148	35.18 N	10.45 E
Mahe	122	11.42 N	75.32 E
Mahébourg	157c	20.24 S	57.42 E
Mahé Island I	138	4.40 S	55.28 E
Mahendraganj	124	25.20 N	89.45 E
Mahendragarh	124	28.17 N	76.09 E
Mahendra Giri ∧	122	18.58 N	84.21 E
Mahendranagar	124	28.52 N	80.17 E
Mahenge, Tan.	154	7.38 S	36.16 E
Mahenge, Tan.	154	8.41 S	36.43 E
Maheno	172	45.10 S	170.50 E
Maheriv	78	50.08 N	23.43 E
Mahesāna	120	23.36 N	72.24 E
Mahesgādi	272b	22.39 N	88.33 E
Maheshmunda	126	24.13 N	86.24 E
Maheshtala	272b	22.30 N	88.15 E
Maheshwar	120	22.11 N	75.35 E
Mahespur	124	23.21 N	88.55 E
Mahgawān	124	26.29 N	78.37 E
Mahi ≃	120	22.16 N	72.58 E
Mahia Peninsula ≻ [1]	172	39.10 S	177.53 E
Mahiāri	272b	22.35 N	88.14 E
Māhikpur	272b	22.32 N	88.14 E
Mahilāra	126	22.56 N	90.16 E
Māhīm ✦ [8]	272c	19.03 N	72.49 E
Māhīm ≃	272c	19.03 N	72.51 E
Māhīm Bay ⊂	272c	19.02 N	72.50 E
Mahina, Mali	150	13.46 N	10.51 W

Symbol	English	Deutsch	Español	Français	Português
≃	River	Fluß	Río	Rivière	Rio
≌	Canal	Kanal	Canal	Canal	Canal
⌞	Waterfall, Rapids	Wasserfall, Stromschnellen	Cascada, Rápidos	Chute d'eau, Rapides	Cascata, Rápidos
⊔	Strait	Meeresstraße	Estrecho	Détroit	Estreito
⊂	Bay, Gulf	Bucht, Golf	Bahía, Golfo	Baie, Golfe	Baía, Golfo
⊜	Lake, Lakes	See, Seen	Lago, Lagos	Lac, Lacs	Lago, Lagos
≡	Swamp	Sumpf	Pantano	Marais	Pântano
⊓	Ice Features, Glacier	Eis- und Gletscherformen	Accidentes Glaciales	Formes glaciaires	Acidentes glaciares
╤	Other Hydrographic Features	Andere Hydrographische Objekte	Otros Elementos Hidrográficos	Autres données hydrographiques	Outros acidentes hidrográficos
✣	Submarine Features	Untermeerische Objekte	Accidentes Submarinos	Formes de relief sous-marin	Acidentes submarinos
□	Political Unit	Politische Einheit	Unidad Política	Entité politique	Unidade política
ʊ	Cultural Institution	Kulturelle Institution	Institución Cultural	Institution culturelle	Instituição cultural
⊥	Historical Site	Historische Stätte	Sitio Histórico	Site historique	Sitio histórico
♠	Recreational Site	Erholungs- und Ferienort	Sitio de Recreo	Centre de loisirs	Area de Lazer
⊠	Airport	Flughafen	Aeropuerto	Aéroport	Aeroporto
■	Military Installation	Militäranlage	Instalación Militar	Installation militaire	Instalação militar
✦	Miscellaneous	Verschiedenes	Misceláneo	Divers	Diversos

Mahina, Poly. fr. 174s 17.31 S 149.30 W
Mahinerangi, Lake @ 172 45.51 S 169.57 E
Mahinog 116 9.09 N 124.47 E
Mahīshādal 126 22.11 N 87.59 E
Mahishdānga 272b 22.54 N 88.11 E
Mahlabatini 158 28.14 S 31.30 E
Mahlangasi 158 27.37 S 31.42 E
Mahlberg 58 48.17 N 7.48 E
Mahlow 54 52.22 N 13.24 E
Mahlsdorf 54 52.47 N 11.13 E
Mahlsdorf ✦⁸ 264a 52.31 N 13.37 E
Mahlsdorf-Süd ✦⁸ 264a 52.29 N 13.36 E
Mahmūdābād, India 124 27.18 N 81.07 E
Mahmūdābād, Īrān 128 36.38 N 52.15 E
Mahmūd-e Rāqī 120 35.01 N 69.20 E
Mahmūdīyah, Tur'at al- ≃ 142 31.11 N 29.53 E
Mahmudiye 130 39.30 N 31.00 E
Mahmūdpur, India 272a 28.46 N 77.22 E
Mahmūdpur, India 272b 22.41 N 88.09 E
Mahmutbey ✦⁸ 267b 41.03 N 28.49 E
Mahmutşevketpaşa 130 41.05 N 29.19 E
Mahmutşevketpaşa ✦⁸ 267b 41.09 N 29.11 E
Mahnomen 198 47.18 N 95.58 W
Mahoba 124 25.17 N 79.52 E
Mahogany Mountain ʌ 202 43.14 N 117.16 W
Mahomet 216 40.11 N 88.24 W
Mahone Bay 186 44.27 N 64.23 W
Mahone Bay ⊂ 186 44.30 N 64.15 W
Mahoning □⁶ 214 41.06 N 80.39 W
Mahoning ≃ 214 40.58 N 80.23 W
Mahoning, West Branch ≃ 214 41.12 N 80.57 W
Mahoning Creek ≃ 214 40.55 N 79.27 W
Mahoning Creek Lake @¹ 214 40.50 N 79.10 W
Mahony Lake @ 180 65.30 N 125.20 W
Mahood Falls 182 51.50 N 120.39 W
Mahood Lake @ 182 51.55 N 120.24 W
Mahopac 210 41.22 N 73.44 W
Mahopac Falls 210 41.22 N 73.46 W
Mahora 34 39.13 N 1.44 W
Mahoras Brook ≃ 276 40.25 N 74.08 W
Mahrāt, Jabal ʌ¹ 144 17.05 N 51.30 E
Mahrauli ✦⁸ 272a 28.31 N 77.11 E
Mahrauni 124 24.35 N 78.43 E
Mähren → Morava □⁹ 30 49.20 N 17.00 E
Mahres 148 34.32 N 10.30 E
Mähring 60 49.55 N 12.32 E
Mahuiling 100 29.24 N 115.48 E
Māhul ✦⁸ 272c 19.01 N 72.53 E
Mahulia 126 22.39 N 86.24 E
Mahur Island I 164 2.50 S 152.40 E
Mahuta 154 10.52 S 39.27 E
Mahuva 120 21.05 N 71.48 E
Mahwa 124 27.03 N 76.56 E
Mahwah 276 41.06 N 74.09 W
Mahwah ≃ 276 41.06 N 74.10 W
Mai, Île de I 275a 45.36 N 73.50 W
Maia, Am. Sam. 174y 14.13 S 169.28 W
Maia, Port. 34 41.14 N 8.37 W
Mai Aini 144 14.47 N 39.06 E
Maiala National Park ✦ 171a 27.19 S 152.46 E
Maianga 152 14.12 S 21.45 E
Maiano 64 46.11 N 13.04 E
Maiauatá 250 1.51 S 49.02 W
Maicao 246 11.23 N 72.13 W
Maîche 58 47.15 N 6.48 E
Maichen 102 20.29 N 109.59 E
Maici ≃ 248 6.30 S 61.43 W
Maicuru ≃ 250 2.14 S 54.17 W
Maida 68 38.51 N 16.22 E
Maidan ✦ 272b 22.33 N 88.21 E
Maiden 192 35.34 N 81.12 W
Maidenhead 42 51.32 N 0.44 W
Maiden Newton 42 50.46 N 2.35 W
Maidstone, Austl. 274b 37.47 S 144.52 E
Maidstone, On., Can. 214 42.13 N 82.53 W
Maidstone, Sk., Can. 184 53.06 N 109.18 W
Maidstone, Eng., U.K. 42 51.17 N 0.32 E
Maidstone □⁸ 260 51.17 N 0.35 E
Maiduguri 146 11.51 N 13.10 E
Maie 154 2.46 N 30.34 E
Maiella, Montagna della ʌ 66 42.05 N 14.07 E
Maienfeld 58 47.00 N 9.32 E
Maierato 68 38.42 N 16.11 E
Maifeld ✦¹ 56 50.20 N 7.20 E
Maigatari 150 12.46 N 9.27 E
Maignelay 50 49.33 N 2.31 E
Maigo 116 8.10 N 123.57 E
Mai Gudo ʌ 144 7.29 N 37.12 E
Maigue ≃ 48 52.39 N 8.48 W
Maihar 124 24.16 N 80.45 E
Maihara 94 35.19 N 136.17 E
Maijoma 196 28.55 N 104.21 W
Maikala Plateau ✦¹ 124 22.30 N 81.00 E
Maikala Range ʌ 122 22.30 N 81.30 E
Maikammer 56 49.18 N 8.08 E
Maiko ≃ 154 0.14 N 25.33 E
Maiko, Parc National de la ✦ 154 3.30 N 27.45 E
Maikoor, Pulau I 164 6.15 S 134.15 E
Mailand → Milano 62 45.28 N 9.12 E
Mailāni 124 28.17 N 80.21 E
Mailasqui 256 23.33 S 47.04 W
Maili 229c 21.25 N 158.10 W
Maillane 62 43.50 N 4.47 E
Mailley-et-Chazelot 58 47.32 N 6.03 E
Maillezais 32 46.22 N 0.44 W
Mailly-le-Camp 50 48.40 N 4.13 E
Mailly-le-Château 50 47.36 N 3.38 E
Mailly-Maillet 50 50.04 N 2.36 E
Mailsi 123 29.48 N 72.11 E
Maimbung 116 5.56 N 121.02 E
Mai Mefales 144 14.59 N 38.16 E
Mā'ln 132 31.41 N 35.44 E
Main ≃, Dtsch. 30 50.00 N 8.18 E
Main ≃, N. Ire., U.K. 48 54.43 N 6.18 W
Maināguri 124 26.34 N 88.49 E
Mainar 58 47.42 N 9.11 E
Mainburg 60 48.38 N 11.47 E
Main Camp 174o 2.01 N 157.25 W
Main Canal ≍, Ca., U.S. 226 37.25 N 121.05 W
Main Canal ≍, Ca., U.S. 226 37.23 N 120.26 W
Main Canal ≍, Wa., U.S. 224 47.07 N 120.44 W
Main Channel ʮ 190 45.22 N 81.50 W
Maincourt-sur-Yvette 261 48.43 N 1.58 E
Main Creek ≃ 276 40.34 N 74.11 W
Maincy 261 48.33 N 2.42 E
Mai-Ndombe, Lac @ 152 2.00 S 18.20 E
Main-Donau-Kanal ≍ 60 49.02 N 11.36 E
Main Duck Island I 212 43.56 N 76.37 W
Maine 210 42.11 N 76.03 W
Maine □⁹ 32 48.15 N 0.05 W
Maine □³, U.S. 178 45.15 N 69.15 W
Maine □³, U.S. 188 45.15 N 69.15 W
Maine ≃ 48 52.09 N 9.45 W
Maine, Gulf of ⊂ 178 43.00 N 68.00 W
Maine-et-Loire □⁵ 32 47.25 N 0.30 W
Mainesburg 210 41.47 N 77.07 W
Mainé-Soroa 146 13.12 N 12.02 E
Maineville 218 39.18 N 84.13 W
Mainguerin 261 48.32 N 1.51 E
Mainhardt 56 49.04 N 9.33 E
Mainit 116 9.32 N 125.32 E
Mainit, Lake @ 116 9.26 N 125.32 E
Mainland 285 40.15 N 75.22 W
Mainland I, Scot., U.K. 46 59.00 N 3.15 W
Mainland I, Scot., U.K. 46a 60.16 N 1.16 W
Mainleus 54 50.06 N 11.22 E
Mainoru 164 14.02 S 134.05 E
Mainpuri 124 27.14 N 79.01 E
Main Range National Park ✦ 171a 28.01 S 152.22 E
Maintal 56 50.09 N 8.54 E
Maintenon 50 48.35 N 1.35 E
Maintirano 157b 18.03 S 44.01 E
Main Topsail ʌ 186 49.08 N 56.33 W
Mainvilliers 50 48.27 N 1.28 E
Mainz 56 50.01 N 8.16 E
Maio I 150a 15.15 N 23.10 W
Maiolati Spontini 66 43.28 N 13.06 E
Maiori 68 40.39 N 14.38 E
Maiori, Nuraghe ⊥ 71 40.56 N 9.06 E
Maipa 164 8.21 S 146.33 E
Maipo ≃ 252 33.37 S 71.39 W
Maipo, Volcán ʌ¹ 252 34.10 S 69.50 W
Maipú, Arg. 252 36.52 S 57.52 W
Maipú, Arg. 252 32.58 S 68.47 W
Maipú, Chile 252 33.31 S 70.46 W
Maiqihamiao 89 43.22 N 120.46 E
Maiquetía 246 10.36 N 66.57 W
Maira ≃ 62 44.49 N 7.38 E
Maira, Valle V 62 44.30 N 7.15 E
Mairābāri 120 26.28 N 92.26 E
Mairi 250 11.43 S 40.08 W
Mairinque 256 23.33 S 47.10 W
Mairiporã 256 23.19 S 46.35 W
Mairiporã □⁷ 287b 23.24 S 46.37 W
Mairipotaba 255 17.18 S 49.28 W
Maisach 60 48.13 N 11.16 E
Maisaka 94 34.41 N 137.37 E
Maishi 100 29.11 N 113.58 E
Maišiagala 76 54.52 N 25.04 E
Maiskhāl Island I 120 21.36 N 91.56 E
Maison de Pierre, Lac de la @ 206 46.53 N 74.42 W
Maisonneuve, Parc ✦ 275a 45.33 N 73.34 W
Maisons-Alfort 261 48.48 N 2.26 E
Maisons-Laffitte 50 48.57 N 2.09 E
Maisons-Laffitte, Château de ⊥ 261 48.57 N 2.09 E
Maisse 50 48.24 N 2.23 E
Maissin 56 49.58 N 5.11 E
Maitani 270 34.49 N 135.22 E
Maitengwe 156 20.06 S 27.13 E
Maitengwe ≃ 156 19.59 S 26.26 E
Maithon Reservoir @¹ 126 23.50 N 86.43 E
Maitland, Austl. 168b 34.22 S 137.40 E
Maitland, Austl. 170 32.44 S 151.33 E
Maitland, N.S., Can. 186 45.19 N 63.30 W
Maitland, On., Can. 212 44.38 N 75.37 W
Maitland, Fl., U.S. 220 28.37 N 81.21 W
Maitland ≃ 190 43.45 N 81.43 W
Maitland ≃ 162 27.11 S 121.03 E
Maitland, Lake @ 162 27.38 N 115.29 E
Maixie 100 27.38 N 115.29 E
Maíz ≃ 236 11.17 N 83.52 W
Maíz, Islas del II 236 12.15 N 83.00 W
Maizefield 158 26.28 S 29.31 E
Maizhokunggar 120 29.50 N 91.45 E
Maizières-lès-Metz 56 49.13 N 6.09 E
Maizières-lès-Vic 58 48.43 N 6.46 E
Maizuru 96 35.28 N 135.24 E
Maja ≃, Ross. 74 60.24 N 134.30 E
Maja ≃, Ross. 89 54.31 N 134.41 E
Majābirah, Minqār al- ʌ¹ 142 30.16 N 29.49 E
Majačnyj 86 52.41 N 55.44 E
Majadahonda 266a 40.29 N 3.52 W
Majagua 240p 21.55 N 79.00 W
Majagual 246 8.33 N 74.38 W
Majalaya 115a 7.03 S 107.45 E
Majalengka 115a 6.50 S 108.13 E
Majana, Ensenada de ⊂ 240p 22.41 N 82.45 W
Majanji 154 0.15 N 33.59 E
Majari ≃ 246 3.29 N 60.58 W
Majayjay 116 14.09 N 121.28 E
Majchura 85 39.02 N 68.35 E
Majdantal 84 43.41 N 68.02 E
Majd el Kurūm 132 32.55 N 35.15 E
Majé 256 22.39 S 43.02 W
Majeigha 140 11.33 N 24.40 E
Majenang 115a 7.18 S 108.45 E
Majene 112 3.33 S 118.57 E
Majenica 216 40.46 N 85.27 W
Majevica ʌ 72 44.40 N 18.55 E
Majī 144 6.11 N 35.38 E
Majia 100 32.32 N 118.50 E
Majia ≃ 100 38.09 N 117.53 E
Majiacun 106 30.08 N 119.58 E
Majiahe 102 35.20 N 104.46 E
Majian, Zhg. 100 29.19 N 119.36 E
Majian, Zhg. 102 29.43 N 120.00 E
Majiang, Zhg. 102 23.48 N 111.09 E
Majiang, Zhg. 110 26.28 N 107.28 E
Majiangzong 120 30.27 N 90.03 E
Majiaoba 102 32.14 N 104.35 E
Majiaping 106 36.31 N 103.20 E
Majiasi 100 39.03 N 117.05 E
Majiawopu 104 41.46 N 121.06 E
Majiayan 100 27.26 N 112.56 E
Majiazhai 104 42.22 N 124.04 E
Majiazhou 100 26.46 N 114.47 E
Majidun Creek ≃ 273a 6.38 N 3.28 E
Majie, Zhg. 102 23.50 N 105.07 E
Majie, Zhg. 102 25.20 N 103.01 E
Majie 100 29.18 N 118.24 E
Majin ≃ 100 29.00 N 118.21 E
Majinzhuangzi 104 41.55 N 123.53 E
Maji Shan I 106 31.26 N 120.06 E
Majitha 123 31.46 N 74.57 E
Majitun 74 61.44 N 130.18 E
Majja 86 51.27 N 75.52 E
Majkain 84 44.35 N 40.07 E
Majkop 86 59.01 N 55.54 E
Majkor 86 45.49 N 62.39 E
Majlibaš 86 41.17 N 72.29 E
Majli-Saj 126 24.13 N 90.53 E
Majlisipur 85 42.40 N 71.15 E
Majmak 80 54.07 N 47.37 E
Majna, Ross. 86 53.00 N 91.28 E
Majna, Ross. 272b 22.59 N 88.09 E
Majnan 180 63.15 N 176.40 E
Majnic, ozero @ 180 63.36 N 176.30 E
Majno-Gytkino 180 39.06 N 127.07 E
Majon-ni, C.M.I.K. 271b 37.36 N 126.41 E
Majon-ni, Taehan 34 39.48 N 2.48 E
Major, Puig ʌ
Majorca → Mallorca I 34 39.30 N 3.00 E
Major Creek ≃ 169 36.51 S 145.05 E
Major Isidoro 250 9.32 S 37.00 W
Majorque, Île → Mallorca I 34 39.30 N 3.00 E
Majrūr 140 14.01 N 30.27 E
Majrūr, Wādī V 140 15.44 N 29.26 E
Majsk 86 57.49 N 77.16 E
Majskij, Ross. 82 47.43 N 43.01 E
Majskij, Ross. 84 43.38 N 44.04 E
Majskij, Ross. 89 52.18 N 129.38 E
Majskij, Ross. 180 35.39 N 140.03 E
Majskoje, Kaz. 86 50.55 N 78.15 E
Majskoje, Ross. 86 55.41 N 76.11 E
Majtan 86 45.46 N 74.20 E
Majtobe 85 43.01 N 70.35 E
Māju 126 22.37 N 88.05 E
Majuba Hill ⊥ 158 27.38 S 29.51 E
Majuqiao 105 39.46 N 116.32 E
Majuro I¹ 14 7.09 N 171.12 E
Majuzigou 104 41.49 N 121.38 E
Maka 150 13.40 N 14.17 W
Makabana 152 3.28 S 12.29 E
Makabe 94 36.16 N 140.06 E
Makadassa ≃ 116 7.22 N 124.36 E
Makaha, Hi., U.S. 229c 21.28 N 158.13 W
Makaha, Zimb. 154 17.17 S 32.37 E
Makaha Point > 229b 22.08 N 159.44 W
Makah Indian Reservation ✦⁴ 224 48.20 N 124.41 W
Makahuena Point > 229b 21.52 N 159.27 W
Makak 152 3.33 N 11.02 E
Makala 273b 4.25 S 15.17 E
Makalamabedi 156 20.19 S 23.51 E
Makale 112 3.06 S 119.51 E
Makallé 252 27.13 S 59.17 W
Makālu ʌ 124 27.54 N 87.06 E
Makamba 154 4.08 S 29.49 E
Makanapur 272a 28.38 N 77.21 E
Makanči 86 46.48 N 82.00 E
Makanya 154 4.20 S 37.51 E
Makanza 152 1.36 N 19.07 E
Makaoo Indian Reserve ✦⁴ 184 53.40 N 110.02 W
Makapu Point > 174v 18.59 S 169.56 W
Makapuu Head > 229c 21.19 N 157.39 W
Makarakomburu, Mount ʌ 175e 9.43 S 160.02 E
Makarakskij 86 55.36 N 88.03 E
Makarapan Mountain ʌ 246 4.00 N 58.51 W
Makarewa 172 46.20 S 168.21 E
Makari 146 12.35 N 14.28 E
Makar-Ib 24 63.39 N 49.24 E
Makaricha 24 66.15 N 58.20 E
Makariv 78 50.28 N 29.49 E
Makarje 80 58.35 N 48.11 E
Makarjev 80 57.52 N 43.48 E
Makarjevo 80 56.06 N 45.06 E
Makarov 89 48.38 N 142.48 E
Makarovo, Ross. 80 52.52 N 45.20 E
Makarovo, Ross. 82 54.22 N 36.40 E
Makarovo, Ross. 88 57.29 N 107.52 E
Makarska 36 43.18 N 17.02 E
Makasar → Ujungpandang 112 5.07 S 119.24 E
Makasar, Selat (Makassar Strait) ʮ 112 2.00 S 117.30 E
Makaševka 80 51.30 N 42.36 E
Makassar Strait → Makasar, Selat ʮ 112 2.00 S 117.30 E
Makasuko 154 6.00 S 34.56 E
Makat 80 47.39 N 53.19 E
Makatea I 14 15.50 S 148.15 W
Makati 269f 14.34 N 121.02 E
Makaw, Mya. 110 26.27 N 96.42 E
Makaw, Zaïre 152 3.29 S 18.19 E
Makawao 229a 20.51 N 156.18 W
Makaweli 229b 21.55 N 159.38 W
Makay, Massif du ✦ 157b 21.15 S 45.15 E
Makaya 152 3.22 S 18.02 E
Makedonija → Macedonia □¹ 38 41.50 N 22.00 E
Makefu 174v 18.59 S 169.55 W
Makemie Park 208 37.55 N 75.34 W
Makemo I¹ 16 16.35 S 143.40 W
Makena 229a 20.39 N 156.27 W
Makeni 150 8.53 N 12.03 W
Makere 154 4.17 S 30.25 E
Makeru 172 37.46 S 176.27 E
Makeyevka → Makiyivka, Ukr. 83 48.02 N 37.58 E
Makeyevka → Makiyivka, Ukr. 83 48.02 N 37.58 E
Makgadikgadi ≃ 156 20.45 S 25.30 E
Makgadikgadi Pans Game Reserve ✦⁴ 156 20.30 S 24.45 E
Makhachkala → Machačkala 84 42.58 N 47.30 E
Makhad 123 33.08 N 71.44 E
Makhaleng ≃ 158 30.20 S 27.23 E
Makhālpur 272b 22.56 N 88.10 E
Makham 110 12.40 N 102.12 E
Makhdūmnagar 124 26.28 N 82.46 E
Makhfar al-Quwayrah 132 29.48 N 35.19 E
Makhfar Ramn 130 29.42 N 35.25 E
Makhrūq, Wādī al- V 132 31.30 N 37.10 E
Makhyah, Wādī V 144 17.40 N 49.01 E
Maki, Indon. 164 3.11 S 134.12 E
Maki, Nihon 92 37.45 N 138.53 E
Maki, Nihon 94 37.05 N 138.23 E
Maki, Nihon 270 34.52 N 135.04 E
Makiang 120 30.20 N 99.24 E
Makika, Lua ±⁶ 229a 20.34 N 156.34 W
Makikihi 172 44.38 S 171.09 E
Makilala 116 6.55 N 125.05 E
Makindu 154 2.17 S 37.49 E
Makino, Nihon 94 35.28 N 136.05 E
M'akino, Ross. 265b 55.48 N 37.22 E
Makinsk 86 52.37 N 70.26 E
Makio-dam ±⁶ 94 35.50 N 137.36 E
Makioka 94 35.45 N 138.43 E
Makira □⁴ 175e 11.00 S 162.30 E
Makira Harbour ⊂ 175e 10.25 S 161.29 E
M'akiševo 76 56.34 N 28.53 E
M'akit 74 61.24 N 152.09 E
Makiyivka, Ukr. 78 50.40 N 31.50 E
Makiyivka, Ukr. 83 49.14 N 37.59 E
Makiyivka, Ukr. 83 48.02 N 37.58 E
Makkah (Mecca) 144 21.27 N 39.49 E
Makkavejevo 88 51.44 N 113.58 E
Makkum 52 53.04 N 5.24 E
Maklakovo 30 46.13 N 20.29 E
Makó, Magy. 152 12.52 N 12.21 W
Mako, Sén. 158 29.47 S 28.57 E
Makoaneng ✦ 190 47.27 N 80.25 W
Makobe Lake @ 154 2.34 S 25.29 E
Makoka 271b 37.43 N 126.38 E
Makok-ni 152 0.34 N 12.52 E
Makokou 154 17.27 S 26.05 E
Makoli 175g 17.27 S 178.58 E
Makongai Island I 154 3.25 N 26.22 E
Makongo 154 8.24 S 33.09 E
Makongolosi 84 43.59 N 39.13 E
Makopse 172 39.09 S 176.02 E
Makorako ʌ 154 3.08 N 29.44 E
Makoro
Makoshika State Park ✦ 198 47.03 N 104.41 W
Makoshyne 78 51.27 N 32.18 E
Makotuku 172 40.07 S 176.14 E
Makouak 152 0.01 S 15.39 E
Makov 30 49.23 N 18.30 E
Makovskoje 86 58.12 N 90.52 E
Maków Mazowiecki 30 52.52 N 21.06 E
Maków Podhalański 30 49.44 N 19.41 E
Makrai 124 22.04 N 77.06 E
Makrampur 124 28.23 N 80.19 E
Makran 120 27.03 N 74.43 E
Makran Coast ±² 128 25.15 N 60.15 E
M'aksa 76 58.54 N 38.12 E
Maksatiha 76 57.48 N 35.53 E
Maksimicha 88 53.15 N 108.43 E
Maksimkin Jar 86 58.42 N 86.48 E
Maksimovka, Ross. 89 46.04 N 137.51 E
Maksimovka, Ross. 86 55.02 N 76.00 E
Maksimovo 82 56.20 N 43.15 E
Maksudangarh 124 24.03 N 77.15 E
Maksymovychi 78 51.13 N 29.37 E
Maktar 148 35.51 N 9.12 E
Maktau 154 3.24 S 38.08 E
Mākū, Īrān 128 39.17 N 44.31 E
Maku, Zhg. 105 39.33 N 114.46 E
Makubetsu 92a 42.54 N 143.21 E
Makuliro 154 9.35 S 37.26 E
Makumbako 154 8.51 S 34.50 E
Makumbi 152 5.51 S 20.41 E
Makung (P'enghu) 100 23.34 N 119.34 E
Makunudu I 122 6.20 N 73.06 E
Makunudu Atoll I¹ 122 6.20 N 73.06 E
Makuragi-san ʌ 96 31.16 N 130.19 E
Makurazaki 96 31.16 N 130.19 E
Makurdi 150 7.44 N 8.32 E
Makushin Volcano ʌ¹ 180 53.53 N 166.50 W
Makušino 86 55.13 N 67.13 E
Makuyuni 154 3.33 S 36.06 E
Makwa Lake @ 184 54.04 N 109.15 W
Makwassie 158 27.26 S 26.00 E
Makwende-Bayo 154 7.08 S 28.06 E
Makwiro 154 17.58 S 30.28 E
Māl, India 124 26.52 N 88.44 E
Mal, Maur. 150 16.58 N 13.23 W
Mala, Perú 248 12.39 S 76.38 W
Malå, Sve. 26 65.11 N 18.44 E
Mala ≃ 248 12.40 S 76.41 W
Mala, Punta > 246 7.28 N 80.00 W
Malabang 116 7.38 N 124.03 E
Malabar, Austl. 274a 33.58 S 151.15 E
Malabar, Fl., U.S. 220 28.00 N 80.33 W
Malabar Coast ±² 122 11.00 N 75.00 E
Malabar Farm State Park ✦ 214 40.38 N 82.25 W
Malabar Hill ʌ² 272c 18.57 N 72.48 E
Malabar Point > 272c 18.57 N 72.47 E
Mala Bilozirka 78 47.14 N 34.56 E
Malabo 152 3.45 N 8.47 E
Mal Abrigo 258 34.09 S 56.57 W
Malabrigo Point > 116 13.36 N 121.15 E
Malabuyoc 116 9.39 N 123.19 E
Malaca, Estrecho de → Malacca, Strait of ʮ 110 2.30 N 101.20 E
Malacacheta 255 17.50 S 42.05 W
Malacañang Palace ⊌ 269f 14.36 N 120.59 E
Malacatepec, Volcán ʌ¹ 286a 19.10 N 99.16 W
Malacca, Strait of ʮ 110 2.30 N 101.20 E
Malachovka 82 55.39 N 38.00 E
Malachovo, Ross. 82 54.45 N 37.27 E
Malachovo, Ross. 82 54.22 N 37.31 E
Malachovskij 80 49.08 N 41.43 E
Malacky 30 48.27 N 17.00 E
Māläd ✦⁸ 272c 19.11 N 72.51 E
Malad ≃ 200 41.35 N 112.07 W
Malad City 202 42.11 N 112.15 W
Malad Creek ≃ 272c 19.08 N 72.48 E
Mala Divytsya 78 50.41 N 32.10 E
Malafede ≃ 267a 41.47 N 12.24 E
Malaga, Col. 246 6.42 N 72.44 W
Málaga, Esp. 34 36.43 N 4.25 W
Malaga, Ca., U.S. 226 36.42 N 119.46 W
Malaga, N.J., U.S. 208 39.34 N 75.02 W
Malaga, N.M., U.S. 196 32.13 N 104.04 W
Málaga □⁴ 34 36.50 N 4.40 W
Malagarasi 154 5.06 S 30.50 E
Malagarasi ≃ 154 5.12 S 29.47 E
Malagash 186 45.46 N 63.23 W
Malagasy Republic → Madagascar □¹ 157b 19.00 S 46.00 E
Malago ≃ 116 10.55 N 123.02 E
Malagón 34 39.10 N 3.51 W
Malagón ≃ 34 37.35 N 7.29 W
Malagrotta ✦⁸ 66 41.53 N 12.20 E
Mal'agurt 80 57.39 N 52.32 E
Malahat 224 48.32 N 123.34 W
Malahide 48 53.27 N 6.09 W
Mălăiești 38 46.59 N 29.33 E
Malaimbandy 157b 20.20 S 45.36 E
Malaisie → Malaysia □¹ 112 2.30 N 112.30 E
Malaita □⁴ 175e 9.00 S 161.00 E
Malaita I 175e 9.00 S 161.00 E
Malaja Bessergenovka 83 47.09 N 38.36 E
Malaja Borščovka 82 56.30 N 36.53 E
Malaja Bykovka 80 51.54 N 47.45 E
Malaja Čuja ≃ 88 58.56 N 112.13 E
Malaja Doroginka 82 54.06 N 38.56 E
Malaja Dubna 82 55.52 N 38.58 E
Malaja Istra ≃ 82 55.54 N 36.50 E
Malaja Ižmora 80 53.32 N 42.48 E
Malaja Jekaterinovka 80 51.26 N 44.17 E
Malaja Kinel' ≃ 80 53.29 N 51.30 E
Malaja Kokšaga ≃ 80 56.09 N 47.53 E
Malaja Konkudera ≃ 88 57.26 N 112.37 E
Malaja Kuril'skaja Gr'ada (Habomai-Shotō) II 92a 43.30 N 146.10 E
Malaja Laba ≃ 84 44.16 N 40.53 E
Malaja Neva ≃¹ 265a 59.57 N 30.15 E
Malaja Ochta ✦⁸ 265a 59.56 N 30.24 E
Malaja Orlovka 80 47.18 N 41.24 E
Malaja Pera 24 64.11 N 54.47 E
Malaja Serdoba 80 52.28 N 44.56 E
Malaja Sestra ≃ 82 56.17 N 35.57 E
Malaja Višera 76 58.51 N 32.14 E
Malaka → Melaka 114 2.12 N 102.15 E
Malaka, Sempitan ʮ 114 5.44 N 95.30 E
Malakāl 140 9.31 N 31.39 E
Malakand 123 34.34 N 71.56 E
Mala Kapela ʌ 36 44.50 N 15.30 E
Malakka, Strasse von → Malacca, Strait of ʮ 110 2.30 N 101.20 E
Malakoff, Fr. 261 48.49 N 2.19 E
Malakoff, Tx., U.S. 222 32.10 N 96.00 W
Malakpur ✦⁸ 272a 28.42 N 77.12 E
Malakula □⁸ 175f 16.20 S 167.20 E
Malakula I 175f 16.15 S 167.30 E
Malakwāl 123 32.34 N 73.13 E
Malala 164 5.15 S 147.10 E
Malalag 116 6.36 N 125.24 E
Malalbergo 64 44.43 N 11.32 E
Malamala 112 3.21 S 120.55 E
Mala Mala Game Reserve ✦⁴ 156 24.52 S 31.30 E
Malamaui Island I 116 6.44 N 121.58 E
Malambo 246 10.52 N 74.47 W
Malambo, Arroyo ≃ 258 33.43 S 58.46 W
Malambunga 116 9.02 N 117.38 E
Malamocco 64 45.22 N 12.20 E
Malampaya Sound ʮ 116 10.51 N 119.20 E
Malān 120 25.37 N 96.21 E
Malān, Rās > 128 25.18 N 65.12 E
Malanao Island I 116 9.27 N 118.37 E
Malanbang 116 17.41 N 120.43 E
Mālancha 272b 22.55 N 88.26 E
Malang ≃¹ 126 21.40 N 89.20 E
Mālandighi 126 23.33 N 87.24 E
Malandji 152 5.56 S 22.18 E
Malang 115a 7.59 S 112.37 E
Malang, Gunung ʌ 115a 7.02 S 107.01 E
Malangali 154 8.34 S 34.51 E
Malangas 116 7.37 N 123.01 E
Malanggwā 124 26.52 N 85.34 E
Malangka, Tanjung > 112 1.20 N 120.48 E
Malan Guan ʌ 105 40.16 N 117.39 E
Malanipa Island I 116 6.53 N 122.16 E
Malanje 152 9.32 S 16.20 E
Malanje □⁵ 152 9.30 S 16.30 E
Malanut Bay ⊂ 116 9.16 N 117.59 E
Malanville 150 11.52 N 3.23 E
Malanyu 105 40.13 N 117.42 E
Malanzhuang 105 40.05 N 117.37 E
Malao 175f 15.05 S 166.57 E
Malappuram 122 11.03 N 76.03 E
Malar ≃ 128 25.37 N 66.37 E
Mala Panew ≃ 30 50.44 N 17.52 E
Malapantao, Mount ʌ 116 9.54 N 122.37 E
Malapardis Brook ≃ 276 40.49 N 74.25 W
Mälaren @ 40 59.30 N 17.12 E
Malargüe 252 35.28 S 69.35 W
Mälar-See → Mälaren @ 40 59.30 N 17.12 E
Malartic 190 48.08 N 78.08 W
Malartic, Lac @ 190 48.15 N 78.07 W
Malasia → Malaysia □¹ 112 2.30 N 112.30 E
Malasiqui 116 15.55 N 120.25 E
Malaspina 254 44.56 S 66.54 W
Malaspina Glacier ⊓ 180 59.50 N 140.30 W
Malaspina Strait ʮ 182 49.44 N 124.24 W
Malassis 261 48.49 N 2.03 E
Malātīyah 142 28.42 N 30.51 E
Mala Tokmachivka 78 47.32 N 35.54 E
Malatya 130 38.21 N 38.19 E
Malatya □⁴ 130 38.30 N 38.10 E
Malatya 175f 15.10 S 166.48 E
Malau 62 44.10 N 5.08 E
Malaucène 50 49.32 N 1.02 E
Malaunay 94 35.40 N 139.21 E
Malaut 123 30.13 N 74.29 E
Malavalli 122 12.23 N 77.05 E
Malavalli 78 48.39 N 31.38 E
Mala Vyska 116 9.39 N 123.33 E
Malawali, Pulau I 116 7.03 N 117.18 E
Malawi □¹, Afr. 138 13.30 S 34.00 E
Malawi □¹, Afr. 154 13.30 S 34.00 E

ENGLISH / DEUTSCH

Name	Page	Lat.°′	Long.°′

Name	Seite	Breite°′	Länge°′ E = Ost

Malawi, Lake → Nyasa, Lake @ 154 12.00 S 34.30 E
Malawiya 140 15.16 N 36.12 E
Malaya → Semenanjung Malaysia □⁹ 114 4.00 N 102.00 E
Malayagiri ʌ 120 21.23 N 85.16 E
Malayal 116 7.12 N 121.57 E
Malaybalay 116 8.09 N 125.05 E
Malāyer 128 34.17 N 48.50 E
Malay Peninsula >¹ 110 6.00 N 101.00 E
Malay Reef ✦² 166 17.59 S 149.18 E
Malaysia □¹, Asia 108 2.30 N 112.30 E
Malaysia □¹, Asia 112 2.30 N 112.30 E
Malazgirt 130 39.09 N 42.31 E
Malbaie ≃ 186 47.39 N 70.09 W
Malbaie, La ⊂ 186 48.35 N 64.14 W
Malbon 166 21.04 S 140.18 E
Malbooma 162 30.41 S 134.11 E
Malborghetto Valbruna 64 46.30 N 13.26 E
Malbork 30 54.02 N 19.01 E
Malbrán 252 29.21 S 62.27 W
Malbuisson 58 46.48 N 6.18 E
Malbun 58 47.35 N 9.33 E
Malcesine 64 45.46 N 10.48 E
Mal'cevo 265b 55.56 N 37.57 E
Mal'čevskaja 78 49.04 N 40.21 E
Mal'čevsko-Polnenskaja 83 48.58 N 40.12 E
Malchanskij chrebet ʌ 88 50.45 N 109.30 E
Malchin 54 53.44 N 12.46 E
Malchiner See @ 54 53.43 N 12.42 E
Malching 60 48.19 N 13.12 E
Malchow 54 53.28 N 12.25 E
Malchow ✦⁸ 264a 52.35 N 13.29 E
Malčin 88 49.44 N 93.18 E
Malcolm 162 28.56 S 121.30 E
Malcolm, Point > 162 33.48 S 123.45 E
Malcolm Island I 182 50.40 N 127.00 W
Malcom 190 41.42 N 92.33 W
Malcompeth → Mahābaleshwar 122 17.55 N 73.40 E
Malcontenta 64 45.25 N 12.13 E
Malczyce 30 51.14 N 16.29 E
Māldah 124 25.02 N 88.09 E
Maldegem 50 51.13 N 3.27 E
Malden, Ma., U.S. 207 42.25 N 71.04 W
Malden, Mo., U.S. 194 36.33 N 89.57 W
Malden I 14 4.03 S 154.59 W
Malden ≃ 283 42.24 N 71.05 W
Malden Bridge 210 42.28 N 73.35 W
Malden on Hudson 210 42.06 N 73.56 W
Maldivas → Maldives □¹ 12 3.15 N 73.00 E
Maldive Islands → Maldives □¹ 12 3.15 N 73.00 E
Mal di Ventre, Isola di I 71 39.59 N 8.18 E
Maldives □¹ 12 3.15 N 73.00 E
Maldon, Austl. 169 37.00 S 144.04 E
Maldon, Eng., U.K. 42 51.45 N 0.40 E
Maldon □⁸ 260 51.43 N 0.40 E
Maldonado 252 34.54 S 54.57 W
Maldonado, Punta > 234 16.20 N 98.35 W
Male, It. 64 46.21 N 10.55 E
Male', Mald. 12 4.10 N 73.30 E
Male, Mya. 110 23.02 N 95.58 E
Maléa, Ákra > 38 36.26 N 23.12 E
Malea, Dolok ʌ 114 0.56 N 99.38 E
Malebo, Pool @ 152 4.17 S 15.20 E
Malediven → Maldives □¹ 12 3.15 N 73.00 E
Malegaon 122 20.33 N 74.32 E
Malegno, It. 64 45.56 N 10.14 E
Malegno, It. 64 46.40 N 11.08 E
Malehra 124 24.34 N 79.19 E
Maleit, Lake @ 140 7.55 N 28.35 E
Malek, Kaz. 85 40.47 N 68.37 E
Malek, Süd. 140 6.04 N 31.36 E
Malé Karpaty ʌ 30 48.30 N 17.20 E
Malek Dīn 120 32.25 N 68.04 E
Malek Kandī 128 37.09 N 46.06 E
Malek Sīāh, Kūh-e ʌ 128 29.51 N 60.52 E
Malela, Zaïre 154 2.28 S 26.09 E
Malela, Zaïre 154 4.22 S 26.08 E
Malema 154 14.57 S 37.20 E
Malen'ga 24 63.50 N 36.25 E
Malengoya 154 3.32 N 25.25 E
Malente 54 54.10 N 10.33 E
Maleo 62 45.10 N 9.46 E
Male Polissya ✦¹ 78 50.10 N 25.00 E
Maler Kotla 124 30.31 N 75.53 E
Malesco 58 46.08 N 8.30 E
Malesherbes 50 48.18 N 2.25 E
Malestroit 32 47.49 N 2.23 W
Maleta 88 50.50 N 108.25 E
Maletto 70 37.49 N 14.52 E
Malfa 70 38.35 N 14.50 E
Malgas 158 34.18 S 20.35 E
Malgersdorf 60 48.32 N 12.45 E
Malgobek 84 43.32 N 44.34 E
Malgomaj @ 26 64.47 N 16.12 E
Malha Wells 140 15.08 N 26.12 E
Malheur ≃ 202 44.03 N 116.59 W
Malheur, North Fork ≃ 202 43.48 N 118.04 W
Malheur, South Fork ≃ 202 43.33 N 118.10 W
Malheureux, Cap > 157c 19.59 S 57.36 E
Malheur Lake @ 202 43.20 N 118.45 W
Mali, Guinée 150 12.05 N 12.18 W
Mali, Zaïre 154 2.48 S 26.08 E
Mali □¹, Afr. 134 17.00 N 4.00 W
Mali □¹, Afr. 150 17.00 N 4.00 W
Mali ≃ 102 25.43 N 97.29 E
Maliangping 102 31.29 N 111.20 E
Maliangjingzi 102 41.32 N 95.23 E
Malibamatšo ≃ 158 29.20 S 29.28 E
Malibu 228 34.02 N 118.42 W
Malibu Lake @¹ 228 34.07 N 118.45 W
Malien ≃ 102 36.06 N 107.50 E
Malienkang 269d 25.11 N 121.41 E
Malienkeng 269d 25.10 N 121.39 E
Maligay Bay ⊂ 116 7.30 N 123.14 E
Malighati 126 22.33 N 87.40 E
Maligne ≃ 182 52.56 N 118.02 W
Maligne Lake @ 182 52.40 N 117.31 W
Malīhābād 124 26.55 N 80.43 E
Mālihah, Wādī V 142 29.21 N 32.35 E
Malik 112 0.34 S 123.04 E
Malik, Wādī al- V 140 18.02 N 30.58 E
Mali Kyun I 110 13.06 N 98.16 E
Mālili 112 2.38 S 121.06 E
Målilla 26 57.23 N 15.48 E
Malimba, Monts ʌ 154 7.32 S 29.30 E
Malim Nawar 114 4.21 N 101.07 E
Malimono 116 9.34 N 125.25 E
Malin, Ire. 48 55.18 N 7.16 W
Malin, Or., U.S. 202 42.00 N 121.24 W
Malinalco 234 18.57 N 99.30 W
Malinaltepec 234 17.03 N 98.40 W
Malinau 112 3.35 N 116.38 E
Malin Beg 48 54.40 N 8.48 W
Malindang, Mount ʌ 116 8.13 N 123.38 E
Malindi 154 3.13 S 40.07 E
Malindi Marine National Park ✦ 154 3.25 S 40.10 E
Malines → Mechelen 50 51.02 N 4.28 E
Malinga 152 2.25 S 12.14 E
Malingping 115a 6.46 S 105.01 E
Malingsbosjön @ 40 59.55 N 15.27 E
Malin Head > 48 55.23 N 7.24 W
Malinki 82 54.05 N 38.59 E
Malinniki 82 56.17 N 38.24 E
Malino, Indon. 112 1.35 N 119.51 E
Malino, Ross. 82 55.06 N 38.11 E
Malino, Ross. 265b 55.58 N 37.13 E
Malino, Bukit ʌ 112 0.45 N 120.47 E
Malinovka, Kaz. 174w 21.02 S 175.08 W
Malinovka, Ross. 80 51.47 N 43.26 E
Malinovka, Ross. 86 53.24 N 87.17 E
Malinta 216 41.19 N 84.02 W
Malinyi 154 8.56 S 36.08 E
Malīpāra 272b 22.57 N 88.14 E
Mali Rajinac ʌ 36 44.48 N 15.02 E
Malita 116 6.25 N 125.36 E
Malitbog 116 10.10 N 125.00 E
Maliuchang 107 29.05 N 104.07 E
Maliuping 107 29.55 N 106.23 E
Ma Liu Shui 271d 22.25 N 114.12 E
Malivo 82 55.07 N 39.02 E
Maliwun 110 10.14 N 98.37 E
Maliyivka 78 47.29 N 32.43 E
Malizhen 102 23.10 N 104.35 E
Maljamar 196 32.51 N 103.46 W
Malka, Ross. 74 53.20 N 157.30 E
Malka, Ross. 84 43.47 N 43.21 E
Malka ≃ 84 43.44 N 44.15 E
Malkāpur 120 20.53 N 76.12 E
Malkara 130 40.53 N 26.54 E
Malkerns 158 26.32 S 31.11 E
Malko Tărnovo 38 41.59 N 27.32 E
Mallāh 132 32.30 N 36.51 E
Mallaig, Ab., Can. 182 54.13 N 111.22 W
Mallaig, Scot., U.K. 46 57.00 N 5.50 W
Mallala 168b 34.26 S 138.30 E
Mallaoua 150 13.02 N 9.36 E
Mallapunyah 164 16.59 S 135.49 E
Mallaranny 48 53.54 N 9.49 W
Mallard Reservoir @¹ 282 38.01 N 122.03 W
Mallawī 142 27.44 N 30.50 E
Mallee Cliffs National Park ✦ 166 34.15 S 142.40 E
Mallemort 62 43.44 N 5.11 E
Mallersdorf 60 48.47 N 12.16 E
Mallery Lake @ 176 63.55 N 98.25 W
Malles Venosta (Mals) 64 46.41 N 10.32 E
Mallet 252 25.55 S 50.50 W
Mallig 116 17.08 N 121.41 E
Malligasta 252 29.11 S 67.26 W
Mallina 162 20.53 S 118.02 E
Malling 41 56.02 N 10.10 E
Mallnitz 64 46.59 N 13.10 E
Mallorca I 34 39.30 N 3.00 E
Mallorytown 212 44.29 N 75.53 W
Mallow 48 52.08 N 8.39 W
Mallwood 216 42.51 N 89.02 W
Malm 26 64.04 N 11.13 E
Malmbäck 26 57.35 N 14.28 E
Malmberget 24 67.10 N 20.40 E
Malmédy 56 50.25 N 6.02 E
Malmesbury, S. Afr. 158 33.28 S 18.44 E
Malmesbury, Eng., U.K. 42 51.36 N 2.06 W
Malmesbury, Vale of V 42 51.22 N 2.10 W
Malmköping 40 59.08 N 16.44 E
Malmlången @ 40 59.27 N 14.42 E
Malmö 41 55.36 N 13.00 E
Malmöhus Län □⁶ 41 55.45 N 13.30 E
Malmsbury 169 37.12 S 144.23 E
Malmsbury Reservoir @¹ 169 37.13 S 144.22 E
Malmslätt 26 58.25 N 15.30 E
Malmstrom Air Force Base ■ 202 47.30 N 111.10 W
Malmyž 80 56.31 N 50.41 E
Malna 116 8.08 N 124.27 E
Malnate 62 45.48 N 8.53 E
Malnoue 261 48.50 N 2.36 E
Malo 64 45.39 N 11.24 E
Malo I 175f 15.40 S 167.11 E
Malo, Arroyo ≃ 258 33.43 S 58.52 W
Maloarchangel'sk 82 52.24 N 36.30 E
Maloarchangel'skoje 88 50.24 N 108.50 E
Maloba 154 6.18 S 27.39 E
Malodel'skaja 80 50.11 N 43.53 E
Maloduša 76 52.09 N 30.14 E
Maloelap I¹ 14 8.45 N 171.03 E
Maloja 58 46.24 N 9.41 E
Malojapass ≍ 58 46.24 N 9.41 E
Malojaroslavec 82 55.01 N 36.28 E
Malojaz 86 55.13 N 58.09 E
Maloje Goloustnoje 88 52.18 N 105.18 E
Maloje Kozino 80 56.26 N 43.41 E
Maloje-Ščerbedino 80 51.59 N 42.50 E
Maloje Skuratovo 76 53.33 N 37.00 E
Malokamenyannika 78 47.39 N 35.13 E
Malokirsanovka 83 47.28 N 38.31 E
Malokrasnojarka 86 56.28 N 76.01 E
Malo-les-Bains 50 51.03 N 2.24 E
Malolo 154 7.18 S 36.35 E
Malolos, Guam 174p 13.18 N 144.46 E
Malolos, Pil. 116 14.51 N 120.49 E
Malolotja 164 3.10 S 151.50 E
Malom 158 27.00 S 31.40 E
Malombe, Lake @ 154 14.38 S 35.12 E
Malomykhaylivka 78 48.06 N 36.23 E
Malomykolaivka 83 48.18 N 39.01 E
Malonabatovskij 80 48.57 N 43.40 E
Malone, Fl., U.S. 192 30.57 N 85.09 W
Malone, N.Y., U.S. 188 44.50 N 74.17 W
Malone, Tx., U.S. 222 31.55 N 96.54 W
Malone, Wa., U.S. 224 46.58 N 123.20 W
Malonga 152 10.24 S 23.10 E
Malonno 64 46.07 N 10.18 E
Malonty 61 48.41 N 14.35 E
Malopolska ✦¹ 30 50.10 N 21.30 E
Malorita 78 51.47 N 24.05 E
Malorossijskij 86 53.12 N 62.30 E
Malošujka 24 63.45 N 37.22 E
Malott 182 48.16 N 119.42 W
Måløy 41 55.45 N 12.20 E
Malowice 30 51.34 N 15.27 E
Måløy 26 61.56 N 5.07 E
Malozemel'skaja Tundra ✦¹ 24 67.50 N 51.00 E
Malpaisillo 236 12.35 N 86.41 W
Malpartida de Plasencia 34 39.59 N 6.02 W
Malpas, Austl. 166 34.43 S 140.37 E
Malpas, Eng., U.K. 44 53.01 N 2.46 W
Malpaso 234 22.37 N 102.46 W
Malpe 122 13.21 N 74.43 E
Malpelo, Isla de I 242 3.59 N 81.35 W
Malpensa, Aeroporto della ■ 62 45.38 N 8.44 E
Malpeque Bay ⊂ 186 46.30 N 63.47 W
Malprabha ≃ 122 16.12 N 76.03 E
Malpura 120 26.17 N 75.23 E
Mals → Malles Venosta 64 46.41 N 10.32 E
Målsåker slott ⊥ 40 59.23 N 17.18 E
Malsch 56 48.53 N 8.19 E
Malše (Maltsch) ≃ 61 48.58 N 14.28 E
Målselva ≃ 24 69.14 N 18.30 E
Malta, Bra. 250 6.54 S 37.31 W
Malta, Lat. 76 56.21 N 27.10 E
Malta, Port. 64 46.57 N 13.30 E
Malta, Il., U.S. 216 41.56 N 88.52 W
Malta, Mt., U.S. 202 48.21 N 107.52 W
Malta, Oh., U.S. 188 39.38 N 81.51 W
Malta □¹, Europe 22 35.50 N 14.35 E
Malta □¹, Europe 36 35.50 N 14.35 E
Malta I 36 35.53 N 14.27 E
Malta ≃ 76 56.44 N 26.53 E
Malta Channel ʮ 36 36.20 N 15.00 E
Maltahöhe 156 24.50 S 17.00 E
Maltahöhe □⁵ 156 25.00 S 16.30 E
Maltatal V 64 47.03 N 13.24 E
Maltby 44 53.26 N 1.11 W
Malte → Malta □¹ 36 35.50 N 14.35 E
Malte Brun ʌ 172 43.34 S 170.18 E
Maltepe ✦⁸ 267b 40.55 N 29.08 E
Malton 44 54.08 N 0.48 W
Malton ✦⁸ 275b 43.42 N 79.38 W
Maltrata 234 18.48 N 97.16 W
Maltsch (Malše) ≃ 61 48.58 N 14.28 E
Malugou 89 43.39 N 128.27 E

Symbols in the index entries represent the broad categories identified in the key at the right. Symbols with superior numbers (ʌ¹) identify subcategories (see complete key on page I · 1).

Symbole im Register stellen die rechts im Schlüssel erklärten Kategorien dar. Symbole mit hochgestellten Ziffern (ʌ¹) bezeichnen Unterabteilungen einer Kategorie (vgl. vollständiger Schlüssel auf Seite I · 1).

Los símbolos incluidos en el texto del índice representan las grandes categorías identificadas con la clave a la derecha. Los símbolos con números en su parte superior (ʌ¹) identifican las subcategorías (véase la clave completa en la página I · 1).

Les symboles de l'index représentent les catégories indiquées dans la légende à droite. Les symboles suivis d'un indice (ʌ¹) représentent des sous-catégories (voir légende complète à la page I · 1).

Os símbolos incluídos no texto do índice representam as grandes categorias identificadas com a chave à direita. Os símbolos com números em sua parte superior (ʌ¹) identificam as subcategorias (veja-se a chave completa à página I · 1).

ʌ Mountain	Berg	Montaña	Montagne	Montanha		
ʌ Mountains	Gebirge	Montañas	Montagnes	Montanhas		
≍ Pass	Paß	Paso	Col	Passo		
V Valley, Canyon	Tal, Cañon	Valle, Cañón	Vallée, Canyon	Vale, Canhão		
≃ Plain	Ebene	Llano	Plaine	Planície		
> Cape	Kap	Cabo	Cap	Cabo		
I Island	Insel	Isla	Île	Ilha		
II Islands	Inseln	Islas	Îles	Ilhas		
± Other Topographic Features	Andere Topographische Objekte	Otros Elementos Topográficos	Autres données topographiques	Outros acidentes topográficos		

ESPAÑOL — Nombre / Página / Lat.°' / Long.°' W = Oeste
FRANÇAIS — Nom / Page / Lat.°' / Long.°' W = Ouest
PORTUGUÊS — Nome / Página / Lat.°' / Long.°' W = Oeste

Maluku □4 164 5.00 S 130.00 E
Maluku (Moluccas) II 108 2.00 S 128.00 E
Maluku, Laut (Molucca Sea) ⚲2 108 0.00 125.00 E
Maluku-Maes 152 4.06 S 15.31 E
Ma'lūlā 130 33.50 N 36.33 E
Ma'lūlā, Jabal ∧ 132 33.54 N 36.36 E
Malu Mare 38 44.15 N 23.51 E
Malumfashi 150 11.47 N 7.37 E
Malunda 112 3.00 S 118.50 E
Malung 26 60.40 N 13.44 E
Maluso 116 6.33 N 121.53 E
Malūt 140 10.26 N 32.12 E
Maluti 126 24.09 N 87.41 E
Maluwe 150 8.40 N 2.17 W
Maluzhen 106 31.20 N 121.16 E
Malvaglia 58 46.25 N 8.59 E
Malvaglio 266b 45.31 N 8.47 E
Malvagna 70 37.55 N 15.04 E
Mālvan 122 16.04 N 73.28 E
Malveira 266c 38.45 N 9.27 W
Malvern, Austl. 274b 37.52 S 145.02 E
Malvern, Ar., U.S. 194 34.21 N 92.48 W
Malvern, Ia., U.S. 198 41.00 N 95.35 W
Malvern, Oh., U.S. 214 40.41 N 81.10 W
Malvern, Pa., U.S. 285 40.02 N 75.31 W
Malvern ✢8 273d 26.12 S 28.06 E
Malverne 276 40.40 N 73.40 W
Malvern Hills ⁂2 42 52.05 N 2.21 W
Malvérnia 156 22.06 S 31.42 E
Malvern Link 42 52.08 N 2.18 W
Malvinas 252 29.37 S 58.59 W
Malvinas, Islas → Falkland Islands □2 254 51.45 S 59.00 W
Malvito 68 39.36 N 16.03 E
Malwal 140 9.19 N 31.35 E
Mālwa Plateau ⁂1 124 23.50 N 77.30 E
Malybaj 85 43.30 N 78.25 E
Malý Dunaj ≃ 30 47.45 N 18.09 E
Malyj Nesvetaj ≃ 83 47.32 N 39.49 E
Malyj, ostrov I 76 60.02 N 28.02 E
Malyj An'uj ≃ 74 68.30 N 160.49 E
Malyj Čeremšan ≃ 80 54.18 N 50.01 E
Malyj Chamar-Daban, chrebet ⁂ 88 51.00 N 105.00 E
Malyj Civil' ≃ 80 55.54 N 47.28 E
Malyje Alabuchi 80 51.33 N 42.10 E
Malyje Čany, ozero ⊜ 86 54.33 N 78.02 E
Malyje Gorod'atiči 76 52.33 N 28.20 E
Malyje Jagury 80 45.26 N 43.01 E
Malyje Kamkaly 86 44.44 N 71.31 E
Malyje Karmakuly 72 72.23 N 52.44 E
Malyje Porogi 265a 59.47 N 30.42 E
Malyj Irgiz ≃ 80 52.12 N 47.58 E
Malyj Jenisej (Ka-Chem) ≃ 88 51.43 N 94.26 E
Malyj Jugan ≃ 86 60.40 N 73.54 E
Malyj Kundyš ≃ 80 56.22 N 47.53 E
Malyj Šantar, ostrov I 89 54.30 N 137.36 E
Malyj Sarybulak 86 52.10 N 72.35 E
Malyj Tajmyr, ostrov I 74 78.08 N 107.12 E
Malyj T'uters, ostrov I 76 59.49 N 26.56 E
Malyj Uran ≃ 80 52.30 N 53.01 E
Malyj Uzen' ≃ 80 48.50 N 49.39 E
Malyj Zelenčuk ≃ 84 44.24 N 41.56 E
Malyn', Ross. 82 54.36 N 38.40 E
Malyn, Ukr. 78 50.46 N 29.15 E
Malynivka 78 49.47 N 36.43 E
Malyševo 76 57.50 N 35.36 E
Malzéville 58 48.43 N 6.12 E
Mama 88 58.18 N 112.54 E
Mama ≃ 88 58.18 N 112.55 E
Ma Ma Creek ≃ 171a 27.35 S 152.13 E
Mamadyš 80 55.44 N 51.25 E
Mamagota 175e 6.46 S 155.24 E
Mamahuolang 104 42.24 N 124.12 E
Mamajiecun 104 41.26 N 122.51 E
Mamakan 88 57.48 N 114.01 E
Mamaku 172 38.06 S 176.05 E
Mamakwash Lake ⊜ 184 51.38 N 92.56 W
Mamala Bay c 229a 21.18 N 157.57 W
Mamalu Bay c 229a 20.37 N 156.09 W
Mamanguape 250 6.50 S 35.07 W
Mama'o, Hakau ✢2 174w 21.00 S 175.12 W
Mamara 248 14.14 S 72.35 W
Mamaroneck 210 40.56 N 73.43 W
Mamaroneck ≃ 276 40.57 N 73.44 W
Mamaroneck Harbor c 276 40.56 N 73.43 W
Mamasa 112 2.56 S 119.22 E
Mamasa ≃ 112 3.30 S 119.42 E
Mamba 94 36.07 N 138.55 E
Mambai 255 14.28 S 46.07 W
Mambajao 116 9.15 N 124.43 E
Mambajao, Mount ∧ 116 9.10 N 124.44 E
Mambali 154 4.33 S 32.41 E
Mambalot 116 8.51 N 117.55 E
Mambare ≃ 164 8.20 S 147.55 E
Mambasa 154 1.21 N 29.03 E
Mamberamo ≃ 164 1.26 S 137.53 E
Mambéré ≃ 152 3.31 N 16.03 E
Mambili ≃ 152 0.07 N 16.08 E
Mambrui 154 3.07 S 40.09 E
Mambucaba 256 23.01 S 44.31 W
Mambucaba ≃ 256 23.02 S 44.32 W
Mamburao 116 13.14 N 120.35 E
Mambusao ≃ 116 11.24 N 122.41 E
Mamdūh, Rujm ∧ 132 32.14 N 36.15 E
Mamedkala 84 42.10 N 48.06 E
Mamehaktebo 112 0.08 N 115.32 E
Mamelodi 158 25.42 S 28.21 E
Ma-Me-O Beach 182 52.58 N 113.59 W
Mamera 286c 10.27 N 66.59 W
Mamera, Quebrada ≃ 286c 10.27 N 66.59 W
Mamers 50 48.21 N 0.23 E
Mamfe 152 5.46 N 9.17 E
Mamiá ≃ 250 1.55 S 55.07 W
Mamiá, Lago ⊜ 246 4.15 S 63.03 W
Mamiao 98 35.04 N 116.10 E
Mamie 192 36.07 N 75.50 W
Mamiña 248 20.05 S 69.14 W
Mamingui 150 7.24 N 5.50 W
Mamirolle 58 47.12 N 6.10 E
Mamisonskij, pereval)(84 42.43 N 43.48 E
Maml'utka 86 54.57 N 68.35 E
Mammendorf 60 48.12 N 11.09 E
Mammola 68 38.22 N 16.15 E
Mammoth, Az., U.S. 200 32.43 N 110.38 W
Mammoth, W.V., U.S. 188 38.15 N 81.22 W
Mammoth Cave National Park ♦ 194 37.08 N 86.13 W
Mammoth Lakes 204 37.38 N 118.58 W
Mammoth Pool Reservoir ⊜1 226 37.20 N 119.20 W
Mammoth Spring 194 36.29 N 91.32 W
Mamoiada 71 40.13 N 9.17 E
Mamonovo, Ross. 76 54.28 N 19.57 E
Mamonovo, Ross. 265b 55.36 N 37.49 E
Mamonovo, Ross. 265b 55.41 N 37.19 E
Mamont 279b 40.29 N 79.36 W
Mamontovo, Ross. 86 52.43 N 81.37 E
Mamontovo, Ross. 86 51.45 N 81.25 E
Mamoré ≃ 248 10.23 S 65.23 W
Mamori, Lago ⊜ 246 3.38 S 60.07 W
Mamoriá ≃ 248 7.30 S 66.21 W
Mamou, Guinée 150 10.23 N 12.05 W
Mamou, La., U.S. 194 30.38 N 92.25 W
Mamoutzou 157a 12.47 S 45.14 E
Mampikony 157b 16.06 S 47.38 E
Mampong 150 7.04 N 1.24 W
Mamrš 84 41.44 N 48.19 E
Mamre 158 33.30 S 18.29 E
Mamry, Jezioro ⊜ 30 54.08 N 21.42 E
Mamuchi 98 35.41 N 118.17 E
Mamué 152 13.35 S 13.13 E
Mamuil, Paso de)(254 39.35 S 71.28 W
Mamuju 112 2.41 S 118.54 E
Mamulique 196 26.08 N 100.20 W
Ma'mūn 140 12.15 N 22.41 E
Mamuno 156 22.16 S 20.01 E
Mamuripi (Manuripe) ≃ 248 11.06 S 67.36 W
Mamuru ≃ 250 2.42 S 56.44 W
Mamykovo 80 54.38 N 50.37 E
Mamyt' 24 61.57 N 56.41 E
Man, C. Iv. 150 7.24 N 7.33 W
Man, India 120 33.51 N 78.32 E
Man, W.V., U.S. 192 37.44 N 81.52 W
Man (Île de) → Isle of Man □2 44 54.15 N 4.30 W
Man, Isle of → Isle of Man □2 44 54.15 N 4.30 W
Mana, Guy. fr. 250 5.40 N 53.47 W
Mana, Hi., U.S. 229b 22.02 N 159.46 W
Mana ≃, Guy. fr. 250 5.44 N 53.54 W
Mana ≃, Ross. 86 55.57 N 92.28 E
Manabí □4 246 0.40 S 80.05 W
Manacacías ≃ 246 4.23 N 72.04 W
Manacapuru 246 3.18 S 60.37 W
Manacapuru ≃ 246 3.18 S 60.38 W
Manacle Point > 42 50.03 N 5.03 W
Manacor 34 39.34 N 3.12 E
Manado 112 1.29 N 124.51 E
Managua 236 12.09 N 86.17 W
Managua □5 236 12.00 N 86.25 W
Managua, Aeropuerto ✈ 286b 23.00 N 82.17 W
Managua, Lago de ⊜ 236 12.20 N 86.20 W
Manahawkin 208 39.41 N 74.15 W
Manahawkin Bay c 208 39.40 N 74.12 W
Manaia 172 39.33 S 174.08 E
Manā'if, Bi'r al- ⚲4 142 30.31 N 32.12 E
Manajenki 76 53.42 N 36.27 E
Manakalampona ∧ 157b 15.23 S 48.50 E
Manakara 157b 22.08 S 48.01 E
Manakau 172 40.43 S 175.13 E
Manakau ∧ 172 42.14 S 173.37 E
Manākhah 144 15.07 N 43.44 E
Manalapan Brook ≃ 276 40.24 N 74.23 W
Manāli 123 32.15 N 77.10 E
Manama → Al-Manāmah 128 26.13 N 50.35 E
Manamansalo I 26 64.21 N 27.04 E
Manambaho ≃ 157b 17.41 S 44.04 E
Manambato, Madag. 157b 13.14 S 49.54 E
Manambato, Madag. 157b 13.43 S 49.07 E
Manambolo ≃ 157b 19.18 S 44.24 E
Manambolosy 157b 16.02 S 49.40 E
Manam Island I 164 4.05 S 145.05 E
Mánamo, Caño ≃1 246 9.55 N 62.16 W
Manamoc Island I 116 11.19 N 120.41 E
Manana Island I 229c 21.20 N 157.40 W
Mananantanana ≃ 157b 21.25 S 45.33 E
Mananao 116 13.30 N 120.34 E
Mananara 157b 16.10 S 49.46 E
Mananara ≃ 157b 23.21 S 47.42 E
Manandaza 157b 19.19 S 45.23 E
Mananjary 157b 21.13 S 48.20 E
Manankoro 150 10.28 N 7.27 W
Manantenina 157b 24.17 S 47.19 E
Manantiales Behr 254 45.41 S 67.31 W
Manaoag 116 16.03 N 120.29 E
Manáos → Manaus 246 3.08 S 60.01 W
Manapatrana 157b 21.40 S 47.35 E
Manapiare ≃ 246 5.04 N 66.30 W
Manapire ≃ 246 7.42 N 66.07 W
Manapla 116 10.58 N 123.07 E
Mana Point > 229b 22.03 N 159.47 W
Mana Pools National Park ♦ 154 16.00 S 28.35 E
Manapouri 172 45.34 S 167.36 E
Manapouri, Lake ⊜ 172 45.30 S 167.30 E
Manappārai 122 10.36 N 78.25 E
Manaquiri, Lago ⊜ 246 3.29 S 60.31 W
Manār ≃ 122 18.39 N 77.44 E
Manaravolo 157b 23.59 S 45.39 E
Manas, Som. 144 2.57 N 43.28 E
Manas, Zhg. 86 44.18 N 86.13 E
Manās ≃, Asia 120 26.13 N 90.38 E
Manas ≃, Zhg. 86 45.38 N 85.12 E
Manas, gora ∧ 85 42.18 N 71.01 E
Manasarowar Lake → Mapam Yumco ⊜ 120 30.42 N 81.27 E
Manas Hu ⊜ 86 45.45 N 85.55 E
Manāslu ∧ 124 28.33 N 84.33 E
Manasota Key I 220 26.58 N 82.23 W
Manasquan 208 40.07 N 74.02 W
Manasquan ≃ 208 40.06 N 74.02 W
Manassa 200 37.10 N 105.56 W
Manassas 208 38.45 N 77.28 W
Manassas National Battlefield Park ♦ 208 38.50 N 77.32 W
Manassas Park 208 38.46 N 77.27 W
Manastash Creek ≃ 224 46.59 N 120.35 W
Manastash Creek, North Fork ≃ 224 46.57 N 120.44 W
Manastash Creek, South Fork ≃ 224 46.57 N 120.44 W
Manastash Ridge ∧ 224 46.55 N 120.30 W
Mănăstirea 38 44.13 N 26.54 E
Manatang 112 8.25 S 124.28 E
Manatawny 208 40.17 N 75.41 W
Manatawny Creek ≃ 208 40.14 N 75.39 W
Manatee □6 220 27.26 N 82.25 W
Manatee ≃ 220 27.32 N 82.38 W
Manatee, Lake ⊜1 220 27.29 N 82.20 W
Manatí, Col. 246 10.27 N 74.58 W
Manatí, Cuba 240p 21.19 N 76.56 W
Manatí, P.R. 240m 18.26 N 66.29 W
Manatí ≃ 240p 21.40 N 79.50 W
Manatí, Bahía de c 240p 21.24 N 76.48 W
Manatuto 112 8.30 S 126.01 E
Manaul 116 12.27 N 121.25 E
Manaung 110 18.51 N 93.44 E
Manaus 246 3.08 S 60.01 W
Manavgat 130 36.47 N 31.26 E
Manawa 190 44.27 N 88.55 W
Mānāwāla 123 31.35 N 73.41 E
Manawan Lake ⊜ 184 55.24 N 103.14 W
Manāwar 120 22.14 N 75.05 E
Manawatu ≃ 172 40.28 S 175.13 E
Manawoka, Pulau I 164 4.05 S 131.20 E
Manay 116 7.13 N 126.32 E
Manayunk ✢8 285 40.01 N 75.13 W
Manazuru 94 35.09 N 139.08 E
Manazuru-misaki > 94 35.08 N 139.10 E
Manban 102 23.04 N 103.11 E
Mānbāzār 126 23.04 N 86.39 E
Manbian 102 24.19 N 100.32 E
Manbij 130 36.31 N 37.57 E
Manby 44 53.22 N 0.06 E
Mancelona 190 44.54 N 85.03 W
Mancha Blanca 254 40.47 S 65.27 W
Mancha Real 34 37.47 N 3.37 W
Manchaug 207 42.05 N 71.44 W
Manche □5 32 49.00 N 1.10 W
Mancheng 105 38.56 N 115.20 E
Mancherāl 122 18.52 N 79.26 E
Manchester, Eng., U.K. 44 53.28 N 2.15 W
Manchester, Eng., U.K. 262 53.28 N 2.15 W
Manchester, Ct., U.S. 207 41.46 N 72.31 W
Manchester, Ga., U.S. 192 32.51 N 84.37 W
Manchester, Il., U.S. 219 39.33 N 90.20 W
Manchester, Ia., U.S. 190 42.29 N 91.27 W
Manchester, Ky., U.S. 192 37.09 N 83.45 W
Manchester, Md., U.S. 208 39.39 N 76.53 W
Manchester, Ma., U.S. 207 42.34 N 70.46 W
Manchester, Mi., U.S. 216 42.09 N 84.02 W
Manchester, N.H., U.S. 188 42.59 N 71.27 W
Manchester, N.Y., U.S. 210 42.58 N 77.13 W
Manchester, Oh., U.S. 218 38.41 N 83.36 W
Manchester, Pa., U.S. 208 40.03 N 76.43 W
Manchester, Tn., U.S. 194 35.28 N 86.05 W
Manchester, Vt., U.S. 210 43.09 N 73.04 W
Manchester, Wa., U.S. 224 47.33 N 122.33 W
Manchester □8 262 53.27 N 2.13 W
Manchester Airport ✈ 44 53.21 N 2.15 W
Manchester Bridge 210 41.41 N 73.52 W
Manchester City Football Ground ♦ 262 53.27 N 2.14 W
Manchester Docks ✢5 262 53.28 N 2.17 W
Manchester Race Course ♦ 262 53.30 N 2.16 W
Manchester Ship Canal ≍ 262 53.19 N 2.57 W
Manchester United Football Ground ♦ 262 53.28 N 2.18 W
Manching 60 48.43 N 11.30 E
Manchioneal 241q 18.02 N 76.17 W
Manchón 236 14.23 N 92.02 W
Manchouli → Manzhouli 88 49.35 N 117.22 E
Manchuria □9 90 47.00 N 125.00 E
Manciano 66 42.35 N 11.31 E
Mancieulles 56 49.17 N 5.53 E
Máncora 246 4.06 S 81.05 W
Mancos 200 37.20 N 108.17 W
Mancos ≃ 200 36.59 N 108.59 W
Mand 128 26.07 N 62.03 E
Mānd ≃, India 120 21.42 N 83.15 E
Mand ≃, Īrān 128 28.11 N 51.17 E
Manda, India 126 22.06 N 86.14 E
Manda, Tan. 154 7.58 S 32.26 E
Manda, Tan. 154 8.30 S 32.44 E
Manda, Tan. 154 10.28 S 34.35 E
Manda, Tchad 146 9.12 N 18.10 E
Manda, Jabal ∧ 140 8.39 N 24.27 E
Mandabe, Madag. 157b 21.03 S 44.55 E
Mandabe, Madag. 157b 20.55 S 45.49 E
Mandach 102 44.28 N 108.11 E
Mandaguari 255 23.32 S 51.42 W
Mandai Orchard Gardens ♦ 271c 1.24 N 103.47 E
Manda Island I 154 2.15 S 40.57 E
Mandal 26 58.02 N 7.27 E
Mandal, Jibāl ∧2 140 12.09 N 29.31 E
Mandala, Puncak ∧ 164 4.44 S 140.20 E
Mandalay 110 22.00 N 96.05 E
Mandalay □5 110 21.00 N 96.00 E
Mandale 216 41.01 N 84.20 W
Mandale Station ✢5 272c 19.03 N 72.56 E
Mandalgov' 102 45.45 N 106.12 E
Mandalī 128 33.45 N 45.32 E
Mandalkia 272b 22.43 N 88.08 E
Mandal-Ovoo 102 44.35 N 104.05 E
Mandalselva ≃ 26 58.02 N 7.28 E
Mandaluyong 269f 14.35 N 121.02 E
Mandan 198 46.49 N 100.53 W
Mandanici 70 38.00 N 15.19 E
Mandāoli ✢8 272a 28.38 N 77.18 E
Mandaon 116 12.14 N 123.17 E
Mandapur 126 23.00 N 88.29 E
Mandar, Teluk c 112 3.40 S 119.15 E
Mandara Mountains (Monts Mandara) ⁂ 146 10.45 N 13.40 E
Mandas 71 39.38 N 9.07 E
Mandatoriccio 68 39.28 N 16.50 E
Mandau ≃ 114 0.48 N 101.47 E
Mandaue 116 10.20 N 123.56 E
Mandāwar 124 29.30 N 78.08 E
Mandeb, Bab el ɤ 144 12.40 N 43.20 E
Mandehu 104 42.07 N 121.33 E
Mandel 128 33.17 N 61.52 E
Mandélia 146 11.43 N 15.15 E
Mandelieu 62 43.33 N 6.56 E
Mandello del Lario 58 45.54 N 9.19 E
Mandera 154 3.56 N 41.52 E
Manderfeld 56 50.20 N 6.20 E
Manderscheid 56 50.05 N 6.49 E
Manderson 202 44.16 N 107.57 W
Mandeure 58 47.27 N 6.48 E
Mandeville, P.Q., Can. 206 46.22 N 73.22 W
Mandeville, Jam. 241q 18.02 N 77.30 W
Mandeville, N.Z. 172 46.00 S 168.49 E
Mandeville, La., U.S. 194 30.21 N 90.03 W
Mandi 123 31.43 N 76.55 E
Mandiana 150 10.38 N 8.41 W
Mandiangin 112 2.01 S 102.58 E
Mandi Angin, Gunong ∧ 114 4.42 N 102.52 E
Mandi Bahāuddīn 123 32.35 N 73.30 E
Mandi Būrewāla 123 30.09 N 72.41 E
Mandi Dabwāli 123 29.58 N 74.42 E
Mandié 154 16.30 S 33.30 E
Mandimba 154 14.21 S 35.39 E
Mandini 158 29.09 S 31.25 E
Mandioli, Pulau I 108 0.44 S 127.14 E
Mandioré, Lagoa ⊜ 248 18.08 S 57.33 W
Mandira ⊜1 124 22.20 N 84.35 E
Mandiri ≃ 115a 7.02 S 106.32 E
Mandi Sādiqganj 123 30.10 N 73.44 E
Mandjé, Lac ⊜ 152 2.50 S 10.22 E
Mandji 152 1.36 S 10.26 E
Mandla 124 22.36 N 80.23 E
Mandora 162 19.44 S 120.51 E
Mandoto 157b 19.34 S 46.17 E
Mandoul ≃ 146 8.56 N 17.58 E
Mandouri 150 10.51 N 0.49 E
Mándra, Ellás 267c 38.04 N 23.30 E
Māndra, India 272b 22.55 N 88.07 E
Mandra, Pāk. 123 33.22 N 73.14 E
Mandrare ≃ 157b 25.10 S 46.27 E
Mandres-les-Roses 261 48.42 N 2.33 E
Mandriola ✢8 267a 41.45 N 12.30 E
Mandriole 64 44.33 N 12.14 E
Mandrioli, Passo dei)(66 43.48 N 11.55 E
Mandritsara 157b 15.50 S 48.49 E
Mandronarivo 157b 21.07 S 45.38 E
Mandsaur 120 24.04 N 75.04 E
Māndu 122 22.22 N 75.23 E
Mandu, Ribeirão do ≃ 256 22.14 S 45.55 W
Manduba, Ponta > 256 24.05 S 46.18 W
Manduhu 104 41.46 N 122.38 E
Mandurah 168a 32.32 S 115.43 E
Manduria 68 40.24 N 17.38 E
Māndvi, India 120 21.15 N 73.18 E
Māndvi, India 120 22.50 N 69.22 E
Mandvi ✢8 272c 18.57 N 72.50 E
Mandya 122 12.33 N 76.54 E
Mané 150 12.59 N 1.21 W
Måne ≃ 26 59.00 N 9.40 E
Manea 42 52.30 N 0.11 E
Manebach 54 50.41 N 10.51 E
Manek Urai 114 5.23 N 102.14 E
Manendragarh 124 23.13 N 82.13 E
Manera 157b 22.55 S 44.20 E
Manerbio 64 45.21 N 10.08 E
Manětín 60 49.59 N 13.14 E
Manevychi 78 51.17 N 25.33 E
Manfalūt 142 27.19 N 30.58 E
Manfredonia 68 41.38 N 15.55 E
Manfredonia, Golfo di c 68 41.35 N 16.05 E
Manga, Bra. 255 14.46 S 43.56 W
Manga, Burkina 150 11.40 N 1.04 W
Manga, Ur. 258 34.49 S 56.06 W
Manga ✢1 146 15.00 N 14.00 E
Mangabeiras, Chapada das ⁂2 250 10.00 S 46.30 W
Mangagoy 116 8.11 N 126.21 E
Mangahao ≃ 172 40.23 S 175.50 E
Mangai 164 2.45 S 151.05 E
Mangaia I 14 21.55 S 157.55 W
Mangakino 172 38.22 S 175.47 E
Mangala 152 1.02 N 23.50 E
Mangalagiri 122 16.26 N 80.33 E
Mangaldai 120 26.26 N 92.02 E
Mangaldan 116 16.04 N 120.24 E
Mangalia 38 43.50 N 28.35 E
Mangalkot 126 23.33 N 87.54 E
Mangalmé 146 12.21 N 19.37 E
Mangalore 122 12.52 N 74.53 E
Mangalpaita 126 23.19 N 89.11 E
Mangalvedha 122 17.31 N 75.28 E
Mangamahu 172 39.49 S 175.22 E
Manganês ≃ 250 10.21 S 48.27 W
Manganji 268 35.40 N 139.26 E
Mangaoka 157b 12.19 S 49.07 E
Mangapehi 172 38.31 S 175.18 E
Mangaratiba 256 22.57 S 44.02 W
Mangart, Monte (Mangrt) ∧ 64 46.25 N 13.40 E
Mangatarem 116 15.47 N 120.17 E
Mangawān 124 24.41 N 81.33 E
Mangaweka 172 39.48 S 175.47 E
Mangaweka ∧ 172 39.49 S 176.05 E
Mangcao Point > 116 11.02 N 123.54 E
Mangchang 102 25.08 N 107.31 E
Mangde ≃ 124 27.35 N 90.28 E
Mange, S.L. 150 8.55 N 12.51 W
Mange, Zaïre 152 0.54 N 20.30 E
Mange, Zhg. 120 32.25 N 83.35 E
Mangeigne 146 10.31 N 21.19 E
Mangerton Mountain ∧ 48 51.57 N 9.29 W
Mangfall ≃ 64 47.51 N 12.08 E
Manggar 112 2.53 S 108.16 E
Manggeng 114 3.36 N 96.55 E
Manggonggri 164 3.30 S 133.19 E
Mangguar, Tanjung > 164 2.53 S 134.51 E
Mangham 194 32.18 N 91.46 W
Mangichu ≃ 126 23.24 N 90.48 E
Mangindrano 157b 14.17 S 48.58 E
Mangin Range ⁂ 110 24.20 N 95.42 E
Mangistau □8 86 44.00 N 54.30 E
Mangkalihat, Tanjung > 112 1.02 N 118.59 E
Mangkutana 112 2.24 S 120.48 E
Manglares, Cabo > 246 1.36 N 79.02 W
Mangla Reservoir ⊜1 123 33.10 N 73.40 E
Manglaur 124 29.48 N 77.52 E
Manglisi 84 41.43 N 44.24 E
Mangnai 120 37.40 N 91.50 E
Mangniu ≃, Zhg. 104 41.45 N 120.53 E
Mangniu ≃, Zhg. 105 39.04 N 116.26 E
Mangnuiyingzi 104 41.37 N 120.42 E
Mango 220 28.00 N 82.19 W
Mangochi 154 14.28 S 35.16 E
Mango Island I 175g 17.27 S 179.09 W
Mangoky ≃, Madag. 157b 21.29 S 43.41 E
Mangoky ≃, Madag. 157b 23.27 S 45.13 E
Mangole, Pulau I 112 1.53 S 125.50 E
Mangombe 154 1.25 S 26.54 E
Mangone 68 39.12 N 16.20 E
Mangonia Park 220 26.46 N 80.05 W
Mangonui 172 34.59 S 173.32 E
Mangoplah 171b 35.23 S 147.15 E
Mangoro ≃ 157b 20.00 S 48.45 E
Mangotsfield 42 51.28 N 2.28 W
Mangoupa 140 5.53 N 24.40 E
Mangrol 120 21.07 N 70.07 E
Mangrove Cay I 238 24.10 N 77.45 W
Mangrove Creek ≃ 170 33.28 S 151.10 E
Mangrove Creek Dam ✢6 170 33.13 S 151.07 E
Mangrove Mountain 170 33.19 S 151.14 E
Mangrove Point > 220 26.56 N 82.08 W
Mangrt (Monte Mangart) ∧ 64 46.25 N 13.40 E
Mangrullo, Cuchilla ⁂2 258 34.34 S 56.42 W
Mangrūl Pīr 122 20.19 N 77.21 E
Mångsälven ≃ 40 59.59 N 14.36 E
Mangsang 112 2.10 S 104.00 E
Mangu ≃ 273b 4.24 S 15.24 E
Mangualde 34 40.36 N 7.46 W
Mangueira, Lagoa c 252 33.06 S 52.48 W
Mangueirinha 252 25.57 S 52.09 W
Manguéni, Plateau du ⁂1 146 22.35 N 12.40 E
Mangui 89 52.03 N 122.13 E
Manguito 240p 22.35 N 80.55 W
Mangulile 236 15.03 N 86.49 W
Mangum 196 34.52 N 99.30 W
Mangungu 152 5.13 S 19.35 E
Mangut, Ross. 86 55.47 N 70.46 E
Mangut, Ross. 88 49.46 N 112.38 E
Mangya 90 37.40 N 90.50 E
Man'gyŏng 98 35.52 N 126.48 E
Manhan ≃ 207 42.17 N 72.38 W
Manhartsberg ∧ 61 48.32 N 15.44 E
Manhasset 276 40.47 N 73.42 W
Manhasset Bay c 276 40.50 N 73.43 W
Manhasset Hills 276 40.46 N 73.41 W
Manhasset Neck >1 276 40.50 N 73.42 W
Manhattan, Il., U.S. 216 41.25 N 87.59 W
Manhattan, Ks., U.S. 198 39.11 N 96.34 W
Manhattan, Mt., U.S. 202 45.51 N 111.19 W
Manhattan □8 276 40.46 N 73.55 W
Manhattan Beach 228 33.53 N 118.24 W
Manhattan Beach State Park ♦ 280 33.54 N 118.25 W
Manhattan Bridge ✢5 276 40.42 N 73.59 W
Manhattan College ✢2 276 40.53 N 73.54 W
Manheim 208 40.09 N 76.23 W
Manhiça 156 25.24 S 32.48 E
Manhuaçu 255 20.15 S 42.02 W
Manhuaçu ≃ 255 19.30 S 41.06 W
Manhumirim 255 20.22 S 41.57 W
Maní, P.R. 240m 18.15 N 67.10 W
Mani, Zaïre 154 6.27 S 25.20 E
Mani', Jabal al- ∧ 132 33.19 N 36.17 E
Mania ≃ 157b 19.42 S 44.22 E
Maniago 64 46.10 N 12.43 E
Maniamba 154 12.43 S 35.00 E
Manianga 273b 4.45 S 15.19 E
Manica □5 156 19.00 S 33.15 E
Manicahan 116 7.01 N 122.12 E
Manicaland □4 154 19.30 S 32.15 E
Manicani Island I 116 11.00 N 125.38 E
Manicaragua 240p 22.09 N 79.58 W
Manic Deux, Réservoir ⊜1 186 49.25 N 68.25 W
Manicoré 248 5.49 S 61.17 W
Manicoré ≃ 248 5.51 S 61.19 W
Manicouagan ≃ 186 49.11 N 68.13 W
Manicouagan, Réservoir ⊜1 186 51.30 N 68.19 W
Manic Trois, Réservoir ⊜1 186 50.00 N 68.40 W
Manifold ≃ 44 53.03 N 1.47 W
Maniganggo 102 32.01 N 99.11 E
Manignan 150 10.00 N 7.50 W
Manigotagan 184 51.06 N 96.18 W
Manigotagan ≃ 184 51.07 N 96.20 W
Manihāri 124 25.21 N 87.38 E
Manihiki I1 14 10.24 S 161.01 W
Manika, Plateau de la ⁂1 154 10.00 S 26.00 E
Manikanāli 126 23.19 N 87.03 E
Mānikganj 124 23.52 N 90.00 E
Mānikpur 124 25.04 N 81.07 E
Manila, Pil. 116 14.35 N 121.00 E
Manila, Pil. 269f 14.35 N 121.00 E
Manila, Ar., U.S. 194 35.52 N 90.10 W
Manila, Ut., U.S. 200 40.59 N 109.43 W
Manila Bay c 116 14.30 N 120.45 E
Manila Cathedral ✢1 269f 14.35 N 120.59 E
Manila International Airport ✈ 269f 14.31 N 121.01 E
Manilla, Austl. 166 30.45 S 150.43 E
Manilla, In., U.S. 218 39.34 N 85.37 W
Manilla, Ia., U.S. 198 41.53 N 95.13 W
Manille → Manila 116 14.35 N 121.00 E
Manily 74 62.29 N 165.36 E
Mani Majra 123 30.43 N 76.50 E
Manimbaya, Tanjung > 112 0.01 N 119.36 E
Manimpé 150 14.09 N 5.31 W
Maningory ≃ 157b 17.13 S 49.28 E
Maningrida 164 12.03 S 134.13 E
Maninjau, Danau ⊜ 112 0.20 S 100.11 E
Manino 76 53.58 N 34.20 E
Manipa, Pulau I 164 3.17 S 127.35 E
Manipa, Selat ɤ 164 3.20 S 127.23 E
Manipur □3 120 25.00 N 94.00 E
Manipur ≃ 110 22.52 N 94.05 E
Manique de Baixo 266c 38.44 N 9.22 W
Maniquin Island I 116 11.36 N 121.45 E
Manirāmpur 126 23.01 N 89.14 E
Manisa 130 38.36 N 27.26 E
Manisa □4 130 38.50 N 28.10 E
Manissauá-Miçu ≃ 250 10.58 S 53.20 W
Manistee 190 44.14 N 86.19 W
Manistee ≃ 190 44.15 N 86.21 W
Manistique 190 45.57 N 86.14 W
Manistique ≃ 190 45.57 N 86.15 W
Manistique, West Branch ≃ 190 46.02 N 86.09 W
Manistique Lake ⊜ 190 46.15 N 85.45 W
Manito 190 40.25 N 89.46 W
Manitoba □4, Can. 176 54.00 N 97.00 W
Manitoba □4, Can. 184 54.00 N 97.00 W
Manitoba, Lake ⊜ 184 51.00 N 98.45 W
Manitou 184 49.15 N 98.31 W
Manitou ≃, On., Can. 184 48.58 N 93.20 W
Manitou ≃, P.Q., Can. 186 50.18 N 65.15 W
Manitou, Lac ⊜, P.Q., Can. 186 50.29 N 63.54 W
Manitou, Lac ⊜, P.Q., Can. 186 50.54 N 65.18 W
Manitou, Lac ⊜, P.Q., Can. 206 46.03 N 74.23 W
Manitou, Lake ⊜, On., Can. 190 45.48 N 82.00 W
Manitou, Lake ⊜, In., U.S. 216 41.03 N 86.11 W
Manitou Beach, Sk., Can. 184 51.43 N 105.26 W
Manitou Beach, Mi., U.S. 216 41.58 N 84.19 W
Manitou Lake ⊜, On., Can. 190 46.01 N 79.00 W
Manitou Lake ⊜, Sk., Can. 184 52.45 N 109.45 W
Manitoulin Island I 190 45.50 N 82.20 W
Manitou Springs 200 38.51 N 104.55 W
Manitouwabing Lake ⊜ 212 45.29 N 79.54 W
Manitowaning 190 45.45 N 81.49 W
Manitowik Lake ⊜ 190 48.10 N 84.24 W
Manitowish Waters 190 46.09 N 89.53 W
Manitowoc 190 44.05 N 87.39 W
Manitowoc ≃ 190 44.05 N 87.39 W
Maniwaki 188 46.23 N 75.58 W
Ma'nīyā 142 30.50 N 30.39 E
Manizales 246 5.05 N 75.32 W
Manja, Madag. 157b 21.26 S 44.20 E
Manjā, Urd. 132 31.45 N 35.51 E
Manjacaze 156 24.44 S 33.53 E
Manjakandriana 157b 18.55 S 47.47 E
Manjeri 122 11.07 N 76.07 E
Manjiang 98 41.57 N 127.36 E
Manjimup 162 34.14 S 116.09 E
Manjing 107 29.55 N 104.07 E
Mānjra ≃ 122 18.49 N 77.52 E
Manjuyod 116 9.41 N 123.09 E
Mank 61 48.06 N 15.20 E
Mankanaj 86 48.58 N 60.58 E
Månkarbo 40 60.14 N 17.28 E
Mān Kāt 110 22.05 N 98.01 E
Mankato, Ks., U.S. 198 39.47 N 98.12 W
Mankato, Mn., U.S. 190 44.09 N 93.59 W
Mankayane 158 26.42 S 31.00 E
Mankent 85 42.25 N 69.50 E
Mankera 123 31.23 N 71.26 E
Mankim 152 5.01 N 12.00 E
Mankinholes 262 53.42 N 2.03 W
Man'kivka, Ukr. 78 48.58 N 30.20 E
Man'kivka, Ukr. 83 49.34 N 38.27 E
Mankono 150 8.04 N 6.12 W
Mankota 184 49.25 N 107.04 W
Man'kovo 83 49.24 N 40.17 E
Man'kovo-Ber'ozovskaja 80 48.47 N 41.33 E
Mankoya 154 14.47 S 24.48 E
Mānkundu 272b 22.50 N 88.22 E
Mānkur, India 126 22.30 N 87.54 E
Mānkur, India 126 23.20 N 87.33 E
Manlaj 102 44.07 N 106.50 E
Manley 262 53.14 N 2.45 W
Manley Hot Springs 180 65.00 N 150.37 W
Manleys Corner 283 42.03 N 71.04 W
Manlius 210 43.00 N 75.58 W
Manlleu 34 42.00 N 2.17 E
Manly, Austl. 170 33.48 S 151.17 E
Manly, Austl. 171a 27.28 S 153.15 E
Manly, Ia., U.S. 190 43.17 N 93.12 W
Manly Warringah War Memorial Park ♦ 274a 33.46 S 151.15 E
Manmād 122 20.15 N 74.27 E
Mann ≃ 164 12.20 S 134.07 E
Mann, Mount ∧ 162 25.59 S 129.42 E
Manna, Indon. 112 4.27 S 102.55 E
Mān Na, Mya. 110 23.27 N 97.14 E
Mannahill 166 32.26 S 139.59 E
Mannar 122 8.59 N 79.54 E
Mannar, Gulf of c 122 8.30 N 79.00 E
Mannārgudi 122 10.40 N 79.26 E
Mannar Island I 122 9.03 N 79.50 E
Mann Creek ≃ 281 42.32 N 83.44 W
Männedorf 58 47.15 N 8.42 E
Mannersdorf am Leithagebirge 61 47.58 N 16.36 E
Mannersdorf an der Rabnitz 61 47.25 N 16.31 E
Mannford 196 36.09 N 96.23 W
Mannheim 56 49.29 N 8.29 E
Manni 120 34.48 N 87.15 E
Manning, Ia., U.S. 198 41.54 N 95.03 W
Manning, N.D., U.S. 198 47.13 N 102.46 W
Manning, S.C., U.S. 192 33.41 N 80.12 W
Manning, Cape > 174o 2.02 N 157.26 W
Manning Provincial Park ♦ 224 49.07 N 120.54 W
Manning Strait ɤ 175e 7.24 S 158.00 E
Mannington 188 39.31 N 80.20 W
Manningtree 42 51.57 N 1.04 E
Mannō 96 34.11 N 133.51 E
Mann Ranges ∧ 162 26.00 S 129.30 E
Mannsville 212 43.42 N 76.03 W
Mannswörth ✢8 264b 48.09 N 16.31 E
Mannu ≃ 71 39.16 N 9.00 E
Mannu ≃, It. 71 39.35 N 8.49 E
Mannu ≃, It. 71 40.50 N 8.23 E
Mannu, Capo > 71 40.02 N 8.22 E
Mannu, Monte ∧ 71 40.23 N 8.25 E
Mannum 166 34.55 S 139.18 E
Mannus 171b 35.48 S 147.57 E
Mannus Creek ≃ 171b 35.58 S 148.03 E
Mannville 182 53.20 N 111.10 W
Mano 150 8.02 N 12.06 W
Mano ≃ 150 6.56 N 11.31 W
Manoa 248 9.40 S 65.27 W
Manoel Ribas 252 24.31 S 51.39 W
Manohardi 126 24.08 N 90.43 E
Manoharpur, India 124 22.23 N 85.12 E
Manoharpur, India 126 21.59 N 87.18 E
Manokin ≃ 208 38.05 N 75.55 W
Manokotak 180 58.40 N 159.09 W
Manokwari 164 0.52 S 134.05 E
Manolo Fortich (Maluko) 116 8.25 N 124.58 E
Manoma ≃ 89 49.18 N 136.37 E
Manombo 157b 22.57 S 43.28 E
Manomet 207 41.55 N 70.34 W
Manomet Hill ∧2 207 41.55 N 70.36 W
Manong 114 4.36 N 100.53 E
Manonga ≃ 154 4.08 S 34.12 E
Manono 154 7.18 S 27.25 E
Manono I 175a 13.50 S 172.05 W
Manoora 168b 34.00 S 138.49 E
Manoppello 66 42.15 N 14.03 E
Manor, Sk., Can. 184 49.36 N 102.05 W
Manor, Pa., U.S. 214 40.20 N 79.40 W
Manor, Tx., U.S. 222 30.20 N 97.33 W
Manorbier 42 51.39 N 4.48 W
Manorhamilton 48 54.18 N 8.10 W
Manorhaven 276 40.50 N 73.42 W
Manor Hill 214 40.38 N 77.55 W
Manori ✢8 272c 19.12 N 72.47 E
Manori Creek c 272c 19.12 N 72.48 E
Manorina National Park ♦ 171a 27.23 S 152.47 E
Manori Point > 272c 19.11 N 72.47 E
Manoron 110 11.38 N 99.04 E
Manorville 214 40.47 N 79.31 W
Manosque 62 43.50 N 5.47 E
Manotick 212 45.13 N 75.41 W
Manouane ≃ 186 49.30 N 71.11 W
Manouane, Lac ⊜ 186 50.41 N 70.45 W
Manouanis ≃ 186 50.28 N 70.08 W
Manouanis, Lac ⊜ 186 50.51 N 70.20 W
Manown 279b 40.13 N 79.54 W
Manpaka 273b 4.18 S 15.12 E
Manpitou 100 22.17 N 112.52 E
Manp'o 98 41.10 N 126.17 E
Mānpur, India 122 20.22 N 80.43 E
Mānpur, India 124 23.46 N 81.08 E
Manqabād 142 27.12 N 31.07 E
Manqatīn 142 28.20 N 30.40 E
Manquehue, Cerro ∧ 286e 33.21 S 70.36 W
Manra I1 14 4.27 S 171.15 W
Manresa 34 41.44 N 1.50 E
Manresa Island I 276 41.04 N 73.25 W
Mānsa, India 120 23.26 N 72.40 E
Mānsa, India 123 29.59 N 75.23 E
Mansa (Fort Rosebery), Zam. 154 11.12 S 28.53 E
Mansabá 150 12.18 N 15.15 W
Mansafīs 142 28.00 N 30.49 E
Mansalay 116 12.31 N 121.26 E
Mansara 150 13.20 N 4.39 W
Manse ≃ 50 47.08 N 0.25 E
Manseau 206 46.22 N 72.00 W
Mansehra 123 34.20 N 73.12 E
Mansein 110 25.12 N 95.58 E
Mansel Island I 176 62.00 N 79.50 W
Mansfeld 54 51.35 N 11.27 E
Mansfield, Austl. 169 37.03 S 146.05 E
Mansfield, Eng., U.K. 44 53.09 N 1.11 W
Mansfield, Ar., U.S. 194 35.04 N 94.13 W
Mansfield, Ga., U.S. 192 33.31 N 83.44 W
Mansfield, Il., U.S. 216 40.12 N 88.30 W
Mansfield, La., U.S. 194 32.02 N 93.42 W
Mansfield, Ma., U.S. 207 42.02 N 71.13 W
Mansfield, Mo., U.S. 194 37.06 N 92.34 W
Mansfield, N.J., U.S. 285 40.05 N 74.43 W
Mansfield, Oh., U.S. 214 40.45 N 82.30 W
Mansfield, Pa., U.S. 210 41.48 N 77.04 W
Mansfield, Tx., U.S. 222 32.33 N 97.08 W
Mansfield, Mount ∧ 188 44.33 N 72.49 W
Mansfield Center 207 41.45 N 72.11 W
Mansfield Hollow Lake ⊜1 207 41.45 N 72.11 W
Mansfield Hollow State Park ♦ 207 41.46 N 72.10 W
Mansfield Municipal Airport ✈ 283 42.00 N 71.12 W
Mansfield Woodhouse 44 53.11 N 1.12 W
Man Shan I 106 31.14 N 120.17 E
Mansieville Location 273d 26.05 S 27.45 E
Mānsinhapur 272b 22.39 N 88.09 E
Mansión 236 10.06 N 85.22 W
Manskoje belogorje ∧ 88 54.35 N 94.00 E
Mansle 32 45.53 N 0.11 E
Manso ≃ 248 14.42 S 56.16 W
Mansôa 150 12.10 N 14.36 W
Manson, Ia., U.S. 198 42.32 N 94.32 W
Manson, Wa., U.S. 182 47.53 N 120.09 W
Manson ≃ 182 55.42 N 123.47 W
Manson Creek 182 55.41 N 124.29 W
Mansonville 206 45.03 N 72.23 W
Mansourah 34 36.04 N 4.28 E
Mansucum 246 9.02 N 77.49 W
Mansura → Al-Manṣūrah, Miṣr 142 31.03 N 31.23 E
Mansura, La., U.S. 194 31.03 N 92.02 W
Manṣūrīyah, Tur'at al- ≍ 142 31.03 N 31.24 E
Mansurovo 82 55.52 N 36.36 E
Manta, Ec. 246 0.57 S 80.44 W
Manta, It. 62 44.37 N 7.29 E
Manta, Bahía de c 246 0.54 S 80.42 W
Mantabuan Island I 116 5.02 N 120.13 E
Mantagao ≃ 184 51.50 N 97.48 W
Mantalingajan, Mount ∧ 116 8.48 N 117.40 E
Mantalingajan Range ⁂ 116 8.46 N 117.40 E
Mantanani Besar, Pulau I 112 6.45 N 116.17 E
Mantangule Island I 116 8.10 N 117.10 E
Mantantale 152 2.10 S 20.06 E
Mantare 154 2.43 S 33.13 E
Mantaro ≃ 248 12.15 S 73.58 W
Manteca 226 37.47 N 121.12 W
Mantecal 246 7.33 N 69.09 W
Mantel 60 49.39 N 12.03 E
Mantena 255 18.47 S 40.59 W
Manteno 216 41.15 N 87.49 W
Manteo 192 35.54 N 75.40 W
Mantes-Chérence, Aérodrome de ✈ 261 49.05 N 1.41 E
Mantes-la-Jolie 50 48.59 N 1.43 E
Mantes-la-Ville 261 48.58 N 1.42 E
Manteswar 126 23.26 N 88.06 E
Manteuil-le-Haudouin 50 49.08 N 2.48 E
Manthelan 50 47.08 N 0.47 E
Manti 200 39.16 N 111.38 W
Manticao 116 8.24 N 124.17 E
Mantilla ✢8 286b 23.04 N 82.20 W
Mantin 114 2.49 N 101.54 E
Mantiqueira, Serra da ⁂ 256 22.00 S 44.45 W
Mantok 112 1.09 S 123.14 E
Manton 190 44.24 N 85.23 W
Mantorville 190 44.04 N 92.45 W
Mantos Blancos 252 23.25 S 70.05 W
Mantou 104 42.27 N 122.26 E
Mantova 64 45.09 N 10.48 E
Mantova □4 64 45.10 N 10.47 E
Māntri 126 21.39 N 86.49 E
Mänttä 26 62.02 N 24.38 E
Mantua, Cuba 240p 22.17 N 84.17 W
Mantua → Mantova, It. 64 45.09 N 10.48 E
Mantua, N.J., U.S. 208 39.47 N 75.10 W
Mantua, Oh., U.S. 214 41.17 N 81.13 W

≃	River	Fluß	Río	Rivière	Rio
≍	Canal	Kanal	Canal	Canal	Canal
ɩ	Waterfall, Rapids	Wasserfall, Stromschnellen	Cascada, Rápidos	Chute d'eau, Rapides	Cascata, Rápidos
ɤ	Strait	Meeresstraße	Estrecho	Détroit	Estreito
c	Bay, Gulf	Bucht, Golf	Bahía, Golfo	Baie, Golfe	Baía, Golfo
⊜	Lake, Lakes	See, Seen	Lago, Lagos	Lac, Lacs	Lago, Lagos
⊞	Swamp	Sumpf	Pantano	Marais	Pântano
❄	Ice Features, Glacier	Eis- und Gletscherformen	Accidentes Glaciales	Formes glaciaires	Acidentes glaciares
⚲	Other Hydrographic Features	Andere Hydrographische Objekte	Otros Elementos Hidrográficos	Autres données hydrographiques	Outros acidentes hidrográficos

✢	Submarine Features	Untermeerische Objekte	Accidentes Submarinos	Formes de relief sous-marin	Acidentes submarinos
□	Political Unit	Politische Einheit	Unidad Política	Entité politique	Unidade política
✢	Cultural Institution	Kulturelle Institution	Institución Cultural	Institution culturelle	Instituição cultural
⊥	Historical Site	Historische Stätte	Sitio Histórico	Site historique	Sitio histórico
♦	Recreational Site	Erholungs- und Ferienort	Sitio de Recreo	Centre de loisirs	Area de Lazer
✈	Airport	Flughafen	Aeropuerto	Aéroport	Aeroporto
■	Military Installation	Militäranlage	Instalación Militar	Installation militaire	Instalação militar
✢	Miscellaneous	Verschiedenes	Misceláneo	Divers	Diversos

Mantua, Va., U.S. 284c 38.51 N 77.15 W
Mantua ≃ 240p 22.12 N 84.25 W
Mantua Creek ≃ 285 39.51 N 75.14 W
Mantua Creek, Chestnut Branch ≃ 285 39.47 N 75.10 W
Mantua Creek, Porch Branch ≃ 285 39.46 N 75.07 W
Mantua Hills 284c 38.51 N 77.16 W
Mantua Terrace 285 39.48 N 75.10 W
Manturovo, Ross. 78 51.28 N 37.07 E
Manturovo, Ross. 80 58.20 N 44.46 E
Mäntyharju 26 61.25 N 26.53 E
Mäntyluoto 26 61.35 N 21.29 E
Manu 248 12.15 S 70.50 W
Manú ≃ 248 12.16 S 70.51 W
Manu, Parque Nacional del ♦ 248 12.15 S 71.40 W
Manuae I[1], Cook Is. 14 19.21 S 158.56 W
Manuae I[1], Poly. fr. 14 16.30 S 154.40 W
Manua Islands II 174y 14.13 S 169.35 W
Manuel 234 22.44 N 98.19 W
Manuel Alves ≃ 250 11.19 S 48.28 W
Manuel Alves Grande ≃ 250 7.27 S 47.35 W
Manuel Antonio, Parque Nacional ♦ 236 9.25 N 84.10 W
Manuel Avila Camacho, Presa ⊜[1] 234 18.55 N 98.10 W
Manuel Benavides 232 29.05 N 103.55 W
Manuel Derqui 252 27.50 S 58.48 W
Manuel Duarte 256 22.06 S 43.34 W
Manuel Ribeiro 256 22.54 S 42.47 W
Manuel Rodriguez, Isla I 254 52.35 S 73.50 W
Manuel Urbano 248 8.53 S 69.18 W
Manués-Açu ≃ 250 3.22 S 57.44 W
Manuguru 122 17.59 N 80.43 E
Manuhangi I[1] 14 19.12 S 141.16 W
Manuherikia ≃ 172 45.16 S 169.24 E
Manui, Pulau I 112 3.35 S 123.08 E
Manuilovskaja 76 60.29 N 40.40 E
Manu Island I 164 1.17 S 143.35 E
Manūjān 128 27.24 N 57.32 E
Manuk ≃ 115a 6.14 S 108.13 E
Manuk, Pulau I 164 5.33 S 130.18 E
Manukan 116 8.31 N 123.06 E
Manukau 172 37.02 S 174.54 E
Manukau Harbour ⊂ 172 37.01 S 174.44 E
Manulla ≃ 48 53.57 N 9.12 W
Manulu Lagoon ⊂ 174o 1.56 N 157.20 W
Manumuskin ≃ 208 39.18 N 75.00 W
Manundi, Tanjung > 164 0.38 S 135.22 E
Manunui 172 38.53 S 175.20 E
Manuoha ∧ 172 38.39 S 177.07 E
Manuripe (Mamuripi) ≃ 248 11.06 S 67.36 W
Manuripi ≃ 248 11.42 S 67.16 W
Manursing Island I 276 40.58 N 73.40 W
Manursing Island Park ♦ 276 40.58 N 73.40 W
Manus □[5] 164 2.00 S 147.00 E
Mānushmuria 126 22.22 N 86.47 E
Manus Island I 164 2.05 S 147.00 E
Manutahi 172 39.40 S 174.24 E
Manutuke 172 38.41 S 177.55 E
Manvel, N.D., U.S. 198 48.04 N 97.10 W
Manvel, Tx., U.S. 222 29.28 N 95.22 W
Manville, N.J., U.S. 210 40.32 N 74.35 W
Manville, R.I., U.S. 207 41.58 N 71.28 W
Mānwat 122 19.18 N 76.30 E
Many 194 31.34 N 93.29 W
Manyal Shīhah 273c 29.57 N 31.14 E
Manyana 156 23.23 S 21.44 E
Manyani 154 3.05 S 38.30 E
Manyara, Lake ⊜ 154 3.35 S 35.50 E
Manyberries 184 49.24 N 110.42 W
Manyč ≃ 72 47.15 N 40.00 E
Manyč-Gudilo, ozero ⊜ 80 46.24 N 42.38 E
Manyeleti Game Reserve ⊕[4] 156 25.42 S 31.30 E
Many Island Lake ⊜ 184 50.08 N 110.03 W
Manyoni 154 5.45 S 34.50 E
Many Peaks 166 24.33 S 151.23 E
Manytsch → Manyč ≃ 72 47.15 N 40.00 E
Manz'a 86 58.29 N 96.15 E
Mānzai 120 30.07 N 68.52 E
Manzanares 34 39.00 N 3.22 W
Manzanares ≃ 34 40.19 N 3.32 W
Manzanares, Canal del ≃ 266a 40.23 N 3.41 W
Manzanillo, Cuba 240p 20.21 N 77.07 W
Manzanillo, Méx. 234 19.03 N 104.20 W
Manzanillo, Bahía ⊂ 234 19.04 N 104.22 W
Manzanillo, Bahía de ⊂ 234 19.12 N 104.43 W
Manzanillo, Punta >, Pan. 236 9.38 N 79.32 W
Manzanillo, Punta >, Ven. 241s 11.32 N 69.17 W
Manzanillo Bay ⊂ 238 19.45 N 71.46 W
Manzanita, Or., U.S. 224 45.43 N 123.56 W
Manzanita, Wa., U.S. 224 47.42 N 122.33 W
Manzano, It. 64 45.59 N 13.23 E
Manzano, N.M., U.S. 200 34.38 N 106.20 W
Manzanola 198 38.06 N 103.51 W
Manzano Peak ∧ 200 34.35 N 106.26 W
Manzheliya 78 49.19 N 33.38 E
Manzhouli 88 49.35 N 117.22 E
Manziana 66 42.08 N 12.08 E
Manzil 128 29.15 N 63.05 E
Manzilah, Birkat al- ⊜ 142 31.08 N 31.56 E
Manzilah, Buḥayrat al- ⊜ 142 31.15 N 32.00 E
Manzini 158 26.30 S 31.25 E
Manzone 258 34.29 S 58.52 W
Manzurka 88 53.30 N 106.04 E
Maó, Esp. 34 39.53 N 4.15 E
Mao, Rep. Dom. 238 19.34 N 71.05 W
Mao, Tchad 136 14.07 N 15.19 E
Maoba 102 30.02 N 108.59 E
Maocifan 100 31.40 N 112.53 E
Maocun 98 34.25 N 117.16 E
Maodianzi, Zhg. 107 30.42 N 104.25 E
Maodianzi, Zhg. 107 29.45 N 104.55 E
Mao'ertuo 107 29.19 N 106.24 E
Maojiagou 104 40.58 N 120.51 E
Maojiaji 100 31.32 N 114.16 E
Maojiakou 100 29.53 N 112.58 E
Maojiaping 105 40.34 N 114.43 E
Maojiapuzi 104 41.10 N 123.32 E
Maojiatun 104 41.05 N 121.58 E
Maojiazao 98 39.53 N 113.26 E
Maoke, Pegunungan ⩕ 164 4.00 S 138.00 E
Maolin, Zhg. 89 43.58 N 123.24 E
Maolin, Zhg. 100 30.32 N 118.14 E
Maomao Shan ∧ 102 37.12 N 103.10 E
Maoming 102 21.39 N 110.54 E
Maomu 102 40.18 N 99.28 E
Ma On Shan ∧ 271d 22.25 N 114.15 E
Ma On Shan Tsuen 271d 22.24 N 114.14 E
Maoping 102 30.23 N 110.33 E
Maopora, Pulau I 112 7.35 S 127.35 E
Maoshan 105 40.17 N 117.26 E
Mao Shan ⩕ 106 31.43 N 119.17 E
Maoshi 100 26.57 N 113.05 E
Maospati 115a 7.36 S 111.26 E
Maouri, Dallol V 150 12.05 N 3.32 E
Maowen 102 31.30 N 103.39 E
Maoxing 89 45.32 N 124.33 E
Mao Yü I 100 23.19 N 119.19 E
Maozhou 105 38.51 N 116.06 E
Mapaga 112 0.06 S 119.48 E
Mapam Yumco ⊜ 120 30.42 N 81.27 E
Mapan 112 2.21 S 111.10 E
Mapanda 152 9.32 S 24.16 E
Mapane 112 1.24 S 120.40 E
Mapanza 154 16.15 S 26.55 E
Mapaoni ≃ 250 1.55 N 54.13 W
Mapari ≃, Bra. 246 1.49 S 66.48 W
Mapari ≃, Bra. 250 0.45 N 53.07 W
Mapastepec 234 15.26 N 92.54 W
Mapaville 219 38.14 N 90.29 W
Mapi 164 7.07 S 139.23 E
Mapi ≃ 164 7.00 S 139.16 E
Mapia, Kepulauan II 108 0.50 N 134.20 E
Mapida 112 0.33 S 119.46 E
Mapimí 232 25.49 N 103.51 W
Mapimí, Bolsón de ⊕[2] 232 26.30 N 104.00 W
Mapimí, Bufa de ∧ 196 25.47 N 103.48 W
Maping, Zhg. 100 24.16 N 117.54 E
Maping, Zhg. 100 31.36 N 113.32 E
Mapinga 154 6.36 S 39.04 E
Mapinhane 156 22.19 S 35.03 E
Mapire 246 7.45 N 64.42 W
Mapiri 248 15.15 S 68.10 W
Mapiri ≃ 248 9.52 S 66.21 W
Mapixari, Ilha I 246 2.10 S 65.08 W
Maple ⊕[8] 275b 43.51 N 79.31 W
Maple ≃, U.S. 198 45.47 N 98.33 W
Maple ≃, Ia., U.S. 198 42.00 N 95.59 W
Maple ≃, Mi., U.S. 190 42.59 N 84.57 W
Maple ≃, Mn., U.S. 190 44.05 N 94.00 W
Maple ≃, N.D., U.S. 198 46.56 N 96.55 W
Maple Airfield ⊠ 275b 43.51 N 79.32 W
Maple Bay 224 48.49 N 123.36 W
Maple Bluff 216 43.07 N 89.22 W
Maple Creek 184 49.55 N 109.27 W
Maple Creek ≃ 198 41.33 N 96.27 W
Maplecrest 210 42.17 N 74.11 W
Maple Cross 260 51.37 N 0.30 W
Mapledale 214 41.23 N 79.51 W
Maple Falls 224 48.55 N 122.04 W
Maple Glen 285 40.11 N 75.11 W
Maple Grove, On., Can. 212 43.55 N 78.44 W
Maple Grove, P.Q., Can. 206 45.19 N 73.50 W
Maple Heights 214 41.24 N 81.33 W
Maple Lake 190 45.13 N 94.00 W
Maple Lake ⊜ 212 45.06 N 78.40 W
Maple Lane 216 41.45 N 86.14 W
Maple Leaf Gardens ♦ 275b 43.40 N 79.23 W
Maple Meadow Brook ≃ 283 42.33 N 71.09 W
Maple Mount 194 37.42 N 87.26 W
Maple Park 216 41.55 N 88.36 W
Maples 216 41.01 N 84.58 W
Maple Shade 285 39.57 N 74.59 W
Maple Springs 214 42.12 N 79.25 W
Maplesville 194 32.47 N 86.52 W
Mapleton, S. Afr. 158 26.20 S 28.14 E
Mapleton, Ia., U.S. 198 42.09 N 95.47 W
Mapleton, Mn., U.S. 190 43.55 N 93.57 W
Mapleton, Or., U.S. 202 44.01 N 123.51 W
Mapleton, Ut,. U.S. 200 40.07 N 111.34 W
Mapleton Depot 214 40.24 N 77.57 W
Maple Valley 224 47.25 N 122.03 W
Mapleville 207 41.56 N 71.38 W
Maplewood, Mo., U.S. 219 38.36 N 90.19 W
Maplewood, N.J., U.S. 276 40.43 N 74.14 W
Maplewood, Oh., U.S. 216 40.23 N 84.02 W
Maplewood, Wa., U.S. 224 47.30 N 122.07 W
Maplewood Terrace 279b 40.17 N 79.32 W
Mapocho ≃ 286e 33.25 S 70.47 W
Mapocho, Estación ⊕[5] 286e 33.26 S 70.40 W
Mapoi 154 5.28 N 27.40 E
Mapoon Aboriginal Reserve ⊕[4] 164 11.40 S 142.25 E
Mappsville 208 37.51 N 75.34 W
Maprik 164 3.40 S 143.05 E
Mapuera ≃ 250 1.05 S 57.02 W
Mapujiang 105 40.24 N 114.56 E
Mapulanguene 156 24.29 S 32.06 E
Mapumulo 158 29.11 S 31.02 E
Maputa 158 26.59 S 32.46 E
Maputo 156 25.58 S 32.35 E
Maputo □[5] 156 26.00 S 32.25 E
Maputo (Great Usutu) (Lusutfu) ≃ 158 26.11 S 32.42 E
Maputo, Baia de ⊂ 158 25.48 S 32.51 E
Maqên Gangri ∧ 102 34.55 N 99.18 E
Maqiangou 105 39.30 N 115.02 E
Maqiao, Zhg. 100 29.48 N 114.22 E
Maqiao, Zhg. 106 30.28 N 120.42 E
Maqna 128 28.24 N 34.45 E
Maqṭeïr ⊤[4] 148 22.10 N 10.50 W
Maquan ≃ 124 29.35 N 84.10 E
Maqueda 34 40.04 N 4.22 W
Maqueda Bay ⊂ 116 11.44 N 124.58 E
Maqueda Channel ⊔ 116 13.42 N 124.01 E
Maquela do Zombo 152 6.03 S 15.07 E
Maquereau, Pointe au > 186 48.12 N 64.47 W
Maquilaú ≃ 246 1.23 N 63.24 W
Maquiling, Mount ∧ 116 14.08 N 121.12 E
Maquinchao 254 41.15 S 68.44 W
Maquinchao ≃ 254 41.13 S 69.25 W
Maquoketa 190 42.04 N 90.39 W
Maquoketa ≃ 190 42.11 N 90.19 W
Maquoketa, North Fork ≃ 190 42.05 N 90.40 W
Mar, Laguna ⊂ 286b 23.05 N 82.30 W
Mar, Serra do ±[4] 252 26.00 S 48.00 W
Mara, India 120 28.11 N 94.06 E
Mara, Perú 248 14.06 S 72.07 W
Mara, Zhg. 120 28.11 N 94.08 E
Mara □[4] 154 1.45 S 34.30 E
Mara ≃, Afr. 154 1.31 S 33.56 E
Mara ≃, Ross. 88 58.06 N 104.06 E
Maraã, Bra. 246 1.50 S 65.22 W
Maraa, Poly. fr. 174s 17.46 S 149.34 W
Marabá 250 5.21 S 49.07 W
Marabahan 112 3.00 S 114.45 E
Marabut 116 11.07 N 125.13 E
Maracá, Ilha de I, Bra. 246 3.25 N 61.40 W
Maracá, Ilha de I, Bra. 250 2.05 N 50.25 W
Maracaçumé ≃ 250 1.23 S 45.42 W
Maracaí 255 22.36 S 50.39 W
Maracaibo 246 10.40 N 71.37 W
Maracaibo, Lago de ⊜ 246 9.50 N 71.30 W
Maracaju 255 21.38 S 55.09 W
Maracaju, Serra de ⩕[2] 255 20.45 S 55.00 W
Maracalagonis 71 39.17 N 9.13 E
Maracanã 250 0.46 S 47.27 W
Maracanã ⊕[8] 287a 22.54 S 43.14 W
Maracanã ≃ 248 8.22 S 59.41 W
Maracanã, Estádio do ♦ 287a 22.55 S 43.14 W
Maracanaú 250 3.52 S 38.38 W
Maracás 255 13.26 S 40.27 W
Maracay 246 10.15 N 67.36 W
Maracossic Creek ≃ 208 37.53 N 77.11 W
Marādah 146 29.14 N 19.13 E
Maradi 150 13.29 N 7.06 E
Maradi □[5] 150 14.00 N 7.00 E
Maradi, Goulbin ≃ 150 13.38 N 6.20 E
Marāghah, Sabkhat al- ⊜ 130 35.39 N 37.39 E
Marāgheh 128 37.23 N 46.13 E
Maragiu, Capo > 71 40.20 N 8.23 E
Maragogi 250 9.01 S 35.13 W
Maragogipe 255 12.46 S 38.55 W
Marahoué, Parc National de la ♦ 150 7.00 N 6.00 W
Mārahra 124 27.44 N 78.35 E
Marahuaca, Cerro ∧ 246 3.34 N 65.27 W
Maraial 250 8.47 S 35.50 W
Maraiche Lake ⊜ 184 54.28 N 102.01 W
Marainviller 58 48.35 N 6.36 E
Maraisburg → Roodepoort-Maraisburg 273d 26.11 S 27.56 E
Marais des Cygnes ≃ 194 38.02 N 94.14 W
Marais Temps Clair ⊜ 219 38.54 N 90.24 W
Marajó, Baía de ⊂ 250 1.00 S 48.30 W
Marajó, Ilha de I 250 1.00 S 49.30 W
Marakabei 158 29.32 S 28.09 E
Ma'rakah 132 33.16 N 35.18 E
Mārākand 84 38.52 N 45.14 E
Marakwini 164 3.42 S 141.31 E
Maralal 154 1.06 N 36.42 E
Maralaleng 156 25.47 S 22.45 E
Maralal Game Sanctuary ⊕[4] 154 1.09 N 36.38 E
Maraldy 86 52.26 N 77.45 E
Marali 152 6.01 N 18.24 E
Maralik 84 40.35 N 43.52 E
Maralinga 162 30.10 S 131.35 E
Maralinga Lands ⊕[4] 162 29.15 S 130.50 E
Maram 120 25.25 N 94.06 E
Maramag 116 7.46 N 125.00 E
Maramasike I 175e 9.32 S 161.27 E
Marambaia ≃ 256 21.44 S 46.25 W
Marambaia, Ilha da I 256 23.04 S 43.58 W
Marambaia, Pico da ∧ 256 23.04 S 43.59 W
Marambaia, Restinga de ±[2] 256 23.04 S 43.45 W
Marambio ʋ[3] 9 64.14 S 56.43 W
Marampa 150 8.41 N 12.28 W
Maramsilli Reservoir ⊜[1] 122 20.32 N 81.41 E
Maramureș □[6] 38 47.40 N 24.00 E
Maran 114 3.35 N 102.46 E
Mārān, Koh-i- ∧ 120 29.26 N 66.48 E
Marana, Mali 150 14.38 N 11.55 W
Marana, Az., U.S. 200 32.26 N 111.13 W
Maranalgo 162 29.23 S 117.48 E
Maranboy 164 14.30 S 132.45 E
Maranchón 34 41.03 N 2.12 W
Marand 128 38.26 N 45.46 E
Maranello 64 44.32 N 10.52 E
Marang, Malay. 114 5.12 N 103.13 E
Marang, Mya. 110 10.27 N 98.47 E
Marangá ≃ 287a 22.51 S 43.23 W
Marangani 248 14.22 S 71.10 W
Marangas 116 8.40 N 117.38 E
Marange-Zondrange 56 49.07 N 6.32 E
Maranguape 250 3.53 S 38.40 W
Maranhão □[3] 250 5.00 S 45.00 W
Maranhão ≃ 255 13.51 S 48.20 W
Marano 266b 45.38 N 8.38 E
Marano, Laguna di ⊂ 64 45.44 N 13.10 E
Maranoa ≃ 166 27.50 S 148.37 E
Marano di Napoli 68 40.54 N 14.11 E
Marano Lagunare 64 45.46 N 13.10 E
Marañón ≃ 242 4.30 S 73.27 W
Marano sul Panaro 64 44.27 N 10.58 E
Marano Vicentino 64 45.41 N 11.25 E
Marans 32 46.19 N 1.00 W
Maraoli ⊕[8] 272c 19.03 N 72.54 E
Marapanim 250 0.42 S 47.42 W
Marapendi, Lagoa de ⊂ 287a 23.01 S 43.24 W
Marapi ≃ 250 0.37 N 55.58 W
Marapicu, Morro do ∧ 287a 22.50 S 43.36 W
Mararoa ≃ 172 45.34 S 167.36 E
Mararui 154 1.56 S 41.18 E
Maras, Perú 248 13.20 S 72.09 W
Maraş → Kahramanmaraş, Tür. 130 37.36 N 36.55 E
Marasany 80 57.27 N 54.25 E
Marasende, Pulau I 112 5.08 S 118.09 E
Mărășești 38 45.52 N 27.14 E
Maratasã ≃ 250 4.14 S 42.15 W
Maratea 68 39.59 N 15.45 E
Marathon, Austl. 166 20.49 S 143.34 E
Marathon, On., Can. 190 48.43 N 86.23 W
Marathón, Ellás 38 38.10 N 23.58 E
Marathon, Fl., U.S. 220 24.42 N 81.05 W
Marathon, N.Y., U.S. 210 42.26 N 76.01 W
Marathon, Tx., U.S. 196 30.12 N 103.15 W
Marathon, Wi., U.S. 190 44.55 N 89.50 W
Maratua, Pulau I 112 2.15 N 118.36 E
Marau, Bra. 252 28.27 S 52.12 W
Maraú, Bra. 255 14.06 S 39.00 W
Marauiá ≃ 246 0.23 S 65.13 W
Marausa 70 37.56 N 12.30 E
Maravari 175e 7.51 S 156.42 E
Maravatío de Ocampo 234 19.54 N 100.27 W
Maravilha 252 26.47 S 53.09 W
Maravillas 232 27.22 N 104.29 W
Maravillas Creek ≃ 196 29.34 N 102.47 W
Mara Vista 207 41.33 N 70.34 W
Marav Lake ⊜ 120 29.04 N 69.18 E
Maravovo 175e 9.17 S 159.38 E
Marāwah 146 32.29 N 21.25 E
Marawi, Pil. 116 8.01 N 124.18 E
Marawī, Sūd. 140 18.29 N 31.49 E
Marawwah I 128 24.18 N 53.18 E
Maraye-en-Othe 50 48.10 N 3.51 E
Marayes 252 31.29 S 67.20 W
Marayong 274a 33.45 S 150.54 E
Märäzä 84 40.33 N 48.56 E
Marazion 42 50.08 N 5.28 W
Marbach, Dtsch. 54 51.02 N 13.13 E
Marbach, Dtsch. 56 50.37 N 9.43 E
Marbach, Schw. 58 46.52 N 7.55 E
Marbach am Neckar 56 48.56 N 9.14 E
Marbache 56 48.48 N 6.05 E
Marbais 50 50.33 N 4.31 E
Marbeck 52 51.49 N 6.52 E
Marbella 34 36.31 N 4.53 W
Marble, Mn., U.S. 190 47.19 N 93.17 W
Marble, N.C., U.S. 192 35.10 N 83.55 W
Marble, Pa., U.S. 214 41.20 N 79.26 W
Marble Arch ⊥ 146 30.29 N 18.35 E
Marble Bar 162 21.11 S 119.44 E
Marble Canyon V 200 36.30 N 111.50 W
Marble Falls 196 30.34 N 98.16 W
Marble Hall 156 24.57 S 29.13 E
Marblehead, Il., U.S. 219 39.50 N 91.22 W
Marblehead, Ma., U.S. 207 42.30 N 70.51 W
Marblehead, Oh., U.S. 214 41.32 N 82.44 W
Marblehead Neck >[1] 283 42.29 N 70.51 W
Marble Hill 194 37.18 N 89.58 W
Marble Lake ⊜ 216 41.54 N 84.54 W
Marblemount 224 48.31 N 121.26 W
Marble Rock 190 42.57 N 92.52 W
Marbleton 206 45.37 N 71.35 W
Marburg, Austl. 171a 27.34 S 152.35 E
Marburg, Dtsch. 56 50.49 N 8.46 E
Marburg, S. Afr. 158 30.44 S 30.26 E
Marburg, Lake ⊜[1] 208 39.48 N 76.53 W
Marburg an der Drau → Maribor 36 46.33 N 15.39 E
Marbury 208 38.34 N 77.09 W
Marc ≃ 50 50.43 N 3.50 E
Marca, Ponta da > 152 16.31 S 11.42 E
Marcal ≃ 30 47.41 N 17.32 E
Marcala 236 14.07 N 88.00 W
Marcali 30 46.35 N 17.25 E
Marcallo con Casone 266b 45.29 N 8.52 E
Marcaria 64 45.07 N 10.32 E
Marceau, Lac ⊜ 186 51.25 N 66.41 W
Marcedusa 68 39.02 N 16.50 E
Marcelin 184 52.55 N 106.47 W
Marceline 194 39.42 N 92.56 W
Marcelino Ramos 252 27.28 S 51.54 W
Marcella 276 40.59 N 74.28 W
Marcellina 66 42.01 N 12.48 E
Marcellus, Mi., U.S. 216 42.01 N 85.48 W
Marcellus, N.Y., U.S. 210 42.59 N 76.20 W
Marcellus Falls 210 43.00 N 76.20 W
Marcevo 83 47.15 N 38.53 E
March 42 52.33 N 0.06 E
March (Morava) ≃ 30 48.10 N 16.59 E
Marcha 74 60.37 N 123.18 E
Marcha ≃ 74 63.28 N 118.50 E
March Air Force Base ■ 228 33.54 N 117.15 W
Marchais 261 48.31 N 2.03 E
Marchal 152 5.16 S 14.58 E
Marchamat 85 40.30 N 72.19 E
Marchand 214 40.51 N 79.02 W
Marchaux 58 47.19 N 6.08 E
Marche □[4] 66 43.30 N 13.15 E
Marche □[9] 32 46.05 N 2.10 E
Marche-en-Famenne 56 50.12 N 5.20 E
Marchegg 61 48.17 N 16.55 E
Marche-les-Dames 56 50.29 N 4.58 E
Marchémoret 261 49.03 N 2.46 E
Marchena 34 37.20 N 5.24 W
Marchena, Isla I 246a 0.21 N 90.29 W
Marchenoir 50 47.49 N 1.24 E
Marchesato ⊕[1] 68 39.07 N 16.58 E
Marchfeld ⊕[1] 264b 48.17 N 16.31 E
Marchienne-au-Pont 50 50.24 N 4.23 E
Marchinbar Island I 164 11.15 S 136.45 E
Marching 60 48.49 N 11.43 E
Mar Chiquita, Laguna ⊂ 252 37.37 S 57.24 W
Mar Chiquita, Laguna ⊜ 252 30.42 S 62.36 W
Marchtrenk 61 48.11 N 14.07 E
Marchykhyna Buda 78 51.58 N 34.03 E
Marciana 66 42.47 N 10.10 E
Marciana Marina 66 42.48 N 10.12 E
Marcianise 68 41.02 N 14.17 E
Marciano della Chiana 66 43.18 N 11.47 E
Marcigny 32 46.17 N 4.02 E
Marcillac-Vallon 32 44.29 N 2.28 E
Marcilloles 62 45.20 N 5.11 E
Marcilly 261 49.02 N 2.53 E
Marcilly-la-Campagne 50 48.50 N 1.13 E
Marcilly-le-Hayer 50 48.21 N 3.38 E
Marcilly-sur-Eure 50 48.49 N 1.21 E
Marck 50 50.57 N 1.57 E
Marckolsheim 58 48.10 N 7.33 E
Marco, Bra. 250 3.08 S 40.09 W
Marco, It. 64 45.51 N 11.01 E
Marco, Fl., U.S. 220 25.58 N 81.43 W
Marcoing 50 50.07 N 3.11 E
Marco Island I 220 25.55 N 81.45 W
Marcola 202 44.10 N 122.51 W
Marcolino, Igarapé ≃ 250 11.03 S 58.35 W
Marcona 248 15.03 S 75.01 W
Marco Polo, Aeroporto ⊠ 64 45.30 N 12.21 E
Marco Polo Bridge ⊕[5] 271a 39.52 N 116.12 E
Marcos Juárez 252 32.42 S 62.06 W
Marcos Paz 258 34.46 S 58.50 W
Marcos Paz □[5] 288 34.49 S 58.49 W
Marcotte, Lac ⊜ 206 46.47 N 73.12 W
Marcoussis 261 48.39 N 2.14 E
Marcq 261 48.52 N 1.49 E
Marcq-en-Barœul 50 50.40 N 3.05 E
Marčugi 82 55.21 N 38.33 E
Mârculești 38 47.52 N 28.14 E
Marcus 198 42.49 N 95.48 W
Marcus Baker, Mount ∧ 180 61.26 N 147.45 W
Marcus Hook 208 39.49 N 75.25 W
Marcus Hook Creek ≃ 285 39.49 N 75.25 W
Marcus Island → Minami-Tori-shima I 14 24.18 N 153.58 E
Marcy, Mount ∧ 188 44.07 N 73.56 W
Marda 162 30.13 S 119.17 E
Mardalsfossen ∟ 26 62.30 N 8.07 E
Mardān 123 34.12 N 72.02 E
Mardarivka 78 47.32 N 29.44 E
Mar de Cães, Vala de ≊ 266c 38.51 N 8.59 W
Mar de Espanha 256 21.52 S 43.00 W
Mardela Springs 208 38.27 N 75.45 W
Mar del Plata 252 38.00 S 57.33 W
Marden 42 51.10 N 0.29 E
Mardie 162 21.11 S 115.57 E
Mardin 130 37.18 N 40.44 E
Mardin □[4] 128 37.25 N 41.00 E
Mar Dyke ≃ 260 51.29 N 0.14 E
Maré I 175f 21.30 S 168.00 E
Mare a Brăilei, Insula I 38 45.00 N 28.00 E
Marea de Portillo 240p 19.55 N 77.11 W
Marecchia ≃ 66 44.04 N 12.34 E
Marechal Cândido Rondon 252 24.34 S 54.04 W
Marechal Deodoro 250 9.43 S 35.54 W
Marechal Taumaturgo 248 8.57 S 72.48 W
Maree, Loch ⊜ 46 57.42 N 5.30 W
Mareeba 166 17.00 S 145.26 E
Mareetsane 158 26.09 S 25.25 E
Mareil-en-France 261 49.04 N 2.26 E
Mareil-le-Guyon 261 48.47 N 1.51 E
Mareil-Marly 261 48.53 N 2.05 E
Mare Island I 226 38.06 N 122.16 W
Mare Island Naval Shipyard ■ 226 38.06 N 122.17 W
Mare Island Strait ⊔ 282 38.06 N 122.17 W
Mareje, Gunung ∧ 115b 8.46 S 116.08 E
Marek 112 4.48 S 120.21 E
Maremma ⊕[1] 66 42.30 N 11.30 E
Marene 62 44.39 N 7.44 E
Marengo, Il., U.S. 216 42.14 N 88.36 W
Marengo, In., U.S. 218 38.22 N 86.20 W
Marengo, Ia., U.S. 190 41.47 N 92.04 W
Marengo, Mi., U.S. 216 42.17 N 84.51 W
Marengo, Oh., U.S. 214 40.24 N 82.49 W
Marengo ⊥ 62 44.49 N 8.40 E
Marengo Cave ±[5] 218 38.23 N 86.21 W
Marenisco 190 46.22 N 89.41 W
Marennes 32 45.50 N 1.06 W
Marerano 157b 21.23 S 44.52 E
Maresias 256 23.48 S 45.33 W
Marettimo 70 37.58 N 12.04 E
Marettimo, Isola I 70 37.58 N 12.03 E
Mareuil-en-Brie 50 48.57 N 3.45 E
Mareuil-lès-Meaux 261 48.56 N 2.52 E
Mareuil-sur-Aÿ 50 49.03 N 4.02 E
Mareuil-sur-Belle 32 45.28 N 0.28 E
Marevo 76 57.19 N 32.05 E
Marey-sur-Tille 58 47.35 N 5.03 E
Marfa 196 30.18 N 104.01 W
Marfinka 83 47.36 N 38.32 E
Marfino 80 46.25 N 48.44 E
Mar Forest ⊕[3] 46 57.00 N 3.35 W
Margai Caka ⊜ 120 35.00 N 87.00 E
Margam, Īrān 84 39.09 N 44.57 E
Margam, Wales, U.K. 42 51.34 N 3.44 W
Margao → Madgaon 122 15.18 N 73.57 E
Margaree 186 46.24 N 61.05 W
Margaree Harbour 186 46.26 N 61.07 W
Margaret ≃ 162 18.10 S 125.37 E
Margaret, Mount ∧ 224 46.18 N 122.08 W
Margaret Bay 182 51.20 N 127.29 W
Margaret Creek ≃ 166 29.26 S 137.07 E
Margarethenhöhe ⊕[8] 263 51.26 N 6.58 E
Margaret River, Austl. 162 33.57 S 115.04 E
Margaret River, Austl. 162 18.38 S 126.52 E
Margaret Roding 260 51.47 N 0.19 E
Margaretting 260 51.41 N 0.25 E
Margarettsville 208 36.32 N 77.21 W
Margaretville 210 42.08 N 74.38 W

ENGLISH Name	Page	Lat.°'	Long.°'

Margarita, Bahía → Marguerite Bay ⊂ 9 68.30 S 68.30 W
Margarita, Isla I 246 9.05 N 74.30 W
Margarita, Isla de I 246 11.00 N 64.00 W
Margarita Belén 252 27.16 S 58.58 W
Margarita Peak ∧ 228 33.26 N 117.23 W
Margaritovka 83 46.55 N 38.52 E
Margate, S. Afr. 158 30.55 S 30.15 E
Margate, Eng., U.K. 42 51.24 N 1.24 E
Margate, Fl., U.S. 220 26.14 N 80.12 W
Margate City 208 39.19 N 74.30 W
Margecany 30 48.54 N 21.01 E
Margelan → Margilan 85 40.28 N 71.44 E
Margeride, Monts de la ⩕ 32 44.50 N 3.30 E
Margès 62 45.09 N 5.03 E
Mārgherita, India 120 27.17 N 95.41 E
Margherita → Jamaame, Som. 144 0.04 N 42.45 E
Margherita di Savoia 68 41.23 N 16.09 E
Margherita Peak ∧ 154 0.22 N 29.51 E
Marghī 120 34.58 N 66.31 E
Marghita 38 47.21 N 22.21 E
Margi ≃ 70 37.16 N 14.58 E
Margilan 85 40.28 N 71.44 E
Margit Híd ⊕[5] 264c 47.31 N 19.02 E
Margit-sziget I 264c 47.32 N 19.03 E
Margny-lès-Compiègne 50 49.26 N 2.49 E
Margone 62 45.13 N 7.11 E
Margonin 30 52.59 N 17.05 E
Margos 248 10.04 S 76.26 W
Margosatubig 116 7.34 N 123.10 E
Margot Lake ⊜ 184 52.28 N 93.10 W
Māŗgow, Dasht-e ⊕[2] 128 30.45 N 63.10 E
Margreid → Magrè 64 46.17 N 11.12 E
Marguerite, Pic → Margherita Peak ∧ 154 0.22 N 29.51 E
Marguerite Bay ⊂ 9 68.30 S 68.30 W
Marguerittes 62 43.51 N 4.27 E
Margut 56 49.35 N 5.16 E
Margyang 124 29.57 N 90.09 E
Marhanets' 78 47.38 N 34.40 E
Mari 164 9.10 S 141.40 E
Maria 116 9.12 N 123.39 E
Maria, Îles II 14 21.48 S 154.41 W
Mariabrunn ⊕[8] 264b 48.12 N 16.14 E
María Cleofas, Isla I 234 21.16 N 106.14 W
Maria da Fé 256 22.18 S 45.23 W
María Elena 252 22.21 S 69.40 W
Maria Enzersdorf 61 48.06 N 16.17 E
Maria Gail 64 46.36 N 13.52 E
Mariager 26 56.39 N 10.00 E
Mariāhu 124 25.37 N 82.37 E
María Ignacia (Vela) 252 37.24 S 59.30 W
Maria Island I, Austl. 164 14.52 S 135.40 E
Maria Island I, Austl. 166 42.39 S 148.04 E
Maria Island National Park ♦ 166 42.39 S 148.06 E
Mariakani 154 3.52 S 39.28 E
Maria Laach ʋ[1] 56 50.24 N 7.14 E
María la Baja 246 9.59 N 75.17 W
Maria Lanzendorf 264b 48.06 N 16.25 E
Maria Luggau 64 46.42 N 12.45 E
María Madre, Isla I 234 21.35 N 106.33 W
María Magdalena, Isla I 234 21.25 N 106.24 W
Marian, Lake ⊜ 220 27.52 N 81.06 W
Mariana 255 20.23 S 43.25 W
Mariana Basin ⊹[1] 14 17.30 N 145.00 E
Mariana Islands II 108 16.00 N 145.30 E
Mariana Ridge ⊹[3] 14 17.00 N 146.00 E
Mariana Trench ⊹[1] 14 15.00 N 147.30 E
Mariāni 120 26.40 N 94.20 E
Marian Lake ⊜ 176 63.00 N 116.10 W
Marianna, Ar., U.S. 194 34.46 N 90.45 W
Marianna, Fl., U.S. 192 30.46 N 85.13 W
Mariannelund 26 57.37 N 15.34 E
Mariannhill 158 29.52 S 30.50 E
Mariano Acosta 258 34.43 S 58.48 W
Mariano Comense 62 45.42 N 9.11 E
Mariano del Friuli 64 45.55 N 13.27 E
Mariano I. Loza 252 29.22 S 58.12 W
Mariano J. Haedo 288 34.38 S 58.36 W
Mariano Moreno, Arg. 252 38.44 S 70.01 W
Mariano Moreno → Moreno, Arg. 258 34.39 S 58.48 W
Marianopoli 70 37.36 N 13.55 E
Mariánské Lázně 60 49.59 N 12.43 E
Mariar 164 2.48 S 132.50 E
Mariarano 157b 15.29 S 46.42 E
Marias ≃ 202 47.56 N 110.30 W
Marias, Dry Fork ≃ 202 48.22 N 111.45 W
Marías, Islas II 234 21.25 N 106.28 W
Maria Saal 61 46.41 N 14.21 E
Marias Pass)(202 48.19 N 113.21 W
Maria Stein 216 40.24 N 84.28 W
María Teresa 252 34.01 S 61.54 W
Maria-Theresiopel → Subotica 38 46.06 N 19.39 E
Mariato, Punta > 246 7.13 N 80.53 W
Maria van Diemen, Cape > 172 34.28 S 172.39 E
Mariaville 210 42.49 N 74.08 W
Mariazell 61 47.47 N 15.19 E
Ma'rib 144 15.30 N 45.20 E
Maribo 41 54.46 N 11.31 E
Maribojoc Bay ⊂ 116 9.42 N 123.50 E
Maribor 36 46.33 N 15.39 E
Maribyrnong 274b 37.46 S 144.54 E
Maricá, Bra. 256 22.55 S 42.49 W
Marica, Ross. 78 51.45 N 35.16 E
Maricá □[7] 287a 22.57 S 42.59 W
Marica (Évros) (Meriç) ≃ 38 40.52 N 26.12 E
Maricá, Lagoa de ⊂ 256 22.56 S 42.50 W
Maricaban Island I 116 13.39 N 120.53 E
Maricao 240m 18.11 N 66.59 W
Maricás, Ilhas II 256 23.01 S 42.55 W
Maricha Bil ⊜ 272b 22.55 N 88.31 E
Marico ≃ 156 24.12 S 26.52 E
Maricopa, Az., U.S. 200 33.03 N 112.02 W
Maricopa, Ca., U.S. 204 35.03 N 119.24 W
Maricopa Indian Reservation ⊕[4] 200 33.02 N 112.05 W
Maricunga, Salar de ≚ 252 26.55 S 69.05 W
Maridagao ≃ 116 7.13 N 124.41 E
Marīdī 154 4.55 N 29.28 E
Maridi ≃ 140 6.05 N 29.24 E
Marié ≃ 246 0.27 S 66.26 W
Marie Byrd Land ⊕[1] 9 80.00 S 120.00 W
Marie Curtis Park ♦ 275b 43.35 N 79.33 W
Mariedamm 40 58.51 N 15.09 E
Mariefred 40 59.16 N 17.13 E
Marie-Galante I 241o 15.56 N 61.16 W
Mariehamn 26 60.06 N 19.57 E
Marieholm 41 55.52 N 13.09 E
Mariel 240p 22.59 N 82.45 W
Mari El → Marij El □[3] 80 56.30 N 48.00 E
Marie Lake ⊜ 184 54.37 N 110.18 W
Marie-Lefranc, Lac ⊜ 206 46.08 N 75.00 W
Mariembourg 50 50.06 N 4.31 E
Marienbad → Mariánské Lázně 60 49.59 N 12.43 E
Marienbaum 52 51.41 N 6.22 E
Marienberg, Dtsch. 54 50.39 N 13.10 E
Marienberg, Dtsch. 56 50.39 N 7.57 E
Marienberg, Pap. N. Gui. 164 3.55 S 144.15 E
Marien-Berg ∧[2] 264a 52.22 N 13.32 E
Marienborn 54 52.12 N 11.08 E
Marienburg → Malbork 30 54.02 N 19.01 E

DEUTSCH Name	Seite	Breite°'	Länge°' E = Ost

Mariendorf ⊕[8] 264a 52.26 N 13.23 E
Marienfelde ⊕[8] 54 52.25 N 13.22 E
Marienhafe 52 53.31 N 7.16 E
Marienheide 56 51.05 N 7.32 E
Mariental, Dtsch. 54 52.16 N 10.59 E
Mariental, Namibia 156 24.36 S 17.59 E
Mariental □[5] 156 25.00 S 19.00 E
Marienville 214 41.28 N 79.07 W
Maries □[6] 219 38.15 N 91.56 W
Maries ≃ 194 38.30 N 92.01 W
Mariestad 40 58.43 N 13.51 E
Marieta ≃ 246 5.02 N 66.38 W
Marietta, Ga., U.S. 192 33.57 N 84.33 W
Marietta, In., U.S. 218 39.26 N 85.53 W
Marietta, Mn., U.S. 198 45.00 N 96.25 W
Marietta, Oh., U.S. 188 39.24 N 81.27 W
Marietta, Ok., U.S. 196 33.56 N 97.06 W
Marietta, Pa., U.S. 208 40.03 N 76.33 W
Marietta, Tx., U.S. 222 33.10 N 94.33 W
Marietta, Wa., U.S. 224 48.47 N 122.34 W
Marieville 206 45.26 N 73.10 W
Mariga ≃ 150 9.40 N 5.55 E
Marignane 62 43.25 N 5.13 E
Marignier 58 46.06 N 6.31 E
Marigny-le-Châtel 50 48.24 N 3.44 E
Marigny-L'Église 50 47.22 N 3.56 E
Marigot, Dom. 240d 15.32 N 61.18 W
Marigot, Guad. 238 18.04 N 63.06 W
Marihatag 116 8.48 N 126.18 E
Mariinsk 86 56.13 N 87.45 E
Mariinskoje 89 51.43 N 140.13 E
Marijampole 76 54.33 N 23.21 E
Marijec 80 56.32 N 49.50 E
Marij El □[3] 80 56.30 N 48.00 E
Marikana 158 25.42 S 27.30 E
Marikina 269f 14.38 N 121.06 E
Marikina ≃ 269f 14.33 N 121.04 E
Marília 255 22.13 S 49.56 W
Marilla 210 42.50 N 78.33 W
Mari-Malmyž 80 56.30 N 50.52 E
Marimari ≃ 246 3.58 S 58.49 W
Marimba 152 8.28 S 17.08 E
Marín 34 42.23 N 8.42 W
Marin □[6] 226 38.03 N 122.33 W
Marina 226 36.41 N 121.48 W
Marina ⊕[8] 282 37.47 N 122.27 W
Marina del Rey 280 33.50 N 118.25 W
Marina del Rey ⊂ 280 33.58 N 118.27 W
Marina di Andora 62 43.57 N 8.08 E
Marina di Campo 66 42.44 N 10.14 E
Marina di Caronia 70 38.02 N 14.28 E
Marina di Carrara 64 44.02 N 10.02 E
Marina di Cecina 66 43.18 N 10.29 E
Marina di Gioiosa Ionica 68 38.18 N 16.20 E
Marina di Grosseto 66 42.43 N 10.59 E
Marina di Massa 64 44.00 N 10.06 E
Marina di Minturno 66 41.16 N 13.45 E
Marina di Orosei 71 40.22 N 9.43 E
Marina di Palma ⊕[8] 70 37.10 N 13.43 E
Marina di Pietrasanta 64 43.56 N 10.12 E
Marina di Pisa 66 43.40 N 10.16 E
Marina di Ragusa 70 36.47 N 14.33 E
Marina di Ravenna 66 44.29 N 12.17 E
Marina Fall ∟ 246 5.22 N 59.29 W
Marin City 282 37.52 N 122.21 W
Marinduque □[4] 116 13.25 N 121.55 E
Marinduque Island I 116 13.24 N 121.58 E
Marine 219 38.47 N 89.46 W
Marine City 214 42.43 N 82.29 W
Marine-Ehrenmal ⊥ 54 54.23 N 10.15 E
Marineland of the Pacific ʋ[3] 228 33.44 N 118.24 W
Marinella 70 37.35 N 12.50 E
Marine Museum ʋ 280 33.43 N 118.17 W
Marineo 70 37.57 N 13.25 E
Marine Park ♦ 283 42.20 N 71.01 W
Marine Parkway Bridge ⊕[5] 276 40.34 N 73.53 W
Mariners Museum ʋ 208 37.03 N 76.30 W
Marines 50 49.09 N 1.59 E
Marinette 190 45.06 N 87.37 W
Maringá 255 23.25 S 51.55 W
Maringa ≃ 152 1.14 N 19.48 E
Maringouin 194 30.29 N 91.31 W
Marínguè 154 17.55 S 34.24 E
Marinha Grande 34 39.45 N 8.56 W
Marinho ≃ 287a 23.00 S 43.27 W
Marin Mall ⊕[9] 282 37.56 N 122.31 W
Marino, It. 66 41.46 N 12.39 E
Marino, Vanuatu 175f 15.00 S 168.09 E
Marinovka 80 48.41 N 43.49 E
Marin Peninsula >[1] 282 37.51 N 122.31 W
Marinskij Posad 80 56.07 N 47.43 E
Marintu 112 0.34 N 110.00 E
Marinwood 226 38.02 N 122.32 W
Mario, Monte ∧[2] 267a 41.55 N 12.27 E
Marion, Austl. 168b 35.01 S 138.34 E
Marion, Al., U.S. 194 32.37 N 87.19 W
Marion, Ar., U.S. 194 35.12 N 90.11 W
Marion, Ct., U.S. 207 41.33 N 72.55 W
Marion, Il., U.S. 194 37.43 N 88.55 W
Marion, In., U.S. 216 40.33 N 85.39 W
Marion, Ia., U.S. 190 42.02 N 91.35 W
Marion, Ks., U.S. 198 38.20 N 97.01 W
Marion, Ky., U.S. 194 37.19 N 88.04 W
Marion, La., U.S. 194 32.54 N 92.14 W
Marion, Ma., U.S. 207 41.42 N 70.45 W
Marion, Mi., U.S. 190 44.06 N 85.08 W
Marion, Ms., U.S. 194 32.25 N 88.38 W
Marion, N.Y., U.S. 210 43.08 N 77.11 W
Marion, N.C., U.S. 192 35.41 N 82.00 W
Marion, N.D., U.S. 198 46.36 N 98.19 W
Marion, Oh., U.S. 214 40.35 N 83.07 W
Marion, S.C., U.S. 192 34.10 N 79.24 W
Marion, S.D., U.S. 198 43.25 N 97.15 W
Marion, Va., U.S. 192 36.50 N 81.30 W
Marion, Wi., U.S. 190 44.40 N 88.53 W
Marion □[6], Fl., U.S. 220 29.00 N 82.03 W
Marion □[6], Il., U.S. 219 38.38 N 88.57 W
Marion □[6], In., U.S. 218 39.46 N 86.09 W
Marion □[6], Mo., U.S. 219 39.50 N 91.37 W
Marion □[6], Oh., U.S. 214 40.35 N 83.08 W
Marion □[6], Or., U.S. 224 45.06 N 122.47 W
Marion □[6], Tx., U.S. 222 32.48 N 94.33 W
Marion, Lake ⊜ 220 28.05 N 81.32 W
Marion, Lake ⊜[1] 192 33.30 N 80.25 W
Marion Bay ⊂ 166 42.48 S 147.55 E
Marion Center 214 40.46 N 79.03 W
Marion Downs 166 23.22 S 139.39 E
Marion Heights 210 40.48 N 76.28 W
Marion Hill 214 40.44 N 80.18 W
Marion Junction 194 32.26 N 87.14 W
Marion Lake ⊜[1] 198 38.24 N 97.08 W
Marion Reef ⊹[2] 166 19.10 S 152.17 E
Marion Station 208 38.02 N 75.46 W
Marionville 194 37.00 N 93.38 W
Mariópolis 252 26.20 S 52.33 W
Maripa 246 7.26 N 65.09 W
Maripá de Minas 256 21.48 S 42.58 W
Maripasoula 250 3.38 N 54.02 W
Maripipi Island I 116 11.47 N 124.19 E
Mariposa 226 37.29 N 119.57 W
Mariposa □[6] 226 37.29 N 119.58 W
Mariposa Creek ≃ 226 37.14 N 120.26 W
Mariposa Slough ≃ 226 37.12 N 120.46 W
Mariquita 246 5.12 N 74.54 W
Marisa 112 0.28 N 121.56 E
Marisa ≃ 112 0.28 N 121.56 E
Mariscal Estigarribia 252 22.02 S 60.38 W
Marisco, Ponta do > 287a 23.01 S 43.17 W
Mariškino 82 55.21 N 38.37 E
Marissa 219 38.15 N 89.45 W
Maritime Alps (Alpes Maritimes) (Alpi Marittime) ⩕ 62 44.15 N 7.10 E
Maritime Atlas → Atlas Tellien ⩕ 148 36.00 N 3.00 E
Maritimes, Alpes → Maritime Alps ⩕ 62 44.15 N 7.10 E

Symbols in the index entries represent the broad categories identified in the key at the right. Symbols with superscript numbers (⩕[1]) identify subcategories (see complete key on page I · 1).

Symbole im Register stellen die rechts im Schlüssel erklärten Kategorien dar. Symbole mit hochgestellten Ziffern (⩕[1]) bezeichnen Unterabteilungen einer Kategorie (vgl. vollständiger Schlüssel auf Seite I · 1).

Los símbolos incluídos en el texto del índice representan las grandes categorías identificadas con la clave a la derecha. Los símbolos con numeros en su parte superior (⩕[1]) identifican las subcategorías (véase la clave completa en la página I · 1).

Les symboles de l'index représentent les catégories indiquées dans la légende à droite. Les symboles suivis d'un indice (⩕[1]) représentent des sous-catégories (voir légende complète à la page I · 1).

Os símbolos incluídos no texto do índice representam as grandes categorias identificadas com a chave à direita. Os símbolos com números em sua parte superior (⩕[1]) identificam as subcategorias (veja-se a chave completa à página I · 1).

∧	Mountain	Berg	Montaña	Montagne	Montanha
⩕	Mountains	Gebirge	Montañas	Montagnes	Montanhas
)(	Pass	Paß	Paso	Col	Passo
V	Valley, Canyon	Tal, Cañon	Valle, Cañón	Vallée, Canyon	Vale, Canhão
≚	Plain	Ebene	Llano	Plaine	Planície
>	Cape	Kap	Cabo	Cap	Cabo
I	Island	Insel	Isla	Île	Ilha
II	Islands	Inseln	Islas	Îles	Ilhas
±	Other Topographic Features	Andere Topographische Objekte	Otros Elementos Topográficos	Autres données topographiques	Outros acidentes topográficos

ESPAÑOL — Nombre | Página | Lat.°′ | Long.°′ W = Oeste

FRANÇAIS — Nom | Page | Lat.°′ | Long.°′ W = Ouest

PORTUGUÊS — Nome | Página | Lat.°′ | Long.°′ W = Oeste

Nombre / Nom / Nome	Página	Lat.°′	Long.°′
Marittime, Alpi → Maritime Alps ⋏	62	44.15 N	7.10 E
Mari-Turek	80	56.47 N	49.36 E
Maritzburg → Pietermaritzburg	158	29.37 S	30.16 E
Mariupol'	83	47.06 N	37.33 E
Mariusa, Caño ≃ [1]	246	9.43 N	61.26 W
Mariusa, Isla I	241r	9.39 N	61.19 W
Marīvān	128	35.31 N	46.10 E
Mariveles	116	14.26 N	120.29 E
Märjamaa	76	58.54 N	24.26 E
Marjanovka	86	54.58 N	72.38 E
Marjanskaja	78	45.06 N	38.38 E
Marjevka	86	53.46 N	67.24 E
Marjina Gorka	76	53.31 N	28.09 E
Marjino, Ross.	82	54.28 N	37.12 E
Marjino, Ross.	89	48.31 N	130.38 E
Marjino, Ross.	265a	59.50 N	29.56 E
Marjino, Ross.	265a	59.54 N	31.00 E
Marjino, Ross.	265b	55.52 N	37.18 E
Marjinskaja	84	43.53 N	43.29 E
Marjinsko	76	58.49 N	28.32 E
Mār Jirjis, Jūn ⊂	132	33.54 N	35.33 E
Marj 'Uyūn	132	33.22 N	35.35 E
Marka, Som.	144	1.43 N	44.53 E
Mārkā, Urd.	132	31.59 N	35.59 E
Markā I	144	18.13 N	41.19 E
Mark Acres	279b	40.21 N	79.42 W
Markakol', ozero ⊜	86	48.45 N	85.48 E
Markala	150	13.41 N	6.05 W
Markam	102	29.40 N	98.30 E
Markansu	85	39.18 N	73.20 E
Mārkāpur	122	15.44 N	79.17 E
Markaryd	26	56.26 N	13.36 E
Markazī ◻ [4]	128	34.30 N	50.30 E
Markdale	212	44.19 N	80.39 W
Markdorf	58	47.43 N	9.23 E
Marked Tree	194	35.31 N	90.25 W
Markelo	52	52.14 N	6.30 E
Markelovo	86	56.42 N	83.33 E
Marken I	52	52.28 N	5.03 E
Markendorf	54	51.59 N	13.10 E
Markermeer ⊜	52	52.33 N	5.15 E
Markesan	190	43.42 N	88.59 W
Märket I	40	60.18 N	19.08 E
Market Bosworth	42	52.37 N	1.24 W
Market Deeping	42	52.41 N	0.19 W
Market Drayton	42	52.54 N	2.29 W
Market Harborough	42	52.29 N	0.55 W
Markethill	48	54.18 N	6.31 W
Market Lavington	42	51.18 N	1.59 W
Market Rasen	44	53.24 N	0.21 W
Market Weighton	44	53.52 N	0.40 W
Markfield	42	52.40 N	1.17 W
Markgröningen	56	48.54 N	9.05 E
Markham, On., Can.	212	43.52 N	79.16 W
Markham, Il., U.S.	278	41.35 N	87.41 W
Markham, Tx., U.S.	222	28.57 N	96.04 W
Markham ≃	164	6.35 S	146.25 E
Markham, Mount ∧	9	82.51 S	161.21 E
Markham Bay ⊂	176	63.30 N	71.48 W
Markinch	46	56.12 N	3.08 W
Märkisch Buchholz	54	52.07 N	13.46 E
Markit	85	38.55 N	77.38 E
Markivka	83	49.31 N	39.34 E
Markkleeberg	54	51.17 N	12.23 E
Markland Dam ◆ [6]	218	38.47 N	84.58 W
Markle, In., U.S.	216	40.50 N	85.20 W
Markle, Pa., U.S.	279b	40.34 N	79.39 W
Markleeville	226	38.41 N	119.46 W
Markleville	218	39.58 N	85.36 W
Markley Canyon V	282	38.00 N	121.50 W
Marknesse	52	52.43 N	5.52 E
Markneukirchen	54	50.18 N	12.19 E
Markoldendorf	52	51.48 N	9.46 E
Markópoulon	267c	37.54 N	23.54 E
Markounda	152	7.37 N	16.59 E
Markovo, Ross.	74	64.40 N	170.25 E
Markovo, Ross.	80	57.01 N	40.30 E
Markovo, Ross.	82	55.52 N	39.17 E
Markovo, Ross.	88	57.20 N	107.04 E
Markoy	150	14.39 N	0.02 E
Markranstädt	54	51.18 N	12.13 E
Marks, Ross.	80	51.42 N	46.46 E
Marks, Ms., U.S.	194	34.15 N	90.16 W
Marks Tey	42	51.52 N	0.47 E
Marksuhl	56	50.55 N	10.11 E
Marksville	194	31.07 N	92.03 W
Markt Bibart	56	49.39 N	10.26 E
Marktbreit	56	49.40 N	10.08 E
Markt Erlbach	56	49.29 N	10.38 E
Marktheidenfeld	56	49.50 N	9.36 E
Markt Indersdorf	60	48.22 N	11.23 E
Marktl	60	48.15 N	12.51 E
Marktleugast	54	50.10 N	11.38 E
Marktleuthen	54	50.08 N	12.00 E
Marktoberdorf	58	47.47 N	10.37 E
Marktredwitz	60	50.00 N	12.06 E
Markt Rettenbach	58	47.57 N	10.23 E
Marktschellenberg	64	47.42 N	13.02 E
Markt Schwaben	60	48.11 N	11.51 E
Mark Twain Cave ⌓ [5]	219	39.42 N	91.21 W
Mark Twain Lake ⊜ [1]	219	39.30 N	91.45 W
Mark Twain State Park ♦	219	39.29 N	91.48 W
Markundi	140	11.33 N	23.49 E
Markvue Manor	279b	40.20 N	79.46 W
Mark West Creek ≃	226	38.30 N	122.42 W
Marl	52	51.38 N	7.05 E
Marlasi	164	5.30 S	134.38 E
Marlboro, Ab., Can.	182	53.33 N	116.45 W
Marlboro, N.J., U.S.	208	40.18 N	74.14 W
Marlboro, N.Y., U.S.	210	41.36 N	73.58 W
Marlboro, Oh., U.S.	214	40.53 N	81.12 W
Marlboro, Pa., U.S.	285	39.54 N	75.42 W
Marlborough, Austl.	166	22.49 S	149.53 E
Marlborough, Guy.	246	7.29 N	58.38 W
Marlborough, Eng., U.K.	42	51.26 N	1.43 W
Marlborough, Ct., U.S.	207	41.37 N	72.27 W
Marlborough, Ma., U.S.	207	42.20 N	71.33 W
Marlborough Downs ⋏ [1]	42	51.30 N	1.45 W
Marldon	42	50.28 N	3.36 W
Marle	50	49.44 N	3.46 E
Marlenheim	58	48.37 N	7.30 E
Marles-en-Brie	261	48.44 N	2.53 E
Marles-les-Mines	50	50.30 N	2.31 E
Marlette	190	43.19 N	83.04 W
Marlette Lake ⊜	226	39.10 N	119.54 W
Marley, Il., U.S.	278	41.33 N	87.55 W
Marley, Md., U.S.	208	39.09 N	76.35 W
Marley Creek ≃	278	41.31 N	87.57 W
Marley Neck ≻ [1]	284b	39.12 N	76.33 W
Marlieux	58	46.04 N	5.04 E
Marlin	222	31.18 N	96.53 W
Marlinton	188	38.13 N	80.05 W
Marl-Loemühle, Flughafen ⊠	263	51.39 N	7.10 E
Marlow, Dtsch.	54	54.09 N	12.34 E
Marlow, Eng., U.K.	42	51.35 N	0.48 W
Marlow, Ok., U.S.	196	34.38 N	97.57 W
Marlpit Hill	260	51.13 N	0.04 E
Marlton	208	39.53 N	74.55 W
Marlton Heights	285	39.40 N	75.21 W
Marly	50	50.20 N	3.32 E
Marly, Forêt de ♦	261	48.52 N	2.03 E
Marly-la-Ville	261	49.05 N	2.30 E
Marly-le-Roi	50	48.52 N	2.05 E
Marma, Sve.	26	61.16 N	16.52 E
Marma, Sve.	40	60.30 N	17.25 E
Marmaduke	194	36.11 N	90.22 W
Marmagne	58	46.50 N	4.21 E
Marmande	32	44.30 N	0.10 E
Marmara, Sea of → Marmara Denizi ⫧ [2]	130	40.40 N	28.15 E
Marmara Adası I	130	40.38 N	27.37 E
Marmara Denizi (Sea of Marmara) ⫧ [2]	130	40.40 N	28.15 E
Marmara Ereğlisi	130	40.58 N	27.57 E
Marmara Gölü ⊜	130	38.37 N	28.02 E
Marmaris	130	36.51 N	28.16 E
Marmarītā	130	34.47 N	36.15 E
Marmarth	198	46.17 N	103.55 W
Marmaton ≃	194	38.00 N	94.19 W
Marmelopolis	256	22.27 S	45.10 W
Marmelos	248	6.08 S	61.50 W
Marmelos, Rio dos ≃	248	6.06 S	61.46 W
Marmet	188	38.14 N	81.34 W
Marmion Lake ⊜ [1]	190	48.54 N	91.30 W
Marmirolo	64	45.13 N	10.45 E
Marmolada ∧	64	46.26 N	11.51 E
Marmora, On., Can.	212	44.29 N	77.41 W
Marmora, N.J., U.S.	208	39.16 N	74.38 W
Marmore	66	42.33 N	12.43 E
Marmore ≃	62	45.44 N	7.37 E
Marmore, Cascàta delle ʟ	66	42.33 N	12.43 E
Marmot Bay ⊂	180	58.00 N	152.20 W
Marmot Island I	180	58.13 N	151.51 W
Marmoutier	58	48.41 N	7.23 E
Mar Muerto, Laguna ⊂	234	16.10 N	94.10 W
Marnate	266b	45.38 N	8.54 E
Marnay	58	47.17 N	5.46 E
Marnaz	58	46.04 N	6.32 E
Marne, Dtsch.	52	53.57 N	9.00 E
Marne, Mi., U.S.	216	43.02 N	85.49 W
Marne ◻ [5]	32	48.55 N	4.10 E
Marne ≃, Austl.	168b	34.40 S	139.18 E
Marne ≃, Fr.	32	48.49 N	2.24 E
Marne à la Saône, Canal de la ≍	58	48.44 N	4.36 E
Marne au Rhin, Canal de la ≍	56	48.35 N	7.47 E
Marneuli	84	41.28 N	44.50 E
Marnhull	42	50.58 N	2.18 W
Marnitz	54	53.19 N	11.56 E
Maroa, Il., U.S.	219	40.02 N	88.57 W
Maroa, Ven.	246	2.43 N	67.33 W
Maroala	157b	15.23 S	47.59 E
Maroantsetra	157b	15.26 S	49.44 E
Marobi Raghza	120	32.36 N	69.52 E
Maroc → Morocco ◻ [1]	148	32.00 N	5.00 W
Maroelaboom	156	19.15 S	18.53 E
Marofandilia	157b	20.07 S	44.34 E
Maroglio ≃	70	37.03 N	14.15 E
Marokko → Morocco ◻ [1]	148	32.00 N	5.00 W
Marol ◆ [8]	272c	19.07 N	72.53 E
Marolambo	157b	20.02 S	48.07 E
Maroldsweisach	56	50.12 N	10.39 E
Marolles-en-Brie	261	48.44 N	2.33 E
Marolles-en-Hurepoix	261	48.34 N	2.18 E
Marolles-les-Braults	50	48.15 N	0.19 E
Maromandia	157b	14.13 S	48.08 E
Maromme	50	49.28 N	1.02 E
Maromokotro ∧	157b	14.01 S	48.59 E
Marondera	154	18.10 S	31.36 E
Marone	64	45.44 N	10.05 E
Marong	102	31.07 N	99.20 E
Maronghi Creek ≃	171a	26.58 S	152.22 E
Maroni (Marowijne) ≃	250	5.45 N	53.58 W
Maroon	171a	28.10 S	152.44 E
Maroon, Mount ∧	171a	28.13 S	152.44 E
Maroondah Aqueduct ≍ [1]	274b	37.42 S	145.01 E
Maros	112	5.00 S	119.34 E
Maros (Mureș) ≃	38	46.15 N	20.13 E
Maroseranana	157b	18.32 S	48.51 E
Marostica	64	45.45 N	11.39 E
Marosvásárhely → Târgu Mureș	38	46.33 N	24.33 E
Marotandrano	157b	16.10 S	48.50 E
Marotiri, Îles II	14	27.55 S	143.26 W
Marotta	66	43.46 N	13.08 E
Maroua	146	10.36 N	14.20 E
Maroubra	274a	33.57 S	151.16 E
Marouini ≃	250	3.18 N	54.04 W
Marovato, Madag.	157b	13.59 S	48.36 E
Marovato, Madag.	157b	15.48 S	48.05 E
Marovato, Madag.	157b	16.28 S	48.25 E
Marovoay	157b	16.06 S	46.39 E
Marovoay Nord	157b	16.57 S	44.34 E
Marowijne ◻ [5]	250	5.40 N	54.20 W
Marowijne (Maroni) ≃	250	5.45 N	53.58 W
Marpent	50	50.18 N	4.05 E
Marple	44	53.24 N	2.03 W
Marquam	224	45.04 N	122.41 W
Marquand	194	37.25 N	90.10 W
Marquard	158	28.54 S	27.28 E
Marquardt	54	52.27 N	12.57 E
Marquartstein	64	47.45 N	12.28 E
Marquesas Islands → Marquises, Îles II	6	9.00 S	139.30 W
Marquesas Keys II	220	24.34 N	82.08 W
Marquette, Ks., U.S.	198	38.33 N	97.50 W
Marquette, Mi., U.S.	190	46.32 N	87.23 W
Marquette Park ♦	278	41.46 N	87.42 W
Márquez, Perú	286d	11.57 S	77.08 W
Marquez, Tx., U.S.	222	31.14 N	96.15 W
Marquion	50	50.13 N	3.05 E
Marquis	241k	12.06 N	61.37 W
Marquis, Cape ≻	241f	14.03 N	60.54 W
Marquise	50	50.49 N	1.42 E
Marquises, Îles (Marquesas Islands) II	6	9.00 S	139.30 W
Marrabel	168b	34.08 S	138.53 E
Marra Creek ≃	166	30.05 S	147.05 E
Marradi	66	44.04 N	11.37 E
Marradong	168a	32.52 S	116.27 E
Marrah, Jabal ∧	140	13.04 N	24.21 E
Marra Hills ⋏ [2]	140	6.05 N	27.33 E
Marrakech	148	31.38 N	8.00 W
Marrakech ◻ [4]	148	31.30 N	8.05 W
Marramarra National Park ♦	170	33.32 S	151.04 E
Marrawah	166	40.56 S	144.41 E
Marree	166	29.39 S	138.04 E
Marrero	194	29.53 N	90.06 W
Marrickville	274a	33.55 S	151.09 E
Marromeu	156	18.20 S	35.56 E
Marrowstone Island I	224	48.04 N	122.41 W
Marrubiu	71	39.45 N	8.38 E
Marruecos → Morocco ◻ [1]	148	32.00 N	5.00 W
Marrupa	154	13.08 S	37.30 E
Mars	214	40.41 N	80.00 W
Marsā al-Burayqah	146	30.25 N	19.34 E
Marsabit	154	2.20 N	37.59 E
Marsabit National Park ♦	154	2.20 N	38.00 E
Marsac-en-Livradois	62	45.29 N	3.44 E
Marṣafā wa Kafr Aḥmad Ḥashīsh	142	30.25 N	31.15 E
Marsal	56	48.48 N	6.36 E
Marsala	70	37.48 N	12.26 E
Marsā Maṭrūḥ	140	31.21 N	27.14 E
Marsā Maṭrūḥ ◻ [4]	142	29.00 N	30.00 E
Marsange ≃	261	48.43 N	2.45 E
Marsangue ≃	261	48.40 N	2.47 E
Marsannay-la-Côte	58	47.16 N	4.59 E
Marsanne	62	44.39 N	4.52 E
Marsassoum	150	12.50 N	16.00 W
Mars'aty	86	60.05 N	60.29 E
Marsberg	52	51.28 N	8.50 E
Marscheid ◆ [8]	263	51.14 N	7.14 E
Marsciano	66	42.54 N	12.20 E
Marsden, Austl.	166	33.45 S	147.32 E
Marsden, Eng., U.K.	262	53.36 N	1.56 W
Marsden, Point ≻	168b	35.35 S	137.38 E
Marsden Park	274a	33.42 S	150.50 E
Marsdiep ⋓	52	52.59 N	4.45 E
Marseille	62	43.18 N	5.24 E
Marseille-en-Beauvaisis	50	49.35 N	1.57 E
Marseille-Marignane, Aéroport de ⊠	62	43.27 N	5.13 E
Marseilles, Il., U.S.	216	41.19 N	88.42 W
Marseilles, Oh., U.S.	214	40.42 N	83.23 W
Marsella → Marseille	62	43.18 N	5.24 E
Marsfield	274a	33.47 S	151.07 E
Marsfjället ∧	24	65.05 N	15.28 E
Marshall, Liber.	150	6.10 N	10.23 W
Marshall, Ar., U.S.	194	35.54 N	92.37 W
Marshall, Il., U.S.	194	39.23 N	87.41 W
Marshall, Mi., U.S.	216	42.16 N	84.57 W
Marshall, Mn., U.S.	198	44.26 N	95.47 W
Marshall, Mo., U.S.	194	39.07 N	93.11 W
Marshall, N.C., U.S.	192	35.47 N	82.41 W
Marshall, Tx., U.S.	194	32.32 N	94.22 W
Marshall, Va., U.S.	188	38.51 N	77.51 W
Marshall, Wi., U.S.	216	43.10 N	89.04 W
Marshall ◻ [6], Il., U.S.	216	41.02 N	89.24 W
Marshall ◻ [6], In., U.S.	216	41.21 N	86.19 W
Marshall ≃	162	22.59 S	136.59 E
Marshall Bennett Islands II	164	8.50 S	151.50 E
Marshallberg	192	34.43 N	76.30 W
Marshall Canyon Regional Park ♦	280	34.09 N	117.43 W
Marshall Gold Discovery State Historical Park ♦	226	38.48 N	120.53 W
Marshall Hall	208	38.41 N	77.06 W
Marshall Islands ◻ [1]	14	11.00 N	168.00 E
Marshall Islands II	14	9.00 N	168.00 E
Marshalls Creek	210	41.03 N	75.08 W
Marshallton, De., U.S.	208	39.43 N	75.39 W
Marshallton, Pa., U.S.	210	40.47 N	76.33 W
Marshallton, Pa., U.S.	285	39.57 N	75.41 W
Marshalltown	190	42.02 N	92.54 W
Marshallville, Ga., U.S.	192	32.27 N	83.56 W
Marshallville, Oh., U.S.	214	40.54 N	81.44 W
Marshbank Metropolitan Park ♦	281	42.36 N	83.23 W
Marsh Creek ≃, Ca., U.S.	282	37.53 N	121.49 W
Marsh Creek ≃, Mi., U.S.	281	42.06 N	83.13 W
Marsh Creek ≃, Pa., U.S.	214	41.03 N	77.36 W
Marsh Creek ≃, Pa., U.S.	285	40.03 N	75.43 W
Marsh Creek ≃, Wi., U.S.	216	42.13 N	89.04 W
Marsh Creek Lake ⊜ [1]	208	40.04 N	75.44 W
Marshes Creek ≃	276	40.36 N	74.13 W
Marshfield, Eng., U.K.	42	51.28 N	2.19 W
Marshfield, Ma., U.S.	207	42.05 N	70.42 W
Marshfield, Mo., U.S.	194	37.20 N	92.54 W
Marshfield, Wi., U.S.	190	44.40 N	90.10 W
Marshfield Airport ⊠	283	42.06 N	70.40 W
Marshfield Center	283	42.07 N	70.43 W
Marshfield Hills	207	42.08 N	70.44 W
Marsh Harbour	238	26.33 N	77.03 W
Marsh Hill	210	41.29 N	76.58 W
Mars Hill, In., U.S.	218	39.43 N	86.09 W
Mars Hill, Me., U.S.	186	46.30 N	67.52 W
Mars Hill, N.C., U.S.	192	35.49 N	82.32 W
Marsh Island I	194	29.35 N	91.53 W
Marsh Lake ⊜	180	60.25 N	134.18 W
Marsh Peak ∧	200	40.43 N	109.50 W
Marshside	262	53.40 N	2.58 W
Marshville	192	34.59 N	80.22 W
Marshyhope Creek ≃	208	38.32 N	75.45 W
Marsica ◆ [1]	66	41.50 N	13.45 E
Marsico Nuovo	68	40.25 N	15.44 E
Marsico Vetere	68	40.23 N	15.49 E
Marsillargues	62	43.40 N	4.11 E
Marsimang, Tanjung ≻	164	3.27 S	130.49 E
Marsing	202	43.32 N	116.48 W
Marske-by-the-Sea	44	54.36 N	1.01 W
Mars-la-Tour	56	49.06 N	5.54 E
Marson	56	48.55 N	4.32 E
Marssum	52	53.12 N	5.42 E
Märsta	40	59.37 N	17.51 E
Marstal	41	54.51 N	10.31 E
Marsteller	214	40.39 N	78.48 W
Märstetten	58	47.36 N	9.04 E
Marston	262	53.16 N	2.30 W
Marston Moor ⩪	44	53.57 N	1.17 W
Marston Moor Battlesite ⊥	44	53.57 N	1.17 W
Marstons Mills	207	41.39 N	70.25 W
Marstrand	26	57.53 N	11.35 E
Marsyāṅgdī ≃	124	28.05 N	84.28 E
Mart	222	31.32 N	96.50 W
Marta	66	42.32 N	11.55 E
Marta ≃	66	42.14 N	11.42 E
Martaban	110	16.32 N	97.37 E
Martaban, Gulf of ⊂	110	16.30 N	97.00 E
Martano	68	40.12 N	18.18 E
Martap	152	6.54 N	13.03 E
Martapura, Indon.	112	3.25 S	114.51 E
Martapura, Indon.	112	4.19 S	104.22 E
Marte	146	12.22 N	13.51 E
Marteg ≃	42	52.20 N	3.33 W
Martel, Fr.	32	44.56 N	1.37 E
Martel, Oh., U.S.	214	40.40 N	82.55 W
Martelange	56	49.50 N	5.44 E
Martell	226	38.22 N	120.48 W
Martello	64	46.34 N	10.47 E
Martello, Val V	64	46.31 N	10.45 E
Martemjanovskij	86	55.54 N	80.22 E
Marten ◆ [8]	263	51.31 N	7.23 E
Marten Lake ⊜	190	46.42 N	79.41 W
Marten Mountain ∧	182	55.28 N	114.43 W
Marte R. Gomez, Presa ⊜ [1]	196	26.10 N	99.00 W
Martfeld	52	52.52 N	9.04 E
Marthaguy Creek ≃	166	30.16 S	147.35 E
Martha Lake	224	47.51 N	122.20 W
Marthall	262	53.17 N	2.18 W
Martham	42	52.42 N	1.38 E
Marthasville	219	38.37 N	91.03 W
Martha's Vineyard I	207	41.25 N	70.40 W
Martí, Cuba	240p	21.09 N	77.27 W
Martí, Cuba	240p	22.57 N	80.55 W
Martí, Pico ∧	240p	20.01 N	76.35 W
Martignacco	64	46.05 N	13.08 E
Martignat	58	46.13 N	5.36 E
Martigny	58	46.06 N	7.04 E
Martigny-les-Bains	58	48.06 N	5.49 E
Martigues	62	43.24 N	5.03 E
Martil	34	35.37 N	5.17 W
Martim Francisco	256	22.31 S	46.57 W
Martin, Slvk.	30	49.05 N	18.55 E
Martin, Ky., U.S.	192	37.34 N	82.45 W
Martin, Mi., U.S.	216	42.32 N	85.38 W
Martin, N.D., U.S.	198	47.49 N	100.06 W
Martin, Oh., U.S.	214	41.33 N	83.20 W
Martin, S.D., U.S.	198	43.10 N	101.43 W
Martin, Tn., U.S.	194	36.20 N	88.51 W
Martin ◻ [6]	220	27.07 N	80.31 W
Martín ≃	34	41.18 N	0.19 W
Martín, Arroyo ≃	288	34.51 S	58.04 W
Martin, Isle I	46	57.55 N	5.14 W
Martina	58	46.53 N	10.30 E
Martina Franca	68	40.42 N	17.21 E
Martinborough	172	41.13 S	175.28 E
Martín Chico, Punta ≻	258	34.10 S	58.13 W
Martindale	196	29.50 N	97.51 W
Martindale Creek ≃, Austl.	170	32.32 S	150.42 E
Martindale Creek ≃, In., U.S.	218	39.48 N	85.09 W
Martindale Pond ⊜	284a	43.11 N	79.16 W
Martin-Église	50	49.54 N	1.09 E
Martinengo	62	45.34 N	9.46 E
Mărtinești	38	45.30 N	27.18 E
Martinez, Ca., U.S.	226	38.01 N	122.07 W
Martinez, Ga., U.S.	192	33.31 N	82.04 W
Martínez ◆ [8]	258	34.29 S	58.30 W
Martínez de la Torre	234	20.04 N	97.03 W
Martín García, Isla I	258	34.13 S	58.15 W
Martinho Campos	255	19.20 S	45.13 W
Martinica → Martinique ◻ [2]	240e	14.40 N	61.00 W
Martini Creek ≃	282	37.33 N	122.31 W
Martinique ◻ [2], N.A.	230	14.40 N	61.00 W
Martinique ◻ [2], N.A.	240e	14.40 N	61.00 W
Martinique Passage ⋓	238	15.10 N	61.15 W
Martin Lake ⊜ [1], Al., U.S.	194	32.50 N	85.55 W
Martin Lake ⊜ [1], Tx., U.S.	222	32.15 N	94.35 W
Martin Marietta Corporation ⊍ [3]	284b	39.20 N	76.26 W
Martinniemi	26	65.13 N	25.18 E
Martinópole	250	3.15 S	40.41 W
Martin Peninsula ≻ [1]	9	74.25 S	114.10 W
Martín Pérez ≃	286b	23.07 N	82.20 W
Martin Point ≻	180	70.08 N	143.16 W
Martin Run ≃	279a	41.27 N	82.12 W
Martins	250	6.05 S	37.55 W
Martinsberg	61	48.22 N	15.09 E
Martins Brook ≃	283	42.34 N	71.06 W
Martinsburg, Mo., U.S.	219	39.06 N	91.38 W
Martinsburg, N.Y., U.S.	212	43.44 N	75.28 W
Martinsburg, Oh., U.S.	214	40.16 N	82.21 W
Martinsburg, Pa., U.S.	214	40.18 N	78.19 W
Martinsburg, W.V., U.S.	188	39.27 N	77.57 W
Martins Creek	208	40.47 N	75.11 W
Martins Creek ≃	210	41.37 N	75.46 W
Martinscroft	262	53.24 N	2.31 W
Martins Ferry	214	40.05 N	80.43 W
Martins Mills	222	32.25 N	95.47 W
Martins Pond ⊜	283	42.36 N	71.08 W
Martinstein	56	49.48 N	7.32 E
Martinsthal	56	50.03 N	8.07 E
Martinsville, Austl.	170	33.03 S	151.25 E
Martinsville, Il., U.S.	194	39.20 N	87.52 W
Martinsville, In., U.S.	218	39.25 N	86.25 W
Martinsville, N.J., U.S.	276	40.36 N	74.34 W
Martinsville, Oh., U.S.	218	39.19 N	83.48 W
Martinsville, Va., U.S.	192	36.41 N	79.52 W
Martinton	216	40.55 N	87.44 W
Martintown	206	45.09 N	74.42 W
Martin Van Buren National Historic Site ⊥	210	42.22 N	73.43 W
Martin Vaz, Ilhas II	244	20.30 S	28.51 W
Martis	71	40.47 N	8.49 E
Martisovo	76	56.34 N	31.55 E
Martock	42	50.59 N	2.46 W
Martofte	41	55.33 N	10.40 E
Marton, N.Z.	172	40.05 S	175.23 E
Marton, Eng., U.K.	262	53.12 N	2.13 W
Martorell	266d	41.28 N	1.56 E
Martorelles de Baix	266d	41.32 N	2.14 E
Martos	34	37.43 N	3.58 W
Martova	78	49.57 N	36.57 E
Martre, Lac la ⊜	176	63.15 N	117.55 W
Martti	24	67.28 N	28.28 E
Martūbah	146	32.35 N	22.46 E
Martuk	86	50.46 N	56.31 E
Martuni	84	40.08 N	45.19 E
Martvili	84	42.25 N	42.22 E
Martville	210	43.17 N	76.38 W
Martynivka	78	49.38 N	31.18 E
Martynovo	80	50.43 N	50.23 E
Martynovskij	80	50.29 N	42.18 E
Martynovychi	78	51.17 N	29.37 E
Maru	150	12.22 N	6.22 E
Marua	164	9.30 S	149.20 E
Marudi	112	4.11 N	114.19 E
Marudu, Telukan ⊂	112	6.45 N	116.55 E
Marugame	96	34.17 N	133.47 E
Maruggio	68	40.19 N	17.34 E
Maruia	172	42.11 S	172.13 E
Maruia ≃	172	41.47 S	172.12 E
Maruim	250	10.45 S	37.05 W
Maruko	94	36.19 N	138.16 E
Marula	154	20.26 S	28.06 E
Marulan	170	34.43 S	150.00 E
Marulan South	170	34.46 S	150.02 E
Marum	52	53.08 N	6.16 E
Marum, Mont ∧	175f	16.15 S	168.07 E
Marunga	152	17.27 S	20.02 E
Marungu	154	3.44 S	30.48 E
Marungu ⋏	154	7.42 S	30.00 E
Maruoka	94	36.09 N	136.16 E
Mårup	41	55.57 N	10.35 E
Marusino	265b	55.42 N	37.59 E
Maruškino	82	55.36 N	37.12 E
Ma'rūt	120	31.34 N	67.03 E
Marutea I [1]	14	17.00 S	143.10 W
Maruyama	94	35.01 N	139.58 E
Maruyama ≃	96	35.39 N	134.50 E
Marv Dasht	128	29.50 N	52.40 E
Marve ◆ [8]	272c	19.12 N	72.49 E
Marvejols	32	44.33 N	3.18 E
Marvell	194	34.33 N	90.54 W
Marvel Loch	162	31.28 S	119.28 E
Marviken	40	58.34 N	16.51 E
Marvila ◆ [8]	266c	38.44 N	9.06 W
Marville	56	49.27 N	5.27 E
Marvin Creek ≃	214	41.48 N	78.26 W
Marvine, Mount ∧	200	38.40 N	111.39 W
Mar Vista ◆ [8]	280	34.00 N	118.27 W
Mārwār	120	25.44 N	73.36 E
Marwayne	184	53.32 N	110.20 W
Marwitz	264a	52.41 N	13.09 E
Marwitzer Heide ◆ [3]	264a	52.40 N	13.06 E
Marwood	214	40.48 N	79.47 W
Marxhagen	54	53.37 N	12.36 E
Marxloh ◆ [8]	263	51.31 N	6.46 E
Mary	128	37.36 N	61.50 E
Mary ◻ [8]	128	37.30 N	62.30 E
Mary ≃, Austl.	164	12.53 S	131.38 E
Mary ≃, Austl.	166	25.26 S	152.55 E
Mar'yanivka	78	50.28 N	24.48 E
Mary Anne Group II	162	21.13 S	115.32 E
Maryborough, Austl.	166	25.32 S	152.42 E
Maryborough, Austl.	169	37.03 S	143.45 E
Maryborough → Port Laoise, Ire.	48	53.02 N	7.17 W
Mary D	208	40.45 N	76.04 W
Marydale	158	29.23 S	22.05 E
Marydel	208	39.06 N	75.44 W
Maryfield	184	49.48 N	101.32 W
Maryhill	224	45.41 N	120.49 W
Mar'yinka	83	47.56 N	37.31 E
Mary Jane, Lake ⊜	220	28.22 N	81.11 W
Mary Kathleen	166	20.49 S	139.58 E
Maryknoll	210	41.11 N	73.50 W
Mary Lake ⊜	212	45.15 N	79.15 W
Maryland	210	42.32 N	74.53 W
Maryland ◻ [3], U.S.	178	39.00 N	76.45 W
Maryland ◻ [3], U.S.	188	39.00 N	76.45 W
Maryland, University of (Baltimore County Campus) ⊍ [2], Md., U.S.	284b	39.15 N	76.43 W
Maryland, University of ⊍ [2], Md., U.S.	284c	38.59 N	76.57 W
Maryland City	208	39.05 N	76.49 W
Maryland Gardens Park ♦	275b	43.47 N	79.32 W
Maryland Heights	219	38.42 N	90.25 W
Maryland Historical Society ⊍	284b	39.18 N	76.37 W
Maryland Line	208	39.42 N	76.39 W
Maryland Park	284c	38.53 N	76.54 W
Marylebone	262	53.34 N	2.38 W
Maryneal	196	32.14 N	100.27 W
Marynivka	78	47.46 N	30.53 E
Marypark	46	57.26 N	3.21 W
Maryport	44	54.43 N	3.30 W
Marys ≃, Il., U.S.	194	37.53 N	89.47 W
Marys ≃, Nv., U.S.	204	41.04 N	115.16 W
Marys Creek ≃	202	42.18 N	115.48 W
Mary's Igloo	180	65.09 N	165.04 W
Marys Peak ∧	202	44.30 N	123.33 W
Marystown	186	47.10 N	55.09 W
Marysvale	200	38.26 N	112.13 W
Marysville, Austl.	169	37.31 S	145.45 E
Marysville, B.C., Can.	182	49.38 N	115.57 W
Marysville, N.B., Can.	186	45.59 N	66.35 W
Marysville, Ca., U.S.	226	39.08 N	121.35 W
Marysville, Ks., U.S.	198	39.50 N	96.38 W
Marysville, Mi., U.S.	214	42.54 N	82.29 W
Marysville, Oh., U.S.	214	40.14 N	83.22 W
Marysville, Pa., U.S.	208	40.20 N	76.55 W
Marysville, Wa., U.S.	224	48.03 N	122.10 W
Maryūṭ, Buḥayrat ⊜	142	31.08 N	29.56 E
Maryvale	171a	28.05 S	152.15 E
Maryvale ◆ [8]	275b	43.46 N	79.18 W
Maryville, Mo., U.S.	194	40.20 N	94.52 W
Maryville, Tn., U.S.	192	35.45 N	83.58 W
Marywell	46	57.02 N	2.42 W
Marywood	216	41.48 N	88.18 W
Marzabotto	64	44.20 N	11.12 E
Marzagão	255	17.59 S	48.39 W
Marzahn ◆ [8]	264a	52.33 N	13.33 E
Marzahna	54	52.00 N	12.46 E
Marzahne	54	52.31 N	12.31 E
Marzal, Aven de ⌓ [5]	62	44.22 N	4.31 E
Marzo, Punta ≻	246	6.50 N	77.42 W
Marzolara	64	44.38 N	10.10 E
Marzūq	146	25.55 N	13.55 E
Marzūq, Ḥamādat ◆ [2]	146	26.10 N	12.45 E
Marzūq, Ṣaḥrā' ◆ [2]	146	24.30 N	13.00 E
Masa	152	3.45 S	15.29 E
Masachapa	236	11.47 N	86.31 W
Masada → Meẕada, Ḥorvot ⊥	132	31.19 N	35.21 E
Mas'adah (Cæsarea Philippi)	132	33.14 N	35.45 E
Más Afuera, Isla → Alejandro Selkirk, Isla I	244	33.45 S	80.46 W
Masagua	236	14.12 N	90.51 W
Masaguisi	116	12.41 N	121.32 E
Masai	114	1.29 N	103.53 E
Masai Mara Game Reserve ◆ [4]	154	1.15 S	35.15 E
Masai Steppe ⋏ [1]	154	4.45 S	37.00 E
Masak	85	43.37 N	78.18 E
Masaka	154	0.20 S	31.44 E
Masaki, Nihon	96	33.47 N	132.42 E
Masaki, Nihon	268	35.13 N	140.02 E
Masalembu Besar, Pulau I	112	5.34 S	114.26 E
Masallı	84	39.03 N	48.40 E
Masalok, Puntan ≻	174n	15.01 N	145.41 E
Masamba	112	2.32 S	120.20 E
Masan	98	35.11 N	128.32 E
Masandra	78	44.32 N	34.12 E
Masangwe ∧	154	5.28 S	30.05 E
Masānjor	126	24.07 N	87.19 E
Masapelid Island I	116	9.42 N	125.39 E
Masapun	112	7.47 S	126.38 E
Masāraḥ	142	27.29 N	30.50 E
Masaran	115a	7.28 S	110.55 E
Ma'ṣarat Samālūṭ	142	28.19 N	30.43 E
Masaryktown	220	28.26 N	82.27 W
Masasi	154	10.43 S	38.48 E
Masatepe	236	11.55 N	86.09 W
Más a Tierra, Isla → Róbinson Crusoe, Isla I	244	33.38 S	78.52 W
Masaya	236	11.58 N	86.06 W
Masaya ◻ [5]	236	12.00 N	86.10 W
Masba	146	11.30 N	13.00 E
Masbate	116	12.22 N	123.36 E
Masbate ◻ [4]	116	12.20 N	123.30 E
Masbate Island I	116	12.15 N	123.30 E
Masbate Pass ⋓	116	12.30 N	123.35 E
Mascali	70	37.45 N	15.12 E
Mascarene Basin ✢ [1]	12	15.00 S	56.00 E
Mascarene Islands II	157c	21.00 S	57.00 E
Mascarene Plateau ✢ [3]	12	10.00 S	60.00 E
Mascasín	252	31.22 S	66.59 W
Maschen	52	53.24 N	10.02 E
Maschito	68	40.54 N	15.50 E
Mascot, Austl.	274a	33.56 S	151.12 E
Mascot, Tn., U.S.	192	36.03 N	83.44 W
Mascota	234	20.32 N	104.49 W
Mascota ≃	234	20.38 N	104.59 W
Mascotte	220	28.35 N	81.53 W
Mascouche	206	45.45 N	73.36 W
Mascouche ≃	206	45.41 N	73.40 W
Mascoutah	219	38.29 N	89.47 W
Mascuppic Lake ⊜	283	42.41 N	71.23 W
Mase	102	27.16 N	104.08 E
Masefield	184	49.09 N	107.48 W
Masela, Pulau I	164	8.09 S	129.50 E
Masenberg ∧	61	47.21 N	15.53 E
Maser	64	45.48 N	11.59 E
Maserada sul Piave	64	45.45 N	12.17 E
Maseru	158	29.28 S	27.30 E
Masevaux	58	47.47 N	7.00 E
Masha	100	27.26 N	117.50 E
Mashaba	154	20.02 S	30.29 E
Mashaba Mountains ⋏	154	18.45 S	30.32 E
Mash'abbe' Sade	132	31.00 N	34.47 E
Mashābih I	128	25.37 N	36.29 E
Mashalah	142	30.44 N	31.08 E
Masham	44	54.13 N	1.40 W
Mashan, Zhg.	89	45.13 N	130.35 E
Mashan, Zhg.	100	27.33 N	113.46 E
Mashan, Zhg.	102	23.50 N	108.16 E
Mashar	140	9.14 N	26.52 E
Mashbury	260	51.47 N	0.24 E
Mashel ≃	224	46.51 N	122.20 W
Mashenqiao	105	40.04 N	117.36 E
Masherbrum ∧	123	35.43 N	76.18 E
Masheve	78	52.06 N	32.48 E
Mashgharah	132	33.32 N	35.39 E
Mashhad, Īrān	128	36.18 N	59.36 E
Mash-had, Yis.	132	32.44 N	35.19 E
Mashi, Nig.	150	13.00 N	7.54 E
Mashi, Zhg.	100	29.05 N	114.22 E
Mashi, Zhg.	100	25.01 N	114.09 E
Mashike	92a	43.51 N	141.31 E
Mashiko	94	36.28 N	140.06 E
Mashita ≃	94	35.40 N	137.10 E
Mashivka	78	49.26 N	34.52 E
Mashīz	128	29.56 N	56.37 E
Mashkai ≃	128	26.02 N	65.19 E
Māshkel, Hāmūn-i- ⊜	128	28.15 N	63.00 E
Māshkel, Rūd-i- (Māshkīd) ≃	128	28.02 N	63.25 E
Mashki Chāh	128	29.01 N	62.27 E
Māshkīd (Rūd-i-Māshkel) ≃	128	28.02 N	63.25 E
Mashonaland North ◻ [4]	154	16.30 S	30.00 E
Mashonaland South ◻ [4]	154	18.15 S	30.45 E
Mashpee	207	41.38 N	70.28 W
Mashra'ur-Raqq	140	8.25 N	29.16 E
Mashtūl as-Sūq	142	30.22 N	31.22 E
Mashū-ko ⊜	92a	43.35 N	144.32 E
Masibi	152	11.08 S	22.42 E
Masihi	114	2.47 N	99.40 E
Masīlah, Wādī al- V	144	15.10 N	51.08 E
Masi-Manimba	152	4.46 S	17.55 E
Masin	164	6.15 S	139.19 E
Masina	272b	22.55 N	88.32 E
Masindi	154	1.41 N	31.43 E
Masini Port	154	1.42 N	32.05 E
Masinloc	116	15.32 N	119.57 E
Masīr	142	31.03 N	31.00 E
Maṣīrah I	118	20.25 N	58.50 E
Maṣīrah, Khalīj ⊂	118	20.10 N	58.15 E
Masis	84	40.00 N	44.29 E
Masisea	248	8.36 S	74.19 W
Masisi	154	1.24 S	28.49 E
Masjed-e Soleymān	128	31.58 N	49.18 E
Masjid Tanah	114	2.21 N	102.07 E
Mask, Lough ⊜	48	53.35 N	9.20 W
Maska	150	11.20 N	7.20 E
Maskan, Ras ≻	144	11.10 N	43.33 E
Maskanah	130	36.01 N	38.05 E
Maskin	128	23.35 N	56.39 E
Maškino	82	54.53 N	36.08 E
Maskinongé ◻ [6]	206	46.35 N	73.30 W
Maskinongé ≃, P.Q., Can.	206	46.10 N	73.01 W
Maskinongé ≃, P.Q., Can.	206	45.49 N	74.40 W
Maskinongé, Lac ⊜	206	46.19 N	73.23 W
Maškoviči	82	54.11 N	36.17 E
Masku	26	60.34 N	22.06 E
Maskūtān	128	26.51 N	59.49 E
Maskwa ≃	184	50.33 N	96.08 W
Masl'anino	86	54.20 N	84.13 E
Masl'anskaja	86	55.56 N	70.08 E
Maslova	265a	59.47 N	30.48 E
Maslovka	78	51.33 N	39.14 E
Maslovo	86	60.07 N	60.30 E
Masnières	50	50.07 N	3.13 E
Maso	150	7.14 N	2.53 W
Masoala	157b	15.59 S	50.10 E
Masoala, Cap ≻	157b	15.59 S	50.13 E
Masoala, Presqu'île de ≻ [1]	157b	15.40 S	50.12 E
Masoarivo	157b	19.03 S	44.19 E
Masomeloka	157b	20.17 S	48.37 E
Mason, Mi., U.S.	216	42.34 N	84.26 W
Mason, Oh., U.S.	218	39.21 N	84.18 W
Mason, Tn., U.S.	194	35.24 N	89.31 W
Mason, Tx., U.S.	196	30.44 N	99.13 W
Mason, W.V., U.S.	188	39.01 N	82.01 W
Mason ◻ [6], Il., U.S.	219	40.18 N	90.04 W
Mason ◻ [6], Ky., U.S.	218	38.35 N	83.48 W
Mason ◻ [6], Wa., U.S.	224	47.20 N	123.09 W
Mason, Lake ⊜	162	27.39 S	119.34 E
Mason Bay ⊂	172	46.56 S	167.44 E
Mason City, Il., U.S.	219	40.12 N	89.41 W
Mason City, Ia., U.S.	190	43.09 N	93.12 W
Mason City, Ne., U.S.	198	41.13 N	99.18 W
Masone	62	44.30 N	8.42 E
Masonicus Brook ≃	276	41.06 N	74.09 W
Mason Lake ⊜	224	47.20 N	122.57 W
Masons Creek ≃	285	39.59 N	74.51 W
Mason Valley V	226	39.07 N	119.10 W
Masonville, N.J., U.S.	285	39.59 N	74.52 W
Masonville, N.Y., U.S.	210	42.15 N	75.23 W
Maspeth ◆ [8]	276	40.43 N	73.55 W
Masqaṭ (Muscat)	128	23.37 N	58.35 E
Maṣra'	142	27.14 N	31.02 E
Massa	64	44.01 N	10.09 E
Massa-Carrara ◻ [4]	64	44.15 N	10.03 E
Massachusetts ◻ [3], U.S.	178	42.15 N	71.50 W
Massachusetts ◻ [3], U.S.	207	42.15 N	71.50 W
Massachusetts (Boston), University of ⊍ [2]	283	42.19 N	71.03 W
Massachusetts Bay ⊂	207	42.20 N	70.50 W
Massachusetts Correctional Institution ⊍	283	42.07 N	71.18 W
Massachusetts Institute of Technology ⊍ [2]	283	42.21 N	71.06 W
Massaciuccoli, Lago di ⊜	66	43.50 N	10.20 E
Massacre Lake ⊜	204	41.39 N	119.35 W
Massa Fermana	66	43.09 N	13.28 E
Massa Fiscaglia	66	44.48 N	12.01 E
Massafra	68	40.35 N	17.07 E
Massaguet	146	12.28 N	15.26 E
Massakory	146	13.00 N	15.44 E
Massalassef	146	11.43 N	17.08 E
Massa Lombarda	66	44.27 N	11.49 E
Massa Lubrense	68	40.36 N	14.20 E
Massa Marittima	66	43.03 N	10.53 E
Massa Martana	66	42.46 N	12.31 E
Massangano	152	9.37 S	14.15 E
Massangena	156	21.32 S	32.57 E
Massapê	250	3.31 S	40.19 W
Massapequa	210	40.40 N	73.28 W
Massapequa Park	276	40.40 N	73.27 W
Massapequa Reserve County Park ♦	276	40.42 N	73.27 W
Massapoag Brook ≃	283	42.09 N	71.09 W
Massapoag Lake ⊜	283	42.06 N	71.11 W
Massara	156	18.20 S	34.09 E
Massarosa	66	43.52 N	10.20 E
Massasoit State Park ♦	207	41.53 N	71.01 W
Massaua → Mitsiwa	144	15.38 N	39.28 E
Massawa → Mitsiwa	144	15.38 N	39.28 E
Massawippi ≃	206	45.22 N	71.51 W
Massawippi, Lake ⊜	206	45.14 N	72.00 W
Massay	50	47.09 N	2.00 E
Massé, Ruisseau ≃	275a	45.28 N	73.17 W
Massello	62	44.57 N	7.04 E
Massen	52	51.32 N	7.38 E
Massena, Ia., U.S.	198	41.15 N	94.46 W
Massena, N.Y., U.S.	206	44.55 N	74.53 W
Massenya	146	11.24 N	16.10 E
Masset	182	54.02 N	132.09 W
Masset Inlet ⊂	182	53.42 N	132.20 W
Masseube	32	43.26 N	0.35 E
Massey	190	46.12 N	82.05 W
Massiac	32	45.15 N	3.12 E
Massiaru	76	58.00 N	24.35 E
Massico, Monte ∧	68	41.10 N	13.55 E
Massieville	218	39.16 N	82.58 W
Massif Central → Central, Massif ⋏	32	45.00 N	3.10 E
Massillon	214	40.48 N	81.32 W
Massima Camp	152	1.27 S	11.42 E
Massina	273b	4.22 S	15.22 E
Massina ◆ [1]	150	14.30 N	5.00 W
Massinga	156	23.20 S	35.25 E
Massingir	156	23.51 S	32.04 E
Massive, Mount ∧	200	39.12 N	106.28 W
Masson, Lac ⊜	206	46.03 N	74.02 W
Masson Island I	9	66.08 S	96.34 E
Massy	261	48.44 N	2.17 E
Mastābah	144	20.49 N	39.20 E
Maştağa	84	40.32 N	50.00 E
Masterson	196	35.38 N	101.58 W
Masterton	172	40.57 S	175.40 E
Mas-Thibert	62	43.34 N	4.44 E
Mastic Point	192	25.03 N	77.57 W
Mastigouche ≃	206	46.20 N	73.24 W
Mastigouche Nord ≃	206	46.24 N	73.25 W
Mastūj	123	36.17 N	72.31 E
Mastūj ≃	123	35.54 N	71.49 E
Mastung	120	29.48 N	66.51 E
Mastūrah	128	23.06 N	38.50 E
Masu	146	12.10 N	13.19 E

Symbol	English	Deutsch	Español	Français	Português
≃	River	Fluß	Río	Rivière	Rio
≍	Canal	Kanal	Canal	Canal	Canal
ʟ	Waterfall, Rapids	Wasserfall, Stromschnellen	Cascada, Rápidos	Chute d'eau, Rapides	Cascata, Rápidos
⋓	Strait	Meeresstraße	Estrecho	Détroit	Estreito
⊂	Bay, Gulf	Bucht, Golf	Bahía, Golfo	Baie, Golfe	Baía, Golfo
⊜	Lake, Lakes	See, Seen	Lago, Lagos	Lac, Lacs	Lago, Lagos
⩪	Swamp	Sumpf	Pantano	Marais	Pântano
⍓	Ice Features, Glacier	Eis- und Gletscherformen	Accidentes Glaciales	Formes glaciaires	Acidentes glaciares
⫧	Other Hydrographic Features	Andere Hydrographische Objekte	Otros Elementos Hidrográficos	Autres données hydrographiques	Outros acidentes hidrográficos
✢	Submarine Features	Untermeerische Objekte	Accidentes Submarinos	Formes de relief sous-marin	Acidentes submarinos
◻	Political Unit	Politische Einheit	Unidad Politica	Entité politique	Unidade política
⊍	Cultural Institution	Kulturelle Institution	Institución Cultural	Institution culturelle	Instituição cultural
⊥	Historical Site	Historische Stätte	Sitio Histórico	Site historique	Sitio histórico
♦	Recreational Site	Erholungs- und Ferienort	Sitio de Recreo	Centre de loisirs	Area de Lazer
⊠	Airport	Flughafen	Aeropuerto	Aéroport	Aeroporto
■	Military Installation	Militäranlage	Instalación Militar	Installation militaire	Instalação militar
◆	Miscellaneous	Verschiedenes	Misceláneo	Divers	Diversos

Name	Page	Lat.°′	Long.°′
Masua	126	24.16 N	90.46 E
Masuda	96	34.40 N	131.51 E
Masuho	94	35.34 N	138.28 E
Masuika	152	7.37 S	22.32 E
Masuku	154	17.12 S	27.07 E
Māsūleh	128	37.10 N	48.59 E
Masulipatam → Machilīpatnam	122	16.10 N	81.08 E
Masura	126	23.16 N	90.24 E
Masurai, Gunung ∧	112	2.30 S	101.51 E
Masury	214	41.12 N	80.32 W
Masvingo	154	20.05 S	30.50 E
Maṣyāf	130	35.03 N	36.21 E
Maszewo, Pol.	30	53.29 N	15.02 E
Maszewo, Pol.	54	52.06 N	14.55 E
Mat ≃	38	41.39 N	19.34 E
Mata, Indon.	115b	8.12 S	122.56 E
Mata, Zaïre	152	7.53 S	21.58 E
Mata Amarilla	254	49.36 S	71.13 W
Mataba, Mount ∧	269f	14.42 N	121.10 E
Matabeleland North □[4]	154	19.00 S	27.15 E
Matabeleland South □[4]	154	21.00 S	29.15 E
Mātābhānga	124	26.20 N	89.13 E
Matabuena	34	41.10 N	3.40 W
Matachel ≃	34	38.50 N	6.17 W
Matachewan	190	47.56 N	80.39 W
Matacuni ≃	246	3.02 N	65.16 W
Matad	88	46.58 N	115.18 E
Mata de Plátano, Quebrada ≃	286c	10.35 N	66.46 W
Matadero Creek ≃	282	37.26 N	122.08 W
Mata de São João	255	12.31 S	38.17 W
Matadi	152	5.49 S	13.27 E
Matador	196	34.00 N	100.49 W
Matagalpa	236	12.55 N	85.55 W
Matagalpa □[5]	236	13.00 N	85.30 W
Matagami	176	49.45 N	77.38 W
Matag-ob	116	11.07 N	124.29 E
Matagorda	196	28.41 N	95.58 W
Matagorda □[6]	222	28.57 N	96.00 W
Matagorda Bay c	196	28.35 N	96.20 W
Matagorda Island I	196	28.15 N	96.30 W
Matagorda Peninsula ≻[1]	196	28.32 N	96.07 W
Mata Grande	250	9.07 S	37.44 W
Matahiae, Pointe ≻	174s	17.49 S	149.17 W
Mataiea	174s	17.45 S	149.23 W
Mataiva I[1]	14	14.53 S	148.40 W
Mataj	86	45.53 N	78.43 E
Matajing	107	29.32 N	104.00 E
Matak, Pulau I	112	3.18 N	106.16 E
Matakana, Austl.	166	33.00 S	145.54 E
Matakana, N.Z.	172	36.21 S	174.43 E
Matakana Island I	172	37.35 S	176.05 E
Matakitaki ≃	172	41.48 S	172.19 E
Matala	152	14.46 S	15.04 E
Matale	122	7.28 N	80.37 E
Matam	150	15.40 N	13.15 W
Matama	96	33.36 N	131.28 E
Matama, Cerro ∧	236	9.47 N	83.15 W
Matamata	172	37.49 S	175.47 E
Matameye	150	13.26 N	8.28 E
Matamoras	210	41.22 N	74.42 W
Matamoros, Méx.	232	25.53 N	97.30 W
Matamoros, Méx.	232	25.32 N	103.15 W
Matan	112	1.52 S	110.00 E
Matana	154	3.46 S	29.41 E
Matana, Danau ⊜	112	2.28 S	121.20 E
Matanalem, Cape ≻	164	2.28 S	149.57 E
Matandu ≃	154	8.45 S	39.19 E
Matane	186	48.51 N	67.32 W
Matang, Malay.	114	4.49 N	100.41 E
Matang, Zhg.	100	29.17 N	113.05 E
Matang, Zhg.	100	32.20 N	121.04 E
Matangi	172	37.49 S	175.25 E
Matani	84	42.06 N	45.13 E
Matanni	123	33.48 N	71.34 E
Matanuska ≃	180	61.30 N	149.15 W
Matanza → San Justo	258	34.40 S	58.33 W
Matanza, Aeródromo ⊠	288	34.44 S	58.30 W
Matanza, Río de la ≃	258	34.42 S	58.28 W
Matanzas, Cuba	240p	23.03 N	81.35 W
Matanzas, Méx.	234	21.37 N	101.38 W
Matanzas □[4]	240p	22.40 N	81.20 W
Matanzas, Bahía de c	240p	23.04 N	81.30 W
Matapa	156	23.11 S	24.39 E
Matapalo, Cabo ≻	236	8.23 N	83.19 W
Matape ≃	232	28.25 N	110.26 W
Matapédia	186	47.58 N	66.57 W
Matapédia, Lac ⊜	186	48.33 N	67.33 W
Matapi ≃	250	0.03 S	51.12 W
Mata Point ≻	174v	19.07 S	169.51 W
Matapu	172	39.29 S	174.14 E
Mataquito ≃	252	34.59 S	72.12 W
Matará, Perú	248	7.16 S	78.16 W
Matara, S. Lan.	122	5.56 N	80.33 E
Mataram	115b	8.35 S	116.07 E
Matarani	248	17.00 S	72.06 W
Mataranka	164	14.56 S	133.07 E
Matārimah, Ra's ≻	142	29.27 N	32.42 E
Matarinao Bay c	116	11.14 N	125.34 E
Mataró	34	41.32 N	2.27 E
Matarraña ≃	34	41.14 N	0.22 E
Matas ∧	266d	41.30 N	2.16 E
Matasiri, Pulau I	112	4.48 S	115.48 E
Mätäsvaara	26	63.26 N	29.36 E
Matata	172	37.53 S	176.45 E
Matatepai, Pointe ≻	174x	9.43 S	139.02 W
Matatiele	158	30.24 S	28.43 E
Mātātīla Dam ◆[6]	124	25.06 N	78.22 E
Matatindoc Point ≻	116	9.43 N	122.23 E
Matatula, Cape ≻	174u	14.15 S	170.34 W
Mataura	172	46.11 S	168.52 E
Mataurá ≃, Bra.	248	5.30 S	60.45 W
Mataura ≃, N.Z.	172	46.34 S	168.43 E
Matāutu	175a	13.57 S	171.56 W
Mataval, Baie de c	174s	17.30 S	149.30 W
Matavera	174k	21.13 S	159.44 W
Mataveri	174z	27.10 S	109.27 E
Mataveri Airstrip ⊠	174z	27.10 S	109.25 W
Matawai	172	38.21 S	177.32 E
Matawan	208	40.24 N	74.13 W
Matawin ≃	206	46.54 N	72.56 W
Matāy	142	28.25 N	30.46 E
Matbūl	142	31.05 N	31.02 E
Matča	85	39.27 N	69.39 E
Matchaponix Brook ≃	276	40.23 N	74.23 W
Matchi-Manitou, Lac ⊜	190	48.00 N	77.04 W
Matching	260	51.47 N	0.13 E
Matching Green	260	51.47 N	0.14 E
Matching Tye	260	51.47 N	0.12 E
Mateare	236	12.14 N	86.26 W
Mateba, Île de I	152	5.54 S	12.50 E
Matehuala	234	23.39 N	100.39 W
Mateke Hills ⋀[2]	154	21.48 S	31.00 E
Mateko	152	4.03 S	18.55 E
Matelica	66	43.15 N	13.00 E
Matemo, Ilha I	154	12.13 S	40.36 E
Matera	68	40.40 N	16.37 E
Matera □[4]	68	40.30 N	16.25 E
Materborn	52	51.46 N	6.06 E
Matese, Lago del ⊜	68	41.25 N	14.25 E
Matese, Monti del ⋀	66	41.27 N	14.22 E
Mátészalka	30	47.57 N	22.19 E
Matete ≃	273b	4.24 S	15.20 E
Matetsi	154	18.16 S	25.56 E
Mateur	148	37.03 N	9.40 E
Matewan	192	37.37 N	82.09 W
Matfield	207	42.02 N	70.59 W
Matfors	26	62.21 N	17.02 E
Matha	32	45.52 N	0.19 W
Mathbaria	126	22.18 N	89.57 E
Mathematicians Seamounts ✦[3]	16	15.00 N	111.00 W
Mather, Mb., Can.	184	49.06 N	99.07 W
Mather, Ca., U.S.	226	37.53 N	119.52 W
Mather, Pa., U.S.	188	39.56 N	80.04 W
Mather Air Force Base ■	226	38.34 N	121.18 W
Mather Gorge V	284c	38.59 N	77.15 W
Matheson	190	48.32 N	80.28 W
Matheson Island	184	51.44 N	96.56 W
Matheu	258	34.22 S	58.50 W
Mathews	208	37.26 N	76.19 W
Mathews □[6]	208	37.25 N	76.20 W
Mathews, Lake ⊜	228	33.51 N	117.26 W
Mathi	62	45.15 N	7.32 E
Mathis	196	28.05 N	97.49 W
Māthle	272b	22.35 N	88.14 E
Mathry	42	51.57 N	5.05 W
Mathura, India	122	10.57 N	78.27 E
Mathura, India	124	27.30 N	77.41 E
Mathura Bil ⊜	272b	22.56 N	88.29 E
Mathurai → Madurai	122	9.56 N	78.07 E
Mathurāpur, Bngl.	126	24.02 N	88.47 E
Mathurāpur, Bngl.	126	23.17 N	89.15 E
Mati	116	6.57 N	126.13 E
Matiacoali	150	12.22 N	1.02 E
Matiakhola	126	23.16 N	86.56 E
Mātiāli	124	26.56 N	88.49 E
Matiāri	120	25.36 N	68.27 E
Matias Barbosa	256	21.53 S	43.20 W
Matías Romero	234	16.53 N	95.02 W
Mātibhānga	126	22.49 N	89.56 E
Matícora ≃	246	11.03 N	71.09 W
Matiere	172	38.45 S	175.06 E
Matignon	32	48.36 N	2.18 W
Matiguás	236	12.50 N	85.28 W
Matinecock	276	40.53 N	73.38 W
Matinenda Lake ⊜	190	46.22 N	82.57 W
Matinha	250	3.06 S	45.02 W
Matinicock Point ≻	276	40.54 N	73.38 W
Matinicus Island I	188	43.54 N	68.55 W
Matino	68	40.02 N	18.08 E
Matipó	255	20.17 S	42.21 W
Maṭir Ṭāris	142	29.22 N	30.54 E
Matiyure ≃	246	7.36 N	67.39 W
Matjiesfontein	158	33.14 S	20.35 E
Matkasel'kja	26	61.58 N	30.33 E
Mātla ≃[1]	126	22.04 N	88.38 E
Matlab Bāzār	126	23.20 N	90.43 E
Matlacha	220	26.37 N	82.05 W
Matlacha Pass ʮ	220	26.37 N	82.04 W
Matlamanyane	156	19.33 S	25.57 E
Matlapa	234	21.15 N	98.50 W
M'atlevo	76	54.54 N	35.39 E
Mātli	120	25.02 N	68.39 E
Matlock, Eng., U.K.	44	53.08 N	1.32 W
Matlock, Wa., U.S.	224	47.14 N	123.25 W
Matlock, Mount ∧	169	37.35 S	146.11 E
Matmata	148	33.33 N	9.58 E
Matnog	116	12.35 N	124.05 E
Mato	154	8.01 S	24.55 E
Mato ≃	246	7.09 N	65.07 W
Mato, Cerro ∧	246	7.15 N	65.14 W
Matoaca	208	37.13 N	77.28 W
Matobe	112	2.42 S	100.11 E
Matočkin Šar	72	73.16 N	56.27 E
Matočkin Šar, proliv ʮ	72	73.20 N	55.21 E
Mato Grosso □[3]	242	12.00 S	57.00 W
Mato Grosso, Planalto do ⋀[1]	242	15.30 S	56.00 W
Mato Grosso do Sul □[3]	242	20.00 S	55.00 W
Matola-Rio	156	25.58 S	32.26 E
Matombo	154	7.03 S	37.46 E
Mato Mole, Serra do ⋀[2]	256	23.00 S	46.12 W
Matong	164	5.35 S	151.45 E
Matonipi ≃	186	51.21 N	69.45 W
Matope	154	15.20 S	34.59 E
Matopo Hills ⋀[2]	154	20.36 S	28.28 E
Matopos	154	20.24 S	28.28 E
Matos ≃	248	14.07 S	65.25 W
Matosinhos	34	41.11 N	8.42 W
Matoso, Ponta do ≻	287a	22.50 S	43.11 W
Matou, T'aiwan	100	23.11 N	120.14 E
Matou, Zhg.	98	36.29 N	114.26 E
Matou, Zhg.	100	25.14 N	118.22 E
Matou, Zhg.	100	29.49 N	115.35 E
Matou, Zhg.	100	30.48 N	118.29 E
Matou, Zhg.	105	39.46 N	116.49 E
Matou, Zhg.	105	39.18 N	116.45 E
Matou, Zhg.	105	39.33 N	116.07 E
Matouji	98	35.02 N	115.07 E
Matour	58	46.18 N	4.29 E
Matoury	250	4.51 N	52.20 W
Matouxi	107	30.15 N	106.31 E
Matouying	98	39.18 N	118.47 E
Matouzhen, Zhg.	98	34.39 N	118.18 E
Matouzhen, Zhg.	100	33.32 N	118.56 E
Mato Verde	255	15.23 S	42.52 W
Matozinhos	255	19.35 S	44.07 W
Mátra ⋀	30	47.55 N	20.00 E
Maṭraḥ	128	23.38 N	58.34 E
Matraville	274a	33.54 S	151.18 E
Matrei am Brenner	64	47.08 N	11.27 E
Matrei in Osttirol	64	47.00 N	12.32 E
Matru	150	7.36 N	12.11 W
Matsap	158	28.38 S	22.47 E
Matsapha	158	26.29 S	31.23 E
Matsari	152	5.21 N	12.14 E
Matsena	150	13.05 N	10.05 E
Matsiatra ≃	157b	21.25 S	45.33 E
Matsieng	158	29.36 S	27.32 E
Matsknutsgårdarna	40	60.28 N	15.22 E
Matsqui	224	49.12 N	122.25 W
Matsu → Matsu Tao I	100	26.09 N	119.56 E
Matsubara	96	34.34 N	135.33 E
Matsubushi	268	35.55 N	139.49 E
Matsuda	94	35.21 N	139.09 E
Matsudai	94	37.08 N	138.37 E
Matsudo	94	35.47 N	139.54 E
Matsudo Race Track ♠	268	35.48 N	139.55 E
Matsue	96	35.28 N	133.04 E
Matsugasaki	268	35.53 N	139.58 E
Matsuida	94	36.19 N	138.48 E
Matsukawa, Nihon	94	36.25 N	137.51 E
Matsukawa, Nihon	94	35.36 N	137.55 E
Matsumae	92	41.26 N	140.07 E
Matsumoto	94	36.14 N	137.58 E
Matsuno	96	33.13 N	132.42 E
Matsunoyama	94	37.05 N	138.37 E
Matsuo	94	35.38 N	140.28 E
Matsuōji	268	35.08 N	140.01 E
Matsuoka	94	36.05 N	136.18 E
Matsuo-san ∧	270	34.38 N	135.44 E
Matsusaka	94	34.34 N	136.32 E
Matsushima	92	38.22 N	141.04 E
Matsu Tao I	100	26.09 N	119.56 E
Matsutō	94	36.31 N	136.34 E
Matsuura	92	33.22 N	129.42 E
Matsuyama	96	33.50 N	132.45 E
Matsuzaki	94	34.45 N	138.47 E
Matta ≃	208	38.07 N	77.26 W
Mattagami ≃	176	50.43 N	81.29 W
Mattagami Heights	190	48.29 N	81.22 W
Mattagami Lake ⊜	190	47.54 N	81.35 W
Mattamuskeet, Lake ⊜	192	35.30 N	76.11 W
Mattapan ◆[8]	283	42.16 N	71.06 W
Mattapoisett	207	41.39 N	70.49 W
Mattaponi	208	37.32 N	76.46 W
Mattaponi ≃	208	37.31 N	76.47 W
Mattarana	62	44.15 N	9.37 E
Mattarello	64	46.00 N	11.07 E
Mattawa, On., Can.	190	46.19 N	78.42 W
Mattawa, Wa., U.S.	202	46.44 N	119.54 W
Mattawa ≃	190	46.19 N	78.43 W
Mattawamkeag	188	45.30 N	68.21 W
Mattawamkeag ≃	188	45.30 N	68.24 W
Mattawan	216	42.12 N	85.47 W
Mattawana	214	40.30 N	77.44 W
Mattawoman Creek ≃	208	38.34 N	77.12 W
Matterhorn (Cervino) ∧, Europe	58	45.59 N	7.43 E
Matterhorn ∧, Nv., U.S.	204	41.49 N	115.23 W
Mattersburg	61	47.44 N	16.25 E
Mattertal V	58	46.10 N	7.49 E
Matteson	216	41.30 N	87.42 W
Matteson Lake ⊜	216	41.56 N	85.12 W
Matthew Flinders Memorial ⊥	169	38.19 S	145.04 E
Matthews	216	40.23 N	85.29 W
Matthews Mountain ∧[2]	194	37.29 N	90.21 W
Matthews Ridge	246	7.30 N	60.10 W
Matthew Town	238	20.57 N	73.40 W
Matthias Church ɤ[1]	264c	47.30 N	19.02 E
Matthiessen State Park ♠	216	41.17 N	89.01 W
Maṭṭī, Sabkhat ⊜	128	23.30 N	52.00 E
Mattie, Lake ⊜	220	28.08 N	81.46 W
Mattig ≃	60	48.16 N	13.04 E
Mattighofen	60	48.06 N	13.09 E
Mattinata	68	41.42 N	16.03 E
Mattishall	42	52.39 N	1.02 E
Mattituck	207	40.59 N	72.32 W
Mattole ≃	204	40.18 N	124.21 W
Mattoon, Il., U.S.	194	39.28 N	88.22 W
Mattoon, Wi., U.S.	190	45.00 N	89.02 W
Mattox Creek ≃	208	38.12 N	76.58 W
Mattox Draw V	198	38.03 N	101.11 W
Mattsee	64	47.58 N	13.06 E
Mattsee ⊜	60	47.59 N	13.07 E
Mattydale	210	43.05 N	76.08 W
Matu	112	2.41 N	111.32 E
Matua	112	2.59 S	110.45 E
Matuba	156	24.27 S	32.55 E
Matucana	248	11.51 S	76.24 W
Matudo → Matsudo	94	35.47 N	139.54 E
Matue → Matsue	96	35.28 N	133.04 E
Matuku Island I	175g	19.10 S	179.46 E
Matumoto → Matsumoto	94	36.14 N	137.58 E
Matungo ≃	152	16.25 S	21.27 E
Matunuck	207	41.23 N	71.32 W
Matuog	116	9.55 N	123.09 E
Matura Bay c	241r	10.38 N	61.01 W
Maturín	246	9.45 N	63.11 W
Maturino	76	59.06 N	37.55 E
Matusadona National Park ♠	154	16.25 S	28.35 E
Matutina	255	19.13 S	45.58 W
Matuto	154	14.46 S	35.59 E
Matutum, Mount ∧	116	6.22 N	125.05 E
Matuzaka → Matsusaka	94	34.34 N	136.32 E
Matvejevka	80	53.32 N	53.29 E
Matvejev Kurgan	83	47.35 N	38.52 E
Matvejevo, Ross.	76	58.38 N	43.30 E
Matvejevo, Ross.	86	57.47 N	57.51 E
Mátyásföld ◆[8]	264c	47.31 N	19.13 E
Matyra ≃	76	52.38 N	39.38 E
Matyševo	80	50.49 N	44.12 E
Matysiv	78	49.03 N	31.34 E
Mau	124	25.17 N	81.23 E
Maú (Ireng) ≃	246	3.33 N	59.51 W
Mauá, Bra.	256	23.40 S	46.27 W
Maúa, Moç.	154	13.51 S	37.10 E
Mauá □[7]	287b	23.40 S	46.27 W
Mau Aimma	124	25.42 N	81.55 E
Mauban	116	14.12 N	121.44 E
Maubara	112	8.37 S	125.12 E
Maubeuge	50	50.17 N	3.58 E
Mauchamps	261	48.32 N	2.12 E
Mauchline	46	55.31 N	4.24 W
Maud, Scot., U.K.	46	57.31 N	2.06 W
Maud, Mo., U.S.	219	39.37 N	92.15 W
Maud, Oh., U.S.	218	39.21 N	84.23 W
Maud, Ok., U.S.	196	35.08 N	96.46 W
Maud, Tx., U.S.	194	33.20 N	94.21 W
Maud, Point ≻	162	23.06 S	113.45 E
Maudaha	124	25.41 N	80.07 E
Maude	166	34.28 S	144.18 E
Maudétour-en-Vexin	261	49.06 N	1.47 E
Mau-é-ele	156	24.21 S	34.07 E
Mauensee	58	47.10 N	8.04 E
Mauer ◆[8]	264b	48.09 N	16.16 E
Mauerbach	264b	48.15 N	16.10 E
Mauerbach ≃	264b	48.12 N	16.14 E
Mauerkirchen	60	48.11 N	13.08 E
Maués	250	3.24 S	57.42 W
Maués ≃	246	3.22 S	57.44 W
Maug ≃	116	8.20 N	125.53 E
Mauganj	124	24.41 N	81.53 E
Mauga Silisili ∧	175a	13.35 S	172.27 W
Maughold	44	54.18 N	4.17 W
Maug Islands II	108	20.01 N	145.13 E
Mauguio	62	43.37 N	4.01 E
Mauguio, Étang de c	62	43.35 N	4.02 E
Maui □[6]	229a	20.53 N	156.30 W
Maui I	229a	20.45 N	156.15 W
Mauk	115a	6.04 S	106.30 E
Mauke I	14	20.09 S	157.23 W
Maulbach	56	50.43 N	9.04 E
Maulbronn	56	49.00 N	8.49 E
Maulde	50	50.30 N	3.26 E
Mauldin	192	34.46 N	82.18 W
Mauldre ≃	261	48.58 N	1.49 E
Maule	50	48.55 N	1.51 E
Maule □[4]	252	35.30 S	71.30 W
Maule ≃	252	35.19 S	72.25 W
Maule, Laguna del ⊜	252	36.04 S	70.30 W
Mauléon	32	46.56 N	0.45 W
Mauléon-Licharre	32	43.14 N	0.53 W
Maulette	261	48.48 N	1.37 E
Maullín	254	41.38 S	73.37 W
Maulvi Bāzār	120	24.29 N	91.47 E
Maumaupaki ∧	172	36.58 S	175.35 E
Maumee	214	41.33 N	83.39 W
Maumee ≃	216	41.42 N	83.28 W
Maumee Bay c	214	41.43 N	83.26 W
Maumelle, Lake ⊜[1]	194	34.55 N	92.40 W
Maumere	115b	8.37 S	122.14 E
Maun	156	20.00 S	23.25 E
Maunabo	240m	18.01 N	65.54 W
Mauna Kea ∧[1]	229d	19.50 N	155.28 W
Maunaloa	229a	21.08 N	157.13 W
Mauna Loa ∧[1]	229d	19.29 N	155.36 W
Maunalua Bay c	229c	21.17 N	157.44 W
Maunath Bhanjan	124	25.57 N	83.33 E
Maunatlala	156	22.32 S	27.28 E
Maunesha ≃	216	43.13 N	88.57 W
Maungahaumi ∧	172	38.18 S	177.40 E
Maunga Roa ∧	174k	21.13 S	159.48 W
Maungatapere	172	35.45 S	174.12 E
Maungaturoto	172	36.06 S	174.22 E
Maungdaw	110	20.50 N	92.21 E
Maungmagan	110	14.09 N	98.06 E
Maungu	154	3.33 S	38.45 E
Maunoir, Lac ⊜	180	67.30 N	125.00 W
Maupihaa I[1]	14	16.50 S	153.55 W
Maupin	224	45.10 N	121.04 W
Maur	123	30.05 N	75.15 E
Mau Rānīpur	124	25.15 N	79.08 E
Maurecourt	261	49.00 N	2.04 E
Maure-de-Bretagne	32	47.54 N	1.59 W
Mauregard	261	49.02 N	2.35 E
Maurepas	261	48.45 N	1.55 E
Maurepas, Lake ⊜	194	30.15 N	90.30 W
Maures ⋀	62	43.16 N	6.23 E
Mauretanien → Mauritania □[1]	134	20.00 N	12.00 W
Mauri ≃	248	17.18 S	68.41 W
Mauria, Passo della)(	64	46.27 N	12.31 E
Mauriac	32	45.13 N	2.20 E
Maurice (Île) → Mauritius □[1]	157c	20.17 S	57.33 E
Maurice ≃	208	39.13 N	75.02 W
Maurice, Lake ⊜	162	29.28 S	130.58 E
Maurice K. Goddard State Park ♠	214	41.23 N	81.10 W
Mauricetown	208	39.17 N	74.58 W
Mauriceville	172	40.47 S	175.42 E
Mauricio → Mauritius □[1]	157c	20.17 S	57.33 E
Maurienne V	62	45.13 N	6.30 E
Maurino, Canal ≅	286e	33.34 S	70.32 W
Mauritania (Mauritanie) □[1]	134	20.00 N	12.00 W
Mauritanie → Mauritania □[1]	134	20.00 N	12.00 W
Mauriti	250	7.23 S	38.46 W
Mauritius □[1], Afr.	138	20.17 S	57.33 E
Mauritius □[1], Afr.	157c	20.17 S	57.33 E
Mauritius I	157c	20.17 S	57.33 E
Mauron	32	48.05 N	2.18 W
Maurs	32	44.43 N	2.11 E
Maurui	154	5.07 S	38.23 E
Maury ≃	192	37.37 N	79.27 W
Maury Channel ʮ	176	75.44 N	94.40 W
Maury Island ≻[1]	224	47.20 N	122.24 W
Maussane	62	43.43 N	4.48 E
Mauston	190	43.47 N	90.04 W
Mautala	126	22.25 N	89.05 E
Mautau, Pointe ≻	174x	9.42 S	138.58 W
Mautern an der Donau	61	48.24 N	15.35 E
Mauterndorf	64	47.08 N	13.40 E
Mautern in Steiermark	61	47.24 N	14.50 E
Mauth	60	48.53 N	13.35 E
Mauthausen	61	48.14 N	14.32 E
Mauthen	64	46.40 N	13.00 E
Mauvais Coulee V	198	48.21 N	99.06 W
Mauvaise Terre Creek ≃	219	39.43 N	90.38 W
Mauvaise Terre Lake ⊜[1]	219	39.42 N	90.12 W
Mauvezin	32	43.44 N	0.55 E
Mava	164	6.50 S	141.25 E
Mavaca ≃	246	2.31 N	65.11 W
Mavanza	156	22.43 S	35.08 E
Māvelikara	122	9.16 N	76.33 E
Maverick	200	33.43 N	109.32 W
Mavinga	152	15.50 S	20.21 E
Mavita	156	19.33 S	33.10 E
Mavonde	156	18.32 S	33.02 E
Mavuradona Mountains ⋀	154	16.30 S	31.20 E
Mawa	154	2.43 N	26.42 E
Mawai	114	1.52 N	103.57 E
Ma Wan I	271d	22.21 N	114.03 E
Mawāna	124	29.06 N	77.55 E
Mawangkanli Shan ∧	120	34.19 N	80.03 E
Mawangtang	106	30.42 N	120.42 E
Mawasangka	112	5.17 S	122.18 E
Mawchi	110	18.49 N	97.09 E
Maw-daung Pass)(	110	11.47 N	99.39 E
Mawdesley	262	53.38 N	2.46 W
Mawdesley Lake ⊜	184	54.01 N	100.39 W
Mawgan	42	50.06 N	5.12 W
Mawi	272a	28.39 N	77.25 E
Mawiwi	154	3.06 N	27.40 E
Māwiyah	144	13.35 N	44.21 E
Mawjib, Wādī al- V	132	31.28 N	35.34 E
Mawkhi	110	16.17 N	98.53 E
Mawlaik	110	23.38 N	94.24 E
Mawlamyaing → Mawlamyine	110	16.30 N	97.38 E
Mawlamyine (Moulmein)	110	16.30 N	97.38 E
Mawr, Wādī V	144	15.41 N	42.42 E
Mawshij	144	13.43 N	43.17 E
Mawson ɤ[3]	9	67.40 S	63.43 E
Mawson Escarpment ±[4]	9	73.05 S	68.10 E
Mawson Peninsula ≻[1]	9	68.35 S	154.11 E
Maw Taung ∧	110	11.39 N	99.35 E
Mawuba	102	29.50 N	108.11 E
Max	198	47.49 N	101.17 W
Maxaranguape	250	5.31 S	35.16 W
Maxatawny	208	40.33 N	75.41 W
Maxcanú	232	20.35 N	89.59 W
Maxéville	58	48.43 N	6.10 E
Maxglan, Flughafen ⊠	64	47.48 N	13.02 E
Maxhütte Haidhof	60	49.12 N	12.05 E
Maxiang	100	24.41 N	118.15 E
Maximo	214	40.53 N	81.11 W
Maximo Paz	258	34.56 S	58.37 W
Maxinkuckee, Lake ⊜	216	41.12 N	86.24 W
Maxixe	156	23.51 S	35.21 E
Maxon Creek ≃	196	29.53 N	102.24 W
Maxton	192	34.44 N	79.20 W
Maxville	206	45.17 N	74.51 W
Maxwell, Ca., U.S.	226	39.16 N	122.11 W
Maxwell, In., U.S.	218	39.51 N	85.46 W
Maxwell, Ia., U.S.	190	41.53 N	93.23 W
Maxwell, Ne., U.S.	198	41.04 N	100.31 W
Maxwell, N.M., U.S.	196	36.32 N	104.32 W
Maxwell, Tx., U.S.	222	29.53 N	97.48 W
Maxwell Air Force Base ■	194	32.23 N	86.21 W
Maxwell Bay c	176	74.35 N	89.00 W
May	196	31.59 N	98.55 W
May ≃, Austl.	162	17.07 S	123.50 E
May ≃, Ab., Can.	182	55.43 N	111.22 W
May ≃, Pap. N. Gui.	164	4.35 S	141.35 E
May, Cape ≻[1]	208	38.58 N	74.55 W
May, Isle of I	46	56.11 N	2.34 W
May, Mount ∧	182	54.02 N	119.58 W
Maya, Pulau I	112	1.10 S	109.35 E
May Aché	146	12.00 N	15.44 E
Mayachka ≃	83	48.44 N	37.33 E
Mayaguana I	238	22.23 N	72.57 W
Mayaguana Passage ʮ	238	22.32 N	73.15 W
Mayagüez	240m	18.12 N	67.09 W
Mayagüez, Aeropuerto ⊠	240m	18.15 N	67.09 W
Mayagüez, Bahía de c	240m	18.12 N	67.10 W
Mayahi	150	13.58 N	7.40 E
Mayajigua	240p	22.14 N	79.04 W
Mayaka	152	5.17 N	16.52 E
Mayaky, Ukr.	78	46.25 N	30.16 E
Mayaky, Ukr.	83	48.57 N	37.37 E
Mayala	273b	4.21 S	15.09 E
Mayales, Punta ≻	236	11.52 N	85.26 W
Mayama	152	3.51 S	14.54 E
Mayamba	152	4.46 S	16.52 E
Mayāmey	128	36.24 N	55.42 E
Maya Mountains ⋀	232	16.40 N	88.50 W
Mayang	102	27.41 N	109.35 E
Mayang-do I	98	40.00 N	128.12 E
Mayantoc	116	15.37 N	120.23 E
Mayao	106	30.50 N	120.23 E
Mayapan ⊥	232	20.38 N	89.27 W
Māyāpur	272b	22.27 N	88.08 E
Mayarí	240p	20.40 N	75.41 W
Mayarí Arriba	240p	20.25 N	75.32 W
Mayaro Bay c	241r	10.15 N	60.58 W
Maya-san ∧	96	34.44 N	135.12 E
Maybee	216	42.00 N	83.30 W
Maybeury	192	37.22 N	81.22 W
Maybole	44	55.21 N	4.41 W
Maybrook	210	41.29 N	74.13 W
Maychew	144	13.02 N	39.34 E
Maydelle	222	31.48 N	95.18 W
Maydena	166	42.55 S	146.30 E
Maydh	144	11.00 N	47.07 E
Maydī	144	16.20 N	42.46 E
Maydolong	116	11.30 N	125.30 E
Maydūm	142	29.22 N	31.10 E
Mayen	56	50.19 N	7.13 E
Mayence → Mainz	56	50.01 N	8.16 E
Mayenne	32	48.18 N	0.37 W
Mayenne □[5]	32	48.05 N	0.40 W
Mayenne ≃	32	47.30 N	0.33 W
Mayer	200	34.23 N	112.14 W
Mayerling	61	48.03 N	16.06 E
Mayersville	194	32.54 N	91.03 W
Mayerthorpe	182	53.57 N	115.08 W
Mayet	50	47.46 N	0.17 E
Mayfair ◆[8], S. Afr.	273d	26.12 S	28.01 E
Mayfair ◆[8], Pa., U.S.	285	40.02 N	75.03 W
Mayfield, N.Z.	172	43.49 S	171.25 E
Mayfield, Eng., U.K.	42	51.01 N	0.15 E
Mayfield, Eng., U.K.	44	53.01 N	1.45 W
Mayfield, Scot., U.K.	46	55.52 N	3.02 W
Mayfield, In., U.S.	218	40.11 N	85.21 W
Mayfield, Ky., U.S.	194	36.44 N	88.38 W
Mayfield, N.Y., U.S.	210	43.06 N	74.15 W
Mayfield, Oh., U.S.	279a	41.33 N	81.26 W
Mayfield, Pa., U.S.	210	41.32 N	75.32 W
Mayfield, Ut,. U.S.	200	39.06 N	111.42 W
Mayfield Creek ≃	194	36.57 N	89.05 W
Mayfield Dam ◆[6]	224	46.30 N	122.35 W
Mayfield Heights	214	41.31 N	81.27 W
Mayfield Lake ⊜[1]	224	46.31 N	122.32 W
Mayflower	194	34.57 N	92.25 W
Mayford	260	51.18 N	0.34 W
May Inlet c	176	76.15 N	100.45 W
Māyir, Sūrīy.	130	36.28 N	37.11 E
Māyir, Sūrīy.	130	36.23 N	37.02 E
May Jirgui	150	13.44 N	8.08 E
Maykop → Majkop	84	44.35 N	40.07 E
Mayland	42	51.39 N	0.47 E
Maymont	184	52.33 N	107.40 W
Maymūn, Wādī V	146	30.10 N	10.27 E
Maymyo	110	22.02 N	96.28 E
Mayna	126	22.14 N	87.47 E
Maynāmati	124	23.29 N	91.07 E
Maynard, Ia., U.S.	190	42.46 N	91.52 W
Maynard, Ma., U.S.	207	42.26 N	71.27 W
Maynard, Oh., U.S.	214	40.07 N	80.53 W
Maynardville	192	36.15 N	83.47 W
Mayne	224	48.51 N	123.18 W
Mayne ≃	166	23.34 S	141.18 E
Mayne Island I	224	48.51 N	123.17 W
Maynooth	48	53.23 N	6.35 W
Mayo, Yk., Can.	180	63.35 N	135.54 W
Mayo, Fl., U.S.	192	30.03 N	83.10 W
Mayo, Md., U.S.	208	38.53 N	76.30 W
Mayo □[6]	48	53.54 N	9.15 W
Mayo ≃, Arg.	254	45.46 S	69.43 W
Mayo ≃, Col.	246	1.40 N	77.21 W
Mayo ≃, Méx.	232	26.45 N	109.47 W
Mayo ≃, Perú	248	6.37 S	76.16 W
Mayoba	154	17.13 S	26.16 E
Mayo Bay c	116	6.56 N	126.22 E
Mayodan	192	36.24 N	79.58 W
Mayo Faran	146	8.57 N	12.04 E
Mayo-Kébbi □[5]	146	10.00 N	15.30 E
Mayoko, Congo	152	2.18 S	12.49 E
Mayoko, Zaïre	152	1.05 S	23.49 E
Mayo Lake ⊜	180	63.46 N	135.10 W
Mayo Ndaga	146	6.54 N	11.25 E
Mayon Volcano ∧[1]	116	13.15 N	123.41 E
Mayor Buratovich	252	39.15 S	62.37 W
Mayo Reservoir ⊜[1]	192	36.00 N	78.53 W
Mayor Island I	172	37.18 S	176.16 E
Mayor Pablo Lagerenza	248	19.58 S	60.45 W
Mayotte □[2], Afr.	138	12.50 S	45.10 E
Mayotte □[2], Afr.	157a	12.50 S	45.10 E
Mayoyao	116	16.59 N	121.14 E
Mayoyoque	246	0.41 N	75.18 W
Maypearl	222	32.19 N	97.01 W
May Pen	241q	17.58 N	77.14 W
Mayport Naval Station ■	192	30.22 N	81.24 W
Mayraira Point ≻	116	18.39 N	120.51 E
Mayrán, Desierto de ◆[2]	196	25.45 N	102.45 W
Mayres	62	44.40 N	4.07 E
Mayrhofen	64	47.10 N	11.52 E
Mays	218	39.45 N	85.26 W
Maysah, Tall al- ∧	132	31.08 N	35.40 E
Maysān □[4]	128	32.00 N	47.00 E
Maysfield	222	30.54 N	96.51 W
Mays Landing	208	39.27 N	74.43 W
Mays Lick	218	38.31 N	83.50 W
Maysville, Ky., U.S.	218	38.38 N	83.44 W
Maysville, Mo., U.S.	194	39.53 N	94.21 W
Maysville, N.C., U.S.	192	34.54 N	77.13 W
Maysville, Ok., U.S.	196	34.49 N	97.24 W
Maythalūn	132	32.21 N	35.16 E
Maytiguid Island I	116	11.03 N	119.36 E
Maytown	208	40.04 N	76.35 W
Mayu	100	27.48 N	120.26 E
Mayumba	152	3.25 S	10.39 E
Mayung	114	0.49 N	103.03 E
Māyūram	122	11.06 N	79.40 E
Mayville, Mi., U.S.	190	43.20 N	83.21 W
Mayville, N.Y., U.S.	214	42.15 N	79.30 W
Mayville, N.D., U.S.	198	47.29 N	97.19 W
Mayville, Wi., U.S.	190	43.29 N	88.32 W
Maywood, Ca., U.S.	280	33.59 N	118.11 W
Maywood, Il., U.S.	216	41.52 N	87.50 W
Maywood, Mo., U.S.	219	39.57 N	91.36 W
Maywood, Ne., U.S.	198	40.39 N	100.37 W
Maywood, N.J., U.S.	276	40.54 N	74.03 W
Maywood, N.Y., U.S.	210	42.42 N	73.52 W
Maywood Race Track ♠	278	41.44 N	87.50 W
Mayyit, Al-Baḥr al- → Dead Sea ⊜	132	31.30 N	35.30 E
Maza, Arg.	252	36.50 S	63.19 W
Maza, Ross.	80	57.14 N	44.13 E
Mazabuka	154	15.51 S	27.46 E
Mazagan → El-Jadida	148	33.16 N	8.30 W
Mazagão	250	0.07 S	51.17 W
Mazagaon ◆[8]	272c	18.57 N	72.50 E
Mazagão Velho	250	0.13 S	51.25 W
Ma'zah, Jabal ∧	130	35.51 N	40.38 E
Mazamet	32	43.30 N	2.24 E
Mazamitla	234	19.55 N	103.02 W
Mazán ≃	246	3.28 S	73.11 W
Māzandarān □[4]	128	36.30 N	53.30 E
Mazanovo	89	51.40 N	128.52 E
Mazār, Jabal ∧	132	33.34 N	36.03 E
Mazar, Oued V	148	31.50 N	1.36 E
Mazara, Val di ◆[1]	70	37.50 N	13.00 E
Mazara del Vallo	70	37.39 N	12.35 E
Mazār-e Sharīf	120	36.42 N	67.06 E
Mazargues	62	43.15 N	5.24 E
Mazaro ≃	70	37.39 N	12.35 E
Mazarredo	254	47.05 S	66.42 W
Mazarrón	34	37.36 N	1.19 W
Mazarrón, Golfo de c	34	37.30 N	1.18 W
Mazarsu	85	41.56 N	72.40 E
Mazaruni ≃	246	6.25 N	58.38 W
Mazatenango	236	14.32 N	91.30 W
Mazatlán	234	23.13 N	106.25 W
Mazatlán Villa de Flores	234	18.02 N	96.54 W
Mazatzal Mountains ⋀	200	34.00 N	111.55 W
Mazatzal Peak ∧	200	34.03 N	111.28 W
Maze	94	35.52 N	137.10 E
Maze ≃	94	35.40 N	137.10 E
Mažeikiai	76	56.19 N	22.20 E
Mazenod	184	49.53 N	106.14 W
Mazeppa, Mn., U.S.	190	44.16 N	92.32 W
Mazeppa, Pa., U.S.	210	40.59 N	76.59 W
Mazha	100	23.27 N	114.00 E
Māzhān, Īrān	128	32.35 N	59.01 E
Mazhan, Zhg.	98	36.04 N	118.45 E
Mazhangfang, Zhg.	104	42.23 N	122.26 E
Mazhangfang, Zhg.	104	40.44 N	120.53 E
Mazhuang, Zhg.	98	37.47 N	115.17 E
Mazhuang, Zhg.	100	32.54 N	114.03 E
Mazhuang, Zhg.	105	39.11 N	116.15 E
Maẓhūr, Khubb al- ±[8]	128	27.45 N	43.55 E
Mazıdağı	130	37.30 N	40.30 E
Mazigou	105	40.28 N	114.48 E
Mazilovo ◆[8]	265b	55.44 N	37.26 E
Mazīnān	128	36.18 N	56.46 E
Mazinaw Lake ⊜	212	44.55 N	77.12 W
Mazirbe	76	57.41 N	22.21 E
Mazoco	154	11.40 S	35.48 E
Mazoe ≃	154	16.32 S	33.25 E
Mazomanie	190	43.10 N	89.47 W
Mazomba ≃	256	22.53 S	43.45 W
Mazon	216	41.14 N	88.25 W
Mazon ≃	216	41.21 N	88.25 W
Mazon, East Fork ≃	216	41.11 N	88.18 W
Mazon, West Fork ≃	216	41.15 N	88.21 W
Mazong Shan ∧	102	41.28 N	97.10 E
Mazong Shan ⋀	102	41.30 N	97.30 E
Mazou ≃	50	47.15 N	2.59 E
Mazra'at-Bayt Jinn	132	33.19 N	35.55 E
Mazsalaca	76	57.52 N	25.03 E
Mazul'skij	86	56.16 N	90.28 E
Mazunga	154	21.45 S	29.52 E
Mazury ◆[1]	30	53.45 N	21.00 E
Mazzarino	70	37.18 N	14.13 E
Mazzarrà Sant'andrea	70	38.05 N	15.08 E
Mazzin	64	46.27 N	11.42 E
Mba	175g	17.33 S	177.41 E
Mbabala Island I	154	11.18 S	29.44 E
Mbabane	158	26.18 S	31.06 E
Mbabo, Tchabal ∧	152	7.16 N	12.09 E
Mbacké	150	14.48 N	15.55 W
Mbaéré ≃	152	3.47 N	17.31 E
Mbage	140	5.30 N	25.13 E
M'bahiakro	150	7.27 N	4.20 W
Mbaïki	152	3.53 N	18.00 E
Mbakaou, Barrage de ◆[5]	152	6.15 N	12.46 E
Mbala, Centraf.	152	7.48 N	20.51 E
Mbala (Abercorn), Zam.	154	8.50 S	31.22 E
Mbalam	152	2.13 N	13.49 E
Mbale	154	1.05 N	34.10 E
Mbali	152	2.50 S	16.12 E
Mbali ≃	152	4.26 N	18.20 E
Mbalizi	154	8.56 S	33.22 E
Mbalmayo	152	3.31 N	11.30 E
Mbalouro ≃	273b	4.09 S	15.21 E
Mbalourou	273b	4.09 S	15.21 E
Mbam ≃	152	4.24 N	11.17 E
Mbamba Bay	154	11.17 S	34.46 E
Mbamou, Île I	152	4.13 S	15.25 E
Mbamou, Pointe ≻	273b	4.16 S	15.19 E
Mbandaka (Coquilhatville)	152	0.04 N	18.16 E
Mbanga	152	4.30 N	9.34 E
Mbanika Island I	175e	9.05 S	159.12 E
M'banza Congo	152	6.16 S	14.15 E
Mbanza-Ngungu	152	5.15 S	14.52 E
Mbarangandu ≃	154	8.57 S	37.24 E
Mbarara	154	0.37 S	30.39 E
Mbari ≃	152	4.34 N	22.43 E
Mbarizunga Game Reserve ◆[4]	154	4.45 N	28.06 E
Mbashe ≃	158	32.15 S	28.53 E
Mbassay	146	7.39 N	15.40 E
Mbate	154	8.52 S	39.10 E
M'batto	150	6.28 N	4.22 W
Mbava Island I	175e	7.49 S	156.33 E
Mbé, Cam.	152	7.43 N	13.30 E
Mbé, Congo	152	3.18 S	15.54 E
Mbé ≃	152	0.27 N	9.41 E
Mbemba	154	10.03 S	38.36 E
Mbengga I	175g	18.23 S	178.08 E
M'bengué	150	10.00 N	5.54 W
Mbéré	146	10.49 N	15.44 E
Mbéré ≃	152	7.45 N	15.36 E
Mberengwa	154	20.30 S	29.53 E
Mbereshi Mission	154	9.45 S	28.46 E
Mberubu	150	6.10 N	7.38 E
Mbeya	154	8.54 S	33.27 E
Mbeya □[4]	154	8.00 S	33.30 E
Mbi ≃	152	4.26 N	18.16 E
Mbia	140	6.15 N	29.19 E
M'bigou	152	1.53 S	11.56 E
Mbinda	152	2.00 S	12.55 E
Mbindawina	152	15.57 S	23.18 E
Mbinga	154	10.56 S	35.01 E
Mbini	152	1.35 N	9.37 E
Mbini ≃	152	1.35 N	9.37 E
Mbirira	154	4.21 S	30.10 E
Mbirizi	154	0.23 S	31.27 E
Mbogo	154	7.26 S	33.26 E
Mboie	152	6.56 S	21.54 E
Mbola	175e	9.37 S	160.39 E
Mboli	152	4.08 N	23.09 E
Mbomou □[5]	152	5.00 N	23.30 E
Mbomou (Bomu) ≃	136	4.08 N	22.26 E
Mbonge	152	4.33 N	9.05 E
Mboro, Sén.	150	15.09 N	16.54 W
Mboro, Sūd.	140	6.18 N	28.45 E
Mborokua I	175e	9.00 S	158.40 E
Mborong	115b	8.49 S	120.37 E
Mboté	152	3.56 S	12.43 E
Mbotou ≃	152	6.49 N	24.14 E
Mbouda	152	5.38 N	10.15 E
Mboula	152	4.27 N	16.29 E
Mbour	150	14.24 N	16.58 W
Mbout	150	16.02 N	12.35 W
Mbrès	152	6.40 N	19.48 E
M'Bridge ≃	152	7.14 S	12.52 E
Mbua	175g	16.48 S	178.37 E
Mbua Bay c	175g	16.49 S	178.35 E
Mbuji-Mayi (Bakwanga)	152	6.09 S	23.38 E
Mbulu	154	3.51 S	35.32 E
Mbulula	154	5.26 S	27.26 E
Mbuluzane ≃	158	26.08 S	31.52 E
Mbuluzi ≃	158	26.08 S	31.52 E
Mbuma	154	3.32 N	24.50 E
Mburucuyá	252	28.03 S	58.14 W
Mbutha	175g	16.39 S	179.50 E
Mbwemkuru ≃	154	9.29 S	39.39 E
McAdam	186	45.36 N	67.20 W
McAdam National Park ♠	164	7.15 S	145.40 E
McAdams Peak ∧[2]	219	38.58 N	90.32 W
McAdoo	210	40.54 N	75.59 W
McAdoo Heights	210	40.54 N	76.01 W
McAfee	210	41.10 N	74.32 W
McAlester	196	34.56 N	95.46 W
McAlisterville	208	40.38 N	77.16 W
McAllen	196	26.12 N	98.13 W
McAlpine	208	39.16 N	76.50 W
McAlpine Dam ◆[6]	218	38.16 N	85.47 W
McAlveys Fort	214	40.39 N	77.50 W
McArthur	188	39.14 N	82.28 W
McArthur ≃	164	15.54 S	136.40 E
McArthur River	164	16.27 S	136.07 E
McAuley	184	50.16 N	101.23 W
McBain	190	44.11 N	85.12 W
McBee	192	34.28 N	80.15 W
McBeth	222	29.11 N	95.30 W
McBeth Fjord c[2]	176	69.38 N	68.30 W
McBride	182	53.18 N	120.10 W
McCall	202	44.54 N	116.05 W
McCall Creek	194	31.30 N	90.41 W
McCallum	186	47.38 N	56.15 W
McCallum Creek ≃	169	37.03 S	143.49 E
McCamey	196	31.08 N	102.13 W
McCammon	202	42.39 N	112.11 W
McCandless, Pa., U.S.	214	40.35 N	80.01 W
McCandless, Pa., U.S.	279b	40.34 N	80.02 W
McCarteney Creek ≃	202	47.13 N	120.05 W
McCarthy	180	61.26 N	142.55 W
McCauley Island I	182	53.40 N	130.15 W
McCaysville	192	34.59 N	84.22 W

Symbols in the index entries represent the broad categories identified in the key at the right. Symbols with superior numbers (⋀[1]) identify subcategories (see complete key on page *I · 1)*.

Symbole im Register stellen die rechts im Schlüssel erklärten Kategorien dar. Symbole mit hochgestellten Ziffern (⋀[1]) bezeichnen Unterabteilungen einer Kategorie (vgl. vollständiger Schlüssel auf Seite *I · 1)*.

Los símbolos incluídos en el texto del índice representan las grandes categorías identificadas con la clave a la derecha. Los símbolos con numeros en su parte superior (⋀[1]) identifican las subcategorías (véase la clave completa en la página *I · 1)*.

Les symboles de l'index représentent les catégories indiquées dans la légende à droite. Les symboles suivis d'un indice (⋀[1]) représentent des sous-catégories (voir légende complète à la page *I · 1)*.

Os símbolos incluídos no texto do índice representam as grandes categorias identificadas com a chave à direita. Os símbolos com números em sua parte superior (⋀[1]) identificam as subcategorias (veja-se a chave completa à página *I · 1)*.

	English	Deutsch	Español	Français	Português
∧	Mountain	Berg	Montaña	Montagne	Montanha
⋀	Mountains	Gebirge	Montañas	Montagnes	Montanhas
)(	Pass	Paß	Paso	Col	Passo
V	Valley, Canyon	Tal, Cañon	Valle, Cañón	Vallée, Canyon	Vale, Canhão
≚	Plain	Ebene	Llano	Plaine	Planície
≻	Cape	Kap	Cabo	Cap	Cabo
I	Island	Insel	Isla	Île	Ilha
II	Islands	Inseln	Islas	Îles	Ilhas
±	Other Topographic Features	Andere Topographische Objekte	Otros Elementos Topográficos	Autres données topographiques	Outros acidentes topográficos

ESPAÑOL — Nombre | Página | Lat.°′ | Long.°′ W = Oeste
FRANÇAIS — Nom | Page | Lat.°′ | Long.°′ W = Ouest
PORTUGUÊS — Nome | Página | Lat.°′ | Long.°′ W = Oeste

McChord Air Force Base ■ 224 47.08 N 122.29 W
McClarens Run ≃ 279b 40.27 N 80.12 W
McClarty Lake ⊜ 184 54.28 N 100.20 W
McCleary 224 47.03 N 123.15 W
McClees Creek ≃ 276 40.22 N 74.03 W
McClellan Air Force Base ■ 226 38.39 N 121.23 W
McClellan Creek ≃ 196 35.22 N 100.34 W
McClellanville 192 33.05 N 79.27 W
McClintock, Mount ∧ 9 80.13 S 157.26 E
McCloud 204 41.15 N 122.08 W
McCloud ≃ 204 40.46 N 122.18 W
McClure, Il., U.S. 194 37.19 N 89.26 W
McClure, Oh., U.S. 216 41.22 N 83.56 W
McClure, Pa., U.S. 210 40.42 N 77.18 W
McClure, Lake ⊜[1] 226 37.37 N 120.16 W
McClusky 198 47.29 N 100.26 W
McColl 192 34.40 N 79.32 W
McComas 192 37.23 N 81.17 W
McComb, Ms., U.S. 194 31.14 N 90.27 W
McComb, Oh., U.S. 216 41.06 N 83.47 W
McConaughy, Lake ⊜[1] 198 41.15 N 101.50 W
McConnell Air Force Base ■ 198 37.38 N 97.15 W
McConnell Range ⋏ 180 64.00 N 123.50 W
McConnellsburg 188 39.55 N 77.59 W
McConnells Mill 279b 40.15 N 80.15 W
McConnells Mill State Park ♠ 214 40.57 N 80.11 W
McConnellstown 214 40.27 N 78.05 W
McConnellsville 210 43.16 N 75.42 W
McConnelsville 188 39.38 N 81.51 W
McCook, Il., U.S. 278 41.48 N 87.50 W
McCook, Ne., U.S. 198 40.12 N 100.37 W
McCordsville 218 39.53 N 85.55 W
McCormick 192 33.54 N 82.17 W
McCormick Place ⊌ 278 41.51 N 87.37 W
McCoy 224 45.03 N 123.13 W
McCoy Creek ≃ 202 43.02 N 118.50 W
McCoy Lake ⊜ 184 52.35 N 92.19 W
McCraney Creek ≃ 219 39.39 N 91.12 W
McCreary 184 50.46 N 99.30 W
McCrory 194 35.15 N 91.12 W
McCulloch, Mount ∧ 162 25.10 S 129.52 E
McCullom Lake 216 42.22 N 88.18 W
McCullough 279b 40.22 N 79.38 W
McCullough Mountain ∧ 204 35.36 N 115.11 W
McCune 198 37.21 N 95.00 W
McCurtain 196 35.08 N 94.58 W
McCusker ≃ 184 55.32 N 108.40 W
McCutchenville 214 40.59 N 83.15 W
McDade 222 30.17 N 97.15 W
McDavid 194 30.51 N 87.19 W
McDermitt 204 41.59 N 117.43 W
McDermott 218 38.50 N 83.03 W
McDonald, Ks., U.S. 198 39.47 N 101.22 W
McDonald, Pa., U.S. 214 40.22 N 80.14 W
McDonald, Lac ⊜ 206 45.52 N 74.35 W
McDonald, Lake ⊜ 202 48.35 N 113.55 W
McDonald Park ♠ 282 37.18 N 122.17 W
McDonogh 284b 39.24 N 76.46 W
McDonough, Ga., U.S. 192 33.26 N 84.08 W
McDonough, N.Y., U.S. 210 42.30 N 75.46 W
McDouall Peak 162 29.51 S 134.55 E
McDougal, Mount ∧ 200 42.54 N 110.36 W
McDowell Peak ∧ 200 33.40 N 111.50 W
McElhattan 210 41.09 N 77.22 W
McElmo Creek ≃ 200 37.13 N 109.12 W
Mc Ennen Airport ⊠ 281 42.12 N 83.37 W
Mcensk 76 53.17 N 36.35 E
McEwen 194 36.06 N 87.37 W
McEwensville 210 41.05 N 76.49 W
McFadden 200 41.39 N 106.07 W
McFarland, Ca., U.S. 226 35.40 N 119.13 W
McFarland, Wi., U.S. 216 43.00 N 89.17 W
McGavock Lake ⊜ 184 56.32 N 101.25 W
McGehee 194 33.37 N 91.23 W
McGill 204 39.24 N 114.46 W
McGill, Université ⊌[2] 275a 45.30 N 73.35 W
McGillivray, Lac ⊜ 190 46.04 N 77.06 W
McGinnis Slough Wildlife Refuge ◆[4] 278 41.39 N 87.52 W
McGovern 214 40.14 N 80.13 W
McGrann 214 40.47 N 79.31 W
McGrath 180 62.58 N 155.38 W
McGraw 210 42.35 N 76.05 W
McGregor, On., Can. 214 42.09 N 82.58 W
McGregor, S. Afr. 158 33.57 S 19.50 E
McGregor, Ia., U.S. 190 43.01 N 91.10 W
McGregor, Tx., U.S. 222 31.26 N 97.24 W
McGregor ≃ 182 54.11 N 122.00 W
McGregor Creek ≃ 214 42.24 N 82.11 W
McGregor Lake ⊜ 182 50.31 N 112.53 W
McGregor Range ⋏ 166 26.40 S 142.45 E
McGuffey 216 40.41 N 83.47 W
McGuire, Mount ∧ 202 45.10 N 114.36 W
McGuire Air Force Base ■ 208 40.02 N 74.35 W
McGuire Reservoir ⊜ 224 45.19 N 123.26 W
M'Chedallah 34 36.21 N 4.16 E
McHenry, Il., U.S. 216 42.20 N 88.16 W
McHenry, Ms., U.S. 194 30.42 N 89.08 W
McHenry □[6] 216 42.19 N 88.27 W
Mcherrah ◆[1] 148 27.00 N 4.40 W
Mchinga 154 9.44 S 39.42 E
Mchinji 154 13.41 S 32.55 E
Mchungo 154 7.42 S 39.17 E
McInnes Lake ⊜ 184 52.12 N 93.45 W
McIntosh, Al., U.S. 194 31.15 N 88.01 W
McIntosh, Il., U.S. 216 42.03 N 88.23 W
McIntosh, Mn., U.S. 198 47.38 N 95.53 W
McIntosh, S.D., U.S. 198 45.55 N 101.20 W
McIntosh Lake ⊜ 184 55.45 N 105.08 W
McIntyre 214 40.34 N 79.17 W
McIntyre Bay ⊂ 182 54.05 N 131.55 W
McKay, Mount ∧ 162 22.26 S 120.01 E
McKay Creek ≃ 202 45.40 N 118.50 W
McKean 214 41.59 N 80.09 W
McKean □[6] 214 41.49 N 78.27 W
McKeand ≃ 176 65.26 N 68.10 W
McKee 192 37.25 N 83.59 W
McKee City 208 39.27 N 74.38 W
McKee Creek ≃ 219 39.46 N 90.36 W
McKeesport 214 40.20 N 79.51 W
McKees Rocks 214 40.27 N 80.03 W
McKenna 224 46.56 N 122.33 W
McKenzie, Al., U.S. 194 31.32 N 86.42 W
McKenzie, Tn., U.S. 194 36.07 N 88.31 W
McKenzie ≃ 202 44.07 N 123.06 W
McKenzie Bridge 202 44.10 N 122.09 W
McKenzie Creek ≃ 212 43.02 N 79.53 W
McKenzie Island 184 51.05 N 93.48 W
McKenzie Lake ⊜, On., Can. 212 45.22 N 78.02 W
McKenzie Lake ⊜, Sk., Can. 184 54.12 N 102.30 W
McKerrow, Lake ⊜ 172 44.26 S 168.03 E
McKillip Ditch ≡ 216 40.50 N 86.51 W
McKinlay 166 21.16 S 141.17 E
McKinlay ≃ 166 20.50 S 141.28 E
McKinley, Mount ∧ 180 63.04 N 151.00 W
McKinley Airport ⊠ 281 42.33 N 82.58 W
McKinley Park ♠ 279b 40.25 N 80.00 W
McKinleyville, Ca., U.S. 204 40.56 N 124.05 W
McKinleyville, W.V., U.S. 214 40.15 N 80.36 W
McKinney 222 33.11 N 96.36 W
McKittrick, Ca., U.S. 226 35.18 N 119.37 W
McKittrick, Mo., U.S. 219 38.44 N 91.27 W
McKittrick Summit ∧ 226 35.18 N 119.46 W
McKnight Lake ⊜ 184 56.03 N 101.08 W
McKnightstown 208 39.52 N 77.20 W
McKnight Village 279b 40.31 N 80.00 W
McKownville 210 42.41 N 73.50 W
McLain 194 31.06 N 88.49 W
McLaren Vale 168b 35.14 S 138.32 E
McLarty Hills ⋏[2] 162 19.29 S 123.33 E
McLaughlin 198 45.48 N 100.48 W
McLaughlin ≃ 184 53.46 N 97.38 W
McLaughlin Run ≃ 279b 40.22 N 80.07 W
McLaurin 194 31.10 N 89.13 W
McLean, Sk., Can. 184 50.30 N 104.04 W
McLean, Il., U.S. 194 40.18 N 89.10 W
McLean, N.Y., U.S. 210 42.33 N 76.17 W
McLean, Tx., U.S. 196 35.13 N 100.35 W
McLean, Va., U.S. 208 38.56 N 77.10 W
McLean □[6] 216 40.29 N 88.45 W
McLean Hamlet 284c 38.56 N 77.13 W
McLean Lake ⊜ 184 56.27 N 109.15 W
McLean Mountain ∧ 186 47.07 N 68.50 W
McLeansboro 194 38.05 N 88.32 W
McLennan 182 55.42 N 116.54 W
McLennan □[6] 222 31.35 N 97.13 W
McLeod ≃ 182 54.08 N 115.42 W
McLeod Bay ⊂ 176 62.53 N 110.00 W
McLeodganj 123 30.15 N 73.42 E
McLeod Lake 182 54.59 N 123.02 W
M'Clintock Channel ʮ 176 72.00 N 102.00 W
McLoughlin, Mount ∧ 202 42.27 N 122.19 W
McLoughlin Bay ⊂ 176 67.50 N 99.00 W
McLoughlin House National Historic Site ⊥ 224 45.20 N 122.33 W
McLouth 198 39.11 N 95.12 W
McLure 182 51.03 N 120.14 W
M'Clure Strait ʮ 176 74.30 N 116.00 W
McMahan 222 29.51 N 97.31 W
McMahon 184 50.05 N 107.32 W
McMasterville 206 45.33 N 73.15 W
McMichael Art Collection ⊌ 275b 43.50 N 79.37 W
McMillan, Lake ⊜[1] 196 32.40 N 104.20 W
McMinnville, Or., U.S. 224 45.12 N 123.11 W
McMinnville, Tn., U.S. 194 35.41 N 85.46 W
McMurdo ⊌[3] 9 77.50 S 166.25 E
McMurdo Sound ʮ 9 77.30 S 165.00 E
McMurray 214 40.17 N 80.05 W
McNair 222 29.48 N 95.02 W
McNary 200 34.04 N 109.51 W
McNeil, Ar., U.S. 194 33.20 N 93.12 W
McNeil, Tx., U.S. 222 30.27 N 97.43 W
McNeil, Mount ∧ 182 54.35 N 130.14 W
McNeil Island I 224 47.13 N 122.41 W
McNeill 194 30.40 N 89.38 W
McNulty 224 45.50 N 122.50 W
McPhail ≃ 184 52.44 N 96.31 W
McPhee Bay ⊂ 212 44.35 N 79.19 W
McPhee Reservoir ⊜[1] 200 37.32 N 108.35 W
McPherson 198 38.22 N 97.39 W
McPherson Range ⋏ 166 28.20 S 153.00 E
McQueeney 196 29.35 N 98.02 W
McRae, Ar., U.S. 194 35.06 N 91.49 W
McRae, Ga., U.S. 192 32.04 N 82.54 W
McRae, Mount ∧ 162 22.17 S 117.35 E
McRae Point Provincial Park ♠ 212 44.34 N 79.19 W
McRoberts 192 37.12 N 82.40 W
McSherrystown 208 39.48 N 77.00 W
McVeigh 192 37.32 N 82.15 W
McVeytown 214 40.30 N 77.44 W
McVickers Brook ≃ 276 40.45 N 74.38 W
McVille 198 47.45 N 98.10 W
McWilliams 194 31.49 N 87.05 W
Mdandu 154 9.09 S 34.42 E
Mdantsana 158 32.56 S 27.42 E
M'Daourouch 36 36.05 N 7.49 E
Meacham 184 52.08 N 105.45 W
Mead 198 41.14 N 96.30 W
Mead, Lake ⊜[1] 200 36.05 N 114.25 W
Meade, Ks., U.S. 198 37.17 N 100.20 W
Meade, Mi., U.S. 214 42.43 N 82.52 W
Meade ≃ 180 70.50 N 156.25 W
Meaden Peak ∧ 200 40.46 N 107.03 W
Meade Peak ∧ 202 42.30 N 111.15 W
Meadie, Loch ⊜ 46 58.20 N 4.33 W
Meadow, Tx., U.S. 196 33.20 N 102.12 W
Meadow, Ut,. U.S. 200 38.53 N 112.24 W
Meadowbank Park ♠ 274a 33.49 S 151.06 E
Meadowbrook, Il., U.S. 219 38.54 N 90.01 W
Meadowbrook, In., U.S. 216 41.03 N 85.03 W
Meadow Brook ≃, Ma., U.S. 283 42.03 N 70.58 W
Meadow Brook ≃, Pa., U.S. 285 40.07 N 75.04 W
Meadow Creek ≃ 202 46.03 N 115.18 W
Meadow Flat 170 33.26 S 149.56 E
Meadow Island I 276 40.36 N 73.33 W
Meadow Lake 184 54.08 N 108.26 W
Meadow Lake ⊜, Sk., Can. 184 54.07 N 108.20 W
Meadow Lake ⊜, N.Y., U.S. 276 40.44 N 73.50 W
Meadow Lake Provincial Park ♠ 184 54.28 N 109.10 W
Meadow Lands 214 40.13 N 80.13 W
Meadowlands Race Track ♠ 276 40.49 N 74.05 W
Meadowlark Airport ⊠ 280 33.43 N 118.02 W
Meadowood, De., U.S. 285 39.43 N 75.47 W
Meadowood, Md., U.S. 284c 39.04 N 77.00 W
Meadows 168b 35.11 S 138.46 E
Meadows, Island of I 276 40.34 N 74.12 W
Meadows Field ⊠ 226 35.26 N 119.03 W
Meadowvale ◆[8] 275b 43.37 N 79.43 W
Meadow Valley Wash ∨ 204 36.39 N 114.35 W
Meadowview 192 36.46 N 81.52 W
Meadow Vista 226 39.06 N 121.01 W
Meads Creek ≃ 210 42.10 N 77.07 W
Meadville, Ms., U.S. 194 31.28 N 90.53 W
Meadville, Mo., U.S. 194 39.47 N 93.18 W
Meadville, Pa., U.S. 214 41.38 N 80.09 W
Meaford 212 44.36 N 80.35 W
Meaghers Grant 186 44.55 N 63.15 W
Me-akan-dake ∧ 92a 43.23 N 144.01 E
Mealasta Isle I 46 58.05 N 7.08 W
Mealhada 34 40.22 N 8.27 W
Méan 56 50.22 N 5.20 E
Meana 128 36.55 N 60.30 E
Meana Sardo 71 39.57 N 9.04 E
Meandarra 166 27.20 S 149.53 E
Meander Creek Reservoir ⊜[1] 214 41.09 N 80.47 W
Meander River 176 59.02 N 117.42 W
Mearim ≃ 250 3.04 S 44.35 W
Measham 42 52.43 N 1.29 W
Meath □[6] 48 53.35 N 6.40 W
Meath □[9] 48 53.40 N 7.00 W
Meaux 50 48.57 N 2.52 E
Meaux-Esbly, Aérodrome de ⊠ 261 48.55 N 2.50 E
Mebane 192 36.05 N 79.16 W
Mebisere 273a 6.42 N 3.31 E
Mebtoûh, Oued el ≃ 34 35.16 N 0.32 W
Meča ≃ 82 54.50 N 39.10 E
Meca, La → Makkah 144 21.27 N 39.49 E
Mecanhelas 154 15.12 S 35.54 E
Mecatán 234 21.32 N 105.08 W
Mecatlán 234 20.13 N 97.41 W
Mecaya ≃ 246 0.29 N 75.11 W
Mecca → Makkah 144 21.27 N 39.49 E
Mečetinskaja 78 46.46 N 40.27 E
Mečetka 78 50.54 N 40.05 E
Mechanic Falls 188 44.06 N 70.23 W
Mechanicsburg, Il., U.S. 219 39.48 N 89.24 W
Mechanicsburg, In., U.S. 218 40.09 N 86.28 W
Mechanicsburg, Oh., U.S. 218 40.04 N 83.33 W
Mechanicsburg, Pa., U.S. 208 40.12 N 77.00 W
Mechanicstown, N.Y., U.S. 210 41.27 N 74.24 W
Mechanicstown, Oh., U.S. 214 40.37 N 80.57 W
Mechanicsville, Ia., U.S. 190 41.54 N 91.15 W
Mechanicsville, Md., U.S. 208 38.26 N 76.44 W
Mechanicsville, Va., U.S. 192 37.36 N 77.22 W
Mechanicville 210 42.54 N 73.41 W
Mechara 144 8.32 N 40.22 E
Mechebylove 78 49.04 N 36.41 E
Mechelen (Malines) 50 51.02 N 4.28 E
Mechel'ta 84 42.48 N 46.30 E
Mechernich 56 50.35 N 6.38 E
Mechī □[8] 124 27.15 N 87.45 E
Mechī ≃ 124 26.14 N 87.58 E
Mechita 252 35.04 S 60.24 W
Mechlin → Mechelen 50 51.02 N 4.28 E
Mechonskoje 86 56.09 N 64.34 E
Mechra Safsaf 34 34.52 N 2.36 W
Mechren'ga 24 61.46 N 40.57 E
Mechrenga ≃ 24 63.15 N 41.20 E
Mechriyya 148 33.35 N 0.18 W
Mechroha 36 36.21 N 7.51 E
Mecidiye, Tür. 130 38.53 N 27.42 E
Mecidiye, Tür. 130 40.38 N 26.32 E
Mečigmen 180 65.28 N 172.05 W
Mečigmeskij zaliv ⊂ 180 65.25 N 172.00 W
Meçitözü 130 40.31 N 35.19 E
Meckelfeld 52 53.25 N 10.01 E
Meckenbeuren 58 47.42 N 9.34 E
Meckenheim 56 50.37 N 7.07 E
Meckering 162 31.38 S 117.01 E
Meckesheim 56 49.19 N 8.49 E
Meckinghoven 263 51.37 N 7.19 E
Mecklenburg, Dtsch. 54 53.47 N 11.28 E
Mecklenburg, N.Y., U.S. 210 42.27 N 76.43 W
Mecklenburg □[9] 54 53.30 N 13.00 E
Mecklenburger Bucht ⊂ 54 54.20 N 11.40 E
Mecklenburgische Seenplatte ◆[1] 54 53.30 N 12.00 E
Mecklenburg-Vorpommern □[3] 54 53.45 N 12.30 E
Meclov 60 49.31 N 12.52 E
Meco 210 43.03 N 74.23 W
Mecoacán 234 18.23 N 93.07 W
Mecoacán, Laguna ⊂ 234 18.22 N 93.09 W
Meconta 154 14.49 S 39.50 E
Mecox Bay ⊂ 207 40.54 N 72.20 W
Mecque, La → Makkah 144 21.27 N 39.49 E
Mecsek ⋏ 30 46.15 N 18.05 E
Mecubúri 154 14.39 S 38.54 E
Mecubúri ≃ 154 14.10 S 40.31 E
Mecúfi 154 13.17 S 40.30 E
Mecula 154 12.04 S 37.40 E
Meda, It. 62 45.40 N 9.09 E
Meda, Port. 34 40.58 N 7.16 W
Medak 122 18.02 N 78.16 E
Medākul 126 23.03 N 90.11 E
Médan, Fr. 261 48.57 N 2.00 E
Medan, Indon. 114 3.35 N 98.40 E
Medang 114 2.06 N 101.38 E
Medang, Pulau I 115b 8.09 S 117.23 E
Medang, Tanjung › 114 2.08 N 101.39 E
Médanos 252 38.50 S 62.41 W
Medanosa, Punta › 254 48.06 S 65.55 W
Medaryville 216 41.04 N 86.53 W
Mede 62 45.06 N 8.44 E
Medebach 56 51.12 N 8.42 E
Medeiros Neto 255 17.20 S 40.14 W
Medel, Val ∨ 58 46.37 N 8.50 E
Medellín, Col. 246 6.15 N 75.35 W
Medellin, Pil. 116 11.08 N 123.58 E
Medelpad □[9] 26 62.40 N 16.15 E
Medemblik 52 52.46 N 5.06 E
Měděnec 54 50.25 N 13.05 E
Médenine 148 33.21 N 10.30 E
Médenine □[8] 148 32.00 N 10.00 E
Medenytsya 78 49.26 N 23.45 E
Mederdra 150 16.55 N 15.39 W
Medesano 64 44.45 N 10.08 E
Medevi 40 58.40 N 14.57 E
Medfield 207 42.11 N 71.18 W
Medford, Ma., U.S. 207 42.25 N 71.06 W
Medford, N.J., U.S. 208 39.54 N 74.49 W
Medford, N.Y., U.S. 210 40.49 N 73.00 W
Medford, Ok., U.S. 196 36.48 N 97.44 W
Medford, Or., U.S. 202 42.19 N 122.52 W
Medford, Wi., U.S. 190 45.08 N 90.20 W
Medford Farms 285 39.52 N 74.45 W
Medford Lakes 285 39.51 N 74.48 W
Medfra 180 63.06 N 154.44 W
Medgidia 38 44.15 N 28.16 E
Medgyes → Mediaș 38 46.10 N 24.21 E
Medi 154 5.04 N 30.44 E
Media 208 39.55 N 75.23 W
Mediapolis 190 41.00 N 91.09 W
Mediaș 38 46.10 N 24.21 E
Medical Lake 202 47.34 N 117.40 W
Medicina 66 44.28 N 11.38 E
Medicine Bow 200 41.53 N 106.12 W
Medicine Bow ≃ 200 42.00 N 106.40 W
Medicine Bow Mountains ⋏ 200 41.10 N 106.10 W
Medicine Bow Peak ∧ 200 41.21 N 106.19 W
Medicine Creek ≃, Mo., U.S. 194 39.43 N 93.24 W
Medicine Creek ≃, Ne., U.S. 198 40.17 N 100.10 W
Medicine Creek ≃, S.D., U.S. 198 44.06 N 99.42 W
Medicine Hat 184 50.03 N 110.40 W
Medicine Knoll Creek ≃ 198 44.19 N 100.05 W
Medicine Lake 198 48.30 N 104.30 W
Medicine Lake ⊜ 198 48.28 N 104.24 W
Medicine Lodge 198 37.16 N 98.34 W
Medicine Lodge ≃ 196 36.49 N 98.20 W
Medicine Rocks State Park ♠ 198 46.01 N 104.35 W
Medina → Al-Madīnah, Ar. Su. 128 24.28 N 39.36 E
Medina, Bra. 255 16.15 S 41.29 W
Medina, Pil. 116 8.55 N 125.01 E
Medina, N.Y., U.S. 210 43.13 N 78.23 W
Medina, N.D., U.S. 198 46.53 N 99.17 W
Medina, Oh., U.S. 214 41.08 N 81.51 W
Medina, Tx., U.S. 196 29.48 N 99.15 W
Medina, Wa., U.S. 224 47.37 N 122.13 W
Medina □[6] 214 41.08 N 81.52 W
Medina ≃ 196 29.12 N 98.20 W
Medinaceli 34 41.10 N 2.26 W
Medina del Campo 34 41.18 N 4.55 W
Medina de Ríoseco 34 41.53 N 5.02 W
Médina Gonasse 150 13.08 N 13.45 W
Medinah 278 41.59 N 88.01 W
Medina Lake ⊜[1] 196 29.35 N 98.58 W
Médina Sabak 150 13.36 N 15.35 W
Medina-Sidonia 34 36.27 N 5.55 W
Medinat al-Faiyum → Al-Fayyūm 142 29.19 N 30.50 E
Medininkai 76 54.32 N 25.40 E
Medinīpur 126 22.26 N 87.20 E
Medino 164 9.40 S 149.40 E
Medio, Arroyo del ≃ 258 33.49 S 57.43 W
Medio, Punta › 252 27.07 S 70.57 W
Medio Creek ≃ 196 28.19 N 97.19 W
Mediterranean Sea ⫧[2] 10 35.00 N 20.00 E
Mediterraneo, Mare → Mediterranean Sea ⫧[2] 10 35.00 N 20.00 E
Medjana 34 36.08 N 4.41 E
Medje 154 2.25 N 27.18 E
Medjerda, Monts de la ⋏ 36 36.35 N 8.15 E
Medkovec 38 43.37 N 23.10 E
Mednogorsk 86 51.24 N 57.37 E
Mednoje 76 56.56 N 35.29 E
Mednyj, ostrov I 74 54.45 N 167.35 E
Médoc ◆[1] 32 45.20 N 1.00 W
Mêdog 120 29.20 N 95.15 E
Medolla 64 44.51 N 11.04 E
Medora, Il., U.S. 219 39.11 N 90.09 W
Medora, In., U.S. 218 38.49 N 86.10 W
Medora, N.D., U.S. 198 46.54 N 103.31 W
Médouneu 152 0.57 N 10.47 E
Medow 54 53.50 N 13.32 E
Medstead, Sk., Can. 184 53.19 N 108.02 W
Medstead, Eng., U.K. 42 51.08 N 1.04 W
Medua 126 22.38 N 90.44 E
Meductic 186 46.00 N 67.29 W
Medulla 220 27.58 N 81.58 W
Međumurje ◆[1] 61 46.25 N 16.30 E
Meduna ≃ 64 45.49 N 12.34 E
Medveđa 38 42.50 N 21.35 E
Medvedevo, Ross. 76 60.02 N 43.01 E
Medvedevo, Ross. 80 56.37 N 47.47 E
Medvedevo, Ross. 86 60.37 N 77.21 E
Medvedevskoje 76 58.58 N 35.58 E
Medvedica ≃, Ross. 76 57.05 N 37.32 E
Medvedica ≃, Ross. 80 49.35 N 42.41 E
Medvedickij 80 50.47 N 44.43 E
Medvědí hora ∧ 60 48.59 N 13.25 E
Medvedkovo ◆[8] 265b 55.53 N 37.38 E
Medvedok 80 57.23 N 50.05 E
Medvedovskaja 78 45.27 N 39.01 E
Medvenka, Ross. 78 51.26 N 36.07 E
Medvenka, Ross. 82 54.15 N 37.42 E
Medvežij, ostrov I 89 54.41 N 136.18 E
Medvežje, ozero ⊜ 86 55.07 N 68.00 E
Medvežjegorsk 24 62.55 N 34.23 E
Medvežji ostrova II 74 70.52 N 161.26 E
Medvežji ozera ⊜ 265b 55.52 N 38.00 E
Medvežji Oz'ora 265b 55.52 N 37.59 E
Medvežskaja 24 64.57 N 57.34 E
Medviagalis ∧[2] 76 55.38 N 22.45 E
Medv'onka ≃ 265b 55.44 N 37.12 E
Medvyn 78 49.23 N 30.47 E
Medway, Ma., U.S. 207 42.08 N 71.23 W
Medway, Oh., U.S. 218 39.53 N 83.59 W
Medway □[8] 260 51.24 N 0.31 E
Medway ≃, N.S., Can. 186 44.08 N 64.36 W
Medway ≃, Eng., U.K. 42 51.27 N 0.44 E
Medyn' 82 54.58 N 35.52 E
Medynka ≃ 82 54.44 N 36.02 E
Medynskij Zavorot, mys › 24 68.58 N 59.17 E
Medzhybizh 78 49.26 N 27.25 E
Medzilaborce 30 49.16 N 21.55 E
Meeberrie 162 26.58 S 115.58 E
Meekatharra 162 26.36 S 118.29 E
Meeker, Co., U.S. 200 40.02 N 107.54 W
Meeker, Oh., U.S. 214 40.39 N 83.18 W
Meeks Bay 226 39.02 N 120.08 W
Meelpaeg Lake ⊜[1] 186 48.16 N 56.35 W
Meenaar 168a 31.38 S 116.53 E
Meentheena 162 21.17 S 120.28 E
Meer 56 51.27 N 4.44 E
Meeralpen → Maritime Alps ⋏ 62 44.15 N 7.10 E
Meerane 54 50.51 N 12.28 E
Meerbeck 263 51.28 N 6.39 E
Meerbeke 50 50.50 N 4.02 E
Meerbusch 56 51.15 N 6.41 E
Meerhout 56 51.08 N 5.05 E
Meerhusener Moor ◆[3] 52 53.35 N 7.30 E
Meerkerk 52 51.55 N 5.00 E
Meerle 52 51.28 N 4.48 E
Meersburg 58 47.41 N 9.16 E
Meerssen 56 50.53 N 5.45 E
Meerut 124 28.59 N 77.42 E
Meese ≃ 42 52.40 N 2.39 W
Meeteetse 202 44.09 N 108.52 W
Mega, Indon. 164 0.41 S 131.53 E
Mega, Ityo. 144 4.07 N 38.16 E
Mega, Pulau I 112 4.00 S 101.02 E
Megalo 144 6.55 N 41.48 E
Megálon Khoríon 38 36.27 N 27.21 E
Megalópolis 38 37.24 N 22.08 E
Mégantic □[6] 206 46.10 N 71.30 W
Mégantic, Lac ⊜ 188 45.32 N 70.53 W
Mégantic, Mont ∧ 206 45.28 N 71.09 W
Mégara 38 38.01 N 23.21 E
Megargel 196 33.27 N 98.56 W
Mégaron, Kólpos ⊂ 267c 37.56 N 23.20 E
Megaruma ≃ 154 13.28 S 40.32 E
Megasini ∧ 126 21.38 N 86.21 E
Meget 88 52.24 N 104.03 E
Megève 62 45.52 N 6.37 E
Mégevette 58 46.12 N 6.30 E
Megezez ∧ 144 9.17 N 39.32 E
Megget Reservoir ⊜[1] 46 55.29 N 3.17 W
Meghālaya □[3] 120 25.30 N 91.15 E
Meghna ≃ 120 22.50 N 90.50 E
Megi-jima I 96 34.24 N 134.03 E
Mégiscane ≃ 190 48.29 N 77.08 W
Mégiscane, Lac ⊜ 190 48.35 N 75.55 W
Meglino, ozero ⊜ 76 58.25 N 35.07 E
Megra, Ross. 24 66.09 N 41.37 E
Megra, Ross. 76 60.10 N 37.13 E
Megri 84 38.56 N 46.16 E
Meguro ◆[8] 268 35.38 N 139.42 E
Meguro ≃ 268 35.37 N 139.45 E
Mehadia 38 44.55 N 22.22 E
Méhaigne ≃ 56 50.32 N 5.13 E
Mehaïguene, Oued ∨ 148 32.15 N 2.59 E
Mehakit 112 2.51 S 115.57 E
Mehanom, mys › 78 44.48 N 35.05 E
Mehar 120 27.11 N 67.49 E
Meharry, Mount ∧ 162 22.59 S 118.35 E
Mehdia 148 35.26 N 1.40 E
Mehede 40 60.27 N 17.24 E
Mehedinți □[6] 38 44.30 N 22.50 E
Meheisa 140 19.37 N 32.57 E
Mehekar 122 20.09 N 76.34 E
Mehendiganj 126 22.49 N 90.32 E
Meherpur 124 23.46 N 88.38 E
Meherrin ≃ 192 36.26 N 76.57 W
Mehetia I 14 17.52 S 148.03 W
Mehidpur 120 23.49 N 75.40 E
Mehikoorma 76 58.14 N 27.28 E
Mehlteuer 54 50.32 N 12.02 E
Mehlville 219 38.30 N 90.19 W
Mehnagar 124 25.53 N 83.07 E
Mehndāwal 124 26.59 N 83.07 E
Mehoopany 210 41.34 N 76.04 W
Mehoopany Creek ≃ 210 41.34 N 76.03 W
Mehpālpur ◆[8] 272a 28.33 N 77.08 E
Mehrābād 128 36.53 N 47.55 E
Mehrābād ◆[8] 267d 35.40 N 51.20 E
Mehram Nagar ◆[8] 272a 28.34 N 77.07 E
Mehrān 128 33.07 N 46.10 E
Mehrān ≃ 128 26.52 N 55.24 E
Mehring 56 49.48 N 6.49 E
Mehrīz 128 31.35 N 54.28 E
Mehrow 264a 52.34 N 13.37 E
Mehrum 263 51.35 N 6.37 E
Mè-hsa-tè 110 19.33 N 97.38 E
Mehtarlām 120 34.39 N 70.10 E
Mehun-sur-Yèvre 50 47.09 N 2.13 E
Mei ≃, Zhg. 100 24.24 N 116.34 E
Mei ≃, Zhg. 100 26.00 N 115.23 E
Mei ≃, Zhg. 105 39.21 N 117.50 E
Meia Meia 154 5.49 S 35.48 E
Meia Ponte, Rio da ≃ 255 18.32 S 49.36 W
Meichang 105 39.22 N 117.10 E
Meichuan 100 30.10 N 115.36 E
Meicun, Zhg. 100 25.30 N 116.56 E
Meicun, Zhg. 106 30.22 N 119.01 E
Meicun, Zhg. 106 30.40 N 119.04 E
Meicun, Zhg. 106 31.33 N 120.24 E
Meide 263 51.11 N 6.55 E
Meiderich ◆[8] 263 51.28 N 6.46 E
Meidling ◆[8] 264b 48.11 N 16.20 E
Meierij ◆[1] 52 51.35 N 5.40 E
Meierkaisong 120 30.54 N 84.31 E
Meiersberg 263 51.17 N 6.57 E
Meig ≃ 46 57.34 N 4.41 W
Meiganga 152 6.31 N 14.11 E
Meigle 46 56.35 N 3.09 W
Meigs 192 31.04 N 84.05 W
Meigs Field ⊠ 278 41.51 N 87.36 W
Meihsien → Meixian 100 24.21 N 116.08 E
Meihua 100 26.02 N 119.40 E
Meihuajie 100 25.14 N 113.05 E
Meijel 52 51.21 N 5.53 E
Meijino-Mori-Minō-kokutei-kōen ♠ 94 34.51 N 135.29 E
Meiji Shrine ⊌[1] 268 35.41 N 139.42 E
Meikeng 100 23.59 N 114.05 E
Meikle Millyea ∧ 44 55.07 N 4.19 W
Meikle Says Law ∧ 46 55.55 N 2.40 W
Meiktila 110 20.52 N 95.52 E
Meila 54 51.09 N 13.13 E
Meilen 58 47.16 N 8.38 E
Meili 106 31.42 N 120.53 E
Meilie 100 26.18 N 117.38 E
Meilin, Zhg. 100 23.18 N 115.58 E
Meilin, Zhg. 106 30.35 N 119.04 E
Meillerie 58 46.24 N 6.43 E
Meilong 100 22.56 N 115.17 E
Meilunyingzi 104 42.18 N 122.10 E
Meina 62 45.47 N 8.32 E
Meine 52 52.23 N 10.32 E
Meiners Oaks 228 34.26 N 119.17 W
Meinerzhagen 56 51.06 N 7.38 E
Meiningen 54 50.34 N 10.25 E
Meinung 100 22.54 N 120.32 E
Meio, Ilha do I 287a 23.02 S 43.17 W
Meiringen 58 46.43 N 8.12 E
Meisburg 56 50.06 N 6.41 E
Meisenheim 56 49.42 N 7.40 E
Meishan, Zhg. 106 31.06 N 119.43 E
Meishan, Zhg. 107 30.02 N 103.49 E
Meissen 54 51.10 N 13.28 E
Meissendorf 52 52.43 N 9.50 E
Meiss Lake ⊜ 204 41.52 N 122.04 W
Meissner ∧ 56 51.12 N 9.50 E
Meitan 102 27.46 N 107.35 E
Meitian 100 25.21 N 112.47 E
Meitingen 56 48.32 N 10.50 E
Meiwa 94 34.33 N 136.39 E
Meixi 106 30.48 N 119.45 E
Meixian, Zhg. 100 24.21 N 116.08 E
Meixian, Zhg. 100 28.52 N 113.38 E
Meiyao 89 49.37 N 124.30 E
Meiyino 140 6.12 N 34.40 E
Meizhai 102 25.30 N 108.50 E
Meizhou 100 23.50 N 117.20 E
Meizhou Dao I 100 25.06 N 119.07 E
Meizhou Wan ⊂ 100 25.06 N 119.00 E
Meizhu 106 31.16 N 119.13 E
Meječkyn, ostrov I 180 65.26 N 178.00 W
Mejerda, Oued (Oued Medjerda) ≃ 36 37.07 N 10.13 E
Mejez el Bab 148 36.39 N 9.37 E
Mejia 126 23.34 N 87.06 E
Mejicanos 236 13.43 N 89.12 W
Mejillones 252 23.06 S 70.27 W
Mejillones, Península ›[1] 252 23.17 S 70.34 W
Mejillones del Sur, Bahía de ⊂ 252 23.03 S 70.27 W
Mejnypil'gyno 74 62.32 N 177.02 E
Mejorada del Campo 266a 40.24 N 3.29 W
Meka 162 27.26 S 116.48 E
Mekada, Garaet el ⁘ 36 36.48 N 8.00 E
Mékambo 152 1.01 N 13.56 E
Mekele 144 13.33 N 39.30 E
Mekerra, Oued ≃ 34 35.00 N 0.45 W
Mekhé 150 15.07 N 16.38 W
Mekhliganj 124 26.21 N 88.55 E
Mekhtar 120 30.28 N 69.22 E
Mékinac ≃ 206 46.51 N 72.46 W
Mekka → Makkah 144 21.27 N 39.49 E
Meknès 148 33.53 N 5.37 W
Meknès □[4] 148 33.50 N 5.30 W
Mekong ≃ 12 10.33 N 105.24 E
Mekongga, Gunung ∧ 112 3.38 S 121.15 E
Mekongga, Pegunungan ⋏ 112 3.35 S 121.15 E
Mékôngk → Mekong ≃ 12 10.33 N 105.24 E
Mekoryuk 180 60.23 N 166.12 W
Mékrou ≃ 150 12.24 N 2.49 E
Mel 64 46.04 N 12.05 E
Melado ≃ 252 35.43 S 71.05 W
Melah, Oued el ∨, Alg. 148 28.21 N 6.00 E
Melah, Oued el ∨, Tun. 148 34.03 N 8.06 E
Melah, Sebkhet el ⊜ 148 29.05 N 1.10 W
Melaka 114 2.12 N 102.15 E
Melaka □[3] 114 2.15 N 102.15 E
Melalap 112 5.14 N 116.00 E
Melandro ≃ 68 40.37 N 15.27 E
Melanesia II 14 13.00 S 164.00 E
Melanesian Basin ✤[1] 14 0.05 N 160.35 E
Melappālaiyam 122 8.42 N 77.43 E
Melara 64 45.03 N 11.11 E
Melaune 54 51.11 N 14.44 E
Melawi ≃ 112 0.05 N 111.29 E
Melayu ≃ 271c 1.27 N 103.42 E
Melbern 216 41.28 N 84.39 W
Melbost 46 58.15 N 6.22 W
Melbourn 42 52.05 N 0.01 E
Melbourne, Austl. 169 37.49 S 144.58 E
Melbourne, Austl. 274b 37.49 S 144.58 E
Melbourne, On., Can. 214 42.49 N 81.33 W
Melbourne, Eng., U.K. 42 52.49 N 1.25 W
Melbourne, Ar., U.S. 194 36.03 N 91.54 W
Melbourne, Fl., U.S. 220 28.04 N 80.36 W
Melbourne, Ia., U.S. 190 41.56 N 93.06 W
Melbourne, University of ⊌[2] 274b 37.48 S 144.58 E
Melbourne Beach 220 28.04 N 80.33 W
Melbourne Island I 176 68.30 N 104.45 W
Melbourne Regional Airport ⊠ 220 28.06 N 80.38 W
Mel'cany 80 54.28 N 44.43 E
Melcher 190 41.13 N 93.14 W
Melchor, Isla I 254 45.08 S 73.57 W
Melchor Múzquiz 232 27.53 N 101.31 W
Melchor Ocampo 196 26.03 N 99.33 W
Melchor Romero ◆[8] 258 34.56 S 58.03 W
Melchtal 58 46.50 N 8.17 E
Melcroft 214 40.03 N 79.24 W
Melderskin ∧ 26 60.01 N 6.05 E
Meldola 66 44.07 N 12.05 E
Meldorf 30 54.05 N 9.05 E
Meldrum Bay 190 45.56 N 83.07 W
Meldrum Creek 182 52.07 N 122.20 W
Mélé, Centraf. 146 9.46 N 21.33 E
Mele, India 272b 22.49 N 88.09 E
Mele, It. 62 44.27 N 8.45 E
Mélé, Baie ⊂ 175f 17.43 S 168.15 E
Mele, Capo › 62 43.57 N 8.10 E
Melechovo 80 56.17 N 41.17 E
Meleck 86 57.25 N 90.12 E
Meleden 144 10.25 N 49.51 E
Melegnano 62 45.21 N 9.19 E
Melekeok 175b 7.29 N 134.38 E
Melekess → Dimitrovgrad 80 54.14 N 49.39 E
Melela ≃ 154 17.04 S 38.36 E
Melena del Sur 240p 22.47 N 82.09 W
Melendiz Dağı ∧ 130 38.07 N 34.25 E
Melendugno 68 40.16 N 18.20 E
Melenki 80 55.20 N 41.38 E
Meleškoviči 78 51.56 N 28.59 E
Meleuz 86 52.58 N 55.55 E
Mélèzes, Rivière aux ≃ 176 57.40 N 69.29 W
Melfa 208 37.39 N 75.45 W
Melfa ≃ 66 41.30 N 13.35 E
Melfi, It. 68 41.00 N 15.39 E
Melfi, Tchad 146 11.04 N 17.56 E
Melfort, Sk., Can. 184 52.52 N 104.36 W
Melfort, Zimb. 154 17.59 S 31.19 E
Melfort, Loch ⊂ 46 56.15 N 5.31 W
Melgaço, Bra. 250 1.47 S 50.44 W
Melgaço, Port. 34 42.07 N 8.16 W
Melgar 246 4.12 N 74.39 W
Melghir, Chott ⊜ 148 34.20 N 6.20 E
Mel'guny 80 52.09 N 40.52 E
Melhus 26 63.17 N 10.16 E
Meli ≃ 150 8.16 N 10.42 W
Meliane, Oued ≃ 36 36.46 N 10.18 E
Meliau 112 0.08 S 110.18 E
Meliau, Gunong ∧ 116 5.50 N 117.14 E
Melibocus ∧ 56 49.42 N 8.40 E
Melichovo, Ross. 78 50.42 N 36.48 E
Melichovo, Ross. 82 55.07 N 37.39 E
Melicuccà 68 38.18 N 15.53 E
Melide, Esp. 34 42.55 N 8.00 W
Melide, Schw. 58 45.57 N 8.57 E
Meligalás 38 37.13 N 21.59 E
Melilla 34 35.19 N 2.58 W
Melilli 70 37.11 N 15.07 E
Melimoyu, Cerro ∧ 254 44.05 S 72.52 W
Melincué 252 33.39 S 61.27 W
Melipilla 252 33.42 S 71.13 W
Mélisey 58 47.45 N 6.35 E
Melissa 68 39.18 N 17.01 E
Melissano 68 39.58 N 18.07 E
Melíssia 267c 38.03 N 23.50 E
Melita 184 49.16 N 101.00 W
Melito di Porto Salvo 68 37.55 N 15.47 E
Melitopol' 78 46.50 N 35.22 E
Melívoia 38 39.45 N 22.48 E
Melk 61 48.14 N 15.20 E
Melk ≃ 61 48.14 N 15.19 E
Melk ⊌[1] 61 48.14 N 15.20 E
Melka Teka 144 6.05 N 43.08 E
Melkbosstrand 158 33.43 S 18.27 E
Melksham 42 51.23 N 2.09 W
Mella ≃ 64 45.13 N 10.13 E
Mellansel 26 63.26 N 18.19 E
Mellau 58 47.21 N 9.53 E
Melle, Dtsch. 52 52.12 N 8.20 E
Melle, Fr. 32 46.13 N 0.09 W
Melleck 64 47.40 N 12.45 E
Mellègue, Oued ≃ 36 36.32 N 8.51 E
Mellen 190 46.19 N 90.39 W
Mellendorf 52 52.33 N 9.43 E
Mellenville 210 42.15 N 73.40 W
Mellerud 26 58.42 N 12.28 E
Mellette 198 45.09 N 98.29 W
Mellier ≃ 56 49.43 N 5.32 E
Melling 262 53.30 N 2.56 W
Mellingen 54 50.56 N 11.23 E
Mellish Reef I[1] 160 17.25 S 155.50 E
Mellish Rise ✤[3] 14 17.00 S 156.00 E
Mellit 140 14.08 N 25.33 E
Mellone, Monte ∧[2] 267a 41.50 N 12.43 E
Mellong Range ⋏ 170 33.06 S 150.43 E
Mellon Udrigle 46 57.55 N 5.39 W
Mellor 262 53.46 N 2.32 W
Mellor Brook 262 53.47 N 2.33 W
Mellösa 40 59.06 N 16.33 E
Mellrichstadt 56 50.26 N 10.18 E
Mellum I 52 53.40 N 8.10 E
Melmerby 44 54.44 N 2.35 W
Melmore 214 41.02 N 83.07 W
Melmoth 158 28.38 S 31.24 E
Mělník 54 50.20 N 14.29 E
Mel'nikovo, Ross. 26 61.05 N 29.22 E
Mel'nikovo, Ross. 86 56.34 N 84.05 E
Mel'nikovo, Taj. 85 40.19 N 70.19 E
Mel'nytsya-Podil's'ka 78 48.37 N 26.10 E
Melo 252 32.22 S 54.11 W
Melo ≃ 248 21.27 S 57.52 W
Melo, Ilha de I 150 11.02 N 15.13 W
Melocheville 206 45.19 N 73.56 W
Meloco 154 13.25 S 39.08 E
Melolo 115b 9.53 S 120.40 E
Melolo ≃ 115b 9.52 S 120.41 E
Melong 152 5.07 N 9.57 E
Melos → Mílos I 38 36.41 N 24.15 E
Melovaja ≃ 83 49.23 N 40.16 E
Melovoj Syrt ∧ 80 52.15 N 52.35 E
Melozitna ≃ 180 64.46 N 155.29 W
Melrose, Austl. 162 27.56 S 121.19 E
Melrose, Austl. 166 32.42 S 146.58 E
Melrose, Scot., U.K. 46 55.36 N 2.44 W
Melrose, Ma., U.S. 207 42.27 N 71.04 W
Melrose, Mn., U.S. 198 45.40 N 94.48 W
Melrose, N.M., U.S. 196 34.25 N 103.37 W
Melrose, N.Y., U.S. 210 42.50 N 73.37 W
Melrose, Oh., U.S. 216 41.05 N 84.25 W
Melrose, Wi., U.S. 190 44.07 N 90.59 W
Melrose ◆[8] 276 40.49 N 73.55 W
Melrose Abbey ⊌[1] 46 55.37 N 2.45 W
Melrose Park, Fl., U.S. 220 26.06 N 80.12 W
Melrose Park, Il., U.S. 216 41.54 N 87.51 W
Melrose Park, N.Y., U.S. 212 42.54 N 76.32 W
Melrose Park, Pa., U.S. 285 40.04 N 75.08 W
Mels 58 47.03 N 9.25 E
Melstone 202 46.35 N 107.52 W
Melsungen 56 51.08 N 9.32 E
Meltaus 24 66.54 N 25.22 E
Meltham, Eng., U.K. 44 53.35 N 1.51 W
Meltham, Eng., U.K. 262 53.36 N 1.51 W
Melton, Austl. 168b 34.05 S 137.59 E
Melton, Austl. 169 37.41 S 144.35 E
Melton Constable 42 52.53 N 1.01 E
Melton Hill Lake ⊜[1] 192 36.00 N 84.15 W
Melton Mowbray 42 52.46 N 0.53 W
Melton Reservoir ⊜[1] 169 37.43 S 144.32 E
Melúa 246 3.55 N 72.50 W
Meluan 112 1.52 N 111.56 E
Meluco 154 12.36 S 39.38 E
Melúli ≃ 154 16.28 S 39.44 E
Melun, Fr. 50 48.32 N 2.40 E
Melun, Mya. 110 20.14 N 93.24 E
Melunga 152 17.16 S 16.24 E
Melūr 122 10.03 N 78.20 E
Melvaig 46 57.48 N 5.49 W
Melvern 198 38.30 N 95.38 W
Melvern Lake ⊜[1] 198 38.30 N 95.50 W
Melvich 46 58.33 N 3.55 W
Melville, Austl. 168a 32.03 S 115.49 E
Melville, Sk., Can. 184 50.55 N 102.48 W
Melville, La., U.S. 194 30.41 N 91.44 W
Melville, N.Y., U.S. 276 40.47 N 73.24 W
Melville ◆[8] 273d 26.11 S 28.00 E
Melville, Cape ›, Austl. 164 14.11 S 144.30 E
Melville, Cape ›, Pil. 116 7.49 N 117.01 E

Symbol	English	Deutsch	Español	Français	Português
≃	River	Fluß	Río	Rivière	Rio
≡	Canal	Kanal	Canal	Canal	Canal
⌞	Waterfall, Rapids	Wasserfall, Stromschnellen	Cascada, Rápidos	Chute d'eau, Rapides	Cascata, Rápidos
ʮ	Strait	Meeresstraße	Estrecho	Détroit	Estreito
⊂	Bay, Gulf	Bucht, Golf	Bahía, Golfo	Baie, Golfe	Baía, Golfo
⊜	Lake, Lakes	See, Seen	Lago, Lagos	Lac, Lacs	Lago, Lagos
⁘	Swamp	Sumpf	Pantano	Marais	Pântano
⍓	Ice Features, Glacier	Eis- und Gletscherformen	Accidentes Glaciales	Formes glaciaires	Acidentes glaciares
⫧	Other Hydrographic Features	Andere Hydrographische Objekte	Otros Elementos Hidrográficos	Autres données hydrographiques	Outros acidentes hidrográficos
✤	Submarine Features	Untermeerische Objekte	Accidentes Submarinos	Formes de relief sous-marin	Acidentes submarinos
□	Political Unit	Politische Einheit	Unidad Politica	Entité politique	Unidade política
⊌	Cultural Institution	Kulturelle Institution	Institución Cultural	Institution culturelle	Institução cultural
⊥	Historical Site	Historische Stätte	Sitio Histórico	Site historique	Sitio histórico
♠	Recreational Site	Erholungs- und Ferienort	Sitio de Recreo	Centre de loisirs	Area de Lazer
⊠	Airport	Flughafen	Aeropuerto	Aéroport	Aeroporto
■	Military Installation	Militäranlage	Instalación Militar	Installation militaire	Instalação militar
◆	Miscellaneous	Verschiedenes	Misceláneo	Divers	Diversos

Melville, Détroit de
— Viscount Melville Sound ⊔ 176 74.10 N 108.00 W
Melville, Lake ◎ 176 53.45 N 59.30 W
Melville Bugt c 16 75.30 N 63.00 W
Melville Hall Airport ⊠ 240d 15.33 N 61.18 W
Melville Hills ⋌² 180 69.15 N 124.00 W
Melville Island I, Austl. 164 11.40 S 131.00 E
Melville Island I, N.T., Can. 16 75.15 N 110.00 W
Melville Island Aboriginal Reserve ◆⁴ 164 11.40 S 131.00 E
Melville Peninsula >¹ 176 68.00 N 84.00 W
Melville Sound ⊔, N.T., Can. 176 68.05 N 107.30 W
Melville Sound ⊔, On., Can. 212 44.57 N 81.05 W
Melvin, Il., U.S. 216 40.34 N 88.15 W
Melvin, Ky., U.S. 192 37.21 N 82.41 W
Melvin, Tx., U.S. 196 31.13 N 99.35 W
Melvin, Lough ◎ 48 54.26 N 8.10 W
Melvindale 214 42.16 N 83.10 W
Melvin Lake ◎ 184 57.08 N 100.15 W
Melyana 148 36.15 N 2.15 E
Mélykút 30 46.13 N 19.24 E
Melzo 62 45.30 N 9.25 E
Memala 112 1.44 S 112.36 E
Mêmar Co ◎ 120 34.15 N 82.20 E
Memāri 126 23.12 N 88.07 E
Memba 154 14.11 S 40.30 E
Membalong 112 3.09 S 107.38 E
Memboro 115b 9.22 S 119.32 E
Membre 56 49.52 N 4.54 E
Même ≐ 50 48.11 N 0.39 E
Memel
— Klaipėda, Liet. 76 55.43 N 21.07 E
Memel, S. Afr. 158 27.43 S 29.30 E
Memel
— Nemunas ≐ 76 55.18 N 21.23 E
Mēmele ≐ 76 56.24 N 24.10 E
Memewin, Lac ◎ 190 46.29 N 78.42 W
Memmert I 52 53.39 N 6.53 E
Memmingen 58 47.59 N 10.11 E
Memo ≐ 246 9.16 N 66.40 W
Memori, Tanjung > 164 0.52 S 134.08 E
Memorial Bridge ◆⁵ 269a 13.44 N 100.30 E
Memorial Stadium ◆ 284b 39.20 N 76.36 W
Memōt 110 11.49 N 106.11 E
Mempawah 112 0.22 N 108.58 E
Memphis, Fl., U.S. 220 27.32 N 82.33 W
Memphis, In., U.S. 218 38.29 N 85.45 W
Memphis, Mi., U.S. 214 42.54 N 82.46 W
Memphis, Mo., U.S. 194 40.27 N 92.10 W
Memphis, Tn., U.S. 194 35.08 N 90.02 W
Memphis, Tx., U.S. 196 34.43 N 100.32 W
Memphis
— Mīt Ruhaynah ⊥ 142 29.51 N 31.15 E
Memphis Naval Air Station ⊠ 194 35.21 N 89.52 W
Memphremagog, Lake ◎ 206 45.05 N 72.15 W
Memsie 46 57.39 N 2.02 W
Mena, Ityo. 144 6.25 N 39.51 E
Mena, Ukr. 78 51.31 N 32.13 E
Mena, Ar., U.S. 194 34.35 N 94.14 W
Menado
— Manado 112 1.29 N 124.51 E
Menaggio 58 46.01 N 9.14 E
Menahga 198 46.45 N 95.06 W
Menai 274a 34.01 S 151.01 E
Menai Bridge 44 53.14 N 4.10 W
Menai Strait ⊔ 44 53.12 N 4.12 W
Ménaka 150 15.55 N 2.24 E
Menaldum 52 53.12 N 5.39 E
Menan 202 43.43 N 111.59 W
Menands 210 42.41 N 73.43 W
Menangina 162 29.50 S 121.54 E
Menantico Creek ≐ 208 39.20 N 75.00 W
Menarandra ≐ 157b 25.17 S 44.30 E
Menard 196 30.55 N 99.47 W
Menard □⁶ 219 40.01 N 89.51 W
Menard Creek ≐ 222 30.29 N 94.50 W
Menars 50 47.38 N 1.24 E
Menasha 190 44.12 N 88.26 W
Menate 112 0.14 S 113.02 E
Menawashei 140 12.40 N 24.59 E
Menchang 105 38.54 N 117.01 E
Menchykury 78 47.04 N 34.48 E
Mencué 254 40.25 S 69.38 W
Mend 89 43.40 N 123.08 E
Mendanau, Pulau I 112 2.51 S 107.26 E
Mendarik, Pulau I 112 1.18 N 107.02 E
Mendatai 102 38.51 N 94.39 E
Mendatica 62 44.05 N 7.49 E
Mendawai 112 2.59 S 113.16 E
Mendawai ≐ 112 3.17 S 113.21 E
Mendaya 115a 8.23 S 114.42 E
Mende 32 44.30 N 3.30 E
Mendebo ∧ 144 6.50 N 39.40 E
Mendel' ≐ 86 58.13 N 90.08 E
Mendelejevsk 80 55.54 N 52.20 E
Menden 56 51.26 N 7.47 E
Menden ◆⁸ 263 51.24 N 6.54 E
Mendenhall, Ms., U.S. 194 31.57 N 89.52 W
Mendenhall, Pa., U.S. 285 39.51 N 75.38 W
Mendenhall, Cape > 180 59.51 N 166.15 W
Mendes 256 22.32 S 43.44 W
Méndez 232 25.07 N 98.34 W
Mendez-Nuñez 116 14.08 N 120.54 E
Mendham 210 40.46 N 74.36 W
Mendi, Ityo. 144 9.50 N 35.06 E
Mendi, Pap. N. Gui. 164 6.10 S 143.40 E
Mendig 56 50.21 N 7.15 E
Mendip Hills ⋌² 42 51.15 N 2.40 W
Mendlesham 42 52.16 N 1.05 E
Mendocino 204 39.18 N 123.47 W
Mendocino, Cape > 204 40.25 N 124.25 W
Mendocino Fracture Zone ✦⁸ 16 40.00 N 145.00 W
Mendola ≐ 70 37.44 N 13.32 E
Mendon, Il., U.S. 219 40.05 N 91.17 W
Mendon, Ma., U.S. 207 42.06 N 71.33 W
Mendon, Mi., U.S. 216 42.00 N 85.27 W
Mendon, N.Y., U.S. 210 43.00 N 77.34 W
Mendon, Oh., U.S. 216 40.40 N 84.31 W
Mendon, Pa., U.S. 279b 40.11 N 79.41 W
Mendota, Ca., U.S. 226 36.45 N 120.22 W
Mendota, Il., U.S. 216 41.32 N 89.07 W
Mendota, Lake ◎ 216 43.05 N 89.25 W
Mendoza, Arg. 252 32.53 S 68.49 W
Mendoza, Perú 248 6.20 S 77.24 W
Mendoza, Ur. 258 34.17 S 56.13 W
Mendoza □⁴ 252 34.30 S 68.30 W
Mendoza ≐ 252 32.21 S 68.18 W
Mendoza, Arroyo de ≐ 258 34.21 S 56.18 W
Mendrisio 58 45.52 N 8.59 E
Mend'ukino 82 54.47 N 38.51 E
Mendung 112 0.31 N 103.13 E
Ménéac 32 48.09 N 2.28 W
Mene de Mauroa 246 10.43 N 71.01 W
Mene Grande 246 9.49 N 70.56 W
Menemen 130 38.36 N 27.04 E
Menen 50 50.48 N 3.07 E
Meneng Point > 174b 0.32 S 166.57 E
Menes 115a 6.23 S 105.55 E
Menfi 70 37.36 N 12.58 E
Mengalum, Pulau I 112 6.16 N 115.12 E
Mengban 102 23.08 N 100.19 E
Mengbang 102 21.28 N 101.19 E
Mengcheng 100 33.17 N 116.33 E
Mengchi ≐ 107 29.47 N 104.56 E
Mengcun 98 38.06 N 117.05 E
Mengdapu 104 41.35 N 123.12 E
Mengede ◆⁸ 263 51.34 N 7.23 E
Mengeh Jek 120 37.02 N 66.07 E
Mengen, Dtsch. 58 48.03 N 9.20 E
Mengen, Tür. 130 40.56 N 32.04 E
Mengeringhausen 56 51.22 N 8.59 E
Mengersgereuth-Hämmern 54 50.24 N 11.07 E
Menges Mills 208 39.52 N 76.54 W
Menggala 112 4.28 S 105.17 E
Menggu 102 26.34 N 102.57 E
Menggubao 104 42.27 N 122.23 E
Menggudai 102 38.10 N 108.15 E
Menghai 102 22.00 N 100.26 E
Menghe 106 32.03 N 119.47 E
Menghun 102 21.44 N 100.23 E
Mengjiacun 106 31.33 N 118.46 E
Mengjiagang 89 46.22 N 130.40 E
Mengjiatai 104 42.06 N 123.21 E
Mengjiawan 102 38.35 N 109.25 E
Mengjiawopeng 104 41.22 N 121.51 E
Mengjiayuanjia 105 40.52 N 118.08 E
Mengjiazhai 269b 31.18 N 121.19 E
Mengka 102 25.10 N 98.01 E
Mengkibol 114 1.58 N 103.20 E
Mengkuang 114 3.11 N 103.24 E
Menglian 102 22.20 N 99.38 E
Menglinghausen ◆⁸ 263 51.28 N 7.25 E
Mengluchang 107 29.19 N 103.35 E
Mengmucun 106 31.59 N 119.01 E
Mengong 152 2.56 N 11.25 E
Mengqigou 104 42.00 N 121.08 E
Mengshan 102 24.18 N 110.30 E
Meng Shan ⋌, Zhg. 98 35.44 N 117.45 E
Meng Shan ⋌, Zhg. 104 41.50 N 121.10 E
Mengtong 107 30.44 N 105.53 E
Mengulek, gora ∧ 86 50.58 N 89.30 E
Mengwang 102 22.26 N 100.34 E
Mengyin 98 35.45 N 117.57 E
Mengzhe 102 22.02 N 100.15 E
Mengzhi 102 24.10 N 99.46 E
Mengzi 102 23.22 N 103.20 E
Menihek Lakes ◎ 176 54.00 N 66.35 W
Ménil-la-Tour 56 48.46 N 5.52 E
Menindee 166 32.24 S 142.26 E
Menindee Lake ◎ 166 32.21 S 142.20 E
Meningie 166 35.42 S 139.20 E
Menjiaqiangzi 104 42.29 N 121.19 E
Menkoutang 106 31.01 N 119.27 E
Menlo 224 46.37 N 123.38 W
Menlo Park 226 37.27 N 122.10 W
Menlo Park Mall ◆⁹ 276 40.32 N 74.20 W
Menlo Park Terrace 276 40.32 N 74.20 W
Mennecy 261 48.34 N 2.26 E
Mennetou-sur-Cher 50 47.16 N 1.53 E
Menninghüffen 52 52.13 N 8.43 E
Menno 198 43.14 N 97.34 W
Meno, Indon. 164 3.52 S 135.31 E
Meno, Ok., U.S. 196 36.23 N 98.10 W
Menominee 190 45.06 N 87.36 W
Menominee ≐ 190 45.05 N 87.36 W
Menominee Indian Reservation ◆⁴ 190 45.00 N 88.45 W
Menomonee ≐ 216 43.02 N 87.54 W
Menomonee Falls 216 43.10 N 88.07 W
Menomonie 190 44.52 N 91.55 W
Menongue 152 14.36 S 17.48 E
Menor, Mar c 34 37.43 N 0.48 W
Menorca I 34 40.00 N 4.00 E
Mens 62 44.49 N 5.45 E
Menslage 52 52.41 N 7.49 E
Menston 44 53.53 N 1.44 W
Menstrup 41 55.13 N 11.36 E
Mentana 66 42.02 N 12.38 E
Mentasta Lake 180 62.55 N 143.45 W
Mentasta Mountains ⋌ 180 62.40 N 143.07 W
Mentawai, Kepulauan II 108 2.00 S 99.30 E
Mentawai, Selat ⊔ 108 1.45 S 100.00 E
Menteleke 114 3.29 N 102.21 E
Menteke, peski ⋌² 80 47.20 N 50.40 E
Menteng ◆⁸ 269e 6.12 S 106.50 E
Menteroda 54 51.18 N 10.33 E
Menthon-Saint-Bernard 62 45.51 N 6.12 E
Menton 62 43.47 N 7.30 E
Mentone, Austl. 274b 37.59 S 145.05 E
Mentone
— Menton, Fr. 62 43.47 N 7.30 E
Mentone, Ca., U.S. 228 34.05 N 117.08 W
Mentone, In., U.S. 216 41.10 N 86.02 W
Mentone, Tx., U.S. 196 31.42 N 103.36 W
Mentor, Ky., U.S. 218 38.53 N 84.14 W
Mentor, Oh., U.S. 214 41.39 N 81.20 W
Mentor-on-the-Lake 214 41.42 N 81.21 W
Mentougou 105 39.56 N 116.03 E
Mentzdam ◎¹ 158 33.10 S 25.09 E
Menucourt 261 49.02 N 1.59 E
Menuma 94 36.13 N 139.23 E
Men'uša 76 58.23 N 30.42 E
Menyamya 164 7.10 S 146.00 E
Menyapa, Gunung ∧ 112 1.05 N 116.05 E
Menyuan 102 37.27 N 101.48 E
Menza ≐ 88 50.14 N 108.38 E
Menzel Bourguiba 148 37.10 N 9.48 E
Menzel Bou Zelfa 36 36.41 N 10.36 E
Menzel Djemil 36 37.14 N 9.55 E
Menzelen 56 51.37 N 6.32 E
Menzelerheide 263 51.37 N 6.31 E
Menzelinsk 80 55.43 N 53.08 E
Menzel Temime 148 36.47 N 10.59 E
Menzenschwand 58 47.49 N 8.04 E
Menzies 162 29.41 S 121.02 E
Menzies, Mount ∧ 24 73.30 S 61.50 E
Menziken 58 47.14 N 8.12 E
Meobbaai c 156 24.25 S 14.34 E
Meola Āgri 272a 28.42 N 77.23 E
Meolo 64 45.37 N 12.27 E
Meon ≐ 42 50.48 N 1.15 W
Meopham 260 51.22 N 0.22 E
Meopham Station 260 51.23 N 0.21 E
Meoqui 232 28.17 N 105.29 W
Meota 184 53.02 N 108.27 W
Méouge ≐ 62 44.16 N 5.50 E
Méounes-lès-Montrieux 62 43.17 N 5.58 E
Mepal 42 52.24 N 0.07 E
Mepiskaro, gora ∧ 84 41.50 N 42.40 E
Meppel 52 52.42 N 6.11 E
Meppen 52 52.41 N 7.17 E
Meqerghane, Sebkha ≐ 148 26.19 N 1.20 E
Meqruur 174q 9.31 N 138.09 E
Mequinenza, Embalse de ◎¹ 34 41.20 N 0.05 E
Mequon 216 43.13 N 87.59 W
Mer 50 47.42 N 1.30 E
Mera ≐ 58 46.11 N 9.25 E
Merah 112 0.50 N 116.48 E
Merai 164 4.05 S 152.19 E
Merak 115a 5.56 S 106.00 E
Meråker 26 63.26 N 11.45 E
Merakurak 115a 6.53 S 111.59 E
Meramangye, Lake ◎ 162 28.25 S 132.13 E
Merambéllou, Kólpos c 38 35.14 N 25.47 E
Meramec ≐ 194 38.23 N 90.21 W
Meramec Caverns ⊥⁵ 219 38.15 N 91.06 W
Meramec State Park ◆ 219 38.14 N 91.05 W
Meran
— Merano, It. 64 46.40 N 11.09 E
Meran, Nig. 273a 6.38 N 3.16 E
Meranggau 112 0.12 S 110.17 E
Merangin ≐ 112 2.09 S 102.47 E
Merano (Meran) 64 46.40 N 11.09 E
Merapi, Gunung ∧ 115a 8.03 S 114.15 E
Merapoh 114 4.41 N 101.59 E
Merasheen 186 47.25 N 54.21 W
Merasheen Island I 186 47.30 N 54.15 W
Merate 62 45.42 N 9.25 E
Meratus, Pegunungan ⋌ 112 2.45 S 115.40 E
Merauke 164 8.28 S 140.20 E
Merauke ≐ 164 8.30 S 140.24 E
Merbabu, Gunung ∧ 115a 7.27 S 110.26 E
Merbau, Indon. 114 2.16 N 99.50 E
Merbau, Indon. 114 1.07 N 102.33 E
Merbein 166 34.11 S 142.04 E
Merca
— Marka 144 1.43 N 44.53 E
Mercaderes 246 1.47 N 77.10 W
Mercantour, Parc National du ◆ 62 44.10 N 7.00 E
Mercāra 122 12.25 N 75.44 E
Mercatale 66 43.15 N 12.08 E
Mercato San Severino 68 40.47 N 14.46 E
Mercato Saraceno 66 43.57 N 12.12 E
Merced 226 37.18 N 120.28 W
Merced □⁶ 226 37.15 N 120.40 W
Merced ≐ 226 37.21 N 120.58 W
Merced, Lake ◎ 282 37.43 N 122.29 W
Merced, North Fork ≐ 226 37.37 N 120.03 W
Merced, South Fork ≐ 226 37.39 N 119.53 W
Merced Airport ⊠ 226 37.17 N 120.31 W
Mercedario, Cerro ∧ 252 31.59 S 70.07 W
Mercedes, Arg. 252 29.12 S 58.05 W
Mercedes, Arg. 252 33.40 S 65.28 W
Mercedes, Arg. 258 34.39 S 59.27 W
Mercedes, Pil. 116 14.07 N 123.01 E
Mercedes, Tx., U.S. 196 26.08 N 97.54 W
Mercedes, Ur. 252 33.16 S 58.01 W
Mercer, N.Z. 172 37.16 S 175.03 E
Mercer, Mo., U.S. 194 40.30 N 93.31 W
Mercer, Oh., U.S. 216 40.40 N 84.35 W
Mercer, Pa., U.S. 214 41.13 N 80.14 W
Mercer, Wi., U.S. 190 46.09 N 90.03 W
Mercer □⁶, N.J., U.S. 208 40.13 N 74.45 W
Mercer □⁶, Oh., U.S. 216 40.33 N 84.34 W
Mercer □⁶, Pa., U.S. 214 41.14 N 80.15 W
Mercer Island 224 47.35 N 122.15 W
Mercersburg 188 39.49 N 77.54 W
Mercerville 208 40.14 N 74.41 W
Mercês, Bra. 256 21.12 S 43.21 W
Mercês, Port. 266c 38.47 N 9.19 W
Merchants Bay c 176 67.10 N 62.50 W
Merchants Millpond ◎ 208 36.26 N 76.41 W
Merchantville 285 39.56 N 75.04 W
Merchong ≐ 114 3.03 N 103.27 E
Merchtem 50 50.58 N 4.14 E
Mercier (Saint-Philomène) 275a 45.19 N 73.45 W
Mercier, Pont ◆⁵ 275a 45.25 N 73.39 W
Mercoal 182 53.10 N 117.05 W
Mercogliano 68 40.55 N 14.44 E
Mercury 204 36.40 N 115.59 W
Mercury Islands II 172 36.35 S 175.55 E
Mercy, Cape > 176 64.53 N 63.32 W
Mercy Bay c 176 74.05 N 119.00 W
Mercy-le-Bas 56 49.23 N 5.45 E
Merdeka Bridge ◆⁵ 271c 1.18 N 103.53 E
Mére, Fr. 261 48.47 N 1.49 E
Mere, Eng., U.K. 42 51.06 N 2.16 W
Mere, Eng., U.K. 262 53.20 N 2.25 W
Mere Brow 262 53.40 N 2.53 W
Mereckij 85 43.48 N 74.42 E
Mereclough 262 53.46 N 2.11 W
Meredale 273d 26.17 S 27.59 E
Meredith, Austl. 169 37.51 S 144.04 E
Meredith, N.H., U.S. 188 43.39 N 71.30 W
Meredith, Cape > 254 52.15 S 60.39 W
Meredith, Lake ◎¹ 196 35.36 N 101.42 W
Meredosia 219 39.50 N 90.34 W
Meredosia Lake ◎ 219 39.52 N 90.33 W
Mereeg 144 3.46 N 47.18 E
Merefa 78 49.49 N 36.03 E
Méré Lava I 175f 14.25 S 168.03 E
Merelbeke 50 51.00 N 3.45 E
Mereni 38 46.58 N 29.04 E
Merenkurkku (Norra Kvarken) ⊔ 26 63.36 N 20.43 E
Merevari ≐ 246 4.28 N 63.57 W
Méréville 50 48.19 N 2.05 E
Merewa 144 7.40 N 37.00 E
Merewether 170 32.57 S 151.46 E
Mereworth 260 51.15 N 0.23 E
Mergenevo 80 49.56 N 51.17 E
Mergozzo 58 45.58 N 8.26 E
Mergui (Myeik) 110 12.26 N 98.36 E
Mergui Archipelago II 110 12.00 N 98.00 E
Merḫavya 132 32.36 N 35.19 E
Meria 272b 22.59 N 88.20 E
Meribah 166 34.42 S 140.51 E
Méribel 62 45.25 N 6.34 E
Meriç 130 41.11 N 26.25 E
Meriç (Marica) (Évros) ≐ 38 40.52 N 26.12 E
Méricourt 50 50.24 N 2.52 E
Mérida, Esp. 34 38.55 N 6.20 W
Mérida, Méx. 200 32.39 N 114.58 W
Mérida, Méx. 232 20.58 N 89.37 W
Merida, Pil. 116 10.55 N 124.32 E
Mérida, Ven. 246 8.36 N 71.08 W
Mérida □³ 246 8.30 N 71.10 W
Mérida, Cordillera de ⋌ 246 8.40 N 71.00 W
Meridale 210 42.22 N 74.57 W
Meriden, Eng., U.K. 42 52.26 N 1.37 W
Meriden, Ct., U.S. 207 41.32 N 72.48 W
Meriden, N.J., U.S. 276 40.57 N 74.28 W
Meridian, Id., U.S. 202 43.36 N 116.23 W
Meridian, Ms., U.S. 194 32.21 N 88.42 W
Meridian, N.Y., U.S. 210 43.09 N 76.32 W
Meridian, Pa., U.S. 214 40.51 N 79.58 W
Meridian, Tx., U.S. 222 31.55 N 97.39 W
Meridian Hills 218 39.53 N 86.09 W
Meridian Naval Air Station ⊠ 194 32.33 N 88.34 W
Meridianville 194 34.51 N 86.34 W
Mériel 261 49.05 N 2.12 E
Mérignac 32 44.50 N 0.42 W
Merigold 194 33.50 N 90.43 W
Merikarvia 26 61.51 N 21.30 E
Merimbula 166 36.53 S 149.54 E
Merín, Laguna (Lagoa Mirim) c 252 32.45 S 52.50 W
Merinda 166 20.01 S 148.10 E
Mering 60 48.16 N 10.59 E
Meringa 146 10.44 N 12.09 E
Merin Gubai 144 1.26 N 44.20 E
Meringur 166 34.24 S 141.16 E
Merino 198 40.28 N 103.21 W
Merinos 252 32.24 S 56.54 W
Merion Station 285 39.59 N 75.15 W
Merir I 108 4.19 N 132.19 E
Merishausen 58 47.45 N 8.37 E
Merit 222 33.13 N 96.17 W
Merivale Gardens 212 45.19 N 75.44 W
Meriwether Farms 285 39.58 N 75.34 W
Merizo 174p 13.16 N 144.40 E
Merke 85 42.52 N 73.11 E
Merkel 196 32.28 N 100.00 W
Merken 56 50.50 N 6.24 E
Merkendorf 56 49.12 N 10.42 E
Merkinė 76 54.10 N 24.10 E
Merklin 60 49.34 N 13.07 E
Merklingen 58 48.30 N 9.44 E
Merkourovoúni ∧ 267c 37.54 N 23.48 E
Merksem 50 51.15 N 4.27 E
Merksplas 56 51.22 N 4.52 E
Merkulovići 76 52.58 N 30.36 E
Merkys ≐ 76 54.10 N 24.11 E
Merlara 64 45.10 N 11.26 E
Merlejevo 82 55.05 N 37.13 E
Merlimau, Pulau I 271c 1.17 N 103.42 E
Merlimont-Plage 50 50.28 N 1.35 E
Merlin, On., Can. 214 42.14 N 82.14 W
Merlin, Or., U.S. 202 42.31 N 123.25 W
Merlin Seamount ✦³ 14 9.05 S 150.44 W
Merlo, Arg. 252 32.21 S 65.02 W
Merlo, Arg. 258 34.40 S 58.45 W
Merlo □⁵ 288 34.40 S 58.45 W
Merlo, Aeródromo ⊠ 288 34.41 S 58.45 W
Merlynston 274b 37.43 S 144.58 E
Mermaid Beach 171a 28.03 S 153.27 E
Mern 41 55.03 N 12.04 E
Merna 198 41.29 N 99.45 W
Mernye 30 46.30 N 17.50 E
Meroe ⊥ 140 16.56 N 33.43 E
Meron 132 32.59 N 35.26 E
Meron, Hare ∧ 132 32.58 N 35.25 E
Meros, Ponta dos > 256 23.13 S 44.21 W
Merotai Besar 112 4.26 N 117.46 E
Merouana 34 35.38 N 5.55 E
Merouane, Chott ◎ 148 34.00 N 6.02 E
Mer'oža 76 59.02 N 36.23 E
Merredin 162 31.29 S 118.16 E
Merrick 276 40.39 N 73.33 W
Merrick ∧ 46 55.08 N 4.29 W
Merrick Bay c 276 40.38 N 73.33 W
Merrickville 212 44.55 N 75.50 W
Merri Creek ≐ 169 37.48 S 145.01 E
Merriewold Lake 210 41.22 N 74.12 W
Merrifield 284c 38.52 N 77.13 W
Merrill, Ia., U.S. 198 42.43 N 96.14 W
Merrill, Mi., U.S. 190 43.24 N 84.19 W
Merrill, Or., U.S. 202 42.01 N 121.35 W
Merrill, Wi., U.S. 190 45.10 N 89.41 W
Merrillan 190 44.27 N 90.50 W
Merrill C. Meigs Field ⊠ 278 41.52 N 87.37 W
Merrill Lake ◎ 212 44.55 N 77.24 W
Merrillville 216 41.28 N 87.19 W
Merrimac 207 42.49 N 71.00 W
Merrimack ≐ 188 42.49 N 70.49 W
Merrimack College ⊻² 283 42.40 N 71.08 W
Merrimac Terrace 283 42.49 N 71.00 W
Merriman, S. Afr. 158 31.13 S 23.38 E
Merriman, Ne., U.S. 198 42.55 N 101.42 W
Merrionette Park 278 41.41 N 87.42 W
Merriott 42 50.54 N 2.48 W
Merritt, B.C., Can. 182 50.07 N 120.47 W
Merritt, Wa., U.S. 224 47.47 N 120.51 W
Merritt, Lake ◎¹ 282 37.48 N 122.16 W
Merritt Island 220 28.21 N 80.42 W
Merritt Island I 220 28.33 N 80.40 W
Merritt Reservoir ◎¹ 198 42.35 N 100.55 W
Merriwa 166 32.08 S 150.21 E
Mer Rouge 194 32.46 N 91.47 W
Merrow 207 41.49 N 72.18 W
Merrygoen 166 31.50 S 149.14 E
Merrylands 274a 33.50 S 150.59 E
Merrymount Park ◆ 283 42.16 N 71.01 W
Merryville 194 30.45 N 93.32 W
Mersa Fatma 144 14.55 N 40.20 E
Mersa Matruh
— Marsā Matrūh 140 31.21 N 27.14 E
Mersch 56 49.46 N 6.06 E
Merscheid ◆⁸ 263 51.10 N 7.01 E
Merse V 46 55.39 N 2.15 W
Mersea Island I 42 51.47 N 0.55 E
Merseburg 54 51.21 N 11.59 E
Mersey ≐, Austl. 166 41.10 S 146.22 E
Mersey ≐, N.S., Can. 186 44.02 N 64.43 W
Mersey ≐, Eng., U.K. 44 53.25 N 3.00 W
Merseyside □⁶ 44 53.25 N 2.50 W
Mersey Tunnel ◆⁵ 262 53.24 N 3.00 W
Mersin
— İçel 130 36.48 N 34.38 E
Mersing 114 2.26 N 103.50 E
Mers-les-Bains 50 50.04 N 1.23 E
Mērsrags 76 57.21 N 23.07 E
Merstham 260 51.16 N 0.09 W
Merta 120 26.39 N 74.02 E
Merta Road 120 26.43 N 73.55 E
Merthyr Tydfil 42 51.46 N 3.23 W
Merti 154 1.04 N 38.40 E
Mertingen 56 48.39 N 10.47 E
Mértola 34 37.38 N 7.40 W
Merton, Austl. 169 36.59 S 145.42 E
Merton, Wi., U.S. 216 43.08 N 88.18 W
Merton ◆⁸ 42 51.25 N 0.12 W
Mertz Glacier Tongue ⊓ 9 67.40 S 144.45 E
Mertzon 196 31.16 N 100.49 W
Mertztown 208 40.30 N 75.40 W
Méru, Fr. 50 49.14 N 2.08 E
Meru, Kenya 154 0.03 N 37.39 E
Meru, Mount ∧ 154 3.14 S 36.45 E
Meru National Park ◆ 154 0.10 N 38.15 E
Meruoca 250 3.28 S 40.28 W
Merv
— Mary 128 37.36 N 61.50 E
Mervans 58 46.48 N 5.11 E
Merville 50 50.38 N 2.38 E
Mervin 184 53.20 N 108.53 W
Merwede 158 31.38 S 23.48 E
Merweville 158 32.40 S 21.31 E
Merwin, Lake ◎¹ 224 45.59 N 122.26 W
Merxleben 54 51.07 N 10.40 E
Mery 82 55.49 N 36.36 E
Méry-la-Bataille 50 49.33 N 2.38 E
Méry-sur-Oise 261 49.04 N 2.11 E
Méry-sur-Seine 50 48.30 N 3.53 E
Merzdorf 54 51.23 N 14.32 E
Merzhausen 58 47.58 N 7.49 E
Merzifon 130 40.53 N 35.29 E
Merzig 56 49.27 N 6.38 E
Mesa, Micron. 175c 7.21 N 151.51 E
Mesa, Moç. 154 13.00 S 39.33 E
Mesa, S. Afr. 158 26.29 S 26.59 E
Mesa, Az., U.S. 200 33.25 N 111.49 W
Mesa ≐ 34 41.15 N 1.48 W
Mesabi Range ⋌ 190 47.30 N 92.50 W
Mesachie Lake 224 48.49 N 124.07 W
Mesa del Nayar 234 22.16 N 104.35 W
Mesa de Santa Rita 234 23.04 N 105.31 W
Mesagne 68 40.33 N 17.49 E
Mes'agutovo 86 55.35 N 58.20 E
Mesamēna 152 3.44 N 12.50 E
Mesa Mountain ∧ 200 37.55 N 106.38 W
Mesarás, Kólpos c 38 34.58 N 24.36 E
Mesa Verde National Park ◆ 200 37.13 N 108.30 W
Mescalero 200 33.09 N 105.46 W
Mescalero Apache Indian Reservation ◆⁴ 200 33.12 N 105.40 W
Meščerino, Ross. 76 53.37 N 37.23 E
Meščerino, Ross. 82 55.11 N 38.21 E
Meščerskij 265b 55.40 N 37.25 E
Meščerskoje 82 55.17 N 37.38 E
Meschede 56 51.20 N 8.17 E
Meschetskij chrebet ⋌ 84 41.48 N 42.30 E
Mescit Tepe ∧ 130 40.22 N 41.11 E
Meščovsk 76 54.19 N 35.17 E
Meščura 24 63.20 N 50.52 E
Mese 58 46.17 N 9.21 E
Mèsè Atet 110 18.38 N 97.39 E
Mesen-Bucht
— Mezenskaja guba c 24 66.40 N 43.45 E
Mesero 266b 45.30 N 8.51 E
Mesewa
— Mitsiwa 144 15.38 N 39.28 E
Mesfinto 144 13.20 N 37.19 E
Mesgarābād 267d 35.37 N 51.31 E
Mesgouez, Lac ◎ 176 51.24 N 75.05 W
Meshed
— Mashhad 128 36.18 N 59.36 E
Meshgīn Shahr 128 38.24 N 47.40 E
Meshomasic Mountain ∧ 207 41.38 N 72.32 W
Meshoppen 210 41.34 N 76.03 W
Meshoppen Creek ≐ 210 41.37 N 76.03 W
Mesick 190 44.24 N 85.42 W
Mesier, Canal ⊔ 254 48.20 S 74.33 W
Mesilinka ≐ 182 56.09 N 124.28 W
Mesilla 200 32.16 N 106.48 W
Mesillas, Méx. 234 23.14 N 106.03 W
Mesillas, Méx. 234 23.33 N 103.35 W
Mesima ≐ 68 38.30 N 15.55 E
Meskiana 148 35.39 N 7.41 E
Meskiana, Oued ≐ 36 35.49 N 7.53 E
Meskine 146 11.25 N 15.21 E
Meškuičiai 76 56.05 N 23.28 E
Meskum 114 1.34 N 102.01 E
Meslay-du-Maine 32 47.57 N 0.33 W
Meslay-le-Grenet 50 48.22 N 1.23 E
Mesnil-Val-Plage 50 50.03 N 1.20 E
Mesocco 58 46.23 N 9.14 E
Mesola 66 44.55 N 12.14 E
Mesolcina, Valle V 58 46.20 N 9.10 E
Mesolóngion 38 38.21 N 21.17 E
Mesomikenda Lake ◎ 190 47.40 N 81.53 W
Mesopotamia 214 41.27 N 80.57 W
Mesopotamia □⁹ 128 34.00 N 44.00 E
Mesoraca 68 39.05 N 16.48 E
Mesóyia □⁹ 267c 37.56 N 23.53 E
Mespelbrunn ⊥ 56 49.54 N 9.19 E
Mesquita, Bra. 255 19.13 S 42.35 W
Mesquita, Bra. 256 22.48 S 43.26 W
Mesquite, Nv., U.S. 204 36.48 N 114.03 W
Mesquite, Tx., U.S. 222 32.46 N 96.35 W
Messach Mellet ⋌² 146 24.30 N 11.35 E
Messalo ≐ 154 11.40 S 40.26 E
Messaoud, Oued V 148 27.28 N 0.21 W
Messdorf 54 52.43 N 11.33 E
Messina, It. 68 38.11 N 15.33 E
Messina, S. Afr. 156 22.23 S 30.00 E
Messina □⁴ 68 38.03 N 14.52 E
Messina, Stretto di ⊔ 70 38.15 N 15.35 E
Messinge ≐ 154 11.34 S 35.25 E
Messingham 44 53.32 N 0.39 W
Messini 38 37.04 N 22.00 E
Messinía □⁵ 38 37.11 N 21.57 E
Messiniakós Kólpos c 38 36.58 N 22.00 E
Messix Peak ∧ 202 41.29 N 112.31 W
Messkirch 58 47.59 N 9.07 E
Messojacha ≐ 74 67.52 N 77.27 E
Messondo 152 3.43 N 10.28 E
Messstetten 58 48.11 N 8.58 E
Messy 261 48.58 N 2.42 E
Mestá 38 38.15 N 25.55 E
Mesta (Néstos) ≐ 38 40.41 N 24.44 E
Mestasa 148 35.07 N 4.25 W
Městečko 60 50.03 N 13.52 E
Mesteghanem 148 35.51 N 0.07 E
Mesteghanem □⁵ 148 36.00 N 0.30 E
Mestia 84 43.03 N 42.43 E
Mestlin 54 53.35 N 11.56 E
Město Touškov 60 49.46 N 13.15 E
Mestre 64 45.29 N 12.15 E
Mestrino 64 45.26 N 11.45 E
Mesudiye 130 40.28 N 37.46 E
Mesuji ≐ 112 4.08 S 105.52 E
Mesum 52 52.13 N 7.29 E
Meszah Peak ∧ 180 58.28 N 131.26 W
Meta, It. 68 40.39 N 14.24 E
Meta, Mo., U.S. 219 38.18 N 92.09 W
Meta □⁵ 246 3.30 N 73.00 W
Meta ≐ 246 6.12 N 67.28 W
Métabief 58 46.47 N 6.21 E
Metagācha 272b 22.38 N 88.31 E
Metahara 144 8.54 N 39.55 E
Meta Incognita Peninsula >¹ 176 62.45 N 68.30 W
Metairie 194 29.59 N 90.09 W
Metaline Falls 202 48.51 N 117.22 W
Metallifere, Colline ⋌ 66 43.15 N 11.00 E
Metallostroj 265a 59.47 N 30.33 E
Metamora, Il., U.S. 190 40.47 N 89.21 W
Metamora, In., U.S. 218 39.26 N 85.08 W
Metamora, Mi., U.S. 216 42.56 N 83.17 W
Metamora, Oh., U.S. 216 41.42 N 83.54 W
Metán 252 25.29 S 64.57 W
Metangula 154 12.43 S 34.49 E
Metapán 236 14.20 N 89.27 W
Metapontum ⊥ 68 40.23 N 16.50 E
Metarica 154 14.20 S 36.48 E
Metates 234 23.46 N 106.02 W
Metaurilia 66 43.49 N 13.03 E
Metauro ≐ 66 43.50 N 13.03 E
Metcalfe 212 45.14 N 75.28 W
Metchosin 224 48.22 N 123.33 W
Metechi 84 41.55 N 44.21 E
Metedeconk, South Branch ≐ 208 40.04 N 74.09 W
Meteghan 186 44.11 N 66.10 W
Metelen 52 52.08 N 7.12 E
Metema 144 12.57 N 36.12 E
Metéora ✦¹ 38 39.43 N 21.38 E
Meteor Crater ⊥⁶ 200 35.02 N 111.02 W
Meteor Seamount ✦³ 8 48.00 S 8.30 E
Metepec, Méx. 234 19.15 N 99.36 W
Metepec, Méx. 234 18.56 N 98.28 W
Metharaw 110 16.12 N 98.08 E
Metheringham 44 53.08 N 0.24 W
Methil 46 56.10 N 3.01 W
Methler 263 51.35 N 7.37 E
Methlick 46 57.25 N 2.14 W
Methóni 38 36.50 N 21.43 E
Methow 182 48.07 N 120.00 W
Methow ≐ 202 48.03 N 119.53 W
Methuen 207 42.43 N 71.11 W
Methven, N.Z. 172 43.38 S 171.39 E
Methven, Scot., U.K. 46 56.25 N 3.34 W
Methwold 42 52.31 N 0.33 E
Metica ≐ 246 4.09 N 72.55 W
Metiskow 184 52.24 N 110.38 W
Metković 36 43.03 N 17.39 E
Metlakatla, B.C., Can. 182 54.20 N 130.27 W
Metlakatla, Ak., U.S. 182 55.08 N 131.35 W
Metlaoui 148 34.20 N 8.24 E
Metlatonoc 234 17.11 N 98.20 W
Metlika 36 45.39 N 15.19 E
Metlili, Oued V 148 31.54 N 4.53 E
Metlili ech Chaâmba 148 32.18 N 3.40 E
Metnitz 58 46.59 N 14.13 E
Meto, Bayou ≐ 194 34.05 N 91.26 W
Metolius ≐ 202 44.36 N 121.17 W
Metompkin Bay c 208 37.45 N 75.35 W
Metompkin Inlet c 208 37.41 N 75.35 W
Metro 115a 5.05 S 105.20 E
Metropolis 194 37.09 N 88.43 W
Metropolitan 190 46.00 N 87.53 W
Metropolitan Beach ◆ 281 42.35 N 82.48 W
Metropolitan Museum of Art ⊻ 276 40.47 N 73.58 W
Metropolitan Oakland International Airport ⊠ 226 37.43 N 122.13 W
Metschow 54 53.49 N 12.58 E
Metsematluku 156 24.01 S 24.40 E
Metsera 154 2.35 S 26.07 E
Métsovon 38 39.46 N 21.11 E
Mettawa 278 42.14 N 87.56 W
Metten 60 48.51 N 12.55 E
Mettendorf 56 49.57 N 6.19 E
Metter 192 32.23 N 82.03 W
Mettet 56 50.19 N 4.40 E
Mettetal Airport ⊠ 281 42.21 N 83.27 W
Mettingen 52 52.18 N 7.46 E
Mettlach 56 49.30 N 6.36 E
Mettmach 60 48.10 N 13.21 E
Mettmann 56 51.15 N 6.58 E
Mettray 50 47.27 N 0.39 E
Mettuppālaiyam 122 11.18 N 76.57 E
Mettūr 122 11.48 N 77.48 E
Metu 144 8.20 N 35.36 E
Metuchen 276 40.32 N 74.21 W
Metuge 154 12.53 S 40.34 E
Metulla 132 33.17 N 35.35 E
Metundo, Ilha I 154 11.10 S 40.41 E
Metz 56 49.08 N 6.10 E
Metzervisse 56 49.19 N 6.17 E
Metzger 224 45.26 N 122.45 W
Metzingen 56 48.32 N 9.17 E
Metzkausen 263 51.16 N 6.57 E
Metztitlán 234 20.36 N 98.45 W
Metztitlán, Laguna ◎ 234 20.40 N 98.50 W
Meu ≐ 32 48.02 N 1.47 W
Meudon 261 48.48 N 2.14 E
Meudon, Bois de ◆ 261 48.47 N 2.12 E
Meul ≐ 158 27.56 S 28.50 E
Meulaboh 114 4.09 N 96.08 E
Meulan 50 49.01 N 1.54 E
Meulebeke 50 50.57 N 3.17 E
Meung-sur-Loire 50 47.50 N 1.42 E
Meureubo ≐ 114 4.09 N 96.09 E
Meureudu 114 5.16 N 96.16 E
Meursault 58 46.59 N 4.46 E
Meurthe ≐ 32 48.47 N 6.09 E
Meurthe-et-Moselle □⁵ 32 48.35 N 6.10 E
Meuse 58 47.59 N 5.33 E
Meuse □⁵ 32 49.00 N 5.30 E
Meuse (Maas) ≐ 30 51.49 N 5.01 E
Meuselwitz 54 51.02 N 12.17 E
Meuvette ≐ 50 48.45 N 1.08 E
Meux Creek ≐ 212 44.07 N 81.02 W
Mevagissey 42 50.16 N 4.48 W
Mevang 152 0.07 N 11.05 E
Mewāt Plain ≐ 124 27.40 N 77.15 E
Mexborough 44 53.30 N 1.17 W
Mexia 222 31.40 N 96.28 W
Mexia Lake ◎¹ 222 31.39 N 96.36 W
Mexiana, Ilha I 250 0.02 S 49.35 W
Mexicali 232 32.40 N 115.29 W
Mexican Hat 200 37.09 N 109.52 W
Mexico, In., U.S. 216 40.49 N 86.06 W
Mexico, Me., U.S. 188 44.33 N 70.32 W
Mexico, Mo., U.S. 219 39.10 N 91.52 W
Mexico, N.Y., U.S. 212 43.27 N 76.13 W
Mexico, Pa., U.S. 208 40.32 N 77.21 W
México □³ 234 19.20 N 99.45 W
Mexico (México) □¹, N.A. 230 23.00 N 102.00 W
Mexico (México) □¹, N.A. 232 23.00 N 102.00 W
México, Golfo de
— Mexico, Gulf of c 230 25.00 N 90.00 W
Mexico, Gulf of c 230 25.00 N 90.00 W
Mexico Basin ✦¹ 16 25.00 N 92.00 W
Mexico Bay c 212 43.31 N 76.17 W
Mexico Beach 192 29.58 N 85.24 W
Mexico City
— Ciudad de México 234 19.24 N 99.09 W
Mexiko
— Ciudad de México 234 19.24 N 99.09 W
Mexiko
— Mexico □¹ 232 23.00 N 102.00 W
Mexiko, Golf von
— Mexico, Gulf of c 230 25.00 N 90.00 W
Meximieux 58 45.54 N 5.12 E
Mexique
— Mexico □¹ 230 23.00 N 102.00 W
Mexique, Golfe du
— Mexico, Gulf of c 230 25.00 N 90.00 W
Mexticacán 234 21.13 N 102.43 W
Mey, Castle of ⊥ 46 58.38 N 3.14 W
Meyanodas 164 7.38 S 131.38 E
Meycauayan 116 14.44 N 120.58 E
Meydan 130 38.21 N 41.47 E
Meydancık 130 41.25 N 42.14 E
Meydān-e Gel ≐ 128 29.04 N 54.50 E
Meydān Khvolah 120 33.36 N 69.51 E
Meyenburg 54 53.18 N 12.14 E
Meyers Chuck 182 55.44 N 132.15 W
Meyersdale 188 39.48 N 79.01 W
Meyers Lake 214 40.52 N 81.24 W
Meyersville 222 28.55 N 97.21 W
Meyerton 158 26.33 S 28.01 E
Meyisti 130 36.08 N 29.34 E
Meyisti I 130 36.08 N 29.34 E
Meymac 32 45.32 N 2.09 E
Meymaneh 120 35.55 N 64.47 E
Meymeh 128 33.27 N 51.10 E
Meymeh ≐ 128 32.05 N 47.16 E
Meynypilgino 180 62.32 N 177.02 E
Meyo Centre 152 2.33 N 11.02 E
Meyrargues 62 43.38 N 5.32 E
Meyrin 58 46.14 N 6.05 E
Meyronne 184 49.39 N 106.50 W
Meyrueis 32 44.10 N 3.26 E
Meyungs 175b 7.20 N 134.27 E
Meža ≐ 61 46.35 N 15.02 E
Mezada, Horvot (Masada) ⊥ 132 31.19 N 35.21 E
Mezapa 236 15.33 N 87.23 W
Mezcala 234 17.56 N 99.37 W
Mezcala ≐ 234 18.00 N 99.47 W
Mezcalapa 234 17.37 N 93.22 W
Mezcalapa ≐ 234 18.00 N 92.54 W
Mezdra 38 43.09 N 23.42 E
Meždurečensk 86 53.42 N 88.03 E
Meždurečenskij 86 59.36 N 65.53 E
Mèze 32 43.25 N 3.36 E
Mézel 62 43.59 N 6.12 E
Mezen' 24 65.50 N 44.13 E
Mezen' ≐ 24 66.11 N 43.59 E
Mézenc, Mont ∧ 62 44.55 N 4.11 E
Mezenskaja guba c 24 66.40 N 43.45 E
Mezhova 78 48.16 N 36.44 E
Mezhyrich 78 50.43 N 34.29 E
Meziadin Lake ◎ 182 56.04 N 129.18 W
Mežica 61 46.31 N 14.52 E
Mézières-en-Brenne 32 46.49 N 1.13 E
Mézières-sur-Seine 261 48.58 N 1.48 E
Mézilhac 62 44.48 N 4.21 E
Mézin 32 44.03 N 0.16 E
Mezinovskij 76 55.30 N 40.21 E
Mezőberény 30 46.50 N 21.02 E
Mezőcsát 30 47.49 N 20.55 E
Mezőkovácsháza 30 46.25 N 20.55 E
Mezőkövesd 30 47.50 N 20.34 E
Mezőtúr 30 47.00 N 20.38 E
Mežoz'ornyj 86 54.09 N 59.23 E
Mezquital 234 23.29 N 104.23 W
Mezquital ≐ 232 22.35 N 104.54 W
Mezquital del Oro 234 21.10 N 103.25 W
Mezquitic 234 22.23 N 103.41 W
Mezraa 130 41.12 N 35.08 E
Mézy 261 49.00 N 1.53 E
Mezzana 64 46.19 N 10.48 E
Mezzano 64 46.09 N 11.48 E
Mezzenile 62 45.17 N 7.23 E
Mezzocorona 64 46.13 N 11.07 E
Mezzoiuso 70 37.52 N 13.28 E
Mezzola, Lago di ◎ 58 46.12 N 9.26 E
Mezzolombardo 64 46.13 N 11.05 E
Mezzomerico 266b 45.37 N 8.36 E
Mfangano Island I 154 0.28 S 34.01 E
Mfolozi ≐ 158 28.25 S 32.26 E
Mfou 152 3.43 N 11.38 E
Mfuwe 154 13.04 S 31.46 E
Mgači 89 51.05 N 142.17 E
Mgeni ≐ 158 29.48 S 31.02 E
Mgeta 154 8.19 S 36.08 E
Mglin 76 53.04 N 32.51 E
M'goun, Irhil ∧ 148 31.31 N 6.25 W
M'hai, B'nom ∧ 110 11.21 N 107.50 E
Mhasvād 122 17.38 N 74.47 E
Mhlatuze ≐ 158 28.47 S 32.06 E
Mhlume 158 26.02 S 31.50 E
Mholach, Beinn ∧² 46 58.14 N 6.31 W
Mhòr, Beinn ∧ 46 57.17 N 7.19 W
Mhòr, Loch ◎ 46 57.13 N 4.28 W
Mhow 120 22.33 N 75.46 E
Mi ≐, Zhg. 98 37.12 N 119.10 E
Mi ≐, Zhg. 100 27.09 N 112.51 E
Mia, Oued V 148 30.47 N 4.54 E

Symbols in the index entries represent the broad categories identified in the key at the right. Symbols with superior numbers (⋌¹) identify subcategories (see complete key on page *I · 1).*

Symbole im Register stellen die rechts im Schlüssel erklärten Kategorien dar. Symbole mit hochgestellten Ziffern (⋌¹) bezeichnen Unterabteilungen einer Kategorie (vgl. vollständiger Schlüssel auf Seite *I · 1).*

Los símbolos incluidos en el texto del índice representan las grandes categorías identificadas con la clave a la derecha. Los símbolos con numeros en su parte superior (⋌¹) identifican las subcategorías (véase la clave completa en la página *I · 1).*

Les symboles de l'index représentent les catégories indiquées dans la légende à droite. Les symboles suivis d'un indice (⋌¹) représentent des sous-catégories (voir légende complète à la page *I · 1).*

Os símbolos incluídos no texto do índice representam as grandes categorias identificadas com a chave à direita. Os símbolos com números em sua parte superior (⋌¹) identificam as subcategorias (veja-se a chave completa à página *I · 1).*

∧ Mountain	Berg	Montaña	Montagne	Montanha
⋌ Mountains	Gebirge	Montañas	Montagnes	Montanhas
)(Pass	Paß	Paso	Col	Passo
V Valley, Canyon	Tal, Cañon	Valle, Cañón	Vallée, Canyon	Vale, Canhão
≐ Plain	Ebene	Llano	Plaine	Planície
> Cape	Kap	Cabo	Cap	Cabo
I Island	Insel	Isla	Île	Ilha
II Islands	Inseln	Islas	Îles	Ilhas
⊥ Other Topographic Features	Andere Topographische Objekte	Otros Elementos Topográficos	Autres données topographiques	Outros acidentes topográficos

ESPAÑOL — Nombre · Página · Lat.°' · Long.°' W = Oeste
FRANÇAIS — Nom · Page · Lat.°' · Long.°' W = Ouest
PORTUGUÊS — Nome · Página · Lat.°' · Long.°' W = Oeste

Nombre	Página	Lat.°'	Long.°' W = Oeste
Miacatlán	234	18.46 N	99.22 W
Mia-dong ⬥[8]	271b	37.37 N	127.01 E
Miagao	116	10.39 N	122.14 E
Miahuatlán de Porfirio Díaz	234	16.20 N	96.36 W
Miajadas	34	39.09 N	5.54 W
Miaméré	146	8.52 N	19.50 E
Miami, Mb., Can.	184	49.21 N	98.11 W
Miami, Az., U.S.	200	33.23 N	110.52 W
Miami, Fl., U.S.	220	25.46 N	80.11 W
Miami, In., U.S.	216	40.36 N	86.06 W
Miami, Ok., U.S.	196	36.52 N	94.52 W
Miami, Tx., U.S.	196	35.42 N	100.38 W
Miami □[6], In., U.S.	216	40.45 N	86.04 W
Miami □[6], Oh., U.S.	218	40.02 N	84.13 W
Miami ≃	224	45.33 N	123.53 W
Miami Beach, On., Can.	212	44.13 N	79.29 W
Miami Beach, Fl., U.S.	220	25.47 N	80.07 W
Miami Canal ≋	220	25.47 N	80.15 W
Miami Creek ≃	226	37.21 N	119.44 W
Miami International Airport ⊠	220	25.48 N	80.17 W
Miami Lakes	220	25.53 N	80.18 W
Miamisburg	218	39.38 N	84.17 W
Miamisburg Mound State Memorial ⊥	218	39.38 N	84.17 W
Miami Shores	220	25.51 N	80.11 W
Miami Springs	220	25.49 N	80.17 W
Miami State Recreation Area ♦	216	40.40 N	85.55 W
Miamiville	218	39.13 N	84.18 W
Miān Channūn	123	30.27 N	72.22 E
Mianchi	102	34.48 N	111.49 E
Miāndoāb	128	36.58 N	46.06 E
Miandrivazo	157b	19.31 S	45.28 E
Mianduhe	89	49.05 N	121.06 E
Miane	64	45.57 N	12.06 E
Miāneh	128	37.26 N	47.42 E
Miang, Phu ∧	110	17.42 N	101.01 E
Miangas, Pulau I	108	5.35 N	126.35 E
Mianhu	100	23.28 N	116.09 E
Mianhuadi	104	41.15 N	120.49 E
Miāni	123	32.32 N	73.04 E
Miāni Hōr ⊂	120	25.34 N	66.19 E
Mianning	102	28.39 N	102.09 E
Mianus ≃	207	41.03 N	73.35 W
Mianus, East Branch ≃	276	41.06 N	73.35 W
Mianus Reservoir ◎[1]	276	41.08 N	73.37 W
Miānwāli	123	32.35 N	71.33 E
Mianxian	102	33.09 N	106.48 E
Mianyang, Zhg.	100	30.23 N	113.25 E
Mianyang, Zhg.	102	31.30 N	104.49 E
Mianzhu	102	31.20 N	104.09 E
Miao Dao I	98	37.56 N	120.45 E
Miaodao Qundao II	98	38.10 N	120.40 E
Miao'ergou	86	45.32 N	83.52 E
Miaofengshan	105	40.04 N	116.13 E
Miaogou	104	41.12 N	120.40 E
Miaojiagou	104	42.16 N	123.22 E
Miaojiatun	104	40.54 N	120.55 E
Miaokou	98	35.48 N	114.09 E
Miaoli	100	24.34 N	120.49 E
Miao Ling ⋀	102	26.15 N	107.26 E
Miaopu	106	31.00 N	118.44 E
Miaoqian	100	30.33 N	117.44 E
Miaotou	106	30.58 N	120.33 E
Miaowan	100	33.07 N	114.41 E
Miaoyang	98	40.49 N	124.24 E
Miaozhen	106	31.43 N	121.21 E
Miaozigou	107	30.17 N	104.35 E
Miarayon	116	8.04 N	124.50 E
Miarinarivo, Madag.	157b	16.38 S	48.15 E
Miarinarivo, Madag.	157b	18.57 S	46.55 E
Miarinavaratra	157b	20.13 S	47.31 E
Miasa	94	36.34 N	137.53 E
Miass	86	54.59 N	60.06 E
Miass ≃	86	56.06 N	64.30 E
Miasteczko Krajeńskie	30	53.06 N	17.01 E
Miastko	30	54.01 N	17.00 E
Miboro-dam ⬥[6]	94	36.08 N	136.55 E
Mibu	94	36.25 N	139.48 E
Mibu ≃	94	35.49 N	137.57 E
Mica	156	24.10 S	30.48 E
Mica Mountain ∧	200	32.13 N	110.33 W
Micang Shan ⋀	102	32.45 N	107.20 E
Micanopy	192	29.30 N	82.16 W
Micaúne	156	18.18 S	36.35 E
Mičavičevnik	24	64.14 N	57.58 E
Miccosukee, Lake ◎[1]	192	30.34 N	83.58 W
Miccosukee Indian Reservation ⬥[4]	220	26.10 N	80.50 W
Michael, Mount ∧	164	6.25 S	145.20 E
Michael J. Kirwan Reservoir ◎[1]	214	41.10 N	81.10 W
Michajlov	82	54.14 N	39.02 E
Michajlovka, Kaz.	85	43.06 N	71.36 E
Michajlovka, Kaz.	85	42.50 N	75.42 E
Michajlovka, Kaz.	86	53.51 N	76.32 E
Michajlovka, Kyrg.	85	42.37 N	78.20 E
Michajlovka, Ross.	78	49.53 N	39.38 E
Michajlovka, Ross.	80	47.38 N	46.54 E
Michajlovka, Ross.	80	50.05 N	43.15 E
Michajlovka, Ross.	86	51.49 N	79.45 E
Michajlovka, Ross.	86	56.26 N	78.53 E
Michajlovka, Ross.	88	50.26 N	104.10 E
Michajlovka, Ross.	88	55.30 N	114.09 E
Michajlovka, Ross.	88	51.07 N	119.20 E
Michajlovka, Ross.	88	52.57 N	103.18 E
Michajlovka, Ross.	89	49.13 N	129.56 E
Michajlovka, Ross.	89	43.56 N	132.00 E
Michajlovka, Ross.	265a	60.04 N	30.14 E
Michajlovka, Ross.	265a	59.43 N	30.01 E
Michajlovo	80	56.56 N	45.04 E
Michajlovo-Aleksandrovskij	83	49.13 N	40.15 E
Michajlovskaja	80	50.58 N	41.52 E
Michajlovskij, Kaz.	86	50.17 N	55.23 E
Michajlovskij, Ross.	76	60.05 N	43.29 E
Michajlovskij, Ross.	86	51.41 N	79.47 E
Michajlovskoje, Ross.	76	58.23 N	37.40 E
Michajlovskoje, Ross.	80	56.11 N	45.47 E
Michajlovskoje, Ross.	82	55.50 N	36.20 E
Michajlovskoje, Ross.	265b	55.35 N	37.35 E
Michalevo	82	55.27 N	38.26 E
Michali	82	55.17 N	39.05 E
Michalkovo	82	54.11 N	37.33 E
Michalovce	30	48.45 N	21.55 E
Michalovy Hory	60	49.55 N	12.47 E
Michanoviči	76	53.45 N	27.40 E
Michaud, Point ›	186	45.34 N	60.40 W
Micheal Peak ∧	182	53.35 N	126.26 W
Michejevo	88	57.10 N	104.53 E
Michel	182	49.43 N	114.49 W
Michelago	171b	35.43 S	149.10 E
Michelau	56	50.10 N	11.06 E
Micheldever	42	51.09 N	1.15 W
Micheldorf in Oberösterreich	61	47.52 N	14.08 E
Michelsneukirchen	60	49.08 N	12.33 E
Michelson, Mount ∧	180	69.19 N	144.17 W
Michel'sonovskij	265b	55.42 N	37.54 E
Michelstadt	56	49.41 N	9.00 E
Michendorf	54	52.18 N	13.01 E
Miches	238	18.59 N	69.03 W
Micheta	84	41.52 N	44.44 E
Michiana	216	41.46 N	86.48 W
Michiana Regional Airport ⊠	216	41.42 N	86.19 W
Michigamme ≃	190	46.04 N	88.13 W
Michigan	198	48.01 N	98.07 W
Michigan □[3], U.S.	178	44.00 N	85.00 W
Michigan □[3], U.S.	190	44.00 N	85.00 W
Michigan ≃	200	40.52 N	106.20 W
Michigan, Lake ◎	190	44.00 N	87.00 W
Michigan, University of ✝[2]	281	42.17 N	83.44 W
Michigan Center	216	42.13 N	84.19 W
Michigan City	216	41.42 N	86.53 W
Michigan International Speedway ♦	216	42.03 N	84.15 W
Michigan Stadium ♦	281	42.16 N	83.45 W
Michigan State Fair Grounds ♦	281	42.27 N	83.07 W
Michigantown	216	40.19 N	86.23 W
Michika	146	10.38 N	13.24 E
Michillinda	280	34.07 N	118.05 W
Michinmahuida, Volcán ∧[1]	254	42.49 S	72.28 W
Michipicoten Bay ⊂	190	47.55 N	84.56 W
Michipicoten Island I	190	47.45 N	85.45 W
Michnevo	82	55.07 N	37.58 E
Michninskaja	24	60.26 N	46.14 E
Michoacán	204	32.28 N	115.20 W
Michoacán □[3]	234	19.10 N	101.50 W
Michoacanejo	234	21.33 N	102.36 W
Michów	30	51.32 N	22.19 E
Michurinsk → Mičurinsk	80	52.54 N	40.30 E
Mickle Fell ∧	44	54.37 N	2.18 W
Mickleham	260	51.16 N	0.19 W
Mickleover	42	52.54 N	1.32 W
Mickleton, Eng., U.K.	42	52.05 N	1.46 W
Mickleton, N.J., U.S.	285	39.47 N	75.14 W
Mickle Trafford	262	53.13 N	2.50 W
Mickleyville	218	39.45 N	86.16 W
Mico ≃	236	12.11 N	84.16 W
Mico, Montañas del ⋀	236	15.30 N	88.55 W
Miconge	152	4.26 S	12.51 E
Micoud	241f	13.50 N	60.54 W
Micronesia II	14	11.00 N	159.00 E
Micronesia, Federated States of □[1]	14	5.00 N	152.00 E
Mičurinsk	80	52.54 N	40.30 E
Midai, Pulau I	112	3.00 N	107.47 E
Midale	184	49.22 N	103.27 W
Midar	148	34.58 N	3.30 W
Mid-Atlantic Ridge ✢[3]	8	0.00	20.00 W
Midbar Yehuda → Wilderness of Judæa ⬥[2]	132	31.30 N	35.18 E
Middalya	162	23.55 S	114.45 E
Middelburg, Ned.	52	51.30 N	3.37 E
Middelburg, S. Afr.	158	31.30 S	25.00 E
Middelburg, S. Afr.	158	25.47 S	29.28 E
Middelfart	41	55.30 N	9.45 E
Middelharnis	52	51.45 N	4.11 E
Middelkerke	50	51.11 N	2.49 E
Middelkerke, Vliegveld ⊠	50	51.12 N	2.52 E
Middelpos	158	31.55 S	20.13 E
Middelstum	52	53.20 N	6.38 E
Middelwater	156	23.17 S	30.16 E
Middelwit	156	24.58 S	27.00 E
Middenbeemster	52	52.33 N	4.55 E
Middenin	158	27.43 S	28.02 E
Middenmeer	52	52.47 N	5.00 E
Middle ≃, B.C., Can.	182	54.50 N	125.08 W
Middle ≃, Ca., U.S.	226	38.03 N	121.31 W
Middle ≃, Ia., U.S.	194	41.29 N	93.24 W
Middle ≃, Mn., U.S.	198	48.22 N	97.04 W
Middle ≃, Mo., U.S.	219	38.39 N	91.53 W
Middle Alkali Lake ◎	204	41.28 N	120.04 W
Middle America Trench ✢[1]	16	15.00 N	95.00 W
Middle Andaman I	110	12.30 N	92.50 E
Middle Barton	42	51.56 N	1.22 W
Middle Bass	214	41.41 N	82.50 W
Middle Bass Island I	214	41.41 N	82.49 W
Middle-Bay	186	51.28 N	57.30 W
Middle Bay ⊂	276	40.37 N	73.36 W
Middleboro	207	41.53 N	70.54 W
Middle Bosque ≃	222	31.31 N	97.16 W
Middlebourne	188	39.29 N	80.54 W
Middlebranch	214	40.54 N	81.20 W
Middle Breakwater ⬥[5]	280	33.43 N	118.13 W
Middlebro	184	49.01 N	95.21 W
Middle Brook	186	48.45 N	54.13 W
Middle Brook ≃, N.J., U.S.	276	40.39 N	74.41 W
Middle Brook ≃, N.J., U.S.	276	40.33 N	74.33 W
Middle Brook, East Branch ≃	276	40.35 N	74.33 W
Middle Brook, West Branch ≃	276	40.35 N	74.33 W
Middleburg, Md., U.S.	208	39.35 N	77.12 W
Middleburg, N.Y., U.S.	210	42.36 N	74.20 W
Middleburg, Oh., U.S.	216	40.17 N	83.34 W
Middleburg, Pa., U.S.	208	40.47 N	77.02 W
Middleburg Heights	214	41.22 N	81.48 W
Middlebury, Ct., U.S.	207	41.31 N	73.07 W
Middlebury, In., U.S.	216	41.40 N	85.42 W
Middlebury, Vt., U.S.	188	44.00 N	73.10 W
Middlebush	276	40.29 N	74.32 W
Middle Caicos I	238	21.47 N	71.43 W
Middle Cape ›	220	25.09 N	81.09 W
Middle Castor ≃	212	45.16 N	75.24 W
Middle Channel ≃[1], N.T., Can.	180	69.21 N	135.33 W
Middle Channel ≃[1], Mi., U.S.	281	42.33 N	82.42 W
Middle Concho ≃	196	31.27 N	100.25 W
Middle Creek ≃, U.S.	208	39.41 N	76.18 W
Middle Creek ≃, Pa., U.S.	210	40.46 N	76.52 W
Middle Creek ≃, Pa., U.S.	210	41.28 N	75.11 W
Middle Fabius ≃	194	39.58 N	91.35 W
Middle Falls	210	43.07 N	73.32 W
Middlefield, Ct., U.S.	207	41.31 N	72.42 W
Middlefield, N.Y., U.S.	210	42.41 N	74.50 W
Middlefield, Oh., U.S.	214	41.27 N	81.04 W
Middle Fork Reservoir ◎[1]	218	39.51 N	84.51 W
Middle Ground I	272c	18.55 N	72.51 E
Middle Ground ✢[2]	174g	28.15 N	177.25 W
Middle Grove, Mo., U.S.	219	39.24 N	92.16 W
Middle Grove, N.Y., U.S.	210	43.05 N	73.55 W
Middle Haddam	207	41.33 N	72.33 W
Middleham	44	54.17 N	1.49 W
Middle Harbour ⊂	274a	33.48 S	151.14 E
Middle Head ›	274a	33.50 S	151.16 E
Middle Hope	210	41.34 N	74.01 W
Middle Island	210	40.53 N	72.56 W
Middle Island I	162	34.07 S	123.12 E
Middle Level Main Drain ≋	42	52.43 N	0.22 E
Middle Loup ≃	198	41.17 N	98.23 W
Middle Maitland ≃	212	43.53 N	81.19 W
Middlemarch	172	45.31 S	170.07 E
Middlemount	166	22.49 S	148.40 E
Middle Musquodoboit	186	45.03 N	63.09 W
Middle Nodaway ≃	194	40.54 N	95.00 W
Middle Pease ≃	196	34.15 N	100.07 W
Middle Point	216	40.51 N	84.27 W
Middleport, N.Y., U.S.	210	43.12 N	78.28 W
Middleport, Oh., U.S.	188	39.00 N	82.02 W
Middleport, Pa., U.S.	208	40.44 N	76.05 W
Middle Raccoon ≃	198	41.34 N	94.12 W
Middle Reservoir ◎[1]	283	42.27 N	71.07 W
Middle River	208	39.20 N	76.26 W
Middle River ⊂	208	39.19 N	76.25 W
Middle River Neck ›[1]	284b	39.22 N	76.23 W
Middle River Rouge ≃	281	42.20 N	83.15 W
Middle Rouge Parkway ♦	281	42.21 N	83.21 W
Middle Run ≃	285	39.41 N	75.43 W
Middlesboro	192	36.36 N	83.43 W
Middlesbrough	44	54.35 N	1.14 W
Middlesex, Belize	232	17.02 N	88.31 W
Middlesex, N.J., U.S.	276	40.34 N	74.29 W
Middlesex, N.Y., U.S.	210	42.42 N	77.16 W
Middlesex, N.C., U.S.	192	35.47 N	78.12 W
Middlesex □[6], On., Can.	212	43.00 N	81.08 W
Middlesex □[6], Ct., U.S.	207	41.33 N	72.39 W
Middlesex □[6], Ma., U.S.	207	42.30 N	71.25 W
Middlesex □[6], N.J., U.S.	208	40.29 N	74.27 W
Middlesex □[6], Va., U.S.	208	37.40 N	76.35 W
Middlesex Fells Reservation ♦	283	42.27 N	71.07 W
Middlesex Reservoir ◎[1]	276	40.37 N	74.19 W
Middle Stewiacke	186	45.13 N	63.08 W
Middle Swan	168a	31.52 S	116.00 E
Middle Thames ≃	212	42.59 N	80.58 W
Middleton, Austl.	166	22.22 S	141.32 E
Middleton, N.S., Can.	186	44.57 N	65.04 W
Middleton, Eng., U.K.	42	52.43 N	0.28 E
Middleton, Eng., U.K.	44	53.33 N	2.13 W
Middleton, Ma., U.S.	207	42.35 N	71.01 W
Middleton, Mi., U.S.	190	43.11 N	84.42 W
Middleton, Tn., U.S.	194	35.03 N	88.53 W
Middleton, Wi., U.S.	216	43.05 N	89.30 W
Middleton-in-Teesdale	44	54.38 N	2.04 W
Middleton Island I	180	59.25 N	146.25 W
Middleton-on-the-Wolds	44	53.56 N	0.33 W
Middleton Pond ◎	283	42.36 N	71.02 W
Middleton Reef I[1]	160	29.28 S	159.06 E
Middleton Saint George	44	54.30 N	1.28 W
Middletown, N. Ire., U.K.	48	54.18 N	6.50 W
Middletown, Ca., U.S.	226	38.45 N	122.36 W
Middletown, Ct., U.S.	207	41.33 N	72.39 W
Middletown, De., U.S.	208	39.26 N	75.43 W
Middletown, Il., U.S.	219	40.11 N	89.35 W
Middletown, In., U.S.	218	40.03 N	85.32 W
Middletown, Ky., U.S.	218	38.14 N	85.32 W
Middletown, Md., U.S.	208	39.26 N	77.32 W
Middletown, Mo., U.S.	219	39.07 N	91.24 W
Middletown, N.J., U.S.	208	40.23 N	74.07 W
Middletown, N.Y., U.S.	210	41.26 N	74.25 W
Middletown, Oh., U.S.	218	39.30 N	84.23 W
Middletown, Pa., U.S.	208	40.11 N	76.43 W
Middletown, R.I., U.S.	207	41.32 N	71.17 W
Middletown, Va., U.S.	188	39.01 N	78.16 W
Middletown Park	218	40.09 N	85.26 W
Middle Tuolumne ≃	226	37.50 N	120.01 W
Middleville, Mi., U.S.	216	42.42 N	85.27 W
Middleville, N.Y., U.S.	210	43.08 N	74.58 W
Middleville, N.Y., U.S.	276	43.08 N	74.58 W
Middlewich	44	53.11 N	2.27 W
Middle Yegua Creek ≃	222	30.19 N	96.47 W
Middle Yuba ≃	226	39.22 N	121.12 W
Midelt	148	32.41 N	4.43 W
Midfield	222	28.56 N	96.13 W
Midge Hall	262	53.42 N	2.45 W
Midgic	186	45.59 N	64.18 W
Mid Glamorgan □[6]	42	51.40 N	3.30 W
Midgley	262	53.44 N	1.58 W
Midhurst, On., Can.	212	44.27 N	79.44 W
Midhurst, Eng., U.K.	42	50.59 N	0.45 W
Midi, Aiguille du ∧	62	45.52 N	6.53 E
Midi, Canal du ≋	32	43.26 N	1.58 E
Midi de Bigorre, Pic du ∧	32	42.56 N	0.08 E
Mid Illovo	158	29.59 S	30.25 E
Mid-Indian Basin ✢[1]	12	10.00 S	80.00 E
Mid-Indian Ridge ✢[3]	6	12.00 S	66.00 E
Midland, Austl.	168a	31.53 S	116.00 E
Midland, On., Can.	212	44.45 N	79.53 W
Midland, Ca., U.S.	204	33.52 N	114.48 W
Midland, Mi., U.S.	190	43.36 N	84.14 W
Midland, N.C., U.S.	192	35.13 N	80.30 W
Midland, Oh., U.S.	218	39.18 N	83.54 W
Midland, Pa., U.S.	214	40.37 N	80.26 W
Midland, Pa., U.S.	214	40.37 N	80.26 W
Midland, S.D., U.S.	198	44.04 N	101.09 W
Midland, Tx., U.S.	196	31.59 N	102.04 W
Midland, Wa., U.S.	224	47.10 N	122.24 W
Midland Bay ⊂	212	44.47 N	79.52 W
Midland Beach ⬥[8]	276	40.34 N	74.05 W
Midland City	219	40.09 N	89.08 W
Midland Park, Mi., U.S.	216	42.23 N	85.22 W
Midland Park, N.J., U.S.	276	40.59 N	74.08 W
Midland Park Lake ◎	212	44.44 N	79.53 W
Midlands □[4]	154	19.00 S	29.45 E
Midleton	48	51.55 N	8.10 W
Midlothian, Il., U.S.	216	41.37 N	87.43 W
Midlothian, Tx., U.S.	222	32.28 N	96.59 W
Midlothian Creek ≃	278	41.39 N	87.40 W
Midlum	52	53.43 N	8.37 E
Midnapore	182	50.55 N	114.05 W
Midnapore Canal ≋	126	22.25 N	87.53 E
Midnapore Plain ≚	126	22.00 N	87.45 E
Mid-Ohio Sports Car Course ♦	214	40.40 N	82.38 W
Midongy Nord	157b	20.45 S	46.13 E
Midongy Sud	157b	23.35 S	47.01 E
Midori	96	34.43 N	132.37 E
Midori ⬥[8]	268	35.32 N	139.34 E
Midori ≃	92	32.42 N	130.37 E
Midou ≃	32	43.54 N	0.30 W
Mid-Pacific Mountains ✢[3]	14	20.00 N	170.00 E
Midpines	226	37.32 N	119.55 W
Midreshet Ben Gurion	132	30.51 N	34.46 E
Midsayap	116	7.12 N	124.32 E
Midshipman Point ›	282	38.07 N	122.27 W
Midsland	52	53.22 N	5.16 E
Midsomer Norton	42	51.18 N	2.28 W
Midu	102	25.22 N	100.31 E
Midvale, De., U.S.	285	39.39 N	75.37 W
Midvale, Id., U.S.	202	44.28 N	116.44 W
Midvale, Oh., U.S.	214	40.26 N	81.22 W
Midville	192	32.49 N	82.14 W
Midway, B.C., Can.	182	49.01 N	118.47 W
Midway, B.C., Can.	202	49.01 N	118.46 W
Midway, Al., U.S.	194	32.04 N	85.31 W
Midway, In., U.S.	216	41.37 N	85.55 W
Midway, Ky., U.S.	218	38.09 N	84.41 W
Midway, Pa., U.S.	279b	40.22 N	80.17 W
Midway, Tx., U.S.	222	31.02 N	95.45 W
Midway, Ut,. U.S.	200	40.30 N	111.28 W
Midway City	280	33.45 N	118.00 W
Midway Islands □[2], Oc.	6	28.13 N	177.22 W
Midway Islands □[2], Oc.	174g	28.13 N	177.22 W
Midway Mall ⬥[9]	279a	41.24 N	82.07 W
Midway Naval Station ■	174g	28.13 N	177.26 W
Midway Park	192	34.43 N	77.21 W
Midwest	200	43.24 N	106.16 W
Midwest City	196	35.26 N	97.23 W
Midwolda	52	53.12 N	7.00 E
Midyan ⬥[1]	128	27.40 N	35.35 E
Midyat	130	37.25 N	41.23 E
Midyobe	152	1.21 N	10.18 E
Midžor (Midžur) ∧	38	43.23 N	22.42 E
Mie	96	32.58 N	131.35 E
Mie □[5]	92	34.30 N	136.30 E
Miechów	30	50.23 N	20.01 E
Miedwie, Jezioro ◎	54	53.17 N	14.52 E
Międzybórz	30	51.24 N	17.40 E
Międzychód	30	52.36 N	15.55 E
Międzylesie	30	50.10 N	16.40 E
Międzyrzec Podlaski	30	52.00 N	22.47 E
Międzyrzecz	30	52.28 N	15.35 E
Międzyzdroje	30	53.55 N	14.28 E
Miehuapu	105	39.11 N	117.44 E
Miejska Górka	30	51.40 N	16.58 E
Miélan	32	43.26 N	0.19 E
Mielec	30	50.18 N	21.25 E
Mielno	30	54.16 N	16.01 E
Mien ◎	26	56.25 N	14.51 E
Mienga	152	17.17 S	19.48 E
Mienhua Yü I	100	25.29 N	122.06 E
Mient'ienhuo Shan ∧	269d	25.11 N	121.30 E
Mier	232	26.26 N	99.09 W
Miercurea-Ciuc	38	46.22 N	25.48 E
Mieres	34	43.15 N	5.46 W
Mierlo	52	51.27 N	5.37 E
Mieroszów	30	50.41 N	16.10 E
Miersdorf	264a	52.20 N	13.37 E
Miersig	38	46.53 N	21.51 E
Mier y Noriega	234	23.25 N	100.07 W
Miesaituo	120	35.52 N	93.40 E
Miesbach	64	47.47 N	11.50 E
Miesenbach	61	47.22 N	15.46 E
Mieso	144	9.15 N	40.48 E
Mieste	54	52.28 N	11.11 E
Miesterhorst	54	52.27 N	11.09 E
Mieszkowice	30	52.46 N	14.30 E
Mifflin, Oh., U.S.	214	40.47 N	82.22 W
Mifflin, Pa., U.S.	208	40.34 N	77.24 W
Mifflin □[6]	210	40.40 N	77.33 W
Mifflinburg	210	40.55 N	77.02 W
Mifflintown	208	40.34 N	77.23 W
Mifflinville	210	41.01 N	76.18 W
Miftāḥ, Wādī V	142	30.15 N	31.46 E
Migdal	132	32.50 N	35.30 E
Migdal Ha'Emeq	132	32.41 N	35.15 E
Migdol	158	26.54 S	25.27 E
Migennes	50	47.58 N	3.31 E
Migliarino	66	44.46 N	11.56 E
Migliaro	64	44.48 N	11.58 E
Miglionico	68	40.34 N	16.30 E
Mignano Monte Lungo	68	41.23 N	13.58 E
Mignone ≃	66	42.11 N	11.44 E
Mignovillard	58	46.48 N	6.08 E
Migori ≃	154	0.59 S	34.15 E
Miguel Alemán, Presa ◎[1]	234	18.13 N	96.32 W
Miguel Alves	250	4.10 S	42.54 W
Miguel Auza	232	24.18 N	103.25 W
Miguel Calmon	250	11.26 S	40.36 W
Miguel Couto	287a	22.43 S	43.27 W
Miguel de la Borda	236	9.09 N	80.19 W
Migueles, Arroyo de los ≃	266a	40.20 N	3.32 W
Miguelete	258	34.01 S	57.39 W
Miguelete, Arroyo ≃	258	34.14 S	57.54 W
Miguel Hidalgo, Presa ◎[1]	232	26.30 N	108.35 W
Miguelópolis	255	20.12 S	48.03 W
Miguel Pereira	256	22.27 S	43.22 W
Miguel Riglos	252	36.51 S	63.42 W
Migulinskaja	80	49.42 N	41.16 E
Migvie	46	57.08 N	2.56 W
Migyaunglaung	110	14.40 N	98.09 E
Mihăești	38	45.07 N	25.00 E
Mihai Viteazu	38	44.39 N	28.41 E
Mihajlovgrad □[4]	38	43.32 N	23.32 E
Mihalgazi	130	40.02 N	30.34 E
Mihalıççık	130	39.52 N	31.30 E
Mihama, Nihon	94	35.36 N	135.56 E
Mihama, Nihon	94	34.46 N	136.54 E
Mihama, Nihon	96	33.54 N	135.08 E
Mihara, Nihon	96	34.32 N	135.34 E
Mihara, Nihon	96	34.24 N	133.05 E
Mihara, Nihon	96	34.17 N	134.46 E
Mihara-yama ∧	94	34.43 N	139.23 E
Mihla	54	51.04 N	10.20 E
Miho	94	36.00 N	140.18 E
Mihonoseki	96	35.34 N	133.19 E
Miho-wan ⊂	96	35.30 N	133.23 E
Mihuangzhuang	105	39.07 N	116.12 E
Mijaly	86	48.57 N	53.42 E
Mijares ≃	34	39.55 N	0.01 W
Mijdaḥah	144	14.00 N	48.26 E
Mijdrecht	52	52.13 N	4.52 E
Mijiang	98	43.01 N	130.08 E
Mijoux	58	46.22 N	6.00 E
Mikabo-yama ∧	94	36.09 N	138.55 E
Mikame	96	33.25 N	132.27 E
Mikamo, Nihon	96	35.09 N	133.37 E
Mikamo, Nihon	96	34.05 N	133.57 E
Mikasa	92a	43.14 N	141.53 E
Mikaševiči	76	52.13 N	27.28 E
Mikata	94	35.33 N	135.55 E
Mikata-ko ◎	94	35.34 N	135.53 E
Mikatou	273b	4.16 S	15.08 E
Mikawa, Nihon	94	36.29 N	136.29 E
Mikawa, Nihon	96	33.37 N	132.58 E
Mikawa-wan ⊂	94	34.43 N	137.10 E
Mikawa-wan-kokutei-kōen ♦	94	34.42 N	137.10 E
Mikazuki	96	34.58 N	134.27 E
Mikese	154	6.46 S	37.54 E
Mikhaylo-Kotsyubyns'ke	78	51.27 N	31.04 E
Mikhaylov, Cape ›	9	66.51 S	118.33 E
Mikhrot Shelomo Hamelekh (Timna') (King Solomon's Mines) ⊥	132	29.45 N	34.56 E
Miki, Nihon	96	34.48 N	134.59 E
Miki, Nihon	96	34.17 N	134.05 E
Mikínai ⊥	38	37.44 N	22.45 E
Mikindani	154	10.17 S	40.07 E
Mikinduri	154	0.07 N	37.50 E
Mikkabi	94	34.48 N	137.33 E
Mikkaichi	270	34.26 N	135.35 E
Mikkeli	26	61.41 N	27.15 E
Mikkelin lääni □[4]	26	62.00 N	27.30 E
Mikkwa ≃	176	58.25 N	114.45 W
Mikołajki	30	53.49 N	21.36 E
Mikołów	30	50.11 N	18.55 E
Mikomeseng	152	2.08 N	10.37 E
Mikomoto-jima I	94	34.34 N	138.56 E
Míkonos	38	37.26 N	25.20 E
Míkonos I	38	37.29 N	25.25 E
Mikope	152	5.03 S	20.48 E
Mikrá Préspa, Límni ◎	38	40.46 N	21.04 E
Mikre	38	43.02 N	24.31 E
Miksimil	126	22.52 N	89.23 E
Mikšino	76	57.15 N	35.43 E
Mikstat	30	51.32 N	17.59 E
Mikulášovice	54	50.58 N	14.20 E
Mikulino	76	55.02 N	31.07 E
Mikulkin, mys ›	24	67.48 N	46.40 E
Mikulov	61	48.49 N	16.39 E
Mikumi	154	7.24 S	36.59 E
Mikumi National Park ♦	154	7.12 S	37.05 E
Mikun'	24	62.21 N	50.06 E
Mikuni	94	36.13 N	136.09 E
Mikuni-sammyaku ⋀	94	36.50 N	138.40 E
Mikuni-tōge)(	94	36.46 N	138.50 E
Mikuni-yama ∧	94	35.59 N	138.43 E
Mikura-jima I	92	33.52 N	139.36 E
Mila	34	36.27 N	6.16 E
Milaca	190	45.45 N	93.39 W
Miladummadulu Atoll I[1]	122	6.15 N	73.15 E
Milagre	256	21.18 S	47.00 W
Milagres	250	7.17 S	38.57 W
Milagro	246	2.07 S	79.36 W
Milagros	116	12.13 N	123.30 E
Milam □[6]	222	30.47 N	96.57 W
Milan → Milano, It.	62	45.28 N	9.12 E
Milan, Ga., U.S.	192	32.01 N	83.03 W
Milan, In., U.S.	218	39.07 N	85.07 W
Milan, Mi., U.S.	216	42.05 N	83.40 W
Milan, Mn., U.S.	198	45.06 N	95.54 W
Milan, Mo., U.S.	194	40.12 N	93.07 W
Milan, N.M., U.S.	200	35.10 N	107.53 W
Milan, Oh., U.S.	214	41.17 N	82.36 W
Milan, Pa., U.S.	210	41.54 N	76.32 W
Milan, Tn., U.S.	194	35.55 N	88.45 W
Milando	152	8.45 S	17.36 E
Milan Federal Correctional Institution ✝	281	42.06 N	83.40 W
Milang	168b	35.25 S	138.58 E
Milano (Milan), It.	62	45.28 N	9.12 E
Milano (Milan), It.	266b	45.28 N	9.12 E
Milano, Tx., U.S.	222	30.43 N	96.52 W
Milano □[4]	62	45.30 N	9.30 E
Milanoa	157b	13.35 S	49.47 E
Milano Marittima	66	44.16 N	12.21 E
Milanville	210	41.40 N	75.04 W
Milâs	130	37.19 N	27.47 E
Milaševiči	78	51.39 N	27.56 E
Mil'atino, Ross.	76	54.29 N	34.18 E
Mil'atino, Ross.	82	55.41 N	35.48 E
Milazzo	70	38.13 N	15.14 E
Milazzo, Capo di ›	70	38.16 N	15.14 E
Milazzo, Golfo di ⊂	70	38.15 N	15.20 E
Milbank	198	45.13 N	96.38 W
Milbanke Sound ⩀	182	52.18 N	128.33 W
Milborne Port	42	50.58 N	2.27 W
Milbuk	116	6.10 N	124.16 E
Milburn	196	34.14 N	96.32 W
Milburn Creek ≃	276	40.38 N	73.36 W
Milden	184	51.30 N	107.31 W
Mildenau	54	50.35 N	13.04 E
Mildenhall	42	52.21 N	0.30 E
Milders	64	47.06 N	11.16 E
Mildmay	212	44.03 N	81.07 W
Mildred, Il., U.S.	219	39.46 N	89.38 W
Mildred, Pa., U.S.	210	41.28 N	76.22 W
Mildura	166	34.12 S	142.09 E
Mil düzü ≚	84	40.00 N	48.00 E
Mile	102	24.26 N	103.26 E
Miléai	38	39.20 N	23.09 E
Milena	70	37.28 N	13.44 E
Milendella	168b	34.49 S	139.12 E
Milepa	154	11.43 S	36.20 E
Miles, Austl.	166	26.40 S	150.11 E
Miles, Tx., U.S.	196	31.35 N	100.10 W
Miles ≃	283	42.40 N	70.51 W
Milesburg	214	40.56 N	77.47 W
Miles City	202	46.24 N	105.50 W
Miles Creek ⊂	208	38.46 N	76.12 W
Miles Creek ≃	226	37.12 N	120.21 W
Mile Seven Hundred Thirty Three	180	60.03 N	131.07 W
Milešovka ∧	54	50.33 N	13.56 E
Milestone	184	50.00 N	104.30 W
Milesville	279b	40.12 N	79.52 W
Milet (Miletus) ⊥	130	37.28 N	27.15 E
Mileto	68	38.36 N	16.04 E
Miletto, Monte ∧	68	41.27 N	14.22 E
Miletus → Milet ⊥	130	37.28 N	27.15 E
Mileura	162	26.23 S	117.20 E
Milevsko	30	49.27 N	14.22 E
Milford, Eng., U.K.	42	51.11 N	0.38 W
Milford, Ct., U.S.	207	41.13 N	73.04 W
Milford, De., U.S.	208	38.54 N	75.25 W
Milford, Il., U.S.	216	40.37 N	87.41 W
Milford, In., U.S.	216	41.24 N	85.50 W
Milford, Ia., U.S.	198	43.19 N	95.08 W
Milford, Ky., U.S.	218	38.34 N	84.09 W
Milford, Me., U.S.	188	44.56 N	68.38 W
Milford, Md., U.S.	284b	39.21 N	76.44 W
Milford, Ma., U.S.	207	42.08 N	71.31 W
Milford, Mi., U.S.	216	42.35 N	83.35 W
Milford, N.H., U.S.	207	42.50 N	71.38 W
Milford, N.J., U.S.	210	40.34 N	75.05 W
Milford, N.Y., U.S.	210	42.35 N	74.56 W
Milford, Oh., U.S.	218	39.10 N	84.17 W
Milford, Pa., U.S.	210	41.19 N	74.48 W
Milford, Tx., U.S.	222	32.07 N	96.57 W
Milford, Ut,. U.S.	200	38.23 N	113.00 W
Milford, Va., U.S.	208	38.01 N	77.22 W
Milford Brook ≃	276	40.19 N	74.17 W
Milford Center	218	40.10 N	83.26 W
Milford Cross Roads	285	39.43 N	75.44 W
Milford Haven	42	51.40 N	5.02 W
Milford Haven ⊂	42	51.42 N	5.03 W
Milford Lake ◎[1]	198	39.15 N	97.00 W
Milford on Sea	42	50.44 N	1.36 W
Milford Ridge	284b	39.21 N	76.45 W
Milford Sound	172	44.40 S	167.54 E
Milford Sound ⩀	172	44.35 S	167.47 E
Milford Station	186	45.03 N	63.26 W
Milgis ≃	154	1.48 N	38.06 E
Milgoo ∧	162	28.51 S	118.07 E
Mil'guvejem ≃	180	68.22 N	171.30 E
Milḥ, Baḥr al- ◎	128	32.40 N	43.35 E
Milḥat Ashqar ≡, 'Īrāq	128	35.18 N	41.55 E
Milḥat Ashqar ≡, 'Īrāq	130	35.18 N	41.55 E
Milhaud	62	43.47 N	4.18 E
Mili I[1]	14	6.08 N	171.55 E
Milian ≃	112	5.13 N	117.25 E
Milibangalala, Ponta ›	158	26.26 S	32.56 E
Milicia ≃	70	38.04 N	13.33 E
Milicz	30	51.32 N	17.17 E
Milieu, Rivière du ≃	206	46.47 N	73.56 W
Milīj	142	30.36 N	31.03 E
Milim	164	5.10 S	152.00 E
Milín	60	49.39 N	14.02 E
Miling	162	30.30 S	116.21 E
Milis	71	40.03 N	8.38 E
Militello in Val di Catania	70	37.16 N	14.48 E
Militello Rosmarino	70	38.03 N	14.41 E
Milk ≃	202	48.05 N	106.15 W
Milk Creek ≃, Co., U.S.	200	40.24 N	107.45 W
Milk Creek ≃, Or., U.S.	224	45.15 N	122.41 W
Milk Hill ∧[2]	42	51.23 N	1.51 W
Mil'kovo	74	54.43 N	158.37 E
Milk River	182	49.09 N	112.05 W
Milk River Ridge Reservoir ◎[1]	182	49.22 N	112.35 W
Mill	52	51.41 N	5.47 E
Mill ≃, Ct., U.S.	276	41.08 N	73.16 W
Mill ≃, Ma., U.S.	207	42.18 N	72.37 W
Mill ≃, Ma., U.S.	283	42.38 N	70.41 W
Mill ≃, Ma., U.S.	283	42.12 N	70.57 W
Mill ≃, Ma., U.S.	283	42.08 N	71.21 W
Mill ≃, Ma., U.S.	283	42.44 N	70.52 W
Mill ≃, N.Y., U.S.	276	40.38 N	73.39 W
Millard	198	41.13 N	96.07 W
Millau	32	44.06 N	3.05 E
Mill Bay	224	48.39 N	123.34 W
Millboro	192	37.59 N	79.36 W
Millbourne	285	39.58 N	75.15 W
Millbrae	226	37.35 N	122.23 W
Millbrook, On., Can.	212	44.09 N	78.27 W
Millbrook, Eng., U.K.	42	50.20 N	4.13 W
Millbrook, Ma., U.S.	283	42.03 N	70.41 W
Millbrook, N.J., U.S.	276	40.52 N	74.33 W
Millbrook, N.Y., U.S.	210	41.47 N	73.41 W
Mill Brook ≃, Ma., U.S.	283	42.31 N	71.18 W
Mill Brook ≃, N.J., U.S.	276	40.53 N	74.32 W
Mill Brook ≃, N.J., U.S.	276	40.25 N	74.06 W
Mill Brook ≃, N.J., U.S.	276	40.29 N	74.23 W
Millburn	276	40.44 N	74.18 W
Millbury, Ma., U.S.	207	42.11 N	71.45 W
Millbury, Oh., U.S.	214	41.33 N	83.25 W
Mill City	202	44.45 N	122.29 W
Mill Creek, Pa., U.S.	214	40.26 N	77.56 W
Millcreek, Ut,. U.S.	200	40.27 N	111.54 W
Mill Creek, W.V., U.S.	188	38.43 N	79.58 W
Mill Creek ≃, Austl.	274a	33.59 S	151.01 E
Mill Creek ≃, Ca., U.S.	226	36.49 N	119.21 W
Mill Creek ≃, Ca., U.S.	228	34.05 N	117.06 W
Mill Creek ≃, De., U.S.	285	39.42 N	75.39 W
Mill Creek ≃, Il., U.S.	219	39.50 N	91.24 W
Mill Creek ≃, In., U.S.	194	39.30 N	86.57 W
Mill Creek ≃, In., U.S.	216	41.01 N	86.36 W
Mill Creek ≃, Ia., U.S.	198	42.47 N	95.31 W
Mill Creek ≃, Ks., U.S.	198	39.55 N	96.56 W
Mill Creek ≃, Ky., U.S.	218	38.28 N	84.20 W
Mill Creek ≃, N.J., U.S.	276	40.48 N	74.03 W
Mill Creek ≃, N.J., U.S.	285	40.02 N	74.55 W
Mill Creek ≃, N.Y., U.S.	212	43.57 N	76.08 W
Mill Creek ≃, Oh., U.S.	214	40.14 N	83.09 W
Mill Creek ≃, Oh., U.S.	214	41.06 N	80.40 W
Mill Creek ≃, Oh., U.S.	218	39.06 N	84.32 W
Mill Creek ≃, Oh., U.S.	279a	41.25 N	81.38 W
Mill Creek ≃, Or., U.S.	224	45.36 N	121.11 W
Mill Creek ≃, Pa., U.S.	208	40.00 N	76.18 W
Mill Creek ≃, Pa., U.S.	210	41.53 N	77.08 W
Mill Creek ≃, Pa., U.S.	214	41.09 N	79.03 W
Mill Creek ≃, Pa., U.S.	285	40.03 N	75.16 W
Mill Creek ≃, Pa., U.S.	285	40.08 N	74.52 W
Mill Creek ≃, Tx., U.S.	222	32.46 N	95.46 W
Mill Creek ≃, Tx., U.S.	222	29.50 N	96.07 W
Mill Creek ≃, Tx., U.S.	222	30.08 N	95.37 W
Mill Creek ≃, Va., U.S.	208	38.09 N	77.10 W
Mill Creek, North Fork ≃	224	45.33 N	121.18 W
Mill Creek, South Fork ≃	224	45.36 N	121.12 W
Millcreek Township	214	42.05 N	80.10 W
Milldale	207	41.33 N	72.53 W
Milledgeville, Ga., U.S.	192	33.04 N	83.13 W
Milledgeville, Il., U.S.	190	41.57 N	89.46 W
Milledgeville, Oh., U.S.	218	39.36 N	83.35 W
Mille Îles, Rivière des ≃	206	45.42 N	73.32 W
Mille Lacs, Lac des ◎	190	48.50 N	90.30 W
Mille Lacs Kathio State Park ♦	190	46.08 N	93.43 W
Mille Lacs Lake ◎	190	46.15 N	93.40 W
Millemont	261	48.49 N	1.45 E
Millen	192	32.48 N	81.56 W
Millendon	168a	31.48 S	116.02 E
Miller, Mo., U.S.	194	37.13 N	93.50 W
Miller, S.D., U.S.	198	44.31 N	98.59 W
Miller □[6]	219	38.15 N	92.15 W
Miller, Mount ∧	180	60.25 N	142.23 W
Miller City	216	41.06 N	84.08 W
Miller Creek ≃	282	38.02 N	122.30 W
Miller House	180	65.32 N	145.11 W
Miller Mountain ∧	204	38.03 N	118.12 W
Millerovo, Ross.	78	48.55 N	40.25 E
Millerovo, Ross.	83	47.49 N	39.15 E
Miller Peak ∧	200	31.23 N	110.17 W
Miller Place	210	40.58 N	73.00 W
Millers ≃	207	42.35 N	72.30 W
Millersburg, In., U.S.	216	41.31 N	85.41 W
Millersburg, In., U.S.	218	41.31 N	85.41 W
Millersburg, Ky., U.S.	218	38.18 N	84.08 W
Millersburg, Mi., U.S.	190	45.20 N	84.03 W
Millersburg, Oh., U.S.	214	40.33 N	81.55 W
Millersburg, Pa., U.S.	208	40.32 N	76.57 W
Millers Creek ≃	196	33.27 N	99.14 W
Miller Seamount ✢[3]	16	53.30 N	144.20 W
Millers Falls	207	42.34 N	72.29 W
Millers Ferry	194	32.05 N	87.22 W
Millers Flat	172	45.40 S	169.25 E
Millers Island	284b	39.14 N	76.24 W
Millers Pond ◎	276	40.51 N	73.12 W
Millersport	188	39.54 N	82.32 W
Millers Run ≃	279b	40.22 N	80.07 W
Millerstown	210	40.32 N	77.09 W
Millersville, Il., U.S.	219	39.25 N	89.07 W
Millersville, Oh., U.S.	214	41.18 N	83.16 W
Millersville, Pa., U.S.	208	39.59 N	76.21 W
Millerton, N.Y., U.S.	210	41.57 N	73.30 W
Millerton, Pa., U.S.	210	41.59 N	76.56 W
Millerton Lake ◎[1]	226	37.01 N	119.41 W
Millerton Lake State Recreation Area ♦	226	37.02 N	119.37 W
Millertown	186	48.49 N	56.33 W
Millertown Junction	186	49.01 N	56.21 W
Millesimo	62	44.22 N	8.12 E
Millet	182	53.06 N	113.28 W
Millett, Mi., U.S.	216	42.42 N	84.38 W
Millett, Tx., U.S.	196	28.35 N	99.12 W
Milleur Point ›	44	55.01 N	5.06 W
Millevaches, Plateau de ⋀[1]	32	45.30 N	2.10 E
Millford	48	55.07 N	7.43 W
Mill Green	260	51.41 N	0.22 E
Mill Grove	216	40.25 N	85.17 W
Mill Hall	210	41.06 N	77.29 W
Millheim	210	40.53 N	77.28 W
Mill Hill ⬥[8]	260	51.37 N	0.13 W
Mill Hill ∧[2]	262	53.25 N	1.54 W
Millhousen	218	39.13 N	85.26 W
Millican	222	30.28 N	96.12 W
Millicent	166	37.36 S	140.22 E
Milligan, Fl., U.S.	194	30.45 N	86.38 W
Milligan, Ne., U.S.	198	40.30 N	97.23 W
Milligan Gulch V	200	33.37 N	107.02 W
Milligantown	279b	40.33 N	79.41 W
Milliken	275b	43.49 N	79.18 W
Millingen aan de Rijn	52	51.52 N	6.02 E
Millington, Il., U.S.	216	41.34 N	88.36 W
Millington, Md., U.S.	208	39.15 N	75.50 W
Millington, Mi., U.S.	190	43.16 N	83.31 W
Millington, N.J., U.S.	210	40.40 N	74.31 W
Millington, Tn., U.S.	194	35.20 N	89.53 W
Millinocket	188	45.39 N	68.42 W
Millionnyj	89	54.30 N	126.19 E
Millis	207	42.10 N	71.21 W
Mill Island I, Ant.	9	65.30 S	100.40 E
Mill Island I, N.T., Can.	176	64.00 N	78.00 W
Millisle	48	54.36 N	5.32 W
Mill Lake ◎	212	45.22 N	80.00 W
Millmerran	166	27.52 S	151.16 E

≃	River	Fluß	Río	Rivière	Rio
≋	Canal	Kanal	Canal	Canal	Canal
⌊	Waterfall, Rapids	Wasserfall, Stromschnellen	Cascada, Rápidos	Chute d'eau, Rapides	Cascata, Rápidos
⩀	Strait	Meeresstraße	Estrecho	Détroit	Estreito
⊂	Bay, Gulf	Bucht, Golf	Bahía, Golfo	Baie, Golfe	Baía, Golfo
◎	Lake, Lakes	See, Seen	Lago, Lagos	Lac, Lacs	Lago, Lagos
≡	Swamp	Sumpf	Pantano	Marais	Pântano
⌸	Ice Features, Glacier	Eis- und Gletscherformen	Accidentes Glaciales	Formes glaciaires	Acidentes glaciares
⊤	Other Hydrographic Features	Andere Hydrographische Objekte	Otros Elementos Hidrográficos	Autres données hydrographiques	Outros acidentes hidrográficos

✢	Submarine Features	Untermeerische Objekte	Accidentes Submarinos	Formes de relief sous-marin	Acidentes submarinos
□	Political Unit	Politische Einheit	Unidad Politica	Entité politique	Unidade política
✝	Cultural Institution	Kulturelle Institution	Institución Cultural	Institution culturelle	Instituição cultural
⊥	Historical Site	Historische Stätte	Sitio Histórico	Site historique	Sitio histórico
♦	Recreational Site	Erholungs- und Ferienort	Sitio de Recreo	Centre de loisirs	Area de Lazer
⊠	Airport	Flughafen	Aeropuerto	Aéroport	Aeroporto
■	Military Installation	Militäranlage	Instalación Militar	Installation militaire	Instalação militar
⬥	Miscellaneous	Verschiedenes	Misceláneo	Divers	Diversos

ENGLISH | DEUTSCH

Name / Name	Page / Seite	Lat.°′ / Breite°′	Long.°′ / Länge°′ E = Ost
Millmont	210	40.53 N	77.08 W
Mill Neck	276	40.52 N	73.34 W
Mill Neck ≻[1]	276	40.53 N	73.33 W
Mill Neck Creek c	276	40.54 N	73.33 W
Millom	44	54.13 N	3.18 W
Mill Pond ⊜	276	40.53 N	73.22 W
Millport, Scot., U.K.	46	55.46 N	4.55 W
Millport, Al., U.S.	194	33.33 N	88.04 W
Millport, N.Y., U.S.	210	42.16 N	76.50 W
Millport, Pa., U.S.	214	41.55 N	78.07 W
Millrift	210	41.25 N	74.45 W
Mill River	207	42.06 N	73.16 W
Mill Run Acres	284c	38.58 N	77.17 W
Millry	194	31.38 N	88.18 W
Mills, Pa., U.S.	214	41.57 N	77.41 W
Mills, Wy., U.S.	202	42.50 N	106.21 W
Mills, Lake ⊜[1]	224	47.59 N	123.36 W
Millsboro	208	38.35 N	75.17 W
Mills Creek ≃, Austl.	166	22.23 S	143.05 E
Mills Creek ≃, Ca., U.S.	282	37.27 N	122.25 W
Mills Lake ⊜	176	61.30 N	118.10 W
Mills Mansion State Historic Site ⊥	210	41.52 N	73.57 W
Millstadt	219	38.27 N	90.05 W
Millstatt	64	46.48 N	13.35 E
Millstätter See ⊜	64	46.47 N	13.35 E
Millstone	276	40.29 N	74.35 W
Millstone ≃	276	40.33 N	74.34 W
Millstream, Austl.	162	21.35 S	117.04 E
Millstream, B.C., Can.	224	48.30 N	123.31 W
Millstream Chichester National Park ♠	162	21.25 S	117.20 E
Millstreet	48	52.03 N	9.04 W
Milltown, Scot., U.K.	46	57.14 N	2.52 W
Milltown, In., U.S.	218	38.20 N	86.16 W
Milltown, Mt., U.S.	202	46.52 N	113.52 W
Milltown, N.J., U.S.	208	40.27 N	74.26 W
Milltown, Wi., U.S.	190	45.31 N	92.30 W
Milltown Malbay	48	52.50 N	9.23 W
Millvale	279b	40.28 N	79.58 W
Mill Valley	226	37.54 N	122.32 W
Mill Village	214	41.53 N	79.58 W
Millville, Ma., U.S.	207	42.01 N	71.34 W
Millville, N.J., U.S.	208	39.24 N	75.02 W
Millville, Oh., U.S.	218	39.24 N	84.40 W
Millville, Pa., U.S.	210	41.07 N	76.31 W
Millville Lake	283	42.48 N	71.13 W
Millville Lake ⊜	283	42.48 N	71.13 W
Millwood, Md., U.S.	284c	38.53 N	76.53 W
Millwood, N.Y., U.S.	210	41.11 N	73.48 W
Millwood, Va., U.S.	188	39.04 N	78.02 W
Millwood Lake ⊜[1]	194	33.45 N	94.00 W
Milly-la-Forêt	50	48.24 N	2.28 E
Milly-Lamartine	58	46.21 N	4.42 E
Milmay	208	39.26 N	74.51 W
Milmersdorf	54	53.06 N	13.38 E
Milmine	219	39.54 N	88.39 W
Milmont Park	285	39.53 N	75.20 W
Milne Bay □[5]	164	10.00 S	152.30 E
Milne Bay c	164	10.22 S	150.30 E
Milner	224	49.20 N	122.42 W
Milnesville	210	40.59 N	75.59 W
Milngavie	46	55.57 N	4.20 W
Milnor	198	46.15 N	97.27 W
Milnrow	44	53.37 N	2.06 W
Milnthorpe	44	54.14 N	2.46 W
Milo, Ab., Can.	182	50.34 N	112.53 W
Milo, Ia., U.S.	190	41.17 N	93.26 W
Milo, Me., U.S.	188	45.15 N	68.59 W
Milo ≃	150	11.04 N	9.14 W
Milon-la-Chapelle	261	48.44 N	2.03 E
Mílos	38	36.45 N	24.27 E
Mílos I	38	36.41 N	24.15 E
Miloslaviči	76	53.41 N	32.15 E
Miloslavskoje	76	53.34 N	39.24 E
Miłosław	30	52.13 N	17.29 E
Milove	83	49.22 N	40.06 E
Milow, Dtsch.	54	53.11 N	11.32 E
Milow, Dtsch.	54	52.31 N	12.18 E
Milpa Alta ◆[8]	286a	19.11 N	99.01 W
Milparinka	166	29.44 S	141.53 E
Milpitas	226	37.25 N	121.54 W
Milpitas Wash V	204	33.18 N	114.44 W
Milroy, In., U.S.	218	39.29 N	85.28 W
Milroy, Pa., U.S.	208	40.42 N	77.35 W
Milseburg ∧	56	50.32 N	9.53 E
Milspe	263	51.18 N	7.21 E
Miltach	60	49.09 N	12.46 E
Miltenberg	56	49.42 N	9.15 E
Miltitz	54	51.19 N	12.16 E
Milton, Austl.	170	35.19 S	150.26 E
Milton, On., Can.	212	43.31 N	79.53 W
Milton, N.Z.	172	46.07 S	169.58 E
Milton, Eng., U.K.	42	52.14 N	0.09 E
Milton, De., U.S.	208	38.46 N	75.18 W
Milton, Fl., U.S.	194	30.37 N	87.02 W
Milton, Il., U.S.	219	39.34 N	90.39 W
Milton, In., U.S.	218	39.47 N	85.09 W
Milton, In., U.S.	218	38.58 N	85.01 W
Milton, Ia., U.S.	190	40.40 N	92.09 W
Milton, Ky., U.S.	218	38.43 N	85.22 W
Milton, Ma., U.S.	207	42.15 N	71.05 W
Milton, N.J., U.S.	276	41.02 N	74.32 W
Milton, N.Y., U.S.	210	41.39 N	73.57 W
Milton, N.D., U.S.	198	48.37 N	98.02 W
Milton, Pa., U.S.	210	41.00 N	76.50 W
Milton, Vt., U.S.	188	44.38 N	73.06 W
Milton, Wa., U.S.	224	47.14 N	122.18 W
Milton, W.V., U.S.	188	38.26 N	82.07 W
Milton, Wi., U.S.	216	42.46 N	88.56 W
Milton, Lake ⊜	214	41.06 N	80.58 W
Milton Abbot	42	50.35 N	4.15 W
Milton-Freewater	202	45.55 N	118.23 W
Milton Harbor c	276	40.57 N	73.42 W
Milton Keynes	42	52.02 N	0.42 W
Milton Point ≻	276	40.57 N	73.42 W
Miltonvale	198	39.20 N	97.26 W
Miltou	146	10.14 N	17.26 E
Miltzow	54	54.12 N	13.13 E
Milumba	154	7.06 S	31.04 E
Miluo	100	28.50 N	113.04 E
Miluo ≃	100	28.50 N	113.06 E
Mil'utinskaja	80	48.38 N	41.40 E
Mil'utkej, gora ∧	180	65.42 N	178.03 W
Miluvatka	83	49.21 N	38.11 E
Milverton, On., Can.	212	43.34 N	80.55 W
Milverton, Eng., U.K.	42	51.02 N	3.16 W
Milwaukee	216	43.02 N	87.54 W
Milwaukee □[6]	216	43.02 N	87.58 W
Milwaukee ≃	190	43.02 N	87.54 W
Milwaukee Bay c	216	43.02 N	87.53 W
Milwaukie	224	45.26 N	122.38 W
Mim	150	6.54 N	2.34 W
Mima	96	33.17 N	132.36 E
Mimasaka	96	35.00 N	134.10 E
Mimbres ≃	200	32.13 N	107.28 W
Mimbres Mountains ⋌	200	32.45 N	107.45 W
Mimi ≃	92	32.20 N	131.37 E
Mimico ◆[8]	275b	43.37 N	79.30 W
Mimico Creek ≃	275b	43.37 N	79.29 W
Mimizan	32	44.12 N	1.14 W
Mimmaya	92	41.12 N	140.26 E
Mimoň	54	50.40 N	14.44 E
Mimongo	152	1.11 S	11.36 E
Mimoso, Bra.	248	16.17 S	55.48 W
Mimoso, Bra.	255	15.10 S	48.05 W
Mimoso do Sul	255	21.04 S	41.22 W
Mims	220	28.39 N	80.50 W
Mimuro-yama ∧	96	35.14 N	134.28 E
Min ≃, Zhg.	100	26.05 N	119.32 E
Min ≃, Zhg.	102	28.46 N	104.38 E
Mina, Méx.	196	26.01 N	100.32 W
Mina, Nv., U.S.	204	38.23 N	118.06 W
Mina ≃	112	10.09 S	124.12 E
Mina, Oued ≃	34	35.47 N	0.30 E
Mīnā' al-Ahmadī	128	29.04 N	48.08 E
Mīnāb	128	27.09 N	57.05 E
Mīnāb ≃	128	27.01 N	56.53 E
Minabe	96	33.46 N	135.19 E
Minabegawa	96	33.47 N	135.20 E
Mina El Limón	236	12.45 N	86.44 W
Minago ≃	184	54.34 N	98.08 W
Minahasa ≻[1]	112	1.00 N	124.35 E
Mināj ≃[1]	126	22.31 N	89.22 E
Minakami	94	36.46 N	138.58 E
Minakuchi	94	34.58 N	136.10 E
Minam ≃	202	45.37 N	117.43 W
Minamata	92	32.13 N	130.24 E
Minami	94	35.39 N	136.57 E
Minami ◆[8], Nihon	268	35.24 N	139.36 E
Minami ◆[8], Nihon	270	34.40 N	135.31 E
Minami ◆[8], Nihon	270	34.58 N	135.45 E
Minami ≃	94	35.30 N	135.49 E
Minamiaiki	94	36.02 N	138.33 E
Minami-Alps-kokuritsu-kōen ♠	94	35.40 N	138.13 E
Minamiashigara	94	35.19 N	139.07 E
Minami-Bōsō-kokutei-kōen ♠	94	35.10 N	140.05 E
Minamichita	94	34.44 N	136.52 E
Minami-Daitō-jima I	90	25.50 N	131.15 E
Minami-Iō-jima I	14	24.14 N	141.28 E
Minamiizu	94	34.39 N	138.50 E
Minamimaki	94	36.00 N	138.30 E
Minaminasu	94	36.39 N	140.06 E
Minamisenju ◆[8]	268	35.44 N	139.48 E
Minamishinano	94	35.19 N	137.56 E
Minami-Tori-shima (Marcus Island) I	14	24.18 N	153.58 E
Minano	94	36.04 N	139.06 E
Mina Pirquitas	252	22.41 S	66.31 W
Minard, S. Afr.	158	31.17 S	27.35 E
Minard, Scot., U.K.	46	56.07 N	5.15 W
Minas, Cuba	240p	21.29 N	77.37 W
Minas, Indon.	114	0.50 N	101.29 E
Minas, Ur.	252	34.23 S	55.14 W
Minas, Sierra de las ⋌	236	15.10 N	89.40 W
Minas Basin c	186	45.20 N	64.00 W
Minas Channel ⊍	186	45.15 N	64.45 W
Minas de Barroterán	232	27.40 N	101.20 W
Minas de Corrales	252	31.35 S	55.28 W
Minas de Matahambre	240p	22.35 N	83.57 W
Minas de Oro	236	14.46 N	87.20 W
Minas de Ríotinto	34	37.42 N	6.35 W
Minas Gerais □[3]	255	18.00 S	44.00 W
Minas Novas	255	17.15 S	42.36 W
Minatare	198	41.48 N	103.30 W
Minatitlán	234	17.59 N	94.31 W
Minato	268	35.13 N	139.52 E
Minato ◆[8], Nihon	268	35.39 N	139.45 E
Minato ◆[8], Nihon	270	34.39 N	135.26 E
Minato ≃	268	35.13 N	139.52 E
Minbāl	142	28.24 N	30.41 E
Minbu	110	20.11 N	94.52 E
Minbulak	85	41.30 N	75.53 E
Minbya	110	20.22 N	93.15 E
Minbyin	110	19.17 N	93.32 E
Minchinābād	123	30.10 N	73.34 E
Minchinhampton	42	51.42 N	2.10 W
Minchumina, Lake ⊜	180	63.52 N	152.15 W
Mincio ≃	64	45.04 N	10.59 E
Mincivan	84	39.03 N	46.42 E
Minco	196	35.18 N	97.56 W
Minčol ∧	30	49.15 N	20.59 E
Mind'ak	86	54.02 N	58.48 E
Mindanao I	116	8.00 N	125.00 E
Mindanao ≃	116	7.07 N	124.24 E
Mindego Creek ≃	282	37.18 N	122.15 W
Mindego Hill ∧[2]	282	37.18 N	122.13 W
Mindel ≃	58	48.31 N	10.23 E
Mindelheim	58	48.03 N	10.29 E
Mindelo	150a	16.53 N	25.00 W
Mindemoya	190	45.44 N	82.10 W
Minden, On., Can.	212	44.55 N	78.43 W
Minden, Dtsch.	52	52.17 N	8.55 E
Minden, La., U.S.	194	32.36 N	93.17 W
Minden, Ne., U.S.	198	40.29 N	98.56 W
Minden, Nv., U.S.	226	38.57 N	119.45 W
Minden, W.V., U.S.	188	37.58 N	81.07 W
Minden City	190	43.40 N	82.46 W
Mindenmines	194	37.28 N	94.35 W
Minderoo	162	22.00 S	115.02 E
Mindif	146	10.24 N	14.26 E
Mindiptana	164	5.45 S	140.42 E
Mindon	110	19.21 N	94.44 E
Mindoro I	116	12.50 N	121.05 E
Mindoro Occidental □[4]	116	13.00 N	121.00 E
Mindoro Oriental □[4]	116	13.00 N	121.20 E
Mindoro Strait ⊍	116	12.20 N	120.40 E
Mindouli	152	4.17 S	14.21 E
Mindourou, Cam.	152	3.25 N	13.32 E
Mindourou, Cam.	152	4.06 N	14.34 E
Minduri	256	21.41 S	44.37 W
Mine, Ityo.	144	8.20 N	40.09 E
Mine, Nihon	96	33.17 N	130.26 E
Mine, Nihon	96	34.10 N	131.13 E
Minear Lake ⊜	278	42.17 N	87.57 W
Minebank Run ≃	284b	39.25 N	76.32 W
Mine Brook ≃, Ma., U.S.	283	42.08 N	71.26 W
Mine Brook ≃, Ma., U.S.	283	42.09 N	71.15 W
Mine Brook ≃, N.J., U.S.	276	40.41 N	74.38 W
Mine Centre	190	48.45 N	92.37 W
Minehead	42	51.13 N	3.29 W
Mine Hill	210	40.52 N	74.35 W
Mineiros	255	17.34 S	52.34 W
Mineo	70	37.16 N	14.42 E
Mineola, N.Y., U.S.	210	40.44 N	73.38 W
Mineola, Tx., U.S.	222	32.39 N	95.29 W
Miner ≃	180	66.30 N	138.25 W
Mineral	224	46.43 N	122.10 W
Mineral City	214	40.36 N	81.21 W
Mineral Creek ≃	224	46.45 N	122.08 W
Mineral de Cucharas	234	22.52 N	105.19 W
Mineral del Monte	234	20.08 N	98.40 W
Mineral de Pozos	234	21.14 N	100.29 W
Mineral'nyje Vody	84	44.12 N	43.08 E
Mineral Point, Pa., U.S.	214	40.23 N	78.50 W
Mineral Point, Wi., U.S.	190	42.51 N	90.10 W
Mineral Ridge	214	41.08 N	80.46 W
Mineral Springs, Ar., U.S.	194	33.52 N	93.54 W
Mineral Springs, Pa., U.S.	214	41.00 N	78.22 W
Mineral Wells	196	32.48 N	98.06 W
Minerbe	64	45.14 N	11.20 E
Minerbio	64	44.37 N	11.29 E
Minersville, Pa., U.S.	208	40.41 N	76.16 W
Minersville, Ut,. U.S.	200	38.12 N	112.55 W
Mine Run ≃	285	40.15 N	75.28 W
Minerva, Ky., U.S.	218	38.42 N	83.55 W
Minerva, Oh., U.S.	214	40.43 N	81.06 W
Minerva, Tx., U.S.	222	30.46 N	96.59 W
Minerva, Embalse ⊜[1]	240p	22.25 N	79.48 W
Minerva Park	214	40.04 N	83.00 W
Minervino Murge	68	41.05 N	16.05 E
Minesing Swamp ≡	212	44.23 N	79.51 W
Minetto	210	43.23 N	76.28 W
Mineville	188	44.05 N	73.31 W
Mineyama	96	35.37 N	135.04 E
Minfeng	120	37.05 N	82.40 E
Minga	154	11.08 S	27.57 E
Mingäçevir	84	40.45 N	47.03 E
Mingäçevir su anbarı ⊜[1]	84	40.50 N	46.50 E
Mingala	152	5.06 N	21.49 E
Mingan	186	50.18 N	64.02 W
Mingan ≃	186	50.18 N	63.59 W
Mingan, Îles de II	186	50.12 N	63.35 W
Mingan Archipelago National Park ♠	186	50.12 N	63.35 W
Mingan Mountains ⋌	116	15.29 N	121.24 E
Mingāora	123	34.47 N	72.22 E
Mingardo ≃	68	40.02 N	15.18 E
Mingary	166	32.08 S	140.44 E
Mingcheng	89	43.11 N	125.59 E
Mingela	166	19.53 S	146.38 E
Mingenew	162	29.11 S	115.26 E
Mingera Creek ≃	166	20.38 S	138.10 E
Minggang	100	32.29 N	114.03 E
Minggao	100	34.20 N	112.15 E
Minghuang	106	31.41 N	119.56 E
Mingin	110	22.52 N	94.39 E
Mingir	38	46.40 N	28.19 E
Mingjuesi	106	31.34 N	118.53 E
Minglanilla	34	39.32 N	1.36 W
Ming Ming	164	5.30 S	146.10 E
Mingo, Congo	152	1.55 S	14.59 E
Mingo, Oh., U.S.	216	40.13 N	83.38 W
Mingo Creek ≃, Pa., U.S.	279b	40.13 N	79.57 W
Mingo Creek ≃, Pa., U.S.	285	40.10 N	75.32 W
Mingo Junction	214	40.19 N	80.36 W
Mingorría	34	40.45 N	4.40 W
Mingoville	214	40.56 N	77.39 W
Mingoyo	154	10.06 S	39.38 E
Mingrel'skaja	78	45.01 N	38.20 E
Mingshantou	100	29.18 N	112.33 E
Mingshui, Zhg.	89	47.10 N	125.55 E
Mingshui, Zhg.	102	42.06 N	96.04 E
Mingulay I	46	56.49 N	7.38 W
Mingwan	106	31.04 N	120.17 E
Mingxi	100	26.24 N	117.13 E
Mingyuegou	89	43.07 N	128.54 E
Mingyuelu	85	39.34 N	75.26 E
Minhang	106	31.01 N	121.24 E
Minhla, Mya.	110	19.58 N	95.03 E
Minhla, Mya.	110	17.59 N	95.43 E
Minho □[9]	34	41.40 N	8.30 W
Minho (Miño) ≃	34	41.52 N	8.51 W
Minhou	100	26.12 N	119.06 E
Minianko	150	9.58 N	8.22 W
Minićevo	38	43.41 N	22.18 E
Minicoy Island I	122	8.17 N	73.02 E
Minier	194	40.26 N	89.18 W
Minigwal, Lake ⊜	162	29.35 S	123.12 E
Minija ≃	76	55.21 N	21.17 E
Minilya	162	23.51 S	113.58 E
Minilya ≃	162	23.56 S	113.51 E
Minimarg	123	34.47 N	75.05 E
Minīn	132	33.39 N	36.18 E
Miniota	184	50.08 N	101.00 W
Minisinakwa Lake ⊜	190	47.40 N	81.43 W
Ministikwan Lake ⊜	184	54.01 N	109.39 W
Ministro Ramos Mexía	254	40.30 S	67.17 W
Ministro Rivadavia	288	34.51 S	58.22 W
Minitonas	184	52.07 N	101.00 W
Minj	164	5.54 S	144.39 E
Minjar	86	55.04 N	57.33 E
Minjary, Mount ∧	171b	35.14 S	148.08 E
Minjiadianzi	104	41.35 N	121.41 E
Minjiaji	100	31.08 N	115.01 E
Minkamman	140	6.03 N	31.32 E
Min'kovo	76	59.42 N	43.28 E
Min-Kuš	85	41.41 N	74.28 E
Minlaton	168b	34.46 S	137.36 E
Minle, Zhg.	100	22.59 N	112.58 E
Minle, Zhg.	102	38.27 N	100.56 E
Minna	150	9.37 N	6.33 E
Minna Bluff ≻[1]	9	78.32 S	166.30 E
Minna-shima I, Nihon	174m	26.39 N	127.49 E
Minna-shima I, Nihon	175d	24.45 N	124.42 E
Minneapolis, Ks., U.S.	198	39.07 N	97.42 W
Minneapolis, Mn., U.S.	190	44.58 N	93.15 W
Minnechaduza Creek ≃	198	42.54 N	100.29 W
Minnedosa	184	50.14 N	99.51 W
Minnehaha	224	45.39 N	122.37 W
Minnehaha, Lake ⊜	220	28.31 N	81.46 W
Minneola, Fl., U.S.	220	28.35 N	81.45 W
Minneola, Ks., U.S.	198	37.26 N	100.00 W
Minneola, Lake ⊜	220	28.34 N	81.46 W
Minneosa Creek ≃	196	35.31 N	102.48 W
Minneota	198	44.34 N	95.59 W
Minnertsga	52	53.15 N	5.35 E
Minnesota □[3]	178	46.00 N	94.15 W
Minnesota ≃	178	44.54 N	93.10 W
Minnesota Lake	190	43.50 N	93.49 W
Minnewanka, Lake ⊜	182	51.15 N	115.20 W
Minnewaukan	198	48.04 N	99.15 W
Minnie Creek	162	24.02 S	115.42 E
Minnigaff	44	54.58 N	4.30 W
Minnipa	162	32.51 S	135.09 E
Minnitaki Lake ⊜	184	49.58 N	92.00 W
Minnoch, Water of ≃	44	55.02 N	4.33 W
Mino, Nihon	94	35.32 N	136.55 E
Minō, Nihon	96	34.50 N	135.28 E
Miño (Minho) ≃, Europe	34	41.52 N	8.51 W
Minō ≃, Nihon	270	34.47 N	134.57 E
Minoa	210	43.04 N	76.00 W
Minobu	94	35.22 N	138.26 E
Minobu-san ∧	94	35.24 N	138.25 E
Minobu-sanchi ⋌	94	35.14 N	138.20 E
Minocqua	190	45.52 N	89.42 W
Minokamo	94	35.26 N	137.01 E
Mino-Mikawa-kōgen ⋌[1]	94	35.11 N	137.23 E
Minong	190	46.05 N	91.49 W
Minonk	216	40.54 N	89.02 W
Minooka	216	41.27 N	88.16 W
Minorca → Menorca I	34	40.00 N	4.00 E
Minori	94	36.14 N	140.21 E
Minorsville	218	38.20 N	84.42 W
Minoshō	270	34.39 N	135.49 E
Minot, Ma., U.S.	283	42.14 N	70.45 W
Minot, N.D., U.S.	198	48.13 N	101.17 W
Minot Air Force Base ■	198	48.26 N	101.21 W
Minowa	94	35.55 N	137.59 E
Minqiao	100	32.53 N	119.13 E
Minqin	102	38.42 N	103.11 E
Minqing	100	26.12 N	118.51 E
Minquadale	285	39.42 N	75.34 W
Minquan	98	34.41 N	115.11 E
Minquiers, Plateau des II	32	48.57 N	2.09 W
Minsen	52	53.42 N	7.58 E
Min Shan ⋌	102	33.35 N	103.00 E
Minshāt adh-Dhahab	142	28.00 N	30.42 E
Minshat al-Amir Muhammad 'Ali	142	29.10 N	30.38 E
Minshāt al-Bakkārī	273c	30.01 N	31.08 E
Minshāt al-Ikhwah	142	30.56 N	31.21 E
Minshāt al-Mughālaqah	142	27.44 N	30.47 E
Minshāt Būlīn	142	31.11 N	30.10 E
Minshāt Sulṭān	142	30.32 N	30.55 E
Minsk	76	53.54 N	27.34 E
Minsk □[8]	76	53.45 N	27.45 E
Minskaja vozvyšennost' ⋌[1]	76	54.00 N	27.10 E
Mińsk Mazowiecki	30	52.11 N	21.34 E
Minster, Eng., U.K.	42	51.20 N	1.19 E
Minster, Eng., U.K.	42	51.26 N	0.49 E
Minster, Oh., U.S.	216	40.24 N	84.23 W
Minsterley	42	52.39 N	2.55 W
Minta	152	4.35 N	12.48 E
Mintaka Pass)(	123	37.00 N	74.50 E
Mintard	263	51.22 N	6.54 E
Mintaro	168b	33.55 S	138.43 E
Mint Canyon	228	34.26 N	118.25 W
Mintlaw	46	57.31 N	2.00 W
Minto, Austl.	274a	34.01 S	150.51 E
Minto, Mb., Can.	184	49.25 N	100.01 W
Minto, N.B., Can.	186	46.05 N	66.05 W
Minto, Yk., Can.	180	62.34 N	136.51 W
Minto, Ak., U.S.	180	65.09 N	149.21 W
Minto, N.D., U.S.	198	48.17 N	97.22 W
Minto, Lac ⊜	176	57.13 N	75.00 W
Minto, Mount ∧	9	71.55 S	169.33 E
Minto Inlet c	176	71.20 N	117.00 W
Mintom II	152	2.42 N	13.17 E
Minton	184	49.10 N	104.35 W
Mintoum	152	0.27 N	12.16 E
Minturn	200	39.35 N	106.25 W
Minturnae ⊥	68	41.14 N	13.45 E
Minturno	66	41.15 N	13.45 E
Minūf	142	30.28 N	30.56 E
Minulovo	265a	60.03 N	30.45 E
Minumadai-yōsui ≡	268	35.50 N	139.42 E
Minur'uk	85	40.56 N	73.22 E
Minusinsk	86	53.43 N	91.42 E
Minutang	120	28.13 N	96.32 E
Minute Man National Historical Park ♠	207	42.27 N	71.17 W
Minvoul	152	2.09 N	12.08 E
Minwakh	144	16.50 N	48.05 E
Minxian	102	34.26 N	104.02 E
Minya → Al-Minyā	142	28.06 N	30.45 E
Minyā al-Qamḥ	142	30.31 N	31.21 E
Minya Konka → Gongga Shan ∧	102	29.35 N	101.51 E
Minyat an-Naṣr	142	31.07 N	31.39 E
Minyat as-Sīrij ◆[8]	273c	30.05 N	31.15 E
Minyat Sandūb	142	31.00 N	31.23 E
Minzow	54	53.23 N	12.30 E
Mio	190	44.39 N	84.07 W
Mioglia	62	44.29 N	8.25 E
Mionica	38	44.15 N	20.05 E
Miory	76	55.37 N	27.38 E
Mipi	120	28.57 N	95.48 E
Miquan	86	44.06 N	87.35 E
Miquelon I	186	47.03 N	56.20 W
Miquihuana	234	23.34 N	99.47 W
Miquon	285	40.04 N	75.16 W
Mir, Bela.	76	53.27 N	26.28 E
Mir, Cuba	240p	20.46 N	76.36 W
Mīr, Miṣr	142	27.27 N	30.44 E
Mir, Niger	146	14.05 N	11.59 E
Mira	34	40.26 N	8.44 W
Mira ≃, N.S., Can.	186	46.03 N	60.00 W
Mira ≃, Col.	246	1.36 N	79.01 W
Mira ≃, Port.	34	37.43 N	8.47 W
Mīrābād	128	30.25 N	61.50 E
Mira Bay c	186	46.02 N	59.56 W
Mirabeau	62	43.42 N	5.39 E
Mirabel	206	45.39 N	74.05 W
Mirabel, Aéroport International de ⊠	206	45.41 N	74.02 W
Mirabella Eclano	68	41.02 N	14.59 E
Mirabella Imbaccari	70	37.19 N	14.27 E
Mirabello, Ippodromo ♠	266b	45.36 N	9.17 E
Mirabello Monferrato	62	45.02 N	8.31 E
Miracema do Tocantins	250	9.33 S	48.24 W
Mirada Hills → La Mirada	228	33.54 N	118.01 W
Mirador	250	6.22 S	44.22 W
Mirador, Cerro ∧	286d	11.57 S	77.02 W
Mirador, Paso de)(	254	40.42 S	71.56 W
Miradouro	255	20.53 S	42.21 W
Miraflores, Arg.	252	28.36 S	65.55 W
Miraflores, Col.	246	5.12 N	73.12 W
Miraflores, Col.	246	1.25 N	72.13 W
Miraflores, Perú	286d	12.07 S	77.02 W
Miraflores, Esclusas de ◆[5]	236	9.00 N	79.36 W
Miraflores, Palacio ⊌	286c	10.31 N	66.55 W
Mīrah, Wādī al- V	128	32.26 N	41.42 E
Miraí	256	21.12 S	42.37 W
Miraj	122	16.50 N	74.38 E
Miraki	85	39.02 N	67.10 E
Miraleste	228	33.46 N	118.19 W
Mira Loma	228	34.01 N	117.31 W
Miramar, Arg.	252	38.16 S	57.51 W
Miramar, Arg.	252	30.54 S	62.40 W
Miramar, C.R.	236	10.06 N	84.44 W
Miramar, Fr.	62	43.30 N	6.57 E
Miramar, Moç.	156	23.50 S	35.34 E
Miramar, Fl., U.S.	220	25.59 N	80.13 W
Miramar ◆[8]	286b	23.07 N	82.25 W
Miramar, Laguna ⊜	236	16.23 N	91.16 W
Miramare	66	44.02 N	12.38 E
Miramare, Aeroporto di ⊠	66	44.02 N	12.35 E
Miramare, Castello di ⊥	64	45.42 N	13.43 E
Miramar Naval Air Station ■	228	32.52 N	117.07 W
Miramas	62	43.35 N	5.00 E
Mirambeau	32	45.23 N	0.34 W
Miramichi Bay c	186	47.08 N	65.08 W
Mira Monte	228	36.42 N	119.03 W
Mīram Shāh	120	33.01 N	70.04 E
Mīrān	123	31.24 N	70.43 E
Miranda, Austl.	274a	34.02 S	151.06 E
Miranda, Bra.	248	20.14 S	56.22 W
Miranda, Col.	246	3.15 N	76.14 W
Miranda, Ca., U.S.	204	40.14 N	123.49 W
Miranda □[3]	246	10.15 N	66.25 W
Miranda ≃	248	19.25 S	57.20 W
Miranda, Aerodromo ⊠	286c	10.29 N	66.50 W
Miranda de Ebro	34	42.41 N	2.57 W
Miranda do Douro	34	41.30 N	6.16 W
Mirande	32	43.31 N	0.25 E
Mirandela	34	41.29 N	7.11 W
Mirando City	196	27.26 N	99.00 W
Mirandola	64	44.53 N	11.04 E
Mirano	64	45.30 N	12.07 E
Mirantão	256	22.15 S	44.30 W
Mirante do Paranapanema	255	22.17 S	51.54 W
Mirapuxi ≃	255	13.06 S	51.10 W
Mirasaka	96	34.46 N	132.58 E
Mira Taglio	64	45.26 N	12.08 E
Miravalles, Volcán ∧[1]	236	10.45 N	85.10 W
Miravete, Puerto de)(	34	39.43 N	5.43 W
Mīr Bacheh Kowt	120	34.45 N	69.08 E
Mirbāṭ	118	17.00 N	54.45 E
Mirboo North	169	38.24 S	146.10 E
Mirebeau-sur-Bèze	58	47.24 N	5.19 E
Mirecourt	58	48.18 N	6.08 E
Miren	64	45.54 N	13.37 E
Mirfield	44	53.40 N	1.41 W
Mirgorodka	80	50.58 N	53.33 E
Miri	112	4.23 N	113.59 E
Miriam Vale	166	24.20 S	151.34 E
Mirim, Lagoa (Laguna Merín) c	252	32.45 S	52.50 W
Mirimichi, Lake ⊜	283	42.02 N	71.18 W
Mírina	38	39.52 N	25.04 E
Miriñay ≃	252	30.10 S	57.39 W
Mirinzal	250	2.01 S	44.43 W
Miritiparaná ≃	246	1.11 S	70.02 W
Miriyama	164	3.57 S	141.45 E
Mīrjāveh	128	29.01 N	61.28 E
Mirke ◆[8]	263	51.16 N	7.09 E
Mirna ≃	64	45.19 N	13.36 E
Mirnock ∧	64	46.46 N	13.43 E
Mirnoje Ozero	86	57.44 N	78.45 E
Mirnyj, Ross.	74	62.33 N	113.53 E
Mirnyj, Ross.	80	53.30 N	50.18 E
Mirnyy ⊌[3]	9	66.33 S	93.00 E
Mirond Lake ⊜	184	55.06 N	102.47 W
Mironeasa	38	46.58 N	27.25 E
Mironovo	88	58.19 N	109.38 E
Miroslav	61	48.57 N	16.18 E
Mirosławiec	30	53.21 N	16.05 E
Mirošov	60	49.41 N	13.40 E
Mirove	78	47.45 N	34.45 E
Mirovice	60	49.31 N	14.02 E
Mirow	54	53.16 N	12.49 E
Mīrpur, Bngl.	126	23.47 N	90.21 E
Mīrpur, Bngl.	126	23.56 N	88.59 E
Mīrpur, Pāk.	123	33.11 N	73.47 E
Mīrpur Batoro	120	24.44 N	68.16 E
Mīrpur Bībīwāri	120	28.32 N	67.44 E
Mīrpur Khās	120	25.32 N	69.00 E
Mīrpur Sakro	120	24.33 N	67.37 E
Mirria	150	13.43 N	9.07 E
Mirror	182	52.28 N	113.07 W
Mirror Lake ⊜, Ma., U.S.	283	42.05 N	71.20 W
Mirror Lake ⊜, N.J., U.S.	276	40.29 N	74.22 W
Mirtağ	130	38.23 N	41.56 E
Mirto	70	38.05 N	14.45 E
Mirtóön Pélagos ▾[2]	38	36.51 N	23.18 E
Miryang	98	35.31 N	128.44 E
Miry Run ≃	285	40.15 N	74.49 W
Mirza-Aki	85	40.45 N	73.25 E
Mirzaani	84	41.23 N	46.09 E
Mirzāganj	126	22.21 N	90.14 E
Mīrzākalu	126	22.29 N	90.48 E
Mirzāpur, Bngl.	126	24.06 N	90.06 E
Mirzāpur, India	124	25.09 N	82.35 E
Mirzāpur, India	272b	22.50 N	88.24 E
Mis, It.	64	46.12 N	11.57 E
Mis, It.	64	46.09 N	12.05 E
Misa ≃	66	43.43 N	13.14 E
Misāḥah, Bi'r ▾[4]	140	22.12 N	27.57 E
Misailovo	265b	55.34 N	37.49 E
Misaka	94	35.38 N	138.40 E
Misaka-tōge)(	96	33.42 N	132.52 E
Misaki, Nihon	94	35.18 N	140.22 E
Misaki → Miura, Nihon	94	35.08 N	139.37 E
Misaki, Nihon	96	33.23 N	132.07 E
Misaki, Nihon	96	34.19 N	135.09 E
Misakubo	94	35.09 N	137.52 E
Misallah, Ra's ≻	142	29.50 N	32.36 E
Misamis Occidental □[4]	116	8.20 N	123.42 E
Misamis Oriental □[4]	116	8.45 N	125.00 E
Misano Adriatico	66	43.57 N	12.39 E
Misantla	234	19.56 N	96.50 W
Misasa	96	35.24 N	133.54 E
Misasagi → Fujiidera	96	34.34 N	135.36 E
Misato, Nihon	94	36.23 N	138.57 E
Misato, Nihon	94	34.43 N	136.24 E
Misato, Nihon	94	36.15 N	137.54 E
Misato, Nihon	96	34.09 N	135.22 E
Misato, Nihon	268	35.50 N	139.53 E
Misawa	92	40.41 N	141.24 E
Misbourne ≃	260	51.34 N	0.29 W
Misburg	52	52.23 N	9.51 E
Miscou Centre	186	47.57 N	64.34 W
Miscou Island I	186	47.57 N	64.33 W
Miscou Point ≻	186	48.03 N	64.32 W
Mišelevka	88	52.51 N	103.09 E
Misema ≃	190	47.54 N	79.53 W
Mi-sen ∧	96	34.16 N	132.19 E
Misenheimer	192	35.29 N	80.17 W
Miseno	68	40.47 N	14.05 E
Misericórdia, Serra da ∧	287a	22.51 S	43.17 W
Misery, Mount ∧	169	37.24 S	143.36 E
Misgār	123	36.47 N	74.47 E
Mish'āb, Ra's al- ≻	128	28.12 N	48.39 E
Mishagua ≃	248	11.13 S	72.59 W
Mishan	89	45.33 N	131.52 E
Mishawaka	216	41.39 N	86.09 W
Mishawum Lake ⊜	283	42.30 N	71.08 W
Mishbiḥ, Jabal ∧	140	22.38 N	34.44 E
Misheguk Mountain ∧	180	68.15 N	161.03 W
Mishe-Mokwa, Lake ⊜	285	39.52 N	74.48 W
Mishibishu Lake ⊜	190	48.05 N	85.25 W
Mishicot	190	44.14 N	87.38 W
Mishima, Nihon	94	35.07 N	138.55 E
Mishima → Settsu, Nihon	96	34.46 N	135.33 E
Mi-shima I	96	34.46 N	131.09 E
Mishmar HaNegev	132	31.21 N	34.43 E
Mishmi Hills ⋌[2]	120	29.00 N	96.00 E
Mishō	96	32.57 N	132.34 E
Mishqal, Jabal al- ∧	132	31.53 N	36.08 E
Mišicha	88	51.38 N	105.35 E
Misikan	120	35.45 N	89.25 E
Misilmeri	70	38.02 N	13.27 E
Misima Island I	164	10.40 S	152.45 E
Misinto	266b	45.40 N	9.05 E
Misiones □[4]	252	27.00 S	55.00 W
Misiones □[5]	252	27.00 S	57.00 W
Misión San Francisco de Laishí	252	26.14 S	58.38 W
Misión San Vicente	232	31.20 N	116.15 W
Misirevo	82	56.16 N	36.45 E
Miskī	140	14.51 N	24.13 E
Miski, Enneri V	146	20.00 N	17.55 E
Miškino, Ross.	86	55.20 N	63.55 E
Miškino, Ross.	265a	59.42 N	30.45 E
Miskito Channel ⊍	236	14.20 N	83.08 W
Miskitos, Cayos II	236	14.23 N	82.46 W
Miskitos Reef ✦[2]	236	14.28 N	82.42 W
Miskolc	30	48.06 N	20.47 E
Misli	130	38.10 N	34.52 E
Mislinja	61	46.28 N	15.14 E
Mislinja ≃	61	46.35 N	15.02 E
Mislippi	146	10.00 N	15.37 E
Mislivna ∧	61	48.40 N	14.44 E
Mismār	140	18.13 N	35.38 E
Mismār, Jabal ∧	140	18.06 N	35.42 E
Mismi, Nevado ∧	248	15.30 S	71.42 W
Mišn'ovo	76	53.58 N	36.21 E
Misoke	154	1.06 S	28.38 E
Misool, Pulau I	164	1.52 S	130.10 E
Mispillion ≃	208	38.57 N	75.20 W
Misquamaebin Lake ⊜	184	53.30 N	91.05 W
Misquamicut	207	41.20 N	71.49 W
Miṣr → Egypt □[1]	140	27.00 N	30.00 E
Miṣr al-Jadīdah (Heliopolis) ◆[8]	273c	30.06 N	31.20 E
Miṣr al-Qadīmah (Old Cairo) ◆[8]	273c	30.00 N	31.14 E
Misrātah	146	32.23 N	15.06 E
Miṣr Baḥrī □[9]	140	31.00 N	31.00 E
Misrikh	124	27.27 N	80.31 E
Missanello	68	40.17 N	16.10 E
Missão Santa Cruz	152	16.14 S	21.57 E
Missão Velha	250	7.15 S	39.08 W
Misserghin	34	35.37 N	0.45 W
Missinaibi ≃	176	50.44 N	81.29 W
Missinaibi Lake ⊜	190	48.23 N	83.40 W
Missinaibi Lake Provincial Park ♠	190	48.25 N	83.35 W
Mission, S.D., U.S.	198	43.18 N	100.39 W
Mission, Tx., U.S.	196	26.12 N	98.19 W
Mission ◆[8]	282	37.45 N	122.25 W
Mission Bay c	228	32.47 N	117.15 W
Mission Beach	166	17.52 S	146.06 E
Mission City	224	49.08 N	122.18 W
Mission Creek ≃	282	37.32 N	121.55 W
Mission Hills ◆[8]	280	34.16 N	118.27 W
Mission Mountain ∧[2]	194	36.02 N	94.35 W
Mission Peak ∧	282	37.31 N	121.53 W
Mission Range ⋌	202	47.30 N	113.55 W
Mission Texas State Historic Park ♠	222	31.33 N	95.15 W
Mission Valley	222	28.54 N	97.12 W
Mission Viejo	228	33.36 N	117.40 W
Missisquoi □[6]	206	45.10 N	72.55 W
Missisquoi ≃	206	45.00 N	73.08 W
Missisquoi Bay c	206	45.05 N	73.10 W
Missisquoi-Nord ≃	206	45.02 N	72.26 W
Mississagagon Lake ⊜	212	44.52 N	77.05 W
Mississagi ≃	190	46.10 N	83.01 W
Mississagi Provincial Park ♠	190	46.35 N	82.45 W
Mississauga	212	44.34 N	78.20 W
Mississauga Lake ⊜	212	44.42 N	78.21 W
Mississauga	212	43.35 N	79.39 W
Mississinewa ≃	216	40.46 N	86.02 W
Mississinewa Lake ⊜[1]	216	40.42 N	85.52 W
Mississippi □[3], U.S.	178	32.50 N	89.30 W
Mississippi □[3], U.S.	194	32.50 N	89.30 W
Mississippi ≃, On., Can.	212	45.26 N	76.16 W
Mississippi ≃, U.S.	178	29.00 N	89.15 W
Mississippi Bay c	162	34.00 S	122.17 E
Mississippi Delta ≚[2]	194	29.10 N	89.15 W
Mississippi Lake ⊜	212	45.05 N	76.12 W
Mississippi Sound ⊍	194	30.15 N	88.40 W
Mississippi State	194	33.26 N	88.47 W
Missolonghi → Mesolóngion	38	38.21 N	21.17 E
Missoula	202	46.52 N	113.59 W
Missouri □[3], U.S.	178	38.30 N	93.30 W
Missouri □[3], U.S.	194	38.30 N	93.30 W
Missouri ≃	178	38.50 N	90.08 W
Missouri, Coteau du ⋌[2]	198	46.00 N	99.30 W
Missouri Buttes ∧	198	44.37 N	104.47 W
Missouri City	222	29.37 N	95.32 W
Missouri Creek ≃	219	40.07 N	90.43 W
Missouri Valley	198	41.33 N	95.53 W
Mistake, Mount ∧	171a	27.52 S	152.20 E
Mistake Creek	164	17.06 S	129.04 E
Mistake Creek ≃	166	21.38 S	146.50 E
Mistake Mountains ⋌	171a	27.52 S	152.22 E
Mistaken Point ≻	186	46.38 N	53.10 W
Mistanipisipou ≃	186	51.32 N	61.50 W
Mistassibi ≃	176	48.53 N	72.13 W
Mistassibi Nord-Est ≃	186	49.50 N	71.56 W
Mistassini	176	50.25 N	73.52 W
Mistassini, Lac ⊜	176	51.00 N	73.37 W
Mistatim	184	52.52 N	103.22 W
Mistawasis Indian Reserve ◆[4]	184	53.06 N	106.48 W
Mistelbach, Dtsch.	60	49.55 N	11.31 E
Mistelbach, Öst.	61	48.34 N	16.35 E
Mistelgau	60	49.55 N	11.28 E
Misteln ⊜	40	59.07 N	16.57 E
Misterbianco	70	37.31 N	15.00 E
Misterei	140	13.07 N	22.09 E
Misteriosa Bank ✦[2]	238	18.50 N	83.50 W
Misterton, Eng., U.K.	42	50.52 N	2.47 W
Misterton, Eng., U.K.	44	53.27 N	0.51 W
Misti, Volcán ∧[1]	248	16.18 S	71.24 W
Mistikokan ≃	184	57.01 N	91.27 W
Mistky	83	49.19 N	38.30 E
Mistley	42	51.56 N	1.05 E
Mistrás ⊥	38	37.04 N	22.21 E
Mistretta	70	37.56 N	14.22 E
Misugi	94	34.33 N	136.16 E
Misumi, Nihon	92	32.37 N	130.27 E
Misumi, Nihon	96	34.46 N	131.58 E
Misumi, Nihon	96	34.22 N	131.15 E
Misumi ≃	96	34.47 N	131.56 E
Misurina	64	46.35 N	12.15 E
Mišutino, Ross.	76	59.31 N	36.01 E
Mišutino, Ross.	82	56.23 N	38.06 E
Mita, Punta ≻	234	20.47 N	105.33 W
Mīt Abū Ghālib	142	31.17 N	31.40 E
Mita Hills Dam ◆[6]	154	14.15 S	29.06 E
Mit'ajevo, Ross.	82	55.16 N	36.32 E
Mit'ajevo, Ross.	86	60.17 N	61.06 E
Mitaka	94	35.40 N	139.33 E
Mitake, Nihon	94	35.25 N	137.08 E
Mitake, Nihon	94	35.51 N	137.37 E
Mit'akinka ≃	83	48.35 N	39.50 E
Mit'akino	82	54.24 N	38.50 E
Mit'akinskaja	83	48.36 N	39.47 E
Mīt al-'Āmil	142	30.54 N	31.21 E
Mitatib	140	16.03 N	36.11 E
Mitau → Jelgava	76	56.39 N	23.42 E
Mīt Badr Ḥalāwah	142	30.51 N	31.14 E
Mīt Bashshār	142	30.31 N	31.24 E
Mitcham, Austl.	168b	34.59 S	138.36 E
Mitcham, Austl.	274b	37.49 S	145.12 E
Mitcham ◆[8]	260	51.24 N	0.10 W
Mitcheldean	42	51.53 N	2.30 W
Mitchell, Austl.	166	26.29 S	147.58 E
Mitchell, On., Can.	212	43.28 N	81.12 W
Mitchell, Il., U.S.	219	38.46 N	90.06 W
Mitchell, In., U.S.	218	38.43 N	86.28 W
Mitchell, Ne., U.S.	198	41.56 N	103.48 W
Mitchell, Or., U.S.	202	44.34 N	120.09 W
Mitchell, S.D., U.S.	198	43.42 N	98.01 W
Mitchell ≃, Austl.	164	15.12 S	141.35 E
Mitchell ≃, Austl.	164	14.28 S	125.43 E
Mitchell ≃, Austl.	166	37.53 S	147.41 E
Mitchell, Lake ⊜[1]	194	32.50 N	86.30 W
Mitchell, Mount ∧	192	35.46 N	82.16 W
Mitchell and Alice Rivers National Park ♠	164	15.30 S	142.05 E
Mitchell Bay c	214	42.28 N	82.26 W
Mitchell Corners	212	43.57 N	78.48 W
Mitchell Field ⊠	278	41.55 N	88.15 W
Mitchell Lake ⊜, B.C., Can.	182	52.53 N	120.36 W
Mitchell Lake ⊜, On., Can.	212	44.34 N	78.58 W
Mitchell Point ≻	214	42.26 N	82.26 W
Mitchellville	190	41.40 N	93.21 W
Mitchelstown	48	52.16 N	8.16 W
Mīt Fāris	142	31.02 N	31.36 E
Mīt Ghamr	142	30.43 N	31.16 E
Mīt Ḥalfah	273c	30.10 N	31.14 E
Mīt Ḥamal	142	30.26 N	31.32 E
Mithapur	120	22.25 N	69.00 E
Mitha Tiwāna	123	32.15 N	72.07 E
Mithi	120	24.44 N	69.48 E
Míthimna	38	39.22 N	26.10 E
Mitiaro I	14	19.49 S	157.43 W
Mitidja, Plaine de la ≚	34	36.45 N	3.00 E
Mitilíni	38	39.06 N	26.32 E
Mitino	265b	55.51 N	37.21 E
Mitis, Lac ⊜	186	48.17 N	67.45 W
Mitishto ≃	184	54.50 N	98.58 W
Mitiškovo	76	54.40 N	33.31 E
Mitiwanga	214	41.22 N	82.27 W
Mitkof Island I	180	56.45 N	132.50 W
Mitla ⊥	234	16.55 N	96.17 W
Mitla, Laguna c	234	17.03 N	100.25 W
Mitla, Mamarr (Mitla Pass))(	142	30.00 N	32.53 E
Mitla Pass → Mitla, Mamarr)(	142	30.00 N	32.53 E
Mito, Nihon	94	34.49 N	137.19 E
Mito, Nihon	94	36.22 N	140.28 E
Mito, Nihon	96	34.40 N	131.59 E
Mitō, Nihon	96	34.13 N	131.21 E
Mito, Nihon	268	35.10 N	139.37 E
Mitomi	94	35.47 N	138.44 E
Mitoya	96	35.17 N	132.52 E
Mitra, Monte ∧	152	1.23 N	9.57 E
Mitra do Bispo ∧	256	22.10 S	44.34 W
Mitre ∧	172	40.48 S	175.27 E
Mitre, Península ≻[1]	254	54.48 S	65.40 W
Mitre Peak ∧	172	44.38 S	167.50 E
Mitrofania Island I	180	55.51 N	158.49 W
Mitrofanovka	78	49.58 N	39.42 E
Mitrofanovo	24	63.13 N	56.00 E
Mīt Ruhaynah	273c	29.51 N	31.15 E
Mīt Ruhaynah (Memphis) ⊥	142	29.51 N	31.15 E
Mitry-le-Neuf	261	48.57 N	2.36 E
Mitry-Mory	261	48.59 N	2.37 E
Mitsamiouli	157a	11.23 S	43.18 E
Mitsinjo	157b	16.01 S	45.52 E
Mitsio, Nosy I	157b	12.54 S	48.36 E
Mitsiwa (Massawa)	144	15.38 N	39.28 E
Mitsiwa Channel ⊍	144	15.30 N	40.00 E
Mitsu, Nihon	94	[illegible]	[illegible]
Mitsu, Nihon	96	34.48 N	133.56 E
Mitsubori	268	35.56 N	139.56 E

Symbols in the index entries represent the broad categories identified in the key at the right. Symbols with superior numbers (⋌[1]) identify subcategories (see complete key on page I · 1).

Symbole im Register stellen die rechts im Schlüssel erklärten Kategorien dar. Symbole mit hochgestellten Ziffern (⋌[1]) bezeichnen Unterabteilungen einer Kategorie (vgl. vollständiger Schlüssel auf Seite I · 1).

Los símbolos incluidos en el texto del índice representan las grandes categorías identificadas con la clave a la derecha. Los símbolos con numeros en su parte superior (⋌[1]) identifican las subcategorías (véase la clave completa en la página I · 1).

Les symboles de l'index représentent les catégories indiquées dans la légende à droite. Les symboles suivis d'un indice (⋌[1]) représentent des sous-catégories (voir légende complète à la page I · 1).

Os símbolos incluídos no texto do índice representam as grandes categorias identificadas com a chave à direita. Os símbolos com números em sua parte superior (⋌[1]) identificam as subcategorias (veja-se a chave completa à página I · 1).

∧ Mountain	Berg	Montaña	Montagne	Montanha
⋌ Mountains	Gebirge	Montañas	Montagnes	Montanhas
)(Pass	Paß	Paso	Col	Passo
V Valley, Canyon	Tal, Cañon	Valle, Cañón	Vallée, Canyon	Vale, Canhão
≚ Plain	Ebene	Llano	Plaine	Planície
≻ Cape	Kap	Cabo	Cap	Cabo
I Island	Insel	Isla	Île	Ilha
II Islands	Inseln	Islas	Îles	Ilhas
⊥ Other Topographic Features	Andere Topographische Objekte	Otros Elementos Topográficos	Autres données topographiques	Outros acidentes topográficos

ESPAÑOL — Nombre | Página | Lat.°′ | Long.°′ W = Oeste
FRANÇAIS — Nom | Page | Lat.°′ | Long.°′ W = Ouest
PORTUGUÊS — Nome | Página | Lat.°′ | Long.°′ W = Oeste

Mitsue 94 34.29 N 136.10 E
Mitsugi 96 34.30 N 133.09 E
Mitsuike Park ♦ 268 35.31 N 139.39 E
Mitsukaidō 94 36.01 N 139.59 E
Mitsuke 92 37.32 N 138.56 E
Mitsumarenge-dake ∧ 94 36.23 N 137.35 E
Mitsushima 92 34.16 N 129.19 E
Mitsuzaku 268 35.25 N 140.00 E
Mitsuzawa Park Race Track ♦ 268 35.27 N 139.36 E
Mitta, Oued el ∨ 148 34.20 N 6.44 E
Mittagong 170 34.27 S 150.27 E
Mittagskogel (Kepa) ∧ 61 46.31 N 13.57 E
Mittainville 261 48.40 N 1.39 E
Mitta Mitta ≃ 171b 36.12 S 147.11 E
Mitte ✦[8] 264a 52.31 N 13.24 E
Mittelberg, Dtsch. 58 47.38 N 10.25 E
Mittelberg, Öst. 58 47.20 N 10.10 E
Mittelfischach 56 49.02 N 9.52 E
Mittelfranken □[5] 56 49.20 N 10.40 E
Mittellandkanal ≊ 30 52.16 N 11.41 E
Mittelmeer → Mediterranean Sea ⊤[2] 10 35.00 N 20.00 E
Mittelsaida 54 50.46 N 13.18 E
Mittelstetten 60 48.15 N 11.06 E
Mittenwald 64 47.27 N 11.15 E
Mittenwalde, Dtsch. 54 53.11 N 13.39 E
Mittenwalde, Dtsch. 54 52.16 N 13.32 E
Mitterndorf 64 47.33 N 13.55 E
Mittersill 64 47.16 N 12.29 E
Mitterskirchen 60 48.21 N 12.44 E
Mitterteich 60 49.57 N 12.15 E
Mittewald an der Drau 64 46.46 N 12.36 E
Mittweida 54 50.59 N 12.59 E
Mitú 246 1.08 N 70.03 W
Mitumba, Monts ⋏ 154 6.00 S 29.00 E
Mituo 107 28.53 N 105.37 E
Mitwaba 154 8.38 S 27.20 E
Mitwitz 56 50.15 N 11.12 E
Mityana 154 0.24 N 32.03 E
Mīt Yazīd 142 30.30 N 31.20 E
Mitzic 152 0.47 N 11.34 E
Miura 94 35.08 N 139.37 E
Miura-chosuichi ◎[1] 94 35.49 N 137.23 E
Miura-dam ✦[6] 94 35.49 N 137.24 E
Miura-hantō ›[1] 94 35.15 N 139.39 E
Mius 80 51.26 N 47.56 E
Mius ≃ 83 47.18 N 38.49 E
Miusskij liman ⊂[1] 83 47.15 N 38.40 E
Miusyns'k 83 48.05 N 38.53 E
Miwa, Nihon 94 35.11 N 136.47 E
Miwa, Nihon 94 36.39 N 140.18 E
Miwa, Nihon 96 35.12 N 135.14 E
Miwa, Nihon 96 34.13 N 132.06 E
Miwa, Nihon 96 34.39 N 132.51 E
Miwa, Nihon 270 34.31 N 135.51 E
Mi-Wuk Village 226 38.05 N 120.13 W
Mixcoac ✦[8] 286a 19.23 N 99.12 W
Mixcoac, Presa de ◎[1] 286a 19.22 N 99.14 W
Mixco Viejo ⊥ 236 14.52 N 90.40 W
Mixian 100 34.31 N 113.22 E
Mixin 107 30.23 N 105.46 E
Mixquiahuala 234 20.14 N 99.13 W
Mixtán 234 17.55 N 95.51 W
Mixteco ≃ 234 18.11 N 98.30 W
Mixtlán 234 20.26 N 104.25 W
Miya 94 36.05 N 137.15 E
Miya ≃, Nihon 94 34.32 N 136.44 E
Miya ≃, Nihon 94 36.28 N 137.15 E
Miyagawa, Nihon 94 36.19 N 137.09 E
Miyagawa, Nihon 94 34.22 N 136.21 E
Miyagi □[5] 92 38.22 N 140.52 E
Miyagi-jima I 174m 26.21 N 127.57 E
Miyāh, Wādī al- ∨ 140 25.00 N 33.23 E
Miyahara 268 35.56 N 139.37 E
Miyajima 96 34.18 N 132.19 E
Miyake 270 34.35 N 135.47 E
Miyake-jima I 92 34.05 N 139.32 E
Miyako 92 39.38 N 141.57 E
Miyakojima ✦[8] 270 34.43 N 135.33 E
Miyako-jima I 175d 24.47 N 125.20 E
Miyakonojō 92 31.44 N 131.04 E
Miyako-rettō II 175d 24.24 N 125.00 E
Miyama, Nihon 92 34.06 N 136.14 E
Miyama, Nihon 94 36.00 N 136.22 E
Miyama, Nihon 94 35.33 N 136.45 E
Miyama, Nihon 96 35.16 N 135.33 E
Miyama, Nihon 96 33.59 N 135.22 E
Miyāni 120 21.51 N 69.23 E
Miyanojō 92 31.54 N 130.27 E
Miyanoura-dake ∧ 93b 30.20 N 130.31 E
Miyara 175d 24.20 N 124.14 E
Miyata 96 33.44 N 130.40 E
Miyazaki, Nihon 92 31.54 N 131.26 E
Miyazaki, Nihon 94 35.56 N 136.05 E
Miyazakino-hana › 96 34.04 N 135.05 E
Miyazu 96 35.32 N 135.11 E
Miyi 102 27.00 N 102.08 E
Miyoshi, Nihon 96 33.57 N 133.03 E
Miyoshi, Nihon 96 34.48 N 132.51 E
Miyoshi, Nihon 96 34.02 N 133.52 E
Miyoshi, Nihon 268 35.50 N 139.31 E
Miyota 94 36.18 N 138.30 E
Miyun 105 40.22 N 116.50 E
Miyun Shuiku ◎[1] 105 40.30 N 116.58 E
Mizan Teferi 144 6.53 N 35.28 E
Mizdah 146 31.26 N 12.59 E
Mize 194 31.52 N 89.33 W
Mizen Head ›, Ire. 48 52.51 N 6.01 W
Mizen Head ›, Ire. 48 51.27 N 9.49 W
Miževiči 76 52.59 N 25.05 E
Mizhhir'ya 78 48.32 N 23.30 E
Mizhi 102 37.49 N 110.02 E
Mizil 38 45.00 N 26.26 E
Mizoch 78 50.24 N 26.09 E
Mizoguchi 96 35.21 N 133.26 E
Mizonokuchi 268 35.36 N 139.37 E
Mizonuma 268 35.48 N 139.36 E
Mizoram □[3] 120 23.30 N 93.00 E
Mizpah 208 39.29 N 74.50 W
Mizpah Creek ≃ 198 46.16 N 105.17 W
Mizpé Ramon 132 30.36 N 34.48 E
Mizque 248 17.56 S 65.19 W
Mizque ≃ 248 18.39 S 64.20 W
Mizue ✦[8] 268 35.41 N 139.54 E
Mizuho, Nihon 94 35.46 N 139.21 E
Mizuho, Nihon 96 35.10 N 135.22 E
Mizuho, Nihon 96 34.51 N 132.31 E
Mizukaidō → Mitsukaidō 94 36.01 N 139.59 E
Mizuko 268 35.50 N 139.34 E
Mizumaki 96 33.51 N 130.42 E
Mizunami 94 35.22 N 137.15 E
Mizunoko-jima I 96 33.02 N 132.11 E
Mizusawa 92 39.08 N 141.08 E
Mizushima-nada ⊂ 96 34.25 N 133.40 E
Mizutori 270 34.47 N 135.45 E
Mizuwake-tōge)(96 33.15 N 131.17 E
Mjälgen 40 60.33 N 15.07 E
Mjällom 26 62.59 N 18.26 E
Mjangad 86 48.15 N 91.57 E
Mjanyana 158 31.50 S 28.10 E
Mjölby 26 58.19 N 15.08 E
Mjøndalen 26 59.45 N 10.01 E
Mjörn ◎ 26 57.54 N 12.25 E
Mjøsa ◎ 26 60.40 N 11.00 E
Mkalama 154 4.07 S 34.38 E
Mkata 154 5.47 S 38.17 E
Mkhondvo ≃ 158 26.39 S 31.25 E
Mkokotoni 154 5.52 S 39.15 E
Mkomazi ≃ 158 30.12 S 30.50 E
Mkomazi Game Reserve ✦[4] 154 4.10 S 38.10 E
Mkulwe 154 8.35 S 32.19 E
Mkumvura ≃ 154 15.55 S 31.07 E
Mkunumbi 154 2.18 S 40.42 E
Mkushi 154 13.40 S 29.20 E
Mkushi ≃ 154 14.40 S 29.07 E
Mkushi River 154 13.32 S 29.45 E
Mkuze 158 27.37 S 32.02 E
Mkuze ≃ 158 27.53 S 32.29 E
Mkuzi Game Reserve ✦[4] 158 27.40 S 32.15 E
Mkwaja 154 5.47 S 38.51 E
Mkwaya 154 10.06 S 39.40 E
Mladá Boleslav 54 50.23 N 14.59 E
Mladenovac 38 44.26 N 20.42 E
Mladotice 60 49.58 N 13.18 E
Mlala Hills ⋏[2] 154 6.47 S 31.45 E
M'Lang 116 6.55 N 124.53 E
M'Lang ≃ 116 6.52 N 124.45 E
Mlanje Peak → Sapitwa ∧ 154 15.57 S 35.36 E
Mlava ≃ 38 44.45 N 21.13 E
Mława 30 53.06 N 20.23 E
Mlawula 158 26.11 S 32.01 E
Mliba 158 26.14 S 31.36 E
Mljet, Otok I 36 42.45 N 17.30 E
Mljet Nacionalni Park ♦ 36 42.47 N 17.25 E
Mljetski Kanal ⊍ 36 42.48 N 17.35 E
Mlyniv 78 50.31 N 25.37 E
Mmabatho 0 25.51 S 25.38 E
Mmadinare 156 21.57 S 27.52 E
Mnazi 154 8.54 S 39.06 E
Mnevniki ✦[8] 265b 55.45 N 37.28 E
Mnichov 60 50.03 N 12.49 E
Mníšek pod Brdy 30 49.52 N 14.16 E
Mo 24 66.15 N 14.08 E
Mo ≃ 150 8.45 N 0.11 E
Moa 240p 20.40 N 74.56 W
Moa ≃, Afr. 150 6.59 N 11.36 W
Moa ≃, Bra. 248 7.39 S 72.41 W
Moa, Pulau I 164 8.10 S 127.56 E
Moab 200 38.34 N 109.32 W
Moabi 152 2.15 S 11.00 E
Moaco ≃ 248 7.41 S 68.18 W
Moa Island I 164 10.12 S 142.16 E
Moala Island I 175g 18.36 S 179.53 E
Moalboal 116 9.56 N 123.23 E
Moama 166 36.07 S 144.47 E
Moamba 156 25.35 S 32.13 E
Moana 168b 35.13 S 138.29 E
Moanda 152 1.34 S 13.11 E
Moanza 152 5.25 S 17.30 E
Moar Lake ◎ 184 52.00 N 95.09 W
Moate 48 53.23 N 7.43 W
Moatize 154 16.08 S 33.45 E
Moawhango 172 39.35 S 175.52 E
Moba, Nig. 273a 6.27 N 3.28 E
Moba, Zaïre 154 7.03 S 29.47 E
Mobara 94 35.25 N 140.18 E
Mobārakpur 126 22.58 N 89.10 E
Mobaye 152 4.19 N 21.11 E
Mobayi-Mbongo 152 4.18 N 21.11 E
Mobberley 262 53.19 N 2.20 W
Mobeetie 196 35.31 N 100.26 W
Mobeka 152 1.53 N 19.46 E
Mobenzélé 152 0.54 N 17.51 E
Moberly 194 39.25 N 92.26 W
Moberly ≃ 182 56.12 N 120.55 W
Moberly Lake 182 55.48 N 121.45 W
Moberly Lake ◎ 182 55.49 N 121.45 W
Mobile, Al., U.S. 194 30.41 N 88.02 W
Mobile, Az., U.S. 200 33.03 N 112.16 W
Mobile ≃ 194 30.29 N 88.01 W
Mobile Bay ⊂ 194 30.25 N 88.00 W
Mobjack 208 37.23 N 76.21 W
Mobjack Bay ⊂ 208 37.19 N 76.21 W
Mobridge 198 45.32 N 100.25 W
Moca, P.R. 240m 18.24 N 67.07 W
Moca, Rep. Dom. 238 19.24 N 70.31 W
Moča ≃ 82 55.25 N 37.28 E
Mocajuba 250 2.35 S 49.30 W
Mocal ≃ 236 14.00 N 88.33 W
Močalejevka 80 53.38 N 51.46 E
Močališče 80 56.21 N 48.23 E
Moçambique 154 15.03 S 40.45 E
Moçambique → Mozambique □[1] 138 18.15 S 35.00 E
Mocanaqua 210 41.08 N 76.08 W
Mocanguê Grande, Ilha I 287a 22.52 S 43.08 W
Mocassins, Lac des ◎ 206 46.35 N 74.25 W
Mo Cay 110 10.08 N 106.20 E
Moccasin, Ca., U.S. 226 37.49 N 120.18 W
Moccasin, Il., U.S. 219 39.09 N 88.45 W
Moc Chau 110 20.51 N 104.37 E
Moccoidumis 144 1.36 N 44.26 E
Mocha → Al-Makhā' 144 13.19 N 43.15 E
Mocha, Isla I 252 38.22 S 73.56 W
Moche ≃ 248 8.10 S 79.03 W
Moche ⊥ 248 8.06 S 79.05 W
Mocheng 106 31.35 N 120.43 E
Mochh 123 32.45 N 71.31 E
Mochigase 96 35.20 N 134.12 E
Mochitlan 234 17.30 N 99.18 W
Mochizuki 94 36.16 N 138.22 E
Mocho, Arroyo ≃ 226 37.41 N 121.55 W
Mochov 54 50.08 N 14.50 E
Mochtín 60 49.22 N 13.21 E
Mochudi 156 24.28 S 26.05 E
Močily 82 54.20 N 38.41 E
Mocímboa da Praia 154 11.20 S 40.21 E
Mocímboa do Rovuma 154 11.20 S 39.18 E
Möckeln ◎, Sve. 26 56.40 N 14.10 E
Möckeln ◎, Sve. 40 59.18 N 14.30 E
Möckern 54 52.08 N 11.57 E
Mockfjärd 40 60.30 N 14.58 E
Mockhorn Island I 208 37.13 N 75.53 W
Möckmühl 56 49.19 N 9.22 E
Mockrehna 54 51.30 N 12.49 E
Mocksville 192 35.53 N 80.33 W
Moclips 224 47.14 N 124.12 W
Môco, Serra do ∧ 152 12.28 S 15.10 E
Mocoa 246 1.09 N 76.37 W
Mococa 256 21.28 S 47.01 W
Mocoduene 156 23.40 S 35.10 E
Mocoretá 252 30.38 S 57.58 W
Mocorito 232 25.29 N 107.55 W
Moctezuma, Méx. 232 29.48 N 109.42 W
Moctezuma, Méx. 234 22.45 N 101.05 W
Moctezuma ≃, Méx. 232 29.09 N 109.40 W
Moctezuma ≃, Méx. 234 21.59 N 98.34 W
Mocuba 154 16.50 S 36.59 E
Močurica ≃ 38 42.31 N 26.32 E
Modane 62 45.12 N 6.40 E
Modāsa 120 23.28 N 73.18 E
Modau ≃ 56 49.49 N 8.28 E
Modbury 42 50.21 N 3.53 W
Modder ≃ 158 29.02 S 24.37 E
Modderbee 273d 26.10 S 28.24 E
Modder East 273d 26.11 S 28.26 E
Modderfontein 273d 26.06 S 28.09 E
Modderfontein ≃ 273d 26.13 S 28.10 E
Modderrivier 158 29.02 S 24.38 E
Model City 284a 43.11 N 78.59 W
Modena, It. 64 44.40 N 10.55 E
Modena, N.Y., U.S. 210 41.40 N 74.07 W
Modena □[4] 64 44.30 N 10.54 E
Moder ≃ 56 48.49 N 8.06 E
Möderbrugg 61 47.17 N 14.29 E
Modern Art, Museum of ʋ 276 40.46 N 73.58 W
Modeste, Mount ∧ 224 48.37 N 124.06 W
Modesto, Ca., U.S. 226 37.38 N 120.59 W
Modesto, Il., U.S. 219 39.29 N 89.59 W
Modesto City-County Airport ⊠ 226 37.39 N 120.57 W
Modesto Main Canal ≊ 226 37.39 N 120.27 W
Modesto Reservoir ◎[1] 226 37.26 N 121.58 W
Modica 70 36.52 N 14.46 E
Modigliana 66 44.09 N 11.47 E
Modinagar 124 28.51 N 77.37 E
Modione ≃ 70 37.34 N 12.49 E
Modjamboli 152 2.28 N 22.06 E
Modjeska 280 33.43 N 117.37 W
Mödling 61 48.05 N 16.17 E
Mödling ≃ 264b 48.04 N 16.22 E
Modoc 218 40.02 N 85.07 W
Modon ≃ 50 47.16 N 1.27 E
Modowi 164 4.05 S 134.39 E
Modra, Slvk. 30 48.21 N 17.17 E
Modra, Tchad 146 20.43 N 17.42 E
Modra špilja ⏊[5] 36 43.00 N 16.02 E
Mödrath 56 50.53 N 6.43 E
Modriča 38 44.57 N 18.18 E
Modřice 61 49.07 N 16.37 E
Mo Duc 110 14.57 N 108.53 E
Modugno 68 41.05 N 16.47 E
Moe 169 38.10 S 146.15 E
Moe ≃, Austl. 169 38.08 S 146.17 E
Moe ≃, P.Q., Can. 206 45.19 N 71.49 W
Moecherville 216 41.44 N 88.17 W
Moeda 255 20.20 S 44.03 W
Moehau ∧ 172 36.35 S 175.24 E
Moel Fferna ∧ 42 52.57 N 3.18 W
Moelv 26 60.56 N 10.42 E
Moema 255 19.50 S 45.24 W
Moen 50 50.46 N 3.24 E
Moen I 175c 7.26 N 151.52 E
Moena 64 46.22 N 11.39 E
Moengo 250 5.37 N 54.24 W
Moen-jo-Daro ⊥ 120 27.18 N 68.15 E
Moenkopi 200 36.06 N 111.13 W
Moenkopi Wash ∨ 200 35.54 N 111.26 W
Moeraki Point › 172 45.22 S 170.52 E
Moerbeke, Bel. 50 50.45 N 3.55 E
Moerbeke, Bel. 50 51.10 N 3.56 E
Moerdijk 52 51.43 N 4.38 E
Moerewa 172 35.23 S 174.02 E
Moergestel 52 51.33 N 5.11 E
Moero, Lago → Mweru, Lake ◎ 154 9.00 S 28.45 E
Moers 56 51.27 N 6.37 E
Moersbach ≃ 263 51.33 N 6.36 E
Moesa ≃ 58 46.13 N 9.03 E
Moffat 44 55.20 N 3.27 W
Moffat Peak ∧ 172 45.02 S 168.07 E
Moffatt 222 31.12 N 97.28 W
Moffatt, Lac ◎ 206 45.34 N 71.19 W
Moffat Water ≃ 44 55.18 N 3.25 W
Moffet Point › 180 55.26 N 162.32 W
Moffett Field Naval Air Station ■ 226 37.24 N 122.03 W
Moffit 198 46.40 N 100.17 W
Mofoluku 273a 6.33 N 3.20 E
Moga 123 30.48 N 75.10 E
Mogadiscio → Muqdisho 144 2.04 N 45.22 E
Mogadishu → Muqdisho 144 2.04 N 45.22 E
Mogador → Essaouira 148 31.30 N 9.47 W
Mogadore 214 41.02 N 81.23 W
Mogadore Reservoir ◎[1] 214 41.04 N 81.21 W
Mogadouro 34 41.20 N 6.39 W
Mogalakwena ≃ 156 23.00 S 28.40 E
Mogalo 152 3.10 N 19.04 E
Mogami ≃ 92 38.55 N 139.48 E
Mogan Shan ∧ 106 30.36 N 119.52 E
Mogapinyana 156 22.19 S 27.27 E
Mogaung 110 25.18 N 96.56 E
Mogdy 89 50.35 N 133.51 E
Mogees 285 40.06 N 75.19 W
Møgeltønder 41 54.56 N 8.49 E
Mogenstrup 41 55.11 N 11.53 E
Mogent ≃ 266d 41.33 N 2.15 E
Moggio Udinese 64 46.25 N 13.12 E
Mogi, Serra do ⋏ 287b 23.47 S 46.20 W
Mogielnica 30 51.42 N 20.43 E
Mogilev → Mogil'ov 76 53.54 N 30.21 E
Mogilno 30 52.40 N 17.58 E
Mogil'ov 76 53.54 N 30.21 E
Mogil'ov □[8] 76 53.45 N 30.30 E
Mogincual 154 15.35 S 40.25 E
Moglal, Wādī ∨ 140 19.18 N 34.29 E
Moglia 64 44.56 N 10.55 E
Mogliano Veneto 64 45.33 N 12.14 E
Mogoča 88 53.44 N 119.44 E
Mogoča ≃ 76 58.00 N 36.26 E
Mogočin 86 57.43 N 83.34 E
Mogod 88 48.24 N 103.00 E
Mogogh 140 8.26 N 31.19 E
Mogojto 88 54.25 N 110.27 E
Mogojtuj 88 51.17 N 114.55 E
Mogok 110 22.55 N 96.30 E
Mogollon Mountains ⋏ 200 33.25 N 108.40 W
Mogollon Rim ⏊[4] 200 34.25 N 110.50 W
Mogor 120 32.52 N 67.47 E
Mogorella 71 39.52 N 8.51 E
Mogoro 71 39.41 N 8.47 E
Mogotes 246 6.30 N 72.58 W
Mogotón ∧ 236 13.45 N 86.23 W
Mograt Island I 140 19.30 N 33.15 E
Mogroum 146 11.06 N 15.25 E
Moguer 34 37.16 N 6.50 W
Mogyoród 264c 47.36 N 19.15 E
Mogyoródi-patak ≃ 264c 47.36 N 19.05 E
Mogzon 88 51.45 N 111.58 E
Mohács 30 45.59 N 18.42 E
Mohaka 172 39.07 S 177.11 E
Mohaka ≃ 172 39.07 S 177.12 E
Mohall 198 48.45 N 101.30 W
Moḥammadābād 128 30.53 N 61.28 E
Mohammedia (Fedala) 148 33.44 N 7.24 W
Mohana 124 25.54 N 77.45 E
Mohangi 154 0.03 N 29.05 E
Mohania 124 25.11 N 83.37 E
Mohanpur, Bngl. 126 23.24 N 90.36 E
Mohanpur, India 126 21.51 N 87.26 E
Mohanpur, India 272a 28.44 N 77.10 E
Mohave, Lake ◎[1] 204 35.25 N 114.38 W
Mohawk, Mi., U.S. 190 47.18 N 88.21 W
Mohawk, N.Y., U.S. 210 43.00 N 75.00 W
Mohawk ≃ 210 42.47 N 73.42 W
Mohawk, East Branch ≃ 212 43.22 N 75.28 W
Mohawk, Lake ◎ 276 41.02 N 74.41 W
Mohawk Dam ✦[6] 214 40.20 N 82.05 W
Mohawk Mountain ∧ 207 41.49 N 73.17 W
Mohawk Point › 212 42.51 N 79.29 W
Mohe 89 53.29 N 122.19 E
Moheda 26 57.00 N 14.34 E
Mohegan 207 41.28 N 72.06 W
Mohegan Lake 210 41.19 N 73.51 W
Mohelnice 30 49.46 N 16.55 E
Moher, Cliffs of ⏊[4] 48 52.57 N 9.26 W
Mohican ≃ 214 40.22 N 82.09 W
Mohican, Black Fork ≃ 214 40.35 N 82.17 W
Mohican, Cape › 180 60.12 N 167.28 W
Mohican, Clear Fork ≃ 214 40.35 N 82.12 W
Mohican, Jerome Fork ≃ 214 40.45 N 82.23 W
Mohican, Lake Fork ≃ 214 40.27 N 82.12 W
Mohican, Muddy Fork ≃ 214 40.45 N 82.08 W
Mohican State Park ♦ 214 40.37 N 82.16 W
Mohicanville Dam ✦[6] 214 40.44 N 82.09 W
Mohili ✦[8] 272c 19.06 N 72.53 E
Mohill 48 53.54 N 7.52 W
Mohlakeng 273d 26.13 S 27.42 E
Möhlau 54 51.44 N 12.21 E
Möhlin 58 47.34 N 7.51 E
Möhne ≃ 52 51.27 N 7.57 E
Möhnestausee ◎[1] 52 51.29 N 8.08 E
Mohns Ridge ✣[3] 16 72.30 N 5.00 E
Mohnton 208 40.17 N 75.59 W
Mohnyin 110 24.47 N 96.22 E
Moho ≃ 236 16.04 N 88.52 W
Mohokare (Caledon) ≃ 158 30.31 S 26.05 E
Moholm 40 58.37 N 14.02 E
Mohon 56 49.45 N 4.44 E
Mohorn 54 51.00 N 13.28 E
Mohoro 154 8.08 S 39.10 E
Möhringen 58 47.57 N 8.46 E
Mohrsville 208 40.28 N 75.59 W
Mohyla-Bel'mak, hora ∧[2] 78 47.20 N 36.35 E
Mohyla-Mechetna, hora ∧[2] 83 48.16 N 38.53 E
Mohyliv 78 48.52 N 34.29 E
Mohyliv-Podil's'kyy 78 48.27 N 27.48 E
Moi 26 58.28 N 6.32 E
Moiano, It. 68 40.39 N 14.28 E
Moiano, It. 68 41.05 N 14.32 E
Moindou 175f 21.42 S 165.41 E
Moinești 38 46.28 N 26.29 E
Moingbi 140 5.46 N 28.49 E
Moinkum 85 43.48 N 73.41 E
Mointy 86 47.13 N 73.21 E
Moio Alcantara 70 37.54 N 15.03 E
Moiporá 255 16.34 S 50.42 W
Moira 48 54.30 N 6.17 W
Moira ≃ 212 44.09 N 77.23 W
Moiraba 250 2.27 S 49.25 W
Moira Lake ◎ 212 44.29 N 77.27 W
Moirans 62 45.20 N 5.34 E
Moirans-en-Montagne 58 46.26 N 5.44 E
Mõisaküla 76 58.06 N 25.11 E
Moisdon 32 47.37 N 1.22 W
Moisejeviči 76 53.13 N 28.17 E
Moisejevka 86 58.05 N 76.16 E
Moisejevo Alabuška 76 51.54 N 42.06 E
Moisenay 261 48.34 N 2.44 E
Moisés Ville 252 30.43 S 61.29 W
Moisie 186 50.11 N 66.05 W
Moisie ≃ 176 50.11 N 66.05 W
Moisie, Baie de ⊂ 186 50.16 N 65.56 W
Moisling ✦[8] 54 53.50 N 10.38 E
Moison Creek ≃ 281 42.18 N 82.40 W
Moissac 32 44.06 N 1.05 E
Moïssala 146 8.21 N 17.46 E
Moisselles 261 49.03 N 2.20 E
Moisson 261 49.05 N 1.40 E
Moisson, Forêt de ♦ 261 49.03 N 1.39 E
Moissy-Cramayel 261 48.38 N 2.36 E
Moita 34 38.39 N 8.59 W
Moitaco 246 8.01 N 64.21 W
Moivre ≃ 56 48.52 N 4.28 E
Mojácar 34 37.08 N 1.51 W
Mojana, Brazo ≃[1] 246 9.02 N 74.46 W
Mojave 228 35.03 N 118.10 W
Mojave ≃ 204 35.06 N 116.04 W
Mojave Desert ✦[2] 204 35.00 N 117.00 W
Mojave River Forks Reservoir ◎[1] 228 34.20 N 117.15 W
Moji 85 38.59 N 74.24 E
Mojiang 102 23.28 N 101.39 E
Mojicuaçu ≃ 255 20.53 S 48.10 W
Moji das Cruzes 256 23.31 S 46.11 W
Mojiguaçu 256 22.22 S 46.57 W
Mojimirim 256 22.26 S 46.57 W
Mojjero ≃ 74 68.44 N 103.42 E
Mojnalyk 88 51.18 N 95.33 E
Mojo 144 8.36 N 39.07 E
Mojoagung 115a 7.34 S 112.21 E
Mojokerto 115a 7.28 S 112.26 E
Mojosari 115a 7.31 S 112.33 E
Mojstrana 64 46.27 N 13.56 E
Moju 250 1.53 S 48.46 W
Moju ≃ 250 1.40 S 48.25 W
Mōka 94 36.26 N 140.01 E
Mokai 172 38.32 S 175.54 E
Mokāma 124 25.24 N 85.55 E
Mokambo 154 12.25 S 28.21 E
Mokane 219 38.40 N 91.52 W
Mokapu Peninsula ›[1] 229c 21.27 N 157.45 W
Mokaria 152 2.00 N 23.20 E
Mokarta, Castello di ⊥ 70 37.48 N 12.45 E
Mokau 172 38.41 S 174.37 E
Mokau ≃ 172 38.42 S 174.37 E
Moke 102 30.14 N 100.01 E
Mokelumne ≃ 226 38.13 N 121.28 W
Mokelumne, Middle Fork ≃ 226 38.22 N 120.37 W
Mokelumne, North Fork ≃ 226 38.22 N 120.37 W
Mokelumne, South Fork ≃ 226 38.23 N 120.35 W
Mokelumne Aqueduct ≊[1] 226 37.54 N 122.07 W
Mokelumne Hill 226 38.18 N 120.42 W
Mokena 216 41.31 N 87.53 W
Mokhotlong 158 29.22 S 29.02 E
Mokil I[1] 14 6.40 N 159.47 E
Mokimbo 154 6.20 S 28.42 E
Mokino 80 57.27 N 49.11 E
Moklakan 88 54.56 N 118.56 E
Möklinta 40 60.05 N 16.32 E
Moknine 148 35.38 N 10.54 E
Mokochu, Khao ∧ 110 15.56 N 99.06 E
Mokohinau Islands II 172 35.55 S 175.07 E
Mokokchūng 120 26.20 N 94.32 E
Mokolo, Cam. 146 10.45 N 13.48 E
Mokolo, Zaïre 152 1.57 N 18.05 E
Mokolo ≃ 156 23.14 S 27.43 E
Mokombe 152 0.14 S 23.48 E
Mokoreta ≃ 172 46.21 S 168.51 E
Mokou 273b 4.13 S 15.13 E
Mokpalin 110 17.26 N 96.53 E
Mokp'o 98 34.48 N 126.22 E
Mokraja Jel'muta 80 46.51 N 41.41 E
Mokraja Ol'chovka 80 50.28 N 44.59 E
Mokrany 78 51.50 N 24.14 E
Mokra Sura ≃ 78 48.19 N 35.09 E
Mokra Volnovakha ≃ 83 47.30 N 37.15 E
Mokrisset 34 34.59 N 5.20 W
Mokri Yaly ≃ 78 48.05 N 36.44 E
Mokrous 80 51.14 N 47.37 E
Mokrousovo 86 55.48 N 66.45 E
Mokroyelanchyk 83 47.42 N 38.31 E
Mokrušinskoje 86 57.31 N 93.11 E
Mokryj Gašun 80 46.53 N 42.45 E
Mokryj Jelančik ≃ 83 47.08 N 38.20 E
Mokryj Kor 82 54.34 N 37.58 E
Mokša ≃ 80 54.44 N 41.53 E
Mokšan 80 53.26 N 44.37 E
Moku 154 2.57 N 29.22 E
Mokuleia 229c 21.35 N 158.09 W
Mokumbusu 152 1.44 N 21.04 E
Mokvyn 78 50.57 N 26.48 E
Mokwa 150 9.20 N 5.02 E
Mol 56 51.11 N 5.06 E
Mola di Bari 68 41.04 N 17.05 E
Molale 144 10.08 N 39.42 E
Molalla 224 45.08 N 122.34 W
Molalla ≃ 224 45.18 N 122.43 W
Molalla, North Fork ≃ 224 45.05 N 122.29 W
Molanda 152 2.28 N 20.48 E
Molango 234 20.53 N 98.46 W
Molanosa 184 54.30 N 105.33 W
Moláoi 38 36.48 N 22.52 E
Molara, Isola I 71 40.52 N 9.43 E
Molaretto 62 45.10 N 7.00 E
Molat, Otok I 36 44.15 N 14.49 E
Molbergen 52 52.51 N 7.55 E
Molčanovka 83 46.52 N 38.37 E
Molčanovo 86 57.35 N 83.48 E
Mold 44 53.10 N 3.08 W
Moldary 86 50.47 N 78.29 E
Moldau → Vltava ≃ 30 50.21 N 14.30 E
Moldavia □[9] 38 47.00 N 27.15 E
Moldavia → Moldova □[1] 38 47.00 N 29.00 E
Moldavija → Moldova □[1] 38 47.00 N 29.00 E
Molde 26 62.44 N 7.11 E
Moldotau, chrebet ⋏ 85 41.35 N 74.40 E
Moldova □[1], Europe 22 47.00 N 29.00 E
Moldova □[1], Europe 38 47.00 N 29.00 E
Moldova ≃ 38 46.54 N 26.58 E
Moldova Nouă 38 44.44 N 21.40 E
Moldoveanu, Vârful ∧ 38 45.36 N 24.44 E
Môle ≃, Fr. 62 43.15 N 6.32 E
Mole ≃, Eng., U.K. 42 50.57 N 3.54 W
Mole ≃, Eng., U.K. 42 51.24 N 0.21 W
Môle, Cap du › 238 19.50 N 73.25 W
Mole Creek 166 41.33 S 146.24 E
Moledet 132 32.35 N 35.26 E
Molega Lake ◎ 186 44.22 N 64.53 W
Mole Game Reserve ✦[4] 150 9.30 N 2.00 W
Molegbe 152 4.14 N 20.53 E
Molenbeek-St.-Jean 50 50.51 N 4.19 E
Molepolole 156 24.25 S 25.30 E
Moléson ∧ 58 46.33 N 7.01 E
Molėtai 76 55.14 N 25.25 E
Mole Valley □[8] 260 51.16 N 0.18 W
Molfetta 68 41.12 N 16.36 E
Molibagu 112 0.23 N 123.59 E
Molières-sur-Cèze 62 44.15 N 4.09 E
Molimiao 89 43.34 N 121.54 E
Molina 252 35.07 S 71.17 W
Molina de Aragón 34 40.51 N 1.53 W
Molina de Segura 34 38.03 N 1.12 W
Molina di Ledro 64 45.56 N 10.46 E
Molinara 68 41.18 N 14.54 E
Moline, Il., U.S. 190 41.30 N 90.30 W
Moline, Ks., U.S. 198 37.21 N 96.18 W
Moline, Mi., U.S. 216 42.44 N 85.39 W
Molinella 64 44.37 N 11.40 E
Molinges 58 46.21 N 5.46 E
Molingguan 106 31.50 N 118.50 E
Molini di Tures (Mühlen) 64 46.54 N 11.56 E
Molinière Point › 241k 12.05 N 61.45 W
Molino 194 30.43 N 87.18 W
Molino de Rosas ✦[8] 286a 19.22 N 99.13 W
Molinos 252 25.25 S 66.19 W
Molins de Rei 34 41.25 N 2.01 E
Moliro 154 8.13 S 30.34 E
Molise □[4] 66 41.35 N 14.30 E
Moliterno 68 40.14 N 15.52 E
Mölkau 54 51.20 N 12.26 E
Molkom 40 59.36 N 13.43 E
Möll ≃ 64 46.50 N 13.26 E
Mollahasan 130 39.22 N 42.37 E
Mollāhāt 126 22.56 N 89.48 E
Mollakendi 130 38.36 N 39.20 E
Mollaro 64 46.16 N 11.05 E
Möllbrücke 64 46.50 N 13.22 E
Mölle 41 56.17 N 12.29 E
Möllen 263 51.35 N 6.42 E
Möllenbeck, Dtsch. 54 53.17 N 11.44 E
Möllenbeck, Dtsch. 54 53.23 N 13.20 E
Mollendo 248 17.02 S 72.01 W
Möllensee ◎ 264a 52.26 N 13.51 E
Mollepata 248 13.31 S 72.32 W
Moller, Port ⊂ 180 55.51 N 160.25 W
Möllersdorf 264b 48.02 N 16.18 E
Mollet del Vallès 266d 41.33 N 2.13 E
Mollia 62 45.49 N 8.02 E
Molliens-Vidame 50 49.53 N 2.01 E
Mollington 262 53.13 N 2.55 W
Mollis 58 47.05 N 9.04 E
Mölln, Dtsch. 54 53.37 N 10.41 E
Molln, Öst. 61 47.53 N 14.15 E
Mollösund 26 58.04 N 11.28 E
Mollusk 208 37.43 N 76.32 W
Molly Ann Brook ≃ 276 40.55 N 74.11 W
Mölnbo 40 59.03 N 17.25 E
Mölndal 26 57.39 N 12.01 E
Mölnlycke 26 57.39 N 12.09 E
Mölntorp 40 59.33 N 16.15 E
Molocaboc Island I 116 10.58 N 123.34 E
Molochans'k 78 47.12 N 35.36 E
Molochio 68 38.18 N 16.02 E
Molochna ≃ 78 46.42 N 35.20 E
Molochnyy lyman ◎ 78 46.30 N 35.20 E
Moločnoje 76 59.17 N 39.41 E
Molócuè ≃ 154 17.03 S 38.52 E
Molodečno 76 54.19 N 26.49 E
Molodežnaja ʋ[3] 9 67.35 S 46.35 E
Molodi 82 55.17 N 37.31 E
Molodo 150 14.14 N 6.02 W
Molodohvariys'k 83 48.20 N 39.40 E
Molodoj Tud 76 56.26 N 33.36 E
Molod'ožnyj 89 50.23 N 136.48 E
Mologa ≃ 76 58.50 N 37.11 E
Molokai I 229a 21.07 N 157.00 W
Molokai Fracture Zone ✣ 16 23.00 N 130.00 W
Molokča ≃ 82 56.15 N 38.45 E
Molokini I 229a 20.38 N 156.30 W
Molokovo, Ross. 76 58.10 N 36.45 E
Molokovo, Ross. 82 55.34 N 37.52 E
Moloma ≃ 24 58.20 N 48.28 E
Molong 166 33.06 S 148.52 E
Molonglo ≃ 171b 35.15 S 148.58 E
Molopo ≃ 156 28.30 S 20.13 E
Molotkoviči 76 52.07 N 25.56 E
Molotov → Perm' 86 58.00 N 56.15 E
Molotovsk → Severodvinsk 24 64.34 N 39.50 E
Molou 146 13.42 N 21.44 E
Moloundou 152 2.03 N 15.10 E
Molowaie 152 5.47 S 23.20 E
Moloy 58 47.32 N 4.55 E
Molsheim 58 48.32 N 7.29 E
Molson Lake ◎ 184 54.12 N 96.45 W
Molteno 158 31.22 S 26.22 E
Moltrasio 58 45.52 N 9.05 E
Molu, Pulau I 164 6.45 S 131.33 E
Moluca, Mar de la → Maluku, Laut ⊤[2] 108 0.00 125.00 E
Molucas, Islas → Maluku II 108 2.00 S 128.00 E
Moluccas → Maluku II 108 2.00 S 128.00 E
Molucca Sea → Maluku, Laut ⊤[2] 108 0.00 125.00 E
Molukken → Maluku II 108 2.00 S 128.00 E
Molumbo 154 15.27 S 30.15 E
Molundo 116 7.56 N 124.23 E
Moluques → Maluku II 108 2.00 S 128.00 E
Molveno, Lago di ◎ 64 46.08 N 10.57 E
Molvoticy 76 57.25 N 32.20 E
Molžaninovo 82 55.56 N 37.22 E
Moma, Moç. 154 16.44 S 39.14 E
Moma, Zaïre 152 1.36 S 23.57 E
Moma ≃ 74 66.26 N 143.06 E
Momanga 156 18.12 S 21.42 E
Momats ≃ 164 5.20 S 137.47 E
Momax 234 21.56 N 103.19 W
Momba ≃ 154 8.28 S 32.40 E
Mombaça 250 5.45 S 39.38 W
Mombaça, Corrego ≃ 287b 23.46 S 46.47 W
Mombachito, Cerro ∧ 236 12.24 N 85.34 W
Mombacho, Volcán ∧[1] 236 11.50 N 85.58 W
Mombango 152 1.45 N 24.26 E
Mombaruzzo 62 44.46 N 8.27 E
Mombasa 154 4.03 S 39.40 E
Mombetsu 92a 44.21 N 143.22 E
Mombo 154 4.53 S 38.17 E
Mombongo 152 1.39 N 23.09 E
Momboyo ≃ 152 0.16 S 19.00 E
Mombuey 34 42.02 N 6.20 W
Mombum 164 8.23 S 138.51 E
Momčilgrad 38 41.32 N 25.25 E
Momence 216 41.10 N 87.39 W
Momfafa, Tanjung › 164 0.18 S 131.20 E
Momi 175g 17.55 S 177.17 E
Momignies 50 50.02 N 4.10 E
Mommark 41 54.55 N 10.03 E
Mommenheim 56 48.45 N 7.39 E
Momo 152 1.52 N 11.48 E
Momotombo, Volcán ∧[1] 236 12.26 N 86.33 W
Momozaka 270 34.51 N 135.02 E
Mompog Island I 116 13.31 N 122.11 E
Mompog Pass ⊍ 116 13.34 N 122.13 E
Mompono 152 0.04 N 21.48 E
Mompós 246 9.14 N 74.26 W
Momskij chrebet ⋏ 74 66.00 N 146.00 E
Mon 110 18.31 N 96.38 E
Mon □[8] 110 17.30 N 97.00 E
Møn I 41 55.00 N 12.20 E
Mon ≃ 110 20.20 N 94.54 E
Mona 200 39.48 N 111.51 W
Mona, Canal de la ⊍ 238 18.30 N 67.45 W
Mona, Isla de I 238 18.05 N 67.54 W
Mona, Punta › 236 9.38 N 82.37 W
Monaca 214 40.41 N 80.16 W
Monach, Sound of ⊍ 46 57.34 N 7.35 W
Monach Islands II 46 57.31 N 7.40 W
Monaci, Fiume dei ≃ 70 37.24 N 14.48 E
Monaco 62 43.42 N 7.23 E
Monaco □[1], Europe 22 43.45 N 7.25 E
Monaco □[1], Europe 62 43.45 N 7.25 E
Monadhliath Mountains ⋏ 46 57.10 N 4.00 W
Monadnock Mountain ∧ 207 42.52 N 72.07 W
Monagas □[3] 246 9.20 N 63.00 W
Monaghan 48 54.15 N 6.58 W
Monaghan □[6] 48 54.10 N 7.00 W
Monagrillo 236 7.59 N 80.26 W
Monahans 196 31.35 N 102.53 W
Monahans Draw ∨ 196 31.55 N 101.46 W
Monahans Sandhills State Park ♦ 196 31.38 N 102.50 W
Monakino 89 43.24 N 133.29 E
Mona Lake ◎ 216 43.11 N 86.17 W
Monamolin 48 52.33 N 6.20 W
Monango 198 46.10 N 98.35 W
Monapo 154 14.57 S 40.17 E
Monapo ≃ 154 15.07 S 40.33 E
Mona Quimbundo 152 9.55 S 19.58 E
Monar, Loch ◎ 46 57.25 N 5.06 W
Monarch 192 34.43 N 81.35 W
Monarch Mountain ∧ 182 51.54 N 125.53 W
Monarch Pass)(200 38.30 N 106.19 W
Monaro Range ⋏ 171b 36.22 S 149.03 E
Monarto South 168b 35.08 S 139.08 E
Monaš 80 46.58 N 50.36 E
Monashee Mountains ⋏ 182 50.30 N 118.30 W
Monashee Provincial Park ♦ 182 50.28 N 118.11 W
Monash University ʋ[2] 274b 37.55 S 145.08 E
Monasterace 68 38.27 N 16.33 E
Monasterevin 48 53.07 N 7.02 W
Monasterolo di Savigliano 62 44.40 N 7.37 E
Monastir, It. 71 39.23 N 9.02 E
Monastir → Bitola, Mak. 38 41.01 N 21.20 E
Monastir, Tun. 148 35.47 N 10.50 E
Monastir □[8] 148 35.15 N 10.45 E
Monastyrščina 76 54.21 N 31.50 E
Monastyryshche 78 49.00 N 29.49 E
Monastyrys'ka 78 49.06 N 25.11 E
Monatélé 152 4.16 N 11.12 E
Mona Vale 170 33.41 S 151.18 E
Monbulk 274b 37.52 S 145.25 E
Monbulk Creek ≃ 274b 37.54 S 145.15 E
Moncada 116 15.44 N 120.34 E
Moncalieri 62 45.00 N 7.41 E
Moncalvo 62 45.03 N 8.16 E
Monção, Bra. 250 3.30 S 45.15 W
Moncão, Port. 34 42.05 N 8.29 W
Monceau-sur-Sambre 50 50.25 N 4.22 E
Mončegorsk 24 67.54 N 32.58 E
Mönchdorf 61 48.21 N 14.48 E
Mönchengladbach 56 51.12 N 6.28 E
Mönchengladbach, Flughafen ⊠ 263 51.14 N 6.29 E
Mönchhof 61 47.52 N 16.56 E
Monchique 34 37.19 N 8.33 W
Mönchweiler 58 48.06 N 8.25 E
Moncks Corner 192 33.11 N 80.00 W
Monclova 232 26.54 N 101.25 W
Moncontour 32 48.21 N 2.39 W
Moncoutant 32 46.43 N 0.35 W
Moncton 186 46.06 N 64.47 W
Mondaí 252 27.05 S 53.25 W
Mondaino 66 43.51 N 12.41 E
Mondavio 66 43.40 N 12.58 E
Monday ≃ 252 25.33 S 54.41 W
Mondego ≃ 34 40.09 N 8.52 W
Mondego, Cabo › 34 40.11 N 8.55 W
Mondello 70 38.13 N 13.20 E
Mondeodo 112 3.33 S 122.12 E
Mondeor 273d 26.17 S 28.00 E
Mondimbi 152 1.43 N 22.58 E
Mondo, Tan. 154 4.59 S 35.54 E
Mondo, Tchad 146 13.47 N 15.32 E
Mondolè, Monte ∧ 62 44.13 N 7.46 E
Mondolfo 66 43.45 N 13.06 E
Mondombe 152 0.53 S 22.45 E
Mondoñedo 34 43.26 N 7.22 W
Mondorf-les-Bains 56 49.31 N 6.16 E
Mondoro 150 14.40 N 1.57 W
Mondoubleau 50 47.59 N 0.54 E
Mondovi 190 44.34 N 91.40 W
Mondragon, Fr. 62 44.14 N 4.43 E
Mondragon, Pil. 116 12.31 N 124.45 E
Mondragone 68 41.07 N 13.53 E
Mondrain Island I 162 34.08 S 122.15 E
Mondsee 64 47.52 N 13.21 E
Mondsee ◎ 64 47.49 N 13.23 E
Monds Island I 285 39.50 N 75.19 W
Mondy 88 51.40 N 100.59 E
Monee 216 41.25 N 87.45 W
Moneglia 62 44.14 N 9.30 E
Monemvasía 38 36.41 N 23.03 E
Monero 200 36.54 N 106.52 W
Moneron, ostrov I 89 46.17 N 141.15 E
Monesiglio 62 44.28 N 8.07 E
Monessen 214 40.08 N 79.53 W
Monesterio 34 38.05 N 6.16 W
Monestier-de-Clermont 62 44.54 N 5.38 E
Monetnyj 86 57.03 N 60.53 E
Monett 194 36.55 N 93.55 W
Monette 194 35.53 N 90.20 W
Money Creek ≃ 216 40.40 N 88.58 W
Moneygall 48 52.53 N 7.57 W
Moneymore 48 54.42 N 6.40 W
Monfalcone 64 45.49 N 13.32 E
Monferrato □[9] 62 44.55 N 8.05 E
Monflanquin 32 44.32 N 0.46 E
Monforte 34 39.03 N 7.26 W
Monforte de Lemos 34 42.31 N 7.30 W
Monforte San Giorgio 70 38.09 N 15.23 E
Monfort Heights 218 39.12 N 84.37 W
Monga 152 4.12 N 22.49 E
Mongaguá 256 24.06 S 46.37 W
Mongai-Musenge 152 4.04 S 19.34 E
Mongala ≃ 152 1.53 N 19.46 E
Mongalla 154 5.12 N 31.46 E

	English	Deutsch	Español	Français	Português
≃	River	Fluß	Río	Rivière	Rio
≊	Canal	Kanal	Canal	Canal	Canal
∟	Waterfall, Rapids	Wasserfall, Stromschnellen	Cascada, Rápidos	Chute d'eau, Rapides	Cascata, Rápidos
⊍	Strait	Meeresstraße	Estrecho	Détroit	Estreito
⊂	Bay, Gulf	Bucht, Golf	Bahía, Golfo	Baie, Golfe	Baía, Golfo
◎	Lake, Lakes	See, Seen	Lago, Lagos	Lac, Lacs	Lago, Lagos
≡	Swamp	Sumpf	Pantano	Marais	Pântano
⊓	Ice Features, Glacier	Eis- und Gletscherformen	Accidentes Glaciales	Formes glaciaires	Acidentes glaciares
⊤	Other Hydrographic Features	Andere Hydrographische Objekte	Otros Elementos Hidrográficos	Autres données hydrographiques	Outros acidentes hidrográficos
✣	Submarine Features	Untermeerische Objekte	Accidentes Submarinos	Formes de relief sous-marin	Acidentes submarinos
□	Political Unit	Politische Einheit	Unidad Política	Entité politique	Unidade política
ʋ	Cultural Institution	Kulturelle Institution	Institución Cultural	Institution culturelle	Institução cultural
⊥	Historical Site	Historische Stätte	Sitio Histórico	Site historique	Sitio histórico
♦	Recreational Site	Erholungs- und Ferienort	Sitio de Recreo	Centre de loisirs	Area de Lazer
⊠	Airport	Flughafen	Aeropuerto	Aéroport	Aeroporto
■	Military Installation	Militäranlage	Instalación Militar	Installation militaire	Instalação militar
✦	Miscellaneous	Verschiedenes	Misceláneo	Divers	Diversos

Mongalla Game Reserve ◆4 154 5.12 N 31.33 E
Mongandjo 152 1.21 N 24.20 E
Mongarlowe ≐ 170 35.15 S 149.52 E
Mongat 266d 41.28 N 2.17 E
Mongaup ≐ 210 41.25 N 74.45 W
Mongaup Valley 210 41.40 N 74.47 W
Mongbwalu 154 1.57 N 30.02 E
Mongbyŏn-ni 271b 37.40 N 126.44 E
Mong Cai 110 21.32 N 107.58 E
Monge ∧ 266c 38.46 N 9.26 W
Monger, Îles II 186 51.05 N 58.45 W
Mongeri 150 8.19 N 11.44 W
Mongers Lake ⊜ 162 29.15 S 117.05 E
Monggon Qulu 89 48.35 N 119.49 E
Monggŭmp'o 98 38.09 N 124.47 E
Möng Hai 110 20.46 N 99.49 E
Möng Hawm 110 23.51 N 98.20 E
Monghidoro 66 44.13 N 11.19 E
Möng Hpāyak 110 20.53 N 99.54 E
Möng Hsat 110 20.32 N 99.15 E
Monghyr → Munger 124 25.23 N 86.28 E
Mongi ≐ 164 6.35 S 147.35 E
Mongiana 68 38.31 N 16.19 E
Mongibello → Etna, Monte ∧1 70 37.46 N 15.00 E
Mongiuffi 70 37.55 N 15.17 E
Möng Küng 110 21.36 N 97.32 E
Möng Ma 110 21.37 N 99.54 E
Möng Mit 110 23.07 N 96.41 E
Möng Nai 110 20.31 N 97.52 E
Möng Nawng 110 21.39 N 98.08 E
Mongo, Tchad 146 12.11 N 18.42 E
Mongo, In., U.S. 216 41.41 N 85.17 W
Mongo ≐ 150 9.34 N 12.11 W
Mongoj 88 53.57 N 113.50 E
Mongol Altajn nuruu ⋏ 90 46.30 N 93.00 E
Mongol Ard Uls → Mongolia □1 90 46.00 N 105.00 E
Mongolei → Mongolia □1 90 46.00 N 105.00 E
Mongol els ◆2 88 47.45 N 94.30 E
Mongolia (Mongol Ard Uls) □1 90 46.00 N 105.00 E
Mongolie → Mongolia □1 90 46.00 N 105.00 E
Mongomo 152 1.38 N 11.19 E
Möngön Mor't 88 48.11 N 108.29 E
Mongororo 146 12.01 N 22.28 E
Mongoumba 152 3.38 N 18.36 E
Möng Pai 110 19.44 N 97.05 E
Möng Pan 110 20.19 N 98.22 E
Möng Pawn 110 20.49 N 97.28 E
Möng Ping 110 22.22 N 99.02 E
Mongpong ≐ 116 12.44 N 120.48 E
Mongrando 62 45.31 N 8.00 E
Möng Si 110 23.40 N 98.23 E
Mong Tung Hang 271d 22.20 N 114.02 E
Mongu 152 15.15 S 23.09 E
Môngua 152 16.43 S 15.23 E
Monguelfo (Welsberg) 64 46.45 N 12.06 E
Monguno 146 12.40 N 13.38 E
Möng Yai 110 22.25 N 98.02 E
Möng Yawng 110 21.11 N 100.22 E
Monheim, Dtsch. 56 48.50 N 10.51 E
Monheim, Dtsch. 56 51.05 N 6.52 E
Moniaive 44 55.12 N 3.55 W
Mönichkirchen 61 47.31 N 16.02 E
Monico 190 45.34 N 89.09 W
Monida Pass)(202 44.33 N 112.18 W
Mon Idée 50 49.53 N 4.23 E
Monie 152 4.00 S 17.22 E
Monie Bay ⊂ 208 38.13 N 75.51 W
Monie Creek ≐ 208 38.14 N 75.50 W
Monifieth 46 56.29 N 2.49 W
Monimail 46 56.18 N 3.08 W
Moninger 214 40.14 N 80.13 W
Monino 82 55.50 N 38.11 E
Moniquirá 246 5.52 N 73.36 W
Mõniste 76 57.35 N 26.33 E
Monistrol-d'Allier 62 44.57 N 3.38 E
Monistrol-sur-Loire 62 45.17 N 4.10 E
Monitor Range ⋏ 204 38.45 N 116.30 W
Monitor Valley V 204 39.00 N 116.40 W
Monívea 48 53.23 N 8.43 W
Monjolo 256 22.49 S 42.57 W
Monk, Pointe > 275a 45.29 N 73.57 W
Monkayo 116 7.50 N 126.03 E
Mönkebude 54 53.46 N 13.57 E
Monken Hadley ◆8 260 51.40 N 0.11 W
Monkey Bay 154 14.05 S 34.55 E
Monkey River 236 16.22 N 88.29 W
Mońki 30 53.24 N 22.49 E
Monkira 166 24.49 S 140.34 E
Monkoto 152 1.38 S 20.39 E
Monks Heath 262 53.16 N 2.14 W
Monkton 212 43.35 N 81.05 W
Monmouth, Wales, U.K. 42 51.50 N 2.43 W
Monmouth, Il., U.S. 190 40.54 N 90.38 W
Monmouth, In., U.S. 216 40.52 N 84.57 W
Monmouth, Or., U.S. 202 44.50 N 123.13 W
Monmouth □6 208 40.16 N 74.17 W
Monmouth Beach 276 40.19 N 73.58 W
Monmouth Hills 276 40.24 N 74.00 W
Monmouth Junction 208 40.22 N 74.32 W
Monmouth Mountain ∧ 182 51.00 N 123.47 W
Monnickendam 52 52.27 N 5.02 E
Monnow ≐ 42 51.48 N 2.42 W
Mono □5 150 6.45 N 1.50 E
Mono □6 226 38.18 N 119.22 W
Mono ≐ 150 6.17 N 1.51 E
Mono, Caño ≐ 246 4.25 N 67.47 W
Mono, Punta > 236 11.36 N 83.39 W
Monobe 96 33.42 N 133.53 E
Monobe ≐ 96 33.32 N 133.41 E
Monocacy ≐ 208 39.13 N 77.27 W
Monocacy Station 208 40.16 N 75.46 W
Monogarovo 82 54.42 N 38.45 E
Mono Island I 175e 7.21 S 155.34 E
Mono Lake ⊜ 204 38.00 N 119.00 W
Monolith 228 35.07 N 118.22 W
Monomoy Island I 207 41.35 N 69.59 W
Monomoy Point > 207 41.33 N 70.02 W
Monon 216 40.52 N 86.52 W
Monona, Ia., U.S. 190 43.03 N 91.23 W
Monona, Wi., U.S. 216 43.03 N 89.20 W
Monona, Lake ⊜ 216 43.03 N 89.22 W
Monongahela 214 40.12 N 79.55 W
Monongahela ≐ 188 40.27 N 80.00 W
Monongahela Brook ≐ 285 39.47 N 75.09 W
Monopoli 68 40.57 N 17.19 E
Monor 30 47.21 N 19.27 E
Mono Road Station 275b 43.51 N 79.51 W
Monòver 34 38.26 N 0.50 W
Monowai, Lake ⊜ 172 45.52 S 167.27 E
Monponsett 207 42.01 N 70.50 W
Monponsett Pond ⊜ 283 42.01 N 70.51 W
Monreal 34 42.42 N 1.30 W
Monreal del Campo 34 40.47 N 1.21 W
Monreale 70 38.05 N 13.17 E
Monreale, Castello di ⊥ 71 39.38 N 8.49 E
Monroe, Ct., U.S. 207 41.19 N 73.12 W
Monroe, Fl., U.S. 220 25.52 N 81.06 W
Monroe, Ga., U.S. 192 33.47 N 83.42 W
Monroe, In., U.S. 216 40.44 N 84.56 W
Monroe, Ia., U.S. 190 41.31 N 93.06 W
Monroe, La., U.S. 194 32.30 N 92.07 W
Monroe, Mi., U.S. 214 41.54 N 83.23 W
Monroe, Ne., U.S. 198 41.28 N 97.35 W
Monroe, N.J., U.S. 276 41.06 N 74.38 W
Monroe, N.Y., U.S. 210 41.19 N 74.11 W
Monroe, N.C., U.S. 192 34.59 N 80.32 W
Monroe, Oh., U.S. 218 39.26 N 84.21 W
Monroe, Or., U.S. 202 44.18 N 123.17 W
Monroe, Ut,. U.S. 200 38.37 N 112.07 W
Monroe, Va., U.S. 192 37.30 N 79.07 W
Monroe, Wa., U.S. 224 47.51 N 121.58 W
Monroe, Wi., U.S. 190 42.36 N 89.38 W
Monroe □6, Fl., U.S. 220 25.10 N 81.10 W
Monroe □6, Il., U.S. 219 38.20 N 90.09 W
Monroe □6, In., U.S. 218 39.10 N 86.26 W
Monroe □6, Mi., U.S. 216 41.55 N 83.26 W
Monroe □6, Mo., U.S. 219 39.30 N 92.00 W
Monroe □6, N.Y., U.S. 210 43.10 N 77.36 W
Monroe □6, Pa., U.S. 210 40.59 N 75.12 W
Monroe, Lake ⊜ 220 28.52 N 81.16 W
Monroe Bridge 207 42.43 N 72.56 W
Monroe Center, Ct., U.S. 207 41.20 N 73.12 W
Monroe Center, Il., U.S. 216 42.06 N 89.00 W
Monroe City, In., U.S. 194 38.36 N 87.21 W
Monroe City, Mo., U.S. 219 39.39 N 91.44 W
Monroe City, Tx., U.S. 222 29.47 N 94.35 W
Monroe Lake ⊜1 218 39.05 N 86.25 W
Monroe Manor 216 41.36 N 86.40 W
Monroeton 210 41.43 N 76.30 W
Monroeville, Al., U.S. 194 31.31 N 87.19 W
Monroeville, In., U.S. 216 40.58 N 84.52 W
Monroeville, N.J., U.S. 208 39.37 N 75.09 W
Monroeville, Oh., U.S. 214 41.14 N 82.41 W
Monroeville, Pa., U.S. 214 40.26 N 79.47 W
Monroeville Mall ◆9 279b 40.26 N 79.48 W
Monrovia, Liber. 150 6.18 N 10.47 W
Monrovia, Ca., U.S. 228 34.08 N 117.59 W
Monrovia, In., U.S. 218 39.34 N 86.28 W
Monrovia Mountain Park ♦ 280 34.10 N 118.10 W
Monrovia Peak ∧ 280 34.13 N 117.58 W
Mons (Bergen), Bel. 50 50.27 N 3.56 E
Mons, Fr. 62 43.41 N 6.43 E
Monschau 56 50.33 N 6.14 E
Monse 112 4.07 S 123.15 E
Monsefú 248 6.52 S 79.52 W
Monselice 64 45.14 N 11.45 E
Monsenhor Hipólito 250 6.59 S 41.07 W
Monsenhor Paulo 256 21.46 S 45.33 W
Monsenhor Tabosa 250 4.47 S 40.04 W
Monsey 210 41.06 N 74.04 W
Monsheim, Dtsch. 56 49.38 N 8.12 E
Mönsheim, Dtsch. 56 48.52 N 8.52 E
Møns Klint ⊥4 41 54.58 N 12.33 E
Monsols 58 46.13 N 4.31 E
Monson, Me., U.S. 188 45.17 N 69.30 W
Monson, Ma., U.S. 207 42.06 N 72.19 W
Monster 52 52.02 N 4.10 E
Mönsterås 26 57.02 N 16.26 E
Monsummano Terme 66 43.52 N 10.49 E
Montà 62 44.48 N 7.57 E
Montabaur 56 50.26 N 7.50 E
Montafon V 58 47.02 N 9.57 E
Montagano 66 41.39 N 14.40 E
Montagnana 64 45.14 N 11.28 E
Montagnareale 70 38.07 N 14.57 E
Montagne d'Ambre, Parque National de la ♦ 157b 12.40 S 49.05 E
Montagnola ⋏ 66 43.17 N 11.11 E
Montagrier 32 45.16 N 0.29 E
Montagu 158 33.45 S 20.08 E
Montague, P.E., Can. 186 46.10 N 62.39 W
Montague, Ca., U.S. 204 41.43 N 122.31 W
Montague, Ma., U.S. 207 42.32 N 72.32 W
Montague, Mi., U.S. 190 43.25 N 86.21 W
Montague, Tx., U.S. 196 33.40 N 97.43 W
Montague, Isla I 232 31.45 N 114.48 W
Montague City 207 42.35 N 72.35 W
Montague Island I 180 60.00 N 147.30 W
Montague Peak ∧ 180 60.15 N 147.01 W
Montagu Island I 18 58.25 S 26.20 W
Montaigle, Château de ⊥ 56 50.18 N 4.49 E
Montaigu 32 46.59 N 1.19 W
Montaigut-en-Combraille 32 46.11 N 2.48 E
Montainville 261 48.53 N 1.52 E
Montaione 66 43.33 N 10.55 E
Montaj-Taš 85 42.06 N 68.58 E
Montalba 222 31.53 N 95.38 W
Montalbán 34 40.50 N 0.48 W
Montalbancito 286c 10.28 N 66.59 W
Montalbano Elicona 70 38.02 N 15.01 E
Montalbano Ionico 68 40.17 N 16.34 E
Montalcino 66 43.03 N 11.29 E
Montaldo di Cosola 62 44.40 N 9.11 E
Montale 66 43.56 N 11.01 E
Montalegre 34 41.49 N 7.48 W
Montalet-le-Bois 261 49.03 N 1.50 E
Montalieu-Vercieu 62 45.49 N 5.24 E
Montallegro 70 37.23 N 13.21 E
Mont Alto 208 39.50 N 77.33 W
Montalto ∧ 68 38.10 N 15.55 E
Montalto delle Marche 66 42.59 N 13.36 E
Montalto di Castro 66 42.21 N 11.37 E
Montalto Ligure 62 43.56 N 7.51 E
Montalto Uffugo 68 39.25 N 16.10 E
Montalvin Manor 226 37.59 N 122.21 W
Montalvo 228 34.15 N 119.12 W
Montana, Blg. 38 43.25 N 23.13 E
Montana, Schw. 58 46.18 N 7.29 E
Montana, Ak., U.S. 180 62.05 N 150.04 W
Montana □3, U.S. 178 47.00 N 110.00 W
Montana □3, U.S. 202 47.00 N 110.00 W
Montana de Oro State Park ♦ 226 35.15 N 120.50 W
Montana Indian Reserve ◆4 182 52.43 N 113.25 W
Montanaro 62 45.14 N 7.51 E
Montánchez 34 39.13 N 6.09 W
Montandon 210 40.58 N 76.51 W
Montanha 255 18.08 S 40.21 W
Montano Antilia 68 40.10 N 15.22 E
Montara 226 37.33 N 122.31 W
Montara Beach ♦ 282 37.33 N 122.31 W
Montara Mountain ⋏ 282 37.32 N 122.27 W
Montargil 34 39.05 N 8.10 W
Montargis 50 48.00 N 2.45 E
Montataire 50 49.16 N 2.26 E
Montauban 32 44.01 N 1.21 E
Montauban, Lac ⊜ 206 46.52 N 72.10 W
Montauban-les-Mines 206 46.50 N 72.20 W
Montauk 207 41.02 N 71.57 W
Montauk, Lake ⊜ 207 41.04 N 71.55 W
Montauk Point > 207 41.04 N 71.52 W
Montauroux 62 43.37 N 6.46 E
Monta Vista 226 37.19 N 122.03 W
Montazzoli 66 41.57 N 14.26 E
Montbard 50 47.37 N 4.20 E
Montbarrey 58 47.01 N 5.39 E
Montbazon 50 47.17 N 0.43 E
Montbéliard 58 47.31 N 6.48 E
Mont Belvieu 222 29.50 N 94.53 W
Montbenoît 58 46.59 N 6.28 E
Montblanc 34 41.22 N 1.10 E
Mont Blanc, Tunnel du ◆5 58 45.50 N 6.53 E
Mont-Bonvillers 56 49.20 N 5.51 E
Montbovon 58 46.29 N 7.03 E
Montbozon 58 47.28 N 6.16 E
Montbrison 62 45.36 N 4.03 E
Montbron 32 45.40 N 0.30 E
Montbronn 56 48.59 N 7.19 E
Montcada i Reixas 266d 41.29 N 2.11 E
Montcalm □6 206 46.20 N 74.20 W
Montceau-les-Mines 58 46.40 N 4.22 E
Montcenis 58 46.47 N 4.23 E
Mont Cenis, Col du)(62 45.15 N 6.54 E
Mont Cenis, Lac du ⊜ 62 45.14 N 6.55 E
Montcevelles, Lac ⊜ 186 51.07 N 60.38 W
Montchanin, Fr. 58 46.45 N 4.27 E
Montchanin, De., U.S. 285 39.47 N 75.35 W
Montchauvet 261 48.54 N 1.38 E
Montclair, Ca., U.S. 228 34.06 N 117.41 W
Montclair, N.J., U.S. 210 40.49 N 74.12 W
Montclair State College ʊ2 276 40.51 N 74.12 W
Mont Clare 285 40.08 N 75.30 W
Montcornet 50 49.41 N 4.01 E
Montdale 210 41.32 N 75.37 W
Mont-de-Marsan 32 43.53 N 0.30 W
Montdidier 50 49.39 N 2.34 E
Mont-Dore 175f 22.16 S 166.34 E
Monte, Castel del ⊥ 68 41.05 N 16.16 E
Monte, Cima del ∧ 66 42.47 N 10.23 E
Monte, Laguna del ⊜, Arg. 252 37.00 S 62.28 W
Monte, Laguna del ⊜, Arg. 258 35.28 S 58.49 W
Montea ∧ 68 39.40 N 15.57 E
Monte Adone, Galleria di ◆5 64 44.21 N 11.25 E
Monteagle 194 35.15 N 85.50 W
Monteagudo 248 19.49 S 63.59 W
Monte Albán ⊥ 234 17.02 N 96.45 W
Monte Alegre, Bra. 250 2.01 S 54.04 W
Monte Alegre, Bra. 250 6.04 S 35.20 W
Monte Alegre de Goiás 255 13.14 S 47.10 W
Monte Alegre de Minas 255 18.52 S 48.52 W
Monte Alegre de Sergipe 250 10.02 S 37.33 W
Monte Alegre do Piauí 250 9.46 S 45.18 W
Monte Alegre do Sul 256 22.40 S 46.41 W
Monte Azul 255 15.09 S 42.53 W
Monte Azul Paulista 255 20.55 S 48.38 W
Montebello, P.Q., Can. 206 45.39 N 74.56 W
Montebello, It. 62 45.00 N 9.06 E
Montebello, P.R. 240m 18.22 N 66.31 W
Montebello, Ca., U.S. 228 34.00 N 118.06 W
Montebello Iónico 68 37.59 N 15.45 E
Monte Bello Islands II 162 20.25 S 115.32 E
Montebello Vicentino 64 45.27 N 11.23 E
Montebelluna 64 45.47 N 12.03 E
Monte Belo 256 21.20 S 46.23 W
Montebruno 62 44.31 N 9.15 E
Monte Buey 252 32.55 S 62.27 W
Montecalvo Irpino 68 41.11 N 15.02 E
Monte Campatri 267a 41.48 N 12.44 E
Montecarlo 252 26.34 S 54.47 W
Monte Carlo ◆8 62 43.44 N 7.25 E
Monte Carmelo 255 18.43 S 47.29 W
Montecarotto 66 43.31 N 13.04 E
Monte Caseros 252 30.15 S 57.39 W
Montecassiano 66 43.21 N 13.26 E
Montecassino, Abbazia di ʊ1 66 41.29 N 13.48 E
Montecastrilli 66 42.39 N 12.29 E
Montecatini-Terme 66 43.53 N 10.46 E
Monte Cavallo 66 42.59 N 13.00 E
Montecchio 66 43.51 N 12.46 E
Montecchio Emilia 64 44.42 N 10.27 E
Montecchio Maggiore 64 45.30 N 11.24 E
Montecelio 66 42.01 N 12.44 E
Monte Ceneri, Passo)(58 46.08 N 8.55 E
Montechiaro d'Asti 62 45.01 N 8.07 E
Montechiarugolo 64 44.42 N 10.25 E
Monte Chingolo ◆8 288 34.45 S 58.20 W
Monteciccardo 66 43.49 N 12.48 E
Montecilfone 66 41.54 N 14.50 E
Montecillos, Cordillera de ⋏ 236 14.25 N 87.51 W
Montecito 204 34.26 N 119.37 W
Monte Comán 252 34.36 S 67.54 W
Montecorice 68 40.14 N 14.59 E
Montecorvino Pugliano 68 40.41 N 14.57 E
Montecorvino Rovella 68 40.42 N 14.59 E
Montecosaro 66 43.19 N 13.37 E
Monte Creek 182 50.39 N 119.57 W
Montecreto 64 44.14 N 10.41 E
Montecristi, Ec. 246 1.03 S 80.40 W
Monte Cristi, Rep. Dom. 238 19.52 N 71.39 W
Monte Cristo 248 14.43 S 61.14 W
Montecristo, Isola di I 36 42.20 N 10.19 E
Montecuccolo ʊ1 64 44.19 N 10.50 E
Montedinove 66 42.58 N 13.35 E
Monte di Procida 68 40.48 N 14.03 E
Monte do Carmo 250 10.45 S 48.07 W
Montedoro 70 37.27 N 13.49 E
Monte Escobedo 234 22.18 N 103.35 W
Monte Estoril 266c 38.42 N 9.24 W
Montefalcione 68 40.58 N 14.53 E
Montefalco 66 42.54 N 12.39 E
Montefalcone di Val Fortore 68 41.20 N 15.00 E
Montefano 66 43.25 N 13.26 E
Montefeltro ◆1 66 43.50 N 12.15 E
Montefiascone 66 42.32 N 12.02 E
Montefiorino 64 44.22 N 10.37 E
Monteforte d'Alpone 64 45.25 N 11.17 E
Monteforte Irpino 68 40.54 N 14.42 E
Montefrío 34 37.19 N 4.01 W
Montegallo 66 42.50 N 13.19 E
Montegiordano 68 40.02 N 16.32 E
Montegiorgio 66 43.08 N 13.32 E
Monte Giovi, Passo di (Jaufen Pass))(64 46.50 N 11.19 E
Montego Bay 241q 18.28 N 77.55 W
Montegranaro 66 43.14 N 13.38 E
Monte Grande 252 30.06 S 70.31 W
Monte Grimano 66 43.52 N 12.29 E
Montegrotto Terme 64 45.19 N 11.46 E
Montegut 194 29.28 N 90.33 W
Monteiasi 68 40.30 N 17.23 E
Monteiro 250 7.53 S 37.07 W
Monteiro Lobato 256 22.58 S 45.50 W
Monteith, Mount ∧ 182 55.45 N 122.30 W
Montejicar 34 37.34 N 3.30 W
Montejinni 164 16.40 S 131.45 E
Montelavar 266c 38.51 N 9.20 W
Monteleone di Puglia 68 41.10 N 15.15 E
Monteleone di Spoleto 66 42.39 N 12.58 E
Monteleone Rocco Doria 71 40.29 N 8.34 E
Monteleone Sabino 66 42.14 N 12.51 E
Montelepre 70 38.05 N 13.10 E
Montelíbano 246 8.05 N 75.29 W
Montélimar 62 44.34 N 4.45 E
Montelindo ≐ 252 23.56 S 57.12 W
Montella 68 40.51 N 15.01 E
Montellano 34 37.00 N 5.34 W
Montello, Nv., U.S. 204 41.15 N 114.11 W
Montello, Wi., U.S. 190 43.47 N 89.19 W
Monteluco ʊ1 66 42.43 N 12.45 E
Montelungo 64 44.24 N 9.54 E
Montelupo Fiorentino 66 43.44 N 11.01 E
Montemaggiore Belsito 70 37.51 N 13.46 E
Montemagno 62 44.59 N 8.20 E
Monte Maíz 252 33.12 S 62.36 W
Montemarano 68 40.55 N 15.00 E
Montemarciano 66 43.38 N 13.19 E
Montemayor, Meseta de ⋏1 254 44.20 S 66.10 W
Montemesola 68 40.34 N 17.20 E
Montemiletto 68 41.01 N 14.54 E
Montemilone 68 41.02 N 15.58 E
Montemor 266c 38.49 N 9.12 W
Montemor ∧ 266c 38.49 N 9.12 W
Montemorelos 232 25.12 N 99.49 W
Montemor-o-Novo 34 38.39 N 8.13 W
Montemor-o-Velho 34 40.10 N 8.41 W
Montemuro ∧ 34 40.58 N 7.56 W
Montemurro 68 40.18 N 15.59 E
Montendre 32 45.17 N 0.24 W
Montenegro 252 29.42 S 51.28 W
Montenegro → Crna Gora □3 38 42.30 N 19.18 E
Montenero 66 43.30 N 10.21 E
Montenero ∧ 68 39.13 N 16.35 E
Montenero di Bisaccia 66 41.57 N 14.47 E
Monteodorisio 66 42.05 N 14.39 E
Monte Oliveto Maggiore, Abbazia del ʊ1 66 43.12 N 11.32 E
Monte Pascoal, Parque Nacional de ♦ 255 16.54 S 39.24 W
Monte Patria 252 30.42 S 70.58 W
Montepescali 66 42.53 N 11.05 E
Monte Porzio Catone 267a 41.49 N 12.43 E
Monteprandone 66 42.55 N 13.50 E
Montepuez 154 13.07 S 39.00 E
Montepuez ≐ 154 12.32 S 40.27 E
Montepulciano 66 43.05 N 11.47 E
Monte Quemado 252 25.48 S 62.52 W
Monterado 112 0.45 N 109.08 E
Monterchi 66 43.29 N 12.07 E
Montereale 66 42.31 N 13.15 E
Montereale Valcellina 64 46.10 N 12.39 E
Montereau 50 47.51 N 2.34 E
Montereau-Faut-Yonne 50 48.23 N 2.57 E
Montereau-sur-le-Jard 261 48.35 N 2.40 E
Monterey, Ca., U.S. 226 36.36 N 121.53 W
Monterey, In., U.S. 216 41.09 N 86.28 W
Monterey, Ky., U.S. 218 38.25 N 84.52 W
Monterey, Ma., U.S. 207 42.10 N 73.12 W
Monterey, N.Y., U.S. 210 42.18 N 77.03 W
Monterey, Tn., U.S. 194 36.08 N 85.16 W
Monterey, Va., U.S. 188 38.24 N 79.34 W
Monterey □6 226 36.40 N 121.38 W
Monterey Bay ⊂ 226 36.45 N 121.55 W
Monterey Park 228 34.03 N 118.07 W
Monterey Peninsula Airport ⊠ 226 36.35 N 121.51 W
Montería 246 8.46 N 75.53 W
Monteriggioni 66 43.23 N 11.13 E
Montero 248 17.20 S 63.15 W
Monte Romano 66 42.16 N 11.54 E
Monteroni d'Arbia 66 43.14 N 11.25 E
Monteroni di Lecce 68 40.19 N 18.06 E
Monteros 252 27.10 S 65.30 W
Monterosso al Mare 62 44.09 N 9.39 E
Monterosso Almo 70 37.05 N 14.46 E
Monterosso Calabro 68 38.43 N 16.17 E
Monterotondo 66 42.03 N 12.37 E
Monterotondo Marittimo 66 43.09 N 10.51 E
Monterrey, Méx. 232 25.40 N 100.19 W
Monterrey, Méx. 234 16.05 N 93.23 W
Monterrico, Hipódromo de ♦ 286d 12.06 S 76.59 W
Monterubbiano 66 43.05 N 13.43 E
Montes Altos 250 5.50 S 47.04 W
Monte San Biagio 66 41.21 N 13.21 E
Monte San Giovanni Campano 66 41.38 N 13.31 E
Montesano 224 46.58 N 123.36 W
Montesano sulla Marcellana 68 40.16 N 15.42 E
Monte San Savino 66 43.20 N 11.43 E
Monte Santa Maria Tiberina 66 43.26 N 12.09 E
Monte Sant'Angelo 68 41.42 N 15.57 E
Monte Santo 250 10.26 S 39.20 W
Monte Santo de Minas 256 21.12 S 46.59 W
Monte Santu, Capo di > 71 40.05 N 9.44 E
Montesarchio 68 41.04 N 14.38 E
Montescaglioso 68 40.33 N 16.40 E
Montes Claros 255 16.43 S 43.52 W
Montescudaio 66 43.18 N 10.40 E
Montese 64 44.16 N 10.56 E
Monte Sereno 226 37.15 N 122.01 W
Monte Sião 256 22.26 S 46.34 W
Montesilvano Marina 66 42.31 N 14.09 E
Montespaccato ◆8 267a 41.54 N 12.23 E
Montespertoli 66 43.38 N 11.04 E
Montespluga 58 46.30 N 9.21 E
Montets, Col des)(58 46.00 N 6.55 E
Monteux 62 44.02 N 5.00 E
Montevago 70 37.42 N 12.58 E
Montevallo 194 33.06 N 86.51 W
Montevarchi 66 43.31 N 11.34 E
Monteverde 68 41.00 N 15.32 E
Monte Verde ≐ 256 21.55 S 43.33 W
Monteverde Nuovo ◆8 267a 41.51 N 12.27 E
Montevergine, Santuario di ʊ1 68 40.55 N 14.45 E
Montevideo, Mn., U.S. 198 44.56 N 95.43 W
Montevideo, Ur. 258 34.53 S 56.11 W
Montevideo □5 258 34.50 S 56.12 W
Montevideo, Cerro de ∧2 258 33.54 S 56.15 W
Monte Vista 200 37.34 N 106.08 W
Montévrain 261 48.53 N 2.45 E
Montezemolo 62 44.22 N 8.08 E
Montezuma, Ga., U.S. 192 32.18 N 84.01 W
Montezuma, In., U.S. 194 39.47 N 87.22 W
Montezuma, Ia., U.S. 190 41.35 N 92.31 W
Montezuma, Ks., U.S. 198 37.35 N 100.26 W
Montezuma, N.Y., U.S. 210 43.00 N 76.42 W
Montezuma, Oh., U.S. 216 40.29 N 84.33 W
Montezuma Castle National Monument ♦ 200 34.38 N 110.49 W
Montezuma Creek ≐ 200 37.17 N 109.20 W
Montezuma Hills ⋏2 282 38.07 N 121.51 W
Montezuma Slough ≐ 226 38.04 N 121.52 W
Montfaucon, Fr. 56 49.17 N 5.08 E
Montfaucon, Fr. 62 45.10 N 4.18 E
Montfaucon, Schw. 58 47.17 N 7.03 E
Montfermeil 261 48.54 N 2.34 E
Montfleur 58 46.19 N 5.26 E
Montfort, Fr. 32 48.08 N 1.58 W
Montfort, Wi., U.S. 190 42.58 N 90.25 W
Montfort-l'Amaury 50 48.47 N 1.49 E
Montfort-le-Rotrou 50 48.03 N 0.25 E
Montfort-sur-Risle 50 49.18 N 0.40 E
Montfrin 62 43.53 N 4.36 E
Montgé 261 49.02 N 2.45 E
Montgenèvre 62 44.56 N 6.43 E
Montgenèvre, Col de)(62 44.56 N 6.44 E
Montgeron 261 48.42 N 2.27 E
Montgeroult 261 49.05 N 2.00 E
Montgesoye 58 47.05 N 6.12 E
Montgomery → Sāhīwāl, Pāk. 123 30.40 N 73.06 E
Montgomery, Wales, U.K. 42 52.33 N 3.03 W
Montgomery, Al., U.S. 194 32.23 N 86.18 W
Montgomery, Il., U.S. 216 41.43 N 88.20 W
Montgomery, La., U.S. 194 31.40 N 92.53 W
Montgomery, Mi., U.S. 216 41.46 N 84.48 W
Montgomery, Mn., U.S. 190 44.26 N 93.34 W
Montgomery, N.Y., U.S. 210 41.31 N 74.14 W
Montgomery, Oh., U.S. 218 39.13 N 84.21 W
Montgomery, Pa., U.S. 210 41.10 N 76.52 W
Montgomery, Tx., U.S. 222 30.23 N 95.42 W
Montgomery, W.V., U.S. 188 38.11 N 81.19 W
Montgomery □6, Il., U.S. 219 39.09 N 89.29 W
Montgomery □6, Md., U.S. 208 39.05 N 77.09 W
Montgomery □6, Mo., U.S. 219 38.57 N 91.27 W
Montgomery □6, N.Y., U.S. 210 42.57 N 74.22 W
Montgomery □6, Oh., U.S. 218 39.45 N 84.15 W
Montgomery □6, Pa., U.S. 208 40.07 N 75.21 W
Montgomery □6, Tx., U.S. 222 30.18 N 95.30 W
Montgomery City 219 38.58 N 91.30 W
Montgomery Dam ◆6 214 40.39 N 80.24 W
Montgomery Knolls 284b 39.14 N 76.48 W
Montgomery Mall ◆9 284c 39.01 N 77.09 W
Montgomery Square 284c 39.04 N 77.09 W
Montgomeryville 285 40.15 N 75.15 W
Montgomeryville Airport ⊠ 285 40.15 N 75.14 W
Montguyon 32 45.13 N 0.11 W
Monthermé 56 49.53 N 4.44 E
Monthey 58 46.15 N 6.57 E
Monthois 56 49.19 N 4.43 E
Monthureux-sur-Saône 58 48.02 N 5.58 E
Monthyon 261 49.00 N 2.50 E
Monti 71 40.49 N 9.19 E
Monticelli d'Ongina 64 45.05 N 9.56 E
Monticello, Ar., U.S. 194 33.37 N 91.47 W
Monticello, Fl., U.S. 192 30.32 N 83.52 W
Monticello, Ga., U.S. 192 33.18 N 83.41 W
Monticello, Il., U.S. 194 40.01 N 88.34 W
Monticello, In., U.S. 216 40.44 N 86.45 W
Monticello, Ia., U.S. 190 42.14 N 91.11 W
Monticello, Ky., U.S. 194 36.49 N 84.50 W
Monticello, Mn., U.S. 190 45.18 N 93.47 W
Monticello, Ms., U.S. 194 31.33 N 90.06 W
Monticello, Mo., U.S. 219 40.07 N 91.42 W
Monticello, N.Y., U.S. 210 41.39 N 74.41 W
Monticello, Ut,. U.S. 200 37.52 N 109.20 W
Monticello, Wi., U.S. 190 42.44 N 89.35 W
Monticello ⊥ 188 38.00 N 78.30 W
Monticello Conte Otto 64 45.35 N 11.35 E
Monticello Dam ◆6 226 38.30 N 122.07 W
Monticello Woods 284c 38.47 N 77.10 W
Montichiari 64 45.25 N 10.23 E
Monticiano 66 43.08 N 11.11 E
Montiel, Campo de ≐ 34 38.46 N 2.44 W
Montier-en-Der 58 48.29 N 4.46 E
Montieri 66 43.08 N 11.01 E
Montieri, Poggio di ∧ 66 43.08 N 11.00 E
Montiers-sur-Saulx 58 48.32 N 5.16 E
Montignac 32 45.04 N 1.10 E
Montigny 58 48.31 N 6.48 E
Montigny-Devant-Sassey 56 49.26 N 5.09 E
Montigny-le-Bretonneux 261 48.46 N 2.02 E
Montigny-le-Roi 58 48.00 N 5.30 E
Montigny-lès-Cormeilles 261 48.59 N 2.12 E
Montigny-lès-Metz 56 49.06 N 6.09 E
Montigny-sur-Aube 58 47.57 N 4.46 E
Montijo, Esp. 34 38.55 N 6.37 W
Montijo, Pan. 236 7.59 N 81.03 W
Montijo, Port. 34 38.42 N 8.58 W
Montijo, Aeroporto ⊠ 266c 38.42 N 9.02 W
Montijo, Golfo de ⊂ 246 7.40 N 81.07 W
Montilla 34 37.35 N 4.38 W
Montividiu 255 17.24 S 51.14 W
Montivilliers 50 49.33 N 0.12 E
Montjay-la-Tour 261 48.55 N 2.40 E
Montjoie, Lac ⊜, P.Q., Can. 206 46.17 N 75.08 W
Montjoie, Lac ⊜, P.Q., Can. 206 45.25 N 72.06 W
Mont-Joli 186 48.35 N 68.11 W
Montjovet 62 45.43 N 7.40 E
Montjuich, Estadio de ♦ 266d 41.22 N 2.09 E
Montjuich, Faro de ◆5 266d 41.21 N 2.11 E
Montjuich, Parque de ♦ 266d 41.21 N 2.09 E
Mont-Laurier 176 46.33 N 75.30 W
Montlebon 58 47.02 N 6.37 E
Montlhéry 50 48.38 N 2.16 E
Montlhéry, Tour de ♦ 261 48.38 N 2.16 E
Montlignon 261 49.01 N 2.17 E
Montlouet 261 48.31 N 1.43 E
Mont-Louis 32 42.31 N 2.07 E
Montlouis-sur-Loire 50 47.23 N 0.50 E
Montluçon 32 46.21 N 2.36 E
Montluel 62 45.51 N 5.03 E
Montmagny, P.Q., Can. 186 46.59 N 70.33 W
Montmagny, Fr. 261 48.58 N 2.21 E
Montmajour, Abbaye de ʊ1 62 43.43 N 4.40 E
Montmartre ◆8 261 48.53 N 2.21 E
Montmédy 56 49.31 N 5.22 E
Montmélian 62 45.30 N 6.04 E
Montmeló 266d 41.33 N 2.15 E
Montmerle-sur-Saône 58 46.05 N 4.46 E
Montmin 62 45.48 N 6.16 E
Montmirail, Fr. 50 48.52 N 3.32 E
Montmirail, Fr. 50 48.06 N 0.48 E
Montmirey-le-Château 58 47.13 N 5.32 E
Montmoreau-Saint-Cybard 32 45.24 N 0.08 E
Montmorenci 216 40.28 N 87.02 W
Montmorency, Austl. 274b 37.43 S 145.07 E
Montmorency → Beauport, P.Q., Can. 186 46.52 N 71.11 W
Montmorency, Fr. 261 49.00 N 2.20 E
Montmorency ≐ 186 46.53 N 71.07 W
Montmorency, Forêt de ♦ 261 49.02 N 2.16 E
Montmorillon 32 46.26 N 0.52 E
Montmort 50 48.55 N 3.49 E
Monto 166 24.52 S 151.07 E
Montodine 62 45.17 N 9.42 E
Montoggio 62 44.31 N 9.03 E
Montoire-sur-le-Loir 50 47.45 N 0.52 E
Montone 66 43.22 N 12.20 E
Montone ≐ 66 44.24 N 12.14 E
Montopoli in Val d'Arno 66 43.40 N 10.45 E
Mont Orford, Parc du ♦ 206 45.22 N 72.05 W
Montorio al Vomano 66 42.35 N 13.38 E
Montorio nei Frentani 66 41.46 N 14.55 E
Montoro 34 38.01 N 4.23 W
Mont'Orso, Galleria di ◆5 66 41.20 N 13.15 E
Montour □6 210 40.58 N 76.37 W
Montour Falls 210 42.20 N 76.50 W
Montour Run ≐, Pa., U.S. 279b 40.36 N 79.57 W
Montour Run ≐, Pa., U.S. 279b 40.31 N 80.08 W
Montoursville 210 41.15 N 76.55 W
Mont Park 274b 37.43 S 145.04 E
Montparnasse, Gare ◆5 261 48.51 N 2.19 E
Mont Peko, Parc National du ♦ 150 7.00 N 7.15 W
Montpelier, Jam. 241q 18.22 N 77.56 W
Montpelier, Id., U.S. 202 42.19 N 111.17 W
Montpelier, In., U.S. 216 40.33 N 85.16 W
Montpelier, Md., U.S. 284c 39.04 N 76.51 W
Montpelier, Ms., U.S. 194 33.43 N 88.56 W
Montpelier, Oh., U.S. 216 41.35 N 84.36 W
Montpelier, Vt., U.S. 188 44.15 N 72.34 W
Montpellier 62 43.36 N 3.53 E
Montpellier-Fréjorgues, Aéroport de ⊠ 62 43.33 N 4.00 E
Montpezat-sous-Bauzon 62 44.43 N 4.12 E
Mont-Pichet 261 48.53 N 2.54 E
Montpon-Ménesterol 32 45.00 N 0.10 E
Montpont-en-Bresse 58 46.33 N 5.09 E
Montréal, P.Q., Can. 206 45.31 N 73.34 W
Montréal, P.Q., Can. 275a 45.31 N 73.34 W
Montréal, Fr. 50 47.32 N 4.02 E
Montreal, Wi., U.S. 190 46.25 N 90.14 W
Montreal ≐, On., Can. 190 47.14 N 84.39 W
Montreal ≐, On., Can. 190 47.08 N 79.27 W
Montreal ≐, Sk., Can. 184 55.06 N 105.19 W
Montreal ≐, U.S. 190 46.44 N 90.25 W
Montréal, Base des Forces Canadiennes ■ 275a 45.31 N 73.25 W
Montréal, Île de I 206 45.30 N 73.40 W
Montréal, Université de ʊ2 275a 45.30 N 73.37 W
Montréal-Est 206 45.38 N 73.31 W
Montreal International Airport ⊠ 206 45.28 N 73.45 W
Montreal Lake 184 54.03 N 105.46 W
Montreal Lake ⊜ 184 54.20 N 105.40 W
Montreal Lake Indian Reserve ◆4 184 54.00 N 105.45 W
Montréal-Nord 206 45.36 N 73.38 W
Montréal-Ouest 275a 45.27 N 73.39 W
Montreal Water Works Aqueduct ≍1 275a 45.26 N 73.36 W
Montrésor 50 47.09 N 1.12 E
Montresta 71 40.22 N 8.30 E
Montret 58 46.41 N 5.07 E
Montreuil 261 48.52 N 2.26 E
Montreuil-Bellay 32 47.08 N 0.09 W
Montreuil-sous-Bois 50 48.52 N 2.26 E
Montreuil-sur-Mer 50 50.28 N 1.46 E
Montreux 58 46.26 N 6.55 E
Montrevel-en-Bresse 58 46.20 N 5.08 E
Montrichard 50 47.21 N 1.11 E
Montriond 58 46.12 N 6.41 E
Mont-Rolland 206 45.57 N 74.07 W
Montrond-les-Bains 62 45.38 N 4.14 E
Montrose, Austl. 274b 37.49 S 145.21 E
Montrose, Scot., U.K. 46 56.43 N 2.29 W
Montrose, Ca., U.S. 228 34.12 N 118.13 W
Montrose, Co., U.S. 200 38.28 N 107.52 W
Montrose, Ia., U.S. 190 40.31 N 91.24 W
Montrose, Mi., U.S. 190 43.10 N 83.53 W
Montrose, N.Y., U.S. 210 41.15 N 73.56 W
Montrose, Oh., U.S. 214 41.08 N 81.37 W
Montrose, Pa., U.S. 210 41.50 N 75.52 W
Montrose, S.D., U.S. 198 43.41 N 97.11 W
Montrose Harbor ⊂ 278 41.58 N 87.38 W
Montrose Hill 279b 40.30 N 79.51 W
Montross 208 38.05 N 76.49 W
Montrouge 261 48.49 N 2.19 E
Mont-Royal 206 45.31 N 73.39 W
Mont Royal, Parc ♦ 275a 45.31 N 73.35 W
Mont Royal Tunnel ◆5 275a 45.31 N 73.38 W
Montry 261 48.53 N 2.50 E
Monts 50 47.17 N 0.37 E
Monts, Pointe des > 186 49.20 N 67.23 W
Mont-Saint-Aignan 50 49.28 N 1.05 E
Mont-Sainte-Anne, Parc du ♦ 186 47.08 N 70.55 W
Mont-Saint-Hilaire 206 45.34 N 73.11 W
Mont-Saint-Martin 56 49.32 N 5.47 E
Mont-Saint-Michel → Le Mont-Saint-Michel ʊ1 32 48.38 N 1.32 W
Mont-Saint-Vincent 58 46.38 N 4.29 E
Montsauche 50 47.13 N 4.01 E
Montsec 56 48.53 N 5.43 E
Montserrat □2, N.A. 230 16.45 N 62.12 W
Montserrat □2, N.A. 238 16.45 N 62.12 W
Montserrat, Monasterio de ʊ1 34 41.36 N 1.49 E
Montsoult 261 49.04 N 2.19 E
Montsûrs 28 48.08 N 0.33 W
Mont-sur-Vaudrey 58 46.58 N 5.36 E
Mont-Tremblant, Parc provincial du ♦ 206 46.42 N 74.20 W
Montuenga 34 41.03 N 4.37 W
Montvale, N.J., U.S. 276 41.02 N 74.01 W
Montvale, Va., U.S. 192 37.23 N 79.43 W
Montverde 220 28.36 N 81.41 W
Montville, Ct., U.S. 207 41.27 N 72.08 W
Montville, N.J., U.S. 276 40.54 N 74.23 W
Montville, Oh., U.S. 214 41.36 N 81.03 W
Montville Airpark ⊠ 276 40.56 N 74.20 W
Monument, S. Afr. 273d 26.06 S 27.43 E
Monument, Or., U.S. 202 44.49 N 119.25 W
Monument, Pa., U.S. 214 41.07 N 77.42 W
Monument Beach 207 41.43 N 70.36 W
Monument Draw V, U.S. 196 32.27 N 102.20 W
Monument Draw V, Tx., U.S. 196 30.51 N 102.33 W
Monument Hill State Historic Site ⊥ 222 29.53 N 96.54 W
Monumento 256 22.44 S 43.51 W
Monument Peak ∧, Co., U.S. 200 39.43 N 107.55 W
Monument Peak ∧, Id., U.S. 202 42.07 N 114.14 W
Monument Valley V 200 37.05 N 110.20 W
Monundilla, Mount ∧ 170 32.45 S 150.29 E
Monveda 152 2.57 N 21.27 E
Monymusk 46 57.13 N 2.31 W
Monyo 110 17.59 N 95.30 E
Monywa 110 22.05 N 95.08 E
Monza 62 45.35 N 9.16 E
Monze 154 16.16 S 27.28 E
Monzen 92 37.17 N 136.46 E
Monzie 46 56.24 N 3.48 W
Monzón, Esp. 34 41.55 N 0.12 E
Monzón, Perú 248 9.10 S 76.23 W
Moóca ◆8 287b 23.33 S 46.35 W
Moóca, Ribeirão da ≐ 287b 23.36 S 46.35 W
Moodie Island I 176 64.37 N 65.30 W
Moodus 207 41.30 N 72.27 W
Moodus Reservoir ⊜1 207 41.30 N 72.24 W
Moody 222 31.18 N 97.21 W
Moody Air Force Base ■ 192 30.59 N 83.11 W
Moody Wood Dale Airport ⊠ 278 41.59 N 87.58 W
Mooers 206 44.58 N 73.35 W
Mooi ≐, S. Afr. 158 28.45 S 30.34 E
Mooi ≐, S. Afr. 158 26.53 S 26.56 E
Mooirivier 158 29.13 S 29.50 E
Mook 52 51.45 N 5.54 E
Mookane 156 24.59 S 24.33 E
Mooketsi 156 23.35 S 30.05 E
Moolawatana 166 29.55 S 139.43 E
Moolman 158 27.10 S 30.53 E
Mooloogool 162 26.06 S 119.05 E
Moon 214 40.31 N 80.14 W
Moon ≐ 212 45.08 N 79.59 W

Symbols in the index entries represent the broad categories identified in the key at the right. Symbols with superior numbers (⋏1) identify subcategories (see complete key on page *I · 1)*.

Symbole im Register stellen die rechts im Schlüssel erklärten Kategorien dar. Symbole mit hochgestellten Ziffern (⋏1) bezeichnen Unterabteilungen einer Kategorie (vgl. vollständiger Schlüssel auf Seite *I · 1)*.

Los símbolos incluídos en el texto del índice representan las grandes categorías identificadas con la clave a la derecha. Los símbolos con numeros en su parte superior (⋏1) identifican las subcategorías (véase la clave completa en la página *I · 1)*.

Les symboles de l'index représentent les catégories indiquées dans la légende à droite. Les symboles suivis d'un indice (⋏1) représentent des sous-catégories (voir légende complète à la page *I · 1)*.

Os símbolos incluídos no texto do índice representam as grandes categorias identificadas com a chave à direita. Os símbolos com números em sua parte superior (⋏1) identificam as subcategorias (veja-se a chave completa à página *I · 1)*.

∧ Mountain	Berg	Montaña	Montagne	Montanha
⋏ Mountains	Gebirge	Montañas	Montagnes	Montanhas
)(Pass	Paß	Paso	Col	Passo
V Valley, Canyon	Tal, Cañon	Valle, Cañón	Vallée, Canyon	Vale, Canhão
≐ Plain	Ebene	Llano	Plaine	Planície
> Cape	Kap	Cabo	Cap	Cabo
I Island	Insel	Isla	Île	Ilha
II Islands	Inseln	Islas	Îles	Ilhas
⊥ Other Topographic Features	Andere Topographische Objekte	Otros Elementos Topográficos	Autres données topographiques	Outros acidentes topográficos

ESPAÑOL · FRANÇAIS · PORTUGUÊS

Nombre / Nom / Nome	Página / Page	Lat.°′	Long.°′ W = Oeste / Ouest
Moon, Mountains of the → Ruwenzori Range ⩘	154	0.23 N	29.54 E
Moonachie	276	40.50 N	74.02 W
Moonah Creek ≃	166	22.03 S	138.33 E
Moon Crest	279b	40.32 N	80.11 W
Moondarra Reservoir ⊜[1]	169	38.04 S	146.22 E
Moonee Valley Racecourse ♠	274b	37.46 S	144.56 E
Moonie	166	27.43 S	150.22 E
Moonie ≃	166	29.19 S	148.43 E
Moon Island I, On., Can.	212	45.09 N	80.01 W
Moon Island I, Ma., U.S.	283	42.18 N	71.00 W
Moon Run	214	40.27 N	80.06 W
Moonta	168b	34.04 S	137.35 E
Moor, Kepulauan II	164	2.57 S	135.45 E
Moora	162	30.39 S	116.00 E
Moorabbin	169	37.56 S	145.02 E
Moorabbin Airport ⊠	274b	37.59 S	145.09 E
Mooraberree	166	25.14 S	140.59 E
Moorabool ≃	169	38.09 S	144.19 E
Moorarie	162	25.56 S	117.35 E
Moorburg	52	53.17 N	7.53 E
Moorcroft	198	44.15 N	104.56 W
Moordorf	52	53.28 N	7.23 E
Moordrecht	52	51.59 N	4.40 E
Moore, Austl.	171a	26.53 S	152.18 E
Moore, Eng., U.K.	262	53.21 N	2.38 W
Moore, Id., U.S.	202	43.44 N	113.21 W
Moore, Mt., U.S.	202	46.58 N	109.41 W
Moore, Ok., U.S.	196	35.20 N	97.29 W
Moore, Tx., U.S.	196	29.03 N	99.01 W
Moore ≃	162	31.22 S	115.29 E
Moore, Lake ⊜	162	29.50 S	117.35 E
Moorea I	174s	17.32 S	149.50 W
Moorebank	274a	33.56 S	150.56 E
Moore Creek ≃	212	45.29 N	77.58 W
Moorefield, Ky., U.S.	218	38.16 N	83.55 W
Moorefield, Oh., U.S.	214	40.12 N	81.10 W
Moorefield, W.V., U.S.	188	39.03 N	78.58 W
Moore Haven	220	26.49 N	81.05 W
Moore Haven Lock ◆[5]	220	26.51 N	81.05 W
Moore Lake ⊜, On., Can.	212	45.26 N	78.01 W
Moore Lake ⊜, On., Can.	212	44.48 N	78.48 W
Moore Lake ⊜, Mi., U.S.	281	42.37 N	83.36 W
Mooreland, In., U.S.	218	39.59 N	85.15 W
Mooreland, Ok., U.S.	196	36.26 N	99.12 W
Moore Point ›	275b	43.48 N	79.03 W
Moore Reservoir ⊜[1]	188	44.25 N	71.50 W
Mooresburg	210	40.59 N	76.43 W
Moores Creek National Battlefield ♠	192	34.24 N	78.08 W
Moores Hill	218	39.06 N	85.05 W
Moore Station	222	32.11 N	95.35 W
Moorestown	208	39.58 N	74.56 W
Moorestown Mall ◆[9]	285	39.56 N	74.58 W
Mooresville, In., U.S.	218	39.36 N	86.22 W
Mooresville, N.C., U.S.	192	35.35 N	80.48 W
Mooreville	281	42.06 N	83.44 W
Moorfoot Hills ⩘[2]	46	55.45 N	3.02 W
Moorhead, Mn., U.S.	198	46.52 N	96.46 W
Moorhead, Ms., U.S.	194	33.27 N	90.30 W
Mooring	222	30.41 N	96.33 W
Mooringsport	194	32.41 N	93.57 W
Moormerland	52	53.20 N	7.27 E
Moornanyah Lake ⊜	166	33.02 S	143.58 E
Moorooka	171a	27.32 S	153.02 E
Mooroolbark	274b	37.47 S	145.19 E
Moorpark	228	34.17 N	118.53 W
Moorreesburg	158	33.08 S	18.40 E
Moorrege	52	53.40 N	9.39 E
Moorriem	52	53.15 N	8.19 E
Moorsel	50	50.57 N	4.06 E
Moorside	262	53.34 N	2.04 W
Moorslede	50	50.53 N	3.04 E
Moos → Moso, It.	64	46.41 N	12.23 E
Moos → Moso in Passiria, It.	64	46.50 N	11.10 E
Moosach ◆[8]	60	48.11 N	11.31 E
Moosbrunn	264b	48.01 N	16.28 E
Moosburg	61	46.39 N	14.10 E
Moosburg an der Isar	60	48.29 N	11.57 E
Moose ≃, Me., U.S.	188	45.40 N	69.42 W
Moose ≃, N.Y., U.S.	212	43.37 N	75.22 W
Moose Creek	206	45.15 N	74.58 W
Moose Creek ≃	206	45.23 N	75.04 W
Moosehead Lake ⊜	188	45.40 N	69.40 W
Mooseheart	216	41.49 N	88.20 W
Moose Heights	182	53.05 N	122.30 W
Moose Hill ∧[2]	283	42.07 N	71.13 W
Moose Island I	184	51.42 N	97.10 W
Moose Jaw	184	50.23 N	105.32 W
Moose Jaw ≃	184	50.34 N	105.17 W
Moose Lake, Mb., Can.	184	53.43 N	100.20 W
Moose Lake, Mn., U.S.	190	46.27 N	92.45 W
Moose Lake ⊜, Ab., Can.	182	54.15 N	110.55 W
Moose Lake ⊜, Mb., Can.	184	53.55 N	99.45 W
Moose Lake ⊜, On., Can.	212	45.09 N	78.28 W
Mooselookmeguntic Lake ⊜	188	44.53 N	70.48 W
Moose Mountain ∧	184	49.45 N	102.37 W
Moose Mountain Creek ≃	184	49.12 N	102.10 W
Moose Mountain Provincial Park ♠	184	49.48 N	102.25 W
Moose Pass	180	60.29 N	149.22 W
Moosomin	184	50.07 N	101.40 W
Moosomin Indian Reserve ◆[4]	184	53.06 N	108.14 W
Moosonee	176	51.17 N	80.39 W
Moosup	207	41.42 N	71.52 W
Mooti	144	0.35 N	41.56 E
Moots Creek ≃	216	40.32 N	86.47 W
Mootwingee National Park ♠	166	31.07 S	142.23 E
Mopane	156	22.37 S	29.52 E
Mopeia Velha	156	17.59 S	35.44 E
Mopipi	156	21.07 S	24.55 E
Mopo	100	33.07 N	113.02 E
Moppo → Mokp'o	98	34.48 N	126.22 E
Mopti	150	14.30 N	4.12 W
Mopti □[4]	150	14.40 N	4.15 W
Moqokorei	144	4.04 N	46.08 E
Moquegua	248	17.12 S	70.56 W
Moquegua □[5]	248	16.50 S	70.55 W
Mór	30	47.23 N	18.12 E
Mor ≃	126	24.01 N	88.03 E
Mòr, Glen V	46	57.10 N	4.40 W
Mor, Sgurr ∧	46	57.42 N	5.03 W
Mora, Cam.	146	11.03 N	14.09 E
Mora, Esp.	34	39.41 N	3.46 W
Mora, India	272c	18.54 N	72.56 E
Mora, Port.	34	38.56 N	8.10 W
Mora, Sve.	26	61.00 N	14.33 E
Mora, Mn., U.S.	190	45.52 N	93.17 W
Mora, N.M., U.S.	200	35.58 N	105.19 W
Mora ≃	196	35.44 N	104.23 W
Mora, Arroyo de la ≃	196	34.05 N	104.18 W
Moraby	40	60.23 N	15.35 E
Morača, Manastir ʊ[1]	38	42.44 N	19.20 E
Morada	226	38.01 N	121.15 W
Morādābād	124	28.50 N	78.47 E
Morada Nova	250	5.07 S	38.23 W
Morada Nova de Minas	255	18.37 S	45.22 W
Moradel, Montaña de ∧	236	15.06 N	86.16 W
Mora de Rubielos	34	40.15 N	0.45 W
Moraduccio	66	44.10 N	11.29 E
Morafenobe	157b	17.49 S	44.55 E
Morąg	30	53.56 N	19.56 E
Moraga	226	37.50 N	122.08 W
Mórahalom	30	46.13 N	19.54 E
Moraine	218	39.42 N	84.13 W
Moraine Hills State Park ♠	216	42.18 N	88.15 W
Moraine State Park ♠	214	40.56 N	80.07 W
Morainvilliers	261	48.56 N	1.56 E
Morākhi ≃	126	24.01 N	88.10 E
Morākhi Reservoir ⊜[1]	126	24.10 N	87.15 E
Mor'akovskij Zaton	86	56.45 N	84.41 E
Moral de Calatrava	34	38.50 N	3.35 W
Moraleda, Canal ʮ	254	44.30 S	73.30 W
Morales, Guat.	236	15.29 N	88.49 W
Morales, Perú	248	6.28 S	76.28 W
Morales, Arroyo ≃	258	34.48 S	58.36 W
Morales, Laguna c	234	23.35 N	97.47 W
Moramanga	157b	18.56 S	48.12 E
Moran, Ks., U.S.	198	37.54 N	95.10 W
Moran, Mi., U.S.	190	45.59 N	84.49 W
Moran, Tx., U.S.	196	32.33 N	99.10 W
Moran ≃	164	15.16 S	125.33 E
Moranbah	166	22.00 S	148.02 E
Morangis	261	48.42 N	2.20 E
Morangup Hill ∧[2]	168a	31.41 S	116.19 E
Morann	214	40.48 N	78.21 W
Morano Calabro	68	39.50 N	16.08 E
Morano sul Po	62	45.10 N	8.22 E
Moran State Park ♠	224	48.41 N	122.52 W
Morant Bay	241q	17.53 N	76.25 W
Morant Cays II	238	17.24 N	75.59 W
Morant Point ›	241q	17.55 N	76.10 W
Morar, Loch ⊜	46	56.57 N	5.43 W
Mörarp	41	56.04 N	12.52 E
Morasverdes	34	40.36 N	6.16 W
Morat, Lac de (Murtensee) ⊜	58	46.55 N	7.05 E
Moratalla	34	38.12 N	1.53 W
Morattico	208	37.47 N	76.37 W
Moratuwa	122	6.46 N	79.53 E
Morava □[9]	30	49.30 N	17.00 E
Morava (March) ≃	30	48.10 N	16.59 E
Morāveh Tappeh	128	37.55 N	55.57 E
Moravia, C.R.	236	9.51 N	83.26 W
Moravia, Ia., U.S.	190	40.53 N	92.48 W
Moravia, N.Y., U.S.	210	42.42 N	76.25 W
Moravia → Morava □[9]	30	49.20 N	17.00 E
Moravian Indian Reserve ◆[4]	214	42.34 N	81.53 W
Moravská Dyje ≃	61	48.51 N	15.30 E
Moravská Ostrava → Ostrava	30	49.50 N	18.17 E
Moravská Třebová	30	49.45 N	16.40 E
Moravské Budějovice	61	49.03 N	15.49 E
Moravský Krumlov	61	49.03 N	16.19 E
Morawa	162	29.13 S	116.00 E
Morawhanna	246	8.16 N	59.45 W
Moraya	248	21.45 S	65.32 W
Morayfield	171a	27.07 S	152.57 E
Moray Firth c[1]	46	57.50 N	3.30 W
Morazán, Guat.	236	14.56 N	90.09 W
Morazán, Hond.	236	15.17 N	87.34 W
Morbach	56	49.48 N	7.07 E
Morbegno	58	46.08 N	9.34 E
Morbi	120	22.49 N	70.50 E
Morbihan □[5]	32	47.55 N	2.50 W
Mörbisch am See	61	47.45 N	16.40 E
Morbras ≃	261	48.47 N	2.29 E
Mörbylånga	26	56.31 N	16.23 E
Morcenx	32	44.02 N	0.55 W
Morciano di Romagna	66	43.55 N	12.38 E
Morcone	68	41.20 N	14.40 E
Morcote	58	45.56 N	8.55 E
Morcy	80	51.18 N	47.51 E
Morden	184	49.11 N	98.05 W
Morden ◆[8]	260	51.24 N	0.12 W
Mordialloc	169	38.00 S	145.05 E
Mordino	24	61.21 N	51.52 E
Mordoğan	130	38.30 N	26.37 E
Mordovija □[3]	80	54.30 N	44.00 E
Mordovo, Ross.	80	51.07 N	45.48 E
Mordovo, Ross.	80	52.05 N	40.46 E
Mordovo-Adel'akovo	80	53.47 N	51.36 E
Mordovskij Buguruslan	80	53.48 N	52.31 E
Mordovskij zapovednik ◆[4]	80	54.48 N	43.20 E
Mordves	82	54.34 N	38.13 E
Mordvinia → Mordovija □[3]	80	54.30 N	44.00 E
Mordy	30	52.13 N	22.31 E
More, Ben ∧, Scot., U.K.	46	56.25 N	6.01 W
More, Ben ∧, Scot., U.K.	46	56.21 N	4.35 W
More, Loch ⊜	46	58.17 N	4.52 W
More Assynt, Ben ∧	46	58.08 N	4.53 W
Moreau ≃, Mo., U.S.	219	38.33 N	92.06 W
Moreau ≃, S.D., U.S.	198	45.18 N	100.43 W
Moreau, North Fork ≃	198	45.09 N	102.50 W
Moreau, South Fork ≃	198	45.09 N	102.50 W
Moreau Peak ∧	198	45.21 N	103.43 W
Moreauville	194	31.02 N	91.58 W
Morec	80	51.03 N	44.03 E
Morecambe	44	54.04 N	2.53 W
Morecambe Bay c	44	54.07 N	3.00 W
Moree, Austl.	166	29.28 S	149.51 E
Morée, Fr.	50	47.54 N	1.14 E
Morehead, Pap. N. Gui.	164	8.40 S	141.35 E
Morehead, Ky., U.S.	218	38.11 N	83.25 W
Morehead ≃	164	9.00 S	141.25 E
Morehead City	192	34.43 N	76.43 W
Morehouse	194	36.50 N	89.41 W
Moreira César	256	22.55 S	45.22 W
Moreland, Austl.	274b	37.45 S	144.58 E
Moreland, Ga., U.S.	192	33.17 N	84.46 W
Moreland, Ky., U.S.	194	37.30 N	84.48 W
Moreland Hills	279a	41.27 N	81.29 W
Morelia	234	19.42 N	101.07 W
Morell	186	46.25 N	62.42 W
Morella, Austl.	166	22.59 S	143.52 E
Morella, Esp.	34	40.37 N	0.06 W
Morello ≃	70	37.29 N	14.08 E
Morelos, Méx.	196	28.25 N	100.53 W
Morelos, Méx.	232	26.42 N	107.40 W
Morelos, Méx.	234	22.53 N	102.37 W
Morelos □[3]	234	18.45 N	99.00 W
Moremi Wildlife Reserve ◆[4]	156	19.10 S	23.15 E
Morena	124	26.30 N	78.09 E
Morena, Sierra ∧	282	37.25 N	122.18 W
Morena, Sierra ⩘	34	38.00 N	5.00 W
Morenci, Az., U.S.	200	33.04 N	109.21 W
Morenci, Mi., U.S.	216	41.43 N	84.13 W
Moreni	38	45.00 N	25.39 E
Moreno, Arg.	258	34.39 S	58.48 W
Moreno, Ca., U.S.	228	33.55 N	117.09 W
Moreno □[5]	288	34.36 S	58.48 W
Moreno, Bahía c	252	23.35 S	70.30 W
Møre og Romsdal □[6]	26	62.40 N	7.50 E
Mores	71	40.33 N	8.50 E
Moresby Island I, B.C., Can.	182	52.50 N	131.55 W
Moresby Island I, B.C., Can.	224	48.40 N	123.20 W
Mores Island I	238	26.18 N	77.33 W
Moresnet	56	50.43 N	5.59 E
Morestel	62	45.40 N	5.28 E
Moreton, Austl.	164	12.28 S	142.38 E
Moreton, Eng., U.K.	44	53.24 N	3.07 W
Moreton, Eng., U.K.	260	51.44 N	0.14 E
Moreton, Cape ›	171a	27.02 S	153.28 E
Moreton Bay c	171a	27.20 S	153.15 E
Moretonhampstead	42	50.40 N	3.45 W
Moreton-in-Marsh	42	51.59 N	1.42 W
Moreton Island I	171a	27.10 S	153.25 E
Moreton Island National Park ♠	171a	27.09 S	153.25 E
Moret-sur-Loing	50	48.22 N	2.49 E
Moretta	62	44.46 N	7.32 E
Moreuil	50	49.46 N	2.29 E
Morey Park	210	42.33 N	73.43 W
Morey Peak ∧	204	38.37 N	116.17 W
Morez	58	46.31 N	6.02 E
Morfa Nefyn	42	52.56 N	4.33 W
Mörfelden-Walldorf	56	49.58 N	8.34 E
Morga	80	54.26 N	46.29 E
Morgan, Austl.	166	34.02 S	139.40 E
Morgan, Ga., U.S.	192	31.32 N	84.35 W
Morgan, Ky., U.S.	218	38.36 N	84.23 W
Morgan, Mn., U.S.	198	44.25 N	94.55 W
Morgan, Pa., U.S.	279b	40.22 N	80.08 W
Morgan, Tx., U.S.	222	32.01 N	97.37 W
Morgan, Ut,. U.S.	200	41.02 N	111.40 W
Morgan □[6], Il., U.S.	219	39.44 N	90.14 W
Morgan □[6], In., U.S.	218	39.30 N	86.25 W
Morgan, Mount ∧	171b	35.44 S	148.47 E
Morgan City, Al., U.S.	194	34.28 N	86.34 W
Morgan City, La., U.S.	194	29.41 N	91.12 W
Morgan Creek ≃	196	32.19 N	100.55 W
Morganfield	194	37.41 N	87.55 W
Morgan Hill	226	37.07 N	121.39 W
Morganito	246	5.04 N	67.44 W
Morgan Park ◆[8]	278	41.42 N	87.40 W
Morgan's Bay	158	32.43 S	28.20 E
Morgan's Point	222	29.41 N	94.59 W
Morgans Point ›	212	42.52 N	79.21 W
Morgan State College ʊ[2]	284b	39.21 N	76.35 W
Morgantina ⊥	70	37.25 N	14.29 E
Morganton	192	35.44 N	81.41 W
Morgantown, In., U.S.	218	39.22 N	86.15 W
Morgantown, Ky., U.S.	194	37.13 N	86.41 W
Morgantown, Md., U.S.	208	38.21 N	76.58 W
Morgantown, Ms., U.S.	194	31.34 N	91.20 W
Morgantown, Ms., U.S.	194	31.18 N	89.54 W
Morgantown, Oh., U.S.	218	39.08 N	83.13 W
Morgantown, Pa., U.S.	208	40.09 N	75.54 W
Morgantown, W.V., U.S.	188	39.37 N	79.57 W
Morganville	208	40.23 N	74.15 W
Morgan Whyalla Pipeline ≍[1]	168b	33.48 S	138.56 E
Morganza	194	30.44 N	91.35 W
Morgårdshammar	40	60.09 N	15.23 E
Morgauši	80	55.58 N	46.47 E
Morgenzon	158	26.45 S	29.36 E
Morges	58	46.31 N	6.30 E
Morgex	62	45.45 N	7.02 E
Morghāb (Murgab) ≃	128	38.18 N	61.12 E
Morghar	126	23.40 N	89.37 E
Morghūm, Kūh-e ∧	128	33.06 N	57.30 E
Morgongåva	40	59.56 N	16.57 E
Morgongiori	71	39.45 N	8.46 E
Morguilla, Punta ›	252	37.46 S	73.40 W
Morhange	56	48.55 N	6.38 E
Mori, It.	64	45.51 N	10.59 E
Mori, Nihon	92a	42.06 N	140.35 E
Mori, Nihon	94	34.50 N	137.56 E
Mori, Nihon	270	34.32 N	135.00 E
Mori ≃	164	10.00 S	148.30 E
Moriah	241r	11.15 N	60.43 W
Moriah, Mount ∧	204	39.17 N	114.12 W
Morialta Conservation Park ♠	168b	34.55 S	138.40 E
Moriarty	200	34.59 N	106.02 W
Moriarty, Mount ∧	224	49.08 N	124.26 W
Morib	114	2.45 N	101.26 E
Moribaya	150	9.53 N	9.33 W
Morice ≃	182	54.24 N	126.45 W
Morice Lake ⊜	182	54.00 N	127.37 W
Morichal Largo ≃	246	9.27 N	62.25 W
Moricsala rezervāts ♠	76	57.17 N	22.11 E
Morie, Loch ⊜	46	57.44 N	4.28 W
Morienval	50	49.18 N	2.56 E
Morigerati	68	40.08 N	15.33 E
Moriguchi	96	34.44 N	135.34 E
Morija	158	29.34 S	27.31 E
Moriki	150	12.52 N	6.30 E
Morin Dawa	89	48.28 N	124.27 E
Moringen	52	51.42 N	9.52 E
Morino, It.	66	41.53 N	13.25 E
Morino, Ross.	76	57.54 N	30.22 E
Morinville	182	53.48 N	113.39 W
Morioka	92	39.42 N	141.09 E
Morīri, Tso ⊜	120	32.54 N	78.20 E
Morisset	170	33.06 S	151.29 E
Moriston ≃	46	57.12 N	4.36 W
Moritzburg ⊥	54	51.09 N	13.40 E
Morivione ◆[8]	266b	45.26 N	9.12 E
Morivs'k	78	51.06 N	30.50 E
Moriya	94	35.56 N	140.00 E
Moriyama	94	35.04 N	135.59 E
Moriyama-chūtonchi, Rikujō-jieitai- ■	94	35.12 N	136.57 E
Moriyoshi-zan ∧	92	39.58 N	140.33 E
Morki	80	56.25 N	49.01 E
Morkill ≃	182	53.42 N	120.30 W
Morkiny Gory	76	57.33 N	36.18 E
Mörkö I	40	58.59 N	17.40 E
Morkoka ≃	74	65.10 N	115.52 E
Mørkøv	41	55.40 N	11.32 E
Morlaix	32	48.35 N	3.50 W
Morlanwelz	50	50.27 N	4.14 E
Morles	56	50.38 N	9.51 E
Morley, Eng., U.K.	44	53.46 N	1.36 W
Morley, Mi., U.S.	190	43.29 N	85.26 W
Morley, N.Y., U.S.	212	44.40 N	75.12 W
Morley Green	262	53.20 N	2.16 W
Mörlunda	26	57.19 N	15.51 E
Mormal'	76	52.45 N	29.53 E
Mormanno	68	39.53 N	16.00 E
Mormant	50	48.36 N	2.53 E
Mormoiron	62	44.04 N	5.11 E
Mormon Bar	226	37.28 N	119.57 W
Mormon Lake ⊜	200	34.57 N	111.27 W
Mormon Peak ∧	204	36.57 N	114.30 W
Mormon Reservoir ⊜[1]	202	43.16 N	114.49 W
Mormon Slough ≃	226	37.57 N	121.18 W
Mormon Station Historical State Monument ♠	226	39.00 N	119.50 W
Mormugao	122	15.24 N	73.48 E
Morna	272a	28.35 N	77.22 E
Mornant	62	45.37 N	4.40 E
Mornas	62	44.12 N	4.44 E
Morne-à-l'Eau	241o	16.21 N	61.31 W
Morne Trois Pitons National Park ♠	240d	15.19 N	61.19 W
Morney	166	25.22 S	141.28 E
Morningdale	207	42.18 N	71.45 W
Morningside	284c	38.50 N	76.53 W
Morningside Park ♠	275b	43.47 N	79.12 W
Morningstar ≃	48	52.27 N	8.41 W
Morning Sun	190	41.05 N	91.15 W
Mornington	169	38.13 S	145.03 E
Mornington, Isla I	254	49.45 S	75.23 W
Mornington Island I	164	16.33 S	139.24 E
Mornington Island Aboriginal Land Trust ◆[4]	164	16.20 S	139.20 E
Mornington Peninsula ›[1]	169	38.20 S	145.05 E
Morno	150	8.41 N	1.31 W
Mornou, Hadjer ∧	146	17.12 N	23.08 E
Moro, Indon.	114	0.46 N	103.43 E
Moro, Or., U.S.	224	45.29 N	120.43 W
Moro ≃	150	7.25 N	11.03 W
Morobe	164	7.45 S	147.35 E
Morobe □[5]	164	7.00 S	146.30 E
Moroč'	76	52.34 N	27.36 E
Moroč' ≃	76	52.35 N	27.35 E
Morocco	216	40.56 N	87.27 W
Morocco (Al-Magreb) □[1], Afr.	134	32.00 N	5.00 W
Morocco (Al-Magreb) □[1], Afr.	148	32.00 N	5.00 W
Morococala	248	18.10 S	66.44 W
Morococha	248	11.37 S	76.09 W
Moro Creek ≃	194	33.18 N	92.22 W
Morogoro	154	6.49 S	37.40 E
Morogoro □[4]	154	8.00 S	37.15 E
Moro Gulf c	116	6.51 N	123.00 E
Moroka	273d	26.16 S	27.52 E
Morokweng	158	26.12 S	23.45 E
Moroleón	234	20.08 N	101.12 W
Morombe	157b	21.45 S	43.22 E
Morón, Arg.	258	34.39 S	58.37 W
Morón, Cuba	240p	22.06 N	78.38 W
Mörön, Mong.	88	48.15 N	100.23 E
Mörön, Mong.	88	47.24 N	110.16 E
Mörön, Mong.	88	49.38 N	100.10 E
Morón, Ven.	246	10.29 N	68.11 W
Morón □[5]	288	34.37 S	58.37 W
Mörön ≃	88	47.14 N	110.37 E
Morón, Aeródromo ⊠	288	34.41 S	58.38 W
Morón, Arroyo ≃	288	34.33 S	58.37 W
Morona ≃	246	4.45 S	77.04 W
Morona-Santiago □[4]	246	2.30 S	78.00 W
Morondava	157b	20.17 S	44.17 E
Morón de Almazán	34	41.25 N	2.25 W
Morón de la Frontera	34	37.08 N	5.27 W
Morones, Sierra ⩘	234	21.45 N	103.10 W
Morong	116	14.41 N	120.16 E
Morongo Indian Reservation ◆[4]	204	33.59 N	116.50 W
Moroni, Comores	157a	11.41 S	43.16 E
Moroni, Ut,. U.S.	200	39.31 N	111.35 W
Moron Us ≃, Zhg.	90	34.42 N	94.50 E
Moron Us ≃, Zhg.	120	34.42 N	94.50 E
Moros ≃	34	41.03 N	4.15 W
Morošečnoje	74	56.24 N	156.12 E
Morotai I	108	2.20 N	128.25 E
Moroto	154	2.32 N	34.39 E
Moroto ∧	154	2.32 N	34.46 E
Morouba	152	6.11 N	20.13 E
Morovis	240m	18.20 N	66.24 W
Morowali	112	1.52 S	121.30 E
Moroyama	94	35.56 N	139.19 E
Morozivka	83	49.28 N	39.54 E
Morozkovo	86	59.29 N	61.01 E
Morozovka	78	50.09 N	39.38 E
Morozovsk	80	48.22 N	41.50 E
Morozovskaja	24	61.10 N	50.18 E
Morpeth, On., Can.	214	42.23 N	81.51 W
Morpeth, Eng., U.K.	44	55.10 N	1.41 W
Morphett Vale	168b	35.07 S	138.31 E
Morra, Monte ∧	267a	42.02 N	12.50 E
Morral	214	40.41 N	83.12 W
Morral, Arroyo del ≃	266d	41.29 N	2.03 E
Morrelganj	126	22.28 N	89.51 E
Morrice	216	42.50 N	84.11 W
Morrill	198	41.57 N	103.55 W
Morrilton	194	35.09 N	92.44 W
Morrin	182	51.40 N	112.47 W
Morrinhos, Bra.	250	3.14 S	40.07 W
Morrinhos, Bra.	255	17.44 S	49.07 W
Morrinsville	172	37.39 S	175.32 E
Morris, Mb., Can.	184	49.21 N	97.22 W
Morris, Ct., U.S.	207	41.41 N	73.11 W
Morris, Il., U.S.	216	41.21 N	88.25 W
Morris, In., U.S.	218	39.16 N	85.10 W
Morris, Mn., U.S.	198	45.35 N	95.54 W
Morris, N.Y., U.S.	210	42.32 N	75.14 W
Morris, Ok., U.S.	196	35.36 N	95.51 W
Morris, Pa., U.S.	210	41.36 N	77.18 W
Morris □[6], N.J., U.S.	210	40.48 N	74.29 W
Morris □[6], Tx., U.S.	222	33.05 N	94.45 W
Morris ≃	184	49.21 N	97.22 W
Morris, Mount ∧	162	26.09 S	131.04 E
Morrisburg	212	44.54 N	75.11 W
Morrisdale	214	40.56 N	78.13 W
Morris Dam ◆[6]	280	34.11 N	117.53 W
Morris Jesup, Kap ›	16	83.38 N	33.52 W
Morris Lake ⊜	276	41.03 N	74.37 W
Morrison, Arg.	252	32.36 S	62.50 W
Morrison, Il., U.S.	190	41.48 N	89.57 W
Morrison, Mo., U.S.	219	38.40 N	91.38 W
Morrison, Point ›	168b	35.44 S	137.47 E
Morrison Creek ≃	275b	43.28 N	79.39 W
Morrison Lake ⊜, On., Can.	212	44.52 N	79.28 W
Morrison Lake ⊜, Mi., U.S.	216	42.53 N	85.13 W
Morrisonville	219	39.25 N	89.27 W
Morris Park ♠	285	39.59 N	75.15 W
Morris Plains	210	40.49 N	74.28 W
Morris Reservoir ⊜[1]	228	34.12 N	117.52 W
Morris Run	210	41.40 N	77.01 W
Morristown, Az., U.S.	200	33.51 N	112.37 W
Morristown, Il., U.S.	216	42.10 N	89.03 W
Morristown, In., U.S.	218	39.40 N	85.41 W
Morristown, Mn., U.S.	190	44.14 N	93.26 W
Morristown, N.J., U.S.	210	40.47 N	74.28 W
Morristown, N.Y., U.S.	212	44.35 N	75.38 W
Morristown, Oh., U.S.	214	40.04 N	81.05 W
Morristown, S.D., U.S.	198	45.56 N	101.43 W
Morristown, Tn., U.S.	192	36.12 N	83.17 W
Morristown Airport ⊠	276	40.48 N	74.25 W
Morristown National Historical Park ♠	210	40.46 N	74.32 W
Morrisville, N.Y., U.S.	210	42.53 N	75.38 W
Morrisville, Pa., U.S.	208	40.12 N	74.47 W
Morrisville, Vt., U.S.	188	44.33 N	72.35 W
Morrito	236	11.37 N	85.05 W
Morro	246	2.39 S	80.19 W
Morro, Castillo del (Morro Castle) ⊥	286b	23.09 N	82.21 W
Morro, Punta ›	232	19.39 N	90.42 W
Morro Agudo	287a	22.45 S	43.29 W
Morro Bay	226	35.21 N	120.50 W
Morro Bay c	226	35.20 N	120.51 W
Morro Bay State Park ♠	226	35.20 N	120.52 W
Morro Creek ≃	226	35.23 N	120.52 W
Morro do Chapéu	250	11.33 S	41.09 W
Morro d'Oro	66	42.39 N	13.54 E
Morro Mazatán	234	16.07 N	95.27 W
Morrone del Sannio	66	41.43 N	14.47 E
Morropón	248	5.15 S	80.00 W
Morros	250	2.52 S	44.03 W
Morrosquillo, Golfo de c	246	9.35 N	75.40 W
Morrow, La., U.S.	194	30.49 N	92.04 W
Morrow, Oh., U.S.	218	39.21 N	84.07 W
Morrow □[6]	214	40.33 N	82.50 W
Morrow Island I	282	38.07 N	122.05 W
Morrow Mountain State Park ♠	192	35.23 N	80.05 W
Morrow Point Reservoir ⊜[1]	200	38.25 N	107.30 W
Mörrum	26	56.11 N	14.45 E
Morrumbala	154	17.22 S	35.36 E
Morrumbene	156	23.39 S	35.20 E
Mörrumsån ≃	26	56.09 N	14.44 E
Mors I	26	56.50 N	8.45 E
Morsains	50	48.48 N	3.32 E
Morsang-sur-Orge	261	48.40 N	2.21 E
Moršansk	80	53.26 N	41.49 E
Morsbach	56	50.52 N	7.43 E
Mörsch	56	48.58 N	8.17 E
Morschwiller-le-Bas	58	47.45 N	7.16 E
Morščichino	265b	55.56 N	37.20 E
Morse, Sk., Can.	184	50.25 N	107.03 W
Morse, La., U.S.	194	30.07 N	92.29 W
Morse, Tx., U.S.	196	36.04 N	101.29 W
Morse Mill	219	38.17 N	90.40 W
Mörsenbroich ◆[8]	263	51.15 N	6.48 E
Morse Reservoir ⊜[1]	218	40.06 N	86.02 W
Morses Pond ⊜	283	42.18 N	71.19 W
Morsi	120	21.21 N	78.00 E
Morskaja Masel'ga	24	63.06 N	34.54 E
Morskoj Bir'učok, ostrov I	84	44.42 N	47.02 E
Morson	184	49.03 N	94.18 W
Morsott	36	35.40 N	8.01 E
Morstein	285	40.01 N	75.35 W
Mort	272a	28.43 N	77.25 E
Morta	272a	28.44 N	77.27 E
Mortagne	32	48.31 N	0.33 E
Mortagne ≃	58	48.33 N	6.27 E
Mortagne-au-Perche	50	48.31 N	0.33 E
Mortagne-sur-Sèvre	32	47.00 N	0.57 W
Mortain	32	48.39 N	0.56 W
Mortana	162	33.02 S	134.07 E
Mortara	62	45.15 N	8.44 E
Morteau	58	47.04 N	6.37 E
Mortefontaine	50	49.07 N	2.36 E
Mortegliano	64	45.57 N	13.10 E
Morte Point ›	42	51.11 N	4.13 W
Morteratsch, Piz ∧	58	46.22 N	9.51 E
Morteros	252	30.42 S	62.00 W
Mortes, Rio das ≃, Bra.	255	11.45 S	50.44 W
Mortes, Rio das ≃, Bra.	256	21.18 S	43.58 W
Mortesoro	140	10.12 N	34.09 E
Mort-Homme, Forêt du ◆[3]	56	49.15 N	5.15 E
Mortimer	42	51.22 N	1.04 W
Mortlach	184	50.28 N	106.03 W
Mortlake, Austl.	166	38.05 S	142.48 E
Mortlake, Austl.	274a	33.51 S	151.07 E
Mortlake ◆[8]	260	51.28 N	0.16 W
Mortlock ≃	168a	31.42 S	116.55 E
Mortlock Islands II	14	5.27 N	153.40 E
Mortlock North ≃	168a	31.38 S	116.42 E
Mortola Inferiore	62	43.47 N	7.33 E
Morton, Il., U.S.	190	40.36 N	89.27 W
Morton, Mn., U.S.	198	44.33 N	94.59 W
Morton, Ms., U.S.	194	32.21 N	89.39 W
Morton, N.Y., U.S.	210	43.20 N	78.00 W
Morton, Pa., U.S.	285	39.55 N	75.20 W
Morton, Tx., U.S.	196	33.43 N	102.45 W
Morton, Wa., U.S.	224	46.33 N	122.16 W
Morton, Mount ∧[2]	274b	37.56 S	145.20 E
Morton Arboretum ♠	278	41.49 N	88.04 W
Morton Craig Range ⩘	162	28.12 S	124.41 E
Morton Grove	216	42.02 N	87.46 W
Morton National Park ♠	170	35.00 S	150.10 E
Mortons Gap	194	37.14 N	87.28 W
Mortorio, Isola I	71	41.05 N	9.36 E
Mortornès del Vallès	266d	41.33 N	2.16 E
Mortrée	50	48.38 N	0.05 E
Mörtschach	64	46.55 N	12.55 E
Mortsel	50	51.10 N	4.28 E
M'ortvyj Donec ≃	83	47.15 N	39.14 E
Morty	80	55.49 N	51.44 E
Morua	175f	16.54 S	168.32 E
Morumbi ◆[8]	287b	23.36 S	46.42 E
Morumbi, Estádio do ♠	287b	23.37 S	46.43 W
Morungaba	256	22.52 S	46.48 W
Morungole ∧	154	3.49 N	34.02 E
Moruya	166	35.55 S	150.05 E
Morvan ⩘	32	47.05 N	4.00 E
Morvant	241r	10.39 N	61.28 W
Morven, Austl.	166	26.25 S	147.07 E
Morven, N.Z.	172	44.50 S	171.07 E
Morven, Ga., U.S.	192	30.56 N	83.29 W
Morven, N.C., U.S.	192	34.51 N	80.00 W
Morven ∧, Scot., U.K.	46	58.14 N	3.42 W
Morven ∧, Scot., U.K.	46	57.07 N	3.02 W
Morwell	169	38.14 S	146.24 E
Morwell ≃	169	38.10 S	146.23 E
Morwenstow	42	50.54 N	4.33 W
Moryń	30	52.49 N	14.13 E
Morženga	76	59.37 N	40.12 E
Morzhovoi	180	54.55 N	163.18 W
Morzine	58	46.11 N	6.43 E
Moržovec, ostrov I	24	66.44 N	42.35 E
Moša ≃, Ross.	24	62.25 N	39.46 E
M'oša ≃, Ross.	80	55.25 N	49.22 E
Mosal'sk	76	54.29 N	34.59 E
Mosambik → Mozambique □[1]	138	18.15 S	35.00 E
Mošanicy	82	54.56 N	38.23 E
Mosås	40	59.12 N	15.08 E
Mosbach	56	49.21 N	9.08 E
Mosborough	44	53.19 N	1.22 W
Mosby	26	58.14 N	7.54 E
Mosby Woods	284c	38.52 N	77.18 W
Moscavide	266c	38.47 N	9.06 W
Mosciano Sant'Angelo	66	42.45 N	13.53 E
Moščnyj, ostrov I	76	60.01 N	27.50 E
Moscos Islands II	110	14.00 N	97.45 E
Moscou → Moskva	82	55.45 N	37.35 E
Moscow → Moskva, Ross.	82	55.45 N	37.35 E
Moscow, Id., U.S.	202	46.43 N	116.59 W
Moscow, In., U.S.	218	39.29 N	85.34 W
Moscow, Oh., U.S.	218	38.51 N	84.13 W
Moscow, Pa., U.S.	210	41.20 N	75.31 W
Moscow, Tx., U.S.	222	30.55 N	94.50 W
Moscow Air Terminal ⊠	265b	55.48 N	37.32 E
Moscow Circus ♠	265b	55.43 N	37.33 E
Moscow Mills	219	38.56 N	90.55 W
Moscow Station ◆[5]	265a	59.56 N	30.22 E
Moscow Victory Park ♠	265a	59.52 N	30.20 E
Moscow Zoo ♠	265b	55.46 N	37.34 E
Moscú → Moskva	82	55.45 N	37.35 E
Moscufo	66	42.25 N	14.03 E
Mosel	54	50.47 N	12.28 E
Mosel (Moselle) ≃	32	50.22 N	7.36 E
Moselebe ≃	156	25.03 S	23.13 E
Moselle, Ms., U.S.	194	31.30 N	89.16 W
Moselle, Mo., U.S.	219	38.23 N	90.54 W
Moselle □[5]	56	49.00 N	6.30 E
Moselle (Mosel) ≃	32	50.22 N	7.36 E
Moselotte ≃	58	48.01 N	6.38 E
Mošenskoje	76	58.31 N	34.35 E
Mosermandl ∧	64	47.12 N	13.24 E
Mosers River	186	44.59 N	62.15 W
Moses Lake	202	47.07 N	119.16 W
Moses Lake ⊜[1]	202	47.10 N	119.20 W
Moses Point	180	64.42 N	162.03 W
Moses Power Plant ◆[6]	284a	43.09 N	79.02 W
Mosetse	156	20.37 S	26.32 E
Mosgiel	172	45.53 S	170.21 E
Moshannon	214	41.02 N	78.00 W
Moshannon Creek ≃	214	41.04 N	78.06 W
Moshanpu	100	29.34 N	112.41 E
Moshaweng ≃	158	26.35 S	22.50 E
Mosheim, Tn., U.S.	192	36.11 N	82.57 W
Mosheim, Tx., U.S.	222	31.38 N	97.36 W
Moshi	154	3.21 S	37.20 E
Moshi ≃	150	9.18 N	4.38 E
Moshiyu	104	41.15 N	124.05 E
Moshny	78	49.32 N	31.44 E
Mosier	224	45.41 N	121.23 W
Mosier Hill ∧[2]	214	40.06 N	80.24 W
Mosina	30	52.16 N	16.51 E
Mosinee	190	44.47 N	89.42 W
Mosjøen	24	65.50 N	13.10 E
Moskal'onki	86	54.59 N	71.54 E
Moskal'vo	89	53.35 N	142.30 E
Moskau → Moskva	82	55.45 N	37.35 E
Moskenesøya I	24	67.59 N	13.00 E
Moskháton	267c	37.57 N	23.41 E
Moškino	80	57.45 N	45.20 E
Moskito-Golf → Mosquitos, Golfo de los c	236	9.00 N	81.15 W
Moškovo	86	55.18 N	83.37 E
Moskovskaja Slav'anka	265a	59.45 N	30.30 E
Moskovskaja vozvyšennost' ⩘[1]	76	56.15 N	37.30 E
Moskva (Moscow), Ross.	82	55.45 N	37.35 E
Moskva (Moscow), Ross.	265b	55.45 N	37.35 E
Moskva ≃	76	55.05 N	38.50 E
Moskva, Gorod □[7]	265b	55.45 N	37.35 E
Moskva, pik ∧	85	38.57 N	71.49 E
Moskva Oblast' □[4]	76	55.30 N	37.30 E
Moskvy, kanal imeni ≍	82	56.43 N	37.08 E
Mosman	170	33.49 S	151.14 E
Mosman Park	168a	32.01 S	115.46 E
Moso (Moos)	64	46.41 N	12.23 E
Moso in Passiria (Moos)	64	46.50 N	11.10 E
Mošok	80	55.48 N	41.17 E
Mosolovo	80	54.17 N	40.32 E
Mosomane	156	24.04 S	26.15 E
Mosoni-Duna ≃	61	47.54 N	17.17 E
Mosonmagyaróvár	30	47.51 N	17.17 E
Mosonszolnok	61	47.51 N	17.11 E
Mosopa	156	24.50 S	25.31 E
Mospyne	83	47.53 N	38.03 E
Mosqueiro	250	1.10 S	48.28 W
Mosquera	246	2.30 N	78.29 W
Mosquero	196	35.46 N	103.57 W
Mosquic, Lac ⊜	206	46.39 N	74.28 W
Mosquito, Punta ›	246	9.07 N	77.53 W
Mosquito, Riacho ≃	252	22.02 S	57.57 W
Mosquito Brook ≃	283	42.40 N	71.02 W
Mosquito Creek ≃, Ia., U.S.	198	41.11 N	95.50 W
Mosquito Creek ≃, Oh., U.S.	214	41.10 N	80.45 W
Mosquito Creek ≃, Pa., U.S.	214	41.07 N	78.07 W
Mosquito Creek Lake ⊜[1]	214	41.22 N	80.45 W
Mosquito Creek State Park ♠	214	41.22 N	80.45 W
Mosquito Indian Reserve ◆[4]	184	52.30 N	108.15 W
Mosquito Lagoon c	220	28.45 N	80.45 W
Mosquitos, Costa de □[9]	236	13.00 N	83.45 W
Mosquitos, Golfo de los c	236	9.00 N	81.15 W
Moss	26	59.26 N	10.42 E
Mossaka	152	1.13 S	16.48 E
Mossâmedes	255	16.07 S	50.11 W
Mossbank, Sk., Can.	184	49.55 N	105.59 W
Moss Bank, Eng., U.K.	262	53.29 N	2.44 W
Mossbank, Scot., U.K.	46a	60.27 N	1.12 W
Moss Bank Park ♠	262	53.36 N	2.28 W
Moss Beach	282	37.32 N	122.31 W
Mossburn	172	45.40 S	168.15 E
Mosselbaai (Mossel Bay)	158	34.11 S	22.08 E
Mosselbaai c	158	34.06 S	22.20 E
Mossendjo	152	2.57 S	12.44 E
Mosses, Col des)(	58	46.24 N	7.06 E
Mossgiel	166	33.15 S	144.34 E
Moss Hill	222	30.15 N	94.45 W
Mossig ≃	58	48.33 N	7.30 E
Mössingen	58	48.24 N	9.03 E
Moss Landing	226	36.48 N	121.47 W
Mossleigh	182	50.43 N	113.20 W
Mossley	262	53.32 N	2.02 W
Mossley Hill ◆[8]	262	53.23 N	2.55 W
Mossman	164	16.28 S	145.22 E
Mossmans Brook ≃	276	41.03 N	74.27 W
Moss Moor ◆[3]	262	53.37 N	2.00 W
Moss Mountain ∧	194	34.50 N	92.40 W
Mossø ⊜	41	56.02 N	9.48 E
Mosson ≃	62	43.33 N	3.54 E
Mossoró	250	5.11 S	37.20 W
Mosso Santa Maria	62	45.38 N	8.08 E
Moss Point	194	30.24 N	88.32 W
Moss Point ›	279a	41.37 N	81.32 W
Moss Side	262	53.46 N	2.57 W
Mossuril	154	14.58 S	40.42 E
Moss Vale	170	34.33 S	150.22 E
Mossy ≃, Mb., Can.	184	51.39 N	99.55 W
Mossy ≃, Sk., Can.	184	54.05 N	103.00 W
Mossyrock	224	46.31 N	122.29 W
Mossyrock Dam ◆[6]	224	46.32 N	122.25 W
Most	54	50.32 N	13.39 E
Mosta	80	56.32 N	42.10 E
Mostar	36	43.20 N	17.49 E
Mostardas, Bra.	252	31.06 S	50.57 W
Mostardas, Bra.	256	23.44 S	46.38 W
Møsting, Kap ›	176	64.00 N	41.00 W
Mostiștea ≃	38	44.15 N	27.10 E
Mostizzolo	64	46.24 N	11.01 E
Most na Soči	64	46.09 N	13.44 E
Mostok	76	53.59 N	30.28 E
Móstoles	266a	40.19 N	3.51 W
Mostoos Hills ⩘[2]	184	55.00 N	109.15 W
Mostovaja	76	56.13 N	33.08 E
Mostove	78	47.24 N	30.59 E
Mostovka	86	58.10 N	65.31 E
Mostovskoj	84	44.25 N	40.48 E
Mostovskoje	86	55.46 N	66.22 E
Mostrim (Edgeworthstown)	48	53.42 N	7.36 W
Mosty	76	53.25 N	24.32 E
Mostyn, Malay.	112	4.40 N	118.11 E
Mostyn, Wales, U.K.	44	53.19 N	3.16 W
Mostys'ka	78	49.48 N	23.09 E
Mosul → Al-Mawṣil	128	36.20 N	43.08 E
Møsvatnet ⊜	26	59.52 N	8.05 E
Mota	144	11.02 N	37.52 E
Mota I	175f	13.49 S	167.42 E
Motaba ≃	152	2.03 N	18.03 E
Mota del Cuervo	34	39.30 N	2.52 W
Mota del Marqués	34	41.38 N	5.10 W
Motagua ≃	236	15.44 N	88.14 W
Motala	26	58.33 N	15.03 E
Motala ström ≃	40	58.38 N	16.10 E
Mota Lava I	175f	13.40 S	167.40 E
Motane I	174x	9.59 S	138.49 W
Motatán	246	9.24 N	70.36 W
Motaze	156	24.48 S	32.52 E
Motegi	94	36.32 N	140.11 E
Mote Park ♠	260	51.17 N	0.34 E
Moteve, Cap ›	174x	9.58 S	139.02 W
Moth	124	25.43 N	78.57 E
Mother Brook ≍	283	42.15 N	71.10 W
Motherwell	46	55.48 N	4.00 W
Motihāri	124	26.39 N	84.55 E

Symbol	English	Deutsch	Español	Français	Português
≃	River	Fluß	Río	Rivière	Rio
≍	Canal	Kanal	Canal	Canal	Canal
⌊	Waterfall, Rapids	Wasserfall, Stromschnellen	Cascada, Rápidos	Chute d'eau, Rapides	Cascata, Rápidos
ʮ	Strait	Meeresstraße	Estrecho	Détroit	Estreito
c	Bay, Gulf	Bucht, Golf	Bahía, Golfo	Baie, Golfe	Baía, Golfo
⊜	Lake, Lakes	See, Seen	Lago, Lagos	Lac, Lacs	Lago, Lagos
⩸	Swamp	Sumpf	Pantano	Marais	Pântano
⌧	Ice Features, Glacier	Eis- und Gletscherformen	Accidentes Glaciales	Formes glaciaires	Acidentes glaciares
⊤	Other Hydrographic Features	Andere Hydrographische Objekte	Otros Elementos Hidrográficos	Autres données hydrographiques	Outros acidentes hidrográficos
✢	Submarine Features	Untermeerische Objekte	Accidentes Submarinos	Formes de relief sous-marin	Acidentes submarinos
□	Political Unit	Politische Einheit	Unidad Politica	Entité politique	Unidade política
ʊ	Cultural Institution	Kulturelle Institution	Institución Cultural	Institution culturelle	Instituição cultural
⊥	Historical Site	Historische Stätte	Sitio Histórico	Site historique	Sitio histórico
♠	Recreational Site	Erholungs- und Ferienort	Sitio de Recreo	Centre de loisirs	Area de Lazer
⊠	Airport	Flughafen	Aeropuerto	Aéroport	Aeroporto
■	Military Installation	Militäranlage	Instalación Militar	Installation militaire	Instalação militar
◆	Miscellaneous	Verschiedenes	Misceláneo	Divers	Diversos

Motilla del Palancar 34 39.34 N 1.53 W
Motiong 116 11.47 N 125.00 E
Motiti Island I 172 37.38 S 176.26 E
Motjärnshyttan 40 59.56 N 13.58 E
Motloutse 156 21.28 S 27.24 E
Motloutse ≃ 156 22.15 S 29.00 E
Moto-ara ≃ 94 35.53 N 139.50 E
Motobu 174m 26.39 N 127.54 E
Motol' 76 52.19 N 25.36 E
Motola, Monte ▲ 68 40.22 N 15.26 E
Motopu 174x 9.55 S 139.03 W
Motor Island I 284a 42.58 N 78.56 W
Motorki 80 56.53 N 51.29 E
Motorovo 86 56.31 N 71.10 E
Motosu 94 35.29 N 136.40 E
Motosu-ko ⊜ 94 35.28 N 138.35 E
Motou 106 32.18 N 120.34 E
Motovilovo 80 55.36 N 43.51 E
Motovun 64 45.20 N 13.50 E
Motoyama 96 33.45 N 133.35 E
Moto-yama ▲2 174f 24.48 N 141.20 E
Motozintla de Mendoza 232 15.22 N 92.14 W
Motril 34 36.45 N 3.31 W
Motrone 64 43.54 N 10.12 E
Motru 38 44.50 N 23.00 E
Mott 198 46.22 N 102.19 W
Motta 64 45.36 N 11.29 E
Motta Camastra 70 37.54 N 15.10 E
Motta d'Affermo 70 37.59 N 14.18 E
Motta di Livenza 64 45.47 N 12.36 E
Mottafollone 68 39.39 N 16.04 E
Motta Montecorvino 68 41.30 N 15.07 E
Motta San Giovanni 68 38.00 N 15.41 E
Motta Sant'Anastasia 70 37.31 N 14.58 E
Motta Visconti 62 45.17 N 8.59 E
Möttingen 56 48.48 N 10.35 E
Mottingham ✦8 260 51.26 N 0.03 E
Mottisfont 42 51.02 N 1.32 W
Mottola 68 40.38 N 17.03 E
Mottram in Longdendale 262 53.27 N 2.01 W
Motts Creek ≃ 276 40.38 N 73.45 W
Mottville, Mi., U.S. 216 41.48 N 85.45 W
Mottville, N.Y., U.S. 210 42.59 N 76.27 W
Motu ≃ 172 37.51 S 177.35 E
Motueka 172 41.07 S 173.00 E
Motueka ≃ 172 41.05 S 173.01 E
Motul [de Felipe Carrillo Puerto] 232 21.06 N 89.17 W
Motu One I1 14 15.48 S 154.33 W
Motupe 248 6.09 S 79.44 W
Motupena Point ≻ 175e 6.32 S 155.09 E
Motutapu I 174k 21.14 S 159.43 W
Motygino 86 58.11 N 94.40 E
Motyklejka 74 59.26 N 148.38 E
Motyzhyn 78 50.23 N 29.55 E
Motyzlej 80 54.54 N 42.54 E
Mou 175f 21.05 S 165.26 E
Mouanko 152 3.39 N 9.49 E
Mouans-Sartoux 62 43.37 N 6.58 E
Mouaskar 148 35.45 N 0.01 E
Mouaskar □5 148 35.10 N 0.00
Mouchard 58 46.58 N 5.48 E
Mouchoir Bank ✦2 238 20.57 N 70.42 W
Mouchoir Passage ⊻ 238 21.10 N 71.00 W
Moúdhros 38 39.52 N 25.16 E
Mouding 102 25.24 N 101.35 E
Moudjéria 150 17.53 N 12.20 W
Moudon 58 46.40 N 6.48 E
Moudongouma ≃ 152 1.36 N 17.24 E
Mouila 152 1.52 S 11.01 E
Mouit 150 16.35 N 13.05 W
Mouka 152 7.16 N 21.52 E
Moukden — Shenyang 104 41.48 N 123.27 E
Moulamein 166 35.05 S 144.02 E
Moulay-bou-Selham 34 34.53 N 6.15 W
Moulay-Idriss 148 34.02 N 5.27 W
Mouldsworth 262 53.14 N 2.44 W
Moule à Chique, Cap ≻ 241f 13.43 N 60.57 W
Moulhoulé 144 12.36 N 43.12 E
Moulin, Île du I 275a 45.41 N 73.32 W
Moulin-des-Ponts 58 46.20 N 5.19 E
Moulineaux 50 49.21 N 0.58 E
Moulinet 62 43.57 N 7.25 E
Moulins 32 46.34 N 3.20 E
Moulins-la-Marche 50 48.39 N 0.29 E
Moulmein — Mawlamyine 110 16.30 N 97.38 E
Moulmeingyun 110 16.23 N 95.16 E
Moulouya, Oued ≃ 148 35.05 N 2.25 W
Moulton, Eng., U.K. 44 53.13 N 2.31 W
Moulton, Al., U.S. 194 34.28 N 87.17 W
Moulton, Ia., U.S. 190 40.41 N 92.40 W
Moulton, Tx., U.S. 222 29.34 N 97.09 W
Moultrie 192 31.10 N 83.47 W
Moultrie □6 219 39.36 N 88.37 W
Moultrie, Lake ⊜1 192 33.20 N 80.05 W
Mouly 175f 20.42 S 166.25 E
Mound 222 31.21 N 97.38 W
Mound Bayou 194 33.52 N 90.43 W
Mound City, Il., U.S. 194 37.05 N 89.09 W
Mound City, Ks., U.S. 198 38.08 N 94.48 W
Mound City, Mo., U.S. 194 40.07 N 95.13 W
Mound City, S.D., U.S. 198 45.43 N 100.04 W
Mound City Group National Monument ✦ 218 39.23 N 83.00 W
Mound Lake ⊜ 219 40.05 N 90.17 W
Moundou 146 8.34 N 16.05 E
Moundridge 198 38.12 N 97.31 W
Mounds, Il., U.S. 194 37.06 N 89.11 W
Mounds, Ok., U.S. 196 35.52 N 96.03 W
Mounds State Park ✦ 218 40.07 N 85.37 W
Mounds State Recreation Area ✦ 218 39.30 N 84.59 W
Moundsville 188 39.55 N 80.44 W
Moundville 194 32.59 N 87.37 W
Moungali ✦8 273b 4.15 S 15.17 E
Moung Roessei 110 12.46 N 103.27 E
Mounianzé ≃ 152 0.32 N 12.52 E
Mounier, Mont ▲ 62 44.09 N 6.58 E
Mounlapamôk 110 14.20 N 105.52 E
Mount Aetna 208 40.25 N 76.18 W
Mountain 190 45.11 N 88.28 W
Mountain □4 116 17.20 N 121.10 E
Mountain ≃ 180 65.41 N 128.50 W
Mountainair 200 34.31 N 106.14 W
Mountainaire 200 35.05 N 111.39 W
Mountain Ash 42 51.42 N 3.24 W
Mountain Brook 194 33.30 N 86.45 W
Mountain Chute Dam ✦6 212 45.11 N 76.54 W
Mountain City, Ga., U.S. 192 34.55 N 83.23 W
Mountain City, Nv., U.S. 204 41.50 N 115.57 W
Mountain City, Tn., U.S. 192 36.28 N 81.48 W
Mountain Creek 194 32.43 N 86.29 W
Mountain Creek ≃, Pa., U.S. 208 40.09 N 77.11 W
Mountain Creek ≃, Tx., U.S. 222 32.42 N 96.58 W
Mountain Creek Lake ⊜1 222 32.43 N 96.58 W
Mountain Dale 210 41.41 N 74.31 W
Mountain Grove 194 37.07 N 92.15 W
Mountain Home, Ar., U.S. 194 36.20 N 92.23 W
Mountain Home, Id., U.S. 202 43.07 N 115.41 W
Mountainhome, Pa., U.S. 210 41.11 N 75.17 W
Mountain Home Air Force Base ■ 202 43.03 N 115.52 W
Mountain Iron 190 47.31 N 92.37 W
Mountain Lake, Fl., U.S. 220 27.57 N 81.36 W
Mountain Lake, Mn., U.S. 198 43.56 N 94.55 W
Mountain Lake ⊜, On., Can. 212 44.42 N 81.03 W
Mountain Lake ⊜, On., Can. 212 44.59 N 78.43 W
Mountain Lake ⊜, N.J., U.S. 276 40.53 N 74.27 W
Mountain Lakes 210 40.53 N 74.26 W
Mountain Lodge 210 41.23 N 74.09 W
Mountain Nile (Bahr al-Jabal) ≃ 136 9.30 N 30.30 E
Mountain Park 182 52.55 N 117.14 W
Mountain Pine 194 34.34 N 93.10 W
Mountain Point 182 55.18 N 131.32 W
Mountain Ranch 226 38.14 N 120.33 W
Mountainside 208 40.40 N 74.21 W
Mountain Spring Lakes 276 41.02 N 74.23 W
Mountain Valley Lake ⊜ 279b 40.18 N 79.35 W
Mountain View, Ar., U.S. 194 35.52 N 92.07 W
Mountain View, Ca., U.S. 226 37.23 N 122.04 W
Mountain View, Mo., U.S. 194 36.59 N 91.42 W
Mountain View, Ok., U.S. 196 35.05 N 98.44 W
Mountain View, Wy., U.S. 200 41.16 N 110.20 W
Mountain View, Wy., U.S. 200 42.51 N 106.23 W
Mountain View Acres 228 34.31 N 117.24 W
Mountain Village 180 62.05 N 163.44 W
Mountain Zebra National Park ✦ 158 32.16 S 25.29 E
Mount Airy, Md., U.S. 208 39.22 N 77.09 W
Mount Airy, N.C., U.S. 192 36.29 N 80.36 W
Mount Airy ✦8 285 40.04 N 75.12 W
Mount Albert 212 44.08 N 79.19 W
Mount Alford 171a 28.04 S 152.36 E
Mount Alida 158 29.09 S 30.18 E
Mount Angel 224 45.04 N 122.47 W
Mount Ann Park ✦ 283 42.37 N 70.44 W
Mount Arlington 210 40.55 N 74.38 W
Mount Assiniboine Provincial Park ✦ 182 50.54 N 115.40 W
Mount Auburn 219 39.46 N 89.16 W
Mount Augustus 162 24.19 S 116.54 E
Mount Ayliff 158 30.54 S 29.20 E
Mount Ayr, In., U.S. 216 40.57 N 87.18 W
Mount Ayr, Ia., U.S. 198 40.42 N 94.14 W
Mount Baldy 280 34.14 N 117.40 W
Mount Barker, Austl. 162 34.38 S 117.40 E
Mount Barker, Austl. 168b 35.04 S 138.52 E
Mount Bellew Bridge 48 53.28 N 8.29 W
Mount Berry 194 34.17 N 85.11 W
Mount Bethel 210 40.54 N 75.07 W
Mount Blanchard 216 40.53 N 83.33 W
Mount Bold Reservoir ⊜1 168b 35.07 S 138.42 E
Mount Brydges 214 42.54 N 81.29 W
Mount Buffalo National Park ✦ 166 36.45 S 146.45 E
Mount Buller 169 37.10 S 146.27 E
Mount Calm 222 31.45 N 96.53 W
Mount Carleton Provincial Park ✦ 186 47.23 N 66.50 W
Mount Carmel, Nf., Can. 186 47.09 N 53.29 W
Mount Carmel, Il., U.S. 194 38.24 N 87.45 W
Mount Carmel, Ky., U.S. 218 38.29 N 83.38 W
Mount Carmel, Oh., U.S. 218 39.06 N 84.18 W
Mount Carmel, Pa., U.S. 208 40.47 N 76.24 W
Mount Carmel Heights 218 39.07 N 84.18 W
Mount Carroll 190 42.05 N 89.58 W
Mount Cavenagh 162 25.58 S 133.15 E
Mount Charles 275b 43.41 N 79.40 W
Mount Clare 188 39.13 N 80.21 W
Mount Clemens 214 42.35 N 82.52 W
Mount Colah 274a 33.41 S 151.07 E
Mount Compass 168b 35.22 S 138.37 E
Mount Cook 172 43.44 S 170.06 E
Mount Cook National Park ✦ 172 43.35 S 170.15 E
Mount Coot-tha Park ✦ 171a 27.28 S 152.56 E
Mount Cory 216 40.56 N 83.50 W
Mount Crawford 168b 34.40 S 138.57 E
Mount Crosby 171a 27.32 S 152.48 E
Mount Currie Indian Reserve ✦4 182 50.19 N 122.42 W
Mount Dandenong 274b 37.50 S 145.22 E
Mount Dennis ✦8 275b 43.42 N 79.30 W
Mount Desert Island I 188 44.20 N 68.20 W
Mount Diablo Creek ≃ 282 38.02 N 122.02 W
Mount Diablo State Park ✦ 226 37.51 N 121.55 W
Mount Dora 220 28.48 N 81.38 W
Mount Doreen 162 22.03 S 131.18 E
Mount Druitt 274a 33.46 S 150.49 E
Mount Eaton 214 40.42 N 81.42 W
Mount Eba 166 30.12 S 135.40 E
Mount Eden 226 37.38 N 122.06 W
Mount Edgecumbe 180 57.03 N 135.21 W
Mount Edwards 171a 28.01 S 152.31 E
Mount Elgon National Park ✦ 154 1.07 N 34.44 E
Mount Elizabeth 164 16.15 S 126.12 E
Mount Emu Creek ≃ 169 38.18 S 142.55 E
Mount Enterprise 222 31.55 N 94.41 W
Mount Ephraim 285 39.52 N 75.05 W
Mount Evelyn 274b 37.47 S 145.23 E
Mount Fern 276 40.52 N 74.34 W
Mount Field National Park ✦ 166 42.40 S 146.35 E
Mount Fletcher 158 30.40 S 28.30 E
Mount Forest 212 43.59 N 80.44 W
Mount Freedom 210 40.49 N 74.34 W
Mount Frere 158 31.00 S 28.58 E
Mount Gambier 166 37.50 S 140.46 E
Mount Garnet 166 17.41 S 145.07 E
Mount Gay 188 37.51 N 82.00 W
Mount Gilead, N.C., U.S. 192 35.12 N 80.00 W
Mount Gilead, Oh., U.S. 214 40.32 N 82.49 W
Mount Gravatt 171a 27.33 S 153.06 E
Mount Greenwood ✦8 278 41.42 N 87.43 W
Mount Gunson 162 31.27 S 137.11 E
Mount Hagen 164 5.50 S 144.15 E
Mount Hawke 42 50.17 N 5.12 W
Mount Hawthorn 168a 31.55 S 115.50 E
Mount Healthy 218 39.14 N 84.32 W
Mount Hebron 284b 39.18 N 76.50 W
Mount Helena 168a 31.53 S 116.13 E
Mount Hermon, Ca., U.S. 226 37.03 N 122.04 W
Mount Hermon, Ma., U.S. 207 42.40 N 72.29 W
Mount Holly, N.J., U.S. 208 39.59 N 74.47 W
Mount Holly, N.C., U.S. 192 35.17 N 81.00 W
Mount Holly Springs 208 40.07 N 77.11 W
Mount Hope, Austl. 166 34.07 S 135.23 E
Mount Hope, On., Can. 212 43.09 N 79.55 W
Mount Hope, Ks., U.S. 198 37.52 N 97.39 W
Mount Hope, N.J., U.S. 276 40.56 N 74.33 W
Mount Hope, Oh., U.S. 214 40.38 N 81.47 W
Mount Hope, W.V., U.S. 188 37.53 N 81.09 W
Mount Hope Lake ⊜ 276 40.56 N 74.32 W
Mount Horeb 190 43.00 N 89.44 W
Mount Houston 222 29.54 N 95.18 W
Mount Howitt 166 26.31 S 142.16 E
Mount Hunter Rivulet ≃ 274a 34.02 S 150.40 E
Mount Ida 194 34.33 N 93.38 W
Mount Isa 166 20.44 S 139.30 E
Mount Jackson, Pa., U.S. 214 40.58 N 80.26 W
Mount Jackson, Va., U.S. 188 38.44 N 78.38 W
Mount Jewett 214 41.43 N 78.38 W
Mount Juliet 194 36.12 N 86.31 W
Mount Kaputar National Park ✦ 166 30.16 S 150.10 E
Mount Kenya National Park ✦ 154 0.09 S 37.19 E
Mount Kisco 210 41.12 N 73.43 W
Mount Kokeby 168a 32.13 S 116.58 E
Mountlake Terrace 224 47.47 N 122.18 W
Mount Laurel 285 39.56 N 74.54 W
Mount Lebanon 214 40.21 N 80.02 W
Mount Liberty 214 40.21 N 82.38 W
Mount Lofty Ranges ⋏ 168b 34.45 S 139.00 E
Mount Magnet 162 28.04 S 117.49 E
Mount Manara 166 32.29 S 143.56 E
Mount Margaret, Austl. 162 28.47 S 122.11 E
Mount Margaret, Austl. 166 26.54 S 143.21 E
Mount Marion 210 42.02 N 73.59 W
Mount Martha 169 38.17 S 145.01 E
Mount Maunganui 172 37.37 S 176.11 E
Mount McKinley National Park — Denali National Park ✦ 180 63.15 N 150.30 W
Mount Mee 171a 27.04 S 152.46 E
Mountmellick 48 53.07 N 7.20 W
Mount Misery Point ≻ 276 40.58 N 73.05 W
Mount Mistake National Park ✦ 171a 27.53 S 152.20 E
Mount Molloy 164 16.41 S 145.20 E
Mount Monger 162 30.59 S 121.53 E
Mount Moorosi 158 30.16 S 27.53 E
Mount Morgan 166 23.39 S 150.23 E
Mount Morris, Il., U.S. 190 42.03 N 89.25 W
Mount Morris, Mi., U.S. 190 43.07 N 83.41 W
Mount Morris, N.Y., U.S. 210 42.43 N 77.52 W
Mount Morris Dam ✦6 210 42.44 N 77.53 W
Mount Mulligan 166 16.51 S 144.52 E
Mount Nebo 279b 40.33 N 80.06 W
Mountnessing 260 51.39 N 0.21 E
Mount Olive, Il., U.S. 219 39.04 N 89.43 W
Mount Olive, Ms., U.S. 194 31.45 N 89.39 W
Mount Olive, N.C., U.S. 192 35.11 N 78.04 W
Mount Oliver 279b 40.28 N 79.59 W
Mount Olivet 218 38.31 N 84.02 W
Mount Orab 218 39.01 N 83.55 W
Mount Penn 208 40.20 N 75.54 W
Mount Perry 166 25.11 S 151.39 E
Mount Pleasant, Austl. 168b 34.47 S 139.02 E
Mount Pleasant, On., Can. 212 43.05 N 80.19 W
Mount Pleasant, In., U.S. 218 38.07 N 86.31 W
Mount Pleasant, Ia., U.S. 190 40.57 N 91.33 W
Mount Pleasant, Mi., U.S. 190 43.35 N 84.46 W
Mount Pleasant, N.C., U.S. 192 35.23 N 80.26 W
Mount Pleasant, Oh., U.S. 214 40.11 N 80.48 W
Mount Pleasant, Pa., U.S. 214 40.08 N 79.32 W
Mount Pleasant, S.C., U.S. 192 32.47 N 79.51 W
Mount Pleasant, Tn., U.S. 194 35.32 N 87.12 W
Mount Pleasant, Tx., U.S. 222 33.09 N 94.58 W
Mount Pleasant, Ut., U.S. 200 39.32 N 111.27 W
Mount Pleasant Mills 208 40.43 N 77.01 W
Mount Pleasant Park ✦ 284b 39.22 N 76.35 W
Mount Pocono 210 41.07 N 75.21 W
Mount Pritchard 274a 33.54 S 150.54 E
Mount Prospect, S. Afr. 158 27.29 S 29.53 E
Mount Prospect, Il., U.S. 216 42.03 N 87.56 W
Mount Pulaski 219 40.00 N 89.16 W
Mount Rainier 284c 38.56 N 76.57 W
Mount Rainier National Park ✦ 224 46.52 N 121.43 W
Mountrath 48 53.00 N 7.27 W
Mount Repose 218 39.10 N 84.14 W
Mount Revelstoke National Park ✦ 182 51.06 N 118.00 W
Mount Riddock 162 23.03 S 134.40 E
Mount Robson Provincial Park ✦ 182 52.58 N 118.50 W
Mount Rogers National Recreation Area ✦ 192 36.42 N 81.30 W
Mount Roskill 172 36.55 S 174.45 E
Mount Royal 285 39.49 N 75.13 W
Mount Rushmore National Memorial ⊥ 198 43.50 N 103.24 W
Mount Saint Helens National Volcanic Monument ✦ 224 46.12 N 122.11 W
Mount Sandiman 162 24.24 S 115.23 E
Mount Sarah 162 26.57 S 135.22 E
Mount Savage 188 39.41 N 78.52 W
Mount's Bay c 42 50.03 N 5.25 W
Mount Selinda 154 20.25 S 32.43 E
Mount Selman 222 32.04 N 95.17 W
Mount Seymour Provincial Park ✦ 182 49.23 N 122.57 W
Mount Shasta 204 41.18 N 122.18 W
Mount Sinai 276 40.57 N 73.02 W
Mount Sinai Harbor c 276 40.57 N 73.02 W
Mount Sinai Ridge ▲ 218 39.04 N 84.58 W
Mount Somers 172 43.43 S 171.24 E
Mountsorrel 42 52.44 N 1.07 W
Mount Spokane State Park ✦ 202 47.58 N 117.13 W
Mount Sterling, Il., U.S. 219 39.59 N 90.45 W
Mount Sterling, Ky., U.S. 192 38.03 N 83.56 W
Mount Sterling, Mo., U.S. 219 38.28 N 91.38 W
Mount Sterling, Oh., U.S. 218 39.43 N 83.15 W
Mount Stewart, P.E., Can. 186 46.22 N 62.52 W
Mount Stewart, S. Afr. 158 33.10 S 24.26 E
Mount Stromlo Observatory ✪3 171b 35.20 S 149.00 E
Mount Summit 218 40.00 N 85.23 W
Mount Surprise 166 18.09 S 144.19 E
Mount Sylvia 171a 27.44 S 152.14 E
Mount Tamalpais State Park ✦ 226 37.54 N 122.34 W
Mount Torrens 168b 34.52 S 138.57 E
Mount Tremper 210 42.03 N 74.17 W
Mount Uniacke 186 44.54 N 63.50 W
Mount Union 214 40.23 N 77.52 W
Mount Upton 210 42.25 N 75.23 W
Mount Vernon, Austl. 162 24.13 S 118.14 E
Mount Vernon, Al., U.S. 194 31.05 N 88.00 W
Mount Vernon, Ga., U.S. 192 32.10 N 82.35 W
Mount Vernon, Il., U.S. 219 38.19 N 88.54 W
Mount Vernon, In., U.S. 194 37.55 N 87.53 W
Mount Vernon, Ia., U.S. 190 41.55 N 91.25 W
Mount Vernon, Ky., U.S. 192 37.21 N 84.20 W
Mount Vernon, Md., U.S. 208 38.14 N 75.49 W
Mount Vernon, Mo., U.S. 194 37.06 N 93.49 W
Mount Vernon, N.Y., U.S. 210 42.45 N 78.53 W
Mount Vernon, N.Y., U.S. 210 40.54 N 73.50 W
Mount Vernon, Oh., U.S. 214 40.23 N 82.29 W
Mount Vernon, Or., U.S. 202 44.25 N 119.06 W
Mount Vernon, Pa., U.S. 279b 40.17 N 79.48 W
Mount Vernon, S.D., U.S. 198 43.42 N 98.15 W
Mount Vernon, Tx., U.S. 222 33.11 N 95.13 W
Mount Vernon, Wa., U.S. 224 48.25 N 122.19 W
Mount Vernon ⊥ 208 38.47 N 77.06 W
Mount Victoria 170 33.35 S 150.15 E
Mount Victory 216 40.32 N 83.31 W
Mount View 207 41.38 N 71.24 W
Mountville 208 40.02 N 76.26 W
Mount Vision 210 42.35 N 75.04 W
Mount Washington 284b 39.23 N 76.41 W
Mount Washington ✦8 284b 39.22 N 76.40 W
Mount Waverley 274b 37.53 S 145.08 E
Mount Wedge, Austl. 162 22.45 S 132.09 E
Mount Wedge, Austl. 162 33.29 S 135.10 E
Mount Wellington 172 36.54 S 174.51 E
Mount Wilhelm National Park ✦ 164 5.45 S 145.05 E
Mount William National Park ✦ 166 40.56 S 148.15 E
Mount Willoughby 162 27.58 S 134.08 E
Mount Wilson Observatory ✪3 228 34.14 N 118.03 W
Mount Wolf 208 40.03 N 76.42 W
Mount Zion 219 39.46 N 88.53 W
Mounyaz 146 10.41 N 21.18 E
Moura, Austl. 166 24.35 S 149.58 E
Moura, Bra. 246 1.27 S 61.38 W
Moura, Port. 34 38.08 N 7.27 W
Moura, Tchad 146 13.47 N 21.13 E
Moura Brasil 256 22.07 S 43.09 W
Mouraya 146 11.27 N 20.59 E
Mourdi, Dépression du ⊥7 146 18.10 N 23.00 E
Mourdiah 150 14.28 N 7.28 W
Mouriès 62 43.41 N 4.52 E
Mourindi 152 2.32 S 10.48 E
Mourmelon-le-Grand 50 49.08 N 4.22 E
Mourne ≃ 48 54.49 N 7.28 W
Mourne Beg ≃ 48 54.41 N 7.39 W
Mourne Mountains ⋏ 48 54.10 N 6.04 W
Mousa I 46a 60.00 N 1.11 W
Mouscron 50 50.44 N 3.13 E
Mousgougou 146 10.47 N 16.09 E
Moussa Ali ▲ 144 12.28 N 42.24 E
Mousseaux-sur-Seine 261 49.03 N 1.39 E
Moussey 58 48.40 N 6.47 E
Moussoro 146 13.39 N 16.29 E
Moussy-le-Neuf 261 49.04 N 2.36 E
Moussy-le-Vieux 261 49.03 N 2.38 E
Moustiers-Sainte-Marie 62 43.51 N 6.13 E
Moustique, Morne ▲ 241o 16.06 N 61.44 W
Mouthe 58 46.43 N 6.12 E
Mouthier-Haute-Pierre 58 47.02 N 6.16 E
Moutier 58 47.17 N 7.23 E
Moûtiers 62 45.29 N 6.32 E
Moutiers-au-Perche 50 48.29 N 0.51 E
Moutnice 61 49.02 N 16.46 E
Moutohora 172 38.17 S 177.32 E
Moutoumoukadi 152 4.41 S 13.15 E
Moutong 112 0.28 N 121.13 E
Mouy 50 49.19 N 2.19 E
Mouydir ⋏ 148 24.45 N 4.05 E
Mouyondzi 152 3.58 S 13.57 E
Mouzákion 38 39.26 N 21.40 E
Mouzarak 146 13.11 N 15.58 E
Mouzon 56 49.36 N 5.05 E
Mouzon ≃ 58 48.21 N 5.41 E
Moville, Ire. 48 55.11 N 7.03 W
Moville, Ia., U.S. 198 42.29 N 96.04 W
Mowang 100 30.31 N 113.34 E
Moweaqua 219 39.37 N 89.01 W
Mowein 140 7.36 N 28.11 E
Mowry Slough ≃ 282 37.29 N 122.03 W
Mowrystown 218 39.02 N 83.44 W
Mowu 100 26.50 N 117.42 E
Moxhe 56 50.38 N 5.05 E
Moxi 107 30.18 N 105.41 E
Moxico □5 152 13.00 S 20.30 E
Moxotó ≃ 250 9.19 S 38.14 W
Moy 48 54.27 N 6.42 W
Moy ≃ 48 54.12 N 9.08 W
Moy, Cnoc ▲2 46 55.22 N 5.46 W
Moya, Comores 157a 12.18 S 44.27 E
Moya, Perú 248 12.24 S 75.10 W
Moyagee 162 27.45 S 117.54 E
Moyahua 234 21.16 N 103.10 W
Moyale, Ityo. 144 3.30 N 39.07 E
Moyale, Kenya 154 3.32 N 39.03 E
Moyamba 150 8.10 N 12.26 W
Moycullen 48 53.21 N 9.09 W
Moydans 62 44.24 N 5.30 E
Moÿ-de-l'Aisne 50 49.45 N 3.22 E
Moye Dao I 98 36.55 N 122.32 E
Moyen Atlas ⋏ 148 33.30 N 5.00 W
Moyen-Chari □5 146 9.00 N 18.00 E
Moyenmoutier 58 48.23 N 6.55 E
Moyenne-Sido 146 8.13 N 18.43 E
Moyenneville 50 50.04 N 1.45 E
Moyen-Ogooué □4 152 0.30 S 10.30 E
Moyenvic 56 48.47 N 6.33 E
Moyeuvre-Grande 56 49.15 N 6.02 E
Moyie 182 49.17 N 115.50 W
Moyie ≃ 202 48.42 N 116.11 W
Moyie Springs 202 48.43 N 116.11 W
Moylan 285 39.54 N 75.23 W
Moyle ≃ 48 52.24 N 7.39 W
Moyo 154 3.39 N 31.43 E
Moyo ≃ 115b 8.26 S 117.28 E
Moyo, Pulau I 115b 8.15 S 117.34 E
Moyobamba 248 6.03 S 76.58 W
Moyock 208 36.31 N 76.10 W
Moyogalpa 236 11.32 N 85.42 W
Moyowosi ≃ 154 4.50 S 31.24 E
Moyseyyivka 83 49.14 N 39.51 E
Moyu 120 37.17 N 79.44 E
Moyuta, Volcán ▲1 236 14.02 N 90.06 W
M'oža ≃, Europe 76 55.27 N 30.43 E

ENGLISH

Name	Page	Lat.°′	Long.°′
M'oža ≃, Ross.	80	58.23 N	44.54 E
Možajevka	83	48.44 N	39.45 E
Možajsk	82	55.30 N	36.01 E
Možajskij	265a	59.43 N	30.07 E
Možajskoje vodochranilišče ⊜1	82	55.35 N	35.50 E
Mozambique — Moçambique	154	15.03 S	40.42 E
Mozambique (Moçambique) □1	138	18.15 S	35.00 E
Mozambique Channel ⊻	138	19.00 S	41.00 E
Mozambique Plateau ✦3	10	32.00 S	35.00 E
Mozarlândia	255	14.47 S	50.35 W
Možarovka	86	51.09 N	59.05 E
Možarov Majdan	80	55.37 N	45.53 E
Možary	80	53.53 N	41.02 E
Mozdok	84	43.44 N	44.38 E
Možga	80	56.23 N	52.17 E
Mozhabong Lake ⊜	190	46.57 N	82.05 W
Mozia ⊥	70	37.52 N	12.28 E
Mozichang	107	29.20 N	103.53 E
Mozolevo	76	59.19 N	33.51 E
Mozu	270	34.34 N	135.29 E
Mozuli	76	56.36 N	28.11 E
Mozyr'	78	52.03 N	29.14 E
Mozzanica	62	45.29 N	9.41 E
Mozzano	66	42.50 N	13.31 E
Mozzate	266b	45.41 N	8.57 E
Mpaka	158	26.26 S	31.47 E
Mpala	154	6.45 S	29.31 E
Mpama ≃	152	0.57 S	15.39 E
Mpanda	154	6.22 S	31.02 E
Mpé	152	2.54 S	14.43 E
Mpese	152	5.14 S	15.33 E
Mpessoba	150	12.40 N	5.43 W
Mphoengs	154	21.10 S	27.51 E
Mpigi	154	0.13 N	32.42 E
Mpika	154	11.54 S	31.26 E
Mpila ✦8	273b	4.14 S	15.18 E
Mpoka	152	1.26 S	17.02 E
Mpoko ≃	152	4.19 N	18.33 E
Mporokoso	154	9.23 S	30.05 E
Mpouya	152	2.37 S	16.13 E
Mpraeso	150	6.35 N	0.44 W
Mpui	154	8.21 S	31.50 E
Mpulungu	154	8.46 S	31.07 E
Mpwapwa	154	6.21 S	36.29 E
Mqanduli	158	31.48 S	28.46 E
Mrągowo	30	53.52 N	21.19 E
Mrakovo	86	52.43 N	56.38 E
M'Ramani	157a	12.21 S	44.32 E
Mranggen	115a	7.01 S	110.31 E
Mras-Su ≃	86	53.45 N	87.49 E
Mrhila, Jebel ▲	36	35.25 N	9.14 E
Mrijo	154	5.10 S	36.15 E
Mrkonjić Grad	36	44.25 N	17.05 E
Mrkopalj	36	45.19 N	14.51 E
Mrocza	30	53.14 N	17.36 E
Msagali	154	6.21 S	36.18 E
M'Saken	148	35.44 N	10.35 E
Msata	154	6.20 S	38.23 E
Mšec	54	50.10 N	13.54 E
Mšeno	54	50.27 N	14.38 E
M'Sila	148	35.46 N	4.31 E
M'Sila □5	148	35.00 N	4.20 E
M'Sila, Oued ≃	34	35.46 N	4.34 E
Mšinskaja	76	59.01 N	29.57 E
Msoro	154	13.36 S	31.55 E
Msta	76	57.55 N	34.29 E
Msta ≃	76	58.25 N	31.20 E
Mstera	80	56.23 N	41.56 E
Mstislavl'	76	54.02 N	31.42 E
Mstiž	76	54.34 N	28.10 E
Mszana Dolna	30	49.42 N	20.05 E
Mszczonów	30	51.58 N	20.31 E
Mtakataka	154	14.12 S	34.32 E
Mtakuja	154	7.22 S	30.37 E
Mtama	154	10.18 S	39.22 E
Mtamvuna ≃	158	31.06 S	30.12 E
Mtarazi National Park ✦	154	18.36 S	32.50 E
Mtata ≃	158	31.58 S	29.10 E
Mtelo ▲	154	1.39 N	35.23 E
Mtilikwe ≃	154	21.09 S	31.30 E
Mtito Andei	154	2.41 S	38.10 E
Mtowabaga	154	2.30 S	35.53 E
Mtsensk — Mcensk	76	53.17 N	36.35 E
Mtubatuba	158	28.30 S	32.08 E
Mtunzini	158	28.57 S	31.46 E
Mtwara	154	10.16 S	40.11 E
Mtwara □4	154	11.00 S	39.00 E
Mtyangimbori	154	10.16 S	35.31 E
Mu ≃, Mya.	110	21.56 N	95.38 E
Mu ≃, Nihon	92a	42.33 N	141.56 E
Mu, Cerro ▲	246	9.29 N	73.07 W
Mu'a	174w	21.11 S	175.07 W
Muacandala	152	10.02 S	19.40 E
Mualama	154	16.53 S	38.17 E
Mualang	112	0.42 N	111.18 E
Mu'allaqah, Lubnān	132	33.50 N	35.54 E
Mu 'Allaqāh, Sūd.	140	13.28 N	23.57 E
Muan	98	34.58 N	126.26 E
Muaná	250	1.32 S	49.13 W
Muanda	152	5.56 S	12.21 E
Muangai	152	12.32 S	19.51 E
Muang Bèng	110	20.22 N	101.44 E
Muang Hay	110	21.03 N	101.49 E
Muang Hinboun	110	17.35 N	104.36 E
Muang Hôngsa	110	19.43 N	101.20 E
Muang Houn	110	20.09 N	101.27 E
Muang Hounxianghoung	110	21.37 N	102.18 E
Muang Huang	110	18.45 N	103.42 E
Muang Khammouan	110	17.24 N	104.48 E
Muang Khao	110	19.47 N	103.29 E
Muang Khi	110	18.27 N	101.46 E
Muang Không	110	14.07 N	105.51 E
Muang Khôngxédôn	110	15.34 N	105.49 E
Muang La	110	20.52 N	102.07 E
Muang Liap	110	18.29 N	101.40 E
Muang Long	110	20.57 N	100.48 E
Muang Meung	110	20.43 N	100.28 E
Muang Ngoy, Lao	102	20.43 N	102.41 E
Muang Ngoy, Lao	110	20.43 N	102.41 E
Muang Nong	110	16.22 N	106.30 E
Muang Ou Nua	110	22.18 N	101.48 E
Muang Ou Tai	110	22.07 N	101.48 E
Muang Pakbèng	110	19.54 N	101.08 E
Muang Pak-Lay	110	18.12 N	101.25 E
Muang Paktha	110	20.06 N	100.36 E
Muang Pakxan	110	18.22 N	103.39 E
Muang Peun	110	20.13 N	103.52 E
Muang Phalan	110	16.39 N	105.34 E
Muang Phiang	110	19.06 N	101.32 E
Muang Phônthong	110	15.05 N	105.39 E
Muang Phoun	110	19.07 N	102.43 E
Muang Sam Sip	110	15.31 N	104.44 E
Muang Sing	110	21.11 N	101.09 E
Muang Soum	110	18.45 N	102.36 E
Muang Souvannakhili	110	15.23 N	105.49 E
Muang Souy	110	19.33 N	102.52 E
Muang Sung	110	20.19 N	102.27 E
Muang Thadua	110	19.26 N	101.50 E
Muang Thatèng	110	15.26 N	106.23 E
Muang Thathôm	110	19.00 N	103.36 E
Muang Va	110	21.53 N	102.19 E
Muang Vangviang	110	18.56 N	102.27 E
Muang Vapi	110	15.40 N	105.55 E
Muang Xaignabouri	110	19.15 N	101.45 E
Muang Xamtong	110	19.51 N	103.51 E
Muang Xay	110	20.42 N	101.59 E
Muang Xépôn	110	16.41 N	106.14 E
Muang Xon	110	20.27 N	103.19 E
Muang Yo	110	21.31 N	101.51 E
Muang You	110	19.49 N	102.50 E
Muanza	156	18.59 S	34.48 E
Muar (Bandar Maharani)	114	2.02 N	102.34 E

DEUTSCH

Name	Seite	Breite°′	Länge°′ E = Ost
Muar ≃	114	2.03 N	102.35 E
Muara	112	5.02 N	115.02 E
Muaraaman	112	3.07 S	102.12 E
Muaraancalung	112	0.27 N	116.41 E
Muarabeliti	112	3.15 S	103.02 E
Muarabenangin	112	0.58 S	115.19 E
Muarabinuangeun	115a	6.50 S	105.53 E
Muarabulian	112	1.43 S	103.15 E
Muarabungo	112	1.28 S	102.07 E
Muaradua	112	4.32 S	104.05 E
Muaraenim	112	3.39 S	103.48 E
Muaragusung	112	1.35 N	117.17 E
Muarajuloi	112	0.12 S	114.03 E
Muarakaman	112	0.09 S	116.43 E
Muarakelingi	112	3.05 S	103.14 E
Muarakumpe	112	1.24 S	104.00 E
Muaralabuh	112	1.29 S	101.03 E
Muaralakitan	112	2.51 S	103.19 E
Muaralasan	112	1.48 N	117.12 E
Muaralembu	112	0.24 S	101.21 E
Muaramawai	112	0.37 N	116.49 E
Muarapangean	112	2.38 N	116.41 E
Muarapantai	112	0.45 S	101.43 E
Muarapayang	112	1.32 S	115.48 E
Muararupit	112	2.44 S	102.54 E
Muarasabak	112	1.08 S	103.51 E
Muarasiberut	108	1.36 S	99.11 E
Muarasipongi	112	0.37 N	99.51 E
Muaratais	114	1.17 N	99.21 E
Muaratebo	112	1.30 S	102.26 E
Muarateladang	112	2.50 S	103.58 E
Muaratembesi	112	1.42 S	103.07 E
Muaratewe	112	0.57 S	114.53 E
Muaratuhup	112	0.37 S	114.50 E
Muaratunan	112	1.24 S	116.39 E
Muarawahau	112	1.02 N	116.52 E
Muāri, Rās ≻	120	24.49 N	66.40 E
Muasdale	46	55.36 N	5.41 W
Muá Ximica	152	9.50 S	18.41 E
Mubārakpur	124	26.05 N	83.18 E
Mubārakpur Dabās ✦8	272a	28.43 N	77.03 E
Mubayyad ⊤4	142	30.55 N	32.48 E
Mubende	154	0.35 N	31.23 E
Mubi	146	10.18 N	13.20 E
Mubur, Pulau I	112	3.20 N	106.12 E
Mucaitá ≃	250	6.59 S	42.40 W
Mucajaí ≃	246	2.25 N	60.52 W
Mucambo	250	3.54 S	40.44 W
Mucári	152	9.30 S	16.54 E
Muccan	162	20.38 S	120.04 E
Muccia	66	43.05 N	13.02 E
Much	56	50.54 N	7.25 E
Mucha	269d	24.59 N	121.34 E
Muchangpu	100	31.55 N	116.35 E
Muchanovo	82	56.31 N	38.20 E
Muchavec ≃	76	52.05 N	23.39 E
Much Dewchurch	42	51.59 N	2.46 W
Muchea	168a	31.35 S	115.59 E
Mücheln	54	51.18 N	11.48 E
Muchen	89	48.10 N	136.13 E
Muchengzhen	107	29.47 N	103.29 E
Much Hoole	262	53.42 N	2.48 W
Muchinga Escarpment ⊥4	154	14.45 S	29.30 E
Muchinga Mountains ⋏	154	12.20 S	31.00 E
Muchino, Ross.	80	58.11 N	51.02 E
Muchino, Ross.	89	52.16 N	127.14 E
Muchor-Konduj	88	52.25 N	113.16 E
Muchrani	84	41.56 N	44.35 E
Muchtolovo	80	55.27 N	43.13 E
Muchuan	107	28.55 N	103.58 E
Much Wenlock	42	52.36 N	2.34 W
Mucifal	266c	38.48 N	9.26 W
Mučikan	88	53.02 N	120.27 E
Muck I	46	56.50 N	6.15 W
Mücka	54	51.18 N	14.40 E
Muckadilla	166	26.35 S	148.23 E
Muckalee Creek ≃	192	31.38 N	84.09 W
Muckamore	48	54.41 N	6.10 W
Mučkapskij	80	51.52 N	42.28 E
Mučkas	24	64.02 N	48.27 E
Mücke	56	50.38 N	9.03 E
Muckendorf an der Donau	264b	48.20 N	16.09 E
Mucking	260	51.30 N	0.26 E
Muckle Roe I	46a	60.22 N	1.27 W
Muckleshoot Indian Reservation ✦4	224	47.16 N	122.09 W
Muckno Lough ⊜	48	54.07 N	6.42 W
Mucojo	154	12.04 S	40.28 E
Mucoma	152	15.18 S	13.39 E
Muconda	152	10.34 S	21.17 E
Mucope, Ang.	152	16.24 S	14.53 E
Mucope, Ang.	152	8.42 S	21.43 E
Mucrone, Monte ▲	62	45.36 N	7.56 E
Mucubela	154	16.55 S	37.52 E
Mucuchíes	246	8.45 N	70.55 W
Mucugê	255	13.00 S	41.23 W
Mucuim ≃	248	6.33 S	64.18 W
Muculo	152	16.47 S	14.51 E
Muçum	252	29.10 S	51.53 W
Mucumbura	154	16.09 S	31.31 E
Mucun	100	26.44 N	114.00 E
Mucupia	156	18.01 S	36.48 E
Mucupina, Monte ▲	236	15.08 N	86.38 W
Mucur	130	39.04 N	34.23 E
Mucuri	255	18.05 S	39.34 W
Mucuri ≃	255	18.05 S	39.34 W
Mucusso	152	18.01 S	21.25 E
Mud ≃, Ky., U.S.	194	37.13 N	86.54 W
Mud ≃, W.V., U.S.	188	38.25 N	82.17 W
Muda ≃	114	5.33 N	100.22 E
Mudan ≃	89	46.22 N	129.33 E
Mudanjiang	89	44.35 N	129.36 E
Mudanya	130	40.22 N	28.52 E
Mudau	56	49.32 N	9.11 E
Mudaysīsāt, Jabal ▲	132	31.39 N	36.14 E
Mud Creek ≃, N.A.	206	45.01 N	72.24 W
Mud Creek ≃, U.S.	198	43.17 N	96.15 W
Mud Creek ≃, Il., U.S.	219	38.21 N	89.48 W
Mud Creek ≃, In., U.S.	216	41.06 N	86.21 W
Mud Creek ≃, In., U.S.	216	40.26 N	85.55 W
Mud Creek ≃, Ne., U.S.	198	41.01 N	98.54 W
Mud Creek ≃, N.Y., U.S.	210	42.17 N	77.13 W
Mud Creek ≃, N.Y., U.S.	210	42.59 N	77.23 W
Mud Creek ≃, N.Y., U.S.	210	43.05 N	78.43 W
Mud Creek ≃, Ok., U.S.	196	33.55 N	97.28 W
Mud Creek ≃, S.D., U.S.	198	45.11 N	98.24 W
Mud Creek ≃, Tx., U.S.	222	31.48 N	94.58 W
Muddus Nationalpark ✦	24	67.00 N	20.16 E
Muddy ≃, Nv., U.S.	204	36.27 N	114.22 W
Muddy ≃, Wa., U.S.	224	46.04 N	122.01 W
Muddy Boggy Creek ≃	196	34.03 N	95.47 W
Muddy Branch ≃	284c	39.03 N	77.18 W
Muddy Brook ≃	276	41.07 N	73.20 W
Muddy Creek ≃, U.S.	276	41.03 N	74.02 W
Muddy Creek ≃, Mo., U.S.	194	38.51 N	93.03 W
Muddy Creek ≃, Mt., U.S.	202	47.56 N	111.46 W
Muddy Creek ≃, Oh., U.S.	214	41.27 N	83.03 W
Muddy Creek ≃, Pa., U.S.	208	39.47 N	76.18 W
Muddy Creek ≃, Ut,. U.S.	200	38.24 N	110.42 W

Symbols in the index entries represent the broad categories identified in the key at the right. Symbols with superior numbers (⋏1) identify subcategories (see complete key on page *I · 1)*.

Symbole im Register stellen die rechts im Schlüssel erklärten Kategorien dar. Symbole mit hochgestellten Ziffern (⋏1) bezeichnen Unterabteilungen einer Kategorie (vgl. vollständiger Schlüssel auf Seite *I · 1)*.

Los símbolos incluídos en el texto del índice representan las grandes categorías identificadas con la clave a la derecha. Los símbolos con numeros en su parte superior (⋏1) identifican las subcategorías (véase la clave completa en la página *I · 1)*.

Les symboles de l'index représentent les catégories indiquées dans la légende à droite. Les symboles suivis d'un indice (⋏1) représentent des sous-catégories (voir légende complète à la page *I · 1)*.

Os símbolos incluídos no texto do índice representam as grandes categorias identificadas com a chave à direita. Os símbolos com números em sua parte superior (⋏1) identificam as subcategorias (veja-se a chave completa à página *I · 1)*.

▲ Mountain	Berg	Montaña	Montagne	Montanha
⋏ Mountains	Gebirge	Montañas	Montagnes	Montanhas
)(Pass	Paß	Paso	Col	Passo
V Valley, Canyon	Tal, Cañon	Valle, Cañón	Vallée, Canyon	Vale, Canhão
≚ Plain	Ebene	Llano	Plaine	Planície
≻ Cape	Kap	Cabo	Cap	Cabo
I Island	Insel	Isla	Île	Ilha
II Islands	Inseln	Islas	Îles	Ilhas
⊥ Other Topographic Features	Andere Topographische Objekte	Otros Elementos Topográficos	Autres données topographiques	Outros acidentes topográficos

ESPAÑOL: Nombre — Página — Lat.°′ — Long.°′ W = Oeste
FRANÇAIS: Nom — Page — Lat.°′ — Long.°′ W = Ouest
PORTUGUÊS: Nome — Página — Lat.°′ — Long.°′ W = Oeste

Muddy Creek ≃, Wy., U.S. 198 42.35 N 104.57 W
Muddy Creek ≃, Wy., U.S. 200 41.59 N 106.08 W
Muddy Creek ≃, Wy., U.S. 200 41.32 N 110.13 W
Muddy Creek ≃, Wy., U.S. 200 41.01 N 107.42 W
Muddy Creek ≃, Wy., U.S. 202 43.17 N 108.14 W
Muddy Fork ≃ 224 46.22 N 121.34 W
Muddy Gut ⊂ 284b 39.17 N 76.26 W
Muddy Peak ∧ 204 36.18 N 114.42 W
Müden, Dtsch. 52 52.52 N 10.07 E
Müden, Dtsch. 54 52.31 N 10.22 E
Mudgee 166 32.36 S 149.35 E
Mudgeeraba 171a 28.04 S 153.22 E
Mudhol 122 16.21 N 75.17 E
Mud Island I 171a 27.20 S 153.15 E
Mud Islands II 169 38.17 S 144.45 E
Mudjatik ≃ 184 56.02 N 107.36 W
Mudjuga 24 63.46 N 39.15 E
Mud Lake ⊜, Id., U.S. 202 43.53 N 112.24 W
Mud Lake ⊜, Nv., U.S. 204 37.52 N 117.04 W
Mud Lake ⊜, N.Y., U.S. 212 44.30 N 75.28 W
Mud Lake Reservoir ⊜1 198 45.50 N 98.10 W
Mudon 110 16.15 N 97.44 E
Mudongzhen 102 29.35 N 106.51 E
Mudu 106 31.15 N 120.30 E
Mudug □4 144 6.15 N 48.00 E
Mudurnu 130 40.28 N 31.13 E
Mudurnu ≃ 130 40.49 N 30.33 E
M'ud'ur'um ≃ 85 40.53 N 76.36 E
Mueda 154 11.39 S 39.33 E
Muelle de los Bueyes 236 12.04 N 84.32 W
Mueller, Mount ∧2 162 19.54 S 127.51 E
Muenster 196 33.39 N 97.23 W
Mu'er 107 29.48 N 106.37 E
Muerte, Valle de la — Death Valley ∨ 204 36.30 N 117.00 W
Muerto ≃ 252 23.02 S 62.29 W
Muerto, Mar — Dead Sea ⊜ 132 31.30 N 35.30 E
Mufulira 154 12.33 S 28.14 E
Mufuma 152 9.04 S 17.06 E
Mufu Shan ∧ 100 29.02 N 113.54 E
Mufu Shan ∧ 100 29.00 N 114.00 E
Muğan düzü ≚ 84 39.40 N 48.15 E
Mugang 100 29.44 N 115.14 E
Mugazine 158 26.07 S 32.30 E
Mugegawa 94 35.31 N 136.51 E
Mugello ∨ 66 43.55 N 11.30 E
Mugeln 54 51.14 N 13.02 E
Muger ≃ 144 9.54 N 37.57 E
Müggelberge ∧2 264a 52.25 N 13.39 E
Müggelheim ⯈8 264a 52.25 N 13.40 E
Muggia 64 45.36 N 13.46 E
Muggio 266b 45.36 N 9.14 E
Mughal Sarāi 124 25.18 N 83.07 E
Mugi, Nihon 94 35.34 N 137.01 E
Mugi, Nihon 96 33.40 N 134.25 E
Mu Gia, Deo)(110 17.40 N 105.47 E
Muginga 152 8.20 S 17.37 E
Muğla 130 37.12 N 28.22 E
Muğla □4 130 37.10 N 28.30 E
Mugodžarskaja 86 48.36 N 58.27 E
Mugodžary, gory ∧2 86 49.00 N 58.40 E
Mugombazi 154 5.50 S 30.14 E
Mugo-ri 98 38.58 N 126.31 E
Mugrejevskij 80 56.36 N 42.21 E
Mugron 32 43.45 N 0.45 W
Mugu Karnāli ≃ 124 29.38 N 81.52 E
Mugur-Aksy 86 50.21 N 90.30 E
Muḥ, Sabkhat al- ⊜ 130 34.30 N 38.20 E
Muhala 154 5.40 S 28.43 E
Muhamdi 124 27.57 N 80.13 E
Muhammad, Ra's ⯈ 140 27.44 N 34.15 E
Muhammadābād 124 26.02 N 83.23 E
Muhammadpur 126 23.24 N 89.36 E
Muhammad Qawl 140 20.54 N 37.05 E
Muhayshir, Birkat ⊜ 142 30.43 N 31.56 E
Muheza 154 5.10 S 38.47 E
Muḥīṭ, Maṣrif al- ≅ 273c 30.07 N 31.06 E
Mühlacker 56 48.57 N 8.50 E
Mühlau 54 50.54 N 12.45 E
Mühlbach am Hochkönig 64 47.22 N 13.08 E
Mühlbach-sur-Munster 58 48.02 N 7.05 E
Mühlberg 54 51.26 N 13.13 E
Mühldorf 61 48.22 N 15.21 E
Mühldorf am Inn 60 48.15 N 12.32 E
Mühlen — Molini di Tures 64 46.54 N 11.56 E
Mühlenbeck 54 52.40 N 13.22 E
Mühlenbecker See ⊜ 264a 52.41 N 13.24 E
Mühlenberg 210 41.14 N 76.09 W
Mühlen-Berg ∧2 264a 52.23 N 13.15 E
Mühlen Eichsen 54 53.45 N 11.15 E
Mühlenfliess ≃ 264a 52.26 N 13.41 E
Mühlenrahmede 263 51.16 N 7.40 E
Mühlhausen, Dtsch. 54 51.12 N 10.27 E
Mühlhausen, Dtsch. 263 51.33 N 7.44 E
Mühlhausen im Täle 56 48.34 N 9.39 E
Mühlheim 56 50.07 N 8.50 E
Mühlheim an der Donau 58 48.01 N 8.53 E
Mühlig-Hofmann Mountains ∧ 9 72.00 S 5.20 E
Mühlleiten 264b 48.10 N 16.34 E
Mühltroff 54 50.32 N 11.55 E
Mühlviertel ⯈1 30 48.25 N 14.10 E
Muhola 26 63.20 N 25.05 E
Muhoro 154 1.01 S 34.07 E
Muhos 26 64.48 N 25.59 E
Muhradah 130 35.15 N 36.35 E
Mühringen 58 48.25 N 8.46 E
Muhu I 76 58.38 N 23.15 E
Muhula 154 13.53 S 39.30 E
Muhulu 154 1.03 S 27.17 E
Muhutwe 154 1.33 S 31.42 E
Muhu väin ≚ 76 58.45 N 23.20 E
Muhuwesi ≃ 154 11.16 S 37.58 E
Muick, Loch ⊜ 46 56.55 N 3.10 W
Muiden 52 52.19 N 5.04 E
Muiderslot ⊥ 52 52.20 N 5.10 E
Muides-sur-Loire 50 47.40 N 1.31 E
Muié 152 14.25 S 20.36 E
Mui Hopohoponga Point ⯈ 174w 21.09 S 175.02 W
Muikaichi 96 34.21 N 131.56 E
Muikamachi 94 37.04 N 138.53 E
Muine Bheag (Bagenalstown) 48 52.41 N 6.58 W
Muir, Mi., U.S. 216 42.59 N 84.56 W
Muir, Pa., U.S. 208 40.36 N 76.31 W
Muir, Mount ∧ 180 61.06 N 148.24 W
Muir Beach 282 37.52 N 122.35 W
Muirdrum 46 56.31 N 2.42 W
Muirkirk, Scot., U.K. 46 55.31 N 4.04 W
Muirkirk, Md., U.S. 284c 39.03 N 76.53 W
Muir of Ord 46 57.31 N 4.27 W
Muiron Islands II 162 21.35 S 114.20 E
Muir Seamount ⯈3 16 33.41 N 62.30 W
Muirtown 46 56.16 N 3.45 W
Muir Woods 282 37.53 N 122.34 W
Muir Woods National Monument ♦ 226 37.54 N 122.33 W
Muiskraal 158 33.56 S 21.13 E
Muisne 246 0.36 N 80.02 W
Muite 154 14.02 S 39.02 E
Mui Wo 271d 22.16 N 113.59 E
Muizen, Bel. 50 51.01 N 4.31 E
Muizen, Bel. 56 50.46 N 5.10 E
Muja, Ityo. 144 12.02 N 39.29 E
Muja, Ross. 88 56.24 N 115.39 E
Muja ≃ 88 56.24 N 115.39 E
Mujāhidpur ⯈8 272a 28.34 N 77.13 E
Mujang-ni 98 35.26 N 126.32 E
Mujezerskij 24 63.57 N 31.55 E
Mujiapucun 104 41.06 N 122.48 E
Mujiayu 105 40.24 N 116.55 E
Mujimbeji Mission 154 12.11 S 24.57 E
Mujnak 86 43.48 N 59.02 E
Muju 98 36.02 N 127.40 E
Mujunkum, peski ⯈2 86 44.20 N 71.00 E
Mukacheve 78 48.27 N 22.45 E
Mukah 112 2.54 N 112.06 E
Mukaishima 96 34.20 N 133.10 E
Mukalla — Al-Mukallā 144 14.32 N 49.08 E
Mukandpur ⯈8 272a 28.44 N 77.11 E
Mukandwara 120 24.49 N 75.59 E
Mukawa 94 35.47 N 138.23 E
Mukāwir 132 31.34 N 35.38 E
Mukāwir ⊥ 132 31.34 N 35.38 E
Mukawwar I 140 20.48 N 37.13 E
Mukdahan 110 16.32 N 104.43 E
Mukden — Shenyang 104 41.48 N 123.27 E
Muke Arba 144 8.57 N 42.09 E
Mukebo 154 6.49 S 28.03 E
Mukeriān 123 31.57 N 75.37 E
Mukharram al-Fawqānī 130 34.49 N 37.04 E
Mukhmās 132 31.52 N 35.17 E
Mukho 98 37.33 N 129.06 E
Mukilteo 224 47.56 N 122.18 W
Mukinbudin 162 30.54 S 118.13 E
Mukinge Hill 154 13.29 S 25.52 E
Mukō 96 34.56 N 135.42 E
Muko ≃ 96 34.41 N 135.23 E
Mukomuko 112 2.35 S 101.07 E
Mukomwenze 154 6.52 S 27.16 E
Mukoshima-rettō II 14 27.37 N 142.10 E
Mukry 128 37.36 N 65.44 E
Muksi-ri 98 39.52 N 125.54 E
Muksu ≃ 85 39.15 N 71.23 E
Muksūdpur 126 23.18 N 89.51 E
Muktāgācha 124 24.46 N 90.14 E
Muktsar 123 30.29 N 74.31 E
Mukuku 154 12.09 S 29.49 E
Mukuleshi ≃ 154 10.21 S 24.30 E
Mukur 86 48.03 N 54.30 E
Mukusaki 115b 8.33 S 121.37 E
Mukutan 154 0.38 N 36.16 E
Mukutawa ≃ 184 53.10 N 97.28 W
Mukwela 154 17.02 S 26.39 E
Mukwonago 216 42.51 N 88.19 W
Mūl 122 20.04 N 79.40 E
Mula, Esp. 34 38.03 N 1.30 W
Mula, Zhg. 102 29.40 N 100.39 E
Mula ≃, India 122 18.34 N 74.20 E
Mula ≃, India 122 19.32 N 74.50 E
Mūla ≃, Pāk. 120 27.57 N 67.36 E
Mulādi 126 22.54 N 90.25 E
Muladu I 122 7.01 N 72.59 E
Mulaly 86 45.27 N 78.19 E
Mulan 89 45.57 N 128.03 E
Muland ⯈8 272c 19.10 N 72.57 E
Mulanda 152 14.41 S 21.48 E
Mulanje, Malaŵi 154 16.03 S 35.31 E
Mulanje, Moç. 154 16.03 S 35.45 E
Mulargia, Lago ⊜1 71 39.37 N 9.14 E
Mulas, Punta ⯈ 240m 18.09 N 65.27 W
Mulas, Punta de ⯈ 240p 21.01 N 75.35 W
Mulatos 232 28.39 N 108.51 W
Mulayit Taung ∧ 110 16.11 N 98.32 E
Mulazzo 64 44.19 N 9.53 E
Mulbāgal 122 13.10 N 78.24 E
Mulben 46 57.31 N 3.06 W
Mulberry, Ar., U.S. 194 35.30 N 94.03 W
Mulberry, Fl., U.S. 220 27.53 N 81.58 W
Mulberry, In., U.S. 216 40.20 N 86.39 W
Mulberry, Oh., U.S. 218 39.11 N 84.14 W
Mulberry ≃ 194 35.28 N 94.03 W
Mulberry Creek ≃, Al., U.S. 194 32.27 N 86.52 W
Mulberry Creek ≃, Tx., U.S. 196 34.37 N 100.55 W
Mulberry Fork ≃ 194 33.33 N 87.11 W
Mulberry Grove 219 38.55 N 89.16 W
Mulberry Mountain ∧ 194 35.42 N 92.56 W
Mulchatna ≃ 180 59.39 N 157.08 W
Mulchén 252 37.43 S 72.14 W
Mulda, Dtsch. 54 50.48 N 13.25 E
Mul'da, Ross. 24 67.28 N 63.34 E
Mulde ≃ 54 51.52 N 12.15 E
Muldenstein 54 51.40 N 12.19 E
Muldersdrif se Loop ≃ 273d 26.06 S 27.51 E
Muldersvlei 158 30.41 S 22.13 E
Muldoon 222 29.49 N 97.04 W
Muldraugh 194 37.56 N 85.59 W
Muldrow 194 35.24 N 94.35 W
Mule, Lac la ⊜ 186 51.33 N 65.35 W
Muleba 154 1.49 S 31.40 E
Mule Creek ≃ 198 37.05 N 99.00 W
Mulegé 232 26.53 N 112.01 W
Mulegns 58 46.33 N 9.37 E
Mulei 86 43.49 N 90.11 E
Mules (Mauls) 64 46.51 N 11.31 E
Mules, Pulau I 115b 8.54 S 120.17 E
Muleshoe 196 34.13 N 102.43 W
Mulevala 154 16.30 S 37.30 E
Mulga Downs 162 22.08 S 118.26 E
Mulgathing 162 30.15 S 134.00 E
Mulgathing Rocks ∧ 162 30.14 S 133.58 E
Mulghar 126 22.46 N 89.45 E
Mulgoa 170 33.50 S 150.40 E
Mulgoa Creek ≃ 274a 33.45 S 150.39 E
Mulgowie 171a 27.43 S 152.22 E
Mulgrave, Austl. 274b 37.56 S 145.12 E
Mulgrave, N.S., Can. 186 45.37 N 61.23 W
Mulgrave Hills ∧2 180 67.42 N 163.24 W
Mulgul 162 24.49 S 118.26 E
Mulhacén ∧ 34 37.03 N 3.19 W
Mulhall 196 36.03 N 97.24 W
Mülhausen — Mulhouse 58 47.45 N 7.20 E
Mülheim 56 49.54 N 7.01 E
Mülheim an der Ruhr 56 51.24 N 6.54 E
Mülheim-Ruhrtalbrüke ⯈5 263 51.23 N 6.54 E
Mülheim-Kärlich 56 50.21 N 7.28 E
Mulhouse (Mülhausen) 58 47.45 N 7.20 E
Muli 102 27.50 N 101.15 E
Muling, Zhg. 89 44.56 N 130.31 E
Muling, Zhg. 89 44.31 N 130.13 E
Muling ≃ 89 45.53 N 133.30 E
Mulini, Capo ⯈ 70 37.34 N 15.10 E
Mulino 224 45.13 N 122.34 W
Mulinu'u, Cape ⯈ 175a 13.26 S 172.43 W
Mulita ≃ 116 7.18 N 124.52 E
Mulkear ≃ 48 52.40 N 8.33 W
Mülki 122 13.06 N 74.48 E
Mull, Island of I 46 56.27 N 6.00 W
Mull, Sound of ≚ 46 56.32 N 5.50 W
Mullagh 48 53.49 N 6.57 W
Mullaghareirk Mountains ∧ 48 52.20 N 9.10 W
Mullaghcleevaun ∧ 48 53.06 N 6.24 W
Mullaghmore ∧ 48 54.52 N 6.51 W
Mullaloo Point ⯈ 168a 31.48 S 115.44 E
Mullan 202 47.28 N 115.48 W
Mullen 198 42.02 N 101.02 W
Müllenbach 56 50.19 N 6.55 E
Mullengudgery 166 31.47 S 147.26 E
Mullens 192 37.34 N 81.22 W
Müller, Pegunungan ∧ 112 0.40 N 113.50 E
Muller Creek ≃ 162 22.29 S 134.30 E
Muller Range ∧ 164 5.35 S 142.15 E
Mullerup 41 55.30 N 11.12 E
Mullet Key I 220 27.37 N 82.44 W
Mullet Peninsula ⯈1 48 54.12 N 10.00 W
Mullett Lake ⊜ 190 45.30 N 84.30 W
Mullewa 162 28.33 S 115.31 E
Mull Head ⯈, Scot., U.K. 46 59.23 N 2.54 W
Mull Head ⯈, Scot., U.K. 46 58.58 N 2.43 W
Müllheim 58 47.48 N 7.38 E
Mullhyttan 40 59.09 N 14.41 E
Mullica ≃ 208 39.33 N 74.25 W
Mullica, Alquatka Branch ≃ 285 39.47 N 74.48 W
Mullica, Sleeper Branch ≃ 285 39.39 N 74.40 W
Mullica Hill 208 39.44 N 75.13 W
Mulligan ≃ 166 25.00 S 138.30 E
Mulliken 216 42.45 N 84.53 W
Mullin 196 31.33 N 98.40 W
Mullinahone 48 52.30 N 7.30 W
Mullinavat 48 52.21 N 7.10 W
Mullingar 48 53.32 N 7.20 W
Mullins 192 34.12 N 79.15 W
Mullinville 198 37.35 N 99.28 W
Mullion 42 50.01 N 5.15 W
Mulloon Creek ≃ 171b 35.12 S 149.38 E
Mullovka 80 54.13 N 49.25 E
Müllrose 54 52.14 N 14.25 E
Mullsjö 26 57.55 N 13.53 E
Mullumbimby 166 28.33 S 153.30 E
Mullum Mullum Creek ≃ 274b 37.44 S 145.10 E
Mulobezi 154 16.48 S 25.09 E
Mulonda Funda 154 11.06 S 25.28 E
Mulondo 152 15.39 S 15.14 E
Mulongo 154 7.50 S 27.00 E
Mulshi Lake ⊜ 122 18.30 N 73.30 E
Multai 120 21.46 N 78.15 E
Multān 123 30.11 N 71.29 E
Multen ⊜ 40 59.10 N 14.37 E
Multia 26 62.25 N 24.47 E
Multnomah □6 224 45.30 N 122.22 W
Multnomah Channel ≚1 224 45.51 N 122.52 W
Multnomah Falls ∟ 224 45.35 N 122.07 W
Mulu, Gunong ∧ 112 4.04 N 114.56 E
Mulumbe, Monts ∧ 154 8.16 S 28.16 E
Mulungushi 154 14.40 S 28.50 E
Mulungushi Dam ⯈6 154 14.40 S 28.50 E
Mulvane 198 37.28 N 97.14 W
Mulwad 140 18.39 N 30.35 E
Mulyah Mountain ∧ 166 30.37 S 144.31 E
Muma 152 3.24 N 23.15 E
Mumbles Head ⯈ 42 51.35 N 3.59 W
Mumbondo 152 10.09 S 14.15 E
Mumbra 272c 19.11 N 73.01 E
Mumbwa 154 14.59 S 27.04 E
Mumcular 130 37.05 N 27.40 E
Mume 154 9.40 S 27.26 E
Mumen 102 32.09 N 106.28 E
Mumeng 164 7.00 S 146.35 E
Mumford, N.Y., U.S. 210 42.59 N 77.52 W
Mumford, Tx., U.S. 222 30.44 N 96.34 W
Mumias 154 0.20 N 34.29 E
Mümling ≃ 56 49.50 N 9.09 E
Mumoni ∧ 154 0.31 S 38.01 E
Mumra 80 45.47 N 47.41 E
Mumu 140 12.06 N 23.42 E
Mumungwe 154 21.59 S 26.24 E
Mun ≃ 110 15.19 N 105.30 E
Mun, Jabal ∧ 140 14.08 N 22.42 E
Munā, Ar. Su. 144 21.25 N 39.52 E
Muna, Méx. 232 20.29 N 89.43 W
Muna ≃ 74 67.52 N 123.06 E
Muna, Pulau I 112 5.00 S 122.30 E
Muna, Selat ≚ 112 5.15 S 122.10 E
Munā al-Amīr 142 29.54 N 31.15 E
Munābāo 120 25.45 N 70.17 E
Munajly 86 46.47 N 54.31 E
Munakata 96 33.50 N 130.35 E
Munam-ni 98 38.41 N 126.54 E
Munam-san ∧ 98 40.26 N 127.22 E
Munbong-ni 271b 37.43 N 126.49 E
Muncar 115a 8.26 S 114.20 E
Münchberg 54 50.11 N 11.47 E
Müncheberg 54 52.30 N 14.08 E
Münchehofe 264a 52.30 N 13.40 E
München (Munich) 60 48.08 N 11.34 E
Münchenbernsdorf 54 50.49 N 11.56 E
Münchenbuchsee 58 47.01 N 7.27 E
Münchendorf 264b 48.02 N 16.23 E
München-Erding, Flughafen ⊠ 60 48.22 N 11.48 E
München-Gladbach — Mönchengladbach 56 51.12 N 6.28 E
München-Riem, Flughafen ⊠ 60 48.08 N 11.41 E
Münchenstein 58 47.31 N 7.37 E
Münchhausen 56 50.57 N 8.43 E
Munchique, Cerro ∧ 246 2.32 N 76.57 W
Munchique, Parque Nacional ♦ 246 2.30 N 77.10 W
Munch'ŏn 98 39.16 N 127.15 E
Muncie 216 40.11 N 85.23 W
Muncusun 130 38.54 N 35.38 E
Muncy 210 41.12 N 76.47 W
Muncy Creek ≃ 210 41.13 N 76.48 W
Muncy Valley 210 41.21 N 76.35 W
Mundare 182 53.36 N 112.20 W
Mundaring 168a 31.54 S 116.10 E
Munday 196 33.26 N 99.37 W
Mundelein 216 42.15 N 88.00 W
Mündelheim ⯈8 263 51.21 N 6.41 E
Münden 56 51.25 N 9.39 E
Munderfing 60 48.05 N 13.11 E
Munderkingen 58 48.14 N 9.38 E
Munderoo ⯈ 171b 35.48 S 147.47 E
Mundesley 42 52.53 N 1.26 E
Mundijong 168a 32.18 S 115.59 E
Mundiwindi 162 23.52 S 120.09 E
Mundka ⯈8 272a 28.41 N 77.02 E
Mundo ≃ 34 38.19 N 1.40 W
Mundolsheim 58 48.39 N 7.42 E
Mundo Novo 255 11.52 S 40.28 W
Mundra 120 22.51 N 69.44 E
Mundrabilla 162 31.52 S 127.51 E
Mundubbera 166 25.36 S 151.18 E
Mundybaš 86 53.14 N 87.19 E
Mundytau, gora ∧ 85 38.00 N 68.27 E
Munene 154 20.38 S 30.03 E
Munenga 152 10.02 S 14.41 E
Munera 34 39.02 N 2.28 W
Munford 194 35.26 N 89.48 W
Munfordville 194 37.16 N 85.53 W
Mungallala 166 26.27 S 147.33 E
Mungallala Creek ≃ 166 28.05 S 147.15 E
Mungana 166 17.07 S 144.24 E
Mungaoli 124 24.25 N 78.06 E
Mungari 154 17.12 S 33.31 E
Mungar Junction 166 25.36 S 152.36 E
Mungau 154 15.56 S 21.55 E
Mungbere 154 2.38 N 28.30 E
Mungeli 124 22.04 N 81.41 E
Munger 124 25.23 N 86.28 E
Mungeranie 162 28.00 S 138.36 E
Mungindi 166 28.58 S 148.59 E
Munglinup 162 33.43 S 120.51 E
Mungo 152 11.40 S 16.16 E
Mungo National Park ♦ 166 33.44 S 143.02 E
Mungra Badshāhpur 124 25.40 N 82.11 E
Mungun-Tajga, gora ∧ 86 50.16 N 90.05 E
Mun'gyŏng 98 36.44 N 128.07 E
Munhall 214 40.23 N 79.54 W
Munhamade 154 16.37 S 36.58 E
Munhango 152 12.13 S 18.42 E
Munhango ≃ 152 11.20 S 19.50 E
Munhoz 256 22.37 S 46.22 W
Munhye-ri 98 38.10 N 127.19 E
Munich — München 60 48.08 N 11.34 E
Muniesa 34 41.02 N 0.48 W
Munim ≃ 250 2.45 S 44.04 W
Munirka ⯈8 272a 28.34 N 77.10 E
Munising 190 46.24 N 86.38 W
Munith 216 42.23 N 84.15 W
Muñiz 258 34.33 S 58.42 W
Muniz Freire 255 20.28 S 41.25 W
Munkács — Mukacheve 78 48.27 N 22.45 E
Munka-Ljungby 41 56.15 N 12.58 E
Munkebjerg ∧2 41 55.41 N 9.37 E
Munkebo 41 55.27 N 10.34 E
Munkedal 26 58.29 N 11.41 E
Munkerud 40 59.50 N 13.31 E
Munkfors 40 59.50 N 13.32 E
Munksund 26 65.17 N 21.29 E
Munktorp 40 59.32 N 16.08 E
Munku-Sardyk, gora ∧ 88 51.45 N 100.32 E
Munlochy 46 57.32 N 4.15 W
Münnerstadt 56 50.15 N 10.11 E
Munnsville 210 42.58 N 75.35 W
Muñoz 116 15.43 N 120.54 E
Munozero 24 67.05 N 34.12 E
Muñoz Gamero, Peninsula ⯈1 254 52.30 S 73.10 W
Munpal-li 271b 37.45 N 126.43 E
Munro ⯈8 288 34.32 S 58.31 W
Munroe Falls 214 41.08 N 81.26 W
Munro Lake ⊜ 184 54.38 N 95.16 W
Munsan 98 37.51 N 126.48 E
Munsarpur 126 24.18 N 88.26 E
Munsey Park 276 40.48 N 73.41 W
Munshiganj 124 23.33 N 90.32 E
Münsing 64 47.54 N 11.22 E
Münsingen, Dtsch. 58 48.25 N 9.29 E
Münsingen, Schw. 58 46.53 N 7.34 E
Munsö I 40 59.23 N 17.35 E
Munson, Ab., Can. 182 51.34 N 112.45 W
Munson, Pa., U.S. 214 40.57 N 78.10 W
Munson Knob ∧2 214 40.40 N 81.54 W
Munsons Corners 210 42.35 N 76.13 W
Münster, Dtsch. 52 51.57 N 7.37 E
Münster, Dtsch. 52 52.59 N 10.05 E
Münster, Dtsch. 56 49.55 N 8.52 E
Munster, Fr. 56 48.55 N 6.54 E
Munster, Fr. 58 48.03 N 7.08 E
Münster, Schw. 58 46.29 N 8.16 E
Munster, In., U.S. 216 41.33 N 87.30 W
Munster □5 52 51.50 N 7.25 E
Munster □9 48 52.25 N 8.20 W
Munster ≃ 48 52.33 N 7.12 W
Münsterkirche ⯈1 263 51.27 N 7.01 E
Münsterland ⯈1 52 52.00 N 7.30 E
Münsterlingen 58 47.38 N 9.14 E
Münstermaifeld 56 50.15 N 7.22 E
Muntadgin 162 31.45 S 118.34 E
Muntahak ∧ 114 1.52 N 103.47 E
Munte 112 0.30 N 119.55 E
Muntele Mare, Vârful ∧ 38 46.29 N 23.14 E
Muntendam 52 53.07 N 6.53 E
Muntok 112 2.04 S 105.11 E
Mununzi 154 0.36 N 29.15 E
Munuscong Lake ⊜ 190 46.10 N 84.08 W
Münzenberg 56 50.27 N 8.46 E
Münzkirchen 60 48.29 N 13.34 E
Munzur Dağları ∧ 130 39.30 N 39.10 E
Munzur Vadisi Milli Parkı ♦ 130 39.25 N 39.30 E
Muolea Point ⯈ 229a 20.41 N 156.01 W
Muong Het 110 20.49 N 104.01 E
Muong Hinh 110 19.49 N 105.03 E
Muong Khoua 110 21.05 N 102.31 E
Muong Saiapoun 110 18.24 N 101.31 E
Muong Te 110 22.28 N 102.37 E
Muonio 24 67.57 N 23.42 E
Muotathal 58 46.59 N 8.46 E
Mupa 152 16.10 S 15.44 E
Mupa, Parque Nacional da ♦ 152 16.00 S 15.35 E
Muping 98 37.24 N 121.35 E
Mupini 156 17.50 S 19.40 E
Mup'ungjang 98 35.58 N 127.49 E
Muqaddam, Wādī ∨ 140 18.04 N 31.30 E
Muqaṭṭa' 140 14.40 N 35.51 E
Muqaybirah, Bi'r al- ⯈4 142 30.53 N 32.50 E
Muqayshiṭ I 128 24.10 N 53.45 E
Muqdisho (Mogadishu) 144 2.04 N 45.22 E
Muqi 98 41.46 N 124.39 E
Muqsam, Jabal ∧ 140 13.38 N 27.42 E
Müqtädir 84 41.41 N 48.46 E
Muquequete 152 14.50 S 14.16 E
Muqui 255 20.57 S 41.20 W
Mur (Mura) ≃ 30 46.18 N 16.53 E
Mura (Mur) ≃, Europe 30 46.18 N 16.53 E
Mura ≃, Ross. 88 58.27 N 98.34 E
Muradiye, Tür. 84 38.59 N 43.46 E
Muradiye, Tür. 130 38.39 N 27.21 E
Murādnagar 124 28.47 N 77.30 E
Murafa ≃ 78 48.13 N 28.14 E
Murāgācha 126 23.32 N 88.24 E
Muraglione, Passo del)(66 43.56 N 11.39 E
Murai Reservoir ⊜1 271c 1.24 N 103.41 E
Murajá 250 0.47 S 47.57 W
Murakami 92 38.14 N 139.29 E
Murallón, Cerro ∧ 254 49.48 S 73.25 W
Murambi 154 1.46 S 30.23 E
Muramvya 154 3.16 S 29.37 E
Murana 164 3.33 S 133.49 E
Murang'a 154 0.43 S 37.09 E
Murano, Isola di I 64 45.28 N 12.21 E
Muranskij porog ∟ 88 58.02 N 112.16 E
Muraoka 96 35.28 N 134.35 E
Murași 24 59.24 N 48.55 E
Muraški 265b 55.59 N 37.45 E
Murat 32 45.07 N 2.52 E
Murat ≃ 84 38.39 N 39.50 E
Murat Dağı ∧ 130 38.55 N 29.43 E
Muratkovo 86 58.26 N 62.23 E
Muratlı 130 41.10 N 27.30 E
Muratove 83 48.48 N 38.45 E
Muratpur 272b 22.59 N 88.27 E
Murau 61 47.07 N 14.10 E
Muravera 71 39.25 N 9.34 E
Muravjovka 89 49.50 N 127.44 E
Muravjovo 76 56.14 N 34.14 E
Murayama 92 38.29 N 140.22 E
Murayama-chosuichi ⊜1 268 35.45 N 139.25 E
Muraysah, Ra's al- ⯈ 146 31.55 N 25.02 E
Murça 34 41.24 N 7.27 W
Murcanyo 144 11.41 N 50.27 E
Mürchen Khvort 128 33.06 N 51.30 E
Murchin 54 53.54 N 13.44 E
Murchison, Austl. 169 36.37 S 145.14 E
Murchison, N.Z. 172 41.48 S 172.20 E
Murchison, Tx., U.S. 222 32.17 N 95.45 W
Murchison ≃ 162 27.42 S 114.09 E
Murchison, Mount ∧, Austl. 162 26.46 S 116.25 E
Murchison, Mount ∧, N.Z. 172 43.01 S 171.22 E
Murchison Falls ∟ — Kabalega Falls ∟ 154 2.17 N 31.41 E
Murchison Range ∧ 162 20.22 S 134.26 E
Murcia, Esp. 34 37.59 N 1.07 W
Murcia, Pil. 116 10.36 N 123.02 E
Murcia □4, Esp. 34 38.05 N 1.45 W
Murcia □4, Esp. 148 37.55 N 1.30 W
Murciélago, Isla I 236 10.51 N 85.57 W
Murcielagos Bay ⊂ 116 8.39 N 123.33 E
Mur-de-Barrez 32 44.51 N 2.39 E
Murdeduke, Lake ⊜ 169 38.11 S 143.53 E
Murder Creek ≃, Al., U.S. 194 31.04 N 87.06 W
Murder Creek ≃, N.Y., U.S. 210 43.05 N 78.31 W
Murderkill ≃ 208 39.03 N 75.24 W
Murdo 198 43.53 N 100.42 W
Murdock 220 27.00 N 82.08 W
Mure 94 36.45 N 138.14 E
Mureaux, Aérodrome des ⊠ 261 49.00 N 1.57 E
Mureck 61 46.42 N 15.46 E
Mürefte 130 40.40 N 27.14 E
Mureș □6 38 46.35 N 24.40 E
Mureș (Maros) ≃ 38 46.15 N 20.13 E
Muret 32 43.28 N 1.21 E
Murewa 154 17.39 S 31.47 E
Murfreesboro, Ar., U.S. 194 34.03 N 93.41 W
Murfreesboro, N.C., U.S. 192 36.26 N 77.05 W
Murfreesboro, Tn., U.S. 194 35.50 N 86.23 W
Murg 58 47.33 N 8.01 E
Murg ≃ 56 48.55 N 8.10 E
Murgab 85 38.10 N 73.59 E
Murgab (Morghāb) ≃, Asia 128 38.18 N 61.12 E
Murgab ≃, Taj. 120 38.20 N 72.30 E
Murgenella 164 11.33 S 132.55 E
Murgeni 38 46.12 N 28.01 E
Murgenthal 58 47.16 N 7.50 E
Murgha Faqīrzai 120 31.03 N 67.48 E
Murgha Kibzai 120 30.44 N 69.25 E
Murgon 166 26.15 S 151.57 E
Muri, Cook Is. 174k 21.14 S 159.43 W
Muri, Nig. 146 9.11 N 10.53 E
Muri, Schw. 58 46.56 N 7.29 E
Muri, Schw. 58 47.16 N 8.21 E
Muria, Gunung ∧ 115a 6.36 S 110.53 E
Muriaé 255 21.08 S 42.22 W
Muriaé ≃ 255 21.43 S 41.22 W
Murias de Paredes 34 42.51 N 6.11 W
Muribeca 250 10.26 S 36.59 W
Muribeca dos Guararapes 250 8.10 S 35.01 W
Murici 250 9.19 S 35.56 W
Muricizal ≃ 250 6.40 S 48.40 W
Murīdke 123 31.48 N 74.16 E
Muriége 152 9.58 S 21.11 E
Muriel Lake ⊜ 182 54.10 N 110.40 W
Murih, Pulau I 112 1.54 N 108.38 E
Murila 152 10.44 S 20.20 E
Murilo I1 14 8.40 N 152.11 E
Mūrinda 123 30.47 N 76.29 E
Murinja 88 54.47 N 107.21 E
Murino, Ross. 88 51.30 N 104.23 E
Murino, Ross. 265a 60.03 N 30.27 E
Murinskij ≃ 265a 60.01 N 30.28 E
Muriqui 256 22.56 S 43.57 W
Muriqui ≃ 287a 22.52 S 43.02 W
Murisengo 62 45.05 N 8.08 E
Mūrītāniyā — Mauritania □1 134 20.00 N 12.00 W
Müritz ⊜ 54 53.25 N 12.43 E
Muriwai 172 38.46 S 177.55 E
Murkong Selek 120 27.49 N 95.16 E
Murlīganj 124 25.54 N 86.59 E
Murlo 66 43.09 N 11.23 E
Murmansk 24 68.58 N 33.05 E
Murmansk Oblast' □4 24 68.00 N 35.00 E
Murmansk Rise ⯈3 12 75.00 N 37.00 E
Murmerwoude 52 53.16 N 6.00 E
Murmino 80 54.36 N 40.03 E
Murnau 64 47.40 N 11.12 E
Murnei 140 12.57 N 22.52 E
Murō 94 34.34 N 136.02 E
Murō-Akame-Aoyama-kokutei-kōen ♦ 94 34.30 N 136.10 E
Muro Lucano 68 40.45 N 15.29 E
Murom 80 55.34 N 42.02 E
Muromcevo 86 56.23 N 75.14 E
Muroran 92a 42.18 N 140.59 E
Muros 34 42.47 N 9.02 W
Muros y Noya, Ría de ⊂1 34 42.45 N 9.00 W
Muroto 96 33.18 N 134.09 E
Muroto-Anan-kaigan-kokutei-kōen ♦ 96 33.41 N 134.32 E
Muroto-zaki ⯈ 96 33.15 N 134.11 E
Murovani Kurylivtsi 78 48.43 N 27.31 E
Murowana Goślina 30 52.35 N 17.01 E
Murphy, Id., U.S. 202 43.13 N 116.33 W
Murphy, Mo., U.S. 219 38.29 N 90.29 W
Murphy, N.C., U.S. 192 35.05 N 84.02 W
Murphy Lake ⊜ 182 52.03 N 121.14 W
Murphys 226 38.08 N 120.27 W
Murphysboro 194 37.45 N 89.20 W
Murphy Slough ≃ 226 36.28 N 120.00 W
Murr ≃ 56 48.57 N 9.16 E
Murr, Wādī ∨ 140 22.27 N 32.18 E
Murrah, Qārat al- ∧2 142 30.00 N 32.41 E
Murrah al-Kubrā, Al-Buhayrah al- (Great Bitter Lake) ⊜ 142 30.20 N 32.23 E
Murrah as-Sughrā, Al-Buhayrah al- (Little Bitter Lake) ⊜ 142 30.13 N 32.33 E
Murra Murra 166 28.16 S 146.48 E
Murrāt, Ābār ⯈4 140 21.03 N 32.55 E
Murray, Ia., U.S. 190 41.02 N 93.56 W
Murray, Ky., U.S. 194 36.36 N 88.18 W
Murray, Ut., U.S. 200 40.40 N 111.53 W
Murray ≃, Austl. 166 35.22 S 139.22 E
Murray ≃, Austl. 168a 32.35 S 115.46 E
Murray ≃, B.C., Can. 182 55.40 N 121.10 W
Murray, Lake ⊜ 164 7.00 S 141.30 E
Murray, Lake ⊜1 192 34.04 N 81.23 W
Murray, Mount ∧, Yk., Can. 180 60.54 N 128.49 W
Murray, Mount ∧, Pap. N. Gui. 164 6.46 S 144.01 E
Murray Bay — La Malbaie 186 47.39 N 70.10 W
Murray Bridge 168b 35.07 S 139.17 E
Murray Canal ≅ 212 44.04 N 77.35 W
Murray City 188 39.30 N 82.09 W
Murray Downs 162 21.04 S 134.40 E
Murray Fracture Zone ⯈ 16 34.00 N 135.00 W
Murray Harbour 186 46.00 N 62.31 W
Murray Head ⯈ 186 46.00 N 62.28 W
Murray Maxwell Bay ⊂ 176 70.00 N 80.00 W
Murray Mouth ≚1 168b 35.33 S 138.54 E
Murray River 186 46.01 N 62.37 W
Murraysburg 158 31.58 S 23.47 E
Murrayville, B.C., Can. 224 49.10 N 122.36 W
Murrayville, Il., U.S. 194 39.35 N 90.15 W
Murrèbuè 154 13.02 S 40.30 E
Murree 123 33.54 N 73.24 E
Mürren 58 46.34 N 7.54 E
Murrhardt 56 48.59 N 9.34 E
Murrí ≃ 246 6.33 N 76.52 W
Murrieta 228 33.33 N 117.12 W
Murrieta di Porca, Capo ⯈ 70 37.00 N 15.20 E
Murrumbidgee ≃ 166 34.43 S 143.12 E
Murrumburrah 166 34.33 S 148.21 E
Murrupula 154 15.27 S 38.47 E
Murrurundi 166 31.46 S 150.50 E
Murry Hill 279b 40.17 N 80.09 W
Murrysville 279b 40.25 N 79.41 W
Mursala, Pulau I 114 1.38 N 98.32 E
Murshidābād 126 24.11 N 88.16 E
Mürşitpınar 130 36.54 N 38.19 E
Murska Sobota 36 46.40 N 16.10 E
Murskij, porog ∟ 88 58.27 N 98.30 E
Mursko Središće 61 46.31 N 16.27 E
Murtajāpur 122 20.44 N 77.23 E
Murtal 266c 38.42 N 9.22 W
Murtee 166 31.35 S 143.30 E
Murten 58 46.56 N 7.07 E
Murtensee — Morat, Lac de ⊜ 58 46.55 N 7.05 E
Murter, Otok I 36 43.48 N 15.37 E
Murtle Lake ⊜ 182 52.08 N 119.38 W
Murtoa 166 36.37 S 142.28 E
Murton 44 54.49 N 1.24 W
Murtosa 34 40.44 N 8.38 W
Muru 140 6.36 N 29.15 E
Muru ≃ 248 8.09 S 70.45 W
Muru, Capu di ⯈ 36 41.44 N 8.40 E
Murud 122 18.19 N 72.58 E
Murud, Gunong ∧ 112 3.52 N 115.30 E
Murukta 74 67.46 N 102.01 E
Murung ≃ 112 0.12 S 114.03 E
Murupara 172 38.28 S 176.42 E
Mururoa I1 6 21.52 S 138.55 W
Murutinga 246 3.26 S 59.12 W
Murvaul, Lake ⊜1 222 32.03 N 94.28 W
Murvaul Creek ≃ 194 32.05 N 94.12 W
Murwāra 124 23.51 N 80.24 E
Murwillumbah 166 28.19 S 153.24 E
Mürz ≃ 61 47.24 N 15.17 E
Mürzsteg 61 47.40 N 15.29 E
Mürzzuschlag 61 47.36 N 15.41 E
Muş 130 38.44 N 41.30 E
Muş □4 130 39.00 N 42.00 E
Musa 152 2.40 N 19.18 E
Mūša ≃, Europe 76 56.24 N 24.12 E
Musa ≃, Pap. N. Gui. 164 9.25 S 148.50 E
Mūsā, Jabal (Mount Sinai) ∧ 140 28.32 N 33.59 E
Mūsā, 'Uyūn (Springs of Moses) ⯈4 142 29.52 N 32.39 E
Musabeyli 130 39.51 N 34.37 E
Musadi 152 2.34 S 22.47 E
Musaid 146 31.35 N 25.03 E
Mūsa Khel 123 32.38 N 71.44 E
Mūsa Khel Bāzār 120 30.52 N 69.49 E
Musala ∧ 38 42.11 N 23.34 E
Musan 98 42.14 N 129.13 E
Musandam Peninsula ⯈1 128 26.18 N 56.24 E
Musao 154 7.43 S 26.17 E
Mūsā Qal'eh 120 32.22 N 64.46 E
Mūsā Qal'eh ≃ 128 32.05 N 64.51 E
Musar 272b 22.54 N 88.14 E
Musasa 154 3.21 S 31.33 E
Musashi — Iruma, Nihon 94 35.50 N 139.24 E
Musashi, Nihon 96 33.30 N 131.43 E
Musashimurayama 268 35.45 N 139.23 E
Musashino 94 35.42 N 139.34 E
Musashino-daichi ⯈1 268 35.45 N 139.35 E
Musau 58 47.32 N 10.40 E
Musay'īd 128 24.59 N 51.32 E
Musaymīr 144 13.27 N 44.37 E
Mūsāzai 120 30.23 N 66.32 E
Muscat — Masqaṭ 128 23.37 N 58.35 E
Muscat and Oman — Oman □1 118 22.00 N 58.00 E
Muscatatuck ≃ 218 38.46 N 86.10 W
Muscatatuck, Grassy Fork ≃ 218 38.45 N 85.07 W
Muscatatuck, Vernon Fork ≃ 218 38.46 N 85.54 W
Muscatine 190 41.25 N 91.03 W
Müsch 56 50.23 N 6.49 E
Mus-Chaja, gora ∧ 74 62.35 N 140.50 E
Muschu Island I 164 3.25 S 143.35 E
Muschwitz 54 51.11 N 12.07 E
Muscle Shoals 194 34.44 N 87.40 W
Musclow, Mount ∧ 182 53.17 N 127.09 W
Musclow Lake ⊜ 184 51.25 N 94.56 W
Muscoda 190 43.11 N 90.26 W
Musconetcong ≃ 210 40.36 N 75.11 W
Musconetcong, Lake ⊜ 276 40.54 N 74.42 W
Muscongus Bay ⊂ 188 43.55 N 69.20 W
Muscote Bay ⊂ 212 44.06 N 77.18 W
Muscowpetung Indian Reserve ⯈4 184 50.45 N 104.15 W
Muscoy 228 34.09 N 117.20 W
Muse 214 40.17 N 80.12 W
Musengezi ≃ 154 15.43 S 31.14 E
Musgrave, Austl. 164 14.47 S 143.30 E
Musgrave, B.C., Can. 224 48.45 N 123.32 W
Musgrave, Mount ∧ 172 43.48 S 170.43 E
Musgrave Ranges ∧ 162 26.10 S 131.50 E
Musgravetown 186 48.24 N 53.53 W
Mushā 142 27.08 N 31.18 E
Mushābani 126 22.31 N 86.27 E
Mushash, Jabal al- ∧2 142 28.54 N 31.11 E
Mushenge 152 4.32 S 21.21 E
Mushie 152 3.01 S 16.54 E
Mushima 154 14.13 S 25.05 E
Mushin 150 6.32 N 3.22 E
Mūsi ≃, India 122 16.41 N 79.40 E
Musi ≃, Indon. 112 2.20 S 104.56 E
Musicians Seamounts ⯈3 6 31.00 N 162.00 W
Muskauer Heide ⯈3 54 51.25 N 14.40 E
Muskeg ≃ 182 54.01 N 119.03 W
Muskeget Channel ≚ 207 41.25 N 70.20 W
Muskeget Island I 207 41.20 N 70.18 W
Muskeg Lake Indian Reserve ⯈4 184 52.58 N 106.57 W
Muskego 216 42.54 N 88.08 W
Muskego Lake ⊜ 216 42.53 N 88.07 W
Muskegon 216 43.14 N 86.14 W
Muskegon □6 216 43.12 N 86.08 W
Muskegon ≃ 216 43.14 N 86.20 W
Muskegon County Airport ⊠ 216 43.10 N 86.14 W
Muskegon Heights 216 43.12 N 86.14 W
Muskegon Lake ⊜ 216 43.14 N 86.17 W
Muskegon State Park ♦ 216 43.14 N 86.20 W
Muškètova, gora ∧ 88 53.35 N 113.32 E
Muskingum □6 214 40.06 N 81.51 W
Muskingum ≃ 188 39.27 N 81.30 W
Muskingum Brook ≃ 285 39.48 N 74.44 W
Muskira 124 25.40 N 79.48 E
Muskö I 40 59.00 N 18.06 E
Muskoday Indian Reserve ⯈4 184 53.06 N 105.30 W
Muskogee 196 35.44 N 95.22 W
Muskoka □6 212 45.05 N 79.03 W
Muskoka, Lake ⊜ 212 45.00 N 79.25 W
Muskoka, North Branch ≃ 212 45.02 N 79.19 W
Muskoka, South Branch ≃ 212 45.02 N 79.19 W
Muskosh Channel ≚ 212 44.55 N 79.53 W
Muskowekwan Indian Reserve ⯈4 184 51.19 N 104.06 W
Muskrat Creek ≃ 202 43.09 N 108.11 W
Muskrat Dam Lake ⊜ 184 53.25 N 91.40 W
Muskrat Lake ⊜ 190 45.40 N 76.55 W
Muskwa 182 58.45 N 122.35 W
Muskwa Lake ⊜ 182 56.09 N 114.38 W
Muslimbāgh 120 30.49 N 67.45 E
Musl'umovo 80 55.18 N 53.12 E
Musmus 132 32.32 N 35.09 E
Musocco ⯈8 266b 45.30 N 9.08 E
Musofu Mission 154 13.31 S 29.02 E
Musoma 154 1.30 S 33.48 E
Musone ≃, It. 64 45.50 N 11.55 E
Musone ≃, It. 66 43.28 N 13.38 E
Musoshi 154 11.54 S 27.46 E
Musquanousse, Lac ⊜ 186 50.22 N 61.05 W

Symbol	Deutsch	Español	Français	Português
≃ River	Fluß	Río	Rivière	Rio
≅ Canal	Kanal	Canal	Canal	Canal
∟ Waterfall, Rapids	Wasserfall, Stromschnellen	Cascada, Rápidos	Chute d'eau, Rapides	Cascata, Rápidos
≚ Strait	Meeresstraße	Estrecho	Détroit	Estreito
⊂ Bay, Gulf	Bucht, Golf	Bahía, Golfo	Baie, Golfe	Baía, Golfo
⊜ Lake, Lakes	See, Seen	Lago, Lagos	Lac, Lacs	Lago, Lagos
Swamp	Sumpf	Pantano	Marais	Pântano
Ice Features, Glacier	Eis- und Gletscherformen	Accidentes Glaciales	Formes glaciaires	Acidentes glaciares
Other Hydrographic Features	Andere Hydrographische Objekte	Otros Elementos Hidrográficos	Autres données hydrographiques	Outros acidentes hidrográficos
Submarine Features	Untermeerische Objekte	Accidentes Submarinos	Formes de relief sous-marin	Acidentes submarinos
□ Political Unit	Politische Einheit	Unidad Política	Entité politique	Unidade política
Cultural Institution	Kulturelle Institution	Institución Cultural	Institution culturelle	Instituição cultural
⊥ Historical Site	Historische Stätte	Sitio Histórico	Site historique	Sítio histórico
♦ Recreational Site	Erholungs- und Ferienort	Sitio de Recreo	Centre de loisirs	Área de Lazer
⊠ Airport	Flughafen	Aeropuerto	Aéroport	Aeroporto
Military Installation	Militäranlage	Instalación Militar	Installation militaire	Instalação militar
Miscellaneous	Verschiedenes	Misceláneo	Divers	Diversos

Musquapsink Brook ≃ 276 40.59 N 74.01 W
Musquaro, Lac ⊜ 186 50.38 N 61.05 W
Musquash ≃ 212 44.57 N 79.52 W
Musquash Brook ≃ 283 42.42 N 71.26 W
Musquashcut Pond ⊜ 283 42.13 N 70.46 W
Musquodoboit Harbour 186 44.47 N 63.09 W
Mussau Island I 164 1.30 S 149.40 E
Musselburgh 46 55.57 N 3.04 W
Musselkanaal 52 52.56 N 7.00 E
Musselshell ≃ 202 47.21 N 107.58 W
Mussende 152 10.32 S 16.05 E
Mussidan 32 45.02 N 0.22 E
Mussolo 152 9.59 S 17.19 E
Mussomeli 70 37.35 N 13.45 E
Mussoorie 124 30.27 N 78.05 E
Mussuco 152 17.08 S 19.05 E
Mussum 52 51.48 N 6.34 E
Mussuma 152 14.14 S 21.59 E
Mussy-sur-Seine 58 47.58 N 4.30 E
Mustafakemalpaşa 130 40.02 N 28.24 E
Mustafa Kemal Paşa ≃ 130 40.07 N 28.33 E
Mustafino 80 55.01 N 53.38 E
Mustahil 144 5.12 N 44.17 E
Müstair 58 46.37 N 10.27 E
Mustajevo 80 51.48 N 53.25 E
Mustajõe 76 57.59 N 26.58 E
Mustāng 124 29.11 N 83.58 E
Mustang Draw V 196 32.12 N 101.36 W
Mustang Island I 196 27.45 N 97.10 W
Mustāy 142 30.37 N 31.09 E
Musters, Lago ⊜ 254 45.27 S 69.13 W
Mustinka ≃ 198 45.45 N 96.38 W
Mustjala 76 58.28 N 22.14 E
Mustla 76 58.14 N 25.52 E
Musṭurud 273c 30.08 N 31.17 E
Mustvee 76 58.51 N 26.56 E
Musu-dan › 98 40.50 N 129.43 E
Musun 84 39.42 N 43.49 E
Müsuslü 84 40.28 N 47.55 E
Muswellbrook 166 32.16 S 150.53 E
Muszyna 30 49.21 N 20.54 E
Mūt, Miṣr 140 25.29 N 28.59 E
Mut, Tür. 130 36.39 N 33.27 E
Muta 61 46.37 N 15.10 E
Mutá, Ponta do › 255 13.52 S 38.56 W
Mu'tah 132 31.06 N 35.42 E
Mutalau 174v 18.56 S 169.50 W
Mutambara 154 19.36 S 32.33 E
Mutanchiang → Mudanjiang 89 44.35 N 129.36 E
Mutanda, Moç. 156 21.02 S 33.31 E
Mutanda, Zaïre 152 5.17 S 16.34 E
Mutanda Mission 154 12.24 S 26.16 E
Mutankiang → Mudanjiang 89 44.35 N 129.36 E
Mutarammil, Jabal al- ∧ 132 31.04 N 36.06 E
Mutare 154 18.58 S 32.40 E
Mutbīn 132 33.09 N 36.15 E
Mutějovice 54 50.09 N 13.41 E
Mutha 154 1.48 S 38.26 E
Muthill 46 56.19 N 3.50 W
Mutiko 154 1.39 S 28.12 E
Muting 164 7.23 S 140.20 E
Mutis, Gunung ∧ 112 9.34 S 124.14 E
Mutlu (Rezovska) ≃ 38 41.59 N 28.01 E
Mutoko 154 17.24 S 32.13 E
Mutombo-Mukulu 152 7.58 S 24.00 E
Mutoraj 74 61.20 N 100.30 E
Mutoto 152 5.42 S 22.42 E
Mutouchengzi 98 41.20 N 119.59 E
Mutouhao 107 28.49 N 105.04 E
Mutsamudu 157a 12.09 S 44.25 E
Mutshatsha 152 10.39 S 24.27 E
Mutsu 92 41.17 N 141.10 E
Mutsuai 268 35.08 N 139.38 E
Mutsumi 96 34.26 N 131.34 E
Mutsuura ●[8] 268 35.19 N 139.37 E
Mutsu-wan ⊂ 92 41.05 N 140.55 E
Muttaburra 166 22.36 S 144.33 E
Mutte Kopf ∧ 58 47.16 N 10.39 E
Muttenz 58 47.32 N 7.39 E
Mutters 64 47.14 N 11.23 E
Mutterstadt 56 49.26 N 8.21 E
Muttonbird Islands II 172 47.15 S 167.24 E
Muttontown 276 40.49 N 73.33 W
Muttra → Mathura 124 27.30 N 77.41 E
Mutual, Oh., U.S. 218 40.05 N 83.38 W
Mutual, Pa., U.S. 279b 40.14 N 79.30 W
Muṭūbis 142 31.18 N 30.31 E
Mutuca, Ribeirão da ≃ 256 21.36 S 45.39 W
Mutuco, Lago ⊜ 250 1.21 N 50.24 W
Mutuípe 255 13.15 S 39.31 W
Mutum 255 19.49 S 41.26 W
Mutum ≃ 246 4.25 S 68.03 W
Mutum Biyu 146 8.38 N 10.46 E
Mutumbo 152 13.14 S 17.17 E
Mutunópolis 255 13.40 S 49.15 W
Muturi 164 2.06 S 133.43 E
Muturi ≃ 164 2.13 S 133.40 E
Mututi, Ilha do I 250 0.45 S 51.00 W
Mutzig 58 48.32 N 7.28 E
Mutzschen 54 51.16 N 12.53 E
Mu Us Shamo ●[2] 102 38.45 N 109.10 E
Mūvattupula 122 9.58 N 76.35 E
Muvukoni 154 0.24 S 38.14 E
Muwopu 104 41.03 N 121.12 E
Muxaluando 152 8.07 S 14.17 E
Muxihe 100 31.03 N 115.21 E
Muxima 152 9.31 S 13.56 E
Muyaga 154 3.14 S 30.33 E
Muyang 100 27.06 N 119.34 E
Muyang ≃ 100 27.00 N 119.41 E
Muyinga 154 2.51 S 30.20 E
Muymano ≃ 248 11.27 S 69.03 W
Muy Muy 236 12.46 N 85.38 W
Muyua Island I 164 9.05 S 152.50 E
Muyuka 152 4.17 N 9.25 E
Muyumba 154 7.15 S 26.59 E
Mužač' 82 54.22 N 36.21 E
Muzaffarābād 123 34.22 N 73.28 E
Muzaffargarh 123 30.04 N 71.12 E
Muzaffarnagar 124 29.28 N 77.41 E
Muzaffarpur 124 26.07 N 85.24 E
Muzambinho 256 21.22 S 46.32 W
Muzambinho ≃ 256 21.15 S 46.26 W
Muzambo ≃ 256 21.17 S 46.16 W
Muzat ≃ 90 41.15 N 83.27 E
Muzayrīb 132 32.42 N 36.01 E
Muzbek, gora ∧ 85 40.23 N 69.39 E
Muzbel' ●[1] 86 50.15 N 70.50 E
Muzeze 152 15.03 S 17.43 E
Muzhen 100 30.43 N 117.56 E
Muži 74 65.22 N 64.40 E
Mužiči 84 43.03 N 44.59 E
Mužiksu 86 47.42 N 84.58 E
Muzillac 32 47.33 N 2.29 W
Muzkol, chrebet ⋏ 85 38.25 N 73.30 E
Muzoka 154 16.41 S 27.19 E
Muzon, Cape › 182 54.41 N 132.44 W
Muztag ∧, Zhg. 120 36.25 N 87.25 E
Muztag ∧, Zhg. 120 36.03 N 80.07 E
Muztagata ∧ 85 38.17 N 75.11 E
Muz Tau ∧ 86 43.50 N 85.40 E
Muzūrah 142 28.53 N 30.48 E
Muzzana del Turgnano 64 45.49 N 13.08 E
Mvam 152 0.13 S 9.39 E
Mvangan 152 2.38 N 11.44 E
Mvela 154 14.46 S 35.16 E
Mvengué 152 3.17 N 11.01 E
Mvolo 140 6.03 N 29.56 E
Mvomero 154 6.20 S 37.25 E
Mvoti ≃ 158 29.24 S 31.22 E
Mvoung ≃ 152 0.04 N 12.18 E
Mvouti 152 4.15 S 12.29 E
Mvuha 154 7.12 S 37.51 E
Mvuma 154 19.19 S 30.35 E
Mwadi-Kalumba 152 7.53 S 18.46 E
Mwadui 154 3.33 S 33.36 E
Mwali (Mohéli) I 157a 12.15 S 43.45 E
Mwami 154 16.40 S 29.46 E
Mwanangumune 152 15.31 S 23.30 E
Mwango 152 6.51 S 24.13 E
Mwanza, Malaŵi 154 15.37 S 34.31 E
Mwanza, Tan. 154 2.31 S 32.54 E
Mwanza, Zaïre 154 7.54 S 26.45 E
Mwanza, Zam. 152 17.02 S 24.27 E
Mwanza □[4] 154 2.45 S 32.45 E
Mwanza Gulf ⊂ 154 2.35 S 32.51 E
Mwaya, Tan. 154 9.33 S 33.57 E
Mwaya, Tan. 154 8.55 S 36.50 E
Mweelrea ∧ 48 53.38 N 9.50 W
Mwehu 154 5.44 S 26.40 E
Mweka 152 4.51 S 21.34 E
Mwemena 154 10.19 S 27.28 E
Mwenda 154 12.01 S 28.44 E
Mwendjila 152 7.12 S 18.51 E
Mwene-Ditu 152 7.03 S 23.27 E
Mwenezi 154 21.22 S 30.45 E
Mwenga 154 3.02 S 28.26 E
Mwepo 154 11.56 S 26.11 E
Mwerasandu 154 0.59 S 30.23 E
Mwereni 154 4.20 S 39.08 E
Mweru, Lake ⊜ 154 9.00 S 28.45 E
Mweru Wantipa, Lake ⊜ 154 8.45 S 29.40 E
Mweru Wantipa National Park ♦ 154 8.45 S 29.30 E
Mwetshi 152 4.42 S 22.39 E
Mwilambwe 154 8.07 S 25.00 E
Mwilitau Islands II 164 2.50 S 146.20 E
Mwimbi 154 8.39 S 31.40 E
Mwingi 154 0.56 S 38.04 E
Mwinilunga 152 11.44 S 24.26 E
Mwitikira 154 6.31 S 35.39 E
Mwombezhi ≃ 154 12.52 S 25.00 E
Myaing 110 21.37 N 94.51 E
Myājlār 120 26.15 N 70.23 E
Myakka ≃ 220 26.56 N 82.11 W
Myakka, Lake ⊜ 220 27.16 N 82.17 W
Myakka City 220 27.20 N 82.09 W
Myakka River State Park ♦ 220 27.15 N 82.17 W
Myall Lakes National Park ♦ 166 32.28 S 152.22 E
Myall Range ⋏ 170 32.58 S 151.22 E
Myanaung 110 18.17 N 95.19 E
Myanmar (Burma) □[1] 110 22.00 N 98.00 E
Myaungmya 110 16.36 N 94.56 E
Myawadi 110 16.41 N 98.31 E
Mybster 46 58.27 N 3.25 W
Myckelgensjö 26 63.34 N 17.37 E
Myebon 110 20.03 N 93.22 E
Myeik → Mergui 110 12.26 N 98.36 E
Myers, Ky., U.S. 218 38.21 N 83.57 W
Myers, N.Y., U.S. 210 42.32 N 76.32 W
Myerstown 208 40.22 N 76.19 W
Myingyan 110 21.28 N 95.23 E
Myinmoletkat Taung ∧ 110 13.28 N 98.48 E
Myitkyinā 110 25.23 N 97.24 E
Myitnge ≃ 110 21.52 N 95.59 E
Myitta 110 14.10 N 98.31 E
Myittha 110 21.25 N 96.08 E
Myittha ≃ 110 23.12 N 94.17 E
Myjava 30 48.45 N 17.34 E
Myjeldino 24 61.46 N 54.48 E
Myjlybulak 86 48.57 N 75.13 E
Mykhaylivka, Ukr. 78 49.19 N 36.28 E
Mykhaylivka, Ukr. 78 47.16 N 35.14 E
Mykhaylivka, Ukr. 83 48.44 N 37.16 E
Mykil's'ke-na-Dnipri 78 48.12 N 35.12 E
Mykolayiv, Ukr. 78 46.58 N 32.00 E
Mykolayiv, Ukr. 78 49.32 N 23.58 E
Mykolayiv □[4] 78 47.15 N 31.45 E
Mykolayivka, Ukr. 78 47.38 N 33.12 E
Mykolayivka, Ukr. 78 47.06 N 34.14 E
Mykolayivka, Ukr. 78 44.58 N 33.37 E
Mykolayivka, Ukr. 78 46.23 N 29.24 E
Mykolayivka, Ukr. 78 47.33 N 30.25 E
Mykolayivka, Ukr. 78 51.04 N 34.02 E
Mykolayivka, Ukr. 83 48.51 N 37.46 E
Mykolayivka, Ukr. 83 47.39 N 37.41 E
Mykulyntsi 78 49.24 N 25.38 E
Myla 24 65.25 N 50.48 E
Mylau 54 50.37 N 12.16 E
Myl'džino 86 59.03 N 78.29 E
Myllendonk, Schloss ⊥ 263 51.13 N 6.29 E
Myllykoski 26 60.47 N 26.48 E
Myllymäki 26 62.32 N 24.17 E
Mylor 168b 35.03 S 138.45 E
Mymensingh 124 24.45 N 90.24 E
Mynämäki 26 60.40 N 22.00 E
Mynaral 86 45.25 N 73.41 E
Mynbulak, gora ∧ 85 41.43 N 69.49 E
Mynfontein 158 30.55 S 23.57 E
Mynydd Bach ∧[2] 42 52.15 N 4.05 W
Mynydd Eppynt ∧ 42 52.05 N 3.30 W
Mynydd Hiraethog ∧ 44 53.05 N 3.33 W
Mynydd Pencarreg ∧[2] 42 52.04 N 4.04 W
Mynydd Preseli ∧ 42 51.58 N 4.42 W
Myōgata 94 35.51 N 137.02 E
Myōgi 94 36.17 N 138.49 E
Myōgi-Arafune-Saku-kōgen-kokutei-kōen ♦ 94 36.12 N 138.10 E
Myōgi-san ∧ 94 36.17 N 138.44 E
Myo-gyi 110 21.27 N 96.22 E
Myohaung 110 20.36 N 93.10 E
Myohyang-san ∧ 98 40.02 N 126.17 E
Myohyang-sanmaek ⋏ 98 40.30 N 127.00 E
Myojin-dake ∧ 270 34.57 N 135.36 E
Myōjin-san ∧ 96 33.34 N 133.04 E
Myōken-san ∧ 96 35.24 N 134.39 E
Myōken-zan ∧ 270 34.56 N 135.28 E
Myōken-zan ∧[2] 270 34.30 N 134.57 E
Myōkō 94 36.56 N 138.13 E
Myōkō-kōgen 94 36.52 N 138.12 E
Myōkō-san ∧ 94 36.52 N 138.07 E
Myŏnmong-ni ●[8] 271b 37.35 N 127.05 E
Myponga 168b 35.24 S 138.28 E
Myponga Reservoir ⊜[1] 168b 35.24 S 138.26 E
Myra ⊥ 130 36.15 N 29.54 E
Mýrdalsjökull ⊓ 24a 63.40 N 19.05 W
Myrhorod 78 49.58 N 33.36 E
Myrivs'ke 78 48.05 N 33.23 E
Myrnam 182 53.40 N 111.14 W
Myrnyy 78 50.57 N 28.34 E
Myronivka 78 49.39 N 30.59 E
Myronivs'kyy 83 48.29 N 38.17 E
Myroodah 162 18.08 S 124.16 E
Myropil' 78 50.07 N 27.41 E
Myropillya 78 51.02 N 35.16 E
Myrskylä (Mörskom) 26 60.40 N 25.51 E
Myrtle Beach 192 33.41 N 78.53 W
Myrtle Beach Air Force Base ■ 192 33.41 N 78.56 W
Myrtle Beach State Park ♦ 192 33.37 N 78.58 W
Myrtle Creek 202 43.01 N 123.17 W
Myrtle Grove 194 30.25 N 87.18 W
Myrtle Point 202 43.03 N 124.08 W
Myrtle Springs 222 32.37 N 95.56 W
Myrtletowne 204 40.47 N 124.04 W
Myrtleville 170 34.29 S 149.49 E
Myšega 82 54.31 N 37.02 E
Mysen 26 59.33 N 11.20 E
Myshuryn Rih 78 48.50 N 33.58 E
Mysia □[9] 130 39.15 N 28.00 E
Mysingen ʊ 40 59.00 N 18.15 E
Myski 86 53.42 N 87.48 E
Myškino 76 57.47 N 38.27 E
Myśla ≃ 54 52.40 N 14.29 E
Myślenice 30 49.51 N 19.56 E
Myślibórz 30 52.55 N 14.52 E
Mysłowice 30 50.15 N 19.07 E
Mysore 122 12.18 N 76.39 E
Mys Šmidta 180 68.56 N 179.26 W
Mystic, Ct., U.S. 207 41.21 N 71.58 W
Mystic, Ia., U.S. 190 40.46 N 92.56 W
Mystic ≃ 283 42.23 N 71.03 W
Mystic Seaport ⊕ 207 41.22 N 71.58 W
Mys Vchodnoj 74 73.53 N 86.43 E
Mysy 24 60.34 N 53.57 E
Mys Želanija 72 76.56 N 68.35 E
Myszków 30 50.36 N 19.20 E
Myszyniec 30 53.24 N 21.21 E
Myt 80 56.48 N 42.21 E
My Tho 110 10.21 N 106.21 E
Mytholm 262 53.44 N 2.01 W
Mytholmroyd 262 53.44 N 1.59 W
Mytilene → Mitilíni 38 39.06 N 26.32 E
Mytišči 82 55.55 N 37.46 E
Mytishchi → Mytišči 82 55.55 N 37.46 E
Mytišino 76 54.48 N 34.01 E
Mýto 60 49.47 N 13.44 E
Myton 200 40.11 N 110.03 W
Mývatn ⊜ 24a 65.37 N 16.58 W
Myzove 78 51.22 N 24.31 E
M'zab, Oued V 148 32.19 N 5.24 E
Mže ≃ 60 49.46 N 13.24 E
Mzenga 154 6.56 S 38.43 E
Mziha 154 5.54 S 37.47 E
Mzimba 154 11.52 S 33.34 E
Mzimkulu ≃ 158 30.44 S 30.28 E
Mzimvubu ≃ 158 31.38 S 29.32 E
Mzintlava ≃ 158 31.12 S 29.18 E
Mzuzu 154 11.27 S 33.55 E
Mzymta ≃ 84 43.27 N 39.56 E

N

Na I 174r 6.52 N 158.22 E
Na (Tengtiao) ≃ 110 22.05 N 103.09 E
Naab ≃ 60 49.01 N 12.02 E
Naach, Jbel ∧ 34 34.53 N 3.22 W
Naachtpunkt Brook ≃ 276 40.54 N 74.15 W
Naaldwijk 52 52.00 N 4.12 E
Naalehu 229d 19.03 N 155.35 W
Na'ām 140 9.42 N 28.27 E
Na'âma, Sebkhet en ≡ 148 33.20 N 0.16 W
Naaman Creek ≃ 285 39.48 N 75.27 W
Naaman Creek, South Branch ≃ 285 39.49 N 75.27 W
Naamans Garden 285 39.49 N 75.31 W
Naantali 26 60.27 N 22.02 E
Naarden 52 52.17 N 5.09 E
Naarn ≃ 61 48.11 N 14.49 E
Naas 48 53.13 N 6.39 W
Naas ≃ 171b 35.36 S 149.04 E
Naast, Bel. 50 50.33 N 4.05 E
Naast, Scot., U.K. 46 57.47 N 5.39 W
Na'azuz, Har ∧ 132 30.01 N 35.00 E
Nabā, Jabal an- (Mount Nebo) ∧ 132 31.46 N 35.45 E
Nababiep 156 29.36 S 17.46 E
Nabābpur 272b 22.42 N 88.12 E
Nabaganga ≃[1] 126 22.59 N 89.34 E
Nabagram 126 24.12 N 88.06 E
Nabalat Al-Ḥajanah 140 13.13 N 29.02 E
Nabari 94 34.37 N 136.05 E
Nabari ≃ 94 34.45 N 136.01 E
Nabarūh 142 31.06 N 31.18 E
Nabas 116 11.50 N 122.05 E
Nabasta 126 23.15 N 88.01 E
Nabawa 162 28.31 S 114.47 E
Nabb 218 38.36 N 85.38 W
Nabberu, Lake ⊜ 162 25.36 S 120.30 E
Nabburg 60 49.28 N 12.11 E
Nabeina 174t 1.26 N 173.05 E
Naberera 154 4.12 S 36.56 E
Naberežnoje 265b 55.57 N 37.58 E
Naberežnyje Čelny 80 55.42 N 52.19 E
Nabesna 180 62.22 N 143.00 W
Nabesna ≃ 180 63.03 N 141.52 W
Nabeul 148 36.27 N 10.44 E
Nabeul □[8] 148 36.35 N 10.45 E
Nābha 123 30.22 N 76.09 E
Nab Hill ∧[2] 262 53.47 N 1.57 W
Nabigou 152 1.12 S 9.31 E
Nabī Hārūn, Jabal an- ∧ 132 30.19 N 35.24 E
Nabileque ≃ 248 20.55 S 57.49 W
Nabire 164 3.22 S 135.29 E
Nabī Shu'ayb, Jabal an- ∧ 144 15.17 N 43.59 E
Nabisipi ≃ 186 50.14 N 62.13 W
Nabiswera 154 1.28 N 32.16 E
Nabī Yūnus, Ra's an- › 132 33.39 N 35.24 E
Nabnasset 207 42.36 N 71.25 W
Nabnasset Pond ⊜ 283 42.37 N 71.26 W
Nabogame 232 26.14 N 106.57 W
Naboomspruit 156 24.32 S 28.36 E
Nabordo 150 10.10 N 9.20 E
Nabou 150 11.27 N 2.43 W
Nabq 140 28.04 N 34.25 E
Nabua 116 13.24 N 123.22 E
Nabula 120 31.55 N 80.10 E
Nābulus 132 32.13 N 35.16 E
Nabunturan 116 7.35 N 125.58 E
Nacajuca 234 18.08 N 93.01 W
Nacala 154 14.34 S 40.41 E
Nacala-Velha 154 14.32 S 40.37 E
Načalovo 80 46.20 N 48.11 E
Nacaome 236 13.31 N 87.30 W
Nacastillo 234 19.35 N 104.55 W
Nacchie 144 7.23 N 40.10 E
Nacereddine 34 36.08 N 3.26 E
Nachabinka ≃ 265b 55.51 N 37.12 E
Nachabino 82 55.51 N 37.11 E
Naches 224 46.43 N 120.41 W
Naches ≃ 202 46.38 N 120.31 W
Nachi-katsuura 92 33.30 N 135.55 E
Nāchinda 126 21.53 N 87.46 E
Nachingwea 154 10.23 S 38.46 E
Nāchna 120 27.30 N 71.43 E
Náchod 30 50.25 N 16.10 E
Nachodka 89 42.48 N 132.52 E
Nachrodt-Wiblingwerde 263 51.19 N 7.37 E
Nächstebreck ●[8] 263 51.18 N 7.14 E
Nachterstedt 54 51.49 N 11.20 E
Nachuge 110 10.45 N 92.22 E
Nachvak Fiord ⊂[2] 176 59.03 N 63.45 W
Naci, Pil. 116 14.19 N 120.46 E
Naci, Pil. 116 6.19 N 124.46 E
Nacimiento 252 37.30 S 72.40 W
Nacimiento ≃ 226 35.49 N 120.45 W
Nacimiento, Lake ⊜[1] 226 35.45 N 121.00 W
Načinskij Golec, gora ∧ 89 52.24 N 118.53 E
Nacka 40 59.18 N 18.10 E
Naco, Méx. 232 31.20 N 109.56 W
Naco, Az., U.S. 200 31.20 N 109.56 W
Nacogdoches 222 31.36 N 94.39 W
Nacogdoches □[6] 222 31.40 N 94.45 W
Nacogdoches, Lake ⊜[1] 222 31.37 N 94.50 W
Nácori Chico 232 29.39 N 109.01 W
Nacozari de García 232 30.24 N 109.39 W
Ñacunday 252 26.01 S 54.46 W
Nada 222 29.24 N 96.23 W
Nada ●[8] 270 34.44 N 135.14 E
Nadābhānga 272b 22.24 N 88.14 E
Nadachi 94 37.09 N 138.06 E
Nadaleen Mountain ∧ 180 64.15 N 133.04 W
Nadasaki 96 34.32 N 133.52 E
Nádasd 61 46.58 N 16.37 E
Nadbai 124 27.14 N 77.12 E
Nadder ≃ 42 51.03 N 1.48 W
Nadela 34 42.58 N 7.30 W
Nadelkap → Agulhas, Cape › 158 34.52 S 20.00 E
Naden Harbour ⊂ 182 54.00 N 132.35 W
Nadeždinskoje 89 48.18 N 133.11 E
Nadi 140 18.40 N 33.42 E
Nadiād 120 22.42 N 72.52 E
Nādir, Miṣr 142 30.33 N 30.51 E
Nadir, Vir. Is., U.S. 240m 18.19 N 64.53 W
Nădlac 38 46.10 N 20.45 E
Nador 148 35.12 N 2.55 W
Nador □[4] 148 35.09 N 3.04 W
Nadporožje 76 60.28 N 34.17 E
Nadrin 56 50.10 N 5.41 E
Nadterečnaja 84 43.37 N 45.22 E
Nadvirna 78 48.38 N 24.34 E
Nadvoicy 24 63.52 N 34.15 E
Nadym 72 65.35 N 72.42 E
Nadym ≃ 74 66.12 N 72.00 E
Nadyrovo 80 54.53 N 52.28 E
Naeba-san ∧ 94 36.51 N 138.41 E
Nae-dong 98 37.16 N 126.27 E
Naejang-san Kukrip Kongwŏn ♦ 98 35.28 N 126.52 E
Naenwa 120 25.46 N 75.51 E
Nærbø 26 58.40 N 5.39 E
Næsby 41 55.25 N 10.22 E
Næstved 41 55.14 N 11.46 E
Nafada 146 11.08 N 11.20 E
Nafadji 150 12.37 N 11.37 W
Nafarros 266c 38.49 N 9.25 W
Nafāzah, 'Alam ∧[2] 142 30.30 N 29.42 E
Näfels 58 47.06 N 9.04 E
Nafī 128 24.57 N 43.42 E
Nafīshah 142 30.34 N 32.15 E
Naftalan 84 40.31 N 46.50 E
Naftan, Puntan I › 174n 15.05 N 145.45 E
Nāfūrah 146 29.20 N 21.20 E
Nafūsah, Jabal ⋏[2] 146 31.50 N 12.00 E
Nāg 120 27.24 N 65.08 E
Naga, Nihon 96 34.16 N 135.26 E
Naga, Pil. 116 13.37 N 123.11 E
Naga, Pil. 116 10.13 N 123.45 E
Nâga, Kreb en ⊥[4] 148 24.00 N 6.00 W
Naga, Oued en V 148 27.53 N 7.10 W
Nagaga 154 10.54 S 39.07 E
Nagahama, Nihon 94 35.23 N 136.16 E
Nagahama, Nihon 96 33.36 N 132.29 E
Nagahama, Nihon 174m 26.25 N 127.44 E
Naga Hills ⋏ 110 26.00 N 95.00 E
Nagai, Nihon 92 38.06 N 140.02 E
Nagai, Nihon 268 35.12 N 139.37 E
Nagai Island I 180 55.11 N 159.55 W
Nagai Park ♦ 270 34.36 N 135.31 E
Nagaizumi 94 35.08 N 138.54 E
Nāgāland □[3] 120 26.00 N 95.00 E
Nagambie 169 36.47 S 145.10 E
Nagannu-shima I 174m 26.16 N 127.33 E
Nagano 94 36.39 N 138.11 E
Nagano □[5] 94 36.00 N 138.00 E
Nagano-dam ●[6] 94 35.50 N 136.33 E
Naganohara 94 36.33 N 138.38 E
Nagao, Nihon 96 34.16 N 134.10 E
Nagao, Nihon 270 34.50 N 135.43 E
Nagao-hana › 96 35.32 N 134.01 E
Nagaoka 92 37.27 N 138.51 E
Nagaokakyō 94 34.55 N 135.42 E
Nagaon 120 26.20 N 92.40 E
Nāgappattinam 122 10.46 N 79.50 E
Nagar, India 123 32.07 N 77.10 E
Nagar, India 124 27.26 N 77.06 E
Nagara 270 34.26 N 135.44 E
Nagara ≃ 94 35.01 N 136.43 E
Nagareyama 94 35.51 N 139.54 E
Nāgārjuna Sāgar ⊜[1] 122 16.35 N 79.21 E
Nagarote 236 12.16 N 86.34 W
Nagar Pārkar 120 24.22 N 70.45 E
Nāgarpur 124 24.03 N 89.53 E
Nagar Untāri 124 24.17 N 83.30 E
Nagarzê 124 28.59 N 90.25 E
Nagas 116 13.06 N 123.18 E
Nagasaka 94 35.49 N 138.22 E
Nagasaki 92 32.48 N 129.55 E
Nagasawa 268 35.12 N 139.41 E
Nagashima 94 35.05 N 136.42 E
Naga-shima I, Nihon 96 33.49 N 132.05 E
Naga-shima I, Nihon 96 34.41 N 134.15 E
Nagashino ⊥ 94 34.56 N 137.32 E
Nagasin Lake ⊜ 190 47.44 N 83.37 W
Nagasu → Usa, Nihon 96 33.31 N 131.22 E
Nagasu, Nihon 96 32.56 N 130.27 E
Nagata ●[8] 270 34.40 N 135.09 E
Nagataki 270 34.23 N 135.20 E
Nagatino ●[8] 265b 55.41 N 37.41 E
Nagato, Nihon 94 36.15 N 138.16 E
Nagato, Nihon 96 34.21 N 131.10 E
Nagatsuda ●[8] 268 35.32 N 139.30 E
Nāgaur 120 27.12 N 73.44 E
Nāgāvali ≃ 122 18.13 N 83.56 E
Nagavskaja 80 47.47 N 42.50 E
Nagawa 94 36.05 N 137.41 E
Nagawicka Lake ⊜ 216 43.05 N 88.23 W
Nagcarlan 116 14.08 N 121.25 E
Nagda 120 23.27 N 75.25 E
Nagele 52 52.37 N 5.44 E
Nāgercoil 122 8.10 N 77.26 E
Nagi 96 35.07 N 134.11 E
Nagiba 116 13.41 N 120.53 E
Nagibino 86 55.46 N 72.43 E
Nagichot 154 4.16 N 33.34 E
Nagīna 124 29.27 N 78.27 E
Nāgirāt 126 23.38 N 89.18 E
Nagi-san ∧ 96 35.10 N 134.11 E
Nagiso 94 35.36 N 137.37 E
Nagla 272a 28.31 N 77.22 E
Naglarby 40 60.25 N 15.34 E
Nagles Mountains ⋏ 48 52.05 N 8.30 W
Nagłowice 30 50.41 N 20.06 E
Nago 174m 26.35 N 127.59 E
Nāgod 124 24.34 N 80.36 E
Nagog Pond ⊜ 283 42.31 N 71.26 W
Nagoja → Nagoya 94 35.10 N 136.55 E
Nagold 56 48.33 N 8.43 E
Nagold ≃ 56 48.52 N 8.42 E
Nagorje 76 56.55 N 38.16 E
Nagorno-Karabakh □[9] 84 40.00 N 46.40 E
Nagornyj, Ross. 74 55.58 N 124.57 E
Nagornyj, Ross. 265a 59.43 N 30.16 E
Nagorsk 24 59.18 N 50.48 E
Nagorskoje 82 56.54 N 38.06 E
Nago-wan ⊂ 174m 26.34 N 127.57 E
Nagoya 94 35.10 N 136.55 E
Nagoya-kūkō ⊠ 94 35.15 N 136.55 E
Nāgpur 120 21.09 N 79.06 E
Nagqu 120 31.34 N 92.00 E
Nagrai 123 34.23 N 72.41 E
Nāgrākāta 124 26.54 N 88.55 E
Nagrota 123 32.03 N 76.05 E
Nagu I 26 60.10 N 21.48 E
Nagua 238 19.23 N 69.50 W
Naguabo 240m 18.13 N 65.44 W
Naguilian 116 17.01 N 121.50 E
Nagumbuaya Point › 116 13.34 N 124.21 E
Naguri 94 35.53 N 139.11 E
Naguri I 122 6.39 N 72.55 E
Nagyatád 30 46.14 N 17.22 E
Nagybajom 30 46.23 N 17.31 E
Nagybánya → Baia Mare 38 47.40 N 23.35 E
Nagycenk 61 47.36 N 16.42 E
Nagyecsed 30 47.52 N 22.24 E
Nagykálló 30 47.53 N 21.51 E
Nagykanizsa 30 46.27 N 17.00 E
Nagykáta 30 47.25 N 19.45 E
Nagy-Kevély ∧[2] 264c 47.37 N 18.59 E
Nagykőrös 30 47.02 N 19.43 E
Nagy-Milic ∧ 30 48.35 N 21.28 E
Nagytarcsa 264c 47.32 N 19.17 E
Nagytétény ●[8] 264c 47.24 N 18.58 E
Nagyvarad → Oradea 38 47.03 N 21.57 E
Naha 174m 26.13 N 127.40 E
Naha Airfield ⊠ 174m 26.13 N 127.40 E
Nahabuan 112 0.49 N 114.05 E
Nahakki 123 34.25 N 71.20 E
Nahalal 132 32.41 N 35.12 E
Naḥal 'Oz 132 31.28 N 34.30 E
Naḥam 132 31.46 N 35.00 E
Nāhan 124 30.33 N 77.18 E
Nahang (Nihing) ≃ 128 26.00 N 62.44 E
Nahanni National Park ♦ 180 61.40 N 126.00 W
Nahant 207 42.25 N 70.55 W
Nahant Bay ⊂ 207 42.27 N 70.55 W
Nahant Beach ⊥[2] 283 42.27 N 70.56 W
Nahari 96 33.25 N 134.01 E
Nahari ≃ 96 33.25 N 134.01 E
Nahariyya 132 33.00 N 35.05 E
Naharpur ●[8] 272a 28.42 N 77.07 E
Nahāta 126 23.20 N 89.31 E
Nahāvand 128 34.12 N 48.22 E
Nahcotta 224 46.30 N 124.02 W
Nahe 89 48.28 N 124.52 E
Nahe ≃ 56 49.58 N 7.57 E
Naḥf 132 32.56 N 35.19 E
Nahirne 78 45.26 N 28.27 E
Nahma 190 45.50 N 86.39 W
Nahmer ●[8] 263 51.20 N 7.35 E
Nahmer ≃ 263 51.21 N 7.35 E
Nahoe 174x 9.45 S 138.55 W
Nahoï, Cap › 175f 14.39 S 166.37 E
Nahol'chyk 83 48.01 N 39.04 E
Nahol'na ≃ 83 47.57 N 38.58 E
Nahol'no-Tarasivka 83 48.00 N 39.29 E
Nahon ≃ 50 47.14 N 1.39 E
Nahrīn 120 36.01 N 69.06 E
Nahr Ouassel, Oued ≃ 148 35.42 N 2.33 E
Nahualate ≃ 236 14.03 N 91.32 W
Nahuatzén 234 19.42 N 101.50 W
Nahuel Huapi 254 41.03 S 71.09 W
Nahuel Huapi, Lago ⊜ 254 40.58 S 71.30 W
Nahuel Huapi, Parque Nacional ♦ 254 41.00 S 71.48 W
Nahuel Niyeu 254 40.30 S 66.33 W
Nahunta 192 31.12 N 81.58 W
Nāhyā 142 30.03 N 31.07 E
Naia ≃ 66 42.46 N 12.22 E
Naica 232 27.53 N 105.31 W
Naicam 184 52.25 N 104.30 W
Nai Ga 102 27.48 N 97.30 E
Naiguatá, Pico ∧ 286c 10.33 N 66.46 W
Naihāti, Bngl. 126 22.49 N 89.37 E
Naihāti, India 126 22.54 N 88.25 E
Naij Gol ≃, Zhg. 102 36.20 N 94.49 E
Naij Gol ≃, Zhg. 120 36.20 N 94.49 E
Naikliu 112 9.30 S 123.50 E
Naikoon Provincial Park ♦ 182 53.50 N 131.50 W
Naila 54 50.19 N 11.42 E
Nailin 98 41.53 N 119.15 E
Nails Creek ≃ 222 30.16 N 96.44 W
Nailsea 42 51.26 N 2.43 W
Nailsworth 42 51.42 N 2.14 W
Nā'im, Jabal an- ∧ 132 31.04 N 35.55 E
Naiman Qi 89 42.55 N 120.43 E
Nain, Nf., Can. 176 56.32 N 61.41 W
Nā'īn, Īrān 128 32.52 N 53.05 E
Nain ⊜ 40 60.14 N 13.50 E
Naini Tāl 124 29.23 N 79.27 E
Nainpur 124 22.26 N 80.07 E
Nairai I 175g 17.49 S 179.24 E
Nairn, Scot., U.K. 46 57.35 N 3.53 W
Nairn, La., U.S. 194 29.27 N 89.38 W
Nairn ≃ 46 57.35 N 3.52 W
Nairne 168b 35.02 S 138.54 E
Nairobi 154 1.17 S 36.49 E
Nairobi Airport ⊠ 276 41.08 N 74.21 W
Nairobi National Park ♦ 154 1.24 S 36.50 E
Naissaar I 76 59.33 N 24.32 E
Naita ∧ 144 5.30 N 35.18 E
Naitamba Island I 175g 17.31 S 179.17 W
Naivasha 154 0.43 S 36.26 E
Naivasha, Lake ⊜ 154 0.46 S 36.21 E
Naivos 114 2.30 N 96.10 E
Naizifang 105 39.36 N 116.47 E
N'aizishen 89 43.41 N 127.29 E
Najac 32 44.13 N 1.59 E
Najafābād 128 32.37 N 51.21 E
Najafgarh ●[8] 272a 28.37 N 76.59 E
Najafgarh Drain ≍ 272a 28.43 N 77.14 E
Najasa ≃ 240p 20.42 N 77.55 W
Najd □[8] 144 21.00 N 46.00 E
Najd □[9] 118 25.00 N 44.30 E
Nájera 34 42.25 N 2.44 W
Najhā 132 33.23 N 36.22 E
Naj' Ḥammādī 140 26.03 N 32.15 E
Najībābād 124 29.38 N 78.20 E
Najin 98 42.15 N 130.18 E
Najinkouzi 89 50.23 N 126.57 E
Najio 270 34.50 N 135.18 E
Najstenjarvi 24 62.16 N 32.38 E
Naju 98 35.03 N 126.43 E
Najza, gora ∧ 86 49.24 N 70.42 E
Naka, Nihon 94 36.27 N 140.30 E
Naka, Nihon 96 35.02 N 134.55 E
Naka, Nihon 268 35.49 N 140.03 E
Naka, Nihon 270 34.50 N 135.48 E
Naka, Nihon 270 34.42 N 135.45 E
Naka, Nihon 270 34.50 N 135.56 E
Naka ●[8] 268 35.27 N 139.39 E
Naka ≃, Nihon 94 36.20 N 140.36 E
Naka ≃, Nihon 96 33.56 N 134.42 E
Naka ≃, Nihon 268 35.39 N 139.51 E
Nakadōri-shima I 92 32.57 N 129.04 E
Nakagami 268 35.49 N 139.21 E
Nakagawa 94 35.38 N 137.56 E
Nakagawa ●[8] 268 35.33 N 139.35 E
Nakagō 94 36.58 N 138.14 E
Nakagusuku 174m 26.15 N 127.49 E
Nakagusuku-wan ⊂ 174m 26.14 N 127.53 E
Nakagyō ●[8] 270 35.01 N 135.45 E
Nakaheji 96 33.47 N 135.31 E
Nakai 94 35.20 N 139.14 E
Nakaizu 94 34.57 N 139.00 E
Nakajima, Nihon 94 37.07 N 136.51 E
Nakajima, Nihon 96 33.58 N 132.07 E
Nakajima, Nihon 268 35.26 N 139.56 E
Nakajima, Nihon 268 35.18 N 139.58 E
Naka-jima I 96 33.58 N 132.37 E
Nakajō, Nihon 92 38.03 N 139.24 E
Nakajō, Nihon 94 36.36 N 138.02 E
Nakakawane 94 35.03 N 138.05 E
Nāka Khārari 120 25.15 N 66.44 E
Nakalele Point › 229a 21.02 N 156.35 W
Nākālia 126 24.02 N 89.40 E
Nakama, Nihon 96 33.50 N 130.43 E
Nakama, Nihon 174m 26.16 N 127.44 E
Nakaminato 94 36.21 N 140.36 E
Nakamura 96 32.59 N 132.56 E
Nakanai Mountains ⋏ 164 5.35 S 151.10 E
Nakano, Nihon 94 36.45 N 138.22 E
Nakano, Nihon 268 35.20 N 139.54 E
Nakano, Nihon 270 34.58 N 135.58 E
Nakano ●[8] 268 35.42 N 139.42 E
Nakanobu ●[8] 268 35.36 N 139.43 E
Nakanojō 94 36.35 N 138.51 E
Nakano-shima I 93b 29.49 N 129.52 E
Nakanoshima-suidō ʊ 93b 29.44 N 129.49 E
Nakanougan-jima I 175d 24.11 N 123.33 E
Nakaosu 174m 26.37 N 128.02 E
Nakaōzō ●[8] 270 34.51 N 135.11 E
Nakape 140 5.47 N 28.37 E
Nakashibetsu 92a 43.33 N 144.59 E
Nākāsipāra 126 23.35 N 88.21 E
Nakasongola 154 1.19 N 32.28 E
Nakatō 268 35.45 N 139.24 E
Nakatomi, Nihon 94 35.28 N 138.26 E
Nakatomi, Nihon 268 35.49 N 139.30 E
Nakatosa 96 33.20 N 133.14 E
Nakatsu, Nihon 96 33.34 N 131.13 E
Nakatsu, Nihon 96 33.57 N 135.18 E
Nakatsu, Nihon 268 35.30 N 139.20 E
Nakatsu ≃ 94 37.00 N 138.39 E
Nakatsue 96 33.08 N 130.56 E
Nakatsugawa 94 35.29 N 137.30 E
Nakatsumine-yama ∧ 96 33.58 N 134.31 E
Nakauchigami 270 34.56 N 135.10 E
Naka-umi ⊂ 96 35.28 N 133.12 E
Nakayama, Nihon 96 33.38 N 132.42 E
Nakayama, Nihon 96 35.31 N 133.35 E
Nakayama ●[8] 268 35.31 N 139.33 E
Nakayama ≃ 96 33.55 N 133.08 E
Nakazato, Nihon 94 36.05 N 138.50 E
Nakazato, Nihon 94 37.03 N 138.42 E
Nakazuma 268 35.58 N 139.35 E
Nakéty 175f 21.33 S 166.03 E
Nakfa 144 16.43 N 38.32 E
Nakhola 120 26.07 N 92.11 E
Nakhon Nayok 110 14.12 N 101.13 E
Nakhon Pathom 110 13.49 N 100.03 E
Nakhon Phanom 110 17.24 N 104.47 E
Nakhon Ratchasima 110 14.58 N 102.07 E
Nakhon Sawan 110 15.41 N 100.07 E
Nakhon Si Thammarat 110 8.26 N 99.58 E
Nakhon Thai 110 17.07 N 100.50 E
Nakhtarana 120 23.20 N 69.15 E
Nakina 176 50.10 N 86.42 W
Nakkaş ≃ 267b 41.00 N 28.45 E
Nakło nad Notecią 30 53.08 N 17.35 E
Naknek 180 58.44 N 157.02 W
Naknek Lake ⊜ 180 58.40 N 156.15 W
Nako 150 10.38 N 3.04 W
Nakodar 123 31.07 N 75.29 E
Nakonde 154 9.20 S 32.42 E
Nakoso-no-seki-ato ⊥ 94 36.53 N 140.46 E
Nakou 100 27.09 N 117.38 E
Nakskov 41 54.50 N 11.09 E
Nakskov Fjord ⊂ 41 54.50 N 11.02 E
Näkten ⊜ 26 62.52 N 14.38 E
Naktong-gang ≃ 98 35.07 N 128.57 E
Nakūr 124 29.55 N 77.18 E
Nakuru 154 0.17 S 36.04 E
Nakuru, Lake ⊜ 154 0.22 S 36.05 E
Nakusp 182 50.15 N 117.48 W
Nāl ≃ 120 26.02 N 65.19 E
Nālāgarh 123 31.03 N 76.43 E
Nalajch 88 47.45 N 107.16 E
Nālanda 124 25.07 N 85.25 E
Nalao 102 24.22 N 105.23 E
Nalázi 156 24.03 S 33.20 E
Nalbāri 120 26.25 N 91.26 E
Nalcayec, Isla I 254 46.06 S 73.49 W
Nalchik → Nal'čik 84 43.29 N 43.37 E
Nālchiti 124 22.38 N 90.17 E
Nal'čik 84 43.29 N 43.37 E
Naldānga 126 23.26 N 89.11 E
Nāldera 123 31.11 N 77.11 E
Näldsjön ⊜ 26 63.23 N 14.17 E
Nałęczów 30 51.18 N 22.11 E
Nalgonda 122 17.03 N 79.16 E
Nalgora 126 22.52 N 90.39 E
Nalhāti 126 24.18 N 87.49 E
Naliagrām 126 23.36 N 89.37 E
Naliang 102 21.43 N 107.51 E
Nālikul 272b 22.49 N 88.11 E
Nalinnes 50 50.19 N 4.26 E
Nalisan 104 42.06 N 122.12 E
Nallamalla Hills ⋏ 122 15.30 N 78.45 E
Nalles (Nals) 64 46.32 N 11.12 E
Nallıhan 130 40.11 N 31.21 E
Na Logu 64 46.23 N 13.45 E
Nalolo 152 15.35 S 23.07 E
Nalón ≃ 34 43.32 N 6.04 W
Nalong 102 23.35 N 106.05 E
Nalusa 152 14.55 S 22.13 E
Nālūt 146 31.52 N 10.59 E
Nalžovské Hory 60 49.20 N 13.33 E
Nam ≃ 110 21.33 N 98.38 E
Namaacha 156 25.58 S 32.01 E
Namachire 152 11.26 S 22.43 E
Namacunde 152 17.18 S 15.50 E
Namacurra 154 17.29 S 37.01 E
Namadgi National Park ♦ 171b 35.45 S 148.57 E
Namak, Daryācheh-ye ⊜ 128 34.30 N 51.50 E
Namak, Kavīr-e ●[2] 128 34.45 N 57.45 E
Namakan Lake ⊜ 190 48.27 N 92.35 W
Nāmakkal 122 11.14 N 78.10 E
Namaksār, Kowl-e ⊜ 128 34.00 N 64.30 E
Namakula 174v 18.57 S 169.54 W
Namaland □[5] 156 25.50 S 18.00 E
Namamugi ●[8] 268 35.29 N 139.41 E
Namanga 154 2.33 S 36.46 E
Namangan 85 41.00 N 71.40 E
Namangan □[4] 85 41.00 N 71.15 E
Namanyere 154 7.31 S 31.03 E
Namapa 154 13.43 S 39.50 E
Namarodu, Cape › 164 3.38 S 152.30 E
Namarrói 154 15.58 S 36.55 E
Namasagali 154 1.01 N 32.57 E
Namatanai 164 3.40 S 152.25 E
Nambe Indian Reservation ●[4] 200 35.52 N 105.57 W
Namber 164 1.04 S 134.49 E
Nambi 162 28.54 S 121.41 E
Nambour 166 26.38 S 152.58 E
Nambouwalu 175g 16.59 S 178.42 E
Nambuangongo 152 8.01 S 14.12 E
Nambucca Heads 166 30.39 S 153.00 E
Nam Can 110 8.46 N 104.59 E
Namcha Barwa → Namjagbarwa Feng ∧ 102 29.38 N 95.04 E
Namch'ang 98 35.26 N 129.16 E
Nam Co ⊜ 120 30.42 N 90.30 E
Namdae-ch'ŏn ≃ 98 40.26 N 128.57 E
Namdanak 85 41.11 N 69.42 E
Nam Dinh 110 20.25 N 106.10 E
Nämdö I 40 59.12 N 18.41 E
Nämdöfjärden ʊ 40 59.12 N 18.34 E
Nam Du, Quan Dao II 110 9.42 N 104.22 E
Namegawa 94 36.04 N 139.22 E
Nameh 112 2.34 N 116.21 E
Nameigos Lake ⊜ 190 48.46 N 84.43 W
Namekagon ≃ 190 46.05 N 92.06 W
Namen → Namur 56 50.28 N 4.52 E
Namerikawa 94 36.46 N 137.20 E
Náměšť 61 49.12 N 16.10 E
Nametil 154 15.43 S 39.21 E
Namew Lake ⊜ 184 54.13 N 101.56 W
Nam-gang ≃ 98 39.03 N 125.52 E
Namhae 98 34.50 N 127.54 E
Namhae-do I 98 34.48 N 127.57 E
Namhan-gang ≃ 98 37.31 N 127.18 E
Namhkam 110 23.50 N 97.41 E
Namho-ri 98 38.07 N 125.10 E
Namhsan 110 22.58 N 97.10 E
Namiai 94 35.22 N 137.41 E
Namib Desert ●[2] 156 23.00 S 15.00 E
Namibe 152 15.10 S 12.09 E
Namibe □[5] 152 15.20 S 12.30 E
Namibia □[1], Afr. 138 22.00 S 17.00 E
Namibia □[1], Afr. 156 22.00 S 17.00 E
Namibie → Namibia □[1] 156 22.00 S 17.00 E
Namib-Naukluft Park ♦ 156 23.30 S 15.30 E

Symbols in the index entries represent the broad categories identified in the key at the right. Symbols with superior numbers (⋏[1]) identify subcategories (see complete key on page I · 1).

Symbole im Register stellen die rechts im Schlüssel erklärten Kategorien dar. Symbole mit hochgestellten Ziffern (⋏[1]) bezeichnen Unterabteilungen einer Kategorie (vgl. vollständiger Schlüssel auf Seite I · 1).

Los símbolos incluídos en el texto del índice representan las grandes categorías identificadas con la clave a la derecha. Los símbolos con numeros en su parte superior (⋏[1]) identifican las subcategorías (véase la clave completa en la página I · 1).

Les symboles de l'index représentent les catégories indiquées dans la légende à droite. Les symboles suivis d'un indice (⋏[1]) représentent des sous-catégories (voir légende complète à la page I · 1).

Os símbolos incluídos no texto do índice representam as grandes categorias identificadas com a chave à direita. Os símbolos com números em sua parte superior (⋏[1]) identificam as subcategorias (veja-se a chave completa à página I · 1).

	English	Deutsch	Español	Français	Português
∧	Mountain	Berg	Montaña	Montagne	Montanha
⋏	Mountains	Gebirge	Montañas	Montagnes	Montanhas
)(	Pass	Paß	Paso	Col	Passo
V	Valley, Canyon	Tal, Cañon	Valle, Cañón	Vallée, Canyon	Vale, Canhão
≚	Plain	Ebene	Llano	Plaine	Planície
›	Cape	Kap	Cabo	Cap	Cabo
I	Island	Insel	Isla	Île	Ilha
II	Islands	Inseln	Islas	Îles	Ilhas
⊥	Other Topographic Features	Andere Topographische Objekte	Otros Elementos Topográficos	Autres données topographiques	Outros acidentes topográficos

ESPAÑOL — Nombre | Página | Lat.°′ | Long.°′ W = Oeste

FRANÇAIS — Nom | Page | Lat.°′ | Long.°′ W = Ouest

PORTUGUÊS — Nome | Página | Lat.°′ | Long.°′ W = Oeste

Nombre	Página	Lat.°′	Long.°′ W = Oeste
Namie	92	37.29 N	141.00 E
Namies	158	29.18 S	19.13 E
Namīn	128	38.25 N	48.30 E
Naminga	88	56.33 N	118.41 E
Namjagbarwa Feng ʌ	102	29.38 N	95.04 E
Nāmja La)(	124	29.27 N	82.34 E
Namji-ri	98	35.23 N	128.29 E
Nāmkhāna	126	21.46 N	88.14 E
Nam Kwo Chau I	271d	22.15 N	114.21 E
Namlan	110	22.15 N	97.24 E
Nāmlāng ≃	124	29.28 N	82.50 E
Namlea	164	3.18 S	127.06 E
Namling	120	29.41 N	89.04 E
Namlos	58	47.21 N	10.40 E
Nam Ngum Reservoir ⊜[1]	110	18.30 N	102.40 E
Namnoi, Khao ʌ	110	10.36 N	98.38 E
Namo	112	1.24 S	119.57 E
Namoi ≃	166	30.00 S	148.07 E
Namoluk I[1]	14	5.55 N	153.08 E
Namonuito I[1]	14	8.46 N	150.02 E
Namorik I[1]	14	5.36 N	168.07 E
Namoruputh	154	4.34 N	35.57 E
Namounou	150	11.52 N	1.42 E
Namous, Oued en V	148	31.00 N	0.15 W
Namoya	154	4.01 S	27.34 E
Nampa, Ab., Can.	182	56.02 N	117.08 W
Nampa, Id., U.S.	202	43.32 N	116.33 W
Nampala	150	15.17 N	5.33 W
Nam Pat	110	17.43 N	100.41 E
Nampawng	110	22.45 N	97.52 E
Nam Phan □[9]	110	11.00 N	107.00 E
Nam Phong	110	16.42 N	102.52 E
Nampicuan	116	15.44 N	120.38 E
Namp'o	98	38.45 N	125.23 E
Nampont-Saint-Martin	50	50.21 N	1.45 E
Namp'ot'ae-san ʌ	98	41.44 N	128.24 E
Nampuecha	154	13.59 S	40.18 E
Nampula	154	15.07 S	39.15 E
Nampula □[5]	154	15.00 S	39.00 E
Namsang	110	20.53 N	97.43 E
Namsan Park ♦	271b	37.34 N	126.59 E
Namsanyŏng-ni	98	38.59 N	127.26 E
Namsen ≃	24	64.27 N	11.28 E
Namsi	98	39.54 N	124.36 E
Namsos	24	64.29 N	11.30 E
Nam Tok	110	14.14 N	99.04 E
Namtu	110	23.05 N	97.24 E
Namu	182	51.49 N	127.52 W
Namu I[1]	14	8.00 N	168.10 E
Namuka-I-Lau I	175g	18.51 S	178.38 W
Namúli, Serra ⩘	154	15.15 S	37.08 E
Namur, Bel.	56	50.28 N	4.52 E
Namur, P.Q., Can.	206	45.54 N	74.56 W
Namur □[4]	56	50.20 N	4.50 E
Namuruputh	154	4.34 N	35.57 E
Namutoni	156	18.49 S	16.55 E
Namwala	154	15.45 S	26.26 E
Namwera	154	14.22 S	35.30 E
Namwŏn	98	35.25 N	127.21 E
Namyang, C.M.I.K.	98	42.57 N	129.53 E
Namyang, Taehan	98	37.14 N	126.44 E
Namyit Island I	108	10.11 N	114.22 E
Namysłów	30	51.05 N	17.42 E
Nan	110	18.47 N	100.47 E
Nan ≃, Thai	110	15.42 N	100.09 E
Nan ≃, Zhg.	100	28.15 N	120.43 E
Nana ≃	152	5.00 N	15.50 E
Nana Barya ≃	146	7.59 N	17.43 E
Nana Barya, Réserve de Faune de la ✦[4]	146	7.30 N	17.30 E
Nanacamilpa	234	19.29 N	98.33 W
Nanaimo	224	49.10 N	123.56 W
Nanaimo ≃	224	49.08 N	123.54 W
Nanaimo Lakes ⊜	224	49.07 N	124.11 W
Nānakheri ✦[8]	272a	28.31 N	76.59 E
Nana Kru	150	4.50 N	8.44 W
Nanakuli	229c	21.23 N	158.09 W
Nanam	98	41.43 N	129.41 E
Nana-Mambéré □[5]	152	5.30 N	15.30 E
Nan'an	100	24.58 N	118.23 E
Nan'anba	107	28.46 N	104.38 E
Nanango	166	26.40 S	152.00 E
Nanantun	110	24.45 N	95.41 E
Nanao, Nihon	94	37.03 N	136.58 E
Nanao, T'aiwan	100	24.28 N	121.48 E
Nan'ao, Zhg.	100	23.27 N	117.02 E
Nan'ao Dao I	100	23.26 N	117.03 E
Nanao-wan c	94	37.06 N	137.00 E
Nanas Channel ʯ	271c	1.25 N	103.58 E
Nanatsu-jima II	92	37.36 N	136.53 E
Nanatsuka	94	36.44 N	136.41 E
Nanay ≃	246	3.42 S	73.16 W
Nanba	102	32.20 N	104.58 E
Nanbaita	105	38.58 N	115.39 E
Nanbaixia	98	35.45 N	117.23 E
Nanbaozhen	106	31.32 N	121.37 E
Nanbu, Nihon	94	35.17 N	138.27 E
Nanbu, Zhg.	102	31.23 N	106.02 E
Nancaicun	105	39.28 N	117.01 E
Nancefield	273d	26.17 S	27.53 E
Nancha	89	47.08 N	129.19 E
Nanchang, Zhg.	100	28.41 N	115.53 E
Nanchang (Liantang), Zhg.	100	28.34 N	115.56 E
Nancheng, Zhg.	100	25.39 N	118.26 E
Nancheng, Zhg.	100	27.35 N	116.40 E
Nancheng → Hanzhong, Zhg.	102	33.08 N	107.02 E
Nanching → Nanjing	106	32.03 N	118.47 E
Nanchital	234	18.04 N	94.24 W
Nanchong	107	30.48 N	106.04 E
Nanchuan	102	29.08 N	107.07 E
Nanchuang	100	24.36 N	120.59 E
Nanch'ung → Nanchong	107	30.48 N	106.04 E
Nancowry Island I	110	7.59 N	93.32 E
Nancroix	62	45.32 N	6.46 E
Nancun, Zhg.	98	36.32 N	120.06 E
Nancun, Zhg.	98	39.46 N	114.07 E
Nancy	58	48.41 N	6.12 E
Nanda Devi ʌ	124	30.23 N	79.59 E
Nāndāha	272b	22.50 N	88.17 E
Nandaime	236	11.46 N	86.03 W
Nanda Kot ʌ	124	30.17 N	80.05 E
Nandan	96	34.15 N	134.43 E
Nandarivatu	175g	17.34 S	177.58 E
Nandashan	100	29.01 N	112.43 E
Nānded	122	19.09 N	77.20 E
Nāndgaon, India	122	20.19 N	74.39 E
Nāndgaon, India	272c	18.58 N	73.08 E
Nandi	175g	17.48 S	177.25 E
Nandi Bay c	175g	17.44 S	177.25 E
Nandi Drug ʌ	122	13.25 N	77.42 E
Nandigrām	126	22.01 N	87.58 E
Nandikotkūr	122	15.52 N	78.16 E
Nanding ≃, Asia	102	23.25 N	98.41 E
Nanding ≃, Asia	110	23.25 N	98.41 E
Nandlstadt	60	48.32 N	11.48 E
Nandom	150	10.51 N	2.45 W
N'andoma	24	61.40 N	40.12 E
Nandu	106	31.27 N	119.19 E
Nandu ≃	110	20.04 N	110.22 E
Nanduluohe	105	40.11 N	117.13 E
Nāndūra	122	20.50 N	76.27 E
Nandurbār	122	21.22 N	74.15 E
Nanduri	175g	16.27 S	179.09 E
Nandy	261	48.35 N	2.34 E
Nandyāl	122	15.29 N	78.29 E
Nanfangquan	106	31.26 N	120.16 E
Nanfen	104	41.06 N	123.44 E
Nanfeng, Zhg.	100	27.15 N	116.32 E
Nanfeng, Zhg.	100	29.16 N	116.32 E
Nangabadau	112	1.02 N	111.54 E
Nangade	154	11.05 S	39.36 E
Nanga Eboko	152	4.41 N	12.22 E
Nangahale	115b	8.34 S	122.32 E
Nangakelawit	112	0.23 N	112.26 E
Nāngal	123	31.24 N	76.14 E
Nangalangki	112	1.15 S	111.40 E
Nangalao Island I	116	11.27 N	120.11 E
Nangal Dewat ✦[8]	272a	28.33 N	77.06 E
Nangamau	112	0.06 S	111.55 E
Nangamesi, Teluk c	115b	9.37 S	120.20 E
Nangamuntatai	112	0.22 S	112.23 E
Nangang	100	31.22 N	116.59 E
Nan Gang c	100	23.30 N	117.00 E
Nan'gangwa	105	39.46 N	116.09 E
Nangaobat	112	0.57 N	113.13 E
Nangaocun	105	39.25 N	115.58 E
Nanga Parbat ʌ	123	35.15 N	74.36 E
Nangapinoh	112	0.20 S	111.44 E
Nangaraun	112	0.38 N	113.11 E
Nangarhār □[4]	120	34.15 N	70.30 E
Nangatayap	112	1.32 S	110.34 E
Nangezhuang	105	39.31 N	116.23 E
Nanggala Hill ʌ	175e	8.16 S	157.43 E
Nanggulan	115a	7.46 S	110.12 E
Nangi	272b	22.31 N	88.13 E
Nangin	110	10.31 N	98.31 E
Nangis	50	48.33 N	3.00 E
Nangka ≃	269f	14.41 N	121.06 E
Nanglal ≃	126	24.20 N	90.04 E
Nangloi ✦[8], India	272a	28.41 N	77.05 E
Nāngloi ✦[8], India	272a	28.40 N	77.02 E
Nangloi Jat ✦[8]	272a	28.41 N	77.04 E
Nangnim	98	40.58 N	127.08 E
Nangnim-sanmaek ⩘	98	40.00 N	127.00 E
Nangō, Nihon	92	31.32 N	131.23 E
Nangō, Nihon	94	37.13 N	139.33 E
Nangola	150	12.40 N	6.36 W
Nangoma	152	15.30 S	23.08 E
Nangong	98	37.24 N	115.22 E
Nangou	89	43.17 N	128.37 E
Nangō-yama-tunnel ✦[6]	94	35.12 N	139.10 E
Nangqên	102	32.22 N	96.21 E
Nang Rong	110	14.38 N	102.48 E
Nanguan	102	37.00 N	112.31 E
Nangweshi	152	16.26 S	23.17 E
Nanhai → Foshan	100	23.03 N	113.09 E
Nanhai → South China Sea ⊤[2]	108	10.00 N	113.00 E
Nanhe	98	37.01 N	114.41 E
Nanhedian	100	33.23 N	112.25 E
Nanhekan	107	30.24 N	103.27 E
Nanhezhao	105	39.05 N	115.56 E
Nanhsi	100	23.11 N	120.29 E
Nanhu	102	39.57 N	94.13 E
Nanhua	102	25.14 N	101.13 E
Nanhualou	104	42.30 N	123.53 E
Nanhuang	98	36.58 N	121.47 E
Nanhui	106	31.03 N	121.45 E
Nan Hulsan Hu ⊜	102	36.39 N	96.20 E
Nanhuta Shan ʌ	100	24.22 N	121.26 E
Nanhutou	89	43.44 N	128.55 E
Nanika Lake ⊜	182	53.45 N	127.40 W
Naniwa ✦[8]	270	34.39 N	135.30 E
Nanjangūd	122	12.06 N	76.42 E
Nanjemoy	208	38.27 N	77.13 W
Nanjemoy Creek c	208	38.25 N	77.07 W
Nanji I	100	27.28 N	121.04 E
Nanjiang, Zhg.	100	32.44 N	120.52 E
Nanjiang, Zhg.	102	32.33 N	107.30 E
Nanjiangqiao	100	28.58 N	113.44 E
Nanjie	107	29.11 N	105.00 E
Nanjing, Zhg.	100	24.41 N	114.25 E
Nanjing, Zhg.	100	24.32 N	117.22 E
Nanjing (Nanking), Zhg.	106	32.03 N	118.47 E
Nanjing, Zhg.	107	28.49 N	105.12 E
Nanjinyi	107	30.02 N	104.42 E
Nanjirinji	154	9.39 S	39.04 E
Nanjō	94	35.50 N	136.13 E
Nanjuma ≃	105	39.24 N	115.43 E
Nankan	96	33.03 N	130.32 E
Nankāna Sāhib	123	31.27 N	73.42 E
Nankang	100	25.42 N	114.44 E
Nankang ✦[8]	269d	25.03 N	121.36 E
Nankin	214	40.55 N	82.17 W
Nanking → Nanjing	106	32.03 N	118.47 E
Nanko-kōen ♦	94	37.05 N	140.14 E
Nankoku	96	33.39 N	133.44 E
Nankou	100	26.38 N	117.24 E
Nankouzhen	105	40.14 N	116.07 E
Nanku	106	31.06 N	120.37 E
Nankye	110	14.20 N	98.11 E
Nanle	98	36.04 N	115.10 E
Nanling, Zhg.	100	30.56 N	118.20 E
Nanling, Zhg.	100	23.21 N	115.25 E
Nanling, Zhg.	104	41.37 N	120.56 E
Nan Ling ⩘	90	25.00 N	112.00 E
Nanlinqiao	100	29.35 N	114.19 E
Nanliu ≃	102	21.38 N	109.00 E
Nanliucun	105	40.10 N	116.04 E
Nanlongba	102	28.02 N	107.31 E
Nanlou Shan ʌ	89	43.27 N	126.42 E
Nanma	102	24.17 N	101.03 E
Nanmatang	106	32.18 N	120.38 E
Nanmeng	105	39.11 N	116.22 E
Nanmoku	94	36.10 N	138.44 E
Nannerch	262	53.13 N	3.15 W
Nannine	162	26.53 S	118.20 E
Nanning	102	22.48 N	108.20 E
Nanniwan	102	36.29 N	109.40 E
Nannō	94	35.13 N	136.36 E
Nannup	162	33.59 S	115.45 E
Nanny ≃	48	53.40 N	6.14 W
Na Noi	110	18.19 N	100.43 E
Nānole ✦[8]	272c	19.01 N	72.55 E
Nanoose Bay	224	49.16 N	124.12 W
Nanoose Harbour c	224	49.20 N	124.10 W
Nanoshi	272c	18.56 N	73.05 E
Nanowin ≃	184	53.13 N	97.13 W
Nanpan ≃, Zhg.	102	25.07 N	106.00 E
Nanpan ≃, Zhg.	102	24.34 N	103.04 E
Nānpāra	124	27.52 N	81.30 E
Nanpengchang	107	29.21 N	106.38 E
Nanpi	98	38.02 N	116.42 E
Nanpiao	104	41.12 N	120.39 E
Nanping, Zhg.	89	43.24 N	129.05 E
Nanping, Zhg.	98	42.16 N	129.09 E
Nanping, Zhg.	100	26.38 N	118.10 E
Nanping, Zhg.	102	21.50 N	107.28 E
Nanping, Zhg.	102	33.07 N	104.20 E
Nanpingji	100	33.30 N	116.51 E
Nanpu	105	39.16 N	118.12 E
Nanpu ≃	100	27.02 N	118.18 E
Nanqingtuo	105	39.37 N	117.53 E
Nanqu	104	40.44 N	122.08 E
Nanquan	98	36.24 N	120.17 E
Nanri Dao I	100	25.13 N	119.30 E
Nansa ≃	34	43.22 N	4.29 W
Nansei	92	34.22 N	136.41 E
Nansei-shotō (Ryukyu Islands) II	90	26.30 N	128.00 E
Nansemond □[6]	208	36.43 N	76.40 W
Nansen, Lago ⊜	254	47.57 S	72.21 W
Nan Sha I	106	31.36 N	121.22 E
Nanshahe	98	35.03 N	117.12 E
Nanshan, Zhg.	100	26.38 N	118.20 E
Nanshan, Zhg.	105	39.21 N	115.34 E
Nanshan → Qilian Shan ⩘	102	39.06 N	98.40 E
Nanshanba	100	25.34 N	116.32 E
Nanshanchengzi	98	42.09 N	125.19 E
Nanshan Island I	108	10.45 N	115.49 E
Nanshankou	102	43.09 N	93.41 E
Nanshanlingcun	105	39.09 N	117.26 E
Nanshuang Dao I	100	26.35 N	120.08 E
Nanshui	100	22.02 N	113.16 E
Nansifa	105	39.27 N	116.27 E
Nansio	154	2.08 S	33.03 E
Nans-les-Pins	62	43.22 N	5.47 E
Nansunzhai	269b	31.21 N	121.27 E
Nant	32	44.01 N	3.18 E
Nant ≃	50	47.32 N	1.41 E
Nantai	104	40.55 N	122.47 E
Nantais, Lac ⊜	176	60.59 N	74.00 W
Nantai-san ʌ	94	36.43 N	140.26 E
Nantai-zan ʌ	94	36.46 N	139.29 E
Nantang	100	26.08 N	115.12 E
Nantangdun	106	31.15 N	120.56 E
Nantangmei	105	38.51 N	114.56 E
Nantasket Beach	283	42.16 N	70.52 W
Nantawarra	168b	34.00 S	138.14 E
Nant Bran ≃	42	51.57 N	3.28 W
Nanterre	50	48.53 N	2.12 E
Nantes	32	47.13 N	1.33 W
Nanteuil-le-Haudouin	50	49.08 N	2.48 E
Nanteuil-lès-Meaux	261	48.56 N	2.54 E
Nantian, Zhg.	100	27.57 N	119.56 E
Nantian, Zhg.	100	29.08 N	121.56 E
Nantianmen	104	40.56 N	123.04 E
Nanticoke, On., Can.	212	42.54 N	80.11 E
Nanticoke, Md., U.S.	208	38.16 N	75.54 W
Nanticoke, Pa., U.S.	210	41.12 N	76.00 W
Nanticoke ≃	208	38.16 N	75.56 W
Nanticoke Creek ≃, On., Can.	212	42.48 N	80.04 W
Nanticoke Creek ≃, N.Y., U.S.	210	42.05 N	76.05 W
Nantmeal Village	285	40.08 N	75.42 W
Nanto	92	34.20 N	136.31 E
Nanton	182	50.21 N	113.46 W
Nantong	106	32.02 N	120.53 E
Nant'ou, T'aiwan	100	23.55 N	120.41 E
Nantou, Zhg.	100	22.33 N	113.55 E
Nantouillet	261	49.00 N	2.42 E
Nantschang → Nanchang	100	28.41 N	115.53 E
Nantua	58	46.09 N	5.37 E
Nantuantingzhuang	105	40.17 N	118.17 E
Nantucket	207	41.17 N	70.06 W
Nantucket □[6]	207	41.17 N	70.06 W
Nantucket Island I	207	41.16 N	70.03 W
Nantucket Sound ʯ	207	41.30 N	70.15 W
Nantuego	154	11.21 S	38.24 E
Nantulo	154	12.17 S	39.03 E
Nantung → Nantong	106	32.02 N	120.53 E
Nantwich	44	53.04 N	2.32 W
Nanty Glo	214	40.28 N	78.50 W
Nant-y-moch Reservoir ⊜[1]	42	52.27 N	3.50 W
Nanu	164	8.50 S	142.40 E
Nanuet	210	41.05 N	74.00 W
Nanuet Mall ✦[9]	276	41.06 N	74.01 W
Nanuku Passage ʯ	175g	16.45 S	179.15 W
Nanumanga I	14	6.18 S	176.20 E
Nanumea I[1]	14	5.39 S	176.08 E
Nanuque	255	17.50 S	40.21 W
Nānūr	126	23.42 N	87.52 E
Nanusa, Kepulauan II	108	4.42 N	127.06 E
Nanushuk ≃	180	69.18 N	151.00 W
Nanwan	100	32.09 N	113.57 E
Nan Wan c	100	21.55 N	120.47 E
Nanwengkouzi	89	51.10 N	125.25 E
Nanwenquan	107	29.26 N	106.35 E
Nanxi, Zhg.	100	31.31 N	115.38 E
Nanxi, Zhg.	100	26.24 N	118.24 E
Nanxi, Zhg.	107	28.51 N	104.58 E
Nanxian	102	29.20 N	112.19 E
Nanxiang	106	31.17 N	121.18 E
Nanxikou	107	30.43 N	106.07 E
Nanxin, Zhg.	98	35.33 N	117.12 E
Nanxin, Zhg.	105	39.11 N	115.38 E
Nanxing Hu ⊜	106	31.08 N	120.48 E
Nanxinzhuang	98	36.39 N	115.15 E
Nanxiong	100	25.10 N	114.20 E
Nanxun	106	30.53 N	120.26 E
Nanya	100	26.52 N	118.19 E
Nanyandang Shan ʌ	100	27.36 N	120.04 E
Nanyang, Zhg.	100	27.24 N	119.39 E
Nanyang, Zhg.	100	33.00 N	112.32 E
Nanyang, Zhg.	100	33.25 N	120.13 E
Nanyangcun	106	31.53 N	121.43 E
Nanyanggangzi	89	48.43 N	125.27 E
Nanyang Hu ⊜	98	35.12 N	116.41 E
Nanyang Shan ʌ	106	31.20 N	120.28 E
Nanyang Technological Institute ʋ[2]	271c	1.21 N	103.41 E
Nanyi Hu ⊜	106	31.07 N	118.57 E
Nan-yō	92	38.03 N	140.10 E
Nanyu	100	25.59 N	119.14 E
Nanyuan	105	39.48 N	116.23 E
Nanyuan Airport ⊠	271a	39.47 N	116.23 E
Nanyue	100	27.13 N	112.43 E
Nanyuki	154	0.01 N	37.04 E
Nanyulin	105	40.09 N	115.23 E
Nanzamu	98	41.56 N	124.23 E
Nanzha	106	31.51 N	120.15 E
Nanzhai	106	31.34 N	120.02 E
Nanzhang, Zhg.	102	31.50 N	111.41 E
Nanzhang, Zhg.	105	39.03 N	115.46 E
Nanzhao	100	33.30 N	112.27 E
Nanzhaoji	100	32.38 N	115.58 E
Nanzhen	100	26.59 N	119.57 E
Nanzhenjie	106	31.48 N	119.17 E
Nanzhila	154	16.05 S	26.07 E
Nanzhuang, Zhg.	105	40.22 N	116.21 E
Nanzhuang, Zhg.	105	40.43 N	114.58 E
Nao	152	4.35 N	15.09 E
Naoābād	272b	22.28 N	88.27 E
Naoāpāra	126	22.45 N	89.39 E
Naococane, Lac ⊜	176	52.52 N	70.40 W
Naoetsu	94	37.11 N	138.15 E
Naogaon	124	24.47 N	88.56 E
Naoiri	96	33.04 N	131.23 E
Naokot	120	24.51 N	69.27 E
Naoli ≃	89	47.20 N	134.10 E
Naolinco	234	19.39 N	96.51 W
Não-me-Toque	252	28.28 S	52.49 W
Naong, Bukit ʌ	112	2.40 N	112.45 E
Nāopāra	126	24.09 N	88.54 E
Naopukuria	272b	22.55 N	88.16 E
Naosap Lake ⊜	184	54.51 N	101.24 W
Naoshima	96	34.27 N	133.59 E
Naours	50	50.02 N	2.17 E
Náousa	38	40.37 N	22.05 E
Naozhou Dao I	102	20.57 N	110.34 E
Napa	226	38.17 N	122.17 W
Napa □[6]	226	38.18 N	122.17 W
Napa ≃	226	38.07 N	122.18 W
Napacao Point ›	116	9.43 N	124.31 E
Napajedla	30	49.10 N	17.31 E
Napakiak	180	60.42 N	161.57 W
Napaku	112	2.32 N	115.58 E
Na Pali Coast State Park ♦	229b	22.09 N	159.41 W
Napalkovo	74	70.03 N	73.47 E
Napamute	180	61.33 N	158.42 W
Napanee	212	44.15 N	76.57 W
Napanee ≃	212	44.12 N	77.02 W
Napanoch	210	41.44 N	74.22 W
Napareuli	84	42.03 N	45.31 E
Napas	86	59.53 N	81.58 E
Napaskiak	180	60.42 N	161.45 W
Napa Valley V	226	38.18 N	122.18 W
Napavine	224	46.34 N	122.54 W
Napayauan Island I	116	12.22 N	123.14 E
Napè	110	18.18 N	105.06 E
Napenay	252	26.44 S	60.37 W
Naperville	216	41.47 N	88.08 W
Napetipi ≃	186	51.21 N	58.08 W
Napf ʌ	58	47.00 N	7.56 E
Napido	164	0.41 S	135.23 E
Napiéolédougou	150	9.18 N	5.35 W
Napier, N.Z.	172	39.29 S	176.55 E
Napier, S. Afr.	158	34.29 S	19.53 E
Napier, Mount ʌ[2]	162	17.32 S	129.10 E
Napier Mountains ⩘	9	66.30 S	53.40 E
Napierville	206	45.11 N	73.25 W
Napierville □[6]	206	45.10 N	73.35 W
Napinka	184	49.17 N	100.50 W
Naplate	216	41.20 N	88.54 W
Naples → Napoli, It.	68	40.51 N	14.17 E
Naples, Fl., U.S.	220	26.08 N	81.47 W
Naples, Id., U.S.	202	48.34 N	116.23 W
Naples, Il., U.S.	219	39.45 N	90.36 W
Naples, N.Y., U.S.	210	42.36 N	77.24 W
Naples, Tx., U.S.	222	33.12 N	94.40 W
Naples Park	220	26.16 N	81.48 W
Napo	102	23.16 N	105.54 E
Napo □[4]	246	0.30 S	77.00 W
Napo ≃	246	3.20 S	72.40 W
Napola	70	37.59 N	12.38 E
Napoleon, In., U.S.	218	39.12 N	85.19 W
Napoleon, Ky., U.S.	218	38.46 N	84.47 W
Napoleon, Mi., U.S.	216	42.10 N	84.15 W
Napoleon, N.D., U.S.	198	46.30 N	99.46 W
Napoleon, Oh., U.S.	216	41.23 N	84.07 W
Napoleonville	194	29.56 N	91.01 W
Nápoles → Napoli	68	40.51 N	14.17 E
Napoli (Naples)	68	40.51 N	14.17 E
Napoli □[4]	68	40.53 N	14.25 E
Napoli, Golfo di c	68	40.43 N	14.10 E
Napopo	154	4.12 N	28.02 E
Nappamerry	166	27.36 S	141.07 E
Nappanee	216	41.26 N	86.00 W
Nappan Island I	212	44.23 N	77.49 W
Napton on the Hill	42	52.15 N	1.24 W
Napu	115b	9.24 S	119.56 E
Napudalutai Shan ʌ	89	51.06 N	122.13 E
Naqādah	140	25.54 N	32.43 E
Naqadeh	128	36.57 N	45.23 E
Naqb, Ra's an- ʌ	132	29.50 N	35.40 E
Nar ≃	42	52.45 N	0.24 E
Nara, Mali	150	15.10 N	7.17 W
Nara, Nihon	96	34.41 N	135.50 E
Nara □[5]	96	34.30 N	135.50 E
Nāra ≃, Pāk.	120	24.07 N	69.07 E
Nara ≃, Ross.	82	54.53 N	37.26 E
Nara-bonchi ≚[1]	270	34.38 N	135.50 E
Naracoorte	166	36.58 S	140.44 E
Naradhan	166	33.37 S	146.19 E
Narai ≃	94	36.20 N	137.55 E
Narāil	126	23.10 N	89.30 E
Naraina ✦[8]	272a	28.37 N	77.08 E
Naraini	124	25.11 N	80.29 E
Narainpur	126	24.03 N	86.36 E
Narakawa	94	35.59 N	137.50 E
Naramata	182	49.36 N	119.35 W
Naran	88	48.34 N	98.17 E
Naran Bulag	86	49.22 N	92.33 E
Nārang	123	31.54 N	74.31 E
Narangba	171a	27.12 S	152.58 E
Naranja	220	25.31 N	80.25 W
Naranjal, Ec.	246	2.42 S	79.37 W
Naranjal, Ven.	286c	10.28 N	67.02 W
Naranjito, Hond.	236	14.57 N	88.41 W
Naranjito, P.R.	240m	18.18 N	66.15 W
Naranjo	236	10.06 N	84.22 W
Naranjo ≃	236	14.30 N	92.11 W
Naranjo Islands II	116	12.23 N	124.03 E
Naranjos	234	21.21 N	97.41 W
Narao	92	32.50 N	129.04 E
Nara Park ♦	270	34.41 N	135.52 E
Narasannapeta	122	18.25 N	84.03 E
Narasapur	122	16.27 N	81.40 E
Narasaraopet	122	16.15 N	80.04 E
Narashino	94	35.41 N	140.02 E
Narasun	88	50.06 N	112.58 E
Narat	86	43.28 N	83.44 E
Narathiwat	110	6.26 N	101.50 E
Nara Visa	196	35.36 N	103.05 W
Nara Women's University ʋ[2]	270	34.42 N	135.49 E
Nārāyanganj	124	23.37 N	90.30 E
Nārāyaṇī □[8]	124	27.15 N	85.00 E
Nārāyaṇi ≃	124	25.39 N	85.13 E
Nārāyanpāra	272b	22.54 N	88.19 E
Nārāyanpet	122	16.44 N	77.30 E
Nārāyanpur	272b	22.29 N	88.34 E
Narazeni	84	42.27 N	41.57 E
Narberth, Wales, U.K.	42	51.48 N	4.45 W
Narberth, Pa., U.S.	285	40.00 N	75.15 W
Narbonne	32	43.11 N	3.00 E
Narcao	71	39.10 N	8.40 E
Narcea ≃	34	43.28 N	6.06 W
Narcondam Island I	110	13.20 N	94.16 E
Narcosli Creek ≃	182	52.49 N	122.28 W
Nardò	68	40.11 N	18.02 E
Nare ≃	246	6.12 N	74.35 W
Narellan	170	34.02 S	150.44 E
Narembeen	162	32.04 S	118.24 E
Narenbulake	89	49.52 N	120.23 E
Narendranagar	124	30.10 N	78.18 E
Nares Strait ʯ	16	80.30 N	68.00 W
Naretha	162	31.00 S	124.50 E
Narew ≃	30	52.26 N	20.42 E
Nargund	122	15.43 N	75.23 E
Narhan	272c	19.08 N	73.07 E
Nāri ≃	120	28.35 N	67.50 E
Naria	124	23.18 N	90.25 E
Nariai	270	34.53 N	135.38 E
Nariel	171b	36.26 S	147.50 E
Narijn ≃	88	50.20 N	93.24 E
Narijnteel	102	45.57 N	101.29 E
Nārikelbāria	126	23.17 N	89.21 E
Nariman	85	40.34 N	72.48 E
Närimanabad	84	38.53 N	48.52 E
Narimba, Her Majesty's Air Station (Royal Australian Navy Airfield) ■	274a	33.43 S	150.53 E
Narin ≃	120	36.54 N	92.51 E
Narince	130	37.52 N	38.46 E
Narinda, Baie de c	157b	14.55 S	47.30 E
Nariño □[5]	246	1.30 N	78.00 W
Narita	94	35.47 N	140.19 E
Nariwa	96	34.47 N	133.33 E
Nariwa ≃	96	34.46 N	133.36 E
Nar'jan-Mar	24	67.39 N	53.00 E
Nārkanda	123	31.16 N	77.27 E
Narkatiāganj	124	27.06 N	84.28 E
Närke □[9]	40	59.06 N	15.03 E
Närkes Marieberg	40	59.12 N	15.10 E
Narlı	130	37.27 N	37.09 E
Narma	80	54.46 N	42.01 E
Narmada ≃	120	21.38 N	72.36 E
Narmada Valley V	124	22.30 N	77.00 E
Narmak ✦[8]	267d	35.43 N	51.29 E
Narman	130	40.21 N	41.52 E
Narmušad'	80	54.40 N	41.07 E
Nar-Nar-Goon	169	38.05 S	145.34 E
Nārnaul	124	28.03 N	76.07 E
Narni	66	42.31 N	12.31 E
Naro	70	37.18 N	13.47 E
Naro ≃	70	37.14 N	13.37 E
Naroč' ≃	76	54.26 N	26.39 E
Naroč', ozero ⊜	76	54.52 N	26.45 E
Narodnaja, gora ʌ	24	65.04 N	60.09 E
Narodychi	78	51.13 N	29.03 E
Naro-Fominsk	82	55.23 N	36.43 E
Naro Island I	116	11.53 N	123.40 E
Narok	154	1.05 S	35.52 E
Narol	30	50.22 N	23.21 E
Narón	34	43.32 N	8.10 W
Narooma	166	36.14 S	150.03 E
Naro-Osakovo	82	55.33 N	36.33 E
Narovčat	80	53.52 N	43.41 E
Narovl'a	78	51.48 N	29.29 E
Nārowāl	123	32.06 N	74.53 E
Närpes (Närpiö)	26	62.28 N	21.20 E
Närpiö → Närpes	26	62.28 N	21.20 E
Narrabeen	170	33.43 S	151.18 E
Narrabeen Lagoon c	274a	33.43 S	151.17 E
Narrabri	166	30.19 S	149.47 E
Narragansett	207	41.25 N	71.27 W
Narragansett Bay c	207	41.40 N	71.20 W
Narran ≃	166	29.45 S	147.20 E
Narra Narra ʌ	171b	35.50 S	147.27 E
Narrandera	166	34.45 S	146.33 E
Narraway ≃	182	54.48 N	119.56 W
Narraweena	274a	33.45 S	151.16 E
Narre Warren	274b	38.02 S	145.19 E
Narre Warren North	274b	37.59 S	145.19 E
Narrogin	162	32.56 S	117.10 E
Narromine	166	32.14 S	148.15 E
Narrows, Md., U.S.	208	38.58 N	76.15 W
Narrows, Va., U.S.	192	37.19 N	80.48 W
Narrowsburg	210	41.36 N	75.03 W
Närsen ⊜	40	60.17 N	14.23 E
Narsimhapur	124	22.57 N	79.12 E
Narsinghdi	124	23.55 N	90.43 E
Narsinghgarh	124	23.42 N	77.06 E
Narsīpatnam	122	17.40 N	82.37 E
Narskije Prudy, ozero ⊜[1]	82	55.32 N	36.36 E
Narssaq	176	60.54 N	46.00 W
Nartkala	84	43.33 N	43.50 E
Nartuby ≃	62	43.28 N	6.34 E
Naru	92	32.49 N	128.56 E
Narubis, Namibia	158	26.55 S	18.35 E
Narubis, Namibia	158	27.10 S	19.05 E
Naruko	92	38.44 N	140.43 E
Naruksovo	80	54.37 N	44.33 E
Naruo	270	34.43 N	135.23 E
Narusawa	94	35.29 N	138.41 E
Narutō, Nihon	94	35.36 N	140.25 E
Naruto, Nihon	96	34.11 N	134.37 E
Naruto-kaikyō ʯ	96	34.14 N	134.39 E
Narva, Eesti	76	59.23 N	28.12 E
Narva, Ross.	86	55.25 N	93.39 E
Narva ≃	76	59.27 N	28.02 E
Narvacan	116	17.25 N	120.28 E
Narva-Jõesuu	76	59.27 N	28.03 E
Narva laht (Narvskij zaliv) c	76	59.30 N	27.40 E
Narvan	85	40.15 N	67.12 E
Narvik	24	68.26 N	17.25 E
Narvskij zaliv (Narva laht) c	76	59.30 N	27.40 E
Narvskoje vodochranilišče ⊜[1]	76	59.18 N	28.14 E
Narwāna	124	29.37 N	76.07 E
Narwietooma	162	23.15 S	132.35 E
Narym	86	58.58 N	81.30 E
Naryn, Kyrg.	85	41.26 N	75.59 E
Naryn, Ross.	88	50.13 N	96.27 E
Naryn □[4]	85	41.30 N	76.00 E
Naryn ≃	85	40.54 N	71.45 E
Narynkol	72	42.43 N	80.12 E
Naryntau, gory ⩘	85	41.25 N	76.50 E
Naryškino	76	52.58 N	35.44 E
Naryū-zaki ›	96	35.36 N	135.28 E
Narzole	62	44.35 N	7.52 E
Nås, Sve.	40	60.27 N	14.29 E
Näs, Sve.	40	58.41 N	15.50 E
Nasadkino	82	56.29 N	37.21 E
Näsåker	26	63.26 N	16.54 E
Na San, Thai	110	8.48 N	99.22 E
Na San, Viet	110	21.12 N	104.02 E
Nasarawa	150	8.30 N	7.40 E
Năsăud	38	47.17 N	24.24 E
Nasawa	175f	15.13 S	168.09 E
NASA Wallops Station ʋ[3]	208	37.52 N	75.28 W
Nasbinals	32	44.40 N	3.03 E
Naschel	252	32.55 S	65.23 W
Nase → Naze	93b	28.23 N	129.30 E
Naseby, N.Z.	172	45.02 S	170.09 E
Naseby, Eng., U.K.	42	52.25 N	0.58 W
Naselle	224	46.21 N	123.48 W
Naselle ≃	224	46.25 N	123.55 W
Nash	194	33.27 N	94.08 W
Nashawena Island I	207	41.26 N	70.53 W
Nāshik	122	19.59 N	73.48 E
Nashoba Brook ≃	283	42.28 N	71.24 W
Nashport	214	40.04 N	82.09 W
Nashū', Wādī an- V	146	26.25 N	14.15 E
Nashua, Ia., U.S.	190	42.57 N	92.32 W
Nashua, Mt., U.S.	202	48.07 N	106.21 W
Nashua, N.H., U.S.	207	42.45 N	71.28 W
Nashua ≃	207	42.46 N	71.27 W
Nashuixi	102	30.09 N	108.40 E
Näshultasjön ⊜	40	59.14 N	16.21 E
Nashville, On., Can.	275b	43.50 N	79.40 W
Nashville, Ar., U.S.	194	33.56 N	93.50 W
Nashville, Ga., U.S.	192	31.12 N	83.15 W
Nashville, Il., U.S.	219	38.20 N	89.22 W
Nashville, In., U.S.	218	39.12 N	86.15 W
Nashville, Mi., U.S.	216	42.36 N	85.05 W
Nashville, N.C., U.S.	192	35.58 N	77.57 W
Nashville, Oh., U.S.	214	40.36 N	82.07 W
Nashville, Tn., U.S.	194	36.09 N	86.47 W
Nashwaak ≃	186	45.57 N	66.37 W
Nashwaaksis	186	45.59 N	66.39 W
Nashwah	142	30.30 N	31.29 E
Nashwauk	190	47.22 N	93.10 W
Nasia	150	10.09 N	0.48 W
Naṣīb	132	32.33 N	36.11 E
Našice	38	45.29 N	18.06 E
Nasielsk	30	52.36 N	20.48 E
Näsijärvi ⊜	26	61.37 N	23.42 E
Nāṣir	140	8.36 N	33.04 E
Nāṣir, Buḥayrat (Lake Nasser) ⊜[1]	140	22.40 N	32.00 E
Nasīrābād, India	120	26.18 N	74.44 E
Nasīrābād, Pāk.	120	28.23 N	68.24 E
Naskaftym	80	52.57 N	45.38 E
Naskaupi ≃	176	53.45 N	60.50 W
Näsnaren ⊜	40	58.51 N	16.18 E
Naso	70	38.07 N	14.47 E
Nasondoye	154	10.22 S	25.06 E
Naso Point ›	116	10.25 N	121.57 E
Nasorolevu ʌ	175g	16.38 S	178.42 E
Naṣr	142	30.36 N	30.23 E
Naṣrābād	128	34.08 N	51.26 E
Naṣrānī, Jabal an- ʌ	130	34.06 N	37.24 E
Nasriddinbek	85	40.41 N	71.55 E
Nāsriganj	124	25.03 N	84.20 E
Nass ≃	182	55.00 N	129.50 W
Nassau, Ba.	240b	25.05 N	77.21 W
Nassau, Dtsch.	54	50.46 N	13.32 E
Nassau, Dtsch.	56	50.19 N	7.47 E
Nassau, N.Y., U.S.	210	42.30 N	73.36 W
Nassau □[6]	210	40.45 N	73.38 W
Nassau, Bahía c	254	55.25 S	67.40 W
Nassau Bay	222	29.32 N	95.05 W
Nassau Coliseum ♦	276	40.43 N	73.36 W
Nassau International Airport ⊠	240b	25.02 N	77.28 W
Nassau Island I	14	11.33 S	165.25 W
Nassau Shores	276	40.39 N	73.26 W
Nassawadox	208	37.28 N	75.51 W
Nassawango Creek ≃	208	38.10 N	75.25 W
Nassenfels	60	48.48 N	11.16 E
Nassenheide	54	52.49 N	13.12 E
Nasser, Lake → Nāṣir, Buḥayrat ⊜[1]	140	22.40 N	32.00 E
Nassereith	58	47.19 N	10.50 E
Nassian	150	8.27 N	3.29 W
Nässjö	26	57.39 N	14.41 E
Nastapoca ≃	176	56.55 N	76.33 W
Nastapoka Islands II	176	57.00 N	76.50 W
Nastashka	78	49.39 N	30.19 E
Nastasjino	82	54.28 N	38.16 E
Nastätten	56	50.12 N	7.51 E
Nastauli	272a	28.43 N	77.22 E
Nastf, Bi'r ⊤[4]	142	30.18 N	30.28 E
Nasu	94	37.01 N	140.07 E
Nasu-dake ʌ, Nihon	92	37.07 N	139.58 E
Nasu-dake ʌ, Nihon	94	37.09 N	139.58 E
Nasugbu	116	14.05 N	120.38 E
Nasukoin Mountain ʌ	202	48.48 N	114.35 W
Nasva	76	56.35 N	30.10 E
Nat ≃	190	48.48 N	82.07 W
Nata, Bots.	156	20.12 S	26.12 E
Natá, Pan.	236	8.20 N	80.31 W
Nata ≃	156	20.14 S	26.10 E
Natagaima	246	3.37 N	75.06 W
Nātāgarh	272b	22.42 N	88.25 E
Natal, Bra.	250	5.47 S	35.13 W
Natal, B.C., Can.	182	49.44 N	114.50 W
Natal, Indon.	110	0.33 N	99.07 E
Natal □[4]	158	28.40 S	30.40 E
Natal Basin ✣[1]	10	30.00 S	40.00 E
Natalia	196	29.11 N	98.51 W
Nataljevka	83	47.10 N	38.29 E
Nataljin Jar	80	51.46 N	50.35 E
Nataljino	80	52.56 N	49.02 E
Natalkuz Lake ⊜	182	53.26 N	125.20 W
Natalspruit ≃	273d	26.19 S	28.10 E
Natanes Plateau ⩘[1]	200	33.35 N	110.15 W
Natash, Wādī V	140	24.25 N	33.26 E
Natashō	96	35.24 N	135.38 E
Natashquan	186	50.12 N	61.49 W
Natashquan ≃	176	50.06 N	61.49 W
Natashquan, Pointe de ›	186	50.06 N	61.44 W
Natashquan Est ≃	186	51.20 N	61.40 W
Natchez	194	31.33 N	91.24 W
Natchez Trace Parkway ♦	194	32.00 N	91.00 W
Natchitoches	194	31.45 N	93.05 W
Natco Lake ⊜	276	40.26 N	74.09 W
Natércia	256	22.07 S	45.30 W
Naters	58	46.20 N	7.59 E
Natewa Bay c	175g	16.35 S	179.40 E
Na Thawi	110	6.45 N	100.42 E
Nāthdwāra	120	24.56 N	73.49 E
Nathia Gali	123	34.04 N	73.24 E
Nathkaw	102	26.53 N	96.13 E
Nathula I	175g	16.53 S	177.25 E
Natick	207	42.17 N	71.21 W
Natick Laboratories ■	283	42.17 N	71.22 W
Natimuk	166	36.45 S	141.57 E
Nation ≃	182	55.28 N	123.35 W
National Agricultural Research Center ʋ[3]	284c	39.02 N	76.52 W
National Airport ⊠	281	42.19 N	83.25 W
National Arboretum ♦	284c	38.54 N	76.58 W
National Assembly ʋ	269a	13.46 N	100.31 E
National Baseball Hall of Fame and Museum ʋ	210	42.42 N	74.57 W
National City	228	32.40 N	117.05 W
National Gallery ʋ	260	51.31 N	0.08 W
National Institute of Health ʋ	284c	39.00 N	77.06 W
National Maritime Museum ʋ	260	51.29 N	0.00
National Park	285	39.51 N	75.10 W
National Taiwan Normal University ʋ[2]	269d	25.02 N	121.31 E
National Taiwan University ʋ[2]	269d	25.01 N	121.32 E
National Zoological Park ♦	284c	38.56 N	77.03 W
Natipi, Lac ⊜	186	51.27 N	71.23 W
Natisone ≃	64	45.57 N	13.22 E
Natitingou	150	10.19 N	1.22 E
Native Bay c	176	63.52 N	82.30 W
Natividade	250	11.43 S	47.47 W
Natividade da Serra	256	23.24 S	45.26 W
Natívitas ✦[8]	286a	19.14 N	99.05 W
Nativity, Church of the ʋ[1]	132	31.43 N	35.12 E
Natkyizin	110	14.55 N	97.57 E
Natl	132	31.39 N	35.52 E
Natoma	198	39.11 N	99.01 W
Natong	102	23.01 N	107.50 E
Nator	124	24.25 N	88.59 E
Natori	92	38.08 N	140.55 E
Natorp	263	51.30 N	7.38 E
Natron, Lake ⊜	154	2.25 S	36.00 E
Natrona Heights	214	40.37 N	79.43 W
Naṭrūn, Wādī an- ⍛[7]	142	30.25 N	30.13 E
Natsui ≃	94	37.03 N	140.59 E
Nattai ≃	170	34.05 S	150.25 E
Nattai River	170	34.04 S	150.27 E
Nattam	122	10.14 N	78.14 E
Nåttarö I	40	58.52 N	18.07 E
Nattaset ʌ	24	68.12 N	27.20 E
Nattaung ʌ	110	18.48 N	97.02 E
Natters	64	47.14 N	11.22 E
Nattwerder	264a	52.26 N	12.56 E
Natuchajevskaja	78	44.54 N	37.34 E
Nātudaha	126	23.39 N	88.41 E
Natukanaoka Pan ≚	156	18.40 S	15.45 E
Natuna Besar I	112	4.00 N	108.15 E
Natuna Besar, Kepulauan II	112	4.40 N	108.00 E
Natuna Selatan, Kepulauan II	112	2.45 N	109.00 E
Natural Bridge	212	44.04 N	75.29 W
Natural Bridge ♦	192	37.38 N	79.33 W
Natural Bridges National Monument ♦	200	37.30 N	110.08 W
Natural Bridge State Resort Park ♦	192	37.47 N	83.42 W
Naturaliste, Cape ›	162	33.32 S	115.01 E
Naturaliste Channel ʯ	162	25.25 S	113.00 E
Naturita	200	38.13 N	108.34 W
Naturita Creek ≃	200	38.13 N	108.32 W
Naturno (Naturns)	64	46.39 N	11.00 E
Natzungen	52	51.36 N	9.14 E
Nau	85	40.09 N	69.22 E
Nau, Cap de la ›	34	38.44 N	0.14 E
Naucalpan de Juárez	286a	19.28 N	99.14 W
Naucelle	32	44.12 N	2.20 E
Nauchnyy	78	44.44 N	34.01 E
Naude	272c	19.03 N	73.06 E
Nauders	58	46.53 N	10.30 E
Nauen	54	52.36 N	12.52 E
Nauener Luch ≋	264a	52.37 N	12.55 E
Nauener Stadtforst ♦	264a	52.38 N	12.58 E
Naugachhia	124	25.24 N	87.06 E
Naugatuck	207	41.30 N	73.05 W
Naugatuck ≃	207	41.19 N	73.05 W
Naughton	190	46.24 N	81.12 W
Naugol'noje	82	56.22 N	38.11 E
Naui	140	18.28 N	30.43 E
Naujamiestis	76	55.41 N	24.04 E
Naujan	116	13.20 N	121.18 E
Naujan, Lake ⊜	116	13.10 N	121.21 E
Naujoji Akmenė	76	56.19 N	22.55 E
Naukan	180	66.01 N	169.43 W
Naulavaara ʌ[2]	26	63.53 N	28.13 E
Naulila	152	17.12 S	14.42 E
Naumburg, Dtsch.	54	51.09 N	11.48 E
Naumburg, Dtsch.	56	51.15 N	9.10 E
Naumovščina	76	58.23 N	28.20 E
Naunak	86	59.00 N	80.13 E
Naundorf	54	50.56 N	13.25 E
Naunglon	110	16.48 N	97.45 E
Naungpale	110	19.33 N	97.08 E
Naunhof	54	51.16 N	12.35 E
Naupada ✦[8]	272c	19.04 N	72.50 E
Nā'ūr	132	31.53 N	35.50 E
Nauraushaun Brook ≃	276	41.03 N	73.59 W
Nauroth	56	50.42 N	7.52 E
Nauroz Kalāt	128	28.47 N	65.38 E
Naurskaja	84	43.38 N	45.19 E
Nauru □[1], Oc.	14	0.32 S	166.55 E
Nauru □[1], Oc.	174b	0.32 S	166.55 E
Naurzumskij zapovednik ♦	86	51.30 N	64.20 E
Naushahro Fīroz	120	26.50 N	68.07 E
Naushon Island I	207	41.29 N	70.45 W
Nauški	88	50.28 N	106.07 E
Nausori	175g	18.02 S	178.32 E

Symbol	English	Deutsch	Español	Français	Português
≃	River	Fluß	Río	Rivière	Rio
≍	Canal	Kanal	Canal	Canal	Canal
⌞	Waterfall, Rapids	Wasserfall, Stromschnellen	Cascada, Rápidos	Chute d'eau, Rapides	Cascata, Rápidos
ʯ	Strait	Meeresstraße	Estrecho	Détroit	Estreito
c	Bay, Gulf	Bucht, Golf	Bahía, Golfo	Baie, Golfe	Baía, Golfo
⊜	Lake, Lakes	See, Seen	Lago, Lagos	Lac, Lacs	Lago, Lagos
≋	Swamp	Sumpf	Pantano	Marais	Pântano
≚	Ice Features, Glacier	Eis- und Gletscherformen	Accidentes Glaciales	Formes glaciaires	Acidentes glaciares
⊤	Other Hydrographic Features	Andere Hydrographische Objekte	Otros Elementos Hidrográficos	Autres données hydrographiques	Outros acidentes hidrográficos
✣	Submarine Features	Untermeerische Objekte	Accidentes Submarinos	Formes de relief sous-marin	Acidentes submarinos
□	Political Unit	Politische Einheit	Unidad Politica	Entité politique	Unidade política
ʋ	Cultural Institution	Kulturelle Institution	Institución Cultural	Institution culturelle	Instituição cultural
ı	Historical Site	Historische Stätte	Sitio Histórico	Site historique	Sitio histórico
♦	Recreational Site	Erholungs- und Ferienort	Sitio de Recreo	Centre de loisirs	Area de Lazer
⊠	Airport	Flughafen	Aeropuerto	Aéroport	Aeroporto
■	Military Installation	Militäranlage	Instalación Militar	Installation militaire	Instalação militar
✦	Miscellaneous	Verschiedenes	Misceláneo	Divers	Diversos

Name	Page	Lat.°′	Long.°′
Naussac, Barrage de •[6]	62	44.46 N	3.49 E
Naustdal	26	61.31 N	5.43 E
Nauta	246	4.32 S	73.33 W
Nautanwa	124	27.26 N	83.25 E
Nautilus Park	207	41.22 N	72.05 W
Nautla	234	20.13 N	96.47 W
Nauvoo	190	40.33 N	91.23 W
Nava, It.	62	44.06 N	7.22 E
Nava, Méx.	232	28.25 N	100.46 W
Nava, Arroyo de la ≃	266a	40.31 N	3.46 W
Nava, Colle di)(	62	44.05 N	7.53 E
Nava del Rey	34	41.20 N	5.05 W
Navadwip	126	23.25 N	88.22 E
Navahermosa	34	39.38 N	4.28 W
Navajo	200	35.55 N	109.01 W
Navajo ≃	200	37.01 N	107.10 W
Navajo Creek ≃	200	36.59 N	111.24 W
Navajo Hopi Joint Use Area •[4]	200	36.15 N	110.30 W
Navajo Indian Reservation •[4]	200	36.25 N	110.00 W
Navajo Mountain ∧	200	37.02 N	110.52 W
Navajo National Monument ♦	200	36.40 N	110.33 W
Navajo Reservoir ⊜[1]	200	36.55 N	107.30 W
Naval	116	11.34 N	124.23 E
Navalmoral de la Mata	34	39.54 N	5.32 W
Naval Ordnance Test Station ■	228	35.32 N	117.05 W
Navalvillar de Pela	34	39.06 N	5.28 W
Navan	48	53.39 N	6.41 W
Navāpur	122	21.09 N	73.48 E
Navarin, mys ›	180	62.16 N	179.10 E
Navarino → Pílos	38	36.55 N	21.43 E
Navarino, Isla I	254	55.05 S	67.40 W
Navarra □[4]	34	42.40 N	1.30 W
Navarre, Austl.	169	36.54 S	143.07 E
Navarre, Oh., U.S.	214	40.43 N	81.31 W
Navarro	258	35.01 S	59.16 W
Navarro □[6]	222	32.05 N	96.30 W
Navarro ≃	204	39.11 N	123.45 W
Navarro, Cañada ≃	258	35.00 S	59.18 W
Navarro, Laguna ⊜	258	35.01 S	59.18 W
Navarro Mills Lake ⊜[1]	222	31.56 N	96.45 W
Navašino	80	55.32 N	42.12 E
Navasota	222	30.23 N	96.05 W
Navasota ≃	222	30.20 N	96.09 W
Navassa	192	34.15 N	78.00 W
Navassa Island I	238	18.24 N	75.01 W
Nave	64	45.35 N	10.17 E
Nävekvarn	40	58.38 N	16.49 E
Navenne	58	47.36 N	6.10 E
Naver ≃	46	58.32 N	4.15 W
Naver, Loch ⊜	46	58.17 N	4.23 W
Navesink	276	40.23 N	74.02 W
Navesink River ⊂	276	40.23 N	73.58 W
Navesnoje	76	52.17 N	37.57 E
Nâves-Parmelan	58	45.56 N	6.11 E
Navesti ≃	76	58.30 N	24.54 E
Navestock	260	51.39 N	0.13 E
Navestock Side	260	51.39 N	0.16 E
Navia, Arg.	252	34.47 S	66.35 W
Navia, Esp.	34	43.32 N	6.43 W
Navia ≃	34	43.33 N	6.44 W
Navidad	252	33.57 S	71.50 W
Navidad ≃	196	28.41 N	96.35 W
Navidad, Bahía de ⊂	234	19.17 N	104.50 W
Navidad Bank ✢[3]	238	20.00 N	68.50 W
Navio, Riacho do ≃	250	8.39 S	38.36 W
Naviraí	255	23.08 S	54.13 W
Navis	64	47.07 N	11.32 E
Naviti I	175g	17.07 S	177.15 E
Navl'a	76	52.51 N	34.30 E
Navl'a ≃	76	52.42 N	34.01 E
Năvodari	38	44.19 N	28.36 E
Navoi	72	40.15 N	65.15 E
Navojoa	232	27.06 N	109.26 W
Navolato	232	24.47 N	107.42 W
Navoloki	80	57.28 N	41.59 E
Navotas	269f	14.39 N	120.57 E
Návpaktos	38	38.23 N	21.50 E
Návplion	38	37.34 N	22.48 E
Navrongo	150	10.54 N	1.06 W
Navsāri	120	20.51 N	72.55 E
Navua	175g	18.14 S	178.10 E
Navy Island I	284a	43.04 N	79.01 W
Navy Pier •[5]	278	41.53 N	87.36 W
Navy Yard City	224	47.32 N	122.41 W
Nawa, Nihon	96	35.30 N	133.30 E
Nawa → Naha, Nihon	174m	26.13 N	127.40 E
Nawá, Sūrīy.	132	32.53 N	36.03 E
Nawābganj, Bngl.	124	24.36 N	88.17 E
Nawābganj, Bngl.	126	23.40 N	90.10 E
Nawābganj, India	124	28.33 N	79.38 E
Nawābganj, India	124	26.52 N	82.08 E
Nawābganj, India	124	26.56 N	81.13 E
Nawābshāh	120	26.15 N	68.25 E
Nawāda	124	24.53 N	85.32 E
Nāwah	120	32.19 N	67.53 E
Nawa Kot	120	28.20 N	71.22 E
Nawalapitiya	122	7.03 N	80.32 E
Nawalgarh	120	27.51 N	75.16 E
Nawān Kot	123	31.06 N	71.32 E
Nawanshahr	123	31.07 N	76.08 E
Nawāpāra, Bngl.	126	23.02 N	89.23 E
Nawāpāra, India	122	20.58 N	81.51 E
Nawāpāra, India	126	23.29 N	88.15 E
Nawasā al-Ghayṭ	142	30.58 N	31.19 E
Nawāshahr	123	34.10 N	73.16 E
Nawāṣīf, Ḥarrat ⊥[9]	144	21.20 N	42.10 E
Nawāy	142	27.47 N	30.46 E
Nawiliwili Bay ⊂	229b	21.57 N	159.21 W
Nawinda Kuta	152	16.25 S	24.28 E
Nawŏn-ni	98	36.25 N	126.40 E
Naxçıvan	84	39.13 N	45.24 E
Naxçıvan Muxtar Respublikası □[3]	84	39.20 N	45.30 E
Naxera	208	37.20 N	76.27 W
Naxi	107	28.47 N	105.22 E
Náxos	38	37.06 N	25.23 E
Náxos I	38	37.02 N	25.35 E
Naxos ⊥	70	37.49 N	15.17 E
Nayābās	272a	28.35 N	77.19 E
Nayāgaon	126	23.32 N	90.46 E
Nayāgarh	120	20.08 N	85.06 E
Nayāgrām	126	22.02 N	87.11 E
Nayak	120	34.44 N	66.57 E
Nayāpāra	126	21.35 N	87.01 E
Nayarit	204	32.20 N	115.19 W
Nayarit □[3]	234	22.00 N	105.00 W
Nayau Island I	175g	17.58 S	179.03 W
Nāy Band, Īrān	128	32.20 N	57.34 E
Nāy Band, Īrān	128	27.23 N	52.38 E
Nāy Band, Kūh-e ∧	128	32.26 N	57.22 E
Nayland	42	51.59 N	0.52 E
Naylor	194	36.34 N	90.36 W
Nayong	102	26.50 N	105.13 E
Nayoro	92a	44.21 N	142.28 E
Nazālī Ṭāhā'	142	28.11 N	30.42 E
Nazaré, Bra.	250	6.23 S	47.40 W
Nazaré, Bra.	255	13.02 S	39.00 W
Nazaré, Port.	34	39.36 N	9.04 W
Nazaré da Mata	250	7.44 S	35.14 W
Nazaré do Piauí	250	6.59 S	42.40 W
Nazareno	256	21.13 S	44.37 W
Nazaré Paulista	256	23.11 S	46.24 W
Nazareth, Bel.	50	50.58 N	3.36 E
Nazareth, Pa., U.S.	208	40.44 N	75.18 W
Nazareth, Vanuatu	175f	15.29 S	168.10 E
Nazareth → Naẕerat, Yis.	132	32.42 N	35.18 E
Nazareth Bank ✢[4]	12	14.30 S	60.45 E
Nazário	255	16.36 S	49.54 W
Nazarjevo, Ross.	82	55.22 N	36.24 E
Nazarjevo, Ross.	265b	55.59 N	37.16 E
Nazarovo	86	56.01 N	90.26 E
Nazarovskij	78	49.33 N	40.56 E
Nazas	232	25.14 N	104.08 W
Nazas ≃	232	25.35 N	105.00 W
Nazca	248	14.50 S	74.57 W
Nazca Ridge ✢[3]	18	22.00 S	82.00 W
Naze	93b	28.23 N	129.30 E
Nazeing	260	51.44 N	0.03 E
N'azepetrovsk	86	56.03 N	59.36 E
Naẕerat (Nazareth)	132	32.42 N	35.18 E
Naẕerat ʿIllit	132	32.42 N	35.19 E
Nazija	76	59.50 N	31.35 E
Nazik Gölü ⊜	130	38.50 N	42.16 E
Nazilli	130	37.55 N	28.21 E
Nazimicha	265b	55.59 N	38.08 E
Nazımiye	130	39.11 N	39.50 E
Nazimovo	86	59.30 N	90.58 E
Nazina	86	60.07 N	78.52 E
Nāzira	120	26.55 N	94.44 E
Nāzir Hāt	120	22.38 N	91.47 E
Nāzirpur	126	22.43 N	89.58 E
Nazko ≃	182	53.07 N	123.34 W
Nazlat al-ʿAmūdayn	142	28.14 N	30.42 E
Nazlat al-Badramān	142	27.40 N	30.44 E
Nazlat as-Sammān	273c	29.59 N	31.08 E
Nazlat Khalīfah	273c	30.01 N	31.10 E
Nazlat Quftan Bāshā	142	28.57 N	30.49 E
Nazlat Thābit	142	28.25 N	30.47 E
Nazran'	84	43.13 N	44.46 E
Nazret	144	8.33 N	39.16 E
Nazyvajevsk	86	55.34 N	71.21 E
N. B. C. Studios ⊛[3]	280	34.09 N	118.20 W
Nchanga	154	12.30 S	27.53 E
Nchelenge	154	9.20 S	28.50 E
Ncue	152	2.01 N	10.28 E
Ndabala	154	13.28 S	29.50 E
Ndala	154	4.46 S	33.16 E
N'dalatando	152	9.18 S	14.54 E
Ndali	150	9.51 N	2.43 E
Ndanda	152	5.12 N	22.21 E
Ndande	150	15.16 N	16.30 W
Ndarassa	152	6.49 N	22.15 E
Ndélé	146	8.24 N	20.39 E
Ndélélé	152	4.02 N	14.56 E
Ndemba	152	0.11 N	14.19 E
Ndendé	152	2.23 S	11.23 E
Ndikiniméki	152	4.46 N	10.50 E
Ndindi	152	3.46 S	11.09 E
N'Djamena	146	12.07 N	15.03 E
Ndji ≃	152	6.47 N	22.14 E
Ndjili •[8]	273b	4.20 S	15.22 E
Ndjili ≃	273b	4.19 S	15.24 E
Ndjili, Grande Île de la I	273b	4.19 S	15.24 E
Ndjim ≃	152	4.38 N	11.24 E
Ndjo	152	1.15 S	14.30 E
Ndjolé	152	0.11 S	10.45 E
Ndogo, Lagune ⊂	152	2.35 S	10.00 E
Ndola	154	12.58 S	28.38 E
Ndolo •[8]	273b	4.19 S	15.19 E
Ndona	115b	8.46 S	121.45 E
Ndongo	152	2.19 S	13.38 E
Ndouba	152	0.11 S	14.09 E
Ndougou	152	1.39 S	9.40 E
Ndu	152	4.41 N	22.49 E
Nduguti	154	4.18 S	34.42 E
Nduindui	175f	15.24 S	167.46 E
Ndumbwe	154	10.14 S	39.58 E
Ndumu Game Reserve •[4]	158	26.53 S	32.15 E
Nduye	154	1.50 N	29.01 E
Ne	268	35.47 N	140.03 E
Nea ≃	26	63.13 N	11.02 E
Neabul Creek ≃	166	27.45 S	147.32 E
Néa Erithraía	267c	38.05 N	23.49 E
Néa Filadhélfia	267c	38.02 N	23.44 E
Neagari	94	36.27 N	136.27 E
Neagh, Lough ⊜	48	54.38 N	6.24 W
Neah Bay	224	48.22 N	124.37 W
Néa Ionía	267c	38.02 N	23.45 E
Neajlov ≃	38	44.11 N	26.12 E
Néa Khalkidhón	267c	38.02 N	23.43 E
Neale, Lake ⊜	162	24.22 S	130.00 E
Neales ≃	162	28.08 S	136.47 E
Neales Flat	168b	34.15 S	139.10 E
Néa Liósia	267c	38.02 N	23.42 E
Neamț □[6]	38	47.00 N	26.30 E
Neandertal, Naturschutzgebiet ♦	263	51.15 N	7.00 E
Néa Páfos (Paphos)	130	34.45 N	32.25 E
Neapel → Napoli	68	40.51 N	14.17 E
Néa Pendéli	267c	38.04 N	23.52 E
Néa Péramos	267c	38.00 N	23.26 E
Neápolis, Ellás	38	36.30 N	23.04 E
Neápolis, Ellás	38	35.15 N	25.37 E
Neapolis, Oh., U.S.	216	41.29 N	83.52 W
Near Islands II	181a	52.40 N	173.30 E
Near North Side •[8]	278	41.54 N	87.38 W
Néa Smírni	267c	37.57 N	23.43 E
Neasons Hill	214	41.37 N	80.08 W
Neatahwanta, Lake ⊜	210	43.18 N	76.27 W
Neath	42	51.40 N	3.48 W
Neath ≃	42	51.37 N	3.50 W
Neauphle-le-Château	50	48.49 N	1.54 E
Neauphle-le-Vieux	261	48.49 N	1.52 E
Neavitt	208	38.43 N	76.16 W
Neba	94	35.15 N	137.35 E
Nebbi	150	2.29 N	31.06 E
Nebbou	150	11.18 N	1.53 W
Nebelhorn ∧	58	47.25 N	10.20 E
Nebesnaja, gora ∧	86	43.19 N	80.44 E
Nebeur	36	36.17 N	8.47 E
Nebine Creek ≃	166	29.07 S	146.56 E
Nebit-Dag	128	39.30 N	54.22 E
Neblina, Pico da ∧	246	0.48 N	66.02 W
Nebo	194	39.27 N	90.47 W
Nebo, Mount ∧, Ut,. U.S.	200	39.49 N	111.46 W
Nebo, Mount → Nabā, Jabal an- ∧, Urd.	132	31.46 N	35.45 E
Nebolči	76	59.08 N	33.18 E
Nebra	54	51.17 N	11.34 E
Nebraska	218	39.04 N	85.28 W
Nebraska □[3], U.S.	178	41.30 N	100.00 W
Nebraska □[3], U.S.	198	41.30 N	100.00 W
Nebraska City	198	40.40 N	95.51 W
Nebrodi ⋏	70	37.54 N	14.35 E
Nebyloje	80	56.22 N	39.59 E
Nečajevka	80	53.17 N	44.27 E
Nečajevo	82	54.42 N	37.23 E
Necaxa ≃	234	20.16 N	97.27 W
Necedah	190	44.01 N	90.04 W
Nechajevskij	80	50.25 N	41.44 E
Nechako ≃	182	53.56 N	122.42 W
Nechako Plateau ⋏[1]	182	54.00 N	124.30 W
Nechako Range ⋏	182	53.20 N	124.30 W
Nechako Reservoir ⊜[1]	182	53.25 N	125.10 W
Nechayane	78	46.57 N	31.33 E
Neche	198	48.59 N	97.33 W
Neches	222	31.52 N	95.30 W
Neches ≃	194	29.55 N	93.52 W
Nechí	246	8.07 N	74.46 W
Nechí ≃	246	8.08 N	74.46 W
Nechisar National Park ♦	144	6.00 N	37.50 E
Nechmeya	36	36.36 N	7.31 E
Nechranická Přehradová Nádrž ⊜[1]	54	50.20 N	13.20 E
Neckar ≃	30	49.31 N	8.26 E
Neckarbischofsheim	56	49.17 N	8.57 E
Neckarelz	56	49.20 N	9.06 E
Neckargemünd	56	49.23 N	8.47 E
Neckarsteinach	56	49.25 N	8.53 E
Neckarsulm	56	49.12 N	9.13 E
Neckartailfingen	56	48.36 N	9.16 E
Neckartenzlingen	56	48.35 N	9.14 E
Neck Creek ≃	276	40.36 N	74.12 W
Necker	284b	39.23 N	76.29 W
Necker Island I, Br. Vir. Is.	240m	18.33 N	64.21 W
Necker Island I, Hi., U.S.	14	23.35 N	164.42 W
Necker Ridge ✢[3]	14	22.00 N	167.15 W
Necochea	252	38.33 S	58.45 W
Necrópolis •	266a	40.25 N	3.38 W
Nedalssjön ⊜	26	62.56 N	12.11 E
Nedanchychi	78	51.30 N	30.37 E
Ned Brown Preserve ♦	278	42.02 N	88.01 W
Nedel'noje	82	54.50 N	36.39 E
Nederland	194	29.58 N	93.59 W
Nederland → Netherlands □[1]	30	52.15 N	5.30 E
Nederlandse Antillen → Netherlands Antilles □[2]	241s	12.15 N	69.00 W
Neder-Rijn ≃[1]	52	51.58 N	5.20 E
Nederweert	52	51.17 N	5.45 E
Nederzwalm-Hermelgem	50	50.53 N	3.41 E
Nedlands	168a	31.59 S	115.49 E
Nedlitz	54	52.04 N	12.14 E
Nedlitz •[8]	264a	52.26 N	13.03 E
Nêdong	120	29.14 N	91.46 E
Nedre Soppero	24	68.01 N	21.44 E
Nedre Vättern ⊜	40	59.49 N	15.40 E
Nédroma	148	35.01 N	1.45 W
Nedrow	210	42.58 N	76.08 W
Nedryhayliv	78	50.50 N	33.53 E
Nedstrand	26	59.21 N	5.51 E
Neebish Island I	190	46.16 N	84.09 W
Neede	52	52.08 N	6.36 E
Needham, In., U.S.	218	39.32 N	85.58 W
Needham, Ma., U.S.	207	42.17 N	71.14 W
Needham Market	42	52.09 N	1.03 E
Needhams Point ›	241g	13.05 N	59.36 W
Needle Mountain ∧	202	44.05 N	109.37 W
Needles	204	34.50 N	114.36 W
Needling Hill ∧[2]	168a	31.53 S	116.56 E
Needville	222	29.23 N	95.50 W
Neelyton	214	40.10 N	77.50 W
Ñeembucú □[5]	252	27.00 S	58.00 W
Neenah	190	44.11 N	88.27 W
Neepawa	184	50.13 N	99.29 W
Neerabup National Park ♦	168a	31.41 S	115.43 E
Neerim South	169	38.01 S	145.58 E
Neermoor	52	53.18 N	7.26 E
Neeroeteren	56	51.05 N	5.42 E
Neerpelt	56	51.13 N	5.25 E
Neersen	263	51.15 N	6.29 E
Nee Soon	271c	1.24 N	103.49 E
Neetze	52	53.15 N	10.39 E
Neetze ≃	54	53.20 N	10.28 E
Nefedjevo, Ross.	82	54.39 N	37.56 E
Nefedjevo, Ross.	265b	55.54 N	37.10 E
Neffs	208	40.42 N	75.37 W
Neffsville	208	40.06 N	76.18 W
Nef'odovo	86	58.48 N	72.34 E
Nefta	148	33.52 N	7.33 E
Neftçala	84	39.23 N	49.16 E
Nefteabad	85	40.12 N	70.34 E
Neftegorsk	84	44.22 N	39.42 E
Neftekumsk	84	44.45 N	44.48 E
Nefyn	42	52.57 N	4.31 W
Nefza	36	36.58 N	9.05 E
Negage	152	7.45 S	15.16 E
Négala	150	12.52 N	8.27 W
Negapatam → Nāgappattinam	122	10.46 N	79.50 E
Negara, Indon.	112	2.37 S	115.06 E
Negara, Indon.	115a	8.22 S	114.37 E
Negara ≃	112	3.00 S	114.45 E
Negast	54	54.15 N	13.01 E
Negaunee	190	46.29 N	87.36 W
Negba	132	31.40 N	34.41 E
Negele	144	5.20 N	39.36 E
Negenborn	52	51.53 N	9.34 E
Negeribatin	112	4.35 S	104.32 E
Negeri Sembilan □[3]	114	2.45 N	102.10 E
Negev Desert → HaNegev •[1]	132	30.30 N	34.55 E
Negishi	268	35.51 N	139.23 E
Negley	214	40.47 N	80.32 W
Negola	152	14.10 S	14.30 E
Negomano	154	11.27 S	38.31 E
Negombo	122	7.13 N	79.50 E
Negoreloje	76	53.36 N	27.04 E
Negotin	38	44.14 N	22.32 E
Negra, Laguna ⊜	252	34.03 S	53.40 W
Negra, Ponta ›	256	22.58 S	42.42 W
Negra, Punta ›, Belize	232	16.17 N	88.34 W
Negra, Punta ›, Perú	248	6.06 S	81.09 W
Negrais	266c	38.53 N	9.17 W
Negras, Lomas ∧[2]	286d	11.55 S	77.06 W
Negreira	34	42.54 N	8.44 W
Nègres, Pointe des ›	240e	14.36 N	61.06 W
Negrești	38	46.50 N	27.27 E
Negrești-Oaș	38	47.52 N	23.25 E
Negrine	148	34.30 N	7.30 E
Negritos	246	4.38 S	81.19 W
Negro ≃, Arg.	254	41.02 S	62.47 W
Negro ≃, Bol.	248	9.49 S	65.42 W
Negro ≃, Bol.	248	14.11 S	63.07 W
Negro ≃, Bra.	248	5.15 S	70.53 W
Negro ≃, Bra.	248	19.13 S	57.17 W
Negro ≃, Bra.	250	9.15 S	47.34 W
Negro ≃, Bra.	252	26.01 S	50.30 W
Negro ≃, Col.	246	5.44 N	74.39 W
Negro ≃, N.A.	236	13.02 N	87.17 W
Negro ≃, Para.	252	24.23 S	57.11 W
Negro ≃, S.A.	246	3.08 S	59.55 W
Negro ≃, S.A.	252	33.24 S	58.22 W
Negro, Baia del ⊂	144	7.55 N	49.55 E
Negro, Cerro ∧, Arg.	254	46.55 S	70.12 W
Negro, Cerro ∧, Arg.	254	44.09 S	69.30 W
Negro, Cerro ∧, Méx.	234	17.19 N	97.25 W
Negro, Mar → Black Sea ≂[2]	22	43.00 N	35.00 E
Negros I	116	10.00 N	123.00 E
Negros Occidental □[4]	116	10.20 N	123.00 E
Negros Oriental □[4]	116	9.40 N	123.00 E
Negru Vodă	38	43.50 N	28.12 E
Neguac	186	47.15 N	65.05 W
Nehalem	224	45.43 N	123.53 W
Nehalem ≃	224	45.40 N	123.56 W
Nehawka	198	40.49 N	95.59 W
Nehbandān	128	31.32 N	60.02 E
Neheim-Hüsten	56	51.27 N	7.57 E
Nehonsey Brook ≃	285	39.49 N	75.18 W
Néhoué, Baie de ⊂	175f	20.21 S	164.09 E
Nehru Planetarium ⊛	272c	18.59 N	72.49 E
Neiba	238	18.28 N	71.25 W
Neichiang → Neijiang	107	29.35 N	105.03 E
Neidpath	184	50.13 N	107.15 W
Neige, Crêt de la ∧	58	46.16 N	5.56 E
Neiges, Piton des ∧	157c	21.05 S	55.29 E
Neihart	202	46.56 N	110.44 W
Neihe ≃	100	22.54 N	115.38 E
Neihu	269d	25.05 N	121.34 E
Neihuang	98	35.59 N	114.55 E
Neijiang	107	29.35 N	105.03 E
Neikiang → Neijiang	107	29.35 N	105.03 E
Neilburg	184	52.50 N	109.38 W
Neillsville	190	44.33 N	90.35 W
Neilston	46	55.47 N	4.27 W
Neimen	263	51.29 N	7.48 E
Nei Monggol Zizhiqu (Inner Mongolia) □[4]	90	43.00 N	115.00 E
Nein	132	32.38 N	35.21 E
Neindorf	54	52.20 N	10.50 E
Neinstedt	54	51.45 N	11.05 E
Neiqiu	98	37.17 N	114.31 E
Neira	246	5.10 N	75.32 W
Neirone	62	44.27 N	9.11 E
Neishuishan	269d	25.09 N	121.43 E
Neisse (Nysa Łużycka) (Nisa) ≃	30	52.04 N	14.46 E
Neiva	246	2.56 N	75.18 W
Neiwufuquan	105	40.11 N	117.39 E
Neixiang	102	33.12 N	111.57 E
Neixpa ≃	234	18.05 N	102.46 W
Neizeng Shan ∧	100	24.02 N	117.32 E
Neja, Ross.	80	58.24 N	46.31 E
Neja, Ross.	80	58.18 N	43.54 E
Neja ≃	80	57.48 N	43.42 E
Nejapa de Madero	234	16.37 N	95.59 W
Nejd → Najd □[9]	118	25.00 N	44.30 E
Nejdek	54	50.17 N	12.42 E
Nejo	144	9.30 N	35.30 E
Nejva ≃	86	57.54 N	62.18 E
Nejvo-Šajtanskij	86	57.44 N	61.15 E
Nekalagba	154	2.50 N	28.01 E
Nekemte	144	9.02 N	36.31 E
Nekhab ⊥	140	25.10 N	32.48 E
Nekhvoroshcha	78	49.09 N	34.44 E
Nekoosa	190	44.18 N	89.54 W
Nekor, Oued ≃	34	35.14 N	3.45 W
Neko-zaki ›	96	35.40 N	134.46 E
Nekrasino	82	56.18 N	36.33 E
Nekrasovka	265b	55.41 N	37.56 E
Nekrasovo, Ross.	80	51.10 N	45.18 E
Nekrasovo, Ross.	82	54.30 N	38.57 E
Nekrasovskoje	80	57.41 N	40.22 E
Nekselø I	41	55.47 N	11.18 E
Neksø	26	55.04 N	15.09 E
Nela Park ♦	279a	41.33 N	81.33 W
Nel'aty	88	56.29 N	115.41 E
Nelichu ∧	140	6.08 N	34.25 E
Nelidovo	76	56.13 N	32.46 E
Neligh	198	42.07 N	98.01 W
Nel'kan	74	57.40 N	136.13 E
Nellie	214	40.20 N	82.04 W
Nellikuppam	122	11.46 N	79.41 E
Nellingen	56	48.33 N	9.47 E
Nellis Air Force Base ■	204	36.14 N	115.02 W
Nelliston	210	42.56 N	74.37 W
Nellis Weapons Range ■	204	37.15 N	116.20 W
Nellore	122	14.26 N	79.58 E
Nel'ma	89	47.39 N	139.09 E
Nelson, B.C., Can.	182	49.29 N	117.17 W
Nelson, N.Z.	172	41.17 S	173.17 E
Nelson, Eng., U.K.	44	53.51 N	2.13 W
Nelson, Ne., U.S.	198	40.12 N	98.04 W
Nelson, Pa., U.S.	210	41.59 N	77.14 W
Nelson ≃	184	57.04 N	92.30 W
Nelson, Cape ›, Austl.	166	38.26 S	141.33 E
Nelson, Cape ›, Pap. N. Gui.	164	9.00 S	149.15 E
Nelson, Estrecho ⋃	254	51.37 S	75.00 W
Nelson Creek ≃	222	30.56 N	95.31 W
Nelson House	184	55.47 N	98.51 W
Nelson Island I	180	60.35 N	164.45 W
Nelson-Kennedy Ledges State Park ♦	214	41.18 N	81.04 W
Nelson Lake ⊜	184	55.44 N	100.00 W
Nelson Lakes National Park ♦	172	41.50 S	172.40 E
Nelson Reservoir ⊜[1]	202	48.30 N	107.34 W
Nelson's Dockyard ⊥	240c	17.00 N	61.46 W
Nelsonville, N.Y., U.S.	210	41.25 N	73.57 W
Nelsonville, Oh., U.S.	188	39.27 N	82.14 W
Nelspoort	158	32.07 S	23.00 E
Nelspoortjie	158	29.58 S	22.25 E
Nelspruit	156	25.30 S	30.58 E
Néma, Maur.	150	16.37 N	7.15 W
Nema, Ross.	80	57.31 N	50.31 E
Néma, Dahr ⊥[4]	150	16.40 N	7.13 W
Nemadji ≃	190	46.41 N	92.02 W
Nemah	224	46.31 N	123.51 W
Nemaha	198	40.20 N	95.40 W
Neman	76	55.02 N	22.02 E
Neman (Nemunas) ≃	76	55.18 N	21.23 E
Nematābād •[8]	267d	35.38 N	51.21 E
Nembe	150	4.35 N	6.26 E
Nembrala	112	10.53 S	122.50 E
Nembro	62	45.45 N	9.45 E
Nemčinovka	265b	55.43 N	37.23 E
Nemda ≃, Ross.	80	57.35 N	48.56 E
Nemda ≃, Ross.	80	57.21 N	43.08 E
Nemegosenda ≃	190	48.31 N	82.53 W
Nemegt uul ⋏	102	43.40 N	101.10 E
Nemeiben Lake ⊜	184	55.20 N	105.20 W
Nemenčinė	76	54.51 N	25.29 E
Nementcha, Monts de ⋏	148	34.52 N	7.05 E
Nemeriči	76	53.51 N	33.59 E
Nemi	66	41.43 N	12.43 E
Nemi, Lago di ⊜	267a	41.43 N	12.42 E
Nemira Mare, Vârful ∧	38	46.15 N	26.19 E
Nemirovo	82	55.54 N	36.12 E
Nemo	222	32.16 N	97.39 W
Nemoli	68	40.04 N	15.48 E
Nemor ≃	89	48.23 N	124.32 E
Nemours	50	48.16 N	2.42 E
Nemovychi	78	51.16 N	26.38 E
Nemrut Gölü ⊜	130	38.37 N	42.12 E
Nemuna, Bjeshkët e ⋏	38	42.27 N	19.47 E
Nemunas (Neman) ≃	76	55.18 N	21.23 E
Nemuro	92a	43.20 N	145.35 E
Nemuro-hantō ›[1]	92a	43.21 N	145.42 E
Nemuro Strait ⋃	92a	44.00 N	145.20 E
Nemyriv, Ukr.	78	50.07 N	23.25 E
Nemyriv, Ukr.	78	48.58 N	28.50 E
Nemzeti Museum ⊛	264c	47.29 N	19.05 E
Nen ≃	89	45.25 N	124.40 E
Nena Creek ≃	224	45.07 N	121.07 W
Nenagh	48	52.52 N	8.12 W
Nenagh ≃	48	52.56 N	8.17 W
Nenana	180	64.34 N	149.07 W
Nenana ≃	180	64.30 N	149.00 W
Nenaševo	82	54.34 N	37.28 E
Nenasi	114	3.08 N	103.27 E
Nendaz	58	46.11 N	7.18 E
Nendeln	58	47.12 N	9.32 E
Nendo I	14	10.45 S	165.54 E
Nene ≃	42	52.48 N	0.13 E
Neneckij □[3]	72	67.30 N	54.00 E
Nenetsia → Neneckij □[3]	72	67.30 N	54.00 E
Nenggiri ≃	114	4.53 N	101.48 E
Nengjia	104	41.38 N	120.46 E
Nengo ≃	152	14.27 S	22.09 E
Nengonengo I[1]	14	18.47 S	141.48 W
Nenneper Fleuth ≃	263	51.32 N	6.26 E
Neno	154	15.24 S	34.39 E
Nentón ≃	236	15.48 N	91.52 W
Nenzing	58	47.11 N	9.42 E
Neo	94	35.38 N	136.37 E
Neo ≃	94	35.24 N	136.34 E
Neodesha	198	37.25 N	95.40 W
Neoga	194	39.19 N	88.27 W
Neola, Ia., U.S.	198	41.26 N	95.36 W
Neola, Ut,. U.S.	200	40.26 N	110.01 W
Neoneli	71	40.04 N	8.57 E
Néon Fáliron	267c	37.57 N	23.40 E
Néon Karlovásion	38	37.48 N	26.44 E
Néon Psikhikón	267c	38.00 N	23.47 E
Neopit	190	44.58 N	88.49 W
Neópolis	250	10.18 S	36.35 W
Neoshera	123	33.09 N	74.14 E
Neosho	194	36.52 N	94.22 W
Neosho ≃	194	35.48 N	95.18 W
Neotsu	224	45.00 N	123.58 W
Nepa ≃	88	59.16 N	108.16 E
Nepal (Nepāl) □[1], Asia	118	28.00 N	84.00 E

ENGLISH

Name	Page	Lat.°′	Long.°′
Nepal (Nepāl) □[1], Asia	124	28.00 N	84.00 E
Nepālgañj	124	28.03 N	81.37 E
Nepa Nagar	120	21.28 N	76.23 E
Nepaug Reservoir ⊜[1]	207	41.48 N	72.57 W
Nepean	212	45.18 N	75.47 W
Nepean ≃	170	33.27 S	150.53 E
Nepean, Point ›	169	38.18 S	144.39 E
Nepean Bay ⊂	168b	35.42 S	137.44 E
Nepean Island I	174c	29.04 S	167.58 E
Nepean Reservoir ⊜[1]	170	34.22 S	150.35 E
Nepecino	82	55.12 N	38.37 E
Nepeña	248	9.10 S	78.23 W
Nepewassi Lake ⊜	190	46.20 N	80.40 W
Nephi	200	39.42 N	111.50 W
Nephin ∧	48	54.01 N	9.22 W
Nephin Beg Range ⋏	48	54.00 N	9.35 W
Nepi	66	42.14 N	12.21 E
Nepisiguit ≃	186	47.37 N	65.38 W
Nepisiguit Bay ⊂	186	47.46 N	65.32 W
Népliget ♦	264c	47.29 N	19.07 E
Nepoko ≃	154	1.40 N	27.01 E
Nepomuceno	256	21.14 S	45.15 W
Nepomuk	60	49.29 N	13.36 E
Neponset ≃	283	42.17 N	71.02 W
Neponset Reservoir ⊜[1]	283	42.05 N	71.15 W
Neponset River Reservation ♦	283	42.13 N	71.08 W
Neppermin	54	53.56 N	14.02 E
Nepr'advа ≃	76	53.40 N	38.39 E
Nép-sziget I	264c	47.34 N	19.05 E
Neptune, N.J., U.S.	208	40.12 N	74.02 W
Neptune, Oh., U.S.	216	40.36 N	84.30 W
Neptune Beach	192	30.18 N	81.23 W
Neptune City	208	40.12 N	74.02 W
Neqarot, Naḥal V	132	30.40 N	35.15 E
Nera ≃, Europe	38	44.49 N	21.22 E
Nera ≃, It.	66	42.26 N	12.24 E
Nérac	32	44.08 N	0.20 E
Nerákion	267c	38.01 N	23.27 E
Nerang	171a	28.00 S	153.20 E
Nerang ≃	171a	28.03 S	153.17 E
Neratovice	54	50.14 N	14.31 E
Nerča ≃	88	51.56 N	116.40 E
Nerchau	54	51.16 N	12.47 E
Nerčinsk	88	51.58 N	116.35 E
Nerčinskij Zavod	88	51.19 N	119.36 E
Nère ≃	50	47.34 N	2.18 E
Nerechta	80	57.28 N	40.34 E
Nerenstetten	56	48.31 N	10.06 E
Neresheim	56	48.45 N	10.15 E
Nereta	76	56.13 N	25.18 E
Nereto	66	42.49 N	13.49 E
Neretva ≃	36	43.01 N	17.27 E
Nerevoznoje	80	56.53 N	53.54 E
Nerima •[8]	268	35.44 N	139.39 E
Neris (Vilija) ≃	76	54.54 N	23.53 E
Nerito	66	42.32 N	13.28 E
Nerja	34	36.44 N	3.52 W
Nerka, Lake ⊜	180	59.30 N	158.45 W
Nerl', Ross.	76	57.03 N	37.59 E
Nerl', Ross.	80	56.40 N	40.24 E
Nerl' ≃, Ross.	76	57.07 N	37.39 E
Nerl' ≃, Ross.	80	56.11 N	40.34 E
Nero, ozero ⊜	80	57.07 N	39.27 E
Neroj	88	54.28 N	97.49 E
Néronde	62	45.50 N	4.14 E
Nérondes	32	47.00 N	2.49 E
Nerópolis	255	16.25 S	49.14 W
Nerriga	170	35.07 S	150.05 E
Nerrima	162	18.24 S	124.29 E
Nerrimunga Creek ≃	170	34.57 S	150.04 E
Nersingen	58	48.25 N	10.07 E
Nerskaja ≃	82	55.23 N	38.35 E
Nerul	272c	19.02 N	73.01 E
Nerus ≃	114	5.20 N	103.05 E
Nerussa ≃	76	52.33 N	33.47 E
Nerva	34	37.42 N	6.32 W
Nervi	62	44.23 N	9.02 E
Nervia ≃	62	43.47 N	7.38 E
Nerviano	266b	45.33 N	8.58 E
Nerville-la-Forêt	261	49.05 N	2.17 E
Nes, Ned.	52	53.04 N	5.51 E
Nes, Ned.	52	53.26 N	5.45 E
Nes, Nor.	26	60.34 N	9.59 E
Nes', Ross.	24	66.37 N	44.36 E
Nes, Har ∧	132	30.22 N	34.37 E
Nesbyen	26	60.34 N	9.09 E
Neščerdo, ozero ⊜	76	55.54 N	29.04 E
Nesco	208	39.38 N	74.41 W
Nescochague Creek ≃	285	39.39 N	74.41 W
Nescochague Creek, Great Swamp Branch ≃	285	39.41 N	74.43 W
Nesconset	276	40.51 N	73.09 W
Nescopeck	210	41.03 N	76.13 W
Nescopeck Creek ≃	210	41.03 N	76.14 W
Nescopeck Mountain ∧	210	41.03 N	76.05 W
Nesebăr	38	42.39 N	27.44 E
Neshaminy Creek ≃	208	40.04 N	74.55 W
Neshaminy Hills	285	40.10 N	74.57 W
Neshaminy Mall •[9]	285	40.08 N	74.57 W
Neshaminy State Park ♦	285	40.05 N	74.55 W
Neshaminy Woods	285	40.10 N	74.57 W
Neshannock Creek ≃	214	40.59 N	80.21 W
Neshcheretove	83	49.24 N	38.48 E
Nesher	132	32.46 N	35.03 E
Nesjøen ⊜[1]	26	63.02 N	12.01 E
Neškan	180	67.03 N	173.01 W
Neskaupstaður	24a	65.10 N	13.43 W
Neskowin	224	45.06 N	123.58 W
Neskynpil'gyn, laguna ⊂	180	66.57 N	172.45 W
Nesle	50	49.46 N	2.55 E
Nesna	24	66.12 N	13.02 E
Nespelem	182	48.10 N	118.58 W
Nesque ≃	62	43.59 N	4.59 E
Nesquehoning	210	40.51 N	75.48 W
Ness	262	53.17 N	3.03 W
Ness, Loch ⊜	46	57.15 N	4.30 W
Ness City	198	38.27 N	99.54 W
Nesse ≃	54	50.59 N	10.32 E
Nesselrode, Mount ∧	180	58.58 N	134.18 W
Nesselwang	58	47.37 N	10.30 E
Nesselwängle	58	47.29 N	10.37 E
Nesslau	58	47.13 N	9.13 E
Nessmersiel	52	53.40 N	7.21 E
Nesso	58	45.55 N	9.08 E
Neštěmice	54	50.40 N	14.07 E
Nesterkovo	76	59.10 N	30.33 E
Nesterov	76	54.38 N	22.34 E
Nesterovka	80	52.26 N	53.42 E
Nesterovo, Ross.	80	54.31 N	41.49 E
Nesterovo, Ross.	82	56.45 N	36.30 E
Nesterovo, Ross.	88	52.22 N	107.53 E
Nestiary	80	56.34 N	45.21 E
Neston	44	53.18 N	3.04 W
Nestore ≃	66	43.21 N	12.15 E
Néstos (Mesta) ≃	38	40.41 N	24.44 E
Nestoyita	78	47.47 N	29.21 E
Nesttun	26	60.19 N	5.20 E
Nestucca ≃	224	45.12 N	123.57 W
Nesvetaj	83	47.27 N	39.40 E
Nesviž	76	53.13 N	26.40 E
Nes Ẓiyyona	132	31.55 N	34.48 E
Netanya	132	32.20 N	34.51 E
Netarhāt	124	23.29 N	84.16 E
Netarts	224	45.26 N	123.56 W
Netarts Bay ⊂	224	45.24 N	123.56 W
Netcong	210	40.53 N	74.42 W
Nethan ≃	46	55.42 N	3.52 W
Nether Alderley	262	53.17 N	2.14 W
Netherdale	166	21.08 S	148.32 E
Netherlands (Nederland) □[1], Europe	22	52.15 N	5.30 E

DEUTSCH

Name	Seite	Breite°′	Länge°′ E = Ost
Netherlands (Nederland) □[1], Europe	30	52.15 N	5.30 E
Netherlands Antilles (Nederlandse Antillen) □[2], N.A.	230	12.15 N	68.45 W
Netherlands Antilles (Nederlandse Antillen) □[2], N.A.	241s	12.15 N	68.45 W
Netherton	262	53.30 N	2.58 W
Nethy Bridge	46	57.16 N	3.38 W
Netia	154	14.48 S	39.59 E
Netley Marsh	42	50.53 N	1.32 W
Neto ≃	68	39.13 N	17.08 E
Netolice	61	49.03 N	14.12 E
Netphen	56	50.55 N	8.06 E
Netra	56	51.06 N	10.05 E
Netrakona	124	24.53 N	90.43 E
Netstal	58	47.03 N	9.03 E
Nettancourt	56	48.52 N	4.57 E
Nette	52	52.02 N	10.05 E
Nette •[8]	263	51.33 N	7.25 E
Nettelstedt	52	52.18 N	8.41 E
Nettetal	56	51.18 N	6.16 E
Nettilling Fiord ⊂[2]	176	66.02 N	68.12 W
Nettilling Lake ⊜	176	66.30 N	70.40 W
Nett Lake ⊜	190	48.10 N	93.10 W
Nett Lake Indian Reservation •[4]	190	48.06 N	93.10 W
Nettlebed	42	51.35 N	1.00 W
Nettle Creek ≃	218	40.03 N	83.48 W
Nettleden	260	51.47 N	0.32 W
Nettleham	44	53.16 N	0.29 W
Nettlestead	260	51.15 N	0.25 E
Nettlestead Green	260	51.14 N	0.25 E
Nettleton	194	34.05 N	88.37 W
Nettuno	66	41.27 N	12.39 E
Nettuno, Grotta di ⊥[5]	71	40.34 N	8.09 E
Netzschkau	54	50.36 N	12.14 E
Neualbenreuth	60	49.59 N	12.27 E
Neu-Anspach	56	50.17 N	8.29 E
Neuastenberg	56	51.10 N	8.29 E
Neubeckum	52	51.48 N	8.01 E
Neubrandenburg	54	53.33 N	13.15 E
Neubraunschweig → New Brunswick □[4]	186	46.30 N	66.15 W
Neubritannien → New Britain I	164	6.00 S	150.00 E
Neu Büddenstedt	54	52.11 N	11.02 E
Neubukow	54	54.02 N	11.40 E
Neuburg am Inn	60	48.30 N	13.27 E
Neuburg an der Donau	60	48.44 N	11.11 E
Neuchâtel	58	46.59 N	6.56 E
Neuchâtel □[3]	58	47.00 N	6.55 E
Neuchâtel, Lac de ⊜	58	46.52 N	6.50 E
Neu-Delhi → New Delhi	124	28.36 N	77.12 E
Neudenau	56	49.17 N	9.16 E
Neudietendorf	54	50.55 N	10.55 E
Neudorf, Sk., Can.	184	50.44 N	102.59 W
Neudorf, Dtsch.	54	50.29 N	12.58 E
Neudorf •[8]	263	51.25 N	6.47 E
Neudörfl	61	47.48 N	16.17 E
Neue Hebriden → Vanuatu □[1]	175f	16.00 S	167.00 E
Neuemühle	264a	52.18 N	13.39 E
Neuenburg, Dtsch.	52	53.23 N	7.57 E
Neuenbürg, Dtsch.	56	48.50 N	8.35 E
Neuenburg, Dtsch.	58	47.49 N	7.35 E
Neuenburg → Neuchâtel, Schw.	58	46.59 N	6.56 E
Neuendettelsau	56	49.17 N	10.47 E
Neuendorf	54	54.31 N	13.05 E
Neuendorfer See ⊜	54	52.07 N	13.55 E
Neuenegg	58	46.54 N	7.18 E
Neuenhagen bei Berlin	54	52.32 N	13.41 E
Neuenhaus	52	52.30 N	6.59 E
Neuenhof •[8]	263	51.10 N	7.13 E
Neuenhoven	263	51.08 N	6.31 E
Neue Niers ≃	263	51.16 N	6.26 E
Neuenkamp •[8]	263	51.26 N	6.44 E
Neuenkirchen, Dtsch.	52	52.30 N	8.04 E
Neuenkirchen, Dtsch.	52	51.50 N	8.26 E
Neuenkirchen, Dtsch.	52	53.14 N	8.31 E
Neuenkirchen, Dtsch.	52	53.02 N	9.42 E
Neuenkirchen, Dtsch.	52	52.14 N	7.22 E
Neuenkirchen, Dtsch.	52	53.46 N	8.53 E
Neuenkirchen, Dtsch.	54	54.32 N	13.20 E
Neuenrade	56	51.17 N	7.47 E
Neuensalz	54	50.30 N	12.13 E
Neuenstadt am Kocher	56	49.14 N	9.20 E
Neuenwalde	52	53.40 N	8.40 E
Neuerburg	56	50.00 N	6.17 E
Neu-Erlaa •[8]	264b	48.08 N	16.19 E
Neues Palais ⊥	264a	52.24 N	13.01 E
Neu Fahrland	264a	52.26 N	13.03 E
Neufahrn bei Freising	60	48.19 N	11.40 E
Neufahrn in Niederbayern	60	48.44 N	12.11 E
Neuf-Brisach	58	48.01 N	7.32 E
Neufchâteau, Bel.	56	49.50 N	5.26 E
Neufchâteau, Fr.	58	48.21 N	5.42 E
Neufchâtel-en-Bray	50	49.44 N	1.27 E
Neufchâtel-sur-Aisne	50	49.26 N	4.02 E
Neufelden	61	48.29 N	14.00 E
Neuffen	56	48.33 N	9.22 E
Neuffossé, Canal de ≍	50	50.45 N	2.15 E
Neufmanil	56	49.49 N	4.48 E
Neuf-Marché	50	49.25 N	1.43 E
Neufmontiers-lès-Meaux	261	48.58 N	2.50 E
Neufundland → Newfoundland □[4]	176	52.00 N	56.00 W
Neufvilles	50	50.34 N	4.00 E
Neugersdorf	54	50.59 N	14.36 E
Neuglobsow	54	53.09 N	13.02 E
Neugraben-Fischbek •[8]	52	53.28 N	9.52 E
Neuguinea → New Guinea I	164	5.00 S	140.00 E
Neuharlingersiel	52	53.42 N	7.42 E
Neu-Hartmannsdorf	264a	52.22 N	13.51 E
Neuhaus, Dtsch.	54	50.30 N	11.08 E
Neuhaus, Dtsch.	54	53.17 N	10.55 E
Neuhaus, Dtsch.	58	47.48 N	8.34 E
Neuhaus, Öst.	61	47.47 N	15.11 E
Neuhaus an der Oste	52	53.48 N	9.02 E
Neuhausen, Dtsch.	54	50.41 N	13.28 E
Neuhausen, Dtsch.	58	47.58 N	8.55 E
Neuhausen, Schw.	58	47.41 N	8.37 E
Neuhaus im Solling	52	51.45 N	9.31 E
Neuhaus-Schierschnitz	54	50.19 N	11.14 E
Neuheum	114	5.34 N	95.32 E
Neuhof	56	50.27 N	9.40 E
Neuhof an der Zenn	56	49.27 N	10.38 E
Neuhofen	56	49.25 N	8.26 E
Neuhofen an der Krems	61	48.08 N	14.14 E
Neuillé-Pont-Pierre	50	47.33 N	0.33 E
Neuilly-en-Thelle	50	49.13 N	2.17 E
Neuilly-L'Évêque	58	47.55 N	5.26 E
Neuilly-Saint-Front	50	49.10 N	3.16 E
Neuilly-sur-Marne	261	48.51 N	2.32 E
Neuilly-sur-Seine	50	48.53 N	2.16 E
Neuirland → New Ireland I	164	3.20 S	152.00 E
Neu-Isenburg	56	50.03 N	8.41 E
Neukagran •[8]	264b	48.14 N	16.27 E
Neu-Kaledonien → New Caledonia □[2]	175f	21.30 S	165.30 E
Neukalen	54	53.49 N	12.47 E
Neu Kaliss	54	53.10 N	11.17 E

Symbols in the index entries represent the broad categories identified in the key at the right. Symbols with superior numbers (⋏[1]) identify subcategories (see complete key on page I · 1).

Symbole im Register stellen die rechts im Schlüssel erklärten Kategorien dar. Symbole mit hochgestellten Ziffern (⋏[1]) bezeichnen Unterabteilungen einer Kategorie (vgl. vollständiger Schlüssel auf Seite I · 1).

Los símbolos incluídos en el texto del índice representan las grandes categorías identificadas con la clave a la derecha. Los símbolos con numeros en su parte superior (⋏[1]) identifican las subcategorías (véase la clave completa en la página I · 1).

Les symboles de l'index représentent les catégories indiquées dans la légende à droite. Les symboles suivis d'un indice (⋏[1]) représentent des sous-catégories (voir légende complète à la page I · 1).

Os símbolos incluídos no texto do índice representam as grandes categorias identificadas com a chave à direita. Os símbolos com números em sua parte superior (⋏[1]) identificam as subcategorias (veja-se a chave completa à página I · 1).

Symbol	English	Deutsch	Español	Français	Português
∧	Mountain	Berg	Montaña	Montagne	Montanha
⋏	Mountains	Gebirge	Montañas	Montagnes	Montanhas
)(	Pass	Paß	Paso	Col	Passo
V	Valley, Canyon	Tal, Cañon	Valle, Cañón	Vallée, Canyon	Vale, Canhão
≐	Plain	Ebene	Llano	Plaine	Planície
›	Cape	Kap	Cabo	Cap	Cabo
I	Island	Insel	Isla	Île	Ilha
II	Islands	Inseln	Islas	Îles	Ilhas
⊥	Other Topographic Features	Andere Topographische Objekte	Otros Elementos Topográficos	Autres données topographiques	Outros acidentes topográficos

ESPAÑOL

Nombre	Página	Lat.°′	Long.°′ W = Oeste
Neukieritzsch	54	51.10 N	12.25 E
Neukirch, Dtsch.	54	51.17 N	13.58 E
Neukirch, Dtsch.	54	51.05 N	14.20 E
Neukirch, Dtsch.	58	47.39 N	9.41 E
Neukirchen, Dtsch.	41	54.52 N	8.44 E
Neukirchen, Dtsch.	54	51.05 N	12.32 E
Neukirchen, Dtsch.	54	50.47 N	12.22 E
Neukirchen, Dtsch.	54	50.46 N	12.52 E
Neukirchen, Dtsch.	54	54.19 N	11.01 E
Neukirchen, Dtsch.	56	50.52 N	9.20 E
Neukirchen, Dtsch.	56	50.46 N	9.41 E
Neukirchen, Dtsch.	56	49.29 N	6.50 E
Neukirchen, Dtsch.	60	49.05 N	11.45 E
Neukirchen, Dtsch.	263	51.07 N	6.41 E
Neukirchen, Öst.	64	47.15 N	12.17 E
Neukirchen am Walde	60	48.24 N	13.46 E
Neukirchen bei Sulzbach-Rosenberg	60	49.32 N	11.38 E
Neukirchen-Vluyn	56	51.27 N	6.33 E
Neukloster	54	53.52 N	11.41 E
Neukölln ➸[8]	54	52.29 N	13.27 E
Neu Kosenow	54	53.47 N	13.46 E
Neulangerwisch	264a	52.19 N	13.04 E
Neulengbach	61	48.12 N	15.55 E
Neulienken	54	53.27 N	14.22 E
Neu Lübbenau	54	52.04 N	13.53 E
Neulussheim	56	49.17 N	8.31 E
Neumagen	56	49.51 N	6.53 E
Neuman Creek ≃	284a	42.42 N	78.48 W
Neumark	54	50.39 N	12.21 E
Neumarkt → Târgu Secuiesc, Rom.	38	46.00 N	26.08 E
Neumarkt → Târgu Mureş, Rom.	38	46.33 N	24.33 E
Neumarkt am Wallersee	64	47.57 N	13.14 E
Neumarkt im Hausruckkreis	60	48.16 N	13.45 E
Neumarkt in der Oberpfalz	60	49.16 N	11.28 E
Neumarkt in Steiermark	61	47.04 N	14.25 E
Neumarkt-Sankt Veit	60	48.22 N	12.30 E
Neumünster	30	54.04 N	9.59 E
Neun ≃	110	19.42 N	104.03 E
Neunburg vorm Wald	60	49.21 N	12.24 E
Neundorf	54	51.49 N	11.34 E
Neung-sur-Beuvron	50	47.32 N	1.48 E
Neunkirchen, Dtsch.	56	50.32 N	8.06 E
Neunkirchen, Dtsch.	56	49.20 N	7.10 E
Neunkirchen, Dtsch.	56	50.48 N	8.00 E
Neunkirchen, Öst.	61	47.43 N	16.05 E
Neunkirchen am Brand	60	49.37 N	11.08 E
Neunkirchen am Potzberg	56	49.30 N	7.29 E
Neunkirchen-Seelscheid	56	50.51 N	7.20 E
Neuötting	60	48.14 N	12.42 E
Neupetershain	54	51.36 N	14.09 E
Neuquén	252	38.57 S	68.04 W
Neuquén □[4]	254	39.00 S	70.00 W
Neuquén ≃	252	38.59 S	68.00 W
Neurara	252	24.10 S	68.29 W
Neuravensburg	58	47.38 N	9.46 E
Neureisenberg	264b	48.01 N	16.30 E
Neurode → Nowa Ruda	30	50.35 N	16.31 E
Neuruppin	54	52.55 N	12.48 E
Neusalz → Nowa Sól	30	51.48 N	15.44 E
Neusalza-Spremberg	54	51.02 N	14.32 E
Neu Sankt Johann	58	47.14 N	9.12 E
Neusatz → Novi Sad	38	45.15 N	19.50 E
Neuschottland → Nova Scotia □[4]	186	45.00 N	63.00 W
Neuschwanstein, Schloss ʊ	64	47.35 N	10.44 E
Neuse ≃	192	35.06 N	76.30 W
Neuseddin	264a	52.18 N	12.59 E
Neuseeland → New Zealand □[1]	172	41.00 S	174.00 E
Neusibirische Inseln → Novosibirskije ostrova II	74	75.00 N	142.00 E
Neusiedl am See	61	47.57 N	16.51 E
Neusiedler See (Fertő) ⊜	61	47.50 N	16.45 E
Neusohl → Banská Bystrica	30	48.44 N	19.07 E
Neusorg	60	49.56 N	11.58 E
Neuss	56	51.12 N	6.41 E
Neusserweyhe	263	51.13 N	6.39 E
Neustadt, On., Can.	212	44.05 N	81.00 W
Neustadt, Dtsch.	54	52.52 N	12.25 E
Neustadt, Dtsch.	54	51.01 N	14.13 E
Neustadt, Dtsch.	54	50.44 N	11.44 E
Neustadt, Dtsch.	56	50.51 N	9.07 E
Neustadt, Dtsch.	56	50.37 N	7.26 E
Neustadt ➸[8]	52	53.04 N	8.47 E
Neustadt am Rübenberge	52	52.30 N	9.28 E
Neustadt an der Aisch	56	49.34 N	10.37 E
Neustadt an der Donau	60	48.48 N	11.46 E
Neustadt an der Waldnaab	60	49.44 N	12.11 E
Neustadt an der Weinstrasse	56	49.21 N	8.08 E
Neustadt bei Coburg	56	50.19 N	11.07 E
Neustädter Bucht ⊂	54	54.02 N	10.50 E
Neustadt-Glewe	54	53.25 N	11.36 E
Neustadt in Holstein	54	54.06 N	10.48 E
Neustettin → Szczecinek	30	53.43 N	16.42 E
Neustift am Walde ➸[8]	264b	48.15 N	16.18 E
Neustift im Stubaital	64	47.07 N	11.19 E
Neustrelitz	54	53.21 N	13.04 E
Neu Töplitz	264a	52.27 N	12.54 E
Neutral Hills ⩘[2]	184	52.10 N	110.50 W
Neutraubling	60	48.59 N	12.12 E
Neutrebbin	54	52.40 N	14.13 E
Neu-Ulm	58	48.23 N	10.01 E
Neuve-Chapelle	50	50.35 N	2.47 E
Neuves-Maisons	58	48.37 N	6.06 E
Neuvic	32	45.23 N	2.16 E
Neuville-aux-Bois	50	48.04 N	2.03 E
Neuville-de-Poitou	32	46.41 N	0.15 E
Neuville-en-Condroz	56	50.32 N	5.27 E
Neuville-lès-Dieppe	50	49.55 N	1.06 E
Neuville-sur-Oise	261	49.01 N	2.04 E
Neuville-sur-Saône	62	45.52 N	4.51 E
Neuvy-le-Roi	50	47.36 N	0.36 E
Neuvy-sur-Barangeon	50	47.19 N	2.15 E
Neuvy-sur-Loire	50	47.31 N	2.53 E
Neuwaldegg ➸[8]	264b	48.14 N	16.17 E
Neuwerk ➸[8]	263	51.13 N	6.28 E
Neuwerk I	52	53.55 N	8.30 E
Neuwied	56	50.25 N	7.27 E
Neuwiller-lès-Saverne	56	48.49 N	7.24 E
Neu Wulmstorf	52	53.28 N	9.48 E
Neuzelle	54	52.05 N	14.38 E
Neu Zittau	54	52.23 N	13.44 E
Neva ≃	265a	59.57 N	30.20 E
Névache	62	45.01 N	6.37 E
Nevada, Ia., U.S.	190	42.01 N	93.27 W
Nevada, Mo., U.S.	194	37.50 N	94.21 W
Nevada, Oh., U.S.	214	40.49 N	83.07 W
Nevada, Tx., U.S.	222	33.02 N	96.22 W
Nevada □[6]	226	39.16 N	121.01 W
Nevada □[3], U.S.	178	39.00 N	117.00 W
Nevada □[3], U.S.	204	39.00 N	117.00 W

FRANÇAIS

Nom	Page	Lat.°′	Long.°′ W = Ouest
Nevada, Sierra ⩘, Esp.	34	37.05 N	3.10 W
Nevada, Sierra ⩘, Ca., U.S.	204	38.00 N	119.15 W
Nevada City	226	39.15 N	121.00 W
Nevada Creek ≃	202	46.54 N	113.02 W
Nevado, Cerro ʌ, Arg.	252	35.35 S	68.30 W
Nevado, Cerro ʌ, Col.	246	3.59 N	74.04 W
Nevado de Colima, Parque Nacional del ♦	234	19.30 N	103.35 W
Nevado de Toluca, Parque Nacional ♦	234	19.10 N	99.44 W
Neval'cevo	86	58.38 N	81.53 E
Nevali	272c	19.01 N	73.07 E
Nevanka	88	56.30 N	98.54 E
Neve, Serra da ⩘	152	13.52 S	13.26 E
Nevel'	76	56.02 N	29.55 E
Nevel'sk	89	46.40 N	141.53 E
Nevel'skogo, proliv ⊔	89	52.05 N	141.35 E
Nevendon	260	51.36 N	0.30 E
Never	89	53.58 N	124.05 E
Neverkino	80	52.47 N	46.44 E
Neverovo	80	55.07 N	44.24 E
Nevers	32	47.00 N	3.09 E
Neversink ≃	210	41.21 N	74.42 W
Neversink Reservoir ⊜[1]	210	41.48 N	74.42 W
Nevertire	166	31.52 S	147.39 E
Neves	256	22.51 S	43.06 W
Nevesinje	38	43.15 N	18.07 E
Nevėžis ≃	76	54.56 N	23.46 E
Nevežkino	80	53.07 N	43.19 E
Neviano	68	40.06 N	18.06 E
Neviano degli Arduini	64	44.35 N	10.19 E
Neviges	56	51.19 N	7.05 E
Neville Island	279b	40.31 N	80.08 W
Neville Island I	279b	40.31 N	80.08 W
Nevinnomyssk	84	44.38 N	41.56 E
Nevis I	238	17.10 N	62.34 W
Nevis ≃	46	56.50 N	5.00 W
Nevis, Ben ʌ	46	56.48 N	5.01 W
Nevis, Loch ⊂	46	57.01 N	5.43 W
Nevjansk	86	57.32 N	60.13 E
Nevlunghamn	26	58.58 N	9.52 E
Nevon	88	58.07 N	102.49 E
Nevşehir	130	38.38 N	34.43 E
Nevşehir □[4]	130	38.50 N	34.40 E
Nevs'ke	83	49.09 N	37.58 E
Nevskoje	76	58.08 N	30.26 E
New ≃, Belize	232	18.22 N	88.24 W
New ≃, Guy.	246	3.23 N	57.36 W
New ≃, N.A.	204	33.08 N	115.44 W
New ≃, Eng., U.K.	260	51.40 N	0.01 W
New ≃, U.S.	192	38.10 N	81.12 W
New ≃, Az., U.S.	200	33.31 N	112.18 W
New ≃, Fl., U.S.	192	29.50 N	84.40 W
New ≃, Fl., U.S.	192	29.55 N	82.25 W
New ≃, N.C., U.S.	192	34.32 N	77.20 W
New ≃, S.C., U.S.	192	32.09 N	80.50 W
New ≃, Tn., U.S.	192	36.25 N	84.38 W
New, North Fork ≃	192	36.33 N	81.21 W
Newabāgam	272b	22.48 N	88.24 E
New Abbey	44	54.59 N	3.38 W
New Addington ➸[8]	260	51.21 N	0.01 W
Newala	154	10.56 S	39.18 E
New Albany, In., U.S.	218	38.17 N	85.49 W
New Albany, Ms., U.S.	194	34.29 N	89.00 W
New Albany, Oh., U.S.	214	40.05 N	82.49 W
New Albany, Pa., U.S.	210	41.36 N	76.27 W
New Albin	190	43.29 N	91.17 W
New Alexandria, Oh., U.S.	214	40.17 N	80.40 W
New Alexandria, Pa., U.S.	214	40.24 N	79.25 W
New Alexandria, Va., U.S.	284c	38.47 N	77.03 W
New Alfa	140	15.10 N	35.40 E
New Almaden	226	37.11 N	121.49 W
New Alresford	42	51.06 N	1.10 W
New Amsterdam	246	6.15 N	57.31 W
New Angledool	166	29.07 S	147.57 E
Newark, Ar., U.S.	194	35.42 N	91.26 W
Newark, Ca., U.S.	226	37.31 N	122.02 W
Newark, De., U.S.	208	39.41 N	75.45 W
Newark, Il., U.S.	216	41.32 N	88.35 W
Newark, Md., U.S.	208	38.15 N	75.17 W
Newark, Mo., U.S.	219	39.59 N	91.59 W
Newark, N.J., U.S.	210	40.44 N	74.10 W
Newark, N.Y., U.S.	210	43.02 N	77.05 W
Newark, Oh., U.S.	214	40.04 N	82.24 W
Newark, Tx., U.S.	222	33.00 N	97.29 W
Newark Bay ⊂, U.S.	276	40.39 N	74.09 W
Newark Bay ⊂, N.J., U.S.	276	40.40 N	74.08 W
Newark Bay Bridge ➸[5]	276	40.42 N	74.07 W
Newark International Airport ⊠	210	40.42 N	74.10 W
Newark Lake ⊜	204	39.41 N	115.44 W
Newark-on-Trent	44	53.05 N	0.49 W
Newark Slough ≃	282	37.31 N	122.05 W
Newark Valley	210	42.13 N	76.11 W
New Athens, Il., U.S.	219	38.19 N	89.52 W
New Athens, Oh., U.S.	214	40.11 N	80.59 W
New Augusta	194	31.12 N	89.02 W
Newaukum, North Fork ≃	224	46.36 N	122.51 W
Newaukum, South Fork ≃	224	46.36 N	122.51 W
Newaygo	190	43.25 N	85.48 W
New Baden, Il., U.S.	219	38.32 N	89.42 W
New Baden, Tx., U.S.	222	31.03 N	96.26 W
New Baltimore, Mi., U.S.	214	42.40 N	82.44 W
New Baltimore, N.Y., U.S.	210	42.26 N	73.47 W
New Bavaria	216	41.12 N	84.10 W
New Bedford, Ma., U.S.	207	41.38 N	70.56 W
New Bedford, Pa., U.S.	214	41.06 N	80.30 W
New Bedford ≃	42	52.35 N	0.20 E
Newberg	224	45.18 N	122.58 W
New Berlin, Il., U.S.	219	39.43 N	89.54 W
New Berlin, N.Y., U.S.	210	42.37 N	75.19 W
New Berlin, Pa., U.S.	210	40.53 N	76.59 W
New Berlin, Wi., U.S.	216	42.58 N	88.06 W
New Berlinville	208	40.20 N	75.38 W
Newbern, Al., U.S.	194	32.35 N	87.31 W
Newbern, Il., U.S.	219	39.01 N	90.20 W
New Bern, N.C., U.S.	192	35.06 N	77.02 W
Newbern, Tn., U.S.	194	36.06 N	89.15 W
Newberry, Fl., U.S.	192	29.38 N	82.36 W
Newberry, Mi., U.S.	190	46.21 N	85.30 W
Newberry, S.C., U.S.	192	34.16 N	81.37 W
Newbery, Aeroparque ⊠, Arg.	258	34.35 S	58.24 W
Newbery, Aeroparque ⊠, Arg.	288	34.35 S	58.24 W
New Bethlehem	214	41.00 N	79.19 W
Newbiggin-by-the-Sea	44	55.11 N	1.30 W
New Bight	238	24.19 N	75.24 W
New Bloomfield, Mo., U.S.	219	38.43 N	92.05 W
New Bloomfield, Pa., U.S.	208	40.25 N	77.11 W
New Bloomington	214	40.35 N	83.19 W
Newbold Island I	285	40.08 N	74.45 W
Newboro	212	44.39 N	76.19 W
Newboro Lake ⊜	212	44.38 N	76.20 W

PORTUGUÊS

Nome	Página	Lat.°′	Long.°′ W = Oeste
Newborough, Austl.	169	38.11 S	146.17 E
Newborough, Wales, U.K.	44	53.09 N	4.22 W
New Boston, Il., U.S.	190	41.10 N	90.59 W
New Boston, Mi., U.S.	216	42.09 N	83.24 W
New Boston, Oh., U.S.	218	38.45 N	82.56 W
New Boston, Tx., U.S.	194	33.27 N	94.24 W
New Braintree	207	42.19 N	72.07 W
New Braunfels	196	29.42 N	98.07 W
New Bremen	216	40.26 N	84.22 W
Newbridge → Droichead Nua	48	53.11 N	6.48 W
Newbridge on Wye	42	52.13 N	3.27 W
New Brighton, N.Z.	172	43.31 S	172.44 E
New Brighton, Eng., U.K.	262	53.26 N	3.03 W
New Brighton, Pa., U.S.	214	40.43 N	80.18 W
New Brighton ➸[8]	276	40.38 N	74.06 W
New Britain, Ct., U.S.	207	41.39 N	72.46 W
New Britain, Pa., U.S.	208	40.18 N	75.11 W
New Britain I	164	6.00 S	150.00 E
New Britain Trench ✢[1]	14	6.00 S	153.00 E
New Brockton	194	31.23 N	85.55 W
Newbrook	182	54.19 N	112.57 W
New Brooklyn County Park ♦	285	39.43 N	74.57 W
New Brunswick, In., U.S.	218	39.57 N	86.31 W
New Brunswick, N.J., U.S.	208	40.29 N	74.27 W
New Brunswick □[4], Can.	176	46.30 N	66.15 W
New Brunswick □[4], Can.	186	46.30 N	66.15 W
New Buffalo, Mi., U.S.	216	41.47 N	86.44 W
New Buffalo, Pa., U.S.	208	40.27 N	76.58 W
New Buildings	48	54.57 N	7.21 W
New Bullards Bar Lake ⊜[1]	226	39.25 N	121.08 W
Newburg, Mo., U.S.	194	37.54 N	91.54 W
Newburg, Pa., U.S.	208	40.08 N	77.32 W
Newburg, Pa., U.S.	214	40.31 N	78.25 W
Newburgh, On., Can.	212	44.19 N	76.52 W
Newburgh, Eng., U.K.	262	53.35 N	2.47 W
Newburgh, Scot., U.K.	46	57.18 N	2.00 W
Newburgh, Scot., U.K.	46	56.20 N	3.15 W
Newburgh, In., U.S.	194	37.56 N	87.24 W
Newburgh, N.Y., U.S.	210	41.30 N	74.00 W
Newburgh Heights	279a	41.27 N	81.39 W
Newburn	44	54.59 N	1.43 W
Newbury, On., Can.	214	42.41 N	81.48 W
Newbury, Eng., U.K.	42	51.25 N	1.20 W
Newbury, Ma., U.S.	207	42.49 N	70.53 W
Newbury Old Town	207	42.46 N	70.51 W
Newbury Park	228	34.11 N	118.53 W
Newburyport	207	42.48 N	70.52 W
Newby	44	54.20 N	0.28 W
Newby Bridge	44	54.16 N	2.58 W
New Caledonia (Nouvelle-Calédonie) □[2], Oc.	14	21.30 S	165.30 E
New Caledonia (Nouvelle-Calédonie) □[2], Oc.	175f	21.30 S	165.30 E
New Caledonia Basin ✢[1]	14	30.00 S	165.00 E
New Canaan	207	41.08 N	73.29 W
New Canada ➸[8]	273d	26.13 S	27.57 E
New Caney	222	30.09 N	95.13 W
New Canton	219	39.38 N	91.06 W
New-Carlisle, P.Q., Can.	186	48.01 N	65.20 W
New Carlisle, In., U.S.	216	41.42 N	86.30 W
New Carlisle, Oh., U.S.	218	39.56 N	84.01 W
New Carrollton	284c	38.58 N	76.52 W
New Cassel	276	40.45 N	73.34 W
Newcastle, Austl.	170	32.56 S	151.46 E
Newcastle, N.B., Can.	186	47.00 N	65.34 W
Newcastle, On., Can.	212	43.55 N	78.35 W
Newcastle, Ire.	48	52.16 N	7.48 W
Newcastle, S. Afr.	158	27.49 S	29.55 E
Newcastle, Eng., U.K.	42	52.26 N	3.06 W
Newcastle, N. Ire., U.K.	48	54.12 N	5.54 W
Newcastle, Ca., U.S.	226	38.53 N	121.08 W
New Castle, Co., U.S.	200	39.34 N	107.32 W
New Castle, De., U.S.	208	39.39 N	75.34 W
New Castle, In., U.S.	218	39.55 N	85.22 W
New Castle, Ky., U.S.	218	38.26 N	85.10 W
Newcastle, Ne., U.S.	198	42.33 N	96.42 W
Newcastle, Oh., U.S.	214	40.20 N	82.10 W
Newcastle, Ok., U.S.	196	35.15 N	97.36 W
New Castle, Pa., U.S.	214	41.00 N	80.20 W
Newcastle, Tx., U.S.	196	33.11 N	98.44 W
New Castle, Va., U.S.	192	37.30 N	80.06 W
Newcastle, Wy., U.S.	198	43.51 N	104.12 W
New Castle □[6]	208	39.44 N	75.33 W
Newcastle Airport ⊠	44	55.03 N	1.43 W
Newcastle Bay ⊂	164	10.50 S	142.37 E
Newcastle Bight ⊂[3]	170	32.51 S	151.54 E
Newcastle Creek ≃	164	17.20 S	133.23 E
Newcastle Emlyn	42	52.02 N	4.28 W
Newcastle Mine	182	51.28 N	112.46 W
Newcastleton	44	55.11 N	2.49 W
Newcastle-under-Lyme	44	53.00 N	2.14 W
Newcastle upon Tyne	44	54.59 N	1.35 W
Newcastle Waters	162	17.24 S	133.24 E
Newcastle West	48	52.27 N	9.03 W
Newcestown	48	51.47 N	8.51 W
New Chicago	216	41.34 N	87.16 W
Newchurch, Wales, U.K.	42	52.09 N	3.08 W
New Church, Va., U.S.	208	37.59 N	75.32 W
New City	210	41.08 N	73.59 W
Newclare ➸[8]	273d	26.11 S	27.58 E
New Columbia	210	41.02 N	76.52 W
New Columbus	210	41.10 N	76.18 W
Newcomerstown	214	40.16 N	81.36 W
New Concord	188	39.59 N	81.44 W
New Corydon	216	40.34 N	84.51 W
New Croton Aqueduct ≍[1]	276	41.11 N	73.49 W
New Croton Reservoir ⊜[1]	210	41.14 N	73.46 W
New Cumberland, Pa., U.S.	208	40.13 N	76.53 W
New Cumberland, W.V., U.S.	214	40.29 N	80.36 W
New Cumberland Dam ➸[6]	214	40.32 N	80.37 W
New Cumnock	44	55.24 N	4.12 W
New Dayton	182	49.25 N	112.23 W
New Deer	46	57.30 N	2.12 W
Newdegate	162	33.06 S	119.01 E
New Delhi, India	124	28.36 N	77.12 E
New Delhi, India	272a	28.36 N	77.12 E
New Delhi Railroad Station ➸[5]	272a	28.39 N	77.13 E
New Denver	182	49.59 N	117.22 W

New Derry	214	40.21 N	79.19 W
New Dundee	212	43.21 N	80.31 W
New Eagle	214	40.12 N	79.56 W
New Edinburg	194	33.45 N	92.14 W
New Effington	198	45.51 N	96.55 W
New Egypt	208	40.04 N	74.31 W
Newell, Ia., U.S.	198	42.36 N	95.00 W
Newell, S.D., U.S.	198	44.42 N	103.25 W
Newell, W.V., U.S.	214	40.37 N	80.36 W
Newell, Lake ⊜, Austl.	162	24.50 S	126.10 E
Newell, Lake ⊜, Ab., Can.	182	50.25 N	111.56 W
New Ellenton	192	33.25 N	81.41 W
Newellton	194	32.04 N	91.14 W
New Eltham ➸[8]	260	51.26 N	0.04 E
New England	198	46.32 N	102.52 W
New England National Park ♦	166	30.30 S	152.15 E
New England Range ⩘	166	30.00 S	151.50 E
Newenham, Cape ›	180	58.37 N	162.12 W
Newent	42	51.56 N	2.24 W
New Enterprise	214	40.10 N	78.25 W
New Ermelo	158	26.32 S	30.02 E
New Falconwood	284a	42.59 N	78.58 W
Newfane, N.Y., U.S.	210	43.17 N	78.42 W
Newfane, Vt., U.S.	188	42.59 N	72.39 W
New Ferry	262	53.22 N	2.59 W
Newfield, N.J., U.S.	208	39.32 N	75.01 W
Newfield, N.Y., U.S.	210	42.22 N	76.35 W
Newfield Pond ⊜	283	42.38 N	71.22 W
New Florence, Mo., U.S.	219	38.54 N	91.26 W
New Florence, Pa., U.S.	214	40.22 N	79.04 W
New Forest ➸[3]	42	50.53 N	1.35 W
New Fork ≃	200	42.33 N	109.58 W
Newfound Gap)(	192	35.37 N	83.25 W
Newfoundland, N.J., U.S.	276	40.44 N	74.29 W
Newfoundland, Pa., U.S.	210	41.19 N	75.19 W
Newfoundland □[4]	176	52.00 N	56.00 W
Newfoundland I	186	48.30 N	56.00 W
Newfoundland Basin ✢[1]	8	45.00 N	40.00 W
Newfoundland Ridge ✢[3]	8	40.30 N	48.00 W
New Franklin	194	39.01 N	92.44 W
New Freedom	208	39.44 N	76.42 W
New Galilee	214	40.50 N	80.24 W
New Galloway	44	55.05 N	4.10 W
New Garden	285	39.49 N	75.45 W
Newgate	182	49.00 N	115.10 W
Newgate Street	260	51.44 N	0.07 W
New Georgia I	175e	8.15 S	157.30 E
New Georgia Group II	175e	8.30 S	157.20 E
New Georgia Sound ⊔	175e	8.00 S	158.10 E
New Germantown	208	40.18 N	77.34 W
New Germany	186	44.33 N	64.43 W
New Glarus	190	42.48 N	89.38 W
New Glasgow	186	45.35 N	62.39 W
New Gretna	208	39.35 N	74.27 W
New Guinea I	164	5.00 S	140.00 E
Newgulf	222	29.16 N	95.54 W
Newhalem	224	48.40 N	121.14 W
Newhalen	180	59.43 N	154.54 W
Newhall, Eng., U.K.	42	52.48 N	1.34 W
Newhall, Ca., U.S.	228	34.23 N	118.31 W
Newham ➸[8]	42	51.32 N	0.03 E
New Hamburg, On., Can.	212	43.23 N	80.42 W
New Hamburg, N.Y., U.S.	210	41.35 N	73.57 W
New Hampshire	216	40.33 N	83.57 W
New Hampshire □[3], U.S.	178	43.35 N	71.40 W
New Hampshire □[3], U.S.	188	43.35 N	71.40 W
New Hampton, Ia., U.S.	190	43.03 N	92.19 W
New Hampton, N.Y., U.S.	210	41.25 N	74.24 W
New Hanover, S. Afr.	158	29.28 S	30.28 E
New Hanover, Il., U.S.	219	38.23 N	90.13 W
New Hanover I	164	2.30 S	150.15 E
New Harmony	194	38.07 N	87.56 W
New Hartford, Ct., U.S.	207	41.52 N	72.58 W
New Hartford, Ia., U.S.	190	42.34 N	92.37 W
New Hartford, Mo., U.S.	219	39.12 N	91.16 W
New Hartford, N.Y., U.S.	210	43.04 N	75.18 W
Newhaven, Eng., U.K.	42	50.47 N	0.03 E
New Haven, Ct., U.S.	207	41.18 N	72.56 W
New Haven, Il., U.S.	194	37.54 N	88.07 W
New Haven, In., U.S.	216	41.04 N	85.00 W
New Haven, Ky., U.S.	194	37.39 N	85.35 W
New Haven, Mi., U.S.	214	42.43 N	82.48 W
New Haven, Mo., U.S.	219	38.36 N	91.13 W
New Haven, N.Y., U.S.	212	43.29 N	76.19 W
New Haven, Oh., U.S.	214	41.02 N	82.41 W
New Haven, W.V., U.S.	188	38.59 N	81.58 W
New Haven □[6]	207	41.18 N	72.56 W
New Hazelton	182	55.15 N	127.35 W
New Hebrides → Vanuatu □[1]	175f	16.00 S	167.00 E
New Hebrides II	175f	16.00 S	167.00 E
New Hebrides Trench ✢[1]	14	22.30 S	170.00 E
Newhebron	194	31.44 N	89.58 W
New Hempstead	276	41.08 N	74.03 W
New Hey	262	53.36 N	2.06 W
New Hogan Lake ⊜[1]	226	38.09 N	120.48 W
New Holland, Eng., U.K.	44	53.42 N	0.22 W
New Holland, Il., U.S.	219	40.11 N	89.36 W
New Holland, Oh., U.S.	218	39.33 N	83.15 W
New Holland, Pa., U.S.	208	40.06 N	76.05 W
New Holstein	190	43.57 N	88.05 W
New Hope, Al., U.S.	194	34.32 N	86.23 W
New Hope, Pa., U.S.	208	40.21 N	74.57 W
New Hudson	281	42.30 N	83.36 W
New Hyde Park	276	40.44 N	73.41 W
New Hythe	260	51.19 N	0.27 E
New Iberia	194	30.00 N	91.49 W
Newick	42	50.58 N	0.01 E
Newington, On., Can.	206	45.07 N	75.01 W
Newington, Eng., U.K.	42	51.05 N	1.08 E
Newington, Eng., U.K.	260	51.21 N	0.40 E
Newington, Ct., U.S.	207	41.42 N	72.43 W
Newinn	48	52.26 N	7.53 W
New Ipswich	207	42.44 N	71.51 W
New Ireland □[5]	164	3.00 S	151.30 E
New Ireland I	164	3.20 S	152.00 E
New Island I	126	21.31 N	88.12 E
New Jersey □[3], U.S.	178	40.15 N	74.30 W
New Jersey □[3], U.S.	188	40.15 N	74.30 W
New Jersey Institute of Technology ʊ[2]	276	40.45 N	74.11 W
New Johnsonville	194	36.01 N	87.58 W
New Kensington	214	40.34 N	79.45 W
New Kent	208	37.31 N	76.58 W
New Kent □[6]	208	37.30 N	77.00 W
New Kingstown	208	40.13 N	77.07 W

Newkirk	196	36.52 N	97.03 W
Newkirk Estates	285	39.42 N	75.36 W
New Knoxville	216	40.29 N	84.18 W
New Kowloon (Xinjiulong)	271d	22.20 N	114.10 E
New Lagos ➸[8]	273a	6.30 N	3.22 E
New Lake ⊜	192	35.38 N	76.20 W
Newland	192	36.05 N	81.55 W
Newland Head ›	168b	35.39 S	138.31 E
Newland Range ⩘	162	27.53 S	123.58 E
Newlands	166	21.11 S	147.54 E
Newlands ➸[8]	273d	26.11 S	27.58 E
New Lane	262	53.37 N	2.52 W
New Lebanon, N.Y., U.S.	210	42.27 N	73.23 W
New Lebanon, Oh., U.S.	218	39.45 N	84.23 W
New Lebanon, Pa., U.S.	214	41.25 N	80.04 W
New Lebanon Center	210	42.28 N	73.25 W
New Leipzig	198	46.22 N	101.56 W
New Lenox	216	41.30 N	87.57 W
New Lexington	188	39.42 N	82.12 W
New Liberty	218	38.36 N	84.54 W
New Lisbon	190	43.52 N	90.09 W
New Liskeard	190	47.30 N	79.40 W
Newllano	194	31.06 N	93.16 W
New London, Ct., U.S.	207	41.21 N	72.07 W
New London, Ia., U.S.	190	40.55 N	91.23 W
New London, Mn., U.S.	198	45.18 N	94.56 W
New London, Mo., U.S.	219	39.35 N	91.24 W
New London, N.H., U.S.	188	43.24 N	71.59 W
New London, Oh., U.S.	214	41.05 N	82.24 W
New London, Pa., U.S.	208	39.47 N	75.52 W
New London, Tx., U.S.	222	32.15 N	94.56 W
New London, Wi., U.S.	190	44.23 N	88.44 W
New London □[6]	207	41.21 N	72.07 W
New London Submarine Base ■	207	41.24 N	72.05 W
New Longton	262	53.44 N	2.45 W
Newlonsburg	279b	40.25 N	79.40 W
New Lyme	214	41.36 N	80.47 W
Newlyn, Austl.	169	37.25 S	143.59 E
Newlyn, Eng., U.K.	42	50.06 N	5.33 W
Newlyn East	42	50.22 N	5.03 W
Newmachar	46	57.16 N	2.11 W
New Machavie	158	26.48 S	26.57 E
New Madison	218	39.58 N	84.42 W
New Madrid	194	36.35 N	89.31 W
Newmains	44	55.47 N	3.53 W
Newman, Austl.	162	23.20 S	119.46 E
Newman, Ca., U.S.	226	37.18 N	121.01 W
Newman, Il., U.S.	194	39.47 N	87.59 W
Newman, Mount ʌ	162	23.16 S	119.33 E
New Manchester	214	40.31 N	80.34 W
Newman Grove	198	41.45 N	97.46 W
Newmanstown	208	40.20 N	76.12 W
Newmansville	219	40.00 N	90.01 W
New Marion	218	39.00 N	85.22 W
Newmarket, Austl.	171a	27.25 S	153.01 E
Newmarket, On., Can.	212	44.03 N	79.28 W
Newmarket, Ire.	48	52.13 N	9.00 W
Newmarket, S. Afr.	273d	26.17 S	28.08 E
Newmarket, Eng., U.K.	42	52.15 N	0.25 E
New Market, Al., U.S.	194	34.54 N	86.25 W
New Market, Ia., U.S.	198	40.43 N	94.53 W
New Market, Md., U.S.	208	39.22 N	77.16 W
Newmarket, N.H., U.S.	188	43.04 N	70.56 W
New Market, N.J., U.S.	276	40.34 N	74.27 W
New Market, Va., U.S.	188	38.39 N	78.40 W
Newmarket on Fergus	48	52.45 N	8.53 W
Newmarket Race Course ♦	273d	26.17 S	28.08 E
New Marske	44	54.34 N	1.02 W
New Martinsville	188	39.38 N	80.51 W
New Meadows	202	44.58 N	116.16 W
New Melle	219	38.42 N	90.52 W
New Melones Lake ⊜[1]	226	38.00 N	120.32 W
New Memphis	219	38.29 N	89.41 W
New Mexico □[3]	178	34.30 N	106.00 W
New Miami	218	39.26 N	84.32 W
New Middletown	214	40.58 N	80.34 W
New Milford, Ct., U.S.	207	41.34 N	73.24 W
New Milford, Il., U.S.	216	42.11 N	89.04 W
New Milford, N.J., U.S.	276	40.56 N	74.01 W
New Milford, Pa., U.S.	210	41.52 N	75.43 W
New Millpond ⊜	276	40.50 N	73.13 W
New Millport	214	40.54 N	78.32 W
New Mills	44	53.23 N	2.00 W
Newmilns	46	55.37 N	4.20 W
New Milton	42	50.44 N	1.40 W
New Minden	219	38.26 N	89.22 W
New Munster	216	42.34 N	88.13 W
Newnan	192	33.22 N	84.47 W
Newnans Lake ⊜	192	29.39 N	82.13 W
Newnham	42	51.49 N	2.27 W
New Norcia	162	30.58 S	116.13 E
New Norfolk	166	42.47 S	147.03 E
New Norway	182	52.53 N	112.58 W
New Orleans	194	29.57 N	90.04 W
New Orleans Naval Air Station ■	194	29.51 N	90.01 W
New Oxford	208	39.51 N	77.03 W
New Palestine	218	39.43 N	85.53 W
New Paltz	210	41.44 N	74.05 W
New Paris, In., U.S.	216	41.30 N	85.49 W
New Paris, Oh., U.S.	218	39.51 N	84.47 W
New Paris, Pa., U.S.	214	40.06 N	78.39 W
New Philadelphia, Oh., U.S.	214	40.30 N	81.27 W
New Philadelphia, Pa., U.S.	208	40.43 N	76.06 W
New Pine Creek	202	41.59 N	120.17 W
New Pitsligo	46	57.35 N	2.11 W
New Pittsburg	214	40.50 N	82.06 W
New Plymouth, N.Z.	172	39.04 S	174.05 E
New Plymouth, Id., U.S.	202	43.58 N	116.49 W
New Point	218	39.18 N	85.19 W
New Point Comfort ›	208	37.18 N	76.17 W
Newport, Austl.	274a	33.40 S	151.19 E
Newport, Austl.	274b	37.51 S	144.53 E
Newport, P.Q., Can.	186	48.16 N	64.45 W
Newport, Ire.	48	53.53 N	9.34 W
Newport, Ire.	48	52.42 N	8.24 W
Newport, Eng., U.K.	42	50.42 N	1.18 W
Newport, Eng., U.K.	42	52.47 N	2.22 W
Newport, Eng., U.K.	42	51.59 N	0.15 E
Newport, Wales, U.K.	42	52.01 N	4.51 W
Newport, Wales, U.K.	42	51.35 N	3.00 W
Newport, Ar., U.S.	194	35.36 N	91.16 W
Newport, De., U.S.	208	39.42 N	75.36 W
Newport, In., U.S.	194	39.53 N	87.24 W
Newport, Ky., U.S.	218	39.05 N	84.29 W
Newport, Me., U.S.	188	44.50 N	69.16 W
Newport, Md., U.S.	208	38.25 N	76.54 W
Newport, Mi., U.S.	216	42.00 N	83.18 W
Newport, N.H., U.S.	188	43.21 N	72.10 W
Newport, N.J., U.S.	208	39.17 N	75.10 W

Newport, N.Y., U.S.	210	43.11 N	75.00 W
Newport, N.C., U.S.	192	34.47 N	76.51 W
Newport, Oh., U.S.	216	39.23 N	81.13 W
Newport, Or., U.S.	202	44.38 N	124.03 W
Newport, Pa., U.S.	208	40.28 N	77.07 W
Newport, R.I., U.S.	207	41.29 N	71.18 W
Newport, Tn., U.S.	192	35.58 N	83.11 W
Newport, Vt., U.S.	206	44.56 N	72.12 W
Newport, Wa., U.S.	202	48.11 N	117.02 W
Newport □[6]	207	41.35 N	71.15 W
Newport Bay ⊂	208	38.14 N	75.13 W
Newport Beach	228	33.37 N	117.55 W
Newport Center	206	44.57 N	72.18 W
Newport Hills	224	47.32 N	122.10 W
Newport News	208	36.58 N	76.25 W
Newport-on-Tay	46	56.26 N	2.55 W
Newport Pagnell	42	52.05 N	0.44 W
New Port Richey	220	28.14 N	82.43 W
Newportville	285	40.09 N	74.53 W
Newportville Terrace	285	40.07 N	74.54 W
New Prague	190	44.32 N	93.34 W
New Preston	207	41.40 N	73.21 W
New Providence, N.J., U.S.	210	40.41 N	74.24 W
New Providence, Pa., U.S.	208	39.56 N	76.12 W
New Providence, Tn., U.S.	194	36.32 N	87.23 W
New Providence I	240b	25.02 N	77.24 W
Newquay, Eng., U.K.	42	50.25 N	5.05 W
New Quay, Wales, U.K.	42	52.13 N	4.22 W
New Redruth	273d	26.16 S	28.07 E
New Richland	190	43.53 N	93.29 W
New-Richmond, P.Q., Can.	186	48.10 N	65.52 W
New Richmond, Oh., U.S.	218	38.56 N	84.16 W
New Richmond, Wi., U.S.	190	45.07 N	92.32 W
New Riegel	214	41.03 N	83.19 W
New Rim Ditch ≍	228	35.08 N	118.58 W
New Ringgold	208	40.41 N	76.00 W
New Road	186	44.45 N	63.28 W
New Roads	194	30.42 N	91.26 W
New Rochelle	210	40.54 N	73.46 W
New Rockford	198	47.40 N	99.08 W
New Romney	42	50.59 N	0.57 E
New Ross, N.S., Can.	186	44.44 N	64.27 W
New Ross, Ire.	48	52.24 N	6.56 W
New Rossington	44	53.29 N	1.04 W
Newry, N. Ire., U.K.	48	54.11 N	6.20 W
Newry, Pa., U.S.	214	40.24 N	78.26 W
Newry, S.C., U.S.	192	34.43 N	82.54 W
New Salem, In., U.S.	218	39.32 N	85.22 W
New Salem, N.D., U.S.	198	46.50 N	101.24 W
New Salisbury	218	38.19 N	86.06 W
New Sarum → Salisbury	42	51.05 N	1.48 W
New Schwabenland ➸[1]	9	72.30 S	1.00 E
New Scone	46	56.25 N	3.24 W
Newsham Park ♦	262	53.25 N	2.56 W
New Sharon	190	41.28 N	92.39 W
New Sheffield	214	40.36 N	80.17 W
New Siberian Islands → Novosibirskoje ostrova II	74	75.00 N	142.00 E
New Smyrna Beach	220	29.01 N	80.55 W
Newsome	222	32.59 N	95.08 W
Newsoms	208	36.37 N	77.07 W
New South Wales □[3]	166	33.00 S	146.00 E
New South Wales, University of ʊ[2]	274a	33.55 S	151.14 E
New South Wales Lawn Tennis Association Courts ♦	274a	33.53 S	151.14 E
New Springfield	214	40.55 N	80.36 W
New Square	276	41.08 N	74.02 W
New Stanton	214	40.13 N	79.37 W
Newstead	169	37.07 S	144.04 E
New Stuyahok	180	59.29 N	157.20 W
New Suffolk	207	41.00 N	72.28 W
New Summerfield	222	31.59 N	95.06 W
New Tazewell	192	36.27 N	83.33 W
New Terrell City Lake ⊜[1]	222	32.44 N	96.14 W
New Territories □[8]	271d	22.24 N	114.10 E
New Thunderchild Indian Reserve ➸[4]	184	53.30 N	108.50 W
Newtok	180	60.56 N	164.38 W
Newton, Eng., U.K.	44	53.57 N	2.27 W
Newton, Eng., U.K.	262	53.16 N	2.43 W
Newton, Ga., U.S.	192	31.18 N	84.20 W
Newton, Il., U.S.	194	38.59 N	88.09 W
Newton, Ia., U.S.	190	41.41 N	93.02 W
Newton, Ks., U.S.	198	38.02 N	97.20 W
Newton, Ma., U.S.	207	42.20 N	71.12 W
Newton, Ms., U.S.	194	32.19 N	89.09 W
Newton, N.J., U.S.	210	41.03 N	74.45 W
Newton, N.C., U.S.	192	35.40 N	81.13 W
Newton, Tx., U.S.	194	30.50 N	93.45 W
Newton □[6]	216	40.46 N	87.27 W
Newton Abbot	42	50.32 N	3.36 W
Newton Arlosh	44	54.53 N	3.15 W
Newton Aycliffe	44	54.36 N	1.32 W
Newton Brook ➸[8]	275b	43.48 N	79.24 W
Newton Center	283	42.20 N	71.12 W
Newton Falls, N.Y., U.S.	188	44.12 N	74.59 W
Newton Falls, Oh., U.S.	214	41.11 N	80.58 W
Newton Ferrers	42	50.18 N	4.02 W
Newton Flotman	42	52.32 N	1.16 E
Newton Hamilton	214	40.24 N	77.51 W
Newton Highlands	283	42.19 N	71.13 W
Newton-le-Willows	44	53.28 N	2.37 W
Newton Longville	42	51.58 N	0.46 W
Newton Lower Falls	283	42.19 N	71.23 W
Newtonmore	46	57.04 N	4.08 W
Newton Stewart	44	54.57 N	4.29 W
Newtonsville	218	39.11 N	84.05 W
Newton Upper Falls	283	42.19 N	71.13 W
Newtonville, On., Can.	212	43.56 N	78.30 W
Newtonville, Ma., U.S.	283	42.21 N	71.13 W
Newtonville, N.J., U.S.	208	39.33 N	74.51 W
New Toronto ➸[8]	275b	43.36 N	79.30 W
Newtown, Austl.	169	38.09 S	144.20 E
Newtown, Nf., Can.	186	49.12 N	53.31 W
Newtown, Eng., U.K.	262	53.21 N	2.00 W
Newtown, Wales, U.K.	42	52.32 N	3.19 W
Newtown, Ct., U.S.	207	41.24 N	73.18 W
Newtown, In., U.S.	216	40.12 N	87.08 W
Newtown, Ky., U.S.	218	38.13 N	84.57 W
New Town, N.D., U.S.	198	47.58 N	102.29 W
Newtown, Pa., U.S.	208	40.14 N	74.56 W
Newtown ➸[8]	274a	33.54 S	151.11 E
Newtownabbey	48	54.42 N	5.54 W
Newtownards	48	54.36 N	5.41 W
Newtownbutler	48	54.12 N	7.23 W
Newtown Creek ≃, N.Y., U.S.	276	40.44 N	73.58 W
Newtown Creek ≃, Pa., U.S.	285	40.13 N	74.56 W
Newtown Crommelin	48	54.59 N	6.13 W
Newtown Forbes	48	53.46 N	7.50 W
Newtownhamilton	48	54.12 N	6.35 W
Newtown Mount Kennedy	48	53.05 N	6.07 W
Newtown Saint Boswells	46	55.34 N	2.40 W
Newtown Square	208	39.59 N	75.24 W

Symbol	English	Deutsch	Español	Français	Português
≃	River	Fluß	Río	Rivière	Rio
≍	Canal	Kanal	Canal	Canal	Canal
ʟ	Waterfall, Rapids	Wasserfall, Stromschnellen	Cascada, Rápidos	Chute d'eau, Rapides	Cascata, Rápidos
⊔	Strait	Meeresstraße	Estrecho	Détroit	Estreito
⊂	Bay, Gulf	Bucht, Golf	Bahía, Golfo	Baie, Golfe	Baía, Golfo
⊜	Lake, Lakes	See, Seen	Lago, Lagos	Lac, Lacs	Lago, Lagos
⁞	Swamp	Sumpf	Pantano	Marais	Pântano
⊓	Ice Features, Glacier	Eis- und Gletscherformen	Accidentes Glaciales	Formes glaciaires	Acidentes glaciares
⊤	Other Hydrographic Features	Andere Hydrographische Objekte	Otros Elementos Hidrográficos	Autres données hydrographiques	Outros acidentes hidrográficos

Symbol	English	Deutsch	Español	Français	Português
✢	Submarine Features	Untermeerische Objekte	Accidentes Submarinos	Formes de relief sous-marin	Acidentes submarinos
□	Political Unit	Politische Einheit	Unidad Politica	Entité politique	Unidade política
ʊ	Cultural Institution	Kulturelle Institution	Institución Cultural	Institution culturelle	Instituição cultural
⊥	Historical Site	Historische Stätte	Sitio Histórico	Site historique	Sitio histórico
♦	Recreational Site	Erholungs- und Ferienort	Sitio de Recreo	Centre de loisirs	Area de Lazer
⊠	Airport	Flughafen	Aeropuerto	Aéroport	Aeroporto
■	Military Installation	Militäranlage	Instalación Militar	Installation militaire	Instalação militar
➸	Miscellaneous	Verschiedenes	Misceláneo	Divers	Diversos

ENGLISH — Name / Page / Lat.°′ / Long.°′
DEUTSCH — Name / Seite / Breite°′ / Länge°′ E = Ost

Newtownstewart 48 54.43 N 7.24 W
New Tredegar 42 51.43 N 3.14 W
New Tripoli 208 40.41 N 75.45 W
New Troy 216 41.53 N 86.33 W
New Truxton 219 38.58 N 91.15 W
New Ulm, Mn., U.S. 190 44.18 N 94.27 W
New Ulm, Tx., U.S. 222 29.53 N 96.29 W
New Utrecht ◆⁸ 276 40.36 N 73.59 W
New Vernon 276 40.45 N 74.30 W
New Vienna 218 39.19 N 83.41 W
Newville, In., U.S. 216 41.21 N 84.51 W
Newville, Pa., U.S. 208 40.10 N 77.23 W
New Vineyard 188 44.48 N 70.07 W
New Waltham 44 53.32 N 0.04 W
New Washington, Pil. 116 11.39 N 122.26 E
New Washington, In., U.S. 218 38.33 N 85.32 W
New Washington, Oh., U.S. 214 40.57 N 82.51 W
New Waterford, N.S., Can. 186 46.15 N 60.05 W
New Waterford, Oh., U.S. 214 40.50 N 80.36 W
New Waverly, In., U.S. 216 40.46 N 86.12 W
New Waverly, Tx., U.S. 222 30.32 N 95.29 W
New Westminster 224 49.12 N 122.55 W
New Whiteland 218 39.33 N 86.05 W
New Wilmington 214 41.07 N 80.19 W
New Windsor
— Windsor, Eng., U.K. 42 51.29 N 0.38 W
New Windsor, Md., U.S. 208 39.32 N 77.06 W
New Windsor, N.Y., U.S. 210 41.30 N 74.01 W
New Woodbine Racetrack ♦ 275b 43.43 N 79.36 W
New Woodstock 210 42.50 N 75.51 W
New World Island I 186 49.35 N 54.40 W
New Year Creek ≏ 222 30.08 N 96.12 W
New York, N.Y., U.S. 210 40.43 N 74.01 W
New York, N.Y., U.S. 276 40.43 N 74.01 W
New York □⁶ 276 40.47 N 73.58 W
New York □³, U.S. 178 43.00 N 75.00 W
New York □³, U.S. 188 43.00 N 75.00 W
New York, City College of ⱴ² 276 40.49 N 73.57 W
New York, Polytechnic Institute of ⱴ² 276 40.42 N 73.59 W
New York, State University of (Stony Brook) ⱴ², N.Y., U.S. 276 40.55 N 73.08 W
New York, State University of (Buffalo) ⱴ², N.Y., U.S. 284a 42.57 N 78.49 W
New York, State University of, College at Buffalo ⱴ² 284a 42.56 N 78.53 W
New York at Buffalo, State University of ⱴ² 284a 42.56 N 78.49 W
New York Mills, Mn., U.S. 198 46.31 N 95.22 W
New York Mills, N.Y., U.S. 210 43.06 N 75.18 W
New York State Barge Canal ≏ 210 43.05 N 78.43 W
New York Stock Exchange ⱴ 276 40.42 N 74.01 W
New Zealand □¹ 172 41.00 S 174.00 E
Nexapa ≏ 234 18.07 N 98.46 W
Nexon 32 45.41 N 1.11 E
Ney 216 41.23 N 84.32 W
Neyagawa 96 34.46 N 135.38 E
Neye 263 51.07 N 7.22 E
Neyestausee ◎¹ 263 51.08 N 7.24 E
Ney Lake ◎ 184 54.38 N 92.25 W
Neyland 42 51.43 N 4.57 W
Neylandville 222 33.12 N 96.00 W
Neyrīz 128 29.12 N 54.19 E
Neyshābūr 128 36.12 N 58.50 E
Neyyāttinkara 122 8.24 N 77.05 E
Nezahualcóyotl 234 19.27 N 99.03 W
Nezahualcóyotl, Presa ◎¹ 234 17.10 N 93.40 W
Nezamajevskaja 78 46.09 N 40.16 E
Nezameno-toko ◆ 94 35.46 N 137.42 E
Nežárka ≏ 61 49.11 N 14.41 E
Nezavertailovca 38 46.37 N 29.56 E
Nezlobnaja 84 44.08 N 43.23 E
Neznanka ≏ 265b 55.34 N 37.21 E
Neznanovo 80 54.02 N 40.06 E
Nezperce 202 46.14 N 116.14 W
Nez Perce Indian Reservation ◆⁴ 202 46.20 N 116.30 W
Nez Perce National Historical Park ♦ 202 45.50 N 116.15 W
Nezpique, Bayou ≏ 194 30.12 N 92.35 W
Nezvěstice 60 49.39 N 13.32 E
Ngabang 112 0.23 N 109.57 E
Ngabé 152 3.12 S 16.11 E
Ngabordamlu, Tanjung ≻ 164 6.56 S 134.11 E
Ngadda ≏ 146 12.40 N 13.50 E
Ngadirojo 115a 8.13 S 111.19 E
Ngadza 152 5.10 N 20.12 E
Ngahere 172 42.24 S 171.27 E
Ngala 146 12.20 N 14.10 E
Ngale 152 2.56 N 21.20 E
Ngali 152 2.27 S 19.20 E
Ngaliema, Baie de c 273b 4.19 S 15.16 E
Ngalipaeng 112 3.24 N 125.37 E
Ngaloa Harbour c 175g 19.06 S 178.11 E
Ngamaba 273b 4.14 S 15.16 E
Ngamba ◆⁸ 273b 4.15 S 15.18 E
Ngambé 152 4.14 N 10.37 E
Ngamdu 146 11.48 N 12.18 E
Ngami, Lake ◎ 156 20.37 S 22.40 E
Ngamiland □⁵ 156 19.09 S 22.47 E
Ngamo 154 19.08 S 27.32 E
Ngamouéri 273b 4.14 S 15.14 E
Ngamring 124 29.14 N 87.10 E
Nganda ≏ 154 10.25 S 33.50 E
Ngandu 154 4.42 N 31.55 E
Ngangala 154 4.42 N 31.55 E
Ngangla Ringco ◎ 120 31.40 N 83.00 E
Nganglong Kangri ∧ 120 32.45 N 81.12 E
Nganglong Kangri ∧ 120 32.00 N 83.00 E
Ngangzê Co ◎ 120 31.05 N 86.55 E
Nganjuk 115a 7.36 S 111.55 E
Ngao 110 18.46 N 99.59 E
Ngaoui, Mont ∧ 152 6.40 N 14.57 E
Ngaoundéré 152 7.19 N 13.35 E
Ngapali 110 18.26 N 94.19 E
Ngapara 172 44.57 S 170.45 E
Ngape 110 20.04 N 94.38 E
Ngaputaw 110 16.32 N 94.42 E
Ngara 154 2.28 S 30.39 E
Ngarasmach 175b 6.54 N 134.08 E
Ngarimbi 154 8.28 S 38.36 E
Ngaruawahia 172 37.40 S 175.09 E
Ngaruroro ≏ 172 39.34 S 176.56 E
Ngasamo 154 2.33 S 33.53 E
Ngat ≏ 110 19.09 N 99.01 E
Ngatangiia 174k 21.14 S 159.43 W
Ngatangiia Harbour c 174k 21.14 S 159.43 W
Ngatea 172 37.17 S 175.30 E
Ngathainggyaung 110 17.24 N 95.05 E
Ngatik I¹ 14 5.51 N 157.16 E
Ngau I 175g 18.02 S 179.18 E
Ngauruhoe, Mount ∧ 172 39.09 S 175.38 E
Ngau Tau Kok
— Kwun Tong 271d 22.19 N 114.12 E
Ngawen 115a 7.00 S 111.18 E
Ngawi 115a 7.24 S 111.26 E
Ngay Nua 110 21.50 N 101.54 E
Ngebel 115a 7.46 S 111.37 E
Ngele 152 0.29 S 20.25 E
Ngemelis Islands II 175b 7.06 N 134.15 E
Ngerengere 154 6.45 S 38.07 E
Ngerkeel 175b 7.25 N 134.30 E
Ngermechau 175b 7.35 N 134.39 E
Ngeruktabel I 175b 7.15 N 134.24 E
Ngetbong 175b 7.37 N 134.35 E
Ngetera 146 12.31 N 12.38 E
Nggamea Island I 175g 16.46 S 179.46 W
Nggatokae Island I 175e 8.46 S 158.11 E
Nggela Pile I 175e 9.05 S 160.15 E
Nggela Sule I 175e 9.05 S 160.15 E
Nggelelevu I 175g 16.05 S 179.09 W
Nggwavuma ≏ 158 26.58 S 32.17 E
Nghia Dan 110 19.18 N 105.26 E
Nghia Hanh 110 15.03 N 108.47 E
Nghia Lo 110 21.36 N 104.31 E
Ngiap ≏ 110 18.24 N 103.36 E
Ngidinga 152 5.37 S 15.17 E
Ngimbang 115a 7.15 S 112.12 E
Ng'iro ∧ 154 2.08 N 36.51 E
Ng'iro, Ewaso ≏, Kenya 154 0.28 N 39.55 E
Ngiro, Ewaso ≏, Kenya 154 2.04 S 36.07 E
Ngo 152 2.29 S 15.45 E
Ngoangoa ≏ 140 5.48 N 25.09 E
Ngoboli 154 4.57 N 32.37 E
Ngoko ≏, Afr. 152 1.40 N 16.03 E
Ngoko ≏, Congo 152 0.25 S 15.29 E
Ngol-Kedju Hill ∧² 152 6.20 N 9.45 E
Ngolo 146 9.56 N 22.16 E
Ngom ≏ 102 31.11 N 97.15 E
Ngomahuru 154 20.26 S 30.43 E
Ngomba 154 8.23 S 32.53 E
Ngomba ∧ 154 5.43 S 35.52 E
Ngombe, Zaïre 152 6.35 S 20.42 E
Ngombe, Zaïre 273b 4.24 S 15.11 E
Ngome 158 27.46 S 31.28 E
Ngomedzap 152 3.15 N 11.12 E
Ngomeni, Ras ≻ 154 2.59 S 40.14 E
Ngong 154 1.22 S 36.39 E
Ngongotaha 172 38.05 S 176.12 E
Ngono ≏ 154 1.08 S 31.35 E
Ngonye Falls ∟ 152 16.40 S 23.35 E
Ngop 140 6.16 N 30.12 E
Ngora 154 1.27 N 33.46 E
Ngorengore 154 1.02 S 35.30 E
Ngoring Hu ◎ 102 34.50 N 97.35 E
Ngoro 115a 7.41 S 112.16 E
Ngorongoro Crater ⁂⁶ 154 3.10 S 35.35 E
Ngote 154 2.14 N 30.48 E
Ngoto 152 4.00 N 17.21 E
Ngotwane ≏ 156 23.35 S 26.58 E
Ngoulémakong 152 3.07 N 11.25 E
Ngouma 150 15.38 N 3.22 W
Ngounié □⁴ 152 1.30 S 11.00 E
Ngounié ≏ 152 0.37 S 10.18 E
Ngouri 146 13.38 N 15.22 E
Ngouroundou 152 6.27 N 22.37 E
Ngourti 146 15.19 N 13.12 E
Ngoywa 154 5.56 S 32.48 E
Ngozi 154 2.54 S 29.50 E
Ngqeleni 158 31.40 S 29.02 E
Ngudiabaka ≏ 273b 4.25 S 15.11 E
Nguélémendouka 152 4.23 N 12.55 E
Nguigha ≏ 156 19.21 S 23.15 E
Nguigmi 146 14.15 N 13.07 E
Nguila 152 4.43 N 11.41 E
Nguiu 164 11.45 S 130.38 E
Ngulu I¹ 108 8.27 N 137.29 E
Ngum ≏ 110 18.09 N 103.06 E
Nguna, Île I 175f 17.26 S 168.21 E
Ngunga 154 3.41 S 33.34 E
Ngunju, Tanjung ≻ 115b 10.19 S 120.28 E
Ngunut 115a 8.06 S 112.01 E
Ngurore 146 9.18 N 12.14 E
Nguru 146 12.52 N 10.27 E
Ngwempisi ≏ 158 26.42 S 31.26 E
Ngweni 158 27.56 S 32.15 E
Ngwenya ∧ 158 26.11 S 31.02 E
Ngwerere 154 15.18 S 28.20 E
Ngweze ≏ 154 17.40 S 25.07 E
Nha Be 269c 10.42 N 106.44 E
Nhabe ≏, Bots. 156 20.22 S 22.58 E
Nha Be ≏, Viet 269c 10.39 N 106.44 E
Nhacoongo 156 24.18 S 35.14 E
Nhamacolomo 156 18.05 S 34.26 E
Nhamundá 250 2.14 S 56.43 W
Nhamundá ≏ 246 2.12 S 56.41 W
Nha Nam 110 21.27 N 106.06 E
Nhandeara 255 20.40 S 50.02 W
Nhareia 152 11.25 S 17.03 E
Nha Trang 110 12.15 N 109.11 E
Nhia ≏ 152 10.15 S 14.12 E
Nhill 166 36.20 S 141.39 E
Nhlangano 158 27.06 S 31.12 E
Nhlazatshe 158 28.10 S 31.14 E
Nhoma ≏ 156 18.52 S 20.53 E
Nhon Trach 269c 10.43 N 106.53 E
Nhulunbuy 164 12.11 S 136.47 E
Nhundo 152 14.25 S 21.23 E
Nhunguaçu 256 22.21 S 42.53 W
Niabembe 154 2.14 S 27.44 E
Niafounké 150 15.56 N 4.00 W
Niagara 190 45.46 N 87.59 W
Niagara □⁶, On., Can. 212 43.05 N 79.20 W
Niagara □⁶, N.Y., U.S. 210 43.10 N 78.42 W
Niagara ≏ 212 43.15 N 79.04 W
Niagara County Historical Center ⱴ 284a 43.10 N 78.43 W
Niagara Falls, On., Can. 212 43.06 N 79.04 W
Niagara Falls, On., Can. 284a 43.06 N 79.04 W
Niagara Falls, N.Y., U.S. 210 43.05 N 79.03 W
Niagara Falls, N.Y., U.S. 284a 43.05 N 79.03 W
Niagara Falls ∟ 212 43.05 N 79.04 W
Niagara Falls Airport ⁂ 284a 43.02 N 79.08 W
Niagara Falls International Airport ⁂ 284a 43.06 N 78.56 W
Niagara-on-the-Lake 212 43.15 N 79.04 W
Niagara University ⱴ² 284a 43.08 N 79.02 W
Niagassola 150 12.19 N 9.07 W
Niah 112 3.52 N 113.44 E
Niakaramandougou 150 8.40 N 5.17 W
Niamey 150 13.31 N 2.07 E
Niamey □⁵ 150 14.00 N 2.00 E
Niamtougou 150 9.46 N 1.06 E
Nianbadu 100 28.17 N 118.28 E
Niandan ≏ 150 10.30 N 10.26 W
Niandan Koro 150 11.05 N 9.15 W
Nianforando 150 9.32 N 10.31 W
Niangara 154 3.42 N 27.52 E
Niangay, Lac ◎ 150 15.50 N 3.00 W
Niangmake 102 30.14 N 99.40 E
Niangniangdong 114 41.00 N 121.13 E
Niangniangmiao 98 42.34 N 118.05 E
Niangniangmiao 105 40.33 N 117.32 E
Niangoloko 150 10.17 N 4.55 W
Niangua ≏ 194 37.58 N 92.48 W
Niangzizhuang 105 40.02 N 118.05 E
Nia-Nia 154 1.24 N 27.36 E
Nianpan 104 41.48 N 124.02 E
Niantic, Ct., U.S. 207 41.19 N 72.11 W
Niantic, Il., U.S. 219 39.51 N 89.10 W
Nianyugou 104 42.00 N 123.59 E
Nianyushan 100 29.11 N 117.04 E
Nianzhuang 98 34.19 N 117.47 E
Nianzigang 100 31.03 N 114.18 E
Nianzishan 89 47.32 N 122.52 E
Niapu 154 2.25 N 26.28 E
Niari □⁵ 152 3.15 S 12.30 E
Niari ≏ 152 3.56 S 12.12 E
Niaro 140 10.38 N 31.31 E
Nias, Pulau I 114 1.05 N 97.35 E
Niassa □⁵ 154 13.30 S 36.00 E
Niatupo 246 9.33 N 78.54 W
Nibbiano 62 44.54 N 9.19 E
Nibe 26 56.59 N 9.38 E
Nibong Tebal 114 5.10 N 100.29 E
Nibra 272b 22.36 N 88.16 E
Nic 84 40.56 N 47.41 E
Nīca 76 56.19 N 21.04 E
Nica ≏ 86 57.29 N 64.33 E
Nicaea
— Iznik 130 40.26 N 29.43 E
Nicaragua □¹, N.A. 230 13.00 N 85.00 W
Nicaragua □¹, N.A. 236 13.00 N 85.00 W
Nicaragua, Lago de ◎ 236 11.30 N 85.30 W
Nicaro 240p 20.42 N 75.33 W
Nicastro 68 38.59 N 16.20 E
Ničatka, ozero ◎ 88 57.45 N 117.30 E
Nice 62 43.42 N 7.15 E
Nice-Côte d'Azur, Aéroport de ⁂ 62 43.40 N 7.14 E
Niceville 194 30.31 N 86.28 W
Nichelino 62 44.59 N 7.38 E
Nicheng 106 30.55 N 121.49 E
Nichihara 96 34.33 N 131.50 E
Nichinan, Nihon 92 31.36 N 131.23 E
Nichinan, Nihon 96 35.09 N 133.16 E
Nicholas □⁶ 218 38.20 N 84.02 W
Nicholas Channel Ψ 238 23.25 N 80.05 W
Nicholasville 192 37.52 N 84.34 W
Nicholls 192 31.31 N 82.38 W
Nicholl's Town 238 25.08 N 78.00 W
Nichols, Ca., U.S. 282 38.02 N 121.59 W
Nichols, Fl., U.S. 220 27.54 N 82.02 W
Nichols, N.Y., U.S. 210 42.01 N 76.22 W
Nichols Brook ≏ 283 42.37 N 70.59 W
Nicholson, Austl. 162 18.02 S 128.54 E
Nicholson, Ky., U.S. 218 38.54 N 84.33 W
Nicholson, Ms., U.S. 194 30.28 N 89.41 W
Nicholson, Pa., U.S. 210 41.37 N 75.46 W
Nicholson ≏, Austl. 162 17.34 S 128.38 E
Nicholson ≏, Austl. 166 17.31 S 139.36 E
Nicholson Island I 212 43.56 N 77.31 W
Nicholson Range ∧ 162 27.15 S 116.45 E
Nicholson River Aboriginal Reserve ◆⁴ 162 18.00 S 137.30 E
Nichols Run ≏ 284b 39.03 N 77.18 W
Nickerie □⁵ 250 5.40 N 56.50 W
Nickerie ≏ 250 5.59 N 57.00 W
Nickerson 198 38.08 N 98.05 W
Nickol Bay c 162 20.39 S 116.52 E
Nicktown 214 40.37 N 78.48 W
Nicobar Islands II 110 8.00 N 93.30 E
Nicola 182 50.10 N 120.40 W
Nicola ≏ 182 50.25 N 121.18 W
Nicolae Bălcescu 38 47.34 N 26.52 E
Nicola Mountain ∧ 224 46.05 N 123.28 W
Nicola Lake ◎ 182 50.10 N 120.25 W
Nicola Mameet Indian Reserve ◆⁴ 182 50.11 N 120.49 W
Nicolaus 226 38.54 N 121.35 W
Nicolet 206 46.13 N 72.37 W
Nicolet □⁶ 206 46.15 N 72.20 W
Nicolet ≏ 206 46.14 N 72.39 W
Nicolet, Lac ◎ 206 45.50 N 71.33 W
Nicolet, Lake ◎ 190 46.20 N 84.15 W
Nicolet Centre ≏ 206 45.46 N 71.50 W
Nicolet Sud-Ouest ≏ 206 46.13 N 72.36 W
Nicoll Bay c 276 40.43 N 73.07 W
Nicollet 190 44.16 N 94.11 W
Nicoll Point ≻ 276 40.42 N 73.09 W
Nicolosi 70 37.37 N 15.01 E
Nicosia, It. 70 37.45 N 14.24 E
Nicosia (Levkosía), Kípros 130 35.10 N 33.22 E
Nicosia (Lefkoşa), Kıbrıs 130 35.10 N 33.22 E
Nicotera 68 38.34 N 15.57 E
Nicoya 236 10.09 N 85.27 W
Nicoya, Golfo de c 236 9.47 N 84.48 W
Nicoya, Peninsula de ≻¹ 236 10.00 N 85.25 W
Nictheroy
— Niterói 256 22.53 S 43.07 W
Nida 76 55.18 N 21.01 E
Nida ≏ 30 50.18 N 20.52 E
Nidadavole 122 16.55 N 81.40 E
Nidau 58 47.07 N 7.14 E
Nidd ≏ 44 54.01 N 1.12 W
Nidda 56 50.24 N 9.00 E
Nidda ≏ 56 50.06 N 8.34 E
Nidder ≏ 56 50.12 N 8.47 E
Nidderau 56 50.14 N 8.52 E
Nide 102 31.51 N 96.19 E
Nideggen 56 50.47 N 6.29 E
Nidelva ≏ 26 58.24 N 8.48 E
Nidwalden □³ 58 46.55 N 8.28 E
Nidzica 30 53.22 N 20.26 E
Niebüll 41 54.48 N 8.50 E
Nied ≏ 56 49.23 N 6.40 E
Nied Allemande ≏ 56 49.10 N 6.26 E
Nieddu, Monte ∧ 71 40.45 N 9.34 E
Niederanven 56 49.39 N 6.16 E
Niederau 54 51.10 N 13.32 E
Niederaula 56 50.48 N 9.36 E
Niederbayern □⁵ 60 48.45 N 12.45 E
Niederbipp 58 47.16 N 7.39 E
Niederbobritzsch 54 50.54 N 13.26 E
Niederbonsfeld 263 51.23 N 7.08 E
Niederbronn-Les-Bains 56 48.57 N 7.38 E
Niederdonk 263 51.14 N 6.41 E
Niederelfringhausen 263 51.21 N 7.10 E
Niedere Tauern ∧ 30 47.18 N 14.00 E
Niederfinow 54 52.50 N 13.55 E
Niederfrohna 54 50.53 N 12.43 E
Niederhaverbeck 52 53.09 N 9.54 E
Niederheimbach 56 50.02 N 7.48 E
Niederhone 56 51.13 N 10.06 E
Niederkassel 56 50.49 N 7.02 E
Nieder-Kassel ◆⁸ 263 51.14 N 6.45 E
Niederkrüchten 56 51.12 N 6.13 E
Niederlande
— Netherlands □¹ 30 52.15 N 5.30 E
Niederländische Antillen
— Netherlands Antilles □² 241s 12.15 N 69.00 W
Niederlausitz □⁹ 54 51.40 N 14.15 E
Niederlehme 54 52.19 N 13.39 E
Niedermarsberg 56 51.27 N 8.51 E
Niedermerschacht 52 53.25 N 10.21 E
Nieder-Mörlen 56 50.23 N 8.43 E
Niederndodeleben 54 52.08 N 11.30 E
Nieder-Neuendorf 264a 52.37 N 13.12 E
Niedernhall 56 49.17 N 9.36 E
Niedernwöhren 52 52.21 N 9.08 E
Niederoderwitz 54 50.57 N 14.44 E
Nieder-Ohmen 56 50.38 N 9.02 E
Nieder-Olm 56 49.55 N 8.11 E
Niederorschel 54 51.22 N 10.25 E
Niederösterreich □³ 61 48.20 N 15.50 E
Niedersachsen □³ 30 52.40 N 9.00 E
Niedersachswerfen 54 51.33 N 10.46 E
Niederschöneweide ◆⁸ 264a 52.27 N 13.31 E
Niederschönhausen ◆⁸ 264a 52.35 N 13.23 E
Niedersonthofen 58 47.38 N 10.13 E
Niederstetten 56 49.24 N 9.55 E
Niederstotzingen 56 48.32 N 10.14 E
Niedersulz 61 48.29 N 16.40 E
Niederurnen 58 47.07 N 9.03 E
Niederwald 58 46.26 N 8.12 E
Niederwalgern 56 50.44 N 8.41 E
Niederweningen 58 47.30 N 8.23 E
Niederwiesa 54 50.51 N 13.01 E
Niederwürschnitz 54 50.43 N 12.45 E
Nied Française ≏ 56 49.10 N 6.26 E
Niedu 100 25.28 N 114.08 E
Niefang 152 1.50 N 10.14 E
Nieheim 52 51.48 N 9.06 E
Niekerkshoop 158 29.19 S 22.51 E
Niel 50 51.07 N 4.20 E
Niellé 150 10.12 N 5.38 W
Niellim 146 9.42 N 17.49 E
Niem 152 6.12 N 15.14 E
Niemba 154 5.57 S 28.26 E
Niemegk 54 52.04 N 12.41 E
Niemeyer ◆⁸ 287a 23.00 S 43.15 W
Niemodlin 30 50.39 N 17.37 E
Niena 150 11.26 N 6.21 W
Nienberge 52 52.00 N 7.34 E
Nienborg-Wigbold 52 52.08 N 7.06 E
Nienburg, Dtsch. 52 52.38 N 9.13 E
Nienburg, Dtsch. 54 51.50 N 11.46 E
Niendorf 54 53.59 N 10.50 E
Nienhagen, Dtsch. 52 52.33 N 10.05 E
Nienhagen, Dtsch. 54 51.57 N 11.09 E
Niénokoué, Mont ∧² 150 5.26 N 7.10 W
Niepkuhlen ≏ 263 51.29 N 6.31 E
Niepołomice 30 50.03 N 20.13 E
Nieppe 50 50.42 N 2.50 E
Nier ≏ 48 52.17 N 7.48 W
Niéré 146 14.30 N 21.09 E
Niéré, Hadjer ∧ 146 14.21 N 21.40 E
Niéri Ko ≏ 150 13.21 N 13.23 W
Niers ≏ 50 51.43 N 5.57 E
Nierst 263 51.19 N 6.43 E
Nierstein 56 49.52 N 8.20 E
Niesen ∧ 58 46.39 N 7.39 E
Niesky 54 51.17 N 14.49 E
Nieszawa 30 52.50 N 18.55 E
Nieto, Cañada de ≏ 258 34.00 S 58.15 W
Nieu Bethesda 158 31.51 S 24.34 E
Nieuw-Amsterdam, Ned. 52 52.44 N 6.51 E
Nieuw Amsterdam, Sur. 250 5.53 N 55.05 W
Nieuw-Buinen 52 52.57 N 6.55 E
Nieuwefontein 158 28.01 S 19.06 E
Nieuwegein 52 52.03 N 5.05 E
Nieuwe-Niedorp 52 52.45 N 4.54 E
Nieuwe-Pekela 52 53.04 N 6.58 E
Nieuweschans 52 53.11 N 7.12 E
Nieuwkoop 52 52.08 N 4.47 E
New Nickerie 250 5.57 N 56.59 W
Nieuwolda 52 53.14 N 6.59 E
Nieuwoudtville 158 31.23 S 19.07 E
Nieuwpoort, Bel. 50 51.08 N 2.45 E
Nieuwpoort, Ned. Ant. 241s 12.03 N 68.49 W
Nieuwpoort-Bad 50 51.09 N 2.42 E
Nieuw-Schoonebeek 52 52.38 N 6.59 E
Nieuw-Vennep 52 52.16 N 4.38 E
Nieuw-Weerdinge 52 52.52 N 6.59 E
Nieva ≏ 246 4.35 S 77.52 W
Nievenheim 56 51.07 N 6.46 E
Nieveria 286d 11.59 S 76.55 W
Nièvre □⁵ 32 47.05 N 3.30 E
Nièvre ≏ 50 47.10 N 3.13 E
Niga 150 13.38 N 5.27 W
Nigan 126 23.30 N 87.59 E
Nigde 130 37.59 N 34.42 E
Nigde □⁴ 130 38.15 N 34.15 E
Nigei Island I 182 50.55 N 127.50 W
Nigel 158 26.30 S 28.28 E
Niger □³ 150 10.00 N 6.00 E
Niger □¹ 134 16.00 N 8.00 E
Niger ≏ 150 5.33 N 6.33 E
Niger Delta ≐² 150 5.00 N 6.00 E
Nigeria □¹ 134 10.00 N 8.00 E
Nigerian Museum ⱴ 273a 6.20 N 3.24 E
Nigg 46 57.43 N 4.00 W
Nighāsan 124 28.14 N 80.52 E
Nightcaps 172 45.58 S 168.02 E
Nighthawk 182 48.58 N 119.38 W
Night Hawk Lake ◎ 190 48.28 N 81.00 W
Nightingale Island I 10 37.24 S 12.28 W
Nightmute 180 60.29 N 164.43 W
Nigrita 38 40.55 N 23.30 E
Nihe 104 41.27 N 121.13 E
Nihing (Nahang) ≏ 128 26.00 N 62.44 E
Nihoa I 14 23.06 N 161.58 W
Nihommatsu 92 37.35 N 140.26 E
Nihon
— Japan □¹ 92 36.00 N 138.00 E
Nihonbashi ◆⁸ 268 35.41 N 139.47 E
Nihon-kai
— Japan, Sea of ▼² 90 40.00 N 135.00 E
Nihon University ⱴ² 268 35.42 N 139.45 E
Nihtaur 124 29.20 N 78.23 E
Nihuil, Embalse del ◎¹ 252 35.05 S 68.45 W
Niida ≏ 96 33.11 N 132.58 E
Niigata 92 37.55 N 139.03 E
Niigata □⁵ 92 37.08 N 138.30 E
Niihama 96 33.58 N 133.16 E
Niihari 94 36.07 N 140.09 E
Niiharu 94 36.41 N 138.55 E
Niihau I 229b 21.55 N 160.10 W
Nii-jima I 92 34.22 N 139.16 E
Niimi 96 34.59 N 133.28 E
Niinisalo 26 61.50 N 22.29 E
Niitsu 92 37.48 N 139.07 E
Niiza 94 35.48 N 139.34 E
Nijar 34 36.58 N 2.12 W
Nijiaqiao 269b 31.14 N 121.21 E
Nijil 132 30.31 N 35.33 E
Nijkerk 52 52.13 N 5.28 E
Nijlen 56 51.10 N 4.39 E
Nijmegen 52 51.50 N 5.50 E
Nijo Castle ⊥ 270 35.01 N 135.45 E
Nijvel
— Nivelles 50 50.36 N 4.20 E
Nijverdal 52 52.22 N 6.27 E
Nikaia 267c 37.58 N 23.38 E
Nikei 24 69.24 N 30.12 E
Nikel'tau 86 50.23 N 58.13 E
Nikiforovo 265b 55.50 N 38.05 E
Nikiniki 112 9.49 S 124.28 E
Nikip Lake ◎ 184 53.02 N 91.53 W
Nikitovka 78 50.23 N 38.25 E
Nikitskoje, Ross. 61 47.32 N 16.40 E
Nikitskoje, Ross. 82 55.18 N 38.28 E
Nikitskoje, Ross. 82 55.13 N 35.46 E
Nikki 150 9.56 N 3.12 E
Nikkō 94 36.45 N 139.37 E
Nikkō-kokuritsu-kōen ⁂ 94 36.49 N 139.33 E
Niklā al-'Inab 142 30.55 N 30.46 E
Niklasdorf 61 47.24 N 15.10 E
Nikobaren
— Nicobar Islands II 110 8.00 N 93.30 E
Nikolai 180 62.58 N 154.09 W
Nikolajevka, Kaz. 86 53.02 N 65.42 E
Nikolajevka, Ross. 80 46.21 N 47.44 E
Nikolajevka, Ross. 80 52.28 N 49.14 E
Nikolajevka, Ross. 82 52.11 N 48.04 E
Nikolajevka, Ross. 80 53.08 N 47.12 E
Nikolajevka, Ross. 83 47.18 N 38.50 E
Nikolajevka, Ross. 86 54.57 N 75.44 E
Nikolajevka, Ross. 86 56.29 N 95.06 E
Nikolajevka, Ross. 88 48.55 N 131.39 E
Nikolajevka, Ross. 89 48.34 N 134.47 E
Nikolajevo 76 58.16 N 29.29 E
Nikolajevo-Kozlovskij 83 47.13 N 38.21 E
Nikolajevsk 80 50.01 N 45.28 E
Nikolajevsk-Na-Amure 89 53.08 N 140.44 E
Nikolajevskoje, Ross. 78 45.08 N 39.36 E
Nikolajevskoje, Ross. 88 51.04 N 111.48 E
Nikolajevskoje, Ross. 89 52.21 N 117.00 E
Nikolassee ◆⁸ 264a 52.26 N 13.12 E
Nikolajev
— Mykolayiv 78 46.58 N 32.00 E
Nikolo-Berezovec 76 58.38 N 42.17 E
Nikolo-Berjozovka 80 56.06 N 54.17 E
Nikolo-Chovanskoje 265b 55.36 N 37.27 E
Nikologory 80 56.09 N 41.59 E
Nikolo-Kropotki 82 56.44 N 37.55 E
Nikolo-L'vovsk 89 43.54 N 131.23 E
Nikolo-Makarovo 80 57.38 N 43.34 E
Nikolsdorf 64 46.47 N 12.55 E
Nikol'sk, Ross. 24 59.30 N 45.27 E
Nikol'sk, Ross. 80 53.45 N 46.05 E
Nikolski 180 52.56 N 168.52 W
Nikol'skij, Ross. 24 60.55 N 34.00 E
Nikol'skij, Ross. 86 56.18 N 68.58 E
Nikol'skij Toržok 76 59.53 N 38.46 E
Nikol'skoje, Ross. 74 55.12 N 166.00 E
Nikol'skoje, Ross. 76 52.39 N 36.04 E
Nikol'skoje, Ross. 76 55.26 N 35.04 E
Nikol'skoje, Ross. 76 59.23 N 44.36 E
Nikol'skoje, Ross. 76 59.30 N 42.32 E
Nikol'skoje, Ross. 78 50.35 N 41.10 E
Nikol'skoje, Ross. 80 47.46 N 46.24 E
Nikol'skoje, Ross. 80 52.37 N 43.49 E
Nikol'skoje, Ross. 82 54.51 N 35.53 E
Nikol'skoje, Ross. 82 54.27 N 36.24 E
Nikol'skoje, Ross. 82 54.30 N 36.50 E
Nikol'skoje, Ross. 82 54.03 N 37.10 E
Nikol'skoje, Ross. 82 54.18 N 35.53 E
Nikol'skoje, Ross. 82 55.37 N 36.41 E
Nikol'skoje, Ross. 82 55.15 N 36.04 E
Nikol'skoje, Ross. 82 56.09 N 36.43 E
Nikol'skoje, Ross. 82 55.53 N 36.26 E
Nikol'skoje, Ross. 86 57.12 N 84.21 E
Nikol'skoje, Ross. 86 52.02 N 55.43 E
Nikol'skoje, Ross. 265a 59.41 N 30.47 E
Nikol'skoje, Ross. 265b 55.46 N 37.54 E
Nikol'skoje-na-Čeremšane 80 54.03 N 49.14 E
Nikol'skoje-Ur'upino 265b 55.48 N 37.13 E
Nikonga ≏ 154 4.40 S 31.28 E
Nikonorovka 83 49.07 N 39.59 E
Nikonova Gora 76 60.22 N 36.07 E
Nikonovskoje 82 55.17 N 38.10 E
Nikopol, Blg. 38 43.42 N 24.54 E
Nikopol', Ukr. 78 47.35 N 34.25 E
Niksar 130 40.36 N 36.58 E
Nīkshahr 128 26.13 N 60.12 E
Nikšić 38 42.46 N 18.56 E
Nikulino, Ross. 76 55.16 N 33.46 E
Nikulino, Ross. 80 58.05 N 44.14 E
Nikulino, Ross. 82 56.48 N 35.50 E
Nikulino ◆⁸ 265b 55.40 N 37.28 E
Nikulkino 82 56.07 N 38.38 E
Nikul'skoje 82 55.10 N 38.41 E
Nikumaroro I¹ 14 4.40 S 174.32 W
Nikunau I 14 1.23 S 176.26 E
Nil
— Nile ≏ 140 30.10 N 31.06 E
Nīl, Nahr an-
— Nile ≏ 140 30.10 N 31.06 E
Nila, Pulau I 164 6.44 S 129.31 E
Nilakka ◎ 26 63.07 N 26.33 E
Niland 204 33.14 N 115.31 W
Nil Blanc
— White Nile ≏ 140 15.38 N 32.31 E
Nile □⁵ 154 3.00 N 31.30 E
Nile (Nahr an-Nīl) ≏ 140 30.10 N 31.06 E
Niles, Il., U.S. 216 42.01 N 87.48 W
Niles, Mi., U.S. 216 41.49 N 86.15 W
Niles, Oh., U.S. 214 41.10 N 80.45 W
Niles Canyon V 282 37.36 N 121.56 W
Niles Pond ◎ 283 42.35 N 70.40 W
Nilgani 272b 22.46 N 88.26 E
Nilgaut, Lac ◎ 190 46.36 N 77.15 W
Nilgiri 126 21.28 N 86.46 E
Nilka 86 43.47 N 82.20 E
Nilkitkwa ≏ 182 55.27 N 126.43 W
Nillahcootie, Lake ◎¹ 169 36.54 S 146.00 E
Nilo
— Nile ≏ 140 30.10 N 31.06 E
Nilo Azul
— Blue Nile ≏ 140 15.38 N 32.31 E
Nilo Blanco
— White Nile ≏ 140 15.38 N 32.31 E
Nilópolis 256 22.49 S 43.25 W
Nilópolis □⁷ 287a 22.49 S 43.26 W
Nilphāmāri 124 25.56 N 88.51 E
Nilsiä 26 63.12 N 28.05 E
Niltepec 234 16.34 N 94.37 W
Nilüfer ≏ 130 40.18 N 28.27 E
Nilwāl ◆⁸ 272a 28.40 N 76.59 E
Nilwood 219 39.24 N 89.49 W
Nima 96 35.09 N 132.24 E
Nimach 120 24.28 N 74.52 E
Niman ≏ 89 51.24 N 132.45 E
Nimančik 89 52.09 N 133.47 E
Nimba, Mount ∧ 150 7.37 N 8.25 W
Nimbāhera 120 24.37 N 74.41 E
Nimba Range ∧ 150 7.30 N 8.30 W
Nimboran, Pegunungan ∧ 164 2.45 S 140.20 E
Nimelen ≏ 89 52.27 N 136.32 E
Nîmes 62 43.50 N 4.21 E
Nimis 64 46.12 N 13.16 E
Nimishillen Creek ≏ 214 40.38 N 81.22 W
Nimisila ≏ 214 40.56 N 81.34 W
Nimisila Reservoir ◎¹ 214 40.57 N 81.31 W
Nīm Ka Thāna 120 27.44 N 75.48 E
Nimmitabel 166 36.31 S 149.16 E
Nimmonsburg 210 42.09 N 75.55 W
Nimpkish Lake ◎ 182 50.25 N 126.59 W
Nimrod Lake ◎¹ 194 34.55 N 93.20 W
Nimrūz □⁴ 128 30.30 N 62.00 E
Nims ≏ 56 49.51 N 6.28 E
Nimta 272b 22.40 N 88.25 E
Nimule 154 3.36 N 32.03 E
Nimule National Park ⁂ 154 3.50 N 31.35 E
Nimy 50 50.28 N 3.57 E
Niña Bonita, Presa ◎¹ 286b 23.02 N 82.29 W
Ninah, Wādī V 146 30.02 N 15.22 E
Nīnawā □⁴ 128 36.10 N 42.35 E
Nīnawā (Nineveh) ⊥ 128 36.25 N 43.10 E
Nin Bay c 116 12.13 N 123.15 E
Ninda 152 14.47 S 21.24 E
Nindigully 166 28.21 S 148.49 E
Nindiri 236 12.00 N 86.08 W
Nine Ashes 260 51.42 N 0.18 E
Nine Degree Channel Ψ 122 9.00 N 73.00 E
Ninemile Creek ≏, N.Y., U.S. 210 43.11 N 75.20 W
Ninemile Creek ≏, N.Y., U.S. 210 43.06 N 76.14 W
Ninemile Creek ≏, N.Y., U.S. 210 43.24 N 76.38 W
Nine Mile Creek ≏, Ut., U.S. 200 39.50 N 109.53 W
Ninemile Island I 214 40.29 N 79.52 W
Nine Mile Lake ◎ 212 44.57 N 79.34 W
Nine Mile Point ≻ 212 44.09 N 76.34 W
Ninepin Group II 271d 22.16 N 114.21 E
Nineteen Hundred Five Memorial Cemetery ◆ 265a 59.51 N 30.27 E
Ninette 184 49.24 N 99.38 W
Ninetyeast Ridge ◆³ 6 4.00 S 90.00 E
Ninety Mile Beach ⁂², Austl. 166 38.13 S 147.23 E
Ninety Mile Beach ⁂², N.Z. 172 34.48 S 173.00 E
Ninety Six 192 34.10 N 82.01 W
Nineveh, In., U.S. 218 39.22 N 86.05 W
Nineveh, N.Y., U.S. 210 42.12 N 75.36 W
Nineveh
— Nīnawā ⊥ 128 36.25 N 43.10 E
Ninfa ⊥ 66 41.36 N 12.58 E
Ninfas, Punta ≻ 254 42.56 S 64.20 W
Ninfield 42 50.53 N 0.25 E
Ninga 184 49.13 N 99.51 W
Ningaloo 162 22.42 S 113.40 E
Ning'an 89 44.22 N 129.25 E
Ningari 150 14.40 N 3.16 W
Ningbo 100 29.52 N 121.31 E
Ningcheng (Tianyi) 98 41.33 N 119.20 E
Ningde 100 26.43 N 119.33 E
Ningdu 100 26.31 N 115.58 E
Ningerum 164 5.41 S 141.08 E
Ninggang 100 26.50 N 114.02 E
Ningguo 106 30.38 N 118.58 E
Ninghai 100 29.17 N 121.25 E
Ninghe (Lutai) 105 39.20 N 117.48 E
Ninghepu 105 40.43 N 116.07 E
Ninghua 100 26.15 N 116.38 E
Ningi 150 11.04 N 9.32 E
Ningjin, Zhg. 98 37.37 N 114.55 E
Ningjin, Zhg. 98 37.39 N 116.48 E
Ningjing Shan ∧ 102 29.45 N 98.45 E
Ningling 98 34.27 N 115.21 E
Ningming 102 22.07 N 107.05 E
Ningnan 102 27.11 N 102.36 E
Ningpo
— Ningbo 100 29.52 N 121.31 E
Ningqiang 102 32.44 N 106.19 E
Ningshan 102 33.04 N 108.39 E
Ningsia
— Yinchuan 102 38.30 N 106.18 E
Ningsia Hui Autonomous Region
— Ningxia Huizu Zizhiqu □⁴ 102 37.00 N 106.00 E
Ningwu 102 39.01 N 112.21 E
Ningxi 100 28.35 N 121.00 E
Ningxia Huizu Zizhiqu (Ningsia Hui) □⁴ 102 37.00 N 106.00 E
Ningxian 102 35.31 N 108.01 E
Ningxiang 100 28.15 N 112.33 E
Ningyang 98 35.47 N 116.47 E
Ningyō-tōge ⲭ 96 35.19 N 133.56 E
Ningyuan 102 25.37 N 111.46 E
Ningyuanbao 102 38.38 N 102.30 E
Ningyuanpu 105 40.44 N 114.54 E
Ninh Binh 110 20.15 N 105.59 E
Ninh Hoa 110 12.29 N 109.08 E
Ninhue 252 36.24 S 72.24 W
Ningo Group II 164 1.15 S 144.15 E
Ninilchik 180 60.03 N 151.41 W
Ninnescah ≏ 198 37.20 N 97.10 W
Ninnescah, North Fork ≏ 198 37.34 N 97.42 W
Ninnescah, South Fork ≏ 198 37.34 N 97.42 W
Ninnis Glacier Tongue ⊓ 9 68.12 S 147.12 E
Ninocminda 84 41.18 N 43.35 E
Ninohe 92 40.16 N 141.18 E
Ninomiya, Nihon 94 35.18 N 139.16 E
Ninomiya, Nihon 94 36.22 N 139.58 E
Ninove 50 50.50 N 4.01 E
Niny 84 44.29 N 43.57 E
Nio 96 34.12 N 133.39 E
Nioaque 248 21.08 S 55.48 W
Nioaque ≏ 248 20.46 S 56.04 W
Niobe 214 42.01 N 79.27 W
Niobrara 198 42.45 N 98.01 W
Niobrara ≏ 198 42.45 N 98.00 W
Nioka 154 2.10 N 30.39 E
Nioki 152 2.43 S 17.41 E
Niokolo Koba 150 13.04 N 12.43 W
Niokolo Koba, Parc National du ♦ 150 13.00 N 13.00 W
Niono 150 14.15 N 6.00 W
Nionsamoridougou 150 8.43 N 8.50 W
Nioro du Rip 150 13.45 N 15.48 W
Nioro du Sahel 150 15.15 N 9.35 W
Niort 32 46.19 N 0.27 W
Niota 192 35.30 N 84.32 W
Nioût ▼⁴ 150 16.03 N 6.52 W
Nipan 166 24.47 S 150.01 E
Nipāni 122 16.24 N 74.23 E
Nipawin 184 53.22 N 104.00 W
Nipawin Provincial Park ♦ 184 54.00 N 104.40 W
Nipe, Bahía de c 240p 20.47 N 75.42 W
Nipekamew ≏ 184 54.59 N 104.52 W
Nipekamew Lake ◎ 184 54.24 N 104.58 W
Nipepe 154 14.01 S 37.55 E
Nipigon 190 49.01 N 88.16 W
Nipigon, Lake ◎ 176 49.50 N 88.30 W
Nipigon Bay c 190 48.53 N 87.50 W
Nipin ≏ 184 55.45 N 109.02 W
Nipisi Lake ◎ 182 55.47 N 114.57 W
Nipissing □⁶ 212 45.30 N 78.50 W
Nipissing, Lake ◎ 190 46.17 N 80.00 W
Nipissis, Lac ◎ 186 51.02 N 66.10 W
Nipisso, Lac ◎ 186 50.52 N 65.50 W
Nipomo 204 35.02 N 120.28 W
Nippenicket, Lake ◎ 283 41.58 N 71.03 W
Nippers Harbour 186 49.48 N 55.52 W
Nippersink Creek ≏ 216 42.23 N 88.22 W
Niqiu 100 33.25 N 115.38 E
Niquelândia 255 14.27 S 48.27 W
Niquero 240p 20.03 N 77.35 W
Niquivil 252 30.25 S 68.42 W
Nīr 128 38.02 N 47.59 E
Nīr, Jabal an- ∧² 128 24.10 N 43.20 E
Nīra ≏ 122 17.59 N 75.07 E
Nir'am 132 31.31 N 34.35 E
Nirasaki 94 35.42 N 138.27 E
Nirayama 94 35.03 N 138.57 E
Nirgua 246 10.09 N 68.34 W
Nirim 132 31.20 N 34.24 E
Nirmal 122 19.06 N 78.21 E
Nirmāli 124 26.19 N 86.35 E
Nirsa 126 23.47 N 86.43 E
Niš 38 43.19 N 21.54 E
Nisa 34 39.31 N 7.39 W
Nisa (Neisse) (Nysa Łużycka) ≏ 30 52.04 N 14.46 E
Nisāb, Ar. Su. 128 29.11 N 44.43 E
Nisāb, Yaman 144 14.31 N 46.30 E
Nišava ≏ 38 43.22 N 21.46 E
Nisbet 210 41.13 N 77.07 W
Niscemi 70 37.09 N 14.23 E
Nischintāpur 272b 22.26 N 88.22 E
Nisf Thānī Bashbīsh 142 31.07 N 31.11 E
Niš
— Niš 38 43.19 N 21.54 E
Nishi 120 33.35 N 85.30 E
Nishi ◆⁸, Nihon 268 35.27 N 139.38 E
Nishi ◆⁸, Nihon 270 34.41 N 135.30 E
Nishiarai ◆⁸ 268 35.47 N 139.47 E
Nishiarai 94 35.31 N 136.10 E
Nishibetsuin 270 34.58 N 135.31 E
Nishi-Chūgoku-sanchi-kokutei-kōen ⁂ 96 34.40 N 132.10 E
Nishigō 94 37.09 N 140.10 E
Nishihiyayama 96 33.53 N 133.49 E
Nishiizu 94 34.46 N 138.47 E
Nishi-jima I 96 34.39 N 134.29 E
Nishikata 94 36.28 N 139.45 E
Nishikatsura 94 35.31 N 138.51 E
Nishiki 96 34.16 N 131.57 E
Nishiki ≏ 96 34.09 N 132.15 E
Nishikiori 270 34.29 N 135.34 E
Nishikujō ◆⁸ 270 34.59 N 135.40 E
Nishimori ◆⁸ 270 34.45 N 135.01 E
Nishinari ◆⁸ 270 34.38 N 135.30 E
Nishinasuno 94 36.53 N 139.59 E
Nishinomiya 96 34.43 N 135.20 E
Nishinoomote 93b 30.44 N 131.00 E
Nishio 94 34.52 N 137.03 E
Nishitōda ◆⁸ 270 34.43 N 135.33 E
Nishitosa 96 33.09 N 132.47 E
Nishiwaki 96 34.59 N 134.58 E
Nishiyodogawa ◆⁸ 270 34.42 N 135.27 E
Nisinomiya
— Nishinomiya 96 34.43 N 135.20 E
Nisiros I 38 36.35 N 27.10 E
Niska Lake ◎ 184 55.35 N 108.38 W

Symbols in the index entries represent the broad categories identified in the key at the right. Symbols with superior numbers (∧¹) identify subcategories (see complete key on page I · 1).

Symbole im Register stellen die rechts im Schlüssel erklärten Kategorien dar. Symbole mit hochgestellten Ziffern (∧¹) bezeichnen Unterabteilungen einer Kategorie (vgl. vollständiger Schlüssel auf Seite I · 1).

Los símbolos incluídos en el texto del índice representan las grandes categorias identificadas con la clave a la derecha. Los símbolos con numeros en su parte superior (∧¹) identifican las subcategorias (véase la clave completa en la página I · 1).

Les symboles de l'index représentent les catégories indiquées dans la légende à droite. Les symboles suivis d'un indice (∧¹) représentent des sous-catégories (voir légende complète à la page I · 1).

Os símbolos incluídos no texto do índice representam as grandes categorias identificadas com a chave à direita. Os símbolos com números em sua parte superior (∧¹) identificam as subcategorias (veja-se a chave completa à página I · 1).

∧ Mountain	Berg	Montaña	Montagne	Montanha
∧ Mountains	Gebirge	Montañas	Montagnes	Montanhas
ⲭ Pass	Paß	Paso	Col	Passo
V Valley, Canyon	Tal, Cañon	Valle, Cañón	Vallée, Canyon	Vale, Canhão
≐ Plain	Ebene	Llano	Plaine	Planície
≻ Cape	Kap	Cabo	Cap	Cabo
I Island	Insel	Isla	Île	Ilha
II Islands	Inseln	Islas	Îles	Ilhas
⁂ Other Topographic Features	Andere Topographische Objekte	Otros Elementos Topográficos	Autres données topographiques	Outros acidentes topográficos

ESPAÑOL Nombre / FRANÇAIS Nom / PORTUGUÊS Nome	Página / Page	Lat.°′	Long.°′ W = Oeste / W = Ouest
Niskayuna	210	42.46 N	73.50 W
Nisling ≃	180	62.27 N	139.30 W
Nismes	56	50.05 N	4.33 E
Nispen	52	51.29 N	4.28 E
Nisporeni	38	47.06 N	28.11 E
Nisqually ≃	224	47.06 N	122.42 W
Nisqually Indian Reservation ◆[4]	224	47.02 N	122.42 W
Nisqually Reach c	224	47.07 N	122.45 W
Nissan ≃	26	56.40 N	12.51 E
Nissequogue	276	40.54 N	73.12 W
Nissequogue ≃	276	40.54 N	73.13 W
Nissequogue, Northeast Branch ≃	276	40.50 N	73.13 W
Nissequogue River State Park ♠	276	40.51 N	73.13 W
Nisser ⊜	26	59.10 N	8.30 E
Nisshin	94	35.08 N	137.02 E
Nissoria	70	37.39 N	14.27 E
Nissum Bredning c	26	56.38 N	8.22 E
Nissum Fjord c[2]	26	56.21 N	8.14 E
Nisswa	190	46.31 N	94.17 W
Nistelrode	52	51.43 N	5.33 E
Nister ≃	56	50.47 N	7.43 E
Nistru (Dnister) ≃	78	46.18 N	30.17 E
Nisutlin ≃	180	60.10 N	132.30 W
Nita, Indon.	115b	8.40 S	122.11 E
Nita, Nihon	96	35.12 N	133.01 E
Nitalas	272c	19.06 N	73.08 E
Nītaure	76	57.10 N	25.10 E
Niterói	256	22.53 S	43.07 W
Niterói □[7]	287a	22.56 S	43.04 W
Nith ≃, On., Can.	212	43.12 N	80.22 W
Nith ≃, Scot., U.K.	44	55.00 N	3.35 W
Nithāri	272a	28.35 N	77.21 E
Nithāri ◆[8]	272a	28.42 N	77.03 E
Nithi River	182	54.01 N	125.01 W
Nithsdale V	44	55.14 N	3.46 W
Nitibe	112	9.19 S	124.12 E
Nitinat	224	48.55 N	124.29 W
Nitinat ≃	224	48.49 N	124.37 W
Nitinat Lake ⊜	182	48.45 N	124.45 W
Niton	42	50.35 N	1.16 W
Nitra	30	48.20 N	18.05 E
Nitra ≃	30	47.46 N	18.10 E
Nitro	188	38.24 N	81.50 W
Nitry	50	47.40 N	3.53 E
Nitta	94	36.17 N	139.18 E
Nittälven ≃	40	59.51 N	14.50 E
Nittany Mountain ∧	210	41.00 N	77.25 W
Nittedal	26	60.04 N	10.53 E
Nittenau	60	49.12 N	12.16 E
Nittendorf	60	49.02 N	11.58 E
Niu Aunfo Point ›	174w	21.04 S	175.20 W
Niubaotun	105	39.46 N	116.41 E
Niubu	100	31.02 N	117.39 E
Niuchutuncun	104	41.28 N	122.58 E
Niudouguang	100	24.51 N	115.44 E
Niue □[2], Oc.	14	19.02 S	169.52 W
Niue □[2], Oc.	174v	19.02 S	169.52 W
Niu'erhe	89	51.30 N	121.49 E
Niufentai	89	47.05 N	120.02 E
Niufozhen	107	29.23 N	105.02 E
Niuhang	100	28.44 N	115.51 E
Niuhuaxi	107	29.29 N	103.48 E
Niujie	102	27.47 N	104.16 E
Niujingjie	110	25.46 N	100.33 E
Niuke	120	30.41 N	82.01 E
Niulakita I	14	10.45 S	179.30 E
Niulan ≃	102	27.28 N	103.10 E
Niulanshan	105	40.13 N	116.39 E
Niumaowu	98	40.58 N	124.59 E
Niupeng	106	31.32 N	121.50 E
Niupichang	107	30.35 N	103.40 E
Niushitun	98	35.18 N	114.24 E
Niut, Gunung ∧	112	1.00 N	109.55 E
Niutan	107	29.05 N	105.21 E
Niutao I	14	6.06 S	177.17 E
Niuti	100	32.58 N	113.35 E
Niutian	100	27.17 N	115.44 E
Niutoushan	89	45.09 N	126.45 E
Niutou Shan I	100	29.07 N	121.56 E
Niutuo	105	39.15 N	116.20 E
Niutuoshan	106	31.04 N	119.37 E
Niuxichang	107	28.47 N	104.31 E
Niuxintai	104	41.21 N	123.53 E
Niuxintun	104	41.56 N	121.21 E
Niuyuanzi	105	40.20 N	117.47 E
Niuzhuang, Zhg.	98	37.21 N	118.29 E
Niuzhuang, Zhg.	104	40.58 N	122.32 E
Nivå	41	55.56 N	12.31 E
Nivala	26	63.55 N	24.58 E
Nive ≃, Austl.	166	26.02 S	146.25 E
Nive ≃, Fr.	32	43.30 N	1.29 W
Nivelles (Nijvel)	50	50.36 N	4.20 E
Nivernais □[9]	32	47.00 N	3.30 E
Nivernais, Canal du ≅	50	47.40 N	3.40 E
Niverville, Mb., Can.	184	49.37 N	97.01 W
Niverville, N.Y., U.S.	210	42.26 N	73.40 W
Nivillers	50	49.28 N	2.10 E
Nivnoje	76	53.11 N	32.35 E
Nivskij	24	67.16 N	32.23 E
Niwāno	128	26.22 N	62.43 E
Nixa	194	37.02 N	93.17 W
Nixi	102	27.58 N	99.27 E
Nixis	107	30.08 N	106.19 E
Nixizhen	107	29.02 N	104.16 E
Nixon, Nv., U.S.	204	39.49 N	119.21 W
Nixon, Pa., U.S.	214	40.45 N	79.56 W
Nixon, Tx., U.S.	222	29.16 N	97.45 W
Niyodo	96	33.32 N	133.08 E
Niyodo ≃	96	33.27 N	133.29 E
Niyor	114	2.05 N	103.17 E
Niyu Shan I	100	27.51 N	121.03 E
Niža	24	66.20 N	43.16 E
Nizāmābād	122	18.40 N	78.07 E
Nizamghāt	120	28.16 N	95.42 E
Nizām Sāgar ⊜[1]	122	18.10 N	77.55 E
Nīzgān ≃	128	33.13 N	63.40 E
Nizhniy Tagil → Nižnij Tagil	86	57.55 N	59.57 E
Nizhyn	78	51.03 N	31.54 E
Nižin	76	52.38 N	28.10 E
Nizino	265a	59.50 N	29.53 E
Nizip	130	37.01 N	37.46 E
Nízke Tatry ⟑	30	48.54 N	19.40 E
Nízke Tatry, národní park ♠	30	47.48 N	19.35 E
Nižn'aja	80	56.34 N	49.07 E
Nižn'aja Čvorovaja	86	59.11 N	77.31 E
Nižnaja Dobrinka	80	50.18 N	45.42 E
Nižn'aja Grajvoronka	78	51.47 N	37.45 E
Nižn'aja Irga	86	56.51 N	57.26 E
Nižn'aja Karelina	88	57.55 N	107.44 E
Nižn'aja Keul'skaja, šivera ∟	88	58.25 N	102.46 E
Nižnaja Matrenka	80	52.16 N	40.06 E
Nižn'aja Omka	86	55.26 N	74.55 E
Nižn'aja Omra	24	62.46 N	55.46 E
Nižn'aja Ošma	80	55.44 N	51.18 E
Nižn'aja Peša	24	66.43 N	47.36 E
Nižn'aja Pojma	88	56.11 N	97.13 E
Nižn'aja Pokrovka	80	51.40 N	50.07 E
Nižn'aja Šachtama	88	51.24 N	117.40 E
Nižn'aja Salda	86	58.05 N	60.43 E
Nižn'aja Syzran'	80	53.04 N	48.34 E
Nižn'aja Tavda	86	57.40 N	66.12 E
Nižn'aja Tunguska ≃	74	65.48 N	88.04 E
Nižn'aja Tura	86	58.37 N	59.49 E
Nižn'aja Vol'dža	86	58.19 N	79.20 E
Nižn'aja Zaimka	88	56.09 N	98.14 E
Nižneangarsk	88	55.47 N	109.33 E
Nižnebakanskij	78	44.52 N	37.52 E
Nižnečujskij	85	43.12 N	74.21 E
Nižnedevick	78	51.33 N	38.20 E
Nižne-Gnilovskoj ◆[8]	83	47.11 N	39.36 E
Nižnegnutov	80	48.02 N	42.22 E
Nižneilimsk	88	57.11 N	103.16 E
Nižneje Al'kejevo	80	54.46 N	50.03 E
Nižn'eje Gir'unino	88	51.12 N	116.58 E
Nižneje Kučukovo	80	56.13 N	52.57 E
Nižneje Kujto, ozero ⊜	24	64.58 N	31.38 E
Nižneje M'ačkovo	82	55.33 N	37.59 E
Nižneje Romanovo	86	59.47 N	69.35 E
Nižneje Sančelejevo	80	53.40 N	49.27 E
Nižnekamsk	80	55.32 N	51.58 E
Nižnekamskoje vodochranilišče ⊜[1]	24	55.50 N	53.00 E
Nižnekundr'učen-Skaja	80	47.45 N	40.57 E
Nižnelemskij	24	64.01 N	56.16 E
Nižne-Mit'akin Pervyj	83	48.41 N	40.02 E
Nižne-Nagol'naja	83	49.00 N	39.59 E
Nižneoz'ornoje	80	51.37 N	53.56 E
Nižne-Podpol'nyj	83	47.12 N	40.01 E
Nižnetambovskoje	89	50.54 N	138.13 E
Nižnetroickij	80	54.20 N	53.41 E
Nižneudinsk	88	54.54 N	99.03 E
Nižnevartovsk	74	60.56 N	76.31 E
Nižnij Baskunčak	80	48.13 N	46.50 E
Nižnij Časučej	88	50.31 N	115.08 E
Nižnij Čir	80	48.22 N	43.03 E
Nižnij Čulym	86	54.37 N	78.56 E
Nižnije Černi	80	47.41 N	43.26 E
Nižnije Čeršely	80	54.40 N	52.08 E
Nižnije Ostrovcy	82	55.35 N	38.01 E
Nižnije Sergi	86	56.40 N	59.18 E
Nižnije Timers'any	80	54.34 N	47.45 E
Nižnije V'azovyje	80	55.49 N	48.32 E
Nižnij Ingaš	88	56.12 N	96.31 E
Nižnij Kisl'aj	78	50.50 N	40.11 E
Nižnij Kuranach	74	58.49 N	125.32 E
Nižnij Lomov	80	53.32 N	43.41 E
Nižnij Mamon	78	50.11 N	40.30 E
Nižnij Novgorod (Gorky)	80	56.20 N	44.00 E
Nižnij Novgorod Oblast' □[4]	80	56.30 N	45.00 E
Nižnij Odes	24	63.40 N	54.52 E
Nižnij Ol'šan	78	50.45 N	38.55 E
Nižnij P'andž	120	37.08 N	68.32 E
Nižnij Paramonov	80	47.57 N	41.55 E
Nižnij Šerebr'akov	80	47.58 N	41.02 E
Nižnij Škaft	80	53.36 N	45.40 E
Nižnij Stan	88	52.18 N	115.44 E
Nižnij Tagil	86	57.55 N	59.57 E
Nižnij Takanyš	80	55.57 N	51.04 E
Nižnij Ufalej	86	55.55 N	59.59 E
Nižnij V'aloz'orskij	24	66.44 N	35.10 E
Nizwā	128	22.56 N	57.32 E
Nizy-le-Comte	50	49.34 N	4.03 E
Nizza Monferrato	62	44.46 N	8.21 E
Nizzana	132	30.53 N	34.27 E
Nizzana, Nahal V	132	30.57 N	34.23 E
Nizzanim	132	31.43 N	34.38 E
Njassa-See → Nyasa, Lake ⊜	154	12.00 S	34.30 E
Njazidja (Grande Comore) I	157a	11.35 S	43.20 E
Njinjo	154	8.48 S	38.54 E
Njoko ≃	152	17.10 S	24.05 E
Njombe	154	9.20 S	34.46 E
Njombe ≃	154	6.56 S	35.06 E
Njupeskär ∟	26	61.38 N	12.41 E
Njurunda	26	62.16 N	17.22 E
Nkambe	152	6.38 N	10.40 E
Nkandla	158	28.37 S	31.05 E
Nkawkaw	150	6.33 N	0.47 W
Nkayi	154	19.00 S	28.54 E
Nkhata Bay	154	11.33 S	34.18 E
Nkhotakota	154	12.57 S	34.17 E
Nkolabona	152	1.14 N	11.43 E
Nkomi, Lagune c	152	1.35 S	9.17 E
Nkongsamba	152	4.57 N	9.56 E
Nkonko	154	6.20 S	34.58 E
Nkoso	152	2.42 S	22.39 E
Nkoto	152	1.56 S	19.41 E
Nkunga	152	4.41 S	18.34 E
Nkurenkuru	152	17.38 S	18.35 E
Nkwalini	158	28.45 S	31.33 E
Nmai ≃	102	25.42 N	97.30 E
Nnewi	150	6.00 N	6.59 E
Nō	94	37.06 N	137.59 E
Noābād	272b	22.34 N	88.31 E
Noailles	50	49.20 N	2.12 E
Noākhāli	124	22.49 N	91.06 E
Noak Hill ◆[8]	260	51.37 N	0.14 E
Noale	64	45.32 N	12.04 E
Noāmundi	124	22.09 N	85.32 E
Noank	207	41.19 N	71.59 W
Noarlunga	168b	35.11 S	138.30 E
Noasca	62	45.27 N	7.19 E
Noatak	180	67.34 N	162.59 W
Noatak ≃	180	67.00 N	162.30 W
Nobby	171a	27.51 S	151.54 E
Nobel	212	45.25 N	80.06 W
Nobeoka	92	32.35 N	131.40 E
Nobidome	268	35.48 N	139.35 E
Nobidome-yōsui ≅[1]	268	35.44 N	139.27 E
Nōbi-heiya ≚	94	35.15 N	136.45 E
Nobili	150	11.33 N	1.12 W
Nobitz	54	50.58 N	12.29 E
Noble, Il., U.S.	194	38.41 N	88.13 W
Noble, Ok., U.S.	196	35.08 N	97.23 W
Noble □[6]	216	41.24 N	85.25 W
Noble Park	274b	37.58 S	145.10 E
Noblestown	279b	40.24 N	80.12 W
Noblesville	218	40.02 N	86.00 W
Nobleton, On., Can.	212	43.54 N	79.40 W
Nobleton, Fl., U.S.	220	28.38 N	82.15 W
Noboribetsu	92a	42.27 N	141.11 E
Noborito	268	35.37 N	139.34 E
Nobres	248	14.44 S	56.20 W
Nobsa	246	5.46 N	72.57 W
Nocatee	220	27.09 N	81.52 W
Noccundra	166	27.50 S	142.36 E
Nocé	50	48.22 N	0.42 E
Noce ≃	64	46.09 N	11.04 E
Nocera Inferiore	68	40.44 N	14.38 E
Nocera Superiore	68	40.44 N	14.40 E
Nocera Tirinese	68	39.02 N	16.09 E
Nocera Umbra	66	43.05 N	12.47 E
Noceto	64	44.48 N	10.11 E
Nochistlán	234	21.22 N	102.51 W
Nochten	54	51.26 N	14.36 E
Noci	68	40.48 N	17.08 E
Nociglia	68	40.02 N	18.20 E
Nockamixon Lake ⊜[1]	208	40.28 N	75.14 W
Nockamixon State Park ♠	208	40.27 N	75.16 W
Nockatunga	166	27.43 S	142.43 E
Nocona	196	33.47 N	97.43 W
Nocupétaro	234	18.48 N	101.04 W
Noda	94	35.56 N	139.52 E
Nodagawa	96	35.31 N	135.06 E
Nodaway ≃	194	39.54 N	94.58 W
Nodera	270	34.45 N	134.56 E
Nods	58	47.06 N	6.20 E
Noé, Ouadi V	146	15.39 N	21.19 E
Noel	194	36.32 N	94.29 W
Noenieput	158	27.29 S	20.06 E
Noepoli	68	40.05 N	16.20 E
Noer	41	54.27 N	10.00 E
Noetinger	252	32.22 S	62.19 W
Nœux-les-Mines	50	50.29 N	2.40 E
Nofels	58	47.15 N	9.34 E
Nogah	132	31.37 N	34.42 E
Nogajskaja step' ≚	84	44.17 N	46.05 E
Nogales, Chile	252	32.44 S	71.15 W
Nogales, Méx.	232	31.20 N	110.56 W
Nogales, Méx.	234	18.49 N	97.10 W
Nogales, Az., U.S.	200	31.20 N	110.56 W
Nogami	94	36.07 N	139.07 E
Nogangjin	98	39.30 N	125.23 E
Nogara, It.	64	45.11 N	11.04 E
Nogara, Ityo.	144	13.53 N	36.32 E
Nogaro	32	43.46 N	0.02 W
Nōgata	96	33.44 N	130.44 E
Nogent-en-Bassigny	58	48.02 N	5.21 E
Nogent-le-Roi	50	48.39 N	1.32 E
Nogent-le-Rotrou	50	48.19 N	0.50 E
Nogent-sur-Marne	261	48.50 N	2.29 E
Nogent-sur-Oise	50	49.16 N	2.28 E
Nogent-sur-Seine	50	48.29 N	3.30 E
Nogent-sur-Vernisson	50	47.51 N	2.45 E
Nogi	94	36.14 N	139.44 E
Nogies Creek ≃	212	44.35 N	78.31 W
Noginsk	82	55.51 N	38.27 E
Nogisaki	268	35.57 N	139.58 E
Nogliki	89	51.48 N	143.10 E
Nogmung	102	27.30 N	97.49 E
Nogoa ≃	166	23.33 S	148.32 E
Nōgohaku-san ∧	94	35.46 N	136.31 E
Nogoon Nuur	86	49.33 N	90.17 E
Nogoyá	252	32.24 S	59.48 W
Nógrád □[6]	30	48.00 N	19.35 E
Noguera Pallaresa ≃	34	42.15 N	0.54 E
Noguera Ribagorzana ≃	34	41.40 N	0.43 E
Nohain ≃	50	47.24 N	2.55 E
Nohar	123	29.11 N	74.46 E
Noheji	92	40.52 N	141.08 E
Nohili Point ›	229b	22.04 N	159.47 W
Nohjhīl	124	27.51 N	77.39 E
Nohta	124	23.40 N	79.34 E
Nohwa-do I	98	34.12 N	126.35 E
Noicattaro	68	41.02 N	16.59 E
Noichi	96	33.33 N	133.42 E
Noir, Causse ⟑[1]	32	44.10 N	3.15 E
Noir, Isla I	254	54.29 S	73.02 W
Noire ≃, P.Q., Can.	190	45.54 N	76.57 W
Noire ≃, P.Q., Can.	206	45.33 N	72.58 W
Noire ≃, P.Q., Can.	206	46.39 N	72.08 W
Noire, Mer du → Black Sea ⊤[2]	22	43.00 N	35.00 E
Noire, Montagne ∧	206	46.14 N	74.18 W
Noire, Montagne ⟑	32	43.28 N	2.18 E
Noirétable	62	45.49 N	3.46 E
Noirmoutier	32	47.00 N	2.14 W
Noirmoutier, Île de I	32	47.00 N	2.15 W
Noiseau	261	48.47 N	2.33 E
Noisiel	261	48.51 N	2.37 E
Noisy ≃	212	44.19 N	80.08 W
Noisy-le-Grand	261	48.51 N	2.33 E
Noisy-le-Roi	261	48.51 N	2.04 E
Noisy-le-Sec	261	48.53 N	2.28 E
Nojember'an	84	41.12 N	45.01 E
Nojima-zaki ›	94	34.56 N	139.53 E
Nojiri-ko ⊜	94	36.49 N	138.13 E
Nojon	102	43.10 N	102.07 E
Nojon uul ⟑	102	43.10 N	101.30 E
Nokami	96	34.15 N	135.20 E
Nokaneng	156	19.40 S	22.16 E
Nōke	270	34.26 N	135.29 E
Nokha Mandi	120	27.35 N	73.29 E
Nokia	26	61.28 N	23.30 E
Nokilalaki, Bulu ∧	112	1.13 S	120.08 E
Nok Kundi	128	28.46 N	62.46 E
Nokogiri-yama ∧[2]	268	35.09 N	139.51 E
Nokomis, Sk., Can.	184	51.30 N	105.00 W
Nokomis, Fl., U.S.	220	27.07 N	82.26 W
Nokomis, Il., U.S.	219	39.18 N	89.17 W
Nokomis Lake ⊜	184	56.58 N	103.02 W
Nokou	146	14.35 N	14.47 E
Nokpan-ni ◆[8]	271b	37.36 N	126.56 E
Nokrek ∧	124	25.27 N	90.20 E
Nokuku	175f	14.53 S	166.35 E
Nola, Centraf.	152	3.32 N	16.04 E
Nola, It.	68	40.55 N	14.33 E
Nolan ≃	222	32.07 N	97.26 W
Nolan Creek ≃	222	31.02 N	97.26 W
Nolands Fork ≃	218	39.41 N	85.07 W
Nolanville	222	31.05 N	97.36 W
Nolay	58	46.57 N	4.38 E
Nole	62	45.15 N	7.35 E
Noli	62	44.12 N	8.26 E
Noli, Capo di ›	62	44.12 N	8.25 E
Nolichucky ≃	192	36.07 N	83.14 W
Nolin ≃	194	37.13 N	86.15 W
Nolin Lake ⊜[1]	194	37.20 N	86.10 W
Nolinsk	80	57.33 N	49.57 E
Nomad	164	6.18 S	142.14 E
Nomahegan Brook ≃	276	40.41 N	74.18 W
Nomans Land I	207	41.15 N	70.49 W
Nombre de Dios, Méx.	234	23.51 N	104.14 W
Nombre de Dios, Pan.	236	9.35 N	79.28 W
Nombre de Dios, Cordillera ⟑	236	15.35 N	86.55 W
Nome	180	64.30 N	165.24 W
Nomény	56	48.54 N	6.14 E
Nomexy	58	48.18 N	6.23 E
Nomgon, Mong.	102	42.50 N	105.07 E
Nomgon, Mong.	102	45.26 N	105.08 E
Nomgon uul ⟑	102	42.50 N	104.20 E
Nomingue, Petit lac ⊜	206	46.21 N	75.00 W
Nomini Bay c	208	38.09 N	76.43 W
Nominingue	206	46.24 N	75.02 W
Nominingue, Lac ⊜	206	46.26 N	74.59 W
Nomoneas II	175c	7.24 N	151.53 E
Nomozaki	92	32.35 N	129.45 E
Nomtsas	156	24.22 S	16.47 E
Nomura	96	33.22 N	132.38 E
Nona, Lake ⊜	220	28.24 N	81.15 W
Nonacho Lake ⊜	176	61.42 N	109.40 W
Nonancourt	50	48.46 N	1.12 E
Nonant-le-Pin	50	48.42 N	0.13 E
Nonantola	64	44.41 N	11.02 E
Nonburg	24	65.34 N	50.32 E
Nonceveux	56	50.28 N	5.44 E
Nondalton	180	60.00 N	154.49 W
Nondwa	154	6.26 S	35.20 E
Nondweni	158	28.11 S	30.49 E
None	62	44.56 N	7.32 E
Nonette ≃	50	49.12 N	2.24 E
None-yama ∧	96	33.29 N	134.10 E
Nong'an	89	44.25 N	125.10 E
Nong Bua Lamphu	110	17.11 N	102.25 E
Nong Han	110	17.21 N	103.07 E
Nong Hèt	110	19.29 N	103.59 E
Nong Khai	110	17.52 N	102.44 E
Nongoma	158	27.58 S	31.35 E
Nongpoh	120	25.54 N	91.53 E
Nongstoin	120	25.31 N	91.16 E
Nonnenhorn	58	47.34 N	9.36 E
Nonnevitz	54	54.39 N	13.17 E
Nonning	166	32.30 S	136.30 E
Nonnweiler	56	49.36 N	6.58 E
Nono	144	8.32 N	37.26 E
Nonoai	252	27.21 S	52.47 W
Nonoava	232	27.28 N	106.44 W
Nonoc Island I	116	9.51 N	125.37 E
Nono de Julho, Túnel ◆[5]	287b	23.34 S	46.39 W
Nonogasta	252	29.18 S	67.30 W
Nonoichi	94	36.32 N	136.37 E
Nonouti I[1]	14	0.40 S	174.21 E
Nonsan	98	36.12 N	127.05 E
Nonsuch Bay c	240c	17.03 N	61.42 W
Non Sung	110	15.11 N	102.16 E
Nonthaburi	110	13.50 N	100.29 E
Nonthaburi □[4]	269a	13.52 N	100.27 E
Nontron	32	45.32 N	0.40 E
Nonvianuk Lake ⊜	180	59.00 N	155.15 W
Noojee	169	37.55 S	146.00 E
Nookawarra	162	26.19 S	116.52 E
Nooksack	224	48.55 N	122.19 W
Nooksack ≃	224	48.46 N	122.35 W
Nooksack, Middle Fork ≃	224	48.50 N	122.08 W
Nooksack, North Fork ≃	224	48.50 N	122.11 W
Nooksack, South Fork ≃	224	48.50 N	122.11 W
Noonamah	164	12.38 S	131.04 E
Noonan	198	48.53 N	103.00 W
Noon Hill ∧[2]	283	42.09 N	71.19 W
Noonkanbah	162	18.30 S	124.50 E
Noorat	169	38.12 S	142.56 E
Noord-Beveland I	52	51.35 N	3.45 E
Noord-Brabant □[4]	52	51.30 N	5.00 E
Noord-Holland □[4]	52	52.40 N	4.50 E
Noordhollands Kanaal ≅	52	52.33 N	4.50 E
Noordhorn	52	53.16 N	6.24 E
Noordoewer	156	28.45 S	17.37 E
Noordoost Polder ◆[1]	52	52.42 N	5.45 E
Noordpunt ›	241s	12.23 N	69.10 W
Noord-Scharwoude	52	52.43 N	4.47 E
Noordwijk aan Zee	52	52.14 N	4.26 E
Noordwijk-Binnen	52	52.13 N	4.27 E
Noordwijkerhout	52	52.15 N	4.30 E
Noordwolde	52	52.54 N	6.09 E
Noormarkku	26	61.35 N	21.52 E
Noorvik	180	66.50 N	161.12 W
Noosaville	166	26.24 S	153.04 E
Nootka Island I	182	49.32 N	126.42 W
Nootka Sound ⊌	182	49.33 N	126.38 W
Nopaltepec	234	18.17 N	95.59 W
No Point, Point ›	276	41.09 N	73.08 W
Nóqui	152	5.51 S	13.25 E
Nora, Sve.	40	59.31 N	15.02 E
Nora, In., U.S.	218	39.55 N	86.08 W
Nora ≃	89	52.26 N	129.58 E
Nora ⊥	71	39.00 N	9.01 E
Nor Ačin	84	40.19 N	44.35 E
Norah Head ›	170	33.17 S	151.35 E
Nora Islands II	144	16.02 N	40.03 E
Norala	116	6.28 N	124.38 E
Noralee	182	53.59 N	126.26 W
Noranda	190	48.15 N	79.02 W
Noraskög ⟑	40	59.39 N	14.50 E
Nora Springs	190	43.08 N	93.00 W
Norberg	40	60.04 N	15.56 E
Norberto de la Riestra	252	35.16 S	59.46 W
Norborne	194	39.18 N	93.40 W
Norcan Lake ⊜	212	45.10 N	76.53 W
Norcatur	198	39.50 N	100.11 W
Norchia ⊥	66	42.20 N	11.57 E
Norcia	66	42.48 N	13.05 E
Norco	228	33.56 N	117.33 W
Norcott, Mount ∧	162	32.07 S	121.59 E
Norcross	192	33.56 N	84.12 W
Nord □[4]	146	9.00 N	13.30 E
Nord □[5]	50	50.20 N	3.40 E
Nord, Canal du ≅	50	50.16 N	3.05 E
Nord, Cap → Nordkapp ›	24	71.11 N	25.48 E
Nord, Gare ◆[5]	261	48.53 N	2.21 E
Nord, Grand lac du ⊜	186	50.54 N	67.06 W
Nord, Petit lac du ⊜	186	50.50 N	67.10 W
Nord, Rivière du ≃	206	45.31 N	74.20 W
Nordamerika → North America ⊥[1]	16	45.00 N	100.00 W
Nordanholen	40	60.30 N	14.57 E
Nordausques	50	50.49 N	2.05 E
Nordaustlandet I	12	79.48 N	22.24 E
Nordbögge	263	51.37 N	7.44 E
Nordborg	41	55.03 N	9.45 E
Nordby	41	55.58 N	10.34 E
Nord Dakota → North Dakota □[3]	198	47.30 N	100.15 W
Norddeich	52	53.37 N	7.09 E
Nordegg	182	52.28 N	116.04 W
Nordegg ≃	182	52.53 N	115.18 W
Norden, Dtsch.	52	53.36 N	7.12 E
Norden, Eng., U.K.	262	53.38 N	2.13 W
Norden, Ca., U.S.	226	39.20 N	120.22 W
Nordendorf	56	48.36 N	10.50 E
Nordenham	52	53.29 N	8.28 E
Nordenšel'da, archipelag II	74	76.45 N	96.00 E
Nordenskiold ≃	180	62.05 N	136.18 W
Norderney	52	53.42 N	7.08 E
Norderney I	52	53.42 N	7.10 E
Norderstapel	41	54.21 N	9.14 E
Norderstedt	52	53.43 N	10.00 E
Nordfjord c[2]	26	61.54 N	5.12 E
Nordfjordeid	26	61.54 N	6.00 E
Nordfold	24	67.46 N	15.12 E
Nordfriesische Inseln → North Frisian Islands II	24	54.50 N	8.12 E
Nordfriesland ◆[1]	41	54.40 N	9.10 E
Nordgermersleben	54	52.13 N	11.20 E
Nordhalben	54	50.22 N	11.30 E
Nordhausen	54	51.30 N	10.47 E
Nordheim	222	28.55 N	97.36 W
Nordheim von der Rhön	56	50.28 N	10.11 E
Nordhelle ∧[2]	263	51.09 N	7.46 E
Nordhorn	52	52.27 N	7.05 E
Nordic Park	278	41.57 N	88.02 W
Nordingrå	26	62.56 N	18.16 E
Nordirland → Northern Ireland □[8]	48	54.40 N	6.45 W
Nordiyya	132	32.19 N	34.54 E
Nordkanal ≅	263	51.10 N	6.42 E
Nordkapp ›	24	71.11 N	25.48 E
Nordkinnhalvøya ›[1]	24	70.55 N	27.45 E
Nordkirchen	52	51.44 N	7.31 E
Nordkjosbotn	24	69.13 N	19.30 E
Nord-Korea → Korea, North □[1]	98	40.00 N	127.00 E
Nordland	224	48.03 N	122.41 W
Nordland □[6]	24	67.00 N	14.40 E
Nördliche Dwina → Severnaja Dvina ≃	24	64.32 N	40.30 E
Nördliches Eismeer → Arctic Ocean ⊤[1]	16	85.00 N	170.00 E
Nördlingen	56	48.51 N	10.30 E
Nordmaling	26	63.34 N	19.30 E
Nordmark	40	59.50 N	14.06 E
Nordmarka ◆[1]	26	60.00 N	10.25 E
Nordostrundingen ›	16	81.36 N	12.09 W
Nord-Ostsee-Kanal ≅	30	53.53 N	9.08 E
Nord-Ouest □[4]	152	6.30 N	10.30 E
Nordpfälzer Bergland ⟑	56	49.40 N	7.40 E
Nordradde ≃	52	52.43 N	7.17 E
Nordreisa	24	69.46 N	21.03 E
Nordre Strømfjord c[2]	176	67.50 N	52.00 W
Nordrhein-Westfalen □[3]	30	51.30 N	7.30 E
Nordsee → North Sea ⊤[2]	22	55.20 N	3.00 E
Nordstemmen	52	52.09 N	9.46 E
Nordstrand I	41	54.30 N	8.53 E
Nordstrandischmoor I	41	54.33 N	8.48 E
Nord-Trøndelag □[6]	24	64.25 N	12.00 E
Nordvik	74	74.02 N	111.32 E
Nordwalde	52	52.05 N	7.28 E
Nordwest-Kap → North West Cape ›	162	21.45 S	114.10 E
Nore	26	60.10 N	9.01 E
Nore ≃	48	52.25 N	6.58 W
Noremberg → Nürnberg	60	49.27 N	11.04 E
Norf	263	51.09 N	6.43 E
Norf ≃	263	51.11 N	6.44 E
Norfolk, Ct., U.S.	207	41.59 N	73.12 W
Norfolk, Ma., U.S.	283	42.07 N	71.19 W
Norfolk, Ne., U.S.	198	42.02 N	97.25 W
Norfolk, Va., U.S.	208	36.50 N	76.17 W
Norfolk □[6], On., Can.	214	42.48 N	80.25 W
Norfolk □[6], Eng., U.K.	42	52.35 N	1.00 E
Norfolk □[6], Ma., U.S.	207	42.10 N	71.15 W
Norfolk Broads ◆[1]	42	52.40 N	1.30 E
Norfolk-Insel → Norfolk Island □[2]	174c	29.02 S	167.57 E
Norfolk International Airport ⊠	208	36.54 N	76.12 W
Norfolk Island □[2], Oc.	14	29.02 S	167.57 E
Norfolk Island □[2], Oc.	174c	29.02 S	167.57 E
Norfolk Island Aerodome ⊠	174c	29.03 S	167.56 E
Norfolk Naval Shipyard ■	208	36.49 N	76.18 W
Norfolk Naval Station ■	208	36.57 N	76.18 W
Norfolk Ridge ✣[3]	14	29.00 S	168.00 E
Norfork Lake ⊜[1]	194	36.25 N	92.10 W
Norg	52	53.04 N	6.27 E
Norge	208	37.22 N	76.46 W
Norge → Norway □[1]	24	62.00 N	10.00 E
Norham	44	55.43 N	2.10 W
Norheimsund	26	60.22 N	6.08 E
Noria de Ángeles	234	22.27 N	101.56 W
Norikura-dake ∧	94	36.06 N	137.33 E
Noril'sk	74	69.20 N	88.06 E
Noring, Gunong ∧	114	5.24 N	101.44 E
Norland, On., Can.	212	44.43 N	78.49 W
Norland, Fl., U.S.	220	25.57 N	80.12 W
Norlane	169	38.06 S	144.21 E
Norley	262	53.15 N	2.39 W
Norlina	192	36.26 N	78.11 W
Norma, It.	66	41.35 N	12.58 E
Norma, N.J., U.S.	208	39.29 N	75.05 W
Normal, Al., U.S.	194	34.47 N	86.34 W
Normal, Il., U.S.	216	40.30 N	88.59 W
Norman, Ar., U.S.	194	34.27 N	93.40 W
Norman, In., U.S.	218	38.57 N	86.16 W
Norman, Ok., U.S.	196	35.13 N	97.26 W
Norman ≃	166	17.28 S	140.49 E
Norman, Lake ⊜[1]	192	35.35 N	80.55 W
Normanby, Austl.	171a	27.28 S	153.01 E
Normanby, N.Z.	172	39.32 S	174.17 E
Normanby ≃	164	14.25 S	144.08 E
Normanby Island I	164	10.05 S	151.05 E
Norman Creek c	284b	39.18 N	76.25 W
Normandie □[9]	32	49.00 N	0.05 W
Normandie, Collines de ⟑[2]	32	48.40 N	0.30 W
Normandien	158	27.57 S	29.47 E
Normandy → Normandie □[9]	32	49.00 N	0.05 W
Normandy Heights	284b	39.17 N	76.48 W
Normandy Park	224	47.27 N	122.21 W
Normangee	222	31.02 N	96.07 W
Normanhurst	274a	33.43 S	151.06 E
Normanhurst, Mount ∧	162	25.04 S	122.32 E
Norman Island I	240m	18.20 N	64.37 W
Normannische Inseln → Channel Islands II	28	49.20 N	2.20 W
Norman Park	192	31.16 N	83.41 W
Normans Kill ≃	210	42.36 N	73.44 W
Normanton, Austl.	166	17.40 S	141.05 E
Normanton, Eng., U.K.	44	53.41 N	1.27 W
Normanville	168b	35.27 S	138.19 E
Norman Wells	180	65.17 N	126.51 W
Nor Marsh ⁝	260	51.24 N	0.38 E
Nornalup	162	35.00 S	116.49 E
Norogachi	232	27.15 N	107.07 W
Noroton ≃	276	41.03 N	73.31 W
Noroton Point ›	276	41.03 N	73.26 W
Norovlin	88	48.40 N	112.00 E
Noroy-le-Bourg	58	47.37 N	6.18 E
Norphlet	194	33.18 N	92.39 W
Norquay	184	51.53 N	102.05 W
Ñorquinco	254	41.51 S	70.54 W
Norra Barken ⊜	40	60.07 N	15.31 E
Norra Björkfjärden c	40	59.27 N	17.28 E
Norrahammar	26	57.42 N	14.06 E
Norra Hörken ⊜	40	60.04 N	14.53 E
Norra Kvarken (Merenkurkku) ⊌	26	63.36 N	20.43 E
Norra Kvills Nationalpark ♠	26	57.44 N	15.37 E
Norrälgen ⊜	40	59.50 N	14.34 E
Norra Rörum	41	56.01 N	13.30 E
Norra Storfjället ∧	24	65.52 N	15.18 E
Norra Yngern ⊜	40	59.09 N	17.22 E
Norrboda	40	60.28 N	18.25 E
Norrbotten □[9]	26	66.45 N	23.00 E
Norrbottens Län □[6]	24	66.00 N	20.00 E
Nørre Åby	41	55.27 N	9.54 E
Nørre Alslev	41	54.54 N	11.54 E
Nørre Broby	41	55.15 N	10.14 E
Nørre Nærå	41	55.34 N	10.17 E
Norrent-Fontes	50	50.35 N	2.24 E
Nørre Snede	41	55.58 N	9.25 E
Nørresundby	26	57.04 N	9.55 E
Nørre Vejrup	41	55.31 N	8.47 E
Norrfjärden	26	65.25 N	21.27 E
Norridge	216	41.57 N	87.49 W
Norridgewock	188	44.42 N	69.47 W
Norris	192	36.11 N	84.04 W
Norris, Lake ⊜	220	28.57 N	81.32 W
Norris Arm	186	49.05 N	55.15 W
Norris Bridge ◆[5]	208	37.37 N	76.26 W
Norris City	194	37.58 N	88.19 W
Norris Dam State Park ♠	192	36.14 N	84.07 W
Norrish Creek ≃	224	49.10 N	122.08 W
Norris Lake ⊜[1]	192	36.20 N	83.55 W
Norris Point	186	49.31 N	57.53 W
Norristown	208	40.07 N	75.20 W
Norrköping	40	58.36 N	16.11 E
Norroway Brook ≃	283	42.11 N	71.03 W
Norrskedika	40	60.17 N	18.17 E
Norrsundet	26	60.56 N	17.08 E
Norrtälje	40	59.46 N	18.42 E
Norrtäljeviken c	40	59.47 N	18.53 E
Norseman	162	32.12 S	121.46 E
Norsewood	172	40.04 S	176.13 E
Norsjå ⊜	26	59.18 N	9.20 E
Norsjö	26	64.55 N	19.29 E
Norsk	89	52.20 N	129.55 E
Norsminde	41	56.01 N	10.16 E
Norsup	175f	16.05 S	167.23 E
Norte, Cabo ›, Bra.	250	1.40 N	49.55 W
Norte, Cabo ›, Chile	174z	27.03 S	109.24 W
Norte, Cabo → Nordkapp ›, Nor.	24	71.11 N	25.48 E
Norte, Canal ⊌	288	34.37 S	58.15 W
Norte, Canal do ⊌	250	0.30 N	50.30 W
Norte, Cayo I	240m	18.20 N	65.15 W
Norte, Estación del ◆[5], Esp.	266a	40.25 N	3.43 W
Norte, Estación del ◆[5], Esp.	266d	41.24 N	2.02 E
Norte, Mar del → North Sea ⊤[2]	22	55.20 N	3.00 E
Norte, Punta ›	254	42.04 S	63.45 W
Norte, Serra do ⟑[1]	248	11.20 S	59.00 W
Norte de Santander □[3]	238	9.15 N	73.00 W
Norte de Santander □[5]	246	8.00 N	73.00 W
Nortelândia	248	14.25 S	56.48 W
Nörten-Hardenberg	52	51.38 N	9.56 E
North, S.C., U.S.	192	33.36 N	81.06 W
North, Va., U.S.	208	37.26 N	76.24 W
North ≃, Nf., Can.	176	57.30 N	62.05 W
North ≃, On., Can.	212	44.44 N	79.39 W
North ≃, Al., U.S.	194	33.15 N	87.30 W
North ≃, Ia., U.S.	194	41.31 N	93.27 W
North ≃, Ma., U.S.	283	42.10 N	70.43 W
North ≃, Mo., U.S.	219	39.52 N	91.27 W
North ≃, Wa., U.S.	224	46.45 N	123.53 W
North, Cape ›	186	47.02 N	60.25 W
North Abington	207	42.07 N	70.57 W
North Adams, Ma., U.S.	207	42.42 N	73.06 W
North Adams, Mi., U.S.	216	41.58 N	84.32 W
North Albany	202	44.39 N	123.06 W
Northallerton	44	54.20 N	1.26 W
Northam, Austl.	168a	31.39 S	116.40 E
Northam, S. Afr.	156	25.03 S	27.11 E
Northam, Eng., U.K.	42	51.02 N	4.12 W
North America ⊥[1]	4	45.00 N	100.00 W
North America ⊥[1]	16	45.00 N	100.00 W
North American Basin ✣[1]	8	30.00 N	60.00 W
North Amherst	207	42.24 N	72.31 W
North Amityville	276	40.41 N	73.25 W
Northampton, Austl.	162	28.21 S	114.37 E
Northampton, Eng., U.K.	42	52.14 N	0.54 W
Northampton, Md., U.S.	284c	38.52 N	76.49 W
Northampton, Ma., U.S.	207	42.19 N	72.38 W
Northampton, N.Y., U.S.	207	40.54 N	72.40 W
Northampton, Pa., U.S.	208	40.41 N	75.29 W
Northampton □[6], N.C., U.S.	208	36.28 N	77.21 W
Northampton □[6], Pa., U.S.	210	40.45 N	75.18 W
Northampton □[6], Va., U.S.	208	37.20 N	75.50 W
Northamptonshire □[6]	42	52.20 N	0.50 W
North Andaman I	110	13.15 N	92.55 E
North Andover	207	42.41 N	71.08 W
North Andrews Gardens	220	26.12 N	80.07 W
North Anna ≃	192	37.48 N	77.25 W
North Anson	188	44.51 N	69.54 W
North Apollo	214	40.35 N	79.33 W
North Arlington	276	40.47 N	74.08 W
North Arm ≃[1]	224	49.12 N	123.10 W
North Asheboro	192	35.44 N	79.49 W
North Atlanta	192	33.51 N	84.20 W
North Attleboro	207	41.59 N	71.20 W
North Attleboro National Fish Hatchery ♠	283	42.00 N	71.17 W
North Auburn	274a	33.50 S	151.02 E
North Augusta	192	33.30 N	81.57 W
North Aulatsivik Island I	176	59.50 N	64.00 W
North Aurora	216	41.48 N	88.19 W
North Australian Basin ✣[1]	14	14.30 S	116.30 E
Northaw	260	51.42 N	0.09 W
North Babylon	276	40.42 N	73.19 W
North Balabac Strait ⊌	116	8.10 N	117.04 E
North Baltimore	216	41.10 N	83.40 W
North Balwyn	274b	37.48 S	145.05 E
North Bannister	168a	32.35 S	116.26 E
North Bārākpur	126	22.46 N	88.22 E
North Bass Island I	214	41.43 N	82.49 W
North Battleford	184	52.47 N	108.17 W
North Bay, On., Can.	190	46.19 N	79.28 W
North Bay, N.Y., U.S.	210	43.14 N	75.45 W
North Bay, Wi., U.S.	216	42.46 N	87.47 W
North Bay c, On., Can.	212	44.53 N	79.48 W
North Bay c, Wa., U.S.	224	46.59 N	124.04 W
North Bay Shore	276	40.45 N	73.16 W
North Bay Village	220	25.51 N	80.08 W
North Beach	168a	31.52 S	115.45 E
North Beach ◆[8]	282	37.48 N	122.25 W
North Beach Peninsula ›[1]	224	46.30 N	124.02 W
North Belle Vernon	214	40.08 N	79.52 W
North Bellmore	276	40.41 N	73.32 W
North Bend, B.C., Can.	182	49.53 N	121.27 W
North Bend, Ne., U.S.	198	41.27 N	96.46 W
North Bend, Oh., U.S.	218	39.09 N	84.44 W
North Bend, Or., U.S.	202	43.24 N	124.13 W
North Bend, Pa., U.S.	214	41.21 N	77.42 W
North Bend, Wa., U.S.	224	47.29 N	121.47 W
North Benfleet	260	51.35 N	0.32 E
North Bengal Plains ≚	124	26.20 N	88.30 E
North Bennington	210	42.55 N	73.14 W
North Bergen	276	40.47 N	74.02 W
North Berwick, Scot., U.K.	46	56.04 N	2.44 W
North Berwick, Me., U.S.	188	43.18 N	70.44 W
North Bethlehem	210	42.40 N	73.50 W
North Bihar Plains ≚	124	26.20 N	86.00 E
North Billerica	207	42.35 N	71.17 W
North Bloomfield	214	41.27 N	80.52 W
North Boggy Creek ≃	196	34.23 N	96.04 W
North Bonneville	224	45.38 N	121.58 W
Northborough	207	42.19 N	71.38 W
North Bosque ≃	196	31.40 N	97.24 W
North Boston	210	42.41 N	78.47 W
North Bourke	166	30.03 S	145.57 E
North Box Hill	274b	37.48 S	145.07 E
North Braddock	279b	40.23 N	79.50 W
North Branch, Mi., U.S.	190	43.13 N	83.11 W
North Branch, Mn., U.S.	190	45.30 N	92.58 W
North Branch, N.J., U.S.	210	40.36 N	74.41 W
North Branch Canal ≅	224	47.12 N	120.40 W
North Branford	207	41.19 N	72.46 W
North Breakers ✣[2]	174g	28.14 N	177.25 W
Northbridge, Austl.	274a	33.49 S	151.13 E
Northbridge, Ma., U.S.	207	42.09 N	71.39 W
North Bristol	214	41.24 N	80.52 W
Northbrook, On., Can.	212	44.44 N	77.10 W
Northbrook, Il., U.S.	216	42.07 N	87.49 W
Northbrook, Pa., U.S.	285	39.55 N	75.41 W
North Brookfield, Ma., U.S.	207	42.16 N	72.05 W
North Brookfield, N.Y., U.S.	210	42.51 N	75.24 W
North Brunswick	208	40.28 N	74.28 W
North Buganda □[5]	154	1.00 N	32.15 E
North Caicos I	238	21.56 N	71.59 W
North Caldwell	276	40.51 N	74.16 W
North Canadian ≃	196	35.17 N	95.31 W
North Canton, Ct., U.S.	207	41.53 N	72.53 W
North Canton, Ga., U.S.	192	34.14 N	84.29 W
North Canton, Oh., U.S.	214	40.52 N	81.24 W
North Cape	216	42.47 N	88.05 W
North Cape ›, P.E., Can.	186	47.05 N	64.00 W
North Cape ›, N.Z.	172	34.25 S	173.02 E
North Cape → Nordkapp ›, Nor.	24	71.11 N	25.48 E
North Cape ›, Pap. N. Gui.	164	2.32 S	150.49 E
North Cape ›, Mi., U.S.	216	41.44 N	83.25 W
North Cape May	208	38.58 N	74.57 W
North Captiva Island I	220	26.35 N	82.13 W
North Caribou Lake ⊜	176	52.50 N	90.40 W

≃	River	Fluß	Río	Rivière	Rio
≅	Canal	Kanal	Canal	Canal	Canal
∟	Waterfall, Rapids	Wasserfall, Stromschnellen	Cascada, Rápidos	Chute d'eau, Rapides	Cascata, Rápidos
⊌	Strait	Meeresstraße	Estrecho	Détroit	Estreito
c	Bay, Gulf	Bucht, Golf	Bahía, Golfo	Baie, Golfe	Baía, Golfo
⊜	Lake, Lakes	See, Seen	Lago, Lagos	Lac, Lacs	Lago, Lagos
⁝	Swamp	Sumpf	Pantano	Marais	Pântano
⊓	Ice Features, Glacier	Eis- und Gletscherformen	Accidentes Glaciales	Formes glaciaires	Acidentes glaciares
⊤	Other Hydrographic Features	Andere Hydrographische Objekte	Otros Elementos Hidrográficos	Autres données hydrographiques	Outros acidentes hidrográficos

✣	Submarine Features	Untermeerische Objekte	Accidentes Submarinos	Formes de relief sous-marin	Acidentes submarinos
□	Political Unit	Politische Einheit	Unidad Politica	Entité politique	Unidade política
ʊ	Cultural Institution	Kulturelle Institution	Institución Cultural	Institution culturelle	Instituição cultural
⊥	Historical Site	Historische Stätte	Sitio Histórico	Site historique	Sitio histórico
♠	Recreational Site	Erholungs- und Ferienort	Sitio de Recreo	Centre de loisirs	Area de Lazer
⊠	Airport	Flughafen	Aeropuerto	Aéroport	Aeroporto
■	Military Installation	Militäranlage	Instalación Militar	Installation militaire	Instalação militar
◆	Miscellaneous	Verschiedenes	Misceláneo	Divers	Diversos

ENGLISH

DEUTSCH

Name	Page	Lat.°′	Long.°′
North Carolina □[3], U.S.	178	35.30 N	80.00 W
North Carolina □[3], U.S.	192	35.30 N	80.00 W
North Carver	207	41.55 N	70.48 W
North Cascades National Park ♠	224	48.30 N	121.00 W
North Castor ≃	212	45.16 N	75.24 W
North Catasauqua	208	40.40 N	75.29 W
North Chagrin Reservation ♠	279a	41.34 N	81.26 W
North Channel ʮ, On., Can.	190	46.02 N	82.50 W
North Channel ʮ, On., Can.	212	44.10 N	76.45 W
North Channel ʮ, U.K.	44	55.10 N	5.40 W
North Channel ʮ, N.Y., U.S.	276	40.36 N	73.53 W
North Channel ≃[1]	281	42.38 N	82.40 W
North Charleroi	214	40.09 N	79.54 W
North Charleston	192	32.51 N	79.58 W
North Chatham	210	42.29 N	73.38 W
North Chelmsford	207	42.38 N	71.23 W
North Chicago	216	42.19 N	87.50 W
North Chili	210	43.06 N	77.45 W
Northchurch	260	51.46 N	0.36 W
North City	224	47.45 N	122.18 W
North Cleveland	222	30.21 N	95.06 W
Northcliff ◆[8]	273d	26.09 S	27.58 E
Northcliffe	162	34.36 S	116.07 E
North Clymer	214	42.04 N	79.34 W
North Cohasset	283	42.15 N	70.50 W
North Cohocton	210	42.34 N	77.28 W
North College Hill	218	39.13 N	84.33 W
North Collins	210	42.35 N	78.56 W
North Commerce Lake ⊜	281	42.35 N	83.30 W
North Concho ≃	196	31.27 N	100.25 W
North Conway	188	44.03 N	71.07 W
North Cotabato □[4]	116	7.15 N	124.50 E
Northcote	274b	37.46 S	145.00 E
North Cray ◆[8]	260	51.26 N	0.08 E
North Creek	188	43.41 N	73.59 W
North Creek ≃	278	41.33 N	87.37 W
Northcrest	222	31.38 N	97.06 W
North Crossett	194	33.09 N	91.56 W
North Crosswicks	285	40.10 N	74.39 W
North Croton Creek ≃	196	33.24 N	100.00 W
North Dakota □[3], U.S.	178	47.30 N	100.15 W
North Dakota □[3], U.S.	198	47.30 N	100.15 W
North Dandalup	168a	32.31 S	115.58 E
North Dandalup ≃	168a	32.36 S	115.53 E
North Dartmouth	207	41.38 N	70.58 W
North Dighton	207	41.51 N	71.07 W
North Dorset Downs ⋏[1]	42	50.47 N	2.30 W
North Downs ⋏[1]	42	51.20 N	0.10 E
North Dum Dum	126	22.38 N	88.23 E
North Eagle Butte	198	45.02 N	101.15 W
North East, Md., U.S.	208	39.36 N	75.56 W
North East, Pa., U.S.	214	42.12 N	79.50 W
North-East □[5]	156	21.00 S	27.30 E
Northeast Cape	180	63.18 N	168.42 W
Northeast Cape >	180	63.17 N	168.45 W
Northeast Cape Fear ≃	192	34.11 N	77.57 W
Northeast Creek ≃	284b	39.18 N	76.29 W
North Eastern □[4]	154	1.00 N	40.15 E
Northeastern University ʋ[2]	283	42.20 N	71.05 W
North Eastham	207	41.51 N	69.59 W
Northeast Henrietta	210	43.04 N	77.36 W
Northeast Islands II	175c	7.36 N	151.57 E
North Easton	207	42.04 N	71.06 W
Northeast Pass ʮ	175c	7.30 N	151.59 E
North East Point >, Ba.	238	21.20 N	73.01 W
North East Point >, Ba.	238	22.43 N	73.50 W
North East Point >, Kiribati	174o	1.57 N	157.16 W
Northeast Point >, St. Vin.	241h	13.03 N	61.13 W
Northeast Providence Channel ʮ	238	25.40 N	77.09 W
North Edwards	228	35.01 N	117.44 W
North Egremont	207	42.11 N	73.26 W
Northeim	52	51.42 N	10.00 E
North Elkhorn Creek ≃	218	38.13 N	84.48 W
North Elm Creek ≃	222	30.53 N	97.00 W
North English	190	41.30 N	92.04 W
Northern □[4], Ghana	150	9.30 N	1.00 W
Northern □[4], Malaŵi	154	11.00 S	34.00 E
Northern □[4], S.L.	150	9.15 N	11.45 W
Northern □[4], Zam.	154	11.00 S	31.00 E
Northern □[5], Pap. N. Gui.	164	9.00 S	148.30 E
Northern □[5], Ug.	154	2.50 N	32.45 E
Northern Arm	186	49.10 N	55.23 W
Northern Cape □[4]	156	29.00 S	21.00 E
Northern Cheyenne Indian Reservation ◆[4]	202	45.31 N	106.45 W
Northern Circārs ⋏[2]	122	18.00 N	83.15 E
Northern Cook Islands II	14	10.00 S	161.00 W
Northern Division □[5]	175g	16.30 S	179.30 E
Northern Dvina → Severnaja Dvina ≃	24	64.32 N	40.30 E
Northern Indian Lake ⊜	176	57.20 N	97.20 W
Northern Ireland □[8]	48	54.40 N	6.45 W
Northern Light Lake ⊜	190	48.15 N	90.38 W
Northern Mariana Islands □[2]	14	16.00 N	149.00 E
Northern Samar □[4]	116	12.30 N	124.30 E
Northern Territory □[8]	160	20.00 S	134.00 E
Northern Transvaal □[4]	156	23.30 S	29.30 E
North Esk ≃, Scot., U.K.	46	56.44 N	2.28 W
North Esk ≃, Scot., U.K.	46	55.54 N	3.04 W
North Essendon	274b	37.45 S	144.54 E
North Evans	210	42.42 N	78.56 W
Northey Island I	260	51.44 N	0.43 E
North Fabius ≃	194	39.54 N	91.30 W
North Fairfield	214	41.06 N	82.36 W
North Fair Oaks	282	37.28 N	122.12 W
North Falmouth	207	41.38 N	70.37 W
North Ferriby	44	53.43 N	0.30 W
Northfield, B.C., Can.	224	49.11 N	123.59 W
Northfield, Ct., U.S.	207	41.41 N	73.06 W
Northfield, Il., U.S.	278	42.05 N	87.46 W
Northfield, Ma., U.S.	207	42.41 N	72.27 W
Northfield, Mn., U.S.	190	44.27 N	93.09 W
Northfield, N.J., U.S.	208	39.22 N	74.33 W
Northfield, Oh., U.S.	214	41.20 N	81.32 W
Northfield, Vt., U.S.	188	44.09 N	72.39 W
Northfield Airport ⊠	279a	41.17 N	81.31 W
Northfield Center	279a	41.19 N	81.32 W
Northfield Park Race Track ♠	279a	41.21 N	81.31 W
Northfield Village	279a	41.21 N	81.31 W
Northfield Woods	278	42.05 N	87.52 W
North Fiji Basin ✣[1]	14	16.00 S	174.00 E
North Fillmore	228	34.24 N	118.56 W
North Fitzroy	274b	37.47 S	144.59 E
Northfleet	42	51.27 N	0.21 E
North Flinders Range ⋏	166	31.00 S	139.00 E
North Fond du Lac	190	43.48 N	88.29 W
Northford	207	41.23 N	72.47 W
North Foreland >	42	51.23 N	1.27 E
North Fork	226	37.13 N	119.30 W
North Fork ≃	194	36.13 N	92.17 W
North Fork Lake ⊜[1]	226	38.56 N	121.00 W
North Fork Reservoir ⊜[1]	224	45.13 N	122.15 W
North Fork Village	218	39.21 N	83.02 W
North Fort Myers	220	26.40 N	81.52 W
North Freedom	190	43.27 N	89.52 W
North Frisian Islands II	24	54.50 N	8.12 E
Northgate	216	43.01 N	85.36 W
Northgate ◆[9]	282	38.00 N	122.33 W
North Georgetown	214	40.51 N	80.59 W
North Glanford	212	43.11 N	79.54 W
North Glen Ellyn	278	41.54 N	88.04 W
Northglenn	200	39.53 N	104.59 W
North Gower	212	45.08 N	75.43 W
North Grafton	207	42.14 N	71.42 W
North Granby	207	41.59 N	72.49 W
North Grand Island Bridge ◆[5]	284a	43.04 N	78.59 W
North Great River	276	40.44 N	73.10 W
North Greece	212	43.15 N	77.44 W
North Grosvenordale	207	41.59 N	71.53 W
North Grove	216	40.37 N	85.58 W
North Gulfport	194	30.24 N	89.06 W
North Hadley	207	42.23 N	72.36 W
North Haledon	276	40.57 N	74.11 W
North Hampton	218	39.59 N	83.56 W
North Hanover	283	42.08 N	70.52 W
North Harbor ⊂	269f	14.36 N	120.57 E
North Harbour ⊂	274a	33.49 S	151.17 E
North Haven	207	41.23 N	72.51 W
North Head >, Austl.	274a	33.49 S	151.18 E
North Head >, N.Z.	172	36.25 S	174.03 E
North Henderson	192	36.21 N	78.22 W
North Henik Lake ⊜	176	61.45 N	97.40 W
North Hero	188	44.49 N	73.17 W
North Highlands	226	38.41 N	121.22 W
North Hill	42	50.34 N	4.25 W
North Hills, De., U.S.	285	39.46 N	75.30 W
North Hills, Il., U.S.	278	42.18 N	88.01 W
North Hills, N.Y., U.S.	276	40.47 N	73.41 W
North Hinksey	42	51.45 N	1.16 W
North Hogan Creek ≃	218	39.03 N	84.54 W
North Hollywood ◆[8]	280	34.10 N	118.23 W
North Holmwood	260	51.13 N	0.20 W
North Honcut Creek ≃	226	39.19 N	121.36 W
North Hoosick	210	42.56 N	73.21 W
North Hornell	210	42.21 N	77.40 W
North Horr	154	3.19 N	37.04 E
North Houston	222	29.54 N	95.31 W
Northiam	42	50.59 N	0.36 E
North Industry	214	40.44 N	81.22 W
North Irwin	279b	40.20 N	79.43 W
North Island I, India	122	10.08 N	72.20 E
North Island I, Kenya	154	4.04 N	36.03 E
North Island I, N.Z.	172	39.00 S	176.00 E
North Island Naval Air Station ■	228	32.42 N	117.12 W
North Islet I	116	8.56 N	120.02 E
North Jackson	214	41.06 N	80.52 W
North Java	210	42.41 N	78.20 W
North Judson	216	41.12 N	86.46 W
North Kenai	180	60.44 N	151.19 W
North Kingstown	207	41.38 N	71.25 W
North Kingsville	214	41.54 N	80.42 W
North Knife Lake ⊜	176	58.05 N	97.05 W
North Knob ∧	210	41.43 N	75.33 W
North Korea → Korea, North □[1]	98	40.00 N	127.00 E
North La Junta	198	37.59 N	103.31 W
North Lake	216	43.09 N	88.22 W
North Lake ⊜, N.Y., U.S.	276	41.09 N	73.41 W
North Lake ⊜, Tx., U.S.	222	32.57 N	96.58 W
North Lakhimpur	120	27.14 N	94.07 E
Northland ◆[9]	281	42.27 N	83.13 W
North Landing ≃	208	36.31 N	76.01 W
North Laramie ≃	198	42.08 N	104.56 W
North Las Vegas	204	36.11 N	115.07 W
North La Veta Pass)(	200	37.37 N	105.11 W
North Lawrence	214	40.51 N	81.38 W
Northleach	42	51.51 N	1.50 W
North Lewisburg	216	40.13 N	83.33 W
North Liberty	216	41.32 N	86.25 W
North Lima	214	40.56 N	80.39 W
North Lindenhurst	276	40.42 N	73.22 W
North Line Island I	276	40.38 N	73.29 W
Northline Terrace	222	29.55 N	95.25 W
North Little Rock	194	34.46 N	92.16 W
North Llano ≃	196	30.30 N	99.46 W
North Logan	202	41.46 N	111.48 W
North Loma Linda	228	34.02 N	117.05 W
North Loon Mountain ∧	202	45.07 N	115.52 W
North Loup	198	41.29 N	98.46 W
North Loup ≃	198	41.17 N	98.23 W
North Luangwa National Park ♠	154	11.50 S	32.15 E
North Luconia Shoals ✣[2]	108	5.40 N	112.35 E
North Macmillan ≃	180	63.03 N	133.18 W
North Madison	214	41.48 N	81.03 W
North Magnetic Pole ◆	16	77.19 N	101.49 W
North Malosmadulu Atoll I[1]	122	5.35 N	72.55 E
North Mamm Peak ∧	200	39.23 N	107.52 W
North Manchester	216	41.00 N	85.46 W
North Manitou Island I	190	45.06 N	86.01 W
North Mankato	190	44.10 N	94.02 W
North Manly	274a	33.46 S	151.16 E
North Maroota	170	33.29 S	150.56 E
North Marshfield	283	42.08 N	70.46 W
North Marysville	224	48.07 N	122.09 W
North Massapequa	276	40.42 N	73.27 W
Northmead, Austl.	274a	33.47 S	151.00 E
Northmead, S. Afr.	273d	26.10 S	28.20 E
North Merrick	276	40.41 N	73.33 W
North Miami	220	25.53 N	80.11 W
North Miami Beach	220	25.55 N	80.09 W
North Middleboro	207	41.56 N	70.58 W
North Milk ≃	202	49.08 N	112.23 W
North Mokelumne ≃	226	38.08 N	121.35 W
North Moose Lake ⊜	184	54.08 N	100.13 W
North Moreau Creek ≃	194	38.30 N	92.18 W
North Muskegon	216	43.15 N	86.16 W
North Myrtle Beach	192	33.49 N	78.40 W
North Nahanni ≃	180	62.05 N	124.30 W
North Naples	220	26.13 N	81.47 W
North Narrabeen	274a	33.42 S	151.18 E
North Nemah ≃	224	46.30 N	123.53 W
North New Hyde Park	276	40.44 N	73.41 W
North New River Canal ≊	220	26.05 N	80.12 W
North Newton	198	38.04 N	97.21 W
North Niles	216	41.52 N	86.15 W
North Norwich	210	42.37 N	75.31 W
North Oaks	222	30.22 N	97.41 W
North Ockendon ◆[8]	260	51.32 N	0.18 E
North Ogden	200	41.18 N	111.57 W
North Olmsted	214	41.24 N	81.55 W
Northolt Aerodrome ⊠	260	51.33 N	0.23 W
Northome	190	47.52 N	94.16 W
Northop	262	53.12 N	3.08 W
North Ore Creek ≃	281	42.43 N	83.47 W
North Orwell	210	41.55 N	76.19 W
North Ossetia → Severnaja Osetija □[3]	84	43.00 N	44.15 E
Northowram	262	53.44 N	1.50 W
North Oxford	207	42.09 N	71.52 W
North Palisade ∧	204	37.06 N	118.31 W
North Palm Beach	220	26.49 N	80.04 W
North Para ≃	168b	34.36 S	138.45 E
North Park ◆[8]	278	41.59 N	87.43 W
North Park ♠	279b	40.36 N	80.00 W
North Park Lake ⊜	279b	40.36 N	80.00 W
North Parramatta	274a	33.48 S	151.00 E
North Pass ʮ	175c	7.41 N	151.48 E
North Patchogue	276	40.47 N	73.00 W
North Peak ∧, Ak., U.S.	180	62.34 N	162.23 W
North Peak ∧, Ca., U.S.	282	37.33 N	122.28 W
North Pease ≃	196	34.15 N	100.07 W
North Pelham, N.H., U.S.	283	42.46 N	71.21 W
North Pelham, N.Y., U.S.	276	40.55 N	73.48 W
North Pembroke	207	42.05 N	70.47 W
North Pender Island I	224	48.49 N	123.17 W
North Perry	214	41.47 N	81.07 W
North Petherton	42	51.06 N	3.01 W
North Philadelphia ◆[8]	285	39.58 N	75.09 W
North Philadelphia Airport ⊠	285	40.05 N	75.01 W
North Pine ≃	171a	27.17 S	153.01 E
North Pine Grove	214	41.24 N	79.13 W
North Piney Creek ≃	200	42.31 N	110.05 W
North Pitcher	210	42.37 N	75.49 W
North Plainfield	210	40.37 N	74.25 W
North Plains	224	45.35 N	122.59 W
North Plains ≚	200	34.40 N	108.15 W
North Platte	198	41.07 N	100.45 W
North Platte ≃	178	41.07 N	100.42 W
North Pleasureville	218	38.22 N	85.07 W
North Plympton	283	41.59 N	70.48 W
North Point, H.K.	271d	22.17 N	114.12 E
Northpoint, Pa., U.S.	214	40.54 N	79.08 W
North Point >, Barb.	241g	13.20 N	59.36 W
North Point >, Md., U.S.	284b	39.12 N	76.27 W
North Point >, Mi., U.S.	190	45.02 N	83.16 W
North Pole	180	64.45 N	147.21 W
North Pole ◆	16	90.00 N	0.00
Northport, Al., U.S.	194	33.13 N	87.34 W
North Port, Fl., U.S.	220	27.03 N	82.15 W
Northport, Mi., U.S.	190	45.07 N	85.37 W
Northport, N.Y., U.S.	210	40.53 N	73.20 W
Northport, Wa., U.S.	202	48.54 N	117.46 W
North Portal	184	49.00 N	102.33 W
Northport Bay ⊂	276	40.55 N	73.23 W
Northport Harbor ⊂	276	40.53 N	73.22 W
North Powder	202	45.01 N	117.55 W
North Pownal	207	42.47 N	73.15 W
North Prairie	216	42.56 N	88.24 W
North Providence	207	41.50 N	71.25 W
North Puyallup	224	47.12 N	122.17 W
North Queensferry	46	56.01 N	3.25 W
North Quincy	219	39.58 N	91.24 W
North Raccoon ≃	198	41.50 N	94.08 W
North Raisin ≃	206	45.09 N	74.43 W
North Ram ≃	182	52.16 N	115.38 W
North Randall	279a	41.27 N	81.32 W
North Reading	207	42.34 N	71.04 W
North Reservoir ⊜[1]	283	42.28 N	71.07 W
North Rhine-Westphalia → Nordrhein-Westfalen □[3]	30	51.30 N	7.30 E
North Richland Hills	222	32.50 N	97.13 W
North Richmond	282	37.57 N	122.22 W
Northridge, Oh., U.S.	218	39.59 N	83.46 W
Northridge, Oh., U.S.	218	39.48 N	84.11 W
Northridge ◆[8]	280	34.14 N	118.33 W
Northridge Fashion Center ◆[9]	280	34.13 N	118.33 W
North Ridge Village	218	39.57 N	86.09 W
North Ridgeville	214	41.23 N	82.01 W
North Rim	200	36.12 N	112.03 W
North River ⊂	208	37.25 N	76.25 W
North Riverside	278	41.50 N	87.49 W
North Riverside Park Mall ◆[9]	278	41.51 N	87.49 W
North Robinson	214	40.48 N	82.51 W
North Rocks	274a	33.46 S	151.02 E
North Ronaldsay I	46	59.22 N	2.26 W
North Ronaldsay Firth ʮ	46	59.20 N	2.25 W
North Rose	210	43.11 N	76.53 W
North Royalton	214	41.18 N	81.43 W
North Rustico	186	46.27 N	63.19 W
North Ryde	274a	33.48 S	151.07 E
North Salem	214	40.09 N	81.33 W
North Salt Lake	200	40.50 N	111.54 W
North San Juan	226	39.22 N	121.06 W
North Santiam ≃	202	44.41 N	123.00 W
North Saskatchewan ≃	176	53.15 N	105.05 W
North Saugeen ≃	212	44.19 N	81.17 W
North Scituate, Ma., U.S.	207	42.13 N	70.47 W
North Scituate, R.I., U.S.	207	41.49 N	71.35 W
North Sea ⫪[2]	22	56.00 N	3.00 E
North Seaton Colliery	44	55.11 N	1.32 W
North Sentinel Island I	110	11.33 N	92.15 E
North Shafter	226	35.31 N	119.18 W
North Shields	44	55.01 N	1.27 W
Norths Highland ⋏[1]	9	66.40 S	126.00 E
North Shoal Lake ⊜	184	50.29 N	97.40 W
North Shore	216	42.16 N	88.23 W
Northshore ◆[9]	283	42.32 N	70.57 W
North Shore Channel ≊	278	42.05 N	87.41 W
North Shores	216	41.50 N	83.25 W
North Shoshone Peak ∧	204	39.09 N	117.29 W
North Siberian Lowland → Severo-Sibirskaja nizmennost' ≚	74	73.00 N	100.00 E
Northside	174h	2.47 S	171.43 W
North Singa	126	23.16 N	89.30 E
North Sioux City	198	42.31 N	96.28 W
North Skunk ≃	190	41.15 N	92.02 W
North Somercotes	44	53.28 N	0.08 E
North Sound ʮ, Antig.	240c	17.07 N	61.45 W
North Sound ʮ, Ire.	48	53.11 N	9.43 W
North Sound ʮ, Scot., U.K.	46	59.18 N	2.46 W
North Spicer Island I	176	68.30 N	78.55 W
North Spirit Lake ⊜	184	52.30 N	92.53 W
North Spot I	236	16.15 N	88.11 W
North Springfield, Pa., U.S.	214	41.59 N	80.26 W
North Springfield, Va., U.S.	284c	38.48 N	77.12 W
North Stamford Reservoir ⊜[1]	276	41.08 N	73.32 W
North Star, De., U.S.	285	39.46 N	75.43 W
North Star, Oh., U.S.	216	40.19 N	84.34 W
North Sterling Reservoir ⊜[1]	198	40.47 N	103.17 W
North Stradbroke Island I	171a	27.35 S	153.28 E
North Sudbury	283	42.24 N	71.24 W
North Sulphur ≃	196	33.23 N	95.18 W
North Sunday Creek ≃	202	46.27 N	105.54 W
North Sunderland	44	55.34 N	1.39 W
North Swansea	207	41.46 N	71.15 W
North Sydenham ≃	214	42.35 N	82.23 W
North Sydney, Austl.	274a	33.50 S	151.13 E
North Sydney, N.S., Can.	186	46.13 N	60.15 W
North Syracuse	210	43.08 N	76.07 W
North Tamborine	171a	27.56 S	153.11 E
North Taranaki Bight ⊂[3]	172	38.42 S	174.15 E
North Tarrytown	276	41.05 N	73.51 W
North Tawton	42	50.48 N	3.53 W
North Tea Lake ⊜	190	45.56 N	79.03 W
North Terre Haute	194	39.31 N	87.21 W
North Tewksbury	283	42.38 N	71.14 W
North Thames ≃	212	42.59 N	81.16 W
North Thompson ≃	182	50.41 N	120.21 W
North Thoresby	44	53.28 N	0.03 W
North Tidworth	42	51.16 N	1.40 W
North Toe ≃	192	36.00 N	82.16 W
North Tolsta	46	58.20 N	6.13 W
North Tonawanda	210	43.02 N	78.51 W
North Towanda	210	41.47 N	76.28 W
North Troy	206	44.59 N	72.24 W
North Truro	207	42.02 N	70.05 W
North Tule Draw V	196	34.30 N	101.36 W
North Tunica	194	34.42 N	90.23 W
North Turlock	226	37.31 N	120.51 W
North Turramurra	274a	33.43 S	151.09 E
North Twin Lake ⊜	186	49.16 N	55.56 W
North Tyne ≃	44	54.59 N	2.08 W
North Ubian Island I	116	6.09 N	120.27 E
North Uist I	46	57.36 N	7.18 W
Northumberland	210	40.53 N	76.47 W
Northumberland □[6], On., Can.	212	44.10 N	78.00 W
Northumberland □[6], Eng., U.K.	44	55.15 N	2.05 W
Northumberland □[6], Pa., U.S.	210	40.49 N	76.39 W
Northumberland □[6], Va., U.S.	208	37.50 N	76.25 W
Northumberland Isles II	166	21.40 S	150.00 E
Northumberland National Park ♠	44	55.15 N	2.20 W
Northumberland Strait ʮ	186	46.00 N	63.30 W
North Umpqua ≃	202	43.16 N	123.27 W
North Uxbridge	207	42.05 N	71.38 W
Northvale	276	41.00 N	73.56 W
North Valley Hills ⋏[2]	285	40.02 N	75.40 W
North Valley Stream	276	40.41 N	73.42 W
North Vancouver	224	49.19 N	123.04 W
North Vandergrift	279b	40.36 N	79.34 W
North Vernon	218	39.00 N	85.37 W
North Versailles	279b	40.22 N	79.48 W
North Vietnam → Vietnam □[1]	108	16.00 N	108.00 E
Northville, Mi., U.S.	216	42.25 N	83.29 W
Northville, N.Y., U.S.	210	43.13 N	74.10 W
Northville Downs ♠	281	42.26 N	83.29 W
Northvue	214	40.54 N	79.56 W
North Wabasca Lake ⊜	182	56.00 N	113.55 W
North Wales	208	40.12 N	75.16 W
Northwall	46	59.16 N	2.17 W
North Walsham	42	52.50 N	1.24 E
North Wantagh	276	40.41 N	73.30 W
North Warren	214	41.52 N	79.09 W
North Washington, Pa., U.S.	214	41.03 N	79.49 W
North Washington, Pa., U.S.	279b	40.32 N	79.36 W
North Watuppa Pond ⊜	207	41.42 N	71.06 W
Northway	180	62.58 N	141.56 W
North Weald Bassett	42	51.43 N	0.10 E
North Webster	216	41.19 N	85.41 W
North Weissport	210	40.50 N	75.41 W
North West □[4]	156	26.30 S	25.00 E
Northwest ≃	208	36.31 N	76.05 W
North West Cape >, Austl.	162	21.45 S	114.10 E
Northwest Cape >, Ak., U.S.	180	63.46 N	171.45 W
Northwest Cape >, Fl., U.S.	220	25.13 N	81.11 W
North Westchester	207	41.34 N	72.24 W
North Western	210	43.20 N	75.22 W
North-Western □[4]	154	13.00 S	25.00 E
Northwestern University ʋ[2], Il., U.S.	278	42.04 N	87.40 W
Northwestern University (Chicago Campus) ʋ[2], Il., U.S.	278	41.54 N	87.37 W
Northwest Frontier □[4]	120	34.30 N	72.00 E
Northwest Gander ≃	186	48.50 N	55.00 W
Northwest Harbor ⊂	284b	39.16 N	76.35 W
Northwest Head >	116	10.08 N	118.45 E
Northwest Miramichi ≃	186	46.58 N	65.35 W
Northwest Pacific Basin ✣[1]	6	40.00 N	155.00 E
North West Point >	174o	2.02 N	157.29 W
Northwest Providence Channel ʮ	238	26.10 N	78.20 W
North West River	176	53.32 N	60.08 W
Northwest Territories □[4]	176	70.00 N	100.00 W
North Weymouth	283	42.15 N	70.57 W
Northwich	44	53.16 N	2.32 W
North Wichita ≃	196	33.43 N	99.29 W
North Wilbraham	207	42.09 N	72.25 W
North Wildwood	208	39.00 N	74.47 W
North Wilkesboro	192	36.09 N	81.08 W
North Willow Creek ≃	202	46.51 N	107.54 W
North Wilmington	283	42.34 N	71.09 W
North Windham, Ct., U.S.	207	41.44 N	72.09 W
North Windham, Me., U.S.	188	43.50 N	70.26 W
Northwold	42	52.33 N	0.35 E
Northwood, Eng., U.K.	42	50.44 N	1.19 W
Northwood, Ia., U.S.	190	43.26 N	93.13 W
Northwood, Mi., U.S.	216	42.19 N	85.38 W
Northwood, N.D., U.S.	198	47.44 N	97.33 W
Northwood, Oh., U.S.	214	41.36 N	83.28 W
Northwood ◆[8]	260	51.37 N	0.25 W
North Woodslee	281	42.13 N	82.43 W
Northwood Village	284c	39.02 N	77.01 W
North Yamhill ≃	224	45.13 N	123.08 W
North Yelta	168b	34.03 S	137.37 E
North York	212	43.46 N	79.25 W
North York Moors ⋏[2]	44	54.24 N	0.53 W
North York Moors National Park ♠	44	54.23 N	0.50 W
North Yorkshire □[6]	44	54.15 N	1.30 W
North Yuba ≃	226	39.22 N	121.08 W
North Zulch	222	30.55 N	96.07 W
Norton, N.B., Can.	186	45.38 N	65.42 W
Norton, Eng., U.K.	44	54.09 N	0.47 W
Norton, Eng., U.K.	262	53.20 N	2.40 W
Norton, Ks., U.S.	198	39.50 N	99.53 W
Norton, Ma., U.S.	207	41.58 N	71.11 W
Norton, Oh., U.S.	214	41.01 N	81.39 W
Norton, Vt., U.S.	206	45.00 N	71.47 W
Norton, Va., U.S.	192	36.56 N	82.37 W
Norton, Zimb.	154	17.53 S	30.42 E
Norton Air Force Base ■	228	34.06 N	117.14 W
Norton Basin ⊂	276	40.36 N	73.47 W
Norton Bay ⊂	180	64.45 N	161.15 W
Norton Creek ≃	281	42.34 N	83.34 W
Norton Fitzwarren	42	51.02 N	3.09 W
Norton Grove	207	42.00 N	71.12 W
Norton Heath	260	51.43 N	0.19 E
Norton Hill	210	42.25 N	74.04 W
Norton Pond ⊜	206	44.56 N	71.51 W
Norton Reservoir ⊜[1]	283	41.59 N	71.12 W
Norton Shores	216	43.10 N	86.15 W
Norton Sound ʮ	180	63.50 N	164.00 W
Nortonville, On., Can.	275b	43.43 N	79.44 W
Nortonville, Ks., U.S.	198	39.25 N	95.20 W
Nortorf, Dtsch.	30	54.10 N	9.50 E
Nortorf, Dtsch.	52	53.55 N	9.16 E
Nort-sur-Erdre	32	47.26 N	1.30 W
Noruega → Norway □[1]	24	62.00 N	10.00 E
Noruega, Mar de → Norwegian Sea ⫪[2]	10	70.00 N	2.00 E
Norumbega Reservoir ⊜[1]	283	42.20 N	71.18 W
Nørup	41	55.43 N	9.19 E
Norval	212	43.39 N	79.51 W
Norvalspont	158	30.38 S	25.27 E
Norvège → Norway □[1]	24	62.00 N	10.00 E
Norvegia, Cape >	9	71.25 S	12.18 W
Norvell	216	42.10 N	84.11 W
Norvelt	214	40.12 N	79.32 W
Norvin Green State Forest ♠	276	41.03 N	74.20 W
Norwalk, Ca., U.S.	228	33.54 N	118.04 W
Norwalk, Ct., U.S.	207	41.07 N	73.24 W
Norwalk, Ia., U.S.	190	41.28 N	93.40 W
Norwalk, Oh., U.S.	214	41.14 N	82.36 W
Norwalk ≃	207	41.06 N	73.25 W
Norwalk Harbor ⊂	276	41.06 N	73.24 W
Norwalk Islands II	276	41.03 N	73.23 W
Norway, In., U.S.	216	40.47 N	86.46 W
Norway, Ia., U.S.	190	41.54 N	91.55 W
Norway, Me., U.S.	188	44.12 N	70.32 W
Norway, Mi., U.S.	190	45.47 N	87.54 W
Norway (Norge) □[1], Europe	22	62.00 N	10.00 E
Norway (Norge) □[1], Europe	24	62.00 N	10.00 E
Norway Bay ⊂	176	71.08 N	104.35 W
Norway House	184	53.59 N	97.50 W
Norway Lake ⊜	212	45.20 N	76.43 W
Norwegen → Norway □[1]	24	62.00 N	10.00 E
Norwegian Basin ✣[1]	10	68.00 N	2.00 W
Norwegian Sea ⫪[2]	10	70.00 N	2.00 E
Norwegian Trench ✣[1]	10	59.00 N	4.30 E
Norwell	283	42.09 N	70.47 W
Norwich, On., Can.	212	42.59 N	80.36 W
Norwich, Eng., U.K.	42	52.38 N	1.18 E
Norwich, Ct., U.S.	207	41.32 N	72.05 W
Norwich, Ks., U.S.	198	37.27 N	97.50 W
Norwich, N.Y., U.S.	210	42.31 N	75.31 W
Norwich Airport ⊠	42	52.41 N	1.15 E
Norwin Heights	279b	40.20 N	79.44 W
Norwood, On., Can.	212	44.23 N	77.59 W
Norwood, Co., U.S.	200	38.07 N	108.17 W
Norwood, Ma., U.S.	207	42.11 N	71.12 W
Norwood, Mn., U.S.	190	44.46 N	93.55 W
Norwood, N.J., U.S.	276	40.59 N	73.57 W
Norwood, N.Y., U.S.	188	44.45 N	74.59 W
Norwood, N.C., U.S.	192	35.13 N	80.07 W
Norwood, Oh., U.S.	218	39.10 N	84.27 W
Norwood, Pa., U.S.	285	39.53 N	75.17 W
Norwood ◆[8]	273d	26.10 S	28.04 E
Norwood Memorial Airport ⊠	283	42.11 N	71.10 W
Norwood Park ◆[8]	278	41.59 N	87.48 W
Norwood Pond ⊜	283	42.35 N	70.52 W
Norwoodville	190	41.39 N	93.33 W
Noryang	98	34.56 N	127.52 E
Nosaka	94	35.39 N	140.34 E
Nosappu-misaki >	92a	43.23 N	145.49 E
Nosate	266b	45.33 N	8.43 E
Nosbonsing, Lake ⊜	190	46.12 N	79.13 W
Nose	96	34.58 N	135.24 E
Nose ◆[8]	270	34.49 N	135.09 E
Nose Creek ≃	182	54.52 N	119.38 W
Noshiro	92	40.12 N	140.02 E
Nosivka	78	50.55 N	31.35 E
Noska ≃	86	58.53 N	68.40 E
Nosop (Nossob) ≃	156	26.55 S	20.37 E
Nosova	86	59.30 N	63.13 E
Nosovaja, Ross.	24	68.15 N	54.35 E
Nosovaja, Ross.	80	57.15 N	45.35 E
Nosovo, Ross.	76	57.07 N	27.50 E
Nosovo, Ross.	83	47.16 N	38.40 E
Nosovščina	24	62.56 N	37.03 E
Noșratābād	128	29.54 N	59.59 E
Noss, Isle of I	46a	60.09 N	1.01 W
Nossa Senhora da Aparecida	256	22.02 S	42.48 W
Nossa Senhora das Dores	250	10.29 S	37.13 W
Nossa Senhora do Amparo	256	22.22 S	44.05 W
Nossa Senhora do Livramento	248	15.48 S	56.22 W
Nossa Senhora do Ó ◆[8]	287b	23.30 S	46.41 W
Nossebro	26	58.11 N	12.43 E
Nossen	54	51.03 N	13.17 E
Nossentiner Heide ◆[3]	54	53.35 N	12.25 E
Noss Head >	46	58.28 N	3.04 W
Nossob	156	22.18 S	17.10 E
Nossob (Nosop) ≃	156	26.55 S	20.37 E
Nossombougou	150	13.06 N	7.56 W
Nošul'	24	60.09 N	49.28 E
Nosy Varika	157b	20.35 S	48.32 E
Notasulga	194	32.33 N	85.40 W
Notch Cliff	284b	39.27 N	76.31 W
Notch Hill	182	50.52 N	119.26 W
Notch Peak ∧	200	39.08 N	113.24 W
Noteć ≃	30	52.44 N	15.26 E
Notigi Lake ⊜	184	55.57 N	99.18 W
Notikewin ≃	176	57.15 N	117.05 W
Nótion Aiyaíon □[4]	38	37.00 N	25.30 E
Noto, It.	70	36.53 N	15.04 E
Noto, Nihon	92	37.18 N	137.09 E
Noto, Golfo di ⊂	70	36.50 N	15.12 E
Noto, Val di ◆[1]	70	37.05 N	14.35 E
Noto Antica ⊥	70	36.56 N	15.02 E
Notodden	26	59.34 N	9.17 E
Notogawa	94	35.10 N	136.10 E
Noto-hantō >[1]	92	37.20 N	137.00 E
Noto-hantō-kokutei-kōen ♠	94	37.10 N	136.50 E
Noto-jima	94	37.08 N	137.00 E
Noto-jima I	94	37.07 N	137.00 E
Nōtori-dake ∧	94	35.37 N	138.15 E
Notoro-ko ⊜	92a	44.05 N	144.10 E
Notozero, ozero ⊜	24	66.28 N	32.05 E
Notre-Dame	186	46.19 N	64.43 W
Notre-Dame ʋ[1]	261	48.51 N	2.21 E
Notre-Dame, Bois ♠	261	48.45 N	2.35 E
Notre-Dame, Monts ⋏	186	48.10 N	68.00 W
Notre-Dame, Ruisseau ≃	275a	45.41 N	73.26 W
Notre Dame Bay ⊂	186	49.45 N	55.15 W
Notre-Dame-de-Bellecombe	62	45.48 N	6.31 E
Notre-Dame-de-Lorette ʋ[1]	50	50.25 N	2.42 E
Notre-Dame-de-Lourdes	184	49.32 N	98.33 W
Notre-Dame-de-Pierreville	206	46.06 N	72.53 W
Notre-Dame-des-Victoires ◆[8]	275a	45.35 N	73.34 W
Notre-Dame-du-Haut ʋ[1]	58	47.43 N	6.37 E
Notre-Dame-du-Laus	188	46.05 N	75.37 W
Notre-Dame-du-Nord	190	47.36 N	79.30 W
Notrees	196	31.55 N	102.45 W
Notreure ≃	50	47.41 N	2.36 E
Notsu	96	33.02 N	131.42 E
Notsuharu	96	33.09 N	131.32 E
Nottawa	216	41.55 N	85.27 W
Nottawa Creek ≃	216	42.01 N	85.24 W
Nottawasaga ≃	212	44.32 N	80.01 W
Nottawasaga Bay ⊂	212	44.35 N	80.15 W
Nottaway ≃	176	51.22 N	79.55 W
Nottingham, Eng., U.K.	42	52.58 N	1.10 W
Nottingham, Pa., U.S.	208	39.45 N	76.01 W
Nottingham, Pa., U.S.	285	40.07 N	74.58 W
Nottingham Island I	176	63.20 N	77.55 W
Nottingham Park	278	41.46 N	87.48 W
Nottingham Road	158	29.22 S	30.00 E
Nottinghamshire □[6]	44	53.00 N	1.00 W
Notting Hill	274b	37.54 S	145.08 E
Nottleben	54	50.58 N	10.50 E
Nottoway	192	37.08 N	78.05 W
Nottoway ≃	192	36.33 N	76.55 W
Nottuln	52	51.55 N	7.22 E
Notukeu Creek ≃	184	49.55 N	106.30 W
Nouâdhibou	148	20.54 N	17.04 W
Nouâdhibou, Râs >	148	20.46 N	17.03 W
Nouakchott	150	18.06 N	15.57 W
Nouâmghâr	150	19.22 N	16.31 W
Nouan-le-Fuzelier	50	47.32 N	2.02 E
Nouans-les-Fontaines	50	47.08 N	1.18 E
Nouméa	175f	22.16 S	166.27 E
Noun ≃	152	4.55 N	11.06 E
Nouna	150	12.44 N	3.52 W
Nounsley	260	51.46 N	0.36 E
Noupoort	158	31.10 S	24.57 E
Nous	158	28.44 S	19.52 E
Nouveau Brunswick → New Brunswick □[4]	186	46.30 N	66.15 W
Nouveau Mexique → New Mexico □[3]	178	34.30 N	106.00 W
Nouveau-Québec, Cratère du ±[6]	176	61.17 N	73.40 W
Nouvelle	186	48.08 N	66.19 W
Nouvelle ≃	186	48.07 N	66.18 W
Nouvelle-Calédonie → New Caledonia □[2]	175f	21.30 S	165.30 E
Nouvelle-Calédonie (New Caledonia) I	175f	21.30 S	165.30 E
Nouvelle Écosse → Nova Scotia □[4]	186	45.00 N	63.00 W
Nouvelle-France, Cap de >	176	62.27 N	73.42 W
Nouvelle Galles du Sud → New South Wales □[3]	166	33.00 S	146.00 E
Nouvelle-Orléans → New Orleans	194	29.58 N	90.07 W
Nouvelles-Hébrides → Vanuatu □[1]	175f	16.00 S	167.00 E
Nouvelle Zélande → New Zealand □[1]	172	41.00 S	174.00 E
Nouvelle Zemble → Novaja Zeml'a II	72	74.00 N	57.00 E
Nouvion-en-Ponthieu	50	50.12 N	1.47 E
Nouvion-sur-Meuse	56	49.42 N	4.48 E
Nouzonville	56	49.49 N	4.45 E
Nova, Magy.	61	46.41 N	16.41 E
Nova, Oh., U.S.	214	41.02 N	82.18 W
Nova América	255	15.01 S	49.56 W
Nova Andradina	255	22.10 S	53.15 W
Nova Astrakhan'	83	49.07 N	38.36 E
Novabad, Taj.	85	38.37 N	68.45 E
Novabad, Taj.	85	39.01 N	70.09 E
Nová Baňa	30	48.26 N	18.39 E
Nova Bila	78	49.46 N	39.11 E
Nova Borova	78	50.42 N	28.39 E
Nová Bystřice	61	49.01 N	15.06 E
Nova Cachoeirinha ◆[8]	287b	23.28 S	46.40 W
Nova Caipemba	152	7.26 S	14.38 E
Novacella ʋ[1]	64	46.44 N	11.39 E
Nova Era	255	19.45 S	43.03 W
Nova Esperança	255	23.08 S	52.13 W
Novafeltria	66	43.53 N	12.17 E
Nova Friburgo	256	22.16 S	42.32 W
Nova Goa → Panaji	122	15.29 N	73.50 E
Nova Gorica	64	45.57 N	13.39 E
Nova Gradiška	36	45.16 N	17.23 E
Nova Granada	255	20.29 S	49.19 W
Nova Iguaçu	256	22.45 S	43.27 W
Nova Iguaçu □[7]	287a	22.45 S	43.29 W
Nova Ivanivka	78	45.55 N	29.05 E
Novaja, Ross.	82	55.13 N	38.54 E
Novaja, Ross.	265b	55.48 N	38.03 E
Novaja ◆[8]	265a	60.02 N	30.28 E
Novaja Binaradka	80	53.48 N	49.56 E
Novaja Čigla	78	51.13 N	40.28 E
Novaja Derevn'a, Ross.	82	54.01 N	38.53 E
Novaja Derevn'a, Ross.	88	57.15 N	103.08 E
Novaja Kalitva	78	50.06 N	40.01 E
Novaja Kazanka	80	48.57 N	49.36 E
Novaja Kazmaska	80	56.49 N	53.31 E
Novaja Kriuša	78	50.16 N	41.16 E
Novaja Ladoga	76	60.05 N	32.16 E
Novaja L'al'a	86	59.03 N	60.36 E
Novaja Maluksa	76	59.39 N	31.21 E
Novaja Malykla	80	54.13 N	49.57 E
Novaja Mojgora	82	54.27 N	38.32 E
Novaja Porubežka	80	51.45 N	49.40 E
Novaja Ropša	265a	59.45 N	29.53 E
Novaja Sibir', ostrov I	74	75.00 N	149.00 E
Novaja Slobodka	82	54.56 N	36.47 E
Novaja Šul'ba	86	50.33 N	81.20 E
Novaja Uda	88	54.07 N	103.33 E
Novaja Usman'	78	51.37 N	39.24 E
Novaja Zeml'a II	72	74.00 N	57.00 E
Nova Kakhovka	78	46.45 N	33.23 E
Nováky	30	48.43 N	18.34 E
Nova Lamego	150	12.19 N	14.11 W
Novale (Rauth)	64	46.24 N	11.30 E
Novalesa	62	45.11 N	7.01 E
Novaliches Reservoir ⊜[1]	269f	14.43 N	121.05 E
Nova Lima	255	19.59 S	43.51 W
Nova Lisboa → Huambo	152	12.44 S	15.47 E
Nova Lusitânia	156	19.54 S	34.35 E
Nova Mambone	156	20.59 S	35.01 E
Nova Mayachka	78	46.36 N	33.14 E
Nova Milanese	266b	45.35 N	9.12 E
Nova Nabúri	154	16.46 S	38.57 E
Nova Odesa	78	47.19 N	31.47 E
Nova Odessa	256	23.09 S	46.51 W
Nova Olinda	250	7.06 S	39.40 W
Nova Olinda do Norte	246	3.45 S	59.03 W
Nová Paka	30	50.29 N	15.31 E
Nova Ponente (Deutschnofen)	64	46.25 N	11.25 E
Nova Ponte	255	19.08 S	47.41 W
Nova Praha	78	48.33 N	32.54 E
Nova Prata	252	28.47 S	51.36 W
Novar	212	45.27 N	79.15 W
Novara	62	45.28 N	8.38 E
Novara □[4]	62	45.40 N	8.30 E
Novara di Sicilia	70	38.01 N	15.08 E
Nová Role	54	50.15 N	12.47 E
Nova Roma	255	13.51 S	46.57 W
Nova Russas	250	4.42 S	40.34 W
Nova Scotia □[4], Can.	176	45.00 N	63.00 W
Nova Scotia □[4], Can.	186	45.00 N	63.00 W
Nova Siri	68	40.09 N	16.32 E
Nova Sloboda	78	51.23 N	34.08 E
Nova Sofala	156	20.09 S	34.42 E
Nova Soure	250	11.14 S	38.29 W
Novate Mezzola	58	46.15 N	9.27 E
Novate Milanese	266b	45.32 N	9.08 E
Nova Timboteua	250	1.12 S	47.24 W
Novato	226	38.06 N	122.34 W
Novato Creek ≃	282	38.06 N	122.29 W
Nova Ushytsya	78	48.49 N	27.16 E
Nova Vandúzi	156	18.57 S	33.16 E
Nova Varoš	38	43.28 N	19.48 E
Nova Venécia	255	18.43 S	40.24 W
Nova Viçosa	255	17.53 S	39.22 W

(DEUTSCH column headings: Name | Seite | Breite°′ | Länge°′ E = Ost)

Symbols in the index entries represent the broad categories identified in the key at the right. Symbols with superior numbers (⋏[1]) identify subcategories (see complete key on page *I · 1).*

Symbole im Register stellen die rechts im Schlüssel erklärten Kategorien dar. Symbole mit hochgestellten Ziffern (⋏[1]) bezeichnen Unterabteilungen einer Kategorie (vgl. vollständiger Schlüssel auf Seite *I · 1).*

Los símbolos incluídos en el texto del índice representan las grandes categorías identificadas con la clave a la derecha. Los símbolos con numeros en su parte superior (⋏[1]) identifican las subcategorías (véase la clave completa en la página *I · 1).*

Les symboles de l'index représentent les catégories indiquées dans la légende à droite. Les symboles suivis d'un indice (⋏[1]) représentent des sous-catégories (voir légende complète à la page *I · 1).*

Os símbolos incluídos no texto do índice representam as grandes categorias identificadas com a chave à direita. Os símbolos com números em sua parte superior (⋏[1]) identificam as subcategorias (veja-se a chave completa à página *I · 1).*

∧ Mountain	Berg	Montaña	Montagne	Montanha
⋏ Mountains	Gebirge	Montañas	Montagnes	Montanhas
)(Pass	Paß	Paso	Col	Passo
V Valley, Canyon	Tal, Cañon	Valle, Cañón	Vallée, Canyon	Vale, Canhão
≚ Plain	Ebene	Llano	Plaine	Planície
> Cape	Kap	Cabo	Cap	Cabo
I Island	Insel	Isla	Île	Ilha
II Islands	Inseln	Islas	Îles	Ilhas
± Other Topographic Features	Andere Topographische Objekte	Otros Elementos Topográficos	Autres données topographiques	Outros acidentes topográficos

ESPAÑOL

Nombre	Página	Lat.°′	Long.°′ W = Oeste
Nova Vida	248	10.11 S	62.47 W
Nova Vida, Cachoeira ∟	248	9.25 S	63.36 W
Nova Vodolaha	78	49.43 N	35.52 E
Novayanysol'	83	47.17 N	37.16 E
Nova Zagora	38	42.29 N	26.01 E
Nova Zburivka	78	46.28 N	32.24 E
Nove	64	45.43 N	11.40 E
Nové Hrady	61	48.47 N	14.37 E
Novelda	34	38.23 N	0.46 W
Novellara	64	44.51 N	10.44 E
Novelty	219	40.00 N	92.12 W
Nové Město	30	50.21 N	16.09 E
Nové Město nad Váhom	30	48.46 N	17.49 E
Nové Město na Moravě	30	49.34 N	16.04 E
Nové Mlýny, údolní nádrž ⊜[1]	61	48.54 N	16.34 E
Noventa di Piave	64	45.39 N	12.31 E
Noventa Padovana	64	45.24 N	11.58 E
Noventa Vicentina	64	45.17 N	11.32 E
Noves	62	43.52 N	4.54 E
Nové Sedlo	54	50.10 N	12.42 E
Nové Strašecí	54	50.07 N	13.53 E
Nové Údoli	60	48.48 N	13.48 E
Nové Zámky	30	47.59 N	18.11 E
Novgorod	76	58.31 N	31.17 E
Novgorod Oblast' □[4]	76	58.15 N	33.00 E
Novhorodka	78	48.21 N	32.39 E
Novhorod-Sivers'kyy	78	51.59 N	33.16 E
Novhorods'ke	83	48.20 N	37.50 E
Novi	216	42.28 N	83.28 W
Novi Basy	78	50.53 N	34.51 E
Novi Bečej	38	45.36 N	20.08 E
Novi Beograd	38	44.49 N	20.27 E
Novi Bilokorovychi	78	51.07 N	28.02 E
Novice	196	31.59 N	99.37 W
Novičicha	86	52.13 N	81.24 E
Novi di Modena	64	44.54 N	10.54 E
Novigrad, Hrv.	36	45.19 N	13.34 E
Novigrad, Hrv.	36	44.11 N	15.33 E
Novikovo, Ross.	86	58.15 N	80.39 E
Novikovo, Ross.	89	46.23 N	143.20 E
Novi Ligure	62	44.46 N	8.47 E
Noville	56	50.40 N	5.23 E
Novi Lyon Drain ≍	281	42.30 N	83.38 W
Novinger	194	40.13 N	92.42 W
Novinka	76	59.49 N	33.20 E
Novion-Porcien	50	49.36 N	4.25 E
Novi Pazar, Blg.	38	43.21 N	27.12 E
Novi Pazar, Jugo.	38	43.08 N	20.31 E
Novi Sad	38	45.15 N	19.50 E
Novi Sanzhary	78	49.21 N	34.19 E
Novi Vinodolski	36	45.08 N	14.48 E
Novka	76	55.27 N	30.24 E
Novki	80	56.22 N	41.06 E
Novl'anka	80	55.48 N	41.44 E
Novlenskoje	76	59.37 N	39.20 E
Novo ≃, Bra.	248	4.55 S	70.33 W
Novo ≃, Bra.	250	4.30 S	53.50 W
Novo ≃, Bra.	250	6.22 S	55.42 W
Novo ≃, Bra.	256	21.23 S	42.44 W
Novo, Lago ⊜	250	1.30 N	50.40 W
Nôvo Acôrdo	255	13.10 S	46.48 W
Novoaleksandrovka, Kaz.	86	51.47 N	68.49 E
Novoaleksandrovka, Ross.	80	51.56 N	52.26 E
Novoaleksandrovo	265b	55.59 N	37.33 E
Novoaleksandrovsk	80	45.29 N	41.16 E
Novoaleksejevka, Kaz.	86	52.56 N	64.41 E
Novoaleksejevka, Kaz.	86	52.47 N	74.54 E
Novoaleksejevka, Kaz.	86	50.08 N	55.39 E
Novoaltajsk	86	53.24 N	83.58 E
Novoamvrosiyivs'ke	83	47.49 N	38.29 E
Novoanninskij	80	50.32 N	42.41 E
Novoarchangel'skoje	265b	55.55 N	37.33 E
Novo Aripuanã	246	5.08 S	60.22 W
Novoarkhanhel's'k	78	48.39 N	30.48 E
Novoasbest	86	57.44 N	60.45 E
Novoaydar	83	48.57 N	39.00 E
Novoazovs'k	83	47.08 N	38.05 E
Novobatajsk	83	46.54 N	39.47 E
Novobelaja	78	49.49 N	39.18 E
Novobessergenovka	83	47.11 N	38.51 E
Novobogatinskoje	80	47.22 N	51.11 E
Novobogordskoje	80	53.11 N	53.56 E
Novobohdanivka	78	47.06 N	35.29 E
Novoborove	83	49.15 N	38.33 E
Novo Brasil	255	16.11 S	50.38 W
Novobratcevskij	82	55.51 N	37.23 E
Novoburejskij	89	49.49 N	129.54 E
Novočeboksarsk	80	56.08 N	47.30 E
Novo Čeremšansk	80	54.21 N	50.10 E
Novočerkassk	83	47.25 N	40.06 E
Novočernorečenskij	86	56.16 N	91.06 E
Novocharitonovo	82	55.35 N	38.30 E
Novocherkassk → Novočerkassk	83	47.25 N	40.06 E
Novochop'orsk	80	51.07 N	41.37 E
Novochop'orskij	80	51.06 N	41.33 E
Novochovrino ◆[8]	265b	55.52 N	37.30 E
Novociml'anskaja	80	47.59 N	42.17 E
Novo Cruzeiro	255	17.29 S	41.53 W
Novodanylivka	78	46.38 N	35.00 E
Novoderev'ankov-Skaja	78	46.19 N	38.45 E
Novodevičje	80	53.37 N	48.52 E
Novodolinka	86	51.12 N	72.33 E
Novodolinskij	86	49.44 N	72.45 E
Novodoroninskoje	88	51.08 N	112.08 E
Novodruzhes'k	83	48.58 N	38.21 E
Novodubovoje	76	52.19 N	39.13 E
Novodugino	76	55.38 N	34.18 E
Novodvinsk	24	64.26 N	40.47 E
Novodžerelijevskaja	78	45.46 N	38.41 E
Novoekonomichne	83	48.18 N	37.15 E
Novofetinino	82	56.14 N	39.17 E
Novogaritovo	80	52.47 N	40.07 E
Novogirejevo ◆[8]	265b	55.45 N	37.49 E
Novogorbovo	82	55.43 N	36.29 E
Novogornyj	86	55.37 N	60.47 E
Novogrigorjevskaja	80	49.26 N	43.37 E
Novogroznenskij	84	43.15 N	46.15 E
Novogrudok	76	53.36 N	25.50 E
Novo Hamburgo	252	29.41 S	51.08 W
Novo Horizonte	255	21.28 S	49.13 W
Novohrad-Volyns'kyy	78	50.36 N	27.36 E
Novohrodivka	83	48.13 N	37.20 E
Novohryhorivka, Ukr.	78	46.24 N	34.59 E
Novohryhorivka, Ukr.	83	48.34 N	37.25 E
Novohupalivka	78	48.02 N	35.26 E
Novoiljinsk	88	51.42 N	108.41 E
Novoiljinskij	86	57.54 N	55.30 E
Novoivanivka	78	49.44 N	33.28 E
Novoivanovka	85	43.08 N	71.26 E
Novoivanovskoje	265b	55.43 N	37.22 E
Novoizborsk	76	57.50 N	27.59 E
Novojampol'	89	52.55 N	127.38 E
Novojamskoje	76	52.14 N	34.28 E
Novoje, Ross.	82	55.38 N	38.55 E
Novoje, Ross.	86	58.53 N	68.40 E
Novoje Alechnovo	82	56.02 N	36.49 E
Novojegorjevskoje	86	51.46 N	80.53 E
Novoje Koval'ovo	265a	59.59 N	30.34 E
Novoje Leušino	80	56.48 N	40.32 E
Novojel'n'a	76	53.28 N	25.35 E
Novojenisejsk	86	58.16 N	92.24 E
Novoje Pavšino	82	54.15 N	37.07 E
Novoje Zarečje	76	57.43 N	34.22 E
Novokačalinsk	89	45.06 N	132.01 E
Novokadinsk	88	54.46 N	101.24 E
Novokamala	88	55.58 N	94.58 E
Novokarasuk	86	56.16 N	71.46 E
Novokaširovo	80	54.58 N	52.32 E
Novokaširsk	82	54.51 N	38.15 E

FRANÇAIS

Nom	Page	Lat.°′	Long.°′ W = Ouest
Novokazalinsk	86	45.50 N	62.10 E
Novokijevskij	80	50.27 N	43.08 E
Novokorsunskaja	78	45.38 N	39.09 E
Novokrasne	78	48.01 N	31.21 E
Novokrasnyanka	83	49.08 N	38.18 E
Novokručininskij	88	51.46 N	113.48 E
Novokubanka	86	51.40 N	70.44 E
Novokujbyševsk	80	53.07 N	49.58 E
Novokurovka	89	48.51 N	134.20 E
Novokuzneck	86	53.45 N	87.06 E
Novokuznetsk → Novokuzneck	86	53.45 N	87.06 E
Novolakskoje	84	43.07 N	46.29 E
Novolazarevskaja ᴗ[3]	9	70.45 S	11.50 E
Novoleuškovskaja	78	45.59 N	39.58 E
Novoli	68	40.23 N	18.03 E
Novolukoml'	76	54.40 N	29.08 E
Novol'vovsk	76	53.55 N	38.47 E
Novomalorossijskaja	78	45.38 N	39.53 E
Novomansurkino	80	53.52 N	51.52 E
Novomargaritovka	83	46.54 N	38.50 E
Novomariinka	88	55.27 N	96.01 E
Novomarkovka	86	51.44 N	72.17 E
Novomel'nikov	84	43.56 N	45.09 E
Novomelovatka	78	50.27 N	40.46 E
Novomelovoje	78	51.23 N	38.13 E
Novo Mesto	36	45.48 N	15.10 E
Novomichajlovka	86	55.13 N	81.57 E
Novomichajlovskij	78	44.15 N	38.51 E
Novomichajlovskoje	82	55.25 N	37.10 E
Novominskaja	78	46.19 N	38.57 E
Novomoskovsk, Ross.	82	54.05 N	38.13 E
Novomoskovs'k, Ukr.	78	48.37 N	35.12 E
Novomykhaylivka, Ukr.	78	47.19 N	36.04 E
Novomykhaylivka, Ukr.	83	47.51 N	37.29 E
Novomykil's'ke	83	49.21 N	39.51 E
Novomykolayivka, Ukr.	78	47.59 N	35.55 E
Novomykolayivka, Ukr.	78	46.13 N	32.45 E
Novomyrhorod	78	48.47 N	31.39 E
Novomyšastovskaja	78	45.12 N	38.35 E
Novonagajevo	80	55.56 N	54.15 E
Novonikolajevka, Kaz.	85	42.26 N	70.28 E
Novonikolajevka, Ross.	83	46.59 N	39.36 E
Novonikolajevskij	80	50.58 N	42.22 E
Novonikolayevsk → Novosibirsk	86	55.02 N	82.55 E
Novonikol'skoje, Ross.	76	59.25 N	33.13 E
Novonikol'skoje, Ross.	80	49.09 N	45.00 E
Novonikol'skoje, Ross.	86	59.46 N	79.12 E
Novonikol'skoje, Ross.	265b	55.50 N	37.15 E
Novookhtyrka	83	48.55 N	38.49 E
Novooleksandrivka, Ukr.	83	48.17 N	39.37 E
Novooleksandrivka, Ukr.	83	49.08 N	39.17 E
Novooleksiyivka, Ukr.	78	46.06 N	32.30 E
Novooleksiyivka, Ukr.	78	46.13 N	34.39 E
Novo Oriente	250	5.32 S	40.42 W
Novoorsk	86	51.23 N	58.58 E
Novopavlovka	88	51.13 N	109.14 E
Novopavlovskaja	84	43.58 N	43.38 E
Novopavlovskoje	88	50.56 N	111.35 E
Novopetrovo	86	57.11 N	69.10 E
Novopetrovskoje	82	55.59 N	36.28 E
Novopiscovo	76	57.19 N	41.54 E
Novopodrezkovo	82	55.57 N	37.21 E
Novopokrovka, Kaz.	86	50.41 N	80.28 E
Novopokrovka, Kaz.	86	53.43 N	67.45 E
Novopokrovka, Kyrg.	85	42.52 N	74.45 E
Novopokrovka, Ross.	89	45.52 N	134.28 E
Novopokrovka, Ukr.	78	48.03 N	34.37 E
Novopokrovskoje	80	51.35 N	43.36 E
Novopolevodino	80	51.46 N	47.29 E
Novopolock	76	55.31 N	28.38 E
Novopskov	83	49.33 N	39.05 E
Novorajčichinsk	89	49.47 N	129.38 E
Novor'ažsk	80	53.44 N	40.07 E
Novorepnoje	80	51.06 N	48.24 E
Novorossijka	85	42.44 N	76.07 E
Novorossijsk	78	44.45 N	37.45 E
Novorossijskoje	86	50.13 N	58.00 E
Novorossiysk → Novorossijsk	78	44.45 N	37.45 E
Novorozsosh	83	49.32 N	39.15 E
Novorudnyj	86	51.30 N	58.10 E
Novorybinka	86	51.51 N	71.14 E
Novorybnoje	74	72.50 N	105.50 E
Novoržev	76	57.02 N	29.20 E
Novošachtinsk	83	47.47 N	39.56 E
Novosaratovka	265a	59.50 N	30.32 E
Novoščerbinovskaja	78	46.28 N	38.38 E
Novosel'e	86	54.10 N	76.53 E
Novoselenginsk	88	51.06 N	106.37 E
Novoselickoje	84	44.45 N	43.26 E
Novoselivka	83	49.04 N	37.42 E
Novoselivs'ke	78	45.26 N	33.34 E
Novoselje	265a	59.48 N	30.05 E
Novoselki, Ross.	82	55.08 N	37.33 E
Novoselki, Ross.	82	54.49 N	38.55 E
Novosel'nyj	86	50.00 N	54.38 E
Novoselovo	82	56.04 N	39.04 E
Novoselytsya, Ukr.	78	48.14 N	26.17 E
Novoselytsya, Ukr.	78	49.48 N	25.03 E
Novosemejkino	80	53.23 N	50.22 E
Novosergijevka, Ross.	80	52.06 N	53.39 E
Novosergijevka, Ross.	265a	59.54 N	30.34 E
Novoseslavino	80	53.21 N	40.26 E
Novošešminsk	80	55.04 N	51.15 E
Novoshakhtinsk → Novošachtinsk	83	47.47 N	39.56 E
Novosibirsk	86	55.02 N	82.55 E
Novosibirskije ostrova II	74	75.00 N	142.00 E
Novosibirsk Oblast' □[4]	86	55.00 N	80.00 E
Novosibirskoje vodochranilišče ⊜[1]	86	54.35 N	82.35 E
Novosil'	76	52.58 N	37.03 E
Novosil's'ke	78	45.20 N	28.33 E
Novosil'skoje	78	51.56 N	38.31 E
Novosokol'niki	76	56.21 N	30.10 E
Novos'olki, Bela.	76	52.24 N	28.33 E
Novos'olki, Bela.	76	52.02 N	24.21 E
Novos'olki, Ross.	76	56.01 N	33.37 E
Novos'olki, Ross.	80	55.48 N	42.41 E
Novos'olki, Ross.	80	54.50 N	39.46 E
Novos'olki, Ross.	265a	59.42 N	30.17 E
Novos'olovo, Ross.	86	55.04 N	91.07 E
Novos'olovo, Ross.	88	56.04 N	107.42 E
Novospasovka	83	47.42 N	39.04 E
Novospasskoje	80	53.08 N	47.45 E
Novostril'tsivka	83	49.20 N	39.55 E
Novostrojevo	76	54.27 N	21.50 E
Novosvitlivka	83	48.30 N	39.30 E
Novosysojevka	89	44.14 N	133.22 E
Novotavolžanka	78	50.22 N	36.50 E
Novotitarovskaja	78	45.14 N	39.00 E
Novotroick, Ross.	86	56.11 N	78.41 E
Novotroick, Ross.	86	51.12 N	58.20 E
Novotroickoje, Kaz.	85	43.42 N	73.46 E
Novotroickoje, Ross.	80	58.28 N	47.06 E
Novo-Troitsk → Novotroick	86	51.12 N	58.20 E
Novotroyits'ke, Ukr.	78	46.22 N	34.20 E
Novotroyits'ke, Ukr.	83	47.43 N	37.35 E
Novotulka, Ross.	80	52.38 N	48.45 E
Novotulka, Ross.	80	50.50 N	47.34 E

PORTUGUÊS

Nome	Página	Lat.°′	Long.°′ W = Oeste
Novotul'skij	82	54.10 N	37.43 E
Novoukolovo	78	51.02 N	38.25 E
Novoukrayinka	78	48.19 N	31.32 E
Novouljanovsk	80	54.08 N	48.24 E
Novoural'sk	86	51.15 N	57.16 E
Novouzensk	80	50.28 N	48.08 E
Novovaršavka	86	54.11 N	74.42 E
Novovasylivka, Ukr.	78	46.51 N	36.46 E
Novovasylivka, Ukr.	78	46.48 N	35.44 E
Novov'atsk	80	58.29 N	49.44 E
Novov'azniki	80	56.12 N	42.10 E
Novovolyns'k	78	50.50 N	24.05 E
Novovoronežskij	78	51.16 N	39.11 E
Novovorontsovka	78	47.29 N	33.54 E
Novovoskresenovka	85	42.50 N	73.32 E
Novovoskresens'ke	78	47.21 N	33.37 E
Novozacharkino	80	52.11 N	48.29 E
Novozagorje	82	55.39 N	38.38 E
Novozavidovskij	82	56.33 N	36.26 E
Novožilovskaja	24	64.50 N	51.20 E
Novozizevka	80	50.48 N	49.08 E
Novozybkov	76	52.32 N	31.56 E
Novska	36	45.21 N	16.59 E
Nový Bohumín	30	49.56 N	18.20 E
Nový Bor	54	50.45 N	14.33 E
Novyj	86	55.39 N	86.39 E
Novyj Afon	84	43.06 N	40.48 E
Novyj Bor	24	66.43 N	52.16 E
Novyj Bujan	80	53.41 N	50.04 E
Novyj Dvor	76	52.50 N	24.21 E
Novyje Ajbesi	80	54.49 N	47.02 E
Novyje Burasy	80	52.08 N	46.06 E
Novyje Denisoviči	76	54.12 N	29.13 E
Novyje Gorki	80	56.42 N	41.06 E
Novyje Maty	80	55.15 N	54.04 E
Novyje Salty	80	54.06 N	53.26 E
Novyje Z'atcy	80	57.27 N	52.36 E
Nový Jičín	30	49.36 N	18.00 E
Novyj Jegorlyk	80	46.24 N	41.54 E
Novyj Karačaj	84	43.49 N	41.56 E
Novyj Karamass	80	56.11 N	48.58 E
Novyj Kiner	80	56.24 N	49.44 E
Novyj Multan	80	57.09 N	52.19 E
Novyj Nekouz	76	57.54 N	38.04 E
Novyj Oskol	78	50.46 N	37.53 E
Novyj Pogost	76	55.30 N	27.29 E
Novyj Port	74	67.40 N	72.52 E
Novyj Put'	85	43.29 N	73.52 E
Novyj Ropsk	76	52.18 N	32.19 E
Novyj Stan	82	56.18 N	37.00 E
Novyj Tap	86	57.04 N	67.49 E
Novyj Terek ≃	84	43.37 N	47.25 E
Novyj Tevriz	86	59.04 N	78.08 E
Novyj Uzen	72	43.18 N	52.48 E
Novyj Vas'ugan	86	58.34 N	76.29 E
Novy Torjal	80	57.00 N	48.44 E
Novyy Buh	78	47.41 N	32.30 E
Novyy Bykiv	78	50.36 N	31.39 E
Novyy Svit	83	47.48 N	38.00 E
Novyy Yarychiv	78	49.55 N	24.18 E
Nowa Dęba	30	50.26 N	21.46 E
Nowaja Semlja → Novaja Zeml'a II	72	74.00 N	57.00 E
Nowa Ruda	30	50.35 N	16.31 E
Nowa Sól (Neusalz)	30	51.48 N	15.44 E
Nowata	196	36.42 N	95.38 W
Nowater Creek ≃	202	43.57 N	108.00 W
Nowbarān	128	35.08 N	48.42 E
Nowe	30	53.40 N	18.43 E
Nowe Miasto Lubawskie	30	53.27 N	19.35 E
Nowe Miasto nad Pilicą	30	51.38 N	20.35 E
Nowendoc	166	31.32 S	151.43 E
Nowe Warpno	30	53.44 N	14.16 E
Nowfel low Shātow	128	34.23 N	50.32 E
Nowgong	124	25.04 N	79.27 E
Nowingi	166	34.36 S	142.14 E
Nowitna ≃	180	65.55 N	154.17 W
Nowogard	30	53.40 N	15.08 E
Nowogród	30	53.15 N	21.53 E
Nowogrodziec	30	51.12 N	15.25 E
Nowokusnezk → Novokuzneck	86	53.45 N	87.06 E
Nowood ≃	202	44.17 N	107.58 W
Nowosibirsk → Novosibirsk	86	55.02 N	82.55 E
Nowra	170	34.53 S	150.36 E
Nowrangapur	122	19.14 N	82.33 E
Nowshāk ∧	123	36.26 N	71.50 E
Nowshera	123	34.01 N	71.59 E
Nowy Dwór Gdański	30	54.13 N	19.06 E
Nowy Dwór Mazowiecki	30	52.26 N	20.43 E
Nowy Sącz	30	49.38 N	20.42 E
Nowy Sącz □[4]	30	49.30 N	20.15 E
Nowy Staw	30	54.09 N	19.00 E
Nowy Targ	30	49.29 N	20.02 E
Nowy Tomyśl	30	52.20 N	16.07 E
Now Zād	120	32.24 N	64.28 E
Noxapater	194	32.59 N	89.03 W
Noxe ≃	50	48.33 N	3.35 E
Noxen	210	41.25 N	76.03 W
Noxon	202	48.00 N	115.47 W
Noxon Reservoir ⊜[1]	202	47.54 N	115.40 W
Noxubee ≃	194	32.50 N	88.10 W
Noy ≃	110	17.05 N	105.02 E
Noya	34	42.47 N	8.53 W
Noya ≃	152	0.58 N	9.48 E
Noyant	50	47.31 N	0.08 E
Noye ≃	50	49.51 N	2.20 E
Noyelles-sur Mer	50	50.11 N	1.43 E
Noyers	50	47.42 N	4.00 E
Noyers, Ruisseau des ≃	275a	45.21 N	73.22 W
Noyers-sur-Jabron	62	44.10 N	5.50 E
Noyes Island I	182	55.30 N	133.40 W
Noyon	50	49.35 N	3.00 E
Nožaj-Jurt	84	43.05 N	46.24 E
Nozawa-onsen	94	36.55 N	138.27 E
Nozay, Fr.	32	47.34 N	1.38 W
Nozay, Fr.	261	48.40 N	2.14 E
Nozeroy	58	46.47 N	6.02 E
Nozori-dam ◆[6]	94	36.43 N	138.39 E
Nozori-ko ⊜	94	36.42 N	138.39 E
Nozuta	268	35.35 N	139.27 E
Nqamakwe	158	32.12 S	27.56 E
Nqutu	158	28.13 S	30.32 E
N'Riquinha	152	15.45 S	21.42 E
N'Rougas	158	29.07 S	21.09 E
Nsa, Oued en V	148	32.28 N	5.24 E
Nsaba	150	5.39 N	0.45 W
Nsah	152	2.22 S	15.19 E
Nsang	152	2.02 N	10.56 E
Nsanje	154	16.55 S	35.12 E
Nsawam	150	5.50 N	0.20 W
Nsefu Game Reserve ◆[4]	154	13.07 S	32.10 E
Nsele ≃	152	4.14 S	15.33 E
Nseleni	158	28.33 S	31.39 E
Nsok	152	1.08 N	11.16 E
Nsoko	158	27.02 S	31.57 E
Nsontin	152	3.09 S	18.00 E
Nsouélé	273b	4.12 S	15.11 E
Nsukka	150	6.52 N	7.24 E
Nsuta	150	5.17 N	1.58 W
Ntakat	150	16.49 N	11.43 W
Ntambanana	158	28.36 S	31.45 E
Ntandembele	152	2.11 S	17.08 E
Ntcheu	154	14.49 S	34.38 E
Ntem ≃	152	2.15 N	9.45 E
Ntoum	152	0.23 N	9.47 E
Ntsama	152	0.32 S	14.38 E
N'Tsaoueni	157a	11.27 S	43.18 E
Ntui	152	4.27 N	11.38 E
Ntumba	154	8.20 S	32.05 E
Ntusi	154	0.03 N	31.13 E
Ntwetwe Pan ≚	156	20.30 S	25.20 E
Nuala	154	13.27 S	28.16 E
Nuanchitang	104	41.02 N	120.41 E

Nuanetsi ≃	156	22.40 S	31.50 E
Nuangola	210	41.09 N	75.58 W
Nuanli	102	23.26 N	100.51 E
Nuannuan	269d	25.06 N	121.44 E
Nuanshui	100	28.53 N	117.51 E
Nuanzhouying	100	25.22 N	117.22 E
Nuasjärvi ⊜	26	64.10 N	28.05 E
Nuatabu	174t	1.33 N	172.59 E
Nuatja	150	6.57 N	1.10 E
Nu'aymah	132	32.38 N	36.10 E
Nūbah	142	30.29 N	31.33 E
Nūbah, Jibāl an- ⩘	140	11.00 N	30.45 E
Nūbārīyah, Tur'at an- ≍	142	30.43 N	30.46 E
Nubian Desert ◆[2]	140	20.30 N	33.00 E
Ñuble ≃	252	36.39 S	72.27 W
Nubra ≃	123	34.39 N	77.36 E
Nucet	38	46.28 N	22.35 E
Nucetto	62	44.20 N	8.04 E
Nucha → Şeki	84	41.12 N	47.12 E
Nuchatlitz Inlet ⊂	182	49.45 N	126.55 W
N'uchča	24	63.27 N	46.28 E
Nuch'ŏn-ni	98	38.14 N	126.16 E
Nucla	200	38.16 N	108.32 W
Núcleo Colonial São Bento	287a	22.44 S	43.18 W
N'učpas	24	60.51 N	51.18 E
Nucuray ≃	246	5.02 S	75.34 W
Nuda, Monte la ∧	64	44.17 N	10.15 E
Nudaybah	142	30.59 N	30.22 E
Nudol' ≃	82	56.07 N	36.42 E
Nudol'-Šarino	82	56.06 N	36.31 E
Nudow	264a	52.20 N	13.10 E
Nueces ≃	196	27.50 N	97.30 W
Nueces Plains ≚	196	28.30 N	99.15 W
Nueltin Lake ⊜	176	60.20 N	99.50 W
Nuenen	52	51.29 N	5.33 E
Nü'er ≃	98	40.57 N	121.19 E
Nü'erhe	104	41.04 N	121.00 E
Nuestra Señora de Talavera	252	25.26 S	63.48 W
Nueva, Isla I	254	55.13 S	66.30 W
Nueva Antioquia	246	6.05 N	69.26 W
Nueva Asunción □[5]	248	21.00 S	61.00 W
Nueva Atzacoalco ◆[8]	286a	19.29 N	99.05 W
Nueva Brunswick → New Brunswick □[4]	186	46.30 N	66.15 W
Nueva Caledonia → New Caledonia □[2]	175f	21.30 S	165.30 E
Nueva Chicago ◆[8]	288	34.40 S	58.30 W
Nueva Ciudad Guerrero	232	26.35 N	99.15 W
Nueva Concepción	236	14.08 N	89.18 W
Nueva Cuadrilla	234	18.04 N	101.33 W
Nueva Ecija □[4]	116	15.35 N	121.00 E
Nueva Escocia → Nova Scotia □[4]	186	45.00 N	63.00 W
Nueva Esparta □[3]	246	11.00 N	64.00 W
Nueva Francia	252	28.11 S	64.12 W
Nueva Galia	252	35.07 S	65.15 W
Nueva Germania	252	23.54 S	56.45 W
Nueva Gerona	240p	21.53 N	82.48 W
Nueva Guinea, Isla → New Guinea I	164	5.00 S	140.00 E
Nueva Hébridas → Vanuatu □[1]	175f	16.00 S	167.00 E
Nueva Helvecia	258	34.19 S	57.13 W
Nueva Imperial	252	38.44 S	72.57 W
Nueva Italia de Ruiz	234	19.01 N	102.06 W
Nueva Loja	246	0.06 N	76.52 W
Nueva Lubecka	254	44.32 S	70.24 W
Nueva Ocotepeque	236	14.24 N	89.13 W
Nueva Palmira	258	33.53 S	58.25 W
Nueva Paz	240p	22.46 N	81.45 W
Nueva Pompeya ◆[8]	288	34.39 S	58.25 W
Nueva Rosita	232	27.57 N	101.13 W
Nueva San Salvador	236	13.41 N	89.17 W
Nueva Segovia □[5]	236	13.40 N	86.10 W
Nueva Siberia, Islas → Novosibirskije ostrova II	74	75.00 N	142.00 E
Nueva Venecia	236	14.03 N	91.33 W
Nueva Vizcaya □[4]	116	16.25 N	121.10 E
Nueva Zelandia → New Zealand □[1]	172	41.00 S	174.00 E
Nueva Zembla, Isla de → Novaja Zeml'a II	72	74.00 N	57.00 E
Nueve, Canal Numero ≍	252	36.11 S	57.18 W
Nueve de Julio	252	35.27 S	60.52 W
Nuevitas	240p	21.33 N	77.16 W
Nuevitas, Bahía de ⊂	240p	21.30 N	77.12 W
Nuevo	228	33.48 N	117.09 W
Nuevo, Bajo ✢[4]	238	15.55 N	78.30 W
Nuevo, Cayo I	232	21.51 N	92.05 W
Nuevo, Golfo ⊂	254	42.42 S	64.36 W
Nuevo Berlín	252	32.59 S	58.03 W
Nuevo Camarón	196	27.05 N	99.55 W
Nuevo Casas Grandes	232	30.25 N	107.55 W
Nuevo Chagres	236	9.14 N	80.05 W
Nuevo Delicias	232	26.15 N	102.50 W
Nuevo Laredo	232	27.30 N	99.31 W
Nuevo Léon	204	32.20 N	115.12 W
Nuevo León □[3]	232	25.40 N	100.00 W
Nuevo Morelos	234	17.31 N	95.02 W
Nuevo Necaxa	234	20.13 N	98.00 W
Nuevo Poblado el Oro	196	26.50 N	101.19 W
Nuevo Primero de Mayo	196	26.01 N	98.02 W
Nuevo Progreso	232	18.38 N	92.18 W
Nuevo Rocafuerte	246	0.56 S	75.24 W
Nuevo Saucillo	196	27.20 N	104.54 W
Nufcor	273d	26.17 S	27.44 E
Nugaal □[4]	144	8.30 N	49.00 E
Nugaaleed, Dooxo V	144	8.35 N	48.35 E
Nugget Point ›	172	46.27 S	169.49 E
Nûgssuaq ›[1]	176	70.25 N	52.30 W
Nugu ⊜[1]	122	11.58 N	76.28 E
Nuguria Islands II	14	3.20 S	154.45 E
Nūh	124	28.07 N	77.01 E
Nūh, Rās ›	128	25.05 N	62.24 E
Nuhaka	172	39.03 S	177.45 E
Nuhaydāt as-Sūd, Jabal an- ∧	142	28.01 N	32.21 E
Nuhūd, Jabal an- ∧	140	14.50 N	29.53 E
Nui I[1]	14	7.15 S	177.10 E
Nuia	76	58.04 N	25.33 E
Nuits-Saint-Georges	58	47.08 N	4.57 E
Nuits-sur-Armançon	50	47.44 N	4.12 E
N'uja	74	60.32 N	116.14 E
N'uja ≃	74	60.32 N	116.20 E
Nujiang	102	29.58 N	97.25 E
N'uk, ozero ⊜	24	64.27 N	31.45 E
Nuka Island I	180	59.21 N	150.42 W
Nukan	175c	7.23 N	151.53 E
Nukata	94	34.55 N	137.17 E
Nukatl', chrebet ⩘	84	42.15 N	46.35 E
Nukey Bluff ⩘[4]	166	32.33 S	135.40 E
Nukhayb	128	32.02 N	42.15 E
Nukhaylah ⫪[4]	140	19.03 N	26.19 E
Nukhaylah, Wādī an- V	132	31.27 N	35.49 E
Nukiki	175e	6.46 S	156.28 E
N'uksenica	24	60.25 N	44.13 E
Nuku'alofa	174w	21.08 S	175.12 W
Nukufetau I[1]	14	8.00 S	178.22 E
Nukuhu	164	5.35 S	149.25 E
Nukulaelae I[1]	14	9.23 S	179.52 E
Nukumanu Islands II	14	4.30 S	159.30 E
Nukunonu I	14	9.12 S	171.54 W
Nukunuku	174w	21.08 S	175.18 W
Nukuoro I[1]	14	3.51 N	154.58 E
Nukus	72	42.50 N	59.29 E

Nul	175f	16.49 S	168.24 E
Nulato	180	64.43 N	158.06 W
Nullagine	162	21.53 S	120.06 E
Nullagine ≃	162	20.43 S	120.33 E
Nullarbor	162	31.26 S	130.55 E
Nullarbor National Park ♠	162	31.30 S	130.30 E
Nullarbor Plain ≚	162	31.00 S	129.00 E
Nulltown	218	39.35 N	85.10 W
Nul'vand	85	38.16 N	70.32 E
Nulvi	71	40.47 N	8.45 E
Num, Mios I	164	1.30 S	135.13 E
Numabin Bay ⊂	184	56.30 N	103.08 W
Numakuma	96	34.23 N	133.20 E
Numan	146	9.28 N	12.02 E
Numana	66	43.31 N	13.37 E
Numancia	116	9.52 N	125.58 E
Numancia ⊥	34	41.48 N	2.25 W
Numansdorp	52	51.44 N	4.26 E
Numara I	122	6.26 N	73.03 E
Numata, Nihon	92a	43.48 N	141.57 E
Numata, Nihon	94	36.38 N	139.03 E
Numata, Nihon	96	34.27 N	132.24 E
Numatinna ≃	140	7.14 N	27.37 E
Numazu	94	35.06 N	138.52 E
Numbargulme, Mount ∧	164	14.56 S	145.03 E
Number 5 Mine	214	41.08 N	80.11 W
Numedal V	26	60.06 N	9.06 E
Numeralla	171b	36.11 S	149.20 E
Numeralla ≃	171b	36.06 S	149.11 E
Numfoor, Pulau I	164	1.03 S	134.54 E
Numidia	210	40.53 N	76.24 W
Numila	229b	21.54 N	159.33 W
Nu Mine	214	40.48 N	79.18 W
Numto	74	63.40 N	71.20 E
Numurkah	166	36.06 S	145.26 E
Nun ≃[1]	150	4.20 N	6.00 E
Nun'amo	180	65.37 N	170.40 W
Nunapitchuk	180	60.54 N	162.29 W
Nunawading	169	37.49 S	145.10 E
Nünchritz	54	51.18 N	13.23 E
Nunda	210	42.34 N	77.56 W
Nundah	171a	27.24 S	153.04 E
Nundu	154	3.49 S	29.05 E
Nuneaton	42	52.32 N	1.28 W
Núñes, Isla I	254	53.31 S	73.48 W
Núñez ◆[8]	288	34.33 S	58.27 W
Nunez ≃	150	10.36 N	14.40 W
Nungarin	162	31.11 S	118.06 E
Nungesser Lake ⊜	184	51.28 N	93.35 W
Nungwe	154	2.46 S	32.01 E
Nunica	216	43.04 N	86.04 W
Nunivak Island I	180	60.00 N	166.30 W
Nunjiang	89	49.10 N	125.11 E
Nunjikompita	162	32.16 S	134.19 E
Nunkini	232	20.20 N	90.11 W
Nunkun ∧	123	33.59 N	76.01 E
Nunligran	180	64.48 N	175.24 W
Nunnelly	194	35.51 N	87.28 W
Ñuñoa	286e	33.28 S	70.36 W
Nunshan	89	48.59 N	125.14 E
Nunspeet	52	52.23 N	5.46 E
Nuomin ≃	89	48.06 N	124.26 E
Nuomin Dashan ∧	89	50.15 N	122.46 E
Nuon ≃	150	6.30 N	8.36 W
Nuoro	71	40.19 N	9.20 E
Nuoro □[4]	71	40.10 N	9.20 E
Nuqruș, Jabal ∧	140	24.49 N	34.36 E
Nuquí	246	5.42 N	77.17 W
Nura	86	48.53 N	62.20 E
Nura ≃	86	50.30 N	69.59 E
Nurallao	71	39.47 N	9.05 E
Nuraminis	71	39.26 N	9.01 E
Nuratau, chrebet ⩘	85	40.20 N	67.15 E
Nuraxi, Nuraghe su ⊥	71	39.42 N	9.00 E
N'urba	74	63.17 N	118.20 E
Nürburg	56	50.21 N	6.57 E
Nürburgring ♠	56	50.21 N	6.58 E
Nur Dağları ⩘	130	36.45 N	36.20 E
Nure ≃	62	45.03 N	9.49 E
Nurek	85	38.23 N	69.19 E
Nurekskoje vodochranilišče ⊜[1]	85	38.30 N	69.30 E
Nuremberg → Nürnberg, Dtsch.	60	49.27 N	11.04 E
Nuremberg, Pa., U.S.	210	40.56 N	76.10 W
Nürenbei	107	30.11 N	106.04 E
Nūrestān □[9]	123	35.30 N	70.45 E
Nurettin	130	39.14 N	42.25 E
Nurhak	130	37.58 N	37.25 E
Nuria, Monte ∧	66	42.21 N	13.05 E
Nuriootpa	168b	34.29 S	139.00 E
Nurlat	80	54.26 N	50.46 E
Nurlaty	80	55.37 N	48.18 E
Nūrmahal	123	31.06 N	75.36 E
Nurmes	26	63.33 N	29.07 E
Nurmijärvi	26	60.28 N	24.48 E
Nūrnagar	126	22.20 N	89.03 E
Nürnberg	60	49.27 N	11.04 E
Nürnberg, Flughafen ⊠	60	49.30 N	11.06 E
Nūrpur, India	123	31.10 N	76.29 E
Nūrpur, India	123	32.18 N	75.54 E
Nurpur, India	126	22.13 N	88.05 E
Nūrpur, Pāk.	123	31.53 N	71.54 E
Nurrari Lakes ⊜	162	29.01 S	130.05 E
Nurri	71	39.43 N	9.14 E
Nurri, Mount ∧[2]	166	31.42 S	146.02 E
Nursery	222	28.56 N	97.06 W
Nürtingen	56	48.38 N	9.20 E
Nus	62	45.45 N	7.28 E
Nūsah	144	14.00 N	46.43 E
Nusa Tenggara Barat □[4]	115b	8.50 S	117.30 E
Nusa Tenggara Timur □[4]	112	9.30 S	122.00 E
Nusaybin	130	37.03 N	41.13 E
Nuṣayrīyah, Jabal an- ⩘	130	35.30 N	36.12 E
Nusco	68	40.53 N	15.05 E
Nushagak ≃	180	59.00 N	158.30 W
Nushagak Bay ⊂	180	58.40 N	158.40 W
Nushagak Peninsula ›[1]	180	58.30 N	159.00 W
Nu Shan ⩘	102	27.00 N	99.00 E
Nüshan Hu ⊜	100	32.57 N	118.03 E
Nu-shima I	96	34.10 N	134.50 E
Nushki	120	29.33 N	66.01 E
Nusplingen	58	48.08 N	8.53 E
Nušpoly	82	56.39 N	37.44 E
Nussdorf ◆[8]	264b	48.15 N	16.22 E
Nussdorf am Attersee	64	47.53 N	13.31 E
Nuta ≃	96	34.23 N	133.04 E
Nutauge, laguna ⊂	180	67.55 N	176.45 W
Nutepel'men, Ross.	180	67.26 N	174.56 W
Nutepelmen, Ross.	180	65.31 N	178.30 W
Nutfield	260	51.14 N	0.07 W
Nuth	56	50.55 N	5.54 E
Nuthe ≃, Dtsch.	54	51.58 N	11.53 E
Nuthe ≃, Dtsch.	54	52.23 N	13.04 E
Nut Lake Indian Reserve ◆[4]	184	52.20 N	103.30 W
Nutley	210	40.49 N	74.09 W
Nutrioso	200	33.57 N	109.12 W
Nut Swamp Brook ≃	276	40.21 N	74.06 W
Nuttby Mountain ∧[2]	186	45.33 N	63.13 W
Nutter Fort	188	39.15 N	80.19 W
Nutting Lake	207	42.32 N	71.16 W
Nutting Lake ⊜	283	42.32 N	71.16 W
Nutwood	219	39.05 N	90.39 W
Nutwood Downs	164	15.49 S	134.10 E
Nutzotin Mountains ⩘	180	62.10 N	141.40 W
Nu'ūmīyah, Wādī an- V	142	29.31 N	31.17 E
Nuupere, Pointe ›	174s	17.36 S	149.47 W
Nu'uuli	174u	14.18 S	170.42 W
N'uvčim	24	61.22 N	50.42 E

Nuwākoṭ	124	28.08 N	83.53 E
Nuwaybi' al-Muzayyinah	140	28.58 N	34.39 E
Nuwerus	158	31.08 S	18.24 E
Nuweveldberge ⩘	158	32.13 S	22.10 E
Nuxis	71	39.09 N	8.44 E
Nuyakuk Lake ⊜	180	60.00 N	158.40 W
Nuyts, Point ›	162	35.04 S	116.37 E
Nuyts Archipelago II	162	32.35 S	133.17 E
Nūzvīd	122	16.47 N	80.51 E
N'Vinda	152	13.04 S	18.57 E
Nwa	152	6.30 N	11.00 E
Nxainxai	156	19.50 S	21.13 E
Nxai Pan National Park ♠	156	19.45 S	24.50 E
Nxaunxau	156	18.19 S	21.04 E
Nyaake	150	4.52 N	7.37 W
Nyabéssan	152	2.24 N	10.24 E
Nyabing	162	33.32 S	118.09 E
Nyac	180	61.01 N	159.57 W
Nyack	210	41.05 N	73.55 W
Nyack Beach State Park ♠	276	41.07 N	73.55 W
Nyadiri ≃	154	16.44 S	32.33 E
Nyahanga	154	2.23 S	33.33 E
Nyahua	154	5.24 S	33.19 E
Nyahururu Falls	154	0.02 N	36.22 E
Nyah West	166	35.11 S	143.22 E
Nyainqêntanglha Feng ∧	124	30.22 N	90.35 E
Nyainqêntanglha Shan ⩘	120	30.00 N	90.00 E
Nyainrong	120	32.09 N	92.11 E
Nyakabindi	154	2.38 S	33.59 E
Nyakakiri	154	2.15 S	31.28 E
Nyakanazi	154	3.00 S	31.15 E
Nyakrom	150	5.37 N	0.48 W
Nyakulenga	152	13.03 S	23.29 E
Nyala	140	12.03 N	24.53 E
Nyalam	120	28.11 N	85.58 E
Nyalas	114	2.26 N	102.28 E
Nyamandhlovu	154	19.50 S	28.16 E
Nyamina	150	13.19 N	6.59 W
Nyamlell	140	9.07 N	26.58 E
Nyamougo	154	1.29 S	34.33 E
Nyamtumbo	154	10.29 S	36.02 E
Nyamwage	154	8.08 S	39.00 E
Nyandekwa	154	3.55 S	32.30 E
Nyanding, Khawr V	140	8.40 N	32.41 E
Nyang ≃	124	29.25 N	94.22 E
Nyanga □[4]	152	3.00 S	11.00 E
Nyanga ≃	152	2.58 S	10.15 E
Nyanga, Lake ⊜	162	29.57 S	126.10 E
Nyangana	156	18.00 S	20.41 E
Nyangui ∧	154	17.53 S	32.44 E
Nyanji Mission	154	14.23 S	31.48 E
Nyanza □[4]	154	0.30 S	34.30 E
Nyanza-Lac	154	4.21 S	29.36 E
Nyasa, Lake (Lake Malawi) ⊜	154	12.00 S	34.30 E
Nyaunglebin	110	17.57 N	96.44 E
Nyavikungu	154	11.26 S	25.54 E
Nyazura	154	18.43 S	32.10 E
Nyazvidzi ≃	154	20.00 S	32.17 E
Nybergsund	26	61.15 N	12.19 E
Nyborg	41	55.19 N	10.48 E
Nybro	26	56.45 N	15.54 E
Nyda	74	66.36 N	72.54 E
Nyêmo	124	29.25 N	90.08 E
Nyengo Swamp ≡	152	14.51 S	22.07 E
Nyeri	154	0.25 S	36.57 E
Nyerol	140	8.41 N	32.02 E
Nyfer ≃	42	52.02 N	4.50 W
Nygčigen, mys ›	180	65.05 N	172.06 W
Nyhammar	40	60.17 N	14.58 E
Nyhyttan	40	59.40 N	14.48 E
Nyiel	140	6.06 N	31.13 E
Nyika National Park ♠	154	10.48 S	33.48 E
Nyika Plateau ⩘[1]	154	10.40 S	33.50 E
Nyimba	154	14.35 S	30.52 E
Nyingchi	120	29.32 N	94.25 E
Nyíradony	30	47.41 N	21.55 E
Nyírbátor	30	47.50 N	22.08 E
Nyíregyháza	30	47.59 N	21.43 E
Nykøbing, Dan.	26	56.48 N	8.52 E
Nykøbing, Dan.	41	55.55 N	11.41 E
Nykøbing, Dan.	41	54.46 N	11.53 E
Nyköping	40	58.45 N	17.00 E
Nykroppa	40	59.38 N	14.18 E
Nykvarn	40	59.11 N	17.26 E
Nyland	26	63.00 N	17.46 E
Nyland Acres	228	34.14 N	119.09 W
Nylga, Ross.	80	56.46 N	52.22 E
Nylga, Ross.	89	51.38 N	127.35 E
Nylstroom	156	24.42 S	28.20 E
Nymagee	166	32.04 S	146.20 E
Nymboida ≃	166	29.39 S	152.30 E
Nymburk	30	50.11 N	15.03 E
Nymphenburg ◆[8]	60	48.09 N	11.30 E
Nynäshamn	40	58.54 N	17.57 E
Nyngan	166	31.34 S	147.11 E
Nyoma	120	33.11 N	78.38 E
Nyon	58	46.23 N	6.14 E
Nyong ≃	152	3.17 N	9.54 E
Nyons	62	44.22 N	5.08 E
Nyord I	41	55.03 N	12.13 E
Nyou	150	12.46 N	1.56 W
Nýřany	60	49.43 N	13.12 E
Nyrov	24	60.42 N	56.40 E
Nýrsko	60	49.18 N	13.09 E
Nyš	89	51.31 N	142.46 E
Nysa, Pol.	30	50.29 N	17.20 E
Nyša, Ross.	80	56.23 N	51.51 E
Nysa Kłodzka ≃	30	50.49 N	17.50 E
Nysa Łużycka (Neisse) (Nisa) ≃	30	52.04 N	14.46 E
Nyslott → Savonlinna	26	61.52 N	28.53 E
Nysø	41	55.08 N	12.02 E
Nyssa	202	43.52 N	116.59 W
Nysted	41	54.40 N	11.45 E
Nytva	86	57.56 N	55.20 E
Nyūdō-zaki ›	92	40.00 N	139.42 E
Nyugati Pályaudvar ◆[5]	264c	47.31 N	19.04 E
Nyūkawa	94	36.10 N	137.19 E
Nyumba ya Mungu Dam ◆[6]	154	3.51 S	37.28 E
Nyungwe	154	10.16 S	34.07 E
Nyunzu	154	5.57 S	28.01 E
Nyuri	120	27.42 N	92.13 E
Nyūzen	94	36.56 N	137.30 E
Nyvång	41	56.08 N	12.54 E
Nyvrovo	89	54.19 N	142.36 E
Nyzhankovychi	78	49.40 N	22.47 E
Nyzhni Sirohozy	78	46.50 N	34.23 E
Nyzhniy Rohachyk	78	47.21 N	34.02 E
Nyzhn'obaranykivka	83	49.05 N	39.51 E
Nyzhn'ohirs'kyy	78	45.27 N	34.44 E
Nyzhn'oteple	83	48.48 N	39.23 E
Nyzhnya Duvanka	83	49.35 N	38.10 E
Nyzhnya Krynka	83	48.07 N	38.11 E
Nyzhnya Vil'khova	83	48.44 N	39.35 E
Nyzhnye	83	48.46 N	38.37 E
Nyzy	78	50.47 N	34.46 E
Nzaba	273b	4.06 S	15.16 E
Nzébéla	150	8.05 N	9.06 W
Nzega	154	4.13 S	33.11 E
Nzéla	152	1.25 S	12.39 E
Nzérékoré	150	7.45 N	8.49 W
N'zeto	152	7.14 S	12.52 E
Nzheleledam ⊜[1]	156	22.44 S	30.06 E
Nzi ≃	150	5.57 N	4.50 W
Nzima	154	3.03 S	32.48 E
Nziro	152	3.17 N	24.06 E
Nzo ≃	150	6.16 N	7.03 W
Nzoia ≃	154	0.03 N	33.57 E
Nzubuka	154	4.45 S	32.50 E
Nzwani (Anjouan) I	157a	12.15 S	44.25 E

≃	River	Fluß	Río	Rivière	Rio
≍	Canal	Kanal	Canal	Canal	Canal
∟	Waterfall, Rapids	Wasserfall, Stromschnellen	Cascada, Rápidos	Chute d'eau, Rapides	Cascata, Rápidos
ʞ	Strait	Meeresstraße	Estrecho	Détroit	Estreito
⊂	Bay, Gulf	Bucht, Golf	Bahía, Golfo	Baie, Golfe	Baía, Golfo
⊜	Lake, Lakes	See, Seen	Lago, Lagos	Lac, Lacs	Lago, Lagos
≡	Swamp	Sumpf	Pantano	Marais	Pântano
⊓	Ice Features, Glacier	Eis- und Gletscherformen	Accidentes Glaciales	Formes glaciaires	Acidentes glaciares
⫪	Other Hydrographic Features	Andere Hydrographische Objekte	Otros Elementos Hidrográficos	Autres données hydrographiques	Outros acidentes hidrográficos

✢	Submarine Features	Untermeerische Objekte	Accidentes Submarinos	Formes de relief sous-marin	Acidentes submarinos
□	Political Unit	Politische Einheit	Unidad Politica	Entité politique	Unidade política
ᴗ	Cultural Institution	Kulturelle Institution	Institución Cultural	Institution culturelle	Instituição cultural
⊥	Historical Site	Historische Stätte	Sitio Histórico	Site historique	Sitio histórico
♠	Recreational Site	Erholungs- und Ferienort	Sitio de Recreo	Centre de loisirs	Area de Lazer
⊠	Airport	Flughafen	Aeropuerto	Aéroport	Aeroporto
■	Military Installation	Militäranlage	Instalación Militar	Installation militaire	Instalação militar
◆	Miscellaneous	Verschiedenes	Misceláneo	Divers	Diversos

ENGLISH / DEUTSCH

O

Name / Name	Page / Seite	Lat.°′ / Breite°′	Long.°′ / Länge°′ E = Ost
Oa, Mull of ›	46	55.35 N	6.20 W
Oacoma	198	43.47 N	99.23 W
Oadby	42	52.36 N	1.04 W
Oad Street	260	51.20 N	0.41 E
Oahe, Lake ⊜[1]	198	45.30 N	100.25 W
Oahe Dam ◆[6]	198	44.21 N	100.23 W
Oahu I	229c	21.30 N	158.00 W
Oak ≃	184	49.51 N	100.28 W
O-Akan-dake ∧	92a	43.27 N	144.10 E
Oakbank, Austl.	162	33.03 S	140.35 E
Oakbank, Austl.	168b	34.59 S	138.51 E
Oak Bay	224	48.27 N	123.18 W
Oak Beach	276	40.38 N	73.17 W
Oak Bluffs	207	41.27 N	70.33 W
Oakboro	192	35.13 N	80.19 W
Oak Brook	278	41.49 N	87.55 W
Oakbrook Center ◆[9]	278	41.52 N	87.57 W
Oakbrook Terrace	278	41.52 N	87.58 W
Oakburn	184	50.35 N	100.32 W
Oak City, N.C., U.S.	192	35.57 N	77.18 W
Oak City, Ut,. U.S.	200	39.22 N	112.20 W
Oak Creek, Co., U.S.	200	40.16 N	106.57 W
Oak Creek, Wi., U.S.	216	42.53 N	87.55 W
Oak Creek ≃, U.S.	198	45.39 N	100.31 W
Oak Creek ≃, Az., U.S.	200	34.41 N	111.56 W
Oak Creek ≃, Co., U.S.	200	40.25 N	106.50 W
Oak Creek ≃, Ks., U.S.	198	39.29 N	98.28 W
Oak Creek ≃, N.D., U.S.	198	48.38 N	100.24 W
Oak Creek ≃, Tx., U.S.	196	31.48 N	100.13 W
Oakdale, Ca., U.S.	226	37.46 N	120.50 W
Oakdale, Ct., U.S.	207	41.27 N	72.09 W
Oakdale, Il., U.S.	219	38.16 N	89.30 W
Oakdale, La., U.S.	194	30.48 N	92.39 W
Oakdale, Ma., U.S.	207	42.23 N	71.47 W
Oakdale, Ne., U.S.	198	42.04 N	97.58 W
Oakdale, N.J., U.S.	285	39.59 N	74.49 W
Oakdale, N.Y., U.S.	210	40.44 N	73.08 W
Oakdale, Pa., U.S.	214	40.23 N	80.11 W
Oakdale, Tn., U.S.	192	35.59 N	84.33 W
Oakdale Woods	278	41.56 N	87.58 W
Oakengates	42	52.42 N	2.28 W
Oakes	198	46.08 N	98.05 W
Oakesdale	202	47.07 N	117.14 W
Oakey	171a	27.26 S	151.43 E
Oakeys Brook ≃	276	40.25 N	74.30 W
Oakfield, Me., U.S.	188	46.05 N	68.09 W
Oakfield, N.Y., U.S.	210	43.03 N	78.16 W
Oakfield, Wi., U.S.	190	43.41 N	88.32 W
Oakford, Il., U.S.	219	40.06 N	89.58 W
Oakford, In., U.S.	216	40.25 N	86.06 W
Oakford, Pa., U.S.	208	40.09 N	74.58 W
Oak Forest	216	41.36 N	87.44 W
Oakgrove, Eng., U.K.	262	53.13 N	2.07 W
Oak Grove, La., U.S.	194	32.51 N	91.23 W
Oak Grove, Or., U.S.	224	45.25 N	122.38 W
Oak Hall	208	37.56 N	75.33 W
Oakham	42	52.40 N	0.43 W
Oak Harbor, Oh., U.S.	214	41.30 N	83.09 W
Oak Harbor, Wa., U.S.	224	48.17 N	122.38 W
Oak Hill, De., U.S.	285	39.44 N	75.36 W
Oak Hill, Fl., U.S.	220	28.51 N	80.51 W
Oak Hill, Mi., U.S.	190	44.13 N	86.18 W
Oak Hill, N.Y., U.S.	210	42.25 N	74.09 W
Oak Hill, Oh., U.S.	188	38.54 N	82.34 W
Oak Hill, W.V., U.S.	188	37.58 N	81.08 W
Oakhurst, Ca., U.S.	226	37.19 N	119.40 W
Oakhurst, N.J., U.S.	208	40.16 N	74.01 W
Oakhurst, Tx., U.S.	222	30.44 N	95.19 W
Oak Island I, N.S., Can.	186	44.31 N	64.18 W
Oak Island I, N.Y., U.S.	276	40.39 N	73.18 W
Oak Knolls	204	34.51 N	120.27 W
Oak Lake	184	49.47 N	100.38 W
Oak Lake ⊜, Mb., Can.	184	49.40 N	100.45 W
Oak Lake ⊜, On., Can.	184	50.26 N	93.50 W
Oak Lake ⊜, On., Can.	212	44.36 N	77.55 W
Oakland, On., Can.	214	42.09 N	82.36 W
Oakland, Ca., U.S.	226	37.48 N	122.16 W
Oakland, Ca., U.S.	282	37.48 N	122.16 W
Oakland, Fl., U.S.	220	28.33 N	81.38 W
Oakland, Il., U.S.	194	39.39 N	88.01 W
Oakland, Ia., U.S.	198	41.18 N	95.23 W
Oakland, Me., U.S.	188	44.32 N	69.43 W
Oakland, Md., U.S.	188	39.24 N	79.24 W
Oakland, Md., U.S.	284c	38.51 N	76.55 W
Oakland, Ms., U.S.	194	34.03 N	89.54 W
Oakland, Ne., U.S.	198	41.50 N	96.28 W
Oakland, N.J., U.S.	210	41.00 N	74.15 W
Oakland, Or., U.S.	202	43.25 N	123.17 W
Oakland, Pa., U.S.	210	41.57 N	75.36 W
Oakland, Pa., U.S.	214	40.59 N	80.22 W
Oakland, Tx., U.S.	222	29.36 N	96.50 W
Oakland ◻[6]	216	42.40 N	83.23 W
Oakland ◆[8]	279b	40.26 N	79.58 W
Oakland-Alameda County Coliseum ♠	282	37.45 N	122.12 W
Oakland Army Base ■	282	37.49 N	122.19 W
Oakland Beach	214	41.37 N	80.18 W
Oakland City	194	38.20 N	87.20 W
Oakland Gardens ◆[8]	276	40.45 N	73.45 W
Oakland Mall ◆[9]	281	42.32 N	83.07 W
Oakland Park	220	26.10 N	80.07 W
Oakland-Pontiac Airport ⊠	281	42.40 N	83.24 W
Oaklands	168b	35.00 S	137.41 E
Oaklands ◆[8]	273d	26.09 S	28.04 E
Oakland Southwest Airport ⊠	281	42.30 N	83.37 W
Oakland University ♉[2]	281	42.41 N	83.13 W
Oak Lane Manor	285	39.47 N	75.32 W
Oak Lawn, Il., U.S.	216	41.43 N	87.45 W
Oaklawn, Ks., U.S.	198	37.36 N	97.17 W
Oaklawn, Md., U.S.	284c	38.47 N	76.57 W
Oakleigh	169	37.54 S	145.06 E
Oakleigh South	274b	37.56 S	145.05 E
Oakley, Eng., U.K.	42	51.15 N	1.11 W
Oakley, Scot., U.K.	46	56.04 N	3.33 W
Oakley, Ca., U.S.	226	37.58 N	121.43 W
Oakley, Id., U.S.	202	42.14 N	113.52 W
Oakley, Il., U.S.	219	39.53 N	88.48 W
Oakley, Ks., U.S.	198	39.08 N	100.51 W
Oakley Park	216	42.34 N	83.30 W
Oaklyn	285	39.54 N	75.05 W
Oakman	194	33.42 N	87.23 W
Oakmont	214	40.31 N	79.50 W
Oak Mountain State Park ♠	194	33.22 N	86.41 W
Oakmulgee Creek ≃	194	32.28 N	87.09 W
Oak Neck ›[1]	276	40.54 N	73.34 W
Oak Neck Point ›	276	40.55 N	73.34 W
Oakohay Creek ≃	194	31.44 N	89.25 W
Oak Orchard Creek ≃	210	43.22 N	78.12 W
Oak Orchard Swamp ⩩	210	43.07 N	78.18 W
Oakover ≃	162	20.43 S	120.33 E
Oak Park, Austl.	274b	37.43 S	144.55 E
Oak Park, Ca., U.S.	228	34.11 N	118.45 W
Oak Park, Il., U.S.	216	41.53 N	87.47 W
Oak Park, Mi., U.S.	216	42.27 N	83.10 W
Oak Park, Pa., U.S.	285	40.15 N	75.18 W
Oak Point	184	50.30 N	98.00 W
Oakridge, Ca., U.S.	226	38.03 N	121.20 W
Oak Ridge, N.J., U.S.	210	41.03 N	74.29 W
Oakridge, Or., U.S.	202	43.44 N	122.27 W
Oak Ridge, Pa., U.S.	214	41.00 N	79.18 W
Oak Ridge, Tn., U.S.	192	36.00 N	84.16 W
Oak Ridge Lake	276	41.00 N	74.32 W
Oak Ridge National Laboratory ♉[3]	192	36.00 N	84.15 W
Oak Ridge Reservoir ⊜[1]	276	41.03 N	74.30 W
Oaks	285	40.08 N	81.28 W
Oaks Corners	210	42.56 N	77.01 W
Oak Shades	276	40.26 N	74.13 W
Oakton	284c	38.52 N	77.18 W
Oaktown	194	38.52 N	87.26 W
Oakura	172	39.07 S	173.57 E
Oak Valley, N.J., U.S.	208	39.48 N	75.09 W
Oak Valley, Va., U.S.	284c	38.54 N	77.18 W
Oak View, Ca., U.S.	228	34.24 N	119.18 W
Oak View, Md., U.S.	284c	39.01 N	76.59 W
Oakview, N.J., U.S.	285	39.51 N	75.09 W
Oakview Beach	212	44.29 N	80.03 W
Oakville, Mb., Can.	184	49.56 N	97.58 W
Oakville, On., Can.	212	43.27 N	79.41 W
Oakville, Ct., U.S.	207	41.35 N	73.05 W
Oakville, In., U.S.	218	40.05 N	85.23 W
Oakville, Mo., U.S.	219	38.28 N	90.18 W
Oakville, Wa., U.S.	224	46.50 N	123.13 W
Oakwood, On., Can.	212	44.20 N	78.53 W
Oakwood, N.J., U.S.	285	39.52 N	74.50 W
Oakwood, Oh., U.S.	214	41.23 N	81.29 W
Oakwood, Oh., U.S.	216	41.05 N	84.22 W
Oakwood, Oh., U.S.	218	39.44 N	84.10 W
Oakwood, Tx., U.S.	222	31.35 N	95.50 W
Oakwood Beach	208	39.33 N	75.31 W
Oakwood Park ♠	279a	41.26 N	82.06 W
Oamaru	172	45.06 S	170.58 E
Ōamishirasato	94	35.31 N	140.19 E
Ōana	268	35.45 N	140.04 E
Oancea	38	45.55 N	28.06 E
Ōarai	94	36.18 N	140.34 E
Oaro	172	42.31 S	173.30 E
Ōasa	96	34.46 N	132.28 E
Oat Creek ≃	226	38.50 N	121.56 W
Oates Coast ⏏[2]	9	70.00 S	160.00 E
Oatka Creek ≃	210	43.01 N	77.44 W
Oatlands	166	42.18 S	147.21 E
Oatley	274a	33.59 S	151.05 E
Oatley Park ♠	274a	33.59 S	151.04 E
Oatman	200	35.01 N	114.22 W
Oaxaca ◻[3]	234	17.00 N	96.30 W
Oaxaca [de Juárez]	234	17.03 N	96.43 W
Ob' ≃	72	66.45 N	69.30 E
Oba ≃	190	48.55 N	84.17 W
Obaba	152	2.00 S	16.10 E
Obabika Lake ⊜	190	47.05 N	80.17 W
Obala	152	4.10 N	11.32 E
Oba Lake ⊜	190	48.38 N	84.18 W
Obama, Nihon	92	32.43 N	130.13 E
Obama, Nihon	94	35.30 N	135.45 E
Obama-wan c	94	35.30 N	135.42 E
Oban, Austl.	166	21.14 S	139.03 E
Oban, Nig.	150	5.17 N	8.35 E
Oban, Scot., U.K.	46	56.25 N	5.29 W
Obanazawa	92	38.36 N	140.24 E
Obando	269f	14.43 N	120.56 E
Oban Hills ⋏[2]	150	5.35 N	8.35 E
Obara	94	35.15 N	137.18 E
Obata	94	34.30 N	136.40 E
Ob' Bay c	9	70.35 S	163.22 E
Obbo	144	3.36 N	38.54 E
Obbola	26	63.42 N	20.19 E
Občuga	76	54.30 N	29.22 E
Obdach	61	47.04 N	14.41 E
Obed	182	53.33 N	117.12 W
Obed ≃	192	36.04 N	84.39 W
Obeliai	76	55.56 N	25.48 E
Obelisk ∧	172	45.20 S	169.12 E
Oberá	252	27.29 S	55.08 W
Oberägeri	58	47.08 N	8.37 E
Oberalppass)(	58	46.39 N	8.40 E
Oberalpstock ∧	58	46.44 N	8.46 E
Oberammergau	64	47.35 N	11.04 E
Oberau	64	47.33 N	11.08 E
Oberaudorf	64	47.39 N	12.10 E
Oberbauer	263	51.17 N	7.26 E
Oberbayern ◻[5]	60	48.15 N	11.45 E
Oberbieber	56	50.28 N	7.29 E
Oberbonsfeld	263	51.22 N	7.08 E
Oberbrügge	263	51.11 N	7.34 E
Obercunnersdorf	54	51.02 N	14.40 E
Oberdiessbach	58	46.51 N	7.38 E
Oberdolling	60	48.50 N	11.35 E
Oberdorla	54	51.10 N	10.25 E
Oberdrauburg	64	46.45 N	12.58 E
Oberelfringhausen	263	51.20 N	7.11 E
Ober Engadin V	58	46.37 N	9.58 E
Oberengstringen	58	47.25 N	8.28 E
Oberer See → Superior, Lake ⊜	190	48.00 N	88.00 W
Oberfranken ◻[5]	60	49.50 N	11.20 E
Obergeis	56	50.54 N	9.35 E
Ober-Grafendorf	61	48.09 N	15.33 E
Obergum	52	53.20 N	6.31 E
Obergünzburg	58	47.51 N	10.25 E
Obergurgl	64	46.52 N	11.01 E
Obergurig	54	51.07 N	14.24 E
Oberhaan	263	51.13 N	7.02 E
Oberhaching	60	48.02 N	11.37 E
Oberharmersbach	58	48.22 N	8.07 E
Oberhaslach	58	48.33 N	7.20 E
Oberhausen	56	51.28 N	6.50 E
Oberhof	54	50.41 N	10.44 E
Oberhofen	58	46.44 N	7.40 E
Oberinntal V	64	47.13 N	10.45 E
Oberjettingen	56	48.34 N	8.46 E
Oberjoch	58	47.31 N	10.23 E
Ober-Kassel ◆[8]	263	51.14 N	6.46 E
Oberkirch	58	48.31 N	8.05 E
Oberkirchbach	264b	48.17 N	16.12 E
Oberkirchen	56	51.09 N	8.22 E
Oberkochen	56	48.47 N	10.06 E
Oberkotzau	54	50.16 N	11.56 E
Oberlaa ◆[8]	264b	48.08 N	16.24 E
Oberlaapark ♠	264b	48.08 N	16.25 E
Oberlausitz ◻[9]	54	51.15 N	14.00 E
Oberlin, Ks., U.S.	198	39.49 N	100.31 W
Oberlin, La., U.S.	194	30.37 N	92.45 W
Oberlin, Oh., U.S.	214	41.17 N	82.13 W
Oberlin, Pa., U.S.	208	40.14 N	76.49 W
Oberloisdorf	61	47.27 N	16.30 E
Oberlungwitz	54	50.47 N	12.44 E
Obermarchtal	58	48.14 N	9.34 E
Obermeiser	56	51.26 N	9.19 E
Obermieming	64	47.18 N	10.59 E
Obermodern	56	48.51 N	7.32 E
Obermoschel	56	49.44 N	7.46 E
Obermühl	61	48.27 N	13.55 E
Obermünstertal	58	47.52 N	7.49 E
Obernai	58	48.28 N	7.29 E
Obernbeck	52	52.12 N	8.41 E
Obernberg am Inn	60	48.19 N	13.20 E
Obernburg am Main	56	49.50 N	9.08 E
Oberndorf	52	53.45 N	9.08 E
Oberndorf am Neckar	58	48.18 N	8.34 E
Oberndorf bei Salzburg	64	47.57 N	12.56 E
Oberndorf in Tirol	64	47.30 N	12.23 E
Oberne	171b	35.24 S	147.50 E
Oberne Hill ∧[2]	171b	35.26 S	147.53 E
Obernhausen	56	50.29 N	9.56 E
Obernkirchen	52	52.16 N	9.07 E
Obernzell	60	48.34 N	13.39 E
Oberoderwitz	54	50.58 N	14.42 E
Oberon	170	33.43 S	149.52 E
Oberösterreich ◻[3]	30	48.15 N	14.00 E
Oberpfalz ◻[5]	60	49.30 N	12.10 E
Oberpleis	56	50.43 N	7.16 E
Oberpullendorf	61	47.31 N	16.31 E
Ober-Ramstadt	56	49.49 N	8.44 E
Oberried	58	46.44 N	7.58 E
Oberriet	58	47.19 N	9.33 E
Oberrimsingen	58	47.59 N	7.40 E
Oberröblingen	54	51.26 N	11.18 E
Ober Sankt Veit ◆[8]	264b	48.11 N	16.16 E
Oberscheidental	56	49.30 N	9.09 E
Oberscheinfeld	56	49.42 N	10.26 E
Oberscheld	56	50.44 N	8.20 E
Oberschleissheim	60	48.15 N	11.34 E
Oberschöneweide ◆[8]	264a	52.28 N	13.31 E
Oberseebach	56	48.58 N	7.59 E
Obersickte	54	52.13 N	10.38 E
Oberspier	54	51.19 N	10.51 E
Oberstadtfeld	56	50.10 N	6.46 E
Oberstaufen	58	47.33 N	10.01 E
Oberstdorf	58	47.24 N	10.16 E
Obersteinbach	56	49.02 N	7.41 E
Oberstreu	56	50.24 N	10.17 E
Obersuhl	56	50.56 N	10.02 E
Obersulm	56	49.08 N	9.27 E
Obertheres	56	50.01 N	10.26 E
Obertilliach	64	46.42 N	12.37 E
Obertraubling	60	48.58 N	12.10 E
Obertraun	64	47.33 N	13.41 E
Obertrum	64	47.56 N	13.05 E
Obertrumer See ⊜	60	47.58 N	13.06 E
Obertürken	60	48.19 N	12.50 E
Obertyn	78	48.42 N	25.11 E
Oberueckersee ⊜	54	53.12 N	13.52 E
Oberursel	56	50.11 N	8.35 E
Oberuzwil	58	47.26 N	9.08 E
Obervellach	64	46.56 N	13.12 E
Oberviechtach	60	49.28 N	12.25 E
Obervolta → Burkina Faso ◻[1]	150	13.00 N	1.30 W
Oberwald	58	46.32 N	8.21 E
Oberwart	61	47.17 N	16.13 E
Oberweissbach	54	50.35 N	11.08 E
Oberwengern	263	51.23 N	7.22 E
Oberwesel	56	50.06 N	7.43 E
Oberwiesenthal	54	50.25 N	12.59 E
Oberwolfach	58	48.19 N	8.12 E
Oberwölz Stadt	61	47.13 N	14.17 E
Oberzeiring	61	47.15 N	14.29 E
Obetz	218	39.52 N	82.57 W
Obey, East Fork ≃	192	36.27 N	85.07 W
Obey, West Fork ≃	192	36.27 N	85.09 W
Obgruiten	263	51.13 N	7.01 E
Obhausen	54	51.23 N	11.39 E
Obi	150	8.22 N	8.46 E
Obi, Kepulauan II	164	1.30 S	127.45 E
Obi, Pulau I	164	1.30 S	127.45 E
Obi, Selat ⊍	164	0.52 S	127.33 E
Obiaruku	150	5.51 N	6.09 E
Obichingou ≃	85	38.53 N	70.01 E
Óbidos	250	1.55 S	55.31 W
Obi-Garm	85	38.43 N	69.42 E
Obihiro	92a	42.55 N	143.12 E
Obikanda	85	39.10 N	67.10 E
Obikhody	78	51.02 N	28.59 E
Obilatu, Pulau I	108	1.25 S	127.20 E
Obil'noje	80	47.31 N	44.25 E
Obing	60	48.00 N	12.24 E
Obion	194	36.15 N	89.11 W
Obion ≃	194	35.55 N	89.39 W
Obion, Middle Fork ≃	194	36.13 N	88.56 W
Obion, Rutherford Fork ≃	194	36.17 N	89.01 W
Obion, South Fork ≃	194	36.17 N	89.03 W
Obion Creek ≃	194	36.35 N	89.11 W
Obiou, Grande Tête de l' ∧	62	44.46 N	5.50 E
Obira	92a	44.00 N	141.35 E
Obitsu ≃	94	35.24 N	139.54 E
Objačevo	24	60.20 N	49.34 E
Oblačnaja, gora ∧	89	43.45 N	134.10 E
Öblarn	61	47.27 N	13.59 E
Oblastnaja	80	56.59 N	52.37 E
Oblivskaja	80	48.32 N	42.30 E
Oblong	194	39.00 N	87.54 W
Oblučje	89	49.03 N	131.04 E
Obninsk	82	55.05 N	36.37 E
Obnora ≃	76	58.14 N	40.58 E
Obnova	38	43.26 N	24.59 E
Obo	154	5.24 N	26.30 E
Obobogorap	158	27.18 S	20.04 E
Obock	144	11.59 N	43.16 E
Obojan'	78	51.13 N	36.16 E
Ō-boke ♠	96	33.55 N	133.46 E
Obokote	154	0.52 S	26.19 E
Obol'	76	55.22 N	29.17 E
Obol' ≃	76	55.24 N	29.02 E
Oboldino	265b	55.53 N	37.56 E
Obolon'	78	49.36 N	32.52 E
Oborniki	30	52.39 N	16.51 E
Obot	144	4.30 N	37.20 E
Obouya	152	0.56 S	15.43 E
Oboz'orskij	24	63.28 N	40.18 E
Obra ≃	30	52.36 N	15.28 E
Obrazcovo-Travino	80	45.58 N	48.02 E
Obree, Mount ∧	164	9.30 S	148.05 E
Obrenovac	38	44.39 N	20.12 E
O'Brien	202	42.04 N	123.42 W
O'Brien Coulee V	202	48.38 N	110.22 W
Obrighoven-Lackhausen	52	51.40 N	6.38 E
Obrovac	36	44.12 N	15.41 E
Obrovo	76	52.30 N	25.34 E
Obručeva, gora ∧	88	53.36 N	113.52 E
Obručevka	85	42.30 N	69.05 E
Obruk	130	38.10 N	33.12 E
Obryta	54	53.13 N	14.59 E
Obryvistoje	89	48.46 N	144.40 E
Obša ≃	76	55.55 N	32.32 E
Obšarovka	80	53.07 N	48.52 E
Obščij Syrt ∧	80	52.00 N	51.30 E
Observation Peak ∧	204	40.46 N	120.10 W
Observatoire, Caye de l' I	160	21.25 S	158.50 E
Observatory Inlet c	182	55.10 N	129.54 W
Obskaja guba c	72	69.00 N	73.00 E
Obsteig	64	47.18 N	10.56 E
Obtove	78	51.37 N	33.13 E
Ob' Trench ⊹[1]	14	33.00 S	98.00 E
Ōbu	94	35.00 N	136.58 E
Obu ◆[8]	270	34.44 N	135.09 E
Obuasi	150	6.14 N	1.39 W
Obubra	150	6.05 N	8.21 E
Obuchova	76	56.06 N	32.22 E
Obuchovka	86	46.13 N	81.05 E
Obuchovo, Ross.	82	55.50 N	38.16 E
Obuchovo, Ross.	82	56.09 N	36.55 E
Óbuda ◆[8]	264c	47.33 N	19.02 E
Óbudai-sziget I	264c	47.33 N	19.04 E
Obudu	150	6.40 N	9.09 E
Obukhiv	78	50.08 N	30.37 E
Obukhovychi	78	51.00 N	29.46 E
Obuse	94	36.42 N	138.19 E
Obushkong Lake ⊜	190	47.42 N	80.48 W
Obuškovo	82	55.47 N	37.02 E
Obu-tōge)(	270	34.44 N	135.10 E
Obva ≃	86	58.32 N	55.18 E
Obvinsk	86	58.29 N	54.51 E
Obwalden ◻[3]	58	46.50 N	8.14 E
Obytichna kosa ›[2]	78	46.33 N	36.13 E
Obytichna zatoka c	78	46.35 N	36.00 E
Obžericha	80	57.11 N	42.58 E
Očakovo ◆[8]	265b	55.41 N	37.27 E
Ocala	192	29.11 N	82.08 W
Ocallí	248	6.09 S	78.18 W
Očamčira	84	42.44 N	41.28 E
Ocamo ≃	246	2.48 N	65.14 W
Ocampo, Méx.	232	28.11 N	108.23 W
Ocampo, Méx.	232	27.20 N	102.21 W
Ocampo, Méx.	234	21.39 N	101.30 W
Ocampo, Méx.	234	22.50 N	99.20 W
Ocaña, Col.	246	8.15 N	73.20 W
Ocaña, Esp.	34	39.56 N	3.31 W
Ocate Creek ≃	196	36.17 N	104.30 W
Occaquan ≃	208	38.40 N	77.14 W
Occaquan Reservoir ⊜[1]	208	38.43 N	77.22 W
Očchamuri	84	41.52 N	41.50 E
Occhieppo Inferiore	62	45.33 N	8.01 E
Occhiobello	64	44.55 N	11.35 E
Occhito, Lago di ⊜[1]	66	41.35 N	14.54 E
Occidental, Cordillera ⋏, Col.	246	5.00 N	76.00 W
Occidental, Cordillera ⋏, Perú	248	10.00 S	77.00 W
Occidental College ♉[2]	280	34.08 N	118.13 W
Occidental de Zapata, Ciénaga ⩩	240p	22.25 N	81.20 W
Occimiano	62	45.03 N	8.30 E
Occoquan	208	38.41 N	77.15 W
Occoquan Bay c	208	38.37 N	77.13 W
Ocean ◻[6]	208	39.58 N	74.12 W
Oceana	192	37.41 N	81.37 W
Oceana Naval Air Station ■	208	36.50 N	76.02 W
Ocean Bay Park	276	40.39 N	73.08 W
Ocean Beach	276	40.38 N	73.18 W
Ocean Bluff	207	42.05 N	70.39 W
Ocean Breeze Park	220	27.15 N	80.14 W
Ocean Cape ›	180	59.30 N	139.45 W
Ocean City, Md., U.S.	208	38.20 N	75.05 W
Ocean City, N.J., U.S.	208	39.16 N	74.34 W
Ocean City, Wa., U.S.	224	47.04 N	124.09 W
Ocean Falls	182	52.21 N	127.40 W
Ocean Gate	208	39.55 N	74.08 W
Ocean Grove, Austl.	169	38.16 S	144.32 E
Ocean Grove, Ma., U.S.	207	41.43 N	71.12 W
Ocean Heights	207	41.24 N	70.33 W
Ocean Island → Banaba I	174d	0.52 S	169.35 E
Ocean Lake ⊜[1]	202	43.11 N	108.36 W
Oceano	204	35.06 N	120.37 W
Ocean Park, B.C., Can.	224	49.02 N	122.53 W
Ocean Park, Wa., U.S.	224	46.29 N	124.02 W
Ocean Park ♠	271d	22.15 N	114.09 E
Ocean Port	276	40.19 N	74.00 W
Ocean Shores	224	47.01 N	124.09 W
Oceanside, Ca., U.S.	228	33.11 N	117.22 W
Oceanside, N.Y., U.S.	210	40.38 N	73.38 W
Ocean Springs	194	30.24 N	88.49 W
Ocean View, De., U.S.	208	38.32 N	75.05 W
Ocean View, N.J., U.S.	208	39.10 N	74.44 W
Oceanville	208	39.28 N	74.27 W
Oceola	214	40.51 N	83.06 W
Očer	80	57.53 N	54.42 E
O. C. Fisher Lake ⊜[1]	196	31.30 N	100.30 W
Ocha	89	53.34 N	142.56 E
Ochagavía, Canal ≊	286e	33.30 S	70.49 W
Ochakiv	78	46.37 N	31.33 E
Ochanomizu Women's University ♉[2]	268	35.43 N	139.44 E
Ochansk	86	57.43 N	55.23 E
Ochapowace Indian Reserve ◆[4]	184	50.30 N	102.24 W
Ocheretyne	83	48.14 N	37.36 E
Ocheyedan	198	43.24 N	95.32 W
Ocheyedan ≃	198	43.08 N	95.09 W
Ōchi, Nihon	96	34.16 N	134.18 E
Ochi, Nihon	96	33.32 N	133.15 E
Ōchi, Nihon	96	35.04 N	132.36 E
Ochiai	96	35.01 N	133.45 E
Ochiai ◆[8]	268	35.43 N	139.42 E
O'Chiese Indian Reserve ◆[4]	182	52.50 N	115.28 W
Ochil Hills ⋏[2]	46	56.14 N	3.40 W
Ochiltree	44	55.28 N	4.23 W
Ōchise ≃	94	35.03 N	137.46 E
Ochlocknee	192	30.58 N	84.03 W
Ochlockonee ≃	192	29.58 N	84.21 W
Ochoco Creek ≃	202	44.19 N	120.53 W
Ochoco Mountains ⋏	202	44.30 N	120.35 W
Ochopee	220	25.54 N	81.18 W
Ocho Rios	241q	18.25 N	77.07 W
Ochota ≃	74	59.20 N	143.04 E
Ochotsk	74	59.23 N	143.18 E
Ochotskisches Meer → Okhotsk, Sea of ⫧[2]	74	53.00 N	150.00 E
Ochotskoje more → Okhotsk, Sea of ⫧[2]	74	53.00 N	150.00 E
Ochre River	184	51.03 N	99.47 W
Ochsenfurt	56	49.40 N	10.03 E
Ochsenhausen	58	48.04 N	9.56 E
Ochsenwerder ◆[8]	52	53.28 N	10.05 E
Ochta ≃	265a	59.57 N	30.24 E
Ochtrup	52	52.13 N	7.11 E
Ochvat	76	56.46 N	32.27 E
Oci ≃	152	15.14 S	15.16 E
Ocilla	192	31.35 N	83.15 W
Ock ≃	42	51.39 N	1.17 W
Ockelbo	26	60.53 N	16.43 E
Öckerö	26	57.43 N	11.39 E
Ockham	260	51.18 N	0.27 W
Ockholm	41	54.40 N	8.49 E
Ockies	158	31.31 S	21.41 E
Ocklawaha, Lake ⊜[1]	192	29.30 N	81.50 W
Ocmulgee ≃	192	31.58 N	82.32 W
Ocmulgee National Monument ♠	192	32.43 N	83.38 W
Ocna Mureș	38	46.23 N	23.51 E
Ocnița	38	48.24 N	27.29 E
Ocoa, Bahía de c	238	18.22 N	70.39 W
Ocoee	220	28.34 N	81.32 W
Ocoee (Toccoa) ≃	192	35.12 N	84.40 W
Ocoña	248	16.26 S	73.07 W
Ocoña ≃	248	16.28 S	73.07 W
Oconee	219	39.17 N	89.07 W
Oconee ≃	192	31.58 N	82.32 W
Oconee, Lake ⊜[1]	192	33.30 N	83.15 W
Ocongate	248	13.38 S	71.24 W
O'Connell	170	33.32 S	149.44 E
Oconomowoc	216	43.06 N	88.29 W
Oconomowoc ≃	216	43.07 N	88.37 W
Oconomowoc Lake	216	42.37 N	88.28 W
Oconomowoc Lake ⊜	216	43.06 N	88.27 W
Oconto	190	44.53 N	87.51 W
Oconto ≃	190	44.53 N	87.50 W
Oconto, North Branch ≃	190	45.00 N	88.23 W
Oconto Falls	190	44.52 N	88.08 W
Ocós	236	14.31 N	92.11 W
Ocosingo	232	16.54 N	92.07 W
Ocotal	236	13.38 N	86.29 W
Ocotepec	234	17.13 N	93.09 W
Ocotepeque ◻[5]	236	14.30 N	89.00 W
Ocotlán	234	20.21 N	102.46 W
Ocotlán de Morelos	234	16.48 N	96.40 W
Ocoyoacac	234	19.16 N	99.26 W
Ocozocoautla [de Espinosa]	234	16.46 N	93.22 W
Ocracoke	192	35.06 N	75.58 W
Ocracoke Island I	192	35.09 N	75.53 W
Ocre, Monte ∧	66	42.15 N	13.26 E
Ocros	248	10.24 S	77.24 W
Octoraro Creek ≃	208	39.39 N	76.09 W
Octoraro Creek, East Branch ≃	208	39.49 N	76.02 W
Octoraro Creek, West Branch ≃	208	39.49 N	76.05 W
Octoraro Lake ⊜[1]	208	39.48 N	76.02 W
Ocú	236	7.57 N	80.47 W
Ocuilán de Arteaga	234	18.58 N	99.25 W
Ocumare del Tuy	246	10.07 N	66.46 W
Ocuri	248	18.50 S	65.50 W
Ocussi	112	9.12 S	124.21 E
Oda, Ghana	150	5.55 N	0.59 W
Oda, Nihon	96	33.34 N	132.48 E
Ōda, Nihon	96	35.11 N	132.30 E
Oda ≃	96	34.37 N	133.44 E
Oda, Jabal ∧	140	20.21 N	36.39 E
Ŏdaejin	98	41.34 N	129.40 E
Odae-san Kukrip Kongwŏn ♠	98	37.46 N	128.37 E
Ōdai	94	34.24 N	136.25 E
Ōdaigahara-zan ∧	92	34.11 N	136.05 E
Odaka	92	37.34 N	141.00 E
Ödåkra	41	56.06 N	12.44 E
Odanakumadona	156	20.53 S	24.45 E
Ōdate	92	40.16 N	140.34 E
Odawara	94	35.15 N	139.10 E
Odayeri ◆[8]	267b	41.14 N	28.51 E
Odda	26	60.04 N	6.33 E
Odden	41	55.58 N	11.22 E
Odder	41	55.58 N	10.10 E
Oddville	218	38.27 N	84.15 W
Odebolt	198	42.18 N	95.15 W
Ödeby	40	59.24 N	15.25 E
Odei ≃	184	56.06 N	96.55 W
Odeleite, Ribeira de ≃	34	37.21 N	7.27 W
Odell, Il., U.S.	216	41.00 N	88.31 W
Odell, Ne., U.S.	198	40.03 N	96.48 W
Odell, Or., U.S.	224	45.37 N	121.32 W
Odell, Tx., U.S.	196	34.21 N	99.25 W
Odell Lake ⊜	202	43.34 N	122.00 W
Odelzhausen	60	48.19 N	11.12 E
Odem	196	27.57 N	97.34 W
Odemira	34	37.36 N	8.38 W
Ödemiş	130	38.13 N	27.59 E
Ödenburg → Sopron	30	47.41 N	16.36 E
Odendaalsrus	158	27.48 S	26.45 E
Odensbacken	40	59.10 N	15.32 E
Odense	41	55.24 N	10.23 E
Odense ≃	41	55.26 N	10.26 E
Odense Fjord c	41	55.30 N	10.34 E
Odenthal	56	51.02 N	7.07 E
Odenton	208	39.05 N	76.42 W
Odenwald ⋏	56	49.40 N	9.00 E
Oder ≃, Dtsch.	52	51.40 N	10.06 E
Oder (Odra) ≃, Europe	30	53.32 N	14.38 E
Oderberg	54	52.52 N	14.02 E
Oderbruch ◆[1]	54	52.40 N	14.15 E
Oderen	58	47.55 N	6.59 E
Oderhaff (Zalew Szczeciński) c	54	53.46 N	14.14 E
Oder-Havel-Kanal ≊	54	52.52 N	14.02 E
Oder-Spree-Kanal ≊	54	52.23 N	13.41 E
Odertalsperre ◆[6]	54	51.38 N	10.30 E
Oderzo	64	45.47 N	12.29 E
Odesa	78	46.28 N	30.44 E
Odesa ◻[4]	78	47.30 N	30.00 E
Ödeshög	26	58.14 N	14.39 E
Odessa, On., Can.	212	44.17 N	76.43 W
Odessa → Odesa, Ukr.	78	46.28 N	30.44 E
Odessa, De., U.S.	208	39.27 N	75.39 W
Odessa, Fl., U.S.	220	28.11 N	82.35 W
Odessa, Mo., U.S.	194	38.59 N	93.57 W
Odessa, N.Y., U.S.	210	42.20 N	76.47 W
Odessa, Tx., U.S.	196	31.50 N	102.22 W
Odessa, Wa., U.S.	202	47.20 N	118.41 W
Odessa Lake ⊜	212	44.19 N	76.41 W
Odesskoje	86	54.13 N	72.58 E
Odiakwe	156	20.01 S	25.17 E
Odib, Wādī V	140	22.38 N	36.06 E
Odiel ≃	34	37.10 N	6.54 W
Odienné	150	9.30 N	7.34 W
Odiham	42	51.15 N	0.57 W
Odin	219	38.37 N	89.03 W
Odin, Mount ∧	182	50.33 N	118.08 W
Odincovo, Ross.	82	55.41 N	37.17 E
Odincovo, Ross.	82	54.40 N	38.00 E
Odiongan	116	12.24 N	121.59 E
Odiongan Bay c	116	12.25 N	121.58 E
Odivelas	266c	38.47 N	9.11 W
Odobești	38	45.45 N	27.04 E
Odojev	76	53.56 N	36.41 E
Odolanów	30	51.35 N	17.39 E
Ōdomari-chosuichi ⊜	96	34.43 N	132.18 E
Odon	194	38.50 N	86.59 W
Ŏdŏngk	110	11.48 N	104.45 E
O'Donnell	196	32.57 N	101.49 W
O'Donnell ≃	162	18.22 S	126.36 E
Odoorn	52	52.51 N	6.51 E
Odorheiu Secuiesc	38	46.18 N	25.18 E
Odra (Oder) ≃	30	53.32 N	14.38 E
Odra Port	54	53.52 N	14.14 E
Odrinhas	266c	38.53 N	9.22 W
Odrzywół	30	51.32 N	20.33 E
Ødsted	41	55.39 N	9.25 E
Odum	192	31.39 N	82.01 W
Odžaci	38	45.30 N	19.16 E
Odzala, Parc National d' ♠	152	1.00 S	15.00 E
Odzi	154	18.58 S	32.23 E
Odzi ≃	154	19.45 S	32.24 E
Odziba	152	3.35 S	15.31 E
Ōe	96	35.23 N	135.09 E
Oebisfelde	54	52.25 N	10.59 E
Oedelem	50	51.10 N	3.20 E
Oederan	54	50.52 N	13.09 E
Oeding	52	51.56 N	6.49 E
Oedt	56	51.19 N	6.22 E
Oegstgeest	52	52.10 N	4.29 E
Oeiras, Bra.	250	7.01 S	42.08 W
Oeiras, Port.	266c	38.41 N	9.21 W
Oeiras do Pará	250	1.58 S	49.51 W
Oelde	52	51.49 N	8.08 E
Oelemari ≃	250	3.13 N	54.09 W
Oella	284b	39.16 N	76.47 W
Oels → Oleśnica	30	51.13 N	17.23 E
Oelsig	54	51.41 N	13.22 E
Oelsnitz, Dtsch.	54	50.24 N	12.10 E
Oelsnitz, Dtsch.	54	50.43 N	12.41 E
Oelwein	190	42.40 N	91.54 W
Oenpelli	164	12.20 S	133.04 E
Oensingen	58	47.17 N	7.44 E
Oepping	60	48.36 N	13.56 E
Oeraro-do I	98	34.27 N	127.30 E
Oer-Erkenschwick	52	51.39 N	7.15 E
Oerlinghausen	52	51.57 N	8.39 E
Oermten	263	51.29 N	6.27 E
Oesede	52	52.12 N	8.04 E
Oeslau	54	50.17 N	11.01 E
Oespel ◆[8]	263	51.30 N	7.23 E
Oeste, Canal del ≊	266a	40.32 N	3.42 W
Oeste, Parque del ♠	266a	40.26 N	3.44 W
Oesterdam ◆[5]	52	51.29 N	4.15 E
Oestrich	263	51.22 N	7.38 E
Oestrich ◆[8]	263	51.34 N	7.22 E
Oestrum ◆[8]	263	51.25 N	6.40 E
Ōetaka-yama ∧	96	35.04 N	132.26 E
Oettingen in Bayern	56	48.57 N	10.36 E
Oetz	64	47.12 N	10.54 E
Oeuf ≃	50	48.11 N	2.21 E
Oeventrop	56	51.23 N	8.08 E
Oeversee	41	54.42 N	9.26 E
Ōe-yama ∧	96	35.27 N	135.07 E
Oeyŏn-do I	98	36.14 N	126.05 E
Of	130	40.57 N	40.18 E
O'Fallon, Il., U.S.	219	38.35 N	89.54 W
O'Fallon, Mo., U.S.	219	38.48 N	90.41 W
O'Fallon Creek ≃	198	46.50 N	105.09 W
Ofanto ≃	68	41.22 N	16.13 E
Ofaqim	132	31.17 N	34.37 E
Ofenpass → Fuorn, Pass dal)(	58	46.37 N	10.15 E
Offa	150	8.09 N	4.44 E
Offaly ◻[6]	48	53.20 N	7.30 W
Offanengo	62	45.22 N	9.44 E
Offemont	58	47.40 N	6.53 E
Offenbach	56	50.08 N	8.47 E
Offenburg	58	48.28 N	7.57 E
Offendorf	58	48.43 N	7.55 E
Offerdal	26	63.28 N	14.00 E
Offham	260	51.17 N	0.23 E
Officer	274b	38.04 S	145.25 E
Officer Creek ≃	162	27.45 S	132.24 E
Offida	66	42.56 N	13.41 E
Offingen	58	48.29 N	10.21 E
Offranville	50	49.52 N	1.03 E
Offutt Air Force Base ■	198	41.08 N	95.56 W
Oficina Alemania	252	25.10 S	69.55 W
Oficina Alianza	248	20.46 S	69.42 W
Oficina Chile	252	25.09 S	69.54 W
Oficina Pedro de Valdivia	252	22.36 S	69.40 W
Oficina Victoria	248	20.44 S	69.42 W
Ofin	273a	6.33 N	3.30 E
Öflingen	58	47.35 N	7.55 E
Ofotfjorden c[2]	24	68.23 N	16.10 E
Oftringen	58	47.19 N	7.56 E
Ofu	174y	14.10 S	169.42 W
Ofu I	174y	14.11 S	169.42 W
Ōfukuroshinden	268	35.53 N	139.27 E
Ōfuna	268	35.21 N	139.32 E
Ōfunato	92	39.04 N	141.43 E
Oga	92	39.53 N	139.51 E
Ogaden ◆[1]	144	8.00 N	44.00 E
Oga-hantō ›[1]	92	39.55 N	139.50 E
Ōgaki, Nihon	94	35.21 N	136.37 E
Ōgaki, Nihon	96	34.06 N	132.30 E
Ogallala	198	41.07 N	101.43 W
Ogan ≃	112	3.01 S	104.44 E
Ogano	94	36.01 N	139.00 E
Ogasa	94	34.41 N	138.06 E
Ogasawara-guntō (Bonin Islands) II	14	27.00 N	142.10 E
Ōgata, Nihon	94	37.13 N	138.20 E
Ōgata, Nihon	96	33.01 N	133.01 E
Ogata, Nihon	96	32.58 N	131.29 E
Ōga-tō ∧	94	36.13 N	138.06 E
Ogatsu	92	38.31 N	141.28 E
Ogawa, Nihon	92	32.35 N	130.43 E
Ogawa, Nihon	94	36.10 N	140.21 E
Ogawa, Nihon	94	36.37 N	137.58 E
Ogawa, Nihon	94	36.03 N	139.16 E
Ogawa, Nihon	94	36.45 N	140.08 E
Ogawa, Nihon	268	35.44 N	139.28 E
Ogawara-ko ⊜	92	40.47 N	141.20 E
Ogbomosho	150	8.08 N	4.15 E
Ogden, Ia., U.S.	190	42.02 N	94.01 W
Ogden, Ks., U.S.	198	39.06 N	96.42 W
Ogden, Pa., U.S.	208	39.49 N	75.27 W
Ogden, Ut,. U.S.	200	41.13 N	111.58 W
Ogden, Mount ∧	180	58.26 N	133.23 W
Ogden Dunes	216	41.38 N	87.12 W
Ogden Island I	212	44.52 N	75.12 W
Ogden Reservoir ⊜[1]	262	53.42 N	2.22 W
Ogdensburg, N.J., U.S.	210	41.04 N	74.35 W
Ogdensburg, N.Y., U.S.	212	44.41 N	75.29 W
Ogeechee ≃	192	31.51 N	81.06 W
Ōge-jima I	96	34.12 N	134.38 E
Ogema	184	49.35 N	104.55 W
Oggersheim	56	49.29 N	8.22 E
Oghi Fort	123	34.31 N	73.01 E
Ogibalovo	76	60.34 N	39.40 E
Ogidaki Mountain ∧[2]	190	46.58 N	83.58 W
Ogies	158	26.02 S	29.04 E
Ogi-jima I	96	34.26 N	134.04 E
Ogijo	273a	6.42 N	3.31 E
Ogilvie, Austl.	162	28.09 S	114.38 E
Ogilvie, Mn., U.S.	190	45.49 N	93.25 W
Ogilvie ≃	180	65.52 N	137.16 W
Ogilvie Mountains ⋏	180	65.00 N	139.30 W
Ogilville	218	39.08 N	86.01 W
Ōgimi	174m	26.42 N	128.07 E
Ōgino-sen ∧	96	35.26 N	134.26 E
Ogle ◻[6]	216	42.01 N	89.20 W
Oglesby, Il., U.S.	216	41.17 N	89.03 W
Oglesby, Tx., U.S.	222	31.25 N	97.31 W
Oglethorpe	192	32.17 N	84.03 W
Ogliastra ◆[1]	71	39.56 N	9.37 E
Ogliastro Cilento	68	40.21 N	15.03 E
Oglio ≃	64	45.02 N	10.39 E
Ogmore	166	22.37 S	149.40 E
Ogmore ≃	42	51.28 N	3.38 W
Ogmore Vale	42	51.38 N	3.31 W
Ogni	86	51.54 N	83.31 E
Ognica	54	53.07 N	14.27 E
Ognon ≃	58	47.20 N	5.29 E
Ogn'ov Jar	86	58.23 N	76.29 E
Ogn'ovka	86	49.36 N	83.25 E
Ōgo	94	36.25 N	139.10 E
Ōgo ◆[8]	270	34.49 N	135.06 E
Ōgo ≃	270	34.47 N	135.04 E
Ogoamas, Bulu ∧	112	0.40 N	120.12 E
Ogōchi-dam ◆[6]	94	35.47 N	139.04 E
Ogodža	89	52.44 N	132.31 E
Ogoja	150	6.40 N	8.48 E
Ogoki ≃	176	51.38 N	85.57 W
'Ogol, Khaṭṭ el V	150	20.01 N	15.29 W
Ogooué ≃	152	0.49 S	9.00 E
Ogooué-Ivindo ◻[4]	152	1.00 N	13.00 E
Ogooué-Lolo ◻[4]	152	1.00 S	12.30 E
Ogooué-Maritime ◻[4]	152	2.00 S	9.30 E
Ogōri, Nihon	96	33.22 N	130.32 E
Ogōri, Nihon	96	34.06 N	131.24 E
Ogose	94	35.58 N	139.18 E
Ogosta ≃	38	43.45 N	23.51 E
Ogou ≃	150	7.50 N	1.19 E
Ogoyo	273a	6.26 N	3.29 E
Ogr	140	12.02 N	27.06 E
Ogre	76	56.51 N	24.36 E
Ogre ≃	76	56.48 N	24.36 E
Ogrodzieniec	30	50.27 N	19.31 E
Ogrosen	54	51.42 N	14.02 E
Ōguchi	94	35.20 N	136.55 E
Ŏgu-dong	98	38.57 N	126.56 E
Ogudu	273a	6.34 N	3.24 E
Ogulin	36	45.16 N	15.14 E
Ogun ◻[3]	150	6.45 N	3.25 E
Ogun ≃	150	6.36 N	3.27 E
Ogun Forest Reserve ♠	273a	6.37 N	3.26 E
Oguni, Nihon	92	38.04 N	139.45 E
Oguni, Nihon	96	33.07 N	131.04 E
Ogunlogun	273a	6.41 N	3.28 E
Ogunquit	188	43.14 N	70.35 W
Ogura-san ∧	94	36.02 N	138.37 E
Ogurčinskij, ostrov I	128	38.55 N	53.02 E
Oguta	150	5.44 N	6.44 E
Oğuz, Azer.	84	41.06 N	47.28 E
Oğuz, Tür.	130	39.32 N	38.51 E
Oğuz, Tür.	130	37.49 N	41.22 E
Oğuzeli	130	36.59 N	37.30 E
Ogwashi-Uku	150	6.10 N	6.31 E
Ohakune	172	39.25 S	175.24 E
Ohanapecosh ≃	224	46.38 N	121.37 W
Ohanet	148	28.45 N	8.55 E
Ohār	124	27.21 N	84.37 E
Ōhara, Nihon	94	35.15 N	140.23 E
Ōhara, Nihon	96	35.07 N	134.20 E
Ōharano ◆[8]	270	34.58 N	135.40 E
Ōhara-tunnel ◆[5]	94	35.12 N	137.50 E
Ōhata	92	41.24 N	141.10 E
Ōhatake	268	35.57 N	139.46 E
Ohau, Lake ⊜	172	44.15 S	169.51 E
Ohaupo	172	37.55 S	175.19 E
Ohey	56	50.26 N	5.08 E
O'Higgins, Cabo ›	174z	27.05 S	109.15 W
O'Higgins, Cerro ∧	254	48.48 S	73.11 W
O'Higgins, Lago (Lago San Martín) ⊜	254	49.00 S	72.40 W
Ohingaiti	172	39.52 S	175.43 E
Ohio	190	41.34 N	89.28 W
Ohio ◻[6], In., U.S.	218	38.57 N	84.51 W
Ohio ◻[6], W.V., U.S.	214	40.09 N	80.35 W
Ohio ◻[3], U.S.	178	40.15 N	82.45 W
Ohio ◻[3], U.S.	188	40.15 N	82.45 W
Ohio ≃	178	36.59 N	89.08 W
Ohio Brush Creek ≃	218	38.41 N	83.27 W

Symbols in the index entries represent the broad categories identified in the key at the right. Symbols with superior numbers (⋏[1]) identify subcategories (see complete key on page I · 1).

Symbole im Register stellen die rechts im Schlüssel erklärten Kategorien dar. Symbole mit hochgestellten Ziffern (⋏[1]) bezeichnen Unterabteilungen einer Kategorie (vgl. vollständiger Schlüssel auf Seite I · 1).

Los símbolos incluídos en el texto del índice representan las grandes categorías identificadas con la clave a la derecha. Los símbolos con numeros en su parte superior (⋏[1]) identifican las subcategorías (véase la clave completa en la página I · 1).

Les symboles de l'index représentent les catégories indiquées dans la légende à droite. Les symboles suivis d'un indice (⋏[1]) représentent des sous-catégories (voir légende complète à la page I · 1).

Os símbolos incluídos no texto do índice representam as grandes categorias identificadas com a chave à direita. Os símbolos com números em sua parte superior (⋏[1]) identificam as subcategorias (veja-se a chave completa à página I · 1).

∧ Mountain	Berg	Montaña	Montagne	Montanha
⋏ Mountains	Gebirge	Montañas	Montagnes	Montanhas
)(Pass	Paß	Paso	Col	Passo
V Valley, Canyon	Tal, Cañon	Valle, Cañón	Vallée, Canyon	Vale, Canhão
≚ Plain	Ebene	Llano	Plaine	Planície
› Cape	Kap	Cabo	Cap	Cabo
I Island	Insel	Isla	Île	Ilha
II Islands	Inseln	Islas	Îles	Ilhas
⏏ Other Topographic Features	Andere Topographische Objekte	Otros Elementos Topográficos	Autres données topographiques	Outros acidentes topográficos

ESPAÑOL — Nombre | Página | Lat. °′ | Long. °′ W = Oeste
FRANÇAIS — Nom | Page | Lat. °′ | Long. °′ W = Ouest
PORTUGUÊS — Nome | Página | Lat. °′ | Long. °′ W = Oeste

Ohio Brush Creek, Baker Fork ≐ 218 39.02 N 83.26 W
Ohio Brush Creek, Little West Fork ≐ 218 38.58 N 83.34 W
Ohio Brush Creek, West Fork ≐ 218 38.56 N 83.28 W
Ohio Canal ≡ 279a 41.26 N 81.40 W
Ohio Caverns ⊥⁵ 216 40.14 N 83.43 W
Ohio City 216 40.46 N 84.36 W
Ohio Peak ∧ 200 38.49 N 107.07 W
Ohiopyle State Park ♦ 188 39.50 N 79.31 W
Ohioville, N.Y., U.S. 210 41.45 N 74.03 W
Ohioville, Pa., U.S. 214 40.40 N 80.29 W
Ōhira 94 36.20 N 139.42 E
Ōhira-yama ∧ 96 34.20 N 133.57 E
Ōhito 94 35.01 N 138.56 E
Ohlau — Oława 30 50.57 N 17.17 E
Ohligs ✈⁸ 263 51.09 N 7.00 E
Ohlman 219 39.21 N 89.13 W
Ohlsdorf 64 47.57 N 13.47 E
Ohm ≐ 56 50.51 N 8.48 E
Ōho 94 36.08 N 140.06 E
Ohoitom 164 5.56 S 132.41 E
'Ohonua 174w 21.20 S 174.57 W
Ohoopee ≐ 192 31.54 N 82.07 W
Ōhori 268 35.20 N 139.52 E
Ohorn 54 51.10 N 14.02 E
Ohra Stausee ⊜¹ 54 50.46 N 10.42 E
Ohrdruf 54 50.50 N 10.44 E
Ohre ≐, Dtsch. 54 52.18 N 11.47 E
Ohře (Eger) ≐, Europe 54 50.32 N 14.08 E
Ohrid 38 41.07 N 20.47 E
Ohrid, Lake ⊜ 38 41.02 N 20.43 E
Ohrigstad 156 24.49 S 30.33 E
Öhringen 56 49.12 N 9.29 E
Ohrnberg 56 49.15 N 9.27 E
Ohuira, Bahía c 232 25.38 N 108.58 W
Ohura 172 38.50 S 174.59 E
Ōi, Nihon 96 35.28 N 135.37 E
Ōi, Nihon 268 35.51 N 139.30 E
Ōi ✈⁸ 268 35.35 N 139.45 E
Ōi ≐, Nihon 94 34.46 N 138.18 E
Ōi ≐, Nihon 96 35.01 N 135.39 E
Oiapoque 250 3.50 N 51.50 W
Oiapoque (Oyapock) ≐ 250 4.08 N 51.40 W
Oies, Île aux I 186 47.07 N 70.30 W
Ōigawa 94 34.48 N 138.17 E
Oignies 50 50.28 N 2.59 E
Oil Center 196 32.29 N 103.15 W
Oil City, La., U.S. 194 32.44 N 93.58 W
Oil City, Pa., U.S. 214 41.26 N 79.42 W
Oil Creek ≐ 214 41.26 N 79.42 W
Oil Creek State Park ♦ 214 41.33 N 79.40 W
Oildale 226 35.25 N 119.01 W
Oilmont 182 48.44 N 111.50 W
Oil Springs 214 42.47 N 82.07 W
Oilton, Ok., U.S. 196 36.05 N 96.35 W
Oilton, Tx., U.S. 196 27.33 N 98.59 W
Oil Trough 194 35.37 N 91.27 W
Oinville-sur-Montcient 261 49.02 N 1.51 E
Oir, Beinn an ∧ 46 55.54 N 6.00 W
Oirschot 52 51.30 N 5.18 E
Oise □⁵ 50 49.30 N 2.30 E
Oise ≐ 50 49.00 N 2.04 E
Oise à l'Aisne, Canal de l' ≡ 50 49.36 N 3.11 E
Oisemont 50 49.57 N 1.46 E
Ōiso, Nihon 94 35.18 N 139.19 E
Ōiso, Nihon 270 34.33 N 135.01 E
Oissel 50 49.20 N 1.06 E
Oissery 261 49.04 N 2.49 E
Oisterwijk 52 51.35 N 5.12 E
Oistins 241g 13.04 N 59.32 W
Ōita 96 33.14 N 131.36 E
Ōita □⁵ 96 33.15 N 131.30 E
Ōita ≐ 96 33.15 N 131.37 E
Oiticica 250 5.03 S 41.05 W
Oituz, Pasul)(38 46.03 N 26.23 E
Ōiwa 270 34.53 N 135.33 E
Oiyung 124 29.39 N 89.46 E
Ōizumi, Nihon 94 36.15 N 139.25 E
Ōizumi, Nihon 94 35.52 N 138.23 E
Ōizuruga-dake ∧ 94 36.18 N 136.47 E
Öja I 40 58.45 N 17.52 E
Oja ≐ 86 53.26 N 91.55 E
Ojai 228 34.26 N 119.14 W
Öjaren ⊜ 40 60.43 N 16.50 E
Ojat' ≐ 76 60.31 N 33.00 E
Ojcowski Park Narodowy ♦ 30 50.15 N 19.50 E
Öje 26 60.49 N 13.51 E
Ojgon nuur ⊜ 88 49.10 N 96.36 E
Ojgor 86 49.10 N 89.17 E
Oji 96 34.35 N 135.42 E
Ōjima 94 36.15 N 139.20 E
Ojinaga 232 29.34 N 104.25 W
Ojiya 92 37.18 N 138.48 E
Ojm'akon 74 63.28 N 142.49 E
Ojocaliente 234 22.34 N 102.15 W
Ojo de la Casa 200 31.23 N 106.32 W
Ojo del Carrizo 232 29.58 N 105.16 W
Ojo de Liebre, Laguna c 232 27.45 N 114.15 W
Ojok 88 52.35 N 104.27 E
Ojos del Salado, Nevado ∧ 252 27.06 S 68.32 W
Ojos Negros 232 31.52 N 116.16 W
Ojota 273a 6.35 N 3.23 E
Ojtal, Kaz. 85 42.55 N 73.17 E
Ojtal, Kyrg. 85 40.24 N 74.06 E
Oju 150 6.53 N 8.26 E
Ojuelos de Jalisco 234 21.52 N 101.35 W
Ojus 220 25.57 N 80.09 W
Oka 150 7.29 N 5.49 E
Oka ≐, Ross. 80 56.20 N 43.59 E
Oka ≐, Ross. 88 55.15 N 102.10 E
Okaba 164 8.06 S 139.42 E
Okabe, Nihon 94 36.12 N 139.15 E
Okabe, Nihon 94 34.55 N 138.17 E
Okagaki 96 33.50 N 130.38 E
Okahandja 156 21.59 S 16.58 E
Okahandja □⁵ 156 21.30 S 17.00 E
Okahukura 172 38.47 S 175.13 E
Okahumpka 220 28.45 N 81.54 W
Okaihau 172 35.19 S 173.47 E
Okalataka 152 0.20 S 14.59 E
Okaloacoochee Slough ≐ 220 26.16 N 81.17 W
Okamoto 270 34.59 N 135.58 E
Okamoto ✈⁸ 270 34.44 N 135.16 E
Okanagan (Okanogan) ≐ 182 48.06 N 119.43 W
Okanagan Centre 182 50.03 N 119.27 W
Okanagan Falls 182 49.21 N 119.34 W
Okanagan Indian Reserve ✈⁴ 182 50.21 N 119.17 W
Okanagan Lake ⊜ 182 50.00 N 119.28 W
Okanagan Landing 182 50.14 N 119.22 W
Okanagan Mountain Provincial Park ♦ 182 49.45 N 119.40 W
Okanagan Range (Okanogan Range) ∧ 182 49.00 N 120.00 W
Okanogan 202 48.21 N 119.34 W
Okanogan □⁶ 224 48.39 N 120.41 W
Okanogan (Okanagan) ≐ 182 48.06 N 119.43 W
Okanogan Range (Okanagan Range) ∧ 182 49.00 N 120.00 W
Okapilco Creek ≐ 192 30.45 N 83.30 W
Okaputa 156 20.09 S 16.56 E
Okāra 123 30.49 N 73.27 E
Okarche 196 35.44 N 97.58 W
Okarito 172 43.14 S 170.11 E
Okasaki 270 34.46 N 135.52 E
Okatibbee Reservoir ⊜¹ 194 32.30 N 88.47 W
Okato 172 39.12 S 173.53 E
Okauchee 216 43.06 N 88.26 W
Okauchee Lake ⊜ 216 43.07 N 88.26 W
Okaukuejo 156 19.10 S 15.54 E
Okavango (Cubango) ≐ 138 18.50 S 22.25 E
Okavango Delta ≐² 156 18.45 S 22.45 E
Ōkawa, Nihon 92 33.12 N 130.23 E
Ōkawa, Nihon 94 35.05 N 138.15 E
Ōkawa, Nihon 96 33.47 N 133.26 E
Ōkawachi 96 35.04 N 134.45 E
Ōkawado 268 35.56 N 139.50 E
Okawville 219 38.26 N 89.33 W
Okaya 94 36.03 N 138.03 E
Okayama 96 34.39 N 133.55 E
Okayama □⁵ 96 35.00 N 134.00 E
Okazaki 94 34.57 N 137.10 E
Okch'ŏn 98 36.20 N 127.34 E
Oke-Aro 273a 6.41 N 3.19 E
Okeechobee 220 27.14 N 80.49 W
Okeechobee □⁶ 220 27.25 N 80.52 W
Okeechobee, Lake ⊜ 220 26.55 N 80.45 W
O'Keefe Centre ᵾ 275b 43.37 N 79.22 W
Okeene 196 36.06 N 98.19 W
Okefenokee Swamp ⩨ 192 30.42 N 82.20 W
Okegawa 94 36.00 N 139.35 E
Okehampton 42 50.44 N 4.00 W
Okeigbo 150 7.09 N 4.43 E
Okemah 196 35.25 N 96.18 W
Okement ≐ 42 50.50 N 4.01 W
Okemos 216 42.43 N 84.25 W
Okene 150 7.33 N 6.15 E
Oke-Ode 150 8.33 N 5.02 E
Oke Ogbe 273a 6.24 N 3.23 E
Oker 52 51.54 N 10.29 E
Oker ≐ 54 52.30 N 10.22 E
Okere ≐ 154 2.07 N 33.55 E
Okhaldunggā 124 27.19 N 86.30 E
Okhla ✈⁸ 272a 28.34 N 77.18 E
Okhotsk, Sea of (Ochotskoje more) ⌐² 74 53.00 N 150.00 E
Okhotsk Basin ✈¹ 12 53.00 N 148.00 E
Okhtyrka 78 50.19 N 34.55 E
Okiep 156 29.39 S 17.53 E
Okinawa 174m 26.20 N 127.50 E
Okinawa □⁵ 93b 26.31 N 127.59 E
Okinawa-jima I 174m 26.30 N 128.00 E
Okinawa-shotō II 93b 26.40 N 128.00 E
Okino-Daitō-jima I 90 24.28 N 131.11 E
Okino-Erabu-shima I 93b 27.22 N 128.35 E
Okino-Kl'uči 88 50.36 N 107.06 E
Okino-shima I, Nihon 94 35.12 N 136.04 E
Okino-shima I, Nihon 96 34.07 N 135.06 E
Okino-Tori-shima (Parece Vela) I 90 20.25 N 136.00 E
Oki-shotō II 92 36.15 N 133.15 E
Okitipupa 150 6.29 N 4.46 E
Okitsu-zaki ⊱ 96 33.09 N 133.14 E
Okkang-ni 98 40.18 N 124.22 E
Okkerbil' ≐ 265a 59.56 N 30.26 E
Okladnevo 76 58.36 N 33.39 E
Oklahoma, Pa., U.S. 214 41.07 N 78.44 W
Oklahoma, Pa., U.S. 279b 40.35 N 79.35 W
Oklahoma □³, U.S. 178 35.30 N 98.00 W
Oklahoma □³, U.S. 196 35.30 N 98.00 W
Oklahoma City 196 35.28 N 97.30 W
Oklawaha 220 29.02 N 81.55 W
Oklawaha ≐, Fl., U.S. 192 29.28 N 81.41 W
Oklawaha ≐, Fl., U.S. 220 29.03 N 81.52 W
Oklee 198 47.50 N 95.51 W
Okmulgee 196 35.37 N 95.57 W
Oko, Wādī V 140 21.15 N 35.56 E
Okobojo Creek ≐ 198 44.38 N 100.28 W
Okok ≐ 154 2.06 N 33.53 E
Okoka 152 2.57 S 23.27 E
Okola 152 4.01 N 11.23 E
Okollo 154 2.40 N 31.08 E
Okolo 152 3.46 S 23.55 E
Okolona, Ar., U.S. 194 33.59 N 93.20 W
Okolona, Ky., U.S. 194 38.08 N 85.41 W
Okolona, Ms., U.S. 194 34.00 N 88.45 W
Okombahe 156 21.23 S 15.22 E
Okondja 152 0.41 S 13.47 E
Okonek 30 53.33 N 16.50 E
Okoneŝnikovo 86 54.50 N 75.05 E
Okotoks 182 50.44 N 113.59 W
Okoyo 152 1.28 S 15.04 E
Okpara ≐ 150 7.40 N 2.35 E
Okrika 150 4.47 N 7.04 E
Oksbøl 26 55.38 N 8.17 E
Okskij zapovednik ✈⁴ 80 54.45 N 40.45 E
Oksko-Donskaja ravnina ≡ 80 53.00 N 40.30 E
Oksovskij 24 62.37 N 39.55 E
Okskolten ∧ 24 65.59 N 14.15 E
Oksu ≐, Asia 85 40.12 N 69.16 E
Oksu ≐, Taj. 120 38.09 N 73.57 E
Okt'abr', Kaz. 85 43.41 N 77.12 E
Okt'abr', Kaz. 86 45.41 N 76.28 E
Okt'abr', Ross. 76 57.50 N 37.26 E
Okt'abr'sk, Kaz. 86 49.28 N 57.25 E
Okt'abr'sk, Ross. 80 53.11 N 48.40 E
Okt'abr'skij, Bela. 76 52.38 N 28.53 E
Okt'abr'skij, Kaz. 86 52.35 N 62.40 E
Okt'abr'skij, Ross. 24 61.04 N 43.08 E
Okt'abr'skij, Ross. 24 59.29 N 48.50 E
Okt'abr'skij, Ross. 76 53.47 N 39.29 E
Okt'abr'skij, Ross. 78 50.26 N 36.22 E
Okt'abr'skij, Ross. 78 44.56 N 39.00 E
Okt'abr'skij, Ross. 80 54.28 N 53.28 E
Okt'abr'skij, Ross. 80 56.17 N 44.12 E
Okt'abr'skij, Ross. 80 57.08 N 40.20 E
Okt'abr'skij, Ross. 80 58.19 N 44.19 E
Okt'abr'skij, Ross. 80 56.35 N 53.58 E
Okt'abr'skij, Ross. 80 47.58 N 43.38 E
Okt'abr'skij, Ross. 82 55.37 N 37.58 E
Okt'abr'skij, Ross. 82 54.14 N 38.54 E
Okt'abr'skij, Ross. 82 56.04 N 35.45 E
Okt'abr'skij, Ross. 86 56.31 N 57.12 E
Okt'abr'skij, Ross. 88 50.04 N 118.04 E
Okt'abr'skij, Ross. 88 56.05 N 99.26 E
Okt'abr'skij, Ross. 89 53.01 N 128.37 E
Okt'abr'skij, Ross. 89 49.02 N 140.11 E
Okt'abr'skij, Taj. 85 38.33 N 68.22 E
Okt'abr'skoje, Kaz. 86 52.07 N 65.40 E
Okt'abr'skoje, Ross. 74 62.28 N 66.03 E
Okt'abr'skoje, Ross. 76 52.18 N 39.44 E
Okt'abr'skoje, Ross. 80 45.37 N 42.49 E
Okt'abr'skoje, Ross. 80 52.54 N 46.30 E
Okt'abr'skoje, Ross. 86 52.20 N 55.30 E
Okt'abr'skoje, Ross. 86 54.26 N 62.44 E
Okt'abr'skoj Revol'ucii, ostrov I 74 79.30 N 97.00 E
Ok Tedi 164 5.44 S 141.09 E
Oktember'an 84 40.09 N 44.02 E
Oktong-ni 98 38.27 N 127.07 E
Oktwin 110 18.49 N 96.26 E
Oktyabrs'ke, Ukr. 78 45.18 N 34.09 E
Oktyabrs'ke, Ukr. 83 48.28 N 37.22 E
Oktyabr'skiy — Okt'abr'skij 80 54.28 N 53.28 E
Oku, Nihon 96 34.40 N 134.05 E
Oku, Nihon 174m 26.50 N 128.17 E
Ōkubo, Nihon 268 35.21 N 139.56 E
Ōkubo, Nihon 270 34.41 N 134.57 E
Ōkubo ✈⁸ 268 35.42 N 139.42 E
Okučani 36 45.16 N 17.12 E
Ōkuchi, Nihon 92 32.04 N 130.37 E
Ōkuchi, Nihon 94 36.17 N 136.39 E
Okuku ≐ 172 43.16 S 172.28 E
Okulovka 76 58.26 N 33.18 E
Okumi 84 42.43 N 41.45 E
Okundi 150 6.22 N 8.44 E
Okun'ov Nos 24 66.15 N 52.28 E
Ōkura-yama ∧ 96 35.08 N 133.22 E
Okusawa ✈⁸ 268 35.36 N 139.40 E
Okushiri 92a 42.10 N 139.31 E
Okushiri-tō I 92a 42.10 N 139.27 E
Ōkusu-yama ∧² 268 35.15 N 139.38 E
Okuta 150 9.14 N 3.15 E
Okutadami Dam ✈⁶ 94 37.09 N 139.15 E
Okutama 94 35.47 N 139.02 E
Okutama-ko ⊜ 94 35.47 N 139.02 E
Okutsu 96 35.14 N 133.56 E
Ōkuwa 94 35.41 N 137.40 E
Okwa (Chapman's) ≐ 156 22.30 S 23.00 E
Okwoga 150 7.01 N 7.50 E
Olá, Pan. 236 8.25 N 80.39 W
Ola, Ross. 74 59.35 N 151.17 E
Ola, Ar., U.S. 194 35.01 N 93.13 W
Ola ≐ 76 52.41 N 29.39 E
Ólafsfjördur 24a 66.06 N 18.38 W
Olambwe Valley Game Reserve ✈⁴ 154 0.37 S 34.15 E
Olancha 204 36.16 N 118.00 W
Olancha Peak ∧ 204 36.16 N 118.07 W
Olanchito 236 15.30 N 86.35 W
Olancho □⁵ 236 14.45 N 86.00 W
Öland I 26 56.45 N 16.38 E
Olandsån ≐ 40 60.20 N 18.14 E
Olango Island I 116 10.16 N 124.03 E
Olanta 192 33.56 N 79.55 W
Olar 192 33.10 N 81.11 W
Olarevo 76 59.22 N 40.04 E
Olaria, Bra. 256 21.52 S 43.56 W
Olaria, Bra. 287a 22.41 S 43.08 W
Olaria ✈⁸ 287a 22.52 S 43.15 W
Olary 166 32.17 S 140.19 E
Olascoaga 252 35.12 S 60.36 W
Olasore 273a 6.40 N 3.17 E
Olathe, Co., U.S. 200 38.36 N 107.58 W
Olathe, Ks., U.S. 198 38.52 N 94.49 W
Olavarría 252 36.54 S 60.17 W
Olavinlinna ⊥ 26 61.52 N 29.00 E
Oława 30 50.57 N 17.17 E
Olbernhau 54 50.39 N 13.20 E
Olbersdorf 54 50.52 N 14.46 E
Olbersleben 54 51.09 N 11.20 E
Olbia 71 40.55 N 9.31 E
Olbia, Golfo di c 71 40.55 N 9.39 E
Ølby Lyng 41 55.29 N 12.09 E
Olca, Volcán ∧¹ 248 20.57 S 68.30 W
Ol'chi 80 53.53 N 41.28 E
Olching 60 48.12 N 11.20 E
Ol'chon, ostrov I 88 53.09 N 107.24 E
Ol'chovaja ≐ 88 48.47 N 40.51 E
Ol'chovatka 78 50.18 N 39.17 E
Ol'chovka, Ross. 80 49.52 N 44.34 E
Ol'chovka, Ross. 86 56.22 N 63.46 E
Olcott 210 43.20 N 78.42 W
Old ≐, Ca., U.S. 226 38.04 N 121.35 W
Old ≐, Tx., U.S. 222 30.25 N 96.19 W
Old Bahama Channel ⵡ 238 22.30 N 78.50 W
Old Bedford ≐ 42 52.35 N 0.20 E
Old Bennington 210 42.52 N 73.12 W
Old Bethpage 276 40.45 N 73.27 W
Old Bethpage Village ⊥ 276 40.47 N 73.28 W
Old Brazoria 222 29.04 N 95.34 W
Old Bridge 276 40.24 N 74.21 W
Old Brookville 276 40.49 N 73.36 W
Oldbury 42 52.30 N 2.00 W
Old Cairo — Miṣr al-Qadīmah ✈⁸ 273c 30.00 N 31.14 E
Oldcastle 48 53.46 N 7.10 W
Old Colwyn 44 53.18 N 3.43 W
Old Cork 166 22.56 S 141.52 E
Old Creek Estates 284c 38.50 N 77.16 W
Old Crow 180 67.35 N 139.50 W
Old Crow ≐ 180 67.35 N 139.28 W
Oldeani 154 3.21 S 35.33 E
Oldebroek 52 52.26 N 5.54 E
Old Economy ⊥ 279b 40.36 N 80.14 W
Olden, Nor. 26 61.50 N 6.49 E
Olden, Tx., U.S. 196 32.25 N 98.45 W
Oldenburg 52 53.17 N 8.23 E
Oldenburg, Dtsch. 54 53.08 N 8.13 E
Oldenburg, In., U.S. 218 39.20 N 85.12 W
Oldenburg □⁹ 52 53.00 N 8.00 E
Oldenburg in Holstein 54 54.17 N 10.52 E
Oldendorf 52 53.35 N 9.14 E
Oldenstadt 52 52.58 N 10.35 E
Oldensworth 41 54.22 N 8.56 E
Oldenzaal 52 52.19 N 6.56 E
Oldersum 52 53.20 N 7.20 E
Old Faithful Geyser ⌐⁴ 202 44.30 N 110.45 W
Old Farm 284c 39.03 N 77.09 W
Old Field 276 40.57 N 73.08 W
Old Field Point ⊱ 276 40.58 N 73.07 W
Old Forge, N.Y., U.S. 188 43.42 N 74.58 W
Old Forge, Pa., U.S. 210 41.22 N 75.44 W
Old Forge Village 276 40.49 N 74.29 W
Old Fort 214 41.15 N 83.09 W
Old Fort Erie ⊥ 284a 42.53 N 78.56 W
Old Fort Henry ⊥ 212 44.14 N 76.28 W
Old Fort Mountain ∧ 182 55.05 N 126.30 W
Old Fort Niagara ⊥ 284a 43.16 N 79.03 W
Old Fort Parker State Historic Site ⊥ 222 31.34 N 96.34 W
Old Fort Point ⊱ 240b 25.03 N 77.29 W
Old Greenwich 276 41.02 N 73.34 W
Oldham, Eng., U.K. 44 53.33 N 2.07 W
Oldham, S.D., U.S. 198 44.13 N 97.18 W
Oldham □⁶ 218 38.23 N 85.27 W
Oldham □⁸ 262 53.34 N 2.03 W
Oldham Pines 283 42.05 N 70.50 W
Oldham Pond ⊜ 283 42.03 N 70.51 W
Oldham Village 207 42.04 N 70.49 W
Old Harbor 180 57.12 N 153.18 W
Old Harbour 241q 17.56 N 77.07 W
Old Hickory Lake ⊜¹ 194 36.18 N 86.30 W
Old Howe ≐ 44 53.57 N 0.21 W
Oldisleben 54 51.18 N 11.10 E
Old Lyme 207 41.18 N 72.19 W
Old Malden ✈⁸ 260 51.23 N 0.15 W
Oldman ≐ 182 49.56 N 111.42 W
Old Man House ⊥ 224 47.43 N 122.34 W
Old Man Mountain ∧ 186 49.08 N 57.23 W
Old Manor 276 40.24 N 74.11 W
Oldmeldrum 46 57.20 N 2.20 W
Old Mkushi 154 14.22 S 29.22 E
Old Monroe 219 38.55 N 90.44 W
Old Mystic 207 41.23 N 71.57 W
Old Nene ≐ 42 52.31 N 0.08 W
Old North Bridge ⊥ 283 42.28 N 71.21 W
Old North Church ᵾ¹ 283 42.22 N 71.03 W
Old Ocean 222 29.05 N 95.45 W
Ol Doinyo Sapuk National Park ♦ 154 1.09 S 37.12 E
Ol'doj ≐ 89 53.33 N 123.21 E
Old Orchard ✈⁹ 278 42.04 N 87.45 W
Old Orchard Beach 188 43.31 N 70.22 W
Old Perlican 186 48.05 N 53.01 W
Old Place Creek ≐ 276 40.38 N 74.12 W
Old Point Comfort ⊱ 208 37.00 N 76.19 W
Old Rhodes Key I 220 25.22 N 80.14 W
Old Ripley 219 38.54 N 89.34 W
Old Road Bay c 284b 39.12 N 76.27 W
Old Road Bluff ⊱ 240c 16.59 N 61.52 W
Old Round Rock 222 30.31 N 97.41 W
Olds 182 51.47 N 114.06 W
Old Saybrook 207 41.17 N 72.22 W
Oldsmar 220 28.02 N 82.39 W
Old Speck Mountain ∧ 188 44.34 N 70.57 W
Old Sturbridge Village ⊥ 207 42.07 N 72.07 W
Old Swamp ≐ 283 42.11 N 70.57 W
Old Swedes Church ᵾ¹ 285 39.44 N 75.32 W
Old Tampa Bay c 220 27.56 N 82.35 W
Old Tappan 276 41.00 N 73.59 W
Old Tate 156 21.22 S 27.46 E
Old Town 188 44.56 N 68.38 W
Old Trafford Cricket Ground ♦ 262 53.28 N 2.17 W
Old Trap 192 36.15 N 76.02 W
Olduvai Gorge V 154 2.58 S 35.22 E
Old Westbury 276 40.47 N 73.37 W
Old Westbury Gardens ♦ 276 40.46 N 73.36 W
Oldwick 210 40.40 N 74.44 W
Old Windsor 260 51.28 N 0.35 W
Old Wives Lake ⊜ 184 50.06 N 106.00 W
Old Woman Creek ≐ 198 43.19 N 104.21 W
Öldzijt, Mong. 88 48.07 N 102.34 E
Öldzijt, Mong. 102 45.18 N 106.12 E
Old Zoinsville 208 40.29 N 75.31 W
Olean 210 42.04 N 78.25 W
Olean Creek ≐ 210 42.04 N 78.25 W
O'Leary 186 46.42 N 64.13 W
Olecko 30 54.03 N 22.30 E
Olegário Maciel 256 22.19 S 45.35 W
Oleggio 62 45.36 N 8.38 E
Olekma — Ol'okma ≐ 74 60.22 N 120.42 E
Oleksandrivka, Ukr. 78 48.43 N 36.55 E
Oleksandrivka, Ukr. 78 48.57 N 32.14 E
Oleksandrivka, Ukr. 78 47.42 N 31.16 E
Oleksandrivka, Ukr. 78 46.32 N 35.29 E
Oleksandrivka, Ukr. 83 47.55 N 37.35 E
Oleksandrivka, Ukr. 83 47.47 N 37.41 E
Oleksandrivs'k 83 48.35 N 39.12 E
Oleksandriya 78 48.40 N 33.07 E
Oleksandro-Kalynove 83 48.25 N 37.40 E
Oleksiyevo-Druzhkivka 83 48.34 N 37.36 E
Oleksiyivka, Ukr. 78 47.14 N 36.32 E
Oleksiyivka, Ukr. 78 49.25 N 38.46 E
Oleksiyivka, Ukr. 83 49.01 N 39.11 E
Olema 24 64.30 N 46.08 E
Olen, Bel. 56 51.09 N 4.51 E
Ølen, Nor. 26 59.36 N 5.48 E
Ølen ⊜ 40 59.13 N 14.31 E
Olenegorsk 24 68.09 N 33.15 E
Olenica 24 66.29 N 35.20 E
Olenij, ostrov I 74 72.25 N 77.45 E
Olenino 76 56.12 N 33.29 E
Olenivka 78 45.23 N 32.32 E
Olenja Rečka 86 52.48 N 93.14 E
Olen'ok 74 68.33 N 112.18 E
Olen'ok ≐ 74 73.00 N 119.55 E
Olen'okskij zaliv c 74 73.20 N 121.00 E
Olentangy ≐ 214 39.58 N 83.06 W
Olenty 80 50.02 N 52.07 E
Olenty ≐ 80 49.50 N 52.03 E
Oleopolis 214 41.27 N 79.37 W
Oléron, Île d' I 32 45.56 N 1.15 W
Oles'ko 78 49.58 N 24.53 E
Olešná 60 49.46 N 13.48 E
Oleśnica 30 51.13 N 17.23 E
Olesno 30 50.53 N 18.25 E
Olevano Romano 66 41.52 N 13.02 E
Olevano sul Tusciano 68 40.40 N 15.01 E
Olevsk 78 51.13 N 27.39 E
Oley 208 40.23 N 75.47 W
Olfen 52 51.42 N 7.23 E
Ol'ga, Ross. 89 43.45 N 135.18 E
Olga, Wa., U.S. 224 48.37 N 122.50 W
Olga, Mount ∧, Austl. 162 25.19 S 130.46 E
Olga, Mount ∧, Vt., U.S. 207 42.51 N 72.48 W
Olgiata 267a 42.02 N 12.22 E
Olgiate Comasco 62 45.48 N 8.58 E
Olgiate Olona 62 45.38 N 8.53 E
Ölgij, Mong. 86 48.56 N 89.57 E
Ölgij, Mong. 86 48.59 N 92.01 E
Ølgod 26 55.49 N 8.37 E
Olginate 62 45.48 N 9.24 E
Ol'ginka 78 44.14 N 38.53 E
Ol'gino 89 52.53 N 125.47 E
Ol'gino ✈⁸ 265a 60.00 N 30.09 E
Ol'ginskaja, Ross. 78 45.57 N 38.34 E
Ol'ginskaja, Ross. 83 47.11 N 39.56 E
Ol'govo 82 56.16 N 37.21 E
Olhão 34 37.02 N 7.50 W
Olho d'Água das Cunhãs 250 4.43 S 44.34 W
Olho d'Água das Flores 250 9.33 S 37.17 W
Ol'hopil' 78 48.12 N 29.29 E
Ol'hynka 83 47.42 N 37.31 E
Oli ≐ 150 9.45 N 4.38 E
Olib, Otok I 36 44.22 N 14.48 E
Oliden 258 35.11 S 57.57 W
Oliena 71 40.16 N 9.24 E
Olifants (Rio dos Elefantes) ≐, Afr. 156 24.10 S 32.40 E
Olifants ≐, Namibia 156 25.30 S 19.30 E
Olifants ≐, S. Afr. 158 29.39 S 21.10 E
Olifants ≐, S. Afr. 158 33.41 S 21.42 E
Olifants ≐, S. Afr. 158 31.42 S 18.12 E
Olifantshoek 158 27.57 S 22.42 E
Olifantsrivierberge ∧ 158 32.10 S 19.00 E
Oliki 265a 59.46 N 29.55 E
Olimarao I¹ 108 7.41 N 145.52 E
Olimbia ⊥ 38 37.38 N 21.41 E
Ólimbos 38 35.44 N 27.11 E
Ólimbos ∧ 130 34.56 N 32.52 E
Ólimbos (Mount Olympus) ∧ 38 40.05 N 22.21 E
Olímpia 255 20.44 S 48.54 W
Olímpico, Estadio ♦ 286a 19.20 N 99.12 W
Olímpico, Stadio ♦ 267a 41.56 N 12.27 E
Olímpio Noronha 256 22.04 S 45.16 W
Olimpo — Ólimbos, Óros ∧ 38 40.05 N 22.21 E
Olin 190 41.59 N 91.08 W
Olinalá 234 17.50 N 98.51 W
Olinda, Austl. 170 32.50 S 150.08 E
Olinda, Austl. 274b 37.51 S 145.22 E
Olinda, Bra. 250 8.01 S 34.51 W
Olinda, Bra. 256 22.49 S 43.25 W
Olinda, Mount ∧ 274b 37.52 S 145.21 E
Olinda Creek ≐ 274b 37.41 S 145.21 E
Olindina 250 11.22 S 38.21 W
Olinsk 88 52.24 N 116.13 E
Olio 166 21.54 S 143.13 E
Olite 34 42.29 N 1.39 W
Oliva, Arg. 252 32.03 S 63.34 W
Oliva, Esp. 34 38.55 N 0.07 W
Oliva de la Frontera 34 38.16 N 6.55 W
Olivais ✈⁸ 266c 38.46 N 9.06 W
Olival Basto 266c 38.47 N 9.10 W
Olivares, Cerro de ∧ 252 30.18 S 69.55 W
Olive Branch 194 34.57 N 89.49 W
Olivebridge 210 41.55 N 74.13 W
Olive Hill 218 38.18 N 83.10 W
Olivehurst 226 39.05 N 121.33 W
Oliveira 255 20.41 S 44.49 W
Oliveira dos Brejinhos 255 12.19 S 42.54 W
Oliveira Fortes 256 21.20 S 43.27 W
Olivelifuri I 122 5.17 N 73.35 E
Olive Mount ✈⁸ 262 53.24 N 2.55 W
Olivença 34 38.41 N 7.06 W
Olivenza 34 38.41 N 7.06 W
Oliver 182 49.11 N 119.33 W
Olivera 258 34.38 S 59.15 W
Oliver Creek ≐ 222 33.06 N 97.17 W
Oliver Ditch ≡ 216 41.00 N 87.10 W
Oliverea 210 42.03 N 74.27 W
Oliver Estates 284c 38.51 N 77.07 W
Oliveri 70 38.07 N 15.03 E
Oliver Lake ⊜ 184 56.56 N 103.22 W
Oliver Springs 192 36.02 N 84.20 W
Olivet, Fr. 50 47.52 N 1.54 E
Olivet, Mi., U.S. 216 42.26 N 84.55 W
Olivet, S.D., U.S. 198 43.14 N 97.40 W
Oliveto Citra 68 40.41 N 15.14 E
Oliveto Lucano 68 40.32 N 16.11 E
Olivette 219 38.39 N 90.22 W
Olivia 198 44.46 N 94.59 W
Olivine Range ∧ 172 44.18 S 168.30 E
Olivo 116 10.52 N 123.53 E
Olivo ≐ 70 37.22 N 14.15 E
Olivone 58 46.32 N 8.57 E
Olivos ✈⁸ 258 34.32 S 58.29 W
Öljaren ⊜ 40 59.08 N 16.02 E
Olji Moron ≐ 89 44.16 N 121.42 E
Olla 194 31.54 N 92.14 W
Ollagüe 248 21.14 S 68.16 W
Ollagüe, Volcán ∧¹ 248 21.18 S 68.12 W
Ollainville 261 48.35 N 2.13 E
Ollantaitambo 248 13.16 S 72.16 W
Ollatrim ≐ 48 52.52 N 8.13 W
Ollei 175b 7.43 N 134.37 E
Ollerton 262 53.17 N 2.20 W
Ollerup 41 55.04 N 10.30 E
Olliergues 62 45.40 N 3.38 E
Ollioules 62 43.08 N 5.51 E
Ollomont 62 45.50 N 7.22 E
Ollon 58 46.18 N 7.00 E
Olloua 152 0.56 S 14.34 E
Olmedillo de Roa 34 41.47 N 3.56 W
Olmedo, Esp. 34 41.23 N 4.41 W
Olmedo, It. 71 40.39 N 8.23 E
Olmo al Brembo 58 45.58 N 9.39 E
Olmos 248 5.59 S 79.46 W
Olmsted 214 41.24 N 81.44 W
Olmsted Falls 279a 41.22 N 81.54 W
Olmütz — Olomouc 30 49.36 N 17.16 E
Olney, Eng., U.K. 42 52.09 N 0.42 W
Olney, Il., U.S. 194 38.43 N 88.05 W
Olney, Md., U.S. 208 39.09 N 77.04 W
Olney, Mo., U.S. 219 39.05 N 91.15 W
Olney, Mt., U.S. 182 48.32 N 114.34 W
Olney, Tx., U.S. 196 33.22 N 98.45 W
Olney ✈⁸ 285 40.02 N 75.08 W
Oloči 89 51.21 N 119.55 E
Olofström 26 56.16 N 14.30 E
Oloj ≐ 74 66.29 N 159.29 E
Ol'okma ≐ 74 60.22 N 120.42 E
Ol'okminsk 74 60.24 N 120.24 E
Ol'okminskij Stanovik ∧ 88 54.30 N 120.00 E
Olokui ∧ 229a 21.08 N 156.51 W
Olomane ≐ 186 50.14 N 60.37 W
Olombo 152 1.18 S 15.53 E
Olomega, Laguna ⊜ 236 13.19 N 88.04 W
Olomouc 30 49.36 N 17.16 E
Olona ≐ 62 45.06 N 9.21 E
Olonec 24 61.00 N 32.57 E
Olongapo 116 14.50 N 120.16 E
Olonki 88 52.54 N 103.45 E
Olorgasailie National Monument ♦ 154 1.40 S 36.22 E
Oloron, Gave d' ≐ 32 43.33 N 1.05 W
Oloron-Sainte-Marie 32 43.12 N 0.36 W
Olosega 174y 14.11 S 169.39 W
Olosega I 174y 14.11 S 169.39 W
Olot 34 42.11 N 2.29 E
Olov'annaja, Ross. 88 50.56 N 115.35 E
Olov'annaja, Ross. 180 66.10 N 178.59 W
Oloví 54 50.11 N 12.33 E
Olpe, Dtsch. 56 51.02 N 7.52 E
Olpe, Ks., U.S. 198 38.15 N 96.10 W
Olperer ∧ 64 47.03 N 11.39 E
Olsabach ≐ 61 46.56 N 14.25 E
Ol'šanka 78 51.46 N 35.25 E
Ol'šany, Bela. 78 52.05 N 27.20 E
Olšany, Česká Rep. 60 49.24 N 13.38 E
Olsberg 56 51.21 N 8.29 E
Ølsemagle 41 55.30 N 12.10 E
Olshammar 40 58.45 N 14.48 E
Ol'shana 78 50.48 N 34.02 E
Olst 52 52.20 N 6.06 E
Ølstykke 41 55.47 N 12.11 E
Olsufjevo 76 53.36 N 33.40 E
Olsztyn (Allenstein) 30 53.48 N 20.29 E
Olsztyn □⁴ 30 53.50 N 20.40 E
Olsztynek 30 53.36 N 20.17 E
Olt □⁶ 38 44.20 N 24.30 E
Olt ≐ 38 43.43 N 24.51 E
Olta 252 30.37 S 66.16 W
Olten 58 47.21 N 7.54 E
Olteni 38 44.10 N 25.18 E
Oltenița 38 44.05 N 26.39 E
Oltet ≐ 38 44.14 N 24.27 E
Olton 196 34.11 N 102.08 W
Oltre il Colle 64 45.54 N 9.46 E
Oltu 130 40.33 N 41.59 E
Oltu ≐ 130 40.49 N 41.40 E
Oluan Pi ⊱ 100 21.54 N 120.51 E
Olukonda 156 18.03 S 16.00 E
Olur 130 40.50 N 42.08 E
Olustee, Fl., U.S. 192 30.12 N 82.26 W
Olustee, Ok., U.S. 196 34.32 N 99.25 W
Olustee Creek ≐ 192 29.57 N 82.32 W
Oluta 234 17.55 N 94.54 W
Olutanga (Suba Nipa) 116 7.26 N 122.54 E
Olutanga Island I 116 7.22 N 122.52 E
Olutayan Island I 116 11.39 N 122.50 E
Olute 273a 6.28 N 3.16 E
Ol'utorskij, mys ⊱ 74 59.55 N 170.27 E
Ol'utorskij zaliv c 74 60.15 N 168.30 E
Oluwo 273a 6.42 N 3.18 E
Olvenstedt 54 52.09 N 11.34 E
Olvera 34 36.56 N 5.16 W
Olyka 78 50.42 N 25.51 E
Olykhovatka 78 50.12 N 37.31 E
Olym 78 51.42 N 38.10 E
Olymp — Ólimbos, Óros ∧ 38 40.05 N 22.21 E
Olympe, Mont — Ólimbos, Óros ∧ 38 40.05 N 22.21 E
Olympia 224 47.02 N 122.53 W
Olympia — Olimbía ⊥ 38 37.38 N 21.41 E
Olympia Fields 216 41.32 N 87.42 W
Olympia Heights 220 25.43 N 80.21 W
Olympia Park ♦ 273d 26.15 S 28.26 E
Olympia-Stadion ♦ 264a 52.31 N 13.14 E
Olympic Mountains ∧ 224 47.50 N 123.45 W
Olympic National Park ♦ 224 47.48 N 123.30 W
Olympic Valley 226 39.13 N 120.14 W
Olympic View 224 47.43 N 122.45 W
Olympieion ⊥ 267c 37.58 N 23.44 E
Olympique, Stade ♦ 275a 45.33 N 73.33 W
Olympus, Mount — Ólimbos, Óros ∧, Ellás 38 40.05 N 22.21 E
Olympus, Mount ∧, Wa., U.S. 224 47.48 N 123.43 W
Olympus, Mount ∧² 192 38.03 N 83.39 W
Olyphant 210 41.28 N 75.36 W
Olyshivka 78 51.13 N 31.18 E
Olzai 71 40.11 N 9.09 E
Ol'zony 88 52.57 N 105.15 E
Om ≐, Pap. N. Gui. 164 5.09 S 142.22 E
Om' ≐, Ross. 86 54.59 N 73.22 E
Ōma 92 41.32 N 140.55 E
Ōmachi, Nihon 94 36.30 N 137.52 E
Ōmachi, Nihon 270 34.28 N 135.25 E
Ōmaezaki 94 34.35 N 138.13 E
Omae-zaki ⊱ 94 34.36 N 138.14 E
Ōmagari 92 39.27 N 140.29 E
Omagh, On., Can. 275b 43.30 N 79.49 W
Omagh, N. Ire., U.K. 48 54.36 N 7.18 W
Omagi 268 35.52 N 139.42 E
Omaguas 248 4.08 S 73.15 W
Omaha, Ne., U.S. 198 41.15 N 95.56 W
Omaha, Tx., U.S. 222 33.11 N 94.45 W
Omaha Indian Reservation ✈⁴ 198 42.08 N 96.22 W
Omak 202 48.24 N 119.31 W
Omakau 172 45.05 S 169.36 E
Omak Lake ⊜ 202 48.16 N 119.23 W
Omalo 84 42.23 N 45.38 E
Ōmama 94 36.26 N 139.17 E
Oman ('Umān) □¹ 118 22.00 N 58.00 E
Oman, Gulf of c 118 24.30 N 58.30 E
Omapere, Lake ⊜ 172 35.21 S 173.47 E
Omar 192 37.45 N 81.59 W
Omarama 172 44.29 S 169.58 E
Omaruru 156 21.28 S 15.56 E
Omaruru □⁵ 156 21.00 S 16.00 E
Omaruru ≐ 156 22.07 S 14.15 E
Omas 248 12.31 S 76.17 W
Omatako ∧ 156 21.07 S 16.43 E
Omatako ≐ 156 17.59 S 20.30 E
Omate 248 16.41 S 70.59 W
Omatena 115b 9.53 S 119.47 E
Ōma-zaki ⊱ 92 41.32 N 140.55 E
Ombai, Selat ⵡ 112 8.30 S 125.00 E
Ombella-Mpoko □⁵ 152 5.00 N 18.00 E
Omberg ∧² 26 58.20 N 14.39 E
Ombersley 42 52.17 N 2.13 W
Ombombo 156 18.43 S 13.53 E
Omboué 152 1.34 S 9.15 E
Ombrone ≐ 66 42.39 N 11.00 E
Ombúes de Lavalle 258 33.55 S 57.47 W
Ombutosu ∧ 156 21.22 S 16.50 E
Ombwe 154 4.22 S 25.35 E
Omčak 74 61.38 N 147.55 E
Omčaly 128 40.47 N 53.43 E
Omdraaisvlei 158 30.08 S 23.08 E
Omdurman — Umm Durmān 140 15.38 N 32.30 E
Ōme 94 35.47 N 139.15 E
Omega, Ga., U.S. 192 31.20 N 83.35 W
Omega, Oh., U.S. 218 39.09 N 82.55 W
Omegna 62 45.53 N 8.24 E
Omel'nyk 78 49.12 N 33.32 E
Omelyanivka 78 45.32 N 34.53 E
Omemee 212 44.18 N 78.33 W
Omeo 166 37.06 S 147.36 E
Ömerköy 130 39.48 N 28.03 E
Ömerli 130 37.24 N 40.58 E
Ömerli Baraji ⊜¹ 130 41.00 N 29.20 E
Omerville 206 45.17 N 72.07 W
Ometepe, Isla de I 236 11.30 N 85.35 W
Ometepec 234 16.41 N 98.25 W
Ometepec ≐ 234 16.30 N 98.45 W
Om Hajer 144 14.24 N 36.46 E
Ōmi, Nihon 94 36.27 N 138.03 E
Ōmi, Nihon 94 37.01 N 137.48 E
Ōmi, Nihon 94 35.20 N 136.24 E
Ōmigawa 94 35.51 N 140.37 E
Ōmi-hachiman 94 35.08 N 136.06 E
Ōminato — Mutsu 92 41.17 N 141.10 E
Omineca ≐ 182 56.05 N 124.30 W
Omineca Mountains ∧ 182 56.00 N 125.00 W
Ōmin-ni ✈⁸ 271b 37.27 N 127.01 E
Ōmino 270 34.32 N 135.33 E
Omišalj 36 45.13 N 14.34 E
Ōmi-shima I, Nihon 96 34.25 N 131.13 E
Ōmi-shima I, Nihon 96 34.15 N 133.00 E
Omitara 156 22.18 S 18.01 E
Omitlán ≐ 234 17.06 N 99.34 W
Ōmiya, Nihon 94 36.33 N 140.25 E
Ōmiya, Nihon 94 35.54 N 139.38 E
Ōmiya, Nihon 96 35.35 N 135.06 E
Ōmiya-daichi ∧¹ 268 35.56 N 139.38 E
Ōmiya Park Race Track ♦ 268 35.55 N 139.38 E
Øm Kloster ⊥ 41 56.03 N 9.45 E
Ommaney, Cape ⊱ 180 56.10 N 134.39 W
Ommanney Bay c 176 73.07 N 100.11 W
Omme ≐ 41 55.53 N 8.40 E
Ommen 52 52.32 N 6.25 E
Ömnödelger 88 47.52 N 109.55 E
Ömnögov' 86 49.06 N 91.43 E
Ömnögov' □⁴ 102 43.00 N 104.00 E
Omø I 41 55.09 N 11.10 E
Omo ≐ 144 43.10 N 35.59 E
Omoa, Bahía de c 236 15.45 N 88.10 W
Omodeo, Lago ⊜ 71 40.08 N 8.55 E
Omogo 96 33.41 N 133.02 E
Omoi ≐ 94 36.09 N 139.41 E
Omoko 150 5.20 N 6.39 E
Omole 273a 6.38 N 3.22 E
Omoloj ≐ 74 71.10 N 132.08 E
Omolon ≐ 74 68.42 N 158.36 E
Omo National Park ♦ 144 6.00 N 35.45 E
Omono ≐ 92 39.46 N 140.03 E
Omont 56 49.36 N 4.44 E
Omo Ranch 226 38.35 N 120.35 W
Ōmori ✈⁸ 268 35.34 N 139.44 E
Omotegō 94 37.03 N 140.18 E
Omoy 152 1.21 S 13.09 E
Omrel'kaj ≐ 180 68.34 N 170.30 E
Omro 190 44.02 N 88.44 W
Omsino 80 58.36 N 50.28 E
Omsk 86 55.00 N 73.24 E
Omsk Oblast' □⁴ 86 56.00 N 73.00 E
Omsukčan 74 62.32 N 155.48 E
O-mu, Mya. 110 22.58 N 99.18 E
Ōmu, Nihon 92a 44.34 N 142.58 E
Omu-Aran 150 8.09 N 5.07 E
Ōmuda — Ōmuta 96 33.02 N 130.27 E
Omul, Vârful ∧ 38 45.26 N 25.26 E
Omulew ≐ 30 53.05 N 21.32 E
Ōmura 92 32.54 N 129.57 E
Ōmura-wan c 92 32.57 N 129.52 E
Ōmuro 268 35.54 N 139.58 E
Omurtag 38 43.06 N 26.25 E
Ōmuta 96 33.02 N 130.27 E
Omutinskij 86 56.31 N 67.41 E
Omutninsk 86 58.40 N 52.12 E
Ŏmyŏnbo 98 41.16 N 127.36 E
On 110 21.40 N 106.35 E
Ona, Nor. 26 62.52 N 6.34 E
Ona, Fl., U.S. 220 27.28 N 81.55 W
Ona ≐, Ross. 86 52.34 N 89.50 E
Ona — Bir'usa ≐, Ross. 88 57.43 N 95.24 E
Onabas 232 29.27 N 109.32 W
Onadikondo 152 3.52 S 24.10 E
Onaga 198 39.29 N 96.10 W
Onagawa 92 38.26 N 141.27 E
Onahama 94 36.57 N 140.54 E
Onalaska, Tx., U.S. 222 30.48 N 95.07 W
Onalaska, Wa., U.S. 224 46.34 N 122.43 W
Onamia 190 46.04 N 93.40 W
Onancock 208 37.42 N 75.44 W
Onangué, Lac ⊜ 152 0.57 S 10.04 E
Onaping ≐ 190 46.37 N 81.18 W
Onaping Lake ⊜ 190 47.00 N 81.30 W
Onarga 216 40.42 N 88.00 W
Ōnari 268 35.55 N 139.37 E
Onatchiway, Lac ⊜ 186 49.00 N 71.03 W
Onawa 198 42.01 N 96.05 W
Onaway 190 45.21 N 84.13 W
Oncativo 252 31.55 S 63.40 W
Once, Canal Numero ≡ 252 36.09 S 58.36 W
Onchāi 272b 22.57 N 88.19 E
Onchan 44 54.11 N 4.27 W
Onch'ŏn-dong 98 40.51 N 129.07 E
Oncócua 152 16.34 S 13.28 E
Onda, Esp. 34 39.58 N 0.15 W
Onda, India 126 23.08 N 87.12 E
Ondangwa 156 17.55 S 16.00 E
Ondas, Rio de ≐ 255 12.08 S 45.00 W
Ondava ≐ 30 48.27 N 21.48 E
Onderdijk 52 52.45 N 5.07 E
Onderstedorings 158 30.13 S 20.37 E
Ondjiva 152 17.03 S 15.47 E
Ondo, Nig. 150 7.04 N 4.47 E
Ondo, Nihon 96 34.11 N 132.32 E

≐	River	Fluß	Río	Rivière	Rio
≡	Canal	Kanal	Canal	Canal	Canal
⌊	Waterfall, Rapids	Wasserfall, Stromschnellen	Cascada, Rápidos	Chute d'eau, Rapides	Cascata, Rápidos
ⵡ	Strait	Meeresstraße	Estrecho	Détroit	Estreito
c	Bay, Gulf	Bucht, Golf	Bahía, Golfo	Baie, Golfe	Baía, Golfo
⊜	Lake, Lakes	See, Seen	Lago, Lagos	Lac, Lacs	Lago, Lagos
⩨	Swamp	Sumpf	Pantano	Marais	Pântano
⌐	Ice Features, Glacier	Eis- und Gletscherformen	Accidentes Glaciales	Formes glaciaires	Acidentes glaciares
⌐	Other Hydrographic Features	Andere Hydrographische Objekte	Otros Elementos Hidrográficos	Autres données hydrographiques	Outros acidentes hidrográficos
✈	Submarine Features	Untermeerische Objekte	Accidentes Submarinos	Formes de relief sous-marin	Acidentes submarinos
□	Political Unit	Politische Einheit	Unidad Política	Entité politique	Unidade política
ᵾ	Cultural Institution	Kulturelle Institution	Institución Cultural	Institution culturelle	Instituição cultural
⊥	Historical Site	Historische Stätte	Sitio Histórico	Site historique	Sítio histórico
♦	Recreational Site	Erholungs- und Ferienort	Sitio de Recreo	Centre de loisirs	Área de Lazer
⊠	Airport	Flughafen	Aeropuerto	Aéroport	Aeroporto
■	Military Installation	Militäranlage	Instalación Militar	Installation militaire	Instalação militar
✈	Miscellaneous	Verschiedenes	Misceláneo	Divers	Diversos

ENGLISH / DEUTSCH

Name	Page	Lat. °′	Long. °′
Ondo □[3]	150	7.00 N	5.15 E
Ondo-ōhashi ◂[5]	96	34.12 N	132.33 E
Öndörchaan	88	47.19 N	110.39 E
Öndörchangaj	88	49.20 N	94.50 E
Öndör-Önc	102	45.51 N	103.11 E
Öndöršireet	88	47.27 N	104.50 E
Öndör-Ulaan	88	48.03 N	100.30 E
Ondozero, ozero ⊜	24	63.48 N	33.20 E
O'Neals	226	37.08 N	119.42 W
One Arrow Indian Reserve ◂[4]	184	52.48 N	106.03 W
Oneco, Ct., U.S.	207	41.41 N	71.48 W
Oneco, Fl., U.S.	220	27.26 N	82.32 W
Onega	24	63.55 N	38.05 E
Onega ≃	24	63.58 N	37.55 E
Onega, Lake → Onežskoje ozero ⊜	24	61.30 N	35.45 E
Oneglia	62	43.53 N	8.02 E
One Hundred and Two ≃	194	39.44 N	94.43 W
One Hundred and Two, West Fork ≃	194	40.26 N	94.49 W
One Hundred Fifty Mile House	182	52.06 N	121.55 W
One Hundred Mile House	182	51.39 N	121.18 W
Oneida, Il., U.S.	190	41.04 N	90.13 W
Oneida, Ky., U.S.	192	37.16 N	83.38 W
Oneida, N.Y., U.S.	210	43.05 N	75.39 W
Oneida, Oh., U.S.	218	39.28 N	84.23 W
Oneida, Pa., U.S.	210	40.54 N	76.08 W
Oneida, Tn., U.S.	192	36.29 N	84.30 W
Oneida □[6]	210	43.10 N	75.20 W
Oneida ≃	210	43.12 N	76.17 W
Oneida Castle	210	43.05 N	75.40 W
Oneida County Airport ⊠	210	43.09 N	75.23 W
Oneida Creek ≃	210	43.10 N	75.44 W
Oneida Indian Reservation ◂[4]	190	44.30 N	88.10 W
Oneida Indian Reserve ◂[4]	214	42.49 N	81.24 W
Oneida Lake ⊜	210	43.13 N	76.00 W
O'Neil Forebay ⊜[1]	226	37.05 N	121.03 W
O'Neill	198	42.27 N	98.38 W
Onekama	190	44.21 N	86.12 W
Onekotan, ostrov I	74	49.25 N	154.45 E
Onema	152	4.33 S	24.31 E
Onemen, zaliv c	180	64.45 N	176.35 E
Oneonta, Al., U.S.	194	33.56 N	86.28 W
Oneonta, N.Y., U.S.	210	42.27 N	75.03 W
Oneroa I	174k	21.15 S	159.43 W
Onești	38	46.14 N	26.44 E
One Tree Hill	168b	34.43 S	138.46 E
One Tree Hill ∧[2]	274b	37.52 S	145.19 E
One Tree Hill Lookout ♦	169	36.48 S	144.18 E
Onevai I	174w	21.05 S	175.07 W
Onex	58	46.10 N	6.06 E
Onežskaja guba c	24	64.20 N	36.30 E
Onežskij poluostrov >[1]	24	64.35 N	38.00 E
Onežskoje ozero (Lake Onega) ⊜	24	61.30 N	35.45 E
Onga ≃	96	33.54 N	130.39 E
Ongaonga	172	39.55 S	176.25 E
Ongarue	172	38.43 S	175.17 E
Ong Con, Cu Lao I	269c	10.45 N	106.50 E
Ongea Levu I	175g	19.08 S	178.24 W
Ongeluks ≃	158	32.24 S	19.46 E
Ongers ≃	158	31.04 S	23.13 E
Ongerup	162	33.58 S	118.29 E
Ongijn ≃	102	44.30 N	103.40 E
Ongjin	98	37.57 N	125.21 E
Ongoka	154	1.23 S	26.02 E
Ongole	122	15.31 N	80.04 E
Ongon	102	45.21 N	113.09 E
Ongudaj	86	50.45 N	86.09 E
Oni	84	42.34 N	43.27 E
Onich	46	56.42 N	5.13 W
Onida	198	44.42 N	100.03 W
Onifai	71	40.24 N	9.39 E
Oniferi	71	40.16 N	9.10 E
Onigajō-yama ∧	96	33.07 N	132.41 E
Onilahy ≃	157b	23.34 S	43.45 E
Onin, Jazirah >[1]	164	2.50 S	132.05 E
Onion Creek ≃	222	30.12 N	97.35 W
Onion Peak ∧	224	45.49 N	123.53 W
Onishi	94	36.09 N	139.04 E
Onistagane, Lac ⊜	186	50.42 N	71.19 W
Onitsha	150	6.09 N	6.47 E
Onji	270	34.37 N	135.38 E
Onjuku	94	35.11 N	140.22 E
Onkaparinga ≃	168b	35.10 S	138.28 E
Onkivesi ⊜	26	63.18 N	27.18 E
Onko	152	4.07 S	19.59 E
Onley	208	37.41 N	75.42 W
Onna	174m	26.30 N	127.51 E
Onnaing	50	50.23 N	3.36 E
Onno	58	45.55 N	9.17 E
Onny ≃	42	52.23 N	2.45 W
Ōno, Nihon	94	35.59 N	136.29 E
Ōno, Nihon	94	35.28 N	136.38 E
Ōno, Nihon	96	34.18 N	132.17 E
Ono, Nihon	96	34.51 N	134.56 E
Ōno, Nihon	96	33.02 N	131.30 E
Ono, Nihon	270	34.57 N	135.14 E
Ono, Pa., U.S.	208	40.24 N	76.32 W
Ono I	175g	18.55 S	178.29 E
Ōno ≃	96	33.15 N	131.43 E
Onochoj	88	51.58 N	108.01 E
Onoda	96	33.59 N	131.11 E
Ōno-dam ◂[6]	96	35.15 N	135.27 E
Onogami	94	36.33 N	138.56 E
Ōnohara	96	34.05 N	133.40 E
Ono-I-Lau I	14	20.39 S	178.42 W
Ōnojō	96	33.32 N	130.28 E
Onolimbu	114	1.03 N	97.53 E
Ōnomi	96	33.21 N	133.09 E
Onomichi	96	34.25 N	133.12 E
Onon	88	49.08 N	112.38 E
Onon ≃	88	51.42 N	115.50 E
Onondaga, Mi., U.S.	216	42.26 N	84.33 W
Onondaga, N.Y., U.S.	210	43.00 N	76.11 W
Onondaga □[6]	210	43.03 N	76.09 W
Onondaga Creek ≃	210	43.04 N	76.11 W
Onondaga Indian Reservation ◂[4]	210	42.55 N	76.09 W
Onor	89	50.11 N	142.40 E
Onota Lake ⊜	207	42.28 N	73.17 W
Onoto	246	9.36 N	65.12 W
Onotoa I[1]	14	1.52 S	175.34 E
Onoway	182	53.42 N	114.12 W
Ons, Isla de I	34	42.23 N	8.56 W
Onsbjerg	41	55.51 N	10.35 E
Onseepkans	158	28.46 S	19.14 E
Onsen	96	35.33 N	134.29 E
Onset	207	41.44 N	70.39 W
Onslow	162	21.39 S	115.06 E
Onslow Bay c	192	34.20 N	77.20 W
Onslow Village	260	51.14 N	0.36 W
Onsted	216	42.00 N	84.11 W
Onstmettingen	58	48.17 N	9.00 E
Onstwedde	52	53.02 N	7.02 E
On-take ∧	92	31.35 N	130.39 E
Ontake-san ∧	94	35.53 N	137.29 E
Ontario, Ca., U.S.	228	34.03 N	117.39 W
Ontario, In., U.S.	216	41.43 N	85.23 W
Ontario, N.Y., U.S.	210	43.13 N	77.17 W
Ontario, Oh., U.S.	214	40.45 N	82.35 W
Ontario, Or., U.S.	202	44.01 N	116.57 W
Ontario □[6]	210	42.54 N	77.17 W
Ontario □[4]	176	51.00 N	85.00 W
Ontario, Lake ⊜	212	43.45 N	78.00 W
Ontario Agricultural Museum ⚘	212	43.30 N	79.56 W
Ontario Center	210	43.14 N	77.19 W
Ontario International Airport ⊠	228	34.04 N	117.36 W
Ontario Place ♦	275b	43.38 N	79.25 W
Ontario Science Centre ⚘	275b	43.43 N	79.21 W
Ontelaunee, Lake ⊜	208	40.27 N	75.55 W
Ontinyent (Onteniente)	34	38.49 N	0.37 W
Ontojärvi ⊜	26	64.08 N	29.09 E
Ontonagon	190	46.52 N	89.18 W
Ontonagon ≃	190	46.52 N	89.20 W
Ontonagon, East Branch ≃	190	46.42 N	89.11 W
Ontonagon, Middle Branch ≃	190	46.42 N	89.10 W
Ontonagon, West Branch ≃	190	46.42 N	89.11 W
Ontong Java I[1]	175e	5.20 S	159.30 E
Onufrijevo	82	55.51 N	36.31 E
Onufriyivka	78	48.54 N	33.26 E
Ōnuma	268	35.32 N	139.25 E
Onverwacht	250	5.36 N	55.12 W
Onward	216	40.42 N	86.12 W
Ŏnyang, Taehan	98	36.47 N	127.00 E
Ŏnyang, Taehan	98	35.34 N	129.07 E
Onzain	50	47.30 N	1.11 E
Onzo ≃	152	8.12 S	13.16 E
Oobagooma	162	16.46 S	123.59 E
Oodnadatta	162	27.33 S	135.28 E
Ood Weyne	144	9.25 N	45.04 E
Ōoka	94	36.30 N	137.59 E
Ooldea	162	30.27 S	131.50 E
Oolitic	218	38.54 N	86.31 W
Oologah	196	36.26 N	95.42 W
Oologah Lake ⊜[1]	196	36.33 N	95.36 W
Ooma	174d	0.53 S	169.36 E
Oombergen	50	50.54 N	3.50 E
Oona River	182	53.57 N	130.18 W
Ooratippra	162	22.00 S	136.00 E
Ooratippra Creek ≃	162	21.55 S	136.05 E
Oorlogskloof ≃	158	31.52 S	19.01 E
Oos	56	48.47 N	8.11 E
Oos-Londen → East London	158	33.00 S	27.55 E
Oostakker	50	51.06 N	3.46 E
Oostburg, Ned.	52	51.20 N	3.30 E
Oostburg, Wi., U.S.	190	43.37 N	87.47 W
Oost-Cappel	50	50.55 N	2.36 E
Oostduinkerke	50	51.07 N	2.41 E
Oostelijk Flevoland ◂[1]	52	52.30 N	5.40 E
Oostende (Ostende)	50	51.13 N	2.55 E
Oosterbeek	52	52.00 N	5.50 E
Oosterend	52	53.05 N	4.52 E
Oosterhout	52	51.38 N	4.51 E
Oosterschelde c	52	51.33 N	4.00 E
Oosterscheldedam ◂[6]	52	51.38 N	3.42 E
Oosterwolde	52	52.59 N	6.17 E
Oosterzele	50	50.57 N	3.48 E
Oosthuizen	52	52.35 N	5.00 E
Oostkamp	50	51.09 N	3.14 E
Oostmahorn	52	53.24 N	6.09 E
Oostmalle	56	51.18 N	4.44 E
Oostpunt >	241s	12.02 N	68.45 W
Oostrozebeke	50	50.55 N	3.20 E
Oost-Souburg	52	51.27 N	3.35 E
Oost-Vlaanderen □[4]	50	51.00 N	3.45 E
Oostvleteren	50	50.56 N	2.44 E
Oost-Vlieland	52	53.17 N	5.04 E
Oostvoorne	52	51.55 N	4.06 E
Ootmarsum	52	52.25 N	6.54 E
Ootsa Lake	182	53.47 N	126.03 W
Ootsa Lake ⊜	182	53.49 N	126.18 W
Ootsi	156	25.02 S	25.45 E
Ootua, Mont ∧	174x	9.47 S	138.58 W
Opaka	38	43.27 N	26.10 E
Opala	152	0.37 S	24.21 E
Opalaca, Cordillera ⋏	236	14.30 N	88.20 W
Opal Cliffs	226	36.57 N	121.57 W
Opale, Côte d' ⩡[2]	50	50.40 N	1.35 E
Opalenica	30	52.19 N	16.23 E
Opalicha	265b	55.49 N	37.15 E
Opa-Locka	220	25.54 N	80.15 W
Opari	154	3.56 N	32.03 E
Oparino	24	59.52 N	48.17 E
Opasatica, Lac ⊜	190	48.05 N	79.18 W
Opasatika Lake ⊜	190	49.04 N	83.08 W
Opasquia	184	53.16 N	93.35 W
Opasquia Lake ⊜	184	53.18 N	93.34 W
Opatija	36	45.21 N	14.19 E
Opatów	30	50.49 N	21.26 E
Opava	30	49.56 N	17.54 E
Opava ≃	30	49.50 N	18.13 E
Opečenskij Posad	76	58.16 N	34.07 E
Opeepeesway Lake ⊜	190	47.38 N	82.14 W
Opeilu	273a	6.42 N	3.18 E
Opelika	194	32.38 N	85.22 W
Opelousas	194	30.32 N	92.04 W
Open Bay c	164	4.50 S	151.20 E
Open Door	258	34.30 S	59.05 W
Opeongo ≃	190	45.30 N	77.57 W
Opeongo Lake ⊜	190	45.42 N	78.23 W
Opequon Creek ≃	188	39.35 N	77.52 W
Opfikon	58	47.26 N	8.35 E
Ophain-Bois-Seigneur-Isaac	50	50.40 N	4.21 E
Ophasselt	50	50.49 N	3.53 E
Opheim	202	48.51 N	106.24 W
Opherdicke	263	51.29 N	7.38 E
Opheusden	52	51.56 N	5.38 E
Ophir, Ak., U.S.	180	63.10 N	156.31 W
Ophir, Or., U.S.	202	42.33 N	124.22 W
Ophirton ◂[8]	273d	26.14 S	28.01 E
Ophthalmia Range ⋏	162	23.17 S	119.30 E
Opi	66	41.47 N	13.50 E
Opienge	154	0.12 N	27.30 E
Opihikao	229d	19.25 N	154.53 W
Opinaca ≃	176	52.15 N	78.02 W
Opinan	46	57.43 N	5.47 W
Opinicon Lake ⊜	212	44.33 N	76.20 W
Opiscotéo, Lac ⊜	176	53.10 N	68.10 W
Opishnya	78	49.58 N	34.37 E
Opladen	56	51.04 N	7.00 E
Opmeer	52	52.43 N	4.56 E
Opobo	150	4.34 N	7.27 E
Opobo Town	150	4.30 N	7.30 E
Opočka	76	56.43 N	28.38 E
Opoczno	30	51.23 N	20.17 E
Opol	116	8.31 N	124.34 E
Opole (Oppeln)	30	50.41 N	17.55 E
Opole □[4]	30	50.30 N	17.45 E
Opole Lubelskie	30	51.09 N	21.58 E
Opon → Lapu-Lapu	116	10.19 N	123.57 E
Oponono, Lake ⊜	156	18.08 S	15.45 E
Opopeo	234	19.24 N	101.36 W
Oporto → Porto	34	41.11 N	8.36 W
Opotiki	172	38.00 S	177.17 E
Opp	194	31.16 N	86.15 W
Oppach	54	51.03 N	14.30 E
Oppdal	26	62.36 N	9.40 E
Oppelhain	54	51.33 N	13.35 E
Oppeln → Opole	30	50.41 N	17.55 E
Oppenau	58	48.28 N	8.10 E
Oppenberg	61	47.29 N	14.16 E
Oppenheim, Dtsch.	56	49.51 N	8.21 E
Oppenheim, N.Y., U.S.	210	43.04 N	74.42 W
Oppenheim Park ♦	284a	43.06 N	78.54 W
Oppenhuizen	52	53.00 N	5.42 E
Oppido Lucano	68	40.47 N	16.00 E
Oppido Mamertina	68	38.16 N	16.00 E
Oppio	66	44.03 N	10.50 E
Oppland □[6]	26	61.10 N	9.40 E
Opportunity, Mt., U.S.	202	46.07 N	112.49 W
Opportunity, Wa., U.S.	202	47.39 N	117.14 W
Oppum ◂[8]	263	51.19 N	6.37 E
Opsa	76	55.32 N	26.47 E
Opsaheden	40	60.28 N	13.59 E
Optic Lake	184	54.46 N	101.13 W
Optima Lake ⊜[1]	196	36.40 N	101.10 W
Opua	172	35.19 S	174.07 E
Opunake	172	39.27 S	173.51 E
Opunohu, Baie d' c	174s	17.30 S	149.51 W
Opuwo	152	18.03 S	13.45 E
Opwijk	50	50.58 N	4.11 E
Oquawka	190	40.55 N	90.56 W
Oquendo, Perú	286d	11.58 S	77.08 W
Oquendo, Pil.	116	12.08 N	124.32 E
O'Quinn	222	29.50 N	96.58 W
Or' ≃	86	51.12 N	58.30 E
Or, Côte d' ∧	58	47.10 N	4.50 E
Or, Étang d' ⊜	261	48.38 N	1.51 E
Ora (Auer), It.	64	46.21 N	11.18 E
Ora, Lībiyā	146	28.33 N	19.24 E
Ōra, Nihon	174m	26.33 N	128.02 E
Ora Banda	162	30.22 S	121.04 E
Oracle	200	32.36 N	110.46 W
Oradea	38	47.03 N	21.57 E
Oradell	276	40.57 N	74.02 W
Oradell Reservoir ⊜[1]	276	40.58 N	74.01 W
Öræfajökull ⊓	24a	64.03 N	16.38 W
Orahovica	38	45.31 N	17.53 E
Orai	124	25.59 N	79.28 E
Oraibi Wash V	200	35.26 N	110.49 W
Oraison	62	43.55 N	5.55 E
Oran → Wahran, Alg.	148	35.43 N	0.43 W
Oran, Mo., U.S.	194	37.05 N	89.39 W
Oran, Sebkha d' ⊜	34	35.32 N	0.48 W
Orange, Austl.	166	33.17 S	149.06 E
Orange, Fr.	62	44.08 N	4.48 E
Orange, Ca., U.S.	228	33.47 N	117.51 W
Orange, Ct., U.S.	207	41.16 N	73.01 W
Orange, Ma., U.S.	207	42.35 N	72.18 W
Orange, N.J., U.S.	276	40.46 N	74.13 W
Orange, Oh., U.S.	279a	41.26 N	81.29 W
Orange, Tx., U.S.	194	30.05 N	93.44 W
Orange, Va., U.S.	188	38.14 N	78.06 W
Orange □[6], Ca., U.S.	228	33.43 N	117.54 W
Orange □[6], Fl., U.S.	220	28.32 N	81.16 W
Orange □[6], In., U.S.	218	38.33 N	86.28 W
Orange □[6], N.Y., U.S.	210	41.24 N	74.20 W
Orange (Oranje) ≃	156	28.41 S	16.28 E
Orange, Cabo >	250	4.24 N	51.33 W
Orange Bowl ♦	220	25.46 N	80.14 W
Orangeburg, Ky., U.S.	218	38.35 N	83.39 W
Orangeburg, N.Y., U.S.	210	41.03 N	73.57 W
Orangeburg, S.C., U.S.	192	33.29 N	80.51 W
Orange City, Fl., U.S.	220	28.57 N	81.17 W
Orange City, Ia., U.S.	198	43.00 N	96.03 W
Orange County Airport ⊠	228	33.40 N	117.51 W
Orange Cove	226	36.37 N	119.19 W
Orange Free State □[4]	158	28.30 S	27.00 E
Orange Grove	196	27.57 N	97.56 W
Orange Grove ◂[8]	273d	26.10 S	28.05 E
Orange Lake, Fl., U.S.	192	29.25 N	82.13 W
Orange Lake, N.Y., U.S.	210	41.33 N	74.06 W
Orange Lake ⊜	192	29.29 N	82.10 W
Orangemouth → Oranjemund	156	28.38 S	16.24 E
Orange Park	192	30.09 N	81.42 W
Orange Park Acres	280	33.48 N	117.47 W
Orange Reservoir ⊜[1]	276	40.46 N	74.17 W
Orangevale	226	38.40 N	121.13 W
Orangeville, On., Can.	212	43.55 N	80.06 W
Orangeville, Oh., U.S.	214	41.20 N	80.31 W
Orangeville, Pa., U.S.	210	41.05 N	76.25 W
Orangeville, Ut,. U.S.	200	39.13 N	111.03 W
Orange Walk	232	18.06 N	88.33 W
Orango Grande I	150	11.10 N	16.08 W
Orani, It.	71	40.15 N	9.11 E
Orani, Pil.	116	14.49 N	120.32 E
Oranienbaum	54	51.48 N	12.24 E
Oranienburg	54	52.45 N	13.14 E
Oranje	52	52.55 N	6.28 E
Oranje → Orange ≃	156	28.41 S	16.28 E
Oranjefontein	156	23.25 S	27.41 E
Oranje Gebergte ⋏	250	3.00 N	55.05 W
Oranjemund	156	28.38 S	16.24 E
Oranjerivier	158	29.40 S	24.12 E
Oranjestad	241s	12.33 N	70.06 W
Oranjeville	158	27.00 S	28.15 E
Oranki	80	55.53 N	43.44 E
Oranmore	48	53.16 N	8.54 W
Ŏran-ni	98	34.22 N	126.29 E
Oranžerei	80	45.50 N	47.36 E
Or 'Aqiva	132	32.30 N	34.55 E
Orarak	140	6.15 N	32.23 E
Orari ≃	172	44.15 S	171.25 E
Oras	116	12.09 N	125.26 E
Oras ≃	116	12.08 N	125.26 E
Oras Bay c	116	12.07 N	125.28 E
Orăștie	38	45.50 N	23.12 E
Orașul Stalin → Brașov	38	45.39 N	25.37 E
Orativ	78	49.12 N	29.32 E
Oratório, Ribeirão do ≃	287b	23.37 S	46.32 W
Oravais (Oravainen)	26	63.18 N	22.23 E
Oravița	38	45.02 N	21.41 E
Orawia	172	46.03 S	167.49 E
Orb ≃	32	43.15 N	3.18 E
Orba ≃	62	44.53 N	8.37 E
Orba Co ⊜	120	34.32 N	81.03 E
Orbassano	62	45.01 N	7.32 E
Orbe	58	46.43 N	6.32 E
Orbe ≃	58	46.47 N	6.39 E
Orbec-en-Auge	50	49.01 N	0.25 E
Orbetello	66	42.27 N	11.13 E
Orbetello, Laguna di c	66	42.27 N	11.14 E
Orbey	58	48.08 N	7.10 E
Orbieu ≃	32	43.14 N	2.54 E
Orbigny	50	47.12 N	1.14 E
Órbigo ≃	34	41.58 N	5.40 W
Orbiquet ≃	50	49.09 N	0.14 E
Orbisonia	214	40.15 N	77.54 W
Orbost	166	37.42 S	148.27 E
Örbyhus	40	60.14 N	17.42 E
Orcadas ⚘[3]	9	60.45 S	44.43 W
Orcadas, Islas → Orkney Islands II	46	59.00 N	3.00 W
Orcadas del Sur, Islas → South Orkney Islands II	9	60.35 S	45.30 W
Orcades du Sud, Îles → South Orkney Islands II	9	60.35 S	45.30 W
Orcas	224	48.36 N	122.57 W
Orcas Island I	224	48.39 N	122.55 W
Orcemont	261	48.35 N	1.49 E
Orcera	34	38.19 N	2.39 W
Orchamps	58	47.09 N	5.40 E
Orchard, Ne., U.S.	198	42.20 N	98.14 W
Orchard, Tx., U.S.	222	29.36 N	95.58 W
Orchard City	200	38.49 N	107.58 W
Orchard Hills, Austl.	274a	33.47 S	150.43 E
Orchard Hills, Pa., U.S.	279b	40.35 N	79.32 W
Orchard Homes	202	46.51 N	114.02 W
Orchard Island	216	40.28 N	83.53 W
Orchard Lake ⊜	281	42.35 N	83.22 W
Orchard Lake Village	281	42.35 N	83.21 W
Orchard Mesa	200	39.02 N	108.33 W
Orchard Park	210	42.46 N	78.44 W
Orchard Park Airport ⊠	284a	42.48 N	78.45 W
Orchard Peak ∧	226	35.44 N	120.08 W
Orchards	224	45.40 N	122.33 W
Orchard Valley	200	41.05 N	104.48 W
Orchard View	285	40.04 N	74.53 W
Orchha	124	25.21 N	78.39 E
Orchies	50	50.28 N	3.14 E
Orchon	88	49.09 N	105.21 E
Orchon ≃	88	50.21 N	106.05 E
Orchon Tuul	88	48.58 N	104.59 E
Orchyk ≃	78	49.10 N	35.04 E
Orcia ≃	66	42.58 N	11.21 E
Orcières	62	44.41 N	6.20 E
Orco ≃	62	45.10 N	7.52 E
Ord	198	41.36 N	98.55 W
Ord ≃	160	15.30 S	128.21 E
Ord, Mount ∧	162	17.20 S	125.34 E
Orda	86	57.12 N	56.54 E
Ordenes	34	43.04 N	8.24 W
Orderville	200	37.16 N	112.38 W
Ordesa, Parque Nacional de ♦	34	42.39 N	0.02 E
Ord Mountain ∧	204	34.40 N	116.49 W
Ord Mountains ⋏	228	34.42 N	117.10 W
Ordoqui	252	35.54 S	61.10 W
Ord River	162	17.23 S	128.51 E
Ordu	130	41.00 N	37.53 E
Ordu □[4]	130	40.45 N	37.30 E
Ordubad	84	38.56 N	46.02 E
Ordway	198	38.13 N	103.45 W
Ordynskoje	86	54.22 N	81.56 E
Ordzhonikidze → Vladikavkaz, Ross.	84	43.03 N	44.40 E
Ordžhonikidze → Vladikavkaz, Ross.	84	43.03 N	44.40 E
Ordzhonikidze, Ukr.	78	47.40 N	34.04 E
Ordzhonikidze → Yenakiyeve, Ukr.	83	48.14 N	38.13 E
Ordžonikidze	86	52.28 N	61.46 E
Ordžonikidzeabad	85	38.34 N	69.01 E
Ordžonikidzevskaja	84	43.18 N	45.03 E
Ordžonikidzevskij, Ross.	84	43.51 N	41.54 E
Ordžonikidzevskij, Ross.	86	54.46 N	88.59 E
Ore	150	6.44 N	4.52 E
Ore ≃	46	56.10 N	3.15 W
Öreälven ≃	26	63.32 N	19.44 E
Oreana	219	39.56 N	88.51 W
Örebro	40	59.17 N	15.13 E
Örebro Län □[6]	40	59.30 N	15.00 E
Orechovka	80	52.56 N	48.14 E
Orechovo	80	58.28 N	41.58 E
Orechovo-Zujevo	82	55.49 N	38.59 E
Orechovsk	76	54.41 N	30.30 E
Ore City	222	32.48 N	94.43 W
Oredež	76	58.49 N	30.20 E
Oredež ≃	76	58.49 N	30.00 E
Orefield	208	40.38 N	75.35 W
Oregon, Il., U.S.	190	42.00 N	89.19 W
Oregon, Mo., U.S.	194	39.59 N	95.08 W
Oregon, Oh., U.S.	214	41.38 N	83.29 W
Oregon, Wi., U.S.	216	42.55 N	89.23 W
Oregon □[3], U.S.	178	44.00 N	121.00 W
Oregon □[3], U.S.	202	44.00 N	121.00 W
Oregon Caves National Monument ♦	202	42.06 N	123.24 W
Oregon City	224	45.21 N	122.36 W
Oregon Creek ≃	226	39.23 N	121.05 W
Oregon Dunes National Recreation Area ♦	202	43.45 N	124.12 W
Oregon House	226	39.21 N	121.17 W
Öregrund	40	60.20 N	18.26 E
Öregrundsgrepen c	40	60.27 N	18.18 E
Orehoved	41	54.57 N	11.52 E
Orekhovo-Zuyevo → Orechovo-Zujevo	82	55.49 N	38.59 E
Orel	76	52.59 N	36.05 E
Orel', ozero ⊜	89	53.30 N	139.42 E
Oreland	285	40.07 N	75.10 W
Orellana	248	6.54 S	75.04 W
Orellana, Embalse de ⊜[1]	34	39.00 N	5.25 W
Orel Oblast' □[4]	76	53.00 N	36.20 E
Orem	200	40.17 N	111.41 W
Ören	130	37.02 N	27.57 E
Orenburg	86	51.54 N	55.06 E
Orenburg Oblast' □[4]	86	52.30 N	54.00 E
Örencik	130	39.16 N	29.33 E
Oreng, Indon.	114	4.03 N	97.28 E
Oreng, Indon.	114	4.33 N	96.49 E
Orense, Arg.	252	38.40 S	59.47 W
Orense, Esp.	34	42.20 N	7.51 W
Orense □[4]	34	42.15 N	7.30 W
Örenşehir	130	39.00 N	36.39 E
Orepuki	172	46.17 S	167.44 E
Oreški	82	55.43 N	36.21 E
Oressa ≃	76	52.33 N	28.45 E
Orestes	216	40.16 N	85.43 W
Orestes Pereyra	232	26.31 N	105.40 W
Orestiás	38	41.30 N	26.31 E
Orestimba Creek ≃	226	37.25 N	121.00 W
Øresund → The Sound Ʉ	41	55.50 N	12.40 E
Oreti ≃	172	46.28 S	168.17 E
Oreto ≃	70	38.06 N	13.24 E
Orewa	172	36.34 S	174.42 E
Oreye	56	50.44 N	5.22 E
Orfanoú, Kólpos c	38	40.40 N	23.50 E
Orford, Eng., U.K.	42	52.06 N	1.31 E
Orford, Eng., U.K.	262	53.25 N	2.35 W
Orford, Mont ∧	206	45.19 N	72.15 W
Orford Ness >	42	52.05 N	1.34 E
Orfordville	190	42.37 N	89.15 W
Organ Needle ∧	200	32.21 N	106.33 W
Organ Pipe Cactus National Monument ♦	200	32.00 N	112.55 W
Órgãos, Serra dos ⋏	256	22.22 S	42.45 W
Orgaz	34	39.39 N	3.54 W
Orge ≃	50	48.42 N	2.24 E
Orgelet	58	46.31 N	5.37 E
Orgères-en-Beauce	50	48.09 N	1.42 E
Orgerus	261	48.50 N	1.42 E
Orgeval	50	48.55 N	1.59 E
Orgeval ≃	261	49.00 N	1.54 E
Orgiano	64	45.21 N	11.28 E
Orgnac, Aven d' ⩡[5]	62	44.19 N	4.27 E
Orgnac-l'Aven	62	44.19 N	4.27 E
Orgof	144	3.03 N	41.44 E
Orgon	62	43.47 N	5.02 E
Orgosolo	71	40.12 N	9.21 E
Orgtrud	80	56.12 N	40.37 E
Orgūn	120	32.51 N	69.07 E
Orhaneli	130	39.54 N	29.00 E
Orhangazi	130	40.30 N	29.18 E
Orhanlar	130	39.54 N	27.37 E
Orhei	38	47.23 N	28.48 E
Oria, It.	68	40.30 N	17.38 E
Oria, Zaïre	154	3.17 N	30.41 E
Orica	236	14.41 N	86.56 W
Oriçanga, Rio do ≃	256	22.18 S	47.03 W
Orichuna ≃	246	7.25 N	68.58 W
Oriči	80	58.24 N	49.05 E
Orick	204	41.17 N	124.03 W
Oricola	66	42.02 N	13.02 E
Orient, Ia., U.S.	198	41.12 N	94.24 W
Orient, N.Y., U.S.	207	41.08 N	72.18 W
Orient, Oh., U.S.	218	39.48 N	83.09 W
Orient, Wa., U.S.	182	48.53 N	118.13 W
Oriental, Méx.	234	19.22 N	97.37 W
Oriental, N.C., U.S.	192	35.01 N	76.41 W
Oriental, Cordillera ⋏, Col.	246	6.00 N	73.00 W
Oriental, Cordillera ⋏, Perú	248	11.00 S	74.00 W
Oriental, Pico ∧	286c	10.32 N	66.50 W
Oriental de Zapata, Ciénaga ≡	240p	22.15 N	80.50 W
Oriental Park	214	42.09 N	79.22 W
Oriente	252	38.44 S	60.37 W
Orientos	166	28.05 S	141.14 E
Origgio	266b	45.36 N	9.01 E
Origny-en-Thiérache	50	49.54 N	4.01 E
Origny-Sainte-Benoite	50	49.50 N	3.30 E
Orikhiv	78	47.34 N	35.47 E
Orikhivka	83	48.17 N	39.13 E
Oril' ≃	78	48.30 N	34.54 E
Orillia	212	44.37 N	79.25 W
Orimattila	26	60.48 N	25.45 E
Orinda	226	37.52 N	122.10 W
Orinduik	246	4.42 N	60.01 W
Orini	172	37.34 S	175.18 E
Orinoco ≃	246	8.37 N	62.15 W
Orinoco, Delta del ≚[2]	246	9.15 N	61.30 W
Oriola (Orihuela)	34	38.05 N	0.57 W
Oriole, Md., U.S.	208	38.10 N	75.48 W
Oriole, Pa., U.S.	210	41.08 N	77.13 W
Oriole Park ♦	284b	39.18 N	76.37 W
Oriolo	68	40.03 N	16.27 E
Oriomo	164	8.50 S	143.15 E
Orion, Pil.	116	14.37 N	120.34 E
Orion, Il., U.S.	190	41.21 N	90.22 W
Oripää	26	60.51 N	22.41 E
Oriskany	210	43.09 N	75.19 W
Oriskany Battlefield State Historic Site ⊥	210	43.11 N	75.23 W
Oriskany Creek ≃	210	43.10 N	75.20 W
Oriskany Falls	210	42.56 N	75.27 W
Orissa □[3]	118	20.00 N	84.00 E
Orissaare	76	58.34 N	23.05 E
Orissa Coast Canal ≊	126	21.51 N	87.41 E
Oristano	71	39.54 N	8.36 E
Oristano □[4]	71	39.55 N	8.40 E
Oristano, Golfo di c	71	39.50 N	8.29 E
Őriszentpéter	61	46.51 N	16.25 E
Orituco ≃	246	8.45 N	67.27 W
Orivesi	26	61.41 N	24.21 E
Orivesi ⊜	26	62.16 N	29.24 E
Oriximiná	250	1.45 S	55.52 W
Orizaba	234	18.51 N	97.06 W
Orizaba, Pico de (Volcán Citlatépetl) ∧[1]	234	19.01 N	97.16 W
Orizona	255	17.03 S	48.18 W
Orjahovo	38	43.45 N	23.57 E
Ørje	26	59.29 N	11.39 E
Orjen ∧	38	42.30 N	18.38 E
Orjiva	34	36.54 N	3.25 W
Ork, Ness of >	46	59.05 N	2.48 W
Orkanger	26	63.19 N	9.52 E
Örkelljunga	41	56.17 N	13.17 E
Orken	263	51.06 N	6.34 E
Orkla ≃	26	63.18 N	9.50 E
Orkney, Sk., Can.	184	49.08 N	107.55 W
Orkney, S. Afr.	158	27.00 S	26.39 E
Orkney □[4]	46	59.00 N	3.00 W
Orkney Islands II	46	59.00 N	3.00 W
Orl'a	76	53.30 N	24.59 E
Orla ≃	54	50.46 N	11.31 E
Orlamünde	54	50.47 N	11.31 E
Orland, Ca., U.S.	204	39.44 N	122.11 W
Orland, In., U.S.	216	41.43 N	85.10 W
Orlândia	255	20.43 S	47.53 W
Orland Lake ⊜	278	41.38 N	87.52 W
Orlando, S. Afr.	273d	26.14 S	27.55 E
Orlando, Fl., U.S.	220	28.32 N	81.22 W
Orlando, Capo d' >	70	38.10 N	14.45 E
Orlando Dam ⊜[1]	273d	26.16 S	27.56 E
Orlando International Airport ⊠	220	28.26 N	81.19 W
Orlando Naval Training Center ■	220	28.34 N	81.20 W
Orlando West Extension	273d	26.15 S	27.54 E
Orland Park	216	41.37 N	87.51 W
Orland Square ◂[9]	278	41.36 N	87.51 W
Orléanais □[9]	50	47.50 N	2.00 E
Orléans, On., Can.	212	45.28 N	75.31 W
Orléans, Fr.	50	47.55 N	1.54 E
Orleans, Ca., U.S.	204	41.18 N	123.32 W
Orleans, In., U.S.	218	38.39 N	86.27 W
Orleans, Ma., U.S.	207	41.47 N	69.59 W
Orleans, Ne., U.S.	198	40.07 N	99.27 W
Orleans, Vt., U.S.	188	44.48 N	72.12 W
Orleans □[6], N.Y., U.S.	210	43.15 N	78.12 W
Orleans □[6], Vt., U.S.	206	44.57 N	72.12 W
Orléans, Canal d' ≊	50	47.54 N	1.55 E
Orléans, Île d' I	186	46.55 N	70.58 W
Orléansville → Ech Cheliff	148	36.10 N	1.20 E
Orlik, Kaz.	80	48.17 N	51.32 E
Orlik, Ross.	88	52.30 N	99.55 E
Orlinaja, gora ∧	180	62.35 N	178.30 E
Orlinga	88	56.03 N	105.53 E
Orlinga ≃	88	56.03 N	105.53 E
Orlivka, Ukr.	78	51.54 N	32.47 E
Orlivka, Ukr.	78	45.40 N	33.21 E
Orlivka, Ukr.	83	48.10 N	37.39 E
Orlov	80	58.33 N	48.50 E
Orlová	30	49.50 N	18.24 E
Orlov Gaj	80	50.57 N	48.12 E
Orlovista	220	28.32 N	81.28 W
Orlovka, Ross.	78	51.02 N	40.32 E
Orlovka, Ross.	86	59.03 N	85.59 E
Orlovka ≃	86	58.40 N	86.08 E
Orlovo, Ross.	78	51.45 N	39.35 E
Orlovo, Ross.	265b	55.38 N	37.23 E
Orlovskij	80	46.52 N	42.03 E
Orlu	150	5.47 N	7.02 E
Orly	261	48.45 N	2.24 E
Ormanlı	130	41.10 N	31.39 E
Ormāra	128	25.12 N	64.38 E
Ormāra, Rās >	128	25.09 N	64.35 E
Orme, Rivière à l' ≃	275a	45.27 N	73.56 W
Ormea	62	44.09 N	7.54 E
Ormesby	44	54.33 N	1.11 W
Ormesby Saint Margaret	42	52.40 N	1.42 E
Ormiston	184	49.45 N	105.22 W
Ormoc	116	11.00 N	124.37 E
Ormoc Bay c	116	10.58 N	124.35 E
Ormond	274b	37.54 S	145.03 E
Ormond Beach	192	29.17 N	81.03 W
Ormož	36	46.25 N	16.09 E
Ormsby	214	41.48 N	78.33 W
Ormsby □[6]	226	39.11 N	119.46 W
Ormsjön ⊜	26	64.23 N	16.03 E
Ormskirk	44	53.35 N	2.54 W
Ormstown	206	45.08 N	74.00 W
Ormtjernkampen Nasjonalpark ♦	26	61.12 N	9.48 E
Ornain ≃	56	48.46 N	4.47 E
Ornans	58	47.06 N	6.09 E
Ornäs	40	60.31 N	15.32 E
Ornavasso	58	45.58 N	8.24 E
Orne □[5]	32	48.40 N	0.05 E
Orne ≃, Fr.	32	49.19 N	0.14 W
Orne ≃, Fr.	50	48.08 N	0.11 E
Orne ≃, Fr.	56	49.17 N	6.11 E
Ornes	26	61.18 N	7.22 E
Orneta	30	54.08 N	20.08 E
Ornö I	40	59.04 N	18.24 E
Örnsköldsvik	26	63.18 N	18.43 E
Oro	98	40.02 N	127.26 E
Orø I	41	55.46 N	11.49 E
Orobie, Alpi ⋏	64	46.00 N	10.00 E
Oročanskij Golec, gora ∧	88	53.29 N	114.18 E
Oročen	74	58.28 N	125.26 E
Orocovis	240m	18.14 N	66.23 W
Orocué	246	4.48 N	71.20 W
Orocuina	236	13.26 N	87.06 W
Orodara	150	10.59 N	4.55 W
Orofino	202	46.28 N	116.15 W
Orogen Zizhiqi	89	50.34 N	123.40 E
Örög nuur ⊜, Mong.	86	50.10 N	91.00 E
Orog nuur ⊜, Mong.	102	45.03 N	100.42 E
Oro Grande	228	34.35 N	117.20 W
Orohena, Mont ∧	174s	17.37 S	149.28 W
Orok, Oldoinyo ∧	154	2.29 S	36.46 E
Oroku	174m	26.12 N	127.39 E
Or'ol	86	59.21 N	56.35 E
Oroluk I[1]	14	7.32 N	155.18 E
Oromocto	186	45.51 N	66.29 W
Oromocto Lake ⊜	186	45.36 N	67.00 W
Oron, Nig.	150	4.48 N	8.14 E
Oron, Ross.	88	57.11 N	116.28 E
Oron ≃	62	45.18 N	4.47 E
Oron, ozero ⊜	88	57.06 N	116.30 E
Orona I[1]	14	4.29 S	172.10 W
Oron-la-Ville	58	46.34 N	6.50 E
Orono, On., Can.	212	43.59 N	78.37 W
Orono, Me., U.S.	188	44.52 N	68.40 W
Oronoque ≃	246	2.45 N	57.25 W
Oronsay I	46	56.01 N	6.16 W
Orontes → Asi ≃	130	36.02 N	35.58 E
Oropa, Santuario di ⚘[1]	62	45.38 N	7.58 E
Oropeo	234	18.50 N	101.48 W
Oroquieta	116	8.29 N	123.48 E
Orós	250	6.15 S	38.55 W
Orós, Açude ⊜[1]	250	6.15 S	39.05 W
Orosei	71	40.23 N	9.42 E
Orosei, Golfo di c	71	40.15 N	9.44 E
Orosháza	30	46.34 N	20.40 E
Orosi	226	36.33 N	119.17 W
Orosí, Volcán ∧[1]	236	10.59 N	85.29 W
Oroszlány	30	47.30 N	18.19 E
Orotelli	71	40.18 N	9.07 E
Orote Peninsula >[1]	174p	13.26 N	144.38 E
Oroville, Ca., U.S.	226	39.30 N	121.33 W
Oroville, Wa., U.S.	202	48.56 N	119.26 W
Oroville, Lake ⊜[1]	204	39.32 N	121.25 W
Orowoc Creek ≃	276	40.43 N	73.13 W
Orpheus Island I	166	18.37 S	146.30 E
Orphin	261	48.35 N	1.47 E
Orpierre	62	44.19 N	5.41 E
Orpington ◂[8]	260	51.23 N	0.06 E
Orrefors	26	56.50 N	15.45 E
Orrell	44	53.32 N	2.42 W
Orrick	194	39.12 N	94.07 W
Orrin	198	48.05 N	100.09 W
Orrin, Glen V	46	57.30 N	4.46 W
Orrin Reservoir ⊜[1]	46	57.30 N	4.45 W
Òrrius	266d	41.33 N	2.21 E
Orr Lake ⊜, Mb., Can.	184	56.07 N	97.11 W
Orr Lake ⊜, On., Can.	212	44.37 N	79.47 W
Orroroo	166	32.44 S	138.37 E
Orrs Island	188	43.45 N	69.58 W
Orrtanna	208	39.51 N	77.22 W
Orrville, Al., U.S.	194	32.18 N	87.14 W
Orrville, Oh., U.S.	214	40.50 N	81.45 W
Orrville, Pa., U.S.	279b	40.33 N	79.47 W
Orša, Bela.	76	54.30 N	30.24 E
Orsa, Sve.	26	61.07 N	14.37 E
Orša ≃	82	56.48 N	36.11 E
Orsago	64	45.56 N	12.25 E
Orsan	62	44.08 N	4.40 E
Oršanka	80	56.55 N	47.53 E
Orsara di Puglia	68	41.17 N	15.16 E
Orsasjön ⊜	26	61.07 N	14.34 E
Orsay	50	48.42 N	2.11 E
Orsett	260	51.31 N	0.22 E
Orsières	58	46.02 N	7.09 E
Orsjön ⊜	26	61.35 N	16.20 E
Orsk	86	51.12 N	58.34 E
Örskär I	40	60.31 N	18.23 E
Ørslev	41	55.02 N	11.59 E
Orsogna	66	42.13 N	14.17 E
Orsomarso	68	39.48 N	15.55 E
Orson	210	41.49 N	75.27 W
Orșova	38	44.42 N	22.24 E
Ørsta	26	62.12 N	6.09 E
Ørsted	41	55.20 N	10.04 E
Örsundaån ≃	40	59.44 N	17.21 E
Örsundsbro	40	59.44 N	17.18 E
Orta	130	40.38 N	33.06 E
Orta, Lago d' ⊜	62	45.49 N	8.24 E
Ortaca	130	36.49 N	28.47 E
Ortakent	130	37.02 N	27.21 E
Ortaklar	130	37.53 N	27.30 E
Ortaköy, Tür.	130	40.17 N	35.16 E
Ortaköy, Tür.	130	38.44 N	34.03 E
Ortaköy, Tür.	130	38.00 N	34.23 E
Ortaköy, Tür.	130	40.27 N	38.02 E
Ortaköy ◂[8]	267b	41.03 N	29.01 E
Orta Nova	68	41.19 N	15.42 E
Orta San Giulio	62	45.48 N	8.25 E
Orte	66	42.27 N	12.23 E
Ortega	246	3.56 N	75.13 W
Ortegal, Cabo >	34	43.45 N	7.53 W
Orteguaza ≃	246	0.43 N	75.16 W
Ortelsburg → Szczytno	30	53.34 N	21.00 E
Ortenberg, Dtsch.	56	50.21 N	9.02 E
Ortenberg, Dtsch.	58	48.27 N	7.58 E
Ortenburg	60	48.33 N	13.14 E
Orth	54	54.27 N	11.03 E
Orthez	32	43.29 N	0.46 W
Orthon ≃	248	10.50 S	66.04 W
Ortigalita Creek ≃	226	36.57 N	120.52 W
Ortigalita Peak ∧	226	36.48 N	120.55 W
Ortigara, Monte ∧	64	46.00 N	11.29 E
Ortigueira	34	43.41 N	7.51 W
Ortigueira, Ría de c[1]	34	43.42 N	7.51 W
Orting	224	47.05 N	122.12 W
Ortisei (Sankt Ulrich)	64	46.34 N	11.40 E
Ortiz, Méx.	232	28.17 N	110.43 W
Ortiz, Ven.	246	9.37 N	67.17 W
Ortles (Otler) ∧	64	46.31 N	10.33 E
Ortles ⋏	64	46.30 N	10.40 E
Örtofta	41	55.47 N	13.14 E
Ortolo ≃	71	41.30 N	8.55 E
Ortona	66	42.21 N	14.24 E
Ortona Lock ◂[5]	220	26.47 N	81.18 W
Orton Park ♦	275b	43.46 N	79.12 W
Ortonura	85	41.29 N	76.12 E
Ortonville, Mi., U.S.	216	42.51 N	83.26 W
Ortonville, Mn., U.S.	198	45.18 N	96.26 W
Ortonville State Recreation Area ♦	216	42.52 N	83.26 W
Ortoterek	85	41.56 N	71.21 E
Orto-Tokoj	85	42.21 N	76.01 E
Ortovero	62	44.03 N	8.07 E
Ortrand	54	51.22 N	13.45 E
Örträsk	26	64.08 N	18.59 E
Ortueri	71	40.02 N	8.59 E
Ortúzar, Canal ≊	286e	33.33 S	70.47 W
Örtze ≃	52	52.40 N	9.57 E
Oruanui	172	38.35 S	176.02 E
Oruba	273a	6.35 N	3.25 E
Orudjevo	82	56.26 N	37.32 E
Orūmīyeh (Reẕā'īyeh)	128	37.33 N	45.04 E
Orūmīyeh, Daryācheh-ye (Lake Urmia) ⊜	128	37.40 N	45.30 E
Orune	71	40.24 N	9.22 E
Oruro	248	17.59 S	67.09 W
Oruro □[5]	248	18.40 S	67.30 W
Or'us-Mijele ≃	88	58.35 N	121.30 E
Orust I	26	58.10 N	11.38 E
Orūzgān (Qala-i-Hazār Qadam)	120	32.56 N	66.38 E
Orūzgān □[4]	120	33.15 N	66.00 E
Orval, Abbaye d' ⚘[1]	56	49.38 N	5.22 E
Orvanne ≃	50	48.22 N	2.50 E
Orvieto	66	42.43 N	12.07 E
Orvilla	208	40.16 N	75.17 W
Orvilliers	261	48.52 N	1.39 E
Orvin ≃	50	48.28 N	3.23 E
Orvinio	66	42.08 N	12.56 E
Orviston	214	41.06 N	77.45 W

Symbols in the index entries represent the broad categories identified in the key at the right. Symbols with superior numbers (⋏[1]) identify subcategories (see complete key on page I · 1).

Symbole im Register stellen die rechts im Schlüssel erklärten Kategorien dar. Symbole mit hochgestellten Ziffern (⋏[1]) bezeichnen Unterabteilungen einer Kategorie (vgl. vollständiger Schlüssel auf Seite I · 1).

Los símbolos incluídos en el texto del índice representan las grandes categorías identificadas con la clave a la derecha. Los símbolos con numeros en su parte superior (⋏[1]) identifican las subcategorías (véase la clave completa en la página I · 1).

Les symboles de l'index représentent les catégories indiquées dans la légende à droite. Les symboles suivis d'un indice (⋏[1]) représentent des sous-catégories (voir légende complète à la page I · 1).

Os símbolos incluídos no texto do índice representam as grandes categorias identificadas com a chave à direita. Os símbolos com números em sua parte superior (⋏[1]) identificam as subcategorias (veja-se a chave completa à página I · 1).

Symbol	English	Deutsch	Español	Français	Português
∧	Mountain	Berg	Montaña	Montagne	Montanha
⋏	Mountains	Gebirge	Montañas	Montagnes	Montanhas
)(	Pass	Paß	Paso	Col	Passo
V	Valley, Canyon	Tal, Cañon	Valle, Cañón	Vallée, Canyon	Vale, Canhão
≚	Plain	Ebene	Llano	Plaine	Planície
>	Cape	Kap	Cabo	Cap	Cabo
I	Island	Insel	Isla	Île	Ilha
II	Islands	Inseln	Islas	Îles	Ilhas
⩡	Other Topographic Features	Andere Topographische Objekte	Otros Elementos Topográficos	Autres données topographiques	Outros acidentes topográficos

ESPAÑOL · FRANÇAIS · PORTUGUÊS

Nombre / Nom / Nome	Página / Page	Lat.°′	Long.°′ W = Oeste / W = Ouest
Orvyn, gora ∧	180	65.14 N	175.20 W
Orwell, On., Can.	214	42.46 N	81.02 W
Orwell, N.Y., U.S.	212	43.35 N	76.00 W
Orwell, Oh., U.S.	214	41.32 N	80.52 W
Orwell ≃	42	51.57 N	1.17 E
Orwigsburg	208	40.39 N	76.06 W
Orwin	208	40.35 N	76.31 W
Orxon ≃	88	49.00 N	117.41 E
Or Yehuda	132	32.01 N	34.51 E
Orynyn	78	48.46 N	26.24 E
Oryu-dong ◆ [8]	271b	37.29 N	126.51 E
Orževka	80	52.43 N	42.55 E
Orzhiv	78	50.45 N	26.07 E
Orzhytsya	78	49.48 N	32.42 E
Orzinuovi	62	45.24 N	9.55 E
Orzyc ≃	30	52.47 N	21.13 E
Orzysz	30	53.49 N	21.56 E
Oš, Kyrg.	85	40.33 N	72.48 E
Os, Nor.	26	62.30 N	11.12 E
Oš □ [4]	85	40.00 N	72.30 E
Ōsa, Nihon	96	35.05 N	133.34 E
Osa, Ross.	86	57.17 N	55.26 E
Osa, Ross.	88	53.24 N	103.53 E
Oša ≃	86	57.13 N	73.41 E
Osa, Península de ≻ [1]	236	8.34 N	83.31 W
Osage, Ia., U.S.	190	43.17 N	92.48 W
Osage, Mo., U.S.	219	38.25 N	92.02 W
Osage, N.J., U.S.	285	39.51 N	75.01 W
Osage, Wy., U.S.	198	43.58 N	104.25 W
Osage □ [6]	219	38.27 N	91.50 W
Osage ≃	194	38.35 N	91.57 W
Osage Beach	194	38.09 N	92.37 W
Osage City	198	38.38 N	95.49 W
Osaka, Nihon	94	35.57 N	137.16 E
Ōsaka, Nihon	96	34.40 N	135.30 E
Ōsaka, Nihon	270	34.40 N	135.30 E
Ōsaka □ [5]	96	34.30 N	135.30 E
Osaka Castle ⊥	270	34.41 N	135.32 E
Ōsaka-heiya ≚	270	34.43 N	135.30 E
Ōsaka International Airport ⊠	270	34.47 N	135.26 E
Ōsaka-kō ⊂	270	34.38 N	135.26 E
Ōsaka-kokusai-kūkō ⊠	96	34.47 N	135.26 E
Osakarovka	86	50.32 N	72.39 E
Ōsaka-tōge)(	270	34.56 N	135.18 E
Osaka University ✿ [2]	270	34.42 N	135.30 E
Ōsaka-wan ⊂	96	34.30 N	135.18 E
Ōsakiga-hana ≻	96	35.11 N	132.25 E
Ōsaki-Kami-jima I	96	34.14 N	132.54 E
Osakis	198	45.52 N	95.09 W
Ōsaki-Shimo-jima I	96	34.10 N	132.50 E
Osăm ≃	38	43.42 N	24.51 E
Osan	98	37.11 N	127.04 E
Osanovo	82	54.12 N	38.41 E
Osasco	256	23.32 S	46.46 W
Osasco □ [7]	287b	23.32 S	46.46 W
Ōsawano	94	36.34 N	137.12 E
Osawatomie	198	38.29 N	94.57 W
Ōsa-yama ∧	96	34.45 N	132.12 E
Osbaldeston	262	53.47 N	2.32 W
Osborne, Ks., U.S.	198	39.26 N	98.41 W
Osborne, Pa., U.S.	279b	40.32 N	80.10 W
Osbourn Seamount ✢ [3]	14	26.00 S	174.50 W
Osburger Hochwald ⋏	56	49.40 N	6.50 E
Osburn	202	47.30 N	115.59 W
Osby	26	56.22 N	13.59 E
Osbyholm	41	55.51 N	13.36 E
Oscar Peak ∧	182	54.51 N	129.07 W
Oscarville	180	60.43 N	161.46 W
Oscawana Lake	210	41.23 N	73.52 W
Osceola, Ar., U.S.	194	35.42 N	89.58 W
Osceola, In., U.S.	216	41.39 N	86.04 W
Osceola, Ia., U.S.	190	41.02 N	93.45 W
Osceola, Mo., U.S.	194	38.02 N	93.42 W
Osceola, Ne., U.S.	198	41.10 N	97.32 W
Osceola, Pa., U.S.	210	41.59 N	77.21 W
Osceola, Tx., U.S.	222	32.08 N	97.14 W
Osceola, Wi., U.S.	190	45.19 N	92.42 W
Osceola □ [6]	220	28.00 N	81.15 W
Osceola Mills	214	40.51 N	78.16 W
Oščepkovo	86	56.29 N	70.42 E
Oschatz	54	51.17 N	13.07 E
Oschersleben	54	52.01 N	11.13 E
Oschiri	71	40.43 N	9.06 E
Oscoda	190	44.26 N	83.20 W
Öse ≃	263	51.26 N	7.49 E
Osečenka	76	57.33 N	34.48 E
Osečina	38	44.23 N	19.36 E
Osejevskaja	82	55.53 N	38.10 E
Ošejkino	82	56.15 N	35.54 E
Osek	54	50.37 N	13.40 E
Ösel → Saaremaa I	76	58.25 N	22.30 E
Osen	24	64.17 N	10.30 E
Osetrovo	88	56.47 N	105.47 E
Ōse-zaki ≻	94	35.02 N	138.47 E
Osgood, In., U.S.	218	39.07 N	85.17 W
Osgood, Oh., U.S.	216	40.20 N	84.30 W
Osgoode	212	45.08 N	75.36 W
Osh → Oš	85	40.33 N	72.48 E
Oshamambe	92a	42.30 N	140.22 E
O'Shanassy ≃	166	18.59 S	138.46 E
O'Shaughnessy Dam ◆ [6]	226	37.57 N	119.47 W
O'Shaughnessy Reservoir ◎ [1]	214	40.12 N	83.09 W
Oshawa	212	43.54 N	78.51 W
Oshawa Creek ≃	212	43.52 N	78.49 W
Oshibe ◆ [8]	270	34.45 N	135.04 E
Oshigambo	156	17.47 S	16.05 E
Oshika, Nihon	92	38.16 N	141.32 E
Ōshika, Nihon	94	35.34 N	138.02 E
Oshika-hantō ≻ [1]	92	38.20 N	141.30 E
Oshikango	156	17.25 S	15.56 E
Ōshima, Nihon	92	33.03 N	129.33 E
Ōshima, Nihon	94	37.07 N	138.30 E
Ōshima, Nihon	94	34.45 N	139.22 E
Ōshima, Nihon	96	33.55 N	132.15 E
Ō-shima I, Nihon	92a	41.30 N	139.22 E
Ō-shima I, Nihon	94	34.43 N	139.23 E
Ō-shima I, Nihon	94	36.15 N	136.07 E
Ō-shima I, Nihon	96	33.54 N	130.26 E
Ō-shima I, Nihon	96	34.30 N	131.25 E
Ō-shima I, Nihon	96	34.00 N	133.22 E
Ō-shima I, Nihon	96	34.09 N	133.04 E
Ō-shima I, Nihon	96	33.38 N	134.30 E
Oshima-hantō ≻ [1]	92a	42.00 N	140.30 E
Oshimizu	94	36.49 N	136.46 E
Oshino	94	35.28 N	138.51 E
Oshivre ◆ [8]	272c	19.09 N	72.51 E
Oshkosh, Ne., U.S.	198	41.24 N	102.20 W
Oshkosh, Wi., U.S.	190	44.01 N	88.32 W
Oshnovīyeh	128	37.02 N	45.06 E
Oshodi	273a	6.34 N	3.21 E
Oshoek	158	26.13 S	30.59 E
Oshogbo	150	7.47 N	4.34 E
Oshtemo	216	42.15 N	85.41 W
Oshtorān Kūh ∧	128	33.20 N	49.16 E
Oshtorīnān	128	34.01 N	48.38 E
Oshwe	152	3.24 S	19.30 E
Osi	150	8.08 N	5.14 E
Osica de Jos	38	44.15 N	24.17 E
Osich'ŏn-ni	98	41.25 N	128.16 E
Osiek	30	50.31 N	21.28 E
Osiglia	62	44.17 N	8.12 E
Osijek	38	45.33 N	18.41 E
Osilinka ≃	182	56.05 N	124.29 W
Osilo	71	40.45 N	8.40 E
Osimo	66	43.29 N	13.29 E
Osini	71	39.50 N	9.29 E
Osinki	80	52.51 N	49.30 E
Osinniki, Ross.	80	58.03 N	47.02 E
Osinniki, Ross.	86	53.37 N	87.21 E
Osinovka, Ross.	88	50.34 N	109.27 E
Osinovka, Ross.	88	56.19 N	101.56 E
Osinovskij chrebet ⋏	180	67.10 N	175.00 E
Osinów Dolny	54	52.48 N	14.10 E
Osintorf	76	54.42 N	30.39 E
Osio Sotto	62	45.36 N	9.35 E
Osipaonica	38	44.33 N	21.04 E
Osipenko → Berdyans'k	78	46.45 N	36.49 E
Osipoviči	76	53.18 N	28.38 E
Osipovo Selo	76	56.51 N	30.30 E
Osire	156	20.59 S	17.19 E
Osivān	120	26.43 N	72.55 E
Oskaloosa, Ia., U.S.	190	41.17 N	92.38 W
Oskaloosa, Ks., U.S.	198	39.12 N	95.18 W
Oskar-Fredriksborg	40	59.24 N	18.26 E
Oskarshamn	26	57.16 N	16.26 E
Oskarström	26	56.48 N	12.58 E
Os'kino	78	51.14 N	39.02 E
Oskol ≃	78	49.06 N	37.25 E
Oskolkovo	24	67.58 N	53.42 E
Oskū	128	37.55 N	46.06 E
Oskuj	76	59.17 N	32.05 E
Oskuja ≃	76	59.14 N	31.54 E
Osl'anka, gora ∧	86	59.10 N	58.33 E
Oslava ≃	61	49.05 N	16.22 E
Ösling ◆ [1]	56	49.55 N	6.00 E
Oslo	26	59.55 N	10.45 E
Oslob	116	9.31 N	123.26 E
Oslofjorden ⊂ [2]	26	59.20 N	10.35 E
Os'ma ≃, Ross.	76	54.55 N	33.24 E
Ošma ≃, Ross.	80	57.52 N	47.45 E
Osmānābād	122	18.10 N	76.02 E
Osmancık	130	40.59 N	34.49 E
Osmaneli	130	40.22 N	30.01 E
Osmaniye	130	37.05 N	36.14 E
Osmanpaşa	130	39.38 N	34.58 E
Ošm'anskaja vozvyšennost' ⋏ [1]	76	54.20 N	26.00 E
Ošm'any	76	54.25 N	25.56 E
Osmeña	116	10.11 N	125.31 E
Osmington	42	50.38 N	2.22 W
Os'mino	76	59.01 N	29.06 E
Osminog, gora ∧	180	67.54 N	176.50 E
Ösmo	40	58.59 N	17.54 E
Osmond	198	42.21 N	97.35 W
Osmore ≃	248	17.33 S	71.12 W
Osmoy	261	48.52 N	1.43 E
Osmussaar I	76	59.18 N	23.22 E
Osnabrück	52	52.16 N	8.02 E
Ośno	30	52.28 N	14.50 E
Osny	261	49.04 N	2.04 E
Oso	224	48.16 N	121.56 W
Oso ≃	154	1.09 S	27.22 E
Oso, Gran Lago del → Great Bear Lake ◎	176	66.00 N	120.00 W
Ošoba	85	40.44 N	70.26 E
Osogna	58	46.18 N	9.00 E
Osoppo	64	46.15 N	13.05 E
Osorakan-zan ∧	96	34.36 N	132.08 E
Osore-yama ∧	92	41.18 N	141.05 E
Osorio, Quebrada ≃	286c	10.36 N	66.56 W
Osório Fonseca	250	3.40 S	58.13 W
Osorno, Chile	254	40.34 S	73.09 W
Osorno, Esp.	34	42.24 N	4.22 W
Osorno, Volcán ∧ [1]	254	41.06 S	72.30 W
Osorun	273a	6.33 N	3.29 E
Os'otr ≃	82	54.58 N	38.46 E
Osoyoos	182	49.02 N	119.28 W
Osoyoos Indian Reserve ◆ [4]	182	49.08 N	119.30 W
Osoyoos Lake ◎	182	49.00 N	119.26 W
Osøyra	26	60.11 N	5.28 E
Ospedaletti	62	43.48 N	7.43 E
Ospedaletto, It.	64	46.17 N	13.07 E
Ospedaletto, It.	64	46.03 N	11.33 E
Ospino	246	9.18 N	69.27 W
Ospitale di Cadore	64	46.20 N	12.19 E
Ospitaletto	64	45.33 N	10.04 E
Osprey	220	27.11 N	82.29 W
Osprey Reef ✢ [2]	164	13.55 S	146.38 E
Ospwagan Lake ◎	184	55.35 N	98.03 W
Oss	52	51.46 N	5.31 E
Ossa, Mount ∧	166	41.54 S	146.01 E
Ossabaw Island I	192	31.47 N	81.06 W
Osse ≃, Fr.	32	44.07 N	0.17 E
Osse ≃, Nig.	150	6.10 N	5.20 E
Ossenberg	263	51.34 N	6.35 E
Ossendrecht	52	51.24 N	4.19 E
Osseo, Mi., U.S.	216	41.53 N	84.33 W
Osseo, Wi., U.S.	190	44.34 N	91.13 W
Ossett	44	53.41 N	1.35 W
Ossi	71	40.40 N	8.35 E
Ossiacher See ◎	64	46.40 N	13.55 E
Ossian, In., U.S.	216	40.52 N	85.09 W
Ossian, Ia., U.S.	190	43.08 N	91.45 W
Ossian, Loch ◎	46	56.46 N	4.38 W
Ossining	210	41.09 N	73.51 W
Ossipee	188	43.41 N	71.07 W
Ossjøen ◎	26	61.13 N	11.53 E
Ossling	54	51.21 N	14.09 E
Ossona	266b	45.30 N	8.54 E
Ossora	74	59.20 N	163.13 E
Ossum-Bösinghoven	263	51.18 N	6.39 E
Ošta	24	60.49 N	35.32 E
Ostaboningue, Lac ◎	190	47.09 N	78.53 W
Östanå, Sve.	40	59.33 N	18.35 E
Östanå, Sve.	40	60.38 N	16.48 E
Östanbyn	40	60.39 N	16.48 E
Ostankino ◆ [8]	265b	55.49 N	37.37 E
Östansjö	40	59.03 N	14.59 E
Ostap'ye	78	49.33 N	33.46 E
Ostaškov	76	57.09 N	33.06 E
Ostašovo	82	55.52 N	35.52 E
Ostbevern	52	52.02 N	7.50 E
Østbirk	41	55.58 N	9.46 E
Ostbüren	263	51.31 N	7.46 E
Østby	26	61.15 N	12.32 E
Ostchinesisches Meer → East China Sea ⊤ [2]	90	30.00 N	126.00 E
Oste ≃	52	53.51 N	8.59 E
Osted	41	55.34 N	11.58 E
Osteen	220	28.50 N	81.09 W
Ostellato	66	44.45 N	11.56 E
Ostende → Oostende	50	51.13 N	2.55 E
Ostenfelde	52	51.52 N	8.04 E
Oster	78	50.57 N	30.53 E
Oster ≃, Dtsch.	60	48.43 N	13.29 E
Oster ≃, Ukr.	78	50.56 N	30.52 E
Osterath	56	51.16 N	6.37 E
Osterbönen	263	51.37 N	7.48 E
Osterburg, Dtsch.	54	52.47 N	11.44 E
Osterburg, Pa., U.S.	214	40.16 N	78.31 W
Osterburken	56	49.26 N	9.26 E
Österbybruk	40	60.12 N	17.54 E
Österbymo	26	57.50 N	15.16 E
Ostercappeln	52	52.20 N	8.13 E
Österdalälven ≃	26	60.33 N	15.08 E
Østerdalen V	26	61.15 N	11.10 E
Österfärnebo	40	60.18 N	16.48 E
Osterfeld	54	51.05 N	11.56 E
Osterfeld ◆ [8]	263	51.30 N	6.53 E
Östergötland □ [9]	26	58.24 N	15.34 E
Östergötlands Län □ [6]	26	58.25 N	15.45 E
Österhaninge	40	59.08 N	18.12 E
Osterhofen	60	48.42 N	13.01 E
Øster Højst	41	55.00 N	9.03 E
Osterholz-Scharmbeck	52	53.14 N	8.47 E
Osterley Park ♠	260	51.30 N	0.21 W
Österlövsta	40	60.26 N	17.47 E
Ostermundigen	58	46.58 N	7.29 E
Osternienburg	54	51.48 N	12.01 E
Osterode, Dtsch.	52	51.44 N	10.11 E
Osterode → Ostróda, Pol.	30	53.43 N	19.59 E
Osterøya I	26	60.33 N	5.35 E
Österreich → Austria □ [1]	30	47.20 N	13.20 E
Österreichisches Freilichtmuseum ✿	61	47.10 N	15.19 E
Osterrönfeld	41	54.17 N	9.41 E
Östersjön → Baltic Sea ⊤ [2]	24	57.00 N	19.00 E
Österskär	40	59.28 N	18.18 E
Östersund	26	63.11 N	14.39 E
Östervåla	40	60.11 N	17.11 E
Osterville	207	41.37 N	70.23 W
Osterwick	52	52.01 N	7.13 E
Osterwieck	54	51.58 N	10.42 E
Ostfeld ◆ [8]	263	51.40 N	7.45 E
Østfold □ [6]	26	59.20 N	11.30 E
Ostfriesische Inseln II	52	53.44 N	7.25 E
Ostfriesland □ [9]	52	53.20 N	7.40 E
Ost-Ghats → Eastern Ghāts ⋏	122	14.00 N	78.50 E
Östhammar	40	60.16 N	18.22 E
Ostheim vor der Rhön	56	50.27 N	10.14 E
Osthofen	56	49.42 N	8.19 E
Ostia, Bonifica di ◆ [1]	267a	41.46 N	12.18 E
Ostia Antica ⊥	66	41.45 N	12.16 E
Ostiano	64	45.13 N	10.15 E
Ostiglia	64	45.04 N	11.08 E
Ostky	78	51.16 N	27.22 E
Östliche Sierra Madre → Madre Oriental, Sierra ⋏	232	22.00 N	99.30 W
Östmark	26	60.17 N	12.45 E
Ost'or	76	54.01 N	32.48 E
Ost'or ≃	76	53.47 N	31.46 E
Ostpeene ≃	54	53.43 N	12.46 E
Ostra	66	43.37 N	13.09 E
Östraby	41	55.46 N	13.41 E
Ostrach	58	47.57 N	9.23 E
Ostrach ≃	58	48.04 N	9.24 E
Östra Grevie	41	55.28 N	13.08 E
Östra Husby	40	58.35 N	16.33 E
Östra Laxsjön ◎	40	58.54 N	14.42 E
Östra Ljungby	41	56.11 N	13.04 E
Ostrander	214	40.15 N	83.12 W
Östra Ringsjön ◎	41	55.52 N	13.32 E
Ostrau → Ostrava, Česká Rep.	30	49.50 N	18.17 E
Ostrau, Dtsch.	54	51.12 N	13.09 E
Ostrava	30	49.50 N	18.17 E
Ostra Vetere	66	43.36 N	13.03 E
Ostrhauderfehn	52	53.08 N	7.37 E
Östrich	263	51.40 N	6.55 E
Ostricourt	50	50.27 N	3.02 E
Östringen	56	49.13 N	8.43 E
Ostritz	54	51.01 N	14.56 E
Ostróda	30	53.43 N	19.59 E
Ostrogožsk	78	50.52 N	39.05 E
Ostroh	78	50.20 N	26.31 E
Ostrokonje	76	59.52 N	42.02 E
Ostrołęka	30	53.06 N	21.34 E
Ostrołęka □ [4]	30	53.00 N	21.30 E
Ostroróg	30	52.39 N	16.27 E
Ostrošickij Gorodok	76	54.04 N	27.42 E
Ostrov, Bela.	76	52.53 N	25.59 E
Ostrov, Česká Rep.	54	50.17 N	12.57 E
Ostrov, Rom.	38	44.06 N	27.22 E
Ostrov, Ross.	76	57.20 N	28.22 E
Ostrov, Ross.	76	60.34 N	37.55 E
Ostrov, Ross.	265b	55.35 N	37.51 E
Ostrov I	30	47.55 N	17.35 E
Ostrov'anskij	80	46.45 N	42.13 E
Ostrovec	76	54.37 N	25.57 E
Ostrovki	265a	59.48 N	30.50 E
Ostrovno	76	55.08 N	29.53 E
Ostrovskaja	80	50.26 N	44.27 E
Ostrovskoje	80	57.48 N	42.15 E
Ostrov-Zalit	76	58.01 N	28.04 E
Ostrowiec Świętokrzyski	30	50.57 N	21.23 E
Ostrów Lubelski	30	51.30 N	22.52 E
Ostrów Mazowiecka	30	52.49 N	21.54 E
Ostrów Wielkopolski	30	51.39 N	17.49 E
Ostryna	76	53.44 N	24.32 E
Ostrzeszów	30	51.25 N	17.57 E
Ostsee → Baltic Sea ⊤ [2]	24	57.00 N	19.00 E
Ostseebad Ahrenshoop	54	54.23 N	12.25 E
Ostseebad Boltenhagen	54	54.00 N	11.12 E
Ostseebad Dierhagen	54	54.18 N	12.22 E
Ostseebad Graal-Müritz	54	54.15 N	12.12 E
Ostseebad Nienhagen	54	54.09 N	11.58 E
Ostseebad Rerik	54	54.06 N	11.37 E
Ostseebad Wustrow	54	54.21 N	12.23 E
Ost-Sümmern	263	51.26 N	7.44 E
Osttirol □ [9]	64	46.55 N	12.30 E
Ostúa ≃	236	14.17 N	89.33 W
Ostuacán	234	17.25 N	93.18 W
Ostula	234	18.30 N	103.28 W
Ostuni	68	40.44 N	17.35 E
Ostwald	58	48.33 N	7.43 E
Osu	98	35.31 N	127.18 E
Osuga	76	56.02 N	34.18 E
Osuga ≃	76	57.16 N	34.49 E
Ōsuka	94	34.41 N	137.59 E
O'Sullivan, Lac ◎	190	47.37 N	76.05 W
Osum ≃	38	40.48 N	19.52 E
Ōsumi	270	34.50 N	135.45 E
Ōsumi-hantō ≻ [1]	92	31.20 N	130.55 E
Ōsumi-kaikyō ⊔	92	31.00 N	131.00 E
Ōsumi-shotō II	93b	30.30 N	130.00 E
Osuna	34	37.14 N	5.07 W
Osupugo ∧	154	1.40 N	35.49 E
Osvaldo Cruz	255	21.47 S	50.50 W
Osveja	76	56.01 N	28.06 E
Osvejskoje, ozero ◎	76	56.03 N	28.08 E
Ošvor	24	66.58 N	62.53 E
Oswaldtwistle	44	53.43 N	2.26 W
Oswaldtwistle Moor ◆ [3]	262	53.43 N	2.23 W
Oswald West State Park ♠	224	45.45 N	123.58 W
Oswayo	214	41.55 N	78.01 W
Oswayo Creek ≃	210	42.02 N	78.21 W
Oswegatchie ≃	188	44.42 N	75.30 W
Oswegatchie, Middle Branch ≃	212	44.07 N	75.19 W
Oswegatchie, West Branch ≃	188	44.18 N	75.20 W
Oswego, Il., U.S.	216	41.40 N	88.21 W
Oswego, In., U.S.	216	41.19 N	85.47 W
Oswego, Ks., U.S.	198	37.10 N	95.06 W
Oswego, N.Y., U.S.	212	43.27 N	76.30 W
Oswego □ [6]	212	43.22 N	76.15 W
Oswego ≃, N.J., U.S.	208	39.40 N	74.32 W
Oswego ≃, N.Y., U.S.	212	43.28 N	76.31 W
Oswestry	42	52.52 N	3.04 W
Oświęcim	30	50.03 N	19.12 E
Osyka	194	31.00 N	90.28 W
Osynyve	83	49.34 N	39.05 E
Osypenko	78	46.54 N	36.49 E
Ota, Nihon	94	35.58 N	136.04 E
Ōta, Nihon	94	36.18 N	139.22 E
Ōta, Nihon	96	33.31 N	131.33 E
Ōta ◆ [8]	268	35.34 N	139.43 E
Ōta ≃, Nihon	94	34.40 N	137.54 E
Ōta ≃, Nihon	96	34.22 N	132.25 E
Otaci	38	48.25 N	27.47 E
Otago Peninsula ≻ [1]	172	45.52 S	170.40 E
Otahuhu	172	36.57 S	174.51 E
Ōtake	96	34.12 N	132.13 E
Otaki, N.Z.	172	40.45 S	175.09 E
Ōtaki, Nihon	94	35.17 N	140.15 E
Ōtaki, Nihon	94	35.48 N	137.33 E
Ōtaki, Nihon	94	35.57 N	138.56 E
Ōtaki ≃	94	35.49 N	137.40 E
Ōtaki-yama ∧	96	34.07 N	134.08 E
Ōta-Koizumi-hikojō ♠	94	36.16 N	139.24 E
Otane	172	39.53 S	176.38 E
Otanmäki	26	64.07 N	27.06 E
Otar	85	43.33 N	75.13 E
Otari	94	36.46 N	137.54 E
Otaru	92a	43.13 N	141.00 E
Otatara	172	46.26 S	168.18 E
Otatitlán	234	18.12 N	96.02 W
Otautau	172	46.09 S	168.00 E
Otava	26	61.39 N	27.04 E
Otava ≃	30	49.27 N	14.12 E
Otavalo	246	0.14 N	78.16 W
Otavi	156	19.39 S	17.20 E
Ōtawara	94	36.52 N	140.02 E
Otawa-yama ∧	270	34.28 N	135.53 E
Otay	228	32.35 N	117.03 W
Otchinjau	152	16.30 S	13.57 E
Oteapan	234	18.00 N	94.39 W
Otego	210	42.23 N	75.10 W
Otego Creek ≃	210	42.25 N	75.07 W
Otélé	152	3.35 N	11.15 E
Otematata	172	44.37 S	170.16 E
Oteotea	175e	9.05 S	161.11 E
Otepää	76	58.03 N	26.30 E
Oteros ≃	232	26.55 N	108.22 W
Otford, Austl.	170	34.12 S	151.01 E
Otford, Eng., U.K.	42	51.19 N	0.12 E
Otgon	88	47.11 N	97.33 E
Otgon Tenger uul ∧	88	47.36 N	97.36 E
Otham	260	51.15 N	0.35 E
Othello	202	46.49 N	119.10 W
Othery	42	51.05 N	2.53 W
Othfresen	52	52.00 N	10.23 E
Óthiris, Óros ⋏	38	39.02 N	22.37 E
Othis	261	49.04 N	2.41 E
Othonoí I	38	39.50 N	19.26 E
Oti ≃	150	8.40 N	0.13 E
Otibanda	164	7.15 S	146.30 E
Otinapa	232	24.11 N	105.02 W
Otira	172	42.50 S	171.33 E
Otis, Co., U.S.	198	40.08 N	102.57 W
Otis, In., U.S.	216	41.36 N	86.54 W
Otis, Ks., U.S.	198	38.32 N	99.03 W
Otis, Ma., U.S.	207	42.11 N	73.05 W
Otisco	218	38.32 N	85.40 W
Otisco Lake ◎	210	42.52 N	76.18 W
Otish, Monts ⋏	176	52.22 N	70.30 W
Otis Reservoir ◎ [1]	207	42.09 N	73.02 W
Otisville	210	41.28 N	74.32 W
Otjassy	80	53.14 N	41.39 E
Otjikondo	156	19.50 S	15.23 E
Otjimbingue	156	22.19 S	16.10 E
Otjinene	156	21.13 S	18.42 E
Otjiwarongo	156	20.29 S	16.36 E
Otjiwarongo □ [5]	156	20.45 S	16.30 E
Otjozondjou ≃	156	20.18 S	20.50 E
Otley	44	53.54 N	1.41 W
Otmanlı	130	41.52 N	34.37 E
Otm'ok, pereval)(	85	42.20 N	73.10 E
Otmuchów	30	50.28 N	17.10 E
Otnes	26	61.45 N	11.14 E
Otnice	61	49.05 N	16.49 E
Ōtō	96	33.41 N	135.35 E
Otočac	36	44.52 N	15.14 E
Otog Qi	102	39.08 N	108.00 E
Ōtomi	175d	24.19 N	123.54 E
Oton	116	10.42 N	122.29 E
Otonabee ≃	212	44.08 N	78.14 W
Otoque, Isla I	236	8.36 N	79.36 W
Ōtori-kita	270	34.33 N	135.27 E
Otorma	80	53.32 N	42.32 E
Otoro ≃	236	15.00 N	88.16 W
Otorohanga	172	38.11 S	175.12 E
Otoskwin ≃	176	52.13 N	88.06 W
Otowa	94	34.51 N	137.18 E
Otowa-yama ∧	270	34.58 N	135.51 E
Otowa-yama-tunnel ◆ [5]	94	34.58 N	135.51 E
Ōtoyo	96	33.46 N	133.40 E
Otra ≃	26	58.09 N	8.00 E
Otradnaja	84	44.23 N	41.31 E
Otradnoje	265a	59.47 N	30.49 E
Otradnyj	80	53.22 N	51.21 E
Otranto	68	40.09 N	18.30 E
Otranto, Capo d' ≻	68	40.06 N	18.31 E
Otranto, Strait of ⊔	38	40.00 N	19.00 E
Otricoli	66	42.25 N	12.29 E
Otrokovice	30	49.13 N	17.31 E
Ötscher ∧	61	47.52 N	15.12 E
Otsego	216	42.27 N	85.41 W
Otsego □ [6]	210	42.42 N	74.56 W
Otsego Lake ◎	210	42.45 N	74.52 W
Otselic ≃	210	42.20 N	75.58 W
Ōtsu, Nihon	96	35.00 N	135.52 E
Ōtsu, Nihon	268	35.16 N	139.42 E
Ōtsu ≃	270	34.30 N	135.24 E
Ōtsuchi	92	39.21 N	141.54 E
Ōtsuki	94	35.36 N	138.57 E
Ōtsu-shima I	96	34.00 N	131.42 E
Otta, Nig.	150	6.42 N	3.10 E
Otta, Nor.	26	61.46 N	9.32 E
Otta ≃	26	61.46 N	9.31 E
Ottakring ◆ [8]	264b	48.12 N	16.19 E
Ottana	71	40.14 N	9.02 E
Otta Pass ⊔	175c	7.09 N	151.53 E
Ottarnic Pond ◎	283	42.46 N	71.25 W
Ottati	68	40.28 N	15.19 E
Ottavia ◆ [8]	267a	41.58 N	12.24 E
Ottaviano	68	40.51 N	14.28 E
Ottawa, On., Can.	212	45.25 N	75.42 W
Ottawa, Il., U.S.	216	41.20 N	88.50 W
Ottawa, Ks., U.S.	198	38.36 N	95.16 W
Ottawa, Oh., U.S.	216	41.01 N	84.02 W
Ottawa □ [6], Mi., U.S.	216	42.57 N	86.02 W
Ottawa □ [6], Oh., U.S.	214	41.31 N	82.56 W
Ottawa ≃, Can.	176	45.20 N	73.58 W
Ottawa ≃, Oh., U.S.	214	41.44 N	83.28 W
Ottawa ≃, Oh., U.S.	216	41.00 N	84.15 W
Ottawa-Carleton □ [6]	212	45.15 N	75.45 W
Ottawa Hills	214	41.39 N	83.38 W
Ottawa International Airport ⊠	212	45.19 N	75.40 W
Ottawa Islands II	176	59.30 N	80.10 W
Ottbergen	52	51.42 N	9.18 E
Ottenby	26	56.14 N	16.25 E
Ottendorf-Okrilla	54	51.11 N	13.50 E
Ottenhöfen	58	48.34 N	8.09 E
Ottenschlag	61	48.25 N	15.13 E
Ottensheim	61	48.20 N	14.11 E
Ottenstein Stausee ◎ [1]	61	48.37 N	15.17 E
Otter ≃	42	50.46 N	3.17 W
Otterbach ≃	56	49.07 N	8.21 E
Otterbäcken	40	58.57 N	14.02 E
Otterbein	216	40.29 N	87.06 W
Otterburn	44	55.14 N	2.10 W
Otterburne	184	49.30 N	97.03 W
Otterburn Park	206	45.33 N	73.13 W
Otter Creek	192	29.19 N	82.46 W
Otter Creek ≃, On., Can.	212	44.06 N	81.07 W
Otter Creek ≃, Il., U.S.	219	39.18 N	90.07 W
Otter Creek ≃, In., U.S.	218	38.58 N	85.37 W
Otter Creek ≃, Ia., U.S.	190	41.20 N	93.30 W
Otter Creek ≃, Mo., U.S.	219	39.31 N	91.51 W
Otter Creek ≃, Mt., U.S.	202	45.36 N	106.17 W
Otter Creek ≃, N.Y., U.S.	212	43.43 N	75.23 W
Otter Creek ≃, Ut,. U.S.	200	38.10 N	112.02 W
Otter Creek ≃, Vt., U.S.	188	44.13 N	73.17 W
Otter Creek Reservoir ◎ [1]	200	38.12 N	111.59 W
Otterhöfen	56	48.33 N	8.12 E
Otter-Lake, P.Q., Can.	188	45.51 N	76.26 W
Otter Lake, Mi., U.S.	190	43.13 N	83.28 W
Otter Lake ◎, On., Can.	212	44.47 N	76.07 W
Otter Lake ◎, On., Can.	212	45.17 N	79.56 W
Otter Lake ◎, Sk., Can.	184	55.35 N	104.39 W
Otter Lake ◎ [1]	219	39.26 N	89.54 W
Otterlo	52	52.06 N	5.45 E
Otterndorf	52	53.48 N	8.53 E
Otterøya I	26	62.42 N	6.48 E
Otter River	207	42.35 N	72.03 W
Ottersberg	52	53.06 N	9.08 E
Ottershaw	260	51.22 N	0.32 W
Ottersleben ◆ [8]	54	52.05 N	11.34 E
Otter Tail ≃	198	46.16 N	96.36 W
Otter Tail Lake ◎	198	46.23 N	95.40 W
Otterup	41	55.31 N	10.24 E
Otterville, On., Can.	212	42.55 N	80.36 W
Otterville, Il., U.S.	219	39.03 N	90.24 W
Otterville, Mo., U.S.	194	38.41 N	93.00 W
Ottery ≃	42	50.39 N	4.20 W
Ottery Saint Mary	42	50.45 N	3.17 W
Ottignies	56	50.40 N	4.34 E
Ottine	222	29.36 N	97.35 W
Ottleben	54	52.05 N	11.07 E
Ottmarsbocholt	52	51.49 N	7.32 E
Ottnang	60	48.06 N	13.40 E
Ottnaren ◎	40	60.29 N	16.37 E
Otto, N.Y., U.S.	210	42.21 N	78.50 W
Otto, Tx., U.S.	222	31.27 N	96.49 W
Ottobeuren	58	47.56 N	10.18 E
Ottobeuren, Klosterkirche ✿ [1]	58	47.56 N	10.18 E
Ottobiano	62	45.09 N	8.50 E
Ottobrunn	60	48.04 N	11.40 E
Ottone	62	44.37 N	9.20 E
Ottoschwanden	58	48.12 N	7.52 E
Ottosdal	158	26.58 S	26.00 E
Ottoshoop	156	25.45 S	25.59 E
Ottoville	216	40.55 N	84.20 W
Ottuk, Kyrg.	85	42.18 N	76.18 E
Ottuk, Kyrg.	85	41.38 N	75.51 E
Ottumwa	190	41.00 N	92.22 W
Ottweiler	56	49.24 N	7.09 E
Otty Lake ◎	212	44.50 N	76.13 W
Otu, Nig.	150	8.14 N	3.24 E
Otu → Ōtsu, Nihon	96	35.00 N	135.52 E
Otukpa	150	7.09 N	7.41 E
Otumpa	252	27.19 S	62.13 W
Otun	273a	6.42 N	3.22 E
Otuquis, Bañados de ☷	248	19.20 S	58.30 W
Oturkpo	150	7.14 N	8.08 E
Otway, Bahía ⊔	254	53.20 S	74.00 W
Otway, Cape ≻	166	38.52 S	143.31 E
Otway, Seno ⊂	254	53.05 S	71.30 W
Otway Range ⋏	169	38.30 S	143.50 E
Otwock	30	52.07 N	21.16 E
Otyniya	78	48.44 N	24.51 E
Ötztal V	64	47.05 N	10.55 E
Ötztaler Ache ≃	64	47.14 N	10.50 E
Ötztaler Alpen (Alpi Venoste) ⋏	64	46.45 N	10.55 E
Ou ≃, Lao	110	20.04 N	102.13 E
Ou ≃, Zhg.	100	26.02 N	113.09 E
Ou ≃, Zhg.	100	28.01 N	120.44 E
Oua ≃	152	0.43 N	12.55 E
Ouachita ≃	194	31.38 N	91.49 W
Ouachita, Lake ◎ [1]	194	34.40 N	93.25 W
Ouachita Mountains ⋏	194	34.40 N	94.25 W
Ouaco	175f	20.50 S	164.29 E
Ouadâne	148	20.56 N	11.37 W
Ouadda	152	8.04 N	22.24 E
Ouaddaï □ [5]	146	13.00 N	21.00 E
Ouadey, Ouadi el V	146	13.34 N	18.03 E
Ouagadougou	150	12.22 N	1.31 W
Ouahigouya	150	13.35 N	2.25 W
Ouahran → Wahran	148	35.43 N	0.43 W
Ouaka □ [5]	152	6.00 N	21.00 E
Ouaka ≃	152	4.59 N	19.56 E
Oualâta	150	17.18 N	7.02 W
Ouâlata, Ḍahr ⊥ [4]	150	17.48 N	7.24 W
Oualé ≃	150	10.52 N	0.51 E
Oualidia	148	32.44 N	9.08 W
Ouallam	150	14.19 N	2.05 E
Ouallene	148	24.37 N	1.14 E
Oualto	150	9.01 N	10.06 W
Ouanary	250	4.13 N	51.40 W
Ouanda Djallé	146	8.54 N	22.48 E
Ouandago	146	7.10 N	18.42 E
Ouandja ≃	146	9.35 N	21.43 E
Ouandja-Vakaga, Réserve de la ◆ [4]	146	9.00 N	21.30 E
Ouango	152	4.19 N	22.33 E
Ouangolodougou	150	9.58 N	5.09 W
Ouaninou	150	8.11 N	7.51 W
Ouanne ≃	50	47.57 N	2.47 E
Ouan Taredert	148	27.33 N	9.32 E
Ouaquaga	210	42.08 N	75.39 W
Ouara ≃	154	5.05 N	24.26 E
Ouarâne ◆ [1]	134	21.00 N	10.30 W
Ouararda, Passe de)(	148	21.01 N	13.03 W
Ouareau ≃	206	45.56 N	73.25 W
Ouareau, Lac ◎ [1]	206	46.17 N	74.09 W
Ouargaye	150	11.32 N	0.01 E
Ouarkoye	150	12.05 N	3.40 W
Ouarkziz, Jbel ⋏	148	28.50 N	9.00 W
Ouarsenis, Djebel ∧	34	35.53 N	1.38 E
Ouarville	50	48.21 N	1.46 E
Ouarzazate	148	30.57 N	6.50 W
Ouarzazate □ [4]	148	30.55 N	6.45 W
Ouassoulou ≃	150	11.35 N	8.11 W
Ouatcha	150	13.22 N	9.18 E
Oubangui (Ubangi) ≃	152	0.30 S	17.42 E
Ouche ≃	58	47.06 N	5.16 E
Oucques	50	47.49 N	1.18 E
Ōuda	94	34.28 N	135.56 E
Oudaze Lake ◎	212	45.27 N	79.11 W
Oud-Beijerland	52	51.49 N	4.25 E
Ouddorp	52	51.48 N	3.56 E
Oude IJssel (Issel) ≃	52	52.00 N	6.10 E
Oudenaarde	50	50.51 N	3.36 E
Oudenbosch	52	51.35 N	4.31 E
Oudenburg	50	51.11 N	3.00 E
Oude-Pekela	52	53.04 N	6.58 E
Oude Rijn ≃	52	52.05 N	4.20 E
Oudeschild	52	53.02 N	4.50 E
Oude-Tonge	52	51.41 N	4.12 E
Oudewater	52	52.02 N	4.52 E
Oud-Gastel	52	51.35 N	4.27 E
Oudjda → Oujda	148	34.41 N	1.45 W
Oud-Loosdrecht	52	52.13 N	5.04 E
Oudtshoorn	158	33.35 S	22.14 E
Oudyoumoudi	150	14.04 N	0.28 W
Oued Athmenia	34	36.15 N	6.17 E
Oued Cheham	36	36.23 N	7.46 E
Oued edh Dheheb, Khlij ⊂	148	23.45 N	15.47 W
Oued Fodda	34	36.11 N	1.32 E
Oued Meliz	36	36.27 N	8.34 E
Oued Rhiou	34	35.58 N	0.55 E
Oued Tlelat	34	35.34 N	0.27 W
Oued Zarga	36	36.40 N	9.25 E
Oued-Zem	148	32.55 N	6.33 W
Ouellé	150	7.18 N	4.01 W
Ouémé □ [5]	150	7.00 N	2.35 E
Ouémé ≃	150	6.29 N	2.32 E
Ouen, Île I	175f	22.26 S	166.49 E
Ouenkoro	150	13.23 N	3.50 W
Ouenza, Djebel ∧	36	35.57 N	8.05 E
Ouenzé ◆ [8]	273b	4.14 S	15.17 E
Ouessa	150	11.03 N	2.47 W
Ouessant, Île d' (Ushant) I	32	48.28 N	5.05 W
Ouesso	152	1.37 N	16.04 E
Ouest □ [4]	152	5.23 N	10.45 E
Ouest, Pointe de l' ≻	186	49.52 N	64.31 W
Ouest, Rivière de l' ≃	206	45.39 N	74.21 W
Ouezzane	148	34.52 N	5.35 W
Ouffet	56	50.26 N	5.28 E
Ouganda → Uganda □ [1]	154	1.00 N	32.00 E
Ougarou	150	12.09 N	0.56 E
Oughter, Lough ◎	48	54.00 N	7.30 W
Oughterard	48	53.25 N	9.17 W
Oughtibridge	44	53.26 N	1.33 W
Ouham □ [5]	152	7.00 N	18.00 E
Ouham ≃	136	9.18 N	18.14 E
Ouham-Pendé □ [5]	152	7.00 N	16.00 E
Ouidah	150	6.22 N	2.05 E
Ouidi	146	14.07 N	12.58 E
Ouimet Canyon V	190	48.47 N	88.40 W
Ouistreham	32	49.17 N	0.15 W
Oujda	148	34.41 N	1.45 W
Oujda □ [4]	148	34.05 N	2.10 W
Oulad Naïl, Monts des ⋏	148	34.33 N	3.28 E
Oulainen	26	64.16 N	24.48 E
Oulangan kansallispuisto ♠	24	66.12 N	29.30 E
Oulchy-le-Château	50	49.12 N	3.21 E
Oule ≃	62	44.25 N	5.21 E
Ouled Agla	34	35.58 N	4.45 E
Ouleout Creek ≃	210	42.20 N	75.18 W
Oulins	50	48.52 N	1.28 E
Oullins	62	45.43 N	4.48 E
Oulou, Bahr ≃	146	9.48 N	21.32 E
Oulton Broad	42	52.31 N	1.42 E
Oulu	26	65.01 N	25.28 E
Oulujärvi ◎	26	64.20 N	27.15 E
Oulujoki ≃	26	65.01 N	25.25 E
Oulun lääni □ [4]	24	65.00 N	27.00 E
Oulx	62	45.02 N	6.50 E
Oumba	152	4.55 N	19.04 E
Oum-Chalouba	146	15.48 N	20.46 E
Oumé	150	6.23 N	5.25 W
Oum El Bouagui	148	35.53 N	7.07 E
Oum El Bouagui □ [5]	148	35.50 N	7.15 E
Oum er Rbia, Oued ≃	148	33.19 N	8.21 W
Oum-Hadjer	146	13.18 N	19.41 E
Oum Hadjer, Ouadi V	146	16.38 N	20.14 E
Oumiao	102	31.55 N	112.09 E
Oumm ed Droûs Guebli, Sebkhet ◎	148	24.03 N	11.45 W
Oumm ed Droûs Telli, Sebkhet ◎	148	24.20 N	11.30 W
Ounâne, Bîr ⊤ [4]	148	21.28 N	3.56 W
Ounara	148	31.33 N	9.28 W
Ounasjoki ≃	24	66.30 N	25.45 E
Oundle	42	52.29 N	0.29 W
Ounianga Kébir	146	19.04 N	20.29 E
Ouolossébougou	150	12.00 N	7.55 W
Our ≃	56	49.53 N	6.18 E
Ouragahio	150	6.19 N	5.56 W
Ōura-wan ⊂	174m	26.32 N	128.04 E
Ouray	200	38.01 N	107.40 W
Ouray, Mount ∧	200	38.25 N	106.14 W
Ource ≃	58	48.06 N	4.23 E
Ourcq ≃	50	49.01 N	3.01 E
Ourcq, Canal de l' ≊	50	48.51 N	2.22 E
Ourém	250	1.33 S	47.06 W
Ouri	146	21.34 N	19.13 E
Ouri, Tarso ∧	146	21.25 N	18.56 E
Ouricuri	250	7.53 S	40.05 W
Ourimbah	170	33.22 S	151.23 E
Ourinhos	255	22.59 S	49.52 W
Ourique	34	37.39 N	8.13 W
Ournie	171b	35.56 S	147.51 E
Ouro, Paraná do ≃	248	8.29 S	70.30 W
Ouro, Ponta do ≻	158	26.51 S	32.54 E
Ouro Branco	250	6.42 S	36.57 W
Ouro Fino	256	22.17 S	46.22 W
Ouro Preto	255	20.23 S	43.30 W
Ouro Preto ≃	248	11.02 S	65.13 W
Ouroufa, Vallée d' V	150	14.42 N	7.00 E
Ours, Grand Lac de l' → Great Bear Lake ◎	176	66.00 N	120.00 W
Oursi	150	14.41 N	0.27 W
Ourthe ≃	56	50.38 N	5.35 E
Ourthe Occidentale ≃	56	50.08 N	5.41 E
Ourthe Orientale ≃	56	50.08 N	5.41 E
Ourville-en-Caux	50	49.44 N	0.36 E
Ōu-sammyaku ⋏	92	38.45 N	140.50 E
Ouse ≃, On., Can.	212	44.17 N	78.03 W
Ouse ≃, Eng., U.K.	42	50.47 N	0.03 E
Ouse ≃, Eng., U.K.	44	53.42 N	0.41 W
Oust ≃	32	47.39 N	2.06 W
Outaouais, Rivière des → Ottawa ≃	176	45.20 N	73.58 W
Outardes, Baie aux ⊂	186	49.02 N	68.30 W
Outardes, Rivière aux ≃	176	49.04 N	68.28 W
Outardes Est, Rivière aux ≃	206	45.06 N	74.04 W
Outardes Quatre, Réservoir ◎ [1]	186	49.50 N	68.58 W
Outardes Trois, Barrage ◆ [6]	186	49.34 N	68.48 W
Outarville	50	48.13 N	2.01 E
Outcalt	276	40.23 N	74.24 W
Outeniekwaberge ⋏	158	33.53 S	22.35 E
Outerbridge Crossing ◆ [5]	276	40.31 N	74.15 W
Outer Harbour	168b	34.47 S	138.30 E
Outer Hebrides II	46	57.45 N	7.00 W
Outer Island I	190	47.03 N	90.30 W
Outer Santa Barbara Passage ⊔	228	33.10 N	118.30 W
Outer Sister Island I	166	39.39 S	148.00 E
Outjo	156	20.08 S	16.08 E
Outjo □ [5]	156	19.30 S	15.30 E
Outlane	262	53.39 N	1.53 W
Outlet Bay ⊂	208	37.22 N	75.49 W
Outlook, Sk., Can.	184	51.30 N	107.03 W
Outlook, Mt., U.S.	198	48.53 N	104.46 W
Outokumpu	26	62.44 N	29.01 E
Outpost Mountain ∧	180	69.08 N	151.12 W
Outreau	50	50.42 N	1.35 E
Outremont	206	45.31 N	73.38 W
Outside Canal ≊	226	37.13 N	121.02 W
Out Skerries II	46a	60.25 N	0.42 W
Outwell	42	52.37 N	0.14 E
Ouvéa I	175f	20.30 S	166.35 E
Ouvéa, Lagon d' ⊂	175f	20.33 S	166.27 E
Ouvèze ≃	62	43.59 N	4.51 E
Ouvidor	255	18.14 S	47.50 W
Ouye, Forêt de l' ♠	261	48.32 N	2.00 E
Ouyen	166	35.04 S	142.20 E
Ouzinkie	180	57.55 N	152.30 W
Ouzouer-le-Marché	50	47.55 N	1.32 E
Ouzouer-sur-Loire	50	47.46 N	2.29 E
Ouzzal, Oued i-n- V	148	21.35 N	2.00 E
Ovabağ	130	37.43 N	39.59 E
Ovacık, Tür.	130	39.22 N	39.13 E
Ovacık, Tür.	130	41.05 N	32.55 E
Ovada	62	44.38 N	8.38 E
Ovakent	130	38.06 N	28.02 E
Oval	210	41.09 N	77.11 W
Ovalau I	175g	17.40 S	178.48 E
Ovalle	252	30.36 S	71.12 W
Ovamboland □ [9]	156	17.45 S	16.30 E
Ovana, Cerro ∧	246	4.38 N	66.57 W
Ovar	34	40.52 N	8.38 W
Ovaro	64	46.29 N	12.52 E
Ovčinino	82	56.02 N	39.03 E

≃	River	Fluß	Río	Rivière	Rio
≊	Canal	Kanal	Canal	Canal	Canal
⌊	Waterfall, Rapids	Wasserfall, Stromschnellen	Cascada, Rápidos	Chute d'eau, Rapides	Cascata, Rápidos
⊔	Strait	Meeresstraße	Estrecho	Détroit	Estreito
⊂	Bay, Gulf	Bucht, Golf	Bahía, Golfo	Baie, Golfe	Baía, Golfo
◎	Lake, Lakes	See, Seen	Lago, Lagos	Lac, Lacs	Lago, Lagos
☷	Swamp	Sumpf	Pantano	Marais	Pântano
⊞	Ice Features, Glacier	Eis- und Gletscherformen	Accidentes Glaciales	Formes glaciaires	Acidentes glaciares
⊤	Other Hydrographic Features	Andere Hydrographische Objekte	Otros Elementos Hidrográficos	Autres données hydrographiques	Outros acidentes hidrográficos

✢	Submarine Features	Untermeerische Objekte	Accidentes Submarinos	Formes de relief sous-marin	Acidentes submarinos
□	Political Unit	Politische Einheit	Unidad Politica	Entité politique	Unidade política
✿	Cultural Institution	Kulturelle Institution	Institución Cultural	Institution culturelle	Instituição cultural
⊥	Historical Site	Historische Stätte	Sitio Histórico	Site historique	Sítio histórico
♠	Recreational Site	Erholungs- und Ferienort	Sitio de Recreo	Centre de loisirs	Área de Lazer
⊠	Airport	Flughafen	Aeropuerto	Aéroport	Aeroporto
■	Military Installation	Militäranlage	Instalación Militar	Installation militaire	Instalação militar
◆	Miscellaneous	Verschiedenes	Misceláneo	Divers	Diversos

Ovcyno 265a 59.48 N 30.37 E
Övedskloster 41 55.41 N 13.38 E
Ovejas 246 9.32 N 75.14 W
Ovelgönne 52 53.20 N 8.25 E
Ovenden 262 53.44 N 1.53 W
Oveng 152 2.25 N 12.16 E
Overath 56 50.55 N 7.14 E
Overberge 263 51.37 N 7.41 E
Overbrook 198 38.46 N 95.33 W
Overbrook ◆[8], Pa., U.S. 279b 40.24 N 79.59 W
Overbrook ◆[8], Pa., U.S. 285 39.58 N 75.16 W
Overdinkel 52 52.14 N 7.01 E
Overflakkee I 52 51.45 N 4.10 E
Overflowing ≃ 184 53.10 N 101.05 W
Overhalla 24 64.30 N 11.57 E
Overijse 56 50.46 N 4.32 E
Overijssel □[4] 52 52.25 N 6.30 E
Over Jerstal 41 55.12 N 9.18 E
Överkalix 24 66.21 N 22.56 E
Overland 219 38.42 N 90.21 W
Overland Park 198 38.58 N 94.40 W
Overlea 208 39.22 N 76.31 W
Overloon 52 51.35 N 5.57 E
Övermark (Ylimarkku) 26 62.38 N 21.30 E
Overpeck Creek ≃ 276 40.51 N 74.02 W
Overpelt 56 51.13 N 5.25 E
Overseal 42 52.44 N 1.34 W
Overstrand 42 52.56 N 1.20 E
Overton, Eng., U.K. 42 51.15 N 1.15 W
Overton, Ne., U.S. 198 40.44 N 99.32 W
Overton, Nv., U.S. 204 36.32 N 114.26 W
Overton, Tx., U.S. 222 32.16 N 94.58 W
Overton Arm c 204 36.20 N 114.25 W
Övertorneå 24 66.23 N 23.40 E
Överum 26 57.59 N 16.19 E
Over Wallop 42 51.09 N 1.35 W
Ovett 194 31.29 N 89.01 W
Ovid, Mi., U.S. 216 43.00 N 84.22 W
Ovid, N.Y., U.S. 210 42.40 N 76.49 W
Ovidiopol' 78 46.17 N 30.27 E
Oviedo, Esp. 34 43.22 N 5.50 W
Oviedo, Fl., U.S. 220 28.40 N 81.13 W
Oviglio 62 44.52 N 8.29 E
Oviken 26 62.59 N 14.24 E
Oviksfjällen ⋏ 26 63.02 N 13.51 E
Ovilla 222 32.32 N 96.53 W
Ovindoli 66 42.08 N 13.31 E
Ovinišče 76 58.22 N 37.02 E
Ovino 76 59.41 N 33.11 E
Ovīši 76 57.34 N 21.45 E
Övörchangaj □[4] 102 46.00 N 102.30 E
Øvre Anarjokka Nasjonalpark ♦ 24 69.00 N 25.00 E
Øvre Årdal 26 61.19 N 7.48 E
Øvre Dividal Nasjonalpark ♦ 24 68.39 N 19.45 E
Øvre Pasvik Nasjonalpark ♦ 24 69.06 N 28.55 E
Øvre Rendal 26 61.53 N 11.05 E
Övre Vättern ⊜ 40 59.52 N 15.40 E
Ovruch 78 51.21 N 28.49 E
Ovs'anikovo 76 60.09 N 45.16 E
Ovs'anka, Ross. 86 55.57 N 92.33 E
Ovs'anka, Ross. 89 53.35 N 126.57 E
Ovs'annikovo 82 56.54 N 37.33 E
Ovstug 76 53.24 N 33.52 E
Ōwada 268 35.49 N 139.33 E
Owaka 172 46.27 S 169.40 E
Owambo □[5] 156 18.00 S 16.00 E
Owambo ≃ 156 18.45 S 17.03 E
Owando 152 0.29 S 15.55 E
Owaneco 219 39.29 N 89.12 W
Owariashi 94 35.12 N 137.02 E
Owasco 210 42.51 N 76.28 W
Owasco Inlet ≃ 210 42.45 N 76.28 W
Owasco Lake ⊜ 210 42.52 N 76.32 W
Owasco Outlet ≃ 210 43.04 N 76.39 W
Owase 92 34.04 N 136.12 E
Owasso 196 36.16 N 95.51 W
Owatonna 190 44.05 N 93.13 W
Owbeh 128 34.22 N 63.10 E
Owe 272c 19.04 N 73.04 E
Owego 210 42.06 N 76.15 W
Owego Creek, East Branch ≃ 210 42.10 N 76.15 W
Owego Creek, West Branch ≃ 210 42.10 N 76.15 W
Owel, Lough ⊜ 48 53.34 N 7.25 W
Owen, Austl. 168b 34.16 S 138.33 E
Owen, Dtsch. 56 48.35 N 9.27 E
Owen, In., U.S. 218 38.27 N 85.34 W
Owen, Wi., U.S. 190 44.57 N 90.33 W
Owen □[6] 218 38.33 N 84.49 W
Owen, Mount ∧ 172 41.33 S 172.32 E
Owenboy ≃ 48 51.48 N 8.18 W
Owendo 152 0.17 N 9.30 E
Owenea ≃ 48 54.47 N 8.26 W
Owen Falls Dam ◆[6] 154 0.27 N 33.11 E
Owen Fracture Zone ✦ 12 12.00 N 58.00 E
Owenkillew ≃ 48 54.44 N 7.18 W
Owenmore ≃ 48 54.07 N 9.50 W
Owen River 172 41.39 S 172.27 E
Owens ≃ 204 36.31 N 117.57 W
Owensboro 194 37.46 N 87.06 W
Owens Creek ≃, Ca., U.S. 226 37.13 N 120.42 W
Owens Creek ≃, Md., U.S. 208 39.33 N 77.20 W
Owens Lake ⊜ 204 36.25 N 117.56 W
Owen Sound 212 44.34 N 80.56 W
Owen Sound c 212 44.40 N 80.55 W
Owen Stanley Range ⋏ 164 9.20 S 147.55 E
Owensville, In., U.S. 194 38.16 N 87.41 W
Owensville, Mo., U.S. 219 38.20 N 91.30 W
Owensville, Oh., U.S. 218 39.07 N 84.08 W
Owenton, Ky., U.S. 218 38.32 N 84.50 W
Owenton, Va., U.S. 208 37.53 N 77.06 W
Owentown 222 32.26 N 95.12 W
Owerri 150 5.29 N 7.02 E
Owhango 172 39.00 S 175.23 E
Owikeno Lake ⊜ 182 51.41 N 127.00 W
Owings 208 38.43 N 76.36 W
Owings Mills 284b 39.25 N 76.46 W
Owingsville 188 38.08 N 83.45 W
Owl ≃, Ab., Can. 182 54.54 N 111.57 W
Owl ≃, Mb., Can. 176 57.51 N 92.44 W
Owl Creek ≃, U.S. 198 44.41 N 103.29 W
Owl Creek ≃, Mt., U.S. 202 45.18 N 107.21 W
Owl Creek ≃, Wy., U.S. 202 43.41 N 108.11 W
Owl Creek, South Fork ≃ 202 43.43 N 108.32 W
Owl Creek Mountains ⋏ 202 43.30 N 108.35 W
Owo 150 7.15 N 5.37 E
Oworonsoki 273a 6.33 N 3.24 E
Owosso 216 42.59 N 84.10 W
Owuru ≃ 273a 6.39 N 3.27 E
Owyhee 204 41.56 N 116.05 W
Owyhee ≃ 202 43.46 N 117.02 W
Owyhee, Lake ⊜[1] 202 43.28 N 117.20 W
Owyhee, South Fork ≃ 202 42.26 N 116.53 W
Oxapampa 248 10.34 S 75.24 W
Öxarfjörður c 24a 66.15 N 16.45 W
Oxbow, Sk., Can. 184 49.14 N 102.11 W
Oxbow, Mi., U.S. 281 42.38 N 83.28 W
Oxbow, N.Y., U.S. 212 44.17 N 75.37 W
Oxbow Lake ⊜ 281 42.38 N 83.28 W
Ox Creek ≃ 198 48.37 N 100.17 W
Oxelösund 40 58.40 N 17.06 E
Oxford, N.S., Can. 186 45.44 N 63.52 W
Oxford, N.Z. 172 43.18 S 172.11 E
Oxford, Eng., U.K. 42 51.46 N 1.15 W
Oxford, Al., U.S. 194 33.36 N 85.50 W
Oxford, Ct., U.S. 207 41.26 N 73.07 W
Oxford, Fl., U.S. 220 28.55 N 82.02 W
Oxford, In., U.S. 216 40.31 N 87.14 W
Oxford, Ia., U.S. 190 41.43 N 91.47 W
Oxford, Ks., U.S. 198 37.16 N 97.10 W
Oxford, Ky., U.S. 218 38.16 N 84.30 W
Oxford, Me., U.S. 188 44.07 N 70.29 W
Oxford, Md., U.S. 208 38.41 N 76.10 W
Oxford, Ma., U.S. 207 42.07 N 71.51 W
Oxford, Mi., U.S. 216 42.49 N 83.15 W
Oxford, Ms., U.S. 194 34.21 N 89.31 W
Oxford, Ne., U.S. 198 40.15 N 99.38 W
Oxford, N.J., U.S. 210 40.48 N 74.59 W
Oxford, N.Y., U.S. 210 42.26 N 75.35 W
Oxford, N.C., U.S. 192 36.18 N 78.35 W
Oxford, Oh., U.S. 218 39.30 N 84.44 W
Oxford, Pa., U.S. 208 39.47 N 75.58 W
Oxford, Wi., U.S. 190 43.46 N 89.34 W
Oxford □[6] 212 43.08 N 80.50 W
Oxford Falls 274a 33.44 S 151.15 E
Oxford House 184 54.56 N 95.16 W
Oxford House Indian Reserve ◆[4] 184 54.54 N 95.15 W
Oxford Junction 190 41.59 N 90.57 W
Oxford Lake ⊜ 184 54.51 N 95.37 W
Oxford Peak ∧ 202 42.16 N 112.06 W
Oxfordshire □[6] 42 51.50 N 1.15 W
Oxford Valley Mall ◆[9] 285 40.11 N 74.53 W
Oxhey 260 51.39 N 0.23 W
Oxie 41 55.33 N 13.04 E
Oxkutzcab 232 20.18 N 89.25 W
Oxley 166 34.12 S 144.06 E
Oxley Creek ≃ 171a 27.32 S 153.00 E
Oxnard 228 34.11 N 119.10 W
Oxnard Beach 228 34.09 N 119.13 W
Oxon Hill 284c 38.48 N 76.59 W
Oxon Run ≃ 284b 38.49 N 77.00 W
Ox Pasture Brook ≃ 283 42.45 N 70.54 W
Oxshott 260 51.20 N 0.21 W
Oxted 42 51.16 N 0.01 W
Oxtongue ≃ 212 45.19 N 79.01 W
Oxtongue Lake ⊜ 212 45.22 N 78.55 W
Oxus → Amu Darya ≃ 72 43.40 N 59.01 E
Oy 58 47.38 N 10.28 E
Oya, Malay. 112 2.52 N 111.53 E
Ōya, Nihon 96 35.20 N 134.40 E
Oya ≃ 112 2.52 N 111.52 E
Oyabe 94 36.40 N 136.52 E
Oyabe ≃ 94 36.48 N 137.04 E
Ōya-ji ⊍[1] 94 36.38 N 139.48 E
Ōyake-yama ∧[2] 270 34.48 N 135.51 E
Oyalı 130 37.14 N 41.45 E
Oyama, B.C., Can. 182 50.07 N 119.22 W
Oyama, Nihon 94 35.21 N 139.00 E
Oyama, Nihon 94 36.18 N 139.48 E
Ōyama, Nihon 94 36.36 N 137.18 E
Oyama, Nihon 268 35.36 N 139.22 E
Ōyamada 94 34.46 N 136.13 E
Ōyamazaki 270 34.54 N 135.42 E
Oyameyo, Volcán ∧[1] 286a 19.10 N 99.11 W
Oyan 152 0.02 N 10.17 E
Ōyano 92 32.35 N 130.26 E
Oyapock (Oiapoque) ≃ 250 4.08 N 51.40 W
Oyashirazu ♦ 94 36.59 N 137.40 E
Oybin 54 50.50 N 14.44 E
Oye-et-Pallet 58 46.51 N 6.20 E
Oyem 152 1.37 N 11.35 E
Oyen 184 51.22 N 110.28 W
Øyeren ⊜ 26 59.48 N 11.14 E
Oykel ≃ 46 57.56 N 4.25 W
Oykel Bridge 46 57.58 N 4.43 W
Oymyakon → Ojm'akon 74 63.28 N 142.49 E
Oyo, Congo 152 0.01 N 15.54 E
Oyo, Nig. 150 7.51 N 3.56 E
Oyo □[3] 150 8.00 N 3.50 E
Oyo ≃ 115a 7.57 S 110.22 E
Ōyodo 96 34.23 N 135.48 E
Oyodo ◆[8] 270 34.43 N 135.30 E
Ōyodo ≃ 92 31.53 N 131.28 E
Oyón 248 10.39 S 76.47 W
Oyonnax 58 46.15 N 5.40 E
Ōyorogi-san ∧ 96 35.05 N 132.51 E
Oyotún 248 6.51 S 79.19 W
Oyster 208 37.17 N 75.55 W
Oyster Bay 210 40.51 N 73.31 W
Oyster Bay c 276 40.55 N 73.30 W
Oyster Bay Cove 276 40.52 N 73.31 W
Oyster Bay Harbor c 276 40.53 N 73.32 W
Oyster Creek 222 29.00 N 95.20 W
Oyster Creek ≃ 222 28.59 N 95.18 W
Oyster Point ∧ 282 37.50 N 121.52 W
Oyster Point > 168b 34.55 S 137.48 E
Oyster Rock I[2] 272c 18.54 N 72.50 E
Oysterville 224 46.33 N 124.02 W
Øystese 26 60.23 N 6.13 E
Oyten 52 53.04 N 9.01 E
Ozaki 268 35.59 N 139.51 E
Ozamiz 116 8.08 N 123.50 E
Ozanne ≃ 50 48.11 N 1.22 E
Ozariči 76 52.28 N 29.16 E
Ozark, Al., U.S. 194 31.27 N 85.38 W
Ozark, Ar., U.S. 194 35.29 N 93.49 W
Ozark, Mo., U.S. 194 37.01 N 93.12 W
Ozark National Scenic Riverways ♦ 194 37.10 N 91.10 W
Ozark Plateau ⋏[1] 194 37.00 N 93.00 W
Ozark Reservoir ⊜[1] 194 35.35 N 94.00 W
Ozarks, Lake of the ⊜[1] 194 38.10 N 92.50 W
Ozaukee □[6] 216 44.14 N 88.00 W
Ózd 30 48.14 N 20.18 E
Ozd'atiči 76 54.06 N 28.50 E
Oze ≃ 96 34.12 N 132.14 E
Ozeblin ∧ 36 44.35 N 15.53 E
Ozek 86 46.35 N 60.41 E
Ozereckoje 82 56.04 N 37.23 E
Ožerelje 82 54.48 N 38.17 E
Ožerelki 82 55.51 N 38.52 E
Ozerišče 76 54.48 N 33.13 E
Ozerki, Ross. 80 51.13 N 53.56 E
Ozerki, Ross. 80 51.32 N 45.16 E
Ozerki, Ross. 80 52.01 N 45.29 E
Ozerki, Ross. 86 53.38 N 83.44 E
Ozerki, Ross. 265a 59.54 N 30.44 E
Ozerna ≃ 82 55.44 N 36.08 E
Ozerne 78 50.11 N 28.42 E
Ozerninskoje vodochranilišče ⊜[1] 82 55.45 N 36.15 E
Ozernovskij 74 51.30 N 156.31 E
Ozernyj 180 66.24 N 179.06 W
Ozero 80 56.58 N 44.43 E
Ozery 82 54.51 N 38.34 E
Ozette Lake ⊜ 224 48.06 N 124.38 W
Ozgoryš 85 41.15 N 74.45 E
Ozieri 71 40.35 N 9.00 E
Ozimek 30 50.41 N 18.13 E
Ozinki 80 51.12 N 49.45 E
Ozirs'k 78 51.43 N 26.24 E
Ožogino, ozero ⊜ 74 69.16 N 146.36 E
Ozoir-la-Ferrière 261 48.46 N 2.40 E
Ozona, Fl., U.S. 220 28.04 N 82.46 W
Ozona, Tx., U.S. 196 30.42 N 101.12 W
Ozone Park ◆[8] 276 40.40 N 73.51 W
Ozorków 30 51.58 N 19.19 E
Oz'ornaja, Kaz. 86 53.25 N 63.15 E
Oz'ornaja, Ross. 86 51.08 N 60.50 E
Oz'ornoje, Ross. 80 51.41 N 44.55 E
Oz'ornoje, Ross. 80 51.46 N 51.28 E
Oz'ornoje, Ross. 86 56.48 N 71.15 E
Oz'ornyj 80 57.10 N 40.59 E
Oz'orsk 76 54.25 N 22.01 E
Oz'orskij 89 46.36 N 143.08 E
Oz'ory 76 53.43 N 24.11 E
Ozouer-le-Voulgis 261 48.40 N 2.47 E
Özpınar 130 37.57 N 42.16 E
Ōzu, Nihon 92 32.52 N 130.52 E
Ōzu, Nihon 96 33.30 N 132.33 E
Ozubulu 150 5.57 N 6.51 E
Ozuluama 234 21.40 N 97.51 W
Ozumba 234 19.03 N 98.48 W
Ozurgeti 84 41.56 N 42.00 E

P

Pâ 150 11.33 N 3.15 W
Paagoumène 175f 20.29 S 164.11 E
Paal 56 51.02 N 5.11 E
Paama □[8] 175f 16.28 S 168.18 E
Paama I 175f 16.28 S 168.14 E
Paar ≃ 60 48.45 N 11.33 E
Paardekraal Monument ⊥ 273d 26.06 S 27.47 E
Paaren 264a 52.39 N 12.59 E
Paarl 158 33.45 S 18.56 E
Paasbach ≃ 263 51.25 N 7.11 E
Paauilo 229d 20.02 N 155.22 W
Pabarabuk 164 6.05 S 144.05 E
Pabbay I, Scot., U.K. 46 56.51 N 7.35 W
Pabbay I, Scot., U.K. 46 57.46 N 7.15 W
Pabbi 123 34.01 N 71.47 E
Pabbiring, Kepulauan II 112 4.55 S 119.25 E
Pabean 112 6.50 S 115.19 E
Pabellón, Punta > 254 43.14 S 74.23 W
Pabellón de Arteaga 234 22.10 N 102.21 W
Pabellones, Ensenada c 232 24.27 N 107.36 W
Pabianice 30 51.40 N 19.22 E
Pabillonis 71 39.35 N 8.43 E
Pablo 202 47.36 N 114.07 W
Pābna 124 24.00 N 89.15 E
Pabo 154 3.00 N 32.09 E
Pabradė 76 54.59 N 25.44 E
Paca 115b 8.29 S 120.11 E
Pacaás Novas, Parque Nacional ♦ 248 11.10 S 63.30 W
Pacaás Novos ≃ 248 10.51 S 65.20 W
Pacaás Novos, Serra dos ⋏ 248 10.45 S 64.15 W
Pacaembu 255 21.34 S 51.17 W
Pacaembú, Estádio do ♦ 287b 23.33 S 46.39 W
Pacajá ≃ 250 1.56 S 50.50 W
Pacajus 250 4.10 S 38.28 W
Pacaltsdorp 158 34.00 S 22.28 E
Pacaraima, Sierra de → Pakaraima Mountains ⋏ 246 5.30 N 60.40 W
Pacarán 248 12.52 S 76.03 W
Pacaraos 248 11.11 S 76.44 W
Pacasmayo 248 7.24 S 79.34 W
Pacatuba 250 3.58 S 38.37 W
Pace, Fl., U.S. 194 30.35 N 87.09 W
Pace, Ms., U.S. 194 33.47 N 90.51 W
Paceco 70 37.59 N 12.33 E
Pačelma, Ross. 80 53.15 N 43.21 E
Pačelma, Ross. 80 53.20 N 43.20 E
Pacet 115a 6.45 S 107.03 E
Pachača 74 60.34 N 169.03 E
Pachacamac ⊥ 248 12.14 S 76.52 W
Pachamba 126 24.12 N 86.16 E
Pachaug Pond ⊜ 207 41.34 N 71.54 W
Pacheco 226 37.59 N 122.04 W
Pacheco, Isla I 254 52.17 S 74.45 W
Pacheco Creek ≃ 226 36.58 N 121.28 W
Pacheco Pass)(226 37.03 N 121.13 W
Pāchh Elāsin 126 24.08 N 89.54 E
Pachino 70 36.43 N 15.05 E
Pachitea ≃ 248 8.46 S 74.32 W
Pachiza 248 7.16 S 76.46 W
Pachkoli ◆[8] 272c 19.08 N 72.54 E
Pachmarhi 124 22.28 N 78.26 E
Pacho 246 5.08 N 74.10 W
Pachomovo 82 54.38 N 37.33 E
Pachor 124 23.42 N 76.44 E
Pāchora 122 20.40 N 75.21 E
Pachotnyj Ugol 80 52.58 N 41.56 E
Pachra ≃ 82 55.32 N 37.59 E
Pachtaabad 85 38.28 N 68.10 E
Pachuca [de Soto] 234 20.07 N 98.44 W
Paciência ◆[8] 256 22.55 S 43.38 W
Pacific, B.C., Can. 182 54.46 N 128.17 W
Pacific, Mo., U.S. 219 38.28 N 90.44 W
Pacific, Wa., U.S. 224 47.15 N 122.14 W
Pacific □[6] 224 46.30 N 123.39 W
Pacifica 226 37.37 N 122.29 W
Pacific-Antarctic Ridge ✦[3] 6 62.00 S 157.00 W
Pacific Beach 224 47.12 N 124.12 W
Pacific City 224 45.12 N 123.57 W
Pacific Creek ≃ 200 42.08 N 109.24 W
Pacific Gardens 226 37.58 N 121.20 W
Pacific Grove 226 36.38 N 121.56 W
Pacific Islands, Trust Territory of the → Palau □[2] 14 5.00 N 137.00 E
Pacific Missile Test Center ■ 228 34.07 N 119.07 W
Pacífico, Océano → Pacific Ocean ⊤[1] 6 10.00 S 150.00 W
Pacific Ocean ⊤[1] 4 10.00 S 150.00 W
Pacific Ocean ⊤[1] 6 10.00 S 150.00 W
Pacifico Mountain ∧ 228 34.23 N 118.02 W
Pacific Palisades ◆[8] 280 34.03 N 118.32 W
Pacific Ranges ⋏ 182 50.45 N 125.30 W
Pacific Rim National Park ♦ 182 48.45 N 125.40 W
Pacifique, Océan → Pacific Ocean ⊤[1] 6 10.00 S 150.00 W
Pacijan Island I 116 10.39 N 124.20 E
Pacinan, Tanjung > 115a 7.36 S 114.02 E
Paciran 115a 6.52 S 112.20 E
Pacitan 115a 8.12 S 111.07 E
Pack 61 46.58 N 14.59 E
Packanack Lake ⊜ 276 40.56 N 74.15 W
Packard Mountain ∧[2] 207 42.28 N 72.21 W
Páckevei-Duna ≃[1] 264c 47.19 N 19.02 E
Pack Monadnock Mountain ∧ 207 42.52 N 71.52 W
Packsattel)(61 46.58 N 14.58 E
Packwood 224 46.36 N 121.40 W
Packwood Lake ⊜ 224 46.35 N 121.34 W
Pacllón 248 10.18 S 77.07 W
Pacock Brook ≃ 276 41.05 N 74.31 W
Paço de Arcos 266c 38.42 N 9.17 W
Paço do Lumiar 250 2.31 S 44.07 W
Pacohuaras ≃ 248 10.04 S 65.46 W
Pacoima ◆[8] 280 34.16 N 118.26 W
Pacolet ≃ 192 34.50 N 81.27 W
Pacolet Mills 192 34.55 N 81.44 W
Pacora 246 9.05 N 79.17 W
Pacov 30 49.28 N 15.00 E
Pacquet 186 49.59 N 55.53 W
Pacuare ≃ 236 10.14 N 83.17 W
Pacuí ≃ 255 16.46 S 45.01 W
Pacuneiro ≃ 255 13.02 S 53.25 W
Pacy-sur-Eure 50 49.01 N 1.23 E
Paczkow 30 50.27 N 17.00 E
Padada 116 6.42 N 125.22 E
Padada ≃ 116 6.42 N 125.23 E
Padaido, Kepulauan II 164 1.15 S 136.30 E
Padam 123 33.28 N 76.53 E
Padamarang, Pulau I 112 4.07 S 121.24 E
Padamo ≃ 246 2.54 N 65.17 W
Padampur 120 20.59 N 83.04 E
Padang, Indon. 112 1.39 S 108.55 E
Padang, Indon. 112 2.59 N 105.40 E
Padang, Indon. 112 6.11 S 120.26 E
Padang, Indon. 112 0.57 S 100.21 E
Padang, Pulau I 114 1.10 N 102.20 E
Padang Besar 114 6.40 N 100.19 E
Padangbetuah 112 3.39 S 102.13 E
Padang Endau 114 2.40 N 103.37 E
Padangpanjang 112 0.27 S 100.25 E
Padangsidempuan 114 1.22 N 99.16 E
Padangtiji 114 5.22 N 95.50 E
Padangtikar, Pulau I 112 0.50 S 109.30 E
Padang Tungku 114 4.14 N 101.59 E
Padany 24 63.17 N 33.22 E
Padas 115a 7.25 S 111.32 E
Padas ≃ 112 5.14 N 115.34 E
Padasjoki 26 61.21 N 25.17 E
Padauari ≃ 246 0.15 S 64.05 W
Padborg 41 54.49 N 9.22 E
Padcaya 248 21.52 S 64.48 W
Paddington ◆[8] 260 51.31 N 0.10 W
Paddington Station ◆[5] 260 51.31 N 0.11 W
Paddle ≃ 182 54.05 N 114.15 W
Paddle Prairie 176 57.57 N 117.29 W
Paddock Lake 216 42.34 N 88.06 W
Paddock Wood 42 51.11 N 0.23 E
Padea 38 44.01 N 23.52 E
Padea-besar I 112 3.30 S 123.05 E
Padeghar 272c 18.58 N 73.03 E
Paden City 188 39.36 N 80.56 W
Paderborn 52 51.43 N 8.45 E
Paderno Dugnano 266b 45.34 N 9.10 E
Paderno Ponchielli 64 45.14 N 9.55 E
Padghe 272c 19.03 N 73.07 E
Padibe 154 3.28 N 32.50 E
Padiham 44 53.49 N 2.19 W
Padilla 248 19.19 S 64.20 W
Padilla Bay c 224 48.35 N 122.32 W
Padjelanta Nationalpark ♦ 24 67.28 N 16.41 E
Padle 272c 19.09 N 73.03 E
Padloping Island I 176 67.07 N 62.35 W
Padma → Ganges ≃ 124 23.22 N 90.32 E
Padola 64 46.36 N 12.28 E
Padoue → Padova 64 45.25 N 11.53 E
Padova 64 45.25 N 11.53 E
Padova □[4] 64 45.21 N 11.49 E
Padovka 80 52.28 N 49.31 E
Pādra 120 22.14 N 73.05 E
Padrão, Ponta do > 152 6.03 S 12.18 E
Padrauna 124 26.55 N 83.59 E
Padre Bernardo 255 15.21 S 48.30 W
Padre Brito 256 21.18 S 43.59 W
Padre Burgos 116 10.02 N 125.01 E
Padre Island I 196 27.00 N 97.15 W
Padre Island National Seashore ♦ 196 27.00 N 97.25 W
Padre Miguel ◆[8] 287a 22.53 S 43.26 W
Padre Paraíso 255 17.06 S 41.31 W
Padria 71 40.24 N 8.38 E
Padrón 34 42.44 N 8.40 W
Padrone, Cape > 158 33.46 S 26.30 E
Padrt' 60 49.40 N 13.46 E
Padstow, Austl. 274a 33.57 S 151.02 E
Padstow, Eng., U.K. 42 50.33 N 4.56 W
Padua → Padova 64 45.25 N 11.53 E
Paducah, Ky., U.S. 194 37.05 N 88.36 W
Paducah, Tx., U.S. 196 34.00 N 100.18 W
Padula 68 40.20 N 15.39 E
Paduli 68 41.10 N 14.53 E
Padunskaja 86 55.02 N 85.02 E
Paea 174s 17.41 S 149.35 W
Paedun 98 35.03 N 128.21 E
Paekakariki 172 40.59 S 174.57 E
Paektu-san ∧ 98 42.00 N 128.03 E
Paengaroa 172 37.49 S 176.25 E
Paengnyŏng-do I 98 37.57 N 124.40 E
Paerdegat Basin c 276 40.37 N 73.54 W
Paeroa 172 37.23 S 175.40 E
Paesana 62 44.41 N 7.16 E
Paese 64 45.40 N 12.10 E
Paestum ⊥ 68 40.25 N 15.00 E
Paete 116 14.23 N 121.29 E
Páez ≃ 246 2.28 N 75.34 W
Pafúri 156 22.27 S 31.21 E
Pag 36 44.27 N 15.04 E
Pag, Otok I 36 44.30 N 15.00 E
Paga 150 10.58 N 1.06 W
Pagadenbaru 115a 6.28 S 107.48 E
Pagadian 116 7.49 N 123.25 E
Pagadian Bay c 116 7.48 N 123.31 E
Pagai Selatan, Pulau I 112 3.00 S 100.20 E
Pagai Utara, Pulau I 112 2.42 S 100.07 E
Pagalungan 116 7.04 N 124.41 E
Pagan 110 21.10 N 94.51 E
Pagan I 108 18.07 N 145.46 E
Pagancillo 252 29.34 S 68.03 W
Paganella ∧ 64 46.08 N 11.02 E
Pagani 68 40.45 N 14.37 E
Paganica 66 42.21 N 13.28 E
Paganico 66 42.56 N 11.16 E
Pagaralam 112 4.01 S 103.16 E
Pagasitikós Kólpos c 38 39.15 N 22.51 E
Pagatan 112 3.36 S 115.56 E
Pagato ≃ 184 55.49 N 102.05 W
Pagato Lake ⊜ 184 56.08 N 102.30 W
Pagbilao 116 13.58 N 121.41 E
Pagbilao Grande Island I 116 13.55 N 121.46 E
Pagdanan Bay c 116 10.31 N 119.15 E
Page, Az., U.S. 200 36.54 N 111.28 W
Page, N.D., U.S. 198 47.09 N 97.34 W
Page Field ⊠ 220 26.35 N 81.52 W
Pagėgiai 76 55.09 N 21.54 E
Pageland 192 34.46 N 80.23 W
Page Manor 218 39.45 N 84.06 W
Pager ≃ 154 3.09 N 32.30 E
Pagerdewa 112 3.46 S 105.18 E
Paget, Mount ∧ 244 54.26 S 36.33 W
Paghmān 120 34.36 N 68.57 E
Paglia ≃ 66 42.42 N 12.11 E
Pagliara 70 37.59 N 15.22 E
Paglieta 66 42.10 N 14.30 E
Pagliete, Bonifica delle ◆[1] 267a 41.53 N 12.12 E
Pagny-sur-Moselle 56 48.59 N 6.01 E
Pago Bay c 174p 13.25 N 144.48 E
Pagoda Peak ∧ 200 40.10 N 107.20 W
Pagoda Point > 110 15.57 N 94.15 E
Pagon, Bukit ∧ 112 4.18 N 115.19 E
Pago Pago 174u 14.16 S 170.42 W
Pago Pago Harbor c 174u 14.17 S 170.40 W
Pago Pago International Airport ⊠ 174u 14.20 S 170.43 W
Pagosa Springs 200 37.16 N 107.00 W
Pagote 272c 18.54 N 72.59 E
Pagouda 150 9.45 N 1.19 E
Pagri 124 27.44 N 89.09 E
Pagsangahan 116 13.13 N 122.33 E
Pagsanjan 116 14.15 N 121.25 E
Paguate 200 35.08 N 107.22 W
Pagudpud 116 18.34 N 120.47 E
Pagueras, Torrente de ≃ 266d 41.28 N 1.58 E
Paguyaman ≃ 112 0.31 N 122.38 E
Pagwi 164 4.03 S 143.02 E
Pah 84 39.08 N 39.40 E
Pahādi ◆[8] 272c 19.10 N 72.51 E
Pahala 229d 19.12 N 155.28 W
Pahalgam 123 34.02 N 75.20 E
Pahang □[3] 114 3.30 N 102.45 E
Pahang ≃ 114 3.32 N 103.28 E
Páhara, Laguna c 236 14.18 N 83.15 W
Pahāsu 124 28.11 N 78.03 E
Pahau Point > 229b 21.49 N 160.15 W
Pahi 114 5.28 N 102.13 E
Pahia Point > 172 46.19 S 167.41 E
Pahiatua 172 40.27 S 175.50 E
Pahlād Garhi 272a 28.40 N 77.21 E
Pahlavī → Bandar-e Anzalī 128 37.28 N 49.27 E
Pahoa 229d 19.29 N 154.57 W
Pahokee 220 26.49 N 80.39 W
Pahrump 204 36.12 N 115.58 W
Pahsimeroi ≃ 202 44.41 N 114.03 W
Pahuatlán de Valle 234 20.17 N 98.09 W
Pahvant Range ⋏ 200 38.45 N 112.15 W
Pai 110 19.19 N 98.27 E
Pai ≃ 110 19.09 N 97.33 E
Pai, Ilha do I 287a 22.59 S 43.05 W
Paia 229a 20.54 N 156.22 W
Paianía 267c 37.57 N 23.51 E
Paicines 226 36.44 N 121.17 W
Paico 248 14.02 S 73.39 W
Paide 76 58.54 N 25.33 E
Paidorzu, Monte ∧ 71 40.30 N 9.05 E
Paifangchang 107 30.31 N 106.38 E
Paige 222 30.13 N 97.07 W
Paignton 42 50.26 N 3.34 W
Paiguano 252 30.01 S 70.32 W
Paihia 172 35.17 S 174.05 E
Paiho 100 23.21 N 120.25 E
Paiján 248 7.44 S 79.19 W
Päijänne ⊜ 26 61.35 N 25.30 E
Pāikgācha 126 22.35 N 89.20 E
Paikü Co ⊜ 124 28.48 N 85.36 E
Pail 123 32.38 N 72.27 E
Paila ≃ 248 16.02 S 64.12 W
Paila, Sierra la ⋏ 196 25.50 N 101.30 W
Pailīn 110 12.51 N 102.36 E
Pailitas 246 8.58 N 73.38 W
Paillaco 254 40.04 S 72.53 W
Pailolo Channel ц 229a 21.05 N 156.42 W
Pailoutou 106 30.56 N 121.16 E
Pailoutun 104 40.44 N 122.49 E
Paimboeuf 32 47.17 N 2.02 W
Paimio 26 60.27 N 22.42 E
Paimpol 32 48.46 N 3.03 W
Painan 112 1.21 S 100.34 E
Paincourt 214 42.23 N 82.17 W
Painesdale 190 47.02 N 88.40 W
Painesville 214 41.43 N 81.14 W
Painscastle 42 52.07 N 3.12 W
Painshawfield 44 54.56 N 1.54 W
Painswick 42 51.48 N 2.11 W
Paint ≃ 190 45.58 N 88.15 W
Paint Creek ≃, Mi., U.S. 281 42.06 N 83.36 W
Paint Creek ≃, Oh., U.S. 218 39.18 N 82.56 W
Paint Creek ≃, Pa., U.S. 214 41.10 N 79.28 W
Paint Creek ≃, Tx., U.S. 196 30.18 N 99.54 W
Paint Creek, East Fork ≃ 218 39.32 N 83.25 W
Paint Creek, North Fork ≃ 218 39.18 N 83.02 W
Paint Creek Lake ⊜[1] 218 39.15 N 83.22 W
Painted Desert ◆[2] 200 36.00 N 111.20 W
Painted Post 210 42.09 N 77.05 W
Painted Rock Reservoir ⊜[1] 200 33.00 N 112.50 W
Painten 60 49.00 N 11.49 E
Painter 208 37.35 N 75.47 W
Painter Creek ≃ 218 40.05 N 84.21 W
Paintertown 279b 40.21 N 79.42 W
Paint Lake ⊜ 184 55.28 N 97.57 W
Paint Rock 196 31.30 N 99.55 W
Paint Rock ≃ 194 34.28 N 86.28 W
Paintsville 192 37.48 N 82.48 W
Paiolinho 256 21.52 S 45.54 W
Pai Pobre, Morro do ∧ 287b 23.40 S 46.55 W
Paisco 64 46.04 N 10.17 E
Paisha 100 23.40 N 119.35 E
Paisley, Austl. 274b 37.51 S 144.51 E
Paisley, On., Can. 212 44.18 N 81.16 W
Paisley, Scot., U.K. 46 55.50 N 4.26 W
Paisley, Fl., U.S. 220 28.59 N 81.32 W
Paisley, Or., U.S. 202 42.41 N 120.32 W
Païta, N. Cal. 175f 22.08 S 166.22 E
Paita, Perú 248 5.06 S 81.07 W
Paita, Bahía de c 248 5.04 S 81.05 W
Paitan 100 23.31 N 113.46 E
Paitan ≃ 116 6.30 N 117.30 E
Paitan, Teluk c 116 6.45 N 117.20 E
Paiton 115a 7.43 S 113.30 E
Paiva 256 21.18 S 43.25 W
Paiva ≃ 34 41.04 N 8.16 W
Paizhou 100 30.13 N 113.56 E
Paj 24 61.13 N 34.24 E
Pajala 24 67.11 N 23.22 E
Pajan 246 1.34 S 80.25 W
Pajapan 234 18.15 N 94.42 W
Pajares, Puerto de)(34 43.00 N 5.46 W
Pajaro 226 36.54 N 121.39 W
Pajaro ≃ 226 36.51 N 121.48 W
Pajaros Point > 240m 18.31 N 64.18 W
Paj-Choj ⋏[2] 72 69.00 N 63.00 E
Pajdugina ≃ 86 58.50 N 81.47 E
Pajęczno 30 51.09 N 19.00 E
Pajeú ≃ 250 8.55 S 38.42 W
Pajiangkou 100 23.46 N 113.14 E
Pajjer, gora ∧ 24 66.42 N 64.25 E
Pajtug 85 40.53 N 72.15 E
Pak ≃ 110 21.05 N 102.31 E
Páka, Magy. 61 46.36 N 16.39 E
Paka, Malay. 114 4.39 N 103.26 E
Paka ≃ 114 4.40 N 103.27 E
Pākāla 122 13.28 N 79.07 E
Pakaraima Mountains ⋏ 246 5.30 N 60.40 W
Pākaur 124 24.38 N 87.51 E
Pak Ban 110 21.14 N 102.28 E
Pakch'ŏn 98 39.45 N 125.35 E
Pak Chong 110 14.42 N 101.25 E
Pakeng 140 6.55 N 30.40 E
Pakenham, Austl. 169 38.04 S 145.29 E
Pakenham, On., Can. 212 45.20 N 76.17 W
Pākhāl ⊜[1] 122 17.57 N 79.59 E
Pákhi 267c 37.59 N 23.22 E
Pákhi I 267c 37.58 N 23.22 E
Pákhna 130 34.46 N 32.48 E
Pakhoi → Beihai 102 21.29 N 109.05 E
Pakin I[1] 14 7.04 N 157.48 E
Pakipaki 172 39.41 S 176.48 E
Pakistan (Pākistān) □[1], Asia 118 30.00 N 70.00 E
Pakistan (Pākistān) □[1], Asia 120 30.00 N 70.00 E
Pakistan, East → Bangladesh □[1] 120 24.00 N 90.00 E
Pak Kong 271d 22.23 N 114.15 E
Pak Kret 269a 13.55 N 100.30 E
Pak Kwo Chau I 271d 22.16 N 114.20 E
Paklenica Nacionalni Park ♦ 36 44.21 N 15.23 E
Pakokku 110 21.20 N 95.05 E
Pakość 30 52.49 N 18.05 E
Pakouabo 150 7.10 N 5.48 W
Pakowki Lake ⊜ 184 49.22 N 110.57 W
Pākpattan 123 30.21 N 73.24 E
Pak Phanang 110 8.21 N 100.12 E
Pak Phayun 110 7.21 N 100.19 E
Pak Phraek 110 8.13 N 100.12 E
Pakrac 36 45.26 N 17.12 E
Pākrāganj 126 24.00 N 90.41 E
Pakruojis 76 55.58 N 23.52 E
Paks 30 46.39 N 18.53 E
Pak Sane → Muang Pakxan 110 18.22 N 103.39 E
Pāksey 126 24.05 N 89.03 E
Pak Thong Chai 110 14.43 N 102.01 E
Paktīā □[4] 120 33.30 N 69.30 E
Paktīkā □[4] 120 32.30 N 68.45 E
Pākundia 126 24.20 N 90.42 E
P'akupur ≃ 74 65.00 N 77.48 E
Pakwach 154 2.28 N 31.30 E
Pakwash Lake ⊜ 184 50.45 N 93.30 W
Pakxé 110 15.07 N 105.47 E
Pala, Mya. 110 12.51 N 98.40 E
Pala, Tchad 146 9.22 N 14.54 E
Pala, Ca., U.S. 228 33.22 N 117.05 W
Palaau State Park ♦ 229a 21.11 N 157.00 W
Palabek 154 3.26 N 32.34 E
Palacca Point > 238 21.15 N 73.26 W
Palacios 196 28.42 N 96.13 W
Palacios ≃ 248 16.36 S 64.18 W
Paladru 62 45.28 N 5.33 E
Palagano 64 44.20 N 10.39 E
Palagianello 68 40.37 N 16.58 E
Palagiano 68 40.35 N 17.02 E
Palagonia 70 37.19 N 14.45 E
Palagruža, Otoci II 36 42.24 N 16.15 E
Palai 122 9.44 N 76.41 E
Palai, Punta ∧ 71 40.20 N 8.55 E
Palaia 66 43.36 N 10.46 E
Palaiá Epídhavros 38 37.38 N 23.09 E
Palaiá Psará 38 38.46 N 25.36 E
Palaikhóri 130 34.55 N 33.05 E
Pala Indian Reservation ◆[4] 228 33.21 N 117.04 W
Palaiokhóra 38 35.14 N 23.41 E
Palaión Fáliron 267c 37.55 N 23.41 E
Palaiseau 50 48.43 N 2.15 E
Pālakodu 122 16.32 N 81.44 E
Pālam ◆[8] 272a 28.35 N 77.05 E
Palam Airport ⊠ 123 28.35 N 77.07 E
Palamás 38 39.28 N 22.05 E
Palamós 34 41.51 N 3.08 E
Pālampur 123 32.07 N 76.32 E
Palamuse 76 58.41 N 26.35 E
Palamut 130 38.59 N 27.41 E
Palana 74 59.07 N 159.58 E
Palanan, Mount ∧ 116 17.03 N 122.15 E
Palanan Bay c 116 17.09 N 122.27 E
Palanan Point > 116 17.09 N 122.30 E
Palanas 116 12.09 N 123.55 E
Palandöken Dağları ⋏ 130 39.47 N 41.15 E
Pālang 126 23.13 N 90.21 E
Pālang ≃[1] 126 23.15 N 90.21 E
Palanga 76 55.55 N 21.03 E
Palanganene 152 6.26 S 18.50 E
Palangkaraya 112 2.16 S 113.56 E
Palani 122 10.28 N 77.32 E
Pālanpur 120 24.10 N 72.26 E
Palanquinos 34 42.27 N 5.31 W
Palanzano 64 44.26 N 10.11 E
Palaoa Point > 229a 20.44 N 156.58 W
Palapag 116 12.33 N 125.07 E
Palapye 156 22.37 S 27.06 E
Pālār ≃ 122 12.28 N 80.10 E
Palasan Island I 116 14.52 N 122.03 E
Palas de Rei 34 42.52 N 7.52 W
Palāshdānga 126 23.24 N 87.22 E
Palāspol 126 22.43 N 89.05 E
Palasthali 126 23.51 N 87.03 E
Palata 66 41.53 N 14.47 E
Palatcy 86 49.09 N 83.43 E
Palatine 216 42.06 N 88.02 W
Palatine Bridge 210 42.55 N 74.35 W
Palatka, Ross. 74 60.06 N 150.54 E
Palatka, Fl., U.S. 192 29.38 N 81.38 W
Palau, It. 71 41.11 N 9.23 E
Palau, Méx. 196 27.54 N 101.26 W
Palau (Belau) □[2], Oc. 14 5.00 N 137.00 E
Palau (Belau) □[2], Oc. 175b 7.30 N 134.30 E
Palauig 116 15.26 N 119.54 E
Palaui Island I 116 18.33 N 122.08 E
Palau Islands II 175b 7.30 N 134.30 E
Palauk 110 13.16 N 98.38 E
Pal'avaam ≃ 180 68.50 N 170.45 E
Pal'avaamskij chrebet ⋏ 180 68.20 N 177.00 E
Palavas-les-Flots 62 43.32 N 3.56 E
Palaw 110 12.58 N 98.39 E
Palawai Basin ≚[1] 229a 20.47 N 156.55 W
Palawan □[4] 116 10.00 N 118.50 E
Palawan I 116 9.30 N 118.30 E
Palawan Passage ц 116 10.00 N 118.00 E
Palayan 116 15.33 N 121.06 E
Pālayankottai 122 8.43 N 77.44 E
Palazzo Adriano 70 37.41 N 13.23 E
Palazzolo Acreide 70 37.04 N 14.54 E
Palazzolo dello Stella 64 45.48 N 13.05 E
Palazzolo sull'Oglio 62 45.36 N 9.53 E
Palazzolo Vercellese 62 45.11 N 8.14 E
Palazzo San Gervasio 68 40.56 N 16.00 E
Palazzuolo sul Senio 66 44.07 N 11.33 E
P'albong-san ∧ 98 40.16 N 127.57 E
Palca, Bol. 248 16.34 S 67.59 W
Palca, Perú 248 11.21 S 75.31 W
Palcamayo 248 11.18 S 75.46 W
Pal'co 76 53.17 N 34.56 E
Paldi 224 48.48 N 123.51 W
Paldiski 76 59.20 N 24.06 E
Pāldor ∧ 124 28.16 N 85.11 E
Palech 80 56.48 N 41.51 E
Palel 120 24.27 N 94.02 E
Paleleh 112 1.04 N 121.57 E
Palembang 112 2.55 S 104.45 E
Palena 66 41.59 N 14.08 E
Palena ≃ 254 43.50 S 72.59 W
Palena, Lago (Lago General Vintter) ⊜ 254 43.55 S 71.40 W
Palencia 34 42.01 N 4.32 W
Palencia □[4] 34 42.25 N 4.35 W
Palen Lake ⊜ 204 33.46 N 115.12 W
Palenque 232 17.31 N 91.58 W
Palenque ⊥ 232 17.30 N 92.00 W
Palenque, Punta > 238 18.14 N 70.09 W
Palenville 210 42.10 N 74.01 W
Paleparto, Monte ∧ 68 39.28 N 16.34 E
Palermo, Col. 246 2.54 N 75.26 W
Palermo, It. 70 38.07 N 13.21 E
Palermo, Ca., U.S. 226 39.26 N 121.33 W
Palermo, Ur. 252 33.48 S 55.59 W
Palermo □[4] 70 37.49 N 13.35 E
Palermo ◆[8] 288 34.35 S 58.25 W
Palermo, Golfo di c 70 38.08 N 13.26 E
Palese, Aeroporto di ⊠ 68 41.10 N 16.47 E
Palestina, Bra. 255 20.23 S 49.25 W
Palestina, Méx. 196 29.10 N 100.55 W
Palestine, Ar., U.S. 194 34.58 N 90.54 W
Palestine, Il., U.S. 194 39.00 N 87.36 W
Palestine, Oh., U.S. 218 40.03 N 84.45 W
Palestine, Tx., U.S. 222 31.45 N 95.37 W
Palestine □[9] 132 32.00 N 35.15 E
Palestine, Lake ⊜[1] 222 32.06 N 95.27 W
Palestrina 66 41.50 N 12.53 E
Paletwa 110 21.18 N 92.51 E
Palézieux 58 46.33 N 6.50 E
Palfau 61 47.42 N 14.48 E
Pālghāt 122 10.47 N 76.39 E
Palgrave, Mount ∧ 162 23.22 S 115.58 E
Palgrave Point > 156 20.45 S 13.20 E
Palhais 266c 38.37 N 9.03 W
Palhano 250 4.44 S 37.57 W
Palhano ≃ 250 4.33 S 37.42 W
Pāli, India 120 25.46 N 73.20 E
Pali, India 124 25.51 N 76.33 E
Paliano 66 41.48 N 13.03 E
Palidoro ◆[8] 66 41.56 N 12.11 E
Palikea ∧ 229c 21.26 N 158.06 W
Palima 112 4.20 S 120.22 E
Palimanan 115a 6.42 S 108.26 E
Palimbang 116 6.12 N 124.12 E
Palimé 150 6.54 N 0.38 E
Palín 236 14.24 N 90.42 W
Palinges 32 46.33 N 4.13 E
Palinuro 68 40.02 N 15.17 E
Palinuro, Capo > 68 40.02 N 15.16 E
Palisade, Co., U.S. 200 39.06 N 108.21 W
Palisade, Ne., U.S. 198 40.20 N 101.06 W
Palisades, Id., U.S. 202 43.21 N 111.13 W
Palisades, N.Y., U.S. 276 41.01 N 73.55 W
Palisades Amusement Park ♦ 276 40.50 N 73.59 W
Palisades Interstate Park ♦ 210 40.56 N 73.55 W
Palisades Park, Mi., U.S. 216 42.18 N 86.19 W

Symbols in the index entries represent the broad categories identified in the key at the right. Symbols with superior numbers (⋏[1]) identify subcategories (see complete key on page *I · 1).*

Symbole im Register stellen die rechts im Schlüssel erklärten Kategorien dar. Symbole mit hochgestellten Ziffern (⋏[1]) bezeichnen Unterabteilungen einer Kategorie (vgl. vollständiger Schlüssel auf Seite *I · 1).*

Los símbolos incluídos en el texto del índice representan las grandes categorías identificadas con la clave a la derecha. Los símbolos con numeros en su parte superior (⋏[1]) identifican las subcategorías (véase la clave completa en la página *I · 1).*

Les symboles de l'index représentent les catégories indiquées dans la légende à droite. Les symboles suivis d'un indice (⋏[1]) représentent des sous-catégories (voir légende complète à la page *I · 1).*

Os símbolos incluídos no texto do índice representam as grandes categorias identificadas com a chave à direita. Os símbolos com números em sua parte superior (⋏[1]) identificam as subcategorias (veja-se a chave completa à página *I · 1).*

	English	Deutsch	Español	Français	Português
∧	Mountain	Berg	Montaña	Montagne	Montanha
⋏	Mountains	Gebirge	Montañas	Montagnes	Montanhas
)(	Pass	Paß	Paso	Col	Passo
V	Valley, Canyon	Tal, Cañon	Valle, Cañón	Vallée, Canyon	Vale, Canhão
≚	Plain	Ebene	Llano	Plaine	Planície
>	Cape	Kap	Cabo	Cap	Cabo
I	Island	Insel	Isla	Île	Ilha
II	Islands	Inseln	Islas	Îles	Ilhas
⊥	Other Topographic Features	Andere Topographische Objekte	Otros Elementos Topográficos	Autres données topographiques	Outros acidentes topográficos

ESPAÑOL · FRANÇAIS · PORTUGUÊS

Nombre / Nom / Nome	Página / Page	Lat.°′	Long.°′ W = Oeste / Ouest
Palisades Park, N.J., U.S.	276	40.50 N	73.59 W
Palisades Reservoir ⊜[1]	202	43.15 N	111.05 W
Paliseul	56	49.54 N	5.08 E
Pālitāna	120	21.31 N	71.50 E
Palivere	76	58.59 N	23.52 E
Palizada	232	18.15 N	92.05 W
Palizzi	68	37.58 N	15.59 E
Paljakka ∧[2]	26	64.41 N	28.08 E
Pälkäne	26	61.20 N	24.16 E
Palk Bay c	122	9.30 N	79.15 E
Palkino, Ross.	76	57.32 N	28.01 E
Palkino, Ross.	80	58.15 N	42.56 E
Pālkonda	122	18.36 N	83.45 E
Pālkonda Range ⋌	122	14.05 N	79.05 E
Palk Strait ʮ	122	10.00 N	79.45 E
Palla Bianca (Weisskugel) ∧	64	46.48 N	10.44 E
Pallagorio	68	39.18 N	16.54 E
Pallamana	168b	35.02 S	139.12 E
Pallasca	248	8.15 S	78.01 W
Pallas Grean	48	52.33 N	8.22 W
Pallaskenry	48	52.39 N	8.52 W
Pallas-Ounastunturin kansallispuisto ▲	24	68.06 N	24.00 E
Pallasovka	80	50.03 N	46.53 E
Pallastunturi ∧	24	68.06 N	24.00 E
Pallejà	266d	41.25 N	2.00 E
Pallës, Bishti i >	38	41.24 N	19.24 E
Palling	182	54.21 N	125.55 W
Pallíni	267c	38.00 N	23.53 E
Pallinup ≃	162	34.29 S	118.54 E
Pallisa	154	1.10 N	33.42 E
Palliser, Cape >	172	41.37 S	175.17 E
Palliser Bay c	172	41.25 S	175.05 E
Pallu	123	28.56 N	74.13 E
Palluau	32	46.48 N	1.37 W
Palma, Bra.	255	21.22 S	42.19 W
Palma, Moç.	154	10.46 S	40.29 E
P'al'ma, Ross.	24	62.26 N	35.53 E
Palma ≃	255	12.33 S	47.52 W
Palma, Badia de c	34	39.27 N	2.35 E
Palmácia	250	4.08 S	38.50 W
Palma del Río	34	37.42 N	5.17 W
Palma [de Mallorca]	34	39.34 N	2.39 E
Palma di Montechiaro	70	37.11 N	13.46 E
Palmaḥim	132	31.56 N	34.42 E
Palmanova	64	45.54 N	13.19 E
Palma Pegada	234	22.42 N	101.48 W
Palmar ≃	246	10.10 N	71.50 W
Palmar, Lago Artificial del ⊜[1]	252	33.05 S	57.10 W
Palmar Camp	232	16.26 N	88.53 W
Palmar de Cariaco	286c	10.34 N	66.55 W
Palmar de los Sepúlveda	232	25.43 N	107.55 W
Palmar de Varela	246	10.45 N	74.45 W
Palmarejo	240m	18.03 N	67.05 W
Palmares, Bra.	250	8.41 S	35.36 W
Palmares, C.R.	236	10.03 N	84.26 W
Palmares, C.R.	236	9.21 N	83.40 W
Palmares do Sul	252	30.16 S	50.31 W
Palmaria, Isola I	62	44.02 N	9.51 E
Palmarito	246	7.37 N	70.10 W
Palmarola, Isola I	66	40.56 N	12.51 E
Palmar Sur	236	8.58 N	83.29 W
Palmas, Bra.	250	10.08 S	48.18 W
Palmas, Bra.	252	26.30 S	52.00 W
Palmas, Méx.	234	22.49 N	103.57 W
Palmas, Golfo di c	71	39.02 N	8.31 E
Palmas, Ilha das I, Bra.	287a	23.02 S	43.12 W
Palmas, Ilha das I, Bra.	287a	23.04 S	43.31 W
Palmas Bellas	236	9.14 N	80.05 W
Palmas de Monte Alto	255	14.16 S	43.10 W
Palma Sola	220	27.31 N	82.38 W
Palma Soriano	240p	20.13 N	76.00 W
Palm Bay	220	28.02 N	80.35 W
Palm Beach, Austl.	170	33.36 S	151.19 E
Palm Beach, Austl.	171a	28.08 S	153.28 E
Palm Beach, Fl., U.S.	220	26.42 N	80.02 W
Palm Beach □[6]	220	26.38 N	80.27 W
Palm Beach Gardens	220	26.49 N	80.06 W
Palm Beach International Airport ⊠	220	26.41 N	80.05 W
Palm City	220	27.09 N	80.16 W
Palmdale, Ca., U.S.	228	34.34 N	118.06 W
Palmdale, Fl., U.S.	220	26.56 N	81.18 W
Palmdale, Pa., U.S.	208	40.18 N	76.37 W
Palmdale, Lake ⊜[1]	228	34.33 N	118.07 W
Palm Desert	204	33.43 N	116.23 W
Palmeira, Bra.	252	25.25 S	50.00 W
Palmeira, C.V.	150a	16.46 N	22.59 W
Palmeira das Missões	252	27.55 S	53.17 W
Palmeira d'Oeste	255	20.23 S	50.47 W
Palmeira dos Índios	250	9.25 S	36.37 W
Palmeirais	250	5.58 S	43.04 W
Palmeiral	256	21.38 S	46.31 W
Palmeiras	255	12.31 S	41.34 W
Palmeiras ≃, Bra.	250	12.22 S	47.08 W
Palmeiras ≃, Bra.	255	15.25 S	51.10 W
Palmeirina	250	8.56 S	36.17 W
Palmeirinhas, Ponta das >	152	9.05 S	13.00 E
Palmela ≃	256	21.38 S	45.23 W
Palmelo	255	17.20 S	48.27 W
Palmer, Austl.	168b	34.51 S	139.10 E
Palmer, P.R.	240m	18.22 N	65.46 W
Palmer, Ak., U.S.	180	61.36 N	149.07 W
Palmer, Il., U.S.	219	39.27 N	89.24 W
Palmer, Ma., U.S.	207	42.09 N	72.19 W
Palmer, Ms., U.S.	194	31.16 N	89.15 W
Palmer, Ne., U.S.	198	41.13 N	98.15 W
Palmer, Tn., U.S.	194	35.21 N	85.34 W
Palmer, Tx., U.S.	222	32.26 N	96.40 W
Palmer ≃, Austl.	162	24.46 S	133.25 E
Palmer ≃, Austl.	164	15.34 S	142.26 E
Palmer ≃, P.Q., Can.	206	46.19 N	71.27 W
Palmer ⛫[3]	9	64.46 S	64.03 W
Palmerah ◆[8]	269e	6.12 S	106.47 E
Palmer Heights	208	40.42 N	75.16 W
Palmer Lake	200	38.52 N	104.48 W
Palmer Land ◆[1]	9	71.30 S	65.00 W
Palmer Mill Brook ≃	283	41.58 N	70.52 W
Palmer Park	284c	38.55 N	76.52 W
Palmer Park ▲	281	42.26 N	83.07 W
Palmerston, On., Can.	212	43.50 N	80.51 W
Palmerston, N.Z.	172	45.29 S	170.43 E
Palmerston I[1]	14	18.04 S	163.10 W
Palmerston, Cape >	166	21.32 S	149.29 E
Palmerston Lake ⊜	212	45.01 N	76.50 W
Palmerston North	172	40.21 S	175.37 E
Palmerton	210	40.48 N	75.36 W
Palmerville	164	15.59 S	144.05 E
Palmetto, Fl., U.S.	220	27.31 N	82.34 W
Palmetto, Ga., U.S.	192	33.31 N	84.40 W
Palmetto, La., U.S.	194	30.43 N	91.54 W
Palmford	158	27.11 S	29.42 E
Palm Harbor	220	28.04 N	82.45 W
Palmi	68	38.21 N	15.51 E
Palminópolis	255	16.47 S	50.08 W
Palmira, Arg.	252	33.03 S	68.34 W
Palmira, Col.	246	3.32 N	76.16 W
Palmira, Cuba	240p	22.14 N	80.23 W
Palmira, Ec.	246	2.05 S	78.43 W
Palmira, Méx.	196	28.58 N	100.47 W
Palmitas	252	33.31 S	57.49 W
Palmitos	252	27.05 S	53.08 W
Palmnicken → Jantarnyj	76	54.52 N	19.57 E
Palmoli	66	41.56 N	14.32 E
Palm River	220	27.56 N	82.23 W
Palms ◆[8]	280	34.02 N	118.25 W
Palm Shores	220	28.11 N	80.35 W
Palm Springs, Ca., U.S.	204	33.49 N	116.32 W
Palm Springs, Fl., U.S.	220	26.39 N	80.06 W
Palmyra → Tudmur, Sūrīy.	130	34.33 N	38.17 E
Palmyra, Il., U.S.	219	39.26 N	89.59 W
Palmyra, In., U.S.	218	38.24 N	86.06 W
Palmyra, Mi., U.S.	216	41.52 N	83.56 W
Palmyra, Mo., U.S.	219	39.47 N	91.31 W
Palmyra, N.J., U.S.	208	40.00 N	75.01 W
Palmyra, N.Y., U.S.	210	43.03 N	77.14 W
Palmyra, Oh., U.S.	214	41.07 N	81.02 W
Palmyra, Pa., U.S.	208	40.18 N	76.35 W
Palmyra, Va., U.S.	192	37.51 N	78.15 W
Palmyra, Wi., U.S.	216	42.52 N	88.35 W
Palmyra ⊥	130	34.33 N	38.17 E
Palmyra Atoll I[1]	14	5.52 N	162.06 W
Palo, It.	66	41.56 N	12.06 E
Palo, Pil.	116	11.10 N	124.59 E
Palo Alto, Méx.	196	26.32 N	99.45 W
Palo Alto, Ca., U.S.	226	37.26 N	122.08 W
Palo Alto, Pa., U.S.	208	40.41 N	76.11 W
Palo Alto Airport ⊠	282	37.28 N	122.07 W
Palo Blanco, Méx.	196	26.45 N	101.32 W
Palo Blanco, P.R.	240m	18.26 N	66.39 W
Palo Blanco Creek ≃	196	27.10 N	97.52 W
Paločka	86	58.25 N	84.32 E
Palo del Colle	68	41.03 N	16.42 E
Palo Duro Canyon State Park ▲	196	34.55 N	101.42 W
Palo Duro Creek ≃, U.S.	196	36.39 N	100.58 W
Palo Duro Creek ≃, Tx., U.S.	196	35.00 N	101.54 W
Paloe, Pulau I	115b	8.20 S	121.43 E
Paloemeu ≃	250	3.21 N	55.26 W
Palo Flechado Pass)(	200	36.25 N	105.20 W
Paloh, Indon.	112	1.43 N	109.18 E
Paloh, Malay.	112	2.25 N	111.15 E
Paloh, Malay.	114	2.11 N	103.12 E
Paloich, Sūd.	140	6.45 N	30.08 E
Paloich, Sūd.	140	10.28 N	32.32 E
Palojoensuu	24	68.17 N	23.05 E
Paloma Creek ≃	226	36.15 N	121.26 W
Palomares Creek ≃	282	37.42 N	122.02 W
Palomar Mountain ∧	204	33.22 N	116.50 W
Palomar Mountain State Park ▲	228	33.19 N	116.53 W
Palomar Park	282	37.29 N	122.16 W
Palomas	196	28.43 N	103.45 W
Palomas Viejo	232	31.44 N	107.37 W
Palombara Sabina	66	42.04 N	12.46 E
Palominos, Isla I	240m	18.21 N	65.34 W
Palomonte	68	40.40 N	15.17 E
Palompon	116	11.03 N	124.23 E
Palo Negro	246	10.11 N	67.33 W
Palo Pinto	196	32.46 N	98.18 W
Palo Pinto Reservoir ⊜[1]	196	32.38 N	98.18 W
Palopo	112	3.00 S	120.12 E
Palora ≃	246	1.51 S	77.49 W
Palos, Cuba	240p	22.48 N	81.44 W
Palos → Palos de la Frontera, Esp.	34	37.14 N	6.53 W
Palos, Cabo de >	34	37.38 N	0.41 W
Palo Santo	252	25.34 S	59.21 W
Palos de la Frontera	34	37.14 N	6.53 W
Palos Gardens	278	41.40 N	87.48 W
Palos Heights	216	41.40 N	87.47 W
Palos Hills	278	41.41 N	87.49 W
Palos Hills ▲	278	41.42 N	87.53 W
Palos Park	278	41.40 N	87.49 W
Palos Verdes Estates	228	33.48 N	118.23 W
Palos Verdes Hills ⋌[2]	280	33.46 N	118.21 W
Palos Verdes Point >	228	33.47 N	118.26 W
Palotai-sziget I	264c	47.35 N	19.05 E
Paloúkia	267c	37.58 N	23.31 E
Palouse	202	46.54 N	117.04 W
Palouse ≃	202	46.35 N	118.13 W
Palouse, South Fork ≃	202	46.53 N	117.22 W
Palo Verde	204	33.25 N	114.43 W
Palo Verde, Parque Nacional ▲	236	10.15 N	85.10 W
P'alovskoje vodochranilišče ⊜[1]	82	56.03 N	37.40 E
Palpa	248	14.32 S	75.11 W
Palpalá	252	24.15 S	65.12 W
Pålsboda	40	59.04 N	15.20 E
Pālsit	126	23.12 N	88.03 E
Paltamo	26	64.25 N	27.50 E
Paltenbach ≃	61	47.34 N	14.20 E
Palu, Indon.	112	0.53 S	119.53 E
Palu, Tür.	130	38.42 N	39.57 E
Palu ≃	112	0.52 S	119.51 E
Palu, Teluk c	112	0.40 S	119.45 E
Paluan	116	13.25 N	120.28 E
Paluan Bay c	116	13.23 N	120.25 E
Palù del Fersina	64	46.08 N	11.21 E
Paludi	68	39.32 N	16.41 E
Paluga	24	65.16 N	45.11 E
Paluke	150	5.02 N	8.06 W
Paluška ∧	61	48.45 N	14.24 E
Paluxy ≃	196	32.15 N	97.43 W
Paluzza	64	46.32 N	13.01 E
Palvantaš	85	40.34 N	72.12 E
Palvār, Kūh-e ∧	128	30.04 N	57.28 E
Palvart	128	38.11 N	64.34 E
Palwal	124	28.09 N	77.20 E
Pal-Waukee Airport ⊠	278	42.07 N	87.54 W
Pam	175f	20.16 S	164.19 E
Pama	150	11.15 N	0.42 E
Pama ≃	152	4.23 N	18.27 E
Pamaluan	112	1.04 S	116.39 E
Pamanukan	115a	6.16 S	107.49 E
Pamarayan	115a	6.16 S	106.17 E
Pam'ati 13 Borcov	86	56.13 N	92.20 E
Pam'atnaja	86	56.01 N	65.42 E
Pam'at' Parižskoj Kommuny	80	56.06 N	44.31 E
Pāmban Channel ʮ	122	9.17 N	79.10 E
Pāmban Island I	122	9.15 N	79.20 E
Pambeguwa	150	10.40 N	8.19 E
Pambuhan	116	13.59 N	123.05 E
Pambuhan ≃	116	12.34 N	124.55 E
Pambujan	116	12.34 N	124.56 E
Pamekasan	115a	7.10 S	113.28 E
Pamenang	112	2.07 S	102.31 E
Pameungpeuk	115a	7.38 S	107.43 E
Pamiers	32	43.07 N	1.36 E
Pamir ⋌	118	38.00 N	73.00 E
Pamlico ≃	192	35.20 N	76.30 W
Pamlico Sound ʮ	192	35.20 N	75.55 W
Pamotan	115a	6.46 S	111.29 E
Pampa	196	35.32 N	100.57 W
Pampã ≃	255	17.43 S	40.36 W
Pampa ◆[1]	252	35.00 S	63.00 W
Pampa Almirón	252	26.42 S	59.08 W
Pampacolca	248	15.43 S	72.33 W
Pampa del Castillo	254	45.48 S	68.05 W
Pampa del Chañar	252	30.11 S	68.43 W
Pampa del Indio	252	26.02 S	59.55 W
Pampa del Infierno	252	26.31 S	61.10 W
Pampa de los Guanacos	252	26.14 S	61.51 W
Pampa Grande	248	18.05 S	64.06 W
Pampana ≃	150	8.24 N	12.00 W
Pampanga □[4]	116	15.05 N	120.40 E
Pampanga ≃	116	14.47 N	120.39 E
Pampanua	112	4.14 S	120.08 E
Pamparato	62	44.17 N	7.55 E
Pampas	248	12.24 S	74.54 W
Pampas ≃	248	13.23 S	73.15 W
Pampas del Heath, Santuario Nacional ▲	248	12.40 S	68.15 W
Pampeluna → Pamplona	34	42.49 N	1.38 W
Pamphylia □[9]	130	37.00 N	31.00 E
Pamplico	192	33.59 N	79.34 W
Pamplona, Col.	246	7.23 N	72.39 W
Pamplona, Esp.	34	42.49 N	1.38 W
Pampoenpoort	158	31.03 S	22.40 E
Pampow	54	53.32 N	14.15 E
Pāmpur	123	34.01 N	74.56 E
Pamukkale (Hierapolis) ⊥	130	37.58 N	29.19 E
Pamukova	130	40.31 N	30.09 E
Pamunkey ≃	208	37.32 N	76.48 W
Pana	219	39.23 N	89.04 W
Panabá	232	21.17 N	88.16 W
Panabo	116	7.19 N	125.42 E
Panaca	204	37.47 N	114.23 W
Panacan	116	9.16 N	118.25 E
Panacea	192	30.02 N	84.23 W
Panache, Lake ⊜	190	46.15 N	81.20 W
Panadura	122	6.43 N	79.54 E
Panaeati Island I	164	10.40 S	152.20 E
Panāgar	124	23.18 N	79.59 E
Panagjurište	38	42.30 N	24.11 E
Panagtaran Point >	116	9.41 N	118.45 E
Panahan	112	1.44 S	111.49 E
Panaitan, Pulau I	115a	6.36 S	105.12 E
Panaitan, Selat ʮ	115a	6.40 S	105.16 E
Panaji (Panjim)	122	15.29 N	73.50 E
Pānākua	272b	22.23 N	88.21 E
Panamá, Bra.	255	18.11 S	49.21 W
Panamá, Pan.	236	8.58 N	79.32 W
Panama, Il., U.S.	219	39.02 N	89.32 W
Panama, N.Y., U.S.	214	42.04 N	79.29 W
Panama, Ok., U.S.	194	35.10 N	94.40 W
Panamá □[4]	236	8.48 N	79.55 W
Panama (Panamá) □[1], N.A.	230	9.00 N	80.00 W
Panama (Panamá) □[1], N.A.	246	9.00 N	80.00 W
Panamá, Bahía de c	246	8.50 N	79.20 W
Panamá, Canal de ≋	236	9.20 N	79.55 W
Panamá, Golfo de c	246	8.00 N	79.30 W
Panamá, Istmo de ⊥[3]	246	9.00 N	80.00 W
Panama Basin ✢[1]	18	5.00 N	83.30 W
Panama City	194	30.09 N	85.39 W
Panamá Vieja ⊥	236	9.00 N	79.29 W
Panambi	252	28.18 S	53.30 W
Panamint Range ⋌	204	36.30 N	117.20 W
Panamint Valley V	204	36.15 N	117.20 W
Pan'an	100	29.06 N	120.27 E
Panao, Perú	248	9.49 S	76.00 W
Pan'ao, Zhg.	107	30.09 N	103.37 E
Panaon Island I	116	10.03 N	125.13 E
Panarea, Isola I	70	38.38 N	15.04 E
Panaro ≃	64	44.55 N	11.25 E
Panarukan	115a	7.42 S	113.56 E
Panasoffkee, Lake ⊜	220	28.47 N	82.08 W
Panatinane Island I	164	11.15 S	153.10 E
Panay I	116	11.15 N	122.30 E
Panay ≃	116	11.35 N	122.43 E
Panay Gulf c	116	10.15 N	122.15 E
Panayía	38	39.59 N	25.24 E
Panay Island I	116	13.58 N	124.20 E
Pancalieri	62	44.50 N	7.35 E
Pancas	266c	38.48 N	8.55 W
Pančevo	38	44.52 N	20.39 E
Panchagarh	124	26.20 N	88.34 E
Pānchāl	126	23.15 N	87.18 E
Pānchet Hill ∧[2]	126	23.37 N	86.47 E
Pānchet Reservoir ⊜[1]	126	23.40 N	86.45 E
Pancheve	78	48.44 N	31.51 E
Pānchghara	272b	22.44 N	88.16 E
Panchgram	126	24.12 N	88.01 E
Panch'iao	269d	25.01 N	121.27 E
Panchla	126	22.32 N	88.09 E
Panchor	114	2.10 N	102.43 E
Pancho Simón ≃	286b	23.03 N	82.21 W
Pānchur	272b	22.32 N	88.16 E
Pānchuria	272b	22.33 N	88.29 E
Panciu	38	45.55 N	27.05 E
Panda	156	24.02 S	34.45 E
Pandakan	115a	7.39 S	112.41 E
Pandamatenga	156	18.35 S	25.42 E
Pandan, Malay.	112	3.09 N	113.22 E
Pandan, Pil.	116	11.43 N	122.06 E
Pandan, Pil.	116	14.03 N	124.10 E
Pandan, Selat ʮ	271c	1.15 N	103.44 E
Pandanan Island I	116	8.17 N	117.13 E
Pandan Bay c	116	11.43 N	122.04 E
Pandan Reservoir ⊜[1]	271c	1.19 N	103.44 E
Pandaria	124	22.14 N	81.25 E
Pandarochan Bay c	116	12.12 N	121.10 E
Pandasan	112	6.28 N	116.32 E
Pan de Azúcar	252	34.48 S	55.14 W
Pan de Azucar, Cerro ∧	286e	33.19 S	70.42 W
Pan de Azucar Island I	116	11.17 N	123.10 E
Pandegelang	115a	6.18 S	106.06 E
Pandėlys	76	56.01 N	25.13 E
Pāndharkawada	122	20.01 N	78.32 E
Pandharpur	122	17.40 N	75.20 E
Pāndhurna	122	21.36 N	78.31 E
Pandian	98	36.38 N	116.27 E
Pandino	62	45.24 N	9.33 E
Pando	252	34.43 S	55.57 W
Pando □[5]	248	11.20 S	67.40 W
Pando, Cerro ∧	236	8.55 N	82.43 W
Pandora	216	40.56 N	83.57 W
Pandu	152	5.01 N	19.16 E
Pandua, India	124	25.08 N	88.10 E
Pāndua, India	126	23.05 N	88.17 E
P'andž (Panj) ≃	120	37.06 N	68.20 E
Panebianco ≃	70	37.24 N	15.04 E
Panelas	250	8.40 S	36.01 W
Paneveggio	64	46.18 N	11.44 E
Panevėžys	76	55.44 N	24.21 E
Panfang	100	27.54 N	115.57 E
Panfilov	86	44.10 N	80.01 E
Panfilovo	80	50.26 N	42.55 E
Pāng ≃	110	20.58 N	98.30 E
Panga	154	1.51 N	26.25 E
Pangala	152	3.19 S	14.34 E
Pangalanes, Canal des ≋	157b	22.40 S	47.50 E
Pangandaran	115a	7.41 S	108.39 E
Pangani	154	5.26 S	38.58 E
Pangani ≃	154	5.26 S	38.58 E
Panganiran	116	13.02 N	123.26 E
Pangantocan	116	7.50 N	124.49 E
Panganuran	116	7.24 N	122.03 E
Pangasinan □[4]	116	16.00 N	120.20 E
Pangbourne	42	51.29 N	1.05 W
Pangburn	194	35.25 N	91.50 W
Pange	56	49.05 N	6.22 E
Pangfou → Bengbu	100	32.58 N	117.24 E
Pangga, Tanjung >	115b	8.55 S	116.02 E
Panggezhuang, Zhg.	105	39.38 N	116.19 E
Panggezhuang, Zhg.	105	39.16 N	115.49 E
Panghkam	110	23.53 N	97.37 E
Pangi	154	3.11 S	26.38 E
Pangian	112	1.06 S	119.24 E
Pangjiabu	105	40.36 N	115.27 E
Pangkah	115a	6.58 S	109.10 E
Pangkajene	112	4.50 S	119.32 E
Pangkalanbrandan	114	4.01 N	98.17 E
Pangkalanbuun	112	2.41 S	111.37 E
Pangkalansusu	114	4.06 N	98.14 E
Pangkalaseang, Tanjung >	112	0.42 S	123.26 E
Pangkalpinang	112	2.08 S	106.08 E
Pangkatan	114	2.09 N	100.00 E
Pangke	114	1.01 N	103.10 E
Pangkor, Pulau I	114	4.13 N	100.33 E
Panglao	116	9.35 N	123.45 E
Panglao Island I	116	9.35 N	123.48 E
Pangman	184	49.39 N	104.38 W
Pangnirtung	176	66.08 N	65.44 W
Pango Aluquém	152	8.43 S	14.27 E
Pangŏjin	98	35.29 N	129.26 E
Pangong Tso ⊜	120	33.45 N	78.43 E
Pangp'u → Bengbu	100	32.58 N	117.24 E
Pāngsa	126	23.47 N	89.25 E
Pangtara	110	20.57 N	96.40 E
Pangubatan	116	6.57 N	125.47 E
Panguil Bay c	116	8.01 N	123.43 E
Panguipulli	254	39.38 S	72.20 W
Panguipulli, Lago ⊜	254	39.43 S	72.13 W
Panguiranan	116	12.04 N	123.19 E
Panguitch	200	37.49 N	112.26 W
Pangururan	114	2.37 N	98.42 E
Pangutaran	116	6.18 N	120.35 E
Pangutaran Group II	116	6.15 N	120.30 E
Pangutaran Island I	116	6.18 N	120.34 E
Pangutaran Passage ʮ	116	6.13 N	120.30 E
Pangzidian	107	30.38 N	105.04 E
Panhandle	196	35.20 N	101.22 W
Paniai, Danau ⊜	164	3.50 S	136.15 E
Pania-Mutombo	152	5.11 S	23.51 E
Paniau ∧	229b	21.57 N	160.05 W
Panié, Mont ∧	175f	20.36 S	164.46 E
Pānihāti	126	22.42 N	88.22 E
Panika	80	50.59 N	50.11 E
Panindícuaro	234	19.59 N	101.46 W
Panino, Ross.	76	56.25 N	34.34 E
Panino, Ross.	78	51.38 N	40.08 E
Panino-Nesterovo	82	55.23 N	38.11 E
Panīpāt	124	29.23 N	76.58 E
Paniqui	116	15.40 N	120.35 E
Panissières	62	45.47 N	4.20 E
Panitan	116	11.28 N	122.46 E
Panitian	116	9.05 N	118.05 E
Panj (P'andž) ≃	120	37.06 N	68.20 E
Panjāb	120	34.22 N	67.01 E
Panjang	115a	5.28 S	105.18 E
Panjang, Pulau I	112	2.44 N	108.55 E
Panjang, Selat ʮ	114	0.40 N	102.30 E
Panje	272c	18.54 N	72.57 E
Panjgūr	128	26.58 N	64.06 E
Panji	114	2.34 N	97.50 E
Panjiapie	100	32.54 N	120.42 E
Panjiatun	104	41.04 N	121.38 E
Panjim → Panaji	122	15.29 N	73.50 E
Pānjkora ≃	123	34.39 N	71.44 E
Panjnad ≃	123	28.57 N	70.30 E
Panjpāi	120	29.55 N	66.30 E
Panjshār ≃	120	34.38 N	69.42 E
Pankakoski	26	63.19 N	30.09 E
Panke ≃	264a	52.32 N	13.22 E
Panker	54	54.20 N	10.34 E
Pānkhāli	126	22.37 N	89.31 E
Pankof, Cape >	180	54.40 N	163.04 W
Pankow ◆[8]	54	52.34 N	13.25 E
Pankratovo	76	59.10 N	43.30 E
Pankshin	150	9.20 N	9.24 E
Panlong, Zhg.	100	25.52 N	114.52 E
Panlong, Zhg.	106	31.58 N	121.35 E
Panlong, Zhg.	106	31.11 N	121.16 E
Panlong (Lo) ≃	110	21.18 N	105.25 E
Panlongzhen	107	29.31 N	105.17 E
P'anmunjŏm	98	37.57 N	126.40 E
Panna	124	24.43 N	80.12 E
Pannawonica	162	21.44 S	116.22 E
Panni	68	41.13 N	15.16 E
Panningen	52	51.20 N	5.59 E
Pannonhalma ⛫[1]	30	47.28 N	17.50 E
Panoche Creek ≃	226	36.44 N	120.31 W
Panola	194	31.58 N	86.23 W
Panola □[6]	222	32.07 N	94.30 W
Páno Lévkara	130	34.52 N	33.18 E
Panopah	112	1.56 S	111.11 E
Páno Panayiá	130	34.55 N	32.38 E
Páno Plátres	130	34.53 N	32.52 E
Panora	198	41.41 N	94.21 W
Panorama	255	21.21 S	51.51 W
Pánormos	38	37.38 N	25.02 E
Panovo, Ross.	24	59.48 N	46.27 E
Panovo, Ross.	88	58.58 N	101.58 E
P'anp'yŏng-ni	98	40.28 N	125.49 E
Panruti	122	11.46 N	79.33 E
Pansfelde	54	51.39 N	11.16 E
Panshan	104	41.12 N	122.04 E
Panshanger Aerodrome ⊠	260	51.48 N	0.08 W
Pansik, Rápido ⌊	236	14.30 N	85.15 W
Pansionat	265b	55.59 N	37.41 E
Pānskura	126	22.25 N	87.42 E
Pantabañgan	116	15.50 N	121.09 E
Pantalica, Necropoli di ⊥	70	37.08 N	15.01 E
Pantanal Matogrossense, Parque Nacional do ▲	248	17.35 S	57.40 W
Pantanaw	110	16.59 N	95.28 E
Pântano	256	22.23 S	46.01 W
Pântano, Ribeirão do ≃	256	22.15 S	45.59 W
Pantar, Pulau I	112	8.25 S	124.07 E
Pantayivka	78	48.41 N	32.53 E
Panteleymonivka	83	48.12 N	37.59 E
Pantelleria	70	36.50 N	11.57 E
Pantelleria, Isola di I	70	36.47 N	12.00 E
Panteón Nacional ⊥	286c	10.31 N	66.55 W
Pantepec ≃	234	20.56 N	97.44 W
Pantha	110	23.49 N	94.33 E
Pantheon ⊥	267a	41.55 N	12.29 E
Panther Creek ≃, Id., U.S.	202	45.19 N	114.24 W
Panther Creek ≃, Ky., U.S.	194	37.45 N	87.19 W
Panther Creek, South Fork ≃	194	37.42 N	87.05 W
Panther Lake	210	43.19 N	75.54 W
Pantin	50	48.54 N	2.24 E
Pantitlán ◆[8]	286a	19.25 N	99.05 W
Panto, Tanjung >	115a	6.51 S	105.54 E
Panton, Mount ∧[2]	162	17.21 S	129.13 E
Pantonlabu	114	5.08 N	97.28 E
Pantry Brook ≃	283	42.24 N	71.22 W
Panu	152	3.48 S	19.07 E
Pánuco	234	22.03 N	98.10 W
Pánuco ≃	234	22.16 N	97.47 W
Panuke Lake ⊜	186	44.48 N	64.07 W
Panukulan	116	14.56 N	121.49 E
Pānuria	126	23.49 N	86.58 E
Panvel	122	18.59 N	73.06 E
Panvel ≃	272c	19.01 N	73.04 W
Panvel Creek ≃	272c	18.59 N	73.00 E
Panwāri	124	25.27 N	79.29 E
Panxi	106	30.35 N	119.20 E
Panxian	102	25.50 N	104.36 E
Panxidu	98	35.39 N	115.52 E
Panyabungan	114	0.51 N	99.33 E
Panyam	150	9.25 N	9.13 E
Panyang	140	10.04 N	29.58 E
Panyčevo	86	57.05 N	81.49 E
Panyu	100	22.57 N	113.20 E
Panyutyne	78	48.56 N	36.17 E
Panzerstausee ⊜[1]	263	51.11 N	7.16 E
Panzhuang	105	39.20 N	117.28 E
Panzi	152	7.13 S	17.58 E
Panzós	236	15.24 N	89.40 W
Pao ≃, Thai	110	16.13 N	103.43 E
Pao ≃, Ven.	246	8.33 N	68.01 W
Pao ≃, Ven.	246	8.06 N	64.17 W
Paochi → Baoji	102	34.23 N	107.09 E
Pão de Açúcar	250	9.45 S	37.26 W
Pão de Açúcar (Sugar Loaf) ∧	287a	22.57 S	43.09 W
Paoki → Baoji	102	34.23 N	107.09 E
Paola, It.	68	39.22 N	16.03 E
Paola, Ks., U.S.	198	38.34 N	94.52 W
Paoli, In., U.S.	218	38.33 N	86.28 W
Paoli, Pa., U.S.	208	40.02 N	75.28 W
Paoli, Wi., U.S.	216	42.56 N	89.32 W
Paonia	200	38.52 N	107.35 W
Pāonta Sāhib	124	30.27 N	77.37 E
Paopao	174s	17.31 S	149.49 W
Paoshenmiao	98	41.12 N	118.17 E
Paotai Yingzi	98	41.48 N	115.12 E
Paoting → Baoding	105	38.52 N	115.29 E
Paotow → Baotou	102	40.40 N	109.59 E
Paoua	152	7.15 N	16.26 E
Paoying → Baoying	100	33.16 N	119.20 E
P'aozero, ozero ⊜	24	66.05 N	30.58 E
Paozi	104	42.13 N	122.19 E
Pap	85	40.53 N	71.07 E
Pápa	30	47.19 N	17.28 E
Papa, Sound of ʮ	46a	60.18 N	1.41 W
Papagaio	250	6.01 S	45.21 W
Papagaio ≃, Bra.	246	1.53 S	62.35 W
Papagaio ≃, Bra.	248	12.56 S	58.18 W
Papagayo ≃	234	16.46 N	99.43 W
Papagayo, Golfo de c	236	10.42 N	85.50 W
Papago Indian Reservation ◆[4]	200	32.20 N	112.00 W
Papaikou	229d	19.47 N	155.05 W
Papakating Creek ≃	276	41.11 N	74.38 W
Papakura	172	37.04 S	174.57 E
Papalia	112	5.58 S	124.01 E
Papaloapan ≃	234	18.42 N	95.38 W
Papanoa	234	17.21 N	101.02 W
Papantla [de Olarte]	234	20.27 N	97.19 W
Papar, Indon.	115a	7.41 S	112.04 E
Papar, Malay.	112	5.44 N	115.56 E
Papara, Poly. fr.	174s	17.44 S	149.21 W
Papara, Sol.Is.	175e	7.02 S	156.48 E
Paparoa	172	36.06 S	174.14 E
Paparoa National Park ▲	172	42.05 S	171.25 E
Paparoa Range ⋌	172	42.00 S	171.35 E
Papasidero	68	39.52 N	15.54 E
Papa Stour I	46a	60.20 N	1.42 W
Papatoetoe	172	36.58 S	174.52 E
Papawai Point >	229a	20.47 N	156.33 W
Papa Westray I	46	59.21 N	2.54 W
Papeari	174s	17.45 S	149.21 W
Papeete	174s	17.32 S	149.34 W
Papelón	286c	10.27 N	66.47 W
Papenburg	52	53.05 N	7.23 E
Papendrecht	52	51.50 N	4.40 E
Papenoo	174s	17.30 S	149.25 W
Papenoo ≃	174s	17.30 S	149.25 W
Papetoai	174s	17.29 S	149.52 W
Papey I	24a	64.37 N	14.11 W
Paphlagonia □[9]	130	41.10 N	32.45 E
Paphos → Néa Páfos	130	34.45 N	32.25 E
Papilė	76	56.09 N	22.48 E
Papillion	198	41.09 N	96.02 W
Papineau	216	40.58 N	87.43 W
Papineau □[6]	206	45.50 N	75.00 W
Papineau, Lac ⊜	206	45.48 N	74.46 W
Papineau Creek ≃	212	45.13 N	77.43 W
Papineau-Labelle, Réserve ▲	188	45.55 N	75.20 W
Papineau Lake ⊜	212	45.20 N	77.50 W
Papineauville	206	45.37 N	75.01 W
Paposo	252	25.01 S	70.28 W
Papouasie Nouvelle-Guinée → Papua New Guinea □[1]	164	6.00 S	150.00 E
Papozze	64	44.59 N	12.02 E
Pappenheim, Dtsch.	54	50.47 N	10.27 E
Pappenheim, Dtsch.	56	48.56 N	10.58 E
Paps of Jura ⋌	46	55.55 N	6.00 W
Papua, Gulf of c	164	8.30 S	145.00 E
Papua Neuguinea → Papua New Guinea □[1]	164	6.00 S	150.00 E
Papua New Guinea □[1]	164	6.00 S	147.00 E
Papuasia Nueva Guinea → Papua New Guinea □[1]	164	6.00 S	150.00 E
Papucaia	256	22.37 S	42.44 W
Papudo	252	32.31 S	71.27 W
Papulovo	24	60.34 N	48.00 E
Papun	110	18.04 N	97.27 E
Papunáua ≃	246	2.09 N	70.32 W
Papunya	162	23.16 S	131.54 E
Papurí ≃	246	0.36 N	69.11 W
Paquequer ≃	256	22.12 S	42.54 W
Paquequer, Serra do ⋌	256	22.12 S	42.40 W
Paquera	236	9.50 N	84.56 W
Paquetá, Ilha de I	287a	22.46 S	43.06 W
Par	42	50.21 N	4.43 W
Pará → Belém	250	1.27 S	48.29 W
Pará □[3]	250	4.00 S	53.00 W
Para □[5]	250	5.30 N	55.15 W
Pará ≃, Bra.	250	1.30 S	48.55 W
Pará ≃, Bra.	255	19.13 S	45.07 W
Para ≃, Ross.	80	54.23 N	40.52 E
Pará, Ilha do I	250	0.18 S	51.15 W
Para, Pulau I	112	3.05 N	125.30 E
Parabel'	86	58.43 N	81.31 E
Parabel' ≃	86	58.44 N	81.35 E
Parabiago	62	45.33 N	8.57 E
Parabita	68	40.03 N	18.08 E
Paraburdoo	162	23.14 S	117.48 E
Paracale	116	14.17 N	122.48 E
Paracambi	256	22.37 S	43.43 W
Paracari ≃	250	4.36 S	57.47 W
Paracas, Bahía de c	248	13.50 S	76.17 W
Paracas, Península de >[1]	248	13.48 S	76.24 W
Paracatu	255	17.13 S	46.52 W
Paracatu ≃, Bra.	255	16.30 S	45.04 W
Paracatu ≃, Bra.	255	16.35 S	45.06 W
Paracel Islands → Xisha Qundao II	108	16.30 N	112.15 E
Parachilna	166	31.08 S	138.23 E
Pārachinār	120	33.54 N	70.06 E
Paracho de Verduzco	234	19.39 N	102.04 W
Parachute	200	39.27 N	108.03 W
Paraćin	38	43.52 N	21.24 E
Parácuaro	234	20.09 N	100.46 W
Paracuellos de Jarama	266a	40.30 N	3.32 W
Paracuru	250	3.24 S	39.04 W
Parád	30	47.55 N	20.02 E
Parada, Punta >	248	15.22 S	75.12 W
Paradas	34	37.18 N	5.30 W
Paradino	76	53.59 N	31.51 E
Paradise, Guy.	246	6.45 N	58.00 W
Paradise, Ca., U.S.	204	39.44 N	121.38 W
Paradise, Mt., U.S.	202	47.23 N	114.48 W
Paradise, Nv., U.S.	204	36.09 N	115.10 W
Paradise, Pa., U.S.	208	40.01 N	76.08 W
Paradise, Tx., U.S.	222	33.09 N	97.41 W
Paradise Hill, Sk., Can.	184	53.32 N	109.28 W
Paradise Hill, Ak., U.S.	180	62.25 N	160.03 W
Paradise Island I	240b	25.05 N	77.19 W
Paradise Mountain ∧	171a	27.45 S	152.02 E
Paradise Valley, Az., U.S.	200	33.31 N	111.56 W
Paradise Valley, Nv., U.S.	204	41.29 N	117.32 W
Parado	115b	8.45 S	118.36 E
Parado ≃	250	10.17 S	55.39 W
Pāradwīp	120	20.16 N	86.37 E
Parafield	168b	34.47 S	138.38 E
Parafiyivka	78	50.53 N	32.38 E
Parağaçay	84	39.07 N	45.56 E
Paragon	218	39.23 N	86.33 W
Paragonah	200	37.53 N	112.46 W
Paragould	194	36.03 N	90.30 W
Paraguá ≃, Bol.	248	13.34 S	61.53 W
Paragua ≃, Ven.	246	6.55 N	62.55 W
Paraguaçu	256	21.33 S	45.44 W
Paraguaçu ≃	255	12.45 S	38.54 W
Paraguaçu Paulista	255	22.25 S	50.34 W
Paraguaipoa	246	11.21 N	71.57 W
Paraguaná, Península de >[1]	246	11.55 N	70.00 W
Paraguarí	252	25.38 S	57.09 W
Paraguarí □[5]	252	26.00 S	57.10 W
Paraguay □[1], S.A.	244	23.00 S	58.00 W
Paraguay □[1], S.A.	252	23.00 S	58.00 W
Paraguay (Paraguai) ≃	18	27.18 S	58.38 W
Parahyba → João Pessoa	250	7.07 S	34.52 W
Parai, Reprêsa do ⊜[1]	256	23.20 S	45.35 W
Paraíba □[3]	250	7.15 S	36.30 W
Paraíba do Sul	256	22.09 S	43.17 W
Paraíba do Sul ≃	255	21.37 S	41.03 W
Paraibano	250	6.30 S	44.01 W
Paraibuna	256	23.23 S	45.39 W
Paraibuna ≃, Bra.	256	22.06 S	43.08 W
Paraibuna ≃, Bra.	256	23.22 S	45.40 W
Paraibuna, Reprêsa do ⊜[1]	256	23.25 S	45.30 W
Paraíso, Bra.	255	19.03 S	52.59 W
Paraíso, Bra.	256	22.19 S	45.42 W
Paraíso, C.R.	236	9.50 N	83.51 W
Paraíso, Méx.	234	18.24 N	93.14 W
Paraiso, Pan.	236	9.02 N	79.38 W
Paraíso do Norte	255	23.13 S	52.38 W
Paraíso Garcia	256	21.32 S	43.53 W
Paraíso Novillero	234	18.16 N	95.59 W
Paraisópolis	256	22.33 S	45.47 W
Paraitinga ≃, Bra.	256	23.34 S	46.02 W
Paraitinga ≃, Bra.	256	23.22 S	45.40 W
Parakan	115a	7.17 S	110.06 E
Parakou	150	9.21 N	2.37 E
Paralía Aspropírgos	267c	38.02 N	23.35 E
Paralímni	130	35.02 N	33.59 E
Parama Island I	164	9.00 S	143.25 E
Paramakkudi	122	9.33 N	78.36 E
Paramaribo	250	5.50 N	55.10 W
Parambu	250	6.13 S	40.43 W
Paramillo, Parque Nacional ▲	246	7.15 N	76.15 W
Paramirim	255	13.26 S	42.15 W
Paramirim ≃	250	11.34 S	43.18 W
Paramithiá	38	39.28 N	20.30 E
Paramonga	248	10.40 S	77.50 W
Paramoti	250	4.06 S	39.15 W
Paramount	228	33.53 N	118.09 W
Paramus	210	40.56 N	74.04 W
Paramušir, ostrov I	74	50.25 N	155.50 E
Paramus Park ◆[9]	276	40.57 N	74.04 W
Paran, Naḥal (Wādī al-Jirāfī) V	132	30.24 N	35.10 E
Paraná, Arg.	252	31.44 S	60.32 W
Paranã, Bra.	255	12.33 S	47.52 W
Paraná □[3]	252	24.00 S	51.00 W
Paranã ≃, Bra.	255	12.30 S	48.14 W
Paraná ≃, S.A.	18	33.43 S	59.15 W
Paraná, Pico ∧	252	25.16 S	48.48 W
Paranabi	256	23.54 S	45.14 W
Paraná Bravo ≃[1]	258	33.53 S	58.27 W
Paranacito ≃	258	33.44 S	58.33 W
Paraná de las Palmas ≃[1]	258	34.18 S	58.33 W
Paranaguá	252	25.31 S	48.30 W
Paranaguá, Baía de c	252	25.29 S	48.33 W
Paraná Guazú ≃[1]	258	34.00 S	58.25 W
Paranaíba	255	19.40 S	51.11 W
Paranaíba ≃	255	20.07 S	51.05 W
Paranaidji	250	6.33 S	47.27 W
Paranaíta ≃	250	9.28 S	56.43 W
Paranam	250	5.37 N	55.06 W
Paraná Miní ≃[1]	258	34.13 S	58.25 W
Paranapanema ≃	255	22.40 S	53.09 W
Paranapiacaba	256	23.47 S	46.19 W
Paranapiacaba, Serra do ⋌	252	24.20 S	49.00 W
Parañaque	269f	14.30 N	120.59 E
Paranavaí	255	23.04 S	52.28 W
Parang, Pil.	116	7.23 N	124.16 E
Parang, Pil.	116	5.55 N	120.54 E
Parang, Pulau I	115a	5.45 S	110.14 E
Paran'ga	80	56.43 N	49.24 E
Parângu Mare, Vârful ∧	38	45.22 N	23.33 E
Paranhos	255	23.55 S	55.25 W
Paranjang	98	37.08 N	126.55 E
Paranoá, Lago do ⊜	255	15.48 S	47.50 W
Párao de Masa, Puerto de)(	34	42.38 N	3.46 W
Paraopeba	255	19.18 S	44.25 W
Parapara	246	9.44 N	67.18 W
Paraparaumu	172	40.55 S	175.01 E
Paraparaumu Beach	172	40.54 S	174.59 E
Parapayè	58	45.55 N	7.32 E
Parapetí ≃	248	18.58 S	62.21 W
Parara	112	2.37 S	120.07 E
Parás, Méx.	196	26.30 N	99.31 W
Paras, Perú	248	13.30 S	74.35 W
Parasan	116	8.05 N	123.33 E
Parāsī	124	27.32 N	83.40 E
Parāsia	124	22.12 N	78.46 E
Parasida	126	23.46 N	87.20 E
Parasnāth	124	23.59 N	86.02 E
Paratei	256	23.14 S	46.00 W
Parateí ≃	256	23.12 S	46.00 W
Parati	256	23.13 S	44.43 W
Paratico	64	45.39 N	9.57 E
Parati-Mirim	256	23.14 S	44.38 W
Paratinga	255	12.42 S	43.10 W
Paratoo	166	32.42 S	139.22 E
Parauapebas ≃	250	5.35 S	49.41 W
Parauari ≃	250	4.36 S	57.47 W
Paraúna	255	17.02 S	50.26 W
Paravani, ozero ⊜	84	41.26 N	43.48 E
Para Wirra Recreation Park ▲	168b	34.43 S	138.50 E
Paray-le-Monial	32	46.27 N	4.07 E
Parbakalan	114	2.38 N	98.27 E
Pārbati ≃	124	25.51 N	76.36 E
Pārbatipur	124	25.39 N	88.55 E
Parbhani	122	19.16 N	76.47 E
Parbig	86	57.14 N	81.24 E
Parbig ≃	86	57.37 N	82.18 E
Parbold	262	53.36 N	2.46 W
Parburuan	114	1.52 N	99.55 E
Parcani	38	46.49 N	29.31 E
Parchen	54	52.21 N	12.05 E
Parchim	54	53.25 N	11.51 E
Parchment	216	42.19 N	85.34 W
Parcines (Partschins)	64	46.41 N	11.04 E
Parczew	30	51.39 N	22.54 E
Pardee Reservoir ⊜[1]	226	38.16 N	120.51 W
Pardeeville	190	43.32 N	89.18 W
Pardes Hanna-Karkur	132	32.28 N	34.58 E
Pārdi	122	20.31 N	72.57 E
Parding	120	32.52 N	88.39 E
Pardo ≃, Bra.	250	5.21 S	52.53 W
Pardo ≃, Bra.	252	29.59 S	52.23 W
Pardo ≃, Bra.	255	15.48 S	44.48 W
Pardo ≃, Bra.	255	20.10 S	48.38 W
Pardo ≃, Bra.	255	22.55 S	49.58 W
Pardo ≃, Bra.	255	15.39 S	38.57 W
Pardo ≃, Bra.	255	21.46 S	52.09 W
Pardo ≃, Bra.	256	23.32 S	45.30 W
Pardo ≃, Bra.	256	21.25 S	42.39 W
Pardomuan	114	2.06 N	98.20 E
Pardubice	30	50.02 N	15.47 E

Symbol	English	Deutsch	Español	Français	Português
≃	River	Fluß	Río	Rivière	Rio
≋	Canal	Kanal	Canal	Canal	Canal
⌊	Waterfall, Rapids	Wasserfall, Stromschnellen	Cascada, Rápidos	Chute d'eau, Rapides	Cascata, Rápidos
ʮ	Strait	Meeresstraße	Estrecho	Détroit	Estreito
c	Bay, Gulf	Bucht, Golf	Bahía, Golfo	Baie, Golfe	Baía, Golfo
⊜	Lake, Lakes	See, Seen	Lago, Lagos	Lac, Lacs	Lago, Lagos
⊞	Swamp	Sumpf	Pantano	Marais	Pântano
⊟	Ice Features, Glacier	Eis- und Gletscherformen	Accidentes Glaciales	Formes glaciaires	Acidentes glaciares
⊤	Other Hydrographic Features	Andere Hydrographische Objekte	Otros Elementos Hidrográficos	Autres données hydrographiques	Outros acidentes hidrográficos
✢	Submarine Features	Untermeerische Objekte	Accidentes Submarinos	Formes de relief sous-marin	Acidentes submarinos
□	Political Unit	Politische Einheit	Unidad Política	Entité politique	Unidade política
⛫	Cultural Institution	Kulturelle Institution	Institución Cultural	Institution culturelle	Instituição cultural
⊥	Historical Site	Historische Stätte	Sitio Histórico	Site historique	Sitio histórico
▲	Recreational Site	Erholungs- und Ferienort	Sitio de Recreo	Centre de loisirs	Area de Lazer
⊠	Airport	Flughafen	Aeropuerto	Aéroport	Aeroporto
■	Military Installation	Militäranlage	Instalación Militar	Installation militaire	Instalação militar
◆	Miscellaneous	Verschiedenes	Misceláneo	Divers	Diversos

Name	Page	Lat.°′	Long.°′
Pare	115a	7.46 S	112.11 E
Parece Vela → Okino-Tori-shima I	90	20.25 N	136.00 E
Parecis	248	14.09 S	56.56 W
Parecis ≃	248	12.56 S	56.43 W
Parecis, Chapada dos ⋏	248	13.00 S	60.00 W
Parede	266c	38.41 N	9.21 W
Paredes de Nava	34	42.09 N	4.41 W
Paredón	232	25.56 N	100.58 W
Parelhas	250	6.41 S	36.39 W
Parelheiros ✦ [8]	256	23.51 S	46.44 W
Pareloup, Lac de ⊜	32	44.15 N	2.45 E
Paremata	172	41.07 S	174.52 E
Parempei I	174r	7.01 N	158.15 E
Paren'	74	62.28 N	163.05 E
Paren' ≃	74	62.25 N	163.10 E
Parengarenga Harbour ⊂	172	34.31 S	172.57 E
Parent	176	47.55 N	74.37 W
Parent, Lac ⊜	190	48.38 N	77.03 W
Parentis-en-Born	32	44.21 N	1.05 W
Pareora	172	44.30 S	171.12 E
Parepare	112	4.01 S	119.38 E
Parera	252	35.08 S	64.32 W
Parets del Vallès	266d	41.34 N	2.14 E
Parey	54	52.22 N	11.59 E
Parfenjevo, Ross.	24	61.21 N	42.43 E
Parfenjevo, Ross.	80	58.29 N	43.25 E
Parfentevo	82	55.06 N	38.49 E
Parfino	76	57.58 N	31.41 E
Parforce-Heide ✦ [3]	264a	52.22 N	13.10 E
Párga	38	39.17 N	20.23 E
Pārgaon	272c	18.59 N	73.05 E
Pargarutan	114	1.28 N	99.20 E
Pargas (Parainen)	26	60.18 N	22.18 E
Pargey Creek ≃	285	39.49 N	75.18 W
Pargny-sur-Saulx	56	48.46 N	4.50 E
Pargolovo ✦ [8]	265a	60.04 N	30.18 E
Parham	240c	17.05 N	61.46 W
Parhebangan	114	2.15 N	98.45 E
Pari ✦ [8]	287b	23.32 S	46.37 W
Paria ≃	200	36.52 N	111.36 W
Paria, Gulf of ⊂	246	10.20 N	62.00 W
Paria, Península de > [1]	241r	10.40 N	62.10 W
Pariaguán	246	8.51 N	64.43 W
Pariaman	112	0.38 S	100.08 E
Pariamanu ≃	248	12.26 S	69.16 W
Pariči	76	52.48 N	29.25 E
Paricutín ∧ [1]	234	19.28 N	102.15 W
Parida, Isla I	236	8.07 N	82.20 W
Pariette Draw V	200	40.02 N	109.45 W
Parigi, Indon.	112	0.48 S	120.10 E
Parigi, Indon.	115a	6.12 S	106.22 E
Parigné-L'Évêque	50	47.56 N	0.22 E
Parika	246	6.52 N	58.25 W
Parikkala	26	61.33 N	29.30 E
Parima ≃	246	3.34 N	63.47 W
Parima, Sierra ⋏	246	2.30 N	64.00 W
Pariñas, Punta >	246	4.40 S	81.20 W
Parintins	250	2.36 S	56.44 W
Paripiranga	250	10.41 S	37.52 W
Pariquera-Açu	252	24.43 S	47.53 W
Paris, On., Can.	212	43.12 N	80.23 W
Paris, Fr.	50	48.52 N	2.20 E
Paris, Fr.	261	48.52 N	2.20 E
Paris, Ar., U.S.	194	35.17 N	93.43 W
Paris, Id., U.S.	202	42.13 N	111.24 W
Paris, Il., U.S.	194	39.36 N	87.41 W
Paris, Ky., U.S.	218	38.12 N	84.15 W
Paris, Me., U.S.	188	44.15 N	70.30 W
Paris, Mo., U.S.	219	39.28 N	92.00 W
Paris, Oh., U.S.	214	40.48 N	81.10 W
Paris, Pa., U.S.	214	40.24 N	80.31 W
Paris, Tn., U.S.	194	36.18 N	88.19 W
Paris, Tx., U.S.	196	33.39 N	95.33 W
Paris □ [5]	261	48.52 N	2.20 E
Paris, Port de ⊂	261	48.57 N	2.17 E
Parish	210	43.24 N	76.07 W
Parisien de Pantin, Cimetière ✦	261	48.54 N	2.23 E
Parisienne, Ile I	190	46.41 N	84.44 W
Paris-le-Bourget, Aéroport de ⊠	50	48.52 N	2.25 E
Parismina	236	10.12 N	83.38 W
Parismina ≃	236	10.19 N	83.21 W
Paris-Orly, Aéroport de ⊠	50	48.43 N	2.22 E
Paris-Plage, Aéroport ⊠	50	50.31 N	1.38 E
Parit	112	3.10 S	104.38 E
Parita, Bahía de ⊂	236	8.08 N	80.24 W
Parit Bunga	114	2.04 N	102.33 E
Parit Buntar	114	5.07 N	100.30 E
Pariti	112	10.01 S	123.43 E
Parit Jawa	114	1.57 N	102.39 E
Park ≃	198	48.28 N	97.09 W
Park, North Branch ≃	198	48.26 N	97.27 W
Park, South Branch ≃	198	48.26 N	97.27 W
Parka	154	4.31 N	27.20 E
Parkano	26	62.01 N	23.01 E
Parkchester	285	40.00 N	75.35 W
Park City, Il., U.S.	216	42.21 N	87.53 W
Park City, Ks., U.S.	198	37.48 N	97.19 W
Park City, Mt., U.S.	202	45.37 N	108.55 W
Park City, Ut,. U.S.	200	40.38 N	111.29 W
Park Creek ≃	285	40.13 N	75.08 W
Parkdale, P.E., Can.	186	46.15 N	63.07 W
Parkdale, Mo., U.S.	219	38.29 N	90.32 W
Parkdale, Or., U.S.	224	45.31 N	121.35 W
Parkdene	273d	26.14 S	28.16 E
Parkent	85	41.18 N	69.40 E
Parker, Az., U.S.	200	34.09 N	114.17 W
Parker, Co., U.S.	198	39.31 N	104.45 W
Parker, Fl., U.S.	194	30.07 N	85.36 W
Parker, Pa., U.S.	214	41.05 N	79.41 W
Parker, S.D., U.S.	198	43.23 N	97.08 W
Parker □ [6]	222	32.48 N	97.42 W
Parker ≃	207	42.45 N	70.49 W
Parker, Cape >	176	75.04 N	79.40 W
Parker, Lake ⊜	220	28.04 N	81.56 W
Parker City	218	40.11 N	85.12 W
Parker Dam	204	34.17 N	114.08 W
Parker Dam ✦ [6]	200	34.18 N	114.10 W
Parker Ford	285	40.12 N	75.35 W
Parker Peak ∧	198	43.24 N	103.41 W
Parker Range	162	31.38 S	119.35 E
Parker River National Wildlife Refuge ✦ [4]	283	42.45 N	70.48 W
Parkersburg, Il., U.S.	194	38.36 N	88.03 W
Parkersburg, Ia., U.S.	190	42.34 N	92.47 W
Parkersburg, W.V., U.S.	188	39.16 N	81.33 W
Parkers Creek ≃	285	40.00 N	74.53 W
Parkers Prairie	198	46.09 N	95.19 W
Parkerville	168a	31.53 S	116.09 E
Parker Volcano ∧ [1]	116	6.07 N	124.54 E
Parkes	166	33.08 S	148.11 E
Parkesburg	208	39.57 N	75.55 W
Park Falls	190	45.56 N	90.26 W
Park Forest	216	41.28 N	87.38 W
Parkgate, Eng., U.K.	262	53.18 N	3.05 W
Parkgate, Eng., U.K.	262	53.16 N	2.20 W
Park Hall	208	38.13 N	76.25 W
Parkhill, On., Can.	190	43.09 N	81.41 W
Parkhill, Pa., U.S.	214	40.22 N	78.52 W
Parkhill Gardens	273d	26.14 S	28.11 E
Parkhomenko	83	48.34 N	39.43 E
Parkhomivka	78	50.08 N	35.01 E
Parkin	194	35.15 N	90.34 W
Park Lake	216	42.48 N	84.27 W
Parkland, Pa., U.S.	285	40.09 N	74.56 W
Parkland, Wa., U.S.	224	47.09 N	122.25 W
Parklawn	284c	38.50 N	77.09 W
Park Layne	218	39.53 N	84.03 W
Parklea	274a	33.44 S	150.57 E
Parkman	214	41.22 N	81.03 W
Park Meadows	279b	40.18 N	79.44 W
Park Orchards	274b	37.46 S	145.13 E
Park Plateau ⋏ [1]	198	37.15 N	104.45 W
Park Range ⋏	200	40.40 N	106.40 W
Park Rapids	198	46.55 N	95.03 W
Park Ridge, Il., U.S.	216	42.00 N	87.50 W
Park Ridge, N.J., U.S.	276	41.02 N	74.02 W
Park Ridge Farms	285	40.10 N	74.42 W
Park River	198	48.23 N	97.44 W
Parkrose	224	45.33 N	122.33 W
Park Rynie	158	30.25 S	30.35 E
Parks	180	57.38 N	154.00 W
Parks Creek ≃	212	44.17 N	77.21 W
Park Shore Resort	216	41.55 N	85.59 W
Parkside, Md., U.S.	284c	39.02 N	77.06 W
Parkside, Pa., U.S.	285	39.52 N	75.23 W
Parksley	208	37.46 N	75.39 W
Park Station ✦ [5]	273d	26.12 S	28.03 E
Parkstein	60	49.44 N	12.04 E
Parkstetten	60	48.55 N	12.36 E
Parkston	198	43.23 N	97.59 W
Parksville, B.C., Can.	182	49.19 N	124.19 W
Parksville, N.Y., U.S.	210	41.51 N	74.45 W
Parktown ✦ [8]	273d	26.11 S	28.03 E
Parktown North ✦ [8]	273d	26.09 S	28.02 E
Parkview	279b	40.30 N	79.56 W
Parkville, Md., U.S.	208	39.22 N	76.32 W
Parkville, Mo., U.S.	194	39.11 N	94.40 W
Parkwater	202	47.40 N	117.19 W
Parkway, Ca., U.S.	226	38.29 N	121.27 W
Parkway, Mo., U.S.	219	38.20 N	90.57 W
Parkwood	284c	39.01 N	77.05 W
Parla	34	40.14 N	3.46 W
Parlākimidi	122	18.47 N	84.06 E
Parle, Lac qui ⊜	198	45.07 N	96.00 W
Parli	122	18.51 N	76.32 E
Parliament, Houses of ⚜	260	51.30 N	0.07 W
Parlier	226	36.36 N	119.31 W
Parma, It.	64	44.48 N	10.20 E
Parma, Id., U.S.	202	43.47 N	116.56 W
Parma, Mi., U.S.	216	42.15 N	84.35 W
Parma, Mo., U.S.	194	36.36 N	89.48 W
Parma, Oh., U.S.	214	41.24 N	81.43 W
Parma □ [4]	64	44.40 N	10.10 E
Parma ≃	64	44.56 N	10.26 E
Parma Heights	214	41.23 N	81.45 W
Parmain	261	49.07 N	2.12 E
Parmatown Mall ✦ [9]	279a	41.23 N	81.44 W
Parnaguá	250	10.13 S	44.38 W
Parnahyba → Parnaíba	250	2.54 S	41.47 W
Parnaíba	250	2.54 S	41.47 W
Parnaíba ≃	250	3.00 S	41.50 W
Parnaìbinha ≃	250	9.17 S	45.55 W
Parnamirim	250	8.05 S	39.34 W
Parnarama	250	5.41 S	43.06 W
Parnassós ∧	38	38.32 N	22.35 E
Parnassus	172	42.43 S	173.18 E
Parndorf	61	47.59 N	16.51 E
Parnell	216	40.14 N	88.42 W
Párnis ∧	38	38.11 N	23.42 E
Párnis Óros ⋏	267c	38.07 N	23.44 E
Parnon ⋏	38	37.05 N	22.40 E
Pärnu	76	58.24 N	24.32 E
Pärnu ≃	76	58.23 N	24.29 E
Pärnu-Jaagupi	76	58.37 N	24.30 E
Pärnu laht ⊂	76	58.15 N	24.25 E
Paro	124	27.26 N	89.25 E
Pārola	120	20.53 N	75.07 E
Paromaj	89	52.50 N	143.02 E
Paroo	162	26.16 S	119.46 E
Paroo ≃	166	31.28 S	143.32 E
Parorā	272b	22.48 N	88.09 E
Páros	38	37.04 N	25.08 E
Páros I	38	37.08 N	25.12 E
Parow	158	33.53 S	18.37 E
Parowan	200	37.50 N	112.49 W
Parpaillon ⋏	62	44.30 N	6.40 E
Parpan	58	46.46 N	9.33 E
Parr	216	41.02 N	87.13 W
Parral, Chile	252	36.09 S	71.50 W
Parral → Hidalgo del Parral, Méx.	232	26.56 N	105.40 W
Parral, Oh., U.S.	214	40.33 N	81.30 W
Parral ≃	232	27.39 N	105.07 W
Parramatta	170	33.49 S	151.00 E
Parramatta ≃	274a	33.51 S	151.14 E
Parramatta Park ♠	274a	33.49 S	151.00 E
Parramore Island I	208	37.32 N	75.38 W
Parras de la Fuente	232	25.25 N	102.11 W
Parrett ≃	42	51.13 N	3.01 W
Parrish, Al., U.S.	194	33.43 N	87.17 W
Parrish, Fl., U.S.	220	27.35 N	82.25 W
Parris Island Marine Corps Recruit Depot ■	192	32.21 N	80.41 W
Parrita	236	9.30 N	84.19 W
Parrita ≃	236	9.29 N	84.19 W
Parrsboro	186	45.24 N	64.20 W
Parry, Cape >	176	70.08 N	124.24 W
Parry, Mount ∧	182	52.53 N	128.45 W
Parry Bay ⊂	176	68.07 N	82.00 W
Parry Channel)(	16	74.20 N	98.00 W
Parry Island I	212	45.18 N	80.10 W
Parry Island Indian Reserve ✦ [4]	212	45.18 N	80.10 W
Parry Peninsula > [1]	180	69.45 N	124.30 W
Parry Sound	212	45.21 N	80.02 W
Parry Sound □ [6]	212	45.25 N	79.55 W
Parry Sound)(	212	45.21 N	80.06 W
Parryville	208	40.49 N	75.40 W
Parsberg	60	49.09 N	11.43 E
Parsdorf	60	48.09 N	11.47 E
Parseier Spitze ∧	58	47.10 N	10.28 E
Parsęta ≃	30	54.12 N	15.33 E
Parshād	120	24.11 N	73.42 E
Parshall	198	47.57 N	102.08 W
Parshallville	281	42.41 N	83.46 W
Paršino	88	59.10 N	111.48 E
Parsippany	210	40.51 N	74.25 W
Parsippany, Lake ⊜	276	40.51 N	74.26 W
Parsnāth ∧	124	23.53 N	86.08 E
Parsnip ≃	182	55.10 N	123.00 W
Parsoburan	114	2.19 N	99.20 E
Parsonage Island I	276	40.37 N	73.37 W
Parsons, Ks., U.S.	198	37.20 N	95.15 W
Parsons, Tn., U.S.	194	35.38 N	88.07 W
Parsons, W.V., U.S.	188	39.05 N	79.40 W
Parsons, Mount ∧ [2]	164	13.33 S	135.09 E
Parson's Pond	186	50.02 N	57.43 W
Parsons Pond ⊜	186	50.00 N	57.35 W
Parsons Range ⋏	164	13.30 S	135.15 E
Parsteiner See ⊜	54	52.55 N	13.59 E
Pärsti	76	58.25 N	25.32 E
Partābpur	124	23.29 N	83.13 E
Partanna	70	37.43 N	12.53 E
Partāppur	126	21.48 N	86.44 E
Partenen	58	46.58 N	10.03 E
Parthala	272a	28.36 N	77.24 E
Parthe ≃	54	51.22 N	12.21 E
Parthenay	32	46.39 N	0.15 W
Partington	262	53.25 N	2.26 W
Partinico	70	38.03 N	13.07 E
Partizansk	89	43.08 N	133.09 E
Partizánske	30	48.39 N	18.23 E
Partizanskoje	86	55.30 N	94.24 E
Parton	44	54.34 N	3.35 W
Partridge, Point >	224	48.13 N	122.46 W
Partridge Creek ≃	212	44.44 N	77.13 W
Partridge Crop Lake ⊜	184	55.38 N	97.27 W
Partridge Point >	186	50.09 N	56.10 W
Partry	48	53.41 N	9.19 W
Partschins → Parcines	64	46.41 N	11.04 E
Paru ≃, Bra.	250	1.33 S	52.38 W
Parú ≃, Ven.	246	4.20 N	66.27 W
Parubcan	116	13.43 N	123.45 E
Paru de Este ≃	250	1.10 N	54.40 W
Paru de Oeste ≃	250	1.30 S	56.00 W
Parung	115a	6.25 S	106.42 E
Pårup, Dan.	41	55.24 N	10.20 E
Pårup, Dan.	41	56.08 N	9.21 E
Parūr	122	10.09 N	76.14 E
Paruro	248	13.46 S	71.51 W
Parutyne	78	46.43 N	31.53 E
Parvān □ [4]	120	35.15 N	69.30 E
Pārvatīpuram	122	18.47 N	83.26 E
Parvin State Park ♠	208	39.30 N	75.09 W
Pŭrvomaj	38	42.06 N	25.13 E
Paryang	120	30.11 N	83.09 E
Påryd	26	56.34 N	15.55 E
Parys	158	27.04 S	27.16 E
Paša ≃	76	60.29 N	32.55 E
Paşabahçe ✦ [8]	267b	41.06 N	29.05 E
Pasacao	116	13.31 N	123.03 E
Pasaco	236	13.59 N	90.12 W
Pasadena, Nf., Can.	186	49.01 N	57.36 W
Pasadena, Ca., U.S.	228	34.08 N	118.08 W
Pasadena, Md., U.S.	208	39.06 N	76.34 W
Pasadena, Tx., U.S.	222	29.41 N	95.12 W
Pasado, Cabo >	246	0.22 S	80.30 W
Pasaje	246	3.20 S	79.49 W
Pasaje ≃	252	25.35 S	63.57 W
Pasaje Talavera ≃ [1]	258	33.53 S	58.55 W
Pa Sak ≃	110	14.21 N	100.35 E
Paşaköy	130	35.09 N	33.36 E
Pasaleng Bay ⊂	116	18.36 N	120.56 E
Paşalimanı Adası I	130	40.28 N	27.37 E
Pasān	124	22.51 N	82.12 E
Pasanauri	84	42.21 N	44.41 E
Pasangkayu	112	1.10 S	119.20 E
Pasarbantal	112	2.45 S	101.20 E
Pasarseluma	112	4.09 S	102.32 E
Pasar Senen Station ✦ [5]	269e	6.10 S	106.50 E
Pasarsorkam	114	1.53 N	98.34 E
Pasarwajo	112	5.29 S	122.50 E
Pasatiempo	226	37.02 N	122.02 W
Pasaunda	272a	28.42 N	77.21 E
Pasawng	110	18.52 N	97.18 E
Pasay	269f	14.33 N	121.00 E
Pasayten ≃	224	49.08 N	120.35 W
Pasayten, Middle Fork ≃	224	48.53 N	120.37 W
Pasayten, West Fork ≃	224	48.53 N	120.37 W
Pascack Brook ≃	276	40.59 N	73.59 W
Pascagama, Lac ⊜	190	48.34 N	75.36 W
Pascagoula	194	30.21 N	88.33 W
Pascagoula ≃	194	30.21 N	88.34 W
Pascalis, Lac ⊜	190	48.16 N	77.24 W
Paşcani	38	47.15 N	26.44 E
Pasching	61	48.15 N	14.12 E
Pasco	202	46.13 N	119.05 W
Pasco □ [5]	248	10.30 S	75.15 W
Pasco □ [6]	220	28.20 N	82.27 W
Pascoag	207	41.57 N	71.42 W
Pascoe Vale	274b	37.44 S	144.56 E
Pascua ≃	254	48.13 S	73.22 W
Pascua, Isla de (Easter Island) (Rapa Nui) I	174z	27.07 S	109.22 W
Pas-de-Calais □ [5]	50	50.30 N	2.20 E
Pas-en-Artois	50	50.09 N	2.30 E
Pasewalk	54	53.30 N	14.00 E
Pashmāl	123	35.26 N	72.36 E
Pasian di Prato	64	46.03 N	13.11 E
Pasiano di Pordenone	64	45.51 N	12.37 E
Pasig	116	14.33 N	121.05 E
Pasig ≃	269f	14.36 N	120.58 E
Pāsighāt	120	28.04 N	95.20 E
Pašija	86	58.26 N	58.16 E
P'asina ≃	74	73.50 N	87.10 E
Pasinler (Hasankale)	130	39.59 N	41.41 E
Pašino	86	55.11 N	83.00 E
P'asino, ozero ⊜	74	69.45 N	87.45 E
P'asinskij zaliv ⊂	74	74.00 N	86.00 E
Pasirganting	112	2.02 S	100.53 E
Pasir Gudang	271c	1.27 N	103.53 E
Pasirian	115a	8.13 S	113.06 E
Pasir Mas	114	6.02 N	102.08 E
Pasir Panjang	271c	1.17 N	103.47 E
Pasirpengarayan	114	0.51 N	100.16 E
Pasir Puteh, Malay.	114	5.50 N	102.24 E
Pasir Puteh, Malay.	271c	1.26 N	103.56 E
Påskallavik	26	57.10 N	16.27 E
Paskeville	168b	34.02 S	137.54 E
Paškovo, Ross.	80	53.39 N	42.25 E
Paškovo, Ross.	89	48.54 N	130.42 E
Paškovskij	78	45.02 N	39.06 E
Pasłęk	30	54.05 N	19.39 E
Pasłęka ≃	30	54.26 N	19.45 E
Pasley, Cape >	162	33.57 S	123.31 E
Pasley Bay ⊂	176	70.40 N	96.27 W
Pašman, Otok I	36	43.58 N	15.21 E
Pasmore ≃	166	31.07 S	139.48 E
Pašn'a	24	63.21 N	56.28 E
Pasni	128	25.16 N	63.28 E
Paso de Indios	254	43.52 S	69.06 W
Paso del Cerro	252	31.29 S	55.50 W
Paso del Macho	234	18.58 N	96.43 W
Paso de los Libres	252	29.43 S	57.05 W
Paso de los Toros	252	32.49 S	56.31 W
Paso del Rey	288	34.39 S	58.46 W
Paso del Toro	234	19.02 N	96.07 W
Paso de Ovejas	234	19.17 N	96.26 W
Paso de Patria	252	27.13 S	58.35 W
Paso de San Antonio	196	29.05 N	103.55 W
Paso Hondo	232	15.49 N	92.02 W
Paso Limay	254	40.33 S	70.26 W
Pasorapa	248	18.16 S	64.37 W
Paso Robles	226	35.37 N	120.41 W
Paso Seco	240m	17.59 N	66.23 W
Paso Severino, Embalse ⊜ [1]	258	34.15 S	56.18 W
Pašozero	76	60.02 N	34.37 E
Pasqua Indian Reserve ✦ [4]	184	50.45 N	104.02 W
Pasque Island I	207	41.27 N	70.50 W
Pasquel, Punta >	232	25.30 N	111.01 W
Pasquia Hills ⋏ [2]	184	53.13 N	102.37 W
Pasquotank □ [6]	208	36.26 N	76.26 W
Pasquotank ≃	192	36.10 N	76.03 W
Pasrūr	123	32.16 N	74.40 E
Passadumkeag	188	45.11 N	68.37 W
Passadumkeag Mountain ∧ [2]	188	45.10 N	68.20 W
Passage East	48	52.13 N	6.59 W
Passagem Franca	250	6.10 S	43.47 W
Passage Point >	176	73.29 N	115.17 W
Passage West	48	51.52 N	8.20 W
Passaic	210	40.51 N	74.07 W
Passaic □ [6]	210	40.55 N	74.10 W
Passaic ≃	276	40.43 N	74.07 W
Passaic Falls ∟	276	40.55 N	74.11 W
Passamaquoddy Bay ⊂	186	45.06 N	66.59 W
Passa Quatro	256	22.23 S	44.58 W
Passa Três	256	22.42 S	44.00 W
Passau	60	48.35 N	13.28 E
Passa Vinte	256	22.13 S	44.15 W
Pass Creek ≃	198	43.45 N	101.28 W
Passero, Capo >	70	36.40 N	15.09 E
Passignano sul Trasimeno	66	43.11 N	12.08 E
Passirio (Passer) ≃	64	46.41 N	11.10 E
Pass Island	186	47.29 N	56.11 W
Pašskij Perevoz	76	60.24 N	32.59 E
Passo Corese	66	42.09 N	12.39 E
Passo Fundo	252	28.15 S	52.24 W
Passopisciaro	70	37.52 N	15.02 E
Passo Real, Représa do ⊜ [1]	252	28.55 S	53.10 W
Passos	255	20.43 S	46.37 W
Passow	54	53.08 N	14.06 E
Passy	58	45.55 N	6.41 E
Passy ✦ [8]	261	48.52 N	2.17 E
Pastaza □ [4]	246	1.45 S	76.50 W
Pastaza ≃	246	4.50 S	76.25 W
Pastecho ≃	182	56.07 N	114.15 W
Pasteur, Lac ⊜	186	50.13 N	66.58 W
Pastillo	240m	17.59 N	66.29 W
Pasto	246	1.13 N	77.17 W
Pastol Bay ⊂	180	63.07 N	163.15 W
Pastora Peak ∧	200	36.47 N	109.10 W
Pastoria Creek ≃	228	35.01 N	118.51 W
Pastos Bons	250	6.36 S	44.05 W
Pastrana	34	40.25 N	2.55 W
Pastrengo	64	45.29 N	10.48 E
Pašukovo	82	55.55 N	38.16 E
Pasuquin	116	18.20 N	120.37 E
Pasuruan	115a	7.38 S	112.54 E
Pasvalys	76	56.04 N	24.24 E
Pásztó	30	47.55 N	19.42 E
Pata	116	5.51 N	121.10 E
Patacamaya	248	17.14 S	67.55 W
Pātāchārkuchi	120	26.31 N	91.16 E
Patagonia	200	31.32 N	110.45 W
Patagonia ✦ [1]	254	44.00 S	68.00 W
Pataha Creek ≃	202	46.31 N	117.59 W
Pata Island I	116	5.49 N	121.10 E
Pātan, India	120	23.50 N	72.07 E
Pātan, India	124	23.18 N	79.42 E
Patapsco	208	39.32 N	76.53 W
Patapsco ≃	208	39.09 N	76.27 W
Patapsco, Cooks Branch ≃	284b	39.27 N	76.53 W
Patapsco, Davis Branch ≃	284b	39.19 N	76.51 W
Patapsco, North Branch ≃	208	39.21 N	76.53 W
Patapsco, Rockburn Branch ≃	284b	39.14 N	76.43 W
Patapsco, Soapstone Branch ≃	284b	39.13 N	76.43 W
Patapsco, South Branch ≃	208	39.21 N	76.53 W
Patapsco River Neck > [1]	284b	39.14 N	76.27 W
Patapsco Valley State Park ♠	208	39.20 N	76.55 W
Patargān, Daqq-e ≡	128	33.30 N	60.40 E
Pătârlagele	38	45.19 N	26.22 E
Pataudi	124	28.19 N	76.47 E
Pataula Creek ≃	192	31.46 N	85.02 W
Patay	50	48.03 N	1.42 E
Pataz	248	7.44 S	77.37 W
Patchewollock	166	35.23 S	142.11 E
Patchogue	210	40.45 N	73.00 W
Patchogue Bay ⊂	276	40.44 N	73.01 W
Patchway	42	51.32 N	2.34 W
Pat Cleburne, Lake ⊜ [1]	222	32.25 N	97.30 W
Pate	154	2.08 S	41.00 E
Patea	172	39.45 S	174.28 E
Patea ≃	172	39.46 S	174.29 E
Patearoa	172	45.16 S	170.03 E
Pategi	150	8.44 N	5.44 E
Pate Island I	154	2.07 S	41.03 E
Pateley Bridge	44	54.05 N	1.45 W
Patel Nagar ✦ [8]	272a	28.39 N	77.10 E
Patensie	158	33.46 S	24.49 E
Patéras Óros ⋏	267c	38.07 N	23.25 E
Patergassen	64	46.49 N	13.52 E
Paterna	34	39.30 N	0.26 W
Paternal ✦ [8]	288	34.36 S	58.28 W
Paternion	64	46.43 N	13.38 E
Paternò	70	37.34 N	14.54 E
Pateros, Pil.	269f	14.33 N	121.04 E
Pateros, Wa., U.S.	202	48.03 N	119.54 W
Patersdorf	60	49.01 N	12.59 E
Paterson, Austl.	170	32.36 S	151.37 E
Paterson, S. Afr.	158	33.26 S	25.58 E
Paterson, N.J., U.S.	210	40.55 N	74.10 W
Paterson ≃	170	32.43 S	151.39 E
Paterson, Cape >	169	38.40 S	145.36 E
Paterson Inlet ⊂	172	46.55 S	168.03 E
Paterswolde	52	53.08 N	6.35 E
Pātghāti	126	22.53 N	89.55 E
Pathalgaon	124	22.34 N	83.28 E
Pathānkot	123	32.17 N	75.39 E
Pathānkot Airport ⊠	123	32.15 N	75.37 E
Pātharghāra	272b	22.34 N	88.35 E
Patharia	124	23.54 N	79.12 E
Pathein (Bassein)	110	16.47 N	94.44 E
Pathfinder Reservoir ⊜ [1]	200	42.30 N	106.50 W
Pathfinder Seamount ✣ [3]	16	50.55 N	143.15 W
Pathiong	140	6.46 N	30.54 E
Pathiu	110	10.42 N	99.19 E
Path of Condie	46	56.15 N	3.30 W
Pāthrāil	126	24.12 N	89.56 E
Pathro ≃	126	24.12 N	86.48 E
Pathum Thani	110	14.01 N	100.32 E
Pati, Indon.	112	0.33 S	111.19 E
Pati, Indon.	115a	6.45 S	111.01 E
Patía	246	2.04 N	77.04 W
Patía ≃	246	2.13 N	78.40 W
Patiāla	123	30.19 N	76.24 E
Patiāla ∧	123	32.32 N	72.11 E
Pati do Alferes	256	22.25 S	43.25 W
P'atigorsk	84	44.03 N	43.04 E
Pātihāl	272b	22.39 N	88.08 E
Patikul	116	6.04 N	121.06 E
Patillas	240m	18.00 N	66.01 W
P'atimar	80	49.31 N	50.32 E
Patinti, Selat)(	164	0.30 S	127.45 E
Patipāda	272c	19.04 N	73.05 E
Pati Point >	174p	13.36 N	144.57 E
Pātiram	124	25.19 N	88.45 E
Patire, Convento del ⚜ [1]	68	39.34 N	16.35 E
Pativilca	248	10.42 S	77.47 W
Pativilca ≃	248	10.44 S	77.48 W
Pātkai Range ⋏	120	27.00 N	96.00 E
Pat Mayse Reservoir ⊜ [1]	196	33.40 N	95.35 W
Pátmos I	38	37.20 N	26.33 E
Patna, India	124	25.36 N	85.07 E
Patna, India	126	21.56 N	87.52 E
Pātna, India	272b	22.59 N	88.18 E
Patna, Scot., U.K.	44	55.21 N	4.30 W
Patnāgarh	122	20.43 N	83.09 E
Patnanongan Island I	116	14.48 N	122.11 E
P'atnica, Ross.	82	54.46 N	38.09 E
P'atnica, Ross.	82	56.05 N	36.48 E
P'atnickoje, Ross.	78	50.25 N	37.51 E
P'atnickoje, Ross.	82	54.20 N	35.53 E
Pātnoli	272c	18.57 N	73.05 E
Patnoñgon	116	10.55 N	122.00 E
Patnos	84	39.14 N	42.52 E
Pato Branco	252	26.13 S	52.40 W
Patoka	219	38.45 N	89.05 W
Patoka ≃	194	38.25 N	87.44 W
Patoka Lake ⊜ [1]	194	38.20 N	86.40 W
Patokino	82	56.27 N	39.06 E
Patomskoje nagorje ⋏ [1]	88	59.00 N	115.00 E
Paton, Île I	275a	45.31 N	73.45 W
Patonga	154	2.46 N	33.18 E
Patos	250	7.01 S	37.16 W
Patos, Lagoa dos ⊂	252	31.06 S	51.15 W
Patos, Río de los ≃	252	31.18 S	69.25 W
Patos, Rio dos ≃	248	13.33 S	56.29 W
Patos de Minas	255	18.35 S	46.32 W
Patos Island I	224	48.47 N	122.56 W
P'atovskij	82	54.41 N	36.04 E
Patquía	252	30.03 S	66.53 W
Pátrai	38	38.15 N	21.44 E
Patraïkós Kólpos ⊂	38	38.14 N	21.15 E
Patras → Pátrai	38	38.15 N	21.44 E
Pātrasāer	124	23.13 N	87.31 E
Patricio Lynch, Isla I	254	48.37 S	75.26 W
Patrick Air Force Base ■	220	28.15 N	80.36 W

ENGLISH

Name	Page	Lat.°′	Long.°′
Patrick Henry International Airport ⊠	208	37.08 N	76.30 W
Patrick Point >	214	42.35 N	81.28 W
Patrington	44	53.41 N	0.02 W
Patriot	218	38.50 N	84.49 W
Patrocínio	255	18.57 S	46.59 W
Patrocínio Paulista	255	20.38 S	47.17 W
Patsaliga Creek ≃	194	31.22 N	86.31 W
Patscherkofel ∧	64	47.13 N	11.28 E
Pattada	71	40.35 N	9.06 E
Pattani	110	6.52 N	101.16 E
Pattani ≃	110	6.53 N	101.16 E
Patten	188	45.59 N	68.26 W
Pattenburg	210	40.38 N	75.01 W
Pattensen	52	52.15 N	9.46 E
Pattenville	283	42.35 N	71.14 W
Patterdale	44	54.32 N	2.56 W
Patterson, Ca., U.S.	226	37.28 N	121.07 W
Patterson, Ga., U.S.	192	31.23 N	82.08 W
Patterson, Il., U.S.	219	39.29 N	90.29 W
Patterson, La., U.S.	194	29.41 N	91.18 W
Patterson, N.Y., U.S.	210	41.30 N	73.36 W
Patterson, Oh., U.S.	216	40.47 N	83.32 W
Patterson ≃	274b	38.05 S	145.07 E
Patterson, Mount ∧	180	64.04 N	134.39 W
Patterson Creek ≃	188	39.34 N	78.44 W
Patterson Gardens	216	41.56 N	83.25 W
Patterson Heights	214	40.45 N	80.19 W
Patterson Island I	190	48.39 N	87.00 W
Patterson Park ♠	284b	39.17 N	76.35 W
Pattersonville	210	42.53 N	74.05 W
Patti, India	123	31.17 N	74.51 E
Patti, India	124	25.55 N	82.12 E
Patti, It.	70	38.08 N	14.58 E
Patti, Golfo di ⊂	36	38.12 N	15.05 E
Pattison, Ms., U.S.	194	31.53 N	90.53 W
Pattison, Tx., U.S.	222	29.49 N	95.60 W
Pattoki	123	31.01 N	73.51 E
Patton	214	40.37 N	78.39 W
Patton, Cape >	169	38.42 S	143.50 E
Patton Park ♠	281	42.19 N	83.10 W
Pattonsburg	194	40.02 N	94.08 W
Patton Seamounts ✣ [3]	16	54.20 N	149.30 W
Pattscheid ✦ [8]	263	51.05 N	7.03 E
Pattukkottai	122	10.26 N	79.19 E
Pattullo, Mount ∧	180	56.14 N	129.39 W
Patu	250	6.06 S	37.38 W
Pātua	126	22.06 N	90.23 E
Patuākhāli	124	22.21 N	90.21 E
Patuca ≃	236	15.50 N	84.17 W
Patuca, Punta >	236	15.51 N	84.18 W
Patuha, Gunung ∧	115a	7.10 S	107.23 E
Pātul	272b	22.45 N	88.10 E
Patul, Cerro ∧	246	2.40 S	79.03 W
Pātuli	126	23.33 N	88.15 E
Patulul	236	14.25 N	91.10 W
Patumahoe	172	37.11 S	174.50 E
Pātūr	122	20.27 N	76.56 E
Patusi	164	2.10 S	147.10 E
Patutu ∧	172	39.15 S	175.51 E
Patuxent ≃	208	38.18 N	76.25 W
Patuxent, Western Branch ≃	208	38.47 N	76.43 W
Patuxent River Naval Air Test Center ■	208	38.17 N	76.25 W
Patuxent Wildlife Research Center ⚜ [3]	284c	39.03 N	76.48 W
Patvinsuon kansallispuisto ♠	24	63.10 N	30.55 E
Patwāri	272a	28.35 N	77.27 E
Pátzcuaro	234	19.31 N	101.36 W
Pátzcuaro, Lago de ⊜	234	19.35 N	101.35 W
Patzicía	236	14.38 N	90.56 W
Patzig	54	54.28 N	13.24 E
Patzún	236	14.41 N	91.01 W
Pau	32	43.18 N	0.22 W
Pau, Gave de ≃	32	43.33 N	1.12 W
Pau Brasil	255	15.27 S	39.39 W
Paucarbamba	248	12.25 S	74.36 W
Paucarpata	248	16.26 S	71.30 W
Paucartambo	248	13.18 S	71.40 W
Paudash Lake ⊜	212	44.58 N	78.04 W
Pau dos Ferros	250	6.07 S	38.10 W
Pauh	112	2.08 S	102.48 E
Pauhunri ∧	124	27.58 N	88.50 E
Pauini	248	7.40 S	66.58 W
Pauini ≃, Bra.	246	1.42 S	62.50 W
Pauini ≃, Bra.	248	7.47 S	67.05 W
Pauk	110	21.27 N	94.27 E
Pauksa Taung ∧	110	19.55 N	94.18 E
Paul	202	42.36 N	113.46 W
Paul, Lac à ⊜	186	49.52 N	70.46 W
Paula Lima	256	21.35 S	43.29 W
Paularo	64	46.32 N	13.07 E
Paulaya ≃	236	15.51 N	85.06 W
Paulding, Ms., U.S.	194	32.01 N	89.02 W
Paulding, Oh., U.S.	216	41.08 N	84.34 W
Paulding □ [6]	216	41.08 N	84.35 W
Paulhan	32	43.32 N	3.27 E
Paulicéia	255	21.17 S	51.51 W
Paulilatino	71	40.05 N	8.46 E
Paulina Peak ∧	202	43.41 N	121.15 W
Pauline, Mount ∧	182	53.33 N	119.54 W
Paulinenaue	54	52.40 N	12.43 E
Paulínia	256	22.45 S	47.10 W
Paulino Neves	250	2.43 S	42.33 W
Paulins Kill	210	41.03 N	74.49 W
Paulins Kill ≃	210	40.55 N	75.05 W
Paulinzella ⊥	54	50.42 N	11.06 E
Paulis → Isiro	154	2.47 N	27.37 E
Paulistana	250	8.09 S	41.09 W
Paulistas	255	18.25 S	42.52 W
Paullina	198	42.58 N	95.41 W
Paull Lake ⊜	184	56.08 N	104.50 W
Paullo	62	45.25 N	9.24 E
Paulo Afonso	250	9.21 S	38.14 W
Paulo Afonso, Cachoeira de ∟	250	9.24 S	38.13 W
Paulo de Faria	255	20.02 S	49.24 W
Pauloff Harbor (Pavlof Harbor)	180	54.27 N	162.42 W
Paulpietersburg	158	27.30 S	30.51 E
Paul Roux	158	28.18 S	27.59 E
Paul-Sauvé, Parc ♠	275a	45.28 N	74.02 W
Paulsboro	208	39.49 N	75.14 W
Pauls Cross Roads	208	37.52 N	76.53 W
Paul Seamount ✣ [3]	14	23.26 N	172.36 W
Paulstown → Whitehall	48	52.41 N	7.01 W
Pauls Valley	196	34.44 N	97.13 W
Paulton, Eng., U.K.	42	51.18 N	2.30 W
Paulton, Pa., U.S.	279b	40.34 N	79.34 W
Pauma Indian Reservation ✦ [4]	228	33.22 N	116.58 W
Pāunān	272b	22.57 N	88.17 E
Paung	110	16.37 N	97.28 E
Paungbyin	110	24.16 N	94.49 E
Paungde	110	18.29 N	95.30 E
Paunggyi	110	17.19 N	96.11 E
Paup	164	3.15 S	142.35 E
Paupack	210	41.24 N	75.14 W
Pauri	124	30.09 N	78.47 E
Pausa, Dtsch.	54	50.35 N	12.00 E
Pausa, Perú	248	15.16 S	73.20 W
Pausin	264a	52.38 N	13.03 E
Paute	246	2.47 S	78.50 W
Paute ≃	246	2.46 S	78.16 W
Pauto ≃	246	5.09 N	70.55 W
Pautou → Baotou	102	40.40 N	109.59 E
Pauwalu Point >	229a	20.52 N	156.08 W
Pauwela	229a	20.56 N	156.19 W
Pauwela Point >	229a	20.57 N	156.19 W
Pavai ✦ [8]	272c	19.07 N	72.55 E
Pavai Lake ⊜	272c	19.07 N	72.55 E
Pavda	86	59.15 N	59.30 E

DEUTSCH

Name	Seite	Breite°′	Länge°′ E = Ost
Pāveh	128	35.03 N	46.22 E
Pavel'cevo	82	56.15 N	36.26 E
Pavelec	76	53.50 N	39.16 E
Pavelec Station ✦ [5]	265b	55.44 N	37.38 E
Pavia	62	45.10 N	9.10 E
Pavia □ [4]	62	45.07 N	9.08 E
Pavia, Naviglio di ≋	266b	45.27 N	9.11 E
Pavia di Udine	64	45.59 N	13.17 E
Pavilion, B.C., Can.	182	50.52 N	121.50 W
Pavilion, N.Y., U.S.	210	42.52 N	78.01 W
Pavilion Key I	220	25.42 N	81.22 W
Pavillion	200	43.14 N	108.41 W
Pavilly	50	49.34 N	0.58 E
Pāvilosta	76	56.53 N	21.14 E
Pavino	24	59.07 N	46.07 E
Pavione, Monte ∧	64	46.07 N	11.50 E
Pavlice	61	48.59 N	15.53 E
Pavlikeni	38	43.14 N	25.18 E
Pavliščevo, Ross.	82	55.11 N	35.59 E
Pavliščevo, Ross.	82	55.34 N	35.59 E
Pavlivka, Ukr.	78	47.45 N	37.14 E
Pavlivka, Ukr.	83	48.08 N	39.33 E
Pavlivka, Ukr.	83	49.36 N	38.42 E
Pavlodar	86	52.18 N	76.57 E
Pavlodar □ [8]	86	52.00 N	76.00 E
Pavlof Bay ⊂	180	55.30 N	161.32 W
Pavlof Volcano ∧ [1]	180	55.24 N	161.52 W
Pavlogradka	86	54.12 N	73.33 E
Pavlohrad	78	48.32 N	35.53 E
Pavlopil'	83	47.16 N	37.47 E
Pavlovka, Ross.	80	52.41 N	47.09 E
Pavlovka, Ross.	86	55.25 N	56.33 E
Pavlovka, Ross.	86	51.55 N	54.47 E
Pavlovo, Ross.	76	60.05 N	45.17 E
Pavlovo, Ross.	80	55.58 N	43.04 E
Pavlovo, Ross.	265a	59.56 N	30.40 E
Pavlovo, Ross.	265a	59.49 N	30.54 E
Pavlovsk, Ross.	76	59.41 N	30.27 E
Pavlovsk, Ross.	78	50.27 N	40.08 E
Pavlovsk, Ross.	86	53.20 N	82.59 E
Pavlovskaja	78	46.08 N	39.48 E
Pavlovskaja Sloboda	82	55.49 N	37.05 E
Pavlovskij, Kaz.	86	52.32 N	63.06 E
Pavlovskij, Ross.	80	57.50 N	54.51 E
Pavlovskij Posad	82	55.47 N	38.40 E
Pavlysh	78	48.55 N	33.21 E
Pavne	272c	19.05 N	73.01 E
Pavo	192	31.02 N	84.04 W
Pavón, Arg.	258	34.23 S	59.03 W
Pavón, Col.	246	3.37 N	72.15 W
Pavón, Arroyo ≃	258	34.30 S	57.05 W
Pavona	267a	41.43 N	12.37 E
Pavonia	214	40.49 N	82.26 W
Pavšino	265b	55.49 N	37.21 E
Pavšozero	76	60.38 N	35.34 E
Pavullo nel Frignano	64	44.20 N	10.50 E
Pavuna, Arroio ≃	287a	22.58 S	43.23 W
Pavuvu Island I	175e	9.03 S	159.06 E
Pavy	76	58.03 N	29.30 E
Pawai, Pulau I	271c	1.12 N	103.43 E
Pawan ≃	112	1.51 S	109.57 E
Pawāyān	124	28.04 N	80.06 E
Pawcatuck	207	41.22 N	71.50 W
Paw Creek	192	35.16 N	80.56 W
Päwesin	54	52.31 N	12.42 E
Pawhuska	196	36.40 N	96.20 W
Pawling	210	41.33 N	73.36 W
Pawn ≃	110	18.53 N	97.19 E
Pawnee, Il., U.S.	219	39.35 N	89.34 W
Pawnee, Ok., U.S.	196	36.20 N	96.48 W
Pawnee ≃	198	38.10 N	99.06 W
Pawnee City	198	40.06 N	96.09 W
Pawnee Creek ≃	198	40.34 N	103.14 W
Pawnee Rock	198	38.15 N	98.58 W
Pawni	122	20.47 N	79.38 E
Pawota	110	17.46 N	97.17 E
Paw Paw, Il., U.S.	216	41.41 N	88.59 W
Paw Paw, Mi., U.S.	216	42.13 N	85.53 W
Paw Paw, W.V., U.S.	188	39.31 N	78.27 W
Paw Paw ≃	216	42.07 N	86.29 W
Paw Paw Creek ≃	216	40.52 N	85.58 W
Paw Paw Lake	216	42.12 N	86.15 W
Paw Paw Lake ⊜	216	42.12 N	86.16 W
Pawtucket	207	41.52 N	71.22 W
Pawtucket Falls ∟	207	42.39 N	71.20 W
Paxoí I	38	39.12 N	20.12 E
Paxson	180	63.02 N	145.30 W
Paxton, Austl.	170	32.54 S	151.16 E
Paxton, Il., U.S.	216	40.27 N	88.05 W
Paxton, Ma., U.S.	207	42.18 N	71.55 W
Paxton, Ne., U.S.	198	41.07 N	101.21 W
Paxtonia	208	40.19 N	76.48 W
Paxtonville	208	40.46 N	77.05 W
Paya	236	15.37 N	85.17 W
Paya Besar	114	3.47 N	103.16 E
Payadapu	114	3.05 N	97.23 E
Payāgpur	124	27.25 N	81.48 E
Payagyi	110	17.29 N	96.32 E
Payakumbuh	112	0.14 S	100.38 E
Paya Lebar	271c	1.22 N	103.53 E
Paya Lebar Airport ⊠	271c	1.21 N	103.54 E
Payamlı	130	37.01 N	38.35 E
Payangan	115b	8.26 S	115.15 E
Payas, Cerro ∧	236	15.50 N	85.00 W
Payerne	58	46.49 N	6.56 E
Payeti	115b	9.41 S	120.20 E
Payette	202	44.04 N	116.55 W
Payette ≃	202	44.05 N	116.57 W
Payette, Middle Fork ≃	202	44.05 N	116.07 W
Payette, North Fork ≃	202	44.05 N	116.07 W
Payette, South Fork ≃	202	44.06 N	116.00 W
Payette Lake ⊜ [1]	202	44.57 N	116.05 W
Paylampur	272b	22.47 N	88.16 E
Payne	216	41.04 N	84.43 W
Payne ≃	206	45.14 N	75.08 W
Payne, Lac ⊜	176	59.25 N	74.00 W
Payne Bay ⊂	176	60.00 N	70.00 W
Payneham	168b	34.53 S	138.38 E
Paynes Creek ≃	204	40.16 N	122.11 W
Paynes Find	162	29.15 S	117.41 E
Paynesville, S. Afr.	273d	26.14 S	28.28 E
Paynesville, Mn., U.S.	198	45.22 N	94.42 W
Paynesville, Mo., U.S.	219	39.16 N	90.54 W
Paynetown State Recreation Area ♠	218	39.05 N	86.27 W
Paynton	184	53.01 N	108.56 W
Paysandú	252	32.19 S	58.05 W
Pays-Bas → Netherlands □ [1]	30	52.15 N	5.30 E
Payson, Az., U.S.	200	34.13 N	111.19 W
Payson, Il., U.S.	219	39.49 N	91.14 W
Payson, Ut,. U.S.	200	40.02 N	111.43 W
Payún, Cerro ∧	252	36.30 S	69.18 W
Paz ≃	236	13.45 N	90.08 W
Paz, Cañada de la ≃	288	34.53 S	58.38 W
Paz, Rio da ≃	250	9.14 S	52.01 W
Pazar, Tür.	130	41.11 N	40.53 E
Pazar, Tür.	130	40.17 N	36.18 E
Pazarbaşi >	130	41.10 N	30.11 E
Pazarcık	130	37.31 N	37.19 E
Pazardžik	38	42.12 N	24.20 E
Pazarköy, Tür.	130	40.55 N	32.11 E
Pazarköy, Tür.	130	39.51 N	27.24 E
Pazarören	130	38.41 N	36.11 E
Pazaryeri, Tür.	130	38.05 N	28.14 E
Pazaryeri, Tür.	130	40.00 N	29.54 E
Paz de Ariporo	246	5.53 N	71.54 W
Paz de Río	246	5.59 N	72.47 W
Pazifischer Ozean → Pacific Ocean ⊤ [1]	6	10.00 S	150.00 W
P'ažijeva Sel'ga	24	61.29 N	34.29 E
Pazin	36	45.14 N	13.56 E
Pazña	248	18.36 S	66.55 W
Paznaun V	58	47.03 N	10.20 E
Pčevža	76	59.23 N	32.20 E
Pčevža ≃	76	59.21 N	31.54 E
Pchery	54	50.10 N	14.08 E

Symbols in the index entries represent the broad categories identified in the key at the right. Symbols with superior numbers (⋏ [1]) identify subcategories (see complete key on page *I · 1*).

Symbole im Register stellen die rechts im Schlüssel erklärten Kategorien dar. Symbole mit hochgestellten Ziffern (⋏ [1]) bezeichnen Unterabteilungen einer Kategorie (vgl. vollständiger Schlüssel auf Seite *I · 1*).

Los símbolos incluídos en el texto del índice representan las grandes categorías identificadas con la clave a la derecha. Los símbolos con numeros en su parte superior (⋏ [1]) identifican las subcategorías (véase la clave completa en la página *I · 1*).

Les symboles de l'index représentent les catégories indiquées dans la légende à droite. Les symboles suivis d'un indice (⋏ [1]) représentent des sous-catégories (voir légende complète à la page *I · 1*).

Os símbolos incluídos no texto do índice representam as grandes categorias identificadas com a chave à direita. Os símbolos com números em sua parte superior (⋏ [1]) identificam as subcategorias (veja-se a chave completa à página *I · 1*).

Symbol	English	Deutsch	Español	Français	Português
∧	Mountain	Berg	Montaña	Montagne	Montanha
⋏	Mountains	Gebirge	Montañas	Montagnes	Montanhas
)(	Pass	Paß	Paso	Col	Passo
V	Valley, Canyon	Tal, Cañon	Valle, Cañón	Vallée, Canyon	Vale, Canhão
≚	Plain	Ebene	Llano	Plaine	Planície
>	Cape	Kap	Cabo	Cap	Cabo
I	Island	Insel	Isla	Île	Ilha
II	Islands	Inseln	Islas	Îles	Ilhas
⊥	Other Topographic Features	Andere Topographische Objekte	Otros Elementos Topográficos	Autres données topographiques	Outros acidentes topográficos

ESPAÑOL — FRANÇAIS — PORTUGUÊS

Nombre / Nom / Nome	Página / Page	Lat.°′	Long.°′ W = Oeste / W = Ouest
Pe	110	13.28 N	98.31 E
Pea	174w	21.10 S	175.14 W
Pea ≃	194	31.01 N	85.51 W
Peabody, Ks., U.S.	198	38.10 N	97.06 W
Peabody, Ma., U.S.	207	42.31 N	70.55 W
Peace ≃, Can.	176	59.00 N	111.25 W
Peace ≃, Fl., U.S.	220	26.55 N	82.05 W
Peace Arch ⊥	224	49.00 N	122.45 W
Peace Bridge ◆[5]	284a	42.54 N	78.55 W
Peace Canyon Dam ◆[6]	182	55.59 N	121.59 W
Peace Dale	207	41.27 N	71.29 W
Peacehaven	42	50.47 N	0.01 E
Peace River	182	56.14 N	117.17 W
Peach Creek	188	37.52 N	81.59 W
Peach Creek ≃, Tx., U.S.	222	29.24 N	97.19 W
Peach Creek ≃, Tx., U.S.	222	30.07 N	95.10 W
Peach Creek, Sandy Fork ≃	222	29.34 N	97.19 W
Peachdale	158	26.30 S	24.42 E
Peachland	182	49.46 N	119.44 W
Peach Orchard	192	33.28 N	82.04 W
Peach Springs	200	35.31 N	113.25 W
Peacock Hills ⋏[2]	176	66.05 N	110.45 W
Peacock Point >, On., Can.	212	42.47 N	79.59 W
Peacock Point >, Wake I.	174a	19.16 N	166.37 E
Peacock Sound ⋓	9	72.55 S	100.00 W
Pea Hill Branch ≃	284c	38.45 N	76.57 W
Peak Charles National Park ♠	162	32.55 S	121.06 E
Peak Crossing	171a	27.47 S	152.44 E
Peak Dale	262	53.17 N	1.52 W
Peak District National Park ♠	44	53.17 N	1.45 W
Peak Downs	166	22.12 S	148.10 E
Peake Creek ≃	162	28.05 S	136.07 E
Peaked Mountain ∧	186	46.34 N	68.49 W
Peak Forest	262	53.19 N	1.50 W
Peak Forest Canal ≊	262	53.29 N	2.06 W
Peak Hill, Austl.	162	25.38 S	118.43 E
Peak Hill, Austl.	166	32.44 S	148.12 E
Peakhurst	274a	33.58 S	151.04 E
Peakview	171b	36.04 S	149.24 E
Peäldoajvi ∧	24	69.11 N	26.36 E
Peale, Mount ∧	200	38.26 N	109.14 W
Peale Island I	174a	19.19 N	166.35 E
Peapack Brook ≃	276	40.41 N	74.39 W
Pearblossom	228	34.30 N	117.55 W
Pearce	200	31.54 N	109.49 W
Pearce, Royal Australian Air Force Station ■	168a	31.41 S	116.01 E
Pearce Point >	164	14.25 S	129.21 E
Peard Bay c	180	70.51 N	159.10 W
Pea Ridge ∧	218	38.25 N	83.36 W
Pea Ridge National Military Park ♠	194	36.29 N	94.06 W
Pearisburg	192	37.19 N	80.44 W
Pearl, Il., U.S.	194	39.28 N	90.38 W
Pearl, Ms., U.S.	194	32.16 N	90.07 W
Pearl ≃	194	30.11 N	89.32 W
Pearl, Lake ⊜	283	42.04 N	71.21 W
Pearland	222	29.33 N	95.17 W
Pearl and Hermes Atoll I[1]	14	27.55 N	175.45 W
Pearl Bank ✢[4]	116	5.49 N	119.42 E
Pearl Beach	214	42.37 N	82.35 W
Pearl City	229c	21.23 N	157.58 W
Pearl Creek ≃	198	44.15 N	98.08 W
Pearl Harbor c	229c	21.22 N	157.58 W
Pearl Harbor Naval Station ■	229c	21.21 N	157.57 W
Pearl Peak ∧	204	40.14 N	115.32 W
Pearl River, La., U.S.	194	30.22 N	89.44 W
Pearl River, N.Y., U.S.	210	41.03 N	74.01 W
Pearns Point >	240c	17.05 N	61.54 W
Pearsall	196	28.53 N	99.05 W
Pearse Island I	182	54.51 N	130.21 W
Pearsoll Peak ∧	202	42.18 N	123.50 W
Pearson	192	31.17 N	82.51 W
Pearson Lake ⊜	184	56.15 N	97.15 W
Pearston	158	32.35 S	25.08 E
Peary Land ◆[1]	16	83.00 N	35.00 W
Pease ≃	196	34.12 N	99.07 W
Pease Air Force Base ■	188	43.06 N	70.49 W
Peasedown Saint John	42	51.19 N	2.27 W
Peaster	222	32.52 N	97.52 W
Peat Inn	46	56.17 N	2.53 W
Pebane	154	17.10 S	38.08 E
Pebas	246	3.20 S	71.49 W
Pebble Beach	226	36.34 N	121.57 W
Pebble Island I	254	51.18 S	59.35 W
Peć	38	42.40 N	20.19 E
Pecan Bayou ≃	196	31.28 N	98.43 W
Pecangakan	115a	6.41 S	110.42 E
Pecan Gap	196	33.26 N	95.51 W
Peçanha	255	18.33 S	42.34 W
Peças, Ilha das I	252	25.26 S	48.19 W
Pecatonica	190	42.18 N	89.21 W
Pecatonica ≃	190	42.27 N	89.05 W
Pecatu	115b	8.50 S	115.07 E
Peccioli	66	43.33 N	10.43 E
Pécel	264c	47.29 N	19.21 E
Peçenek	130	40.25 N	32.19 E
Pečenga	24	69.33 N	31.07 E
Pečerniki	82	54.39 N	39.14 E
Pečernikovskije Vyselki	82	54.10 N	39.10 E
Pechanga Indian Reservation ◆[4]	228	33.27 N	117.04 W
Peche Island I	281	42.21 N	82.56 W
Pechenihy	78	49.52 N	36.55 E
Pechenizhyn	78	48.32 N	24.54 E
Pecheniz'ke vodoskhovyshche ⊜[1]	78	50.05 N	36.47 E
Pechera	78	48.52 N	28.42 E
Pechincha ◆[8]	287a	22.56 S	43.21 W
Pechora → Pečora ≃	24	68.13 N	54.15 E
Pechorka ≃	265b	55.35 N	38.03 E
Pechra-Jakovlevskaja	265b	55.48 N	37.58 E
Pechra-Pokrovskoje	265b	55.50 N	37.57 E
Pechu	84	43.24 N	40.49 E
Peči	80	54.48 N	44.19 E
Pecica	38	46.10 N	21.05 E
Pečicy	82	55.36 N	38.27 E
Pecixe, Ilha de I	150	11.50 N	16.05 W
Peck	190	43.15 N	82.49 W
Peck Bay c	208	39.16 N	74.37 W
Peck-Berge ⋏[2]	264a	52.36 N	13.34 E
Peckeloh	52	52.01 N	8.07 E
Peckelsheim	52	51.36 N	9.07 E
Pecket Well	262	53.46 N	2.00 W
Peck Lake ⊜	210	43.07 N	74.25 W
Peckman ≃	276	40.53 N	74.13 W
Peconic ≃	207	40.55 N	72.37 W
Pečora	24	65.10 N	57.11 E
Pečora ≃	24	68.13 N	54.15 E
Pecora, Capo >	71	39.27 N	8.23 E
Pecoraro, Monte ∧	68	38.32 N	16.20 E
Pečoro-Ilyčskij zapovednik ◆[4]	24	62.20 N	59.00 E
Pečorskaja guba c	24	68.40 N	54.45 E
Pečorskoje more ⫪[2]	24	70.00 N	54.00 E
Pečory	76	57.49 N	27.36 E
Pecos, N.M., U.S.	200	35.34 N	105.40 W
Pecos, Tx., U.S.	196	31.25 N	103.29 W
Pecos ≃	178	29.42 N	101.22 W
Pecos National Monument ♠	200	35.26 N	105.56 W
Pecos Plains ≚	196	33.20 N	104.30 W
Pecq	50	50.41 N	3.20 E
Pecquencourt	50	50.23 N	3.13 E
Pecqueuse	261	48.39 N	2.03 E
Pécs	30	46.05 N	18.13 E
Pedana	122	16.16 N	81.10 E
Pedara	70	37.38 N	15.04 E
Pedas	114	2.37 N	102.04 E
Pedasí	246	7.32 N	80.02 W
Pedaso	66	43.06 N	13.50 E
Peddāpuram	122	17.05 N	82.08 E
Pedder, Lake ⊜[1]	166	42.54 S	146.12 E
Peddie	158	33.12 S	27.07 E
Peddocks Island I	283	42.17 N	70.56 W
Pededze ≃	76	56.56 N	26.54 E
Pedernales, Arg.	252	35.15 S	59.39 W
Pedernales, Méx.	234	19.08 N	101.28 W
Pedernales, Rep. Dom.	238	18.02 N	71.45 W
Pedernales, Ven.	246	9.58 N	62.16 W
Pedernales ≃	196	30.26 N	98.04 W
Pedernales, Salar de ≚	252	26.15 S	69.10 W
Pedernales Falls State Park ♠	196	30.20 N	98.14 W
Pederobba	64	45.53 N	11.58 E
Pedersborg	41	55.27 N	11.34 E
Pederstrup	41	54.54 N	11.16 E
Pedesina	58	46.05 N	9.33 E
Pedhoulás	130	34.58 N	32.50 E
Pedja ≃	76	58.25 N	26.11 E
Pedley	228	33.59 N	117.28 W
Pé do Morro	256	22.20 S	44.57 W
Pedra	250	8.30 S	36.57 W
Pedra Azul	255	16.01 S	41.16 W
Pedra Bela	256	22.47 S	46.27 W
Pedra Branca	250	5.27 S	39.43 W
Pedra de Guaratiba ◆[8]	256	23.00 S	43.39 W
Pedra Grande, Recifes da ✢[2]	255	17.45 S	38.58 W
Pedra Lume	150a	16.46 N	22.54 W
Pedralva	256	22.14 S	45.28 W
Pedras	250	2.48 S	57.16 W
Pedras, Rio das ≃	287a	22.51 S	43.01 W
Pedras de Fogo	250	7.23 S	35.07 W
Pedra Selada	256	22.21 S	44.26 W
Pedras Negras	248	12.51 S	62.54 W
Pedras Salgadas	34	41.32 N	7.36 W
Pedraza	246	10.11 N	74.55 W
Pedregal, Pan.	236	8.22 N	82.26 W
Pedregal, Ven.	246	11.01 N	70.08 W
Pedregulho	255	20.16 S	47.29 W
Pedreira	256	22.43 S	46.55 W
Pedreira ≃	250	0.12 N	50.47 W
Pedreiras	250	4.34 S	44.39 W
Pedriceña	232	25.06 N	103.47 W
Pedricktown	208	39.46 N	75.24 W
Pedrinhas	250	11.12 S	37.41 W
Pedro, Point >	122	9.50 N	80.14 E
Pedro Afonso	250	8.59 S	48.11 W
Pedro Antonio de los Santos	234	21.36 N	98.58 W
Pedro Avelino	250	5.31 S	36.23 W
Pedro Bay	180	59.47 N	154.07 W
Pedro Betancourt	240p	22.44 N	81.17 W
Pedro Cays II	238	17.00 N	77.50 W
Pedro de Olla, Cerro ∧	234	17.07 N	97.40 W
Pedro do Rio	256	22.20 S	43.09 W
Pedrógão Grande	34	39.55 N	8.09 W
Pedro Gomes	255	18.04 S	54.32 W
Pedro II	250	4.25 S	41.28 W
Pedro II, Ilha I	246	1.10 N	66.40 W
Pedro Juan Caballero	252	22.34 S	55.37 W
Pedro Leopoldo	255	19.38 S	44.03 W
Pedro Luro	252	39.29 S	62.41 W
Pedro Muñoz	34	39.24 N	2.58 W
Pedro Osório	252	31.51 S	52.45 W
Pedro R. Fernández	252	28.45 S	58.39 W
Pedro Teixeira	256	21.43 S	43.44 W
Pedro Velho	250	6.26 S	35.14 W
Peebinga	166	34.56 S	140.55 E
Peebles, Scot., U.K.	46	55.39 N	3.12 W
Peebles, Oh., U.S.	218	38.56 N	83.24 W
Peedamullah	162	21.50 S	115.38 E
Pee Dee ≃	192	34.43 N	79.52 W
Peekaboo Mountain ∧[2]	188	45.45 N	67.53 W
Peekskill	210	41.17 N	73.55 W
Peel, Austl.	170	33.19 S	149.38 E
Peel, I. of Man	44	54.13 N	4.40 W
Peel □[6]	212	43.45 N	79.47 W
Peel ≃	180	67.37 N	134.40 W
Peel Channel ≃[1]	180	68.13 N	135.00 W
Peel Fell ∧	44	55.17 N	2.35 W
Peel Inlet c	168a	32.35 S	115.44 E
Peel Island I	171a	27.30 S	153.22 E
Pe Ell	224	46.34 N	123.17 W
Peel Point >	176	73.22 N	114.35 W
Peel Sound ⋓	176	73.15 N	96.30 W
Peene ≃	54	54.09 N	13.46 E
Peenemünde	54	54.08 N	13.46 E
Peepeekisis Indian Reserve ◆[4]	184	50.52 N	103.24 W
Peer	56	51.08 N	5.28 E
Peerless	202	48.46 N	105.49 W
Peers	182	53.40 N	116.00 W
Peesane	184	52.52 N	103.36 W
Peetz	198	40.57 N	103.06 W
Peetzsee ⊜	264a	52.26 N	13.50 E
Pefferlaw	212	44.19 N	79.12 W
Pefferlaw Brook ≃	212	44.15 N	79.13 W
Pegasus, Port c	172	47.12 S	167.41 E
Pegasus Bay c	172	43.20 S	173.00 E
Pegau	54	51.10 N	12.14 E
Pegli	62	44.26 N	8.48 E
Peglia, Monte ∧	66	42.49 N	12.13 E
Pegnitz	60	49.45 N	11.33 E
Pegnitz ≃	60	49.29 N	11.00 E
Pego	34	38.51 N	0.07 W
Pegolotte	64	45.12 N	12.02 E
Pegswood	44	55.11 N	1.38 W
Pegtymel' ≃	180	69.25 N	174.35 E
Pegtymel'skij chrebet ⋏	180	68.30 N	177.00 E
Pegu → Bago	110	17.20 N	96.29 E
Pegu ≃	110	16.47 N	96.13 E
Pegueros	234	20.57 N	102.40 W
Peguis Indian Reserve ◆[4]	184	51.20 N	97.35 W
Pegu Yoma ⋏	110	19.00 N	95.50 E
Pegwell Bay c	42	51.18 N	1.26 E
Pegyš	24	63.26 N	50.30 E
Pehčevo	38	41.46 N	22.54 E
Pehladpur ◆[8]	272a	28.35 N	77.06 E
Pehlivanköy	130	41.21 N	26.55 E
Pehowa	124	29.59 N	76.35 E
Pehuajó	252	35.48 S	61.53 W
Pehula	26	61.17 N	22.42 E
Peian → Bei'an	89	48.16 N	126.36 E
Peiching → Beijing	105	39.55 N	116.25 E
Peigan Indian Reserve ◆[4]	182	49.35 N	113.40 W
Peihai → Beihai	102	21.29 N	109.05 E
Peij	52	51.06 N	5.53 E
Peijiatun	98	39.19 N	121.41 E
Peikang	100	23.34 N	120.18 E
Peikang ≃	100	23.31 N	120.08 E
Peikant'ang Tao I	100	26.13 N	119.59 E
Peilstein im Mühlviertel	60	48.37 N	13.53 E
Peinan	100	22.47 N	121.07 E
Peinan ≃	100	22.46 N	121.10 E
Peine	52	52.19 N	10.13 E
Peine, Pointe à >	240d	15.23 N	61.15 W
Peinnechaung I	110	19.59 N	93.04 E
Peio	64	46.22 N	10.40 E
Peip'ing → Beijing	105	39.55 N	116.25 E
Peipsi järv (Čudskoje ozero) ⊜	76	58.45 N	27.25 E
Peipus, Lake → Čudskoje ozero ⊜	76	58.45 N	27.25 E
Peïra-Cava	62	43.56 N	7.22 E
Peirce, Cape >	180	58.35 N	161.47 W
Peisey-Nancroix	62	45.33 N	6.45 E
Peissenberg	64	47.48 N	11.04 E
Peissenberg ∧, Dtsch.	60	47.48 N	11.01 E
Peissenberg ∧, Dtsch.	64	47.48 N	11.01 E
Peiting	58	47.47 N	10.55 E
Peit'ou ◆[8]	269d	25.08 N	121.30 E
Peitz	54	51.51 N	14.24 E
Peixe	255	12.03 S	48.32 W
Peixe, Rio do ≃, Bra.	255	14.06 S	50.51 W
Peixe, Rio do ≃, Bra.	255	21.31 S	51.58 W
Peixe, Rio do ≃, Bra.	256	23.24 S	45.28 W
Peixe, Rio do ≃, Bra.	256	21.55 S	43.21 W
Peixe, Rio do ≃, Bra.	256	22.23 S	46.51 W
Peixe, Rio do ≃, Bra.	256	23.12 S	46.06 W
Peixe, Rio do ≃, Bra.	256	21.38 S	45.11 W
Peixe-Boi	250	1.12 S	47.18 W
Peixes, Rio dos ≃	250	10.42 S	57.56 W
Peixian (Yunhe), Zhg.	98	34.21 N	117.59 E
Peixian, Zhg.	98	34.44 N	116.59 E
Peixoto, Reprêsa de ⊜[1]	255	20.10 S	47.20 W
Peixoto de Azevedo ≃	250	10.06 S	55.31 W
Peiziyan	98	35.07 N	115.01 E
Pejantan, Pulau I	112	0.07 N	107.14 E
Pejelagartero	234	18.04 N	93.45 W
Pek ≃	38	44.46 N	21.33 E
Pekalongan	115a	6.53 S	109.40 E
Pekan	114	3.30 N	103.25 E
Pekanbaru	112	0.32 N	101.27 E
Pekanheran	112	0.21 S	102.26 E
Pekin, Il., U.S.	190	40.34 N	89.38 W
Pekin, In., U.S.	218	38.29 N	86.01 W
Pekin, N.Y., U.S.	284a	43.10 N	78.53 W
Pekin, Oh., U.S.	214	40.43 N	81.07 W
Pékin → Beijing, Zhg.	105	39.55 N	116.25 E
Peking → Beijing	105	39.55 N	116.25 E
Peking National Library ʋ	271a	39.56 N	116.22 E
Peking Railway Station ◆[5]	271a	39.54 N	116.26 E
Peking University ʋ[2]	271a	39.59 N	116.18 E
Peking Zoo ♠	271a	39.56 N	116.19 E
Peklino	76	53.33 N	33.32 E
Pekša ≃	80	55.53 N	39.40 E
Pektubajevo	80	57.02 N	48.23 E
Pekul'nej, chrebet ⋏	180	66.00 N	175.00 E
Pekul'nejskoje, ozero ⊜	180	62.40 N	177.00 E
Péla	150	7.37 N	9.07 W
Pelabuhandagang	112	1.08 S	103.05 E
Pelabuhan Kelang	114	3.00 N	101.24 E
Pelabuhanratu	115a	6.59 S	106.33 E
Pelabuhanratu, Teluk c	115a	7.03 S	106.27 E
Pel'a-Chovanskaja	80	54.36 N	44.56 E
Pelado, Volcán ∧[1]	286a	19.09 N	99.13 W
Pelagie, Isole II	70a	35.40 N	12.40 E
Pelago	66	43.46 N	11.30 E
Pelahatchie	194	32.18 N	89.47 W
Pelahiyivka	83	48.06 N	38.36 E
Pelaihari	112	3.48 S	114.45 E
Pelalawan	112	0.27 N	102.05 E
Pelat, Mont ∧	62	44.16 N	6.42 E
Pelawan	114	2.47 N	102.55 E
Pełczyce	30	53.03 N	15.18 E
Pélé, Mont ∧	152	3.15 S	11.14 E
Pelechuco	248	14.48 S	69.04 W
Peleduj	74	59.36 N	112.45 E
Pelée, Montagne ∧	240e	14.48 N	61.10 W
Pelee, Point >	214	41.54 N	82.30 W
Pelee Island I	214	41.46 N	82.39 W
Pelee Passage ⋓	214	41.52 N	82.37 W
Pelega, Vârful ∧	38	45.22 N	22.54 E
Pelekech ∧	154	3.48 N	35.04 E
Peleliu I	175b	7.01 N	134.15 E
Peleng, Pulau I	112	1.20 S	123.10 E
Peleng, Selat ⋓	112	1.10 S	122.45 E
Pelf, Monte ∧	64	46.14 N	12.12 E
Pelham, On., Can.	212	43.02 N	79.17 W
Pelham, Al., U.S.	194	33.17 N	86.48 W
Pelham, Ga., U.S.	192	31.07 N	84.09 W
Pelham, Ma., U.S.	207	42.23 N	72.24 W
Pelham, N.H., U.S.	207	42.44 N	71.19 W
Pelham, N.Y., U.S.	276	40.54 N	73.48 W
Pelham Bay c	276	40.52 N	73.47 W
Pelham Bay Park ♠	276	40.52 N	73.49 W
Pelham Manor	276	40.53 N	73.48 W
Pelhřimov	30	49.26 N	15.13 E
Pelican	180	57.57 N	136.14 W
Pelican ≃	198	46.17 N	96.08 W
Pelican, Punta >	200	31.19 N	113.43 W
Pelican Bay c	184	52.45 N	100.20 W
Pelican Island I, Mo., U.S.	219	38.52 N	90.18 W
Pelican Island I, Tx., U.S.	222	29.20 N	94.48 W
Pelican Lagoon c	168b	35.50 S	137.47 E
Pelican Lake	190	45.30 N	89.10 W
Pelican Lake ⊜, Ab., Can.	182	55.47 N	113.15 W
Pelican Lake ⊜, Mb., Can.	184	53.50 N	96.08 W
Pelican Lake ⊜, Mb., Can.	184	52.30 N	100.20 W
Pelican Lake ⊜, Mb., Can.	184	49.20 N	99.35 W
Pelican Lake ⊜, Sk., Can.	184	50.32 N	106.00 W
Pelican Lake ⊜, Sk., Can.	184	55.08 N	103.00 W
Pelican Lake ⊜, Mn., U.S.	190	48.05 N	92.54 W
Pelican Lake ⊜, S.D., U.S.	198	44.52 N	97.11 W
Pelican Mountain ∧	182	55.35 N	113.40 W
Pelican Narrows	184	55.10 N	102.56 W
Pelican Point >	168b	34.48 S	138.29 E
Pelican Rapids, Mb., Can.	184	52.45 N	100.42 W
Pelican Rapids, Mn., U.S.	198	46.34 N	96.04 W
Pelileo	246	1.19 S	78.32 W
Pelinia	38	47.53 N	27.50 E
Pelister ∧	38	41.00 N	21.12 E
Pelješac, Poluotok >[1]	36	42.58 N	17.20 E
Pelkosenniemi	24	67.07 N	27.30 E
Pelkum, Dtsch.	52	51.39 N	7.46 E
Pelkum, Dtsch.	263	51.40 N	7.24 E
Pella, S. Afr.	158	29.01 S	19.06 E
Pella, Ia., U.S.	190	41.24 N	92.54 W
Pélla ⊥	38	40.45 N	22.33 E
Pellaro	68	38.01 N	15.39 E
Pell City	194	33.35 N	86.17 W
Pellechia, Monte ∧	66	42.07 N	12.52 E
Pellegrini	252	36.16 S	63.09 W
Pellegrini, Lago ⊜	252	38.40 S	68.00 W
Pellegrino, Cozzo ∧	68	39.45 N	16.03 E
Pellegrino, Monte ∧	70	38.10 N	13.21 E
Pellegrino Parmense	64	44.44 N	9.55 E
Pellendorf	264b	48.06 N	16.27 E
Peller, Monte ∧	64	46.18 N	10.57 E
Pellestrina, Litorale di ⩋[2]	64	45.16 N	12.18 E
Pelletier Lake ⊜	184	56.30 N	97.00 W
Pellice ≃	62	44.50 N	7.38 E
Pellingen	56	49.40 N	6.40 E
Pell Lake	216	42.32 N	88.21 W
Pello	24	66.47 N	24.00 E
Pellston	190	45.33 N	84.47 W
Pellworm I	30	54.31 N	8.38 E
Pelly	184	51.52 N	101.55 W
Pelly ≃	180	62.47 N	137.19 W
Pelly Bay c	176	68.53 N	89.51 W
Pelly Crossing	180	62.50 N	136.35 W
Pelly Lake ⊜	176	65.59 N	101.12 W
Pelly Mountains ⋏	180	62.00 N	133.00 W
Pelón, Cerro ∧	234	20.05 N	99.55 W
Peloncillo Mountains ⋏	200	32.15 N	109.00 W
Pelopónnisos □[4]	38	37.30 N	22.30 E
Pelopónnisos (Peloponnesus) >[1]	38	37.30 N	22.00 E
Peloritani, Monti ⋏	70	38.03 N	15.20 E
Pelotas	252	31.46 S	52.20 W
Pelotas ≃	252	27.28 S	51.55 W
Pelplin	30	53.56 N	18.42 E
Pelque ≃	254	51.03 S	70.58 W
Pelsin	54	53.48 N	13.40 E
Pelusium Bay → Ţīnah, Khalīj aţ- c	140	31.08 N	32.40 E
Pel'ušn'a	76	58.56 N	32.52 E
Pélussin	62	45.25 N	4.41 E
Pelvo d'Elva ∧	62	44.33 N	7.02 E
Pelym	86	59.38 N	63.05 E
Pemadumcook Lake ⊜	188	45.40 N	68.55 W
Pemalang	115a	6.54 S	109.22 E
Pemalang, Ujung >	115a	6.47 S	109.29 E
Pemali ≃	115a	6.47 S	109.01 E
Pemangkat	112	1.10 N	108.58 E
Pematang	112	0.12 S	102.04 E
Pematangsiantar	114	2.57 N	99.03 E
Pematangtanahjawa	114	2.53 N	99.12 E
Pemba, Moç.	154	12.58 S	40.30 E
Pemba, Zam.	154	16.31 S	27.22 E
Pemba I	154	5.10 S	39.48 E
Pemba Channel ⋓	154	5.10 S	39.20 E
Pembarisan, Pegunungan ⋏	115a	7.13 S	108.45 E
Pemberton, Austl.	162	34.28 S	116.01 E
Pemberton, B.C., Can.	182	50.20 N	122.48 W
Pemberton, Eng., U.K.	262	53.32 N	2.41 W
Pemberton, N.J., U.S.	208	39.58 N	74.41 W
Pemberton, Oh., U.S.	216	40.18 N	84.02 W
Pemberton Airport ⊠	285	39.59 N	74.41 W
Pemberton Heights	285	39.58 N	74.41 W
Pemberville	214	41.24 N	83.27 W
Pembina	198	48.57 N	97.14 W
Pembina ≃, Ab., Can.	182	54.45 N	114.15 W
Pembina ≃, N.A.	184	48.57 N	97.14 W
Pembina Hills ⋏[2]	198	49.10 N	98.25 W
Pembine	190	45.38 N	87.59 W
Pembrey	42	51.42 N	4.16 W
Pembroke, On., Can.	190	45.49 N	77.07 W
Pembroke, Wales, U.K.	42	51.41 N	4.55 W
Pembroke, Ga., U.S.	192	32.08 N	81.37 W
Pembroke, Ky., U.S.	194	36.46 N	87.21 W
Pembroke, Me., U.S.	188	44.57 N	67.09 W
Pembroke, N.Y., U.S.	210	43.00 N	78.27 W
Pembroke, N.C., U.S.	192	34.40 N	79.11 W
Pembroke, Va., U.S.	192	37.19 N	80.38 W
Pembroke, Cape >	176	62.56 N	81.55 W
Pembroke Castle ⊥	42	51.41 N	4.56 W
Pembroke Dock	42	51.42 N	4.56 W
Pembroke Pines	220	26.00 N	80.13 W
Pembrokeshire Coast National Park ♠	42	51.47 N	5.06 W
Pembuang	112	2.34 S	112.19 E
Pembuang ≃	112	3.24 S	112.33 E
Pembury	42	51.09 N	0.20 E
Pemfling	60	49.16 N	12.37 E
Pemichigamau Lake ⊜	184	56.16 N	99.33 W
Pemigewasset ≃	188	43.26 N	71.40 W
Pemmican Portage	184	53.56 N	102.17 W
Pemuco	252	36.58 S	72.06 W
Pemynoos Indian Reserve ◆[4]	182	50.29 N	121.15 W
Pemzašen	84	40.35 N	43.57 E
Pena, Parque de ♠	266c	38.47 N	9.23 W
Peña Barroza	248	22.10 S	67.25 W
Peña Blanca	236	8.27 N	81.40 W
Peñafiel, Esp.	34	41.36 N	4.07 W
Penafiel, Port.	34	41.12 N	8.17 W
Pen'agino	265b	55.50 N	37.21 E
Peña Gorda, Cerro ∧	234	20.44 N	104.50 W
Peña Grande ◆[8]	266a	40.29 N	3.44 W
Pen'akša	80	56.22 N	44.56 E
Peñalara ∧	34	40.51 N	3.57 W
Peñalolén	286e	33.29 S	70.32 W
Pena-Lunanga	154	4.16 S	28.10 E
Penalva	250	3.18 S	45.10 W
Penambulai, Pulau I	164	6.24 S	134.48 E
Penang → George Town	114	5.25 N	100.20 E
Penanjung, Teluk c	115a	7.45 S	108.37 E
Penápolis	255	21.24 S	50.04 W
Peñaranda de Bracamonte	34	40.54 N	5.12 W
Pen Argyl	210	40.52 N	75.15 W
Penaron	114	4.38 N	97.40 E
Peñarroya-Pueblonuevo	34	38.18 N	5.16 W
Penarth	42	51.27 N	3.11 W
Peñas, Cabo de >	34	43.39 N	5.51 W
Penas, Golfo de c	254	47.22 S	74.50 W
Penasco	200	36.10 N	105.41 W
Peñasco, Rio ≃	196	32.45 N	104.19 W
Penataquit Creek ≃	276	40.43 N	73.14 W
Penbrook	208	40.16 N	76.50 W
Pencader	42	52.01 N	4.16 W
Pencahue	252	35.24 S	71.49 W
Pence	190	46.25 N	90.16 W
Pen Centre ◆[9]	284a	43.08 N	79.14 W
Penchard	261	48.59 N	2.52 E
Penck Trough V	9	73.00 S	2.45 W
Penco	252	36.44 S	72.59 W
Pencoed	42	51.32 N	3.30 W
Pendang, Indon.	112	1.28 S	114.51 E
Pendang, Malay.	114	6.00 N	100.28 E
Pendé ≃	146	7.55 N	16.36 E
Pendéli	267c	38.03 N	23.52 E
Pendelikón Óros ⋏	267c	38.06 N	23.54 E
Pendembu, S.L.	150	8.06 N	10.42 W
Pendembu, S.L.	150	9.06 N	12.12 W
Pendências	250	5.15 S	36.43 W
Pendeng	114	4.06 N	97.36 E
Pender	198	42.06 N	96.42 W
Pender Bay c	162	16.45 S	122.42 E
Pendhar	272c	19.04 N	73.06 E
Pendjari ≃	150	10.54 N	0.51 E
Pendjari, Parc National de la ♠	150	11.20 N	1.15 E
Pendlebury	262	53.31 N	2.20 W
Pendle Hill	274a	33.48 S	150.57 E
Pendle Hill ∧[2]	44	53.52 N	2.17 W
Pendleton, In., U.S.	218	39.59 N	85.44 W
Pendleton, N.Y., U.S.	284a	43.05 N	78.44 W
Pendleton, Or., U.S.	202	45.40 N	118.47 W
Pendleton, S.C., U.S.	192	34.39 N	82.47 W
Pendleton □[6]	218	38.42 N	84.22 W
Pendolo	112	2.05 S	120.42 E
Pendopo	112	3.17 S	103.52 E
Pend Oreille ≃	202	49.04 N	117.37 W
Pend Oreille, Lake ⊜	202	48.10 N	116.11 W
Pend Oreille, Mount ∧	202	48.25 N	116.10 W
Pendotiba ≃	287a	22.53 S	43.02 W
Pendžikent	85	39.29 N	67.35 E
Penebel	115b	8.25 S	115.09 E
Penedo	250	10.17 S	36.36 W
Penedono	34	40.59 N	7.24 W
Penela	34	40.02 N	8.23 W
Penelope	222	31.52 N	96.56 W
Penetang Harbour c	212	44.47 N	79.57 W
Penetanguishene	212	44.47 N	79.55 W
Penfield, Il., U.S.	216	40.18 N	87.57 W
Penfield, N.Y., U.S.	210	43.07 N	77.28 W
Penfield, Oh., U.S.	214	41.10 N	82.08 W
Penfield, Pa., U.S.	214	41.13 N	78.34 W
Penganga ≃	122	19.53 N	79.09 E
Pengastulan	115b	8.11 S	114.55 E
Peng Chau I	271d	22.17 N	114.02 E
P'engchia Yü I	100	25.38 N	122.04 E
Penge, S. Afr.	156	24.22 S	30.13 E
Penge, Zaïre	154	5.31 S	24.37 E
Penge ◆[8]	260	51.25 N	0.04 W
Penggong	106	30.27 N	119.57 E
Penggongmiao	100	26.07 N	113.34 E
Penghu	100	25.24 N	118.11 E
P'enghu Ch'üntao (Pescadores) II	100	23.30 N	119.30 E
P'enghu Shuitao ⋓	100	23.30 N	119.50 E
Pengiki, Pulau I	112	0.15 N	108.03 E
Pengjiachang	107	30.36 N	103.53 E
Pengjialouzi	104	41.56 N	123.40 E
Pengjiawan	100	32.16 N	114.04 E
Pengjiawu	105	39.41 N	117.10 E
Pengkalan Baharu	114	4.28 N	100.38 E
Pengkou	100	25.32 N	116.42 E
Penglai (Dengzhou)	98	37.48 N	120.42 E
Penglaizhen	107	30.36 N	105.14 E
Penglang	106	31.23 N	121.05 E
Pengnan	107	30.25 N	105.53 E
Pengpu → Bengbu	100	32.58 N	117.24 E
Pengshan	107	30.13 N	103.52 E
Pengshi	100	30.28 N	113.10 E
Pengshui	102	29.18 N	108.09 E
Penguin	166	41.07 S	146.04 E
Pengwaluote Shan ∧	120	33.30 N	86.35 E
Pengxi	102	30.49 N	105.40 E
Pengxian	102	31.00 N	103.50 E
Pengze	100	29.53 N	116.33 E
Pengzhai	100	24.23 N	115.06 E
Pengzhuangzi	105	40.06 N	114.51 E
Penha	252	26.46 S	48.39 W
Penha ◆[8]	287a	22.49 S	43.17 W
Penha de França ◆[8]	287b	23.32 S	46.32 W
Penha Longa, Bra.	256	22.04 S	43.05 W
Penhalonga, Zimb.	154	18.54 S	32.40 E
Penhold	182	52.08 N	113.52 W
Penhold, Canadian Forces Base ■	182	52.12 N	113.53 W
Penhorn Creek ≃	276	40.45 N	74.05 W
Penhsi → Benxi	104	41.18 N	123.45 E
Peniche	34	39.21 N	9.23 W
Penicuik	46	55.50 N	3.14 W
Penida, Nusa I	115b	8.44 S	115.32 E
Penig	54	50.56 N	12.41 E
Peningo Neck >[1]	276	40.57 N	73.41 W
Peninjai	112	1.26 S	101.50 E
Peninsula Lake ⊜	212	45.20 N	79.05 W
Peninsula State Park ♠	190	45.09 N	87.14 W
Peníscola	34	40.21 N	0.25 E
Penistone	44	53.32 N	1.37 W
Penitas	196	26.17 N	98.27 W
Penitencia Creek ≃	282	37.27 N	121.55 W
Penitente, Serra do ⋏[2]	250	8.45 S	46.20 W
Penjamillo [de Degollado]	234	20.06 N	101.54 W
Pénjamo	234	20.26 N	101.44 W
Penketh	262	53.23 N	2.40 W
Penki → Benxi	104	41.18 N	123.45 E
Penkino	82	54.50 N	38.53 E
Penkridge	42	52.44 N	2.07 W
Penkun	54	53.17 N	14.14 E
Pen Lake ⊜	212	45.28 N	78.23 W
Penllyn	285	40.10 N	75.15 W
Penmaenmawr	44	53.16 N	3.54 W
Penmarc'h, Pointe de >	32	47.48 N	4.22 W
Penn	279b	40.20 N	79.38 W
Penna, Punta della >	66	42.10 N	14.43 E
Pennabilli	66	43.49 N	12.16 E
Penn Acres	285	39.40 N	75.34 W
Pennant Hills	274a	33.44 S	151.04 E
Pennant Hills Park ♠	274a	33.45 S	151.06 E
Pennant Point >	186	44.26 N	63.39 W
Pennant Station	184	50.33 N	108.12 W
Pennask Lake ⊜	182	50.00 N	120.05 W
Pennask Mountain ∧	182	49.53 N	120.07 W
Penn Brook ≃	283	42.44 N	70.59 W
Penn Cove c	224	48.14 N	122.41 W
Penn Cove Park	224	48.14 N	122.41 W
Penndel	285	40.09 N	74.55 W
Penne	66	42.27 N	13.55 E
Penne, Punta >	68	40.41 N	17.56 E
Penne-d'Agenais	32	44.23 N	0.49 E
Pennedepie	50	49.25 N	0.11 E
Pennel Creek ≃	198	46.34 N	104.52 W
Penneru ≃	122	14.35 N	80.10 E
Pennes (Pens)	64	46.47 N	11.25 E
Pennes, Val di V	64	46.47 N	11.25 E
Penneshaw	168b	35.44 S	137.56 E
Penngrove	226	38.18 N	122.40 W
Penn Hills	214	40.28 N	79.51 W
Penn Hills Center ◆[9]	279b	40.28 N	79.50 W
Pennines ⋏	44	54.10 N	2.05 W
Pennines, Alpes ⋏	58	46.05 N	7.50 E
Penningby	40	59.41 N	18.40 E
Penningby slott ⊥	40	59.41 N	18.40 E
Pennington, N.J., U.S.	208	40.19 N	74.47 W
Pennington, Tx., U.S.	222	31.11 N	95.14 W
Pennington ≃[1]	150	4.45 N	5.35 E
Pennington Gap	192	36.45 N	83.01 W
Pennino, Monte ∧	66	43.06 N	12.53 E
Penn Run	214	40.37 N	79.01 W
Pennsauken	208	39.58 N	75.04 W
Pennsauken Creek ≃	285	39.59 N	75.03 W
Pennsauken Creek, North Branch ≃	285	39.58 N	75.01 W
Pennsauken Creek, South Branch ≃	285	39.58 N	75.01 W
Pennsboro	188	39.17 N	80.58 W
Penns Brook ≃	276	40.43 N	74.32 W
Pennsburg	208	40.23 N	75.29 W
Pennsbury Heights	285	40.12 N	74.49 W
Pennsbury Manor ⊥	285	40.08 N	74.46 W
Penn's Cave ⩋[5]	210	40.53 N	77.36 W
Penns Creek	210	40.52 N	77.04 W
Penns Creek ≃	210	40.48 N	76.51 W
Pennsdale	210	41.15 N	76.48 W
Penns Grove	208	39.43 N	75.28 W
Pennside	208	40.20 N	75.53 W
Penns Neck	276	40.20 N	74.38 W
Pennsuco	220	25.53 N	80.22 W
Pennsville	208	39.39 N	75.31 W
Penns Woods	279b	40.21 N	79.46 W
Pennsylvania □[3], U.S.	178	40.45 N	77.30 W
Pennsylvania □[3], U.S.	188	40.45 N	77.30 W
Pennsylvania, University of ʋ[2]	285	39.57 N	75.12 W
Pennsylvania Canal ≊	285	40.13 N	74.47 W
Pennsylvania Station ◆[5]	276	40.45 N	74.00 W
Penn Valley, Ca., U.S.	226	39.12 N	121.11 W
Penn Valley, Pa., U.S.	285	40.01 N	75.16 W
Penn Valley Terrace	285	40.11 N	74.47 W
Pennville	216	40.29 N	85.08 W
Penn Wynne	285	39.59 N	75.16 W
Penny	182	53.50 N	121.17 W
Penn Yan	210	42.39 N	77.03 W
Pennycutaway ≃	184	56.43 N	92.44 W
Penny Hill	285	39.46 N	75.30 W
Penny Ice Cap ⊼	176	67.10 N	66.00 W
Pennypack Creek ≃	285	40.02 N	75.00 W
Pennypack Park ♠	285	40.04 N	75.03 W
Penny Strait ⋓	176	76.30 N	97.00 W
Peno	76	56.55 N	32.45 E
Penobscot	210	41.10 N	75.52 W
Penobscot ≃	188	44.30 N	68.50 W
Penobscot, East Branch ≃	186	45.35 N	68.32 W
Penobscot, West Branch ≃	188	45.35 N	68.32 W
Penobscot Bay c	188	44.15 N	68.52 W
Peno Creek ≃	219	39.32 N	91.16 W
Pen'ok	86	55.30 N	81.34 E
Penola	166	37.23 S	140.50 E
Peñoles	196	25.39 N	104.30 W
Peñón Blanco	232	24.47 N	104.02 W
Penong	162	31.55 S	133.01 E
Penonomé	236	8.31 N	80.22 W
Penrhyn I[1]	14	9.00 S	158.00 W
Penrhyn Bay	44	53.19 N	3.45 W
Penrhyndeudraeth	42	52.56 N	4.04 W
Penrith, Austl.	170	33.45 S	150.42 E
Penrith, Eng., U.K.	44	54.40 N	2.44 W
Penryn, Eng., U.K.	42	50.09 N	5.06 W
Penryn, Ca., U.S.	226	38.51 N	121.10 W
Penryn, Pa., U.S.	208	40.12 N	76.22 W
Pens → Pennes	64	46.47 N	11.25 E
Pensacola	194	30.25 N	87.13 W
Pensacola Bay c	194	30.25 N	87.06 W
Pensacola Mountains ⋏	9	83.45 S	55.00 W
Pensacola Naval Air Station ■	194	30.21 N	87.19 W
Pensacola Seamount ✢[3]	14	18.17 N	157.20 W
Pensaukee ≃	190	44.49 N	87.55 W
Pensby	262	53.21 N	3.06 W
Pense	184	50.25 N	105.00 W
Penshaw	44	54.53 N	1.29 W
Pensiangan	112	4.33 N	116.19 E
Pensilva	42	50.30 N	4.25 W
Pensilvania	246	5.31 N	75.05 W
Pentagna	256	22.09 S	43.45 W
Pentagon ʋ	284c	38.52 N	77.03 W
Pentagon Mountain ∧	202	47.56 N	113.07 W
Pentecost □[8]	175f	15.45 S	168.12 E
Pentecoste	250	3.48 S	39.17 W
Pentecôte I	175f	15.42 S	168.10 E
Pentecôte ≃	186	49.47 N	67.10 W
Pentecôte, Lac ⊜	186	49.53 N	67.20 W
Penticton	182	49.30 N	119.35 W
Penticton Indian Reserve ◆[4]	182	49.30 N	119.40 W
Pentire Point >	42	50.36 N	4.55 W
Pentland	166	20.32 S	145.24 E
Pentland Firth ⋓	46	58.44 N	3.07 W
Pentland Hills ⋏[2]	46	55.48 N	3.23 W
Pentraeth	44	53.17 N	4.12 W
Pentre Halkyn	262	53.15 N	3.12 W
Pentucket, Lake ⊜	283	42.47 N	71.05 W
Pentucket Pond ⊜	283	42.44 N	71.00 W
Pentwater	190	43.46 N	86.25 W
Penuba	112	0.20 S	104.28 E
Peñuelas	240m	18.03 N	66.43 W
Penuguan	112	2.27 S	104.31 E
Penukonda	122	14.05 N	77.35 E
Penunjok, Tanjong >	114	4.22 N	103.29 E
Pènwègon	110	18.13 N	96.34 E
Penwell	196	31.44 N	102.35 W
Peny	78	51.04 N	35.54 E
Penyagolosa ∧	34	40.13 N	0.21 W
Penyal d'Ifac ♠	34	38.38 N	0.05 E
Penyengat	114	0.54 N	102.20 E
Pen-y-Ghent ∧	44	54.09 N	2.14 W
Penygroes, Wales, U.K.	42	51.49 N	4.02 W
Penygroes, Wales, U.K.	44	53.04 N	4.17 W
Penyu, Kepulauan II	164	5.22 S	127.46 E
Penyu, Teluk c	115a	7.45 S	109.15 E
Penza	80	53.13 N	45.00 E
Penzance	42	50.07 N	5.33 W
Penza Oblast' □[4]	80	53.00 N	45.00 E
Penzberg	64	47.45 N	11.23 E
Penžina ≃	74	62.28 N	165.18 E
Penzing ◆[8]	264b	48.12 N	16.18 E
Penzino	80	52.07 N	50.27 E
Penžinskaja guba c	74	61.00 N	162.00 E
Penžinskij chrebet ⋏	74	62.30 N	167.00 E
Penzlin	54	53.30 N	13.05 E
Péone	62	44.07 N	6.54 E
Peoples Creek ≃	202	48.24 N	108.19 W
Peoples Ditch ≊	226	36.15 N	119.41 W
Peoria, Az., U.S.	200	33.34 N	112.14 W
Peoria, Il., U.S.	190	40.41 N	89.35 W
Peoria, Oh., U.S.	216	40.19 N	83.27 W
Peoria Heights	190	40.44 N	89.34 W
Peotillos	234	22.30 N	100.37 W
Peotone	216	41.19 N	87.47 W
Peover Eye ≃	262	53.15 N	2.31 W
Peover Heath	262	53.15 N	2.19 W
Pepa	154	7.42 S	29.47 E
Pepacton Reservoir ⊜[1]	210	42.06 N	74.54 W
Pepaw ≃	184	52.40 N	102.23 W
Pepel	150	8.35 N	13.03 W
Peper	140	7.04 N	33.00 E
Pepin	190	44.26 N	92.08 W
Pepin, Lake ⊜	190	44.30 N	92.15 W
Pepinster	56	50.34 N	5.49 E
Pepperell	207	42.40 N	71.35 W
Pepper Park State Recreation Area ♠	220	27.30 N	80.18 W
Pepper Pike	279a	41.28 N	81.27 W
Peqi'in Hadasha	132	32.59 N	35.20 E
Peqin	38	41.03 N	19.45 E
Pequannock	210	40.57 N	74.17 W
Pequannock ≃	276	40.58 N	74.17 W
Pequanticut Brook ≃	283	42.01 N	71.08 W
Pequea Creek ≃	208	39.53 N	76.22 W
Pequeno ≃	287a	22.55 S	43.25 W
Pequeri	256	21.50 S	43.06 W
Pequest ≃	210	40.50 N	75.05 W
Pequez	208	39.53 N	76.22 W
Pequizeiro	250	8.32 S	48.58 W
Pequop Mountains ⋏	204	40.45 N	114.40 W
Pequot Lakes	190	46.36 N	94.18 W
Perabumulih	112	3.27 S	104.15 E
Perak □[3]	114	5.00 N	101.00 E
Perak ≃	114	3.58 N	100.53 E
Perak, Kuala c	114	4.00 N	100.47 E
Peralba, Monte ∧	64	46.37 N	12.43 E
Perales de Alfambra	34	40.38 N	1.00 W
Perales del Rio	266a	40.19 N	3.38 W
Peralillo	252	34.29 S	71.29 W
Peralta	200	34.50 N	106.41 W
Pérama	267c	37.58 N	23.34 E
Perambalur	122	11.14 N	78.53 E
Perämeri (Bottenviken) c	26	65.00 N	23.00 E
Peranāmbattu	122	12.56 N	78.43 E
Peraní, Ákra >	267c	37.54 N	23.31 E
Perarolo di Cadore	64	46.24 N	12.21 E
Peräseinäjoki	26	62.34 N	23.04 E
Percé	186	48.31 N	64.13 W
Percée, Pointe ∧	58	45.57 N	6.33 E
Perch ≃	212	44.00 N	76.05 W
Perchas	240m	18.19 N	66.59 W
Perchau	61	47.06 N	14.27 E
Perchauer Sattel)(	61	47.07 N	14.27 E
Perche, Collines du ⋏[2]	50	48.25 N	0.40 E
Perche Creek ≃	194	38.49 N	92.24 W
Perch Lake ⊜	212	44.07 N	75.54 W
Perchtoldsdorf	61	48.07 N	16.17 E
Perchuškovo	265b	55.41 N	37.10 E

Symbol	English	Deutsch	Español	Français	Português
≃	River	Fluß	Río	Rivière	Rio
≊	Canal	Kanal	Canal	Canal	Canal
ʟ	Waterfall, Rapids	Wasserfall, Stromschnellen	Cascada, Rápidos	Chute d'eau, Rapides	Cascata, Rápidos
⋓	Strait	Meeresstraße	Estrecho	Détroit	Estreito
c	Bay, Gulf	Bucht, Golf	Bahía, Golfo	Baie, Golfe	Baía, Golfo
⊜	Lake, Lakes	See, Seen	Lago, Lagos	Lac, Lacs	Lago, Lagos
⩰	Swamp	Sumpf	Pantano	Marais	Pântano
⊼	Ice Features, Glacier	Eis- und Gletscherformen	Accidentes Glaciales	Formes glaciaires	Acidentes glaciares
⫪	Other Hydrographic Features	Andere Hydrographische Objekte	Otros Elementos Hidrográficos	Autres données hydrographiques	Outros acidentes hidrográficos
✢	Submarine Features	Untermeerische Objekte	Accidentes Submarinos	Formes de relief sous-marin	Acidentes submarinos
□	Political Unit	Politische Einheit	Unidad Politica	Entité politique	Unidade política
ʋ	Cultural Institution	Kulturelle Institution	Institución Cultural	Institution culturelle	Instituição cultural
⊥	Historical Site	Historische Stätte	Sitio Histórico	Site historique	Sitio histórico
♠	Recreational Site	Erholungs- und Ferienort	Sitio de Recreo	Centre de loisirs	Area de Lazer
⊠	Airport	Flughafen	Aeropuerto	Aéroport	Aeroporto
■	Military Installation	Militäranlage	Instalación Militar	Installation militaire	Instalação militar
◆	Miscellaneous	Verschiedenes	Misceláneo	Divers	Diversos

ENGLISH — DEUTSCH

Name	Page	Lat.°′	Long.°′
Percival Lakes ⊜	162	21.25 S	125.00 E
Percy Creek ≃	212	44.15 N	77.49 W
Percy Isles II	166	21.39 S	150.16 E
Percy Lake ⊜	212	45.13 N	78.22 W
Percy Reach ⊜	212	44.15 N	77.45 W
Perdagangan-tomuon	114	3.09 N	99.20 E
Perdasdefogu	71	39.41 N	9.26 E
Perdeberg	158	28.59 S	25.05 E
Perdekop	158	27.13 S	29.38 E
Perdices, Arroyo de las ≃	288	34.41 S	58.22 W
Perdida ≃	250	9.13 S	47.59 W
Perdido	194	31.00 N	87.37 W
Perdido ≃, Bra.	248	22.10 S	57.33 W
Perdido ≃, U.S.	194	30.29 N	87.26 W
Perdido, Arroyo ≃	254	42.55 S	67.00 W
Perdido, Arroyo del ≃	258	33.37 S	57.23 W
Perdido, Cuchilla del ⋏[2]	258	33.43 S	57.17 W
Perdido, Monte ∧	34	42.40 N	0.05 E
Perdido Bay ⊂	194	30.21 N	87.27 W
Perdifumo	68	40.16 N	15.01 E
Perdix	208	40.22 N	76.57 W
Perdizes	255	19.21 S	47.17 W
Perdreauville	261	48.58 N	1.38 E
Perdu, Lac ⊜	186	50.44 N	70.14 W
Perdue	184	52.04 N	107.32 W
Perebrody	78	51.43 N	27.00 E
Perechyn	78	48.44 N	22.26 E
Peredel	76	55.12 N	35.41 E
Peredel'cy	82	55.36 N	37.21 E
Peredelkino	265b	55.39 N	37.21 E
Peredmistne	78	45.57 N	34.37 E
Peregino	76	57.27 N	31.21 E
Perehins'ke	78	48.49 N	24.12 E
Perehonivka	78	48.32 N	30.31 E
Pereira	246	4.49 N	75.43 W
Pereira Barreto	255	20.38 S	51.07 W
Pereiro	250	6.03 S	38.28 W
Perejaslavka	89	47.58 N	135.06 E
Perejaslavskaja	78	45.51 N	39.02 E
Perejež'na	24	59.43 N	48.12 E
Perekopivka	78	50.37 N	33.25 E
Perekopnoje	80	51.13 N	48.04 E
Perekopskaja	80	49.21 N	43.20 E
Père-Lachaise, Cimetière du ◆	261	48.51 N	2.25 E
Perelazovskij	80	49.09 N	42.33 E
Perelazy	76	53.02 N	31.28 E
Perelesinskij	78	51.44 N	40.07 E
Perel'ub	80	51.52 N	50.22 E
Pere Marquette ≃	190	43.57 N	86.27 W
Pere Marquette, Big South Branch ≃	190	43.56 N	86.10 W
Pere Marquette State Park ♦	219	39.00 N	90.30 W
Perem'otnoje	80	51.11 N	50.49 E
Peremyshlyany	78	49.41 N	24.33 E
Peremyšl'	82	54.16 N	36.10 E
Perené ≃	248	11.09 S	74.18 W
Perenjori	162	29.26 S	116.17 E
Pereputje	92a	46.17 N	141.54 E
Pererov	78	52.04 N	28.00 E
Pereščepnoje	80	50.32 N	45.06 E
Pereshchepyne	78	49.01 N	35.22 E
Pereslavl'-Zalesskij	82	56.44 N	38.51 E
Peresypkino Pervoje	80	52.55 N	42.55 E
Peretrusovo	82	56.51 N	36.53 E
Perevals'k	83	48.26 N	38.47 E
Perevoz, Ross.	80	55.36 N	44.32 E
Perevoz, Ross.	88	59.00 N	116.57 E
Perevoz, Ross.	265a	59.43 N	30.47 E
Pereyaslav-Khmel'nyts'kyy	78	50.06 N	31.30 E
Pereyra, Arroyo ≃	288	34.47 S	58.08 W
Pereyra, Punta ›	258	34.14 S	58.04 W
Pérez	252	33.00 S	60.46 W
Perfugas	71	40.50 N	8.53 E
Perg	61	48.15 N	14.37 E
Pergamino	252	33.53 S	60.35 W
Pergamum ⊥	130	39.10 N	27.13 E
Pergau ≃	114	5.23 N	102.02 E
Pergine Valdarno	66	43.28 N	11.41 E
Pergine Valsugana	64	46.04 N	11.14 E
Pergola	66	43.34 N	12.50 E
Pergusa, Lago di ⊜	70	37.31 N	14.18 E
Perham	198	46.35 N	95.34 W
Perho	26	63.13 N	24.25 E
Peri	64	45.39 N	10.54 E
Peri ≃	130	38.50 N	39.35 E
Peribán de Ramos	234	19.32 N	102.28 W
Péribonca ≃	176	48.45 N	72.05 W
Péribonca, Lac ⊜	186	50.04 N	71.15 W
Perico, Arg.	252	24.23 S	65.06 W
Perico, Cuba	240p	22.46 N	81.01 W
Pericos	232	25.03 N	107.42 W
Pericumã ≃	250	2.17 S	44.42 W
Peridot	200	33.18 N	110.27 W
Périers	32	49.11 N	1.25 W
Perigiraja	112	0.16 S	103.30 E
Périgord □[9]	32	45.20 N	1.00 E
Perigoso, Canal ⋃	250	0.05 N	49.40 W
Périgueux	32	45.11 N	0.43 E
Perijá, Serranía De ⋏	246	10.00 N	73.00 W
Perim → Barīm I	144	12.39 N	43.25 E
Peri-Mirim	250	2.38 S	44.54 W
Perinaldo	62	43.52 N	7.40 E
Peringat	114	6.02 N	102.17 E
Periprava	38	45.24 N	29.32 E
Perisher Valley ♦	171b	36.23 S	145.24 E
Peristérion	267c	38.01 N	23.42 E
Perito	68	40.18 N	15.09 E
Perito Moreno	254	46.36 S	70.56 W
Peritoró	250	4.20 S	44.18 W
Perivale ◆[8]	260	51.32 N	0.19 W
Periyakulam	122	10.07 N	77.33 E
Periyār ≃	122	10.11 N	76.13 E
Perkasie	208	40.22 N	75.17 W
Perkins	196	35.58 N	97.02 W
Perkinsfield	212	44.42 N	79.57 W
Perkins Observatory ⊕[3]	214	40.14 N	83.02 W
Perkinston	194	30.46 N	89.08 W
Perkinsville, In., U.S.	218	40.09 N	85.52 W
Perkinsville, N.Y., U.S.	210	42.32 N	77.38 W
Perkiomen Creek ≃	208	40.07 N	75.28 W
Perkiomen Creek, East Branch ≃	208	40.15 N	75.27 W
Perkiomen Junction	285	40.06 N	75.28 W
Perkiomen Valley Airport ⊠	285	40.12 N	75.25 W
Perl	56	49.28 N	6.23 E
Perlas, Archipiélago de las II	246	8.25 N	79.00 W
Perlas, Laguna de ⊂	236	12.30 N	83.40 W
Perlas, Punta de ›	236	12.23 N	83.30 W
Perleberg	54	53.04 N	11.51 E
Perlez	38	45.12 N	20.24 E
Perlis □[3]	114	6.30 N	100.15 E
Perl'ovka	78	51.51 N	38.51 E
Perm'	86	58.00 N	56.15 E
Permanente Creek ≃	282	37.25 N	122.05 W
Permas	24	59.20 N	45.34 E
Përmet	38	40.14 N	20.21 E
Permisi	80	54.06 N	45.48 E
Perm' Oblast' □[4]	86	58.00 N	58.00 E
Pernambuco → Recife	250	8.03 S	34.54 W
Pernambuco □[3]	250	8.00 S	37.00 W
Pernate	266b	45.27 N	8.41 E
Pernatty Lagoon ⊜	166	31.31 S	137.14 E
Pernay	50	47.27 N	0.30 E
Pernegg an der Mur	61	47.22 N	15.21 E
Pernes-les-Fontaines	62	44.00 N	5.03 E
Pernik	38	42.36 N	23.02 E
Pernink	54	50.20 N	12.45 E
Perniö	26	60.12 N	23.08 E
Pernitz	61	47.54 N	15.58 E
Pernovo	82	55.58 N	39.10 E
Pero	266b	45.31 N	9.05 E
Peroba, Ribeirão do ≃	287b	23.27 S	46.22 W
Pérols, Étang de ⊂	62	43.33 N	3.56 E
Peron, Cape ›	168a	32.17 S	115.41 E
Péronne	50	49.56 N	2.56 E
Peron Peninsula ›[1]	162	25.55 S	113.30 E
Pero Pinheiro	266c	38.51 N	9.20 W
Perosa Argentina	62	44.58 N	7.10 E
Perote	234	19.34 N	97.14 W
Peroto	248	14.50 S	64.31 W
Pérou → Peru □[1]	242	10.00 S	76.00 W
Pérouges	58	45.54 N	5.11 E
Peroulaz	62	45.42 N	7.19 E
Perovo ◆[8]	265b	55.44 N	37.46 E
Perow	182	54.31 N	126.26 W
Perpendicular, Point ›	170	35.06 S	150.48 E
Perpignan	32	42.41 N	2.53 E
Perranporth	42	50.20 N	5.09 W
Perrault Falls	184	50.19 N	93.11 W
Perray ≃	261	48.31 N	1.42 E
Perrero	62	44.56 N	7.05 E
Perriers-sur-Andelle	50	49.25 N	1.22 E
Perrignier	58	46.18 N	6.27 E
Perrigny	58	46.40 N	5.35 E
Perrin	196	33.02 N	98.04 W
Perrine	220	25.36 N	80.21 W
Perrineville	208	40.13 N	74.26 W
Perris	228	33.46 N	117.13 W
Perris, Lake ⊜[1]	228	33.50 N	117.10 W
Perro, Laguna del ⊜	200	34.40 N	105.57 W
Perro, Punta del ›	34	36.45 N	6.25 W
Perros, Bahía de ⊂	240p	22.25 N	78.30 W
Perros-Guirec	32	48.49 N	3.27 W
Perrot, Île I	206	45.22 N	73.57 W
Perry, Fl., U.S.	192	30.07 N	83.34 W
Perry, Ga., U.S.	192	32.27 N	83.43 W
Perry, Il., U.S.	219	39.47 N	90.45 W
Perry, Ia., U.S.	190	41.50 N	94.06 W
Perry, Ks., U.S.	198	39.04 N	95.23 W
Perry, Me., U.S.	186	44.58 N	67.04 W
Perry, Mi., U.S.	216	42.49 N	84.13 W
Perry, Mo., U.S.	219	39.25 N	91.40 W
Perry, N.Y., U.S.	210	42.42 N	78.00 W
Perry, Oh., U.S.	214	41.45 N	81.08 W
Perry, Ok., U.S.	196	36.17 N	97.17 W
Perry, Tx., U.S.	222	31.25 N	96.55 W
Perry, Ut,. U.S.	200	41.27 N	112.02 W
Perry □[6]	208	40.25 N	77.11 W
Perrydale	224	45.02 N	123.15 W
Perry Hall	208	39.24 N	76.27 W
Perry Heights	214	40.47 N	81.28 W
Perry-Jōriku-kinenhi ⊥	94	35.14 N	139.43 E
Perry Lake ⊜[1]	198	39.20 N	95.30 W
Perryman	208	39.28 N	76.12 W
Perrymont	279b	40.33 N	80.02 W
Perryopolis	214	40.05 N	79.45 W
Perry Park	218	38.33 N	85.00 W
Perry Point	208	39.33 N	76.04 W
Perrysburg, N.Y., U.S.	210	42.27 N	79.00 W
Perrysburg, Oh., U.S.	214	41.33 N	83.37 W
Perry's Landing Monument ⊥	268	35.13 N	139.43 E
Perry's Victory and International Peace Memorial ⊥	214	41.33 N	82.50 W
Perrysville	214	40.39 N	82.18 W
Perryton	196	36.24 N	100.48 W
Perryville, Ak., U.S.	180	55.54 N	159.10 W
Perryville, Ar., U.S.	194	35.00 N	92.48 W
Perryville, Ky., U.S.	192	37.39 N	84.57 W
Perryville, Md., U.S.	208	39.33 N	76.04 W
Perryville, Mo., U.S.	194	37.43 N	89.51 W
Perryville, N.Y., U.S.	210	43.01 N	75.48 W
Peršaj	76	54.02 N	26.41 E
Persan	50	49.09 N	2.16 E
Perșani, Munții ⋏	38	45.40 N	25.15 E
Persberg	40	59.45 N	14.15 E
Perschling ≃	61	48.20 N	15.58 E
Perşembe	130	41.04 N	37.46 E
Persepolis → Takht-e Jamshīd ⊥	128	29.57 N	52.52 E
Perseverance, Mount ∧	171a	27.25 S	152.10 E
Perseverancia	248	14.44 S	62.48 W
Pershagen	40	59.10 N	17.39 E
Pershing	218	39.49 N	84.53 W
Pershore	42	52.07 N	2.05 W
Pershotravens'k, Ukr.	78	50.12 N	27.39 E
Pershotravens'k, Ukr.	78	48.22 N	36.24 E
Pershotravneve, Ukr.	78	51.24 N	28.53 E
Pershotravneve, Ukr.	83	47.03 N	37.18 E
Pershyttan	40	59.30 N	15.00 E
Persia	198	41.34 N	95.34 W
Persia → Iran □[1]	128	32.00 N	53.00 E
Persian Gulf (Arabian Gulf) ⊂	128	27.00 N	51.00 E
Pérsico, Golfo → Persian Gulf ⊂	128	27.00 N	51.00 E
Persimmon Creek ≃	194	31.31 N	86.50 W
Persique, Golfe → Persian Gulf ⊂	128	27.00 N	51.00 E
Persischer Golf → Persian Gulf ⊂	128	27.00 N	51.00 E
Perštejn	54	50.23 N	13.08 E
Perstorp	41	56.08 N	13.23 E
Pertandangan, Tanjung ›	114	2.41 N	100.14 E
Pertek	130	38.50 N	39.22 E
Perth, Austl.	168a	31.56 S	115.50 E
Perth, On., Can.	212	44.54 N	76.15 W
Perth, Scot., U.K.	46	56.24 N	3.28 W
Perth, N.Y., U.S.	210	43.03 N	74.12 W
Perth □[6]	212	43.30 N	81.05 W
Perth Amboy	210	40.30 N	74.15 W
Perth-Andover	186	46.45 N	67.42 W
Perth Basin ✢[1]	14	28.30 S	110.00 E
Perthes	58	48.39 N	4.49 E
Perth International Airport ⊠	168a	31.57 S	115.58 E
Perthois ◆[1]	58	48.40 N	4.45 E
Pertokar	144	16.59 N	37.28 E
Pertominsk	24	64.47 N	38.25 E
Pertovo	80	54.22 N	41.31 E
Pertuis	62	43.41 N	5.30 E
Pertusato, Capo ›	71	41.21 N	9.10 E
Peru, Il., U.S.	216	41.19 N	89.07 W
Peru, In., U.S.	216	40.45 N	86.04 W
Peru, Ne., U.S.	198	40.28 N	95.44 W
Peru, N.Y., U.S.	188	44.34 N	73.31 W
Peru (Perú) □[1], S.A.	242	10.00 S	76.00 W
Peru (Perú) □[1], S.A.	248	10.00 S	76.00 W
Peruaçu ≃	255	15.11 S	44.07 W
Peru Basin ✢[1]	18	15.00 S	85.00 W
Peruc	54	50.19 N	13.59 E
Perućac, Jezero ⊜[1]	38	43.55 N	19.10 E
Peru-Chile Trench ✢[1]	18	20.00 S	73.00 W
Perugia	66	43.08 N	12.22 E
Perugia □[4]	66	43.03 N	12.33 E
Perugorría	252	29.20 S	58.37 W
Peruíbe	252	24.19 S	47.00 W
Peruípe ≃	255	17.43 S	39.16 W
Perumalpār I[1]	122	11.10 N	72.04 E
Peruque Creek ≃	219	38.53 N	90.39 W
Perus ◆[8]	256	23.25 S	46.45 W
Perušić	36	44.39 N	15.23 E
Péruwelz	50	50.31 N	3.35 E
Pervaja Maja	86	48.55 N	67.25 E
Pervari	128	37.54 N	42.36 E
Pervenchères	50	48.26 N	0.26 E
Pervesinka	80	52.13 N	43.15 E
Pervijze	50	51.05 N	2.47 E
Pervoavgustovskij	76	52.14 N	35.03 E
Pervoje Pole	180	63.05 N	179.19 E
Pervomajka	86	51.17 N	70.08 E
Pervomajsk, Ross.	80	54.53 N	43.49 E
Pervomajsk, Ross.	88	58.02 N	94.05 E
Pervomajskij, Bela.	76	53.54 N	25.23 E
Pervomajskij, Kyrg.	85	42.51 N	74.04 E
Pervomajskij, Ross.	76	54.04 N	32.29 E
Pervomajskij, Ross.	80	53.22 N	51.38 E
Pervomajskij, Ross.	80	51.22 N	48.54 E
Pervomajskij, Ross.	80	53.15 N	40.18 E
Pervomajskij, Ross.	82	55.57 N	37.52 E
Pervomajskij, Ross.	82	54.03 N	37.32 E
Pervomajskij, Ross.	82	55.32 N	37.09 E
Pervomajskij, Ross.	86	51.32 N	55.06 E
Pervomajskij, Ross.	86	53.41 N	55.57 E
Pervomajskij, Ross.	86	59.29 N	61.24 E
Pervomajskij, Ross.	86	54.52 N	61.08 E
Pervomajskij, Ross.	88	51.44 N	115.39 E
Pervomajskoje, Kaz.	85	42.05 N	69.53 E
Pervomajskoje, Ross.	76	52.56 N	33.36 E
Pervomajskoje, Ross.	80	55.05 N	47.22 E
Pervomajskoje, Ross.	80	46.03 N	42.13 E
Pervomajskoje, Ross.	80	46.21 N	43.37 E
Pervomajskoje, Ross.	80	48.50 N	41.14 E
Pervomajskoje, Ross.	80	51.28 N	47.37 E
Pervomajskoje, Ross.	80	50.56 N	46.46 E
Pervomajskoje, Ross.	86	53.45 N	84.08 E
Pervomajskoje, Ross.	86	57.06 N	86.12 E
Pervomays'k, Ukr.	78	48.04 N	30.52 E
Pervomays'k, Ukr.	83	48.37 N	38.35 E
Pervomays'ke	78	45.43 N	33.51 E
Pervomays'kyy, Ukr.	78	49.24 N	36.12 E
Pervomays'kyy, Ukr.	83	47.58 N	38.47 E
Pervoural'sk	86	56.54 N	59.58 E
Pervušino	80	58.02 N	41.56 E
Pervyj Kuril'skij proliv ⋃	74	50.50 N	156.36 E
Perwenitz	264a	52.40 N	13.01 E
Pes'	76	58.55 N	34.19 E
Pes' ≃	76	59.08 N	35.18 E
Pesa ≃	66	43.44 N	11.01 E
Pes'akov, ostrov I	24	68.47 N	57.35 E
Pesangrohan ≃	269e	6.11 S	106.45 E
Pesaro	66	43.54 N	12.55 E
Pesaro e Urbino □[4]	66	43.40 N	12.38 E
Pesca	246	5.33 N	73.03 W
Pescadero	226	37.15 N	122.22 W
Pescadero Creek ≃, Ca., U.S.	226	36.42 N	121.17 W
Pescadero Creek ≃, Ca., U.S.	226	37.16 N	122.25 W
Pescadores → P'enghu Ch'üntao II	100	23.30 N	119.30 E
Pescadores, Punta ›, Méx.	232	23.46 N	109.43 W
Pescadores, Punta ›, Perú	248	16.21 S	73.15 W
Pescaglia	66	43.58 N	10.25 E
Pesčanka	80	51.18 N	43.40 E
Pesčanoje, Kaz.	86	53.01 N	76.19 E
Pesčanoje, Ross.	24	62.09 N	35.48 E
Pesčanokopskoje	80	46.12 N	41.04 E
Pescantina	64	45.29 N	10.51 E
Pesčanyje, ostrova II	83	46.52 N	38.17 E
Pescara	66	42.28 N	14.13 E
Pescara □[4]	66	42.20 N	13.57 E
Pescara ≃	66	42.28 N	14.13 E
Pescasseroli	66	41.48 N	13.47 E
Pesch	263	51.11 N	6.32 E
Pesch, Schloss ⊥	263	51.18 N	6.39 E
Peschici	68	41.57 N	16.01 E
Peschiera del Garda	64	45.26 N	10.42 E
Peschio, Monte ∧	267a	41.43 N	12.46 E
Pescia	66	43.54 N	10.41 E
Pescina	66	42.02 N	13.39 E
Pescocostanzo	66	41.53 N	14.04 E
Pescolanciano	66	41.41 N	14.20 E
Pescopagano	68	40.50 N	15.24 E
Pescorocchiano	66	42.12 N	13.09 E
Pesco Sannita	68	41.14 N	14.49 E
Pesé	236	7.54 N	80.37 W
Pesek, Pulau I	271c	1.17 N	103.41 E
Peseux	58	46.59 N	6.53 E
Peshastin	224	47.34 N	120.36 W
Peshastin Creek ≃	224	47.33 N	120.35 W
Peshāwar	123	34.01 N	71.33 E
Peshīn Jān	128	33.25 N	61.28 E
Peshkopi	38	41.41 N	20.26 E
Peshtigo	190	45.03 N	87.44 W
Peshtigo ≃	190	44.58 N	87.40 W
Pesio ≃	62	44.28 N	7.53 E
Pesjane	82	56.01 N	38.48 E
Peski, Bela.	76	53.21 N	24.38 E
Peski, Ross.	80	51.16 N	42.27 E
Peski, Ross.	82	55.13 N	38.46 E
Peški, Ross.	82	56.08 N	37.04 E
Peskovatskoje	82	54.03 N	36.16 E
Peskovka	86	59.04 N	52.22 E
Peškovo	83	47.02 N	39.24 E
Peškovo Grecovo	82	54.26 N	37.36 E
Peškovskoje	86	53.45 N	62.23 E
Pesmes	58	47.17 N	5.34 E
Pesnica	61	46.36 N	15.41 E
Pesnica ≃	61	46.24 N	16.05 E
Pešnoj, poluostrov ›[2]	80	46.52 N	51.42 E
Pesočenskij	82	54.10 N	36.06 E
Pesočn'a	80	54.07 N	40.50 E
Pesočnoje, Bela.	76	53.20 N	27.06 E
Pesočnoje, Ross.	80	58.01 N	39.10 E
Pesočnyj	76	60.07 N	30.08 E
Peso da Régua	34	41.10 N	7.47 W
Pespire	236	13.35 N	87.22 W
Pesqueira	250	8.22 S	36.42 W
Pesquería	196	25.47 N	100.03 W
Pesquería ≃	196	25.54 N	99.11 W
Pessac	32	44.48 N	0.38 W
Pessin	54	52.38 N	12.40 E
Pessinetto	62	45.17 N	7.24 E
Pest □[6]	30	47.25 N	19.20 E
Pest ◆[8]	264c	47.30 N	19.04 E
Pest'aki	80	56.43 N	42.40 E
Peštera	38	42.02 N	24.18 E
Pesterzsébet ◆[8]	264c	47.26 N	19.07 E
Pesthidegkút ◆[8]	264c	47.34 N	18.58 E
Pestimre ◆[8]	264c	47.24 N	19.12 E
Pestlőrinc ◆[8]	264c	47.26 N	19.12 E
Pestovo, Ross.	76	58.36 N	35.48 E
Pestovo, Ross.	80	57.12 N	46.44 E
Pestovskoje vodochranilišče ⊜[1]	82	56.06 N	37.40 E
Pestravka	80	52.24 N	49.58 E
Pestrecy	80	55.46 N	49.39 E
Pestrikovo	82	55.05 N	38.53 E
Pestújhely ◆[8]	264c	47.32 N	19.07 E
Petacalco, Bahía ⊂	234	17.57 N	102.05 W
Petah Tiqwa	132	32.05 N	34.53 E
Petäjävesi	26	62.15 N	25.12 E
Petal	194	31.20 N	89.15 W
Petalcingo	232	17.17 N	92.27 W
Petaling Jaya	114	3.05 N	101.39 E
Petalión, Kólpos ⊂	38	37.59 N	24.02 E
Petaluma	226	38.13 N	122.38 W
Petaluma ≃	226	38.06 N	122.30 W
Pétange	56	49.34 N	5.52 E
Petare	246	10.29 N	66.49 W
Petatlán	234	17.31 N	101.16 W
Petauke	154	14.15 S	31.20 E
Petawawa	190	45.54 N	77.17 W
Petawawa ≃	190	45.55 N	77.15 W
Pété	146	10.58 N	14.30 E
Petegem	50	50.58 N	3.32 E
Petén □[5]	236	16.15 N	89.50 W
Petén Itzá, Lago ⊜	232	16.59 N	89.50 W
Petenwell Lake ⊜[1]	190	44.10 N	89.57 W
Peter and Paul Fortress ⊥	265a	59.57 N	30.19 E
Peterboro	210	42.58 N	75.41 W
Peterborough, Austl.	166	32.58 S	138.50 E
Peterborough, On., Can.	212	44.18 N	78.19 W
Peterborough, Eng., U.K.	42	52.35 N	0.15 W
Peterborough, N.H., U.S.	188	42.52 N	71.57 W
Peterborough □[6]	212	44.33 N	78.15 W
Peterculter	46	57.05 N	2.16 W
Peterhead	46	57.30 N	1.49 W
Peter Hill ∧	46	56.58 N	2.42 W
Peter I Island I	9	68.47 S	90.35 W
Peter Island I	240m	18.22 N	64.35 W
Peter Lake ⊜, N.T., Can.	176	63.08 N	92.48 W
Peter Lake ⊜, Sk., Can.	184	57.15 N	103.53 W
Peterlee	44	54.46 N	1.19 W
Peter Lougheed Provincial Park ♦	182	50.45 N	115.15 W
Peterman	194	31.35 N	87.15 W
Petermann Ranges ⋏	162	25.00 S	129.46 E
Petermann Reserve ◆[4]	162	25.00 S	130.15 E
Peter Pond Lake ⊜	184	55.55 N	108.44 W
Peter Pond Lake Indian Reserve ◆[4]	184	55.55 N	109.00 W
Petersberg	56	50.33 N	9.43 E
Peters Brook ≃	276	40.33 N	74.37 W
Petersburg, Ak., U.S.	180	56.49 N	132.57 W
Petersburg, Il., U.S.	219	40.00 N	89.50 W
Petersburg, In., U.S.	194	38.29 N	87.16 W
Petersburg, Mi., U.S.	216	41.54 N	83.42 W
Petersburg, Ne., U.S.	198	41.51 N	98.04 W
Petersburg, N.J., U.S.	208	39.15 N	74.43 W
Petersburg, N.Y., U.S.	210	42.44 N	73.20 W
Petersburg, Oh., U.S.	214	40.54 N	80.31 W
Petersburg, Pa., U.S.	214	40.34 N	78.03 W
Petersburg, Tn., U.S.	194	35.19 N	86.38 W
Petersburg, Tx., U.S.	196	33.52 N	101.36 W
Petersburg, Va., U.S.	208	37.13 N	77.24 W
Petersburg, W.V., U.S.	188	38.59 N	79.07 W
Petersburg National Battlefield ♦	208	37.14 N	77.22 W
Peters Canyon Reservoir ⊜[1]	280	33.47 N	117.45 W
Peters Creek ≃, Ca., U.S.	282	37.15 N	122.13 W
Peters Creek ≃, Pa., U.S.	279b	40.18 N	79.52 W
Peters Creek, Piney Fork ≃	279b	40.16 N	79.58 W
Petersdorf	54	54.29 N	11.04 E
Petersfield, S. Afr.	273d	26.14 S	28.26 E
Petersfield, Eng., U.K.	42	51.00 N	0.56 W
Petershagen, Dtsch.	52	52.23 N	8.58 E
Petershagen, Dtsch.	54	52.24 N	14.20 E
Petershagen bei Berlin	54	52.31 N	13.46 E
Petersham, Austl.	274a	33.54 S	151.09 E
Petersham, Ma., U.S.	207	42.29 N	72.11 W
Peters Hill ∧[2]	168b	34.11 S	138.50 E
Peterson	198	42.55 N	95.20 W
Peterson Air Force Base ■	198	38.49 N	104.42 W
Peters Pond ⊜	283	42.43 N	71.16 W
Peterswald Hill ∧[2]	162	26.43 S	123.39 E
Peter the Great Bay → Petra Velikogo, zaliv ⊂	89	42.40 N	132.00 E
Peter the Great Monument ⊥	265a	59.56 N	30.18 E
Pétervására	30	48.01 N	20.06 E
Petilia Policastro	68	39.07 N	16.47 E
Pétionville	238	18.31 N	72.17 W
Petit	273d	26.06 S	28.22 E
Petit Bois Island I	194	30.12 N	88.26 W
Petit-Bourg	241o	16.12 N	61.36 W
Petit-Canal	241o	16.23 N	61.29 W
Petitcodiac	186	45.56 N	65.10 W
Petitcodiac ≃	186	45.50 N	64.33 W
Petit Cul-de-Sac Marin ⊂	241o	16.12 N	61.33 W
Petite Nation, Rivière de la ≃	206	45.35 N	75.06 W
Petite Rivière du Chêne ≃	206	46.34 N	72.02 W
Petite Rivière Noire, Piton de la ∧	157c	20.24 S	57.24 E
Petite Rivière Rouge ≃	206	45.45 N	75.00 W
Petites-Anses	241o	15.51 N	61.39 W
Petite Sauldre ≃	50	47.26 N	2.05 E
Petite Terre, Îles de la II	241o	16.10 N	61.07 W
Petit Forte	186	47.24 N	54.40 W
Petit-Fort-Philippe	50	51.00 N	2.07 E
Petit-Goâve	238	18.26 N	72.52 W
Petit Jean ≃	194	35.10 N	92.56 W
Petit Jean State Park ♦	194	35.06 N	92.57 W
Petit Loango	152	2.16 S	9.35 E
Petit Loango, Parc National du ♦	152	2.15 S	9.36 E
Petit Mécatina, Île du I	186	50.33 N	59.20 W
Petit Morin ≃	50	48.56 N	3.07 E
Petitot ≃	176	60.14 N	123.29 W
Petit Piton ∧	241f	13.50 N	61.04 W
Petit Rhône ≃	62	43.27 N	4.24 E
Petit-Saint-Bernard, Col du)(	62	45.41 N	6.53 E
Petitsikapau Lake ⊜	176	54.45 N	66.25 W
Petkeljärven kansallispuisto ♦	24	62.35 N	31.12 E
Petkus	54	51.59 N	13.21 E
Petlād	120	22.28 N	72.48 E
Petlalcingo	234	18.05 N	97.54 W
Peto	232	20.08 N	88.55 W
Petoh	114	2.53 N	103.15 E
Petone	172	41.13 S	174.52 E
Petorca	252	32.15 S	70.56 W
Petoskey	190	45.22 N	84.57 W
Petownikip Lake ⊜	184	52.56 N	92.02 W
Petra → Batrā ⊥	132	30.20 N	35.26 E
Petralia Soprana	70	37.47 N	14.06 E
Petralia Sottana	70	37.48 N	14.05 E
Petras, Mount ∧	9	75.52 S	128.38 W
Petra Velikogo, zaliv (Peter the Great Bay) ⊂	89	42.40 N	132.00 E
Petre, Point ›	212	43.50 N	77.09 W
Petrecovo	24	61.18 N	57.07 E
Petrella, Monte ∧	66	41.18 N	13.40 E
Petrella Salto	66	42.18 N	13.04 E
Petrella Tifernina	66	41.41 N	14.42 E
Petrič	38	41.24 N	23.13 E
Petrie	171a	27.16 S	152.59 E
Petrified Forest National Park ♦	200	34.55 N	109.49 W
Petrikov	76	52.08 N	28.30 E
Petrila	38	45.27 N	23.25 E
Petrinja	36	45.26 N	16.17 E
Petriščevo, Ross.	82	54.37 N	36.57 E
Petriščevo, Ross.	82	55.30 N	36.18 E
Petrítis, Ákra ›	267c	37.56 N	23.24 E
Petrivka, Ukr.	78	46.54 N	30.44 E
Petrivka, Ukr.	83	48.53 N	39.52 E
Petrivka, Ukr.	83	48.48 N	39.16 E
Petrivs'ke	78	49.10 N	36.54 E
Petrodvorec	76	59.53 N	29.54 E
Petroglyphs Provincial Park ♦	212	44.33 N	77.53 W
Petrograd → Sankt-Peterburg	76	59.55 N	30.15 E
Petrohué	254	41.08 S	72.25 W
Petrolândia	250	9.05 S	38.18 W
Petrólea	246	8.30 N	72.35 W
Petroleum	216	40.36 N	85.09 W
Petrolia, On., Can.	214	42.52 N	82.09 W
Petrolia, Pa., U.S.	214	41.01 N	79.43 W
Petrolia, Tx., U.S.	196	34.01 N	98.14 W
Petrolina	250	9.24 S	40.30 W
Petrolina de Goiás	255	16.06 S	49.20 W
Petronà	68	39.03 N	16.45 E
Petrona, Punta ›	240m	17.56 N	66.23 W
Petronila Creek ≃	196	27.32 N	97.32 W
Petropavlivka, Ukr.	78	48.27 N	36.26 E
Petropavlivka, Ukr.	83	49.43 N	37.42 E
Petropavlovka, Ross.	78	50.06 N	40.54 E
Petropavlovka, Ross.	88	50.38 N	105.19 E
Petropavlovsk, Kaz.	86	54.54 N	69.06 E
Petropavlovsk, Ross.	86	56.20 N	57.09 E
Petropavlovsk-Kamčatskij	74	53.01 N	158.39 E
Petropavlovskoje, Ross.	86	52.04 N	84.08 E
Petropavlovskoje, Ross.	88	58.13 N	108.59 E
Petrópolis	256	22.31 S	43.10 W
Petros	192	36.05 N	84.26 W
Petroșani	38	45.25 N	23.22 E
Petrosino	70	37.43 N	12.29 E
Petro-Slav'anka	265a	59.48 N	30.31 E
Petroso, Monte ∧	66	41.44 N	13.55 E
Petroúpolis	267c	38.03 N	23.41 E
Petrovac	38	44.22 N	21.27 E
Petrove	78	48.20 N	33.16 E
Petrovgrad → Zrenjanin	38	45.23 N	20.24 E
Petrovka	80	53.13 N	51.58 E
Petrovo, Ross.	76	58.22 N	35.09 E
Petrovo, Ross.	82	55.00 N	38.08 E
Petrovo, Ross.	88	54.30 N	105.15 E
Petrovo-Dal'neje	265b	55.45 N	37.11 E
Petrovsk	80	52.19 N	45.23 E
Petrovskaja	78	45.25 N	37.57 E
Petrovs'ke	83	48.18 N	38.52 E
Petrovskij, Ross.	80	56.39 N	40.19 E
Petrovskij, Ross.	80	50.45 N	41.59 E
Petrovskij, Ross.	82	54.29 N	36.59 E
Petrovskoje, Ross.	80	52.39 N	40.15 E
Petrovskoje, Ross.	80	57.01 N	39.16 E
Petrovskoje, Ross.	82	55.27 N	38.21 E
Petrovskoje, Ross.	82	55.32 N	36.59 E
Petrovskoje, Ross.	265b	55.36 N	37.53 E
Petrovsko-Razumovskoje ◆[8]	265b	55.50 N	37.34 E
Petrovsk-Zabajkal'skij	88	51.17 N	108.50 E
Petrov Val	80	50.09 N	45.12 E
Petrozavodsk	24	61.47 N	34.20 E
Petrozsény → Petroșani	38	45.25 N	23.22 E
Petrun'	24	66.28 N	60.43 E
Petrusburg	158	29.08 S	25.27 E
Petrušino	265a	59.48 N	30.50 E
Petrus Steyn	158	27.38 S	28.08 E
Petrusville	158	30.05 S	24.41 E
Petrykivka	78	48.43 N	34.37 E
Petschora → Pečora ≃	24	68.13 N	54.15 E
Petten	52	52.45 N	4.39 E
Pettenbach	61	47.57 N	14.01 E
Petteril ≃	44	54.54 N	2.55 W
Petticoat Creek ≃	275b	43.48 N	79.06 W
Pettigoe	48	54.33 N	7.50 W
Pettinascura, Monte ∧	68	39.22 N	16.37 E
Pettineo	70	37.58 N	14.17 E
Pettisville	216	41.31 N	84.13 W
Pettnau	64	47.18 N	11.08 E
Pettneu am Arlberg	58	47.09 N	10.20 E
Pettus	196	28.37 N	97.48 W
Petty Harbour	186	47.28 N	52.43 W
Petty Island I	285	39.58 N	75.07 W
Petua	272b	22.25 N	88.27 E
Petuchovo	86	55.06 N	67.58 E
Petuški	80	55.55 N	39.28 E
Petworth	42	50.59 N	0.38 W
Petzow	264a	52.21 N	12.56 E
Peudada	114	5.12 N	96.35 E
Peuerbach	60	48.20 N	13.46 E
Peuetsagoe, Gunung ∧	114	4.55 N	96.20 E
Peureulak	114	4.48 N	97.53 E
Peureulak ≃	114	4.54 N	97.53 E
Peureulak, Ujung ›	114	4.54 N	97.54 E
Peusangan ≃	114	5.16 N	96.51 E
Peusangan, Ujung ›	114	5.16 N	96.50 E
Pevek	74	69.42 N	170.17 E
Pevely	219	38.17 N	90.23 W
Pevensey	42	50.49 N	0.20 E
Pevensey Levels ⩦	42	50.50 N	0.20 E
Peveragno	62	44.20 N	7.37 E
Pewamo	216	43.00 N	84.50 W
Pewaukee	216	43.04 N	88.15 W
Pewaukee Lake ⊜	216	43.04 N	88.19 W
Pewee Valley	218	38.18 N	85.29 W
Pews Creek ≃	276	40.27 N	74.06 W
Pewsey	42	51.21 N	1.46 W
Pewsey, Vale of V	42	51.20 N	1.48 W
Péyia	130	34.53 N	32.23 E
Peyrolles-en-Provence	62	43.39 N	5.35 E
Peyruis	62	44.02 N	5.56 E
Peza ≃	24	65.36 N	44.35 E
Pezas	86	54.39 N	87.46 E
Pezawa Taung ∧	110	19.33 N	94.31 E
Pézenas	32	43.27 N	3.25 E
Peženga	76	59.10 N	44.16 E
Pezinok	30	48.18 N	17.17 E
Pezu	123	32.19 N	70.44 E
Pezzana	62	45.16 N	8.29 E
Pfäfers	58	46.59 N	9.30 E
Pfaffenhausen	58	48.07 N	10.27 E
Pfaffenhofen an der Ilm	60	48.31 N	11.30 E
Pfaffenhoffen	56	48.51 N	7.37 E
Pfaffenöden ∧[2]	264b	48.04 N	16.33 E
Pfäffikersee ⊜	58	47.21 N	8.48 E
Pfäffikon	58	47.22 N	8.47 E
Pfaffnau	58	47.14 N	7.54 E
Pfaffstätten	264b	48.01 N	16.16 E
Pfalzdorf	52	51.42 N	6.11 E
Pfalzel	56	49.47 N	6.41 E
Pfänder ∧	58	47.30 N	9.47 E
Pfarrkirchen	60	48.27 N	12.56 E
Pfarrweisach	56	50.09 N	10.44 E
Pfastatt	58	47.47 N	7.18 E
Pfatter	60	48.58 N	12.23 E
Pfaueninsel, Schloss ⊥	264a	52.26 N	13.07 E
Pfeddersheim	56	49.38 N	8.16 E
Pfeffenhausen	60	48.40 N	11.58 E
Pfeiffer-Big Sur State Park ♦	226	36.15 N	121.47 W
Pferderennbahn ♦	263	51.31 N	7.32 E
Pflugerville	222	30.26 N	97.37 W
Pforzen	58	47.55 N	10.37 E
Pforzheim	56	48.54 N	8.42 E
Pfreimd ≃	60	49.29 N	12.11 E
Pfrimm ≃	56	49.39 N	8.22 E
Pfronten	58	47.34 N	10.33 E
Pfuhl	58	48.24 N	10.02 E
Pfullendorf	58	47.55 N	9.15 E
Pfullingen	58	48.28 N	9.13 E
Pfunds	58	46.58 N	10.33 E
Pfungstadt	56	49.48 N	8.36 E
Pfyn	58	47.36 N	8.57 E
Pha-an	110	16.53 N	97.38 E
Phachi ≃	110	13.56 N	99.24 E
Phaéton, Port ⊂	174s	17.44 S	149.21 W
Phagwāra	123	31.14 N	75.46 E
Phala	156	23.45 S	26.57 E
Phalaborwa	156	23.55 S	31.13 E
Phalanx	214	41.15 N	80.58 W
Phalempin	50	50.31 N	3.01 E
Phālia	123	32.26 N	73.35 E
Phalodi	120	27.08 N	72.22 E
Phalsbourg	56	48.46 N	7.16 E
Phalta	126	22.17 N	88.07 E
Phaltan	122	17.59 N	74.26 E
Phalti	272b	22.46 N	88.34 E
Phan	110	19.28 N	99.43 E
Phanat Nikhom	110	13.27 N	101.11 E
Phangan, Ko I	110	9.45 N	100.04 E
Phang Hoei, Khao ∧	110	15.15 N	101.23 E
Phangnga	110	8.28 N	98.32 E
Phaniang ≃	110	16.49 N	102.24 E
Phanom Dongrak, Thiu Khao ⋏	110	14.25 N	103.30 E
Phanom Thuan	110	14.07 N	99.42 E
Phan Rang	110	11.34 N	108.59 E
Phan Thiet	110	10.56 N	108.06 E
Phan Thong	110	13.28 N	101.06 E
Phantom Lake	216	42.52 N	88.21 W
Pharenda	124	27.06 N	83.17 E
Phariāro	120	27.12 N	68.59 E
Pharr	196	26.11 N	98.11 W
Phasi Charoen	269a	13.43 N	100.26 E
Phasi Charoen, Khlong ≋	269a	13.44 N	100.30 E
Phat Diem	110	20.06 N	106.06 E
Phato	110	9.48 N	98.48 E
Phatthalung	110	7.37 N	100.05 E
Phayao	110	19.10 N	99.55 E
Pheasant Creek ≃	184	50.35 N	103.28 W
Pheba	194	33.35 N	88.56 W
Phelan	228	34.25 N	117.34 W
Phelps, N.Y., U.S.	210	42.57 N	77.03 W
Phelps, Tx., U.S.	222	30.42 N	95.27 W
Phelps, Wi., U.S.	190	46.03 N	89.05 W
Phelps Lake ⊜	192	35.46 N	76.27 W
Phenix City	192	32.28 N	85.00 W
Phepane ≃	156	25.50 S	22.45 E
Phet Buri ≃	110	13.13 N	99.59 E
Phetchabun	110	16.25 N	101.08 E
Phetchabun, Thiu Khao ⋏	110	16.20 N	100.55 E
Phetchaburi	110	13.06 N	99.57 E
Phibun Mangsahan	110	15.14 N	105.14 E
Phichai	110	17.17 N	100.05 E
Phichit	110	16.26 N	100.22 E
Philadelphia, S. Afr.	158	33.40 S	18.36 E
Philadelphia, Il., U.S.	219	39.58 N	90.07 W
Philadelphia, Ms., U.S.	194	32.46 N	89.07 W
Philadelphia, Mo., U.S.	219	39.50 N	91.44 W
Philadelphia, N.Y., U.S.	212	44.09 N	75.42 W
Philadelphia, Pa., U.S.	208	39.57 N	75.09 W
Philadelphia, Pa., U.S.	285	39.57 N	75.09 W
Philadelphia, Tn., U.S.	192	35.40 N	84.24 W
Philadelphia □[6]	285	39.57 N	75.07 W
Philadelphia International Airport ⊠	208	39.53 N	75.14 W
Philadelphia Museum of Art ⊕	285	39.58 N	75.11 W
Philadelphia Naval Shipyard ■	285	39.53 N	75.11 W
Philadelphia Park Race Track ♦	285	40.07 N	74.57 W
Philae ⊥	140	24.01 N	32.53 E
Phil Campbell	194	34.21 N	87.42 W
Philip	198	44.02 N	101.39 W
Philipp	194	33.45 N	90.12 W
Philippeville → Skikda, Alg.	148	36.50 N	6.58 E
Philippeville, Bel.	50	50.12 N	4.32 E
Philippi	188	39.09 N	80.02 W
Philippi, Lake ⊜	166	24.22 S	139.00 E
Philippine Basin ✢[1]	14	17.00 N	132.00 E
Philippine International Convention Center ♦	269f	14.32 N	120.59 E
Philippinen → Philippines □[1]	116	13.00 N	122.00 E
Philippines (Pilipinas) □[1], Asia	108	13.00 N	122.00 E
Philippines (Pilipinas) □[1], Asia	116	13.00 N	122.00 E
Philippines, University of the ⊕[2]	269f	14.39 N	121.04 E
Philippine Sea ⊤[2]	14	20.00 N	135.00 E
Philippine Trench ✢[1]	14	9.00 N	127.00 E
Philippolis	158	30.19 S	25.13 E
Philippopolis → Plovdiv	38	42.09 N	24.45 E
Philippsreut	60	48.52 N	13.41 E
Philippsthal	264a	52.20 N	13.09 E
Philipsburg, P.Q., Can.	206	45.02 N	73.05 W
Philipsburg, Ned. Ant.	238	17.59 N	63.10 W
Philipsburg, Mt., U.S.	202	46.19 N	113.17 W
Philipsburg, Pa., U.S.	214	40.53 N	78.13 W
Philipsburg Manor ⊥	276	41.05 N	73.52 W
Philipse Manor Hall State Historic Site ⊥	276	40.56 N	73.54 W
Philip Smith Mountains ⋏	180	68.30 N	148.00 W
Philipstown	158	30.26 S	24.29 E
Phillaur	123	31.01 N	75.47 E
Phillip Island I	169	38.29 S	145.14 E
Phillips, Me., U.S.	188	44.49 N	70.20 W
Phillips, Tx., U.S.	196	35.41 N	101.21 W
Phillips, Wi., U.S.	190	45.41 N	90.24 W
Phillipsburg, Ga., U.S.	192	31.34 N	83.31 W
Phillipsburg, Ks., U.S.	198	39.45 N	99.19 W
Phillipsburg, N.J., U.S.	210	40.41 N	75.11 W
Philmont	210	42.14 N	73.39 W
Philo, Il., U.S.	194	40.01 N	88.09 W
Philo, Oh., U.S.	188	39.51 N	81.54 W
Philomath	202	44.32 N	123.21 W
Philpots Island I	176	74.48 N	80.00 W
Phimai	110	15.13 N	102.30 E
Phinga	272b	22.41 N	88.25 E
Phitsanulok	110	16.50 N	100.15 E
Phnom Penh → Phnum Pénh	110	11.33 N	104.55 E
Phnum Pénh	110	11.33 N	104.55 E
Phnum Tbêng Méanchey	110	13.49 N	104.58 E
Pho ≃	124	27.41 N	89.53 E
Phoenicia	210	42.05 N	74.18 W
Phoenix, Az., U.S.	200	33.26 N	112.04 W
Phoenix, Il., U.S.	278	41.36 N	87.38 W
Phoenix, Md., U.S.	208	39.30 N	76.36 W
Phoenix, N.Y., U.S.	210	43.13 N	76.18 W
Phoenix Islands II	14	4.00 S	172.00 W
Phoenix Lake ⊜[1]	282	37.57 N	122.35 W
Phoenix Park ♦	281	42.24 N	83.27 W
Phoenixville	208	40.07 N	75.30 W
Phon	110	15.49 N	102.36 E
Phong ≃	110	16.23 N	102.56 E
Phôngsali	110	21.41 N	102.06 E
Phong Tho	110	22.32 N	103.21 E
Phon Phisai	110	18.01 N	103.05 E
Phosphate Hill	166	21.52 S	139.51 E
Phrae	110	18.09 N	100.08 E
Phra Khanong ◆[8]	269a	13.42 N	100.35 E
Phra Nakhon → Krung Thep	110	13.45 N	100.31 E
Phra Nakhon Si Ayutthaya	110	14.21 N	100.33 E
Phran Kratai	110	16.40 N	99.36 E
Phrao	110	19.22 N	99.13 E
Phra Pradaeng	269a	13.40 N	100.32 E
Phra Rop, Khao ∧	110	13.11 N	99.31 E
Phrom Phiram	110	17.02 N	100.12 E
Phrygia □[9]	130	39.00 N	30.00 E
Phsar Réam	110	10.30 N	103.37 E
Phu Cat	110	14.01 N	109.03 E
Phu Huu, Viet	110	18.58 N	105.31 E
Phu Huu, Viet	269c	10.43 N	106.47 E

Symbols in the index entries represent the broad categories identified in the key at the right. Symbols with superior numbers (⋏[1]) identify subcategories (see complete key on page I · 1).

Symbole im Register stellen die rechts im Schlüssel erklärten Kategorien dar. Symbole mit hochgestellten Ziffern (⋏[1]) bezeichnen Unterabteilungen einer Kategorie (vgl. vollständiger Schlüssel auf Seite I · 1).

Los símbolos incluídos en el texto del índice representan las grandes categorías identificadas con la clave a la derecha. Los símbolos con numeros en su parte superior (⋏[1]) identifican las subcategorías (véase la clave completa en la página I · 1).

Les symboles de l'index représentent les catégories indiquées dans la légende à droite. Les symboles suivis d'un indice (⋏[1]) représentent des sous-catégories (voir légende complète à la page I · 1).

Os símbolos incluídos no texto do índice representam as grandes categorias identificadas com a chave à direita. Os símbolos com números em sua parte superior (⋏[1]) identificam as subcategorias (veja-se a chave completa à página I · 1).

	English	Deutsch	Español	Français	Português
∧	Mountain	Berg	Montaña	Montagne	Montanha
⋏	Mountains	Gebirge	Montañas	Montagnes	Montanhas
)(	Pass	Paß	Paso	Col	Passo
V	Valley, Canyon	Tal, Cañon	Valle, Cañón	Vallée, Canyon	Vale, Canhão
⩦	Plain	Ebene	Llano	Plaine	Planície
›	Cape	Kap	Cabo	Cap	Cabo
I	Island	Insel	Isla	Île	Ilha
II	Islands	Inseln	Islas	Îles	Ilhas
⩡	Other Topographic Features	Andere Topographische Objekte	Otros Elementos Topográficos	Autres données topographiques	Outros acidentes topográficos

ESPAÑOL — FRANÇAIS — PORTUGUÊS

Nombre / Nom / Nome	Página / Page	Lat.°′	Long.°′ W = Oeste / W = Ouest
Phuket	110	7.53 N	98.24 E
Phuket, Ko I	110	8.00 N	98.22 E
Phularwān	123	32.22 N	73.00 E
Phulbari	126	21.52 N	88.08 E
Phulbāria	126	23.22 N	89.50 E
Phuljhuri	126	22.12 N	90.04 E
Phulkusma	126	22.43 N	86.52 E
Phu Loc	110	16.16 N	107.53 E
Phūlpur	124	25.33 N	82.06 E
Phulra	123	34.20 N	73.03 E
Phultala	126	22.59 N	89.28 E
Phu Ly	110	20.32 N	105.56 E
Phum Duang ≃	110	9.10 N	99.20 E
Phumĭ Bâ Khăm	110	13.51 N	107.22 E
Phumĭ Banam	110	11.19 N	105.18 E
Phumĭ Béng	110	13.05 N	104.18 E
Phumĭ Châmbák	110	11.14 N	104.49 E
Phumĭ Chângho Ândêng	110	12.39 N	104.35 E
Phumĭ Chhuk	110	10.50 N	104.28 E
Phumĭ Chruŏy Slêng	110	13.14 N	105.57 E
Phumĭ Dăk Dăm	110	12.20 N	107.21 E
Phumĭ Kâmpóng Srâlau	110	14.05 N	105.46 E
Phumĭ Kâmpóng Trâbâk	110	13.06 N	105.14 E
Phumĭ Kântuŏt Sâmraông	110	14.12 N	104.37 E
Phumĭ Kaôh Kért	110	13.47 N	104.32 E
Phumĭ Kaôh Kŏng	110	11.26 N	103.11 E
Phumĭ Khpôb	110	11.02 N	105.12 E
Phumĭ Krêk	110	11.46 N	105.56 E
Phumĭ Lvéa Kraôm	110	13.21 N	102.54 E
Phumĭ Moŭng	110	13.45 N	103.33 E
Phumĭ Narŭng	110	13.53 N	105.34 E
Phumĭ Phnum Srâlau	110	11.03 N	103.42 E
Phumĭ Prêk Kák	110	12.15 N	105.32 E
Phumĭ Prêk Sândêk	110	11.51 N	105.22 E
Phumĭ Prey Toch	110	12.54 N	103.23 E
Phumĭ Puŏk Chăs	110	13.26 N	103.44 E
Phumĭ Rôluŏs Chăs	110	13.19 N	104.00 E
Phumĭ Sâmraông	110	14.11 N	103.31 E
Phumĭ Spœ Tbong	110	12.20 N	105.19 E
Phumĭ Srê Kôkir	110	13.08 N	106.04 E
Phumĭ Srê Rônéam	110	12.16 N	106.25 E
Phumĭ Tbêng	110	13.35 N	104.55 E
Phumĭ Thalabârĭvăt	110	13.33 N	105.57 E
Phumĭ Thmâ Pôk	110	13.57 N	103.04 E
Phumĭ Tnaôt	110	12.56 N	104.34 E
Phumĭ Tœk Choŭ	110	13.36 N	103.24 E
Phu My	110	14.10 N	109.03 E
Phung Hiep	110	9.49 N	105.50 E
Phuntsholing	124	26.53 N	89.23 E
Phuoc Binh	110	11.50 N	106.58 E
Phuoc Khanh	269c	10.40 N	106.48 E
Phuoc Long	110	9.26 N	105.28 E
Phuoc Long Xa	269c	10.49 N	106.46 E
Phuoc Luong	269c	10.45 N	106.48 E
Phu Quoc	110	10.13 N	103.58 E
Phu Quoc, Dao I	110	10.12 N	104.00 E
Phurphura	272b	22.44 N	88.08 E
Phu Tho	110	21.24 N	105.13 E
Phu Tho Hoa	269c	10.46 N	106.38 E
Phu Tho Race Track ♦	269c	10.46 N	106.40 E
Phutthaisong	110	15.32 N	103.01 E
Phu Vang	110	16.31 N	107.37 E
Phu Yen	110	21.16 N	104.39 E
Pi ≃	100	32.26 N	116.34 E
Pia	154	4.00 N	26.17 E
Piaanu Pass Ʉ	175c	7.20 N	151.26 E
Piabas	250	1.12 S	46.54 W
Piabetá	256	22.37 S	43.10 W
Piabonha ≃	256	22.07 S	43.08 W
Piaçabuçu	250	10.24 S	36.25 W
Piacatuba	256	21.29 S	42.47 W
Piacenza	62	45.01 N	9.40 E
Piacenza □[4]	62	44.53 N	9.35 E
Piacouadie, Lac ⊜	186	51.16 N	70.54 W
Piadena	64	45.08 N	10.22 E
Piaggine	68	40.21 N	15.23 E
Piako ≃	172	37.12 S	175.30 E
Pialba	166	25.17 S	152.51 E
Piāli ≃	272b	22.23 N	88.35 E
Piana	36	42.14 N	8.38 E
Piana, Isola I	71	40.58 N	8.13 E
Piana Crixia	62	44.29 N	8.18 E
Piana degli Albanesi	70	38.00 N	13.17 E
Piana degli Albanesi, Lago di ⊜	70	37.58 N	13.18 E
Piana Mwanga	154	7.40 S	28.10 E
Piancastagnaio	66	42.51 N	11.41 E
Piancó	250	7.12 S	37.57 W
Pian Creek ≃	166	30.02 S	148.12 E
Pian di Sco	66	43.38 N	11.33 E
Pianella	66	42.24 N	14.02 E
Pianello Val Tidone	62	44.57 N	9.24 E
Pianezza	62	45.06 N	7.33 E
Pianguan	102	39.24 N	111.30 E
Pianjiaojie	102	26.01 N	100.32 E
Piankatank ≃	208	37.32 N	76.18 W
Pianling	104	41.24 N	123.58 E
Piano	64	45.46 N	11.08 E
Piano d'Arta	64	46.29 N	13.01 E
Piano del Voglio	66	44.10 N	11.13 E
Pianoro	64	44.22 N	11.20 E
Pianosa, Isola I, It.	36	42.35 N	10.04 E
Pianosa, Isola I, It.	66	42.13 N	15.45 E
Pianosinatico	66	44.07 N	10.44 E
Pianottoli-Caldarello	71	41.29 N	9.03 E
Pians	58	47.08 N	10.30 E
Piapot	184	49.59 N	109.07 W
Piapot Indian Reserve ➔[4]	184	50.45 N	104.26 W
Piasa	219	39.07 N	90.07 W
Piasa Creek ≃	219	38.56 N	90.17 W
Piaseczno	30	52.05 N	21.01 E
Piashti, Lac ⊜	186	50.29 N	62.52 W
Piaski	30	51.08 N	22.51 E
Piat	116	17.48 N	121.29 E
Piatã	255	13.09 S	41.48 W
Piatra-Neamț	38	46.56 N	26.22 E
Piatra-Olt	38	44.24 N	24.16 E
Piatt □[6]	219	40.00 N	88.35 W
Piau	256	21.31 S	43.19 W
Piauí □[3]	250	7.00 S	43.00 W
Piauí ≃, Bra.	250	6.38 S	42.42 W
Piauí ≃, Bra.	255	16.41 S	41.53 W
Piauí, Morro do ∧	255	14.59 S	47.31 W
Piaus ≃	255	12.27 S	49.32 W
Piave ≃	64	45.32 N	12.44 E
Piawaning	162	30.51 S	116.22 E
Piaxtla ≃	232	23.42 N	106.49 W
Piazza Armerina	70	37.23 N	14.22 E
Piazzi, Isla I	254	51.45 S	74.05 W
Piazzola sul Brenta	64	45.32 N	11.47 E
Piberegg	61	47.05 N	15.05 E
Pibor ≃	140	8.26 N	33.13 E
Pibor Post	140	6.48 N	33.08 E
Pibroch	182	54.16 N	113.52 W
Pic ≃	190	48.36 N	86.18 W
Pica	248	20.30 S	69.21 W
Picacho	200	32.42 N	111.29 W
Picacho, Cerro del ∧	286a	19.35 N	99.08 W
Pičajevo	80	53.15 N	42.12 E
Picanoc ≃	190	46.05 N	76.03 W
Picardie □[9]	50	49.45 N	2.50 E
Picatinny Arsenal ■	276	40.57 N	74.33 W
Picatinny Lake ⊜	276	40.57 N	74.33 W
Picayune	194	30.31 N	89.40 W
Piccadilly	186	48.34 N	58.55 W
Piccadilly Station ➔[5]	262	53.28 N	2.14 W
Piccione	66	43.11 N	12.31 E
Piccolo, Mar ⊤[2]	68	40.29 N	17.16 E
Piccotts End	260	51.46 N	0.28 W
Pic de Tio ∧	150	8.52 N	8.54 W
Piceance Creek ≃	200	40.05 N	108.14 W
Picentini, Monti ⋀	68	40.45 N	15.00 E
Picerno	68	40.38 N	15.38 E
Pičeury	80	54.19 N	45.50 E
Pīch ≃	123	34.52 N	71.09 E
Pichana ≃	246	3.31 S	71.43 W
Pichanal	252	23.19 S	64.13 W
Picheng	106	32.07 N	119.42 E
Picher	196	36.59 N	94.49 W
Pichhor	124	25.58 N	78.24 E
Pichilemu	252	34.23 S	72.00 W
Pichileufú, Arroyo ≃	254	40.35 S	70.39 W
Pichimá	246	4.24 N	77.21 W
Pichi-Mahuída	252	38.50 S	64.57 W
Pichincha □[4]	246	0.10 S	78.40 W
Pichis ≃	248	9.59 S	74.59 W
Pichl bei Wels	60	48.11 N	13.54 E
Pichor	124	25.11 N	78.11 E
Pichtovka	86	56.00 N	82.42 E
Pichucalco	234	17.31 N	93.09 W
Picinguaba	256	23.22 S	44.50 W
Picinisco	66	41.39 N	13.52 E
Pic Island I	190	48.43 N	86.38 W
Pickardville	182	54.03 N	113.53 W
Pickaway □[6]	218	39.36 N	82.57 W
Pickens, Ms., U.S.	194	32.53 N	89.58 W
Pickens, S.C., U.S.	192	34.53 N	82.42 W
Pickens, W.V., U.S.	188	38.39 N	80.12 W
Pickensville	194	33.14 N	88.16 W
Pickerel ≃	190	45.55 N	80.50 W
Pickerel Lake ⊜	184	52.36 N	99.30 W
Pickering, On., Can.	212	43.52 N	79.02 W
Pickering, Eng., U.K.	44	54.14 N	0.46 W
Pickering, Vale of V	44	54.12 N	0.45 W
Pickering Beach	212	43.50 N	78.59 W
Pickering Brook	168a	32.03 S	116.08 E
Pickering Creek ≃	285	40.08 N	75.30 W
Pickering Creek Reservoir ⊜[1]	285	40.07 N	75.30 W
Pickett, Lake ⊜	220	28.36 N	81.07 W
Pickford	190	46.09 N	84.21 W
Pičkir'ajevo	80	54.12 N	42.27 E
Pickle Crow	176	51.30 N	90.04 W
Pickmere	262	53.17 N	2.28 W
Pick Mere ⊜	262	53.17 N	2.29 W
Pickstown	198	43.04 N	98.31 W
Pickton	222	33.02 N	95.24 W
Pickwick Lake ⊜[1]	194	34.55 N	88.10 W
Pickwick Landing Dam ➔[6]	194	35.00 N	88.21 W
Picnic Point ›	274b	37.57 S	145.00 E
Pico	66	41.27 N	13.34 E
Pico ∧	150a	14.56 N	24.21 W
Pico I	148a	38.28 N	28.20 W
Pico, Ponta do ∧	148a	38.28 N	28.25 W
Pico da Neblina, Parque Nacional ♦	246	0.30 N	66.00 W
Pico de Orizaba, Parque Nacional ♦	234	19.05 N	97.16 W
Pico Rivera	228	33.58 N	118.05 W
Picos	250	7.05 S	41.28 W
Picota	248	6.55 S	76.20 W
Pico Truncado	254	46.48 S	67.58 W
Picquigny	50	49.57 N	2.09 E
Picton, Austl.	170	34.11 S	150.36 E
Picton, On., Can.	212	44.00 N	77.08 W
Picton, N.Z.	172	41.18 S	174.01 E
Picton, Eng., U.K.	262	53.14 N	2.51 W
Picton, Isla I	254	55.02 S	66.57 W
Picton Bay ⊂	212	44.03 N	77.08 W
Picton Junction	168a	33.21 S	115.41 E
Pictou	186	45.41 N	62.43 W
Pictou Island I	186	45.50 N	62.34 W
Picture Butte	182	49.53 N	112.47 W
Pictured Rocks National Lakeshore ♦	190	46.35 N	86.20 W
Picture Rocks	210	41.17 N	76.43 W
Picúa, Punta ›	240m	18.25 N	65.46 W
Picuí	250	6.31 S	36.21 W
Picunda	84	43.12 N	40.21 E
Picún Leufú	254	39.31 S	69.15 W
Picún Leufú, Arroyo ≃	254	39.31 S	69.08 W
Picuris Indian Reservation ➔[4]	200	36.12 N	105.42 W
Pidálion, Akrotírion ›	130	34.56 N	34.05 E
Pidarak	128	25.51 N	63.14 E
Pidbyzh	78	49.22 N	23.15 E
Piddle ≃	42	50.42 N	2.04 W
Piddletrenthide	42	50.48 N	2.25 W
Pide Adası I	267b	40.53 N	29.04 E
Pidhaytsi	78	49.16 N	25.08 E
Pidhorodna	78	48.07 N	30.51 E
Pidhorodne	78	48.34 N	35.08 E
Pidie, Ujung ›	114	5.30 N	95.53 E
Piding	64	47.46 N	12.55 E
Pidkamin'	78	49.57 N	25.19 E
Pidlisne	78	48.47 N	32.15 E
Pidurutalagala ∧	122	7.00 N	80.46 E
Pidvolochys'k	78	49.33 N	26.09 E
Piedade	287a	22.41 S	43.05 W
Piedade ➔[8]	287a	22.53 S	43.19 W
Piedade do Baruel	287b	23.37 S	46.18 W
Piedade do Rio Grande	256	21.28 S	44.12 W
Piedecuesta	246	6.59 N	73.03 W
Piedicavallo	62	45.42 N	7.57 E
Piedicroce	36	42.23 N	9.23 E
Piediluco	66	42.32 N	12.45 E
Piedimonte Etneo	70	37.48 N	15.12 E
Piedimonte Matese	68	41.21 N	14.22 E
Piedimonte San Germano	66	41.30 N	13.45 E
Piedimulera	58	46.01 N	8.16 E
Piè di Ripa	66	43.15 N	13.29 E
Piedmont, Al., U.S.	194	33.55 N	85.36 W
Piedmont, Ca., U.S.	226	37.49 N	122.13 W
Piedmont, Mo., U.S.	194	37.09 N	90.41 W
Piedmont, Oh., U.S.	214	40.11 N	81.12 W
Piedmont, S.C., U.S.	192	34.54 N	82.21 W
Piedmont Lake ⊜[1]	214	40.08 N	81.11 W
Piedra, C.R.	236	9.29 N	83.40 W
Piedra, Ca., U.S.	226	36.48 N	119.22 W
Piedra ≃	200	37.01 N	107.24 W
Piedra, Cerro ∧	252	37.41 S	73.07 W
Piedra Azul, Quebrada ≃	286c	10.36 N	66.57 W
Piedrabuena	34	39.02 N	4.10 W
Piedra del Águila	254	40.03 S	70.05 W
Piedra del Águila, Embalse ⊜[1]	254	40.30 S	70.20 W
Piedrafita, Puerto de)(	34	42.40 N	7.01 W
Piedrahita	34	40.28 N	5.19 W
Piedra Roja	236	8.38 N	81.48 W
Piedras, Arroyo de las ≃	288	34.43 S	58.19 W
Piedras, Punta ›, Arg.	258	35.25 S	57.08 W
Piedras, Punta ›, Ven.	246	10.40 N	61.40 W
Piedras Blancas	252	31.11 S	59.56 W
Piedras Blancas, Point ›	226	35.40 N	121.17 W
Piedras Coloradas	252	32.23 S	57.36 W
Piedras Negras, Guat.	232	17.11 N	91.15 W
Piedras Negras, Méx.	232	28.42 N	100.31 W
Piedras Negras ⊥	232	17.12 N	91.15 W
Piedra Sola	252	32.04 S	56.21 W
Piegaro	66	42.58 N	12.05 E
Pie Island I	190	48.15 N	89.05 W
Pieksämäki	26	62.18 N	27.08 E
Piéla	150	12.42 N	0.08 W
Pielach ≃	61	48.15 N	15.22 E
Pielavesi	26	63.14 N	26.45 E
Pielavesi ⊜	26	63.18 N	26.35 E
Pielinen ⊜	26	63.15 N	29.40 E
Pieljekaise Nationalpark ♦	24	66.18 N	16.58 E
Piemonte □[4]	36	45.00 N	8.00 E
Pienaarsrivier	156	25.15 S	28.18 E
Piendamó	246	2.38 N	76.30 W
Pieniężno	30	54.15 N	20.08 E
Pieniński Park Narodowy ♦	30	49.25 N	20.25 E
Pieni-Salpausselkä ∧	26	61.08 N	27.20 E
Piennes	56	49.19 N	5.47 E
Pieńsk	30	51.15 N	15.03 E
Pienza	66	43.04 N	11.41 E
Pierce, Co., U.S.	200	40.38 N	104.45 W
Pierce, Fl., U.S.	220	27.50 N	81.58 W
Pierce, Id., U.S.	202	46.29 N	115.47 W
Pierce, Ne., U.S.	198	42.11 N	97.31 W
Pierce, Tx., U.S.	222	29.14 N	96.12 W
Pierce □[6]	224	47.04 N	122.07 W
Pierce, Lake ⊜	220	27.58 N	81.31 W
Pierce City	194	36.56 N	94.00 W
Pierce Lake ⊜, Can.	184	54.10 N	92.56 W
Pierce Lake ⊜, Sk., Can.	184	54.30 N	109.42 W
Pierceton	216	41.12 N	85.42 W
Piermont	210	41.03 N	73.55 W
Pierowall	46	59.20 N	2.59 W
Pierpont, Oh., U.S.	214	41.45 N	80.34 W
Pierpont, S.D., U.S.	198	45.29 N	97.49 W
Pierre	198	44.22 N	100.21 W
Pierre, Bayou ≃, La., U.S.	194	31.51 N	93.06 W
Pierre, Bayou ≃, Ms., U.S.	194	31.55 N	91.11 W
Pierre-Buffière	32	45.42 N	1.21 E
Pierreclos	58	46.20 N	4.41 E
Pierre-de-Bresse	58	46.53 N	5.15 E
Pierrefeu-du-Var	62	43.13 N	6.08 E
Pierrefitte-sur-Aire	56	48.54 N	5.20 E
Pierrefitte-sur-Sauldre	50	47.30 N	2.09 E
Pierrefitte-sur-Seine	261	48.58 N	2.22 E
Pierrefonds, P.Q., Can.	206	45.29 N	73.52 W
Pierrefonds, Fr.	50	49.21 N	2.59 E
Pierrefontaine-les-Varans	58	47.13 N	6.33 E
Pierrelatte	62	44.23 N	4.42 E
Pierrelaye	261	49.01 N	2.09 E
Pierre Part	194	29.57 N	91.12 W
Pierre Pertuis, Col de)(	58	47.12 N	7.11 E
Pierrepont Manor	212	43.44 N	76.04 W
Pierre-sur-Haute ∧	62	45.39 N	3.49 E
Pierreville, P.Q., Can.	206	46.04 N	72.49 W
Pierreville, Trin.	241r	10.18 N	61.01 W
Pierron	219	38.47 N	89.36 W
Pierron, Lac ⊜	206	46.53 N	74.20 W
Pierry	50	49.01 N	3.56 E
Pierson	192	29.14 N	81.27 W
Piersonville	285	40.10 N	74.42 W
Pierz	190	45.58 N	94.06 W
Piesendorf	64	47.17 N	12.43 E
Piešt'any	30	48.36 N	17.50 E
Piesting ≃	61	48.02 N	16.30 E
Pietarsaari → Jakobstad	26	63.40 N	22.42 E
Pieterburen	52	53.24 N	6.27 E
Pieterlen	58	47.11 N	7.20 E
Pietermaritzburg	158	29.37 S	30.16 E
Pietersburg	156	23.54 S	29.25 E
Pietrabbondante	66	41.45 N	14.23 E
Pietracamela	66	42.31 N	13.33 E
Pietracatella	66	41.35 N	14.52 E
Pietra del Pertusillo, Lago di ⊜	68	40.17 N	15.58 E
Pietragalla	68	40.45 N	15.53 E
Pietra Ligure	62	44.09 N	8.17 E
Pietralunga	66	43.26 N	12.26 E
Pietramala	66	44.10 N	11.20 E
Pietramelara	68	41.16 N	14.11 E
Pietramontecorvino	68	41.32 N	15.07 E
Pietrapaola	68	39.29 N	16.49 E
Pietrapertosa	68	40.31 N	16.04 E
Pietraperzia	70	37.25 N	14.08 E
Pietrasanta	64	43.57 N	10.14 E
Pietrelcina	68	41.12 N	14.51 E
Piet Retief	158	27.01 S	30.50 E
Pietrosu, Vârful ∧, Rom.	38	47.08 N	25.11 E
Pietrosu, Vârful ∧, Rom.	38	47.36 N	24.38 E
Pieve	64	45.46 N	10.45 E
Pieve d'Alpago	64	46.10 N	12.21 E
Pieve del Cairo	62	45.03 N	8.48 E
Pieve di Cadore	64	46.26 N	12.22 E
Pieve di Cento	64	44.43 N	11.18 E
Pieve di Soligo	64	45.53 N	12.10 E
Pieve di Teco	62	44.03 N	7.56 E
Pieve Fosciana	64	44.08 N	10.25 E
Pievepelago	64	44.12 N	10.37 E
Pieve Porto Morone	62	45.07 N	9.26 E
Pieve Santo Stefano	66	43.40 N	12.02 E
Piffard	210	42.50 N	77.51 W
Pigari	80	51.24 N	49.42 E
Pigeon, Mi., U.S.	190	43.49 N	83.16 W
Pigeon, Pa., U.S.	214	41.32 N	79.03 W
Pigeon ≃, Mb., Can.	184	52.15 N	97.00 W
Pigeon ≃, On., Can.	212	44.22 N	78.31 W
Pigeon ≃, N.A.	190	48.00 N	89.34 W
Pigeon ≃, U.S.	192	36.00 N	83.11 W
Pigeon ≃, U.S.	216	41.46 N	85.47 W
Pigeon ≃, Mi., U.S.	190	43.56 N	83.17 W
Pigeon ≃, Mi., U.S.	190	45.27 N	84.33 W
Pigeon ≃, Mi., U.S.	216	42.54 N	86.11 W
Pigeon Bay ⊂	214	42.01 N	82.40 W
Pigeon Cove	207	42.40 N	70.38 W
Pigeon Creek ≃, Al., U.S.	194	31.20 N	86.42 W
Pigeon Creek ≃, In., U.S.	194	37.59 N	87.35 W
Pigeon Creek ≃, In., U.S.	216	41.41 N	85.17 W
Pigeon Creek ≃, Pa., U.S.	279b	40.12 N	79.55 W
Pigeon Creek ≃, Pa., U.S.	285	40.12 N	75.35 W
Pigeon Forge	192	35.47 N	83.33 W
Pigeon Lake ⊜, Ab., Can.	182	53.00 N	114.00 W
Pigeon Lake ⊜, On., Can.	212	44.30 N	78.30 W
Pigeon Run ≃	285	40.06 N	75.35 W
Pigeon Swamp ⠿	276	40.23 N	74.29 W
Pigezhuang	105	39.39 N	116.15 E
Pigg ≃	192	37.00 N	79.29 W
Piggott	194	36.22 N	90.11 W
Piggs Peak	158	25.38 S	31.15 E
Pigkawagan	116	7.12 N	124.32 E
Piglio	66	41.49 N	13.08 E
Pigna	62	43.56 N	7.40 E
Pignans	62	43.18 N	6.13 E
Pignataro Maggiore	68	41.11 N	14.10 E
Pignola	68	40.34 N	15.47 E
Pigs, Bay of → Cochinos, Bahía de ⊂	240p	22.07 N	81.10 W
Pigüé	252	37.37 S	62.25 W
Pigŭm-do I	98	34.45 N	125.55 E
Pihama	172	39.30 S	173.56 E
Piha Passage Ʉ	174w	21.07 S	175.05 W
Pihāri	124	27.38 N	80.12 E
Pihlajavesi ⊜	26	61.45 N	28.50 E
Pihlava	26	61.33 N	21.36 E
Pihtipudas	26	63.23 N	25.34 E
Pihuamo	234	19.15 N	103.23 W
P'ihyŏn	98	40.01 N	124.37 E
Piikkiö	26	60.26 N	22.31 E
Piippola	26	64.10 N	25.58 E
Pijijiapan	234	15.42 N	93.14 W
Pijnacker	52	52.02 N	4.27 E
Pijol, Pico ∧	236	15.06 N	87.35 W
Pikal'ovo	76	59.31 N	34.06 E
Pikangikum	184	51.49 N	94.00 W
Pikangikum Lake ⊜	184	51.48 N	94.00 W
Pike	210	42.33 N	78.09 W
Pike □[6], Il., U.S.	219	39.36 N	90.48 W
Pike □[6], Mo., U.S.	219	39.21 N	91.10 W
Pike □[6], Oh., U.S.	218	39.05 N	83.06 W
Pike □[6], Pa., U.S.	210	41.19 N	74.48 W
Pike ≃, N.A.	206	45.04 N	73.06 W
Pike ≃, Wi., U.S.	190	45.26 N	87.52 W
Pike, North Branch ≃	190	45.30 N	88.01 W
Pike, South Branch ≃	190	45.30 N	88.01 W
Pike Creek ≃, On., Can.	281	42.19 N	82.51 W
Pike Creek ≃, De., U.S.	285	39.42 N	75.42 W
Pike Lake ⊜	212	44.46 N	76.21 W
Pikelot I	14	8.05 N	147.38 E
Pike Lowe ∧[2]	262	53.42 N	2.34 W
Pike Run ≃	276	40.25 N	74.38 W
Pikes Peak	218	39.08 N	86.09 W
Pikes Peak ∧	200	38.51 N	105.03 W
Pikes Rocks ∧[2]	214	41.56 N	79.24 W
Pikesville	208	39.22 N	76.43 W
Piketberg	158	32.54 S	18.46 E
Piketon	218	39.04 N	83.00 W
Piketown	208	40.23 N	76.45 W
Pikeville, Ky., U.S.	192	37.28 N	82.31 W
Pikeville, Tn., U.S.	194	35.36 N	85.11 W
Pikkola	265a	59.42 N	30.08 E
Pikou	98	39.24 N	122.20 E
Pikounda	152	0.33 N	16.42 E
Pikwitonei	184	55.35 N	97.09 W
Pila, Arg.	252	36.01 S	58.08 W
Pila, It.	62	45.41 N	7.18 E
Piła (Schneidemühl), Pol.	30	53.10 N	16.44 E
Piła □[4]	30	53.15 N	16.30 E
Pilanesberg ∧	156	25.14 S	27.04 E
Pilanesberg Game Reserve ➔[4]	156	25.15 S	27.05 E
Pilão Arcado	250	9.56 S	42.29 W
Pilar, Arg.	252	31.41 S	63.54 W
Pilar, Arg.	252	31.27 S	61.15 W
Pilar, Arg.	258	34.27 S	58.54 W
Pilar, Bra.	250	9.36 S	35.56 W
Pilar, Bra.	287a	22.42 S	43.19 W
Pilar, Para.	252	26.52 S	58.23 W
Pilar, Pil.	116	11.29 N	123.00 E
Pilar, Pil.	116	9.52 N	126.06 E
Pilar □[5]	288	34.28 S	58.52 W
Pilar Bay ⊂	116	11.34 N	123.00 E
Pilarcitos Creek ≃	282	37.28 N	122.27 W
Pilarcitos Lake ⊜	282	37.33 N	122.25 W
Pilar de Goiás	255	14.41 S	49.27 W
Pilar do Sul	255	23.49 S	47.42 W
Pilares	196	30.24 N	104.52 W
Pilas Group II	116	6.45 N	121.35 E
Pilas Island I	116	6.38 N	121.37 E
Pilatus ∧	58	46.59 N	8.15 E
Pilawa	30	51.58 N	21.31 E
Pilaya ≃	248	20.55 S	64.04 W
Pilcher Park ♦	278	41.32 N	88.01 W
Pilchuck ≃	224	47.55 N	122.02 W
Pilchuck Creek ≃	224	48.12 N	122.13 W
Pilcomayo ≃	18	25.21 S	57.42 W
Pilcomayo, Brazo Norte ≃	252	24.56 S	58.16 W
Pilcomayo, Brazo Sur ≃	252	24.56 S	58.16 W
Pil'dozero	24	65.43 N	33.28 E
Piles Creek ≃	276	40.37 N	74.12 W
Pilga	162	21.29 S	119.25 E
Pilger	198	42.00 N	97.03 W
Pilgrim Gardens	285	39.57 N	75.19 W
Pilgrim Memorial Monument ⊥	207	42.04 N	70.12 W
Pilgrims Hatch	260	51.38 N	0.17 E
Pilgrim's Rest	156	24.55 S	30.44 E
Pil'gyn	180	69.18 N	179.08 E
Pili	116	13.33 N	123.16 E
Pīlībhīt	124	28.38 N	79.48 E
Pilica ≃	30	51.52 N	21.17 E
Pilipinas → Philippines □[1]	116	13.00 N	122.00 E
Pilis ⋀	264c	47.37 N	18.59 E
Pilisborosjenő	264c	47.36 N	19.00 E
Pilkhua	124	28.43 N	77.39 E
Pillaro	246	1.10 S	78.32 W
Pillar Point ›	282	37.30 N	122.30 W
Pillar Point ›[1]	212	43.59 N	76.09 W
Pillau → Baltijsk	76	54.39 N	19.55 E
Pilley's Island	186	49.31 N	55.44 W
Pilliga	166	30.21 S	148.54 E
Pillings Pond ⊜	283	42.32 N	71.02 W
Pillnitz ➔[8]	54	51.00 N	13.52 E
Pillon, Col du)(	58	46.22 N	7.13 E
Pillow	208	40.38 N	76.48 W
Pillsbury Sound Ʉ	240m	18.20 N	64.49 W
Pil'na	80	55.33 N	45.55 E
Pílos	38	36.55 N	21.43 E
Pilot ∧	166	36.45 S	148.13 E
Pilot Butte	184	50.28 N	104.25 W
Pilot Grove	194	38.52 N	92.54 W
Pilot Hill	226	38.50 N	121.02 W
Pilot Knob	194	37.37 N	90.38 W
Pilot Knob ∧, Ar., U.S.	194	35.42 N	93.57 W
Pilot Knob ∧, Id., U.S.	202	45.54 N	115.42 W
Pilot Mound	184	49.16 N	98.55 W
Pilot Mountain	192	36.23 N	80.28 W
Pilot Peak ∧, Nv., U.S.	204	38.21 N	117.58 W
Pilot Peak ∧, Nv., U.S.	204	41.02 N	114.06 W
Pilot Peak ∧, Wy., U.S.	202	44.58 N	109.53 W
Pilot Point, Ak., U.S.	180	57.34 N	157.35 W
Pilot Point, Tx., U.S.	196	33.23 N	96.57 W
Pilot Rock	202	45.29 N	118.49 W
Pilot Rock ∧	200	35.09 N	109.53 W
Pilot Station	180	61.56 N	162.54 W
Pilottown	194	29.10 N	89.15 W
Pilpah Range ⋀	166	20.23 S	138.34 E
Pilsen → Plzeň	60	49.45 N	13.23 E
Pilsensee ⊜	60	48.01 N	11.11 E
Pilsum	52	53.29 N	7.04 E
Piltene	76	57.13 N	21.40 E
Pilu ≃	110	19.33 N	97.24 E
Piluchang	107	29.13 N	105.37 E
Pil'ugino	80	53.25 N	52.26 E
Pilusi	106	32.05 N	120.05 E
Pilzno	30	49.59 N	21.17 E
Pim ≃	74	61.18 N	71.57 E
Pima	200	32.53 N	109.49 W
Pimah	110	15.36 N	107.25 E
Pimba	166	31.15 S	136.47 E
Pimelles	50	47.50 N	4.10 E
Pimenta Bueno ≃	248	11.39 S	61.11 W
Pimenteira, Vereda ≃	250	9.58 S	42.46 W
Pimenteiras	250	6.14 S	41.25 W
Pimentel, Bra.	250	3.43 S	45.30 W
Pimentel, Perú	248	6.50 S	79.57 W
Pimlico Race Course ♦	284b	39.21 N	76.40 W
Pimmit Hills	284c	38.54 N	77.12 W
Pimmit Run ≃	284c	38.55 N	77.07 W
Pimu-Lendo	152	1.46 N	20.54 E
Pimville ➔[8]	273d	26.16 S	27.54 E
Pina	34	41.29 N	0.32 W
Pina ≃	76	52.10 N	26.14 E
Pinacanauan ≃	116	17.37 N	121.44 E
Pináculo, Cerro ∧	254	50.45 S	72.16 W
Pinalón, Cerro ∧	236	15.05 N	89.55 W
Pinamalayan	116	13.02 N	121.29 E
Pinang → George Town	114	5.25 N	100.20 E
Pinang □[3]	114	5.20 N	100.20 E
Pinang, Pulau I	114	5.23 N	100.15 E
Pinangah	112	5.12 N	116.50 E
Pınarbaşı, Tür.	130	41.36 N	33.07 E
Pınarbaşı, Tür.	130	38.44 N	36.24 E
Pinar del Río	240p	22.25 N	83.42 W
Pinar del Río □[4]	240p	22.30 N	83.45 W
Pinardville	188	42.59 N	71.30 W
Pınarhisar	130	41.37 N	27.30 E
Pınarlar	130	38.53 N	39.29 E
Pinas, Arg.	252	31.09 S	65.29 W
Piñas, Ec.	246	3.42 S	79.42 W
Piñas, Cerro ∧	236	15.25 N	85.47 W
Pinatubo, Mount ∧	116	15.08 N	120.21 E
Pinazo, Arroyo ≃	288	34.24 S	58.48 W
Pinchbeck	42	52.48 N	0.09 W
Pincher Creek	182	49.29 N	113.57 W
Pinchi Lake ⊜	182	54.35 N	124.20 W
Pinckney	216	42.27 N	83.56 W
Pinckney State Recreation Area ♦	216	42.25 N	84.04 W
Pinckneyville	194	38.04 N	89.22 W
Pinconning	190	43.51 N	83.57 W
Pincourt	206	45.23 N	74.00 W
Pinčuga	86	58.23 N	96.59 E
Pińczów	30	50.32 N	20.35 E
Pindaíba, Ribeirão ≃	255	14.18 S	51.45 W
Pindale	110	21.11 N	95.51 E
Pindamonhangaba	256	22.55 S	45.28 W
Pindar	162	28.29 S	115.48 E
Pindaré ≃	250	3.17 S	44.47 W
Pindaré-Mirim	250	3.37 S	45.21 W
Pind Dādan Khān	123	32.35 N	73.03 E
Pinde → Píndhos Óros ⋀	38	39.49 N	21.14 E
Pinder Point ›	192	26.28 N	78.39 W
Píndhos Óros (Pindus Mountains) ⋀	38	39.49 N	21.14 E
Pindi Bhattiān	123	31.54 N	73.16 E
Pindiga	146	9.59 N	10.54 E
Pindi Gheb	123	33.14 N	72.16 E
Pindo → Píndhos Óros ⋀	38	39.49 N	21.14 E
Pindobaçu	250	10.44 S	40.21 W
Pindorama de Goiás	250	10.55 S	47.40 W
Pinduši	24	62.56 N	34.35 E
Pindus Mountains → Píndhos Óros ⋀	38	39.49 N	21.14 E
Pindwāra	120	24.48 N	73.04 E
Pine ≃, B.C., Can.	182	56.08 N	120.41 W
Pine ≃, Mb., Can.	184	52.00 N	100.09 W
Pine ≃, On., Can.	212	44.20 N	79.52 W
Pine ≃, Mi., U.S.	190	44.15 N	85.55 W
Pine ≃, Mi., U.S.	190	46.03 N	84.40 W
Pine ≃, Mi., U.S.	190	44.26 N	83.21 W
Pine ≃, Mi., U.S.	190	43.35 N	84.08 W
Pine ≃, Mi., U.S.	214	42.49 N	82.29 W
Pine ≃, Wi., U.S.	190	44.08 N	88.54 W
Pine ≃, Wi., U.S.	190	45.50 N	88.08 W
Pine ≃, Wi., U.S.	190	43.12 N	90.18 W
Pine Apple	194	31.52 N	86.59 W
Pine Banks Park ♦	283	42.26 N	71.04 W
Pine Barrens ➔[1]	208	39.48 N	74.35 W
Pine Beach	206	45.32 N	73.57 W
Pine Bluff	194	34.13 N	92.00 W
Pine Bluffs	198	41.10 N	104.04 W
Pine Brook	276	40.52 N	74.20 W
Pine Brook ≃, U.S.	276	41.04 N	74.05 W
Pine Brook ≃, Ma., U.S.	283	42.00 N	70.47 W
Pine Brook ≃, N.J., U.S.	276	40.19 N	74.20 W
Pine Bush	210	41.36 N	74.17 W
Pine Castle	220	28.28 N	81.22 W
Pine City, Mn., U.S.	190	45.49 N	92.58 W
Pine City, N.Y., U.S.	210	42.02 N	76.52 W
Pinecliff Lake ⊜	276	41.08 N	74.23 W
Pinecraft	220	27.19 N	82.30 W
Pine Creek	164	13.49 S	131.49 E
Pine Creek ≃, Ab., Can.	182	54.56 N	112.31 W
Pine Creek ≃, Ca., U.S.	204	40.40 N	120.46 W
Pine Creek ≃, Ca., U.S.	282	37.58 N	122.02 W
Pine Creek ≃, Nv., U.S.	204	40.36 N	116.10 W
Pine Creek ≃, Pa., U.S.	210	41.10 N	77.16 W
Pine Creek ≃, Pa., U.S.	279b	40.30 N	79.57 W
Pine Creek ≃, Pa., U.S.	285	40.05 N	75.37 W
Pine Creek, West Branch ≃	210	41.43 N	77.38 W
Pine Creek Indian Reserve ➔[4]	184	52.03 N	100.14 W
Pine Creek Lake ⊜[1]	196	34.05 N	95.05 W
Pine Creek Point ›	276	41.07 N	73.16 W
Pine Crest, Fl., U.S.	220	28.01 N	82.32 W
Pinecrest, Va., U.S.	208	38.50 N	77.09 W
Pinecrest Lake ⊜	226	38.12 N	119.58 W
Pine Crest Point ›	284a	42.52 N	79.11 W
Pinedale, Ca., U.S.	226	36.50 N	119.48 W
Pinedale, Wy., U.S.	200	42.52 N	109.51 W
Pine Falls	184	50.35 N	96.15 W
Pine Flat Lake ⊜[1]	226	36.52 N	119.18 W
Pinega	24	64.42 N	43.19 E
Pinega ≃	24	64.08 N	41.54 E
Pine Glen	212	45.19 N	75.43 W
Pine Grove, On., Can.	275b	43.48 N	79.35 W
Pine Grove, Ca., U.S.	226	38.25 N	120.39 W
Pine Grove, Fl., U.S.	220	28.16 N	81.11 W
Pine Grove, N.J., U.S.	285	39.53 N	74.52 W
Pine Grove, Pa., U.S.	208	40.32 N	76.23 W
Pine Grove, W.V., U.S.	188	39.33 N	80.40 W
Pine Grove Mills	214	40.44 N	77.53 W
Pine Hill, Austl.	166	23.39 S	146.58 E
Pine Hill, Al., U.S.	194	31.58 N	87.35 W
Pine Hill, N.J., U.S.	208	39.47 N	74.59 W
Pine Hill, N.Y., U.S.	210	42.08 N	74.29 W
Pinehill, Tx., U.S.	222	32.06 N	94.36 W
Pine Hills	220	28.33 N	81.27 W
Pinehouse Lake	184	55.31 N	106.36 W
Pinehouse Lake ⊜	184	55.32 N	106.35 W
Pinehurst, Ga., U.S.	192	32.11 N	83.45 W
Pinehurst, Id., U.S.	202	45.15 N	116.20 W
Pinehurst, Ma., U.S.	207	42.31 N	71.13 W
Pinehurst, N.Y., U.S.	284a	42.44 N	78.57 W
Pinehurst, N.C., U.S.	192	35.11 N	79.28 W
Pinehurst, Tx., U.S.	222	30.10 N	95.41 W
Pinehurst Lake ⊜	182	54.39 N	111.25 W
Pine Island, Mn., U.S.	190	44.12 N	92.38 W
Pine Island, N.Y., U.S.	210	41.17 N	74.27 W
Pine Island I	220	26.35 N	82.06 W
Pine Island Bay ⊂	9	74.50 S	102.05 W
Pine Island Bayou ≃	194	30.10 N	94.07 W
Pine Island Creek ≃	283	42.47 N	70.48 W
Pine Island Dam ➔[6]	214	40.08 N	80.43 W
Pine Island Sound Ʉ	220	26.33 N	82.10 W
Pine Lake, In., U.S.	216	41.38 N	86.45 W
Pine Lake, Ma., U.S.	283	42.23 N	71.27 W
Pine Lake ⊜, On., Can.	212	44.57 N	79.27 W
Pine Lake ⊜, Mi., U.S.	281	42.35 N	83.20 W
Pine Lake ⊜, N.Y., U.S.	210	43.12 N	74.31 W
Pineland	194	31.14 N	93.58 W
Pine Lawn	219	38.41 N	90.16 W
Pinellas □[6]	220	27.53 N	82.43 W
Pinellas, Point ›	220	27.42 N	82.38 W
Pinellas Park	220	27.50 N	82.41 W
Pine Marsh ⠿	276	40.37 N	73.34 W
Pine Meadow Lake ⊜	276	41.11 N	74.07 W
Pine Mountain ∧, U.S.	192	36.55 N	83.20 W
Pine Mountain ∧, Ca., U.S.	226	35.41 N	121.05 W
Pine Mountain ∧, Ca., U.S.	280	34.13 N	117.54 W
Pine Mountain ∧, Ct., U.S.	207	41.58 N	72.56 W
Pine Mountain ∧, Ga., U.S.	192	32.51 N	84.47 W
Pine Mountain ∧, Or., U.S.	202	43.47 N	120.54 W
Pine Mountain ∧, Wy., U.S.	200	41.02 N	109.01 W
Pine Nut Mountains ⋀	226	39.00 N	119.25 W
Pine Orchard Meadows	284b	39.17 N	76.52 W
Pine Pass)(	182	55.22 N	122.40 W
Pine Plains	210	41.59 N	73.40 W
Pine Point, Austl.	168b	34.34 S	137.52 E
Pine Point, N.T., Can.	176	61.01 N	114.15 W
Pine Point Park ♦	275b	43.43 N	79.33 W
Pine Portage Dam ➔[6]	176	49.18 N	88.19 W
Pine Prairie	194	30.47 N	92.25 W
Piner	218	38.50 N	84.32 W
Pine Rest	283	42.23 N	71.26 W
Pine Ridge, Pa., U.S.	285	39.55 N	75.22 W
Pine Ridge, S.D., U.S.	198	43.01 N	102.33 W
Pine Ridge, Va., U.S.	284c	38.52 N	77.14 W
Pine Ridge ∧	198	42.40 N	103.00 W
Pine Ridge Estates	276	41.02 N	73.41 W
Pine Ridge Indian Reservation ➔[4]	198	43.25 N	102.21 W
Pine River, Mb., Can.	184	51.47 N	100.32 W
Pine River, Mn., U.S.	190	46.43 N	94.24 W
Piñero	258	34.32 S	58.45 W
Pinerolo	62	44.53 N	7.21 E
Piñeros, Isla I	240m	18.15 N	65.35 W
Pinerovka	80	51.34 N	43.04 E
Pine Run ≃	279b	40.37 N	79.35 W
Pines ≃	283	42.27 N	70.58 W
Pines, Isle of → Juventud, Isla de la I	240p	21.40 N	82.50 W
Pines, Lake o' the ⊜[1]	222	32.46 N	94.35 W
Pines, Point of ›	283	42.26 N	70.58 W
Pine Shores	220	27.17 N	82.32 W
Pines Lake ⊜	276	41.00 N	74.16 W
Pines Run ≃	285	39.50 N	75.05 W
Pine Swamp Knob ∧	188	39.33 N	79.31 W
Pineto	66	42.36 N	14.04 E
Pinetop	200	34.07 N	109.56 W
Pinetops	192	35.47 N	77.38 W
Pinetown	158	29.52 S	30.46 E
Pine Tree Hill ∧	114	3.43 N	101.42 E
Pine Valley, Md., U.S.	284b	39.26 N	76.39 W
Pine Valley, N.Y., U.S.	210	42.14 N	76.51 W
Pine Valley V	204	38.25 N	113.40 W
Pine Village	216	40.27 N	87.15 W
Pineville, Ky., U.S.	192	36.45 N	83.41 W
Pineville, La., U.S.	194	31.19 N	92.26 W
Pineville, Mo., U.S.	194	36.35 N	94.23 W
Pineville, N.C., U.S.	192	35.04 N	80.53 W
Pineville, Pa., U.S.	208	40.18 N	75.00 W
Pineville, W.V., U.S.	192	37.34 N	81.32 W
Pinewood, Fl., U.S.	220	25.53 N	80.14 W
Pinewood, S.C., U.S.	192	33.44 N	80.27 W
Piney	50	48.22 N	4.20 E
Piney ≃	194	35.49 N	87.33 W
Piney Branch ≃	284c	38.56 N	77.18 W
Piney Creek ≃, Tx., U.S.	222	31.03 N	94.34 W
Piney Creek ≃, Wy., U.S.	202	44.34 N	106.32 W
Piney Fork	214	40.15 N	80.50 W
Piney Point	222	29.46 N	95.31 W
Piney Point ›	208	38.08 N	76.32 W
Piney Run ≃	284c	38.58 N	77.17 W
Piney Woods	194	32.03 N	89.59 W
Pinfold	262	53.36 N	2.55 W
Ping ≃, Thai	110	15.42 N	100.09 E
Ping ≃, Zhg.	100	25.59 N	115.07 E
Pinga	154	1.01 S	28.42 E
Ping'an, Zhg.	89	45.20 N	123.42 E
Ping'an, Zhg.	104	41.11 N	123.26 E
Ping'an, Zhg.	107	30.36 N	104.42 E
Ping'anbu	98	41.45 N	116.13 E
Ping'ancheng	105	40.03 N	117.48 E
Ping'andi	104	42.34 N	121.52 E
Pingaring	162	32.45 S	118.37 E
Pingba, Zhg.	100	31.19 N	113.18 E
Pingba, Zhg.	102	26.22 N	106.09 E
Pingchang	102	31.35 N	107.03 E
Pingchao	106	32.07 N	120.45 E
Pingding	98	37.48 N	113.37 E
Pingdingpu	104	42.22 N	123.55 E
Pingdingshan, Zhg.	98	41.26 N	124.45 E
Pingdingshan, Zhg.	100	33.45 N	113.17 E
Pingding Shan ∧	89	46.38 N	128.27 E
Pingdu	98	36.47 N	119.54 E
Pingelap I[1]	14	6.13 N	160.42 E
Pingelly	162	32.32 S	117.05 E
Pingfang, Zhg.	100	30.07 N	113.48 E
Pingfang, Zhg.	104	41.17 N	120.40 E
Pingfang, Zhg.	104	41.28 N	120.48 E
Pingfang, Zhg.	104	42.14 N	120.38 E
Pingfang, Zhg.	104	42.27 N	120.38 E
Pingfang, Zhg.	271a	39.56 N	116.33 E
Pingfangdu	104	41.45 N	121.12 E
Pingfangzi	104	41.31 N	121.21 E
Pinggau	61	47.27 N	16.04 E
Pinggu	105	40.09 N	117.07 E
Pingguo	102	23.19 N	107.39 E
Pinghai, Zhg.	100	25.14 N	119.15 E
Pinghai, Zhg.	100	22.39 N	114.53 E
Pinghe, Zhg.	100	24.25 N	117.22 E
Pinghe, Zhg.	102	22.51 N	102.30 E
Pinghe ≃	100	24.25 N	116.36 E
P'inghsiang → Pingxiang	102	22.09 N	106.43 E
Pinghu, Zhg.	100	26.46 N	118.48 E
Pinghu, Zhg.	100	30.56 N	115.22 E
Pinghu, Zhg.	100	22.42 N	114.08 E
Pinghu, Zhg.	106	30.42 N	121.01 E
Pingjiang	100	28.44 N	113.34 E
Pingjing	105	39.20 N	116.06 E
Pinglan	100	22.22 N	113.27 E
Pingle, Zhg.	102	24.37 N	110.40 E
Pingle, Zhg.	102	24.31 N	106.59 E
Pingli	102	32.19 N	109.21 E
Pingliang	102	35.32 N	106.41 E
Pinglidian	98	37.17 N	119.59 E
Pingling	100	23.39 N	114.23 E
Pinglucheng	102	39.50 N	112.19 E
Pingluo	102	38.57 N	106.35 E
Pingluopu	104	41.56 N	123.20 E
Pingnan, Zhg.	100	26.56 N	119.02 E
Pingnan, Zhg.	102	23.30 N	110.30 E
Pingqiao	100	33.24 N	119.13 E
Pingquan	98	40.59 N	118.34 E
Pingrup	162	33.32 S	118.31 E
Ping Shan, H.K.	271d	22.27 N	114.00 E
Pingshan, Zhg.	100	25.36 N	117.52 E
Pingshan, Zhg.	100	23.26 N	113.15 E
Pingshan, Zhg.	100	22.43 N	114.22 E
Pingshan, Zhg.	102	38.15 N	114.10 E
Pingshang	98	35.11 N	119.07 E
Pingshi, Zhg.	100	32.32 N	113.03 E
Pingshi, Zhg.	100	25.20 N	113.02 E
Pingshui	100	29.53 N	120.38 E
Pingtaizi	105	40.44 N	116.25 E
Pingtan, Zhg.	100	25.31 N	119.47 E
Pingtan, Zhg.	100	23.04 N	114.38 E
Pingtan, Zhg.	107	29.50 N	105.56 E
Pingtan, Zhg.	107	29.38 N	105.16 E
Pingtan Dao I	100	25.33 N	119.48 E
Pingtang	102	25.50 N	107.19 E
Pingtian	100	25.19 N	113.31 E
P'ingtung	100	22.40 N	120.29 E
Pingües, Cayos II	240p	20.47 N	78.15 W
Pingwang	106	30.59 N	120.38 E

Symbol	English	Deutsch	Español	Français	Português
≃	River	Fluß	Río	Rivière	Rio
≍	Canal	Kanal	Canal	Canal	Canal
⌊	Waterfall, Rapids	Wasserfall, Stromschnellen	Cascada, Rápidos	Chute d'eau, Rapides	Cascata, Rápidos
Ʉ	Strait	Meeresstraße	Estrecho	Détroit	Estreito
⊂	Bay, Gulf	Bucht, Golf	Bahía, Golfo	Baie, Golfe	Baía, Golfo
⊜	Lake, Lakes	See, Seen	Lago, Lagos	Lac, Lacs	Lago, Lagos
⠿	Swamp	Sumpf	Pantano	Marais	Pântano
⊓	Ice Features, Glacier	Eis- und Gletscherformen	Accidentes Glaciales	Formes glaciaires	Acidentes glaciares
⊤	Other Hydrographic Features	Andere Hydrographische Objekte	Otros Elementos Hidrográficos	Autres données hydrographiques	Outros acidentes hidrográficos
✣	Submarine Features	Untermeerische Objekte	Accidentes Submarinos	Formes de relief sous-marin	Acidentes submarinos
□	Political Unit	Politische Einheit	Unidad Politica	Entité politique	Unidade política
▿	Cultural Institution	Kulturelle Institution	Institución Cultural	Institution culturelle	Instituição cultural
⊥	Historical Site	Historische Stätte	Sitio Histórico	Site historique	Sitio histórico
♦	Recreational Site	Erholungs- und Ferienort	Sitio de Recreo	Centre de loisirs	Area de Lazer
⊠	Airport	Flughafen	Aeropuerto	Aéroport	Aeroporto
■	Military Installation	Militäranlage	Instalación Militar	Installation militaire	Instalação militar
➔	Miscellaneous	Verschiedenes	Misceláneo	Divers	Diversos

ENGLISH | DEUTSCH

Name / Name	Page / Seite	Lat.°′ / Breite°′	Long.°′ / Länge°′ E = Ost
Pingwu	102	32.29 N	104.37 E
Pingxiang, Zhg.	100	27.38 N	113.50 E
Pingxiang, Zhg.	102	22.09 N	106.43 E
Pingyang, Zhg.	89	48.13 N	124.23 E
Pingyang, Zhg.	100	27.41 N	120.33 E
Pingyao, Zhg.	102	37.16 N	112.09 E
Pingyao, Zhg.	106	30.24 N	119.58 E
Pingyi	98	35.34 N	117.37 E
Pingyin	98	36.19 N	116.22 E
Pingyu	100	32.57 N	114.41 E
Pingyuan, Zhg.	98	37.11 N	116.25 E
Pingyuan, Zhg.	100	24.36 N	115.54 E
Pingzhai	102	24.07 N	104.22 E
Pingzhuang	98	42.03 N	119.22 E
Pinhal	256	22.12 S	46.45 W
Pinhal, Ribeirão do ≃	256	22.42 S	46.42 W
Pinhal Novo	34	38.38 N	8.55 W
Pinhalzinho	256	22.46 S	46.36 W
Pinhão	250	10.34 S	37.44 W
Pinheiral	256	22.31 S	43.59 W
Pinheirinhos	256	22.26 S	44.59 W
Pinheiro	250	2.31 S	45.05 W
Pinheiro de Loures	266c	38.50 N	9.12 W
Pinheiro Machado	252	31.34 S	53.23 W
Pinheiros, Bra.	255	18.21 S	40.14 W
Pinheiros, Bra.	256	22.32 S	44.54 W
Pinheiros ≃	287b	23.32 S	46.44 W
Pinhel	34	40.46 N	7.04 W
Pinhoe	42	50.44 N	3.27 W
Pinhuã ≃	248	6.21 S	65.00 W
Pini, Pulau I	110	0.08 N	98.40 E
Pinillos	246	8.55 N	74.28 W
Piniós ≃	38	39.54 N	22.45 E
Pinitos, Sierra de ⋏	200	31.08 N	110.50 W
Pinjar, Lake ⊜	168a	31.38 S	115.49 E
Pinjarra	168a	32.37 S	115.53 E
Pinjor Garden ♦	123	30.47 N	76.47 E
Pinka ≃	61	47.00 N	16.35 E
Pinkafeld	61	47.22 N	16.07 E
Pinkiang → Harbin	89	45.45 N	126.41 E
Pinlaung	110	20.08 N	96.47 E
Pinlebu	110	24.05 N	95.21 E
Pinn ≃	260	51.31 N	0.29 W
Pinnacle ∧, N.Z.	172	41.49 S	173.17 E
Pinnacle ∧, N.Y., U.S.	188	43.13 N	74.23 W
Pinnacle ∧, Va., U.S.	188	39.08 N	78.26 W
Pinnacle Buttes ∧	202	43.44 N	109.57 W
Pinnacle Island I	180	60.12 N	172.46 W
Pinnacle Peak ∧	224	46.45 N	121.43 W
Pinnacles National Monument ♦	226	36.28 N	121.19 W
Pinnaroo	166	35.16 S	140.55 E
Pinneberg	52	53.40 N	9.47 E
Pinner ◆[8]	260	51.36 N	0.23 W
Pino, Sierra del ⋏	196	28.15 N	103.03 W
Pin Oak Creek ≃	222	31.57 N	96.28 W
Pinocchio	66	43.35 N	13.30 E
Pinochle Peak ∧	224	45.43 N	123.36 W
Pinole	226	38.00 N	122.17 W
Pinole Creek ≃	282	38.01 N	122.18 W
Pinole Point >	282	38.01 N	122.22 W
Pinole Ridge ∧	282	37.59 N	122.15 W
Pinos	234	22.18 N	101.34 W
Pinos, Mount ∧	228	34.50 N	119.09 W
Pinos, Point >	226	36.38 N	121.56 W
Pinos-Puente	34	37.15 N	3.45 W
Pinotepa de Don Luis	234	16.25 N	97.55 W
Pinrang	112	3.48 S	119.38 E
Pins, Île de → Juventud, Isla de la I	240p	21.40 N	82.50 W
Pins, Île des I	175f	22.37 S	167.30 E
Pins, Pointe aux >	214	42.15 N	81.51 W
Pins, Rivière des ≃	206	46.01 N	72.03 W
Pinsk	76	52.07 N	26.04 E
Pinson	194	33.41 N	86.41 W
Pinsot	62	45.21 N	6.06 E
Pinta, Isla I	246a	0.35 N	90.44 W
Pintada Arroyo V	196	34.53 N	104.39 W
Pintado	258	33.50 S	56.18 W
Pintado ≃	255	13.33 S	50.16 W
Pintado, Arroyo de ≃	258	34.08 S	56.14 W
Pintado, Cuchilla del ⋏[2]	258	34.12 S	56.25 W
Pintados	248	20.37 S	69.38 W
Pintados, Salar de ≚	248	20.30 S	69.42 W
Pintasan	112	5.26 N	117.43 E
Pinteus	266c	38.52 N	9.09 W
Pintlala Creek ≃	194	32.21 N	86.30 W
Pinto Butte ∧	184	49.22 N	107.25 W
Pinto Creek ≃, Ab., Can.	182	53.51 N	117.35 W
Pinto Creek ≃, Sk., Can.	184	49.40 N	106.42 W
Pintos, Arroyo de ≃	258	33.55 S	56.51 W
Pintos Negreiros	256	22.18 S	45.13 W
Pintoyacu ≃, Ec.	246	2.07 S	76.03 W
Pintoyacu ≃, Perú	246	3.35 S	73.55 W
Pinturas ≃	254	46.35 S	70.18 W
Pintuyan	116	9.57 N	125.15 E
Pin'ug	24	60.15 N	47.48 E
Pinukpuk	116	17.35 N	121.22 E
Pinwherry	44	55.09 N	4.50 W
Pinxton	44	53.06 N	1.19 W
Pinzano al Tagliamento	64	46.11 N	12.57 E
Pinzgau V	64	47.15 N	12.40 E
Pinzón, Isla I	246a	0.36 S	90.40 W
Piobbico	66	43.35 N	12.31 E
Pioche	204	37.55 N	114.27 W
Pio IX	250	6.50 S	40.37 W
Piolenc	62	44.11 N	4.46 E
Piombino	66	42.55 N	10.32 E
Piombino, Canale di ⊔	66	42.53 N	10.30 E
Pioneer, Austl.	162	31.48 S	121.43 E
Pioneer, Ca., U.S.	226	38.25 N	120.33 W
Pioneer, Oh., U.S.	216	41.40 N	84.33 W
Pioneer Mine	182	50.46 N	122.46 W
Pioneer Mountains ⋏	202	45.40 N	113.00 W
Pioneer Park ♦	273d	26.14 S	28.04 E
Pioner, ostrov I	74	79.50 N	92.30 E
Pionerskij	76	54.57 N	20.20 E
Pionierbivak	164	2.16 S	138.02 E
Pionki	30	51.30 N	21.27 E
Pio Pico State Historical Monument ♦	280	33.59 N	118.04 W
Piopio	172	38.28 S	175.01 E
Pioppo	70	38.03 N	13.14 E
Piora, Mount ∧	164	6.45 S	146.00 E
Pioraco	66	43.11 N	12.59 E
Piorini ≃	246	3.23 S	63.30 W
Piorini, Lago ⊜	246	3.34 S	63.15 W
Piotrków Trybunalski	30	51.25 N	19.42 E
Piotrków Trybunalski □[4]	30	51.30 N	19.45 E
Piotta	58	46.31 N	8.40 E
Pio V. Corpus (Limbujan)	116	11.53 N	124.03 E
Piove di Sacco	64	45.18 N	12.02 E
Piovene-Rocchette	64	45.45 N	11.25 E
Pio XII	250	3.53 S	45.17 W
Pipa	107	29.07 N	105.05 E
Pipalkoti	124	30.26 N	79.27 E
Pipanaco, Salar de ≚	252	28.07 S	66.25 W
Pīpār	120	26.23 N	73.32 E
Piparia	124	22.45 N	78.21 E
Pīpar Road	120	26.27 N	73.27 E
Pipas	152	14.56 S	12.12 E
Pipe Creek ≃, In., U.S.	194	40.08 N	85.52 W
Pipe Creek ≃, In., U.S.	216	40.45 N	86.13 W
Pipe Creek ≃, In., U.S.	218	39.26 N	85.06 W
Piper City	216	40.45 N	88.11 W
Pipe Spring National Monument ♦	200	36.43 N	112.33 W
Pipestem Creek ≃	198	46.54 N	98.43 W
Pipestem State Park ♦	192	37.32 N	81.00 W
Pipestone	198	44.00 N	96.19 W
Pipestone ≃	176	52.53 N	89.23 W
Pipestone Creek ≃, Can.	184	49.42 N	100.45 W
Pipestone Creek ≃, Mi., U.S.	216	42.04 N	86.24 W
Pipestone National Monument ♦	198	44.00 N	96.18 W
Pipi ≃	146	7.27 N	22.48 E
Pipinas	258	35.32 S	57.20 W
Piping Brook ≃	276	41.08 N	73.37 W
Pipiriki	172	39.29 S	175.03 E
Piplān	123	32.17 N	71.21 E
Piplūn	126	23.21 N	88.07 E
Pipmuacan, Réservoir ⊜[1]	186	49.35 N	70.30 W
Pipri	124	23.58 N	82.40 E
Pipriac	28	47.49 N	1.57 W
Piqiang	85	40.20 N	77.38 E
Piqiao	106	31.34 N	119.27 E
Piqua	218	40.08 N	84.14 W
Piquet Carneiro	250	5.48 S	39.25 W
Piquete	256	22.36 S	45.11 W
Piquete, Ribeirão ≃	256	22.36 S	45.01 W
Piquiri ≃, Bra.	248	17.39 S	55.09 W
Piquiri ≃, Bra.	248	17.18 S	56.44 W
Piquiri ≃, Bra.	252	24.03 S	54.14 W
Pira	150	8.30 N	1.44 E
Piracaia	256	23.03 S	46.21 W
Piracanjuba	255	17.18 S	49.01 W
Piracanjuba ≃	255	18.14 S	48.48 W
Piracão ≃	287a	23.02 S	43.36 W
Piracicaba	255	22.43 S	47.38 W
Piracicaba ≃	255	22.36 S	48.19 W
Piraçununga	255	21.59 S	47.25 W
Piracuruca	250	3.56 S	41.42 W
Pirae	174s	17.32 S	149.33 W
Piraeus → Piraiévs	38	37.57 N	23.38 E
Pirahmet	130	38.11 N	39.51 E
Piraí	256	22.38 S	43.54 W
Piraí ≃	256	22.28 S	43.50 W
Piraí do Sul	252	24.31 S	49.56 W
Piraiévs (Piraeus)	38	37.57 N	23.38 E
Piraino	70	38.10 N	14.52 E
Piraju	255	23.12 S	49.23 W
Pirajuba	255	19.54 S	48.42 W
Pirajucara, Ribeirão ≃	287b	23.34 S	46.43 W
Pirajuí	255	21.59 S	49.29 W
Pirakata	126	22.34 N	87.11 E
Piramida, gora ∧	88	54.15 N	95.45 E
Piramidal'nyj, pik ∧	85	39.34 N	69.57 E
Pirámide de Cuicuilco ⊥	286a	19.18 N	99.11 W
Pirámide de Santa Cecilia ⊥	286a	19.33 N	99.09 W
Pirámide de Tenayuca ⊥	286a	19.32 N	99.11 W
Piram Island I	120	21.36 N	72.41 E
Piran	36	45.32 N	13.34 E
Piraña, Arroyo ≃	288	34.24 S	58.30 W
Pirané	252	25.43 S	59.06 W
Piranga	255	20.41 S	43.18 W
Pirangaí	256	22.34 S	44.37 W
Piranguçu	256	22.31 S	45.30 W
Piranguinho	256	22.24 S	45.32 W
Piranhas	255	16.31 S	51.51 W
Piranhas ≃, Bra.	250	5.15 S	36.45 W
Piranhas ≃, Bra.	250	8.40 S	49.28 W
Piranhas ≃, Bra.	250	5.56 S	48.15 W
Piranji ≃	250	4.23 S	37.48 W
Pīrān Shahr	128	36.41 N	45.08 E
Pirapemas	250	3.43 S	44.14 W
Pirapetinga ≃	256	21.37 S	42.32 W
Pirapetinga, Ribeirão ≃	256	21.49 S	43.36 W
Pirapó ≃	255	22.30 S	52.01 W
Pirapora	255	17.21 S	44.56 W
Pirapora do Bom Jesus	256	23.24 S	47.00 W
Pirapora do Bom Jesus □[7]	287b	23.24 S	46.56 W
Piraputanga	255	20.26 S	55.32 W
Piraquara	252	25.26 S	49.04 W
Piraquê ≃	287a	23.01 S	43.37 W
Pirarajá	252	33.44 S	54.45 W
Pirata, Monte ∧[2]	240m	18.06 N	65.33 W
Pirate Creek ≃	282	37.33 N	121.52 W
Piratinga ≃	255	15.41 S	46.07 W
Piratini	252	31.27 S	53.06 W
Piratini ≃	252	28.06 S	55.27 W
Piratininga	287a	22.57 S	43.04 W
Piratininga, Lagoa c	256	22.57 S	43.05 W
Piratuba	252	27.27 S	51.48 W
Piratuba, Lago c	250	1.37 N	50.10 W
Piratucu ≃	250	1.59 S	56.58 W
Piraúba	256	21.17 S	43.02 W
Piraube, Lac ⊜	186	50.33 N	71.42 W
Piray ≃	248	16.32 S	63.45 W
Piraziz	130	40.58 N	38.08 E
Pirbright	260	51.18 N	0.39 W
Pirdop	38	42.42 N	24.11 E
Pirenópolis	255	15.51 S	48.57 W
Pires, Ribeirão ≃	287b	23.43 S	46.25 W
Pires do Rio	255	17.18 S	48.17 W
Pírgos	38	37.41 N	21.28 E
Piriá	250	1.40 S	50.02 W
Piriápolis	252	34.54 S	55.17 W
Piribebuy	252	25.29 S	57.03 W
Pirin ⋏	38	41.40 N	23.30 E
Pirinççi ◆[8]	267b	41.10 N	28.50 E
Pirineos → Pyrenees ⋏	34	42.40 N	1.00 E
Piripiri	250	4.16 S	41.47 W
Piritiba	250	11.44 S	40.34 W
Píritu, Ven.	246	11.22 N	69.08 W
Píritu, Ven.	246	9.23 N	69.12 W
Pirituba ◆[8]	287b	23.29 S	46.43 W
Pirk	54	50.25 N	12.04 E
Pīr Mahal	123	30.46 N	72.26 E
Pirmasens	56	49.12 N	7.36 E
Pirna	54	50.58 N	13.56 E
Piroči	82	55.04 N	38.57 E
Pirogovskij	265b	55.59 N	37.44 E
Pirogovskoje vodochranilišče ⊜[1]	82	55.58 N	37.40 E
Pirojpur	126	22.34 N	89.59 E
Pirón ≃	34	41.23 N	4.31 W
Pirongia	172	38.00 S	175.12 E
Pirot	38	43.09 N	22.35 E
Pirovano	252	36.30 S	61.34 W
Pirovskoje	86	57.37 N	92.16 E
Pīr Panjāl Range ⋏	123	33.37 N	74.32 E
Pirpirituba	250	6.46 S	35.30 W
Pirreşit Tepe ∧	84	38.56 N	43.55 E
Pirsaat	84	39.54 N	49.24 E
Pirsaatçay ≃	84	39.53 N	49.19 E
Pirtleville	200	31.22 N	109.34 W
Piru, Indon.	164	3.04 S	128.12 E
Piru, Ca., U.S.	228	34.25 N	118.48 W
Piru, Lake ⊜[1]	228	34.30 N	118.45 W
Piru, Teluk c	164	3.10 S	128.08 E
Piru Creek ≃	228	34.23 N	118.47 W
Pisa	66	43.43 N	10.23 E
Pisa □[4]	66	43.25 N	10.43 E
Pisa ∧[2]	26	63.13 N	28.18 E
Pisa ≃	30	53.15 N	21.52 E
Pisa, Certosa di ʊ[1]	66	43.45 N	10.31 E
Pisa, Mount ∧	172	44.52 S	169.11 E
Pisagua	248	19.36 S	70.13 W
Pisam-bong ∧	98	40.41 N	126.34 E
Pisang, Pulau I	164	1.23 S	128.55 E
Pisarevka	78	49.53 N	40.12 E
Pisarve	272c	19.06 N	73.05 E
Pisau, Tanjong >	116	6.04 N	118.03 E
Piščalje	80	58.14 N	48.42 E
Piscasaw Creek ≃	216	42.16 N	88.49 W
Piscataway	210	40.29 N	74.23 W
Piscataway Creek ≃, Md., U.S.	208	38.42 N	77.02 W
Piscataway Creek ≃, Va., U.S.	208	37.54 N	76.50 W
Pișchia	38	45.55 N	21.20 E
Pisciotta	68	40.06 N	15.14 E
Pisco	248	13.42 S	76.13 W
Pisco ≃	248	13.42 S	76.15 W
Pișcolt	38	47.35 N	22.18 E
Piscovo	80	57.11 N	40.32 E
Piseco Lake ⊜	210	43.23 N	74.36 W
Písek	30	49.19 N	14.10 E
Pisgah, Md., U.S.	208	38.32 N	77.08 W
Pisgah, Oh., U.S.	218	39.19 N	84.22 W
Pisgah Forest	192	35.15 N	82.42 W
Pishan	120	37.37 N	78.18 E
Pishchana	78	48.08 N	29.44 E
Pishchane, Ukr.	78	49.44 N	31.50 E
Pishchane, Ukr.	83	49.34 N	37.51 E
Pishchanka	78	48.12 N	28.53 E
Pishīn	120	30.35 N	67.00 E
Pishīn Lora (Lowrah) ≃	120	29.09 N	64.55 E
Pisidia □[9]	130	37.30 N	31.00 E
Pisinemo	200	32.02 N	112.18 W
Pising	112	5.05 S	121.54 E
Piskivka	78	50.42 N	29.38 E
Pisky, Ukr.	78	50.23 N	33.27 E
Pisky, Ukr.	83	49.26 N	38.59 E
Pisky-Rad'kivs'ki	83	49.17 N	37.36 E
Pismo Beach	226	35.08 N	120.38 W
Pišnur	80	57.47 N	47.58 E
Piso, Lake ⊜	150	6.48 N	11.17 W
Pisogne	64	45.48 N	10.06 E
Pisqui ≃	248	7.45 S	75.01 W
Pissila	150	13.10 N	0.49 W
Pissos	32	44.19 N	0.47 W
Pistakee Highlands	216	42.25 N	88.11 W
Pistakee Lake ⊜	216	42.23 N	88.12 W
Pisticci	68	40.23 N	16.34 E
Pistoia	66	43.55 N	10.54 E
Pistoia □[4]	64	43.58 N	10.50 E
Pistolet Bay c	186	51.32 N	55.50 W
Pistuk Peak ∧	180	59.43 N	159.42 W
Pisuerga ≃	34	41.33 N	4.52 W
Pisz	30	53.38 N	21.49 E
Pit ≃	204	40.45 N	122.22 W
Pit, North Fork ≃	204	41.28 N	120.33 W
Pit, South Fork ≃	204	41.28 N	120.33 W
Pita	150	11.05 N	12.24 W
Pital	246	2.16 N	75.49 W
Pitalito	246	1.51 N	76.02 W
Pitampura Kālan ◆[8]	272a	28.42 N	77.08 E
Pitanga	252	24.46 S	51.44 W
Pitangueiras	255	21.02 S	48.13 W
Pitangueiras, Ribeirão das ≃	256	21.27 S	44.27 W
Pitangui	255	19.40 S	44.54 W
Pitcairn	279b	40.24 N	79.46 W
Pitcairn □[2], Oc.	6	25.04 S	130.05 W
Pitcairn □[2], Oc.	174e	25.04 S	130.05 W
Pitcher	210	42.35 N	75.52 W
Pitch Place	260	51.16 N	0.36 W
Piteå	26	65.20 N	21.30 E
Piteälven ≃	24	65.14 N	21.32 E
Piteglio	66	44.01 N	10.46 E
Pitelino	80	54.34 N	41.49 E
Piterka	80	50.42 N	47.27 E
Pitești	38	44.52 N	24.52 E
Pithapuram	122	17.07 N	82.16 E
Pithara	162	30.24 S	116.40 E
Pithiviers	50	48.10 N	2.15 E
Pithorāgarh	124	29.35 N	80.13 E
Piti, Lagoa ⊜	158	26.34 S	32.53 E
Pitigliano	66	42.38 N	11.40 E
Pitim	80	53.12 N	42.21 E
Pitinga ≃	246	1.32 S	59.49 W
Pitiquito	232	30.42 N	112.02 W
Pitjantjatjara Lands ◆[4]	162	27.00 S	130.30 E
Pitk'aranta	24	61.34 N	31.27 E
Pitkas Point	180	62.02 N	163.17 W
Pitlochry	46	56.43 N	3.45 W
Pitman	208	39.43 N	75.07 W
Pitman Airport ⊠	285	39.45 N	75.08 W
Pitmedden	46	57.20 N	2.11 W
Pitner Ditch ≍	216	41.14 N	86.53 W
Pitogo	116	10.08 N	124.33 E
Pitomača	36	45.57 N	17.14 E
Pitou, Zhg.	100	25.01 N	114.35 E
Pitou, Zhg.	100	23.34 N	116.05 E
Pitou, Zhg.	100	24.26 N	114.22 E
Pitrufquén	254	38.59 S	72.39 W
Pitsea	260	51.34 N	0.31 E
Pitseng	158	28.58 S	28.16 E
Pitsford Reservoir ⊜[1]	42	52.20 N	0.52 W
Pitt ≃	224	49.12 N	122.47 W
Pitt, Mount ∧	174c	29.01 S	167.56 E
Pittem	50	51.00 N	3.16 E
Pitten ≃	61	47.44 N	16.14 E
Pittenweem	46	56.12 N	2.44 W
Pitti Island I	122	10.50 N	72.38 E
Pitt Island I	182	53.35 N	129.45 W
Pitt Lake ⊜	182	49.25 N	122.32 W
Pittsboro, In., U.S.	218	39.51 N	86.28 W
Pittsboro, Ms., U.S.	194	33.56 N	89.20 W
Pittsboro, N.C., U.S.	192	35.43 N	79.10 W
Pittsburg, Ca., U.S.	226	38.01 N	121.53 W
Pittsburg, In., U.S.	216	40.37 N	86.42 W
Pittsburg, Ks., U.S.	198	37.24 N	94.42 W
Pittsburg, N.H., U.S.	206	45.03 N	71.23 W
Pittsburg, Tx., U.S.	222	32.59 N	94.57 W
Pittsburgh, Pa., U.S.	214	40.26 N	79.59 W
Pittsburgh, Pa., U.S.	279b	40.26 N	79.59 W
Pittsburgh, University of ʊ[2]	279b	40.27 N	79.58 W
Pittsburgh-Monroeville Airport ⊠	279b	40.27 N	79.46 W
Pittsfield, Il., U.S.	219	39.36 N	90.48 W
Pittsfield, Me., U.S.	188	44.46 N	69.23 W
Pittsfield, Ma., U.S.	207	42.27 N	73.14 W
Pittsfield, N.H., U.S.	188	43.18 N	71.19 W
Pittsfield, Pa., U.S.	214	41.50 N	79.23 W
Pittsford, Mi., U.S.	216	41.52 N	84.28 W
Pittsford, N.Y., U.S.	210	43.05 N	77.31 W
Pitt Stadium ♦	279b	40.27 N	79.58 W
Pittston	210	41.19 N	75.47 W
Pittsview	194	32.11 N	85.09 W
Pittsville	208	38.23 N	75.24 W
Pittsworth	166	27.43 S	151.38 E
Pitt Water c	170	33.37 S	151.18 E
Pituil	252	28.34 S	67.27 W
Pitumarca	248	13.59 S	71.25 W
Pituri Creek ≃	166	22.58 S	138.50 E
Pitzbach ≃	64	47.13 N	10.46 E
Pitztal V	64	47.07 N	10.47 E
Pium	250	10.27 S	49.11 W
Pium ≃	250	10.12 S	49.57 W
Piura	248	5.12 S	80.38 W
Piura □[5]	248	5.10 S	80.00 W
Piura ≃	248	5.32 S	80.53 W
Piute Peak ∧	204	35.27 N	118.24 W
Piute Reservoir ⊜[1]	200	38.17 N	112.12 W
Piva ≃	38	43.21 N	18.51 E
Pivan'	89	50.29 N	137.06 E
Pivdennyy Buh ≃	78	46.59 N	31.58 E
Piverone	62	45.27 N	8.00 E
Pivijay	246	10.28 N	74.37 W
Piwniczna	30	49.27 N	20.42 E
Pixian	102	30.49 N	103.49 E
Pixley	226	35.58 N	119.17 W
Pižanka	80	57.28 N	48.33 E
Pižma	80	57.52 N	47.06 E
Pižma ≃	80	57.37 N	48.58 E
Pizzighettone	62	45.11 N	9.47 E
Pizzillo, Monte ∧	70	37.48 N	15.01 E
Pizzo	68	38.44 N	16.10 E
Pizzoferrato	66	41.55 N	14.14 E
Pizzoli	66	42.26 N	13.18 E
Pizzone	66	41.40 N	14.02 E
Pjalka	24	66.43 N	40.59 E
Pjana ≃	80	55.40 N	45.57 E
Pjöngjang → P'yŏngyang	98	39.01 N	125.45 E
P. K. le Rouxdam ⊜[1]	158	30.12 S	24.54 E
Placanica	68	38.25 N	16.27 E
Place Bonaventure ◆[9]	275a	45.30 N	73.34 W
Placentia, Nf., Can.	186	47.14 N	53.58 W
Placentia, Ca., U.S.	228	33.52 N	117.52 W
Placentia Bay c	186	47.15 N	54.30 W
Placer, Pil.	116	11.52 N	123.55 E
Placer, Pil.	116	9.39 N	125.36 E
Placer □[6]	226	38.54 N	121.04 W
Placeres del Oro ≃	234	18.27 N	100.57 W
Placeres de Picacho	234	23.11 N	105.42 W
Placerville	226	38.43 N	120.47 W
Placetas	240p	22.19 N	79.40 W
Place Versailles ◆[9]	275a	45.35 N	73.32 W
Plachino	76	54.28 N	39.20 E
Placid, Lake ⊜	220	27.14 N	81.22 W
Placida	220	26.49 N	82.15 W
Plácido de Castro	248	10.20 S	67.11 W
Plácido Rosas	252	32.45 S	53.44 W
Placita de Morelos	234	18.31 N	103.42 W
Plačkovica ⋏	38	41.45 N	22.35 E
Plaffeien	58	46.44 N	7.17 E
Plages, Lac des ⊜	206	45.59 N	74.54 W
Plage-Sainte-Cécile	50	50.34 N	1.35 E
Plailly	261	49.06 N	2.35 E
Plai Mat ≃	110	15.22 N	102.45 E
Plain	224	47.46 N	120.39 W
Plain City, Oh., U.S.	214	40.06 N	83.16 W
Plain City, Ut,. U.S.	200	41.17 N	112.05 W
Plain Dealing	194	32.54 N	93.41 W
Plaines, Île aux I	275a	45.21 N	73.50 W
Plainfield, Ct., U.S.	207	41.40 N	71.54 W
Plainfield, Il., U.S.	216	41.37 N	88.12 W
Plainfield, In., U.S.	218	39.42 N	86.23 W
Plainfield, Ma., U.S.	207	42.30 N	72.55 W
Plainfield, N.J., U.S.	210	40.37 N	74.26 W
Plainfield, Oh., U.S.	214	40.13 N	81.43 W
Plainfield, Pa., U.S.	208	40.12 N	77.17 W
Plainfield, Wi., U.S.	190	44.12 N	89.29 W
Plainfield Heights	216	43.01 N	85.37 W
Plains, Ga., U.S.	192	32.02 N	84.23 W
Plains, Ks., U.S.	198	37.15 N	100.35 W
Plains, Mt., U.S.	202	47.27 N	114.52 W
Plains, Tx., U.S.	196	33.11 N	102.50 W
Plainsboro	208	40.20 N	74.36 W
Plainview, Ca., U.S.	226	36.08 N	119.08 W
Plainview, Il., U.S.	219	39.10 N	89.59 W
Plainview, Mn., U.S.	190	44.09 N	92.10 W
Plainview, Ne., U.S.	198	42.20 N	97.47 W
Plainview, N.Y., U.S.	210	40.46 N	73.28 W
Plainview, Tx., U.S.	196	34.11 N	101.42 W
Plainville, Ct., U.S.	207	41.40 N	72.51 W
Plainville, Il., U.S.	219	39.47 N	91.11 W
Plainville, In., U.S.	194	38.48 N	87.09 W
Plainville, Ks., U.S.	198	39.14 N	99.17 W
Plainville, Ma., U.S.	207	42.00 N	71.20 W
Plainville, N.Y., U.S.	210	43.10 N	76.27 W
Plainwell	216	42.26 N	85.38 W
Plaisance, Baie de c	186	47.18 N	61.53 W
Plaisir	261	48.49 N	1.57 E
Plaistow	207	42.50 N	71.05 W
Plakhtiyivka	78	46.07 N	29.43 E
Plaksino	76	56.11 N	30.42 E
Plamondon	182	54.51 N	112.19 W
Plampang	115b	8.48 S	117.48 E
Planá	60	49.52 N	12.44 E
Plana, Illa I	34	38.10 N	0.28 W
Planada	226	37.18 N	120.19 W
Planalto, Bra.	252	27.20 S	53.03 W
Planalto, Bra.	255	14.39 S	40.29 W
Planches	50	48.42 N	0.22 E
Plandome	276	40.48 N	73.42 W
Plandome Heights	276	40.48 N	73.42 W
Plandome Manor	276	40.49 N	73.42 W
Plan-d'Orgon	62	43.48 N	5.00 E
Plane ≃	54	52.23 N	12.30 E
Planegg	60	48.06 N	11.25 E
Planers'ke	78	44.57 N	35.14 E
Planeta Rica	246	8.25 N	75.36 W
Plangeross	64	46.59 N	10.52 E
Plankenfels	60	49.53 N	11.20 E
Plankinton	198	43.42 N	98.29 W
Plano, Il., U.S.	216	41.39 N	88.32 W
Plano, Tx., U.S.	222	33.01 N	96.41 W
Plansee ⊜	64	47.28 N	10.48 E
Plantagenet	206	45.32 N	75.00 W
Plantation, Fl., U.S.	220	26.07 N	80.14 W
Plantation, Fl., U.S.	220	24.59 N	80.33 W
Plantation, Ky., U.S.	218	38.17 N	85.36 W
Plantation Key I	220	24.58 N	80.33 W
Plant City	220	28.01 N	82.06 W
Plantersville, Al., U.S.	194	32.39 N	86.55 W
Plantersville, Ms., U.S.	194	34.12 N	88.39 W
Plantersville, Tx., U.S.	222	30.20 N	95.52 W
Planting Fields Arboretum State Park ♦	276	40.52 N	73.33 W
Plantsite	200	33.03 N	109.19 W
Plantsville	207	41.35 N	72.53 W
Plaquemine	194	30.17 N	91.14 W
Plaridel, Pil.	116	10.32 N	124.46 E
Plaridel, Pil.	116	8.37 N	123.43 E
Plasencia	34	40.02 N	6.05 W
Plaški	36	45.05 N	15.22 E
Plassenburg ⊥	60	50.06 N	11.28 E
Plassey	126	23.47 N	88.15 E
Plast	86	54.22 N	60.50 E
Plaster Rock	186	46.54 N	67.24 W
Plastovo	82	54.17 N	37.03 E
Plastun	89	44.45 N	136.19 E
Plastunovskaja	78	45.18 N	39.16 E
Plasy	60	49.56 N	13.24 E
Plata, Isla de la I	246	1.16 S	81.06 W
Plata, Río de la c[1]	258	35.00 S	57.00 W
Plata, Río de la ≃	240m	18.29 N	66.15 W
Platani ≃	70	37.24 N	13.16 E
Platania	68	39.00 N	16.19 E
Plátanos	288	34.47 S	58.11 W
Plátanos, Arroyo ≃	288	34.45 S	58.08 W
Plate, Île I	275a	45.22 N	73.48 W
Platea	214	41.57 N	80.20 W
Plateau □[3]	150	8.45 N	8.30 E
Plateau Creek ≃	200	39.11 N	108.18 W
Plateaux □[5]	152	2.15 S	15.30 E
Platì	68	38.13 N	16.03 E
Platinum	180	59.01 N	161.49 W
Platnirovskaja	78	45.23 N	39.23 E
Plato	246	9.47 N	74.47 W
Platono-Petrovka	83	46.59 N	39.28 E
Platonovka	80	52.43 N	41.57 E
Platón Sánchez	234	21.17 N	98.22 W
Platovo	83	48.05 N	39.53 E
Platrand	158	27.08 S	29.29 E
Platt	260	51.17 N	0.20 E
Platta	58	46.40 N	8.51 E
Platte	198	43.23 N	98.50 W
Platte ≃, U.S.	194	39.16 N	94.50 W
Platte ≃, Mn., U.S.	190	45.47 N	94.17 W
Platte ≃, Ne., U.S.	198	41.04 N	95.53 W
Platte ≃, Wi., U.S.	190	42.37 N	90.40 W
Platte Center	198	41.32 N	97.29 W
Platte City	194	39.22 N	94.46 W
Platte Creek ≃	198	43.19 N	99.00 W
Platte Island I	138	5.52 S	55.23 E
Plattekill	210	41.37 N	74.05 W
Platteville, Co., U.S.	200	40.12 N	104.49 W
Platteville, Wi., U.S.	190	42.44 N	90.28 W
Platt Hall ⊥	262	53.27 N	2.13 W
Plattling	60	48.47 N	12.53 E
Plattsburg	194	39.33 N	94.26 W
Plattsburgh	188	44.41 N	73.27 W
Plattsburgh Air Force Base ■	188	44.40 N	73.28 W
Plattsmouth	198	41.00 N	95.52 W
Plattsville	212	43.18 N	80.37 W
Platveld	156	19.58 S	17.07 E
Plau	54	53.27 N	12.16 E
Plaue, Dtsch.	54	52.24 N	12.25 E
Plaue, Dtsch.	54	50.47 N	10.54 E
Plauen	54	50.30 N	12.08 E
Plauer See ⊜	54	53.30 N	12.20 E
Plav	38	42.36 N	19.56 E
Plave	64	46.02 N	13.36 E
Plaviņas	76	56.37 N	25.43 E
Plavsk	76	53.43 N	37.18 E
Plaxtol	260	51.15 N	0.18 E
Playa Azul	234	17.59 N	102.24 W
Playa Baracoa	286b	23.03 N	82.34 W
Playa Bonita	236	9.39 N	84.27 W
Playa de Fajardo	240m	18.20 N	65.38 W
Playa de Guayanés	240m	18.04 N	65.49 W
Playa de Guayanilla	240m	18.01 N	66.46 W
Playa del Carmen	232	20.36 N	87.06 W
Playa del Rey ◆[8]	280	33.58 N	118.26 W
Playa de Naguabo	240m	18.12 N	65.43 W
Playa de Ponce	240m	17.59 N	66.37 W
Playa Noriega, Laguna ⊜	232	29.10 N	111.50 W
Playas Lake ⊜	200	31.50 N	108.34 W
Playa Vicente	234	17.50 N	95.49 W
Play Cu	110	13.59 N	108.00 E
Playford ≃	162	19.03 S	135.35 E
Playgreen Lake ⊜	184	54.00 N	98.10 W
Playland ♦	276	40.58 N	73.41 W
Plaza	198	48.01 N	101.57 W
Plaza at Mid Island ◆[9]	276	40.46 N	73.32 W
Plaza de Caisán	236	8.46 N	82.45 W
Plaza de Mayo ♦	288	34.36 S	58.23 W
Plaza de Toros ♦	266a	40.26 N	3.39 W
Plaza de Toros Las Arenas ♦	266d	41.23 N	2.09 W
Plaza de Toros Monumental ♦	266d	41.24 N	2.11 E
Plaza Huincul	252	38.55 S	69.09 W
Plaza Park	285	40.04 N	74.53 W
Plazas de Soberanía en el Norte de África → Spanish North Africa □[2]	34	35.53 N	5.19 W
Pleasant	275b	43.41 N	79.49 W
Pleasant, Lake ⊜[1]	200	33.53 N	112.16 W
Pleasant, Mount ∧	192	37.44 N	79.10 W
Pleasant, Mount ∧[2]	186	45.26 N	66.49 W
Pleasant Bay	186	46.49 N	60.48 W
Pleasantdale, Sk., Can.	184	52.35 N	104.30 W
Pleasantdale, N.Y., U.S.	210	42.47 N	73.40 W
Pleasant Gap	214	40.52 N	77.44 W
Pleasant Garden	192	35.57 N	79.45 W
Pleasant Grove, Ca., U.S.	226	38.49 N	121.29 W
Pleasant Grove, Ut,. U.S.	200	40.21 N	111.44 W
Pleasant Grove Creek ≃	226	38.48 N	121.32 W
Pleasant Hill, Ca., U.S.	226	37.56 N	122.03 W
Pleasant Hill, Il., U.S.	219	39.26 N	90.52 W
Pleasant Hill, La., U.S.	194	31.49 N	93.31 W
Pleasant Hill, Mo., U.S.	194	38.47 N	94.16 W
Pleasant Hill, N.C., U.S.	208	36.32 N	77.32 W
Pleasant Hill, Oh., U.S.	218	40.03 N	84.20 W
Pleasant Hill Lake ⊜[1]	214	40.38 N	82.21 W
Pleasant Hills	214	40.20 N	79.57 W
Pleasant Lake, In., U.S.	216	41.34 N	85.00 W
Pleasant Lake, Mi., U.S.	216	42.23 N	84.22 W
Pleasant Lake ⊜	216	42.13 N	83.56 W
Pleasant Mills	216	40.47 N	84.51 W
Pleasant Mount	210	41.44 N	75.26 W
Pleasanton, Ca., U.S.	226	37.39 N	121.52 W
Pleasanton, Ks., U.S.	198	38.10 N	94.42 W
Pleasanton, Tx., U.S.	196	28.58 N	98.28 W
Pleasanton Ridge ∧	282	37.40 N	121.55 W
Pleasant Plains, Il., U.S.	219	39.52 N	89.55 W
Pleasant Plains, N.J., U.S.	208	40.00 N	74.13 W
Pleasant Point	172	44.16 S	171.08 E
Pleasant Prairie	216	42.33 N	87.57 W
Pleasant Ridge	281	42.31 N	83.10 W
Pleasant Unity	214	40.15 N	79.28 W
Pleasant Valley, N.Y., U.S.	210	41.44 N	73.49 W
Pleasant Valley, Oh., U.S.	218	39.22 N	83.03 W
Pleasant Valley, Pa., U.S.	279b	40.31 N	75.18 W
Pleasantville, Ia., U.S.	190	41.23 N	93.16 W
Pleasantville, Md., U.S.	284b	39.11 N	76.38 W
Pleasantville, N.J., U.S.	208	39.23 N	74.31 W
Pleasantville, N.Y., U.S.	210	41.07 N	73.47 W
Pleasantville, Pa., U.S.	214	41.35 N	79.34 W
Pleasington	262	53.44 N	2.34 W
Pleasure Beach	207	41.18 N	72.08 W
Pleasure Ridge Park	218	38.09 N	85.51 W
Pleasureville	218	38.33 N	85.04 W
Pléaux	32	45.08 N	2.14 E
Plechanovo	82	54.14 N	37.33 E
Plechanovskoje	76	52.39 N	39.50 E
Plechovo	78	51.07 N	35.18 E
Plechý (Plöckenstein) ∧	60	48.46 N	13.51 E
Pledger	222	29.11 N	95.55 W
Pleebo	150	4.35 N	7.40 W
Pleiku → Play Cu	110	13.59 N	108.00 E
Pleinfeld	56	49.06 N	10.59 E
Pleissa	54	50.50 N	12.46 E
Pleisse ≃	54	51.20 N	12.22 E
Pléneuf	32	48.36 N	2.33 W
Plenty	184	51.47 N	108.36 W
Plenty ≃, Austl.	162	23.25 S	136.31 E
Plenty ≃, Austl.	274b	37.45 S	145.07 E
Plenty, Bay of c	172	37.40 S	177.00 E
Plentywood	198	48.46 N	104.33 W
Plered	115a	6.38 S	107.23 E
Pleščejevo, ozero ⊜	82	56.46 N	38.47 E
Pleščenicy	76	54.25 N	27.50 E
Pleseck	24	62.43 N	40.20 E
Plešivka	82	54.23 N	37.09 E
Plesna ≃	54	50.07 N	12.28 E
Pless, Dtsch.	58	48.05 N	10.08 E
Pless → Pszczyna, Pol.	30	49.59 N	18.57 E
Plessa	54	51.28 N	13.37 E
Plessisville	206	46.14 N	71.47 W
Pleszew	30	51.54 N	17.48 E
Pletenevka	82	54.31 N	36.06 E
Pletenyy Tashlyk	78	48.29 N	31.40 E
Pleternica	38	45.17 N	17.48 E
Plétipi, Lac ⊜	176	51.44 N	70.06 W
Plettenberg	56	51.13 N	7.52 E
Plettenbergbaai	158	34.04 S	23.22 E
Pleurs	50	48.41 N	3.52 E
Pleven	38	43.25 N	24.37 E
Plevna, Mo., U.S.	219	39.58 N	92.05 W
Plevna, Mt., U.S.	198	46.25 N	104.31 W
Pleyben	32	48.14 N	3.58 W
Pleystein	60	49.39 N	12.25 E
Pliening	60	48.12 N	11.48 E
Pliezhausen	56	48.33 N	9.12 E
Plimmerton	172	41.05 S	174.52 E
Plimoth Plantation ⊥	207	41.57 N	70.38 W
Plintovka	265a	60.01 N	30.46 E
Pliszka ≃	54	52.14 N	14.42 E
Plitvička Jezera Nacionalni Park ♦	36	44.53 N	15.38 E
Plješevica ⋏	36	44.40 N	15.45 E
Pljevlja	38	43.21 N	19.21 E
Ploaghe	71	40.40 N	8.45 E
Plochingen	56	48.42 N	9.25 E
Płock	30	52.33 N	19.43 E
Płock □[4]	30	52.25 N	19.45 E
Plöckenpass)(	64	46.36 N	12.58 E
Plöckenstein (Plechý) ∧	60	48.46 N	13.51 E
Plockton	46	57.20 N	5.39 W
Pločno ∧	36	43.36 N	17.34 E
Plodorodnoje	80	46.44 N	41.06 E
Ploegsteert	50	50.43 N	2.53 E
Ploërmel	32	47.56 N	2.24 W
Ploești → Ploiești	38	44.56 N	26.02 E
Plogastel-Saint-Germain	28	47.59 N	4.16 W
Ploiești	38	44.56 N	26.02 E
Plomárion	38	38.59 N	26.22 E
Plomb du Cantal ∧	32	45.03 N	2.46 E
Plombières-les-Bains	58	47.58 N	6.29 E
Plombières-lès-Dijon	58	47.20 N	4.58 E
Plomer	258	34.48 S	59.02 W
Plomer, Point >	166	31.19 S	152.58 E
Plön	54	54.09 N	10.25 E
Plonge, Lac la ⊜	184	55.08 N	107.25 W
Płońsk	30	52.38 N	20.23 E
Pl'os	80	57.27 N	41.31 E
Plose, Cima delle ∧	64	46.42 N	11.44 E
Ploskij	78	46.17 N	40.15 E
Ploskoje	76	52.45 N	38.21 E
Ploskoš'	76	56.46 N	31.16 E
Pl'oso	76	59.47 N	35.43 E
Plotbišče	80	56.50 N	50.35 E
Plotina	83	48.33 N	40.05 E
Plotnica	76	52.03 N	26.39 E
Plottier	252	38.58 S	68.14 W
Płoty	30	53.49 N	15.16 E
Plötz	54	51.38 N	11.56 E
Plouay	32	47.55 N	3.20 W
Ploučnice ≃	54	50.47 N	14.13 E
Ploudalmézeau	32	48.32 N	4.39 W
Plouguenast	32	48.17 N	2.43 W
Plouha	32	48.41 N	2.56 W
Plovdiv	38	42.09 N	24.45 E
Plovdiv □[4]	38	42.08 N	24.32 E
Plover ≃	190	44.29 N	89.35 W
Plover Islands II	180	71.15 N	155.30 W
Pluckemin	276	40.39 N	74.39 W
Plum, Pa., U.S.	214	40.31 N	79.45 W
Plum, Pa., U.S.	214	41.35 N	79.51 W
Plum, Tx., U.S.	222	29.56 N	96.58 W
Pluma Hidalgo	234	15.55 N	96.25 W
Plumas	184	50.25 N	99.02 W
Plumbridge	48	54.46 N	7.15 W
Plum Brook ≃	281	42.34 N	82.58 W
Plum Creek ≃, Il., U.S.	278	41.33 N	87.29 W
Plum Creek ≃, Ne., U.S.	198	41.52 N	96.44 W
Plum Creek ≃, Oh., U.S.	279a	41.18 N	82.09 W
Plum Creek ≃, Pa., U.S.	279b	40.31 N	79.51 W
Plum Creek ≃, S.D., U.S.	198	44.13 N	100.43 W
Plum Creek ≃, Tx., U.S.	196	29.38 N	97.36 W
Plum Creek, Clear Fork ≃	222	29.45 N	97.37 W
Plumerville	194	35.09 N	92.38 W
Plum Grove	222	30.15 N	95.05 W
Plum Grove Estates	278	42.04 N	88.02 W
Plum Island	283	42.49 N	70.59 W
Plum Island I, Ma., U.S.	207	42.45 N	70.48 W
Plum Island I, N.Y., U.S.	207	41.11 N	72.12 W
Plum Island Airport ⊠	283	42.48 N	70.50 W
Plum Island Sound ⊔	283	42.45 N	70.48 W
Plum Island State Park ♦	283	42.42 N	70.47 W
Plumley	262	53.17 N	2.25 W
Plummer	202	47.20 N	116.53 W
Plummers Landing	218	38.19 N	83.33 W
Plumper Sound ⊔	224	48.47 N	123.13 W
Plum Point >	276	40.50 N	40.43 W
Plumpton	274a	33.45 S	150.50 E
Plumridge Lakes ⊜	162	29.30 S	125.25 E
Plum Run ≃	279b	40.15 N	80.13 W
Plumsteadville	208	40.23 N	75.09 W
Plumtree	154	20.30 S	27.50 E
Plumville	214	40.48 N	79.11 W
Plumwood	218	40.01 N	83.23 W
Plungė	76	55.55 N	21.51 E
Pl'uskovo	76	52.46 N	33.49 E
Pl'ussa	76	58.26 N	29.21 E
Pl'ussa ≃	76	59.19 N	28.11 E
Plutarco Elías Calles, Presa ⊜[1]	232	29.10 N	109.40 W
Pluvigner	32	47.46 N	3.01 E
Plym ≃	42	50.22 N	4.07 W
Plymouth, Monts.	238	16.42 N	62.13 W
Plymouth, Trin.	241r	11.13 N	60.47 W
Plymouth, Eng., U.K.	42	50.23 N	4.10 W
Plymouth, Ca., U.S.	226	38.29 N	120.51 W
Plymouth, Ct., U.S.	207	41.40 N	73.03 W
Plymouth, Il., U.S.	194	40.17 N	90.55 W
Plymouth, In., U.S.	216	41.20 N	86.18 W
Plymouth, Ma., U.S.	207	41.57 N	70.40 W
Plymouth, Mi., U.S.	216	42.22 N	83.28 W
Plymouth, Ne., U.S.	198	40.18 N	96.59 W
Plymouth, N.H., U.S.	188	43.45 N	71.41 W
Plymouth, N.Y., U.S.	210	42.37 N	75.36 W
Plymouth, N.C., U.S.	192	35.52 N	76.44 W
Plymouth, Oh., U.S.	214	41.00 N	82.40 W
Plymouth, Pa., U.S.	210	41.14 N	75.56 W
Plymouth, Wi., U.S.	190	43.44 N	87.58 W
Plymouth □[6]	207	41.58 N	70.41 W
Plymouth ≃	283	42.12 N	70.54 W
Plymouth Airport ⊠	42	50.25 N	4.06 W
Plymouth Bay c	207	41.57 N	70.37 W
Plymouth Harbor c	283	41.58 N	70.39 W
Plymouth Meeting	285	40.06 N	75.16 W
Plymouth Meeting Mall ◆[9]	285	40.07 N	75.17 W
Plymouth Rock ⊥	207	41.57 N	70.39 W
Plymouth Valley	285	40.07 N	75.23 W
Plympton, Eng., U.K.	42	50.23 N	4.03 W
Plympton, Ma., U.S.	207	41.57 N	70.48 W
Plymptonville	214	41.03 N	78.28 W
Plymstock	42	50.22 N	4.04 W
Plynlimon ∧	42	52.28 N	3.47 W
Plyskiv	78	49.23 N	29.18 E
Plysky	78	51.07 N	32.24 E
Plzeň	60	49.45 N	13.23 E
Pniewy	30	52.31 N	16.15 E
Pô	150	11.10 N	1.09 W
Po ≃, It.	36	44.57 N	12.04 E
Po ≃, Zhg.	100	28.57 N	116.39 E
Po, Foci del (Mouths of the Po) ≃[1]	64	44.52 N	12.30 E
Pô, Parc National de ♦	150	11.30 N	1.15 W
Poá	256	23.32 S	46.20 W
Poá ≃	287b	23.37 S	46.45 W
Poana ≃	250	0.56 N	57.03 W
Poarta Orientală, Pasul)(	38	45.06 N	22.18 E
Poás, Volcán ∧[1]	236	10.11 N	84.13 W
Pobé, Bénin	150	6.58 N	2.41 E
Pobé, Burkina	150	13.53 N	1.45 W
Pobeda, gora ∧	74	65.12 N	146.12 E
Pobeda Ice Island I	9	64.30 S	97.00 E
Pobedino	74	49.51 N	142.49 E

Symbols in the index entries represent the broad categories identified in the key at the right. Symbols with superior numbers (⋏[1]) identify subcategories (see complete key on page *I · 1).*

Symbole im Register stellen die rechts im Schlüssel erklärten Kategorien dar. Symbole mit hochgestellten Ziffern (⋏[1]) bezeichnen Unterabteilungen einer Kategorie (vgl. vollständiger Schlüssel auf Seite *I · 1).*

Los símbolos incluídos en el texto del índice representan las grandes categorías identificadas con la clave a la derecha. Los símbolos con numeros en su parte superior (⋏[1]) identifican las subcategorías (véase la clave completa en la página *I · 1).*

Les symboles de l'index représentent les catégories indiquées dans la légende à droite. Les symboles suivis d'un indice (⋏[1]) représentent des sous-catégories (voir légende complète à la page *I · 1).*

Os símbolos incluídos no texto do índice representam as grandes categorias identificadas com a chave à direita. Os símbolos com números em sua parte superior (⋏[1]) identificam as subcategorias (veja-se a chave completa à página *I · 1).*

∧ Mountain	Berg	Montaña	Montagne	Montanha
⋏ Mountains	Gebirge	Montañas	Montagnes	Montanhas
)(Pass	Paß	Paso	Col	Passo
V Valley, Canyon	Tal, Cañon	Valle, Cañón	Vallée, Canyon	Vale, Canhão
≚ Plain	Ebene	Llano	Plaine	Planície
> Cape	Kap	Cabo	Cap	Cabo
I Island	Insel	Isla	Île	Ilha
II Islands	Inseln	Islas	Îles	Ilhas
⊥ Other Topographic Features	Andere Topographische Objekte	Otros Elementos Topográficos	Autres données topographiques	Outros acidentes topográficos

ESPAÑOL Nombre	Página	Lat.°′	Long.°′ W = Oeste

FRANÇAIS Nom	Page	Lat.°′	Long.°′ W = Ouest

PORTUGUÊS Nome	Página	Lat.°′	Long.°′ W = Oeste

Pobedy, pik ▲ 72 42.02 N 80.05 E
Pobershau 54 50.38 N 13.13 E
Poběžovice 60 49.31 N 12.48 E
Poblado Cerro Gordo 240m 18.11 N 66.20 W
Poblado Jacaguas 240m 18.03 N 66.32 W
Poblado Medianía Alta 240m 18.26 N 65.50 W
Poblado Sábalos 240m 18.11 N 67.09 W
Poblado Santana 240m 18.27 N 66.40 W
Poblet 258 35.04 S 57.57 W
Pocahontas, Ar., U.S. 194 36.15 N 90.58 W
Pocahontas, Il., U.S. 219 38.49 N 89.32 W
Pocahontas, Ia., U.S. 198 42.44 N 94.40 W
Pocahontas State Park ♦ 208 37.23 N 77.34 W
Pocantico Hills 276 41.06 N 73.50 W
Pocantico Lake ⊜ 276 41.07 N 73.50 W
Poção 250 8.11 S 36.42 W
Pocasset 207 41.41 N 70.37 W
Pocatalico ≐ 188 38.29 N 81.49 W
Pocatello 202 42.52 N 112.26 W
Počep 76 52.56 N 33.27 E
Počepy 76 53.17 N 31.20 E
Pocé-sur-Cisse 50 47.26 N 0.59 E
Pochayiv 78 50.01 N 25.31 E
Pöchlarn 61 48.12 N 15.13 E
Pochvistnevo 80 53.38 N 52.08 E
Pocinhos, Bra. 250 7.04 S 36.03 W
Pocinhos, Bra. 256 21.56 S 46.25 W
Počinki 80 54.42 N 44.51 E
Počinnaja Sopka 76 58.25 N 34.22 E
Počinok 76 54.25 N 32.27 E
Pocitos, Salar ⊻ 252 24.30 S 67.03 W
Pockau 54 50.42 N 13.14 E
Pocking 60 48.24 N 13.19 E
Pocklington 44 53.56 N 0.46 W
Pocoata 248 18.41 S 66.11 W
Poço da Cruz, Açude ⊜ 1 250 8.30 S 37.35 W
Poço do Bispo ✈ 8 266c 38.44 N 9.06 W
Poções 255 14.31 S 40.21 W
Poço Fundo 256 21.48 S 45.58 W
Poço Fundo, Cachoeira do ⌞ 256 22.10 S 44.13 W
Pocol 64 46.31 N 12.07 E
Pocola 194 35.13 N 94.28 W
Pocomoke ≐ 208 37.58 N 75.39 W
Pocomoke City 208 38.04 N 75.34 W
Pocomoke Sound ⊻ 208 37.52 N 75.49 W
Pocona 248 17.39 S 65.24 W
Poconé 248 16.15 S 56.37 W
Pocono International Raceway ♦ 210 41.03 N 75.31 W
Pocono Lake 210 41.06 N 75.31 W
Pocono Manor 210 41.06 N 75.22 W
Pocono Mountains ⋀ 2 210 41.10 N 75.20 W
Pocono Pines 210 41.05 N 75.29 W
Pocono Summit 210 41.07 N 75.25 W
Pocopson 285 39.54 N 75.37 W
Pocopson Creek ≐ 285 39.54 N 75.37 W
Poço Redondo 250 9.49 S 37.41 W
Poços de Caldas 256 21.48 S 46.34 W
Poço Verde 250 10.42 S 38.11 W
Pocrane 255 19.37 S 41.37 W
Pocrí 236 8.16 N 80.33 W
Podbel'skaja 80 53.37 N 51.50 E
Podberezje, Ross. 76 56.57 N 30.38 E
Podberezje, Ross. 82 56.46 N 37.10 E
Podbořany 54 50.11 N 13.25 E
Podborki 82 54.11 N 35.56 E
Podborovje 76 59.30 N 35.02 E
Podbužje 76 53.30 N 34.56 E
Podčerje 24 63.57 N 57.34 E
Podchoževe 82 54.19 N 38.34 E
Podčinnyj 80 50.52 N 45.13 E
Poddebice 30 51.53 N 18.58 E
Poddemjur 24 64.05 N 53.26 E
Poddolgoje 76 53.12 N 38.04 E
Poddorje 76 57.28 N 31.07 E
Podébrady 30 50.08 N 15.07 E
Po della Donzella ≐ 64 44.48 N 12.25 E
Po delle Tolle ≐ 64 44.50 N 12.28 E
Podensac 32 44.39 N 0.22 W
Podenzano 62 44.57 N 9.41 E
Podersdorf am See 61 47.51 N 16.50 E
Podgorenskij 78 50.24 N 39.39 E
Podgorica 38 42.26 N 19.14 E
Podgornaja 78 50.28 N 41.10 E
Podgornoje, Kaz. 85 42.55 N 72.25 E
Podgornoje, Ross. 78 51.43 N 39.07 E
Podgornoje, Ross. 78 50.27 N 39.37 E
Podgornoje, Ross. 80 46.33 N 43.07 E
Podgornoje, Ross. 86 57.47 N 82.36 E
Podhůří 60 49.28 N 13.40 E
Podi 112 1.08 S 121.16 E
Po di Goro ≐ 64 44.48 N 12.27 E
Podillya ⌂ 9 78 48.50 N 27.30 E
Podil's'ka vysochyna ⋀ 1 78 49.00 N 27.00 E
Po di Volano ≐ 64 44.49 N 12.15 E
Podjom-Michajlovka 80 52.49 N 50.32 E
Podjuchy ✈ 8 54 53.20 N 14.36 E
Podkamennaja Tunguska ≐ 74 61.36 N 90.09 E
Podkamennaja Tunguska ≐ 74 61.36 N 90.18 E
Podkoren 64 46.30 N 13.45 E
Podkumok ≐ 84 44.14 N 43.36 E
Podlasie ✈ 1 30 52.30 N 23.00 E
Podlesnoje 80 51.50 N 47.03 E
Podlipatki 88 50.55 N 107.05 E
Podmošje 82 56.23 N 37.24 E
Podol'sk 82 55.26 N 37.33 E
Podor, Maur. 150 16.40 N 15.00 W
Podor, Sén. 150 16.40 N 14.57 W
Podora 24 62.22 N 54.19 E
Podosinovec 24 60.17 N 47.04 E
Podoz'orskij 80 57.14 N 40.20 E
Podporožje 24 60.53 N 34.07 E
Podravina ✈ 1 36 45.40 N 17.40 E
Podravska Slatina 38 45.42 N 17.42 E
Podrezčicha 24 59.22 N 51.28 E
Podstepnyj 80 51.08 N 51.28 E
Podsvilje 76 55.09 N 27.58 E
Podt'osovo 88 58.36 N 92.06 E
Pod'uga 24 61.06 N 40.53 E
Podujevo 38 42.55 N 21.11 E
Poduškino 265b 55.43 N 37.17 E
Podu Turcului 38 46.12 N 27.23 E
Podymachino 88 56.59 N 106.11 E
Podyvotje 78 52.03 N 34.08 E
Poe 216 40.56 N 85.05 W
Poechos, Embalse ⊜ 1 246 4.40 S 80.30 W
Poel I 54 54.00 N 11.26 E
Poeldijk 52 52.01 N 4.12 E
Poelela, Lagoa ⊜ 156 24.38 S 35.00 E
Poelkapelle 50 50.55 N 2.57 E
Poestenkill 210 42.41 N 73.34 W
Poesten Kill ≐ 210 42.43 N 73.42 W
Poetto 71 39.12 N 9.10 E
Pofadder 158 29.10 S 19.22 E
Pogamasing Lake ⊜ 190 46.57 N 81.50 W
Pogan, Zhg. 100 28.18 N 116.46 E
Pogan, Zhg. 100 27.40 N 116.46 E
Pogăniș ≐ 38 45.41 N 21.22 E
Pogar 76 52.33 N 33.16 E
Poge, Cape ⟩ 207 41.25 N 70.27 W
Poggendorf 54 54.03 N 13.07 E
Poggiardo 68 40.03 N 18.23 E
Poggibonsi 66 43.28 N 11.09 E
Poggio 64 44.30 N 10.00 E
Poggio Berni 66 44.02 N 12.24 E
Poggio Bustone 66 42.30 N 12.53 E
Poggio Imperiale 68 41.49 N 15.22 E
Poggiomarino 68 40.48 N 14.32 E
Poggio Mirteto 66 42.16 N 12.41 E
Poggio Moiano 66 42.12 N 12.53 E
Poggioreale 70 37.47 N 13.01 E
Poggio Renatico 64 44.46 N 11.29 E
Poggiorsini 68 40.55 N 16.15 E
Poggio Rusco 64 44.59 N 11.07 E
Poggio Sannita 66 41.47 N 14.25 E
Pöggstall 61 48.19 N 15.12 E
Pogibi 89 52.12 N 141.42 E
Pogil-to I 98 34.09 N 126.33 E
Pogliano 266b 45.32 N 8.59 E
Pogny 56 48.52 N 4.29 E
Pogoanele 38 44.54 N 27.00 E
Pogodajev 80 51.37 N 51.04 E
Pogoniani 38 40.00 N 20.25 E
Pogoreloje Gorodišče 76 56.08 N 34.56 E
Pogoso 152 6.46 S 17.12 E
Pogost, Bela. 76 52.51 N 27.39 E
Pogost, Bela. 76 53.51 N 29.09 E
Pogost, Ross. 80 57.39 N 42.33 E
Pogost, Ross. 82 56.52 N 39.04 E
Pogožeje 78 51.36 N 37.16 E
Pogradec 38 40.54 N 20.39 E
Po Grande ≐ 64 44.57 N 12.26 E
Pograničnoje 80 50.32 N 48.38 E
Pograničnyj, Ross. 80 46.57 N 45.46 E
Pograničnyj, Ross. 89 44.25 N 131.24 E
Pogromni Volcano ▲ 1 180 54.33 N 164.45 W
Pogromnoje 80 52.35 N 52.32 E
Pogruznaja 80 54.14 N 50.29 E
Poh 112 0.46 S 122.49 E
P'ohang 98 36.03 N 129.20 E
Pohatcong Creek ≐ 210 40.37 N 75.11 W
Pohénégamook 186 47.31 N 69.16 W
Pohick Creek ≐ 284c 38.46 N 77.14 W
Pohick Creek, Rabbit Branch ≐ 284c 38.48 N 77.17 W
Pohick Creek, Sideburn Branch ≐ 284c 38.48 N 77.17 W
Pohjanmaa ✈ 1 26 64.00 N 25.00 E
Pohjois-Karjalan lääni ⌂ 4 24 63.00 N 30.00 E
Pöhl, Talsperre ✈ 6 54 50.33 N 12.12 E
Pöhla 54 50.31 N 12.49 E
Pöhlde 52 51.37 N 10.18 E
Pohl-Göns 56 50.28 N 8.39 E
Pohlheim 56 50.34 N 8.45 E
Pohnpei I 174r 6.55 N 158.15 E
Pohořelice 61 48.59 N 16.32 E
Pohorje ⋀ 61 46.30 N 15.20 E
Pohrebyshche 78 49.29 N 29.16 E
Pohri 124 25.32 N 77.21 E
Pohsien — Boxian 100 33.53 N 115.45 E
Pohue Bay c 229d 19.00 N 155.48 W
Poiana Mare 38 43.55 N 23.04 E
Poiana Ruscă, Munții ⋀ 38 45.41 N 22.30 E
Pöide 76 58.31 N 23.03 E
Poigny-la-Forêt 261 48.41 N 1.45 E
Poim 80 53.01 N 43.11 E
Poinsett, Cape ⟩ 9 65.42 S 113.18 E
Poinsett, Lake ⊜, Fl., U.S. 220 28.20 N 80.50 W
Poinsett, Lake ⊜, S.D., U.S. 198 44.34 N 97.05 W
Point 222 32.56 N 95.52 W
Point Arena 204 38.54 N 123.41 W
Point Au Fer Island I 194 29.15 N 91.15 W
Point Baker 180 56.21 N 133.37 W
Pointblank 222 30.45 N 95.13 W
Point Chautauqua 214 42.14 N 79.28 W
Point Comfort 196 28.41 N 96.33 W
Point Cook 274b 37.56 S 144.45 E
Point Cook Royal Australian Air Force Station ■ 169 37.56 S 144.45 E
Point du Jour, Ruisseau du ≐ 206 45.50 N 73.25 W
Pointe-à-la-Frégate 186 49.12 N 64.55 W
Pointe-à-la-Garde 186 48.05 N 66.32 W
Pointe à la Hache 194 29.34 N 89.47 W
Pointe-à-Maurier 186 50.20 N 59.48 W
Pointe-à-Pitre 241o 16.14 N 61.32 W
Pointe-à-Pitre-le Raizet, Aéroport de ≋ 241o 16.17 N 61.32 W
Pointe-au-Chêne 206 45.38 N 74.45 W
Pointe Aux Peaux Farms 216 41.57 N 83.16 W
Pointe-aux-Trembles 206 45.39 N 73.30 W
Pointe-Calumet 275a 45.30 N 73.58 W
Pointe-Claire 206 45.26 N 73.50 W
Pointe-des-Cascades 275a 45.20 N 73.58 W
Pointe-des-Galets — Le Port 157c 20.55 S 55.18 E
Pointe-du-Moulin 275a 45.22 N 73.52 W
Point Edward 214 43.00 N 82.24 W
Pointe-Noire, Congo 152 4.48 S 11.51 E
Pointe-Noire, Guad. 241o 16.14 N 61.47 W
Point Enterprise 222 31.40 N 96.26 W
Pointers 208 39.35 N 75.26 W
Point Fortin 241r 10.11 N 61.41 W
Point Hope 180 68.21 N 166.41 W
Point Imperial ▲ 200 36.16 N 111.58 W
Point Independence 207 41.44 N 70.39 W
Point Lake ⊜ 176 65.15 N 113.04 W
Point Leamington 186 49.20 N 55.24 W
Point Lookout, Md., U.S. 208 38.02 N 76.19 W
Point Lookout, N.Y., U.S. 276 40.35 N 73.35 W
Point Marion 188 39.44 N 79.53 W
Point McLeay 168b 35.32 S 139.06 E
Point Nepean National Park ♦ 169 38.25 S 144.45 E
Point of Rocks 208 39.16 N 77.32 W
Point O'Woods 276 40.39 N 73.08 W
Point Pass 168b 34.05 S 139.03 E
Point Pelee National Park ♦ 214 41.57 N 82.30 W
Point Peninsula ⟩ 1 212 44.01 N 76.15 W
Point Pleasant, Md., U.S. 284b 39.11 N 76.35 W
Point Pleasant, N.J., U.S. 208 40.04 N 74.04 W
Point Pleasant, Oh., U.S. 218 38.54 N 84.14 W
Point Pleasant, Pa., U.S. 208 40.25 N 75.04 W
Point Pleasant, W.V., U.S. 188 38.50 N 82.08 W
Point Pleasant Beach 208 40.05 N 74.02 W
Point Reyes National Seashore ♦ 204 38.00 N 122.58 W
Point Roberts 224 48.59 N 123.04 W
Point Salines International Airport ≋ 241k 12.01 N 61.47 W
Point Samson 162 20.36 S 117.12 E
Point Sapin 186 46.58 N 64.50 W
Point View Reservoir ⊜ 1 276 40.58 N 74.15 W
Point Whitehead 180 60.28 N 145.57 W
Poirino 62 44.55 N 7.51 E
Poisevo 80 55.32 N 53.30 E
Poison Creek ≐ 202 43.15 N 108.09 W
Poison Spider Creek ≐ 200 42.46 N 106.31 W
Poisson Blanc, Réservoir du ⊜ 1 188 46.00 N 75.45 W
Poissonnier Point ⟩ 162 19.57 S 119.11 E
Poissons 58 48.25 N 5.13 E
Poissy 50 48.56 N 2.03 E
Poitiers 32 46.35 N 0.20 E
Poitou ⌂ 9 32 46.20 N 0.10 W
Poix 50 49.47 N 1.59 E
Poix-Terron 56 49.39 N 4.39 E
Pojarkovo 89 49.38 N 128.38 E
Pojma ≐ 88 56.54 N 97.48 E
Pojo 248 17.45 S 64.49 W
Pojoaque Valley 200 35.59 N 106.00 W
Pojuca 255 12.25 S 38.20 W
Pojuca ≐ 255 12.34 S 38.03 W
Pokagon State Park ♦ 216 41.43 N 85.01 W
Pokaran 120 26.55 N 71.55 E
Pokataroo 166 29.35 S 148.42 E
Pokatejeva 88 56.59 N 97.25 E
Pokatilovka, Kaz. 80 51.06 N 51.53 E
Pokatilovka, Kaz. 86 45.23 N 80.10 E
Poke Run ≐ 279b 40.30 N 79.33 W
Pokharā 124 28.14 N 83.59 E
Pokharia 126 23.55 N 86.37 E
Poko, Süd. 140 5.38 N 31.50 E
Poko, Zaïre 154 3.09 N 26.53 E
Pokoinu 174k 21.12 S 159.49 W
Pokojnoje 84 44.48 N 44.16 E
Pokok Sena 114 6.10 N 100.32 E
Pokol'ubiči 76 52.30 N 31.02 E
Pokrov 82 55.55 N 39.10 E
Pokrovka, Kaz. 86 54.17 N 68.15 E
Pokrovka, Kaz. 86 49.28 N 81.28 E
Pokrovka, Kyrg. 85 42.20 N 78.01 E
Pokrovka, Kyrg. 85 42.45 N 71.36 E
Pokrovka, Ross. 80 48.22 N 46.04 E
Pokrovka, Ross. 83 53.47 N 53.19 E
Pokrovka, Ross. 89 43.57 N 131.39 E
Pokrovsk 74 61.29 N 129.06 E
Pokrovskaja Arčada 80 52.56 N 44.13 E
Pokrovs'ke, Ukr. 78 49.44 N 38.13 E
Pokrovs'ke, Ukr. 78 47.59 N 36.14 E
Pokrovs'ke, Ukr. 78 46.32 N 31.38 E
Pokrovs'ke, Ukr. 78 47.27 N 38.09 E
Pokrovskoje, Ross. 76 52.38 N 36.51 E
Pokrovskoje, Ross. 80 54.04 N 43.37 E
Pokrovskoje, Ross. 80 53.54 N 40.26 E
Pokrovskoje, Ross. 82 56.25 N 37.03 E
Pokrovskoje, Ross. 82 55.53 N 36.19 E
Pokrovskoje, Ross. 83 47.25 N 38.54 E
Pokrovskoje, Ross. 86 57.14 N 66.48 E
Pokrovskoje, Ross. 265a 59.44 N 30.46 E
Pokrovskoje ✈ 8 265b 55.37 N 37.37 E
Pokrovskoje-Strešnevo ✈ 8 265b 55.49 N 37.29 E
Pokrovsk-Ural'skij 86 60.10 N 59.49 E
Pokur 74 61.02 N 75.26 E
Pola — Pula, Hrv. 64 44.52 N 13.50 E
Pola, Pil. 116 13.09 N 121.26 E
Pola, Ross. 76 57.56 N 31.50 E
Pola ≐ 76 58.04 N 31.37 E
Pola Bay c 116 13.10 N 121.28 E
Polacca 200 35.50 N 110.22 W
Polacca Wash ∨ 200 35.22 N 110.50 W
Pola de Laviana 34 43.15 N 5.34 W
Pola de Lena 34 43.10 N 5.49 W
Pola de Siero 34 43.23 N 5.40 W
Polān 128 25.35 N 61.12 E
Polanco 252 33.54 S 55.09 W
Poland, Kiribati 174o 1.59 N 157.32 W
Poland, N.Y., U.S. 210 43.13 N 75.03 W
Poland, Oh., U.S. 214 41.01 N 80.37 W
Poland (Polska) ⌂ 1, Europe 22 52.00 N 19.00 E
Poland (Polska) ⌂ 1, Europe 30 52.00 N 19.00 E
Polangui 116 13.17 N 123.29 E
Polanów 30 54.08 N 16.39 E
Polapane ✈ 115b 9.43 S 119.06 E
Pol'arnik 180 67.03 N 178.53 W
Pol'arnyj, Ross. 24 69.12 N 33.22 E
Pol'arnyj, Ross. 74 69.10 N 178.48 E
Pol'arnyj Ural ⋀ 24 66.55 N 64.30 E
Polatli 130 39.36 N 32.09 E
Polba 272b 22.57 N 88.18 E
Polbain 46 58.02 N 5.23 W
Polbeth 46 55.52 N 3.33 W
Polch 56 50.18 N 7.18 E
Polcirkeln 24 66.34 N 21.05 E
Polcura 252 37.17 S 71.43 W
Połczyn Zdrój 30 53.46 N 16.06 E
Polden Hills ⋀ 2 42 51.08 N 2.50 W
Poldnevica 80 58.37 N 46.38 E
Pol'dorak 85 39.25 N 69.56 E
Poleang 112 4.42 S 121.46 E
Polebridge 182 48.45 N 114.17 W
Polecat Creek ≐ 196 36.00 N 95.57 W
Polednik ▲ 60 49.04 N 13.24 E
Polee, Pulau I 164 2.12 S 130.15 E
Polegate 42 50.49 N 0.15 E
Pol-e Khomrī 120 35.56 N 68.43 E
Pole Moor 262 53.39 N 1.54 W
Polen — Poland ⌂ 1 30 52.00 N 19.00 E
Polenezköy ✈ 8 267b 41.07 N 29.12 E
Pol-e Safīd 128 36.06 N 53.01 E
Polesden Lacey ⊥ 260 51.15 N 0.22 W
Polesella 64 44.58 N 11.45 E
Polesine ✈ 1 64 45.00 N 11.45 E
Polesine Parmense 64 45.01 N 10.04 E
Polesje 76 53.05 N 31.17 E
Polesje ✈ 1 78 52.00 N 27.00 E
Polessk [Labiau] 76 54.52 N 21.05 E
Polesworth 42 52.37 N 1.36 W
Polevaja 78 51.37 N 36.30 E
Polevskoj 86 56.26 N 60.11 E
Polewali 112 3.25 S 119.20 E
Pole Žahāb 128 34.28 N 45.52 E
Polgár 30 47.52 N 21.08 E
Polgooth 42 50.19 N 4.48 W
Polgyo 98 34.52 N 127.21 E
Poli, Cam. 146 8.29 N 13.15 E
Poli, Zhg. 98 45.43 N 119.47 E
Poli, Zhg. 98 35.57 N 118.17 E
Polia 68 38.45 N 16.19 E
Poliaigos I 38 36.46 N 24.38 E
Policastro, Golfo di c 68 40.00 N 15.30 E
Policastro Bussentino 68 40.09 N 15.32 E
Police 30 53.35 N 14.33 E
Polička 30 49.43 N 16.16 E
Policoro 68 40.13 N 16.41 E
Poligna c 62 45.04 N 3.22 E
Polignano a Mare 68 41.00 N 17.13 E
Poligny 58 46.50 N 5.43 E
Polihale State Park ♦ 229b 22.05 N 159.45 W
Polikastron 38 41.00 N 22.34 E
Polikhnitos 38 39.05 N 26.11 E
Polillo 116 14.43 N 121.56 E
Polillo Island I 116 14.50 N 121.57 E
Polillo Islands II 116 14.50 N 122.05 E
Polillo Strait ⊻ 116 14.44 N 121.51 E
Polinésia Francesa — French Polynesia ⌂ 2 14 15.00 S 140.00 W
Polinik ▲ 64 46.54 N 13.09 E
Polinyà de Vallès 266d 41.33 N 2.09 E
Pólis 130 35.02 N 32.25 E
Polis'ke 78 51.14 N 29.22 E
Polist' ≐ 76 58.06 N 31.31 E
Polistena 68 38.25 N 16.05 E
Politécnico Nacional, Instituto ▾ 2 286a 19.30 N 99.08 W
Politotdel'skoje 83 47.33 N 39.05 E
Pölitz — Police 30 53.35 N 14.33 E
Polivanovo 82 55.36 N 47.23 E
Polïyiros 38 40.23 N 23.27 E
Polizzi Generosa 70 37.49 N 14.00 E
Polizzo, Monte ▲ 70 37.52 N 12.47 E
Polk, Ne., U.S. 198 41.04 N 97.47 W
Polk, Oh., U.S. 214 40.57 N 82.13 W
Polk, Pa., U.S. 214 41.22 N 79.55 W
Polk ⌂ 6, Fl., U.S. 220 28.00 N 81.37 W
Polk ⌂ 6, Or., U.S. 224 45.00 N 123.23 W
Polk ⌂ 6, Tx., U.S. 222 30.45 N 94.48 W
Polk City 220 28.10 N 81.49 W
Pol'kino 74 71.10 N 99.15 E
Polkowice 30 51.31 N 16.04 E
Polla 68 40.30 N 15.30 E
Polläch 122 10.40 N 77.01 E
Pollanten 60 49.09 N 11.28 E
Pöllau 61 47.18 N 15.51 E
Pöllauberg 61 47.19 N 15.52 E
Polleben 54 51.34 N 11.36 E
Pollenfeld 60 48.57 N 11.12 E
Pollenza 66 43.16 N 13.21 E
Pollica 68 40.11 N 15.03 E
Pollina 70 37.59 N 14.09 E
Polling 64 47.48 N 11.09 E
Pollino, Monte ▲ 68 39.55 N 16.11 E
Polloc Harbor c 116 7.23 N 124.12 E
Pollock, La., U.S. 194 31.31 N 92.24 W
Pollock, S.D., U.S. 198 45.54 N 100.17 W
Pollock Pines 226 38.46 N 120.34 W
Pollock Run ≐ 279b 40.14 N 79.47 W
Pollok 222 31.27 N 94.52 W
Pollutri 66 42.08 N 14.35 E
Pollux ▲ 172 44.14 S 168.53 E
Polmak 24 70.04 N 28.00 E
Polmont 46 55.59 N 3.42 W
Polná 30 49.29 N 15.43 E
Polnaja ≐ 83 48.54 N 39.50 E
Pol'noje-Jaltunovo 80 53.59 N 41.52 E
Polnovo-Seliger 76 57.32 N 32.55 E
Polo, Il., U.S. 190 41.59 N 89.34 W
Polo, Mo., U.S. 194 39.33 N 94.02 W
Polochic ≐ 236 15.28 N 89.22 W
Polock, Bela. 76 55.31 N 28.46 E
Polock, Ross. 86 52.46 N 59.42 E
Pologne — Poland ⌂ 1 30 52.00 N 19.00 E
Pologoje Zajmišče 80 48.29 N 45.57 E
Pologrudovo 86 57.07 N 74.13 E
Polohy 78 47.29 N 36.15 E
Polom, Ross. 24 59.13 N 50.50 E
Polom, Ross. 80 57.47 N 53.29 E
Polo Magnético del Sur — South Magnetic Pole ✈ 9 65.18 S 139.30 E
Polomäki ▲ 2 26 63.21 N 27.03 E
Polomet' ≐ 76 57.41 N 32.12 E
Polomolok 116 6.14 N 125.03 E
Polonia — Poland ⌂ 1 30 52.00 N 19.00 E
Polonia, Arroyo ≐ 258 34.10 S 57.15 W
Polonio, Cabo ⟩ 252 34.24 S 53.46 W
Polonnaruwa 122 7.56 N 81.00 E
Polonnaruwa ⊥ 122 7.56 N 81.00 E
Polonne 78 50.07 N 27.30 E
Pološkovo 82 54.08 N 35.53 E
Polo Sur — South Pole ✈ 9 90.00 S 0.00
Polotn'anyj 82 54.45 N 36.00 E
Polotsk — Polock 76 55.31 N 28.46 E
Polovinnoje, Ross. 86 54.43 N 63.50 E
Polovinnoje, Ross. 86 53.46 N 79.15 E
Polovo 76 57.03 N 32.27 E
Polovynkyne 83 49.14 N 38.55 E
Polperro 42 50.19 N 4.31 W
Polruan 42 50.19 N 4.36 W
Pöls 61 47.13 N 14.35 E
Pölsbach ≐ 61 47.11 N 14.45 E
Polska — Poland ⌂ 1 30 52.00 N 19.00 E
Polski Trămbeš 38 43.22 N 25.38 E
Polson 202 47.41 N 114.09 W
Polster ▲ 61 47.32 N 14.58 E
Polsum 52 51.37 N 7.03 E
Poltava 78 49.35 N 34.34 E
Poltava ⌂ 4 78 49.45 N 34.00 E
Poltavka 86 54.22 N 71.45 E
Poltevy Pen'ki 80 54.35 N 42.06 E
Poltimore 188 45.47 N 75.43 W
Põltsamaa 76 58.38 N 25.58 E
Põltsamaa ≐ 76 58.27 N 26.09 E
Poludino 86 54.51 N 69.55 E
Poluj ≐ 74 66.31 N 66.33 E
Polunočnoje 72 60.52 N 60.25 E
Polur 122 12.30 N 79.08 E
Polur'adinki 82 54.51 N 38.41 E
Poluškino 265b 55.41 N 37.18 E
Pol'ustrovo ✈ 8 265a 59.58 N 30.25 E
Põlva 76 58.03 N 27.03 E
Polvaredas 258 35.35 S 59.30 W
Polverigi 66 43.31 N 13.23 E
Polvijärvi 26 62.51 N 29.22 E
Polvilho 287b 23.23 S 46.50 W
Polvoreda 266a 40.19 N 3.46 W
Polyesinia II 14 4.00 S 156.00 W
Polynesian Cultural Center ▾ 229c 21.39 N 157.55 W
Polynésie française — French Polynesia ⌂ 2 14 15.00 S 140.00 W
Polynoje 80 46.51 N 46.56 E
Polysajevo 86 54.35 N 86.14 E
Pölzig 54 50.57 N 12.11 E
Poma, Lago ⊜ 1 70 37.55 N 13.06 E
Pomabamba 248 8.50 S 77.28 W
Pomacanchi 248 14.02 S 71.34 W
Pomahaka ≐ 172 46.09 S 169.34 E
Pomarance 66 43.18 N 10.52 E
Pomarico 68 40.31 N 16.33 E
Pomarkku 26 61.42 N 22.00 E
Pomata 248 16.16 S 69.18 W
Pomáz 264c 47.39 N 19.02 E
Pombal, Bra. 250 6.46 S 37.48 W
Pombal, Port. 256 21.24 S 42.32 W
Pombais, Ribeira de ≐ 266c 38.48 N 9.07 W
Pombal, Bra. 250 6.46 S 37.47 W
Pombal, Port. 34 39.55 N 8.38 W
Pombia 266b 45.39 N 8.38 E
Pomellen 54 53.20 N 14.23 E
Pomene 156 22.53 S 35.33 E
Pomerania ⌂ 9 30 54.00 N 16.00 E
Pomeranian Bay c 54 54.00 N 14.15 E
Pomerene 200 31.59 N 110.17 W
Pomerode 252 26.45 S 49.11 W
Pomeroon ≐ 246 7.37 N 58.45 W
Pomeroon-Supenaam ⌂ 4 246 7.20 N 58.50 W
Pomeroy, S. Afr. 158 28.33 S 30.26 E
Pomeroy, N. Ire., U.K. 48 54.36 N 6.55 W
Pomeroy, Ia., U.S. 198 42.33 N 94.41 W
Pomeroy, Oh., U.S. 188 39.01 N 82.02 W
Pomeroy, Pa., U.S. 208 39.58 N 75.53 W
Pomeroy, Wa., U.S. 202 46.28 N 117.36 W
Pomezia 66 41.40 N 12.30 E
Pomfret 158 25.50 S 23.32 E
Pomfret, S. Afr. 156 25.50 S 23.32 E
Pomfret, Ct., U.S. 207 41.53 N 71.57 W
Pomfret, Md., U.S. 208 38.34 N 77.01 W
Pomi 38 47.42 N 23.19 E
Pomichna 78 48.14 N 31.26 E
Pomigliano d'Arco 68 40.54 N 14.23 E
Pominovo 82 55.26 N 39.11 E
Pomio 164 5.30 S 151.30 E
Pommard 58 47.01 N 4.47 E
Pomme de Terre ≐, Mn., U.S. 198 45.10 N 96.05 W
Pomme de Terre ≐, Mo., U.S. 194 38.11 N 93.24 W
Pomme de Terre Lake ⊜ 1 194 37.51 N 93.19 W
Pommern — Pomerania ⌂ 9 50 50.10 N 2.26 E
30 54.00 N 16.00 E
Pommersche Bucht — Pomeranian Bay c 54 54.00 N 14.15 E
Pommersfelden 56 49.46 N 10.49 E
Pomona, Namibia 156 27.09 S 15.18 E
Pomona, Ca., U.S. 228 34.03 N 117.45 W
Pomona, Ks., U.S. 198 38.36 N 95.27 W
Pomona, N.J., U.S. 208 39.28 N 74.34 W
Pomona, N.Y., U.S. 276 41.10 N 74.02 W
Pomona College ▾ 2 280 34.06 N 117.44 W
Pomona Estates 273d 26.06 S 28.15 E
Pomona Lake ⊜ 1 198 38.40 N 95.35 W
Pomona Park 192 29.30 N 81.35 W
Pomongo 152 5.00 S 19.08 E
Pomorie 38 42.33 N 27.39 E
Pomorskij proliv ⊻ 24 68.30 N 50.00 E
Pomoryany 78 49.38 N 24.56 E
Pomorze — Pomerania ⌂ 9 30 54.00 N 16.00 E
Pomozdino 24 62.12 N 54.06 E
Pompano Beach 220 26.14 N 80.07 W
Pompano Beach Highlands 220 26.16 N 80.06 W
Pompei 68 40.45 N 14.30 E
Pompei ⊥ 68 40.45 N 14.30 E
Pompéia 255 22.08 S 50.10 W
Pompejevka 89 48.23 N 130.46 E
Pompeston Creek ≐ 285 40.01 N 75.01 W
Pompéu 255 19.12 S 44.59 W
Pompey, Fr. 56 48.46 N 6.07 E
Pompey, N.Y., U.S. 210 42.54 N 76.01 W
Pomponio Creek ≐ 282 37.18 N 122.25 W
Pomponio State Beach ♦ 282 37.17 N 122.24 W
Pomponne 261 48.53 N 2.41 E
Pompon-yama ▲ 270 34.56 N 135.37 E
Pomposa 64 44.49 N 12.11 E
Pomposa, Abbazia di ▾ 1 64 44.49 N 12.11 E
Pompton ≐ 276 40.54 N 74.16 W
Pompton Lakes 210 41.00 N 74.17 W
Pompton Lakes ⊜ 276 41.00 N 74.17 W
Pomquet 186 45.38 N 61.51 W
Pomssen 54 51.14 N 12.37 E
Ponape — Pohnpei I 174r 6.55 N 158.15 E
Ponask Lake ⊜ 184 54.00 N 92.41 W
Ponass Lakes ⊜ 184 52.18 N 103.58 W
Ponazyrevo 80 58.21 N 46.19 E
Ponca 198 42.33 N 96.42 W
Ponca City 196 36.42 N 97.05 W
Ponca Creek ≐ 198 42.48 N 98.05 W
Ponce 240m 18.01 N 66.37 W
Ponce, Aeropuerto ≋ 240m 18.01 N 66.34 W
Ponce de Leon 194 30.43 N 85.56 W
Ponce de Leon Bay c 220 25.21 N 81.07 W
Ponce de Leon Inlet c 192 29.04 N 80.55 W
Poncé-sur-le-Loir 50 47.46 N 0.40 E
Poncha Pass ⟩⟨ 200 38.25 N 106.05 W
Ponchatoula 194 30.26 N 90.26 W
Poncin 58 46.05 N 5.24 E
Poncitlán 234 20.22 N 102.55 W
Pond ≐ 194 37.32 N 87.21 W
Pond Brook ≐, N.J., U.S. 276 41.02 N 74.15 W
Pond Brook ≐, Oh., U.S. 279a 41.17 N 81.24 W
Pondcreek 196 36.40 N 97.48 W
Pond Creek ≐, U.S. 196 36.40 N 97.33 W
Pond Creek ≐, Tx., U.S. 222 31.02 N 96.46 W
Pond Eddy 210 41.27 N 74.49 W
Ponder 222 33.11 N 97.17 W
Pondera Coulee ∨ 202 48.16 N 111.03 W
Ponders End ✈ 8 260 51.39 N 0.03 W
Pondicherry 122 11.56 N 79.53 E
Pondicherry ⌂ 8 122 11.56 N 79.50 E
Pond Inlet 176 72.41 N 78.00 W
Pond Inlet c 176 72.46 N 77.00 W
Pondok Tanjong 114 5.00 N 100.44 E
Pondoland ⌂ 9 158 31.10 S 29.30 E
Pondosa 204 41.12 N 121.41 W
Pond Run ≐ 285 40.13 N 74.44 W
Poneas Island I 116 9.55 N 125.57 E
Ponente, Capo ⟩ 70a 35.31 N 12.31 E
Ponente, Riviera di ⋀ 2 62 44.10 N 8.20 E
Ponérihouen 175f 21.05 S 165.24 E
Poneto 216 40.39 N 85.13 W
Ponežukaj 78 44.53 N 39.22 E
Ponferrada 34 42.33 N 6.35 W
Pong 110 19.10 N 100.17 E
Pongani 164 9.05 S 148.35 E
Pongara, Pointe ⟩ 152 0.21 N 9.21 E
Pongaroa 172 40.33 S 176.11 E
Pongau ∨ 64 47.21 N 13.14 E
Pong Dam ✈ 6 123 31.59 N 75.57 E
Ponghyon 98 37.49 N 125.36 E
Pongo ≐ 140 8.42 N 27.40 E
Pongola ≐ 158 26.57 S 32.17 E
Pong'goma 24 65.21 N 34.25 E
Pong Tamale 150 9.41 N 0.49 W
Ponhook Lake ⊜ 186 44.19 N 64.53 W
Poni ≐ 208 38.07 N 77.26 W
Poniatowa 30 51.11 N 22.05 E
Poniec 30 51.47 N 16.50 E
Ponil Creek ≐ 196 36.29 N 104.48 W
Poninka 78 50.12 N 27.32 E
Ponino 80 58.16 N 52.49 E
Ponitz, Dtsch. 54 50.51 N 12.25 E
Pönitz, Dtsch. 54 54.03 N 10.40 E
Ponizovje 76 55.17 N 31.04 E
Ponkapoag Pond ⊜ 283 42.12 N 71.06 W
Pönley 110 12.26 N 104.27 E
Ponnaiyār ≐ 122 11.46 N 79.47 E
Ponnāni 122 10.46 N 75.54 E
Ponnūru Nidubrolu 122 16.04 N 80.34 E
Pono 164 6.22 S 134.36 E
Ponoj 24 67.05 N 41.07 E
Ponoj ≐ 24 66.59 N 41.17 E
Ponoka 182 52.42 N 113.35 W
Ponomar'ovka, Ross. 80 53.19 N 54.08 E
Ponomar'ovka, Ross. 86 56.08 N 82.23 E
Ponornytsya 78 51.43 N 32.49 E
Ponorogo 115a 7.52 S 111.27 E
Ponpāj 272b 22.56 N 88.16 E
Pons 32 45.35 N 0.33 W
Ponsacco 66 43.37 N 10.38 E
Ponson Island I 116 10.46 N 124.32 E
Ponsul ≐ 34 39.40 N 7.31 W
Pont 62 45.34 N 7.07 E
Pont-à-Celles 50 50.30 N 4.21 E
Ponta Delgada 148a 37.44 N 25.40 W
Ponta Delgada ⌂ 5 148a 37.40 N 25.30 W
Ponta de Pedras 250 1.23 S 48.52 W
Ponta Grossa 252 25.05 S 50.09 W
Pontalete 266c 38.41 N 9.04 W
Pontalina 255 17.31 S 49.27 W
Pontailler-sur-Saône 58 47.18 N 5.25 E
Pont-à-Marcq 50 50.31 N 3.07 E
Pont-à-Mousson 56 48.54 N 6.04 E
Ponta Negra 256 22.57 S 35.10 W
Pontão 34 39.55 N 8.22 W
Ponta Porã 252 22.32 S 55.43 W
Pontardawe 42 51.44 N 3.51 W
Pontarddulais 42 51.43 N 4.02 W
Pontarlier 58 46.54 N 6.22 E
Pontas de Pedra 250 7.38 S 34.48 W
Pontassieve 66 43.46 N 11.26 E
Pontaubert 50 47.29 N 3.52 E
Pont-Audemer 50 49.21 N 0.31 E
Pontault-Combault 261 48.47 N 2.36 E
Pontaumur 32 45.52 N 2.40 E
Pont-Aven 32 47.51 N 3.45 W
Pontbriand 206 46.09 N 71.15 W
Pont Canavese 62 45.25 N 7.36 E
Pontcarré 261 48.48 N 2.42 E
Pontcharra 62 45.26 N 6.01 E
Pontchartrain, Lake ⊜ 194 30.10 N 90.10 W
Pontchâteau 32 47.26 N 2.05 W
Pont-Croix 32 48.02 N 4.29 W
Pont-d'Ain 58 46.03 N 5.20 E
Pont-d'Arc ▲ 62 44.23 N 4.24 E
Pont-de-Bonne 56 50.27 N 5.17 E
Pont-de-Chéruy 58 45.45 N 5.11 E
Pont-de-l'Arche 50 49.18 N 1.10 E
Pont-de-Pany 58 47.18 N 4.49 E
Pont-de-Poitte 58 46.35 N 5.41 E
Pont-de-Roide 58 47.23 N 6.46 E
Pont-de-Ruan 50 47.15 N 0.35 E
Pont-de-Salars 32 44.17 N 2.44 E
Pont-de-Vaux 58 46.26 N 4.56 E
Pont-de-Veyle 58 46.16 N 4.53 E
Ponte a Elsa 66 43.41 N 10.54 E
Ponte Alta do Bom Jesus 255 12.06 S 46.29 W
Ponte Alta do Norte 250 10.45 S 47.34 W
Ponte a Moriano 66 43.54 N 10.31 E
Pontecaeas 34 42.11 N 8.30 W
Pontebba 64 46.30 N 13.18 E
Ponte Branca 255 16.27 S 52.40 W
Ponte Caffaro 64 45.50 N 10.32 E
Pontecagnano 68 40.39 N 14.52 E
Ponte Caldelas 34 42.23 N 8.30 W
Pontecchio Marconi 64 44.25 N 11.15 E
Pontecchio Polesine 64 45.01 N 11.49 E
Pontecorvo 66 41.27 N 13.40 E
Pontecurone 62 44.57 N 8.56 E
Ponte da Barca 34 41.48 N 8.25 W
Ponte d'Arbia 66 43.10 N 11.28 E
Ponte dell'Arche 64 46.02 N 10.52 E
Ponte dell'Olio 62 44.52 N 9.39 E
Pontedera 66 43.40 N 10.38 E
Ponte de Sor 34 39.15 N 8.01 W
Pontedeume 34 43.24 N 8.10 W
Ponte di Barbarano 64 45.23 N 11.34 E
Ponte di Legno 64 46.16 N 10.31 E
Ponte di Nava 62 44.08 N 7.53 E
Ponte di Piave 64 45.43 N 12.28 E
Ponte do Lima 34 41.46 N 8.35 W
Ponte do Púngoè 156 19.30 S 34.32 E
Pontefract 44 53.42 N 1.18 W
Ponte Galeria ✈ 8 267a 41.49 N 12.21 E
Ponte Gardena (Waidbruck) 64 46.36 N 11.32 E
Ponte Ghiereto 66 43.59 N 11.15 E
Pontegrande 68 45.59 N 8.09 E
Ponte in Valtellina 64 46.12 N 9.59 E
Ponteix 184 49.45 N 107.29 W
Pontelagoscuro 64 44.53 N 11.36 E
Pontelland 44 55.03 N 1.44 W
Pontelandolfo 68 41.17 N 14.41 E
Pontelongo 64 45.15 N 12.02 E
Ponte nell'Alpi 64 46.11 N 12.16 E
Ponte Nova 255 20.24 S 42.54 W
Pont-en-Royans 62 45.04 N 5.21 E
Ponte Nuovo 66 43.01 N 12.28 E
Pontenure 62 44.59 N 9.47 E
Pontepetri 66 44.02 N 10.53 E
Ponte ricciolo 66 43.26 N 12.38 E
Ponte Rocchetta 64 46.14 N 11.04 E
Ponterwyd 42 52.25 N 3.50 W
Ponte San Giovanni 66 43.05 N 12.26 E
Ponte San Pietro 62 45.42 N 9.35 E
Pontesbury 42 52.39 N 2.54 W
Ponte Selva 64 45.52 N 9.54 E
Ponte Serrada 252 26.52 S 51.58 W
Pontestura 62 45.08 N 8.20 E
Ponte Tresa 62 45.58 N 8.52 E
Pontevedra, Arg. 258 34.45 S 58.42 W
Pontevedra, Esp. 34 42.26 N 8.38 W
Pontevedra, Pil. 116 10.22 N 122.52 E
Pontevedra ⌂ 4 34 42.30 N 8.40 W
Pontevedra, Ría de c 1 34 42.22 N 8.45 W
Ponte Vedra Beach 192 30.14 N 81.23 W
Pont-Évêque 62 45.32 N 4.55 E
Pontevico 64 45.16 N 10.05 E
Pontfaverger-Moronvilliers 50 49.18 N 4.19 E
Pontgibaud 32 45.50 N 2.52 E
Ponthévrard 261 48.33 N 1.55 E
Ponthierry 261 48.32 N 2.33 E
Ponthierville — Ubundu 154 0.21 S 25.29 E
Pontiac, Il., U.S. 216 40.52 N 88.37 W
Pontiac, Mi., U.S. 216 42.38 N 83.17 W
Pontiac ⌂ 6 212 46.30 N 77.00 W
Pontiac Lake 281 42.40 N 83.28 W
Pontiac Lake ⊜ 281 42.40 N 83.28 W
Pontiac Lake State Recreation Area ♦ 216 42.41 N 83.28 W
Pontiac Mall ✈ 9 281 42.39 N 83.20 W
Pontiac State Recreation Area ♦ 281 42.41 N 83.28 W
Pontianak 112 0.02 S 109.20 E
Pontian Kechil 114 1.29 N 103.23 E
Pontida 62 45.43 N 9.30 E
Pontigny 50 47.55 N 3.43 E
Pontinha ✈ 8 266c 38.46 N 9.11 W
Pontinia 66 41.24 N 13.02 E
Pontivy 32 48.04 N 2.59 W
Pont-l'Abbé 32 47.52 N 4.13 W
Pont-lès-Moulins 58 47.19 N 6.22 E
Pont-l'Évêque 50 49.18 N 0.11 E
Pontlevoy 50 47.23 N 1.15 E
Pontoise 50 49.03 N 2.05 E
Pontoise-Cormeilles-en-Vexin, Aérodrome ≋ 261 49.06 N 2.02 E
Ponton Creek ≐ 162 31.10 S 124.25 E
Pontonnyj 265a 59.47 N 30.38 E
Pontoon Beach 219 38.43 N 90.04 W
Pontorson 32 48.33 N 1.31 W
Pontotoc, Ms., U.S. 194 34.14 N 88.59 W
Pontotoc, Tx., U.S. 196 30.54 N 98.59 W
Pontremoli 62 44.22 N 9.53 E
Pont-Remy 50 50.03 N 1.55 E
Pontresina 58 46.28 N 9.53 E
Pontrhydfendigaid 42 52.17 N 3.51 W
Pont-Rouge 206 46.45 N 71.42 W
Pont-Royal 62 43.43 N 5.11 E
Ponts 34 41.55 N 1.12 E
Pont-Sainte-Marie 50 48.19 N 4.06 E
Pont-Sainte-Maxence 50 49.18 N 2.36 E
Pont-Saint-Esprit 62 44.15 N 4.39 E
Pont-Saint-Martin 62 45.36 N 7.48 E
Pont-Scorff 28 47.50 N 3.24 W
Ponts Quentin, Ruisseau des ≐ 261 48.44 N 1.48 E
Pont-sur-Yonne 50 48.17 N 3.12 E
Pontuda, Ilha I 287a 23.02 S 43.18 W
Pontus ⌂ 9 130 40.15 N 38.00 E
Pontvallain 50 47.45 N 0.12 E
Pont-Viau ✈ 8 275a 45.34 N 73.41 W
Pontyberem 42 51.47 N 4.09 W
Pontycymer 42 51.37 N 3.34 W
Pontypool 42 51.43 N 3.02 W
Pontypridd 42 51.37 N 3.22 W
Pony 202 45.39 N 111.53 W
Ponyri 76 52.19 N 36.20 E
Ponza 66 40.54 N 12.58 E
Ponza, Isola di I 66 40.55 N 12.57 E
Ponziane, Isole II 66 40.55 N 12.57 E
Ponzone 62 44.35 N 8.27 E
Poochera 162 32.43 S 134.51 E
Pool ⌂ 5 152 3.30 S 15.00 E
Poole 42 50.43 N 1.59 W
Poole, Mount ▲ 166 29.37 S 141.46 E
Poole Bay c 42 50.42 N 1.52 W
Pooler 192 32.06 N 81.14 W
Poole's Cavern ♦ 5 262 53.14 N 1.55 W
Pooles Island I 208 39.17 N 76.16 W
Poolesville 208 39.08 N 77.25 W
Poolewe 46 57.45 N 5.37 W
Pooley Island I 182 52.44 N 128.16 W
Pool's Cove 186 47.41 N 55.26 W
Poolville 222 32.58 N 97.52 W
Poona — Pune 122 18.32 N 73.52 E
Pooncarie 166 33.23 S 142.34 E
Poondinna, Mount ▲ 162 27.20 S 129.59 E
Poopó 248 18.23 S 66.59 W
Poopó, Lago ⊜ 248 18.45 S 67.07 W
Pooraka 168b 34.50 S 138.37 E
Poor Knights Islands II 172 35.30 S 174.45 E
Poor Man Indian Reserve ✈ 4 184 51.30 N 104.23 W

≐ River	Fluß	Río	Rivière	Rio
≐ Canal	Kanal	Canal	Canal	Canal
⌞ Waterfall, Rapids	Wasserfall, Stromschnellen	Cascada, Rápidos	Chute d'eau, Rapides	Cascata, Rápidos
⊻ Strait	Meeresstraße	Estrecho	Détroit	Estreito
c Bay, Gulf	Bucht, Golf	Bahía, Golfo	Baie, Golfe	Baía, Golfo
⊜ Lake, Lakes	See, Seen	Lago, Lagos	Lac, Lacs	Lago, Lagos
Swamp	Sumpf	Pantano	Marais	Pântano
Ice Features, Glacier	Eis- und Gletscherformen	Accidentes Glaciales	Formes glaciaires	Acidentes glaciares
Other Hydrographic Features	Andere Hydrographische Objekte	Otros Elementos Hidrográficos	Autres données hydrographiques	Outros acidentes hidrográficos

✈ Submarine Features	Untermeerische Objekte	Accidentes Submarinos	Formes de relief sous-marin	Acidentes submarinos
⌂ Political Unit	Politische Einheit	Unidad Política	Entité politique	Unidade política
▾ Cultural Institution	Kulturelle Institution	Institución Cultural	Institution culturelle	Instituição cultural
⊥ Historical Site	Historische Stätte	Sitio Histórico	Site historique	Sítio histórico
♦ Recreational Site	Erholungs- und Ferienort	Sitio de Recreo	Centre de loisirs	Area de Lazer
≋ Airport	Flughafen	Aeropuerto	Aéroport	Aeroporto
■ Military Installation	Militäranlage	Instalación Militar	Installation militaire	Instalação militar
✈ Miscellaneous	Verschiedenes	Misceláneo	Divers	Diversos

ENGLISH | DEUTSCH

Name / Name	Page / Seite	Lat.°' / Breite°'	Long.°' / Länge°' E = Ost
Poor Meadow Brook ≃	**283**	42.01 N	70.55 W
Poortjie	**158**	30.13 S	22.44 E
Poowong	**169**	38.21 S	145.46 E
Popa, Isla I	**236**	9.11 N	82.07 W
Popasna	**83**	48.37 N	38.20 E
Popasne	**78**	48.48 N	35.31 E
Popayán	**246**	2.27 N	76.36 W
Pope	**194**	34.12 N	89.56 W
Pope Creek ≃	**226**	38.37 N	122.17 W
Popelnaste	**78**	48.39 N	33.43 E
Poperečnoje	**88**	52.23 N	110.42 E
Poperinge	**50**	50.51 N	2.43 E
Popeşti	**38**	47.14 N	22.25 E
Popeşti-Leordeni	**38**	44.23 N	26.10 E
Pope Valley	**226**	38.37 N	122.26 W
Popham Bay c	**176**	64.10 N	65.10 W
Popigaj	**74**	71.55 N	110.47 E
Popigaj ≃	**74**	72.54 N	106.36 E
Popil'nya	**78**	49.57 N	29.27 E
Popiltah Lake ⊜	**166**	33.10 S	141.43 E
Popinci	**38**	42.25 N	24.17 E
Popki	**80**	50.11 N	44.30 E
Popkum	**224**	49.12 N	121.44 W
Poplar, Ca., U.S.	**226**	36.03 N	119.08 W
Poplar, Mt., U.S.	**198**	48.06 N	105.11 W
Poplar, Wi., U.S.	**190**	46.35 N	91.47 W
Poplar ◆[8]	**260**	51.31 N	0.01 W
Poplar ≃, Can.	**184**	53.00 N	97.24 W
Poplar ≃, N.A.	**198**	48.05 N	105.11 W
Poplar ≃, Mn., U.S.	**198**	47.51 N	96.04 W
Poplar, West Fork ≃	**198**	48.31 N	105.22 W
Poplar Bluff	**194**	36.45 N	90.23 W
Poplar Grove	**216**	42.22 N	88.49 W
Poplar Heights	**284c**	38.53 N	77.12 W
Poplar Hill	**184**	52.05 N	94.18 W
Poplar Mountain ʌ	**194**	36.43 N	85.03 W
Poplar Point	**184**	50.04 N	97.57 W
Poplar Ridge	**210**	42.44 N	76.37 W
Poplar Springs	**208**	39.21 N	77.06 W
Poplarville	**194**	30.50 N	89.32 W
Poplevinskij	**76**	53.41 N	39.33 E
Popocatépetl, Volcán ʌ[1]	**234**	19.02 N	98.38 W
Popof Island I	**180**	55.17 N	160.25 W
Popoh	**115a**	8.15 S	111.48 E
Popokabaka	**152**	5.42 S	16.35 E
Popoli	**66**	42.10 N	13.50 E
Popondetta	**164**	8.46 S	148.14 E
Popova	**89**	42.58 N	131.42 E
Popovka, Ross.	**76**	60.08 N	39.21 E
Popovka, Ross.	**80**	49.14 N	41.12 E
Popovkino	**82**	56.07 N	36.01 E
Popovo	**38**	43.21 N	26.13 E
Poppberg ʌ	**60**	49.25 N	11.35 E
Poppel	**56**	51.27 N	5.02 E
Poppenbüttel ◆[8]	**52**	53.39 N	10.04 E
Poppenhausen	**56**	50.06 N	10.08 E
Poppi	**66**	43.43 N	11.46 E
Popple ≃	**190**	45.50 N	88.21 W
Poprad	**30**	49.03 N	20.18 E
Poprad ≃	**30**	49.38 N	20.42 E
Popricani	**38**	47.18 N	27.31 E
Pŏpsŏng	**98**	35.22 N	126.27 E
Pŏptong	**98**	38.59 N	127.05 E
Poptún	**236**	16.21 N	89.26 W
Populonia	**66**	42.59 N	10.29 E
Poputnaja	**84**	44.31 N	41.27 E
Poquessing Creek ≃	**285**	40.03 N	74.58 W
Poquetanuck	**207**	41.29 N	72.02 W
Poquonock	**207**	41.54 N	72.40 W
Poquonock Bridge	**207**	41.20 N	72.01 W
Poquoson	**208**	37.07 N	76.21 W
Poquoson ≃	**208**	37.10 N	76.24 W
Poquott	**276**	40.57 N	73.05 W
Porādaha	**126**	23.51 N	89.01 E
Porādiha	**126**	21.33 N	86.26 E
Porāli Nai ≃	**120**	25.58 N	66.26 E
Poranga	**250**	4.44 S	40.55 W
Porangahau	**172**	40.18 S	176.37 E
Porangatu	**255**	13.26 S	49.10 W
Porbandar	**120**	21.38 N	69.36 E
Porce ≃	**246**	7.28 N	74.53 W
Porchaman	**128**	33.08 N	63.51 E
Porcher Island I	**182**	53.57 N	130.30 W
Porcheville	**261**	48.58 N	1.47 E
Porchov	**76**	57.46 N	29.34 E
Porcia	**64**	45.57 N	12.36 E
Porciúncula	**255**	20.58 S	42.02 W
Porco	**248**	19.50 S	65.59 W
Porcos, Rio dos ≃	**255**	12.42 S	45.07 W
Porcuna	**34**	37.52 N	4.11 W
Porcupine ≃	**180**	66.35 N	145.15 W
Porcupine Brook ≃	**283**	42.46 N	71.13 W
Porcupine Creek ≃	**202**	48.07 N	106.20 W
Porcupine Creek, Middle Fork ≃	**202**	48.31 N	106.30 W
Porcupine Creek, West Fork ≃	**202**	48.31 N	106.30 W
Porcupine Dome ʌ	**180**	65.31 N	145.31 W
Porcupine Hills ʎ[2]	**184**	52.30 N	101.45 W
Porcupine Mountains State Park ♠	**190**	46.47 N	89.50 W
Pordenone	**64**	45.57 N	12.39 E
Pordenone □[4]	**64**	46.00 N	12.45 E
Pordim	**38**	43.23 N	24.51 E
Poreč	**36**	45.13 N	13.37 E
Porecatu	**255**	22.43 S	51.24 W
Porečje, Bela.	**76**	53.55 N	24.07 E
Porečje, Ross.	**76**	55.43 N	35.33 E
Porečje, Ross.	**76**	56.06 N	30.29 E
Porečje-Rybnoje	**80**	57.06 N	39.23 E
Poreckoje	**80**	55.12 N	46.20 E
Porez	**80**	57.40 N	51.10 E
Pori	**26**	61.29 N	21.47 E
Poricy Brook ≃	**276**	40.21 N	74.05 W
Poringland	**42**	52.33 N	1.21 E
Porirua	**172**	41.08 S	174.51 E
Porjaguba	**24**	66.47 N	33.45 E
Porkkala	**26**	59.59 N	24.26 E
Porlamar	**246**	10.57 N	63.51 W
Porlezza	**58**	46.03 N	9.07 E
Porlock	**42**	51.14 N	3.36 W
Porma ≃	**34**	42.29 N	5.28 W
Pornassio	**62**	44.04 N	7.52 E
Pörnbach	**60**	48.37 N	11.28 E
Pornic	**32**	47.07 N	2.06 W
Poro ʌ	**154**	1.14 N	36.37 E
Porog, Ross.	**24**	63.50 N	38.29 E
Porog, Ross.	**76**	59.16 N	33.24 E
Porogi	**265a**	59.46 N	30.47 E
Poro Island I	**116**	10.40 N	124.27 E
Porokylä	**26**	63.33 N	29.06 E
Poroma	**248**	18.29 S	65.30 W
Poronaj ≃	**89**	49.14 N	143.06 E
Poronajsk	**89**	49.14 N	143.04 E
Porong	**115a**	7.32 S	112.41 E
Porong ≃	**115a**	7.32 S	112.51 E
Poropotank ≃	**208**	37.27 N	76.42 W
Poroshkove	**78**	48.41 N	22.45 E
Porosozero	**24**	62.43 N	32.42 E
Poroto Mountains ʎ	**154**	9.00 S	33.45 E
Porozovo	**76**	52.56 N	24.22 E
Porožskij	**88**	56.04 N	101.46 E
Porpoise Bay c	**9**	66.30 S	128.30 E
Porpoise Channel ʊ	**276**	40.55 N	73.09 W
Porquerolles	**62**	43.00 N	6.12 E
Porquerolles, Île de I	**62**	43.00 N	6.13 E
Porrentruy	**58**	47.25 N	7.05 E
Porretta Terme	**64**	44.09 N	10.59 E
Porsangen c[2]	**24**	70.58 N	27.00 E
Porsangerhalvøya ≻[1]	**24**	70.50 N	25.00 E
Porsea	**114**	2.27 N	99.09 E
Porsgrunn	**26**	59.09 N	9.40 E
Porsuk ≃	**130**	39.42 N	31.59 E
Port → Le Port	**157c**	20.55 S	55.18 E
Portachuelo	**248**	17.21 S	63.24 W
Portacloy	**48**	54.19 N	9.48 W
Port Adelaide	**168b**	34.51 S	138.30 E
Portadown	**48**	54.26 N	6.27 W
Portaferry	**48**	54.23 N	5.33 W
Portage, In., U.S.	**216**	41.34 N	87.10 W
Portage, Mi., U.S.	**216**	42.12 N	85.34 W
Portage, Oh., U.S.	**216**	41.20 N	83.39 W
Portage, Pa., U.S.	**214**	40.23 N	78.40 W
Portage, Ut,. U.S.	**200**	41.58 N	112.14 W
Portage, Wi., U.S.	**190**	43.32 N	89.27 W
Portage □[6]	**214**	41.09 N	81.15 W
Portage ≃, Mi., U.S.	**216**	41.57 N	85.38 W
Portage ≃, Oh., U.S.	**214**	41.31 N	83.05 W
Portage, East Branch ≃	**216**	41.17 N	83.31 W
Portage, Middle Branch ≃	**216**	41.22 N	83.28 W
Portage, North Branch ≃	**216**	41.25 N	83.27 W
Portage, South Branch ≃	**216**	41.22 N	83.30 W
Portage Bay c	**184**	51.33 N	98.50 W
Portage Des Sioux	**219**	38.55 N	90.20 W
Portage Lake ⊜, Mi., U.S.	**190**	47.04 N	88.30 W
Portage Lake ⊜, Mi., U.S.	**216**	42.25 N	83.54 W
Portage Lake ⊜, Mi., U.S.	**216**	42.03 N	85.31 W
Portage Lakes	**214**	40.59 N	81.32 W
Portage Lakes ⊜	**214**	40.59 N	81.32 W
Portage Lakes State Park ♠	**214**	40.57 N	81.32 W
Portage-la-Prairie	**184**	49.59 N	98.18 W
Portage Park ◆[8]	**278**	41.57 N	87.46 W
Portageville, Mo., U.S.	**194**	36.25 N	89.41 W
Portageville, N.Y., U.S.	**210**	42.34 N	78.02 W
Portal, Ga., U.S.	**192**	32.32 N	81.55 W
Portal, N.D., U.S.	**198**	48.59 N	102.32 W
Port Alberni	**224**	49.14 N	124.48 W
Portal del Infierno ⌊	**236**	14.22 N	85.38 W
Portalegre, Bra.	**250**	6.02 S	38.00 W
Portalegre, Port.	**34**	39.17 N	7.26 W
Portales	**196**	34.11 N	103.20 W
Port Alexander	**180**	56.15 N	134.39 W
Port Alfred (Kowie)	**158**	33.36 S	26.55 E
Port Alice	**182**	50.23 N	127.27 W
Port Allegany	**214**	41.48 N	78.16 W
Port Allen	**194**	30.27 N	91.12 W
Port Alma, Austl.	**166**	23.35 S	150.51 E
Port Alma, On., Can.	**214**	42.11 N	82.15 W
Port Alsworth	**180**	60.12 N	154.20 W
Port Angeles	**224**	48.07 N	123.25 W
Port Angeles Harbor c	**224**	48.07 N	123.24 W
Port Anson	**186**	49.32 N	55.50 W
Port Antonio	**241q**	18.11 N	76.28 W
Port Aransas	**196**	27.50 N	97.04 W
Portarlington, Austl.	**169**	38.07 S	144.39 E
Portarlington, Ire.	**48**	53.10 N	7.11 W
Port Arthur, Austl.	**166**	43.09 S	147.51 E
Port Arthur → Thunder Bay, On., Can.	**190**	48.23 N	89.15 W
Port Arthur, Tx., U.S.	**194**	29.53 N	93.55 W
Port Arthur → Lüshun, Zhg.	**98**	38.48 N	121.16 E
Port Ashton	**180**	60.04 N	148.01 W
Port Askaig	**46**	55.51 N	6.07 W
Port Augusta	**166**	32.30 S	137.46 E
Port au Port	**186**	48.33 N	58.44 W
Port au Port Bay c	**186**	48.40 N	58.45 W
Port au Port Peninsula ≻[1]	**186**	48.35 N	59.00 W
Port-au-Prince	**238**	18.32 N	72.20 W
Port-au-Prince, Baie de c	**238**	18.40 N	72.30 W
Port Austin	**190**	44.02 N	82.59 W
Port-aux-Basques → Channel-Port-aux-Basques	**186**	47.34 N	59.09 W
Portavogie	**48**	54.27 N	5.27 W
Porta Westfalica	**52**	52.14 N	8.55 E
Porta Westfalica ♠	**52**	52.14 N	8.55 E
Port Bannatyne	**46**	55.52 N	5.05 W
Port Barre	**194**	30.33 N	91.57 W
Port Bell	**154**	0.17 N	32.39 E
Port-Bergé	**157b**	15.33 S	47.40 E
Port Blair	**110**	11.40 N	92.45 E
Port Blakely	**224**	47.37 N	122.28 W
Port Blandford	**186**	48.21 N	54.10 W
Port Bolivar	**222**	29.23 N	94.46 W
Port Borden	**186**	46.15 N	63.42 W
Port-Bouët	**150**	5.15 N	3.58 W
Port Broughton	**166**	33.36 S	137.56 E
Port Burwell	**212**	42.39 N	80.49 W
Port Byron, Il., U.S.	**190**	41.36 N	90.20 W
Port Byron, N.Y., U.S.	**210**	43.02 N	76.37 W
Port Campbell	**169**	38.37 S	143.00 E
Port Campbell National Park ♠	**169**	38.38 S	142.55 E
Port Canning	**126**	22.18 N	88.40 E
Port Carbon	**208**	40.42 N	76.10 W
Port Carling	**212**	45.07 N	79.35 W
Port-Cartier	**186**	50.01 N	66.52 W
Port-Cartier Sept-Îles, Réserve ♠	**186**	50.35 N	67.10 W
Port Chalmers	**172**	45.49 S	170.37 E
Port Charlotte	**220**	26.58 N	82.05 W
Port Chester	**210**	41.00 N	73.39 W
Port Chester Harbor c	**276**	40.59 N	73.40 W
Port Chicago	**226**	38.03 N	122.01 W
Port Clements	**182**	53.42 N	132.11 W
Port Clinton, Austl.	**168b**	34.14 S	138.01 E
Port Clinton, Oh., U.S.	**214**	41.30 N	82.56 W
Port Clinton, Pa., U.S.	**208**	40.35 N	76.02 W
Port Clyde	**188**	43.55 N	69.15 W
Port Colborne	**212**	42.53 N	79.14 W
Port Colden	**210**	40.45 N	74.57 W
Port Columbus International Airport ⊠	**218**	40.00 N	82.53 W
Port Coquitlam	**224**	49.16 N	122.46 W
Port Costa	**226**	38.03 N	122.11 W
Port Crane	**210**	42.10 N	75.50 W
Port Credit	**212**	43.33 N	79.35 W
Port-Cros	**62**	43.00 N	6.23 E
Port-Cros, Île de I	**62**	43.00 N	6.24 E
Port-Cros, Parc National de ♠	**62**	43.01 N	6.24 E
Port-Daniel, Réserve ♠	**186**	48.18 N	64.55 W
Port-de-Bouc	**62**	43.24 N	4.59 E
Port-de-Paix	**238**	19.57 N	72.50 W
Port Deposit	**208**	39.36 N	76.06 W
Port Dickinson	**210**	42.08 N	75.53 W
Port Dickson	**114**	2.31 N	101.48 E
Porte Crayon, Mount ʌ	**188**	38.56 N	79.27 W
Port Edward, B.C., Can.	**182**	54.14 N	130.18 W
Port Edward, S. Afr.	**158**	31.02 S	30.13 E
Port Edward → Weihai, Zhg.	**98**	37.28 N	122.07 E
Port Edwards	**190**	44.21 N	89.51 W
Portegolpe	**236**	10.20 N	85.46 W
Porteiras	**250**	7.31 S	39.07 W
Porteirinha	**255**	15.44 S	43.02 W
Portel, Bra.	**250**	1.57 S	50.49 W
Portel, Port.	**34**	38.18 N	7.42 W
Portela, Aeroporto da ⊠	**266c**	38.46 N	9.08 W
Port Elgin, N.B., Can.	**186**	46.03 N	64.05 W
Port Elgin, On., Can.	**190**	44.26 N	81.24 W
Port Elizabeth, St. Vin.	**241h**	13.03 N	61.13 W
Port Elizabeth, S. Afr.	**158**	33.58 S	25.40 E
Port Elizabeth, N.J., U.S.	**208**	39.18 N	74.58 W
Port Ellen	**46**	55.39 N	6.12 W
Port Elliot	**168b**	35.32 S	138.41 E
Port-en-Bessin	**32**	49.21 N	0.45 W
Porter, In., U.S.	**216**	41.36 N	87.04 W
Porter, Ok., U.S.	**196**	35.52 N	95.31 W
Porter, Tx., U.S.	**222**	30.06 N	95.14 W
Porter, Wa., U.S.	**224**	46.56 N	123.18 W
Porter □[6]	**216**	41.28 N	87.04 W
Port'Ercole	**66**	42.23 N	11.12 E
Porter Corners	**210**	43.09 N	73.53 W
Porter Creek ≃	**279a**	41.41 N	81.56 W
Port Erin	**44**	54.06 N	4.44 W
Porter Lake ⊜	**184**	56.21 N	107.20 W
Porter Point ≻	**241h**	13.23 N	61.11 W
Porter Springs	**222**	31.16 N	95.36 W
Porters Retreat	**170**	34.00 S	149.48 E
Porters Run ≃	**279b**	40.27 N	79.33 W
Portersville	**214**	40.56 N	80.09 W
Porterville, S. Afr.	**158**	33.00 S	19.00 E
Porterville, Ca., U.S.	**204**	36.03 N	119.00 W
Porterville, Ms., U.S.	**194**	32.41 N	88.28 W
Portes-lés-Valence	**62**	44.52 N	4.53 E
Port Essington	**182**	54.09 N	129.57 W
Portete, Bahía c	**246**	12.13 N	71.55 W
Port-Étienne → Nouâdhibou	**148**	20.54 N	17.04 W
Port Ewen	**210**	41.54 N	73.58 W
Port-Eynon	**42**	51.33 N	4.13 W
Port-Eynon Point ≻	**42**	51.32 N	4.12 W
Portezuelo	**234**	20.25 N	102.31 W
Port Fairy	**166**	38.23 S	142.14 E
Port Fitzroy	**172**	36.10 S	175.21 E
Port Gamble	**224**	47.51 N	122.34 W
Port Gamble Indian Reservation ◆[4]	**224**	47.53 N	122.34 W
Port Gentil	**152**	0.43 S	8.47 E
Port Germein	**166**	33.01 S	138.00 E
Port Gibson, Ms., U.S.	**194**	31.57 N	90.59 W
Port Gibson, N.Y., U.S.	**210**	43.02 N	77.09 W
Port Glasgow	**46**	55.57 N	4.41 W
Portglenone	**48**	54.52 N	6.29 W
Port Graham	**180**	59.21 N	151.50 W
Port Greville	**186**	45.24 N	64.33 W
Porth	**42**	51.38 N	3.25 W
Port Hacking	**274a**	34.04 S	151.08 E
Port Hacking Point ≻	**170**	34.05 S	151.10 E
Port Hammond	**224**	49.13 N	122.39 W
Port Harcourt	**150**	4.43 N	7.05 E
Port Hardy	**182**	50.43 N	127.29 W
Port Hawkesbury	**186**	45.37 N	61.21 W
Porthcawl	**42**	51.29 N	3.43 W
Port Hedland	**162**	20.19 S	118.34 E
Port Heiden	**180**	56.55 N	158.41 W
Port Henry	**188**	44.02 N	73.27 W
Port Hill	**186**	46.35 N	63.53 W
Porthleven	**42**	50.05 N	5.19 W
Porthmadog	**42**	52.55 N	4.08 W
Porth Neigwl c	**42**	52.48 N	4.34 W
Port Hood	**186**	46.01 N	61.32 W
Port Hope, On., Can.	**212**	43.57 N	78.18 W
Port Hope, Mi., U.S.	**190**	43.56 N	82.42 W
Port Howe	**238**	24.15 N	75.21 W
Port Hueneme	**228**	34.08 N	119.11 W
Port Hughes	**168b**	34.04 S	137.32 E
Port Huron	**214**	42.58 N	82.25 W
Portici	**68**	40.49 N	14.20 E
Portico di Romagna	**66**	44.01 N	11.47 E
Portigliola	**68**	38.14 N	16.13 E
Port-Iliç	**84**	38.53 N	48.48 E
Portimão	**34**	37.08 N	8.32 W
Portinho, Rio do ≃	**287a**	23.03 S	43.35 W
Port Isaac	**42**	50.35 N	4.49 W
Port Isabel	**196**	26.04 N	97.12 W
Portishead	**42**	51.30 N	2.46 W
Port Jefferson, N.Y., U.S.	**210**	40.56 N	73.03 W
Port Jefferson, Oh., U.S.	**216**	40.19 N	84.05 W
Port Jefferson Harbor c	**276**	40.58 N	73.05 W
Port Jefferson Station	**210**	40.55 N	73.02 W
Port Jervis	**210**	41.22 N	74.41 W
Port Julia	**168b**	34.40 S	137.52 E
Port-Katon	**83**	46.52 N	38.46 E
Port Kembla	**170**	34.29 S	150.54 E
Port Kennedy	**285**	40.06 N	75.25 W
Port Kenny	**162**	33.10 S	134.42 E
Portknockie	**46**	57.41 N	2.51 W
Port Láirge → Waterford	**48**	52.15 N	7.06 W
Port Lambton	**214**	42.39 N	82.30 W
Portland, Austl.	**166**	38.21 S	141.36 E
Portland, Austl.	**170**	33.22 S	150.00 E
Portland, N.Z.	**172**	35.48 S	174.19 E
Portland, Ar., U.S.	**194**	33.14 N	91.30 W
Portland, Ct., U.S.	**207**	41.34 N	72.38 W
Portland, In., U.S.	**216**	40.26 N	84.58 W
Portland, Me., U.S.	**188**	43.39 N	70.15 W
Portland, Mi., U.S.	**216**	42.52 N	84.54 W
Portland, Mo., U.S.	**219**	38.42 N	91.43 W
Portland, N.Y., U.S.	**214**	42.22 N	79.28 W
Portland, N.D., U.S.	**198**	47.29 N	97.22 W
Portland, Or., U.S.	**224**	45.31 N	122.40 W
Portland, Pa., U.S.	**210**	40.55 N	75.06 W
Portland, Tn., U.S.	**194**	36.34 N	86.30 W
Portland, Tx., U.S.	**196**	27.52 N	97.19 W
Portland, Wi., U.S.	**216**	43.12 N	88.58 W
Portland, Bill of ≻	**42**	50.31 N	2.27 W
Portland, Cape ≻	**166**	40.45 S	147.57 E
Portland, Isle of I	**42**	50.33 N	2.27 W
Portland Bay c	**166**	38.19 S	141.47 E
Portland Bight c[3]	**241q**	17.53 N	77.08 W
Portland Canal c	**182**	55.10 N	130.08 W
Portland Creek Pond ⊜	**186**	50.12 N	57.34 W
Portland Inlet c	**182**	54.50 N	130.15 W
Portland International Airport ⊠	**224**	45.35 N	122.36 W
Portland Island I	**172**	39.17 S	177.52 E
Portland Mills	**214**	41.23 N	78.50 W
Portland Point ≻	**241q**	17.42 N	77.11 W
Portlandville	**210**	42.32 N	74.58 W
Port Laoise (Maryborough)	**48**	53.02 N	7.17 W
Port Lavaca	**196**	28.36 N	96.37 W
Portlaw	**48**	52.17 N	7.19 W
Port-Lesney	**58**	47.00 N	5.49 E
Portlethen	**46**	57.03 N	2.06 W
Port Leyden	**212**	43.35 N	75.21 W
Port Lincoln	**166**	34.44 S	135.52 E
Port Lions	**180**	57.52 N	152.53 W
Portlock Reefs ✧[2]	**164**	9.30 S	144.45 E
Port Logan	**44**	54.43 N	4.56 W
Port Loko	**150**	8.46 N	12.47 W
Port-Louis, Fr.	**32**	47.43 N	3.21 W
Port-Louis, Guad.	**241o**	16.25 N	61.32 W
Port Louis, Maus.	**157c**	20.10 S	57.30 E
Port Ludlow	**224**	47.55 N	122.40 W
Port-Lyautey → Kenitra	**148**	34.16 N	6.40 W
Port MacDonnell	**166**	38.03 S	140.42 E
Port Macquarie	**166**	31.26 S	152.55 E
Port Madison Indian Reservation ◆[4]	**224**	47.45 N	122.35 W
Portmahomack	**46**	57.49 N	3.50 W
Port Maitland, N.S., Can.	**186**	43.59 N	66.09 W
Port Maitland, On., Can.	**214**	42.52 N	79.34 W
Port Maria	**241q**	18.22 N	76.54 W
Portmarnock	**48**	53.25 N	6.08 W
Port Matilda	**214**	40.48 N	78.03 W
Port Mayaca	**220**	27.08 N	80.12 W
Port McNeill	**182**	50.35 N	127.06 W
Port McNicoll	**212**	44.45 N	79.49 W
Port Melbourne	**274b**	37.51 S	144.56 E
Port Mellon	**182**	49.32 N	123.29 W
Port-Menier	**186**	49.48 N	64.20 W
Port Moller	**180**	55.59 N	160.34 W
Port Monmouth	**276**	40.25 N	74.05 W
Port Moody	**224**	49.17 N	122.51 W
Port Morant	**241q**	17.54 N	76.19 W
Portmore	**241q**	17.58 N	76.53 W
Port Moresby	**164**	9.30 S	147.10 E
Port Moresby □[5]	**164**	9.30 S	147.10 E
Port Morien	**186**	46.08 N	59.52 W
Port Morris	**276**	40.54 N	74.41 W
Port Mouton	**186**	43.56 N	64.51 W
Port Murray	**210**	40.47 N	74.54 W
Portnaguran	**46**	58.17 N	6.13 W
Portnahaven	**46**	55.41 N	6.31 W
Port Neches	**194**	29.59 N	93.57 W
Port Neill	**166**	34.07 S	136.20 E
Port Nelson	**184**	57.03 N	92.36 W
Portneuf	**206**	46.42 N	71.53 W
Portneuf □[6]	**206**	46.45 N	72.00 W
Portneuf ≃, P.Q., Can.	**186**	48.38 N	69.05 W
Portneuf ≃, P.Q., Can.	**206**	46.42 N	71.53 W
Portneuf ≃, Id., U.S.	**202**	42.58 N	112.35 W
Portneuf, Lac ⊜	**186**	49.08 N	70.18 W
Portneuf-Station	**206**	46.43 N	71.54 W
Portneuf-sur-Mer	**186**	48.37 N	69.06 W
Port Neville	**182**	50.29 N	126.05 W
Port Noarlunga	**168b**	35.09 S	138.28 E
Port Nolloth	**156**	29.17 S	16.51 E
Port Norris	**208**	39.14 N	75.02 W
Porto, Bra.	**250**	3.54 S	42.42 W
Porto, Port.	**34**	41.11 N	8.36 W
Porto, Bonifica di ◆[1]	**267a**	41.48 N	12.16 E
Porto Acre	**248**	9.34 S	67.31 W
Porto Alegre, Bra.	**252**	30.04 S	51.11 W
Porto Alegre, S. Tom./P.	**152**	0.02 N	6.32 E
Porto Amboim	**152**	10.44 S	13.44 E
Porto Azzurro	**66**	42.46 N	10.24 E
Portobello	**46**	55.58 N	3.07 W
Porto Belo, Bra.	**252**	27.10 S	48.33 W
Portobelo, Pan.	**236**	9.33 N	79.39 W
Porto Calvo	**250**	9.04 S	35.24 W
Porto Ceresio	**58**	45.54 N	8.55 E
Port O'Connor	**196**	28.27 N	96.24 W
Porto das Caixas	**256**	22.42 S	42.53 W
Porto d'Ascoli	**66**	42.55 N	13.53 E
Porto das Flôres	**256**	22.05 S	43.34 W
Porto das Gabarras	**250**	3.07 S	44.34 W
Pôrto de Mós	**34**	39.36 N	8.39 W
Porto de Moz	**250**	1.45 S	52.14 W
Porto de Pedras	**250**	9.10 S	35.17 W
Porto di Potenza Picena	**66**	43.21 N	13.42 E
Porto di Traiano, Necropoli del ⊥	**267a**	41.46 N	12.16 E
Porto dos Gaúchos	**250**	11.29 S	57.22 W
Porto Empedocle	**70**	37.17 N	13.32 E
Porto Esperança	**248**	19.37 S	57.27 W
Porto Esperidião	**248**	15.51 S	58.28 W
Porto Farina	**36**	37.10 N	10.12 E
Porto Feliz	**255**	23.13 S	47.32 W
Portoferraio	**66**	42.49 N	10.19 E
Porto Ferreira	**255**	21.51 S	47.28 W
Portofino	**62**	44.18 N	9.12 E
Port of Ness	**46**	58.29 N	6.13 W
Porto Franco	**250**	6.20 S	47.24 W
Port of Spain	**241r**	10.39 N	61.31 W
Porto Garibaldi	**66**	44.41 N	12.14 E
Porto Grande	**250**	0.42 N	51.24 W
Portogruaro	**64**	45.47 N	12.50 E
Porto Inglês	**150a**	15.08 N	23.13 W
Portola	**204**	39.48 N	120.28 W
Portola State Park ♠	**226**	37.15 N	122.13 W
Portola Valley	**226**	37.23 N	122.13 W
Porto Lucena	**252**	27.51 S	55.01 W
Pörtom (Pirttikylä)	**26**	62.42 N	21.37 E
Portomaggiore	**64**	44.42 N	11.48 E
Porto Maurizio	**62**	43.52 N	8.01 E
Porto Mendes	**252**	24.30 S	54.20 W
Porto Murtinho	**248**	21.42 S	57.52 W
Porto Nacional	**250**	10.42 S	48.25 W
Porto-Novo, Bénin	**150**	6.29 N	2.37 E
Porto Novo, Bra.	**256**	23.40 S	45.28 W
Porto Novo, India	**122**	11.29 N	79.46 E
Porto Novo Creek c	**273a**	6.26 N	3.20 E
Portopalo, It.	**70**	36.41 N	15.08 E
Porto Palo, It.	**70**	37.34 N	12.54 E
Port Orange	**192**	29.06 N	80.59 W
Port Orchard	**224**	47.32 N	122.38 W
Porto Real	**256**	22.25 S	44.20 W
Porto Real do Colégio	**250**	10.11 S	36.49 W
Porto Recanati	**66**	43.26 N	13.40 E
Port Orford	**202**	42.44 N	124.29 W
Porto Rico	**152**	6.08 S	12.30 E
Porto Rico → Puerto Rico □[2]	**240m**	18.15 N	66.30 W
Portorož	**64**	45.31 N	13.36 E
Porto Salvo	**266c**	38.43 N	9.18 W
Porto San Giorgio	**66**	43.11 N	13.48 E
Porto Santana	**250**	0.03 S	51.11 W
Porto Sant'Elpidio	**66**	43.15 N	13.45 E
Porto Santo I	**148**	33.04 N	16.20 W
Porto Santo Stefano	**66**	42.26 N	11.07 E
Porto São José	**255**	22.43 S	53.10 W
Portoscuso	**71**	39.12 N	8.23 E
Porto Seguro, Bra.	**255**	16.26 S	39.05 W
Porto-Séguro, Togo	**150**	6.12 N	1.29 E
Porto Torres	**71**	40.50 N	8.24 E
Porto União	**252**	26.15 S	51.05 W
Porto Válter	**248**	8.15 S	72.45 W
Porto Valtravaglia	**58**	45.58 N	8.41 E
Porto-Vecchio	**36**	41.35 N	9.16 E
Porto Velho	**248**	8.46 S	63.54 W
Porto Velho do Cunha	**256**	21.50 S	42.32 W
Portovenere	**62**	44.03 N	9.51 E
Portoviejo	**246**	1.03 S	80.27 W
Portpatrick, Scot., U.K.	**44**	54.51 N	5.07 W
Port Patrick, Vanuatu	**175f**	20.08 S	169.47 E
Port Penn	**208**	39.31 N	75.34 W
Port Perry	**212**	44.06 N	78.57 W
Port Phillip Bay c	**169**	38.07 S	144.48 E
Port Pirie	**166**	33.11 S	138.01 E
Port Providence	**285**	40.08 N	75.30 W
Portraine	**48**	53.30 N	6.07 W
Port Reading	**276**	40.33 N	74.15 W
Portree	**46**	57.24 N	6.12 W
Port Renfrew	**224**	48.33 N	124.25 W
Port Republic	**208**	39.31 N	74.29 W
Port Rexton	**186**	48.23 N	53.20 W
Port Richey	**220**	28.16 N	82.43 W
Port Richmond	**208**	37.33 N	76.49 W
Port Robinson	**284a**	43.02 N	79.13 W
Port Rowan	**214**	42.37 N	80.28 W
Port Royal, Jam.	**241q**	17.56 N	76.51 W
Port Royal, Ky., U.S.	**218**	38.33 N	85.04 W
Port Royal, Pa., U.S.	**208**	40.32 N	77.23 W
Port Royal, S.C., U.S.	**192**	32.22 N	80.41 W
Port Royal, Va., U.S.	**208**	38.10 N	77.11 W
Port-Royal-des-Champs, Abbaye de ☩[1]	**261**	48.45 N	2.01 E
Port Royal National Historic Park ♠	**186**	44.44 N	65.40 W
Portrush	**48**	55.12 N	6.40 W
Port Said → Būr Sa'īd	**142**	31.16 N	32.18 E
Port-Sainte-Marie	**32**	44.15 N	0.24 E
Port Saint Joe	**192**	29.49 N	85.18 W
Port Saint Johns	**158**	31.38 S	29.33 E
Port-Saint-Louis	**62**	43.23 N	4.48 E
Port Saint Lucie	**220**	27.20 N	80.20 W
Port Saint Mary	**44**	54.05 N	4.43 W
Port-Saint-Servan	**186**	51.19 N	58.02 W
Port Salerno	**220**	27.08 N	80.12 W
Portsalon	**48**	55.13 N	7.37 W
Port Sanilac	**190**	43.25 N	82.32 W
Port Saunders	**186**	50.39 N	57.18 W
Pörtschach	**61**	46.37 N	14.08 E
Portsea	**169**	38.19 S	144.43 E
Port Seton	**46**	55.58 N	2.57 W
Port Shepstone	**158**	30.46 S	30.22 E
Portslade	**42**	50.50 N	0.11 W
Portsmouth, Dom.	**240d**	15.35 N	61.28 W
Portsmouth, Eng., U.K.	**42**	50.48 N	1.05 W
Portsmouth, N.H., U.S.	**188**	43.04 N	70.45 W
Portsmouth, Oh., U.S.	**218**	38.43 N	82.59 W
Portsmouth, R.I., U.S.	**207**	41.36 N	71.15 W
Portsmouth, Va., U.S.	**208**	36.50 N	76.17 W
Portsmouth Naval Shipyard ■	**188**	43.05 N	70.45 W
Portsoy	**46**	57.41 N	2.41 W
Port Stanley, On., Can.	**214**	42.40 N	81.13 W
Port Stanley → Stanley, Falk. Is.	**254**	51.42 S	57.51 W
Portstewart	**48**	55.11 N	6.43 W
Port Sudan → Būr Sūdān	**140**	19.37 N	37.14 E
Port Sulphur	**194**	29.28 N	89.41 W
Port Sunlight	**262**	53.21 N	2.59 W
Port-sur-Saône	**58**	47.41 N	6.03 E
Port Talbot	**42**	51.36 N	3.47 W
Port Taufiq → Būr Tawfīq	**128**	29.57 N	32.34 E
Porttipahdan tekojärvi ⊜[1]	**24**	68.08 N	26.40 E
Port Tobacco River c	**208**	38.27 N	77.02 W
Port Townsend	**224**	48.07 N	122.45 W
Port Trevorton	**208**	40.42 N	76.52 W
Portugal □[1], Europe	**22**	39.30 N	8.00 W
Portugal □[1], Europe	**34**	39.30 N	8.00 W
Portugal, Cachoeira ⌊	**248**	9.55 S	64.16 W
Portugal Cove South	**186**	46.42 N	53.15 W
Portugalete	**34**	43.19 N	3.01 W
Portuguesa □[3]	**246**	9.10 N	69.15 W
Portuguesa ≃	**246**	7.57 N	67.32 W
Portuguese Guinea → Guinea-Bissau □[1]	**150**	12.00 N	15.00 W
Portumna	**48**	53.06 N	8.13 W
Port Union, Nf., Can.	**186**	48.30 N	53.05 W
Port Union, On., Can.	**275b**	43.47 N	79.08 W
Port-Vendres	**32**	42.31 N	3.07 E
Port Victoria → Victoria	**138**	4.38 S	55.27 E
Port Vila	**175f**	17.44 S	168.19 E
Portville	**210**	42.02 N	78.20 W
Port Vincent	**168b**	34.47 S	137.51 E
Port-Vladimir	**24**	69.25 N	33.06 E
Port Vue	**279b**	40.20 N	79.52 W
Port Waikato	**172**	37.23 S	174.44 E
Port Wakefield, Austl.	**168b**	34.11 S	138.09 E
Port Wakefield, Ak., U.S.	**180**	58.03 N	153.03 W
Port Washington, B.C., Can.	**224**	48.49 N	123.19 W
Port Washington, N.Y., U.S.	**210**	40.49 N	73.41 W
Port Washington, Oh., U.S.	**214**	40.27 N	81.37 W
Port Washington, Wi., U.S.	**190**	43.23 N	87.52 W
Port Weld	**114**	4.50 N	100.38 E
Port Welshpool	**169**	38.42 S	146.28 E
Port Wentworth	**192**	32.08 N	81.09 W
Port William, Scot., U.K.	**44**	54.46 N	4.35 W
Port William, Oh., U.S.	**218**	39.33 N	83.47 W
Port Wing	**190**	46.46 N	91.23 W
Porum	**196**	35.21 N	95.15 W
Porus	**241q**	18.02 N	77.25 W
Porvenir, Chile	**254**	53.18 S	70.22 W
Porvenir, Méx.	**232**	31.15 N	105.51 W
Porvoo (Borgå)	**26**	60.24 N	25.40 E
Porvoonjoki ≃	**26**	60.23 N	25.40 E
Porz	**56**	50.53 N	7.03 E
Porzdni	**80**	57.00 N	42.33 E
Porzuna	**34**	39.09 N	4.09 W
Posada	**71**	40.38 N	9.43 E
Posada ≃	**71**	40.39 N	9.45 E
Posadas, Arg.	**252**	27.23 S	55.53 W
Posadas, Esp.	**34**	37.48 N	5.06 W
Posavina V	**36**	45.10 N	17.20 E
Poščharv	**85**	38.24 N	71.10 E
Poschiavino ≃	**58**	46.12 N	10.10 E
Poschiavo	**58**	46.18 N	10.04 E
Pošechon'e	**76**	58.30 N	39.07 E
Posen → Poznań, Pol.	**30**	52.25 N	16.55 E
Posen, Il., U.S.	**278**	41.37 N	87.40 W
Posen, Mi., U.S.	**190**	45.15 N	83.41 W
Poseritz	**54**	54.18 N	13.16 E
Posesión, Bahía c	**254**	52.17 S	69.14 W
Posevnaja	**86**	54.18 N	83.20 E
Poshan → Boshan	**98**	36.29 N	117.50 E
Poshiwu	**106**	30.22 N	119.36 E
Posieux	**58**	46.46 N	7.06 E
Posina	**64**	45.47 N	11.15 E
Pösing	**60**	49.14 N	12.33 E
Posio	**26**	66.06 N	28.09 E
Positano	**68**	40.38 N	14.29 E
Posjet	**89**	42.39 N	130.50 E
Poso	**112**	1.23 S	120.44 E
Poso, Danau ⊜	**112**	1.52 S	120.35 E
Poso, Teluk c	**112**	1.15 S	120.55 E
Poso Creek ≃	**226**	35.41 N	119.22 W
Posof	**130**	41.31 N	42.42 E
Pos'olki	**80**	53.08 N	46.29 E
Pos'olok	**265a**	59.43 N	30.12 E
Posŏng	**98**	34.47 N	127.04 E
Posooy, Mount ʌ	**116**	17.21 N	120.48 E
Pospelicha	**86**	51.57 N	81.46 E
Possagno	**64**	45.51 N	11.51 E
Posse, Bra.	**255**	14.05 S	46.22 W
Posse, Bra.	**256**	22.16 S	43.06 W
Possel	**152**	5.01 N	19.15 E
Possendorf	**54**	50.57 N	13.42 E
Posses	**256**	21.43 S	46.08 W
Possession Islands II	**9**	71.27 S	171.08 E
Possession Sound ʊ	**224**	48.00 N	122.20 W
Possidhonia ⊥	**38**	37.40 N	24.00 E
Pössneck	**54**	50.42 N	11.37 E
Possruck (Kozjak) ʎ	**61**	46.37 N	15.28 E
Possum Kingdom Lake ⊜[1]	**196**	32.55 N	98.28 W
Post	**196**	33.11 N	101.22 W
Posta	**66**	42.31 N	13.06 E
Postal (Burgstall)	**64**	46.36 N	11.11 E
Postau	**60**	48.39 N	12.20 E
Postavy	**76**	55.07 N	26.50 E
Postbauer	**60**	49.19 N	11.21 E
Post Creek ≃	**210**	42.09 N	77.02 W
Poste-de-la-Baleine	**176**	55.17 N	77.45 W
Postelle	**192**	35.02 N	84.22 W
Poste Ramartina	**157b**	19.38 S	45.58 E
Posterholt	**52**	51.07 N	6.03 E
Post Falls	**202**	47.43 N	116.57 W
Postiglione	**68**	40.33 N	15.13 E
Postmasburg	**158**	28.18 S	23.05 E
Postojna	**36**	45.47 N	14.13 E
Postojnska jama ⊥[7]	**36**	45.47 N	14.12 E
Postoloprty	**54**	50.20 N	13.40 E
P'ostraja Dresva	**74**	61.34 N	156.41 E
Postrevalle	**248**	18.29 S	63.51 W
Postsee ⊜	**54**	54.13 N	10.13 E
Poststadion ♠	**264a**	52.32 N	13.21 E
Postville	**190**	43.05 N	91.34 W
Pota	**115b**	8.20 S	120.46 E
Potaizi	**104**	41.34 N	121.08 E
Potake Pond ⊜	**276**	41.08 N	74.13 W
Pótam	**232**	27.36 N	110.23 W
Potanino	**76**	60.16 N	32.47 E
Potaro ≃	**246**	5.22 N	58.54 W
Potaro Landing	**246**	5.23 N	59.08 W
Potaro-Siparuni □[4]	**246**	5.00 N	59.30 W
Potato Creek ≃, Ga., U.S.	**192**	32.47 N	84.21 W
Potato Creek ≃, Pa., U.S.	**214**	41.53 N	78.23 W
Potawatomie Woods ♠	**278**	42.08 N	87.53 W
Potchefstroom	**158**	26.46 S	27.01 E
Poté	**255**	17.49 S	41.49 W
Poteau	**194**	35.03 N	94.37 W
Poteau ≃	**194**	35.23 N	94.26 W
Poteet	**196**	29.02 N	98.34 W
Potengi ≃	**250**	5.47 S	35.16 W
Pötenitz	**54**	53.57 N	10.58 E
Pötenitzer Wiek c	**54**	53.55 N	10.55 E
Potenji	**250**	7.06 S	40.00 W
Potenza	**68**	40.38 N	15.49 E
Potenza □[4]	**68**	40.30 N	15.50 E
Potenza ≃	**66**	43.25 N	13.40 E
Potenza Picena	**66**	43.22 N	13.37 E
Poteriteri, Lake ⊜	**172**	46.06 S	167.08 E
Potes	**34**	43.09 N	4.37 W
Potfontein	**158**	30.12 S	24.08 E
Potgietersrus	**156**	24.15 S	28.55 E
Poth	**196**	29.04 N	98.05 W
Potholes Reservoir ⊜[1]	**202**	47.01 N	119.19 W
Poti	**84**	42.09 N	41.40 E
Poti ≃	**250**	5.02 S	42.50 W
Potic Creek ≃	**210**	42.16 N	73.55 W
Potiraguá	**255**	15.36 S	39.53 W
Potirendaba	**255**	21.08 S	49.08 W
Potiskum	**146**	11.43 N	11.05 E
Potiyivka	**78**	50.37 N	28.58 E
Potlatch	**202**	46.55 N	116.53 W
Potlatch ≃	**202**	46.28 N	116.46 W
Po Toi Island I	**271d**	22.10 N	114.15 E
Po Toi Island Group II	**271d**	22.11 N	114.16 E
Potol Point ≻	**116**	11.56 N	121.57 E
Potomac, Il., U.S.	**216**	40.18 N	87.48 W
Potomac, Md., U.S.	**284c**	39.01 N	77.12 W
Potomac ≃	**188**	38.00 N	76.18 W
Potomac, South Branch ≃	**188**	39.31 N	78.35 W
Potomac, South Branch, North Fork ≃	**188**	38.59 N	79.11 W
Potomac, South Branch, South Fork ≃	**188**	39.04 N	78.59 W
Potomac Creek ≃	**208**	38.21 N	77.18 W
Potomac Creek, Long Branch ≃	**208**	38.23 N	77.29 W
Potomac Heights	**208**	38.36 N	77.08 W
Poto-Poto ◆[8]	**273b**	4.15 S	15.18 E
Potosí, Bol.	**248**	19.35 S	65.45 W
Potosi, Mo., U.S.	**194**	37.56 N	90.47 W
Potosí □[5]	**248**	20.40 S	67.00 W
Pototan	**116**	10.55 N	122.40 E
Potrerillos, Chile	**252**	26.26 S	69.29 W
Potrerillos, Hond.	**236**	15.11 N	87.58 W
Potrerillos Arriba	**236**	8.41 N	82.30 W
Potrero	**236**	10.28 N	85.47 W
Potrero ◆[8]	**282**	37.48 N	122.24 W
Potrero de Gallegos	**234**	22.38 N	103.41 W
Potrero del Llano	**196**	29.12 N	104.28 W
Potrero Grande	**236**	9.00 N	83.11 W
Potrite	**248**	61.32 S	16.10 W
Potro, Cerro del ʌ	**252**	28.24 S	69.39 W
Potsdam, Dtsch.	**54**	52.24 N	13.04 E
Potsdam, N.Y., U.S.	**188**	44.40 N	74.58 W
Potsdam, Oh., U.S.	**218**	39.58 N	84.25 W
Potsdam, Staatsforst ♠	**264a**	52.26 N	13.04 E
Potshausen	**52**	53.11 N	7.37 E
Pott, Île I	**175f**	19.35 S	163.36 E
Pottawatomie Creek ≃	**198**	38.29 N	94.55 W
Pottawatomi Indian Reservation ◆[4]	**198**	39.20 N	95.50 W
Pottendorf	**61**	47.55 N	16.23 E
Potten End	**260**	51.46 N	0.31 W
Pottenhofen	**61**	48.46 N	16.33 E
Pottenstein	**60**	49.46 N	11.25 E
Potter	**198**	41.13 N	103.18 W
Potter □[6]	**214**	41.47 N	78.01 W
Potter Hollow	**210**	42.25 N	74.13 W
Potter Lake	**216**	42.50 N	88.21 W
Potter Point ≻	**274a**	34.03 S	151.13 E
Potters Bar	**42**	51.42 N	0.11 W
Potters Mills	**208**	40.48 N	77.32 W
Potter Street	**260**	51.46 N	0.08 E
Pottersville	**276**	40.42 N	74.43 W
Potterville	**216**	42.38 N	84.45 W
Pöttmes	**60**	48.35 N	11.06 E
Potton	**42**	52.08 N	0.14 W
Potts Camp	**194**	34.38 N	89.18 W
Potts Creek ≃	**192**	37.45 N	80.00 W
Potts Grove	**210**	41.00 N	76.48 W
Potts Hill Reservoirs ⊜[1]	**274a**	33.54 S	151.02 E
Pott Shrigley	**262**	53.19 N	2.05 W
Pottstown	**208**	40.14 N	75.39 W
Pottstown Landing	**285**	40.14 N	75.40 W
Pottstown Limerick Airport ⊠	**285**	40.14 N	75.34 W
Pottstown Municipal Airport ⊠	**285**	40.16 N	75.40 W
Pottsville	**208**	40.41 N	76.11 W
Potwin	**198**	37.56 N	97.01 W
Pötzleinsdorf ◆[8]	**264b**	48.15 N	16.19 E
Pötzleinsdorfer Park ♠	**264b**	48.14 N	16.18 E
P'otzu	**100**	23.28 N	120.14 E
Pouancé	**32**	47.44 N	1.11 W
Pouce-Coupe	**182**	55.43 N	120.08 W
Pouce Coupé ≃	**182**	56.08 N	119.52 W
Pouch	**54**	51.37 N	12.24 E
Pouch Cove	**186**	47.46 N	52.46 W
Pouembout	**175f**	21.08 S	164.53 E
Poughkeepsie	**210**	41.42 N	73.55 W
Poughquag	**210**	41.37 N	73.41 W
Pouilly-en-Auxois	**58**	47.16 N	4.33 E
Pouilly-sur-Loire	**50**	47.17 N	2.57 E
Pouilly-sur-Meuse	**56**	49.32 N	5.07 E
Poulain, Étang ⊜	**261**	48.43 N	1.44 E
Poulan	**192**	31.30 N	83.47 W
Poulaphouca Reservoir ⊜[1]	**48**	53.08 N	6.31 W
Poulin-de-Courval, Lac ⊜	**186**	48.52 N	70.27 W
Poulsbo	**224**	47.44 N	122.38 W
Poulter, Lac ⊜	**190**	47.07 N	76.45 W
Poultney	**188**	43.31 N	73.14 W
Poulton-le-Fylde	**44**	53.51 N	2.59 W
Poum	**175f**	20.14 S	164.02 E
Poŭn	**98**	36.29 N	127.43 E
Pound	**192**	37.07 N	82.36 W
Poundmaker Indian Reserve ◆[4]	**184**	52.51 N	109.00 W
Poundstock	**42**	50.46 N	4.33 W
Pouoanuu, Mont ʌ	**174x**	9.49 S	139.07 W
Pourri, Mont ʌ	**62**	45.32 N	6.52 E
Pouru-Saint-Rémy	**56**	49.41 N	5.05 E
Pourville-sur-Mer	**50**	49.55 N	1.02 E
Pouso Alegre	**256**	22.13 S	45.56 W
Pouso Alto	**256**	22.11 S	44.58 W
Pouso Redondo	**252**	27.15 S	49.57 W
Pouso Sêco	**256**	22.41 S	44.10 W
Pouss	**146**	10.51 N	15.03 E
Poutasi	**175a**	14.01 S	171.41 W
Poŭthĭsăt	**110**	12.32 N	103.55 E
Poŭthĭsăt ≃	**110**	12.41 N	104.09 E

Symbols in the index entries represent the broad categories identified in the key at the right. Symbols with superior numbers (ʎ[1]) identify subcategories (see complete key on page *I · 1).*

Symbole im Register stellen die rechts im Schlüssel erklärten Kategorien dar. Symbole mit hochgestellten Ziffern (ʎ[1]) bezeichnen Unterabteilungen einer Kategorie (vgl. vollständiger Schlüssel auf Seite *I · 1).*

Los símbolos incluídos en el texto del índice representan las grandes categorías identificadas con la clave a la derecha. Los símbolos con numeros en su parte superior (ʎ[1]) identifican las subcategorías (véase la clave completa en la página *I · 1).*

Les symboles de l'index représentent les catégories indiquées dans la légende à droite. Les symboles suivis d'un indice (ʎ[1]) représentent des sous-catégories (voir légende complète à la page *I · 1).*

Os símbolos incluídos no texto do índice representam as grandes categorias identificadas com a chave à direita. Os símbolos com números em sua parte superior (ʎ[1]) identificam as subcategorias (veja-se a chave completa à página *I · 1).*

ʌ Mountain	Berg	Montaña	Montagne	Montanha
ʎ Mountains	Gebirge	Montañas	Montagnes	Montanhas
)(Pass	Paß	Paso	Col	Passo
V Valley, Canyon	Tal, Cañon	Valle, Cañón	Vallée, Canyon	Vale, Canhão
≚ Plain	Ebene	Llano	Plaine	Planície
≻ Cape	Kap	Cabo	Cap	Cabo
I Island	Insel	Isla	Île	Ilha
II Islands	Inseln	Islas	Îles	Ilhas
⊥ Other Topographic Features	Andere Topographische Objekte	Otros Elementos Topográficos	Autres données topographiques	Outros acidentes topográficos

Pouxeux 58 48.06 N 6.34 E
Pouzauges 32 46.47 N 0.50 W
Považská Bystrica 30 49.08 N 18.27 E
Povenec 24 62.51 N 34.45 E
Poverello, Monte ∧ 70 38.05 N 15.22 E
Poverennyj 80 46.45 N 43.12 E
Poverty Bay c 172 38.42 S 177.58 E
Povetkino 82 54.20 N 38.23 E
Poviglio 64 44.51 N 10.32 E
Povljen ∧ 38 43.55 N 19.30 E
Póvoa, Mouchão da I 266c 38.51 N 9.03 W
Povoação 148a 37.45 N 25.15 W
Póvoa de Santa Iria 266c 38.52 N 9.04 W
Póvoa de Santo Adrião 266c 38.48 N 9.10 W
Póvoa de Varzim 34 41.23 N 8.46 W
Povorino 80 51.12 N 42.14 E
Povorotnyj, mys > 89 42.42 N 133.04 E
Povorsk 78 51.16 N 25.07 E
Povrly 54 50.40 N 14.10 E
Povungnituk 176 60.02 N 77.10 W
Povungnituk, Rivière de ≃ 176 60.03 N 77.15 W
Powassan 190 46.05 N 79.22 W
Poway 228 32.57 N 117.02 W
Powder ≃, U.S. 178 46.44 N 105.26 W
Powder ≃, Or., U.S. 202 44.45 N 117.03 W
Powder, Dry Fork ≃ 200 43.47 N 106.15 W
Powder, Middle Fork ≃ 200 43.42 N 106.33 W
Powder, North Fork ≃ 202 43.42 N 106.33 W
Powder, Red Fork ≃ 202 43.39 N 106.47 W
Powder, South Fork ≃ 202 43.40 N 106.30 W
Powder Horn Lake ⊜ 278 41.38 N 87.32 W
Powderly, Ky., U.S. 194 37.09 N 87.10 W
Powderly, Tx., U.S. 196 33.49 N 95.31 W
Powdermaker Ditch ≋ 279a 41.30 N 82.02 W
Powder Mill Village 284c 39.03 N 76.57 W
Powder River Pass × 202 44.09 N 107.04 W
Powell, Oh., U.S. 214 40.09 N 83.05 W
Powell, Pa., U.S. 210 41.42 N 76.31 W
Powell, Tx., U.S. 222 32.07 N 96.20 W
Powell, Wy., U.S. 202 44.45 N 108.45 W
Powell ≃ 192 36.29 N 83.42 W
Powell, Lake ⊜[1] 200 37.25 N 110.45 W
Powell, Mount ∧ 200 39.46 N 106.20 W
Powell Creek ≃, Austl. 166 25.02 S 143.40 E
Powell Creek ≃, Oh., U.S. 216 41.17 N 84.21 W
Powellhurst 224 45.30 N 122.32 W
Powell Lake ⊜ 182 50.11 N 124.24 W
Powell River 182 49.52 N 124.33 W
Powells Valley 208 40.26 N 76.56 W
Powellton 188 38.05 N 81.19 W
Powellville 208 38.19 N 75.22 W
Powers, Mi., U.S. 190 45.41 N 87.31 W
Powers, Or., U.S. 202 42.53 N 124.04 W
Powers Lake, N.D., U.S. 198 48.33 N 102.38 W
Powers Lake, Wi., U.S. 216 42.33 N 88.17 W
Powers Lookout ♦ 169 36.50 S 146.22 E
Powhatan, La., U.S. 194 31.52 N 93.12 W
Powhatan, Va., U.S. 192 37.32 N 77.55 W
Powhatan Mill 284b 39.20 N 76.43 W
Powhatan Point 188 39.51 N 80.48 W
Powis, Vale of V 42 52.38 N 3.08 W
Powissett Brook ≃ 283 42.16 N 71.14 W
Powlett ≃ 169 38.35 S 145.32 E
Pownal 210 42.45 N 73.14 W
Powys □[6] 42 52.17 N 3.20 W
Poxoréo 255 15.50 S 54.23 W
Poya 175f 21.19 S 165.07 E
Poyang Hu ⊜ 100 29.00 N 116.25 E
Poyan Reservoir ⊜[1] 271c 1.23 N 103.40 E
Poyen 194 34.19 N 92.38 W
Poygan, Lake ⊜ 190 44.09 N 88.50 W
Poyle 260 51.28 N 0.31 W
Poynette 190 43.23 N 89.24 W
Poynor 222 32.04 N 95.36 W
Poynton 44 53.21 N 2.07 W
Poyntz Pass 48 54.18 N 6.23 W
Poyraz ◆[8] 267b 41.12 N 29.07 E
Poyraz Burnu > 267b 41.12 N 29.08 E
Poysdorf 61 48.40 N 16.38 E
Pozantı 130 37.25 N 34.52 E
Požarevac 38 44.37 N 21.11 E
Poza Rica 234 20.33 N 97.27 W
Požarskoje 89 46.16 N 134.04 E
Pozdejevka 89 50.36 N 128.56 E
Požega 38 43.50 N 20.02 E
Poznań 30 52.25 N 16.55 E
Poznań □[4] 30 52.20 N 16.55 E
Pozo Alcón 34 37.42 N 2.56 W
Pozo Almonte 248 20.16 S 69.48 W
Pozoblanco 34 38.22 N 4.51 W
Pozo-Cañada 34 38.48 N 1.45 W
Pozo Colorado 252 23.28 S 58.51 W
Pozo del Molle 252 32.02 S 62.55 W
Pozo del Tigre 252 24.54 S 60.19 W
Pozo Hondo 252 27.10 S 64.30 W
Pozos, Punta > 254 47.57 S 65.47 W
Pozsony — Bratislava 30 48.09 N 17.07 E
Pozuelo de Alarcón, Esp. 34 40.26 N 3.49 W
Pozuelo de Alarcón, Esp. 266a 40.26 N 3.49 W
Pozuelos 246 10.11 N 64.39 W
Pozuelos, Laguna ⊜ 252 22.22 S 66.01 W
Pozuzo 248 10.04 S 75.32 W
Pozuzo ≃ 248 9.52 S 75.12 W
Požva 86 59.05 N 56.05 E
Pozzallo 70 36.43 N 14.51 E
Pozzillo, Lago di ⊜ 70 37.40 N 14.35 E
Pozzolo Formigaro 62 44.48 N 8.47 E
Pozzomaggiore 71 40.24 N 8.39 E
Pozzuoli 68 40.49 N 14.07 E
Pozzuolo del Friuli 64 45.59 N 13.12 E
Pra ≃, Ghana 150 5.01 N 1.37 W
Pra ≃, Ross. 80 54.45 N 41.01 E
Prabuty 30 53.46 N 19.10 E
Praça Cruzeiro 256 22.43 S 42.38 W
Praça Sêca ◆[8] 287a 22.54 S 43.21 W
Prachatice 30 49.01 N 14.00 E
Prachin Buri 110 14.03 N 101.22 E
Prachuap Khiri Khan 110 11.49 N 99.48 E
Prackenbach 60 49.06 N 12.50 E
Pracuí ≃ 250 2.26 S 51.19 W
Pracuí ≃ 250 2.06 S 51.30 W
Pradelles 62 44.46 N 3.53 E
Pradera 246 3.25 N 76.15 W
Prades 32 42.37 N 2.26 E
Pradleves 62 44.25 N 7.17 E
Prado 255 17.21 S 39.13 W
Prado, Museo del ʋ 266a 40.25 N 3.41 W
Prado Dam ◆[6] 280 33.54 N 117.39 W
Prado Flood Control Basin ≃[1] 280 33.54 N 117.38 W
Prados 255 21.03 S 44.05 W
Prads 62 44.13 N 6.27 E
Præstø 41 55.07 N 12.03 E
Prag — Praha 54 50.05 N 14.26 E
Praga — Praha 54 50.05 N 14.26 E
Pragelato 62 45.01 N 6.57 E
Pragersko 61 46.23 N 15.40 E
Praglia, Monastero di ʋ[1] 64 45.23 N 11.45 E
Prägraten 64 47.01 N 12.23 E
Prague — Praha, Česká Rep. 54 50.05 N 14.26 E
Prague, Ne., U.S. 198 41.18 N 96.48 W
Prague, Ok., U.S. 196 35.29 N 96.41 W
Praha (Prague) 54 50.05 N 14.26 E
Praha ∧ 60 49.40 N 13.49 E
Prahova □[6] 38 45.00 N 26.00 E
Prahova ≃ 38 44.43 N 26.27 E
Prahran 274b 37.51 S 144.59 E
Praia 150a 14.55 N 23.31 W
Praia a Mare 68 39.54 N 15.47 E
Praia da Cruz Quebrada 266c 38.42 N 9.14 W
Praia da Enseada 256 23.29 S 45.05 W
Praia das Maçãs 266c 38.51 N 9.28 W
Praia da Vitória 148a 38.44 N 27.04 W
Praia de Araçatiba 256 23.15 S 44.21 W
Praia Funda, Ponta da > 287a 23.05 S 43.33 W
Praia Grande, Bra. 252 29.12 S 49.57 W
Praia Grande, Bra. 256 24.01 S 46.25 W
Praiano 68 40.37 N 14.32 E
Praikalogu 115b 9.45 S 119.25 E
Prainha 250 1.48 S 53.29 W
Prainha Nova 248 7.16 S 60.23 W
Prairie 166 20.52 S 144.36 E
Prairie ≃, Mi., U.S. 216 41.55 N 85.38 W
Prairie ≃, Mn., U.S. 190 47.18 N 93.29 W
Prairie ≃, Wi., U.S. 190 45.10 N 89.42 W
Prairie City, Il., U.S. 190 40.37 N 90.28 W
Prairie City, Ia., U.S. 190 41.35 N 93.14 W
Prairie City, Or., U.S. 202 44.27 N 118.42 W
Prairie Creek ≃, Fl., U.S. 220 26.59 N 81.56 W
Prairie Creek ≃, Il., U.S. 216 41.21 N 88.12 W
Prairie Creek ≃, Il., U.S. 216 40.55 N 87.49 W
Prairie Creek ≃, Il., U.S. 278 41.36 N 87.40 W
Prairie Creek ≃, Mi., U.S. 216 42.59 N 85.01 W
Prairie Creek ≃, Ne., U.S. 198 41.22 N 97.32 W
Prairie Creek Reservoir ⊜[1] 218 40.08 N 85.17 W
Prairie Dog Creek ≃ 198 40.00 N 99.23 W
Prairie du Chien 190 43.03 N 91.08 W
Prairie du Sac 190 43.17 N 89.43 W
Prairie Elk Creek ≃ 198 48.00 N 105.51 W
Prairie Grove 194 35.58 N 94.19 W
Prairie Hill 222 31.39 N 96.47 W
Prairie Lea 222 29.44 N 97.45 W
Prairie River 184 52.52 N 103.00 W
Prairies, Coteau des ∧[2] 198 44.30 N 96.45 W
Prairies, Lake of the ⊜[1] 184 51.05 N 101.25 W
Prairies, Rivière des ≃ 275a 45.42 N 73.29 W
Prairie View, Il., U.S. 278 42.12 N 87.57 W
Prairie View, Tx., U.S. 222 30.05 N 95.59 W
Prairie Village 198 38.59 N 94.38 W
Prajekan 115a 7.47 S 113.59 E
Prakhon Chai 110 14.37 N 103.05 E
Pralboino 64 45.16 N 10.13 E
Prali 62 44.54 N 7.03 E
Pralls Island I 276 40.37 N 74.12 W
Pralognan-la-Vanoise 62 45.23 N 6.43 E
Pram 60 48.14 N 13.37 E
Pram ≃ 60 48.28 N 13.26 E
Pramaggiore, Monte ∧ 64 46.22 N 12.33 E
Prambachkirchen 60 48.19 N 13.55 E
Prambanan 115a 7.45 S 110.30 E
Pr'amicyno 78 51.39 N 35.56 E
Pramort 54 54.26 N 12.55 E
Prampram 150 5.42 N 0.07 E
Pran Buri 110 12.23 N 99.55 E
Pran Buri ≃ 110 12.24 N 100.00 E
Prang 150 7.59 N 0.53 W
Prangli I 76 59.38 N 25.02 E
Prānhita ≃ 122 18.49 N 79.55 E
Pranzo 64 45.55 N 10.48 E
Prapa, Khlong ≋ 269a 13.46 N 100.32 E
Prapat 114 2.40 N 98.56 E
Praraye 58 45.55 N 7.32 E
Prärien — Great Plains ≡ 16 42.00 N 100.00 W
Praskoveja 84 44.43 N 44.12 E
Praslin, Lac ⊜ 186 50.03 N 69.48 W
Praslin Island I 138 4.19 S 55.44 E
Prasonisi, Ákra > 38 35.52 N 27.46 E
Praszka 30 51.04 N 18.26 E
Prat, Isla I 254 48.15 S 75.00 W
Prata, Bra. 250 7.41 S 37.06 W
Prata, Bra. 255 19.18 S 48.55 W
Prata, Bra. 287a 22.45 S 43.25 W
Prata, Rio da ≃, Bra. 255 17.28 S 46.35 W
Prata, Rio da ≃, Bra. 255 18.49 S 49.54 W
Prata, Rio da ≃, Bra. 287a 22.56 S 43.34 W
Pratāpgarh, India 120 24.02 N 74.47 E
Pratāpgarh, India 124 25.54 N 81.58 E
Pratāpnagar 126 22.23 N 89.13 E
Pratápolis 255 20.45 S 46.52 W
Pratas Island — Tungsha Tao I 90 20.42 N 116.43 E
Pratau 54 51.50 N 12.38 E
Pratella 68 41.24 N 14.11 E
Prater ♦ 264b 48.12 N 16.25 E
Prathet Thai — Thailand □[1] 110 15.00 N 100.00 E
Pratinha 255 19.46 S 46.24 W
Prato 66 43.53 N 11.06 E
Prato allo Stelvio 64 46.37 N 10.35 E
Pratola Peligna 66 42.06 N 13.52 E
Pratola Serra 68 40.59 N 14.51 E
Pratolino 66 43.52 N 11.18 E
Pratomagno ∧ 66 43.39 N 11.39 E
Pratt 198 37.38 N 98.44 W
Prattein 58 47.31 N 7.42 E
Prattico 58 46.55 N 9.45 E
Prättigau V 58 46.55 N 9.45 E
Pratt's Bottom ◆[8] 260 51.20 N 0.07 E
Prattsburg 210 42.31 N 77.17 W
Prattsville 210 42.18 N 74.26 W
Prattville 194 32.27 N 86.27 W
Pratudão ≃ 255 13.56 S 44.55 W
Prauthoy 58 47.40 N 5.17 E
Pravaja Mama ≃ 88 57.10 N 111.54 E
Pravda 89 47.50 N 142.09 E
Pravdinsk, Ross. 76 54.27 N 21.01 E
Pravdinsk, Ross. 80 56.32 N 43.34 E
Pravdinskij 82 56.04 N 37.51 E
Pravia 34 43.29 N 6.07 W
Prawet Buri Rom, Khlong ≋ 269a 13.42 N 100.35 E
Prawle Point > 42 50.13 N 3.42 W
Praya 115b 8.42 S 116.17 E
Pr'aža 24 61.42 N 33.35 E
Praz-sur-Arly 62 45.50 N 6.34 E
Prazzo 62 44.29 N 7.03 E
Preakness Brook ≃ 276 40.54 N 74.15 W
Preakness Mountain ∧ 276 40.58 N 74.13 W
Preakness Valley Park ♦ 276 40.55 N 74.14 W
Preble, In., U.S. 216 40.50 N 85.01 W
Preble, N.Y., U.S. 210 42.44 N 76.09 W
Preble □[6] 218 39.45 N 84.38 W
Preci 66 42.53 N 13.02 E
Prečistoje, Ross. 76 55.31 N 32.22 E
Prečistoje, Ross. 80 58.27 N 40.19 E
Précy-sous-Thil 50 47.23 N 4.19 E
Précy-sur-Marne 261 48.56 N 2.47 E
Précy-sur-Oise 50 49.12 N 2.22 E
Preda 58 46.36 N 9.46 E
Predappio 66 44.06 N 11.58 E
Predazzo 64 46.19 N 11.36 E
Predeal 38 45.30 N 25.35 E
Prédecelle ≃ 261 48.35 N 2.07 E
Předenice 60 49.37 N 13.24 E
Predești 38 44.21 N 23.36 E
Predgornoje 86 47.10 N 81.02 E
Predigtstuhl ∧ 61 48.48 N 15.22 E
Předín 61 49.12 N 15.40 E
Predivinsk 86 57.04 N 93.27 E
Predlitz [-Turrach] 64 47.04 N 13.55 E
Predoi (Prettau) 64 47.02 N 12.06 E
Predore 64 45.40 N 10.01 E
Preeceville 184 51.58 N 102.40 W
Pré-en-Pail 32 48.27 N 0.12 W
Preesall 44 53.55 N 2.58 W
Preetz 54 54.14 N 10.16 E
Pregarten 61 48.21 N 14.32 E
Pregel — Pregol'a ≃ 76 54.41 N 20.22 E
Pregnana 266b 45.31 N 9.00 E
Pregol'a ≃ 76 54.41 N 20.22 E
Pregonero 246 8.01 N 71.46 W
Pregos 256 21.46 S 42.54 W
Pregradnaja 84 43.58 N 41.12 E
Pregradnoje 80 45.49 N 41.45 E
Preguiças ≃ 250 2.34 S 42.44 W
Preila 76 55.22 N 21.04 E
Preiļi 76 56.18 N 26.43 E
Preissac, Lac ⊜ 190 48.20 N 78.20 W
Prekestolen ♦ 26 59.00 N 6.01 E
Preko 36 44.05 N 15.11 E
Prekomurje ◆[1] 61 46.40 N 16.10 E
Prěk Pouthi 110 11.51 N 105.07 E
Prelate 184 50.51 N 109.23 W
Přelouč 30 50.02 N 15.34 E
Premana 58 46.03 N 9.25 E
Prembun 115a 7.43 S 109.48 E
Prémery 50 47.10 N 3.20 E
Premià de Dalt 266d 41.31 N 2.21 E
Premià de Mar 266d 41.29 N 2.21 E
Premnitz 54 52.32 N 12.19 E
Prémont, P.Q., Can. 206 46.22 N 73.03 W
Premont, Tx., U.S. 196 27.21 N 98.07 W
Prémontré 50 49.33 N 3.24 E
Premuda, Otok I 36 44.20 N 14.37 E
Prenestini, Monti ∧ 66 41.50 N 12.55 E
Prenjas 38 41.04 N 20.32 E
Prentice 190 45.32 N 90.17 W
Prentiss 194 31.35 N 89.52 W
Prenton 262 53.22 N 3.03 W
Prenzlau 54 53.19 N 13.52 E
Prenzlauer Berg ◆[8] 264a 52.32 N 13.26 E
Preobraženije 89 42.57 N 133.55 E
Preobraženovka 89 48.04 N 131.55 E
Preobrazhenne 83 49.32 N 38.10 E
Preparis Island I 110 14.52 N 93.41 E
Preparis North Channel ʁ 110 15.27 N 94.05 E
Preparis South Channel ʁ 110 14.40 N 94.00 E
Přerov 30 49.27 N 17.27 E
Prerow 54 54.26 N 12.35 E
Pré-Saint-Didier 62 45.46 N 6.59 E
Presanella, Cima ∧ 64 46.13 N 10.40 E
Prescot 44 53.26 N 2.48 W
Prescott, On., Can. 212 44.43 N 75.31 W
Prescott, Az., U.S. 200 34.32 N 112.28 W
Prescott, Ar., U.S. 194 33.48 N 93.22 W
Prescott, Or., U.S. 224 46.02 N 122.53 W
Prescott, Wi., U.S. 190 44.44 N 92.48 W
Prescott and Russell □[6] 206 45.25 N 75.00 W
Prescott Island I 176 73.01 N 96.50 W
Preševo 38 42.18 N 21.39 E
Presho 198 43.54 N 100.03 W
Presicce 68 39.54 N 18.16 E
Presidencia de la Plaza 252 27.01 S 59.51 W
Presidencia Roca 252 26.08 S 59.36 W
Presidencia Roque Sáenz Peña 252 26.47 S 60.27 W
Presidente Costa e Silva, Ponte ◆[5] 287a 22.53 S 43.10 W
Presidente Derqui 258 34.29 S 58.51 W
Presidente Dutra 250 5.15 S 44.30 W
Presidente Epitácio 255 21.46 S 52.06 W
Presidente Getúlio 252 27.03 S 49.37 W
Presidente Hayes □[5] 252 24.00 S 59.00 W
Presidente Nicolás Avellaneda, Parque ♦ 288 34.39 S 58.29 W
Presidente Olegário 255 18.25 S 46.25 W
Presidente Prudente 255 22.07 S 51.22 W
Presidente Ríos, Lago ⊜ 254 46.28 S 74.25 W
Presidente Roosevelt, Estação ◆[5] 287b 23.33 S 46.36 W
Presidente Venceslau 255 21.52 S 51.50 W
Presidential Heights 279b 40.34 N 80.03 W
President Roxas 116 11.26 N 122.56 E
Presidio 196 29.33 N 104.22 W
Presidio ≃ 234 23.06 N 106.17 W
Presidio of San Francisco ■ 226 37.48 N 122.28 W
Presles 56 50.23 N 4.35 E
Presles-en-Brie 261 48.43 N 2.45 E
Presnogor'kovka 86 54.30 N 65.45 E
Presnovka 86 54.40 N 67.09 E
Presolana, Passo della × 64 45.55 N 10.06 E
Prešov 30 49.00 N 21.15 E
Prespa, Lake ⊜ 38 40.55 N 21.00 E
Prespansko Jezero — Prespa, Lake ⊜ 38 40.55 N 21.00 E
Presque Isle 186 46.40 N 68.00 W
Presque Isle > 216 42.09 N 80.06 W
Presque Isle ≃ 190 46.43 N 89.59 W
Presque Isle State Park ♦ 214 42.09 N 80.06 W
Presqu'ile Bay c 212 44.01 N 77.43 W
Presqu'ile Peninsula >[1] 212 44.00 N 77.41 W
Presqu'ile Provincial Park ♦ 212 44.00 N 77.42 W
Pressana 64 45.17 N 11.24 E
Pressath 60 49.46 N 11.56 E
Pressbaum 61 48.11 N 16.05 E
Pressburg — Bratislava 30 48.09 N 17.07 E
Pressel 54 51.34 N 12.41 E
Presteigne 44 53.20 N 3.24 W
Prestatyn 42 52.17 N 3.00 W
Prestbury 262 53.17 N 2.09 W
Prestbury 44 52.16 N 2.00 W
Prestice 60 49.34 N 13.20 E
Prestice 60 49.34 N 13.20 E
Prestice ≃ 60 49.32 N 6.58 E
Presto 279b 40.23 N 80.07 W
Preston, Austl. 169 37.45 S 145.01 E
Preston, Eng., U.K. 42 50.39 N 2.25 W
Preston, Eng., U.K. 44 53.46 N 2.42 W
Preston, Eng., U.K. 260 51.34 N 0.18 W
Preston, Ga., U.S. 192 32.03 N 84.32 W
Preston, Id., U.S. 202 42.05 N 111.52 W
Preston, Ia., U.S. 190 42.03 N 90.24 W
Preston, Ks., U.S. 198 37.45 N 98.33 W
Preston, Md., U.S. 208 38.42 N 75.54 W
Preston, Mn., U.S. 190 43.40 N 92.04 W
Preston, Wa., U.S. 224 47.31 N 121.56 W
Preston □[8] 262 53.48 N 2.42 W
Preston ≃, Austl. 168a 33.20 S 115.40 E
Preston ≃, P.Q., Can. 206 46.05 N 75.04 W
Preston, Cape > 162 20.51 S 116.12 E
Preston, Lac ⊜ 206 46.05 N 75.04 W
Preston, Lake ⊜, Austl. 168a 32.59 S 115.42 E
Preston, Lake ⊜, Fl., U.S. 220 28.18 N 81.08 W
Preston Airport ⊗ 276 40.22 N 74.15 W
Preston Brook 262 53.19 N 2.39 W
Preston Brook Canal Tunnel ◆[5] 262 53.19 N 2.38 W
Preston Heights 216 41.28 N 88.08 W
Preston Hollow 210 42.27 N 74.13 W
Preston North End Football Ground ♦ 262 53.47 N 2.42 W
Prestonpans 46 55.57 N 3.00 W
Preston Peak ∧ 204 41.50 N 123.37 W
Prestonsburg 192 37.39 N 82.46 W
Prestrud Inlet c 9 78.18 S 156.00 W
Prestranda 26 59.06 N 9.04 E
Prestville 182 55.44 N 118.37 W
Prestwich 44 53.32 N 2.17 W
Prestwick 46 55.29 N 4.37 W
Prestwick Airport ⊗ 46 55.30 N 4.36 W
Preto ≃, Bra. 246 1.41 S 63.48 W
Preto ≃, Bra. 248 8.03 S 62.54 W
Preto ≃, Bra. 250 11.21 S 43.52 W
Preto ≃, Bra. 250 3.32 S 43.46 W
Preto ≃, Bra. 255 13.37 S 48.06 W
Preto ≃, Bra. 255 17.00 S 46.12 W
Preto ≃, Bra. 255 18.44 S 50.23 W
Preto ≃, Bra. 255 20.08 S 49.38 W
Preto ≃, Bra. 256 22.14 S 43.07 W
Preto ≃, Bra. 256 22.01 S 43.20 W
Preto do Igapó-açu ≃ 246 4.26 S 59.48 W
Pretoria 158 25.45 S 28.10 E
Pretoria-Witwatersrand-Vereeniging □[4] 156 26.00 S 28.15 E
Pretoriusvlei 158 28.30 S 22.59 E
Prettau — Predoi 64 47.02 N 12.06 E
Prettin 54 51.39 N 12.55 E
Prettyboy Reservoir ⊜[1] 208 39.38 N 76.45 W
Pretty Prairie 198 37.46 N 98.01 W
Pretzfeld 60 49.45 N 11.11 E
Pretzier 54 52.49 N 11.15 E
Pretzsch 54 51.42 N 12.48 E
Preussisch Eylau — Bagrationovsk 76 54.23 N 20.39 E
Preussisch-Oldendorf 52 52.18 N 8.30 E
Preussisch-Ströhen 52 52.29 N 8.40 E
Prevalje 61 46.32 N 14.55 E
Préveza 38 38.57 N 20.44 E
Prévost 206 45.52 N 74.05 W
Prevost Island I 224 48.50 N 123.22 W
Prey Lvéa 110 11.10 N 104.57 E
Prey Nŏb 110 10.38 N 103.47 E
Prey Vêng 110 11.29 N 105.19 E
Prezza, Monte ∧ 66 42.02 N 13.49 E
Priaral'skije Karakumy ◆[2] 86 47.00 N 63.30 E
Priargunsk 88 50.27 N 119.00 E
Priay 58 46.00 N 5.17 E
Pribilof Islands II 180 57.00 N 170.00 W
Priboj 38 43.35 N 19.31 E
Příbram 30 49.42 N 14.01 E
Pribylovo 76 60.26 N 28.40 E
Priccio, Cozzo ∧ 70 37.01 N 14.46 E
Price, Austl. 168b 34.17 S 138.00 E
Price, Tx., U.S. 222 32.08 N 94.57 W
Price, Ut., U.S. 200 39.35 N 110.48 W
Price ≃ 200 39.10 N 110.06 W
Price, Cape > 110 13.34 N 93.03 E
Price Bend c 276 40.55 N 73.24 W
Price Island I 182 52.23 N 128.36 W
Prichard 194 30.44 N 88.04 W
Prickly Point > 241k 11.59 N 61.45 W
Priddy 196 31.40 N 98.31 W
Priego 34 40.27 N 2.18 W
Priego de Córdoba 34 37.26 N 4.11 W
Priekule, Lat. 76 56.26 N 21.35 E
Priekule, Liet. 76 55.33 N 21.19 E
Prienai 76 54.38 N 23.57 E
Prien am Chiemsee 64 47.51 N 12.20 E
Prieros 54 52.13 N 13.46 E
Prieska 158 29.40 S 22.42 E
Priest ≃ 202 48.11 N 116.53 W
Priestewitz 54 51.15 N 13.30 E
Priest Island I 46 57.58 N 5.30 W
Priest Lake ⊜ 202 48.34 N 116.52 W
Priestley, Mount ∧ 182 55.13 N 128.53 W
Priest Rapids Lake ⊜[1] 202 46.45 N 119.55 W
Priest River 202 48.10 N 116.54 W
Prieta, Loma ∧ 226 37.07 N 121.51 W
Prieta, Peña ∧ 34 43.01 N 4.44 W
Prieto ≃ 240m 18.15 N 66.54 W
Prieto Diaz 116 13.02 N 124.12 E
Prievidza 30 48.47 N 18.37 E
Prignitz ◆[1] 54 53.10 N 12.15 E
Priiskovyj, Ross. 86 54.39 N 88.42 E
Priiskovyj, Ross. 88 51.57 N 116.39 E
Prijedor 36 44.59 N 16.43 E
Prijepolje 38 43.23 N 19.39 E
Prijutnoje 80 46.06 N 43.31 E
Prijutovo 80 53.54 N 53.56 E
Prikaspijskaja nizmennost' ≡ 80 48.00 N 52.00 E
Prikro 150 7.39 N 3.59 W
Prilep 38 41.20 N 21.33 E
Prilepy 82 54.03 N 37.42 E
Prilly 58 46.32 N 6.36 E
Priluki, Ross. 76 59.16 N 39.53 E
Priluki, Ross. 82 54.51 N 37.53 E
Prima Porta ◆[8] 267a 42.00 N 12.29 E
Primavera 250 0.56 S 47.06 W
Přimda 60 49.41 N 12.41 E
Primeira Cruz 250 2.30 S 43.26 W
Primeiro de Maio 255 22.48 S 51.01 W
Primera 196 26.14 N 97.43 W
Primero ≃ 252 31.00 S 63.12 W
Primero de Mayo 196 27.12 N 101.15 W
Primghar 198 43.05 N 95.37 W
Primolano 64 45.58 N 11.42 E
Primorje [Warnicken] 76 54.57 N 20.02 E
Primorka 83 47.16 N 39.03 E
Primorsk, Ross. 76 54.44 N 20.01 E
Primorsk, Ross. 76 60.22 N 28.36 E
Primorsk, Ross. 80 49.16 N 45.03 E
Primorskij 89 43.07 N 131.38 E
Primorskij chrebet ∧ 88 52.30 N 106.00 E
Primorskij Kraj □[8] 89 45.25 N 135.25 E
Primorsko 38 42.10 N 27.51 E
Primorsko-Achtarsk 78 46.03 N 38.11 E
Primos 285 39.55 N 75.18 W
Primrose, S. Afr. 273d 26.12 S 28.10 E
Primrose, Pa., U.S. 210 40.42 N 76.17 W
Primrose, Pa., U.S. 279b 40.21 N 80.16 W
Primrose Brook ≃ 276 40.43 N 74.31 W
Primrose Lake ⊜ 184 54.55 N 109.45 W
Prims ≃ 56 49.20 N 6.44 E
Primstal 56 49.32 N 6.58 E
Prince, Lake ⊜[1] 208 36.48 N 76.38 W
Prince Albert, On., Can. 212 44.05 N 78.58 W
Prince Albert, Sk., Can. 184 53.12 N 105.46 W
Prince Albert, S. Afr. 158 33.13 S 22.02 E
Prince Albert Mountains ∧ 9 76.00 S 161.30 E
Prince Albert National Park ♦ 184 54.00 N 106.25 W
Prince Albert Road 158 33.01 S 21.40 E
Prince Albert Sound ʁ 176 70.25 N 115.00 W
Prince Alexander Mountains ∧ 164 3.30 S 142.50 E
Prince Alfred Hamlet 158 33.18 S 19.20 E
Prince Charles Island I 176 67.50 N 76.00 W
Prince Charles Mountains ∧ 9 72.00 S 67.00 E
Prince-de-Galles, Île du — Prince of Wales Island I, Austl. 164 10.40 S 142.10 E
Prince-de-Galles, Île du — Prince of Wales Island I, N.T., Can. 176 72.40 N 99.00 W
Prince Edward □[6] 212 44.00 N 77.15 W
Prince Edward Bay c 212 43.57 N 76.57 W
Prince Edward Island □[4], Can. 176 46.20 N 63.20 W
Prince Edward Island □[4], Can. 186 46.20 N 63.20 W
Prince Edward Island National Park ♦ 186 46.31 N 63.26 W
Prince Edward Islands II 6 46.35 S 37.56 E
Prince Edward Park ♦ 274a 34.02 S 151.03 E
Prince Edward Point > 212 43.56 N 76.52 W
Prince Frederick 208 38.32 N 76.35 W
Prince Gallitzin State Park ♦ 214 40.40 N 78.32 W
Prince George, B.C., Can. 182 53.55 N 122.45 W
Prince George, Va., U.S. 208 37.13 N 77.17 W
Prince George □[6] 208 37.13 N 77.10 W
Prince Georges □[6] 208 38.49 N 76.45 W
Prince Georges Plaza ◆[9] 284c 38.58 N 76.57 W
Prince Leopold Island I 176 74.02 N 89.55 W
Prince of Wales, Cape > 180 65.40 N 168.05 W
Prince of Wales Island I, Austl. 164 10.40 S 142.10 E
Prince of Wales Island I, N.T., Can. 176 72.40 N 99.00 W
Prince of Wales Island I, Ak., U.S. 180 55.47 N 132.50 W
Prince of Wales Strait ʁ 176 73.00 N 117.00 W
Prince Olav Coast ⚓[2] 9 68.30 S 42.30 E
Prince Patrick Island I 16 76.45 N 119.30 W
Prince Regent ≃ 164 15.28 S 125.05 E
Prince Regent Inlet c 176 73.00 N 90.30 W
Prince Regent Nature Reserve ♦ 164 15.30 S 125.30 E
Prince Rupert 182 54.19 N 130.19 W
Prince Rupert Bay c 240d 15.34 N 61.29 W
Prince Rupert Bluff Point > 240d 15.35 N 61.29 W
Princesa, Puerto c 116 9.45 N 118.43 E
Princesa Astrid, Costa — Princess Astrid Coast ⚓[2] 9 70.45 S 12.30 E
Princesa Carlota, Bahía — Princess Charlotte Bay c 164 14.25 S 144.00 E
Princesa Isabel 250 7.44 S 38.00 W
Princesa Marta, Costa — Princess Martha Coast ⚓[2] 9 72.00 S 7.30 W
Princesa Ragnhild, Costa — Princess Ragnhild Coast ⚓[2] 9 70.15 S 27.30 E
Princes Bay c 276 40.30 N 74.12 W
Princes Risborough 42 51.44 N 0.51 W
Princess Anne 208 38.12 N 75.41 W
Princess Astrid Coast ⚓[2] 9 70.45 S 12.30 E
Princess Charlotte Bay c 164 14.25 S 144.00 E
Princess Martha Coast ⚓[2] 9 72.00 S 7.30 W
Princess Ragnhild Coast ⚓[2] 9 70.15 S 27.30 E
Princess Ranges ∧ 162 26.08 S 121.55 E
Princess Royal Channel ʁ 182 53.10 N 128.37 W
Princess Royal Island I 182 52.57 N 128.49 W
Princes Town 241r 10.16 N 61.23 W
Princeton, B.C., Can. 182 49.27 N 120.31 W
Princeton, Nf., Can. 186 48.25 N 53.36 W
Princeton, On., Can. 212 43.10 N 80.32 W
Princeton, Ca., U.S. 226 39.24 N 122.00 W
Princeton, Fl., U.S. 220 25.32 N 80.24 W
Princeton, Il., U.S. 190 41.22 N 89.27 W
Princeton, In., U.S. 194 38.21 N 87.34 W
Princeton, Ky., U.S. 194 37.06 N 87.52 W
Princeton, Me., U.S. 188 45.13 N 67.34 W
Princeton, Mi., U.S. 190 46.17 N 87.28 W
Princeton, Mn., U.S. 190 45.34 N 93.34 W
Princeton, Mo., U.S. 194 40.24 N 93.34 W
Princeton, N.J., U.S. 208 40.20 N 74.39 W
Princeton, N.C., U.S. 192 35.27 N 78.09 W
Princeton, Tx., U.S. 222 33.11 N 96.30 W
Princeton, W.V., U.S. 192 37.21 N 81.06 W
Princeton, Wi., U.S. 190 43.51 N 89.07 W
Princeton Airfield ⊗ 276 40.24 N 74.39 W
Princeton Battlefield Park ♦ 276 40.20 N 74.41 W
Princeton Junction 208 40.19 N 74.37 W
Princeton Township 276 40.22 N 74.40 W
Princeton University ʋ[2] 276 40.21 N 74.39 W
Princetown 42 50.33 N 4.00 W
Princeville, P.Q., Can. 206 46.10 N 71.53 W
Princeville, Il., U.S. 190 40.56 N 89.45 W
Princeville, N.C., U.S. 192 35.53 N 77.31 W
Prince William □[6] 208 38.42 N 77.27 W
Prince William Forest Park ♦ 208 38.36 N 77.23 W
Prince William Sound ʁ 180 60.40 N 147.00 W
Príncipe I 152 1.37 N 7.25 E
Príncipe Alberto, Montes — Prince Albert Mountains ∧ 9 76.00 S 161.30 E
Príncipe Carlos, Montes — Prince Charles Mountains ∧ 9 72.00 S 67.00 E
Principe Channel ʁ 182 53.28 N 130.00 W
Príncipe da Beira 248 12.25 S 64.25 W
Príncipe de Gales, Isla — Prince of Wales Island I, Austl. 164 10.40 S 142.10 E
Príncipe de Gales, Isla — Prince of Wales Island I, N.T., Can. 176 72.40 N 99.00 W
Príncipe Eduardo, Isla — Prince Edward Island □[4] 186 46.20 N 63.20 W
Príncipe Olav, Costa — Prince Olav Coast ⚓[2] 9 68.30 S 42.30 E
Príncipe Patricio, Isla — Prince Patrick Island I 16 76.45 N 119.30 W
Prineville 202 44.18 N 120.51 W
Prineville Reservoir ⊜[1] 202 44.08 N 120.42 W
Prineville Southeast 202 44.17 N 120.53 W
Pringgabaja 115b 8.34 S 116.37 E
Pringsewu 112 5.24 S 104.55 E
Pringy 261 48.31 N 2.34 E
Prinsenbeek 52 51.36 N 4.42 E
Prinses Margrietkanaal ≋ 52 53.10 N 5.55 E
Prinshof 158 32.06 S 20.53 E
Prinzapolka 236 13.24 N 83.34 W
Prinzapolka ≃ 236 13.24 N 83.34 W
Prinzessin Astrid-Küste — Princess Astrid Coast ⚓[2] 9 70.45 S 12.30 E
Prinzessin Charlotte Bucht — Princess Charlotte Bay c 164 14.25 S 144.00 E
Prinzessin Martha-Küste — Princess Martha Coast ⚓[2] 9 72.00 S 7.30 W
Prinzessin Ragnhild-Küste — Princess Ragnhild Coast ⚓[2] 9 70.15 S 27.30 E
Priobskoje plato ∧[1] 86 52.40 N 83.00 E
Priokso-Terrasnyj zapovednik ◆[4] 82 54.51 N 37.36 E
Priolo Gargallo 70 37.09 N 15.11 E
Prior, Cabo > 34 43.34 N 8.19 W
Priort 264a 52.31 N 12.58 E
Priozernyj 80 47.23 N 45.14 E
Prioz'ornyj 86 47.50 N 84.13 E
Prioz'orsk 24 61.02 N 30.04 E
Pripet — Pryp'yat' ≃ 78 51.21 N 30.09 E
Pripet Marshes — Polesje ◆[1] 72 52.00 N 27.00 E
Pripol'arnyj Ural ∧ 24 65.00 N 60.00 E
Prirečje 88 55.07 N 101.03 E
Prirečnyj 80 51.03 N 52.26 E
Přísečnice 54 50.27 N 13.06 E
Priselje 76 55.09 N 32.49 E
Prislon 82 56.48 N 37.16 E
Pristan'-Prževal'sk 85 42.34 N 78.18 E
Pristen' 78 51.15 N 36.41 E
Priština 38 42.39 N 21.10 E
Pritchett 198 37.22 N 102.51 W
Přítluky 61 48.51 N 16.46 E
Pritzerbe 54 52.30 N 12.27 E
Pritzier 54 53.22 N 11.04 E
Pritzwalk 54 53.09 N 12.10 E
Priural'nyj 80 51.29 N 53.06 E
Privas 62 44.44 N 4.36 E
Priverno 66 41.28 N 13.11 E
Privodino 24 61.05 N 46.28 E
Privokzal'nyj, Ross. 82 55.59 N 35.56 E
Privokzal'nyj, Ross. 86 58.53 N 60.43 E
Privol'naja 78 46.09 N 38.42 E
Privol'noje 80 50.57 N 46.06 E
Privolžje 80 52.52 N 48.37 E
Privolžsk 80 57.23 N 41.17 E
Privolžskaja vozvyšennost' ∧[1] 80 52.00 N 46.00 E
Privolžskij, Ross. 80 46.24 N 48.00 E
Privolžskij, Ross. 80 51.24 N 46.02 E
Privolžskoje 80 51.06 N 45.57 E
Prizren 38 42.12 N 20.44 E
Prizzi 70 37.43 N 13.25 E
Prizzi, Lago di ⊜ 70 37.44 N 13.25 E
Prnjavor 36 44.52 N 17.40 E
Probolinggo 115a 7.45 S 113.13 E
Proboštov 54 50.39 N 13.50 E
Probstzella 54 50.32 N 11.22 E
Probus 42 50.17 N 4.57 W
Procchio 66 42.47 N 10.15 E
Prochladnoje 88 48.30 N 82.41 E
Prochladnyj 84 43.46 N 44.00 E
Prochorkino 86 59.34 N 79.26 E
Prochorovka 82 54.07 N 38.11 E
Prochowice 30 51.17 N 16.22 E
Procida 68 40.46 N 14.02 E
Procida, Isola di I 68 40.45 N 14.01 E
Procter 182 49.37 N 116.57 W
Proctor, Mn., U.S. 190 46.44 N 92.13 W
Proctor, Vt., U.S. 188 43.39 N 73.02 W
Proctor Brook ≃ 283 42.32 N 70.54 W
Proctor Lake ⊜ 228 35.07 N 118.21 W
Proctor Lake ⊜[1] 196 32.02 N 98.32 W
Proddatūr 122 14.44 N 78.33 E
Proença-a-Nova 34 39.45 N 7.55 W
Profen 54 51.07 N 12.13 E
Pro Football Hall of Fame ♦ 214 40.49 N 81.25 W
Progonoj 83 48.45 N 39.51 E
Progreso, Méx. 196 27.28 N 100.59 W
Progreso, Méx. 232 21.17 N 89.40 W
Progreso, Méx. 234 20.15 N 99.12 W
Progreso, Méx. 234 23.48 N 103.18 W
Progreso, Ur. 258 34.40 S 56.13 W
Progress, Ross. 89 49.42 N 129.39 E
Progress, Or., U.S. 224 45.28 N 122.47 W
Progress, Pa., U.S. 208 40.08 N 76.34 W
Project City 204 40.41 N 122.21 W
Prokopjeva 88 58.03 N 100.39 E
Prokopjevsk 86 53.53 N 86.45 E
Prokopjevsk — Prokopjevsk 86 53.53 N 86.45 E
Prokuplje 38 43.14 N 21.36 E
Prokuševo 76 59.55 N 34.56 E
Prokutkino 86 56.19 N 69.46 E
Proletarij 76 58.26 N 31.44 E
Proletarsk, Ross. 80 46.42 N 41.44 E
Proletarsk, Taj. 85 40.10 N 69.30 E
Proletarskij, Ross. 78 50.47 N 35.47 E
Proletarskij, Ross. 82 55.01 N 37.23 E
Prolysovo 76 52.54 N 34.09 E
Prome (Pyè) 110 18.49 N 95.13 E
Promised Land State Park ♦ 210 41.18 N 75.11 W
Promissão 255 21.32 S 49.52 W
Promontogno 58 46.21 N 9.34 E
Prompton 210 41.35 N 75.19 W
Prompton Lake ⊜[1] 210 41.36 N 75.20 W
Prompton Lake State Park ♦ 210 41.37 N 75.22 W
Promyšlennaja 86 54.55 N 85.40 E
Promyšlennovskij 86 55.29 N 86.12 E
Promyšlennyj 24 67.35 N 63.55 E
Promyslovka 80 45.44 N 47.10 E
Pron'a ≃, Bela. 76 53.25 N 31.01 E
Pron'a ≃, Ross. 80 54.21 N 40.24 E
Pron'a Gorodišče 82 54.15 N 38.43 E
Pronin 80 49.12 N 42.11 E
Pronsfeld 56 50.10 N 6.20 E
Pronsk 80 54.07 N 39.37 E
Prony, Baie du c 175f 22.22 S 166.53 E
Prophet ≃ 176 58.45 N 122.45 W
Prophetstown 190 41.40 N 89.56 W
Propriá 250 10.13 S 36.51 W
Propriano 36 41.40 N 8.55 E
Prorer Wiek c 54 54.27 N 13.38 E
Prorva 86 46.03 N 53.15 E
Proryvnoje 86 54.23 N 64.26 E
Prösen 54 51.25 N 13.29 E
Proserpine 166 20.24 S 148.34 E
Prosigk 54 51.42 N 12.05 E
Proskurov — Khmel'nyts'kyy 78 49.25 N 27.00 E
Prosna ≃ 30 52.10 N 17.39 E
Prosnica 86 58.26 N 50.15 E
Prosotsáni 38 41.10 N 23.59 E
Prospect, Austl. 168b 34.54 S 138.35 E
Prospect, Austl. 274a 33.48 S 150.56 E
Prospect, Ct., U.S. 207 41.30 N 72.58 W
Prospect, N.Y., U.S. 210 43.18 N 75.09 W
Prospect, Oh., U.S. 214 40.27 N 83.11 W
Prospect, Pa., U.S. 214 40.54 N 80.03 W
Prospect Bay c 208 38.56 N 76.14 W
Prospect Creek ≃ 274a 33.55 S 150.59 E
Prospect Heights 278 42.05 N 87.56 W
Prospect Hill 168b 35.13 S 138.44 E
Prospect Hill ∧[2], Ma., U.S. 207 41.21 N 70.45 W
Prospect Hill ∧[2], Ma., U.S. 283 42.23 N 71.15 W
Prospect Hill Park ♦ 283 42.23 N 71.15 W
Prospect Park, N.J., U.S. 276 40.56 N 74.10 W
Prospect Park, Pa., U.S. 214 41.31 N 78.13 W
Prospect Park, Pa., U.S. 285 39.53 N 75.18 W

≃ River / Fluß / Río / Rivière / Rio
≋ Canal / Kanal / Canal / Canal / Canal
ʟ Waterfall, Rapids / Wasserfall, Stromschnellen / Cascada, Rápidos / Chute d'eau, Rapides / Cascata, Rápidos
ʁ Strait / Meeresstraße / Estrecho / Détroit / Estreito
c Bay, Gulf / Bucht, Golf / Bahía, Golfo / Baie, Golfe / Baía, Golfo
⊜ Lake, Lakes / See, Seen / Lago, Lagos / Lac, Lacs / Lago, Lagos
ⵣ Swamp / Sumpf / Pantano / Marais / Pântano
⚘ Ice Features, Glacier / Eis- und Gletscherformen / Accidentes Glaciales / Formes glaciaires / Acidentes glaciares
◆ Other Hydrographic Features / Andere Hydrographische Objekte / Otros Elementos Hidrográficos / Autres données hydrographiques / Outros acidentes hidrográficos

◆ Submarine Features / Untermeerische Objekte / Accidentes Submarinos / Formes de relief sous-marin / Acidentes submarinos
□ Political Unit / Politische Einheit / Unidad Política / Entité politique / Unidade política
ʋ Cultural Institution / Kulturelle Institution / Institución Cultural / Institution culturelle / Instituição cultural
⊥ Historical Site / Historische Stätte / Sitio Histórico / Site historique / Sitio histórico
♦ Recreational Site / Erholungs- und Ferienort / Sitio de Recreo / Centre de loisirs / Area de Lazer
⊗ Airport / Flughafen / Aeropuerto / Aéroport / Aeroporto
■ Military Installation / Militäranlage / Instalación Militar / Installation militaire / Instalação militar
◆ Miscellaneous / Verschiedenes / Misceláneo / Divers / Diversos

ENGLISH / DEUTSCH

Name	Page / Seite	Lat. °′ / Breite °′	Long. °′ / Länge °′ E = Ost
Prospect Park ♦	276	40.40 N	73.58 W
Prospect Park Lake ⊜	276	40.39 N	73.57 W
Prospect Plains	276	40.19 N	74.28 W
Prospect Point	276	40.58 N	74.38 W
Prospect Point ›	276	40.52 N	73.43 W
Prospect Reservoir ⊜[1]	274a	33.49 S	150.54 E
Prospectville	285	40.13 N	75.11 W
Prosper	222	33.14 N	96.48 W
Prosperi Airport ⊠	278	41.33 N	87.47 W
Prosperidad	116	8.34 N	125.52 E
Prosser	202	46.12 N	119.46 W
Prosser Creek Reservoir ⊜[1]	226	39.22 N	120.08 W
Prostějov	30	49.29 N	17.07 E
Prostki	30	53.43 N	22.26 E
Proston	166	26.10 S	151.36 E
Prosyana	78	48.07 N	36.23 E
Prosyane	78	49.42 N	35.47 E
Proszowice	30	50.12 N	20.18 E
Protasovo, Ross.	82	54.48 N	38.35 E
Protasovo, Ross.	82	54.11 N	37.00 E
Protasovo, Ross.	82	56.08 N	37.36 E
Protasy	76	52.47 N	29.05 E
Protea	273d	26.17 S	27.51 E
Protection	198	37.12 N	99.29 W
Protection Island I	224	48.07 N	122.55 W
Protem	158	34.16 S	20.05 E
Protivín	61	49.12 N	14.13 E
Protoka ≃	78	45.43 N	37.46 E
Protva	82	55.01 N	36.41 E
Protva ≃	82	54.51 N	37.16 E
Protville	36	36.54 N	10.01 E
Prötzel	54	52.38 N	13.59 E
Proud Lake State Recreation Area ♦	281	42.34 N	83.33 W
Proulxville	206	46.40 N	72.30 W
Provadija	38	43.11 N	27.26 E
Provencal	194	31.39 N	93.12 W
Provence □[9]	62	44.00 N	6.00 E
Provence, Alpes de ⋏	62	43.40 N	6.00 E
Provenchères-sur-Fave	58	48.19 N	7.05 E
Providence, Ky., U.S.	194	37.23 N	87.45 W
Providence, R.I., U.S.	207	41.49 N	71.24 W
Providence, Ut,. U.S.	200	41.42 N	111.48 W
Providence □[6]	207	41.52 N	71.36 W
Providence ≃	207	41.43 N	71.21 W
Providence Forge	208	37.26 N	77.02 W
Providence Island I	138	9.14 S	51.02 E
Providência, Bra.	256	21.40 S	42.35 W
Providencia, Chile	286e	33.26 S	70.37 W
Providencia, Méx.	196	27.06 N	103.32 W
Providencia, Isla de I	236	13.21 N	81.22 W
Providenciales I	238	21.47 N	72.17 W
Providenija	180	64.23 N	173.18 W
Providenija, buchta c	180	64.30 N	173.20 W
Provincetown	207	42.03 N	70.10 W
Provins	50	48.33 N	3.18 E
Provo	200	40.14 N	111.39 W
Provo ≃	200	40.14 N	111.44 W
Provost	184	52.21 N	110.16 W
Provost, Lac ⊜	206	46.22 N	74.00 W
Proyizhdzhe	83	49.25 N	38.58 E
Prozor	36	43.49 N	17.37 E
Pru ≃	150	7.58 N	0.53 W
Prudence Island I	207	41.37 N	71.19 W
Prudentópolis	252	25.12 S	50.57 W
Prudentov	80	49.39 N	46.19 E
Prudhoe	44	54.58 N	1.51 W
Prudhoe Bay c	180	70.20 N	148.20 W
Prudhoe Island I	166	21.19 S	149.40 E
Prudišči	82	54.24 N	38.26 E
Prudki	82	54.46 N	36.29 E
Prudnik	30	50.19 N	17.34 E
Prudy	76	53.47 N	26.32 E
Prudyanka	78	50.14 N	36.09 E
Pruggern	64	47.25 N	13.52 E
Prüm	56	50.12 N	6.25 E
Prüm ≃	56	49.49 N	6.28 E
Pruna, Punta sa ∧	71	40.11 N	9.26 E
Prunay-le-Temple	261	48.52 N	1.40 E
Prunay-sous-Ablis	261	48.32 N	1.48 E
Prunedale	226	36.47 N	121.40 W
Prunéřov	54	50.25 N	13.16 E
Prunières	62	44.33 N	6.20 E
Prunn, Schloss ⊥	60	48.57 N	11.44 E
Pruszków	30	52.11 N	20.48 E
Prut ≃	78	45.30 N	28.12 E
Pruth → Prut ≃	78	45.30 N	28.12 E
Prutting	64	47.53 N	12.11 E
Prutz	58	47.05 N	10.40 E
Pružany	76	52.33 N	24.28 E
Pryadivka	78	48.55 N	34.41 E
Pryazovs'ka vysochyna ⋏[1]	83	47.30 N	37.30 E
Pryazovs'ke	78	46.43 N	35.38 E
Prychornomors'ka nyzovyna ≍	78	47.00 N	33.00 E
Prydniprovs'ka nyzovyna ≍	78	50.00 N	32.00 E
Prydniprovs'ka vysochyna ⋏[1]	78	49.00 N	32.00 E
Prydz Bay c	9	69.00 S	76.00 E
Prykolotne	78	50.09 N	37.21 E
Pryluky	78	50.36 N	32.24 E
Prymors'k	78	46.44 N	36.20 E
Prymors'ke	83	47.11 N	37.42 E
Prymors'kyy	78	45.07 N	35.29 E
Pryor	196	36.19 N	95.19 W
Pryor Creek ≃	202	45.54 N	108.19 W
Pryor Mountain ∧[2]	222	31.43 N	95.12 W
Pryputni	78	50.57 N	32.14 E
Pryp'yat'	78	51.26 N	30.10 E
Pryp'yat' ≃	78	51.21 N	30.09 E
Pryshyb	78	47.16 N	35.21 E
Prysor ≃	42	52.56 N	4.00 W
Prystin	83	49.36 N	37.38 E
Pryvillya, Ukr.	83	49.01 N	38.18 E
Pryvillya, Ukr.	83	48.52 N	37.16 E
Pryvil'ne	78	47.29 N	32.17 E
Pryvitne	78	44.50 N	34.41 E
Przasnysz	30	53.01 N	20.55 E
Przedbórz	30	51.06 N	19.53 E
Przemków	30	51.32 N	15.48 E
Przemocze	54	53.27 N	14.55 E
Przemyśl	30	49.47 N	22.47 E
Przemyśl □[4]	30	50.00 N	22.40 E
Przeworsk	30	50.05 N	22.29 E
Przewóz	54	51.29 N	14.59 E
Przybiernów	54	53.46 N	14.46 E
Przysucha	30	51.22 N	20.38 E
Pšagar	85	39.58 N	68.08 E
Psakhná	38	38.35 N	23.38 E
Psará I	38	38.35 N	25.37 E
Psárion	38	37.20 N	21.51 E
Psebaj	84	44.07 N	40.47 E
Pšecha ≃	78	44.47 N	39.48 E
Psekups ≃	78	45.00 N	39.09 E
Pselec	78	51.17 N	36.32 E
Psikhikón	267c	38.01 N	23.46 E
Pšiš ≃	78	45.01 N	39.18 E
Pšiš, gora ∧	84	43.24 N	41.12 E
Psittália I	267c	37.56 N	23.35 E
Pskem	85	41.56 N	70.22 E
Pskem ≃	85	41.38 N	70.01 E
Pskent	85	40.54 N	69.20 E
Pskov	76	57.50 N	28.20 E
Pskov Oblast' □[4]	76	57.00 N	29.00 E
Pskovskoje ozero ⊜	76	58.00 N	28.00 E
Pskowsee → Pskovskoje ozero ⊜	76	58.00 N	28.00 E
Ps'ol ≃	78	49.02 N	33.33 E
Pšov	54	50.10 N	13.29 E
Pszczyna	30	49.59 N	18.57 E
Ptarmigan, Cape ›	176	71.04 N	118.07 W
Ptič'	76	52.09 N	28.52 E
Ptič' ≃	76	52.09 N	28.52 E
Ptolemaís	38	40.31 N	21.41 E
Ptolemais ⊥	146	32.43 N	20.57 E
Ptuj	36	46.25 N	15.52 E
Pu ≃, Zhg.	104	41.21 N	122.47 E
Pu ≃, Zhg.	107	30.25 N	103.49 E
Puah, Pulau I	112	0.30 S	122.34 E
Puakonikai	174d	0.52 S	169.36 E
Puamau, Baie c	174x	9.46 S	138.52 W
Puán, Arg.	252	37.33 S	62.43 W
Puan, Taehan	98	35.45 N	126.44 E
Pubāil	126	23.56 N	90.29 E
Pubnico	186	43.42 N	65.47 W
Pucallpa	248	8.23 S	74.32 W
Pucara	248	18.43 S	64.11 W
Pucarani	248	16.23 S	68.30 W
Puccha ≃	248	9.05 S	76.54 W
Puccia, Serra di ∧	70	37.44 N	13.56 E
Puce	214	42.18 N	82.47 W
Puces ≃	281	42.18 N	82.47 W
Pučevejem ≃	180	68.48 N	170.30 E
Pučež	80	56.59 N	43.11 E
Puchberg am Schneeberg	61	47.47 N	15.54 E
Pucheng, Zhg.	100	27.55 N	118.31 E
Pucheng, Zhg.	102	34.59 N	109.29 E
Pucheta	252	29.54 S	57.34 W
Puchheim	60	48.09 N	11.20 E
Púchov	30	49.08 N	18.20 E
Puchoviči	76	53.32 N	28.15 E
Pucioasa	38	45.04 N	25.26 E
Pucio Point ›	116	11.46 N	121.51 E
Pučišća	36	43.21 N	16.44 E
Puck	30	54.44 N	18.27 E
Puckapunyal	169	37.01 S	145.03 E
Pucketa Creek ≃	279b	40.33 N	79.45 W
Pudahuel	286e	33.26 S	70.46 W
Pudding ≃	224	45.18 N	122.43 W
Puddingstone Reservoir ⊜[1]	280	34.05 N	117.48 W
Puddington	262	53.15 N	3.00 W
Puddletown	42	50.45 N	2.21 W
Pūdeh Tal ≃	128	31.03 N	62.15 E
Pudem	80	58.18 N	52.10 E
Pudi	102	27.58 N	99.05 E
Pudimoe	158	27.26 S	24.44 E
Puding	102	26.21 N	105.40 E
Pudino	86	57.34 N	79.24 E
Pudops Dam ◈[6]	186	48.09 N	56.50 W
Pudož	24	61.48 N	36.32 E
Pudsey	44	53.48 N	1.40 W
Pudu ≃	102	26.19 N	102.45 E
Puduari ≃	246	2.08 S	61.15 W
Puduhe	102	25.39 N	102.39 E
Pudukkottai	122	10.23 N	78.49 E
Puebla □[3]	234	18.50 N	98.00 W
Puebla de Alcocer	34	38.59 N	5.15 W
Puebla de Don Fadrique	34	37.58 N	2.26 W
Puebla de Don Rodrigo	34	39.05 N	4.37 W
Puebla de Sanabria	34	42.03 N	6.38 W
Puebla de Trives	34	42.20 N	7.15 W
Puebla [de Zaragoza]	234	19.03 N	98.12 W
Pueblito de Ponce	240m	18.26 N	66.58 W
Pueblo	198	38.15 N	104.36 W
Pueblo Libertador	252	30.13 S	59.23 W
Pueblo Libre	286d	12.05 S	77.04 W
Pueblo Mountain ∧	202	42.06 N	118.39 W
Pueblo Nuevo, Col.	246	8.31 N	75.15 W
Pueblo Nuevo, Méx.	234	20.31 N	101.22 W
Pueblo Nuevo, Nic.	236	13.23 N	86.29 W
Pueblo Nuevo, P.R.	240m	18.28 N	66.51 W
Pueblo Nuevo, Ur.	258	34.26 S	56.29 W
Pueblo Nuevo, Ven.	246	11.58 N	69.55 W
Pueblo Nuevo ◈[8]	266a	40.26 N	3.39 W
Pueblo Nuevo Tiquisate	236	14.17 N	91.22 W
Pueblo of Acoma	200	35.03 N	107.35 W
Pueblo Reservoir ⊜[1]	198	38.15 N	104.45 W
Puebloviejo, Ec.	246	1.34 S	79.30 W
Pueblo Viejo, Méx.	234	17.33 N	100.05 W
Pueblo Viejo, Méx.	234	16.14 N	94.39 W
Pueblo Viejo, Laguna c	234	22.10 N	97.53 W
Pueblo Yaqui	232	27.19 N	110.01 W
Puelches	252	38.09 S	65.55 W
Puente Alto	252	33.37 S	70.35 W
Puente de Arganda	266a	40.19 N	3.31 W
Puente de Ixtla	234	18.37 N	99.20 W
Puente-Genil	34	37.23 N	4.47 W
Puente Hills ⋏[2]	280	34.00 N	117.55 W
Puente Hills Mall ◈[9]	280	33.59 N	117.56 W
Puente la Reina	34	42.40 N	1.49 W
Puente Negro	196	27.55 N	101.01 W
Puente Nuevo, Embalse de ⊜[1]	34	38.00 N	5.00 W
Puente Piedra	286d	11.57 S	77.05 W
Pueo Point ›	229b	21.54 N	160.04 W
Pu'er	102	23.07 N	101.00 E
Puerca, Punta ›	240m	18.14 N	65.36 W
Puerco ≃	200	34.53 N	110.07 W
Puerco, Rio ≃	200	34.22 N	106.50 W
Pu'erdu	102	28.08 N	104.24 E
Puerto Acosta	248	15.32 S	69.15 W
Puerto Adela	252	24.33 S	54.22 W
Puerto Aisén	254	45.24 S	72.42 W
Puerto Alegre	248	13.53 S	61.36 W
Puerto Ángel	234	15.40 N	96.29 W
Puerto Arista	234	15.56 N	93.48 W
Puerto Armuelles	236	8.17 N	82.52 W
Puerto Asís	246	0.30 N	76.31 W
Puerto Ayacucho	246	5.40 N	67.35 W
Puerto Ayora, Ec.	246a	0.45 S	90.19 W
Puerto Ayora, Ec.	246a	0.45 S	90.19 W
Puerto Bahía Negra	248	20.15 S	58.12 W
Puerto Baquerizo Moreno	246a	0.54 S	89.36 W
Puerto Barrios	236	15.43 N	88.36 W
Puerto Bermejo	252	26.56 S	58.30 W
Puerto Bermúdez	248	10.20 S	74.54 W
Puerto Berrío	246	6.29 N	74.24 W
Puerto Bolívar, Col.	246	12.15 N	71.58 W
Puerto Bolívar, Ec.	246	3.16 S	79.59 W
Puerto Boyacá	246	5.45 N	74.39 W
Puerto Busch	248	20.02 S	57.55 W
Puerto Cabello	246	10.28 N	68.01 W
Puerto Cabezas	236	14.02 N	83.23 W
Puerto Carreño	246	6.12 N	67.22 W
Puerto Casado	252	22.20 S	57.55 W
Puerto Castilla	236	16.01 N	86.01 W
Puerto Chicama	248	7.42 S	79.27 W
Puerto Colombia	246	10.59 N	74.58 W
Puerto Constanza	258	33.50 S	59.03 W
Puerto Cortés	236	15.48 N	87.56 W
Puerto Cumarebo	246	11.29 N	69.21 W
Puerto de Eten	248	6.54 S	79.52 W
Puerto Delicia	252	26.12 S	54.35 W
Puerto de Lomas	248	15.34 S	74.50 W
Puerto Delón	236	14.22 N	85.53 W
Puerto del Rosario	148	28.30 N	13.52 W
Puerto Deseado	254	47.45 S	65.54 W
Puerto El Triunfo	236	13.17 N	88.33 W
Puerto Escondido	234	15.50 N	97.10 W
Puerto España → Port of Spain	241r	10.39 N	61.31 W
Puerto Esperanza	252	26.01 S	54.39 W
Puerto Felipe, Bahía → Port Phillip Bay c	169	38.07 S	144.48 E
Puerto Fonciere	252	22.29 S	57.48 W
Puerto Francisco de Orellana	246	0.28 S	76.58 W
Puerto Gonzalo Moreno	248	11.06 S	66.10 W
Puerto Guaraní	248	21.18 S	57.55 W
Puerto Heath	248	12.30 S	68.40 W
Puerto Iguazú	252	25.34 S	54.34 W
Puerto Inca	248	9.22 S	74.58 W
Puerto Ingeniero Ibáñez	254	46.18 S	71.56 W
Puerto Inírida	246	3.53 N	67.52 W
Puerto Jiménez	236	8.33 N	83.19 W
Puerto Juárez	232	21.11 N	86.49 W
Puerto la Cruz	246	10.13 N	64.38 W
Puerto la Plata, Zona Nacional □[5]	288	34.52 S	57.52 W
Puerto Leda	248	20.41 S	58.02 W
Puerto Leguízamo	246	0.12 S	74.46 W
Puerto Lempira	236	15.13 N	83.47 W
Puerto Libertad, Arg.	252	25.55 S	54.36 W
Puerto Libertad, Méx.	232	29.55 N	112.43 W
Puerto Limón, Col.	246	3.23 N	73.30 W
Puerto Limón, C.R.	236	10.00 N	83.02 W
Puertollano	34	38.41 N	4.07 W
Puerto Lobos	254	42.00 S	65.06 W
Puerto López	246	4.05 N	72.58 W
Puerto Madero	236	14.44 N	92.25 W
Puerto Madryn	254	42.46 S	65.03 W
Puerto Maldonado	248	12.36 S	69.11 W
Puerto Manatí	240p	21.22 N	76.50 W
Puerto Mihanovich	248	20.52 S	57.59 W
Puerto Montt	254	41.28 S	72.57 W
Puerto Morazán	236	12.51 N	87.11 W
Puerto Morelos	232	20.50 N	86.52 W
Puerto Nariño	246	4.56 N	67.48 W
Puerto Natales	254	51.44 S	72.31 W
Puerto Nuevo, Punta ›	240m	18.30 N	66.24 W
Puerto Octay	254	40.58 S	72.54 W
Puerto Ordaz → Ciudad Guayana	246	8.22 N	62.40 W
Puerto Padre	240p	21.12 N	76.36 W
Puerto Páez	246	6.13 N	67.28 W
Puerto Palmer, Pico ∧	196	27.08 N	101.47 W
Puerto Peñasco	232	31.20 N	113.33 W
Puerto Pilón	236	9.22 N	79.48 W
Puerto Pinasco	252	22.43 S	57.50 W
Puerto Pirámide	254	42.34 S	64.17 W
Puerto Piray	252	26.28 S	54.42 W
Puerto Píritu	246	10.04 N	65.03 W
Puerto Plata	238	19.48 N	70.41 W
Puerto Portillo	248	9.46 S	72.45 W
Puerto Princesa, Pil.	116	9.44 N	118.44 E
Puerto Princesa, Pil.	116	10.06 N	125.29 E
Puerto Real, Esp.	34	36.32 N	6.11 W
Puerto Real, P.R.	240m	18.05 N	67.11 W
Puerto Rico, Arg.	252	26.48 S	55.02 W
Puerto Rico, Bol.	248	11.05 S	67.38 W
Puerto Rico, Col.	246	1.54 N	75.10 W
Puerto Rico □[2], N.A.	230	18.15 N	66.30 W
Puerto Rico □[2], N.A.	240m	18.15 N	66.30 W
Puerto Rico Trench ✢[1]	16	20.00 N	66.00 W
Puerto Rondón	246	6.17 N	71.06 W
Puerto Saavedra	252	38.47 S	73.24 W
Puerto Salgar	246	5.28 N	74.39 W
Puerto Sandino	236	12.12 N	86.46 W
Puerto San José	236	13.55 N	90.49 W
Puerto San Julián	254	49.18 S	67.43 W
Puerto Santa Cruz	254	50.01 S	68.31 W
Puerto Sastre	252	22.06 S	57.59 W
Puerto Siles	248	12.48 S	65.05 W
Puerto Suarez	248	18.57 S	57.51 W
Puerto Supe	248	10.49 S	77.45 W
Puerto Tejada	246	3.14 N	76.24 W
Puerto Tolosa	246	0.59 S	74.09 W
Puerto Umbría	246	0.52 N	76.33 W
Puerto Vallarta	234	20.37 N	105.15 W
Puerto Varas	254	41.19 S	72.59 W
Puerto Victoria, Arg.	252	26.20 S	54.39 W
Puerto Victoria, Perú	248	9.54 S	74.58 W
Puerto Viejo, C.R.	236	10.26 N	83.59 W
Puerto Viejo, C.R.	236	9.39 N	82.45 W
Puerto Villamil	246a	0.56 S	91.01 W
Puerto Villamizar	246	8.19 N	72.26 W
Puerto Villarroel	248	16.50 S	64.47 W
Puerto Visser	254	45.24 S	67.08 W
Puerto Wilches	246	7.21 N	73.54 W
Puerto Williams	254	54.56 S	67.37 W
Puerto Ybapobó	252	23.42 S	57.12 W
Pueyrredón, Lago (Lago Cochrane) ⊜	254	47.20 S	72.00 W
Puffendorf	56	50.56 N	6.13 E
Puffing Billy Railroad Station ◈[5]	274b	37.55 S	145.21 E
Pugačov	80	52.01 N	48.50 E
Pugač'ovo	80	56.35 N	53.02 E
Puge, Tan.	154	4.45 S	33.07 E
Puge, Zhg.	102	27.28 N	102.31 E
Puget, Cape ›	180	59.52 N	148.26 W
Puget Island I	224	46.10 N	123.23 W
Puget Sound ⋓	224	47.50 N	122.30 W
Puget Sound Naval Shipyard ■	224	47.33 N	122.38 W
Puget-sur-Argens	62	43.27 N	6.41 E
Puget-Théniers	62	43.57 N	6.54 E
Puget-Ville	62	43.17 N	6.08 E
Pugh Mountain ∧	224	48.08 N	121.22 W
Pughtown	285	40.10 N	75.40 W
Puglia □[4]	68	41.15 N	16.15 E
Pugong-ni	271b	37.43 N	126.58 E
Pugŏ-ri	98	42.01 N	129.59 E
Pugwash	186	45.51 N	63.40 W
Puhe	104	41.57 N	123.36 E
Puhi	229b	21.58 N	159.23 W
Puhja	76	58.20 N	26.19 E
Puhos	26	62.05 N	29.54 E
Puhosjärvi ⊜	26	65.19 N	27.55 E
Puica	248	15.04 S	72.42 W
Puiești	38	46.25 N	27.33 E
Puigcerdá	34	42.26 N	1.56 E
Puigmal ∧	34	42.23 N	2.07 E
Puimoisson	62	43.52 N	6.08 E
Puinahua, Canal de ≃[1]	248	5.20 S	74.13 W
Puinān	272b	22.56 N	88.13 E
Puir	89	53.10 N	141.25 E
Puisaye, Collines de la ⋏[2]	50	47.40 N	3.15 E
Puiseaux	50	48.12 N	2.28 E
Puiseaux ≃	50	48.00 N	2.44 E
Puiseux-en-France	261	49.04 N	2.29 E
Puiseux-Pontoise	261	49.03 N	2.01 E
Puisieux	50	50.07 N	2.42 E
Puits ≃	50	48.31 N	4.15 E
Pujada Bay c	116	6.51 N	126.14 E
Pujehun	150	7.21 N	11.42 W
Puji, Zhg.	100	27.59 N	113.25 E
Puji, Zhg.	100	29.58 N	112.32 E
Pujiang, Zhg.	100	29.28 N	119.53 E
Pujiang, Zhg.	107	30.12 N	103.30 E
Pujilí	246	0.57 S	78.41 W
Pujon	115a	7.50 S	112.28 E
Pujun	112	1.20 S	114.20 E
Pujut	114	1.25 N	100.39 E
Pujut, Tanjung ›	115a	5.52 S	106.02 E
Pukaki, Lake ⊜	172	44.07 S	170.10 E
Pukalani	229a	20.50 N	156.20 W
Pukaskwa ≃	190	48.00 N	85.53 W
Pukaskwa National Park ♦	190	48.20 N	85.50 W
Pukch'ang	98	39.36 N	126.17 E
Pukchin	98	40.10 N	125.43 E
Pukch'ŏn	98	36.13 N	126.45 E
Pukch'ŏng	98	40.15 N	128.20 E
Pukë	38	42.03 N	19.54 E
Pukeashun Mountain ∧	182	51.12 N	119.14 W
Pukekohe	172	37.12 S	174.55 E
Puketeraki Range ⋏	172	42.58 S	172.12 E
Puketoi Range ⋏	172	40.30 S	176.05 E
Pukeuri Junction	172	45.02 S	171.02 E
Pukhan-gang ≃	98	37.31 N	127.18 E
Pŭkhan-san ∧	271b	37.41 N	127.00 E
Pukhrāyān	124	26.14 N	79.51 E
Pukoo	229d	21.04 N	156.48 W
Pukou, Zhg.	100	26.16 N	119.35 E
Pukou, Zhg.	106	32.07 N	118.43 E
Puksoozero	24	62.38 N	40.36 E
Puksubaek-san ∧	98	40.42 N	127.44 E
Puktae-ch'ŏn ≃	98	40.28 N	129.00 E
Pula, Hrv.	36	44.52 N	13.50 E
Pula, It.	71	39.01 N	9.00 E
Pulacayo	248	20.25 S	66.41 W
Pulandian Wan c	98	39.18 N	121.35 E
Pulanduta Point ›	116	11.54 N	123.10 E
Pulangi ≃	116	7.18 N	124.50 E
Pulangpisau	112	2.46 S	114.14 E
Pulap I[1]	14	7.35 N	149.24 E
Púlar, Cerro ∧	252	24.11 S	68.04 W
Pulaski, In., U.S.	216	40.59 N	86.40 W
Pulaski, Mi., U.S.	216	42.07 N	84.40 W
Pulaski, N.Y., U.S.	212	43.34 N	76.07 W
Pulaski, Oh., U.S.	216	41.30 N	84.26 W
Pulaski, Pa., U.S.	214	41.07 N	80.26 W
Pulaski, Tn., U.S.	194	35.11 N	87.01 W
Pulaski, Va., U.S.	192	37.02 N	80.46 W
Pulaski, Wi., U.S.	190	44.40 N	88.14 W
Pulaski □[6]	216	41.03 N	86.36 W
Pulau ≃	164	5.50 S	138.15 E
Pulaukida	112	2.44 S	102.34 E
Pulaukijang	112	0.42 S	103.12 E
Pulaumerak, Indon.	115a	5.56 S	106.00 E
Pulaumerak, Indon.	115a	5.56 S	106.00 E
Pulauraja	114	2.42 N	99.37 E
Puławy	30	51.25 N	21.57 E
Pulborough	42	50.58 N	0.30 W
Pul'chakim	85	38.10 N	67.21 E
Pulehu Gulch V	229a	20.50 N	156.28 W
Pulfero	64	46.11 N	13.29 E
Pulga	123	31.59 N	77.26 E
Pulgaon	122	20.44 N	78.20 E
Pulham Market	42	52.26 N	1.14 E
Pulheim	56	51.00 N	6.47 E
Puli	100	23.58 N	120.57 E
Pulicat	122	13.25 N	80.19 E
Pulicat Lake c	122	13.40 N	80.10 E
Pulichatum	128	35.57 N	61.07 E
Puliciano	66	43.23 N	11.51 E
Puliyangudi	122	9.10 N	77.25 E
Pulj → Pula	64	44.52 N	13.50 E
Pulkau	61	48.42 N	15.51 E
Pulkau ≃	61	48.43 N	16.21 E
Pulkkila	26	64.16 N	25.52 E
Pulkovo ◈[8]	265a	59.46 N	30.20 E
Pullman, Mi., U.S.	216	42.29 N	86.05 W
Pullman, Wa., U.S.	202	46.43 N	117.10 W
Pullman ◈[8]	278	41.43 N	87.36 W
Púllo	248	15.14 S	73.50 W
Pully	58	46.31 N	6.39 E
Pul'mo	78	51.31 N	23.47 E
Pulo ⊥	68	41.12 N	16.34 E
Pulo Anna I	108	4.40 N	131.58 E
Pulog, Mount ∧	116	16.36 N	120.54 E
Pulogadung ◈[8]	269e	6.11 S	106.54 E
Pulon'ga	24	66.17 N	40.02 E
Púlpito do Sul	152	15.46 S	12.00 E
Pulsano	68	40.23 N	17.22 E
Pulsen	54	51.23 N	13.26 E
Pulsnitz	54	51.11 N	14.01 E
Pulsnitz ≃	54	51.27 N	13.30 E
Pulteney	210	42.31 N	77.10 W
Pultneyville	210	43.17 N	77.11 W
Pułtusk	30	52.43 N	21.05 E
Pulü, Zhg.	107	29.50 N	106.11 E
Pulu, Zhg.	120	36.11 N	81.30 E
Pulupandan	116	10.31 N	122.48 E
Pulur	130	40.10 N	39.53 E
Pulusuk I	14	6.42 N	149.19 E
Pulversheim	58	47.51 N	7.18 E
Puma Yumco ⊜	124	28.35 N	90.20 E
Pumbi	152	3.26 N	22.11 E
Pumei	102	23.28 N	105.15 E
Pumphrey	284b	39.13 N	76.38 W
Pumpkin Buttes ∧	200	43.44 N	105.54 W
Pumpkin Center	228	35.18 N	119.05 W
Pumpkin Creek ≃, Mt., U.S.	198	46.15 N	105.45 W
Pumpkin Creek ≃, Ne., U.S.	198	41.38 N	103.01 W
Pumsaint	42	52.03 N	3.58 W
Pumsi	80	57.12 N	51.39 E
Puná, Isla I	246	2.50 S	80.08 W
Punaauia	174s	17.38 S	149.36 W
Punaauia, Pointe de ›	174s	17.38 S	149.36 W
Punakha	124	27.37 N	89.52 E
Punaluu	229c	21.35 N	157.53 W
Punan, Indon.	112	1.20 N	115.34 E
Punan, Indon.	112	3.24 N	116.16 E
Punan, Zhg.	100	24.39 N	117.41 E
Punata	248	17.32 S	65.50 W
Pūnch	123	33.46 N	74.06 E
Pūnch ≃	123	33.12 N	73.40 E
Puncha	126	23.10 N	86.39 E
Punchaw	182	53.28 N	123.13 W
Punchbowl	274a	33.56 S	151.03 E
Pundaguitan	116	6.22 N	126.10 E
Punda Maria	156	22.40 S	31.05 E
Pünderich	56	50.02 N	7.08 E
Pūndri	124	29.45 N	76.33 E
Punduga	76	60.08 N	40.12 E
Pune (Poona)	122	18.32 N	73.52 E
P'ungam-ni	98	37.43 N	128.11 E
Pungan	85	40.45 N	70.49 E
Punganūru	122	13.22 N	78.35 E
Pungarancho ≃	234	18.47 N	100.41 W
Pungești	38	46.42 N	27.20 E
Punggol	271c	1.25 N	103.55 E
Punggol ≃	271c	1.25 N	103.54 E
Pungki	114	4.17 N	96.13 E
Pungo ≃	192	35.23 N	76.33 W
Pungo Andongo	152	9.40 S	15.35 E
Púngoè ≃	154	19.50 S	34.48 E
P'ungsan, C.M.I.K.	98	40.47 N	128.10 E
P'ungsan, C.M.I.K.	98	38.28 N	125.01 E
P'ungsong-ni	98	39.56 N	127.11 E
Punia	154	1.28 S	26.27 E
Punilla, Sierra de la ⋏	252	28.55 S	69.00 W
Puning	100	23.18 N	116.12 E
Punitaqui	252	30.50 S	71.16 W
Punjab □[3]	123	31.00 N	75.30 E
Punjab □[4]	120	31.00 N	72.00 E
Punkaharju ♦	26	61.47 N	29.20 E
Punkalaidun	26	61.07 N	23.06 E
Punnichy	184	51.23 N	104.18 W
Puno	248	15.50 S	70.02 W
Puno □[5]	248	15.00 S	70.00 W
Punta, Castillo de la ⊥	286b	23.09 N	82.21 W
Punta, Cerro de ∧	240m	18.10 N	66.36 W
Punta Alegre	240p	22.23 N	78.49 W
Punta Alta	254	38.53 S	62.05 W
Punta Arenas	254	53.09 S	70.55 W
Punta Banda, Cabo ›	232	31.45 N	116.45 W
Punta Brava ◈[8]	286b	23.01 N	82.30 W
Punta Cardón	246	11.38 N	70.14 W
Punta Colnett	232	31.05 N	116.05 W
Punta de Agua Creek (Tramperos Creek) ≃	196	35.32 N	102.27 W
Punta de Bombón	248	17.11 S	71.48 W
Punta de Díaz	252	28.03 S	70.37 W
Punta del Cobre	252	27.30 S	70.16 W
Punta del Este	252	34.58 S	54.57 W
Punta Delgada	254	42.46 S	63.38 W
Punta de los Llanos	252	30.09 S	66.33 W
Punta de Mata	246	9.43 N	63.38 W
Punta de Piedras	246	10.54 N	64.06 W
Punta Flecha	116	7.23 N	123.25 E
Punta Gorda, Belize	232	16.07 N	88.48 W
Punta Gorda, Nic.	236	11.31 N	83.47 W
Punta Gorda, Fl., U.S.	220	26.55 N	82.02 W
Punta Gorda ≃	236	11.30 N	83.47 W
Punta Gorda, Bahía de c	236	11.15 N	83.45 W
Punta Negra, Salar de ≍	252	24.35 S	69.00 W
Punta Prieta	232	28.58 N	114.17 W
Punta Raisi, Aeroporto di ⊠	70	38.11 N	13.06 E
Puntarenas	236	9.58 N	84.50 W
Puntarenas □[4]	236	9.00 N	83.15 W
Punta Santiago	240m	18.10 N	65.45 W
Puntas del Sauce	258	33.51 S	57.01 W
Punto Fijo	246	11.42 N	70.13 W
Puntzi Lake ⊜	182	52.12 N	124.02 W
Punung	115a	8.08 S	111.01 E
Punxsutawney	214	40.56 N	78.58 W
Puolanka	26	64.52 N	27.40 E
Puolo Point ›	229b	21.54 N	159.36 W
Puper	164	0.10 S	131.18 E
Pup'yŏng	271b	37.30 N	126.43 E
Puqi, Zhg.	100	28.11 N	121.01 E
Puqi, Zhg.	100	29.43 N	113.53 E
Puqian, Zhg.	100	23.34 N	114.38 E
Puqian, Zhg.	102	20.03 N	110.36 E
Puquio	248	14.42 S	74.08 W
Pur ≃	74	67.31 N	77.55 E
Purabiya Plain ≍	124	25.50 N	82.30 E
Puracé, Volcán ∧[1]	246	2.21 N	76.23 W
Purandarpur	126	23.51 N	87.36 E
Pūranpur	124	28.31 N	80.09 E
Purari ≃	164	7.25 S	145.05 E
Purba	114	2.54 N	98.42 E
Purbashthāli	126	23.28 N	88.21 E
Purbeck, Isle of I	42	50.38 N	2.00 W
Purbolinggo	115a	7.24 S	109.22 E
Purcell	196	35.00 N	97.21 W
Purcell Mountains ⋏	182	50.00 N	116.30 W
Purcellville	188	39.08 N	77.42 W
Purchase	276	41.02 N	73.43 W
Purchena	34	37.21 N	2.22 W
Purdon	222	31.57 N	96.37 W
Purdoški	80	54.40 N	43.32 E
Purdy	194	36.49 N	93.55 W
Purech	80	56.39 N	43.05 E
Pureora ∧	172	38.33 S	175.38 E
Purépero	234	19.55 N	102.01 W
Purfleet	42	51.29 N	0.15 E
Purga	171a	27.43 S	152.44 E
Purga Creek ≃	171a	27.42 S	152.45 E
Purgatoire ≃	198	38.04 N	103.10 W
Purgatory Brook ≃	283	42.11 N	71.11 W
Pürgg	61	47.32 N	14.04 E
Purgstall an der Erlauf	61	48.03 N	15.08 E
Puri	120	19.48 N	85.51 E
Purial, Sierra del ⋏	240p	20.12 N	74.42 W
Purificación, Col.	246	3.51 N	74.55 W
Purificación, Méx.	234	19.43 N	104.38 W
Purificación ≃, Méx.	232	23.58 N	98.42 W
Purificación ≃, Méx.	234	19.18 N	104.54 W
Purikari neem ›	76	59.40 N	25.43 E
Purísima	196	29.09 N	100.46 W
Purísima, Sierra de la ⋏	196	26.30 N	101.44 W
Purisima Creek ≃	282	37.24 N	122.26 W
Purísima de Bustos	234	21.02 N	101.52 W
Purkersdorf	61	48.12 N	16.11 E
Purleigh	260	51.41 N	0.40 E
Purley	222	33.05 N	95.16 W
Purley ◈[8]	260	51.20 N	0.07 W
Purling	210	42.17 N	74.00 W
Purmerend	52	52.31 N	4.57 E
Pūrna ≃, India	122	19.07 N	77.02 E
Pūrna ≃, India	122	21.05 N	76.00 E
Pūrnia	124	25.47 N	87.31 E
Puronga	76	60.09 N	40.54 E
Purranque	254	40.55 S	73.10 W
Purrorumba Hill ∧	171b	35.10 S	149.23 E
Purros	156	18.38 S	12.59 E
Purrumbete, Lake ⊜	169	38.17 S	143.14 E
Pursat → Poŭthĭsăt	110	12.32 N	103.55 E
Purton	42	51.36 N	1.52 W
Puruándiro	234	20.05 N	101.30 W
Puruarán	234	19.06 N	101.32 W
Puruí ≃	246	1.40 S	68.08 W
Purukcahu	112	0.35 S	114.35 E
Puruliya	126	23.20 N	86.22 E
Puruni ≃	246	6.00 N	59.12 W
Purus (Purús) ≃	242	3.42 S	61.28 W
Puruvesi ⊜	26	61.50 N	29.27 E
Purvis	194	31.08 N	89.24 W
Purwakarta	115a	6.34 S	107.26 E
Purwantoro	115a	7.51 S	111.15 E
Purwareja	115a	7.28 S	109.25 E
Purwodadi, Indon.	115a	7.49 S	110.00 E
Purwodadi, Indon.	115a	7.05 S	110.54 E
Purwokerto	115a	7.25 S	109.14 E
Purworejo	115a	7.43 S	110.01 E
Pusa	112	1.36 N	111.17 E
Pusad	122	19.54 N	77.35 E
Pusan	98	35.06 N	129.03 E
Pusan □[4]	98	35.10 N	129.05 E
Pūsa Road	124	25.59 N	85.41 E
Pusat Gayo, Pegunungan ⋏	114	4.15 N	97.05 E
Puščino	82	54.50 N	37.36 E
Pusgo Point ›	116	13.31 N	122.38 E
Pushang	98	36.08 N	119.42 E
Pushkar	120	26.30 N	74.33 E
Pushkarivka	78	48.40 N	34.16 E
Pushkin → Puškin	76	59.43 N	30.25 E
Pushkin Airport ⊠	265a	59.41 N	30.21 E
Pushkin Drama Theatre ʊ	265a	59.56 N	30.21 E
Pushthrough	186	47.39 N	56.10 W
Puskiakiwenin Indian Reserve ◈[4]	184	53.57 N	110.26 W
Puškin	76	59.43 N	30.25 E
Puškino, Ross.	80	51.14 N	46.59 E
Puškino, Ross.	82	56.01 N	37.51 E
Puškino, Ross.	82	56.36 N	35.46 E
Puškinskij	265a	59.43 N	30.18 E
Puškinskije Gory	76	57.01 N	28.54 E
Puskwaskau ≃	182	55.29 N	118.10 W
Puslinch Lake ⊜	212	43.25 N	80.16 W
Pusŏng-ni	98	40.19 N	127.19 E
Püspökladány	30	47.19 N	21.07 E
Pussay	50	48.21 N	2.00 E
Püssi	76	59.24 N	27.01 E
Pustertal V	64	46.45 N	12.20 E
Pustin'	76	59.54 N	35.32 E
Pustomyty	78	49.42 N	23.56 E
Pustoš'	76	60.07 N	42.45 E
Pustoška	76	56.20 N	29.22 E
Pustozersk	24	67.33 N	52.27 E
Pusur ≃[1]	126	21.45 N	89.30 E
Puszczykowo	30	52.17 N	16.52 E
Putaendo	252	32.38 S	70.44 W
Putah Creek ≃	226	38.33 N	121.42 W
Putai	100	23.23 N	120.09 E
Putana, Volcán ∧[1]	252	22.43 S	67.54 W
Putang ≃	269e	6.13 S	106.54 E
Putangqiao	106	31.34 N	118.59 E
Putao	102	27.21 N	97.24 E
Putaruru	172	38.03 S	175.47 E
Put'atin	89	42.52 N	132.25 E
Put'atino	80	54.10 N	41.07 E
Putbus	54	54.21 N	13.28 E
Puteaux	261	48.53 N	2.14 E
Puteran, Pulau I	115a	7.05 S	114.00 E
Putfontein Landbouhoewes	273d	26.08 S	28.24 E
Putgarten	54	54.40 N	13.25 E
Puth Kalān ◈[8]	272a	28.43 N	77.05 E
Putian, Zhg.	100	25.26 N	119.01 E
Putian, Zhg.	100	29.16 N	114.58 E
Putifigari	71	40.34 N	8.27 E
Putignano	68	40.51 N	17.07 E
Putilkovo	265b	55.52 N	37.23 E
Putina	248	14.55 S	69.52 W
Put-in-Bay	214	41.39 N	82.49 W
Putincevo	86	49.50 N	84.22 E
Puting, Tanjung ›	112	3.31 S	111.46 E
Putla de Guerrero	234	17.02 N	97.56 W
Putlitz	54	53.15 N	12.02 E
Putnam, Ct., U.S.	207	41.54 N	71.54 W
Putnam, Tx., U.S.	196	32.22 N	99.12 W
Putnam □[6], N.Y., U.S.	210	41.26 N	73.41 W
Putnam □[6], Oh., U.S.	216	41.01 N	84.03 W
Putnam Lake	210	41.28 N	73.35 W
Putnam Lake ⊜	276	41.05 N	73.38 W
Putnam Valley	210	41.20 N	73.52 W
Putnamville Reservoir ⊜[1]	283	42.36 N	70.57 W
Putney, Ga., U.S.	192	31.29 N	84.07 W
Putney, Vt., U.S.	188	42.58 N	72.31 W
Putney ◈[8]	260	51.28 N	0.13 W
Putney Island I	126	21.42 N	89.20 E
Puto	175e	5.41 S	154.43 E
Putorana, plato ⋏[1]	74	69.00 N	95.00 E
Putorino	172	39.08 S	177.00 E
Putre	248	18.12 S	69.35 W
Putri Narrows ⋓	271c	1.27 N	103.42 E
Putsonderwater	158	29.09 S	21.51 E
Pütt	263	51.11 N	6.59 E
Puttalam	122	8.02 N	79.49 E
Puttalam Lagoon c	122	8.07 N	79.47 E
Putte, Bel.	56	51.04 N	4.38 E
Putte, Ned.	52	51.22 N	4.23 E
Puttelange-lès-Farschviller	56	49.03 N	6.56 E
Putten	52	52.15 N	5.36 E
Putten I	52	51.50 N	4.15 E
Puttgarden	54	54.30 N	11.13 E
Püttlingen	56	49.17 N	6.53 E
Puttūr	122	13.27 N	79.33 E
Putty	170	32.57 S	150.40 E
Putty Creek ≃	170	33.05 S	150.37 E
Putú	252	35.13 S	72.17 W
Putumayo □[8]	246	0.30 N	76.00 W
Putumayo (Içá) ≃	246	3.07 S	67.58 W
Putuo	100	29.58 N	122.17 E
Putu Range ⋏	150	5.30 N	8.10 W
Pütürge	130	38.12 N	38.53 E
Putussibau	112	0.50 N	112.56 E
Putyla	78	48.01 N	25.03 E
Putyvl'	78	51.21 N	33.52 E
Putzkau	54	51.06 N	14.13 E
Putzu Idu	71	40.02 N	8.25 E
Pu'uhonua o Honaunau National Historical Park ♦	229d	19.25 N	155.54 W
Puu Kaaumakua ∧	229c	21.30 N	157.54 W
Puu Keahiakahoe ∧	229c	21.23 N	157.49 W
Puukohola Heiau National Historic Site ⊥	229d	20.00 N	155.46 W
Puukolii	229a	20.56 N	156.40 W
Puu Kukui ∧	229a	20.52 N	156.35 W
Puula ⊜	26	61.50 N	26.42 E
Puumala	26	61.32 N	28.11 E
Puunene	229a	20.51 N	156.27 W
Pu'upu'a	175a	13.34 S	172.09 W
Puurmani	76	58.34 N	26.17 E
Puurs	50	51.05 N	4.17 E
Puuwai	229b	21.54 N	160.12 W
Puxi	100	25.10 N	119.08 E
Puxian	102	36.30 N	111.02 E
Puxico	194	36.56 N	90.09 W
Puxingchang	107	30.41 N	105.06 E
Puyallup	224	47.11 N	122.17 W
Puyallup ≃	224	47.15 N	122.24 W
Puyang	98	35.42 N	114.59 E
Puyang ≃	100	30.05 N	120.11 E
Puyango (Tumbes) ≃	246	3.30 S	80.27 W
Puy-de-Dôme □[5]	32	45.45 N	3.05 E
Puyehue	254	40.40 S	72.37 W
Puyehue, Volcán ∧[1]	254	40.35 S	72.08 W
Puylaurens	32	43.34 N	2.01 E
Puy-l'Évêque	32	44.30 N	1.08 E
Puyloubier	62	43.31 N	5.41 E
Puymorens, Col de)(	32	42.30 N	1.50 E
Puyo, Ec.	246	1.28 S	77.59 W
Puyŏ, Taehan	98	36.18 N	126.54 E
Puysegur Point ›	172	46.09 S	166.36 E
Puyuan	106	30.41 N	120.38 E
Puyuguapi, Canal ⋓	254	44.45 S	72.48 W
Puyun-dong	98	41.55 N	129.30 E
Pūzak, Hāmūn-e ⊜	128	31.30 N	61.45 E
Puzhen	106	32.09 N	118.41 E
Puzzle Creek ≃	162	17.58 S	135.41 E
Puzzle Lake ⊜, On., Can.	212	44.36 N	76.58 W
Puzzle Lake ⊜, Fl., U.S.	220	28.41 N	81.02 W
Pwalagu	150	10.35 N	0.50 W
Pwani □[4]	154	7.00 S	39.00 E
Pweto	154	8.28 S	28.54 E
Pwinbyu	110	20.22 N	94.40 E
Pwllheli	42	52.53 N	4.25 W
Pyalo	110	19.09 N	95.11 E
Pyalong	169	37.07 S	144.54 E
Pyamalaw ≃[1]	110	15.49 N	94.42 E
Pyapon	110	16.17 N	95.41 E
Pyatigorsk → P'atigorsk	84	44.03 N	43.04 E
P'yatykhatky	78	48.24 N	33.42 E
Pyawbwe	110	20.35 N	96.04 E
Pyaye	110	19.15 N	95.06 E
Pyčas	80	56.29 N	52.28 E
Pye Islands II	180	59.22 N	150.25 W
Pygmalion Point ›	110	6.45 N	93.49 E
Pyhäjärvi ⊜, Europe	26	61.53 N	30.00 E
Pyhäjärvi ⊜, Suomi	26	62.46 N	25.30 E
Pyhäjärvi ⊜, Suomi	26	63.35 N	25.57 E
Pyhäjärvi ⊜, Suomi	26	61.28 N	23.35 E
Pyhäjärvi ⊜, Suomi	26	61.00 N	22.18 E
Pyhäjoki	26	64.28 N	24.14 E
Pyhäjoki ≃	26	64.28 N	24.13 E
Pyhämaa I	26	60.57 N	21.20 E
Pyhän-Häkin kansallispuisto ♦	26	62.52 N	25.30 E
Pyhäsalmi	26	63.41 N	25.59 E
Pyhäselkä	26	62.26 N	29.58 E
Pyhäselkä ⊜	26	62.26 N	29.58 E
Pyhätunturi ∧	24	67.01 N	27.09 E
Pyhätunturin kansallispuisto ♦	24	67.01 N	27.10 E
Pyhra	61	48.10 N	15.41 E
Pyhtää (Pyttis)	26	60.29 N	26.32 E
Pyinbongyi	110	17.34 N	96.34 E
Pyingaing	110	23.09 N	94.51 E
Pyinkayaing	110	15.58 N	94.24 E
Pyinmana	110	19.44 N	96.13 E
Pyle	42	51.32 N	3.42 W
Pylos → Pílos	38	36.55 N	21.43 E
Pymatuning Creek ≃	214	41.18 N	80.27 W
Pymatuning Reservoir ⊜[1]	214	41.37 N	80.30 W
Pymatuning State Park ♦, Oh., U.S.	214	41.38 N	80.33 W
Pymatuning State Park ♦, Pa., U.S.	214	41.30 N	80.27 W
Pymble	274a	33.45 S	151.09 E
Pyngopil'gyn, laguna c	180	67.24 N	175.10 W
Pyŏktong	98	40.35 N	125.20 E
Pyŏlch'ang-ni	98	39.17 N	126.26 E
P'yŏngan Namdo □[4]	98	39.20 N	126.00 E
P'yŏngan Pukdo □[4]	98	40.10 N	125.20 E
P'yŏngch'ang	98	37.23 N	128.22 E
P'yŏngdong-ni	98	37.10 N	128.02 E
P'yŏnggang	98	38.26 N	127.16 E
P'yonghae	98	36.46 N	129.28 E
P'yŏngsan	98	38.19 N	126.23 E
P'yŏngt'aek	98	37.00 N	127.05 E
P'yŏngyang	98	39.01 N	125.45 E
P'yŏngyang □[4]	98	39.05 N	125.50 E
Pyŏrha-ri	98	40.48 N	126.32 E
Pyote	196	31.32 N	103.08 W
Pyramid Head ›	228	32.49 N	118.21 W
Pyramid Lake ⊜	204	40.00 N	119.35 W
Pyramid Lake ⊜[1]	228	34.39 N	118.47 W
Pyramid Lake Indian Reservation ◈[4]	204	40.20 N	119.35 W

Symbols in the index entries represent the broad categories identified in the key at the right. Symbols with superior numbers (⋏[1]) identify subcategories (see complete key on page *I · 1*).

Symbole im Register stellen die rechts im Schlüssel erklärten Kategorien dar. Symbole mit hochgestellten Ziffern (⋏[1]) bezeichnen Unterabteilungen einer Kategorie (vgl. vollständiger Schlüssel auf Seite *I · 1*).

Los símbolos incluídos en el texto del índice representan las grandes categorías identificadas con la clave a la derecha. Los símbolos con numeros en su parte superior (⋏[1]) identifican las subcategorías (véase la clave completa en la página *I · 1*).

Les symboles de l'index représentent les catégories indiquées dans la légende à droite. Les symboles suivis d'un indice (⋏[1]) représentent des sous-catégories (voir légende complète à la page *I · 1*).

Os símbolos incluídos no texto do índice representam as grandes categorias identificadas com a chave à direita. Os símbolos com números em sua parte superior (⋏[1]) identificam as subcategorias (veja-se a chave completa à página *I · 1*).

English	Deutsch	Español	Français	Português
∧ Mountain	Berg	Montaña	Montagne	Montanha
⋏ Mountains	Gebirge	Montañas	Montagnes	Montanhas
)(Pass	Paß	Paso	Col	Passo
V Valley, Canyon	Tal, Cañon	Valle, Cañón	Vallée, Canyon	Vale, Canhão
≍ Plain	Ebene	Llano	Plaine	Planície
› Cape	Kap	Cabo	Cap	Cabo
I Island	Insel	Isla	Île	Ilha
II Islands	Inseln	Islas	Îles	Ilhas
⊥ Other Topographic Features	Andere Topographische Objekte	Otros Elementos Topográficos	Autres données topographiques	Outros acidentes topográficos

ESPAÑOL — Nombre · Página · Lat.°′ · Long.°′ W = Oeste
FRANÇAIS — Nom · Page · Lat.°′ · Long.°′ W = Ouest
PORTUGUÊS — Nome · Página · Lat.°′ · Long.°′ W = Oeste

Nombre / Nom / Nome	Página / Page	Lat.°′	Long.°′
Pyramid Peak ∧, Ca., U.S.	226	38.50 N	120.19 W
Pyramid Peak ∧, Wa., U.S.	224	47.07 N	121.24 W
Pyramid Peak ∧, Wy., U.S.	200	43.27 N	110.28 W
Pyramid Point ➤	174h	2.52 S	171.37 W
Pyramids of Giza → Jīzah, Ahrāmāt al- ⊥	142	29.59 N	31.08 E
Pyrenäen → Pyrenees ⋏	34	42.40 N	1.00 E
Pyrenees ⋏	34	42.40 N	1.00 E
Pyrénées-Atlantiques □[5]	32	43.15 N	0.50 W
Pyrénées Occident, Parc National des ♠	32	42.48 N	0.08 W
Pyrénées-Orientales □[5]	32	42.30 N	2.20 E
Pyre Peak ∧	180	52.20 N	172.31 W
Pyrford	260	51.19 N	0.30 W
Pyrgi ⊥	66	42.01 N	11.58 E
Pyrgos → Pírgos	38	37.41 N	21.28 E
Pyrkanajjan, gora ∧	180	69.14 N	175.50 E
Pyrkino	80	53.29 N	45.07 E
Pyrmont	216	40.28 N	86.41 W
Pyrohivka	78	51.54 N	33.18 E
Pyryatyn	78	50.15 N	32.30 E
Pyrzyce	30	53.10 N	14.55 E
Pyšma	86	56.56 N	63.13 E
Pyšma ≃	86	57.08 N	66.18 E
Pys'menne	78	48.13 N	35.48 E
Pytalovo	76	57.04 N	27.56 E
Pythonga, Lac ⊜	190	46.23 N	76.25 W
Pyu	110	18.29 N	96.26 E
Pyuntaza	110	17.52 N	96.44 E
Pyūthān	124	28.06 N	82.54 E
Pyvėsa ≃	76	56.06 N	24.27 E
Pyzdry	30	52.11 N	17.41 E
Q			
Qäbälä	84	40.59 N	47.50 E
Qabātīyah	132	32.25 N	35.17 E
Qabbāsīn	130	36.25 N	37.34 E
Qabb Ilyās	132	33.48 N	35.49 E
Qabırrı (Iori) ≃	84	41.03 N	46.17 E
Qabr Hūd	144	16.08 N	49.37 E
Qacentina (Constantine)	148	36.22 N	6.37 E
Qacentina □[5]	148	36.20 N	6.40 E
Qaddīs Anṭūn, Dayr al- (Monastery of Saint Anthony) ʊ[1]	142	28.55 N	32.21 E
Qaddīs Būlus, Dayr al- (Monastery of Saint Paul) ʊ[1]	142	28.52 N	32.33 E
Qāderābād	128	30.17 N	53.16 E
Qādiān	123	31.49 N	75.23 E
Qā'emshahr	128	36.28 N	52.53 E
Qā'en	128	33.44 N	59.11 E
Qāfilah	142	31.04 N	30.16 E
Qagan	88	49.14 N	118.08 E
Qagan Nur ⊜, Zhg.	98	41.23 N	113.55 E
Qagan Nur ⊜, Zhg.	102	43.37 N	114.40 E
Qahā	142	30.17 N	31.12 E
Qahar Youyi Zhongqi	102	41.09 N	112.38 E
Qahbûna	142	30.48 N	31.54 E
Qaidam ≃	102	36.39 N	96.20 E
Qaidam Pendi ⊻[1]	120	37.00 N	95.00 E
Qakar	120	36.32 N	80.43 E
Qalaʿ an-Naḥl	140	13.38 N	34.57 E
Qalabshū	142	31.26 N	31.19 E
Qalamshāh	142	29.10 N	30.50 E
Qalandīyah	132	31.50 N	35.14 E
Qalandūl	142	27.49 N	30.50 E
Qalāt	120	32.07 N	66.54 E
Qalʿat ash-Shaqīf (Beaufort Castle) ⊥	132	33.19 N	35.32 E
Qalʿat Bīshah	144	20.01 N	42.36 E
Qalʿat Ṣāliḥ	128	31.31 N	47.16 E
Qalʿat Sukkar	128	31.51 N	46.05 E
Qalʿeh Shahr	120	35.33 N	65.34 E
Qalʿeh-ye Deh-e Bārez	128	27.26 N	57.12 E
Qalʿeh-ye Now, Afg.	120	35.27 N	67.08 E
Qalʿeh-ye Now, Afg.	128	34.59 N	63.08 E
Qalʿeh-ye Panjeh	123	37.00 N	72.36 E
Qalʿeh-ye Sarkārī	120	35.54 N	67.17 E
Qallābāt, Sūd.	140	12.43 N	23.26 E
Qallābāt, Sūd.	140	12.58 N	36.09 E
Qallīn	142	31.03 N	30.51 E
Qalqilīya	132	32.11 N	34.58 E
Qalyūb	142	30.11 N	31.12 E
Qamar, Ghubbat al- ⊂	118	16.00 N	52.30 E
Qamata	158	32.00 S	27.21 E
Qamdo	102	31.11 N	97.15 E
Qamīnis	146	31.39 N	20.03 E
Qamr-ud-dīn Kārez	120	31.39 N	68.25 E
Qamṣar	128	33.45 N	51.26 E
Qanā, Ar. Su.	128	27.47 N	41.25 E
Qānā, Lubnān	132	33.13 N	35.18 E
Qanāyah	132	33.01 N	36.11 E
Qandahār	120	31.32 N	65.30 E
Qandahār □[4]	120	31.00 N	65.45 E
Qandala	144	11.28 N	49.52 E
Qanṭarah, Jabal ∧[2]	142	30.09 N	30.15 E
Qantur	140	9.45 N	25.52 E
Qarabağlar	84	39.26 N	45.12 E
Qarabağ silsilăsi ⋏	84	39.42 N	46.36 E
Qaraçala	84	39.48 N	48.57 E
Qaraçay ≃	84	41.28 N	49.00 E
Qaracinar	84	40.26 N	46.34 E
Qārah, Ar. Su.	128	29.52 N	40.15 E
Qārah, Sūrīy.	130	34.09 N	36.44 E
Qarah Bāgh	128	34.56 N	61.46 E
Qarak	85	38.23 N	76.58 E
Qarasu	84	40.11 N	48.41 E
Qarāvol	120	37.14 N	68.46 E
Qardho	144	9.30 N	49.05 E
Qareh ≃	128	34.52 N	51.25 E
Qareh Sū ≃	128	39.27 N	47.23 E
Qareh Ẕīā' od Dīn	84	38.54 N	45.02 E
Qarqan ≃	90	39.25 N	88.20 E
Qarqīn	120	37.25 N	66.03 E
Qarṭabā	130	34.06 N	35.51 E
Qārūn, Birkat (Lake Moeris) ⊜	142	29.28 N	30.40 E
Qaryat al-Qaddāḥīyah	146	31.22 N	15.14 E
Qaryat al-Zuwaytīnah	146	30.58 N	20.07 E
Qasa-e Qand	128	26.12 N	60.45 E
Qāsh, Nahr al- (Gash) ≃	140	16.48 N	35.51 E
Qashqeh, Kūh-e ∧	128	28.23 N	55.18 E
Qāsim	132	32.59 N	36.05 E
Qāsimwāla	123	30.09 N	73.50 E
Qaṣr ad-Dayr, Jabal ∧	132	30.48 N	35.34 E
Qaṣr al-Azraq ⊥	132	31.53 N	36.49 E
Qasr al-Dubārā (Garden City) ✥[8]	273c	30.02 N	31.14 E
Qaṣr al-Farāfirah	140	27.03 N	27.58 E
Qaṣr al-Jibālī	142	29.20 N	30.38 E
Qaṣr al-Kharānah ⊥	132	31.44 N	36.28 E
Qaṣr al-Mushāsh ⊥	132	31.49 N	36.19 E
Qaṣr al-Mushattā ⊥	132	31.44 N	36.01 E
Qaṣr al Qarābūllī	146	32.45 N	13.43 E
Qaṣr ʿAmrah ⊥	132	31.48 N	36.35 E
Qaṣr aṭ-Ṭūbah ⊥	132	31.20 N	36.34 E
Qaṣr Baghdād	142	30.44 N	30.53 E
Qaṣr Bū-Hādī	146	31.03 N	16.40 E
Qaṣr Ḍabʿah ⊥	132	31.36 N	36.03 E
Qaṣr-e Fīrūzeh	267d	35.40 N	51.32 E
Qasr el-Boukhari	148	35.51 N	2.52 E
Qaṣr-e Shīrīn	128	34.31 N	45.35 E
Qaṣr Qārūn	142	29.25 N	30.25 E
Qaʿṭabah	144	13.51 N	44.42 E
Qaṭanā	132	33.26 N	36.05 E
Qatar (Qaṭar) □[1], Asia	118	25.00 N	51.10 E
Qatar (Qaṭar) □[1], Asia	128	25.00 N	51.10 E
Qaṭia, Bi'r ⫪[4]	142	30.58 N	32.45 E
Qaṭmah	130	36.36 N	36.57 E
Qaṭrānī, Jabal ∧[2]	142	29.41 N	30.35 E
Qattāntyah, Ghurd al- ⩦[8]	142	29.50 N	30.17 E
Qattara Depression → Qaṭṭārah, Munkhafaḍ al- ⩦[7]	140	30.00 N	27.30 E
Qaṭṭārah, Munkhafaḍ al- (Qattara Depression) ⩦[7]	140	30.00 N	27.30 E
Qaṭṭīnah, Buḥayrat ⊜[1]	130	34.39 N	36.34 E
Qawz Rajab	140	16.04 N	35.34 E
Qāy	142	29.09 N	30.57 E
Qayṭah	132	33.04 N	36.08 E
Qazanbulag	84	40.38 N	46.41 E
Qazangöldağ ∧	84	39.13 N	46.00 E
Qazax	84	41.06 N	45.22 E
Qāzigund	123	33.38 N	75.09 E
Qazımämmäd	84	40.03 N	48.56 E
Qazvīn	128	36.16 N	50.00 E
Qeh	102	42.18 N	100.59 E
Qena → Qinā	140	26.10 N	32.43 E
Qeqertaq I	176	71.55 N	55.30 W
Qesari, Ḥorbat (Cæsarea) ⊥	132	32.30 N	34.53 E
Qeshm	128	26.58 N	56.16 E
Qeshm, Jazīreh-ye I	128	26.45 N	55.45 E
Qetura	132	29.58 N	35.03 E
Qeydār	128	36.07 N	48.35 E
Qeyṣār	120	35.41 N	64.17 E
Qezel Owzan ≃	128	36.45 N	49.22 E
Qezel Qeshlāq	84	39.08 N	45.21 E
Qi ≃, Zhg.	98	35.30 N	114.17 E
Qi ≃, Zhg.	100	30.09 N	115.20 E
Qi ≃, Zhg.	107	30.38 N	105.26 E
Qi ≃, Zhg.	107	29.15 N	106.24 E
Qiakemake	85	40.05 N	75.24 E
Qian ≃	102	23.25 N	110.10 E
Qian'an, Zhg.	89	45.00 N	124.01 E
Qian'an, Zhg.	98	39.59 N	118.40 E
Qiancaijiatun	104	41.14 N	121.38 E
Qiandiwu	105	39.16 N	116.38 E
Qiandong	100	23.41 N	116.55 E
Qiandun	106	31.16 N	121.00 E
Qianertaizi	104	42.04 N	122.42 E
Qianfang	100	28.32 N	116.13 E
Qian Gorlos	89	45.08 N	124.47 E
Qiangzilu	105	40.26 N	117.13 E
Qianhonghepu	104	41.23 N	123.07 E
Qianhuang	106	31.36 N	119.58 E
Qianji	100	33.55 N	118.56 E
Qianjiadian	89	43.42 N	122.35 E
Qianjiang, Zhg.	100	30.25 N	112.51 E
Qianjiang, Zhg.	102	23.37 N	109.00 E
Qianjian'gangzi	104	41.34 N	122.26 E
Qianjiangtai	104	41.46 N	122.03 E
Qianjiaqiao	106	30.53 N	121.31 E
Qianjiaying	105	39.35 N	118.21 E
Qianjiazhuang	106	32.16 N	120.17 E
Qianjing	106	31.33 N	121.15 E
Qianjinmiao	100	25.09 N	118.20 E
Qiankeng	106	30.43 N	119.47 E
Qiankoutou	105	39.42 N	117.01 E
Qianlijiazhuang	105	39.25 N	118.17 E
Qianluanshanzi	104	42.17 N	122.27 E
Qianmajiagushanzi	104	42.23 N	123.33 E
Qianmintun	104	41.49 N	123.15 E
Qianning	102	30.30 N	101.31 E
Qianpai	102	22.22 N	111.11 E
Qianqi	100	27.20 N	120.20 E
Qianqianjianglugou	104	41.59 N	120.58 E
Qiansandaoliangzi	104	42.06 N	120.44 E
Qianshahezi	104	41.46 N	123.01 E
Qianshan, Zhg.	100	30.38 N	116.33 E
Qianshan, Zhg.	106	31.06 N	120.24 E
Qian Shan ⋏	104	40.52 N	123.25 E
Qianshuangshanzi	104	41.22 N	121.13 E
Qiansuo	100	28.44 N	121.27 E
Qiantang ≃	106	30.23 N	120.33 E
Qiantangzhen	107	30.12 N	106.18 E
Qianwei, Zhg.	98	40.12 N	120.06 E
Qianwei, Zhg.	107	29.12 N	103.57 E
Qianxi, Zhg.	102	26.57 N	106.00 E
Qianxi, Zhg.	105	40.09 N	118.19 E
Qianxiatazi	104	42.23 N	123.53 E
Qianyamen	104	42.04 N	121.26 E
Qianyang	102	27.11 N	110.04 E
Qianyaopu	104	42.02 N	123.37 E
Qi'anzhen	106	32.11 N	121.03 E
Qianzhou	106	31.42 N	120.13 E
Qiaodun	100	27.29 N	120.18 E
Qiaoershan ⋏	102	31.48 N	99.10 E
Qiaogou	100	32.26 N	115.45 E
Qiaohengjin	102	29.30 N	99.50 E
Qiaojia	102	26.57 N	102.52 E
Qiaojiang	269b	31.15 N	121.19 E
Qiaokou	100	25.55 N	113.10 E
Qiaolima	120	34.35 N	81.00 E
Qiaolin	100	31.57 N	118.32 E
Qiaomu	98	39.34 N	114.27 E
Qiaopurikebazha	85	38.48 N	76.19 E
Qiaoqi	106	31.49 N	120.18 E
Qiaoshe	100	28.48 N	115.58 E
Qiaosi	106	30.21 N	120.18 E
Qiaotou, Zhg.	100	33.05 N	112.46 E
Qiaotou, Zhg.	102	28.17 N	99.22 E
Qiaotou, Zhg.	104	41.13 N	123.44 E
Qiaotou, Zhg.	106	32.11 N	119.14 E
Qiaotou, Zhg.	107	29.18 N	104.39 E
Qiaotoucun	106	30.36 N	119.08 E
Qiaotouji	100	31.45 N	117.34 E
Qiaotoupu	106	30.33 N	118.50 E
Qiaotouyi	100	28.24 N	112.58 E
Qiaotouzhen	106	30.49 N	119.13 E
Qiaowan	102	40.36 N	96.55 E
Qiaowei	102	22.51 N	109.50 E
Qiaoxia	106	31.09 N	119.35 E
Qiaoxiajie	100	28.10 N	120.34 E
Qiaozhen	106	31.39 N	121.24 E
Qibao	106	31.09 N	121.20 E
Qibyā	132	31.59 N	35.01 E
Qichun	100	30.17 N	115.26 E
Qiddīsah Kātrīnā, Dayr al- (Monastery of Saint Catherine) ʊ[1]	140	28.29 N	34.01 E
Qidong, Zhg.	102	26.44 N	112.04 E
Qidong, Zhg.	106	31.49 N	121.40 E
Qidu	100	30.16 N	117.46 E
Qiemo	120	38.08 N	85.32 E
Qiesanglinzi	104	41.42 N	123.30 E
Qieshikou	271a	39.59 N	116.24 E
Qiezixi	107	29.25 N	106.30 E
Qifosi	107	29.27 N	105.58 E
Qifṭ (Coptos)	140	26.00 N	32.49 E
Qigong	102	28.38 N	100.38 E
Qigongtai	104	41.50 N	123.08 E
Qihe (Yancheng)	98	36.48 N	116.44 E
Qiji	98	37.16 N	115.21 E
Qijiadian	89	46.48 N	125.36 E
Qijian	107	30.14 N	106.09 E
Qijiang	107	29.02 N	106.39 E
Qijiapuzi	104	40.54 N	122.31 E
Qijiawan	100	30.53 N	114.13 E
Qijiawopeng	104	41.02 N	121.26 E
Qijiazi	104	41.54 N	122.58 E
Qika	89	50.35 N	119.16 E
Qikou	98	38.35 N	117.31 E
Qila Abdullāh	120	30.43 N	66.38 E
Qila Dīdār Singh	123	32.08 N	74.01 E
Qilaguganni Shan ∧	124	28.46 N	87.38 E
Qila Lādgasht	128	27.54 N	62.57 E
Qila Saifullāh	120	30.43 N	68.21 E
Qila Sobha Singh	123	32.14 N	74.46 E
Qilian	102	38.05 N	100.12 E
Qilian Shan ∧	102	39.12 N	98.35 E
Qilian Shan ⋏	102	39.06 N	98.40 E
Qili Hai ≣	105	39.19 N	117.33 E
Qilihe, Zhg.	104	41.21 N	121.16 E
Qilihe, Zhg.	104	41.30 N	121.15 E
Qilihezi	104	40.56 N	121.02 E
Qiling	100	24.05 N	115.27 E
Qilingzicun	104	41.05 N	123.06 E
Qilinmen	106	32.04 N	118.55 E
Qilinzhen	106	31.56 N	121.21 E
Qiliping	100	31.27 N	114.39 E
Qiliqiao	106	31.35 N	120.48 E
Qilizhen, Zhg.	102	35.43 N	108.59 E
Qilizhen, Zhg.	106	32.19 N	121.05 E
Qilṭ, ʿAyn al- ⫪[4]	132	31.50 N	35.23 E
Qimafang	98	40.08 N	114.31 E
Qiman al-ʿArūs	142	29.18 N	31.10 E
Qimen, Zhg.	100	29.52 N	117.42 E
Qimen, Zhg.	100	25.18 N	113.15 E
Qimoudi	105	39.35 N	115.32 E
Qimu Jiao ➤	98	37.46 N	120.12 E
Qin ≃, Zhg.	100	23.58 N	115.47 E
Qin ≃, Zhg.	100	26.16 N	115.52 E
Qin ≃, Zhg.	102	35.01 N	113.25 E
Qinā	140	26.10 N	32.43 E
Qinā, Wādī ∨, Miṣr	140	26.12 N	32.44 E
Qinā, Wādī ∨, Miṣr	142	29.39 N	31.53 E
Qincaigou	104	40.38 N	120.37 E
Qing ≃, Zhg.	98	42.26 N	123.50 E
Qing ≃, Zhg.	102	30.22 N	111.20 E
Qing'an	89	46.52 N	127.30 E
Qingbaikou	105	40.01 N	115.50 E
Qingcaoge	100	30.50 N	116.46 E
Qingcheng	98	37.12 N	117.40 E
Qingchengzi	104	40.44 N	123.36 E
Qingchuan	102	32.36 N	105.09 E
Qingcungang	106	30.56 N	121.34 E
Qingdao (Tsingtao)	98	36.06 N	120.19 E
Qingdian	105	39.51 N	117.22 E
Qingduizi, Zhg.	98	39.50 N	123.18 E
Qingduizi, Zhg.	104	41.28 N	121.53 E
Qingfeng	98	35.54 N	115.07 E
Qingfengtuo	98	40.59 N	116.04 E
Qingfu	102	28.29 N	104.35 E
Qinggang	89	46.43 N	126.07 E
Qingguang	105	39.11 N	117.02 E
Qingguji	98	34.45 N	115.47 E
Qinghai (Tsinghai) □[4]	90	36.00 N	96.00 E
Qinghai Hu ⊜	102	36.50 N	100.20 E
Qinghai Nanshan ⋏	102	37.06 N	99.05 E
Qinghe, Zhg.	86	46.36 N	90.39 E
Qinghe, Zhg.	98	40.02 N	122.35 E
Qinghe, Zhg.	104	42.32 N	124.09 E
Qinghe, Zhg.	105	40.01 N	116.20 E
Qinghecheng	104	41.28 N	124.15 E
Qinghechengzi	104	41.44 N	121.25 E
Qinghemen	104	41.45 N	121.25 E
Qinghezhen	98	37.16 N	117.39 E
Qinghu	100	28.40 N	118.34 E
Qinghua	100	29.24 N	117.46 E
Qinghuayuan	105	40.00 N	116.19 E
Qinghuazhen	100	32.55 N	112.19 E
Qingjian	102	37.10 N	110.00 E
Qingjiang, Zhg.	100	28.05 N	115.29 E
Qingjiang, Zhg.	100	28.16 N	121.06 E
Qingjiang, Zhg.	100	33.35 N	119.02 E
Qingjiang, Zhg.	107	29.17 N	105.34 E
Qingjujie	107	30.42 N	106.07 E
Qinglian	100	24.27 N	112.45 E
Qingliu	100	26.12 N	116.52 E
Qingliuzhen	107	29.56 N	105.19 E
Qinglong, Zhg.	98	40.24 N	118.54 E
Qinglong, Zhg.	100	25.28 N	114.28 E
Qinglong, Zhg.	102	25.50 N	105.10 E
Qinglong ≃, Zhg.	98	39.51 N	118.51 E
Qinglong ≃, Zhg.	105	39.35 N	117.46 E
Qinglongchang, Zhg.	107	28.50 N	106.31 E
Qinglongchang, Zhg.	107	29.51 N	105.40 E
Qinglongchang, Zhg.	107	30.20 N	103.51 E
Qinglonggang	106	31.51 N	121.15 E
Qinglongguan	107	30.25 N	104.48 E
Qinglongji	98	34.05 N	116.37 E
Qinglongwan ≃	105	39.19 N	117.32 E
Qingmuguan	107	29.41 N	106.18 E
Qingningsi	106	31.16 N	121.33 E
Qingping, Zhg.	98	36.47 N	116.06 E
Qingping, Zhg.	107	29.00 N	106.21 E
Qingping, Zhg.	107	30.14 N	106.12 E
Qingpu	106	31.09 N	121.06 E
Qingshan, Zhg.	100	31.33 N	116.22 E
Qingshan, Zhg.	100	30.38 N	114.23 E
Qingshan, Zhg.	106	30.15 N	119.52 E
Qingshan, Zhg.	106	30.36 N	119.41 E
Qingshan, Zhg.	106	30.43 N	120.03 E
Qingshanpu	100	29.27 N	114.01 E
Qingshen	107	29.50 N	103.50 E
Qingshui, Zhg.	102	34.42 N	106.21 E
Qingshui, Zhg.	102	39.23 N	99.09 E
Qingshui, Zhg.	107	30.10 N	104.03 E
Qingshui ≃, Zhg.	102	37.30 N	105.30 E
Qingshui ≃, Zhg.	102	27.08 N	109.36 E
Qingshuihe	86	44.12 N	80.45 E
Qingshuijian	105	39.59 N	115.58 E
Qingshuilang Shan ⋏	102	26.15 N	99.35 E
Qingshuixi	102	29.09 N	103.55 E
Qingtan	100	31.48 N	112.48 E
Qingtang, Zhg.	100	26.28 N	115.48 E
Qingtang, Zhg.	100	24.14 N	113.51 E
Qingtian	100	28.10 N	120.17 E
Qingtong	107	29.28 N	103.27 E
Qingtongxia	102	37.53 N	105.54 E
Qingtuosi	98	35.29 N	118.20 E
Qingtuozi, Zhg.	104	41.05 N	121.28 E
Qingtuozi, Zhg.	105	39.08 N	117.45 E
Qingxi, Zhg.	89	49.19 N	127.10 E
Qingxi, Zhg.	100	31.40 N	118.00 E
Qingxi, Zhg.	107	30.40 N	106.14 E
Qingxian	98	38.34 N	116.46 E
Qingxizhen	107	29.09 N	103.55 E
Qingyang, Zhg.	89	45.20 N	128.47 E
Qingyang, Zhg.	100	30.38 N	117.48 E
Qingyang, Zhg.	102	36.06 N	107.47 E
Qingyangzhen	106	31.46 N	120.15 E
Qingyi ≃	107	29.34 N	103.42 E
Qingyuan, Zhg.	98	42.13 N	124.56 E
Qingyuan, Zhg.	100	27.38 N	119.04 E
Qingyuan, Zhg.	100	23.42 N	113.02 E
Qingyuan → Baoding, Zhg.	105	38.52 N	115.29 E
Qingyun (Xiejiaji)	98	37.52 N	117.21 E
Qingyunbao	104	42.34 N	123.50 E
Qingyundian	105	39.38 N	116.29 E
Qing Zang Gaoyuan ⋏[1]	12	33.00 N	92.00 E
Qingzhen, Zhg.	102	26.29 N	106.22 E
Qingzhen, Zhg.	106	30.45 N	120.30 E
Qingzhou	100	23.39 N	116.57 E
Qinhuai ≃	106	32.01 N	118.50 E
Qinhuangdao (Chinwangtao)	98	39.56 N	119.36 E
Qinjia	89	46.47 N	127.00 E
Qinlan	100	32.37 N	119.08 E
Qin Ling (Tsinlingshan) ⋏	102	34.00 N	108.00 E
Qinnan	100	33.16 N	119.55 E
Qinshui	102	35.41 N	112.11 E
Qintong	100	32.39 N	120.08 E
Qinxian	102	36.48 N	112.41 E
Qinyang	102	35.06 N	112.57 E
Qinyuan	102	36.30 N	112.15 E
Qinzhou	102	21.59 N	108.36 E
Qionghai (Jiaji)	110	19.20 N	110.30 E
Qionglai	107	30.25 N	103.27 E
Qionglaishan ⋏	102	31.21 N	102.50 E
Qionglong Shan ∧	106	31.15 N	120.25 E
Qiongzhong, Zhg.	90	19.02 N	109.49 E
Qiongzhong, Zhg.	110	19.04 N	109.48 E
Qiongzhou Haixia ⊍	102	20.10 N	110.15 E
Qipandi	105	39.46 N	115.12 E
Qipanshan	98	42.05 N	117.30 E
Qiqian	89	52.12 N	120.49 E
Qiqihar (Tsitsihar)	89	47.19 N	123.55 E
Qira	120	37.00 N	80.47 E
Qirʿawn, Buḥayrat al- ⊜[1]	132	33.34 N	35.42 E
Qırmızı Bazar	84	39.41 N	46.58 E
Qiryat	132	32.49 N	35.06 E
Qiryat ʿAnavim	132	31.48 N	35.07 E
Qiryat Ata	132	32.48 N	35.06 E
Qiryat Bialik	132	32.50 N	35.05 E
Qiryat Gat	132	31.36 N	34.46 E
Qiryat Ḥayyim	132	32.49 N	35.04 E
Qiryat Mal'akhi	132	31.44 N	34.44 E
Qiryat Motzkin	132	32.50 N	35.04 E
Qiryat Ono	132	32.04 N	34.51 E
Qiryat Shemona	132	33.13 N	35.34 E
Qiryat Tivʿon	132	32.43 N	35.08 E
Qiryat Yam	132	32.51 N	35.04 E
Qirzah, Wādī ∨	146	30.56 N	14.31 E
Qiseqi Shan ∧	89	48.37 N	122.32 E
Qishn	144	15.26 N	51.40 E
Qishon ≃	132	32.49 N	35.02 E
Qishrān I	144	20.14 N	40.05 E
Qishudang	107	29.13 N	104.39 E
Qishuyan	106	31.44 N	120.04 E
Qiṣrāyā	130	34.53 N	36.26 E
Qitai	86	44.01 N	89.28 E
Qitaihe	89	45.48 N	130.53 E
Qitaizi	104	41.33 N	122.11 E
Qitamu	89	44.22 N	126.20 E
Qitangzhen	107	29.47 N	106.16 E
Qiting	100	31.02 N	114.44 E
Qitingqiao	106	31.26 N	119.52 E
Qitou	100	24.54 N	117.29 E
Qiubei	102	24.07 N	104.12 E
Qiuchang	107	28.59 N	104.42 E
Qiuji	100	33.51 N	118.01 E
Qiujia	106	31.49 N	121.51 E
Qiujiatun	104	41.20 N	121.00 E
Qiujin	100	29.10 N	115.42 E
Qiuxi ≃	107	29.58 N	104.40 E
Qiuxizhen	107	29.56 N	104.41 E
Qiweigang	106	32.01 N	119.59 E
Qixia	98	37.17 N	120.48 E
Qixian (Zhaoge), Zhg.	98	35.38 N	114.11 E
Qixian, Zhg.	100	34.33 N	114.47 E
Qixianji	100	33.28 N	117.01 E
Qixiashan	106	32.10 N	118.57 E
Qi Xia Si ʊ[1]	106	32.12 N	118.58 E
Qixingqiao	106	30.49 N	120.51 E
Qiyahe	89	53.02 N	120.33 E
Qiyang	102	26.29 N	111.43 E
Qiyi	100	32.30 N	112.54 E
Qiying	102	36.38 N	106.25 E
Qizhou	100	30.04 N	115.20 E
Qızılağaç körfäzi ⊂	84	39.09 N	49.03 E
Qizil Jilga	120	35.21 N	78.52 E
Qizil Langar	120	35.13 N	77.59 E
Qnadsa	148	31.48 N	2.26 W
Qobustan	84	40.06 N	49.24 E
Qogir Feng (K2) ∧	123	35.53 N	76.30 E
Qolhak ✥[8]	267d	35.47 N	51.26 E
Qom	128	34.39 N	50.54 E
Qom ≃	128	34.48 N	51.02 E
Qomolangma Feng → Everest, Mount ∧	124	27.59 N	86.56 E
Qomsheh	128	32.01 N	51.52 E
Qonaqkänd	84	41.04 N	48.37 E
Qondūz ≃	120	37.00 N	68.16 E
Qorveh	128	35.10 N	47.48 E
Qoṭbābād	128	28.42 N	53.34 E
Qoṭūr	128	38.28 N	44.25 E
Qu ≃, Zhg.	100	29.12 N	119.27 E
Qu ≃, Zhg.	102	30.01 N	106.24 E
Quabbin Reservoir ⊜[1]	207	42.22 N	72.18 W
Quaddick Reservoir ⊜[1]	207	41.57 N	71.49 W
Quadra Island I	182	50.08 N	125.16 W
Quadraro ✥[8]	267a	41.51 N	12.33 E
Quadrath-Ichendorf	56	50.56 N	6.41 E
Quadros, Lagoa dos ⊂	252	29.42 S	50.05 W
Quāidābād	123	32.20 N	71.52 E
Quail Lake ⊜[1]	228	34.47 N	118.45 W
Quail Valley	228	33.43 N	117.15 W
Quairading	162	32.01 S	117.25 E
Quakake	210	40.51 N	76.02 W
Quakenbrück	52	52.40 N	7.57 E
Quaker Hill, Ct., U.S.	207	41.22 N	72.06 W
Quaker Hill, N.Y., U.S.	210	41.35 N	73.33 W
Quakers Hill	170	33.43 S	150.53 E
Quakers Knob ∧[2]	214	40.21 N	80.24 W
Quaker Street	210	42.44 N	74.11 W
Quakertown, N.J., U.S.	210	40.33 N	74.56 W
Quakertown, Pa., U.S.	208	40.26 N	75.20 W
Qualicum Beach	182	49.21 N	124.27 W
Quambatook	166	35.51 S	143.31 E
Quanah	196	34.17 N	99.44 W
Quanbao Shan ∧	102	34.09 N	111.29 E
Quangang	100	28.10 N	115.34 E
Quang Ngai	110	15.07 N	108.48 E
Quang Trach	110	17.45 N	106.27 E
Quanjiang	100	27.43 N	113.59 E
Quanjiao	100	32.06 N	118.16 E
Quan Long → Ca Mau	110	9.11 N	105.08 E
Quanmian	104	42.02 N	122.13 E
Quannan	100	24.44 N	114.31 E
Quannapowitt, Lake ⊜	283	42.31 N	71.05 W
Quanshang	100	26.25 N	116.55 E
Quanshengpu	104	41.59 N	123.22 E
Quanshui	104	41.18 N	124.11 E
Quanshuitou	105	40.24 N	116.39 E
Quantico, Md., U.S.	208	38.22 N	75.44 W
Quantico, Va., U.S.	208	38.31 N	77.17 W
Quantico Marine Corps Air Station ■	208	38.31 N	77.19 W
Quantock Hills ⋏[2]	42	51.07 N	3.10 W
Quantou	89	42.52 N	124.07 E
Quanxishi	100	26.51 N	112.45 E
Quanyanhezi	104	40.52 N	123.26 E
Quanzhou (Chuanchou)	100	24.54 N	118.35 E
Quanzhou Gang ⊂	100	24.52 N	118.37 E
Qu'Appelle	184	50.33 N	103.52 W
Qu'Appelle ≃	184	50.25 N	101.20 W
Qu'Appelle Dam ✥[6]	184	51.00 N	106.25 W
Quaraí	252	30.23 S	56.27 W
Quaraí ≃	252	30.12 S	57.36 W
Quaregnon	50	50.26 N	3.51 E
Quarles, Pegunungan ⋏	112	2.55 S	119.30 E
Quarrata	66	43.51 N	10.58 E
Quarré-les-Tombes	50	47.22 N	3.59 E
Quarry	222	30.18 N	96.30 W
Quarry Heights	276	41.04 N	73.45 W
Quarryville, Ct., U.S.	207	41.51 N	72.25 W
Quarryville, Pa., U.S.	208	39.53 N	76.09 W
Quartu Sant'Elena	71	39.14 N	9.11 E
Quartz Hill	228	34.39 N	118.13 W
Quartz Lake ⊜	176	70.55 N	80.33 W
Quartz Mountain ∧	202	43.10 N	122.40 W
Quartzsite	200	33.39 N	114.13 W
Quatis	256	22.25 S	44.16 W
Quatre, Isle à I	241h	12.57 N	61.15 W
Quatsino Sound ⊍	182	50.25 N	127.55 W
Quba	84	41.22 N	48.31 E
Qubadlı	84	39.22 N	46.34 E
Qubei	124	28.18 N	86.53 E
Qūchān	128	37.06 N	58.30 E
Quchijie	102	28.03 N	111.53 E
Qudaym	130	35.03 N	38.25 E
Qudi	98	37.06 N	117.15 E
Qudsia Gardens ♠	272a	28.40 N	77.13 E
Quê ≃	152	14.45 S	14.45 E
Queanbeyan	171b	35.21 S	149.14 E
Queanbeyan ≃	171b	35.20 S	149.14 E
Québec	206	46.49 N	71.14 W
Québec □[6]	206	46.50 N	71.20 W
Québec □[4]	176	52.00 N	72.00 W
Quebec Airport ⊠	206	46.47 N	71.23 W
Quebec House ⊥	260	51.14 N	0.05 E
Quebeck	194	35.49 N	85.34 W
Quebra-Anzol ≃	255	19.09 S	47.38 W
Quebra-Cangalha, Serra do ⋏	256	22.55 S	45.10 W
Quebracho	252	31.57 S	57.53 W
Quebrada Seca	240m	18.14 N	65.40 W
Quebradillas	240m	18.29 N	66.56 W
Quebrangulo	250	9.20 S	36.29 W
Quecholac	234	18.57 N	97.40 W
Quechultenango	234	17.25 N	99.13 W
Quecreek	214	40.06 N	79.05 W
Quedal, Cabo ➤	254	40.59 S	73.59 W
Quedas	156	19.30 S	33.29 E
Quedlinburg	54	51.48 N	11.09 E
Queen	214	40.16 N	78.31 W
Queen Alexandra Range ⋏	9	84.00 S	168.00 E
Queen Alia International Airport ⊠	132	31.44 N	35.59 E
Queen Anne	208	38.55 N	75.57 W
Queen Anne Creek ≃	285	40.08 N	74.53 W
Queen Annes □[6]	208	39.03 N	76.04 W
Queen Bess, Mount ∧	182	51.16 N	124.34 W
Queenborough	42	51.26 N	0.45 E
Queen Charlotte	182	53.16 N	132.05 W
Queen Charlotte Bay ⊂	254	51.50 S	60.40 W
Queen Charlotte Islands II	182	53.00 N	132.00 W
Queen Charlotte Mountains ⋏	182	53.00 N	132.00 W
Queen Charlotte Sound ⊍	182	51.30 N	129.30 W
Queen Charlotte Strait ⊍	182	50.50 N	127.25 W
Queen City, Mo., U.S.	194	40.24 N	92.34 W
Queen City, Tx., U.S.	194	33.08 N	94.09 W
Queen Elizabeth II Reservoir ⊜[1]	260	51.23 N	0.24 W
Queen Elizabeth Islands II	16	78.00 N	95.00 W
Queen Fabiola Mountains ⋏	9	71.30 S	35.40 E
Queen Mary ʊ	280	33.45 N	118.12 W
Queen Mary Coast ⩦[2]	9	67.00 S	96.00 E
Queen Mary Reservoir ⊜[1]	260	51.25 N	0.28 W
Queen Maud Gulf ⊂	176	68.25 N	102.30 W
Queen Maud Land ✥[1]	9	72.30 S	12.00 E
Queen Maud Mountains ⋏	9	86.00 S	160.00 W
Queens □[6]	210	40.34 N	73.52 W
Queensbury	44	53.46 N	1.50 W
Queens Channel ⊍, Austl.	164	14.46 S	129.24 E
Queens Channel ⊍, N.T., Can.	176	76.11 N	96.00 W
Queenscliff	169	38.16 S	144.40 E
Queensferry, Scot., U.K.	46	55.59 N	3.25 W
Queensferry, Wales, U.K.	44	53.12 N	3.01 W
Queensland □[3]	160	22.00 S	145.00 E
Queensland Plateau ✣[3]	14	17.00 S	150.00 E
Queens Park ♠, Austl.	274a	33.54 S	151.16 E
Queens Park ♠, On., Can.	275b	43.40 N	79.24 W
Queens Park ♠, Eng., U.K.	262	53.35 N	2.27 W
Queen's Park ♠, Eng., U.K.	262	53.44 N	2.28 W
Queensport	186	45.20 N	61.16 W
Queens Sound ⊍	182	51.55 N	128.11 W
Queenston	284a	43.10 N	79.03 W
Queenston Chippawa Power Canal ≅	284a	43.08 N	79.03 W
Queenstown, Austl.	166	42.05 S	145.33 E
Queenstown, Guy.	246	7.12 N	58.29 W
Queenstown → Cobh, Ire.	48	51.51 N	8.17 W
Queenstown, N.Z.	172	45.02 S	168.40 E
Queenstown, S. Afr.	158	31.52 S	26.52 E
Queenstown, Md., U.S.	208	38.59 N	76.09 W
Queensville	212	44.08 N	79.28 W
Queen Victoria Park ♠	284a	43.05 N	79.05 W
Que'er'ao I	100	28.48 N	121.51 E
Queerhe	104	40.57 N	121.35 E
Queets	224	47.32 N	124.19 W
Queets ≃	224	47.33 N	124.21 W
Queguay Grande ≃	252	32.09 S	58.09 W
Queich ≃	56	49.14 N	8.23 E
Queige	62	45.43 N	6.28 E
Queimada, Ilha I	250	0.10 S	50.50 W
Queimada Nova	250	8.35 S	41.25 W
Queimadas	250	10.58 S	39.38 W
Queimados	256	22.42 S	43.34 W
Queiros, Cap ➤	175f	14.55 S	167.01 E
Quela	152	9.16 S	17.02 E
Quelimane	156	17.53 S	36.51 E
Quelizhen	106	30.54 N	121.26 E
Quelle	52	52.00 N	8.29 E
Quellendorf	54	51.45 N	12.07 E
Quellón	254	43.07 S	73.37 W
Quelo	152	6.27 S	12.48 E
Quelpart Island → Cheju-do I	90	33.20 N	126.30 E
Queluz → Conselheiro Lafaiete, Bra.	255	20.40 S	43.48 W
Queluz, Bra.	256	22.32 S	44.46 W
Queluz, Port.	266c	38.45 N	9.15 W
Quemado, N.M., U.S.	200	34.20 N	108.29 W
Quemado, Tx., U.S.	196	28.56 N	100.38 W
Quemado, Punta de ➤	240p	20.13 N	74.08 W
Quemado de Güines	240p	22.48 N	80.15 W
Quemahoning Reservoir ⊜[1]	214	40.09 N	78.57 W
Quembo ≃	152	14.57 S	20.22 E
Quemchi	254	42.09 S	73.29 W
Quemoy → Chinmen Tao I	100	24.27 N	118.23 E
Quemú Quemú	252	36.03 S	63.33 W
Quend	50	50.19 N	1.38 E
Quend Plage	50	50.19 N	1.33 E
Queñi, Nevado de ∧	254	40.14 S	71.49 W
Quenouilles, Lac aux ⊜	206	46.10 N	74.23 W
Quentin	208	40.17 N	76.26 W
Quepos	236	9.27 N	84.09 W
Quepos, Punta ➤	236	9.23 N	84.10 W
Quequén	252	38.32 S	58.42 W
Querary ≃	246	1.04 N	69.51 W
Quercianella	66	43.27 N	10.22 E
Quercy □[9]	32	44.30 N	1.25 E
Querecotillo	248	4.50 S	80.40 W
Querenburg ✥[8]	263	51.27 N	7.16 E
Querenhorst	54	52.20 N	10.57 E
Querétaro	234	20.36 N	100.23 W
Querétaro □[3]	234	21.00 N	99.55 W
Querfurt	54	51.23 N	11.36 E
Quero	64	45.55 N	11.56 E
Querobabi	232	30.03 N	111.01 W
Quesada, C.R.	236	10.19 N	84.26 W
Quesada, Esp.	34	37.51 N	3.04 W
Queset Brook ≃	283	42.02 N	71.04 W
Queshan	100	32.48 N	114.01 E
Quesnel	182	52.59 N	122.30 W
Quesnel ≃	182	53.00 N	122.30 W
Quesnel Lake ⊜	182	52.32 N	121.05 W
Quesnoy	50	50.43 N	3.00 E
Que Son	110	15.40 N	108.14 E
Questa	200	36.42 N	105.35 W
Questembert	32	47.40 N	2.27 W
Quetico Lake ⊜	190	48.34 N	91.52 W
Quetico Provincial Park ♠	190	48.30 N	91.30 W
Quetta	120	30.12 N	67.00 E
Quettehou	32	49.36 N	1.18 W
Quetzala ≃	234	16.35 N	98.30 W
Quetzaltenango	236	14.50 N	91.31 W
Quetzaltenango □[5]	236	14.45 N	91.40 W
Quevedo	246	1.02 S	79.29 W
Quezaltepeque, El Sal.	236	13.50 N	89.17 W
Quezaltepeque, Guat.	236	14.38 N	89.27 W
Quezon, Pil.	116	15.34 N	120.49 E
Quezon, Pil.	116	14.01 N	122.11 E
Quezon □[4]	116	13.58 N	122.02 E
Quezon City	116	14.38 N	121.03 E
Quezon Memorial ⊥	269f	14.39 N	121.03 E
Qufu	98	35.36 N	117.02 E
Qugou, Zhg.	102	36.10 N	100.56 E
Qugou, Zhg.	105	39.17 N	116.15 E
Quibala	152	10.46 S	14.59 E
Quibaxi	152	8.29 S	14.36 E
Quibdó	246	5.42 N	76.40 W
Quiberon	32	47.29 N	3.07 W
Quiberville	50	49.54 N	0.55 E
Quíbor	246	9.56 N	69.37 W
Quibray Bay ⊂	274a	34.01 S	151.11 E
Quibú ≃	286b	23.05 N	82.27 W
Quiçama, Parque Nacional de ♠	152	9.45 S	13.30 E
Qui Chau	110	19.33 N	105.06 E
Quiches	248	8.25 S	77.27 W
Quickborn	52	53.44 N	9.53 E
Quiculungo	152	8.31 S	15.19 E
Quidapil Point ➤	116	6.49 N	123.57 E
Quidnessett	207	41.37 N	71.27 W
Quidnick	207	41.41 N	71.32 W
Quiechapa ≃	234	16.37 N	95.59 W
Quien Sabe Creek ≃	226	36.43 N	121.09 W
Quiévrain	50	50.24 N	3.41 E
Quiévy	50	50.10 N	3.25 E
Quiindy	252	25.58 S	57.16 W
Quila	232	24.23 N	107.13 W
Quilalí	236	13.34 N	86.02 W
Quilates, Cap ➤	34	35.20 N	3.45 W
Quilcene	224	47.49 N	122.52 W
Quilenda	152	10.33 S	14.22 E
Quilengues	152	14.05 S	14.04 E
Quileute Indian Reservation ✥[4]	224	47.55 N	124.38 W
Quilicura	286e	33.22 S	70.45 W
Quilimarí	252	32.07 S	71.30 W
Quilino	252	30.12 S	64.29 W
Quillabamba	248	12.49 S	72.43 W
Quillacollo	248	17.26 S	66.17 W
Quillagua	248	21.39 S	69.33 W
Quillan	32	42.52 N	2.11 E
Quillebeuf-sur-Seine	50	49.29 N	0.31 E
Quill Lake	184	52.05 N	104.15 W
Quillota	252	32.53 S	71.16 W
Quilmes	258	34.44 S	58.16 W
Quilmes □[5]	288	34.44 S	58.16 W
Quilmes, Aeródromo ⊠	288	34.42 S	58.15 W
Quilombo ≃	256	23.52 S	46.21 W
Quilon	122	8.53 N	76.36 E
Quilotosa Wash ∨	200	32.56 N	112.46 W
Quilpie	166	26.37 S	144.15 E
Quilpué	252	33.03 S	71.27 W
Quilty	48	52.47 N	9.26 W
Quimarí, Alto de ∧	246	8.07 N	76.23 W
Quimbango	152	11.01 S	17.26 E
Quimbaya	246	4.38 N	75.47 W
Quimbele	152	6.28 S	16.13 E
Quimbo	152	13.59 S	16.05 E
Quimbonge	152	8.36 S	18.30 E
Quimbumbe	152	7.50 S	14.03 E
Quimby	198	42.37 N	95.38 W
Quime	248	17.02 S	67.15 W
Quimichis	234	22.21 N	105.32 W
Quimilí	252	27.38 S	62.25 W
Quimper	32	48.00 N	4.06 W
Quimperlé	32	47.52 N	3.33 W
Quinalasag Island I	116	13.56 N	123.38 E
Quinault	224	47.28 N	123.50 W
Quinault ≃	224	47.23 N	124.18 W
Quinault, North Fork ≃	224	47.32 N	123.40 W
Quinault Indian Reservation ✥[4]	224	47.24 N	124.10 W
Quinault Lake ⊜	224	47.28 N	123.52 W
Quinby Inlet ⊂	208	37.28 N	75.40 W
Quincampoix	50	49.32 N	1.11 E
Quince Mil	248	13.16 S	70.38 W
Quinches	248	12.13 S	76.05 W
Quincy, Ca., U.S.	204	39.56 N	120.56 W
Quincy, Fl., U.S.	192	30.35 N	84.35 W
Quincy, Il., U.S.	219	39.56 N	91.24 W
Quincy, Ky., U.S.	218	38.37 N	83.07 W
Quincy, Ma., U.S.	207	42.15 N	71.00 W
Quincy, Mi., U.S.	216	41.56 N	84.53 W
Quincy, Oh., U.S.	216	40.17 N	83.58 W
Quincy, Or., U.S.	224	46.08 N	123.09 W
Quincy, Pa., U.S.	208	39.48 N	77.35 W
Quincy, Wa., U.S.	202	47.14 N	119.51 W
Quincy Bay ⊂	283	42.17 N	70.58 W
Quincy-sous-Sénart	261	48.40 N	2.33 E
Quincy-Voisins	261	48.54 N	2.53 E
Quindanning	168a	33.03 S	116.34 E
Quindío □[5]	246	4.30 N	75.40 W
Quinebaug	207	42.01 N	71.57 W
Quinebaug ≃	207	41.33 N	72.03 W
Quines	252	32.13 S	65.48 W
Quinga	154	15.49 S	40.15 E
Quingey	58	47.06 N	5.53 E
Quingyi ≃	100	31.12 N	118.29 E
Quinhagak	180	59.45 N	161.43 W
Qui Nhon	110	13.46 N	109.14 E
Quiniluban Islands II	116	11.27 N	120.48 E
Quinjenje	152	12.49 S	14.55 E
Quinlan	222	32.55 N	96.08 W
Quinn ≃	204	40.52 N	119.03 W
Quiñones, Arroyo de los ≃	266a	40.33 N	3.34 W
Quinson	62	43.42 N	6.02 E
Quinta da Boa Vista ♠	287a	22.54 S	43.15 W
Quintanar de la Orden	34	39.34 N	3.03 W
Quintana Roo □[3]	232	19.40 N	88.30 W
Quinta Normal	286e	33.27 S	70.42 W
Quinta Normal de Agricultura ʊ[2]	286e	33.27 S	70.42 W
Quinte, Bay of ⊂	212	44.07 N	77.15 W
Quinter	198	39.04 N	100.13 W
Quintero	252	32.47 S	71.32 W
Quintette Mountain ∧	182	54.52 N	120.53 W
Quintin	32	48.24 N	2.55 W
Quintino Sella, Canale ≅	266b	45.29 N	8.38 E
Quinto	34	41.25 N	0.29 W
Quinto ≃	252	34.14 S	64.10 W
Quinto Creek ≃	226	37.11 N	121.02 W

Symbol	English	Deutsch	Español	Français	Português
≃	River	Fluß	Río	Rivière	Rio
≅	Canal	Kanal	Canal	Canal	Canal
⌊	Waterfall, Rapids	Wasserfall, Stromschnellen	Cascada, Rápidos	Chute d'eau, Rapides	Cascata, Rápidos
⊍	Strait	Meeresstraße	Estrecho	Détroit	Estreito
⊂	Bay, Gulf	Bucht, Golf	Bahía, Golfo	Baie, Golfe	Baía, Golfo
⊜	Lake, Lakes	See, Seen	Lago, Lagos	Lac, Lacs	Lago, Lagos
≣	Swamp	Sumpf	Pantano	Marais	Pântano
⍓	Ice Features, Glacier	Eis- und Gletscherformen	Accidentes Glaciales	Formes glaciaires	Acidentes glaciares
⫪	Other Hydrographic Features	Andere Hydrographische Objekte	Otros Elementos Hidrográficos	Autres données hydrographiques	Outros acidentes hidrográficos
✣	Submarine Features	Untermeerische Objekte	Accidentes Submarinos	Formes de relief sous-marin	Acidentes submarinos
□	Political Unit	Politische Einheit	Unidad Politica	Entité politique	Unidade política
ʊ	Cultural Institution	Kulturelle Institution	Institución Cultural	Institution culturelle	Instituição cultural
⊥	Historical Site	Historische Stätte	Sitio Histórico	Site historique	Sitio histórico
♠	Recreational Site	Erholungs- und Ferienort	Sitio de Recreo	Centre de loisirs	Area de Lazer
⊠	Airport	Flughafen	Aeropuerto	Aéroport	Aeroporto
■	Military Installation	Militäranlage	Instalación Militar	Installation militaire	Instalação militar
✥	Miscellaneous	Verschiedenes	Misceláneo	Divers	Diversos

Name	Page	Lat. °′	Long. °′
Quinto de Noviembre, Presa ✦[6]	236	13.59 N	88.44 W
Quinton, Sk., Can.	184	51.23 N	104.24 W
Quinton, N.J., U.S.	208	39.32 N	75.24 W
Quinton, Ok., U.S.	196	35.07 N	95.22 W
Quinto Romano ✦[8]	266b	45.29 N	9.05 E
Quinzano d'Oglio	64	45.19 N	10.00 E
Quinzáu	152	6.51 S	12.46 E
Quinze, Lac des ⊜	190	47.35 N	79.05 W
Quionga	154	10.37 S	40.30 E
Quipapá	250	8.50 S	36.02 W
Quipar ≃	34	38.14 N	1.36 W
Quipeio	152	12.26 S	15.30 E
Quipemba	152	7.12 S	15.06 E
Quipit ≃	116	8.04 N	122.29 E
Quipungo	152	14.51 S	14.30 E
Quiquive ≃	248	14.39 S	67.38 W
Quirauk Mountain ∧	208	39.42 N	77.31 W
Quiriguá ⊥	236	15.17 N	89.04 W
Quirihue	252	36.17 S	72.32 W
Quirima	152	10.48 S	18.09 E
Quirimba, Ilha I	154	12.20 S	40.36 E
Quirimbo	152	10.36 S	14.12 E
Quirindi	166	31.31 S	150.41 E
Quirino □[4]	116	16.25 N	121.35 E
Quirinópolis	255	18.32 S	50.30 W
Quiriquire	246	9.59 N	63.13 W
Quiriri ≃	152	15.13 S	18.47 E
Quiririm	256	23.02 S	45.38 W
Quirke Lake ⊜	190	46.28 N	82.33 W
Quiroga, Esp.	34	42.29 N	7.16 W
Quiroga, Méx.	234	19.40 N	101.32 W
Quirós	252	28.47 S	65.07 W
Quirpon Island I	186	51.35 N	55.25 W
Quirra, Salto di ✦[1]	71	39.35 N	9.33 E
Quissac	62	43.55 N	4.00 E
Quissanga	154	12.25 S	40.29 E
Quissico	156	24.42 S	34.44 E
Quissongo	152	10.01 S	15.07 E
Quistello	64	45.00 N	10.59 E
Quitapa	152	10.23 S	18.14 E
Quitaque	196	34.22 N	101.04 W
Quitasueño ✧[4]	236	14.20 N	81.15 W
Quiterajo	154	11.48 S	40.25 E
Quitilipi	252	26.52 S	60.13 W
Quitman, Ga., U.S.	192	30.47 N	83.33 W
Quitman, Ms., U.S.	194	32.02 N	88.43 W
Quitman, Tx., U.S.	222	32.47 N	95.27 W
Quitman, Lake ⊜[1]	222	32.52 N	95.27 W
Quito	246	0.13 S	78.30 W
Quitzdorf, Speicherbecken ⊜[1]	54	51.17 N	14.45 E
Quivilla	248	9.32 S	76.41 W
Quixadá	250	4.58 S	39.01 W
Quixeramobim	250	5.12 S	39.17 W
Quixeré	250	5.05 S	37.59 W
Quixico	152	7.59 S	14.25 E
Quixinge	152	9.52 S	14.23 E
Quixito ≃	246	4.29 S	70.18 W
Quizenga	152	9.21 S	15.28 E
Qujiadian	89	43.13 N	123.53 E
Qujiang, Zhg.	100	28.15 N	115.45 E
Qujiang, Zhg.	100	24.48 N	113.17 E
Qujiang, Zhg.	100	24.41 N	113.35 E
Qujing	102	25.32 N	103.41 E
Qujiu	102	22.28 N	107.40 E
Qukou	105	39.46 N	117.07 E
Qulay'ah, Ra's al- >	128	28.53 N	48.18 E
Qulin	194	36.35 N	90.14 W
Qulubbā	142	27.45 N	30.50 E
Qulūd, Jabal ∧[2]	140	11.41 N	29.31 E
Qulūṣanā	142	28.21 N	30.44 E
Qulzum, Baḥr al- ⊂	142	29.55 N	32.31 E
Qumar ≃, Zhg.	90	34.42 N	94.50 E
Qumar ≃, Zhg.	120	34.39 N	95.00 E
Qumarlêb	102	34.35 N	95.27 E
Qumbu	158	31.10 S	28.48 E
Qumrān, Khirbat ⊥	132	31.44 N	35.27 E
Qunayfidhah, Nafūd ⩡[8]	128	24.45 N	45.30 E
Qunbush Al-Ḥamrā'	142	29.00 N	30.59 E
Qungtag	120	29.59 N	87.33 E
Qunshen'guan	105	39.49 N	117.59 E
Quobba, Point >	162	24.23 S	113.24 E
Quoich ≃	176	64.00 N	93.30 W
Quoich, Loch ⊜	46	57.04 N	5.17 W
Quoile ≃	48	54.21 N	5.42 W
Quoin Point >	158	34.46 S	19.37 E
Quonochontaug	207	41.21 N	71.43 W
Quorn	166	32.21 S	138.03 E
Quorndon	42	52.45 N	1.09 W
Quoxo ≃	156	22.16 S	24.02 E
Qurayyah, Wādī V	132	30.26 N	34.01 E
Qurayyāt	128	23.17 N	58.55 E
Qurdūd	140	10.17 N	29.56 E
Qurrāṣah	140	14.38 N	32.12 E
Qurūn Ḥarḥash ∧[2]	142	28.09 N	31.42 E
Qūṣ	140	25.55 N	32.45 E
Qusar	84	41.25 N	48.26 E
Quṣayr ad-Daffah ⊥	146	30.20 N	23.57 E
Qūshchī	128	37.59 N	45.03 E
Qushui	107	30.41 N	106.02 E
Qutang	100	32.30 N	120.21 E
Qutbapur ✦[8]	272a	28.35 N	77.01 E
Qutb Minar ʋ[1]	272a	28.32 N	77.11 E
Qutdligssat	176	70.04 N	53.01 W
Quthing	158	30.30 S	27.36 E
Quṭūr	142	30.59 N	30.57 E
Quwaysinā	142	30.34 N	31.09 E
Quxi, Zhg.	100	28.00 N	120.31 E
Quxi, Zhg.	100	23.36 N	116.26 E
Quxia	106	32.06 N	120.09 E
Quxian, Zhg.	100	28.58 N	118.52 E
Quxian, Zhg.	102	30.51 N	106.59 E
Quxingji	98	34.52 N	114.39 E
Quxiong	102	31.09 N	96.00 E
Qüxü	120	29.22 N	90.43 E
Quyang	98	38.34 N	114.42 E
Qūyjāq-e-Bālā	84	39.16 N	47.07 E
Quyon	188	45.31 N	76.14 W
Quyquyó	252	26.14 S	57.01 W
Quzaymah, Jabal ∧	132	30.34 N	36.21 E
Quzhou	98	36.46 N	114.57 E
Quzong	102	30.08 N	96.00 E

R

Name	Page	Lat. °′	Long. °′
Råå	41	56.00 N	12.44 E
Raab → Győr, Magy.	30	47.42 N	17.38 E
Raab, Öst.	60	48.21 N	13.39 E
Raab (Rába) ≃	30	47.42 N	17.38 E
Raabs an der Thaya	61	48.51 N	15.30 E
Raadt ✦[8]	263	51.24 N	6.56 E
Raahe	26	64.41 N	24.29 E
Rääkkylä	26	62.19 N	29.37 E
Raalte	52	52.24 N	6.16 E
Raamsdonksveer	52	51.42 N	4.56 E
Ra'ananna	132	32.11 N	34.53 E
Raas, Pulau I	115a	7.09 S	114.32 E
Raasay I	46	57.23 N	6.04 W
Raasay, Sound of ʮ	46	57.27 N	6.06 W
Raasdorf	264b	48.15 N	16.34 E
Raasiku	76	59.22 N	25.11 E
Rab	36	44.46 N	14.46 E
Rab, Otok I	36	44.47 N	14.45 E
Raba	115b	8.27 S	118.46 E
Rába (Raab) ≃, Europe	30	47.42 N	17.38 E
Raba ≃, Pol.	30	50.09 N	20.30 E
Rabaable	144	8.17 N	48.18 E
Rabaçal ≃	34	41.30 N	7.12 W
Rábade	34	43.07 N	7.37 W
Rábahidvég	61	47.04 N	16.45 E
Rabai	154	3.58 S	39.37 E
Rabak	140	13.09 N	32.44 E
Rabal	164	6.22 S	134.52 E
Rabaraba	164	10.00 S	149.50 E
Rabat, Magreb	148	34.02 N	6.51 W
Rabat, Malta	36	35.52 N	14.25 E
Rabat (Victoria), Malta	36	36.02 N	14.14 E
Rabat □[4]	148	33.57 N	6.50 W
Rabaul	164	4.12 S	152.12 E
Rabbit ≃	216	42.38 N	86.06 W
Rabbit, Lac ⊜	190	47.30 N	78.22 W
Rabbit Creek ≃, S.D., U.S.	198	45.13 N	102.10 W
Rabbit Creek ≃, Tx., U.S.	222	32.26 N	94.47 W
Rabbit Ears Pass)(	200	40.23 N	106.37 W
Rabbit Lake ⊜, On., Can.	190	47.00 N	79.37 W
Rabbit Lake ⊜, Ca., U.S.	228	34.27 N	117.01 W
Rabbs Creek ≃	222	29.59 N	96.55 W
Rábca ≃	61	47.43 N	17.17 E
R'abcevo	76	54.39 N	32.19 E
Rabeira, Ponta da >	287a	22.49 S	43.10 W
Rabenau	54	50.57 N	13.38 E
Rabette, Ruisseau la ≃	261	48.35 N	2.00 E
Rābi', Ash-Shallāl ar- (Fourth Cataract) ∟	140	18.47 N	32.03 E
Rābigh	128	22.48 N	39.01 E
Rabinal	236	15.06 N	90.27 W
Rabiusa ≃	58	46.48 N	9.20 E
Rabka	30	49.36 N	19.56 E
Rabkavi Banhatti	122	16.28 N	75.06 E
Rabnābād Channel ʮ	126	21.50 N	90.19 E
Rabnābād Islands II	126	21.58 N	90.24 E
Râbniţa (Rybnica)	38	47.45 N	29.01 E
Raboćeostrovsk	24	64.59 N	34.48 E
Rabočij	86	59.07 N	79.00 E
Rabong, Gunong ∧	114	4.48 N	102.07 E
Rabotki	80	56.03 N	44.38 E
R'abovskij	80	50.01 N	41.53 E
Rabun Bald ∧	192	34.58 N	83.18 W
Rabwāh	123	31.44 N	72.50 E
Raby	262	53.19 N	3.02 W
Rabyānah ⫧[4]	146	24.15 N	22.00 E
Rabyānah, Ṣaḥrā' ✦[2]	146	24.30 N	21.00 E
Racale	68	39.57 N	18.06 E
Racalmuto	70	37.24 N	13.44 E
Răcari	38	44.38 N	25.45 E
Raccoon ≃	194	41.35 N	93.37 W
Raccoon Creek ≃, N.J., U.S.	208	39.48 N	75.23 W
Raccoon Creek ≃, Oh., U.S.	188	38.43 N	82.11 W
Raccoon Creek ≃, Oh., U.S.	214	40.02 N	82.24 W
Raccoon Creek ≃, Pa., U.S.	214	40.38 N	80.22 W
Raccoon Creek ≃, Pa., U.S.	285	39.48 N	75.23 W
Raccoon Creek ≃, Va., U.S.	208	36.48 N	77.10 W
Raccoon Creek, South Branch ≃	285	39.44 N	75.15 W
Raccoon Creek State Park ♦	214	40.30 N	80.27 W
Raccoon Island I	285	39.49 N	75.22 W
Raccuia	70	38.03 N	14.54 E
Race, Cape >	186	46.40 N	53.10 W
Raceland	194	29.43 N	90.35 W
Race Point >	207	42.04 N	70.14 W
Racette, Lac ⊜	206	46.34 N	74.03 W
Racette, Ruisseau ≃	206	46.36 N	74.04 W
Raceview	273d	26.17 S	28.08 E
Rach'a	76	60.05 N	30.49 E
Rach Gia	110	10.01 N	105.05 E
Rach Gia, Vinh ⊂	110	10.00 N	105.00 E
Rachmanovka	80	51.57 N	49.29 E
Rachmanovo	82	55.44 N	38.37 E
Raciąż	30	52.47 N	20.06 E
Racibórz (Ratibor)	30	50.06 N	18.13 E
Racine, Pa., U.S.	214	40.49 N	80.20 W
Racine, Wi., U.S.	216	42.43 N	87.46 W
Racine □[6]	216	42.45 N	88.05 W
Racines	64	46.52 N	11.18 E
Račinskij chrebet ⋏	84	42.30 N	43.30 E
Rackerby	226	39.26 N	121.20 W
Ráckeve	30	47.10 N	18.56 E
Rackwick	46	58.52 N	3.23 W
R'ad	76	57.56 N	35.04 E
Råda	40	60.00 N	13.36 E
Radama, Nosy II	157b	14.00 S	47.47 E
Radama, Presqu'île >[1]	157b	14.16 S	47.53 E
Rådasjön ⊜	40	59.58 N	13.38 E
Radaur	124	30.02 N	77.09 E
Rădăuți	38	47.51 N	25.55 E
Radbuza ≃	60	49.46 N	13.24 E
Radčenskoje	78	49.48 N	40.32 E
Radcliff	194	37.50 N	85.56 W
Radcliffe	44	53.34 N	2.20 W
Radcliffe on Trent	42	52.57 N	1.03 W
Radda in Chianti	66	43.29 N	11.22 E
Raddusa	70	37.28 N	14.32 E
Råde	26	59.21 N	10.51 E
Radebaugh	279b	40.19 N	79.35 W
Radeberg	54	51.07 N	13.55 E
Radebeul	54	51.06 N	13.40 E
Radeburg	54	51.13 N	13.43 E
Radeče	36	46.04 N	15.11 E
Radegast	54	51.39 N	12.05 E
Radekhiv	78	50.18 N	24.37 E
Radenci	61	46.38 N	16.03 E
Radenthein	64	46.48 N	13.43 E
Radevormwald	56	51.12 N	7.21 E
Radford	192	37.07 N	80.34 W
Rādhānagar, India	126	23.09 N	87.19 E
Rādhānagar, India	272b	22.27 N	88.28 E
Rādhanpur	120	23.50 N	71.36 E
Radici, Foce delle)(	64	44.12 N	10.31 E
Radicofani	66	42.54 N	11.46 E
Radicondoli	66	43.16 N	11.02 E
Rădinești	38	44.48 N	23.46 E
Radiščevo	80	52.51 N	47.53 E
Radisson	184	52.27 N	107.23 W
Radiumbad Brambach	54	50.13 N	12.19 E
Radium Hot Springs	182	50.38 N	116.03 W
Rad'kovka	78	51.06 N	36.58 E
Radlett	42	51.42 N	0.20 W
Radlett Aerodrome ⊠	260	51.43 N	0.19 W
Radley Run ≃	285	39.54 N	75.37 W
Radlje ob Dravi	61	46.37 N	15.13 E
Rådmansö >[1]	40	59.45 N	18.55 E
Radnevo	38	42.18 N	25.56 E
Radnice	60	49.51 N	13.37 E
Radnor, Oh., U.S.	214	40.23 N	83.09 W
Radnor, Pa., U.S.	285	40.02 N	75.21 W
Radnor Forest ∧	42	52.18 N	3.10 W
Radnor Mere ⊜	262	53.17 N	2.14 W
Rădoaia	38	47.44 N	28.09 E
Radofinnikovo	76	59.09 N	30.55 E
Radogošča	76	59.47 N	34.51 E
Radolfzell	58	47.44 N	8.58 E
Radom, Pol.	30	51.25 N	21.10 E
Radom, Il., U.S.	219	38.17 N	89.12 W
Radom □[4]	30	51.25 N	21.15 E
Radomicko	54	52.10 N	14.58 E
Radomir	38	42.33 N	22.58 E
Radomka	78	51.56 N	32.32 E
Radomka ≃	30	51.43 N	21.26 E
Radomsko	30	51.05 N	19.25 E
Radomyshl'	78	50.30 N	29.14 E
Radomyśl Wielki	30	50.12 N	21.16 E
Radošice	60	49.33 N	13.39 E
Radoškoviči	76	54.09 N	27.14 E
Radotin	30	50.00 N	14.22 E
Radovicy	80	55.06 N	39.32 E
Radoviš	38	41.38 N	22.28 E
Radovljica	36	46.21 N	14.11 E
Radstadt	64	47.23 N	13.27 E
Radstädter Tauern)(	64	47.15 N	13.34 E
Radstock	42	51.18 N	2.28 W
Radstock, Cape >	162	33.12 S	134.20 E
Raduha ∧	61	46.25 N	14.45 E
Radul'	78	51.49 N	30.42 E
Radun'	76	54.03 N	25.00 E
Radushne	78	47.49 N	33.29 E
Radutino	76	52.39 N	33.57 E
Radvaniči	76	52.02 N	24.02 E
Radviliškis	76	55.50 N	23.31 E
Radville	184	49.27 N	104.17 W
Radway	182	54.04 N	112.57 W
Radykovskoje	80	45.56 N	41.57 E
Radymno	30	49.57 N	22.48 E
Radyr	42	51.31 N	3.15 W
Radziejów	30	52.38 N	18.32 E
Radzyń Chełmiński	30	53.24 N	18.56 E
Radzyń Podlaski	30	51.48 N	22.38 E
Rae	176	62.50 N	116.03 W
Rae ≃	176	67.55 N	115.30 W
Rāe Bareli	124	26.13 N	81.14 E
Raeford	192	34.58 N	79.13 W
Rae Isthmus ⩡[3]	176	66.55 N	86.10 W
Rāenda	126	22.18 N	89.51 E
Raeren	56	50.41 N	6.07 E
Raesfeld	52	51.46 N	6.50 E
Raeside, Lake ⊜	162	29.30 S	122.00 E
Rae Strait ʮ	176	68.45 N	95.00 W
Raetihi	172	39.26 S	175.17 E
Rafaela	252	31.16 S	61.29 W
Rafael Calzada	258	34.48 S	58.22 W
Rafael Castillo	288	34.43 S	58.37 W
Rafael Perazza	258	34.32 S	56.47 W
Rafaḥ	132	31.18 N	34.15 E
Rafaï	152	4.58 N	23.56 E
Rafalivka	78	51.19 N	25.59 E
Raffadali	70	37.24 N	13.32 E
Raffelberg, Rennbahn ♦	263	51.26 N	6.50 E
Raffili Mission	140	6.53 N	27.58 E
Rafḥā'	128	29.42 N	43.30 E
Rafinesque, Mount ∧[2]	210	42.47 N	73.37 W
Rafsanjān	128	30.24 N	56.01 E
Raft ≃	202	42.37 N	113.15 W
Raft River Mountains ⋏	200	41.55 N	113.25 W
Rafz	58	47.37 N	8.32 E
Raga	140	8.28 N	25.41 E
Ragada	64	46.10 N	10.38 E
Ragang, Mount ∧	116	7.43 N	124.32 E
Ragay	116	13.49 N	122.47 E
Ragay Gulf ⊂	116	13.30 N	122.45 E
Rågeleje	41	56.06 N	12.10 E
Rägelin	54	53.01 N	12.38 E
Ragewitz	54	51.14 N	12.51 E
Ragged, Mount ∧	162	33.27 S	123.25 E
Ragged Island I	238	22.12 N	75.44 W
Ragged Island Range II	238	22.40 N	75.54 W
Ragged Lake ⊜	212	45.28 N	78.38 W
Ragged Top Mountain ∧	200	41.27 N	105.20 W
Raghabpur	272b	22.25 N	88.21 E
Rāghogarh	124	24.27 N	77.12 E
Raghumāthbāri	126	22.22 N	87.47 E
Raghunāthpur, Bngl.	126	23.12 N	89.31 E
Raghunāthpur, India	126	23.33 N	86.40 E
Raglan, Austl.	170	33.26 S	149.36 E
Raglan, N.Z.	172	37.48 S	174.53 E
Raglan, Wales, U.K.	42	51.47 N	2.51 W
Ragland	194	33.44 N	86.09 W
Ragnitz	61	46.50 N	15.35 E
Rago Nasjonalpark ♦	24	67.26 N	16.00 E
Ragow	264a	52.17 N	13.33 E
Ragozino	86	59.15 N	77.52 E
Rågsveden	40	60.29 N	14.05 E
Raguda, Ghubbet ⊂	144	10.45 N	46.34 E
Raguhn	54	51.42 N	12.17 E
Raguli	80	45.38 N	43.42 E
Ragusa → Dubrovnik, Hrv.	38	42.38 N	18.07 E
Ragusa, It.	70	36.55 N	14.44 E
Ragusa □[4]	70	36.55 N	14.36 E
Raguva	76	55.34 N	24.36 E
Raha	112	4.51 S	122.43 E
Rahad, Nahr ar- (Rahad) ≃	140	14.28 N	33.31 E
Rahad al-Bardī	140	11.18 N	23.53 E
Rahad Game Reserve ✦[4]	140	13.06 N	35.05 E
Rahaṭ, Ḥarrat ⩡[9]	144	22.20 N	40.05 E
Rahatgaon	124	22.15 N	77.14 E
Rāhatgarh	124	23.47 N	78.22 E
Raḥbah	130	34.30 N	36.09 E
Rahden	52	52.26 N	8.36 E
Rahimatpur	122	17.36 N	74.12 E
Rahīm Ki Bāzār	120	24.19 N	69.09 E
Rahīmyār Khān	120	28.25 N	70.18 E
Rahlstedt ✦[8]	52	53.36 N	10.09 E
Rahm	263	51.26 N	6.26 E
Rahm ✦[8], Dtsch.	263	51.32 N	7.23 E
Rahm ✦[8], Dtsch.	263	51.21 N	6.47 E
Rahmede ≃	263	51.17 N	7.41 E
Rahmer See ⊜	264a	52.45 N	13.25 E
Rahns	285	40.12 N	75.27 W
Rahnsdorf ✦[8]	264a	52.26 N	13.42 E
Rāhon	123	31.03 N	76.07 E
Rahotu	172	39.20 S	173.48 E
Rahouia	34	35.32 N	1.01 E
Rāhwāli	123	32.15 N	74.10 E
Rahway	210	40.36 N	74.16 W
Rahway ≃	276	40.35 N	74.12 W
Rahway, East Branch ≃	276	40.42 N	74.18 W
Rahway, Robinsons Branch ≃	276	40.37 N	74.17 W
Rahway, South Branch ≃	276	40.36 N	74.17 W
Rahway, West Branch ≃	276	40.42 N	74.18 W
Rahway River Parkway ♦	276	40.41 N	74.19 W
Raiano	66	42.06 N	13.49 E
Raiatea I	14	16.50 S	151.25 W
Rāichūr	122	16.12 N	77.22 E
Raidak ≃	124	26.22 N	89.45 E
Rāidighi	126	22.00 N	88.26 E
Raiding	61	47.34 N	16.32 E
Raiford	192	30.03 N	82.14 W
Raiganj	124	25.37 N	88.07 E
Raigarh	122	21.54 N	83.24 E
Raijua, Pulau I	112	10.37 S	121.36 E
Rāikot	123	30.39 N	75.36 E
Railroad	208	39.46 N	76.42 W
Railroad Canyon Reservoir ⊜[1]	228	33.42 N	117.16 W
Railroad Creek ≃	224	48.12 N	120.36 W
Rail Road Flat	226	38.20 N	120.30 W
Railroad Valley V	204	38.25 N	115.40 W
Railton	166	41.21 S	146.25 E
Raimangal ≃	126	21.47 N	89.08 E
Rain, Dtsch.	56	48.41 N	10.55 E
Rain → Riva di Tures, It.	64	46.57 N	12.04 E
Rainbach im Innkreis	60	48.27 N	13.32 E
Rainbow	228	33.24 N	117.10 W
Rainbow Bridge ✦[5]	284a	43.05 N	79.04 W
Rainbow Bridge National Monument ♦	200	37.06 N	110.57 W
Rainbow Falls ∟	182	52.23 N	119.59 W
Rainbow Lakes	276	40.52 N	74.28 W
Rainbow Park ♦	278	41.46 N	87.33 W
Rainbow Shores	212	43.37 N	76.12 W
Rainelle	188	37.58 N	80.46 W
Rainford	44	53.30 N	2.48 W
Rainham	42	51.23 N	0.36 E
Rainham ✦[8]	260	51.31 N	0.12 E
Rainhill	262	53.26 N	2.46 W
Rainhill Stoops	262	53.24 N	2.45 W
Rainier, Or., U.S.	224	46.05 N	122.56 W
Rainier, Wa., U.S.	224	46.53 N	122.41 W
Rainier, Mount ∧	224	46.52 N	121.46 W
Rainow	262	53.17 N	2.04 W
Rains □[6]	222	32.50 N	95.47 W
Rainsboro	218	39.13 N	83.25 W
Rainsford Island I	283	42.18 N	70.57 W
Rainworth	44	53.07 N	1.08 W
Rainy ≃, N.A.	184	48.50 N	94.41 W
Rainy ≃, Mi., U.S.	190	45.27 N	84.13 W
Rainy Lake ⊜, On., Can.	212	45.32 N	79.30 W
Rainy Lake ⊜, N.A.	184	48.42 N	93.10 W
Rainy Pass)(	224	48.32 N	120.39 W
Rainy River	190	48.43 N	94.34 W
Rāipur, Bngl.	126	23.03 N	90.46 E
Raipur, India	122	21.14 N	81.38 E
Raipur, India	124	30.19 N	78.06 E
Raipur, India	126	22.48 N	86.57 E
Raipur, India	272a	28.32 N	77.20 E
Raipur, India	272b	22.24 N	88.09 E
Rāipura	126	23.59 N	90.53 E
Raipur Uplands ⋏[1]	122	21.00 N	82.20 E
Rairākhol	120	21.04 N	84.21 E
Ra'īs	128	23.34 N	38.36 E
Raisdorf	54	54.17 N	10.16 E
Raisen	124	23.20 N	77.48 E
Ráisi, Punta >	70	38.11 N	13.06 E
Raisin	226	36.36 N	119.54 W
Raisin ≃, On., Can.	206	45.08 N	74.29 W
Raisin ≃, Mi., U.S.	216	41.53 N	83.20 W
Rāisinghnagar	123	29.32 N	73.27 E
Raismes	50	50.23 N	3.29 E
Raita	126	24.07 N	88.57 E
Raitenbuch	60	49.01 N	11.08 E
Raití	236	14.35 N	85.02 W
Raivavae I	14	23.52 S	147.40 W
Rāiwind	123	31.15 N	74.13 E
Raizeux	261	48.37 N	1.41 E
Raja, Gili I	115a	7.14 S	113.47 E
Raja, Ujung >	114	3.45 N	96.33 E
Rājābāri	126	23.23 N	90.28 E
Rajabasa	112	5.25 S	104.24 E
Rājābhāt Khāwa	124	26.37 N	89.32 E
Rājābhita	126	23.52 N	86.20 E
Rājahmundry	122	16.59 N	81.47 E
Rajāj	140	10.55 N	24.43 E
Rāja Jang	123	31.13 N	74.16 E
Raja-Jooseppi	24	68.28 N	28.21 E
Rājākhera	124	26.55 N	78.11 E
Rājaldesar	120	28.02 N	74.28 E
Rājāluka	126	22.09 N	86.38 E
Rajamäki	26	60.32 N	24.45 E
Rājampet	122	14.11 N	79.10 E
Rajang ≃	112	2.04 N	111.12 E
Rājanpur	120	29.06 N	70.19 E
Rājapālaiyam	122	9.27 N	77.34 E
Rājāpur, Bngl.	126	22.34 N	90.09 E
Rājāpur, India	122	16.40 N	73.31 E
Rājāpur, India	124	25.23 N	81.09 E
Rājāpur, India	272b	22.39 N	88.11 E
Rājapur Canal ≋	272b	22.30 N	88.07 E
Rājasthān □[3]	120	27.00 N	74.00 E
Rājauri	123	33.23 N	74.18 E
Rājbāri, Bngl.	124	23.46 N	89.39 E
Rājbāri, India	126	22.25 N	88.48 E
Raj Bhavan ʋ	272b	22.34 N	88.21 E
Rājbirāj	124	26.32 N	86.44 E
Rajčichinsk	89	49.46 N	129.25 E
Rājendrapur	126	24.06 N	90.27 E
Rajevskij	86	54.04 N	54.56 E
Rāj Gangpur	124	22.11 N	84.36 E
Rājganj ≃[1]	126	22.21 N	90.16 E
Rājgarh, India	123	28.38 N	75.23 E
Rājgarh, India	124	23.56 N	76.58 E
Rājgarh, India	124	27.14 N	76.38 E
Rajghat ʋ[1]	272a	28.39 N	77.15 E
Rājgīr	124	25.02 N	85.25 E
Rajgorod	80	48.26 N	44.55 E
Rajgorodok	80	48.48 N	52.53 E
Rajgród	30	53.44 N	22.42 E
Rājhāt	272b	22.56 N	88.21 E
Rajhrad	61	49.05 N	16.37 E
Rājibpur	272b	22.49 N	88.34 E
Rajik	112	2.36 S	105.56 E
Rajka	30	48.00 N	17.12 E
Rājkot	120	22.18 N	70.47 E
Rajkuzi	265a	59.47 N	29.57 E
Rājmahāl	124	25.03 N	87.50 E
Rājmahāl Hills ⋏[2]	124	24.40 N	87.25 E
Rājnagar	126	23.57 N	87.19 E
Rāj Nāndgaon	120	21.06 N	81.02 E
Rajokri ✦[8]	272a	28.31 N	77.07 E
Raj-Oleksandrivka	83	48.48 N	37.51 E
Rājpipla	120	21.47 N	73.34 E
Rājpur, India	120	21.56 N	75.08 E
Rājpur, India	126	22.25 N	88.25 E
Rājpur, India	272a	28.44 N	77.22 E
Rājpur ✦[8]	272a	28.41 N	77.12 E
Rājpura	124	30.29 N	76.36 E
Rājshāhi	124	24.22 N	88.36 E
Rājshāhi □[5]	124	25.15 N	89.15 E
Rājula	122	21.03 N	71.26 E
Raka	124	29.26 N	85.50 E
Raka ≃	124	29.24 N	87.58 E
Rakaia	172	43.45 S	172.01 E
Rakaia ≃	172	43.56 S	172.13 E
Rakamaz	30	48.08 N	21.30 E
Rakaposhi ∧	123	36.10 N	74.30 E
Rakata, Pulau I	115a	6.10 S	105.26 E
Rakha La)(	124	27.53 N	87.34 E
Rakhawt, Wādī V	144	17.40 N	51.40 E
Rakhine □[8]	110	19.00 N	94.15 E
Rakhiv	78	48.03 N	24.12 E
Rakhmanivka	78	47.48 N	33.13 E
Rakhneh	128	31.39 N	59.13 E
Rakhni	120	30.03 N	69.55 E
Rakhny-Lisovi	78	48.47 N	28.29 E
Rakhshān ≃	128	27.10 N	63.25 E
Rākīn	132	31.14 N	35.42 E
Rakitnoje, Ross.	78	50.51 N	35.50 E
Rakitnoje, Ross.	89	45.36 N	134.17 E
Rakke	76	58.59 N	26.15 E
Rakkestad	26	59.26 N	11.21 E
Rakoniewice	30	52.10 N	16.16 E
Rakops	156	21.00 S	24.32 E
Rákoscsaba ✦[8]	264c	47.29 N	19.17 E
Rákoshegy ✦[8]	264c	47.28 N	19.14 E
Rákoskeresztúr ✦[8]	264c	47.29 N	19.15 E
Rákoskert ✦[8]	264c	47.28 N	19.19 E
Rákosliget ✦[8]	264c	47.30 N	19.16 E
Rákospalota ✦[8]	264c	47.34 N	19.08 E
Rákos-patak ≃	264c	47.33 N	19.04 E
Rákosszentmihály ✦[8]	264c	47.32 N	19.11 E
Rakovnická plošina ⋏[1]	54	50.08 N	13.47 E
Rakovník	54	50.05 N	13.43 E
Rakovski	38	42.18 N	24.58 E
Rakša	80	53.33 N	41.37 E
Raksakiny	86	60.37 N	73.52 E
Rakuša	80	47.03 N	52.47 E
Råkvåg	26	63.46 N	10.05 E
Rakvere	76	59.22 N	26.20 E
Rakwa	164	2.42 S	134.30 E
Raleigh, Nf., Can.	186	51.34 N	55.44 W
Raleigh, Ms., U.S.	194	32.02 N	89.31 W
Raleigh, N.C., U.S.	192	35.46 N	78.38 W
Raleigh Hills	224	45.29 N	122.45 W
Raleighvallen Voltz Berg, Natuurreservaat ♦, Sur.	246	4.45 N	56.05 W
Raleighvallen Voltz Berg, Natuurreservaat ♦, Sur.	250	4.50 N	55.10 W
Ralik Chain II	14	8.00 N	167.00 E
Ralls	196	33.40 N	101.23 W
Ralls □[6]	219	39.34 N	91.30 W
Ralsko ∧	54	50.42 N	14.47 E
Ralston, Ne., U.S.	198	41.12 N	96.02 W
Ralston, Pa., U.S.	210	41.31 N	76.57 W
Ram ≃	182	52.23 N	115.25 W
Rama, Nic.	236	12.09 N	84.15 W
Rama, Yis.	132	32.56 N	35.22 E
Rama ≃	236	12.08 N	84.13 W
Ramacca	70	37.23 N	14.42 E
Rāmachandrapuram	122	16.51 N	82.01 E
Ramādah	144	13.38 N	43.56 E
Ramah	200	35.07 N	108.29 W
Ramah Indian Reservation ✦[4]	200	34.50 N	108.25 W
Rama Indian Reserve ✦[4]	212	44.41 N	79.15 W
Ramales de la Victoria	34	43.15 N	3.27 W
Rām Allāh	132	31.54 N	35.12 E
Rāman	123	29.58 N	74.58 E
Rāmanagaram	122	12.43 N	77.18 E
Rāmanāthapuram	122	9.23 N	78.50 E
Ramānāthpur	272b	22.41 N	88.14 E
Ramanbāti	272b	22.47 N	88.08 E
Rāmānuj Ganj	124	23.48 N	83.42 E
Ramapo	276	41.08 N	74.10 W
Ramapo ≃	276	40.58 N	74.17 W
Ramapo Lake ⊜	276	41.02 N	74.16 W
Ramapo Mountains ⋏	276	41.08 N	74.12 W
Ramas, Cape >	122	15.07 N	73.55 E
Ramasaig	46	57.24 N	6.44 W
Ramasucha	76	52.46 N	33.33 E
Ramat Gan	132	32.05 N	34.49 E
Ramat HaSharon	132	32.09 N	34.50 E
Ramat HaShofét	132	32.37 N	35.06 E
Ramathlabama	156	25.40 S	25.35 E
Ramatuelle	62	43.13 N	6.37 E
Rama VI Bridge ✦[5]	269a	13.48 N	100.31 E
Rāmban	123	33.15 N	75.15 E
Rambervillers	58	48.21 N	6.38 E
Rambi I	175g	16.30 S	179.59 E
Rambipuji	115a	8.13 S	113.36 E
Rambleton Acres	208	39.39 N	75.38 W
Ramblewood	285	39.55 N	74.56 W
Rambouillet	50	48.39 N	1.50 E
Rambouillet, Château de ⊥	261	48.39 N	1.49 E
Rambouillet, Forêt de ♦	261	48.40 N	1.50 E
Rambutyo Island I	164	2.20 S	147.50 E
Rām Dās	123	31.58 N	74.54 E
Rāmdia	126	23.42 N	89.32 E
Rāmdurg	122	15.57 N	75.18 E
Ramea	186	47.31 N	57.23 W
Ramea Islands II	186	47.31 N	57.21 W
Rāmechhāp	124	27.20 N	86.05 E
Rame Head >, S. Afr.	158	31.48 S	29.22 E
Rame Head >, Eng., U.K.	42	50.19 N	4.13 W
Rämen ⊜	40	60.18 N	15.10 E
Ramenje, Ross.	76	60.17 N	43.46 E
Ramenje, Ross.	82	56.34 N	37.13 E
Ramenka ✦[8]	265b	55.41 N	37.30 E
Ramenskoje	82	55.34 N	38.14 E
Ramer	194	32.03 N	86.13 W
Ramerupt	50	48.31 N	4.18 E
Rameški	76	57.21 N	36.03 E
Rāmeswaram	122	9.17 N	79.18 E
Ramey	214	40.48 N	78.24 W
Rāmganj	126	23.06 N	90.51 E
Rāmgarh, Bngl.	120	22.59 N	91.44 E
Rāmgarh, India	120	27.22 N	70.30 E
Rāmgarh, India	120	27.15 N	75.11 E
Rāmgarh, India	124	23.38 N	85.31 E
Rāmgarh, India	124	24.34 N	87.15 E
Rāmgarh, India	126	22.42 N	87.04 E
Rāmgarh Hills ⋏[2]	124	22.50 N	83.10 E
Ram Head >	240m	18.18 N	64.42 W
Rāmhormoz	128	31.16 N	49.36 E
Ramingining	164	12.19 S	135.03 E
Ramingstein	64	47.04 N	13.50 E
Ramírez, Méx.	196	27.20 N	100.58 W
Ramírez, Méx.	196	25.57 N	97.46 W
Ramiriquí	246	5.24 N	73.20 W
Ramis ≃	144	7.59 N	41.34 E
Rāmjībanpur	126	22.50 N	87.37 E
Rāmkānāli	126	23.35 N	86.45 E
Raml, Qārat ar- ∧[2]	142	30.02 N	30.39 E
Ramla	132	31.55 N	34.52 E
Ramlu ∧	144	13.24 N	41.51 E
Ramm, Jabal ∧	132	29.35 N	35.24 E
Rämmen	40	60.07 N	14.08 E
Râmna ≃	38	45.39 N	27.19 E
Rāmnagar, India	123	32.49 N	75.19 E
Rāmnagar, India	124	25.17 N	83.02 E
Rāmnagar, India	124	29.24 N	79.07 E
Rāmnagar, India	126	21.41 N	87.33 E
Rāmnagar, India	272b	22.23 N	88.19 E
Ramnäs	40	59.46 N	16.12 E
Râmnicu Sărat	38	45.23 N	27.03 E
Râmnicu Vâlcea	38	45.06 N	24.22 E
Ramo	144	6.42 N	41.23 E
Ramon'	78	51.54 N	39.20 E
Ramon, Har ∧	132	30.30 N	34.38 E
Ramon, Makhtésh ⩡[7]	132	30.36 N	34.49 E
Ramon, Naḥal V	132	30.36 N	34.55 E
Ramona, Ca., U.S.	228	33.02 N	116.52 W
Ramona, Ok., U.S.	196	36.31 N	95.55 W
Ramona, S.D., U.S.	198	44.07 N	97.12 W
Ramor, Lough ⊜	48	53.49 N	7.05 W
Ramos	234	22.50 N	101.55 W
Ramos ✦[8]	287a	22.51 S	43.15 W
Ramos ≃[1]	150	5.08 N	5.22 E
Ramosch	58	46.50 N	10.22 E
Ramos Island I	116	8.06 N	117.02 E
Ramos Mejía	258	34.38 S	58.34 W
Ramot	132	32.46 N	35.40 E
Ramotswa	156	24.56 S	25.50 E
Rāmpāl	126	22.34 N	89.39 E
Rampart	180	65.30 N	150.11 W
Ramparts ≃	180	66.11 N	129.03 W
Rampillon	50	48.33 N	3.04 E
Rampside	44	54.05 N	3.10 W
Rāmpur, India	120	31.27 N	77.38 E
Rāmpur, India	123	29.49 N	77.27 E
Rāmpur, India	124	28.49 N	79.02 E
Rāmpura	120	24.28 N	75.26 E
Rāmpura Phūl	123	30.17 N	75.14 E
Rampur Boalia → Rājshāhi	124	24.22 N	88.36 E
Rāmpur Hāt	126	24.10 N	87.47 E
Ramrath	263	51.06 N	6.41 E
Ramree Island I	110	19.06 N	93.48 E
Rāmsāgar	126	23.05 N	87.17 E
Ramsau	64	47.36 N	12.54 E
Ramsay Range ⋏	162	18.31 S	127.03 E
Ramsbeck	56	51.18 N	8.24 E
Ramsberg	40	59.46 N	15.17 E
Ramsbottom	44	53.40 N	2.19 W
Ramsden Bellhouse	260	51.37 N	0.29 E
Ramsden Heath	260	51.38 N	0.28 E
Ramsdorf	52	51.54 N	6.55 E
Ramsele	26	63.33 N	16.29 E
Ramsenthal	60	50.01 N	11.35 E
Ramseur	192	35.44 N	79.39 W
Ramsey, I. of Man	44	54.20 N	4.21 W
Ramsey, Eng., U.K.	42	51.56 N	1.14 E
Ramsey, Eng., U.K.	42	52.27 N	0.07 W
Ramsey, Il., U.S.	219	39.08 N	89.06 W
Ramsey, N.J., U.S.	210	41.03 N	74.08 W
Ramsey Bay ⊂	44	54.20 N	4.20 W
Ramsey Brook ≃	276	41.02 N	74.08 W
Ramsey Creek ≃	219	39.03 N	89.04 W
Ramsey Island I	42	51.52 N	5.10 W
Ramsey Lake ⊜	190	47.15 N	82.16 W
Ramsey Lake State Park ♦	219	39.10 N	89.08 W
Ramsgate, Austl.	274a	33.59 S	151.08 E
Ramsgate, S. Afr.	158	30.55 S	30.20 E
Ramsgate, Eng., U.K.	42	51.20 N	1.25 E
Rāmshai	124	26.44 N	88.51 E
Rāmshīr	128	30.54 N	49.24 E
Ramshorn Peak ∧	202	45.09 N	111.06 W
Rämshyttan	40	60.18 N	15.13 E
Ramsjö	26	62.11 N	15.39 E
Ramsloh	52	53.06 N	7.40 E
Ramstein	56	49.27 N	7.33 E
Rāmtek	120	21.24 N	79.20 E
Rāmu, Bngl.	120	21.25 N	92.07 E
Ramu, Kenya	154	3.56 N	41.13 E
Ramu ≃	164	4.02 S	144.41 E
Ramuševo	76	57.50 N	31.37 E
Ramvik	26	62.49 N	17.51 E
Ramville, Îlet I	240e	14.42 N	60.53 W
Ramygala	76	55.31 N	24.18 E
Ramzaj	80	53.18 N	44.44 E
Rānāghāt	126	23.11 N	88.35 E
Rana Kao, Volcán ∧[1]	174z	27.11 S	109.27 W
Ranalt	64	47.02 N	11.13 E
Rāna Pratāp Sāgar ⊜[1]	120	24.50 N	75.35 E
Rånäs	40	59.48 N	18.17 E
Ranau	112	5.58 N	116.41 E
Ranau, Danau ⊜	112	4.50 S	103.55 E
Ranbīrsinghpura	123	32.38 N	74.44 E
Ranburne	194	33.31 N	85.20 W
Rancabali	115a	7.08 S	107.21 E
Rancagua	252	34.10 S	70.45 W
Rancah	115a	7.12 S	108.30 E
Rance ≃	32	48.31 N	1.59 W
Rancevo, Ross.	76	56.56 N	34.03 E
Rancevo, Ross.	76	56.40 N	33.02 E
Rancharia	255	22.15 S	50.55 W
Rancheria	180	60.05 N	130.40 W
Ranchería ≃	246	11.34 N	72.54 W
Rancheria Rock ∧	202	44.53 N	120.08 W
Ranches of Taos	200	36.22 N	105.37 W
Ranchester	202	44.54 N	107.09 W
Rānchi	124	23.21 N	85.20 E
Ranchillos	252	26.57 S	65.03 W
Rānchi Plateau ⋏[1]	124	23.20 N	84.50 E
Ranch Lake ⊜	184	52.30 N	104.46 W
Rancho Colorado, Presa de ⊜[1]	286a	19.29 N	99.17 W
Rancho Cordova	226	38.35 N	121.18 W
Rancho Del Mar	226	38.10 N	122.15 W
Rancho Nuevo, Méx.	196	26.22 N	99.54 W
Rancho Nuevo, Méx.	234	23.12 N	97.48 W
Rancho Palos Verdes	228	33.45 N	118.24 W
Rancho Rinconado	226	37.18 N	122.01 W
Rancho Santa Fe	228	33.01 N	117.12 W
Rancho Veloz	240p	22.53 N	80.23 W
Ranchuelo	240p	22.23 N	80.09 W
Ranco, Lago ⊜	254	40.14 S	72.24 W
Rancocas	208	40.00 N	74.52 W
Rancocas Creek ≃	285	40.02 N	74.59 W
Rancocas Creek, North Branch ≃	208	40.00 N	74.52 W
Rancocas Creek, South Branch ≃	208	40.00 N	74.52 W
Rancocas Creek, Southwest Branch ≃	285	39.57 N	74.48 W
Rancocas Heights	285	39.59 N	74.51 W
Rancocas State Park ♦	285	40.00 N	74.50 W
Rancocas Woods	285	39.59 N	74.51 W
Rancul	252	35.03 S	64.42 W
Rand	166	35.36 S	146.35 E
Rand (Germiston) Airport ⊠	273d	26.15 S	28.09 E
Randa	58	46.07 N	7.47 E
Randall Lake ⊜	216	41.57 N	85.02 W
Randall Park Mall ✦[9]	279a	41.26 N	81.32 W
Randalls Island I	276	40.48 N	73.55 W
Randallstown	284b	39.22 N	76.48 W
Randalstown	48	54.45 N	6.19 W
Randan	32	46.01 N	3.21 E
Rāndaveswar	126	23.43 N	87.17 E
Randazzo	70	37.53 N	14.57 E
Randbøl	41	55.42 N	9.16 E
Randburg	273d	26.06 S	27.59 E
Randers	26	56.28 N	10.03 E
Randfontein	158	26.11 S	27.42 E
Randfontein □[5]	273d	26.13 S	27.40 E
Randgate	273d	26.11 S	27.41 E
Randhurst ✦[9]	278	42.05 N	87.56 W
Randle	224	46.32 N	121.57 W
Randleman	192	35.49 N	79.48 W
Randlett	196	34.10 N	98.27 W
Randolph, Az., U.S.	200	32.55 N	111.30 W
Randolph, Me., U.S.	188	44.13 N	69.46 W
Randolph, Ma., U.S.	207	42.09 N	71.02 W
Randolph, Ne., U.S.	198	42.22 N	97.21 W
Randolph, N.Y., U.S.	210	42.09 N	78.58 W
Randolph, Oh., U.S.	214	41.01 N	81.14 W
Randolph, Ut,. U.S.	200	41.39 N	111.10 W
Randolph, Vt., U.S.	188	43.55 N	72.39 W
Randolph, Wi., U.S.	190	43.32 N	89.00 W
Randolph □[6], In., U.S.	218	40.10 N	85.00 W
Randolph □[6], Mo., U.S.	219	39.22 N	92.20 W
Randolph Air Force Base ■	196	29.32 N	98.16 W
Randolph Hills	284c	39.03 N	77.05 W
Randolph Village	284c	38.53 N	76.52 W
Random Island I	186	48.08 N	53.45 W
Random Lake	190	43.33 N	87.57 W
Randow ≃	54	53.41 N	14.04 E
Randowaya	164	1.52 S	136.31 E
Randowbruch ≡	54	53.15 N	14.10 E
Randsburg	228	35.22 N	117.39 W
Randse Afrikaanse Universiteit ʋ[2]	273d	26.11 S	27.50 E
Randsfjorden ⊜	26	60.25 N	10.24 E
Rand Stadium ♦	273d	26.14 S	28.03 E
Randublatung	115a	7.12 S	111.23 E
Randudongkal	115a	7.06 S	109.19 E
Randwick	170	33.55 S	151.15 E
Randwick Racecourse ♦	274a	33.54 S	151.14 E
Råneå	26	65.52 N	22.18 E
Ranelagh	258	34.48 S	58.12 W
Rāner	123	28.53 N	73.17 E
Ranérou	150	15.18 N	13.58 W
Rāneswar	126	24.02 N	87.25 E
Raneue	114	5.03 N	95.20 E
Ranford	168a	32.48 S	116.31 E
Ranfurly, N.Z.	172	45.08 S	170.06 E
Ranfurly, Scot., U.K.	46	55.52 N	4.33 W
Rangae	114	6.17 N	101.44 E
Rāngāmāti	120	22.38 N	92.12 E
Rangantemiang	112	0.35 S	113.19 E
Rangas, Tanjung >	112	2.38 S	118.49 E
Rangasa, Tanjung >	112	3.33 S	118.56 E
Rangaunu Bay ⊂	172	34.50 S	173.15 E
Range Creek ≃	200	39.18 N	110.04 W
Range Indian Reserve ✦[4]	182	49.09 N	119.50 W
Rangeley	188	44.57 N	70.38 W
Rangely	200	40.05 N	108.48 W
Ranger	196	32.28 N	98.40 W
Ranger Lake ⊜	190	46.54 N	83.35 W
Rangersdorf	64	46.51 N	12.58 E
Ranghe	100	33.43 N	112.51 E
Rangia	120	26.28 N	91.38 E
Rangiora	172	43.18 S	172.36 E
Rangitaiki ≃	172	37.54 S	176.53 E
Rangitata ≃	172	44.12 S	171.30 E
Rangitikei ≃	172	40.18 S	175.14 E
Rangitukia	172	37.46 S	178.27 E
Rangkasbitung	115a	6.21 S	106.15 E
Rangkul'	85	38.29 N	74.22 E
Rangoon → Yangon	110	16.47 N	96.10 E
Rangoon ≃	110	16.29 N	96.21 E
Rangpo	124	27.11 N	88.32 E
Rangpur, Bngl.	124	25.45 N	89.15 E
Rangpur, Pāk.	123	30.31 N	71.34 E
Rangpuri ⊥	272a	28.33 N	77.08 E
Rangsang, Pulau I	114	1.00 N	102.55 E

Symbols in the index entries represent the broad categories identified in the key at the right. Symbols with superior numbers (⋏[1]) identify subcategories (see complete key on page *I · 1).*

Symbole im Register stellen die rechts im Schlüssel erklärten Kategorien dar. Symbole mit hochgestellten Ziffern (⋏[1]) bezeichnen Unterabteilungen einer Kategorie (vgl. vollständiger Schlüssel auf Seite *I · 1).*

Los símbolos incluídos en el texto del índice representan las grandes categorías identificadas con la clave a la derecha. Los símbolos con numeros en su parte superior (⋏[1]) identifican las subcategorías (véase la clave completa en la página *I · 1).*

Les symboles de l'index représentent les catégories indiquées dans la légende à droite. Les symboles suivis d'un indice (⋏[1]) représentent des sous-catégories (voir légende complète à la page *I · 1).*

Os símbolos incluídos no texto do índice representam as grandes categorias identificadas com a chave à direita. Os símbolos com números em sua parte superior (⋏[1]) identificam as subcategorias (veja-se a chave completa à página *I · 1).*

∧	Mountain	Berg	Montaña	Montagne	Montanha
⋏	Mountains	Gebirge	Montañas	Montagnes	Montanhas
)(	Pass	Paß	Paso	Col	Passo
V	Valley, Canyon	Tal, Cañon	Valle, Cañón	Vallée, Canyon	Vale, Canhão
=	Plain	Ebene	Llano	Plaine	Planície
>	Cape	Kap	Cabo	Cap	Cabo
I	Island	Insel	Isla	Île	Ilha
II	Islands	Inseln	Islas	Îles	Ilhas
⊥	Other Topographic Features	Andere Topographische Objekte	Otros Elementos Topográficos	Autres données topographiques	Outros acidentes topográficos

ESPAÑOL

Nombre	Página	Lat.°′	Long.°′ W = Oeste

FRANÇAIS

Nom	Page	Lat.°′	Long.°′ W = Ouest

PORTUGUÊS

Nome	Página	Lat.°′	Long.°′ W = Oeste

Rangsdorf 54 52.17 N 13.25 E
Rangsdorfer See ⊜ 264a 52.17 N 13.24 E
Ranguana Cay I 236 16.20 N 88.09 W
Ranguana Entrance ʊ 236 16.19 N 88.09 W
Rangun → Yangon 110 16.47 N 96.10 E
Ranholas 266c 38.47 N 9.22 W
Rānībāndh 126 22.52 N 86.47 E
Rānībennur 122 14.37 N 75.37 E
Rānīganj 126 23.37 N 87.08 E
Rānikhet 124 29.39 N 79.25 E
Ranino 80 52.58 N 40.15 E
Ranis 54 50.39 N 11.34 E
Rānīwāra 120 24.45 N 72.13 E
Rāniyah 128 36.15 N 44.53 E
Rankamhaeng National Park ♠ 110 17.10 N 99.58 E
Ranken ≃ 166 20.31 S 137.36 E
Ranken Store 166 19.35 S 136.55 E
Rankin, Il., U.S. 216 40.27 N 87.53 W
Rankin, Mi., U.S. 216 42.55 N 83.46 W
Rankin, Pa., U.S. 279b 40.24 N 79.52 W
Rankin, Tx., U.S. 196 31.13 N 101.56 W
Rankin Inlet 176 62.45 N 92.10 W
Rankins Springs 166 33.50 S 146.16 E
Rankūs 132 33.45 N 36.23 E
Rankweil 58 47.17 N 9.39 E
Ranlo 192 35.17 N 81.07 W
Ranneje 80 51.29 N 52.37 E
Rannersdorf 264b 48.08 N 16.28 E
Rannoch, Loch ⊜ 46 56.41 N 4.20 W
Rannoch Moor ◆[3] 46 56.38 N 4.40 W
Rann of Kutch → Kutch, Rann of ◆[1] 120 24.05 N 70.10 E
Ranobe ≃ 157b 17.10 S 44.08 E
Ranohira 157b 22.29 S 45.24 E
Ranomafana, Madag. 157b 18.57 S 48.50 E
Ranomafana, Madag. 157b 24.36 S 46.58 E
Ranomena 157b 23.25 S 47.17 E
Ranong 110 9.58 N 98.38 E
Ranongga Island I 175e 8.05 S 156.34 E
Ranopiso 157b 25.03 S 46.40 E
Ranot 110 7.46 N 100.19 E
Ranotsara Nord 157b 22.48 S 46.36 E
Rānsai 272c 18.53 N 73.05 E
Ransäter 40 59.46 N 13.26 E
Ransiki 164 1.30 S 134.10 E
Ransom, Il., U.S. 216 41.09 N 88.39 W
Ransom, Ks., U.S. 198 38.38 N 99.56 W
Ransom, Pa., U.S. 210 41.24 N 75.50 W
Ransom Creek ≃ 284a 43.04 N 78.45 W
Ransomville 210 43.14 N 78.54 W
Ranson 188 39.17 N 77.51 W
Ransta 40 59.48 N 16.38 E
Ranstadt 56 50.21 N 8.59 E
Rantabe 157b 15.42 S 49.39 E
Rantasalmi 26 62.04 N 28.18 E
Rantau, Indon. 112 2.56 S 115.09 E
Rantau, Malay. 114 2.35 N 101.58 E
Rantaukampar 114 1.24 N 100.59 E
Rantaupanjang, Indon. 112 1.51 S 102.19 E
Rantaupanjang, Indon. 112 1.16 S 101.49 E
Rantaupanjang, Indon. 114 0.58 N 99.13 E
Rantauprapat 114 2.06 N 99.50 E
Rantekombola, Bulu ∧ 112 3.21 S 120.01 E
Ranten 61 47.09 N 14.05 E
Rantepao 112 2.59 S 119.54 E
Rantigny 50 49.20 N 2.26 E
Rantoul 216 40.09 N 88.20 W
Rantsila 26 64.31 N 25.39 E
Rantzau 54 54.15 N 10.30 E
Ranua 26 65.55 N 26.32 E
Rānvād 272c 18.53 N 72.55 E
Ranwanalenaus 156 19.35 S 22.47 E
Råö 26 57.24 N 11.56 E
Rao'er 100 28.48 N 117.40 E
Raohe 89 46.47 N 134.00 E
Raon-L'Étape 58 48.24 N 6.51 E
Raon-sur-Plaine 58 48.31 N 7.06 E
Raoping 100 23.43 N 117.01 E
Raoui, 'Erg er ◆[2] 148 29.17 N 2.20 W
Raoul 192 34.27 N 83.36 W
Raoul Island I 14 29.16 S 177.54 W
Raoyang 98 38.16 N 115.44 E
Raoyang ≃ 104 41.50 N 122.35 E
Raoyanghe 104 41.46 N 122.26 E
Rapa I 14 27.36 S 144.20 W
Rapa, Ponta do › 252 27.22 S 48.26 W
Rapallo 62 44.21 N 9.14 E
Rapang 112 3.50 S 119.48 E
Rāpar 120 23.34 N 70.38 E
Raparo, Monte ∧ 68 40.12 N 15.59 E
Rapatovo 80 55.04 N 54.37 E
Rāpch ≃ 128 25.28 N 59.21 E
Rapel ≃ 252 33.55 S 71.51 W
Rapel, Embalse ⊜[1] 252 34.12 S 71.30 W
Rapelli 252 26.24 S 64.29 W
Raphoe 48 54.52 N 7.36 W
Rapid ≃, Mi., U.S. 190 45.55 N 86.58 W
Rapid ≃, Mn., U.S. 198 48.42 N 94.26 W
Rapid ≃, Wa., U.S. 224 47.48 N 121.18 W
Rapidan ≃ 188 38.22 N 77.37 W
Rapid Bay 168b 35.32 S 138.12 E
Rapid City, Mb., Can. 184 50.08 N 100.02 W
Rapid City, Mi., U.S. 190 44.50 N 85.16 W
Rapid City, S.D., U.S. 198 44.04 N 103.13 W
Rapid Creek ≃ 198 43.54 N 102.37 W
Rapide Taureau, Barrage du ◆[6] 206 46.52 N 73.39 W
Rapid River 190 45.55 N 86.58 W
Räpina 76 58.06 N 27.27 E
Rapkan 85 40.22 N 70.40 E
Rapla 76 59.01 N 24.47 E
Rapness 46 59.14 N 2.51 W
Rapolano Terme 66 43.17 N 11.36 E
Rapolla 68 40.58 N 15.41 E
Rapone 68 40.51 N 15.30 E
Raposo ∧[2] 266c 38.40 N 9.11 W
Rappahannock ≃ 208 37.34 N 76.18 W
Rappbodestausee ⊜[1] 54 51.44 N 10.53 E
Rappenlochschlucht ʟ 58 47.23 N 9.47 E
Rappottenstein 61 48.31 N 15.05 E
Rāptī □[8] 124 28.15 N 82.30 E
Rāpti (Raptī) ≃, Asia 124 26.18 N 83.41 E
Rāptī ≃, Nepāl 124 27.33 N 84.07 E
Rapulo ≃ 248 13.43 S 65.32 W
Rapu-Rapu 116 13.11 N 124.08 E
Rapu Rapu Island I 116 13.12 N 124.09 E
Raqabah, Khashm ar- ∧[2] 142 28.18 N 31.43 E
Raquette ≃ 206 45.00 N 74.42 W
Raraka I[1] 14 16.10 S 144.54 W
Rara National Park ♠ 124 29.35 N 82.05 E
Rārh Plains ⩦ 126 23.13 N 87.20 E
Rāribahāl 126 24.05 N 87.21 E
Raritan 210 40.34 N 74.38 W
Raritan ≃ 208 40.29 N 74.17 W
Raritan, North Branch ≃ 210 40.33 N 74.41 W
Raritan, South Branch ≃ 210 40.33 N 74.41 W
Raritan Bay ⊂ 208 40.28 N 74.12 W
Raroïa I 14 16.01 S 142.27 W
Raron 58 46.19 N 7.48 E
Rarotonga I 174k 21.14 S 159.46 W
Rarotonga International Airport ⊠ 174k 21.12 S 159.49 W
Rarz 85 39.23 N 68.44 E
Rasa, Ilha I 287a 23.04 S 43.09 W
Rasa, Punta ›, Arg. 252 36.17 S 56.47 W
Rasa, Punta ›, Arg. 254 40.51 S 62.19 W
Rašaant 88 49.07 N 101.25 E
Rasa de Guaratiba, Ilha I 256 23.05 S 43.34 W
Rasa Island I 116 9.14 N 118.27 E
Ra's al-'Ayn 130 36.51 N 40.04 E
Ra's al-Barr 142 31.31 N 31.50 E
Ra's al-Khalīj 142 31.15 N 31.39 E
Ra's al-Khaymah 128 25.47 N 55.57 E
Ra's al-Unūf 146 30.31 N 18.34 E
Ra's al-Ushsh ◆[8] 142 31.08 N 32.18 E
Ra's an-Naqb, Miṣr 132 29.36 N 34.51 E
Ra's an-Naqb, Urd. 132 30.00 N 35.29 E
Rasawi 164 2.04 S 134.01 E
Ra's Ba'labakk 130 34.15 N 36.25 E
Rasbo 40 59.57 N 17.53 E
Râșcani 38 47.58 N 27.32 E
Raschau 54 50.32 N 12.50 E
Rașcov 38 47.57 N 28.50 E
Ras Dashen Terara ∧ 144 13.16 N 38.24 E
Rasdorf 56 50.43 N 9.53 E
Raseborg 26 59.59 N 23.39 E
Raseiniai 76 55.24 N 23.07 E
Râs el Aïoun 36 35.30 N 8.18 E
Ras el Ma, Alg. 148 34.31 N 0.46 W
Râs el Mâ, Mali 150 16.37 N 4.28 W
Ras el Oued 34 35.57 N 5.03 E
Rasen-Antholz → Anterselva di Sopra 64 46.52 N 12.08 E
Rashād 140 11.51 N 31.04 E
Rāshayyā 132 33.30 N 35.51 E
Rashīd (Rosetta) 142 31.24 N 30.25 E
Rashīd, Far' (Rosetta Branch) ≃ 142 31.30 N 30.21 E
Rashīd, Maṣabb (Rosetta Mouth) ≃[1] 142 31.30 N 30.20 E
Rashīd Qal'eh 120 31.31 N 67.31 E
Rashin → Najin 98 42.15 N 130.18 E
Rashivka 78 50.14 N 33.54 E
Rasht 128 37.16 N 49.36 E
Rashtrapati Bhawan ♁ 272a 28.37 N 77.12 E
Rasina ≃ 38 43.37 N 21.22 E
Rāsipuram 122 11.28 N 78.10 E
Rasi Salai 110 15.20 N 104.09 E
Rāsk 128 26.13 N 61.25 E
Raška 38 43.17 N 20.37 E
Rask Mølle 41 55.52 N 9.37 E
Rās Koh ∧ 128 28.50 N 65.12 E
Raskunda 126 22.48 N 87.26 E
Rasm al-Arwām, Sabkhat ⊜ 130 35.53 N 37.40 E
R'asna 76 54.01 N 31.12 E
Râșnov 38 45.36 N 25.28 E
Raso, Cabo › 266c 38.43 N 9.29 W
Raso, Ilhéu I 150a 16.37 N 24.36 W
Rasocolmo, Capo › 70 38.18 N 15.31 E
Rason Lake ⊜ 162 28.46 S 124.20 E
Raspberry Peak ∧ 194 34.23 N 94.01 W
Raspopinskaja 80 49.24 N 42.52 E
Rasra 124 25.51 N 83.51 E
Rass Jebel 36 37.13 N 10.09 E
Rasskazovka 265b 55.38 N 37.20 E
Rasskazovo 80 52.40 N 41.53 E
Rasšua, ostrov I 74 47.45 N 153.01 E
Rassudovo 82 55.29 N 36.54 E
Rassvet, Ross. 84 43.58 N 46.44 E
Rassvet, Ross. 84 43.58 N 46.44 E
Rassvet, Ross. 86 57.02 N 91.34 E
Rassvet, Ross. 88 57.02 N 91.34 E
Rassypnaja 80 51.35 N 53.37 E
Rast 38 43.53 N 23.17 E
Rastälven ≃ 40 59.37 N 14.56 E
Ra's Tannūrah 128 26.42 N 50.06 E
Rastatt 56 48.51 N 8.12 E
Rastede 52 53.15 N 8.11 E
Rastegai'sa ∧ 24 70.00 N 26.18 E
Rastenberg 54 51.10 N 11.25 E
Rastenburg → Kętrzyn 30 54.06 N 21.23 E
Rastorf 54 54.16 N 10.19 E
Rastorgujevo 82 55.33 N 37.41 E
Rastovcy 82 56.39 N 37.35 E
Rastunovo 82 55.16 N 37.50 E
Rasu, Monte ∧ 71 40.25 N 9.00 E
Rasūl 123 32.42 N 73.34 E
Rasūlnagar 123 32.20 N 73.47 E
Rasulpur 272a 28.37 N 77.22 E
Rasulpur ◆[8] 272a 28.42 N 77.01 E
Rasun di sopra 64 46.48 N 12.03 E
Rasun di sotto 64 46.47 N 12.02 E
Rasura 58 46.06 N 9.33 E
Råsvalen ⊜ 40 59.40 N 15.10 E
Rat ≃, Mb., Can. 184 49.35 N 97.08 W
Rat ≃, Mb., Can. 184 55.41 N 99.04 W
Ratahan 112 1.04 N 124.48 E
Ratak Chain II 14 9.00 N 171.00 E
Ratangarh 120 28.05 N 74.36 E
Ratanpur, India 126 23.07 N 87.04 E
Ratanpur, India 272b 22.50 N 88.14 E
Rätansbyn 26 62.29 N 14.32 E
Rat Burana 269a 13.41 N 100.30 E
Ratčino, Ross. 80 53.02 N 39.55 E
Ratčino, Ross. 82 55.16 N 38.39 E
Ratcliff 222 31.24 N 95.08 W
Rateče 64 46.30 N 13.43 E
Ratekau 54 53.57 N 10.44 E
Rāth 124 25.35 N 79.34 E
Rath ◆[8] 263 51.17 N 6.49 E
Rathangan 48 53.12 N 6.59 W
Rathbone 210 42.08 N 77.19 W
Rathbun Lake ⊜ 212 44.47 N 78.12 W
Rathbun Lake ⊜[1] 190 40.54 N 93.05 W
Rathcoole 48 53.16 N 6.28 W
Rathcormack 48 52.05 N 8.17 W
Rathdowney, Austl. 171a 28.12 S 152.52 E
Rathdowney, Ire. 48 52.50 N 7.34 W
Rathdrum, Ire. 48 52.56 N 6.13 W
Rathdrum, Id., U.S. 202 47.48 N 116.53 W
Rathebur 54 53.44 N 13.46 E
Ratheim 52 51.04 N 6.10 E
Rathen 46 57.38 N 2.02 W
Rathenow 54 52.36 N 12.20 E
Rathfriland 48 54.14 N 6.10 W
Rathkeale 48 52.32 N 8.56 W
Rathlin Island I 48 55.18 N 6.13 W
Rathlin Sound ʊ 48 55.15 N 6.15 W
Ráth Luirc (Charleville) 48 52.21 N 8.41 W
Rathmecke 263 51.15 N 7.38 E
Rathmelton 48 55.02 N 7.38 W
Rathmore 48 52.03 N 9.13 W
Rathmullan 48 55.06 N 7.33 W
Rathnew 48 53.00 N 6.05 W
Ratho 46 55.55 N 3.22 W
Rathowen 48 53.40 N 7.31 W
Rathstock 54 52.31 N 14.32 E
Rathwell 184 49.40 N 98.32 W
Ratibor → Racibórz 30 50.06 N 18.13 E
Raticosa, Passo della)(66 44.10 N 11.20 E
Rätikon ⋀ 58 47.03 N 9.40 E
Ratingen 56 51.18 N 6.51 E
Ratisbon → Regensburg 60 49.01 N 12.06 E
Rätische Alpen → Rhaetian Alps ⋀ 58 46.30 N 10.00 E
Rat Island I 181a 51.55 N 178.20 E
Rat Islands II 181a 51.40 N 178.30 E
Rat'kovo 82 56.01 N 38.38 E
Rat Lake ⊜ 184 56.10 N 99.40 W
Ratlām 120 23.19 N 75.04 E
Ratmanova, ostrov I 180 65.46 N 169.02 W
Ratnāgiri 122 16.59 N 73.18 E
Ratnapura 122 6.41 N 80.24 E
Ratne 78 51.40 N 24.31 E
Ratodero 120 27.48 N 68.18 E
Ratomka 76 53.56 N 27.21 E
Raton 196 36.54 N 104.26 W
Raton Pass)(196 36.59 N 104.29 W
Ratqah, Wādī ar- V 130 34.25 N 40.55 E
Ratt ≃ 224 47.27 N 124.21 W
Rattanaburi 110 15.19 N 103.51 E
Rattaphum 110 7.08 N 100.16 E
Ratten 61 47.29 N 15.43 E
Rattlesnake 202 46.56 N 113.59 W
Rattlesnake Creek ≃, Ks., U.S. 198 38.13 N 98.22 W
Rattlesnake Creek ≃, Oh., U.S. 218 39.16 N 83.23 W
Rattlesnake Creek ≃, Or., U.S. 202 42.44 N 117.47 W
Rattlesnake Creek ≃, Wa., U.S. 224 46.45 N 120.55 W
Rattlesnake Creek ≃, Wa., U.S. 224 45.48 N 121.29 W
Rattlesnake Mountain ∧ 207 41.42 N 72.50 W
Rattlesnake Peak ∧ 280 34.16 N 117.47 W
Rattling Brook 186 49.38 N 56.10 W
Rattling Run ≃ 279b 40.33 N 79.32 W
Rattray 46 56.35 N 3.19 W
Rattray Head › 46 57.37 N 1.49 W
Rattu 123 35.08 N 74.48 E
Rättvik 26 60.53 N 15.06 E
Ratz, Mount ∧ 180 57.23 N 132.19 W
Ratzeburg 54 53.42 N 10.46 E
Ratzeburger See ⊜ 54 53.45 N 10.47 E
Rätzlingen 54 52.23 N 11.08 E
Rau 112 0.34 N 100.01 E
Raub, Malay. 114 3.48 N 101.52 E
Raub, In., U.S. 216 40.44 N 87.29 W
Raubsville 208 40.38 N 75.12 W
Rauch 252 36.46 S 59.06 W
Raucheck ∧ 64 47.30 N 13.14 E
Rauchenwarth 264b 48.05 N 16.32 E
Rauchtown 210 41.07 N 77.14 W
Raucourt-et-Flaba 56 49.36 N 4.57 E
Rauen 54 52.20 N 14.01 E
Rauenstein 54 50.24 N 11.03 E
Raufarhöfn 24a 66.30 N 15.57 W
Raufoss 26 60.43 N 10.37 E
Rauhe Ebrach ≃ 56 49.50 N 10.56 E
Raukumara Range ⋀ 172 37.47 S 178.02 E
Raul Soares 255 20.05 S 42.22 W
Rauma 26 61.08 N 21.30 E
Rauma ≃ 26 62.33 N 7.43 E
Raumünzach 56 48.38 N 8.21 E
Rauna 76 57.20 N 25.43 E
Raunds 42 52.21 N 0.33 W
Raung, Gunung ∧ 115a 8.08 S 114.03 E
Raunheim 56 50.01 N 8.28 E
Raupal'an 180 65.28 N 171.59 W
Raurimu 172 39.07 S 175.24 E
Rauris 64 47.13 N 13.00 E
Raurkela 124 22.13 N 84.53 E
Rauschenberg 56 50.53 N 8.55 E
Rausu 92a 44.01 N 145.12 E
Räut ≃ 38 47.15 N 29.09 E
Rautalampi 26 62.38 N 26.50 E
Rāutara 272b 22.51 N 88.28 E
Rautavaara 26 63.29 N 28.18 E
Ravahere I[1] 14 18.14 S 142.09 W
Ravalgaon 122 20.38 N 74.25 E
Ravanica, Manastir ♁[1] 38 43.58 N 21.26 E
Ravānsar 128 34.43 N 46.40 E
Ravanusa 70 37.16 N 13.58 E
Rāvar 128 31.15 N 56.53 E
Ravarano 64 44.35 N 10.04 E
Ravarino 64 44.44 N 11.06 E
Rava-Rus'ka 78 50.14 N 23.37 E
Ravascletto 64 46.32 N 12.57 E
Ravat 85 39.54 N 70.12 E
Ravello 68 40.39 N 14.37 E
Ravelo 248 18.48 S 65.32 W
Raven 192 37.05 N 81.51 W
Ravena 210 42.28 N 73.49 W
Ravenglass 44 54.21 N 3.24 W
Raven Lake ⊜ 212 45.13 N 78.51 W
Ravenna, It. 66 44.25 N 12.12 E
Ravenna, Ky., U.S. 192 37.41 N 83.57 W
Ravenna, Mi., U.S. 216 43.11 N 85.56 W
Ravenna, Ne., U.S. 198 41.01 N 98.54 W
Ravenna, Oh., U.S. 214 41.09 N 81.14 W
Ravenna □[4] 66 44.25 N 11.59 E
Ravensbourne 171a 27.22 S 152.10 E
Ravensbourne National Park ♠ 171a 27.21 S 152.15 E
Ravensburg 58 47.47 N 9.37 E
Ravenscrag 184 49.30 N 109.05 W
Ravensdale 224 47.21 N 121.58 W
Ravenshoe 166 17.37 S 145.29 E
Ravensthorpe 162 33.35 S 120.02 E
Ravenswood, S. Afr. 273d 26.11 S 28.15 E
Ravenswood, Mi., U.S. 216 42.45 N 84.36 W
Ravenswood, W.V., U.S. 188 38.56 N 81.45 W
Ravenswood Park ♠ 283 42.36 N 70.42 W
Ravenswood Point › 282 37.30 N 122.08 W
Ravensworth 284c 38.48 N 77.13 W
Rāver 120 21.15 N 76.02 E
Ravernet ≃ 48 54.30 N 6.04 W
Rāvi ≃ 123 30.35 N 71.49 E
Ravières 50 47.45 N 4.17 E
Ravine 208 40.34 N 76.24 W
Ravine Lake ⊜[1] 276 40.43 N 74.38 W
Ravinia Park ♠ 278 42.09 N 87.46 W
Ravna Gora 36 45.23 N 14.57 E
Ravne 61 46.33 N 14.58 E
Ravnina 128 37.57 N 62.40 E
Ravsted 41 55.01 N 9.08 E
Rāwah 128 34.28 N 41.55 E
Rawaki I[1] 14 3.43 S 170.43 W
Rāwala Kot 123 33.52 N 73.46 E
Rāwalpindi 123 33.36 N 73.04 E
Rawa Mazowiecka 30 51.46 N 20.16 E
Rāwāndūz 128 36.37 N 44.31 E
Rawang 114 3.19 N 101.35 E
Rawas ≃ 112 2.42 S 103.24 E
Rāwatsar 123 29.17 N 74.23 E
Rawāwiṣ, Wādī V 146 30.26 N 15.24 E
Rawḍah ⊜ 130 35.15 N 41.05 E
Rawḍah, Wādī ar- V 130 34.22 N 37.21 E
Rawd al-Faraj ◆[8] 273c 30.05 N 31.14 E
Rawḍaw, Jazīrat ar- I 273c 30.01 N 31.13 E
Rawdon 206 46.03 N 73.43 W
Rawene 172 35.24 S 173.30 E
Rawḥah 144 19.28 N 41.48 E
Rawhide Creek ≃ 198 42.06 N 104.20 W
Rawhide Lake ⊜ 190 46.39 N 82.37 W
Rawhide Mountain ∧ 204 38.17 N 116.25 W
Rawi 112 2.07 S 113.56 E
Rawi, Ko I 114 6.33 N 99.14 E
Rawicz 30 51.37 N 16.52 E
Rawlinna 162 31.01 S 125.20 E
Rawlins 200 41.47 N 107.14 W
Rawlinson, Mount ∧ 162 25.58 S 127.28 E
Rawlinson Range ⋀ 162 24.51 S 128.00 E
Rawmarsh 44 53.27 N 1.21 W
Rawreth 260 51.37 N 0.35 E
Rawson, Arg. 252 34.36 S 60.04 W
Rawson, Arg. 254 43.18 S 65.06 W
Rawson, Oh., U.S. 216 40.57 N 83.47 W
Rawsonville 158 33.41 S 19.20 E
Rawtenstall 44 53.42 N 2.18 W
Rawu 102 29.30 N 96.45 E
Rax ⋀ 61 47.42 N 15.43 E
Raxāul 124 26.59 N 84.51 E
Ray, Il., U.S. 219 40.12 N 90.29 W
Ray, In., U.S. 216 41.45 N 84.53 W
Ray, N.D., U.S. 198 48.20 N 103.09 W
Ray ≃ 42 51.48 N 1.15 W
Ray, Cape › 186 47.40 N 59.18 W
Raya 112 1.05 N 118.32 E
Raya, Bukit ∧ 112 0.40 S 112.41 E
Raya, Gunong ∧ 114 6.22 N 99.49 E
Raya, Pulau I 114 4.52 N 95.22 E
Rāyachoti 122 14.03 N 78.45 E
Rāyadurg 122 14.42 N 76.52 E
Rāyagarha 122 19.10 N 83.25 E
Rayburn 222 30.25 N 94.56 W
Rayen, Dtsch. 263 51.28 N 6.32 E
Rāyen, Īrān 128 29.34 N 57.26 E
Rayhorodka 83 48.50 N 39.04 E
Rayhorodok 83 48.54 N 37.43 E
Ray Hubbard, Lake ⊜[1] 222 32.53 N 96.35 W
Rāyikhah I 128 26.12 N 36.21 E
Rayland 214 40.11 N 80.41 W
Rayleigh 42 51.36 N 0.36 E
Raymond, Ab., Can. 182 49.27 N 112.39 W
Raymond, Ca., U.S. 226 37.13 N 119.54 W
Raymond, Il., U.S. 219 39.19 N 89.34 W
Raymond, Mn., U.S. 198 45.00 N 95.14 W
Raymond, Ms., U.S. 194 32.15 N 90.25 W
Raymond, Oh., U.S. 216 40.20 N 83.28 W
Raymond, Wa., U.S. 224 46.41 N 123.43 W
Raymond Terrace 170 32.46 S 151.44 E
Raymondville 196 26.29 N 97.47 W
Raymore 184 51.25 N 104.31 W
Ray Mountains ⋀ 180 65.45 N 151.30 W
Rāyna 126 23.05 N 87.54 E
Rayne 194 30.14 N 92.16 W
Raynham 207 41.56 N 71.04 W
Raynham Greyhound Park ♠ 283 41.59 N 71.04 W
Rayón, Méx. 232 29.43 N 110.35 W
Rayón, Méx. 234 17.12 N 93.00 W
Rayón, Méx. 234 21.51 N 99.40 W
Rayones 232 25.01 N 100.05 W
Rayong 110 12.40 N 101.17 E
Rāypur 272b 22.25 N 88.31 E
Rayrah ⫪[4] 140 15.21 N 34.41 E
Rayse Creek ≃ 219 38.13 N 89.00 W
Raystown Lake ⊜[1] 214 40.20 N 78.05 W
Rayton 158 25.45 S 28.32 E
Raytown 194 39.00 N 94.27 W
Rayville 194 32.28 N 91.45 W
Raywood 222 30.02 N 94.40 W
Raz, Pointe du › 32 48.02 N 4.44 W
Raza, Punta › 234 21.02 N 105.20 W
Razan, Īrān 128 35.23 N 49.02 E
R'azan', Ross. 80 54.38 N 39.44 E
R'azancevo 82 56.42 N 39.12 E
Ražanj 38 43.40 N 21.33 E
R'azan' Oblast' □[4] 76 54.30 N 40.30 E
R'azanovo 82 55.29 N 37.31 E
Razbegaj 265a 59.47 N 29.56 E
Războieni 38 47.05 N 26.32 E
Razdan 84 40.30 N 44.46 E
Razdan ≃ 84 39.58 N 44.27 E
Razdolinsk 86 58.25 N 94.38 E
Razdolje 88 52.27 N 103.13 E
Razdol'noje 89 43.30 N 131.52 E
Razdol'nyj 80 46.38 N 42.57 E
Razdorskaja 78 47.33 N 40.38 E
Razdory 265b 55.45 N 37.18 E
Răzeni 38 46.46 N 28.54 E
R'aženoje 83 47.31 N 38.52 E
Raževo 86 56.09 N 68.25 E
Razgrad 38 43.32 N 26.31 E
Razgrad □[4] 38 43.32 N 26.31 E
Razim, Lacul ⊜ 38 44.54 N 28.57 E
Razlog 38 41.53 N 23.28 E
Razmachnino 88 51.47 N 115.28 E
Razmitelevo 265a 59.54 N 30.41 E
Rāznas ezers ⊜ 76 56.20 N 27.27 E
Raznočinovka 80 46.37 N 47.57 E
Raznomojka 86 52.29 N 55.52 E
Razorback Mountain ∧ 182 51.35 N 124.42 W
R'ažsk 80 53.43 N 40.04 E
Răzvani 38 44.25 N 26.53 E
Razvil'noje 80 46.14 N 41.18 E
Razzoli, Isola I 71 41.18 N 9.21 E
Ré, Île de I 32 46.12 N 1.25 W
Rea ≃ 42 52.18 N 2.32 W
Read 262 53.49 N 2.21 W
Reading, Eng., U.K. 42 51.28 N 0.59 W
Reading, Il., U.S. 216 41.05 N 88.51 W
Reading, Ks., U.S. 198 38.31 N 95.57 W
Reading, Ma., U.S. 207 42.31 N 71.05 W
Reading, Mi., U.S. 216 41.50 N 84.44 W
Reading, Oh., U.S. 218 39.13 N 84.26 W
Reading, Pa., U.S. 208 40.20 N 75.55 W
Reading Center 210 42.26 N 76.56 W
Reading Station ◆[5] 285 39.57 N 75.10 W
Readington 210 40.34 N 74.44 W
Readlyn 190 42.42 N 92.13 W
Readsboro 207 42.46 N 72.56 W
Readstown 190 43.26 N 90.45 W
Reagan 222 31.13 N 96.47 W
Real 116 14.40 N 121.36 E
Real ≃ 250 11.27 S 37.22 W
Real, Cordillera ⋀ 248 19.00 S 66.30 W
Real, Estero ≃ 236 12.55 N 87.23 W
Real del Padre 252 34.50 S 67.46 W
Real de San Carlos 258 34.26 S 57.53 W
Realengo ◆[8] 256 22.53 S 43.25 W
Real Felipe, Museo Histórico del ⊥ 286d 12.04 S 77.09 W
Realicó 252 35.02 S 64.15 W
Realitos 196 27.27 N 98.32 W
Realmonte 70 37.18 N 13.28 E
Reamstown 208 40.12 N 76.07 W
Reana del Roiale 64 46.12 N 13.13 E
Reardan 202 47.40 N 117.52 W
Reata 232 26.08 N 101.05 W
Reatini, Monti ⋀ 66 42.28 N 13.00 E
Réau 261 48.37 N 2.38 E
Reay 46 58.33 N 3.47 W
Reay Forest ◆[3] 46 58.19 N 4.47 W
Rebecca, Lake ⊜ 162 29.53 S 122.10 E
Rebecq-Rognon 50 50.40 N 4.08 E
Rebeida, Wādī V 140 20.45 N 34.06 E
Rebel Hill 285 40.04 N 75.20 W
Rebersburg 210 40.57 N 77.27 W
Rebi 164 6.23 S 134.06 E
Rebiana Sand Sea → Rabyānah, Ṣaḥrā' ◆[2] 146 24.20 N 20.37 E
Rebild Bakker ♠ 26 56.50 N 9.51 E
Reboly 24 63.50 N 30.47 E
Rebouças 252 25.36 S 50.42 W
Reboucas, Túnel ◆[5] 287a 22.56 S 43.14 W
Rebricha 86 53.05 N 82.20 E
Rebun-tō I 92a 45.23 N 141.02 E
Recalde 252 36.39 S 61.05 W
Recanati 66 43.24 N 13.32 E
Rečane 76 56.25 N 31.39 E
Recco 62 44.22 N 9.09 E
Recey-sur-Ource 58 47.47 N 4.52 E
Rēchah Lām 120 34.58 N 70.51 E
Rechberghausen 56 48.44 N 9.38 E
Recherche, Archipelago of the II 162 34.05 S 122.45 E
Recherche, Cape › 175e 10.11 S 161.19 E
Réchicourt-le-Château 58 48.40 N 6.51 E
Rechlin 54 53.21 N 12.43 E
Rechna Doāb ⋀[1] 123 31.35 N 73.30 E
Rechnitz 61 47.18 N 16.27 E
Rečica, Bela. 76 52.22 N 30.25 E
Rečica, Bela. 78 51.52 N 26.48 E
Recife 250 8.03 S 34.54 W
Recife, Kaap › 158 34.02 S 25.44 E
Recinto 252 36.48 S 71.44 W
Recke 52 52.22 N 7.43 E
Recklinghausen 52 51.36 N 7.13 E
Recknitz ≃ 54 54.14 N 12.28 E
Recoaro Terme 64 45.42 N 11.13 E
Recogne 56 49.55 N 5.22 E
Recoleta 286e 33.23 S 70.38 W
Recologne 58 47.16 N 5.50 E
Reconquista 252 29.09 S 59.39 W
Reconquista, Río de la ≃ 288 34.25 S 58.35 W
Recovery Glacier ⍓ 9 81.10 S 28.00 W
Recreio 255 21.32 S 42.28 W
Recreo 252 29.16 S 65.04 W
Rector 194 36.15 N 90.17 W
Rectorville 218 38.34 N 83.39 W
Recuay 248 9.43 S 77.28 W
Recz 30 53.16 N 15.33 E
Red (Hong) (Yuan) ≃, Asia 110 20.17 N 106.34 E
Red ≃, N.A. 178 50.24 N 96.48 W
Red ≃, U.S. 178 31.00 N 91.40 W
Red ≃, U.S. 194 36.32 N 87.22 W
Red ≃, Ky., U.S. 192 37.51 N 84.05 W
Red ≃, N.M., U.S. 200 36.39 N 105.42 W
Red ≃, Wi., U.S. 190 44.49 N 88.38 W
Red, Elm Fork ≃ 196 34.53 N 99.19 W
Red, North Fork ≃ 196 34.24 N 99.14 W
Red, Prairie Dog Town Fork ≃ 196 34.35 N 99.58 W
Red, Salt Fork ≃ 196 34.27 N 99.22 W
Red, South Fork ≃ 194 36.41 N 86.56 W
Red, West Fork ≃ 194 36.32 N 87.21 W
Reda 30 54.37 N 18.21 E
Redang, Pulau I 114 5.47 N 103.00 E
Redange 56 49.46 N 5.54 E
Redang Panjang 114 5.07 N 100.47 E
Red Bank, N.J., U.S. 208 40.20 N 74.03 W
Red Bank, Tn., U.S. 194 35.07 N 85.17 W
Red Bank Battle Monument ⊥ 285 39.52 N 75.11 W
Redbank Creek ≃ 214 40.58 N 79.33 W
Red Banks 194 34.49 N 89.33 W
Red Bay, Nf., Can. 186 51.44 N 56.25 W
Red Bay, Al., U.S. 194 34.26 N 88.08 W
Redbay, Fl., U.S. 194 30.35 N 85.56 W
Red Bay ⊂ 48 55.04 N 6.02 W
Redberry Lake ⊜ 184 52.40 N 107.10 W
Redbird 214 41.48 N 81.06 W
Red Bluff 204 40.10 N 122.14 W
Red Bluff Reservoir ⊜[1] 196 31.57 N 103.56 W
Red Boiling Springs 194 36.31 N 85.50 W
Redbourn 42 51.48 N 0.24 W
Redbridge ◆[8] 42 51.34 N 0.05 E
Red Bud 219 38.12 N 89.59 W
Red Canyon V 198 43.18 N 103.49 W
Redcar 44 54.37 N 1.04 W
Red Cedar ≃, Mi., U.S. 216 42.43 N 84.33 W
Red Cedar ≃, Wi., U.S. 190 44.42 N 91.53 W
Red Cedar Lake ⊜ 190 46.45 N 79.54 W
Red Clay Creek ≃ 285 39.43 N 75.39 W
Red Clay Creek, East Branch ≃ 285 39.49 N 75.42 W
Red Clay Creek, West Branch ≃ 285 39.49 N 75.42 W
Redcliff, Ab., Can. 184 50.05 N 110.47 W
Red Cliff, Co., U.S. 200 39.31 N 106.22 W
Redcliff, Zimb. 154 19.02 S 29.50 E
Redcliffe 171a 27.14 S 153.07 E
Redcliffe, Mount ∧ 162 28.25 S 121.32 E
Red Cliff Indian Reservation ◆[4] 190 46.50 N 90.47 W
Red Cliffs 166 34.19 S 142.11 E
Red Cloud 198 40.05 N 98.31 W
Red Creek 210 43.14 N 76.43 W
Red Creek ≃ 194 30.41 N 88.40 W
Red Cross Lake ⊜ 184 55.05 N 92.55 W
Red Deer 182 52.16 N 113.48 W
Red Deer ≃, Can. 176 50.56 N 109.54 W
Red Deer ≃, Can. 184 52.53 N 101.01 W
Red Deer Creek ≃ 196 35.56 N 100.24 W
Red Deer Lake ⊜, Ab., Can. 182 52.43 N 113.02 W
Red Deer Lake ⊜, Mb., Can. 184 52.56 N 101.20 W
Reddersburg 158 29.38 S 26.07 E
Red Devil 180 61.46 N 157.18 W
Red Dial 44 54.48 N 3.10 W
Reddick 216 41.06 N 88.15 W
Redding, Ca., U.S. 204 40.35 N 122.23 W
Redding, Ct., U.S. 207 41.18 N 73.23 W
Redding Ridge 207 41.18 N 73.21 W
Reddish 262 53.26 N 2.09 W
Redditch 42 52.19 N 1.56 W
Rede ≃ 44 55.08 N 2.13 W
Redefin 54 53.21 N 11.11 E
Redelinghuys 158 32.30 S 18.33 E
Redenção 250 4.13 S 38.43 W
Redenção da Serra 256 23.16 S 45.33 W
Redesdale V 44 55.17 N 2.16 W
Redes Mere ⊜ 262 53.15 N 2.14 W
Redeye ≃ 198 46.26 N 94.49 W
Redfield, Ia., U.S. 198 41.35 N 94.11 W
Redfield, N.Y., U.S. 212 43.32 N 75.49 W
Redfield, S.D., U.S. 198 44.52 N 98.31 W
Redfish Lake ⊜ 202 44.07 N 114.56 W
Redford 196 29.47 N 104.10 W
Redford ◆[8] 281 42.25 N 83.16 W
Redford Township 216 42.25 N 83.16 W
Red Fox Forest 284c 38.49 N 77.15 W
Redhead 241r 10.47 N 60.57 W
Red Hill, Austl. 162 21.59 S 116.03 E
Redhill, Eng., U.K. 42 51.14 N 0.11 W
Red Hill, Ca., U.S. 280 33.45 N 117.48 W
Red Hill, Pa., U.S. 208 40.22 N 75.29 W
Red Hill ∧ 172 41.38 S 173.04 E
Redhill Aerodrome ⊠ 260 51.12 N 0.07 W
Red Hill Branch ≃ 284b 39.14 N 76.51 W
Red Hook 210 41.59 N 73.52 W
Redhouse Creek ≃ 284b 39.18 N 76.31 W
Rédics 61 46.36 N 16.30 E
Red Indian Lake ⊜ 186 48.40 N 56.50 W
Redinger Lake ⊜[1] 226 37.09 N 119.26 W
Redington Beach 220 27.49 N 82.49 W
Redington Shores 220 27.50 N 82.50 W
Red Island I 186 47.23 N 54.11 W
Redja ≃ 76 58.05 N 31.33 E
Redkey 216 40.21 N 85.09 W
Redkino 82 56.38 N 36.17 E
Red Lake, On., Can. 184 51.03 N 93.49 W
Redlake, Mn., U.S. 198 47.53 N 95.01 W
Red Lake ⊜, On., Can. 184 51.01 N 94.05 W
Red Lake ⊜, Az., U.S. 200 35.40 N 114.04 W
Red Lake ⊜, S.D., U.S. 198 43.44 N 99.13 W
Red Lake ⊜[1] 222 31.40 N 95.58 W
Red Lake ≃ 198 47.55 N 97.01 W
Red Lake Falls 198 47.52 N 96.16 W
Red Lake Indian Reservation ◆[4] 198 48.05 N 95.05 W
Red Lake Road 184 49.58 N 93.22 W
Redland, Scot., U.K. 46 59.05 N 3.05 W
Redland, Tx., U.S. 222 31.25 N 94.43 W
Redland Bay 171a 27.37 S 153.18 E
Redlands, S. Afr. 158 29.52 S 22.57 E
Redlands, Ca., U.S. 228 34.01 N 117.12 W
Redlands, Co., U.S. 200 39.04 N 108.38 W
Red Level 194 31.24 N 86.36 W
Red Lick 194 31.47 N 90.58 W
Redlin 54 53.22 N 12.01 E
Red Lion, Pa., U.S. 208 39.54 N 76.36 W
Red Lion, Pa., U.S. 285 39.53 N 75.41 W
Red Lion Airport ⊠ 285 39.54 N 74.45 W
Red Lodge 202 45.11 N 109.14 W
Red Mill 206 46.25 N 72.28 W
Redmond, Or., U.S. 202 44.16 N 121.10 W
Redmond, Ut,. U.S. 200 39.00 N 111.51 W
Redmond, Wa., U.S. 224 47.40 N 122.07 W
Red Mountain 228 35.21 N 117.36 W
Red Mountain ∧, Ca., U.S. 204 41.35 N 123.06 W
Red Mountain ∧, Ca., U.S. 228 35.21 N 117.36 W
Red Mountain ∧, Mt., U.S. 202 47.07 N 112.44 W
Red Mountain Pass)(200 37.54 N 107.43 W
Rednitz ≃ 56 49.28 N 10.59 E
Red Oak, Ia., U.S. 198 41.00 N 95.13 W
Red Oak, Ok., U.S. 196 34.57 N 95.04 W
Red Oak, Tx., U.S. 222 32.31 N 96.48 W
Red Oak Creek ≃ 222 32.28 N 96.30 W
Red Oaks Mill 210 41.40 N 73.53 W
Redon 32 47.39 N 2.05 W
Redonda I 238 16.55 N 62.19 W
Redonda, Ilha I 256 23.04 S 43.12 W
Redonda, Isla I 241r 9.52 N 61.35 W
Redonda Islands II 182 50.13 N 124.48 W
Redondela 34 42.17 N 8.36 W
Redondo, Port. 34 38.39 N 7.33 W
Redondo, Wa., U.S. 224 47.20 N 122.19 W
Redondo, Mount ∧ 116 10.21 N 125.38 E
Redondo Beach 228 33.50 N 118.23 W
Redondo Beach State Park ♠ 280 33.50 N 118.24 W
Redoubt, Mount ∧ 224 48.57 N 121.18 W
Redoubt Volcano ∧[1] 180 60.29 N 152.45 W
Red Pass 182 52.59 N 118.59 W
Red Pheasant Indian Reserve ◆[4] 184 52.30 N 108.07 W
Red Pine Lake ⊜ 212 45.12 N 78.42 W
Red Point › 170 34.29 S 150.55 E
Red Rock, B.C., Can. 182 53.39 N 122.41 W
Red Rock, On., Can. 190 48.58 N 88.15 W
Red Rock, Tx., U.S. 222 29.58 N 97.27 W
Red Rock I 282 37.56 N 122.26 W
Red Rock ≃ 202 44.59 N 112.52 W
Red Rock, Lake ⊜[1] 190 41.30 N 93.02 W
Red Rock Canyon State Park ♠ 228 35.23 N 118.00 W
Red Rock Creek ≃ 196 36.36 N 97.03 W
Red Rocks Point › 162 32.13 S 127.32 E
Red Root Creek ≃ 276 40.30 N 74.19 W
Red Run ≃, Md., U.S. 284b 39.24 N 76.47 W
Red Run ≃, Mi., U.S. 281 42.34 N 82.58 W
Redruth 42 50.13 N 5.14 W
Red Sea ⫪[2] 136 20.00 N 38.00 E
Red Springs 192 34.48 N 79.11 W
Redstone 182 52.08 N 123.42 W
Redstone ≃, N.T., Can. 180 64.17 N 124.33 W
Redstone ≃, On., Can. 190 48.27 N 81.03 W
Redstone Arsenal ■ 194 34.38 N 86.38 W
Redstone Creek ≃ 198 44.04 N 98.05 W
Redstone Lake ⊜ 212 45.11 N 78.32 W
Red Sucker ≃ 184 55.19 N 92.31 W
Red Sucker Lake ⊜ 184 54.09 N 93.40 W
Reduction 279b 40.11 N 79.46 W
Redut 80 47.22 N 51.53 E
Redvers 184 49.33 N 101.39 W
Redwater 182 53.57 N 113.06 W
Redwater ≃ 198 48.03 N 105.13 W
Red Wharf Bay ⊂ 44 53.18 N 4.10 W
Redwillow ≃ 182 55.04 N 119.21 W
Red Willow Creek ≃ 198 40.13 N 100.29 W
Red Wing 190 44.33 N 92.32 W
Redwood 212 44.18 N 75.48 W
Redwood ≃ 198 44.34 N 95.05 W
Redwood City 226 37.29 N 122.14 W
Redwood Creek ≃, Ca., U.S. 204 41.18 N 124.05 W
Redwood Creek ≃, Ca., U.S. 226 38.18 N 122.18 W
Redwood Creek ≃, Ca., U.S. 282 37.31 N 122.12 W
Redwood Creek ≃, Ca., U.S. 282 37.52 N 122.35 W
Redwood Estates 226 37.10 N 121.59 W
Redwood Falls 198 44.32 N 95.07 W
Redwood National Park ♠ 204 41.30 N 124.05 W
Redwood Point › 282 37.32 N 122.12 W
Redwood Regional Park ♠ 282 37.38 N 122.10 W
Redwood Terrace 282 37.19 N 122.18 W
Redwood Valley 204 39.15 N 123.12 W
Ree, Lough ⊜ 48 53.35 N 8.00 W
Reed City 190 43.52 N 85.30 W
Reeder 198 46.06 N 102.56 W
Reeders 210 41.01 N 75.20 W
Reed Lake ⊜, Mb., Can. 184 54.37 N 100.30 W
Reed Lake ⊜, Sk., Can. 184 50.24 N 107.05 W
Reedley 226 36.35 N 119.26 W
Reedsburg, Oh., U.S. 214 40.49 N 82.07 W
Reedsburg, Wi., U.S. 190 43.31 N 90.00 W
Reeds Peak ∧ 200 33.09 N 107.51 W
Reedsport 202 43.42 N 124.05 W
Reedsville, Pa., U.S. 208 40.39 N 77.35 W
Reedsville, Wi., U.S. 190 44.09 N 87.57 W
Reedurban 214 40.47 N 81.26 W
Reedville 208 37.50 N 76.16 W
Reedy Creek ≃ 220 28.04 N 81.21 W
Reedy Creek Swamp ⁂ 220 28.17 N 81.31 W
Reedy Lake ⊜ 220 27.44 N 81.22 W
Reefton 172 42.07 S 171.52 E
Reelfoot Lake ⊜ 194 36.25 N 89.22 W
Reepham 42 52.46 N 1.07 E
Reersø ›[1] 41 55.31 N 11.06 E
Rees 52 51.45 N 6.23 E
Reese 190 43.27 N 83.41 W
Reese ≃ 204 40.39 N 116.54 W
Reese Air Force Base ■ 196 33.36 N 102.02 W
Reeseville 190 43.18 N 88.50 W
Reesville 218 39.29 N 83.41 W
Reetz 54 53.11 N 11.52 E
Refaa, Djebel ∧ 34 35.34 N 5.52 E
Refahiye 130 39.54 N 38.46 E
Reform 194 33.22 N 88.00 W
Reforma de Pineda 234 16.24 N 94.28 W
Refton 208 39.57 N 76.14 W
Refuge Cove 182 50.07 N 124.50 W
Refugio 196 28.18 N 97.16 W
Refugio, Isla I 254 43.58 S 73.12 W
Refugio Creek ≃ 282 38.01 N 122.17 W
Rega ≃ 30 54.10 N 15.18 E
Regaïa 34 35.38 N 5.46 W
Regalbuto 70 37.39 N 14.38 E
Regau 64 47.59 N 13.41 E
Regen 60 48.59 N 13.07 E
Regen ≃ 60 49.01 N 12.06 E
Regência 255 19.36 S 39.49 W
Regency Estates 284c 39.03 N 77.10 W
Regeneração 250 6.15 S 42.41 W
Regensburg 60 49.01 N 12.06 E
Regensdorf 58 47.26 N 8.28 E
Regenstauf 60 49.08 N 12.08 E
Regent, Austl. 274b 37.44 S 145.00 E
Regent, N.D., U.S. 198 46.25 N 102.33 W
Regent Park 284c 39.03 N 77.10 W
Regents Park 274a 33.53 S 151.02 E
Regents Park ◆[8] 273d 26.15 S 28.04 E
Regent's Park ♠ 260 51.32 N 0.09 W
Regentville 274a 33.47 S 150.40 E
Reggâne 148 26.42 N 0.10 E
Regge ≃ 52 52.31 N 6.22 E
Reggello 66 43.41 N 11.32 E
Reggio di Calabria 68 38.07 N 15.39 E
Reggio di Calabria □[4] 68 38.10 N 16.00 E
Reggiolo 64 44.55 N 10.48 E
Reggio nell'Emilia 64 44.43 N 10.36 E
Reggio nell'Emilia □[4] 64 44.37 N 10.37 E
Regharen ⊜ 40 58.54 N 15.46 E
Reghin 38 46.47 N 24.42 E
Regina, Sk., Can. 184 50.25 N 104.39 W
Régina, Guy. fr. 250 4.19 N 52.08 W
Regina, S. Afr. 158 27.02 S 26.30 E
Regina Beach 184 50.47 N 105.00 W

Symbol	English	Deutsch	Español	Français	Português
≃	River	Fluß	Río	Rivière	Rio
≅	Canal	Kanal	Canal	Canal	Canal
ʟ	Waterfall, Rapids	Wasserfall, Stromschnellen	Cascada, Rápidos	Chute d'eau, Rapides	Cascata, Rápidos
ʊ	Strait	Meeresstraße	Estrecho	Détroit	Estreito
⊂	Bay, Gulf	Bucht, Golf	Bahía, Golfo	Baie, Golfe	Baía, Golfo
⊜	Lake, Lakes	See, Seen	Lago, Lagos	Lac, Lacs	Lago, Lagos
⁂	Swamp	Sumpf	Pantano	Marais	Pântano
⍓	Ice Features, Glacier	Eis- und Gletscherformen	Accidentes Glaciales	Formes glaciaires	Acidentes glaciares
⫪	Other Hydrographic Features	Andere Hydrographische Objekte	Otros Elementos Hidrográficos	Autres données hydrographiques	Outros acidentes hidrográficos
✢	Submarine Features	Untermeerische Objekte	Accidentes Submarinos	Formes de relief sous-marin	Acidentes submarinos
□	Political Unit	Politische Einheit	Unidad Politica	Entité politique	Unidade política
♁	Cultural Institution	Kulturelle Institution	Institución Cultural	Institution culturelle	Instituição cultural
⊥	Historical Site	Historische Stätte	Sitio Histórico	Site historique	Sitio histórico
♠	Recreational Site	Erholungs- und Ferienort	Sitio de Recreo	Centre de loisirs	Area de Lazer
⊠	Airport	Flughafen	Aeropuerto	Aéroport	Aeroporto
■	Military Installation	Militäranlage	Instalación Militar	Installation militaire	Instalação militar
◆	Miscellaneous	Verschiedenes	Misceláneo	Divers	Diversos

Regina Elena, Canale ≅ 266b 45.41 N 8.39 E
Región Metropolitana □4 252 33.30 S 70.30 W
Regis-Breitingen 54 51.05 N 12.26 E
Registro 252 24.30 S 47.50 W
Registro do Araguaia 255 15.44 S 51.50 W
Regiwar 120 25.57 N 65.44 E
Regla ✈8 286b 23.08 N 82.20 W
Regnéville 32 49.01 N 1.33 W
Regnitz ≐ 56 49.54 N 10.49 E
Rego Park ✈8 276 40.44 N 73.52 W
Regozero 24 65.28 N 31.10 E
Regresso, Cachoeira do ⌊ 250 0.58 S 54.51 W
Regstrup 41 55.40 N 11.37 E
Reguengos de Monsaraz 34 38.25 N 7.32 W
Rehau 54 50.15 N 12.02 E
Rehbach ≐ 56 49.27 N 8.27 E
Rehberg 54 52.43 N 12.10 E
Rehberge ∧2 264a 52.35 N 13.11 E
Rehberge, Volkspark ♦ 264a 52.33 N 13.20 E
Rehburg 52 52.28 N 9.13 E
Rehden 52 52.37 N 8.29 E
Rehe 56 50.38 N 8.07 E
Rehefeld-Zaunhaus 54 50.43 N 13.42 E
Rehfelde 54 52.30 N 13.54 E
Rehli 124 23.38 N 79.05 E
Rehme 52 52.12 N 8.49 E
Rehna 54 53.47 N 11.03 E
Rehoboth, Namibia 156 23.18 S 17.03 E
Rehoboth, Namibia 156 17.53 S 15.04 E
Rehoboth □5 156 23.30 S 17.00 E
Rehoboth Bay ⊂ 208 38.40 N 75.06 W
Rehoboth Beach 208 38.43 N 75.04 W
Rehoboth Seamount ≐3 16 37.30 N 59.50 W
Réhon 56 49.30 N 5.45 E
Rehovot 132 31.54 N 34.49 E
Rehti 124 22.44 N 77.26 E
Reiche Ebrach ≐ 56 49.49 N 10.58 E
Reiche Liesing ≐ 264b 48.08 N 16.16 E
Reichelsheim 56 49.43 N 8.50 E
Reichenau, Dtsch. 58 47.41 N 9.03 E
Reichenau, Schw. 58 46.49 N 9.24 E
Reichenau an der Rax 61 47.42 N 15.50 E
Reichenbach, Dtsch. 54 51.08 N 14.48 E
Reichenbach, Dtsch. 54 50.37 N 12.18 E
Reichenbach — Dzierżoniów, Pol. 30 50.44 N 16.39 E
Reichenbach, Schw. 58 46.38 N 7.42 E
Reichenberg — Liberec 30 50.46 N 15.03 E
Reichenhofen 58 47.50 N 9.58 E
Reichensachsen 56 51.09 N 9.59 E
Reichen Spitze ∧ 64 47.09 N 12.07 E
Reichertshausen 60 48.28 N 11.31 E
Reichertsheim 60 48.12 N 12.17 E
Reichertshofen 60 48.40 N 11.28 E
Reichraming 61 47.53 N 14.27 E
Reichsbrücke ✈5 264b 48.14 N 16.25 E
Reichshoffen 58 48.56 N 7.40 E
Reid 162 30.49 S 128.26 E
Reid, Mount ∧, Austl. 162 17.58 S 130.38 E
Reid, Mount ∧, Ak., U.S. 182 55.42 N 131.15 W
Reid Lake ⊜1 184 50.02 N 108.05 W
Reidsville, Ga., U.S. 192 32.05 N 82.07 W
Reidsville, N.C., U.S. 192 36.21 N 79.39 W
Reiffton 208 40.19 N 75.53 W
Reigate 42 51.14 N 0.13 W
Reigate and Banstead □8 260 51.17 N 0.12 W
Reignac-sur-Indre 50 47.13 N 0.55 E
Reignier 58 46.08 N 6.16 E
Reigoldswil 58 47.24 N 7.41 E
Reihoku 92 32.31 N 130.02 E
Reillanne 62 43.53 N 5.40 E
Reims 50 49.15 N 4.02 E
Reims, Montagne de ∧2 50 49.08 N 4.00 E
Reina Alejandra — Queen Alexandra Range ∧ 9 84.00 S 168.00 E
Reina Carlota, Estrecho de la — Queen Charlotte Sound ⊔ 182 51.30 N 129.30 W
Reinach, Schw. 58 47.30 N 7.35 E
Reinach, Schw. 58 47.15 N 8.11 E
Reina Fabiola — Queen Fabiola Mountains ∧ 9 71.30 S 35.40 E
Reina María, Costa de la — Queen Mary Coast ≐2 9 67.00 S 96.00 E
Reina Maud, Tierras de la — Queen Maud Land ≐1 9 72.30 S 12.00 E
Reinbeck 190 42.19 N 92.35 W
Reinbek 52 53.31 N 10.14 E
Reinberg 54 54.12 N 13.15 E
Reindeer ≐ 184 55.36 N 103.11 W
Reindeer Island I 184 52.25 N 98.00 W
Reindeer Lake ⊜ 176 57.15 N 102.40 W
Reindeer Station 180 68.42 N 134.06 W
Reine Charlotte, Détroit de la — Queen Charlotte Sound ⊔ 182 51.30 N 129.30 W
Reinerton 208 40.36 N 76.34 W
Reinfeld 52 53.49 N 10.28 E
Reinga, Cape > 172 34.25 S 172.41 E
Reinhardswald ∧ 52 51.30 N 9.30 E
Reinhardtsdorf 54 50.53 N 14.11 E
Reinheim 56 49.49 N 8.50 E
Reinickendorf ✈8 264a 52.35 N 13.21 E
Reinosa 34 43.00 N 4.08 W
Reino Unido — United Kingdom □1 28 54.00 N 2.00 W
Reinsdorf, Dtsch. 54 50.42 N 12.33 E
Reinsdorf, Dtsch. 54 51.54 N 12.37 E
Reinshagen ✈8 263 51.10 N 7.09 E
Reinstorf 54 53.50 N 11.38 E
Reis 130 38.16 N 31.35 E
Reisach 64 46.39 N 13.09 E
Reisaelva ≐ 24 69.48 N 21.00 E
Reischach 60 48.17 N 12.44 E
Reisdorf 56 49.53 N 6.15 E
Reisdorf, Camp ■ 273b 4.21 S 15.15 E
Reisholz ✈8 263 51.11 N 6.52 E
Reisjärvi 26 63.37 N 24.54 E
Reiss 46 58.28 N 3.10 W
Reisterstown 208 39.28 N 76.49 W
Reisterstown Road Plaza ✈9 284b 39.02 N 76.42 W
Reitano 70 37.58 N 14.20 E
Reitdiep ≅ 52 53.20 N 6.18 E
Reith bei Seefeld 64 47.18 N 11.12 E
Reit im Winkl 64 47.40 N 12.28 E
Reitz 158 27.53 S 28.31 E
Reitzenhain 54 50.33 N 13.13 E
Reivilo 158 27.36 S 24.08 E
Rejinagar 126 23.53 N 88.15 E
Rejmyra 40 58.50 N 15.55 E
Rejowiec Fabryczny 30 51.08 N 23.13 E
Rejštejn 60 49.09 N 13.31 E
Rekarne 40 59.26 N 16.25 E
Rekarne □9 40 59.17 N 16.25 E
Reken 52 51.50 N 7.02 E
Rekjoäti 272b 22.37 N 88.28 E
Reliance, N.T., Can. 176 62.42 N 109.08 W
Reliance, Wy., U.S. 200 41.40 N 109.11 W
Relief Reservoir ⊜1 226 38.16 N 119.44 W
Religione, Punta > 70 36.42 N 14.46 E
Reliz Creek ≐ 226 36.19 N 121.18 W
Rellingen 52 53.39 N 9.49 E
Rellinghausen ✈8 263 51.25 N 7.04 E
Reloncaví, Seno ⊂ 254 41.40 S 72.35 W
Remada 148 32.19 N 10.24 E
Remagen 56 50.34 N 7.13 E
Rémalard 50 48.26 N 0.47 E
Remanso 250 9.37 S 42.07 W
Remarde ≐ 261 48.35 N 2.15 E
Remarkable, Mount ∧ 162 32.48 S 138.10 E
Rembang 115a 6.42 S 111.20 E
Rembau 114 2.35 N 102.06 E
Rembia 114 2.20 N 102.13 E
Remchi 34 35.04 N 1.26 W
Remecó 252 37.38 S 63.39 W
Remedios, Col. 246 7.02 N 74.41 W
Remedios, Cuba 240p 22.30 N 79.33 W
Remedios, Pan. 236 8.14 N 81.51 W
Remedios, Punta > 236 13.31 N 89.49 W
Remedios, Santuario de los ♦1 286a 19.28 N 99.15 W
Remedios de Escalada ✈8 258 34.43 S 58.23 W
Remels 52 53.18 N 7.44 E
Remennicy 82 56.43 N 36.36 E
Remer 190 47.03 N 93.54 W
Remeshk 128 26.50 N 58.49 E
Remhoogte 158 29.33 S 23.01 E
Remich 56 49.33 N 6.22 E
Remich Airport ⊠ 279b 40.36 N 79.49 W
Rémigny, Lac ⊜ 190 47.51 N 79.12 W
Remilly 56 49.01 N 6.24 E
Remington 214 41.20 N 81.23 W
Remington, In., U.S. 216 40.45 N 87.09 W
Remington, Va., U.S. 188 38.32 N 77.48 W
Rémire 250 4.53 N 52.17 W
Remiremont 58 48.01 N 6.35 E
Remo □8 273a 6.42 N 3.29 E
Remolá, Estany del ⊂ 266d 41.17 N 2.04 E
Remollon 62 44.28 N 6.10 E
Remontnoje 80 46.33 N 43.39 E
Remoray 58 46.46 N 6.14 E
Remoulins 62 43.56 N 4.34 E
Rempang, Pulau I 114 0.51 N 104.10 E
Remptendorf 54 50.31 N 11.39 E
Rems ≐ 56 48.52 N 9.16 E
Remscheid 56 51.11 N 7.11 E
Remscheider-Stausee ⊜1 263 51.10 N 7.14 E
Remsen, Ia., U.S. 198 42.48 N 95.58 W
Remsen, N.Y., U.S. 210 43.19 N 75.11 W
Remsfeld 56 51.00 N 9.29 E
Remuna 126 21.33 N 86.54 E
Remus 190 43.36 N 85.09 W
Rémuzat 62 44.24 N 5.21 E
Rena 26 61.08 N 11.22 E
Renaix — Ronse 50 50.45 N 3.36 E
Renāla Khurd 123 30.53 N 73.36 E
Rena Point > 116 16.10 N 119.45 E
Renard Islands II 164 10.50 S 153.05 E
Renata 182 49.26 N 118.06 W
Renaud Island I 9 65.40 S 66.00 W
Renca 286e 33.24 S 70.44 W
Renca, Cerro ∧ 286e 33.23 S 70.43 W
Renčeni 76 57.44 N 25.26 E
Renchen 56 48.35 N 8.01 E
Rencontre East 186 47.38 N 55.12 W
Rencun 98 36.19 N 113.50 E
Renda, Ityo. 144 14.30 N 39.53 E
Renda, Lat. 76 57.09 N 22.22 E
Rende 68 39.19 N 16.11 E
Rendena, Valle V 64 46.08 N 10.42 E
Rend Lake ⊜1 194 38.05 N 88.58 W
Rendova Island I 175e 8.32 S 157.20 E
Rendsburg 41 54.18 N 9.40 E
Renens 58 46.32 N 6.35 E
Renesse 52 51.44 N 3.46 E
Renews 186 46.56 N 52.56 W
Renfrew, On., Can. 212 45.28 N 76.41 W
Renfrew, Scot., U.K. 46 55.53 N 4.24 W
Renfrew, Pa., U.S. 214 40.46 N 79.58 W
Renfrew □6 46 55.50 N 4.30 W
Rengam 114 1.53 N 103.24 E
Ren'gang 106 32.01 N 120.50 E
Rengasdengklok 115a 6.09 S 107.17 E
Rengat 112 0.24 S 102.33 E
Rengel 115a 7.04 S 112.00 E
Rengen ⊜ 26 64.05 N 14.03 E
Rengezhuang 105 39.45 N 118.10 E
Rengit 114 1.41 N 103.09 E
Rengkang 112 1.07 N 112.10 E
Rengo 252 34.25 S 70.52 W
Rengsdorf 56 50.30 N 7.29 E
Reng Tlāng ∧ 120 21.59 N 92.36 E
Renhe, Zhg. 100 33.32 N 114.02 E
Renhe, Zhg. 100 27.41 N 115.15 E
Renhechang 107 30.30 N 105.56 E
Renheji 100 31.56 N 115.07 E
Renhua 100 25.06 N 113.44 E
Renhuai 102 27.48 N 106.18 E
Reni 78 45.27 N 28.17 E
Renick 188 37.59 N 80.21 W
Renish Point > 46 57.44 N 6.59 W
Renjiawopeng 104 41.27 N 122.18 E
Renjiaxu 106 30.49 N 121.00 E
Renju 100 24.51 N 115.54 E
Renko 26 60.54 N 24.17 E
Renkum 52 51.58 N 5.45 E
Renliuchang 107 29.13 N 106.39 E
Renlong 107 30.32 N 105.47 E
Renmark 166 34.11 S 140.45 E
Renmei 100 25.50 N 117.56 E
Renmin 89 46.37 N 125.32 E
Renna, Monte ∧ 70 36.52 N 14.41 E
Rennau 54 52.17 N 10.55 E
Renne, Lac du — Reindeer Lake ⊜ 176 57.15 N 102.40 W
Renne, Rivière le ≐ 206 45.41 N 72.39 W
Rennell I 160 11.40 S 160.10 E
Rennell, Islas II 254 52.00 S 74.00 W
Rennell Sound ⊔ 182 53.25 N 132.40 W
Renner 222 32.59 N 96.47 W
Rennerdale 279b 40.24 N 80.08 W
Rennerod 56 50.36 N 8.04 E
Renner Springs 162 18.20 S 133.48 E
Rennertshofen 60 48.45 N 11.02 E
Rennes 48 48.05 N 1.41 W
Rennick Bay ⊂ 9 70.18 S 161.45 E
Rennick Glacier ⊓ 9 70.30 S 161.45 E
Rennie 184 49.51 N 95.33 W
Rennie's Mill 271d 22.18 N 114.15 E
Renningen 56 48.46 N 8.56 E
Renntier-See — Reindeer Lake ⊜ 176 57.15 N 102.40 W
Rennweg 64 47.01 N 13.37 E
Reno, Nv., U.S. 226 39.31 N 119.48 W
Reno, Pa., U.S. 214 41.25 N 79.45 W
Reno, Tx., U.S. 222 32.56 N 97.05 W
Reno ≐ 64 44.37 N 12.16 E
Reno Beach 214 41.40 N 83.15 W
Reno Hill ∧ 200 42.35 N 106.03 W
Reno International Airport ⊠ 226 39.30 N 119.46 W
Renoster ≐ 158 31.37 S 20.37 E
Renous ≐ 186 46.50 N 65.50 W
Renovo 210 41.19 N 77.45 W
Renqiao 100 33.27 N 117.16 E
Renqiu 98 38.43 N 116.05 E
Rens 41 54.54 N 9.06 E
Renshan 100 22.50 N 114.48 E
Renshou, Zhg. 100 27.08 N 117.51 E
Renshou, Zhg. 107 30.00 N 104.08 E
Rensjön 24 68.05 N 19.49 E
Rensselaer, In., U.S. 216 40.56 N 87.09 W
Rensselaer, Mo., U.S. 219 39.40 N 91.33 W
Rensselaer, N.Y., U.S. 210 42.38 N 73.44 W
Rensselaer □6 210 42.43 N 73.40 W
Rensselaer Falls 210 44.35 N 75.19 W
Rensselaerville 210 42.30 N 74.08 W
Rentería 34 43.19 N 1.54 W
Rentfort ✈8 263 51.35 N 6.57 E
Renton 224 47.28 N 122.12 W
Rentuo 107 29.14 N 106.23 E
Rentweinsdorf 56 50.04 N 10.47 E
Renun ≐ 114 3.05 N 97.55 E
Renville 198 44.47 N 95.12 W
Renwez 56 49.50 N 4.36 E
Renwick, N.Z. 172 41.30 S 173.50 E
Renwick, Ia., U.S. 190 42.49 N 93.58 W
Renyichang 107 29.29 N 105.28 E
Renziehausen Park ♦ 279b 40.21 N 79.50 W
Réo, Burkina 150 12.19 N 2.28 W
Reo, Indon. 115b 8.19 S 120.30 E
Reola ✈8 272a 28.34 N 76.59 E
Repartimento ≐ 250 6.06 S 50.40 W
Repaupo 285 39.48 N 75.18 W
Repbäcken 40 60.31 N 15.20 E
Répce ≐ 30 47.41 N 17.03 E
Repentigny 206 45.44 N 73.28 W
Repetek 128 38.34 N 63.11 E
Repino 76 60.10 N 29.52 E
Repjovka, Ross. 78 51.05 N 38.39 E
Repjovka, Ross. 80 53.09 N 48.06 E
Repolka 76 59.16 N 29.34 E
Repolovo 86 60.40 N 69.50 E
Reporoa 172 38.26 S 176.21 E
Reposaari 26 61.37 N 21.27 E
Repton 194 31.24 N 87.14 W
Republic, Ks., U.S. 198 39.55 N 97.49 W
Republic, Mi., U.S. 190 46.24 N 87.58 W
Republic, Mo., U.S. 194 37.07 N 93.28 W
Republic, Oh., U.S. 214 41.07 N 83.00 W
Republic, Wa., U.S. 202 48.38 N 118.44 W
República Centroafricana — Central African Republic □1 136 7.00 N 21.00 E
Republic Airport ⊠ 276 40.44 N 73.25 W
Republican ≐ 198 39.03 N 96.48 W
Republican, North Fork ≐ 198 40.01 N 101.59 W
Republican, South Fork ≐ 198 40.03 N 101.31 W
Republic Observatory ⊍3 273d 26.11 S 28.05 E
Republic Steel Corporation ⊍3 279a 41.28 N 81.40 W
République centrafricaine — Central African Republic □1 136 7.00 N 21.00 E
Repueblo de Oriente 196 25.51 N 99.39 W
Repulse Bay 176 66.32 N 86.15 W
Repulse Bay ⊂ 166 20.36 S 148.43 E
Repvåg 24 70.45 N 25.41 E
Requena, Esp. 34 39.29 N 1.06 W
Requena, Perú 248 4.58 S 73.50 W
Réquista 62 44.02 N 2.32 E
Rère ≐ 50 47.22 N 1.50 E
Reriutaba 250 4.10 S 40.35 W
Reşadiye 130 40.24 N 37.21 E
Reşadiye ✈8 267b 41.05 N 29.15 E
Reşadiye Yarımadası >1 130 36.40 N 27.45 E
Resang, Tanjong > 114 2.35 N 103.51 E
Resarö 40 59.26 N 18.20 E
Rescalda 266b 45.38 N 8.56 E
Rescaldina 266b 45.37 N 8.57 E
Reschenpass (Passo di Resia) ≍ 64 46.50 N 10.30 E
Rescue 208 36.59 N 76.33 W
Research 274b 37.42 S 145.11 E
Reseda ✈8 280 34.12 N 118.31 W
Resen 38 41.05 N 21.00 E
Resende 256 22.28 S 44.27 W
Reserva 252 24.38 S 50.52 W
Reserva, Parque de la ♦ 286d 12.04 S 77.02 W
Reserve, La., U.S. 194 30.03 N 90.33 W
Reserve, N.M., U.S. 200 33.42 N 108.45 W
Reserve Township 279b 40.29 N 79.59 W
Reservoir 274b 37.43 S 145.00 E
Reservoir Pond ⊜ 283 42.10 N 71.07 W
Rešetnikovo 82 56.27 N 36.34 E
Reshetylivka 78 49.34 N 34.04 E
Reshui 98 42.09 N 119.18 E
Reshuitang 102 24.10 N 103.09 E
Resia, Lago di ⊜ 64 46.47 N 10.32 E
Resia, Passo di (Reschenpass) ≍ 64 46.50 N 10.30 E
Resipol, Beinn ∧ 46 56.43 N 5.39 W
Resistencia 252 27.27 S 58.59 W
Reşita 38 45.17 N 21.53 E
Resiutta 64 46.23 N 13.13 E
Resko 30 53.47 N 15.25 E
Rešma 80 57.24 N 42.34 E
Resolute 176 74.41 N 94.54 W
Resolution Island I, N.T., Can. 176 61.30 N 65.00 W
Resolution Island I, N.Z. 172 45.40 S 166.40 E
Resolven 42 51.42 N 3.42 W
Resort, Loch ⊂ 46 58.03 N 7.06 W
Rešoty 76 57.09 N 28.30 E
Resplandes 250 6.17 S 45.13 W
Resplendor 255 19.20 S 41.15 W
Ressa ≐ 76 54.45 N 35.10 E
Ressaca, Ribeirão da ≐ 287b 23.38 S 46.51 W
Resse ✈8 263 51.34 N 7.07 E
Resseta ≐ 76 53.49 N 35.15 E
Ressons-sur-Matz 50 49.33 N 2.45 E
Restavan 76 53.36 N 30.56 E
Restavhaven 216 41.16 N 88.09 W
Restigouche (Ristigouche) ≐ 186 48.04 N 66.20 W
Restín, Punta > 246 4.17 S 81.15 W
Restinga 34 35.42 N 5.23 W
Restinga Seca 252 29.49 S 53.23 W
Reston, Mb., Can. 184 49.35 N 101.02 W
Reston, Scot., U.K. 46 55.51 N 2.12 W
Reston, Va., U.S. 208 38.58 N 77.20 W
Restoule Lake ⊜ 190 46.03 N 79.47 W
Restrepo, Col. 246 4.15 N 73.33 W
Restrepo, Col. 246 3.48 N 76.31 W
Resuttano 70 37.41 N 14.02 E
Retalhuleu 236 14.32 N 91.41 W
Retalhuleu □5 236 14.20 N 91.50 W
Retamosa 34 39.33 N 5.44 W
Retem, Oued er V 148 33.30 N 5.45 E
Retenice 54 50.38 N 13.43 E
Retezat, Munții ∧ 38 45.25 N 23.00 E
Retezat, Parcul National ♦ 38 45.20 N 22.50 E
Rethel 50 49.31 N 4.22 E
Rethem 52 52.45 N 9.23 E
Réthimnon 38 35.22 N 24.29 E
Retiche, Alpi — Rhaetian Alps ∧ 58 46.30 N 10.00 E
Retie 56 51.16 N 5.04 E
Retiers 50 47.55 N 1.23 W
Retiro, Estacion ✈5 288 34.36 S 58.22 W
Retiro, Parque del ♦ 266a 40.25 N 3.41 W
Retournac 62 45.12 N 4.02 E
Retreat 222 32.03 N 96.29 W
Retreat ≐ 170 34.07 S 149.38 E
Retsof 210 42.50 N 77.53 W
Rettenberg 58 47.35 N 10.17 E
Rettendon 260 51.39 N 0.33 E
Rettendon Place 260 51.38 N 0.34 E
Rettichovka 89 44.10 N 132.47 E
Rettin 54 54.06 N 10.53 E
Return Creek ≐ 226 37.56 N 119.28 W
Retz 61 48.45 N 15.57 E
Retzow 54 52.37 N 12.41 E
Reuden 54 52.04 N 12.18 E
Reungeut 114 4.34 N 96.22 E
Reunión (Réunion) □2, Afr. 138 21.06 S 55.36 E
Reunion (Réunion) □2, Afr. 157c 21.06 S 55.36 E
Reus 34 41.09 N 1.07 E
Reuschenberg 263 51.10 N 6.42 E
Reusel 52 51.21 N 5.22 E
Reuss ≐ 58 47.28 N 8.14 E
Reuterstadt Stavenhagen 54 53.42 N 12.53 E
Reutlingen 58 48.29 N 9.11 E
Reutov 82 55.46 N 37.52 E
Reutte 58 47.29 N 10.43 E
Reuver 52 51.17 N 6.05 E
Revadim 132 31.46 N 34.48 E
Rev'akino 82 54.22 N 37.40 E
Reval — Tallinn 76 59.25 N 24.45 E
Revda, Ross. 24 67.58 N 34.32 E
Revda, Ross. 86 56.48 N 59.57 E
Réveillon, Ruisseau le ≐ 261 48.42 N 2.30 E
Revel 62 45.11 N 5.52 E
Revelganj 124 25.47 N 84.40 E
Revelstoke 182 50.59 N 118.12 W
Reventazón 248 6.10 S 80.58 W
Reventazón ≐ 236 10.17 N 83.24 W
Revere, It. 64 45.03 N 11.08 E
Revere, Ma., U.S. 207 42.24 N 71.00 W
Revere, Pa., U.S. 208 40.31 N 75.10 W
Revere Beach ≐2 283 42.25 N 70.59 W
Revermont ∧2 58 46.27 N 5.25 E
Revesby 274a 33.57 S 151.01 E
Revest-du-Bion 62 44.05 N 5.33 E
Révia 154 13.23 S 36.31 E
Reviga ≐ 38 44.42 N 27.06 E
Revigny-sur-Ornain 56 48.50 N 4.59 E
Revilla del Campo 34 42.13 N 3.32 W
Revillagigedo, Islas II 232 19.00 N 111.30 W
Revillagigedo Channel ⊔ 182 55.10 N 131.13 W
Revillagigedo Island I 182 55.35 N 131.23 W
Revillo 198 45.01 N 96.34 W
Revin 56 49.56 N 4.38 E
Revloc 214 40.29 N 78.45 W
Řevničov 54 50.08 N 13.45 E
Revò 64 46.23 N 11.03 E
Revol'ucii, pik ∧ 85 38.31 N 72.21 E
Revolución Mexicana 234 16.03 N 93.04 W
Revolution, Museum of the ⊍ 265b 55.46 N 37.36 E
Revsundssjön ⊜ 26 62.49 N 15.17 E
Revúboè ≐ 154 16.13 S 33.37 E
Revuè ≐ 156 19.49 S 34.00 E
Rew 214 41.54 N 78.32 W
Rewa 124 24.32 N 81.18 E
Rewa ≐ 246 3.53 N 58.45 W
Rewāri 124 28.11 N 76.37 E
Rewataya, Taka ≐2 112 6.05 S 118.55 E
Rex, Mount ∧ 9 74.57 S 76.00 W
Rexburg 202 43.49 N 111.47 W
Rexdale ✈8 275b 43.43 N 79.35 W
Rexford, Ks., U.S. 198 39.28 N 100.44 W
Rexford, Mt., U.S. 202 48.52 N 115.13 W
Rexhame 283 42.06 N 70.40 W
Rexton 186 46.39 N 64.52 W
Rexville 210 42.05 N 77.40 W
Rey, Arroyo del ≐ 288 34.46 S 58.27 W
Rey, Embalse del ⊜1 266a 40.18 N 3.32 W
Rey, Estrecho del — King Sound ⊔ 162 17.00 S 123.30 E
Rey, Isla del I 236 8.22 N 78.55 W
Rey, Laguna del ⊜ 196 27.01 N 103.26 W
Rey Bouba 146 8.40 N 14.11 E
Reyes 248 14.19 S 67.23 W
Reyes, Point > 204 38.00 N 123.01 W
Reyes Peak ∧ 228 34.38 N 119.17 W
Reyhanlı 130 36.18 N 36.32 E
Rey Jorge, Estrecho del — King George Sound ⊔ 162 35.03 S 117.57 E
Rey Jorge, Isla — King George Island I 9 62.00 S 58.15 W
Reykjanes >1 24a 63.49 N 22.43 W
Reykjanes Ridge ≐3 10 62.00 N 27.00 W
Reykjavík 24a 64.09 N 21.51 W
Reynella 168b 35.06 S 138.32 E
Reyno 194 36.21 N 90.45 W
Reynolds, Ga., U.S. 192 32.33 N 84.05 W
Reynolds, In., U.S. 216 40.44 N 86.52 W
Reynolds, N.D., U.S. 198 47.57 N 97.45 W
Reynolds Channel ⊔ 276 40.36 N 73.40 W
Reynolds Creek ≐, Austl. 171a 27.56 S 152.36 E
Reynolds Creek ≐, On., Can. 212 43.00 N 80.58 W
Reynoldsville 214 41.05 N 78.53 W
Reynosa 232 26.07 N 98.18 W
Reyssouze ≐ 58 46.27 N 4.54 E
Rež 86 57.23 N 61.24 E
Rež ≐ 86 57.54 N 62.18 E
Reza, gora (Kūh-e Rīzeh) ∧ 128 37.47 N 58.05 E
Rezé 32 47.12 N 1.34 W
Rēzekne 76 56.30 N 27.19 E
Rēzekne ≐ 76 56.46 N 26.58 E
Rezina 38 47.44 N 28.58 E
Rezino 86 55.51 N 55.18 E
Rezovo 38 41.59 N 28.02 E
Rezovska (Mutlu) ≐ 38 41.59 N 28.01 E
Rezvānshahr 128 37.33 N 49.09 E
Rezzato 64 45.31 N 10.19 E
Rezzoaglio 62 44.32 N 9.23 E
Rezzonico 58 46.04 N 9.16 E
Rhade 52 53.19 N 9.07 E
Rhadeswood Reservoir ⊜1 262 53.29 N 1.56 W
Rhaetian Alps (Rätische Alpen) (Alpi Retiche) ∧ 58 46.30 N 10.00 E
Rhallamane, Sebkha de ≅ 148 23.41 N 9.50 W
Rhame 198 46.13 N 103.39 W
Rharbi, Île I 148 34.39 N 11.03 E
Rharbi, Zahrez ⊜ 148 34.50 N 2.50 E
Rhauderfehn 52 53.08 N 7.35 E
Rhaunen 56 49.52 N 7.20 E
Rhayader 42 52.18 N 3.30 W
Rhea Creek ≐ 202 45.30 N 119.46 W
Rheda-Wiedenbrück 52 51.50 N 8.18 E
Rhede, Dtsch. 52 53.03 N 7.16 E
Rhede, Dtsch. 52 51.51 N 6.42 E
Rheden 52 52.01 N 6.02 E
Rheems 208 40.08 N 76.34 W
Rheem Valley 226 37.52 N 122.07 W
Rheidol ≐ 42 52.25 N 4.05 W
Rheims — Reims 50 49.15 N 4.02 E
Rhein 184 51.22 N 102.10 W
Rhein — Rhine ≐ 30 51.52 N 6.02 E
Rheinau 56 48.41 N 7.56 E
Rheinbach 56 50.37 N 6.57 E
Rheinberg 56 51.33 N 6.35 E
Rheinböllen 56 50.00 N 7.40 E
Rheinbrohl 56 50.30 N 7.19 E
Rheinbrücke ✈5 263 51.12 N 6.44 E
Rheindürkheim 56 49.42 N 8.21 E
Rheine 52 52.17 N 7.26 E
Rheineck 58 47.28 N 9.35 E
Rheinen 263 51.27 N 7.38 E
Rheinfall ⌊ 58 47.41 N 8.38 E
Rheinfelden, Dtsch. 58 47.33 N 7.47 E
Rheinfelden, Schw. 58 47.33 N 7.48 E
Rheinhausen 56 51.24 N 6.44 E
Rhein-Herne-Kanal ≅ 263 51.27 N 6.47 E
Rheinhessen-Pfalz □5 56 49.30 N 8.00 E
Rheinkamp 52 51.30 N 6.37 E
Rheinland-Pfalz □3 56 50.00 N 7.00 E
Rheinsberg 54 53.06 N 12.53 E
Rheinstadion ♦ 263 51.16 N 6.44 E
Rheinstein, Burg ⊥ 56 50.00 N 7.50 E
Rheinwald V 58 46.32 N 9.17 E
Rheinwaldhorn ∧ 58 46.30 N 9.02 E
Rheirs, Oued V 148 30.39 N 4.26 W
Rhêmes-Notre-Dame 62 45.34 N 7.07 E
Rhenen 52 51.57 N 5.34 E
Rhens 56 50.17 N 7.37 E
Rheurdt 56 51.27 N 6.28 E
Rheydt 56 51.10 N 6.25 E
Rheydt, Schloss ⊥ 263 51.11 N 6.29 E
Rhin ≐, Dtsch. 54 52.59 N 12.55 E
Rhin — Rhine ≐, Europe 30 51.52 N 6.02 E
Rhinau 58 48.19 N 7.42 E
Rhine 192 31.59 N 83.12 W
Rhine (Rhein) (Rhin) ≐ 30 51.52 N 6.02 E
Rhinebeck 210 41.55 N 73.54 W
Rhinecliff 210 41.55 N 73.57 W
Rhineland 219 38.43 N 91.31 W
Rhinelander 190 45.38 N 89.24 W
Rhin Kanal ≅ 54 52.47 N 12.24 E
Rhinluch ≡ 54 52.50 N 12.50 E
Rhinns of Kells ∧ 44 55.07 N 4.22 W
Rhinns Point > 46 55.40 N 6.30 W
Rhino Camp 154 2.58 N 31.24 E
Rhinow 54 52.45 N 12.20 E
Rhiou, Oued ≐ 34 36.00 N 0.55 E
Rhir, Cap > 148 30.38 N 9.55 W
Rhis, Oued ≐ 34 35.14 N 3.57 W
Rhiw ≐ 42 52.36 N 3.11 W
Rho 62 45.32 N 9.02 E
Rhode Island □3, U.S. 178 41.40 N 71.30 W
Rhode Island □3, U.S. 207 41.40 N 71.30 W
Rhode Island I 207 41.33 N 71.15 W
Rhode Island Sound ⊔ 207 41.25 N 71.15 W
Rhoden 52 51.28 N 9.00 E
Rhodes, Austl. 274a 33.50 S 151.05 E
Rhodes — Ródhos, Ellás 38 36.26 N 28.13 E
Rhodes, S. Afr. 158 30.47 S 27.59 E
Rhodes, Eng., U.K. 262 53.33 N 2.14 W
Rhodes — Ródhos I 38 36.10 N 28.00 E
Rhodesia — Zimbabwe □1 154 20.00 S 30.00 E
Rhodes Inyanga National Park ♦ 154 18.12 S 32.45 E
Rhodes Matopos National Park ♦ 154 20.33 S 28.20 E
Rhodes Park ♦ 273d 26.12 S 28.06 E
Rhodes Peak ∧ 202 46.41 N 114.47 W
Rhodes' Tomb ⊥ 154 20.30 S 28.30 E
Rhododendron 224 45.20 N 121.55 W
Rhododendron State Park ♦ 207 42.47 N 72.12 W
Rhodon 261 48.43 N 2.04 E
Rhodon, Ruisseau le ≐ 261 48.42 N 2.04 E
Rhodope Mountains (Rodopi) (Orosirá Rodhópis) ∧ 38 41.30 N 24.30 E
Rhodt 56 49.16 N 8.07 E
Rhome 222 33.03 N 97.28 W
Rhondda 42 51.40 N 3.27 W
Rhône □5 32 45.55 N 4.40 E
Rhône ≐ 32 43.20 N 4.50 E
Rhône à Sète, Canal du ≅ 62 43.25 N 3.42 E
Rhône au Rhin, Canal du ≅ 58 47.06 N 5.19 E
Rhoose 42 51.24 N 3.20 W
Rhosesmor 262 53.12 N 3.10 W
Rhosllanerchrugog 44 53.00 N 3.03 W
Rhosneigr 44 53.14 N 4.31 W
Rhos-on-Sea 44 53.19 N 3.45 W
Rhossili 42 51.34 N 4.17 W
Rhourde-el-Baguel 148 31.24 N 6.57 E
Rhuddlan 44 53.18 N 3.27 W
Rhue ≐ 32 45.23 N 2.29 E
Rhum I 46 57.00 N 6.20 W
Rhum, Sound of ⊔ 46 56.56 N 6.14 W
Rhyl 44 53.19 N 3.29 W
Rhymney 42 51.46 N 3.18 W
Rhymney ≐ 42 51.28 N 3.10 W
Rhynie 46 57.19 N 2.50 W
Riaba 152 3.23 N 8.46 E
Riace 68 38.25 N 16.29 E
Riachão 250 7.22 S 46.37 W
Riachão das Neves 250 11.04 S 44.55 W
Riachão do Dantas 250 11.04 S 37.44 W
Riachão do Jacuípe 250 11.48 S 39.21 W
Riacho de Santana 255 13.37 S 42.57 W
Riacho Grande 256 23.48 S 46.35 W
Riachos, Islas de los II 254 40.10 S 62.08 W
Riachuelo, Bra. 250 10.44 S 37.11 W
Riachuelo, Chile 254 40.49 S 73.42 W
Riachuelo, Ur. 258 34.28 S 57.43 W
Riachuelo ≐ 288 34.38 S 58.22 W
Riachuelo, Arroyo ≐ 258 34.27 S 57.44 W
Rialma 255 15.18 S 49.34 W
Rialto, Bra. 256 22.35 S 44.16 W
Rialto, Ca., U.S. 228 34.06 N 117.22 W
Riamkanan, Waduk ⊜1 112 3.30 S 115.05 E
Rianápolis 255 15.29 S 49.28 W
Riang 120 27.32 N 92.56 E
Riangnom 140 9.55 N 30.01 E
Riaño 34 42.58 N 5.01 W
Rians 62 43.37 N 5.45 E
Riánsares ≐ 34 39.32 N 3.18 W
Riasi 123 33.05 N 74.50 E
Riau □4 112 1.00 N 102.00 E
Riau, Kepulauan II 112 1.00 N 104.30 E
Riaz 58 46.38 N 7.04 E
Riaza 34 41.17 N 3.28 W
Riaza ≐ 34 41.42 N 3.55 W
Ribadavia 34 42.17 N 8.08 W
Ribadeo 34 43.32 N 7.02 W
Ribadesella 34 43.28 N 5.04 W
Ribas de Jarama 266a 40.23 N 3.31 W
Ribas do Rio Pardo 255 20.27 S 53.46 W
Ribauê 154 14.57 S 38.17 E
Ribble ≐ 44 53.44 N 2.50 W
Ribbleton 262 53.46 N 2.40 W
Ribble Valley □8 262 53.48 N 2.31 W
Ribbon Fall ⌊ 226 37.44 N 119.39 W
Ribchester 262 53.49 N 2.32 W
Ribe 41 55.21 N 8.46 E
Ribe □6 41 55.35 N 8.50 E
Ribe ≐ 41 55.21 N 8.40 E
Ribeauvillé 58 48.12 N 7.19 E
Ribécourt 50 49.31 N 2.55 E
Ribeira 252 24.40 S 49.01 W
Ribeira do Iguape ≐ 252 24.40 S 47.24 W
Ribeira do Pombal 250 10.50 S 38.32 W
Ribeira Grande, C.V. 150a 17.11 N 25.04 W
Ribeira Grande, Port. 148a 37.49 N 25.31 W
Ribeirão 250 8.31 S 35.23 W
Ribeirão das Lajes, Reprêsa do ⊜1 256 22.45 S 43.55 W
Ribeirão de São Joaquim 256 22.17 S 44.11 W
Ribeirão do Pinhal 255 23.24 S 50.18 W
Ribeirão Pires 256 23.43 S 46.25 W
Ribeirão Preto 255 21.10 S 47.48 W
Ribeirão Vermelho 255 21.11 S 45.03 W
Ribeirãozinho 255 16.27 S 52.35 W
Ribeiro Gonçalves 250 7.32 S 45.14 W
Ribeiro Junqueira 256 21.28 S 42.31 W
Ribeiros 256 21.59 S 45.35 W
Ribemont 50 49.48 N 3.28 E
Ribera 70 37.30 N 13.16 E
Riberalta 248 10.59 S 66.06 W
Riberão Pires □7 287b 23.43 S 46.21 W
Ribiers 62 44.14 N 5.52 E
Rib Lake 190 45.19 N 90.12 W
Ribnica, Slvn. 36 45.44 N 14.44 E
Ribnica, Slvn. 61 46.32 N 15.16 E
Ribnitz-Damgarten 54 54.15 N 12.28 E
Ribstone Creek ≐ 184 52.51 N 110.05 W
Ricadi 68 38.37 N 15.52 E
Ricarda, Estany de la ⊂ 266d 41.18 N 2.07 E
Ricardo Flores Magón 232 29.58 N 106.58 W
Ricaurte 246 1.13 N 77.59 W
Riccall 44 53.50 N 1.04 W
Riccarton 172 43.32 S 172.36 E
Riccia 66 41.29 N 14.50 E
Riccione 66 43.59 N 12.39 E
Rice 222 32.15 N 96.30 W
Rice Creek ≐ 216 42.16 N 84.57 W
Rice Lake 190 45.30 N 91.44 W
Rice Lake ⊜, On., Can. 190 47.42 N 82.08 W
Rice Lake ⊜, On., Can. 212 44.08 N 78.13 W
Rice Lake Indian Reserve ♦4 212 44.10 N 78.12 W
Riceville, Ia., U.S. 190 43.22 N 92.33 W
Riceville, Pa., U.S. 214 41.47 N 79.48 W
Riceville, Tn., U.S. 192 35.23 N 84.41 W
Rich, Cape > 212 44.43 N 80.38 W
Richan 184 49.59 N 92.49 W
Richard B. Russell Lake ⊜1 192 34.05 N 82.39 W
Richard Collinson Inlet ⊂ 176 72.45 N 113.45 W
Richards 222 30.32 N 95.51 W
Richard's Bay 158 28.47 S 32.06 E
Richard's Bay ⊂ 158 28.50 S 32.02 E
Richards-Gebaur Air Force Base ■ 194 38.51 N 94.33 W
Richard's Harbour 186 47.37 N 56.24 W
Richards Island I 180 69.20 N 134.30 W
Richardson 222 32.56 N 96.43 W
Richardson ≐ 176 58.30 N 111.30 W
Richardson, Mount ∧ 162 28.49 S 119.59 E
Richardson Bay ⊂ 282 37.52 N 122.29 W
Richardson Mountains ∧, Can. 180 67.15 N 136.30 W
Richardson Mountains ∧, N.Z. 172 44.45 S 168.31 E
Richardson Park 285 39.44 N 75.35 W
Richardsville 214 41.14 N 79.01 W
Richard-Toll 150 16.28 N 15.41 W
Richardton 198 46.53 N 102.18 W
Richāt, Guelb er ∧2 148 21.07 N 11.24 W
Richboro 208 40.13 N 75.01 W
Richburg 210 42.05 N 78.09 W
Riche, Pointe > 186 50.42 N 57.25 W
Richebourg 261 48.49 N 1.38 E
Richelieu, P.Q., Can. 206 45.27 N 73.15 W
Richelieu, Fr. 32 47.01 N 0.19 E
Richelieu □6 206 45.55 N 73.00 W
Richelieu ≐ 206 46.03 N 73.07 W
Richer 184 49.39 N 96.28 W
Richey 198 47.38 N 105.04 W
Richfield, Id., U.S. 202 43.02 N 114.09 W
Richfield, Mn., U.S. 190 44.53 N 93.16 W
Richfield, Oh., U.S. 214 41.14 N 81.39 W
Richfield, Pa., U.S. 208 40.41 N 77.07 W
Richfield, Ut., U.S. 200 38.46 N 112.05 W
Richfield Springs 210 42.51 N 74.59 W
Richford, N.Y., U.S. 210 42.21 N 76.12 W
Richford, Vt., U.S. 206 44.59 N 72.40 W
Rich Fountain 219 38.24 N 91.53 W
Richgrove 226 35.48 N 119.07 W
Richhill, N. Ire., U.K. 48 54.23 N 6.33 W
Rich Hill, Mo., U.S. 194 38.05 N 94.21 W
Richibucto 186 46.41 N 64.52 W
Richisau 58 47.02 N 8.54 E
Richky 78 51.07 N 34.30 E
Richland, Ga., U.S. 192 32.05 N 84.40 W
Richland, Mi., U.S. 216 42.22 N 85.27 W
Richland, Mo., U.S. 194 37.51 N 92.24 W
Richland, N.J., U.S. 208 39.29 N 74.52 W
Richland, N.Y., U.S. 212 43.34 N 76.03 W
Richland, Pa., U.S. 208 40.21 N 76.16 W
Richland, Tx., U.S. 222 31.56 N 96.26 W
Richland, Tx., U.S. 222 32.57 N 95.49 W
Richland, Wa., U.S. 202 46.17 N 119.17 W
Richland □6 214 40.46 N 82.31 W
Richland Center 190 43.20 N 90.23 W
Richland Creek ≐, Il., U.S. 219 38.14 N 89.54 W
Richland Creek ≐, Tn., U.S. 194 35.02 N 86.55 W
Richland Creek ≐, Tx., U.S. 222 31.58 N 96.03 W
Richlands, N.C., U.S. 192 34.53 N 77.32 W
Richlands, Va., U.S. 192 37.05 N 81.47 W
Richland Springs 196 31.16 N 98.57 W
Richmond, Austl. 166 20.44 S 143.08 E
Richmond, Austl. 170 33.36 S 150.46 E
Richmond, Austl. 274b 37.49 S 145.00 E
Richmond, B.C., Can. 224 49.09 N 123.06 W
Richmond, On., Can. 212 45.11 N 75.50 W
Richmond, P.Q., Can. 206 45.40 N 72.09 W
Richmond, N.Z. 172 41.20 S 173.11 E
Richmond, S. Afr. 158 31.23 S 23.56 E
Richmond, S. Afr. 158 29.54 S 30.08 E
Richmond, Eng., U.K. 44 54.24 N 1.44 W
Richmond, Ca., U.S. 226 37.56 N 122.20 W
Richmond, Il., U.S. 216 42.28 N 88.18 W
Richmond, In., U.S. 218 39.49 N 84.53 W
Richmond, Ks., U.S. 198 38.24 N 95.15 W
Richmond, Ky., U.S. 192 37.44 N 84.17 W
Richmond, Me., U.S. 188 44.05 N 69.47 W
Richmond, Ma., U.S. 207 42.22 N 73.22 W
Richmond, Mi., U.S. 214 42.48 N 82.45 W
Richmond, Mn., U.S. 190 45.27 N 94.31 W
Richmond, Mo., U.S. 194 39.16 N 93.58 W
Richmond, Oh., U.S. 214 40.26 N 80.46 W
Richmond, Tx., U.S. 222 29.34 N 95.45 W
Richmond, Ut., U.S. 200 41.55 N 111.48 W
Richmond, Vt., U.S. 188 44.24 N 72.59 W
Richmond, Va., U.S. 208 37.33 N 77.27 W
Richmond □6, P.Q., Can. 206 45.40 N 72.00 W
Richmond □6, N.Y., U.S. 210 40.38 N 74.05 W
Richmond □6, Va., U.S. 208 37.32 N 77.28 W
Richmond ✈8, Eng., U.K. 42 51.28 N 0.18 W
Richmond ✈8, Ca., U.S. 282 37.46 N 122.29 W
Richmond ✈8, Pa., U.S. 285 39.59 N 75.06 W
Richmond, Mount ∧ 172 41.29 S 173.24 E
Richmond, Point > 282 37.55 N 122.23 W
Richmond Beach 224 47.46 N 122.23 W
Richmond Creek ≐ 276 40.34 N 74.11 W
Richmond Heights, Fl., U.S. 220 25.37 N 80.22 W
Richmond Heights, Mo., U.S. 219 38.37 N 90.19 W
Richmond Heights, Oh., U.S. 214 41.33 N 81.30 W
Richmond Highlands 224 47.45 N 122.20 W
Richmond Hill, On., Can. 212 43.52 N 79.27 W
Richmond Hill, Ga., U.S. 192 31.56 N 81.18 W
Richmond Hill ✈8 276 40.42 N 73.49 W
Richmond International Airport ⊠ 208 37.30 N 77.19 W
Richmond Mall ✈9 279a 41.32 N 81.30 W
Richmond National Battlefield Park ♦ 208 37.25 N 77.23 W
Richmond Park ♦ 260 51.26 N 0.16 W
Richmond Peak ∧ 241h 13.17 N 61.13 W

Symbols in the index entries represent the broad categories identified in the key at the right. Symbols with superior numbers (∧1) identify subcategories (see complete key on page I · 1).

Symbole im Register stellen die rechts im Schlüssel erklärten Kategorien dar. Symbole mit hochgestellten Ziffern (∧1) bezeichnen Unterabteilungen einer Kategorie (vgl. vollständiger Schlüssel auf Seite I · 1).

Los símbolos incluidos en el texto del índice representan las grandes categorías identificadas con la clave a la derecha. Los símbolos con números en su parte superior (∧1) identifican las subcategorías (véase la clave completa en la página I · 1).

Les symboles de l'index représentent les catégories indiquées dans la légende à droite. Les symboles suivis d'un indice (∧1) représentent des sous-catégories (voir légende complète à la page I · 1).

Os símbolos incluídos no texto do índice representam as grandes categorias identificadas com a chave à direita. Os símbolos com números em sua parte superior (∧1) identificam as subcategorias (veja-se a chave completa à página I · 1).

ENGLISH	DEUTSCH	ESPAÑOL	FRANÇAIS	PORTUGUÊS
∧ Mountain	Berg	Montaña	Montagne	Montanha
∧∧ Mountains	Gebirge	Montañas	Montagnes	Montanhas
≍ Pass	Paß	Paso	Col	Passo
V Valley, Canyon	Tal, Cañon	Valle, Cañón	Vallée, Canyon	Vale, Canhão
≃ Plain	Ebene	Llano	Plaine	Planície
> Cape	Kap	Cabo	Cap	Cabo
I Island	Insel	Isla	Île	Ilha
II Islands	Inseln	Islas	Îles	Ilhas
≐ Other Topographic Features	Andere Topographische Objekte	Otros Elementos Topográficos	Autres données topographiques	Outros acidentes topográficos

Richmond Range ⋀ 172 41.27 S 173.30 E
Richmond Royal Australian Air Force Base ■ 170 33.37 S 150.48 E
Richmond-San Rafael Bridge ◆[5] 282 37.56 N 122.27 W
Richmondtown Restoration ⊥ 276 40.34 N 74.09 W
Richmond Valley ◆[8] 276 40.31 N 74.13 W
Richmondville 210 42.38 N 74.33 W
Richrath 263 51.08 N 6.56 E
Rich Square 192 36.16 N 77.17 W
Rich Stadium ♦ 284a 42.57 N 78.47 W
Richtenberg 54 54.12 N 12.53 E
Richterswil 58 47.13 N 8.42 E
Richton 194 31.20 N 88.56 W
Richton Park 216 41.29 N 87.42 W
Richvale, On., Can. 212 43.51 N 79.26 W
Richvale, Ca., U.S. 226 39.30 N 121.45 W
Richview 219 38.23 N 89.11 W
Richville, N.Y., U.S. 212 44.25 N 75.23 E
Richville, Oh., U.S. 214 40.45 N 81.27 W
Richwood, N.J., U.S. 285 39.43 N 75.10 W
Richwood, Oh., U.S. 214 40.25 N 83.17 W
Richwood, W.V., U.S. 188 38.13 N 80.32 W
Richwood Village 222 29.04 N 95.25 W
Ricinskij zapovednik ♦ 84 43.25 N 40.30 E
Rickenbacker Air Force Base ■ 218 39.48 N 82.56 W
Rickenpass)(58 47.14 N 9.02 E
Ricken Tunnel ◆[5] 58 47.12 N 9.05 E
Ricketts Glen State Park ♦ 210 41.20 N 76.18 W
Ricketts Point > 274b 38.00 S 145.02 E
Rickleån ≃ 26 64.05 N 20.56 E
Rickling 54 54.01 N 10.13 E
Rickmansworth 42 51.39 N 0.29 W
Rico 200 37.41 N 108.01 W
Ricoa ≃ 241s 11.30 N 69.12 W
Ricobayo, Embalse de ◎[1] 34 41.30 N 5.55 W
Ricupe 152 14.37 S 21.25 E
Ridā' 144 14.38 N 44.54 E
Ridanna (Ridnaun) 64 46.55 N 11.15 E
Riddarhyttan 40 59.48 N 15.33 E
Ridderkerk 52 51.52 N 4.36 E
Riddes 58 46.10 N 7.13 E
Riddle 202 42.57 N 123.21 W
Riddle Mountain ▲ 202 43.07 N 118.30 W
Riddlesburg 214 40.10 N 78.15 W
Riddlewood 285 39.54 N 75.26 W
Riddon, Loch c 46 55.58 N 5.12 W
Rideau ≃ 212 45.27 N 75.42 W
Ridge, Eng., U.K. 260 51.41 N 0.15 W
Ridge, N.Y., U.S. 207 40.54 N 72.53 W
Ridge, Tx., U.S. 222 31.09 N 96.19 W
Ridge Acres 276 40.41 N 74.32 W
Ridgecrest, Ca., U.S. 204 35.37 N 117.40 W
Ridgecrest, Wa., U.S. 224 47.45 N 122.21 W
Ridgedale 184 53.04 N 104.09 W
Ridge Farm 194 39.53 N 87.39 W
Ridgefield, Ct., U.S. 207 41.16 N 73.29 W
Ridgefield, Il., U.S. 216 42.16 N 88.22 W
Ridgefield, N.J., U.S. 210 40.50 N 74.00 W
Ridgefield, Wa., U.S. 224 45.48 N 122.44 W
Ridgefield Park 276 40.51 N 74.01 W
Ridgeland, Ms., U.S. 194 32.25 N 90.07 W
Ridgeland, S.C., U.S. 192 32.28 N 80.58 W
Ridgely, Md., U.S. 208 38.56 N 75.53 W
Ridgely, Tn., U.S. 194 36.15 N 89.29 W
Ridge Manor 220 28.31 N 82.10 W
Ridgemont 210 43.13 N 77.43 W
Ridgetown 214 42.26 N 81.54 W
Ridgeville, Mb., Can. 184 49.04 N 97.01 W
Ridgeville, In., U.S. 216 40.17 N 85.01 W
Ridgeville, S.C., U.S. 192 33.05 N 80.18 W
Ridgeville Corners 216 41.26 N 84.15 W
Ridgeway, On., Can. 284a 42.53 N 79.03 W
Ridgeway, Mi., U.S. 216 41.59 N 83.51 W
Ridgeway, Mo., U.S. 194 40.22 N 93.56 W
Ridgeway, N.J., U.S. 208 40.01 N 74.17 W
Ridgeway, Oh., U.S. 216 40.30 N 83.34 W
Ridgeway, Tx., U.S. 222 33.11 N 95.46 W
Ridgeway, Wi., U.S. 190 43.00 N 89.59 W
Ridgeway Ditch ≡ 279a 41.25 N 82.05 W
Ridgewood 210 40.58 N 74.07 W
Ridgewood ◆[8] 276 40.42 N 73.53 W
Ridgewood Farm 285 39.57 N 75.34 W
Ridgewood Reservoir ◎[1] 276 40.41 N 73.53 W
Ridgway, Co., U.S. 200 38.09 N 107.46 W
Ridgway, Il., U.S. 194 37.47 N 88.15 W
Ridgway, Pa., U.S. 214 41.25 N 78.43 W
Riding Mountain ▲ 184 50.37 N 99.37 W
Riding Mountain National Park ♦ 184 50.55 N 100.25 W
Ridīwajār 124 27.57 N 83.26 E
Ridley Creek ≃ 285 39.51 N 75.21 W
Ridley Creek State Park ♦ 285 39.57 N 75.27 W
Ridley Park 285 39.52 N 75.19 W
Ridnaun
— Ridanna 64 46.55 N 11.15 E
Riebeek-Kasteel 158 33.23 S 18.53 E
Riebeek-Oos 158 33.10 S 26.10 E
Riebeek-Wes 158 33.21 S 18.52 E
Riecawr, Loch ◎ 44 55.13 N 4.27 W
Riedau 60 48.18 N 13.38 E
Riedelbach 56 50.19 N 8.23 E
Rieden 60 49.19 N 11.57 E
Riedenburg 60 48.58 N 11.41 E
Rieder 54 51.44 N 11.10 E
Riederalp 58 46.23 N 8.01 E
Riedern 56 49.40 N 9.23 E
Ried im Innkreis 60 48.13 N 13.30 E
Ried im Oberinntal 58 47.03 N 10.39 E
Riedisheim 58 47.45 N 7.22 E
Riedlingen 58 48.09 N 9.28 E
Riedstadt 56 49.50 N 8.30 E
Riegel 58 48.09 N 7.45 E
Riegelsville, N.J., U.S. 210 40.49 N 74.52 W
Riegelsville, Pa., U.S. 208 40.36 N 75.12 W
Riegelwood 192 34.20 N 78.15 W
Riegersburg 61 47.00 N 15.56 E
Riegersburg, Schloss ⊥ 61 47.01 N 15.56 E
Riegersdorf 64 46.33 N 13.47 E
Riehen 58 47.35 N 7.39 E
Rieka
— Rijeka 36 45.20 N 14.27 E
Rielasingen 58 47.44 N 8.50 E
Riemke ◆[8] 263 51.30 N 7.13 E
Riemst 56 50.48 N 5.36 E
Rieneck 56 50.05 N 9.38 E
Rienza (Rienz) ≃ 64 46.43 N 11.39 E
Rienzi 194 34.45 N 88.31 W
Riesa 54 51.18 N 13.17 E
Riesco, Isla I 254 53.00 S 72.30 W
Rieseby 41 54.32 N 9.48 E
Riesel 222 31.28 N 96.56 W
Riesenbeck 52 52.16 N 7.37 E
Riese Pio X 64 45.44 N 11.55 E
Riesi 70 37.17 N 14.05 E
Riestedt 54 51.29 N 11.21 E
Riet ≃, S. Afr. 158 29.00 S 23.54 E
Riet ≃, S. Afr. 158 31.20 S 20.17 E
Rietavas 76 55.44 N 21.56 E
Rietberg 52 51.47 N 8.25 E
Rietbron 158 32.54 S 23.10 E
Rietfontein 158 21.58 S 20.58 E
Riethuiskraal 158 34.20 S 21.22 E
Rieti 66 42.24 N 12.51 E
Rieti □[4] 66 42.18 N 12.52 E
Rietschen 54 51.23 N 14.47 E
Rietspruit ≃, S. Afr. 273d 26.06 S 27.39 E
Rietspruit ≃, S. Afr. 273d 26.19 S 28.18 E
Rietvlei 158 30.29 S 29.51 E
Rietzer See ◎ 54 52.22 N 12.39 E
Rievaulx Abbey ⊌[1] 44 54.16 N 1.07 W
Riez 62 43.49 N 6.06 E
Riezlern 58 47.21 N 10.11 E
Rif ⋀ 148 35.00 N 4.00 W
Riffle Lake ◎[1] 224 46.30 N 122.20 W
Rifflart 273b 4.25 S 15.21 E
Rifiano (Riffian) 64 46.42 N 11.11 E
Rifle 200 39.32 N 107.46 W
Rifle ≃ 190 44.00 N 83.49 W
Rifstangi > 24a 66.35 N 16.10 W
Rifton 210 41.50 N 74.03 W
Rift Valley □[4] 154 0.30 N 36.00 E
Rift Valley V 10 3.00 S 29.00 E
Rift Valley Lakes National Park ♦ 144 7.30 N 38.30 E
Rīga, Lat. 76 56.57 N 24.06 E
Riga, Ross. 88 56.36 N 106.17 E
Riga, Mi., U.S. 216 41.49 N 83.50 W
Riga, Gulf of (Rīgas jūras līcis) (Riia laht) c 76 57.30 N 23.35 E
Riga, Mount ▲ 162 21.59 S 116.25 E
Rigacikun 150 10.40 N 7.28 E
Rigaih 114 4.40 N 95.34 E
Rigān 128 28.37 N 58.58 E
Rīgas jūras līcis
— Riga, Gulf of c 76 57.30 N 23.35 E
Rīga Station ◆[5] 265b 55.48 N 37.38 E
Rigaud 206 45.29 N 74.18 W
Rigaud ≃ 206 45.29 N 74.18 W
Rigby 202 43.40 N 111.54 W
Rīgestān ◆[1] 128 31.00 N 65.00 E
Riggins 202 45.25 N 116.18 W
Riggisberg 58 46.48 N 7.29 E
Riggston 219 39.42 N 90.25 W
Rigi ▲ 58 47.05 N 8.30 E
Rignano Flaminio 66 42.12 N 12.29 E
Rignano Garganico 68 41.40 N 15.35 E
Rignano sull'Arno 66 43.43 N 11.27 E
Rigney 58 47.23 N 6.11 E
Rigney Bluff 210 43.19 N 77.38 W
Rigny-Ussé 50 47.15 N 0.18 E
Rigo 164 9.47 S 147.34 E
Rigolet 176 54.20 N 58.35 W
Rig-Rig 146 14.16 N 14.21 E
Rigside 46 55.36 N 3.47 W
Riguldi 76 59.08 N 23.34 E
Rīh, Jazīrat ar- I 140 18.10 N 38.27 E
Rihāb 132 32.19 N 36.06 E
Rihand ≃ 124 24.33 N 82.59 E
Rihand Dam ◆[6] 124 24.05 N 82.45 E
Riihimäki 26 60.45 N 24.46 E
Riiser-Larsen Peninsula >[1] 9 68.55 S 34.00 E
Rijau 150 11.07 N 5.14 E
Riječki Zaljev c 36 45.15 N 14.25 E
Rijeka 36 45.20 N 14.27 E
Rijen 52 51.35 N 4.55 E
Rijkevorsel 56 51.21 N 4.46 E
Rijksdorp 52 52.09 N 4.25 E
Rijn
— Rhine ≃ 30 51.52 N 6.02 E
Rijnsburg 52 52.12 N 4.27 E
Rijssel
— Lille 50 50.38 N 3.04 E
Rijssen 52 52.18 N 6.30 E
Rijswijk 52 52.04 N 4.20 E
Rikers Island I 276 40.47 N 73.53 W
Rikers Island Channel ⊔ 276 40.47 N 73.52 W
Rikkavesi ◎ 26 62.50 N 28.44 E
Riksgränsen 24 68.24 N 18.12 E
Rikuchū-kaigan-kokuritsu-kōen ♦ 92 39.25 N 141.57 E
Rikuzen-takata 92 39.01 N 141.38 E
Rila 38 42.08 N 23.33 E
Riley 198 39.17 N 96.49 W
Riley, Mount ▲ 200 31.55 N 107.07 W
Riley, Point > 168b 33.53 S 137.36 E
Riley Creek ≃ 216 41.02 N 84.00 W
Riley Lake ◎ 212 44.50 N 79.11 W
Rileys Range ⋀ 170 34.21 S 150.10 E
Rillevo 72 37.55 N 12.33 E
Rillieux 62 45.49 N 4.54 E
Rillington 44 54.09 N 0.42 W
Rillito 200 32.24 N 111.09 W
Rillton 214 40.17 N 79.44 W
Rilly-la-Montagne 50 49.10 N 4.03 E
Rilski manastir ⊌[1] 38 42.08 N 23.20 E
Rima ≃ 150 13.04 N 5.10 E
Rimac 286d 12.03 S 77.03 W
Rímac ≃ 248 12.02 S 77.09 W
Rimachi, Laguna ◎ 246 4.25 S 76.43 W
Rimah, Jabal ar- ▲ 132 32.19 N 36.52 E
Rima San Giuseppe 62 45.52 N 8.00 E
Rimatara I 14 22.38 S 152.51 W
Rimavská Sobota 30 48.23 N 20.02 E
Rimbey 182 52.38 N 114.14 W
Rimbo 40 59.45 N 18.22 E
Rimé, Ouadi V 146 14.02 N 18.03 E
Rimersburg 214 41.02 N 79.30 W
Rimforsa 26 58.08 N 15.40 E
Rimi 150 12.58 N 7.43 E
Rimini 66 44.04 N 12.34 E
Rimno Glacier ⊞ 123 35.25 N 77.30 E
Rimogne 56 49.50 N 4.33 E
Rimouski 186 48.26 N 68.33 W
Rimouski ≃ 186 48.27 N 68.32 W
Rimouski, Réserve ♦ 186 48.03 N 68.15 W
Rimpar 56 49.51 N 9.57 E
Rimrock Lake ◎[1] 224 46.38 N 121.12 W
Rimsko-Korsakovka 80 51.34 N 48.31 E
Rīn
— Rhine ≃ 30 51.52 N 6.02 E
Rinbung 124 29.21 N 89.57 E
Rinca 115b 8.37 S 119.48 E
Rinca, Pulau I 115b 8.41 S 119.42 E
Rinchnach 60 48.57 N 13.12 E
Rinčin Lchumbe 88 51.07 N 99.40 E
Rincón, C.R. 236 8.42 N 83.29 W
Rincón, P.R. 240m 18.20 N 67.15 W
Rincon, Ga., U.S. 192 32.17 N 81.14 W
Rincon, N.M., U.S. 200 32.40 N 107.03 W
Rincón, Bahía de c 240m 17.58 N 66.20 W
Rinconada 252 22.26 S 66.10 W
Rinconada, Hipódromo de la ♦ 286c 10.26 N 66.56 W
Rincón de la Vieja, Parque Nacional ♦ 236 10.48 N 85.18 W
Rincón del Bonete, Lago Artificial de ◎[1] 252 32.45 S 56.00 W
Rincón del Ocote, Cerro ▲ 236 13.36 N 87.10 W
Rincón de Romos 234 22.14 N 102.18 W
Rincon Indian Reservation ◆[4] 228 33.15 N 116.57 W
Rincon Valley 226 38.28 N 122.39 W
Rindal 26 63.03 N 9.13 E
Rindown Castle ⊥ 48 53.32 N 7.59 W
Ringas 120 27.21 N 75.34 E
Ringdove 175f 16.38 S 168.09 E
Ringe 41 55.14 N 10.29 E
Ringebu 26 61.31 N 10.10 E
Ringenwalde 54 53.03 N 13.42 E
Ringertown 279b 40.25 N 79.36 W
Ringford 44 54.54 N 4.03 W
Ringgau ◆[1] 56 51.04 N 10.04 E
Ringgit, Gunung ▲ 115a 7.43 S 113.50 E
Ringgold, Ga., U.S. 192 34.54 N 85.06 W
Ringgold, La., U.S. 194 32.19 N 93.16 W
Ringgold, Pa., U.S. 279b 40.10 N 79.58 W
Ringgold, Tx., U.S. 196 33.48 N 97.56 W
Ringgold Isles II 175g 16.15 S 179.25 W
Ringim 150 12.08 N 9.10 E
Ringkøbing 26 56.05 N 8.15 E
Ringkøbing □[6] 41 56.10 N 8.50 E
Ringkøbing Fjord c[2] 26 56.00 N 8.15 E
Ringlet 114 4.25 N 101.23 E
Ringling 196 34.10 N 97.35 W
Ringling Museums ⊌ 220 27.23 N 82.34 W
Ringmer 42 50.53 N 0.04 E
Ringoes 208 40.26 N 74.52 W
Rings Island 283 42.49 N 70.52 W
Ringsted, Dan. 41 55.27 N 11.49 E
Ringsted, Ia., U.S. 198 43.17 N 94.30 W
Ringtown 210 40.51 N 76.14 W
Ringvassøy I 24 69.55 N 19.15 E
Ringville 48 52.02 N 7.34 W
Ringwood, Austl. 169 37.49 S 145.14 E
Ringwood, Eng., U.K. 42 50.51 N 1.47 W
Ringwood, N.J., U.S. 210 41.06 N 74.14 W
Ringwood Manor ⊥ 276 41.08 N 74.15 W
Ringwood North 274b 37.48 S 145.14 E
Ringwood State Park ♦ 210 41.08 N 74.16 W
Riñihue 254 39.49 S 72.27 W
Riñihue, Lago ◎ 254 39.50 S 72.18 W
Rinjani, Gunung ▲ 115b 8.24 S 116.28 E
Rinkenæs 41 54.54 N 9.34 E
Rinkerode 52 51.50 N 7.41 E
Rinnes, Ben ▲ 46 57.23 N 3.15 W
Rinnthal 56 49.13 N 7.55 E
Rinsumageest 52 53.18 N 5.57 E
Rinteln 52 52.11 N 9.04 E
Rinxent 50 50.48 N 1.44 E
Rio, Fl., U.S. 220 27.13 N 80.14 W
Rio, Wi., U.S. 190 43.26 N 89.14 W
Rio Azul 252 25.43 S 50.47 W
Riobamba 246 1.40 S 78.38 W
Río Blanco, Chile 252 32.55 S 70.19 W
Río Blanco (Tenango de Río Blanco), Méx. 234 18.50 N 97.09 W
Rio Bonito 256 22.43 S 42.37 W
Rio Bonito ◆[8] 287b 23.43 S 46.41 W
Rio Branco, Bra. 248 9.58 S 67.48 W
Río Branco, Ur. 252 32.34 S 53.25 W
Rio Bravo, Méx. 196 28.17 N 100.55 W
Río Bravo, Méx. 232 25.59 N 98.06 W
Rio Brilhante 255 21.48 S 54.33 W
Río Bueno 254 40.19 S 72.58 W
Río Caribe 246 10.42 N 63.07 W
Rio Casca 255 20.13 S 42.39 W
Río Cauto 240p 20.33 N 76.55 W
Río Ceballos 252 31.10 S 64.20 W
Río Chico, Arg. 254 41.43 S 70.30 W
Río Chico, Ven. 246 10.18 N 65.59 W
Rio Claro, Bra. 255 22.24 S 47.33 W
Rio Claro, Bra. 256 22.43 S 44.09 W
Rio Claro, Trin. 241r 10.18 N 61.11 W
Rio Claro, Represa do ◎[1] 256 23.39 S 45.54 W
Río Colorado 252 39.01 S 64.05 W
Rio Comprido ◆[8] 287a 22.55 S 43.12 W
Río Cuarto 252 33.08 S 64.21 W
Rio das Flores 256 22.10 S 43.35 W
Rio das Pedras 156 23.12 S 35.23 E
Rio de Contas 255 13.36 S 41.48 W
Rio de Janeiro, Bra. 256 22.54 S 43.14 W
Rio de Janeiro, Bra. 287a 22.54 S 43.14 W
Rio de Janeiro □[3] 256 22.00 S 42.30 W
Rio de Janeiro □[3] 287a 22.55 S 43.30 W
Río de Jesús 236 7.59 N 81.10 W
Rio Dell 204 40.29 N 124.06 W
Rio de Mouro 266c 38.46 N 9.20 W
Río de Oro 246 8.17 N 73.23 W
Rio do Prado 255 16.35 S 40.34 W
Rio do Sul 252 27.13 S 49.39 W
Rio Douro 287a 22.39 S 43.32 W
Rio Espera 255 20.51 S 43.29 W
Río Gallegos 254 51.38 S 69.13 W
Río Grande, Arg. 254 53.47 S 67.42 W
Rio Grande, Bra. 252 32.02 S 52.05 W
Río Grande, Méx. 234 15.59 N 97.27 W
Río Grande, Méx. 234 23.50 N 103.02 W
Río Grande, Nic. 236 12.53 N 86.32 W
Rio Grande, P.R. 240m 18.23 N 65.50 W
Rio Grande, N.J., U.S. 208 39.00 N 74.52 W
Río Grande, Ven. 286c 10.35 N 66.57 W
Rio Grande
— Grande, Rio ≃ 178 25.57 N 97.09 W
Rio Grande, Ponte do ◆[5] 287b 23.46 S 46.31 W
Rio Grande City 196 26.22 N 98.49 W
Rio Grande Da Serra, Bra. 256 23.44 S 46.24 W
Rio Grande da Serra, Bra. 287b 23.44 S 46.24 W
Rio Grande da Serra □[7] 287b 23.45 S 46.23 W
Rio Grande do Norte □[3] 250 5.45 S 36.00 W
Rio Grande do Sul
— Rio Grande 252 32.02 S 52.05 W
Rio Grande do Sul □[3] 252 30.00 S 54.00 W
Riogrodina 256 22.11 S 42.30 W
Riohacha 246 11.33 N 72.55 W
Río Hato 236 8.23 N 80.10 W
Río Hondo, Méx. 286a 19.25 N 99.16 W
Rio Hondo, Tx., U.S. 196 26.14 N 97.34 W
Rioja 248 6.05 S 77.09 W
Rio Jaguari, Reservatório do ◎[1] 256 22.55 S 46.25 W
Río Jueyes 240m 18.01 N 66.20 W
Riola 64 44.16 N 11.04 E
Río Lagartos 232 21.36 N 88.10 W
Riolândia 255 19.59 S 49.40 W
Rio Largo 250 9.29 S 35.51 W
Riola Sardo 71 39.59 N 8.32 E
Rio Linda 226 38.41 N 121.26 W
Riolo Terme 66 44.16 N 11.43 E
Río Luján 258 34.17 S 58.54 W
Riom 32 45.54 N 3.07 E
Riomaggiore 62 44.06 N 9.44 E
Rio Marina 66 42.49 N 10.25 E
Río Mayo 254 45.41 S 70.16 W
Río Mulatos 248 19.42 S 66.47 W
Río Muni □[4] 152 1.30 N 10.30 E
Riondel 182 49.46 N 116.52 W
Rio Negro, Bra. 252 26.06 S 49.48 W
Rio Negro, Bra. 255 19.27 S 54.58 W
Río Negro, Chile 254 40.47 S 73.14 W
Rionegro, Col. 246 6.09 N 75.22 W
Rionegro, Col. 246 7.16 N 73.09 W
Río Negro □[4] 254 40.00 S 67.00 W
Rio Negro, Pantanal do ≋ 248 19.00 S 56.00 W
Rionero in Vulture 68 40.56 N 15.41 E
Rionero Sannitico 66 41.42 N 14.08 E
Rioni ≃ 84 42.08 N 41.39 E
Rio Novo 256 21.29 S 43.08 W
Rio Novo do Sul 255 20.52 S 40.56 W
Riópar 34 38.30 N 2.27 W
Rio Pardo 252 29.59 S 52.22 W
Rio Pardo de Minas 255 15.37 S 42.33 W
Río Pico 254 44.13 S 71.21 W
Río Piedras, Arg. 252 25.18 S 64.54 W
Río Piedras, P.R. 240m 18.24 N 66.03 W
Río Pilcomayo, Parque Nacional ♦ 252 25.10 S 58.00 W
Rio Piracicaba 255 19.55 S 43.11 W
Rio Pomba 256 21.17 S 43.11 W
Rio Prêto, Bra. 256 22.06 S 43.50 W
Rio Prêto
— São José do Rio Prêto, Bra. 256 22.10 S 42.57 W
Rio Rancho 200 35.14 N 106.38 W
Rio Real 250 11.28 S 37.56 W
Rio Saliceto 64 44.49 N 10.49 E
Río San Juan □[5] 236 11.10 N 84.30 W
Río Segundo 252 31.40 S 63.55 W
Ríosucio, Col. 246 5.25 N 75.42 W
Ríosucio, Col. 246 7.27 N 77.07 W
Río Tercero 252 32.11 S 64.06 W
Rio Tinto 250 6.48 S 35.05 W
Riotord 62 45.14 N 4.24 E
Rio Tuba 116 8.30 N 117.25 E
Riou, Île de I 62 43.11 N 5.24 E
Rioveggio 64 44.17 N 11.14 E
Rio Verde, Bra. 255 17.43 S 50.56 W
Rioverde, Méx. 234 21.56 N 99.59 W
Rio Verde de Mato Grosso 255 18.56 S 54.52 W
Rio Vermelho 255 18.18 S 43.00 W
Rio Vista, Ca., U.S. 226 38.09 N 121.41 W
Rio Vista, Tx., U.S. 222 32.14 N 97.23 W
Rioz 58 47.25 N 6.04 E
Riozinho ≃, Bra. 246 2.55 S 67.07 W
Riozinho ≃, Bra. 250 10.22 S 49.50 W
Riozinho ≃, Bra. 250 8.25 S 45.43 W
Riozinho ≃, Bra. 250 7.06 S 51.40 W
Říp ▲ 54 50.24 N 14.18 E
Ripacandida 68 40.55 N 15.43 E
Ripalti, Punta dei > 66 42.42 N 10.25 E
Ripatransone 66 43.00 N 13.46 E
Ripky 78 51.48 N 31.05 E
Ripley, Eng., U.K. 44 53.03 N 1.24 W
Ripley, Eng., U.K. 260 51.18 N 0.29 W
Ripley, Il., U.S. 219 40.01 N 90.38 W
Ripley, In., U.S. 216 41.06 N 86.39 W
Ripley, Ms., U.S. 194 34.43 N 88.57 W
Ripley, N.Y., U.S. 214 42.16 N 79.42 W
Ripley, Oh., U.S. 218 38.44 N 83.50 W
Ripley, Tn., U.S. 194 35.44 N 89.31 W
Ripley, W.V., U.S. 188 38.49 N 81.42 W
Ripley □[6] 218 39.04 N 85.15 W
Ripoll 34 42.12 N 2.12 E
Ripoll ≃ 266d 41.29 N 2.12 E
Ripollet 266d 41.30 N 2.10 E
Ripon, P.Q., Can. 206 45.47 N 75.06 W
Ripon, Eng., U.K. 44 54.08 N 1.31 W
Ripon, Ca., U.S. 226 37.44 N 121.07 W
Ripon, Wi., U.S. 190 43.50 N 88.50 W
Riposto 70 37.44 N 15.12 E
Rippling Ridge 284b 39.11 N 76.37 W
Ripponden 44 53.41 N 1.57 W
Rippowam ≃ 276 41.03 N 73.33 W
Riquewihr 58 48.10 N 7.18 E
Ririba, Laga ≃ 154 3.34 N 37.15 E
Ririe 202 43.37 N 111.46 W
Risālpur Cantonment 123 34.04 N 72.00 E
Risaralda □[5] 246 5.00 N 76.00 W
Risasi 154 0.25 S 25.44 E
Risbäck 26 64.42 N 15.32 E
Risca 42 51.37 N 3.07 W
Rischenau 52 51.53 N 9.17 E
Riscle 32 43.40 N 0.05 W
Risco, Ilha do I 246 3.07 S 58.19 W
Rishā', Wādī ar- V 128 25.33 N 44.05 E
Rīshahr 128 28.55 N 50.50 E
Rishīkesh 124 30.07 N 78.19 E
Rishiri-Rebun-Sarobetsu-kokuritsu-kōen ♦ 92a 45.10 N 141.35 E
Rishiri-suidō ⊔ 92a 45.10 N 141.25 E
Rishiri-tō I 92a 45.11 N 141.15 E
Rishiri-zan ▲ 92a 45.11 N 141.15 E
Rishmayyā 132 33.44 N 35.36 E
Rishon LeZiyyon 132 31.58 N 34.48 E
Rishpon 132 32.12 N 34.49 E
Rishra 272b 22.43 N 88.21 E
Rishrāsh, Wādī V 142 29.29 N 31.16 E
Rishton 262 53.46 N 2.25 W
Rishworth 262 53.40 N 1.57 W
Rishworth Moor ◆[3] 262 53.39 N 2.01 W
Risinge 40 58.42 N 15.51 E
Rising Star 196 32.05 N 98.57 W
Rising Sun, In., U.S. 218 38.56 N 84.51 W
Rising Sun, Md., U.S. 208 39.41 N 76.03 W
Risingsun, Oh., U.S. 214 41.16 N 83.25 W
Risle ≃ 50 49.26 N 0.23 E
Risnjak ▲ 36 45.26 N 14.37 E
Risø 41 55.42 N 12.06 E
Rison, Ar., U.S. 194 33.57 N 92.11 W
Rison, Md., U.S. 208 38.32 N 77.10 W
Risør 26 58.43 N 9.14 E
Ris-Orangis 50 48.39 N 2.25 E
Riss ≃ 58 48.17 N 9.49 E
Rissani 148 31.23 N 4.09 W
Risskov ◆[8] 41 56.11 N 10.14 E
Rississen 58 48.16 N 9.49 E
Risti 76 58.59 N 24.03 E
Ristigouche (Restigouche) ≃ 186 48.04 N 66.20 W
Ristiina 26 61.30 N 27.16 E
Ristijärvi 26 64.30 N 28.13 E
Ristinge 41 54.50 N 10.38 E
Ristna 76 58.56 N 22.05 E
Risum-Lindholm 41 54.45 N 8.53 E
Rita Blanca Creek ≃ 196 35.40 N 102.29 W
Ritchie, S. Afr. 158 29.02 S 24.38 E
Ritchie, Md., U.S. 284c 38.52 N 76.52 W
Ritchie Branch ≃ 284c 38.53 N 76.52 W
Rithāla ◆[8] 272a 28.43 N 77.06 E
Ritidian Point > 174p 13.39 N 144.51 E
Ritscher Upland ⋀[1] 9 73.20 S 9.30 W
Ritsumeikan University ⊌[2] 270 35.01 N 135.46 E
Ritsurin-kōen ♦ 96 34.21 N 134.02 E
Ritta Island I 220 26.44 N 80.48 W
Ritter, Mount ▲ 226 37.42 N 119.12 W
Ritterhude 52 53.11 N 8.45 E
Rittersgrün 54 50.29 N 12.47 E
Rittman 214 40.58 N 81.46 W
Rittō 94 35.01 N 136.00 E
Ritzleben 54 52.50 N 11.21 E
Ritzville 202 47.07 N 118.22 W
Riu 120 28.19 N 95.03 E
Riva 208 38.57 N 76.35 W
Rivadavia, Arg. 252 35.28 S 62.57 W
Rivadavia, Arg. 252 33.11 S 68.28 W
Rivadavia, Arg. 252 24.11 S 62.53 W
Rivadavia, Arg. 252 31.33 S 68.37 W
Rivadavia, Chile 252 29.58 S 70.34 W
Riva del Garda 64 45.53 N 10.50 E
Riva del Sole 66 42.46 N 10.52 E
Riva di Tures (Rain) 64 46.57 N 12.04 E
Rivanazzano 62 44.56 N 9.01 E
Rivanna ≃ 192 37.45 N 78.10 W
Rivare 216 40.49 N 84.50 W
Rivarolo Canavese 62 45.19 N 7.43 E
Rivarolo Mantovano 64 45.04 N 10.26 E
Rivas 236 11.26 N 85.50 W
Rivas □[5] 236 11.25 N 85.50 W
Rivasdale 273d 26.17 S 27.56 E
Rīvash 128 35.26 N 58.26 E
Rivas-Vaciamadrid 266a 40.20 N 3.31 W
Riva Trigoso 62 44.16 N 9.26 E
Rive, Île de la I 273b 4.21 S 15.26 E
Rive d'Arcano 64 46.08 N 13.02 E
Rive-de-Gier 62 45.32 N 4.37 E
Rivello 68 40.05 N 15.45 E
Rivera, Arg. 252 37.12 S 63.14 W
Rivera, Col. 246 2.47 N 75.15 W
Rivera, Ur. 252 30.54 S 55.31 W
Riverbank 226 37.44 N 120.56 W
River Cess 150 5.28 N 9.32 W
Riverdale, Ca., U.S. 226 36.25 N 119.51 W
Riverdale, Il., U.S. 278 41.38 N 87.37 W
Riverdale, Md., U.S. 284c 38.57 N 76.55 W
Riverdale, N.J., U.S. 276 40.59 N 74.18 W
Riverdale, N.D., U.S. 198 47.29 N 101.22 W
Riverdale, Or., U.S. 224 45.27 N 122.41 W
Riverdale ◆[8] 276 40.54 N 73.54 W
Riverdale Heights 284c 38.58 N 76.54 W
Riverdale Park ♦ 275b 43.40 N 79.21 W
River Drive Park 212 44.08 N 79.31 W
River Edge, N.J., U.S. 276 40.55 N 74.02 W
River Edge, Oh., U.S. 279a 41.25 N 81.51 W
River Falls, Al., U.S. 194 31.21 N 86.32 W
River Falls, Wi., U.S. 190 44.51 N 92.37 W
River Forest 278 41.53 N 87.48 W
Rivergaro 62 44.55 N 9.36 E
River Grove 278 41.55 N 87.50 W
Riverhaven 216 41.05 N 85.02 W
Riverhead, Eng., U.K. 260 51.17 N 0.10 E
Riverhead, N.Y., U.S. 207 40.55 N 72.39 W
River Hébert 186 45.42 N 64.23 W
River Hill 279b 40.12 N 79.54 W
River Hills 216 43.10 N 87.55 W
Riverhurst 184 50.53 N 106.52 W
Riverina ◆[1] 166 35.30 S 145.30 E
River John 186 45.45 N 63.03 W
River Jordan 224 48.25 N 124.03 W
Riverlea 214 40.05 N 83.02 W
River Lea Navigation ≡ 260 51.32 N 0.02 W
River Meadow Brook ≃ 283 42.38 N 71.17 W
Rivermont 192 35.13 N 77.38 W
Rivero, Isla I 254 45.37 S 74.20 W
River Oaks 284c 38.57 N 77.11 W
River of Ponds 186 50.32 N 57.24 W
River Pines, Ca., U.S. 226 38.33 N 120.45 W
River Pines, Ma., U.S. 207 42.33 N 71.17 W
River Plaza 208 40.21 N 74.05 W
River Ridge Estates 284c 38.47 N 77.00 W
River Road 202 44.03 N 123.05 W
River Rouge 216 42.16 N 83.08 W
River Rouge Park ♦ 281 42.22 N 83.15 W
Rivers 184 50.02 N 100.12 W
Rivers □[3] 150 4.30 N 6.30 E
Rivers, Lake of the ◎ 184 49.45 N 105.45 W
Riversdale, N.Z. 172 45.54 S 168.45 E
Riversdale, S. Afr. 158 34.07 S 21.15 E
Riverside, Ca., U.S. 228 33.57 N 117.23 W
Riverside, Ct., U.S. 276 41.02 N 73.35 W
Riverside, Il., U.S. 278 41.50 N 87.49 W
Riverside, Ia., U.S. 190 41.28 N 91.34 W
Riverside, Mi., U.S. 216 42.11 N 86.23 W
Riverside, Mi., U.S. 216 42.17 N 84.29 W
Riverside, N.J., U.S. 208 40.01 N 74.57 W
Riverside, N.Y., U.S. 210 42.55 N 73.40 W
Riverside, N.Y., U.S. 210 42.08 N 77.01 W
Riverside, Pa., U.S. 210 40.57 N 76.38 W
Riverside, Tx., U.S. 222 30.57 N 95.24 W
Riverside, Wa., U.S. 182 48.30 N 119.30 W
Riverside □[6] 228 33.45 N 117.10 W
Riverside ◆[8] 281 42.20 N 82.57 W
Riverside International Raceway ♦ 228 33.57 N 117.17 W
Riverside Manors 284a 43.11 N 79.03 W
Riverside Park ♦, Mi., U.S. 281 42.22 N 83.26 W
Riverside Park ♦, N.Y., U.S. 284a 42.57 N 78.54 W
Rivers Inlet 182 51.41 N 127.15 W
Rivers Inlet c 182 51.39 N 127.30 W
Riversleigh 166 19.02 S 138.44 E
Riverstone 170 33.40 S 150.52 E
Riverton, Austl. 168b 34.09 S 138.45 E
Riverton, Mb., Can. 184 50.59 N 96.59 W
Riverton, N.Z. 172 46.21 S 168.01 E
Riverton, Il., U.S. 219 39.51 N 89.33 W
Riverton, Ne., U.S. 198 40.05 N 98.45 W
Riverton, N.J., U.S. 208 40.00 N 75.00 W
Riverton, Ut., U.S. 200 40.31 N 111.56 W
Riverton, Va., U.S. 188 38.56 N 78.11 W
Riverton, Wy., U.S. 200 43.01 N 108.22 W
Riverton Heights 224 47.28 N 122.18 W
River Vale 276 40.59 N 74.00 W
Riverview, S. Afr. 158 28.27 S 32.10 E
River View, Al., U.S. 194 32.47 N 85.08 W
Riverview, Fl., U.S. 220 27.51 N 82.19 W
Riverview, Ks., U.S. 198 37.47 N 97.22 W
Riverview, Mi., U.S. 216 42.10 N 83.10 W
Riverview Park ♦ 279b 40.29 N 80.01 W
Riverwood, Austl. 274a 33.57 S 151.03 E
Riverwood, In., U.S. 218 40.06 N 85.58 W
Riverwoods 278 42.10 N 87.54 W
Rives, Fr. 62 45.21 N 5.30 E
Rives, Tn., U.S. 194 36.21 N 89.02 W
Rivesaltes 32 42.46 N 2.52 E
Rives Junction 216 42.23 N 84.27 W
Rive Sud, Canal de la ≡ 275a 45.25 N 73.41 W
Rivesville 188 39.31 N 80.07 W
Riviera, Az., U.S. 204 35.04 N 114.35 W
Riviera, Tx., U.S. 196 27.18 N 97.49 W
Riviera V 58 46.15 N 8.58 E
Riviera Beach, Fl., U.S. 220 26.46 N 80.03 W
Riviera Beach, Md., U.S. 208 39.10 N 76.30 W
Rivière-à-Claude 186 49.13 N 65.54 W
Rivière-au-Tonnerre 186 50.16 N 64.47 W
Rivière-Bleue 186 47.26 N 69.03 W
Rivière-Bois-Clair 206 46.34 N 71.50 W
Rivière-de-la-Chaloupe 186 49.08 N 62.32 W
Rivière-des-Prairies ◆[8] 275a 45.39 N 73.33 W
Rivière-du-Loup 186 47.50 N 69.32 W
Rivière du Rempart 157c 20.06 S 57.41 E
Rivière-Matane 186 48.39 N 67.20 W
Rivière-Mékinac 206 46.47 N 72.48 W
Rivière-Pentecôte 186 49.47 N 67.10 W
Rivière-Pilote 240e 14.29 N 60.54 W
Rivière-Salée 240e 14.32 N 60.59 W
Rivière-Verte 186 47.19 N 68.09 W
Riviersonderend 158 34.09 S 19.55 E
Rivignano 64 45.53 N 13.03 E
Rivington 262 53.37 N 2.34 W
Rivington Reservoirs ◎[1] 262 53.37 N 2.34 W
Rivisondoli 66 41.52 N 14.04 E
Rivne, Ukr. 78 50.37 N 26.15 E
Rivne, Ukr. 78 48.15 N 31.45 E
Rivne □[4] 78 51.00 N 26.30 E
Rivoli 62 45.04 N 7.31 E
Rivoli Bay c 166 37.32 S 140.04 E
Rivolta d'Adda 62 45.28 N 9.31 E
Rivoltella 64 45.27 N 10.33 E
Riwaka 172 41.05 S 173.00 E
Rixford 214 41.55 N 78.30 W
Rixheim 58 47.46 N 7.24 E
Riyadh
— Ar-Riyāḍ 128 24.38 N 46.43 E
Rīyāq 132 33.51 N 36.00 E
Rizal, Pil. 116 15.43 N 121.06 E
Rizal
— Pasay, Pil. 269f 14.33 N 121.00 E
Rizal □[4] 116 14.35 N 121.10 E
Rizal Memorial Stadium ♦ 269f 14.34 N 120.59 E
Rize 130 41.02 N 40.31 E
Rize □[4] 130 40.55 N 40.55 E
Rīzeh, Kūh-e (gora Reza) ▲ 128 37.47 N 58.05 E
Rizhao 98 35.27 N 119.29 E
Rizziconi 68 38.25 N 15.57 E
Rizzuto, Capo > 68 38.54 N 17.06 E
Rjukan 26 59.52 N 8.34 E
Rkîz, Lac ◎ 150 16.50 N 15.19 W
Rô 175f 21.22 S 167.50 E
Roa, Esp. 34 41.42 N 3.55 W
Roa, Nor. 26 60.17 N 10.37 E
Roa, Zaïre 154 3.49 N 24.56 E
Roachdale 194 39.50 N 86.48 W
Roade 42 52.09 N 0.53 W
Roadford Reservoir ◎[1] 42 50.43 N 4.13 W
Roadhead 44 55.04 N 2.46 W
Roadknight, Point > 169 38.26 S 144.11 E
Roadside 158 27.31 S 28.52 E
Road Town 240m 18.27 N 64.37 W
Roag, East Loch c 46 58.14 N 6.48 W
Roag, West Loch c 46 58.13 N 6.53 W
Roaming Rock, Lake ◎[1] 214 41.38 N 80.49 W
Roaming Shores 214 41.39 N 80.49 W
Roana 64 45.52 N 11.28 E
Roan Cliffs ◆[4] 200 39.30 N 109.40 W
Roan Creek ≃ 200 39.20 N 108.13 W
Roan Fell ▲ 44 55.13 N 2.52 W
Roan Mountain 192 36.11 N 82.04 W
Roann 216 40.54 N 85.55 W
Roanne 32 46.02 N 4.04 E
Roanoke, Al., U.S. 194 33.09 N 85.22 W
Roanoke, Il., U.S. 190 40.47 N 89.11 W
Roanoke, In., U.S. 216 40.57 N 85.22 W
Roanoke, Tx., U.S. 222 33.01 N 97.14 W
Roanoke, Va., U.S. 192 37.16 N 79.56 W
Roanoke (Staunton) ≃ 192 35.56 N 76.43 W
Roanoke Island I 192 35.53 N 75.39 W
Roanoke Rapids 192 36.27 N 77.39 W
Roanoke Rapids Dam ◆[6] 192 36.24 N 77.40 W
Roan Plateau ⋀[1] 200 39.30 N 109.40 W
Roans Prairie 222 30.35 N 95.57 W
Roaring ≃ 224 45.13 N 122.12 W
Roaring Branch 210 41.34 N 76.57 W
Roaring Brook ≃ 212 43.44 N 75.24 W
Roaring Fork ≃ 200 39.33 N 107.20 W
Roaring River Slough ≃ 282 38.05 N 121.55 W
Roaring Run ≃ 279b 40.33 N 79.32 W
Roaring Spring 214 40.20 N 78.23 W
Roaring Springs 196 33.54 N 100.52 W
Roaringwater Bay c 48 51.31 N 9.26 W
Roatán 236 16.18 N 86.35 W
Roatán, Isla de I 236 16.23 N 86.30 W
Robāā Oued Yahia 36 36.05 N 9.35 E
Robāṭ Karīm 128 35.28 N 51.05 E
Robbeneiland I 158 33.49 S 18.22 E
Robbers Cave State Park ♦ 196 35.01 N 95.27 W
Robbins, Ca., U.S. 226 38.53 N 121.42 W
Robbins, Il., U.S. 216 41.38 N 87.42 W
Robbins, N.C., U.S. 192 35.26 N 79.35 W
Robbins, Tn., U.S. 192 36.21 N 84.35 W
Robbins Airport ⊠ 283 42.34 N 70.58 W
Robbins Ditch ≡ 216 41.21 N 86.43 W
Robbins Island I 166 40.41 S 144.57 E
Robbins Pond ◎ 283 42.00 N 70.55 W
Robbins Rest 276 40.39 N 73.10 W
Robbinsville, N.J., U.S. 208 40.13 N 74.37 W
Robbinsville, N.C., U.S. 192 35.19 N 83.48 W
Robbio 62 45.17 N 8.35 E
Robe, Austl. 166 37.11 S 139.45 E
Robe, Ityo. 144 7.52 N 39.38 E
Robe ≃, Austl. 162 21.19 S 115.40 E
Robe ≃, Ire. 48 53.37 N 9.16 W
Robe, Mount ▲[2] 166 31.40 S 141.20 E
Robecchetto con Induno 266b 45.32 N 8.46 E
Robecco d'Oglio 64 45.15 N 10.04 E
Robecco sul Naviglio 266b 45.26 N 8.53 E
Röbel 54 53.23 N 12.35 E
Robeline 194 31.41 N 93.18 W
Röberget ▲[2] 40 59.45 N 14.54 E
Robersonville 192 35.49 N 77.15 W
Robert, Havre du c 240e 14.40 N 60.55 W
Roberta 192 32.43 N 84.00 W
Roberta Mills 192 35.22 N 80.38 W
Robert E. Lee Memorial Park ♦ 284b 39.23 N 76.39 W
Robert E. Lee's Birthplace ⊥ 208 38.10 N 76.49 W
Robert-Espagne 56 48.45 N 5.02 E
Robert F. Kennedy Memorial Stadium ♦ 284c 38.53 N 76.58 W
Robert H. Treman State Park ♦ 210 42.24 N 76.35 W
Robert Lee 196 31.54 N 100.29 W
Robert Louis Stevenson Memorial State Park ♦ 226 38.40 N 122.36 W
Robert Louis Stevenson's Tomb ⊥ 175a 13.50 S 171.44 W
Robert Morse College ⊌[2] 279b 40.31 N 80.12 W
Robert Moses State Park ♦ 210 40.37 N 73.16 W
Robert Mueller Municipal Airport ⊠ 222 30.18 N 97.42 W
Roberto Payró 258 35.10 S 57.39 W
Robert Point > 168a 32.31 S 115.42 E
Roberts, Id., U.S. 202 43.43 N 112.07 W
Roberts, Il., U.S. 216 40.37 N 88.11 W
Roberts, Mt., U.S. 202 45.21 N 109.10 W
Roberts, Mount ▲ 171a 28.13 S 152.28 E
Roberts, Point > 224 49.00 N 123.06 W
Robert's Arm 186 49.29 N 55.49 W
Robertsbridge 42 50.59 N 0.29 E
Roberts Canyon V 280 34.11 N 117.54 W
Roberts Creek Mountain ▲ 204 39.52 N 116.18 W
Robertsdale, Al., U.S. 194 30.33 N 87.42 W
Robertsdale, Pa., U.S. 214 40.11 N 78.06 W
Robertsfield 150 6.15 N 10.24 W
Robertsfors 26 64.11 N 20.51 E
Robertsganj 124 24.42 N 83.04 E
Robertsham ◆[8] 273d 26.15 S 28.00 E
Robertsholm 40 60.35 N 16.16 E
Robert S. Kerr Lake ◎[1] 194 35.25 N 95.00 W
Roberts Mountain ▲ 180 60.03 N 166.16 W
Robertson, Austl. 170 34.35 S 150.35 E
Robertson, S. Afr. 158 33.46 S 19.50 E
Robertson □[6], Ky., U.S. 218 38.32 N 84.04 W
Robertson □[6], Tx., U.S. 222 31.00 N 96.30 W
Robertson, Lac ◎ 186 51.00 N 59.10 W
Robertson Bay c 9 71.25 S 170.00 E
Robertson Range ⋀ 162 23.10 S 121.00 E
Robertsonville 206 46.09 N 71.13 W
Roberts Park 278 41.44 N 87.49 W
Roberts Peak ▲ 182 52.57 N 120.32 W
Robertsport 150 6.45 N 11.22 W
Robertstown 168b 34.00 S 139.05 E
Robertsville 214 40.46 N 81.11 W
Robertville 56 50.27 N 6.07 E
Roberval 176 48.31 N 72.13 W
Robin Hood's Bay 44 54.25 N 0.33 W
Robins Air Force Base ■ 192 32.38 N 83.35 W
Robins Island I 207 40.58 N 72.28 W
Robinson, Il., U.S. 194 39.00 N 87.44 W
Robinson, Tx., U.S. 222 31.28 N 97.06 W
Robinson ≃ 164 16.03 S 137.16 E
Robinson, Lake ◎[1] 192 34.26 N 80.10 W
Robinson Brook ≃ 283 43.02 N 71.13 W
Robinson Creek ≃ 226 38.16 N 119.15 W
Róbinson Crusoe, Isla (Isla Más a Tierra) I 244 33.38 S 78.52 W
Robinson Gorge National Park ♦ 166 25.15 S 149.10 E
Robinson Lake ◎ 222 29.35 N 94.36 W
Robinson Lake Aerodrome ⊠ 273d 26.08 S 27.42 E
Robinson Pond ◎ 283 42.48 N 71.23 W
Robinson Range ⋀ 162 25.45 S 119.00 E
Robinson Run ≃ 279b 40.23 N 80.06 W
Robinson Run, North Branch ≃ 279b 40.23 N 80.11 W
Robinsons 186 48.15 N 58.48 W
Robinvale 166 34.36 S 142.46 E
Robleda 34 40.23 N 6.36 W
Robledo 34 38.46 N 2.26 W
Roblin 184 51.14 N 101.21 W
Röblingen 54 51.28 N 11.40 E
Roboré 248 18.20 S 59.45 W
Röbrinken 40 58.36 N 15.53 E
Rob Roy Island I 175e 7.25 S 157.35 E
Robson, Mount ▲ 182 53.07 N 119.09 W
Robstown 196 27.47 N 97.40 W

≃ River / Fluß / Río / Rivière / Rio
≡ Canal / Kanal / Canal / Canal / Canal
Waterfall, Rapids / Wasserfall, Stromschnellen / Cascada, Rápidos / Chute d'eau, Rapides / Cascata, Rápidos
⊔ Strait / Meeresstraße / Estrecho / Détroit / Estreito
c Bay, Gulf / Bucht, Golf / Bahía, Golfo / Baie, Golfe / Baía, Golfo
◎ Lake, Lakes / See, Seen / Lago, Lagos / Lac, Lacs / Lago, Lagos
≋ Swamp / Sumpf / Pantano / Marais / Pântano
⊞ Ice Features, Glacier / Eis- und Gletscherformen / Accidentes Glaciales / Formes glaciaires / Acidentes glaciares
Other Hydrographic Features / Andere Hydrographische Objekte / Otros Elementos Hidrográficos / Autres données hydrographiques / Outros acidentes hidrográficos

Submarine Features / Untermeerische Objekte / Accidentes Submarinos / Formes de relief sous-marin / Acidentes submarinos
□ Political Unit / Politische Einheit / Unidad Política / Entité politique / Unidade política
⊌ Cultural Institution / Kulturelle Institution / Institución Cultural / Institution culturelle / Instituição cultural
⊥ Historical Site / Historische Stätte / Sitio Histórico / Site historique / Sitio histórico
♦ Recreational Site / Erholungs- und Ferienort / Sitio de Recreo / Centre de loisirs / Area de Lazer
⊠ Airport / Flughafen / Aeropuerto / Aéroport / Aeroporto
■ Military Installation / Militäranlage / Instalación Militar / Installation militaire / Instalação militar
◆ Miscellaneous / Verschiedenes / Misceláneo / Divers / Diversos

Roby, Eng., U.K. 262 53.25 N 2.51 W
Roby, Il., U.S. 219 39.44 N 89.24 W
Roby, Tx., U.S. 196 32.44 N 100.22 W
Roby Mill 262 53.34 N 2.44 W
Roca, Cabo da > 34 38.47 N 9.30 W
Roçado 250 6.40 S 44.19 W
Rocafuerte 246 0.55 S 80.28 W
Roça Grande 256 21.36 S 42.58 W
Rocanville 184 50.24 N 101.43 W
Roca Partida, Isla I 232 19.01 N 112.02 W
Roca Partida, Punta > 234 18.42 N 95.10 W
Rocas, Atol das I[1] 250 3.52 S 33.59 W
Roccabernarda 68 39.08 N 16.52 E
Roccacasale 66 42.07 N 13.53 E
Roccadaspide 68 40.26 N 15.12 E
Rocca di Cambio 66 42.14 N 13.29 E
Rocca di Mezzo 66 42.12 N 13.31 E
Rocca di Neto 68 39.11 N 17.00 E
Rocca di Papa 66 41.46 N 12.42 E
Roccafluvione 66 42.51 N 13.29 E
Roccagloriosa 68 40.06 N 15.26 E
Roccalbegna 66 42.47 N 11.30 E
Roccalumera 70 37.58 N 15.24 E
Rocca Massima 66 41.41 N 12.55 E
Roccamena 70 37.50 N 13.09 E
Roccamonfina 68 41.17 N 13.59 E
Roccanova 68 40.13 N 16.12 E
Roccapalumba 70 37.48 N 13.39 E
Rocca Pia 66 41.56 N 13.59 E
Rocca Pietore 64 46.26 N 11.59 E
Roccaprebalza 64 44.31 N 9.57 E
Rocca Priora 267a 41.48 N 12.45 E
Roccaraso 66 41.51 N 14.05 E
Rocca San Casciano 66 44.03 N 11.50 E
Rocca Santa Maria 66 42.41 N 13.30 E
Roccasecca 66 41.33 N 13.40 E
Roccasecca dei Volsci 66 41.29 N 13.13 E
Roccastrada 66 43.00 N 11.10 E
Roccavione 62 44.19 N 7.29 E
Roccavivara 66 41.50 N 14.36 E
Roccelito, Monte ∧ 70 37.50 N 13.47 E
Roccella Ionica 68 38.19 N 16.24 E
Roccella Valdemone 70 37.56 N 15.00 E
Rocchetta Sant'Antonio 68 41.06 N 15.27 E
Rocciamelone ∧ 62 45.12 N 7.05 E
Ročegda 24 62.42 N 43.23 E
Roch ≃ 44 53.34 N 2.18 W
Rocha, Bra. 256 21.28 S 45.49 W
Rocha, Ur. 252 34.29 S 54.20 W
Rocha Miranda ◆[8] 287a 22.52 S 43.22 W
Rocha Sobrinho 287a 22.47 S 43.25 W
Rochdale, Eng., U.K. 44 53.38 N 2.09 W
Rochdale, Ma., U.S. 207 42.11 N 71.54 W
Rochdale, N.Y., U.S. 210 41.43 N 73.50 W
Rochdale □[8] 262 53.37 N 2.08 W
Rochdale Canal ≋ 262 53.43 N 1.54 W
Roche 42 50.24 N 4.48 W
Rochebrune, Grand Pic de ∧ 62 44.49 N 6.51 E
Rochechouart 32 45.50 N 0.50 E
Rochedinho 255 20.14 S 54.33 W
Rochedo 255 19.57 S 54.52 W
Rochedo de Minas 256 21.38 S 43.01 W
Rochefort, Bel. 56 50.10 N 5.13 E
Rochefort, Fr. 32 45.57 N 0.58 W
Rochefort-en-Yvelines 50 48.35 N 1.59 E
Rochefort-Montagne 32 45.41 N 2.48 E
Rochefort-sur-Nenon 58 47.07 N 5.34 E
Roche Harbor 224 48.36 N 123.08 W
Rochehaut 56 49.51 N 5.00 E
Roche-la-Molière 62 45.26 N 4.19 E
Roche-lez-Beaupré 58 47.17 N 6.07 E
Rochelle, Ga., U.S. 192 31.57 N 83.27 W
Rochelle, Il., U.S. 216 41.55 N 89.04 W
Rochelle, Tx., U.S. 196 31.13 N 99.13 W
Rochelle Park 276 40.54 N 74.04 W
Rochemaure 62 44.35 N 4.42 E
Roche-Percée 184 49.03 N 102.45 W
Rochepot, Château de la ⊥ 58 46.57 N 4.40 E
Rocher Fendu, Rapides du ⊔ 275a 45.19 N 73.57 W
Rochester, Austl. 166 36.22 S 144.42 E
Rochester, Eng., U.K. 42 51.24 N 0.30 E
Rochester, Eng., U.K. 44 55.16 N 2.16 W
Rochester, Il., U.S. 219 39.45 N 89.32 W
Rochester, In., U.S. 216 41.03 N 86.12 W
Rochester, Ma., U.S. 207 41.43 N 70.49 W
Rochester, Mi., U.S. 214 42.40 N 83.08 W
Rochester, Mn., U.S. 190 44.01 N 92.28 W
Rochester, N.H., U.S. 188 43.18 N 70.58 W
Rochester, N.Y., U.S. 210 43.09 N 77.36 W
Rochester, Oh., U.S. 214 41.07 N 82.18 W
Rochester, Pa., U.S. 214 40.42 N 80.17 W
Rochester, Tx., U.S. 196 33.19 N 99.51 W
Rochester, Wa., U.S. 224 46.49 N 123.05 W
Rochester, Wi., U.S. 216 42.44 N 88.13 W
Rochester City Airport ⊠ 260 51.21 N 0.30 E
Rochester Hills 214 42.40 N 83.09 W
Rochester Mills 214 40.49 N 78.59 W
Rochester-Monroe County Airport ⊠ 210 43.07 N 77.40 W
Rochester-Utica State Recreation Area ♠ 214 42.39 N 83.04 W
Rochetaillée 62 45.25 N 4.27 E
Rocheuses → Rocky Mountains ⋏ 16 48.00 N 116.00 W
Rochford 42 51.36 N 0.43 E
Rochford □[8] 260 51.36 N 0.39 E
Rochfortbridge 48 53.23 N 7.17 W
Rochlitz 54 51.03 N 12.47 E
Rochon, Lac ⊜ 206 46.43 N 75.14 W
Rock 190 46.04 N 87.09 W
Rock □[6] 216 42.41 N 89.05 W
Rock ≃, U.S. 190 41.29 N 90.37 W
Rock ≃, U.S. 198 43.05 N 96.27 W
Rockall I 22 57.35 N 13.48 W
Rockall Rise ✦[3] 10 59.00 N 14.00 W
Rockanje 52 51.53 N 4.05 E
Rockaway, N.J., U.S. 210 40.54 N 74.30 W
Rockaway, Or., U.S. 224 45.36 N 123.56 W
Rockaway ≃ 210 40.51 N 74.21 W
Rockaway Inlet c 276 40.34 N 73.55 W
Rockaway Neck 276 40.51 N 74.21 W
Rockaway Park ◆[8] 276 40.35 N 73.50 W
Rockaway Point ◆[8] 276 40.33 N 73.55 W
Rockaway Point > 276 40.33 N 73.56 W
Rockaways' Playland ♠ 276 40.35 N 73.49 W
Rockbank 274b 37.43 S 144.39 E
Rock Bay 182 50.20 N 125.29 W
Rockbridge 219 39.16 N 90.12 W
Rock Bridge State Park ♠ 219 38.53 N 92.19 W
Rock Brook ≃ 276 40.25 N 74.40 W
Rock Candy Mountain ∧ 224 47.01 N 123.07 W
Rockcastle ≃ 192 36.58 N 84.21 W
Rock City Falls 210 43.04 N 73.55 W
Rockcliffe Park 212 45.27 N 75.41 W
Rockcorry 48 54.07 N 7.01 W
Rock Creek, B.C., Can. 182 49.06 N 118.58 W
Rock Creek, Oh., U.S. 214 41.39 N 80.51 W
Rock Creek ≃, N.A. 202 48.25 N 107.05 W
Rock Creek ≃, U.S. 208 39.43 N 77.13 W
Rock Creek ≃, U.S. 284c 38.54 N 77.04 W
Rock Creek ≃, Ca., U.S. 226 37.55 N 120.58 W
Rock Creek ≃, Co., U.S. 198 40.20 N 102.31 W
Rock Creek ≃, Il., U.S. 216 41.12 N 87.59 W
Rock Creek ≃, In., U.S. 216 40.42 N 86.35 W
Rock Creek ≃, In., U.S. 216 40.49 N 85.23 W
Rock Creek ≃, Mt., U.S. 202 45.31 N 108.49 W
Rock Creek ≃, Mt., U.S. 202 46.43 N 113.40 W
Rock Creek ≃, Nv., U.S. 204 40.39 N 116.54 W
Rock Creek ≃, Or., U.S. 202 45.34 N 120.25 W
Rock Creek ≃, Or., U.S. 202 42.39 N 119.08 W
Rock Creek ≃, Or., U.S. 224 45.51 N 123.12 W
Rock Creek ≃, S.D., U.S. 198 43.44 N 97.58 W
Rock Creek ≃, Ut,. U.S. 200 40.17 N 110.30 W
Rock Creek ≃, Wa., U.S. 202 46.55 N 117.56 W
Rock Creek ≃, Wa., U.S. 202 45.42 N 120.29 W
Rock Creek ≃, Wy., U.S. 200 41.54 N 106.08 W
Rock Creek Butte ∧ 202 44.49 N 118.07 W
Rock Creek Hills 284c 39.01 N 77.04 W
Rock Creek Park ♠ 284c 38.58 N 77.03 W
Rock Cut State Park ♠ 216 42.20 N 89.00 W
Rockdale, Austl. 170 33.57 S 151.08 E
Rockdale, Il., U.S. 216 41.30 N 88.06 W
Rockdale, Md., U.S. 284b 39.21 N 76.45 W
Rockdale, Pa., U.S. 285 39.53 N 75.26 W
Rockdale, Tx., U.S. 222 30.39 N 97.00 W
Rockdale, W.V., U.S. 214 40.18 N 80.35 W
Rockefeller Center ʋ 276 40.45 N 74.00 W
Rockefeller Park ♠ 279a 41.32 N 81.38 W
Rockefeller Plateau ⋏[1] 9 80.00 S 135.00 W
Rockenhausen 56 49.38 N 7.49 E
Rockensüss 56 51.03 N 9.50 E
Rockfall 207 41.31 N 72.41 W
Rock Falls 190 41.46 N 89.41 W
Rock Ferry 262 53.22 N 3.00 W
Rockfield 216 40.38 N 86.34 W
Rock Flat 171b 36.21 S 149.12 E
Rock Flat Creek ≃ 171b 36.07 S 149.12 E
Rockford, Al., U.S. 194 32.53 N 86.13 W
Rockford, Il., U.S. 216 42.16 N 89.05 W
Rockford, In., U.S. 218 38.59 N 85.54 W
Rockford, Ia., U.S. 190 43.03 N 92.56 W
Rockford, Mi., U.S. 190 43.07 N 85.33 W
Rockford, Oh., U.S. 216 40.41 N 84.38 W
Rockford, Tn., U.S. 192 35.49 N 83.56 W
Rock Forest 206 45.20 N 71.59 W
Rockglen, Sk., Can. 184 49.10 N 105.57 W
Rock Glen, N.Y., U.S. 210 42.41 N 78.07 W
Rock Hall 208 39.08 N 76.14 W
Rockhammar 40 59.32 N 15.26 E
Rockhampton 166 23.23 S 150.31 E
Rockhampton Downs 162 18.57 S 135.01 E
Rock Hill, N.Y., U.S. 210 41.38 N 74.36 W
Rock Hill, S.C., U.S. 192 34.55 N 81.01 W
Rockhill Furnace 214 40.15 N 77.54 W
Rockingham, Austl. 168a 32.17 S 115.44 E
Rockingham, N.C., U.S. 192 34.56 N 79.46 W
Rockingham □[6] 207 42.50 N 71.15 W
Rockingham Bay c 166 18.10 S 146.05 E
Rockingham Forest ◆[3] 42 52.30 N 0.37 W
Rockingham Park ♠ 283 42.47 N 71.14 W
Rockingham State Historic Site ⊥ 276 40.24 N 74.37 W
Rock Island, P.Q., Can. 206 45.01 N 72.06 W
Rock Island, Il., U.S. 190 41.30 N 90.34 W
Rock Island, Tx., U.S. 222 29.32 N 96.35 W
Rocklake 198 48.47 N 99.15 W
Rock Lake ⊜, Mb., Can. 184 49.11 N 99.12 W
Rock Lake ⊜, On., Can. 212 45.30 N 78.23 W
Rock Lake ⊜, Il., U.S. 278 41.40 N 88.03 W
Rock Lake ⊜, N.D., U.S. 198 48.50 N 99.10 W
Rock Lake ⊜, Wi., U.S. 216 43.04 N 88.56 W
Rockland, On., Can. 188 45.33 N 75.17 W
Rockland, De., U.S. 285 39.47 N 75.34 W
Rockland, Id., U.S. 202 42.34 N 112.52 W
Rockland, Me., U.S. 188 44.06 N 69.06 W
Rockland, Ma., U.S. 207 42.07 N 70.55 W
Rockland, Mi., U.S. 190 46.44 N 89.10 W
Rockland, N.Y., U.S. 210 41.58 N 74.54 W
Rockland □[6] 210 41.09 N 73.59 W
Rockland Lake 276 41.09 N 73.55 W
Rockland Lake ⊜ 276 41.08 N 73.55 W
Rockland Lake State Park ♠ 276 41.08 N 73.55 W
Rocklands Reservoir ⊜[1] 166 37.15 S 142.00 E
Rockledge, Fl., U.S. 220 28.21 N 80.43 W
Rockledge, Pa., U.S. 285 40.03 N 75.05 W
Rockleigh 276 41.00 N 73.55 W
Rocklin 226 38.47 N 121.14 W
Rockmart 192 34.00 N 85.02 W
Rock Meadow Brook ≃ 283 42.16 N 71.13 W
Rock of Cashel ⊥ 48 52.31 N 7.53 W
Rock Point 208 38.16 N 76.50 W
Rock Point Provincial Park ♠ 212 42.51 N 79.33 W
Rock Pond ⊜ 283 42.44 N 71.00 W
Rockport, Il., U.S. 219 39.32 N 91.00 W
Rockport, Ky., U.S. 194 37.20 N 86.59 W
Rockport, Me., U.S. 188 44.11 N 69.04 W
Rockport, Ma., U.S. 207 42.39 N 70.37 W
Rock Port, Mo., U.S. 194 40.24 N 95.30 W
Rockport, Tx., U.S. 196 28.01 N 97.03 W
Rock Rapids 198 43.25 N 96.10 W
Rock River 200 41.44 N 105.58 W
Rock Run 208 39.59 N 75.50 W
Rock Run ≃ 284c 38.58 N 77.11 W
Rock Sound 238 24.54 N 76.12 W
Rocksprings, Tx., U.S. 196 30.00 N 100.12 W
Rock Springs, Wy., U.S. 200 41.35 N 109.12 W
Rockstone 246 5.59 N 58.33 W
Rock Stream 210 42.28 N 76.56 W
Rockton, Il., U.S. 216 42.27 N 89.04 W
Rockton, Pa., U.S. 214 41.05 N 78.39 W
Rock Valley 198 43.12 N 96.17 W
Rockville, N.Z. 172 40.44 S 172.38 E
Rockville, Ct., U.S. 207 41.52 N 72.27 W
Rockville, In., U.S. 194 39.45 N 87.13 W
Rockville, Md., U.S. 208 39.05 N 77.09 W
Rockville, Ma., U.S. 283 42.08 N 71.21 W
Rockville, Pa., U.S. 208 40.20 N 76.54 W
Rockville, R.I., U.S. 207 41.27 N 71.30 W
Rockville Centre 210 40.39 N 73.38 W
Rockwall 222 32.55 N 96.27 W
Rockwall □[6] 222 32.55 N 96.23 W
Rockwell, Ia., U.S. 190 42.59 N 93.11 W
Rockwell, N.C., U.S. 192 35.33 N 80.24 W
Rockwell, Lake ⊜ 214 41.12 N 81.19 W
Rockwell City 198 42.23 N 94.38 W
Rockwell International Corporation ʋ[3] 280 33.52 N 117.51 W
Rockwood, On., Can. 212 43.37 N 80.08 W
Rockwood, Me., U.S. 188 45.41 N 69.44 W
Rockwood, Mi., U.S. 216 42.04 N 83.14 W
Rockwood, Or., U.S. 224 45.31 N 122.28 W
Rockwood, Pa., U.S. 188 39.54 N 79.09 W
Rockwood, Tn., U.S. 192 35.51 N 84.41 W
Rockwood Lake ⊜ 276 41.06 N 73.38 W
Rockwood Lake Brook ≃ 276 41.03 N 73.36 W
Rocky 196 35.09 N 99.03 W
Rocky ≃, Ab., Can. 182 53.08 N 117.59 W
Rocky ≃, Mi., U.S. 216 41.57 N 85.39 W
Rocky ≃, N.C., U.S. 192 35.37 N 79.09 W
Rocky ≃, Oh., U.S. 214 41.30 N 81.49 W
Rocky, East Branch ≃ 279a 41.24 N 81.53 W
Rocky, West Branch ≃ 214 41.24 N 81.53 W
Rocky Arroyo V 196 32.32 N 104.21 W
Rocky Boy's Indian Reservation ◆[4] 202 48.18 N 109.45 W
Rocky Branch ≃ 284c 38.53 N 77.19 W
Rocky Cape National Park ♠ 166 40.56 S 145.35 E
Rocky Comfort Creek ≃ 192 32.59 N 82.25 W
Rocky Coulee V 202 47.10 N 119.16 W
Rocky Creek ≃ 192 35.53 N 80.47 W
Rockyford, Ab., Can. 182 51.13 N 113.08 W
Rocky Ford, Co., U.S. 198 38.06 N 103.43 W
Rocky Ford Creek ≃ 216 41.19 N 83.37 W
Rocky Fork Lake ⊜ 218 39.11 N 83.28 W
Rocky Fork State Park ♠ 218 39.11 N 83.30 W
Rocky Gorge Reservoir ⊜[1] 208 39.07 N 76.54 W
Rocky Grove 214 41.25 N 79.49 W
Rocky Gully 162 34.30 S 116.48 E
Rocky Harbour 186 49.36 N 57.55 W
Rocky Harbour c 271d 22.20 N 114.19 E
Rocky Hill, Ct., U.S. 207 41.40 N 72.39 W
Rocky Hill, N.J., U.S. 276 40.24 N 74.38 W
Rocky Island Lake ⊜[1] 190 46.56 N 83.04 W
Rocky Lake ⊜ 184 54.08 N 101.30 W
Rocky Mount, N.C., U.S. 192 35.57 N 77.48 W
Rocky Mount, Va., U.S. 192 36.59 N 79.53 W
Rocky Mountain ∧ 202 47.49 N 112.49 W
Rocky Mountain House 182 52.22 N 114.55 W
Rocky Mountain National Park ♠ 200 40.19 N 105.42 W
Rocky Mountains ⋏ 16 48.00 N 116.00 W
Rocky Point, N.Y., U.S. 207 40.57 N 72.56 W
Rocky Point, Wa., U.S. 224 47.35 N 122.41 W
Rocky Point >, Ba. 192 26.00 N 77.25 W
Rocky Point >, Ire. 48 54.42 N 8.48 W
Rocky Point >, Namibia 156 19.03 S 12.30 E
Rocky Point >, Norf. I. 174c 29.03 S 167.55 E
Rocky Point >, Ak., U.S. 180 64.25 N 163.10 W
Rocky Point >, Ma., U.S. 207 41.57 N 70.35 W
Rocky Point >, N.Y., U.S. 276 40.55 N 73.32 W
Rocky Ridge 214 41.32 N 83.13 W
Rocky Ridge ∧ 282 37.48 N 122.03 W
Rocky River 214 41.28 N 81.50 W
Rocky River Reservation ♠ 279a 41.27 N 81.50 W
Rocky Run ≃, N.D., U.S. 198 47.38 N 99.02 W
Rocky Run ≃, Pa., U.S. 285 39.54 N 75.28 W
Rocky Run ≃, Va., U.S. 284c 38.58 N 77.15 W
Rocky Saugeen ≃ 212 44.13 N 80.53 W
Rocky Top ∧ 202 44.47 N 122.17 W
Roclenge-sur-Geer 56 50.45 N 5.36 E
Rocosas, Montañas → Rocky Mountains ⋏ 16 48.00 N 116.00 W
Rocquencourt 261 48.50 N 2.07 E
Rocroi 50 49.55 N 4.31 E
Roda 192 36.58 N 82.49 W
Roda ≃ 54 50.52 N 11.44 E
Rodach 56 50.20 N 10.46 E
Rodach ≃, Dtsch. 54 50.09 N 11.10 E
Rodach ≃, Dtsch. 56 50.08 N 10.52 E
Rodakove 83 48.33 N 39.02 E
Rodalben 56 49.14 N 7.38 E
Rodalquilar 34 37.40 N 2.08 W
Rodas 240p 22.20 N 80.33 W
Rodas → Ródhos I 38 36.10 N 28.00 E
Rodaun ◆[8] 264b 48.08 N 16.16 E
Rødberg 26 60.16 N 8.58 E
Rødby 41 54.42 N 11.24 E
Rødbyhavn 41 54.39 N 11.21 E
Roddickton 186 50.52 N 56.08 W
Rødding 41 55.23 N 9.06 E
Rodeiro 256 21.12 S 42.52 W
Rødekro 41 55.04 N 9.21 E
Rodel 46 57.41 N 7.05 W
Roden 52 53.07 N 6.26 E
Roden ≃ 42 52.43 N 2.36 W
Rodenberg 52 52.18 N 9.21 E
Rodenkirchen, Dtsch. 52 53.24 N 8.26 E
Rodenkirchen, Dtsch. 56 50.54 N 6.59 E
Rödentel 54 50.17 N 11.01 E
Rodeo, Arg. 252 30.12 S 69.06 W
Rodeo, Méx. 232 25.11 N 104.34 W
Rodeo, Ca., U.S. 226 38.01 N 122.15 W
Rodeo, N.M., U.S. 200 31.50 N 109.01 W
Rodeo Lagoon c 282 37.50 N 122.31 W
Röderau 54 51.19 N 13.19 E
Roderick ≃ 162 26.57 S 116.13 E
Roderick Island I 182 52.40 N 128.22 W
Rödermark 56 49.59 N 8.50 E
Rodewisch 54 50.32 N 12.24 E
Rodez 32 44.21 N 2.35 E
Rodgau 56 50.02 N 8.54 E
Rodheim-Bieber 56 50.37 N 8.35 E
Rodhópis, Orosirá → Rhodope Mountains ⋏ 38 41.30 N 24.30 E
Ródhos (Rhodes) 38 36.26 N 28.13 E
Ródhos (Rhodes) I 38 36.10 N 28.00 E
Rodi Garganico 68 41.55 N 15.53 E
Roding 60 49.12 N 12.32 E
Roding ≃ 42 51.31 N 0.06 E
Rodinka 80 57.24 N 43.34 E
Rodino, Ross. 76 58.57 N 44.59 E
Rodino, Ross. 86 52.30 N 80.15 E
Rodionovo-Nesvetajskaja 83 47.36 N 39.42 E
Rodman 180 57.28 N 135.21 W
Rodman Naval Station ■ 236 8.56 N 79.36 W
Rodn'a 76 56.22 N 34.55 E
Rodnei, Munții ⋏ 38 47.35 N 24.40 E
Rodney, On., Can. 214 42.34 N 81.41 W
Rodney, Ms., U.S. 194 31.51 N 91.11 W
Rodney, Cape >, N.Z. 172 36.17 S 174.49 E
Rodney, Cape >, Ak., U.S. 180 64.39 N 166.24 W
Rodney Bay c 241f 14.05 N 60.58 W
Rodney Village 208 39.07 N 75.31 W
Rodničok 80 51.26 N 42.54 E
Rodniki, Ross. 80 57.06 N 41.44 E
Rodniki, Ross. 265b 55.39 N 38.04 E
Rodnikovskij 86 50.39 N 57.12 E
Rodolfo, Lago → Rudolf, Lake ⊜ 144 3.30 N 36.05 E
Rodonit, Kep i > 38 41.35 N 19.27 E
Rodostov 76 51.58 N 24.57 E
Rødovre 41 55.41 N 12.29 E
Rodrigo de Freitas, Lagoa c 287a 22.58 S 43.13 W
Rodrigues I 12 19.42 S 63.25 E
Rodríguez, Méx. 196 27.10 N 100.01 W
Rodríguez, Ur. 258 34.23 S 56.33 W
Rodríguez, Arroyo ≃ 288 34.52 S 58.02 W
Roduco 208 36.27 N 76.48 W
Rødven 26 62.38 N 7.33 E
Rødvig 41 55.15 N 12.23 E
Rodyns'ke 83 48.25 N 37.19 E
Roe ≃ 48 55.07 N 6.59 W
Roebling 208 40.06 N 74.47 W
Roebourne 162 20.47 S 117.09 E
Roebuck Bay c 162 18.04 S 122.17 E
Roehampton ◆[8] 260 51.27 N 0.14 W
Roe Island I 282 38.04 N 122.02 W
Roeland Park 198 39.02 N 94.37 W
Roelands 168a 33.18 S 115.50 E
Roeliff Jansen Kill ≃ 210 42.11 N 73.52 W
Roelofarendsveen 52 52.12 N 4.38 E
Roelofskamp 158 26.10 S 24.24 E
Roen, Monte ∧ 64 46.22 N 11.11 E
Roer (Rur) ≃ 56 51.12 N 5.59 E
Roermond 52 51.12 N 6.00 E
Roesbrugge-Haringe 50 50.55 N 2.37 E
Roeselare (Roulers) 50 50.57 N 3.08 E
Roesinger, Lake ⊜ 224 47.58 N 121.55 W
Roessleville 210 42.41 N 73.48 W
Roes Welcome Sound ꞷ 176 64.00 N 88.00 W
Roetgen 56 50.39 N 6.12 E
Rœulx 50 50.30 N 4.06 E
Roff 196 34.37 N 96.50 W
Röfors 40 58.57 N 14.37 E
Rofrano 68 40.12 N 15.25 E
Rogačevo 82 56.26 N 37.10 E
Rogačov 76 53.05 N 30.03 E
Rogačovka 78 51.30 N 39.34 E
Rogagua, Laguna ⊜ 248 13.43 S 66.54 W
Rogaguado, Laguna ⊜ 248 12.52 S 65.43 W
Rogaland □[6] 26 59.00 N 6.15 E
Rogalik 83 48.56 N 40.03 E
Rogans Hill 274a 33.44 S 151.01 E
Rogan's Seat ∧ 44 54.25 N 2.07 W
Rogart 46 58.00 N 4.08 W
Rogäsen 54 52.19 N 12.20 E
Rogaška Slatina 36 46.14 N 15.38 E
Rogatica 38 43.48 N 19.00 E
Rogätz 54 52.19 N 11.46 E
Rogen ⊜ 26 62.19 N 12.23 E
Roger, Lac ⊜ 190 47.50 N 78.51 W
Roger Island I 283 42.43 N 70.50 W
Rogers, Ar., U.S. 194 36.19 N 94.07 W
Rogers, Ct., U.S. 207 41.50 N 71.54 W
Rogers, Oh., U.S. 214 40.48 N 80.38 W
Rogers, Tx., U.S. 222 30.55 N 97.13 W
Rogers, Mount ∧ 192 36.39 N 81.33 W
Rogers City 190 45.25 N 83.49 W
Rogers Lake ⊜ 228 34.52 N 117.51 W
Rogers Park ◆[8] 278 42.01 N 87.40 W
Rogers Pass)(182 51.17 N 117.31 W
Rogersville, N.B., Can. 186 46.44 N 65.26 W
Rogersville, Al., U.S. 194 34.49 N 87.17 W
Rogersville, Tn., U.S. 192 36.24 N 83.00 W
Roggeveldberge ⋏ 158 32.17 S 20.08 E
Roggewein, Cabo > 174z 27.07 S 109.15 W
Roggiano Gravina 68 39.37 N 16.09 E
Roghudi 68 38.03 N 15.55 E
Rogliano, Fr. 36 42.57 N 9.25 E
Rogliano, It. 68 39.11 N 16.20 E
Rognac 62 43.29 N 5.14 E
Rognedino 76 53.48 N 33.33 E
Rögnitz ≃ 54 53.19 N 10.57 E
Rognon ≃ 58 48.23 N 5.10 E
Rogny 50 47.45 N 2.53 E
Rogojampi 115a 8.19 S 114.17 E
Rogovatoje 78 51.14 N 38.22 E
Rogovo 82 55.13 N 37.05 E
Rogovskaja 78 45.44 N 38.44 E
Rogovskoje 80 58.33 N 50.43 E
Rogožkino 83 47.10 N 39.21 E
Rogoźno 30 52.46 N 17.00 E
Rogue ≃, Mi., U.S. 190 43.04 N 85.35 W
Rogue ≃, Or., U.S. 202 42.26 N 124.25 W
Rogue River 202 42.26 N 123.10 W
Rohan' 78 49.54 N 36.29 E
Rohatyn 78 49.25 N 24.37 E
Rohdenhaus 263 51.18 N 7.01 E
Rohilkhand Plains ≚ 124 28.20 N 79.30 E
Rohinjan 272c 19.06 N 73.04 E
Rohitpur 126 23.42 N 90.19 E
Rohl ≃ 140 6.22 N 29.46 E
Röhlinghausen ◆[8] 263 51.30 N 7.10 E
Rohnert Park 226 38.20 N 122.42 W
Rohoziv 78 50.14 N 31.03 E
Rohr 60 48.46 N 11.58 E
Rohrbach in Oberösterreich 60 48.34 N 13.59 E
Rohrbach-lès-Bitche 56 49.03 N 7.16 E
Rohrbeck 264a 52.32 N 13.02 E
Rohrberg 54 52.42 N 11.02 E
Röhrenfurth 56 51.09 N 9.32 E
Rohri 120 27.41 N 68.54 E
Röhrsdorf 54 50.51 N 12.50 E
Rohtak 123 28.54 N 76.34 E
Rohunta, Laguna c 236 15.12 N 83.30 W
Roi, Île du → King Island I 166 39.50 S 144.00 E
Roia (Roya) ≃ 62 43.48 N 7.35 E
Roi Et 110 16.03 N 103.40 E
Roi Georges, Îles du II 14 14.32 S 145.08 W
Roi Léopold, Monts du → King Leopold Ranges ⋏ 160 17.30 S 125.45 E
Roine ⊜ 26 61.24 N 24.06 E
Roinville 261 48.32 N 2.03 E
Roisel 50 49.57 N 3.06 E
Roissy 261 48.47 N 2.39 E
Roissy-en-France 261 49.00 N 2.31 E
Roitzsch 54 51.34 N 12.16 E
Roja 76 57.30 N 22.49 E
Rojas 252 34.12 S 60.44 W
Rojo → Red ≃ 178 31.00 N 91.40 W
Rojo, Cabo >, Méx. 234 21.33 N 97.20 W
Rojo, Cabo >, P.R. 240m 17.56 N 67.11 W
Rojo, Mar → Red Sea ⊤[2] 136 20.00 N 38.00 E
Rokan 112 0.34 N 100.25 E
Rokan ≃ 114 2.00 N 100.52 E
Rokan-kanan ≃ 114 1.23 N 100.56 E
Rokan-kiri ≃ 114 1.23 N 100.56 E
Röke 41 56.14 N 13.30 E
Rokeby National Park ♠ 164 13.40 S 142.55 E
Rokel ≃ 150 8.33 N 12.48 W
Rokewood 169 37.54 S 143.43 E
Rokewood Junction 169 37.51 S 143.41 E
Rokhah 120 35.16 N 69.28 E
Rokiškis 76 55.58 N 25.35 E
Rokkō-san ∧ 96 34.46 N 135.16 E
Rokkō-sanchi ⋏ 270 34.45 N 135.13 E
Roklum 54 52.04 N 10.44 E
Rokuan kansallispuisto ♠ 26 64.32 N 26.33 E
Rokugō 94 35.29 N 138.27 E
Rokugō ◆[8] 268 35.33 N 139.43 E
Rokusei 94 36.58 N 136.52 E
Rokycany 60 49.45 N 13.36 E
Rokytná ≃ 61 49.05 N 16.22 E
Rokytne, Ukr. 78 49.42 N 30.27 E
Rokytne, Ukr. 78 51.17 N 27.14 E
Rolampont 58 47.57 N 5.16 E
Roland, Mb., Can. 184 49.25 N 97.55 W
Roland, Ar., U.S. 194 34.54 N 92.29 W
Roland, Ia., U.S. 190 42.09 N 93.30 W
Roland, Lake ⊜[1] 284b 39.23 N 76.38 W
Roland C. Nickerson State Park ♠ 207 41.46 N 70.03 W
Rolândia 255 23.18 S 51.22 W
Roland Park ◆[8] 284b 39.22 N 76.39 W
Roland Run ≃ 284b 39.23 N 76.39 W
Rolava ≃ 54 50.15 N 12.51 E
Røldal 26 59.49 N 6.48 E
Roldán 252 32.54 S 60.54 W
Roldanillo 246 4.24 N 76.09 W
Rolde 52 52.58 N 6.38 E
Roldskov ◆[3] 26 56.48 N 9.50 E
Rolette 198 48.39 N 99.50 W
Roleystone 168a 32.08 S 116.04 E
Rolfe 198 42.48 N 94.31 W
Roll, Az., U.S. 200 32.45 N 113.59 W
Roll, In., U.S. 216 40.33 N 85.23 W
Rolla, B.C., Can. 182 55.54 N 120.09 W
Rolla, Ks., U.S. 198 37.07 N 101.07 W
Rolla, Mo., U.S. 194 37.57 N 91.46 W
Rolla, N.D., U.S. 198 48.51 N 99.37 W
Rolle 58 46.28 N 6.20 E
Rolle, Passo di)(64 46.18 N 11.47 E
Rolleboise 261 49.01 N 1.36 E
Rolleston, Austl. 166 24.28 S 148.37 E
Rolleston, N.Z. 172 43.35 S 172.23 E
Rolling Acres 284b 39.17 N 76.52 W
Rollingbay 224 47.39 N 122.30 W
Rolling Fork 194 32.54 N 90.52 W
Rolling Fork ≃ 194 37.55 N 85.50 W
Rolling Hills 280 33.46 N 118.21 W
Rolling Hills Estates 280 33.47 N 118.21 W
Rolling Meadows 216 42.05 N 88.00 W
Rolling Prairie 216 41.40 N 86.37 W
Rolling River Indian Reserve ◆[4] 184 50.27 N 100.00 W
Rollingstone 166 19.03 S 146.24 E
Rollingwood 226 37.57 N 122.20 W
Rollins 182 47.54 N 114.11 W
Rollins Reservoir ⊜[1] 226 39.08 N 120.57 W
Rolvsøya I 24 71.00 N 24.00 E
Rom → Roma 66 41.54 N 12.29 E
Roma, Austl. 166 26.35 S 148.47 E
Roma (Rome), It. 66 41.54 N 12.29 E
Roma (Rome), It. 267a 41.54 N 12.29 E
Roma, Leso. 158 29.27 S 27.45 E
Roma, Tx., U.S. 196 26.25 N 99.01 W
Roma □[4] 66 41.58 N 12.40 E
Romagna □[9] 64 44.30 N 12.15 E
Romagnano Sesia 62 45.38 N 8.23 E
Romagne-sous-Montfaucon 56 49.20 N 5.05 E
Romain, Cape > 192 33.00 N 79.22 W
Romaine ≃ 176 50.18 N 63.47 W
Romainmôtier 58 46.42 N 6.29 E
Romainville 261 48.53 N 2.26 E
Romakloster 26 57.31 N 18.27 E
Roman 38 46.55 N 26.56 E
Roman ≃ 42 51.51 N 0.57 E
Romanche ≃ 62 45.05 N 5.43 E
Romanche Gap ✦[1] 10 0.10 S 18.15 W
Romang, Pulau I 164 7.35 S 127.26 E
Romang, Selat ꞷ 164 7.30 S 127.00 E
Romania (România) □[1], Europe 22 46.00 N 25.30 E
Romania (România) □[1], Europe 38 46.00 N 25.30 E
Romankivtsi 78 48.29 N 27.13 E
Roman-Kosh, hora ∧ 78 44.37 N 34.15 E
Roman Nose Mountain ∧ 202 43.55 N 123.44 W
Romano, Cape > 220 25.50 N 81.41 W
Romano, Cayo I 240p 22.04 N 77.50 W
Romano Banco 266b 45.25 N 9.06 E
Romano di Lombardia 62 45.31 N 9.45 E
Romanova 88 57.04 N 103.24 E
Romanovka, Ross. 80 51.24 N 47.23 E
Romanovka, Ross. 80 51.45 N 42.45 E
Romanovka, Ross. 80 49.47 N 45.05 E
Romanovka, Ross. 86 54.38 N 76.03 E
Romanovka, Ross. 88 53.14 N 112.46 E
Romanovka, Ross. 265a 60.03 N 30.42 E
Romanovo, Ross. 82 56.39 N 39.14 E
Romanovo, Ross. 86 53.58 N 80.30 E
Romanovo, Ross. 86 52.37 N 81.14 E
Romanovo, Ross. 86 59.09 N 61.30 E
Romans d'Isonzo 64 45.53 N 13.26 E
Romanshorn 58 47.34 N 9.22 E
Romans-sur-Isère 62 45.03 N 5.03 E
Romansville 285 39.57 N 75.45 W
Romanzof Mountains ⋏ 180 69.00 N 144.00 W
Romaški 80 50.13 N 46.41 E
Romaškino 80 52.29 N 51.48 E
Romaškovo 265b 55.44 N 37.20 E
Romayor 222 30.27 N 94.50 W
Rombari 154 4.33 N 31.02 E
Romblon 116 12.35 N 122.15 E
Romblon □[4] 116 12.30 N 122.10 E
Romblon Island I 116 12.33 N 122.17 E
Romblon Passage ꞷ 116 12.27 N 122.12 E
Rombo, Ilhéus do II 150a 14.58 N 24.40 W
Rome → Roma, It. 66 41.54 N 12.29 E
Rome, Ga., U.S. 192 34.15 N 85.09 W
Rome, Il., U.S. 190 40.53 N 89.30 W
Rome, Ms., U.S. 194 33.57 N 90.28 W
Rome, N.Y., U.S. 210 43.12 N 75.27 W
Rome, Oh., U.S. 214 41.36 N 80.52 W
Rome, Pa., U.S. 210 41.51 N 76.21 W
Rome, Wi., U.S. 216 42.58 N 88.38 W
Rome City 216 41.29 N 85.22 W
Romeleåsen ⋏[2] 41 55.34 N 13.33 E
Romenay 58 46.30 N 5.04 E
Romeno 64 46.24 N 11.07 E
Romentino 62 45.28 N 8.42 E
Romeo 214 42.48 N 83.00 W
Romeoville 216 41.38 N 88.05 W
Römerberg 56 49.17 N 8.24 E
Romero, Isla I 258 33.48 S 59.20 W
Rometan 128 39.56 N 64.23 E
Rometta 70 38.10 N 15.25 E
Romfartuna 40 59.44 N 16.35 E
Romford ◆[8] 260 51.35 N 0.11 E
Römhild 54 50.24 N 10.32 E
Romiley 262 53.25 N 2.05 W
Romilly, Mount ∧[2] 162 20.27 S 126.34 E
Romilly-sur-Seine 50 48.31 N 3.43 E
Romit 85 38.44 N 69.17 E
Romit, zapovednik ♠ 85 38.52 N 69.20 E
Romita 234 20.52 N 101.31 W
Romitorio 267a 42.01 N 12.39 E
Rommani 148 34.34 N 6.37 W
Romme 40 60.26 N 15.30 E
Rommerskirchen 56 51.02 N 6.40 E
Romney, In., U.S. 216 40.14 N 86.54 W
Romney, W.V., U.S. 188 39.20 N 78.45 W
Romney Marsh ≡ 42 51.03 N 0.55 E
Romny, Ross. 89 50.44 N 129.15 E
Romny, Ukr. 78 50.45 N 33.30 E
Rømø I 26 55.08 N 8.31 E
Romodan 78 49.59 N 33.19 E
Romodanovo 80 54.26 N 45.20 E
Romoland 228 33.45 N 117.10 W
Romont 58 46.42 N 6.55 E
Romorantin-Lanthenay 50 47.22 N 1.45 E
Rompin, Malay. 114 2.42 N 102.31 E
Rompin, Malay. 114 2.48 N 103.29 E
Rompin ≃ 114 2.49 N 103.29 E
Romrod 56 50.43 N 9.13 E
Romsdalen V 26 62.15 N 8.05 E
Romsdalsfjorden c[2] 26 62.39 N 7.15 E
Romsey, Austl. 169 37.21 S 144.45 E
Romsey, Eng., U.K. 42 50.59 N 1.30 W
Romsø I 41 55.31 N 10.48 E
Romulus, Mi., U.S. 216 42.13 N 83.23 W
Romulus, N.Y., U.S. 210 42.45 N 76.50 W
Røn, Nor. 26 61.03 N 9.03 E
Ron, Viet 110 17.53 N 106.27 E
Ron, Mui > 110 18.07 N 106.27 E
Rona, Schw. 58 46.34 N 9.38 E
Rona, Zaïre 154 2.14 N 30.52 E
Rona I, Scot., U.K. 46 57.34 N 5.59 W
Rona I, Scot., U.K. 46 59.07 N 5.49 W
Ronald 224 47.14 N 121.01 W
Ronan 202 47.31 N 114.06 W
Ronas Hill ∧[2] 46a 60.31 N 1.28 W
Ronas Voe c 46a 60.32 N 1.29 W
Ronay I 46 57.29 N 7.11 W
Roncade 64 45.38 N 12.22 E
Roncador, Cayos de ✦[4] 236 13.32 N 80.03 W
Roncador, Serra do ⋏[1] 242 12.00 S 52.00 W
Roncador Reef ✦[2] 175e 6.13 S 159.22 E
Roncegno 64 46.03 N 11.25 E
Roncesvalles 34 43.01 N 1.19 W
Ronceverte 192 37.44 N 80.27 W
Ronchamp 58 47.42 N 6.39 E
Ronchi dei Legionari 64 45.50 N 13.30 E
Ronchin 50 50.36 N 3.06 E
Ronchis 64 45.49 N 13.00 E
Ronciglione 66 42.17 N 12.13 E
Ronco ≃ 58 46.08 N 8.44 E
Ronco Canavese 62 45.30 N 7.32 E
Roncofreddo 66 44.02 N 12.20 E
Roncone 64 45.59 N 10.40 E
Ronco Scrivia 62 44.37 N 8.59 E
Roncq 50 50.45 N 3.07 E
Rond, Sommet ∧ 206 45.05 N 72.33 W
Ronda 34 36.44 N 5.10 W
Ronda, Serranía de ⋏ 34 36.44 N 5.03 W
Rondane ∧ 26 61.55 N 9.45 E
Rondane Nasjonal Park ♠ 26 61.50 N 9.50 E
Rønde 41 56.18 N 10.29 E
Ronde, Pointe > 240d 15.33 N 61.29 W
Rondeau Harbour c 214 42.18 N 81.53 W
Rondeau Provincial Park ♠ 214 42.16 N 81.51 W
Rondebult 273d 26.18 S 28.14 E
Ronde Island I 241k 12.18 N 61.35 W
Rondissone 62 45.15 N 7.58 E
Rondon 255 23.23 S 52.48 W
Rondônia □[3] 248 11.00 S 63.00 W
Rondonópolis 255 16.28 S 54.38 W
Rondout 278 42.17 N 87.53 W
Rondout Creek ≃ 210 41.55 N 73.53 W
Rondout Reservoir ⊜[1] 210 41.50 N 74.29 W
Rone ≃ 50 50.46 N 3.27 E
Ronehamn 26 57.10 N 18.29 E
Rong ≃ 102 24.32 N 109.15 E
Ronga 80 56.43 N 48.32 E
Rongai 154 0.10 S 35.51 E
Rong'an 102 25.10 N 109.20 E
Rongbaca 102 31.48 N 99.40 E
Rongchang 107 29.24 N 105.36 E
Rongcheng, Zhg. 98 37.08 N 122.23 E
Rongcheng, Zhg. 105 39.03 N 115.52 E
Rongding 107 28.57 N 103.40 E
Ronge, Lac la ⊜ 184 55.10 N 105.00 W
Rongelap I[1] 14 11.20 N 166.50 E
Rongjiang 102 25.52 N 108.37 E
Rongkop 115a 8.10 S 110.45 E
Rongola 158 27.22 S 31.37 E
Rongotea 172 40.18 S 175.25 E
Rõngu 76 58.09 N 26.15 E
Rongui, Ilha I 154 10.50 S 40.40 E
Rongwanshi 100 28.10 N 112.57 E
Rongxian, Zhg. 102 22.50 N 110.38 E
Rongxian, Zhg. 107 29.28 N 104.25 E
Ronkiti Harbor c 174r 6.48 N 158.10 E
Ronkonkoma 276 40.48 N 73.06 W
Ronkonkoma, Lake ⊜ 276 40.50 N 73.07 W
Rønne 26 55.06 N 14.42 E
Rönne ≃ 41 56.16 N 12.50 E
Ronneburg 54 50.51 N 12.10 E
Ronneby 26 56.12 N 15.18 E
Ronne Entrance c 9 72.30 S 74.00 W
Ronne Ice Shelf ⊓ 9 78.30 S 61.00 W
Ronnenberg 52 52.20 N 9.40 E
Rönneshytta 40 58.56 N 15.02 E
Rönninge 40 59.12 N 17.44 E
Ronroni 175e 9.37 S 159.58 E
Rönsahl 263 51.07 N 7.30 E
Ronsdorf ◆[8] 263 51.14 N 7.12 E
Ronse (Renaix-Gleiche) 50 50.45 N 3.36 E
Röntgenmuseum ʋ 263 51.12 N 7.16 E
Ronuro ≃ 255 11.56 S 53.33 W
Roodepoort □[5] 273d 26.10 S 27.52 E
Roodepoort-Maraisburg 158 26.11 S 27.54 E
Roodeschool 52 53.25 N 6.45 E
Roodhouse 219 39.29 N 90.22 W
Roof Butte ∧ 200 36.28 N 109.05 W
Rooiberge ∧ 158 28.27 S 28.26 E
Rooiboklaagte ≃ 156 20.50 S 21.00 E
Rooidam 158 28.07 S 21.15 E
Rooilyf 158 28.49 S 21.57 E
Rooiwal 158 27.18 S 27.32 E
Rooks Creek ≃ 216 40.57 N 88.44 W
Rookwood Cemetery ◆ 274a 33.53 S 151.04 E
Roon, Pulau I 164 2.23 S 134.33 E
Rooniu, Mont ∧ 174s 17.49 S 149.12 W
Roordahuizum 52 53.06 N 5.46 E
Roorkee 124 29.52 N 77.53 E
Roosboom 158 28.36 S 29.44 E
Roosendaal 52 51.32 N 4.28 E
Roosevelt, Az., U.S. 200 33.40 N 111.08 W
Roosevelt, Mn., U.S. 198 48.48 N 95.05 W
Roosevelt, N.J., U.S. 208 40.13 N 74.28 W
Roosevelt, N.Y., U.S. 276 40.40 N 73.35 W
Roosevelt, Ok., U.S. 196 34.50 N 99.01 W
Roosevelt, Ut,. U.S. 200 40.17 N 109.59 W
Roosevelt ≃ 248 7.35 S 60.20 W
Roosevelt Beach 210 43.19 N 78.52 W
Roosevelt Campobello International Park ♠ 186 44.52 N 66.58 W
Roosevelt Field ◆[9] 276 40.45 N 73.37 W
Roosevelt Island I 9 79.30 S 162.00 W
Roosevelt Park 216 43.11 N 86.15 W
Roosevelt Park ♠ 276 40.33 N 74.21 W
Roosevelt Roads Naval Station ■ 240m 18.15 N 65.38 W
Roosevelt Terrace 226 38.08 N 122.16 W
Root 58 47.07 N 8.23 E
Root ≃, N.T., Can. 180 62.50 N 123.40 W
Root ≃, Mn., U.S. 190 43.46 N 91.15 W
Root ≃, Wi., U.S. 216 42.44 N 87.47 W
Root, North Branch ≃ 190 43.49 N 92.10 W
Root, South Branch ≃ 190 43.44 N 91.58 W
Root Lake ⊜ 184 54.04 N 101.24 W
Rootstown 214 41.05 N 81.14 W
Rooty Hill 170 33.46 S 150.50 E
Ropang 115b 8.52 S 117.29 E
Ropaži 76 57.08 N 24.30 E
Ropča 24 63.02 N 52.16 E
Ropczyce 30 50.03 N 21.37 E
Roper 192 35.52 N 76.36 W
Roper ≃ 164 14.43 S 135.27 E
Roper Bar 164 14.44 S 134.44 E
Roper Valley 164 14.56 S 134.00 E
Ropes Creek ≃ 274a 33.43 S 150.47 E
Ropesville 196 33.26 N 102.09 W
Roppe 58 47.40 N 6.55 E
Ropša 265a 59.44 N 29.52 E
Roque 250 3.01 S 45.23 W
Roquebillière 62 44.01 N 7.18 E
Roquebrune-Cap-Martin 62 43.46 N 7.28 E
Roquebrune-sur-Argens 62 43.26 N 6.38 E
Roquefavour, Aqueduc de ≋[1] 62 43.31 N 5.19 E
Roquefort 32 44.02 N 0.19 W
Roquemaure 62 44.03 N 4.47 E
Roque Pérez 258 35.25 S 59.20 W

Symbols in the index entries represent the broad categories identified in the key at the right. Symbols with superior numbers (⋏[1]) identify subcategories (see complete key on page *I · 1*).

Symbole im Register stellen die rechts im Schlüssel erklärten Kategorien dar. Symbole mit hochgestellten Ziffern (⋏[1]) bezeichnen Unterabteilungen einer Kategorie (vgl. vollständiger Schlüssel auf Seite *I · 1*).

Los símbolos incluídos en el texto del índice representan las grandes categorías identificadas con la clave a la derecha. Los símbolos con numeros en su parte superior (⋏[1]) identifican las subcategorías (véase la clave completa en la página *I · 1*).

Les symboles de l'index représentent les catégories indiquées dans la légende à droite. Les symboles suivis d'un indice (⋏[1]) représentent des sous-catégories (voir légende complète à la page *I · 1*).

Os símbolos incluídos no texto do índice representam as grandes categorias identificadas com a chave à direita. Os símbolos com números em sua parte superior (⋏[1]) identificam as subcategorias (veja-se a chave completa à página *I · 1*).

	English	Deutsch	Español	Français	Português
∧	Mountain	Berg	Montaña	Montagne	Montanha
⋏	Mountains	Gebirge	Montañas	Montagnes	Montanhas
)(	Pass	Paß	Paso	Col	Passo
V	Valley, Canyon	Tal, Cañon	Valle, Cañón	Vallée, Canyon	Vale, Canhão
≚	Plain	Ebene	Llano	Plaine	Planície
>	Cape	Kap	Cabo	Cap	Cabo
I	Island	Insel	Isla	Île	Ilha
II	Islands	Inseln	Islas	Îles	Ilhas
⊥	Other Topographic Features	Andere Topographische Objekte	Otros Elementos Topográficos	Autres données topographiques	Outros acidentes topográficos

ESPAÑOL — FRANÇAIS — PORTUGUÊS

Nombre / Nom / Nome	Página / Page / Página	Lat.°′	Long.°′ W = Oeste / W = Ouest / W = Oeste
Roquestéron	62	43.52 N	7.00 E
Roquevaire	62	43.21 N	5.36 E
Rora Head ›	46	58.52 N	3.25 W
Roraima □ [3]	246	1.00 N	61.00 W
Roraima, Mount ∧	246	5.12 N	60.44 W
Rörbäcksnäs	26	61.08 N	12.49 E
Roreto Chisone	62	44.59 N	7.06 E
Rorey Lake ⊜	180	66.55 N	128.25 W
Rorke Lake ⊜	184	54.33 N	92.30 W
Rorke's Drift ⊥	158	28.20 S	30.32 E
Rorketon	184	51.26 N	99.32 W
Røros	26	62.35 N	11.20 E
Rorschach	58	47.29 N	9.30 E
Rørvig	41	55.57 N	11.46 E
Rørvik	24	64.51 N	11.14 E
Ros' ≃	78	49.39 N	31.35 E
Rosà, It.	64	45.43 N	11.45 E
Rosa, Zam.	154	9.38 S	31.21 E
Rosa, Cap ›	36	36.58 N	8.14 E
Rosa, Lake ⊜	238	21.00 N	73.30 W
Rosa, Monte ∧	58	45.55 N	7.53 E
Rosairinho	266c	38.40 N	9.01 W
Rošal'	80	55.40 N	39.51 E
Rosales, Méx.	232	28.12 N	105.33 W
Rosales, Pil.	116	15.54 N	120.38 E
Rosalia	202	47.14 N	117.22 W
Rosalie, Lake ⊜	220	27.58 N	81.28 W
Rosalind Bank ✢ [4]	238	16.30 N	80.30 W
Rosamond, Ca., U.S.	228	34.51 N	118.09 W
Rosamond, Il., U.S.	219	39.23 N	89.10 W
Rosamond Lake ⊜	228	34.50 N	118.04 W
Rosamorada	234	22.08 N	105.12 W
Rosana	255	22.33 S	53.00 W
Rosander, Mount ∧	224	48.46 N	124.42 W
Rosanky	222	29.56 N	97.18 W
Rosanna	274b	37.45 S	145.04 E
Rosans	62	44.23 N	5.28 E
Rosario, Arg.	252	32.57 S	60.40 W
Rosário, Bra.	250	2.57 S	44.14 W
Rosario, Méx.	232	27.37 N	109.16 W
Rosario, Méx.	234	23.00 N	105.52 W
Rosario, Para.	252	24.27 S	57.03 W
Rosario, Pil.	116	13.51 N	121.12 E
Rosario, Pil.	116	16.14 N	120.29 E
Rosario, Ur.	258	34.19 S	57.21 W
Rosario, Ven.	246	10.19 N	72.19 W
Rosario ≃, Arg.	252	24.50 S	65.43 W
Rosario ≃, Ur.	258	34.26 S	57.21 W
Rosario, Bahía ⊂	232	29.52 N	115.45 W
Rosario, Cayo el I	240p	21.38 N	81.53 W
Rosario, Islas del II	246	10.10 N	75.46 W
Rosario Bank ✢ [2]	238	18.30 N	84.05 W
Rosario de Arriba	232	30.01 N	115.40 W
Rosario de la Frontera	252	25.48 S	64.58 W
Rosario de Lerma	252	24.59 S	65.35 W
Rosario del Tala	252	32.18 S	59.09 W
Rosário de Minas	256	21.43 S	43.38 W
Rosário do Sul	252	30.15 S	54.55 W
Rosário Oeste	248	14.50 S	56.25 W
Rosario Strait ⊍	224	48.30 N	122.45 W
Rosarito, Méx.	204	32.20 N	117.02 W
Rosarito, Méx.	232	26.27 N	111.38 W
Rosarito, Embalse de ⊜ [1]	34	40.05 N	5.15 W
Rosarno	68	38.29 N	15.59 E
Rosas	196	26.09 N	103.27 W
Rosazza	62	45.41 N	7.58 E
Rošča	82	54.47 N	36.51 E
Roščino	76	60.15 N	29.37 E
Rosciolo	66	42.07 N	13.20 E
Roscoe, Il., U.S.	216	42.25 N	89.01 W
Roscoe, N.Y., U.S.	210	41.55 N	74.54 W
Roscoe, Pa., U.S.	214	40.04 N	79.51 W
Roscoe, S.D., U.S.	198	45.26 N	99.20 W
Roscoe, Tx., U.S.	196	32.26 N	100.32 W
Roscoe ≃	180	69.40 N	120.57 W
Roscoe Village ⊥	214	40.18 N	81.54 W
Roscoff	32	48.44 N	3.59 E
Roscommon, Ire.	48	53.38 N	8.11 W
Roscommon, Mi., U.S.	190	44.29 N	84.35 W
Roscommon □ [6]	48	53.45 N	8.15 W
Roscrea	48	52.57 N	7.47 W
Rosdorf	52	51.30 N	9.53 E
Rose, It.	68	39.24 N	16.17 E
Rose, N.Y., U.S.	210	43.09 N	76.53 W
Rose, Monte ∧	70	37.39 N	13.25 E
Rose, Mount ∧	226	39.21 N	119.55 W
Rose, Pointe de la ›	240e	14.40 N	60.53 W
Roseau, Dom.	240d	15.18 N	61.24 W
Roseau, Mn., U.S.	198	48.50 N	95.45 W
Roseau ≃, Dom.	240d	15.18 N	61.24 W
Roseau ≃, N.A.	198	49.08 N	97.15 W
Roseau ≃, St. Luc.	241f	13.58 N	61.02 W
Rosebank ◂ [8]	273d	26.09 S	28.02 E
Rosebank Station	275b	43.47 N	79.07 W
Roseberry Lakes ⊜	184	52.40 N	92.30 W
Roseberth	166	25.47 S	139.37 E
Rosebery	166	41.46 S	145.32 E
Rosebery ◂ [8]	274a	33.55 S	151.12 E
Rose-Blanche	186	47.37 N	58.41 W
Roseboom	210	42.45 N	74.47 W
Roseboro	192	34.57 N	78.30 W
Rose Bowl ♠	280	34.10 N	118.09 W
Rosebud, Austl.	169	38.21 S	144.54 E
Rosebud, Mo., U.S.	219	38.23 N	91.24 W
Rosebud, Mt., U.S.	202	46.16 N	106.26 W
Rose Bud, Pa., U.S.	214	40.45 N	78.33 W
Rosebud, S.D., U.S.	198	43.13 N	100.51 W
Rosebud, Tx., U.S.	222	31.04 N	96.58 W
Rosebud ≃	182	51.25 N	112.37 W
Rosebud Creek ≃	202	46.16 N	106.28 W
Rosebud Indian Reservation ◂ [4]	198	43.25 N	100.28 W
Roseburg	202	43.13 N	123.20 W
Rosebush	190	43.41 N	84.46 W
Rose City	190	44.25 N	84.07 W
Rose Creek ≃, U.S.	198	40.04 N	97.07 W
Rose Creek ≃, Ca., U.S.	226	38.07 N	120.24 W
Rosecroft Raceway ♠	284c	38.48 N	76.58 W
Rosedale, Austl.	166	24.38 S	151.55 E
Rosedale, Ab., Can.	182	51.25 N	112.38 W
Rosedale, B.C., Can.	224	49.11 N	121.48 W
Rosedale, In., U.S.	194	39.37 N	87.17 W
Rosedale, La., U.S.	194	30.27 N	91.27 W
Rosedale, Md., U.S.	284b	39.19 N	76.30 W
Rosedale, Ms., U.S.	194	33.51 N	91.01 W
Rosedale ◂ [8], On., Can.	275b	43.41 N	79.22 W
Rosedale ◂ [8], N.Y., U.S.	276	40.39 N	73.45 W
Rosedale Estates	284c	38.47 N	76.58 W
Rosedale Hills	218	39.42 N	86.07 W
Rosedene	158	32.01 S	22.07 E
Rosehall	246	6.16 N	57.21 W
Rosehearty	46	57.42 N	2.07 W
Rose-Hill, Maus.	157c	20.14 S	57.27 E
Rose Hill, N.C., U.S.	192	34.49 N	78.01 W
Rose Hill, Va., U.S.	192	36.40 N	83.22 W
Rose Hill, Wa., U.S.	224	47.42 N	122.10 W
Rosehill Cemetery ◂	278	41.59 N	87.41 W
Rosehill Racecourse ♠	274a	33.49 S	151.02 E
Rose Hills Memorial Park ◂	280	34.01 N	118.02 W
Roseira	256	22.54 S	45.18 W
Rose Island I, Am. Sam.	14	14.32 S	168.08 W
Rose Island I, Ba.	192	25.06 N	77.14 W
Rose Lake	182	54.24 N	126.02 W
Roseland, Ca., U.S.	226	38.30 N	122.55 W
Roseland, In., U.S.	216	41.42 N	86.15 W
Roseland, La., U.S.	194	30.45 N	90.30 W
Roseland, N.J., U.S.	276	40.49 N	74.17 W
Roseland, Oh., U.S.	214	40.47 N	82.32 W
Roseland ◂ [8]	278	41.42 N	87.38 W
Roselawn	216	41.09 N	87.19 W
Roselle, Il., U.S.	216	41.59 N	88.04 W
Roselle, N.J., U.S.	276	40.39 N	74.15 W
Roselle Field ⊠	278	41.59 N	88.06 W
Rosellen	263	51.08 N	6.43 E
Roselle Park	276	40.39 N	74.15 W
Rosellerheide	263	51.07 N	6.44 E
Rose Lodge	224	45.01 N	123.52 W
Rosemary	182	50.46 N	112.05 W
Rosemary Brook ≃	283	42.19 N	71.15 W
Rosemead	280	34.04 N	118.04 W
Rosemère	206	45.38 N	73.48 W
Rosemont, Ca., U.S.	226	38.34 N	121.20 W
Rosemont, Il., U.S.	278	41.59 N	87.52 W
Rosemont, Ky., U.S.	218	38.01 N	84.32 W
Rosemont, Oh., U.S.	214	41.03 N	80.53 W
Rosemont, Pa., U.S.	285	40.01 N	75.19 W
Rosemont Horizon ♠	278	42.00 N	87.53 W
Rosenberg	222	29.33 N	95.48 W
Rosendaël	50	51.02 N	2.24 E
Rosendal, Nor.	26	59.59 N	6.01 E
Rosendal, S. Afr.	158	28.30 S	27.55 E
Rosendale	210	41.51 N	74.05 W
Roseneath	273d	26.17 S	28.11 E
Rosenfeld	58	48.17 N	8.43 E
Rosengarten	52	53.23 N	9.54 E
Rosenhayn	208	39.28 N	75.07 W
Rosenheim	64	47.51 N	12.07 E
Rosenhügel ◂ [8]	263	51.10 N	7.12 E
Rosenthal, Dtsch.	54	50.51 N	14.04 E
Rosenthal, Dtsch.	56	50.58 N	8.52 E
Rosenthal ◂ [8]	264a	52.36 N	13.23 E
Rose Peak ∧	200	33.26 N	109.22 W
Rosepine	194	30.55 N	93.17 W
Rose Point ›	182	54.13 N	131.35 W
Rosersberg	40	59.35 N	17.53 E
Rosersberg ⊥	40	59.34 N	17.50 E
Roses, Golf de ⊂	34	42.10 N	3.15 E
Roseto	210	40.52 N	75.12 W
Roseto Capo Spulico	68	39.59 N	16.36 E
Roseto degli Abruzzi	66	42.41 N	14.01 E
Roseto Valfortore	68	41.22 N	15.06 E
Rosetown	184	51.33 N	108.00 W
Rose Tree	285	39.56 N	75.23 W
Rose Tree Park ♠	285	39.56 N	75.24 W
Rosetta → Rashīd	142	31.24 N	30.25 E
Rosetta Branch → Rashīd, Far'≃	142	31.30 N	30.21 E
Rosetta Mouth → Rashīd, Maṣabb ≃ [1]	142	31.30 N	30.20 E
Rosettenville ◂ [8]	273d	26.15 S	28.03 E
Rosevale	171a	27.51 S	152.29 E
Rose Valley, Sk., Can.	184	52.18 N	103.50 W
Rose Valley, Pa., U.S.	285	39.53 N	75.23 W
Rose Valley, Pa., U.S.	285	40.10 N	75.13 W
Rose Valley, Wa., U.S.	224	46.06 N	122.50 W
Roseville, Austl.	274a	33.47 S	151.11 E
Roseville, Ca., U.S.	226	38.45 N	121.17 W
Roseville, Il., U.S.	190	40.43 N	90.39 W
Roseville, Mi., U.S.	214	42.29 N	82.56 W
Roseville, Mn., U.S.	190	45.00 N	93.09 W
Roseville, Oh., U.S.	188	39.48 N	82.04 W
Roseville, Pa., U.S.	210	41.51 N	76.57 W
Roseville Park	285	39.42 N	75.43 W
Rosewood, Austl.	171a	27.39 S	152.35 E
Rosewood, Austl.	171b	35.41 S	147.52 E
Rosewood, Oh., U.S.	216	40.13 N	83.58 W
Rosewood Heights	219	38.53 N	90.05 W
Roseworthy	168b	34.32 S	138.44 E
Roshage ›	26	57.07 N	8.38 E
Roshanara Gardens ♠	272a	28.40 N	77.12 E
Rosharon	222	29.21 N	95.28 W
Rosheim	58	48.30 N	7.28 E
Rosherville Dam ⊜ [1]	273d	26.14 S	28.07 E
Rosh Ha'Ayin	132	32.06 N	34.57 E
Rosholt, S.D., U.S.	198	45.52 N	96.43 W
Rosholt, Wi., U.S.	190	44.37 N	89.18 W
Rosh Pinna	132	32.58 N	35.32 E
Rosica ≃	38	43.15 N	25.42 E
Rosice	30	49.11 N	16.23 E
Rosiclare	194	37.25 N	88.20 W
Rosières-aux-Salines	58	48.36 N	6.20 E
Rosières-en-Santerre	50	49.49 N	2.43 E
Rosiers, Rivière des ≃	206	45.59 N	72.07 W
Rosignano Marittimo	66	43.24 N	10.28 E
Rosignano Solvay	66	43.23 N	10.26 E
Rosignol	246	6.17 N	57.32 W
Roșiori de Vede	38	44.07 N	25.00 E
Rositz	54	51.01 N	12.22 E
Roskilde	41	55.39 N	12.05 E
Roskilde □ [6]	41	55.30 N	12.05 E
Roskilde Fjord ⊂	41	55.56 N	12.00 E
Roskow	54	52.28 N	12.42 E
Roslagen □ [9]	40	59.30 N	18.40 E
Roslags-Bro	40	59.50 N	18.44 E
Rosl'akovo	24	69.03 N	33.09 E
Rosl'atino	76	59.46 N	44.15 E
Roslavl'	76	53.57 N	32.52 E
Roslev	26	56.42 N	8.59 E
Roslindale ◂ [8]	283	42.18 N	71.07 W
Roslyn, N.Y., U.S.	276	40.48 N	73.39 W
Roslyn, Pa., U.S.	208	40.07 N	75.08 W
Roslyn, Pa., U.S.	285	39.57 N	75.36 W
Roslyn, Wa., U.S.	224	47.13 N	120.59 W
Roslyn Estates	276	40.47 N	73.40 W
Roslyn Harbor	276	40.49 N	73.38 W
Roslyn Heights	276	40.47 N	73.38 W
Rosmalen	52	51.43 N	5.22 E
Rosman	192	35.08 N	82.49 W
Rosmead	158	31.29 S	25.08 E
Ros Mhic Thriúin → New Ross	48	52.24 N	6.56 W
Røsnæs › [1]	41	55.44 N	10.59 E
Rosne, Ruisseau le ≃	261	48.58 N	2.25 E
Rosneath	46	56.01 N	4.49 W
Rosny-sous-Bois	261	48.53 N	2.29 E
Rosny-sur-Seine	50	49.00 N	1.38 E
Rosolina	64	45.05 N	12.15 E
Rosolini	70	36.49 N	14.57 E
Rošore	85	38.20 N	72.19 E
Rosporden	32	47.58 N	3.50 W
Rösrath	56	50.54 N	7.11 E
Ross, Austl.	166	42.02 S	147.29 E
Ross', Bela.	76	53.17 N	24.24 E
Ross, N.Z.	172	42.54 S	170.49 E
Ross, Ca., U.S.	226	37.55 N	122.32 W
Ross, In., U.S.	278	41.32 N	87.23 W
Ross, Oh., U.S.	218	39.19 N	84.39 W
Ross □ [6]	218	39.20 N	83.06 W
Ross ≃	180	61.59 N	132.26 W
Ross, Cape ›	116	10.56 N	119.13 E
Ross, Mount ∧	172	41.28 S	175.21 E
Ross, Point ›	174c	29.04 S	167.56 E
Ross, Pointe ›	275a	45.21 N	73.48 W
Rossa	58	46.22 N	9.08 E
Rossach	56	50.09 N	10.56 E
Rossano	68	39.35 N	16.39 E
Rossasna	76	54.39 N	30.53 E
Rossau	54	52.47 N	11.38 E
Rossbach	54	51.15 N	11.53 E
Ross Behy	48	52.02 N	9.58 W
Ross-Béthio	150	16.16 N	16.08 W
Rossburg	216	40.17 N	84.38 W
Rossburn	184	50.40 N	100.52 W
Ross Carbery	48	51.35 N	9.01 W
Rosscott Manor	285	39.39 N	75.44 W
Ross Dam ◂ [6]	224	48.44 N	121.04 W
Rossdorf	56	49.51 N	8.45 E
Rosseau	212	45.16 N	79.39 W
Rosseau, Lake ⊜	212	45.10 N	79.35 W
Rossel, Cap ›	175f	20.23 S	166.36 E
Rossell y Rius	252	33.11 S	55.42 W
Rossen ⊜	40	60.19 N	16.26 E
Rossendale □ [8]	262	53.43 N	2.14 W
Rosser	222	32.28 N	96.27 W
Rosses Bay ⊂	48	55.02 N	8.27 W
Rosses Point	48	54.18 N	8.33 W
Rossford	214	41.37 N	83.33 W
Ross Fork Creek ≃	202	47.05 N	109.43 W
Rosshaupten	58	47.39 N	10.43 E
Rosshyttan	40	60.04 N	16.21 E
Ross Ice Shelf ⊓	9	81.30 S	175.00 W
Rossiglione	62	44.34 N	8.40 E
Rossignol, Lake ⊜	186	44.10 N	65.10 W
Rossija → Russia □ [1]	72	60.00 N	80.00 E
Rössing	156	22.31 S	14.52 E
Rossio, Estação do ◂ [5]	266c	38.43 N	9.09 W
Ross Island I, Ant.	9	77.30 S	168.00 E
Ross Island I, Mb., Can.	184	54.14 N	97.45 W
Rossiter	214	40.53 N	78.55 W
Rossitten → Rybačij	76	55.09 N	20.51 E
Rossiya → Russia □ [1]	72	60.00 N	80.00 E
Rossla	54	51.28 N	11.04 E
Ross Lake ⊜ [1]	224	48.53 N	121.04 W
Ross Lake National Recreation Area ♠	224	48.45 N	121.00 W
Rossland	182	49.05 N	117.48 W
Rosslare	48	52.17 N	6.23 W
Rosslare Harbour	48	52.15 N	6.22 W
Rosslau	54	51.53 N	12.14 E
Rosslea	48	54.14 N	7.11 W
Rosslyn Farms	279b	40.26 N	80.05 W
Rossmoor	280	33.47 N	118.05 W
Rossmore	274a	33.57 S	150.46 E
Rossmoyne	208	40.13 N	76.57 W
Rosso	150	16.30 N	15.49 W
Rossön	26	63.55 N	16.21 E
Ross-on-Wye	42	51.55 N	2.35 W
Rossony	76	55.53 N	28.49 E
Rossoš', Ross.	78	51.08 N	38.29 E
Rossoš', Ross.	78	50.12 N	39.34 E
Rossouw	158	31.09 S	27.18 E
Ross R. Barnett Reservoir ⊜ [1]	194	32.30 N	90.00 W
Ross River	180	61.59 N	132.27 W
Ross-Schelfeis → Ross Ice Shelf ⊓	9	81.30 S	175.00 W
Ross Sea ⊤ [2]	9	76.00 S	175.00 W
Rosstal	56	49.25 N	10.52 E
Rosston	218	40.03 N	86.17 W
Ross Township	279b	40.32 N	80.01 W
Rossu, Capu ›	36	42.14 N	8.33 E
Røssvatnet ⊜	24	65.45 N	14.00 E
Rossville, Ga., U.S.	192	34.58 N	85.17 W
Rossville, Il., U.S.	216	40.22 N	87.40 W
Rossville, In., U.S.	216	40.25 N	86.35 W
Rossville, Ks., U.S.	198	39.08 N	95.57 W
Rossville, Md., U.S.	284b	39.20 N	76.29 W
Rosswein	54	51.03 N	13.10 E
Røst II	24	67.28 N	11.59 E
Rostāg	120	37.07 N	69.49 E
Röstånga	41	56.00 N	13.17 E
Rostavytsya ≃	78	49.44 N	30.01 E
Rosthern	184	52.40 N	106.17 W
Rostherne	262	53.21 N	2.23 W
Rostherne Mere ⊜	262	53.21 N	2.23 W
Roštkala	120	37.16 N	71.49 E
Rostock	54	54.05 N	12.07 E
Rostov	80	57.11 N	39.25 E
Rostov-na-Donu	83	47.14 N	39.42 E
Rostov Oblast' □ [4]	78	48.00 N	40.00 E
Rostrataville	158	26.49 S	25.39 E
Rostraver Airport ⊠	279b	40.13 N	79.50 W
Rostrevor	48	54.06 N	6.12 W
Rosvinskoje	24	66.32 N	52.26 E
Roswell, Ga., U.S.	192	34.01 N	84.21 W
Roswell, N.M., U.S.	196	33.23 N	104.31 W
Roswell, Oh., U.S.	214	40.28 N	81.21 W
Rosyth	46	56.03 N	3.26 W
Rot ≃	58	48.19 N	9.54 E
Rota	34	36.37 N	6.21 W
Rota I	108	14.10 N	145.12 E
Rot am See	56	49.15 N	10.01 E
Rotan	196	32.51 N	100.27 W
Rotanda	156	19.33 S	32.50 E
Rotary Island I	285	40.14 N	74.49 W
Rotbach ≃	263	51.34 N	6.41 E
Rotberg	264a	52.21 N	13.31 E
Rote-Erde, Stadion ♠	263	51.30 N	7.27 E
Rotenburg	52	53.06 N	9.24 E
Rotenburg an der Fulda	56	51.00 N	9.45 E
Roter Main ≃	60	50.04 N	11.24 E
Rotes Meer → Red Sea ⊤ [2]	136	20.00 N	38.00 E
Roth, Dtsch.	56	50.46 N	7.42 E
Roth, Dtsch.	60	49.15 N	11.06 E
Roth ≃	58	48.27 N	10.10 E
Rötha	54	51.12 N	12.25 E
Rothaargebirge ⋏	56	51.05 N	8.15 E
Rothbury	44	55.19 N	1.55 W
Rothbury Forest ◂ [3]	44	55.18 N	1.54 W
Rothemühl	54	53.36 N	13.49 E
Röthenbach, Dtsch.	58	47.37 N	9.59 E
Röthenbach, Schw.	58	46.51 N	7.45 E
Röthenbach an der Pegnitz	60	49.29 N	11.15 E
Rothenburg	54	51.20 N	14.58 E
Rothenburg ob der Tauber	56	49.23 N	10.10 E
Rothenkirchen	54	50.33 N	12.30 E
Rothenschirmbach	54	51.27 N	11.33 E
Rothenstein ∧ [2]	263	51.07 N	7.41 E
Rother ≃, Eng., U.K.	42	50.57 N	0.32 W
Rother ≃, Eng., U.K.	42	50.54 N	0.42 E
Rothera ⊛ [3]	9	67.34 S	68.08 W
Rotherham, N.Z.	172	42.42 S	172.57 E
Rotherham, Eng., U.K.	44	53.26 N	1.20 W
Rothes	46	57.31 N	3.13 W
Rothesay, N.B., Can.	186	45.23 N	66.00 W
Rothesay, Scot., U.K.	46	55.51 N	5.03 W
Rothneusiedl ◂ [8]	264b	48.08 N	16.23 E
Rothrist	58	47.19 N	7.53 E
Rothsay, Austl.	162	29.17 S	116.53 E
Rothsay, Mn., U.S.	198	46.28 N	96.16 W
Rothschild	190	44.53 N	89.37 W
Rothsville	208	40.09 N	76.15 W
Rothwell, N.B., Can.	186	46.04 N	66.04 W
Rothwell, Eng., U.K.	42	52.25 N	0.48 W
Rothwell, Eng., U.K.	44	53.46 N	1.29 W
Roti, Pulau I	112	10.45 S	123.10 E
Roti, Selat ⊍	112	10.25 S	123.25 E
Roto	166	33.03 S	145.28 E
Rotoiti, Lake ⊜, N.Z.	172	38.02 S	176.25 E
Rotoiti, Lake ⊜, N.Z.	172	41.50 S	172.50 E
Rotomanu	172	42.39 S	171.32 E
Rotonda	68	39.57 N	16.02 E
Rotondella	68	40.10 N	16.32 E
Rotondo, Monte ∧	36	42.13 N	9.03 E
Rotoroa, Lake ⊜	172	41.52 S	172.38 E
Rotorua	172	38.09 S	176.15 E
Rotorua, Lake ⊜	172	38.05 S	176.16 E
Rotowaro	172	37.36 S	175.05 E
Rott	64	47.54 N	10.59 E
Rott ≃	60	48.27 N	13.26 E
Rottach-Egern	64	47.41 N	11.46 E
Rott am Inn	64	47.59 N	12.07 E
Röttenbach	60	49.09 N	11.02 E
Rottenbach-Tremersdorf	56	50.21 N	10.56 E
Rottenbuch	64	47.44 N	10.58 E
Rottenburg am Neckar	58	48.28 N	8.56 E
Rottenburg an der Laaber	60	48.42 N	12.02 E
Rottenmann	61	47.31 N	14.22 E
Rotterdam, Ned.	52	51.55 N	4.28 E
Rotterdam, N.Y., U.S.	210	42.48 N	73.59 W
Rotterdam, Luchthaven ⊠	52	51.58 N	4.30 E
Rotterdam Junction	210	42.52 N	74.03 W
Rotthalmünster	60	48.21 N	13.12 E
Rotthausen ◂ [8]	263	51.30 N	7.05 E
Rottingdean	42	50.48 N	0.04 W
Röttingen	56	49.31 N	9.58 E
Rottleberode	54	51.31 N	10.57 E
Rottnest Island I	168a	32.00 S	115.30 E
Rottofreno	62	45.03 N	9.34 E
Rottum	263	51.36 N	7.42 E
Rottumeroog I	52	53.33 N	6.35 E
Rottumerplaat I	52	53.32 N	6.30 E
Rottweil	58	48.10 N	8.37 E
Rotuma I	14	12.30 S	177.05 E
Rotwand ∧	64	47.39 N	11.56 E
Rötz	60	49.21 N	12.32 E
Roubaix	50	50.42 N	3.10 E
Roubideau Creek ≃	200	38.44 N	108.10 W
Roubidoux Creek ≃	194	37.51 N	92.13 W
Roubion ≃	62	44.31 N	4.42 E
Rouceux	58	48.22 N	5.41 E
Roudnice [nad Labem]	54	50.22 N	14.16 E
Rouen	50	49.26 N	1.05 E
Rougé	32	47.47 N	1.27 W
Rouge ≃, On., Can.	212	43.48 N	79.07 W
Rouge ≃, P.Q., Can.	206	45.39 N	74.42 W
Rouge ≃, P.Q., Can.	206	45.33 N	74.20 W
Rouge → Red ≃, U.S.	178	31.00 N	91.40 W
Rouge, Bell Branch ≃	281	42.23 N	83.16 W
Rouge, Lac ⊜	206	46.56 N	74.38 W
Rouge, Mer → Red Sea ⊤ [2]	136	20.00 N	38.00 E
Rouge, River ≃	281	42.17 N	83.06 W
Rougeau, Forêt de ♠	261	48.35 N	2.30 E
Rougemont, Fr.	58	47.29 N	6.21 E
Rougemont, Schw.	58	46.29 N	7.12 E
Rougemont-le-Château	58	47.44 N	6.58 E
Rough ≃	194	37.29 N	87.08 W
Rough And Ready	226	39.14 N	121.08 W
Rough River Lake ⊜ [1]	194	37.40 N	86.25 W
Rouiba	34	36.44 N	3.17 E
Rouillac	32	45.47 N	0.04 W
Rouillon	261	48.33 N	2.00 E
Roulans	58	47.19 N	6.14 E
Rouleau	184	50.11 N	104.55 W
Roulers → Roeselare	50	50.57 N	3.08 E
Roulette	214	41.46 N	78.09 W
Roumanie → Romania □ [1]	38	46.00 N	25.30 E
Round Harbour	186	49.51 N	55.40 W
Roundhead	216	40.34 N	83.50 W
Round Hill Head ›	166	24.10 S	151.53 E
Round Hill Regional Park ♠	279b	40.15 N	79.51 W
Round Knowe ∧ [2]	48	55.08 N	6.55 W
Round Lake, Il., U.S.	278	42.21 N	88.05 W
Round Lake, Mn., U.S.	198	43.32 N	95.28 W
Round Lake, N.Y., U.S.	210	42.56 N	73.47 W
Round Lake ⊜, Nf., Can.	186	51.08 N	56.33 W
Round Lake ⊜, On., Can.	190	45.38 N	77.32 W
Round Lake ⊜, On., Can.	212	44.30 N	77.52 W
Round Lake ⊜, On., Can.	212	45.28 N	79.24 W
Round Lake ⊜, Sk., Can.	184	50.33 N	102.23 W
Round Lake ⊜, Il., U.S.	278	42.22 N	88.05 W
Round Lake ⊜, Mi., U.S.	216	41.58 N	84.17 W
Round Lake Beach	216	42.22 N	88.05 W
Round Lake Park	216	42.21 N	88.04 W
Round Mound ∧ [2]	198	38.55 N	99.39 W
Round Mountain	204	38.42 N	117.04 W
Round Mountain ∧, Austl.	166	30.27 S	152.14 E
Round Mountain ∧, Austl.	171b	36.15 S	148.34 E
Round Pond ⊜, Nf., Can.	186	48.10 N	56.00 W
Round Pond ⊜, Ma., U.S.	283	42.36 N	70.49 W
Round Rock	222	30.30 N	97.40 W
Roundstone	48	53.23 N	9.53 W
Round Top	210	42.16 N	74.02 W
Round Top ∧ [2]	208	40.30 N	76.42 W
Round Top Regional Park ♠	282	37.51 N	122.12 W
Roundup	202	46.26 N	108.32 W
Round Valley Indian Reservation ◂ [4]	204	39.50 N	123.20 W
Round Valley Reservoir ⊜ [1]	210	40.36 N	74.50 W
Roundwood	48	53.04 N	6.13 W
Roura	250	4.44 N	52.20 W
Rourkela → Raurkela	124	22.13 N	84.53 E
Rousay I	46	59.10 N	3.02 W
Rouse Hill	274a	33.41 S	150.56 E
Rouses Point	206	45.00 N	73.22 W
Rouseville	214	41.28 N	79.41 W
Rousies	50	50.16 N	4.00 E
Rousseau, Lake ⊜ [1]	220	29.02 N	82.32 W
Rousset, Col de)(	62	44.50 N	5.24 E
Roussigny	261	48.39 N	2.06 E
Roussillon, Fr.	62	45.22 N	4.49 E
Roussillon, Fr.	62	43.54 N	5.17 E
Roussillon □ [9]	32	42.30 N	2.30 E
Roussy-le-Village	56	49.27 N	6.10 E
Routhierville	186	48.11 N	67.09 W
Routot	50	49.23 N	0.44 E
Rouveen	52	52.36 N	6.11 E
Rouvignies	50	50.20 N	3.26 E
Rouville □ [6]	206	45.23 N	73.04 W
Rouvray	50	47.25 N	4.06 E
Rouvray, Lac ⊜	186	49.18 N	70.49 W
Rouxville	158	30.29 S	26.46 E
Rouyn	190	48.15 N	79.01 W
Rouzerville	208	39.44 N	77.32 W
Rovaniemi	24	66.34 N	25.48 E
Rovasenda	62	45.32 N	8.19 E
Rovato	64	45.34 N	10.00 E
Rovbickskaja	76	52.40 N	24.05 E
Rove, Tunnel du ◂ [5]	62	43.22 N	5.17 E
Rovegno	62	44.35 N	9.17 E
Rovellasca	62	45.40 N	9.03 E
Rovello Porro	62	45.39 N	9.02 E
Roven'ki	78	49.56 N	38.54 E
Roven'ky	83	48.05 N	39.21 E
Rovenskaja Sloboda	76	52.13 N	30.19 E
Roverbella	64	45.16 N	10.46 E
Rovere	66	42.10 N	13.31 E
Roverè della Luna	64	46.15 N	11.10 E
Roveredo	58	46.14 N	9.08 E
Rovereto	64	45.53 N	11.02 E
Roverè Veronese	64	45.36 N	11.03 E
Rövershagen	54	54.10 N	12.15 E
Roversi	252	27.35 S	61.57 W
Roverud	26	60.15 N	12.03 E
Roviano	66	42.01 N	13.00 E
Rovigo	64	45.04 N	11.47 E
Rovigo □ [4]	64	45.02 N	11.50 E
Rovinj	36	45.05 N	13.38 E
Rovira	246	4.14 N	75.14 W
Rovnoje, Kyrg.	85	42.53 N	73.32 E
Rovnoje, Ross.	80	50.47 N	46.05 E
Rovubu (Ruvubu) ≃	154	2.23 S	30.47 E
Rovuma (Ruvuma) ≃	154	10.29 S	40.28 E
Rów	54	52.58 N	14.45 E
Rowan □ [6]	218	38.17 N	83.26 W
Rowan Lake ⊜	184	49.18 N	93.32 W
Rowanty Creek ≃	208	36.58 N	77.21 W
Rowena, Austl.	166	29.49 S	148.54 E
Rowena, Tx., U.S.	196	31.39 N	100.03 W
Rowe Park ♠	273a	6.30 N	3.23 E
Rowhill	273d	26.14 S	28.26 E
Rowland, N.C., U.S.	192	34.32 N	79.17 W
Rowland, Pa., U.S.	210	41.28 N	75.03 W
Rowland Flat	168b	34.35 S	138.56 E
Rowland Heights	280	33.58 N	117.54 W
Rowlands Gill	44	54.54 N	1.45 W
Rowlesburg	188	39.20 N	79.40 W
Rowlett	222	32.54 N	96.33 W
Rowlett, Isla I	254	44.48 S	74.25 W
Rowlett Creek ≃	222	32.49 N	96.31 W
Rowley	207	42.43 N	70.52 W
Rowley ≃, N.T., Can.	176	70.16 N	77.45 W
Rowley ≃, Ma., U.S.	283	42.43 N	70.49 W
Rowley Island I	176	69.08 N	78.50 W
Rowley Shoals ✢ [2]	162	17.30 S	119.00 E
Rowntree Mill Park ♠	275b	43.45 N	79.35 W
Rowsburg	214	40.52 N	82.10 W
Rowville	274b	37.56 S	145.14 E
Roxa, Ilha I	150	11.15 N	15.40 W
Roxana	219	38.50 N	90.04 W
Roxas, Pil.	108	11.35 N	122.45 E
Roxas, Pil.	116	17.08 N	121.36 E
Roxas, Pil.	116	12.35 N	121.31 E
Roxas, Pil.	116	10.20 N	119.21 E
Roxas (Capiz), Pil.	116	11.35 N	122.45 E
Roxboro, P.Q., Can.	275a	45.31 N	73.48 W
Roxboro, N.C., U.S.	192	36.23 N	78.58 W
Roxborough	241r	11.15 N	60.35 W
Roxborough ◂ [8]	285	40.02 N	75.13 W
Roxburgh, N.Z.	172	45.32 S	169.19 E
Roxburgh, Scot., U.K.	46	55.34 N	2.30 W
Roxbury, Ct., U.S.	207	41.33 N	73.18 W
Roxbury, N.Y., U.S.	210	42.17 N	74.33 W
Roxbury, Pa., U.S.	214	40.07 N	77.40 W
Roxbury, Va., U.S.	208	37.28 N	77.09 W
Roxbury ◂ [8], Ma., U.S.	283	42.20 N	71.06 W
Roxbury ◂ [8], N.Y., U.S.	276	40.34 N	73.54 W
Roxby Downs	162	30.43 S	136.46 E
Roxel	52	51.57 N	7.32 E
Roxen ⊜	26	58.30 N	15.41 E
Roxie	194	31.30 N	91.04 W
Roxo, Cap ›	150	12.20 N	16.43 W
Roxton	196	33.33 N	95.44 W
Roxton Pond (Sainte-Pudentienne)	206	45.29 N	72.40 W
Roxwell	260	51.45 N	0.23 E
Roy, N.M., U.S.	196	35.56 N	104.11 W
Roy, Ut., U.S.	200	41.09 N	112.01 W
Roy, Wa., U.S.	224	47.00 N	122.32 W
Roya (Roia) ≃	62	43.48 N	7.35 E
Royal	198	43.03 N	95.17 W
Royal Albert Hall ⊛	260	51.30 N	0.11 W
Royal Australian Naval College ⊛ [2]	170	35.07 S	150.42 E
Royal Bangkok Sports Club ♠	269a	13.44 N	100.33 E
Royal Botanic Gardens ♠, Austl.	274a	33.52 S	151.13 E
Royal Botanic Gardens ♠, Austl.	274b	37.50 S	144.59 E
Royal Canal ≍	48	53.21 N	6.15 W
Royal Center	216	40.51 N	86.29 W
Royal Chitwan National Park ♠	124	27.30 N	84.30 E
Royal City	202	46.54 N	119.38 W
Royale, Isle I	190	48.00 N	89.00 W
Royal Gorge V	200	38.17 N	105.45 W
Royal Island I	192	25.31 N	76.51 W
Royalla	171b	35.31 S	149.09 E
Royal Leamington Spa	42	52.18 N	1.31 W
Royal Natal National Park ♠	158	28.45 S	28.57 E
Royal National Park ♠	170	34.10 S	151.05 E
Royal Naval College ■	260	51.29 N	0.01 W
Royal Oak, B.C., Can.	224	48.30 N	123.23 W
Royal Oak, Md., U.S.	208	38.44 N	76.10 W
Royal Oak, Mi., U.S.	216	42.29 N	83.08 W
Royal Oak Township	281	42.27 N	83.10 W
Royal Ontario Museum ⊛	275b	43.40 N	79.24 W
Royal Palms State Beach ♠	280	33.44 N	118.19 W
Royal Park ♠	274b	37.47 S	144.57 E
Royal Roads ⊂	224	48.26 N	123.26 W
Royalton, In., U.S.	218	39.56 N	86.21 W
Royalton, Mn., U.S.	190	45.49 N	94.17 W
Royalton, Pa., U.S.	208	40.11 N	76.44 W
Royal Tunbridge Wells	42	51.08 N	0.16 E
Royal Turf Club ♠	269a	13.46 N	100.32 E
Royan	32	45.37 N	1.01 W
Royaume-Uni → United Kingdom □ [1]	28	54.00 N	2.00 W
Roybon	62	45.15 N	5.15 E
Royce Brook ≃	276	40.32 N	70.35 W
Roydon, Eng., U.K.	42	51.46 N	0.03 E
Roydon, Eng., U.K.	42	52.50 N	0.32 E
Roye	50	49.42 N	2.48 E
Royersford	208	40.11 N	75.32 W
Royerton	216	40.15 N	85.21 W
Roy Hill	162	22.38 S	119.57 E
Roylyanka	78	46.17 N	29.46 E
Royse City	222	32.58 N	96.19 W
Royston, Eng., U.K.	42	52.03 N	0.01 W
Royston, Eng., U.K.	44	53.37 N	1.27 W
Royston, Ga., U.S.	192	34.17 N	83.06 W
Royton	44	53.34 N	2.08 W
Rožaj	38	42.50 N	20.10 E
Różan	30	52.53 N	21.25 E
Rozay-en-Brie	50	48.41 N	2.58 E
Roždestvenka, Kaz.	86	50.52 N	71.22 E
Roždestvenka, Ross.	86	55.21 N	77.29 E
Roždestvenka, Ross.	86	55.42 N	70.00 E
Roždestveno, Ross.	76	57.44 N	37.57 E
Roždestveno, Ross.	80	53.15 N	50.04 E
Roždestveno, Ross.	82	56.51 N	36.33 E
Roždestveno, Ross.	82	55.57 N	36.23 E
Roždestvenskaja Chava	78	51.38 N	39.40 E
Roždestvenskoje, Ross.	80	58.09 N	45.35 E
Roždestvenskoje, Ross.	80	52.47 N	42.10 E
Roždestvenskoje, Ross.	80	51.14 N	42.10 E
Roždestvo	76	57.36 N	33.48 E
Rozdil'na	78	46.51 N	30.05 E
Rozdol'ne, Ukr.	78	45.47 N	33.29 E
Rozdol'ne, Ukr.	83	47.37 N	38.01 E
Rozdory	78	48.21 N	35.42 E
Rozel	43b	49.14 N	2.03 W
Rozelle	274a	33.52 S	151.10 E
Roželov	60	49.33 N	13.48 E
Rozewie, Przylądek ›	30	54.51 N	18.21 E
Rozhnof, Cape ›	180	55.58 N	160.58 W
Rozhnyativ	78	48.56 N	24.09 E
Rozhyshche	78	50.54 N	25.15 E
Rozivka	78	47.23 N	37.04 E
Rožki	80	56.41 N	50.31 E
Rozkishne	83	48.30 N	39.18 E
Rožkov	80	51.39 N	52.19 E
Rožmberk ⊜	61	49.04 N	14.47 E
Rožmberk nad Vltavou	61	48.39 N	14.22 E
Rožmitál pod Třemšínem	60	49.36 N	13.52 E
Rožňava	30	48.40 N	20.32 E
Roznov	38	46.50 N	26.31 E
Rožnov pod Radhoštěm	30	49.28 N	18.10 E
Rożnów	30	49.46 N	20.42 E
Rozoy-sur-Serre	50	49.43 N	4.08 E
Rozsypne	83	48.08 N	38.34 E
Roztocze ⋏ [2]	30	50.30 N	23.20 E
Roztoky	54	50.09 N	14.22 E
Rozzano	62	45.20 N	9.06 E
Rrëshen	38	41.47 N	19.54 E
Rrogozhinë	38	41.05 N	19.40 E
Rtiščevo	80	52.16 N	43.47 E
Ru ≃	100	32.43 N	115.01 E
Ru, Tanjong ›	114	2.50 N	101.17 E
Ruabon	42	52.59 N	3.02 W
Ruacaná	152	17.25 S	14.12 E
Ruacana Falls ∟	152	17.22 S	14.12 E
Ruaha National Park ♠	154	7.30 S	34.40 E
Ruahine Range ⋏	172	40.00 S	176.06 E
Ruahmi, Ra's ›	142	28.44 N	32.50 E
Ruanda	154	10.33 S	34.57 E
Ruanda → Rwanda □ [1]	154	2.00 S	30.00 E
Ruango	164	5.35 S	150.10 E
Ruapehu, Mount ∧	172	39.17 S	175.34 E
Ruapuke Island I	172	46.47 S	168.30 E
Ruatahuna	172	38.33 S	176.57 E
Ruatapu	172	42.48 S	170.53 E
Ruathair, Loch an ⊜	46	58.18 N	3.56 W
Ruatoria	172	37.53 S	178.20 E
Ruawai	172	36.08 S	174.02 E
Rub' al Khali → Ar-Rub' al-Khālī ◂ [2]	118	20.00 N	51.00 E
Rubanivka	78	47.00 N	34.10 E
Rubbestadneset	26	59.49 N	5.17 E
Rubcovsk	86	51.33 N	81.10 E
Rubeho Mountains ⋏	154	6.55 S	36.30 E
Rubel'	78	51.58 N	27.04 E
Rübeland	54	51.45 N	10.50 E
Rubelles	261	48.34 N	2.41 E
Rubery ◂ [8]	42	52.24 N	2.00 W
Rubeshibe	92a	43.47 N	143.38 E
Rubežka	80	51.26 N	51.59 E
Rubí, Esp.	266d	41.29 N	2.02 E
Rubi, Zaïre	154	2.49 N	25.14 E
Rubí ≃, Esp.	266d	41.26 N	2.00 E
Rubi ≃, Zaïre	152	2.48 N	23.54 E
Rubiana	62	45.08 N	7.23 E
Rubiataba	255	15.08 S	49.48 W
Rubicon ≃	226	39.00 N	120.44 W
Rubicone ≃	66	44.08 N	12.28 E
Rubidoux	228	33.59 N	117.24 W
Rubiera	64	44.39 N	10.45 E
Rubim	255	16.23 S	40.32 W
Rubino	150	6.04 N	4.18 W
Rubio	246	7.43 N	72.22 W
Rubio Woods ♠	278	41.38 N	87.46 W
Rubizhne	83	49.01 N	38.23 E
Rubl'ovo	82	55.47 N	37.21 E
Rublyivka	78	49.15 N	33.19 E
Ruboani	140	8.06 N	30.45 E
Rubona	154	0.33 N	30.10 E
Rubondo Island I	154	2.20 S	31.52 E
Rubondo Island National Park ♠	154	2.20 S	31.52 E
Rubtsi	83	49.12 N	37.33 E
Rubtsovsk → Rubcovsk	86	51.33 N	81.10 E
Ruby, Ak., U.S.	180	64.44 N	155.30 W
Ruby, N.Y., U.S.	210	42.01 N	74.01 W
Ruby ≃	202	45.34 N	112.21 W
Ruby Creek ≃	224	48.43 N	120.59 W
Ruby Dome ∧	204	40.37 N	115.28 W
Ruby Lake ∷	204	40.10 N	115.30 W
Ruby Mountains ⋏	204	40.25 N	115.35 W
Ruby Valley V	204	40.30 N	115.15 W
Rucava	76	56.09 N	21.10 E
Ruchan'	76	53.33 N	32.48 E
Ruche	261	49.02 N	2.27 E
Rucheng	100	25.34 N	113.41 E
Ruciane-Nida	30	53.39 N	21.35 E
Ručji ◂ [8]	265a	60.01 N	30.24 E
Ručjuvom	24	66.42 N	61.08 E
Rucphen	52	51.32 N	4.34 E
Ruda	64	45.50 N	13.24 E
Rudall	166	33.41 S	136.16 E
Rudall ≃	162	22.16 S	122.47 E
Rudall River National Park ♠	162	22.25 S	122.40 E
Ruda Śląska	30	50.18 N	18.51 E
Rudauli	124	26.45 N	81.45 E
Ruḍaymat al-Liwā'	132	33.01 N	36.35 E
Rūdbār, Afg.	128	30.09 N	62.36 E
Rūdbār, Īrān	128	36.48 N	49.24 E
Rudbøl	41	54.54 N	8.45 E
Ruddervoorde	50	51.06 N	3.12 E
Ruddiman Terrace	216	43.12 N	86.17 W
Rudelsburg ⊥	54	51.07 N	11.43 E
Ruden I	54	54.12 N	13.46 E
Rudensk	76	53.36 N	27.52 E
Rüdersdorf, Dtsch.	54	52.29 N	13.47 E
Rudersdorf, Öst.	61	47.03 N	16.07 E
Rüdersdorf, Forst ◂ [3]	264a	52.26 N	13.50 E
Rüdesheim am Rhein	56	49.59 N	7.56 E
Rudeville	276	41.09 N	74.33 W
Rudewa	154	10.06 S	34.39 E
Rudge Ramos	287b	23.41 S	46.34 W
Rūdiškės	76	54.31 N	24.50 E
Rudivka	83	49.24 N	38.27 E
Rudkino	78	51.27 N	39.01 E
Rudkøbing	41	54.56 N	10.43 E
Rudky	78	49.39 N	23.29 E
Rudn'a, Ross.	76	54.57 N	31.06 E
Rudn'a, Ross.	80	50.48 N	44.33 E
Rudnaja Pristan'	89	44.22 N	135.48 E
Rudnevka ≃	265b	55.43 N	37.56 E
Rudnevo	82	54.44 N	38.09 E
Rudničnyj, Kaz.	86	44.40 N	78.55 E
Rudničnyj, Ross.	24	59.38 N	52.27 E
Rudničnyj, Ross.	86	56.08 N	86.12 E
Rudničnyj, Ross.	86	59.42 N	60.18 E
Rudnik	30	50.28 N	22.15 E
Rüdnitz	54	52.43 N	13.37 E
Rudnyj, Kaz.	86	52.57 N	63.07 E
Rudnyj, Ross.	89	44.21 N	134.58 E
Rudnytsya	78	48.15 N	28.55 E
Rudo	38	43.37 N	19.22 E
Rudolf, Lake (Lake Turkana) ⊜	144	3.30 N	36.00 E
Rudolfov	61	48.59 N	14.34 E
Rudolph	216	41.17 N	83.40 W
Rudolstadt	54	50.43 N	11.20 E
Rudong, Zhg.	102	21.39 N	111.23 E
Rudong, Zhg.	106	32.19 N	121.12 E
Rudovka	80	53.07 N	42.23 E
Rudow ◂ [8]	54	52.25 N	13.30 E
Rudrón ≃	34	42.47 N	3.45 W
Rūdsar	128	37.08 N	50.18 E
Ruds Vedby	41	55.33 N	11.23 E
Rudyard, Mi., U.S.	190	46.13 N	84.36 W
Rudyard, Mt., U.S.	202	48.33 N	110.33 W
Rudyerd Bay ⊂	182	55.35 N	130.44 W
Rue, Fr.	50	50.16 N	1.40 E
Rue, Schw.	58	46.37 N	6.50 E
Ruecas ≃	34	39.00 N	5.55 W
Rueil-Malmaison	261	48.53 N	2.11 E
Ruen ∧	38	42.10 N	22.31 E
Ruenya (Luenha) ≃	154	16.24 S	33.48 E
Rufā'ah	140	14.46 N	33.22 E
Ruffano	68	39.59 N	18.15 E
Ruffec	32	46.01 N	0.12 E
Ruffieu	58	46.00 N	5.40 E
Ruffieux	62	45.51 N	5.50 E
Ruffin	192	33.00 N	80.48 W
Ruffle Bar I	276	40.36 N	46.51 W
Rufford	262	53.38 N	2.49 W

Symbol	English	Deutsch	Español	Français	Português
≃	River	Fluß	Río	Rivière	Rio
≍	Canal	Kanal	Canal	Canal	Canal
∟	Waterfall, Rapids	Wasserfall, Stromschnellen	Cascada, Rápidos	Chute d'eau, Rapides	Cascata, Rápidos
⊍	Strait	Meeresstraße	Estrecho	Détroit	Estreito
⊂	Bay, Gulf	Bucht, Golf	Bahía, Golfo	Baie, Golfe	Baía, Golfo
⊜	Lake, Lakes	See, Seen	Lago, Lagos	Lac, Lacs	Lago, Lagos
∷	Swamp	Sumpf	Pantano	Marais	Pântano
⊓	Ice Features, Glacier	Eis- und Gletscherformen	Accidentes Glaciales	Formes glaciaires	Acidentes glaciares
⊤	Other Hydrographic Features	Andere Hydrographische Objekte	Otros Elementos Hidrográficos	Autres données hydrographiques	Outros acidentes hidrográficos
✢	Submarine Features	Untermeerische Objekte	Accidentes Submarinos	Formes de relief sous-marin	Acidentes submarinos
□	Political Unit	Politische Einheit	Unidad Politica	Entité politique	Unidade política
⊛	Cultural Institution	Kulturelle Institution	Institución Cultural	Institution culturelle	Instituição cultural
⊥	Historical Site	Historische Stätte	Sitio Histórico	Site historique	Sitio histórico
♠	Recreational Site	Erholungs- und Ferienort	Sitio de Recreo	Centre de loisirs	Area de Lazer
⊠	Airport	Flughafen	Aeropuerto	Aéroport	Aeroporto
■	Military Installation	Militäranlage	Instalación Militar	Installation militaire	Instalação militar
◂	Miscellaneous	Verschiedenes	Misceláneo	Divers	Diversos

ENGLISH — Name | Page | Lat.°′ | Long.°′
DEUTSCH — Name | Seite | Breite°′ | Länge°′ E = Ost

Rufford Old Hall ⊥ **262** 53.38 N 2.49 W
Ruffs Dale **279b** 40.10 N 79.37 W
Rufidschi
→ Rufiji ≃ **154** 8.00 S 39.20 E
Rufiji ≃ **154** 8.00 S 39.20 E
Rufina **66** 43.49 N 11.29 E
Rufino **252** 34.16 S 62.42 W
Rufisque **150** 14.43 N 17.17 W
Rufunsa **154** 15.05 S 29.40 E
Rufus **224** 45.41 N 120.44 W
Rufus, Mount ∧ **168b** 34.20 S 139.07 E
Rugāji **76** 57.00 N 27.08 E
Rugao **100** 32.25 N 120.36 E
Rugby, Eng., U.K. **42** 52.23 N 1.15 W
Rugby, N.D., U.S. **198** 48.22 N 99.59 W
Rugeley **42** 52.46 N 1.55 W
Rügen I **54** 54.25 N 13.24 E
Rüggeberg **263** 51.16 N 7.22 E
Rugged Mountain ∧ **182** 50.02 N 126.41 W
Ruggles Beach **214** 41.22 N 82.29 W
Rugles **50** 48.49 N 0.42 E
Rugufu ≃ **154** 5.10 S 30.14 E
Ruguj **76** 59.28 N 32.50 E
Ruḩama **132** 31.30 N 34.42 E
Ruhea **124** 26.10 N 88.25 E
Ruhengeri **154** 1.30 S 29.38 E
Ruhla **54** 50.53 N 10.22 E
Ruhland **54** 51.27 N 13.52 E
Ruhlsdorf **264a** 52.23 N 13.16 E
Ruhmannsfelden **60** 48.59 N 12.59 E
Ruhner Berge ∧[2] **54** 53.17 N 11.55 E
Ruhnu saar I **76** 57.48 N 23.15 E
Ruhpolding **64** 47.45 N 12.38 E
Ruhr ≃ **52** 51.27 N 6.44 E
Ruhrort •[8] **263** 51.26 N 6.45 E
Ruhr-Universität ʊ[2] **263** 51.27 N 7.16 E
Ruhstorf an der Rott **60** 48.26 N 13.20 E
Ruhudji ≃ **154** 8.52 S 36.01 E
Ruhuhu ≃ **154** 10.31 S 34.34 E
Ruhunu National
Park ◆ **122** 6.30 N 81.30 E
Rui'an **100** 27.49 N 120.38 E
Ruichang **100** 29.41 N 115.40 E
Ruicheng **102** 34.45 N 110.45 E
Ruidoso **200** 33.19 N 105.40 W
Ruidoso, Rio ≃ **200** 33.23 N 105.16 W
Ruidoso Downs **200** 33.19 N 105.36 W
Ruifeng Sha I **106** 31.25 N 121.36 E
Ruihong **100** 28.45 N 116.23 E
Ruijin **100** 25.50 N 116.00 E
Ruinen **52** 52.46 N 6.22 E
Ruiselede **50** 51.03 N 3.24 E
Ruislip •[8] **260** 51.34 N 0.25 W
Ruivo, Pico ∧ **148** 32.45 N 16.56 W
Ruiz **234** 21.57 N 105.09 W
Ruiz, Nevado del ∧[1] **246** 4.54 N 75.18 W
Ruiz de Montoya **252** 26.59 S 55.03 W
Rūjiena **76** 57.54 N 25.21 E
Rujm ar-Rashīd,
Jabal ∧ **132** 31.53 N 36.18 E
Rujm aṣ-Ṣakhrī **132** 31.02 N 35.43 E
Rukan-shō ✢[2] **174m** 26.06 N 127.32 E
Ruki ≃ **152** 0.05 N 18.17 E
Rukni **126** 23.33 N 86.33 E
Rukungiri **154** 0.48 S 29.55 E
Rukwa □[4] **154** 7.00 S 31.30 E
Rukwa, Lake ⊜ **154** 8.00 S 32.25 E
Rule **196** 33.11 N 99.53 W
Rule Creek ≃ **198** 38.02 N 103.02 W
Ruleville **194** 33.43 N 90.33 W
Rulle **52** 52.20 N 8.04 E
Rully **58** 46.52 N 4.45 E
Rulo **198** 40.03 N 95.25 W
Rülzheim **56** 49.09 N 8.16 E
Rum **61** 47.08 N 16.51 E
Rum ≃ **190** 45.11 N 93.23 W
Ruma **38** 45.00 N 19.49 E
Rumaat **164** 5.49 S 132.48 E
Rumāh **128** 25.34 N 47.09 E
Rumahtinggih **164** 6.23 S 140.17 E
Rum'ancevo, Ross. **82** 55.38 N 37.26 E
Rum'ancevo, Ross. **82** 55.58 N 36.32 E
Rumänien
→ Romania □[1] **38** 46.00 N 25.30 E
Rumaysh **132** 33.05 N 35.22 E
Rumbek **140** 6.48 N 29.41 E
Rumbeke **50** 50.56 N 3.10 E
Rumberpon, Pulau I **164** 1.50 S 134.15 E
Rumbling Bridge **46** 56.10 N 3.35 W
Rumburk **54** 50.57 N 14.32 E
Rum Cay I **238** 23.40 N 74.53 W
Rumelange **56** 49.28 N 6.02 E
Rumelifeneri •[8] **267b** 41.14 N 29.06 E
Rumelihisarı •[8] **267b** 41.05 N 29.03 E
Rumelihisarı ⊥ **267b** 41.05 N 29.02 E
Rumelikavağı •[8] **267b** 41.11 N 29.04 E
Rumford **188** 44.33 N 70.33 W
Rumford ≃ **283** 41.58 N 71.11 W
Rumia **30** 54.35 N 18.25 E
Rumigny **50** 49.48 N 4.16 E
Rumilly **62** 45.52 N 5.57 E
R'uminskoje **82** 56.31 N 38.47 E
Rum Jungle **164** 13.01 S 131.00 E
R'umki **265a** 59.47 N 30.02 E
Rümlang **58** 47.27 N 8.32 E
Rummah, Wādī ar- V **128** 26.12 N 44.04 E
Rummānah **142** 31.01 N 32.40 E
Rummānah, Bi'r ar-
⊤[4] **142** 31.00 N 32.40 E
Rummel **214** 40.13 N 78.48 W
Rummelsburg •[8] **264a** 52.30 N 13.29 E
Rummenohl •[8] **263** 51.17 N 7.32 E
Rumney **42** 51.31 N 3.07 W
Rumoi **92a** 43.56 N 141.39 E
Rumont **56** 48.50 N 5.17 E
Rumphi **154** 11.01 S 33.52 E
Rump Mountain ∧ **188** 45.12 N 71.04 W
Rumson **208** 40.22 N 73.59 W
Rumst **50** 51.05 N 4.25 E
Rumula **164** 16.35 S 145.20 E
Rumung I **174q** 9.37 N 138.10 E
Rumuruti **154** 0.16 N 36.32 E
Runan **100** 33.01 N 114.22 E
Runanga **172** 42.24 S 171.16 E
Runaway, Cape › **172** 37.32 S 177.59 E
Runazi **154** 2.47 S 31.28 E
Runcorn •[8] **44** 53.20 N 2.44 W
Rundeng **114** 2.39 N 97.52 E
Rundēni **76** 56.16 N 27.50 E
Rundu **156** 17.52 S 19.43 E
Rundvik **26** 63.32 N 19.26 E
Runere **154** 3.06 S 33.16 E
Rŭng, Kaôh I **110** 10.44 N 103.14 E
Rungāni **120** 26.38 N 65.43 E
Runge **222** 28.52 N 97.42 W
Rungis **261** 48.45 N 2.21 E
Rungis-Halles,
Marché de ʊ **261** 48.46 N 2.21 E
Rungsted **41** 55.53 N 12.33 E
Rungus Point › **116** 13.43 N 123.58 E
Rungwa, Tan. **154** 7.21 S 31.40 E
Rungwa, Tan. **154** 6.57 S 33.31 E
Rungwa ≃ **154** 7.36 S 31.50 E
Rungwa Game
Reserve •[4] **154** 7.00 S 34.10 E
Rungwe **154** 9.10 S 33.36 E
Runhällen **40** 60.02 N 16.49 E
Runheji **100** 32.30 N 116.05 E
Runkel **56** 50.24 N 8.10 E
Runmarö I **40** 59.17 N 18.46 E
Runn ⊜ **40** 60.33 N 15.40 E
Runnemede **285** 39.51 N 75.04 W
Running Springs **228** 34.12 N 117.07 W
Running Water Draw
V **196** 33.58 N 101.30 W
Runnymede □[8] **260** 51.24 N 0.32 W
Runnymede ⊥ **42** 51.26 N 0.34 W
Rünthe **263** 51.39 N 7.39 E
Runwell **260** 51.37 N 0.32 E
Ruo ≃, Afr. **154** 16.33 S 35.09 E
Ruo ≃, Zhg. **102** 41.00 N 100.10 E
Ruo'ergai **102** 33.16 N 102.55 E
Ruoheng **100** 28.24 N 121.31 E
Ruokolahti **26** 61.17 N 28.50 E
Ruoms **62** 44.27 N 4.21 E
Ruoqiang **90** 38.30 N 88.05 E
Ruoti **68** 40.43 N 15.41 E
Ruovesi **26** 61.59 N 24.05 E
Ruoxi **100** 29.18 N 115.20 E
Rupanco **254** 40.46 S 72.42 W
Rupanco, Lago ⊜ **254** 40.49 S 72.28 W
Rupari **168b** 35.37 S 139.09 E
Rupat, Pulau I **114** 1.50 N 101.35 E
Rupat, Selat ʯ **114** 1.50 N 101.25 E
Rupdia **126** 23.08 N 89.18 E
Rupea **38** 46.02 N 25.13 E
Rupert, Id., U.S. **202** 42.37 N 113.40 W
Rupert, Vt., U.S. **210** 43.15 N 73.13 W
Rupert, W.V., U.S. **188** 37.57 N 80.41 W
Rupert, Rivière de ≃ **176** 51.29 N 78.45 W
Rupert Creek ≃ **166** 20.53 S 142.23 E
Rupganj **126** 23.48 N 90.31 E
Rūpnagar **123** 30.59 N 76.31 E
Rūpnārāyan ≃ **126** 22.13 N 88.03 E
Ruponda **154** 10.15 S 38.42 E
Ruppertenrod **56** 50.37 N 9.05 E
Ruppiner See ⊜ **54** 52.48 N 12.50 E
Rupprechtseck ∧ **61** 47.14 N 14.00 E
Rupt de Mad ≃ **56** 49.01 N 6.02 E
Rupt-sur-Moselle **58** 47.56 N 6.40 E
Rupununi ≃ **246** 4.03 N 58.34 W
Ruqqād, Wādī ar- V **132** 32.44 N 35.46 E
Rur (Roer) ≃ **56** 51.12 N 5.59 E
Rural Hall **192** 36.14 N 80.17 W
Rural Retreat **192** 36.53 N 81.16 W
Rural Ridge **279b** 40.35 N 79.50 W
Rural Valley **214** 40.48 N 79.18 W
Rurberg **56** 50.37 N 6.22 E
Ruri-kei ◆ **96** 35.03 N 135.26 E
Rurrenabaque **248** 14.28 S 67.34 W
Rurstausee ⊜[1] **56** 50.36 N 6.22 E
Rurutu I **14** 22.26 S 151.20 W
Rusambo **154** 16.35 S 32.12 E
Rušan **120** 37.58 N 71.30 E
Rusaniv **78** 50.29 N 31.09 E
Rusanivka **78** 50.32 N 33.44 E
Rusape **154** 18.32 S 32.07 E
Rusavkina-
Popovščina **265b** 55.42 N 38.04 E
Ruṣayriṣ, Khazzān
ar- ⊜[1] **140** 11.40 N 34.20 E
Ruschuk
→ Ruse **38** 43.50 N 25.57 E
Ruscom ≃ **214** 42.18 N 82.38 W
Ruscom Station **214** 42.13 N 82.39 W
Ruse, Blg. **38** 43.50 N 25.57 E
Ruše, Slvn. **61** 46.32 N 15.31 E
Rusera **124** 25.45 N 86.02 E
Rush, Ire. **48** 53.32 N 6.06 W
Rush, N.Y., U.S. **210** 42.59 N 77.39 W
Rush, Pa., U.S. **210** 41.47 N 76.03 W
Rush □[6] **218** 39.37 N 85.27 W
Rush ≃, N.D., U.S. **198** 47.00 N 96.54 W
Rush ≃, Wi., U.S. **190** 44.34 N 92.19 W
Rushan (Xiacun) **98** 36.54 N 121.29 E
Rush Center **198** 38.27 N 99.18 W
Rush City **190** 45.41 N 92.57 W
Rush Creek ≃, Co.,
U.S. **198** 38.22 N 102.32 W
Rush Creek ≃, Ne.,
U.S. **198** 41.27 N 102.32 W
Rush Creek ≃, N.Y.,
U.S. **284a** 42.00 N 78.52 W
Rush Creek ≃, Oh.,
U.S. **188** 39.38 N 82.33 W
Rush Creek ≃, Oh.,
U.S. **214** 40.34 N 83.20 W
Rush Creek ≃, Ok.,
U.S. **196** 34.42 N 97.10 W
Rushden **42** 52.17 N 0.36 W
Rushford, Mn., U.S. **190** 43.48 N 91.45 W
Rushford, N.Y., U.S. **210** 42.23 N 78.15 W
Rush Hill **219** 39.13 N 91.43 W
Rush Lake ⊜, On.,
Can. **190** 47.48 N 82.12 W
Rush Lake ⊜, Wi.,
U.S. **190** 43.56 N 88.49 W
Rushland **285** 40.15 N 75.02 W
Rushmore **198** 43.37 N 95.48 W
Rusholme •[8] **262** 53.27 N 2.12 W
Rush Springs **196** 34.46 N 97.57 W
Rushsylvania **216** 40.27 N 83.40 W
Rushville, Il., U.S. **219** 40.07 N 90.33 W
Rushville, In., U.S. **218** 39.36 N 85.26 W
Rushville, Ne., U.S. **198** 42.43 N 102.27 W
Rushville, N.Y., U.S. **210** 42.45 N 77.13 W
Rusinga Island I **154** 0.24 S 34.10 E
Rusizi (Ruzizi) ≃ **154** 3.16 S 29.14 E
Rusk **222** 31.47 N 95.09 W
Rusk □[6] **222** 32.10 N 94.50 W
Rusken ⊜ **26** 57.17 N 14.20 E
Ruskin, B.C., Can. **224** 49.12 N 122.28 W
Ruskin, Fl., U.S. **220** 27.43 N 82.26 W
Ruskington **44** 53.02 N 0.23 W
Rusnė **76** 55.18 N 21.22 E
Rušons ⊜ **76** 56.11 N 27.02 E
Rusovce **61** 48.04 N 17.10 E
Russa **272b** 22.29 N 88.21 E
Russas **250** 4.56 S 37.58 W
Russbach ≃ **61** 48.10 N 16.58 E
Russee **41** 54.18 N 10.04 E
Russell, Mb., Can. **184** 50.47 N 101.15 W
Russell, On., Can. **212** 45.15 N 75.22 W
Russell, N.Z. **172** 35.16 S 174.07 E
Russell, Ia., U.S. **190** 40.58 N 93.11 W
Russell, Ks., U.S. **198** 38.53 N 98.51 W
Russell, Ky., U.S. **188** 38.31 N 82.41 W
Russell, Ma., U.S. **207** 42.11 N 72.51 W
Russell, Mn., U.S. **198** 44.19 N 95.57 W
Russell, Pa., U.S. **214** 41.56 N 79.08 W
Russell, Cape › **176** 75.15 N 117.35 W
Russell, Mount ∧ **180** 62.48 N 151.52 W
Russell Cave
National Monument
◆ **194** 34.54 N 85.48 W
Russell Creek ≃ **194** 37.14 N 85.30 W
Russell Gardens **276** 40.47 N 73.43 W
Russell Island I **176** 73.55 N 98.25 W
Russell Islands II **175e** 9.04 S 159.12 E
Russellkonda **120** 19.56 N 84.35 E
Russell Lake ⊜ **184** 56.15 N 101.30 W
Russell Range ⋏ **162** 33.24 S 123.28 E
Russells Point **216** 40.28 N 83.54 W
Russell Springs **194** 37.03 N 85.05 W
Russellton **214** 40.37 N 79.50 W
Russellville, Al., U.S. **194** 34.30 N 87.43 W
Russellville, Ar., U.S. **194** 35.16 N 93.08 W
Russellville, Ky., U.S. **194** 36.50 N 86.53 W
Russellville, Mo., U.S. **194** 38.30 N 92.26 W
Russellville, Oh., U.S. **218** 38.51 N 83.47 W
Russellville, Or., U.S. **224** 45.31 N 122.33 W
Rüsselsheim **56** 50.00 N 8.25 E
Russi **66** 44.22 N 12.02 E
Russia **216** 40.14 N 84.24 W
Russia □[1], Europe **72** 60.00 N 80.00 E
Russia □[1], Europe **74** 60.00 N 100.00 E
Russian ≃ **204** 38.27 N 123.08 W
Russian Mission **180** 61.47 N 161.19 W
Russiaville **216** 40.25 N 86.16 W
Russka **76** 58.59 N 28.30 E
Russkaja Bujlovka **78** 50.22 N 40.03 E
Russkaja Gavan' **74** 76.10 N 62.35 E
Russkaja Pol'ana **86** 53.47 N 73.53 E
Russkaja Talovka **80** 49.59 N 49.05 E
Russkaja Žuravka **80** 50.21 N 40.33 E
Russkij **89** 43.03 N 131.50 E
Russkij, ostrov I **74** 77.00 N 96.00 E
Russkij Aktaš **80** 55.02 N 52.07 E
Russkij Brod **76** 52.36 N 37.22 E
Russkij Kameškir **80** 52.52 N 46.06 E
Russkij Turek **80** 57.03 N 50.13 E
Russkij Vožoj **80** 56.57 N 53.22 E
Russkij Zavorot, mys
› **24** 68.58 N 54.34 E
Russkoje **83** 47.45 N 38.56 E
Russkoje-Dobrino **80** 54.22 N 52.28 E
Russko-Vysockoje **265a** 59.42 N 29.56 E
Rust, Dtsch. **58** 48.16 N 7.43 E
Rust, Öst. **61** 47.48 N 16.41 E
Rustajskij **80** 56.31 N 44.49 E
Rustam **123** 34.21 N 72.17 E
Rustavi **84** 41.33 N 45.02 E
Rustburg **192** 37.16 N 79.06 W
Rustenburg **158** 25.37 S 27.08 E
Rustfontein **158** 30.28 S 29.17 E
Rustic Canyon V **280** 34.04 N 118.31 W
Rustig **158** 27.22 S 27.09 E
Rustington **42** 50.48 N 0.31 W
Ruston, La., U.S. **194** 32.31 N 92.38 W
Ruston, Wa., U.S. **224** 47.17 N 122.30 W
Rusville **273d** 26.10 S 28.18 E
Rutana **154** 3.55 S 30.00 E
Rute **34** 37.19 N 4.22 W
Rütenbrock **52** 52.50 N 7.10 E
Ruteng **115b** 8.36 S 120.27 E
Rutenga **154** 21.08 S 30.45 E
Rutersville **222** 29.57 N 96.48 W
Rutgers University
ʊ[2], N.J., U.S. **276** 40.30 N 74.27 W
Rutgers University
(Newark) ʊ[2], N.J.,
U.S. **276** 40.44 N 74.10 W
Rutgers University
(Camden) ʊ[2], N.J.,
U.S. **285** 39.56 N 75.07 W
Ruth, Ms., U.S. **194** 31.22 N 90.18 W
Ruth, Nv., U.S. **204** 39.16 N 114.59 W
Rüthen **52** 51.29 N 8.25 E
Rutherford, Ca., U.S. **226** 38.28 N 122.25 W
Rutherford, N.J., U.S. **210** 40.49 N 74.06 W
Rutherford, Tn., U.S. **194** 36.07 N 88.59 W
Rutherfordton **192** 35.22 N 81.57 W
Rutherglen, Scot.,
U.K. **46** 55.50 N 4.12 W
Ruther Glen, Va.,
U.S. **208** 37.56 N 77.27 W
Ruthin **44** 53.07 N 3.18 W
Ruthton **198** 44.10 N 96.06 W
Ruthven, On., Can. **214** 42.03 N 82.40 W
Ruthven, Ia., U.S. **198** 43.07 N 94.53 W
Rüti **58** 47.16 N 8.51 E
Rutigliano **68** 41.01 N 17.00 E
Rutino **68** 40.18 N 15.04 E
Rutka ≃ **80** 56.22 N 46.38 E
Rutland, B.C., Can. **182** 49.53 N 119.24 W
Rutland, Fl., U.S. **220** 28.51 N 82.13 W
Rutland, Il., U.S. **216** 40.59 N 89.03 W
Rutland, Ma., U.S. **207** 42.22 N 71.56 W
Rutland, N.D., U.S. **198** 46.03 N 97.30 W
Rutland, Vt., U.S. **188** 43.36 N 72.58 W
Rutland □[6] **210** 43.21 N 73.15 W
Rutland Island I **110** 11.25 N 92.40 E
Rutland State Park ◆ **207** 42.23 N 72.01 W
Rutland Water ⊜[1] **42** 52.39 N 0.38 W
Rutledge, Ga., U.S. **192** 33.37 N 83.36 W
Rutledge, Pa., U.S. **285** 39.54 N 75.20 W
Rutledge, Tn., U.S. **192** 36.16 N 83.30 W
Rutog **120** 33.27 N 79.42 E
Rutshuru **154** 1.11 S 29.27 E
Rüttenscheid •[8] **263** 51.26 N 7.00 E
Rutter **190** 46.06 N 80.40 W
Rutul **84** 41.33 N 47.25 E
Ruukki **26** 64.40 N 25.06 E
Ruurlo **52** 52.05 N 6.26 E
Ruvo del Monte **68** 40.51 N 15.32 E
Ruvo di Puglia **68** 41.07 N 16.29 E
Ruvu **154** 6.48 S 38.39 E
Ruvu ≃ **154** 6.23 S 38.52 E
Ruvubu (Rovubu) ≃ **154** 2.23 S 30.47 E
Ruvuma □[4] **154** 11.00 S 36.00 E
Ruvuma (Rovuma) ≃ **154** 10.29 S 40.28 E
Ruwayān, Wādī ar-
⩡[7] **142** 29.07 N 30.10 E
Ruwaybah ⊤[4] **140** 15.39 N 28.45 E
Ruwayfī, Jabal ar- ∧ **132** 31.12 N 36.00 E
Ruwenzori National
Park ◆ **154** 0.15 S 30.00 E
Ruwenzori Range ⋏ **154** 0.23 N 29.54 E
Ruwer **56** 49.47 N 6.43 E
Ruwer ≃ **56** 49.47 N 6.42 E
Ruya (Luia) ≃ **154** 16.34 S 33.12 E
Ruyang **100** 34.10 N 112.26 E
Ruy Barbosa **255** 12.18 S 40.27 W
Ruyigi **154** 3.29 S 30.15 E
Ruyton-Eleven-Towns **42** 52.48 N 2.54 W
Ruza **82** 55.42 N 36.12 E
Ruza ≃ **82** 55.38 N 36.17 E
Ruzajevka, Kaz. **86** 52.49 N 66.57 E
Ruzajevka, Ross. **80** 54.04 N 44.57 E
Ružany **76** 52.52 N 24.53 E
Ruzhyn **78** 49.43 N 29.14 E
Ruzizi (Rusizi) ≃ **154** 3.16 S 29.14 E
Ružomberok **30** 49.06 N 19.18 E
Ruzskoje
vodochranilišče ⊜[1] **82** 55.47 N 36.00 E
Ruzychna **78** 49.24 N 26.58 E
Ruzyně ⊠ **54** 50.06 N 14.17 E
Ruzzah, Jabal ∧[2] **142** 30.01 N 30.26 E
Rwamagana **154** 1.57 S 30.34 E
Rwanda □[1], Afr. **138** 2.00 S 30.00 E
Rwanda □[1], Afr. **154** 2.00 S 30.00 E
Rwashamaire **154** 0.49 S 30.08 E
Ry **41** 56.05 N 9.46 E
Ryal Fold **262** 53.41 N 2.30 W
Ryan **196** 34.01 N 97.57 W
Ryan ≃ **182** 50.25 N 122.43 W
Ryan, Loch ⊂ **44** 54.58 N 5.02 W
Ryan Peak ∧ **202** 43.54 N 114.25 W
Ryans Creek ≃ **169** 36.43 S 146.12 E
Ryarsh **260** 51.19 N 0.24 E
Ryasnopil' **78** 47.04 N 31.12 E
Ryazan'
→ R'azan' **80** 54.38 N 39.44 E
Rybačij **76** 55.09 N 20.51 E
Rybačij, poluostrov
›[1] **24** 69.42 N 32.36 E
Rybačje **86** 46.27 N 81.32 E
Rybackaja •[8] **265a** 60.00 N 30.30 E
Rybackoje •[8] **265a** 59.50 N 30.30 E
Rybakivka **78** 46.37 N 31.20 E
Rybinsk **76** 58.03 N 38.52 E
Rybinsker Stausee
→ Rybinskoje
vodochranilišče ⊜[1] **76** 58.30 N 38.25 E
Rybinskije Budy **78** 51.13 N 35.57 E
Rybinskoje **86** 55.47 N 94.47 E
Rybinskoje
vodochranilišče ⊜[1] **76** 58.30 N 38.25 E
Rybkino **80** 54.15 N 43.46 E
Rybnaja Sloboda **80** 55.28 N 50.09 E
Rybnik **30** 50.06 N 18.32 E
Rybnoje, Ross. **76** 54.44 N 39.30 E
Rybnoje, Ross. **86** 58.08 N 94.30 E
Rybnovsk **89** 53.12 N 141.50 E
Ryburn ≃ **262** 53.43 N 1.54 W
Rybuška **80** 51.17 N 45.26 E
Rychwał **30** 52.05 N 18.09 E
Ryčkovo **86** 58.09 N 61.43 E
Rycroft **182** 55.45 N 118.43 W
Ryd **26** 56.28 N 14.41 E
Rydaholm **26** 56.59 N 14.16 E
Rydal, Austl. **170** 33.29 S 150.02 E
Rydal, Pa., U.S. **285** 40.06 N 75.06 W
Rydalmere **274a** 33.49 S 151.02 E
Rydbo **40** 59.28 N 18.11 E
Ryde, Austl. **170** 33.49 S 151.06 E
Ryde, Eng., U.K. **42** 50.44 N 1.10 W
Ryder **198** 47.55 N 101.40 W
Ryder's Hill ∧[2] **42** 50.31 N 3.53 W
Ryderwood **224** 46.22 N 123.02 W
Rydsgård **41** 55.28 N 13.35 E
Rydzyna **30** 51.48 N 16.40 E
Rye, Austl. **169** 38.23 S 144.49 E
Rye, Eng., U.K. **42** 50.57 N 0.44 E
Rye, N.Y., U.S. **210** 40.58 N 73.41 W
Rye, Tx., U.S. **222** 30.27 N 94.46 W
Rye ≃ **44** 54.10 N 0.45 W
Ryegate **202** 46.17 N 109.15 W
Rye Hills-Rye Brook **276** 41.00 N 73.41 W
Rye Lake ⊜ **276** 41.04 N 73.43 W
Ryeosu
→ Yŏsu **98** 34.46 N 127.44 E
Rye Patch Reservoir
⊜[1] **204** 40.38 N 118.18 W
Ryer Island I **282** 38.05 N 122.01 W
Ryes **32** 49.19 N 0.37 W
Ryfoss **26** 61.09 N 8.49 E
Ryfylke •[1] **26** 59.30 N 5.30 E
Rygge **26** 59.23 N 10.43 E
Rygnestad **26** 59.16 N 7.29 E
Ryhope **44** 54.52 N 1.21 W
Rykaartspos **158** 26.32 S 26.39 E
Ryker Lake ⊜ **276** 41.03 N 74.33 W
Rykerts **182** 49.00 N 116.35 W
Ryki **30** 51.39 N 21.56 E
Rykonec **76** 59.33 N 36.34 E
Ryley **182** 53.17 N 112.26 W
Rylovići **76** 52.31 N 32.04 E
Ryl'sk **78** 51.36 N 34.43 E
Rylstone **170** 32.48 S 149.58 E
Rymanów **30** 49.34 N 21.53 E
Rýmařov **30** 49.56 N 17.16 E
Ryn **30** 53.56 N 21.33 E
Rynfield **273d** 26.09 S 28.20 E
Rynok **80** 45.39 N 47.34 E
Ryn-Peski •[2] **80** 48.24 N 49.00 E
Ryō **270** 34.44 N 135.55 E
Ryōhaku-sanchi ⋏ **94** 36.09 N 136.45 E
Ryojun
→ Lüshun **98** 38.48 N 121.16 E
Ryōkami **94** 36.00 N 138.58 E
Ryōke **268** 35.58 N 139.33 E
Ryōnan **96** 33.15 N 133.55 E
Ryōtsu **92** 38.05 N 138.26 E
Rypin **30** 53.05 N 19.25 E
Ryshnivka **78** 49.47 N 27.25 E
Ryslinge **41** 55.15 N 10.33 E
Rysy ∧ **30** 49.12 N 20.04 E
Ryton **44** 54.59 N 1.46 W
Ryton ≃ **44** 53.25 N 1.00 W
Ryton-on-Dunsmore **42** 52.22 N 1.26 W
Ryūga-do ⩡[5] **96** 33.39 N 133.45 E
Ryūgasaki **94** 35.54 N 140.11 E
Ryūjin **96** 33.53 N 135.29 E
Ryukyu Islands
→ Nansei-shotō II **90** 26.30 N 128.00 E
Ryukyu Trench ✢[1] **12** 24.45 N 128.00 E
Ryūmon-dake ∧ **270** 34.26 N 135.53 E
Ryūō, Nihon **94** 35.04 N 136.07 E
Ryūō, Nihon **94** 35.39 N 138.30 E
Ryūsen **270** 34.28 N 135.37 E
Ryūyō **94** 34.40 N 137.48 E
Ržaksa **80** 52.09 N 42.02 E
Ržanica **76** 53.26 N 33.55 E
Ržava **78** 51.14 N 36.43 E
Rzepin **30** 52.22 N 14.50 E
Rzeszów **30** 50.03 N 22.00 E
Rzeszów □[4] **30** 50.00 N 22.00 E
Ržev **76** 56.16 N 34.20 E
Rzhyshchiv **78** 49.58 N 31.03 E
Ržovka •[8] **265a** 59.58 N 30.30 E

S

Sa **110** 18.34 N 100.45 E
Sa ≃ **105** 40.22 N 117.58 E
Saa **152** 4.22 N 11.27 E
Sa'ad **132** 31.28 N 34.32 E
Sa'ādatābād **128** 30.06 N 53.08 E
Sääksjärvi ⊜ **26** 61.24 N 22.24 E
Saal **54** 54.19 N 12.29 E
Saalach ≃ **64** 47.51 N 13.00 E
Saal an der Donau **60** 48.54 N 11.56 E
Saal an der Saale **56** 50.19 N 10.21 E
Saalbach **64** 47.23 N 12.38 E
Saalburg **54** 50.30 N 11.43 E
Saaldorf **54** 50.27 N 11.41 E
Saale ≃ **54** 51.57 N 11.55 E
Saaler Bodden ⊂ **54** 54.20 N 12.28 E
Saales **58** 48.21 N 7.07 E
Saaletalsperre •[6] **54** 50.30 N 11.43 E
Saalfeld **54** 50.39 N 11.22 E
Saalfelden **64** 47.25 N 12.51 E
Šaamar **88** 50.08 N 106.10 E
Saâne ≃, Fr. **50** 49.54 N 0.56 E
Saane ≃, Schw. **58** 46.59 N 7.16 E
Saanen **58** 46.29 N 7.16 E
Saanenmöser **58** 46.31 N 7.18 E
Saanich Inlet ⊂ **224** 48.38 N 123.30 W
Saar
→ Saarland □[3] **56** 49.20 N 7.00 E
Saar (Sarre) ≃ **56** 49.42 N 6.34 E
Saarbrücken **56** 49.14 N 6.59 E
Saarburg **56** 49.36 N 6.33 E
Sääre **76** 57.56 N 22.02 E
Saarelouis
→ Saarlouis **56** 49.21 N 6.45 E
Saaremaa I **76** 58.25 N 22.30 E
Saarijärvi **26** 62.43 N 25.16 E
Saaristomeren
kansallispuisto ◆ **26** 59.50 N 21.50 E
Saarland □[3] **56** 49.20 N 7.00 E
Saarlautern
→ Saarlouis **56** 49.21 N 6.45 E
Saarlouis **56** 49.21 N 6.45 E
Saarmund **264a** 52.19 N 13.07 E
Saarn •[8] **263** 51.24 N 6.53 E
Saarnberg •[8] **263** 51.25 N 6.53 E
Saas Almagell **58** 46.07 N 7.58 E
Saas Fee **58** 46.07 N 7.55 E
Saas Grund **58** 46.08 N 7.56 E
Saastal V **58** 46.10 N 7.56 E
Saatlı **84** 39.56 N 48.23 E
Saavedra **252** 37.45 S 62.22 W
Saba I **238** 17.38 N 63.10 W
Saba ≃, Nihon **96** 34.02 N 131.30 E
Saba ≃, Ross. **76** 59.08 N 29.00 E
Sabā', Wādī al- V **128** 28.35 N 36.35 E
Saba Bank ✢[2] **238** 17.30 N 63.30 W
Šabac **38** 44.45 N 19.42 E
Sabadell **34** 41.33 N 2.06 E
Sabae **94** 35.57 N 136.11 E
Sab'ah **142** 30.15 N 32.33 E
Sabah □[3] **112** 5.20 N 117.10 E
Sabajevo **80** 53.59 N 45.43 E
Sabak, Cape › **181a** 52.20 N 173.45 E
Sabak Bernam **114** 3.46 N 100.59 E
Sabal **112** 0.59 S 123.14 E
Sabalān ∧ **128** 38.15 N 47.48 E
Sabalana, Kepulauan
II **112** 6.45 S 118.50 E
Sabalgarh **124** 26.15 N 77.24 E
Sabaluka Game
Reserve •[4] **140** 16.18 N 32.40 E
Sabana **240m** 18.20 N 65.44 W
Sabana, Archipiélago
de II **240p** 23.00 N 80.00 W
Sabana de La Mar **238** 19.04 N 69.23 W
Sabana de Mendoza **246** 9.26 N 70.46 W
Sabanagrande, Hond. **236** 13.50 N 87.15 W
Sabana Grande, P.R. **240m** 18.05 N 66.58 W
Sabanalamar,
Ensenada ⊂ **240p** 21.36 N 78.44 W
Sabanalarga **246** 10.38 N 74.55 W
Sabana Llana **240m** 18.02 N 66.15 W
Sabancuy **232** 18.58 N 91.11 W
Sabaneta, Rep. Dom. **238** 19.30 N 71.21 W
Sabaneta, Ven. **246** 8.46 N 69.56 W
Sabaneta, Puntan › **174n** 15.17 N 145.49 E
Sābang, India **126** 22.11 N 87.36 E
Sabang (Dampelas),
Indon. **112** 0.11 N 119.51 E
Sabang, Indon. **114** 5.55 N 95.19 E
Sabanillas **232** 25.08 N 101.44 W
Šabanovo **82** 55.38 N 38.43 E
Şabanözü **130** 40.29 N 33.18 E
Sabará **255** 19.54 S 43.48 W
Sabarei **154** 4.20 N 36.55 E
Sābari ≃ **122** 17.34 N 81.15 E
Sābarmati ≃ **120** 22.18 N 72.22 E
Sabasṭīyah (Samaria) **132** 32.17 N 35.12 E
Sab'atayn, Ramlat
as- ⩡[8] **144** 15.30 N 46.10 E
Sabathu **123** 30.59 N 76.59 E
Sabatini, Monti ⋏ **66** 42.10 N 12.15 E
Sabato ≃ **66** 41.08 N 14.45 E
Sabaudia **66** 41.18 N 13.01 E
Sabaudia, Lago di ⊂ **66** 41.16 N 13.02 E
Sabaúna **256** 23.29 S 46.05 W
Saba Wanak **144** 10.33 N 44.08 E
Sabaya **248** 19.01 S 68.23 W
Ṣabāyā, Jabal I **144** 18.35 N 41.03 E
Sabažo **84** 42.14 N 41.48 E
Sabbioneta **64** 45.00 N 10.29 E
Şabe **272c** 19.11 N 73.02 E
Šabel'sk **83** 46.51 N 38.29 E
Ṣāberī, Hāmūn-e ⊜ **128** 31.30 N 61.20 E
Sabetha **198** 39.54 N 95.48 W
Sabhā, Lībiyā **146** 27.03 N 14.26 E
Ṣabḩā, Urd. **132** 32.20 N 36.30 E
Sābhār **126** 23.51 N 90.15 E
Sabi (Save) ≃, Afr. **156** 21.00 S 35.02 E
Sabi ≃, Nihon **94** 36.48 N 140.04 E
Sabicy **76** 58.50 N 29.18 E
Sabidana, Jabal ∧ **140** 18.04 N 36.50 E
Sabie **156** 25.10 S 30.48 E
Sábiè ≃ **156** 25.19 S 32.18 E
Sabile **76** 57.03 N 22.35 E
Sabillasville **208** 39.42 N 77.27 W
Sabina **218** 39.29 N 83.38 W
Sabina □[9] **66** 42.15 N 12.42 E
Sabinal **196** 29.19 N 99.27 W
Sabinal ≃ **196** 29.06 N 99.27 W
Sabinal, Cayo I **240p** 21.40 N 77.18 W
Sabiñánigo **34** 42.31 N 0.22 W
Sabinas **232** 27.51 N 101.07 W
Sabinas ≃, Méx. **232** 27.37 N 100.42 W
Sabinas ≃, Méx. **232** 26.51 N 99.34 W
Sabinas ≃, Méx. **234** 22.59 N 98.58 W
Sabinas Hidalgo **232** 26.30 N 100.10 W
Sabine ≃ **178** 30.00 N 93.45 W
Sabine, Mount ∧ **169** 38.38 S 143.44 E
Sabine, South Fork
≃ **222** 32.52 N 96.10 W
Sabine Bay ⊂ **176** 75.35 N 109.30 W
Sabine Lake ⊜ **194** 29.50 N 93.50 W
Sabine Pass ⊂ **194** 29.44 N 93.52 W
Sabine Peninsula ›[1] **176** 76.20 N 109.30 W
Sabini, Monti ⋏ **66** 42.13 N 12.50 E
Sabinópolis **255** 18.40 S 43.06 W
Sabinov **30** 49.06 N 21.06 E
Sabinsville **210** 41.52 N 77.31 W
Sabir, Jabal ∧ **144** 13.30 N 44.03 E
Şabirabad **84** 40.01 N 48.29 E
Šabla **38** 43.32 N 28.32 E
Sabl'a, gora ∧ **24** 64.48 N 58.50 E
Sablayan **116** 12.50 N 120.46 E
Sable, Anse au ⊂ **275a** 45.21 N 73.56 W
Sable, Cape › **186** 43.25 N 65.35 W
Sable, Cape ›[1] **220** 25.12 N 81.05 W
Sable, Île de I **160** 19.15 S 159.56 E
Sable, Rivière du ≃ **176** 55.30 N 68.21 W
Sable Island I **186** 43.55 N 59.50 W
Sables, Lac aux ⊜ **206** 46.53 N 72.22 W
Sables, River aux ≃ **190** 46.13 N 82.04 W
Sablé-sur-Sarthe **32** 47.50 N 0.20 W
Sablinskoje **84** 44.31 N 43.14 E
Sablūkah, Ash-Shallāl
as- (Sixth Cataract)
⌊ **140** 16.20 N 32.42 E
Šablykino **76** 52.51 N 35.12 E
Sabo **152** 7.50 N 17.49 E
Saboeiro **250** 6.32 S 39.54 W
Sabogal ≃ **236** 10.55 N 84.43 W
Sāboli •[8] **272a** 28.43 N 77.18 E
Sabonkafi **150** 14.38 N 8.45 E
Sabor ≃ **34** 41.10 N 7.07 W
Sabou **150** 12.04 N 2.14 W
Sabourin, Lac ⊜ **190** 47.58 N 77.41 W
Sabra, Tanjung › **164** 2.17 S 132.19 E
Şabrātah **146** 32.47 N 12.29 E
Sabres **32** 44.09 N 0.44 W
Sabrevois **206** 45.12 N 73.14 W
Sabrina Coast ⩡[2] **9** 67.00 S 119.30 E
Sabuda, Pulau I **164** 2.38 S 131.36 E
Sabugal **34** 40.21 N 7.05 W
Sabugo **266c** 38.49 N 9.18 W
Sabuka **273b** 4.27 S 15.10 E
Sabula **190** 42.04 N 90.10 W
Sabunçu, Azer. **84** 40.26 N 49.56 E
Sabuncu, Tür. **130** 39.33 N 30.12 E
Saburovo **265b** 55.53 N 37.16 E
Saburovo •[8] **265b** 55.38 N 37.42 E
Şabyā **144** 17.09 N 42.37 E
Sabyin **110** 19.06 N 94.11 E
Sabyndy **86** 50.53 N 70.33 E
Sabzevār **128** 36.13 N 57.42 E
Sac ≃ **194** 38.01 N 93.43 W
Sacaba **248** 17.23 S 66.02 W
Sacaca **248** 18.05 S 66.26 W
Sacacomie, Lac ⊜ **206** 46.31 N 73.14 W
Sacagawea ≃ **202** 47.27 N 107.58 W
Sacajawea Peak ∧ **202** 45.15 N 117.17 W
Sacanche **248** 7.05 S 76.44 W
Sacandaga ≃ **210** 43.19 N 73.50 W
Sacandaga, West
Branch ≃ **210** 43.22 N 74.17 W
Sacandica **152** 5.58 S 15.56 E
Sacaola **152** 12.57 S 22.25 E
Sacariúna ≃ **248** 12.52 S 57.22 W
Sacaton **200** 33.04 N 111.44 W
Sacavém **266c** 38.47 N 9.06 W
Sačchere **84** 42.21 N 43.23 E
Sac City **198** 42.25 N 94.59 W
Sacco ≃ **66** 41.31 N 13.32 E
Sacedón **34** 40.29 N 2.43 W
Săcele **38** 45.37 N 25.42 E
Şaç Geçidi)(**130** 39.54 N 42.22 E
Šacha ≃ **82** 56.45 N 39.10 E
Sachalin, ostrov
(Sakhalin) I **89** 51.00 N 143.00 E
Sachalin Oblast' □[4] **89** 51.00 N 143.00 E
Sachalinskij zaliv ⊂ **89** 53.45 N 141.30 E
Šachand **85** 40.54 N 71.28 E
Sachayoj **252** 26.41 S 61.50 W
Saché **50** 47.14 N 0.33 E
Šache ≃ **84** 43.47 N 39.27 E
Sachicapa **152** 10.21 S 19.59 E
Sachigo ≃ **176** 55.06 N 88.58 W
Sachigo Lake ⊜ **184** 53.49 N 92.08 W
Sachimbo **152** 9.14 S 20.16 E
Šachovskaja **76** 56.02 N 35.29 E
Šachrang **64** 47.41 N 12.15 E
Šachrichan **85** 40.44 N 72.03 E
Šachrinau **85** 38.34 N 68.20 E
Šachrisabz **72** 39.03 N 66.50 E
Šachristan **85** 39.47 N 68.49 E
Šachristan, pereval)(**85** 39.33 N 68.33 E
Šachrovka **80** 58.34 N 52.12 E
Sachse **222** 32.59 N 96.36 W
Sachseln **58** 46.52 N 8.15 E
Sachsen □[3] **30** 51.00 N 13.00 E
Sachsen □[9] **30** 52.45 N 9.30 E
Sachsen-Anhalt □[3] **54** 52.00 N 11.30 E
Sachsenbrunn **54** 50.27 N 10.56 E
Sachsenburg **64** 46.50 N 13.21 E
Sachsenhagen **52** 52.24 N 9.16 E
Sachsenhausen,
Dtsch. **54** 52.47 N 13.14 E
Sachsenhausen,
Dtsch. **56** 51.15 N 9.00 E
Sachs Harbour **176** 72.00 N 125.00 W
Sächsische Schweiz
•[1] **54** 50.55 N 14.10 E
Šachterskij **180** 64.42 N 177.40 E
Šachtinsk **86** 49.40 N 72.37 E
Šacht'orsk **89** 49.11 N 142.07 E
Šachty **83** 47.42 N 40.13 E
Šachunja **80** 57.40 N 46.37 E
Sachy **56** 49.40 N 5.08 E
Şacile **64** 45.57 N 12.30 E
Šack, Bela. **76** 53.25 N 27.41 E
Šack, Ross. **80** 54.01 N 41.43 E
Sackets Harbor **212** 43.56 N 76.07 W
Sackville **186** 45.54 N 64.22 W
Saclay **261** 48.44 N 2.10 E
Saclay, Étang de ⊜ **261** 48.45 N 2.10 E
Saco, Me., U.S. **188** 43.30 N 70.26 W
Saco, Mt., U.S. **202** 48.27 N 107.20 W
Saco ≃ **188** 43.27 N 70.22 W
Saco Bay ⊂ **188** 43.30 N 70.15 W
Sacol Island I **116** 6.58 N 122.13 E
Sacotes **266c** 38.48 N 9.20 W
Sacra, Isola I **267a** 41.45 N 12.15 E
Sacra Família do
Tinguá **256** 22.29 S 43.36 W
Sacramento, Bra. **255** 19.53 S 47.27 W
Sacramento, Ca.,
U.S. **226** 38.34 N 121.29 W
Sacramento □[6] **226** 38.35 N 121.30 W
Sacramento ≃, Ca.,
U.S. **204** 38.03 N 121.56 W
Sacramento ≃, N.M.,
U.S. **200** 32.16 N 105.31 W
Sacramento, Pampa
del ≚ **248** 8.00 S 75.50 W
Sacramento
Metropolitan
Airport ⊠ **226** 38.42 N 121.37 W
Sacramento
Mountains ⋏ **200** 32.45 N 105.30 W
Sacramento River
Deep Water Ship
Channel ≊ **226** 38.15 N 121.40 W
Sacramento South **226** 38.32 N 121.26 W
Sacramento Valley V **204** 39.15 N 122.00 W
Sacramento Wash V **200** 34.43 N 114.28 W
Sacre ≃ **248** 12.56 S 58.18 W
Sacré-Cœur ʊ[1] **261** 48.53 N 2.21 E
Sacred Heart **198** 44.47 N 95.21 W
Sacriston **44** 54.49 N 1.37 W
Sacro, Monte ∧ **68** 40.13 N 15.20 E
Sacro Monte ʊ[1] **62** 45.49 N 8.15 E
Sacrow •[8] **264a** 52.26 N 13.06 E
Sacrower-Paretzer
Kanal ≊ **264a** 52.28 N 12.55 E
Sacrower See ⊜ **264a** 52.27 N 13.06 E
Săcueni **38** 47.21 N 22.06 E
Sacul **222** 31.50 N 94.56 W
Sacupana **246** 8.35 N 61.39 W
Sada, Esp. **34** 43.21 N 8.15 W
Sada, Nihon **96** 35.15 N 132.43 E
Sádaba **34** 42.17 N 1.16 W
Sadābād, India **124** 27.27 N 78.03 E
Sa'dābād, Īrān **128** 29.23 N 51.07 E
Sa'dābād, Īrān **128** 34.51 N 50.36 E
Ṣadad **130** 34.18 N 36.56 E
Ṣa'dah **144** 16.52 N 43.37 E
Sadaik Taung ∧ **110** 15.09 N 98.12 E
Sadali **71** 39.49 N 9.16 E
Sada-misaki › **96** 33.20 N 132.01 E
Sada-misaki-hantō ›[1] **96** 33.26 N 132.13 E
Sadamitsu **96** 34.02 N 134.04 E
Sadane ≃ **115a** 6.01 S 106.37 E
Sadang ≃ **112** 3.43 S 119.27 E
Sadanga **116** 17.09 N 121.02 E
Sadani **154** 6.03 S 38.47 E
Sadao **110** 6.38 N 100.26 E
Sadarpur, Bngl. **126** 23.28 N 90.02 E
Sādarpur, India **272a** 28.33 N 77.21 E
Sadčikovka **86** 53.01 N 63.27 E
Sadda **120** 33.42 N 70.20 E
Saddle ≃ **276** 40.52 N 74.07 W
Saddleback, Mount ∧ **168a** 32.58 S 116.28 E
Saddle Brook **276** 40.54 N 74.06 W
Saddlebunch Keys II **220** 24.37 N 81.37 W
Saddle Lake Indian
Reserve •[4] **182** 54.00 N 111.40 W
Saddle Mountain ∧,
Co., U.S. **200** 38.50 N 105.28 W
Saddle Mountain ∧,
Or., U.S. **224** 45.58 N 123.41 W
Saddle Mountains ⋏ **202** 46.50 N 119.55 W
Saddle Mountain
State Park ◆ **224** 45.58 N 123.41 W
Saddle Peak ∧ **110** 13.09 N 93.01 E
Saddle River **276** 40.54 N 74.05 W
Saddle Rock **276** 40.48 N 73.45 W
Saddleworth, Austl. **168b** 34.05 S 138.47 E
Saddleworth, Eng.,
U.K. **262** 53.33 N 1.59 W
Saddleworth Moor
•[3] **262** 53.33 N 1.57 W
Sa Dec **110** 10.18 N 105.46 E
Sadelkow **54** 53.36 N 13.26 E
Sādhaura **124** 30.23 N 77.13 E
Sādhuhāti **126** 23.34 N 89.01 E
Sadieville **218** 38.23 N 84.32 W
Sadiola **150** 13.53 N 11.42 W
Sādiqābād **120** 28.18 N 70.08 E
Sadiya **120** 27.50 N 95.40 E
Sa'dīyah, Wādī V **144** 20.35 N 39.38 E
Sa'dīyāt, Ra's as- › **132** 33.41 N 35.25 E
Sadler Lake ⊜ **184** 55.17 N 103.45 W
Sado I **92** 38.00 N 138.25 E
Sado ≃ **34** 38.29 N 8.55 W
Sado-kaikyō ʯ **92** 37.50 N 138.40 E
Sadon **84** 42.51 N 44.00 E
Sadovoje, Ross. **80** 46.56 N 44.23 E
Sadovoje, Ross. **80** 47.46 N 44.30 E
Sadovoje Pervoje **78** 51.33 N 40.29 E
Sadowara **92** 32.02 N 131.26 E
Şādri **120** 25.11 N 73.26 E
Šadrina **89** 51.33 N 130.22 E
Šadrino **86** 55.52 N 91.06 E
Šadrinsk **86** 56.05 N 63.38 E
Sadsburyville **208** 39.59 N 75.53 W
Sādulpur **123** 28.38 N 75.24 E
Sädvaluspen **24** 66.24 N 16.51 E
Sæby, Dan. **26** 57.20 N 10.32 E
Sæby, Dan. **41** 55.33 N 11.19 E
Saegertown **214** 41.43 N 80.09 W
Sae Islands II **164** 0.45 S 145.15 E
Saeki, Nihon **96** 34.22 N 132.11 E
Saeki, Nihon **96** 34.51 N 134.06 E
Saeki
→ Saiki, Nihon **96** 32.57 N 131.54 E
Saengil-to I **98** 34.19 N 126.59 E
Saerbeck **52** 52.10 N 7.38 E
Saerluojia Hu ⊜ **120** 33.55 N 86.55 E
Særslev, Dan. **41** 55.31 N 10.11 E
Særslev, Dan. **41** 55.43 N 11.23 E
Saeul **56** 49.44 N 5.59 E
Şafā, Tulūl aṣ- ∧[1] **132** 33.02 N 37.12 E
Safad
→ Ẕefat **132** 32.58 N 35.30 E
Safājah, Jazīrat I **140** 26.45 N 33.59 E
Safakulevo **86** 54.59 N 62.33 E
Şafānīyah **142** 28.49 N 30.48 E
Safdar Jang Airport ⊠ **272a** 28.37 N 77.13 E
Safdar Jang's Tomb
⊥ **272a** 28.36 N 77.13 E
Safed Koh Range ⋏ **123** 33.58 N 70.25 E
Safe Harbor Dam •[6] **208** 39.59 N 76.28 W
Safenbach ≃ **61** 47.06 N 16.05 E
Safety Bay **168a** 32.18 S 115.43 E
Safety Harbor **220** 27.59 N 82.41 W
Säffle **26** 59.08 N 12.56 E
Safford **200** 32.50 N 109.42 W
Saffron Walden **42** 52.01 N 0.15 E
Safi **148** 32.20 N 9.17 W
Safi □[4] **148** 32.05 N 9.00 W

Symbols in the index entries represent the broad categories identified in the key at the right. Symbols with superior numbers (⋏[1]) identify subcategories (see complete key on page *I · 1).*

Symbole im Register stellen die rechts im Schlüssel erklärten Kategorien dar. Symbole mit hochgestellten Ziffern (⋏[1]) bezeichnen Unterabteilungen einer Kategorie (vgl. vollständiger Schlüssel auf Seite *I · 1).*

Los símbolos incluídos en el texto del índice representan las grandes categorías identificadas con la clave a la derecha. Los símbolos con numeros en su parte superior (⋏[1]) identifican las subcategorías (véase la clave completa en la página *I · 1).*

Les symboles de l'index représentent les catégories indiquées dans la légende à droite. Les symboles suivis d'un indice (⋏[1]) représentent des sous-catégories (voir légende complète à la page *I · 1).*

Os símbolos incluídos no texto do índice representam as grandes categorias identificadas com a chave à direita. Os símbolos com números em sua parte superior (⋏[1]) identificam as subcategorias (veja-se a chave completa à página *I · 1).*

	English	Deutsch	Español	Français	Português
∧	Mountain	Berg	Montaña	Montagne	Montanha
⋏	Mountains	Gebirge	Montañas	Montagnes	Montanhas
)(	Pass	Paß	Paso	Col	Passo
V	Valley, Canyon	Tal, Cañon	Valle, Cañón	Vallée, Canyon	Vale, Canhão
≚	Plain	Ebene	Llano	Plaine	Planície
›	Cape	Kap	Cabo	Cap	Cabo
I	Island	Insel	Isla	Île	Ilha
II	Islands	Inseln	Islas	Îles	Ilhas
⩡	Other Topographic Features	Andere Topographische Objekte	Otros Elementos Topográficos	Autres données topographiques	Outros acidentes topográficos

ESPAÑOL — Nombre / Página / Lat.°′ / Long.°′ W = Oeste
FRANÇAIS — Nom / Page / Lat.°′ / Long.°′ W = Ouest
PORTUGUÊS — Nome / Página / Lat.°′ / Long.°′ W = Oeste

Safia 164 9.35 S 148.40 E
Safīābād 128 36.45 N 57.58 E
Safīd ≃ 120 36.44 N 65.38 E
Safīd Kūh, Selseleh-ye ⋏ 128 34.30 N 63.30 E
Safidon 124 29.25 N 76.40 E
Safiental V 58 46.40 N 9.18 E
Safioune, Sebkhet ⊟ 148 32.16 N 5.27 E
Safipur 126 23.01 N 90.22 E
Sāfitā 130 34.49 N 36.07 E
Safonovo, Russ. 24 65.42 N 47.39 E
Safonovo, Ross. 76 55.06 N 33.15 E
Safonovo, Ross. 82 55.33 N 38.17 E
Safrakköyü ◆8 267b 41.00 N 28.47 E
Safranbolu 130 41.15 N 32.45 E
Saft al-'Inab 142 30.49 N 30.41 E
Şaft al-Khammār 142 28.02 N 30.42 E
Şaft al-Laban 273c 30.02 N 31.10 E
Şaft al-Mulūk 142 30.49 N 30.41 E
Saft Rāshīn 142 28.58 N 30.55 E
Saft Turāb 142 30.54 N 31.07 E
Safwān 128 30.07 N 47.43 E
Saga, Kaz. 86 50.23 N 64.15 E
Saga, Kaz. 86 49.25 N 55.17 E
Saga, Nihon 92 33.15 N 130.18 E
Saga, Nihon 96 33.05 N 133.06 E
Saga, Zhg. 120 29.30 N 85.22 E
Saga □5 96 33.21 N 130.28 E
Sagaba 152 11.17 S 23.07 E
Sagae 92 38.22 N 140.17 E
Sagaing 110 21.52 N 95.59 E
Sagaing □8 110 24.00 N 95.00 E
Sagak, Cape ⟩ 180 52.48 N 169.08 W
Sagalaherang 115a 6.40 S 107.39 E
Sagalakasa 80 46.54 N 50.43 E
Sagamāthā □8 124 27.15 N 86.45 E
Sagami ≃ 94 35.19 N 139.22 E
Sagamihara 94 35.34 N 139.23 E
Sagamihara-daichi ⋏1 268 35.27 N 139.27 E
Sagamiko 94 35.37 N 139.12 E
Sagami-ko ◎ 94 35.35 N 139.16 E
Sagami-nada c 94 35.00 N 139.30 E
Sagami-wan c 94 35.15 N 139.25 E
Sagamore, Ma., U.S. 207 41.46 N 70.31 W
Sagamore, Pa., U.S. 214 40.46 N 79.13 W
Sagamore Beach 207 41.47 N 70.31 W
Sagamore Hill National Historic Site ⊥ 276 40.53 N 73.30 W
Sagamore Hills 279a 41.02 N 81.26 W
Sagan → Żagań 30 51.37 N 15.19 E
Šagan ≃, Kaz. 86 50.37 N 79.15 E
Sagån ≃, Sve. 40 59.35 N 16.54 E
Saganaga Lake ◎ 190 48.14 N 90.52 W
Saganashkee Slough ≃ 278 41.41 N 87.53 W
Saganash Lake ◎ 190 49.04 N 82.35 W
Saganoseki 96 33.15 N 131.53 E
Saganthit Kyun I 110 11.56 N 98.29 E
Sagaon 272c 19.12 N 73.06 E
Sāgar, India 122 14.10 N 75.02 E
Sāgar, India 124 23.50 N 78.43 E
Sagara 94 34.41 N 138.12 E
Sagaranten 115a 7.13 S 106.52 E
Sagard 54 54.31 N 13.33 E
Sāgardīghi 126 24.17 N 88.06 E
Sagaredžo 84 41.44 N 45.20 E
Sāgar Island I 126 21.43 N 88.06 E
Sagarmatha → Everest, Mount ⋏ 124 27.59 N 86.56 E
Sagarmatha National Park ♦ 124 27.50 N 86.45 E
Sāgar Plateau ⋏1 124 23.30 N 78.30 E
Sagavanirktok ≃ 180 70.20 N 148.00 W
Sagay 116 10.57 N 123.25 E
Sage, Mount ⋏ 240m 18.25 N 64.39 W
Sage Creek ≃, N.A. 202 48.58 N 110.06 W
Sage Creek ≃, U.S. 202 44.50 N 108.26 W
Sage Creek ≃, Mt., U.S. 202 47.16 N 109.43 W
Sage Creek ≃, Mt., U.S. 202 48.20 N 110.03 W
Sagemace Bay c 184 51.49 N 100.03 W
Sagerton 196 33.05 N 99.58 W
Saggaubach ≃ 61 46.43 N 15.24 E
Sag Harbor 207 40.59 N 72.17 W
Saggart 48 53.17 N 6.27 W
Saghīr, Al-Bahr aş- ⊟ 142 31.09 N 31.56 E
Sagil 86 50.20 N 91.40 E
Saginaw, Mi., U.S. 190 43.25 N 83.56 W
Saginaw, Tx., U.S. 222 32.52 N 97.22 W
Saginaw ≃ 190 43.39 N 83.51 W
Saginaw Bay c 190 43.50 N 83.40 W
Sagiz, Kaz. 80 47.31 N 53.16 E
Sagiz, Kaz. 86 48.12 N 54.56 E
Sagiz ≃ 86 47.32 N 53.20 E
Sağkaya 130 37.11 N 35.41 E
Sagleipie 150 7.00 N 8.52 W
Şaglek Bay c 176 58.35 N 63.00 W
Şaglyteniz, ozero ◎ 86 54.08 N 69.52 E
Šagonar 86 51.32 N 92.48 E
Sagra ⋏ 34 37.57 N 2.34 W
Sagrado 64 45.52 N 13.29 E
Sagres 34 37.00 N 8.56 W
Sag Sag 164 5.35 S 148.20 E
Sagsaj 86 48.54 N 89.37 E
Sagsajn ≃ 102 44.50 N 96.26 E
Sagu, Indon. 112 8.15 S 123.13 E
Şagu, Rom. 38 46.03 N 21.17 E
Saguache 200 38.05 N 106.05 W
Saguache Creek ≃ 200 37.52 N 105.51 W
Sagua de Tánamo 240p 20.35 N 75.14 W
Sagua la Chica ≃ 240p 22.45 N 79.39 W
Sagua la Grande 240p 22.49 N 80.05 W
Saguaro National Monument ♦ 200 32.12 N 110.38 W
Saguenay ≃ 176 48.08 N 69.44 W
Saguna 272b 22.59 N 88.29 E
Sagunay Lake 216 41.43 N 86.34 W
Sagunt 34 39.41 N 0.16 W
Saguny 78 50.36 N 39.43 E
Sagutjevo 76 52.28 N 33.28 E
Sāgwāra 120 23.41 N 74.01 E
Sagy 261 49.03 N 1.57 E
Sa'gya 120 28.55 N 88.05 E
Sagyndyk, mys ⟩ 84 44.02 N 50.52 E
Sah 150 15.38 N 4.03 W
Saḥāb 132 31.53 N 36.00 E
Sahaba 140 18.55 N 30.28 E
Sahagún, Col. 246 8.57 N 75.27 W
Sahagún, Esp. 34 42.22 N 5.02 W
Saḥam 132 32.42 N 35.47 E
Saḥam al-Jawlān 132 32.46 N 35.56 E
Sahana Ambodipont 157b 14.37 S 50.11 E
Sahand, Kūh-e ⋏ 128 37.44 N 46.27 E
Sahara ◆2 10 26.00 N 13.00 E
Sahāranpur 124 29.58 N 77.33 E
Sahara Occidental → Western Sahara □2 148 24.30 N 13.00 W
Sahara Occidentale → Western Sahara □2 148 24.30 N 13.00 W
Saharsa 124 25.53 N 86.36 E
Sahasinaka 157b 21.49 S 47.49 E
Sahasrail 126 23.19 N 89.43 E
Sahaswān 124 28.05 N 78.45 E
Şahbuz 84 39.25 N 45.34 E
Sahel → Sudan ◆1 134 10.00 N 20.00 E
Sahel, Canal du ≍ 150 13.44 N 6.05 W
Sahel, Oued ≃ 34 36.26 N 4.33 E
Sāhibabad 272a 28.40 N 77.22 E
Sāhibābād ◆8 272a 28.45 N 77.05 E
Sāhibganj 124 25.15 N 87.39 E
Sāhibi ≃ 124 28.29 N 76.44 E
Şahin 130 41.01 N 26.50 E
Sāhīwāl, Pāk. 123 30.40 N 73.06 E
Sāhīwāl, Pāk. 123 31.58 N 72.20 E
Sahlenburg 52 53.52 N 8.38 E
Şahneh 128 34.29 N 47.41 E
Sahrā', Bi'r ⊤4 140 22.52 N 28.37 E
Şahrajat al-Kubrā wa Kafr Jirjis Yūsuf 142 30.38 N 31.17 E
Sahtlam 224 48.48 N 123.54 W
Sahuaripa 232 29.03 N 109.14 W
Sahuarita 200 31.57 N 110.58 W
Sahuayo de José María Morelos 234 20.04 N 102.43 W
Sahul Shelf ◆4 14 12.30 S 125.00 E
Sahunivka 78 49.17 N 32.23 E
Sa Huynh 110 14.40 N 109.04 E
Şahwat al-Qamḥ 132 32.36 N 36.23 E
Šahy 30 48.05 N 18.57 E
Saï 150 13.50 N 5.00 W
Sai ≃, India 124 25.39 N 82.47 E
Sai ≃, Nihon 94 36.36 N 136.35 E
Sai ≃, Nihon 94 36.37 N 138.14 E
Saibai Island I 164 9.24 S 142.40 E
Sai Buri 110 6.42 N 101.37 E
Sai Buri ≃ 110 6.43 N 101.39 E
Saïda 148 34.50 N 0.09 E
Saïda □5 148 33.00 N 0.30 W
Saidābād, Bngl. 126 24.18 N 89.43 E
Sa'īdābād, Īrān 267d 35.40 N 51.11 E
Saidaiji 96 34.39 N 134.02 E
Saïdia 148 35.04 N 2.15 W
Sa'īdīyeh 128 36.26 N 48.48 E
Saido 268 35.52 N 139.41 E
Saidor 164 5.35 S 146.30 E
Saidpur, Bngl. 124 25.47 N 88.54 E
Saidpur, India 124 25.33 N 83.11 E
Saidu 123 34.45 N 72.21 E
Saigawa 96 33.39 N 130.57 E
Saignelégier 58 47.15 N 7.00 E
Saignon 62 43.52 N 5.26 E
Saigō 92 36.12 N 133.20 E
Saigon → Thanh Pho Ho Chi Minh 269c 10.45 N 106.40 E
Sai Gon ≃ 269c 10.45 N 106.45 E
Saihaku 96 35.20 N 133.20 E
Saihan Toroi 102 41.41 N 100.26 E
Saijō, Nihon 96 33.55 N 133.11 E
Saijō, Nihon 96 34.56 N 133.07 E
Saijō 96 34.48 N 132.51 E
Saikai-kokuritsu-kōen ♦ 92 33.12 N 129.22 E
Sai Keng 271d 22.26 N 114.16 E
Saiki 96 32.57 N 131.54 E
Saiki-wan c 96 33.00 N 131.58 E
Sai Kung 271d 22.23 N 114.15 E
Saileati 85 38.57 N 74.45 E
Sailkupa 126 23.41 N 89.15 E
Saillans 62 44.42 N 5.11 E
Sailly 261 49.02 N 1.48 E
Sailmouille, Ruisseau ≃ 261 48.37 N 2.17 E
Sailolof 164 1.15 S 130.46 E
Sailor Creek ≃ 202 42.56 N 115.29 W
Sail-sous-Couzan 62 45.44 N 3.57 E
Saim 86 60.21 N 64.14 E
Saima 98 41.00 N 124.14 E
Saimaa ◎ 26 61.15 N 28.15 E
Saimaa Canal ≍ 26 61.05 N 28.18 E
Saimbeyli 130 38.00 N 36.06 E
Saín Alto 234 23.35 N 103.15 W
Saindak 128 29.17 N 61.34 E
Sā'īn Dezh 128 36.40 N 46.33 E
Sainghin-en-Weppes 50 50.33 N 2.54 E
Sainjang 98 39.15 N 125.51 E
Sainō-ha'iji ⊥ 96 35.29 N 133.39 E
Sains-du-Nord 50 50.06 N 4.00 E
Sains-en-Gohelle 50 50.27 N 2.41 E
Sains-Richaumont 50 49.49 N 3.42 E
Saint Abb's Head ⟩ 46 55.54 N 2.09 W
Sainte-Adèle 206 45.57 N 74.07 W
Sainte-Adresse 50 49.30 N 0.05 E
Saint-Adrien 206 45.49 N 71.43 W
Saint-Affrique 32 43.57 N 2.53 E
Saint-Agapit 206 46.34 N 71.27 W
Saint Agatha 212 43.26 N 80.36 W
Sainte-Agathe, Mb., Can. 184 49.34 N 97.10 W
Sainte-Agathe, Fr. 62 45.49 N 3.37 E
Sainte-Agathe [-de-Lotbinière] 206 46.23 N 71.24 W
Sainte-Agathe-des-Monts 206 46.03 N 74.17 W
Sainte-Agnès, Fr. 62 43.48 N 7.28 E
Saint Agnes, Eng., U.K. 42 50.18 N 5.13 W
Saint Agnes I 42a 49.54 N 6.20 W
Saint-Agrève 62 45.01 N 4.24 E
Saint-Aignan 50 47.16 N 1.23 E
Saint-Aimé (Massueville) 206 45.55 N 72.56 W
Saint Albans, Austl. 169 37.44 S 144.48 E
Saint Albans, Austl. 170 33.17 S 150.59 E
Saint Alban's, Nf., Can. 186 47.52 N 55.51 W
Saint Albans, Eng., U.K. 42 51.46 N 0.21 W
Saint Albans, Mo., U.S. 219 38.35 N 90.46 W
Saint Albans, Vt., U.S. 188 44.48 N 73.05 W
Saint Albans, W.V., U.S. 188 38.23 N 81.50 W
Saint Albans □8 260 51.45 N 0.20 W
Saint Albans ◆8 276 40.42 N 73.46 W
Saint Albans, Cape ⟩ 168b 35.49 S 138.07 E
Saint Albans Cathedral ♥1 260 51.45 N 0.20 W
Saint Albert, Ab., Can. 182 53.38 N 113.38 W
Saint-Albert, P.Q., Can. 206 46.00 N 72.05 W
Saint Aldhelm's Head ⟩ 42 50.34 N 2.04 W
Saint-Alexandre-de-Kamouraska 186 47.41 N 69.38 W
Saint-Alexis-des-Monts 206 46.28 N 73.08 W
Saint-Amable 275a 45.39 N 73.18 W
Saint-Amand 56 48.49 N 4.36 E
Saint-Amand-en-Puisaye 50 47.31 N 3.04 E
Saint-Amand-les-Eaux 50 50.26 N 3.26 E
Saint-Amand-Longpré 50 47.41 N 1.01 E
Saint-Amand-Montrond 32 46.44 N 2.30 E
Saint-Amant-Roche-Savine 62 45.34 N 3.38 E
Saint-Amarin 58 47.53 N 7.01 E
Saint-Ambroix 62 44.15 N 4.11 E
Sainte-Amélie 184 50.59 N 99.21 W
Saint-Amour 58 46.26 N 5.21 E
Saint-André 157c 20.57 S 55.39 E
Saint-André, Cap ⟩ 157b 16.11 S 44.27 E
Saint-André, Ruisseau ≃ 275a 45.22 N 73.29 W
Saint-André-Avellin 206 45.43 N 75.03 W
Saint-André-de-l'Eure 50 48.54 N 1.17 E
Saint-André-de-Valborgne 62 44.09 N 3.41 E
St.-André-Est 206 45.34 N 74.20 W
Saint-André-les-Alpes 62 43.58 N 6.30 E
Saint-André-les-Vergers 50 48.17 N 4.03 E
Saint Andrew 241g 13.15 N 59.33 W
Saint Andrew, Mount ⋏ 241h 13.11 N 61.13 W
Saint Andrew Lakes ◎ 212 44.36 N 76.40 W
Saint Andrews, N.B., Can. 186 45.05 N 67.03 W
Saint Andrews, Scot., U.K. 46 56.20 N 2.48 W
Saint Andrews, S.C., U.S. 192 32.46 N 79.59 W
Saint Andrews Bay c 46 56.22 N 2.50 W
Saint Andrew's Cathedral ♥1 271c 1.18 N 103.51 E
Saint Andrews Channel ⩊ 186 46.03 N 60.38 W
Saint Ann 219 38.43 N 90.22 W
Sainte-Anne, Guad. 241o 16.14 N 61.23 W
Saint Anne, Guernsey 43b 49.42 N 2.12 W
Sainte-Anne, Mart. 240e 14.26 N 60.53 W
Saint Anne, Il., U.S. 216 41.01 N 87.42 W
Sainte-Anne ≃ 206 46.33 N 72.12 W
Saint Anne, Cathedral of ♥1 273b 4.18 S 15.19 E
Sainte Anne, Lac ◎, Ab., Can. 182 53.43 N 114.27 W
Sainte-Anne, Lac ◎, P.Q., Can. 186 50.05 N 67.50 W
Sainte-Anne-de-Beaupré 186 47.02 N 70.56 W
Sainte-Anne-de-Bellevue 275a 45.24 N 73.57 W
Sainte-Anne-de-la-Pérade 206 46.35 N 72.12 W
Sainte-Anne-de-Madawaska 186 47.15 N 68.02 W
Sainte-Anne-des-Chênes 184 49.40 N 96.40 W
Sainte-Anne-des-Monts 186 49.08 N 66.30 W
Sainte-Anne-des-Plaines 206 45.46 N 73.48 W
Saint Anne of the Congo ♥1 273b 4.16 S 15.17 E
Saint Anne's 44 53.45 N 3.02 W
Saint Ann's Bay 241q 18.26 N 77.08 W
Saint Anns Bay c 186 46.20 N 60.30 W
Saint Ann's Head ⟩ 42 51.41 N 5.10 W
Saint-Anselme 186 46.37 N 70.58 W
Saint Ansgar 190 43.22 N 92.55 W
Saint-Anthème 62 45.31 N 3.55 E
Saint Anthony, N.B., Can. 186 46.22 N 64.45 W
Saint Anthony, Nf., Can. 186 51.22 N 55.35 W
Saint Anthony, Id., U.S. 202 43.57 N 111.40 W
Saint-Antoine, P.Q., Can. 206 45.46 N 73.59 W
Saint-Antoine, Fr. 62 45.10 N 5.13 E
Saint-Antonin 32 44.09 N 1.45 E
Saint-Apollinaire (Francoeur) 206 46.37 N 71.31 W
Saint Arnaud, Austl. 166 36.37 S 143.15 E
Saint Arnaud, N.Z. 172 41.48 S 172.50 E
Saint-Arnoult, Forêt de ♦ 261 48.35 N 1.55 E
Saint-Arnoult-en-Yvelines 50 48.34 N 1.56 E
Saint Arvans 42 51.40 N 2.41 W
Saint Asaph 44 53.16 N 3.26 W
Saint-Astier 32 45.09 N 0.32 E
Saint Athan 42 51.24 N 3.25 W
Saint-Auban 62 43.51 N 6.44 E
Saint-Aubert, Mont ⋏2 50 50.39 N 3.24 E
Saint Aubert Island I 219 38.40 N 91.52 W
Saint-Aubin, Fr. 50 49.53 N 0.53 E
Saint-Aubin, Fr. 58 47.02 N 5.20 E
Saint Aubin, Jersey 43b 49.11 N 2.10 W
Saint-Aubin, Schw. 58 46.54 N 6.47 E
Saint-Aubin-lès-Elbeuf 50 49.18 N 1.01 E
Saint-Aubin-sur-Aire 58 48.42 N 5.27 E
Saint-Augustin 157b 23.33 S 43.46 E
Saint-Augustin ≃ 176 51.14 N 58.41 W
Saint-Augustin-Deux-Montagnes 275a 45.38 N 73.59 W
Saint Augustine 192 29.53 N 81.18 W
Saint-Augustin Nord-Ouest ≃ 186 51.16 N 58.42 W
Saint-Augustin-Saguenay 186 51.14 N 58.39 W
Saint-Aulaye 32 45.12 N 0.08 E
Saint Austell 42 50.20 N 4.48 W
Saint-Avertin 50 47.22 N 0.44 E
Saint-Avold 56 49.06 N 6.42 E
Saint-Ay 50 47.51 N 1.45 E
Saint-Aygulf 62 43.23 N 6.44 E
Saint Barbe 186 51.12 N 56.46 W
Saint Barnabas Chapel ♥1 174c 29.02 S 167.55 E
Saint-Barthélemy I 238 17.54 N 62.50 W
Saint-Basile 186 47.21 N 68.14 W
Saint-Basile-de-Portneuf 206 46.45 N 71.49 W
Saint-Basile-le-Grand 206 45.32 N 73.17 W
Saint Bathans, Mount ⋏ 172 44.44 S 169.46 E
Sainte-Baume, Chaîne de la ⋏ 62 43.20 N 5.45 E
Saint-Béat 32 42.55 N 0.42 E
Saint Bees 44 54.30 N 3.37 W
Saint Bees Head ⟩ 44 54.32 N 3.38 W
Saint Benedict 214 40.38 N 78.44 W
Saint-Benoît, Fr. 261 48.40 N 1.55 E
Saint-Benoît, Réu. 157c 21.02 S 55.43 E
Saint-Benoît-du-Sault 32 46.27 N 1.23 E
Saint-Benoît-en-Woëvre 56 48.59 N 5.47 E
Saint Bernard 218 39.10 N 84.29 W
Saint-Bernard, Île I 275a 45.23 N 73.45 W
Saint-Bernard-de-Dorchester 206 46.30 N 71.08 W
Saint-Béron 62 45.30 N 5.43 E
Saint-Blaise, P.Q., Can. 206 45.13 N 73.17 W
Saint-Blaise, Schw. 58 47.01 N 6.59 E
Saint-Blaise-la-Roche 58 48.24 N 7.10 E
Saint Blaize, Cape ⟩ 158 34.11 S 22.10 E
Saint Blazey 42 50.22 N 4.43 W
Saint-Blin 58 48.16 N 5.25 E
Saint-Bonaventure, P.Q., Can. 206 45.58 N 72.41 W
Saint Bonaventure, N.Y., U.S. 210 42.05 N 78.28 W
Saint-Boniface-de-Shawinigan 206 46.30 N 72.49 W
Saint-Bonnet 62 44.41 N 6.05 E
Saint-Bonnet-de-Joux 58 46.29 N 4.27 E
Saint-Bonnet-le-Château 62 45.25 N 4.04 E
Saint-Bonnet-le-Froid 62 45.09 N 4.27 E
Saint Boswells 46 55.34 N 2.39 W
Saint Brendan's 186 48.52 N 53.40 W
Saint-Brice-sous-Forêt 261 49.00 N 2.21 E
Saint Bride, Mount ⋏ 182 51.30 N 115.57 W
Saint Bride's 186 46.55 N 54.10 W
Saint Brides Bay c 42 51.48 N 5.15 W
Saint Bride's Major 42 51.28 N 3.38 W
Saint-Brieuc 32 48.31 N 2.47 W
Saint-Brieux 184 52.38 N 104.52 W
Saint-Broing-les-Moines 58 47.41 N 4.50 E
Saint-Bruno 206 45.32 N 73.21 W
Saint-Bruno, Mont ⋏2 275a 45.33 N 73.19 W
Saint-Calais 50 47.55 N 0.45 E
Saint-Calixte-de-Kilkenny 206 45.57 N 73.51 W
Saint-Cannat 62 43.37 N 5.18 E
Saint-Casimir 206 46.40 N 72.08 W
Saint-Cassien, Lac de ◎1 62 43.35 N 6.48 E
Saint Catharines 212 43.10 N 79.15 W
Saint Catharines Airport ⊗ 284a 43.11 N 79.10 W
Saint Catherine 220 28.37 N 82.08 W
Saint Catherine, Monastery of → Qiddīsah Kātrīnā, Dayr al- ♥1 140 28.29 N 34.01 E
Saint Catherine, Mount ⋏ 241k 12.10 N 61.40 W
Sainte-Catherine-de-Fierbois 50 47.09 N 0.39 E
Saint Catherines Island I 192 31.38 N 81.10 W
Saint Catherine's Point ⟩ 42 50.34 N 1.15 W
Saint-Célestin (Annaville) 206 46.13 N 72.26 W
Saint-Céré 32 44.52 N 1.53 E
Saint-Cergue 58 46.27 N 6.09 E
Saint-Césaire 206 45.25 N 73.00 W
Saint-Cézaire-sur-Siagne 62 43.39 N 6.48 E
Saint-Chamas 62 43.33 N 5.02 E
Saint-Chamond 62 45.28 N 4.30 E
Saint-Chaptes 62 43.58 N 4.17 E
Saint Charles, Ar., U.S. 194 34.22 N 91.08 W
Saint Charles, Id., U.S. 202 42.06 N 111.23 W
Saint Charles, Il., U.S. 216 41.54 N 88.18 W
Saint Charles, Md., U.S. 208 38.36 N 76.56 W
Saint Charles, Mi., U.S. 190 43.17 N 84.08 W
Saint Charles, Mn., U.S. 190 43.58 N 92.03 W
Saint Charles, Mo., U.S. 219 38.47 N 90.28 W
Saint Charles □6 219 38.47 N 90.43 W
Saint-Charles ≃ 275a 45.40 N 73.27 W
Saint-Charles, Lac ◎ 206 46.55 N 71.23 W
Saint-Charles-de-Drummond 206 45.54 N 72.28 W
Saint Charles Mesa 198 38.15 N 104.32 W
Saint-Charles-sur-Richelieu 206 45.41 N 73.11 W
Saint-Chef 62 45.38 N 5.22 E
Saint-Chély-d'Apcher 32 44.48 N 3.17 E
Saint-Chéron 261 48.33 N 2.07 E
Saint-Christophe-en-Bazelle 50 47.11 N 1.43 E
Saint-Christophe-Nevis → Saint Kitts and Nevis □1 238 17.20 N 62.45 W
Saint Christopher (Saint Kitts) I 238 17.20 N 62.45 W
Saint Christopher-Nevis → Saint Kitts and Nevis □1 238 17.20 N 62.45 W
Saint-Chrysostome 206 45.06 N 73.46 W
Saint-Ciers-sur-Gironde 32 45.18 N 0.37 W
Saint Clair, Mi., U.S. 214 42.48 N 82.29 W
Saint Clair, Mo., U.S. 219 38.20 N 90.58 W
Saint Clair, Pa., U.S. 208 40.43 N 76.11 W
Saint Clair, Pa., U.S. 279b 40.16 N 79.33 W
Saint Clair □6, Il., U.S. 219 38.31 N 90.00 W
Saint Clair □6, Mi., U.S. 214 42.50 N 82.42 W
Saint Clair ≃ 214 42.37 N 82.31 W
Saint Clair, Lake ◎ 214 42.25 N 82.41 W
Saint Clair Beach 281 42.19 N 82.51 W
Saint Clair Flats 214 42.32 N 82.37 W
Saint Clair Flats ≚ 281 42.35 N 82.36 W
Saint Clair Flats Canal ≍ 214 42.20 N 82.58 W
Saint Clair Flats State Wildlife Area ◆4 281 42.36 N 82.40 W
Saint Clair Haven 214 42.34 N 82.47 W
Saint Clair Shores 214 42.29 N 82.53 W
Saint-Clair-sur-Epte 50 49.12 N 1.41 E
Saint Clairsville, Oh., U.S. 214 40.04 N 80.54 W
Saint Clairsville, Pa., U.S. 214 40.09 N 78.31 W
Saint Clair Tunnel ◆5 214 42.57 N 82.25 W
Saint-Claud 32 45.53 N 0.23 E
Saint-Claude, Mb., Can. 184 49.40 N 98.22 W
Saint-Claude, Fr. 58 46.23 N 5.52 E
Saint-Claude, Guad. 241o 16.02 N 61.42 W
Saint-Claude, Ruisseau ≃ 275a 45.25 N 73.28 W
Saint Clears 42 51.50 N 4.30 W
Saint-Clément 58 48.32 N 6.36 E
Saint Clements 212 43.31 N 80.39 W
Saint Clements Bay c 208 38.17 N 76.42 W
Sainte-Clothilde 206 45.59 N 72.14 W
Sainte-Clotilde-de-Châteauguay 206 45.10 N 73.41 W
Saint-Cloud, Fr. 50 48.50 N 2.11 E
Saint Cloud, Fl., U.S. 220 28.14 N 81.16 W
Saint Cloud, Mn., U.S. 190 45.33 N 94.09 W
Saint-Cloud, Parc de ♦ 261 48.50 N 2.13 E
Saint-Colomban-des-Villards 62 45.18 N 6.14 E
Sainte-Colombe 58 47.52 N 4.32 E
Saint Columb Major 42 50.26 N 4.56 W
Saint Combs 46 57.39 N 1.54 W
Saint Constant 206 45.22 N 73.37 W
Saint-Cosme-en-Vairais 50 48.16 N 0.28 E
Sainte-Croix, P.Q., Can. 206 46.38 N 71.44 W
Sainte-Croix, Schw. 58 46.49 N 6.31 E
Saint Croix I 241n 17.45 N 64.45 W
Saint Croix ≃, N.A. 186 45.10 N 67.10 W
Saint Croix ≃, U.S. 190 44.45 N 92.49 W
Sainte-Croix, Barrage de ◆6 62 43.45 N 6.08 E
Sainte-Croix-aux-Mines 58 48.16 N 7.13 E
Saint Croix Falls 190 45.24 N 92.38 W
Saint Croix Island I 158 33.48 S 25.45 E
Saint Croix Island National Monument ♦ 188 45.08 N 67.08 W
Saint Croix National Scenic Riverway ♦ 190 46.00 N 92.25 W
Saint Croix State Park ♦ 190 46.00 N 92.40 W
Sainte-Croix-Vallée-Francaise 62 44.11 N 3.44 E
Saint-Cuthbert 206 46.09 N 73.14 W
Saint-Cyprien 32 44.52 N 1.02 E
Saint-Cyrille-de-Wendover 206 45.56 N 72.26 W
Saint-Cyr-l'École 261 48.48 N 2.04 E
Saint-Cyr-l'École, Aérodrome de ⊗ 261 48.49 N 2.04 E
Saint Cyr Range ⋏ 180 61.10 N 131.10 W
Saint-Cyr-sous-Dourdan 261 48.34 N 2.02 E
Saint-Cyr-sur-Loire 50 47.24 N 0.40 E
Saint-Cyr-sur-Mer 62 43.11 N 5.42 E
Saint-Dalmas-de-Tende 62 44.03 N 7.35 E
Saint-Damien-de-Brandon 206 46.20 N 73.29 W
Saint David, Az., U.S. 200 31.54 N 110.12 W
Saint David, Il., U.S. 190 40.29 N 90.02 W
Saint David's, Nf., Can. 186 48.12 N 58.52 W
Saint Davids, On., Can. 284a 43.10 N 79.06 W
Saint David's, Wales, U.K. 42 51.54 N 5.16 W
Saint Davids, Pa., U.S. 285 40.02 N 75.22 W
Saint David's Cathedral ♥1 42 51.54 N 5.16 W
Saint David's Head ⟩ 42 51.55 N 5.19 W
Saint David's Island I 240a 32.22 N 64.39 W
Saint Day 42 50.14 N 5.11 W
Saint-Denis, Fr. 50 48.56 N 2.22 E
Saint-Denis, Réu. 157c 20.52 S 55.28 E
Saint-Denis, Basilique ♥1 261 48.56 N 2.22 E
Saint-Denis-de-l'Hôtel 50 47.52 N 2.07 E
Saint-Denis-en-Bugey 58 45.57 N 5.20 E
Saint-Denis-Rivière-Richelieu 206 45.47 N 73.09 W
Saint Dennis 42 50.23 N 4.53 W
Saint-Didier-en-Velay 62 45.18 N 4.17 E
Saint-Didier-les-Bains 62 44.00 N 5.07 E
Saint-Dié 58 48.17 N 6.57 E
Saint-Disdier 62 44.44 N 5.54 E
Saint-Dizier 58 48.38 N 4.57 E
Saint Dogmaels 42 52.05 N 4.40 W
Saint-Donat-de-Montcalm 206 46.19 N 74.13 W
Saint-Donat-sur-l'Herbasse 62 45.07 N 5.00 E
Sainte-Dorothée ◆8 275a 45.32 N 73.49 W
Saint-Dyé-sur-Loire 50 47.39 N 1.29 E
Saint-Édouard-de-Maskinongé 206 46.20 N 73.09 W
Saint Edward 198 41.34 N 97.52 W
Saint-Égrève 62 45.14 N 5.41 E
Saint Eleanor's 186 46.25 N 63.49 W
Saint Elias, Cape ⟩ 180 59.52 N 144.30 W
Saint Elias, Mount ⋏ 180 60.18 N 140.55 W
Saint Elias Mountains ⋏ 180 60.30 N 139.30 W
Saint-Élie 250 4.50 N 53.17 W
Saint Elmo 219 39.01 N 88.50 W
Saint-Éloi 186 48.02 N 69.14 W
Saint-Émile-de-Montcalm 206 46.06 N 74.00 W
Saint-Émile-de-Québec 206 46.52 N 71.20 W
Saint-Émile-de-Suffolk 206 45.56 N 74.55 W
Sainte-Enimie 32 44.22 N 3.26 E
Saint-Épain 50 47.08 N 0.32 E
Saint-Esprit ≃ 206 45.52 N 73.27 W
Saint-Étienne 62 45.26 N 4.24 E
Saint-Étienne-de-Lugdarès 62 44.39 N 3.57 E
Saint-Étienne-de-Saint-Geoirs 62 45.20 N 5.21 E
Saint-Étienne-des-Grès 206 46.26 N 72.46 W
Saint-Étienne-de-Tinée 62 44.15 N 6.55 E
Saint-Étienne-du-Rouvray 50 49.23 N 1.06 E
Saint-Étienne-en-Dévoluy 62 44.42 N 5.56 E
Saint-Étienne-le-Laus 62 44.30 N 6.10 E
Saint-Étienne-les-Orgues 62 44.03 N 5.47 E
Saint-Étienne-lès-Remiremont 58 48.02 N 6.37 E
Saint-Eugène 206 45.30 N 74.28 W
Saint-Eustache 206 45.34 N 73.54 W
Saint-Evroult-Notre-Dame-du-Bois 50 48.48 N 0.28 E
Saint-Fabien 186 48.18 N 68.52 W
Saint Faith's 158 30.30 S 30.12 E
Saint-Fargeau 50 47.38 N 3.04 E
Saint-Fargeau-Ponthierry 261 48.33 N 2.32 E
Saint-Félicien, P.Q., Can. 176 48.39 N 72.26 W
Saint-Félicien, Fr. 62 45.05 N 4.38 E
Sainte-Félicité 186 48.54 N 67.20 W
Saint-Félix 62 45.48 N 5.58 E
Saint-Félix-de-Kingsey 206 45.48 N 72.12 W
Saint-Félix-de-Valois 206 46.10 N 73.26 W
Saint-Ferdinand (Bernierville) 206 46.06 N 71.34 W
Saintfield 48 54.28 N 5.50 W
Saint Fillans 46 56.23 N 4.07 W
Saint-Firmin 62 44.47 N 6.02 E
Saint-Firmin-sur-Loire 50 47.37 N 2.44 E
Saint-Flavien 206 46.31 N 71.36 W
Saint-Florent 36 42.41 N 9.18 E
Saint-Florentin 50 48.00 N 3.44 E
Saint-Florent-sur-Cher 32 46.59 N 2.15 E
Saint-Floris, Parc National ♦ 146 9.40 N 21.35 E
Saint-Flour 32 45.02 N 3.05 E
Saint-Fons 62 45.42 N 4.52 E
Saint-Fortunat 206 45.58 N 71.36 W
Sainte-Foy 206 46.47 N 71.17 W
Sainte-Foy-la-Grande 32 44.50 N 0.13 E
Sainte-Foy-l'Argentière 62 45.42 N 4.28 E
Sainte-Foy-lès-Lyon 62 45.44 N 4.48 E
Saint-François 62 45.35 N 6.53 E
Saint Francis, Ks., U.S. 198 39.46 N 101.47 W
Saint Francis, S.D., U.S. 198 43.08 N 100.54 W
Saint Francis, Wi., U.S. 216 42.58 N 87.52 W
Saint Francis ≃, N.A. 186 47.10 N 68.57 W
Saint Francis ≃, U.S. 194 34.38 N 90.35 W
Saint Francis, Cape ⟩, Nf., Can. 186 47.50 N 52.47 W
Saint Francis, Cape ⟩, S. Afr. 158 34.14 S 24.49 E
Saint Francis, Lake ◎ 206 45.08 N 74.25 W
Saint Francis Bay c 158 34.05 S 25.10 E
Saint Francisville 194 30.46 N 91.22 W
Saint-François 241o 16.15 N 61.17 W
Saint-François ≃ 206 46.07 N 72.55 W
Saint-François, Lac ◎ 206 45.55 N 71.10 W
Saint-François de Boundji 152 1.03 S 15.22 E
Saint-François-de-Laval ◆8 275a 45.40 N 73.34 W
Saint-François-du-Lac 206 46.04 N 72.50 W
Saint Francois Mountains ⋏ 194 37.30 N 90.35 W
Saint-François-sur-Bugeon 62 45.24 N 6.21 E
Saint-Front 62 44.59 N 4.08 E
Saint-Gabriel 206 46.17 N 73.23 W
Saint-Gabriel-de-Gaspé 186 48.31 N 64.32 W
Saint-Gabriel-de-Rimouski 186 48.25 N 68.10 W
Saint-Gall → Sankt Gallen 58 47.25 N 9.23 E
Saint-Galmier 62 45.35 N 4.19 E
Sainte-Gauburge-Sainte-Colombe 50 48.42 N 0.26 E
Saint-Gaudens 32 43.07 N 0.44 E
Saint-Gaudens National Historic Site ⊥ 188 43.29 N 72.19 W
Saint-Gaultier 32 46.38 N 1.25 E
Saint-Gély-du-Fesc 62 43.42 N 3.48 E
Saint-Genest-Lerpt 62 45.27 N 4.20 E
Saint-Genest-Malifaux 62 45.20 N 4.25 E
Sainte-Geneviève, P.Q., Can. 275a 45.29 N 73.52 W
Sainte Genevieve, Mo., U.S. 194 37.59 N 90.03 W
Sainte-Geneviève-de-Batiscan 206 46.32 N 72.20 W
Sainte-Geneviève-des-Bois 50 48.38 N 2.20 E
Saint-Gengoux-le-National 58 46.37 N 4.39 E
Saint-Genis-de-Saintonge 32 45.29 N 0.34 W
Saint-Genis-Laval 62 45.41 N 4.48 E
Saint-Genis-Pouilly 58 46.15 N 6.01 E
Saint-Genix-sur-Guiers 62 45.36 N 5.38 E
Saint-Geoire-en-Valdaine 62 45.27 N 5.38 E
Saint George, Austl. 166 28.02 S 148.35 E
Saint George, Ber. 240a 32.22 N 64.40 W
Saint George, N.B., Can. 186 45.08 N 66.49 W
Saint George, On., Can. 212 43.15 N 80.15 W
Saint George, Pa., U.S. 214 41.15 N 79.47 W
Saint George, S.C., U.S. 192 33.11 N 80.34 W
Saint George, Ut., U.S. 200 37.06 N 113.34 W
Saint George ◆8 276 40.39 N 74.05 W
Saint George, Cape ⟩, Nf., Can. 186 48.27 N 59.15 W
Saint George, Cape ⟩, Pap. N. Gui. 164 4.52 S 152.52 E
Saint George, Cape ⟩, Fl., U.S. 192 29.35 N 85.04 W
Saint George, Point ⟩ 204 41.47 N 124.15 W
Saint George Island, Ak., U.S. 180 56.36 N 169.32 W
Saint George Island, Md., U.S. 208 38.07 N 76.29 W
Saint George Island I, Ak., U.S. 180 56.35 N 169.35 W
Saint George Island I, Fl., U.S. 192 29.39 N 84.55 W
Saint George's, Nf., Can. 186 48.26 N 58.29 W
Saint-Georges, P.Q., Can. 188 46.07 N 70.40 W
Saint-Georges, P.Q., Can. 206 46.37 N 72.40 W
Saint-Georges, Fr. 58 48.40 N 6.56 E
Saint George's, Gren. 241k 12.03 N 61.45 W
Saint-Georges, Guy. fr. 250 3.54 N 51.48 W
Saint Georges, De., U.S. 208 39.33 N 75.39 W
Saint Georges Basin c 170 35.07 S 150.36 E
Saint George's Bay c, Nf., Can. 186 48.20 N 59.00 W
Saint Georges Bay c, N.S., Can. 186 45.50 N 61.45 W
Saint George's Channel ⩊, Europe 28 52.00 N 6.00 W
Saint George's Channel ⩊, Pap. N. Gui. 164 4.30 S 152.30 E
Saint-Georges-de-Reneins 58 46.04 N 4.43 E
Saint-Georges-de-Windsor 206 45.42 N 71.50 W
Saint-Georges-en-Couzan 62 45.42 N 3.56 E
Saint Georges Head ⟩ 170 35.12 S 150.42 E
Saint George's Island I 240a 32.22 N 64.40 W
Saint George Sound ⩊ 192 29.47 N 84.42 W
Saint-Gérard, Bel. 56 50.21 N 4.45 E
Saint-Gérard, P.Q., Can. 206 45.46 N 71.25 W
Saint-Germain ≃ 206 45.55 N 72.30 W
Saint-Germain, Forêt de ♦ 261 48.55 N 2.05 E
Saint-Germain-de-Calberte 62 44.13 N 3.48 E
Saint-Germain-de-Grantham 206 45.50 N 72.34 W
Saint-Germain-de-Joux 58 46.11 N 5.44 E
Saint-Germain-des-Champs 50 47.25 N 3.55 E
Saint-Germain-du-Bois 58 46.45 N 5.15 E
Saint-Germain-du-Plain 58 46.42 N 4.58 E
Saint-Germain-en-Laye 50 48.54 N 2.05 E
Saint-Germain-en-Laye, Château de ⊥ 261 48.54 N 2.06 E
Saint-Germain-Laval 62 45.50 N 4.01 E
Saint-Germain-Laxis 261 48.35 N 2.43 E
Saint-Germain-Lembron 32 45.28 N 3.14 E
Saint-Germain-lès-Arlay 58 46.46 N 5.34 E
Saint-Germain-lès-Corbeil 261 48.37 N 2.29 E
Saint-Germain-l'Herm 32 45.28 N 3.33 E
Saint-Germain-sur-Morin 261 48.53 N 2.51 E
Saint Germans 42 50.24 N 4.18 W
Saint-Germer-de-Fly 50 49.27 N 1.47 E
Saint-Gervais-d'Auvergne 32 46.02 N 2.49 E
Saint-Gervais-les-Bains 62 45.54 N 6.43 E
Saint-Gervasy 62 43.53 N 4.29 E
Saint-Géry 32 44.29 N 1.35 E
Saint-Gilles, Bel. 50 50.49 N 4.20 E
Saint-Gilles, P.Q., Can. 206 46.31 N 71.22 W
Saint-Gilles, Fr. 62 43.41 N 4.26 E
Saint-Gilles-Croix-de-Vie 32 46.42 N 1.57 W
Saint-Gingolph 58 46.24 N 6.52 E
Saint-Girons 32 42.59 N 1.09 E
Saint-Gobain 50 49.36 N 3.23 E
Saint Gotthard Pass → San Gottardo, Passo del ⩉ 58 46.33 N 8.34 E
Saint Govan's Head ⟩ 42 51.36 N 4.55 W
Saint-Gratien 261 48.58 N 2.17 E
Saint-Grégoire (Larochelle) 206 46.16 N 72.30 W
Saint Gregory, Mount ⋏ 186 49.19 N 58.13 W
Saint-Guénolé 32 47.49 N 4.20 W
Saint-Guillaume-d'Upton 206 45.53 N 72.46 W
Saint-Héand 62 45.31 N 4.22 E
Saint Helena 226 38.30 N 122.28 W
Saint Helena □2 10 15.57 S 5.42 W
Saint Helena, Mount ⋏ 226 38.40 N 122.38 W
Saint Helena Sound ⩊ 192 32.27 N 80.25 W
Sainte-Hélène, Île I 275a 45.31 N 73.32 W
Sainte-Hélène-de-Bagot 206 45.44 N 72.44 W
Saint Helens, Austl. 166 41.20 S 148.15 E
Saint Helens, Eng., U.K. 42 50.42 N 1.06 W
Saint Helens, Eng., U.K. 44 53.28 N 2.44 W
Saint Helens, Or., U.S. 224 45.51 N 122.48 W
Saint Helens □8 262 53.28 N 2.45 W

≃	River	Fluß	Río	Rivière	Rio
≍	Canal	Kanal	Canal	Canal	Canal
⌊	Waterfall, Rapids	Wasserfall, Stromschnellen	Cascada, Rápidos	Chute d'eau, Rapides	Cascata, Rápidos
⩊	Strait	Meeresstraße	Estrecho	Détroit	Estreito
c	Bay, Gulf	Bucht, Golf	Bahía, Golfo	Baie, Golfe	Baía, Golfo
◎	Lake, Lakes	See, Seen	Lago, Lagos	Lac, Lacs	Lago, Lagos
⩸	Swamp	Sumpf	Pantano	Marais	Pântano
⊟	Ice Features, Glacier	Eis- und Gletscherformen	Accidentes Glaciales	Formes glaciaires	Acidentes glaciares
⊤	Other Hydrographic Features	Andere Hydrographische Objekte	Otros Elementos Hidrográficos	Autres données hydrographiques	Outros acidentes hidrográficos

◆	Submarine Features	Untermeerische Objekte	Accidentes Submarinos	Formes de relief sous-marin	Acidentes submarinos
□	Political Unit	Politische Einheit	Unidad Política	Entité politique	Unidade política
♥	Cultural Institution	Kulturelle Institution	Institución Cultural	Institution culturelle	Instituição cultural
⊥	Historical Site	Historische Stätte	Sitio Histórico	Site historique	Sitio histórico
♦	Recreational Site	Erholungs- und Ferienort	Sitio de Recreo	Centre de loisirs	Area de Lazer
⊗	Airport	Flughafen	Aeropuerto	Aéroport	Aeroporto
■	Military Installation	Militäranlage	Instalación Militar	Installation militaire	Instalação militar
◆	Miscellaneous	Verschiedenes	Misceláneo	Divers	Diversos

Name	Page	Lat.°′	Long.°′
Saint Helens, Mount ∧[1]	224	46.12 N	122.11 W
Saint Helens Canal ≍	262	53.27 N	2.42 W
Saint Helier	43b	49.11 N	2.06 W
Saint Henry	216	40.25 N	84.38 W
Sainte-Hermine	32	46.33 N	1.04 W
Saint-Hilaire-du-Harcouët	32	48.35 N	1.06 W
Saint-Hilarion	261	48.37 N	1.44 E
Saint-Hippolyte, Fr.	58	47.19 N	6.49 E
Saint-Hippolyte, Fr.	62	43.38 N	4.45 E
Saint-Hippolyte-de-Kilkenny	206	45.56 N	74.01 W
Saint-Hippolyte-du-Fort	62	43.58 N	3.51 E
Saint-Honorat, Mont ∧	62	44.05 N	6.46 E
Saint-Hubert, Bel.	56	50.01 N	5.23 E
Saint-Hubert, P.Q., Can.	206	45.30 N	73.25 W
Saint-Hubert, Étang de ⊜	261	48.43 N	1.51 E
Saint-Hubert-le-Roi	261	48.43 N	1.52 E
Saint-Hugues	206	45.48 N	72.52 W
Saint-Hyacinthe	206	45.37 N	72.57 W
Saint-Hyacinthe □[6]	206	45.40 N	73.05 W
Saint-Ignace, N.B., Can.	186	46.42 N	65.05 W
Saint Ignace, Mi., U.S.	190	45.52 N	84.43 W
Saint Ignace Island I	190	48.48 N	87.55 W
Saint Ignatius, Guy.	246	3.20 N	59.47 W
Saint Ignatius, Mt., U.S.	202	47.19 N	114.05 W
Saint-Imier	58	47.09 N	7.00 E
Saint-Imier, Vallon de V	58	47.10 N	7.00 E
Saint-Isidore	186	47.33 N	65.03 W
Saint-Isidore-d'Auckland	206	45.16 N	71.31 W
Saint-Isidore-de-Laprairie	275a	45.18 N	73.41 W
Saint Ives, Austl.	274a	33.44 S	151.10 E
Saint Ives, Eng., U.K.	32	50.12 N	5.29 W
Saint Ives, Eng., U.K.	42	52.20 N	0.05 W
Saint Ives Bay c	42	50.14 N	5.28 W
Saint Jacob	219	38.43 N	89.46 W
Saint Jacobs	212	43.32 N	80.33 W
Saint-Jacques	206	45.57 N	73.34 W
Saint-Jacques ≃	275a	45.26 N	73.29 W
Saint James, Il., U.S.	219	38.57 N	88.51 W
Saint James, Mi., U.S.	190	45.45 N	85.30 W
Saint James, Mn., U.S.	198	43.58 N	94.37 W
Saint James, Mo., U.S.	194	37.59 N	91.36 W
Saint James, N.Y., U.S.	210	40.52 N	73.09 W
Saint James, Cape ›	182	51.56 N	131.01 W
Saint James City	220	26.29 N	82.04 W
Saint James Islands II	240m	18.19 N	64.50 W
Saint-Janvier	275a	45.43 N	73.56 W
Saint-Jean □[6]	206	45.15 N	73.20 W
Saint-Jean ≃, P.Q., Can.	186	48.46 N	64.26 W
Saint-Jean ≃, P.Q., Can.	186	50.17 N	64.20 W
Saint-Jean, Île I	275a	45.41 N	73.39 W
Saint-Jean, Lac ⊜	176	48.35 N	72.05 W
Saint-Jean, Rapides de ⌊	275a	45.19 N	73.15 W
Saint-Jean Airport ⊠	275a	45.18 N	73.17 W
Saint-Jean-aux-Bois	50	49.21 N	2.55 E
Saint-Jean-Baptiste	184	49.16 N	97.21 W
Saint-Jean-Baptiste-de-Rouville	206	45.31 N	73.07 W
Saint-Jean-Cap-Ferrat	62	43.41 N	7.20 E
Saint-Jean-d'Angély	32	45.57 N	0.31 W
Saint-Jean-d'Assé	50	48.09 N	0.07 E
Saint-Jean-de-Bournay	62	45.29 N	5.08 E
Saint-Jean-de-Braye	50	47.54 N	1.58 E
Saint-Jean-de-la-Roulle	50	47.55 N	1.52 E
Saint-Jean-de-Losne	58	47.06 N	5.15 E
Saint-Jean-de-Luz	32	43.23 N	1.40 W
Saint-Jean-de-Maurienne	62	45.17 N	6.21 E
Saint-Jean-de-Monts	32	46.48 N	2.03 W
Saint-Jean-des-Piles	206	46.41 N	72.45 W
Saint-Jean-du-Gard	62	44.06 N	3.53 E
Saint-Jean-en-Royans	62	45.01 N	5.18 E
Saint-Jean-Pied-de-Port	32	43.10 N	1.14 W
Saint-Jean-Port-Joli	186	47.13 N	70.16 W
Saint-Jean-Soleymieux	62	45.30 N	4.02 E
Saint-Jean-sur-Richelieu	206	45.19 N	73.16 W
Saint-Jeoire	58	46.09 N	6.28 E
Saint-Jérôme	206	45.47 N	74.00 W
Saint Jo	196	33.41 N	97.31 W
Saint Joachim	214	42.16 N	82.38 W
Saint Joe	216	41.18 N	84.54 W
Saint Joe ≃	202	47.21 N	116.42 W
Saint John, N.B., Can.	186	45.16 N	66.03 W
Saint John, Jersey	43b	49.15 N	2.08 W
Saint John, In., U.S.	216	41.27 N	87.28 W
Saint John, Ks., U.S.	198	38.00 N	98.45 W
Saint John, N.D., U.S.	198	48.56 N	99.42 W
Saint John, Wa., U.S.	202	47.05 N	117.34 W
Saint John I	240m	18.20 N	64.45 W
Saint John ≃, Liber.	150	6.40 N	9.10 W
Saint John ≃, N.A.	186	45.15 N	66.04 W
Saint John, Cape ›	186	50.00 N	55.32 W
Saint John, Lake ⊜, Nf., Can.	186	48.23 N	54.41 W
Saint John, Lake ⊜, On., Can.	212	44.41 N	79.20 W
Saint John Bay c	186	50.54 N	57.08 W
Saint John Island I	186	50.49 N	57.14 W
Saint John's, Antig.	240c	17.06 N	61.51 W
Saint John's, Nf., Can.	186	47.34 N	52.43 W
Saint Johns → Saint-Jean-sur-Richelieu, P.Q., Can.	206	45.19 N	73.16 W
Saint John's, I. of Man	44	54.13 N	4.38 W
Saint Johns, Az., U.S.	200	34.30 N	109.21 W
Saint Johns, Mi., U.S.	216	43.00 N	84.33 W
Saint Johns, Mo., U.S.	219	38.42 N	90.20 W
Saint Johns, Oh., U.S.	216	40.33 N	84.05 W
Saint Johns ≃, Ca., U.S.	226	36.25 N	119.25 W
Saint Johns ≃, Fl., U.S.	192	30.24 N	81.24 W
Saint Johnsburg	210	43.05 N	78.53 W
Saint Johnsbury	188	44.25 N	72.00 W
Saint Johns Creek ≃	219	38.34 N	91.01 W
Saint John's Jerusalem ⊥	260	51.25 N	0.14 E
Saint Johns Marsh ≋	220	27.45 N	80.40 W
Saint John's Point ›	48	54.13 N	5.40 W
Saint John's University ⊕[2]	276	40.43 N	73.48 W
Saint Johnsville	210	42.59 N	74.41 W
Saint Joseph, N.B., Can.	186	45.59 N	64.34 W
Saint Joseph, Dom.	240d	15.26 N	61.26 W
Saint-Joseph, Mart.	240e	14.40 N	61.03 W
Saint-Joseph, N. Cal.	175f	20.27 S	166.36 E
Saint-Joseph, Réu.	157c	21.22 S	55.36 E
Saint Joseph, Il., U.S.	194	40.06 N	88.02 W
Saint Joseph, La., U.S.	194	31.55 N	91.14 W
Saint Joseph, Mi., U.S.	216	42.05 N	86.29 W
Saint Joseph, Mn., U.S.	190	45.33 N	94.19 W
Saint Joseph, Mo., U.S.	194	39.46 N	94.50 W
Saint Joseph, Tn., U.S.	194	35.02 N	87.30 W
Saint Joseph □[6], In., U.S.	216	41.41 N	86.15 W
Saint Joseph □[6], Mi., U.S.	216	41.55 N	85.31 W
Saint Joseph ≃, U.S.	216	42.07 N	86.29 W
Saint Joseph ≃, U.S.	216	41.05 N	85.08 W
Saint Joseph, East Branch ≃	216	41.39 N	84.34 W
Saint-Joseph, Île I	275a	45.41 N	73.42 W
Saint-Joseph, Lac ⊜	206	46.54 N	71.38 W
Saint Joseph, Lake ⊜	176	51.05 N	90.35 W
Saint Joseph, West Branch ≃	216	41.39 N	84.34 W
Saint Joseph Bay c	192	29.47 N	85.21 W
Saint Joseph Channel ∪	190	46.19 N	84.04 W
Saint-Joseph-d'Alma → Alma	186	48.33 N	71.39 W
Saint-Joseph-de-Beauce	186	46.18 N	70.53 W
Saint-Joseph-de-Mékinac	206	46.55 N	72.42 W
Saint-Joseph-de-Sorel	206	46.02 N	73.07 W
Saint-Joseph-du-Lac	275a	45.32 N	74.00 W
Saint Joseph Island I	190	46.13 N	83.57 W
Saint Joseph's University ⊕[2]	285	40.00 N	75.14 W
Saint-Jouin-Bruneval	50	49.39 N	0.10 E
Saint-Jovite	206	46.07 N	74.36 W
Sainte-Julie	206	45.35 N	73.19 W
Saint-Julien	58	46.23 N	5.27 E
Saint-Julien-Chapteuil	62	45.02 N	4.04 E
Saint-Julien-du-Sault	50	48.02 N	3.18 E
Saint-Julien-du-Verdon	62	43.55 N	6.32 E
Saint-Julien-en-Beauchêne	62	44.37 N	5.42 E
Saint-Julien-en-Born	32	44.04 N	1.14 W
Saint-Julien-en-Genevois	58	46.08 N	6.05 E
Saint-Julien-en-Jarez	62	45.28 N	4.31 E
Saint-Julien-les-Villas	50	48.16 N	4.06 E
Saint-Julien-Molin-Molette	62	45.19 N	4.37 E
Sainte-Julienne	206	45.58 N	73.43 W
Saint-Junien	32	45.53 N	0.54 E
Saint Just, P.R.	240m	18.23 N	66.00 W
Saint Just, Eng., U.K.	42	50.07 N	5.42 W
Saint-Just-en-Chaussée	50	49.30 N	2.26 E
Saint-Just-en-Chevalet	32	45.55 N	3.50 E
Saint-Justin	206	46.15 N	73.05 W
Saint-Just-Malmont	62	45.20 N	4.19 E
Saint-Just-sur-Loire	62	45.29 N	4.16 E
Saint Keverne	42	50.03 N	5.06 W
Saint Kilda, Austl.	168b	34.44 S	138.32 E
Saint Kilda, Austl.	169	37.52 S	144.59 E
Saint Kilda, N.Z.	172	45.54 S	170.30 E
Saint Kilda I	28	57.49 N	8.36 W
Saint Kitts	168b	34.21 S	139.04 E
Saint Kitts → Saint Christopher I	238	17.20 N	62.45 W
Saint Kitts and Nevis □[1], N.A.	230	17.20 N	62.45 W
Saint Kitts and Nevis □[1], N.A.	238	17.20 N	62.45 W
Saint-Lambert, P.Q., Can.	206	45.30 N	73.30 W
Saint-Lambert, Fr.	261	48.44 N	2.01 E
Saint Landry	194	30.50 N	92.15 W
Saint-Laurent, Mb., Can.	184	50.24 N	97.56 W
Saint-Laurent, P.Q., Can.	206	45.30 N	73.40 W
Saint-Laurent, Fr.	58	48.09 N	6.27 E
Saint-Laurent → Saint Lawrence ≃	176	49.30 N	67.00 W
Saint-Laurent-Blangy	50	50.18 N	2.48 E
Saint-Laurent-de-Chamousset	62	45.44 N	4.28 E
Saint-Laurent-du-Maroni	250	5.30 N	54.02 W
Saint-Laurent-du-Maroni □[8]	250	4.00 N	53.30 W
Saint-Laurent-du-Pont	62	45.23 N	5.44 E
Saint-Laurent-du-Var	62	43.40 N	7.11 E
Saint-Laurent-en-Caux	50	49.45 N	0.53 E
Saint-Laurent-en-Grandvaux	58	46.35 N	5.57 E
Saint-Laurent-et-Benon	32	45.09 N	0.49 W
Saint-Laurent-les-Bains	62	44.37 N	3.58 E
Saint-Laurent-sur-Saône	58	46.18 N	4.50 E
Saint Lawrence, Austl.	166	22.21 S	149.31 E
Saint Lawrence, Nf., Can.	186	46.55 N	55.24 W
Saint Lawrence □[6]	212	44.30 N	75.27 W
Saint Lawrence ≃	176	49.30 N	67.00 W
Saint Lawrence, Cape ›	186	47.03 N	60.37 W
Saint Lawrence, Gulf of c	186	48.00 N	62.00 W
Saint Lawrence, Lake ⊜	206	44.56 N	75.04 W
Saint Lawrence Island I	180	63.30 N	170.30 W
Saint Lawrence Islands National Park ♠	212	44.18 N	76.08 W
Saint-Lawrence Seaway ≍	275a	45.43 N	73.25 W
Saint-Lazare	184	50.26 N	101.16 W
Saint-Lazare, Gare •[5]	261	48.53 N	2.20 E
Saint-Léandre	186	48.44 N	67.36 W
Saint-Léger-en-Yvelines	50	48.43 N	1.46 E
Saint-Léger-sur-Dheune	58	46.51 N	4.38 E
Saint Leo	220	28.20 N	82.15 W
Saint Leon	218	39.17 N	84.57 W
Saint-Léonard, N.B., Can.	186	47.10 N	67.56 W
Saint-Léonard, P.Q., Can.	206	45.35 N	73.35 W
Saint Leonard, Md., U.S.	208	38.28 N	76.30 W
Saint-Léonard-d'Aston	206	46.06 N	72.22 W
Saint Leonards, Eng., U.K.	42	50.51 N	0.34 E
Saint Leonards, Eng., U.K.	42	50.49 N	1.51 W
Saint-Leu-d'Esserent	50	49.13 N	2.25 E
Saint-Leu-la-Forêt	50	49.01 N	2.15 E
Saint-Liboire	206	45.39 N	72.46 W
Saint-Lô	32	49.07 N	1.05 W
Saint-Louis, Sk., Can.	184	52.56 N	105.49 W
Saint-Louis, Fr.	58	47.35 N	7.34 E
Saint-Louis, Guad.	241o	15.57 N	61.19 W
Saint-Louis, Réu.	157c	21.16 S	55.25 E
Saint-Louis, Sén.	150	16.02 N	16.30 W
Saint Louis, Mi., U.S.	190	43.24 N	84.36 W
Saint Louis, Mo., U.S.	219	38.37 N	90.11 W
Saint Louis, Tx., U.S.	222	32.18 N	95.20 W
Saint-Louis □[4]	150	16.00 N	14.30 W
Saint Louis □[6]	219	38.39 N	90.25 W
Saint-Louis ≃, P.Q., Can.	275a	45.19 N	73.53 W
Saint Louis ≃, U.S.	190	46.45 N	92.06 W
Saint-Louis, Lac ⊜	206	45.24 N	73.48 W
Saint-Louis, Pointe ›	275a	45.19 N	73.53 W
Saint Louis Crossing	218	39.19 N	85.51 W
Saint-Louis-de-Champlain	206	46.25 N	72.36 W
Saint-Louis-de-Kent	186	46.44 N	64.58 W
Saint Louis Park	190	44.56 N	93.20 W
Saint Louisville	214	40.10 N	82.25 W
Saint-Loup-sur-Aujon	58	47.53 N	5.05 E
Saint-Loup-sur-Semouse	58	47.53 N	6.16 E
Saint-Luc, P.Q., Can.	206	45.22 N	73.18 W
Saint-Luc, Schw.	58	46.13 N	7.36 E
Sainte-Luce	240e	14.28 N	60.56 W
Saint Lucia □[1], N.A.	230	13.53 N	60.58 W
Saint Lucia □[1], N.A.	241f	13.53 N	60.58 W
Saint Lucia, Cape ›	158	28.25 S	32.25 E
Saint Lucia, Lake ⊜	158	28.05 S	32.26 E
Saint Lucia Channel ∪	238	14.09 N	60.57 W
Saint Lucia Estuary	158	28.22 S	32.25 E
Saint Lucia Game Reserve •[4]	158	28.10 S	32.28 E
Sainte-Lucie, Fr.	36	41.42 N	9.22 E
Saint Lucie, Fl., U.S.	220	27.29 N	80.20 W
Saint Lucie □[6]	220	27.23 N	80.26 W
Saint Lucie Canal ≍	220	27.10 N	80.15 W
Saint Lucie Inlet c	220	27.10 N	80.10 W
Saint Lucie Lock •[5]	220	27.07 N	80.17 W
Saint-Lucien	261	48.39 N	1.38 E
Saint-Lupicin	58	46.24 N	5.47 E
Sainte-Magnance	50	47.27 N	4.04 E
Saint Magnus Bay c	46a	60.24 N	1.34 W
Saint Magnus Cathedral ⊕[1]	46	58.58 N	2.57 W
Saint-Malo, P.Q., Can.	206	45.12 N	71.30 W
Saint-Malo, Fr.	32	48.39 N	2.01 W
Saint-Malo, Golfe de c	32	48.45 N	2.00 W
Saint-Mamert-du-Gard	62	43.53 N	4.12 E
Saint-Mammès	50	48.23 N	2.49 E
Saint-Mandé	261	48.50 N	2.25 E
Saint-Mandrier-sur-Mer	62	43.04 N	5.56 E
Saint-Marc	238	19.07 N	72.42 W
Saint-Marc, Canal de ∪	238	18.50 N	72.45 W
Saint-Marc-des-Carrières	206	46.41 N	72.03 W
Saint-Marcel	58	46.47 N	4.54 E
Saint-Marcellin	62	45.09 N	5.19 E
Saint-Marcelline-de-Kildare	206	46.07 N	73.36 W
Saint-Marc-sur-Richelieu	275a	45.41 N	73.12 W
Saint-Mard	261	49.02 N	2.42 E
Saint Margaret Bay c	186	51.01 N	56.58 W
Saint Margaret's at Cliffe	42	51.09 N	1.24 E
Saint Margarets Bay c	186	44.35 N	64.00 W
Saint Margaret's Hope	46	58.49 N	2.57 W
Sainte-Marguerite ≃	176	50.09 N	66.36 W
Sainte-Marguerite, Baie c	186	50.06 N	66.36 W
Sainte-Marguerite-sur-Mer	50	49.55 N	0.57 E
Sainte-Marie	240e	14.47 N	61.00 W
Sainte-Marie, Cap ›	157b	25.36 S	45.08 E
Sainte-Marie-aux-Mines (Markirch)	58	48.15 N	7.11 E
Saint Maries	202	47.18 N	116.33 W
Saint Maries ≃	202	47.19 N	116.33 W
Saint-Marin → San Marino □[1]	66	43.56 N	12.25 E
Saint Marks, S. Afr.	158	32.01 S	27.22 E
Saint Marks, Fl., U.S.	192	30.09 N	84.12 W
Saint Marks ≃	192	30.08 N	84.12 W
Sainte-Marthe-de-Gaspé	186	49.12 N	66.10 W
Sainte-Marthe-sur-le-Lac	275a	45.32 N	73.56 W
Saint-Martin (Sint Maarten) I	238	18.04 N	63.04 W
Saint-Martin, Cap ›	240e	14.52 N	61.13 W
Saint Martin, Lake ⊜	184	51.37 N	98.29 W
Saint-Martin-Boulogne	50	50.43 N	1.38 E
Saint-Martin-d'Ardèche	62	44.18 N	4.35 E
Saint-Martin-d'Auxigny	50	47.12 N	2.25 E
Saint-Martin-de-Belleville	62	45.23 N	6.30 E
Saint-Martin-de-Bossenay	50	48.26 N	3.41 E
Saint-Martin-de-Bréthencourt	261	48.31 N	1.56 E
Saint-Martin-de-Crau	62	43.38 N	4.49 E
Saint-Martin-de-Londres	62	43.47 N	3.44 E
Saint-Martin-de-Nigelles	261	48.37 N	1.37 E
Saint-Martin-d'Entraunes	62	44.08 N	6.46 E
Saint-Martin-des-Champs	261	48.53 N	1.43 E
Saint-Martin-de-Valamas	62	44.56 N	4.22 E
Saint-Martin-d'Hères	62	45.10 N	5.46 E
Saint-Martin-du-Puy	50	47.20 N	3.52 E
Saint-Martin-du-Tertre	261	49.06 N	2.21 E
Saint-Martin-du-Var	62	43.49 N	7.12 E
Sainte-Martine	206	45.15 N	73.48 W
Saint-Martin-en-Bresse	58	46.49 N	5.04 E
Saint-Martin-la-Garenne	261	49.02 N	1.41 E
Saint-Martin-la-Plaine	62	45.32 N	4.36 E
Saint Martins, N.B., Can.	186	45.21 N	65.32 W
Saint Martin's, Eng., U.K.	42	52.55 N	2.59 W
Saint Martin's I	42a	49.58 N	6.20 W
Saint Martins Keys II	220	28.47 N	82.44 W
Saint-Martin-Vésubie	62	44.04 N	7.15 E
Saint Martinville	194	30.07 N	91.49 W
Saint Mary	194	37.52 N	89.58 W
Saint Mary ≃, B.C., Can.	182	49.37 N	115.38 W
Saint Mary ≃, N.A.	182	49.37 N	112.52 W
Saint Mary, Cape ›	150	13.28 N	16.40 W
Saint Mary, Mount ∧	164	8.10 S	147.00 E
Saint Mary Bourne	42	51.16 N	1.24 W
Saint Mary Cray •[8]	260	51.23 N	0.07 E
Saint Mary Lake ⊜	202	48.40 N	113.30 W
Saint Marylebone •[8]	260	51.31 N	0.10 W
Saint Mary of the Lake Seminary ⊕[2]	278	42.17 N	88.00 W
Saint Mary Peak ∧	166	31.30 S	138.33 E
Saint Mary Reservoir ⊜[1]	182	49.19 N	113.12 W
Saint Marys, Austl.	166	41.35 S	148.10 E
Saint Marys, Austl.	170	33.47 S	150.47 E
Saint Mary's, Nf., Can.	186	46.55 N	53.34 W
Saint Mary's, On., Can.	212	43.16 N	81.08 W
Saint Marys, Ak., U.S.	180	62.04 N	163.10 W
Saint Marys, Ga., U.S.	192	30.43 N	81.32 W
Saint Marys, Ks., U.S.	198	39.11 N	96.04 W
Saint Marys, Oh., U.S.	216	40.32 N	84.23 W
Saint Marys, Pa., U.S.	214	41.25 N	78.33 W
Saint Marys, W.V., U.S.	188	39.23 N	81.12 W
Saint Marys □[6]	208	38.17 N	76.38 W
Saint Mary's I	42a	49.55 N	6.18 W
Saint Marys ≃, N.S., Can.	186	45.02 N	61.54 W
Saint Marys ≃, N.A.	190	45.58 N	83.54 W
Saint Marys ≃, U.S.	192	30.43 N	81.27 W
Saint Marys ≃, U.S.	216	41.05 N	85.08 W
Saint Marys ≃, Md., U.S.	208	38.06 N	76.26 W
Saint Mary's, Cape ›, Nf., Can.	186	46.49 N	54.12 W
Saint Marys, Cape ›, N.S., Can.	186	44.05 N	66.13 W
Saint Marys, North Prong ≃	192	30.22 N	82.06 W
Saint Marys, South Prong ≃	192	30.22 N	82.06 W
Saint Mary's Bay	42	51.00 N	0.58 E
Saint Mary's Bay c, Nf., Can.	186	46.50 N	53.47 W
Saint Marys Bay c, N.S., Can.	186	44.25 N	66.10 W
Saint Marys City	208	38.11 N	76.26 W
Saint Mary's Hoo	260	51.28 N	0.36 E
Saint Marys Lake ⊜	278	42.17 N	87.59 W
Saint Mary's Marshes ≋	260	51.28 N	0.35 E
Saint-Mathieu	32	45.42 N	0.46 E
Saint-Mathieu, Pointe de ›	32	48.20 N	4.46 W
Saint-Mathieu-de-Laprairie	275a	45.19 N	73.31 W
Saint Matthew Island I	180	60.30 N	172.45 W
Saint Matthews, Ky., U.S.	218	38.15 N	85.39 W
Saint Matthews, S.C., U.S.	192	33.39 N	80.46 W
Saint Matthias Group II	164	1.30 S	149.40 E
Saint-Maur-des-Fossés	50	48.48 N	2.30 E
Sainte-Maure-de-Touraine	32	47.07 N	0.37 E
Saint-Maurice, Fr.	261	48.49 N	2.25 E
Saint-Maurice, Schw.	58	46.13 N	7.00 E
Saint-Maurice □[6]	206	46.35 N	73.00 W
Saint-Maurice ≃	176	46.21 N	72.31 W
Saint-Maurice, Parc de ♠	206	46.52 N	73.10 W
Saint-Maurice-en-Montagne	58	46.34 N	5.50 E
Saint-Maurice-Montcouronne	261	48.35 N	2.07 E
Saint Mawes	42	50.09 N	5.01 W
Saint Mawgan	42	50.28 N	4.58 W
Saint-Max	58	48.42 N	6.13 E
Sainte-Maxime	62	43.18 N	6.38 E
Saint-Maximin-la-Sainte-Baume	62	43.27 N	5.52 E
Saint-Méen-le-Grand	32	48.11 N	2.12 W
Saint Meinrad	194	38.10 N	86.48 W
Sainte-Menehould	56	49.05 N	4.54 E
Saint-Menges	56	49.44 N	4.56 E
Sainte-Mère-Église	32	49.25 N	1.19 W
Saint Merryn	42	50.31 N	4.58 W
Saint-Méry	261	48.35 N	2.50 E
Sainte-Mesme	261	48.32 N	1.58 E
Saint-Mesmes	261	48.59 N	2.42 E
Saint Michael, Ak., U.S.	180	63.29 N	162.02 W
Saint Michael, Pa., U.S.	214	40.20 N	78.46 W
Saint Michaels	208	38.47 N	76.13 W
Saint-Michel, Fr.	50	49.55 N	4.08 E
Saint-Michel, Fr.	62	45.13 N	6.28 E
Saint-Michel •[8]	275a	45.35 N	73.35 W
Saint-Michel-de-Napierville	206	45.14 N	73.34 W
Saint-Michel-des-Saints	206	46.41 N	73.55 W
Saint-Michel-sur-Meurthe	58	48.19 N	6.54 E
Saint-Michel-sur-Orge	261	48.38 N	2.18 E
Saint-Mihiel	56	48.54 N	5.33 E
Saint Monance	46	56.12 N	2.46 W
Sainte-Monique-des-Deux-Montagnes	275a	45.40 N	74.00 W
Sainte-Montaine	50	47.29 N	2.19 E
Saint-Moritz → Sankt Moritz	58	46.30 N	9.50 E
Saint-Narcisse	206	46.34 N	72.28 W
Saint-Nazaire	32	47.17 N	2.12 W
Saint-Nazaire-en-Royans	62	45.04 N	5.15 E
Saint-Nazaire-le-Désert	62	44.34 N	5.17 E
Saint Nazianz	190	44.00 N	87.55 W
Saint Neots	42	52.14 N	0.17 W
Saint-Nicéphore	206	45.50 N	72.25 W
Saint-Nicolas → Sint-Niklaas, Bel.	50	51.10 N	4.08 E
Saint-Nicolas, Bel.	56	50.38 N	5.32 E
Saint-Nicolas, P.Q., Can.	206	46.42 N	71.24 W
Saint-Nicolas-aux-Bois	50	49.36 N	3.25 E
Saint-Nicolas-d'Aliermont	50	49.53 N	1.13 E
Saint-Nizier-du-Moucherotte	62	45.10 N	5.38 E
Saint-Nom-la-Bretèche	261	48.51 N	2.01 E
Saint Nora Lake ⊜	212	45.08 N	78.49 W
Saint-Norbert-d'Arthabaska	206	46.07 N	71.50 W
Sainte-Odile ⊕[1]	58	48.26 N	7.24 E
Saint-Omer	50	50.45 N	2.15 E
Saintonge □[9]	32	45.30 N	0.30 W
Saint-Ouen, Fr.	50	50.02 N	2.03 E
Saint-Ouen, Fr.	261	48.54 N	2.20 E
Saint-Ouen-l'Aumône	50	49.03 N	2.06 E
Saint-Pacôme	186	47.24 N	69.57 W
Saint-Pamphile	186	46.58 N	69.47 W
Saint Pancras •[8]	260	51.32 N	0.07 W
Saint Paris	218	40.07 N	83.57 W
Saint-Pascal	186	47.32 N	69.49 W
Saint-Paterne	50	48.24 N	0.07 E
Saint-Pathus	261	49.04 N	2.48 E
Saint-Patrice, Lac ⊜	190	46.22 N	77.20 W
Saint Paul, Ab., Can.	182	53.59 N	111.17 W
Saint-Paul, Fr.	62	43.42 N	7.07 E
Saint-Paul, Fr.	62	44.31 N	6.45 E
Saint-Paul, Réu.	157c	21.00 S	55.16 E
Saint Paul, In., U.S.	218	39.25 N	85.28 W
Saint Paul, Ks., U.S.	198	37.31 N	95.10 W
Saint Paul, Mn., U.S.	190	44.57 N	93.05 W
Saint Paul, Ne., U.S.	198	41.13 N	98.27 W
Saint Paul, Or., U.S.	224	45.12 N	122.58 W
Saint Paul, Va., U.S.	192	36.54 N	82.18 W
Saint-Paul ≃, Can.	176	51.26 N	57.40 W
Saint Paul ≃, Liber.	150	6.23 N	10.48 W
Saint Paul, Cape ›	150	5.49 N	0.57 E
Saint-Paul, Île I	6	38.43 S	77.29 E
Saint-Paul, Lac ⊜	206	46.18 N	72.29 W
Saint Paul Bay c	116	10.14 N	118.54 E
Saint-Paul-de-Chester (Chesterville)	206	45.57 N	71.49 W
Saint-Paul-en-Jarez	62	45.29 N	4.35 E
Saint-Paul-et-Valmalle	62	43.38 N	3.40 E
Saint-Paulien	62	45.08 N	3.49 E
Saint-Paulin	206	46.25 N	73.01 W
Saint Paul Island	180	57.07 N	170.17 W
Saint Paul Island I, N.S., Can.	186	47.15 N	60.10 W
Saint Paul Island I, Ak., U.S.	180	57.10 N	170.15 W
Saint Pauls	192	34.48 N	78.58 W
Saint Paul's Cathedral ⊕[1]	260	51.31 N	0.06 W
Saint Paul's Cray •[8]	260	51.24 N	0.07 E
Saint Pauls Inlet c	186	49.50 N	57.45 W
Saint Paul's Point ›	174e	25.04 S	130.05 W
Saint-Paul-Trois-Châteaux	62	44.21 N	4.46 E
Saint-Péravy-la-Colombe	50	48.00 N	1.42 E
Saint-Péray	62	44.57 N	4.50 E
Saint-Père	50	47.28 N	3.46 E
Saint Peter, Il., U.S.	219	38.52 N	88.51 W
Saint Peter, Mn., U.S.	190	44.19 N	93.57 W
Saint Peter, Lake ⊜	212	45.18 N	78.02 W
Saint Peter Island I	162	32.17 S	133.35 E
Saint Peter Port	43b	49.27 N	2.32 W
Saint Peters, N.S., Can.	186	45.40 N	60.52 W
Saint Peters, Mo., U.S.	219	38.48 N	90.37 W
Saint Peters, Pa., U.S.	285	40.11 N	75.44 W
Saint Peters Bay	186	46.25 N	62.35 W
Saint Petersburg → Sankt-Peterburg, Ross.	76	59.55 N	30.15 E
Saint Petersburg, Fl., U.S.	220	27.46 N	82.40 W
Saint Petersburg, Pa., U.S.	214	41.10 N	79.37 W
Saint Petersburg Beach	220	27.43 N	82.44 W
Saint Peter's College ⊕[2]	276	40.44 N	74.05 W
Saint-Philippe-d'Argenteuil	206	45.37 N	74.25 W
Saint-Philippe-de-Laprairie	275a	45.21 N	73.28 W
Saint-Pie	206	45.30 N	72.54 W
Saint-Pierre, P.Q., Can.	275a	45.27 N	73.39 W
Saint-Pierre, Fr.	62	45.40 N	3.45 E
Saint-Pierre, It.	62	45.42 N	7.14 E
Saint-Pierre, Mart.	240e	14.45 N	61.11 W
Saint-Pierre, Réu.	157c	21.19 S	55.29 E
Saint-Pierre, St. P./M.	186	46.47 N	56.11 W
Saint-Pierre I	186	46.47 N	56.11 W
Saint-Pierre ≃	275a	45.23 N	73.34 W
Saint-Pierre, Lac ⊜, P.Q., Can.	186	50.08 N	68.26 W
Saint-Pierre, Lac ⊜, P.Q., Can.	206	46.12 N	72.52 W
Saint Pierre and Miquelon (Saint-Pierre-et-Miquelon) □[2], N.A.	176	46.55 N	56.20 W
Saint Pierre and Miquelon (Saint-Pierre-et-Miquelon) □[2], N.A.	186	46.55 N	56.20 W
Saint-Pierre-d'Albigny	62	45.34 N	6.09 E
Saint-Pierre-de-Bœuf	62	45.22 N	4.45 E
Saint-Pierre-de-Broughton	206	46.15 N	71.12 W
Saint-Pierre-de-Chartreuse	62	45.20 N	5.49 E
Saint-Pierre-des-Corps	50	47.23 N	0.44 E
Saint-Pierre-de-Vacquière	62	43.52 N	4.13 E
Saint-Pierre-du-Vauvray	50	49.14 N	1.13 E
Saint-Pierre-Église	32	49.40 N	1.24 W
Saint-Pierre-en-Port	50	49.48 N	0.29 E
Saint-Pierre-et-Miquelon → Saint Pierre and Miquelon □[2]	186	46.55 N	56.20 W
Saint Pierre Island I	138	9.19 S	50.43 E
Saint Pierre-Jolys	184	49.26 N	96.59 W
Saint Pierre-le-Moûtier	32	46.48 N	3.07 E
Saint-Pierre-lès-Elbeuf	50	49.16 N	1.03 E
Saint-Pierre-sur-Dives	28	49.01 N	0.02 W
Saint-Pierreville	62	44.49 N	4.29 E
Saint-Point, Lac de ⊜	58	46.49 N	6.19 E
Saint-Pol-de-Léon	32	48.41 N	3.59 W
Saint-Pol-sur-Mer	50	51.02 N	2.21 E
Saint-Pol-sur-Ternoise	50	50.23 N	2.20 E
Saint-Polycarpe	206	45.18 N	74.18 W
Saint-Pons	32	43.29 N	2.46 E
Saint-Pourçain-sur-Sioule	32	46.19 N	3.17 E
Saint-Prex	58	46.29 N	6.28 E
Saint-Priest	62	45.42 N	4.57 E
Saint-Priest-en-Jarez	62	45.28 N	4.22 E
Saint-Prix	261	49.01 N	2.16 E
Saint-Prosper-de-Dorchester	188	46.13 N	70.29 W
Saint-Quentin, N.B., Can.	186	47.30 N	67.23 W
Saint-Quentin, Fr.	50	49.51 N	3.17 E
Saint-Quentin, Canal de ≍	50	49.36 N	3.11 E
Saint-Quentin, Étang de ⊜	261	48.47 N	2.01 E
Saint-Rambert-d'Albon	62	45.17 N	4.49 E
Saint-Rambert-en-Bugey	58	45.57 N	5.26 E
Saint-Rambert-sur-Loire	62	45.30 N	4.15 E
Saint-Raphaël	62	43.25 N	6.46 E
Saint-Raymond	206	46.54 N	71.50 W
Saint-Rédempter-de-Lévis	206	46.42 N	71.17 W
Saint Regis	202	47.17 N	115.06 W
Saint-Régis ≃, P.Q., Can.	275a	45.24 N	73.34 W
Saint Regis ≃, N.A.	188	45.00 N	74.39 W
Saint Regis ≃, Mt., U.S.	202	47.18 N	115.05 W
Saint Regis, West Branch ≃	188	44.47 N	74.46 W
Saint Regis Falls	188	44.40 N	74.32 W
Saint Regis Indian Reservation •[4]	206	44.58 N	74.39 W
Saint-Rémi	206	45.16 N	73.37 W
Saint-Rémi-d'Amherst	206	46.01 N	74.46 W
Saint-Rémy (lès-Chevreuse), Fr.	50	48.42 N	2.05 E
Saint-Rémy, Fr.	58	46.46 N	4.50 E
Saint Remy, N.Y., U.S.	210	41.54 N	74.01 W
Saint-Rémy-de-Provence	62	43.47 N	4.50 E
Saint-Rémy-en-Bouzemont	58	48.38 N	4.39 E
Saint-Rémy-l'Honoré	261	48.45 N	1.53 E
Saint-Rémy-sur-Avre	50	48.46 N	1.15 E
Saint-Renan	32	48.26 N	4.37 W
Saint-Révérien	50	47.13 N	3.30 E
Saint-Rhémy	62	45.50 N	7.11 E
Saint-Riquier	50	50.08 N	1.57 E
Saint Robert	194	37.50 N	92.09 W
Saint-Roch-de-l'Achigan	206	45.51 N	73.36 W
Saint-Romain-de-Colbosc	50	49.32 N	0.22 E
Saint-Romain-le-Puy	62	45.33 N	4.07 E
Saint-Romans	62	45.07 N	5.19 E
Saint-Romuald	206	46.45 N	71.14 W
Sainte-Rosalie	206	45.38 N	72.54 W
Sainte-Rose	241o	16.20 N	61.42 W
Sainte-Rose •[8]	275a	45.36 N	73.47 W
Sainte-Rose-du-Lac	184	51.03 N	99.32 W
Saintry-sur-Seine	261	48.36 N	2.30 E
Saintes, Bel.	50	50.42 N	4.10 E
Saintes, Fr.	32	45.45 N	0.38 W
Saint-Saëns	50	49.40 N	1.17 E
Saint Sampson	43b	49.29 N	2.31 W
Saint-Satur	50	47.20 N	2.51 E
Saint-Saturnin-d'Apt	62	43.56 N	5.23 E
Saint-Sauveur, Fr.	50	47.37 N	3.12 E
Saint-Sauveur, Fr.	58	47.48 N	6.23 E
Saint-Sauveur-des-Monts	206	45.52 N	74.10 W
Saint-Sauveur-sur-Tinée	62	44.05 N	7.06 E
Saint-Savin	32	46.34 N	0.52 E
Saint-Savinien	32	45.53 N	0.41 W
Saint Saviour	43b	49.11 N	2.06 W
Saint Sebastian Bay c	158	34.25 S	21.00 E
Saint-Sébastien	206	45.07 N	73.09 W
Saint-Sébastien, Cap ›	157b	12.26 S	48.44 E
Saint-Seine-l'Abbaye	58	47.26 N	4.47 E
Saint Séverin	56	50.32 N	5.25 E
Saint Shotts	186	46.38 N	53.35 W
Sainte-Sigolène	62	45.14 N	4.15 E
Saint-Siméon	186	47.50 N	69.53 W
Saint-Simon	50	49.45 N	3.10 E
Saint Simons Island	192	31.09 N	81.22 W
Saint Simons Island I	192	31.14 N	81.21 W
Saint-Sixte ≃	206	45.39 N	75.08 W
Saintes-Maries, Golfe des c	62	43.25 N	4.31 E
Saintes-Maries-de-la-Mer	62	43.27 N	4.26 E
Sainte-Sophie-de-Mégantic	206	46.09 N	71.42 W
Saint-Soupplets	261	49.02 N	2.48 E
Saint Stanislas Bay c	174o	1.53 N	157.30 W
Saint-Stanislas-de-Kosta	206	45.11 N	74.08 W
Saint Stephen, N.B., Can.	186	45.12 N	67.17 W
Saint Stephen, S.C., U.S.	192	33.24 N	79.55 W
Saint-Sulpice-de-Favières	261	48.33 N	2.11 E
Saint-Sulpice-les-Feuilles	32	46.19 N	1.22 E
Sainte-Suzanne	58	47.30 N	6.46 E
Saint-Sylvestre	206	46.22 N	71.14 W
Saint-Symphorien, Fr.	32	44.26 N	0.30 W
Saint-Symphorien, Fr.	261	48.31 N	1.46 E
Saint-Symphorien-d'Ozon	62	45.38 N	4.52 E
Saint-Symphorien-sur-Coise	62	45.38 N	4.27 E
Sainte-Thècle	206	46.49 N	72.31 W
Saint-Théodore-d'Acton	206	45.41 N	72.35 W
Sainte-Thérèse	206	45.38 N	73.51 W
Sainte-Thérèse, Île I, P.Q., Can.	275a	45.41 N	73.28 W
Sainte-Thérèse, Île I, P.Q., Can.	275a	45.22 N	73.15 W
Saint-Thibault-des-Vignes	261	48.52 N	2.41 E
Saint Thomas, On., Can.	212	42.47 N	81.12 W
Saint Thomas, Mo., U.S.	219	38.22 N	92.13 W
Saint Thomas, N.D., U.S.	198	48.37 N	97.26 W
Saint Thomas → Charlotte Amalie, Vir. Is., U.S.	240m	18.21 N	64.56 W
Saint Thomas I	240m	18.21 N	64.55 W
Saint-Timothée	206	45.18 N	74.02 W
Saint-Tite	206	46.44 N	72.34 W
Saint-Tite-des-Caps	186	47.08 N	70.47 W
Saint-Trivier-de-Courtes	58	46.28 N	5.05 E
Saint-Trivier-sur-Moignans	58	46.04 N	4.54 E
Saint-Tropez	62	43.16 N	6.38 E
Saint Tudy	42	50.33 N	4.43 W
Sainte-Tulle	62	43.47 N	5.46 E
Saint-Ubald	206	46.45 N	72.16 W
Saint-Urbain-de-Charlevoix	186	47.33 N	70.32 W
Saint-Ursanne	58	47.22 N	7.10 E
Saint-Uze	62	45.11 N	4.52 E
Saint-Valérien	50	48.11 N	3.06 E
Saint-Valéry-en-Caux	50	49.52 N	0.44 E
Saint-Valéry-sur-Somme	50	50.11 N	1.38 E
Saint-Vallier, Fr.	58	46.38 N	4.22 E
Saint-Vallier, Fr.	62	45.10 N	4.49 E
Saint-Vallier-de-Thiey	62	43.42 N	6.51 E
Saint-Varent	32	46.53 N	0.14 W
Saint-Venant	50	50.37 N	2.33 E
Saint-Véran	62	44.42 N	6.52 E
Sainte-Victoire, Montagne ∧	62	43.32 N	5.39 E
Saint-Victoret	62	43.25 N	5.14 E
Saint-Vincent, It.	62	45.45 N	7.39 E
Saint Vincent, Mn., U.S.	198	48.58 N	97.13 W
Saint Vincent I	241h	13.15 N	61.12 W
Saint-Vincent, Baie de c	175f	22.00 S	166.05 E
Saint-Vincent, Cap ›	157b	21.57 S	43.16 E
Saint Vincent, Cape ›, Austl.	166	43.18 S	145.50 E
Saint Vincent, Cape → São Vicente, Cabo de ›, Port.	34	37.01 N	9.00 W
Saint Vincent, Gulf c	168b	35.00 S	138.05 E
Saint Vincent and the Grenadines □[1], N.A.	230	13.15 N	61.12 W
Saint Vincent and the Grenadines □[1], N.A.	241h	13.15 N	61.12 W
Saint-Vincent-de-Paul •[8]	275a	45.37 N	73.39 W
Saint-Vincent-de-Tyrosse	32	43.40 N	1.18 W
Saint Vincent Passage ∪	238	13.30 N	61.00 W
Saint Vincent's	186	46.48 N	53.38 W
Saint-Vit	58	47.11 N	5.49 E
Saint-Vith	56	50.17 N	6.08 E
Saint-Vivien-de-Médoc	32	45.26 N	1.02 W
Saint-Vrain	261	48.33 N	2.20 E
Saint Walburg	184	53.39 N	109.12 W
Saint-Wandrille-Rançon	50	49.32 N	0.46 E
Saint-Wenceslas ≃	206	46.18 N	72.23 W
Saint Williams	212	42.40 N	80.25 W
Saint-Witz	261	49.05 N	2.34 E
Saint-Yrieix-la-Perche	32	45.31 N	1.12 E
Saint-Yvon	186	49.10 N	64.48 W
Saint-Zacharie	62	43.23 N	5.43 E
Saint-Zénon	206	46.33 N	73.49 W
Sāinthiya	126	23.57 N	87.40 E
Saipan I	174n	15.12 N	145.45 E
Saipan Channel ∪	174n	15.05 N	145.41 E

Symbols in the index entries represent the broad categories identified in the key at the right. Symbols with superior numbers (∧[1]) identify subcategories (see complete key on page *I · 1).*

Symbole im Register stellen die rechts im Schlüssel erklärten Kategorien dar. Symbole mit hochgestellten Ziffern (∧[1]) bezeichnen Unterabteilungen einer Kategorie (vgl. vollständiger Schlüssel auf Seite *I · 1).*

Los símbolos incluídos en el texto del índice representan las grandes categorías identificadas con la clave a la derecha. Los símbolos con numeros en su parte superior (∧[1]) identifican las subcategorías (véase la clave completa en la página *I · 1).*

Les symboles de l'index représentent les catégories indiquées dans la légende à droite. Les symboles suivis d'un indice (∧[1]) représentent des sous-catégories (voir légende complète à la page *I · 1).*

Os símbolos incluídos no texto do índice representam as grandes categorias identificadas com a chave à direita. Os símbolos com números em sua parte superior (∧[1]) identificam as subcategorias (veja-se a chave completa à página *I · 1).*

	English	Deutsch	Español	Français	Português
∧	Mountain	Berg	Montaña	Montagne	Montanha
∧	Mountains	Gebirge	Montañas	Montagnes	Montanhas
)(	Pass	Paß	Paso	Col	Passo
V	Valley, Canyon	Tal, Cañon	Valle, Cañón	Vallée, Canyon	Vale, Canhão
≃	Plain	Ebene	Llano	Plaine	Planície
›	Cape	Kap	Cabo	Cap	Cabo
I	Island	Insel	Isla	Île	Ilha
II	Islands	Inseln	Islas	Îles	Ilhas
⊥	Other Topographic Features	Andere Topographische Objekte	Otros Elementos Topográficos	Autres données topographiques	Outros acidentes topográficos

ESPAÑOL · FRANÇAIS · PORTUGUÊS

Nombre / Nom / Nome	Página / Page	Lat.°′	Long.°′ W = Oeste / Ouest
Saipan International Airport ⊠	174n	15.07 N	145.43 E
Saiqi	100	27.00 N	119.43 E
Saishu-to → Cheju-do I	90	33.20 N	126.30 E
Saita	96	34.08 N	133.49 E
Saita ≃	96	34.08 N	133.38 E
Saitama □[5]	94	36.00 N	139.30 E
Saitama University ʊ[2]	268	35.52 N	139.36 E
Saito	92	32.06 N	131.24 E
Saiwai ◆[8]	268	35.33 N	139.41 E
Saiwa Swamp National Park ♠	154	1.06 N	35.12 E
Saiyidān ◆[8]	272a	28.40 N	77.05 E
Sai Yok	110	14.07 N	99.08 E
Sajak	86	47.02 N	77.22 E
Sajam	164	0.53 S	132.41 E
Sajama	248	18.07 S	69.00 W
Sajama, Nevado ∧	248	18.06 S	68.54 W
Sajan → Sayan Mountains ⋌	88	52.45 N	96.00 E
Sajanogorsk	86	53.08 N	91.29 E
Sajano-Šušenskoje vodochranilišče ⊜[1]	86	52.20 N	92.25 E
Sajantuj	88	51.44 N	107.30 E
Sajasan	84	43.03 N	46.17 E
Sajat	128	38.47 N	63.53 E
Sajchan	88	48.40 N	102.39 E
Sajchandulaan	102	44.40 N	109.01 E
Sajchan-Ovoo	102	45.27 N	103.54 E
Sajchin	80	48.50 N	46.47 E
Sajen	115a	7.40 S	112.31 E
Šajgino	80	57.46 N	46.51 E
Ṣajīd I	144	16.52 N	41.50 E
Šajmak'	120	37.27 N	74.44 E
Sajnšand	102	44.52 N	110.09 E
Sajó (Slaná) ≃	30	47.56 N	21.08 E
Sajószentpéter	30	48.13 N	20.44 E
Sajram	85	42.18 N	69.45 E
Sajukino	80	52.47 N	41.59 E
Sājūr (Bağırsak) ≃	130	36.40 N	38.05 E
Sak ≃	158	30.02 S	20.40 E
Saka, Kenya	154	0.09 S	39.20 E
Saka, Nihon	96	34.20 N	132.31 E
Sakado	94	35.57 N	139.24 E
Sakae, Nihon	94	35.50 N	140.15 E
Sakae, Nihon	94	36.58 N	138.35 E
Sa Kaeo	110	13.49 N	102.04 E
Sakahogi	94	35.26 N	136.59 E
Sakai, Nihon	94	36.10 N	136.14 E
Sakai, Nihon	94	36.16 N	139.15 E
Sakai, Nihon	94	36.06 N	139.48 E
Sakai, Nihon	96	34.35 N	135.28 E
Sakai, Nihon	268	35.25 N	139.22 E
Sakai ≃	94	35.18 N	139.29 E
Sakaide	96	34.19 N	133.52 E
Sakaigawa	94	35.35 N	138.37 E
Sakaiminato	96	35.33 N	133.15 E
Sakākah	128	29.59 N	40.06 E
Sakakawea, Lake ⊜[1]	198	47.50 N	102.20 W
Sakaki	94	36.28 N	138.11 E
Sakakita	94	36.25 N	138.01 E
Sakala, Pulau I	112	6.54 S	116.15 E
Sakami ≃	176	53.40 N	76.40 W
Sakami, Lac ⊜	176	53.15 N	76.45 W
Sakania	154	12.45 S	28.34 E
Sakar	128	38.56 N	63.45 E
Sakar ⋌	38	41.59 N	26.16 E
Sakaraha	157b	22.55 S	44.32 E
Sakar-Čaga	128	37.38 N	61.40 E
Sakar Island I	164	5.25 S	148.05 E
Sakartvelo → Georgia □[1]	22	42.00 N	44.00 E
Sakarya	130	40.46 N	30.24 E
Sakarya □[4]	130	40.45 N	30.35 E
Sakarya ≃	130	41.07 N	30.39 E
Sakashita	94	35.34 N	137.32 E
Sakassou	150	7.27 N	5.18 W
Sakata	92	38.55 N	139.50 E
Sakauchi	94	35.36 N	136.25 E
Sakawa	96	33.30 N	133.17 E
Sakawa ≃	94	35.15 N	139.11 E
Sakchu	98	40.23 N	125.01 E
Sakesar	123	32.33 N	71.56 E
Sakété	150	6.43 N	2.40 E
Sakhā	142	31.05 N	30.57 E
Sakhalin → Sachalin, ostrov I	89	51.00 N	143.00 E
Sākhar	120	32.57 N	65.32 E
Sakhi Sarwar	120	29.59 N	70.18 E
Sakhnin	132	32.52 N	35.17 E
Sakhnovshchyna	78	49.08 N	35.53 E
Ṣakhrīyāt, Jabal aṣ- ∧	132	31.01 N	36.21 E
Sakht Sar	128	36.53 N	50.41 E
Şāki ◆[8]	272c	19.06 N	72.53 E
Šakiai	76	54.57 N	23.03 E
Sākib	132	32.17 N	35.49 E
Sakiet Sidi Youssef	36	36.13 N	8.22 E
Sakijang Bendera, Pulau I	271c	1.13 N	103.51 E
Sakijang Pelepah, Pulau I	271c	1.13 N	103.52 E
Sakishima-shotō II	175d	24.46 N	124.00 E
Sakito	92	33.02 N	129.32 E
Sakkara → Ṣaqqārah	142	29.51 N	31.13 E
Sakmara ≃	86	51.46 N	55.01 E
Sako	270	34.53 N	135.47 E
Sakon Nakhon	110	17.10 N	104.09 E
Sakonnet	207	41.28 N	71.12 W
Sakonnet Point ›	207	41.27 N	71.12 W
Sakoyra	150	14.17 N	1.24 E
Sakra, Pulau I	271c	1.16 N	103.42 E
Sakrand	120	26.08 N	68.16 E
Sakrivier	158	30.54 S	20.28 E
Saks	194	33.42 N	85.52 W
Saksahan' ≃	78	47.53 N	33.18 E
Saksauldala ◆[2]	86	44.30 N	73.00 E
Sakskøbing	41	54.48 N	11.39 E
Sakti	124	22.02 N	82.58 E
Saku, Nihon	94	36.09 N	138.30 E
Saku, Nihon	94	36.13 N	138.29 E
Sakubva	154	19.00 S	32.10 E
Sakugi	96	34.52 N	132.43 E
Sakuma	94	35.05 N	137.48 E
Sakuma-dam ◆[6]	94	35.05 N	137.47 E
Sakuma-ko ⊜[1]	94	35.08 N	137.47 E
Sakura	94	35.43 N	140.14 E
Sakura ≃	94	36.05 N	140.14 E
Sakurae	96	34.57 N	132.20 E
Sakurai	96	34.30 N	135.51 E
Sakura-tōge)(	270	34.36 N	135.53 E
Saku-shima I	94	34.43 N	137.03 E
Sakutō	96	35.01 N	134.14 E
Sakwaso Lake ⊜	184	53.01 N	91.55 W
Saky	78	45.09 N	33.35 E
Säkylä	26	61.02 N	22.20 E
Sakyō ◆[8]	270	35.02 N	135.48 E
Sal I	150a	16.45 N	22.55 W
Sal ≃	80	47.31 N	40.45 E
Sal, Cay I	238	23.42 N	80.24 W
Sal, Ponta do ›	266c	38.41 N	9.22 W
Sal, Punta ›	236	15.53 N	87.37 W
Šal'a, Ross.	86	57.15 N	58.43 E
Šal'a, Slvk.	30	48.09 N	17.52 E
Sala, Sve.	40	59.55 N	16.36 E
Sala, Ouadi V	146	17.00 N	20.53 E
Sala Baganza	64	44.43 N	10.14 E
Salabangka, Kepulauan II	112	3.02 S	122.25 E
Salaberry, Île de I	206	45.17 N	74.07 W
Salaberry-de-Valleyfield	206	45.15 N	74.08 W
Salaca ≃	76	57.45 N	24.21 E
Salacgrīva	76	57.45 N	24.21 E
Sala Consilina	68	40.24 N	15.36 E
Salada, Laguna ⊜, Arg.	258	35.17 S	59.24 W
Salada, Laguna ⊜, Méx.	232	32.20 N	115.40 W
Saladas	252	28.15 S	58.38 W
Saladillo	252	35.38 S	59.46 W
Saladillo ≃, Arg.	252	33.25 S	63.02 W
Saladillo ≃, Arg.	252	29.05 S	63.25 W
Saladillo, Arroyo ≃	258	35.33 S	59.04 W
Saladillo de Rodríguez, Arroyo ≃	258	35.29 S	59.01 W
Saladillo Dulce, Arroyo ≃	252	31.25 S	60.33 W
Salado, Arg.	252	28.18 S	67.15 W
Salado, Tx., U.S.	222	30.57 N	97.32 W
Salado ≃, Arg.	252	38.49 S	64.57 W
Salado ≃, Arg.	252	31.42 S	60.44 W
Salado ≃, Arg.	252	35.44 S	57.21 W
Salado ≃, Arg.	252	29.13 S	66.34 W
Salado ≃, Cuba	240p	20.36 N	76.56 W
Salado ≃, Méx.	232	26.52 N	99.19 W
Salado ≃, Méx.	234	18.44 N	103.36 W
Salado ≃, Méx.	234	17.55 N	96.58 W
Salado, Arroyo ≃, Arg.	254	40.35 S	66.33 W
Salado, Arroyo ≃, Arg.	254	41.37 S	65.02 W
Salado, Rio ≃	200	34.16 N	106.52 W
Salado Creek ≃, Tx., U.S.	196	29.14 N	98.25 W
Salado Creek ≃, Tx., U.S.	222	30.59 N	97.25 W
Salaga	150	8.33 N	0.31 W
Salagle	144	1.50 N	42.17 E
Sālah	132	32.38 N	36.46 E
Ṣalāh ad-Dīn □[4]	128	34.15 N	43.55 E
Salahin	144	2.57 N	46.26 E
Sala'ilua	175a	13.41 S	172.34 W
Salair	86	54.13 N	85.47 E
Salairskij kr'až ∧	86	54.15 N	85.30 E
Sălaj □[6]	38	47.15 N	23.00 E
Salak	114	2.34 N	98.20 E
Salak, Gunung ∧	115a	6.42 S	106.44 E
Šalakas	76	55.35 N	26.08 E
Šalakuša	24	62.15 N	40.17 E
Salal	146	14.51 N	17.13 E
Salala, Chile	252	30.41 S	71.32 W
Salala, Liber.	150	6.40 N	10.05 W
Salālah, Sūd.	140	21.19 N	36.13 E
Ṣalālah, 'Umān	118	17.00 N	54.06 E
Salamá, Guat.	236	15.06 N	90.16 W
Salamá, Hond.	236	14.50 N	86.36 W
Salamajärven kansallispuisto ♠	26	63.20 N	24.40 E
Salaman	115a	7.35 S	110.08 E
Salamanca, Chile	252	31.47 S	70.58 W
Salamanca, Esp.	34	40.58 N	5.39 W
Salamanca, Méx.	234	20.34 N	101.12 W
Salamanca, Perú	248	15.31 S	72.50 W
Salamanca, Perú	286d	12.05 S	77.00 W
Salamanca, N.Y., U.S.	210	42.09 N	78.42 W
Salamanca □[4]	34	40.45 N	6.00 W
Salamanga	158	26.28 S	32.39 E
Salamat □[5]	146	11.00 N	20.30 E
Salamat, Bahr ≃	146	9.27 N	18.06 E
Salāmbek	120	28.18 N	65.09 E
Salamina	246	5.25 N	75.29 W
Salamínos, Órmos ⊂	267c	37.56 N	23.27 E
Salamís	38	37.58 N	23.29 E
Salamís I	38	37.54 N	23.26 E
Salamis ⊥	130	35.10 N	33.54 E
Salamīyah	130	35.01 N	37.03 E
Salām Khān	120	31.47 N	66.45 E
Salamonia	216	40.23 N	84.52 W
Salamonie ≃	216	40.50 N	85.43 W
Salamonie Lake ⊜[1]	216	40.46 N	85.37 W
Salāmūn	142	31.04 N	31.28 E
Salandra	68	40.31 N	16.19 E
Sālang, Tūnel-e ◆[5]	120	35.19 N	69.02 E
Salani	175a	14.00 S	171.33 W
Salantai	76	56.04 N	21.32 E
Salaparuta	70	37.47 N	13.00 E
Salaquí	246	7.18 N	77.33 W
Salaquí ≃	246	7.27 N	77.07 W
Salāqūs	142	28.44 N	30.50 E
Salar	85	41.21 N	69.22 E
Salara	64	44.59 N	11.25 E
Sălard	38	47.13 N	22.03 E
Salarjovo	265b	55.37 N	37.26 E
Salas	248	6.16 S	79.37 W
Salas de los Infantes	34	42.01 N	3.17 W
Salat ≃	32	43.10 N	0.58 E
Salatiga	115a	7.19 S	110.30 E
Salauš	80	55.59 N	52.53 E
Salavat	86	53.21 N	55.55 E
Salavaux	58	46.55 N	7.02 E
Salaverry	248	8.14 S	78.58 W
Salavina	252	28.48 S	63.25 W
Salawati I	164	1.07 S	130.52 E
Salawe	154	3.19 S	32.52 E
Salay	116	8.52 N	124.47 E
Salāya	120	22.19 N	69.35 E
Sala y Gómez, Isla I	18	26.28 S	105.28 W
Sala y Gomez Ridge ⊹[3]	18	25.00 S	98.00 W
Salazgor'	80	54.07 N	43.09 E
Salba	88	53.14 N	92.36 E
Salbani	126	22.38 N	87.20 E
Salbohed	40	59.55 N	16.19 E
Salbosjön ⊜	40	59.50 N	14.54 E
Salbris	50	47.26 N	2.03 E
Šalbuzdag, gora ∧	84	41.19 N	47.48 E
Salcajá	236	14.53 N	91.27 W
Salccantay, Nevado ∧	248	13.20 S	72.33 W
Salcedo, Pil.	116	11.09 N	125.40 E
Salcedo, Rep. Dom.	238	19.23 N	70.25 W
Salcha ≃	180	64.29 N	147.00 W
Salching	60	48.49 N	12.34 E
Şalcia	38	43.57 N	24.56 E
Šalčininkai	76	54.18 N	25.23 E
Salcombe	42	50.13 N	3.47 W
Şalda ≃	86	58.48 N	61.20 E
Šaldaj	86	51.56 N	78.48 E
Saldaña	34	42.31 N	4.44 W
Saldaña ≃	246	4.01 N	74.52 W
Saldanha	158	33.00 S	17.56 E
Saldanhabaai ⊂	158	33.04 S	18.00 E
Šaldež	80	56.52 N	44.46 E
Saldungaray	252	38.12 S	61.47 W
Saldus	76	56.40 N	22.30 E
Sale, Austl.	166	38.06 S	147.04 E
Sale, It.	62	44.59 N	8.48 E
Salé, Magreb	148	34.04 N	6.50 W
Sale, Eng., U.K.	44	53.26 N	2.19 W
Salebabu, Pulau I	108	3.55 N	126.40 E
Salechard	74	66.33 N	66.40 E
Sale Creek	194	35.22 N	85.06 W
Salée, Rivière ʮ	241o	16.17 N	61.33 W
Saleh, Teluk ⊂	115b	8.34 S	117.57 E
Salelologa	175a	13.44 S	172.10 W
Salem, On., Can.	212	43.42 N	80.27 W
Salem, Dtsch.	58	47.46 N	9.16 E
Salem, India	122	11.39 N	78.10 E
Salem, S. Afr.	158	33.28 S	26.29 E
Salem, Sve.	40	59.13 N	17.44 E
Salem, Ar., U.S.	194	36.22 N	91.49 W
Salem, Il., U.S.	219	38.37 N	88.56 W
Salem, In., U.S.	218	38.03 N	86.15 W
Salem, Ia., U.S.	190	40.51 N	91.37 W
Salem, Ky., U.S.	194	37.15 N	88.14 W
Salem, Ma., U.S.	207	42.31 N	70.53 W
Salem, Mi., U.S.	281	42.24 N	83.34 W
Salem, Mo., U.S.	194	37.38 N	91.32 W
Salem, N.H., U.S.	207	42.47 N	71.12 W
Salem, N.J., U.S.	208	39.34 N	75.28 W
Salem, N.Y., U.S.	210	43.10 N	73.19 W
Salem, Oh., U.S.	214	40.54 N	80.51 W
Salem, Or., U.S.	224	44.56 N	123.02 W
Salem, S.D., U.S.	198	43.43 N	97.23 W
Salem, Ut,. U.S.	200	40.03 N	111.40 W
Salem, Va., U.S.	192	37.17 N	80.03 W
Salem, W.V., U.S.	188	39.16 N	80.33 W
Salem, Wi., U.S.	216	42.33 N	88.06 W
Salem □[6]	208	39.34 N	75.20 W
Salem ≃	208	39.34 N	75.31 W
Salem Airfield ⊠	281	42.25 N	83.34 W
Sale Marasino	64	45.43 N	10.06 E
Salem Canal ≚	285	39.41 N	75.31 W
Salem Depot	283	42.47 N	71.12 W
Salem Harbor ⊂	283	42.31 N	70.53 W
Salem Heights	214	40.54 N	80.53 W
Salemi	70	37.49 N	12.48 E
Salem Maritime National Historic Site ⊥	207	42.31 N	70.53 W
Salem State College ʊ[2]	283	42.30 N	70.54 W
Salem Upland ⋌[1]	194	37.25 N	91.30 W
Sälen, Sve.	26	61.10 N	13.16 E
Salen, Scot., U.K.	46	56.43 N	5.47 W
Salen, Scot., U.K.	46	56.31 N	5.57 W
Salentina, Penisola ›[1]	68	40.25 N	18.00 E
Salentine, Murge ◆[1]	68	40.02 N	18.13 E
Salento	68	40.15 N	15.11 E
Salernes	62	43.33 N	6.14 E
Salerno	68	40.41 N	14.47 E
Salerno □[4]	68	40.27 N	15.16 E
Salerno, Golfo di ⊂	68	40.32 N	14.42 E
Salers	32	45.08 N	2.30 E
Salesbury	262	53.47 N	2.30 W
Salesópolis	256	23.32 S	45.51 W
Salève, Mont ∧	58	46.07 N	6.10 E
Salford	44	53.28 N	2.18 W
Salford □[8]	262	53.28 N	2.23 W
Şalfords	260	51.12 N	0.10 W
Šalgačova	24	62.19 N	39.35 E
Salgado	250	11.02 S	37.28 W
Salgan	80	55.14 N	45.30 E
Şalgar	246	5.58 N	75.59 W
Šalgija	86	47.35 N	70.36 E
Salgótarján	30	48.07 N	19.48 E
Salgueiro	250	8.04 S	39.06 W
Salher ∧	122	20.43 N	73.56 E
Salhyr ≃	78	45.38 N	35.01 E
Sali, Alg.	148	26.58 N	0.01 W
Şali, Hrv.	36	43.56 N	15.10 E
Šali, Ross.	80	55.41 N	49.40 E
Šali, Ross.	84	43.08 N	45.54 E
Salí ≃	252	27.33 S	64.57 W
Salice Salentino	68	40.23 N	17.58 E
Salice Terme	62	44.55 N	9.01 E
Salici, Monte ∧	70	37.44 N	14.38 E
Salida, Ca., U.S.	226	37.42 N	121.05 W
Salida, Co., U.S.	200	38.32 N	105.59 W
Salies-de-Béarn	32	43.29 N	0.55 W
Salīf	144	15.18 N	42.40 E
Salignac-Eyvignes	32	44.59 N	1.19 E
Salihli	130	38.29 N	28.09 E
Şālikha	126	23.18 N	89.22 E
Šalikovo	82	55.30 N	36.13 E
Salim	140	12.52 N	28.40 E
Salima	154	13.47 S	34.26 E
Salīmah, Wāḥat ⊤[4]	140	21.22 N	29.19 E
Salimani	157a	11.47 S	43.17 E
Salimbatu	112	2.57 N	117.21 E
Salimgarh Fort ⊥	272a	28.40 N	77.14 E
Salimi	152	9.24 S	23.35 E
Salin	110	20.35 N	94.39 E
Salina, Ks., U.S.	198	38.50 N	97.36 W
Salina, Ok., U.S.	196	36.17 N	95.09 W
Salina, Pa., U.S.	214	40.31 N	79.30 W
Salina, Ut,. U.S.	200	38.57 N	111.51 W
Salina, Canale di ʮ	70	38.32 N	14.54 E
Salina, Isola I	70	38.34 N	14.50 E
Salina Cruz	234	16.10 N	95.12 W
Salina Point ›	238	22.13 N	74.18 W
Salinas, Bra.	255	16.10 S	42.17 W
Salinas, Ec.	246	2.13 S	80.58 W
Salinas, P.R.	240m	17.59 N	66.18 W
Salinas, Ca., U.S.	226	36.40 N	121.39 W
Salinas ≃, Bra.	255	16.37 S	42.18 W
Salinas (Chixoy) ≃, N.A.	232	16.28 N	90.33 W
Salinas ≃, Ca., U.S.	226	36.45 N	121.48 W
Salinas, Pampa de las ⁙	252	31.58 S	66.42 W
Salinas, Ponta das ›	152	12.50 S	12.56 E
Salinas, Sierra de ⋌	226	36.18 N	121.20 W
Salinas de Garci Mendoza	248	19.38 S	67.43 W
Salinas de Hidalgo	234	22.38 N	101.43 W
Salinas del Rey	196	27.38 N	102.24 W
Salinas Municipal Airport ⊠	226	36.40 N	121.40 W
Salinas National Monument ♠	200	34.05 N	106.14 W
Salinas Valley V	226	36.15 N	121.15 W
Salinas Victoria	196	25.53 N	100.19 W
Salin-de-Giraud	62	43.25 N	4.44 E
Salindres	62	44.10 N	4.10 E
Saline, La., U.S.	194	32.09 N	92.58 W
Saline, Mi., U.S.	216	42.10 N	83.46 W
Saline ≃, Ar., U.S.	194	33.44 N	93.58 W
Saline ≃, Ar., U.S.	194	33.10 N	92.08 W
Saline ≃, Il., U.S.	194	37.35 N	88.08 W
Saline ≃, Ks., U.S.	198	38.51 N	97.30 W
Saline ≃, Mi., U.S.	216	41.59 N	83.37 W
Saline, North Fork ≃	194	37.44 N	88.19 W
Saline Bayou ≃	194	31.45 N	92.58 W
Saline di Volterra	66	43.22 N	10.49 E
Saline Lake ⊜[1]	194	31.55 N	92.55 W
Salines, Point ›	241k	12.00 N	61.48 W
Salines, Pointe des ›	240e	14.24 N	60.53 W
Salineville	214	40.37 N	80.51 W
Salingyi	110	21.58 N	95.03 E
Salinópolis	250	0.37 S	47.20 W
Šalinskoje	86	55.43 N	93.46 E
Salins-les-Bains	58	46.57 N	5.53 E
Salins-les-Thermes	62	45.28 N	6.32 E
Salipolo	112	3.45 S	119.29 E
Salisbury, Austl.	168b	34.46 S	138.38 E
Salisbury, Dom.	240d	15.26 N	61.27 W
Salisbury, Eng., U.K.	42	51.05 N	1.48 W
Salisbury, Ct., U.S.	207	41.59 N	73.25 W
Salisbury, Md., U.S.	208	38.21 N	75.35 W
Salisbury, Ma., U.S.	207	42.50 N	70.51 W
Salisbury, Mo., U.S.	194	39.25 N	92.48 W
Salisbury, N.C., U.S.	192	35.40 N	80.28 W
Salisbury, Pa., U.S.	188	39.45 N	79.04 W
Salisbury → Harare, Zimb.	154	17.50 S	31.03 E
Salisbury Cathedral ʊ[1]	42	51.05 N	1.48 W
Salisbury Center	210	43.09 N	74.47 W
Salisbury Hall ⊥	260	51.43 N	0.16 W
Salisbury Island I, Austl.	162	34.21 S	123.32 E
Salisbury Island I, N.T., Can.	176	63.30 N	77.00 W
Salisbury Mills	210	41.26 N	74.08 W
Salisbury Plain ⁙	42	51.12 N	1.55 W
Salisbury Plain ≃	283	42.02 N	70.58 W
Salish Mountains ⋌	202	48.15 N	114.45 W
Salito ≃	70	37.29 N	13.46 E
Salitpa	194	31.37 N	88.01 W
Salitre ≃	250	9.29 S	40.39 W
Şalix	214	40.18 N	78.46 W
Šalkar, Kaz.	80	48.03 N	48.56 E
Šalkar, Kaz.	80	50.32 N	51.51 E
Šalkar, ozero ⊜	80	50.33 N	51.40 E
Šalkar-Jega-Kara, ozero ⊜	86	50.45 N	60.54 E
Salkehatchie ≃	192	32.37 N	80.53 W
Şalkhad	132	32.29 N	36.43 E
Salkhia	272b	22.35 N	88.21 E
Salkum	224	46.31 N	122.37 W
Salla	24	66.50 N	28.40 E
Salladasburg	210	41.17 N	77.14 W
Sallagriffon	62	43.53 N	6.54 E
Sallanches	58	45.56 N	6.38 E
Salland ◆[1]	52	52.20 N	6.20 E
Salles-Curan	32	44.11 N	2.47 E
Salles-sous-Bois	62	44.27 N	4.56 E
Sallgast	54	51.35 N	13.51 E
Salling ◆[1]	26	56.40 N	9.00 E
Salliqueló	252	36.45 S	62.56 W
Sallisaw	196	35.27 N	94.47 W
Sallisaw Creek ≃	194	35.23 N	94.52 W
Salluit	176	62.14 N	75.38 W
Sallūm	140	19.23 N	37.06 E
Sallūm, Khalīj as- ⊂	146	31.41 N	25.21 E
Salm ≃, Bel.	56	50.22 N	5.52 E
Salm ≃, Dtsch.	56	49.51 N	6.51 E
Salmās	128	38.11 N	44.47 E
Salmchâteau	56	50.16 N	5.54 E
Salme	76	58.10 N	22.15 E
Salmi	24	61.22 N	31.53 E
Salmo	182	49.12 N	117.17 W
Salmon	202	45.10 N	113.53 W
Salmon ≃, B.C., Can.	182	54.05 N	122.34 W
Salmon ≃, N.B., Can.	186	46.06 N	65.56 W
Salmon ≃, On., Can.	212	44.11 N	77.15 W
Salmon ≃, N.A.	188	45.02 N	74.31 W
Salmon ≃, Ct., U.S.	207	41.29 N	72.29 W
Salmon ≃, Id., U.S.	202	45.51 N	116.46 W
Salmon ≃, N.Y., U.S.	212	43.35 N	76.12 W
Salmon ≃, Or., U.S.	224	45.03 N	124.00 W
Salmon ≃, Or., U.S.	224	45.22 N	122.02 W
Salmon, East Fork ≃	202	44.16 N	114.19 W
Salmon, Middle Fork ≃	202	45.18 N	114.36 W
Salmon, North Branch ≃	212	43.32 N	75.48 W
Salmon, South Fork ≃	202	45.23 N	115.31 W
Salmon Arm	182	50.42 N	119.16 W
Salmon-Bay	186	51.26 N	57.36 W
Salmon Creek ≃, N.Y., U.S.	210	43.16 N	77.02 W
Salmon Creek ≃, N.Y., U.S.	210	43.19 N	77.43 W
Salmon Creek ≃, Wa., U.S.	224	46.26 N	122.52 W
Salmon Creek ≃, Wa., U.S.	224	45.44 N	122.45 W
Salmon Falls Creek ≃	202	42.43 N	114.51 W
Salmon Falls Creek Reservoir ⊜[1]	202	42.08 N	114.45 W
Salmon Gums	162	32.59 S	121.38 E
Salmon Lake ⊜	212	44.49 N	78.28 W
Salmon Mountain ∧	188	45.14 N	71.08 W
Salmon Mountains ⋌	204	41.00 N	123.00 W
Salmon Peak ∧	196	29.28 N	100.10 W
Salmon Point ›	212	43.52 N	77.14 W
Salmon River Mountains ⋌	202	44.45 N	115.30 W
Salmon River Reservoir ⊜[1]	212	43.32 N	75.52 W
Salmon Valley	182	54.05 N	122.41 W
Salmyš ≃	86	52.01 N	55.21 E
Sal'nytsya	78	49.44 N	28.02 E
Salo, Centraf.	152	3.12 N	16.07 E
Salò, It.	64	45.36 N	10.31 E
Salo, Suomi	26	60.23 N	23.08 E
Salobel'ak	80	57.07 N	48.05 E
Salobra ≃	248	20.12 S	56.29 W
Salomatino	80	50.01 N	44.50 E
Salome	200	33.46 N	113.36 W
Salomon, Cap ›	240e	14.30 N	61.06 W
Salomon, Îles → Solomon Islands □[1]	175e	8.00 S	159.00 E
Salomón, Islas → Solomon Islands □[1]	175e	8.00 S	159.00 E
Salomone, Monte ∧	267a	41.47 N	12.44 E
Salomon-Inseln → Solomon Islands □[1]	175e	8.00 S	159.00 E
Salon ≃	58	47.32 N	5.41 E
Salona	210	41.05 N	77.28 W
Salon-de-Provence	62	43.38 N	5.06 E
Salonga ≃	152	0.10 S	19.50 E
Salonga, Parc National de la ♠	152	1.45 S	21.20 E
Salonika → Thessaloníki	38	40.38 N	22.56 E
Salonta	38	46.48 N	21.40 E
Salor ≃, Esp.	34	39.39 N	7.03 W
Salor ≃, Esp.	34	39.42 N	6.28 W
Salorno (Salurn)	64	46.14 N	11.13 E
Saloslovo	265b	55.42 N	37.09 E
Şaloum ≃	150	13.50 N	16.45 W
Šalovka ≃	265b	55.47 N	38.12 E
Salpausselkä ∧	26	61.00 N	26.30 E
Şalpazarı	130	40.59 N	39.10 E
Šalqīn	130	36.08 N	36.27 E
Sal Rei	150a	16.11 N	22.55 W
Salsacate	252	31.19 S	65.05 W
Salsette Island I	272c	19.10 N	72.53 E
Salsilgo, Qawz ⁂[8]	140	10.49 N	22.54 E
Salsipuedes, Canal ʮ	232	28.37 N	113.00 W
Salsipuedes, Punta ›, C.R.	236	8.28 N	83.37 W
Salsipuedes, Punta ›, Méx.	232	32.05 N	116.53 W
Şal'sk	80	46.28 N	41.33 E
Šal'skij	24	61.48 N	35.58 E
Sal'sko-Manyčskaja gr'ada ∧	80	46.40 N	42.30 E
Salso ≃	70	37.06 N	13.57 E
Salsomaggiore Terme	64	44.49 N	9.59 E
Salt ≃, U.S.	202	43.08 N	111.02 W
Salt ≃, Az., U.S.	200	33.23 N	112.18 W
Salt ≃, Ky., U.S.	194	38.00 N	85.57 W
Salt ≃, Mi., U.S.	281	42.39 N	82.47 W
Salt ≃, Mo., U.S.	219	39.28 N	91.04 W
Salt, Elk Fork ≃	219	39.28 N	91.53 W
Salt, Middle Fork ≃	219	39.28 N	91.49 W
Salt, North Fork ≃	219	39.30 N	91.47 W
Salt, South Fork ≃	219	39.28 N	91.49 W
Salta	252	24.47 S	65.25 W
Salta □[4]	252	25.00 S	64.30 W
Saltaim, ozero ⊜	86	56.10 N	71.45 E
Saltair	224	48.57 N	123.46 W
Saltaire	276	40.39 N	73.12 W
Saltanovka	76	52.47 N	34.17 E
Saltara	66	43.45 N	12.54 E
Salt Ash, Austl.	170	32.47 S	151.55 E
Saltash, Eng., U.K.	42	50.24 N	4.12 W
Saltbæk Vig ⊂	41	55.43 N	11.12 E
Salt Basin ⊜	196	31.50 N	105.00 W
Saltburn-by-the-Sea	44	54.35 N	0.58 W
Salt Cay I	240b	25.06 N	77.18 W
Saltcoats, Sk., Can.	184	51.03 N	102.12 W
Saltcoats, Scot., U.K.	46	55.38 N	4.47 W
Salt Creek ≃, On., Can.	275b	43.48 N	79.42 W
Salt Creek ≃, Ca., U.S.	204	36.15 N	116.49 W
Salt Creek ≃, Il., U.S.	194	40.08 N	89.50 W
Salt Creek ≃, Il., U.S.	278	41.49 N	87.50 W
Salt Creek ≃, In., U.S.	216	41.37 N	87.09 W
Salt Creek ≃, In., U.S.	218	38.50 N	86.32 W
Salt Creek ≃, In., U.S.	218	39.27 N	85.09 W
Salt Creek ≃, Ks., U.S.	198	39.06 N	97.44 W
Salt Creek ≃, N.M., U.S.	196	33.35 N	104.23 W
Salt Creek ≃, Ok., U.S.	196	36.32 N	96.43 W
Salt Creek ≃, Or., U.S.	202	43.43 N	122.26 W
Salt Creek ≃, Or., U.S.	224	45.09 N	123.13 W
Salt Creek ≃, Wy., U.S.	202	43.41 N	106.20 W
Salt Creek, Middle Fork ≃	218	39.04 N	86.15 W
Salt Creek, North Fork ≃, Il., U.S.	216	40.13 N	88.50 W
Salt Creek, North Fork ≃, In., U.S.	218	39.08 N	86.21 W
Salt Creek, West Branch ≃	278	42.02 N	88.01 W
Salt Creek South Fork ≃	218	39.02 N	86.16 W
Salt Draw V	196	31.19 N	103.28 W
Saltee Islands II	48	52.07 N	6.36 W
Salten	41	56.05 N	9.35 E
Saltfleet	44	53.25 N	0.11 E
Saltford	42	51.24 N	2.27 W
Salt Fork Lake ⊜[1]	214	41.07 N	81.30 W
Salt Fork State Park ♠	214	40.06 N	81.29 W
Saltholm I	41	55.38 N	12.46 E
Saltillo, Méx.	232	25.25 N	101.00 W
Saltillo, Ms., U.S.	194	34.22 N	88.40 W
Saltillo, Pa., U.S.	214	40.13 N	78.01 W
Saltillo, Tn., U.S.	194	35.22 N	88.12 W
Saltillo, Tx., U.S.	222	33.11 N	95.20 W
Salt Island I	240m	18.23 N	64.31 W
Salt Lake	158	29.16 S	24.00 E
Salt Lake ⊜	196	34.05 N	103.05 W
Salt Lake City	200	40.45 N	111.53 W
Salto, Arg.	252	34.17 S	60.15 W
Salto, Ur.	252	31.23 S	57.58 W
Salto ≃	66	42.23 N	12.54 E
Salto, Lago del ⊜	66	42.15 N	13.02 E
Salto da Divisa	255	16.00 S	39.57 W
Salto de las Rosas	252	34.43 S	68.14 W
Salto del Fraile ›	286d	12.11 S	77.03 W
Salto del Guairá	252	24.03 S	54.17 W
Salto Grande	255	22.54 S	49.59 W
Salto Grande, Embalse ⊜[1]	252	31.00 S	57.55 W
Salton City	204	33.19 N	115.59 W
Salton Sea ⊜	204	33.19 N	115.50 W
Salton Sea State Recreation Area ♠	204	33.29 N	115.53 W
Saltonstall, Lake ⊜	283	42.47 N	71.04 W
Sāltora	126	23.32 N	86.56 E
Saltoro Range ⋌	123	35.17 N	77.03 E
Salto Santiago, Represa de ⊜[1]	252	25.40 S	52.30 W
Salt Pan Creek ≃	274a	33.59 S	151.02 E
Saltpeter Creek ⊂	284b	39.20 N	76.22 W
Salt Point	210	41.44 N	73.42 W
Saltpond	150	5.12 N	1.04 W
Salt Range ⋌	123	32.40 N	72.35 E
Salt River Indian Reservation ◆[4]	200	33.31 N	111.48 W
Saltsburg	214	40.29 N	79.27 W
Saltsjöbaden	40	59.17 N	18.18 E
Salt Slough ≃	226	37.18 N	120.54 W
Saltspring Island I	224	48.47 N	123.30 W
Salt Springs Reservoir ⊜[1]	226	38.30 N	120.11 W
Saltville	192	36.52 N	81.45 W
Salt Wells Creek ≃	200	41.39 N	108.59 W
Saltykovka, Ross.	80	52.07 N	44.05 E
Saltykovka, Ross.	265b	55.46 N	37.55 E
Saluda, S.C., U.S.	192	34.00 N	81.46 W
Saluda, Va., U.S.	208	37.36 N	76.35 W
Saluda ≃	192	34.00 N	81.04 W
Saludecio	66	43.52 N	12.40 E
Saluën → Salween ≃	12	16.31 N	97.37 E
Salue Timpaus, Selat ʮ	112	1.55 S	124.00 E
Salug	116	8.07 N	122.47 E
Saluggia	62	45.14 N	8.00 E
Sālūmbar	120	24.08 N	74.03 E
Salunga	208	40.06 N	76.26 W
Saluping Island I	116	6.20 N	122.02 E
Salūq 'Atīq	130	36.36 N	39.07 E
Sālūr	122	18.32 N	83.13 E
Salurn → Salorno	64	46.14 N	11.13 E
Salussola	62	45.27 N	8.07 E
Salutaris	256	22.10 S	43.17 W
Saluzzo	62	44.39 N	7.29 E
Salvación, Bahía ⊂	254	50.55 S	75.05 W
Salvado, Mount ∧	162	25.15 S	121.01 E
Salvador, Bra.	255	12.59 S	38.31 W
Salvador, Pil.	116	7.54 N	123.50 E
Salvador, Ca., U.S.	226	38.20 N	122.18 W
Salvador, El → El Salvador □[1]	236	13.50 N	88.55 W
Salvador, Lake ⊜	194	29.45 N	90.15 W
Salvador Island I	116	15.31 N	119.55 E
Salvador María	258	35.18 S	59.10 W
Salvador Mazza	252	22.04 S	63.43 W
Salvage	186	48.41 N	53.38 W
Salvail ≃	206	45.49 N	72.58 W
Salvaterra	250	0.46 S	48.31 W
Salvaterra de Magos	34	39.01 N	8.48 W
Salvatierra	234	20.13 N	100.53 W
Salve	68	39.51 N	18.17 E
Salviac	32	44.41 N	1.16 E
Salwā, Dawḥat ⊂	128	25.30 N	50.40 E
Salwā Baḥrī	140	24.44 N	32.56 E
Salween ≃	12	16.31 N	97.37 E
Salyan, Azer.	84	39.34 N	48.58 E
Salyān, Nepāl	124	28.22 N	82.10 E
Salyer	204	40.53 N	123.35 W
Salyersville	192	37.45 N	83.04 W
Salza ≃, Dtsch.	54	51.32 N	11.50 E
Salza ≃, Öst.	61	47.40 N	14.43 E
Salzach ≃	30	48.12 N	12.56 E
Salza Irpina	68	40.55 N	14.53 E
Salzbergen	52	52.19 N	7.20 E
Salzböde ≃	56	50.40 N	8.42 E
Salzbrunn	156	24.23 S	18.00 E
Salzburg	64	47.48 N	13.02 E
Salzburg □[3]	64	47.25 N	13.15 E
Salzgitter	52	52.10 N	10.25 E
Salzgitter-Bad ◆[8]	52	52.04 N	10.23 E
Salzgitter-Barum ◆[8]	52	52.07 N	10.25 E
Salzgitter-Immendorf ◆[8]	52	52.09 N	10.26 E
Salzgitter-Lebenstedt ◆[8]	52	52.09 N	10.20 E
Salzgitter-Thiede ◆[8]	52	52.11 N	10.29 E
Salzgitter-Watenstedt ◆[8]	54	52.06 N	10.22 E
Salzhaff ⊂	54	54.06 N	11.36 E
Salzhausen	52	53.13 N	10.09 E
Salzhemmendorf	52	52.04 N	9.35 E
Salzkammergut ◆[1]	64	47.45 N	13.30 E
Salzkotten	52	51.40 N	8.36 E
Salzmünde	54	51.31 N	11.49 E
Salzwedel	54	52.51 N	11.09 E
Sam, Gabon	152	0.58 N	11.16 E
Sām, India	120	26.50 N	70.31 E
Samā	132	32.28 N	36.14 E
Sama ≃	248	18.10 S	70.40 W
Sam A. Baker State Park ♠	194	37.16 N	90.34 W
Samacá	246	5.29 N	73.29 W
Samacimbo	152	13.33 S	16.59 E
Sama [de Langreo]	34	43.18 N	5.41 W
Samādūn	142	30.20 N	30.57 E
Samagaltaj	88	50.36 N	95.03 E
Samah	146	28.12 N	19.09 E
Samāika ◆[8]	272a	28.32 N	77.05 E
Samaipata	248	18.09 S	63.52 W
Samal (Peñaplata)	116	7.05 N	125.42 E
Samalá ≃	236	14.11 N	91.47 W
Samalanga	114	5.13 N	96.22 E
Şamalayuca	200	31.21 N	106.28 W
Šamaldy-Saj	85	41.12 N	72.11 E
Samales Group II	116	6.00 N	121.45 E
Samalga Pass ʮ	180	52.48 N	169.25 W
Samal Island I	116	7.03 N	125.44 E
Sāmalkot	122	17.03 N	82.11 E
Samālūt	142	28.18 N	30.42 E
Samambaia ≃	255	22.45 S	53.21 W
Samāna, India	124	30.09 N	76.12 E
Samaná, Rep. Dom.	238	19.13 N	69.19 W
Samaná, Bahía de ⊂	238	19.10 N	69.25 W
Samaná, Cabo ›	238	19.18 N	69.09 W
Samana Cay I	238	23.06 N	73.42 W
Samandağı	130	36.07 N	35.56 E
Samandıra	130	40.59 N	29.13 E
Samandıra ≃	267b	40.59 N	29.15 E
Samangān	120	36.16 N	68.01 E
Samangān □[4]	120	36.15 N	67.40 E
Samangwa	152	4.24 S	24.10 E
Samani	92a	42.07 N	142.56 E
Samaniego	246	1.20 N	77.35 W
Samanlı Dağları ⋌	130	40.36 N	29.30 E
Samannūd	142	30.58 N	31.15 E
Samar	132	29.49 N	35.01 E
Samar □[4]	116	11.50 N	125.00 E
Samar I	116	12.00 N	125.00 E
Samara	80	53.12 N	50.09 E
Samara ≃, Ross.	80	53.10 N	50.04 E
Samara ≃, Ukr.	78	48.27 N	35.07 E
Samarai	164	10.37 S	150.40 E
Samara Oblast' □[4]	80	53.30 N	50.30 E
Samarate	62	45.38 N	8.47 E
Samarga	89	47.17 N	138.48 E
Samarga ≃	89	47.15 N	138.46 E
Samaria, Id., U.S.	202	42.07 N	112.20 W
Samaria, Mi., U.S.	216	41.48 N	83.35 W
Samaria (As-Sāmirah) □[9]	132	32.15 N	35.10 E
Samaria, Mount ∧	169	36.52 S	146.03 E
Samaria Gorge → Farángi Samariás V	38	35.18 N	24.00 E
Samariapo	246	5.15 N	67.48 W
Samarinda	112	0.30 S	117.09 E
Samarka	89	44.44 N	134.13 E
Samarkand	85	39.40 N	66.48 E
Samarkand □[4]	85	39.40 N	67.15 E
Sāmarrā'	128	34.12 N	43.52 E
Samar Sea ⊤[2]	116	12.15 N	124.15 E
Samarskoje, Kaz.	86	49.00 N	83.23 E
Samarskoje, Ross.	83	46.56 N	39.41 E
Şamarskoje, Ross.	86	52.02 N	58.10 E
Šamary	86	57.21 N	58.14 E
Samasata	123	29.21 N	71.33 E
Samassi	71	39.29 N	8.54 E
Samastīpur	124	25.51 N	85.47 E
Samatya ◆[8]	267b	41.00 N	28.56 E
Samaúna	248	7.50 S	60.02 W
Samawāri	120	28.34 N	66.46 E
Şamaxi	84	40.38 N	48.39 E
Šamba, Centraf.	152	6.49 N	21.12 E
Samba, India	123	32.34 N	75.07 E
Samba, Zaïre	152	0.14 N	21.19 E
Samba, Zaïre	154	4.38 S	26.22 E
Samba Caju	152	8.46 S	15.24 E
Sambaetiba	256	22.41 S	42.48 W
Sambaíba	250	7.08 S	45.21 W
Sambalpur	120	21.27 N	83.58 E
Sambar, Tanjung ›	112	2.59 S	110.19 E
Sambas	112	1.20 N	109.15 E
Sambava	157b	14.16 S	50.10 E
Sambawizi	154	18.21 S	26.16 E
Şambayat	130	37.41 N	38.03 E
Šambāza	120	31.49 N	69.20 E
Sambek, Ross.	83	47.20 N	39.01 E
Sambek, Ross.	83	47.45 N	39.48 E
Sambek ≃	83	47.16 N	39.01 E
Sambesi → Zambezi ≃	138	18.55 S	36.04 E
Sambhal	124	28.35 N	78.33 E
Sāmbhar	120	26.55 N	75.12 E
Sāmbhar Lake ⊜	120	26.58 N	75.05 E
Sambia → Zambia □[1]	154	14.30 S	27.30 E
Sambiase	68	38.58 N	16.17 E
Sambir	78	49.32 N	23.11 E
Sambit, Pulau I	112	1.46 N	119.03 E
Sambito ≃	250	5.40 S	42.10 W
Sambo	152	12.57 S	16.05 E
Samboan	116	9.32 N	123.18 E
Samboja	112	1.02 S	117.02 E
Sambolabbo	152	7.05 N	11.59 E
Sâmbor	110	12.46 N	105.58 E
Samborombón ≃	252	35.43 S	57.20 W
Samborombón, Bahía ⊂	252	36.00 S	57.12 W
Samborondón	246	1.57 S	79.44 W
Sambre ≃	32	50.28 N	4.52 E
Sambre à l'Oise, Canal de la ≚	50	49.39 N	3.20 E
Sambreville	56	50.26 N	4.37 E
Sambriāl	123	32.28 N	74.21 E
Sambú ≃	246	8.05 N	78.18 W
Sambuca di Sicilia	70	37.39 N	13.07 E
Sambuca Pistoiese	66	44.06 N	11.00 E
Sambughetti, Monte ∧	70	37.50 N	14.22 E
Sambungo	152	8.39 S	20.43 E
Sambusu	156	17.50 S	19.20 E
Samch'ŏk	98	37.27 N	129.10 E
Sam Chom, Khao ∧	110	8.07 N	99.26 E
Samch'ŏnp'o	98	34.57 N	128.03 E
Samdžir, gora ∧	88	52.32 N	93.53 E
Same	154	4.04 S	37.44 E
Same ≃	94	36.54 N	140.49 E
Samedan	58	46.33 N	9.52 E
Samegawa	94	37.02 N	140.31 E
Sāmen	128	34.12 N	48.42 E
Samene, Oued V	148	26.49 N	7.08 E
Samer	50	50.38 N	1.45 E
Sameru Dando ∧	124	27.02 N	90.20 E
Samet'	80	57.49 N	40.44 E
Samford	171a	27.23 S	152.53 E
Samfya	154	11.21 S	29.32 E
Samga	98	35.25 N	128.05 E
Samho	98	39.56 N	127.53 E
Saminka ≃	265b	55.45 N	37.17 E
Samiria ≃	246	4.42 S	74.13 W
Samish	224	48.35 N	122.33 W
Samish ≃	224	48.38 N	122.29 W
Samish Bay ⊂	224	48.36 N	122.28 W
Samish Lake ⊜	224	48.39 N	122.24 W
Samj	132	32.27 N	36.30 E
Samka	110	20.09 N	96.57 E
Şämkir	84	40.50 N	46.02 E
Šamlesbury	262	53.46 N	2.38 W
Samlesbury Aerodrome ⊠	262	53.47 N	2.34 W
Samlesbury Bottoms	262	53.45 N	2.34 W
Samlesbury Higher Hall ⊥	262	53.46 N	2.34 W
Şamlı	130	39.48 N	27.51 E
Šammamish, Lake ⊜	224	47.36 N	122.06 W
Sammichele di Bari	68	40.53 N	16.57 E
Samnangjin	98	35.23 N	128.50 E
Samnaun	58	46.56 N	10.22 E
Samnaungruppe ⋌	58	47.00 N	10.25 E
Sam Ngao	110	17.15 N	99.01 E
Samnū	146	27.17 N	14.53 E
Samnye	98	35.55 N	127.05 E
Samo	164	3.58 S	152.51 E
Samoa → Western Samoa □[1]	175a	13.55 S	172.00 W
Samoa → American Samoa □[2]	175a	14.20 S	170.00 W

≃ River	Fluß	Río	Rivière	Rio
≚ Canal	Kanal	Canal	Canal	Canal
⌞ Waterfall, Rapids	Wasserfall, Stromschnellen	Cascada, Rápidos	Chute d'eau, Rapides	Cascata, Rápidos
ʮ Strait	Meeresstraße	Estrecho	Détroit	Estreito
⊂ Bay, Gulf	Bucht, Golf	Bahía, Golfo	Baie, Golfe	Baía, Golfo
⊜ Lake, Lakes	See, Seen	Lago, Lagos	Lac, Lacs	Lago, Lagos
⁙ Swamp	Sumpf	Pantano	Marais	Pântano
⊓ Ice Features, Glacier	Eis- und Gletscherformen	Accidentes Glaciales	Formes glaciaires	Acidentes glaciares
⊤ Other Hydrographic Features	Andere Hydrographische Objekte	Otros Elementos Hidrográficos	Autres données hydrographiques	Outros acidentes hidrográficos

⊹ Submarine Features	Untermeerische Objekte	Accidentes Submarinos	Formes de relief sous-marin	Acidentes submarinos
□ Political Unit	Politische Einheit	Unidad Politica	Entité politique	Unidade política
ʊ Cultural Institution	Kulturelle Institution	Institución Cultural	Institution culturelle	Institução cultural
⊥ Historical Site	Historische Stätte	Sitio Histórico	Site historique	Sitio histórico
♠ Recreational Site	Erholungs- und Ferienort	Sitio de Recreo	Centre de loisirs	Area de Lazer
⊠ Airport	Flughafen	Aeropuerto	Aéroport	Aeroporto
■ Military Installation	Militäranlage	Instalación Militar	Installation militaire	Instalação militar
◆ Miscellaneous	Verschiedenes	Misceláneo	Divers	Diversos

Samoa americane — American Samoa □[2] 175a 14.20 S 170.00 W
Samoa Basin ✦[1] 14 16.00 S 166.00 W
Samoa i Sisifo — Western Samoa □[1] 175a 13.55 S 172.00 W
Samoa Islands II 175a 14.00 S 171.00 W
Samo Alto 252 30.25 S 70.58 W
Samoa Occidental — Western Samoa □[1] 175a 13.55 S 172.00 W
Samoa Occidentales — Western Samoa □[1] 175a 13.55 S 172.00 W
Samobor 36 45.48 N 15.43 E
Samoded 24 63.38 N 40.29 E
Samoëns 58 46.05 N 6.44 E
Samofalovka 80 48.57 N 44.13 E
Samoggia ≃ 64 44.41 N 11.15 E
Samojlovka 80 51.12 N 43.43 E
Samokov 38 42.20 N 23.33 E
Samolaco 58 46.15 N 9.21 E
Samora ≃ 266c 38.50 N 8.57 W
Sámos 38 37.45 N 27.00 E
Sámos I 38 37.48 N 26.44 E
Samosdelka 80 46.02 N 47.53 E
Samoset 220 27.28 N 82.32 W
Samosir, Pulau I 114 2.35 N 98.50 E
Samotevíči 76 53.13 N 31.50 E
Samothrace — Samothráki I 38 40.30 N 25.32 E
Samothráki 38 40.28 N 25.31 E
Samothráki (Samothrace) I 38 40.30 N 25.32 E
Samouco 266c 38.43 N 9.00 W
Šamovo 76 54.12 N 31.22 E
Samovol'no-Ivanovka 80 52.33 N 50.53 E
S'amozero 24 61.54 N 33.18 E
Sampacho 252 33.23 S 64.43 W
Sampaga 112 2.19 S 119.07 E
Sampaio Correia 256 22.52 S 42.36 W
Sampalan 115b 8.41 S 115.34 E
Sampanahan 112 2.38 S 116.11 E
Sampang 115a 7.12 S 113.14 E
Sampara ≃ 112 3.49 S 122.28 E
Sampawams Creek ≃ 276 40.41 N 73.19 W
Sam Pervyj 86 45.28 N 56.06 E
Sampéyre 62 44.34 N 7.11 E
Sampford Peverell 42 50.56 N 3.22 W
Sampieri 70 36.43 N 14.44 E
Sampit 112 2.32 S 112.57 E
Sampit ≃ 112 2.44 S 112.54 E
Sampit, Teluk C 112 3.05 S 113.03 E
Sampolawa 112 5.36 S 122.43 E
Sampson 279b 40.10 N 79.53 W
Sampson State Park ♦ 210 42.44 N 76.55 W
Sampués 246 9.11 N 75.23 W
Sampur 80 52.19 N 41.37 E
Sampwe 154 9.20 S 27.26 E
Samrāla 123 30.51 N 76.11 E
Sam Rayburn Reservoir ⊜[1] 194 31.27 N 94.37 W
Samre 144 13.07 N 39.10 E
Samreboi 150 5.36 N 2.34 W
Samro, ozero ⊜ 76 58.57 N 28.49 E
Samrong, Khlong ≋ 269a 13.39 N 100.34 E
Sams ≃ 224 47.38 N 124.01 W
Samsang 120 30.31 N 82.37 E
Samsø I 41 55.52 N 10.37 E
Samsø Bælt ⊔ 41 55.48 N 10.47 E
Samson, Al., U.S. 194 31.06 N 86.02 W
Sam Son, Viet 110 19.44 N 105.54 E
Samson I 42a 49.56 N 6.22 W
Samson Indian Reserve ◆[4] 182 52.48 N 113.10 W
Samsonovka 85 42.44 N 70.32 E
Samsonvale, Lake ⊜[1] 171a 27.15 S 152.55 E
Samsonville 210 41.53 N 74.18 W
Sams Point ∧ 210 41.40 N 74.22 W
Samsu 98 41.19 N 127.59 E
Samsun 130 41.17 N 36.20 E
Samsun □[4] 130 41.15 N 36.00 E
Samsun Körfezi C 130 41.18 N 36.21 E
Samtens 54 54.21 N 13.17 E
Samthar 124 25.51 N 78.55 E
Samtown 194 31.16 N 92.26 W
Samtredia 84 42.10 N 42.20 E
Samu 112 2.01 S 115.57 E
Samūdragarh 126 23.21 N 88.20 E
Samuel, Mount ∧ 162 19.41 S 134.09 E
Samuel P. Taylor State Park ♦ 226 38.01 N 122.44 W
Samugheo 71 39.57 N 8.56 E
Samuhú 252 27.31 S 60.24 W
Samui, Ko I 110 9.30 N 100.00 E
Samukawa 94 35.22 N 139.23 E
Samundri 123 31.04 N 72.58 E
Samur ≃ 84 41.53 N 48.32 E
Samur-Abşeron kanalı ≋ 84 41.38 N 48.25 E
Samus' 86 56.46 N 84.44 E
Samusele 152 10.06 S 24.05 E
Samut Prakan 110 13.36 N 100.36 E
Samut Prakan □[4] 269a 13.35 N 100.35 E
Samut Sakhon 110 13.32 N 100.17 E
Samut Songkhram 110 13.24 N 100.00 E
Samuyi Shankou)(124 29.55 N 84.46 E
S'amža 76 60.01 N 41.02 E
San 150 13.18 N 4.54 W
San (Xan) ≃, Asia 110 13.32 N 105.58 E
San ≃, Europe 30 50.44 N 21.50 E
San ≃, Zhg. 100 33.02 N 119.21 E
Saña, Perú 248 6.55 S 79.35 W
Şan'ā', Yaman 144 15.23 N 44.12 E
Sana ≃, Bos. 36 45.03 N 16.23 E
San'a ≃, Ross. 82 54.41 N 35.55 E
Sanaag □[4] 144 10.30 N 47.45 E
Sanaba 150 12.25 N 3.49 W
Sanaba ≃ 150 15.06 N 10.55 W
Şanabū 142 27.30 N 30.47 E
Sanada 94 36.27 N 138.20 E
Sanae ʋ[3] 9 70.30 S 2.30 W
Sanafā 142 30.47 N 31.21 E
Şanāfīr I 128 27.55 N 34.40 E
Sanaga ≃ 152 3.35 N 9.38 E
Sanage-yama ∧ 94 35.12 N 137.10 E
Sanagōchi 96 33.59 N 134.28 E
San Agustín, Arg. 252 38.01 S 58.21 W
San Agustín, Arg. 252 31.59 S 64.23 W
San Agustín, Bol. 248 21.05 S 67.45 W
San Agustín, Col. 246 1.53 N 76.16 W
San Agustín, Méx. 200 31.31 N 106.15 W
San Agustin, Pil. 116 16.30 N 121.45 E
San Agustin, Pil. 116 12.25 N 120.59 E
San Agustin, Cape > 116 6.16 N 126.11 E
San Agustin, Plains of ⊻ 200 33.50 N 108.00 W
San Agustín Atenango 234 17.38 N 97.59 W
San Agustín de Valle Fértil 252 30.38 S 67.27 W
San Agustín Loxicha 234 16.01 N 96.38 W
San Agustín Tlaxiaca 234 20.07 N 98.53 W
Sanak Islands II 180 54.25 N 162.35 W
San Alberto 196 27.30 N 101.20 W
San Alejo 236 13.26 N 87.58 W
Şān al-Ḥajar, Birkat ⊜ 142 31.03 N 31.54 E
Şān al-Ḥajar al-Qiblīyah 142 30.58 N 31.52 E
Sanalona, Presa ⊜[1] 232 24.53 N 107.00 W
San Ambrosio, Isla I 244 26.21 S 79.52 W
Sanam Chai, Khlong ≋ 269a 13.38 N 100.27 E
Sanana 112 2.04 S 125.58 E
Sanana, Pulau I 112 2.12 S 125.55 E
Sānand 120 22.59 N 72.23 E
Sanandaj 128 35.19 N 47.00 E
Sanandita 248 21.40 S 63.35 W
San Andreas 226 38.11 N 120.40 W
San Andreas Fault V 282 37.25 N 122.15 W
San Andreas Lake ⊜ 282 37.36 N 122.26 W
San Andrés, Col. 236 12.35 N 81.42 W
San Andrés, Col. 246 6.49 N 72.52 W
San Andrés, Méx. 232 27.14 N 114.14 W
San Andrés, Pan. 236 8.36 N 82.44 W
San Andrés, Isla de I 236 12.32 N 81.42 W
San Andrés, Laguna C 234 22.40 N 97.52 W
San Andrés Calpan 234 19.06 N 98.27 W
San Andrés Cohamiata 234 22.12 N 104.03 W
San Andrés de Giles 258 34.27 S 59.27 W
San Andres Mountains ⋀ 200 32.55 N 106.45 W
San Andres Point > 116 13.34 N 121.52 E
San Andrés Sajcabajá 236 15.13 N 90.55 W
San Andrés Timilpan 234 19.52 N 99.45 W
San Andrés Totoltepec ◆[8] 286a 19.15 N 99.10 W
San Andrés Tuxtla 234 18.27 N 95.13 W
San Andrés y Providencia □[8] 238 12.30 N 81.45 W
Sananduva 252 27.57 S 51.48 W
San Angel — Álvaro Obregón ◆[8] 286a 19.21 N 99.12 W
San Angelo 196 31.27 N 100.26 W
San Anselmo 226 37.58 N 122.33 W
San Antero 246 9.23 N 75.46 W
San Antonio, Arg. 252 28.57 S 65.20 W
San Antonio, Arg. 252 28.56 S 65.06 W
San Antonio, Belize 236 16.15 N 89.02 W
San Antonio, Chile 252 27.53 S 70.03 W
San Antonio, Chile 252 33.35 S 71.38 W
San Antonio, Col. 246 3.55 N 75.28 W
San Antonio, C.R. 236 10.12 N 85.26 W
San Antonio, N. Mar. Is. 174n 15.08 N 145.43 E
San Antonio, Perú 248 6.22 S 76.21 W
San Antonio, Pil. 116 12.25 N 124.17 E
San Antonio, Pil. 116 14.57 N 120.05 E
San Antonio, P.R. 240m 18.30 N 67.07 W
San Antonio, Fl., U.S. 220 28.20 N 82.16 W
San Antonio, N.M., U.S. 200 35.06 N 106.22 W
San Antonio, Tx., U.S. 196 29.25 N 98.29 W
San Antonio, Ur. 252 31.22 S 57.48 W
San Antonio, Ur. 258 34.27 S 56.05 W
San Antonio □[7] 286b 22.55 N 82.29 W
San Antonio ≃, Méx. 196 29.13 N 103.47 W
San Antonio ≃, Méx. 232 31.00 N 116.15 W
San Antonio ≃, Ca., U.S. 226 35.52 N 120.48 W
San Antonio ≃, Tx., U.S. 196 28.30 N 96.50 W
San Antonio ≃[1] 288 34.24 S 58.31 W
San Antonio, Cabo > 252 36.40 S 56.42 W
San Antonio, Cabo de > 240p 21.52 N 84.57 W
San Antonio, Lake ⊜[1] 226 35.55 N 121.00 W
San Antonio, Mount ∧ 228 34.17 N 117.39 W
San Antonio, Punta >, Méx. 232 29.46 N 115.42 W
San Antonio, Punta >, Méx. 232 26.31 N 111.28 W
San Antonio, Rio ≃ 200 37.11 N 105.55 W
San Antonio Bay C, Pil. 116 8.38 N 117.35 E
San Antonio Bay C, Tx., U.S. 196 28.20 N 96.45 W
San Antonio Canyon V 280 34.12 N 117.40 W
San Antonio Creek ≃ 226 38.09 N 122.33 W
San Antonio Dam ◆[6] 280 34.09 N 117.41 W
San Antonio de Areco 258 34.15 S 59.28 W
San Antonio de Galipán 286c 10.33 N 66.53 W
San Antonio de los Baños 240p 22.53 N 82.30 W
San Antonio de los Cobres 252 24.11 S 66.21 W
San Antonio del Táchira 246 7.50 N 72.27 W
San Antonio de Padua, Arg. 258 34.40 S 58.42 W
San Antonio de Padua, Méx. 234 22.35 N 104.30 W
San Antonio de Padua, Mission ʋ[1] 226 36.01 N 121.15 W
San Antonio de Tamanaco 246 9.41 N 66.03 W
San Antonio El Bravo 232 30.10 N 104.42 W
San Antonio Eloxochitlán 234 18.11 N 96.52 W
San Antonio Heights 228 34.10 N 117.40 W
San Antonio Mountain ∧ 200 36.52 N 106.02 W
San Antonio Nogalar 234 23.04 N 98.22 W
San Antonio Oeste 254 40.44 S 64.56 W
San Antonio Reservoir ⊜[1] 226 37.35 N 121.50 W
San Antonio Someyucan 286a 19.27 N 99.16 W
San Antonio Suchitepéquez 236 14.32 N 91.25 W
San Antonio Tecómitl ◆[8] 286a 19.13 N 98.59 W
San Antonio Ticino 266b 45.35 N 8.46 E
San Ardo 226 36.01 N 120.54 W
Sanaroa Island I 164 9.35 S 151.00 E
Sanary-sur-Mer 62 43.07 N 5.48 E
Sanatoga 285 40.15 N 75.36 W
Sanatoga Creek ≃ 285 40.14 N 75.36 W
Sanatorium 194 31.53 N 89.46 W
San Augustine 194 31.31 N 94.06 W
San Augustin Pass)(200 32.26 N 106.34 W
Sanaur 124 30.18 N 76.27 E
Sanāw 144 17.50 N 51.00 E
Sanāwad 120 22.11 N 76.04 E
Sanāwān 123 30.19 N 70.59 E
Sanbao, Zhg. 102 43.00 N 93.19 E
Sanbao, Zhg. 105 40.20 N 116.02 E
Sanbaoyingzi 104 41.34 N 120.56 E
San Bartolomeo in Galdo 68 41.24 N 15.01 E
San Basilio 71 39.32 N 9.11 E
San Benedetto, Alpe di ⋀ 66 43.53 N 11.43 E
San Benedetto del Tronto 66 42.57 N 13.53 E
San Benedetto in Alpe 66 43.59 N 11.41 E
San Benedetto Po 64 45.02 N 10.55 E
San Benedicto, Isla I 232 19.18 N 110.49 W
San Benigno Canavese 62 45.13 N 7.46 E
San Benito, Bol. 248 17.31 S 65.55 W
San Benito, Guat. 232 16.55 N 89.54 W
San Benito, Perú 248 7.26 S 78.56 W
San Benito, Tx., U.S. 196 26.07 N 97.37 W
San Benito □[6] 226 36.51 N 121.24 W
San Benito ≃ 226 36.53 N 121.34 W
San Benito Mountain ∧ 226 36.22 N 120.38 W
San Bernard ≃ 222 28.52 N 95.27 W
San Bernardino, Schw. 58 46.28 N 9.12 E
San Bernardino, Ca., U.S. 228 34.07 N 117.18 W
San Bernardino □[6] 228 34.40 N 117.17 W
San Bernardino, Passo del)(58 46.30 N 9.11 E
San Bernardino Mountains ⋀ 204 34.10 N 116.45 W
San Bernardino National Forest ♦ 280 34.12 N 117.38 W
San Bernardino Strait ⊔ 116 12.32 N 124.10 E
San Bernardo, Arg. 252 27.17 S 60.42 W
San Bernardo, Chile 252 33.36 S 70.43 W
San Bernardo, Méx. 232 25.59 N 105.33 W
San Bernardo, Isla I 236 11.32 N 85.06 W
San Bernardo, Islas de II 246 9.45 N 75.50 W
San Bernardo del Viento 246 9.21 N 75.57 W
Sanbe-yama ∧ 96 35.08 N 132.37 E
San Biagio 66 44.35 N 11.52 E
San Biagio di Callalta 64 45.41 N 12.22 E
San Biagio Platani 70 37.31 N 13.32 E
San Biagio Saracinisco 66 41.37 N 13.55 E
San Blas, Méx. 232 26.05 N 108.46 W
San Blas, Méx. 234 21.31 N 105.16 W
San Blas, Cape > 192 29.40 N 85.22 W
San Blas, Golfo de C 246 9.30 N 79.00 W
San Blas, Serranía De ⋀ 246 9.18 N 79.00 W
San Blas de los Sauces 252 28.24 S 67.05 W
San Bonifacio 64 45.24 N 11.16 E
San Borja 248 14.49 S 66.51 W
Sanborn, Ia., U.S. 198 43.10 N 95.39 W
Sanborn, Mn., U.S. 198 44.12 N 95.07 W
Sanborn, N.Y., U.S. 210 43.08 N 78.53 W
Sanborn, N.D., U.S. 198 46.56 N 98.13 W
San Bovio 266b 45.28 N 9.19 E
San Bruno 226 37.37 N 122.24 W
San Bruno, Point > 282 37.39 N 122.22 W
San Bruno Mountain ∧ 282 37.42 N 122.25 W
Sanbu 94 35.39 N 140.23 E
San Buenaventura, Bol. 248 14.28 S 67.35 W
San Buenaventura, Méx. 232 27.05 N 101.32 W
San Buenaventura — Ventura, Ca., U.S. 228 34.17 N 119.18 W
San Buono 66 41.59 N 14.34 E
San Calogero 68 38.34 N 16.01 E
San Calogero, Monte ∧ 70 37.57 N 13.44 E
San Candido (Innichen) 64 46.44 N 12.17 E
Sancang 100 32.45 N 120.43 E
San Carlo 58 46.25 N 8.32 E
San Carlos, Arg. 252 27.45 S 55.54 W
San Carlos, Arg. 252 33.46 S 69.02 W
San Carlos, Arg. 252 25.56 S 65.56 W
San Carlos, Chile 252 36.25 S 71.58 W
San Carlos, Chile 286e 33.36 S 70.35 W
San Carlos, Méx. 232 29.01 N 100.51 W
San Carlos, Méx. 232 24.35 N 98.56 W
San Carlos, Nic. 236 11.07 N 84.47 W
San Carlos, Pan. 236 8.29 N 79.57 W
San Carlos, Para. 252 22.16 S 57.18 W
San Carlos, Pil. 116 10.30 N 123.25 E
San Carlos, Pil. 116 15.55 N 120.20 E
San Carlos, Az., U.S. 200 33.20 N 110.27 W
San Carlos, Ca., U.S. 226 37.29 N 122.15 W
San Carlos, Ur. 252 34.48 S 54.55 W
San Carlos, Ven. 246 9.40 N 68.36 W
San Carlos ≃, C.R. 236 10.47 N 84.12 W
San Carlos ≃, Az., U.S. 200 33.16 N 110.27 W
San Carlos ≃, Ven. 246 9.07 N 68.25 W
San Carlos, Riacho ≃ 252 22.51 S 57.51 W
San Carlos Airport ⊠ 282 37.31 N 122.15 W
San Carlos Bay C 220 26.28 N 82.03 W
San Carlos Borromeo, Mission ʋ[1] 226 36.34 N 121.55 W
San Carlos Centro 252 31.44 S 61.06 W
San Carlos de Bariloche 254 41.09 S 71.18 W
San Carlos de Bolívar 252 36.15 S 61.06 W
San Carlos de Chena 286e 33.35 S 70.44 W
San Carlos de Guaroa 246 3.44 N 73.14 W
San Carlos del Zulia 246 9.01 N 71.55 W
San Carlos de Río Negro 246 1.55 N 67.04 W
San Carlos Indian Reservation ◆[4] 200 33.23 N 110.09 W
San Carlos Reservoir ⊜[1] 200 33.13 N 110.24 W
San Carlos Viejo, Canal ≋ 286e 33.25 S 70.38 W
San Carpoforo Creek ≃ 226 35.47 N 121.19 W
San Casciano dei Bagni 66 42.52 N 11.53 E
San Casciano in Val di Pesa 66 43.39 N 11.11 E
San Cataldo, It. 68 40.23 N 18.17 E
San Cataldo, It. 70 37.29 N 13.59 E
San Cayetano 252 38.20 S 59.37 W
Sancergues 50 47.09 N 2.55 E
Sancerre 50 47.20 N 2.51 E
Sancerrois, Collines du ⋀[2] 50 47.25 N 2.45 E
San Cesario di Lecce 68 40.18 N 18.10 E
San Cesario sul Panaro 64 44.34 N 11.02 E
Sancey-le-Grand 58 47.18 N 6.35 E
Sancha, Zhg. 105 40.27 N 116.26 E
Sancha, Zhg. 106 31.52 N 119.06 E
Sancha ≃ 102 26.55 N 106.06 E
Sanchaba 107 30.19 N 104.14 E
Sanchahe 89 44.59 N 126.04 E
Sanchakou 105 39.47 N 117.19 E
Sanchang 106 31.54 N 121.15 E
Sanchazi 104 41.07 N 124.15 E
Sanchazicun 104 42.03 N 123.59 E
Sanchenglong 89 44.02 N 120.58 E
Sánchez 238 19.14 N 69.36 W
Sanchez Creek ≃ 222 32.36 N 97.50 W
Sánchez Magallanes 234 18.14 N 93.52 W
Sānchi 124 23.29 N 77.44 E
Sanchih 100 25.16 N 121.30 E
San Chirico Raparo 68 40.11 N 16.05 E
Sanch'ŏng 98 35.26 N 127.54 E
Sanchung 269d 25.04 N 121.30 E
Sanch'ungch'iao 269d 25.12 N 121.35 E
San Cipirello 70 37.58 N 13.10 E
San Ciro de Acosta 234 21.38 N 99.49 W
San Clemente, Esp. 34 39.24 N 2.26 W
San Clemente, Ca., U.S. 228 33.25 N 117.36 W
San Clemente, Arroyo de ≃ 266d 41.20 N 2.00 E
San Clemente, Cerro ∧ 254 46.36 S 73.20 W
San Clemente a Casauria ʋ[1] 66 42.14 N 13.55 E
San Clemente Island I 228 32.54 N 118.29 W
Sancoins 32 46.50 N 2.55 E
San Colombano al Lambro 62 45.11 N 9.29 E
San Cono 70 37.17 N 14.22 E
Sanco Point > 116 8.15 N 126.27 E
San Cosme 252 27.22 S 58.31 W
San Cosmo Albanese 68 39.35 N 16.25 E
San Costantino Albanese 68 40.02 N 16.18 E
San Cristóbal, Arg. 252 30.19 S 61.14 W
San Cristóbal, Cuba 240p 22.43 N 83.03 W
San Cristóbal, Rep. Dom. 238 18.25 N 70.06 W
San Cristóbal, Ven. 246 7.46 N 72.14 W
San Cristobal I 175e 10.36 S 161.45 E
San Cristóbal, Bahía C 232 27.23 N 114.38 W
San Cristóbal, Cerro ∧, Chile 286e 33.25 S 70.39 W
San Cristóbal, Cerro ∧, Perú 286d 12.02 S 77.01 W
San Cristóbal, Isla I 246a 0.50 S 89.26 W
San Cristóbal, Nevis — Saint Kitts and Nevis □[1] 238 17.20 N 62.45 W
San Cristóbal, Volcán ∧[1] 236 12.42 N 87.01 W
San Cristóbal de la Barranca 234 21.03 N 103.26 W
San Cristóbal de la Laguna 148 28.29 N 16.19 W
San Cristóbal de las Casas 234 16.45 N 92.38 W
San Cristóbal Totonicapán 236 14.55 N 91.26 W
San Cristobal Trench ✦[1] 14 11.15 S 162.45 E
San Cristóbal Verapaz 236 15.23 N 90.24 W
San Cristobal Wash V 200 32.47 N 113.44 W
San Croce, Monte ∧ 66 41.17 N 13.58 E
Sancti Spíritus 240p 21.56 N 79.27 W
Sancti Spíritus □[4] 240p 22.00 N 79.20 W
San Cugat, Riera de ≃ 266d 41.29 N 2.11 E
Sančursk 80 56.57 N 47.15 E
Sancy, Puy de ∧ 32 45.32 N 2.49 E
Sand, Dtsch. 56 48.32 N 7.55 E
Sand, Nor. 26 59.29 N 6.15 E
Sand ≃, Ab., Can. 184 54.22 N 111.05 W
Sand ≃, S. Afr. 156 22.25 S 30.05 E
Sand ≃, S. Afr. 158 28.05 S 26.25 E
Sanda, Nihon 96 34.53 N 135.14 E
Sanda, Nihon 268 35.28 N 139.21 E
Sandafā al-Fa'r 142 28.32 N 30.40 E
Sandai 112 1.15 S 110.31 E
Sanda Island I 44 55.18 N 5.34 W
Sandakan 112 5.50 N 118.07 E
Sandakan, Pelabuhan C 116 5.45 N 118.05 E
Sandal, Baie du C 175f 20.50 S 167.05 E
San Damián 248 12.02 S 76.24 W
San Damiano d'Asti 62 44.50 N 8.04 E
San Damiano Macra 62 44.29 N 7.16 E
Sândăn 110 12.42 N 106.01 E
Sandan, Chāh ⊤[4] 128 28.59 N 63.27 E
Sandane 26 61.46 N 6.13 E
San Daniele del Friuli 64 46.09 N 13.00 E
Sandan-kyō ♦ 96 34.38 N 132.13 E
Sandanski 38 41.34 N 23.17 E
Sandaogang 89 46.08 N 130.05 E
Sandaogou, Zhg. 104 41.39 N 121.45 E
Sandaogou, Zhg. 105 39.33 N 115.27 E
Sandaohe 86 44.21 N 85.37 E
Sandaoliangzi 104 41.20 N 122.07 E
Sandaolingzi 104 40.58 N 124.08 E
Sandaozhen 89 47.25 N 126.25 E
Sandaré 150 14.42 N 10.18 W
Sandared 26 57.43 N 12.47 E
Sandarne 26 61.16 N 17.10 E
Sand Arroyo V 196 37.29 N 101.29 W
Sandata 80 46.16 N 41.46 E
Sandau 54 52.47 N 12.02 E
Sanday I 46 59.15 N 2.35 W
Sanday Sound C 46 59.11 N 2.31 W
Sandbach 44 53.09 N 2.22 W
Sandbank 46 55.59 N 4.58 W
Sandbanks Provincial Park ♦ 212 43.55 N 77.17 W
Sandbochum ◆[8] 263 51.40 N 7.41 E
Sand City 226 36.37 N 121.51 W
Sand Coulee 202 47.23 N 111.10 W
Sand Coulee Creek ≃ 202 47.27 N 111.18 W
Sand Creek ≃, U.S. 200 41.13 N 105.43 W
Sand Creek ≃, In., U.S. 218 39.03 N 85.51 W
Sand Creek ≃, Ks., U.S. 198 37.26 N 98.12 W
Sand Creek ≃, Mn., U.S. 190 45.56 N 92.39 W
Sand Creek ≃, Mt., U.S. 202 47.18 N 106.45 W
Sand Creek ≃, S.D., U.S. 198 44.02 N 98.05 W
Sand Creek ≃, Wy., U.S. 200 43.27 N 105.26 W
Sand Creek ≃, Wy., U.S. 200 41.02 N 107.52 W
Sand Creek ≃, Wy., U.S. 202 44.16 N 107.55 W
Sand Cut 220 26.56 N 80.35 W
Sande, Dtsch. 52 51.45 N 8.39 E
Sande, Dtsch. 52 53.30 N 8.01 E
Sandefjord 26 59.08 N 10.14 E
San Demetrio Corone 68 39.34 N 16.22 E
San Demetrio ne'Vestini 66 42.17 N 13.34 E
Sanders, Az., U.S. 200 35.12 N 109.19 W
Sanders, Ky., U.S. 218 38.39 N 84.56 W
Sandersdorf, Dtsch. 54 51.37 N 12.15 E
Sandersdorf, Dtsch. 60 48.54 N 11.37 E
Sandersleben 54 51.40 N 11.34 E
Sanderson 196 30.08 N 102.23 W
Sanderstead ◆[8] 260 51.20 N 0.05 W
Sanderston 168b 34.46 S 139.13 E
Sandersville, Ga., U.S. 192 32.58 N 82.48 W
Sandersville, Ms., U.S. 194 31.47 N 89.01 W
Sandeshkhali 126 22.22 N 88.53 E
Sandesneben 52 53.41 N 10.30 E
Sandfly Lake ⊜ 184 55.45 N 106.05 W
Sand Fork 188 38.54 N 80.45 W
Sandgate, Austl. 171a 27.20 S 153.05 E
Sandgate, Eng., U.K. 42 51.05 N 1.08 E
Sandhammaren > 26 55.23 N 14.12 E
Sandhamn 40 59.17 N 18.55 E
Sandhead 44 54.48 N 4.58 W
Sandheuwel 158 31.46 S 20.48 E
Sandhill, On., Can. 275b 43.50 N 79.49 W
Sand Hill, Ma., U.S. 207 42.13 N 70.44 W
Sand Hill ∧[2] 210 42.31 N 77.37 W
Sand Hill ≃ 198 47.36 N 96.52 W
Sand Hills ⋀[2] 198 42.00 N 101.00 W
Sandhorst 52 53.29 N 7.29 E
Sandhurst 42 51.19 N 0.48 W
Sāndi 124 27.18 N 79.57 E
Sandia 248 14.17 S 69.26 W
Sandia Crest ∧ 200 35.13 N 106.27 W
Sandia Indian Reservation ◆[4] 200 35.15 N 106.30 W
Sandian 100 30.56 N 114.48 E
San Diego, Ca., U.S. 228 32.42 N 117.09 W
San Diego, Tx., U.S. 196 27.45 N 98.14 W
San Diego □[6] 228 33.00 N 117.05 W
San Diego ≃, Cuba 240p 22.20 N 83.16 W
San Diego ≃, Ca., U.S. 204 32.46 N 117.13 W
San Diego, Cabo > 254 54.38 S 65.07 W
San Diego Aqueduct ≋[1] 228 32.55 N 116.55 W
San Diego Bay C 228 32.37 N 117.07 W
San Diego Creek ≃ 196 27.47 N 98.03 W
San Diego de Alcala, Mission ʋ[1] 228 32.48 N 117.06 W
San Diego de la Unión 234 21.28 N 100.52 W
San Diego Naval Training Center ■ 228 32.44 N 117.13 W
San Dieguito ≃ 228 32.58 N 117.16 W
Sandies Creek ≃ 222 29.06 N 97.20 W
Sandıklı 130 38.28 N 30.17 E
Sandīla 124 27.05 N 80.31 E
Sandilands 168b 34.31 S 137.46 E
Sandilands Village 240b 25.02 N 77.18 W
San Dimas 228 34.06 N 117.48 W
San Dimas Canyon V 280 34.10 N 117.46 W
San Dimas Reservoir ⊜[1] 280 34.09 N 117.43 W
San Dionisio, Nic. 236 12.45 N 85.51 W
San Dionisio, Pil. 116 11.16 N 123.06 E
Sand Island I, Mid. Is. 174g 28.12 N 177.23 W
Sand Island I, Hi., U.S. 229c 21.18 N 157.53 W
Sand Islet I 174g 28.16 N 177.23 W
Sandiway 262 53.14 N 2.36 W
Sand Key I 220 27.53 N 82.51 W
Sandkrug 54 52.53 N 13.52 E
Sandl 61 48.33 N 14.38 E
Sand Lake 210 42.38 N 73.32 W
Sand Lake ⊜, On., Can. 184 50.05 N 94.39 W
Sand Lake ⊜, On., Can. 212 44.56 N 77.02 W
Sand Lake ⊜, On., Can. 212 44.34 N 76.15 W
Sandling ∧ 64 47.39 N 13.43 E
Sandnes 26 58.51 N 5.44 E
Sandness 46a 60.17 N 1.38 W
Sandoa 152 9.41 S 22.52 E
Sandogora 80 58.12 N 40.59 E
Sandomierz 30 50.41 N 21.45 E
San Domingo Creek ≃ 226 38.07 N 120.40 W
San Domino, Isola I 66 42.07 N 15.29 E
Sandon 260 51.43 N 0.32 E
Sandoná 246 1.17 N 77.28 W
San Donaci 68 40.27 N 17.55 E
San Donà di Piave 64 45.38 N 12.34 E
San Donato di Lecce 68 40.15 N 18.10 E
San Donato di Ninea 68 39.42 N 16.03 E
San Donato Milanese 62 45.24 N 9.16 E
San Donato Val di Comino 66 41.42 N 13.49 E
Sandongo 152 15.30 S 21.28 E
San Dorligo della Valle 64 45.36 N 13.51 E
Sandouping 102 30.48 N 110.49 E
Sandoval 219 38.36 N 89.06 W
Sandovalina 255 22.27 S 51.44 W
Sandover ≃ 162 21.43 S 136.32 E
Sandovo 76 58.28 N 36.25 E
Sandoway 110 18.28 N 94.22 E
Sandown 42 50.39 N 1.09 W
Sandown Park Racecourse ♦, Austl. 274b 37.57 S 145.10 E
Sandown Park Race Course ♦, Eng., U.K. 260 51.22 N 0.22 W
Sand Point, Ak., U.S. 180 55.20 N 160.30 W
Sandpoint, Id., U.S. 202 48.16 N 116.33 W
Sandrancourt 261 49.02 N 1.39 E
Sandray I 46 56.53 N 7.30 W
Sandridge, Eng., U.K. 260 51.47 N 0.18 W
Sand Ridge, N.Y., U.S. 210 43.15 N 76.14 W
Sandrigo 64 45.39 N 11.36 E
Sandringham, Austl. 166 24.05 S 139.04 E
Sandringham, Austl. 169 37.57 S 145.00 E
Sandringham, Eng., U.K. 42 52.50 N 0.30 E
Sandringham ◆[8] 273d 26.09 S 28.07 E
Sandringham House ⊥ 42 52.50 N 0.30 E
Sand River Valley 158 28.28 S 29.33 E
Sands Key I 220 25.30 N 80.11 W
Sandslån 26 63.01 N 17.47 E
Sandspit 182 53.14 N 131.50 W
Sands Point 276 40.51 N 73.43 W
Sands Point > 276 40.52 N 73.44 W
Sand Springs, Ok., U.S. 196 36.08 N 96.06 W
Sand Springs, Tx., U.S. 196 32.15 N 101.22 W
Sandspruit 158 27.18 S 29.48 E
Sandspruit ≃ 273d 26.07 S 28.04 E
Sandstedt 52 53.21 N 8.31 E
Sandston 208 37.31 N 77.18 W
Sandstone, Austl. 162 27.59 S 119.17 E
Sandstone, Mn., U.S. 190 46.07 N 92.52 W
Sandstone Creek ≃ 216 42.23 N 84.33 W
Sandu, Zhg. 100 29.46 N 120.12 E
Sandu, Zhg. 100 26.02 N 113.16 E
Sandu, Zhg. 100 29.12 N 114.40 E
Sandu, Zhg. 102 25.59 N 107.52 E
Sanduan 104 41.10 N 121.27 E
Sandu Ao C 100 26.35 N 119.50 E
Sandugan Point > 116 9.18 N 123.36 E
Sandumba 152 13.45 S 17.29 E
Sandun, Zhg. 106 31.52 N 121.50 E
Sandun, Zhg. 106 30.19 N 120.05 E
Sanduo 100 32.49 N 119.42 E
Sandusky, In., U.S. 218 39.25 N 85.29 W
Sandusky, Mi., U.S. 190 43.25 N 82.49 W
Sandusky, N.Y., U.S. 210 42.30 N 78.23 W
Sandusky, Oh., U.S. 214 41.26 N 82.42 W
Sandusky □[6] 214 41.21 N 83.07 W
Sandusky ≃ 214 41.27 N 83.00 W
Sandusky Bay C 214 41.27 N 82.52 W
Sand uul ∧ 102 43.27 N 104.04 E
Sandvig 26 55.17 N 14.47 E
Sandvika 26 59.54 N 10.31 E
Sandviken 40 60.37 N 16.46 E
Sandweiler 56 49.37 N 6.13 E
Sandwich, Eng., U.K. 42 51.17 N 1.20 E
Sandwich, Il., U.S. 216 41.38 N 88.37 W
Sandwich, Ma., U.S. 207 41.45 N 70.29 W
Sandwich Bay C, Nf., Can. 176 53.35 N 57.15 W
Sandwich Bay C, Namibia 156 23.22 S 14.30 E
Sandwich del Sur, Islas — South Sandwich Islands II 18 57.45 S 26.30 W
Sandwick, B.C., Can. 182 49.42 N 124.59 W
Sandwick, Scot., U.K. 46a 60.00 N 1.15 W
Sand Wick C 46a 60.42 N 0.52 W
Sandwīp 124 22.29 N 91.26 E
Sandwīp Channel ⊔ 124 22.30 N 91.35 E
Sandwīp Island I 124 22.30 N 91.25 E
Sandy, Eng., U.K. 42 52.08 N 0.18 W
Sandy, Or., U.S. 224 45.23 N 122.15 W
Sandy, Pa., U.S. 214 41.07 N 78.47 W
Sandy, Ut., U.S. 200 40.35 N 111.53 W
Sandy ≃, Me., U.S. 188 44.45 N 69.52 W
Sandy ≃, Or., U.S. 224 45.34 N 122.24 W
Sandy ≃, Va., U.S. 192 36.35 N 79.25 W
Sandy Bay C, Nic. 236 14.28 N 83.16 W
Sandy Bay C, Ma., U.S. 283 42.40 N 70.37 W
Sandy Bay Indian Reserve ◆[4] 184 50.33 N 98.40 W
Sandy Bay Mountain ∧ 188 45.47 N 70.25 W
Sandy Beach 210 43.04 N 78.55 W
Sandy Branch ≃ 284c 39.03 N 77.16 W
Sandy Cape >, Austl. 166 41.25 S 144.45 E
Sandy Cape >, Austl. 166 24.42 S 153.17 E
Sandy Creek 212 43.38 N 76.05 W
Sandy Creek ≃, Austl. 166 32.10 S 144.39 E
Sandy Creek ≃, U.S. 196 34.25 N 99.35 W
Sandy Creek ≃, U.S. 196 36.50 N 98.10 W
Sandy Creek ≃, Il., U.S. 219 39.34 N 90.35 W
Sandy Creek ≃, N.Y., U.S. 212 43.44 N 76.15 W
Sandy Creek ≃, N.Y., U.S. 212 43.20 N 77.55 W
Sandy Creek ≃, N.C., U.S. 192 36.08 N 78.02 W
Sandy Creek ≃, Oh., U.S. 214 40.38 N 81.26 W
Sandy Creek ≃, Pa., U.S. 214 41.18 N 79.51 W
Sandy Creek ≃, Tx., U.S. 196 30.34 N 98.26 W
Sandy Creek ≃, Tx., U.S. 222 29.02 N 96.33 W
Sandy Creek, East Branch ≃ 210 43.17 N 78.03 W
Sandy Creek, North Branch ≃ 212 43.51 N 75.58 W
Sandy Creek, West Branch ≃ 210 43.17 N 78.03 W
Sandy Desert ◆[2] 128 28.40 N 62.30 E
Sandy Hook, Ct., U.S. 207 41.25 N 73.16 W
Sandy Hook, Ky., U.S. 192 38.05 N 83.07 W
Sandy Hook, Ms., U.S. 194 31.02 N 89.48 W
Sandy Hook >[2] 208 40.27 N 74.00 W
Sandy Hook Bay C 276 40.26 N 74.03 W
Sandykači 128 36.33 N 62.34 E
Sandy Key I 220 25.02 N 81.01 W
Sandy Lake 214 41.20 N 80.04 W
Sandy Lake ⊜, Nf., Can. 186 49.16 N 57.00 W
Sandy Lake ⊜, On., Can. 184 53.02 N 93.00 W
Sandy Lake ⊜, On., Can. 212 44.33 N 78.24 W
Sandy Lick Creek ≃ 214 41.09 N 79.05 W
Sandy Point >, Austl. 168b 34.16 S 138.09 E
Sandy Point >, Trin. 241r 11.09 N 60.50 W
Sandy Point >, R.I., U.S. 207 41.14 N 71.35 W
Sandy Point Town 238 17.22 N 62.50 W
Sandy Ridge 214 40.49 N 78.14 W
Sandy Springs 192 33.55 N 84.22 W
Sandyville, Md., U.S. 208 39.31 N 76.55 W
Sandyville, Oh., U.S. 214 40.38 N 81.23 W
Sandžak ◆[1] 38 43.10 N 19.30 E
San Eladio 258 34.46 S 59.11 W
San Elizario 200 31.35 N 106.16 W
San Emigdio Creek ≃ 228 35.02 N 119.11 W
San Emilio 116 17.14 N 120.37 E
Sanen ≃ 115a 8.23 S 113.37 E
San Enrique 252 35.47 S 60.22 W
San Estanislao 252 24.39 S 56.26 W
San Esteban 236 15.17 N 85.52 W
San Esteban, Isla I 232 28.42 N 112.36 W
San Esteban de Gormaz 34 41.35 N 3.12 W
San Fele 68 40.49 N 15.32 E
San Felice (Sankt Felix) 64 46.30 N 11.08 E
San Felice Circeo 66 41.14 N 13.05 E
San Felice sul Panaro 64 44.50 N 11.08 E
San Felipe, Chile 252 32.45 S 70.44 W
San Felipe, Col. 246 1.55 N 67.06 W
San Felipe, Méx. 232 31.00 N 114.52 W
San Felipe, Méx. 234 21.29 N 101.13 W
San Felipe, Pil. 116 15.04 N 120.04 E
San Felipe, Tx., U.S. 222 29.48 N 96.06 W
San Felipe, Ven. 246 10.20 N 68.44 W
San Felipe, Castillo de ⊥ 236 15.39 N 89.01 W
San Felipe, Cayos de II 240p 21.58 N 83.30 W
San Felipe Aztatán 234 22.23 N 105.24 W
San Felipe Creek ≃ 204 33.09 N 115.46 W
San Felipe de Vichayal 248 4.52 S 81.05 W
San Felipe Indian Reservation ◆[4] 200 35.26 N 106.26 W
San Felipe Jalapa de Díaz 234 18.04 N 96.32 W
San Felipe Nuevo Mercurio 232 24.22 N 102.06 W
San Felipe Pueblo 200 35.27 N 106.28 W
San Félix ≃ 236 8.10 N 81.51 W
San Félix, Isla I 244 26.17 S 80.05 W
San Ferdinando di Puglia 68 41.18 N 16.04 E
San Fermín 196 26.20 N 104.49 W
San Fernando, Arg. 258 34.26 S 58.34 W
San Fernando, Chile 252 34.35 S 71.00 W
San Fernando, Esp. 34 36.28 N 6.12 W
San Fernando, Méx. 196 28.32 N 100.54 W
San Fernando, Méx. 200 31.16 N 110.36 W
San Fernando, Méx. 232 24.50 N 98.10 W
San Fernando, Méx. 234 16.52 N 93.13 W
San Fernando, Pil. 116 16.37 N 120.19 E
San Fernando, Pil. 116 12.30 N 123.46 E
San Fernando, Pil. 116 15.01 N 120.41 E
San Fernando, Trin. 241r 10.17 N 61.28 W
San Fernando, Ca., U.S. 228 34.16 N 118.26 W
San Fernando, Ven. 246 7.54 N 67.28 W
San Fernando □[5] 288 34.28 S 58.34 W
San Fernando, Aeródromo ⊠ 288 34.27 S 58.35 W
San Fernando Airport ⊠ 280 34.17 N 118.25 W
San Fernando Creek ≃ 196 27.28 N 97.46 W
San Fernando de Atabapo 246 4.03 N 67.42 W
San Fernando de Henares 266a 40.26 N 3.32 W
San Fernando del Valle de Catamarca 252 28.28 S 65.47 W
San Fernando Mission ʋ[1] 280 34.16 N 118.28 W
San Fernando Point > 116 16.38 N 120.17 E
San Fernando Valley V 280 34.13 N 118.27 W
San Fili 68 39.20 N 16.09 E
San Filippo del Mela, It. 70 38.10 N 15.17 E
San Filippo del Mela, It. 70 38.10 N 15.17 E
Sånfjället ∧ 26 62.17 N 13.32 E
Sånfjällets Nationalpark ♦ 26 62.20 N 13.40 E
San Floriano 64 46.02 N 12.18 E
Sanford, Co., U.S. 200 37.15 N 105.54 W
Sanford, Fl., U.S. 220 28.48 N 81.16 W
Sanford, Me., U.S. 188 43.26 N 70.46 W
Sanford, Mi., U.S. 190 43.40 N 84.22 W
Sanford, N.C., U.S. 192 35.28 N 79.10 W
Sanford, Tx., U.S. 196 35.42 N 101.32 W
Sanford ≃ 162 27.22 S 115.53 E
Sanford, Mount ∧ 180 62.13 N 144.09 W
San Francesco, Convento ʋ[1], It. 66 42.28 N 12.45 E
San Francesco, Convento ʋ[1], It. 267a 42.03 N 12.46 E
San Francisco, Arg. 252 31.26 S 62.05 W
San Francisco, Col. 246 1.11 N 76.53 W
San Francisco, C.R. 236 9.49 N 85.15 W
San Francisco, El Sal. 236 13.42 N 88.06 W
San Francisco, Pan. 236 8.15 N 80.58 W
San Francisco, Pil. 116 8.30 N 125.56 E
San Francisco, Pil. 116 10.04 N 125.09 E
San Francisco, Ca., U.S. 226 37.46 N 122.25 W
San Francisco, Ca., U.S. 282 37.46 N 122.25 W
San Francisco □[6] 226 37.45 N 122.22 W
San Francisco ≃, Arg. 252 23.16 S 64.03 W
San Francisco — São Francisco ≃, Bra. 242 10.30 S 36.24 W

Symbols in the index entries represent the broad categories identified in the key at the right. Symbols with superior numbers (⋀[1]) identify subcategories (see complete key on page *I · 1*).

Symbole im Register stellen die rechts im Schlüssel erklärten Kategorien dar. Symbole mit hochgestellten Ziffern (⋀[1]) bezeichnen Unterabteilungen einer Kategorie (vgl. vollständiger Schlüssel auf Seite *I · 1*).

Los símbolos incluídos en el texto del índice representan las grandes categorías identificadas con la clave a la derecha. Los símbolos con numeros en su parte superior (⋀[1]) identifican las subcategorías (véase la clave completa en la página *I · 1*).

Les symboles de l'index représentent les catégories indiquées dans la légende à droite. Les symboles suivis d'un indice (⋀[1]) représentent des sous-catégories (voir légende complète à la page *I · 1*).

Os símbolos incluídos no texto do índice representam as grandes categorias identificadas com a chave à direita. Os símbolos com números em sua parte superior (⋀[1]) identificam as subcategorias (veja-se a chave completa à página *I · 1*).

∧ Mountain	Berg	Montaña	Montagne	Montanha
⋀ Mountains	Gebirge	Montañas	Montagnes	Montanhas
)(Pass	Paß	Paso	Col	Passo
V Valley, Canyon	Tal, Cañon	Valle, Cañón	Vallée, Canyon	Vale, Canhão
⊻ Plain	Ebene	Llano	Plaine	Planície
> Cape	Kap	Cabo	Cap	Cabo
I Island	Insel	Isla	Île	Ilha
II Islands	Inseln	Islas	Îles	Ilhas
⊥ Other Topographic Features	Andere Topographische Objekte	Otros Elementos Topográficos	Autres données topographiques	Outros acidentes topográficos

ESPAÑOL — Nombre / Página / Lat.°′ / Long.°′ W = Oeste
FRANÇAIS — Nom / Page / Lat.°′ / Long.°′ W = Ouest
PORTUGUÊS — Nome / Página / Lat.°′ / Long.°′ W = Oeste

Nombre	Página	Lat.°′	Long.°′ W = Oeste
San Francisco ≃, U.S.	200	32.59 N	109.22 W
San Francisco, Arroyo ≃	288	34.43 S	58.19 W
San Francisco, Paso de)(	252	26.53 S	68.19 W
San Francisco, University of ʋ[2]	282	37.46 N	122.26 W
San Francisco Bay ⊂	226	37.43 N	122.17 W
San Francisco Creek ≃	196	29.53 N	102.19 W
San Francisco Culhuacán ◆[8]	286a	19.20 N	99.08 W
San Francisco de Borja	232	27.53 N	106.41 W
San Francisco de Horizonte	196	25.56 N	103.26 W
San Francisco de Lajas	234	23.07 N	105.07 W
San Francisco de la Paz	236	14.55 N	86.14 W
San Francisco del Chañar	252	29.47 S	63.56 W
San Francisco del Monte de Oro	252	32.36 S	66.08 W
San Francisco del Oro	232	26.52 N	105.51 W
San Francisco del Rincón	234	21.01 N	101.51 W
San Francisco de Macoris	238	19.18 N	70.15 W
San Francisco de Mostazal	252	33.59 S	70.43 W
San Francisco el Grande, Iglesia de ʋ[1]	266a	40.25 N	3.43 W
San Francisco International Airport ⊠	226	37.37 N	122.23 W
San Francisco Ixhuatán	234	16.22 N	94.29 W
San Francisco Libre	236	12.30 N	86.18 W
San Francisco Maritime National Historical Park ♠	282	37.48 N	122.27 W
San Francisco-Oakland Bay Bridge ◆[5]	282	37.48 N	122.22 W
San Francisco State Fish and Game Refuge ◆[4]	282	37.35 N	122.25 W
San Francisco State University ʋ[2]	282	37.43 N	122.28 W
San Francisco Tlalcilalcalpa	234	19.18 N	99.46 W
San Francisco Tlaltenco ◆[8]	286a	19.17 N	99.01 W
San Francisco Zoological Gardens ♠	282	37.44 N	122.30 W
San Francisquito Creek ≃	282	37.28 N	122.07 W
San Franco, Cerro ∧	236	15.25 N	87.18 W
San Fratello	70	38.01 N	14.36 E
San Fratello ≃	70	38.02 N	14.34 E
Sanga, Ang.	152	11.07 S	15.22 E
Sanga, Burkina	150	11.10 N	0.10 E
Sanga, Mali	150	14.28 N	3.19 W
Sanga, Zaïre	154	7.02 S	28.21 E
San Gabriel, Ec.	246	0.36 N	77.49 W
San Gabriel, Ca., U.S.	228	34.05 N	118.06 W
San Gabriel ≃, Ca., U.S.	280	33.45 N	118.07 W
San Gabriel ≃, Tx., U.S.	222	30.46 N	97.01 W
San Gabriel, Isla I	258	34.28 S	57.54 W
San Gabriel, North Fork ≃, Ca., U.S.	280	34.15 N	117.52 W
San Gabriel, North Fork ≃, Tx., U.S.	196	30.38 N	97.41 W
San Gabriel, South Fork ≃	196	30.38 N	97.41 W
San Gabriel Arcangel, Mission ʋ[1]	280	34.06 N	118.06 W
San Gabriel Chilac	234	18.19 N	97.21 W
San Gabriel Dam ◆[6]	280	34.13 N	117.52 W
San Gabriel Mountains ⋏	228	34.20 N	118.00 W
San Gabriel Peak ∧	280	34.15 N	118.06 W
San Gabriel Reservoir ⊜[1]	228	34.13 N	117.51 W
Sängäçal burnu ›	84	40.07 N	49.30 E
San Galgano, Abbazia di ʋ[1]	66	43.10 N	11.10 E
Šangaly	24	61.08 N	43.19 E
Sangamankanda Point ›	122	7.01 N	81.52 E
Sangamner	122	19.34 N	74.13 E
Sangamon □[6]	219	39.47 N	89.40 W
Sangamon ≃	194	40.07 N	90.20 W
Sangamon, South Fork ≃	219	39.48 N	89.32 W
Sanga Puitã	255	22.40 S	55.36 W
Sangar	74	63.55 N	127.31 E
Sangar Sarāy	120	34.24 N	70.38 E
Sangasanga-dalam	112	0.40 S	117.14 E
Sanga Sanga Island I	116	5.04 N	119.47 E
Sangat	123	30.05 N	74.50 E
Sangatte	50	50.56 N	1.45 E
San Gavino Monreale	71	39.33 N	8.47 E
Sangay ∧[1]	246	2.00 S	78.20 W
Sangay, Parque Nacional ♠	246	1.50 S	78.20 W
Sangayán, Isla I	248	13.51 S	76.28 W
Sang Bast	128	35.59 N	59.46 E
Sangbé	152	6.03 N	12.28 E
Sangchris Lake ⊜[1]	219	39.35 N	89.30 W
Sangchris Lake State Park ♠	219	39.38 N	89.28 W
Sangchungshih	100	25.04 N	121.29 E
Sangeang, Pulau I	115b	8.12 S	119.04 E
Sang-e Māsheh	120	33.08 N	67.27 E
San Gemini	66	42.37 N	12.33 E
San Genesio Atesino	64	46.32 N	11.20 E
Sangenjaya ◆[8]	268	35.38 N	139.40 E
Sanger, Ca., U.S.	226	36.42 N	119.33 W
Sanger, Tx., U.S.	196	33.21 N	97.10 W
Sângera	38	47.38 N	28.09 E
Sangerhausen	54	51.28 N	11.17 E
San Germán	240m	18.05 N	67.03 W
San Germano Vercellese	62	45.21 N	8.15 E
San Geronimo	226	38.01 N	122.39 W
San Gerónimo, Arroyo ≃	258	33.57 S	56.05 W
Sangerville	188	45.09 N	69.21 W
Sanggan ≃	90	40.21 N	115.21 E
Sanggar, Teluk ⊂	115b	8.20 S	118.18 E
Sanggau	112	0.08 N	110.36 E
Sangge-ri ◆[8]	271b	37.41 N	127.05 E
Sanggin Dalai	102	38.11 N	105.17 E
Sanggona	112	3.52 S	121.46 E
Sangha □[5], Centraf.	152	3.35 N	16.20 E
Sangha □[5], Congo	152	1.00 N	15.30 E
Sangha ≃	152	1.13 S	16.49 E
Sanghar	120	26.02 N	68.57 E
San Giacomo (Sankt Jakob in Pfitsch)	64	46.57 N	11.36 E
San Giacomo Filippo	58	46.20 N	9.21 E
Sangihe, Kepulauan II	112	3.00 N	125.30 E
Sangihe, Pulau I	112	3.35 N	125.32 E
Sangijn dalaj nuur ⊜	88	49.17 N	99.00 E
San Gil	246	6.33 N	73.08 W
Sangilen, chrebet ⋏	88	50.18 N	96.30 E
San Gimignano	66	43.28 N	11.02 E
San Ginesio	66	43.06 N	13.19 E
San Gion	58	46.38 N	8.50 E
San Giorgio	68	40.51 N	14.23 E
San Giorgio Canavese	62	45.20 N	7.48 E
San Giorgio della Richinvelda	64	46.03 N	12.52 E
San Giorgio del Sannio	68	41.04 N	14.51 E
San Giorgio di Lomellina	62	45.10 N	8.47 E
San Giorgio di Nogaro	64	45.50 N	13.13 E
San Giorgio di Piano	64	44.39 N	11.22 E
San Giorgio Ionico	68	40.27 N	17.23 E
San Giorgio la Molara	68	41.16 N	14.55 E
San Giorgio Lucano	68	40.07 N	16.23 E
San Giorgio Monferrato	62	45.07 N	8.23 E
San Giorgio Morgeto	68	38.23 N	16.06 E
San Giorgio Piacentino	62	44.57 N	9.44 E
San Giorgio su Legnano	266b	45.34 N	8.55 E
San Giovanni (Sankt Johann)	64	46.38 N	11.44 E
San Giovanni al Timavo (Sankt Johann in Ahrn)	64	46.58 N	11.57 E
San Giovanni a Piro	68	40.03 N	15.27 E
San Giovanni-Bianco	58	45.52 N	9.39 E
San Giovanni d'Asso	66	43.09 N	11.35 E
San Giovanni Gemini	70	37.38 N	13.39 E
San Giovanni Ilarione	64	45.30 N	11.15 E
San Giovanni in Croce	64	45.05 N	10.22 E
San Giovanni in Fiore	68	39.15 N	16.42 E
San Giovanni in Laterano ʋ[1]	267a	41.53 N	12.30 E
San Giovanni in Persiceto	64	44.38 N	11.11 E
San Giovanni la Punta	70	37.35 N	15.07 E
San Giovanni Lupatoto	64	45.23 N	11.03 E
San Giovanni Rotondo	68	41.42 N	15.44 E
San Giovanni Suergiu	71	39.07 N	8.31 E
San Giovanni Valdarno	66	43.34 N	11.32 E
San Giuliano, Lago di ⊜	68	40.37 N	16.30 E
San Giuliano Milanese	266b	45.24 N	9.17 E
San Giuliano Terme	66	43.46 N	10.26 E
San Giuseppe, It.	62	44.22 N	8.18 E
San Giuseppe, It.	70	37.58 N	13.11 E
San Giuseppe Vesuviano	68	40.50 N	14.30 E
San Giustino	66	43.33 N	12.10 E
San Giusto, Aeroporto di ⊠	66	43.41 N	10.21 E
San Giusto Canavese	62	45.19 N	7.49 E
Sangju	98	36.26 N	128.09 E
Sangkapura	115a	5.52 S	112.40 E
Sângkê ≃	110	13.13 N	103.41 E
Sangkhai	110	14.39 N	103.52 E
Sangkulirang	112	0.59 N	117.58 E
Sāngla	123	31.43 N	73.23 E
Sangley Point ›	269f	14.30 N	120.55 E
Sāngli	122	16.52 N	74.34 E
Sanglin	100	27.54 N	114.46 E
Sangluoshu	98	37.31 N	117.43 E
Sangmélima	152	2.56 N	11.59 E
Sangngagqoiling	120	28.33 N	93.00 E
Sangnyŏng-ni	98	38.14 N	126.54 E
Sango	270	34.36 N	135.42 E
San Godenzo	66	43.55 N	11.37 E
Sāngole	122	17.26 N	75.12 E
Sangolquí	246	0.19 S	78.27 W
San Gorgonio Mountain ∧	204	34.06 N	116.50 W
San Gottardo, Passo del)(	58	46.33 N	8.34 E
Sangou	98	41.02 N	118.11 E
Sangre de Cristo Mountains ⋏	200	37.30 N	105.15 W
San Gregorio, Arg.	252	34.19 S	62.02 W
San Gregorio, It.	66	42.19 N	13.29 E
San Gregorio, Ca., U.S.	226	37.19 N	122.23 W
San Gregorio, Ur.	252	32.37 S	55.40 W
San Gregorio, Ur.	258	33.57 S	56.45 W
San Gregorio ◆[8]	286a	19.15 N	99.03 W
San Gregorio, Arroyo ≃	258	33.59 S	56.50 W
San Gregorio Creek ≃	282	37.19 N	122.25 W
San Gregorio Magno	68	40.39 N	15.24 E
San Gregorio State Beach ♠	282	37.19 N	122.24 W
Sangre Grande	241r	10.35 N	61.07 W
Sangro ≃	66	42.14 N	14.32 E
Sangrūr	123	30.14 N	75.50 E
Sangsang	120	29.25 N	86.40 E
Sangshuyuan	86	42.23 N	88.30 E
Sangsues, Lac aux ⊜	190	46.29 N	77.57 W
Sangtuda	85	38.04 N	69.04 E
Sanguandian	100	31.19 N	118.05 E
Sanguang	106	31.47 N	121.16 E
Sanguanmiao	100	32.25 N	114.04 E
Sanguanyingzi	104	41.39 N	120.44 E
Sangudo	182	53.53 N	114.54 W
Sangue, Rio do ≃	248	11.01 S	58.39 W
Sangüesa	34	42.35 N	1.17 W
Sanguinetto	64	45.11 N	11.09 E
Sanguliu	104	40.45 N	124.14 E
Sāngurli	272c	18.56 N	73.07 E
Sangutane ≃	156	24.07 S	33.47 E
Sangvor, Taj.	85	38.47 N	71.12 E
Sangvor, Taj.	85	38.53 N	71.06 E
Sangwa	154	5.30 S	26.00 E
Sangya	120	30.52 N	91.40 E
Sangyuanbao	105	40.15 N	115.32 E
Sangyuanbu	106	31.37 N	118.53 E
Sangyuanzhen	107	30.30 N	103.26 E
Sangzhi	102	29.18 N	110.02 E
Sangzidian	98	36.46 N	116.55 E
Sanhe, Zhg.	100	24.24 N	116.34 E
Sanhe, Zhg.	105	39.59 N	117.04 E
Sanhechang, Zhg.	102	31.22 N	106.48 E
Sanhechang, Zhg.	107	30.04 N	105.01 E
Sanhecun	98	42.28 N	129.39 E
Sanheji	100	32.42 N	117.55 E
Sanhekou	106	31.50 N	120.08 E
Sanhetun	104	42.38 N	123.38 E
Sanhezhan	89	52.34 N	126.02 E
Sanhezhen	100	31.30 N	117.14 E
Sanhezhuang	105	40.04 N	116.18 E
San Hipólito, Punta ›	232	26.59 N	113.59 W
Sanhsient'ai I	100	23.08 N	121.25 E
Sanhsing	100	24.40 N	121.39 E
Sanhu	100	27.55 N	115.24 E
Sanhui, Zhg.	107	30.06 N	106.36 E
Sanhui, Zhg.	107	29.57 N	105.53 E
Sanhūr	142	29.25 N	30.46 E
Sanhūr al-Madīnah	142	31.07 N	30.44 E
Sani	100	24.25 N	120.46 E
Sanibel	220	26.26 N	82.01 W
Sanibel Island I	220	26.27 N	82.06 W
Sānī Bherī ≃	124	28.42 N	82.16 E
San Ignacio, Arg.	252	27.16 S	55.32 W
San Ignacio, C.R.	236	9.48 N	84.09 W
San Ignacio, Hond.	236	14.38 N	87.02 W
San Ignacio, Méx.	232	27.27 N	112.51 W
San Ignacio, Méx.	234	23.12 N	100.12 W
San Ignacio, Méx.	234	23.55 N	106.25 W
San Ignacio, Para.	252	26.52 S	57.03 W
San Ignacio, Perú	248	5.08 S	78.59 W
San Ignacio, Isla I	232	25.25 N	108.54 W
San Ignacio, Laguna ⊜	232	26.54 N	113.13 W
San Ignacio de Moxo	248	14.53 S	65.36 W
San Ignacio de Velasco	248	16.23 S	60.59 W
San Ildefonso, Cape ›	116	16.02 N	121.59 E
San Ildefonso, Cerro ∧	236	15.31 N	88.17 W
San Ildefonso Indian Reservation ◆[4]	200	35.53 N	106.08 W
San Ildefonso o La Granja	34	40.54 N	4.00 W
San Ildefonso Peninsula ›[1]	116	16.10 N	122.05 E
San Ildefonso Villa Alta	234	17.21 N	96.09 W
San'in-kaigan-kokuritsu-kōen ♠	96	35.38 N	134.38 E
Sanino	265a	59.50 N	29.54 E
Sani Pass)(	158	29.34 S	29.19 E
San Isidro, Arg.	252	28.27 S	65.44 W
San Isidro, Arg.	258	34.27 S	58.30 W
San Isidro, C.R.	236	9.22 N	83.42 W
San Isidro, Méx.	200	31.31 N	106.18 W
San Isidro, Nic.	236	12.56 N	86.12 W
San Isidro, Perú	286d	12.07 S	77.03 W
San Isidro, Pil.	116	11.24 N	124.21 E
San Isidro, Tx., U.S.	196	26.42 N	98.27 W
San Isidro □[5]	288	34.29 S	58.33 W
San Isidro el Real, Catedral de ʋ[1]	266a	40.25 N	3.42 W
Sanitaria Springs	210	42.09 N	75.46 W
Sanitatas	156	18.11 S	12.47 E
Sanitz	54	54.04 N	12.22 E
San Jacinto, Col.	246	9.50 N	75.08 W
San Jacinto, Méx.	196	25.29 N	103.44 W
San Jacinto, Pil.	116	12.34 N	123.44 E
San Jacinto, Ca., U.S.	228	33.47 N	116.57 W
San Jacinto □[6]	222	30.35 N	95.10 W
San Jacinto ≃, Ca., U.S.	228	33.43 N	117.16 W
San Jacinto ≃, Tx., U.S.	222	29.46 N	95.05 W
San Jacinto, East Fork ≃	222	30.05 N	95.09 W
San Jacinto, West Fork ≃	222	30.02 N	95.15 W
San Jacinto Monument ⊥	222	29.45 N	95.01 W
San Jacinto Peak ∧	204	33.49 N	116.41 W
San Jacinto Valley V	228	33.50 N	117.05 W
Sanjahā	142	30.50 N	31.38 E
San Javier, Arg.	252	27.53 S	55.08 W
San Javier, Arg.	252	30.35 S	59.57 W
San Javier, Bol.	248	14.34 S	64.42 W
San Javier, Bol.	248	16.20 S	62.38 W
San Javier, Méx.	196	26.16 N	99.27 W
San Javier, Ur.	252	32.41 S	58.08 W
San Javier ≃	252	31.30 S	60.20 W
San Javier de Loncomilla	252	35.35 S	71.45 W
Sanjāwi	120	30.17 N	68.21 E
Sanje	154	0.46 S	31.30 E
San Jeronimito	234	17.33 N	101.20 W
San Jerónimo, Guat.	236	15.03 N	90.12 W
San Jerónimo, Méx.	234	17.08 N	100.28 W
San Jerónimo Norte	252	31.33 S	61.05 W
Sanjiadian, Zhg.	105	40.09 N	116.36 E
Sanjiadian, Zhg.	105	39.58 N	116.06 E
Sanjiadian, Zhg.	105	39.22 N	115.58 E
Sanjiang, Zhg.	102	25.42 N	109.23 E
Sanjiang, Zhg.	107	29.33 N	104.03 E
Sanjiangzhen	107	30.31 N	103.48 E
Sanjiaocheng	102	36.47 N	104.40 E
Sanjiaopao	104	41.22 N	122.17 E
Sanjiaoshancun	104	40.42 N	122.49 E
Sanjiazhen	107	30.17 N	105.32 E
Sanjiazi, Zhg.	104	41.53 N	121.42 E
Sanjiazi, Zhg.	104	40.42 N	123.16 E
Sanjiazi, Zhg.	104	40.54 N	121.59 E
Sanjiazi, Zhg.	104	42.33 N	121.38 E
Sanjiazi, Zhg.	104	42.02 N	122.20 E
Sanjiaziyingzi	104	41.52 N	120.49 E
Sanjie, Zhg.	100	32.35 N	118.08 E
Sanjie, Zhg.	102	25.01 N	101.02 E
Sanjō	92	37.37 N	138.57 E
San Joaquín, Bol.	248	13.04 S	64.49 W
San Joaquín, Chile	286e	33.30 S	70.37 W
San Joaquín, Para.	252	24.57 S	56.07 W
San Joaquin, Pil.	116	10.35 N	122.08 E
San Joaquin, Ca., U.S.	226	36.36 N	120.11 W
San Joaquin □[6]	226	37.57 N	121.17 W
San Joaquín ≃, Bol.	248	13.08 S	63.41 W
San Joaquin ≃, Ca., U.S.	226	38.03 N	121.50 W
San Joaquin, Middle Fork ≃	226	37.32 N	119.11 W
San Joaquin, North Fork ≃	226	37.32 N	119.11 W
San Joaquin, South Fork ≃	226	37.26 N	119.14 W
San Joaquin Valley V	204	36.50 N	120.10 W
San Jon	196	35.06 N	103.19 W
San Jorge, Arg.	252	31.54 S	61.52 W
San Jorge, El Sal.	236	13.25 N	88.21 W
San Jorge, Nic.	236	11.27 N	85.48 W
San Jorge ≃	246	9.07 N	74.44 W
San Jorge, Bahía de ⊂	200	31.12 N	113.15 W
San Jorge, Cabo ›	254	45.47 S	67.21 W
San Jorge, Canal de → Saint George's Channel ⊔	28	52.00 N	6.00 W
San Jorge, Golfo ⊂	254	46.00 S	67.00 W
San Jorge Island I	175e	8.27 S	159.35 E
San José, Arg.	252	27.46 S	55.47 W
San José, C.R.	236	9.56 N	84.05 W
San José, Méx.	196	28.16 N	100.15 W
San Jose, N. Mar. Is.	174n	15.09 N	145.43 E
San José, Para.	252	25.33 S	56.45 W
San Jose, Pil.	116	10.45 N	121.56 E
San Jose, Pil.	116	15.48 N	121.00 E
San Jose, Pil.	116	12.27 N	121.03 E
San Jose, Ca., U.S.	226	37.20 N	121.53 W
San Jose, Ca., U.S.	282	37.20 N	121.53 W
San Jose, Il., U.S.	194	40.18 N	89.36 W
San Jose, N.M., U.S.	200	35.23 N	105.28 W
San José, Ven.	286c	10.34 N	66.57 W
San José □[4]	236	9.40 N	84.00 W
San José □[5]	258	34.15 S	56.45 W
San José □[7]	286b	22.57 N	82.14 W
San Jose ≃, B.C., Can.	182	52.14 N	122.15 W
San José ≃, Ur.	258	34.38 S	56.29 W
San Jose, Arroyo ≃	282	38.03 N	122.30 W
San José, Golfo ⊂	254	42.20 S	64.18 W
San José, Isla I, Méx.	232	25.00 N	110.38 W
San José, Isla I, Pan.	246	8.15 N	79.07 W
San José, Laguna ⊂	240m	18.25 N	66.01 W
San Jose, Mission ʋ[1]	282	37.32 N	121.55 W
San Jose, Rio ≃	200	34.52 N	107.01 W
San Jose Arena ♠	282	37.20 N	121.54 W
San José Ayuquila	234	17.58 N	97.57 W
San José Batuc	232	29.15 N	109.44 W
San José Buena Vista	236	13.49 N	90.19 W
San Jose Creek ≃	280	34.01 N	118.03 W
San José de Aura	196	27.34 N	101.23 W
San José de Bácum	232	27.32 N	110.09 W
San Jose de Buan	116	12.02 N	125.01 E
San José de Chiquitos	248	17.51 S	60.47 W
San José de Copán	236	14.54 N	88.44 W
San José de Feliciano	252	30.23 S	58.45 W
San José de Galipán	286c	10.35 N	66.54 W
San José de Galipán, Quebrada ≃	286c	10.37 N	66.54 W
San José de Gracia	234	20.40 N	102.35 W
San José de Guanipa	246	8.54 N	64.09 W
San José de Guaribe	246	9.52 N	65.48 W
San José de Iturbide	234	21.00 N	100.23 W
San José de Jáchal	252	30.14 S	68.45 W
San José de la Esquina	252	33.06 S	61.42 W
San José de la Parilla	234	23.44 N	104.07 W
San José de la Popa	196	26.10 N	100.47 W
San José de las Flores	234	17.20 N	95.24 W
San José de las Lajas	240p	22.58 N	82.09 W
San José de las Raíces	232	24.35 N	100.14 W
San José del Cabo	232	23.03 N	109.41 W
San José del Guaviare	246	2.35 N	72.38 W
San José de Llanetes	234	22.55 N	103.16 W
San José de los Molinos	248	13.57 S	75.41 W
San José de Lourdes	234	23.18 N	103.01 W
San José del Valle	234	23.20 N	98.24 W
San José de Mayo	258	34.20 S	56.42 W
San José de Ocuné	246	4.15 N	70.20 W
San José de Sisa	248	6.37 S	76.39 W
San José de Tiznados	246	9.23 N	67.33 W
San Jose Hills ⋏[2]	280	34.04 N	117.49 W
San Jose Island I	196	28.10 N	96.45 W
San Jose Municipal Airport ⊠	226	37.22 N	121.56 W
San Jose State University ʋ[2]	282	37.20 N	121.53 W
San Juan, Arg.	252	31.32 S	68.31 W
San Juan, Guat.	236	15.52 N	88.53 W
San Juan, Méx.	196	29.34 N	104.36 W
San Juan, Perú	248	15.21 S	75.10 W
San Juan, Pil.	116	13.50 N	121.24 E
San Juan, Pil.	116	16.40 N	120.20 E
San Juan, Pil.	116	8.25 N	126.20 E
San Juan, P.R.	240m	18.28 N	66.07 W
San Juan □[4]	252	31.00 S	69.00 W
San Juan □[6]	224	48.34 N	122.59 W
San Juan ≃, Arg.	252	32.17 S	67.22 W
San Juan ≃, B.C., Can.	224	48.34 N	124.24 W
San Juan ≃, Col.	246	4.03 N	77.27 W
San Juan ≃, Méx.	232	26.22 N	98.51 W
San Juan ≃, Méx.	234	18.36 N	95.40 W
San Juan ≃, Méx.	234	17.59 N	99.47 W
San Juan ≃, N.A.	236	10.56 N	83.42 W
San Juan ≃, Perú	248	13.27 S	76.11 W
San Juan ≃, Pil.	269f	14.35 N	121.01 E
San Juan ≃, S.A.	246	1.11 N	78.33 W
San Juan ≃, U.S.	200	37.18 N	110.28 W
San Juan ≃, Ur.	258	34.17 S	57.58 W
San Juan ≃, Ven.	246	10.14 N	62.38 W
San Juan, Bahía de ⊂	240m	18.27 N	66.07 W
San Juan, Cabezas de ›	240m	18.23 N	65.37 W
San Juan, Cabo ›, Arg.	254	54.44 S	63.44 W
San Juan, Cabo ›, Gui. Ecu.	152	1.08 N	9.23 E
San Juan, Embalse de ⊜[1]	34	40.30 N	4.15 W
San Juan, Pasaje de ⊔	240m	18.24 N	65.37 W
San Juan, Pico ∧	240p	21.59 N	80.09 W
San Juan, Port ⊂	224	48.34 N	124.27 W
San Juan, Punta ›	174z	27.03 S	109.22 W
San Juan Basin ≚[1]	200	36.15 N	108.20 W
San Juan Bautista, Méx.	196	26.58 N	101.24 W
San Juan Bautista, Para.	252	26.38 S	57.10 W
San Juan Bautista, Ca., U.S.	226	36.51 N	121.32 W
San Juan Bautista State Historical Park ♠	226	36.51 N	121.31 W
San Juan Capistrano	228	33.30 N	117.39 W
San Juan Capistrano Mission ʋ[1]	228	33.31 N	117.40 W
San Juan Cotzal	236	15.26 N	91.01 W
San Juan Creek ≃, Ca., U.S.	226	35.40 N	120.22 W
San Juan Creek ≃, Ca., U.S.	228	33.28 N	117.41 W
San Juan de Abajo	234	20.48 N	105.13 W
San Juan de Aragón, Bosque ♠	286a	19.28 N	99.04 W
San Juan de Aragón, Zoológico de ♠	286a	19.28 N	99.05 W
San Juan de Colón	246	8.02 N	72.16 W
San Juan de Dios	286c	10.35 N	66.55 W
San Juan de Guadalupe	232	24.38 N	102.44 W
San Juan [de la Maguana]	238	18.48 N	71.14 W
San Juan de la Vega	234	20.38 N	100.46 W
San Juan del César	246	10.46 N	73.01 W
San Juan del Monte	269f	14.36 N	121.02 E
San Juan del Norte	236	10.55 N	83.42 W
San Juan del Oro ≃	248	21.02 S	65.19 W
San Juan de los Cayos	246	11.10 N	68.25 W
San Juan de los Lagos	234	21.15 N	102.18 W
San Juan de los Lagos ≃	234	21.18 N	102.33 W
San Juan de los Morros	246	9.55 N	67.21 W
San Juan del Río, Méx.	232	24.47 N	104.27 W
San Juan del Río, Méx.	234	20.23 N	100.00 W
San Juan del Salado	234	23.18 N	101.56 W
San Juan del Sur	236	11.15 N	85.52 W
San Juan de Lurigancho	286d	11.59 S	77.01 W
San Juan de Micay ≃	246	3.05 N	77.32 W
San Juan de Miraflores	286d	12.11 S	76.57 W
San Juan de Payara	246	7.39 N	67.36 W
San Juan de Sabinas	196	27.55 N	101.18 W
San Juan Evangelista	234	17.54 N	95.08 W
San Juan Guichicovi	234	16.58 N	95.06 W
San Juanico	232	26.15 N	112.24 W
San Juanillo	236	10.02 N	85.44 W
San Juan Indian Reservation ◆[4]	200	36.03 N	106.04 W
San Juan Island I	224	48.32 N	123.05 W
San Juan Island National Historical Park ♠	224	48.28 N	123.00 W
San Juan Islands II	224	48.36 N	122.50 W
San Juanito, Isla I	234	21.43 N	106.38 W
San Juan Ixcaquixtla	234	18.27 N	97.49 W
San Juan Ixtayopan ◆[8]	286a	19.14 N	99.00 W
San Juan Lachao	234	16.14 N	97.09 W
San Juan Mazatlán	234	17.02 N	95.25 W
San Juan Mountains ⋏	200	37.35 N	107.10 W
San Juan Nepomuceno, Col.	246	9.57 N	75.05 W
San Juan Nepomuceno, Para.	252	26.06 S	55.58 W
San Juan Peyotán	234	22.24 N	104.21 W
San Juan Quiahije	234	16.17 N	97.20 W
San Juan Sacatepéquez	236	14.43 N	90.39 W
San Juan Teita	234	17.05 N	97.25 W
San Juan y Martínez	240p	22.16 N	83.50 W
San Julián, Méx.	234	21.01 N	102.10 W
San Julian, Pil.	116	11.45 N	125.27 E
San Julian, Quebrada ≃	286c	10.37 N	66.51 W
San Justo, Arg.	252	30.47 S	60.35 W
San Justo, Arg.	258	34.40 S	58.33 W
San Justo, Aeródromo ⊠	288	34.44 S	58.36 W
Sankanbiaiwa ∧	150	8.56 N	10.48 W
Sankarani ≃	150	12.01 N	8.19 W
Sankarankovil	122	9.10 N	77.33 E
Sankarpur	272b	22.51 N	88.27 E
Sānkdaha	126	22.46 N	89.10 E
Sankeng	100	23.36 N	112.48 E
Sankertown	214	40.28 N	78.35 W
Sankeshu	104	42.38 N	122.25 E
Sankeshwar	122	16.16 N	74.29 E
Sankey Brook ≃	262	53.22 N	2.38 W
Sankh ≃	124	22.15 N	84.48 E
Sankheda	120	22.10 N	73.35 E
Sankosh ≃	124	26.48 N	89.56 E
Sānkra	120	21.18 N	82.39 E
Sānkrāil	272b	22.34 N	88.14 E
Sankt Aegyd am Neuwalde	61	47.52 N	15.35 E
Sankt Andrä	61	46.46 N	14.49 E
Sankt Andrä [-vor dem Hagenthale]	61	48.19 N	16.13 E
Sankt Andreasberg	54	51.43 N	10.31 E
Sankt Anton am Arlberg	58	47.08 N	10.16 E
Sankt Antönien	58	46.58 N	9.49 E
Sankt Augustin	56	50.40 N	7.16 E
Sankt Bartholomä ʋ[1]	64	47.32 N	12.58 E
Sankt Blasien	58	47.46 N	8.07 E
Sankt Christopher-Nevis → Saint Kitts and Nevis □[1]	238	17.20 N	62.45 W
Sankt Egidien	54	50.47 N	12.36 E
Sankt Florian ʋ[1]	61	48.12 N	14.23 E
Sankt Gallen, Öst.	61	47.41 N	14.37 E
Sankt Gallen, Schw.	58	47.25 N	9.23 E
Sankt Gallen □[3]	58	47.10 N	9.08 E
Sankt Gallenkirch	58	47.01 N	9.59 E
Sankt Georgen, Dtsch.	58	48.07 N	8.20 E
Sankt Georgen, Dtsch.	58	47.59 N	7.47 E
Sankt Georgen, Öst.	61	46.43 N	14.55 E
Sankt Georgen im Attergau	64	47.56 N	13.29 E
Sankt Gertraud → Santa Gertrude	64	46.29 N	10.53 E
Sankt Gertrud ◆[8]	54	53.52 N	10.47 E
Sankt Gilgen	64	47.46 N	13.22 E
Sankt Goar	56	50.09 N	7.43 E
Sankt Goarshausen	56	50.09 N	7.44 E
Sankt Helena → Saint Helena □[2]	8	15.57 S	5.42 W
Sankt Hubert	56	51.23 N	6.26 E
Sankt Ingbert	56	49.17 N	7.06 E
Sankt Jakob → San Giacomo	64	46.57 N	11.36 E
Sankt Jakob im Lesachtal	64	46.41 N	12.56 E
Sankt Jakob im Rosental	61	46.33 N	14.03 E
Sankt Jakob in Defereggen	64	46.55 N	12.20 E
Sankt Johann → San Giovanni	64	46.38 N	11.44 E
Sankt Johann am Tauern	61	47.22 N	14.29 E
Sankt Johann im Pongau	64	47.21 N	13.12 E
Sankt Johann im Walde	64	46.54 N	12.37 E
Sankt Johann in Tirol	64	47.31 N	12.26 E
Sankt Kanzian	61	46.37 N	14.34 E
Sankt Leonhard → San Leonardo	64	46.49 N	11.15 E
Sankt Leonhard am Forst	61	48.09 N	15.17 E
Sankt Leonhard im Pitztal	64	47.04 N	10.51 E
Sankt Lorenz ◆[8]	54	53.51 N	10.40 E
Sankt Lorenz → Saint Lawrence ≃	176	49.30 N	67.00 W
Sankt Lorenzen → San Lorenzo di Sebato	64	46.47 N	11.54 E
Sankt Lorenzen im Lesachtal	64	46.42 N	12.47 E
Sankt Lorenz-Golf → Saint Lawrence, Gulf of ⊂	186	48.00 N	62.00 W
Sankt Lorenz-Insel → Saint Lawrence Island I	180	63.30 N	170.30 W
Sankt Mang	58	47.44 N	10.21 E
Sankt Margarethen an der Raab	61	47.03 N	15.45 E
Sankt Märgen	58	48.00 N	8.05 E
Sankt Margrethen	58	47.27 N	9.36 E
Sankt Martin	64	47.28 N	13.23 E
Sankt Martin an der Raab	61	46.55 N	16.08 E
Sankt Martin in Gsies → San Martino in Casies	64	46.49 N	12.14 E
Sankt Mauritz	52	51.57 N	7.39 E
Sankt Michael im Lungau	64	47.06 N	13.38 E
Sankt Michael in Obersteiermark	61	47.20 N	15.01 E
Sankt Michel → Mikkeli	26	61.41 N	27.15 E
Sankt Moritz	58	46.30 N	9.50 E
Sankt Niklaus	58	46.11 N	7.48 E
Sankt Nikolaus → San Nicolò d'Ultima	64	46.30 N	10.55 E
Sankt Oswald	60	48.54 N	13.25 E
Sankt Paul im Lavanttal	61	46.42 N	14.52 E
Sankt Peter, Dtsch.	30	54.18 N	8.38 E
Sankt Peter, Dtsch.	58	48.01 N	8.01 E
Sankt Peter ʋ[1]	263	51.37 N	7.12 E
Sankt Peter am Kammersberg	61	47.11 N	14.11 E
Sankt Peter am Ottersbach	61	46.48 N	15.45 E
Sankt-Peterburg (Saint Petersburg), Ross.	76	59.55 N	30.15 E
Sankt-Peterburg (Saint Petersburg), Ross.	265a	59.55 N	30.15 E
Sankt-Peterburg, Gorod □[7]	265a	59.55 N	30.15 E
Sankt Peter in der Au	61	48.03 N	14.37 E
Sankt Pölten	61	48.12 N	15.37 E
Sankt-Quirinus-Dom ʋ[1]	263	51.12 N	6.42 E
Sankt Stefan an der Gail	64	46.37 N	13.31 E
Sankt Stefan im Rosental	61	46.54 N	15.42 E
Sankt Ulrich → Ortisei	64	46.34 N	11.40 E
Sankt Valentin	61	48.10 N	14.32 E
Sankt Veit an der Glan	61	46.46 N	14.21 E
Sankt Veit an der Gölsen	61	48.03 N	15.40 E
Sankt Veit im Pongau	64	47.20 N	13.09 E
Sankt-Viktors-Dom ʋ[1]	263	51.40 N	6.27 E
Sankt Vincent → Saint Vincent and the Grenadines □[1]	241h	13.15 N	61.12 W
Sankt Wallburg → Santa Valburga	64	46.33 N	11.00 E
Sankt Wendel	56	49.28 N	7.10 E
Sankt-Willibrodi-Dom ʋ[1]	263	51.40 N	6.37 E
Sankt Wolfgang im Salzkammergut	64	47.44 N	13.27 E
Sankuru ≃	152	4.17 S	20.25 E
San Lázaro	252	22.10 S	57.55 W
San Lázaro, Cabo ›	232	24.48 N	112.19 W
San Lazaro Race Track ♠	269f	14.37 N	120.59 E
San Lazzaro di Savena	64	44.28 N	11.25 E
San Leandro	226	37.43 N	122.09 W
San Leandro Creek ≃	282	37.45 N	122.12 W
San Leo	66	43.54 N	12.21 E
San Leon	222	29.29 N	94.55 W
San Leonardo (Sankt Leonhard), It.	64	46.49 N	11.15 E
San Leonardo, Méx.	196	27.28 N	104.55 W
San Leonardo ≃	70	37.59 N	13.41 E
San Leone	70	37.16 N	13.35 E
Sanlicheng	100	31.48 N	114.12 E
Sanlidian	100	30.48 N	118.15 E
Sanlifan	100	30.51 N	115.15 E
Sanlintang	106	31.08 N	121.29 E
Sanlipu	106	31.46 N	119.03 E
Sanliuji	100	32.08 N	116.19 E
Şanlıurfa	130	37.08 N	38.46 E
Şanlıurfa □[4]	130	37.20 N	39.15 E
San Lope	246	6.12 N	71.56 W
San Lorenzo, Arg.	252	28.08 S	58.46 W
San Lorenzo, Arg.	252	32.45 S	60.44 W
San Lorenzo, Bol.	248	21.26 S	64.47 W
San Lorenzo, Ec.	246	1.17 N	78.50 W
San Lorenzo, Hond.	236	13.25 N	87.27 W
San Lorenzo, It.	68	38.01 N	15.50 E
San Lorenzo, Méx.	196	25.37 N	97.35 W
San Lorenzo, Méx.	232	25.32 N	102.11 W
San Lorenzo, Nic.	236	12.23 N	85.40 W
San Lorenzo, P.R.	240m	18.11 N	65.58 W
San Lorenzo, Ca., U.S.	226	37.40 N	122.07 W
San Lorenzo, Ven.	246	9.47 N	71.04 W
San Lorenzo ≃, Méx.	232	24.15 N	107.24 W
San Lorenzo → Saint Lawrence ≃, N.A.	176	49.30 N	67.00 W
San Lorenzo ≃, Ca., U.S.	226	36.58 N	122.01 W
San Lorenzo, Bahía de ⊂	236	13.19 N	87.30 W
San Lorenzo, Cabo ›	246	1.04 S	80.56 W
San Lorenzo, Golfo del → Saint Lawrence, Gulf of ⊂	186	48.00 N	62.00 W
San Lorenzo, Isla I, Méx.	232	28.38 N	112.51 W
San Lorenzo, Isla I, Perú	248	12.05 S	77.15 W
San Lorenzo, Monte (Cerro Cochrane) ∧	254	47.37 S	72.19 W
San Lorenzo Bellizzi	68	39.53 N	16.20 E
San Lorenzo Creek ≃, Ca., U.S.	226	36.12 N	120.38 W
San Lorenzo Creek ≃, Ca., U.S.	282	37.39 N	122.09 W
San Lorenzo de El Escorial	34	40.35 N	4.09 W
San Lorenzo de la Parrilla	34	39.51 N	2.22 W
San Lorenzo del Vallo	68	39.40 N	16.18 E
San Lorenzo di Sebato (Sankt Lorenzen)	64	46.47 N	11.54 E
San Lorenzo in Campo	66	43.36 N	12.56 E
San Lorenzo Nuovo	66	42.41 N	11.54 E
San Lorenzo Tezonco ◆[8]	286a	19.18 N	99.04 W
San Luca	68	38.09 N	16.04 E
Sanlúcar de Barrameda	34	36.47 N	6.21 W
Sanlúcar la Mayor	34	37.23 N	6.12 W
San Lucas, Bol.	248	20.06 S	65.07 W
San Lucas, Ec.	246	3.45 S	79.15 W
San Lucas, Méx.	232	22.53 N	109.54 W
San Lucas, Ca., U.S.	226	36.08 N	121.01 W
San Lucas, Cabo ›	232	22.52 N	109.53 W
San Luis, Arg.	252	33.18 S	66.21 W
San Luis, Cuba	240p	20.12 N	75.51 W
San Luis, Cuba	240p	22.17 N	83.46 W
San Luis, Guat.	236	16.14 N	89.27 W
San Luis, Perú	286d	12.04 S	77.00 W
San Luis, Az., U.S.	200	32.04 N	111.57 W
San Luis, Co., U.S.	200	37.12 N	105.25 W
San Luis, Ven.	246	11.07 N	69.42 W
San Luis □[4]	252	34.00 S	66.00 W
San Luis ◆[8]	286b	23.05 N	82.20 W
San Luis ≃	234	17.13 N	100.55 W
San Luis, Arroyo ≃	258	34.10 S	57.44 W
San Luís, Laguna ⊜	248	13.45 S	64.00 W
San Luis, Sierra de ⋏	252	32.40 S	65.50 W
San Luis Acatlán	234	16.48 N	98.45 W
San Luis Creek ≃	200	37.42 N	105.44 W
San Luis de la Loma	234	17.18 N	100.55 W
San Luis de la Paz	234	21.18 N	100.31 W
San Luis del Cordero	232	25.26 N	104.18 W
San Luis del Palmar	252	27.31 S	58.34 W
San Luis Gonzaga	232	24.55 N	111.16 W
San Luis Gonzaga, Bahía ⊂	232	29.48 N	114.22 W
San Luis Jilotepeque	236	14.39 N	89.44 W
San Luis Obispo	226	35.16 N	120.39 W
San Luis Obispo □[6]	226	35.30 N	120.30 W
San Luis Pass ⊂	222	29.05 N	95.08 W
San Luis Peak ∧	200	37.59 N	106.56 W
San Luis Potosí	234	22.09 N	100.59 W
San Luis Potosí □[3]	234	22.30 N	100.30 W
San Luis Reservoir ⊜[1]	226	37.07 N	121.05 W
San Luis Rey	228	33.14 N	117.20 W
San Luis Rey ≃	204	33.12 N	117.24 W
San Luis Rey, Mission ʋ[1]	228	33.14 N	117.20 W
San Luis Río Colorado	232	32.29 N	114.48 W
San Luis Soyatlán	234	20.12 N	103.18 W
San Luis State Recreation Area ♠	226	37.04 N	121.05 W
San Luis Valley V	200	37.25 N	106.00 W
Sanluri	71	39.34 N	8.54 E
San Macario	266b	45.36 N	8.47 E
Sanmaiden	270	34.34 N	135.51 E
San Mamete	58	46.02 N	9.04 E
San Mango d'Aquino	68	39.03 N	16.11 E
San Manuel, Arg.	252	37.47 S	58.50 W
San Manuel, Méx.	234	17.37 N	93.24 W
San Manuel, Az., U.S.	200	32.35 N	110.37 W
San Marcelino	116	14.58 N	120.09 E
San Marcello Pistoiese	66	44.03 N	10.47 E
San Marcial ≃	232	28.04 N	110.44 W
San Marco, Capo ›, It.	70	37.30 N	13.01 E
San Marco, Capo ›, It.	71	39.51 N	8.26 E
San Marco Argentano	68	39.33 N	16.07 E
San Marco dei Cavoti	68	41.18 N	14.53 E
San Marco in Lamis	68	41.43 N	15.38 E

Symbol	English	Deutsch	Español	Français	Português
≃	River	Fluß	Río	Rivière	Rio
≅	Canal	Kanal	Canal	Canal	Canal
↳	Waterfall, Rapids	Wasserfall, Stromschnellen	Cascada, Rápidos	Chute d'eau, Rapides	Cascata, Rápidos
⊔	Strait	Meeresstraße	Estrecho	Détroit	Estreito
⊂	Bay, Gulf	Bucht, Golf	Bahía, Golfo	Baie, Golfe	Baía, Golfo
⊜	Lake, Lakes	See, Seen	Lago, Lagos	Lac, Lacs	Lago, Lagos
⩩	Swamp	Sumpf	Pantano	Marais	Pântano
⊓	Ice Features, Glacier	Eis- und Gletscherformen	Accidentes Glaciales	Formes glaciaires	Acidentes glaciares
⫪	Other Hydrographic Features	Andere Hydrographische Objekte	Otros Elementos Hidrográficos	Autres données hydrographiques	Outros acidentes hidrográficos
✣	Submarine Features	Untermeerische Objekte	Accidentes Submarinos	Formes de relief sous-marin	Acidentes submarinos
□	Political Unit	Politische Einheit	Unidad Politica	Entité politique	Unidade política
ʋ	Cultural Institution	Kulturelle Institution	Institución Cultural	Institution culturelle	Institução cultural
⊥	Historical Site	Historische Stätte	Sitio Histórico	Site historique	Sitio histórico
♠	Recreational Site	Erholungs- und Ferienort	Sitio de Recreo	Centre de loisirs	Area de Lazer
⊠	Airport	Flughafen	Aeropuerto	Aéroport	Aeroporto
■	Military Installation	Militäranlage	Instalación Militar	Installation militaire	Instalação militar
◆	Miscellaneous	Verschiedenes	Misceláneo	Divers	Diversos

San Marco la Catola 68 41.31 N 15.00 E
San Marcos, Chile 252 30.56 S 71.03 W
San Marcos, Col. 246 8.39 N 75.08 W
San Marcos, C.R. 236 9.40 N 84.01 W
San Marcos, El Sal. 236 13.39 N 89.11 W
San Marcos, Guat. 236 14.58 N 91.48 W
San Marcos, Hond. 236 14.24 N 88.56 W
San Marcos, Hond. 236 15.17 N 88.23 W
San Marcos, Méx. 234 16.48 N 99.21 W
San Marcos, Méx. 234 20.02 N 99.20 W
San Marcos, Méx. 234 20.47 N 104.11 W
San Marcos, Ca., U.S. 228 33.08 N 117.09 W
San Marcos, Tx., U.S. 196 29.52 N 97.56 W
San Marcos ▫5 236 15.00 N 91.55 W
San Marcos ≐ 196 29.29 N 97.28 W
San Marcos, Isla I 232 27.13 N 112.06 W
San Marcos, Laguna ⊜ 234 20.17 N 103.33 W
San Marcos, Universidad Nacional de ✓2 286d 12.04 S 77.05 W
San Marcos Arteaga 234 17.45 N 97.58 W
San Marcos de Colón 236 13.26 N 86.48 W
San Marino, S. Mar. 66 43.55 N 12.28 E
San Marino, Ca., U.S. 280 34.07 N 118.06 W
San Marino ▫1, Europe 22 43.56 N 12.25 E
San Marino ▫1, Europe 66 43.56 N 12.25 E
San Martín, Arg. 252 29.14 S 65.46 W
San Martín, Arg. 252 33.04 S 68.28 W
San Martín — General San Martín, Arg. 258 34.34 S 58.32 W
San Martín, Col. 246 3.42 N 73.42 W
San Martin, Ca., U.S. 226 37.05 N 121.37 W
San Martín, Ur. 258 33.45 S 57.37 W
San Martín ▫5 248 7.00 S 76.50 W
San Martín ≐, Bol. 248 13.08 S 63.43 W
San Martín ≐, Bol. 248 11.50 S 67.16 W
San Martín ✓3 9 68.07 S 67.08 W
San Martín, Arroyo ≐ 258 33.49 S 57.44 W
San Martín, Cuchilla ⋏2 258 33.45 S 57.54 W
San Martín, Lago (Lago O'Higgins) ⊜ 254 49.00 S 72.40 W
San Martín, Volcán ∧1 234 18.33 N 95.12 W
San Martín de Bolaños 234 21.29 N 103.58 W
San Martín de las Vacas 196 25.30 N 101.20 W
San Martín de los Andes 254 40.10 S 71.21 W
San Martín de Porras 286d 12.04 S 77.04 W
San Martín de Valdeiglesias 34 40.21 N 4.24 W
San Martín Hidalgo 234 20.27 N 103.57 W
San Martino, It. 62 45.27 N 8.47 E
San Martino (Sankt Martin), It. 64 46.47 N 11.13 E
San Martino, It. 64 45.25 N 10.35 E
San Martino Buon Albergo 64 45.25 N 11.05 E
San Martino d'Agri 68 40.14 N 16.04 E
San Martino di Castrozza 64 46.16 N 11.48 E
San Martino di Lupari 64 45.39 N 11.51 E
San Martino in Badia (Sankt Martin) 64 46.41 N 11.52 E
San Martino in Casies (Sankt Martin in Gsies) 64 46.49 N 12.14 E
San Martino in Rio 64 44.44 N 10.48 E
San Martino Valle Caudina 68 41.01 N 14.39 E
San Martín Peras 234 17.19 N 98.15 W
San Marzano di San Giuseppe 68 40.27 N 17.30 E
San Mateo, Méx. 234 22.59 N 103.30 W
San Mateo, Pil. 269f 14.42 N 121.07 E
San Mateo, Ca., U.S. 226 37.33 N 122.19 W
San Mateo, Fl., U.S. 192 29.36 N 81.35 W
San Mateo, N.M., U.S. 200 35.19 N 107.38 W
San Mateo, Ven. 246 9.45 N 64.33 W
San Mateo ▫6 226 37.25 N 122.20 W
San Mateo Atenco 234 19.16 N 99.32 W
San Mateo Bridge ◆5 282 37.36 N 122.13 W
San Mateo Canyon ∨ 228 33.23 N 117.36 W
San Mateo Creek ≐ 282 37.34 N 122.18 W
San Mateo del Mar 234 16.12 N 95.00 W
San Mateo Ixtatán 236 15.50 N 91.29 W
San Mateo Memorial Park ◆ 282 37.17 N 122.18 W
San Mateo Point > 228 33.23 N 117.36 W
San Mateo Tecoloapan 286a 19.34 N 99.14 W
San Matías 248 16.22 S 58.24 W
San Matías, Golfo ⊂ 254 41.30 S 64.15 W
San Mauro Castelverde 70 37.55 N 14.11 E
San Mauro Forte 68 40.29 N 16.15 E
San Mauro la Bruca 68 40.07 N 15.17 E
San Mauro Marchesato 68 39.06 N 16.56 E
San Mauro Torinese 62 45.06 N 7.46 E
San Medi, Arroyo de ≐ 266d 41.28 N 2.06 E
Sanmen 100 29.06 N 121.24 E
San Menaio 68 41.56 N 15.58 E
Sanmen Wan ⊂ 100 29.08 N 121.44 E
Sanmenxia (Shanxian) 102 34.45 N 111.05 E
San Michele, Sacra di ✓1 62 45.11 N 7.21 E
San Michele all'Adige 64 46.12 N 11.08 E
San Michele al Tagliamento 64 45.46 N 12.59 E
San Michele di Ganzaria 70 37.17 N 14.26 E
San Michele Mondovì 62 44.23 N 7.54 E
San Michele Salentino 68 40.38 N 17.37 E
San Miguel, Arg. 252 28.00 S 57.36 W
San Miguel — General Sarmiento, Arg. 258 34.33 S 58.43 W
San Miguel, Bol. 248 16.42 S 61.01 W
San Miguel, Chile 286e 33.30 S 70.40 W
San Miguel, Ec. 246 1.44 S 79.01 W
San Miguel, El Sal. 236 13.29 N 88.11 W
San Miguel, Esp. 148 28.05 N 16.37 W
San Miguel, Méx. 232 29.10 N 101.28 W
San Miguel, Méx. 234 23.23 N 98.10 W
San Miguel, Pan. 236 8.27 N 78.56 W
San Miguel, Perú 248 13.01 S 73.58 W
San Miguel, Perú 286d 12.06 S 77.07 W
San Miguel, Pil. 116 15.09 N 120.59 E
San Miguel, Ca., U.S. 226 35.45 N 120.41 W
San Miguel ≐, Bol. 248 13.52 S 63.56 W
San Miguel (Cuilco) ≐, N.A. 236 15.56 N 92.10 W
San Miguel ≐, S.A. 246 0.08 N 75.51 W
San Miguel ≐, S.A. 248 19.15 S 59.20 W
San Miguel ≐, Co., U.S. 200 38.23 N 108.48 W
San Miguel, Cerro ∧2 248 19.19 S 60.36 W
San Miguel, Golfo de ⊂ 246 8.22 N 78.17 W
San Miguel, Volcán de ∧1 236 13.26 N 88.16 W
San Miguel Arcángel, Mission ✓1 226 35.44 N 120.42 W
San Miguel Bay ⊂ 116 13.50 N 123.10 E
San Miguel Chimalapa 234 16.43 N 94.41 W
San Miguel Creek ≐ 196 28.30 N 98.25 W
San Miguel de Allende 234 20.55 N 100.45 W
San Miguel de Cruces 232 24.25 N 105.51 W
San Miguel del Monte 258 35.27 S 58.48 W
San Miguel de Pallaques 248 7.00 S 78.51 W
San Miguel de Salcedo 246 1.02 S 78.34 W
San Miguel de Tucumán 252 26.49 S 65.13 W
San Miguel El Alto 234 21.01 N 102.21 W
San Miguel El Grande 234 17.02 N 97.37 W
San Miguel Island I, Pil. 116 13.23 N 123.48 E
San Miguel Island I, Ca., U.S. 204 34.02 N 120.22 W
San Miguel Islands II 116 7.45 N 118.28 E
San Miguelito 236 11.24 N 84.54 W
San Miguel Ixtahuacán 236 15.15 N 91.45 W
San Miguel Mountain ∧ 228 32.42 N 116.56 W
San Miguel Sola de Vega 234 16.31 N 96.59 W
San Miguel Talea de Castro 234 17.22 N 96.15 W
San Miguel Tecuixiapan 234 17.58 N 99.27 W
San Miguel Tenango 234 16.16 N 95.36 W
San Miguel Totolapan 234 18.08 N 100.23 W
Sanming 100 26.14 N 117.36 E
San Miniato 66 43.41 N 10.51 E
San Murezzan — Sankt Moritz 58 46.30 N 9.50 E
Sannahed 40 59.06 N 15.09 E
Sannan 96 35.04 N 135.02 E
Sannār 140 13.33 N 33.38 E
San Narciso, Pil. 116 13.34 N 122.34 E
San Narciso, Pil. 116 15.01 N 120.05 E
Sannazzaro de'Burgondi 62 45.06 N 8.54 E
Sannicandro di Bari 68 41.00 N 16.48 E
Sannicandro Garganico 68 41.50 N 15.34 E
Sannicola 68 40.05 N 18.04 E
San Nicola, Isola I 66 42.07 N 15.30 E
San Nicola, Monte ∧ 68 38.35 N 16.24 E
San Nicola Arcella 68 39.51 N 15.48 E
San Nicola da Crissa 68 38.40 N 16.17 E
San Nicolás, Cuba 240p 22.47 N 81.55 W
San Nicolás, Esp. 148 27.59 N 15.46 W
San Nicolás, Hond. 236 15.00 N 88.45 W
San Nicolás, Méx. 234 16.26 N 98.32 W
San Nicolás, Perú 248 15.13 S 75.12 W
San Nicolas, Pil. 116 18.09 N 120.38 E
San Nicolás ≐ 234 19.40 N 105.14 W
San Nicolás de los Arroyos 252 33.20 S 60.13 W
San Nicolás de los Garza 196 25.45 N 100.18 W
San Nicolas Island I 204 33.15 N 119.31 W
Sânnicolau Mare 38 46.05 N 20.38 E
San Nicolò di Comelico 64 46.35 N 12.31 E
San Nicolò d'Ultimo (Sankt Nikolaus) 64 46.30 N 10.55 E
San Nicolò Ferrarese 64 44.42 N 11.42 E
San Nicolò Gerrei 71 39.30 N 9.18 E
Sannieshof 158 26.30 S 25.47 E
Sannikova, proliv ℍ 74 74.30 N 140.00 E
Sannīn, Jabal ∧ 132 33.57 N 35.52 E
Sannio, Monti del ⋏ 66 41.30 N 14.45 E
Sanniquellie 150 7.22 N 8.43 W
Sannohe 92 40.22 N 141.15 E
Sannois 261 48.58 N 2.15 E
Sanņūr, Wādī ∨ 142 28.58 N 31.03 E
Sano 94 36.19 N 139.35 E
Sañogasta 252 29.18 S 67.36 W
Sanok 30 49.34 N 22.13 E
Sânon ≐ 58 48.38 N 6.20 E
San Onofre 246 9.44 N 75.32 W
San Onofre Mountain ∧ 228 33.22 N 117.30 W
San Pablo, Chile 254 40.24 S 73.01 W
San Pablo, Col. 246 1.40 N 77.00 W
San Pablo, Pil. 116 14.04 N 121.19 E
San Pablo, Pil. 116 7.40 N 123.27 E
San Pablo, Ca., U.S. 226 37.57 N 122.20 W
San Pablo ◆8 286a 19.11 N 99.04 W
San Pablo ≐, Bol. 248 14.52 S 63.42 W
San Pablo ≐, Méx. 234 18.32 N 96.01 W
San Pablo ≐, Pan. 236 7.51 N 81.10 W
San Pablo, Point > 282 37.58 N 122.26 W
San Pablo Autopan 234 19.21 N 99.40 W
San Pablo Bay ⊂ 226 38.06 N 122.22 W
San Pablo Creek ≐ 282 37.58 N 122.30 W
San Pablo Huixtepec 234 16.50 N 96.46 W
San Pablo Reservoir ⊜1 282 37.56 N 122.15 W
San Pablo Ridge ∧ 282 37.55 N 122.15 W
San Pablo Strait ℍ 282 37.58 N 122.26 W
San Pablo Villa de Mitla 234 16.55 N 96.24 W
Sanpada 272c 19.04 N 73.01 E
San Pancrazio Salentino 68 40.25 N 17.50 E
San Paolo 64 46.29 N 11.15 E
San Paolo di Civitate 68 41.44 N 15.15 E
San Pascual 116 13.08 N 122.59 E
San Pasqual Indian Reservation ◆4 228 33.12 N 116.58 W
San Pedro, Arg. 252 33.40 S 59.40 W
San Pedro, Arg. 252 24.14 S 64.52 W
San Pedro, Arg. 252 27.57 S 65.10 W
San Pedro, Chile 252 21.57 S 68.34 W
San Pedro, Chile 252 33.54 S 71.28 W
San Pedro, Col. 246 9.24 N 75.04 W
San Pedro, C.R. 236 9.56 N 84.03 W
San Pedro, C. Iv. 150 4.44 N 6.37 W
San Pedro, Para. 252 24.07 S 56.59 W
San Pedro, Tx., U.S. 196 27.47 N 97.40 W
San Pedro, Ur. 258 34.31 S 57.51 W
San Pedro, Ven. 246 8.50 N 71.58 W
San Pedro ▫5 252 24.15 S 56.30 W
San Pedro ◆8 228 33.44 N 118.18 W
San Pedro ≐, Cuba 240p 21.09 N 78.30 W
San Pedro ≐, Méx. 232 30.50 N 108.08 W
San Pedro ≐, Méx. 234 21.45 N 105.30 W
San Pedro ≐, N.A. 200 32.59 N 110.47 W
San Pedro ≐, N.A. 232 17.45 N 91.23 W
San Pedro ≐, Ven. 286c 10.35 N 66.48 W
San Pedro, Arroyo ≐ 258 34.21 S 57.56 W
San Pedro, Point >, Ca., U.S. 282 37.59 N 122.27 W
San Pedro, Point >, Ca., U.S. 282 37.35 N 122.31 W
San Pedro, Punta > 252 25.30 S 70.38 W
San Pedro, Volcán ∧1 252 21.53 S 68.25 W
San Pedro Amuzgos 234 16.39 N 98.06 W
San Pedro Apóstol 234 16.44 N 96.44 W
San Pedro Ayampuc 236 14.47 N 90.27 W
San Pedro Bay ⊂, Pil. 116 11.13 N 125.05 E
San Pedro Bay ⊂, Ca., U.S. 228 33.45 N 118.11 W
San Pedro Breakwater ◆5 280 33.42 N 118.16 W
San Pedro Carchá 236 15.29 N 90.16 W
San Pedro Channel ℍ 228 33.35 N 118.25 W
San Pedro Creek ≐, Ca., U.S. 282 37.36 N 122.30 W
San Pedro Creek ≐, Tx., U.S. 222 31.34 N 95.14 W
San Pedro de Arriba 258 34.18 S 57.47 W
San Pedro de Atacama 252 22.55 S 68.13 W
San Pedro de Buena Vista 248 18.13 S 65.59 W
San Pedro de Curahuara 248 17.40 S 68.02 W
San Pedro de la Cueva 232 29.18 N 109.44 W
San Pedro de las Colonias 232 25.45 N 102.59 W
San Pedro del Gallo 232 25.33 N 104.18 W
San Pedro de Lloc 248 7.26 S 79.31 W
San Pedro del Norte 236 13.04 N 84.33 W
San Pedro del Paraná 252 26.46 S 56.15 W
San Pedro de Macorís 238 18.27 N 69.18 W
San Pedro El Alto 234 16.01 N 96.28 W
San Pedro Huamelula 234 16.02 N 95.40 W
San Pedro Jicayán 234 16.25 N 97.59 W
San Pedro Juchatengo 234 16.21 N 97.06 W
San Pedro Mártir ◆8 286a 19.16 N 99.10 W
San Pedro Mixtepec 234 16.00 N 97.07 W
San Pedro Peaks ⋏ 200 36.07 N 106.49 W
San Pedro Pinula 236 14.40 N 89.51 W
San Pedro Pochutla 234 15.44 N 96.28 W
San Pedro Sacatepéquez 236 14.58 N 91.46 W
San Pedro Sula 236 15.27 N 88.02 W
San Pedro Tabasco 232 17.47 N 91.10 W
San Pedro Tapanatepec 234 16.21 N 94.12 W
San Pedro Tututepec 234 16.09 N 97.38 W
San Pedro Xalostoc 286a 19.32 N 99.05 W
San Pedro y Miquelón — Saint Pierre and Miquelon ▫2 186 46.55 N 56.20 W
San Pelayo 246 8.58 N 75.51 W
San Pellegrino 62 45.50 N 9.40 E
San Piero a Grado 66 43.41 N 10.21 E
San Piero in Bagno 66 43.51 N 11.58 E
San Pierre 216 41.12 N 86.53 W
San Pietro (Sankt Peter) 64 47.01 N 12.03 E
San Pietro, Isola di I 71 39.08 N 8.17 E
San Pietro a Maida 68 38.50 N 16.20 E
San Pietro di Cadore 64 46.34 N 12.35 E
San Pietro in Casale 64 44.42 N 11.24 E
San Pietro in Gu 64 45.37 N 11.40 E
San Pietro in Guarano 68 39.20 N 16.19 E
San Pietro in Palazzi 66 43.20 N 10.30 E
San Pietro in Vaticano ✓1 267a 41.54 N 12.28 E
San Pietro Vara 62 44.20 N 9.35 E
San Pietro Vernotico 68 40.29 N 18.00 E
San Pitch ≐ 200 39.03 N 111.51 W
Sanpoil ≐ 202 47.53 N 118.41 W
San Policarpio 116 12.11 N 125.30 E
San Polo d'Enza 64 44.38 N 10.26 E
Sanpu 98 34.09 N 117.10 E
Sanqiao 106 30.35 N 119.58 E
San Quentin 282 37.56 N 122.29 W
San Quentin State Prison ◆ 282 37.56 N 122.28 W
Sanquhar 44 55.22 N 3.56 W
Sanquianga, Parque Nacional ◆ 246 2.30 N 78.15 W
San Quintin 116 16.00 N 120.50 E
San Quintín, Cabo > 232 30.21 N 116.00 W
San Quirico d'Orcia 66 43.03 N 11.36 E
Sanqutan 100 27.17 N 115.04 E
Sanquzhen 107 29.39 N 105.37 E
San Rafael, Arg. 252 34.36 S 68.20 W
San Rafael, Chile 252 35.19 S 71.32 W
San Rafael, Méx. 232 25.01 N 100.33 W
San Rafael, Méx. 234 20.12 N 96.51 W
San Rafael, Ca., U.S. 226 37.58 N 122.31 W
San Rafael, N.M., U.S. 200 35.06 N 107.52 W
San Rafael, Ven. 246 10.58 N 71.44 W
San Rafael ≐, Bol. 248 18.38 S 58.55 W
San Rafael ≐, Ut., U.S. 200 38.47 N 110.07 W
San Rafael Bay ⊂ 282 37.58 N 122.28 W
San Rafael de las Tortillas 196 26.49 N 99.32 W
San Rafael del Norte 236 13.12 N 86.06 W
San Rafael del Sur 236 11.51 N 86.27 W
San Rafael Desert ◆2 200 38.40 N 110.30 W
San Rafael Hills ⋏2 280 34.10 N 118.12 W
San Rafael Mountains ⋏ 204 34.45 N 119.50 W
San Rafael Oriente 236 13.23 N 88.21 W
San Rafael Swell ⋏1 200 38.40 N 110.45 W
San Rafael Tasajera 236 13.16 N 88.52 W
San Ramón, Arg. 252 27.42 S 64.17 W
San Ramón, Bol. 248 13.17 S 64.43 W
San Ramón, C.R. 236 10.06 N 84.28 W
San Ramón, Hond. 236 14.41 N 84.43 W
San Ramón, Perú 248 11.08 S 75.20 W
San Ramon, Pil. 116 13.16 N 124.05 E
San Ramon, Ca., U.S. 282 37.47 N 121.59 W
San Ramón, Ur. 252 34.18 S 55.58 W
San Ramon Creek ≐ 282 37.54 N 122.03 W
San Ramón de la Nueva Orán 252 23.08 S 64.20 W
San Ramon Valley ∨ 282 37.46 N 121.58 W
Sanrao 100 23.59 N 116.50 E
San-rei ∧ 96 33.50 N 133.59 E
San Remigio 116 11.05 N 123.56 E
San Remo, Austl. 169 38.31 S 145.22 E
San Remo, It. 62 43.49 N 7.46 E
San Remo, N.Y., U.S. 210 40.52 N 73.13 W
San Roberto 68 38.18 N 15.44 E
San Rodrigo ≐ 196 28.54 N 100.37 W
San Román 236 16.21 N 90.22 W
San Román, Cabo > 246 12.12 N 70.00 W
San Roque, Arg. 252 28.34 S 58.43 W
San Roque, Arg. 252 30.17 S 68.41 W
San Roque, Esp. 34 36.13 N 5.24 W
San Roque, N. Mar. Is. 174n 15.15 N 145.47 E
San Roque, Pil. 269f 14.29 N 120.54 E
San Roque, Cabo — São Roque, Cabo de > 250 5.29 S 35.16 W
San Roque, Punta > 232 27.11 N 114.26 W
San Rosendo 252 37.16 S 72.43 W
San Rufo 68 40.26 N 15.28 E
San Saba 196 31.11 N 98.43 W
San Saba ≐ 196 31.15 N 98.35 W
San Saep, Khlong ≐ 269a 13.45 N 100.36 E
San Salvador, Arg. 252 29.16 S 57.31 W
San Salvador, Arg. 252 31.37 S 58.30 W
San Salvador, El Sal. 236 13.42 N 89.12 W
San Salvador (Watling Island) I 238 24.02 N 74.28 W
San Salvador ≐ 258 33.37 S 58.06 W
San Salvador, Cuchilla ⋏2 258 33.56 S 57.45 W
San Salvador, Volcán de ∧1 236 13.44 N 89.17 W
San Salvador de Jujuy 252 24.11 S 65.18 W
San Salvador el Seco 234 19.08 N 97.39 W
San Salvatore, Monte ∧ 70 37.50 N 14.03 E
San Salvatore Monferrato 62 44.59 N 8.34 E
San Salvatore Telesino 68 41.14 N 14.30 E
San Salvo 66 42.03 N 14.44 E
Sansanné-Mango 150 10.21 N 0.28 E
Sans Bois Creek ≐ 196 35.20 N 94.50 W
San Sebastián, El Sal. 236 13.44 N 88.50 W
San Sebastián — Donostia, Esp. 34 43.19 N 1.59 W
San Sebastián, Guat. 236 14.34 N 91.39 W
San Sebastián, Hond. 236 14.24 N 88.42 W
San Sebastián, Méx. 234 20.47 N 104.51 W
San Sebastián, P.R. 240m 18.20 N 66.59 W
San Sebastián, Bahía ⊂ 254 53.12 S 68.20 W
San Sebastián de la Gomera 148 28.06 N 17.06 W
San Sebastián del Álamo 234 21.26 N 102.21 W
San Sebastián de los Reyes 266a 40.33 N 3.38 W
San Sebastián de Yalí 236 13.18 N 86.11 W
San Sebastiano 64 45.38 N 10.16 E
San Sebastiano Curone 62 44.47 N 9.04 E
San Sebastián Tecomaxtlahuaca 234 17.21 N 98.02 W
San Sebastián Zinacatepec 234 18.20 N 97.15 W
San Secondo Parmense 64 44.55 N 10.14 E
Sansepolcro 66 43.34 N 12.08 E
San Severino Lucano 68 40.01 N 16.08 E
San Severino Marche 66 43.13 N 13.10 E
San Severo 68 41.41 N 15.23 E
Sansha 100 26.58 N 120.12 E
Sanshengchang 89 44.51 N 120.21 E
Sanshierzhan 89 53.16 N 121.49 E
Sanshijia, Zhg. 98 41.44 N 119.15 E
Sanshijia, Zhg. 98 41.05 N 119.03 E
Sanshilibao 98 39.15 N 121.48 E
Sanshiling 106 30.51 N 119.29 E
Sanshisanzhan 89 53.10 N 121.27 E
Sanshui 100 23.11 N 112.53 E
San Sigismondo (Sankt Sigmund) 64 46.49 N 11.46 E
San Simeon 226 35.39 N 121.11 W
San Simon, Méx. 204 30.30 N 115.58 W
San Simon, Az., U.S. 200 32.16 N 109.13 W
San Simón ≐, Bol. 248 13.13 S 63.31 W
San Simon ≐, Az., U.S. 200 32.50 N 109.39 W
San Simon Wash ∨ 200 31.45 N 112.25 W
San Siro ◆8 266b 45.29 N 9.07 E
Sanski Most 36 44.46 N 16.40 E
Sanso 150 11.43 N 6.51 W
San Solano 252 31.29 S 65.55 W
Sansom Park Village 222 32.48 N 97.24 W
Sanson 172 40.13 S 175.25 E
San Sosti 68 39.40 N 16.02 E
San Sperate 71 39.21 N 9.00 E
Sans Souci 274a 33.59 S 151.08 E
Sans-Souci ⊥ 238 19.37 N 72.19 W
Sanssouci, Schloss ✓ 54 52.24 N 13.02 E
San Stefano Ticino 266b 45.29 N 8.55 E
Santa, Perú 248 8.59 S 78.36 W
Santa, Pil. 116 17.29 N 120.26 E
Santa ≐ 248 8.58 S 78.39 W
Santa, Isla del I 248 9.02 S 78.40 W
Santa Adélia 255 21.16 S 48.48 W
Santa Albertina 255 20.02 S 50.44 W
Santa Amalia 34 39.01 N 6.01 W
Santa Ana, Arg. 252 27.22 S 55.34 W
Santa Ana, Bol. 248 13.45 S 65.35 W
Santa Ana, Bol. 248 18.43 S 58.44 W
Santa Ana, Col. 246 9.19 N 74.35 W
Santa Ana, Ec. 246 1.13 S 80.23 W
Santa Ana, El Sal. 236 13.59 N 89.34 W
Santa Ana, Méx. 232 30.33 N 111.07 W
Santa Ana, Méx. 234 24.04 N 100.30 W
Santa Ana, Ca., U.S. 228 33.44 N 117.52 W
Santa Ana, Ven. 246 9.19 N 64.39 W
Santa Ana ≐, Cuba 286b 23.04 N 82.32 W
Santa Ana ≐, Ca., U.S. 228 33.38 N 117.57 W
Santa Ana, Volcán de ∧1 236 13.50 N 89.38 W
Santa Ana Canyon ∨ 280 33.53 N 117.43 W
Santa Ana de Chena 286e 33.34 S 70.47 W
Santa Ana del Alto Beni 248 15.31 S 67.30 W
Santa Ana Heights 228 33.39 N 117.54 W
Santa Ana Indian Reservation ◆4 200 35.28 N 106.37 W
Santa Ana Island I 175e 10.50 S 162.28 E
Santa Ana Maya 234 20.00 N 101.01 W
Santa Ana Mountains ⋏ 228 33.45 N 117.35 W
Santa Ana Race Track ◆ 269f 14.35 N 121.01 E
Santa Ana Tlacotenco ◆8 286a 19.10 N 98.59 W
Santa Anita 234 20.33 N 103.27 W
Santa Anita Canyon ∨ 280 34.12 N 118.01 W
Santa Anita Park ◆ 280 34.08 N 118.03 W
Santa Anna 196 31.44 N 99.19 W
Santa Apolonia 196 25.38 N 97.59 W
Santa Bárbara, Chile 252 37.40 S 72.01 W
Santa Barbara, Col. 246 5.53 N 75.35 W
Santa Bárbara, Hond. 236 14.53 N 88.14 W
Santa Bárbara, Méx. 232 26.48 N 105.49 W
Santa Bárbara, Méx. 234 18.52 N 101.07 W
Santa Barbara, Ca., U.S. 204 34.25 N 119.42 W
Santa Bárbara, Ven. 246 3.57 N 67.06 W
Santa Bárbara, Ven. 246 7.47 N 71.10 W
Santa Bárbara ▫5 236 15.10 N 88.20 W
Santa Barbara ▫6 228 33.28 N 119.02 W
Santa Bárbara ≐ 248 16.58 S 61.39 W
Santa Bárbara, Morro de ∧ 287a 22.57 S 43.28 W
Santa Bárbara, Túnel ◆5 287a 22.56 S 43.12 W
Santa Barbara Channel ℍ 204 34.15 N 119.55 W
Santa Bárbara do Monte Verde 256 21.58 S 43.42 W
Santa Bárbara do Sul 252 28.22 S 53.15 W
Santa Barbara do Tugúrio 256 21.15 S 43.35 W
Santa Barbara Island I 228 33.28 N 119.02 W
Santa Branca 256 23.24 S 45.53 W
Santa Branca, Reprêsa ⊜1 256 23.20 S 45.50 W
Santaca 158 26.36 S 32.32 E
Santa Catalina, Arg. 252 21.57 S 66.04 W
Santa Catalina, Pil. 116 9.20 N 122.51 E
Santa Catalina, Ur. 258 33.49 S 57.29 W
Santa Catalina, Arroyo ≐ 288 34.46 S 58.27 W
Santa Catalina, Gulf of ⊂ 228 33.20 N 117.45 W
Santa Catalina, Isla I 232 25.40 N 110.47 W
Santa Catalina, Laguna ⊜ 288 34.46 S 58.27 W
Santa Catalina Island I 228 33.23 N 118.24 W
Santa Catalina o Calovébora 236 8.47 N 81.20 W
Santa Catarina, Méx. 204 31.37 N 115.48 W
Santa Catarina, Méx. 232 25.41 N 100.28 W
Santa Catarina ▫3 252 27.00 S 50.00 W
Santa Catarina, Ilha de I 252 27.36 S 48.30 W
Santa Catarina Juquila 234 16.14 N 97.18 W
Santa Caterina di Pittinuri 71 40.06 N 8.30 E
Santa Caterina Valfurva 64 46.25 N 10.29 E
Santa Caterina Villarmosa 70 37.35 N 14.02 E
Santa Cecília 252 26.56 S 50.27 W
Santa Cesarea Terme 68 40.02 N 18.29 E

ENGLISH

Name Page Lat.°′ Long.°′
Santa Clara, Col. 246 2.43 S 69.43 W
Santa Clara, Cuba 240p 22.24 N 79.58 W
Santa Clara, Méx. 232 29.17 N 107.01 W
Santa Clara, Méx. 234 19.41 N 102.30 W
Santa Clara, Méx. 286a 19.34 N 99.04 W
Santa Clara, Ca., U.S. 226 37.20 N 121.56 W
Santa Clara, Ut,. U.S. 200 37.07 N 113.39 W
Santa Clara ▫6 226 37.20 N 121.53 W
Santa Clara ≐, Ca., U.S. 228 34.14 N 119.16 W
Santa Clara ≐, Ut,. U.S. 200 37.05 N 113.36 W
Santa Clara, Bahía de ⊂ 240p 23.05 N 80.30 W
Santa Clara, University of ✓2 282 37.21 N 121.56 W
Santa Clara de Olimar 252 32.55 S 54.58 W
Santa Clara Indian Reservation ◆4 200 35.59 N 106.10 W
Santa Clara Valley ∨ 226 37.10 N 121.40 W
Santa Clarita 286d 12.00 S 77.01 W
Santa Clotilde 246 2.34 S 73.44 W
Santa Coloma de Cervelló 266d 41.22 N 2.01 E
Santa Coloma de Farners 34 41.52 N 2.40 E
Santa Coloma de Gramanet 266d 41.27 N 2.13 E
Santa Comba 34 43.02 N 8.49 W
Santa Comba Dão 34 40.24 N 8.08 W
Santa Cristina 64 46.34 N 11.43 E
Santa Cristina d'Aspromonte 68 38.15 N 15.58 E
Santa Croce 64 46.05 N 12.18 E
Santa Croce, Capo > 70 37.14 N 15.15 E
Santa Croce, Lago di ⊜ 64 46.10 N 12.20 E
Santa Croce Camerina 70 36.50 N 14.31 E
Santa Croce del Sannio 68 41.23 N 14.43 E
Santa Croce di Magliano 66 41.42 N 14.59 E
Santa Croce Sull'Arno 66 43.42 N 10.47 E
Santa Cruz, Bra. 250 6.13 S 36.01 W
Santa Cruz, Bra. 255 19.56 S 40.09 W
Santa Cruz, Chile 252 34.38 S 71.22 W
Santa Cruz, C.R. 236 10.16 N 85.36 W
Santa Cruz, Méx. 200 31.14 N 110.35 W
Santa Cruz, Perú 248 6.37 S 78.57 W
Santa Cruz, Pil. 116 6.50 N 125.25 E
Santa Cruz, Pil. 116 14.17 N 121.25 E
Santa Cruz, Pil. 116 13.29 N 122.02 E
Santa Cruz, Pil. 116 13.04 N 120.43 E
Santa Cruz, Pil. 116 15.46 N 119.55 E
Santa Cruz (Tubajon), Pil. 116 10.19 N 125.33 E
Santa Cruz, Ca., U.S. 226 36.58 N 122.01 W
Santa Cruz, Ven. 246 8.25 N 71.39 W
Santa Cruz, Ven. 286c 10.26 N 67.01 W
Santa Cruz ▫4 254 49.00 S 70.00 W
Santa Cruz ▫5 248 17.30 S 61.30 W
Santa Cruz ▫6 226 36.58 N 122.01 W
Santa Cruz ◆8, Bra. 256 22.56 S 43.41 W
Santa Cruz ◆8, India 272c 19.05 N 72.50 E
Santa Cruz ≐, Arg. 254 50.08 S 68.20 W
Santa Cruz ≐, Cuba 286b 23.04 N 82.29 W
Santa Cruz ≐, N.A. 200 32.42 N 111.33 W
Santa Cruz, Ilha I 287a 22.52 S 43.07 W
Santa Cruz, Isla I 246a 0.38 S 90.23 W
Santa Cruz, Sierra de ⋏ 236 15.40 N 89.15 W
Santa Cruz Basin ◆1 14 12.00 S 163.00 E
Santa Cruz Cabrália 255 16.17 S 39.02 W
Santa Cruz da Graciosa 148a 39.05 N 28.01 W
Santa Cruz das Flores 148a 39.27 N 31.07 W
Santa Cruz de Goiás 255 17.19 S 48.30 W
Santa Cruz de Juventino Rosas 234 20.39 N 101.00 W
Santa Cruz de la Palma 148 28.41 N 17.45 W
Santa Cruz de la Sierra 248 17.48 S 63.10 W
Santa Cruz de la Zarza 34 39.58 N 3.10 W
Santa Cruz del Quiché 236 15.02 N 91.08 W
Santa Cruz del Sur 240p 20.43 N 78.00 W
Santa Cruz de Mudela 34 38.38 N 3.28 W
Santa Cruz de Tenerife 148 28.27 N 16.14 W
Santa Cruz de Tenerife ▫4, Esp. 34 28.20 N 16.50 W
Santa Cruz de Tenerife ▫4, Esp. 148 28.15 N 17.00 W
Santa Cruz do Capibaribe 250 7.57 S 36.12 W
Santa Cruz do Piauí 250 7.09 S 41.48 W
Santa Cruz do Prata 256 21.12 S 46.45 W
Santa Cruz do Rio Pardo 255 22.55 S 49.37 W
Santa Cruz do Sul 252 29.43 S 52.26 W
Santa Cruz International Airport ⊠ 272c 19.05 N 72.52 E
Santa Cruz Island I 204 34.01 N 119.45 W
Santa Cruz Islands II 14 11.00 S 166.15 E
Santa Cruz Meyehualco ◆8 286a 19.20 N 99.03 W
Santa Cruz Mountains ⋏ 226 37.15 N 122.00 W
Santa Cruz Point > 116 15.44 N 119.52 E
Santa Cruz Tacache de Mina 234 17.51 N 98.07 W
Santadi 71 39.05 N 8.43 E
Santa Domenica Talao 68 39.49 N 15.51 E
Santa Domenica Vittoria 70 37.55 N 14.58 E
Sant Adrià de Besòs 266d 41.25 N 2.14 E
Santa Elena, Arg. 252 30.57 S 59.48 W
Santa Elena, Ec. 246 2.14 S 80.51 W
Santa Elena, El Sal. 236 13.22 N 88.25 W
Santa Elena, Méx. 196 27.59 N 103.56 W
Santa Elena, Méx. 232 27.28 N 102.33 W
Santa Elena, Méx. 234 18.39 N 101.34 W
Santa Elena ≐ 248 15.42 S 67.13 W
Santa Elena, Bahía de ⊂ 246 2.06 S 80.53 W
Santa Elena, Cabo > 236 10.54 N 85.57 W
Santa Elena, Golfo de ⊂ 236 10.59 N 85.50 W
Santa Elena, Punta > 246 2.11 S 81.00 W
Santa Elena del Gomero 286e 33.29 S 70.46 W
Santa Elena de Uairén 246 4.37 N 61.08 W
Santa Elisabetta 70 37.26 N 13.33 E
Santa Eufemia 34 38.36 N 4.54 W
Santa Eugenia 34 42.33 N 9.00 W
Santa Eulalia, Esp. 34 40.34 N 1.19 W
Santa Eulalia, Guat. 236 15.45 N 91.29 W
Santa Eulària del Riu 34 38.59 N 1.31 E
Santa Fe, Arg. 252 31.38 S 60.42 W
Santa Fé, Bra. 255 15.40 S 51.16 W
Santa Fé, Bra. 255 23.01 S 51.48 W
Santa Fe, Esp. 34 37.11 N 3.43 W
Santa Fe, Hond. 236 15.55 N 86.05 W
Santa Fé, Pan. 236 8.31 N 81.05 W
Santa Fe, Pil. 116 11.09 N 123.47 E
Santa Fe, Pil. 116 16.10 N 120.57 E
Santa Fe, Pil. 116 12.10 N 122.00 E
Santa Fe, Mo., U.S. 219 39.22 N 91.49 W
Santa Fe, N.M., U.S. 200 35.41 N 105.56 W
Santa Fe ▫4 252 31.00 S 61.00 W

DEUTSCH

Name Seite Breite°′ Länge°′ E = Ost
Santa Fé ◆8 286b 23.05 N 82.31 W
Santa Fe ≐, Fl., U.S. 192 29.53 N 82.53 W
Santa Fe ≐, N.M., U.S. 200 35.36 N 106.20 W
Santa Fé, Aeropuerto ⊠ 286b 23.04 N 82.28 W
Santa Fe, Isla I 246a 0.49 S 90.04 W
Santa Fé, Ribeirão ≐ 287b 23.24 S 46.48 W
Santa Fe Baldy ∧ 200 35.50 N 105.46 W
Santa Fe Dam ◆6 280 34.07 N 117.58 W
Santa Fe de Bogotá 246 4.36 N 74.05 W
Santa Fe de Minas 255 16.42 S 45.26 W
Santa Fé do Sul 255 20.13 S 50.56 W
Santa Fe Flood Control Basin ≃1 280 34.07 N 117.58 W
Santa Fe Springs 280 33.56 N 118.04 W
Santa Filomena 250 9.07 S 45.56 W
Santa Fiora 66 42.50 N 11.35 E
Santa Flavia 70 38.05 N 13.31 E
Sant'Agata Bolognese 64 44.40 N 11.08 E
Sant'Agata de'Goti 68 41.05 N 14.30 E
Sant'Agata del Bianco 68 38.05 N 16.05 E
Sant'Agata di Militello 70 38.04 N 14.38 E
Sant'Agata di Puglia 68 41.09 N 15.23 E
Sant'Agata Feltria 66 43.52 N 12.12 E
Sant'Agata sul Santerno 66 44.26 N 11.51 E
Santa Gertrude (Sankt Gertraud) 64 46.29 N 10.53 E
Santa Gertrudis 196 26.09 N 98.44 W
Santa Giusta, Stagno di ⊜ 71 39.52 N 8.35 E
Sant'Agostino 64 44.48 N 11.23 E
Sāntāhār 124 24.48 N 88.59 E
Santa Helena 250 2.14 S 45.18 W
Santa Helena de Goiás 255 17.43 S 50.35 W
Santai, Zhg. 85 39.14 N 77.42 E
Santai, Zhg. 86 44.35 N 81.18 E
Santai, Zhg. 102 31.10 N 105.02 E
Santai, Zhg. 104 41.56 N 123.11 E
Santai, Zhg. 104 41.48 N 121.53 E
Santai, Zhg. 105 38.58 N 115.49 E
Santa Inês 255 13.17 S 39.48 W
Santa Inés, Bahía ⊂ 232 26.59 N 111.59 W
Santa Inés, Isla I 254 53.45 S 72.45 W
Santa Inés Ahuatempan 234 18.25 N 98.01 W
Santa Iria de Azóia 266c 38.51 N 9.05 W
Santa Isabel, Arg. 252 36.15 S 66.56 W
Santa Isabel, Arg. 252 33.54 S 61.42 W
Santa Isabel, Bra. 256 23.19 S 46.14 W
Santa Isabel, Ec. 246 3.21 S 79.19 W
Santa Isabel — Malabo, Gui. Ecu. 152 3.45 N 8.47 E
Santa Isabel, Méx. 234 23.15 N 100.52 W
Santa Isabel, P.R. 240m 17.58 N 66.24 W
Santa Isabel I 175e 8.00 S 159.00 E
Santa Isabel ≐ 236 15.59 N 90.00 W
Santa Isabel, Pico de ∧ 152 3.35 N 8.46 E
Santa Isabel Creek ≐ 196 27.39 N 99.38 W
Santa Isabel de Sihuas 248 16.20 S 72.06 W
Santa Isabel do Araguaia 250 6.07 S 48.19 W
Santa Isabel do Rio Prêto 256 22.14 S 44.05 W
Santaizi 104 41.21 N 121.36 E
Santa Josefa 116 8.02 N 125.57 E
Santa Julia 286e 33.30 S 70.38 W
Santa Juliana 255 19.19 S 47.32 W
Sant'Alberto 66 44.32 N 12.09 E
Sant'Alfio 70 37.44 N 15.08 E
Sāntalpur 120 23.45 N 71.10 E
Santa Luce 66 43.28 N 10.34 E
Santa Lucía, Arg. 252 28.59 S 59.06 W
Santa Lucía, Arg. 252 31.32 S 68.29 W
Santa Lucía, Cuba 240p 21.02 N 76.00 W
Santa Lucía, Cuba 240p 22.40 N 83.58 W
Santa Lucia, It. 64 46.28 N 10.21 E
Santa Lucia, It. 64 45.26 N 10.57 E
Santa Lucía, Ur. 258 34.27 S 56.24 W
Santa Lucía, Ven. 246 8.07 N 69.46 W
Santa Lucía — Saint Lucia ▫1 241f 13.53 N 60.58 W
Santa Lucía ≐ 258 34.48 S 56.22 W
Santa Lucia, Cabo — Saint Lucia, Cape > 158 28.25 S 32.25 E
Santa Lucía, Cuchilla ⋏2 258 34.09 S 56.11 W
Santa Lucía Chico ≐ 258 34.21 S 56.20 W
Santa Lucía Cotzumalguapa 236 14.20 N 91.01 W
Santa Lucia Creek ≐ 226 36.13 N 121.30 W
Santa Lucia del Mela 70 38.09 N 15.17 E
Santa Lucia di Piave 64 45.51 N 12.17 E
Santa Lucia Range ⋏ 226 36.00 N 121.20 W
Santaluz 250 11.15 S 39.22 W
Santa Luzia, Bra. 250 6.53 S 36.56 W
Santa Luzia, Port. 34 37.44 N 8.24 W
Santa Luzia I 150a 16.46 N 24.45 W
Santa Magdalena 252 34.30 S 63.56 W
Santa-Manza, Golfu di ⊂ 71 41.37 N 9.22 E
Santa Margarita 226 35.23 N 120.36 W
Santa Margarita ≐ 228 33.14 N 117.25 W
Santa Margarita, Isla I 232 24.27 N 111.50 W
Santa Margarita Lake ⊜1 226 35.20 N 120.28 W
Santa Margarita Mountains ⋏ 228 33.30 N 117.25 W
Santa Margherita di Belice 70 37.41 N 13.01 E
Santa Margherita Ligure 62 44.20 N 9.12 E
Santa María, Arg. 252 26.41 S 66.02 W
Santa Maria, Bra. 252 29.41 S 53.48 W
Santa Maria, C.V. 150a 16.36 N 22.54 W
Santa María, C.R. 236 9.39 N 83.57 W
Santa María, Méx. 196 28.02 N 101.38 W
Santa María, Pan. 236 8.07 N 80.40 W
Santa Maria, Pil. 116 17.22 N 120.29 E
Santa María, P.R. 240m 18.09 N 65.26 W
Santa Maria, Schw. 58 46.16 N 9.09 E
Santa Maria, Schw. 58 46.36 N 10.24 E
Santa Maria, Ca., U.S. 204 34.57 N 120.26 W
Santa Maria I, Port. 148a 36.58 N 25.06 W
Santa Maria I, Vanuatu 175f 14.15 S 167.30 E
Santa Maria ≐, Bra. 252 29.48 S 54.56 W
Santa Maria ≐, Bra. 252 21.50 S 54.53 W
Santa María ≐, Méx. 232 31.00 N 107.14 W
Santa María ≐, Méx. 234 21.48 N 99.10 W
Santa María ≐, Pan. 236 8.06 N 80.29 W
Santa Maria ≐, Az., U.S. 200 34.19 N 113.31 W
Santa María, Bahía ⊂ 232 25.04 N 108.06 W
Santa María, Cabo — Sainte-Marie, Cap >, Madag. 157b 25.36 S 45.08 E
Santa María, Cabo >, Ur. 252 34.40 S 54.10 W
Santa Maria, Cabo de >, Ang. 152 13.25 S 12.32 E
Santa Maria, Cabo de >, Port. 34 36.58 N 7.54 W
Santa Maria, Cape > 238 23.41 N 75.19 W
Santa María, Cayo I 240p 22.40 N 79.00 W
Santa María, Cerro ∧ 286d 11.56 S 76.57 W
Santa Maria, Giogo di (Pass Umbrail))(64 46.34 N 10.25 E
Santa María, Isla I, Chile 252 37.02 S 73.33 W

Symbols in the index entries represent the broad categories identified in the key at the right. Symbols with superior numbers (⋏1) identify subcategories (see complete key on page I · 1).

Symbole im Register stellen die rechts im Schlüssel erklärten Kategorien dar. Symbole mit hochgestellten Ziffern (⋏1) bezeichnen Unterabteilungen einer Kategorie (vgl. vollständiger Schlüssel auf Seite I · 1).

Los símbolos incluidos en el texto del índice representan las grandes categorías identificadas con la clave a la derecha. Los símbolos con números en su parte superior (⋏1) identifican las subcategorías (véase la clave completa en la página I · 1).

Les symboles de l'index représentent les catégories indiquées dans la légende à droite. Les symboles suivis d'un indice (⋏1) représentent des sous-catégories (voir légende complète à la page I · 1).

Os símbolos incluídos no texto do índice representam as grandes categorias identificadas com a chave à direita. Os símbolos com números em sua parte superior (⋏1) identificam as subcategorias (veja-se a chave completa à página I · 1).

∧ Mountain	Berg	Montaña	Montagne	Montanha
⋏ Mountains	Gebirge	Montañas	Montagnes	Montanhas
)(Pass	Paß	Paso	Col	Passo
∨ Valley, Canyon	Tal, Cañon	Valle, Cañón	Vallée, Canyon	Vale, Canhão
≃ Plain	Ebene	Llano	Plaine	Planície
> Cape	Kap	Cabo	Cap	Cabo
I Island	Insel	Isla	Île	Ilha
II Islands	Inseln	Islas	Îles	Ilhas
≐ Other Topographic Features	Andere Topographische Objekte	Otros Elementos Topográficos	Autres données topographiques	Outros acidentes topográficos

ESPAÑOL · FRANÇAIS · PORTUGUÊS

Nombre / Nom / Nome	Página / Page	Lat. °′	Long. °′ W = Oeste / W = Ouest
Santa María, Isla I, Ec.	246a	1.17 S	90.26 W
Santa Maria, Isola I	71	41.17 N	9.22 E
Santa María, Laguna de ⊜	200	31.07 N	107.16 W
Santa Maria, Ribeirão ≏	250	7.10 S	49.13 W
Santa María, Volcán ∧ [1]	236	14.45 N	91.33 W
Santa María Ajoloapan	234	19.58 N	99.03 W
Santa Maria a Monte	66	43.42 N	10.42 E
Santa Maria Asunción Tlaxiaco	234	17.16 N	97.41 W
Santa Maria a Vico	68	41.02 N	14.29 E
Santa María Ayoquezco	234	16.41 N	96.50 W
Santa Maria Capua Vetere	68	41.05 N	14.15 E
Santa María Chimalapa	234	16.55 N	94.41 W
Santa María Colotepec	234	15.53 N	96.55 W
Santa Maria da Boa Vista	250	8.49 S	39.49 W
Santa Maria da Vitória	255	13.24 S	44.12 W
Santa Maria degli Angeli	66	43.03 N	12.34 E
Santa María de Huazamoto	234	22.30 N	104.30 W
Santa María de Ipire	246	8.49 N	65.19 W
Santa Maria de Itabira	255	19.27 S	43.08 W
Santa Maria del Cedro	68	39.45 N	15.50 E
Santa Maria della Versa	62	44.59 N	9.18 E
Santa Maria delle Grazie ᵾ [1]	266b	45.27 N	9.10 E
Santa María del Oro	232	25.56 N	105.22 W
Santa María de los Ángeles	234	22.11 N	103.14 W
Santa María del Refugio	234	23.44 N	101.14 W
Santa María del Río	234	21.48 N	100.45 W
Santa María del Valle	234	20.54 N	102.22 W
Santa Mariá de Mohovano	232	26.42 N	103.39 W
Santa Maria di Galeria ⬥ [8]	267a	42.01 N	12.19 E
Santa Maria di Leuca, Capo ›	68	39.47 N	18.22 E
Santa Maria di Licodia	70	37.37 N	14.53 E
Santa Maria di Siponto ᵾ [1]	68	41.40 N	15.51 E
Santa Maria do Suaçuí	255	18.12 S	42.25 W
Santa María Huazolotitlán	234	16.17 N	97.56 W
Santa María Jalapa del Marqués	234	16.30 N	95.28 W
Santa María la Real de Nieva	34	41.04 N	4.24 W
Santa Maria Madalena	255	21.57 S	42.01 W
Santa Maria Maggiore	58	46.08 N	8.28 E
Santa Maria Maggiore ᵾ [1]	267a	41.53 N	12.30 E
Santa Maria Nuova	66	43.29 N	13.18 E
Santa-Maria-Siché	36	41.52 N	8.59 E
Santa María Tulpetlac	286a	19.34 N	99.03 W
Santa María Xadani	234	15.56 N	96.04 W
Santa María Zoquitlán	234	16.33 N	96.23 W
Santa Marinella	66	42.02 N	11.51 E
Santa Marta, Col.	246	11.15 N	74.13 W
Santa Marta, Guat.	236	13.58 N	91.18 W
Santa Marta, Cabo de ›, Ang.	152	13.52 S	12.25 E
Santa Marta, Cabo de ›, Moç.	158	26.05 S	32.58 E
Santa Marta, Cerro ∧	234	18.19 N	94.48 W
Santa Marta, Ciénaga Grande ⊂	246	10.50 N	74.25 W
Santa Marta Grande, Cabo de ›	252	28.38 S	48.45 W
Sant'Ambrogio	64	45.31 N	10.50 E
Santa Mónica, Méx.	196	28.12 N	100.37 W
Santa Monica, Ca., U.S.	228	34.01 N	118.29 W
Santa Mónica ⬥ [8]	286c	10.29 N	66.53 W
Santa Monica Bay ⊂	228	33.54 N	118.25 W
Santa Monica Beach State Park ♠	280	34.01 N	118.30 W
Santa Monica Mountains ⋏	228	34.05 N	118.40 W
Santa Monica Mountains National Recreation Area ♠	228	34.05 N	118.45 W
Santa Monica Municipal Airport ⊠	280	34.01 N	118.27 W
Santan	112	0.03 S	117.28 E
Santana, Bra.	255	12.59 S	44.03 W
Sântana, Rom.	38	46.21 N	21.30 E
Santana ⬥ [8]	287b	23.29 S	46.38 W
Santana ≏	255	19.43 S	51.02 W
Santana, Coxilha de ⋏ [2]	252	31.15 S	55.15 W
Santana, Ilha de I	250	2.18 S	43.41 W
Santana, Ribeirão ≏	250	9.47 S	50.13 W
Santana da Boa Vista	252	30.52 S	53.07 W
Santana da Vargem	256	21.15 S	45.30 W
Santana de Caldas	256	21.50 S	46.24 W
Santana de Cataguases	256	21.17 S	42.33 W
Santana de Parnáiba	256	23.27 S	46.55 W
Santana de Parnaíba □ [7]	287b	23.27 S	46.54 W
Santana do Campestre	256	21.16 S	42.56 W
Santana do Capivari	256	22.14 S	44.56 W
Santana do Cariri	250	7.11 S	39.44 W
Santana do Deserto	256	21.57 S	43.11 W
Santana do Garambéu	256	21.36 S	44.06 W
Santana do Ipanema	250	9.22 S	37.14 W
Santana do Livramento	252	30.53 S	55.31 W
Santana do Matos	250	5.57 S	36.39 W
Santander, Col.	246	3.01 N	76.28 W
Santander, Esp.	34	43.28 N	3.48 W
Santander, Pil.	116	9.25 N	123.20 E
Santander □ [5]	246	7.00 N	73.15 W
Santander Jiménez	232	24.13 N	98.28 W
Sant'Andrea, Isola I	68	40.03 N	17.57 E
Sant'Andrea Frius	71	39.29 N	9.10 E
Sant Andreu de la Barca	266d	41.27 N	1.59 E
Santa Nella	226	37.03 N	121.02 W
Santanésia	256	22.30 S	43.49 W
Santang	100	28.44 N	116.32 E
Sant'Angelo, Castel ⊥	267a	41.55 N	12.28 E
Sant'Angelo, Monte ∧	267a	41.56 N	12.49 E
Sant'Angelo dei Lombardi	68	40.56 N	15.11 E
Sant'Angelo in Vado	66	43.40 N	12.25 E
Sant'Angelo Lodigiano	62	45.14 N	9.24 E
Sant'Angelo Muxard	70	37.28 N	13.32 E
Sant'Angelo Romano	267a	42.02 N	12.42 E
Santanghu	102	44.13 N	93.22 E
Santanilla, Islas II	238	17.25 N	83.55 W
Santa Ninfa	70	37.46 N	12.53 E
Sant'Antimo	68	40.56 N	14.14 E
Sant'Antine, Nuraghe ⊥	71	40.29 N	8.46 E
Sant'Antioco	71	39.04 N	8.27 E
Sant'Antioco, Isola di I	71	39.02 N	8.25 E
Sant Antoni de Portmany	34	38.58 N	1.18 E
Sant'Antonio Abate	68	40.43 N	14.32 E
Sant'Antonio di Santadi	71	39.43 N	8.29 E
Sant'Antonio Morignone	64	46.24 N	10.21 E
Santanyi	34	39.22 N	3.07 E
Santa Panagia, Capo ›	70	37.07 N	15.18 E
Santa Paula	228	34.21 N	119.03 W
Santa Paula Creek ≏	228	34.21 N	119.03 W
Santa Perpètua de Mogoda	266d	41.32 N	2.11 E
Santapogue Creek ≏	276	40.40 N	73.21 W
Santa Pola, Cap de ›	34	38.12 N	0.31 W
Sant'Apollinare in Classe ᵾ [1]	66	44.22 N	12.15 E
Santaquin	200	39.58 N	111.47 W
Santa Quitéria	250	4.20 S	40.10 W
Santa Quitéria do Maranhão	250	3.31 S	42.32 W
Sant'Arcangelo	68	40.15 N	16.17 E
Santarcangelo di Romagna	66	44.04 N	12.27 E
Sant'Arcangelo Trimonte	68	41.10 N	14.56 E
Santarém, Bra.	250	2.26 S	54.42 W
Santarém, Port.	34	39.14 N	8.41 W
Santarém □ [5]	266c	38.50 N	8.56 W
Santaren Channel ʯ	238	24.00 N	79.30 W
Santa Rita, Bra.	250	7.08 S	34.58 W
Santa Rita, Bra.	287a	22.41 S	43.28 W
Santa Rita, Col.	246	0.33 N	73.58 W
Santa Rita, Hond.	236	15.09 N	87.53 W
Santa Rita, Méx.	196	27.29 N	100.33 W
Santa Rita, Méx.	232	28.34 N	111.42 W
Santa Rita, Pil.	116	11.27 N	124.56 E
Santa Rita, Mt., U.S.	182	48.42 N	112.19 W
Santa Rita, Ven.	246	10.32 N	71.32 W
Santa Rita, Punta ›	258	34.28 S	57.52 W
Santa Rita de Caldas	256	22.02 S	46.20 W
Santa Rita de Catuna	252	30.57 S	66.13 W
Santa Rita de Jacutinga	256	22.09 S	44.06 W
Santa Rita del Rucio	234	23.04 N	100.19 W
Santa Rita do Araguaia	255	17.20 S	53.12 W
Santa Rita do Ibitipoca	256	21.33 S	43.55 W
Santa Rita do Sapucaí	256	22.15 S	45.42 W
Santa Rita do Weil	246	3.29 S	69.19 W
Santa Rita Park	226	37.02 N	120.35 W
Santa Rosa, Arg.	252	36.37 S	64.17 W
Santa Rosa, Arg.	252	23.22 S	64.30 W
Santa Rosa, Bol.	248	14.10 S	66.53 W
Santa Rosa, Bol.	248	10.36 S	67.25 W
Santa Rosa, Bol.	248	17.07 S	63.35 W
Santa Rosa, Bra.	252	27.52 S	54.29 W
Santa Rosa, Bra.	255	15.01 S	47.13 W
Santa Rosa, Col.	246	2.31 N	68.13 W
Santa Rosa, C.R.	236	10.51 N	85.38 W
Santa Rosa, Ec.	246	3.27 S	79.58 W
Santa Rosa, Méx.	204	31.59 N	116.45 W
Santa Rosa, Méx.	234	22.18 N	104.24 W
Santa Rosa, Para.	248	21.46 S	61.43 W
Santa Rosa, Para.	252	26.52 S	56.49 W
Santa Rosa, Ca., U.S.	226	38.26 N	122.42 W
Santa Rosa, N.M., U.S.	196	34.56 N	104.40 W
Santa Rosa, Tx., U.S.	196	26.15 N	97.50 W
Santa Rosa, Ur.	258	34.30 S	56.03 W
Santa Rosa, Ven.	246	8.26 N	69.24 W
Santa Rosa, Ven.	246	7.03 N	68.28 W
Santa Rosa, Ven.	286c	10.30 N	66.46 W
Santa Rosa □ [5]	236	14.10 N	90.18 W
Santa Rosa, Mount ∧ [2]	174p	13.32 N	144.55 E
Santa Rosa, Parque Nacional ♠	236	10.50 N	85.45 W
Santa Rosa, Presa ⊜ [1]	234	20.58 N	103.35 W
Santa Rosa Beach	194	30.23 N	86.13 W
Santa Rosa Creek ≏	226	35.34 N	121.06 W
Santa Rosa de Aguán	236	15.57 N	85.43 W
Santa Rosa de Amanadona	246	1.29 N	66.55 W
Santa Rosa [de Copán]	236	14.47 N	88.46 W
Santa Rosa de Huechuraba	286e	33.21 S	70.41 W
Santa Rosa del Conlara	252	32.20 S	65.12 W
Santa Rosa de Leales	252	27.09 S	65.15 W
Santa Rosa de Lima	236	13.37 N	87.53 W
Santa Rosa de Locobe	286e	33.26 S	70.33 W
Santa Rosa del Palmar	248	16.54 S	62.24 W
Santa Rosa de Osos	246	6.39 N	75.28 W
Santa Rosa de Río Primero	252	31.09 S	63.23 W
Santa Rosa de Sucumbíos	246	0.22 N	77.10 W
Santa Rosa de Viterbo	246	5.53 N	72.59 W
Santa Rosa Indian Reservation ⬥ [4]	204	33.35 N	116.35 W
Santa Rosa Island I, Ca., U.S.	204	33.58 N	120.06 W
Santa Rosa Island I, Fl., U.S.	194	30.22 N	86.55 W
Santa Rosa Jáuregui	234	20.44 N	100.27 W
Santa Rosalía, Méx.	196	26.08 N	98.59 W
Santa Rosalía, Méx.	232	27.19 N	112.17 W
Santa Rosalía, Ven.	246	9.02 N	69.01 W
Santa Rosa Range ⋏	204	41.35 N	117.40 W
Santa Rosa Wash ∨	200	33.00 N	112.00 W
Santa Rosita	286d	12.03 S	76.59 W
Sant'Arsenio	68	40.28 N	15.29 E
Šantarskije ostrova II	74	55.00 N	137.36 E
Santa Severa	66	42.02 N	11.57 E
Santa Severina	68	39.09 N	16.55 E
Santa Sofia	66	43.57 N	11.54 E
Santa Susana	228	34.16 N	118.43 W
Santa Susana Mountains ⋏	228	34.20 N	118.42 W
Santa Sylvina	252	27.49 S	61.09 W
Santa Tecla → Nueva San Salvador	236	13.41 N	89.17 W
Santa Teresa, Bra.	255	19.55 S	40.36 W
Santa Teresa, Méx.	196	29.34 N	104.39 W
Santa Teresa, Méx.	200	30.52 N	111.33 W
Santa Teresa, Méx.	232	25.17 N	97.51 W
Santa Teresa, Méx.	234	22.28 N	104.44 W
Santa Teresa ≏	255	11.47 S	48.37 W
Santa Teresa, Embalse de ⊜ [1]	34	40.40 N	5.30 W
Santa Teresa de lo Ovalle	286e	33.23 S	70.47 W
Santa Teresa di Riva	70	37.57 N	15.22 E
Santa Teresa Gallura	71	41.14 N	9.11 E
Santa Tereza de Goiás	255	13.38 S	49.01 W
Santa Terezinha	250	10.28 S	50.31 W
Santa Valburga (Sankt Wallburg)	64	46.33 N	11.00 E
Santa Venerina	70	37.41 N	15.08 E
Santa Venetia	226	38.01 N	122.31 W
Santa Vitória	255	18.50 S	50.08 W
Santa Vitória do Palmar	252	33.31 S	53.21 W
Santa Vittoria, Monte ∧	71	39.45 N	9.18 E
Santa Vittoria in Matenano	66	43.01 N	13.29 E
Santa Ynez ≏	204	34.41 N	120.36 W
Santa Ynez Canyon ∨	280	34.04 N	118.34 W
Santa Ysabel Indian Reservation ⬥ [4]	204	33.11 N	116.41 W
Sant Bartomeu de la Quadra	266d	41.26 N	2.02 E
Sant Boi de Llobregat	266d	41.21 N	2.03 E
Sant Carles de la Ràpita	34	40.37 N	0.36 E
Sant Climent de Llobregat	266d	41.20 N	2.00 E
Sant Cugat del Vallès	266d	41.28 N	2.05 E
Santee	228	32.50 N	116.58 W
Santee ≏	192	33.14 N	79.28 W
Santee Dam ⬥ [6]	192	33.24 N	80.12 W
Santee Indian Reservation ⬥ [4]	198	42.45 N	97.50 W
Sant'Egidio alla Vibrata	66	42.49 N	13.42 E
Sant'Elena	64	45.12 N	11.43 E
Sant'Elia a Pianisi	66	41.38 N	14.52 E
Sant'Elia Fiumerapido	66	41.32 N	13.52 E
Sant'Elpidio a Mare	66	43.14 N	13.41 E
Santena	62	44.57 N	7.45 E
Santenay	58	46.55 N	4.41 E
Santeny	261	48.43 N	2.34 E
San Teodoro, It.	70	37.51 N	14.42 E
San Teodoro, It.	71	40.46 N	9.39 E
Santermo in Colle	68	40.48 N	16.45 E
Santerno ≏	64	44.34 N	11.58 E
Santerre □ [9]	50	49.40 N	2.40 E
Sant'Eufemia, Golfo di ⊂	68	38.50 N	16.00 E
Sant'Eufemia a Maiella	66	42.07 N	14.02 E
Sant'Eufemia d'Aspromonte	68	38.16 N	15.52 E
Sant'Eufemia Lamezia	68	38.55 N	16.15 E
Sant Feliu de Guíxols	34	41.47 N	3.02 E
Sant Feliu de Llobregat	266d	41.23 N	2.03 E
Sant Fost de Campsentelles	266d	41.31 N	2.14 E
Sānthia, Bngl.	126	24.03 N	89.33 E
Santhià, It.	62	45.22 N	8.10 E
Santiago, Bol.	248	18.19 S	59.34 W
Santiago, Bra.	252	29.11 S	54.53 W
Santiago, Chile	252	33.27 S	70.40 W
Santiago, Chile	286e	33.27 S	70.40 W
Santiago → Santiago de Compostela, Esp.	34	42.53 N	8.33 W
Santiago, Méx.	232	23.28 N	109.43 W
Santiago, Pan.	236	8.06 N	80.59 W
Santiago, Para.	252	27.09 S	56.47 W
Santiago, Perú	248	14.11 S	75.44 W
Santiago, Pil.	116	16.41 N	121.33 E
Santiago I	150a	15.05 N	23.40 W
Santiago ≏, Arg.	288	34.50 S	57.57 W
Santiago ≏, Méx.	232	25.11 N	105.26 W
Santiago ≏, S.A.	246	4.27 S	77.38 W
Santiago, Cape ›	116	13.46 N	120.39 E
Santiago, Cerro ∧	236	8.33 N	81.44 W
Santiago, Isla I, Arg.	288	34.50 S	57.53 W
Santiago, Isla I, Ec.	246a	0.14 S	90.45 W
Santiago, Serranía de ⋏	248	18.25 S	59.25 W
Santiago Atitlán	236	14.38 N	91.14 W
Santiago Chazumba	234	18.12 N	97.40 W
Santiago Choapan	234	17.20 N	95.57 W
Santiago Creek ≏, Ca., U.S.	228	35.06 N	119.17 W
Santiago Creek ≏, Ca., U.S.	228	33.46 N	117.54 W
Santiago Dam ⬥ [6]	280	33.47 N	117.43 W
Santiago de Cao	248	7.58 S	79.15 W
Santiago de Chocorvos	248	13.50 S	75.16 W
Santiago de Chuco	248	8.09 S	78.11 W
Santiago de Compostela	34	42.53 N	8.33 W
Santiago de Cuba	240p	20.01 N	75.49 W
Santiago de Cuba □ [4]	240p	20.10 N	75.55 W
Santiago de Huari	248	19.00 S	66.48 W
Santiago de Huata	248	16.06 S	68.53 W
Santiago de la Peña	234	20.57 N	97.24 W
Santiago de las Vegas ⬥ [8]	286b	22.58 N	82.23 W
Santiago del Estero	252	27.47 S	64.16 W
Santiago del Estero □ [4]	252	28.00 S	63.30 W
Santiago [de los Caballeros]	238	19.27 N	70.42 W
Santiago de Machaca	248	17.05 S	69.16 W
Santiago de Méndez	246	2.43 S	78.19 W
Santiago de Surco	286d	12.09 S	77.01 W
Santiago do Cacém	34	38.01 N	8.42 W
Santiago Island I	116	16.24 N	119.56 E
Santiago Ixcuintla	234	21.49 N	105.13 W
Santiago Ixtayutla	234	16.33 N	97.39 W
Santiago Jamiltepec	234	16.17 N	97.49 W
Santiago Juxtlahuaca	234	17.20 N	98.01 W
Santiago Lachiguirí	234	16.41 N	95.32 W
Santiago Larre	258	35.34 S	59.10 W
Santiago Maravatío	234	20.10 N	101.00 W
Santiago Papasquiaro	232	25.03 N	105.25 W
Santiago Peak ∧, Ca., U.S.	228	33.42 N	117.32 W
Santiago Peak ∧, Tx., U.S.	196	29.47 N	103.25 W
Santiago Pinotepa Nacional	234	16.19 N	98.01 W
Santiago Reservoir ⊜ [1]	228	33.47 N	117.43 W
Santiago Tepalcatlapan ⬥ [8]	286a	19.15 N	99.08 W
Santiago Tulantepec	234	20.02 N	98.22 W
Santiago Tutla	234	17.10 N	95.26 W
Santiago Tuxtla	234	18.28 N	95.18 W
Santiago Vázquez	258	34.48 S	56.21 W
Santiago Yaveo	234	17.19 N	95.42 W
Santiago Zacatepec	234	17.11 N	95.51 W
Santiaguillo, Laguna ⊜	232	24.48 N	104.48 W
Santiam Pass)(	202	44.25 N	121.51 W
San Tian Zhu (Three Indian Temples) ᵾ [1]	106	30.15 N	120.08 E
Santiao Chiao ›	100	25.02 N	121.59 E
Santiaoqiao	106	31.36 N	121.22 E
Santi Filippo e Giacomo	70	37.51 N	12.31 E
Santiguila	150	12.42 N	7.26 W
Sant'Ilario d'Enza	64	44.46 N	10.27 E
San Timoteo	246	9.48 N	71.04 W
San Timoteo Canyon ∨	228	34.04 N	117.17 W
Säntis ∧	58	47.15 N	9.21 E
Santissima Trinita di Saccargia ᵾ [1]	71	40.41 N	8.42 E
Santissimo ⬥ [8]	287a	22.53 S	43.31 W
Santisteban del Puerto	34	38.15 N	3.12 W
Sant Joan de Labritja	34	39.05 N	1.30 E
Sant Joan Despí	266d	41.22 N	2.04 E
Sant Jordi, Golf de ⊂	34	40.53 N	1.00 E
Sant Just Desvern	266d	41.23 N	2.05 E
Sant Mateu del Maestrat	34	40.28 N	0.11 E
Santō, Nihon	94	35.21 N	136.22 E
Santō, Nihon	96	35.19 N	134.53 E
Santo, Tx., U.S.	196	32.36 N	98.13 W
Santo, Vanuatu	175f	15.32 S	167.08 E
Santo Aleixo	256	22.34 S	43.04 W
Santo Amaro, Bra.	250	2.33 S	43.14 W
Santo Amaro, Bra.	255	12.32 S	38.43 W
Santo Amaro ⬥ [8]	287b	23.39 S	46.42 W
Santo Amaro, Ilha de I	256	23.57 S	46.14 W
Santo Amaro das Brotas	250	10.47 S	37.04 W
Santo Anastácio	255	21.58 S	51.39 W
Santo André	256	23.40 S	46.31 W
Santo Ângelo	252	28.18 S	54.16 W
Santo Antão I	150a	17.05 N	25.10 W
Santo Antônio, Bra.	250	6.18 S	35.27 W
Santo António, S. Tom./P.	152	1.39 N	7.26 E
Santo Antônio ≏, Bra.	250	11.31 S	48.37 W
Santo Antônio ≏, Bra.	255	17.30 S	45.37 W
Santo Antônio ≏, Bra.	287a	22.42 S	43.37 W
Santo António, Ilha de I	156	21.58 S	35.28 E
Santo António da Charneca	266c	38.37 N	9.02 W
Santo Antônio da Patrulha	252	29.50 S	50.32 W
Santo Antônio de Jesus	255	12.58 S	39.16 W
Santo Antônio de Pádua	255	21.32 S	42.11 W
Santo Antonio de Posse	256	22.36 S	46.55 W
Santo Antônio do Amparo	255	20.57 S	44.55 W
Santo Antônio do Aventureiro	256	21.45 S	42.49 W
Santo Antônio do Içá	246	3.05 S	67.57 W
Santo Antônio do Jardim	256	22.07 S	46.41 W
Santo Antônio do Leverger	248	15.52 S	56.05 W
Santo Antônio do Pinhal	256	22.47 S	45.41 W
Santo Antônio do Rio Verde	255	17.57 S	47.27 W
Santo Antônio do Sudoeste	252	26.02 S	53.44 W
Santo Augusto	252	27.51 S	53.47 W
Santo Corazón	248	17.59 S	58.51 W
Santo Domingo, Cuba	240p	22.35 N	80.15 W
Santo Domingo, Méx.	196	25.38 N	101.05 W
Santo Domingo, Méx.	196	25.48 N	104.28 W
Santo Domingo, Méx.	232	25.32 N	112.02 W
Santo Domingo, Nic.	236	12.16 N	85.05 W
Santo Domingo, Rep. Dom.	238	18.28 N	69.54 W
Santo Domingo ≏, Méx.	234	16.41 N	93.00 W
Santo Domingo ≏, Méx.	234	17.40 N	98.07 W
Santo Domingo ≏, Méx.	234	18.10 N	96.08 W
Santo Domingo ≏, Méx.	236	16.15 N	91.17 W
Santo Domingo, Arroyo ≏	204	30.43 N	116.03 W
Santo Domingo, Isla → Hispaniola I	238	19.00 N	71.00 W
Santo Domingo de la Calzada	34	42.26 N	2.57 W
Santo Domingo de los Colorados	246	0.15 S	79.09 W
Santo Domingo Indian Reservation ⬥ [4]	200	35.30 N	106.25 W
Santo Domingo Nuxaá	234	17.08 N	97.02 W
Santo Domingo Pueblo	200	35.30 N	106.21 W
Santo Domingo Tehuantepec	234	16.20 N	95.14 W
Santo Domingo Teojomulco	234	16.36 N	97.14 W
Santo Domingo Zanatepec	234	16.29 N	94.21 W
Santo Estêvão	255	12.26 S	39.13 W
Sant'Olcese	62	44.30 N	8.58 E
Santolea, Embalse de ⊜ [1]	34	40.47 N	0.19 W
Santo / Malo □ [8]	175f	15.20 S	166.55 E
San Tomé	246	8.58 N	64.08 W
San Tommaso	66	42.11 N	13.58 E
Sant'Omobono Imagna	62	45.48 N	9.32 E
Santoña	34	43.27 N	3.27 W
Santong ≏	98	42.39 N	126.03 E
Santo Nino Island I	116	11.55 N	124.27 E
Sant' Onofrio ⬥ [8]	267a	41.56 N	12.25 E
Santo Onofre ≏	255	12.34 S	43.12 W
Santop, Pic ∧	175f	18.39 S	169.03 E
Sant'Oreste	66	42.14 N	12.32 E
Santorini → Thíra I	38	36.24 N	25.29 E
Santorso	64	45.44 N	11.23 E
Santos	256	23.57 S	46.20 W
Santos, Arroyo de los ≏	258	35.28 S	57.29 W
Santos, Baía de ⊂	256	24.00 S	46.21 W
Santos Dumont	256	21.28 S	43.34 W
Santos Dumont, Aeroporto ⊠	256	22.55 S	43.10 W
Santoshpur	272b	22.40 N	88.10 E
Santo Stefano, Isola I	66	40.47 N	13.27 E
Santo Stefano Belbo	62	44.43 N	8.14 E
Santo Stefano d'Aveto	62	44.35 N	9.27 E
Santo Stefano di Cadore	64	46.33 N	12.32 E
Santo Stefano di Camastra	70	38.01 N	14.21 E
Santo Stefano di Magra	64	44.10 N	9.55 E
Santo Stefano Quisquina	70	37.37 N	13.29 E
Santo Stino di Livenza	64	45.44 N	12.41 E
Santos Tomás del Norte	236	13.11 N	86.56 W
Santo Tirso	34	41.21 N	8.28 W
Santo Tomás, Col.	246	10.46 N	74.45 W
Santo Tomás, Méx.	232	31.33 N	116.24 W
Santo Tomás, Nic.	236	12.04 N	85.05 W
Santo Tomás, Perú	248	6.36 S	77.48 W
Santo Tomás, Perú	248	14.29 S	72.06 W
Santo Tomas, Pil.	116	7.29 N	125.38 E
Santo Tomás ≏, Méx.	204	31.32 N	116.40 W
Santo Tomás ≏, Perú	248	13.47 S	72.09 W
Santo Tomás, Punta ›	232	31.34 N	116.42 W
Santo Tomas, University of ᵾ [2]	269f	14.37 N	120.59 E
Santo Tomás, Volcán ∧ [1]	246a	0.48 S	91.07 W
Santo Tomás y Principe → Sao Tome and Principe □ [1]	152	1.00 N	7.00 E
Santo Tomé, Arg.	252	28.33 S	56.03 W
Santo Tomé, Arg.	252	31.40 S	60.46 W
Santo Tomé de Guayana → Ciudad Guayana	246	8.22 N	62.40 W
Sant'pietro, Lago di ⊜	68	41.01 N	15.30 E
Santpoort	52	52.25 N	4.38 E
Sant Quirze de la Serra	266d	41.32 N	2.05 E
Santuanjiang	106	30.54 N	121.43 E
Santuario de Quillacas	248	19.14 S	66.58 W
Santu Lussurgiu	71	40.08 N	8.39 E
Santunying	105	40.14 N	118.12 E
Sant Vicenç dels Horts	266d	41.24 N	2.01 E
San Ubaldo	236	11.51 N	85.20 W
Sanuki	268	35.16 N	139.53 E
Sanuki-sammyaku ⋏	96	34.09 N	134.11 E
Ṣānūr	132	32.21 N	35.15 E
San Valentino in Abruzzo Citeriore	66	42.14 N	13.59 E
San Valentino Torio	68	40.48 N	14.36 E
San Venanzo	66	42.52 N	12.16 E
San Vendemiano	64	45.54 N	12.20 E
San Vicente, Arg.	252	28.30 S	64.09 W
San Vicente, Arg.	258	34.58 S	58.22 W
San Vicente, El Sal.	236	13.38 N	88.48 W
San Vicente □ [5]	288	34.56 S	58.24 W
San Vicente → Saint Vincent and the Grenadines □ [1]	241h	13.15 N	61.12 W
San Vicente, Cabo → São Vicente, Cabo de ›	34	37.01 N	9.00 W
San Vicente, Volcán de ∧ [1]	236	13.36 N	88.51 W
San Vicente Creek ≏	282	37.32 N	122.31 W
San Vicente de Alcántara	34	39.21 N	7.08 W
San Vicente de Cañete	248	13.05 S	76.24 W
San Vicente de Chucurí	246	6.54 N	73.25 W
San Vicente de la Barquera	34	43.26 N	4.24 W
San Vicente del Caguán	246	2.07 N	74.46 W
San Vicente de Tagua-Tagua	252	34.26 S	71.05 W
San Vicente Mountain ∧	280	34.08 N	118.31 W
San Vicente Reservoir ⊜ [1]	228	32.55 N	116.55 W
San Vicente Tancuayalab	234	21.44 N	98.34 W
San Vigilio	64	45.34 N	10.41 E
San Vigilio ᵾ [1]	64	46.37 N	11.07 E
San Vincenzo	66	43.06 N	10.32 E
San Vito, C.R.	236	8.50 N	82.58 W
San Vito, It.	71	39.26 N	9.32 E
San Vito, Capo ›	70	38.11 N	12.44 E
San Vito, Serralta di ∧	68	38.46 N	16.22 E
San Vito al Tagliamento	64	45.54 N	12.52 E
San Vito Chietino	66	42.18 N	14.27 E
San Vito dei Normanni	68	40.39 N	17.42 E
San Vito lo Capo	70	38.10 N	12.45 E
San Vito Romano	66	41.53 N	12.59 E
San Vito sullo Ionio	68	38.43 N	16.25 E
Sanwa, Nihon	94	37.07 N	138.21 E
Sanwa, Nihon	94	36.12 N	139.49 E
Sanwa, Nihon	96	34.42 N	133.15 E
San Xavier Indian Reservation ⬥ [4]	200	32.05 N	111.08 W
Sanxi, Zhg.	100	30.22 N	118.25 E
Sanxi, Zhg.	100	27.42 N	120.04 E
Sanxing, Zhg.	106	31.47 N	121.35 E
Sanxing, Zhg.	106	31.58 N	121.07 E
Sanxingchang, Zhg.	107	30.19 N	104.09 E
Sanxingchang, Zhg.	107	30.32 N	104.38 E
Sanxingjie	106	32.06 N	121.01 E
Sanyang, Zhg.	100	28.37 N	116.15 E
Sanyang, Zhg.	100	31.20 N	113.10 E
Sanyang, Zhg.	100	27.57 N	114.22 E
Sanyangzhen	106	31.55 N	121.29 E
Sanyanjing	104	41.28 N	122.27 E
Sanyanqiao	100	28.39 N	113.43 E
Sanyati ≏	154	16.49 S	28.45 E
San Ygnacio	196	27.03 N	99.27 W
Sanyō, Nihon	96	34.45 N	134.01 E
Sanyō, Nihon	96	34.02 N	131.10 E
Sanyuan	102	34.35 N	108.54 E
Sanyuanpu	98	42.02 N	125.44 E
Sanyuhao	98	42.30 N	117.34 E
Sanyuzhen	106	32.08 N	121.19 E
Sanza	68	40.15 N	15.33 E
Sanzao Dao I	100	22.03 N	113.21 E
Sanza Pombo	152	7.19 S	15.59 E
Sanzar ≏	85	40.00 N	67.40 E
San Zeno di Montagna	64	45.37 N	10.43 E
Sanzha	98	41.44 N	114.39 E
Sanzhan, Zhg.	89	49.42 N	125.20 E
Sanzhan, Zhg.	89	49.36 N	126.38 E
Sanzuodian	98	41.36 N	118.49 E
São Benedito	250	4.03 S	40.53 W
São Benedito ≏	250	9.11 S	57.02 W
São Benedito das Areias	256	21.19 S	47.02 W
São Benedito do Rio Preto	250	3.20 S	43.35 W
São Bento	250	2.42 S	44.50 W
São Bento ≏	256	21.42 S	45.18 W
São Bento, Mosteiro de ᵾ [1]	287a	22.54 S	43.11 W
São Bento Abade	256	21.35 S	45.04 W
São Bento de Caldas	256	22.08 S	46.18 W
São Bento do Norte	250	5.04 S	36.02 W
São Bento do Sapucaí	256	22.42 S	45.43 W
São Bento do Sul	252	26.15 S	49.23 W
São Bento do Una	250	8.32 S	36.22 W
São Bernardino	287a	22.40 S	43.26 W
São Bernardo	250	3.22 S	42.24 W
São Bernardo do Campo	256	23.42 S	46.33 W
São Bernardo do Campo □ [7]	287b	23.44 S	46.33 W
São Borja	252	28.39 S	56.00 W
São Brás	250	10.05 S	36.55 W
São Brás de Alportel	34	37.09 N	7.53 W
Sâo Braz, Cabo de ›	152	9.59 S	13.19 E
São Caetano de Odivelas	250	0.45 S	48.02 W
São Caetano do Sul	256	23.36 S	46.34 W
São Caetano do Sul □ [7]	287b	23.37 S	46.33 W
São Carlos	255	22.01 S	47.54 W
São Cristóvão	250	11.01 S	37.12 W
São Cristóvão ⬥ [8]	287a	22.54 S	43.14 W
Saodatun	104	42.02 N	123.31 E
São Domingos, Bra.	252	26.34 S	52.32 W
São Domingos, Bra.	255	13.24 S	46.19 W
São Domingos, Bra.	256	21.41 S	42.47 W
São Domingos, Gui.-B.	150	12.22 N	16.08 W
São Domingos ≏, Bra.	248	12.28 S	64.13 W
São Domingos ≏, Bra.	255	13.24 S	47.12 W
São Domingos ≏, Bra.	255	19.13 S	50.44 W
São Domingos ≏, Bra.	255	20.03 S	53.13 W
São Domingos da Bocaina	256	21.50 S	44.01 W
São Domingos do Capim	250	1.41 S	47.47 W
São Domingos do Maranhão	250	5.42 S	44.22 W
São Felipe	255	14.49 S	41.23 W
São Félix de Balsas	250	7.08 S	44.52 W
São Félix do Araguaia	250	11.36 S	50.39 W
São Félix do Piauí	250	5.56 S	42.07 W
São Filipe	150a	14.54 N	24.31 W
São Francisco	255	15.57 S	44.52 W
São Francisco ≏, Bra.	242	10.30 S	36.24 W
São Francisco ≏, Bra.	255	16.09 S	40.39 W
São Francisco ≏, Bra.	256	21.50 S	42.42 W
São Francisco ≏, Bra.	287a	22.57 S	43.20 W
São Francisco, Baía de ⊂	252	26.10 S	48.34 W
São Francisco, Ilha de I	252	26.18 S	48.37 W
São Francisco de Assis	252	29.33 S	55.08 W
São Francisco de Goiás	255	15.55 S	49.16 W
São Francisco de Paula	252	29.27 S	50.35 W
São Francisco do Croará	287a	22.42 S	43.08 W
São Francisco do Maranhão	250	6.15 S	42.52 W
São Francisco do Piauí	250	7.15 S	42.32 W
São Francisco do Sul	252	26.14 S	48.39 W
São Francisco Xavier	256	22.54 S	45.58 W
São Gabriel	252	30.20 S	54.19 W
São Gabriel da Palha	255	19.01 S	40.32 W
São Gabriel de Goiás	255	15.12 S	47.34 W
São Gonçalo, Bra.	256	21.36 S	46.19 W
São Gonçalo, Bra.	256	22.51 S	43.04 W
São Gonçalo □ [7]	287a	22.48 S	43.01 W
São Gonçalo do Abaeté	255	18.20 S	45.49 W
São Gonçalo do Sapucaí	256	21.54 S	45.36 W
São Gonçalo dos Campos	255	12.25 S	38.58 W
Sao Hill	154	8.20 S	35.12 E
São Jerônimo	252	29.58 S	51.43 W
São Jerônimo, Serra de ⋏ [1]	255	16.30 S	54.50 W
São Jerônimo da Serra	255	23.43 S	50.44 W
São João	150	11.32 N	15.26 W
São João ≏, Bra.	255	12.27 S	51.07 W
São João ≏, Bra.	256	22.33 S	42.29 W
São João da Barra	255	21.38 S	41.03 W
São João da Boa Vista	256	21.58 S	46.47 W
São João D'Aliança	255	14.42 S	47.32 W
São João da Madeira	34	40.54 N	8.30 W
São João da Mata	256	21.56 S	45.56 W
São João da Ponte	255	15.56 S	44.01 W
São João da Serra	256	21.28 S	43.27 W
São João das Lampas	266c	38.52 N	9.24 W
São João de Côrtes	250	2.12 S	44.32 W
São João del-Rei	255	21.09 S	44.16 W
São João de Meriti	256	22.48 S	43.22 W
São João de Meriti □ [7]	287a	22.48 S	43.21 W
São João de Meriti ≏	287a	22.48 S	43.18 W
São João do Araguaia	250	5.23 S	48.46 W
São João do Jaguaribe	250	5.16 S	38.16 W
São João do Paraíso	255	15.19 S	42.01 W
São João do Piauí	250	8.21 S	42.15 W
São João do Sabugi	250	6.43 S	37.12 W
São João dos Patos	250	6.30 S	43.42 W
São João Evangelista	255	18.32 S	42.45 W
São João Nepomuceno	256	21.33 S	43.01 W
São João Novo	256	23.33 S	47.01 W
São Joaquim	252	28.18 S	49.56 W
São Joaquim, Parque Nacional de ♠	252	28.15 S	49.57 W
São Joaquim da Barra	255	20.35 S	47.53 W
São Jorge I	148a	38.38 N	28.03 W
São Jorge, Castelo de ⊥	266c	38.43 N	9.08 W
São José, Bra.	252	27.38 S	48.39 W
São José, Bra.	256	22.43 S	42.36 W
São José ≏, Bra.	255	19.10 S	40.12 W
São José ≏, Bra.	287a	22.39 S	43.27 W
Sâo José, Ponta de ›	152	12.36 S	13.12 E
São José da Laje	250	9.01 S	36.03 W
São José de Anauá	246	1.00 N	61.23 W
São José de Encoge	152	7.38 S	14.41 E
São José de Mipibu	250	6.05 S	35.15 W
São José de Piranhas	250	7.07 S	38.30 W
São José do Alegre	256	22.19 S	45.32 W
São José do Barreiro	256	22.38 S	44.35 W
São José do Belmonte	250	7.52 S	38.46 W
São José do Campestre	250	6.18 S	35.42 W
São José do Cedro	252	26.30 S	53.30 W
São José do Egito	250	7.28 S	37.16 W
São José do Gurupi	250	1.36 S	46.13 W
São José do Norte	252	32.01 S	52.03 W
São José do Peixe	250	7.24 S	42.34 W
São José do Piriá	250	1.17 S	46.18 W
São José do Rio Pardo	256	21.36 S	46.54 W
São José do Rio Preto, Bra.	255	20.48 S	49.23 W
São José do Rio Prêto, Bra.	256	22.10 S	42.57 W
São José dos Campos	256	23.11 S	45.53 W
São José dos Lopes	256	21.48 S	43.53 W
São José dos Pinhais	252	25.31 S	49.13 W
São José do Turvo	256	22.21 S	43.59 W
São Julião da Barra	266c	38.40 N	9.21 W
São Julião do Tojal	266c	38.51 N	9.08 W
São Leopoldo	252	29.46 S	51.09 W
São Lourenço	256	22.07 S	45.03 W
São Lourenço, Pantanal de ≋	248	17.30 S	56.30 W
São Lourenço da Serra	256	23.52 S	46.57 W
São Lourenço do Oeste	252	26.24 S	52.46 W
São Lourenço do Sul	252	31.22 S	51.58 W
São Luís	250	2.31 S	44.16 W
São Luís de Montes Belos	255	16.32 S	50.20 W
São Luís do Curu	250	3.40 S	39.14 W
São Luís Do Paraitinga	256	23.14 S	45.20 W
São Luís do Quitunde	250	9.20 S	35.33 W
São Luís Gonzaga	252	28.24 S	54.58 W
São Mamede	250	6.56 S	37.06 W
São Manuel	255	22.44 S	48.34 W
São Manuel ≏	242	7.21 S	58.03 W
São Manuel do Guaiaçu	256	21.20 S	42.51 W
São Marcos ≏	255	18.15 S	47.37 W
São Mateus, Bra.	255	18.44 S	39.51 W
São Mateus, Bra.	256	22.49 S	43.23 W
São Mateus, Port.	148a	38.26 N	28.27 W
São Mateus, Braço Norte ≏	255	18.37 S	40.05 W
São Mateus de Minas	256	22.42 S	46.03 W
São Mateus do Sul	252	25.52 S	50.23 W
São Miguel	250	6.13 S	38.30 W
São Miguel I	148a	37.47 N	25.30 W
São Miguel ≏	255	16.26 S	41.00 W

Symbol	English	Deutsch	Español	Français	Português
≏	River	Fluß	Río	Rivière	Rio
≖	Canal	Kanal	Canal	Canal	Canal
∟	Waterfall, Rapids	Wasserfall, Stromschnellen	Cascada, Rápidos	Chute d'eau, Rapides	Cascata, Rápidos
ʯ	Strait	Meeresstraße	Estrecho	Détroit	Estreito
⊂	Bay, Gulf	Bucht, Golf	Bahía, Golfo	Baie, Golfe	Baía, Golfo
⊜	Lake, Lakes	See, Seen	Lago, Lagos	Lac, Lacs	Lago, Lagos
≋	Swamp	Sumpf	Pantano	Marais	Pântano
⊓	Ice Features, Glacier	Eis- und Gletscherformen	Accidentes Glaciales	Formes glaciaires	Acidentes glaciares
⊤	Other Hydrographic Features	Andere Hydrographische Objekte	Otros Elementos Hidrográficos	Autres données hydrographiques	Outros acidentes hidrográficos
✦	Submarine Features	Untermeerische Objekte	Accidentes Submarinos	Formes de relief sous-marin	Acidentes submarinos
□	Political Unit	Politische Einheit	Unidad Politica	Entité politique	Unidade política
ᵾ	Cultural Institution	Kulturelle Institution	Institución Cultural	Institution culturelle	Institução cultural
⊥	Historical Site	Historische Stätte	Sitio Histórico	Site historique	Sitio histórico
♠	Recreational Site	Erholungs- und Ferienort	Sitio de Recreo	Centre de loisirs	Area de Lazer
⊠	Airport	Flughafen	Aeropuerto	Aéroport	Aeroporto
■	Military Installation	Militäranlage	Instalación Militar	Installation militaire	Instalação militar
⬥	Miscellaneous	Verschiedenes	Misceláneo	Divers	Diversos

ENGLISH — Name | Page | Lat.°′ | Long.°′
DEUTSCH — Name | Seite | Breite°′ | Länge°′ E = Ost

São Miguel do Araguaia 255 13.19 S 50.13 W
São Miguel d'Oeste 252 26.45 S 53.34 W
São Miguel do Guamá 250 1.37 S 47.27 W
São Miguel dos Campos 250 9.47 S 36.05 W
São Miguel dos Macacos 250 1.11 S 50.28 W
São Miguel do Tapuio 250 5.30 S 41.20 W
São Miguel Paulista (Baquiriru) ◆[8] 256 23.30 S 46.26 W
Saona, Isla I 238 18.09 N 68.40 W
Saonara 64 45.22 N 11.59 E
Saône ≃ 58 45.44 N 4.50 E
Saône-et-Loire □[5] 32 46.42 N 4.45 E
Saonek 164 0.28 S 130.47 E
Saoner 120 21.23 N 78.54 E
São Nicolau I 150a 16.35 N 24.15 W
São Nicolau ≃ 250 5.45 S 42.02 W
São Paulo, Bra. 256 23.32 S 46.37 W
São Paulo, Bra. 287b 23.32 S 46.37 W
São Paulo □[3] 255 22.00 S 49.00 W
São Paulo □[7] 287b 23.33 S 46.38 W
São Paulo, Ribeirão de ≃ 256 22.16 S 46.37 W
São Paulo de Olivença 246 3.27 S 68.48 W
São Paulo do Potengi 250 5.55 S 35.45 W
São Pedro 255 19.53 S 51.55 W
São Pedro ≃ 255 16.30 S 41.17 W
São Pedro de Caldas 256 21.49 S 46.16 W
São Pedro de Viseu 250 2.33 S 49.33 W
São Pedro do Estoril 266c 38.42 N 9.22 W
São Pedro do Piauí 250 5.56 S 42.43 W
São Pedro do Sul, Bra. 252 29.37 S 54.10 W
São Pedro do Sul, Port. 34 40.45 N 8.04 W
São Rafael 250 5.47 S 36.55 W
São Raimundo das Mangabeiras 250 7.01 S 45.29 W
São Raimundo Nonato 250 9.01 S 42.42 W
Saorge 62 43.59 N 7.33 E
Saori 94 35.11 N 136.44 E
São Romão 255 16.22 S 45.04 W
São Roque, Bra. 256 23.32 S 47.08 W
São Roque, Bra. 256 23.06 S 44.42 W
São Roque, Cabo de > 250 5.29 S 35.16 W
São Roque da Fartura 256 21.51 S 46.45 W
São Salvador → Salvador 255 12.59 S 38.31 W
São Sebastião 256 23.48 S 45.25 W
São Sebastião, Canal de ⊔ 256 23.48 S 45.23 W
São Sebastião, Ilha de I 256 23.50 S 45.18 W
São Sebastião, Pico de ∧ 256 23.52 S 45.23 W
São Sebastião, Ponta > 156 22.07 S 35.30 E
São Sebastião da Bela Vista 256 22.10 S 45.45 W
São Sebastião da Boa Vista 250 1.42 S 49.31 W
São Sebastião da Grama 256 21.43 S 46.49 W
São Sebastião da Vitória 256 21.14 S 44.25 W
São Sebastião do Barreado 256 22.04 S 43.38 W
São Sebastião do Maranhão 255 18.05 S 42.35 W
São Sebastião do Paraíso 255 20.55 S 47.00 W
São Sebastião do Rio Claro 255 15.45 S 51.30 W
São Sebastião do Rio Verde 256 22.13 S 44.58 W
São Sebastião dos Robertos 256 22.13 S 46.32 W
São Sebastião do Umbuzeiro 250 8.09 S 37.01 W
São Sepé 252 30.10 S 53.34 W
São Silvestre do Jacareí 256 23.23 S 46.01 W
São Simão, Bra. 255 18.56 S 50.30 W
São Simão, Bra. 255 21.30 S 47.33 W
São Simão, Reprêsa de ⊜[1] 255 18.40 S 50.00 W
São Tiago 255 20.55 S 44.30 W
São Timóteo 255 13.51 S 42.11 W
São Tomé, Bra. 250 5.58 S 36.04 W
São Tomé, S. Tom./P. 152 0.20 N 6.44 E
São Tomé I 152 0.12 N 6.39 E
São Tomé ≃, Bra. 250 8.10 S 58.13 W
São Tomé ≃, Bra. 256 21.26 S 46.02 W
São Tomé, Cabo de > 255 21.59 S 40.59 W
São Tomé, Pico de ∧ 152 0.16 N 6.33 E
Sao Tome and Principe (São Tomé e Principe) □[1], Afr. 138 1.00 N 7.00 E
Sao Tome and Principe (São Tomé e Principe) □[1], Afr. 152 1.00 N 7.00 E
São Tomé das Letras 256 21.43 S 44.59 W
Sao Tomé-et-Principe → Sao Tome and Principe □[1] 152 1.00 N 7.00 E
Saou 62 44.39 N 5.04 E
Saoura, Oued V 148 29.00 N 0.55 W
São Valério ≃ 250 11.20 S 48.28 W
São Vicente 256 23.58 S 46.23 W
São Vicente I 150a 16.50 N 25.00 W
São Vicente, Cabo de (Cape Saint Vincent) > 34 37.01 N 9.00 W
São Vicente, Ribeirão ≃ 256 21.59 S 45.40 W
São Vicente de Minas 256 21.42 S 44.27 W
São Vicente Ferrer 250 7.35 S 35.30 W
Sa Pa 110 22.21 N 103.50 E
Sápai 38 41.02 N 25.41 E
Sapanca 130 40.41 N 30.16 E
Sapang Baho ≃ 269f 14.33 N 121.06 E
Sapao 116 10.01 N 126.02 E
Sapão ≃ 250 11.01 S 45.32 W
Saparua, Pulau I 164 3.34 S 128.40 E
Sapatgrām 124 26.20 N 90.08 E
Sapé, Bra. 250 7.06 S 35.13 W
Sape, Indon. 115b 8.34 S 118.59 E
Sapé ≃ 287a 22.52 S 43.02 W
Sape, Selat ⊔ 115b 8.39 S 119.18 E
Sapele 150 5.54 N 5.41 E
Sapello ≃ 200 35.47 N 104.59 W
Sapelo Island I 192 31.28 N 81.15 W
Saperkino 80 54.05 N 51.38 E
Şaphane 130 39.01 N 29.14 E
Sapian Bay ⊂ 116 11.33 N 122.37 E
Sapindji 152 9.39 S 23.12 E
Sapitwa ∧ 154 15.57 S 35.36 E
Šapki 76 59.36 N 31.14 E
Šapkina ≃ 24 66.44 N 52.25 E
Šapkino 80 51.42 N 42.24 E
Šapkovo, Ross. 76 55.47 N 33.20 E
Šapkovo, Ross. 82 54.34 N 39.10 E
Sa Pobla 34 39.46 N 3.01 E
Sapodilla Cays I 236 16.08 N 88.15 W
Saponara 70 38.11 N 15.26 E
Saponé 150 12.03 N 1.36 W
Sap'o-ri 98 40.49 N 129.31 E
Sap'ornaja 265a 59.46 N 30.41 E
Saporoschje → Zaporizhzhya 78 47.50 N 35.10 E
Saposoa 248 6.56 S 76.48 W
Sapou 175c 7.18 N 151.53 E
Sapožok 80 53.56 N 40.41 E
Sappa Creek ≃ 198 40.07 N 99.38 W
Sappa Creek, Middle Fork ≃ 198 39.40 N 100.53 W
Sappa Creek, North Fork ≃ 198 39.47 N 100.35 W
Sappa Creek, South Fork ≃ 198 39.47 N 100.35 W
Sappada 64 46.34 N 12.41 E
Sapphire Mountains ⋏ 202 46.20 N 113.45 W
Sappho 224 48.04 N 124.16 W
Sappington 219 38.32 N 90.22 W
Sapporo 92a 43.03 N 141.21 E
Şapri 68 40.04 N 15.38 E
Šapša 76 60.34 N 34.01 E
Sap Songkhla, Thale ⊂ 110 7.13 N 100.30 E
Šapsugskaja 78 44.45 N 38.05 E
Saptajev 86 47.55 N 67.28 E
Saptakośī ≃ 124 26.31 N 86.58 E
Sapta-ri 271b 37.43 N 126.44 E
Sapu 152 12.29 S 19.26 E
Sapucaí 256 22.19 S 46.42 W
Sapucaí ≃ 256 21.33 S 45.40 W
Sapucaia 256 22.00 S 42.54 W
Sapucaí-Mirim 256 22.44 S 45.45 W
Sapucaí-Mirim ≃ 256 22.12 S 45.53 W
Sapudi, Pulau I 115a 7.06 S 114.20 E
Sapulpa 196 35.59 N 96.06 W
Sapulu 115a 6.54 S 112.57 E
Sapuran 115a 7.28 S 109.58 E
Sapwe 154 10.57 S 28.10 E
Sāq, Jabal ∧[2] 128 26.17 N 43.16 E
Sāqiat al-ʿAbd 140 20.48 N 30.19 E
Sāqiyat Makkī 142 30.00 N 31.13 E
Şaqqārah 142 29.51 N 31.13 E
Şaqqārah (Step Pyramid) ⊥ 142 29.52 N 31.13 E
Saqqez 128 36.14 N 46.16 E
Saquarema 256 22.56 S 42.30 W
Saquarema, Lagoa de ⊂ 256 22.55 S 42.33 W
Saquena 248 4.40 S 73.31 W
Saquish Neck >[1] 283 42.00 N 70.37 W
Saquisilí 246 0.51 S 78.40 W
Sāra, Bngl. 126 24.07 N 89.02 E
Sara, Burkina 150 11.43 N 3.50 W
Sara, Pil. 116 11.16 N 123.01 E
Sara, Ross. 80 54.38 N 46.46 E
Sarāb 128 37.56 N 47.32 E
Sarabia, Méx. 234 17.03 N 95.01 W
Sarabia, Méx. 234 20.31 N 101.05 W
Sarabia ≃ 234 17.11 N 94.56 W
Sarābiyūm 142 30.23 N 32.17 E
Saraburi 110 14.32 N 100.55 E
Saracena 68 39.46 N 16.09 E
Saraceno, Monte ∧ 66 41.27 N 14.44 E
Saracura ≃ 255 12.18 S 40.07 W
Saracuruna ≃ 287a 22.41 S 43.13 W
Saraféré 150 15.50 N 3.42 W
Saragosa 196 31.01 N 103.39 W
Saragossa → Zaragoza 34 41.38 N 0.53 W
Saraguay ◆[8] 275a 45.31 N 73.45 W
Saraguro 246 3.36 S 79.13 W
Sarai 80 53.44 N 41.00 E
Sarāi Alamgir 123 32.54 N 73.45 E
Saraikela 124 22.43 N 85.57 E
Sarāi Naurang 123 32.50 N 70.47 E
Saraipāli 120 21.20 N 83.00 E
Säräisniemi 26 64.27 N 26.47 E
Sarajas de Madrid ◆[8] 266a 40.28 N 3.35 W
Sarajčik 80 47.30 N 51.43 E
Sarajevo 38 43.52 N 18.25 E
Saraj-Gir 80 53.36 N 53.24 E
Saraji 166 22.21 S 148.18 E
Sarajskij 80 47.19 N 40.45 E
Sarakhs 128 36.32 N 61.11 E
Saraktaš 86 51.50 N 56.22 E
Sarala 86 54.52 N 89.14 E
Şaraland 194 30.49 N 88.04 W
Šaraldaj 88 51.01 N 107.38 E
Saralžinskaja 80 49.12 N 48.55 E
Saramacca □[5] 250 5.40 N 55.40 W
Saramacca ≃ 250 5.51 N 55.53 W
Saramaguacán ≃ 240p 21.30 N 77.17 W
Saran, Fr. 50 47.57 N 1.53 E
Şaran', Kaz. 86 49.46 N 72.52 E
Šaran, Ross. 80 54.49 N 54.00 E
Saran, Gunung ∧ 112 0.25 S 111.18 E
Saranac 216 42.55 N 85.12 W
Saranac ≃ 188 44.42 N 73.27 W
Saranac Lake 188 44.19 N 74.07 W
Saranakan, gora ∧ 88 52.35 N 113.50 E
Şaranap 226 37.53 N 122.06 W
Šaranbaš-Kn'azevo 80 54.58 N 54.09 E
Saranda 154 5.43 S 34.59 E
Sarandapótamos ≃ 267c 38.03 N 23.34 E
Sarandë 38 39.52 N 20.00 E
Sarandi 252 27.56 S 52.55 W
Sarandí ◆[8] 258 34.40 S 58.21 W
Sarandí del Yi 252 33.21 S 55.38 W
Sarandí Grande 258 33.44 S 56.20 W
Şarandira 256 21.50 S 43.11 W
Šaranga 80 57.11 N 46.34 E
Sarangani Bay ⊂ 116 5.57 N 125.11 E
Sarangani Island I 116 5.27 N 125.28 E
Sarangani Islands II 116 5.25 N 125.26 E
Sarangani Strait ⊔ 116 5.31 N 125.23 E
Sārangarh 120 21.36 N 83.05 E
Sārangpur 124 23.34 N 76.28 E
Sārankhola 126 22.18 N 89.47 E
Saranley 144 2.22 N 42.17 E
Saranpaul' 24 64.14 N 60.53 E
Saransk 80 54.11 N 45.11 E
Sara Peak ∧ 150 9.41 N 9.17 E
Saraphi 110 18.43 N 99.03 E
Sarapiquí ≃ 236 10.43 N 83.56 W
Şarapó ≃ 287a 22.46 S 43.37 W
Šarapovo, Ross. 80 55.17 N 44.42 E
Šarapovo, Ross. 82 55.11 N 37.16 E
Sarapuí ≃ 287a 22.46 S 43.24 W
Sarapuí, Canal de ≍ 287a 22.44 S 43.16 W
Sarapul 80 56.28 N 53.48 E
Sarapul'skaja vozvyšennost' ⋏[1] 80 56.15 N 53.30 E
Sarapul'skoje 89 48.52 N 135.59 E
Sarāqib 130 35.52 N 36.48 E
Sarare 246 9.47 N 69.10 W
Sarare ≃ 246 7.18 N 70.41 W
Sarar Plain = 144 9.25 N 46.17 E
Sara Sara, Nevado ∧ 248 15.19 S 73.27 W
Sarasota 220 27.20 N 82.31 W
Sarasota □[6] 220 27.10 N 82.21 W
Sarasota Bay ⊂ 220 27.23 N 82.39 W
Sarasota-Bradenton Airport ⊠ 220 27.24 N 82.33 W
Sarasota Springs 220 27.17 N 82.28 W
Saraswati ≃ 272b 22.59 N 88.22 E
Sarata 78 46.02 N 29.38 E
Sarath 126 24.14 N 86.50 E
Saratoga, Austl. 170 33.28 S 151.21 E
Saratoga, Ca., U.S. 226 37.15 N 122.01 W
Saratoga, In., U.S. 216 40.14 N 84.55 W
Saratoga, Tx., U.S. 222 30.17 N 94.31 W
Saratoga, Wy., U.S. 200 41.27 N 106.48 W
Saratoga □[6] 210 43.00 N 73.51 W
Saratoga Battlefield Monument ⊥ 210 43.05 N 73.35 W
Saratoga Creek ≃ 282 37.25 N 121.58 W
Saratoga Lake ⊜ 210 43.01 N 73.39 W
Saratoga National Historical Park ♦ 210 43.00 N 73.38 W
Saratoga Passage ⊔ 224 48.10 N 122.30 W
Saratoga Spa State Park ♦ 210 43.03 N 73.50 W
Saratoga Springs 210 43.04 N 73.47 W
Šara-Togot 88 53.01 N 106.43 E
Saratok 112 1.44 N 111.20 E
Saratov 80 51.34 N 46.02 E
Saratovka 86 51.12 N 54.54 E
Saratov Oblast' □[4] 80 51.30 N 47.00 E
Saratovskoje vodochranilišče ⊜[1] 80 52.45 N 48.30 E
Saraurcu ∧ 246 0.06 S 77.55 W
Sarāvān, Īrān 128 27.15 N 62.40 E
Saravan, Lao 110 15.43 N 106.25 E
Sarawak □[3] 112 2.30 N 113.30 E
Saray 130 41.26 N 27.55 E
Saraya, Guinée 150 10.46 N 10.24 W
Saraya, Sén. 150 12.50 N 11.45 W
Sarāyān 128 33.51 N 58.31 E
Saraycık 130 40.57 N 35.08 E
Saraydüzü 130 41.20 N 34.52 E
Sarā-ye Aḥmadī 128 27.56 N 56.42 E
Sarayevo → Sarajevo 38 43.52 N 18.25 E
Sarayköy 130 37.55 N 28.58 E
Sarayönü 130 38.17 N 32.25 E
Sarbaj 80 53.39 N 51.34 E
Sarbāz 128 26.39 N 61.15 E
Sarbinowo 54 52.40 N 14.40 E
Sárbogárd 30 46.53 N 18.38 E
Sarca ≃ 64 45.52 N 10.52 E
Sarce ≃ 50 48.09 N 4.18 E
Sarcee Indian Reserve ◆[4] 182 50.58 N 114.06 W
Sarcelle, Passe de la ⊔ 175f 22.29 S 167.12 E
Sarcelles 50 49.00 N 2.23 E
Sarche di Calavino 64 46.03 N 10.57 E
Şarcidano ◆[1] 71 39.49 N 9.10 E
Šarčino 86 53.09 N 81.45 E
Sarclet 46 58.22 N 3.07 W
Sarcoxie 194 37.04 N 94.06 W
Sārda (Mahākālī) ≃ 124 27.22 N 81.23 E
Sard āb)(123 36.40 N 71.32 E
Sārda Canal ≍ 124 28.08 N 80.24 E
Sardagna 64 46.03 N 11.06 E
Sardah 124 24.18 N 88.44 E
Sardaq 128 34.48 N 58.07 E
Sardara 71 39.37 N 8.49 E
Sardār Chāh 128 27.58 N 64.50 E
Sardārpur 120 22.39 N 74.59 E
Sardārshahr 120 28.26 N 74.29 E
Sar Dasht, Īrān 128 36.09 N 45.28 E
Sar Dasht, Īrān 128 32.32 N 48.52 E
Sardegna □[4] 71 40.00 N 9.00 E
Sardegna (Sardinia) I 71 40.00 N 9.00 E
Sardeh Band 120 33.17 N 68.39 E
Sardhana 124 29.09 N 77.37 E
Sardiha 126 22.22 N 87.09 E
Sardinal 236 10.31 N 85.39 W
Sardinata 246 8.05 N 72.48 W
Sardinia, N.Y., U.S. 210 42.32 N 78.31 W
Sardinia, Oh., U.S. 218 39.00 N 83.48 W
Sardinia → Sardegna I 71 40.00 N 9.00 E
Sardinien → Sardegna I 71 40.00 N 9.00 E
Sardis, B.C., Can. 224 49.08 N 121.57 W
Sardis, Al., U.S. 194 32.17 N 86.59 W
Sardis, Ga., U.S. 192 32.58 N 81.45 W
Sardis, Ky., U.S. 218 38.31 N 83.57 W
Sardis, Ms., U.S. 194 34.26 N 89.55 W
Sardis, Pa., U.S. 279b 40.29 N 79.42 W
Sardis, Tn., U.S. 194 35.27 N 88.18 W
Sardis Lake ⊜[1] 194 34.27 N 89.43 W
Şardona, Piz ∧ 58 46.55 N 9.15 E
Šardonem' 24 63.56 N 44.37 E
Sarek ∧ 24 67.25 N 17.46 E
Sareks Nationalpark ♦ 24 67.15 N 17.30 E
Sārenga, India 126 22.46 N 87.02 E
Sārenga, India 272b 22.31 N 88.13 E
Sarentina, Valle V 64 46.35 N 11.25 E
Sarentino (Sarnthein) 64 46.38 N 11.21 E
Sar-e Pol 120 36.14 N 65.55 E
Sarepta 194 32.53 N 93.26 W
Sarezzo 64 45.39 N 10.12 E
Sargans 58 47.03 N 9.26 E
Sargasso Sea ⊤[2] 8 30.00 N 50.00 W
Sargasso Sea ⊤[2] 8 30.00 N 50.00 W
Sargatskoje 86 55.37 N 73.30 E
Sargé-lès-le-Mans 50 48.02 N 0.14 E
Sargent, Ga., U.S. 192 33.25 N 84.52 W
Sargent, Ne., U.S. 198 41.38 N 99.22 W
Sargent Creek ≃ 226 35.57 N 120.52 W
Şargodha 123 32.05 N 72.40 E
Šargol'džin 88 52.21 N 114.42 E
Sargou ≃ 85 43.25 N 73.50 E
Şargul', ozero ⊜ 86 54.35 N 78.51 E
Šargun 85 38.37 N 67.53 E
Sarh 146 9.09 N 18.23 E
Sarhli, Djebel ∧ 34 36.06 N 0.40 E
Sārī 128 36.34 N 53.04 E
Saría I 38 35.50 N 27.15 E
Saribi, Tanjung > 164 1.36 S 135.25 E
Sarıbuğday 130 40.35 N 35.35 E
Saric 232 31.08 N 111.23 W
Saricumbe 152 12.12 S 19.46 E
Sarigan I 108 16.42 N 145.47 E
Sarıgazi ◆[8] 267b 41.01 N 29.12 E
Sarıgöl 130 38.14 N 28.43 E
Sarıkamış 130 40.20 N 42.35 E
Sarıkaya, Tür. 130 38.47 N 32.15 E
Sarıkaya, Tür. 130 39.30 N 35.24 E
Sarikei 112 2.07 N 111.31 E
Sarıköy 130 40.12 N 27.36 E
Sarilhos Grandes 266c 38.41 N 8.58 W
Sarilhos Pequenos 266c 38.41 N 8.59 W
Sarim 154 0.23 S 40.58 E
Sarimbun, Pulau I 271c 1.26 N 103.41 E
Sarina 166 21.26 S 149.13 E
Sarine ≃ 58 46.54 N 7.14 E
Sariñena 34 41.48 N 0.10 W
Sarıoğlan 130 39.05 N 35.59 E
Saripul' 85 38.26 N 70.08 E
Sarīr 146 27.36 N 22.32 E
Sarısu 84 39.01 N 42.55 E
Sarita 196 27.13 N 97.47 W
Sariwŏn 98 38.31 N 125.44 E
Sarıyar Barajı ⊜[1] 130 40.02 N 31.40 E
Şarız 130 38.30 N 36.30 E
Šarja 80 58.24 N 45.30 E
Sarju (Babaī) ≃ 124 27.42 N 81.16 E
Sark I 43b 49.26 N 2.21 W
Sark ≃ 44 54.58 N 3.04 W
Şarkad 30 46.44 N 21.23 E
Šarkan 80 57.18 N 53.53 E
Sarkand 86 45.26 N 79.54 E
Şarkikaraağaç 130 38.04 N 31.23 E
Şarkışla 130 39.21 N 36.26 E
Šarkovščina 76 55.22 N 27.28 E
Şarköy 130 40.37 N 27.06 E
Şarlat-la-Canéda 32 44.53 N 1.13 E
Šarlauk 128 38.13 N 55.38 E
Şarles 198 48.56 N 98.59 W
Šarlyk 86 52.55 N 54.35 E
Sarmakovo 84 43.43 N 43.12 E
Sarmanovo 80 55.15 N 52.36 E
Sărmaşu 38 46.46 N 24.11 E
Sarmathura 124 26.31 N 77.22 E
Sarmatskaja ≃ 83 47.20 N 38.48 E
Sármellék 30 46.44 N 17.10 E
Sarmi 164 1.51 S 138.44 E
Sarmiento 254 45.36 S 69.05 W
Sarmiento ≃ 288 34.25 S 58.35 W
Sarmiento de Gambia, Cerro ∧ 254 54.27 S 70.50 W
Sarmiento de Gamboa, Lago ⊜ 254 51.04 S 72.45 W
Särna 26 61.41 N 13.08 E
Sarna, ozero ⊜ 80 48.24 N 44.38 E
Sarnano 66 43.02 N 13.18 E
Sārnāth ⊥ 124 25.24 N 83.01 E
Sarnen 58 46.54 N 8.15 E
Sărnena Gora ⋏ 38 42.35 N 25.10 E
Sarner See ⊜ 58 46.52 N 8.13 E
Sarnia 214 42.58 N 82.23 W
Sarnico 64 45.40 N 9.57 E
Sarno 68 40.49 N 14.37 E
Sarnow 54 53.45 N 13.37 E
Sarnowa 30 51.38 N 16.54 E
Sarnthein → Sarentino 64 46.38 N 11.21 E
Šarnutovskij 80 47.40 N 43.46 E
Sarny 78 51.21 N 26.36 E
Şaroako 112 2.31 S 121.22 E
Šaroargun ≃ 84 43.02 N 45.44 E
Sarolangun 112 2.18 S 102.42 E
Saroma-ko ⊜ 92a 44.08 N 143.50 E
Saron 158 33.11 S 19.01 E
Saronikós Kólpos ⊂ 38 37.45 N 23.30 E
Saronno 62 45.38 N 9.02 E
Saros Körfezi ⊂ 130 40.30 N 26.20 E
Sárospatak 30 48.19 N 21.34 E
Sarowbī 120 34.36 N 69.43 E
Sarpa 80 47.07 N 45.29 E
Şarpa, ozero ⊜ 80 47.18 N 45.20 E
Šarpajevka 78 48.34 N 40.59 E
Sar Passage ⊔ 175b 7.12 N 134.23 E
Şarpinskije ozera ⊜ 80 47.30 N 45.00 E
Šar Planina ⋏ 38 42.05 N 20.50 E
Sarpsborg 26 59.17 N 11.07 E
Sarpy Creek ≃ 202 46.15 N 107.09 W
Sárrabus ◆[1] 71 39.23 N 9.21 E
Sarralbe 56 49.00 N 7.01 E
Sarras 62 45.11 N 4.48 E
Sarrath, Oued V 36 35.59 N 8.23 E
Sarratt 260 51.41 N 0.29 W
Sarre 62 45.43 N 7.15 E
Sarre (Saar) ≃ 56 49.42 N 6.34 E
Sarre Blanche ≃ 56 48.41 N 7.01 E
Sarrebourg 58 48.44 N 7.03 E
Sarrebruck → Saarbrücken 56 49.14 N 6.59 E
Sarreguemines 56 49.06 N 7.03 E
Sarre Rouge ≃ 56 48.41 N 7.01 E
Sarre-Union 56 48.56 N 7.05 E
Sarria 34 42.47 N 7.24 W
Sarriá ◆[8] 266d 41.24 N 2.08 E
Sarro 150 13.43 N 5.15 W
Sarroch 71 39.04 N 9.00 E
Sars 86 56.33 N 57.07 E
Sarsfield 212 45.27 N 75.21 W
Sarsina 66 43.55 N 12.08 E
Sarsol 272c 19.02 N 73.01 E
Sarstedt 52 52.14 N 9.51 E
Sarstein ∧ 64 47.36 N 13.41 E
Sarstoon (Sarstún) ≃ 236 15.53 N 88.55 W
Sarstún (Sarstoon) ≃ 236 15.53 N 88.55 W
Sarsuna 272b 22.28 N 88.18 E
Sart 56 50.31 N 5.56 E
Sartang ≃ 74 67.44 N 133.12 E
Sarteano 66 42.59 N 11.52 E
Sartell 190 45.37 N 94.12 W
Sartène 36 41.36 N 8.59 E
Sarthe □[5] 32 48.00 N 0.05 E
Sarthe ≃ 32 47.30 N 0.32 W
Sartičala 84 41.43 N 45.10 E
Sartilly 32 48.45 N 1.27 W
Sartirana Lomellina 62 45.07 N 8.39 E
Sartlan, ozero ⊜ 86 55.00 N 78.35 E
Sartol'gen 80 48.57 N 47.03 E
Sartrouville 261 48.57 N 2.10 E
Saru 85 42.20 N 77.55 E
Sarufutsu 92a 45.16 N 142.12 E
Saruhanlı 130 38.44 N 27.34 E
Şārur, Azer. 84 39.33 N 44.58 E
Şarūr, ʿUmān 128 23.22 N 58.07 E
Šar Us ≃ 88 47.08 N 97.38 E
Saru-shima I 268 35.17 N 139.42 E
Sarvadyk 80 46.07 N 44.07 E
Sárvár 30 47.15 N 16.57 E
Sarver 214 40.44 N 79.45 W
Sarvestān 128 29.16 N 53.13 E
Sárvíz ≃ 30 46.24 N 18.41 E
Saryagač 85 41.27 N 69.10 E
Saryassija 85 38.25 N 67.57 E
Sarybarak 85 43.24 N 71.30 E
Sarybasat 86 46.38 N 60.27 E
Sarybulak, Kaz. 86 49.27 N 76.27 E
Sarybulak, Kyrg. 85 40.54 N 73.49 E
Sarych, mys > 78 44.23 N 33.45 E
Sarychosor 85 38.32 N 69.49 E
Sarydala 85 41.11 N 70.27 E
Saryg-Sep 88 51.30 N 95.36 E
Sary-Išikotrau ◆[2] 86 45.30 N 76.00 E
Sarykamskoje ozero ⊜ 72 41.56 N 57.25 E
Sarykoby 85 43.44 N 72.35 E
Sarykol'skij chrebet ⋏ 120 38.00 N 74.30 E
Sarykomej 86 45.12 N 74.11 E
Sarykopa, ozero ⊜ 86 50.22 N 64.08 E
Sarymogol 85 39.55 N 72.47 E
Sarymoin, ozero ⊜ 86 51.36 N 64.30 E
Şaryozek 86 44.22 N 77.59 E
Šarypovo 86 55.33 N 89.12 E
Saryšagan 86 46.07 N 73.38 E
Sarysu 86 48.23 N 69.59 E
Sarysu ≃ 86 45.12 N 66.36 E
Sary-Taš 85 39.44 N 73.15 E
Sarytau 86 49.54 N 76.41 E
Saryžaz 72 42.55 N 79.38 E
Sarzana 64 44.07 N 9.58 E
Sarzanello, Fortezza di ⊥ 64 44.08 N 9.58 E
Sarzeau 32 47.32 N 2.46 W
S'as' ≃ 76 60.09 N 32.30 E
Saʿsaʿ, Sūrīy. 132 33.17 N 36.02 E
Sasa, Yis. 132 33.02 N 35.24 E
Sasabe 200 31.27 N 111.31 W
Sasabe ≃ 200 30.41 N 111.56 W
Sasabeneh 144 7.55 N 43.39 E
Sasaga-mine ∧ 96 33.49 N 133.17 E
Sasaginnigak Lake ⊜ 184 51.36 N 95.40 W
Sasago-tunnel ◆[5] 94 35.38 N 138.47 E
Sasaguri 96 33.37 N 130.32 E
Sasak 110 0.01 S 99.42 E
Sasakwa 196 34.56 N 96.31 W
Sasamungga 175e 7.02 S 156.47 E
Sasao 270 34.57 N 135.20 E
Sasar, Tanjung > 115b 9.17 S 119.56 E
Sāsarām 124 24.57 N 84.02 E
Sasayama 96 35.04 N 135.13 E
Sasa-yama ∧ 96 33.03 N 132.40 E
Sasbach 58 48.08 N 7.37 E
Sasco Brook ≃ 276 41.07 N 73.18 W
Sásd 30 46.15 N 18.06 E
Sasebo 92 33.10 N 129.43 E
Sasebo Naval Base ▪ 92 33.09 N 129.45 E
Saseenos 224 48.24 N 123.40 W
Saseginaga, Lac ⊜ 190 47.06 N 78.35 W
Sashalom ◆[8] 264c 47.31 N 19.11 E
Sas-hegy ∧[2] 264c 47.23 N 19.18 E
Sashiki 174m 26.10 N 127.47 E
Sashima 94 36.08 N 139.51 E
Saskatchewan □[4], Can. 176 54.00 N 105.00 W
Saskatchewan □[4], Can. 184 54.00 N 105.00 W
Saskatchewan ≃ 184 53.12 N 99.16 W
Saskatoon 184 52.07 N 106.38 W
Saskylach 74 71.55 N 114.01 E
Saslaya, Cerro ∧ 238 13.45 N 85.03 W
Sasmik, Cape > 180 51.36 N 177.55 W
Sāsni 124 27.43 N 78.05 E
Sasolburg 158 26.48 S 27.45 E
Sason 130 38.20 N 41.25 E
Sasovo 80 54.21 N 41.54 E
Saspamco 196 29.14 N 98.18 W
Saspul Gompa 123 34.15 N 77.09 E
Sassafras, Austl. 274b 37.52 S 145.21 E
Sassafras, Ky., U.S. 192 37.14 N 83.06 W
Sassafras ≃ 208 39.23 N 76.02 W
Sassafras Mountain ∧ 192 35.03 N 82.48 W
Sassafras Neck >[1] 208 39.25 N 75.55 W
Sassandra 150 4.58 N 6.05 W
Sassandra ≃ 150 4.58 N 6.05 W
Sassano 68 40.20 N 15.33 E
Sassari 71 40.44 N 8.33 E
Sassari □[4] 71 40.40 N 9.00 E
Sassbach ≃ 61 46.43 N 15.48 E
Sasse ≃ 62 44.15 N 5.55 E
Sassello 62 44.29 N 8.30 E
Sassenage 62 45.12 N 5.40 E
Sassenberg 52 51.59 N 8.02 E
Sassenheim 52 52.13 N 4.31 E
Sassnitz 54 54.31 N 13.38 E
Sassocorvaro 66 43.47 N 12.30 E
Sasso di Castalda 68 40.30 N 15.40 E
Sassoferrato 66 43.26 N 12.51 E
Sasso Marconi 64 44.24 N 11.15 E
S'as'stroj 76 60.08 N 32.34 E
Sassuolo 64 44.33 N 10.47 E
Sastobe 85 42.34 N 70.00 E
Sastown 150 4.40 N 8.26 W
Sastre 252 31.45 S 61.50 W
Sas van Gent 52 51.14 N 3.47 E
Sasyk, ozero ⊜ 78 45.12 N 33.31 E
Sasykkol', ozero ⊜ 86 46.35 N 81.00 E
Şasykoli 80 47.33 N 47.00 E
Šat ≃ 82 54.08 N 37.47 E
Satadougou 150 12.21 N 10.07 W
Satah Mountain ∧ 182 52.29 N 124.41 W
Şatakunta ◆[1] 26 61.30 N 23.00 E
Šatalovka 78 51.09 N 38.16 E
Šatalovo 76 54.20 N 32.27 E
Sata-misaki > 92 30.59 N 130.40 E
Satāna 122 20.35 N 74.12 E
Sataniv 78 49.15 N 26.16 E
Satanta 198 37.26 N 100.59 W
Sátão 34 40.44 N 7.44 W
Sātāra, India 122 17.41 N 73.59 E
Satara, S. Afr. 156 24.29 S 31.47 E
Sataua 175a 13.28 S 172.40 W
Sātbāria, Bngl. 126 23.52 N 89.26 E
Sātbāria, India 272b 22.25 N 88.33 E
Satélite 232 31.43 N 106.23 W
Satellite Beach 220 28.10 N 80.35 W
Satellite Channel ⊔ 224 48.43 N 123.30 W
Satema 152 4.18 N 21.42 E
Satengar, Pulau I 112 7.31 S 117.17 E
Säter 40 60.21 N 15.45 E
Sātgāchia 126 23.16 N 88.08 E
Sātghara 272b 22.44 N 88.21 E
Saticoy 228 34.17 N 119.09 W
Satilla ≃ 192 30.59 N 81.28 W
Satilpa Creek ≃ 194 31.39 N 88.05 W
Satin 222 31.21 N 97.02 W
Satipo 248 11.16 S 74.37 W
Sátiro Dias 250 11.36 S 38.36 W
Satis 80 55.02 N 43.48 E
Satīt (Tekeze) ≃ 140 14.20 N 35.50 E
Satka 86 55.03 N 59.01 E
Satkānia 120 22.04 N 92.03 E
Sātkhira 124 22.43 N 89.06 E
Šatki 80 55.11 N 44.08 E
Satla Bīl ≋ 126 22.54 N 90.04 E
Satluj → Sutlej ≃ 120 29.23 N 71.02 E
Satna 124 24.35 N 80.50 E
Sato, Cañada de ≃ 288 34.35 S 58.38 W
Satomi 94 36.43 N 140.30 E
Sátoraljaújhely 30 48.24 N 21.39 E
Šatov 61 48.48 N 16.01 E
Šatovo 82 54.56 N 37.14 E
Satow 54 53.59 N 11.51 E
Sātpura Range ⋏ 122 22.00 N 78.00 E
Sätrabrunn 40 59.51 N 16.27 E
Şatriano di Lucania 68 40.33 N 15.33 E
Šatrovo 86 56.31 N 64.38 E
Satrup 41 54.41 N 9.35 E
Satsop ≃ 224 47.03 N 123.30 W
Satsop, Middle Fork ≃ 224 47.05 N 123.30 W
Satsop, West Fork ≃ 224 47.02 N 123.32 W
Satsuma 194 30.51 N 88.03 W
Satsuma-hantō >[1] 92 31.25 N 130.25 E
Satsunan-shotō II 93b 29.00 N 130.00 E
Sattahip 110 12.40 N 100.54 E
Sāttānkulam 122 8.27 N 77.56 E
Satte 94 36.04 N 139.43 E
Sattel 58 47.05 N 8.42 E
Sattenapalle 122 16.24 N 80.11 E
Satthwa 110 17.46 N 94.30 E
Sattledt 61 48.04 N 14.03 E
Satui 112 3.47 S 115.27 E
Sātuli 272b 22.33 N 88.34 E
Satu Mare 38 47.48 N 22.53 E
Satu Mare □[6] 38 47.40 N 23.00 E
Şatun 110 6.37 N 100.04 E
Šatura 80 55.34 N 39.32 E
Saturna 224 48.43 N 123.11 W
Saturna Island I 224 48.47 N 123.08 W
Şaturnino M. Laspiur 252 31.42 S 62.29 W
Šaturtorf 76 55.34 N 39.26 E
Satus Creek ≃ 202 46.16 N 120.07 W
Satus Peak ∧ 224 46.15 N 120.45 W
Satyamangalam 122 11.31 N 77.15 E
Satzkorn 264a 52.29 N 12.59 E
Sau ≃ 269c 10.46 N 106.48 E
Saualpe ⋏ 61 46.55 N 14.40 E
Sauble ≃ 212 44.40 N 81.17 W
Sauce, Arg. 252 30.05 S 58.46 W
Sauce, Perú 248 6.44 S 76.10 W
Sauce, Ur. 258 34.39 S 56.04 W
Sauce, Arroyo ≃ 258 34.26 S 57.28 W
Sauce, Arroyo del ≃ 288 34.41 S 58.50 W
Sauce Corto, Arroyo ≃ 252 36.55 S 61.48 W
Saucier 194 30.38 N 89.08 W
Saucillo 232 28.01 N 105.17 W
Sauda 26 59.39 N 6.20 E
Saudade 256 21.56 S 43.03 W
Sauđárkrókur 24a 65.46 N 19.41 W
Saúde 250 10.56 S 40.24 W
Saúde ◆[8] 287b 23.37 S 46.37 W
Saudi Arabia (Al-ʿArabīyah as-Suʿūdīyah) □[1] 118 25.00 N 45.00 E
Saudi-Arabien → Saudi Arabia □[1] 118 25.00 N 45.00 E
Saudron 58 48.30 N 5.20 E
Sauer (Sûre) ≃, Europe 56 49.44 N 6.31 E
Sauer ≃, Europe 56 48.55 N 8.10 E
Sauerkohl-Berge ∧[2] 264a 52.20 N 13.45 E
Sauerlach 64 47.58 N 11.38 E
Sauerland ◆[1] 52 51.10 N 8.00 E
Saueruiná ≃ 248 12.00 S 58.43 W
Sauê-Uiná ≃ 248 12.24 S 58.40 W
Saug ≃ 116 7.27 N 125.44 E
Saugatuck, Ct., U.S. 276 41.08 N 73.23 W
Saugatuck, Mi., U.S. 216 42.39 N 86.12 W
Saugatuck ≃ 276 41.07 N 73.22 W
Saugatuck Reservoir ⊜[1] 207 41.16 N 73.22 W
Saugeen ≃ 190 44.30 N 81.22 W
Saugeen Indian Reserve ◆[4] 212 44.33 N 81.18 W
Saugerties 210 42.04 N 73.57 W
Saughall 262 53.13 N 2.58 W
Saugor → Sāgar 124 23.50 N 78.43 E
Saugstad, Mount ∧ 182 52.15 N 126.31 W
Saugus, Ca., U.S. 228 34.24 N 118.32 W
Saugus, Ma., U.S. 207 42.27 N 71.00 W
Saugus ≃ 283 42.28 N 70.58 W
Saugus Iron Works National Historic Site ⊥ 283 42.28 N 71.01 W
Sauh, Tanjong > 114 3.46 N 100.49 E
Saujil 252 28.11 S 66.14 W
Saujon 32 45.40 N 0.56 W
Sauk ≃, Mn., U.S. 198 45.36 N 94.10 W
Sauk ≃, Wa., U.S. 224 48.30 N 121.37 W
Sauk Centre 198 45.44 N 94.57 W
Sauk City 190 43.16 N 89.43 W
Sauk Rapids 190 45.35 N 94.09 W
Sauksaj ≃ 85 39.11 N 72.15 E
Sauk Village 216 41.29 N 87.34 W
Saukville 190 43.22 N 87.56 W
Şaül 250 3.37 N 53.12 W
Šaul'der 85 42.47 N 68.24 E
Sauldre ≃ 50 47.16 N 1.30 E
Sauldre, Canal de la ≍ 50 47.36 N 2.06 E
Saulgau 58 48.01 N 9.30 E
Saulgrub 64 47.40 N 11.01 E
Saulheim 56 49.51 N 8.09 E
Saulieu 50 47.16 N 4.14 E
Saulkrasti 76 57.17 N 24.25 E
Saulnot 58 47.34 N 6.38 E
Sault-au-Mouton 186 48.33 N 69.15 W
Sault au Récollet ◆[8] 275a 45.34 N 73.39 W
Sault aux Cochons, Rivière du ≃ 186 48.44 N 69.04 W
Sault-de-Vaucluse 62 44.05 N 5.25 E
Saulteaux ≃ 182 55.16 N 114.25 W
Saulteaux Indian Reserve ◆[4] 184 53.08 N 108.18 W
Sault-lès-Rethel 50 49.30 N 4.22 E
Sault Sainte Marie, On., Can. 190 46.31 N 84.20 W
Sault Sainte Marie, Mi., U.S. 190 46.29 N 84.20 W
Saulx ≃, Fr. 56 48.45 N 4.35 E
Saulx ≃, Fr. 261 48.41 N 2.19 E
Saulx-de-Vesoul 58 47.42 N 6.17 E
Saulx-les-Chartreux 261 48.42 N 2.16 E
Saulxures-sur-Moselotte 58 47.57 N 6.46 E
Šaum'ani 84 41.21 N 44.46 E
Saumarez Reef ✦[2] 166 21.50 S 153.40 E
Saumlaki 164 7.57 S 131.19 E
Saumon, Rivière au ≃ 206 45.41 N 71.27 W
Saumons, Rivíere aux ≃ 186 49.25 N 62.15 W
Saumur 32 47.16 N 0.05 W
Saundatti 122 15.47 N 75.07 E
Saundersfoot 42 51.43 N 4.43 W
Saunders Island I, Falk. Is. 254 51.20 S 60.10 W
Saunders Island I, S. Geor. 9 57.47 S 26.27 W
Saunders Point ∧[2] 162 27.52 S 125.38 E
Saunderstown 207 41.30 N 71.25 W
Saunemin 216 40.54 N 88.24 W
Saupite 152 13.54 S 17.43 E
Sauquoit 210 43.00 N 75.16 W
Sauquoit Creek ≃ 210 43.08 N 75.16 W
Saura 84 44.14 N 50.50 E
Sauran 85 43.29 N 67.50 E
Saurimo 152 9.39 S 20.24 E
Sausalito 226 37.51 N 122.29 W
Sausar 120 21.39 N 78.47 E
Sauškin 80 49.30 N 43.32 E
Sausset-les-Pins 62 43.20 N 5.07 E
Saussy 58 47.28 N 4.57 E
Sausu 112 1.00 S 120.30 E
Saútar 152 11.06 S 18.27 E
Sauteurs 241k 12.14 N 61.38 W
Sauvas 62 44.19 N 4.09 E
Sauve 62 43.56 N 3.57 E
Sauveterre 62 44.02 N 4.48 E
Sauveterre-de-Béarn 32 43.24 N 0.56 W
Sauveterre-de-Guyenne 32 44.42 N 0.05 W
Sauvie Island I 224 45.41 N 122.49 W
Sauvo 26 60.21 N 22.42 E
Sauwald ◆[3] 60 48.28 N 13.40 E
Sauzal 200 31.37 N 106.18 W
Sauze di Cesana 62 44.56 N 6.51 E
Sauze d'Oulx 62 45.02 N 6.52 E
Sava, It. 68 40.24 N 17.34 E
S'ava, Ross. 80 58.01 N 46.22 E
Sava ≃ 38 44.50 N 20.26 E
Sävaån ≃ 40 59.45 N 17.24 E
Savage, Md., U.S. 208 39.08 N 76.49 W
Savage, Mt., U.S. 198 47.27 N 104.20 W
Savai'i I 175a 13.35 S 172.25 W
Savala ≃ 80 51.03 N 41.30 E
Savalen ⊜ 26 62.15 N 10.29 E
Savalou 150 7.56 N 1.58 E
Savana Island I 240m 18.20 N 65.05 W
Savana Passage ⊔ 240m 18.21 N 65.04 W
Savane ≃ 186 51.08 N 71.26 W
Savanna, Il., U.S. 190 42.05 N 90.09 W
Savanna, Ok., U.S. 196 34.49 N 95.50 W
Savannah, Ga., U.S. 192 32.05 N 81.06 W
Savannah, Mo., U.S. 194 39.56 N 94.49 W
Savannah, N.Y., U.S. 210 43.04 N 76.45 W
Savannah, Oh., U.S. 214 40.57 N 82.21 W
Savannah, Tn., U.S. 194 35.13 N 88.14 W
Savannah ≃ 192 32.02 N 80.53 W
Savannah River Plant ⊗[3] 192 33.15 N 81.40 W
Savannah Sound 192 25.06 N 76.09 W
Savannakhét 110 16.33 N 104.45 E
Savanna-la-Mar 241q 18.13 N 78.08 W
Savanna Portage State Park ♦ 190 46.51 N 93.10 W
Sāvantvādi 122 15.54 N 73.49 E
Savanūr 122 14.58 N 75.21 E
Sävar 26 63.54 N 20.34 E
Savara ≃ 62 45.42 N 7.12 E
Săvârșin 38 46.01 N 22.14 E
Savasse ≃ 62 45.03 N 5.02 E
Savaştepe 130 39.22 N 27.40 E
Savat 130 38.21 N 40.38 E
Savcılıbüyükoba 130 39.14 N 33.41 E
Savé 150 8.02 N 2.29 E
Save (Sabi) ≃, Afr. 156 21.00 S 35.02 E
Save ≃, Fr. 32 43.47 N 1.17 E
Sāveh 128 35.01 N 50.20 E
Savelli 68 39.19 N 16.47 E
Savelugu 150 9.37 N 0.49 W
Savenay 32 47.22 N 1.57 W
Săveni 38 47.57 N 26.52 E
Saverdun 32 43.14 N 1.35 E
Savernake Forest ◆[3] 42 51.24 N 1.38 W
Saverne 56 48.44 N 7.22 E
Savery Creek ≃ 200 41.01 N 107.27 W
Saviči, Bela. 76 52.25 N 29.03 E
Saviči, Bela. 78 51.37 N 30.17 E
Savick Brook ≃ 262 53.45 N 2.47 W
Savièse 58 46.16 N 7.20 E
Savigliano 62 44.38 N 7.40 E
Savignano Irpino 68 41.14 N 15.11 E
Savignano sul Panaro 64 44.29 N 11.02 E
Savignano sul Rubicone 66 44.05 N 12.24 E
Savignone 62 44.34 N 8.58 E
Savigny-lès-Beaune 58 47.04 N 4.49 E
Savigny-le-Temple 261 48.35 N 2.35 E
Savigny-sur-Braye 50 47.53 N 0.49 E
Savigny-sur-Orge 50 48.40 N 2.21 E
Savill Gardens ♦ 260 51.27 N 0.36 W
Savines 62 44.32 N 6.24 E
Savinjske Alpe ⋏ 61 46.23 N 14.35 E
Savinka, Ross. 80 50.06 N 47.06 E
Savinka, Ross. 82 54.27 N 38.52 E
Savino 80 56.35 N 41.13 E
Savino-Borisovskaja 24 62.38 N 44.34 E
Savinsk 89 52.10 N 140.23 E
Savinskij 24 62.58 N 40.08 E
Savio 66 44.18 N 12.18 E
Savio ≃ 66 44.19 N 12.20 E
Saviore dell'Adamello 64 46.05 N 10.24 E
Şavitaipale 26 61.12 N 27.42 E
Šavnik 38 42.57 N 19.05 E
Savognin 58 46.36 N 9.36 E
Savoie □[5] 32 45.30 N 6.25 E
Savoie □[9] 58 45.55 N 6.30 E
Savo Island I 175e 9.08 S 159.49 E
Savolaks ◆[1] 26 62.00 N 28.00 E

Symbols in the index entries represent the broad categories identified in the key at the right. Symbols with superior numbers (⋏[1]) identify subcategories (see complete key on page I · 1).

Symbole im Register stellen die rechts im Schlüssel erklärten Kategorien dar. Symbole mit hochgestellten Ziffern (⋏[1]) bezeichnen Unterabteilungen einer Kategorie (vgl. vollständiger Schlüssel auf Seite I · 1).

Los símbolos incluídos en el texto del índice representan las grandes categorías identificadas con la clave a la derecha. Los símbolos con numeros en su parte superior (⋏[1]) identifican las subcategorías (véase la clave completa en la página I · 1).

Les symboles de l'index représentent les catégories indiquées dans la légende à droite. Les symboles suivis d'un indice (⋏[1]) représentent des sous-catégories (voir légende complète à la page I · 1).

Os símbolos incluídos no texto do índice representam as grandes categorias identificadas com a chave à direita. Os símbolos com números em sua parte superior (⋏[1]) identificam as subcategorias (veja-se a chave completa à página I · 1).

	English	Deutsch	Español	Français	Português
∧	Mountain	Berg	Montaña	Montagne	Montanha
⋏	Mountains	Gebirge	Montañas	Montagnes	Montanhas
)(	Pass	Paß	Paso	Col	Passo
V	Valley, Canyon	Tal, Cañon	Valle, Cañón	Vallée, Canyon	Vale, Canhão
=	Plain	Ebene	Llano	Plaine	Planície
>	Cape	Kap	Cabo	Cap	Cabo
I	Island	Insel	Isla	Île	Ilha
II	Islands	Inseln	Islas	Îles	Ilhas
⊥	Other Topographic Features	Andere Topographische Objekte	Otros Elementos Topográficos	Autres données topographiques	Outros acidentes topográficos

ESPAÑOL — Nombre | Página | Lat.°′ | Long.°′ W = Oeste
FRANÇAIS — Nom | Page | Lat.°′ | Long.°′ W = Ouest
PORTUGUÊS — Nome | Página | Lat.°′ | Long.°′ W = Oeste

Sav'olovo 82 56.52 N 37.22 E
Sav'olovo Station ●[5] 265b 55.48 N 37.35 E
Savona, B.C., Can. 182 50.45 N 120.50 W
Savona, It. 62 44.17 N 8.30 E
Savona, N.Y., U.S. 210 42.17 N 77.13 W
Savona □[4] 62 44.18 N 8.16 E
Savonlinna 26 61.52 N 28.53 E
Savonnières 50 47.21 N 0.33 E
Savonranta 26 62.11 N 29.12 E
Savoonga 180 63.42 N 170.27 W
Savory Creek ≃ 162 23.22 S 122.37 E
Savoureuse ≃ 58 47.31 N 6.51 E
Savoy 196 33.34 N 96.21 W
Savran' 78 48.09 N 30.04 E
Savruši 80 55.02 N 50.40 E
Sävsjö 26 57.25 N 14.40 E
S'avta 24 67.08 N 61.45 E
Savu Basin ✢[1] 14 9.15 S 123.15 E
Savudrija 64 45.30 N 13.30 E
Savur 130 37.33 N 40.53 E
Savur-Mohyla ⊥ 83 47.56 N 38.46 E
Savusavu 175g 16.16 S 179.21 E
Savusavu Bay c 175g 16.45 S 179.15 E
Savu Sea
— Sawu, Laut ⊤[2] 112 9.40 S 122.00 E
Savuto ≃ 68 39.02 N 16.06 E
Savvatejevka 88 52.20 N 103.39 E
Savvino, Ross. 82 55.43 N 36.48 E
Savvino, Ross. 82 56.33 N 37.47 E
Savvo-Borz'a 88 50.46 N 118.18 E
Savyntsi 78 49.24 N 37.04 E
Şawāb, Wādī aş- V 130 34.36 N 40.25 E
Sawabala Point ≻ 164 10.10 S 151.15 E
Sawah 112 2.23 N 115.14 E
Sawahlunto 112 0.40 S 100.47 E
Sawai 164 2.58 S 129.09 E
Sawai, Teluk c 164 2.52 S 129.12 E
Sawāi Mādhopur 124 25.59 N 76.22 E
Sawākin 140 19.07 N 37.20 E
Sawal, Gunung ʌ 115a 7.12 S 108.16 E
Sawan, Indon. 115b 8.08 S 115.11 E
Sawan, Mya. 110 24.30 N 96.19 E
Sawang 114 0.45 N 103.21 E
Sawankhalok 110 17.19 N 99.50 E
Sawara 94 35.53 N 140.30 E
Sawata 92 38.00 N 138.16 E
Sawatch Range ⋏ 200 39.10 N 106.25 W
Sawbridgeworth 42 51.50 N 0.09 E
Sawdā', Jabal as- ⋏[2] 146 28.40 N 15.30 E
Sawdā', Qurnat as- ʌ 130 34.18 N 36.07 E
Sawdirī 140 14.25 N 29.05 E
Sawel Mountain ʌ 48 54.49 N 7.02 W
Sawhāj 140 26.33 N 31.42 E
Sawi 110 10.14 N 99.07 E
Sawin, Lac ⊜ 206 46.32 N 73.54 W
Sawknah 146 29.04 N 15.47 E
Şawl 142 29.21 N 31.14 E
Sawla 150 9.17 N 2.25 W
Saw Log Creek ≃ 198 38.07 N 99.42 W
Saw Mill ≃ 276 40.56 N 73.53 W
Sawmill Brook ≃, Ma., U.S. 283 42.34 N 70.46 W
Sawmill Brook ≃, N.J., U.S. 276 40.28 N 74.26 W
Sawmill Creek ≃, N.J., U.S. 276 40.46 N 74.05 W
Sawmill Creek ≃, Pa., U.S. 279b 40.10 N 79.58 W
Sawmill Pond Brook ≃ 276 41.10 N 74.23 W
Sawmill Run ≃ 285 40.07 N 75.21 W
Sawmills 154 19.31 S 28.02 E
Şawqirah, Ghubbat c 118 18.35 N 57.00 E
Sawston 42 52.07 N 0.10 E
Sawtayr ⊤[4] 140 17.03 N 30.24 E
Sawtooth National Recreation Area ♠ 202 44.00 N 114.55 W
Sawtry 42 52.27 N 0.17 W
Sawu, Laut (Savu Sea) ⊤[2] 112 9.40 S 122.00 E
Sawu, Pulau ɪ 112 10.30 S 121.54 E
Sawyer, Mi., U.S. 216 41.53 N 86.35 W
Sawyer, N.D., U.S. 198 48.05 N 101.03 W
Sawyers Hill ʌ[2] 186 47.11 N 53.52 W
Sawyers Valley 168a 31.54 S 116.13 E
Sawyerville, P.Q., Can. 206 45.20 N 71.34 W
Sawyerville, Il., U.S. 219 39.05 N 89.48 W
Sawyerwood 214 41.02 N 81.27 W
Saxby ≃ 166 18.25 S 140.53 E
Saxdalen 40 60.09 N 14.57 E
Saxen ⊜ 40 59.46 N 14.25 E
Saxike 120 30.44 N 86.22 E
Saxilby 44 53.17 N 0.40 W
Saxis 208 37.55 N 75.43 W
Saxmundham 42 52.13 N 1.29 E
Saxon, Schw. 58 46.09 N 7.11 E
Saxon, Wi., U.S. 190 46.29 N 90.24 W
Saxonburg 214 40.45 N 79.49 W
Saxon Woods Park ♠ 276 40.59 N 73.45 W
Saxony
— Sachsen □[3] 30 51.00 N 13.00 E
Saxony
— Sachsen □[9] 30 52.45 N 9.30 E
Saxton 214 40.12 N 78.14 W
Say 150 13.07 N 2.21 E
Sāy, Jazīrat ɪ 140 20.42 N 30.20 E
Saya de Malha Bank ✢[4] 12 10.30 S 61.30 E
Sayama, Nihon 94 35.51 N 139.24 E
Sayama, Nihon 270 34.31 N 135.34 E
Sayama-kyūryō ⋏[2] 268 35.47 N 139.24 E
Sayán 248 11.08 S 77.12 W
Sayan Mountains (Sajany) ⋏ 88 52.45 N 96.00 E
Sayansk 88 54.02 N 102.06 E
Sayaxché 232 16.31 N 90.10 W
Saybrook, Il., U.S. 216 40.25 N 88.31 W
Saybrook, Oh., U.S. 214 41.50 N 80.51 W
Saybrook Manor 207 41.17 N 72.23 W
Sayda, Dtsch. 54 50.43 N 13.25 E
Şaydā (Sidon), Lubnān 132 33.33 N 35.22 E
Şaydā □[4] 132 33.15 N 35.15 E
Şaydnāyā 132 33.42 N 36.22 E
Sayghān 120 35.11 N 67.42 E
Sayhūt 144 15.12 N 51.14 E
Sayil ⊥ 232 20.16 N 89.42 W
Saylah 142 29.21 N 30.58 E
Saylorsburg 210 40.54 N 75.19 W
Saylorville Lake ⊜[1] 190 41.48 N 93.46 W
Saylūn, Khirbat (Shiloh) ⊥ 132 32.03 N 35.17 E
Säynätsalo 26 62.08 N 25.46 E
Sayō 96 35.00 N 134.22 E
Şayqal, Baḩr ⊜ 132 33.40 N 37.06 E
Sayram Hu ⊜ 86 44.36 N 81.13 E
Sayre, Ok., U.S. 196 35.17 N 99.38 W
Sayre, Pa., U.S. 210 41.58 N 76.30 W
Sayreville 208 40.27 N 74.21 W
Sayula 234 19.52 N 103.37 W
Sayula, Laguna de ⊜ 234 20.03 N 103.31 W
Sayula de Alemán 234 17.52 N 94.57 W
Sayultepec 234 17.27 N 97.17 W
Sayville 210 40.44 N 73.04 W
Sayward 182 50.22 N 125.55 W
Saywūn 144 15.56 N 48.47 E
Saza 92 33.14 N 129.39 E
Sazanit ɪ 38 40.30 N 19.16 E
Sazdy, Kaz. 80 46.57 N 49.19 E
Sazdy, Kaz. 86 47.22 N 61.48 E
Saze 62 43.56 N 4.41 E
Sažino 86 56.20 N 58.11 E
Sazlijka ≃ 38 42.02 N 25.52 E
Šazonovo 76 59.04 N 35.14 E
Šazud 120 37.43 N 72.11 E
Sazykul', ozero ⊜ 86 55.22 N 67.34 E
Sba 148 28.13 N 0.08 W
Sbeïtla 148 35.14 N 9.08 E
Sbiba 36 35.33 N 9.05 E
Scaddan 162 33.27 S 121.43 E
Scaër 32 48.02 N 3.42 W
Scafati 68 40.45 N 14.31 E
Scafell Pikes ʌ 44 54.27 N 3.12 W
Scaggsville 208 39.09 N 76.54 W
Scajaquada Creek ≃ 284a 42.56 N 78.53 W
Scala, Teatro alla ʋ 266b 45.28 N 9.11 E
Scala Coeli 68 39.27 N 16.53 E
Scalasaig 46 56.04 N 6.11 W
Scalby 44 54.18 N 0.27 W
Scalea 68 39.49 N 15.48 E
Scaletta Zanclea 70 38.03 N 15.28 E
Scalloway 46a 60.08 N 1.18 W
Scalpay ɪ, Scot., U.K. 46 57.17 N 5.59 W
Scalpay ɪ, Scot., U.K. 46 57.52 N 6.40 W
Scalp Level 214 40.14 N 78.50 W
Scalp Mountain ʌ[2] 48 55.04 N 7.24 W
Scammon 198 37.16 N 94.49 W
Scammon Bay 180 61.53 N 165.38 W
Scammon Bay c 180 61.53 N 165.54 W
Scammonden Water ⊜[1] 262 53.38 N 1.56 W
Scampton 44 53.18 N 0.34 W
Scandale 68 39.07 N 16.57 E
Scandia 198 39.47 N 97.47 W
Scandiano 64 44.36 N 10.43 E
Scandicci 66 43.45 N 11.11 E
Scanlon 190 46.42 N 92.25 W
Scanno 66 41.54 N 13.53 E
Scansano 66 42.41 N 11.20 E
Scantic ≃ 207 41.52 N 72.38 W
Scapa 182 51.52 N 111.59 W
Scapa Flow c 46 58.55 N 3.06 W
Scapegoat Mountain ʌ 202 47.19 N 112.50 W
Ščapino 74 55.19 N 159.25 E
Ščapov 80 51.01 N 51.11 E
Ščapovo 82 55.09 N 38.11 E
Scappoose 224 45.45 N 122.52 W
Scar ≃ 44 55.13 N 3.46 W
Ščara ≃ 76 53.27 N 24.45 E
Scaramia, Capo ≻ 70 36.47 N 14.29 E
Scarba ɪ 46 56.11 N 5.43 W
Scarborough, Austl. 168a 31.54 S 115.45 E
Scarborough, On., Can. 212 43.47 N 79.15 W
Scarborough, Trin. 241r 11.11 N 60.44 W
Scarborough, Eng., U.K. 44 54.17 N 0.24 W
Scarborough Centre ●[9] 275b 43.47 N 79.16 W
Scarborough Point ≻ 171a 27.12 S 153.07 E
Scarborough Reef ✢[2] 116 15.08 N 117.46 E
Scardroy 46 57.31 N 4.59 W
Scargill 172 42.56 S 172.57 E
Scarinish 46 56.29 N 6.48 W
Scarisbrick 262 53.37 N 2.56 W
Scărişoara 38 44.00 N 24.35 E
Scarlino 66 42.54 N 10.51 E
Scarp ɪ 46 58.02 N 7.08 W
Scarpe ≃ 50 50.30 N 3.27 E
Scarperia 66 44.00 N 11.21 E
Scarper Peak ʌ 282 37.32 N 122.26 W
Scarriff 48 52.55 N 8.31 W
Scarsdale, Austl. 169 37.40 S 143.40 E
Scarsdale, N.Y., U.S. 210 40.59 N 73.49 W
Scartaglin 48 52.10 N 9.26 W
Scarth Hill 262 53.33 N 2.52 W
Scatarie Island ɪ 186 46.00 N 59.44 W
Scatter Creek ≃ 224 46.48 N 123.06 W
Scauri, It. 66 41.15 N 13.42 E
Scauri, It. 70 36.45 N 11.58 E
Scavaig, Loch c 46 57.09 N 6.10 W
Scawfell Island ɪ 166 20.52 S 149.36 E
Sceaux 50 48.47 N 2.17 E
Sceaux, Château de ⊥ 261 48.46 N 2.18 E
Ščedrin 76 52.53 N 29.33 E
Ščedrovka 83 49.30 N 40.17 E
Ščeglovo 265a 60.02 N 30.46 E
Ščeljajur 24 65.21 N 53.21 E
Ščelkan ≃ 80 50.47 N 43.33 E
Ščelkovo 76 55.55 N 38.00 E
Ščemilovo 265b 55.48 N 38.05 E
Scena 64 46.41 N 11.12 E
Scenery Hill 214 40.05 N 80.04 W
Sceptre 184 50.51 N 109.15 W
Ščerbakovo, Ross. 74 65.15 N 160.30 E
Ščerbakovo, Ross. 86 56.01 N 73.29 E
Ščerbakty 86 52.29 N 78.09 E
Ščerbinka 82 55.31 N 37.35 E
Scerni 66 42.07 N 14.34 E
Scey-sur-Saône-et-Saint-Albin 58 47.40 N 5.58 E
Schaale ≃ 54 53.21 N 10.49 E
Schaalsee ⊜ 54 53.35 N 10.57 E
Schaan 58 47.10 N 9.31 E
Schabs
— Sciaves 64 46.46 N 11.40 E
Schachendorf 61 47.16 N 16.26 E
Schaefferstown 208 40.17 N 76.17 W
Schaephuysen 263 51.26 N 6.29 E
Schaerbeek 50 50.51 N 4.23 E
Schafberg ʌ 64 47.47 N 13.27 E
Schäferberg ʌ[2] 264a 52.25 N 13.08 E
Schaffhausen 58 47.42 N 8.38 E
Schaffhausen □[3] 58 47.40 N 8.35 E
Schafstädt 54 51.23 N 11.46 E
Schäftlarn 64 47.59 N 11.28 E
Schagen 52 52.46 N 4.47 E
Schaghticoke 210 42.54 N 73.35 W
Schalchen 60 48.07 N 13.10 E
Schale 52 52.26 N 7.37 E
Schalkau 54 50.24 N 11.00 E
Schalke ●[8] 263 51.31 N 7.05 E
Schälker Heide ●[3] 263 51.24 N 7.36 E
Schalksmühle 56 51.14 N 7.31 E
Schaller 198 42.30 N 95.18 W
Schanck, Cape ≻ 169 38.30 S 144.53 E
S-Chanf 58 46.36 N 9.59 E
Schanfigg V 58 46.51 N 9.38 E
Schanghai
— Shanghai 106 31.14 N 121.28 E
Schangnau 58 46.50 N 7.52 E
Schapbach 58 48.22 N 8.17 E
Schapen 52 52.24 N 7.33 E
Schaprode 54 54.31 N 13.10 E
Šchara, gora ʌ 84 43.00 N 43.06 E
Scharbeutz 54 54.03 N 10.44 E
Schardenberg 60 48.32 N 13.30 E
Schardenberg ʌ[2] 263 51.27 N 6.28 E
Schärding 60 48.27 N 13.26 E
Scharhörn ɪ 52 53.57 N 8.25 E
Schari
— Chari ≃ 146 12.58 N 14.31 E
Scharmützelsee ⊜ 54 52.15 N 14.03 E
Scharnhorst ●[8] 263 51.32 N 7.32 E
Scharnitz 60 47.23 N 11.17 E
Scharnitzer Klause)(64 47.24 N 11.16 E
Scharrel 52 53.04 N 7.42 E
Scharzfeld 52 51.37 N 10.22 E
Schässburg
— Sighişoara 38 46.13 N 24.48 E
Schauinsland ʌ 58 47.55 N 7.54 E
Schaumburg 216 42.02 N 88.05 W
Schaut 84 43.43 N 42.32 E
Schebeli
— Shabeelle ≃ 144 0.12 S 42.45 E
Scheessel 52 53.10 N 9.29 E
Schefferville 176 54.48 N 66.50 W
Scheggia 66 43.24 N 12.40 E
Scheggino 66 42.43 N 12.50 E
Scheibbs 61 48.00 N 15.10 E
Scheiblingstein 264b 48.16 N 16.13 E
Scheidegg 58 47.35 N 9.51 E
Scheifling 61 47.09 N 14.24 E
Scheinfeld 56 49.40 N 10.27 E
Schelde (Escaut) ≃ 50 51.22 N 4.15 E
Schelklingen 58 48.22 N 9.44 E
Schell Creek Range ⋏ 204 39.10 N 114.40 W
Schellenberg ʌ 60 48.18 N 13.03 E
Schellsburg 214 40.03 N 78.39 W
Schelsen ●[8] 263 51.09 N 6.31 E
Schenectady 210 42.48 N 73.56 W
Schenectady □[6] 210 42.47 N 73.53 W
Schenefeld 52 53.36 N 9.49 E
Schenevus 210 42.32 N 74.49 W
Schenevus Creek ≃ 210 42.29 N 74.59 W
Schenkendorf 264a 52.16 N 13.35 E
Schenkenhorst 264a 52.20 N 13.12 E
Schenklengsfeld 56 50.49 N 9.50 E
Schenley 214 40.41 N 79.40 W
Schenley Park ♠ 279b 40.26 N 79.56 W
Schepsdorf-Lohne 52 52.30 N 7.16 E
Schererville 216 41.30 N 87.27 W
Scherfede 52 51.32 N 9.02 E
Scherlebeck 263 51.37 N 7.08 E
Schermbeck 52 51.41 N 6.52 E
Schermerhorn 52 52.36 N 4.52 E
Schermützelsee ⊜ 54 52.34 N 14.04 E
Scherpenheuvel 56 50.59 N 4.59 E
Scherpenzeel 52 52.05 N 5.30 E
Schertz 196 29.33 N 98.16 W
Schesch, Erg
— Chech, Erg ⋏[2] 148 25.00 N 2.15 W
Schesslitz 60 49.59 N 11.01 E
Schevelinger-Stausee ⊜[1] 263 51.08 N 7.26 E
Scheveningen ●[8] 52 52.06 N 4.18 E
Schiedam 52 51.55 N 4.24 E
Schieder 52 51.55 N 9.09 E
Schiefbahn 56 51.14 N 6.31 E
Schiehallion ʌ 46 56.40 N 4.06 W
Schierke 54 51.46 N 10.40 E
Schierling 60 48.50 N 12.08 E
Schiermonnikoog 52 53.24 N 6.10 E
Schiermonnikoog ɪ 52 53.28 N 6.15 E
Schiers 58 46.59 N 9.41 E
Schiessen 58 48.18 N 10.14 E
Schiffdorf 52 53.32 N 8.39 E
Schiffenensee ⊜ 58 46.50 N 7.10 E
Schifferstadt 56 49.23 N 8.22 E
Schiffshebewerk ●[5] 263 51.37 N 7.19 E
Schihkiatschwang
— Shijiazhuang 98 38.03 N 114.28 E
Schijndel 52 51.37 N 5.25 E
Schikoku
— Shikoku ɪ 92 33.45 N 133.30 E
Schildau 54 51.27 N 12.56 E
Schilde 56 51.14 N 4.34 E
Schilde ≃ 54 53.26 N 10.53 E
Schildow 54 52.38 N 13.23 E
Schildwolde 52 53.14 N 6.49 E
Schiller Park 216 41.57 N 87.52 W
Schillingsfürst 56 49.17 N 10.15 E
Schillingstedt 54 51.14 N 11.11 E
Schilpario 64 46.01 N 10.09 E
Schiltach 58 48.17 N 8.20 E
Schiltigheim 58 48.36 N 7.45 E
Schimborn 56 50.03 N 9.11 E
Schimmert 56 50.55 N 5.50 E
Schinveld 56 50.57 N 5.59 E
Schinznach Bad 58 47.27 N 8.10 E
Schio 64 45.43 N 11.21 E
Schipbeek ≃ 52 52.14 N 6.09 E
Schiphol, Luchthaven ⊠ 52 52.17 N 4.40 E
Schipkau 54 51.31 N 13.53 E
Schirgiswalde 54 51.05 N 14.27 E
Schirmeck 58 48.29 N 7.13 E
Schirnding 54 50.05 N 12.13 E
Schisuoka
— Shizuoka 94 34.58 N 138.23 E
Schjetman Reef ✢[2] 14 15.10 N 178.40 W
Schkeuditz 54 51.24 N 12.13 E
Schkoder-See
— Scutari, Lake ⊜ 38 42.12 N 19.18 E
Schkölen 54 51.02 N 11.49 E
Schkopau 54 51.23 N 11.59 E
Schladen 54 52.01 N 10.32 E
Schladming 64 47.23 N 13.41 E
Schlanders
— Silandro 64 46.38 N 10.46 E
Schlangen 52 51.49 N 8.50 E
Schlangenbad 56 50.05 N 8.05 E
Schlänitz-See ⊜ 264a 52.27 N 12.57 E
Schlanstedt 54 52.00 N 11.02 E
Schlater 194 33.38 N 90.20 W
Schlegel Lake ⊜ 276 40.59 N 74.03 W
Schlei c 41 54.36 N 9.51 E
Schleiden 56 50.31 N 6.28 E
Schleife 54 51.32 N 14.32 E
Schleinitz Range ⋏ 164 3.10 S 151.40 E
Schleithal 56 48.59 N 8.02 E
Schleitheim 58 47.45 N 8.29 E
Schleiz 54 50.34 N 11.49 E
Schlema 54 50.40 N 12.40 E
Schlepzig 54 52.01 N 13.53 E
Schlesien
— Silesia □[9] 30 51.00 N 16.45 E
Schlesischer (Ost) Bahnhof ●[5] 264a 52.30 N 13.26 E
Schleswig, Dtsch. 41 54.31 N 9.33 E
Schleswig, Ia., U.S. 198 42.09 N 95.26 W
Schleswig-Holstein □[3] 30 54.20 N 9.40 E
Schlettau 54 50.33 N 12.56 E
Schlettstadt
— Sélestat 58 48.16 N 7.27 E
Schleusingen 54 50.31 N 10.45 E
Schlicke ʌ 58 47.31 N 10.37 E
Schlieben 54 51.43 N 13.23 E
Schliengen 58 47.46 N 7.35 E
Schlieren 58 47.24 N 8.27 E
Schliersee 64 47.44 N 11.51 E
Schlitz 56 50.40 N 9.33 E
Schloss Holte 52 51.52 N 8.35 E
Schloss Neuhaus 52 51.44 N 8.43 E
Schlossvippach 54 51.06 N 11.08 E
Schloss Zeil 64 47.52 N 10.00 E
Schlotheim 54 51.14 N 10.39 E
Schluchsee 58 47.49 N 8.10 E
Schluchsee ⊜ 58 47.49 N 8.10 E
Schlucht, Col de la)(58 48.04 N 7.02 E
Schlüchtern 56 50.20 N 9.31 E
Schluderns
— Sluderno 64 46.40 N 10.35 E
Schlüsselburg 52 52.29 N 9.04 E
Schlüsselfeld 56 49.45 N 10.37 E
Schlutup ●[8] 54 53.53 N 10.48 E
Schmachtendorf ●[8] 263 51.32 N 6.49 E
Schmalfeld 52 53.52 N 9.58 E
Schmalkalden 54 50.43 N 10.26 E
Schmallenberg 56 51.09 N 8.17 E
Schmalnau 56 50.27 N 9.47 E
Schmannewitz 54 51.24 N 12.58 E
Schmarsau 54 52.54 N 11.21 E
Schmelz 56 49.27 N 6.51 E
Schmida ≃ 61 48.21 N 16.09 E
Schmidmühlen 60 49.16 N 11.56 E
Schmidt 56 50.39 N 6.25 E
Schmidtsdrif 158 28.41 S 24.02 E
Schmiedeberg 54 50.50 N 13.40 E
Schmiedefeld 54 50.37 N 10.49 E
Schmilka 54 50.53 N 14.14 E
Schmöckwitz ●[8] 264a 52.23 N 13.39 E
Schmölln 54 50.53 N 12.20 E
Schmutter ≃ 58 48.42 N 10.46 E
Schnabelwaid 60 49.49 N 11.35 E
Schnackenburg 54 53.02 N 11.32 E
Schnait 56 48.47 N 9.23 E
Schnaitsee 60 48.04 N 12.22 E
Schnaittach 60 49.31 N 11.19 E
Schnaittenbach 60 49.33 N 12.01 E
Schnakenbek 52 53.23 N 10.30 E
Schnecksville 208 40.41 N 75.36 W
Schneealpe ⋏ 61 47.41 N 15.36 E
Schneeberg 54 50.36 N 12.38 E
Schneeberg ʌ, Dtsch. 54 50.03 N 11.51 E
Schneeberg ʌ, Öst. 61 47.47 N 15.47 E
Schneidemühl
— Piła 30 53.10 N 16.44 E
Schneider 216 41.11 N 87.26 W
Schneifel ⋏[1] 56 50.15 N 6.25 E
Schneverdingen 52 53.07 N 9.47 E
Schney 56 50.10 N 11.04 E
Schober Gruppe ⋏ 64 46.55 N 12.42 E
Schobüll 41 54.30 N 9.00 E
Schöckl ʌ 61 47.11 N 15.28 E
Schodn'a 82 55.57 N 37.18 E
Schodn'a ≃ 265b 55.50 N 37.25 E
Schœlcher 240e 14.37 N 61.06 W
Schoenbrunn Village State Memorial ⊥ 214 40.27 N 81.24 W
Schofield 190 44.54 N 89.36 W
Schofield Barracks ■ 229c 21.30 N 158.04 W
Schofields 274a 33.42 S 150.52 E
Schöftland 58 47.18 N 8.03 E
Schoharie 210 42.39 N 74.18 W
Schoharie □[6] 210 42.40 N 74.19 W
Schoharie Creek ≃ 210 42.57 N 74.18 W
Schoharie Reservoir ⊜[1] 210 42.22 N 74.26 W
Scholen 52 52.44 N 8.46 E
Scholes 44 53.49 N 1.25 W
Schollene 54 52.41 N 12.13 E
Schöllenen V 58 46.40 N 8.35 E
Schöller ●[8] 263 51.14 N 7.01 E
Schöllkrippen 56 50.05 N 9.14 E
Schöllnach 60 48.45 N 13.11 E
Scholls 224 45.24 N 122.55 W
Scholven ●[8] 263 51.36 N 7.01 E
Schomberg, On., Can. 212 44.00 N 79.41 W
Schömberg, Dtsch. 56 48.47 N 8.38 E
Schömberg, Dtsch. 58 48.13 N 8.46 E
Schonach 58 48.08 N 8.11 E
Schönaich 56 48.39 N 9.03 E
Schönau, Dtsch. 56 49.26 N 8.49 E
Schönau, Dtsch. 58 47.47 N 7.53 E
Schönau, Dtsch. 64 47.37 N 12.59 E
Schönbeck 54 53.34 N 13.34 E
Schönberg, Dtsch. 54 50.31 N 11.57 E
Schönberg, Dtsch. 54 50.11 N 12.19 E
Schönberg, Dtsch. 54 54.23 N 10.22 E
Schönberg, Dtsch. 54 53.51 N 10.56 E
Schönberg, Dtsch. 60 48.50 N 13.20 E
Schönberger Strand 54 54.25 N 10.24 E
Schönberg im Stubaital 64 47.11 N 11.25 E
Schönbrunn 54 50.32 N 10.53 E
Schönbrunn, Schloss ʋ 264b 48.11 N 16.19 E
Schönbrunner Schlosspark ♠ 264b 48.11 N 16.19 E
Schondra ≃ 56 50.07 N 9.44 E
Schönebeck, Dtsch. 54 53.03 N 12.13 E
Schönebeck, Dtsch. 54 52.01 N 11.44 E
Schönebeck ●[8] 263 51.28 N 6.56 E
Schöneberg ●[8] 264a 52.29 N 13.21 E
Schöneck, Dtsch. 54 50.23 N 12.20 E
Schöneck, Dtsch. 56 50.13 N 8.52 E
Schönecken 56 50.09 N 6.27 E
Schönefeld 264a 52.23 N 13.30 E
Schöneiche 54 52.28 N 13.41 E
Schönenwerd 58 47.22 N 8.00 E
Schönerlinde 264a 52.39 N 13.27 E
Schönewalde 54 51.49 N 13.13 E
Schönfeld 264a 52.41 N 13.44 E
Schönfliess 264a 52.39 N 13.20 E
Schongau 58 47.49 N 10.54 E
Schönhagen, Dtsch. 41 54.38 N 10.01 E
Schönhagen, Dtsch. 52 51.41 N 9.33 E
Schönhausen, Dtsch. 54 52.35 N 12.02 E
Schönhausen, Dtsch. 263 51.37 N 7.38 E
Schönheide 54 50.30 N 12.31 E
Schönholthausen 56 51.11 N 8.00 E
Schöningen 54 52.08 N 10.58 E
Schönkirchen 54 54.20 N 10.15 E
Schönmünzach 56 48.36 N 8.22 E
Schonnebeck ●[8] 263 51.29 N 7.04 E
Schönningstedt 52 53.32 N 10.15 E
Schönow 54 52.40 N 13.32 E
Schönsee 60 49.31 N 12.33 E
Schönthal 60 49.21 N 12.36 E
Schonungen 56 50.03 N 10.18 E
Schönwald, Dtsch. 54 50.12 N 12.05 E
Schönwald, Dtsch. 58 48.06 N 8.11 E
Schönwalde, Dtsch. 54 54.11 N 10.45 E
Schönwalde, Dtsch. 54 52.40 N 13.26 E
Schönwalde, Dtsch. 54 52.37 N 13.07 E
Schönwies 58 47.11 N 10.39 E
Schoodic Lake ⊜ 188 45.21 N 68.54 W
Schoolcraft 216 42.06 N 85.38 W
Schoolhouse Run ≃ 285 40.13 N 75.27 W
Schoombee 158 31.28 S 25.30 E
Schoondijke 52 51.21 N 3.32 E
Schoonebeek 52 52.40 N 6.53 E
Schoonhoven 52 51.56 N 4.51 E
Schoorl 52 52.42 N 4.41 E
Schopfheim 58 47.39 N 7.49 E
Schopfloch 56 49.07 N 10.18 E
Schopp 56 49.21 N 7.41 E
Schöppenstedt 54 52.08 N 10.46 E
Schöppingen 52 52.05 N 7.14 E
Schorfheide 54 52.56 N 13.43 E
Schorfheide ●[3] 54 52.55 N 13.35 E
Schörfling 64 47.56 N 13.36 E
Schorndorf 56 48.48 N 9.31 E
Schortens 52 53.31 N 7.56 E
Schoten 50 51.15 N 4.30 E
Schötmar 52 52.04 N 8.45 E
Schotten 56 50.30 N 9.07 E
Schottland
— Scotland □[8] 28 57.00 N 4.00 W
Schouten, Kepulauan ɪɪ 164 0.55 S 135.55 E
Schouten Island ɪ 166 42.19 S 148.17 E
Schouten Islands ɪɪ 164 3.30 S 144.40 E
Schouwen ɪ 52 51.43 N 3.50 E
Schrader Creek ≃ 210 41.43 N 76.30 W
Schrader Range ⋏ 164 5.05 S 144.15 E
Schramberg 58 48.13 N 8.23 E
Schram City 219 39.09 N 89.27 W
Schrankogel ʌ 64 47.02 N 11.06 E
Schraplau 54 51.26 N 11.40 E
Schreiber 190 48.48 N 87.15 W
Schrems 61 48.47 N 15.04 E
Schrick 61 48.30 N 16.37 E
Schriever 194 29.44 N 90.48 W
Schrobenhausen 60 48.33 N 11.17 E
Schröcken 58 47.15 N 10.05 E
Schroffenstein ʌ 158 27.11 S 18.42 E
Schroon ≃ 188 43.29 N 73.49 W
Schroon Lake ⊜ 188 43.47 N 73.46 W
Schrozberg 56 49.20 N 9.59 E
Schruns 58 47.04 N 9.55 E
Schulenburg, Dtsch. 52 52.12 N 9.47 E
Schulenburg, Tx., U.S. 222 29.40 N 96.54 W
Schuls
— Scuol 58 46.48 N 10.18 E
Schultz Lake ⊜ 176 64.45 N 97.30 W
Schulzendorf 54 52.22 N 13.35 E
Schulzenhöhe 264a 52.29 N 13.47 E
Schumacher 190 48.28 N 81.18 W
Schüpfheim 58 46.57 N 8.01 E
Schüren ●[8] 263 51.30 N 7.32 E
Schurwald ⋏ 56 48.46 N 9.29 E
Schussen ≃ 58 47.37 N 9.32 E
Schussenried 58 48.00 N 9.40 E
Schüttenberg ʌ[2] 61 48.05 N 16.44 E
Schutter ≃ 58 48.34 N 7.50 E
Schüttorf 52 52.19 N 7.13 E
Schuyler, Ne., U.S. 198 41.26 N 97.03 W
Schuyler, Va., U.S. 192 37.47 N 78.41 W
Schuyler □[6], Il., U.S. 219 40.07 N 90.34 W
Schuyler □[6], N.Y., U.S. 210 42.23 N 76.52 W
Schuyler Lake 210 42.47 N 75.02 W
Schuylerville 210 43.06 N 73.34 W
Schuylkill □[6] 210 40.41 N 76.12 W
Schuylkill ≃ 208 39.53 N 75.12 W
Schuylkill Canal ≊ 285 40.14 N 75.42 W
Schuylkill Haven 208 40.37 N 76.10 W
Schwaan 54 53.56 N 12.06 E
Schwabach 60 49.20 N 11.01 E
Schwaben □[5] 58 48.15 N 10.30 E
Schwaben □[9] 30 48.10 N 9.25 E
Schwabing ●[8] 60 48.10 N 11.34 E
Schwäbische Alb ⋏ 58 48.25 N 9.30 E
Schwäbisch Gmünd 56 48.48 N 9.47 E
Schwäbisch Hall 56 49.07 N 9.44 E
Schwabmünchen 58 48.11 N 10.45 E
Schwabstedt 41 54.23 N 9.11 E
Schwadorf 61 48.04 N 16.35 E
Schwafheim 263 51.25 N 6.39 E
Schwagstorf 52 52.31 N 7.45 E
Schwaigern 56 49.08 N 9.03 E
Schwalenberg 52 51.52 N 9.11 E
Schwalm ≃ 56 51.10 N 9.25 E
Schwalmstadt 56 50.55 N 9.11 E
Schwalmtal 56 51.13 N 6.16 E
Schwanden 58 47.00 N 9.04 E
Schwandorf 60 49.20 N 12.08 E
Schwanebeck, Dtsch. 54 52.37 N 13.32 E
Schwanebeck, Dtsch. 54 51.58 N 11.07 E
Schwanenstadt 60 48.03 N 13.46 E
Schwanenwerder ●[8] 264a 52.27 N 13.10 E
Schwaner, Pegunungan ⋏ 112 0.40 S 112.40 E
Schwanewede 52 53.14 N 8.35 E
Schwangau 58 47.35 N 10.44 E
Schwansen ●[1] 41 54.35 N 9.50 E
Schwante 264a 52.44 N 13.05 E
Schwarme 52 52.54 N 9.01 E
Schwarmstedt 52 52.40 N 9.37 E
Schwartau ≃ 54 53.56 N 10.41 E
Schwarza, Dtsch. 54 50.38 N 10.32 E
Schwarza, Dtsch. 54 50.41 N 11.19 E
Schwarza ≃, Dtsch. 54 50.41 N 11.19 E
Schwarza ≃, Öst. 61 47.43 N 16.13 E
Schwarzach, Dtsch. 60 48.55 N 12.49 E
Schwarzach, Öst. 58 47.27 N 9.45 E
Schwarzach ≃ 60 49.36 N 12.08 E
Schwarzach im Pongau 64 47.19 N 13.09 E
Schwarzbach ≃, Dtsch. 56 49.16 N 7.18 E
Schwarzbach ≃, Dtsch. 263 51.19 N 6.44 E
Schwarzburg 54 50.38 N 11.12 E
Schwarze Elster ≃ 54 51.49 N 12.51 E
Schwarze Laber ≃ 60 49.00 N 12.03 E
Schwarzenbach am Wald 54 50.17 N 11.37 E
Schwarzenbach an der Saale 54 50.13 N 11.56 E
Schwarzenbek 52 53.30 N 10.29 E
Schwarzenberg 54 50.32 N 12.47 E
Schwarzenberg ●[8] 263 51.24 N 6.42 E
Schwarzenberg Park ♠ 264b 48.14 N 16.15 E
Schwarzenborn 56 50.55 N 9.27 E
Schwarzenbruck 60 49.21 N 11.14 E
Schwarzenburg 58 46.49 N 7.21 E
Schwarzenfeld 60 49.23 N 12.08 E
Schwarze Pumpe 54 51.32 N 14.20 E
Schwarzer Berg ʌ[2] 263 51.41 N 7.12 E
Schwarzer Mann ʌ 56 50.15 N 6.21 E
Schwarzer Regen ≃ 60 49.10 N 12.50 E
Schwarzes Meer
— Black Sea ⊤[2] 22 43.00 N 35.00 E
Schwarzheide 54 51.29 N 13.51 E
Schwarzkogel ʌ 61 47.25 N 15.25 E
Schwarzrand ⋏ 156 25.37 S 16.50 E
Schwarzriegel ʌ 60 49.14 N 12.56 E
Schwarzsee 58 46.40 N 7.20 E
Schwarzwald (Black Forest) ⋏ 58 48.00 N 8.15 E
Schwarzwälder Hochwald ●[3] 56 49.39 N 6.55 E
Schwatka Mountains ⋏ 180 67.25 N 157.00 W
Schwaz 64 47.20 N 11.42 E
Schwechat 61 48.08 N 16.29 E
Schwechat ≃ 61 48.08 N 16.34 E
Schweden
— Sweden □[1] 24 62.00 N 15.00 E
Schwedeneck 41 54.27 N 10.05 E
Schwedt 54 53.03 N 14.17 E
Schweez 54 53.53 N 12.24 E
Schweflinghausen 263 51.16 N 7.25 E
Schwegenheim 56 49.16 N 8.20 E
Schwei 52 53.24 N 8.21 E
Schweich 56 49.49 N 6.45 E
Schweidnitz
— Świdnica 30 50.51 N 16.29 E
Schweighausen 58 48.13 N 7.57 E
Schweighouse-sur-Moder 56 48.49 N 7.44 E
Schweinfurt 56 50.03 N 10.14 E
Schweinitz 54 51.48 N 13.01 E
Schweinrich 54 53.10 N 12.37 E
Schweiz
— Switzerland □[1] 58 47.00 N 8.00 E
Schweizer Nationalpark ♠ 58 46.38 N 10.11 E
Schweizer-Reneke 158 27.11 S 25.18 E
Schwelm 56 51.17 N 7.17 E
Schwendi 58 48.10 N 9.58 E
Schwenke 263 51.11 N 7.26 E
Schwenksville 285 40.16 N 75.28 W
Schwepnitz 54 51.20 N 13.57 E
Schwerin, Dtsch. 54 53.38 N 11.25 E
Schwerin, Dtsch. 263 51.33 N 7.20 E
Schweriner See ⊜ 54 53.45 N 11.28 E
Schwertberg 61 48.16 N 14.35 E
Schwerte 56 51.26 N 7.34 E
Schwetzingen 56 49.23 N 8.34 E
Schweyen 56 49.10 N 7.24 E
Schwieberdingen 56 48.52 N 9.04 E
Schwielochsee ⊜ 54 52.03 N 14.12 E
Schwielowsee ⊜ 54 52.20 N 12.57 E
Schwitten 263 51.27 N 7.48 E
Schwyz 58 47.02 N 8.40 E
Schwyz □[3] 58 47.05 N 8.40 E
Sciacca 70 37.31 N 13.03 E
Sciara 70 37.55 N 13.45 E
Sciaves (Schabs) 64 46.46 N 11.40 E
Scicli 70 36.47 N 14.42 E
Scie ≃ 50 49.55 N 1.02 E
Science and Industry, Museum of ʋ 278 41.47 N 87.35 W
Sciez 58 46.20 N 6.23 E
Scigliano 68 39.08 N 16.19 E
Ščigry 78 51.53 N 36.55 E
Scilla 68 38.15 N 15.44 E
Scilly, Isles of ɪɪ 42a 49.55 N 6.20 W
Ścinawa 30 51.25 N 16.27 E
Scio, N.Y., U.S. 210 42.10 N 77.59 W
Scio, Oh., U.S. 214 40.23 N 81.05 W
Scio, Or., U.S. 202 44.42 N 122.50 W
Scionzier 58 46.03 N 6.34 E
Sciota 210 40.56 N 75.19 W
Scioto □[6] 218 38.48 N 83.01 W
Scioto ≃ 188 38.44 N 83.01 W
Scioto Brush Creek ≃ 218 38.50 N 83.01 W
Scipio, In., U.S. 218 39.05 N 85.43 W
Scipio, Ut,. U.S. 200 39.14 N 112.06 W
Scipio Center 210 42.47 N 76.34 W
Scippo Creek ≃ 218 39.31 N 82.59 W
Ščit ʌ 36 44.02 N 17.47 E
Ščitkoviči 76 53.13 N 27.59 E
Scituate 207 42.11 N 70.43 W
Scituate Reservoir ⊜[1] 207 41.47 N 71.36 W
Sclafani Bagni 70 37.49 N 13.51 E
Scobey 202 48.47 N 105.25 W
Scoffera, Passo della)(62 44.29 N 9.07 E
Scofield Reservoir ⊜[1] 200 39.47 N 111.09 W
Scoglitti ●[8] 70 36.53 N 14.26 E
Ščokino 76 54.01 N 37.31 E
Scole 42 52.22 N 1.10 E
Ščolkovo 82 55.55 N 38.00 E
Scoltenna ≃ 64 44.15 N 10.50 E
Scolt Head ≻ 42 52.58 N 0.42 E
Scone 166 32.03 S 150.52 E
Scooba 194 32.49 N 88.28 W
Scopello 62 45.46 N 8.06 E
Scordia 70 37.18 N 14.51 E
Scoresby 274b 37.54 S 145.14 E
Scorrano, It. 66 42.35 N 13.49 E
Scorrano, It. 68 40.05 N 18.18 E
Scorzè 64 45.34 N 12.06 E
Scotch ≃ 206 45.27 N 74.59 W
Scotch Plains 210 40.39 N 74.23 W
Scotchtown 210 41.29 N 74.21 W
Scotia, Ne., U.S. 198 41.27 N 98.42 W
Scotia, N.Y., U.S. 210 42.49 N 73.57 W
Scotia Lake ⊜ 190 47.05 N 81.23 W
Scotian Shelf ✢[4] 16 44.00 N 62.00 W
Scotia Ridge ✢[3] 18 54.00 S 50.00 W
Scotia Sea ⊤[2] 9 56.00 S 40.00 W
Scotland, On., Can. 212 43.01 N 80.22 W
Scotland, Pa., U.S. 208 39.58 N 77.35 W
Scotland, S.D., U.S. 198 43.08 N 97.43 W
Scotland, Tx., U.S. 196 33.40 N 98.28 W
Scotland □[8] 28 57.00 N 4.00 W
Scotland Neck 192 36.07 N 77.25 W
Scotland Run ≃ 285 39.39 N 75.03 W
Scotlandville 194 30.31 N 91.10 W
Scotrun 210 41.04 N 75.19 W
Scotsburn 186 45.39 N 62.51 W
Scotstown 206 45.32 N 71.17 W
Scott, Sk., Can. 184 52.23 N 108.50 W
Scott, Ms., U.S. 194 33.35 N 91.04 W
Scott, Oh., U.S. 216 40.59 N 84.35 W
Scott □[6], Il., U.S. 219 39.38 N 90.27 W
Scott □[6], In., U.S. 218 38.41 N 85.46 W
Scott □[6], Ky., U.S. 218 38.18 N 84.35 W
Scott ≃ 204 41.48 N 123.02 W
Scott, Cape ≻ 182 50.47 N 128.26 W
Scott, Mount ʌ, Ok., U.S. 196 34.44 N 98.32 W
Scott, Mount ʌ, Or., U.S. 202 42.56 N 122.01 W
Scott Air Force Base ■ 219 38.32 N 89.52 W
Scott Base ʋ[3] 9 77.50 S 166.25 E
Scottburgh 158 30.19 S 30.40 E
Scott City, Ks., U.S. 198 38.28 N 100.54 W
Scott City, Mo., U.S. 194 37.13 N 89.31 W
Scott Cove c 276 41.03 N 73.28 W
Scott Creek ≃ 226 37.02 N 122.13 W
Scottdale, Mi., U.S. 216 42.03 N 86.27 W
Scottdale, Pa., U.S. 214 40.06 N 79.35 W
Scotter 44 53.29 N 0.40 W
Scott Haven 279b 40.15 N 79.47 W
Scott Island ɪ, Ant. 9 67.24 S 179.55 W
Scott Island ɪ, On., Can. 212 44.36 N 76.20 W
Scott Islands ɪɪ 182 50.48 N 128.40 W
Scott Lake 220 25.56 N 80.13 W
Scott Mountain ʌ 202 44.11 N 115.47 W
Scott Peak ʌ 202 44.21 N 112.50 W
Scott Reef ✢[2] 160 14.00 S 121.50 E
Scott Run ≃ 284c 38.58 N 77.12 W
Scotts 216 42.11 N 85.24 W
Scottsbluff 198 41.52 N 103.40 W
Scotts Bluff National Monument ♠ 198 41.49 N 103.41 W
Scottsboro 194 34.40 N 86.02 W
Scottsburg, In., U.S. 218 38.41 N 85.46 W
Scottsburg, N.Y., U.S. 210 42.40 N 77.43 W
Scottsdale, Austl. 166 41.10 S 147.31 E
Scottsdale, Az., U.S. 200 33.30 N 111.53 W
Scotts Flat Reservoir ⊜[1] 226 39.17 N 120.55 W
Scotts Head ≻ 240d 15.13 N 61.23 W
Scotts Hill 194 35.31 N 88.15 W
Scotts Level Branch ≃ 284b 39.22 N 76.45 W
Scottsmoor 220 28.46 N 80.53 W
Scotts Valley 226 37.03 N 122.00 W
Scottsville, Ky., U.S. 194 36.45 N 86.11 W
Scottsville, N.Y., U.S. 210 43.01 N 77.44 W
Scott Township 279b 40.32 N 80.11 W
Scottville, Il., U.S. 219 39.29 N 90.06 W
Scottville, Mi., U.S. 190 43.57 N 86.16 W
Scourie 46 58.20 N 5.08 W
Scout Lake 184 49.22 N 106.00 W
Scrabster 46 58.37 N 3.32 W
Scranton, Ia., U.S. 198 42.01 N 94.32 W
Scranton, N.Y., U.S. 210 42.44 N 78.50 W
Scranton, N.D., U.S. 198 46.08 N 103.08 W
Scranton, Pa., U.S. 210 41.24 N 75.39 W
Scremerston 44 55.44 N 1.59 W
Screven 192 31.29 N 82.01 W
Screw ≃ 164 3.55 S 142.50 E
Scribner 198 41.40 N 96.39 W
Scridain, Loch c 46 56.21 N 6.07 W
Scripps Institution of Oceanography ʋ[3] 228 32.52 N 117.15 W
Scrivia ≃ 62 45.03 N 8.54 E
Scroggins 222 32.58 N 95.11 W
Scrooby 44 53.25 N 1.01 W
Scrub Island ɪ 240m 18.28 N 64.31 W
Ščučin 76 53.36 N 24.45 E
Ščučinsk 86 52.56 N 70.12 E
Ščučje, Ross. 78 51.45 N 40.29 E
Ščučje, Ross. 80 51.46 N 40.29 E
Ščučje, Ross. 86 55.17 N 63.59 E
Ščučje Ozero 86 56.28 N 56.38 E
Scugog ≃ 212 44.24 N 78.45 W
Scugog, Lake ⊜ 212 44.10 N 78.51 W
Scugog Indian Reserve ●[4] 212 44.11 N 78.54 W
Scugog Island ɪ 212 44.10 N 78.53 W
Ščukino 82 54.28 N 37.01 E
Scunthorpe 44 53.36 N 0.38 W
Scuol (Schuls) 58 46.48 N 10.18 E
Scuppernong ≃ 216 42.54 N 88.42 W
Scurcola Marsicana 66 42.03 N 13.20 E
Ščurovo 82 55.03 N 38.49 E
Scurrival Point ≻ 46 57.04 N 7.31 W
Scurry 222 32.31 N 96.23 W
Scutari
— Shkodër 38 42.05 N 19.30 E
Scutari, Lake ⊜ 38 42.12 N 19.18 E
Sé ●[8] 287b 23.33 S 46.37 W
Seabeck 224 47.38 N 122.51 W
Sea Bird Island ɪ 224 49.15 N 121.45 W
Seabird Island Indian Reserve ●[4] 182 49.17 N 121.42 W
Seaboard 192 36.29 N 77.26 W
Sea Bright 276 40.21 N 73.58 W
Seabrook, Md., U.S. 284c 38.58 N 76.50 W
Seabrook, N.J., U.S. 208 39.30 N 75.13 W
Seabrook, Tx., U.S. 222 29.33 N 95.01 W
Seabrook, Lake ⊜ 162 30.56 S 119.40 E
Sea Cliff 210 40.50 N 73.38 W
Seacock Swamp ≃ 208 36.48 N 76.51 W
Seacombe 262 53.25 N 3.01 W
Sea Dog Island ɪ 276 40.36 N 73.35 W
Seadrift 196 28.30 N 96.47 W
Seaford, Eng., U.K. 42 50.46 N 0.06 E
Seaford, De., U.S. 208 38.38 N 75.36 W
Seaford, N.Y., U.S. 276 40.39 N 73.29 W
Seaford, Va., U.S. 208 37.11 N 76.26 W
Seaford Creek ≃ 276 40.38 N 73.29 W
Seaforth, Austl. 274a 33.48 S 151.15 E
Seaforth, On., Can. 190 43.33 N 81.24 W
Seaforth, Eng., U.K. 262 53.28 N 3.01 W
Seaforth, Loch c 46 57.54 N 6.40 W

Symbol	English	Deutsch	Español	Français	Português
≃	River	Fluß	Río	Rivière	Rio
≊	Canal	Kanal	Canal	Canal	Canal
ʟ	Waterfall, Rapids	Wasserfall, Stromschnellen	Cascada, Rápidos	Chute d'eau, Rapides	Cascata, Rápidos
ʊ	Strait	Meeresstraße	Estrecho	Détroit	Estreito
c	Bay, Gulf	Bucht, Golf	Bahía, Golfo	Baie, Golfe	Baía, Golfo
⊜	Lake, Lakes	See, Seen	Lago, Lagos	Lac, Lacs	Lago, Lagos
≡	Swamp	Sumpf	Pantano	Marais	Pântano
⍓	Ice Features, Glacier	Eis- und Gletscherformen	Accidentes Glaciales	Formes glaciaires	Acidentes glaciares
⊤	Other Hydrographic Features	Andere Hydrographische Objekte	Otros Elementos Hidrográficos	Autres données hydrographiques	Outros acidentes hidrográficos
✢	Submarine Features	Untermeerische Objekte	Accidentes Submarinos	Formes de relief sous-marin	Acidentes submarinos
□	Political Unit	Politische Einheit	Unidad Politica	Entité politique	Unidade política
ʋ	Cultural Institution	Kulturelle Institution	Institución Cultural	Institution culturelle	Instituição cultural
⊥	Historical Site	Historische Stätte	Sitio Histórico	Site historique	Sitio histórico
♠	Recreational Site	Erholungs- und Ferienort	Sitio de Recreo	Centre de loisirs	Area de Lazer
⊠	Airport	Flughafen	Aeropuerto	Aéroport	Aeroporto
■	Military Installation	Militäranlage	Instalación Militar	Installation militaire	Instalação militar
●	Miscellaneous	Verschiedenes	Misceláneo	Divers	Diversos

Seafox Seamount ✦[3] 14 30.30 S 172.45 W
Seager Wheeler Lake ⊜ 184 54.27 N 103.30 W
Seagoville 222 32.38 N 96.32 W
Seagraves 196 32.56 N 102.33 W
Seaham 44 54.52 N 1.21 W
Seaholme 274b 37.52 S 144.50 E
Seahorse Breakers ✦[2] 112 5.30 N 112.37 E
Seahorse Point › 176 63.47 N 80.09 W
Seahouses 44 55.35 N 1.38 W
Seahurst 224 47.28 N 122.22 W
Sea Island I 224 49.12 N 123.10 W
Sea Islands II 192 31.20 N 81.20 W
Sea Isle City 208 39.09 N 74.41 W
Seal 260 51.17 N 0.14 E
Seal ≃ 176 59.04 N 94.48 W
Seal, Cape › 158 34.07 S 23.25 E
Sea Lake 166 35.30 S 142.51 E
Sealand 262 53.12 N 2.58 W
Sealark Channel)(175e 9.18 S 160.20 E
Seal Bay c 9 71.40 S 12.25 W
Seal Beach 228 33.44 N 118.06 W
Seal Beach National Wildlife Refuge ◆[4] 280 33.45 N 118.03 W
Seal Cays II 238 21.10 N 71.38 W
Seal Cove, N.B., Can. 186 44.39 N 66.51 W
Seal Cove, Nf., Can. 186 49.56 N 56.23 W
Sealdah Railroad Station ◆[5] 272b 22.34 N 88.23 E
Seale 194 32.17 N 85.10 W
Sealevel 192 34.51 N 76.23 W
Seal Island I 186 43.25 N 66.01 W
Seal Islands II 282 38.03 N 122.03 W
Seal Lake ⊜ 176 54.18 N 61.40 W
Seal Rocks II[1] 282 37.47 N 122.31 W
Sealston 208 38.15 N 77.19 W
Sealy 222 29.46 N 96.09 W
Seaman 218 38.56 N 83.34 W
Seamer 44 54.14 N 0.26 W
Seanor 214 40.13 N 78.54 W
Seara 252 27.07 S 52.17 W
Searchlight 204 35.27 N 114.55 W
Searcy 194 35.15 N 91.44 W
Searles Lake ⊜ 204 35.43 N 117.20 W
Sears Lake ⊜ 281 42.35 N 83.39 W
Searsport 188 44.27 N 68.55 W
Sears Tower ✤ 278 41.53 N 87.38 W
Searsville Lake ⊜ 282 37.24 N 122.14 W
Seascale 44 54.24 N 3.29 W
Seashore State Park ♠ 208 36.54 N 76.02 W
Seaside, Ca., U.S. 226 36.36 N 121.51 W
Seaside, Or., U.S. 224 45.59 N 123.55 W
Seaside Park 208 39.55 N 74.04 W
Seaside Park ♠ 276 41.10 N 73.12 W
Seaton, Eng., U.K. 42 50.43 N 3.05 W
Seaton, Eng., U.K. 44 54.41 N 3.33 W
Seaton, Eng., U.K. 44 53.54 N 0.14 W
Seaton ≃ 42 50.22 N 4.22 W
Seaton Delaval 44 55.04 N 1.31 W
Seaton Sluice 44 55.05 N 1.28 W
Seat Pleasant 284c 38.53 N 76.54 W
Seattle 224 47.36 N 122.19 W
Seattle, Mount ʌ 180 60.06 N 139.11 W
Seattle Heights 224 47.48 N 122.20 W
Seattle-Tacoma International Airport ⊠ 224 47.27 N 122.18 W
Seatuck National Wildlife Refuge ◆[4] 276 40.43 N 73.13 W
Seaview, Eng., U.K. 42 50.43 N 1.06 W
Sea View, Ma., U.S. 283 42.08 N 70.42 W
Seaview, N.Y., U.S. 276 40.39 N 73.09 W
Seaview, Wa., U.S. 224 46.20 N 124.03 W
Seaward Kaikoura Range ⋏ 172 42.14 S 173.39 E
Seaward Roads)(174g 28.13 N 177.25 W
Sea World ♠, Fl., U.S. 220 28.25 N 81.28 W
Sea World ♠, Oh., U.S. 214 41.21 N 81.23 W
Seba 112 10.29 S 121.50 E
Sébaco 236 12.51 N 86.06 W
Sebago Lake ⊜ 188 43.50 N 70.35 W
Se Bai ≃ 110 15.13 N 104.47 E
Sebakor, Teluk c 164 3.35 S 132.50 E
Sebakung 112 1.37 S 116.26 E
Šebalin 80 47.22 N 43.36 E
Šebalino, Ross. 80 48.16 N 43.21 E
Šebalino, Ross. 86 51.17 N 85.40 E
Sebanga 114 1.24 N 101.10 E
Sebangan, Teluk c 112 3.15 S 113.30 E
Sebangka, Pulau I 112 0.07 N 104.36 E
Sébaou, Oued ≃ 34 36.55 N 3.55 E
Sebarok, Pulau I 271c 1.13 N 103.48 E
Sebastian, Fl., U.S. 220 27.46 N 80.29 W
Sebastian, Tx., U.S. 196 26.20 N 97.47 W
Sebastian, Cape › 202 42.19 N 124.26 W
Sebastian Inlet c 220 27.51 N 80.26 W
Sebastián Vizcaíno, Bahía c 232 28.00 N 114.30 W
Sebastião de Lacerda 256 22.17 S 43.35 W
Sebastopol, Austl. 169 37.36 S 143.51 E
Sebastopol, Ca., U.S. 204 38.24 N 122.49 W
Sebastopol, Ms., U.S. 194 32.34 N 89.20 W
Sebatik, Pulau I 112 4.10 N 117.45 E
Sebba 150 13.26 N 0.32 E
Sebderat 144 15.26 N 36.40 E
Sébé ≃ 152 1.02 S 13.06 E
Sebec Lake ⊜ 188 45.18 N 69.18 W
Sebeka 198 46.38 N 95.05 W
Šebekino 78 50.25 N 36.56 E
Sébékoro 150 12.57 N 8.59 W
Seben 130 40.24 N 31.34 E
Sebenico → Šibenik 36 43.44 N 15.54 E
Sebera, Punta ʌ 71 39.03 N 8.50 E
Seberi 252 27.29 S 53.24 W
Seberida 112 0.43 S 102.31 E
Šeberta 88 54.40 N 99.54 E
Sebeș 38 45.58 N 23.34 E
Sebesi, Pulau I 115a 5.57 S 105.30 E
Sebes Körös (Crișul Repede) ≃ 38 46.55 N 20.59 E
Sebewaing 190 43.43 N 83.27 W
Sebež 76 56.17 N 28.29 E
Sebille Manor 281 42.39 N 82.49 W
Şebinkarahisar 130 40.18 N 38.26 E
Sebiș 38 46.23 N 22.08 E
Sebnitz 54 50.58 N 14.16 E
Sebou, Oued ≃ 148 34.15 N 6.40 W
Sebree 194 37.36 N 87.31 W
Sebrell 208 36.47 N 77.07 W
Sebring, Fl., U.S. 220 27.29 N 81.26 W
Sebring, Oh., U.S. 214 40.55 N 81.01 W
Sebringville 212 43.24 N 81.04 W
Sebuku 112 4.03 N 116.56 E
Sebuku, Pulau I, Indon. 112 3.30 S 116.22 E
Sebuku, Pulau I, Indon. 115a 5.53 S 105.31 E
Sebuku, Teluk c 112 4.00 N 118.26 E
Šebunino 89 46.27 N 141.51 E
Seč 60 49.36 N 13.30 E
Seca, Ilha I 287a 22.50 S 43.11 W
Secane 285 39.55 N 75.18 W
Secang 115a 7.23 S 110.15 E
Secas, Islas II 236 7.58 N 82.02 W
Secaucus 276 40.47 N 74.03 W
Secchia ≃ 64 45.04 N 11.00 E
Sečenovo 80 55.13 N 45.54 E
Secesh ≃ 202 45.02 N 115.43 W
Séchault 56 49.16 N 4.44 E
Sechelt 182 49.28 N 123.45 W
Sechman' 76 52.32 N 40.29 E
Sechura 248 5.33 S 80.51 W
Sechura, Bahía de c 248 5.42 S 81.00 W
Sechura, Desierto de ◆[2] 248 5.50 S 80.40 W
Seckach 56 49.26 N 9.20 E
Seckau 61 47.16 N 14.47 E
Seckau ✤[1] 61 47.16 N 14.47 E
Seckauer Alpen ⋏ 61 47.20 N 14.40 E
Seckauer Zinken ʌ 61 47.20 N 14.44 E
Seclantas 252 25.18 S 66.15 W
Seclin 50 50.33 N 3.02 E
Seco ≃, Arg. 252 23.08 S 63.57 W
Seco ≃, Arg. 254 48.34 S 67.02 W
Seco ≃, Esp. 266d 41.30 N 2.09 E
Seco, Arroyo ≃, Ca., U.S. 226 36.25 N 121.20 W
Seco, Arroyo ≃, Ca., U.S. 280 34.05 N 118.13 W
Seco Creek ≃, N.M., U.S. 200 32.59 N 107.18 W
Seco Creek ≃, Tx., U.S. 196 29.02 N 99.08 W
Seco Island I 116 11.19 N 121.40 E
Second ≃ 276 40.47 N 74.09 W
Second Cliff ⊥[4] 283 42.12 N 70.43 W
Second Han-gang Bridge ◆[5] 271b 37.34 N 126.54 E
Second Herring Brook ≃ 283 42.09 N 70.47 W
Second Lake ⊜ 206 45.09 N 71.10 W
Second Mountain ʌ 208 40.33 N 76.30 W
Second San Diego Aqueduct ≅[1] 228 32.41 N 117.01 W
Second Swamp ≃ 208 37.08 N 77.12 W
Second Valley 168b 35.33 S 138.14 E
Second Watchung Mountain ʌ 276 40.55 N 74.13 W
Sečovce 30 48.43 N 21.40 E
Sečovská Polianka 30 48.47 N 21.42 E
Secretário, Ribeirão do ≃ 256 22.14 S 43.25 W
Secretary 208 38.36 N 75.56 W
Secretary Island I 172 45.15 S 166.55 E
Section 194 34.34 N 85.59 W
Secubun Island I 116 5.06 N 120.18 E
Sécure ≃ 248 15.10 S 64.52 W
Security 198 38.45 N 104.44 W
Security Square ◆[9] 284b 39.19 N 76.45 W
Séd ≃ 30 47.00 N 18.31 E
Seda, Lat. 76 57.40 N 25.46 E
Seda, Liet. 76 56.10 N 22.04 E
Seda, Zhg. 102 32.20 N 100.41 E
Seda ≃ 76 57.47 N 25.15 E
Sedah 112 10.46 S 123.12 E
Sedalia, Ab., Can. 184 51.41 N 110.40 W
Sedalia, In., U.S. 216 40.25 N 86.31 W
Sedalia, Mo., U.S. 194 38.42 N 93.13 W
Sedalia, Oh., U.S. 218 39.44 N 83.29 W
Sedan, Austl. 168b 34.35 S 139.18 E
Sedan, Fr. 56 49.42 N 4.57 E
Sedan, Ks., U.S. 198 37.07 N 96.11 W
Sedanka, Cape › 180 53.49 N 166.06 W
Sedanka Island I 180 53.50 N 166.10 W
Sedano 34 42.43 N 3.45 W
Sedano, Tanjung › 115a 7.49 S 114.27 E
Sedanovo 88 56.58 N 101.22 E
Sedari, Tanjung › 115a 5.57 S 107.18 E
Sedayu 115a 6.59 S 112.33 E
Sedbergh 44 54.20 N 2.31 W
Sedco Hills 228 33.39 N 117.24 W
Seddin 54 52.16 N 13.01 E
Seddin-Berg ʌ[2] 264a 52.24 N 13.40 E
Seddinsee ⊜ 264a 52.23 N 13.41 E
Seddon 172 41.40 S 174.05 E
Seddonville 172 41.33 S 171.59 E
Sedé Boqér 132 30.52 N 34.47 E
Sedel'nikovo 86 56.57 N 75.18 E
Séderon 62 44.12 N 5.32 E
Sederot 132 31.31 N 34.35 E
Sedgefield, Eng., U.K. 44 54.39 N 1.26 W
Sedgefield, N.J., U.S. 276 40.51 N 74.28 W
Sedgefield, N.C., U.S. 192 35.10 N 80.51 W
Sedge Island I 276 40.21 N 73.59 W
Sedgewick 182 52.46 N 111.41 W
Sedgwick, Co., U.S. 198 40.56 N 102.31 W
Sedgwick, Ks., U.S. 198 37.55 N 97.25 W
Sedgwick, Mount ʌ 200 35.11 N 108.06 W
Sédhiou 150 12.44 N 15.33 W
Sedico 64 46.06 N 12.06 E
Sedilo 71 40.10 N 8.55 E
Sedini 71 40.51 N 8.49 E
Sedlčany 30 49.40 N 14.26 E
Sedley 208 36.46 N 76.59 W
Sedlice 60 49.23 N 13.56 E
Sedlitz 54 51.33 N 14.03 E
Sedlo ʌ 54 50.36 N 14.17 E
Sedniv 78 51.39 N 31.34 E
Šedok 84 44.13 N 40.52 E
Sedom (Sodom) ⊥ 132 31.04 N 35.23 E
Sedona 200 34.52 N 111.45 W
Sedot Yam 132 32.29 N 34.53 E
Sedova, pik ʌ 72 73.29 N 54.58 E
Sedrata 36 36.08 N 7.32 E
Sedriano 62 45.29 N 8.58 E
Sedrina 62 45.47 N 9.38 E
Sedro Woolley 224 48.30 N 122.14 W
Sedrun 58 46.41 N 8.46 E
Şedtim 24 66.25 N 56.20 E
Šeduva 76 55.46 N 23.46 E
Sędziszów 30 50.04 N 21.41 E
See 58 47.05 N 10.28 E
Seebad Ahlbeck 54 53.56 N 14.11 E
Seebad Bansin 54 53.57 N 14.07 E
Seebad Heringsdorf 54 53.56 N 14.08 E
Seeberg, Dtsch. 264a 52.33 N 13.41 E
Seeberg, Schw. 58 47.09 N 7.40 E
Seebergsattel)(61 47.38 N 15.18 E
Seeber Lake ⊜ 184 53.52 N 93.03 W
Seeboden 64 46.49 N 13.30 E
Seebruck 64 47.56 N 12.28 E
Seebrugg 58 47.49 N 8.13 E
Seeburg 264a 52.31 N 13.07 E
Seefeld, Dtsch. 52 53.27 N 8.21 E
Seefeld, Dtsch. 54 52.37 N 13.40 E
Seefeld in Tirol 64 47.20 N 11.11 E
Seefin ʌ[2] 48 52.18 N 8.32 W
Seeg 58 47.38 N 10.36 E
Seege ≃ 54 53.04 N 11.23 E
Seegefeld 264a 52.33 N 13.05 E
Seehausen, Dtsch. 54 52.06 N 11.17 E
Seehausen, Dtsch. 54 52.53 N 11.45 E
Seeheim 156 26.50 S 17.45 E
Seeheim-Jugenheim 56 49.45 N 8.38 E
Seehof 264a 52.24 N 13.17 E
Seeis 156 22.29 S 17.39 E
Seekaskootch Indian Reserve ◆[4] 184 53.43 N 109.55 W
Seekoegat 158 33.03 S 22.31 E
Seekoei ≃ 158 30.18 S 25.01 E
Seekonk 207 41.48 N 71.20 W
Seelbach 58 48.18 N 7.56 E
Seeley Lake 202 47.10 N 113.29 W
Seeleys Bay 212 44.29 N 76.14 W
Seelingstädt 54 50.46 N 12.14 E
Seelow 54 52.32 N 14.23 E
Seelyville, In., U.S. 194 39.29 N 87.16 W
Seelyville, Pa., U.S. 210 41.35 N 75.17 W
Seelze 52 52.24 N 9.35 E
Seemade 144 7.10 N 48.36 E
Seemalik Butte ʌ 180 60.09 N 167.08 W
Seemenbach ≃ 56 50.17 N 8.59 E
Seemore Downs 162 30.42 S 125.15 E
Seen 58 47.29 N 8.46 E
Seengen 58 47.19 N 8.13 E
Seeon 64 47.58 N 12.26 E
Seer Green 260 51.37 N 0.36 W
Seergu 102 32.00 N 103.33 E
Seerhausen 54 51.16 N 13.15 E
Sées 50 48.36 N 0.10 E
Seesen 52 51.53 N 10.10 E
Seeshaupt 64 47.49 N 11.18 E
Seest 41 55.29 N 9.27 E
Seetal 61 47.09 N 13.57 E
Seetaler Alpen ⋏ 61 47.05 N 14.35 E
Seevetal 52 53.23 N 9.59 E
Seewalchen am Attersee 64 47.57 N 13.35 E
Seewiesen 61 47.37 N 15.16 E
Seewinkel ◆[1] 61 47.48 N 16.49 E
Seewis 58 47.00 N 9.32 E
Séez 62 45.37 N 6.48 E
Seez ≃ 58 47.07 N 9.18 E
Şefaatli 130 39.31 N 34.46 E
Šefadu 150 8.39 N 10.59 W
Sefar ⊥ 148 24.27 N 9.16 E
Sefare 156 23.02 S 27.28 E
Seferihisar 130 38.11 N 26.51 E
Séféto 150 14.08 N 9.49 W
Seffern 56 50.04 N 6.30 E
Seffner 220 27.59 N 82.17 W
Sefīd ≃ 128 37.26 N 49.55 E
Sefīd Ābeh 128 30.56 N 60.35 E
Sefrou 148 33.50 N 4.50 W
Sefton, N.Z. 172 43.15 S 172.40 E
Sefton, Eng., U.K. 262 53.30 N 2.58 W
Sefton □[8] 262 53.34 N 3.14 W
Sefton, Mount ʌ 172 43.41 S 170.03 E
Sefton Park ♠ 262 53.23 N 2.56 W
Segag 144 7.40 N 42.50 E
Segaliud ≃ 116 5.43 N 117.55 E
Segama ≃ 112 5.27 N 118.48 E
Segamat 114 2.30 N 102.49 E
Segang 100 31.58 N 114.18 E
Segangane 34 35.09 N 3.00 W
Şegarcea 38 44.06 N 23.45 E
Šegarka ≃ 86 57.16 N 84.05 E
Segbana 150 10.56 N 3.42 E
Segbwema 150 8.00 N 10.57 W
Segen ≃ 144 4.49 N 36.57 E
Segera 164 8.15 S 143.30 E
Segeri 112 4.39 S 119.33 E
Segesta ⊥ 70 37.56 N 12.50 E
Segesvár → Sighișoara 38 46.13 N 24.48 E
Segeža 24 63.44 N 34.19 E
Seggiano 66 42.56 N 11.33 E
Seggueur, Oued es V 148 31.39 N 2.26 E
Šegmas 24 64.43 N 49.14 E
Segni 66 41.41 N 13.01 E
Segno 222 30.35 N 94.41 W
Segorbe 34 39.51 N 0.29 W
Ségou 150 13.27 N 6.16 W
Ségou □[4] 150 14.00 N 5.40 E
Šegovary 24 62.23 N 42.57 E
Segovia, Col. 246 7.07 N 74.42 W
Segovia, Esp. 34 40.57 N 4.07 W
Segovia □[4] 34 41.15 N 4.00 W
Segozero, ozero ⊜ 24 63.18 N 33.45 E
Segrate 266b 45.29 N 9.19 E
Segré 32 47.41 N 0.53 W
Segre ≃ 34 41.22 N 0.20 E
Seguam Island I 180 52.17 N 172.30 W
Seguam Pass)(180 52.08 N 172.45 W
Séguédine 146 20.12 N 12.59 E
Séguéla, C. Iv. 150 7.57 N 6.40 W
Séguéla, Mali 150 14.07 N 6.44 W
Séguélon 150 9.25 N 7.09 W
Séguénéga 150 13.27 N 1.58 W
Seguí 252 31.57 S 60.08 W
Seguin 196 29.34 N 97.57 W
Seguin ≃ 212 45.21 N 80.01 W
Seguine Point › 276 40.31 N 74.12 W
Segula Island I 181a 52.01 N 178.07 E
Segundo 198 37.07 N 104.45 W
Segundo ≃ 252 31.21 S 62.59 W
Seguntur 112 1.54 N 117.47 E
Segura 34 39.50 N 6.59 W
Segura ≃ 34 38.06 N 0.38 W
Segura, Sierra de ⋏ 34 38.00 N 2.43 W
Sehāni Kalān 272a 28.41 N 77.25 E
Sehāni Khurd 272a 28.42 N 77.25 E
Sehāra Bāzār 126 23.06 N 87.49 E
Sehithwa 156 20.23 S 22.45 E
Sehlabathebe 158 29.53 S 29.05 E
Sehlabathebe National Park ♠ 158 29.53 S 29.06 E
Sehma 54 50.32 N 13.00 E
Sehnde 52 52.18 N 9.57 E
Sehnkwehn 150 5.13 N 9.12 W
Sehnkwehn ≃ 150 5.12 N 9.21 W
Sehore 124 23.12 N 77.05 E
Sehwān 120 26.26 N 67.52 E
Sehyŏn-ni 98 38.20 N 127.41 E
Seia 34 40.25 N 7.42 W
Seibert 198 39.18 N 102.52 W
Seibu 268 35.50 N 139.22 E
Seiches-sur-le-Loir 32 47.35 N 0.22 W
Seidan 96 34.19 N 134.45 E
Seidersville 210 40.35 N 75.23 W
Seiersberg 61 47.01 N 15.24 E
Seiffen 54 50.39 N 13.26 E
Seifhennersdorf 54 50.56 N 14.36 E
Seignelay 50 47.54 N 3.36 E
Seigneurial, Lac ⊜ 275a 45.33 N 73.20 W
Seika 270 34.46 N 135.48 E
Seikpyu 110 20.55 N 94.47 E
Seil I 46 56.18 N 5.39 W
Seiland I 24 70.25 N 23.15 E
Seilhac 32 45.22 N 1.42 E
Seiling 196 36.08 N 98.55 W
Seillans 62 43.38 N 6.38 E
Seille ≃, Fr. 56 49.07 N 6.11 E
Seille ≃, Fr. 58 46.31 N 4.56 E
Seilo 140 12.20 N 23.50 E
Seim → Sejm ≃ 78 51.27 N 32.34 E
Sein, Île de I 32 48.02 N 4.51 W
Seinaiji 94 35.30 N 137.42 E
Seinäjoki 26 62.47 N 22.50 E
Seine ≃, Mb., Can. 184 49.54 N 97.07 W
Seine ≃, On., Can. 190 48.40 N 92.49 W
Seine ≃, Fr. 32 49.26 N 0.26 E
Seine, Baie de la c 32 49.30 N 0.30 W
Seine-et-Marne □[5] 50 48.30 N 3.00 E
Seine-Maritime □[5] 50 49.45 N 1.00 E
Seine-Port 50 48.33 N 2.33 E
Seine-Saint-Denis □[5] 261 48.55 N 2.30 E
Seip Mound State Memorial ⊥ 218 39.15 N 83.13 W
Seipstown 208 40.35 N 75.40 W
Seis de Septiembre → Morón 258 34.39 S 58.37 W
Seishin → Ch'ŏngjin 98 41.47 N 129.50 E
Seitenstetten 61 48.02 N 14.39 E
Seitovka 80 46.43 N 48.03 E
Seitsemisen kansallispuisto ♠ 26 61.58 N 23.20 E
Seiwa 94 34.29 N 136.30 E
Seixal 34 38.38 N 9.06 W
Seixas, Ponta do › 250 7.09 S 34.47 W
Seiz 61 47.23 N 14.55 E
Seize Îles, Lac des ⊜ 206 45.54 N 74.28 W
Sejaka 112 3.34 S 116.12 E
Sejerø I 41 55.53 N 11.09 E
Sejerø Bugt c 41 55.50 N 11.15 E
Sejm (Seym) ≃ 78 51.27 N 32.34 E
Şejmčan 74 62.53 N 152.26 E
Šejno 80 53.22 N 43.12 E
Sejny 30 54.07 N 23.20 E
Sejorong 115b 9.02 S 116.48 E
Sejs 41 56.09 N 9.36 E
Sekači 80 50.30 N 43.37 E
Sekadau 112 0.01 S 110.54 E
Sekake 158 29.58 S 28.27 E
Sekampung ≃ 115a 5.36 S 105.50 E
Sekayam ≃ 112 0.07 N 110.38 E
Sekayu 112 2.51 S 103.51 E
Seke, Ityo. 144 9.56 N 38.19 E
Seke, Tan. 154 3.20 S 33.31 E
Seke-Banza 152 5.20 S 13.16 E
Sekeladi 112 2.38 S 102.14 E
Sekenke 154 4.16 S 34.10 E
Şekerli 130 37.33 N 39.22 E
Šeki, Azer. 84 41.12 N 47.12 E
Šeki, Nihon 94 35.29 N 136.55 E
Seki, Nihon 94 34.51 N 136.24 E
Seki, Tür. 130 36.24 N 29.13 E
Sekidō-san ʌ 94 36.58 N 136.59 E
Sekigahara 94 35.22 N 136.28 E
Sekigane 96 35.22 N 133.46 E
Sekijō 94 36.14 N 139.55 E
Sekima 112 1.41 S 111.31 E
Sekinomiya 96 35.22 N 134.38 E
Sekiu 224 48.15 N 124.18 W
Sekiya 270 34.27 N 135.42 E
Sekiyado 94 36.06 N 139.47 E
Seki-zaki › 96 33.15 N 131.54 E
Sekoma 156 24.41 S 23.50 E
Sekondi-Takoradi 150 4.59 N 1.43 W
Sekota 144 12.38 N 39.03 E
Sekpiegu 150 9.33 N 0.02 W
Sekretaris ≃ 269e 6.10 S 106.47 E
Şekretarka 80 52.36 N 44.11 E
Šekšema 80 58.22 N 45.11 E
Šeksna 76 59.13 N 38.30 E
Sekudai 114 1.32 N 103.40 E
Sela ≃[1] 126 21.54 N 89.39 E
Şela, Ponta da › 256 23.54 S 45.27 W
Šelabolicha 86 53.25 N 82.37 E
Şela Dingay 144 9.59 N 39.33 E
Šelagskij, mys › 74 70.06 N 170.26 E
Selah 202 46.39 N 120.31 W
Şelai ≃ 114 2.13 N 103.26 E
Šelajevo 88 56.56 N 97.42 E
Şelama 114 5.13 N 100.42 E
Šelanger 80 56.13 N 48.16 E
Selangor □[3] 114 3.20 N 101.30 E
Selangor ≃ 114 3.20 N 101.15 E
Selaön I 40 59.24 N 17.12 E
Selaphum 110 16.02 N 103.57 E
Selargius 71 39.16 N 9.10 E
Selaru, Pulau I 164 8.09 S 131.00 E
Selatan, Tanjung › 112 4.10 S 114.38 E
Selatpanjang 114 1.00 N 102.43 E
Selawik 180 66.37 N 160.03 W
Selawik ≃ 180 66.36 N 160.20 W
Selawik Lake ⊜ 180 66.30 N 160.40 W
Selayar, Pulau I 112 6.05 S 120.30 E
Selayar, Selat)(112 5.42 S 120.28 E
Selb 54 50.10 N 12.08 E
Selbeck ◆[8] 263 51.22 N 6.52 E
Selbecke ◆[8] 263 51.20 N 7.28 E
Selbitz 54 50.19 N 11.44 E
Selborne 42 51.06 N 0.56 W
Selbu 26 63.13 N 11.02 E
Selbusjøen ⊜ 26 63.14 N 10.54 E
Selby, Austl. 274b 37.55 S 145.22 E
Selby, Eng., U.K. 44 53.48 N 1.04 W
Selby, S.D., U.S. 198 45.30 N 100.01 W
Selby ◆[8] 273d 26.13 S 28.02 E
Selbyville 208 38.27 N 75.13 W
Selchow 264a 52.21 N 13.28 E
Sel'co, Ross. 24 63.18 N 41.22 E
Sel'co, Ross. 76 53.22 N 34.06 E
Selcourt 273d 26.18 S 28.27 E
Selčuga ≃ 89 49.42 N 133.20 E
Selçuk 130 37.56 N 27.22 E
Sel'cy, Ross. 76 57.57 N 35.59 E
Sel'cy, Ross. 265a 59.57 N 30.43 E
Selden, Ks., U.S. 198 39.32 N 100.34 W
Selden, N.Y., U.S. 210 40.51 N 73.02 W
Seldovia 180 59.27 N 151.43 W
Sele ≃ 68 40.29 N 14.56 E
Sele, Piana del ≚ 68 40.33 N 14.57 E
Sele, Selat)(164 1.10 S 131.05 E
Sele, Tanjung › 164 1.26 S 130.55 E
Selebi Phikwe 156 22.00 S 27.50 E
Selec 76 52.33 N 33.35 E
Şelec-Cholopejev 76 53.23 N 30.24 E
Šelechov 88 52.13 N 104.08 E
Selečn'a 76 52.23 N 34.23 E
Selection Park 273d 26.18 S 28.27 E
Selegas 71 39.34 N 9.06 E
Selemadeg 115b 8.29 S 115.02 E
Selembao 273b 4.22 S 15.17 E
Selemdža ≃ 89 51.42 N 128.53 E
Şelemdžinsk 89 52.36 N 131.08 E
Šelemeti 80 57.27 N 48.07 E
Selendi 130 38.45 N 28.53 E
Selenduma 88 50.55 N 106.10 E
Selenga (Selenge) ≃ 88 52.16 N 106.16 E
Selenge, Mong. 88 49.25 N 103.59 E
Selenge, Zaïre 152 1.58 S 18.11 E
Selenge □[4] 88 49.30 N 106.30 E
Selenge (Selenga) ≃ 88 52.16 N 106.16 E
Selenginsk 88 52.06 N 107.01 E
Selenicë 38 40.32 N 19.38 E
Selenn'ach ≃ 74 67.48 N 144.54 E
Selent 54 54.17 N 10.26 E
Selenter See ⊜ 54 54.17 N 10.28 E
Sélestat (Schlettstadt) 58 48.16 N 7.27 E
Seletar ≃ 271c 1.25 N 103.52 E
Seletar, Pulau I 271c 1.27 N 103.52 E
Seletar Airport ⊠ 271c 1.16 N 103.53 E
Seletar Hills 271c 1.23 N 103.53 E
Seletar Reservoir ⊜[1] 271c 1.24 N 103.48 E
Selety ≃ 86 53.06 N 73.22 E
Seletyteniz, ozero ⊜ 86 53.15 N 73.15 E
Selezen'ovo, Ross. 26 60.45 N 28.39 E
Selezen'ovo, Ross. 76 59.12 N 42.18 E
Selezni, Ross. 76 55.39 N 31.29 E
Selezni, Ross. 80 52.48 N 41.15 E
Selezn'ovo 76 60.45 N 28.39 E
Self Defense Fleet Headquarters ■ 268 35.18 N 139.38 E
Selfoss 24a 63.56 N 20.57 W
Selfridge 198 46.02 N 100.55 W
Selfridge Air National Guard Base ■ 281 42.36 N 82.49 W
Selghar 272c 18.57 N 73.02 E
Sel'gon 89 49.36 N 135.26 E
Sélibaby 150 15.10 N 12.11 W
Şelichino 89 50.22 N 137.38 E
Šelichova, zaliv c 74 60.00 N 158.00 E
Šelichovo 88 55.42 N 97.41 E
Seligenthal 54 50.45 N 10.28 E
Seliger, ozero ⊜ 76 57.13 N 33.05 E
Seligman, Az., U.S. 200 35.19 N 112.52 W
Seligman, Mo., U.S. 194 36.31 N 93.56 W
Selim 114 3.51 N 101.29 E
Selimbau 112 0.37 N 112.08 E
Selimiye 130 37.24 N 27.40 E
Selim River 114 3.50 N 101.24 E
Selínia 267c 37.56 N 23.32 E
Selinsgrove 208 40.47 N 76.51 W
Selinunte ⊥ 70 37.35 N 12.49 E
Selišče, Ross. 24 64.58 N 46.18 E
Selišče, Ross. 76 56.53 N 33.16 E
Selitrennoje 80 47.11 N 47.27 E
Selivanovskaja 80 48.52 N 41.42 E
Seližarovo 76 56.51 N 33.27 E
Selje 26 62.03 N 5.22 E
Seljord 26 59.29 N 8.37 E
Selkämeri (Bottenhavet) c 26 62.00 N 20.00 E
Selke ≃ 54 51.52 N 11.14 E
Selkirk, Mb., Can. 184 50.09 N 96.52 W
Selkirk, On., Can. 212 42.49 N 79.56 W
Selkirk, Scot., U.K. 46 55.33 N 2.50 W
Selkirk, N.Y., U.S. 210 42.32 N 73.48 W
Selkirk Mountains ⋏ 182 51.00 N 117.40 W
Selkirk Provincial Park ♠ 212 42.49 N 79.58 W
Selkirk Shores State Park ♠ 212 43.33 N 76.12 W
Šelkovka 82 55.32 N 36.22 E
Šelkovskaja 84 43.30 N 46.22 E
Sella 64 46.00 N 11.25 E
Sella, Monte ʌ 64 46.40 N 12.02 E
Sella, Passo di (Sellajoch))(64 46.30 N 11.45 E
Sella di Corno 66 42.21 N 13.14 E
Sellano 66 42.54 N 12.55 E
Selle ≃ 50 49.54 N 2.17 E
Seller Lake ⊜ 184 55.00 N 94.32 W
Sellero 64 46.03 N 10.20 E
Sellers 192 34.17 N 79.28 W
Sellersburg 218 38.23 N 85.45 W
Sellersville 208 40.21 N 75.18 W
Selles-sur-Cher 50 47.16 N 1.33 E
Sellia Marina 68 38.55 N 16.45 E
Sellières 58 46.50 N 5.34 E
Sellin 54 54.22 N 13.41 E
Sells 200 31.54 N 111.52 W
Selly Oak ◆[8] 42 52.25 N 1.52 W
Selm 52 51.42 N 7.28 E
Selma, Al., U.S. 194 32.24 N 87.01 W
Selma, Ca., U.S. 226 36.34 N 119.36 W
Selma, In., U.S. 218 40.11 N 85.16 W
Selma, N.C., U.S. 192 35.32 N 78.17 W
Selman City 222 32.11 N 94.58 W
Selmer 194 35.10 N 88.35 W
Selmigerheide ◆[8] 263 51.38 N 7.47 E
Selmont 194 32.23 N 87.01 W
Selmsdorf 54 53.48 N 10.50 E
Şelommes 50 47.45 N 1.12 E
Šelon' ≃ 76 58.14 N 30.50 E
Seloncourt 58 47.28 N 6.52 E
Selong 115b 8.39 S 116.32 E
Şelongey 58 47.35 N 5.10 E
Šelopugino 88 51.39 N 117.33 E
Selouane 34 35.04 N 2.58 W
Selous, Mount ʌ 180 62.57 N 132.31 W
Selous Game Reserve ◆[4] 154 9.10 S 37.10 E
Selsdon ◆[8] 260 51.21 N 0.04 W
Selsey 42 50.44 N 0.48 W
Selsey Bill › 42 50.43 N 0.48 W
Selsingen 52 53.22 N 9.13 E
Selston 44 53.04 N 1.20 W
Selters 56 50.32 N 7.44 E
Selty 80 57.19 N 52.10 E
Seltz 56 48.53 N 8.06 E
Selu, Pulau I 164 7.32 S 130.54 E
Selva, Arg. 252 29.46 S 62.03 W
Selva, It. 64 46.33 N 11.46 E
Sel'vačevo 82 55.25 N 37.57 E
Selva di Cadore 64 46.27 N 12.02 E
Selvagens, Ilhas II 148 30.05 N 15.55 W
Selvas ◆[3] 242 5.00 S 68.00 W
Selvino 62 45.48 N 9.45 E
Selway ≃ 202 46.08 N 115.36 W
Selwyn 166 21.32 S 140.30 E
Selwyn, Mount ʌ 182 55.59 N 123.36 W
Selwyn, Passage)(175f 16.03 S 168.12 E
Selwyn Lake ⊜ 176 59.55 N 104.35 W
Selwyn Mountains ⋏ 180 63.10 N 130.20 W
Selwyn Range ⋏ 166 21.35 S 140.35 E
Selyatyn 78 47.53 N 25.12 E
Selydove 83 48.08 N 37.18 E
Şelz ≃ 56 49.59 N 8.02 E
Šemacha 86 56.15 N 59.16 E
Semai, Pulau I 164 3.08 S 132.30 E
Semakau, Pulau I 271c 1.12 N 103.46 E
Seman ≃ 38 40.56 N 19.24 E
Semanggol 114 4.57 N 100.38 E
Şemangka, Teluk c 112 5.36 S 104.42 E
Šemanicha 80 57.18 N 45.24 E
Semans 184 51.25 N 104.44 W
Semanu 115a 8.00 S 110.39 E
Semarang 115a 6.58 S 110.25 E
Semaria 124 24.16 N 79.54 E
Sematan 112 1.48 N 109.46 E
Semau, Pulau I 112 10.13 S 123.22 E
Semayang, Kenohan ⊜ 112 0.14 S 116.28 E
Sembabule 154 0.05 S 31.27 E
Sembadel 62 45.16 N 3.41 E
Sembakung ≃ 112 3.47 N 117.30 E
Sembawang 271c 1.27 N 103.50 E
Sembé 152 1.39 N 14.36 E
Semberong ≃ 114 2.27 N 103.37 E
Semblançay 50 47.30 N 0.35 E
Sembo ≃ 152 7.42 S 13.01 E
Semcy 76 52.51 N 33.28 E
Şemdinli 128 37.18 N 44.35 E
Šemeliškės 76 54.40 N 24.40 E
Semenanjung Malaysia □[9] 114 4.00 N 102.00 E
Semendua 152 3.11 S 18.05 E
Semène ≃ 62 45.23 N 4.13 E
Semenicului, Munții ⋏ 38 45.05 N 22.05 E
Semenivka, Ukr. 78 49.36 N 33.10 E
Semenivka, Ukr. 78 52.10 N 32.35 E
Semenyih 114 2.57 N 101.51 E
Semertak 89 52.57 N 132.34 E
Şemeru, Gunung ʌ 115a 8.06 S 112.55 E
Šemetovo 82 54.28 N 38.30 E
Semeževo 76 52.58 N 27.00 E
Semiahmoo Bay c 224 48.58 N 122.48 W
Semibalki 83 47.00 N 39.03 E
Semibratovo 80 57.18 N 39.32 E
Semibugry 80 46.11 N 48.16 E
Semichi Islands II 181a 52.42 N 174.00 E
Semides'atnoje 78 51.21 N 38.44 E
Semidi Islands II 180 56.07 N 156.44 W
Semigorsk 88 56.42 N 104.41 E
Semijarka 86 50.54 N 78.20 E
Semikarakorsk 80 47.31 N 40.48 E
Semilej 80 53.57 N 45.21 E
Semilovo 80 55.04 N 42.10 E
Semiluki 78 51.41 N 39.02 E
Semily 30 50.36 N 15.20 E
Seminara 68 38.20 N 15.52 E
Seminary 194 31.33 N 89.29 W
Seminoe Reservoir ⊜[1] 200 42.00 N 106.50 W
Seminoe State Park ♠ 202 42.05 N 106.55 W
Seminole, Fl., U.S. 220 27.50 N 82.47 W
Seminole, Ok., U.S. 196 35.13 N 96.40 W
Seminole, Tx., U.S. 196 32.43 N 102.38 W
Seminole □[6] 220 28.45 N 81.13 W
Seminole, Lake ⊜[1] 192 30.46 N 84.50 W
Seminole Draw V 196 32.27 N 102.20 W
Seminole Park 220 27.52 N 82.45 W
Seminskij chrebet ⋏ 86 51.05 N 85.50 E
Semiozerje 88 49.52 N 110.23 E
Semioz'ornoje 86 52.22 N 64.08 E
Semioz'ornyj 88 53.44 N 120.25 E
Semipalatinsk 86 50.28 N 80.13 E
Semipalatinsk □[8] 86 49.00 N 80.00 E
Semipolka 86 54.07 N 67.16 E
Semirara Island I 116 12.04 N 121.23 E
Semisopochnoi Island I 181a 52.00 N 179.35 E
Semitau 112 0.33 N 111.58 E
Semizbugy 86 50.12 N 74.48 E
Semizbugy, gora ʌ 86 50.10 N 74.56 E
Semjany 80 56.02 N 45.59 E
Semli Kalān 124 24.10 N 76.39 E
Seml'ovo 76 55.03 N 33.58 E
Semmens Lake ⊜ 184 55.03 N 94.11 W
Semmering 61 47.38 N 15.49 E
Semnān 128 35.33 N 53.24 E
Semnān □[4] 128 35.30 N 54.00 E
Şemois ≃ 56 49.53 N 4.45 E
Šemonaicha 86 50.39 N 81.54 E
Sem'ono-Aleksandrovka 78 51.03 N 40.12 E
Sem'onov 24 56.48 N 44.30 E
Sem'onovka, Kaz. 86 51.20 N 70.46 E
Sem'onovka, Kyrg. 85 42.43 N 77.32 E
Sem'onovskoje, Ross. 82 55.03 N 37.46 E
Sem'onovskoje, Ross. 82 55.18 N 38.21 E
Šemordan 80 56.11 N 50.26 E
Sempach 58 47.08 N 8.11 E
Sempacher See ⊜ 58 47.09 N 8.09 E
Sempang Mangayau, Tanjong › 112 7.02 N 116.45 E
Semple Lake ⊜ 184 55.02 N 95.38 W
Sempol 115a 8.01 S 114.08 E
Semporna 112 4.28 N 118.36 E
Sempu, Pulau I 115a 8.26 S 112.42 E
Semuda 112 2.51 S 112.58 E
Semuliki ≃ 154 1.14 N 30.28 E
Şemur-en-Auxois 50 47.29 N 4.20 E
Šemurša 80 54.53 N 47.32 E
Şemypolky 78 50.43 N 30.56 E
Šemyšejka 80 52.54 N 45.24 E
Semža 24 66.09 N 44.08 E
Sên ≃ 110 12.32 N 104.28 E
Sena, Bol. 248 11.32 S 67.11 W
Sena, Moç. 154 17.27 S 35.00 E
Sena → Seine ≃ 32 49.26 N 0.26 E
Senador Amaral 256 22.35 S 46.11 W
Senador Canedo 255 16.43 S 49.05 W
Senador Côrtes 256 21.48 S 42.56 W
Senador Firmino 255 20.55 S 43.06 W
Senador Guiomard 248 10.14 S 67.36 W
Senador José Bento 256 22.10 S 46.10 W
Senador José Porfírio 250 2.39 S 51.55 W
Senador Pompeu 250 5.35 S 39.22 W
Senago 266b 45.35 N 9.07 E
Senahú 236 15.24 N 89.50 W
Senai 114 1.36 N 103.39 E
Senainville 261 48.30 N 1.37 E
Senaja 112 6.45 N 117.03 E
Senaki 84 42.17 N 42.04 E
Senale 64 46.31 N 11.06 E
Senales, Val di V 64 46.45 N 10.50 E
Sena Madureira 248 9.04 S 68.40 W
Senamaninik 114 0.45 N 100.47 E
Senanayake Samudra ⊜[1] 122 7.11 N 81.29 E
Senang, Pulau I 271c 1.11 N 103.44 E
Senanga 152 16.06 S 23.16 E
Sénart, Forêt de ♠ 261 48.40 N 2.30 E
Sénas 62 43.45 N 5.05 E
Senate 184 49.18 N 109.41 W
Senath 194 36.08 N 90.09 W
Şenatobia 194 34.37 N 89.58 W
Šenber 86 49.46 N 66.09 E
Šenbertal 86 48.43 N 60.20 E
Sencha 78 50.16 N 33.20 E
Send 260 51.17 N 0.31 W
Sendafa 144 9.07 N 39.00 E
Sendai, Nihon 92 31.49 N 130.18 E
Sendai, Nihon 92 38.15 N 140.53 E
Sendai ≃, Nihon 92 31.51 N 130.12 E
Sendai ≃, Nihon 96 35.32 N 134.11 E
Sendai-heiya ≚ 92 38.15 N 141.00 E
Sendelingsdrif 156 28.12 S 16.53 E
Senden, Dtsch. 52 51.51 N 7.29 E
Senden, Dtsch. 58 48.19 N 10.03 E
Sendenhorst 52 51.50 N 7.49 E
Sendhwa 120 21.41 N 75.06 E
Sêndo 102 31.42 N 95.16 E
Sendurjana 120 21.32 N 78.17 E
Senduruhan 112 1.00 S 110.46 E
Sene ≃ 150 7.30 N 0.33 W
Senebui, Tanjung › 114 2.17 N 101.03 E
Senec 30 48.14 N 17.24 E
Seneca, Il., U.S. 216 41.18 N 88.36 W
Seneca, Ks., U.S. 198 39.50 N 96.03 W
Seneca, Md., U.S. 284c 39.04 N 77.17 W
Seneca, Mo., U.S. 194 36.50 N 94.36 W
Seneca, Or., U.S. 202 44.08 N 118.58 W
Seneca, Pa., U.S. 214 41.23 N 79.42 W
Seneca, S.C., U.S. 192 34.41 N 82.57 W
Seneca □[6], N.Y., U.S. 210 42.54 N 76.52 W
Seneca □[6], Oh., U.S. 214 41.07 N 83.11 W
Seneca ≃ 210 43.12 N 76.17 W
Seneca, Mount ʌ 210 42.01 N 78.49 W
Seneca Castle 210 42.53 N 77.06 W
Seneca Caverns ⊥[5] 214 41.11 N 82.53 W
Seneca Creek c 284b 39.19 N 76.22 W
Seneca Creek ≃ 196 36.36 N 102.52 W
Seneca Falls 210 42.54 N 76.47 W
Seneca Lake ⊜ 210 42.40 N 76.57 W
Seneca Mall ◆[9] 284a 42.50 N 78.47 W
Seneca State Park ♠ 208 39.08 N 77.15 W
Senecaville Lake ⊜[1] 188 39.55 N 81.25 W
Seneffe 50 50.31 N 4.15 E
Senegal (Sénégal) □[1], Afr. 134 14.00 N 14.00 W
Senegal (Sénégal) □[1], Afr. 150 14.00 N 14.00 W
Sénégal ≃ 150 15.48 N 16.32 W
Seneghe 71 40.05 N 8.36 E
Senekal 158 28.19 S 27.36 E
Senerchia 68 40.44 N 15.12 E
Senetosa, Capu di › 71 41.33 N 8.47 E
Sénez 62 43.55 N 6.24 E
Senežskoje, ozero ⊜ 82 56.12 N 37.00 E
Senftenberg 54 51.31 N 14.00 E
Senga Hill 154 9.22 S 31.12 E
Sengbachstausee ⊜[1] 263 51.08 N 7.09 E
Şengejskij, ostrov I 24 68.27 N 51.05 E
Šengel'šij 86 48.33 N 57.28 E
Sengés 255 24.06 S 49.29 W
Senggarang 114 1.45 N 103.03 E
Sênggê ≃ 120 32.28 N 79.44 E
Senghenydd 42 51.36 N 3.16 W
Sengilej 80 53.58 N 48.46 E
Sengkamang 114 0.42 N 101.55 E
Sengsengebirge ⋏ 61 47.47 N 14.15 E
Senguer ≃ 254 45.32 S 68.54 W
Sengwa ≃ 154 17.07 S 28.05 E
Sengwarden 52 53.35 N 8.02 E
Senhāti 126 22.53 N 89.33 E
Senhor do Bonfim 250 10.27 S 40.11 W
Senica 30 48.41 N 17.22 E
Senigallia 66 43.43 N 13.13 E
Senirkent 130 38.07 N 30.33 E
Senise 68 40.09 N 16.18 E
Senj 36 44.59 N 14.54 E
Senja I 24 69.20 N 17.30 E
Senjitu 98 41.56 N 116.25 E
Senjō-san ʌ 96 35.26 N 133.36 E
Senkaku-shotō II 90 25.45 N 124.00 E
Senkevychivka 78 50.32 N 25.02 E
Senkobo 154 17.38 S 25.58 E
Sen'kove 83 49.31 N 37.43 E
Şenköy 130 36.05 N 36.05 E
Šenkursk 24 62.08 N 42.53 E
Senlac 184 52.29 N 109.41 W
Şenlikköy ◆[8] 267b 40.59 N 28.47 E
Šenlis 50 49.12 N 2.35 E
Senlisse 261 48.41 N 1.59 E
Senmonorom 110 12.27 N 107.12 E
Senn, Ḑahr ou ⊥[4] 150 18.30 N 11.00 W
Sennaja 78 45.15 N 37.01 E
Sennan 96 34.22 N 135.17 E
Senne (Zenne) ≃ 50 51.04 N 4.26 E
Sennecey-le-Grand 58 46.39 N 4.52 E
Senne II → Sennestadt 52 51.59 N 8.37 E
Sennen 42 50.04 N 5.42 W
Sennestadt 52 51.59 N 8.37 E
Senneterre 190 48.23 N 77.15 W
Senneville 275a 45.27 N 73.57 W
Sennevoy-le-Bas 50 47.48 N 4.17 E
Senno 76 54.49 N 29.43 E
Sennoj, Ross. 80 52.11 N 46.57 E
Sennoj, Ross. 80 50.16 N 43.37 E
Sennokura-yama ʌ 94 36.49 N 138.50 E
Sennori 71 40.47 N 8.35 E
Sennwald 58 47.16 N 9.30 E
Sennybridge 42 51.57 N 3.34 W
Senoia 192 33.18 N 84.33 W
Senonches 50 48.33 N 1.02 E
Senones 58 48.24 N 6.59 E
Senorbì 71 39.32 N 9.08 E
Sénou 150 12.31 N 6.56 W
Sénouire ≃ 62 45.11 N 3.34 E
Şenpazar 130 41.48 N 33.16 E

Symbols in the index entries represent the broad categories identified in the key at the right. Symbols with superior numbers (⋏[1]) identify subcategories (see complete key on page *I · 1).*

Symbole im Register stellen die rechts im Schlüssel erklärten Kategorien dar. Symbole mit hochgestellten Ziffern (⋏[1]) bezeichnen Unterabteilungen einer Kategorie (vgl. vollständiger Schlüssel auf Seite *I · 1).*

Los símbolos incluídos en el texto del índice representan las grandes categorías identificadas con la clave a la derecha. Los símbolos con numeros en su parte superior (⋏[1]) identifican las subcategorías (véase la clave completa en la página *I · 1).*

Les symboles de l'index représentent les catégories indiquées dans la légende à droite. Les symboles suivis d'un indice (⋏[1]) représentent des sous-catégories (voir légende complète à la page *I · 1).*

Os símbolos incluídos no texto do índice representam as grandes categorias identificadas com a chave à direita. Os símbolos com números em sua parte superior (⋏[1]) identificam as subcategorias (veja-se a chave completa à página *I · 1).*

	English	Deutsch	Español	Français	Português
ʌ	Mountain	Berg	Montaña	Montagne	Montanha
⋏	Mountains	Gebirge	Montañas	Montagnes	Montanhas
)(	Pass	Paß	Paso	Col	Passo
V	Valley, Canyon	Tal, Cañon	Valle, Cañón	Vallée, Canyon	Vale, Canhão
≚	Plain	Ebene	Llano	Plaine	Planície
›	Cape	Kap	Cabo	Cap	Cabo
I	Island	Insel	Isla	Île	Ilha
II	Islands	Inseln	Islas	Îles	Ilhas
⊥	Other Topographic Features	Andere Topographische Objekte	Otros Elementos Topográficos	Autres données topographiques	Outros acidentes topográficos

ESPAÑOL

Nombre	Página	Lat.°′	Long.°′ W = Oeste
Senqu → Orange ≃	156	28.41 S	16.28 E
Senqunyane ≃	158	30.03 S	28.10 E
Senriyama	270	34.47 N	135.30 E
Sens	50	48.12 N	3.17 E
Sense ≃	58	46.54 N	7.14 E
Sensée ≃	50	50.16 N	3.06 E
Sensée, Canal de la ≅	50	50.14 N	3.17 E
Sensuntepeque	236	13.52 N	88.38 W
Şenta	38	45.56 N	20.04 E
Šentala	80	54.27 N	51.29 E
Sentani, Danau ⊜	164	2.36 S	140.34 E
Sentarum, Danau ⊜	112	0.51 N	112.06 E
Sentas	86	49.19 N	82.28 E
Sentelek	86	51.13 N	83.44 E
Şentery	154	5.22 S	25.45 E
Šentilj	61	46.41 N	15.40 E
Sentinel	196	35.09 N	99.10 W
Sentinel Butte ʌ	198	46.53 N	103.50 W
Sentinel Peak ʌ	182	54.54 N	121.57 W
Sentinel Range ⩘	9	78.10 S	85.30 W
Şentino ≃	66	43.24 N	12.59 E
Šentjur	36	46.13 N	15.24 E
Sentolo	115a	7.50 S	110.13 E
Sentosa I	271c	1.15 N	103.50 E
Sento Sé	250	9.51 S	41.51 W
Sentsū-zan ʌ	96	35.09 N	133.11 E
Senyavin Islands II	14	6.55 N	158.00 E
Senye	152	1.34 N	9.50 E
Şenyurt	130	37.06 N	40.40 E
Šenzaki-wan ᴄ	96	34.24 N	131.15 E
Sen-zan ʌ	96	34.21 N	134.51 E
Senzig	54	52.17 N	13.39 E
Senzu-dake ʌ	270	34.57 N	135.52 E
Seo de Urgel	34	42.21 N	1.28 E
Seohāra	124	29.13 N	78.35 E
Seolag-san Kukrip Kongwŏn ♦	98	38.09 N	128.24 E
Seon	58	47.21 N	8.10 E
Seonāth ≃	122	21.44 N	82.28 E
Seoni	124	22.05 N	79.32 E
Seoni Mālwa	124	22.27 N	77.28 E
Seorīnārāyan	120	21.44 N	82.35 E
Seoul → Sŏul	98	37.33 N	126.58 E
Seoul Bridge ◆[5]	271b	37.32 N	126.56 E
Seoul National University ʊ[2]	271b	37.28 N	126.57 E
Seoul Stadium ♦	271b	37.35 N	127.02 E
Seoul Station ◆[5]	271b	37.34 N	126.58 E
Sepahat	114	1.34 N	101.53 E
Sepang	114	2.42 N	101.45 E
Sepanjang, Pulau I	112	7.10 S	115.50 E
Separation Creek ≃	200	41.59 N	107.28 W
Separation Point ›	172	40.47 S	173.00 E
Sepasu	112	0.43 N	117.35 E
Sepatini ≃	248	7.36 S	65.24 W
Sépeaux	50	47.57 N	3.14 E
Sepetiba ◆[8]	256	22.58 S	43.42 W
Sepetiba, Baía de ᴄ	256	23.00 S	43.48 W
Sepi	175e	8.33 S	159.50 E
Sepik ≃	164	3.51 S	144.34 E
Sepino	66	41.24 N	14.37 E
Sep'o	98	38.39 N	127.22 E
Sępólno Krajeńskie	30	53.28 N	17.32 E
Sépone → Muang Xépôn	110	16.41 N	106.14 E
Sepopa	156	18.13 S	22.13 E
Sępopol	30	54.15 N	21.00 E
Sepoti ≃	248	6.43 S	61.38 W
Sepotuba ≃	248	15.56 S	57.39 W
Seppeltsfield	168b	34.30 S	138.54 E
Seppenrade	52	51.46 N	7.23 E
Sepphoris → Ẓippori	132	32.45 N	35.17 E
Seppois-le-Bas	58	47.33 N	7.10 E
Septeuil	261	48.54 N	1.41 E
Sept Frères, Lac des ⊜	206	46.20 N	75.10 W
Sept-Îles (Seven Islands)	186	50.12 N	66.23 W
Septvaux	50	49.34 N	3.23 E
Sepulga ≃	194	31.11 N	86.46 W
Sepúlveda	34	41.18 N	3.45 W
Sepulveda ◆[8]	280	34.13 N	118.28 W
Sepulveda Dam ◆[6]	280	34.10 N	118.29 W
Sepulveda Flood Control Basin ≚[1]	228	34.11 N	118.29 W
Seputih ≃	112	4.42 S	105.54 E
Sepyč	80	58.11 N	54.08 E
Sequals	64	46.10 N	12.50 E
Sequatchie ≃	192	35.02 N	85.38 W
Sequeros	34	40.31 N	6.01 W
Sequillo ≃	34	41.45 N	5.30 W
Sequim	224	48.04 N	123.06 W
Sequim Bay ᴄ	224	48.03 N	123.02 W
Sequoia National Park ♦	204	36.30 N	118.30 W
Sera	96	34.36 N	133.03 E
Şera, Pulau I	164	7.40 S	131.05 E
Šerabad	128	37.40 N	67.01 E
Serachs	128	36.32 N	61.13 E
Serafettin Dağları ⩘	130	39.05 N	41.10 E
Şerafimovič	80	49.36 N	42.43 E
Šeragul	88	54.29 N	100.56 E
Seraidi	36	36.55 N	7.41 E
Seraing	56	50.36 N	5.29 E
Seraja ≃	82	56.15 N	38.45 E
Serakhovychi	78	51.25 N	24.40 E
Seram (Ceram) I	164	3.00 S	129.00 E
Seram, Laut (Ceram Sea) ⊤[2]	108	2.30 S	128.00 E
Serampore	126	22.45 N	88.21 E
Serang	115a	6.07 S	106.09 E
Serang ≃	115a	6.43 S	110.35 E
Serangoon	271c	1.22 N	103.54 E
Serangoon ≃	271c	1.24 N	103.56 E
Serangoon, Pulau I	271c	1.25 N	103.56 E
Serangoon Harbour ᴄ	271c	1.23 N	103.57 E
Serapo	66	41.13 N	13.34 E
Serasan, Pulau I	112	2.30 N	109.03 E
Serasan, Selat ⊔	112	2.20 N	109.00 E
Seravalle Sesia	62	45.41 N	8.19 E
Seravezza	64	43.59 N	10.13 E
Seraya, Pulau I	271c	1.16 N	103.43 E
Serayevo → Sarajevo	38	43.52 N	18.25 E
Şerayu ≃	115a	7.41 S	109.06 E
Šerbakul'	86	54.38 N	72.24 E
Serbeulangit, Pegunungan ⩘	114	3.45 N	97.50 E
Serbia → Srbija □[3]	38	44.00 N	21.00 E
Serchio ≃	64	43.47 N	10.16 E
Serdce-Kamen', mys ›	180	66.57 N	171.40 W
Serdež	80	57.17 N	48.17 E
Serdo	144	11.58 N	41.18 E
Serdoba ≃	80	52.34 N	44.01 E
Serdobsk	80	52.28 N	44.13 E
Serdyte	83	48.02 N	38.24 E
Séré'ama, Mont ʌ	175f	13.47 S	167.29 E
Serebr'anka, Ross.	86	57.13 N	70.42 E
Serebr'anka, Ross.	265b	55.45 N	37.55 E
Serebr'anka ≃	265b	55.47 N	37.42 E
Serebr'ansk	86	49.43 N	83.20 E
Serebr'anyj Bor ◆[8]	265b	55.48 N	37.25 E
Serebr'anyje Prudy	82	54.28 N	38.44 E
Serebrovo	88	55.24 N	97.52 E
Serebryans'kyy lis ♦	83	48.55 N	38.00 E
Sered'	30	48.17 N	17.44 E
Sereda, Ross.	76	55.54 N	35.31 E
Şereda, Ross.	80	58.00 N	40.27 E
Šeredar' ≃	82	55.56 N	39.04 E
Seredejskij	76	54.03 N	35.14 E
Seredīči	76	53.35 N	35.51 E
Serednikovo, Ross.	80	55.15 N	39.40 E
Serednikovo, Ross.	265b	55.56 N	37.14 E
Seredn'ovo	265b	55.35 N	37.18 E

FRANÇAIS

Nom	Page	Lat.°′	Long.°′ W = Ouest
Seredyna-Buda	78	52.11 N	34.01 E
Seredžius	76	55.05 N	23.25 E
Şereflikoçhisar	130	38.56 N	33.33 E
Šereges	86	52.57 N	88.02 E
Seregno	62	45.39 N	9.12 E
Serein ≃	50	47.55 N	3.31 E
Şeremban	114	2.43 N	101.56 E
Šeremetjevka	80	55.23 N	51.32 E
Šeremetjevo, Aeroport ⊠	82	55.59 N	37.24 E
Šeremetjevskij	82	55.59 N	37.30 E
Seremuk ≃	164	1.36 S	131.46 E
Serena	216	41.29 N	88.44 W
Seren del Grappa	64	45.59 N	11.51 E
Serengeti National Park ♦	154	2.20 S	34.50 E
Serengeti Plain ≚	154	2.50 S	35.00 E
Serengka	112	1.40 S	110.40 E
Serenje	154	13.15 S	30.14 E
Şereno	256	21.19 S	42.39 W
Šereševo	76	52.33 N	24.13 E
Seret (Siret) ≃, Europe	38	45.24 N	28.01 E
Seret ≃, Ukr.	78	48.38 N	25.52 E
Serfaus	58	47.02 N	10.36 E
Ser'ga	86	57.46 N	56.52 E
Sergač	80	55.32 N	45.28 E
Sergeant	214	41.38 N	78.45 W
Sergeant Bluff	198	42.24 N	96.21 W
Sergeja Kirova, ostrova II	74	77.12 N	89.30 E
Sergejeviči	76	53.30 N	27.45 E
Sergejevka, Kaz.	86	51.39 N	68.13 E
Sergejevka, Kaz.	86	53.51 N	67.25 E
Sergejevka, Ross.	89	44.22 N	131.39 E
Sergejevka, Ross.	89	43.21 N	133.22 E
Sergejevo	86	57.18 N	86.02 E
Sergen	130	41.42 N	27.42 E
Sergijevka	78	51.46 N	41.05 E
Sergijev Posad (Zagorsk)	82	56.18 N	38.08 E
Sergijevskaja, Ross.	76	60.16 N	43.54 E
Sergijevskaja, Ross.	80	50.16 N	43.47 E
Sergijevskij	80	51.56 N	51.54 E
Sergili	85	41.13 N	69.14 E
Sergines	50	48.20 N	3.15 E
Serginskij	72	62.30 N	65.38 E
Sergipe □[3]	250	10.30 S	37.30 W
Sergokala	84	42.27 N	47.40 E
Sergozero, ozero ⊜	24	66.47 N	36.42 E
Serhiyivka	83	48.40 N	37.22 E
Seria	112	4.39 N	114.23 E
Serian	112	1.10 N	110.34 E
Seriana, Valle V	64	45.55 N	9.55 E
Seriate	62	45.41 N	9.43 E
Seribu, Kepulauan II	115a	5.36 S	106.33 E
Seribudolok, Indon.	114	2.51 N	99.04 E
Seribudolok, Indon.	114	2.56 N	98.37 E
Sericho	154	1.05 N	39.05 E
Seridó ≃	250	6.12 S	37.10 W
Sérifontaine	50	49.21 N	1.46 E
Sérifos	38	37.09 N	24.31 E
Sérifos I	38	37.11 N	24.31 E
Sérignan-du-Comtat	62	44.11 N	4.51 E
Sérigny ≃	176	56.47 N	66.00 W
Serik	130	36.55 N	31.06 E
Seringat, Pulau I	271c	1.14 N	103.51 E
Serino	68	40.51 N	14.52 E
Serinyol	130	36.24 N	36.11 E
Serio ≃	62	45.16 N	9.45 E
Seritinga	256	21.54 S	44.30 W
Serjol	24	60.02 N	48.58 E
Serkhe, Cerro ʌ	248	17.22 S	69.22 W
Serkout, Djebel ʌ	148	23.30 N	6.48 E
Serkovo	82	54.28 N	38.46 E
Şerles ʌ	64	47.08 N	11.23 E
Šerlovaja Gora	88	50.34 N	116.15 E
Serm ◆[8]	263	51.21 N	6.42 E
Sermaise	261	48.32 N	2.05 E
Sermaises	50	48.18 N	2.12 E
Sermaize-les-Bains	56	48.47 N	4.55 E
Serman	80	53.34 N	46.22 E
Sermata, Pulau I	164	8.13 S	128.55 E
Sermide	64	45.00 N	11.18 E
Sermilik ᴄ[2]	176	65.37 N	38.03 W
Sermizelles	50	47.32 N	3.48 E
Şermoneta	66	41.33 N	12.59 E
Šerna ≃	82	55.51 N	38.34 E
Sernambetiba, Pontal de ›	287a	23.02 S	43.27 W
Sernambitiba	287a	22.41 S	42.59 W
Sernovodsk	80	53.56 N	51.17 E
Sernur	80	56.56 N	49.09 E
Sernyky	78	51.49 N	26.14 E
Sernyy Zavod	128	39.59 N	58.50 E
Séro	150	14.48 N	11.04 W
Serodino	252	32.37 S	60.57 W
Ser'odka	76	58.10 N	28.12 E
Seroglazka	80	47.01 N	47.29 E
Ser'ogovo	24	62.20 N	50.36 E
Serooskerke	52	51.42 N	3.50 E
Seropédica	256	22.44 S	43.43 W
Serov	86	59.29 N	60.31 E
Serovo	85	40.27 N	71.12 E
Serowe	156	22.25 S	26.44 E
Ser'oža ≃	80	55.34 N	42.29 E
Serpa	34	37.56 N	7.36 W
Serpeddi, Punta ʌ	71	39.22 N	9.18 E
Serpejsk	76	54.20 N	34.59 E
Serpent, Rivière au ≃	186	49.33 N	71.14 W
Serpentine	168a	32.22 S	115.59 E
Serpentine ≃, Austl.	168a	32.33 S	115.46 E
Serpentine ≃, B.C., Can.	224	49.05 N	122.50 W
Serpentine Lakes ⊜	162	28.32 S	129.09 E
Serpentine National Park ♦	168a	32.22 S	116.01 E
Serpentine Reservoir ⊜[1]	168a	32.25 S	116.08 E
Serpent Mound State Memorial ⊥	218	39.02 N	83.26 W
Serpents Mouth ⊔	241r	10.00 N	62.00 W
Serpneve	78	46.18 N	29.02 E
Serpuchov	82	54.55 N	37.25 E
Serpukhov → Serpuchov	82	54.55 N	37.25 E
Serqo → Sark I	43b	49.26 N	2.21 W
Serra	255	20.07 S	40.18 W
Serra, Monte ʌ	66	43.46 N	10.33 E
Serra Branca	250	7.29 S	36.40 W
Serracapriola	68	41.48 N	15.09 E
Serrada	64	45.53 N	11.09 E
Serra da Canastra, Parque Nacional da ♦	255	20.10 S	46.40 W
Serra da Capivara, Parque Nacionl da ♦	250	8.40 S	42.15 W
Serra d'Aiello	68	39.05 N	16.08 E
Serra de'Conti	66	43.33 N	13.02 E
Serra di Corvo, Lago di ⊜[1]	68	40.51 N	16.14 E
Serradifalco	70	37.27 N	13.53 E
Serra do Navio	250	0.59 N	52.03 W
Serra dos Aimorés	255	17.46 S	40.15 W
Serra do Salitre	255	19.06 S	46.41 W
Serra dos Órgãos, Parque Nacional da ♦	256	22.26 S	43.02 W
Sérrai	38	41.05 N	23.32 E
Serramanna	71	39.25 N	8.55 E
Serramazzoni	64	44.25 N	10.47 E
Serramonte Center ◆[9]	282	37.40 N	122.28 W
Serrana	255	21.14 S	47.36 W
Serrana, Cayo de ✣[4]	236	14.23 N	80.12 W
Serra Negra	256	22.36 S	46.42 W
Serra Negra do Norte	250	6.40 S	37.24 W
Serrânia	255	21.33 S	46.03 W

PORTUGUÊS

Nome	Página	Lat.°′	Long.°′ W = Oeste
Serranilla, Cayo de ✣[4]	236	15.50 N	79.50 W
Serranópolis	255	18.16 S	52.00 W
Serranos	256	21.51 S	44.30 W
Serrara	68	40.42 N	13.54 E
Serra San Bruno	68	38.35 N	16.20 E
Serra San Quirico	66	43.27 N	13.01 E
Serrastretta	68	39.01 N	16.25 E
Serrat, Cap ›	36	37.14 N	9.13 E
Serra Talhada	250	7.59 S	38.18 W
Serravalle, It.	66	42.47 N	13.01 E
Serravalle, S. Mar.	66	43.57 N	12.30 E
Serravalle all'Adige	64	45.49 N	11.01 E
Serravalle Scrivia	62	44.43 N	8.51 E
Serre	68	40.35 N	15.11 E
Serre ≃	50	49.41 N	3.23 E
Serrenti	71	39.29 N	8.58 E
Serre-Ponçon, Barrage de ◆[6]	62	44.33 N	6.30 E
Serre-Ponçon, Lac de ⊜[1]	62	44.30 N	6.17 E
Serres	62	44.26 N	5.43 E
Serrezuela	252	30.38 S	65.23 W
Serri	71	39.42 N	9.08 E
Serrières	62	45.19 N	4.45 E
Serrinha	250	11.39 S	39.00 W
Serriola, Bocca)(	66	43.31 N	12.21 E
Serris	261	48.51 N	2.47 E
Serrita	250	7.56 S	39.19 W
Serro	255	18.37 S	43.23 W
Şersale	68	39.01 N	16.44 E
Šerstin	76	52.39 N	31.03 E
Šerstobitovo	86	57.16 N	78.52 E
Sertã	34	39.48 N	8.06 W
Sertânia	250	8.05 S	37.16 W
Sertãozinho	256	22.19 S	46.03 W
Sertig-Dörfli	58	46.44 N	9.51 E
Sertung, Pulau I	115a	6.06 S	105.24 E
Seru	144	7.50 N	40.28 E
Şerua, Pulau I	164	6.18 S	130.01 E
Šerubaj-Nura ≃	86	49.54 N	72.31 E
Serui	164	1.53 S	136.14 E
Seruini ≃	248	7.42 S	66.42 W
Serule	156	21.58 S	27.20 E
Serutu, Pulau I	112	1.42 S	108.45 E
Seruwai	114	4.21 N	98.10 E
Sérvia	38	40.11 N	22.00 E
Servi Burnu ›	130	41.40 N	28.06 E
Servigliano	66	43.05 N	13.29 E
Servon	261	48.43 N	2.35 E
Servoz	58	45.56 N	6.46 E
Serwaru	112	8.10 S	127.42 E
Sêrxü	102	33.04 N	97.45 E
Seryševo	89	51.08 N	128.20 E
şes, Munții ⩘	38	47.05 N	22.30 E
Šešan	180	66.46 N	171.26 W
Sesayap ≃	112	3.36 N	117.15 E
Sesayap Lama	112	3.36 N	117.03 E
Seščа	76	53.45 N	33.23 E
Sese Islands II	154	0.20 S	32.20 E
Seseke ≃	263	51.37 N	7.32 E
Sesfontein	156	19.07 S	13.39 E
Sesheke	152	17.28 S	24.18 E
Seshu	105	39.33 N	115.37 E
Sesia ≃	62	45.05 N	8.37 E
Sesia, Val V	62	45.47 N	8.05 E
Sesibu	112	4.02 N	116.33 E
Sesimbra	34	38.26 N	9.06 W
Seskar, ostrov I	76	60.02 N	28.23 E
Şeskarö	26	65.44 N	23.44 E
Šešma ≃	80	55.27 N	51.05 E
Sesmarias ≃	256	22.28 S	44.27 W
Sesoko-jima I	174m	26.38 N	127.52 E
Sespe	228	34.23 N	118.58 W
Sespe Creek ≃	204	34.23 N	118.57 W
Sessa	152	13.56 S	20.38 E
Sessa Aurunca	68	41.14 N	13.56 E
Ses Salines, Cap de ›	34	39.16 N	3.03 E
Séssé	146	11.30 N	17.34 E
Sessenheim	56	48.48 N	7.59 E
Şesta Godano	62	44.17 N	9.40 E
Šestakovo, Ross.	82	56.21 N	35.49 E
Šestakovo, Ross.	88	56.29 N	103.59 E
Sestao	34	43.18 N	3.00 W
Sestino	66	43.42 N	12.18 E
Sesto (Sexten)	64	46.42 N	12.21 E
Sesto Calende	62	45.44 N	8.38 E
Sesto Fiorentino	66	43.50 N	11.12 E
Sestola	64	44.14 N	10.46 E
Sesto San Giovanni	62	45.32 N	9.14 E
Sestra ≃, Ross.	80	52.11 N	49.36 E
Sestra ≃, Ross.	82	56.43 N	37.14 E
Sestriere	62	44.57 N	6.53 E
Sestri Levante	62	44.16 N	9.24 E
Sestri Ponente	62	44.25 N	8.51 E
Sestroreck	76	60.06 N	29.58 E
Sestroreckij Razliv, ozero ⊜	265a	60.04 N	30.00 E
Şestu	71	39.18 N	9.05 E
Šešupe ≃	76	55.03 N	22.12 E
Šešurga	80	57.29 N	47.35 E
Šešuvis ≃	76	55.13 N	22.15 E
Šėta, Liet.	76	55.17 N	24.15 E
Seta, Nihon	270	34.58 N	135.55 E
Seta ≃	270	34.56 N	135.54 E
Setagaya ◆[8]	268	35.39 N	139.40 E
Setail ≃	115a	8.30 S	114.21 E
Setaka	96	33.09 N	130.28 E
Setana	92a	42.26 N	139.51 E
Setapak	114	3.11 N	101.42 E
Setauket	210	40.57 N	73.07 W
Sète	62	43.24 N	3.41 E
Sete Barras	252	24.23 S	47.55 W
Sete Cidades, Parque Nacional de ♦	250	3.50 S	41.40 W
Sete de Setembro ≃	255	12.56 S	52.51 W
Sete Lagoas	255	19.27 S	44.14 W
Sete Pontes	256	22.51 S	43.05 W
Sete Quedas, Cachoeira das ʟ	250	9.27 S	56.41 W
Sete Quedas, Parque Nacional de ♦	252	24.02 S	54.12 W
Sete Rios ◆[8]	266c	38.45 N	9.10 W
Setesdal V	26	59.25 N	7.25 E
Seth Ward	196	34.13 N	101.42 W
Setī □[8]	124	29.15 N	81.00 E
Setī ≃	124	28.58 N	81.06 E
Setlagodi	158	26.16 S	25.06 E
Set Net, Punta ›	236	12.28 N	83.30 W
Seto, Nihon	94	35.14 N	137.06 E
Seto, Nihon	96	33.27 N	132.15 E
Seto, Nihon	96	34.44 N	134.02 E
Setoda	96	34.18 N	133.05 E
Seto-naikai ⊤[2]	96	34.20 N	133.30 E
Seto-naikai-kokuritsu-kōen ♦	96	34.15 N	133.28 E
Seton Hall University ʊ[2]	276	40.45 N	74.15 W
Seton Lake ⊜	182	50.45 N	122.05 W
Seton Portage	182	50.43 N	122.18 W
Seto-saki ›	174m	26.51 N	128.18 E
Setouchi	93b	28.10 N	129.15 E
Seto-zaki ›	96	33.40 N	135.20 E
Setraki	78	49.23 N	40.49 E
Setta ≃	64	44.22 N	11.14 E
Settat	148	33.04 N	7.37 W
Settat □[4]	148	33.05 N	7.30 W
Setté Cama	152	2.32 S	9.45 E
Settecamini ◆[8]	267a	41.56 N	12.37 E
Sette-Daban, chrebet ⩘	74	62.00 N	138.00 E
Settee Lake ⊜	184	57.03 N	96.55 W
Settepani, Monte ʌ	62	44.15 N	8.12 E
Settimo Milanese	266b	45.29 N	9.03 E
Settimo San Pietro	71	39.17 N	9.11 E
Settimo Torinese	62	45.09 N	7.46 E
Settimo Vittone	62	45.33 N	7.50 E
Settingiano	68	38.55 N	16.31 E
Setting Lake ⊜	184	55.00 N	98.38 W
Settle	44	54.04 N	2.16 W
Settlement Point ›	169	38.25 S	145.25 E
Settlers	156	25.02 S	28.30 E
Settlers Cabin Regional Park ♦	279b	40.26 N	80.10 W
Settons, Lac des ⊜	50	47.11 N	4.04 E
Settsu	96	34.46 N	135.33 E
Setúbal	34	38.32 N	8.54 W
Setúbal □[5]	266c	38.37 N	9.00 W
Setúbal, Baía de ᴄ	34	38.27 N	8.53 W
Setun' ≃	265b	55.44 N	37.33 E
Seui	71	39.50 N	9.19 E
Seúl → Sŏul	98	37.33 N	126.58 E
Seul, Lac ⊜	184	50.20 N	92.30 W
Seul Choix Point ›	190	45.56 N	85.52 W
Seulimeum	114	5.22 N	95.35 E
Seulo	71	39.52 N	9.14 E
Seumanyam	114	3.45 N	96.38 E
Seurre	58	47.00 N	5.09 E
Seuzach	58	47.32 N	8.44 E
Sev ≃	76	52.24 N	34.10 E
Sevan	84	40.34 N	44.57 E
Sevan, ozero ⊜	84	40.20 N	45.20 E
Sévaré	150	14.32 N	4.06 W
Sevastopol'	78	44.36 N	33.32 E
Sevastopol'skij	86	53.08 N	65.44 E
Sevelen, Dtsch.	52	51.29 N	6.25 E
Şevelen, Schw.	58	47.07 N	9.29 E
Ševelevskaja	24	60.52 N	44.12 E
Ševelevskij Majdan	80	54.25 N	42.15 E
Seven ≃	44	54.11 N	0.52 W
Seven Caves ⊥[5]	218	39.13 N	83.23 W
Seven Creeks ≃	169	36.43 S	145.34 E
Seven Harbors	216	42.40 N	83.34 W
Sevenhill	168b	33.53 S	138.38 E
Seven Hills, Austl.	274a	33.46 S	150.57 E
Seven Hills, Oh., U.S.	214	41.23 N	81.40 W
Seven Islands → Sept-Îles	186	50.12 N	66.23 W
Seven Kings ◆[8]	260	51.34 N	0.05 E
Seven Mile	218	39.28 N	84.33 W
Seven Mile Beach National Park ♦	170	34.49 S	150.46 E
Sevenmile Bridge ◆[5]	220	24.41 N	81.11 W
Sevenmile Creek ≃	218	39.28 N	84.33 W
Sevenoaks, Eng., U.K.	42	51.16 N	0.12 E
Seven Oaks, Tx., U.S.	222	30.51 N	94.51 W
Sevenoaks □[8]	260	51.18 N	0.10 E
Sevenoaks Weald	260	51.14 N	0.12 E
Seven Palm Lake ⊜	220	25.12 N	80.44 W
Seven Persons	184	49.52 N	110.54 W
Seven Sisters	42	51.46 N	3.43 W
Seven Sisters Peaks ⩘	182	54.58 N	128.10 W
Seventy Mile House	182	51.18 N	121.24 W
Seven Valleys	208	39.51 N	76.46 W
Sévérac-le-Château	32	44.19 N	3.04 E
Severance Center ◆[9]	279a	41.31 N	81.33 W
Severka ≃	82	55.10 N	38.45 E
Severn, S. Afr.	158	26.36 S	22.52 E
Severn, Md., U.S.	208	39.08 N	76.41 W
Severn, N.C., U.S.	208	36.30 N	77.11 W
Severn, Va., U.S.	208	37.17 N	76.24 W
Severn ≃, On., Can.	176	56.02 N	87.36 W
Severn ≃, On., Can.	212	44.52 N	79.41 W
Severn ≃, U.K.	42	51.35 N	2.40 W
Severn, Mouth of the ≃	42	51.25 N	3.00 W
Severnaja Dvina ≃	24	64.32 N	40.30 E
Severnaja Osetija □[3]	84	43.00 N	44.15 E
Severnaja Sos'va ≃	72	64.10 N	65.28 E
Severnaja Zeml'a II	74	79.30 N	98.00 E
Severna Park	208	39.04 N	76.32 W
Severn Bridge ◆[5]	42	51.39 N	2.42 W
Severne	83	48.04 N	38.44 E
Severn Lake ⊜	184	53.54 N	90.48 W
Severnoje, Ross.	80	58.02 N	41.26 E
Severnoje, Ross.	80	54.06 N	52.32 E
Severnoje, Ross.	84	44.49 N	42.51 E
Severnoje, Ross.	86	56.21 N	78.23 E
Severn River ᴄ, Md., U.S.	208	38.58 N	76.28 W
Severn River ᴄ, Va., U.S.	208	37.19 N	76.25 W
Severn Tunnel ◆[5]	42	51.35 N	2.44 W
Severnyj, Ross.	24	67.38 N	64.06 E
Severnyj, Ross.	265b	55.56 N	37.33 E
Severnyje uvaly ⩘[2]	24	59.30 N	49.00 E
Severnyj Kommunar	80	58.23 N	54.02 E
Severnyj Prijut	84	43.16 N	41.51 E
Severnyj Ural ⩘	24	63.00 N	59.00 E
Severo-Bajkal'skoje nagorje ⩘[1]	88	57.00 N	111.00 E
Severočeský Kraj □[4]	30	50.30 N	14.00 E
Severodvinsk	24	64.34 N	39.50 E
Severo-Dvinskij kanal ≅	76	59.45 N	38.22 E
Severo-Jenisejskij	74	60.22 N	93.01 E
Severo-Kazachstan □[8]	86	54.30 N	69.00 E
Severo-Kuril'sk	74	50.40 N	156.08 E
Severomoravský Kraj □[4]	30	49.45 N	17.50 E
Severomorsk	24	69.05 N	33.24 E
Severo-Mujskij chrebet ⩘	88	56.30 N	114.00 E
Severo-Sibirskaja nizmennost' ≚	74	73.00 N	100.00 E
Severoural'sk	86	60.09 N	59.57 E
Severo-Zadonsk	82	54.02 N	38.24 E
Severskaja	78	44.51 N	38.42 E
Severucha	86	58.28 N	63.25 E
Severy	198	37.37 N	96.13 W
Seveso	62	45.39 N	9.09 E
Şeveso ≃	266b	45.30 N	9.12 E
Ševětin	61	49.06 N	14.35 E
Sevettijärvi	24	69.26 N	28.38 E
Sevier ≃	200	39.04 N	113.06 W
Sevier, East Fork ≃	200	38.14 N	112.12 W
Sevier Bridge Reservoir ⊜[1]	200	39.21 N	111.57 W
Sevier Desert ◆[2]	200	39.25 N	112.50 W
Sevier Lake ⊜	200	38.55 N	113.09 W
Sevierville	192	35.52 N	83.33 W
Sevilla, Col.	246	4.16 N	75.57 W
Sevilla (Seville), Esp.	34	37.23 N	5.59 W
Sevilla □[4]	34	37.25 N	5.35 W
Sevilla, Isla I	236	8.14 N	82.24 W
Seville → Sevilla, Esp.	34	37.23 N	5.59 W
Seville, Fl., U.S.	192	29.19 N	81.29 W
Seville, Oh., U.S.	214	41.00 N	81.51 W
Sevir	130	39.12 N	38.13 E
Şevketiye	130	40.05 N	27.51 E
Ševli ≃	89	54.08 N	133.04 E
Sevlievo	38	43.01 N	25.06 E
Sevran	50	48.56 N	2.32 E
Sevrej	102	43.35 N	102.12 E
Sèvres	50	48.49 N	2.12 E
Sévrier	58	45.52 N	6.08 E
Şevsk	78	52.09 N	34.30 E
Ševykan	88	54.20 N	106.49 E
Sewa ≃	150	7.18 N	12.08 W
Sewanee	194	35.04 N	85.55 W
Sewāni	123	28.55 N	75.37 E
Seward, Ak., U.S.	180	60.06 N	149.26 W
Seward, Ne., U.S.	198	40.54 N	97.05 W
Seward, N.Y., U.S.	210	42.43 N	74.37 W
Seward, Pa., U.S.	214	40.25 N	79.01 W
Seward Glacier ⍓	180	60.22 N	140.15 W
Seward Peninsula ›[1]	180	65.00 N	164.00 W
Sewaren	276	40.33 N	74.15 W
Sewekow	54	53.15 N	12.39 E
Sewell, Chile	252	34.05 S	70.23 W
Sewell, N.J., U.S.	208	39.45 N	75.08 W
Sewen	58	47.48 N	6.54 E
Sewernaja-Semlja → Severnaja Zeml'a II	74	79.30 N	98.00 E
Seweweekspoort	158	33.22 S	21.25 E
Sewickley	214	40.32 N	80.11 W
Sewickley Creek ≃	279b	40.14 N	79.47 W
Sewickley Heights	279b	40.33 N	80.09 W
Sewickley Hills	279b	40.34 N	80.08 W
Sewri ◆[8]	272c	19.00 N	72.51 E
Sexcello	152	3.58 S	11.38 E
Sexsmith	182	55.21 N	118.47 W
Sexten → Sesto	64	46.42 N	12.21 E
Sextin ≃	232	25.44 N	105.14 W
Sexton	218	39.42 N	85.27 W
Sexton Island I	276	40.39 N	73.14 W
Seya ◆[8], Nihon	268	35.29 N	139.29 E
Seya ◆[8], Nihon	268	35.27 N	139.30 E
Seybaplaya	232	19.39 N	90.40 W
Seybothenreuth	60	49.54 N	11.43 E
Seybouse, Oued ≃	148	36.54 N	7.47 E
Seychellen → Seychelles □[1]	138	4.35 S	55.40 E
Seychelles □[1]	138	4.35 S	55.40 E
Seychelles Bank ✣[4]	12	4.45 S	55.30 E
Seyches	32	44.33 N	0.18 E
Seyda	54	51.53 N	12.53 E
Seydim	130	40.33 N	34.45 E
Seydişehir	130	37.25 N	31.51 E
Seyđisfjörđur	24a	65.16 N	14.00 W
Seyfe Gölü ⊜	130	39.13 N	34.23 E
Seyhan ≃	130	36.43 N	34.53 E
Seyhan Barajı ⊜[1]	130	37.05 N	35.15 E
Seyitgazi	130	39.27 N	30.43 E
Seylac	144	11.21 N	43.29 E
Seym ≃	78	51.27 N	32.34 E
Seymour, Austl.	169	37.02 S	145.08 E
Seymour, S. Afr.	158	32.33 S	26.46 E
Seymour, Ct., U.S.	207	41.23 N	73.04 W
Seymour, In., U.S.	218	38.57 N	85.53 W
Seymour, Ia., U.S.	190	40.40 N	93.07 W
Seymour, Mo., U.S.	194	37.08 N	92.46 W
Seymour, Tx., U.S.	196	33.35 N	99.15 W
Seymour, Wi., U.S.	190	44.30 N	88.19 W
Seymour ≃	182	51.05 N	126.50 W
Seymour Inlet ᴄ	182	51.03 N	127.10 W
Seymour Johnson Air Force Base ■	192	35.21 N	77.58 W
Seymour Range ⩘	224	48.40 N	124.00 W
Seymourville	194	30.27 N	91.29 W
Seyne	62	44.21 N	6.21 E
Seynod	58	45.53 N	6.05 E
Seyring	264b	48.20 N	16.29 E
Seyssel	58	45.57 N	5.49 E
Şeytan ≃	267b	41.06 N	28.59 E
Sežana	36	45.42 N	13.52 E
Sézanne	50	48.43 N	3.43 E
Şezela	158	30.24 S	30.42 E
Šežim	24	62.07 N	58.21 E
Sezimovo Ústí	30	49.23 N	14.42 E
Sezze	66	41.30 N	13.03 E
Sfântu Gheorghe	38	45.52 N	25.47 E
Sfântu Gheorghe, Brațul ≃[1]	38	44.53 N	29.36 E
Sfântu Gheorghe, Ostrovul I	38	45.07 N	29.22 E
Sfax	148	34.44 N	10.46 E
Sfax □[8]	148	34.50 N	10.20 E
Sferracavallo ◆[8]	70	38.12 N	13.17 E
Sfizef	148	35.14 N	0.15 W
Sforzesco, Castello ⊥	266b	45.28 N	9.11 E
's-Gravendeel	52	51.46 N	4.37 E
's-Gravenhage (The Hague)	52	52.06 N	4.18 E
's-Gravenzande	52	52.00 N	4.10 E
Sgritheall, Beinn ʌ	46	57.08 N	5.35 W
Sgurgola	66	41.40 N	13.09 E
Sha ≃, Zhg.	98	37.31 N	117.50 E
Sha ≃, Zhg.	100	33.39 N	114.38 E
Sha ≃, Zhg.	100	26.35 N	118.02 E
Sha ≃, Zhg.	104	41.21 N	123.07 E
Sha'alav, Har ʌ	132	30.04 N	35.06 E
Sha'alvim	132	31.52 N	34.59 E
Shaanxi (Shensi) □[4]	102	35.00 N	109.00 E
Sha'ar HaGolan	132	32.41 N	35.36 E
Sha'ar Menashe	132	32.27 N	35.01 E
Shab'ā	132	33.21 N	35.45 E
Shaba □[4]	154	8.00 S	27.00 E
Shābah	142	31.11 N	30.46 E
Shabakunk Creek ≃	285	40.15 N	74.43 W
Shabās al-Milḥ	142	31.12 N	30.39 E
Shabās ash-Shuhadā'	142	31.05 N	30.45 E
Shabās 'Umayr	142	31.06 N	30.48 E
Shabbona	216	41.46 N	88.52 W
Shabeellaha Dhexe □[4]	144	3.00 N	46.00 E
Shabeellaha Hoose □[4]	144	1.30 N	44.15 E
Shabeelle (Shebele) ≃	144	0.12 S	42.45 E
Shabel'kivka	83	48.45 N	37.29 E
Shabestar	128	38.11 N	45.42 E
Shabo	78	46.08 N	30.23 E
Shabomeka Lake ⊜	212	44.54 N	77.09 W
Shabotik ≃	190	48.50 N	85.34 W
Shabqadar	123	34.13 N	71.34 E
Shabrāmant	142	29.56 N	31.12 E
Shabshīr al-Ḥiṣṣah	142	30.52 N	31.04 E
Shabunda	154	2.42 S	27.20 E
Shabwah	144	15.22 N	47.01 E
Shache (Yarkand)	120	38.25 N	77.16 E
Shacheng	105	40.25 N	115.31 E
Shacheng Gang ᴄ	100	27.10 N	120.24 E
Shackan Indian Reserve ◆[4]	182	50.17 N	121.12 W
Shackleton Ice Shelf ⍓	9	66.00 S	100.00 E
Shackleton Range ⩘	9	80.40 S	26.00 W
Shādegān	128	30.40 N	48.38 E
Shade Gap	214	40.11 N	77.52 W
Shadehill Reservoir ⊜[1]	198	45.45 N	102.15 W
Shade Mountain ʌ	208	40.34 N	77.30 W
Shades Glen	210	41.11 N	75.42 W
Shadi	100	26.08 N	114.49 E
Shadian	98	35.30 N	114.26 E
Shading	102	31.20 N	94.40 E
Shadow Lake ⊜, On., Can.	212	44.43 N	78.48 W
Shadow Lake ⊜, Ma., U.S.	283	42.50 N	71.14 W
Shadow Lake ⊜, N.J., U.S.	276	40.21 N	74.06 W
Shado-Wood Village	214	40.35 N	79.12 W
Shadrinsk → Šadrinsk	86	56.05 N	63.38 E
Shadui	102	31.30 N	100.10 E
Shady Cove	202	42.04 N	122.36 W
Shady Grove, Fl., U.S.	192	30.17 N	83.37 W
Shady Grove, Tx., U.S.	222	32.48 N	97.01 W
Shady Hills	216	40.36 N	85.41 W
Shady Shores	222	33.10 N	97.02 W
Shadyside	188	39.58 N	80.45 W
Sha'f	132	32.38 N	36.51 E
Shafer, Lake ⊜	216	40.47 N	86.46 W
Shafer Butte ʌ	202	43.47 N	116.05 W
Shafir	132	31.42 N	34.44 E
Shaft	128	37.12 N	49.24 E
Shafter	226	35.30 N	119.16 W
Shaftesbury	42	51.01 N	2.12 W
Shafton	279b	40.20 N	79.42 W
Shaftsburg	216	42.48 N	84.18 W
Shaftsbury	210	43.00 N	73.11 W
Shafu	100	22.25 N	113.01 E
Shag ≃	172	45.29 S	170.49 E
Shagamu	150	6.51 N	3.39 E
Shageluk	180	62.36 N	159.32 W
Shag Rocks II[1]	244	53.33 S	42.02 W
Shaguotun	104	41.10 N	120.38 E
Shāhābād, India	122	17.08 N	76.56 E
Shāhābād, India	123	30.10 N	76.53 E
Shāhābād, India	124	27.39 N	79.57 E
Shāhābād, India	272c	19.01 N	73.02 E
Shāhābād, Īrān	128	37.32 N	56.54 E
Shāhābād, Īrān	267d	35.47 N	51.31 E
Shāhāda	120	21.28 N	74.18 E
Shah Alam	114	3.04 N	101.33 E
Shahany, ozero ⊜	78	45.43 N	29.53 E
Shahbā'	132	32.51 N	36.37 E
Shāhbandar	120	24.10 N	67.54 E
Shāhbāz Kalāt	128	26.42 N	63.58 E
Shāhbāzpur ⊔	124	22.05 N	90.50 E
Shahdād, Namakzār-e ≚	128	30.30 N	58.30 E
Shāhdādkot	120	27.51 N	67.54 E
Shāhdādpur	120	25.56 N	68.37 E
Shāhdara, India	272a	28.30 N	77.25 E
Shāhdara, Pāk.	123	31.38 N	74.18 E
Shāhdara ◆[8]	272a	28.40 N	77.18 E
Shahdol	124	23.20 N	81.21 E
Shahe, Zhg.	98	36.56 N	114.30 E
Shahe, Zhg.	98	34.44 N	118.58 E
Shahe, Zhg.	98	37.01 N	119.43 E
Shahe, Zhg.	102	22.06 N	109.43 E
Shahedian	100	33.01 N	113.44 E
Shaheji	100	32.26 N	118.14 E
Shahepu	104	41.08 N	121.01 E
Shaheyi	98	39.53 N	118.31 E
Shaheying	104	40.50 N	120.46 E
Shahezhan	98	35.49 N	116.23 E
Shahezhen	105	40.08 N	116.15 E
Shahezi	89	46.05 N	129.20 E
Shāhganj	124	26.03 N	82.41 E
Shāhgarh, India	120	27.07 N	69.54 E
Shāhgarh, India	124	24.19 N	79.08 E
Shaḥḥāt	146	32.49 N	21.52 E
Shāhī Kowt	123	34.16 N	70.34 E
Shāhjahānpur	124	27.53 N	79.55 E
Shāh Jūy	120	32.31 N	67.25 E
Shāh Kot	123	31.34 N	73.29 E
Shāh Kūh ʌ	128	31.37 N	59.16 E
Shāhpur, India	122	16.42 N	76.50 E
Shāhpur, Pāk.	120	28.43 N	68.25 E
Shāhpur, Pāk.	123	32.17 N	72.26 E
Shāhpura, India	120	27.23 N	75.58 E
Shāhpura, India	120	25.38 N	74.56 E
Shāhpura, India	124	23.11 N	80.42 E
Shāhpur Chākar	120	26.09 N	68.39 E
Shahrak	120	34.06 N	64.18 E
Shahr-e Bābak	128	30.07 N	55.09 E
Shahr-e Kord	128	32.19 N	50.50 E
Shahr-e Monjān	120	36.02 N	70.46 E
Shahr-e Ṣafā	128	31.50 N	66.22 E
Shahrestān	120	34.22 N	66.47 E
Shāhrūd ≃	128	36.40 N	49.26 E
Shahryār	128	35.28 N	51.05 E
Shahu	100	30.11 N	113.39 E
Shāhzādpur	126	24.10 N	89.36 E
Shā'ib al-Banāt, Jabal ʌ	140	26.59 N	33.29 E
Shaighālu	120	31.11 N	68.49 E
Shaikou	100	27.19 N	117.35 E
Sha'īrah, Jabal ʌ[2]	132	30.06 N	34.17 E
Sha'īrah, Jabal ash- ⩘	132	29.31 N	34.29 E
Shājāpur	124	23.26 N	76.16 E
Shajian	100	24.46 N	117.38 E
Shajianzi	98	41.01 N	125.26 E
Shajiazhuang	106	32.13 N	120.53 E
Shajing	100	23.36 N	114.06 E
Shajingzi	102	37.42 N	105.09 E
Shakaga-dake ʌ	96	33.11 N	130.53 E
Shakaga-hana ›	96	34.25 N	134.14 E
Shakaga-take-tunnel ◆[5]	96	33.27 N	130.52 E
Shakardarra	123	33.14 N	71.30 E
Shakargarh	123	32.16 N	75.10 E
Shakarpura	272a	28.46 N	77.21 E
Shakarpur Khās ◆[8]	272a	28.38 N	77.17 E
Shakaskraal	158	29.26 S	31.14 E
Shakawe	156	18.23 S	21.50 E
Shakeng	98	42.13 N	116.35 E
Shaker Heights	214	41.28 N	81.32 W
Shaker Heights Park ♦	279a	41.29 N	81.33 W
Shakespeare	212	43.22 N	80.49 W
Shākhen	128	33.22 N	59.32 E
Shakhtars'k	83	48.03 N	38.28 E
Shakhtne	83	47.57 N	38.17 E
Shakhty → Šachty	83	47.42 N	40.13 E
Shaki	150	8.39 N	3.25 E
Shākir, Jazīrat I	140	27.30 N	33.59 E
Shakopee	190	44.47 N	93.31 W
Shakotan-hantō ›[1]	92a	43.20 N	140.30 E
Shakou	100	24.25 N	113.32 E
Shakshūk	142	29.28 N	30.42 E
Shaktoolik	180	64.20 N	161.09 W
Shakujii ◆[8]	268	35.45 N	139.37 E
Shakūrpur ◆[8]	272a	28.41 N	77.09 E
Shala, Lake ⊜	144	7.25 N	38.30 E
Shalalth	182	50.44 N	122.13 W
Shalatayn, Bi'r ⊤[4]	140	23.08 N	35.36 E
Shaleitian Dao I	98	39.03 N	118.44 E
Shaler Mountains ⩘	176	72.35 N	110.45 W
Shaleshanto	156	19.09 S	23.58 E
Shalford	260	51.13 N	0.34 W
Shālimah	142	31.14 N	30.52 E
Shalimar Railroad Station ◆[5]	272b	22.33 N	88.19 E
Shaling, Zhg.	104	41.09 N	122.22 E
Shaling, Zhg.	104	41.20 N	123.01 E
Shalingpu	104	41.47 N	123.11 E
Shalingzi	105	40.42 N	114.55 E
Shaliuhe, Zhg.	102	36.28 N	98.57 E
Shaliuhe, Zhg.	105	39.53 N	117.56 E
Shallotte	192	33.58 N	78.23 W
Shallowater	196	33.41 N	101.59 W
Shallow Brook ≃	276	40.21 N	74.35 W
Shallow Lake	212	44.36 N	81.05 W
Shaluhe	89	51.08 N	126.00 E
Shaluli Shan ⩘	102	30.45 N	99.45 E
Shalyhyne	78	51.34 N	34.07 E
Shām, Bādiyat ash- (Syrian Desert) ◆[2]	128	32.00 N	40.00 E
Shām, Jabal ash- ʌ	128	23.13 N	57.16 E
Shama ≃	154	6.16 S	32.27 E
Shaman	85	38.50 N	75.36 E
Shamattawa	184	55.52 N	92.05 W
Shambe	140	7.07 N	30.46 E
Shambi	152	1.49 S	22.39 E
Shambu	144	9.40 N	37.03 E
Shambuanda	152	6.38 S	20.13 E
Shām Churasi	123	31.30 N	75.45 E
Shamei	100	24.32 N	118.25 E
Shamepūr ◆[8]	272a	28.45 N	77.09 E
Shamīl	128	27.30 N	56.53 E
Shāmli	124	29.27 N	77.19 E
Shammākh	132	30.30 N	35.30 E
Shamokin	208	40.47 N	76.33 W
Shamona Creek ≃	285	40.02 N	75.43 W
Shamrayivka	78	49.46 N	29.49 E
Shamrock, Fl., U.S.	192	29.38 N	83.08 W
Shamrock, Tx., U.S.	196	35.12 N	100.14 W
Shamsābād	124	27.01 N	78.08 E
Shamsher	272a	28.44 N	77.24 E
Shamva	154	17.18 S	31.34 E
Shan □[3]	110	22.00 N	98.00 E
Shanbiao	98	35.28 N	113.57 E
Shancheng	102	37.01 N	107.00 E
Shanchengzhen	98	42.23 N	125.26 E
Shandaken	210	42.07 N	74.23 W
Shandan	102	38.45 N	101.15 E
Shandatgyi	110	19.37 N	94.43 E
Shandī	140	16.42 N	33.26 E
Shandian ≃	98	42.23 N	116.21 E
Shandianhe	98	42.22 N	116.15 E

	English	Deutsch	Español	Français	Português
≃	River	Fluß	Río	Rivière	Rio
≅	Canal	Kanal	Canal	Canal	Canal
ʟ	Waterfall, Rapids	Wasserfall, Stromschnellen	Cascada, Rápidos	Chute d'eau, Rapides	Cascata, Rápidos
⊔	Strait	Meeresstraße	Estrecho	Détroit	Estreito
ᴄ	Bay, Gulf	Bucht, Golf	Bahía, Golfo	Baie, Golfe	Baía, Golfo
⊜	Lake, Lakes	See, Seen	Lago, Lagos	Lac, Lacs	Lago, Lagos
⩩	Swamp	Sumpf	Pantano	Marais	Pântano
⍓	Ice Features, Glacier	Eis- und Gletscherformen	Accidentes Glaciales	Formes glaciaires	Acidentes glaciares
⊤	Other Hydrographic Features	Andere Hydrographische Objekte	Otros Elementos Hidrográficos	Autres données hydrographiques	Outros acidentes hidrográficos
✣	Submarine Features	Untermeerische Objekte	Accidentes Submarinos	Formes de relief sous-marin	Acidentes submarinos
□	Political Unit	Politische Einheit	Unidad Politica	Entité politique	Unidade política
ʊ	Cultural Institution	Kulturelle Institution	Institución Cultural	Institution culturelle	Instituição cultural
⊥	Historical Site	Historische Stätte	Sitio Histórico	Site historique	Sitio histórico
♦	Recreational Site	Erholungs- und Ferienort	Sitio de Recreo	Centre de loisirs	Area de Lazer
⊠	Airport	Flughafen	Aeropuerto	Aéroport	Aeroporto
■	Military Installation	Militäranlage	Instalación Militar	Installation militaire	Instalação militar
◆	Miscellaneous	Verschiedenes	Misceláneo	Divers	Diversos

Name	Page	Lat.°′	Long.°′
Shandīd	**142**	30.55 N	30.40 E
Shandon	**226**	35.39 N	120.22 W
Shandong	**107**	29.31 N	106.25 E
Shandong (Shantung) □[4]	**98**	36.00 N	118.00 E
Shandong Bandao (Shantung Peninsula) ≻[1]	**98**	37.00 N	121.00 E
Shandrivka	**78**	48.57 N	35.46 E
Shaner	**279b**	40.17 N	79.47 W
Shanesville	**214**	40.31 N	81.39 W
Shangalume	**154**	10.49 S	26.34 E
Shangani	**154**	19.47 S	29.22 E
Shangani ≃	**154**	18.41 S	27.10 E
Shang'ao	**106**	30.41 N	119.25 E
Shangba	**106**	32.11 N	118.46 E
Shangbahe	**100**	30.40 N	115.05 E
Shangbai	**106**	30.29 N	119.58 E
Shangbancheng	**105**	40.50 N	118.03 E
Shangbatang	**102**	32.46 N	96.20 E
Shangcai	**100**	33.16 N	114.15 E
Shangcang	**105**	39.54 N	117.23 E
Shangchen	**106**	30.07 N	119.53 E
Shangcheng	**100**	31.48 N	115.24 E
Shangchewan	**100**	29.48 N	113.01 E
Shangch'iu → Shangqiu	**98**	34.27 N	115.42 E
Shangchuan Dao I	**102**	21.42 N	112.47 E
Shangdang	**106**	32.06 N	119.24 E
Shangdayangqi	**89**	51.09 N	124.02 E
Shangdian	**100**	34.07 N	112.23 E
Shangdianmiao	**106**	30.56 N	120.51 E
Shangdouying	**105**	40.36 N	115.33 E
Shangdu	**98**	41.29 N	113.34 E
Shangduichunshi	**104**	41.00 N	123.02 E
Shangdundu	**100**	27.56 N	116.15 E
Shangfu	**100**	28.40 N	114.59 E
Shanggaixin	**102**	23.25 N	100.02 E
Shanggan	**100**	25.56 N	119.22 E
Shanggang	**100**	33.30 N	120.04 E
Shanggangzi	**104**	42.26 N	123.03 E
Shanggao	**100**	28.18 N	114.54 E
Shanggecun	**106**	31.49 N	119.07 E
Shanggu	**98**	40.47 N	118.28 E
Shangguanying	**98**	41.18 N	117.07 E
Shanghai, Va., U.S.	**208**	37.37 N	76.47 W
Shanghai, Zhg.	**106**	31.14 N	121.28 E
Shanghai, Zhg.	**106**	31.07 N	121.22 E
Shanghai, Zhg.	**269b**	31.14 N	121.28 E
Shanghailingao	**104**	41.57 N	120.55 E
Shanghai Museum ✿	**269b**	31.13 N	121.28 E
Shanghai Shi (Shanghai Shih) □[7]	**106**	31.10 N	121.30 E
Shanghai Station ⊸[5]	**269b**	31.15 N	121.28 E
Shanghang	**100**	25.06 N	116.25 E
Shanghe	**98**	37.19 N	117.07 E
Shanghekou	**98**	40.26 N	124.47 E
Shanghetou	**105**	39.12 N	116.59 E
Shanghewantun	**104**	41.42 N	123.23 E
Shang Hu ⊜	**106**	31.39 N	120.41 E
Shanghuang	**106**	31.33 N	119.34 E
Shanghuangqi	**98**	41.29 N	116.31 E
Shanghucun	**105**	40.45 N	115.45 E
Shangjao → Shangrao	**100**	28.26 N	117.58 E
Shangjiafen	**104**	41.18 N	121.10 E
Shangjiahe	**98**	41.51 N	124.28 E
Shangjiaodao	**100**	29.00 N	119.54 E
Shangjiatai	**104**	40.53 N	123.35 E
Shangjie	**100**	27.06 N	116.06 E
Shangjin	**102**	33.09 N	110.03 E
Shangjiuwu	**100**	33.59 N	113.01 E
Shangkasa	**120**	33.45 N	80.12 E
Shangkou	**98**	36.59 N	118.53 E
Shanglanjiagou	**104**	40.52 N	120.37 E
Shanglin, Zhg.	**98**	38.19 N	116.05 E
Shanglin, Zhg.	**102**	23.28 N	108.33 E
Shanglin, Zhg.	**104**	41.31 N	122.14 E
Shanglishi	**100**	27.52 N	113.46 E
Shangliuhezicun	**104**	41.28 N	123.32 E
Shangliulinzi	**104**	41.02 N	123.13 E
Shangmagushan	**104**	41.41 N	124.10 E
Shangmatai	**105**	39.22 N	117.15 E
Shangmatun	**104**	40.57 N	123.22 E
Shangmingdian	**106**	31.12 N	120.57 E
Shangmingju	**105**	39.41 N	115.12 E
Shangnan	**102**	33.31 N	110.45 E
Shangpandaoling	**104**	41.42 N	121.14 E
Shangpeibu	**106**	31.28 N	119.13 E
Shangping, Zhg.	**100**	25.57 N	117.33 E
Shangping, Zhg.	**100**	24.43 N	115.27 E
Shangping, Zhg.	**100**	24.29 N	114.38 E
Shangpuzi	**104**	41.37 N	121.35 E
Shangqianbu	**106**	30.27 N	120.04 E
Shangqiao	**100**	31.02 N	117.42 E
Shangqing, Zhg.	**100**	25.53 N	118.36 E
Shangqing, Zhg.	**100**	28.02 N	117.00 E
Shangqingshuicun	**105**	39.56 N	115.38 E
Shangqiu (Zhuji), Zhg.	**98**	34.27 N	115.42 E
Shangqiu, Zhg.	**98**	34.23 N	115.37 E
Shangrao	**100**	28.26 N	117.58 E
Shangshe	**102**	38.15 N	113.20 E
Shangshibatai	**104**	42.02 N	120.51 E
Shangshui	**100**	33.33 N	114.34 E
Shangsi	**102**	22.09 N	107.57 E
Shangtan	**106**	30.27 N	118.42 E
Shangtang	**100**	33.23 N	118.02 E
Shan Guan)(	**100**	27.30 N	117.06 E
Shangweiniuchang	**104**	40.54 N	120.44 E
Shangxian	**102**	33.51 N	109.54 E
Shangxingzhen	**106**	31.32 N	119.15 E
Shangxinhe	**106**	32.02 N	118.43 E
Shangxinqiu	**104**	42.27 N	121.37 E
Shangyangbao	**98**	42.30 N	124.14 E
Shangyangcun	**106**	30.48 N	118.40 E
Shangye	**98**	35.26 N	117.59 E
Shangyi (Nanhaoqian)	**98**	41.04 N	114.03 E
Shangying	**89**	44.10 N	127.17 E
Shangyinkou	**102**	32.52 N	103.04 E
Shangyou	**100**	25.51 N	114.30 E
Shangyou ≃	**100**	25.49 N	114.50 E
Shangyou Shuiku ⊜[1]	**100**	25.52 N	114.21 E
Shangyu	**100**	30.02 N	120.54 E
Shangyuan	**104**	41.39 N	120.55 E
Shangyun	**102**	23.01 N	99.50 E
Shangzhai	**98**	39.13 N	114.17 E
Shangzhaoshugou	**104**	42.12 N	121.58 E
Shangzhazi	**105**	40.52 N	117.42 E
Shangzhenzhuang	**105**	40.20 N	117.06 E
Shangzhi	**89**	45.13 N	127.59 E
Shangzhuangtai	**105**	39.41 N	115.25 E
Shanhaiguan	**98**	40.01 N	119.44 E
Shanhaikwan → Shanhaiguan	**98**	40.01 N	119.44 E
Shanhecun	**89**	45.38 N	128.27 E
Shanhetun	**89**	44.44 N	127.12 E
Shanjiazhuang	**105**	38.52 N	115.45 E
Shanklin	**42**	50.38 N	1.10 W
Shankou, Zhg.	**100**	26.40 N	117.46 E
Shankou, Zhg.	**100**	28.58 N	115.12 E
Shankou, Zhg.	**100**	28.48 N	114.29 E
Shankou, Zhg.	**102**	21.38 N	109.43 E
Shanlenggang	**102**	28.33 N	103.23 E
Shanli	**100**	29.52 N	117.21 E
Shanlian	**106**	30.42 N	120.19 E
Shanmenjie	**106**	30.40 N	118.52 E
Shanmulong	**102**	24.39 N	98.05 E
Shannanguan	**100**	31.36 N	116.52 E
Shannock	**207**	41.26 N	71.38 W
Shannon, Ire.	**48**	52.43 N	8.53 W
Shannon, N.Z.	**172**	40.33 S	175.25 E
Shannon, S. Afr.	**158**	29.08 S	26.18 E
Shannon, Ga., U.S.	**192**	34.20 N	85.04 W
Shannon, Il., U.S.	**190**	42.09 N	89.44 W
Shannon, Ms., U.S.	**194**	34.06 N	88.42 W
Shannon ≃	**48**	52.36 N	9.41 W
Shannon, Lake ⊜	**224**	48.37 N	121.42 W
Shannon, Mouth of the ≃[1]	**48**	52.30 N	9.50 W
Shannon Airport ⊠	**48**	52.41 N	8.55 W
Shannons Flat	**171b**	35.54 S	148.58 E
Shannontown	**192**	33.53 N	80.21 W
Shannonville	**212**	44.12 N	77.13 W
Shanpo	**100**	30.06 N	114.20 E
Shanrendong	**89**	46.50 N	123.08 E
Shanrenqiao	**106**	31.16 N	120.27 E
Shanshan	**86**	42.52 N	90.10 E
Shanshenmiao	**105**	40.45 N	117.11 E
Shanshūr	**142**	30.21 N	31.00 E
Shansi → Shanxi □[4]	**102**	37.00 N	112.00 E
Shanting	**98**	35.09 N	117.29 E
Shāntipur	**126**	23.15 N	88.26 E
Shantou (Swatow)	**100**	23.23 N	116.41 E
Shantung → Shandong □[4]	**98**	36.00 N	118.00 E
Shantung Peninsula → Shandong Bandao ≻[1]	**98**	37.00 N	121.00 E
Shanty Bay	**212**	44.25 N	79.36 W
Shanwa	**154**	3.10 S	33.46 E
Shanwei	**100**	22.47 N	115.21 E
Shanxi (Shansi) □[4]	**102**	37.00 N	112.00 E
Shanxian, Zhg.	**98**	34.48 N	116.03 E
Shanxian → Sanmenxia, Zhg.	**102**	34.45 N	111.05 E
Shanxiawu	**100**	28.52 N	113.52 E
Shanxu	**102**	22.21 N	107.58 E
Shanyang, Zhg.	**100**	26.43 N	119.13 E
Shanyang, Zhg.	**102**	33.35 N	109.49 E
Shanyang, Zhg.	**106**	31.19 N	120.16 E
Shanyao	**100**	25.13 N	118.55 E
Shanyaqiao	**106**	31.15 N	119.25 E
Shanyin	**102**	39.33 N	112.50 E
Shanzhangjiafen	**105**	40.37 N	116.44 E
Shanzui	**105**	40.48 N	118.13 E
Shanzuizi	**104**	41.55 N	120.30 E
Shaobo	**100**	32.30 N	119.32 E
Shaodenggao	**104**	42.13 N	121.47 E
Shaodian, Zhg.	**98**	34.08 N	118.25 E
Shaodian, Zhg.	**100**	33.10 N	114.18 E
Shaoguan	**100**	24.50 N	113.37 E
Shaogudian	**98**	36.57 N	115.32 E
Shaoguyingzi	**104**	41.33 N	120.27 E
Shaohing → Shaoxing	**100**	30.00 N	120.35 E
Shaohsing → Shaoxing	**100**	30.00 N	120.35 E
Shaojiaolou	**106**	31.05 N	121.32 E
Shaokuan → Shaoguan	**100**	24.50 N	113.37 E
Shaowu	**100**	27.20 N	117.28 E
Shaoxing	**100**	30.00 N	120.35 E
Shaoyang, Zhg.	**102**	27.15 N	111.28 E
Shaoyang, Zhg.	**102**	27.00 N	111.18 E
Shaoyun	**107**	29.30 N	105.57 E
Shaozihe	**98**	40.13 N	123.33 E
Shap	**44**	54.32 N	2.41 W
Shapinsay I	**46**	59.03 N	2.53 W
Shāpūr ≃	**128**	29.39 N	51.03 E
Shaq'ah, Ra's ash- ≻	**130**	34.19 N	35.41 E
Shaqqā	**132**	32.53 N	36.42 E
Shaqq al-Ju'ayfir, Wādī ∨	**140**	15.16 N	26.00 E
Shaqrā', Ar. Su.	**128**	25.15 N	45.15 E
Shaqrā, Lubnān	**132**	33.12 N	35.28 E
Shaqrā', Sūrīy.	**132**	32.54 N	36.14 E
Shaqrā', Yaman	**144**	13.21 N	45.42 E
Shaquan	**86**	44.33 N	83.25 E
Shaquzhen	**107**	30.33 N	103.45 E
Sharafābād	**272a**	28.36 N	77.23 E
Sharafkhāneh	**128**	38.11 N	45.29 E
Sharan Jogīzai	**120**	31.02 N	68.33 E
Sharatin Mountain ∧	**180**	57.49 N	152.41 W
Sharbatāt, Ra's ash- ≻	**118**	17.56 N	56.21 E
Sharbīn, Jabal ∧	**132**	33.43 N	36.21 E
Sharbot Lake	**212**	44.46 N	76.41 W
Sharbot Lake ⊜	**212**	44.46 N	76.41 W
Share	**150**	8.50 N	4.56 E
Sharhorod	**78**	48.44 N	28.05 E
Shari	**92a**	43.55 N	144.50 E
Shari-dake ∧	**92a**	43.46 N	144.43 E
Sharīṭah, Ra's ≻	**128**	26.23 N	56.23 E
Sharivka	**78**	50.01 N	35.27 E
Shark ≃	**220**	25.21 N	81.05 W
Shark Bay ⊂	**162**	25.30 S	113.30 E
Shark Point ≻, Austl.	**274a**	33.55 S	151.17 E
Shark Point ≻, Fl., U.S.	**220**	25.23 N	81.09 W
Shark River Hills	**208**	40.12 N	74.03 W
Sharktooth Mountain ∧	**180**	58.35 N	127.57 W
Sharm ash-Shaykh	**140**	27.51 N	34.17 E
Sharnbrook	**42**	52.13 N	0.32 W
Sharnūb	**142**	31.01 N	30.35 E
Sharon, On., Can.	**214**	42.53 N	81.22 W
Sharon, Ct., U.S.	**207**	41.52 N	73.28 W
Sharon, Ma., U.S.	**207**	42.07 N	71.10 W
Sharon, N.D., U.S.	**198**	47.35 N	97.53 W
Sharon, Pa., U.S.	**214**	41.13 N	80.29 W
Sharon, Tn., U.S.	**194**	36.14 N	88.49 W
Sharon, Wi., U.S.	**216**	42.30 N	88.43 W
Sharon Center	**214**	41.06 N	81.44 W
Sharon Hill	**285**	39.54 N	75.16 W
Sharon Park	**218**	39.23 N	84.35 W
Sharon Springs, Ks., U.S.	**198**	38.53 N	101.45 W
Sharon Springs, N.Y., U.S.	**210**	42.48 N	74.37 W
Sharon Valley	**207**	41.53 N	73.29 W
Sharonville	**218**	39.16 N	84.24 W
Sharpe, Lake ⊜[1]	**198**	44.05 N	99.55 W
Sharpe Lake ⊜	**184**	54.24 N	93.30 W
Sharpes	**220**	28.25 N	80.45 W
Sharp Island I	**271d**	22.22 N	114.17 E
Sharpley	**285**	39.48 N	75.33 W
Sharp Park ♦	**282**	37.37 N	122.29 W
Sharp Peak ∧	**116**	5.58 N	125.31 E
Sharpsburg, Il., U.S.	**219**	39.37 N	89.21 W
Sharpsburg, Ky., U.S.	**218**	38.12 N	83.55 W
Sharpsburg, Pa., U.S.	**279b**	40.29 N	79.55 W
Sharps Hill	**279b**	40.30 N	79.56 W
Sharps Run ≃	**285**	39.54 N	74.49 W
Sharpsville, In., U.S.	**216**	40.22 N	86.05 W
Sharpsville, Pa., U.S.	**214**	41.15 N	80.28 W
Sharptown, Md., U.S.	**208**	38.32 N	75.43 W
Sharptown, N.J., U.S.	**285**	39.39 N	75.21 W
Sharqī, Al-Jabal ash- (Anti-Lebanon) ⋀	**132**	33.35 N	36.00 E
Sharqīyah, Aṣ-Ṣaḥrā' ash- (Arabian Desert) ⊸[2]	**140**	28.00 N	32.00 E
Sharqpur	**123**	31.28 N	74.06 E
Sharshar, Jabal ∧[2]	**140**	23.52 N	30.20 E
Shartlesville	**208**	40.31 N	76.06 W
Shārūnah	**142**	28.36 N	30.51 E
Shārūnah, Wādī ∨	**142**	28.36 N	30.52 E
Shasha	**144**	6.20 N	35.57 E
Shashe ≃	**156**	22.14 S	29.20 E
Shashemene	**144**	7.12 N	38.43 E
Shashi	**102**	30.19 N	112.14 E
Shashibu	**100**	25.48 N	114.54 E
Shasi → Shashi	**102**	30.19 N	112.14 E
Shasta	**204**	40.36 N	122.29 W
Shasta ≃	**204**	41.50 N	122.35 W
Shasta, Mount ∧[1]	**204**	41.20 N	122.20 W
Shasta Lake ⊜[1]	**204**	40.50 N	122.25 W
Shatangjiang	**106**	31.25 N	120.01 E
Shaṭānūf	**142**	30.14 N	31.04 E
Shatawī	**140**	14.39 N	32.06 E
Shāṭi', Wādī ash- ∨	**146**	27.30 N	13.15 E
Shatian, Zhg.	**100**	25.53 N	113.44 E
Shatian, Zhg.	**100**	23.59 N	113.56 E
Shatila	**132**	33.51 N	35.30 E
Sha Tin	**271d**	22.23 N	114.11 E
Shats'k	**78**	51.31 N	23.57 E
Shats'kyy Pryrodnyy Natsional'nyy Park ♦	**78**	51.30 N	23.55 E
Shatt al-Arab → Arab, Shatt al- ≃	**128**	29.57 N	48.34 E
Shattuck	**196**	36.16 N	99.52 W
Shatuji	**98**	35.18 N	115.45 E
Shatuosi	**102**	31.20 N	108.51 E
Shauck	**214**	40.37 N	82.40 W
Shaunavon	**184**	49.40 N	108.25 W
Shaver Lake	**226**	37.09 N	119.18 W
Shaver Lake ⊜[1]	**226**	37.08 N	119.17 W
Shavertown	**210**	41.19 N	75.55 W
Shavé Ẕiyyon	**132**	32.59 N	35.05 E
Shavington	**44**	53.04 N	2.27 W
Shaw, Eng., U.K.	**44**	53.34 N	2.05 W
Shaw, Ms., U.S.	**194**	33.36 N	90.46 W
Shaw ≃	**162**	20.20 S	119.17 E
Shaw Air Force Base ■	**192**	33.58 N	80.29 W
Shawan, Zhg.	**86**	44.34 N	85.48 E
Shawan, Zhg.	**100**	27.52 N	119.28 E
Shawan, Zhg.	**107**	29.25 N	103.33 E
Shawanaga Inlet ⊂	**190**	45.32 N	80.24 W
Shawangunk Kill ≃	**210**	41.41 N	74.10 W
Shawangunk Mountains ⋀	**210**	41.35 N	74.30 W
Shawano	**190**	44.46 N	88.36 W
Shawbury	**42**	52.47 N	2.39 W
Shaw Creek ≃	**192**	33.34 N	81.30 W
Shawforth	**262**	53.41 N	2.10 W
Shawhan	**218**	38.18 N	84.16 W
Shawinigan	**206**	46.33 N	72.45 W
Shawinigan ≃	**206**	46.32 N	72.46 W
Shawinigan, Lac ⊜	**206**	46.41 N	73.10 W
Shawinigan Falls → Shawinigan	**206**	46.33 N	72.45 W
Shawinigan-Sud	**206**	46.31 N	72.45 W
Shaw Island I	**224**	48.34 N	122.57 W
Shawmarī, Wādī ash- ∨	**132**	30.21 N	36.25 E
Shawmere ≃	**190**	48.20 N	82.28 W
Shawnee, Ks., U.S.	**198**	39.02 N	94.43 W
Shawnee, Oh., U.S.	**188**	39.36 N	82.12 W
Shawnee, Ok., U.S.	**196**	35.19 N	96.55 W
Shawnee, Lake ⊜	**276**	40.58 N	74.35 W
Shawnee Hills	**214**	40.07 N	83.09 W
Shawnee On Delaware	**210**	41.01 N	75.07 W
Shawnee State Park ♦	**218**	38.43 N	83.10 W
Shawneetown	**194**	37.42 N	88.11 W
Shawnī	**142**	30.45 N	30.55 E
Shawnigan Lake	**224**	48.38 N	123.35 W
Shawnigan Lake ⊜	**224**	48.37 N	123.37 W
Shawo, Som.	**144**	3.26 N	45.21 E
Shawo, Zhg.	**98**	34.28 N	114.37 E
Shawo, Zhg.	**100**	31.44 N	115.08 E
Shawo, Zhg.	**100**	28.52 N	114.47 E
Shawsheen ≃	**283**	42.42 N	71.08 W
Shawsheen Village	**283**	42.40 N	71.09 W
Shawtown	**279b**	40.20 N	79.42 W
Shawville	**188**	45.36 N	76.30 W
Shaxi, Zhg.	**100**	28.34 N	118.06 E
Shaxi, Zhg.	**100**	26.53 N	115.34 E
Shaxi, Zhg.	**100**	24.38 N	113.42 E
Shaxi, Zhg.	**106**	31.34 N	121.04 E
Shaxian	**100**	26.24 N	117.47 E
Shaxikou	**100**	26.33 N	118.02 E
Shaximiao	**107**	29.57 N	106.19 E
Shayang	**100**	30.42 N	112.33 E
Shaybārā I	**128**	25.27 N	36.48 E
Shay Gap	**162**	20.25 S	120.03 E
Shaykh, Jabal ash- (Mount Hermon) ∧	**132**	33.26 N	35.51 E
Shaykh, Wādī ash- ∨	**142**	28.48 N	30.55 E
Shaykh Al-Ḥadīd	**130**	36.30 N	36.35 E
Shaykh Miskīn	**132**	32.49 N	36.09 E
Shaykh Sa'd	**128**	32.34 N	46.17 E
Shaykh 'Uthmān	**144**	12.52 N	44.59 E
Shayuan	**100**	27.45 N	120.38 E
Shazhen	**98**	36.23 N	115.47 E
Shazhou	**106**	31.52 N	120.32 E
Shazihe	**102**	32.12 N	106.42 E
Shchastya	**83**	48.44 N	39.14 E
Shchekino → Ščokino	**76**	54.01 N	37.31 E
Shchelkovo → Ščolkovo	**76**	55.55 N	38.00 E
Shcherbakov → Rybinsk	**76**	58.03 N	38.52 E
Shchors	**78**	51.49 N	31.59 E
Shchors'k	**78**	48.22 N	34.06 E
Shchotove	**83**	48.09 N	39.04 E
She ≃	**100**	30.41 N	114.32 E
Sheaf ≃	**44**	53.23 N	1.26 W
Shea Island I	**276**	41.03 N	73.24 W
Sheakleyville	**214**	41.27 N	80.13 W
Shea Stadium ♦	**276**	40.45 N	73.51 W
Shebele	**144**	9.43 N	42.43 E
Shebele (Shabeelle) ≃	**144**	0.12 S	42.45 E
Shebelynka	**78**	49.27 N	36.30 E
Sheberghān	**120**	36.41 N	65.45 E
Shebeshekong ≃	**212**	45.26 N	80.19 W
Sheboygan	**190**	43.45 N	87.42 W
Sheboygan ≃	**190**	43.45 N	87.42 W
Sheboygan Falls	**190**	43.43 N	87.48 W
Shebu	**100**	27.40 N	112.48 E
Shechem → Nābulus	**132**	32.13 N	35.16 E
Shechem ⊥	**132**	32.13 N	35.15 E
Shecheng	**102**	37.14 N	113.05 E
Shedd Canyon ∨	**226**	35.39 N	120.26 W
Shedden	**214**	42.44 N	81.21 W
Shediac	**186**	46.13 N	64.32 W
Shedin Peak ∧	**182**	55.55 N	127.32 W
Sheekh	**144**	9.56 N	45.11 E
Sheelin, Lough ⊜	**48**	53.48 N	7.22 W
Sheenjek ≃	**180**	66.45 N	144.33 W
Sheep ≃	**182**	50.44 N	113.51 W
Sheep Creek ≃, Ab., Can.	**182**	54.04 N	119.00 W
Sheep Creek ≃, U.S.	**202**	42.27 N	115.36 W
Sheep Creek ≃, Ut., U.S.	**200**	40.55 N	109.39 W
Sheep Creek ≃, Wy., U.S.	**200**	42.03 N	106.04 W
Sheep Haven ⊂	**48**	55.10 N	7.52 W
Sheepmoor	**158**	26.42 S	30.13 E
Sheep Mountain ∧, Az., U.S.	**200**	32.32 N	114.14 W
Sheep Mountain ∧, Wy., U.S.	**200**	43.33 N	110.32 W
Sheep Peak ∧	**196**	31.14 N	104.59 W
Sheepranch	**226**	38.13 N	120.28 W
Sheep Range ⋀	**204**	36.45 N	115.05 W
Sheepshead Bay ⊸[8]	**276**	40.35 N	73.56 W
's-Heerenberg	**52**	51.53 N	6.15 E
's-Heerenhoek	**52**	51.27 N	3.46 E
Sheerness	**42**	51.27 N	0.45 E
Sheet Harbour	**186**	44.55 N	62.32 W
Shefar'am	**132**	32.48 N	35.10 E
Sheffield, N.Z.	**172**	43.23 S	172.01 E
Sheffield, Eng., U.K.	**44**	53.23 N	1.28 W
Sheffield, Al., U.S.	**194**	34.45 N	87.41 W
Sheffield, Il., U.S.	**190**	41.21 N	89.44 W
Sheffield, Ia., U.S.	**190**	42.53 N	93.12 W
Sheffield, Ma., U.S.	**207**	42.06 N	73.21 W
Sheffield, Oh., U.S.	**214**	41.25 N	82.05 W
Sheffield, Pa., U.S.	**214**	41.42 N	79.02 W
Sheffield, Tx., U.S.	**196**	30.41 N	101.49 W
Sheffield Island I	**276**	41.03 N	73.25 W
Sheffield Island Harbor ⊂	**276**	41.03 N	73.25 W
Sheffield Lake	**214**	41.29 N	82.06 W
Sheffield Lake ⊜	**186**	49.20 N	56.35 W
Shefford	**42**	52.02 N	0.20 W
Shefford □[6]	**206**	45.25 N	72.30 W
Shefu	**100**	26.11 N	115.22 E
Shegangshi	**100**	28.32 N	113.36 E
Shegaon	**122**	20.47 N	76.41 E
Sheho	**184**	51.38 N	103.12 W
Shehong	**102**	30.56 N	105.22 E
Shehongmiao	**107**	30.44 N	106.03 E
Shehy Mountains ⋀	**48**	51.48 N	9.15 W
Sheikh Hasan	**144**	12.04 N	35.53 E
Sheikhpura	**124**	25.09 N	85.51 E
Shekatika	**186**	51.17 N	58.20 W
Shekhūpura	**123**	31.42 N	73.59 E
Sheki → Šeki	**84**	41.12 N	47.12 E
Shekki → Zhongshan	**100**	22.31 N	113.22 E
Shek Kong	**271d**	22.26 N	114.06 E
Shek Kong Airfield ⊠	**271d**	22.27 N	114.05 E
Shek Kwu Chau I	**271d**	22.12 N	113.59 E
Shekou	**100**	30.44 N	114.20 E
Shek Uk Shan ∧	**271d**	22.27 N	114.18 E
Shelagyote Peak ∧	**182**	55.58 N	127.12 W
Shelbina	**219**	39.41 N	92.02 W
Shelbourne	**169**	36.52 S	144.01 E
Shelburn	**194**	39.11 N	87.24 W
Shelburne, N.S., Can.	**186**	43.46 N	65.19 W
Shelburne, On., Can.	**212**	44.04 N	80.12 W
Shelburne Bay ⊂	**164**	11.49 S	143.00 E
Shelburne Falls	**207**	42.36 N	72.44 W
Shelby, In., U.S.	**216**	41.11 N	87.20 W
Shelby, Ia., U.S.	**198**	41.30 N	95.27 W
Shelby, Mi., U.S.	**190**	43.36 N	86.21 W
Shelby, Ms., U.S.	**194**	33.57 N	90.46 W
Shelby, Mt., U.S.	**202**	48.30 N	111.51 W
Shelby, Ne., U.S.	**198**	41.11 N	97.25 W
Shelby, N.C., U.S.	**192**	35.17 N	81.32 W
Shelby, Oh., U.S.	**214**	40.52 N	82.39 W
Shelby □[6], Il., U.S.	**219**	39.24 N	88.48 W
Shelby □[6], In., U.S.	**218**	39.31 N	85.47 W
Shelby □[6], Ky., U.S.	**218**	38.15 N	85.13 W
Shelby □[6], Mo., U.S.	**219**	39.49 N	92.03 W
Shelby □[6], Oh., U.S.	**216**	40.17 N	84.09 W
Shelby Village	**281**	42.38 N	83.04 W
Shelbyville, Il., U.S.	**219**	39.24 N	88.47 W
Shelbyville, In., U.S.	**218**	39.31 N	85.46 W
Shelbyville, Ky., U.S.	**218**	38.12 N	85.13 W
Shelbyville, Mo., U.S.	**219**	39.48 N	92.02 W
Shelbyville, Tn., U.S.	**194**	35.29 N	86.27 W
Shelbyville, Lake ⊜[1]	**219**	39.30 N	88.40 W
Sheldon, Il., U.S.	**216**	40.46 N	87.33 W
Sheldon, Ia., U.S.	**198**	43.10 N	95.51 W
Sheldon, Mi., U.S.	**216**	42.17 N	83.28 W
Sheldon, Mo., U.S.	**194**	37.39 N	94.17 W
Sheldon, Tx., U.S.	**222**	29.52 N	95.08 W
Sheldon Brook ≃	**276**	41.03 N	73.52 W
Sheldon Creek ≃	**212**	44.07 N	79.53 W
Sheldon Point	**180**	62.32 N	164.52 W
Sheldon Reservoir ⊜[1]	**222**	29.52 N	95.10 W
Sheldonville	**283**	42.02 N	71.23 W
Sheldrake ≃	**276**	40.57 N	73.44 W
Sheldrake Lake ⊜, On., Can.	**212**	44.49 N	77.16 W
Sheldrake Lake ⊜, N.Y., U.S.	**276**	40.57 N	73.46 W
Shelikof Strait ⋃	**180**	57.30 N	155.00 W
Shell ≃	**184**	50.58 N	101.24 W
Shell, Loch ⊂	**46**	58.00 N	6.30 W
Shellbrook	**184**	53.13 N	106.24 W
Shell Brook ≃	**184**	53.21 N	106.00 W
Shell Creek ≃, U.S.	**200**	40.56 N	108.37 W
Shell Creek ≃, Ne., U.S.	**198**	41.27 N	96.58 W
Shell Creek ≃, N.D., U.S.	**198**	47.59 N	102.17 W
Shell Creek ≃, Wy., U.S.	**202**	44.31 N	108.03 W
Shellen	**146**	9.54 N	12.00 E
Shelley, B.C., Can.	**182**	54.00 N	122.37 W
Shelley, Id., U.S.	**202**	43.22 N	112.07 W
Shellharbour	**170**	34.35 S	150.52 E
Shell Lake, Sk., Can.	**184**	53.18 N	107.04 W
Shell Lake, Wi., U.S.	**190**	45.44 N	91.55 W
Shell Lakes ⊜	**162**	29.21 S	127.25 E
Shellman	**192**	31.45 N	84.36 W
Shellmouth Dam ⊸[6]	**184**	50.58 N	101.25 W
Shellow Bowells	**260**	51.45 N	0.20 E
Shell Rock	**190**	42.42 N	92.34 W
Shell Rock ≃	**190**	42.38 N	92.30 W
Shellrock Peak ∧	**224**	46.43 N	121.14 W
Shellsburg	**190**	42.05 N	91.52 W
Shelocta	**214**	40.39 N	79.18 W
Shelter, Port ⊂	**271d**	22.21 N	114.17 E
Shelter Island	**207**	41.04 N	72.20 W
Shelter Island I, H.K.	**271d**	22.20 N	114.17 E
Shelter Island I, N.Y., U.S.	**207**	41.04 N	72.20 W
Shelter Island Heights	**207**	41.05 N	72.21 W
Shelter Island Sound ⋃	**207**	41.03 N	72.22 W
Shelton, Ct., U.S.	**207**	41.18 N	73.05 W
Shelton, Ne., U.S.	**198**	40.47 N	98.44 W
Shelton, Wa., U.S.	**224**	47.13 N	123.06 W
Shemanker ≃	**150**	8.12 N	9.45 E
Shemogue	**186**	46.09 N	64.11 W
Shemya Station	**181a**	52.43 N	174.05 E
Shenandoah, Ia., U.S.	**198**	40.45 N	95.22 W
Shenandoah, Pa., U.S.	**208**	40.49 N	76.12 W
Shenandoah, Va., U.S.	**188**	38.29 N	78.37 W
Shenandoah ≃	**188**	39.19 N	77.44 W
Shenandoah, North Fork ≃	**188**	38.57 N	78.12 W
Shenandoah, South Fork ≃	**188**	38.57 N	78.12 W
Shenandoah Heights	**210**	40.49 N	76.12 W
Shenandoah National Park ♦	**188**	38.48 N	78.12 W
Shenango	**214**	41.23 N	80.24 W
Shenango ≃	**214**	40.57 N	80.23 W
Shenango River Lake ⊜[1]	**214**	41.22 N	80.28 W
Shenchi	**102**	39.09 N	112.19 E
Shencottah	**122**	8.58 N	77.16 E
Shencun	**106**	31.04 N	118.51 E
Shendam	**150**	8.53 N	9.32 E
Shendang	**106**	30.34 N	120.49 E
Shending Shan ∧	**89**	46.38 N	133.28 E
Shenduncun	**106**	30.48 N	120.25 E
Shenfield	**260**	51.38 N	0.19 E
Shengang, Zhg.	**100**	27.20 N	116.18 E
Shengang, Zhg.	**106**	31.54 N	120.08 E
Shenge	**150**	7.55 N	12.57 W
Shengfang	**105**	39.04 N	116.42 E
Shenggongjing	**106**	31.07 N	119.48 E
Shenghongqing	**100**	30.12 N	114.56 E
Shengjiachi	**107**	30.28 N	105.03 E
Shengjiaqiao	**106**	31.27 N	121.24 E
Shengjiatun	**104**	41.14 N	121.22 E
Shengjin'gao	**104**	42.04 N	120.43 E
Shengou	**100**	34.08 N	113.13 E
Shengqing	**104**	41.34 N	121.36 E
Shengshan	**106**	30.50 N	120.15 E
Shengshui	**98**	35.45 N	119.39 E
Shengshuihezi	**98**	42.27 N	125.59 E
Shengsi Liedao II	**100**	30.42 N	122.20 E
Shengtian	**100**	27.14 N	113.06 E
Shengxian	**100**	29.36 N	120.48 E
Shengze	**106**	30.55 N	120.39 E
Shengzigou	**104**	41.35 N	124.04 E
Shenhu	**100**	24.38 N	118.39 E
Shenipsit Lake ⊜	**207**	41.53 N	72.26 W
Shenji	**98**	34.47 N	115.09 E
Shenjia	**89**	46.06 N	126.46 E
Shenjiadian	**89**	46.35 N	130.38 E
Shenjiatai	**104**	41.22 N	120.50 E
Shenjiawan	**106**	31.43 N	121.19 E
Shenjiazhuang	**106**	32.18 N	120.26 E
Shenjing, Zhg.	**102**	21.59 N	112.28 E
Shenjing, Zhg.	**105**	40.24 N	114.49 E
Shenjingzi	**104**	41.47 N	123.41 E
Shenk'eng	**269d**	25.00 N	121.36 E
Shenkou	**100**	28.42 N	116.02 E
Shenley	**260**	51.41 N	0.17 W
Shenmu	**102**	38.56 N	110.19 E
Shennan	**105**	38.59 N	114.56 E
Shenorock	**210**	41.20 N	73.44 W
Shenqiu	**100**	33.24 N	115.02 E
Shenquan	**100**	22.59 N	116.20 E
Shenquan Gang ⊂	**100**	22.54 N	116.18 E
Shensi → Shaanxi □[4]	**102**	35.00 N	109.00 E
Shenton, Mount ∧	**162**	28.00 S	123.22 E
Shentuan	**98**	35.30 N	119.17 E
Shenxian, Zhg.	**98**	38.01 N	115.33 E
Shenxian, Zhg.	**98**	36.15 N	115.41 E
Shenxing	**105**	39.02 N	115.19 E
Shenyang (Mukden)	**104**	41.48 N	123.27 E
Shenze	**98**	38.11 N	115.11 E
Shenzhen	**100**	22.34 N	114.07 E
Sheoganj	**120**	25.09 N	73.04 E
Sheokhāla	**126**	22.46 N	88.10 E
Sheopur	**124**	25.40 N	76.42 E
Shepard	**182**	50.57 N	113.55 W
Shepard Island I	**9**	74.25 S	132.30 W
Shepards Brook ≃	**283**	42.08 N	71.25 W
Shepaug ≃	**207**	41.28 N	73.19 W
Shepetivka	**78**	50.11 N	27.04 E
Shepherd, Mi., U.S.	**190**	43.31 N	84.41 W
Shepherd, Tx., U.S.	**222**	30.30 N	95.01 W
Shepherd □[8]	**175f**	17.05 S	168.25 E
Shepherd, Îles II	**175f**	16.55 S	168.36 E
Shepherdstown	**188**	39.25 N	77.48 W
Shepherdsville	**194**	37.59 N	85.42 W
Sheppard Air Force Base ■	**196**	33.58 N	98.30 W
Sheppard Peak ∧	**180**	57.41 N	132.37 W
Sheppard Pond ⊜	**276**	41.08 N	74.13 W
Shepparton	**166**	36.23 S	145.25 E
Shepperd, Lake ⊜	**162**	29.55 S	123.09 E
Shepperton	**260**	51.24 N	0.27 W
Sheppey, Isle of I	**42**	51.24 N	0.50 E
Sheppler Hill ∧[2]	**279b**	40.09 N	79.49 W
Sheppton	**210**	40.53 N	76.07 W
Shepshed	**42**	52.47 N	1.18 W
Shepton Mallet	**42**	51.12 N	2.33 W
Shepway	**260**	51.15 N	0.33 E
Sheqi	**100**	33.03 N	112.57 E
Sherab	**140**	10.43 N	24.47 E
Sherada	**144**	7.21 N	36.32 E
Sheraden ⊸[8]	**279b**	40.28 N	80.05 W
Sherard, Cape ≻	**176**	74.36 N	80.25 W
Sherborn	**283**	42.14 N	71.22 W
Sherborne	**42**	50.57 N	2.31 W
Sherborne Lake ⊜	**212**	45.11 N	78.47 W
Sherborne Saint John	**42**	51.18 N	1.07 W
Sherbro ≃	**150**	7.45 N	12.55 W
Sherbro Island I	**150**	7.45 N	12.55 W
Sherbrooke, N.S., Can.	**186**	45.08 N	61.59 W
Sherbrooke, P.Q., Can.	**206**	45.25 N	71.54 W
Sherbrooke □[6]	**206**	45.25 N	71.55 W
Sherbrooke Lake ⊜	**186**	44.40 N	64.35 W
Sherburn	**198**	43.39 N	94.43 W
Sherburne	**210**	42.40 N	75.29 W
Sherburne Reef ✧[2]	**164**	3.20 S	148.00 E
Sherburn in Elmet	**44**	53.48 N	1.15 W
Shercock	**48**	54.00 N	6.54 W
Shere	**260**	51.13 N	0.28 W
Sheridan, Ar., U.S.	**194**	34.18 N	92.24 W
Sheridan, Ca., U.S.	**226**	38.59 N	121.22 W
Sheridan, Il., U.S.	**216**	41.32 N	88.41 W
Sheridan, In., U.S.	**218**	40.08 N	86.13 W
Sheridan, Mt., U.S.	**202**	45.27 N	112.11 W
Sheridan, Or., U.S.	**202**	45.05 N	123.23 W
Sheridan, Pa., U.S.	**208**	40.21 N	76.14 W
Sheridan, Tx., U.S.	**222**	29.29 N	96.40 W
Sheridan, Wy., U.S.	**202**	44.47 N	106.57 W
Sheridan, Mount ∧	**202**	44.16 N	110.32 W
Sheridan Park ♦	**284a**	42.59 N	78.54 W
Sheringa	**162**	33.51 S	135.15 E
Sheringham	**42**	52.57 N	1.12 E
Sherkston	**284a**	42.53 N	79.08 W
Sherlock ≃	**162**	20.44 S	117.35 E
Sherman, Ct., U.S.	**207**	41.34 N	73.29 W
Sherman, Il., U.S.	**219**	39.54 N	89.36 W
Sherman, Ky., U.S.	**218**	38.44 N	84.36 W
Sherman, Ms., U.S.	**194**	34.21 N	88.50 W
Sherman, N.Y., U.S.	**214**	42.09 N	79.35 W
Sherman, Tx., U.S.	**196**	33.38 N	96.36 W
Sherman □[6]	**224**	45.25 N	120.49 W
Sherman Creek ≃	**208**	40.23 N	77.02 W
Sherman Mills	**188**	45.52 N	68.23 W
Sherman Mountain ∧	**194**	36.01 N	93.17 W
Sherman Oaks ⊸[8]	**280**	34.09 N	118.26 W
Sherman Reservoir ⊜[1]	**198**	41.20 N	98.55 W
Sherman Station	**188**	45.53 N	68.25 W
Sherpur, Bngl.	**124**	24.41 N	89.25 E
Sherpur, Bngl.	**124**	25.01 N	90.01 E
Sher Qila	**123**	36.06 N	74.03 E
Sherrard	**190**	41.19 N	90.31 W
Sherridon	**184**	55.07 N	101.05 W
Sherrill	**210**	43.04 N	75.35 W
Sherrodsville	**214**	40.29 N	81.14 W
Sher Shāh	**123**	30.06 N	71.21 E
Shertallai	**122**	9.42 N	76.20 E
's-Hertogenbosch	**52**	51.41 N	5.19 E
Sherway Centre ⊸[9]	**275b**	43.37 N	79.33 W
Sherwood, On., Can.	**275b**	43.50 N	79.31 W
Sherwood, P.E., Can.	**186**	46.17 N	63.08 W
Sherwood, Ar., U.S.	**194**	34.48 N	92.13 W
Sherwood, Md., U.S.	**208**	38.36 N	76.19 W
Sherwood, Mi., U.S.	**216**	42.00 N	85.14 W
Sherwood, N.D., U.S.	**198**	48.57 N	101.37 W
Sherwood, Oh., U.S.	**216**	41.17 N	84.33 W
Sherwood, Or., U.S.	**224**	45.21 N	122.50 W
Sherwood, Tn., U.S.	**194**	35.04 N	85.55 W
Sherwood, Lake ⊜	**281**	42.36 N	83.33 W
Sherwood Forest, Ca., U.S.	**226**	37.57 N	122.17 W
Sherwood Forest, Md., U.S.	**284c**	39.05 N	77.01 W
Sherwood Forest ⊸[3]	**44**	53.08 N	1.08 W
Sherwood Island State Park ♦	**276**	41.07 N	73.20 W
Sherwood Manor	**207**	42.01 N	72.38 W
Sherwood Park, Ab., Can.	**182**	53.31 N	113.19 W
Sherwood Park, De., U.S.	**285**	39.44 N	75.39 W
Sherwood Park, N.Y., U.S.	**210**	42.36 N	73.43 W
Sherwood Park ♦	**275b**	43.43 N	79.24 W
Sherwood Point ≻	**276**	41.07 N	73.20 W
Sherwood Shores	**196**	30.36 N	98.22 W
She Shan ∧[2]	**106**	31.06 N	121.11 E
Sheshea ≃	**248**	9.36 S	74.10 W
Shesh Gāv	**120**	33.45 N	68.33 E
Shestakivka	**78**	48.32 N	31.58 E
Shesternya	**78**	47.33 N	33.16 E
Shet Bandar	**272c**	18.58 N	72.56 E
Shetek, Lake ⊜	**198**	44.08 N	95.42 W
Shetland □[4]	**46a**	60.30 N	1.15 W
Shetland del Sur, Islas → South Shetland Islands II	**9**	62.00 S	58.00 W
Shetland Islands II	**46a**	60.30 N	1.15 W
Shetou	**106**	31.39 N	119.27 E
Shetrunji ≃	**120**	21.19 N	72.07 E
Shetucket ≃	**207**	41.31 N	72.05 W
Sheva	**272c**	18.56 N	72.57 E
Sheva Nhava	**272c**	18.58 N	72.58 E
Shevaroy Hills ⋀[2]	**122**	11.50 N	78.16 E
Shevchenkove, Ukr.	**78**	49.41 N	37.10 E
Shevchenkove, Ukr.	**78**	45.33 N	29.20 E
Shevchenkove, Ukr.	**78**	51.40 N	33.39 E
Shevchenkove Druhe	**78**	47.29 N	36.08 E
Shevington	**262**	53.34 N	2.42 W
Shevington Moor	**262**	53.35 N	2.41 W
Shewa □[4]	**144**	9.00 N	39.00 E
Shewa Gimira	**144**	7.00 N	35.50 E
Shexian, Zhg.	**98**	36.33 N	113.40 E
Shexian, Zhg.	**100**	29.53 N	118.26 E
Sheyang, Zhg.	**100**	33.20 N	119.38 E
Sheyang, Zhg.	**100**	33.46 N	120.18 E
Sheyenne	**198**	47.49 N	99.07 W
Sheyenne ≃	**198**	47.05 N	96.50 W
Sheykhābād	**120**	34.05 N	68.45 E
Shey-Phoksundo National Park ♦	**124**	29.30 N	82.45 E
Shezhu	**106**	31.19 N	119.16 E
Shḥīm	**132**	33.37 N	35.29 E
Shi ≃, Zhg.	**100**	32.18 N	114.31 E
Shi ≃, Zhg.	**100**	32.32 N	115.52 E
Shiant, Sound of ⋃	**46**	57.55 N	6.25 W
Shiant Islands II	**46**	57.53 N	6.21 W
Shiawassee □[6]	**216**	42.56 N	84.09 W
Shiawassee ≃	**216**	43.06 N	84.10 W
Shiawassee, South Branch ≃	**216**	42.49 N	83.56 W
Shiba	**100**	32.45 N	118.07 E
Shiba ≃	**268**	35.47 N	139.44 E
Shibadu	**102**	28.01 N	110.51 E
Shibakawa	**94**	35.13 N	138.33 E
Shibām	**144**	15.56 N	48.38 E
Shiban	**107**	30.18 N	104.28 E
Shibanxi	**107**	29.17 N	103.51 E
Shibaocheng	**102**	39.48 N	96.10 E
Shibarni	**140**	14.50 N	24.25 E
Shibasaki	**268**	35.39 N	139.34 E
Shibata	**92**	37.57 N	139.20 E
Shibayama	**94**	35.41 N	140.25 E
Shibayama-gata ⊜	**94**	36.21 N	136.23 E
Shibden Hall ⊥	**262**	53.44 N	1.51 W
Shibecha	**92a**	43.17 N	144.36 E
Shibetsu, Nihon	**92a**	43.40 N	145.08 E
Shibetsu, Nihon	**92a**	44.10 N	142.23 E
Shibi	**100**	26.43 N	120.02 E
Shibīn al-Kawm	**142**	30.33 N	31.01 E
Shibīn al-Qanāṭir	**142**	30.19 N	31.19 E
Shibing	**102**	26.50 N	108.04 E
Shibishan	**100**	29.21 N	116.45 E
Shiblanjah	**142**	30.28 N	31.16 E
Shibu	**98**	36.45 N	119.27 E
Shibukawa	**94**	36.29 N	139.00 E
Shibure-yama ∧	**270**	34.45 N	135.05 E
Shibushi	**92**	31.28 N	131.07 E
Shibutsu-san ∧	**94**	36.54 N	139.11 E
Shibuya ⊸[8]	**268**	35.40 N	139.42 E
Shibuzi	**98**	36.09 N	119.06 E
Shicha	**100**	28.24 N	115.50 E
Shichangyu	**104**	41.12 N	123.14 E
Shicheng, Zhg.	**98**	40.39 N	124.17 E
Shicheng, Zhg.	**100**	25.18 N	119.21 E
Shicheng, Zhg.	**100**	26.22 N	116.22 E
Shicheng Dao I	**98**	39.31 N	123.02 E
Shichisō	**94**	35.33 N	137.07 E
Shickley	**198**	40.25 N	97.43 W
Shickshinny	**210**	41.09 N	76.09 W
Shidai	**100**	30.20 N	117.56 E
Shidao	**98**	36.53 N	122.23 E
Shideng	**102**	26.44 N	99.11 E
Shidler	**196**	36.46 N	96.39 W
Shido	**96**	34.19 N	134.10 E
Shidong, Zhg.	**107**	28.59 N	105.27 E
Shidong, Zhg.	**107**	30.25 N	105.20 E
Shidongzigou	**105**	40.41 N	118.23 E
Shiel, Loch ⊜	**46**	56.47 N	5.35 W
Shiel Bridge	**46**	57.12 N	5.25 W
Shieldaig	**46**	57.31 N	5.39 W
Shieldhill	**46**	55.58 N	3.46 W
Shields ≃	**202**	45.43 N	110.28 W
Shiercun	**106**	30.31 N	119.34 E
Shi'er Shan ∧	**100**	29.18 N	118.08 E
Shi'erwei	**106**	32.15 N	119.14 E
Shifang	**100**	25.01 N	116.14 E
Shifnal	**42**	52.40 N	2.21 W
Shifo	**107**	29.58 N	103.50 E
Shifobao	**104**	41.28 N	121.27 E
Shifochang	**107**	30.19 N	105.07 E
Shifodian	**100**	32.06 N	115.46 E
Shifosi	**104**	42.08 N	123.20 E
Shifoya	**98**	40.12 N	123.10 E
Shiga, Nihon	**94**	36.20 N	137.59 E
Shiga, Nihon	**94**	35.09 N	135.55 E
Shiga □[5]	**96**	35.15 N	136.00 E
Shigaib	**140**	15.01 N	23.36 E
Shigang, Zhg.	**100**	32.13 N	120.58 E
Shigang, Zhg.	**106**	32.14 N	121.00 E
Shigangmen	**269b**	31.21 N	121.17 E
Shigaopu	**107**	30.16 N	104.01 E
Shigar ≃, Asia	**123**	34.39 N	75.51 E
Shigar ≃, Pāk.	**123**	34.39 N	75.51 E
Shigaraki	**94**	34.52 N	136.03 E
Shigaraki-gū ✿[1]	**94**	34.54 N	136.04 E
Shigenobu	**96**	33.48 N	132.50 E
Shigenobu ≃	**96**	33.48 N	132.41 E
Shigezhuang, Zhg.	**105**	38.59 N	115.36 E
Shigezhuang, Zhg.	**105**	39.18 N	116.53 E
Shigezhuang, Zhg.	**105**	38.57 N	116.19 E
Shigouyi	**102**	37.44 N	106.26 E
Shigu, Zhg.	**100**	29.27 N	117.14 E
Shigu, Zhg.	**102**	26.50 N	99.55 E
Shiguaigou	**102**	40.42 N	110.20 E
Shiguantun	**104**	41.38 N	123.39 E
Shigulingyu	**105**	40.38 N	116.54 E
Shīḥān ∧	**132**	31.23 N	35.44 E
Shihch'i → Zhongshan	**100**	22.31 N	113.22 E
Shihchiachuang → Shijiazhuang	**98**	38.03 N	114.28 E
Shihe	**98**	39.19 N	121.52 E
Shihengyuanyu	**106**	31.50 N	121.45 E
Shihezi	**86**	44.18 N	86.02 E
Shihkiachwang → Shijiazhuang	**98**	38.03 N	114.28 E
Shihlin ⊸[8]	**269d**	25.06 N	121.31 E
Shihti	**269d**	25.02 N	121.44 E
Shihting	**269d**	24.59 N	121.39 E
Shihu, Zhg.	**98**	41.29 N	126.18 E
Shihu, Zhg.	**105**	40.04 N	117.17 E
Shihuajie	**102**	32.20 N	111.25 E
Shihudang	**106**	30.58 N	121.07 E
Shihuixi	**107**	29.02 N	105.04 E
Shihuiyaozi	**104**	42.08 N	123.47 E
Shihuxia	**105**	40.48 N	117.22 E
Shiida	**96**	33.39 N	131.04 E
Shijiaba	**107**	30.18 N	104.46 E
Shijiagangzi	**104**	42.19 N	123.34 E
Shijiagou	**104**	42.27 N	123.28 E
Shijiao	**100**	23.36 N	112.59 E
Shijiaqiao, Zhg.	**106**	32.18 N	119.26 E
Shijiaqiao, Zhg.	**106**	30.46 N	120.06 E
Shijiawu	**105**	39.21 N	116.15 E
Shijiaxiang	**107**	29.38 N	104.59 E
Shijiayaozhuang	**106**	32.13 N	120.29 E
Shijiazhai, Zhg.	**98**	38.56 N	114.18 E
Shijiazhai, Zhg.	**269b**	31.23 N	121.30 E
Shijiazhen	**106**	31.51 N	121.10 E
Shijiazhuang	**98**	38.03 N	114.28 E
Shijiazi, Zhg.	**104**	42.07 N	122.18 E
Shijiazi, Zhg.	**104**	42.39 N	122.06 E
Shijiedu	**106**	30.57 N	119.13 E
Shijing, Zhg.	**98**	35.30 N	118.57 E
Shijing, Zhg.	**100**	24.40 N	118.24 E
Shijing, Zhg.	**105**	39.54 N	114.58 E
Shijingshan	**105**	39.56 N	116.07 E
Shijiu Hu ⊜	**106**	31.28 N	118.53 E
Shijiusuo	**98**	35.24 N	119.29 E
Shijiu Tuo I	**98**	39.11 N	118.56 E
Shijōnawate	**270**	34.45 N	135.39 E
Shijūmagari-tōge)(	**96**	35.11 N	133.32 E
Shika	**94**	37.01 N	136.47 E
Shikami-yama ∧	**270**	34.47 N	135.10 E
Shikano	**96**	35.28 N	134.04 E
Shikārpur, India	**122**	14.16 N	75.21 E
Shikārpur, India	**124**	28.17 N	78.01 E
Shikārpur, Pāk.	**120**	27.57 N	68.38 E
Shikatsu	**94**	35.14 N	136.53 E

Symbols in the index entries represent the broad categories identified in the key at the right. Symbols with superior numbers (⋀[1]) identify subcategories (see complete key on page *I · 1).*

Symbole im Register stellen die rechts im Schlüssel erklärten Kategorien dar. Symbole mit hochgestellten Ziffern (⋀[1]) bezeichnen Unterabteilungen einer Kategorie (vgl. vollständiger Schlüssel auf Seite *I · 1).*

Los símbolos incluídos en el texto del índice representan las grandes categorías identificadas con la clave a la derecha. Los símbolos con numeros en su parte superior (⋀[1]) identifican las subcategorías (véase la clave completa en la página *I · 1).*

Les symboles de l'index représentent les catégories indiquées dans la légende à droite. Les symboles suivis d'un indice (⋀[1]) représentent des sous-catégories (voir légende complète à la page *I · 1).*

Os símbolos incluídos no texto do índice representam as grandes categorias identificadas com a chave à direita. Os símbolos com números em sua parte superior (⋀[1]) identificam as subcategorias (veja-se a chave completa à página *I · 1).*

∧ Mountain	Berg	Montaña	Montagne	Montanha
⋀ Mountains	Gebirge	Montañas	Montagnes	Montanhas
)(Pass	Paß	Paso	Col	Passo
∨ Valley, Canyon	Tal, Cañon	Valle, Cañón	Vallée, Canyon	Vale, Canhão
⊻ Plain	Ebene	Llano	Plaine	Planície
≻ Cape	Kap	Cabo	Cap	Cabo
I Island	Insel	Isla	Île	Ilha
II Islands	Inseln	Islas	Îles	Ilhas
⊥ Other Topographic Features	Andere Topographische Objekte	Otros Elementos Topográficos	Autres données topographiques	Outros acidentes topográficos

ESPAÑOL

Nombre	Página	Lat.°′	Long.°′ W = Oeste
Shikengkong ∧	100	24.56 N	113.00 E
Shikewusumiao	102	40.13 N	108.52 E
Shiki	94	35.50 N	139.35 E
Shikishima	94	35.41 N	138.32 E
Shikohābād	124	27.06 N	78.36 E
Shikoku I	92	33.45 N	133.30 E
Shikoku-sanchi ⋏	96	33.47 N	133.30 E
Shikoma	268	35.11 N	139.56 E
Shikotsu-ko ◎	92a	42.45 N	141.20 E
Shikotsu-Tōya-kokuritsu-kōen ♠	92a	42.47 N	141.00 E
Shikuang	106	31.54 N	121.24 E
Shil	272c	19.09 N	73.03 E
Shilabo	144	6.05 N	44.48 E
Shilbottle	44	55.23 N	1.42 W
Shildon	44	54.38 N	1.39 W
Shiliangji	100	33.54 N	115.14 E
Shilibao	105	39.55 N	116.29 E
Shiliguri	124	26.42 N	88.26 E
Shilihe	104	41.31 N	123.22 E
Shiling	106	30.26 N	119.35 E
Shilipeng	106	31.14 N	119.35 E
Shilipu, Zhg.	105	39.29 N	116.18 E
Shilipu, Zhg.	105	39.11 N	115.59 E
Shilipu, Zhg.	105	40.15 N	117.58 E
Shiliuban	100	24.08 N	117.33 E
Shillelagh	48	52.45 N	6.32 W
Shillingstone	42	50.54 N	2.14 W
Shillington	208	40.18 N	75.57 W
Shillong	120	25.34 N	91.53 E
Shilo, Canadian Forces Base ■	184	49.49 N	99.38 W
Shiloh, Il., U.S.	219	38.34 N	89.54 W
Shiloh, N.J., U.S.	208	39.27 N	75.17 W
Shiloh, Oh., U.S.	214	40.58 N	82.36 W
Shiloh, Oh., U.S.	218	39.49 N	84.13 W
Shiloh, Oh., U.S.	218	39.49 N	84.13 W
Shiloh, Pa., U.S.	208	39.59 N	76.49 W
Shiloh → Saylūn, Khirbat ⊥	132	32.03 N	35.17 E
Shiloh National Military Park ♠	194	35.06 N	88.21 W
Shilong, Zhg.	100	23.07 N	113.48 E
Shilong, Zhg.	102	23.54 N	109.40 E
Shilong, Zhg.	107	30.15 N	106.34 E
Shilou	100	22.58 N	113.29 E
Shima, Nihon	92	34.13 N	136.51 E
Shima, Nihon	270	34.59 N	135.20 E
Shima, Zhg.	100	24.27 N	117.49 E
Shima, Zhg.	107	29.38 N	105.50 E
Shimabara	92	32.47 N	130.22 E
Shimachang, Zhg.	107	28.59 N	105.55 E
Shimachang, Zhg.	107	29.03 N	105.36 E
Shimada, Nihon	94	34.49 N	138.11 E
Shimada, Nihon	268	35.59 N	139.25 E
Shimagahara	94	34.46 N	136.03 E
Shima-hantō >[1]	94	34.26 N	136.33 E
Shimamiao	106	32.08 N	119.20 E
Shimamoto	96	34.53 N	135.40 E
Shimane □[5]	96	35.00 N	132.30 E
Shimane-hantō >[1]	96	35.30 N	133.00 E
Shimantan	100	33.17 N	113.28 E
Shimanto ≃	96	32.56 N	133.00 E
Shimata ≃	96	33.57 N	131.55 E
Shimber Berris ∧	144	10.44 N	47.15 E
Shimei	106	32.14 N	120.10 E
Shimen, Zhg.	98	39.44 N	118.52 E
Shimen, Zhg.	102	29.28 N	111.17 E
Shimen, Zhg.	105	40.06 N	117.42 E
Shimen, Zhg.	106	30.37 N	120.26 E
Shimen, Zhg.	107	29.36 N	106.27 E
Shimen, Zhg.	107	29.09 N	106.02 E
Shimencun, Zhg.	106	31.21 N	119.34 E
Shimencun, Zhg.	106	30.23 N	119.41 E
Shimendong	100	28.16 N	120.07 E
Shimengou	104	40.40 N	123.43 E
Shimenjie	100	29.34 N	116.44 E
Shimenlou	100	28.58 N	114.51 E
Shimenying	105	39.54 N	116.05 E
Shimenzi	89	48.30 N	121.31 E
Shimian	102	29.18 N	102.22 E
Shimiaozi	104	40.39 N	123.31 E
Shimizu, Nihon	92	35.01 N	138.29 E
Shimizu → Tosa-shimizu, Nihon	92	32.46 N	132.57 E
Shimizu, Nihon	92a	43.01 N	142.53 E
Shimizu, Nihon	94	36.02 N	136.09 E
Shimizu, Nihon	94	35.01 N	138.29 E
Shimizu, Nihon	96	34.05 N	135.26 E
Shimizu-tunnel ◆[5]	94	36.52 N	138.55 E
Shimla	123	31.06 N	77.10 E
Shimminato	94	36.47 N	137.04 E
Shimobe	94	35.27 N	138.29 E
Shimoda	94	34.40 N	138.57 E
Shimodate	94	36.18 N	139.59 E
Shimofusa	94	35.52 N	140.21 E
Shimofusa-daichi ⋏[1]	268	35.45 N	139.58 E
Shimofusa-kōkūkichi, Kaijō-jieitai- ■	94	35.50 N	140.05 E
Shimofusa Naval Air Base ■	268	35.48 N	140.01 E
Shimoga	122	13.55 N	75.34 E
Shimogawara	268	35.56 N	139.21 E
Shimogōri	268	35.21 N	140.03 E
Shimogyō ◆[8]	270	34.59 N	135.45 E
Shimohōya	268	35.45 N	139.34 E
Shimoichi	96	34.22 N	135.47 E
Shimoigusa ◆[8]	268	35.43 N	139.37 E
Shimoji	175d	24.45 N	125.16 E
Shimoji-jima I	175d	24.49 N	125.09 E
Shimojō	94	35.24 N	137.47 E
Shimokawa	92a	44.18 N	142.39 E
Shimokita-hantō >[1]	92	41.15 N	141.00 E
Shimomatsu	270	34.27 N	135.23 E
Shimomizo	268	35.31 N	139.23 E
Shimoni	154	4.39 S	39.23 E
Shimoniikura	268	35.47 N	139.38 E
Shimonita	94	36.13 N	138.47 E
Shimonoseki	96	33.57 N	130.57 E
Shimookudomi	268	35.53 N	139.26 E
Shimoryūzu-zaki >	96	33.30 N	133.34 E
Shimosakamoto	270	35.03 N	135.53 E
Shimosuwa	94	36.04 N	138.05 E
Shimotajiri	270	34.57 N	135.28 E
Shimotomi	268	35.50 N	139.29 E
Shimotsu	96	34.10 N	135.08 E
Shimotsuchidana	268	35.24 N	139.27 E
Shimotsui	96	34.26 N	133.47 E
Shimotsuma	94	36.11 N	139.58 E
Shimotsuruma	268	35.29 N	139.28 E
Shimoya	268	35.23 N	139.21 E
Shimoyama	94	35.02 N	137.19 E
Shimoyugi	268	35.38 N	139.23 E
Shimura ◆[8]	268	35.46 N	139.41 E
Shin, Loch ◎	46	58.06 N	4.34 W
Shinagawa ◆[8]	268	35.37 N	139.45 E
Shinan	102	22.43 N	109.54 E
Shinano	94	36.48 N	138.13 E
Shinano ≃	92	37.56 N	139.03 E
Shinarā	142	28.47 N	30.46 E
Shināṣ	128	24.46 N	56.28 E
Shinawari	123	33.32 N	70.48 E
Shinbārī	273c	30.07 N	31.09 E
Shīndand	128	33.18 N	62.08 E
Shindenbaru-kichi, Kōkū-jieitai- ■	92	32.04 N	131.30 E
Shindo	268	35.21 N	139.21 E
Shiner	222	29.25 N	97.10 W
Shingbwiyang	110	26.41 N	96.13 E
Shingishū → Sinŭiju	98	40.05 N	124.24 E
Shinglehouse	214	41.57 N	78.11 W
Shingle Springs	226	38.40 N	120.56 W
Shing Mun Reservoir ◎[1]	271d	22.23 N	114.08 E
Shingo	96	34.59 N	133.23 E
Shingū, Nihon	92	33.44 N	135.59 E
Shingū, Nihon	96	34.55 N	134.33 E

FRANÇAIS

Nom	Page	Lat.°′	Long.°′ W = Ouest
Shingū, Nihon	96	33.56 N	133.38 E
Shingwidzi	156	23.05 S	31.25 E
Shingwidzi (Singuédeze) ≃	156	23.53 S	32.17 E
Shinichi	96	34.33 N	133.16 E
Shining Tor ∧	262	53.16 N	2.01 W
Shinīrah	132	32.22 N	36.45 E
Shinji	96	35.24 N	132.54 E
Shinji-ko ◎	96	35.27 N	132.58 E
Shinjō, Nihon	92	38.46 N	140.18 E
Shinjō, Nihon	270	34.30 N	135.44 E
Shinjuku ◆[8]	268	35.41 N	139.42 E
Shinkawa	94	35.09 N	136.50 E
Shīnkay	120	31.57 N	67.26 E
Shinkolobwe	154	11.02 S	26.35 E
Shinmachi	94	36.16 N	139.07 E
Shinminato ≃	270	34.38 N	135.09 E
Shinnārah, Minqār ⊥[4]	142	28.52 N	30.38 E
Shinnayō	96	34.04 N	131.47 E
Shinnecock Bay ⊂	207	40.52 N	72.28 W
Shinnel Water ≃	44	55.13 N	3.49 W
Shinness	46	58.05 N	4.28 W
Shinnston	188	39.23 N	80.18 W
Shino-jima I	94	34.39 N	137.00 E
Shinsai-bashi ◆[8]	270	34.40 N	135.31 E
Shinshār	130	34.36 N	36.44 E
Shinshiro	94	34.54 N	137.30 E
Shinshū-shinmachi	94	36.34 N	138.01 E
Shintone	94	35.50 N	140.20 E
Shinyanga	154	3.40 S	33.26 E
Shinyanga □[4]	154	3.45 S	33.00 E
Shin-yōdo ≃[1]	270	34.41 N	135.26 E
Shio	94	36.52 N	136.48 E
Shiobara	94	36.58 N	139.49 E
Shiocton	190	44.26 N	88.34 W
Shiogama	92	38.19 N	141.01 E
Shiojiri	94	36.06 N	137.58 E
Shiojiri-tōge)(	94	36.05 N	138.02 E
Shiomi-dake ∧	94	35.34 N	138.12 E
Shionoe	96	34.10 N	134.05 E
Shiono-misaki >	92	33.26 N	135.45 E
Shioya	94	36.46 N	139.51 E
Shioya ◆[8]	270	34.38 N	135.06 E
Shioya-zaki >, Nihon	92	33.26 N	135.45 E
Shioya-zaki >, Nihon	94	36.59 N	140.59 E
Shiozawa	94	37.02 N	138.51 E
Shipai, Zhg.	100	23.08 N	113.21 E
Shipai, Zhg.	106	31.30 N	120.55 E
Shipanpu	107	30.28 N	104.23 E
Shipantuo	107	30.25 N	106.13 E
Ship Bottom	208	39.38 N	74.10 W
Shipbourne	260	51.15 N	0.17 E
Ship Cove	186	47.06 N	54.05 W
Shipdham	42	52.37 N	0.53 E
Shiping, Zhg.	102	28.20 N	107.42 E
Shiping, Zhg.	102	23.47 N	102.30 E
Shipley	44	53.50 N	1.47 W
Shipman, Il., U.S.	219	39.07 N	90.03 W
Shipman, Va., U.S.	192	37.43 N	78.50 W
Shippan Point >	276	41.01 N	73.32 W
Shippegan	186	47.45 N	64.42 W
Shippensburg	208	40.03 N	77.31 W
Shippenville	214	41.15 N	79.28 W
Shippingport	214	40.38 N	80.25 W
Shippō	94	35.10 N	136.48 E
Shiprock	200	36.47 N	108.41 W
Ship Rock ∧	200	36.42 N	108.50 W
Shipshaw ≃	186	48.27 N	71.12 W
Shipshewana	216	41.40 N	85.34 W
Shipston-on-Stour	42	52.04 N	1.37 W
Shipton-under-Wychwood	42	51.51 N	1.35 W
Shipu, Zhg.	100	29.13 N	121.55 E
Shipu, Zhg.	106	31.15 N	121.03 E
Shiqi → Zhongshan	100	22.31 N	113.22 E
Shiqian	102	27.31 N	108.20 E
Shiqiao, Zhg.	100	26.58 N	114.23 E
Shiqiao, Zhg.	100	33.12 N	112.36 E
Shiqiao, Zhg.	106	30.30 N	119.11 E
Shiqiao, Zhg.	107	30.25 N	104.31 E
Shiqiaopu	107	30.05 N	105.23 E
Shiqiaozi	104	41.27 N	123.43 E
Shiqma ≃	132	31.36 N	34.30 E
Shiquan, Zhg.	102	33.03 N	108.17 E
Shiquan, Zhg.	106	30.30 N	120.48 E
Shirahama, Nihon	94	34.54 N	139.54 E
Shirahama, Nihon	96	33.40 N	135.20 E
Shirahata-yama ∧	96	34.54 N	134.23 E
Shiraitono-taki ↳	94	35.18 N	138.38 E
Shirakami-misaki >	92a	41.24 N	140.12 E
Shirakawa, Nihon	94	37.07 N	140.13 E
Shirakawa, Nihon	94	35.35 N	137.12 E
Shirakawa, Nihon	94	36.16 N	136.54 E
Shirakawa-no-seki-ato ⊥	94	37.03 N	140.15 E
Shirakawa-tōge ∧[2]	270	34.42 N	135.07 E
Shirako	94	35.26 N	140.23 E
Shirākol	126	22.18 N	88.16 E
Shirakura-yama ∧	94	35.00 N	137.46 E
Shirama-yama ∧	96	34.01 N	135.23 E
Shiramine	94	36.10 N	136.37 E
Shirane	94	35.38 N	138.28 E
Shirane-san (Kita-dake) ∧, Nihon	94	35.40 N	138.15 E
Shirane-san ∧, Nihon	94	36.38 N	138.32 E
Shirane-san ∧, Nihon	94	36.48 N	139.22 E
Shiranuka	92a	42.57 N	144.05 E
Shiraoi	92a	42.33 N	141.21 E
Shiraoka	94	36.01 N	139.40 E
Shiraone	272c	19.03 N	73.01 E
Shirasawa	94	36.40 N	139.08 E
Shirati	154	1.08 S	33.59 E
Shīrāz	128	29.36 N	52.32 E
Shirbīn	142	31.11 N	31.32 E
Shirdley Hill	262	53.36 N	2.58 W
Shire (Chire) ≃	154	17.42 S	35.19 E
Shirebrook	44	53.12 N	1.13 W
Shiremanstown	208	40.13 N	76.57 W
Shiretoko-hantō >[1]	92a	44.00 N	145.00 E
Shiretoko-kokuritsu-kōen ♠	92a	44.08 N	145.10 E
Shiretoko-misaki >	92a	44.14 N	145.17 E
Shīrīn ≃	120	36.49 N	65.01 E
Shīr Kūh ∧	128	31.34 N	54.04 E
Shirland	216	42.27 N	89.12 W
Shirley, B.C., Can.	224	48.23 N	123.54 W
Shirley, Il., U.S.	216	40.24 N	89.04 W
Shirley, In., U.S.	218	39.53 N	85.34 W
Shirley, Ma., U.S.	207	42.32 N	71.39 W
Shirley Plantation ⊥	208	37.21 N	77.15 W
Shirleysburg	214	40.18 N	77.53 W
Shiro	222	30.37 N	95.53 W
Shiroi	94	35.48 N	140.04 E
Shiroishi	92	38.00 N	140.37 E
Shirokawa	96	33.23 N	132.46 E
Shirone	92	37.46 N	139.01 E
Shirotori, Nihon	94	35.53 N	136.52 E
Shirotori, Nihon	96	34.15 N	134.20 E
Shirouma-dake ∧	94	36.45 N	137.46 E
Shiroyama	94	35.35 N	139.19 E
Shiro-yama ∧	270	34.38 N	135.53 E
Shirpur	120	21.21 N	74.53 E
Shirrell Heath	42	50.55 N	1.12 W
Shirshābah	142	30.47 N	31.10 E
Shīrvān	128	37.24 N	57.55 E
Shisaka-jima I	96	34.07 N	133.11 E
Shisanling	105	40.19 N	116.16 E
Shi San Ling (Ming Tombs) ⊥	105	40.19 N	116.13 E
Shisanzhan	89	51.21 N	125.43 E
Shisha Hai ◎	271a	39.57 N	116.22 E
Shishaldin Volcano ∧[1]	180	54.45 N	163.57 W
Shishan	104	41.16 N	121.30 E
Shishi	100	24.48 N	118.38 E
Shishikui	96	33.34 N	134.18 E
Shishi Shan ∧	100	24.44 N	117.54 E
Shishmaref	180	66.14 N	166.09 W
Shishmaref Inlet ⊂	180	66.07 N	165.50 W

PORTUGUÊS

Nome	Página	Lat.°′	Long.°′ W = Oeste
Shishou	102	29.43 N	112.19 E
Shisht al-An'ām	142	30.52 N	30.44 E
Shisiazhan	89	51.36 N	125.42 E
Shisixian	104	40.53 N	122.59 E
Shisler Point >	284a	42.52 N	79.08 W
Shisui	94	35.43 N	140.16 E
Shitai	100	30.13 N	117.27 E
Shitan, Zhg.	100	27.44 N	112.42 E
Shitan, Zhg.	100	23.10 N	113.47 E
Shitang, Zhg.	100	28.16 N	121.36 E
Shitang, Zhg.	102	25.38 N	110.50 E
Shitangwan	106	31.40 N	120.13 E
Shitara	94	35.05 N	137.35 E
Shithāthah	128	32.33 N	43.29 E
Shiting, Zhg.	100	27.36 N	113.16 E
Shiting, Zhg.	105	39.31 N	115.41 E
Shitoufangzi	89	48.38 N	126.08 E
Shitougouzi	89	49.19 N	125.55 E
Shitoumiao	102	41.41 N	106.50 E
Shitoumiaozi	104	41.38 N	121.26 E
Shitoushan	105	40.27 N	116.13 E
Shitoushuangmiao	98	41.28 N	118.55 E
Shituan	107	30.09 N	105.01 E
Shitunwei	104	41.07 N	121.31 E
Shiv	120	26.11 N	71.15 E
Shivalya	126	23.50 N	89.47 E
Shively	218	38.12 N	85.49 W
Shivering, Mount ∧	170	34.08 S	150.02 E
Shivpuri	124	25.26 N	77.39 E
Shivta, Horvot (Subeita) ⊥	132	30.53 N	34.38 E
Shivwits Plateau ⋏[1]	200	36.15 N	113.40 W
Shiwaku-shotō II	96	34.20 N	133.45 E
Shiwan, Zhg.	100	27.17 N	112.57 E
Shiwan, Zhg.	100	28.12 N	113.49 E
Shiwan, Zhg.	100	23.01 N	113.04 E
Shiwan, Zhg.	102	37.35 N	109.01 E
Shiwenchang	104	41.43 N	123.54 E
Shiwu	89	43.48 N	124.13 E
Shixi, Zhg.	100	28.16 N	117.45 E
Shixi, Zhg.	100	28.16 N	115.36 E
Shixia	105	40.20 N	114.59 E
Shixian	89	43.05 N	129.47 E
Shixiancun	106	31.12 N	120.29 E
Shixiechang	107	29.51 N	106.41 E
Shixing	100	24.58 N	114.03 E
Shixun	100	24.44 N	118.11 E
Shiyachang	107	30.27 N	106.31 E
Shiyan, Zhg.	102	32.38 N	110.44 E
Shiyan, Zhg.	107	30.22 N	104.27 E
Shiyangchang, Zhg.	107	29.56 N	105.37 E
Shiyangchang, Zhg.	107	30.42 N	105.57 E
Shiyanqiao	107	29.19 N	105.22 E
Shiyiwei	106	31.59 N	120.43 E
Shiyizhan	89	51.13 N	125.52 E
Shiyu	107	29.46 N	106.06 E
Shizhangzi	98	40.24 N	119.48 E
Shizheng	100	24.32 N	115.50 E
Shizhenjie	100	28.51 N	116.56 E
Shizhong, Zhg.	100	24.57 N	117.06 E
Shizhong, Zhg.	106	30.44 N	120.16 E
Shizhongtan	107	30.26 N	104.35 E
Shizhu, Zhg.	100	28.48 N	120.06 E
Shizhu, Zhg.	102	29.56 N	108.09 E
Shizhuang	106	32.08 N	120.31 E
Shizhuangzi, Zhg.	104	42.24 N	122.53 E
Shizhuangzi, Zhg.	105	40.38 N	116.59 E
Shizhuzi	104	41.18 N	121.35 E
Shizichang	107	29.32 N	106.14 E
Shizigu	105	39.23 N	118.08 E
Shizikou	100	24.12 N	113.38 E
Shizilin	106	31.26 N	121.25 E
Shizipo	105	40.21 N	115.07 E
Shizipu	106	30.59 N	119.07 E
Shizuchi-kokutei-kōen ♠	96	33.45 N	133.08 E
Shizugawa	92	38.40 N	141.27 E
Shizui, Zhg.	89	43.08 N	126.06 E
Shizui, Zhg.	98	38.52 N	113.42 E
Shizuma ≃	96	35.12 N	132.28 E
Shizunai	92a	42.20 N	142.22 E
Shizuoka	94	34.58 N	138.23 E
Shizuoka □[5]	94	35.00 N	138.00 E
Shkodër	38	42.05 N	19.30 E
Shkumbin ≃	38	41.01 N	19.26 E
Shō ≃	94	36.47 N	137.04 E
Shoal ≃	194	30.41 N	86.39 W
Shoal Cape >	162	33.53 S	121.07 E
Shoal Creek ≃, U.S.	194	37.05 N	94.42 W
Shoal Creek ≃, U.S.	194	40.28 N	92.42 W
Shoal Creek ≃, U.S.	194	34.50 N	87.33 W
Shoal Creek ≃, Il., U.S.	219	38.28 N	89.35 W
Shoal Creek ≃, Mo., U.S.	194	39.44 N	93.32 W
Shoal Creek, East Fork ≃	219	38.51 N	89.30 W
Shoal Creek, Middle Fork ≃	219	39.05 N	89.33 W
Shoal Creek, West Fork ≃	219	39.05 N	89.33 W
Shoal Harbour	186	48.11 N	53.59 W
Shoalhaven ≃	170	34.52 S	150.44 E
Shoalhaven Bight ⊂[3]	170	34.52 S	150.47 E
Shoal Lake	184	50.26 N	100.34 W
Shoal Lake ◎	184	49.32 N	95.00 W
Shoal Point >	276	41.08 N	73.15 W
Shoals	194	38.39 N	86.47 W
Shoals, Bay of ⊂	168b	35.37 S	137.37 E
Shoalwater Bay ⊂	166	22.02 S	150.25 E
Shōbara	96	34.51 N	133.01 E
Shōboku	96	35.06 N	134.07 E
Shobonier	219	38.52 N	89.05 W
Shōbu	94	36.04 N	139.36 E
Shōdai	270	34.51 N	135.42 E
Shōdo-shima I	96	34.30 N	134.17 E
Shoeburyness	42	51.32 N	0.48 E
Shoe Cove	186	49.55 N	55.33 W
Shoemakersville	208	40.30 N	75.58 W
Shōgawa	94	36.34 N	136.59 E
Shogunle	273a	6.35 N	3.21 E
Shohola	210	41.28 N	74.55 W
Shohola Creek ≃	210	41.28 N	74.55 W
Shokambetsu-dake ∧	92a	43.43 N	141.31 E
Shokan	210	41.58 N	74.13 W
Shōkawa	94	36.02 N	136.57 E
Sholingnur	122	13.07 N	79.25 E
Shomera	132	33.05 N	35.17 E
Shomolu	273a	6.32 N	3.23 E
Shōmyō-no-taki ↳	94	36.35 N	137.24 E
Shona, Eilean I	46	56.47 N	5.52 W
Shōnai	96	33.11 N	131.26 E
Shōnai ≃	94	35.04 N	136.50 E
Shōnan	268	35.50 N	140.02 E
Shongum	276	40.50 N	74.33 W
Shongum Lake ◎	276	40.51 N	74.32 W
Shongwe	158	27.24 S	32.25 E
Shōō	96	35.02 N	134.08 E
Shooters Hill	170	33.54 S	149.52 E
Shooters Island I	276	40.39 N	74.10 W
Shopiere	216	42.34 N	88.57 W
Shoranūr	122	10.46 N	76.17 E
Shorāpur	122	16.31 N	76.45 E
Shoreacres, B.C., Can.	182	49.26 N	117.32 W
Shore Acres, Ca., U.S.	226	38.02 N	121.58 W
Shore Acres, Ma., U.S.	207	42.12 N	70.44 W
Shore Acres, N.J., U.S.	208	40.01 N	74.06 W
Shoreacres, Tx., U.S.	222	29.37 N	95.01 W
Shoreditch ◆[8]	260	51.32 N	0.05 W
Shoreham, Austl.	169	38.25 S	145.03 E
Shoreham, Eng., U.K.	260	51.20 N	0.11 E
Shoreham, Mi., U.S.	216	42.03 N	86.30 W
Shoreham-by-Sea	42	50.49 N	0.16 W
Shorewood, Il., U.S.	216	41.32 N	88.12 W
Shorewood, Wi., U.S.	216	43.05 N	87.53 W
Shorewood Hills	216	43.04 N	89.26 W
Shorkot	123	30.50 N	72.04 E
Shorkot Road	123	30.47 N	72.15 E
Shorne	260	51.25 N	0.26 E
Short Acres	226	36.21 N	119.38 W
Short Beach	207	41.15 N	72.50 W
Short Creek	214	40.11 N	80.55 W
Shortland Islands II	175e	6.55 S	155.53 E
Short Mountain ∧	192	36.23 N	83.10 W
Shortsville	210	42.57 N	77.13 W
Shoshone	202	42.56 N	114.24 W
Shoshone ≃	202	44.52 N	108.11 W
Shoshone, North Fork ≃	202	44.29 N	109.18 W
Shoshone, South Fork ≃	202	44.27 N	109.14 W
Shoshone Basin ≚[1]	202	43.05 N	108.05 W
Shoshone Lake ◎	202	44.22 N	110.43 W
Shoshone Mountains ⋏	204	39.00 N	117.30 W
Shoshone Peak ∧	204	36.56 N	116.16 W
Shoshone Range ⋏	204	40.20 N	116.50 W
Shoshong	156	22.59 S	26.30 E
Shoshoni	200	43.14 N	108.06 W
Shostka	78	51.52 N	33.30 E
Shotley Gate	42	51.58 N	1.15 E
Shotton	262	53.12 N	3.02 W
Shotton Colliery	44	54.44 N	1.20 W
Shotts	46	55.49 N	3.48 W
Shotwick	262	53.14 N	2.59 W
Shou'anzhen	107	30.16 N	103.37 E
Shouchang	100	29.22 N	119.13 E
Shoufeng	100	23.52 N	121.30 E
Shouguang	98	36.53 N	118.42 E
Shouning	100	27.27 N	119.30 E
Shournagh ≃	48	51.53 N	8.35 W
Shoushan	104	41.12 N	123.03 E
Shouwangfen	105	40.35 N	117.48 E
Shouxian	100	32.35 N	116.47 E
Shouyang	102	37.59 N	113.09 E
Shōwa, Nihon	94	36.37 N	139.04 E
Shōwa, Nihon	96	34.43 N	133.39 E
Showell	208	38.23 N	75.12 W
Show Low	200	34.15 N	110.01 W
Shpola	78	49.01 N	31.24 E
Shpykiv	78	48.46 N	28.35 E
Shqipëri → Albania □[1]	38	41.00 N	20.00 E
Shramkivka	78	50.10 N	32.05 E
Shreve	214	40.40 N	82.01 W
Shreveport	194	32.30 N	93.44 W
Shrevewood	284c	38.53 N	77.13 W
Shrewsbury, Eng., U.K.	42	52.43 N	2.45 W
Shrewsbury, Ma., U.S.	207	42.17 N	71.42 W
Shrewsbury, N.J., U.S.	208	40.19 N	74.03 W
Shrewsbury, Pa., U.S.	208	39.46 N	76.40 W
Shrewsbury River ⊂	276	40.21 N	74.00 W
Shrewton	42	51.12 N	1.55 W
Shri Dūngargarh	120	28.05 N	74.00 E
Shri Mohangarh	120	27.17 N	71.14 E
Shriner Mountain ∧	210	40.56 N	77.20 W
Shrīrangapattana	122	12.25 N	76.42 E
Shrivenham	42	51.36 N	1.39 W
Shropshire □[6]	42	52.40 N	2.40 W
Shropshire Union Canal ≍	262	53.17 N	2.53 W
Shrub Oak	210	41.20 N	73.49 W
Shrule	48	53.30 N	9.08 W
Shtormove	83	49.06 N	38.55 E
Shu ≃	98	34.07 N	118.30 E
Shuajingsi	102	32.00 N	103.05 E
Shuanfeng Shan ∧	107	29.26 N	105.47 E
Shuang ≃	269d	25.00 N	121.31 E
Shuangbai	102	24.54 N	101.32 E
Shuangcheng	89	45.21 N	126.17 E
Shuangchengzi	105	40.11 N	118.03 E
Shuangdian	100	32.23 N	120.51 E
Shuangdun	106	32.13 N	121.08 E
Shuangfeng, Zhg.	102	27.24 N	112.05 E
Shuangfeng, Zhg.	106	31.31 N	121.01 E
Shuangfeng, Zhg.	106	31.31 N	121.02 E
Shuangfeng Shan ∧	100	24.28 N	114.43 E
Shuangfengyi	107	29.27 N	105.09 E
Shuangfu	105	39.48 N	117.44 E
Shuangfuchang, Zhg.	107	29.41 N	103.31 E
Shuangfuchang, Zhg.	107	30.08 N	103.32 E
Shuanggang, Zhg.	89	45.07 N	122.59 E
Shuanggang, Zhg.	100	28.11 N	117.30 E
Shuanggetun	89	48.58 N	129.57 E
Shuanggou, Zhg.	98	34.03 N	117.37 E
Shuanggou, Zhg.	100	32.12 N	112.21 E
Shuanggou, Zhg.	100	33.16 N	118.10 E
Shuanggufen	107	29.38 N	104.11 E
Shuanghe, Zhg.	100	31.33 N	116.46 E
Shuanghe, Zhg.	100	31.41 N	112.46 E
Shuanghe, Zhg.	107	29.40 N	104.48 E
Shuanghe, Zhg.	107	30.07 N	105.10 E
Shuanghe, Zhg.	107	30.15 N	104.44 E
Shuanghechang, Zhg.	107	28.51 N	104.51 E
Shuanghechang, Zhg.	107	29.25 N	106.17 E
Shuanghechang, Zhg.	107	29.12 N	105.43 E
Shuanghechang, Zhg.	107	29.18 N	105.36 E
Shuang-hsi	269d	25.01 N	121.39 E
Shuangji ≃	100	34.05 N	114.24 E
Shuangjiang, Zhg.	100	26.48 N	116.28 E
Shuangjiang, Zhg.	102	23.37 N	99.41 E
Shuangjiang, Zhg.	107	30.13 N	105.45 E
Shuangjiangqiao	102	25.19 N	98.51 E
Shuangjianji	100	33.12 N	116.40 E
Shuangjingzi	104	42.28 N	123.42 E
Shuangkou	105	39.15 N	117.02 E
Shuangliao	89	43.31 N	123.30 E
Shuanglin	106	30.47 N	120.19 E
Shuanglingzi, Zhg.	104	40.54 N	124.10 E
Shuanglingzi, Zhg.	104	40.50 N	123.06 E
Shuangliu	107	30.34 N	103.55 E
Shuangliushu	100	31.56 N	115.12 E
Shuanglongtai	104	40.56 N	122.39 E
Shuangmiao, Zhg.	100	28.24 N	120.45 E
Shuangmiao, Zhg.	100	32.09 N	116.52 E
Shuangmiaozi, Zhg.	104	42.25 N	122.17 E
Shuangmiaozi, Zhg.	104	42.02 N	121.52 E
Shuangpai	110	25.57 N	111.32 E
Shuangpaishi	106	31.24 N	118.59 E
Shuangqiao, Zhg.	100	32.29 N	116.41 E
Shuangqiao, Zhg.	105	39.54 N	116.37 E
Shuangqiao, Zhg.	106	30.59 N	118.47 E
Shuangshanzi	98	40.21 N	119.08 E
Shuangshipu	107	29.14 N	104.42 E
Shuangshiqiao, Zhg.	107	29.22 N	105.51 E
Shuangshiqiao, Zhg.	107	29.23 N	104.29 E
Shuangshu	105	39.34 N	117.01 E
Shuangshutai	89	43.50 N	121.15 E
Shuangtaizi, Zhg.	104	41.34 N	121.12 E
Shuangtaizi, Zhg.	104	42.21 N	124.10 E
Shuangtaizi, Zhg.	104	42.25 N	123.11 E
Shuangtaizi, Zhg.	104	41.00 N	122.34 E
Shuangtaizi, Zhg.	104	41.11 N	121.14 E
Shuangtaizi ≃	104	40.59 N	121.51 E
Shuangtaizihe Kou ≃[1]	104	40.55 N	121.50 E
Shuangtang, Zhg.	100	28.01 N	116.44 E
Shuangtang, Zhg.	105	39.03 N	116.17 E
Shuangtang, Zhg.	105	38.53 N	116.54 E
Shuangtangdian	106	30.59 N	118.51 E
Shuangtuo	105	39.14 N	117.20 E
Shuangtuozhen	105	39.29 N	118.23 E
Shuangxi, Zhg.	100	27.01 N	119.03 E
Shuangxi, Zhg.	106	30.24 N	119.50 E
Shuangyang	89	43.32 N	125.42 E
Shuangyangdian	104	41.07 N	121.16 E
Shuangyaocun	105	38.55 N	117.03 E
Shuangyashan	89	46.37 N	131.22 E
Shu'ayb, Wādī ∨	132	31.54 N	35.38 E
Shu'ayt, Wādī ∨	144	18.15 N	52.00 E
Shubenacadie ≃	186	45.20 N	63.30 W
Shublik Mountains ⋏	180	69.31 N	145.40 W
Shubrā al-Khaymah	142	30.06 N	31.15 E
Shubrā Bābil	142	30.54 N	31.11 E
Shubrā Khalfūn	142	30.29 N	31.05 E
Shubrā Khīt	142	31.02 N	30.43 E
Shubuta	194	31.51 N	88.41 W
Shucheng	100	31.27 N	116.57 E
Shufu	85	39.27 N	75.52 E
Shufuka Shan ∧	89	50.28 N	123.10 E
Shugudali	89	52.47 N	124.02 E
Shuheyingzi	104	42.18 N	122.16 E
Shuhezhen	106	31.35 N	121.35 E
Shūhō	96	34.13 N	131.18 E
Shuhong	100	28.39 N	120.09 E
Shuibatang	102	28.39 N	107.03 E
Shuibei, Zhg.	100	28.04 N	115.01 E
Shuibei, Zhg.	106	31.40 N	119.39 E
Shuichaoyang	100	26.22 N	117.57 E
Shuicheng	102	26.41 N	104.50 E
Shuidao	98	37.10 N	121.33 E
Shuidiangou	89	47.43 N	122.40 E
Shuidong, Zhg.	106	31.23 N	119.37 E
Shuidong, Zhg.	106	30.47 N	118.57 E
Shuidongjie	106	31.07 N	119.33 E
Shuiduixia	106	30.17 N	118.50 E
Shuihai	100	33.02 N	120.26 E
Shuihouling	100	30.43 N	116.26 E
Shuiji	100	27.26 N	118.20 E
Shuijiahuangdi	104	42.14 N	123.28 E
Shuijian	105	40.09 N	115.58 E
Shuijing	102	26.10 N	99.09 E
Shuijingtang	102	28.50 N	108.11 E
Shuikou, Zhg.	100	26.59 N	117.41 E
Shuikou, Zhg.	100	26.22 N	118.44 E
Shuikou, Zhg.	100	24.00 N	115.55 E
Shuikou, Zhg.	100	26.18 N	113.46 E
Shuikou, Zhg.	102	25.54 N	109.06 E
Shuikou, Zhg.	107	29.29 N	103.42 E
Shuikouchang	107	29.33 N	103.40 E
Shuikouguan	102	22.30 N	106.34 E
Shuikoushan	102	26.30 N	112.30 E
Shuikouxu	100	25.09 N	114.28 E
Shuiliandong	98	42.12 N	125.09 E
Shuimenzi	98	39.36 N	122.19 E
Shuimingqiao	106	31.03 N	119.09 E
Shuimoqipan	85	39.51 N	76.42 E
Shuiquan'gou	104	41.58 N	121.50 E
Shuiquanzi, Zhg.	104	42.15 N	121.32 E
Shuiquanzi, Zhg.	104	40.53 N	121.05 E
Shuitangzi	102	29.18 N	101.10 E
Shuiting	100	29.10 N	119.14 E
Shuitou, Zhg.	100	24.43 N	118.25 E
Shuitou, Zhg.	100	23.53 N	113.37 E
Shuitou, Zhg.	100	27.38 N	120.16 E
Shuitouwei	100	26.06 N	115.28 E
Shuituzhen	107	29.47 N	106.31 E
Shuiyang	106	31.14 N	118.47 E
Shuiyang ≃	106	31.14 N	118.48 E
Shuiye	98	36.08 N	114.07 E
Shuizhai	98	36.54 N	117.24 E
Shuizhuyang	100	26.59 N	119.13 E
Shujāābād	123	29.53 N	71.18 E
Shujālpur	124	23.24 N	76.43 E
Shujiawazi	104	42.20 N	121.57 E
Shuksan, Mount ∧	224	48.50 N	121.36 W
Shulan	89	44.27 N	126.57 E
Shulaps Peak ∧	182	50.57 N	122.31 W
Shule	85	39.23 N	76.06 E
Shule ≃	102	40.50 N	94.10 E
Shūlgareh	120	36.19 N	66.53 E
Shul'hynka	83	49.08 N	38.56 E
Shullsburg	190	42.34 N	90.13 W
Shulu (Xinji)	98	37.54 N	115.13 E
Shumagin Islands II	180	55.07 N	159.45 W
Shumatuscacant ≃	283	42.03 N	70.51 W
Shumen → Šumen	38	43.16 N	26.55 E
Shums'k	78	50.07 N	26.07 E
Shūnah, Wādī ash- ∨	142	29.38 N	32.13 E
Shun'an	100	30.57 N	117.57 E
Shūnat Nimrīn	132	31.54 N	35.37 E
Shunayn, Sabkhat ◎	146	30.30 N	21.00 E
Shunchang	100	26.50 N	117.48 E
Shunde	100	22.50 N	113.14 E
Shundian	100	34.15 N	113.20 E
Shundianqiao	106	31.24 N	120.41 E
Shunge	102	37.25 N	95.27 E
Shungnak	180	66.53 N	157.02 W
Shunhechang	107	29.57 N	104.42 E
Shunlongchang	107	30.04 N	103.27 E
Shunshanpu	104	42.08 N	122.21 E
Shuntianhu	100	24.08 N	114.48 E
Shunyi	105	40.08 N	116.38 E
Shuoduzong	102	30.48 N	95.47 E
Shuojiaji	100	33.42 N	119.44 E
Shuping	107	29.19 N	104.43 E
Shupiyan	123	33.43 N	74.50 E
Shuqayyiqah, Nafūd ⊥[8]	128	25.45 N	43.55 E
Shuqualak	194	32.58 N	88.34 W
Shūr ≃, Īrān	128	31.45 N	55.15 E
Shūr ≃, Īrān	128	34.38 N	51.46 E
Shūr ≃, Īrān	128	30.57 N	57.42 E
Shūr ≃, Īrān	128	35.57 N	56.24 E
Shuri	174m	26.13 N	127.43 E
Shurkhua	110	22.15 N	93.38 E
Shurugwi	154	19.40 S	30.00 E
Shūsf	128	31.48 N	60.01 E
Shūsh	128	32.11 N	48.15 E
Shushan	210	43.05 N	73.21 W
Shushan Hu ◎	98	35.36 N	116.27 E
Shūshtar	128	32.03 N	48.51 E
Shuswap ≃	182	50.50 N	119.00 W
Shuswap Lake ◎	182	50.57 N	119.15 W
Shuṭab	142	27.08 N	31.14 E
Shutendōji-yama ∧	96	33.06 N	130.54 E
Shuteye Peak ∧	226	37.21 N	119.25 W
Shutlingsloe ∧	262	53.13 N	2.02 W
Shūtō	96	34.05 N	132.05 E
Shuwak	140	14.23 N	35.52 E
Shuwaykah	132	32.20 N	35.02 E
Shuya, Nihon	174m	26.40 N	128.06 E
Shuya → Šuja, Ross.	24	61.55 N	34.12 E
Shuyak Island I	180	58.35 N	152.30 W
Shuyang	98	34.08 N	118.47 E
Shuyūkh Fawqānī	130	36.46 N	38.03 E
Shuzenji	94	34.58 N	138.56 E
Shwangliao → Liaoyuan	89	42.54 N	125.07 E
Shwebo	110	22.34 N	95.42 E
Shwegun	110	17.09 N	97.39 E
Shwegyin	110	17.55 N	96.53 E
Shweli (Longchuan) ≃	102	23.56 N	96.17 E
Shwenyaung	110	20.46 N	96.57 E
Shyamdih	126	23.47 N	86.56 E
Shyok	120	34.11 N	78.08 E
Shyok ≃	120	35.13 N	75.53 E
Shypuvate	78	49.56 N	37.24 E
Shyrmivka	78	49.34 N	29.06 E
Shyroke, Ukr.	78	48.08 N	34.49 E
Shyroke, Ukr.	78	47.41 N	33.14 E
Shyrokolanivka	78	47.10 N	31.24 E
Shyrokyne	83	47.06 N	37.49 E
Shyryaeve	78	47.23 N	30.13 E
Shyshaky	78	49.53 N	34.00 E
Si ≃	98	35.11 N	116.42 E
Sia	164	6.49 S	134.19 E
Siabu	114	1.01 N	99.29 E
Siachen Glacier ⊓	123	35.30 N	77.00 E
Siagne ≃	62	43.32 N	6.57 E
Siāhān Range ⋏	128	27.25 N	64.30 E
Sīāh Kūh, Kavīr-e ≚	128	32.40 N	53.52 E
Sīāh Kūh, Selseleh-ye ⋏	128	34.00 N	64.00 E
Siak ≃	114	1.13 N	102.09 E
Siak Kecil ≃	114	1.16 N	102.08 E
Siak Sri Indrapura	114	0.46 N	102.04 E
Sialang	114	1.31 N	99.27 E
Sialejevskaja P'atina	80	53.49 N	44.32 E
Siālkot	123	32.30 N	74.31 E
Sialsūk	120	23.24 N	92.45 E
Siam → Thailand □[1]	110	15.00 N	100.00 E
Siam, Gulf of → Thailand, Gulf of ⊂	110	10.00 N	101.00 E
Siamanna	71	39.55 N	8.46 E
Sian → Xi'an, Zhg.	102	34.15 N	108.52 E
Si'an, Zhg.	106	30.54 N	119.39 E
Siangtan → Xiangtan	100	27.51 N	112.54 E
Sianhala	150	10.03 N	6.51 W
Sianów	30	54.15 N	16.16 E
Siantan, Pulau I	112	3.10 N	106.15 E
Sianzhuang	100	33.05 N	119.13 E
Siapa ≃	246	2.07 N	66.28 W
Siargao Island I	116	9.53 N	126.02 E
Siari	123	34.56 N	76.44 E
Siasconset	207	41.15 N	69.58 W
Siasi	116	5.33 N	120.49 E
Siasi Island I	116	5.33 N	120.51 E
Šiaškotan, ostrov I	74	48.49 N	154.06 E
Siátista	38	40.16 N	21.33 E
Siaton	116	9.04 N	123.02 E
Siaton ≃	116	9.02 N	123.02 E
Siaton Point >	116	9.03 N	123.01 E
Siau, Pulau I	112	2.42 N	125.24 E
Siaugues-Saint-Romain	62	45.06 N	3.38 E
Šiauliai	76	55.56 N	23.19 E
Sibago Island I	116	6.45 N	122.24 E
Sibā'ī, Jabal as- ∧	140	25.43 N	34.09 E
Sibaj	86	52.42 N	58.39 E
Sibalom	116	10.47 N	122.01 E
Sibanicú	240p	21.14 N	77.31 W
Sibao	100	25.55 N	116.42 E
Sibari	68	39.45 N	16.27 E
Sibari, Piana di ≚	68	39.45 N	16.25 E
Sibasa	156	22.53 S	30.33 E
Sibati	86	47.12 N	88.15 E
Sibayi ◎	158	27.20 S	32.40 E
Sibay Island I	116	11.51 N	121.29 E
Sibbald	184	51.23 N	110.09 W
Sibbald Point Provincial Park ♠	212	44.19 N	79.19 W
Šibbe	85	39.53 N	72.05 E
Sibbo	26	60.22 N	25.16 E
Şibchar	126	23.21 N	90.09 E
Šibenik	36	43.44 N	15.54 E
Siberia → Sibir' ◆[1]	74	65.00 N	110.00 E
Siberia Occidental, Llanura de → Zapadno-Sibirskaja ravnina ≚	72	60.00 N	75.00 E
Sibérie Occidental, Dépression de la → Zapadno-Sibirskaja ravnina ≚	72	60.00 N	75.00 E
Siberut, Pulau I	108	1.20 S	98.55 E
Sibi	120	29.33 N	67.53 E
Sibiči	89	46.04 N	135.22 E
Sibidiri	164	9.00 S	142.15 E
Sibigo	114	2.51 N	95.55 E
Sibillini, Monti ⋏	66	42.54 N	13.13 E
Sibir' (Siberia) ◆[1]	74	65.00 N	110.00 E
Sibir'akova, ostrov I	74	72.50 N	79.00 E
Sibircevo	89	44.12 N	132.26 E
Sibiti	152	3.41 S	13.21 E
Sibiti ≃	154	3.49 S	34.46 E
Sibiu	38	45.48 N	24.09 E
Sibiu □[6]	38	46.00 N	24.15 E
Sible Hedingham	42	51.58 N	0.35 E
Sibley, Il., U.S.	216	40.35 N	88.23 W
Sibley, Ia., U.S.	198	43.23 N	95.45 W
Sibley, La., U.S.	194	32.33 N	93.18 W
Sibley, Ms., U.S.	194	31.22 N	91.23 W
Sibley Peninsula >[1]	190	48.25 N	88.45 W
Sibley Provincial Park ♠	190	48.25 N	88.49 W
Siboa	112	0.30 N	120.02 E
Sibochi	107	28.50 N	104.32 E
Sibolga	114	1.45 N	98.48 E
Siborang	114	1.08 N	99.26 E
Siborongborong	114	2.13 N	98.59 E
Sibpur, Bngl.	124	24.02 N	90.44 E
Sibpur, India	272b	22.24 N	88.33 E
Sibpur, India	272b	22.34 N	88.19 E
Sibsa ≃[1]	126	22.01 N	89.30 E
Sibsāgar	120	26.59 N	94.39 E
Sibu	112	2.18 N	111.49 E
Sibu, Pulau I	114	2.13 N	104.04 E
Sibuatan, Gunung ∧	114	2.56 N	98.24 E
Sibuguey ≃	116	7.38 N	122.48 E
Sibuguey Bay ⊂	116	7.30 N	122.40 E
Sibut	152	5.44 N	19.05 E
Sibuti	112	4.03 N	113.48 E
Sibutu Island I	112	4.46 N	119.29 E
Sibutu Passage ⊔	112	4.50 N	119.35 E
Sibuyan Island I	116	12.25 N	122.34 E
Sibuyan Sea ⊤[2]	116	12.50 N	122.40 E
Siby	150	12.23 N	8.20 W
Sibyŏn	98	38.19 N	126.41 E
Sicamous	182	50.50 N	119.00 W
Sicapoo, Mount ∧	116	18.01 N	120.56 E
Siccus ≃	166	31.26 S	139.30 E
Şichakou	98	41.39 N	116.26 E
Šichany	80	52.07 N	47.13 E
Sichifulo ≃	154	17.26 S	25.02 E
Si Chon	110	9.00 N	99.54 E
Sichote-Alin' ⋏	89	48.00 N	138.00 E
Sichote-Alinskij zapovednik ♠	89	45.15 N	136.15 E
Šichtovo	76	55.43 N	32.18 E
Sichuan (Szechwan) □[4]	102	31.00 N	105.00 E
Sichuan Pendi ≚[1]	102	30.00 N	105.00 E
Sichuanzhai	102	23.02 N	101.44 E
Sicié, Cap >	62	43.03 N	5.51 E
Sicignano degli Alburni	68	40.34 N	15.18 E
Sicilia □[4]	70	37.30 N	14.00 E
Sicilia (Sicily) I	70	37.30 N	14.00 E
Sicilia, Isla de → Sicilia I	70	37.30 N	14.00 E
Sicily → Sicilia I	70	37.30 N	14.00 E
Sicily, Strait of ⊔	36	37.20 N	11.20 E
Sicily Island	194	31.50 N	91.39 W
Sicklerville	208	39.43 N	74.58 W
Sicogon Island I	116	11.27 N	123.16 E
Sico Tinto ≃	236	15.58 N	84.58 W
Sicuani	248	14.16 S	71.13 W
Siculiana	70	37.20 N	13.25 E
Şicun	106	31.55 N	119.18 E
Šid	38	45.08 N	19.13 E
Sīdah, Qārat ∧[2]	142	30.16 N	29.58 E
Sidamo □[4]	144	5.00 N	39.00 E
Sidao	271a	39.51 N	116.26 E
Sidaohe	105	40.24 N	117.17 E
Sidareja	115a	7.29 S	108.47 E
Sidas	112	0.24 N	109.46 E
Sidcup ◆[8]	260	51.25 N	0.06 E
Siddeburen	52	53.15 N	6.52 E
Siddhapur	120	23.55 N	72.23 E
Siddinghausen	263	51.32 N	7.48 E
Siddington	262	53.14 N	2.14 W
Siddipet	122	18.06 N	78.51 E
Sideia Island I	164	10.35 S	150.50 E
Sidel'kino	80	54.32 N	51.08 E
Sidéradougou	150	10.40 N	4.15 W

≃ River	Fluß	Río	Rivière	Rio	◆ Submarine Features	Untermeerische Objekte	Accidentes Submarinos	Formes de relief sous-marin	Acidentes submarinos
≍ Canal	Kanal	Canal	Canal	Canal	□ Political Unit	Politische Einheit	Unidad Politica	Entité politique	Unidade política
↳ Waterfall, Rapids	Wasserfall, Stromschnellen	Cascada, Rápidos	Chute d'eau, Rapides	Cascata, Rápidos	Cultural Institution	Kulturelle Institution	Institución Cultural	Institution culturelle	Institução cultural
⊔ Strait	Meeresstraße	Estrecho	Détroit	Estreito	⊥ Historical Site	Historische Stätte	Sitio Histórico	Site historique	Sitio histórico
⊂ Bay, Gulf	Bucht, Golf	Bahía, Golfo	Baie, Golfe	Baía, Golfo	♠ Recreational Site	Erholungs- und Ferienort	Sitio de Recreo	Centre de loisirs	Area de Lazer
◎ Lake, Lakes	See, Seen	Lago, Lagos	Lac, Lacs	Lago, Lagos	Airport	Flughafen	Aeropuerto	Aéroport	Aeroporto
≚ Swamp	Sumpf	Pantano	Marais	Pântano	■ Military Installation	Militäranlage	Instalación Militar	Installation militaire	Instalação militar
⊓ Ice Features, Glacier	Eis- und Gletscherformen	Accidentes Glaciales	Formes glaciaires	Acidentes glaciares	◆ Miscellaneous	Verschiedenes	Misceláneo	Divers	Diversos
⊤ Other Hydrographic Features	Andere Hydrographische Objekte	Otros Elementos Hidrográficos	Autres données hydrographiques	Outros acidentes hidrográficos					

Name / Name	Page / Seite	Lat.°′ / Breite°′	Long.°′ / Länge°′ E = Ost
Siderno	**68**	38.16 N	16.18 E
Sideropólis	**252**	28.35 S	49.26 W
Šiderty ≏, Kaz.	**80**	50.10 N	52.20 E
Šiderty ≏, Kaz.	**86**	52.32 N	74.50 E
Sidhauli	**124**	27.17 N	80.50 E
Sídheros, Ákra ›	**38**	35.19 N	26.19 E
Sidhi	**124**	24.25 N	81.53 E
Sidhirókastron	**38**	41.14 N	23.22 E
Sīdī ʻAbd ar-Raḥmān	**140**	30.58 N	29.44 E
Sidi Aïch	**34**	36.37 N	4.42 E
Sidi Aïssa	**148**	35.53 N	3.48 E
Sidi Akacha	**34**	36.28 N	1.18 E
Sidi Ali	**34**	36.06 N	0.25 E
Sidi Ali, Oued V	**148**	34.07 N	2.05 W
Sidi Ali Ben Nasrallah	**36**	35.15 N	9.50 E
Sīdī Barrānī	**140**	31.36 N	25.55 E
Sidi bel Abbès	**148**	35.13 N	0.10 W
Sidi bel Abbès □[5]	**148**	35.00 N	1.00 W
Sidi Bennour	**148**	32.30 N	8.30 W
Sidi Bou Zid	**148**	35.02 N	9.30 E
Sidi Bou Zid □[8]	**148**	35.00 N	9.15 E
Sidi Daoud	**36**	37.00 N	10.55 E
Sidi el Hani, Sebkhet ⊜	**36**	35.33 N	10.25 E
Sīdī Ghāzī	**142**	31.12 N	31.03 E
Sīdī Ḥunaysh	**140**	31.10 N	27.37 E
Sidi Ifni	**148**	29.24 N	10.12 W
Sidi Kacem	**148**	34.15 N	5.39 W
Sidikalang	**114**	2.45 N	98.19 E
Sidimo	**144**	2.27 N	41.58 E
Sidi Mohammed Ben Ali	**34**	36.09 N	0.51 E
Sidi Moussa, Oued V	**148**	26.58 N	3.54 E
Sidi Okba	**148**	34.48 N	5.54 E
Sīdī Sālim	**142**	31.17 N	30.48 E
Sidi Slimane	**148**	34.15 N	5.49 W
Sidi Smaïl	**148**	32.49 N	8.30 W
Sidlaghatta	**122**	13.23 N	77.52 E
Sidlaw Hills ⋏[2]	**46**	56.30 N	3.10 W
Sidley, Mount ∧	**9**	77.02 S	126.00 W
Sidli	**124**	26.33 N	90.28 E
Sidman	**214**	40.20 N	78.45 W
Sidmouth	**42**	50.41 N	3.15 W
Sidnaw	**190**	46.30 N	88.42 W
Sidney, B.C., Can.	**224**	48.39 N	123.24 W
Sidney, Il., U.S.	**194**	40.01 N	88.04 W
Sidney, In., U.S.	**216**	41.06 N	85.45 W
Sidney, Ia., U.S.	**198**	40.44 N	95.38 W
Sidney, Mt., U.S.	**198**	47.43 N	104.09 W
Sidney, Ne., U.S.	**198**	41.08 N	102.58 W
Sidney, N.Y., U.S.	**210**	42.18 N	75.23 W
Sidney, Oh., U.S.	**216**	40.17 N	84.09 W
Sidney Center	**210**	42.17 N	75.15 W
Sidney Island I	**224**	48.37 N	123.18 W
Sidney Lanier, Lake ⊜[1]	**192**	34.15 N	83.57 W
Sido	**150**	11.40 N	7.36 W
Sidoan	**112**	0.16 N	120.12 E
Sidoarjo	**115a**	7.27 S	112.43 E
Sidon → Ṣaydā, Lubnān	**132**	33.33 N	35.22 E
Sidon, Ms., U.S.	**194**	33.24 N	90.12 W
Sidorovo	**76**	58.48 N	40.58 E
Sidory	**80**	50.08 N	43.19 E
Sidr, Ra's as- ›	**142**	29.36 N	32.40 E
Sidr, Wādī V	**142**	29.40 N	32.41 E
Sidra, Gulf of → Surt, Khalīj ⊂	**146**	31.30 N	18.00 E
Sidrolândia	**255**	20.55 S	54.58 W
Sidu, Zhg.	**100**	23.48 N	117.18 E
Sidu, Zhg.	**100**	24.12 N	115.15 E
Siduan	**106**	30.59 N	121.48 E
Siebengebirge ⋏[2]	**56**	50.40 N	7.14 E
Siebenlehn	**54**	51.01 N	13.18 E
Sieber	**52**	51.42 N	10.25 E
Siebnen	**58**	47.11 N	8.54 E
Siedenbollentin	**54**	53.44 N	13.23 E
Siedenburg	**52**	52.41 N	8.56 E
Siedlce	**30**	52.11 N	22.16 E
Siedlce □[4]	**30**	52.15 N	22.00 E
Sieg ≏	**56**	50.45 N	7.05 E
Siegburg	**56**	50.47 N	7.12 E
Siegen	**56**	50.52 N	8.02 E
Siegenburg	**60**	48.45 N	11.51 E
Siegendorf im Burgenland	**61**	47.47 N	16.33 E
Siegenfeld	**264b**	48.02 N	16.10 E
Sieghartskirchen	**61**	48.15 N	16.01 E
Siegler Springs	**226**	38.54 N	122.39 W
Siegsdorf	**64**	47.46 N	12.39 E
Sielbeck	**54**	54.11 N	10.37 E
Sielenbach	**60**	48.24 N	11.10 E
Siemens, Cape ›	**164**	1.21 S	149.34 E
Siemensstadt ⊶[8]	**264a**	52.32 N	13.17 E
Siemianowice Śląskie	**30**	50.19 N	19.01 E
Siemiatycze	**30**	52.26 N	22.53 E
Siĕmpang	**110**	14.07 N	106.23 E
Siĕmréab	**110**	13.22 N	103.51 E
Siems-Dänischburg ⊶[8]	**54**	53.55 N	10.44 E
Siena	**66**	43.19 N	11.21 E
Siena □[4]	**66**	43.13 N	11.24 E
Sieniawa	**30**	50.11 N	22.36 E
Sienna → Siena	**66**	43.19 N	11.21 E
Sienyang → Xianyang	**102**	34.22 N	108.42 E
Sieradz	**30**	51.36 N	18.45 E
Sieradz □[4]	**30**	51.40 N	18.45 E
Sieraków	**30**	52.39 N	16.04 E
Sierck-les-Bains	**56**	49.26 N	6.21 E
Sierksdorf	**54**	54.04 N	10.46 E
Sierning	**61**	48.03 N	14.19 E
Sierpc	**30**	52.52 N	19.41 E
Si'erpu	**104**	40.47 N	120.41 E
Sierra □[6]	**226**	39.30 N	120.30 W
Sierra Blanca	**200**	31.11 N	105.21 W
Sierra Blanca Peak ∧	**200**	33.23 N	105.48 W
Sierra-Bullones	**116**	9.51 N	124.20 E
Sierra Chica	**252**	36.50 S	60.13 W
Sierra City	**226**	39.33 N	120.37 W
Sierra Colorada	**254**	40.35 S	67.48 W
Sierra de Agua	**232**	17.32 N	88.54 W
Sierra de Outes	**34**	42.51 N	8.54 W
Sierra Gorda	**252**	22.54 S	69.19 W
Sierra Leona → Sierra Leone □[1]	**150**	8.30 N	11.30 W
Sierra Leone □[1], Afr.	**134**	8.30 N	11.30 W
Sierra Leone □[1], Afr.	**150**	8.30 N	11.30 W
Sierra Leone Basin ⊹[1]	**10**	5.00 N	17.00 W
Sierra Leone Rise ⊹[3]	**10**	5.30 N	21.00 W
Sierra Madre	**228**	34.09 N	118.03 W
Sierra Mojada	**196**	27.17 N	103.42 W
Sierra Nevada, Parque Nacional ♦	**246**	8.36 N	70.50 W
Sierra Peak ∧	**280**	33.51 N	117.39 W
Sierra San Pedro Mártir, Parque Nacional ♦	**204**	31.00 N	115.30 W
Sierras Bayas	**252**	36.57 S	60.09 W
Sierraville	**226**	39.35 N	120.21 W
Sierra Vista	**200**	31.33 N	110.18 W
Sierre	**58**	46.18 N	7.32 E
Siersleben	**54**	51.36 N	11.32 E
Siesta Key	**220**	27.19 N	82.34 W
Siesta Key I	**220**	27.16 N	82.33 W
Siete Puntas ≏	**252**	23.34 S	57.20 W
Siethen	**264a**	52.17 N	13.13 E
Siethener See ⊜	**264a**	52.17 N	13.12 E
Sietow	**54**	53.26 N	12.35 E
Sieve ≏	**66**	43.46 N	11.26 E
Sievering ⊶[8]	**264b**	48.15 N	16.20 E
Siezenheim	**64**	47.48 N	12.59 E
Sifahandra	**114**	1.30 N	97.21 E
Sifangtai, Zhg.	**89**	46.55 N	127.00 E
Sifangtai, Zhg.	**104**	41.33 N	121.19 E
Sifangtai, Zhg.	**104**	41.02 N	122.46 E
Sifangtai, Zhg.	**104**	41.35 N	122.57 E
Sifen	**100**	27.32 N	113.30 E
Sifeni	**144**	12.16 N	40.21 E
Sifentoudun	**106**	32.18 N	121.21 E
Siffu ≏	**116**	17.12 N	121.48 E
Sifié	**150**	7.59 N	6.55 W
Sífnos I	**38**	36.59 N	24.40 E
Sifón Villanueva	**196**	27.17 N	100.17 W
Sifton	**184**	51.21 N	100.07 W
Sig, Alg.	**34**	35.32 N	0.11 W
Sig, Ross.	**24**	65.35 N	34.13 E
Si Galangang	**114**	1.15 N	99.20 E
Šigali	**80**	55.33 N	48.02 E
Sigean	**32**	43.02 N	2.59 E
Sigel	**214**	41.17 N	79.07 W
Sigep	**110**	1.02 S	98.49 E
Siggebohyttan	**40**	59.37 N	15.01 E
Sighetu Marmației	**38**	47.56 N	23.54 E
Sighișoara	**38**	46.13 N	24.48 E
Sighty Crag ∧	**44**	55.07 N	2.37 W
Sigillo	**66**	43.20 N	12.44 E
Sigiriya	**122**	7.57 N	80.45 E
Siglan	**74**	59.02 N	152.25 E
Siglerville	**208**	40.44 N	77.31 W
Sigli	**114**	5.23 N	95.57 E
Sigli, Cap ›	**34**	36.54 N	4.46 E
Sigloy	**50**	47.50 N	2.14 E
Siglufjörður	**24a**	66.10 N	18.56 W
Sigmaringen	**58**	48.05 N	9.13 E
Sigmaringendorf	**58**	48.04 N	9.15 E
Signa	**66**	43.47 N	11.05 E
Signachi	**84**	41.37 N	45.54 E
Signalberg ∧	**60**	49.28 N	12.32 E
Signal Hill, Ca., U.S.	**280**	33.47 N	118.09 W
Signal Hill, Il., U.S.	**219**	38.34 N	90.05 W
Signal Hill National Historic Park ♦	**186**	47.35 N	52.40 W
Signal Mountain	**194**	35.07 N	85.20 W
Signal Mountain ∧	**188**	44.12 N	72.20 W
Signal Peak ∧	**200**	37.19 N	113.29 W
Signau	**58**	46.55 N	7.43 E
Signes	**62**	43.18 N	5.52 E
Signy ʊ[3]	**9**	60.43 S	45.36 W
Signy-l'Abbaye	**50**	49.42 N	4.25 E
Signy-Le-Petit	**50**	49.54 N	4.17 E
Šigony	**80**	53.23 N	48.42 E
Sigourney	**190**	41.20 N	92.12 W
Sigre ≏	**236**	15.49 N	84.38 W
Sigriswil	**58**	46.43 N	7.42 E
Sígsig	**246**	3.01 S	78.45 W
Sigtuna	**40**	59.37 N	17.43 E
Siguanea, Ensenada de la ⊂	**240p**	21.38 N	83.05 W
Siguatepeque	**236**	14.32 N	87.49 W
Siguel ≏	**116**	5.58 N	125.06 E
Sigüenza	**34**	41.04 N	2.38 W
Sigües	**34**	42.38 N	1.00 W
Siguiri	**150**	11.25 N	9.10 W
Sigulda	**76**	57.09 N	24.51 E
Sigurd	**200**	38.50 N	111.58 W
Siguri Falls ⌞	**154**	8.31 S	37.23 E
Sihabuhabu, Dolok ∧	**114**	2.10 N	99.21 E
Sihai	**105**	40.33 N	116.24 E
Sihala → Sri Lanka □[1]	**122**	7.00 N	81.00 E
Sihanoukville → Kâmpóng Saôm	**110**	10.38 N	103.30 E
Sihecun	**105**	39.56 N	117.07 E
Sihepeng	**114**	1.06 N	99.27 E
Sihl ≏	**58**	47.23 N	8.32 E
Sihlepu	**158**	27.42 S	32.06 E
Sihlsee ⊜	**58**	47.07 N	8.47 E
Sihong	**100**	33.28 N	118.11 E
Sihor	**120**	21.42 N	71.58 E
Sihorā	**124**	23.29 N	80.07 E
Sihu	**98**	34.38 N	117.59 E
Sihuas	**248**	8.34 S	77.37 W
Sihuas ≏	**248**	16.37 S	72.19 W
Sihui	**102**	23.19 N	112.40 E
Sihŭng ⊶[8]	**271b**	37.28 N	126.54 E
Šiiči	**76**	52.15 N	29.14 E
Siikajoki ≏	**26**	64.50 N	24.44 E
Siilinjärvi	**26**	63.05 N	27.40 E
Si' īr	**132**	31.35 N	35.09 E
Siirt	**130**	37.56 N	41.57 E
Siirt □[4]	**128**	38.00 N	42.00 E
Sija	**24**	63.38 N	41.38 E
Sijā ≏	**124**	29.08 N	81.35 E
Sijbekarspel	**52**	52.43 N	4.59 E
Sijiaba	**106**	32.02 N	121.18 E
Sijianfang	**104**	42.29 N	122.17 E
Sijiao Shan I	**100**	30.41 N	122.28 E
Sijiazi	**98**	41.47 N	120.06 E
Sijing	**106**	31.07 N	121.16 E
Sijunjung	**112**	0.42 S	100.58 E
Sijupu	**107**	30.02 N	106.18 E
Sik	**114**	5.49 N	100.44 E
Sika	**115b**	8.45 S	122.12 E
Sikalongo	**154**	16.46 S	27.07 E
Sikandarābād	**124**	28.27 N	77.42 E
Sikandarpur, India	**272a**	28.42 N	77.21 E
Sikandarpur, India	**272b**	22.57 N	88.12 E
Sikandra	**124**	24.57 N	86.02 E
Sikandra Rao	**124**	27.42 N	78.24 E
Sikanni Chief ≏	**176**	58.20 N	121.50 W
Sikao	**110**	7.34 N	99.21 E
Sīkar	**120**	27.37 N	75.09 E
Sikarpur	**272b**	22.36 N	88.32 E
Sikasso	**150**	11.19 N	5.40 W
Sikasso □[4]	**150**	10.55 N	7.00 W
Sikelenge	**152**	14.50 S	24.14 E
Sikeli	**112**	5.16 S	121.48 E
Sikensi	**150**	5.40 N	4.34 W
Sikeshu	**86**	44.25 N	84.14 E
Sikeston	**194**	36.52 N	89.35 W
Sikfors	**40**	59.48 N	14.35 E
Si Khiu	**110**	14.53 N	101.44 E
Sikiá	**38**	40.02 N	23.56 E
Sikiang → Xi ≏	**102**	22.25 N	113.23 E
Sikijang	**114**	4.22 N	98.02 E
Siking → Xi'an	**102**	34.15 N	108.52 E
Síkinos	**38**	36.39 N	25.06 E
Síkinos I	**38**	36.39 N	25.06 E
Sikión ⊥	**38**	37.59 N	22.44 E
Sikkim □[3]	**124**	27.35 N	88.35 E
Siklós ⊥	**30**	45.51 N	18.18 E
Sikonge	**154**	5.38 S	32.46 E
Sikosi	**156**	17.59 S	23.19 E
Šikotan, ostrov (Shikotan-tō) I	**92a**	43.47 N	146.45 E
Sikrod	**272a**	28.43 N	77.11 E
Sikt'ach	**74**	69.55 N	125.02 E
Sikuati	**112**	6.53 N	116.40 E
Sikutu	**112**	0.53 N	120.37 E
Sil'	**83**	48.43 N	38.02 E
Sil ≏	**34**	42.27 N	7.43 W
Šila	**86**	56.33 N	93.02 E
Silacayoapan	**234**	17.30 N	98.09 W
Sila Grande ⋏	**68**	39.22 N	16.30 E
Sila Greca ⋏	**68**	39.30 N	16.30 E
Silai ≏	**126**	22.41 N	87.46 E
Silalahi	**114**	2.48 N	98.32 E
Šilalė	**76**	55.28 N	22.12 E
Silam, Gunong ∧	**116**	4.58 N	118.10 E
Silāmpur ⊶[8]	**272a**	28.40 N	77.16 E
Silandro (Schlanders)	**64**	46.38 N	10.46 E
Silang	**116**	14.14 N	120.58 E
Silangcheng	**98**	42.19 N	115.43 E
Silanus	**71**	40.17 N	8.53 E
Silao	**234**	20.56 N	101.26 W
Sila Piccola ⋏	**68**	39.05 N	16.35 E
Silas	**194**	31.45 N	88.19 W
Silat	**112**	0.21 N	111.47 E
Sīlat aẓ-Ẓahr	**132**	32.19 N	35.11 E
Silau ≏	**114**	2.58 N	99.48 E
Silaut	**112**	2.22 S	101.08 E
Silaw Aihagam, Gunung ∧	**114**	5.25 N	95.40 E
Silay	**116**	10.48 N	122.58 E
Silay, Mount ∧	**116**	10.47 N	123.14 E
Silba	**36**	44.23 N	14.42 E
Silbertal	**58**	47.05 N	9.59 E
Silchar	**120**	24.49 N	92.48 E
Šilda, India	**126**	22.37 N	86.49 E
Šil'da, Ross.	**86**	51.46 N	59.45 E
Şile	**130**	41.11 N	29.36 E
Šile ≏	**64**	45.33 N	12.27 E
Sileby	**42**	52.43 N	1.06 W
Šilega	**24**	64.03 N	44.01 E
Silenrieux	**50**	50.14 N	4.24 E
Silent Lake ⊜	**212**	44.55 N	78.04 W
Silent Lake Provincial Park ♦	**212**	44.54 N	78.05 W
Siler City	**192**	35.43 N	79.27 W
Sileru ≏	**122**	17.47 N	81.24 E
Silesia □[9]	**30**	51.00 N	16.45 E
Silet	**148**	22.44 N	4.37 E
Siletz	**202**	44.43 N	123.55 W
Siletz ≏	**202**	44.54 N	124.00 W
Silex	**219**	39.07 N	91.03 W
Silgaḍhī	**124**	29.16 N	80.59 E
Silghāt	**120**	26.37 N	92.56 E
Silhouette I	**138**	4.29 S	55.14 E
Siliana	**148**	36.05 N	9.22 E
Siliana □[8]	**148**	36.00 N	9.20 E
Siliana, Oued ≏	**36**	36.33 N	9.25 E
Silifke	**130**	36.22 N	33.56 E
Şilijiang	**105**	39.43 N	117.28 E
Šilikty	**86**	47.10 N	84.32 E
Silingan, Mount ∧	**116**	7.46 N	122.30 E
Siling Co ⊜	**120**	31.50 N	89.00 E
Siliqua	**71**	39.18 N	8.48 E
Silistra	**38**	44.07 N	27.16 E
Şilivri	**130**	41.04 N	28.15 E
Šiljak ∧	**38**	43.45 N	21.50 E
Siljan ⊜	**26**	60.50 N	14.45 E
Şiljansnäs	**26**	60.45 N	14.42 E
Šilka	**88**	51.51 N	116.02 E
Šilka ≏	**74**	53.22 N	121.32 E
Silkāripāra	**126**	24.14 N	87.28 E
Silkeborg	**41**	56.10 N	9.34 E
Silkworth	**210**	41.16 N	76.05 W
Sill ≏	**64**	47.16 N	11.25 E
Sillamäe	**76**	59.24 N	27.45 E
Sillānwāli	**123**	31.50 N	72.33 E
Sillaro ≏	**64**	44.34 N	11.51 E
Sille	**130**	37.56 N	32.26 E
Sillem Island I	**176**	70.55 N	71.30 W
Sillen ⊜	**40**	58.59 N	17.22 E
Sillenstede	**52**	53.34 N	7.59 E
Sillery, P.Q., Can.	**206**	46.46 N	71.15 W
Sillery, Fr.	**50**	49.12 N	4.08 E
Silli	**150**	11.36 N	2.30 W
Sillian	**64**	46.45 N	12.25 E
Sillil	**144**	10.59 N	43.26 E
Sillon de Talbert ›[1]	**32**	48.53 N	3.05 W
Silloth	**44**	54.52 N	3.23 W
Sillustani ⊥	**248**	15.45 S	70.05 W
Silly-le-Long	**261**	49.06 N	2.48 E
Šil'naja Balka	**80**	50.34 N	49.01 E
Silnice	**60**	48.54 N	13.44 E
Siloam Springs	**194**	36.11 N	94.32 W
Siloam Springs State Park ♦	**219**	39.53 N	90.54 W
Şilogui	**110**	1.14 S	99.00 E
Šiloviči	**76**	55.24 N	32.33 E
Šilovka	**80**	54.03 N	48.40 E
Šilovo, Ross.	**76**	55.00 N	33.46 E
Šilovo, Ross.	**80**	54.19 N	40.53 E
Silowana Plains ≚	**152**	17.00 S	23.15 E
Silphuh	**126**	23.44 N	86.22 E
Silsbee	**194**	30.20 N	94.10 W
Silsby Lake ⊜	**184**	55.29 N	95.46 W
Silschede	**263**	51.21 N	7.19 E
Silsden	**44**	53.55 N	1.55 W
Sils im Engadin	**58**	46.22 N	9.46 E
Silton	**184**	50.48 N	104.55 W
Siluas	**112**	1.17 N	109.51 E
Şiluko	**150**	6.31 N	5.09 E
Šilutė	**76**	55.21 N	21.29 E
Silvacane, Abbaye de ʊ[1]	**62**	43.44 N	5.20 E
Silvan (Miyafarkin)	**130**	38.08 N	41.01 E
Silvana	**224**	48.12 N	122.15 W
Sīlvāneh	**128**	37.25 N	44.51 E
Silvânia	**255**	16.42 S	48.38 W
Silvano d'Orba	**62**	44.41 N	8.40 E
Silvan Reservoir ⊜[1]	**169**	37.50 S	145.25 E
Silvaplana	**58**	46.26 N	9.47 E
Silvassa	**122**	20.17 N	73.00 E
Silveiras	**256**	22.40 S	44.52 W
Silver	**196**	32.04 N	100.40 W
Silverado	**228**	33.45 N	117.35 W
Silver Bank ⊹[2]	**238**	20.30 N	69.45 W
Silver Bank Passage ⋓	**238**	20.45 N	70.15 W
Silver Bay	**190**	47.17 N	91.15 W
Silver Bell	**200**	32.23 N	111.29 W
Silver City, N.M., U.S.	**200**	32.46 N	108.16 W
Silver City, N.C., U.S.	**192**	35.00 N	79.12 W
Silver Creek, Ms., U.S.	**194**	31.36 N	89.59 W
Silver Creek, Ne., U.S.	**198**	41.18 N	97.39 W
Silver Creek, N.Y., U.S.	**214**	42.32 N	79.10 W
Silver Creek ≏, Az., U.S.	**200**	34.44 N	110.02 W
Silver Creek ≏, Ca., U.S.	**226**	38.47 N	120.35 W
Silver Creek ≏, Ca., U.S.	**226**	36.36 N	120.41 W
Silver Creek ≏, Il., U.S.	**219**	38.20 N	89.52 W
Silver Creek ≏, Il., U.S.	**278**	41.54 N	87.50 W
Silver Creek ≏, In., U.S.	**218**	38.17 N	85.47 W
Silver Creek ≏, In., U.S.	**218**	39.36 N	84.59 W
Silver Creek ≏, Ky., U.S.	**192**	37.48 N	84.30 W
Silver Creek ≏, Mi., U.S.	**281**	42.06 N	83.17 E
Silver Creek ≏, Or., U.S.	**202**	43.16 N	119.13 W
Silver Creek ≏, Wa., U.S.	**224**	46.32 N	121.55 W
Silver Creek, Muddy Fork ≏	**218**	38.25 N	86.44 W
Silver Creek, South Fork ≏	**226**	38.49 N	120.27 W
Silverdale, B.C., Can.	**224**	49.09 N	122.24 W
Silverdale, N.Z.	**172**	36.37 S	174.40 E
Silverdale, Eng., U.K.	**44**	54.10 N	2.49 W
Silverdale, Pa., U.S.	**208**	40.21 N	75.16 W
Silverdale, Wa., U.S.	**224**	47.38 N	122.41 W
Silverdalen	**26**	57.32 N	15.44 E
Silverdome ♦	**281**	42.39 N	83.15 W
Silver End	**42**	51.51 N	0.37 E
Silver Falls State Park ♦	**202**	44.48 N	122.50 W
Silverfields	**273d**	26.07 S	27.49 E
Silver Fork ≏	**219**	39.06 N	92.21 W
Silver Grove	**218**	39.02 N	84.23 W
Silver Hill	**284c**	38.50 N	76.56 W
Silverhope Creek ≏	**224**	49.18 N	121.27 W
Silver Lake, Ca., U.S.	**226**	38.38 N	120.07 W
Silver Lake, In., U.S.	**216**	41.04 N	85.53 W
Silver Lake, Ks., U.S.	**198**	39.06 N	95.51 W
Silver Lake, Ma., U.S.	**207**	42.34 N	71.11 W
Silver Lake, Mn., U.S.	**190**	44.54 N	94.11 W
Silver Lake, Oh., U.S.	**214**	41.09 N	81.27 W
Silver Lake, Or., U.S.	**202**	43.07 N	121.02 W
Silverlake, Wa., U.S.	**224**	46.17 N	122.48 W
Silver Lake, Wi., U.S.	**216**	42.32 N	88.09 W
Silver Lake ⊜, Ca., U.S.	**226**	38.39 N	120.07 W
Silver Lake ⊜, De., U.S.	**208**	39.11 N	75.32 W
Silver Lake ⊜, Ma., U.S.	**283**	42.01 N	70.48 W
Silver Lake ⊜, N.Y., U.S.	**210**	42.42 N	78.02 W
Silver Lake ⊜, N.Y., U.S.	**276**	41.03 N	73.45 W
Silver Lake ⊜, Or., U.S.	**202**	43.06 N	120.53 W
Silver Lake ⊜, Or., U.S.	**202**	43.22 N	119.24 W
Silver Lake ⊜, Wa., U.S.	**224**	46.17 N	122.47 W
Silver Lake ⊜, Wa., U.S.	**224**	48.58 N	122.04 W
Silver Lake Park ♦	**276**	41.03 N	73.45 W
Silver Lake Reservoir ⊜[1], Ca., U.S.	**280**	34.06 N	118.16 W
Silver Lake Reservoir ⊜[1], N.Y., U.S.	**276**	40.37 N	74.06 W
Silvermine ≏	**276**	41.08 N	73.26 W
Silver Mine Bay ⊂	**271d**	22.16 N	114.00 E
Silvermine Brook ≏	**276**	41.08 N	73.27 W
Silvermine Mountains ⋏	**48**	52.45 N	8.15 W
Silvermines	**48**	52.47 N	8.13 W
Silver Mountain ∧	**280**	34.12 N	117.52 W
Silver Peak ∧	**228**	33.28 N	118.35 W
Silver Peak Range ⋏	**204**	37.35 N	117.45 W
Silver Spring, Md., U.S.	**208**	38.59 N	77.01 W
Silver Spring, Pa., U.S.	**208**	40.04 N	76.26 W
Silver Springs, Nv., U.S.	**226**	39.24 N	119.13 W
Silver Springs, N.Y., U.S.	**210**	42.39 N	78.05 W
Silver Springs State Park ♦	**216**	41.38 N	88.32 W
Silver Star Mountain ∧	**224**	48.33 N	120.35 W
Silver Star Provincial Park ♦	**182**	50.22 N	119.05 W
Silverstone	**42**	52.05 N	1.02 W
Silver Streams	**158**	28.20 S	23.33 E
Silverthrone Mountain ∧	**182**	51.31 N	126.06 W
Silvertip Mountain ∧	**202**	47.47 N	113.[illegible] W
Silverton, Austl.	**166**	31.53 S	141.13 E
Silverton, B.C., Can.	**182**	49.57 N	117.21 W
Silverton, Eng., U.K.	**42**	50.48 N	3.28 W
Silverton, Co., U.S.	**200**	37.48 N	107.39 W
Silverton, N.J., U.S.	**208**	40.00 N	74.08 W
Silverton, Oh., U.S.	**218**	39.12 N	84.24 W
Silverton, Or., U.S.	**224**	45.00 N	122.46 W
Silverton, Tx., U.S.	**196**	34.28 N	101.19 W
Silverwood Lake ⊜[1]	**228**	34.18 N	117.19 W
Silves	**34**	37.11 N	8.26 W
Silvi	**66**	42.34 N	14.05 E
Silvia	**246**	2.37 N	76.21 W
Silvianópolis	**256**	22.02 S	45.50 W
Silvícola	**164**	8.39 S	126.59 E
Silvies ≏	**202**	43.22 N	118.48 W
Silview	**285**	39.42 N	75.37 W
Silvolde	**52**	51.55 N	6.23 E
Silvretta Gruppe ⋏	**58**	46.50 N	10.10 E
Sim	**86**	54.59 N	57.41 E
Sim, Cap ›	**148**	31.23 N	9.51 W
Sima, Comores	**157a**	12.11 S	44.17 E
Sima, Ross.	**80**	56.41 N	39.33 E
Simaltala	**124**	24.43 N	86.33 E
Simanggang	**112**	1.15 N	111.26 E
Simangumban	**114**	1.42 N	99.10 E
Şimanoviči	**76**	53.05 N	28.38 E
Šimanovsk	**89**	52.00 N	127.42 E
Simao	**102**	22.50 N	101.00 E
Simão Dias	**250**	10.44 S	37.49 W
Simão Pereira	**256**	21.58 S	43.19 W
Simara Island I	**116**	12.48 N	122.03 E
Simard, Lac ⊜	**190**	47.37 N	78.41 W
Simaria Kalān	**124**	24.04 N	84.56 E
Simatang, Pulau I	**112**	1.04 N	120.23 E
Simav	**130**	39.05 N	28.59 E
Simav ≏	**130**	40.23 N	28.31 E
Simav Gölü ⊜	**130**	39.09 N	28.55 E
Simaxis	**71**	39.56 N	8.41 E
Simba, Kenya	**154**	2.10 S	37.36 E
Simba, Tan.	**154**	1.44 S	34.13 E
Simba, Zaïre	**152**	0.36 N	22.55 E
Simbach	**60**	48.34 N	12.45 E
Simbach am Inn	**60**	48.16 N	13.01 E
Simbario	**68**	38.37 N	16.20 E
Simberi Island I	**164**	2.40 S	152.00 E
Simbirsk → Uljanovsk	**80**	54.20 N	48.24 E
Simbo, Tan.	**154**	4.53 S	29.44 E
Simbo, Tan.	**154**	4.40 S	33.27 E
Simbo Island I	**175e**	8.17 S	156.33 E
Simbruini, Monti ⋏	**66**	41.55 N	13.15 E
Simcoe	**212**	42.50 N	80.18 W
Simcoe □[6]	**212**	44.25 N	79.50 W
Simcoe, Lake ⊜	**212**	44.20 N	79.20 W
Simcoe Creek ≏	**224**	46.22 N	120.36 W
Simcoe Island I	**212**	44.10 N	76.31 W
Simcoe Point ›	**275b**	43.49 N	79.01 W
Simdega	**124**	22.37 N	84.31 E
Simen	**104**	40.44 N	123.49 E
Simeng	**107**	29.56 N	103.44 E
Simen Mountains National Park ♦	**144**	13.08 N	38.15 E
Simenti	**150**	13.00 N	13.25 W
Simeonovgrad	**38**	42.02 N	25.50 E
Simeri ≏	**68**	38.52 N	16.43 E
Simeria	**38**	45.51 N	23.01 E
Simeto ≏	**70**	37.24 N	15.06 E
Simeulue, Pulau I	**114**	2.33 N	96.05 E
Simeyiz	**78**	44.26 N	34.01 E
Simeykyne	**83**	48.19 N	39.32 E
Simferopol'	**78**	44.57 N	34.06 E
Sími	**38**	36.36 N	27.50 E
Sími I	**38**	36.35 N	27.52 E
Simi, Arroyo ≏	**228**	34.16 N	118.39 W
Simiane	**62**	43.25 N	5.26 E
Simianshan	**107**	28.49 N	105.09 E
Simikoṭ	**124**	29.58 N	81.50 E
Similkameen ≏	**182**	48.56 N	119.26 W
Simingchang	**107**	29.02 N	105.45 E
Simiri	**150**	14.08 N	2.08 E
Simisa Island I	**116**	5.57 N	121.35 E
Simití	**246**	7.58 N	73.57 W
Simi Valley	**228**	34.16 N	118.47 W
Simiyu ≏	**154**	2.33 S	33.25 E
Simizu → Shimizu	**94**	35.01 N	138.29 E
Simla, India	**272b**	22.47 N	88.16 E
Simla, India	**272b**	22.54 N	88.22 E
Simla, Co., U.S.	**198**	39.08 N	104.05 W
Simla ⊶[8]	**272b**	22.35 N	88.22 E
Simlāpāl	**126**	22.55 N	87.05 E
Şimleu Silvaniei	**38**	47.14 N	22.48 E
Simlipālgarh	**126**	21.51 N	86.23 E
Simme ≏	**58**	46.41 N	7.38 E
Simmelsdorf	**60**	49.36 N	11.21 E
Simmental V	**58**	46.37 N	7.25 E
Simmerath	**56**	50.36 N	6.18 E
Simmerberg	**58**	47.35 N	9.56 E
Simmering ⊶[8]	**264b**	48.11 N	16.25 E
Simmern	**56**	49.59 N	7.31 E
Simmesport	**194**	30.59 N	91.48 W
Simmie	**184**	49.57 N	108.06 W
Simmons Island I	**282**	38.06 N	121.58 W
Simmons Point ›	**282**	38.03 N	121.56 W
Simmonswood Moss ⊶[3]	**262**	53.30 N	2.50 W
Simms	**202**	47.29 N	111.55 W
Simnas	**76**	54.24 N	23.39 E
Simoca	**252**	27.16 S	65.21 W
Simões	**250**	7.36 S	40.49 W
Simojärvi ⊜	**26**	66.06 N	27.03 E
Simojoki ≏	**26**	65.37 N	25.03 E
Simojovel	**234**	17.12 N	92.38 W
Simon, Lac ⊜, P.Q., Can.	**206**	46.10 N	74.45 W
Simon, Lac ⊜, P.Q., Can.	**206**	45.58 N	75.05 W
Simón Bolívar, Aeropuerto Internacional ⊠	**286c**	10.37 N	66.59 W
Simoneti	**84**	42.14 N	42.52 E
Simonette ≏	**182**	55.07 N	118.00 W
Simonhouse Lake ⊜	**184**	54.30 N	101.10 W
Simonicha	**80**	56.31 N	53.50 E
Simoniči	**78**	51.53 N	28.04 E
Simonoseki → Shimonoseki	**96**	33.57 N	130.57 E
Simonsbath	**42**	51.09 N	3.45 W
Simonson Brook ≏	**276**	40.26 N	74.37 W
Simonstone	**262**	53.48 N	2.20 W
Simonstorp	**40**	58.47 N	16.09 E
Simon's Town	**158**	34.14 S	18.26 E
Simonton Lake	**216**	41.44 N	85.59 W
Şimoom Sound	**182**	50.45 N	126.29 W
Šimorskoje	**80**	55.19 N	42.02 E
Simpang, Indon.	**112**	1.16 S	104.05 E
Simpang, Indon.	**112**	1.03 S	110.06 E
Simpang, Indon.	**112**	0.09 N	103.15 E
Simpangampat	**114**	2.55 N	99.43 E
Simpang Empat	**114**	6.20 N	100.11 E
Simpang-kanan ≏	**114**	2.21 N	97.51 E
Simpang-kiri ≏	**114**	2.21 N	97.51 E
Simpang Rengam	**114**	1.50 N	103.19 E
Simpangtiga	**114**	2.23 N	99.47 E
Simpangulim	**114**	5.06 N	97.32 E
Simpele	**26**	61.26 N	29.22 E
Simplício Mendes	**250**	7.51 S	41.54 W
Simplon Pass)(	**58**	46.15 N	8.02 E
Simplon Tunnel ⊶[5]	**58**	46.15 N	8.05 E
Simpnäs	**40**	59.52 N	19.04 E
Simp'o-ri	**98**	38.36 N	127.41 E
Simpson, La., U.S.	**194**	31.14 N	93.00 W
Simpson, Pa., U.S.	**210**	41.35 N	75.29 W
Simpson ≏	**254**	45.25 S	72.32 W
Simpson, Isla I	**254**	45.53 S	73.48 W
Simpson Desert ⊶[2]	**162**	25.00 S	137.00 E
Simpson Desert National Park ♦	**162**	25.40 S	138.15 E
Simpson Island I	**190**	48.48 N	87.40 W
Simpson Lake ⊜	**180**	68.10 N	126.35 W
Simpson Peak ∧	**180**	59.44 N	131.27 W
Simpson Peninsula ›[1]	**176**	68.34 N	88.45 W
Simpsons Gap National Park ♦	**162**	23.40 S	133.45 E
Simpson Strait ⋓	**176**	68.27 N	97.45 W
Simpsonville, Ky., U.S.	**218**	38.13 N	85.21 W
Simpsonville, Md., U.S.	**208**	39.11 N	76.52 W
Simpsonville, S.C., U.S.	**192**	34.44 N	82.15 W
Simrishamn	**26**	55.33 N	14.20 E
Sims	**216**	40.30 N	85.51 W
Şimsbury	**207**	41.52 N	72.48 W
Šimsk	**76**	58.13 N	30.43 E
Simssee ⊜	**64**	47.52 N	12.14 E
Simunjan	**112**	1.23 N	110.45 E
Simurāli	**126**	23.03 N	88.30 E
Simušir, ostrov I	**74**	46.58 N	152.02 E
Sīnā' □[4]	**142**	30.15 N	32.40 E
Sīna ≏	**122**	17.22 N	75.54 E
Sīnā', Shibh Jazīrat (Sinai Peninsula) ›[1]	**140**	29.30 N	34.00 E
Sinabang	**114**	2.29 N	96.23 E
Sinabelkirchen	**61**	47.06 N	15.50 E
Sinabung, Gunung ∧	**114**	3.10 N	98.24 E
Sinadhago	**144**	5.22 N	46.20 E
Sinagra	**70**	38.05 N	14.51 E
Sinai, Mount ∧, Gren.	**241k**	12.04 N	61.42 W
Sinai, Mount → Mūsā, Jabal ∧, Miṣr	**140**	28.32 N	33.59 E
Sinaia	**38**	45.21 N	25.33 E
Sinai Peninsula → Sīnā', Shibh Jazīrat ›[1]	**140**	29.30 N	34.00 E
Sin'aja ≏, Europe	**76**	57.10 N	28.31 E
Sin'aja ≏, Ross.	**74**	61.06 N	126.50 E
Sinajana	**174p**	13.28 N	144.45 E
Sinako, Mount ∧	**116**	7.30 N	125.17 E
Sinaloa □[3]	**232**	25.00 N	107.30 W
Sinaloa ≏	**232**	25.18 N	108.30 W
Sinalunga	**66**	43.12 N	11.44 E
Sinamaica	**246**	11.05 N	71.51 W
Sinamary ≏	**250**	5.27 N	53.00 W
Sinan, Tür.	**130**	37.52 N	41.00 E
Sinan, Zhg.	**102**	27.54 N	108.18 E
Sinanju	**98**	39.36 N	125.36 E
Sinanpaşa	**130**	38.45 N	30.15 E
Sīnarū	**142**	29.22 N	30.45 E
Sinatle	**84**	42.28 N	43.04 E
Sin'avka, Bela.	**76**	52.58 N	26.29 E
Sin'avka, Ross.	**83**	47.17 N	39.17 E
Sīnāwin	**146**	31.02 N	10.36 E
Sinbad Creek ≏	**282**	37.35 N	121.53 W
Sinbaungwe	**110**	19.43 N	95.10 E
Sinbo	**110**	24.46 N	97.03 E
Sinbokchang	**98**	41.01 N	128.54 E
Sincan, Tür.	**130**	39.28 N	37.54 E
Sincan, Tür.	**130**	39.59 N	32.26 E
Sincé	**246**	9.15 N	75.09 W
Sincelejo	**246**	9.18 N	75.24 W
Sinch'ang, C.M.I.K.	**98**	40.07 N	128.28 E
Sinch'ang, C.M.I.K.	**98**	40.19 N	125.27 E
Sinch'ŏn	**98**	38.22 N	125.28 E
Sinch'ŏn-ni	**271b**	37.27 N	126.48 E
Sinclair	**200**	41.46 N	107.06 W
Sinclair, Lake ⊜[1]	**192**	33.11 N	83.16 W
Sinclair, Point ›	**162**	32.06 S	133.00 E
Sinclair Island I	**224**	48.37 N	122.40 W
Sinclair Mills	**182**	54.02 N	121.41 W
Sinclair's Bay ⊂	**46**	58.30 N	3.07 W
Sinclairville	**214**	42.15 N	79.15 W
Sind □[4]	**120**	25.30 N	69.00 E
Sind ≏	**124**	26.26 N	79.13 E
Sinda	**89**	48.57 N	136.18 E
Sindal	**26**	57.28 N	10.13 E
Sindangan	**116**	8.14 N	123.00 E
Sindangan ≏	**116**	8.13 N	123.00 E
Sindangan Bay ⊂	**116**	8.11 N	122.50 E
Sindangan Point ›	**116**	8.10 N	122.40 E
Sindangbarang	**115a**	7.27 S	107.08 E
Sindara	**152**	1.02 S	10.40 E
Sindari	**120**	25.35 N	71.55 E
Sindelfingen	**56**	48.42 N	9.00 E
Sindèr	**150**	14.29 N	1.22 E
Sindhnūr	**122**	15.47 N	76.46 E
Sindhulī Māḿdi	**124**	27.16 N	85.58 E
Sindi	**76**	58.24 N	24.40 E
Sindia	**71**	40.18 N	8.39 E
Sindingale	**110**	18.17 N	94.25 E
Sındıran	**130**	39.17 N	32.41 E
Sındırgı	**130**	39.14 N	28.10 E
Sindiyūn	**142**	30.15 N	31.12 E
Sin-do I	**98**	39.48 N	124.14 E
Sindŏk	**98**	36.47 N	126.10 E
Sindor	**24**	62.50 N	51.57 E
Sindou	**150**	10.40 N	5.10 W
Sindri	**126**	23.45 N	86.42 E
Sind Sāgar Doāb ⋏[1]	**123**	31.30 N	71.30 E
Sine V	**150**	14.10 N	16.28 W
Sinegorje	**24**	59.42 N	50.40 E
Sinegorsk	**89**	47.10 N	142.30 E
Şinegorskij	**78**	48.00 N	40.53 E
Šine-Ider	**88**	48.56 N	99.33 E
Sinekçi	**130**	40.16 N	27.24 E
Sinekli	**130**	41.14 N	28.12 E
Sinendé	**150**	10.21 N	2.23 E
Sinen'kije	**80**	51.15 N	45.46 E
Sinepuxent Bay ⊂	**208**	38.16 N	75.09 W
Sines	**34**	37.57 N	8.52 W
Sines, Cabo de ›	**34**	37.57 N	8.53 W
Sinewit, Mount ∧	**164**	4.40 S	152.00 E
Sinez'orki	**76**	53.02 N	34.26 E
Sinfra	**150**	6.37 N	5.55 W
Singair	**126**	23.49 N	90.08 E
Singako	**146**	9.50 N	19.29 E
Singal	**123**	36.06 N	73.53 E
Singalamwe	**156**	17.41 S	23.23 E
Singālila ∧	**124**	27.13 N	88.01 E
Singālila Range ⋏	**124**	27.25 N	88.05 E
Singaparna	**115a**	7.21 S	108.06 E
Singapore, Sing.	**114**	1.17 N	103.51 E
Singapore, Sing.	**271c**	1.17 N	103.51 E
Singapore □[1], Asia	**108**	1.22 N	103.48 E
Singapore □[1], Asia	**114**	1.22 N	103.48 E
Singapore I	**271c**	1.23 N	103.48 E
Singapore ≏	**271c**	1.17 N	103.51 E
Singapore, National University of ʊ[2]	**271c**	1.18 N	103.46 E
Singapore Station ⊶[5]	**271c**	1.17 N	103.50 E
Singapore Strait ⋓	**112**	1.15 N	104.00 E
Singapour → Singapore □[1]	**114**	1.22 N	103.48 E
Singapur → Singapore	**114**	1.17 N	103.51 E
Singapur → Singapore □[1]	**114**	1.22 N	103.48 E
Singaraja	**115b**	8.07 S	115.06 E
Singarka ≏	**265a**	59.53 N	29.54 E
Singāti	**126**	22.44 N	89.43 E
Singatoka	**175g**	18.08 S	177.30 E
Sing Buri	**110**	14.53 N	100.25 E
Singe	**272b**	22.57 N	88.26 E
Singen (Hohentwiel)	**58**	47.46 N	8.50 E
Singer	**194**	30.39 N	93.24 W
Singhi	**126**	23.37 N	87.48 E
Singida	**154**	4.49 S	34.45 E
Singida □[4]	**154**	5.30 S	34.30 E
Singing, India	**102**	28.59 N	94.50 E
Singing, India	**120**	28.53 N	94.47 E
Singing Tower ♦	**220**	27.57 N	81.34 W
Singkaling Hkāmti	**110**	26.00 N	95.42 E
Singkang	**112**	4.08 S	120.01 E
Singkawang	**112**	0.54 N	109.00 E
Singkep, Pulau I	**112**	0.30 S	104.25 E
Singkil	**114**	2.17 N	97.49 E
Singkuang	**114**	1.03 N	98.56 E
Singleton, Austl.	**170**	32.34 S	151.10 E
Singleton, Eng., U.K.	**42**	50.55 N	0.46 W
Singleton, Mount ∧, Austl.	**162**	29.28 S	117.18 E
Singleton, Mount ∧, Austl.	**162**	22.00 S	130.49 E
Singleton Ditch ≍	**216**	41.10 N	87.37 W
Singlewell or Ifield	**260**	51.25 N	0.23 E
Singö	**40**	60.10 N	18.44 E
Singö I	**40**	60.11 N	18.46 E
Singora → Songkhla	**110**	7.12 N	100.36 E
Şingorkai	**164**	5.55 S	146.55 E
Šingoža	**86**	47.45 N	80.40 E
Singpāra	**272b**	22.40 N	88.31 E
Singrāmau	**124**	25.57 N	82.23 E
Singuédeze (Shingwidzi) ≏	**156**	23.53 S	32.17 E
Singur	**126**	22.49 N	88.14 E
Sin'gye	**98**	38.36 N	126.30 E
Sinhai → Lianyungang	**98**	34.39 N	119.16 E
Sinh Ho	**110**	22.22 N	103.14 E
Sinhŭng	**98**	40.11 N	127.34 E
Siniaka-Minia, Réserve de ■	**146**	10.30 N	18.00 E
Siničká ≏	**265b**	55.50 N	37.19 E
Sinije gory ⋏[2]	**80**	51.10 N	49.25 E
Sinije Lip'agi	**78**	51.23 N	38.29 E
Siniloan	**116**	14.25 N	121.27 E
Sining → Xining	**102**	36.38 N	101.55 E
Siniscola	**71**	40.34 N	9.41 E
Sinj	**36**	43.42 N	16.38 E
Sinjah	**140**	13.09 N	33.56 E
Sinjai	**112**	5.07 S	120.15 E
Sinjang-ni	**98**	39.04 N	127.46 E
Sinjār	**128**	36.19 N	41.52 E
Sinjār, Jabal ⋏	**130**	36.25 N	41.40 E
Sinji-do I	**98**	34.20 N	126.50 E
Sinkan	**110**	24.08 N	97.01 E
Sinkāt	**140**	18.50 N	36.50 E
Sinkiang → Xinjiang Uygur Zizhiqu □[4]	**90**	40.00 N	85.00 E
Sinking ≏	**48**	53.37 N	8.52 W
Sinking Creek ≏	**210**	40.51 N	77.34 W
Sinking Spring, Oh., U.S.	**218**	39.04 N	83.23 W
Sinking Spring, Pa., U.S.	**208**	40.19 N	76.02 W
Şin'kok-ni	**271b**	37.37 N	126.46 E
Šinkovo, Ross.	**76**	56.03 N	31.31 E
Sin'kovo, Ross.	**82**	56.26 N	36.04 E
Sin'kovo, Ross.	**82**	54.37 N	38.56 E
Sin'kovo, Ross.	**82**	56.23 N	37.19 E
Sinks Canyon State Park ♦	**200**	42.45 N	108.50 W
Sin-le-Noble	**50**	50.22 N	3.07 E
Sinmak	**98**	38.25 N	126.14 E
Sinmi-do I	**98**	39.33 N	124.53 E
Sinn ≏	**56**	50.03 N	9.42 E
Sinnahwā	**142**	30.25 N	31.21 E
Sínnai	**71**	39.18 N	9.12 E
Sinnamahoning	**214**	41.19 N	78.06 W
Sinnamary	**250**	5.23 N	52.57 W
Sinnar	**122**	19.51 N	74.00 E
Sinnemahoning Creek ≏	**210**	41.15 N	77.54 W
Sinnemahoning Creek, Bennett Branch ≏	**210**	41.20 N	78.08 W
Sinnemahoning Creek, Driftwood Branch ≏	**210**	41.20 N	78.08 W
Sinnemahoning Creek, First Fork ≏	**210**	41.19 N	78.05 W
Sinnersdorf	**56**	51.01 N	6.49 E
Sinnes	**26**	58.56 N	6.50 E
Sinni ≏	**68**	40.09 N	16.42 E
Sinntal	**56**	50.18 N	9.38 E
Sinnūris	**142**	29.25 N	30.52 E
Sinnyŏng	**98**	36.04 N	128.46 E
Sino, Pedra do ∧	**256**	22.30 S	43.03 W
Sinoie, Lacul ⊜	**38**	44.38 N	28.53 E
Sinop, Bra.	**250**	11.55 S	55.35 W
Sinop, Tür.	**130**	42.01 N	35.09 E
Sinop □[4]	**130**	41.40 N	34.50 E
Sinop Burnu ›	**130**	42.02 N	35.12 E
Sinp'a	**98**	41.24 N	127.46 E
Sinp'o	**98**	40.03 N	128.12 E
Sins	**58**	47.11 N	8.23 E
Sinsang	**98**	39.38 N	127.25 E
Sinsen	**263**	51.40 N	7.11 E
Sinsheim	**56**	49.15 N	8.53 E
Sinsiang → Xinxiang	**98**	35.20 N	113.51 E
Sinsin	**56**	50.17 N	5.15 E
Sinsi-ri	**98**	39.59 N	124.58 E
Sinskoje	**74**	61.08 N	126.48 E
Sinspelt	**56**	49.58 N	6.19 E
Sint-Amandsberg	**50**	51.04 N	3.45 E
Sint-Andries	**50**	51.12 N	3.10 E
Sintang	**112**	0.04 N	111.30 E
Sint Annaland	**52**	51.36 N	4.06 E
Sint Annaparochie	**52**	53.16 N	5.39 E
Sint Anthonis	**52**	51.37 N	5.52 E
Sint Christoffelberg ∧[2]	**241s**	12.20 N	69.08 W
Sint-Denijs-Westrem	**50**	51.01 N	3.40 E
Sint Eustatius I	**238**	17.30 N	62.59 W
Sint-Gillis-Waas	**50**	51.13 N	4.08 E
Sint Helenabaai ⊂	**158**	32.43 S	18.05 E

Symbols in the index entries represent the broad categories identified in the key at the right. Symbols with superior numbers (⋏[1]) identify subcategories (see complete key on page *I · 1).*

Symbole im Register stellen die rechts im Schlüssel erklärten Kategorien dar. Symbole mit hochgestellten Ziffern (⋏[1]) bezeichnen Unterabteilungen einer Kategorie (vgl. vollständiger Schlüssel auf Seite *I · 1).*

Los símbolos incluídos en el texto del índice representan las grandes categorías identificadas con la clave a la derecha. Los símbolos con numeros en su parte superior (⋏[1]) identifican las subcategorías (véase la clave completa en la página *I · 1).*

Les symboles de l'index représentent les catégories indiquées dans la légende à droite. Les symboles suivis d'un indice (⋏[1]) représentent des sous-catégories (voir légende complète à la page *I · 1).*

Os símbolos incluídos no texto do índice representam as grandes categorias identificadas com a chave à direita. Os símbolos com números em sua parte superior (⋏[1]) identificam as subcategorias (veja-se a chave completa à página *I · 1).*

Symbol	English	Deutsch	Español	Français	Português
∧	Mountain	Berg	Montaña	Montagne	Montanha
⋏	Mountains	Gebirge	Montañas	Montagnes	Montanhas
)(	Pass	Paß	Paso	Col	Passo
V	Valley, Canyon	Tal, Cañon	Valle, Cañón	Vallée, Canyon	Vale, Canhão
≚	Plain	Ebene	Llano	Plaine	Planície
›	Cape	Kap	Cabo	Cap	Cabo
I	Island	Insel	Isla	Île	Ilha
II	Islands	Inseln	Islas	Îles	Ilhas
⊥	Other Topographic Features	Andere Topographische Objekte	Otros Elementos Topográficos	Autres données topographiques	Outros acidentes topográficos

ESPAÑOL Nombre	Página	Lat.°′	Long.°′ W = Oeste
Sint-Joris-Weert	56	50.48 N	4.39 E
Sint-Joris-Winge	56	50.55 N	4.52 E
Sint-Katelijne-Waver	56	51.04 N	4.32 E
Sint-Kruis, Bel.	50	51.13 N	3.15 E
Sint Kruis, Ned. Ant.	241s	12.18 N	69.08 W
Sint-Lenaarts	56	51.21 N	4.41 E
Sint Maarten	52	52.46 N	4.44 E
Sint Maarten (Saint-Martin) I	238	18.04 N	63.04 W
Sint Maartensdijk	52	51.33 N	4.05 E
Sint-Michiels	50	51.11 N	3.12 E
Sint Michielsgestel	52	51.38 N	5.21 E
Sint Nicolaas	241s	12.27 N	69.52 W
Sint-Niklaas (Saint-Nicolas)	50	51.10 N	4.08 E
Sint-Oedenrode	52	51.34 N	5.27 E
Sinton	196	28.02 N	97.30 W
Sintong	114	1.31 N	100.58 E
Sint Pancras	52	52.39 N	4.46 E
Sint-Pieters-Leeuw	50	50.47 N	4.14 E
Sintra	34	38.48 N	9.23 W
Sintra, Serra de ⋏[2]	266c	38.47 N	9.25 W
Sintra Granjo do Marquez, Aeroporto ⊠	266c	38.49 N	9.20 W
Sint-Truiden	56	50.48 N	5.12 E
Sint Willebrord	52	51.33 N	4.35 E
Sinú ≃	246	9.24 N	75.49 W
Sin'ucha ≃	84	44.45 N	40.58 E
Sin'uga	88	57.45 N	115.13 E
Sinŭiju	98	40.05 N	124.24 E
Sinujif	144	8.33 N	48.59 E
Sinŭp, C.M.I.K.	98	39.54 N	126.47 E
Sinŭp, Taehan	98	37.54 N	127.12 E
Sinwŏn-ni	98	38.13 N	125.44 E
Sinzig	56	50.32 N	7.15 E
Sinzing	60	49.00 N	12.02 E
Sió ≃, Magy.	30	46.20 N	18.55 E
Sio ≃, Togo	150	6.17 N	1.13 E
Siocon	116	7.42 N	122.08 E
Siófok	30	46.54 N	18.04 E
Sioma	152	16.39 S	23.30 E
Sioma Ngweze National Park ♠	152	17.15 S	23.20 E
Sion (Sitten)	58	46.14 N	7.21 E
Sionascaig, Loch ⊜	46	58.04 N	5.11 W
Sion Mills	48	54.47 N	7.29 W
Sioule ≃	32	46.22 N	3.19 E
Sioux Center	198	43.04 N	96.10 W
Sioux City	198	42.30 N	96.24 W
Sioux Falls	198	43.33 N	96.42 W
Sioux Lookout	184	50.06 N	91.55 W
Sioux Narrows	184	49.25 N	94.06 W
Sioux Rapids	198	42.53 N	95.09 W
Sipalay	116	9.45 N	122.24 E
Sipalay ≃	116	9.46 N	122.24 E
Sipaliwini □[5]	250	4.00 N	56.00 W
Sipaliwini ≃	250	2.22 N	56.50 W
Sipaozi	104	41.26 N	122.13 E
Sipapo ≃	246	5.03 N	67.48 W
Siparia	241r	10.08 N	61.30 W
Šipčenski Prohod)(	38	42.46 N	25.19 E
Şipek	130	40.14 N	41.29 E
Sipes	220	28.48 N	81.14 W
Sipesville	214	40.06 N	79.06 W
Šipicyno, Ross.	24	61.17 N	46.28 E
Šipicyno, Ross.	86	56.04 N	77.18 E
Šipilovo	82	54.49 N	37.32 E
Siping	89	43.12 N	124.20 E
Sipingjie	98	42.31 N	125.08 E
Sipirok	114	1.37 N	99.16 E
Sipitang	112	5.05 N	115.33 E
Sipiwesk	184	55.27 N	97.24 W
Sipiwesk Lake ⊜	184	55.05 N	97.35 W
Siple ♁[3]	9	75.56 S	84.15 W
Siple, Mount ∧	9	73.15 S	126.06 W
Siple Coast ⊥[2]	9	82.00 S	153.00 W
Sipocot	116	13.46 N	122.58 E
Sipofaneni	158	26.41 S	31.41 E
Sipot	114	4.31 N	96.02 E
Şipoteni	38	47.18 N	28.11 E
Šipplingen	58	47.47 N	9.05 E
Si Prachan	110	14.37 N	100.09 E
Sipsey ≃	194	33.00 N	88.10 W
Sipsey Creek ≃	194	33.53 N	88.17 W
Sipu	98	40.48 N	113.43 E
Şipul	164	5.50 S	148.45 E
Šipunovo	86	52.13 N	82.17 E
Šipunskij, mys ›	74	53.06 N	160.02 E
Sipupus	114	1.25 N	99.31 E
Sipura, Pulau I	112	2.12 S	99.40 E
Siqian, Zhg.	100	22.31 N	112.52 E
Siqian, Zhg.	100	24.40 N	114.06 E
Siqueira Campos	255	23.42 S	49.50 W
Siquia ≃	236	12.09 N	84.13 W
Siquijor	116	9.13 N	123.30 E
Siquijor □[4]	116	9.11 N	123.34 E
Siquijor Island I	116	9.11 N	123.34 E
Siquirres	236	10.06 N	83.30 W
Siquisique	246	10.34 N	69.42 W
Sīra, India	122	13.45 N	76.54 E
Şira, Nor.	26	58.25 N	6.38 E
Šira, Ross.	86	54.29 N	89.56 E
Sira ≃	26	58.17 N	6.24 E
Si Racha	110	13.10 N	100.56 E
Siracuas	248	21.03 S	61.46 W
Siracusa (Syracuse)	70	37.04 N	15.17 E
Siracusa □[4]	70	37.03 N	15.00 E
Sir Adam Beck II Reservoir ⊜[1]	284a	43.08 N	79.04 W
Sirāhā	124	26.39 N	86.12 E
Šir'aj	80	49.34 N	44.07 E
Sirājganj	124	24.27 N	89.43 E
Sir Alexander, Mount ∧	182	53.56 N	120.23 W
Sirāmpur	126	24.08 N	86.20 E
Şiran	130	40.12 N	39.08 E
Şirasso	150	9.16 N	6.06 W
Sirault	50	50.30 N	3.47 E
Siraway	116	7.34 N	122.08 E
Sirba ≃	150	13.46 N	1.40 E
Şīr Banī Yās I	128	24.19 N	52.37 E
Sir Colin Mackenzie Wildlife Sanctuary ◆[4]	169	37.40 S	145.32 E
Sirdalsvatn ⊜	26	58.33 N	6.41 E
Sīrdān	128	36.39 N	49.12 E
Sirdar	182	49.15 N	116.37 W
Sir Douglas, Mount ∧	182	50.44 N	115.20 W
Sire	144	9.00 N	36.55 E
Sir Edward Pellew Group II	164	15.40 S	136.48 E
Širega	76	60.10 N	41.15 E
Sireniki	180	64.25 N	173.57 W
Sirente, Monte ∧	66	42.09 N	13.36 E
Siret	38	47.57 N	26.04 E
Siret (Seret) ≃	38	45.24 N	28.01 E
Sirevåg	26	58.30 N	5.47 E
Sir Francis Drake, Mount ∧	182	50.48 N	124.47 W
Sir Francis Drake Channel ⋓	240m	18.25 N	64.30 W
Sirghāyā	132	33.48 N	36.09 E
Sirḥān, Wādī as- V	128	30.30 N	38.00 E
Sirhind	124	30.39 N	76.23 E
Sirhind Canal ≊	123	30.47 N	76.01 E
Siria → Syria □[1]	128	35.00 N	38.00 E
Sirik, Tanjong ›	112	2.46 N	111.19 E
Sirikit Reservoir ⊜[1]	110	17.50 N	100.30 E
Sírina I	130	36.21 N	26.42 E
Širinguši	80	53.51 N	42.46 E
Sirino, Monte ∧	68	40.08 N	15.50 E
Siriya-zaki ›	92	41.26 N	141.28 E
Sir James MacBrien, Mount ∧	180	62.07 N	127.41 W
Sīrjān	128	29.27 N	55.40 E
Sir Joseph Banks Group II	166	34.32 S	136.17 E
Sirkābād	126	23.16 N	86.12 E

FRANÇAIS Nom	Page	Lat.°′	Long.°′ W = Ouest
Sirkeli	130	40.09 N	32.52 E
Sirmaur	124	24.51 N	81.23 E
Sirmione	64	45.30 N	10.36 E
Sirnach	58	47.28 N	9.00 E
Şırnak	128	37.32 N	42.28 E
Şırnak □[4]	128	37.30 N	42.30 E
Širo, Jabal ∧	140	14.23 N	24.23 E
Sirohi	120	24.54 N	72.51 E
Širokaja Pad'	89	50.14 N	142.09 E
Širokij	89	49.45 N	129.30 E
Širokij Bujerak	80	52.07 N	47.46 E
Širokovo	88	55.27 N	99.23 E
Sirolo	66	43.32 N	13.37 E
Sirombu	114	0.57 N	97.25 E
Sironj	124	24.06 N	77.42 E
Síros → Ermoúpolis	38	37.26 N	24.56 E
Síros I	38	37.26 N	24.54 E
Sirotino	76	55.23 N	29.37 E
Sirotinskaja	80	49.16 N	43.39 E
Siroua, Jebel ∧	148	30.41 N	7.37 W
Sırpsındığı	130	41.46 N	26.29 E
Sirrah, Nafūd as- ⊥[8]	128	23.05 N	44.25 E
Sīrrī, Jazīreh-ye I	128	25.55 N	54.32 E
Sirsa, India	123	29.32 N	75.01 E
Sirsa, India	126	22.14 N	86.38 E
Sirsāganj	124	27.03 N	78.42 E
Sirs al-Layyānah	142	30.26 N	30.58 E
Sir Sandford, Mount ∧	182	51.40 N	117.52 W
Sirsi	122	14.37 N	74.51 E
Sirsilla	122	18.23 N	78.50 E
Sirsinā, Mişr	142	30.36 N	30.54 E
Sirsinā, Mişr	142	29.24 N	30.58 E
Sirsiri	154	4.24 N	31.53 E
Sir Thomas, Mount ∧	162	27.10 S	129.45 E
Siruma	116	14.00 N	123.15 E
Sirupa ≃	232	29.10 N	108.35 W
Şirvan	130	38.02 N	42.00 E
Šīrvān (Diyālā) ≃	128	33.14 N	44.31 E
Şirvan düzü ⁞	84	40.15 N	48.00 E
Širvintos	76	55.03 N	24.57 E
Sir Wilfrid Laurier, Mount ∧	182	52.47 N	119.45 W
Sir Wilfrid Laurier's Birthplace National Historic Site ⊥	206	45.51 N	73.45 W
Sirykrabet ⊥	86	44.07 N	62.35 E
Šís ≃, Guat.	236	14.09 N	91.39 W
Šiš ≃, Ross.	86	57.19 N	73.23 E
Sisa, Mount ∧	164	6.08 S	142.45 E
Sisaba ∧	154	6.09 S	29.48 E
Sisaiya Thāna	124	27.35 N	81.20 E
Sisak	36	45.29 N	16.23 E
Şi Sa Ket	110	15.07 N	104.20 E
Šišakovo	76	60.02 N	41.30 E
Şi Satchanalai	110	17.31 N	99.46 E
Šišchid (Kyzyl-Chem) ≃	88	51.21 N	96.58 E
Šiševka	76	58.52 N	38.52 E
Sishangcun	105	40.16 N	116.33 E
Sishen	158	27.55 S	22.59 E
Sishili	106	32.09 N	120.45 E
Sishilijie	100	29.08 N	116.44 E
Sishilipu	105	40.12 N	118.08 E
Sishuang Liedao II	100	26.42 N	120.24 E
Sishui	98	35.39 N	117.15 E
Sisian	84	39.32 N	46.02 E
Şisib Lake ⊜	184	52.35 N	99.22 W
Šišicy	76	53.13 N	27.32 E
Sisikon	58	46.57 N	8.42 E
Sisim ≃	88	55.09 N	91.54 E
Şisipuk Lake ⊜	184	55.45 N	101.50 W
Šiškejevo	80	54.12 N	44.45 E
Šiškino	88	52.18 N	113.35 E
Siskiyou Mountains ⋏	204	41.55 N	123.15 W
Siskiyou Pass)(	202	42.03 N	122.36 W
Şişli ◆[8]	267b	41.04 N	28.59 E
Šišlovo	82	54.14 N	38.33 E
Sison	116	9.40 N	125.31 E
Sisŏphŏn	110	13.35 N	102.59 E
Sisquoc ≃	204	34.54 N	120.18 W
Sissa ≃	115b	8.29 S	121.18 E
Sissach	58	47.28 N	7.49 E
Sissano	164	3.00 S	142.05 E
Sisséla	150	10.49 N	10.37 W
Sisseton	198	45.39 N	97.02 W
Sisseton Indian Reservation ◆[4]	198	45.40 N	97.02 W
Sissili ≃	150	10.16 N	1.15 W
Sisson Branch Reservoir ⊜[1]	186	47.16 N	67.20 W
Sissonne	50	49.34 N	3.54 E
Sissonville	188	38.31 N	81.37 W
Sīstān ◆[1]	128	30.30 N	62.00 E
Sīstān va Balūchestān □[4]	128	28.30 N	60.30 E
Sister Bay	190	45.11 N	87.07 W
Sister Lakes	216	42.05 N	86.12 W
Sisteron	62	44.12 N	5.56 E
Sisters	202	44.17 N	121.32 W
Sistersville	188	39.33 N	80.59 W
Sistig	56	50.29 N	6.30 E
Sisto ≃	66	41.18 N	13.10 E
Sistranda	26	63.43 N	8.50 E
Sit' ≃, Ross.	76	59.59 N	40.10 E
Sit' ≃, Ross.	76	58.16 N	37.54 E
Sitabamba	248	8.02 S	77.44 W
Sitai, Zhg.	85	39.23 N	77.56 E
Sitai, Zhg.	98	41.16 N	114.23 E
Sitaizi, Zhg.	104	42.29 N	123.20 E
Sitaizi, Zhg.	104	41.17 N	122.16 E
Sitaizui	105	40.49 N	115.20 E
Sitakili	150	13.07 N	11.14 W
Sitalike	154	6.38 S	31.08 E
Sitalkuchi	124	26.10 N	89.11 E
Sītāmarhi	124	26.36 N	85.29 E
Sitampiky	157b	16.41 S	46.06 E
Si Tangkay	112	4.40 N	119.24 E
Sītāpur	124	27.34 N	80.41 E
Sītāpur Branch ≊	124	28.10 N	80.25 E
Sitārāmpur	126	23.43 N	86.53 E
Siteki	158	26.32 S	31.58 E
Sites	226	39.19 N	122.20 W
Si Thep ⊥	110	15.30 N	101.10 E
Sithoniá	38	35.12 N	26.07 E
Sithoniá ›[1]	38	40.10 N	23.47 E
Sitidgi Lake ⊜	180	68.32 N	132.42 W
Sítio D'Abadia	255	14.48 S	46.16 W
Sítio Novo	250	5.51 S	46.43 W
Sitka	180	57.03 N	135.02 W
Sitkalidak Island I	180	57.10 N	153.14 W
Sitka National Historical Park ♠	180	57.05 N	135.15 W
Sitka Point ›	180	57.00 N	135.49 W
Sitka Sound ⋓	180	57.00 N	135.30 W
Sitkinak Island I	180	56.35 N	154.12 W
Sitkinak Strait ⋓	180	56.39 N	154.06 W
Šitkino	88	56.23 N	98.21 E
Sitna ≃	38	47.37 N	27.08 E
Sitn'a-Ščelkanovo	82	54.58 N	37.59 E
Sitnica ≃	38	42.45 N	21.01 E
Sitniki	80	56.27 N	44.06 E
Sitnikovo	86	56.23 N	67.53 E
Sitobela	158	26.53 S	31.36 E
Sitona	144	14.28 N	37.27 E
Sitrah	128	26.09 N	50.38 E
Sitrah ⫪[4]	140	28.42 N	26.54 E
Sittard	56	51.00 N	5.53 E
Sitten → Sion	58	46.14 N	7.21 E
Sittendorf	264b	48.05 N	16.10 E
Sittensen	52	53.17 N	9.30 E
Sitter ≃	58	47.29 N	9.14 E
Sittingbourne	42	51.21 N	0.44 E
Sittoung ≃	110	17.10 N	96.58 E
Sittwe (Akyab)	110	20.09 N	92.54 E
Situ	105	39.20 N	115.39 E
Situbondo	115a	7.42 S	114.00 E
Siufaalele Point ›	174y	14.17 S	169.29 W

PORTUGUÊS Nome	Página	Lat.°′	Long.°′ W = Oeste
Si'ufage	174y	14.14 S	169.32 W
Siulakderas	112	1.55 S	101.18 E
Siu Lek Yuen	271d	22.23 N	114.12 E
Siumbatu	112	2.45 S	122.03 E
Siumpu, Pulau I	112	5.40 S	122.31 E
Siuna	236	13.44 N	84.46 W
Siurgus Donigala	71	39.35 N	9.12 E
Siuri	126	23.55 N	87.32 E
Siusi (Seis)	64	46.32 N	11.34 E
Siuslaw ≃	202	44.01 N	124.08 W
Siva ≃	80	56.48 N	53.55 E
Sivaganga	122	9.52 N	78.29 E
Sivakāsi	122	9.27 N	77.49 E
Sivaki	89	52.39 N	126.45 E
Sīvand ≃	128	29.51 N	52.46 E
Sivas	130	39.45 N	37.02 E
Sivas □[4]	130	39.30 N	37.15 E
Sivaslı	130	38.30 N	29.42 E
Sivé	150	15.42 N	13.12 W
Ševeluč, vulkan ∧[1]	74	56.39 N	161.18 E
Siverek	130	37.45 N	39.19 E
Siverskij	76	59.21 N	30.05 E
Sivers'kyy Donets' ≃	72	47.35 N	40.54 E
Sivers'kyy Donets'-Donbas, kanal ≊	83	48.55 N	37.45 E
Sivkovo	82	55.26 N	35.53 E
Sivomaskinskij	24	66.40 N	62.35 E
Sivri Ada I	267b	40.54 N	28.59 E
Sivrice	130	38.27 N	39.19 E
Sivrihisar	130	39.27 N	31.34 E
Sivry-Courtry	261	48.32 N	2.45 E
Sivry-sur-Meuse	56	49.19 N	5.16 E
Sīwah	140	29.12 N	25.31 E
Sīwah, Wāḥat ⫪[4]	140	29.12 N	25.31 E
Siwalik Range ⋏	120	31.00 N	78.00 E
Siwān	124	26.13 N	84.22 E
Siwang ≃	107	29.25 N	103.50 E
Sixaola ≃	236	9.34 N	82.34 W
Six Flags Great America ♠	216	42.21 N	87.55 W
Six Flags over Mid-America ♠	219	38.31 N	90.40 W
Six Flags Over Texas ♠	222	32.45 N	97.05 W
Six-Fours-la-Plage	62	43.06 N	5.51 E
Sixian	100	33.30 N	117.56 E
Sixitou	100	27.31 N	119.57 E
Six Mile Creek ≃, On., Can.	284a	43.15 N	79.10 W
Sixmile Creek ≃, Ky., U.S.	218	38.26 N	84.58 W
Sixmile Creek ≃, N.Y., U.S.	284a	43.17 N	78.58 W
Sixmilecross	48	54.34 N	7.08 W
Six Mile Lake ⊜	212	44.55 N	79.45 W
Sixmile Run ≃	276	40.28 N	74.35 W
Six Mile Water ≃	48	54.42 N	6.14 W
Six Nations Indian Reserve ◆[4]	212	43.03 N	80.07 W
Sixshooter Draw V	196	30.51 N	102.33 W
Sixteen Mile Creek ≃, On., Can.	275b	43.27 N	79.40 W
Sixteenmile Creek ≃, Mt., U.S.	202	46.06 N	111.23 W
Sixth Cataract → Sablūkah, Ash-Shallāl as- ∟	140	16.20 N	32.42 E
Siyāl, Jazā'ir II	140	22.47 N	36.12 E
Siyāna	124	28.38 N	78.03 E
Siyang	100	33.43 N	118.41 E
Si Yat ≃	110	13.42 N	101.26 E
Siyäzän	84	41.05 N	49.06 E
Siyeteb	140	18.00 N	35.01 E
Siz'absk	24	65.05 N	53.49 E
Sizaja	88	58.07 N	100.38 E
Sizhijian	98	42.25 N	114.36 E
Siziano	62	45.20 N	9.12 E
Sizilien → Sicilia I	70	37.30 N	14.00 E
Siziman	89	50.43 N	140.26 E
Siziwang Qi	102	41.33 N	111.31 E
Sizun	32	48.24 N	4.05 W
Sizuoka → Shizuoka	94	34.58 N	138.23 E
Sjælland I	41	55.30 N	11.45 E
Sjællands Odde ›[1]	41	55.58 N	11.22 E
Själevad	26	63.18 N	18.36 E
Sjanovo	82	54.59 N	37.25 E
Sjenica	38	43.16 N	20.00 E
Sjeništa ∧	38	43.42 N	18.37 E
Sjoa ≃	26	61.41 N	9.33 E
Sjöbo	41	55.38 N	13.42 E
Sjøholt	26	62.29 N	6.48 E
Sjösa	40	58.46 N	17.04 E
Sjötorp	40	58.50 N	13.59 E
Skaby	264a	52.19 N	13.51 E
Skaby-Berge ∧[2]	264a	52.19 N	13.49 E
Skåde	41	56.06 N	10.13 E
Skadovs'k	78	46.08 N	32.54 E
Skælskør	41	55.15 N	11.19 E
Skærbæk, Dan.	41	55.31 N	9.38 E
Skærbæk, Dan.	41	55.09 N	8.46 E
Skævinge	41	55.55 N	12.10 E
Skaftafell National Park ♠	24a	64.15 N	17.00 W
Skaftung	26	62.07 N	21.22 E
Skagafjörður ⊂	24a	65.55 N	19.35 W
Skagen	26	57.44 N	10.36 E
Skagern ⊜	40	58.59 N	14.17 E
Skagerrak ⋓	26	57.45 N	9.00 E
Skagersvik	40	58.58 N	14.06 E
Skaggs Creek ≃	194	36.54 N	86.04 W
Skagit □[6]	224	48.29 N	121.45 W
Skagit ≃	224	48.20 N	122.25 W
Skagit Bay ⊂	224	48.19 N	122.24 W
Skagway	180	59.28 N	135.19 W
Skaidi	24	70.25 N	24.30 E
Skaistkalne	76	56.23 N	24.39 E
Skála Oropoú	38	38.20 N	23.46 E
Skala-Podil's'ka	78	48.51 N	26.12 E
Skalat	78	49.26 N	25.59 E
Skalbmierz	30	50.19 N	20.25 E
Skälderviken	41	56.17 N	12.50 E
Skälderviken ⊂	41	56.18 N	12.38 E
Skalica	30	48.51 N	17.14 E
Skalino	76	58.32 N	40.13 E
Skalistaja, gora ∧	84	42.48 N	45.08 E
Skalistyj, gora ∧	180	68.12 N	178.10 E
Skalistyj chrebet ⋏	84	43.15 N	43.00 E
Skalistyj Golec, gora ∧	88	56.24 N	119.12 E
Skalka ⊜	24	66.50 N	18.46 E
Skalka, údolní nádrž ⊜[1]	54	50.06 N	12.19 E
Skalná	54	50.07 N	12.23 E
Skal'nyj	86	58.22 N	57.59 E
Skamania	224	45.37 N	122.02 W
Skamania □[6]	224	45.58 N	121.53 W
Skamlingsbanke ∧[2]	41	55.25 N	9.34 E
Skamokawa	224	46.16 N	123.27 W
Skanderborg	41	56.02 N	9.56 E
Skanderborg Sø ⊜	41	56.01 N	9.56 E
Skåne □[9]	41	55.59 N	13.30 E
Skaneateles	210	42.56 N	76.25 W
Skaneateles Falls	210	43.00 N	76.27 W
Skaneateles Lake ⊜	210	42.53 N	76.24 W
Skånevik	26	59.44 N	5.59 E
Skänninge	26	58.24 N	15.05 E
Skanör	26	55.25 N	12.52 E
Skara	26	58.22 N	13.25 E
Skaraborgs Län □[6]	26	58.20 N	13.30 E
Skaramagás	267c	38.01 N	23.36 E
Skärblacka	40	58.34 N	15.54 E
Skarð	24a	64.03 N	19.50 W
Skardhø ∧	26	62.30 N	8.45 E
Skārdu	123	35.18 N	75.37 E
Skärhamn	26	58.00 N	11.33 E
Skarhult	41	55.49 N	13.23 E
Skarnes	26	60.15 N	11.41 E
Skärplinge	40	60.28 N	17.46 E

Skarszewy	30	54.05 N	18.27 E
Skårup	41	55.05 N	10.42 E
Skaryszew	30	51.19 N	21.15 E
Skarżysko-Kamienna	30	51.08 N	20.53 E
Skášov	60	49.31 N	13.26 E
Skate Creek ≃	224	46.37 N	121.41 W
Skattkärr	40	59.25 N	13.41 E
Skaudvilė	76	55.24 N	22.35 E
Skaugum	26	59.51 N	10.26 E
Skawina	30	49.59 N	19.49 E
Skebobruk	40	59.58 N	18.36 E
Skebokvarn	40	59.04 N	16.42 E
Skedviken ⊜	40	59.46 N	18.16 E
Skedvisjön ⊜	40	59.35 N	15.40 E
Skeena ≃	182	54.09 N	130.02 W
Skeena Crossing	182	55.06 N	127.49 W
Skeena Mountains ⋏	176	57.00 N	128.30 W
Skeen Peak ∧	222	32.59 N	97.48 W
Skegness	44	53.10 N	0.21 E
Skegrie	41	55.24 N	13.04 E
Skei	26	61.38 N	6.30 E
Skeikampen	26	61.20 N	10.07 E
Skelde	41	54.51 N	9.44 E
Skeleton Coast ⊥[2]	156	19.15 S	12.30 E
Skeleton Coast Park ♠	156	19.25 S	12.55 E
Skeleton Creek ≃	196	35.58 N	97.25 W
Skeleton Lake ⊜	212	45.15 N	79.27 W
Skellefteå	26	64.46 N	20.57 E
Skellefteälven ≃	26	64.42 N	21.06 E
Skelleftehamn	26	64.41 N	21.14 E
Skellig Rocks II[1]	48	51.48 N	10.31 W
Skellytown	196	35.34 N	101.11 W
Skelmersdale	44	53.33 N	2.48 W
Skelmorlie	46	55.51 N	4.53 W
Skelton, Eng., U.K.	44	54.33 N	0.59 W
Skelton, Eng., U.K.	44	54.43 N	2.51 W
Skene	26	57.29 N	12.38 E
Skene, Mount ∧	169	37.25 S	146.23 E
Skepptuna	40	59.43 N	18.05 E
Skerne ≃	44	54.29 N	1.34 W
Skerpioensdrif	158	31.05 S	21.33 E
Skerries	48	53.35 N	6.07 W
Skerryvore I[2]	46	56.19 N	7.07 W
Skewen	42	51.40 N	3.51 W
Skhíza I	38	36.44 N	21.46 E
Ski	26	59.43 N	10.50 E
Skíathos	38	39.10 N	23.29 E
Skíathos I	38	39.10 N	23.28 E
Skiatook	196	36.22 N	96.00 W
Skibbereen	48	51.33 N	9.15 W
Skibby	41	55.45 N	11.58 E
Skibotn	24	69.24 N	20.16 E
Skiddaw ∧	44	54.38 N	3.08 W
Skidegate	182	53.15 N	132.00 W
Skidegate Inlet ⊂	182	53.14 N	132.00 W
Skidel'	76	53.34 N	24.15 E
Skidmore	196	28.15 N	97.41 W
Skien	26	59.12 N	9.36 E
Skierniewice	30	51.58 N	20.08 E
Skierniewice □[4]	30	52.10 N	20.15 E
Skiftet ⋓	26	60.15 N	21.05 E
Skihist Mountain ∧	182	50.11 N	121.54 W
Skikda (Philippeville)	148	36.50 N	6.58 E
Skikda □[5]	148	36.45 N	7.00 E
Skilak Lake ⊜	180	60.25 N	150.25 W
Skillet Fork ≃	194	38.08 N	88.07 W
Skillingaryd	26	57.26 N	14.05 E
Şkillman	276	40.25 N	74.42 W
Škin'	82	55.11 N	38.30 E
Skinnastaður	24a	66.07 N	16.24 W
Skinner Reservoir ⊜[1]	228	33.35 N	117.03 W
Skinnskatteberg	40	59.50 N	15.41 E
Skippack	285	40.14 N	75.24 W
Skippack Creek ≃	285	40.09 N	75.27 W
Skippack Creek, West Branch ≃	285	40.14 N	75.23 W
Skippers	208	36.37 N	77.38 W
Skipskop	158	34.33 S	20.25 E
Skipton, Austl.	169	37.41 S	143.22 E
Skipton, Eng., U.K.	44	53.58 N	2.01 W
Skirfare ≃	44	54.07 N	2.01 W
Skirmish Point ›	171a	27.05 S	153.13 E
Skíros	38	38.53 N	24.33 E
Skíros I	38	38.53 N	24.32 E
Skivarp	41	55.25 N	13.34 E
Skive	26	56.34 N	9.02 E
Skjálfandafljót ≃	24a	65.57 N	17.38 W
Skjálfandi ⊂	24a	66.08 N	17.38 W
Skjeberg	26	59.14 N	11.12 E
Skjern	26	55.57 N	8.30 E
Skjern ≃	41	55.57 N	8.40 E
Şklad	74	71.55 N	123.33 E
Šklov	76	54.13 N	30.18 E
Skniga ≃	82	54.53 N	37.24 E
Skobeleva, pik ∧	85	39.49 N	72.44 E
Şkoby	40	60.02 N	18.01 E
Škocjanske jame ⊥[7]	36	45.40 N	14.00 E
Skodborg	41	55.25 N	9.09 E
Skodsborg	41	55.49 N	12.34 E
Şkoenmakerskop	158	34.02 S	25.33 E
Škofije	64	45.34 N	13.48 E
Škofja Loka	36	46.10 N	14.18 E
Skoganvarre	24	69.47 N	25.06 E
Skoghall	40	59.19 N	13.26 E
Skogstorp	40	59.20 N	16.28 E
Skokholm Island I	42	51.42 N	5.16 W
Skoki	30	52.41 N	17.10 E
Skokie	216	42.02 N	87.44 W
Skokie ≃	216	42.05 N	87.46 W
Skokie Lagoons ⊂	278	42.07 N	87.47 W
Skokloster ⊥	40	59.42 N	17.37 E
Skokomish, North Fork ≃	224	47.18 N	123.14 W
Skokomish, South Fork ≃	224	47.18 N	123.14 W
Skokomish Indian Reservation ◆[4]	224	47.21 N	123.12 W
Sköldinge	40	59.02 N	16.26 E
Skole	78	49.02 N	23.29 E
Sköllersta	40	59.09 N	15.20 E
Skolsta	40	59.40 N	17.14 E
Skolwin	54	53.32 N	14.35 E
Skomer Island I	42	51.44 N	5.17 W
Skomoroshky	78	49.20 N	29.26 E
Skomoroški	82	54.05 N	36.57 E
Skón	110	12.04 N	105.04 E
Skookumchuck ≃	224	46.41 N	123.00 W
Skookumchuck Reservoir ⊜[1]	224	47.47 N	122.42 W
Skoonspruit ≃	158	27.00 S	26.38 E
Skootamatta ≃	212	44.32 N	77.20 W
Skootamatta Lake ⊜	212	44.50 N	77.15 W
Skópelos, Ellás	38	39.07 N	23.43 E
Skópelos, Ellás	38	39.02 N	26.26 E
Skópelos I	38	39.10 N	23.40 E
Skopin	76	53.51 N	39.33 E
Skopje	38	41.59 N	21.26 E
Skórcz	30	53.48 N	18.32 E
Skorodnoje, Bela.	78	51.38 N	28.49 E
Skorodnoje, Ross.	78	51.05 N	37.14 E
Skørping	26	56.50 N	9.53 E
Şkotfoss	26	59.12 N	9.30 E
Škotovo	89	43.20 N	132.21 E
Skotterud	26	59.59 N	12.07 E
Skovby	41	54.53 N	10.00 E
Skövde	26	58.24 N	13.50 E
Skovlund	41	55.44 N	8.43 E
Skovorodino	89	53.59 N	123.55 E
Skowhegan	188	44.45 N	69.43 W
Skownan	184	51.57 N	99.36 W
Skradin	36	43.49 N	15.56 E
Skreen	48	54.15 N	8.45 W
Skreia	26	60.39 N	10.56 E
Skriplivka	76	57.32 N	30.38 E
Skrīveri	76	56.39 N	25.08 E
Skromberga	41	56.00 N	12.58 E
Skrudaliena	76	55.49 N	26.43 E
Skrunda	76	56.41 N	22.01 E
Skruv	26	56.41 N	15.22 E

Skrydstrup	41	55.14 N	9.15 E
Skudeneshavn	26	59.09 N	5.17 E
Skukuza	156	25.01 S	31.38 E
Skuleberget ∧[2]	26	63.05 N	18.21 E
Skulforp	26	58.21 N	13.49 E
Skull	48	51.32 N	9.33 W
Skull Creek ≃	222	29.32 N	96.24 W
Skull Valley	200	34.30 N	112.41 W
Skull Valley Indian Reservation ◆[4]	200	40.24 N	112.45 W
Skultuna	40	59.43 N	16.25 E
Skuna ≃	194	33.54 N	89.41 W
Şkunk ≃	190	40.42 N	91.07 W
Škunovka	86	50.45 N	55.27 E
Skuodas	76	56.16 N	21.32 E
Şkuratovskij	82	54.07 N	37.36 E
Škurinskaja	78	46.35 N	39.22 E
Skurišenskaja	80	49.52 N	42.57 E
Skurup	41	55.28 N	13.30 E
Skutskär	40	60.38 N	17.25 E
Skvyra	78	49.44 N	29.40 E
Skwentna	180	61.58 N	151.11 W
Skwentna ≃	180	62.00 N	151.08 W
Skwierzyna	30	52.36 N	15.30 E
Skye, Island of I	46	57.18 N	6.15 W
Sky Harbor Airport ⊠	278	42.09 N	87.51 W
Skykomish	224	47.42 N	121.21 W
Skykomish ≃	224	47.50 N	122.03 W
Skykomish, North Fork ≃	224	47.47 N	121.33 W
Skykomish, South Fork ≃	224	47.47 N	121.33 W
Sky Lake	220	28.28 N	81.24 W
Sky Lake ⊜	212	44.48 N	81.15 W
Skyland, Nv., U.S.	226	39.01 N	119.56 W
Skyland, N.C., U.S.	192	35.29 N	82.31 W
Skylight	218	38.25 N	85.31 W
Skyline	284c	38.50 N	76.54 W
Skyline Lakes ⊜	276	41.04 N	74.16 W
Skyllberg	40	58.57 N	14.59 E
Skyring, Península ›[1]	254	45.58 S	74.53 W
Skyring, Seno ⋓	254	52.35 S	72.00 W
Sky Sailing Airport ⊠	282	37.30 N	121.58 W
Skytop	210	41.14 N	75.15 W
Skyttorp	40	60.05 N	17.44 E
Skyway	224	47.29 N	122.14 W
Slackhall	262	53.20 N	1.53 W
Slackwood	208	40.15 N	74.44 W
Slade Green ◆[8]	260	51.28 N	0.12 E
Sladkij	80	46.10 N	42.17 E
Sladkovo	86	55.32 N	70.20 E
Slagelse	41	55.24 N	11.22 E
Slagnäs	24	65.34 N	18.05 E
Slagovišči	76	53.57 N	35.54 E
Slaithwaite	262	53.37 N	1.53 W
Slamannan	46	55.56 N	3.50 W
Slamet, Gunung ∧	115a	7.14 S	109.12 E
Slaná (Sajó) ≃	30	47.56 N	21.08 E
Slancy	76	59.06 N	28.04 E
Slaney ≃	48	52.21 N	6.30 W
Slangerup	41	55.51 N	12.11 E
Slănic	38	45.15 N	25.57 E
Slănic Moldova	38	46.13 N	26.26 E
Slano	36	42.47 N	17.54 E
Slanské vrchy ⋏	30	48.50 N	21.30 E
Slaný	54	50.11 N	14.04 E
Šlapanice	30	49.10 N	16.44 E
Slaščevskaja	80	49.52 N	42.21 E
Śląsk → Silesia □[9]	30	51.00 N	16.45 E
Slastucha	80	51.57 N	44.32 E
Slate Bottom Creek ≃	284a	42.53 N	78.45 W
Slate Creek ≃, Ks., U.S.	198	37.08 N	97.09 W
Slate Creek ≃, Pa., U.S.	279b	40.28 N	79.32 W
Slatedale	208	40.45 N	75.40 W
Slate Hill	210	41.23 N	74.29 W
Slater, Ia., U.S.	190	41.52 N	93.40 W
Slater, Mo., U.S.	194	39.13 N	93.04 W
Slater Creek ≃	200	40.59 N	107.23 W
Slatersville	207	42.00 N	71.34 W
Slaterville Springs	210	42.24 N	76.21 W
Slatina	38	44.26 N	24.22 E
Slatington	208	40.44 N	75.36 W
Slaton	196	33.26 N	101.38 W
Slattocks	262	53.35 N	2.10 W
Slatyne	78	50.12 N	36.11 E
Slaughter	194	30.43 N	91.08 W
Slaung	115a	8.02 S	111.24 E
Slautnoje	74	63.00 N	167.59 E
Slava	89	52.08 N	129.24 E
Slav'anka, Ross.	89	42.53 N	131.21 E
Slav'anka, Uzb.	85	40.40 N	68.32 E
Slav'anka ≃	265a	59.50 N	30.32 E
Slav'ansk-na-Kubani	78	45.15 N	38.08 E
Slave ≃	176	61.18 N	113.39 W
Slave Coast ⊥[2]	150	6.25 N	3.00 E
Slave Lake	182	55.17 N	114.46 W
Slavgorod, Bela.	76	53.27 N	31.00 E
Slavgorod, Ross.	86	53.00 N	78.40 E
Slavgorod, Ukr.	78	50.36 N	35.21 E
Slavhorod	78	48.06 N	35.31 E
Slavitino	82	56.41 N	39.13 E
Slavkino	80	52.58 N	47.11 E
Slavkoviči	76	57.39 N	29.05 E
Slavkovský les ⋏	54	50.07 N	12.45 E
Slavkov u Brna	61	49.09 N	16.52 E
Slavnoje	76	54.18 N	29.27 E
Slavonia → Slavonija □[9]	36	45.00 N	18.00 E
Slavonice	61	49.00 N	15.21 E
Slavonija □[9]	36	45.00 N	18.00 E
Slavonska Požega	36	45.20 N	17.41 E
Slavonski Brod	38	45.10 N	18.01 E
Slavsk	76	55.03 N	21.41 E
Slavs'ke	78	48.49 N	23.24 E
Slavuta	78	50.18 N	26.52 E
Sława	30	51.53 N	16.04 E
Slawi	115a	6.59 S	109.08 E
Sławno	30	54.22 N	16.40 E
Slayton	198	43.59 N	95.45 W
Slea ≃	44	53.03 N	0.12 W
Sleaford	42	53.00 N	0.24 W
Slea Head ›	48	52.06 N	10.27 W
Sleat, Point of ›	46	57.01 N	6.02 W
Sleat, Sound of ⋓	46	57.06 N	5.49 W
Sledge	194	34.25 N	90.13 W
Sledge Island I	180	64.29 N	166.13 W
Sled Lake ⊜	184	54.27 N	107.25 W
Sledmere	44	54.04 N	0.35 W
Slednevo	82	56.25 N	38.36 E
Sled'uki	76	53.35 N	30.22 E
Sleen	52	52.46 N	6.48 E
Sleeping Bear Dunes National Lakeshore ♠	190	44.50 N	86.08 W
Sleeping Giant State Park ♠	207	41.25 N	72.53 W
Sleepy Eye	198	44.17 N	94.43 W
Sleepy Hollow, Ca., U.S.	226	38.00 N	122.34 W
Sleepy Hollow, Ca., U.S.	280	33.57 N	117.47 W
Sleepy Hollow, Il., U.S.	216	42.06 N	88.24 W
Sleetmute	180	61.42 N	157.11 W
Sleidinge	50	51.08 N	3.41 E
Sleights	44	54.27 N	0.40 W
Sleman	115a	7.42 S	110.20 E
Slepino	76	59.11 N	29.02 E
Ślesin	30	52.23 N	18.19 E
Slessor Glacier ⊓	9	79.50 S	28.30 W
Slickville	214	40.27 N	79.31 W
Slidell	194	30.16 N	89.46 W
Slide Mountain ∧	210	42.00 N	74.23 W
Sliderock Mountain ∧	202	46.35 N	113.33 W
Sliedrecht	52	51.49 N	4.45 E

Slieve Aughty Mountains ⋏	48	53.05 N	8.35 W
Slieve Bloom Mountains ⋏	48	53.05 N	7.35 W
Slievekimalta ∧	48	52.45 N	8.16 W
Slievenamon ∧	48	52.25 N	7.34 W
Sligeach → Sligo	48	54.17 N	8.28 W
Sligo (Sligeach), Ire.	48	54.17 N	8.28 W
Sligo, Pa., U.S.	214	41.06 N	79.29 W
Sligo □[6]	48	54.10 N	8.40 W
Sligo Bay ⊂	48	54.20 N	8.40 W
Sligo Creek ≃	284c	38.57 N	76.58 W
Slikkerveer	52	51.53 N	4.37 E
Slingebeek ≃	52	51.56 N	6.17 E
Şlinger	190	43.20 N	88.17 W
Šlino, ozero ⊜	76	57.40 N	33.23 E
Slioch ∧	46	57.41 N	5.22 W
Slippery Rock	214	41.03 N	80.03 W
Slippery Rock Creek ≃	214	40.51 N	80.15 W
Šlissel'burg	265a	59.57 N	31.02 E
Slite	26	57.43 N	18.48 E
Slīteres Rezervāts ♠	76	57.38 N	22.25 E
Sliven	38	42.40 N	26.19 E
Slivnica	38	42.51 N	23.02 E
Sloan, Ia., U.S.	198	42.13 N	96.13 W
Sloan, Nv., U.S.	204	35.56 N	115.12 W
Sloan, N.Y., U.S.	210	42.53 N	78.47 W
Sloan Peak ∧	224	48.03 N	121.20 W
Sloansville	210	42.46 N	74.20 W
Sloatsburg	210	41.09 N	74.11 W
Slobidka	78	47.53 N	29.21 E
Sloboda, Bela.	76	53.58 N	28.08 E
Sloboda, Ross.	76	55.30 N	31.51 E
Sloboda, Ross.	78	51.09 N	40.17 E
Sloboda, Ukr.	78	51.11 N	33.37 E
Slobodka, Bela.	76	55.41 N	27.11 E
Slobodka, Ross.	82	54.22 N	37.33 E
Slobodskoj	86	58.42 N	50.12 E
Slobozia, Mol.	38	46.44 N	29.43 E
Slobozia, Rom.	38	44.34 N	27.23 E
Slobozia, Rom.	38	43.51 N	25.54 E
Slobozia Mare	38	45.34 N	28.12 E
Slocan	182	49.46 N	117.28 W
Slocan Lake ⊜	182	49.56 N	117.22 W
Slochteren	52	53.12 N	6.47 E
Slocomb	194	31.06 N	85.35 W
Slocum	207	41.32 N	71.31 W
Slocum Mountain ∧	228	35.18 N	117.13 W
Słomniki	30	50.15 N	20.06 E
Slonim	76	53.06 N	25.19 E
Slonovka	78	50.39 N	37.45 E
Słońsk	54	52.35 N	14.50 E
Sloop Channel ⋓	276	40.36 N	73.31 W
Sloping Hills	276	40.42 N	74.34 W
Slosh Indian Reserve ◆[4]	182	50.44 N	122.13 W
Sloten	52	52.54 N	5.38 E
Sloten ◆[8]	52	52.21 N	4.48 E
Slotermeer ⊜	52	52.55 N	5.40 E
Slough	42	51.31 N	0.36 W
Slough □[8]	260	51.32 N	0.35 W
Slough Brook ≃	276	40.45 N	74.21 W
Sloughhouse	226	38.30 N	121.12 W
Slovakia □[1], Europe	22	48.30 N	20.00 E
Slovakia (Slovenská Republika) □[1], Europe	30	48.30 N	20.00 E
Slovan	214	40.21 N	80.23 W
Slovechne	78	51.23 N	28.21 E
Slovečna ≃	78	51.41 N	29.41 E
Slovenia □[1], Europe	22	46.15 N	15.10 E
Slovenia (Slovenija) □[1], Europe	36	46.15 N	15.10 E
Slovenija → Slovenia □[1]	36	46.15 N	15.10 E
Slovenj Gradec	61	46.31 N	15.05 E
Slovenska Bistrica, Slvn.	36	46.23 N	15.34 E
Slovenska Bistrica, Slvn.	61	46.23 N	15.34 E
Slovenske Gorice ⋏[2]	61	46.35 N	15.55 E
Slovenské rudohorie ⋏	30	48.45 N	20.00 E
Slovinka	80	58.02 N	43.07 E
Slov'yanhirs'k	83	49.02 N	37.31 E
Slov'yanka	78	48.24 N	36.43 E
Slov'yanoserbs'k	83	48.42 N	38.59 E
Slov'yans'k	83	48.52 N	37.37 E
Słowiński Park Narodowy ♠	30	54.40 N	17.25 E
Słubice	54	52.20 N	14.32 E
Sluč' ≃	76	52.08 N	27.31 E
Sluch ≃	78	51.37 N	26.38 E
Sluck	76	53.01 N	27.33 E
Sl'ud'anka	88	51.38 N	103.42 E
Sluderno (Schluderns)	64	46.40 N	10.35 E
Sludy	76	58.52 N	36.52 E
Sluis	52	51.18 N	3.24 E
Şluiskil	52	51.16 N	3.50 E
Šluknov	54	51.00 N	14.27 E
Slunj	36	45.07 N	15.35 E
Słupca	30	52.19 N	17.52 E
Słupia ≃	30	54.35 N	16.50 E
Słupsk (Stolp)	30	54.28 N	17.01 E
Słupsk □[4]	30	54.10 N	17.15 E
Şlurry	156	25.49 S	25.52 E
Šl'uz-Mokr'aki	86	59.17 N	88.50 E
Sly, Oued ≃	34	36.04 N	1.08 E
Smachtino	82	54.51 N	36.25 E
Smackover	194	33.21 N	92.43 W
Smackover Creek ≃	194	33.22 N	92.24 W
Småland □[9]	26	57.20 N	15.00 E
Smålandsfarvandet ⋓	41	55.05 N	11.20 E
Smålandsstenar	26	57.10 N	13.24 E
Smalininkai	76	55.05 N	22.35 E
Smallbridge	262	53.38 N	2.08 W
Smalleytown	276	40.39 N	74.28 W
Smallwood	210	41.40 N	74.49 W
Smallwood Reservoir ⊜[1]	176	54.05 N	64.30 W
Smallwood State Park ♠	208	38.33 N	77.12 W
Smara	148	26.44 N	11.41 W
Smartt Syndicate Dam ⊜[1]	158	30.40 S	23.18 E
Smartville	226	39.12 N	121.18 W
Smeaton	184	53.30 N	104.49 W
Smeaton Bay ⊂	182	55.20 N	130.50 W
Smečno	54	50.10 N	14.03 E
Smedby	40	58.33 N	16.16 E
Smědeč	61	48.56 N	14.09 E
Smederevo	38	44.40 N	20.56 E
Smederevska Palanka	38	44.22 N	20.58 E
Şmedjebacken	40	60.08 N	15.25 E
Šmel'ovka	80	54.47 N	49.11 E
Smelt Brook ≃, Ma., U.S.	283	42.00 N	70.43 W
Smelt Brook ≃, Ma., U.S.	283	42.13 N	70.58 W
Smelt Pond ⊜	283	41.58 N	70.43 W
Smeralda, Costa ⊥[2]	71	41.04 N	9.30 E
Smerwick Harbour ⊂	48	52.12 N	10.24 W
Smethport	214	41.48 N	78.26 W
Smethwick	42	52.30 N	1.58 W
Smicksburg	214	40.52 N	79.10 W
Şmidovič	89	48.36 N	133.49 E
Šmidta → Mys Šmidta	180	68.56 N	179.26 W
Šmidta, mys ›	180	68.56 N	179.30 W
Šmidta, ostrov I	74	81.08 N	90.48 E
Šmidta, poluostrov ›[1]	89	54.10 N	142.40 E
Śmigiel	30	52.01 N	16.32 E
Smila	78	49.14 N	31.53 E
Smilde	52	52.57 N	6.27 E
Smile, Ukr.	78	50.55 N	33.36 E
Smile, Ky., U.S.	218	38.15 N	83.29 W

≃	River	Fluß	Río	Rivière	Rio
≊	Canal	Kanal	Canal	Canal	Canal
∟	Waterfall, Rapids	Wasserfall, Stromschnellen	Cascada, Rápidos	Chute d'eau, Rapides	Cascata, Rápidos
⋓	Strait	Meeresstraße	Estrecho	Détroit	Estreito
⊂	Bay, Gulf	Bucht, Golf	Bahía, Golfo	Baie, Golfe	Baía, Golfo
⊜	Lake, Lakes	See, Seen	Lago, Lagos	Lac, Lacs	Lago, Lagos
⁞	Swamp	Sumpf	Pantano	Marais	Pântano
⊓	Ice Features, Glacier	Eis- und Gletscherformen	Accidentes Glaciales	Formes glaciaires	Acidentes glaciares
⫪	Other Hydrographic Features	Andere Hydrographische Objekte	Otros Elementos Hidrográficos	Autres données hydrographiques	Outros acidentes hidrográficos

✥	Submarine Features	Untermeerische Objekte	Accidentes Submarinos	Formes de relief sous-marin	Acidentes submarinos
□	Political Unit	Politische Einheit	Unidad Politica	Entité politique	Unidade política
♁	Cultural Institution	Kulturelle Institution	Institución Cultural	Institution culturelle	Instituição cultural
⊥	Historical Site	Historische Stätte	Sitio Histórico	Site historique	Sitio histórico
♠	Recreational Site	Erholungs- und Ferienort	Sitio de Recreo	Centre de loisirs	Area de Lazer
⊠	Airport	Flughafen	Aeropuerto	Aéroport	Aeroporto
■	Military Installation	Militäranlage	Instalación Militar	Installation militaire	Instalação militar
◆	Miscellaneous	Verschiedenes	Misceláneo	Divers	Diversos

Name	Page	Lat.°'	Long.°'
Smiley, Sk., Can.	184	51.37 N	109.29 W
Smiley, Tx., U.S.	222	29.16 N	97.38 W
Smilovići	76	53.45 N	28.01 E
Smiltene	76	57.26 N	25.56 E
Smirnovskij	86	54.31 N	69.25 E
Smirnych	89	49.43 N	142.38 E
Smite ≃	44	53.04 N	0.48 W
Smith	182	55.10 N	114.02 W
Smith □[6]	222	32.20 N	95.15 W
Smith ≃, U.S.	192	36.29 N	79.45 W
Smith ≃, Ca., U.S.	204	41.56 N	124.12 W
Smith ≃, Mt., U.S.	202	47.25 N	111.29 W
Smith ≃, Or., U.S.	202	43.43 N	124.05 W
Smith, Cape ›	190	45.48 N	81.35 W
Smith Arm c	180	66.15 N	124.00 W
Smith Bay c	180	70.51 N	154.25 W
Smithboro, Il., U.S.	219	38.54 N	89.20 W
Smithboro, N.Y., U.S.	210	42.02 N	76.24 W
Smith Canyon V	198	37.46 N	103.26 W
Smith Center	198	39.46 N	98.47 W
Smith Creek ≃, S.D., U.S.	198	43.58 N	99.20 W
Smith Creek ≃, Wa., U.S.	224	46.45 N	123.53 W
Smithdale	279b	40.14 N	79.48 W
Smithers, B.C., Can.	182	54.47 N	127.10 W
Smithers, W.V., U.S.	188	38.10 N	81.18 W
Smithers Lake ⊜[1]	222	29.29 N	95.38 W
Smithfield, Austl.	168b	34.41 S	138.41 E
Smithfield, Austl.	274a	33.51 S	150.57 E
Smithfield, On., Can.	212	44.04 N	77.41 W
Smithfield, S. Afr.	158	30.09 S	26.30 E
Smithfield, Eng., U.K.	44	54.59 N	2.52 W
Smithfield, N.C., U.S.	192	35.30 N	78.20 W
Smithfield, Oh., U.S.	214	40.16 N	80.46 W
Smithfield, Pa., U.S.	214	39.48 N	79.48 W
Smithfield, Ut,. U.S.	200	41.50 N	111.49 W
Smithfield, Va., U.S.	208	36.58 N	76.37 W
Smithflat	226	38.44 N	120.45 W
Smith Haven Mall ⊸[9]	276	40.52 N	73.08 W
Smithills Hall ⊥	262	53.36 N	2.27 W
Smith Island I, Ant.	9	62.59 S	62.32 W
Smith Island I, N.C., U.S.	192	33.52 N	77.59 W
Smith Island I, Va., U.S.	208	37.10 N	75.51 W
Smith Island I, Wa., U.S.	224	48.19 N	122.50 W
Smith Island II	208	38.01 N	76.02 W
Smithland	194	37.08 N	88.24 W
Smithmill	214	40.46 N	78.25 W
Smith Mountain ∧	280	34.17 N	117.52 W
Smith Mountain Lake ⊜[1]	192	37.10 N	79.40 W
Smith Peak ∧	202	48.50 N	116.39 W
Smith Peninsula ›[1]	9	74.25 S	61.15 W
Smith Point	222	29.27 N	94.45 W
Smith Point ›, N.S., Can.	186	45.51 N	63.25 W
Smith Point ›, Tx., U.S.	222	29.32 N	94.46 W
Smith Point ›, Va., U.S.	208	37.53 N	76.14 W
Smithport	214	40.50 N	78.52 W
Smith River	204	41.55 N	124.08 W
Smiths	194	32.32 N	85.05 W
Smithsburg	208	39.39 N	77.34 W
Smiths Creek	214	42.55 N	82.36 W
Smiths Falls	212	44.54 N	76.01 W
Smiths Fork ≃	202	41.23 N	110.12 W
Smiths Grove	194	37.03 N	86.12 W
Smiths Mills	276	41.01 N	74.22 W
Smith Sound ʯ	182	51.18 N	127.48 W
Smithton, Austl.	166	40.51 S	145.07 E
Smithton, Il., U.S.	219	38.24 N	89.59 W
Smithton, Mo., U.S.	194	38.40 N	93.05 W
Smithton, Pa., U.S.	279b	40.09 N	79.44 W
Smithtown	210	40.52 N	73.13 W
Smithtown Bay c	276	40.57 N	73.12 W
Smith Valley	218	39.36 N	86.12 W
Smithville, On., Can.	212	43.06 N	79.33 W
Smithville, Ga., U.S.	192	31.54 N	84.15 W
Smithville, In., U.S.	218	39.04 N	86.30 W
Smithville, Ms., U.S.	194	34.04 N	88.23 W
Smithville, Mo., U.S.	194	39.23 N	94.34 W
Smithville, N.J., U.S.	208	39.59 N	74.44 W
Smithville, N.J., U.S.	285	39.29 N	74.27 W
Smithville, Oh., U.S.	214	40.51 N	81.51 W
Smithville, Tn., U.S.	194	35.57 N	85.48 W
Smithville, Tx., U.S.	222	30.00 N	97.09 W
Smithville Flats	210	42.24 N	75.49 W
Smithville Lake ⊜[1]	194	39.25 N	94.30 W
Smögen	26	58.21 N	11.13 E
Smoke Creek ≃, Mt., U.S.	198	48.18 N	104.41 W
Smoke Creek ≃, N.Y., U.S.	284a	42.49 N	78.52 W
Smoke Creek, South Branch ≃	284a	42.49 N	78.49 W
Smoke Creek Desert ⊸[2]	204	40.30 N	119.40 W
Smoke Lake ⊜	212	45.32 N	78.41 W
Smokeless	214	40.24 N	76.02 W
Smokerun	214	40.48 N	78.26 W
Smoketown	208	40.02 N	76.12 W
Smokey, Cape ›	186	46.38 N	60.21 W
Smokey Dome ∧	202	43.29 N	114.56 W
Smoky ≃	182	56.10 N	117.21 W
Smoky Bay	162	32.22 S	133.56 E
Smoky Cape ›	166	30.56 S	153.05 E
Smoky Hill ≃	198	39.03 N	96.48 W
Smoky Hill, North Fork ≃	198	38.55 N	101.17 W
Smoky Lake	182	54.07 N	112.28 W
Smøla I	24	63.24 N	8.00 E
Smol'anica	76	52.42 N	24.38 E
Smol'aninovo	89	43.19 N	132.28 E
Smol'any	76	54.36 N	30.04 E
Smolensk	76	54.47 N	32.03 E
Smolenskaja vozvyšennost' ⋏[1]	76	54.30 N	33.00 E
Smolensk Oblast' □[4]	76	55.00 N	33.00 E
Smolenskoje	86	52.20 N	85.05 E
Smoleviči	76	54.02 N	28.05 E
Smólikas ∧	38	40.06 N	20.52 E
Smoljan	38	41.35 N	24.41 E
Smolny ʋ	265a	59.57 N	30.24 E
Smolovka	76	55.33 N	30.13 E
Smoot	200	42.37 N	110.54 W
Smoothstone ≃	184	55.20 N	106.39 W
Smoothstone Lake ⊜	184	54.40 N	106.50 W
Smorgon'	76	54.29 N	26.24 E
Smorodovka	76	57.08 N	29.52 E
Smotrych	78	48.56 N	26.34 E
Smotrych ≃	78	48.34 N	26.38 E
Smuškovoje	80	47.20 N	45.55 E
Smyčka	82	56.04 N	35.56 E
Smygehamn	41	55.21 N	13.22 E
Smygehuk ›	41	55.21 N	13.23 E
Smyley Island I	9	72.55 S	78.00 W
Smyrna → İzmir, Tür.	130	38.25 N	27.09 E
Smyrna, De., U.S.	208	39.17 N	75.36 W
Smyrna, Ga., U.S.	192	33.53 N	84.30 W
Smyrna, N.Y., U.S.	210	42.41 N	75.34 W
Smyrna, Tn., U.S.	194	35.58 N	86.31 W
Smyrna ≃	208	39.22 N	75.31 W
Smyšl'ajevka	80	53.15 N	50.22 E
Smyth, Canal ʯ	254	52.15 S	73.40 W
Smythe, Mount ∧	176	57.54 N	124.53 W
Smythe Park ♦	275b	43.41 N	79.30 W
Smythesdale	169	37.38 S	143.41 E
Sn'adin	78	52.04 N	28.19 E
Snæfell ∧, Ísland	24a	64.48 N	15.32 W
Snaefell ∧, I. of Man	44	54.16 N	4.27 W
Snæfellness ›[1]	24a	64.50 N	23.00 W
Snag	180	62.24 N	140.22 W
Snaght, Slieve ∧	48	55.12 N	7.20 W
Snagost'	78	51.21 N	34.54 E
Snahapish ≃	224	47.38 N	124.11 W
Snaith	44	53.41 N	1.02 W
Šn'ajevo	80	52.34 N	46.11 E
Snake ≃, Yk., Can.	180	65.58 N	134.10 W
Snake ≃, U.S.	202	46.12 N	119.02 W
Snake ≃, Ca., U.S.	226	39.07 N	121.43 W
Snake ≃, Mn., U.S.	190	45.49 N	92.46 W
Snake ≃, Mn., U.S.	198	48.26 N	97.07 W
Snake ≃, Ne., U.S.	198	42.47 N	100.48 W
Snake Bight c[3]	220	25.10 N	80.50 W
Snake Brook ≃	283	42.18 N	71.22 W
Snake Creek ≃, Mt., U.S.	202	48.32 N	108.53 W
Snake Creek ≃, Ne., U.S.	198	42.01 N	102.45 W
Snake Creek ≃, S.D., U.S.	198	44.58 N	98.29 W
Snake Creek, South Fork ≃	198	45.02 N	98.36 W
Snake Creek Canal ≅	220	25.57 N	80.11 W
Snake Indian ≃	182	53.11 N	118.00 W
Snake Range ⋏	204	39.00 N	114.15 W
Snake Rapids ⌊	212	45.14 N	77.20 W
Snake River Plain ≍	202	43.00 N	113.00 W
Snake Valley	169	37.37 S	143.35 E
Snake Valley V	204	39.20 N	113.55 W
Snape	42	52.11 N	1.30 E
Snaptun	41	55.49 N	10.04 E
Snares Islands II	9	48.00 S	166.30 E
Snasahögarna ∧	26	63.13 N	12.21 E
Snay Pôl	110	11.40 N	105.13 E
Sneads	192	30.42 N	84.55 W
Snedsted	26	56.54 N	8.32 E
Sneedville	192	36.31 N	83.13 W
Sneek	52	53.02 N	5.40 E
Sneekermeer ⊜	52	53.02 N	5.45 E
Snee-osh-Beach	224	48.24 N	122.33 W
Sneeuberg ∧	158	32.25 S	19.12 E
Sneeuberg ⋏	158	31.46 S	24.20 E
Snekkersten	41	56.00 N	12.36 E
Snelgrove	275b	43.44 N	79.49 W
Snelling	204	37.31 N	120.26 W
Snettisham	42	52.53 N	0.30 E
Snežnaja ≃	88	51.28 N	104.38 E
Snežnik ∧	36	45.35 N	14.27 E
Śniardwy, Jezioro ⊜	30	53.46 N	21.44 E
Snicarte	219	40.07 N	90.14 W
Snicarte Island I	219	40.08 N	90.12 W
Snihurivka	78	47.06 N	32.47 E
Snina	30	48.59 N	22.07 E
Snipe Keys II	220	24.40 N	81.38 W
Snipe Lake ⊜	182	55.07 N	116.46 W
Snizhne	83	48.01 N	38.46 E
Snizort, Loch c	46	57.34 N	6.28 W
Snøde	41	55.05 N	10.55 E
Snodland	42	51.20 N	0.27 E
Snoghøj	41	55.31 N	9.43 E
Snøhetta ∧	26	62.20 N	9.17 E
Snohomish	224	47.54 N	122.05 W
Snohomish □[6]	224	48.02 N	121.41 W
Snohomish ≃	224	48.01 N	122.13 W
Snønipa ∧	26	61.42 N	6.41 E
Snook	222	30.29 N	96.28 W
Snoqualmie	224	47.31 N	121.49 W
Snoqualmie ≃	224	47.50 N	122.03 W
Snoqualmie, Middle Fork ≃	224	47.31 N	121.46 W
Snoqualmie, North Fork ≃	224	47.31 N	121.46 W
Snoqualmie, South Fork ≃	224	47.31 N	121.46 W
Snoqualmie Falls	224	47.32 N	121.49 W
Snoqualmie Mountain ∧	224	47.27 N	121.25 W
Snoqualmie Pass)(	224	47.25 N	121.25 W
Snøtinden ∧	24	66.38 N	14.00 E
Snov	76	53.13 N	26.24 E
Snov ≃	78	51.45 N	31.45 E
Snover	190	43.27 N	82.58 W
Snowbird Lake ⊜	176	60.41 N	103.00 W
Snow Canyon State Park ♦	200	37.11 N	113.42 W
Snow Creek ≃	224	47.59 N	122.53 W
Snowden, Sk., Can.	184	53.30 N	104.41 W
Snowden, Pa., U.S.	279b	40.16 N	79.58 W
Snowden Oaks	284c	39.04 N	76.52 W
Snowdenville	285	40.11 N	75.36 W
Snowdon ∧	44	53.04 N	4.05 W
Snowdonia National Park ♦	28	53.00 N	3.57 W
Snowdoun	194	32.14 N	86.17 W
Snowdrift	176	62.23 N	110.47 W
Snowflake	200	34.30 N	110.04 W
Snow Hill, Md., U.S.	208	38.10 N	75.23 W
Snow Hill, N.C., U.S.	192	35.27 N	77.40 W
Snowking Mountain ∧	224	48.24 N	121.17 W
Snow Lake	184	54.53 N	100.02 W
Snow Lakes ⊜	224	47.29 N	120.45 W
Snowmass Mountain ∧	200	39.07 N	107.04 W
Snow Mountain ∧	226	39.23 N	122.45 W
Snow Peak ∧	202	48.35 N	118.29 W
Snows Brook ≃	283	42.47 N	71.06 W
Snow Shoe	214	41.02 N	77.57 W
Snowshoe Butte ∧	224	47.13 N	121.22 W
Snowshoe Peak ∧	202	48.13 N	115.41 W
Snowtown	166	33.47 S	138.13 E
Snow Water Lake ⊜	204	41.07 N	115.00 W
Snowy ≃	166	37.48 S	148.32 E
Snowy Mountain ∧	188	43.42 N	74.23 W
Snowy Mountains ⋏	166	36.30 S	148.20 E
Snowyside Peak ∧	202	43.57 N	114.58 W
Snubba Range ⋏	171b	35.40 S	148.10 E
Snuŏl	110	12.04 N	106.26 E
Snyatyn	78	48.28 N	25.34 E
Snyder, Ok., U.S.	196	34.39 N	98.57 W
Snyder, Tx., U.S.	196	32.43 N	100.55 W
Snyder □[6]	210	40.47 N	77.03 W
Snydertown	210	40.53 N	76.40 W
Soacha	246	4.35 N	74.13 W
Soahany	157b	18.42 S	44.13 E
Soaker, Mount ∧	172	45.23 S	167.15 E
Soalala	157b	16.06 S	45.20 E
Soalara	157b	23.36 S	43.44 E
Soaloka	157b	18.32 S	45.15 E
Sŏam	98	38.01 N	126.43 E
Soamanonga	157b	23.52 S	44.47 E
Soān ≃	123	33.01 N	71.44 E
Soan-do I	98	34.09 N	126.39 E
Soanierana Ivongo	157b	16.55 S	49.35 E
Soanindrariny	157b	19.54 S	47.14 E
Soap Creek ≃	190	40.55 N	92.14 W
Soap Lake	202	47.23 N	119.29 W
Soasiu → Tidore	108	0.40 N	127.26 E
Soatá	246	6.20 N	72.41 W
Soavina	157b	20.23 S	46.56 E
Soavinandriana	157b	19.09 S	46.45 E
Soay I	46	57.08 N	6.14 W
Soazza	58	46.22 N	9.13 E
Sob ≃	78	48.42 N	29.17 E
Sobaek-sanmaek ⋏	98	36.00 N	128.00 E
Sobat ≃	140	9.22 N	31.33 E
Sobernheim	56	49.47 N	7.38 E
Soběšice	60	49.12 N	13.41 E
Soběslav	30	49.15 N	14.44 E
Sobger ≃	164	3.44 S	140.20 E
Sobinka	80	55.59 N	40.01 E
Soboba Indian Reservation ⊸[4]	228	33.47 N	116.54 W
Soboko	140	6.49 N	24.50 E
Sobolekovo	80	55.39 N	51.53 E
Sobolev	80	51.56 N	51.43 E
Sobolevo	82	55.31 N	38.43 E
Sobolino	88	53.23 N	119.42 E
Sobolivka	78	48.36 N	29.30 E
Sobótka	30	50.55 N	16.45 E
Sobradinho	252	29.24 S	53.03 W
Sobradinho, Reprêsa de ⊜[1]	250	9.40 S	42.00 W
Sobrado	34	41.02 N	8.16 W
Sobral	250	3.42 S	40.21 W
Sobrance	30	48.45 N	22.11 E
Sobrante Ridge ∧	282	37.58 N	122.15 W
Sobrarbe ⊸[1]	34	42.22 N	0.10 E
Sobue	94	35.15 N	136.43 E
Søby	41	54.56 N	10.16 E
Sobych	78	51.52 N	33.14 E
Soča	64	46.20 N	13.39 E
Soča (Isonzo) ≃	64	45.47 N	13.32 E
Socaire	252	23.36 S	67.51 W
Socchieve	64	46.25 N	12.52 E
Soc Giang	110	22.54 N	106.01 E
Socgorodok	78	50.11 N	38.09 E
Soch	85	39.57 N	71.08 E
Soch ≃	85	40.20 N	71.02 E
Sochaczew	30	52.14 N	20.14 E
Sochaux	58	47.31 N	6.50 E
Soch'e → Shache	120	38.25 N	77.16 E
Sochi → Soči	84	43.35 N	39.45 E
Sŏch'ŏn	98	36.05 N	126.41 E
Sochondo	88	51.49 N	112.32 E
Sochondo, gora ∧	88	49.44 N	111.05 E
Soch'ŏng-do I	98	37.46 N	124.45 E
Sochor, gora ∧	88	51.18 N	105.15 E
Soči	84	43.35 N	39.45 E
Social Circle	192	33.39 N	83.43 W
Social Security Administration ʋ	284b	39.19 N	76.44 W
Sociedade Hípica Paulista ♦	287b	23.36 S	46.41 W
Société, Archipel de la (Society Islands) II	14	17.00 S	150.00 W
Society Hill	192	34.30 N	79.51 W
Society Islands → Société, Archipel de la II	14	17.00 S	150.00 W
Society Ridge ✣[3]	14	17.00 S	151.00 W
Soco ≃	238	18.27 N	69.12 W
Socoltenango	232	16.13 N	92.15 W
Socompa, Paso)(	252	24.27 S	68.18 W
Soconusco, Sierra de → Madre, Sierra ⋏	236	15.20 N	92.20 W
Socorro, Bra.	256	22.36 S	46.32 W
Socorro, Col.	246	6.29 N	73.16 W
Socorro, Pil.	116	9.37 N	125.58 E
Socorro, N.M., U.S.	200	34.03 N	106.53 W
Socorro, Tx., U.S.	200	31.39 N	106.18 W
Socorro ⊸[8]	287b	23.39 S	46.42 W
Socorro, Isla I	232	18.45 N	110.58 W
Socota	248	6.18 S	78.44 W
Socotora, Isla → Suquṭrā I	118	12.30 N	54.00 E
Socotra → Suquṭrā I	118	12.30 N	54.00 E
Soc Trang	110	9.36 N	105.58 E
Socuéllamos	34	39.17 N	2.48 W
Soda Creek	182	52.21 N	122.18 W
Soda Creek ≃	226	38.48 N	122.29 W
Soda Lake ⊜, Ca., U.S.	204	35.08 N	116.04 W
Soda Lake ⊜, Ca., U.S.	226	35.15 N	119.53 W
Sodankylä	24	67.29 N	26.32 E
Soda Springs	202	42.39 N	111.36 W
Soddy-Daisy	194	35.16 N	85.10 W
Sodegaura	94	35.26 N	139.57 E
Söderälgen ⊜	40	59.43 N	14.35 E
Söderåsen ⋏[2]	41	56.04 N	13.05 E
Söderbärke	40	60.05 N	15.33 E
Söderby-Karl	40	59.53 N	18.41 E
Söderfors	40	60.23 N	17.14 E
Söderhamn	26	61.18 N	17.03 E
Söderköping	26	58.29 N	16.18 E
Södermanland □[9]	41	59.12 N	16.49 E
Södermanlands Län □[6]	40	59.15 N	16.40 E
Södernmanland □[9]	40	59.12 N	16.49 E
Söderslätt □[9]	41	55.29 N	13.15 E
Södertälje	40	59.12 N	17.37 E
Södertörn ›[1]	40	59.05 N	18.00 E
Sodhra	123	32.28 N	74.11 E
Sodingen ⊸[8]	263	51.32 N	7.15 E
Sodium	158	30.11 S	23.09 E
Sodo	144	6.52 N	37.47 E
Sodom → Sedom ⊥	132	31.04 N	35.23 E
Sodpur	272b	22.39 N	88.23 E
Södra Björkfjärden c	40	59.18 N	17.32 E
Södra Hörken ⊜	40	60.02 N	15.02 E
Södra Kvarken ʯ	26	60.15 N	19.05 E
Södra Råda	40	59.01 N	14.10 E
Södra Sandby	41	55.43 N	13.20 E
Södra Vi	26	57.45 N	15.48 E
Sodražica	36	45.46 N	14.38 E
Sodus	210	43.14 N	77.03 W
Sodus Bay c	210	43.15 N	76.58 W
Sodus Creek ≃	210	43.13 N	76.56 W
Sodus Point	210	43.16 N	76.59 W
Sŏdu-su ≃	98	42.05 N	129.00 E
Sodwalls	170	33.31 S	149.59 E
Sodwana Bay National Park ♦	158	27.30 S	32.39 E
Soe	112	9.52 S	124.17 E
Soeda	96	33.34 N	130.52 E
Soekmekaar	156	23.28 S	29.58 E
Soela väin ʯ	76	58.40 N	22.35 E
Soerabaja → Surabaya	115a	7.15 S	112.45 E
Soest, Dtsch.	52	51.34 N	8.07 E
Soest, Ned.	52	52.09 N	5.18 E
Soestdijk	52	52.11 N	5.18 E
Soestdijk, Paleis ʋ	52	52.12 N	5.15 E
Soeste ≃	52	53.10 N	7.44 E
Soesterberg	52	52.07 N	5.17 E
Soeurs, Île des I	275a	45.28 N	73.33 W
Sofádhes	38	39.20 N	22.06 E
Sofala	170	33.05 S	149.42 E
Sofala □[5]	156	19.00 S	35.00 E
Sofia → Sofija	38	42.41 N	23.19 E
Sofia ≃	157b	15.27 S	47.23 E
Sofiero	41	56.05 N	12.39 E
Sofija (Sofia)	38	42.41 N	23.19 E
Sofija □[4]	38	42.17 N	23.16 E
Sofijsk, Ross.	89	51.34 N	139.52 E
Sofijsk, Ross.	89	52.15 N	133.58 E
Sofiyivka, Ukr.	78	48.04 N	33.52 E
Sofiyivka, Ukr.	78	46.33 N	34.03 E
Sofiyivs'kyy	83	48.12 N	38.52 E
Sofjanga	24	65.52 N	31.15 E
Sofjino	82	55.30 N	38.11 E
Sofrino	82	56.09 N	37.56 E
Sofronovo	76	59.48 N	36.54 E
Sogakofe	150	6.00 N	0.36 E
Sogamoso	246	5.43 N	72.56 W
Sogamoso ≃	246	7.13 N	73.56 W
Soğanlı ≃	130	41.11 N	32.38 E
Soğanlı Geçidi)(	130	40.33 N	40.16 E
Soğanlıköy ⊸[8]	267b	40.55 N	29.12 E
Sogcho → Sokch'o	98	38.12 N	128.36 E
Sogda	89	50.24 N	132.12 E
Sögel	52	52.50 N	7.31 E
Sogen	164	9.25 S	147.25 E
Sogliano al Rubicone	66	44.00 N	12.18 E
Sognafjorden c[2]	26	61.06 N	5.10 E
Søgne	26	58.05 N	7.49 E
Sogne Fjord → Sognafjorden c[2]	26	61.06 N	5.10 E
Sogn og Fjordane □[6]	26	61.30 N	6.50 E
Sogod, Pil.	116	10.45 N	124.00 E
Sogod, Pil.	116	10.23 N	124.59 E
Sogod Bay c	116	10.15 N	125.02 E
Sogo Nur ⊜	102	42.18 N	101.08 E
Sogoža ≃	76	58.28 N	39.06 E
Sogri-san Kukrip Kongwŏn ♦	98	36.33 N	127.52 E
Soğuksu Milli Parkı ♦	130	40.25 N	32.35 E
Söğüt	130	40.00 N	30.11 E
Söğütalan	130	40.03 N	28.34 E
Söğüt Gölü ⊜	130	37.03 N	29.53 E
Söğütlü	130	40.54 N	30.29 E
Sog Xian	120	31.50 N	93.45 E
Sohāg → Sawhāj	140	26.33 N	31.42 E
Sohāgpur, India	124	23.19 N	81.21 E
Sohāgpur, India	124	22.42 N	78.12 E
Soham	42	52.20 N	0.20 E
Sohano	175e	5.27 S	154.40 E
Soharkha	272a	28.35 N	77.24 E
Soheit-Tinlot	56	50.29 N	5.22 E
Sohland	54	51.02 N	14.25 E
Söhlde	52	52.11 N	10.14 E
Sohna	124	28.15 N	77.04 E
Sŏhŭng	98	38.27 N	126.10 E
Sŏhwa-ri	98	38.15 N	128.13 E
Soignies (Zinnik)	50	50.35 N	4.04 E
Soignolles-en-Brie	261	48.39 N	2.42 E
Soin	150	12.47 N	3.49 W
Soindres	261	48.57 N	1.40 E
Soini	26	62.52 N	24.13 E
Sointula	182	50.38 N	127.01 W
Soira ∧	144	14.45 N	39.32 E
Soisalo ∧	26	62.40 N	28.10 E
Soissons	50	49.22 N	3.20 E
Soisy-sous-Montmorency	261	48.59 N	2.18 E
Soisy-sur-Seine	261	48.39 N	2.27 E
Sōja	96	34.40 N	133.45 E
Sojana	24	65.48 N	43.20 E
Sojat	120	25.55 N	73.40 E
Šojda	24	61.11 N	37.40 E
Sojiji Temple ʋ[1]	268	35.31 N	139.41 E
Sojītra	120	22.33 N	72.43 E
Šojna	24	67.52 N	44.08 E
Sŏjosŏn-man c	98	39.20 N	124.50 E
Sojoton Point ›	116	9.58 N	122.27 E
Sok ≃	80	53.24 N	50.08 E
Sōka, Nihon	94	35.49 N	139.48 E
Soka, Taehan	271b	37.30 N	126.48 E
Sokal'	78	50.29 N	24.17 E
Šokal'skogo, proliv ʯ	74	79.00 N	100.25 E
Sokch'o	98	38.12 N	128.36 E
Söke	130	37.45 N	27.24 E
Sokehs Passage ʯ	174r	7.01 N	158.11 E
Sokele	154	9.55 S	24.36 E
Sokhós	38	40.49 N	23.21 E
Sokna	26	60.14 N	9.54 E
Sokodé	150	8.59 N	1.08 E
Sokol, Ross.	74	72.24 N	126.48 E
Sokol, Ross.	76	59.28 N	40.10 E
Sokol, Ross.	89	47.14 N	142.45 E
Sokol ∧	60	49.03 N	13.31 E
Sokółka, Pol.	30	53.25 N	23.31 E
Sokolka, Ross.	80	55.34 N	51.30 E
Sokol'niki ⊸[8]	265b	55.48 N	37.41 E
Sokolniki Park ♦	265b	55.48 N	37.41 E
Sokol'nikovo	82	55.21 N	35.49 E
Sokolo	150	14.44 N	6.08 W
Sokolohirne	78	46.29 N	34.58 E
Sokolov	54	50.09 N	12.40 E
Sokolova Hora	78	50.19 N	28.36 E
Sokolova Pustyn'	82	54.51 N	38.03 E
Sokolovka	86	55.06 N	69.12 E
Sokolovo, Ross.	24	65.21 N	56.57 E
Sokolovo, Ross.	76	52.55 N	34.39 E
Sokolovo, Ross.	80	52.49 N	42.26 E
Sokolovo, Ross.	82	56.02 N	36.55 E
Sokolovo, Ross.	86	52.33 N	84.46 E
Sokolovo-Kundr'učenskij	83	47.50 N	39.57 E
Sokołów	30	50.14 N	22.07 E
Sokołów Podlaski	30	52.25 N	22.15 E
Sokol'skoje	80	57.08 N	43.13 E
Sokone	150	13.53 N	16.22 W
Sokoto	150	13.04 N	5.16 E
Sokoto □[3]	150	12.05 N	5.30 E
Sokoto ≃	150	11.20 N	4.10 E
Šokpar	85	43.49 N	74.21 E
Sŏkp'o-ri	98	37.46 N	125.27 E
Sokrutovka	80	47.54 N	46.33 E
Šokša	76	58.24 N	42.27 E
Soksa-ri	98	40.40 N	127.17 E
Sokskije jary ⋏[2]	80	54.10 N	51.30 E
Sŏk-to I	98	38.40 N	125.00 E
Sokuluk	85	42.52 N	74.18 E
Sokur, Ross.	80	52.01 N	45.48 E
Sokur, Ross.	86	55.13 N	83.13 E
Sokyryany	78	48.27 N	27.25 E
Sokyryntsi	78	50.42 N	32.46 E
Sol'	30	48.56 N	21.36 E
Sol, Costa del ⊥[2]	34	36.40 N	4.00 W
Sola, Nor.	26	58.53 N	5.36 E
Sola, Vanuatu	175f	13.53 S	167.33 E
Sola, Zaïre	154	5.09 S	27.06 E
Soła ≃	30	50.04 N	19.13 E
Solacolu	38	44.23 N	26.34 E
Solai	154	0.02 N	36.09 E
Šolaksaj	86	51.45 N	64.48 E
Solan	123	30.55 N	77.07 E
Solana	220	26.56 N	82.01 W
Solana Beach	228	32.59 N	117.16 W
Solander, Cape ›	274a	34.01 S	151.14 E
Solander Island I	172	46.34 S	166.53 E
Solânea	250	6.45 S	35.39 W
Solangāri	272b	22.36 N	88.27 E
Sol'anka ≃	80	50.10 N	51.20 E
Solano	116	16.31 N	121.11 E
Solano □[6]	226	38.15 N	121.52 W
Solāpur	122	17.41 N	75.55 E
Solar, Morro ∧[2]	286d	12.11 S	77.02 W
Solarino	70	37.06 N	15.07 E
Solaro	266b	45.37 N	9.05 E
Solaro, Monte ∧	68	40.33 N	14.13 E
Solberg	26	63.47 N	17.38 E
Solbiate Arno	62	45.42 N	8.48 E
Solbiate Olona	266b	45.39 N	8.53 E
Solca, Arg.	252	30.46 S	66.28 W
Solca, Rom.	38	47.42 N	25.50 E
Solčava	61	46.25 N	14.41 E
Sol'cy	76	58.08 N	30.20 E
Solda Gölü ⊜	130	37.33 N	29.42 E
Soldatskaja	84	43.48 N	43.49 E
Soldatskoje	85	40.52 N	68.56 E
Soldatsko-Stepnoje	80	49.32 N	45.30 E
Sölde ⊸[8]	263	51.31 N	7.35 E
Sol de Julio	252	29.33 S	63.27 W
Sölden	64	46.58 N	11.00 E
Sölderholz ⊸[8]	263	51.29 N	7.35 E
Soldier Creek ≃	198	39.04 N	95.39 W
Soldier Field ♦	278	41.52 N	87.37 W
Soldier Key I	220	25.35 N	80.10 W
Soldier Point ›	240c	17.02 N	61.41 W
Soldier Pond	186	47.09 N	68.34 W
Soldiers Grove	190	43.23 N	90.46 W
Soldotna	180	60.29 N	151.04 W
Sole, Val di V	64	46.20 N	10.45 E
Solebury	208	40.23 N	75.02 W
Solec Kujawski	30	53.06 N	18.14 E
Soledad, Col.	246	10.55 N	74.46 W
Soledad, Ca., U.S.	226	36.25 N	121.19 W
Soledad, Ven.	246	8.10 N	63.34 W
Soledad, Cerro ∧	196	26.29 N	103.23 W
Soledad de Doblado	234	19.03 N	96.25 W
Soledad Díez Gutiérrez	234	22.12 N	100.57 W
Soledade	252	28.50 S	52.30 W
Soledade de Minas	256	22.04 S	45.03 W
Soledad Pass)(	228	34.30 N	118.07 W
Soleduck ≃	224	47.55 N	124.35 W
Solemar	256	24.05 S	46.36 W
Solen	198	46.23 N	100.47 W
Sølen ∧	26	61.55 N	11.30 E
Solenoje	80	46.14 N	42.32 E
Solentiname, Archipiélago de II	236	11.10 N	85.00 W
Solenzara	36	41.51 N	9.23 E
Solenzo	150	12.11 N	4.05 W
Solero	62	44.55 N	8.30 E
Solers	261	48.40 N	2.43 E
Solesmes	50	50.11 N	3.30 E
Soleure → Solothurn	58	47.13 N	7.32 E
Solferino	64	45.23 N	10.34 E
Solginskij	24	61.05 N	41.19 E
Solgne	56	48.58 N	6.18 E
Solgonskij kr'až ∧	86	55.30 N	91.00 E
Solhan	130	38.58 N	41.03 E
Solheim, Nor.	26	60.53 N	5.27 E
Solheim, S. Afr.	273d	26.11 S	28.10 E
Soliera	64	44.45 N	10.55 E
Soligalič	76	59.05 N	42.17 E
Solignac-sur-Loire	62	44.58 N	3.53 E
Soligny-la-Trappe	50	48.37 N	0.32 E
Soligorsk	76	52.48 N	27.32 E
Solihull	42	52.25 N	1.45 W
Solikamsk	86	59.39 N	56.47 E
Solila	157b	21.25 S	46.37 E
Sol'-Ileck	86	51.10 N	54.59 E
Soliman	148	36.42 N	10.30 E
Solimões → Amazon ≃	242	0.10 S	49.00 W
Solin ≃	50	48.02 N	2.43 E
Solingen	56	51.10 N	7.05 E
Solís, Arg.	258	34.18 S	59.20 W
Solís, Ur.	252	34.36 S	55.29 W
Solís, Presa ⊜[1]	234	20.05 N	100.36 W
Soliseño	196	26.01 N	97.48 W
Söll	64	47.30 N	12.11 E
Sollar	84	41.40 N	48.38 E
Šollas	46	57.39 N	7.21 W
Sollefteå	26	63.10 N	17.16 E
Sollenau	61	47.53 N	16.15 E
Sollentuna	40	59.28 N	17.54 E
Sóller	34	39.46 N	2.42 E
Søllerød	41	55.49 N	12.31 E
Sollerön I	26	60.55 N	14.37 E
Søllested	41	54.49 N	11.17 E
Solliès-Pont	62	43.11 N	6.03 E
Solling ⋏	52	51.45 N	9.35 E
Söllingen	54	52.05 N	10.55 E
Solln ⊸[8]	60	48.05 N	11.31 E
Sollom	262	53.40 N	2.50 W
Sollstedt	54	51.25 N	10.31 E
Solms	56	50.32 N	8.24 E
Solna	40	59.22 N	18.01 E
Solncedar	78	44.34 N	38.01 E
Solncevo	265b	55.39 N	37.24 E
Solnečnogorsk	82	56.11 N	36.59 E
Solnhofen	56	48.53 N	10.59 E
Solo → Surakarta	115a	7.35 S	110.50 E
Solo ≃	115a	6.47 S	112.33 E
Šolochovskij	80	48.18 N	41.03 E
Solodča	80	49.39 N	44.17 E
Solodniki	80	48.25 N	45.16 E
Solofra	68	40.50 N	14.51 E
Sologne ⊸[1]	50	47.20 N	2.00 E
Šologoncy	74	66.13 N	114.14 E
Solok	112	0.48 S	100.39 E
Sololá, Guat.	236	14.46 N	91.11 W
Solola, Som.	144	0.07 N	41.31 E
Sololá □[5]	236	14.40 N	91.15 W
Solomennikova	86	58.20 N	89.02 E
Solomennoje	24	61.51 N	34.19 E
Solomon, Az., U.S.	200	32.48 N	109.37 W
Solomon, Ks., U.S.	198	38.55 N	97.22 W
Solomon ≃	198	38.54 N	97.22 W
Solomon, North Fork ≃	198	39.29 N	98.26 W
Solomon, South Fork ≃	198	39.29 N	98.26 W
Solomon Basin ✣[1]	14	7.00 S	152.00 E
Solomon Islands □[1]	175e	8.00 S	159.00 E
Solomon Islands II	175e	8.00 S	159.00 E
Solomons	208	38.20 N	76.28 W
Solomon Sea ⊤[2]	14	8.00 S	155.00 E
Solomon's Pools → Sulaymān, Birak ⊥	132	31.41 N	35.10 E
Solon, Ia., U.S.	190	41.48 N	91.29 W
Solon, Me., U.S.	188	44.56 N	69.51 W
Solon, Oh., U.S.	214	41.23 N	81.26 W
Solon, Zhg.	89	46.36 N	121.13 E
Solone, Ukr.	78	48.13 N	34.52 E
Solone, Ukr.	83	49.18 N	37.39 E
Solone Ozero	78	45.53 N	34.27 E
Solonešnoje	86	51.40 N	84.21 E
Solonka	80	50.13 N	41.28 E
Sol'onoje	84	44.03 N	40.53 E
Sol'onoje, ozero ⊜	86	55.20 N	70.05 E
Sol'onoje Zajmišče	80	47.56 N	46.07 E
Solonópole	250	5.44 S	39.01 W
Solon Springs	190	46.21 N	91.49 W
Solopaca	68	41.11 N	14.33 E
Solor, Kepulauan II	112	8.25 S	123.30 E
Solor, Pulau I	112	8.27 S	123.05 E
Solotča	80	54.48 N	39.51 E
Solothurn	58	47.13 N	7.32 E
Solothurn □[3]	58	47.25 N	7.35 E
Solotobe	86	44.38 N	66.05 E
Solotvyn	78	48.42 N	24.25 E
Solotvyna	78	47.57 N	23.52 E
Soloveckije ostrova II	24	65.07 N	35.53 E
Solovjovka	76	60.46 N	30.09 E
Solovjovsk, Ross.	88	49.55 N	115.42 E
Solovjovsk, Ross.	89	54.14 N	124.26 E
Solre-le-Château	50	50.10 N	4.05 E
Solre-sur-Sambre	50	50.18 N	4.08 E
Solrød Strand	41	55.32 N	12.14 E
Solsona	34	41.59 N	1.31 E
Solt	30	46.48 N	19.00 E
Šolta, Otok I	36	43.23 N	16.15 E
Solṭānābād	128	36.23 N	58.02 E
Soltau	52	52.59 N	9.49 E
Solton	86	52.50 N	86.28 E
Solunto ⊥	70	38.06 N	13.32 E
Solus, Mount ∧	168a	32.28 S	116.13 E
Solutré-Pouilly	58	46.18 N	4.43 E
Solva	42	51.52 N	5.11 W
Solva ≃	42	51.52 N	5.17 W
Solvang	204	34.36 N	120.08 W
Solvarbo	40	60.24 N	15.40 E
Solvay	210	43.03 N	76.12 W
Sölvesborg	26	56.03 N	14.33 E
Sol'vyčegodsk	24	61.21 N	46.52 E
Solway Firth c[1]	44	54.50 N	3.35 W
Solwezi	154	12.11 S	26.25 E
Soly	76	54.31 N	26.11 E
Solymár	264c	47.36 N	18.56 E
Solza	24	64.33 N	39.29 E
Sōma, Nihon	92	37.48 N	140.57 E
Soma, Tür.	130	39.10 N	27.36 E
Somabula	154	19.41 S	29.41 E
Sōmahara-chūtonchi, Rikujō-jieitai- ■	94	36.23 N	138.58 E
Somain	50	50.22 N	3.17 E
Somalia (Somaliya) □[1], Afr.	136	6.00 N	48.00 E
Somalia (Somaliya) □[1], Afr.	144	6.00 N	48.00 E
Somali Basin ✣[1]	12	0.00	52.00 E
Somalie → Somalia □[1]	144	6.00 N	48.00 E
Somaliland → Somalia □[1]	144	6.00 N	48.00 E
Somali Republic → Somalia □[1]	144	6.00 N	48.00 E
Somaliya → Somalia □[1]	144	6.00 N	48.00 E
Somalomo	152	3.23 N	12.44 E
Sŏman	98	41.20 N	128.54 E
Somanga	154	8.24 S	39.17 E
Sombernon	58	47.18 N	4.42 E
Sombo	152	8.42 S	20.57 E
Sombor	38	45.46 N	19.07 E
Sombra	214	42.43 N	82.29 W
Sombrerete	234	23.38 N	103.39 W
Sombreretillo	196	26.19 N	99.58 W
Sombrero I	238	18.36 N	63.26 W
Sombrero Channel ʯ	110	7.41 N	93.35 E
Sombrio	252	29.07 S	49.40 W
Sombrio, Lagoa do c	252	29.12 S	49.42 W
Şomcuta Mare	38	47.31 N	23.29 E
Somdari	120	25.49 N	72.35 E
Somenos	224	48.49 N	123.44 W
Somercotes	44	53.04 N	1.22 W
Somerdale, N.J., U.S.	208	39.50 N	75.01 W
Somerdale, Oh., U.S.	214	40.34 N	81.22 W
Someren	52	51.24 N	5.44 E
Somero	26	60.37 N	23.32 E
Sõmerpalu	76	57.51 N	26.48 E
Somers, Austl.	169	38.24 S	145.10 E
Somers, Ct., U.S.	207	41.59 N	72.26 W
Somers, Mt., U.S.	202	48.04 N	114.13 W
Somers, Wi., U.S.	216	42.38 N	87.54 W
Somersby	170	33.25 S	151.17 E
Somerset, Austl.	166	41.03 S	145.49 E
Somerset, Mb., Can.	184	49.24 N	98.39 W
Somerset, Co., U.S.	200	38.55 N	107.28 W
Somerset, Ky., U.S.	192	37.05 N	84.36 W
Somerset, Md., U.S.	284c	38.58 N	77.05 W
Somerset, Ma., U.S.	207	41.46 N	71.07 W
Somerset, N.J., U.S.	208	40.44 N	74.34 W
Somerset, Oh., U.S.	188	39.48 N	82.17 W
Somerset, Pa., U.S.	188	40.00 N	79.04 W
Somerset, Tx., U.S.	196	29.13 N	98.40 W
Somerset, Wi., U.S.	190	45.07 N	92.40 W
Somerset □[6], Eng., U.K.	42	51.08 N	3.00 W
Somerset □[6], Md., U.S.	208	38.12 N	75.41 W
Somerset □[6], N.J., U.S.	208	40.34 N	74.37 W
Somerset □[6], Pa., U.S.	214	40.09 N	79.00 W
Somerset Airport ⊠	276	40.37 N	74.40 W
Somerset Center	216	42.03 N	84.25 W
Somerset East	158	32.42 S	25.35 E
Somerset Hills Airport ⊠	276	40.41 N	74.32 W
Somerset Island I, Ber.	240a	32.17 N	64.52 W
Somerset Island I, N.T., Can.	176	73.15 N	93.30 W
Somerset Reservoir ⊜[1]	171a	27.03 S	152.35 E
Somerset West	158	34.08 S	18.50 E
Somersham	42	52.23 N	0.01 E
Somers Point	208	39.19 N	74.35 W
Somersworth	188	43.15 N	70.51 W
Somerton, Eng., U.K.	42	51.03 N	2.44 W
Somerton, Az., U.S.	200	32.35 N	114.42 W
Somerton ⊸[8]	285	40.06 N	75.01 W
Somerton Creek ≃	208	36.32 N	76.55 W
Somervell □[6]	222	32.15 N	97.45 W
Somerville, Austl.	169	38.13 S	145.10 E
Somerville, Ma., U.S.	207	42.23 N	71.06 W
Somerville, N.J., U.S.	210	40.34 N	74.36 W
Somerville, Oh., U.S.	218	39.33 N	84.38 W
Somerville, Tn., U.S.	194	35.14 N	89.21 W
Somerville, Tx., U.S.	222	30.20 N	96.31 W
Somerville Lake ⊜[1]	222	30.18 N	96.40 W
Someș (Szamos) ≃	38	48.07 N	22.22 E
Someșu Cald ≃	38	46.44 N	23.22 E
Someșu Mare ≃	38	47.12 N	24.12 E
Someșu Mic ≃	38	47.09 N	23.55 E
Someșu Rece ≃	38	46.44 N	23.22 E
Somino	76	59.21 N	34.52 E
Somis	228	34.16 N	119.00 W
Sŏmjin-gang ≃	98	34.58 N	127.46 E
Somma	66	42.40 N	12.44 E
Sommacampagna	64	45.24 N	10.50 E
Somma Lombardo, It.	62	45.41 N	8.42 E
Somma Lombardo, It.	266b	45.41 N	8.42 E
Sommariva	166	26.24 S	146.36 E
Sommariva del Bosco	62	44.46 N	7.47 E
Sommatino	70	37.20 N	13.59 E
Somme □[5]	50	49.55 N	2.30 E
Somme ≃, Fr.	50	49.01 N	4.12 E
Somme ≃, Fr.	50	50.11 N	1.39 E
Somme, Baie de la c	50	50.14 N	1.33 E
Somme, Canal de la ≅	50	49.55 N	2.43 E
Sommedieue	56	49.05 N	5.28 E
Sommelsdijk	52	51.45 N	4.09 E
Sommen ⊜	26	58.01 N	15.15 E
Sommepy-Tahure	56	49.15 N	4.33 E
Sommerberg ⊸[8]	263	51.27 N	7.32 E
Sömmerda	54	51.10 N	11.07 E
Sommersdorf	54	53.17 N	14.11 E
Sommersted	41	55.19 N	9.19 E
Sommesous	50	48.44 N	4.12 E
Somme Woods ♦	278	42.09 N	87.49 W
Somnitel'nyj	89	52.12 N	139.04 E
Somo ≃	190	45.29 N	89.48 W
Somogy □[6]	30	46.25 N	17.35 E
Somonauk	216	41.38 N	88.40 W
Somonauk Creek ≃	216	41.32 N	88.41 W
Somosierra, Puerto de)(	34	41.09 N	3.35 W
Somosomo	175g	16.46 S	179.58 W
Somosomo Strait ʯ	175g	16.47 S	179.58 E
Somotillo	236	13.02 N	86.55 W
Somoto	236	13.28 N	86.35 W
Somovo, Ross.	76	52.53 N	34.58 E
Somovo, Ross.	78	51.44 N	39.23 E
Sompeta	122	18.56 N	84.36 E
Somplago	64	46.21 N	13.04 E
Sompolno	30	52.24 N	18.31 E
Somport, Puerto de)(	34	42.48 N	0.31 W
Sompuis	50	48.41 N	4.23 E
Somuncurá, Meseta de ⋏[1]	254	41.30 S	67.15 W
Somvix	58	46.44 N	8.56 E
Šomyškol'	86	46.30 N	59.53 E
Son, Ned.	52	51.31 N	5.30 E
Son, Nor.	26	59.31 N	10.42 E
Son ≃	124	25.42 N	84.52 E
Soná	236	8.01 N	81.19 W
Sona-Bata	152	4.54 S	15.09 E
Sonādugi	126	22.47 N	90.40 E
Sonaguera	236	15.38 N	86.20 W
Sonahula	124	25.05 N	87.09 E
Sonāmarg	123	34.18 N	75.18 E
Sonāmukhi	126	23.18 N	87.25 E
Sonāpur	126	23.42 N	89.30 E
Sonar	164	2.33 S	133.00 E
Sonār ≃	124	24.24 N	79.56 E
Sonari	272c	18.52 N	72.59 E
Sonarpur	272b	22.26 N	88.25 E
Sonātikri	272b	22.57 N	88.20 E
Sonceboz	58	47.11 N	7.11 E
Sonchamp	261	48.35 N	1.53 E
Sŏnch'ŏn	98	39.48 N	124.55 E
Soncino	62	45.24 N	9.52 E
Sondags ≃, S. Afr.	158	28.43 S	30.16 E
Sondags ≃, S. Afr.	158	33.44 S	25.51 E
Sondalo	64	46.20 N	10.19 E
Sønderå ≃	41	54.53 N	8.59 E
Sønderborg	41	54.55 N	9.47 E
Sønderby	41	55.47 N	10.01 E
Sønder Felding	41	55.57 N	8.47 E
Sønderhav	41	54.51 N	9.30 E
Sønderjylland □[6]	41	55.10 N	9.15 E
Sønder Nærå	41	55.18 N	10.30 E
Sønder Omme	41	55.50 N	8.54 E
Sondershausen	54	51.22 N	10.52 E
Søndersø	41	55.29 N	10.16 E
Sondi	114	2.58 N	98.52 E
Søndre Strømfjord	176	66.59 N	50.40 W
Søndre Strømfjord c[2]	176	66.30 N	52.15 W
Sondrio	64	46.10 N	9.52 E
Sondrio □[4]	58	46.10 N	10.03 E
Sonduga	76	60.08 N	41.55 E
Sone ≃	126	21.34 N	86.54 E
Sonepur	120	20.50 N	83.55 E
Sonestown	210	41.21 N	76.33 W

Symbols in the index entries represent the broad ˈegories identified in the key at the right. Symbols superior numbers (⋏[1]) identify subcategories (see ˈete key on page *I · 1*).

e im Register stellen die rechts im ˈ erklärten Kategorien dar. Symbole mit ˈlten Ziffern (⋏[1]) bezeichnen Unterab- ˈer Kategorie (vgl. vollständiger Schlüssel 1).

Los símbolos incluídos en el texto del índice representan las grandes categorías identificadas con la clave a la derecha. Los símbolos con numeros en su parte superior (⋏[1]) identifican las subcategorías (véase la clave completa en la página *I · 1*).

Les symboles de l'index représentent les catégories indiquées dans la légende à droite. Les symboles suivis d'un indice (⋏[1]) représentent des sous-catégories (voir légende complète à la page *I · 1*).

Os símbolos incluídos no texto do índice representam as grandes categorias identificadas com a chave à direita. Os símbolos com números em sua parte superior (⋏[1]) identificam as subcategorias (veja-se a chave completa à página *I · 1*).

English	Deutsch	Español	Français	Português
∧ Mountain	Berg	Montaña	Montagne	Montanha
⋏ Mountains	Gebirge	Montañas	Montagnes	Montanhas
)(Pass	Paß	Paso	Col	Passo
V Valley, Canyon	Tal, Cañon	Valle, Cañón	Vallée, Canyon	Vale, Canhão
≍ Plain	Ebene	Llano	Plaine	Planície
› Cape	Kap	Cabo	Cap	Cabo
I Island	Insel	Isla	Île	Ilha
II Islands	Inseln	Islas	Îles	Ilhas
⊥ Other Topographic Features	Andere Topographische Objekte	Otros Elementos Topográficos	Autres données topographiques	Outros acidentes topográficos

ESPAÑOL

Nombre	Página	Lat.°′	Long.°′ W = Oeste
Song, Malay.	112	2.01 N	112.33 E
Song, Nig.	146	9.50 N	12.38 E
Song, Thai	110	18.28 N	100.11 E
Song ≃	100	27.02 N	118.18 E
Song'ao	100	29.36 N	121.41 E
Songbahutun	104	41.28 N	121.11 E
Song Bay Hap, Cua c	110	8.46 N	104.52 E
Songbu	100	31.05 N	114.48 E
Sŏngbyŏn-ni	98	38.03 N	125.18 E
Song Cau	110	13.27 N	109.13 E
Sŏng-ch'ŏn-gang ≃	98	39.48 N	127.35 E
Songcun	106	30.26 N	119.43 E
Songe	26	58.41 N	9.00 E
Songea	154	10.41 S	35.39 E
Songeons	50	49.33 N	1.52 E
Songgaizhen	107	29.03 N	105.54 E
Songgang	100	22.49 N	113.51 E
Songgato ≃	164	3.26 S	140.22 E
Songhe	100	31.10 N	113.20 E
Songhua ≃	89	47.44 N	132.32 E
Songhuahu ⊜[1]	89	43.20 N	127.07 E
Songhuajiang	89	44.46 N	125.54 E
Songhwa	98	38.21 N	125.08 E
Songino	88	48.54 N	95.54 E
Sŏngjang-ni	98	41.02 N	126.50 E
Songjiachang	107	28.47 N	104.55 E
Songjiang	106	31.01 N	121.14 E
Songjiangzhen	98	42.12 N	126.56 E
Songjiapu	107	29.38 N	104.44 E
Songjiaying	105	40.38 N	115.14 E
Sŏngjin → Kimch'aek	98	40.41 N	129.12 E
Songjŏng	98	35.10 N	126.46 E
Sŏngju	98	35.55 N	128.16 E
Songkan	102	28.27 N	106.50 E
Songkhla	110	7.12 N	100.36 E
Songkhram ≃	110	17.39 N	104.28 E
Songkou, Zhg.	100	25.48 N	118.36 E
Songkou, Zhg.	100	24.32 N	116.24 E
Songlinba	100	24.00 N	115.59 E
Songlindian	105	39.25 N	115.54 E
Songling	89	48.02 N	121.12 E
Song Ling ⩘	98	41.10 N	120.09 E
Songmen	100	28.19 N	121.34 E
Songming	102	25.24 N	102.59 E
Sŏngmo-do I	98	37.42 N	126.18 E
Sŏngnae-ri	98	39.28 N	126.59 E
Sŏngnam	98	37.26 N	127.08 E
Sŏng-ni	98	39.38 N	127.06 E
Songnim	98	38.44 N	125.38 E
Songo	152	7.22 S	14.51 E
Songololo	152	5.42 S	14.02 E
Songot ʌ	154	3.59 N	34.28 E
Songpan	102	32.40 N	103.24 E
Song Phi Nong	110	14.13 N	100.03 E
Sŏngsa-ri	271b	37.38 N	126.52 E
Songshancun	104	41.02 N	121.09 E
Songshu	98	39.50 N	122.06 E
Songshugou	105	41.02 N	117.49 E
Songtangmiao	106	31.08 N	119.16 E
Songtao	102	28.06 N	109.05 E
Songtun	98	39.54 N	123.56 E
Šonguj	24	68.47 N	33.00 E
Songu-ri	98	37.49 N	127.09 E
Songwe, Zaïre	154	3.24 S	26.16 E
Songwe, Zaïre	154	12.25 S	29.40 E
Songwe ≃	154	9.43 S	33.56 E
Songxi, Zhg.	100	27.33 N	118.46 E
Songxi, Zhg.	100	26.16 N	116.59 E
Songxia, Zhg.	100	25.44 N	119.36 E
Songxia, Zhg.	100	30.07 N	120.51 E
Songxian	102	34.10 N	112.05 E
Songyan	98	37.13 N	113.43 E
Songyin	106	30.54 N	121.13 E
Songyin ≃	100	28.18 N	119.44 E
Songzhangzi	98	41.13 N	119.08 E
Songzhuang	106	32.06 N	121.17 E
Son Ha	110	15.03 N	108.34 E
Soni, Ehi ʌ	146	20.49 N	17.23 E
Sonico	64	46.10 N	10.21 E
Sonid Youqi	102	42.44 N	112.40 E
Sonid Zuoqi	102	43.58 N	113.59 E
Sonīpat	124	28.59 N	77.01 E
Sonkach	124	22.59 N	76.21 E
Sonk'ol', ozero ⊜	85	41.50 N	75.08 E
Sonkovo	76	57.47 N	37.09 E
Son La	110	21.19 N	103.54 E
Sonmiāni	120	25.26 N	66.36 E
Sonmiāni Bay c	120	25.15 N	66.30 E
Sonnberg ʌ	264b	48.20 N	16.15 E
Sonneberg	54	50.22 N	11.10 E
Sonnefeld	56	50.13 N	11.08 E
Sonnen	60	48.41 N	13.43 E
Sonnenberg ʌ[2]	61	47.52 N	16.28 E
Sonnewalde	54	51.42 N	13.38 E
Sonning Common	42	51.31 N	0.59 W
Sonningdale	184	52.24 N	107.40 W
Sonnino	66	41.25 N	13.14 E
Sonntagberg	61	47.59 N	14.45 E
Sono	270	34.48 N	135.55 E
Sono, Rio do ≃, Bra.	250	8.58 S	48.11 W
Sono, Rio do ≃, Bra.	255	17.02 S	45.32 W
Sonobe	96	35.06 N	135.28 E
Sonogno	58	46.21 N	8.47 E
Sonoita Creek ≃	200	31.30 N	110.58 W
Sonoma	226	38.17 N	122.27 W
Sonoma □[6]	226	38.26 N	122.35 W
Sonoma Creek ≃	226	38.10 N	122.24 W
Sonoma Mountains ⩘	226	38.17 N	122.35 W
Sonoma Peak ʌ	204	40.52 N	117.36 W
Sonoma State Historical Park ♠	226	38.18 N	122.28 W
Sononder	158	29.43 S	21.51 E
Sonop	158	25.39 S	27.42 E
Sonora, Ca., U.S.	226	37.59 N	120.22 W
Sonora, Tx., U.S.	196	30.34 N	100.38 W
Sonora □[3]	232	29.20 N	110.40 W
Sonora ≃	232	28.48 N	111.33 W
Sonoran Desert ◆[2]	16	30.00 N	113.00 W
Sonora Pass)(	226	38.19 N	119.37 W
Sonostrov	24	66.09 N	34.10 E
Sonoyta	232	31.51 N	112.50 W
Sonoyta ≃	200	31.16 N	113.26 W
Sonpār Hills ⩘[2]	124	24.20 N	82.15 E
Sonqor	128	34.47 N	47.36 E
Sŏnsan	98	36.16 N	128.17 E
Sonsbeck	52	51.37 N	6.22 E
Sonseca	34	39.42 N	3.57 W
Sonskyn	158	30.47 S	26.28 E
Sonsón	246	5.42 N	75.18 W
Sonsonate	236	13.43 N	89.44 W
Sonsorol Islands II	108	5.20 N	132.13 E
Sonstorp	40	58.45 N	15.36 E
Sonstraal	158	27.07 S	22.28 E
Sontag	194	31.39 N	90.12 W
Son Tay	110	21.08 N	105.30 E
Sonthofen	58	47.31 N	10.17 E
Sontra	56	51.04 N	9.56 E
Sonwān	124	27.40 N	81.45 E
Sonyea	210	42.41 N	77.50 W
Soo → Sault Sainte Marie	190	46.29 N	84.20 W
Soochow → Suzhou	106	31.18 N	120.37 E
Sooke	224	48.23 N	123.43 W
Sooke ≃	224	48.23 N	123.42 W
Sooke Basin c	224	48.23 N	123.40 W
Sooke Lake ⊜	224	48.33 N	123.42 W
Sooner Lake ⊜[1]	196	36.26 N	97.02 W
Soonwald ⩘	56	49.55 N	7.40 E
Sooyaac	144	0.03 N	42.17 E
Sopa Sopa Head ›	164	1.58 S	146.35 E
Sopchoppy	192	30.03 N	84.29 W
Soperton	192	32.22 N	82.35 W
Sop Hao	110	20.33 N	104.27 E
Sophia	192	37.42 N	81.15 W
Sopki	76	57.06 N	30.55 E
Sopockin	76	53.50 N	23.39 E

FRANÇAIS

Nom	Page	Lat.°′	Long.°′ W = Ouest
Sopot	30	54.28 N	18.34 E
Sop Pong	110	22.04 N	102.03 E
Sop Prap	110	17.53 N	99.20 E
Soprabolzano	64	46.32 N	11.24 E
Sopron	30	47.41 N	16.36 E
Sopronhorpács	61	47.29 N	16.44 E
Sopronkövesd	61	47.33 N	16.45 E
Šoptykol'	86	51.16 N	75.45 E
Sopur	123	34.18 N	74.28 E
Sŏp'yŏng-ni	98	35.01 N	127.24 E
Soquel	226	36.59 N	121.57 W
Soquel Creek ≃	226	36.58 N	121.57 W
Sor, Ribeira de ≃	34	39.00 N	8.17 W
Sora	66	41.43 N	13.37 E
Sorada	122	19.45 N	84.26 E
Sorae-san ʌ	271b	37.27 N	126.47 E
Soraga	64	46.22 N	11.39 E
Soragna	64	44.56 N	10.07 E
Söråker	26	62.31 N	17.30 E
Sorano	66	42.41 N	11.43 E
Šorapani	84	42.05 N	43.05 E
Soras	248	14.07 S	73.37 W
Sorata	248	15.47 S	68.40 W
Soratte, Monte ʌ	66	42.15 N	12.30 E
Sorau → Żary	30	51.38 N	15.09 E
Soraya	248	14.10 S	73.19 W
Sorbas	34	37.07 N	2.07 W
Šorbas, gora ʌ	86	47.25 N	84.12 E
Sorbhog	120	26.30 N	90.52 E
Sorbie	44	54.48 N	4.26 W
Sorbo ≃	85	38.45 N	69.20 E
Sorbolo	64	44.51 N	10.28 E
Sorbonne ʋ[2]	261	48.51 N	2.21 E
Sorcier, Lac au ⊜	206	46.42 N	73.24 W
Sordevolo	62	45.34 N	7.59 E
Sore	32	44.20 N	0.35 W
Sorel	206	46.02 N	73.07 W
Sorell	166	42.47 S	147.33 E
Sorell, Cape ›	166	42.12 S	145.10 E
Sorel Point ›	43b	49.16 N	2.10 W
Sörenberg	58	46.50 N	8.03 E
Sorento	219	39.00 N	89.34 W
Soreq ≃	132	31.56 N	34.42 E
Soresina	64	45.17 N	9.51 E
Sörfjärden c	40	59.24 N	16.50 E
Sørfjorden c[2]	26	60.24 N	6.40 E
Sørfold	24	67.28 N	15.22 E
Sörforsa	26	61.40 N	17.00 E
Sorge ≃	41	54.21 N	9.25 E
Sorgono	71	40.01 N	9.06 E
Sorgues	62	44.00 N	4.52 E
Sorgun	130	39.49 N	35.11 E
Sori	62	44.22 N	9.06 E
Soria	34	41.46 N	2.28 W
Soria □[4]	34	41.35 N	2.35 W
Soriano	252	33.24 S	58.19 W
Soriano □[5]	258	33.45 S	57.45 W
Soriano Calabro	68	38.36 N	16.14 E
Soriano nel Cimino	66	42.25 N	12.14 E
Sorico	58	46.10 N	9.22 E
Sorido	164	1.09 S	136.03 E
Sori-do I	98	34.26 N	127.48 E
Sørli	26	64.15 N	13.45 E
Sormonne ≃	56	49.46 N	4.40 E
Sorn	46	55.30 N	4.18 W
Sorne ≃	58	47.22 N	7.22 E
Sorø, Dan.	41	55.26 N	11.34 E
Soro, India	120	21.17 N	86.40 E
Soro, Monte ʌ	70	37.56 N	14.42 E
Soroca	38	48.09 N	28.17 E
Sorocaba	255	23.29 S	47.27 W
Sorocabuçu ≃	256	23.38 S	47.13 W
Soročinka	80	47.30 N	51.44 E
Soročinsk	80	52.26 N	53.10 E
Soročkino	86	57.02 N	68.52 E
Soroco	240m	18.22 N	65.38 W
Sorok	88	52.20 N	100.12 E
Sorok ≃	61	47.07 N	16.50 E
Sorokino, Ross.	86	53.45 N	84.58 E
Sorokino, Ross.	86	54.13 N	91.31 E
Sorokoshychi	78	51.12 N	30.35 E
Soroksár ◆[8]	264c	47.24 N	19.07 E
Sorol I[1]	108	8.08 N	140.23 E
Soron	124	27.53 N	78.45 E
Sorong	164	0.53 S	131.15 E
Sororó ≃	250	5.24 S	49.07 W
Sorot' ≃	76	57.04 N	28.50 E
Soroti	154	1.43 N	33.37 E
Sorovskije	86	59.53 N	71.34 E
Sørøya I	24	70.36 N	22.46 E
Sorpestausee ⊜[1]	56	51.20 N	7.56 E
Sorraia ≃	34	38.56 N	8.53 W
Sorrento, Austl.	169	38.20 S	144.45 E
Sorrento, It.	68	40.37 N	14.22 E
Sorrento, Fl., U.S.	220	28.48 N	81.33 W
Sorrento, La., U.S.	194	30.11 N	90.51 W
Sorris Sorris	156	20.57 S	14.50 E
Sør Rondane Mountains ⩘	9	72.00 S	25.00 E
Sorsakoski	26	62.27 N	27.39 E
Sorsatunturi ʌ	24	67.24 N	29.38 E
Sorsele	24	65.30 N	17.30 E
Sorsk	86	54.01 N	90.12 E
Sorso	71	40.48 N	8.34 E
Sorsogon	116	12.58 N	124.00 E
Sorsogon □[4]	116	12.50 N	123.55 E
Sorsogon Bay c	116	12.55 N	123.55 E
Sörstafors	40	59.35 N	16.13 E
Šorsu	85	40.17 N	70.48 E
Sort	34	42.24 N	1.08 E
Šortandy	86	51.42 N	71.00 E
Sortat	46	58.33 N	3.13 W
Sortavala	24	61.42 N	30.41 E
Sortino	70	37.09 N	15.02 E
Sortland	24	68.40 N	15.20 E
Sør-Trøndelag □[6]	26	63.00 N	10.40 E
Sorunda	40	59.01 N	17.48 E
Sörup	41	54.43 N	9.40 E
Sõrve neem ›	76	57.54 N	22.03 E
Sörvik	40	60.11 N	15.09 E
Sorviži	80	57.52 N	48.32 E
Sosa, Dtsch.	54	50.30 N	12.39 E
Sosa, Taehan	271b	37.29 N	126.47 E
Šoša ≃	82	56.31 N	36.05 E
Sŏsan	98	36.47 N	126.26 E
Sösdala	41	56.02 N	13.40 E
Sos del Rey Católico	34	42.30 N	1.13 W
Sosedka	80	53.15 N	42.40 E
Sosedno	76	58.14 N	28.42 E
Sosenka ≃, Ross.	265b	55.35 N	37.23 E
Sosenka ≃, Ross.	265b	55.47 N	37.42 E
Sosenki	82	55.34 N	37.26 E
Sösetalsperre ◆[6]	52	51.44 N	10.20 E
Soshigaya ◆[8]	268	35.39 N	139.36 E
Sösjöfjällen ⩘	26	63.53 N	13.15 E
Šoška	24	62.42 N	50.40 E
Soskovo	76	52.45 N	35.23 E
Sosna ≃	76	52.42 N	38.55 E
Sosneado, Cerro ʌ	252	34.45 S	69.59 W
Sosnicy	76	57.38 N	30.25 E
Sosnogorsk	24	63.37 N	53.51 E
Sosnovaja Maza	80	52.30 N	47.53 E
Sosnovaja Pol'ana ◆[8]	265a	59.50 N	30.09 E
Sosnove	78	50.49 N	27.00 E
Sosnovec	24	64.26 N	34.27 E
Sosnovica	76	60.21 N	40.50 E
Sosnovka, Kaz.	86	51.26 N	79.28 E
Sosnovka, Kyrg.	85	42.40 N	73.55 E
Sosnovka, Ross.	24	66.30 N	40.32 E
Sosnovka, Ross.	80	56.13 N	47.13 E
Sosnovka, Ross.	80	57.48 N	51.43 E
Sosnovka, Ross.	80	56.17 N	51.17 E
Sosnovka, Ross.	80	53.14 N	41.22 E
Sosnovka, Ross.	80	57.16 N	53.31 E
Sosnovka, Ross.	80	54.06 N	46.38 E
Sosnovka, Ross.	80	52.26 N	43.29 E
Sosnovka, Ross.	82	54.31 N	38.08 E
Sosnovka, Ross.	82	54.54 N	38.41 E

PORTUGUÊS

Nome	Página	Lat.°′	Long.°′ W = Oeste
Sosnovka, Ross.	86	59.10 N	81.18 E
Sosnovka, Ross.	88	54.09 N	109.35 E
Sosnovo, Ross.	76	60.33 N	30.15 E
Sosnovo, Ross.	80	56.42 N	54.35 E
Sosnovoborsk	80	53.18 N	46.16 E
Sosnovo-Oz'orskoje	88	52.31 N	111.30 E
Sosnovskij	86	54.36 N	73.10 E
Sosnovskoje	80	55.48 N	43.10 E
Sosnovyj Bor, Bela.	76	52.32 N	29.36 E
Sosnovyj Bor, Ross.	76	59.55 N	29.07 E
Sosnovyj Bor, Ross.	86	57.07 N	55.03 E
Sosnovyj Solonec	80	53.17 N	49.33 E
Sosnowiec	30	50.18 N	19.08 E
Sosnytsya	78	51.32 N	32.28 E
Soso	194	31.45 N	89.16 W
Sosok	112	0.17 N	110.14 E
Sospel	62	43.53 N	7.27 E
Sospirolo	64	46.09 N	12.04 E
Sossusvlei ⊜	156	24.40 S	15.23 E
Šoštanj	36	46.23 N	15.03 E
Sŏsura	98	42.16 N	130.37 E
Sos'va, Ross.	72	63.40 N	62.06 E
Sos'va, Ross.	86	59.10 N	61.50 E
Sos'va ≃	86	59.32 N	62.20 E
Sosyka ≃	78	46.35 N	39.05 E
Sot' ≃	80	58.00 N	40.39 E
Sota ≃	150	11.52 N	3.24 E
Sotik	154	0.41 S	35.21 E
Sotkamo	26	64.08 N	28.25 E
Sotnicyno	80	54.17 N	41.49 E
Soto de Aldovea	266a	40.26 N	3.27 W
Soto de Pajares	266a	40.17 N	3.32 W
Soto la Marina	234	23.46 N	98.13 W
Soto La Marina ≃	234	23.45 N	97.45 W
Soto la Marina, Barra I	232	24.10 N	97.43 W
Sotomayor	248	19.18 S	65.03 W
Sotonera, Embalse de ⊜[1]	34	42.05 N	0.48 W
Sotouboua	150	8.34 N	0.59 E
Sotta	71	41.32 N	9.12 E
Sottens	58	46.39 N	6.44 E
Sottern ⊜	40	59.02 N	15.29 E
Sotteville	50	49.25 N	1.06 E
Sottile, Punta ›	70a	35.30 N	12.38 E
Sotto il Monte	62	45.43 N	9.30 E
Sottomarina	64	45.13 N	12.17 E
Sottrum	52	53.06 N	9.14 E
Sottunga I	26	60.08 N	20.40 E
Souain-Perthes-lès-Hurlus	56	49.11 N	4.32 E
Souanké	152	2.05 N	14.03 E
Soubakaniédougou	150	10.28 N	5.01 W
Soubré	150	5.47 N	6.36 W
Soudan	166	20.05 S	137.00 E
Soudan → Sudan □[1]	140	15.00 N	30.00 E
Soude ≃	50	48.52 N	4.10 E
Soudersburg	208	40.01 N	76.09 W
Souderton	208	40.18 N	75.19 W
Souesmes	50	47.27 N	2.10 E
Soufflay	152	2.01 N	14.54 E
Soufflenheim	56	48.50 N	7.58 E
Soufflot, Lac ⊜	190	47.24 N	78.31 W
Soufliön	38	41.12 N	26.18 E
Soufrière	241f	13.52 N	61.04 W
Soufrière ʌ, Guad.	241o	16.03 N	61.40 W
Soufrière ʌ, St. Vin.	241h	13.20 N	61.11 W
Soufrière Bay c, Dom.	240d	15.14 N	61.22 W
Soufrière Bay c, St. Luc.	241f	13.51 N	61.04 W
Sougahatchee Creek ≃	194	32.38 N	85.50 W
Sougne-Remouchamps	56	50.29 N	5.40 E
Souguer	148	35.12 N	1.30 E
Souhegan ≃	188	42.51 N	71.29 W
Souillac	32	44.54 N	1.29 E
Souilly	56	49.01 N	5.17 E
Souk-el-Arba-des-Beni-Hassan	34	35.16 N	5.20 W
Souk-Khemis-du-Sahel	34	35.17 N	6.05 W
Souk Larbat Gharb	148	34.43 N	6.01 W
Sŏul (Seoul), Taehan	98	37.33 N	126.58 E
Sŏul (Seoul), Taehan	271b	37.33 N	126.58 E
Sŏul □[4]	98	37.34 N	127.00 E
Soulac-sur-Mer	32	45.31 N	1.07 W
Soulaines-Dhuys	58	48.22 N	4.44 E
Soulanges □[6]	206	45.20 N	74.15 W
Soulanges, Canal de ≅	275a	45.20 N	73.58 W
Soulougou	150	13.01 N	0.23 E
Soulsbyville	226	37.59 N	120.16 W
Soultzeren	58	48.04 N	7.06 E
Soultz-Haut-Rhin	58	47.53 N	7.14 E
Soultzmatt	58	47.58 N	7.14 E
Soultz-sous-Forêts	56	48.56 N	7.53 E
Soummam, Oued ≃	34	36.45 N	5.04 E
Sound Beach	210	40.57 N	72.58 W
Sounding Creek ≃	184	52.06 N	110.28 W
Sounding Lake ⊜	184	52.08 N	110.29 W
Sound View Park ♠	276	40.49 N	73.52 W
Soúnion, Ákra ›	38	37.39 N	24.02 E
Soup Harbour c	212	43.51 N	77.11 W
Souppes-sur-Loing	50	48.11 N	2.44 E
Souq Ahras	148	36.23 N	8.00 E
Sources, Mont aux ʌ	158	28.46 S	28.52 E
Soure, Bra.	250	0.44 S	48.31 W
Soure, Port.	34	40.03 N	8.38 W
Sour el Ghozlane	148	36.10 N	3.45 E
Souris, Mb., Can.	184	49.38 N	100.15 W
Souris, P.E., Can.	186	46.21 N	62.15 W
Souris ≃	198	49.39 N	99.34 W
Sourlake	194	30.09 N	94.25 W
Sourland Mountain ʌ[2]	208	40.29 N	74.43 W
Sourou ≃	150	12.45 N	3.25 W
Souroukaha	150	8.13 N	5.08 W
Souš	54	50.32 N	13.34 E
Sous, Oued V	148	30.27 N	9.31 W
Sousa	250	6.45 S	38.14 W
Sousânia	255	16.11 S	49.05 W
Sousas	256	22.52 S	46.59 W
Sousel	34	38.57 N	7.40 W
Sous-le-Vent, Îles → Leeward Islands II	238	17.00 N	63.00 W
Sousse	148	35.49 N	10.38 E
Sousse □[8]	148	35.40 N	10.30 E
Sout ≃, S. Afr.	158	31.35 S	18.24 E
Sout ≃, S. Afr.	158	33.03 S	23.28 E
Sout ≃, S. Afr.	158	28.56 S	20.40 E
South ≃, Ia., U.S.	190	41.29 N	93.20 W
South ≃, Ma., U.S.	283	42.10 N	70.43 W
South ≃, Mo., U.S.	219	39.52 N	91.26 W
South ≃, N.J., U.S.	208	40.29 N	74.23 W
South ≃, N.C., U.S.	192	34.20 N	78.03 W
South ≃, Va., U.S.	192	37.46 N	79.23 W
South ≃, Va., U.S.	208	38.02 N	77.23 W
South Acton	207	42.27 N	71.27 W
South Africa (Suid-Afrika) □[1], Afr.	138	30.00 S	26.00 E
South Africa (Suid-Afrika) □[1], Afr.	156	30.00 S	26.00 E
Southall ◆[8]	260	51.31 N	0.23 W
South Alligator ≃	164	12.15 S	132.24 E
Southam	42	52.15 N	1.23 W
South Amboy	208	40.28 N	74.17 W
South America ≛[1]	4	15.00 S	60.00 W
South America ≛[1]	18	15.00 S	60.00 W
South Amherst, Ma., U.S.	207	42.20 N	72.30 W
South Amherst, Oh., U.S.	214	41.22 N	82.14 W
Southampton, N.S., Can.	186	45.35 N	64.15 W
Southampton, On., Can.	212	44.29 N	81.23 W

Nome	Página	Lat.°′	Long.°′ W = Oeste
Southampton, Eng., U.K.	42	50.55 N	1.25 W
Southampton, Ma., U.S.	207	42.13 N	72.43 W
Southampton, N.Y., U.S.	207	40.53 N	72.23 W
Southampton, Pa., U.S.	285	40.10 N	75.02 W
Southampton □[6]	208	36.42 N	77.05 W
Southampton (Eastleigh) Airport ⊠	42	50.57 N	1.21 W
Southampton, Cape ›	176	62.09 N	83.40 W
Southampton Island I	176	64.20 N	84.40 W
South Andaman I	110	11.45 N	92.45 E
South Anna ≃	192	37.48 N	77.25 W
South Apopka	220	28.39 N	81.31 W
Southard	208	40.08 N	74.14 W
Southards Pond ⊜	276	40.43 N	73.20 W
South Ashburnham	207	42.36 N	71.56 W
South Aulatsivik Island I	176	56.45 N	61.30 W
South Australia □[3]	162	30.00 S	135.00 E
South Australian Basin ✦[1]	14	38.00 S	126.00 E
Southaven	194	34.59 N	90.02 W
South Bald Mountain ʌ	200	40.45 N	105.41 W
South Baldy ʌ	200	33.59 N	107.11 W
South Banda Basin ✦[1]	14	6.30 S	127.30 E
Southbank	182	54.02 N	125.46 W
South Barre	207	42.23 N	72.05 W
South Barrington	278	42.06 N	88.07 W
South Barrule ʌ[2]	44	54.12 N	4.40 W
South Bass Island I	214	41.39 N	82.49 W
South Bay	220	26.39 N	80.42 W
South Bay c, Mb., Can.	184	56.43 N	99.00 W
South Bay c, N.T., Can.	176	63.58 N	83.30 W
South Bay c, On., Can.	190	45.38 N	81.50 W
South Bay c, On., Can.	212	43.55 N	77.03 W
South Bay c, On., Can.	212	44.52 N	79.47 W
South Bay c, Fl., U.S.	220	26.42 N	80.45 W
South Bay c, Va., U.S.	208	37.14 N	75.52 W
South Bay c, Wa., U.S.	224	46.53 N	124.04 W
South Baymouth	190	45.33 N	82.01 W
South Beach ♠	276	40.35 N	74.05 W
South Beacon Mountain ʌ	210	41.29 N	73.57 W
South Bedias Creek ≃	222	30.54 N	95.42 W
South Bellingham	207	42.03 N	71.28 W
South Belmar	208	40.10 N	74.02 W
South Beloit	216	42.29 N	89.02 W
South Bend, In., U.S.	216	41.41 N	86.15 W
South Bend, Wa., U.S.	224	46.40 N	123.48 W
South Benfleet	42	51.33 N	0.34 E
South Bentinck Arm c	182	52.15 N	126.50 W
South Bethlehem	214	41.00 N	79.20 W
South Bihar Plains ☷	124	25.15 N	84.30 E
South Bloomfield	218	39.43 N	82.59 W
Southborough, Eng., U.K.	42	51.10 N	0.15 E
Southborough, Ma., U.S.	207	42.18 N	71.31 W
South Bosque ≃	222	31.29 N	97.16 W
South Boston	192	36.41 N	78.54 W
South Boston ◆[8]	283	42.20 N	71.03 W
South Bound Brook	276	40.33 N	74.32 W
South Bradenton	220	27.27 N	82.35 W
South Branch, Nf., Can.	186	47.55 N	59.02 W
South Branch, N.J., U.S.	276	40.33 N	74.42 W
South Brent	42	50.25 N	3.50 W
Southbridge, N.Z.	172	43.49 S	172.15 E
Southbridge, Ma., U.S.	207	42.04 N	72.02 W
South Britain	207	41.28 N	73.15 W
Southbrook, Austl.	171a	27.41 S	151.43 E
Southbrook, N.Z.	172	43.20 S	172.36 E
South Brook ≃	285	39.52 N	75.44 W
South Brookfield	186	44.23 N	64.58 W
South Brooklyn ◆[8]	276	40.41 N	73.59 W
South Bruny Island I	166	43.23 S	147.17 E
South Buganda □[5]	154	0.30 S	31.35 E
South Burlington	188	44.28 N	73.10 W
Southbury	207	41.28 N	73.12 W
South Butler	210	43.08 N	76.46 W
South Byfield	283	42.44 N	70.54 W
South Byron	210	43.03 N	78.04 W
South Cairo	210	42.17 N	73.57 W
South Canaan	210	41.30 N	75.25 W
South Cape ›	175g	17.01 S	179.55 E
South Carolina □[3], U.S.	178	34.00 N	81.00 W
South Carolina □[3], U.S.	192	34.00 N	81.00 W
South Carver	207	41.50 N	70.44 W
South Castor ≃	212	45.15 N	75.23 W
South Cave	44	53.46 N	0.35 W
South Cerney	42	51.40 N	1.56 W
South Chagrin Reservation ♠	279a	41.25 N	81.25 W
South Channel ʊ, Pil.	116	14.20 N	120.37 E
South Channel ʊ, Mi., U.S.	190	45.38 N	84.32 W
South Channel ≃[1]	281	42.32 N	82.40 W
South Chaplin	207	41.46 N	72.07 W
South Charleston, Oh., U.S.	218	39.49 N	83.38 W
South Charleston, W.V., U.S.	188	38.22 N	81.41 W
South Chatham	207	41.40 N	70.01 W
South Chelmsford	283	42.34 N	71.23 W
South Chicago ◆[8]	278	41.44 N	87.33 W
South China Basin ✦[1]	12	15.00 N	115.00 E
South China Sea ⊤[2]	108	10.00 N	113.00 E
South Cle Elum	224	47.11 N	120.56 W
South Coast Botanic Garden ♠	280	33.47 N	118.21 W
South Coatesville	208	39.58 N	75.49 W
South Coffeyville	196	36.59 N	95.37 W
South Concho ≃	196	31.21 N	100.28 W
South Corinth	210	43.12 N	73.51 W
South Corning	210	42.07 N	77.02 W
South Cotabato □[4]	116	6.15 N	125.00 E
South Creek ≃	170	33.36 S	150.50 E
South Crest	273d	26.15 S	28.07 E
South Dakota □[3], U.S.	178	44.15 N	100.00 W
South Dakota □[3], U.S.	198	44.15 N	100.00 W
South Dandalup ≃	168a	32.35 S	115.53 E
South Dandalup Dam ◆[6]	168a	32.38 S	116.04 E
South Darenth	260	51.24 N	0.15 E
South Dartmouth	207	41.35 N	70.56 W
South Dayton	210	42.21 N	79.03 W
South Deerfield	207	42.28 N	72.36 W
South Dennis, Ma., U.S.	207	41.41 N	70.09 W
South Dennis, N.J., U.S.	208	39.10 N	74.49 W
South Dorset	210	43.13 N	73.04 W
South Dorset Downs ⩘[1]	42	50.40 N	2.25 W
South Dos Palos	226	36.57 N	120.39 W
South Downs ⩘[1]	42	50.55 N	0.25 W
South Dum Dum	126	22.37 N	88.25 E

Nome	Página	Lat.°′	Long.°′ W = Oeste
South Duxbury	207	42.01 N	70.41 W
South East □[5]	156	25.00 S	25.45 E
Southeast Asia Treaty Organization Headquarters ʋ	269a	13.45 N	100.31 E
South East Cape ›, Austl.	166	43.39 S	146.50 E
Southeast Cape ›, Ak., U.S.	180	62.55 N	169.42 W
Southeast Indian Ridge ✦[3]	6	50.00 S	110.00 E
South Easton	207	42.02 N	71.04 W
Southeast Pacific Basin ✦[1]	6	60.00 S	115.00 W
South East Point ›, Austl.	166	39.00 S	146.20 E
South East Point ›, Kiribati	174o	1.40 N	157.10 W
South Egg Harbor	208	39.31 N	74.39 W
South Egremont	207	42.09 N	73.25 W
South Elgin	216	41.59 N	88.17 W
South Elkhorn Creek ≃	218	38.13 N	84.48 W
South El Monte	280	34.03 N	118.02 W
Southend	46	55.20 N	5.38 W
Southend Municipal Airport ⊠	42	51.34 N	0.41 E
Southend-on-Sea	42	51.33 N	0.43 E
Southend-on-Sea □[8]	260	51.33 N	0.41 E
Southend Pier ◆[5]	260	51.31 N	0.44 E
South English ≃	190	41.30 N	91.56 W
Southern □[4], Malaŵi	154	15.30 S	35.00 E
Southern □[4], S.L.	150	8.00 N	12.15 W
Southern □[4], Zam.	154	16.30 S	27.00 E
Southern □[5], Bots.	156	24.45 S	24.00 E
Southern □[5], Ug.	154	0.30 S	30.30 E
Southern Alps ⩘	172	43.30 S	170.30 E
Southern California, University of ʋ[2]	280	34.02 N	118.17 W
Southern Cook Islands II	14	20.00 S	159.00 W
Southern Cross	162	31.13 S	119.19 E
Southern Ghāts ⩘	122	9.30 N	77.00 E
Southern Highlands □[5]	164	6.00 S	143.30 E
Southern Indian Lake ⊜	176	57.10 N	98.40 W
Southern Leyte □[4]	116	10.50 N	124.55 E
Southern Lueti ≃	152	16.14 S	23.13 E
Southern Pines	192	35.10 N	79.23 W
Southern Ute Indian Reservation ◆[4]	200	37.05 N	107.45 W
Southern View	219	39.46 N	89.39 W
Southern Yemen → Yemen □[1]	144	15.00 N	47.00 E
Southery	42	52.32 N	0.23 E
South Esk ≃, Austl.	166	41.25 S	147.08 E
South Esk ≃, Scot., U.K.	46	56.42 N	2.32 W
South Esk ≃, Scot., U.K.	46	55.53 N	3.04 W
Southesk Tablelands ⩘[1]	162	20.50 S	126.40 E
South Essex	207	42.38 N	70.46 W
South Euclid	214	41.31 N	81.31 W
Southey	184	50.56 N	104.30 W
South Fabius ≃	219	39.54 N	91.30 W
South Fallsburg	210	41.42 N	74.37 W
South Farmbridge	260	51.38 N	0.41 E
South Farmingdale	276	40.43 N	73.26 W
Southfield, Ma., U.S.	207	42.06 N	73.14 W
Southfield, Mi., U.S.	216	42.28 N	83.13 W
Southfields	210	41.15 N	74.11 W
South Fiji Basin ✦[1]	14	26.00 S	175.00 E
Southfleet	260	51.25 N	0.19 E
South Floral Park	276	40.43 N	73.42 W
South Foreland ›	42	51.09 N	1.23 E
South Fork, Co., U.S.	200	37.40 N	106.38 W
South Fork, Pa., U.S.	214	40.22 N	78.47 W
South Fort George	182	53.54 N	122.45 W
South Forty Foot Drain ≅	42	52.56 N	0.15 W
South Fox Island I	190	45.25 N	85.50 W
South Fulton	194	36.30 N	88.52 W
South Gate, Ca., U.S.	228	33.57 N	118.12 W
Southgate, Fl., U.S.	220	27.18 N	82.32 W
Southgate, Mi., U.S.	216	42.12 N	83.11 W
Southgate, Wa., U.S.	224	47.10 N	122.30 W
Southgate ◆[8]	260	51.38 N	0.08 W
Southgate U.S.A. ◆[9]	279a	41.25 N	81.32 W
South Georgia I	244	54.15 S	36.45 W
South Georgia and the South Sandwich Islands □[2]	244	54.00 S	38.00 W
South Gibson	210	41.44 N	75.38 W
South Glamorgan □[6]	42	51.30 N	3.25 W
South Glastonbury	207	41.40 N	72.35 W
South Glens Falls	210	43.17 N	73.38 W
South Grafton	207	42.11 N	71.42 W
South Grand ≃	194	38.18 N	93.28 W
South Grand Island Bridge ◆[5]	284a	43.00 N	78.56 W
South Green	260	51.37 N	0.26 E
South Greensburg	214	40.17 N	79.33 W
South Hackensack	276	40.51 N	74.02 W
South Hadley, Ma., U.S.	188	42.15 N	72.34 W
South Hadley, Ma., U.S.	207	42.15 N	72.34 W
South Hadley Falls	207	42.13 N	72.36 W
South Hamilton	207	42.36 N	70.52 W
South Hams ☷	42	50.22 N	3.50 W
South Hanningfield	260	51.39 N	0.31 E
South Hanover	283	42.05 N	70.51 W
South Harbor c	269f	14.33 N	120.58 E
South Hartford	210	43.21 N	73.25 W
South Harwich	207	41.40 N	70.02 W
South Hātia Island I	124	22.19 N	91.07 E
South Haven, In., U.S.	216	41.32 N	87.08 W
South Haven, Ks., U.S.	198	37.03 N	97.24 W
South Haven, Mi., U.S.	216	42.24 N	86.16 W
South Hayling	42	50.47 N	0.59 W
South Head ›, Austl.	274a	33.50 S	151.17 E
South Head ›, N.Z.	172	36.26 S	174.14 E
South Heart ≃	182	55.34 N	116.11 W
South Heights	279b	40.35 N	80.14 W
South Hempstead	276	40.41 N	73.37 W
South Henderson	192	36.17 N	78.25 W
South Henik Lake ⊜	176	61.30 N	97.30 W
South Hero	188	44.38 N	73.18 W
South Hetton	44	54.48 N	1.24 W
South Hill, N.Y., U.S.	210	42.25 N	76.33 W
South Hill, Va., U.S.	192	36.43 N	78.07 W
South Hills ◆[8]	273d	26.15 S	28.05 E
South Hills Village ◆[9]	279b	40.21 N	80.03 W
South Hingham	207	42.11 N	70.52 W
South Hogan Creek ≃	218	39.03 N	84.54 W
South Holland	216	41.36 N	87.36 W
South Holston Lake ⊜[1]	192	36.35 N	82.00 W
South Honcut Creek ≃	226	39.19 N	121.35 W
South Honshu Ridge ✦[3]	14	24.00 N	142.00 E
South Hopkinton	207	41.24 N	71.45 W
South Horr	154	2.06 N	36.55 E
South Houston	222	29.39 N	95.14 W
South Huntington	276	40.49 N	73.23 W
South Indian Basin ✦[1]	6	60.00 S	120.00 E
South Indian Lake	184	56.46 N	98.57 W

Nome	Página	Lat.°′	Long.°′ W = Oeste
Southington, Ct., U.S.	207	41.35 N	72.52 W
Southington, Oh., U.S.	214	41.19 N	80.57 W
South International Falls	190	48.35 N	93.23 W
South Ionia	216	42.57 N	85.04 W
South Island I, India	122	10.03 N	72.17 E
South Island I, Kenya	154	2.38 N	36.36 E
South Island I, Micron.	175c	6.59 N	151.59 E
South Island I, N.Z.	172	43.00 S	171.00 E
South Islet I	116	8.44 N	119.49 E
South Jacksonville	219	39.42 N	90.13 W
South Kemptville Creek ≃	212	44.54 N	75.41 W
South Kenosha	216	42.32 N	87.50 W
South Kent	207	41.40 N	73.28 W
South Kirkby	44	53.34 N	1.20 W
South Konkan Hills ⩘[2]	122	17.00 N	73.30 E
South Korea → Korea, South □[1]	98	36.30 N	128.00 E
South Ladder Creek ≃	198	38.41 N	101.34 W
South Laguna	228	33.30 N	117.45 W
Southlake	222	32.57 N	97.09 W
South Lake ⊜, On., Can.	212	44.26 N	76.13 W
South Lake ⊜, Fl., U.S.	220	28.37 N	80.52 W
South Lake Tahoe	226	38.56 N	119.58 W
South Lancaster	207	42.26 N	71.41 W
Southland, Ky., U.S.	218	38.01 N	84.31 W
Southland, Mi., U.S.	216	42.13 N	84.24 W
Southland, Tx., U.S.	196	33.22 N	101.33 W
Southland ◆[9]	282	37.39 N	122.06 W
South Laurel	284c	39.05 N	76.52 W
Southlawn, Il., U.S.	219	39.45 N	89.37 W
Southlawn, Md., U.S.	284c	38.48 N	76.59 W
South Layhill	284c	39.04 N	77.03 W
South Lebanon	218	39.22 N	84.12 W
South Lee	207	42.16 N	73.16 W
South Lima	210	42.51 N	77.41 W
South Line Island I	276	40.37 N	73.30 W
South Llano ≃	196	30.30 N	99.46 W
South Lockport	284a	43.09 N	78.42 W
South Lorain	279a	41.27 N	82.08 W
South Loup ≃	198	41.04 N	98.40 W
South Luangwa National Park ♠	154	12.50 S	31.45 E
South Luconia Shoals ✦[2]	112	5.00 N	112.42 E
South Lynnfield	283	42.31 N	71.00 W
South Lyon	216	42.27 N	83.39 W
South Macmillan ≃	180	63.03 N	133.18 W
South Magnetic Pole ◆	9	65.18 S	139.30 E
South Malosmadulu Atoll I[1]	122	5.10 N	72.58 E
South Manitou Island I	190	45.01 N	86.07 W
South Marsh Island I	208	38.06 N	76.02 W
South Medford	202	42.18 N	122.50 W
South Media	285	39.54 N	75.23 W
South Melbourne	274b	37.50 S	144.57 E
South Merrimack	207	42.48 N	71.33 W
South Miami	220	25.42 N	80.17 W
South Miami Heights	220	25.35 N	80.22 W
South Middleboro	207	41.49 N	70.49 W
South Milford	216	41.31 N	85.16 W
South Mills	192	36.26 N	76.19 W
South Milwaukee	216	42.54 N	87.51 W
South Mimms	260	51.42 N	0.14 W
Southminster	42	51.40 N	0.50 E
South Modesto	226	37.38 N	120.58 W
South Mokelumne ≃	226	38.08 N	121.35 W
South Molton	42	51.01 N	3.50 W
South Monroe	216	41.54 N	83.25 W
Southmont	214	40.18 N	78.56 W
South Montrose	210	41.48 N	75.53 W
South Moose Lake ⊜	184	53.46 N	100.08 W
South Mountain	208	39.51 N	77.29 W
South Mountain ʌ, U.S.	208	39.40 N	77.30 W
South Mountain ʌ, Id., U.S.	202	42.44 N	116.54 W
South Mountain Reservation ♠	276	40.45 N	74.18 W
South Mount Vernon	214	40.23 N	82.23 W
South Nahanni ≃	176	61.03 N	123.20 W
South Naknek	180	58.43 N	157.00 W
South Nation ≃	188	45.34 N	75.06 W
South Negril Point ›	241q	18.15 N	78.22 W
South New Berlin	210	42.31 N	75.23 W
South New Castle	214	40.58 N	80.21 W
South New River Canal ≅	220	26.04 N	80.12 W
South Norfolk → Chesapeake	208	36.43 N	76.15 W
South Normanton	44	53.06 N	1.20 W
South Norwalk Reservoir ⊜[1]	276	41.11 N	73.27 W
South Norwood ◆[8]	260	51.24 N	0.04 W
South Nutfield	260	51.14 N	0.08 W
South Nyack	276	41.04 N	73.55 W
South Ockendon	42	51.32 N	0.18 E
South Ogden	200	41.11 N	111.58 W
Southold	207	41.03 N	72.25 W
South Onondaga	210	42.56 N	76.13 W
South Orange	276	40.47 N	74.15 W
South Orkney Islands II	9	60.35 S	45.30 W
South Oroville	226	39.30 N	121.33 W
South Ossetia → Jugo Osetija □[9]	84	42.20 N	44.00 E
South Otselic	210	42.38 N	75.46 W
Southowram	262	53.43 N	1.50 W
South Oxhey	260	51.38 N	0.23 W
South Oyster Bay c	276	40.38 N	73.28 W
South Palo Duro Creek ≃	196	36.06 N	101.29 W
South Para ≃	168b	34.36 S	138.45 E
South Para Reservoir ⊜[1]	168b	34.42 S	138.52 E
South Paris	188	44.13 N	70.30 W
South Park	216	41.44 N	88.18 W
South Park ♠, N.Y., U.S.	284a	42.50 N	78.50 W
South Park ♠, Pa., U.S.	279b	40.19 N	80.01 W
South Pasadena, Ca., U.S.	280	34.06 N	118.08 W
South Pasadena, Fl., U.S.	220	27.46 N	82.43 W
South Pass)(	200	42.22 N	108.55 W
South Pass ʊ	175c	7.14 N	151.48 E
South Passage ʊ, Austl.	171a	27.22 S	153.26 E
South Passage ʊ, Oh., U.S.	214	41.35 N	82.45 W
South Patrick Shores	220	28.12 N	80.35 W
South Pekin	190	40.29 N	89.39 W
South Pender	224	48.45 N	123.14 W
South Pender Island I	224	48.45 N	123.10 W
South Perth	168a	31.59 S	115.52 E
South Petherton	42	50.58 N	2.49 W
South Philadelphia ◆[8]	285	39.56 N	75.10 W
South Philipsburg	214	40.53 N	78.13 W
South Pittsburg	194	35.00 N	85.42 W
South Plainfield	210	40.34 N	74.24 W
South Platte ≃	178	41.07 N	100.42 W
South Platte, North Fork ≃	200	39.25 N	105.10 W
South Point ›, Barb.	241g	13.02 N	59.31 W
South Point ›, Pil.	116	10.24 N	122.30 E
South Pole ◆	9	90.00 S	0.00
South Porcupine	190	48.28 N	81.13 W
Southport, Austl.	166	43.25 S	146.59 E

≃ River	Fluß	Río	Rivière	Rio		
≅ Canal	Kanal	Canal	Canal	Canal		
ʟ Waterfall, Rapids	Wasserfall, Stromschnellen	Cascada, Rápidos	Chute d'eau, Rapides	Cascata, Rápidos		
ʊ Strait	Meeresstraße	Estrecho	Détroit	Estreito		
c Bay, Gulf	Bucht, Golf	Bahía, Golfo	Baie, Golfe	Baía, Golfo		
⊜ Lake, Lakes	See, Seen	Lago, Lagos	Lac, Lacs	Lago, Lagos		
☷ Swamp	Sumpf	Pantano	Marais	Pântano		
⍓ Ice Features, Glacier	Eis- und Gletscherformen	Accidentes Glaciales	Formes glaciaires	Acidentes glaciares		
⊤ Other Hydrographic Features	Andere Hydrographische Objekte	Otros Elementos Hidrográficos	Autres données hydrographiques	Outros acidentes hidrográficos		

✦ Submarine Features	Untermeerische Objekte	Accidentes Submarinos	Formes de relief sous-marin	Acidentes submarinos
□ Political Unit	Politische Einheit	Unidad Politica	Entité politique	Unidade política
ʋ Cultural Institution	Kulturelle Institution	Institución Cultural	Institution culturelle	Instituição cultural
ɪ Historical Site	Historische Stätte	Sitio Histórico	Site historique	Sitio histórico
♠ Recreational Site	Erholungs- und Ferienort	Sitio de Recreo	Centre de loisirs	Area de Lazer
⊠ Airport	Flughafen	Aeropuerto	Aéroport	Aeroporto
■ Military Installation	Militäranlage	Instalación Militar	Installation militaire	Instalação militar
◆ Miscellaneous	Verschiedenes	Misceláneo	Divers	Diversos

Name	Page	Lat.°′	Long.°′
Southport, Austl.	171a	27.58 S	153.25 E
Southport, Eng., U.K.	44	53.39 N	3.01 W
Southport, Ct., U.S.	207	41.08 N	73.17 W
Southport, Fl., U.S.	194	30.17 N	85.38 W
Southport, In., U.S.	218	39.39 N	86.07 W
Southport, N.Y., U.S.	210	42.03 N	76.49 W
Southport, N.C., U.S.	192	33.55 N	78.01 W
South Portland	188	43.38 N	70.14 W
South Portsmouth	218	38.43 N	83.00 W
South Pottstown	208	40.14 N	75.39 W
South Prairie Creek ≃	224	47.08 N	122.10 W
South Raisin ≃	206	45.08 N	74.35 W
South Range	190	47.04 N	88.38 W
South Renovo	214	41.19 N	77.44 W
South Reservoir ⊜[1]	283	42.27 N	71.07 W
South Ribble □[8]	262	53.45 N	2.42 W
South River, On., Can.	190	45.50 N	79.23 W
South River, N.J., U.S.	208	40.26 N	74.23 W
South River c	208	38.57 N	76.29 W
South Rockwood	216	42.04 N	83.16 W
South Ronaldsay I	46	58.46 N	2.58 W
South Roxana	219	38.50 N	90.04 W
South Royalston	207	42.37 N	72.08 W
South Rukuru ≃	154	10.46 S	34.14 E
South Russell	214	41.25 N	81.21 W
South Salmara	124	25.55 N	90.01 E
South Sand Bluff ›	158	31.19 S	30.01 E
South Sandwich Islands II	18	57.45 S	26.30 W
South Sandwich Trench ✦[1]	18	56.30 S	25.00 W
South Sandy Creek ≃	212	43.43 N	76.12 W
South San Francisco	226	37.39 N	122.24 W
South San Gabriel	280	34.03 N	118.05 W
South San Jose Hills	280	34.01 N	117.55 W
South San Ramon Creek ≃	282	37.42 N	121.55 W
South Santiam ≃	202	44.41 N	123.00 W
South Saskatchewan ≃	184	53.15 N	105.05 W
South Saugeen ≃	212	44.08 N	81.02 W
South Seaville	208	39.10 N	74.45 W
South Setauket	210	40.54 N	73.06 W
South Shafter	226	35.28 N	119.17 W
South Shetland Islands II	9	62.00 S	58.00 W
South Shields	44	55.00 N	1.25 W
South Shore	218	38.43 N	82.59 W
South Shore ◆[8]	278	41.46 N	87.35 W
South Shore Mall ◆[9]	276	40.44 N	73.15 W
South Shore Plaza ◆[9]	283	42.13 N	71.01 W
Southside	174h	2.49 S	171.43 W
South Side ◆[8]	279b	40.26 N	79.58 W
Southside Place	222	29.42 N	95.26 W
South Sioux City	198	42.28 N	96.24 W
South Skunk ≃	190	41.15 N	92.02 W
South Slocan	182	49.28 N	117.32 W
South Solon	218	39.44 N	83.36 W
South Sound ᴜ	48	53.02 N	9.28 W
South Spicer Island I	176	68.06 N	79.13 W
South Standard	219	39.21 N	89.47 W
South Station ◆[5]	283	42.21 N	71.04 W
South Sterling	210	41.17 N	75.21 W
South Stony Brook	276	40.53 N	73.07 W
South Stradbroke Island I	171a	27.51 S	153.25 E
South Streator	216	40.39 N	88.23 W
South Suburban → Behāla	126	22.31 N	88.19 E
South Sulphur ≃	196	33.23 N	95.18 W
South Sunday Creek ≃	202	46.27 N	105.54 W
South Superior	200	41.45 N	108.57 W
South Swansea	207	41.43 N	71.12 W
South Taranaki Bight c[3]	172	39.40 S	174.10 E
South Tasman Rise ✦[3]	6	49.00 S	148.00 E
South Temple	208	40.24 N	75.55 W
South Thompson ≃	182	50.41 N	120.21 W
South Toms River	208	39.56 N	74.12 W
South Torrington	198	42.02 N	104.10 W
South Towanda	210	41.45 N	76.27 W
South Tucson	200	32.11 N	110.58 W
South Turkeyfoot Creek ≃	216	41.25 N	83.58 W
South Turlock	226	37.29 N	120.51 W
South Twillingate Island I	186	49.37 N	54.47 W
South Tyne ≃	44	54.59 N	2.08 W
South Ubian	116	5.11 N	120.30 E
South Uist I	46	57.15 N	7.21 W
South Umpqua ≃	202	43.20 N	123.25 W
South Valley	210	42.42 N	74.43 W
South Valley Hills ⩘[2]	285	40.00 N	75.40 W
South Valley Stream	276	40.38 N	73.44 W
South Venice	220	27.03 N	82.25 W
South Ventana Cone ∧	204	36.17 N	121.38 W
South Vestal	210	42.01 N	76.00 W
South Vietnam → Vietnam □[1]	108	16.00 N	108.00 E
Southview	214	40.20 N	80.16 W
Southview Apartments	284c	38.50 N	77.00 W
South Wabasca Lake ⊜	182	55.54 N	113.45 W
South Wales	210	42.43 N	78.35 W
South Walpole	283	42.06 N	71.15 W
Southwark ◆[8]	260	51.30 N	0.06 W
South Warren Reservoir ⊜[1]	168b	34.43 S	138.55 E
Southwater	42	51.01 N	0.21 W
South Waverly	210	41.59 N	76.32 W
South Weald	260	51.37 N	0.16 E
Southwell	44	53.05 N	0.58 W
South Wellfleet	207	41.55 N	69.59 W
South Wellington	224	49.06 N	123.53 W
Southwest	214	40.12 N	79.32 W
South West Bay c	240b	25.00 N	77.32 W
Southwest Branch ≃	284c	38.53 N	76.48 W
South Westbury	276	40.45 N	73.35 W
South West Cape ›, Austl.	166	43.34 S	146.02 E
South West Cape ›, N.Z.	172	47.17 S	167.28 E
Southwest Cape ›, Ak., U.S.	180	63.18 N	171.27 W
Southwest Cape ›, Vir. Is., U.S.	241n	17.41 N	64.54 W
Southwest Channel ᴜ	220	27.34 N	82.45 W
South West City	194	36.30 N	94.36 W
South Westerlo	210	42.27 N	74.02 W
Southwest Greensburg	214	40.17 N	79.33 W
Southwest Harbor	188	44.16 N	68.19 W
Southwest Indian Ridge ✦[3]	6	30.00 S	60.00 E
Southwest Miramichi ≃	186	46.58 N	65.35 W
Southwest Museum ᴗ	280	34.06 N	118.13 W
Southwest National Park ♠	166	43.15 S	146.15 E
Southwest Pacific Basin ✦[1]	6	40.00 S	150.00 W
Southwest Point ›, Ba.	238	25.51 N	77.13 W
South West Point ›, Kiribati	174o	1.52 N	157.33 W
Southwest Point ›, Pap. N. Gui.	164	2.14 S	146.34 E
South Weymouth	283	42.10 N	70.57 W
South Weymouth Naval Air Station ■	207	42.09 N	70.57 W
South Whitley	216	41.05 N	85.37 W
South Whittier	280	33.57 N	118.02 W
South Wichita ≃	196	33.43 N	99.29 W
Southwick, Eng., U.K.	42	50.50 N	0.13 W
Southwick, Ma., U.S.	207	42.03 N	72.46 W
South Williamson	192	37.40 N	82.17 W
South Williamsport	210	41.13 N	76.59 W
South Wilmington	216	41.10 N	88.16 W
South Windham	188	43.44 N	70.25 W
South Windsor	207	41.49 N	72.37 W
Southwold	42	52.20 N	1.40 E
Southwood	210	42.59 N	76.08 W
Southwood Acres	207	41.59 N	72.32 W
South Woodham Ferrers	42	51.39 N	0.37 E
South Woodslee	214	42.14 N	82.43 W
South Woodstock	207	41.56 N	71.57 W
Southworth	224	47.31 N	122.30 W
South Yadkin ≃	192	35.45 N	80.27 W
South Yamhill ≃	224	45.13 N	123.08 W
South Yarmouth	207	41.40 N	70.11 W
South Yarra	274b	37.51 S	145.00 E
South Yorkshire □[6]	44	53.30 N	1.15 W
South Yuba ≃	226	39.17 N	121.12 W
South Zeal	42	50.44 N	3.54 W
Soutpan	158	28.43 S	26.04 E
Soutpansberg ⩘	156	22.55 S	29.30 E
Souttouf, Adrar ⩘	148	22.15 N	15.40 W
Souvigny	32	46.32 N	3.11 E
Souzy-la-Briche	261	48.32 N	2.09 E
Sovata	38	46.35 N	25.04 E
Soverato	68	38.41 N	16.33 E
Sovere	64	45.49 N	10.01 E
Sovereign Hill Historical Park ⊥	169	37.37 S	143.51 E
Sovereign Mountain ∧	180	62.08 N	148.36 W
Soveria Mannelli	68	39.05 N	16.22 E
Sövestad	41	55.30 N	13.47 E
Sovetašen	84	40.06 N	44.33 E
Sovetka	83	47.30 N	39.15 E
Sovetsk, Ross.	76	53.56 N	37.39 E
Sovetsk, Ross.	76	55.05 N	21.53 E
Sovetsk, Ross.	80	57.37 N	48.58 E
Sovetskaja, Ross.	80	49.00 N	42.07 E
Sovetskaja, Ross.	84	44.46 N	41.11 E
Sovetskaja, Ross.	84	44.02 N	44.03 E
Sovetskaja Gavan'	89	48.58 N	140.18 E
Sovetskich Oficerov, pik ∧	85	38.26 N	73.18 E
Sovetskij, Ross.	76	60.32 N	28.41 E
Sovetskij, Ross.	80	56.46 N	48.32 E
Sovetskij, Ross.	86	51.04 N	56.29 E
Sovetskij, Taj.	85	38.02 N	69.35 E
Sovetskij, Taj.	85	40.11 N	71.19 E
Sovetskoje, Kaz.	85	42.17 N	70.15 E
Sovetskoje, Ross.	78	50.21 N	39.01 E
Sovetskoje, Ross.	80	51.27 N	46.44 E
Sovetskoje, Ross.	84	43.19 N	43.36 E
Sovetskoje, Ross.	84	42.52 N	45.41 E
Šovgenovskij	78	45.02 N	40.14 E
Sovicille	66	43.17 N	11.13 E
Sovico	266b	45.39 N	9.16 E
Søvik	26	62.33 N	6.18 E
Søvind	41	55.54 N	10.01 E
Sovpolje	24	65.18 N	43.55 E
Sovyets'kyy	78	45.20 N	34.56 E
Sow ≃	42	52.48 N	2.00 W
Sowa Pan ≍	156	20.45 S	26.00 E
Sowek	164	0.49 S	135.30 E
Sowerby, Eng., U.K.	44	54.13 N	1.21 W
Sowerby, Eng., U.K.	262	53.42 N	1.56 W
Sowerby Bridge	44	53.43 N	1.54 W
Soweto	158	26.14 S	27.54 E
Sowjetisches Ehrenmal ⊥	264a	52.29 N	13.28 E
Soy	56	50.17 N	5.31 E
Sōya-kaikyō → La Perouse Strait ᴜ	89	45.45 N	142.00 E
Sōya-misaki ›	92a	45.31 N	141.56 E
Soyang-chŏsuji ⊜[1]	98	37.56 N	127.53 E
Soyapango	236	13.42 N	89.09 W
Soyers Lake ⊜	212	45.02 N	78.37 W
Soyet	124	24.12 N	76.10 E
Soyland Moor ◆[3]	262	53.40 N	2.02 W
Soyo	152	6.07 S	12.18 E
Soyons	62	44.53 N	4.51 E
Sož (Sozh) ≃, Europe	78	51.57 N	30.48 E
Soz' ≃, Ross.	82	56.48 N	36.44 E
Sozh (Sož) ≃	78	51.57 N	30.48 E
Şozimskij	24	59.44 N	52.16 E
Šožma	24	61.56 N	40.15 E
Sozopol	38	42.25 N	27.42 E
Sozzago	266b	45.24 N	8.43 E
Spa	56	50.30 N	5.52 E
Spaatz Island I	9	73.12 S	75.00 W
Space Needle ᴗ	224	47.38 N	122.23 W
Space Obelisk ⊥	265b	55.49 N	37.38 E
Spadafora	70	38.13 N	15.22 E
Spada Lake ⊜[1]	224	47.57 N	121.40 W
Spaden	52	53.34 N	8.38 E
Spahl	56	50.39 N	9.55 E
Spaichingen	58	48.04 N	8.44 E
Spain (España) □[1], Europe	22	40.00 N	4.00 W
Spain (España) □[1], Europe	34	40.00 N	4.00 W
Spakenburg	52	52.15 N	5.23 E
Spalato → Split	36	43.31 N	16.27 E
Spalding, Austl.	166	33.30 S	138.37 E
Spalding, Sk., Can.	184	52.20 N	104.30 W
Spalding, Eng., U.K.	42	52.47 N	0.10 W
Spalding, Mo., U.S.	219	39.38 N	91.32 W
Spalding, Ne., U.S.	198	41.41 N	98.21 W
Spalt	56	49.10 N	10.55 E
Spam Island I	174h	2.48 S	171.43 W
Spanaway	224	47.06 N	122.26 W
Spandau ◆[8]	54	52.33 N	13.12 E
Spandau, Berliner Forst ◆[3]	264a	52.35 N	13.11 E
Spang	41	54.56 N	9.50 E
Spangenberg	56	51.07 N	9.40 E
Spangler	214	40.38 N	78.46 W
Spaniard's Bay	186	47.37 N	53.17 W
Spanien → Spain □[1]	34	40.00 N	4.00 W
Spanish	190	46.12 N	82.21 W
Spanish ≃	190	46.11 N	82.19 W
Spanish Camp	222	29.23 N	96.10 W
Spanish Fork	200	40.06 N	111.39 W
Spanish Lake	219	38.47 N	90.12 W
Spanish North Africa □[2], Afr.	34	35.53 N	5.19 W
Spanish North Africa □[2], Afr.	134	35.53 N	5.19 W
Spanish Peak ∧	202	44.24 N	119.46 W
Spanish Point ›	240a	32.18 N	64.48 W
Spanish Sahara → Western Sahara □[2]	134	24.30 N	13.00 W
Spanish Town, Br. Vir. Is.	240m	18.27 N	64.26 W
Spanish Town, Jam.	241q	17.59 N	76.57 W
Spannberg	61	48.27 N	16.44 E
Sparagio, Monte ∧	70	38.03 N	12.46 E
Sparbach	264b	48.04 N	16.11 E
Spargi, Isola I	71	41.14 N	9.21 E
Sparkford	42	51.02 N	2.34 W
Sparkill	276	41.02 N	73.56 W
Sparkle Lake	210	41.18 N	73.47 W
Sparkman	194	33.55 N	92.50 W
Sparks, Ga., U.S.	192	31.10 N	83.26 W
Sparks, Nv., U.S.	226	39.32 N	119.45 W
Sparland	190	41.02 N	89.26 W
Sparlingville	214	42.58 N	82.30 W
Sparneck	54	50.09 N	11.50 E
Sparreholm	40	59.04 N	16.49 E
Sparrow Bush	210	41.23 N	74.43 W
Sparrow Lake ⊜	212	44.49 N	79.24 W
Sparrowpit	262	53.19 N	1.52 W
Sparrows Point	208	39.13 N	76.28 W
Sparrows Point ›	284b	39.12 N	76.30 W
Sparta, On., Can.	212	42.42 N	81.05 W
Sparta → Spárti, Ellás	38	37.05 N	22.27 E
Sparta, Ga., U.S.	192	33.16 N	82.58 W
Sparta, Il., U.S.	194	38.07 N	89.42 W
Sparta, Ky., U.S.	218	38.40 N	84.54 W
Sparta, Mi., U.S.	190	43.09 N	85.42 W
Sparta, N.J., U.S.	210	41.02 N	74.38 W
Sparta, N.C., U.S.	192	36.30 N	81.07 W
Sparta, Oh., U.S.	214	40.24 N	82.42 W
Sparta, Tn., U.S.	194	35.55 N	85.27 W
Sparta, Wi., U.S.	190	43.56 N	90.48 W
Sparta Brook ≃	276	41.08 N	73.52 W
Spartak Garden ♠	265a	59.51 N	30.30 E
Sparta Lake	210	41.03 N	74.34 W
Spartanburg, In., U.S.	218	40.03 N	84.51 W
Spartanburg, S.C., U.S.	192	34.56 N	81.55 W
Spartansburg	214	41.49 N	79.41 W
Spartel, Cap ›	34	35.48 N	5.56 W
Spárti (Sparta)	38	37.05 N	22.27 E
Spartivento, Capo ›, It.	68	37.55 N	16.04 E
Spartivento, Capo ›, It.	71	38.53 N	8.50 E
Spas-Demensk	76	54.25 N	34.01 E
Spas-Klepiki	80	55.08 N	40.13 E
Spass	82	55.55 N	35.55 E
Spassk-Dal'nij	89	44.37 N	132.48 E
Spasskij	86	53.42 N	59.12 E
Spasskij Zavod	86	49.32 N	73.17 E
Spasskoje, Ross.	76	53.06 N	36.24 E
Spasskoje, Ross.	80	55.52 N	45.42 E
Spasskoje, Ross.	82	54.05 N	38.28 E
Spassk-R'azanskij	80	54.24 N	40.23 E
Spas-Zaulok	82	56.29 N	36.34 E
Spáta	267c	37.48 N	23.55 E
Spátha, Ákra ›	38	35.42 N	23.44 E
Spaulding	219	39.52 N	89.32 W
Spaulding, Lake ⊜[1]	226	39.20 N	120.37 W
Speaks	222	29.15 N	96.42 W
Spean, Glen V	46	56.53 N	4.45 W
Spean Bridge	46	56.53 N	4.54 W
Spear, Cape ›	186	47.32 N	52.32 W
Spearfish	198	44.29 N	103.51 W
Spearman	196	36.11 N	101.11 W
Spearsville	218	39.21 N	86.11 W
Spearville	198	37.51 N	99.45 W
Spearwood	168a	32.07 S	115.47 E
Speas Artemidos (Rock Tombs) ⊥	142	27.54 N	30.52 E
Specchia	68	39.57 N	18.18 E
Spechtsbrunn	54	50.30 N	11.14 E
Spectacle Island I	283	42.19 N	70.59 W
Spectrum ♠	285	39.54 N	75.10 W
Spectrum Range ⩘	180	57.30 N	130.40 W
Spednic Lake ⊜	186	45.36 N	67.35 W
Speed	218	38.24 N	85.45 W
Speed ≃	212	43.23 N	80.22 W
Speedway	218	39.48 N	86.16 W
Speicher	58	47.24 N	9.27 E
Speichersee ⊜	60	48.13 N	11.45 E
Speightstown	241g	13.15 N	59.39 W
Speigletown	210	42.48 N	73.38 W
Speikkogel ∧	61	47.14 N	15.03 E
Speinshart	60	49.47 N	11.49 E
Speising ◆[8]	264b	48.10 N	16.17 E
Speke ◆[8]	262	53.21 N	2.51 W
Speke Gulf c	154	2.20 S	33.15 E
Speke Hall ⊥	262	53.20 N	2.52 W
Speldorf ◆[8]	263	51.25 N	6.52 E
Spellen	263	51.37 N	6.37 E
Spello	66	42.59 N	12.40 E
Spelthorne □[8]	260	51.25 N	0.28 W
Spelve, Loch c	46	56.22 N	5.46 W
Spenard	180	61.11 N	149.55 W
Spence Bay	176	69.32 N	93.31 W
Spencer, In., U.S.	194	39.17 N	86.45 W
Spencer, Ia., U.S.	198	43.08 N	95.08 W
Spencer, Ma., U.S.	207	42.14 N	71.59 W
Spencer, Ne., U.S.	198	42.52 N	98.42 W
Spencer, N.Y., U.S.	210	42.12 N	76.29 W
Spencer, N.C., U.S.	192	35.41 N	80.26 W
Spencer, Oh., U.S.	214	41.06 N	82.07 W
Spencer, S.D., U.S.	198	43.43 N	97.35 W
Spencer, Tn., U.S.	194	35.44 N	85.28 W
Spencer, W.V., U.S.	188	38.48 N	81.21 W
Spencer, Wi., U.S.	190	44.45 N	90.17 W
Spencer, Cape ›, Austl.	166	35.18 S	136.53 E
Spencer, Cape ›, N.B., Can.	186	45.12 N	65.55 W
Spencer, Cape ›, Ak., U.S.	180	58.14 N	136.40 W
Spencer, Mount ∧	224	49.03 N	124.38 W
Spencer, Point ›	180	65.18 N	166.50 W
Spencer Brook ≃	283	42.28 N	71.22 W
Spencer Creek ≃, On., Can.	212	43.17 N	79.54 W
Spencer Creek ≃, Mo., U.S.	219	39.33 N	91.20 W
Spencer Field ⊠	281	42.31 N	83.33 W
Spencer Gulf c	166	34.00 S	137.00 E
Spencer Lake ⊜	224	47.16 N	122.57 W
Spencerport	210	43.11 N	77.48 W
Spencertown	210	42.20 N	73.33 W
Spencerville, On., Can.	212	44.51 N	75.33 W
Spencerville, In., U.S.	216	41.16 N	84.55 W
Spencerville, Md., U.S.	208	39.06 N	76.58 W
Spencerville, Oh., U.S.	216	40.42 N	84.21 W
Spences Bridge	182	50.25 N	121.21 W
Spenge	52	52.08 N	8.28 E
Spennymoor	44	54.42 N	1.35 W
Spenser Mountains ⩘	172	42.15 S	172.30 E
Sperenberg	54	52.08 N	13.22 E
Sperillen ⊜	26	60.28 N	10.03 E
Sperling	224	49.08 N	122.33 W
Sperlinga	70	37.46 N	14.21 E
Sperlonga	66	41.15 N	13.26 E
Spermaceti Cove c	276	40.26 N	73.59 W
Sperone, Capo ›	71	38.57 N	8.25 E
Sperrin Mountains ⩘	48	54.50 N	7.05 W
Sperry Creek ≃	279a	41.29 N	81.53 W
Sperry Rand Corporation ᴗ[3]	276	40.45 N	73.42 W
Sperryville	188	38.39 N	78.13 W
Spessart ◆[1]	56	50.10 N	9.20 E
Spesutie Island I	208	39.27 N	76.05 W
Spétsai I	38	37.16 N	23.08 E
Spexard	52	51.52 N	8.24 E
Spey ≃	46	57.40 N	3.06 W
Spey Bay c	46	57.41 N	3.00 W
Speyer	56	49.19 N	8.26 E
Speyerbach ≃	56	49.19 N	8.27 E
Speyside	241r	11.18 N	60.32 W
Spezia → La Spezia	62	44.07 N	9.50 E
Spezzano Albanese	68	39.40 N	16.19 E
Spezzano della Sila	68	39.18 N	16.20 E
Sphinx → Abū al-Hawl ⊥	142	29.59 N	31.08 E
Spiazzo	64	46.07 N	10.40 E
Spiceland	218	39.50 N	85.26 W
Spicer	198	45.13 N	94.56 W
Spicer Creek ≃	284a	43.02 N	78.53 W
Spicer Meadow Reservoir ⊜[1]	226	38.23 N	119.59 W
Spicheren	56	49.12 N	6.58 E
Spickard	194	40.14 N	93.35 W
Spicket ≃	283	42.42 N	71.09 W
Spieka	52	53.45 N	8.35 E
Spiekeroog I	52	53.46 N	7.42 E
Spiess Seamount ✦[3]	8	54.40 S	0.15 E
Spiez	58	46.41 N	7.39 E
Spijkenisse	52	51.51 N	4.20 E
Spilamberto	64	44.32 N	11.01 E
Spilimbergo	64	46.07 N	12.54 E
Spilinga	68	38.37 N	15.54 E
Spillersboda	40	59.42 N	18.51 E
Spillimacheen ≃	182	50.55 N	116.20 W
Spillville	190	43.12 N	91.57 W
Spilsby	44	53.11 N	0.06 E
Spinazzola	68	40.58 N	16.06 E
Spīn Būldak	120	31.01 N	66.24 E
Spincourt	56	49.20 N	5.40 E
Spindale	192	35.21 N	81.55 W
Spindoli	66	43.12 N	12.54 E
Spinea-Orgnano	64	45.29 N	12.10 E
Spinetta Marengo	62	44.53 N	8.41 E
Spinnerstown	208	40.26 N	75.26 W
Spinoso	68	40.16 N	15.58 E
Spires → Speyer	56	49.19 N	8.26 E
Spirit Lake, Id., U.S.	202	47.57 N	116.52 W
Spirit Lake, Ia., U.S.	198	43.25 N	95.06 W
Spirit Lake ⊜	224	46.16 N	122.08 W
Spirit River	182	55.47 N	118.50 W
Spiritwood	184	53.22 N	107.31 W
Spiro	194	35.14 N	94.37 W
Spirovo	76	57.26 N	34.59 E
Spišská Nová Ves	30	48.57 N	20.34 E
Spitak	84	40.51 N	44.16 E
Spital am Pyhrn	61	47.39 N	14.20 E
Spithead ᴜ	42	50.45 N	1.05 W
Spit Point ›	162	20.02 S	119.00 E
Spitsbergen I	12	78.45 N	16.00 E
Spitsbergen Bank ✦[4]	12	76.00 N	23.00 E
Spittal an der Drau	64	46.48 N	13.30 E
Spittal of Glenshee	46	56.48 N	3.28 W
Spitz	61	48.22 N	15.25 E
Spitzbergen und Jan Mayen → Svalbard □[2]	12	78.00 N	20.00 E
Spitzer Berg ∧[2]	264a	52.38 N	13.35 E
Spivakivka	83	49.03 N	38.54 E
Spixworth	42	52.40 N	1.20 E
Spjelkavik	26	62.28 N	6.23 E
Splavnucha	80	51.05 N	45.22 E
Splendora	222	30.14 N	95.10 W
Split	36	43.31 N	16.27 E
Split, Cape ›	186	45.20 N	64.30 W
Split Lake ⊜	184	56.08 N	96.15 W
Splitrock Reservoir ⊜[1]	276	40.58 N	74.27 W
Spluga, Passo della (Splügenpass))(	58	46.30 N	9.20 E
Splügen	58	46.33 N	9.20 E
Splügenpass (Passo della Spluga))(	58	46.30 N	9.20 E
Spodsbjerg	41	54.56 N	10.50 E
Spofford	196	29.11 N	100.25 W
Špogi	76	56.05 N	26.44 E
Spokane	202	47.39 N	117.25 W
Spokane ≃	202	47.54 N	118.20 W
Spokane, Mount ∧	202	47.55 N	117.07 W
Spokane Indian Reservation ◆[4]	202	47.55 N	118.00 W
Spokojnaja	84	44.15 N	41.25 E
Spoleto	66	42.44 N	12.44 E
Spoltore	66	42.27 N	14.08 E
Spondigna	64	46.38 N	10.37 E
Spondon	42	52.54 N	1.25 W
Sponds Hill ∧[2]	262	53.19 N	2.03 W
Spóng	110	13.27 N	105.34 E
Spoon ≃	194	40.18 N	90.04 W
Spooner	190	45.49 N	91.53 W
Spořice	54	50.26 N	13.25 E
Spornitz	54	53.24 N	11.43 E
Spornoje	74	62.20 N	151.03 E
Sporovo	76	52.25 N	25.20 E
Spørring	41	56.18 N	10.09 E
Sportforum ♠	264a	52.33 N	13.29 E
Sport Hill	207	41.14 N	73.16 W
Sporting Hill	208	40.09 N	76.26 W
Sportsman's Park Race Track ♠	278	41.50 N	87.46 W
Spotorno	62	44.14 N	8.25 E
Spot Pond ⊜	283	42.27 N	71.06 W
Spotswood, Austl.	274b	37.50 S	144.53 E
Spotswood, N.J., U.S.	208	40.23 N	74.23 W
Spotsylvania	208	38.12 N	77.35 W
Spotsylvania □[6]	208	38.15 N	77.30 W
Spotsylvania Court House Battlefield ⊥	208	38.15 N	77.35 W
Sprague, Mb., Can.	184	49.02 N	95.38 W
Sprague, Wa., U.S.	202	47.18 N	117.58 W
Sprague ≃	202	42.34 N	121.51 W
Sprague, North Fork ≃	202	42.26 N	121.07 W
Sprague, South Fork ≃	202	42.26 N	121.07 W
Spragueville	207	41.53 N	71.32 W
Sprain Ridge Park ♠	276	40.59 N	73.51 W
Sprankle Mills	214	41.00 N	79.07 W
Spratly Islands II	108	10.00 N	114.00 E
Spratt Point ›	212	44.36 N	80.01 W
Spray	202	44.50 N	119.47 W
Spray Lakes Reservoir ⊜[1]	182	50.55 N	115.20 W
Spreča ≃	38	44.45 N	18.06 E
Spreckels	226	36.36 N	121.34 W
Spreckelsville	229a	20.53 N	156.24 W
Spree ≃	54	52.32 N	13.13 E
Spreenhagen	54	52.20 N	13.52 E
Spreeufontein	158	33.22 S	20.45 E
Spreewald ◆[1]	54	51.50 N	14.05 E
Spremberg	54	51.34 N	14.22 E
Sprendlingen	56	49.51 N	7.59 E
Spresiano	64	45.46 N	12.16 E
Spring	222	30.04 N	95.25 W
Spring ≃, U.S.	194	36.52 N	94.44 W
Spring ≃, Ar., U.S.	194	36.08 N	91.05 W
Spring, North Fork ≃	194	37.18 N	94.21 W
Spring, South Fork ≃	194	36.19 N	91.30 W
Spring Arbor	216	42.12 N	84.33 W
Spring Bay c	200	41.40 N	112.50 W
Springbok	156	29.43 S	17.55 E
Springboro, Oh., U.S.	218	39.33 N	84.14 W
Springboro, Pa., U.S.	214	41.48 N	80.22 W
Spring Branch ≃	284b	39.26 N	76.35 W
Springbrook, On., Can.	275b	43.39 N	79.47 W
Springbrook, Md., U.S.	284c	39.03 N	77.00 W
Spring Brook, N.Y., U.S.	210	42.49 N	78.40 W
Spring Brook ≃	278	41.58 N	87.59 W
Springbrook Forest	284c	39.03 N	77.01 W
Springburn	172	43.40 S	171.28 E
Spring City, Pa., U.S.	208	40.10 N	75.32 W
Spring City, Tn., U.S.	192	35.41 N	84.51 W
Spring City, Ut,. U.S.	200	39.28 N	111.29 W
Spring Coulee V	198	48.31 N	100.54 W
Spring Creek, N.Z.	172	41.28 S	173.58 E
Spring Creek, Pa., U.S.	214	41.53 N	79.32 W
Spring Creek ≃, Austl.	166	24.12 S	140.58 E
Spring Creek ≃, U.S.	198	40.30 N	101.21 W
Spring Creek ≃, Ga., U.S.	192	30.54 N	84.45 W
Spring Creek ≃, Il., U.S.	216	40.49 N	87.50 W
Spring Creek ≃, Il., U.S.	219	39.52 N	89.37 W
Spring Creek ≃, Il., U.S.	278	41.32 N	88.04 W
Spring Creek ≃, Mo., U.S.	219	38.21 N	91.10 W
Spring Creek ≃, Nv., U.S.	204	39.55 N	117.50 W
Spring Creek ≃, N.D., U.S.	198	47.15 N	101.48 W
Spring Creek ≃, Pa., U.S.	214	40.56 N	77.47 W
Spring Creek ≃, Pa., U.S.	214	41.24 N	78.57 W
Spring Creek ≃, S.D., U.S.	198	45.54 N	100.18 W
Spring Creek ≃, S.D., U.S.	198	43.52 N	102.42 W
Spring Creek ≃, Tx., U.S.	222	30.02 N	95.16 W
Springdale, Nf., Can.	186	49.30 N	56.04 W
Springdale, Ar., U.S.	194	36.11 N	94.07 W
Springdale, Oh., U.S.	218	39.17 N	84.28 W
Springdale, Pa., U.S.	214	40.32 N	79.47 W
Springdale, S.C., U.S.	192	33.57 N	81.06 W
Springdale, Ut,. U.S.	200	37.11 N	112.59 W
Springdale, Wa., U.S.	202	48.03 N	117.44 W
Spring Dale, W.V., U.S.	192	37.52 N	80.48 W
Springe	52	52.12 N	9.32 E
Springer	196	36.21 N	104.35 W
Springers Brook ≃	285	39.44 N	74.41 W
Springerville	200	34.08 N	109.17 W
Springfield, N.S., Can.	186	44.38 N	64.52 W
Springfield, On., Can.	212	42.50 N	80.56 W
Springfield, N.Z.	172	43.20 S	171.55 E
Springfield, S. Afr.	158	29.02 S	22.53 E
Springfield, Co., U.S.	198	37.24 N	102.36 W
Springfield, Fl., U.S.	194	30.09 N	85.36 W
Springfield, Ga., U.S.	192	32.22 N	81.18 W
Springfield, Il., U.S.	219	39.48 N	89.38 W
Springfield, Ky., U.S.	194	37.41 N	85.13 W
Springfield, Ma., U.S.	207	42.06 N	72.35 W
Springfield, Mi., U.S.	216	42.19 N	85.14 W
Springfield, Mn., U.S.	198	44.14 N	94.58 W
Springfield, Mo., U.S.	194	37.12 N	93.17 W
Springfield, N.J., U.S.	276	40.43 N	74.18 W
Springfield, Oh., U.S.	218	39.55 N	83.48 W
Springfield, Or., U.S.	202	44.02 N	123.01 W
Springfield, Pa., U.S.	285	39.55 N	75.19 W
Springfield, S.C., U.S.	192	33.29 N	81.16 W
Springfield, S.D., U.S.	198	42.51 N	97.53 W
Springfield, Tn., U.S.	194	36.30 N	86.53 W
Springfield, Vt., U.S.	188	43.17 N	72.28 W
Springfield, Va., U.S.	284c	38.45 N	77.13 W
Springfield, Lake ⊜[1]	219	39.44 N	89.36 W
Springfield Center	210	42.50 N	74.53 W
Springfield Estates	284c	38.47 N	77.11 W
Springfield Lake ⊜	285	40.11 N	75.00 W
Springfield Lake ⊜[1]	222	31.36 N	96.33 W
Springfield Mall ◆[9]	284c	38.46 N	77.11 W
Springfield Plateau ⩘[1]	194	37.10 N	93.30 W
Springfontein	158	30.19 S	25.36 E
Spring Garden	246	6.59 N	58.31 W
Spring Garden Brook ≃	276	40.46 N	74.23 W
Spring Garden Township	208	39.57 N	76.44 W
Spring Glen, N.Y., U.S.	210	41.40 N	74.26 W
Spring Glen, Pa., U.S.	208	40.38 N	76.37 W
Spring Glen, Ut,. U.S.	200	39.39 N	110.51 W
Spring Green	190	43.10 N	90.04 W
Spring Grove, Il., U.S.	216	42.26 N	88.13 W
Spring Grove, Mn., U.S.	190	43.33 N	91.38 W
Spring Grove, Pa., U.S.	208	39.52 N	76.51 W
Springhill, N.S., Can.	186	45.39 N	64.03 W
Spring Hill, Ca., U.S.	226	39.15 N	121.03 W
Spring Hill, Fl., U.S.	220	28.33 N	82.27 W
Springhill, La., U.S.	194	33.00 N	93.28 W
Spring Hill, Pa., U.S.	214	40.23 N	78.40 W
Spring Hill, Tn., U.S.	194	35.45 N	86.55 W
Spring Hill, Tx., U.S.	222	32.34 N	94.48 W
Springhills	216	40.16 N	83.22 W
Spring Hope	192	35.56 N	78.06 W
Springhouse, B.C., Can.	182	51.55 N	122.07 W
Spring House, Pa., U.S.	285	40.11 N	75.14 W
Spring Lake, Mi., U.S.	216	43.04 N	86.11 W
Spring Lake, N.J., U.S.	208	40.09 N	74.01 W
Spring Lake, N.C., U.S.	192	35.10 N	78.58 W
Spring Lake ⊜, Mi., U.S.	216	43.06 N	86.11 W
Spring Lake ⊜, N.J., U.S.	276	40.35 N	74.25 W
Spring Lake Heights	208	40.09 N	74.01 W
Spring Mill, Oh., U.S.	214	40.54 N	82.36 W
Spring Mill, Pa., U.S.	285	40.04 N	75.17 W
Spring Mill Reservoir ⊜[1]	262	53.39 N	2.13 W
Spring Mills	210	40.51 N	77.34 W
Spring Mill State Park ♠	218	38.43 N	86.25 W
Spring Mount	208	40.17 N	75.28 W
Spring Mountains ⩘	204	36.10 N	115.40 W
Spring Pond ⊜	283	42.30 N	70.57 W
Springport, In., U.S.	218	40.03 N	85.24 W
Springport, Mi., U.S.	216	42.22 N	84.41 W
Spring Run	214	40.09 N	83.47 W
Springs	158	26.13 S	28.25 E
Springs □[5]	273d	26.14 S	28.30 E
Springs Aerodrome ⊠	273d	26.15 S	28.24 E
Springside	285	40.04 N	74.51 W
Springs Junction	172	42.19 S	172.11 E
Springsure	166	24.07 S	148.05 E
Springton	168b	34.43 S	139.05 E
Springtown	222	32.58 N	97.41 W
Springvale, Austl.	162	17.48 S	127.41 E
Springvale, Austl.	166	23.33 S	140.42 E
Springvale, Austl.	169	37.57 S	145.09 E
Springvale, Me., U.S.	188	43.28 N	70.47 W
Springvale South	274b	37.58 S	145.09 E
Spring Valley, Ca., U.S.	228	32.44 N	116.59 W
Spring Valley, Il., U.S.	190	41.19 N	89.11 W
Spring Valley, Mn., U.S.	190	43.41 N	92.23 W
Spring Valley, N.Y., U.S.	210	41.06 N	74.02 W
Spring Valley, Oh., U.S.	218	39.36 N	84.00 W
Spring Valley, Tx., U.S.	222	29.47 N	95.31 W
Spring Valley, Wi., U.S.	190	44.50 N	92.14 W
Spring Valley V	204	39.15 N	114.25 W
Spring Valley Creek ≃	204	39.20 N	114.25 W
Springview	198	42.49 N	99.44 W
Springville, Al., U.S.	194	33.46 N	86.28 W
Springville, Ca., U.S.	204	36.08 N	118.49 W
Springville, Ia., U.S.	190	42.03 N	91.26 W
Springville, N.J., U.S.	285	39.56 N	74.52 W
Springville, N.Y., U.S.	210	42.30 N	78.40 W
Springville, Pa., U.S.	210	41.42 N	75.55 W
Springville, Ut,. U.S.	200	40.09 N	111.36 W
Springwater	210	42.38 N	77.35 W
Springwood	170	33.42 S	150.33 E
Sprint ≃	44	54.22 N	2.45 W
Sprite Creek ≃	210	43.08 N	74.44 W
Sproat Lake ⊜	182	49.16 N	125.03 W
Sprockhövel	56	51.22 N	7.15 E
Sprogels Run ≃	285	40.14 N	75.37 W
Sprogø I	41	55.20 N	10.58 E
Sprötze	52	53.18 N	9.49 E
Sproul	214	40.16 N	78.28 W
Sprout Brook ≃	276	40.54 N	74.05 W
Spruce ≃	184	53.15 N	105.43 W
Spruce Brook	186	48.45 N	58.11 W
Spruce Creek	214	40.37 N	78.08 W
Spruce Creek ≃	210	43.07 N	74.46 W
Spruce Grove	182	53.32 N	113.55 W
Spruce Knob ∧	188	38.42 N	79.32 W
Spruce Knob-Seneca Rocks National Recreation Area ♠	188	38.50 N	79.20 W
Spruce Lake	184	53.32 N	109.05 W
Spruce Mountain ∧, Az., U.S.	200	34.28 N	112.24 W
Spruce Mountain ∧, Nv., U.S.	204	40.33 N	114.49 W
Spruce Pine, Al., U.S.	194	34.23 N	87.43 W
Spruce Pine, N.C., U.S.	192	35.54 N	82.03 W
Spruce Run Reservoir ⊜[1]	210	40.40 N	74.57 W
Spruce Run State Park ♠	210	40.40 N	74.56 W
Spruce Woods Provincial Park ♠	184	49.42 N	99.05 W
Spry	208	39.55 N	76.41 W
Spry Lake ⊜	212	44.44 N	81.15 W
Spulico, Capo ›	68	39.58 N	16.39 E
Spur	196	33.28 N	100.51 W
Spurfield	182	55.13 N	114.16 W
Spurger	194	30.42 N	94.11 W
Spurn Head ›	44	53.34 N	0.07 E
Spurr, Mount ∧	180	61.18 N	152.15 W
Sputendorf	264a	52.20 N	13.13 E
Spuzzum	182	49.41 N	121.25 W
Spy Hill	184	50.36 N	101.41 W
Spy Pond ⊜	283	42.24 N	71.09 W
Squally Channel ᴜ	182	53.10 N	129.15 W
Squamish	182	49.42 N	123.09 W
Squamish ≃	182	49.45 N	123.09 W
Squam Lake ⊜	188	43.45 N	71.32 W
Square Butte Creek ≃	198	46.55 N	100.55 W
Square Lake ⊜	186	47.03 N	68.20 W
Squatec	186	47.53 N	68.43 W
Squaw Cap Mountain ∧	186	47.53 N	66.53 W
Squaw Creek ≃, Id., U.S.	202	43.51 N	116.22 W
Squaw Creek ≃, Il., U.S.	278	42.21 N	88.07 W
Squaw Creek ≃, Or., U.S.	202	44.27 N	121.20 W
Squaw Creek Lake ⊜[1]	222	32.19 N	97.47 W
Squaw Harbor	180	55.11 N	160.30 W
Squaw Hill ∧	200	41.48 N	105.02 W
Squaw Island I	284a	42.56 N	78.54 W
Squaw Peak ∧, Ca., U.S.	226	39.11 N	120.16 W
Squaw Peak ∧, Mt., U.S.	202	47.10 N	114.21 W
Squaw Rapids	184	53.41 N	103.20 W
Squaw Rapids Dam ◆[6]	184	53.40 N	103.25 W
Squaw Run ≃	279b	40.29 N	79.52 W
Squaw Valley State Recreation Area ♠	226	39.12 N	120.15 W
Squibnocket Point ›	207	41.18 N	70.47 W
Squilax	182	50.52 N	119.35 W
Squillace	68	38.47 N	16.31 E
Squillace, Golfo di c	68	38.50 N	16.50 E
Squinzano	68	40.26 N	18.03 E
Squire	192	37.14 N	81.36 W
Squires, Mount ∧	162	26.12 S	127.28 E
Squirrel ≃	180	66.57 N	160.27 W
Squirrel Hill ◆[8]	279b	40.26 N	79.55 W
Squirrel Hill Tunnel ◆[5]	279b	40.26 N	79.55 W
Squirrel's Heath ◆[8]	260	51.35 N	0.13 E
Sragen	115a	7.26 S	111.02 E
Srbija (Serbia) □[3]	38	44.00 N	21.00 E
Srbobran	38	45.33 N	19.48 E
Srê Âmběl	110	11.07 N	103.46 E
Sredec	38	42.21 N	27.10 E
Sredinnyj chrebet ⩘	74	56.00 N	158.00 E
Sredna Gora ⩘	38	42.30 N	25.00 E
Sredn'aja Achtuba	80	48.43 N	44.52 E
Sredn'aja Mokla ≃	88	55.01 N	119.37 E
Sredn'aja Nanaki, gora ∧	89	52.26 N	132.50 E
Sredn'aja Ol'okma	88	55.26 N	120.33 E
Srednegorje	76	60.34 N	29.25 E
Sredneje Kujto, ozero ⊜	24	65.08 N	31.15 E
Srednekolymsk	74	67.27 N	153.41 E
Srednerusskaja vozvyšennost' ⩘[1]	72	52.00 N	38.00 E
Srednesibirskoje ploskogorje ⩘[1]	74	65.00 N	105.00 E
Srednij Ikorec	78	51.05 N	39.45 E
Srednij Kalar	88	55.51 N	117.24 E
Srednij Ural ⩘	86	58.00 N	59.00 E
Srednij Urgal	89	51.09 N	132.59 E
Srednij Vas'ugan	86	59.16 N	78.15 E
Srê Khtŭm	110	12.10 N	106.52 E
Śrem	30	52.08 N	17.01 E
Srê Moăt	110	13.18 N	107.10 E
Sremska Mitrovica	38	44.58 N	19.37 E
Sremski Karlovci	38	45.12 N	19.57 E
Srêng ≃	110	13.21 N	103.27 E
Srêpŏk ≃	110	13.33 N	106.16 E
Sretensk	88	52.15 N	117.43 E
Sretenskoje	88	56.28 N	96.25 E
Srīdharpur	126	23.04 N	89.25 E
Sri Hargobindpur	123	31.41 N	75.39 E
Sri Jayawardenepura (Kotte)	122	6.54 N	79.54 E
Srīkākulam	122	18.18 N	83.54 E
Sri Kālahasti	122	13.45 N	79.43 E
Sri Lanka □[1], Asia	118	7.00 N	81.00 E
Sri Lanka □[1], Asia	122	7.00 N	81.00 E
Srīnagar, Bngl.	126	23.32 N	90.18 E
Srīnagar, India	123	34.05 N	74.49 E
Srīnagar, India	124	30.13 N	78.47 E
Srīnagar Airport ⊠	123	34.00 N	74.52 E
Srīpur, Bngl.	126	24.12 N	90.29 E
Srīpur, Bngl.	126	23.36 N	89.24 E
Srīrampur, India	122	19.34 N	74.34 E
Srirāmpur, India	272b	22.49 N	88.29 E
Srīrangam	122	10.52 N	78.41 E
Srīvardhan	122	18.02 N	73.01 E
Srīvilliputtūr	122	9.31 N	77.38 E
Środa Śląska	30	51.10 N	16.36 E
Środa Wielkopolski	30	52.14 N	17.17 E
Srpska Crnja	38	45.43 N	20.42 E
Ssangmun-ni ◆[8]	271b	37.39 N	127.02 E
Ssuchunghsi	100	22.06 N	120.44 E
Ssup'ing → Siping	89	43.12 N	124.20 E
Staaken ◆[8]	54	52.32 N	13.08 E
Staaten ≃	164	16.24 S	141.17 E
Staaten River National Park ♠	164	16.40 S	143.00 E
Staatsburg	210	41.50 N	73.55 W
Staatz	61	48.40 N	16.29 E
Stabbursdalen Nasjonalpark ♠	24	70.06 N	24.30 E
Staberhuk ›	54	54.24 N	11.19 E
Stabroek	50	51.20 N	4.22 E
Stachy	60	49.06 N	13.40 E
Stack, Loch ⊜	46	58.20 N	4.55 W
Stack Skerry I[2]	46	59.01 N	4.31 W
Stacksteads	262	53.41 N	2.13 W
Stacyville	190	43.26 N	92.46 W
Stad-Delden	52	52.16 N	6.42 E
Stade	52	53.36 N	9.28 E
Staden, Bel.	50	50.59 N	3.01 E
Staden, Dtsch.	56	50.20 N	8.54 E
Stadion am Zoo ♠	263	51.14 N	7.07 E
Städjan ∧	26	61.55 N	12.52 E
Stadl an der Mur	61	47.05 N	13.58 E
Stadlandet ›[1]	26	62.07 N	5.18 E
Stadlau ◆[8]	264b	48.14 N	16.28 E
Stadl-Paura	64	48.05 N	13.53 E

Symbols in the index entries represent the broad categories identified in the key at the right. Symbols with superior numbers (⩘[1]) identify subcategories (see complete key on page I · 1).

Symbole im Register stellen die rechts im Schlüssel erklärten Kategorien dar. Symbole mit hochgestellten Ziffern (⩘[1]) bezeichnen Unterabteilungen einer Kategorie (vgl. vollständiger Schlüssel auf Seite I · 1).

Los símbolos incluídos en el texto del índice representan las grandes categorías identificadas con la clave a la derecha. Los símbolos con numeros en su parte superior (⩘[1]) identifican las subcategorías (véase la clave completa en la página I · 1).

Les symboles de l'index représentent les catégories indiquées dans la légende à droite. Les symboles suivis d'un indice (⩘[1]) représentent des sous-catégories (voir légende complète à la page I · 1).

Os símbolos incluídos no texto do índice representam as grandes categorias identificadas com a chave à direita. Os símbolos com números em sua parte superior (⩘[1]) identificam as subcategorias (veja-se a chave completa à página I · 1).

∧	Mountain	Berg	Montaña	Montagne	Montanha
⩘	Mountains	Gebirge	Montañas	Montagnes	Montanhas
)(	Pass	Paß	Paso	Col	Passo
V	Valley, Canyon	Tal, Cañon	Valle, Cañón	Vallée, Canyon	Vale, Canhão
≍	Plain	Ebene	Llano	Plaine	Planície
›	Cape	Kap	Cabo	Cap	Cabo
I	Island	Insel	Isla	Île	Ilha
II	Islands	Inseln	Islas	Îles	Ilhas
⊥	Other Topographic Features	Andere Topographische Objekte	Otros Elementos Topográficos	Autres données topographiques	Outros acidentes topográficos

ESPAÑOL / FRANÇAIS / PORTUGUÊS

Nombre / Nom / Nome	Página / Page	Lat.°′	Long.°′ W = Oeste / W = Ouest
Stadskanaal	52	53.00 N	6.55 E
Stadtallendorf	56	50.50 N	9.01 E
Stadtbergen	58	48.22 N	10.50 E
Stadthagen	52	52.19 N	9.13 E
Stadtilm	54	50.47 N	11.05 E
Städtische Rahmede	263	51.17 N	7.40 E
Stadtkyll	56	50.21 N	6.32 E
Stadtlauringen	56	50.11 N	10.22 E
Stadtlengsfeld	56	50.47 N	10.07 E
Stadtlohn	52	51.59 N	6.55 E
Stadtoldendorf	52	51.53 N	9.37 E
Stadtprozelten	56	49.47 N	9.25 E
Stadtroda	54	50.51 N	11.44 E
Stadtsteinach	54	50.09 N	11.30 E
Stadt Wehlen	54	50.58 N	14.02 E
Stadum	41	54.44 N	9.03 E
Stäfa	58	47.15 N	8.44 E
Staffa I	46	56.25 N	6.20 W
Staffanstorp	41	55.38 N	13.13 E
Staffelberg ∧	56	50.06 N	11.02 E
Staffelde	264a	52.44 N	13.00 E
Staffelsee ⊜	64	47.42 N	11.10 E
Staffelstein	56	50.06 N	11.00 E
Staffin	46	57.37 N	6.12 W
Staffora ≃	62	45.04 N	9.01 E
Stafford, Eng., U.K.	42	52.48 N	2.07 W
Stafford, Ct., U.S.	207	41.59 N	72.17 W
Stafford, Ks., U.S.	198	37.57 N	98.36 W
Stafford, N.Y., U.S.	210	42.59 N	78.04 W
Stafford, Tx., U.S.	222	29.37 N	95.34 W
Stafford, Va., U.S.	208	38.25 N	77.24 W
Stafford □[6]	208	38.25 N	77.30 W
Staffordshire □[6]	28	52.50 N	2.00 W
Stafford Springs	207	41.57 N	72.18 W
Staffordsville	188	37.49 N	82.50 W
Staffordville	207	41.59 N	72.15 W
Stagen	112	3.18 S	116.10 E
Stag Pond ⊜	276	40.59 N	74.42 W
Stahl-Berg ∧[2]	264a	52.21 N	13.46 E
Stahlbrode	54	54.14 N	13.17 E
Stahle	52	51.50 N	9.25 E
Stahnsdorf	54	52.23 N	13.13 E
Stahringen	58	47.47 N	8.58 E
Staicele	76	57.50 N	24.45 E
Staines	42	51.26 N	0.31 W
Staines Reservoirs ⊜[1]	260	51.27 N	0.30 W
Stainforth	44	53.36 N	1.01 W
Staining	44	53.49 N	2.59 W
Stainland	262	53.40 N	1.53 W
Stainmore Forest ◆[3]	44	54.30 N	2.10 W
Stains	261	48.57 N	2.23 E
Stainz	61	46.54 N	15.16 E
Stairtown	222	29.43 N	97.44 W
Staked Plain → Estacado, Llano ≚	196	33.30 N	102.40 W
Stäket	40	59.28 N	17.48 E
Stakhanov	83	48.34 N	38.40 E
Stakroge	41	55.53 N	8.51 E
Stalać	38	43.40 N	21.25 E
Stalbridge	42	50.58 N	2.23 W
Stalden	58	46.14 N	7.52 E
Stalettì	68	38.46 N	16.32 E
Stalham	42	52.47 N	1.31 E
Stalheim	26	60.50 N	6.40 E
Stalhofen	61	47.05 N	15.16 E
Stalin → Varna, Blg.	38	43.13 N	27.55 E
Stalin → Brașov, Rom.	38	45.39 N	25.37 E
Stalin → Kuçovë, Shq.	38	40.48 N	19.54 E
Stalinabad → Dušanbe	85	38.35 N	68.48 E
Stalingrad → Volgograd	80	48.44 N	44.25 E
Stalino → Donets'k	83	48.00 N	37.48 E
Stalinogorsk → Novomoskovsk	82	54.05 N	38.13 E
Stalinsk → Novokuzneck	86	53.45 N	87.06 E
Stallarholmen	40	59.22 N	17.12 E
Ställberg	40	59.59 N	14.55 E
Ställdalen	40	59.56 N	14.56 E
Stallwang	60	49.03 N	12.40 E
Stalowa Wola	30	50.35 N	22.02 E
Stalybridge	44	53.29 N	2.03 W
Stambaugh	190	46.04 N	88.37 W
Stamford, Austl.	166	21.16 S	143.49 E
Stamford, Eng., U.K.	42	52.39 N	0.29 W
Stamford, Ct., U.S.	207	41.03 N	73.32 W
Stamford, N.Y., U.S.	210	42.24 N	74.36 W
Stamford, Tx., U.S.	196	32.56 N	99.48 W
Stamford, Vt., U.S.	207	42.45 N	73.04 W
Stamford, Lake ⊜[1]	196	33.05 N	99.35 W
Stamford Bridge	44	53.59 N	0.55 W
Stamford Brige Stadium ♠	260	51.29 N	0.11 W
Stamford Harbor ⊂	276	41.02 N	73.32 W
Stamford Museum ⊍	276	41.07 N	73.33 W
Stammbach	54	50.09 N	11.41 E
Stammersdorf ◆[8]	264b	48.18 N	16.25 E
Stammham, Dtsch.	60	48.52 N	11.28 E
Stammham, Dtsch.	60	48.15 N	12.53 E
Stammheim, Dtsch.	56	48.41 N	8.46 E
Stammheim, Schw.	58	47.38 N	8.47 E
Stampede Reservoir ⊜[1]	226	39.29 N	120.07 W
Stamping Ground	218	38.16 N	84.41 W
Stampriet	156	24.20 S	18.28 E
Stamps	194	33.21 N	93.29 W
Stams	64	47.16 N	10.59 E
Stanaford	188	37.48 N	81.09 W
Stanardsville	188	38.17 N	78.26 W
Stanberry	194	40.13 N	94.32 W
Stanborough	260	51.47 N	0.13 W
Stancija-Gorčakovo	85	40.25 N	71.45 E
Stancionno-Ojašinskij	86	55.28 N	83.53 E
Standard, Ab., Can.	182	51.07 N	112.59 W
Standard, Ak., U.S.	180	64.47 N	148.32 W
Standard, Ca., U.S.	226	37.59 N	120.20 W
Standard, Pa., U.S.	214	40.10 N	79.32 W
Standard Oil Company Refinery ⊍[3]	282	37.57 N	122.24 W
Standard Shaft	279b	40.10 N	79.32 W
Standedge Canal Tunnel ◆[5]	262	53.34 N	2.00 W
Standedge Railway Tunnel ◆[5]	262	53.34 N	2.00 W
Standerton	158	26.58 S	29.07 E
Standiford Field ⊠	218	38.11 N	85.44 W
Standing Rock Indian Reservation ◆[4]	198	45.50 N	101.10 W
Standing Stone Creek ≃	214	40.30 N	78.00 W
Standing Stones ⊥	46	58.12 N	6.48 W
Standish, Eng., U.K.	44	53.36 N	2.41 W
Standish, Mi., U.S.	190	43.58 N	83.57 W
Standish Monument ⊥	283	42.01 N	70.41 W
Standon	42	51.53 N	0.02 E
Stanfield, Az., U.S.	200	32.52 N	111.57 W
Stanfield, Or., U.S.	202	45.46 N	119.12 W
Stanford, S. Afr.	158	34.26 S	19.29 E
Stanford, Ca., U.S.	226	37.25 N	122.08 W
Stanford, Ky., U.S.	192	37.31 N	84.39 W
Stanford, Mt., U.S.	202	47.09 N	110.13 W
Stanford Center ◆[9]	282	37.27 N	122.10 W
Stanford Heights	210	42.46 N	73.53 W
Stanford le Hope	42	51.31 N	0.26 E
Stanford Linear Accelerator ⊍[3]	282	37.25 N	122.12 W
Stanford Rivers	260	51.41 N	0.13 E
Stanford University ⊍[2]	282	37.26 N	122.10 W
Stanfordville	210	41.52 N	73.43 W
Stånga	26	57.17 N	18.28 E
Stångån ≃	26	58.27 N	15.37 E
Stångby	41	55.46 N	13.10 E
Stange	26	60.43 N	11.11 E
Stanger	158	29.27 S	31.14 E
Stanghella	64	45.08 N	11.45 E
Stanhope, Eng., U.K.	44	54.45 N	2.01 W
Stanhope, Ia., U.S.	190	42.17 N	93.47 W
Stanhope, N.J., U.S.	210	40.54 N	74.42 W
Stanislaus □[6]	226	37.39 N	121.00 W
Stanislaus ≃	226	37.40 N	121.14 W
Stanislaus, Clark Fork ≃	226	38.22 N	119.52 W
Stanislaus, Middle Fork ≃	226	38.09 N	120.21 W
Stanislaus, North Fork ≃	226	38.09 N	120.21 W
Stanislaus, South Fork ≃	226	38.04 N	120.25 W
Stanislav → Ivano-Frankivs'k, Ukr.	78	48.55 N	24.43 E
Stanislav, Ukr.	78	46.34 N	32.09 E
Stanislavchyk	78	48.58 N	28.07 E
Stanisławów → Ivano-Frankivs'k	78	48.55 N	24.43 E
Stânișoara, Munții ⨳	38	47.10 N	26.00 E
Staňkov	60	49.34 N	13.04 E
Stanley, Austl.	166	40.46 S	145.18 E
Stanley, N.B., Can.	186	46.17 N	66.44 W
Stanley, Falk. Is.	254	51.42 S	57.51 W
Stanley, H.K.	271d	22.13 N	114.12 E
Stanley, Eng., U.K.	44	54.52 N	1.42 W
Stanley, Scot., U.K.	46	56.28 N	3.27 W
Stanley, N.Y., U.S.	210	42.49 N	77.06 W
Stanley, N.C., U.S.	192	35.21 N	81.05 W
Stanley, N.D., U.S.	198	48.19 N	102.23 W
Stanley, Va., U.S.	188	38.34 N	78.30 W
Stanley, Wi., U.S.	190	44.57 N	90.56 W
Stanley ≃	171a	27.09 S	152.32 E
Stanley, Mont ∧[2]	273b	4.19 S	15.15 E
Stanley Bay ⊂	271d	22.12 N	114.12 E
Stanley Falls ∟	154	0.30 N	25.12 E
Stanley Mills	275b	43.46 N	79.44 W
Stanley Mound ∧	271d	22.14 N	114.12 E
Stanley Park ♠, B.C., Can.	224	49.19 N	123.09 W
Stanley Park ♠, Eng., U.K.	262	53.26 N	2.57 W
Stanley Park ♠, Eng., U.K.	262	53.49 N	3.02 W
Stanley Reservoir ⊜[1]	122	11.54 N	77.50 E
Stanleyville → Kisangani	154	0.30 N	25.12 E
Stanlow	44	53.17 N	2.52 W
Stanmore ◆[8]	260	51.37 N	0.19 W
Stannards	210	42.05 N	77.55 W
Stannington	44	55.06 N	1.40 W
Stanovoj chrebet ⨳	74	56.20 N	126.00 E
Stanovoje nagorje (Stanovoy Mountains) ⨳	88	56.00 N	114.00 E
Stanovoj Kolodez'	76	52.51 N	36.16 E
Stanovoy Mountains → Stanovoje nagorje ⨳	88	56.00 N	114.00 E
Stans	58	46.57 N	8.22 E
Stansbury	168b	34.55 S	137.47 E
Stansmore Range ⨳	162	21.23 S	128.33 E
Stansstad	58	46.59 N	8.20 E
Stanstead	206	45.01 N	72.05 W
Stanstead □[6]	206	45.10 N	72.00 W
Stanstead Abbots	42	51.47 N	0.01 E
Stansted	260	51.20 N	0.18 E
Stansted Mountfitchet	42	51.54 N	0.12 E
Stanthorpe	166	28.39 S	151.57 E
Stanton, Eng., U.K.	42	52.19 N	0.53 E
Stanton, Ca., U.S.	228	33.48 N	117.59 W
Stanton, De., U.S.	208	39.43 N	75.37 W
Stanton, Ia., U.S.	198	41.05 N	95.11 W
Stanton, Ky., U.S.	192	37.50 N	83.51 W
Stanton, Mi., U.S.	190	43.17 N	85.04 W
Stanton, Mo., U.S.	219	38.16 N	91.06 W
Stanton, Ne., U.S.	198	41.57 N	97.13 W
Stanton, N.D., U.S.	198	47.19 N	101.22 W
Stanton, Tn., U.S.	194	35.27 N	89.24 W
Stanton, Tx., U.S.	196	32.07 N	101.47 W
Stantonsburg	192	35.36 N	77.49 W
Stanwell	260	51.27 N	0.29 W
Stanwell Moor	260	51.28 N	0.30 W
Stanwood	224	48.14 N	122.22 W
Stanwyck Estates	285	39.42 N	75.33 W
Stanychno-Luhans'ke	83	48.39 N	39.30 E
Stanzach	58	47.23 N	10.34 E
Stanz im Mürztal	61	47.28 N	15.30 E
Stapelburg	54	51.53 N	10.40 E
Stapelfeld	52	53.36 N	10.13 E
Staphorst	52	52.37 N	6.12 E
Stapleford	42	52.56 N	1.16 W
Stapleford Abbotts	260	51.38 N	0.10 E
Stapleford Aerodrome ⊠	260	51.39 N	0.08 E
Stapleford Tawney	260	51.40 N	0.11 E
Staplehurst	42	51.10 N	0.33 E
Staples	198	46.21 N	94.47 W
Stapleton, Al., U.S.	194	30.44 N	87.47 W
Stapleton, Ne., U.S.	198	41.28 N	100.30 W
Stąporków	30	51.09 N	20.34 E
Star', Ross.	76	53.37 N	34.09 E
Star, Ms., U.S.	194	32.05 N	90.02 W
Star, N.C., U.S.	192	35.24 N	79.47 W
Stará Boleslav	54	50.12 N	14.42 E
Starachowice	30	51.03 N	21.04 E
Stara Fužina	64	46.17 N	13.54 E
Staraja	265a	59.55 N	30.38 E
Staraja Belica, Bela.	76	54.42 N	29.38 E
Staraja Belica, Ross.	78	51.59 N	35.13 E
Staraja Belogorka	80	52.05 N	53.17 E
Staraja Derevn'a ◆[8]	265a	59.59 N	30.15 E
Staraja Duginka	82	54.20 N	38.45 E
Staraja Kriuša	78	50.12 N	41.09 E
Staraja Kulatka	80	52.43 N	47.37 E
Staraja Kupavna	82	55.48 N	38.10 E
Staraja Majna	80	54.36 N	48.57 E
Staraja Poltavka	80	50.28 N	46.28 E
Staraja Porubežka	80	52.03 N	49.11 E
Staraja Račejka	80	53.22 N	48.03 E
Staraja Rudn'a	76	52.50 N	30.17 E
Staraja Russa	76	58.00 N	31.23 E
Staraja Ruza	82	55.39 N	36.20 E
Staraja Sachča	80	54.25 N	49.58 E
Staraja Sitn'a	82	54.56 N	38.09 E
Staraja Terizmorga	80	54.16 N	44.32 E
Staraja Toropa	76	56.17 N	31.40 E
Staraja Veduga	78	51.48 N	38.31 E
Staraja Vičuga	80	57.16 N	41.53 E
Stara Mayachka	78	46.30 N	33.11 E
Staranzano	64	45.49 N	13.30 E
Stara Pazova	38	44.59 N	20.10 E
Stara Planina (Balkan Mountains) ⨳	38	42.45 N	25.00 E
Stará Role	54	50.14 N	12.47 E
Stara Synyava	78	49.36 N	27.37 E
Stara Ushytsya	78	48.35 N	27.07 E
Starav, Ben ∧	46	56.32 N	5.03 W
Stará Voda	60	50.00 N	12.36 E
Stara Vyzhivka	78	51.27 N	24.24 E
Stara Zagora	38	42.25 N	25.38 E
Starbejevo	265b	55.55 N	37.28 E
Starbrick	214	41.50 N	79.12 W
Starbuck, Mb., Can.	184	49.46 N	97.36 W
Starbuck, Mn., U.S.	198	45.36 N	95.31 W
Starbuck, Wa., U.S.	202	46.31 N	118.07 W
Starbuck I	14	5.37 S	155.53 W
Starchenkove	78	47.17 N	36.59 E
Star City, Sk., Can.	184	52.53 N	104.21 W
Star City, Ar., U.S.	194	33.56 N	91.50 W
Star City, In., U.S.	216	40.58 N	86.33 W
Starcross	42	50.38 N	3.27 W
Stare Czarnowo	54	53.16 N	14.45 E
Staré Sedliště	60	49.45 N	12.42 E
Starford	214	40.42 N	78.58 W
Stargard Szczeciński (Stargard in Pommern)	30	53.20 N	15.02 E
Stargo	200	33.04 N	109.21 W
Star Harbour ⊂	175e	10.47 S	162.18 E
Stari Bar	38	42.06 N	19.08 E
Starica, Ross.	76	56.30 N	34.56 E
Starica, Ross.	76	59.04 N	29.30 E
Starica, Ross.	80	48.13 N	45.56 E
Stari Grad	36	43.11 N	16.36 E
Starij R'ad	76	58.05 N	34.54 E
Starina	76	59.37 N	44.42 E
Stari Popylyukhy	78	48.18 N	28.55 E
Stari Sanzhary	78	49.25 N	34.27 E
Stari Vlah ◆[1]	38	43.35 N	20.15 E
Star Junction	214	40.04 N	79.46 W
Stark □[6]	214	40.48 N	81.22 W
Starke	192	29.56 N	82.06 W
Starke □[6]	216	41.18 N	86.37 W
Starkey	210	42.32 N	76.56 W
Starkville	194	33.27 N	88.49 W
Star Lake	224	47.22 N	122.18 W
Star Mountains ⨳	164	5.05 S	141.05 E
Starnberg	60	48.00 N	11.20 E
Starnberger See ⊜	64	47.55 N	11.18 E
Starnikovo	82	55.22 N	38.24 E
Staroalejskoje	86	51.00 N	82.01 E
Starobačaty	86	54.14 N	86.07 E
Starobaltačevo	86	56.01 N	55.56 E
Starobesheve	83	47.44 N	38.03 E
Starobil's'k	83	49.16 N	38.56 E
Starobin	76	52.44 N	27.28 E
Staročerkasskaja	83	47.15 N	40.03 E
Starocuruchajtuj	88	50.12 N	119.15 E
Staroderev'ankov-Skaja	78	46.08 N	38.58 E
Starodub	76	52.35 N	32.46 E
Starod'umejevo	80	55.16 N	54.22 E
Starogan'kino	80	53.55 N	52.15 E
Starogard Gdański	30	53.59 N	18.33 E
Staroihnativka	83	47.32 N	37.47 E
Staroje	76	59.16 N	40.40 E
Staroje Bajsarovo	80	55.31 N	53.54 E
Staroje Drožžanoje	80	54.44 N	47.34 E
Staroje Ibrajkino	80	54.52 N	51.02 E
Staroje Jaškino	80	52.49 N	52.57 E
Staroje Jermakovo	80	54.04 N	51.59 E
Staroje Oleničevo	80	45.34 N	47.11 E
Staroje Rachino	76	58.08 N	32.39 E
Staroje Šajgovo	80	54.18 N	44.26 E
Staroje Šajmurzino	80	54.45 N	47.58 E
Staroje Selo	76	55.14 N	29.54 E
Staroje Sindrovo	80	54.25 N	44.06 E
Staroje Slavkino	80	52.34 N	45.08 E
Staroje Ustje	80	53.28 N	41.51 E
Starojurjevo	80	53.21 N	40.42 E
Starokostyantyniv	78	49.46 N	27.13 E
Starokozache	78	46.21 N	29.59 E
Starokuručevo	80	55.09 N	54.04 E
Starolaspa	83	47.34 N	37.59 E
Staroleuškovskaja	78	45.59 N	39.44 E
Starominskaja	78	46.31 N	39.04 E
Staromlynivka	78	47.42 N	36.49 E
Staromušta	80	55.49 N	54.14 E
Staromykhaylivka	83	47.58 N	37.36 E
Staronikolajevo	82	55.37 N	36.16 E
Staro-Podgorodneje	82	54.46 N	38.57 E
Staropokrovka	85	42.50 N	75.18 E
Staroščerbinovskaja	78	46.37 N	38.40 E
Staroseslavino	80	53.12 N	40.25 E
Starošešminsk	80	55.22 N	51.15 E
Starosiedle	54	51.50 N	14.50 E
Starosoldatskoje	86	56.12 N	72.37 E
Starosubchangulovo	86	53.06 N	57.26 E
Starotimoškino	24	53.43 N	47.32 E
Starotitarovskaja	78	45.14 N	37.09 E
Staroutkinsk	86	57.14 N	59.20 E
Starovirivka	78	49.33 N	35.42 E
Starožilovo	80	54.14 N	39.55 E
Starožil'sk	80	56.34 N	47.17 E
Star Peak ∧	204	40.32 N	118.10 W
Starr	214	41.32 N	79.22 W
Starrucca	210	41.54 N	75.28 W
Start Bay ⊂	42	50.17 N	3.36 W
Start Point ›	42	50.13 N	3.38 W
Startup	224	47.52 N	121.44 W
Starvation Reservoir ⊜[1]	200	40.15 N	110.30 W
Starved Rock State Park ♠	216	41.19 N	88.58 W
Staryj Ajbesi	80	54.57 N	47.03 E
Staryj Bagr'až	80	54.54 N	51.39 E
Staryj Bir'uz'ak	84	44.47 N	46.54 E
Staryj Bol'ševik	265b	55.57 N	37.47 E
Staryj Chop'or	80	51.30 N	42.58 E
Staryj Čindant	88	50.33 N	115.33 E
Staryje Burasy	80	52.16 N	46.09 E
Staryje Dorogi	76	53.02 N	28.16 E
Staryje Maty	80	55.14 N	53.55 E
Staryje Turdaki	80	53.55 N	45.29 E
Staryje Z'atcy	80	57.21 N	52.39 E
Staryj Kazangal	80	50.15 N	47.39 E
Staryj Kistruss	80	54.28 N	40.34 E
Staryj Lesken	84	43.20 N	43.55 E
Staryj Medved'	76	58.18 N	30.30 E
Staryj Oskol	78	51.19 N	37.51 E
Staryj Terek ≃	84	44.00 N	47.24 E
Staryj Tukšum	80	53.42 N	48.33 E
Starý Plzenec	60	49.42 N	13.28 E
Stary Sącz	30	49.34 N	20.38 E
Staryy Chortoryys'k	78	51.15 N	25.54 E
Staryy Krym, Ukr.	78	45.03 N	35.05 E
Staryy Krym, Ukr.	83	47.10 N	37.30 E
Staryy Merchyk	78	49.58 N	35.46 E
Staryy Sambir	78	49.27 N	22.59 E
Stassfurt	54	51.51 N	11.34 E
Staszów	30	50.34 N	21.20 E
State Center	190	42.01 N	93.09 W
State College	214	40.47 N	77.51 W
State Fair Grounds ♠	284b	39.27 N	76.38 W
Stateline, Ca., U.S.	226	38.57 N	119.57 W
State Line, Ms., U.S.	194	31.26 N	88.28 W
Stateline, Nv., U.S.	204	38.58 N	119.56 W
Staten Island I	276	40.35 N	74.09 W
Staten Island Mall ◆[9]	276	40.35 N	74.10 W
Statenville	192	30.42 N	83.01 W
State Park Place	219	38.40 N	90.03 W
State Road	192	36.19 N	80.52 W
Statesboro	192	32.26 N	81.47 W
Statesville	192	35.46 N	80.53 W
Stateville Correctional Center ⊍	278	41.35 N	88.06 W
Station Peak	162	21.10 S	118.11 E
Statte	68	40.34 N	17.12 E
Statue of Liberty National Monument ♠	210	40.41 N	74.03 W
Staubbachfall ∟	58	46.35 N	7.55 E
Staufen	58	47.53 N	7.44 E
Staufenberg	56	50.40 N	8.43 E
Staughton Vale	169	37.51 S	144.17 E
Staunton, Il., U.S.	219	39.00 N	89.47 W
Staunton, Va., U.S.	188	38.08 N	79.04 W
Staunton → Roanoke ≃	192	35.56 N	76.43 W
Stavanger	26	58.58 N	5.45 E
Stave ≃	224	49.10 N	122.26 W
Stave Lake ⊜	182	49.15 N	122.21 W
Staveley	44	53.16 N	1.20 W
Stavelot	56	50.23 N	5.56 E
Stavely, Ab., Can.	182	50.10 N	113.38 W
Stavely, Eng., U.K.	44	54.22 N	2.49 W
Staveren	52	52.53 N	5.22 E
Stavern	26	59.00 N	10.02 E
Stavne	78	48.59 N	22.40 E
Stavropol', Ross.	72	45.02 N	41.59 E
Stavropol → Toljatti, Ross.	80	53.31 N	49.26 E
Stavropol' Kraj □[8]	84	44.38 N	43.30 E
Stavrovo	80	56.08 N	40.00 E
Stavsnäs	40	59.17 N	18.41 E
Stavyshche	78	49.23 N	30.12 E
Stawell	166	37.04 S	142.46 E
Stawell ≃	166	20.38 S	142.55 E
Stawiski	30	53.23 N	22.09 E
Stawiszyn	30	51.55 N	18.07 E
Staxigoe	46	58.28 N	3.04 W
Stayky	78	50.05 N	30.54 E
Stayner	212	44.25 N	80.05 W
Stayton	202	44.48 N	122.47 W
Stazzema	64	43.59 N	10.19 E
Steamboat	226	39.22 N	119.44 W
Steamboat Creek ≃	226	39.31 N	119.42 W
Steamboat Mountain ∧	200	41.58 N	108.58 W
Steamboat Slough ≃	226	38.11 N	121.40 W
Steamboat Springs	200	40.29 N	106.49 W
Steamburg	210	42.07 N	78.54 W
Stearns	192	36.41 N	84.28 W
Stearns Pond ⊜	283	42.37 N	71.04 W
Stębark	30	53.30 N	20.08 E
Stebbins	180	63.32 N	162.18 W
Stebliv	78	49.24 N	31.06 E
Stechow	54	52.38 N	12.28 E
Steckborn	58	47.40 N	8.55 E
Stederdorf	52	52.21 N	10.15 E
Stedten	54	51.26 N	11.41 E
Stedum	52	53.18 N	6.41 E
Steeg	58	47.14 N	10.17 E
Steel ≃	190	48.46 N	86.54 W
Steel City	210	40.38 N	75.20 W
Steele, Mo., U.S.	194	36.05 N	89.49 W
Steele, N.D., U.S.	198	46.51 N	99.54 W
Steele ◆[8]	263	51.27 N	7.05 E
Steele, Mount ∧	200	41.50 N	107.00 W
Steele Creek ≃, Tx., U.S.	222	31.13 N	96.19 W
Steele Creek ≃, Tx., U.S.	222	32.01 N	97.28 W
Steeles Corners	275b	43.48 N	79.25 W
Steeleville	194	38.00 N	89.39 W
Steelhead	224	49.13 N	122.19 W
Steel's Drift	158	27.21 S	29.30 E
Steels Point ›	174c	29.02 S	168.00 E
Steels Run ≃	279b	40.25 N	79.38 W
Steelton, N.Y., U.S.	284a	42.47 N	78.49 W
Steelton, Pa., U.S.	208	40.14 N	76.50 W
Steelville	194	37.58 N	91.21 W
Steenbergen	52	51.35 N	4.19 E
Steenburg Lake ⊜	212	44.50 N	77.41 W
Steenderen	52	52.04 N	6.11 E
Steens Mountain ⨳	202	42.35 N	118.40 W
Steenvoorde	50	50.48 N	2.35 E
Steenwijk	52	52.47 N	6.08 E
Steepbank ≃	184	57.01 N	111.28 W
Steephill Lake ⊜	184	55.58 N	103.08 W
Steep Holm I	42	51.21 N	3.07 W
Steeping ≃	44	53.06 N	0.18 E
Steeple Claydon	42	51.56 N	0.59 W
Steep Point ›	162	26.08 S	113.08 E
Steep Rock	184	51.26 N	98.48 W
Stefanie, Lake (Chew Bahir) ⊜, Afr.	144	4.40 N	36.50 E
Stefanie, Lake → Chew Bahir ⊜, Afr.	144	4.40 N	36.50 E
Stefansson Island I	176	73.20 N	105.45 W
Ştefan Vodă	38	44.19 N	27.19 E
Steffisburg	58	46.47 N	7.39 E
Steg	58	47.21 N	8.56 E
Stegalovka	76	52.24 N	38.19 E
Stege	41	54.59 N	12.18 E
Stegeborg	26	58.26 N	16.35 E
Stege Bugt ⊂	41	55.01 N	12.05 E
Stegelitz	54	53.08 N	13.51 E
Steger	216	41.28 N	87.38 W
Stegersbach	61	47.10 N	16.10 E
Steglitz ◆[8]	264a	52.28 N	13.19 E
Stehag	41	55.54 N	13.23 E
Stehekin	224	48.18 N	120.39 W
Stehekin ≃	224	48.21 N	120.40 W
Ştei	38	46.32 N	22.28 E
Steiermark □[3]	30	47.10 N	15.10 E
Steigerwald ⨳	56	49.40 N	10.20 E
Steigra	54	51.18 N	11.39 E
Steilacoom	224	47.10 N	122.36 W
Steimbke	52	52.40 N	9.22 E
Stein, Dtsch.	60	49.25 N	11.01 E
Stein, Ned.	56	50.57 N	5.46 E
Stein, Schw.	58	47.33 N	7.58 E
Steina	54	51.12 N	14.01 E
Steinach, Dtsch.	54	50.25 N	11.10 E
Steinach, Dtsch.	58	48.18 N	8.04 E
Steinach, Öst.	64	47.05 N	11.28 E
Steinach ≃	54	50.11 N	11.12 E
Steinamanger → Szombathely	30	47.14 N	16.38 E
Stein am Rhein	58	47.40 N	8.51 E
Steinau	56	50.23 N	9.27 E
Steinbach, Mb., Can.	184	49.32 N	96.41 W
Steinbach, Dtsch.	56	48.43 N	8.10 E
Steinbach-Hallenberg	54	50.42 N	10.34 E
Steinberg ∧[2]	263	51.05 N	7.27 E
Steinberger Slough ≃	282	37.33 N	122.13 W
Steinbourg	56	48.46 N	7.25 E
Steindorf	61	46.42 N	14.01 E
Steinen	58	47.38 N	7.44 E
Steinernes Meer ⨳	64	47.30 N	12.58 E
Steinfeld, Dtsch.	52	52.35 N	8.12 E
Steinfeld, Dtsch.	54	50.22 N	10.44 E
Steinfeld, Öst.	64	46.45 N	13.15 E
Steinfort	56	49.40 N	5.55 E
Steinforth	263	51.09 N	6.32 E
Steinfurt	52	52.09 N	7.21 E
Steingaden	58	47.42 N	10.51 E
Steinhagen, Dtsch.	52	52.00 N	8.24 E
Steinhagen, Dtsch.	54	54.13 N	12.59 E
Steinhatchee ≃	192	29.40 N	83.24 W
Steinhausen	156	21.49 S	18.20 E
Steinhausen ⊍[1]	58	48.01 N	9.41 E
Steinheid	54	50.28 N	11.04 E
Steinheim, Dtsch.	52	51.52 N	9.05 E
Steinheim, Dtsch.	56	48.58 N	9.16 E
Steinheim, Dtsch.	58	48.01 N	10.09 E
Steinhöfel	54	52.24 N	14.10 E
Steinhöring	60	48.05 N	12.02 E
Steinhude	52	52.27 N	9.21 E
Steinhuder Meer ⊜	52	52.28 N	9.19 E
Steinkjer	26	64.01 N	11.30 E
Steinkopf	156	29.18 S	17.43 E
Steinloge	52	52.54 N	8.19 E
Stein-Neukirch	56	50.41 N	8.03 E
Steinpass)(	64	47.39 N	12.45 E
Steinsdorf	54	52.02 N	14.40 E
Steinshamn	26	62.47 N	6.29 E
Steinstücken ◆[8]	264a	52.23 N	13.08 E
Steinwiesen	54	50.17 N	11.28 E
Stekene	50	51.12 N	4.02 E
Stekl'anka	76	59.08 N	41.37 E
Steklino	76	56.51 N	32.10 E
Steksovo	80	55.17 N	43.25 E
Stella, It.	62	44.24 N	8.30 E
Stella, S. Afr.	158	26.38 S	24.48 E
Stella, Ne., U.S.	198	40.13 N	95.46 W
Stella Niagara	210	43.12 N	79.02 W
Stella-Plage	50	50.29 N	1.35 E
Stellaquo Indian Reserve ◆[4]	182	54.03 N	124.55 W
Stellarton	186	45.34 N	62.40 W
Stelle	52	53.23 N	10.06 E
Stellenbosch	158	33.58 S	18.50 E
Steller, Mount ∧	180	60.30 N	143.02 W
Stelvio, Parco Nazionale dello ♠	64	46.30 N	10.40 E
Stelvio, Passo dello)(	64	46.32 N	10.27 E
Stemwede	52	52.25 N	8.27 E
Stenay	56	49.29 N	5.11 E
Stendal	54	52.36 N	11.51 E
Stende	76	57.09 N	22.33 E
Stenden	263	51.25 N	6.27 E
Stenhammar slott ⊥	40	59.03 N	16.31 E
Stenhouse Bay	166	35.17 S	136.56 E
Stenhousemuir	46	56.02 N	3.48 W
Stenico	64	46.03 N	10.51 E
Stenlille	41	55.32 N	11.36 E
Stenløse	41	55.46 N	12.12 E
Stenness, Loch of ⊜	46	59.00 N	3.15 W
Stenón	267c	37.58 N	23.25 E
Stenón Návstathmou ⩌	267c	37.58 N	23.33 E
Stensätra	40	60.36 N	16.44 E
Stensele	24	65.05 N	17.09 E
Stenstorp	26	58.16 N	13.43 E
Stenstrup	41	55.07 N	10.31 E
Stentrop	263	51.30 N	7.49 E
Stenungsund	26	58.05 N	11.49 E
Stepan'	78	51.10 N	26.18 E
Stepanakert → Xankändi	84	39.49 N	46.44 E
Stepanavan	84	41.00 N	44.23 E
Stepancevo, Ross.	80	56.08 N	41.42 E
Stepancevo, Ross.	82	56.22 N	36.10 E
Stepancy	78	49.42 N	31.18 E
Stepanivka	78	50.58 N	34.37 E
Stepano-Krynka	83	47.55 N	38.21 E
Stepanovka, Ross.	80	52.04 N	53.02 E
Stepanovka, Ross.	86	57.13 N	67.26 E
Stepanovo	82	55.43 N	38.28 E
Stepanovskoje	265b	55.47 N	37.10 E
Stepanščino	82	55.15 N	38.30 E
Stepenitz ≃	54	53.48 N	11.10 E
Stephans-Dom ⊍[1]	264b	48.12 N	16.23 E
Stephanskirchen	64	47.51 N	12.11 E
Stephen	198	48.27 N	96.52 W
Stephen A. Forbes State Park ♠	219	38.44 N	88.46 W
Stephen F. Austin State Historic Park ♠	222	29.48 N	96.05 W
Stephens	194	33.24 N	93.04 W
Stephens, Cape ›	172	40.42 S	173.57 E
Stephens, Port ⊂	166	32.45 S	152.05 E
Stephens City	188	39.05 N	78.13 W
Stephens Creek	166	31.50 S	141.30 E
Stephens Island I	182	54.10 N	130.45 W
Stephens Knob ∧[2]	192	36.37 N	84.20 W
Stephens Lake ⊜[1]	184	56.26 N	95.07 W
Stephens Mills	210	42.23 N	77.38 W
Stephenson	190	45.24 N	87.36 W
Stephenson, Lake ⊜	222	29.35 N	94.40 W
Stephenson, Mount ∧	9	69.49 S	69.43 W
Stephens Passage ⩌	180	57.50 N	133.50 W
Stephentown	210	42.33 N	73.23 W
Stephentown Center	210	42.34 N	73.25 W
Stephenville, Nf., Can.	186	48.33 N	58.35 W
Stephenville, Tx., U.S.	196	32.13 N	98.12 W
Stephenville Crossing	186	48.30 N	58.26 W
Stepn'ak	86	52.50 N	70.50 E
Stepney ◆[8]	260	51.31 N	0.02 W
Stepnica	54	53.40 N	14.36 E
Stepnoj	80	48.56 N	45.36 E
Stepnoje, Ross.	80	51.24 N	46.52 E
Stepnoje, Ross.	84	44.17 N	44.36 E
Step Pyramid → Şaqqārah ⊥	142	29.52 N	31.14 E
Steps Point ›	174u	14.22 S	170.45 W
Steptoe Valley V	204	39.25 N	114.45 W
Stepurino	76	56.24 N	35.16 E
Sterdyń	30	52.35 N	22.18 E
Stereá Ellás □[4]	38	38.30 N	23.00 E
Sterkaar	158	31.05 S	23.42 E
Sterkrade ◆[8]	263	51.31 N	6.51 E
Sterkspruit	158	30.32 S	27.22 E
Sterkstroom	158	31.32 S	26.32 E
Sterlibaševo	86	53.28 N	55.15 E
Sterling, S. Afr.	158	31.16 S	21.28 E
Sterling, Ak., U.S.	180	60.32 N	150.48 W
Sterling, Co., U.S.	198	40.37 N	103.12 W
Sterling, Ct., U.S.	207	41.42 N	71.49 W
Sterling, Il., U.S.	190	41.47 N	89.41 W
Sterling, Ks., U.S.	198	38.12 N	98.12 W
Sterling, Ma., U.S.	207	42.26 N	71.45 W
Sterling, Mi., U.S.	190	44.02 N	84.01 W
Sterling, Ne., U.S.	198	40.27 N	96.22 W
Sterling, N.Y., U.S.	210	43.20 N	76.39 W
Sterling, Oh., U.S.	214	40.58 N	81.51 W
Sterling, Ok., U.S.	196	34.45 N	98.10 W
Sterling, Va., U.S.	208	39.00 N	77.25 W
Sterling City	196	31.50 N	100.59 W
Sterling Creek ≃	210	43.20 N	76.42 W
Sterling Forest Lake ⊜	276	41.10 N	74.16 W
Sterling Heights	214	42.34 N	83.01 W
Sterling Junction	207	42.24 N	71.46 W
Sterling Park	282	37.41 N	122.26 W
Sterling Run	214	41.25 N	78.12 W
Sterlington	194	32.41 N	92.05 W
Sterlitamak	86	53.37 N	55.58 E
Šternberg	54	53.43 N	11.49 E
Šternberk	30	49.44 N	17.18 E
Sternstein ∧	61	48.34 N	14.16 E
Sterup	41	54.44 N	9.44 E
Sterzing → Vipiteno	64	46.54 N	11.26 E
Stęszew	30	52.18 N	16.42 E
Štětí	54	50.25 N	14.23 E
Stetson Pond ⊜	283	42.02 N	70.50 W
Stetten am kalten Markt	58	48.07 N	9.04 E
Stettin → Szczecin	30	53.24 N	14.32 E
Stettler	182	52.19 N	112.43 W
Steuben □[6], In., U.S.	216	41.38 N	85.00 W
Steuben □[6], N.Y., U.S.	210	42.20 N	77.19 W
Steubenville	214	40.22 N	80.38 W
Stevenage	42	51.55 N	0.14 W
Stevens, N.J., U.S.	285	40.05 N	74.49 W
Stevens, Pa., U.S.	208	40.13 N	76.09 W
Stevens, Lake ⊜	224	48.01 N	122.05 W
Stevens, Mount ∧	172	40.48 S	172.27 E
Stevens Creek ≃, Ca., U.S.	282	37.26 N	122.05 W
Stevens Creek ≃, S.C., U.S.	192	33.34 N	82.03 W
Stevens Creek Park ♠	282	37.17 N	122.04 W
Stevens Creek Reservoir ⊜[1]	282	37.17 N	122.05 W
Stevens Institute of Technology ⊍[2]	276	40.44 N	74.02 W
Stevenson, Al., U.S.	194	34.52 N	85.50 W
Stevenson, Md., U.S.	284b	39.25 N	76.43 W
Stevenson, Wa., U.S.	224	45.42 N	121.53 W
Stevenson Creek ≃	162	27.06 S	135.33 E
Stevenson Entrance ⩌	180	58.45 N	152.20 W
Stevenson Lake ⊜	184	53.56 N	96.09 W
Stevens Pass)(	224	47.45 N	121.04 W
Stevens Peak ∧	202	47.27 N	115.46 W
Stevens Point	190	44.31 N	89.34 W
Stevenston	46	55.39 N	4.45 W
Stevens Village	180	66.00 N	149.05 W
Stevensville, On., Can.	284a	42.57 N	79.04 W
Stevensville, Md., U.S.	208	38.58 N	76.18 W
Stevensville, Mi., U.S.	216	42.00 N	86.31 W
Stevensville, Mt., U.S.	202	46.30 N	114.05 W
Stevensville, Pa., U.S.	210	41.46 N	76.11 W
Stevinson	226	37.20 N	120.51 W
Stevns Klint ⊥[4]	41	55.18 N	12.27 E
Steward	216	41.51 N	89.01 W
Stewardson	219	39.15 N	88.37 W
Stewart, B.C., Can.	182	55.56 N	129.59 W
Stewart, Mn., U.S.	190	44.43 N	94.29 W
Stewart ≃	180	63.18 N	139.25 W
Stewart, Cape ›	164	11.57 S	134.45 E
Stewart, Isla I	254	54.52 S	71.12 W
Stewart, Mount ∧	166	20.12 S	145.29 E
Stewart Island I	172	47.00 S	167.50 E
Stewart Islands II	175e	8.25 S	162.52 E
Stewart Lake ⊜	219	40.09 N	90.16 W
Stewart Manor	276	40.43 N	73.41 W
Stewarton	46	55.41 N	4.31 W
Stewartstown, N. Ire., U.K.	48	54.35 N	6.41 W
Stewartstown, Pa., U.S.	208	39.45 N	76.35 W
Stewartsville, Mo., U.S.	194	39.45 N	94.29 W
Stewartsville, N.J., U.S.	208	40.41 N	75.06 W
Stewartsville, Pa., U.S.	279b	40.21 N	79.46 W
Stewart Valley	184	50.36 N	107.50 W
Stewartville	190	43.51 N	92.29 W
Stewiacke	186	45.08 N	63.21 W
Steyerberg	52	52.34 N	9.01 E
Steyning	42	50.53 N	0.20 W
Steynsburg	158	31.15 S	25.49 E
Steynsrus	158	27.58 S	27.33 E
Steyr	61	48.03 N	14.25 E
Steyr ≃	61	48.02 N	14.25 E
Steyregg	61	48.17 N	14.22 E
Steytlerville	158	33.21 S	24.21 E
Stežki	80	53.06 N	41.13 E
Stezzano	62	45.38 N	9.39 E
Sthal	126	24.12 N	89.44 E
Ştia	66	43.48 N	11.42 E
Štiavnické vrchy ⨳	30	48.40 N	18.45 E
Stickle Pond ⊜	276	40.59 N	74.25 W
Stickney, Eng., U.K.	44	53.05 N	0.01 E
Stickney, Il., U.S.	216	41.49 N	87.46 W
Stickney, S.D., U.S.	198	43.35 N	98.26 W
Stidsvig	41	56.12 N	13.08 E
Stiefingbach ≃	61	46.47 N	15.35 E
Stiege	54	51.40 N	10.53 E
Stiene	76	57.26 N	24.34 E
Stienitzfliess ≃	264a	52.33 N	13.43 E
Stienitz-See ⊜	264a	52.30 N	13.49 E
Stiens	52	53.15 N	5.45 E
Stiepel ◆[8]	263	51.25 N	7.15 E
Stif	148	36.09 N	5.26 E
Stif □[5]	148	36.15 N	5.10 E
Stiftskirche ⊍[1]	263	51.23 N	7.00 E
Stige	41	55.26 N	10.25 E
Stigler	196	35.15 N	95.07 W
Stigliano	68	40.24 N	16.14 E
Stigtomta	40	58.48 N	16.47 E
Stih, hora ∧	78	48.37 N	23.11 E
Stikine ≃	180	56.40 N	132.30 W
Stikine Ranges ⨳	180	58.45 N	130.00 W
Stiklestad	26	63.48 N	11.33 E
Stilbaai	158	34.24 S	21.26 E
Stiles	210	40.40 N	75.30 W
Stiles Pond ⊜	283	42.41 N	71.02 W
Stilesville	210	42.05 N	75.24 W
Stilfontein	158	26.50 S	26.50 E
Stilís	38	38.55 N	22.36 E
Still	148	34.20 N	5.51 E
Stillaguamish ≃	224	48.11 N	122.22 W
Stillaguamish, North Fork ≃	224	48.11 N	122.07 W
Stillaguamish, South Fork ≃	224	48.11 N	122.07 W
Stillhouse Hollow Lake ⊜[1]	222	31.00 N	97.35 W
Stilling	41	56.04 N	10.00 E
Stillman Valley	216	42.07 N	89.11 W
Stillmore	192	32.26 N	82.12 W
Still Pond	208	39.19 N	76.02 W
Still Run ≃	285	39.49 N	75.18 W
Stillwater, B.C., Can.	182	49.46 N	124.18 W
Stillwater, Mn., U.S.	190	45.03 N	92.48 W
Stillwater, N.J., U.S.	210	41.02 N	74.52 W
Stillwater, N.Y., U.S.	210	42.56 N	73.39 W
Stillwater, Oh., U.S.	214	40.20 N	81.18 W
Stillwater, Ok., U.S.	196	36.06 N	97.03 W
Stillwater, Pa., U.S.	210	41.09 N	76.22 W
Stillwater ≃, Mt., U.S.	202	45.38 N	109.17 W
Stillwater ≃, Oh., U.S.	218	39.47 N	84.12 W
Stillwater Creek ≃	214	40.25 N	81.22 W
Stillwater Range ⨳	204	39.50 N	118.15 W
Stillwell, Il., U.S.	219	40.13 N	91.11 W
Stillwell, Ok., U.S.	194	35.49 N	94.38 W
Stilo	68	38.29 N	16.28 E
Stilo, Punta ›	68	38.28 N	16.36 E
Stimberg ∧[2]	263	51.40 N	7.15 E
Stimigliano	66	42.18 N	12.34 E
Stimson, Mount ∧	202	48.31 N	113.36 W
Stînca-Costești, Lacul ⊜[1]	38	47.55 N	27.10 E
Stinchar ≃	44	55.06 N	5.00 W
Stinear Nunataks ⨳	9	69.42 S	64.40 E
Stine Canal ≅	226	35.15 N	119.08 W
Stine Mountain ∧	202	45.44 N	113.07 W
Stingray Point ›	208	37.33 N	76.18 W
Stinking Water Creek ≃	198	40.22 N	101.07 W
Stinnett	196	35.49 N	101.26 W
Stintino	71	40.56 N	8.13 E
Stintonville	273d	26.14 S	28.13 E
Štip	38	41.44 N	22.12 E
Stiperstones ∧	42	52.35 N	2.56 W
Stiring-Wendel	56	49.12 N	6.56 E
Stírka ∧	60	49.24 N	13.34 E
Stirling, Austl.	162	21.44 S	133.45 E
Stirling, Austl.	168a	31.54 S	115.47 E
Stirling, Austl.	168b	35.00 S	138.43 E
Stirling, Ab., Can.	182	49.30 N	112.31 W
Stirling, On., Can.	212	44.18 N	77.33 W
Stirling, Scot., U.K.	46	56.07 N	3.57 W
Stirling, N.J., U.S.	210	40.40 N	74.29 W
Stirling, Mount ∧	162	31.50 S	117.38 E
Stirling Castle ⊥	46	56.07 N	3.57 W
Stirling City	204	39.54 N	121.31 W
Stirling Range ⨳	162	34.23 S	117.50 E
Stirling Range National Park ♠	162	34.22 S	118.00 E
Stirling Reservoir ⊜[1]	168a	33.08 S	116.03 E
Stirrat	192	37.43 N	82.00 W
Stissing Mountain ∧	210	41.57 N	73.42 W
Štitary	61	48.56 N	15.51 E
Stittsville	212	45.15 N	75.55 W
Stittville	210	43.13 N	75.17 W
Stjärnhov	40	59.05 N	17.00 E
Stjärnsund, Sve.	40	60.26 N	16.12 E
Stjärnsund, Sve.	40	58.51 N	14.55 E
Stjernøya I	24	70.18 N	22.45 E
Stjørdalshalsen	26	63.28 N	10.56 E
Stöberhai ∧	54	51.39 N	10.34 E
Stobi ⊥	38	41.33 N	21.59 E
Stock	260	51.40 N	0.27 E
Stock, Étang du ⊜	56	48.45 N	6.55 E
Stockach	58	47.51 N	9.00 E
Stöckalp	58	46.48 N	8.17 E
Stockamöllan	41	55.57 N	13.22 E
Stockbridge, Eng., U.K.	42	51.07 N	1.29 W
Stockbridge, Ga., U.S.	192	33.32 N	84.14 W
Stockbridge, Ma., U.S.	207	42.17 N	73.19 W
Stockbridge, Mi., U.S.	216	42.27 N	84.10 W
Stockbridge Bowl ⊜	207	42.20 N	73.19 W
Stockbridge Indian Reservation ◆[4]	190	44.52 N	88.53 W
Stockbury	260	51.20 N	0.39 E

Symbol	English	Deutsch	Español	Français	Português
≃	River	Fluß	Río	Rivière	Rio
≅	Canal	Kanal	Canal	Canal	Canal
∟	Waterfall, Rapids	Wasserfall, Stromschnellen	Cascada, Rápidos	Chute d'eau, Rapides	Cascata, Rápidos
⩌	Strait	Meeresstraße	Estrecho	Détroit	Estreito
⊂	Bay, Gulf	Bucht, Golf	Bahía, Golfo	Baie, Golfe	Baía, Golfo
⊜	Lake, Lakes	See, Seen	Lago, Lagos	Lac, Lacs	Lago, Lagos
⩩	Swamp	Sumpf	Pantano	Marais	Pântano
≂	Ice Features, Glacier	Eis- und Gletscherformen	Accidentes Glaciales	Formes glaciaires	Acidentes glaciares
≚	Other Hydrographic Features	Andere Hydrographische Objekte	Otros Elementos Hidrográficos	Autres données hydrographiques	Outros acidentes hidrográficos
✤	Submarine Features	Untermeerische Objekte	Accidentes Submarinos	Formes de relief sous-marin	Acidentes submarinos
□	Political Unit	Politische Einheit	Unidad Política	Entité politique	Unidade política
⊍	Cultural Institution	Kulturelle Institution	Institución Cultural	Institution culturelle	Instituição cultural
⊥	Historical Site	Historische Stätte	Sitio Histórico	Site historique	Sitio histórico
♠	Recreational Site	Erholungs- und Ferienort	Sitio de Recreo	Centre de loisirs	Area de Lazer
⊠	Airport	Flughafen	Aeropuerto	Aéroport	Aeroporto
■	Military Installation	Militäranlage	Instalación Militar	Installation militaire	Instalação militar
◆	Miscellaneous	Verschiedenes	Misceláneo	Divers	Diversos

ENGLISH

Name	Page	Lat.°′	Long.°′
Stockby	40	59.20 N	17.41 E
Stockdale, Oh., U.S.	218	38.57 N	82.51 W
Stockdale, Tx., U.S.	196	29.14 N	97.57 W
Stockelsdorf	54	53.54 N	10.38 E
Stöcken	54	53.00 N	10.40 E
Stockerau	61	48.23 N	16.13 E
Stockertown	208	40.45 N	75.15 W
Stockett	202	47.21 N	111.09 W
Stockheim	56	50.19 N	9.01 E
Stockholm, Sve.	40	59.20 N	18.03 E
Stockholm, Me., U.S.	186	47.02 N	68.08 W
Stockholm, N.J., U.S.	210	41.05 N	74.31 W
Stockholm, Lake ⊜	276	41.04 N	74.32 W
Stockholms Län ▫[6]	40	59.30 N	18.20 E
Stock Island	220	24.34 N	81.45 W
Stockland	216	40.37 N	87.36 W
Stockport, Eng., U.K.	44	53.25 N	2.10 W
Stockport, N.Y., U.S.	210	42.19 N	73.45 W
Stockport ▫[8]	262	53.23 N	2.08 W
Stocksbridge	44	53.27 N	1.34 W
Stockstadt	56	49.59 N	9.04 E
Stocksund	40	59.23 N	18.04 E
Stockton, Austl.	170	32.55 S	151.47 E
Stockton, Al., U.S.	194	30.59 N	87.51 W
Stockton, Ca., U.S.	226	37.57 N	121.17 W
Stockton, Il., U.S.	190	42.20 N	90.00 W
Stockton, Ks., U.S.	198	39.26 N	99.15 W
Stockton, Md., U.S.	208	38.03 N	75.24 W
Stockton, Mo., U.S.	194	37.41 N	93.47 W
Stockton, N.J., U.S.	208	40.24 N	74.58 W
Stockton, N.Y., U.S.	214	42.19 N	79.22 W
Stockton, Ut,. U.S.	200	40.27 N	112.21 W
Stockton Heath, Eng., U.K.	44	53.22 N	2.34 W
Stockton Heath, Eng., U.K.	262	53.22 N	2.34 W
Stockton Metropolitan Airport ⊠	226	37.54 N	121.15 W
Stockton-on-Tees	44	54.34 N	1.19 W
Stockton Plateau ⋏[1]	196	30.30 N	102.30 W
Stockton Reservoir ⊜[1]	194	37.40 N	93.45 W
Stockton Springs	188	44.29 N	68.51 W
Stockum, Dtsch.	52	51.40 N	7.42 E
Stockum, Dtsch.	263	51.32 N	7.47 E
Stockum, Dtsch.	263	51.36 N	6.39 E
Stockum, Dtsch.	263	51.28 N	7.22 E
Stockum ◆[8]	263	51.16 N	6.44 E
Stockville	198	40.31 N	100.22 W
Stockwell	216	40.17 N	86.46 W
Stockwell, Lake ⊜	285	39.51 N	74.47 W
Stoco Lake ⊜	212	44.28 N	77.18 W
Stoczek Łukowski	30	51.58 N	21.58 E
Stod	60	49.39 N	13.10 E
Stoddard Mountain ∧	228	34.42 N	117.07 W
Stöde	26	62.25 N	16.35 E
Stodoliči	78	51.44 N	28.30 E
Stodolišče	76	54.11 N	32.39 E
Stœng Tréng	110	13.31 N	105.58 E
Stoer	46	58.12 N	5.20 W
Stoer, Point of ›	46	58.15 N	5.21 W
Stoffberg	156	25.29 S	29.49 E
Stojba	89	52.49 N	131.43 E
Stoke	260	51.27 N	0.37 E
Stoke ≃	206	45.35 N	71.58 W
Stoke, Monts ⋏	206	45.33 N	71.42 W
Stoke D'Abernon	260	51.19 N	0.23 W
Stokenchurch	42	51.40 N	0.55 W
Stoke Newington ◆[8]	260	51.34 N	0.05 W
Stoke-on-Trent	42	53.00 N	2.10 W
Stoke Poges	260	51.33 N	0.35 W
Stokes, Mount ∧	172	41.06 S	174.06 E
Stokes Inlet c	162	33.50 S	121.08 E
Stokesley	44	54.28 N	1.11 W
Stokes Point ›	166	40.10 S	143.56 E
Stokes Range ⋏[2]	164	15.46 S	130.57 E
Stokhid ≃	78	51.52 N	25.38 E
Stokkemarke	41	54.50 N	11.23 E
Stokksnes ›	24a	64.17 N	14.54 W
Stol ∧	38	44.13 N	22.14 E
Stolac	36	43.05 N	17.58 E
Stolbcy	76	53.29 N	26.44 E
Stolberg, Dtsch.	54	51.34 N	10.57 E
Stolberg, Dtsch.	56	50.46 N	6.13 E
Stolbišči	80	55.39 N	49.14 E
Stolboucha	86	49.59 N	84.30 E
Stolbovo	76	52.38 N	34.47 E
Stolbovoj, ostrov I	74	74.05 N	136.00 E
Stolbun	76	52.48 N	31.25 E
Stolby, zapovednik ♠	88	55.45 N	92.45 E
Stolin	78	51.53 N	26.51 E
Stollberg	54	50.42 N	12.47 E
Stöllet	26	60.24 N	13.16 E
Stol'ne	78	51.31 N	31.55 E
Stolp → Słupsk	30	54.28 N	17.01 E
Stolpe	264a	52.40 N	13.16 E
Stolpen	54	51.05 N	14.04 E
Stolper Heide ◆[3]	264a	52.39 N	13.14 E
Stolpino	80	57.24 N	42.55 E
Stolzenau	52	52.31 N	9.04 E
Ston	36	42.50 N	17.42 E
Stondon Massey	260	51.41 N	0.18 E
Stone, Eng., U.K.	42	52.54 N	2.10 W
Stone, Eng., U.K.	260	51.27 N	0.16 E
Stoneboro	214	41.20 N	80.06 W
Stone Canyon Reservoir ⊜[1]	280	34.07 N	118.28 W
Stone Corral Creek ≃	226	39.16 N	122.06 W
Stone Creek	214	40.24 N	81.34 W
Stonecutters Island I	271d	22.19 N	114.08 E
Stonefort	194	37.37 N	88.42 W
Stoneham, Ma., U.S.	283	42.28 N	71.06 W
Stoneham, Pa., U.S.	214	41.49 N	79.07 W
Stone Harbor	208	39.03 N	74.45 W
Stonehaven	46	56.57 N	2.12 W
Stonehenge	166	24.22 S	143.17 E
Stonehenge ⊥	42	51.11 N	1.49 W
Stonehill College ⌂[2]	283	42.03 N	71.05 W
Stonehouse, Eng., U.K.	42	51.45 N	2.17 W
Stonehouse, Scot., U.K.	46	55.43 N	4.00 W
Stone Indian Reserve ◆[4]	182	51.54 N	123.12 W
Stoneleigh	42	52.21 N	1.31 W
Stonelick Creek ≃	218	39.07 N	84.13 W
Stonelick State Park ♠	218	39.13 N	84.04 W
Stone Mountain	192	33.48 N	84.10 W
Stone Mountain ∧, Pa., U.S.	210	40.37 N	77.48 W
Stone Mountain ∧, Vt., U.S.	188	44.34 N	71.40 W
Stone Mountain Memorial State Park ♠	192	33.49 N	84.06 W
Stone Park	278	41.54 N	87.53 W
Stoner	182	53.36 N	122.40 W
Stoner Creek ≃	218	38.18 N	84.14 W
Stone Ridge	210	41.51 N	74.09 W
Stonerstown	214	40.13 N	78.16 W
Stones, East Fork ≃	194	35.59 N	86.27 W
Stones, West Fork ≃	194	35.59 N	86.27 W
Stones River National Battlefield ⊥	194	35.52 N	86.26 W
Stonestown ◆[9]	282	37.44 N	122.28 W
Stonevilla	279b	40.18 N	79.31 W
Stoneville	192	36.27 N	79.54 W
Stonewall, Mb., Can.	184	50.09 N	97.21 W
Stonewall, La., U.S.	194	32.16 N	93.49 W
Stonewall, Ms., U.S.	194	32.07 N	88.47 W
Stonewall, Ok., U.S.	196	34.39 N	96.31 W
Stonewall Manor	284c	38.53 N	77.14 W
Stoney Creek	212	43.13 N	79.46 W
Stoney Point ›	214	42.18 N	82.34 W
Stonington, Ct., U.S.	207	41.20 N	71.54 W
Stonington, Il., U.S.	219	39.38 N	89.11 W
Stonington, Me., U.S.	188	44.09 N	68.40 W
Stony ≃, Ak., U.S.	180	61.45 N	156.35 W
Stony ≃, Mn., U.S.	190	47.44 N	91.47 W
Stony Brook	210	40.55 N	73.08 W
Stony Brook ≃, Ct., U.S.	276	41.04 N	73.28 W
Stony Brook ≃, Ct., U.S.	276	41.08 N	73.22 W
Stony Brook ≃, Ma., U.S.	283	42.38 N	71.22 W
Stony Brook ≃, Ma., U.S.	283	42.22 N	71.16 W
Stony Brook ≃, N.J., U.S.	276	40.19 N	74.41 W
Stony Brook ≃, N.J., U.S.	276	40.56 N	74.26 W
Stony Brook Harbor c	276	40.54 N	73.10 W
Stony Brook Reservation ♠	283	42.16 N	71.09 W
Stony Creek, Ct., U.S.	207	41.15 N	72.44 W
Stony Creek, Va., U.S.	208	36.56 N	77.24 W
Stony Creek ≃, Ca., U.S.	204	39.41 N	121.58 W
Stony Creek ≃, Il., U.S.	278	41.41 N	87.51 W
Stony Creek ≃, Mi., U.S.	216	41.57 N	83.18 W
Stony Creek ≃, Mi., U.S.	216	43.00 N	84.55 W
Stony Creek ≃, N.Y., U.S.	212	43.49 N	76.14 W
Stony Creek ≃, Pa., U.S.	285	40.07 N	75.21 W
Stony Creek ≃, Va., U.S.	208	36.56 N	77.23 W
Stony Creek, Middle Fork ≃	226	39.25 N	122.31 W
Stony Creek, North Fork ≃	226	39.22 N	122.37 W
Stony Creek, South Fork ≃	226	39.22 N	122.39 W
Stony Creek Indian Reserve ◆[4]	182	53.57 N	124.07 W
Stony Creek Mills	208	40.21 N	75.52 W
Stonyford	226	39.22 N	122.32 W
Stony Gorge Reservoir ⊜[1]	226	39.34 N	122.31 W
Stony Indian Reserve ◆[4]	182	51.10 N	114.55 W
Stony Island I, Mi., U.S.	281	42.07 N	83.08 W
Stony Island I, N.Y., U.S.	212	43.53 N	76.25 W
Stony Kill ≃	210	42.24 N	73.38 W
Stony Lake ⊜, Mb., Can.	176	58.51 N	98.35 W
Stony Lake ⊜, On., Can.	212	44.33 N	78.05 W
Stony Plain	182	53.32 N	114.00 W
Stony Plain Indian Reserve ◆[4]	182	53.30 N	113.45 W
Stony Point, Austl.	169	38.22 S	145.13 E
Stony Point, Mi., U.S.	216	41.57 N	83.16 W
Stony Point, N.Y., U.S.	210	41.13 N	73.59 W
Stony Point, N.C., U.S.	192	35.51 N	81.02 W
Stony Point ›	284a	42.50 N	78.52 W
Stony Point ›[1]	212	43.52 N	76.15 W
Stony Prairie	214	41.21 N	83.10 W
Stony Rapids	176	59.16 N	105.50 W
Stony Ridge	214	41.30 N	83.30 W
Stony River	180	61.47 N	156.41 W
Stony Run	284b	39.11 N	76.42 W
Stony Run ≃	285	40.09 N	75.32 W
Stony Stratford	42	52.04 N	0.52 W
Stoober Bach ≃	61	47.27 N	16.35 E
Stop ≃	283	42.10 N	71.19 W
Stopnica	30	50.27 N	20.57 E
Stoppenberg ◆[8]	263	51.29 N	7.02 E
Stör ≃	54	53.50 N	11.29 E
Storå	40	59.43 N	15.08 E
Storå ≃	26	56.19 N	8.19 E
Stora Alvaret ≚	26	56.30 N	16.30 E
Stora Gla ⊜	26	59.30 N	12.30 E
Stora Kloten ⊜	40	59.52 N	15.16 E
Stora Le ⊜	26	59.05 N	11.53 E
Stora Lulevatten ⊜	24	67.10 N	19.16 E
Stora Mellösa	40	59.13 N	15.30 E
Stora Möja I, Sve.	26	59.26 N	18.55 E
Stora Möja I, Sve.	40	59.26 N	18.55 E
Stora Norn ⊜	40	60.14 N	15.42 E
Stora Sjöfallets Nationalpark ♠	24	67.44 N	18.16 E
Stora Skedvi	40	60.24 N	15.48 E
Stora Sundby	40	59.16 N	16.07 E
Storavan ⊜	24	65.40 N	18.15 E
Stora Vika	40	58.56 N	17.48 E
Storby	26	60.13 N	19.34 E
Stord I	26	59.53 N	5.25 E
Store Andst	41	55.29 N	9.14 E
Storebælt ⊔	41	55.30 N	11.00 E
Store Heddinge	41	55.19 N	12.25 E
Store Magleby	41	55.36 N	12.38 E
Store Merløse	41	55.33 N	11.40 E
Støren	26	63.02 N	10.18 E
Store Sotra I	26	60.18 N	5.05 E
Storeton	262	53.21 N	3.03 W
Storey ▫[6]	226	39.28 N	119.30 W
Storfjärden ⊜	40	60.30 N	17.23 E
Storfjorden c[2]	26	62.25 N	6.30 E
Storfors	40	59.32 N	14.16 E
Störitzsee ⊜	264a	52.23 N	13.51 E
Störkanal ≅	54	53.36 N	11.30 E
Storkerson Bay c	176	73.00 N	124.50 W
Storkerson Peninsula ›[1]	176	72.30 N	106.30 W
Storkow, Dtsch.	54	53.19 N	14.17 E
Storkow, Dtsch.	54	52.15 N	13.56 E
Storlien	26	63.19 N	12.06 E
Stormarn ◆[1]	52	53.45 N	10.20 E
Storm Bay c	166	43.10 S	147.32 E
Stormberg ∧	158	30.57 S	26.41 E
Stormberge ⋏	158	31.27 S	26.55 E
Storm King Mountain ∧	224	46.39 N	122.10 W
Storm Lake	198	42.38 N	95.12 W
Storm Mountain ∧	180	59.37 N	150.35 W
Stormont-Dundas and Glengarry ▫[6]	206	45.10 N	75.00 W
Stormsrivier	158	33.59 S	23.52 E
Stormsvlei	158	34.05 S	20.06 E
Stormville	210	41.34 N	73.45 W
Stornara	68	41.17 N	15.46 E
Stornarella	68	41.15 N	15.44 E
Stornorrforsen	26	63.52 N	20.03 E
Stornoway	46	58.12 N	6.23 W
Storo	64	45.51 N	10.35 E
Storoževaja	84	43.53 N	41.27 E
Storoževsk	24	61.57 N	52.16 E
Storozhynets'	78	48.10 N	25.43 E
Storrensjön ⊜	26	63.38 N	12.34 E
Storrington	42	50.55 N	0.28 W
Storrs	207	41.48 N	72.15 W
Storsjøen ⊜, Nor.	26	60.23 N	11.40 E
Storsjøen ⊜, Nor.	26	61.35 N	11.12 E
Storsjön ⊜, Sve.	26	62.48 N	13.07 E
Storsjön ⊜, Sve.	26	63.12 N	14.18 E
Storsjön ⊜, Sve.	40	60.34 N	16.44 E
Storsjön ⊜, Sve.	40	59.04 N	17.12 E
Storsteinsfjellet ∧	24	68.14 N	17.52 E
Storstrøm ▫[6]	41	55.00 N	11.55 E
Storstrømmen ⊔	41	54.58 N	11.55 E
Storstrømsbroen ◆[5]	41	54.58 N	11.50 E
Stort ≃	260	51.46 N	0.01 E
Storthoaks	184	49.22 N	101.38 W
Storuman	24	65.06 N	17.06 E
Storuman ⊜[1]	24	65.14 N	16.54 E
Storuman-See → Storavan ⊜	24	65.40 N	18.15 E
Storvarts gruve	26	62.38 N	11.31 E
Storvätteshågna ∧	26	62.07 N	12.27 E
Storvik	40	60.35 N	16.32 E
Storvindeln ⊜	24	65.43 N	17.05 E
Storvreta	40	59.58 N	17.42 E
Story	202	44.34 N	106.53 W
Story City	190	42.11 N	93.35 W
Stosch, Isla I	254	49.09 S	75.26 W
Stössen	54	51.06 N	11.55 E
Stotfold	42	52.01 N	0.14 W
Stotternheim	54	51.03 N	11.02 E
Stottville	210	42.17 N	73.44 W
Stouchsburg	208	40.23 N	76.14 W
Stough Park ♠	280	34.12 N	118.18 W
Stoughton, Sk., Can.	184	49.41 N	103.03 W
Stoughton, Eng., U.K.	260	51.15 N	0.35 W
Stoughton, Ma., U.S.	207	42.07 N	71.06 W
Stoughton, Wi., U.S.	216	42.55 N	89.13 W
Stoumont	56	50.25 N	5.48 E
Stoŭng ≃	110	12.50 N	104.19 E
Stour ≃, Eng., U.K.	42	51.52 N	1.16 E
Stour ≃, Eng., U.K.	42	50.43 N	1.46 W
Stour ≃, Eng., U.K.	42	51.18 N	1.22 E
Stour ≃, Eng., U.K.	42	52.20 N	2.15 W
Stourbridge	42	52.27 N	2.09 W
Stourport-on-Severn	42	52.21 N	2.16 W
Stout Lake ⊜	184	52.08 N	94.33 W
Stoutsville	219	39.33 N	91.51 W
Stover	194	38.26 N	92.59 W
Stow, Ma., U.S.	207	42.26 N	71.30 W
Stow, N.Y., U.S.	214	42.09 N	79.25 W
Stow, Oh., U.S.	214	41.10 N	81.27 W
Stowe, Pa., U.S.	208	40.15 N	75.40 W
Stowe, Vt., U.S.	188	44.27 N	72.41 W
Stowell	194	29.47 N	94.23 W
Stowe Township	279b	40.29 N	80.04 W
Stow Maries	260	51.40 N	0.39 E
Stowmarket	42	52.11 N	1.00 E
Stow-on-the-Wold	42	51.56 N	1.44 W
Stowupland	42	52.12 N	1.01 E
Stoyoma Mountain ∧	182	49.59 N	121.13 W
Stoystown	214	40.06 N	78.57 W
Stožec	60	48.51 N	13.50 E
Stra	64	45.25 N	12.00 E
Straach	54	51.57 N	12.35 E
Strabane, N. Ire., U.K.	48	54.49 N	7.27 W
Strabane, Pa., U.S.	214	40.15 N	80.11 W
Straberg	263	51.05 N	6.45 E
Strachan	46	57.01 N	2.32 W
Strachan Island I	164	9.00 S	142.10 E
Strachur	46	56.10 N	5.04 W
Stradbally	48	53.00 N	7.08 W
Stradbroke	42	52.19 N	1.16 E
Stradeč'	76	51.56 N	23.40 E
Stradella	62	45.05 N	9.18 E
Stradone	48	53.58 N	7.14 W
Stradovn'a, ozero ⊜	82	56.53 N	36.18 E
Straelen	56	51.27 N	6.16 E
Strafford	285	40.03 N	75.25 W
Straffordville	212	42.45 N	80.47 W
Strahan	166	42.09 S	145.19 E
Straight Creek ≃	218	38.46 N	83.55 W
Strakonice	60	49.16 N	13.55 E
Stralsund	54	54.19 N	13.05 E
Strambino	62	45.23 N	7.53 E
Strand	158	34.06 S	18.50 E
Stranda	26	62.19 N	6.54 E
Strande	54	54.26 N	10.12 E
Strandhill	48	54.17 N	8.36 W
Stranger Creek ≃	198	39.00 N	95.01 W
Strangford	48	54.22 N	5.34 W
Strangford Lough ⊜	48	54.28 N	5.35 W
Strängnäs	40	59.23 N	17.02 E
Strångsjö	40	58.54 N	16.12 E
Strangways ≃	164	14.52 S	133.50 E
Strangways, Mount ∧	162	23.02 S	133.51 E
Stranorlar	48	54.48 N	7.46 W
Stranraer	44	54.55 N	5.02 W
Strasbourg, Sk., Can.	184	51.04 N	104.57 W
Strasbourg, Fr.	58	48.35 N	7.45 E
Strasbourg, Aéroport ⊠	58	48.32 N	7.38 E
Strasburg, Dtsch.	54	53.30 N	13.44 E
Strasburg, Co., U.S.	198	39.44 N	104.20 W
Strasburg, N.D., U.S.	198	46.08 N	100.09 W
Strasburg, Oh., U.S.	214	40.35 N	81.31 W
Strasburg, Pa., U.S.	208	39.58 N	76.11 W
Strasburg, Va., U.S.	188	38.59 N	78.21 W
Străşeni	38	47.08 N	28.36 E
Straševiči	76	56.49 N	34.36 E
Strašín	60	49.08 N	13.38 E
Stråssa	40	59.45 N	15.13 E
Strassburg → Strasbourg	58	48.35 N	7.45 E
Strasshof an der Nordbahn	61	48.19 N	16.39 E
Strasskirchen	60	48.50 N	12.43 E
Strata Florida Abbey ⌂[1]	42	52.16 N	3.51 W
Stratford, On., Can.	212	43.22 N	80.57 W
Stratford, N.Z.	172	39.20 S	174.17 E
Stratford, Ca., U.S.	226	36.11 N	119.49 W
Stratford, Ct., U.S.	207	41.11 N	73.08 W
Stratford, De., U.S.	285	39.40 N	75.38 W
Stratford, Ia., U.S.	190	42.16 N	93.55 W
Stratford, N.J., U.S.	208	39.49 N	75.00 W
Stratford, N.Y., U.S.	210	43.11 N	74.42 W
Stratford, Ok., U.S.	196	34.47 N	96.57 W
Stratford, Tx., U.S.	196	36.20 N	102.04 W
Stratford, Wi., U.S.	190	44.48 N	90.04 W
Stratford Centre	206	45.47 N	71.16 W
Stratford Point ›	276	41.09 N	73.06 W
Stratford-upon-Avon	42	52.12 N	1.41 W
Strathalbyn	168b	35.16 S	138.54 E
Strathaven	46	55.40 N	4.04 W
Strathbogie Ranges ⋏	169	36.55 S	145.45 E
Strathclair	184	50.24 N	100.24 W
Strathclyde ▫[4]	46	56.00 N	5.15 W
Strathcona Provincial Park ♠	182	49.40 N	125.50 W
Strathdearn V	46	57.15 N	4.05 W
Strathdon	46	57.11 N	3.02 W
Strathearn V	46	56.18 N	3.45 W
Strathfield	170	33.52 S	151.06 E
Strathgordon	166	42.46 S	146.03 E
Strath Kanaird	46	57.59 N	5.11 W
Strathlorne	186	46.11 N	61.17 W
Strathminglo	46	56.16 N	3.16 W
Strathmoor ◆[8]	281	42.23 N	83.11 W
Strathmore, Ab., Can.	182	51.03 N	113.23 W
Strathmore, Ca., U.S.	204	36.08 N	119.03 W
Strathmore, N.J., U.S.	276	40.24 N	74.13 W
Strathmore V	46	56.39 N	3.00 W
Strathpeffer	46	57.35 N	4.33 W
Strathpine	171a	27.19 S	152.59 E
Strathroy	214	42.57 N	81.38 W
Strathy ≃	46	58.34 N	4.00 W
Strathy Point ›	46	58.35 N	4.02 W
Strattanville	214	41.12 N	79.19 W
Stratton, Eng., U.K.	42	50.50 N	4.31 W
Stratton, Eng., U.K.	42	51.44 N	1.59 W
Stratton, Co., U.S.	198	39.18 N	102.36 W
Stratton, Me., U.S.	188	45.08 N	70.26 W
Stratton, Ne., U.S.	198	40.08 N	101.13 W
Stratton, Oh., U.S.	214	40.32 N	80.38 W
Stratton Mountain ∧	188	43.05 N	72.56 W
Stratton Saint Margaret	42	51.35 N	1.45 W
Straubing	60	48.53 N	12.34 E
Strauch	263	51.09 N	6.56 E
Straumen	26	63.52 N	11.18 E
Straupitz	54	51.54 N	14.07 E
Strausberg	54	52.35 N	13.53 E
Straus-Berger Stadtforst ♠	264a	52.34 N	13.52 E
Strausberg-Vorstadt	264a	52.32 N	13.51 E
Straussberg	54	51.23 N	10.44 E
Straussee ⊜	264a	52.35 N	13.53 E
Straussfurt	54	51.09 N	10.59 E
Strausstown	208	40.30 N	76.11 W
Stravignano	66	43.05 N	12.49 E
Strawberry	226	38.13 N	118.35 W
Strawberry ≃, Ar., U.S.	194	35.53 N	91.13 W
Strawberry ≃, Ut,. U.S.	200	40.10 N	110.24 W
Strawberry Island I	284a	42.57 N	78.55 W
Strawberry Mountain ∧	202	44.19 N	118.43 W
Strawberry Point, Ca., U.S.	282	37.54 N	122.31 W
Strawberry Point, Ia., U.S.	190	42.41 N	91.32 W
Strawberry Point ›	283	42.15 N	70.46 W
Strawberry Reservoir ⊜[1]	200	40.11 N	111.08 W
Strawberry Valley	226	39.34 N	121.06 W
Strawbridge Lake ⊜	285	39.57 N	74.57 W
Strawn	196	32.33 N	98.29 W
Straw Pump	279b	40.19 N	79.40 W
Stráž	61	49.04 N	14.54 E
Strážnice	30	48.54 N	17.18 E
Strážov	60	49.18 N	13.15 E
Strážske	30	48.53 N	21.50 E
Streaky Bay	162	32.48 S	134.13 E
Streaky Bay c	162	32.36 S	134.08 E
Streamwood	216	42.01 N	88.10 W
Streatham, Austl.	169	37.41 S	143.04 E
Streatham, B.C., Can.	182	53.52 N	126.12 W
Streatham ◆[8]	260	51.26 N	0.08 W
Streator	216	41.07 N	88.50 W
Strebersdorf ◆[8]	264b	48.18 N	16.23 E
Středočeský Kraj ▫[4]	30	49.55 N	14.30 E
Stredoslovenský Kraj ▫[4]	30	48.50 N	19.10 E
Street	42	51.07 N	2.42 W
Streeter	198	46.39 N	99.21 W
Streetman	222	31.53 N	96.19 W
Streetsboro	214	41.14 N	81.20 W
Streets Run ≃	279b	40.23 N	79.56 W
Streetsville	212	43.35 N	79.42 W
Strehaia	38	44.37 N	23.12 E
Strehla	54	51.21 N	13.13 E
Streitberg	60	49.49 N	11.13 E
Střela ≃	60	49.55 N	13.33 E
Strelasund ⊔	54	54.20 N	13.05 E
Streleckije Vyselki	82	54.12 N	38.57 E
Strelica	78	51.37 N	38.55 E
Střelice	61	49.09 N	16.30 E
Strelitzalt	54	53.20 N	13.05 E
Strelka	86	58.05 N	93.01 E
Strelka ≃	265a	59.52 N	30.03 E
Strelka-Čun'a	74	61.45 N	102.48 E
Strelkovo	82	55.28 N	37.37 E
Strel'na, Ross.	24	66.06 N	38.40 E
Strel'na, Ross.	76	59.51 N	30.02 E
Strel'na ≃	24	66.04 N	38.39 E
Strel'skaja	24	59.28 N	47.47 E
Střelské Hoštice	60	49.18 N	13.46 E
Strem ≃	61	47.00 N	16.31 E
Strembo	64	46.09 N	10.44 E
Stremilovo	82	55.09 N	37.09 E
Strenči	76	57.37 N	25.41 E
Strengen	58	47.08 N	10.27 E
Strensall	44	54.03 N	1.02 W
Stresa	62	45.53 N	8.32 E
Strešin	76	52.43 N	30.05 E
Stretford	44	53.27 N	2.19 W
Stretton, Austl.	162	32.32 S	117.41 E
Stretton, Eng., U.K.	42	52.44 N	0.35 W
Stretton, Eng., U.K.	44	53.21 N	2.35 W
Streu ≃	56	50.21 N	10.16 E
Strib	41	55.32 N	9.47 E
Striberg	40	59.33 N	14.56 E
Stříbro	60	49.46 N	13.00 E
Strichen	46	57.34 N	2.05 W
Strickherdicke	263	51.29 N	7.43 E
Strickland ≃	164	6.00 S	142.05 E
Strigno	64	46.04 N	11.31 E
Strijen	52	51.45 N	4.33 E
Striker, Lake ⊜[1]	222	31.57 N	94.59 W
Strilkove	78	45.54 N	34.53 E
Stril'tsivka	83	49.18 N	39.52 E
Strimón (Struma) ≃	38	40.47 N	23.51 E
Stringtown	218	40.05 N	86.29 W
Striven, Loch c	46	55.58 N	5.09 W
Strižament, gora ∧	84	44.46 N	42.01 E
Striži	80	58.30 N	49.13 E
Strjama ≃	38	42.10 N	24.56 E
Strobel	252	32.03 S	60.37 W
Strobel, Lago ⊜	254	48.22 S	71.12 W
Strobl	64	47.43 N	13.29 E
Strobleton	214	41.22 N	79.25 W
Strøby	41	55.23 N	12.18 E
Stroeder	254	40.11 S	62.37 W
Strofádhes, Nísoi II	38	37.15 N	21.00 E
Strogino ◆[8]	265b	55.49 N	37.25 E
Strogonof Point ›	180	56.53 N	158.49 W
Stroh	216	41.34 N	85.11 W
Ströhen	52	52.32 N	8.41 E
Stroitel'	78	50.47 N	36.26 E
Strokestown	48	53.47 N	8.08 W
Strom ≃	54	53.15 N	13.50 E
Stroma I	46	58.41 N	3.08 W
Stromberg, Dtsch.	52	51.48 N	8.12 E
Stromberg, Dtsch.	56	49.57 N	7.46 E
Stromboli, Isola I	70	38.47 N	15.13 E
Strome	182	52.48 N	112.04 W
Stromeferry	46	57.21 N	5.34 W
Strömkendorf	54	53.58 N	11.29 E
Stromness	46	58.57 N	3.18 W
Strömsberg	40	60.24 N	17.35 E
Strömsbro	40	60.42 N	17.10 E
Strömsbruk	26	61.53 N	17.19 E
Stromsburg	198	41.06 N	97.35 W
Strömsholm	40	59.32 N	16.15 E
Strömsnäsbruk	26	56.33 N	13.43 E
Strömstad	26	58.56 N	11.10 E
Strömsund	26	63.51 N	15.35 E
Strömsvattudal ⊜	26	63.56 N	15.28 E
Stromyn'	82	56.03 N	38.29 E
Strong	194	33.06 N	92.20 W
Strong ≃	194	31.51 N	90.08 W
Strong City	198	38.23 N	96.32 W
Stronghurst	190	40.44 N	90.54 W
Strongoli	68	39.15 N	17.03 E
Strongs Creek ≃	276	40.40 N	73.22 W
Strongs Neck ›[1]	276	40.58 N	73.07 W
Strongstown	214	40.33 N	78.55 W
Strongsville	214	41.18 N	81.50 W
Strongsville Airport ⊠	279a	41.19 N	81.52 W
Stronsay I	46	59.07 N	2.37 W
Stronsay Firth ⊔	46	59.02 N	2.41 W
Stronsdorf	61	48.39 N	16.18 E
Strontian	46	56.41 N	5.34 W
Strood	42	51.24 N	0.28 E
Stropkov	30	49.12 N	21.40 E
Stropnice ≃	61	48.52 N	14.30 E
Stroppiana	62	45.14 N	8.27 E
Stroud, Austl.	166	32.20 S	151.56 E
Stroud, Eng., U.K.	42	51.45 N	2.12 W
Stroud, Ok., U.S.	196	35.44 N	96.39 W
Stroudsburg	210	40.59 N	75.11 W
Strövelstorp	41	56.09 N	12.49 E
Strubenvale	273d	26.16 S	28.28 E
Strücklingen	52	53.07 N	7.40 E
Struer	26	56.29 N	8.37 E
Struga	38	41.11 N	20.40 E
Strugi-Krasnyje	76	58.17 N	29.06 E
Struisbaai	158	34.49 S	20.04 E
Struisbult	273d	26.19 S	28.29 E
Strule ≃	48	54.43 N	7.25 W
Strum	190	44.32 N	91.23 W
Struma (Strimón) ≃	38	40.47 N	23.51 E
Strumble Head ›	42	52.02 N	5.04 W
Strumica	38	41.26 N	22.38 E
Strümp	263	51.17 N	6.40 E
Strunino	82	56.23 N	38.34 E
Strupna	82	54.43 N	38.48 E
Struthers	214	41.03 N	80.36 W
Struy	46	57.24 N	4.39 W
Strydenburg	158	29.58 S	23.40 E
Strydomsvlei	158	33.10 S	23.03 E
Strydpoort	158	27.00 S	25.58 E
Stryker, Mt., U.S.	182	48.40 N	114.46 W
Stryker, Oh., U.S.	216	41.30 N	84.24 W
Strykersville	210	42.42 N	78.27 W
Stryków	30	51.55 N	19.37 E
Stryn	26	61.55 N	6.47 E
Strynø I	41	54.54 N	10.37 E
Strypa ≃	78	48.52 N	25.26 E
Stryy	78	49.15 N	23.51 E
Stryy ≃	78	49.24 N	24.13 E
Stryzhavka	78	49.19 N	28.28 E
Strzegom	30	50.57 N	16.21 E
Strzegowo-Osada	30	52.55 N	20.18 E
Strzelce Krajeńskie	30	52.53 N	15.32 E
Strzelce Opolskie	30	50.31 N	18.19 E
Strzelecki Creek ≃	166	29.37 S	139.59 E
Strzelecki Desert ◆[2]	166	28.00 S	140.10 E
Strzeleckie, Mount ∧	162	21.10 S	133.53 E
Strzelecki National Park ♠	166	40.14 S	148.06 E
Strzelin	30	50.47 N	17.03 E
Strzelno	30	52.38 N	18.11 E
Strzyżów	30	49.52 N	21.47 E
Stuart, Fl., U.S.	220	27.11 N	80.15 W
Stuart, Ia., U.S.	198	41.30 N	94.19 W
Stuart, Ne., U.S.	198	42.35 N	99.08 W
Stuart, Va., U.S.	192	36.38 N	80.15 W
Stuart ≃	182	54.00 N	123.32 W
Stuart, Central Mount ∧	162	21.54 S	133.27 E
Stuart, Mount ∧	224	47.29 N	120.54 W
Stuart Channel ⊔	224	48.55 N	123.45 W
Stuart Island I, Ak., U.S.	180	63.35 N	162.30 W
Stuart Island I, Wa., U.S.	224	48.42 N	123.12 W
Stuart Lake ⊜	182	54.32 N	124.35 W
Stuart Mountains ⋏	172	45.00 S	167.37 E
Stuart Range ⋏	162	29.10 S	134.56 E
Stuarts Draft	192	38.01 N	79.02 W
Stubai V	64	47.06 N	11.19 E
Stubaier Alpen ⋏	64	47.10 N	11.05 E
Stubalpe ⋏	61	47.06 N	14.54 E
Stübbecken	263	51.23 N	7.36 E
Stubbekøbing	41	54.53 N	12.03 E
Stubbenfelde	54	54.02 N	14.01 E
Stubbenkammer	54	54.35 N	13.40 E
Stubbington	42	50.50 N	1.13 W
Stubbins	262	53.39 N	2.19 W
Stubenberg	61	47.14 N	15.48 E
Stubla ≃	78	50.50 N	26.04 E
Stubner Kogel ∧	64	47.07 N	13.06 E
Studená	61	49.11 N	15.17 E
Studenec	80	54.52 N	48.16 E
Studenica, Manastir ⌂[1]	38	43.21 N	20.35 E
Studen Kladenec, Jazovir ⊜[1]	38	41.37 N	25.30 E
Studenok	78	51.42 N	34.07 E
Studholme Junction	172	44.44 S	171.08 E
Studi, Università degli ⌂[2]	266b	45.28 N	9.14 E
Studland	42	50.39 N	1.58 W
Studley	42	52.16 N	1.52 W
Stud'onoje, Ross.	80	51.36 N	53.10 E
Stud'onoje, Ross.	86	53.37 N	77.31 E
Studsvik	40	58.46 N	17.23 E
Stugudal	26	62.54 N	11.52 E
Stugun	26	63.10 N	15.36 E
Stuhleck ∧	61	47.34 N	15.47 E
Stühlingen	58	47.44 N	8.26 E
Stuhlweissenburg → Székesfehérvár	30	47.12 N	18.25 E
Stuhr	52	53.01 N	8.45 E
Stuie	182	52.22 N	126.02 W
Stukely, Lac ⊜	206	45.22 N	72.15 W
Stukenbrock	52	51.54 N	8.39 E
Stull ≃	184	55.10 N	92.39 W
Stull Lake ⊜	184	54.23 N	92.34 W
Stülpe	54	52.02 N	13.19 E
Stumm	64	47.17 N	11.53 E
Stump Creek	214	41.01 N	78.50 W
Stump Creek ≃	276	40.28 N	74.16 W
Stumpf	263	51.06 N	7.13 E
Stump Lake ⊜	198	47.54 N	98.24 W
Stumsdorf	54	51.37 N	12.03 E
Stuorre Tjõure ∧	26	63.56 N	13.30 E
Stupart ≃	184	56.00 N	93.22 W
Stupava	61	48.17 N	17.02 E
Stupino	82	54.53 N	38.05 E
Stuppach	56	49.27 N	9.44 E
Stura ≃	62	45.09 N	8.21 E
Stura di Ala ≃	62	45.18 N	7.24 E
Stura di Demonte ≃	62	44.40 N	7.53 E
Stura di Lanzo ≃	62	45.06 N	7.44 E
Stura di Val Grande ≃	62	45.18 N	7.24 E
Stura di Viù ≃	62	45.16 N	7.26 E
Sturbridge	207	42.06 N	72.04 W
Sturdee	162	31.52 S	132.23 E
Sturge Island I	9	67.27 S	164.18 E
Sturgeon, Mo., U.S.	219	39.14 N	92.16 W
Sturgeon, Pa., U.S.	279b	40.23 N	80.13 W
Sturgeon ≃, On., Can.	190	46.19 N	79.58 W
Sturgeon ≃, Sk., Can.	184	53.12 N	105.53 W
Sturgeon ≃, Mi., U.S.	190	45.24 N	84.38 W
Sturgeon ≃, Mi., U.S.	190	45.50 N	86.41 W
Sturgeon ≃, Mi., U.S.	190	47.02 N	88.30 W
Sturgeon Bay	190	44.50 N	87.22 W
Sturgeon Bay c	184	52.00 N	97.50 W
Sturgeon Falls	190	46.22 N	79.55 W
Sturgeon Lake ⊜, Ab., Can.	182	55.06 N	117.30 W
Sturgeon Lake ⊜, On., Can.	184	55.25 N	90.55 W
Sturgeon Lake ⊜, On., Can.	212	44.28 N	78.42 W
Sturgeon Lake ⊜, Wa., U.S.	224	45.44 N	122.48 W
Sturgeon Lake Indian Reserve ◆[4], Ab., Can.	182	55.04 N	117.29 W
Sturgeon Lake Indian Reserve ◆[4], Sk., Can.	184	53.25 N	106.05 W
Sturgeon Landing	184	54.16 N	101.49 W
Sturgeon Point ›	212	42.42 N	79.03 W
Sturgis, Sk., Can.	184	51.58 N	102.32 W
Sturgis, Ky., U.S.	194	37.32 N	87.59 W
Sturgis, Mi., U.S.	216	41.47 N	85.25 W
Sturgis, Ms., U.S.	194	33.20 N	89.02 W
Sturgis, S.D., U.S.	198	44.24 N	103.30 W
Sturla	62	44.24 N	8.59 E
Sturminster Newton	42	50.50 N	2.19 W
Štúrovo	30	47.48 N	18.49 E
Sturry	42	51.18 N	1.07 E
Sturt, Mount ∧	166	29.33 S	141.42 E
Sturt Creek	162	19.10 S	128.10 E
Sturt Creek ≃	162	20.08 S	127.24 E
Sturtevant	216	42.41 N	87.53 W
Sturt National Park ♠	166	29.00 S	141.40 E
Sturt Stony Desert ◆[2]	166	28.30 S	141.00 E
Sturup flygplats ⊠	41	55.34 N	13.21 E
Stürzelberg	263	51.08 N	6.49 E
Stutterheim	158	32.33 S	27.28 E
Stuttgart, Dtsch.	56	48.46 N	9.11 E
Stuttgart, Ar., U.S.	194	34.30 N	91.33 W
Stuttgart ▫[5]	56	49.00 N	9.45 E

DEUTSCH

Name	Seite	Breite°′	Länge°′ E = Ost
Stuttgart, Flughafen ⊠	56	48.41 N	9.12 E
Stützengrün	54	50.32 N	12.31 E
Stützerbach	54	50.38 N	10.51 E
Stuyvesant	210	42.24 N	73.47 W
Stuyvesant Falls	210	42.21 N	73.44 W
Stviga ≃	78	52.04 N	27.54 E
Styal	262	53.21 N	2.15 W
Stykkishólmur	24a	65.06 N	22.48 W
Styr ≃	78	52.07 N	26.35 E
Styrum ◆[8]	263	51.27 N	6.51 E
Styx ≃, On., Can.	212	44.11 N	80.57 W
Styx ≃, Al., U.S.	194	30.31 N	87.27 W
Suaçuí Grande ≃	255	18.50 S	41.46 W
Suai	112	3.48 N	113.38 E
Suain	164	3.20 S	142.55 E
Suaita	246	6.07 N	73.27 W
Suakin Archipelago II	140	18.42 N	38.30 E
Sual	116	16.04 N	120.05 E
Suan	98	38.42 N	126.22 E
Suao, T'aiwan	100	24.36 N	121.51 E
Su'ao, Zhg.	100	25.38 N	119.42 E
Suapure ≃	246	6.25 N	66.23 W
Suaqui Grande	232	28.24 N	109.54 W
Suār	124	29.02 N	79.03 E
Suātala	124	23.09 N	79.02 E
Suatima	114	4.13 N	96.04 E
Šubač	76	60.22 N	38.14 E
Subačius	76	55.46 N	24.47 E
Subah	115a	6.58 S	109.52 E
Subaio	256	22.30 S	42.50 W
Subang	115a	6.34 S	107.45 E
Subansiri ≃	120	26.48 N	93.50 E
Šubarkuduk	86	49.13 N	56.34 E
Subar Laut, Pulau I	271c	1.13 N	103.50 E
Subarnapur	272b	22.58 N	88.34 E
Subarnarekha ≃	120	21.34 N	87.24 E
Šubarši	86	48.35 N	57.12 E
Subashi	85	38.22 N	74.57 E
Subasio, Monte ∧	66	43.03 N	12.40 E
Subate	76	56.01 N	25.56 E
Subay', 'Urūq as- ◆[2]	144	22.15 N	43.05 E
Subbiano	66	43.34 N	11.52 E
Subbotino	86	53.04 N	91.55 E
Subchankulovo	80	54.34 N	53.49 E
Subei	102	39.27 N	95.03 E
Subeita → Shivta, Horvot ⊥	132	30.53 N	34.38 E
Suben	60	48.25 N	13.26 E
Subhepur	272a	28.45 N	77.16 E
Subi, Pulau I	112	2.55 N	108.50 E
Subiaco	66	41.55 N	13.06 E
Subic	116	14.53 N	120.14 E
Subic Bay c	116	14.45 N	120.13 E
Subic Bay Naval Base (U.S.) ■	116	14.47 N	120.16 E
Subipur	272b	22.54 N	88.08 E
Subk al-Ahad	142	30.18 N	31.02 E
Sublette	198	37.28 N	100.50 W
Sublett Range ⋏	202	42.20 N	112.50 W
Sublime	222	29.29 N	96.48 W
Subotica	38	46.06 N	19.39 E
Suburban Airport ⊠	284c	39.05 N	76.50 W
Suburban Village	285	39.58 N	75.34 W
Suca	144	6.31 N	39.14 E
Sucarnoochee ≃	194	32.25 N	88.02 W
Succasunna	210	40.52 N	74.38 W
Succor Creek ≃	202	43.38 N	116.56 W
Suceava	38	47.39 N	26.19 E
Suceava ▫[6]	38	47.30 N	25.45 E
Suceava ≃	38	47.32 N	26.32 E
Sucha [Beskidzka]	30	49.44 N	19.36 E
Suchaja	88	52.32 N	107.06 E
Suchań, Pol.	30	53.17 N	15.19 E
Suchan → Partizansk, Ross.	89	43.08 N	133.09 E
Suchana	74	68.45 N	118.00 E
Suchang	107	30.34 N	103.34 E
Süchbaatar	88	50.15 N	106.12 E
Süchbaatar ▫[4]	102	45.30 N	114.00 E
Suchdol ◆[8]	54	50.08 N	14.21 E
Suchdol nad Lužnicí	61	48.54 N	14.53 E
Suchedniów	30	51.03 N	20.51 E
Suchetgarh	123	32.34 N	74.40 E
Suchiapa	234	16.37 N	93.05 W
Suchiapa ≃	234	16.36 N	93.01 W
Súchil	234	23.38 N	103.55 W
Suchiniči	76	54.06 N	35.20 E
Suchitepéquez ▫[5]	236	14.25 N	91.20 W
Suchitlán	234	19.22 N	103.43 W
Suchitoto	236	13.56 N	89.02 W
Suchobezvodnoje	80	57.03 N	44.50 E
Suchoborka	24	59.06 N	49.58 E
Suchodol, Ross.	80	53.55 N	51.14 E
Suchodol, Ross.	82	54.27 N	37.22 E
Suchodol'skij	76	53.43 N	38.17 E
Suchodrev ≃	82	54.44 N	35.59 E
Suchoj	80	47.06 N	41.21 E
Suchoj Jelančik ≃	83	47.16 N	38.25 E
Suchoj Log	86	56.55 N	62.01 E
Suchoj Pit	86	58.48 N	92.49 E
Suchoj Sambek ≃	83	47.23 N	39.07 E
Suchona ≃	24	60.46 N	46.24 E
Suchorečka	80	52.49 N	52.27 E
Suchotinka	80	52.31 N	41.35 E
Suchou → Suzhou	106	31.18 N	120.37 E
Suchoverkovo	76	56.37 N	35.35 E
Suchov Pervyj	80	49.59 N	43.28 E
Süchow → Xuzhou	98	34.16 N	117.11 E
Süchteln	56	51.17 N	6.22 E
Suchumi	84	43.01 N	41.02 E
Sucio ≃	246	7.27 N	77.07 W
Suck ≃	48	53.16 N	8.03 W
Sucker Creek ≃	212	44.09 N	77.08 W
Sucker Creek Indian Reserve ◆[4]	182	55.28 N	116.10 W
Sucker Lake ⊜	212	44.46 N	78.16 W
Suckling, Mount ∧	164	9.45 S	148.55 E
Sucre, Arg.	258	34.30 S	59.07 W
Sucre, Bol.	248	19.02 S	65.17 W
Sucre, Col.	246	8.49 N	74.44 W
Sucre, Ec.	246	1.16 S	80.26 W
Sucre ▫[3]	246	10.25 N	63.30 W
Sucre ▫[5], Col.	246	9.00 N	75.00 W
Sucre ▫[5], Ven.	286c	10.25 N	66.50 W
Sucúa	246	2.28 S	78.10 W
Sucuaro	246	4.34 N	68.50 W
Sucumbíos ▫[4]	246	0.06 N	76.52 W
Sucunduri ≃	248	5.50 S	59.32 W
Sucuriju	250	1.39 N	49.57 W
Sucuriú ≃	255	20.47 S	51.38 W
Sucy-en-Brie	50	48.46 N	2.32 E
Sud, Canal du ⊔	238	18.40 N	73.05 W
Sud, Grand Récif ✣[2]	175f	23.00 S	167.02 E
Sud, Pointe ›	157a	11.53 S	43.49 E
Sud, Rivière du ≃	206	45.08 N	73.15 W
Suda	76	59.09 N	37.33 E
Suda ≃	76	59.11 N	37.30 E
Südafrika → South Africa ▫[1]	156	30.00 S	26.00 E
Sudaj	76	58.58 N	43.08 E
Sudak	78	44.52 N	34.59 E
Südamerika → South America •[1]	18	15.00 S	60.00 W
Sudan	196	34.04 N	102.31 W
Sudan (As-Sūdān) ▫[1], Afr.	136	15.00 N	30.00 E
Sudan (As-Sūdān) ▫[1], Afr.	140	15.00 N	30.00 E
Sudan ◆[1]	10	10.00 N	20.00 E
Sudañez	248	19.06 S	64.44 W
Sudarsan	272b	22.59 N	88.17 E
Südbahnhof ◆[5]	264b	48.11 N	16.23 E
Sudberg ◆[8]	263	51.11 N	7.08 E
Sudbišči	76	52.57 N	37.39 E
Sud'bodarovka	80	52.19 N	54.07 E
Südbrookmerland	52	53.29 N	7.24 E

Symbols in the index entries represent the broad categories identified in the key at the right. Symbols with superior numbers (⋏[1]) identify subcategories (see complete key on page *I · 1).*

Symbole im Register stellen die rechts im Schlüssel erklärten Kategorien dar. Symbole mit hochgestellten Ziffern (⋏[1]) bezeichnen Unterabteilungen einer Kategorie (vgl. vollständiger Schlüssel auf Seite *I · 1).*

Los símbolos incluídos en el texto del índice representan las grandes categorías identificadas con la clave a la derecha. Los símbolos con numeros en su parte superior (⋏[1]) identifican las subcategorías (véase la clave completa en la página *I · 1).*

Les symboles de l'index représentent les catégories indiquées dans la légende à droite. Les symboles suivis d'un indice (⋏[1]) représentent des sous-catégories (voir légende complète à la page *I · 1).*

Os símbolos incluídos no texto do índice representam as grandes categorias identificadas com a chave à direita. Os símbolos com números em sua parte superior (⋏[1]) identificam as subcategorias (veja-se a chave completa à página *I · 1).*

∧ Mountain	Berg	Montaña	Montagne	Montanha
⋏ Mountains	Gebirge	Montañas	Montagnes	Montanhas
)(Pass	Paß	Paso	Col	Passo
V Valley, Canyon	Tal, Cañon	Valle, Cañón	Vallée, Canyon	Vale, Canhão
≚ Plain	Ebene	Llano	Plaine	Planície
› Cape	Kap	Cabo	Cap	Cabo
I Island	Insel	Isla	Île	Ilha
II Islands	Inseln	Islas	Îles	Ilhas
• Other Topographic Features	Andere Topographische Objekte	Otros Elementos Topográficos	Autres données topographiques	Outros acidentes topográficos

ESPAÑOL — Nombre · Página · Lat.°′ · Long.°′ W = Oeste

FRANÇAIS — Nom · Page · Lat.°′ · Long.°′ W = Ouest

PORTUGUÊS — Nome · Página · Lat.°′ · Long.°′ W = Oeste

Nombre / Nom / Nome	Página / Page	Lat.°′	Long.°′
Sudbury, On., Can.	190	46.30 N	81.00 W
Sudbury, Eng., U.K.	42	52.02 N	0.44 E
Sudbury, Ma., U.S.	207	42.23 N	71.25 W
Sudbury ≃	283	42.28 N	71.22 W
Sudbury Center	283	42.23 N	71.25 W
Sudbury Reservoir ⊜[1]	207	42.19 N	71.31 W
Südchinesisches Meer → South China Sea ⍑[2]	108	10.00 N	113.00 E
Sudd → As-Sudd ◆[1]	140	8.00 N	31.00 E
Sud Dakota → South Dakota □[3]	198	44.15 N	100.00 W
Sudd an-Na'ām, Jabal ∧	142	29.49 N	31.43 E
Suddie	246	7.07 N	58.29 W
Sude ≃	54	53.22 N	10.45 E
Süderbrarup	41	54.38 N	9.46 E
Süderlügum	41	54.52 N	8.55 E
Suderwich	263	51.37 N	7.15 E
Sudeten → Sudety ⋏	30	50.30 N	16.00 E
Sudety ⋏	30	50.30 N	16.00 E
Süd-Georgien → South Georgia I	244	54.15 S	36.45 W
Sudi	154	10.06 S	39.57 E
Sudislavl'	80	57.53 N	41.43 E
Südkamen	263	51.35 N	7.39 E
Süd-Korea → Korea, South □[1]	98	36.30 N	128.00 E
Sudlersville	208	39.11 N	75.51 W
Südlicher Bug → Pivdennyy Buh ≃	78	46.59 N	31.58 E
Südlicher Indianer-See → Southern Indian Lake ⊜	176	57.10 N	98.40 W
Sudnikovo	82	55.53 N	36.02 E
Sudogda	80	55.57 N	40.50 E
Sudomskaja vozvyšennost' ⋏[1]	76	57.25 N	29.25 E
Sudong, Pulau I	271c	1.13 N	103.44 E
Süd-Orkney-Inseln → South Orkney Islands II	9	60.35 S	45.30 W
Sudost' ≃	76	52.19 N	33.24 E
Sud-Ouest □[4]	152	5.10 N	9.00 E
Sud-Ouest, Pointe du ›	186	49.23 N	63.36 W
Sudova Vyshnya	78	49.49 N	23.22 E
Südradde ≃	52	52.41 N	7.34 E
Süd-Sandwich-Inseln → South Sandwich Islands II	18	57.45 S	26.30 W
Süd-Shetland-Inseln → South Shetland Islands II	9	62.00 S	58.00 W
Sudūd	142	30.25 N	30.54 E
Südwest-Kap → South West Cape ›	166	43.34 S	146.02 E
Sudweyhe	52	52.59 N	8.53 E
Sudža	78	51.12 N	35.16 E
Sue	96	33.35 N	130.30 E
Sue ≃	140	7.41 N	28.03 E
Sueca	34	39.12 N	0.19 W
Suecia → Sweden □[1]	24	62.00 N	15.00 E
Sue Creek ᴄ	284b	39.17 N	76.24 W
Suedberg	208	40.32 N	76.28 W
Suède → Sweden □[1]	24	62.00 N	15.00 E
Suemez Island I	182	55.17 N	133.21 W
Suèvres	50	47.40 N	1.28 E
Suez → As-Suways	142	29.58 N	32.33 E
Suez, Gulf of → Suways, Khalīj as- ᴄ	140	29.00 N	32.50 E
Suez Canal → Suways, Qanāt as- ≊	142	29.55 N	32.33 E
Sūf	132	32.19 N	35.50 E
Şufaynah	128	23.09 N	40.32 E
Suffern	210	41.06 N	74.09 W
Suffern Park	276	41.07 N	74.07 W
Suffield, Ab., Can.	184	50.12 N	111.10 W
Suffield, Ct., U.S.	207	41.58 N	72.39 W
Suffield, Oh., U.S.	214	41.01 N	81.21 W
Suffield, Canadian Forces Base ■	184	50.15 N	111.10 W
Suffolk	208	36.43 N	76.35 W
Suffolk □[6], Eng., U.K.	42	52.10 N	1.00 E
Suffolk □[6], Ma., U.S.	207	42.21 N	71.04 W
Suffolk □[6], N.Y., U.S.	210	40.55 N	72.40 W
Suffolk, Ruisseau ≃	206	45.48 N	74.59 W
Şūfīān	128	38.17 N	45.59 E
Sufi-Kurgan	85	40.02 N	73.30 E
Sufu → Kashi	85	39.29 N	75.59 E
Suga-jima I	94	34.29 N	136.53 E
Sugana, Val V	64	46.00 N	11.40 E
Sugandha	272b	22.54 N	88.20 E
Sugandy	85	43.27 N	74.38 E
Sugano	268	35.44 N	139.56 E
Sugar ≃, U.S.	190	42.26 N	89.12 W
Sugar ≃, N.H., U.S.	188	43.24 N	72.24 W
Sugar ≃, N.Y., U.S.	212	43.31 N	75.19 W
Sugar City	202	43.52 N	111.44 W
Sugarcreek, Oh., U.S.	214	40.30 N	81.39 W
Sugarcreek, Pa., U.S.	214	41.25 N	79.52 W
Sugar Creek ≃, U.S.	216	40.47 N	87.45 W
Sugar Creek ≃, Il., U.S.	194	40.09 N	89.38 W
Sugar Creek ≃, Il., U.S.	219	38.28 N	89.37 W
Sugar Creek ≃, Il., U.S.	219	39.48 N	89.32 W
Sugar Creek ≃, In., U.S.	194	39.51 N	87.21 W
Sugar Creek ≃, In., U.S.	218	39.21 N	86.00 W
Sugar Creek ≃, Mi., U.S.	281	42.06 N	83.36 W
Sugar Creek ≃, N.Y., U.S.	210	42.38 N	77.09 W
Sugar Creek ≃, Oh., U.S.	214	40.31 N	81.28 W
Sugar Creek ≃, Oh., U.S.	216	40.57 N	84.11 W
Sugar Creek ≃, Oh., U.S.	218	39.27 N	83.25 W
Sugar Creek ≃, Ok., U.S.	196	35.05 N	98.10 W
Sugar Creek ≃, Pa., U.S.	210	41.47 N	76.27 W
Sugar Creek ≃, Wi., U.S.	216	42.43 N	88.19 W
Sugar Grove, Il., U.S.	216	41.45 N	88.27 W
Sugargrove, Pa., U.S.	214	41.59 N	79.21 W
Sugar Grove, Va., U.S.	192	36.46 N	81.24 W
Sugar Hill	192	34.06 N	84.02 W
Sugar Island I, On., Can.	212	44.26 N	77.17 W
Sugar Island I, Mi., U.S.	190	46.25 N	84.12 W
Sugar Land	222	29.37 N	95.38 W
Sugar Loaf	210	41.19 N	74.17 W
Sugar Loaf → Pão de Açúcar ∧	287a	22.57 S	43.09 W
Sugarloaf ∧[2]	214	41.24 N	81.06 W
Sugarloaf Hill ∧[2]	274b	37.58 S	145.19 E
Sugarloaf Key I	220	24.40 N	81.32 W
Sugarloaf Mountain ∧, Ky., U.S.	218	38.13 N	83.32 W
Sugarloaf Mountain ∧, Me., U.S.	188	45.01 N	70.22 W
Sugar Loaf Mountain ∧, Md., U.S.	208	39.16 N	77.23 W
Sugar Loaf Mountain ∧, Ok., U.S.	194	35.02 N	94.28 W
Sugarloaf Mountain ∧[2]	220	28.39 N	81.44 W
Sugarloaf Peak ∧	280	34.14 N	117.38 W
Sugarloaf Point ›, Austl.	166	32.26 S	152.33 E
Sugar Loaf Point ›, On., Can.	284a	42.52 N	79.17 W
Sugarloaf Reservoir ⊜[1]	169	37.41 S	145.18 E
Sugarloaf Ridge State Park ♠	226	38.26 N	122.29 W
Sugar Notch	210	41.11 N	75.55 W
Sugar Pine Point State Park ♠	226	39.03 N	120.07 W
Sugartown	285	40.00 N	75.31 W
Sugauli	124	26.46 N	84.44 E
Sugbai Passage ʮ	116	5.22 N	120.33 E
Sugbay	116	7.31 N	123.19 E
Sugbuhan Point ›	116	10.04 N	126.04 E
Suggi Lake ⊜	184	54.22 N	102.47 W
Suginami ◆[8]	268	35.42 N	139.38 E
Sugita ◆[8]	268	35.23 N	139.38 E
Sugito	94	36.02 N	139.44 E
Şuğla Gölü ⊜	130	37.20 N	32.02 E
Šugnou	85	38.35 N	70.20 E
Sugod	116	12.03 N	124.09 E
Sugoj ≃	74	64.15 N	154.29 E
Šugonovo	82	54.41 N	36.41 E
Šugozero	76	59.55 N	34.12 E
Šugurovo, Ross.	80	53.25 N	46.29 E
Šugurovo, Ross.	80	54.31 N	52.06 E
Sugut ≃	112	6.26 N	117.43 E
Suguta ≃	154	2.03 N	36.33 E
Suguti	154	1.44 S	33.39 E
Suhai Hu ⊜	102	38.50 N	94.00 E
Suhaitu	102	44.50 N	93.39 E
Şuḩār	128	24.22 N	56.45 E
Suheli Island I[1]	122	10.03 N	72.17 E
Suhl	54	50.37 N	10.41 E
Suhlendorf	54	52.55 N	10.46 E
Suhopolje	36	45.48 N	17.30 E
Suhr	58	47.22 N	8.05 E
Suhr ≃	58	47.25 N	8.04 E
Suhum	150	6.05 N	0.27 W
Şuhut	130	38.32 N	30.33 E
Sūi	120	28.37 N	69.19 E
Suiá-Miçu ≃	250	11.13 S	53.15 W
Suianzhan	89	53.07 N	125.20 E
Suiattle ≃	224	48.20 N	121.33 W
Suichang	100	28.34 N	119.14 E
Suichuan	100	26.26 N	114.32 E
Suichuan ≃	100	26.30 N	114.45 E
Suid Afrika → South Africa □[1]	156	30.00 S	26.00 E
Suide	102	37.32 N	110.12 E
Suiding	86	44.03 N	80.49 E
Suido-suigenchi ⊜[1]	270	34.54 N	135.17 E
Suidvaal	158	26.52 S	29.47 E
Suifenhe	89	44.24 N	131.10 E
Suifu, Nihon	94	36.37 N	140.29 E
Suifu → Yibin, Zhg.	107	28.47 N	104.38 E
Suigō-kokutei-kōen ♠	94	36.05 N	140.20 E
Suigō-Tsukuba-kokutei-kōen ♠	94	36.00 N	140.20 E
Suihua	89	46.37 N	127.00 E
Suijiang	102	28.31 N	104.07 E
Suileng	89	47.18 N	127.10 E
Suining, Zhg.	100	33.54 N	117.56 E
Suining, Zhg.	102	26.21 N	110.00 E
Suining, Zhg.	107	30.31 N	105.34 E
Suipacha	252	34.45 S	59.41 W
Suiping	100	33.10 N	113.57 E
Suippe ≃	50	49.25 N	3.57 E
Suippes	56	49.08 N	4.32 E
Suir ≃	48	52.15 N	7.00 W
Suisse → Switzerland □[1]	58	47.00 N	8.00 E
Suisun Bay ᴄ	226	38.06 N	122.00 W
Suisun City	226	38.14 N	122.02 W
Suisun Creek ≃	226	38.12 N	122.06 W
Suita	96	34.45 N	135.32 E
Suiti burnu ›	84	40.12 N	50.22 E
Suitland	284c	38.50 N	76.55 W
Suixi, Zhg.	100	33.56 N	116.46 E
Suixi, Zhg.	102	21.25 N	110.15 E
Suixian, Zhg.	98	34.26 N	115.05 E
Suixian, Zhg.	100	31.42 N	113.20 E
Suiyang, Zhg.	89	44.26 N	130.53 E
Suiyang, Zhg.	102	27.56 N	107.18 E
Suiyangdian	100	32.04 N	112.55 E
Suiza → Switzerland □[1]	58	47.00 N	8.00 E
Suize ≃	58	48.08 N	5.08 E
Şuizhong	98	40.20 N	120.19 E
Šuja, Ross.	24	61.55 N	34.12 E
Šuja, Ross.	80	56.50 N	41.23 E
Šuja ≃, Ross.	24	61.54 N	34.15 E
Šuja ≃, Ross.	80	57.56 N	43.15 E
Sujānagar	126	23.57 N	89.25 E
Sujāngarh	120	27.42 N	74.28 E
Sujāwal	120	24.36 N	68.05 E
Suji	107	29.35 N	103.37 E
Sujiabu	100	31.38 N	116.22 E
Sujiaqiao	105	39.24 N	116.10 E
Sujiatun	104	41.40 N	123.22 E
Sujiawan	107	29.48 N	104.57 E
Sujiawu	105	39.17 N	115.55 E
Şujiazui	100	33.40 N	119.29 E
Šujskoje	76	59.22 N	40.59 E
Sujutkina Kosa, mys ›	84	44.13 N	47.15 E
Sukabihanawa	112	9.30 S	124.57 E
Sukabumi	115a	6.55 S	106.56 E
Sukadana, Indon.	112	1.15 S	109.57 E
Sukadana, Indon.	115a	5.05 S	105.33 E
Sukadana, Teluk ᴄ	112	1.24 S	109.50 E
Sukagawa	92	37.17 N	140.23 E
Sukamandi	115a	6.20 S	107.39 E
Sukamara	112	2.43 S	111.11 E
Sukanegara	115a	7.06 S	107.07 E
Sukapura	115a	7.52 S	113.03 E
Sukaraja, Indon.	112	2.21 S	110.37 E
Sukaraja, Indon.	115a	7.27 S	108.12 E
Sukaraja, Indon.	115a	7.27 S	109.17 E
Sukarno, Pegunungan → Jaya, Puncak ∧	164	4.05 S	137.11 E
Sukau	112	5.32 N	118.17 E
Sukchar	272b	22.42 N	88.22 E
Sukch'ŏn	98	39.24 N	125.38 E
Sukematsu	270	34.31 N	135.26 E
Sukeva	26	63.52 N	27.26 E
Sukha Volnovakha ≃	83	47.37 N	38.01 E
Sukhnah, 'Ayn ⍑[4]	142	29.35 N	32.15 E
Sukhothai	110	17.01 N	99.49 E
Sukhumi → Suchumi	84	43.01 N	41.02 E
Sukhyy Torets' ≃	83	48.49 N	37.36 E
Sukkertoppen (Maniitsoq)	176	65.25 N	52.53 W
Sukkozero	24	63.11 N	32.18 E
Sukkur	120	27.42 N	68.52 E
Sukkwan Island I	182	55.05 N	132.45 W
Suklāra	126	23.11 N	86.21 E
Sukmanovka	78	51.47 N	41.34 E
Sukodadi	115a	7.06 S	112.19 E
Sukoharjo	115a	7.41 S	110.50 E
Sukovo	82	54.54 N	38.19 E
Sukroml'a	76	56.53 N	34.44 E
Sukses	156	21.01 S	16.52 E
Suksun	86	57.07 N	57.24 E
Sukumo	92	32.56 N	132.44 E
Sukun, Pulau I	115b	8.07 S	122.08 E
Sukunka ≃	182	55.37 N	121.37 W
Sul, Baía ᴄ	252	27.40 S	48.35 W
Sul, Canal do ʮ	250	0.10 S	49.30 W
Sula I	26	61.08 N	4.55 E
Sula ≃, Ross.	24	67.16 N	52.07 E
Sula ≃, Ukr.	78	49.40 N	32.41 E
Sula, Kepulauan II	112	1.52 S	125.22 E
Sulaco ≃	236	15.01 N	87.44 W
Sulaimān Khel	123	33.41 N	71.01 E
Sulaimān Range ⋏	120	30.30 N	70.10 E
Sulak, Ross.	80	51.52 N	48.21 E
Sulak, Ross.	84	43.16 N	47.32 E
Sulak ≃	84	43.20 N	47.34 E
Sulakyurt	130	40.10 N	33.44 E
Sulang	115a	6.48 S	111.23 E
Sulat	116	11.49 N	125.27 E
Sulauan Point ›	116	8.37 N	124.29 E
Sulawesi (Celebes) I	112	2.00 S	121.00 E
Sulawesi Selatan □[4]	112	3.30 S	120.00 E
Sulawesi Tengah □[4]	112	1.00 N	123.00 E
Sulawesi Tenggara □[4]	112	4.00 S	122.00 E
Sulawesi Utara □[4]	112	0.30 N	124.00 E
Sulaymān, Birak (Solomon's Pools) ⊥	132	31.41 N	35.10 E
Sulby	44	54.18 N	4.29 W
Sulcis ◆[1]	71	39.04 N	8.41 E
Suldalsvatnet ⊜	26	59.35 N	6.45 E
Sūldeh	128	36.34 N	52.01 E
Sulechów	30	52.06 N	15.37 E
Sulęcin	30	52.26 N	15.08 E
Suleja	86	55.09 N	58.50 E
Sulejów	30	51.22 N	19.53 E
Sulejówek	30	52.14 N	21.17 E
Sulen, Mount ∧	164	3.25 S	142.15 E
Sule Skerry I[2]	46	59.05 N	4.26 W
Suleymaniye Mosque ʊ[1]	267b	41.00 N	28.57 E
Süleymanlı	130	37.54 N	36.50 E
Şülfeld	52	53.48 N	10.14 E
Šul'gino, Ross.	82	54.33 N	37.35 E
Sulğino, Ross.	82	55.50 N	35.55 E
Sulia	154	1.32 S	26.33 E
Suliki	112	0.06 S	100.27 E
Sulima	150	6.58 N	11.35 W
Sulin	83	48.54 N	40.07 E
Sulina	38	45.09 N	29.40 E
Sulina, Braţul ≃[1]	38	45.09 N	29.41 E
Sulincheer	102	42.41 N	109.20 E
Sulingen	52	52.41 N	8.47 E
Sulinskij	83	47.52 N	40.06 E
Sulitelma ∧	24	67.08 N	16.24 E
Sulkava	26	61.47 N	28.23 E
Sullana	248	4.53 S	80.41 W
Sullane ≃	48	51.53 N	8.56 W
Sulligent	194	33.54 N	88.08 W
Sullivan, Il., U.S.	194	39.35 N	88.36 W
Sullivan, In., U.S.	194	39.06 N	87.24 W
Sullivan, Mo., U.S.	219	38.12 N	91.09 W
Sullivan, Oh., U.S.	214	41.02 N	82.13 W
Sullivan, Wi., U.S.	216	43.00 N	88.35 W
Sullivan □[6], N.Y., U.S.	210	41.39 N	74.42 W
Sullivan □[6], Pa., U.S.	210	41.25 N	76.29 W
Sullivan Canyon V	280	34.03 N	118.30 W
Sullivan Creek ≃	226	37.53 N	120.25 W
Sullivan Lake ⊜	182	52.00 N	112.00 W
Sullivanville	210	42.14 N	76.46 W
Sully-sur-Loire	50	47.46 N	2.22 E
Sulm ≃	61	46.45 N	15.34 E
Sulmona	66	42.03 N	13.55 E
Sulot' ≃	82	56.41 N	38.01 E
Sulphur, Yk., Can.	180	63.47 N	138.53 W
Sulphur, In., U.S.	218	38.14 N	86.28 W
Sulphur, Ky., U.S.	218	38.29 N	85.16 W
Sulphur, La., U.S.	194	30.14 N	93.22 W
Sulphur, Ok., U.S.	196	34.30 N	96.58 W
Sulphur ≃, Ab., Can.	182	53.50 N	119.10 W
Sulphur ≃, U.S.	194	33.07 N	93.52 W
Sulphur Creek ≃	198	44.46 N	102.25 W
Sulphur Draw V	196	33.12 N	102.17 W
Sulphur Springs, In., U.S.	218	40.00 N	85.26 W
Sulphur Springs, Oh., U.S.	214	40.52 N	82.52 W
Sulphur Springs, Tx., U.S.	222	33.08 N	95.36 W
Sulphur Springs Draw V	196	32.12 N	101.36 W
Sulphur Springs Valley V	200	31.50 N	109.50 W
Sulsul	144	5.06 N	44.55 E
Sultan	224	47.51 N	121.48 W
Sultan ≃	224	47.52 N	121.49 W
Sultana	226	36.33 N	119.20 W
Sultanahmet Mosque ʊ[1]	267b	41.00 N	28.58 E
Sultan Alonto, Lake ⊜	116	7.53 N	124.15 E
Sultana Point ›	168b	35.08 S	137.45 E
Sulṭanatābād ◆[8]	267d	35.46 N	51.28 E
Sultançiftligi ◆[8]	267b	41.02 N	29.13 E
Sultandağı	130	38.32 N	31.14 E
Sultan Dağı ∧	130	38.58 N	27.26 E
Sultanhanı	130	38.15 N	33.33 E
Sultanhisar	130	37.53 N	28.10 E
Sultan Kudarat	116	7.17 N	124.16 E
Sultan Kudarat □[4]	116	6.20 N	124.20 E
Sultan Mosque ʊ[1]	271c	1.18 N	103.52 E
Sultānpur, India	123	31.13 N	75.11 E
Sultānpur, India	124	26.16 N	82.04 E
Sultānpur Dabās ◆[8]	272a	28.46 N	77.03 E
Sultan sa Barongis	116	6.46 N	124.38 E
Sultan-Saly	83	47.21 N	39.35 E
Sulu	164	5.25 S	151.00 E
Sulu □[4]	116	6.00 N	121.00 E
Suluan Island I	116	10.46 N	125.57 E
Sulu Archipelago II	116	6.00 N	121.00 E
Sulu Basin ✤[1]	12	8.00 N	121.30 E
Sulu Chi ⊜	124	30.12 N	86.20 E
Sülüklü	130	39.05 N	30.58 E
Sul'ukta	85	39.56 N	69.34 E
Sululta	144	9.10 N	38.48 E
Suluntah	146	32.36 N	21.43 E
Suluova (Suluca)	130	40.47 N	35.42 E
Sulūq	146	31.39 N	20.15 E
Sulusaj	85	38.50 N	67.05 E
Sulusaray	130	40.00 N	36.06 E
Sulu Sea ⍑[2]	116	8.00 N	120.00 E
Suly	86	53.45 N	66.30 E
Sulz	58	48.18 N	7.51 E
Sulz am Neckar	58	48.21 N	8.37 E
Sulzano	64	45.41 N	10.05 E
Sulzbach, Dtsch.	56	49.18 N	7.07 E
Sulzbach, Dtsch.	56	49.00 N	9.30 E
Sulzbach ≃	60	48.36 N	13.02 E
Sulzbach am Kocher	56	48.58 N	9.50 E
Sulzbach-Rosenberg	60	49.30 N	11.45 E
Sulzberger Bay ᴄ	9	77.00 S	152.00 W
Sulzbrunn	58	47.41 N	10.20 E
Sulzburg	58	47.50 N	7.42 E
Şülze	52	52.46 N	10.02 E
Šum, Ross.	76	59.52 N	31.46 E
Šum, Ross.	88	54.51 N	95.18 E
Šuma ◆[8]	270	34.39 N	135.08 E
Šum'ači	76	53.52 N	32.25 E
Šumadija ◆[1]	38	44.10 N	20.50 E
Sumalata	112	0.59 N	122.30 E
Sumallo ≃	224	49.14 N	121.05 W
Şumampa	252	29.22 S	63.28 W
Šumanaj	86	42.37 N	59.08 E
Sumangat, Tanjong ›	116	6.35 N	117.33 E
Sumano-ura ♠	96	34.38 N	135.08 E
Sūmār	128	33.52 N	45.39 E
Sumarokovo	82	55.46 N	35.55 E
Sumas	202	49.00 N	122.15 W
Sumas ≃	224	49.09 N	122.12 W
Sumatera (Sumatra) I	108	0.05 S	102.00 E
Sumatera Barat □[4]	112	0.30 S	100.30 E
Sumatera Selatan □[4]	112	3.00 S	104.00 E
Sumatera Utara □[4]	114	2.20 N	99.00 E
Sum'atino	82	55.00 N	36.21 E
Sumatou	107	30.28 N	104.03 E
Sumatra → Sumatera I	108	0.05 S	102.00 E
Sumava Resorts	216	41.10 N	87.26 W
Sumayḩ	140	12.43 N	30.50 E
Sumba I	115b	10.00 S	120.00 E
Sumba, Île I	152	1.44 N	19.32 E
Sumba, Selat ʮ	115b	9.05 S	120.00 E
Sumbar ≃	128	38.00 N	55.17 E
Sumbawa I	115b	8.40 S	118.00 E
Sumbawa Besar	115b	8.30 S	117.26 E
Sumbawanga	154	7.58 S	31.37 E
Sumbay	248	15.58 S	71.23 W
Sumbe	152	11.13 S	13.50 E
Sümber	90	46.21 N	108.20 E
Sumbilla	34	43.10 N	1.40 W
Sumbing, Gunung ∧	115a	7.23 S	110.04 E
Sumbu National Park ♠	154	8.50 S	30.25 E
Sumburgh Head ›	46a	59.53 N	1.20 W
Şumburgh Roost ʮ	46a	59.49 N	1.19 W
Šumbut	80	55.33 N	50.41 E
Sumbuya	150	7.39 N	11.58 W
Sumdo	120	35.01 N	78.41 E
Sumé	250	7.39 S	36.55 W
Sumedang	115a	6.52 S	107.55 E
Şümeg	30	46.59 N	17.17 E
Šumek	86	48.42 N	85.32 E
Šumen	38	43.16 N	26.55 E
Sumène	62	43.59 N	3.43 E
Şumenep	115a	7.01 S	113.52 E
Šumerl'a	80	55.30 N	46.26 E
Sumgait → Sumqayıt	84	40.36 N	49.38 E
Šumicha	86	55.14 N	63.19 E
Sumida ◆[8]	268	35.42 N	139.48 E
Sumida ≃	268	35.40 N	139.47 E
Sumidouro	256	22.03 S	42.41 W
Şumilao	116	8.18 N	124.57 E
Šumilino	76	55.18 N	29.37 E
Šumilinskaja	80	49.58 N	41.26 E
Suminoe ◆[8]	270	34.36 N	135.28 E
Sumisu-jima I	90	31.27 N	140.03 E
Sumiswald	58	47.02 N	7.45 E
Sumiyoshi ◆[8]	270	34.36 N	135.31 E
Sumki	86	55.03 N	65.44 E
Sumkino	86	58.09 N	68.21 E
Sumlog ≃	116	6.53 N	126.02 E
Summer Bridge	44	54.03 N	1.41 W
Summerdale	208	40.18 N	76.56 W
Summerfield, Fl., U.S.	220	29.00 N	82.02 W
Summerfield, Mo., U.S.	219	38.17 N	91.49 W
Summerfield, N.C., U.S.	192	36.12 N	79.54 W
Summerford, Nf., Can.	186	49.29 N	54.47 W
Summerford, Oh., U.S.	218	39.55 N	83.29 W
Summerhill, Ire.	48	53.29 N	6.44 W
Summerhill, Pa., U.S.	214	40.22 N	78.46 W
Summer Island I	190	45.34 N	86.39 W
Summer Isles II	46	58.02 N	5.28 W
Summer Lake ⊜	202	42.50 N	120.45 W
Summerland	182	49.36 N	119.41 W
Summerland Reserve ◆[4]	169	38.31 S	145.10 E
Sümmern	56	51.25 N	7.43 E
Summer Palace ʊ	265a	59.53 N	29.55 E
Summerseat	262	53.38 N	2.19 W
Summerside	186	46.24 N	63.47 W
Summersville, Mo., U.S.	194	37.10 N	91.39 W
Summersville, W.V., U.S.	188	38.16 N	80.51 W
Summerton	192	33.36 N	80.21 W
Summertown	194	35.26 N	87.18 W
Summerville, On., Can.	275b	43.37 N	79.34 W
Summerville, Ga., U.S.	192	34.28 N	85.20 W
Summerville, Pa., U.S.	214	41.06 N	79.11 W
Summerville, S.C., U.S.	192	33.00 N	80.11 W
Summit, Eng., U.K.	262	53.40 N	2.05 W
Summit, Ak., U.S.	180	63.20 N	149.08 W
Summit, Ca., U.S.	228	34.20 N	117.25 W
Summit, Il., U.S.	216	41.47 N	87.48 W
Summit, Ms., U.S.	194	31.17 N	90.28 W
Summit, N.J., U.S.	210	40.44 N	74.21 W
Summit, N.Y., U.S.	210	42.35 N	74.35 W
Summit, S.D., U.S.	198	45.18 N	97.02 W
Summit, Wa., U.S.	224	47.10 N	122.21 W
Summit □[6]	214	41.05 N	81.31 W
Summit Creek ≃	224	46.00 N	121.10 W
Summit Farms	284b	39.19 N	76.32 W
Summit Hill	210	40.49 N	75.52 W
Summit Lake	182	54.17 N	122.38 W
Summit Lake ⊜	224	47.04 N	123.07 W
Summit Mountain ∧	204	39.23 N	116.28 W
Summit Park	276	41.09 N	74.03 W
Summit Park Mall ◆[9]	284a	43.05 N	78.56 W
Summit Peak ∧	200	37.21 N	106.42 W
Summit Rock ∧	172	45.25 S	170.04 E
Summit Station	208	40.34 N	76.12 W
Summitville, In., U.S.	216	40.20 N	85.38 W
Summitville, N.Y., U.S.	210	41.37 N	74.27 W
Summitville, Oh., U.S.	214	40.41 N	80.53 W
Summt	264a	52.41 N	13.22 E
Şummter See ⊜	264a	52.42 N	13.23 E
Šumná	61	48.56 N	15.52 E
Sumnal	120	35.45 N	78.40 E
Sumner, Ia., U.S.	190	42.50 N	92.05 W
Sumner, Ms., U.S.	194	33.58 N	90.22 W
Sumner, Wa., U.S.	224	47.12 N	122.14 W
Sumner, Lake ⊜	172	42.42 S	172.13 E
Sumner, Lake ⊜[1]	196	34.38 N	104.25 W
Sumner Lake State Park ♠	196	34.38 N	104.24 W
Sumner Strait ʮ	180	56.15 N	133.45 W
Sumoto	96	34.21 N	134.54 E
Şumpangbinangae	112	4.24 S	119.36 E
Šumperk	30	49.58 N	16.58 E
Sumpiuh	115a	7.37 S	109.21 E
Sumprabum	110	26.33 N	97.34 E
Sumpter	281	42.10 N	83.29 W
Sumqayıt	84	40.36 N	49.38 E
Sumqayıt ≃	84	40.37 N	49.37 E
Sumrall	194	31.25 N	89.32 W
Sumsar	85	41.18 N	71.19 E
Ş'umsi	80	57.07 N	51.37 E
Šumskij	88	54.48 N	99.09 E
Şumskij Posad	24	64.15 N	35.25 E
Šumšu, ostrov I	74	50.45 N	156.20 E
Sumter	192	33.55 N	80.20 W
Sumter □[6]	220	28.38 N	82.08 W
Sumusṭā al-Waqf	142	28.55 N	30.51 E
Sumy	78	50.55 N	34.45 E
Sumy □[4]	78	51.00 N	34.00 E
Sumzom	102	29.45 N	96.10 E
S'un' ≃, Ross.	80	55.44 N	54.16 E
Sun ≃, Mt., U.S.	202	47.30 N	111.19 W
Sun ≃, Zhg.	107	29.13 N	106.21 E
Suna, Kenya	154	1.05 S	34.26 E
Suna, Ross.	80	57.51 N	50.05 E
Suna ≃	24	62.08 N	34.12 E
Sunagawa	92a	43.29 N	141.55 E
Sun al-Heteimi ⍑[4]	132	31.05 N	34.00 E
Sun' al-Menī'i ⍑[4]	132	31.07 N	34.12 E
Sunām	123	30.08 N	75.48 E
Sunāmganj	120	25.04 N	91.24 E
Sunami	94	35.25 N	136.40 E
Sunan	98	39.13 N	125.41 E
Sunapee Lake ⊜	188	43.23 N	72.03 W
Sunart, Loch ᴄ	46	56.41 N	5.43 W
Sunashinden	268	35.53 N	139.30 E
Sunbāṭ	142	30.48 N	31.12 E
Sunbright	192	36.14 N	84.40 W
Sunburst	202	48.52 N	111.54 W
Sunbury, Austl.	169	37.35 S	144.44 E
Sunbury, Eng., U.K.	260	51.25 N	0.26 W
Sunbury, N.C., U.S.	192	36.26 N	76.36 W
Sunbury, Oh., U.S.	214	40.14 N	82.51 W
Sunbury, Pa., U.S.	210	40.51 N	76.47 W
Sunchales	252	30.56 S	61.34 W
Sunch'ang	98	35.23 N	127.07 E
Sunchild Indian Reserve ◆[4]	182	52.43 N	115.24 W
Sünching	60	48.53 N	12.21 E
Suncho Corral	252	27.56 S	63.27 W
Sunch'ŏn, C.M.I.K.	98	39.26 N	125.54 E
Sunch'ŏn, Taehan	98	34.57 N	127.28 E
Sun City, Az., U.S.	200	33.35 N	112.16 W
Sun City, Ca., U.S.	228	33.42 N	117.11 W
Sun City, Fl., U.S.	220	27.40 N	82.28 W
Sun City Center	220	27.43 N	82.21 W
Suncook	188	43.07 N	71.27 W
Suncook ≃	188	43.08 N	71.28 W
Sunda, Selat (Sunda Strait) ʮ	112	6.00 S	105.45 E
Sundance	198	44.24 N	104.22 W
Sundar	112	4.54 N	115.12 E
Sundar ∧	124	28.26 N	84.20 E
Sundarbans ◆[1]	126	22.00 N	89.00 E
Sundargarh	124	22.07 N	84.02 E
Sundarnagar	123	31.32 N	76.53 E
Sunda Shelf ✤[4]	14	5.00 N	107.00 E
Sunda Strait → Sunda, Selat ʮ	112	6.00 S	105.45 E
Sunday Creek ≃	169	37.02 S	145.05 E
Sundby, Dan.	41	54.42 N	11.48 E
Sundby, Sve.	40	59.23 N	17.03 E
Sundbyberg	40	59.22 N	17.58 E
Sundbyholm	40	59.27 N	16.37 E
Sundbyholm slott ⊥	40	59.27 N	16.37 E
Sunde	26	59.50 N	5.43 E
Sunderland, On., Can.	212	44.16 N	79.04 W
Sunderland, Eng., U.K.	44	54.55 N	1.23 W
Sunderland, Ma., U.S.	207	42.28 N	72.34 W
Sunderland, Vt., U.S.	210	43.06 N	73.06 W
Sundern	56	51.20 N	8.00 E
Sünderup	41	54.46 N	9.27 E
Sundhausen	54	50.56 N	10.40 E
Sundhouse	58	48.15 N	7.36 E
Sundi-Lutete	152	4.34 S	14.14 E
Sundown, Austl.	162	26.14 S	133.12 E
Sundown, N.Y., U.S.	210	41.53 N	74.28 W
Sundown, Tx., U.S.	196	33.27 N	102.29 W
Sundra	273d	26.11 S	28.33 E
Sundre	182	51.48 N	114.38 W
Sundridge, On., Can.	190	45.46 N	79.24 W
Sundridge, Eng., U.K.	260	51.17 N	0.08 E
Sunds	41	56.12 N	9.01 E
Sundsbruk	26	62.27 N	17.22 E
Sundsvall	26	62.23 N	17.18 E
Sundwig	263	51.23 N	7.47 E
Suneori	268	35.56 N	139.24 E
Sunfield	216	42.45 N	84.59 W
Sunfish Creek ≃	218	39.01 N	83.03 W
Sunflower	194	33.32 N	90.32 W
Sunflower, Mount ∧	198	39.04 N	102.01 W
Sungaianyar	112	2.55 S	116.18 E
Sungaiapit	114	1.09 N	102.10 E
Sungaibamban	114	3.26 N	99.09 E
Sungaibatu	112	0.48 N	110.45 E
Sungai Bayor	114	5.15 N	100.47 E
Sungaibuntu	115a	6.03 S	107.24 E
Sungaidareh	112	0.58 S	101.30 E
Sungaigerong	112	2.59 S	104.52 E
Sungaiguntung	112	0.18 N	103.37 E
Sungaikakap	112	0.04 S	109.10 E
Sungai Kolok	114	6.02 N	101.58 E
Sungailangsat	112	0.52 S	101.18 E
Sungai Lembing	114	3.55 N	103.02 E
Sungailiat	112	1.51 S	106.08 E
Sungailimau	112	0.31 S	100.03 E
Sungaimanasip	114	1.49 N	100.54 E
Sungainipah	114	0.57 N	98.57 E
Sungaipakning	114	1.20 N	102.09 E
Sungaipenuh	112	2.05 S	101.23 E
Sungaipenyu	112	0.16 N	109.04 E
Sungai Petani	114	5.39 N	100.30 E
Sungaipinang	112	0.48 S	114.04 E
Sungairampah	114	3.29 N	99.09 E
Sungairotan, Indon.	112	1.39 S	102.51 E
Sungairotan, Indon.	112	3.06 S	104.18 E
Sungaisalak	112	0.27 S	102.59 E
Sungaiselan	112	2.24 S	105.59 E
Sungai Siput	114	4.49 N	101.04 E
Sungaitampang	114	2.20 N	100.07 E
Şungaitiram	112	0.47 S	117.12 E
Šungaj	80	48.32 N	46.46 E
Sungari → Songhua ≃	89	47.44 N	132.32 E
Sungchiang → Songjiang	106	31.01 N	121.14 E
Sungezhuang	105	40.15 N	116.39 E
Sungguminasa	112	5.12 S	119.27 E
Sungi ≃	115b	8.38 S	115.06 E
Sungi Point ›	116	10.55 N	125.50 E
Sungkai	114	4.00 N	101.19 E
Sung Kong I	271d	22.11 N	114.17 E
Sung Noen	110	14.54 N	101.50 E
Sungsang	112	2.22 S	104.56 E
Sungshan Domestic Airport ⌧	269d	25.04 N	121.33 E
Sungurlu	130	40.10 N	34.23 E
Sunhezhen	105	40.03 N	116.31 E
Suni	71	40.17 N	8.33 E
Suning	98	38.25 N	115.50 E
Sunjiabu	106	30.55 N	118.54 E
Sunjiadizi	104	42.09 N	124.09 E
Sunjiagou	104	40.45 N	120.39 E
Sunjiajiang	105	40.10 N	115.32 E
Sunjiakanzi	104	40.42 N	123.02 E
Sunjiawan	104	41.59 N	121.42 E
Sunjiazhai	106	30.55 N	121.52 E
Sunjikāy	140	12.20 N	29.46 E
Sunkar, gora ∧	86	44.15 N	73.50 E
Sunken Meadow State Park ♠	207	40.54 N	73.16 W
Sunkośī ≃	124	26.55 N	87.09 E
Sunland ◆[8]	280	34.16 N	118.19 W
Sunland Park	200	32.15 N	106.45 W
Sunlight Creek ≃	202	44.47 N	109.23 W
Sunlongwan	104	41.19 N	122.57 E
Sunman	218	39.14 N	85.05 W
Sunnansjö	40	60.13 N	14.57 E
Sunndalsøra	26	62.40 N	8.33 E
Sunne	26	59.50 N	13.09 E
Sunnemo	40	59.53 N	13.43 E
Sunnersta	40	59.48 N	17.39 E
Sunnī, Khawr V	140	7.09 N	28.41 E
Sunningdale	260	51.24 N	0.38 W
Sunninghill	42	51.25 N	0.40 W
Sunnybrae	186	45.24 N	62.30 W
Sunny Corner	170	33.23 S	149.53 E
Sunny Crest	278	41.33 N	87.42 W
Sunnydale	224	47.28 N	122.20 W
Sunnyland	220	27.17 N	82.29 W
Sunnylvsfjorden ᴄ[2]	26	62.17 N	7.01 E
Sunnymead	228	33.56 N	117.14 W
Sunnynook	182	51.17 N	111.40 W
Sunnyridge	273d	26.10 S	28.11 E
Sunnyside, Nf., Can.	186	47.51 N	53.55 W
Sunnyside, Ca., U.S.	226	32.40 N	117.01 W
Sunny Side, Tx., U.S.	222	29.54 N	96.04 W
Sunnyside, Ut,. U.S.	200	39.33 N	110.23 W
Sunnyside, Wa., U.S.	202	46.19 N	120.00 W
Sunnyside ⊥	276	41.03 N	73.52 W
Sunnyslope, Ab., Can.	182	51.40 N	113.32 W
Sunnyslope, Wa., U.S.	224	47.30 N	122.44 W
Sunnyvale, Ca., U.S.	226	37.22 N	122.02 W
Sunnyvale, Tx., U.S.	222	32.48 N	96.33 W
Sunol	282	37.36 N	121.53 W
Sunol Ridge ∧	282	37.38 N	121.56 W
Sun Prairie	216	43.11 N	89.12 W
Sunray	196	36.01 N	101.49 W
Sunrise, Ky., U.S.	218	38.33 N	84.14 W
Sunrise, Tx., U.S.	222	31.17 N	96.53 W
Sunrise, Wy., U.S.	200	42.19 N	104.42 W
Sunrise Heights	216	42.18 N	85.09 W
Sunrise Mall ◆[9]	276	40.41 N	73.26 W
Sunrise Manor	204	36.08 N	115.04 W
Sunrise Peak ∧	224	46.20 N	121.46 W
Sun River Terrace	216	41.06 N	87.45 W
Sunset, La., U.S.	194	30.24 N	92.04 W
Sunset, Tx., U.S.	196	33.27 N	97.46 W
Sunset ◆[8]	282	37.45 N	122.30 W
Sunset Bay	214	42.11 N	79.24 W
Sunset Beach, Ca., U.S.	280	33.43 N	118.04 W
Sunset Beach, Hi., U.S.	229c	21.40 N	158.02 W
Sunset Country ◆[1]	166	35.00 S	141.30 E
Sunset Crater National Monument ♠	200	35.18 N	111.21 W
Sunset Heights	196	31.53 N	102.22 W
Sunset Hill	276	40.26 N	74.35 W
Sunset Hills	279b	40.35 N	80.15 W
Sunset Peak ∧	280	34.13 N	117.42 W
Sunset Prairie	182	55.50 N	120.48 W
Sunset Valley	214	40.18 N	79.44 W
Sunshine, Austl.	166	37.47 S	144.50 E
Sunshine, Austl.	169	37.47 S	144.50 E
Sunshine, Ak., U.S.	180	62.10 N	150.04 W
Sunshine Island I	271d	22.16 N	114.03 E
Sunshine Point ›	281	42.36 N	82.47 W
Sunshine Skyway Bridge ◆[5]	220	27.37 N	82.39 W
Suntai ≃	146	8.05 N	10.04 E
Suntar	74	62.10 N	117.40 E
Suntar-Chajata, chrebet ⋏	74	62.00 N	143.00 E
Suntaug Lake ⊜	283	42.32 N	71.00 W
Süntel ⋏	52	52.12 N	9.25 E
Sun Temple ʊ[1]	273c	29.55 N	31.11 E
Sunter ◆[8]	269e	6.09 S	106.50 E
Sunter, Kali ≊	269e	6.07 S	106.50 E
Sunti ≃	272b	22.37 N	88.34 E
Suntrana	180	63.51 N	148.51 W
Suntsar	128	25.31 N	62.00 E
Suntu	144	8.06 N	36.57 E
Sun Valley, Id., U.S.	202	43.41 N	114.21 W
Sun Valley, Nv., U.S.	226	39.34 N	119.47 W
Sun Valley ◆[8]	280	34.14 N	118.21 W
SunValley Center ◆[9]	282	37.58 N	122.03 W
Sun Village	228	34.35 N	118.03 W
Sunwapta ≃	182	52.32 N	117.41 W
Sunwi-do I	98	37.44 N	125.15 E
Sunwu	89	49.27 N	127.20 E
Sunwui → Jiangmen	100	22.35 N	113.05 E
Sunyani	150	7.20 N	2.20 W
Sunying	98	34.30 N	114.21 E
Sunža ≃	84	43.26 N	46.08 E
Sunženskij chrebet ⋏	84	43.21 N	45.00 E
Sun Zhong Shan Ling (Tomb of Sun Yat Sen) ⊥	106	32.10 N	118.56 E
Suojarvi	24	62.05 N	32.21 E
Suolahti	26	62.34 N	25.52 E
Suomenlahti → Finland, Gulf of ᴄ	26	60.00 N	27.00 E
Suomenselkä ∧	26	63.59 N	27.00 E
Suomi → Finland □[1]	24	64.00 N	26.00 E
Suomussalmi	26	64.53 N	29.05 E
Suō-nada ⍑[2]	96	33.50 N	131.30 E
Suonenjoki	26	62.37 N	27.08 E
Suontee ⊜	26	61.40 N	26.30 E
Suordach	74	66.43 N	132.04 E
Suoshu	106	31.57 N	119.00 E
Supachuy	248	19.29 S	64.31 W
Supamo ≃	246	6.48 N	61.50 W
Supaul	124	26.07 N	86.36 E
Supe	144	8.37 N	35.38 E
Superbe ≃	50	48.35 N	3.53 E
Superga, Basilica di ʊ[1]	62	45.05 N	7.46 E
Superior, Az., U.S.	200	33.17 N	111.05 W
Superior, Mt., U.S.	202	47.11 N	114.53 W
Superior, Ne., U.S.	198	40.01 N	98.04 W
Superior, Wi., U.S.	190	46.43 N	92.06 W
Superior, Laguna ᴄ	234	16.20 N	94.55 W
Superior, Lake ⊜	190	48.00 N	88.00 W
Superior Lake ⊜	228	35.15 N	117.02 W
Superior Valley V	228	35.16 N	117.00 W
Supersano	68	40.01 N	18.14 E
Supetar	36	43.23 N	16.33 E
Suphan Buri	110	14.28 N	100.07 E
Suphan Buri ≃	110	13.29 N	100.17 E
Süphan Dağı ∧	84	38.56 N	42.50 E
Supino	66	41.37 N	13.14 E
Supiori I	164	0.45 S	135.30 E
Supiy ≃	78	49.38 N	31.48 E
Sūpkhār	124	22.12 N	80.56 E
Suponevo	76	53.12 N	34.18 E
Supoqiao	107	30.40 N	103.59 E
Süpplingen	54	52.14 N	10.54 E
Supraśl	30	53.13 N	23.20 E
Supraśl ≃	30	53.04 N	22.56 E
Sup'ung	98	40.27 N	124.57 E
Sup'ung-chŏsuji ⊜[1]	98	40.30 N	125.05 E
Supur	126	23.01 N	86.52 E
Suputinskij zapovednik ♠	89	43.40 N	132.20 E
Sūq-'Abs	144	15.59 N	43.04 E
Sūq ash-Shuyūkh	128	30.53 N	46.28 E
Suq'at al-Jamal	140	12.48 N	27.42 E
Suqian	100	33.59 N	118.18 E
Suqiao, Zhg.	100	34.08 N	113.47 E
Suqiao, Zhg.	105	39.03 N	116.29 E
Sūq Suwayq	128	24.23 N	38.27 E
Suquamish	224	47.43 N	122.33 W
Suquṭrā (Socotra) I	118	12.30 N	54.00 E
Şūr (Tyre), Lubnān	132	33.16 N	35.11 E
Şūr, 'Umān	118	22.35 N	59.31 E
Sur, Cabo ›	174z	27.12 S	109.26 W
Sur, Campos de Hielo ⊡	254	49.10 S	73.30 W
Sur, Canal ʮ	288	34.37 S	58.15 W
Sur, Point ›	226	36.18 N	121.54 W
Sura	80	53.53 N	45.45 E
Sura ◆[8]	272b	22.33 N	88.25 E
Sura ≃	80	56.06 N	46.00 E
Sura, Cape ›	144	11.10 N	47.30 E
Şūrāb, Pāk.	120	28.29 N	66.16 E
Šurab, Taj.	85	40.03 N	70.33 E
Surabaya	115a	7.15 S	112.45 E
S'urachi, Nuraghe ⊥	71	40.01 N	8.33 E
Şurad	142	30.59 N	30.54 E
Surag-san ∧	271b	37.42 N	127.04 E
Surahammar	40	59.43 N	16.13 E
Sūrak	128	25.43 N	58.48 E
Surakarta	115a	7.35 S	110.50 E
Suramana	112	0.50 S	119.33 E
Surami	84	42.01 N	43.34 E
Şūrān, Īrān	128	27.18 N	62.04 E
Šuran, Ross.	80	55.22 N	49.50 E
Şūrān, Sūrīy.	130	36.34 N	37.13 E
Şūrān, Sūrīy.	130	35.17 N	36.45 E
Şuran ≃	58	46.02 N	5.19 E
Šurany	30	48.06 N	18.14 E

Symbol	English	Deutsch	Español	Français	Português
≃	River	Fluß	Río	Rivière	Rio
≊	Canal	Kanal	Canal	Canal	Canal
ʟ	Waterfall, Rapids	Wasserfall, Stromschnellen	Cascada, Rápidos	Chute d'eau, Rapides	Cascata, Rápidos
ʮ	Strait	Meeresstraße	Estrecho	Détroit	Estreito
ᴄ	Bay, Gulf	Bucht, Golf	Bahía, Golfo	Baie, Golfe	Baía, Golfo
⊜	Lake, Lakes	See, Seen	Lago, Lagos	Lac, Lacs	Lago, Lagos
≋	Swamp	Sumpf	Pantano	Marais	Pântano
⊡	Ice Features, Glacier	Eis- und Gletscherformen	Accidentes Glaciales	Formes glaciaires	Acidentes glaciares
⍑	Other Hydrographic Features	Andere Hydrographische Objekte	Otros Elementos Hidrográficos	Autres données hydrographiques	Outros acidentes hidrográficos

Symbol	English	Deutsch	Español	Français	Português
✤	Submarine Features	Untermeerische Objekte	Accidentes Submarinos	Formes de relief sous-marin	Acidentes submarinos
□	Political Unit	Politische Einheit	Unidad Politica	Entité politique	Unidade política
ʊ	Cultural Institution	Kulturelle Institution	Institución Cultural	Institution culturelle	Instituição cultural
⊥	Historical Site	Historische Stätte	Sitio Histórico	Site historique	Sitio histórico
♠	Recreational Site	Erholungs- und Ferienort	Sitio de Recreo	Centre de loisirs	Area de Lazer
⌧	Airport	Flughafen	Aeropuerto	Aéroport	Aeroporto
■	Military Installation	Militäranlage	Instalación Militar	Installation militaire	Instalação militar
◆	Miscellaneous	Verschiedenes	Misceláneo	Divers	Diversos

ENGLISH

Name	Page	Lat.°′	Long.°′
Surar	144	7.27 N	40.57 E
Surat, Austl.	166	27.09 S	149.04 E
Sūrat, India	120	21.10 N	72.50 E
Sūratgarh	123	29.19 N	73.54 E
Surat Thani (Ban Don)	110	9.08 N	99.19 E
Surava	80	52.57 N	41.18 E
Suraž, Bela.	76	55.25 N	30.44 E
Suraż, Pol.	30	52.58 N	22.58 E
Suraž, Ross.	76	53.01 N	32.24 E
Surbiton ◆[8]	260	51.24 N	0.18 W
Surbo	68	40.24 N	18.08 E
Surbourg	56	48.55 N	7.51 E
Surchan	80	46.39 N	49.38 E
Surchandarja □[4]	85	38.00 N	67.30 E
Surchandarja ≃	85	37.58 N	67.50 E
Surchdara	85	38.37 N	69.55 E
Surchob ≃	85	38.53 N	70.03 E
Šurči	85	37.59 N	67.47 E
Surco ≃	286d	12.13 S	77.03 W
Surdulica	38	42.41 N	22.10 E
Sûre (Sauer) ≃	56	49.44 N	6.31 E
Şureanu, Munţii ⋏	38	45.38 N	23.27 E
Šureksor, ozero ⊜	86	52.16 N	75.50 E
Surendorf	41	54.28 N	10.04 E
Surendranagar	120	22.42 N	71.41 E
Suresnes	261	48.52 N	2.14 E
Suretka	236	9.34 N	82.56 W
Surf City	208	39.39 N	74.09 W
Surfers Paradise	171a	28.00 S	153.26 E
Surfside, Fl., U.S.	220	25.52 N	80.07 W
Surfside, Tx., U.S.	222	28.57 N	95.17 W
Surgères	32	46.07 N	0.45 W
Surgidero	240p	22.41 N	82.18 W
Surgijn ≃	88	47.20 N	95.50 E
Surgoinsville	192	36.28 N	82.51 W
Sürgü	130	38.01 N	37.59 E
Sürgücü	130	37.35 N	40.44 E
Surgut	74	61.14 N	73.20 E
Surhuisterveen	52	53.10 N	6.10 E
Suri	164	7.10 S	143.55 E
Suria	272b	22.51 N	88.33 E
Suriāpet	122	17.09 N	79.37 E
Suribachi-yama ∧[2]	174f	24.45 N	141.17 E
Suribao ≃	116	11.33 N	125.28 E
Surigao	116	9.45 N	125.30 E
Surigao del Norte □[4]	116	9.35 N	125.36 E
Surigao del Sur □[4]	116	9.00 N	126.00 E
Surigao Strait ʯ	116	10.15 N	125.23 E
Surikova	86	56.59 N	91.31 E
Surin	110	14.53 N	103.29 E
Surinam → Suriname □[1]	250	4.00 N	56.00 W
Suriname □[1], S.A.	242	4.00 N	56.00 W
Suriname □[1], S.A.	250	4.00 N	56.00 W
Šurinda	88	55.13 N	113.23 E
Suring	190	44.59 N	88.22 W
Sūrīyah → Syria □[1]	128	35.00 N	38.00 E
S'urkum	89	50.08 N	140.31 E
S'urkum, mys ›	89	50.05 N	140.41 E
Šurma	80	56.58 N	50.21 E
Sūrmaq	128	31.03 N	52.48 E
Surmelin ≃	50	49.04 N	3.31 E
Surnadalsøra	26	62.59 N	8.39 E
Surodadi	115a	6.53 S	109.15 E
Surovaticha	80	55.45 N	43.56 E
Surovikino	80	48.36 N	42.51 E
Surovo	88	55.37 N	105.36 E
Surprise	200	33.37 N	112.19 W
Surprise, Lake ⊜	222	29.33 N	94.41 W
Surprise Valley V	204	41.35 N	120.05 W
Surquillo	286d	12.07 S	77.02 W
Surrency	192	31.43 N	82.11 W
Surrey	198	48.14 N	101.07 W
Surrey □[6]	42	51.10 N	0.20 W
Surrey, University of ʊ[2]	260	51.14 N	0.36 W
Surrey Heath □[8]	260	51.23 N	0.35 W
Surry	208	37.08 N	76.50 W
Surry □[6]	208	37.10 N	76.50 W
Sursee	58	47.10 N	8.06 E
Sursés V	58	46.34 N	9.38 E
Sursk	80	53.04 N	45.42 E
Surskij Majdan	80	55.01 N	46.32 E
Surskoje	80	54.30 N	46.44 E
Surt	146	31.12 N	16.35 E
Surt, Khalīj (Gulf of Sidra) c	146	31.30 N	18.00 E
Surtainville	28	49.25 N	1.50 W
Surtanāhu	120	26.22 N	70.00 E
Surte	26	57.49 N	12.01 E
Surtsey I	24a	63.16 N	20.32 W
Suru	164	6.50 S	144.45 E
Suru ≃	123	34.45 N	76.12 E
Surubiú ≃	250	3.58 S	48.52 W
Sürüç	130	36.58 N	38.24 E
Suruga-wan c	94	34.51 N	138.33 E
Suruí	256	22.40 S	43.07 W
Suruí ≃	287a	22.42 S	43.07 W
Surulangun	112	2.37 S	102.45 E
Suru-Lere ◆[8]	273a	6.31 N	3.22 E
Surumu ≃	246	3.22 N	60.19 W
Surveyor Creek ≃	198	40.20 N	102.38 W
Surveyor Point ›	168b	34.47 S	137.51 E
Survilliers	261	49.06 N	2.33 E
Surwold	52	53.00 N	7.30 E
Şury-le-Comtal	62	45.32 N	4.10 E
Šuryškary	74	65.54 N	65.22 E
Şuşa, Azer.	84	39.45 N	46.44 E
Susa, It.	62	45.08 N	7.03 E
Susa, Nihon	96	34.37 N	131.36 E
Suså ≃	41	55.11 N	11.46 E
Susa, Valle di V	62	45.09 N	7.10 E
Sūsah	146	32.54 N	21.58 E
Susak, Otok I	36	44.31 N	14.18 E
Susaki	96	33.22 N	133.17 E
Susami	96	33.33 N	135.30 E
Susamyr	85	42.09 N	73.58 E
Susamyr ≃	85	42.08 N	74.03 E
Susamyrtau, chrebet ⋏	85	42.08 N	73.15 E
Susan	208	37.22 N	76.19 W
Susan ≃	204	40.19 N	120.17 W
Susan, Port c	224	48.10 N	122.25 W
Susana Knolls	228	34.16 N	118.41 W
Sūsangerd	128	31.34 N	48.11 E
Susanino, Ross.	76	59.30 N	30.22 E
Susanino, Ross.	80	58.09 N	41.36 E
Susanino, Ross.	89	52.47 N	140.06 E
Susano	256	23.32 S	46.20 W
Susano □[7]	287b	23.35 S	46.18 W
Susanville	204	40.24 N	120.39 W
Šušary, Ross.	265a	59.46 N	30.21 E
Šušary, Ross.	265a	59.48 N	30.23 E
Susch	58	46.46 N	10.04 E
Susegana	64	45.51 N	12.15 E
Suşehri	130	40.11 N	38.06 E
Süsel	54	54.04 N	10.43 E
Šušenskoje	86	53.19 N	91.58 E
Sušice	60	49.14 N	13.32 E
Susitna	180	61.33 N	150.31 W
Susitna ≃	180	61.16 N	150.30 W
Susleni	38	47.25 N	28.59 E
Suslonger	80	56.18 N	48.13 E
Sušn'aki Pervoje	86	57.53 N	88.47 E
Susobana ≃	94	36.37 N	138.11 E
Susoh	114	3.43 N	96.50 E
Susong	100	30.09 N	116.06 E
Susono	94	35.09 N	138.54 E
Suspiro del Moro, Puerto del)(	34	37.04 N	3.39 W
Susquehanna	210	41.56 N	75.36 W
Susquehanna □[6]	210	41.50 N	75.50 W
Susquehanna ≃	188	39.33 N	76.05 W
Susquehanna, West Branch ≃	210	40.53 N	76.47 W
Susquehanna State Park ♦	208	39.36 N	76.09 W
Susques	252	23.25 S	66.29 W
Sussa ≃	152	7.22 S	17.05 E
Süssen	56	48.41 N	9.45 E
Süssenbrunn ◆[8]	264b	48.17 N	16.30 E
Süsser See ⊜	54	51.30 N	11.40 E
Sussex, N.B., Can.	186	45.43 N	65.31 W
Sussex, N.J., U.S.	210	41.12 N	74.36 W
Sussex, Va., U.S.	208	36.54 N	77.16 W
Sussex, Wi., U.S.	216	43.08 N	88.13 W
Sussex □[6], De., U.S.	208	38.42 N	75.23 W
Sussex □[6], N.J., U.S.	210	41.08 N	74.41 W
Sussex □[6], Va., U.S.	208	36.50 N	77.15 W
Sussex, Vale of V	42	50.57 N	0.17 W
Sussex Inlet	170	35.11 S	150.36 E
Sussey	50	47.13 N	4.22 E
Sustenhorn ∧	58	46.42 N	8.28 E
Susten Pass)(	58	46.44 N	8.27 E
Şusteren	52	51.04 N	5.51 E
Šustikovo	82	55.17 N	35.59 E
Susu	174m	26.47 N	128.19 E
Susubona	175e	8.18 S	159.27 E
Susui	112	4.56 N	116.41 E
Susuman	74	62.47 N	148.10 E
Susurluk	130	39.54 N	28.10 E
Şusuzmüsellim	130	41.06 N	27.03 E
Šušvė ≃	76	55.10 N	23.49 E
Susz	30	53.44 N	19.20 E
Sutāhāta	126	22.08 N	88.07 E
Sutak	123	33.12 N	77.28 E
Sutama	94	35.47 N	138.25 E
Sut-Chol'	86	51.24 N	91.17 E
Sütçüler	130	37.30 N	30.59 E
Sutera	70	37.31 N	13.44 E
Sutersville	214	40.14 N	79.48 W
Suthat, Wat ʊ[1]	269a	13.45 N	100.30 E
Sutherland, Austl.	170	34.02 S	151.04 E
Sutherland, S. Afr.	158	32.24 S	20.40 E
Sutherland, Ia., U.S.	198	42.58 N	95.29 W
Sutherland, Ne., U.S.	198	41.09 N	101.07 W
Sutherland ≃	182	54.29 N	125.05 W
Sutherland, Lake ⊜	224	48.05 N	123.42 W
Sutherland Falls ⌊	172	44.48 S	167.44 E
Sutherlands	168b	34.10 S	139.13 E
Sutherlin	202	43.23 N	123.18 W
Suthiāna	272a	28.31 N	77.26 E
Sutjeska Nacionalni Park ♦	38	43.22 N	18.45 E
Sutlej (Satluj) (Langqên) ≃	120	29.23 N	71.02 E
Sutri	66	42.14 N	12.13 E
Sutrio	64	46.31 N	12.59 E
Sütschou → Xuzhou, Zhg.	98	34.16 N	117.11 E
Sutschou → Suzhou, Zhg.	106	31.18 N	120.37 E
Sutter	226	39.10 N	121.45 W
Sutter □[6]	226	39.08 N	121.37 W
Sutter Buttes ∧	226	39.12 N	121.50 W
Sutter Bypass ≃	226	38.47 N	121.38 W
Sutter Creek	226	38.23 N	120.48 W
Sutter Creek ≃	226	38.22 N	120.59 W
Sutton, Austl.	171b	35.10 S	149.15 E
Sutton, P.Q., Can.	206	45.06 N	72.37 W
Sutton, Eng., U.K.	42	52.23 N	0.07 E
Sutton, Eng., U.K.	260	51.12 N	0.26 W
Sutton, Ak., U.S.	180	61.43 N	148.53 W
Sutton, Ma., U.S.	207	42.09 N	71.45 W
Sutton, Ne., U.S.	198	40.36 N	97.51 W
Sutton, W.V., U.S.	188	38.39 N	80.42 W
Sutton ◆[8]	42	51.22 N	0.12 W
Sutton, Monts ⋏	206	45.05 N	72.30 W
Sutton-at-Home	260	51.25 N	0.14 E
Sutton Bridge	42	52.46 N	0.12 E
Sutton Coldfield	42	52.34 N	1.48 W
Sutton Courtenay	42	51.39 N	1.17 W
Sutton Forest	170	34.35 S	150.19 E
Sutton in Ashfield	44	53.08 N	1.15 W
Sutton Lake ⊜[1]	188	38.40 N	80.40 W
Sutton Lane Ends	262	53.14 N	2.06 W
Sutton Leach	262	53.26 N	2.42 W
Sutton on Sea	44	53.19 N	0.17 E
Sutton on Trent	44	53.10 N	0.49 W
Sutton Park	276	40.49 N	74.42 W
Sutton Place ⊥	260	51.16 N	0.33 W
Suttons Bay	190	44.58 N	85.39 W
Sutton Scotney	42	51.10 N	1.21 W
Sutton Valence	42	51.12 N	0.36 E
Sutton Veny	42	51.11 N	2.08 W
Sutton Weaver	262	53.18 N	2.41 W
Sutton West	212	44.18 N	79.22 W
Suttor ≃	166	21.25 S	147.45 E
Suttrop	56	51.27 N	8.22 E
Suttsu	92a	42.48 N	140.14 E
Sutwik Island I	180	56.34 N	157.05 W
Suunduk ≃	86	51.46 N	58.46 E
Suurberge ⋏	158	33.18 S	25.32 E
Suurbraak	158	34.00 S	20.39 E
Suure-Jaani	76	58.33 N	25.28 E
Suur Munamägi ∧[2]	76	57.43 N	27.04 E
Suur Pakri I	76	59.20 N	23.55 E
Suva	175g	18.08 S	178.25 E
Suvainiškis	76	56.10 N	25.17 E
Şuvälan	84	40.30 N	50.09 E
Šuvalovo Oz'orki ◆[8]	265a	60.02 N	30.18 E
Suva Planina ⋏	38	43.10 N	22.10 E
Suvarlı	130	37.32 N	37.38 E
Suvasvesi ⊜	26	62.39 N	28.12 E
Suvereto	66	43.05 N	10.40 E
Suvo	88	53.39 N	110.00 E
Suvorka	88	56.33 N	103.24 E
Suvorov	82	54.07 N	36.30 E
Suvorove	78	45.34 N	28.59 E
Suvorovo	82	56.07 N	35.54 E
Suwa, Erit.	144	14.17 N	41.06 E
Suwa, Nihon	94	36.02 N	138.08 E
Suwa-ko ⊜	94	36.05 N	138.05 E
Suwałki	30	54.07 N	22.56 E
Suwałki □[4]	30	54.10 N	22.15 E
Suwannaphum	110	15.33 N	103.47 E
Suwannee ≃	192	29.18 N	83.09 W
Suwannee Lake ⊜	184	56.08 N	100.10 W
Suwanose-jima I	93b	29.38 N	129.43 E
Suwanose-suidō ʯ	93b	29.32 N	129.40 E
Suwarrow I[1]	14	13.15 S	163.05 W
Suwaydah	130	35.46 N	39.38 E
Şuwaylih	132	32.02 N	35.50 E
Suways, Khalīj as- (Gulf of Suez) c	140	29.00 N	32.50 E
Suways, Qanāt as- (Suez Canal) ≅	142	29.55 N	32.33 E
Suwŏn	98	37.17 N	127.01 E
Suwon-dong	98	41.54 N	129.43 E
Suxi	100	29.25 N	120.07 E
Suxian	100	33.38 N	116.58 E
Suya	150	9.28 N	3.11 E
Suykbulak	86	49.48 N	80.50 E
Suyo	246	4.30 S	80.00 W
Suzak	86	44.07 N	68.28 E
Suzaka	94	36.39 N	138.19 E
Suzdal'	80	56.25 N	40.26 E
Suze ≃	58	47.08 N	7.14 E
Suze-la-Rousse	62	44.17 N	4.51 E
Suzhi	98	42.17 N	113.42 E
Suzhou (Soochow)	106	31.18 N	120.37 E
Suzhuang	105	40.04 N	116.44 E
Suzi ≃	98	41.55 N	124.17 E
Suzigou	98	40.25 N	123.25 E
S'uzikozero	24	61.48 N	37.20 E
Suz'omka	76	52.19 N	34.05 E
Suzu	92	37.25 N	137.17 E
Suzuka	94	34.51 N	136.35 E
Suzuka ≃	94	34.54 N	136.39 E
Suzuka-kokutei-kōen ♦	94	35.00 N	136.25 E
Suzuka-sammyaku ⋏	94	35.00 N	136.25 E
Suzuki	268	35.43 N	139.31 E
S'uz'um	80	58.02 N	47.32 E
Suzu-misaki ›	92	37.31 N	137.21 E
Suzun	86	53.47 N	82.19 E
Suzzara	64	45.00 N	10.45 E
Sværdborg	41	55.05 N	11.54 E
Svalbard □[2]	12	78.00 N	20.00 E
Svalöv	41	55.55 N	13.06 E
Svalyava	78	48.33 N	22.59 E
Svaneholm	41	55.30 N	13.28 E
Svaneke	26	55.08 N	15.09 E
Svanetskij chrebet ⋏	84	42.55 N	42.42 E
Svängsta	26	56.16 N	14.46 E
Svanninge	41	55.07 N	10.15 E
Svanskog	26	59.11 N	12.33 E
Svapa ≃	78	51.44 N	34.56 E
Şvappavaara	24	67.39 N	21.04 E
Švarcevskij	82	54.06 N	37.59 E
Şvärdsjö	26	60.45 N	15.55 E
Švaricha	80	57.33 N	49.37 E
Svartå	40	59.08 N	14.31 E
Svartälven ≃	40	59.19 N	14.35 E
Svartån ≃	40	59.37 N	16.33 E
Svarte	41	55.25 N	13.43 E
Svartenhuk ›[1]	176	71.55 N	55.00 W
Svärtinge	40	58.39 N	16.00 E
Svartisen ⊓	24	66.38 N	14.00 E
Svartlöga I	40	59.34 N	19.03 E
Svartsjölandet I	40	59.22 N	17.41 E
Svataj	74	67.57 N	151.54 E
Svatava	54	50.11 N	12.35 E
Svatava ≃	54	50.11 N	12.38 E
Sv'atica ≃	80	58.22 N	51.43 E
Sv'atoj Nos, mys ›, Ross.	24	68.10 N	39.45 E
Sv'atoj Nos, mys ›, Ross.	74	72.52 N	140.42 E
Sv'atoj Nos, poluostrov ›[1]	88	53.40 N	108.50 E
Sv'atoslavka	80	51.20 N	43.26 E
Svatove	83	49.23 N	38.13 E
Svay Chék	110	13.48 N	102.58 E
Svay Riĕng	110	11.05 N	105.48 E
Sveafallen ⌊	40	59.10 N	14.22 E
Svebølle	41	55.38 N	11.20 E
Sveča	80	58.16 N	47.32 E
Svedala	41	55.30 N	13.14 E
Svėdasai	76	55.41 N	25.22 E
Sveg	26	62.02 N	14.21 E
Şvegssjön ⊜[1]	26	62.03 N	14.10 E
Švėkšna	76	55.31 N	21.37 E
Svelgen	26	61.47 N	5.15 E
Svelvik	26	59.37 N	10.24 E
Şven'	76	53.09 N	34.21 E
Švenčionėliai	76	55.10 N	26.00 E
Švenčionys	76	55.07 N	26.10 E
Svendborg	41	55.03 N	10.37 E
Svenljunga	26	57.30 N	13.07 E
Svennevad	40	59.01 N	15.22 E
Svensen	224	46.10 N	123.39 W
Svenstorp	41	55.46 N	13.15 E
Svenstrup	26	56.59 N	9.52 E
Šventoji	76	56.02 N	21.05 E
Šventoji ≃	76	55.06 N	24.22 E
Sverbejevo	89	53.36 N	123.15 E
Sverdlovo, Ross.	80	51.16 N	44.34 E
Sverdlovo, Ross.	82	56.38 N	36.37 E
Sverdlovsk → Jekaterinburg, Ross.	86	56.51 N	60.36 E
Sverdlovs'k, Ukr.	83	48.05 N	39.40 E
Sverdrup, ostrov I	74	74.35 N	79.30 E
Sverige → Sweden □[1]	24	62.00 N	15.00 E
Şverkestaån ≃	40	59.28 N	15.28 E
Švermov	54	50.09 N	14.05 E
Svesa	78	51.57 N	33.54 E
Sveti Arhandjel Mihajlo ʊ[1]	38	42.07 N	21.28 E
Sveti Jovan Bigorski ʊ[1]	38	41.38 N	20.37 E
Svetilovičі	76	52.48 N	31.19 E
Sveti Nikole	38	41.52 N	21.58 E
Sveti Petar u Šumi	64	45.11 N	13.52 E
Svetlaja	89	46.33 N	138.18 E
Světlá nad Sázavou	30	49.40 N	15.25 E
Svetlogorsk, Bela.	76	52.38 N	29.42 E
Svetlogorsk, Ross.	76	54.57 N	20.10 E
Svetlograd	72	45.20 N	42.40 E
Svetloje	80	57.03 N	53.38 E
Svetlyj, Ross.	76	54.41 N	20.08 E
Svetlyj, Ross.	86	50.47 N	60.53 E
Svetlyj, Ross.	88	58.26 N	115.55 E
Svetlyj Jar	80	48.29 N	44.46 E
Svetogorsk	24	61.07 N	28.51 E
Svetozarevo	38	43.58 N	21.16 E
Svežen'kaja	80	54.01 N	42.26 E
Şvidník	30	49.18 N	21.35 E
Švihov	60	49.29 N	13.17 E
Svijaga ≃	80	55.47 N	48.40 E
Svilajnac	38	44.14 N	21.13 E
Svilengrad	38	41.46 N	26.12 E
Svindal	26	58.30 N	7.28 E
Svinecea Mare, Vârful ∧	38	44.48 N	22.09 E
Svinesund	26	59.06 N	11.16 E
Svinninge	41	55.43 N	11.28 E
Svir'	76	54.51 N	26.24 E
Svir' ≃	76	60.30 N	32.48 E
Svirica	76	60.29 N	32.51 E
Svirsk	88	53.04 N	103.21 E
Svir'stroj	76	60.48 N	33.43 E
Sviščovka	80	52.51 N	43.44 E
Svisloč', Bela.	76	53.02 N	24.06 E
Svisloč', Bela.	76	53.26 N	28.59 E
Svisloč' ≃	76	53.26 N	28.59 E
Sviştov	38	43.37 N	25.20 E
Svit	30	49.03 N	20.12 E
Svitava ≃	30	49.09 N	16.38 E
Svitávka	30	49.30 N	16.37 E
Svitavy	30	49.45 N	16.27 E
Svitino	82	54.54 N	35.49 E
Svitlovods'k	78	49.04 N	33.15 E
Svobidnyy port	78	46.20 N	31.51 E
Svoboda, Ross.	78	51.58 N	36.17 E
Svoboda, Ross.	78	47.12 N	40.39 E
Svobodnaja	89	46.48 N	143.23 E
Svobodne	83	47.32 N	37.34 E
Svobodnyj, Ross.	80	52.20 N	46.22 E
Svobodnyj, Ross.	89	51.24 N	128.08 E
Svoge	38	42.58 N	23.21 E
Svojna	82	54.09 N	36.39 E
Svol'na ≃	76	55.43 N	28.02 E
Svolvær	24	68.14 N	14.34 E
Svor	54	50.47 N	14.36 E
Svorkmo	26	63.10 N	9.45 E
Svratka ≃	61	49.11 N	16.38 E
Svržno	60	49.35 N	12.46 E
Svullrya	26	60.25 N	12.24 E
Svystunivka	83	49.29 N	38.20 E
Swābi	123	34.07 N	72.28 E
Swadlincote	42	52.47 N	1.33 W
Swaffham	42	52.39 N	0.41 E
Swain	210	42.29 N	77.51 W
Swain Reefs ✢[2]	166	21.40 S	152.15 E
Swainsboro	192	32.35 N	82.20 W
Swains Island I[1]	14	11.03 S	171.05 W
Swakop ≃	156	22.38 S	14.36 E
Swakopmund	156	22.41 S	14.34 E
Swakopmund □[5]	156	23.00 S	15.00 E
Swale □[8]	260	51.21 N	0.41 E
Swale ≃	44	54.06 N	1.20 W
Swale Canyon V	224	45.49 N	121.05 W
Swale Creek ≃	224	45.49 N	121.05 W
Swaledale V	44	54.25 N	1.47 W
Swallowfield	218	38.21 N	84.51 W
Swalmen	52	51.15 N	6.02 E
Swamp City	222	32.29 N	94.56 W
Swampscott	207	42.28 N	70.55 W
Swan	222	32.26 N	95.22 W
Swan ≃, Austl.	168a	32.03 S	115.45 E
Swan ≃, Can.	184	52.30 N	100.47 W
Swan ≃, Ab., Can.	182	55.31 N	115.17 W
Swan ≃, Mn., U.S.	190	47.01 N	93.16 W
Swan ≃, Mt., U.S.	202	48.04 N	114.05 W
Swan Acres	279b	40.33 N	80.02 W
Swanage	42	50.37 N	1.58 W
Swan Bay c	169	38.14 S	144.40 E
Swan Creek ≃, Austl.	171a	28.08 S	152.13 E
Swan Creek ≃, Mi., U.S.	216	41.58 N	85.19 W
Swan Creek ≃, Mi., U.S.	216	41.58 N	83.17 W
Swan Creek ≃, Oh., U.S.	216	41.39 N	83.32 W
Swan Creek ≃, S.D., U.S.	198	45.19 N	100.15 W
Swan Creek, North Branch ≃	281	42.06 N	83.23 W
Swan Creek Point ›	281	42.40 N	82.39 W
Swanee → Suwannee ≃	192	29.18 N	83.09 W
Swan Hill	166	35.21 S	143.34 E
Swan Hills	182	54.43 N	115.24 W
Swan Hills ⋏[2]	182	54.48 N	115.52 W
Swanington	216	40.35 N	87.17 W
Swan Island I	169	38.15 S	144.41 E
Swan Islands → Santanilla, Islas II	238	17.25 N	83.55 W
Swank Creek ≃	224	47.07 N	120.45 W
Swan Lake, Mb., Can.	184	49.24 N	98.46 W
Swan Lake, Mt., U.S.	202	47.55 N	113.50 W
Swan Lake, N.Y., U.S.	210	41.45 N	74.47 W
Swan Lake ⊜, Mb., Can.	184	52.30 N	100.45 W
Swan Lake ⊜, On., Can.	184	54.17 N	91.12 W
Swan Lake ⊜, Il., U.S.	219	38.57 N	90.33 W
Swan Lake ⊜, Mn., U.S.	190	44.19 N	94.15 W
Swanland	44	53.44 N	0.29 W
Swanley	42	51.24 N	0.12 E
Swanlinbar	48	54.10 N	7.42 W
Swannanoa	192	35.36 N	82.23 W
Swannanoa, Lake ⊜	276	41.01 N	74.31 W
Swan Peak ∧	202	47.43 N	113.38 W
Swanquarter	192	35.24 N	76.20 W
Swan Range ⋏	202	47.50 N	113.40 W
Swan Reach	166	34.34 S	139.36 E
Swan River	184	52.06 N	101.16 W
Swansboro	192	34.41 N	77.07 W
Swanscombe	260	51.26 N	0.18 E
Swansea, Austl.	166	42.08 S	148.04 E
Swansea, Austl.	170	33.05 S	151.38 E
Swansea, Wales, U.K.	42	51.38 N	3.57 W
Swansea, Il., U.S.	219	38.32 N	89.59 W
Swansea, Ma., U.S.	207	41.44 N	71.11 W
Swansea, S.C., U.S.	192	33.44 N	81.05 W
Swansea ◆[8]	275b	43.38 N	79.28 W
Swansea Bay c	42	51.35 N	3.52 W
Swans Island I	188	44.10 N	68.25 W
Swanson Lake ⊜[1]	198	40.09 N	101.06 W
Swanton, Oh., U.S.	216	41.35 N	83.53 W
Swanton, Vt., U.S.	206	44.55 N	73.07 W
Swanville	190	45.54 N	94.38 W
Swanzey Center	207	42.49 N	72.10 W
Swarbacks Minn ʯ	46a	60.20 N	1.36 W
Swartberg	158	30.15 S	29.23 E
Swarthmore	208	39.54 N	75.21 W
Swarthmore College ʊ[2]	285	39.54 N	75.21 W
Swart-Kei ≃	158	32.09 S	27.24 E
Swart-Mfolozi ≃	158	28.22 S	31.58 E
Swartplaas	158	26.08 S	26.57 E
Swartruggens	156	25.40 S	26.42 E
Swartruggens ⋏	158	33.02 S	19.35 E
Swartswood Lake	210	41.04 N	74.51 W
Swartswood State Park ♦	210	41.05 N	74.50 W
Swartz Creek	216	42.57 N	83.49 W
Swarupkāti	126	22.45 N	90.06 E
Swarupnagar	126	22.49 N	88.52 E
Swarzędz	30	52.26 N	17.05 E
Swasey Peak ∧	200	39.23 N	113.19 W
Swasey Wash V	200	39.15 N	112.53 W
Swasiland → Swaziland □[1]	158	26.30 S	31.30 E
Swāt ≃	123	34.20 N	71.34 E
Swatara Creek ≃	208	40.11 N	76.44 W
Swa-Tenda	152	7.09 S	17.07 E
Swatow → Shantou	100	23.23 N	116.41 E
Swauger Creek ≃	226	38.16 N	119.16 W
Swauk Pass)(	224	47.21 N	120.40 W
Sway	42	50.47 N	1.37 W
Swayzee	216	40.30 N	85.49 W
Swaziland □[1], Afr.	138	26.30 S	31.30 E
Swaziland □[1], Afr.	158	26.30 S	31.30 E
Swea City	190	43.23 N	94.19 W
Swede Hill	279b	40.17 N	79.34 W
Swedeland	285	40.05 N	75.20 W
Sweden (Sverige) □[1], Europe	22	62.00 N	15.00 E
Sweden (Sverige) □[1], Europe	24	62.00 N	15.00 E
Sweden Valley	214	41.45 N	77.56 W
Swede Run ≃	285	40.02 N	74.58 W
Swedesboro	208	39.44 N	75.18 W
Swedesburg	285	40.06 N	75.20 W
Swedish Knoll ∧	200	39.16 N	111.26 W
Swedru	150	5.32 N	0.43 W
Sween, Loch c	46	55.59 N	5.39 W
Sweeney Plan	279b	40.11 N	79.48 W
Sweeny	222	29.02 N	95.41 W
Sweeny Park ♦	284a	43.02 N	78.52 W
Sweet Briar	192	37.33 N	79.04 W
Sweetgrass	182	49.00 N	111.57 W
Sweet Grass Creek ≃	202	45.47 N	109.47 W
Sweetgrass Hills ⋏[2]	202	48.55 N	111.30 W
Sweet Grass Indian Reserve ◆[4]	184	52.44 N	108.45 W
Sweetheart Abbey ʊ[1]	44	54.59 N	3.38 W
Sweet Home, Or., U.S.	202	44.23 N	122.44 W
Sweet Home, Tx., U.S.	222	29.21 N	97.04 W
Sweetsers	216	40.34 N	85.46 W
Sweet Springs	194	38.57 N	93.24 W
Sweet Valley	210	41.17 N	76.09 W
Sweetwater, Fl., U.S.	220	25.46 N	80.21 W
Sweet Water, Il., U.S.	219	40.03 N	89.42 W
Sweetwater, Tn., U.S.	192	35.36 N	84.27 W
Sweetwater, Tx., U.S.	196	32.28 N	100.24 W
Sweetwater ≃	200	42.31 N	107.02 W
Sweetwater Creek	220	27.59 N	82.33 W
Sweetwater Creek ≃, U.S.	196	35.18 N	99.57 W
Sweetwater Creek ≃, Tx., U.S.	196	32.40 N	100.06 W
Sweetwater Mountains ⋏	226	38.30 N	119.17 W
Swellendam	158	34.02 S	20.26 E
Swepsonville	192	36.01 N	79.21 W
Swerdlovsk → Jekaterinburg	86	56.51 N	60.36 E
Świdnica (Schweidnitz)	30	50.51 N	16.29 E
Świdnik	30	51.14 N	22.41 E
Świdwin	30	53.47 N	15.47 E
Świebodzice	30	50.52 N	16.19 E
Świebodzin	30	52.15 N	15.32 E
Świecie	30	53.25 N	18.28 E
Świerzawa	30	51.01 N	15.54 E
Świerzno	54	53.57 N	14.59 E
Święta	54	53.35 N	14.36 E
Świętokrzyskie, Góry ⋏	30	50.55 N	21.00 E
Świętokrzyski Park Narodowy ♦	30	50.55 N	21.00 E
Swift ≃, Eng., U.K.	42	52.23 N	1.16 W
Swift ≃, Ak., U.S.	180	61.53 N	156.18 W
Swift ≃, Ma., U.S.	207	42.12 N	72.22 W
Swift Creek ≃, Al., U.S.	194	32.25 N	86.38 W
Swift Creek ≃, N.C., U.S.	192	35.12 N	77.05 W
Swift Creek ≃, N.C., U.S.	192	35.57 N	77.35 W
Swift Creek ≃, Va., U.S.	208	37.17 N	77.15 W
Swift Current	184	50.17 N	107.50 W
Swift Current Creek ≃	184	50.40 N	107.44 W
Swifton	194	35.49 N	91.07 W
Swift Reservoir ⊜[1]	224	46.04 N	122.05 W
Swiftwater	210	41.06 N	75.20 W
Swilly ≃	48	54.57 N	7.42 W
Swilly, Lough c	48	55.10 N	7.38 W
Swimming ≃	276	40.21 N	74.05 W
Swimming River Reservoir ⊜[1]	276	40.19 N	74.07 W
Świna ≃[1]	54	53.55 N	14.17 E
Swinburne, Cape ›	176	71.14 N	98.34 W
Swinden Reservoirs ⊜[1]	262	53.48 N	2.10 W
Swindle Island I	182	52.32 N	128.35 W
Swindon	42	51.34 N	1.47 W
Swinemünde → Świnoujście	30	53.53 N	14.14 E
Swineshead	42	52.56 N	0.09 W
Swinford	48	53.57 N	8.57 W
Swinging Bridge Reservoir ⊜[1]	210	41.37 N	74.48 W
Swinomish Indian Reservation ◆[4]	224	48.25 N	122.33 W
Świnoujście (Swinemünde)	30	53.53 N	14.14 E
Swinton, Eng., U.K.	44	53.28 N	1.20 W
Swinton, Eng., U.K.	262	53.31 N	2.20 W
Swinton, Scot., U.K.	46	55.43 N	2.15 W
Swissvale	279b	40.25 N	79.52 W
Swisttal	56	50.40 N	6.54 E
Switzerland □[6]	218	38.45 N	85.04 W
Switzerland □[1], Europe	22	47.00 N	8.00 E
Switzerland □[1], Europe	58	47.00 N	8.00 E
Swona I	46	58.45 N	3.03 W
Swordfish Seamount ✢[3]	14	18.25 N	158.25 W
Swords	48	53.28 N	6.13 W
Swords Range ⋏	166	21.57 S	141.32 E
Swormville	284a	43.02 N	78.42 W
Sworton Heath	262	53.21 N	2.28 W
Swoyerville	210	41.18 N	75.52 W
Syalach	74	66.12 N	124.00 E
Syam	58	46.42 N	5.57 E
Syāmnagar	126	22.21 N	89.07 E
Syāmpur, India	126	22.18 N	88.02 E
Syampur, India	272b	22.29 N	88.13 E
Sybille Creek ≃	198	42.07 N	105.02 W
Syburg ◆[8]	263	51.25 N	7.29 E
Sycamore, Ga., U.S.	192	31.40 N	83.38 W
Sycamore, Il., U.S.	216	41.59 N	88.41 W
Sycamore, Oh., U.S.	214	40.56 N	83.10 W
Sycamore Creek ≃, Az., U.S.	200	33.38 N	111.40 W
Sycamore Creek ≃, Mi., U.S.	216	42.43 N	84.32 W
Sycamore Creek ≃, Oh., U.S.	214	40.59 N	83.12 W
Sycamore Creek ≃, Tx., U.S.	196	29.14 N	100.48 W
Sycamore Gardens	285	39.42 N	75.42 W
Sycamore Island I	279b	40.29 N	79.52 W
Sycamore Slough ≃	226	38.48 N	121.44 W
Sycan ≃	202	42.27 N	121.15 W
Sycaway	210	42.44 N	73.39 W
Syčova	86	57.35 N	69.20 E
Syčovka	76	55.50 N	34.17 E
Syców	30	51.19 N	17.43 E
Sydenham, Austl.	274b	37.42 S	144.46 E
Sydenham, On., Can.	212	44.25 N	76.36 W
Sydenham ◆[8], S. Afr.	273d	26.09 S	28.06 E
Sydenham ◆[8], Eng., U.K.	260	51.26 N	0.03 W
Sydenham ≃, On., Can.	190	42.33 N	82.25 W
Sydenham ≃, On., Can.	212	44.35 N	80.57 W
Sydenham Lake ⊜	212	44.25 N	76.35 W
Sydenham West	274b	37.41 S	144.39 E
Sydney, Austl.	170	33.52 S	151.13 E
Sydney, Austl.	274a	33.52 S	151.13 E
Sydney, N.S., Can.	186	46.09 N	60.11 W
Sydney, Fl., U.S.	220	27.58 N	82.12 W
Sydney, University of ʊ[2]	274a	33.53 S	151.11 E
Sydney Bay c, On., Can.	212	44.54 N	81.05 W
Sydney Bay c, Norf. I.	174c	29.04 S	167.57 E
Sydney Bay Bluff ⊥[4]	212	44.54 N	81.07 W
Sydney Harbour Bridge ◆[5]	170	33.52 S	151.12 E
Sydney Lake ⊜	184	50.40 N	94.24 W
Sydney Mines	186	46.14 N	60.14 W
Sydney Point ›	174d	0.53 S	169.36 E
Syedove	83	47.03 N	38.10 E
Syevernyy	83	48.22 N	39.56 E
Syeverodonets'k	83	48.58 N	38.27 E
Syevero-Hundorivs'kyy	83	48.23 N	39.54 E
Syferbult	158	26.00 S	27.20 E
Sygan	279b	40.21 N	80.08 W
Syke	52	52.54 N	8.49 E
Sykesville, Md., U.S.	208	39.22 N	76.58 W
Sykesville, Pa., U.S.	214	41.03 N	78.49 W
Sykkylven	26	62.24 N	6.35 E
Syktyvkar	24	61.40 N	50.46 E
Sylacauga	194	33.10 N	86.15 W
Sylarna ∧	26	63.02 N	12.13 E
Sylhet	120	24.54 N	91.52 E
Syloga	24	63.50 N	43.39 E
Sylt I	30	54.54 N	8.20 E
Sylva	192	35.22 N	83.13 W
Sylva ≃	86	57.39 N	56.54 E
Sylvan	224	45.30 N	122.41 W
Sylvan Beach	210	43.11 N	75.43 W
Sylvan Glen	285	40.11 N	75.42 W
Sylvan Grove	198	39.00 N	98.23 W
Sylvan Hills	194	34.50 N	92.13 W
Sylvania, Austl.	274a	34.01 S	151.07 E
Sylvania, Ga., U.S.	192	32.45 N	81.38 W
Sylvania, Oh., U.S.	214	41.43 N	83.42 W
Sylvania, Pa., U.S.	210	41.48 N	76.51 W
Sylvania Heights	274a	34.02 S	151.06 E
Sylvan Lake, Ab., Can.	182	52.19 N	114.05 W
Sylvan Lake, Il., U.S.	278	42.15 N	88.03 W
Sylvan Lake, Mi., U.S.	281	42.37 N	83.20 W
Sylvan Lake ⊜, Ab., Can.	182	52.21 N	114.10 W
Sylvan Lake ⊜, In., U.S.	216	41.29 N	85.20 W
Sylvan Lake ⊜, Mi., U.S.	281	42.37 N	83.20 W
Sylvan Pass)(	202	44.28 N	110.08 W
Sylvan Shores	220	28.49 N	81.41 W
Sylvensteinsee ⊜[1]	64	47.34 N	11.32 E
Sylvester, Ga., U.S.	192	31.31 N	83.50 W
Sylvester, Tx., U.S.	196	32.43 N	100.15 W
Sylvester, Mount ∧[2]	186	48.11 N	55.04 W
Sylvia	198	37.57 N	98.24 W
Sym	74	60.20 N	88.23 E
Symmes Creek ≃	188	38.26 N	82.27 W
Syn'a	24	65.22 N	57.42 E
Syndal	274b	37.53 S	145.09 E
Synel'nykove	78	48.20 N	35.31 E

DEUTSCH

Name	Seite	Breite°′	Länge°′ E = Ost
Synevir	78	48.30 N	23.38 E
Synivka	78	50.33 N	34.06 E
Synkovo	82	55.21 N	37.38 E
Synnyr, chrebet ⋏	88	56.50 N	111.10 E
Syntul	80	55.00 N	41.18 E
Synyukha ≃	78	48.03 N	30.51 E
Syon House ⊥	260	51.29 N	0.19 W
Syosset	210	40.49 N	73.30 W
Syowa ʊ[3]	9	69.00 S	39.35 E
Syracuse → Siracusa, It.	70	37.04 N	15.18 E
Syracuse, In., U.S.	216	41.25 N	85.45 W
Syracuse, Ks., U.S.	198	37.58 N	101.45 W
Syracuse, Ne., U.S.	198	40.39 N	96.11 W
Syracuse, N.Y., U.S.	210	43.02 N	76.08 W
Syracuse Hancock International Airport ⊠, N.Y., U.S.	210	43.07 N	76.07 W
Syracuse Hancock International Airport ⊠, N.Y., U.S.	212	43.07 N	76.07 W
Syrčan	80	57.22 N	50.15 E
Syrdarja	85	40.52 N	68.38 E
Syrdarja □[4]	85	40.30 N	68.40 E
Syrdarja (Syr Darya) ≃	72	46.03 N	61.00 E
Syr-Darya → Syrdarja ≃	72	46.03 N	61.00 E
Syre	46	58.22 N	4.14 W
Syre ≃	56	49.42 N	6.29 E
Syria (Sūrīyah) □[1], Asia	118	35.00 N	38.00 E
Syria (Sūrīyah) □[1], Asia	128	35.00 N	38.00 E
Syriam	110	16.46 N	96.15 E
Syrian Desert → Shām, Bādiyat ash- ◆[2]	128	32.00 N	40.00 E
Syrie → Syria □[1]	128	35.00 N	38.00 E
Syrien → Syria □[1]	128	35.00 N	38.00 E
Syrotyne	83	48.55 N	38.31 E
Syrskij	76	52.34 N	39.29 E
Sysert'	86	56.29 N	60.49 E
Sysmä	26	61.30 N	25.41 E
Sysola ≃	24	61.42 N	50.53 E
Sysslebäck	26	60.44 N	12.52 E
Syston	42	52.42 N	1.04 W
Systyg-Chem	88	52.40 N	95.30 E
Sytkivtsi	78	48.54 N	29.12 E
Syt'kovo	76	56.31 N	34.01 E
Sytykanskij, porog ⌊	88	57.49 N	118.33 E
Syukunoshō	270	34.50 N	135.32 E
Syväri ⊜	26	63.16 N	28.06 E
Syvash, zatoka ʯ	78	46.00 N	34.30 E
Syvas'ke	78	46.23 N	34.34 E
Syzran'	80	53.09 N	48.27 E
Syzran' ≃	80	53.04 N	48.26 E
Szabadka → Subotica	38	46.06 N	19.39 E
Szabolcs-Szatmár-Bereg □[6]	30	48.00 N	22.10 E
Szada	264c	47.38 N	19.19 E
Szamocin	30	53.02 N	17.08 E
Szamos (Someș) ≃	38	48.07 N	22.20 E
Szamotuły	30	52.37 N	16.35 E
Szarvas	30	46.52 N	20.34 E
Szatmárnémeti → Satu Mare	38	47.48 N	22.53 E
Százhalombatta	264c	47.20 N	18.56 E
Szczawnica	30	49.26 N	20.30 E
Szczecin (Stettin)	30	53.24 N	14.32 E
Szczecin □[4]	30	53.45 N	15.00 E
Szczecinek (Neustettin)	30	53.43 N	16.42 E
Szczeciński, Zalew (Oderhaff) c	54	53.46 N	14.14 E
Szczekociny	30	50.38 N	19.50 E
Szczuczyn	30	53.34 N	22.18 E
Szczytno	30	53.34 N	21.00 E
Szechwan → Sichuan □[4]	102	31.00 N	105.00 E
Szechwan Basin → Sichuan Pendi ≚[1]	102	30.00 N	105.00 E
Szécsény	30	48.06 N	19.31 E
Szeged	30	46.15 N	20.09 E
Szeghalom	30	47.01 N	21.11 E
Székesfehérvár	30	47.12 N	18.25 E
Szekszárd	30	46.21 N	18.42 E
Szemenyecsörnye	61	46.30 N	16.37 E
Szentendre	30	47.40 N	19.05 E
Szentendrei-Duna ≃[1]	264c	47.36 N	19.05 E
Szentendrei-sziget I	264c	47.39 N	19.07 E
Szentes	30	46.39 N	20.16 E
Szentgotthárd	30	46.57 N	16.17 E
Szentpéterfa	61	47.06 N	16.29 E
Szeping → Siping	89	43.12 N	124.20 E
Szépművészeti Museum ʊ	264c	47.31 N	19.05 E
Szerencs	30	48.09 N	21.13 E
Szigethalom	264c	47.20 N	19.00 E
Szigetszentmiklós	264c	47.21 N	19.03 E
Szilas-patak ≃	264c	47.36 N	19.06 E
Szlichtyngowa	30	51.43 N	16.15 E
Szob	30	47.50 N	18.52 E
Szolnok	30	47.10 N	20.12 E
Szombathely	30	47.14 N	16.38 E
Szprotawa	30	51.34 N	15.33 E
Sztum	30	53.56 N	19.01 E
Szubin	30	53.00 N	17.44 E
Szydłowiec	30	51.14 N	20.51 E
Szypliszki	30	54.15 N	23.05 E

T

Name	Seite	Breite°′	Länge°′ E = Ost
Ta ≃	94	36.17 N	139.54 E
Taacyn ≃	102	45.09 N	101.27 E
Taal	116	13.53 N	120.55 E
Taal, Lake ⊜	116	13.55 N	121.00 E
Taalintehdas → Dalsbruk	26	60.02 N	22.31 E
Taan ≃	100	24.24 N	120.36 E
Taancan Point ›	116	10.00 N	125.01 E
Taavetti	26	60.55 N	27.34 E
Tabacal	252	23.16 S	64.15 W
Tabacal, Quebrada ≃	286c	10.31 N	67.02 W
Tabaco	116	13.23 N	123.44 E
Tabacundo	246	0.03 N	78.12 W
Tabai ≃	164	3.01 S	135.52 E
Tabalosos	248	6.21 S	76.41 W
Tabanan	115b	8.32 S	115.08 E
Tabango	116	11.19 N	124.22 E
Tabankulu	158	30.58 S	29.19 E
Tábara	34	41.49 N	5.57 W
Tabar Island I	164	2.55 S	152.05 E
Tabar Islands II	164	2.50 S	152.00 E
Tabarka	148	36.57 N	8.45 E
Tabarz	54	50.52 N	10.31 E
Ţabas	128	33.36 N	56.54 E
Tabasará ≃	236	8.00 N	81.39 W
Tabasco □[3]	232	18.15 N	93.00 W
Ţabas Masīnā	128	32.48 N	60.14 E
Tabat	86	52.57 N	90.43 E
Tabatinga ≃	255	17.24 S	43.18 W
Tabayama	94	35.47 N	138.55 E
Tabayin	110	22.42 N	95.19 E
Tabb	208	37.08 N	76.29 W
Tabei	98	39.44 N	122.29 E
Tabelbala	148	29.23 N	3.15 W
Tabelbala, Kahal ⊥[8]	148	28.30 N	2.00 W
Taber	182	49.47 N	112.08 W
Taberg, Sve.	26	57.41 N	14.05 E
Taberg, Sve.	40	59.50 N	14.08 E

Symbols in the index entries represent the broad categories identified in the key at the right. Symbols with superior numbers (⋏[1]) identify subcategories (see complete key on page *I · 1)*.

Symbole im Register stellen die rechts im Schlüssel erklärten Kategorien dar. Symbole mit hochgestellten Ziffern (⋏[1]) bezeichnen Unterabteilungen einer Kategorie (vgl. vollständiger Schlüssel auf Seite *I · 1)*.

Los símbolos incluídos en el texto del índice representan las grandes categorías identificadas con la clave a la derecha. Los símbolos con numeros en su parte superior (⋏[1]) identifican las subcategorías (véase la clave completa en la página *I · 1)*.

Les symboles de l'index représentent les catégories indiquées dans la légende à droite. Les symboles suivis d'un indice (⋏[1]) représentent des sous-catégories (voir légende complète à la page *I · 1)*.

Os símbolos incluídos no texto do índice representam as grandes categorias identificadas com a chave à direita. Os símbolos com números em sua parte superior (⋏[1]) identificam as subcategorias (veja-se a chave completa à página *I · 1)*.

∧	Mountain	Berg	Montaña	Montagne	Montanha
⋏	Mountains	Gebirge	Montañas	Montagnes	Montanhas
)(	Pass	Paß	Paso	Col	Passo
V	Valley, Canyon	Tal, Cañon	Valle, Cañón	Vallée, Canyon	Vale, Canhão
≚	Plain	Ebene	Llano	Plaine	Planície
›	Cape	Kap	Cabo	Cap	Cabo
I	Island	Insel	Isla	Île	Ilha
II	Islands	Inseln	Islas	Îles	Ilhas
⊥	Other Topographic Features	Andere Topographische Objekte	Otros Elementos Topográficos	Autres données topographiques	Outros acidentes topográficos

ESPAÑOL — Nombre | Página | Lat.°′ | Long.°′ W = Oeste

FRANÇAIS — Nom | Page | Lat.°′ | Long.°′ W = Ouest

PORTUGUÊS — Nome | Página | Lat.°′ | Long.°′ W = Oeste

Taberg, N.Y., U.S.	210	43.18 N	75.37 W
Tabernacle	285	39.50 N	74.42 W
Tabi	152	8.10 S	13.18 E
Tabiang	174d	0.52 S	169.35 E
Tabiano Terme	64	44.48 N	10.02 E
Tabira	250	7.35 S	37.33 W
Tabiteuea	174t	1.25 N	173.07 E
Tabiteuea I [1]	14	1.20 S	174.50 E
Tabla	150	13.46 N	3.01 E
Tabla, Cerro de la ∧	240m	18.03 N	66.08 W
Tablada	288	34.42 S	58.32 W
Tablas, Cabo ⋗	252	31.51 S	71.34 W
Tablas Island I	116	12.24 N	122.02 E
Tablas Plateau ⋏ [1]	116	9.43 N	122.43 E
Tablas Strait ʊ	116	12.40 N	121.48 E
Tablat	34	36.24 N	3.19 E
Table Bay ⊂	158	33.53 S	18.27 E
Table Cape ⋗	172	39.06 S	178.00 E
Tableland	162	17.17 S	127.00 E
Table Mountain ∧, Nf., Can.	186	47.43 N	59.13 W
Table Mountain ∧, S. Afr.	158	33.57 S	18.25 E
Table Mountain ∧, Az., U.S.	200	32.49 N	110.31 W
Table Rock	198	40.10 N	96.05 W
Table Rock Lake ⊜ [1]	194	36.35 N	93.30 W
Tabletop ∧, Austl.	162	22.32 S	123.55 E
Table Top ∧, Az., U.S.	200	32.46 N	112.07 W
Tabletop Mountain ∧	171b	35.58 S	148.30 E
Tabley Mere ⊜	262	53.17 N	2.25 W
Tabligbo	150	6.35 N	1.30 E
Tablones	240m	18.15 N	65.45 W
Taboan ≃	116	17.57 N	122.11 E
Taboão, Ribeirão do ≃	287b	23.40 S	46.28 W
Taboão da Serra	256	23.38 S	46.46 W
Taboco ≃	248	19.53 S	55.58 W
Taboga	236	8.48 N	79.33 W
Tabogon	116	10.57 N	124.02 E
Tábor, Česká Rep.	30	49.25 N	14.41 E
Tabor, Ross.	74	71.16 N	150.12 E
Tabor, Ia., U.S.	198	40.53 N	95.40 W
Tabor, N.J., U.S.	276	40.52 N	74.29 W
Tabor, S.D., U.S.	198	42.56 N	97.39 W
Tabor, Mount → Tavor, Har ∧	132	32.41 N	35.23 E
Tabora	154	5.01 S	32.48 E
Tabora □ [4]	154	5.15 S	32.45 E
Tabor City	192	34.08 N	78.52 W
Tabory	86	58.31 N	64.33 E
Tabou	150	4.25 N	7.21 W
Tabrīz	128	38.05 N	46.18 E
Tábua, Riacho da ≃	250	9.12 S	44.25 W
Tabuaço	34	41.07 N	7.34 W
Tabuaeran I [1]	14	3.52 N	159.20 W
Tabuão	256	21.59 S	44.02 W
Tábuas	256	22.12 S	43.37 W
Tabu-dong	98	36.03 N	128.31 E
Tabuelan	116	10.49 N	123.52 E
Tabūk, Ar. Su.	128	28.23 N	36.35 E
Tabuk, Pil.	116	17.24 N	121.25 E
Tabuleiro	256	21.22 S	43.15 W
Tabuleiro do Norte	250	5.15 S	38.07 W
Tabuny	86	52.46 N	78.45 E
Tabuse	96	33.57 N	132.03 E
Tabuyung	114	0.51 N	99.00 E
Tabwémasana, Mont ∧	175f	15.20 S	166.44 E
Täby	40	59.30 N	18.03 E
Tacagua, Quebrada ≃	286c	10.37 N	67.02 W
Tacámbaro de Codallos	234	19.14 N	101.28 W
Tacaná	236	15.14 N	92.05 W
Tacaná, Volcán ∧ [1]	236	15.08 N	92.06 W
Tacañitas	252	28.38 S	62.36 W
Tacaratu	250	9.06 S	38.10 W
Taceno	58	46.02 N	9.21 E
Taché, Lac ⊜	176	64.00 N	120.00 W
Tacheng (Qoqek)	86	46.45 N	82.57 E
Tacherting	60	48.05 N	12.34 E
Tachia	100	24.21 N	120.37 E
Tachia ≃	100	24.20 N	120.33 E
Tachiaochang Airport ⊠	107	32.01 N	118.47 E
Tachiataš	72	42.22 N	59.35 E
Tachibana, Nihon	96	33.11 N	130.36 E
Tachibana, Nihon	96	33.54 N	132.17 E
Tachie ≃	182	54.40 N	124.50 W
Tachikawa	94	35.42 N	139.25 E
Tachikawa Air Base ■	268	35.43 N	139.25 E
Tachinger See ⊜	60	47.58 N	12.45 E
Táchira □ [3]	246	7.50 N	72.05 W
Tachoshui	100	24.20 N	121.44 E
Tachov	60	49.48 N	12.38 E
Tachta, Ross.	80	45.54 N	42.07 E
Tachta, Ross.	89	53.08 N	139.53 E
Tachta-Bazar	128	35.57 N	62.50 E
Tachtabrod	86	52.38 N	67.34 E
Tachtakupyr	86	43.02 N	60.17 E
Tachtamygda	89	54.06 N	123.34 E
Tacima	250	6.30 S	35.39 W
Tacina ≃	68	38.56 N	16.53 E
Tacinskij	80	48.13 N	41.17 E
Taciuã, Lago ≃	246	4.29 S	60.35 W
Tacloban	116	11.15 N	125.00 E
Taclobo	116	12.20 N	122.34 E
Tacna, Perú	248	18.01 S	70.15 W
Tacna, Az., U.S.	200	32.41 N	113.57 W
Tacna □ [5]	248	17.40 S	70.20 W
Tacoignières	261	48.50 N	1.40 E
Tacoma	224	47.15 N	122.26 W
Tacoma Narrows Bridge ✦ [5]	224	47.16 N	122.33 W
Taconic	207	42.02 N	73.24 W
Taconic Range ⋏	210	42.30 N	73.20 W
Taconic State Park ♦	210	42.05 N	73.34 W
Tacony ✦ [8]	285	40.02 N	75.03 W
Tacony Creek ≃	285	40.01 N	75.06 W
Tacony Creek Park ♦	285	40.02 N	75.07 W
Tacony Palmyra Bridge ✦ [5]	285	40.01 N	75.02 W
Taco Pozo	252	25.37 S	63.17 W
Tacotalpa	234	17.36 N	92.49 W
Tacotalpa ≃	234	17.50 N	92.52 W
Tacuarembó	252	31.44 S	55.59 W
Tacuarembó ≃	252	32.25 S	55.29 W
Tacuarí ≃	252	32.46 S	53.18 W
Tacuatí	252	23.27 S	56.35 W
Tacuba ✦ [8]	286a	19.28 N	99.12 W
Tacubaya ✦ [8]	286a	19.25 N	99.12 W
Tacuparé, Cachoeira ∟	250	5.20 S	55.50 W
Tacurong	116	6.42 N	124.42 E
Tacuru, Bra.	252	23.38 S	55.01 W
Tacuru, Bra.	255	23.38 S	55.01 W
Tacurú, Laguna ⊜	258	34.58 S	58.25 W
Tacutu (Takutu) ≃	246	3.01 N	60.29 W
Tadain	270	34.52 N	135.24 E
Tadami	92	37.21 N	139.19 E
Tadaoka	270	34.29 N	135.24 E
Tadasuni	71	40.06 N	8.53 E
Tadcaster	44	53.53 N	1.16 W
Tademaït, Plateau du ⋏ [1]	148	28.30 N	2.00 E
Tadenac Lake ⊜	212	45.03 N	79.56 W
Tādepallegūdem	122	16.50 N	81.30 E
Tadía, Ciénaga de ⊜	246	6.48 N	76.49 W
Tadine	175f	21.33 S	167.52 E
Tadio, Lagune ⊂	150	5.11 N	5.15 W
Tadjemout	148	25.37 N	3.48 E
Tadjenanet	34	36.08 N	5.59 E
Tadjeraout, Oued ∨	148	21.17 N	1.19 E
Tadjoura	144	11.47 N	42.54 E
Tadjoura, Golfe de ⊂	144	11.42 N	43.00 E
Tadley	42	51.21 N	1.08 W
Tado	94	35.08 N	136.38 E
Tadok	114	3.58 N	96.19 E
Tadotsu	96	34.16 N	133.45 E
Tadoule Lake ⊜	176	58.36 N	98.20 W
Tadoussac	186	48.09 N	69.43 W
Tādpatri	122	14.55 N	78.01 E
Taduno	112	1.55 S	123.05 E
Tadworth	42	51.17 N	0.14 W
Tadzhikistan → Tajikistan □ [1]	72	39.00 N	71.00 E
Tadžikabad	85	39.07 N	70.50 E
T'aean	98	36.46 N	126.16 E
T'aebaek-san ∧	98	37.06 N	128.55 E
T'aebaek-sanmaek ⋏	98	37.40 N	128.50 E
Taebu-do I	98	37.15 N	126.35 E
Taech'ŏn	98	36.22 N	126.34 E
Taech'ŏng-do I	98	37.49 N	124.43 E
Taedong	98	39.05 N	125.31 E
Taedong-gang ≃	98	38.42 N	125.15 E
Taegu	98	35.52 N	128.35 E
Taegu □ [4]	98	35.50 N	128.35 E
Taegwan	98	40.13 N	125.12 E
Taehan-Min'guk → Korea, South □ [1]	98	36.30 N	128.00 E
Taehŭksan-do I	98	34.40 N	125.25 E
Taehŭng	98	40.06 N	126.56 E
Taehwajŏn	271b	37.36 N	126.52 E
T'aein	98	35.40 N	126.55 E
Taejin	98	36.34 N	129.24 E
Taejŏn	98	36.20 N	127.26 E
Taejujŏm	98	38.24 N	127.58 E
T'aemo-san ∧	271b	37.27 N	127.04 E
Taeng ≃	110	19.06 N	98.57 E
Taer	102	34.09 N	98.50 E
Ta'erwan	100	31.49 N	113.25 E
Taeryanghwa	98	41.14 N	129.42 E
Taf ≃	42	51.47 N	4.26 W
Tafahi I	14	15.51 S	173.43 W
Tafahnā al-ʿAzab	142	30.36 N	31.15 E
Tafalla	34	42.31 N	1.40 W
Tafanlieh	100	21.58 N	120.46 E
Ṭafas	132	32.44 N	36.04 E
Ṭafāsīkh, Ghurd at- ⊥ [8]	142	29.43 N	29.45 E
Tafassasset, Oued (Oued Tafassâsset) ∨	148	20.56 N	10.12 E
Tafassâsset, Ténéré du ✦ [2]	146	21.00 N	11.00 E
Tafea □ [8]	175f	19.30 S	169.00 E
Tafelbaai → Table Bay ⊂	158	33.53 S	18.27 E
Tafelberg ∧	250	3.55 N	56.10 W
Tafermaar	164	6.51 S	134.06 E
Taff ≃	42	51.27 N	3.09 W
Tafiré	150	9.04 N	5.10 W
Tafí Viejo	252	26.44 S	65.16 W
Taflan	130	41.25 N	36.09 E
Tafna, Oued ≃	34	35.17 N	1.30 W
Tafo	150	6.13 N	0.22 W
Tafraoute	148	29.40 N	8.58 W
Taft, Īrān	128	31.45 N	54.14 E
Taft, Pil.	116	11.54 N	125.25 E
Taft, Ca., U.S.	204	35.08 N	119.27 W
Taft, Fl., U.S.	220	28.23 N	81.24 W
Taft, Ok., U.S.	196	35.45 N	95.32 W
Taft, Tx., U.S.	196	27.58 N	97.23 W
Taftān, Kūh-e ∧	128	28.36 N	61.08 E
Tafton	210	41.25 N	75.11 W
Taga, Nihon	94	35.13 N	136.17 E
Taga, Nihon	270	34.49 N	135.49 E
Taga, W. Sam.	175a	13.46 S	172.28 W
Tagabukid	116	7.00 N	126.21 E
Taga Dzong	124	27.04 N	89.53 E
Tagagawik ≃	180	66.30 N	159.00 W
Tagaj	80	54.18 N	47.39 E
Tagajō	92	38.20 N	141.00 E
Tagan	86	54.57 N	77.18 E
Tagana-an	116	9.42 N	125.35 E
Taganrog	83	47.12 N	38.56 E
Taganrogskij zaliv ⊂	78	47.00 N	38.23 E
Tagant □ [4]	150	18.20 N	11.30 W
Tagânt ✦ [1]	150	18.00 N	12.00 W
Tagapula Island I	116	12.04 N	124.12 E
Tågarp	41	55.56 N	12.57 E
Tagauayan Island I	116	10.58 N	121.13 E
Tagawa	96	33.38 N	130.49 E
Tagaytay	116	14.06 N	120.56 E
Tagbara	152	5.56 N	21.09 E
Tagbilaran	116	9.39 N	123.51 E
Tagdempt → Tihert	148	35.28 N	1.21 E
Tage	164	6.20 S	143.20 E
Tageren Canal ≅	174q	9.33 N	138.09 E
Taggia	62	43.52 N	7.51 E
Taghit	148	30.55 N	2.02 W
Taghkanic Creek ≃	210	42.13 N	73.45 W
Taghmon	48	52.18 N	6.39 W
Tagig	269f	14.32 N	121.04 E
Tagig ≃	269f	14.31 N	121.05 E
Tagish Lake ⊜	180	59.45 N	134.15 W
Tagliacozzo	66	42.04 N	13.14 E
Tagliamento ≃	64	45.38 N	13.06 E
Tagliata, Monte della ∧	64	44.34 N	9.48 E
Taglio di Po	64	45.00 N	12.12 E
Tagna	88	53.36 N	101.54 E
Tagna ≃	88	53.38 N	101.53 E
Tago	116	9.02 N	126.13 E
Tago ≃	116	9.01 N	126.14 E
Tagoloan	116	8.32 N	124.45 E
Tagolo Point ⋗	116	8.44 N	123.23 E
Tagon Harbour ⊂	162	33.53 S	123.00 E
Tagounit	148	29.58 N	5.36 W
Tagourâret ⊤ [4]	150	17.45 N	7.43 W
Tagow Bāy	120	35.42 N	66.03 E
Tagrina, Oued ∨	148	21.00 N	6.16 E
Taguatinga	255	12.25 S	46.26 W
Tagubanhan Island I	116	11.08 N	123.07 E
Tagudin	116	16.56 N	120.27 E
Taguedoufat ∨	150	14.50 N	7.42 E
Taguke	120	32.07 N	84.35 E
Tagul ≃	88	55.35 N	97.45 E
Tagula Island I	160	11.30 S	153.30 E
Tagum	116	7.28 N	125.48 E
T'agun	86	53.56 N	85.38 E
Tagun Bay ⊂	116	13.55 N	123.46 E
Tagus (Tejo) (Tajo) ≃	34	38.40 N	9.24 W
T'agyŏng-ni	98	38.04 N	126.03 E
Tah, Sebkha ⊜	148	27.45 N	12.42 W
Taha	89	47.33 N	124.14 E
Tahaa I	14	16.38 S	151.30 W
Tahakopa	172	46.31 S	169.23 E
Tahala	148	34.04 N	4.20 W
Tahan, Gunong ∧	114	4.38 N	102.14 E
Tahanaoute	148	31.24 N	7.54 W
Tahāneh-ye Ney Basteh	128	32.59 N	60.53 E
Tahara	94	34.40 N	137.16 E
Tahart	148	22.51 N	5.12 E
Tahat ∧	148	23.18 N	5.47 E
Taheke	172	35.27 S	173.39 E
Ṭāherī	128	27.42 N	52.21 E
Tahgong, Puntan ⋗	174n	15.06 N	145.39 E
Tahifet	148	22.58 N	5.55 E
Tahiryuak Lake ⊜	176	70.56 N	112.20 W
Tahiti I	174s	17.37 S	149.27 W
Tahkuna neem ⋗	76	59.07 N	22.36 E
Tāhlāb (Ṭālāb) ≃	128	28.09 N	62.45 E
Tahlequah	196	35.54 N	94.58 W
Ṭahmā wa Minshāt ʿAbd as-Sayyid	142	29.38 N	31.14 E
Tahmoor	170	34.13 S	150.36 E
Tahneta Pass)(	180	61.53 N	147.20 W
Tahoe, Lake ⊜	226	39.07 N	120.03 W
Tahoe City	226	39.10 N	120.08 W
Tahoe Lake ⊜	176	70.15 N	108.45 W
Tahoe Paradise	226	38.52 N	120.01 W
Tahoe Valley	226	38.55 N	120.00 W
Tahoka	196	33.10 N	101.47 W
Taholah	224	47.20 N	124.17 W
Tahoua	150	14.54 N	5.16 E
Tahoua □ [5]	150	16.00 N	5.00 E
Tahquamenon ≃	190	46.34 N	85.02 W
Tahquamenon Falls State Park ♦	190	46.29 N	85.05 W
Tahsi	100	24.57 N	121.53 E
Tahsis	182	49.55 N	126.39 W
Ṭahṭā	140	26.46 N	31.30 E
Tahtaköprü	130	39.57 N	29.39 E
Tahtsa Lake ⊜	182	53.42 N	127.26 W
Tahtsa Peak ∧	182	53.33 N	127.47 W
Tahu	100	24.26 N	120.52 E
Tahuamanu ≃	248	11.06 S	67.36 W
Tahuata I	174x	9.57 S	139.05 W
Tahulandang, Pulau I	112	2.20 N	125.25 E
Tahuna	112	3.37 N	125.29 E
Tahuofang ⊜ [1]	104	41.55 N	124.07 E
Tahuya ≃	224	47.23 N	123.03 W
Ṭahwāy	142	30.22 N	30.52 E
Taï, C. Iv.	150	5.52 N	7.27 W
Tai, It.	64	46.25 N	12.20 E
Tai, Nihon	270	34.31 N	135.26 E
Tai ✦ [8]	270	34.45 N	135.00 E
Taiaçupeba	256	23.40 S	46.11 W
Tai'an, Zhg.	98	36.12 N	117.07 E
Tai'an, Zhg.	104	41.23 N	122.27 E
Tai'an, Zhg.	107	30.05 N	105.47 E
Tai'angang	106	31.43 N	121.40 E
Taiarapu, Presqu'île de ⋗ [1]	174s	17.47 S	149.14 W
Taibai	102	34.00 N	107.18 E
Taibai Shan ∧, Zhg.	98	39.19 N	114.11 E
Taibai Shan ∧, Zhg.	102	33.54 N	107.46 E
Taibilla, Sierra de ⋏	34	38.10 N	2.10 W
Taibon Agordino	64	46.18 N	12.00 E
Taibus Qi (Baochang)	98	41.56 N	115.22 E
Taicang	106	31.26 N	121.07 E
T'aichou → Taizhou	100	32.30 N	119.58 E
Taichu → T'aichung	100	24.09 N	120.41 E
T'aichung	100	24.09 N	120.41 E
Taicunzhen	106	31.27 N	119.03 E
Taiden → Taejŏn	98	36.20 N	127.26 E
Taiei	94	35.49 N	140.25 E
Taieri ≃	172	46.03 S	170.11 E
Taif → Aṭ-Ṭā'if	144	21.16 N	40.24 E
Taigu	102	37.28 N	112.30 E
Tai Hang	271d	22.17 N	114.11 E
Taihang Shan ⋏	102	38.00 N	114.00 E
Taihape	172	39.40 S	175.48 E
Taihe, Zhg.	100	33.11 N	115.36 E
Taihe, Zhg.	100	26.49 N	114.55 E
Taihe, Zhg.	107	30.10 N	105.56 E
Taihezhen, Zhg.	89	44.47 N	123.29 E
Taihezhen, Zhg.	107	30.07 N	103.50 E
Taihezhen, Zhg.	107	30.06 N	106.03 E
Taiho	174m	26.39 N	128.07 E
Taihoku → T'aipei	100	25.03 N	121.30 E
T'aihsi	100	23.42 N	120.11 E
T'aihsien → Taizhou	100	32.30 N	119.58 E
Taihu	100	30.26 N	116.16 E
Tai Hu ⊜	106	31.15 N	120.10 E
Taijiang	102	26.32 N	108.22 E
Taijimiao	98	40.55 N	113.46 E
Taijüan → Taiyuan	102	37.55 N	112.30 E
Taikang	98	34.04 N	114.50 E
Taikkyi	110	17.19 N	95.58 E
Taikou	102	31.53 N	111.07 E
Taiko-yama ∧	96	35.46 N	135.12 E
Taikyu → Taegu	98	35.52 N	128.35 E
Tailai	89	46.23 N	123.27 E
Tai Lam Chung	271d	22.22 N	114.01 E
Tai Lam Chung Reservoir ⊜ [1]	271d	22.23 N	114.01 E
Tailem Bend	166	35.16 S	139.27 E
Tailfingen	58	48.15 N	9.01 E
Tai Long, H.K.	271d	22.25 N	114.22 E
Tai Long, H.K.	271d	22.13 N	113.59 E
Tai Long Bay ⊂	271d	22.24 N	114.24 E
Taima, Nihon	96	34.30 N	135.42 E
T'aima, T'aiwan	100	22.37 N	120.59 E
Taimba	74	60.18 N	98.58 E
Taimei	100	23.19 N	114.29 E
Tai Mong Tsai	271d	22.24 N	114.18 E
Tai Mo Shan ∧	271d	22.25 N	114.07 E
Taimyr-Halbinsel → Tajmyr, poluostrov ⋗ [1]	74	76.00 N	104.00 E
Tain	46	57.48 N	4.04 W
Tainaka	270	34.36 N	135.37 E
T'ainan	100	23.00 N	120.12 E
Taínaron, Ákra ⋗	38	36.22 N	22.30 E
Taining	100	26.54 N	117.09 E
Tain-l'Hermitage	62	45.04 N	4.51 E
Tai O, H.K.	100	22.15 N	113.51 E
Taio, It.	64	46.20 N	11.04 E
Taiobeiras	255	15.49 S	42.14 W
Tai Pang Wan ⊂	100	22.30 N	114.24 E
T'aipei, T'aiwan	100	25.03 N	121.30 E
T'aipei, T'aiwan	269d	25.03 N	121.30 E
T'aipei □ [6]	269d	25.00 N	121.40 E
Taipei Bridge ✦ [5]	269d	25.04 N	121.30 E
T'aipeihsien	100	25.00 N	121.27 E
Taipei Institute of Technology ⊍ [2]	269d	25.02 N	121.32 E
Taipei New Park ♦	269d	25.03 N	121.31 E
T'aipei Shih □ [7]	269d	25.05 N	121.33 E
Taiping, Malay.	114	4.51 N	100.44 E
Taiping, Zhg.	100	30.18 N	118.12 E
Taiping, Zhg.	100	22.49 N	113.41 E
Taiping, Zhg.	102	22.40 N	107.05 E
Taiping, Zhg.	107	30.24 N	103.37 E
Taipingchang, Zhg.	102	27.25 N	103.04 E
Taipingchang, Zhg.	107	29.53 N	106.04 E
Taipingchang, Zhg.	107	29.55 N	103.49 E
Taipingchang, Zhg.	107	30.10 N	106.21 E
Taipingchang, Zhg.	107	30.39 N	105.54 E
Taipingchang, Zhg.	107	29.33 N	103.33 E
Taipingchang, Zhg.	107	30.25 N	103.46 E
Taipingchuan, Zhg.	89	44.23 N	123.11 E
Taipingchuan, Zhg.	98	42.36 N	127.20 E
Taipingdian	102	32.08 N	111.45 E
Taipingkou	100	29.50 N	113.35 E
Taipingling	89	43.26 N	128.09 E
Taipingshan, Zhg.	98	40.34 N	122.25 E
Taipingshan, Zhg.	104	41.36 N	123.41 E
Taipingshao	98	40.54 N	125.08 E
Taipingsi	107	29.24 N	103.34 E
Taipingxigou	104	42.36 N	121.13 E
Taipingzhai	104	42.14 N	124.07 E
Taipingzhen, Zhg.	89	46.44 N	130.44 E
Taipingzhen, Zhg.	102	35.42 N	107.37 E
Taipingzhen, Zhg.	107	29.24 N	105.47 E
Taipingzhen, Zhg.	107	30.26 N	104.12 E
Taipingzhuang, Zhg.	104	42.38 N	123.45 E
Taipingzhuang, Zhg.	105	40.03 N	116.24 E
Taipingzhuang, Zhg.	105	40.08 N	117.36 E
Tai Po Hoi ⊂	271d	22.26 N	114.12 E
Tai Po Tsai	271d	22.21 N	114.15 E
Taipu	250	5.37 S	35.36 W
Taira, Nihon	94	36.26 N	136.57 E
Taira → Iwaki, Nihon	94	37.03 N	140.55 E
Taireta	256	22.36 S	43.42 W
Tairiqiao	106	30.59 N	121.33 E
Tais	112	4.06 S	102.34 E
Taisen-zan ∧	96	33.06 N	131.17 E
Taisha → Izumo, Nihon	96	35.22 N	132.46 E
Taisha, Nihon	96	35.24 N	132.40 E
Taishaku-kyō ♦	96	34.53 N	133.13 E
Taishaku-zan ∧, Nihon	94	36.58 N	139.28 E
Taishaku-zan ∧, Nihon	270	34.47 N	135.07 E
Taishan, Zhg.	98	39.01 N	113.36 E
Taishan, Zhg.	102	22.16 N	112.44 E
Taishanchang	107	30.32 N	106.42 E
Taishi, Nihon	96	34.50 N	134.33 E
Taishi, Nihon	270	34.31 N	135.39 E
Taishō	96	33.12 N	132.58 E
Taishō ✦ [8]	270	34.38 N	135.27 E
Tai Shui Hang	271d	22.25 N	14.13 E
Taishun	100	27.33 N	119.43 E
Tai Tam Bay ⊂	271d	22.13 N	114.13 E
Taitao, Península de ⋗ [1]	254	46.30 S	74.25 W
Taitapu	172	43.40 S	172.33 E
Taitō ✦ [8]	268	35.43 N	139.47 E
Tai Tong	271d	22.25 N	114.01 E
Taitouying	98	40.02 N	119.12 E
Taitō-zaki ⋗	94	35.18 N	140.25 E
T'aitung	100	22.45 N	121.09 E
Taivalkoski	26	65.34 N	28.15 E
Tai Wan	271d	22.10 N	114.15 E
Taiwan (T'aiwan) □ [1], Asia	90	23.30 N	121.00 E
Taiwan (T'aiwan) □ [1], Asia	100	23.30 N	121.00 E
T'aiwan I	100	23.30 N	121.00 E
Taiwan Strait ʊ	100	24.00 N	119.00 E
Tai Wan Tau	271d	22.18 N	114.17 E
Taixi	100	24.42 N	116.56 E
Taixian	100	32.31 N	120.09 E
Taixing	106	32.11 N	120.01 E
Taixizhen	106	31.03 N	119.49 E
Taiyang	100	30.12 N	119.19 E
Taiyanggong	271a	39.58 N	116.25 E
Taíyetos Óros ⋏	38	37.00 N	22.20 E
Ṭaiyiba	132	32.16 N	35.01 E
Taiyuan	102	37.55 N	112.30 E
Taizhao	120	30.01 N	93.08 E
Taizhou	100	32.30 N	119.58 E
Taizhou Liedao II	100	28.30 N	121.53 E
Taizi ≃	98	41.00 N	122.26 E
Taʿizz	144	13.38 N	44.04 E
Tāj al-ʿIzz	142	30.57 N	31.35 E
Tajarḥī	146	24.21 N	14.28 E
Tajbola	24	68.26 N	33.19 E
Tajdakovo	82	54.29 N	37.32 E
Tajerouine	36	35.54 N	8.34 E
Tajetteret, Oued ∨	148	21.20 N	7.22 E
Tajga	86	56.04 N	85.37 E
Tajgonos, mys ⋗	74	60.35 N	160.08 E
Tajgonos, poluostrov ⋗ [1]	74	61.20 N	161.00 E
Tajikistan □ [1], Asia	72	39.00 N	71.00 E
Tajikistan □ [1], Asia	85	39.00 N	71.00 E
Tajikstan → Tajikistan □ [1]	72	39.00 N	71.00 E
Tajima	94	37.12 N	139.46 E
Tajimi	94	35.19 N	137.08 E
Tajique	200	34.45 N	106.17 W
Tajiri	270	34.24 N	135.18 E
Tajitos	232	30.58 N	112.18 W
Tajlakdžegen	86	43.54 N	60.29 E
Tajlakovy	86	59.20 N	74.04 E
Tāj Mahal ⊥	124	27.10 N	78.03 E
Tajmura ≃	72	63.46 N	98.01 E
Tajmyr, ozero ⊜	74	74.30 N	102.30 E
Tajmyr, poluostrov ⋗ [1]	74	76.00 N	104.00 E
Tajna	88	56.27 N	95.30 E
Tajninka	265b	55.54 N	37.45 E
Tajo → Tagus ≃	34	38.40 N	9.24 W
Tajožnyj, Ross.	86	56.09 N	94.29 E
Tajožnyj, Ross.	88	56.13 N	94.55 E
Tajpur, India	124	25.51 N	85.41 E
Tajpur, India	124	29.10 N	78.29 E
Tājpur, India	272b	22.44 N	88.16 E
Tajpur Khurd ✦ [8]	272a	28.35 N	77.03 E
Tajšet	88	55.57 N	98.00 E
Tajsojgan	80	48.19 N	53.29 E
Tajturka	88	52.51 N	103.28 E
Tajumulco, Volcán ∧ [1]	236	15.02 N	91.55 W
Tajuña ≃	34	40.07 N	3.35 W
Tājūrā', Lībiyā	146	32.53 N	13.21 E
Tajura, Ross.	88	57.00 N	106.35 E
Tajura ≃	88	57.00 N	106.35 E
Tajžina	86	53.38 N	87.28 E
Tak	110	16.52 N	99.08 E
Takāb	128	36.24 N	47.07 E
Takabanare-jima I	174m	26.22 N	127.59 E
Takabara	150	11.50 N	11.30 W
Takachiho	92	32.42 N	131.18 E
Takachu	156	22.37 S	21.58 E
Takada → Bungo-takada, Nihon	96	33.33 N	131.27 E
Takada → Yamato-takada, Nihon	96	34.31 N	135.45 E
Takagi	268	35.56 N	139.35 E
Takahagi	94	36.43 N	140.43 E
Takahama, Nihon	94	34.55 N	136.59 E
Takahama, Nihon	94	37.00 N	136.46 E
Takahama, Nihon	96	35.29 N	135.33 E
Takahara ≃	94	36.28 N	137.15 E
Takahashi	96	34.47 N	133.37 E
Takahashi ≃	96	34.31 N	133.42 E
Takahe, Mount ∧	9	76.16 S	112.14 W
Takaido ✦ [8]	268	35.40 N	139.37 E
Takaishi	96	34.32 N	135.26 E
Takaka	172	40.51 S	172.48 E
Takakkaw Falls ∟	182	51.30 N	116.28 W
Takalaou	146	10.07 N	19.48 E
Takalar	112	5.28 S	119.24 E
Takamatsu, Nihon	94	36.46 N	136.43 E
Takamatsu, Nihon	96	34.20 N	134.03 E
Takami-shima I	96	34.19 N	133.41 E
Takamiya	96	34.47 N	132.44 E
Takami-yama ∧	94	34.25 N	136.05 E
Takamori	94	35.33 N	137.53 E
Takanabe	92	32.08 N	131.30 E
Takanawa-hantō ⋗ [1]	96	33.58 N	132.56 E
Takanawa-san ∧	96	33.56 N	132.51 E
Takane, Nihon	94	36.02 N	137.29 E
Takane, Nihon	94	35.50 N	138.25 E
Takanezawa	94	36.37 N	139.59 E
Takano	96	35.02 N	132.55 E
Takanosu	92	40.13 N	140.22 E
Takao → Kaohsiung	100	22.38 N	120.17 E
Takaoka	94	36.45 N	137.01 E
Takao-kokutei-kōen ♦	94	35.38 N	139.15 E
Takao-san ∧, Nihon	94	35.38 N	139.15 E
Takao-san ∧, Nihon	270	34.49 N	135.51 E
Takapau	172	40.02 S	176.21 E
Takapuna	172	36.47 S	174.47 E
Takara-jima I	93b	29.09 N	129.13 E
Takarazuka	270	34.49 N	135.21 E
Takasago	96	34.45 N	134.48 E
Takasaki	94	36.20 N	139.01 E
Takase	96	34.10 N	133.45 E
Takase ≃	94	36.28 N	137.52 E
Takashima, Nihon	92	32.39 N	129.45 E
Takashima, Nihon	94	35.18 N	136.01 E
Taka-shima I	96	34.50 N	131.50 E
Takashippu	174m	26.24 N	127.44 E
Takasu	94	35.57 N	136.53 E
Takata → Rikuzen-takata, Nihon	92	39.01 N	141.38 E
Takata → Joetsu, Nihon	94	37.06 N	138.15 E
Takata, Nihon	96	33.06 N	130.28 E
Takatō	94	35.50 N	138.04 E
Takatomi	94	35.29 N	136.47 E
Takatori	96	34.27 N	135.48 E
Takatori-yama ∧	96	33.18 N	130.43 E
Takatori-yama ∧ [2]	268	35.18 N	139.37 E
Takatsu ≃	96	34.42 N	131.49 E
Takatsuki, Nihon	94	35.28 N	136.14 E
Takatsuki, Nihon	96	34.51 N	135.37 E
Takaungu	154	3.41 S	39.51 E
Ta-kaw	110	21.36 N	98.56 E
Takayama, Nihon	94	36.08 N	137.15 E
Takayama, Nihon	94	36.37 N	138.57 E
Takayama, Nihon	94	36.40 N	138.21 E
Takayama, Nihon	270	34.45 N	135.44 E
Takayanagi, Nihon	94	37.13 N	138.38 E
Takayanagi, Nihon	268	35.25 N	139.57 E
Tak Bai	114	6.16 N	102.03 E
Takčijan	85	38.32 N	68.03 E
Takebe	96	34.52 N	133.54 E
Takefu	94	35.54 N	136.10 E
Takehara	96	34.21 N	132.55 E
Takeli	85	40.30 N	69.25 E
Takenake	120	34.11 N	81.20 E
Takengon	114	4.38 N	96.50 E
Takeno ≃	96	35.45 N	135.06 E
Takenotsuka ✦ [8]	268	35.48 N	139.48 E
Takeo	92	33.12 N	130.01 E
Takeoka	268	35.12 N	139.51 E
Tåkern ⊜	26	58.21 N	14.48 E
Takeshi	94	36.17 N	138.14 E
Take-shima I	93b	30.49 N	130.26 E
Take-shima (Tok-to) II	92	37.17 N	131.53 E
Tākestān	128	36.04 N	49.43 E
Taketa	96	32.58 N	131.24 E
Taketoyo	94	34.51 N	136.55 E
Takêv	110	10.59 N	104.47 E
Take-yama ∧ [2]	268	35.13 N	139.39 E
Takhādīd ⊤ [4]	128	29.59 N	44.30 E
Takhār □ [4]	120	36.30 N	69.30 E
Takhatpur	124	22.09 N	81.52 E
Takhli	110	15.15 N	100.21 E
Ta Khoa	110	21.13 N	104.18 E
Takht-e Jamshīd ⊥	128	29.57 N	52.52 E
Takht-i-Bhāi	123	34.17 N	71.56 E
Tāki, India	126	22.36 N	88.55 E
Taki, Nihon	94	34.30 N	136.33 E
Taki, Nihon	96	35.16 N	132.38 E
Taki, Pap. N. Gui.	175e	6.29 S	155.50 E
Takijuk Lake ⊜	176	66.15 N	113.05 W
Takikawa	92a	43.33 N	141.54 E
Takino	96	34.56 N	134.58 E
Takipur	126	24.19 N	87.58 E
Takitimu Mountains ⋏	172	45.41 S	167.53 E
Takla Lake ⊜	182	55.25 N	125.53 W
Takla Landing	182	55.29 N	125.58 W
Takla Makan → Taklimakan Shamo ✦ [2]	90	39.00 N	83.00 E
Taklimakan Shamo ✦ [2]	90	39.00 N	83.00 E
Tako	94	35.44 N	140.28 E
Takob	85	38.50 N	68.57 E
Tako-bana ⋗	96	35.36 N	133.06 E
Takolekaju, Pegunungan ⋏	112	2.00 S	121.00 E
Takoma Park	284c	38.58 N	77.00 W
Takoradi → Sekondi-Takoradi	150	4.59 N	1.43 W
Takotna	180	62.56 N	156.04 W
Takow → Kaohsiung	100	22.38 N	120.17 E
Takpochao, Okso ∧	174n	15.11 N	145.45 E
Takrouna	36	36.09 N	10.20 E
Taksimo	88	51.03 N	107.50 E
Taksino	82	56.19 N	36.10 E
Takslesluk Lake ⊜	180	61.04 N	162.55 W
Taksony	264c	47.20 N	19.04 E
Taku	92	33.17 N	130.08 E
Taku ≃	180	58.26 N	133.59 W
Takuan, Mount ∧	175e	6.27 S	155.36 E
Takua Pa	110	8.53 N	98.21 E
Taku Glacier ⍽	180	58.35 N	134.10 W
Takum	150	7.17 N	9.59 E
Takuma	96	34.13 N	133.40 E
Takundi	152	4.45 S	16.34 E
Takutea I	14	19.49 S	158.18 W
Takut Tangub Bay ⊂	116	6.33 N	122.15 E
Takutu (Tacutu) ≃	246	3.01 N	60.29 W
Takuu Islands II	14	4.45 S	157.00 E
Takysie Lake	182	53.54 N	125.53 W
Tāl	123	34.55 N	72.13 E
Tala, Bngl.	126	22.46 N	89.16 E
Tāla, India	124	23.43 N	81.02 E
Tala, Méx.	234	20.40 N	103.42 W
Talā, Miṣr	142	30.41 N	30.56 E
Tala, Ur.	252	34.21 S	55.46 W
Tala, Arroyo del ≃	258	33.37 S	56.34 W
Ṭālāb (Tāhlāb) ≃	128	28.09 N	62.45 E
Talacogon	116	8.28 N	125.46 E
Talaga	112	2.11 S	125.53 E
Talagang	123	32.55 N	72.25 E
Talagante	252	33.40 S	70.56 W
Talagou	104	41.37 N	120.32 E
Ta Lai	110	11.24 N	107.23 E
Talaimannar	122	9.05 N	79.44 E
Talāja	120	21.21 N	72.03 E
Talak ✦ [1]	150	18.20 N	6.00 E
Talakag	116	8.16 N	124.37 E
Talakan	89	49.38 N	133.18 E
Talakivka	83	47.10 N	37.43 E
Tālāla	120	21.02 N	70.32 E
Talalayivka	78	50.51 N	33.08 E
Talamanca, Cordillera de ⋏	236	9.30 N	83.40 W
Talamba	123	30.32 N	72.14 E
Talamone	66	42.33 N	11.08 E
Talana, It.	71	40.02 N	9.30 E
Talana, S. Afr.	158	28.10 S	30.15 E
Talandža	89	49.27 N	131.35 E
Talang, Gunung ∧	112	0.58 S	100.39 E
Talangbatu	112	4.06 S	105.29 E
Talangbetutu	112	2.53 S	104.41 E
Talangpadang	112	5.21 S	104.11 E
Talangrimbo	112	3.29 S	105.25 E
Talant	58	47.19 N	5.00 E
Talap	80	48.26 N	48.03 E
Talara	246	4.34 S	81.17 W
Talarrubias	34	39.02 N	5.14 W
Talas	85	42.32 N	72.14 E
Talas □ [4]	85	42.30 N	72.00 E
Talas ≃	85	44.02 N	69.37 E
Talasea	164	5.20 S	150.05 E
Talasskij-Alatau, chrebet ⋏	85	42.10 N	72.00 E
Talatakoh, Pulau I	112	0.22 S	122.05 E
Talʿat al-Jamāʿah, Rujm ∧	132	30.23 N	35.30 E
Talata Mafara	150	12.35 N	6.04 E
Talaud, Kepulauan II	108	4.20 N	126.50 E
Talavera	116	15.35 N	120.55 E
Talavera de la Reina	34	39.57 N	4.50 W
Talawdī	140	10.38 N	30.23 E
Talayan	116	6.55 N	124.24 E
Tālbāndh	126	22.03 N	86.20 E
Talbingo	171b	35.34 S	148.18 E
Talbingo Reservoir ⊜ [1]	171b	35.43 S	148.20 E
Talbot	169	37.11 S	143.43 E
Talbot ≃	212	44.28 N	79.10 W
Talbot, Cape ⋗	164	13.48 S	126.43 E
Talbot Brook	168a	32.01 S	116.40 E
Talbot Brook ≃	168a	32.10 S	116.49 E
Talbot Islands II	164	9.15 S	142.08 E
Talbot Lake ⊜, Mb., Can.	184	54.00 N	99.55 W
Talbot Lake ⊜, On., Can.	212	44.42 N	78.51 W
Talbotton	192	32.40 N	84.32 W
Talbotville Royal	214	42.48 N	81.15 W
Talbragar ≃	166	32.12 S	148.37 E
Talca	252	35.26 S	71.40 W
Talcahuano	252	36.43 S	73.07 W
Tālcher	120	20.57 N	85.13 E
Talchichitle, Isla I	232	24.59 N	108.04 W
Talco	196	33.21 N	95.06 W
Talcottville	207	41.49 N	72.30 W
Talcy, Château de ⊥	50	47.46 N	1.27 E
Taldan	89	53.40 N	124.48 E
Tāldāngra	126	23.02 N	87.06 E
Taldom	82	56.44 N	37.32 E
Taldyapan, Kaz.	80	48.07 N	47.08 E
Taldyapan, Kaz.	80	49.46 N	50.14 E
Taldyk, pereval)(	85	39.47 N	73.11 E
Taldykuduk	80	50.09 N	49.33 E
Taldy-Kurgan	86	45.00 N	78.23 E
Taldy-Kurgan □ [8]	86	45.30 N	78.30 E
Tale	150	9.26 N	1.07 W
Taleex	144	9.09 N	48.26 E
Talence	32	44.49 N	0.35 W
Talent	202	42.14 N	122.47 W
Tālesh	128	37.48 N	48.55 E
Taley	152	6.40 N	16.23 E
Talgar	85	43.18 N	77.18 E
Talgar, pik ∧	85	43.05 N	77.20 E
Talgarreg	42	52.08 N	4.18 W
Talgarth	42	52.00 N	3.15 W
Ṭalḥ, ʿIlw aṭ- ∧ [2]	142	28.30 N	29.38 E
Talhār	120	24.53 N	68.49 E
Tali, Pointe de ⋗	241o	15.56 N	61.12 W
Talia, Austl.	162	33.19 S	134.54 E
Talia, Méx.	196	25.44 N	102.26 W
Taliabu, Pulau I	112	1.48 S	124.48 E
Talian Dao I	98	39.03 N	122.52 E
Talibon	116	10.09 N	124.19 E
Talibong, Ko I	110	7.15 N	99.23 E
Talica, Ross.	76	58.44 N	41.34 E
Talica, Ross.	80	58.01 N	51.30 E
Talica, Ross.	86	57.00 N	63.43 E
Talickij Čamlyk	80	52.02 N	40.32 E
Talien → Dalian	98	38.53 N	121.35 E
Talihina	196	34.45 N	95.02 W
Tālīkota	122	16.29 N	76.19 E
Talikud Island I	116	6.56 N	125.42 E
Talim Island I	116	14.21 N	121.14 E
Talimuashili	85	39.08 N	77.03 E
Taling Chan	269a	13.46 N	100.27 E
Taliouine	148	30.36 N	7.49 W
Taliparamba	122	12.03 N	75.21 E
Tali Post	140	5.54 N	30.47 E
Talisay, Pil.	116	14.08 N	122.55 E
Talisay, Pil.	116	10.44 N	122.58 E
Talisay, Pil.	116	10.15 N	123.51 E
Talisayan	116	9.00 N	124.55 E
Talisei, Pulau I	112	1.51 N	125.05 E
Talish-Mikeyli	84	39.23 N	48.22 E
Talish Mountains (Kūhhā-ye Ṭavālesh) ⋏	128	38.42 N	48.18 E
Talisker	46	57.17 N	6.27 W
Taliwang	115b	8.44 S	116.52 E
Tal'ka	76	53.22 N	28.21 E
Talkeetna	180	62.20 N	150.07 W
Talkeetna Mountains ⋏	180	62.10 N	148.15 W
Ṭalkhā	142	31.03 N	31.22 E
Talkheh ≃	128	37.52 N	45.53 E
Talladale	46	57.42 N	5.29 W
Talladega	194	33.26 N	86.06 W
Tall ʿAfar	128	36.22 N	42.27 E
Tallaght	48	53.17 N	6.21 W
Tal Lah, India	126	22.19 N	87.18 E
Tallah, Miṣr	142	28.05 N	30.44 E
Tallahaga Creek ≃	194	32.55 N	88.58 W
Tallahala Creek ≃	194	31.12 N	89.05 W
Tallahassee	192	30.26 N	84.16 W
Tallahatchie ≃	194	33.33 N	90.10 W
Tall al-Abyaḍ	130	36.41 N	38.57 E
Tall al-ʿAmārnah (Akhetatem) ⊥	142	27.38 N	30.54 E
Tall al-Maskhūtah (Succotah) ⊥	142	30.33 N	32.07 E
Tall al-Muqayyar (Ur) ⊥	128	30.57 N	46.09 E
Tallanalla	168a	33.06 S	116.07 E
Tallangatta	166	36.13 S	147.15 E
Tallangatta Creek ≃	171b	36.15 S	147.13 E
Tallapoosa	194	33.44 N	85.17 W
Tallapoosa ≃	194	32.30 N	86.16 W
Tallard	62	44.28 N	6.03 E
Talla Reservoir ⊜ [1]	46	55.29 N	3.24 W
Tall ar-Ratābah (Pithom) ⊥	142	30.32 N	32.06 E
Tall ar-Rubʿ (Mendes) ⊥	142	30.58 N	31.31 E
Tallassee	194	32.32 N	85.53 W
Tall as-Sulṭān ⊥	132	31.52 N	35.27 E
Tall Banī ʿUmrān	142	27.40 N	30.54 E
Tall Basṭah (Bubastis) ⊥	142	30.34 N	31.31 E
Tällberg	26	60.49 N	15.00 E
Tall Bīsah	130	34.50 N	36.44 E
Tall-e Khosrow-ye Soflá	128	30.37 N	51.35 E
Talleyville	208	39.48 N	75.32 W
Tallinn	76	59.25 N	24.45 E
Tall Kalakh	130	34.40 N	36.15 E
Tall Kayf	128	36.29 N	43.08 E
Tall Kūjik	130	36.48 N	42.04 E
Tallmadge	214	41.06 N	81.27 W
Tallman	276	41.07 N	74.06 W
Tallman Mountain State Park ♦	276	41.01 N	73.54 W
Talloires	62	45.51 N	6.13 E
Tallong	170	34.44 S	150.05 E
Tallow	48	52.05 N	8.00 W
Tallowa Dam ✦ [6]	170	34.47 S	150.18 E
Tall Rāk	142	30.54 N	31.43 E
Tall Rifʿat	130	36.28 N	37.06 E
Tall Salḥab	130	35.15 N	36.22 E
Tall Tamir	130	36.39 N	40.22 E
Tallula	219	39.56 N	89.56 W
Tallulah	194	32.24 N	91.11 W
Tally	80	53.08 N	53.04 E
Tally Ho	274b	37.52 S	145.09 E
Tālma	126	23.29 N	89.54 E
Talmage, Ca., U.S.	204	39.08 N	123.10 W
Talmage, Ne., U.S.	198	40.31 N	96.01 W
Talmage, Pa., U.S.	208	40.07 N	76.13 W
Talmalmo	171b	35.56 S	147.30 E
Talmas	50	50.02 N	2.20 E
Talmaz	38	46.38 N	29.40 E
Tal'menka	86	53.51 N	83.35 E
Talmine	46	58.31 N	4.26 W
Talmont	32	46.28 N	1.37 W
Tal'ne	78	48.53 N	30.42 E
Tal'niki	88	52.47 N	102.24 E
Talo ∧	144	10.44 N	37.55 E
Taloda	120	21.34 N	74.13 E
Talofofo	174p	13.21 N	144.45 E
Talofofo Bay ⊂	174p	13.20 N	144.46 E
Taloga	196	36.02 N	98.57 W
Taloje	88	55.24 N	95.40 E
Taloje Budrukh	272c	19.05 N	73.05 E
Talok	112	1.03 N	118.48 E
Talon, Lake ⊜	190	46.18 N	79.05 W
Talonan, Tano ⋗	115b	9.07 S	117.02 E
Tāloqān	120	36.44 N	69.33 E
Taloro ≃	71	40.08 N	8.58 E
Talovaja	78	51.06 N	40.44 E
Talovka, Kaz.	80	50.25 N	47.35 E
Talovka, Ross.	80	49.58 N	45.01 E
Talovka, Ross.	84	44.14 N	46.36 E
Talovka, Ross.	86	51.27 N	81.54 E
Talovka, Ross.	86	57.10 N	93.09 E
Talpa	196	31.47 N	99.43 W
Talpa de Allende	234	20.23 N	104.51 W
Talquin, Lake ⊜ [1]	192	30.26 N	84.33 W
Tālsa	272b	22.49 N	88.33 E
Talsarnau	42	52.54 N	4.03 W
Talsi	76	57.15 N	22.36 E
Talšik	86	53.42 N	71.53 E
Taltal	252	25.24 S	70.29 W
Taltapin Lake ⊜	182	54.19 N	125.20 W
Taltson ≃	176	61.23 N	112.45 W
Talu	112	0.14 N	99.59 E

≃ River	Fluß	Río	Rivière	Rio
≅ Canal	Kanal	Canal	Canal	Canal
∟ Waterfall, Rapids	Wasserfall, Stromschnellen	Cascada, Rápidos	Chute d'eau, Rapides	Cascata, Rápidos
ʊ Strait	Meeresstraße	Estrecho	Détroit	Estreito
⊂ Bay, Gulf	Bucht, Golf	Bahía, Golfo	Baie, Golfe	Baía, Golfo
⊜ Lake, Lakes	See, Seen	Lago, Lagos	Lac, Lacs	Lago, Lagos
⩨ Swamp	Sumpf	Pantano	Marais	Pântano
⍽ Ice Features, Glacier	Eis- und Gletscherformen	Accidentes Glaciales	Formes glaciaires	Acidentes glaciares
⊤ Other Hydrographic Features	Andere Hydrographische Objekte	Otros Elementos Hidrográficos	Autres données hydrographiques	Outros acidentes hidrográficos

✧ Submarine Features	Untermeerische Objekte	Accidentes Submarinos	Formes de relief sous-marin	Acidentes submarinos
□ Political Unit	Politische Einheit	Unidad Politica	Entité politique	Unidade política
⊍ Cultural Institution	Kulturelle Institution	Institución Cultural	Institution culturelle	Instituição cultural
⊥ Historical Site	Historische Stätte	Sitio Histórico	Site historique	Sitio histórico
♦ Recreational Site	Erholungs- und Ferienort	Sitio de Recreo	Centre de loisirs	Area de Lazer
⊠ Airport	Flughafen	Aeropuerto	Aéroport	Aeroporto
■ Military Installation	Militäranlage	Instalación Militar	Installation militaire	Instalação militar
✦ Miscellaneous	Verschiedenes	Misceláneo	Divers	Diversos

Name / Name	Page / Seite	Lat.°′ / Breite°′	Long.°′ / Länge°′ E = Ost
Taludaa	112	0.20 N	123.28 E
Taluk	112	0.32 S	101.35 E
Talumphuk, Laem ›	110	8.30 N	100.10 E
Taluti, Teluk c	164	3.21 S	129.45 E
Talvik'ul'a	24	68.45 N	29.19 E
Talwandi Bhāi	123	30.51 N	74.56 E
Talwood	166	28.30 S	149.30 E
Taly	78	49.51 N	40.04 E
Ṭalyā	142	30.16 N	31.00 E
Tal-y-bont	42	52.29 N	3.59 W
Tama, Arg.	252	30.31 S	66.32 W
Tama, Nihon	94	35.37 N	139.27 E
Tama, Ia., U.S.	190	41.58 N	92.34 W
Tama ≃	94	35.32 N	139.47 E
Tama Cemetery •	268	35.41 N	139.31 E
Tamacuarí, Pico ∧	246	1.15 N	64.45 W
Tamadjert	148	25.36 N	7.20 E
Tamagawa, Nihon	94	37.12 N	140.24 E
Tamagawa, Nihon	96	34.01 N	132.56 E
Tamagawa •[8]	268	35.37 N	139.39 E
Tamagawa-josui ≃	268	35.42 N	139.35 E
Tamakautonga	174v	19.05 S	169.55 W
Tamaki	94	34.29 N	136.38 E
Tāmākośī ≃	124	27.22 N	85.59 E
Tama-kyūryō ⋏[2]	268	35.35 N	139.30 E
Tamala, Austl.	162	26.42 S	113.45 E
Tamala, Ross.	80	52.33 N	43.16 E
Tamalameque	246	8.52 N	73.49 W
Tamalave, Sierra ⋏	234	22.45 N	99.15 W
Ṭamalāy	142	30.30 N	30.51 E
Tamale	150	9.25 N	0.50 W
Tamalea	112	2.29 S	119.19 E
Tamalpais, Mount ∧	226	37.56 N	122.35 W
Tamalpais Valley	226	37.53 N	122.32 W
Tamamura	94	36.18 N	139.07 E
Taman, Indon.	115a	7.25 S	112.41 E
Taman', Ross.	78	45.13 N	36.43 E
Tamana	92	32.55 N	130.33 E
Tamana I	14	2.29 S	175.59 E
Tamaná, Cerro ∧	246	5.02 N	76.17 W
Tamana, Mount ∧[2]	241r	10.28 N	61.12 W
Tamanaco ≃	246	9.25 N	65.23 W
Tamanan	115a	8.01 S	113.49 E
Tamanar	148	31.00 N	9.35 W
Tamandourirt, Oued V	150	19.39 N	2.04 W
Tamanduateí ≃	287b	23.36 S	46.35 W
Tamanhint	146	27.13 N	14.36 E
Tamani	150	13.20 N	6.50 W
Tamaniquá	246	2.38 S	65.44 W
Taman Negara ♦	114	4.43 N	102.23 E
Tamano	96	34.30 N	133.56 E
Tamanquaré, Ilha I	246	0.28 S	64.55 W
Tamanskij zaliv c	78	45.18 N	36.45 E
Tamanthi	110	25.19 N	95.18 E
Tamanusi	112	1.48 S	121.18 E
Tamapatz	234	21.35 N	99.09 W
Tamaqua	208	40.47 N	75.58 W
Tamar ≃, Austl.	166	41.04 S	146.47 E
Tamar ≃, Nepāl	124	26.55 N	87.10 E
Tamar ≃, Eng., U.K.	42	50.22 N	4.10 W
Támara	246	5.50 N	72.10 W
Tamarac ≃	198	48.29 N	97.07 W
Tamarack Lake ⊜[1]	214	41.35 N	80.05 W
Tamarite de Litera	34	41.52 N	0.26 E
Tamaroa	194	38.08 N	89.14 W
Tamarome	164	2.54 S	133.38 E
Tamarugal, Pampa del ≚	248	21.00 S	69.25 W
Tamashima	96	34.32 N	133.40 E
Tamási	30	46.38 N	18.18 E
Tamaské	150	14.49 N	5.39 E
Tamatsukuri	94	36.06 N	140.25 E
Tamaulipas □[3]	232	24.00 N	98.45 W
Tamaya ≃	248	8.31 S	74.13 W
Tamayu	96	35.25 N	133.01 E
Tama Zoological Park ♦	268	35.39 N	139.24 E
Tamazula	232	24.57 N	106.57 W
Tamazula de Gordiano	234	19.38 N	103.15 W
Tamazulapan del Progreso	234	17.41 N	97.34 W
Tamazunchale	234	21.16 N	98.47 W
Tamba	96	35.09 N	135.25 E
Tambach-Dietharz	54	50.48 N	10.36 E
Tambacounda	150	13.47 N	13.40 W
Tambacounda □[4]	150	14.00 N	13.00 W
Tamba Dabatou	150	11.48 N	10.40 W
Tambak	115a	5.45 S	112.37 E
Tambakboyo	115a	6.48 S	111.50 E
Tamba-kōchi ⋏[1]	92	35.20 N	135.30 E
Tambakrejo	115a	7.16 S	111.36 E
Tambalan	112	3.08 N	115.34 E
Tambangsawah	112	3.02 S	102.11 E
Tambara, Moç.	154	16.45 S	34.15 E
Tambara, Nihon	96	33.54 N	133.04 E
Tāmbaram	122	12.55 N	80.07 E
Tambaú ≃	256	21.34 S	47.05 W
Tambault, Île à I	275a	45.20 N	73.51 W
Tambea	112	4.12 S	121.36 E
Tambej	74	71.30 N	71.50 E
Tambelan, Kepulauan II	112	1.00 N	107.30 E
Tambelan Besar, Pulau I	112	0.58 N	107.34 E
Tambellup	162	34.02 S	117.39 E
Tamberías	252	31.28 S	69.25 W
Tambisan, Pulau I	116	5.27 N	119.10 E
Tambler	116	6.03 N	125.09 E
Tambo, Austl.	166	24.53 S	146.15 E
Tambo, Perú	248	12.56 S	74.01 W
Tambo ≃, Austl.	166	37.51 S	147.48 E
Tambo ≃, Perú	248	17.10 S	71.51 W
Tambo ≃, Perú	248	10.43 S	73.45 W
Tamboara	255	23.09 S	52.33 W
Tambo Grande	248	4.56 S	80.21 W
Tambohorano	157b	17.30 S	43.58 E
Tamboli	112	3.57 S	121.20 E
Tambolongang, Pulau I	112	6.36 S	120.24 E
Tambopata ≃	248	12.36 S	69.11 W
Tambor	236	9.43 N	85.01 W
Tambora, Gunung ∧	115b	8.14 S	117.55 E
Tamboril	250	4.50 S	40.20 W
Tamborine	171a	27.53 S	153.08 E
Tamborine Mountain ∧[2]	171a	27.55 S	153.10 E
Tamboritha, Mount ∧	166	37.28 S	146.41 E
Tamboryacu ≃	246	2.31 S	73.40 W
Tambov	80	52.43 N	41.25 E
Tambovka, Ross.	80	47.18 N	47.23 E
Tambovka, Ross.	89	50.06 N	128.04 E
Tambov Oblast' □[4]	80	52.45 N	41.30 E
Tambre ≃	34	42.49 N	8.53 W
Tambu	112	0.02 S	119.52 E
Tambu, Teluk c	112	0.02 N	119.45 E
Tambulian Point ›	116	7.22 N	123.27 E
Tambunan	112	5.40 N	116.22 E
Tambura	140	5.36 N	27.28 E
Tamchaket	150	17.15 N	10.40 W
Tam Chuak, Laem ›	110	8.33 N	98.12 E
Tamdhas	124	28.04 N	83.14 E
Tame	246	6.28 N	71.44 W
Tame ≃	262	53.25 N	2.09 W
Tameapa	232	25.39 N	107.22 W
Tamedda, Djebel ∧	148	32.48 N	0.05 E
Tâmega ≃	34	41.05 N	8.21 W
Tameghza	148	34.23 N	7.57 E
Tamel Aike	254	48.19 S	70.58 W
Tamelelt	148	31.50 N	7.29 W
Tamenghest	148	22.56 N	5.30 E
Tamenghest □[5]	148	25.00 N	5.00 E
Tamenghest, Oued V	148	22.10 N	0.10 E
Tamenuen	164	6.27 S	139.48 E
Tamerton Foliot	42	50.26 N	4.08 W
Tamesí ≃	234	22.13 N	97.52 W
Tameside □[8]	262	53.29 N	2.03 W
Tamga, Kyrg.	85	42.09 N	77.32 E
Tamga, Ross.	89	45.34 N	133.36 E
Tamgak, Monts ⋏	150	19.11 N	8.42 E
Tamgué, Massif du ⋏	150	12.00 N	12.18 W
Tamiahua	234	21.16 N	97.27 W
Tamiahua, Laguna de c	234	21.35 N	97.35 W
Tamiami Canal ≡	220	25.47 N	80.15 W
Tamiang ≃	114	4.25 N	98.16 E
Tamica	24	64.10 N	38.05 E
Tamil Harbor c	174q	9.30 N	138.09 E
Tamil Nādu □[3]	122	11.00 N	78.15 E
Tamiment	210	41.09 N	75.02 W
Tamina	222	30.11 N	96.26 W
Tamir	88	50.24 N	107.25 E
Tamiryn ≃	88	47.48 N	102.36 E
Tamiš (Timiș) ≃	38	44.51 N	20.39 E
Tamitatoala ≃	255	11.56 S	53.36 W
Ṭamīyah	142	29.29 N	30.58 E
Tamkūhi	124	26.41 N	84.11 E
Tam Ky	110	15.34 N	108.29 E
Tamlūk	126	22.18 N	87.55 E
Tāmma	120	25.11 N	93.42 E
Tammaro ≃	68	41.09 N	14.50 E
Tammerfors → Tampere	26	61.30 N	23.45 E
Tammisaari → Ekenäs	26	59.58 N	23.26 E
Tamms	194	37.14 N	89.16 W
Ṭammūh	273c	29.56 N	31.16 E
Tāmna	126	23.15 N	86.21 E
Tämnarån ≃	40	60.31 N	17.39 E
Tämnaren ⊜	40	60.10 N	17.20 E
Tamnum	144	15.07 N	50.49 E
Tamon •[8]	270	34.39 N	135.04 E
Tampa, Ang.	152	15.30 S	13.27 E
Tampa, Fl., U.S.	220	27.56 N	82.27 W
Tampa Bay c	220	27.45 N	82.35 W
Tampa International Airport ⊠	220	27.59 N	82.32 W
Tampamachoco, Laguna c	234	21.00 N	97.21 W
Tampang	112	5.54 S	104.43 E
Tampaón ≃	234	21.59 N	98.36 W
Tamparan	116	8.27 N	117.13 E
Tampere	26	61.30 N	23.45 E
Tampico, Méx.	234	22.13 N	97.51 W
Tampico, Il., U.S.	190	41.37 N	89.47 W
Tampico, In., U.S.	218	38.48 N	85.58 W
Tampin	114	2.28 N	102.14 E
Tampiquito	234	23.52 N	98.14 W
Tampulonanjing, Gunung ∧	114	1.46 N	99.24 E
Tam Quan	110	14.35 N	109.03 E
Tamra	132	32.51 N	35.12 E
Tamrau, Pegunungan ⋏	164	0.30 S	132.27 E
Tamri	148	30.43 N	9.43 W
Tamsagbulag	88	47.14 N	117.21 E
Tamsalu	76	59.10 N	26.06 E
Tamshiyacu	246	4.05 S	72.58 W
Tamsweg	64	47.08 N	13.48 E
Tamu	110	24.13 N	94.18 E
Tamuín	234	21.59 N	98.45 W
Tamuk Island I	116	6.27 N	121.49 E
Tamuning	174p	13.29 N	144.46 E
Tamura	268	35.22 N	139.22 E
Tamusuke	85	38.03 N	76.53 E
Tamworth, Austl.	166	31.05 S	150.55 E
Tamworth, On., Can.	212	44.29 N	77.00 W
Tamworth, Eng., U.K.	42	52.39 N	1.40 W
Tamyang	98	35.21 N	126.58 E
Tan ≃	100	23.57 N	115.47 E
Tana, Chile	248	19.27 S	69.57 W
Tana, Nor.	24	70.28 N	28.18 E
Tana ≃, Cuba	240p	20.42 N	77.25 W
Tana ≃, Kenya	154	2.32 S	40.31 E
T'an'a ≃, Ross.	88	58.40 N	120.30 E
Tana, Lake ⊜	144	12.00 N	37.20 E
Tanabe, Nihon	96	34.49 N	135.46 E
Tanabe, Nihon	96	33.44 N	135.22 E
Tanabi	255	20.37 S	49.37 W
Tanacross	180	63.23 N	143.21 W
Tanafjorden c[2]	24	70.54 N	28.40 E
Tanaga Island I	180	51.50 N	178.00 W
Tanaga Volcano ∧[1]	180	51.53 N	178.09 W
Tanagro ≃	68	40.38 N	15.14 E
Tanaguarena	286c	10.37 N	66.49 W
Tanagura	94	37.02 N	140.23 E
Tanah, Tanjung ›	115a	6.29 S	108.32 E
Tanahbala, Pulau I	110	0.25 S	98.25 E
Tanahgrogot	112	1.55 S	116.12 E
Tanahjampea, Pulau I	112	7.05 S	120.42 E
Tanahmasa, Pulau I	110	0.12 S	98.27 E
Tanahmerah, Indon.	112	3.41 N	117.31 E
Tanahmerah, Indon.	164	6.05 S	140.17 E
Tanah Merah, Malay.	114	5.48 N	102.09 E
Tanah Merah, Malay.	114	2.36 N	101.48 E
Tanahputih	114	1.41 N	101.03 E
Tanaka •[8]	270	34.42 N	134.59 E
Tanakeke, Pulau I	112	5.30 S	119.16 E
Tanakpur	124	29.05 N	80.07 E
Tan'am	128	23.09 N	56.29 E
Tanami	162	19.59 S	129.43 E
Tanami Desert •[2]	162	20.00 S	129.30 E
Ṭanān, Miṣr	142	30.15 N	31.14 E
Tan An, Viet	110	8.46 N	105.11 E
Tan An, Viet	110	10.32 N	106.25 E
Tanana	180	65.10 N	152.05 W
Tanana ≃	180	65.09 N	151.55 W
Tananarive → Antananarivo	157b	18.55 S	47.31 E
Tanapag	174n	15.14 N	145.45 E
Tanapag, Lagunan c	174n	15.14 N	145.44 E
Tanaro ≃	62	45.01 N	8.47 E
Tanārūt, Wādī V	146	30.08 N	9.59 E
Tanashi	94	35.44 N	139.33 E
Tanat ≃	42	52.46 N	3.07 W
Tanauan	116	11.07 N	125.01 E
Tanbar	166	25.50 S	141.55 E
Ṭanbidī	142	28.38 N	30.47 E
Tan Binh	269c	10.48 N	106.40 E
Tanbu, Zhg.	98	35.51 N	118.17 E
Tanbu, Zhg.	100	28.08 N	114.12 E
Tancarville	50	49.29 N	0.28 E
Tancarville, Canal de ≡	50	49.28 N	0.28 E
Tancha	174m	26.28 N	127.50 E
Tan Chau	110	10.48 N	105.15 E
Tancheng	98	34.37 N	118.23 E
Tanchoj	88	51.33 N	105.07 E
Tanch'ŏn	98	40.27 N	128.54 E
Tancítaro	234	19.20 N	102.22 W
Tancítaro, Pico de ∧	234	19.23 N	102.13 W
Tancochapa ≃	234	17.59 N	94.04 W
Tanda, C. Iv.	150	7.48 N	3.10 W
Tānda, India	123	31.42 N	75.38 E
Tānda, India	124	28.59 N	78.56 E
Tānda, India	124	26.33 N	82.39 E
Tānda, Pāk.	123	32.42 N	74.22 E
Tandag	116	9.04 N	126.12 E
Tandah	142	27.41 N	30.46 E
Tandai	154	19.36 S	32.48 E
Tandaj	80	47.33 N	51.30 E
Tandala	154	9.23 S	34.14 E
Tandaltī	140	13.01 N	31.52 E
Ţăndărei	38	44.38 N	27.40 E
Tandaué	152	17.00 S	18.06 E
Tandian	98	40.39 N	124.46 E
Tandil	252	37.19 S	59.09 W
Tandjilé □[5]	146	9.45 N	16.30 E
Tandjilé ≃	146	9.45 N	15.50 E
Tāndliānwāla	123	31.02 N	73.08 E
Tando Ādam	120	25.46 N	68.40 E
Tando Allāhyār	120	25.28 N	68.43 E
Tando Bāgo	120	24.47 N	68.58 E
Tando Muhammad Khān	120	25.08 N	68.32 E
Tandou Bougou	152	3.32 S	10.53 E
Tandou Lake ⊜	166	32.38 S	142.05 E
Tandovo, ozero ⊜	86	55.07 N	78.02 E
Tando Zinze	152	5.22 S	12.26 E
Tandragee	48	54.20 N	6.25 W
Tandridge	260	51.14 N	0.02 W
Tandridge □[8]	260	51.17 N	0.05 W
Tandslet	41	54.55 N	9.59 E
Tandubas	116	5.10 N	120.20 E
Tandubatu Island I	116	5.13 N	120.17 E
Tandula Tank ⊜[1]	122	20.40 N	81.12 E
Tandun	112	0.36 N	100.38 E
Tāndūr	122	17.14 N	77.35 E
Tanduy ≃	115a	7.41 S	108.47 E
Taneatua	172	38.04 S	177.01 E
Tanega-shima I	93b	30.40 N	131.00 E
Taneichi	92	40.26 N	141.43 E
Tan Emellel	148	27.30 N	9.45 E
Tanete	112	4.32 S	119.36 E
Taneum Creek ≃	224	47.10 N	120.40 W
Tanew ≃	30	50.31 N	22.16 E
Taneytown	208	39.39 N	77.10 W
Tanezrouft •[2]	148	24.00 N	0.45 W
Tanezzuft, Wādī V	146	25.51 N	10.19 E
Tanforan Park •[9]	282	37.38 N	122.25 W
Tang ≃, Zhg.	98	38.45 N	115.35 E
Tang ≃, Zhg.	100	32.09 N	112.25 E
Tang ≃, Zhg.	100	33.18 N	117.46 E
Tang ≃, Zhg.	104	41.15 N	123.21 E
Tang ≃, Zhg.	105	40.43 N	116.38 E
Tanga, Ross.	88	51.02 N	111.33 E
Tånga, Sve.	41	56.12 N	12.46 E
Tanga, Tan.	154	5.04 S	39.06 E
Tanga □[4]	154	5.00 S	38.15 E
Tangail	124	24.15 N	89.55 E
Tangainony	157b	22.42 S	47.45 E
Tanga Islands II	14	3.30 S	153.15 E
Tanga Langua ›	241k	12.14 N	61.39 W
Tangalla	122	6.01 N	80.48 E
Tangamong Lake ⊜	212	44.43 N	77.51 W
Tangancícuaro [de Arista]	234	19.54 N	102.08 W
Tanganika, Lago → Tanganyika, Lake ⊜	154	6.00 S	29.30 E
Tanganjika-See → Tanganyika, Lake ⊜	154	6.00 S	29.30 E
Tanganyika, Lake ⊜	154	6.00 S	29.30 E
Tangarana ≃	246	3.02 S	75.08 W
Tangarare	175e	9.35 S	159.39 E
Tanga-shima I	96	34.40 N	134.35 E
Tangba	107	30.00 N	105.46 E
Tangchi	89	47.00 N	123.46 E
Tangchigou	104	41.04 N	124.11 E
Tangcun, Zhg.	100	29.50 N	118.54 E
Tangcun, Zhg.	100	25.26 N	113.10 E
Tangdaohe	98	40.38 N	118.58 E
Tanger (Tangier)	148	35.48 N	5.45 W
Tanger □[4]	148	35.35 N	5.50 W
Tanger ≃	54	52.33 N	11.59 E
Tangerang	115a	6.11 S	106.37 E
Tangerhütte	54	52.26 N	11.48 E
Tangerine	220	28.47 N	81.38 W
Tang'erli	105	39.09 N	116.43 E
Tangermünde	54	52.32 N	11.58 E
Tangfang, Zhg.	102	27.00 N	101.08 E
Tangfang, Zhg.	104	41.20 N	120.34 E
Tangfang, Zhg.	105	39.29 N	118.01 E
Tangfangqiao	106	31.45 N	120.50 E
Tangfeng	98	38.07 N	115.30 E
Tanggangzi	104	41.01 N	122.54 E
Tanggeasinua, Pegunungan ⋏	112	3.24 S	121.42 E
Tanggengtou	106	30.55 N	119.03 E
Tanggou	100	33.59 N	118.57 E
Tanggu	105	39.01 N	117.40 E
Tangguantun	98	38.43 N	116.55 E
Tanggul	115a	8.10 S	113.26 E
Tanggulashan (Tuotuoheyan)	120	34.05 N	92.45 E
Tanggula Shan ⋏	120	33.00 N	92.00 E
Tanggula Shankou)(	120	32.59 N	91.45 E
Tanggushiluke	120	38.45 N	80.55 E
Tanghe	100	32.43 N	112.48 E
Tanghekou	105	40.44 N	116.38 E
Tanghu	105	39.11 N	115.24 E
Tanghuang	106	31.41 N	119.25 E
Tangi	123	34.18 N	71.40 E
Tangier, N.S., Can.	186	44.48 N	62.42 W
Tangier → Tanger, Magreb	148	35.48 N	5.45 W
Tangier, Va., U.S.	208	37.49 N	75.59 W
Tangier Island I	208	37.50 N	76.00 W
Tangier Sound ⊔	208	38.02 N	75.58 W
Tangijatuo	107	29.36 N	106.39 E
Tangipahoa ≃	194	30.20 N	90.18 W
Tangjia	100	22.23 N	113.36 E
Tangjiagou	100	30.48 N	117.28 E
Tangjiang	100	25.51 N	114.44 E
Tangjiapao	104	41.59 N	122.14 E
Tangjiaqiao	106	31.24 N	119.12 E
Tangjin	98	36.54 N	126.37 E
Tangjiqiaozhen	106	31.13 N	121.31 E
Tangkahan	112	1.36 S	113.52 E
Tangkak	114	2.16 N	102.33 E
Tangkou	100	30.06 N	118.11 E
Tanglad	115b	8.47 S	115.35 E
Tanglewood, Fl., U.S.	220	26.37 N	81.53 W
Tanglewood, Tx., U.S.	222	30.30 N	96.59 W
Tanglewood ♦	207	42.21 N	73.20 W
Tangling	100	26.14 N	119.24 E
Tanglitun	104	41.45 N	123.57 E
Tangmai	102	30.08 N	95.08 E
Tangmarg	123	34.02 N	74.26 E
Tangmazhai	104	41.10 N	122.44 E
Tang Nhon Phu	269c	10.50 N	106.47 E
Tang-ni	98	34.12 N	126.52 E
Tango	96	35.44 N	135.06 E
Tango-hantō ›[1]	96	35.40 N	135.10 E
Tangowahine	172	35.52 S	173.56 E
Tangpu, Zhg.	100	29.51 N	120.47 E
Tangpu, Zhg.	100	28.28 N	114.58 E
Tangqi	106	30.29 N	120.11 E
Tangqiao	106	31.13 N	119.15 E
Tangra Yumco ⊜	120	31.00 N	86.20 E
Tangsanying	98	41.38 N	117.40 E
Tangschan → Tangshan	105	39.38 N	118.11 E
Tangse	114	5.01 N	95.55 E
Tangshan, Zhg.	105	40.10 N	116.22 E
Tangshan, Zhg.	105	39.38 N	118.11 E
Tangshan, Zhg.	106	32.05 N	119.03 E
Tang Shan ∧	106	32.03 N	119.02 E
Tangshi	106	31.33 N	120.51 E
Tangtou, Zhg.	98	35.16 N	118.35 E
Tangtou, Zhg.	102	27.42 N	108.17 E
Tangtou, Zhg.	106	31.38 N	120.19 E
Tangtouxia	100	22.50 N	114.06 E
Tangtse	120	34.02 N	78.11 E
Tanguá	256	22.44 S	42.43 W
Tangub	116	8.03 N	123.44 E
Tanguiéta	150	10.37 N	1.16 E
Tanguip Point ›	116	7.43 N	126.32 E
Tanguj	88	55.23 N	100.58 E
Tangulbei	154	0.48 N	36.17 E
Tangusu, Telukan c	116	5.27 N	119.03 E
Tangwang ≃	89	46.40 N	129.54 E
Tangxi	100	29.04 N	119.23 E
Tangxian	98	38.45 N	114.58 E
Tangxianzhen	100	31.59 N	113.07 E
Tangyan	110	22.29 N	98.24 E
Tangyi	98	36.32 N	115.47 E
Tangyin, Zhg.	98	35.55 N	114.21 E
Tangyin, Zhg.	100	27.32 N	116.16 E
Tangyuan	89	46.42 N	129.55 E
Tangzha	106	32.05 N	120.49 E
Tanhuato	234	20.17 N	102.20 W
Taniantaweng Shan ⋏	102	30.00 N	98.00 E
Tanigami •[8]	270	34.46 N	135.10 E
Tanigawa-dake ∧	94	36.50 N	138.56 E
Tanigumi	94	35.31 N	136.36 E
Tanimbar, Kepulauan II	164	7.30 S	131.30 E
Taninges	58	46.07 N	6.36 E
Tanintharyi □[8]	110	12.00 N	99.00 E
Tanır	130	38.26 N	36.55 E
Tanis (Zoan) ⊥	142	30.57 N	31.53 E
Tanishpa ∧	120	31.10 N	68.24 E
Tanjay	116	9.31 N	123.09 E
Tanjiafang	98	36.41 N	118.36 E
Tanjiahe	100	31.58 N	113.56 E
Tanjiang	100	24.07 N	116.32 E
Tanjiaqiao	100	30.11 N	118.15 E
Tanjil ≃	169	38.08 S	146.17 E
Tanjong Dawai	114	5.41 N	100.22 E
Tanjong Malim	114	3.41 N	101.31 E
Tanjore → Thanjāvūr	122	10.48 N	79.09 E
Tanjung, Indon.	112	2.11 S	115.23 E
Tanjung, Indon.	115a	6.52 S	108.52 E
Tanjung, Indon.	115b	8.21 S	116.09 E
Tanjungbalai	114	2.58 N	99.48 E
Tanjungbatu, Indon.	112	0.45 N	117.26 E
Tanjungbatu, Indon.	112	2.17 N	118.05 E
Tanjungbatu, Indon.	112	0.38 N	103.26 E
Tanjungenim	112	3.45 S	103.48 E
Tanjungkarang-Telukbetung	115a	5.27 S	105.16 E
Tanjunglabu	112	2.57 S	106.54 E
Tanjungmedan, Indon.	114	1.26 N	100.34 E
Tanjungmedan, Indon.	114	2.06 N	100.14 E
Tanjungmengedar	114	2.39 N	100.01 E
Tanjungpandan	112	2.45 S	107.39 E
Tanjungpinang	112	0.55 N	104.27 E
Tanjungpriok •[8]	269e	6.06 S	106.53 E
Tanjungpura	114	3.54 N	98.26 E
Tanjungpusu	112	0.01 S	113.30 E
Tanjungraja	112	3.21 S	104.40 E
Tanjungredep	112	2.09 N	117.29 E
Tanjungsamak	114	0.52 N	103.03 E
Tanjungselor	112	2.51 N	117.22 E
Tanjungslamat	114	3.49 N	98.20 E
Tanjunguban	112	1.03 N	104.14 E
Tānk	120	32.13 N	70.23 E
Tan Kena	148	26.33 N	9.35 E
Tan Kien	269c	10.42 N	106.35 E
Tankou	100	25.48 N	114.50 E
Tankwa ≃	158	32.20 S	19.33 E
Tanlay	50	47.50 N	4.05 E
Tann	56	50.38 N	10.01 E
Tanna	54	50.30 N	11.51 E
Tanna I	175f	19.30 S	169.20 E
Tannan	96	35.05 N	135.10 E
Tännäs	26	62.27 N	12.40 E
Tanna-tunnel •[5]	94	35.06 N	139.00 E
Tannay	50	47.21 N	3.36 E
Tanne	54	51.41 N	10.42 E
Tannenberg → Stębark	30	53.30 N	20.08 E
Tannenbergsthal	54	50.26 N	12.27 E
Tanner	194	34.43 N	86.58 W
Tanner, Mount ∧	182	49.40 N	118.34 W
Tannersville, N.Y., U.S.	210	42.12 N	74.08 W
Tannersville, Pa., U.S.	210	41.03 N	75.18 W
Tännesberg	60	49.32 N	12.20 E
Tännforsen ∟	26	63.27 N	12.44 E
Tannhausen	56	48.59 N	10.21 E
Tannheim	58	47.30 N	10.31 E
Tannila	26	65.29 N	25.59 E
Tannis Bugt c	26	57.40 N	10.15 E
Tannu-Ola, chrebet ⋏	74	51.00 N	94.00 E
Tannūrah, Ra's ›	128	26.40 N	50.30 E
Tano, Nihon	96	33.26 N	134.00 E
Tano, Nihon	270	34.57 N	135.36 E
Tano ≃	150	5.07 N	2.56 W
Tanon Strait ⊔	116	10.20 N	123.30 E
Tânout	150	14.58 N	8.53 E
Tanpok ≃	250	3.27 N	54.00 W
Tanque de Dolores	234	23.40 N	101.10 W
Tanque Grande, Ribeirão ≃	287b	23.25 S	46.28 W
Tan Qui Dong	269c	10.44 N	106.42 E
Tanquinho	255	11.58 S	39.06 W
T'an' Šan' → Tien Shan ⋏	90	42.00 N	80.00 E
Tansania → Tanzania □[1]	154	6.00 S	35.00 E
Tansboro	285	39.46 N	74.55 W
Tānsen	124	27.52 N	83.33 E
Tanshui	100	25.10 N	121.26 E
Tanshui ≃	100	25.11 N	121.25 E
Tansilla	150	12.26 N	4.23 W
Tánsin, Isla de I	236	15.17 N	83.54 W
Tánsin, Laguna de c	236	15.19 N	83.58 W
Tan Son Nhut Airport ⊠	269c	10.49 N	106.40 E
Tansyk	86	47.20 N	79.52 E
Ṭanṭā	142	30.47 N	31.00 E
Tantabogue Creek ≃	222	31.00 N	95.21 W
Tan-Tan	148	28.26 N	11.06 W
Tan-Tan □[4]	148	28.05 N	11.00 W
Tantangara Reservoir ⊜[1]	171b	35.45 S	148.39 E
Tan Thoi Nhut	269c	10.50 N	106.36 E
Tan Thuan Dong	269c	10.45 N	106.44 E
Tāntipāra	126	23.54 N	87.22 E
Tantō	96	35.29 N	135.00 E
Tantonville	58	48.28 N	6.08 E
Tantou, Zhg.	100	29.07 N	121.09 E
Tantou, Zhg.	100	26.03 N	119.35 E
Tantou, Zhg.	100	26.53 N	115.26 E
Tantou Shan I	100	29.11 N	122.01 E
Tantoyuca	234	21.21 N	98.14 W
Tanuku	122	16.45 N	81.42 E
Tanuma	94	36.22 N	139.35 E
Tanumshede	26	58.44 N	11.19 E
Tanunda	168b	34.32 S	138.57 E
Tan'urer ≃	180	64.44 N	174.15 E
Tanushimaru	96	33.21 N	130.41 E
Tanvald	30	50.45 N	15.19 E
Tanwax Creek ≃	224	46.52 N	122.27 W
Tanworth-in-Arden	42	52.20 N	1.50 W
Tanxi	100	28.58 N	115.38 E
Tanxia	100	23.58 N	115.34 E
Tanxu Shan I	106	30.37 N	121.37 E
Tanyang	98	36.57 N	128.21 E
Tanyeri	130	39.37 N	39.50 E
Tanyi	98	35.14 N	118.09 E
Tanymas ≃	85	38.25 N	72.39 E
Tanzania □[1], Afr.	138	6.00 S	35.00 E
Tanzania □[1], Afr.	154	6.00 S	35.00 E
Tanzanie → Tanzania □[1]	154	6.00 S	35.00 E
Tanzawa-Ōyama-kokutei-kōen ♦	94	35.30 N	139.10 E
Tanzawa-san ∧	94	35.28 N	139.10 E
Tao ≃, Zhg.	100	25.56 N	115.06 E
Tao ≃, Zhg.	102	35.52 N	103.16 E
Tao, Ko I	110	10.05 N	99.52 E
Tao'an	89	45.22 N	122.47 E
Taochong	100	31.04 N	118.06 E
Taochuan	102	25.07 N	111.06 E
Taocun	98	37.10 N	121.05 E
Taodigou	105	40.52 N	116.14 E
Tao'er ≃	89	45.42 N	124.05 E
Taoerdeng	98	40.44 N	119.02 E
Taohe	105	39.12 N	116.50 E
Taohua	106	31.23 N	120.04 E
Taohuachiyingzi	104	42.18 N	121.06 E
Taohua Dao I	100	29.48 N	122.17 E
Taohuanbuligai	104	42.13 N	122.14 E
Taohuatu	104	41.40 N	120.40 E
Taohuayuan	106	30.34 N	118.42 E
Taohuazhen	105	40.04 N	114.59 E
Taojiagou	107	29.48 N	104.48 E
Taojiahe	100	30.55 N	115.56 E
Taojialiang	104	42.36 N	121.25 E
Taolahusu	98	42.34 N	116.48 E
Taolaizhao	89	44.51 N	125.57 E
Taolakepa	120	32.05 N	85.22 E
Taole	102	38.46 N	106.40 E
Taolin	98	34.30 N	118.30 E
Taoling	100	30.21 N	118.16 E
Taoluo	98	35.17 N	119.24 E
T'aonan → Tao'an	89	45.22 N	122.47 E
Taongi I[1]	14	14.37 N	168.58 E
Taormina	70	37.51 N	15.17 E
Taos, Mo., U.S.	219	38.30 N	92.04 W
Taos, N.M., U.S.	200	36.24 N	105.34 W
Taos Pueblo	200	36.26 N	105.32 W
Taoudenni	148	22.40 N	4.00 W
Taougrite	34	36.15 N	0.55 E
Taounate	148	34.25 N	4.39 W
Taounate □[4]	148	34.30 N	4.40 W
Taoura	36	36.09 N	8.03 E
Taourirt	148	34.25 N	2.53 W
Taourirt ∧	148	24.03 N	5.02 E
Taoussa	150	16.55 N	0.35 W
Taowu	106	31.47 N	118.46 E
Taoxi, Zhg.	100	31.33 N	117.00 E
Taoxi, Zhg.	100	25.18 N	116.05 E
Taoxi, Zhg.	100	28.44 N	119.36 E
Taoxiantun	104	41.39 N	123.27 E
Taoyuan, Zhg.	100	25.48 N	117.32 E
Taoyuan, Zhg.	102	28.46 N	111.20 E
Taozhu	100	28.50 N	121.31 E
Taozhuang	106	30.58 N	120.48 E
Tapa, Eesti	76	59.16 N	25.58 E
Tapa, India	123	30.19 N	75.21 E
Tapaan Island I	116	5.28 N	120.44 E
Tapacari	248	17.31 S	66.36 W
Tapachula	232	14.54 N	92.17 W
Tapaga, Cape ›	175a	14.01 S	171.23 W
Tapah	114	4.11 N	101.16 E
Tapah Road	114	4.10 N	101.12 E
Tapaje ≃	246	2.44 N	78.07 W
Tapajós ≃	250	2.24 S	54.41 W
Tapaktuan	114	3.16 N	97.11 E
Tapalpa	234	19.57 N	103.46 W
Tapalqué	252	36.21 S	60.01 W
Tapan	112	2.10 S	101.04 E
Tapanahony ≃	250	4.22 N	54.27 W
Tapanui	172	45.57 S	169.16 E
Tapanuli, Teluk c	114	1.38 N	98.45 E
Tapasi	126	23.40 N	87.08 E
Tapauá	248	5.45 S	63.04 W
Tapauá ≃	248	5.40 S	64.21 W
Tapawera	172	41.24 S	172.49 E
Tapaz	116	11.16 N	122.32 E
Tapejara	252	28.04 S	52.00 W
Tapera	252	28.38 S	52.52 W
Taperas	248	17.54 S	60.23 W
Taperoá, Bra.	250	7.12 S	36.49 W
Taperoá, Bra.	255	13.31 S	39.06 W
Tapes	252	30.40 S	51.23 W
Tapeta	150	6.29 N	8.51 W
Taphan Hin	110	16.13 N	100.26 E
Taphoen ≃	110	14.07 N	99.25 E
Tāpi ≃, India	120	21.06 N	72.41 E
Ta Pi ≃, Thai	110	9.05 N	99.12 E
Tapiales	288	34.42 S	58.31 W
Tapiantana Channel ⊔	116	6.23 N	122.00 E
Tapiantana Group II	116	6.20 N	122.00 E
Tapiantana Island I	116	6.18 N	121.59 E
Tapiche ≃	248	4.59 S	73.51 W
Tapili	154	3.25 N	27.40 E
Tapilula	234	17.14 N	93.02 W
Taping (Daying) ≃	102	24.17 N	97.14 E
Tapini	164	8.20 S	147.00 E
Tapiraí	255	19.52 S	46.01 W
Tapirapé ≃	250	10.41 S	50.38 W
Tapiratiba	256	21.28 S	46.45 W
Tapis, Gunong ∧	114	4.03 N	102.54 E
Tapiutan Island I	116	11.12 N	119.16 E
Tapiwa	174d	0.52 S	169.35 E
Taplan National Park ♦	110	14.20 N	102.20 E
Tāplejungg	124	27.21 N	87.40 E
Tapoa ≃	150	12.36 N	2.29 E
Tapol	146	8.31 N	15.35 E
Tapolca	30	46.53 N	17.27 E
Tappahannock	208	37.55 N	76.51 W
Tappal	124	28.03 N	77.35 E
Tappan	210	41.01 N	73.56 W
Tappan, Lake ⊜[1]	276	41.01 N	73.59 W
Tappan Lake ⊜[1]	214	40.21 N	81.11 W
Tappan Zee c	276	41.06 N	73.53 W
Tappan Zee Bridge •[5]	276	41.04 N	73.54 W
Tappen	198	46.52 N	99.38 W
Tappernøje	41	55.10 N	11.59 E
Tappi-zaki ›	92	41.15 N	140.21 E
Tappo	150	10.12 N	2.38 W
Tapps, Lake ⊜	224	47.13 N	122.09 W
Tapsiā •[8]	272b	22.32 N	88.22 E
Tapuaenuku ∧	172	42.00 S	173.40 E
Tapuio ≃	250	3.41 S	44.16 W
Tapul Group II	116	5.30 N	121.00 E
Tapul Island I	116	5.43 N	120.55 E
Tapun	110	18.22 N	95.27 E
Tapurucuara	246	0.24 S	65.02 W
Taputapu, Cape ›	174u	14.19 S	170.50 W
Taqātu' Hayyā	140	18.20 N	36.22 E
Taqian	100	29.03 N	117.03 E
Taqiao, Zhg.	100	31.28 N	118.25 E
Taqiao, Zhg.	100	28.24 N	117.02 E
Ṭaqṭaq	128	35.53 N	44.35 E
Taquara	252	29.39 S	50.47 W
Taquara •[8]	287a	22.55 S	43.21 W
Taquara, Serra da ∧	256	22.12 S	43.53 W
Taquaras, Ponta das ›	252	27.01 S	48.34 W
Taquari, Bra.	252	29.48 S	51.51 W
Taquari, Bra.	255	17.50 S	53.17 W
Taquari ≃, Bra.	248	19.15 S	57.17 W
Taquari ≃, Bra.	252	29.56 S	51.44 W
Taquari, Pantanal do ≋	248	18.20 S	56.30 W
Taquaritinga	255	21.24 S	48.30 W
Taquaruçu ≃, Bra.	248	20.30 S	55.49 W
Taquaruçu ≃, Bra.	255	21.35 S	52.07 W
Tar ≃, Kyrg.	85	40.38 N	73.26 E
Tar ≃, N.C., U.S.	192	35.33 N	77.05 W
Tara, Austl.	166	27.17 S	150.28 E
Tara, On., Can.	212	44.28 N	81.09 W
Tara, Ross.	86	56.54 N	74.22 E
Tara, Zam.	154	16.56 S	26.47 E
Tara ⋏	38	43.55 N	19.25 E
Tara ≃, Europe	38	43.21 N	18.51 E
Tara ≃, Ross.	86	56.42 N	74.36 E
Taraba ≃	146	8.30 N	10.15 E
Tarabine, Oued ti-n- V	148	20.50 N	7.25 E
Tarabuco	248	19.10 S	64.57 W
Ṭarābulus (Tripoli), Lībiyā	146	32.54 N	13.11 E
Ṭarābulus (Tripoli), Lubnān	130	34.26 N	35.51 E
Ṭarābulus (Tripolitania) □[9]	146	31.00 N	15.00 E
Tarabusi Creek ≃	281	42.24 N	83.19 W
Tarabya •[8]	267b	41.08 N	29.03 E
Tarach ≃	154	4.09 N	34.56 E
Taraclia, Mol.	38	46.34 N	29.06 E
Taraclia, Mol.	38	45.54 N	28.38 E
Taradale	172	39.32 S	176.51 E
Taragaj ≃	85	41.35 N	77.42 E
Tarāghin	146	25.59 N	14.26 E
Tarago	170	35.04 S	149.39 E
Tara Hills	282	38.00 N	122.19 W
Tarai ≚	124	26.35 N	86.40 E
Taraia	124	26.05 N	84.53 E
Taraira (Traíra) ≃	246	1.04 S	69.26 W
Tara Island I	116	12.17 N	120.22 E
Taraju	115a	7.27 S	107.59 E
Tarakan	112	3.18 N	117.38 E
Tarakan, Pulau I	112	3.21 N	117.36 E
Tarakanovka	82	55.07 N	35.44 E
Tārakeshwar	126	22.54 N	88.02 E
Taraklı	130	40.24 N	30.29 E
Taralga	170	34.24 S	149.49 E
Tarama	175d	24.40 N	124.41 E
Taramakau ≃	172	42.34 S	171.08 E
Taramana	112	8.10 S	124.51 E
Tarama-shima I	175d	24.39 N	124.42 E
Tarana	170	33.32 S	149.54 E
Tārānagar	123	28.41 N	75.02 E
Taranaki, Mount ∧	172	39.18 S	174.04 E
Tarancón	34	40.01 N	3.00 W
Tarandacuao	234	19.59 N	100.32 W
Taranga Island I	172	35.58 S	174.43 E
Tarangire National Park ♦	154	4.00 S	36.00 E
Tarangnan	116	11.54 N	124.45 E
Tarango, Presa ⊜[1]	286a	19.22 N	99.13 W
Taranivka	78	49.37 N	36.08 E
Taransay I	46	57.54 N	7.01 W
Taranta Peligna	66	42.01 N	14.10 E
Tarantine, Murge •[1]	68	40.22 N	17.40 E
Taranto	68	40.28 N	17.15 E
Taranto □[4]	68	40.37 N	17.15 E
Taranto, Golfo di c	68	40.10 N	17.20 E
Tarapacá	246	2.52 S	69.44 W
Tarapoto	248	6.30 S	76.25 W
Ṭaraq al-Hbâri •[1]	130	34.17 N	39.16 E
Ṭaraq an-Na'jah •[1]	130	34.16 N	39.53 E
Ṭaraq Sidâoui •[1]	130	34.33 N	39.54 E
Taraquá	246	0.06 N	68.28 W
Tarare	58	45.54 N	4.26 E
Tarariras	258	34.17 S	57.37 W
Tararua Range ⋏	172	40.46 S	175.23 E
Tarāsa Dwīp I	110	8.15 N	93.10 E
Tarascon, Fr.	32	42.51 N	1.36 E
Tarascon, Fr.	62	43.48 N	4.40 E
Tarashcha	78	49.34 N	30.29 E
Tarasht •[8]	267d	35.42 N	51.21 E
Tarasivka	83	49.40 N	38.23 E
Tarasovka, Ross.	83	49.28 N	40.05 E
Tarasovka, Ross.	265b	55.58 N	37.50 E
Tarasovo, Ross.	24	66.13 N	46.39 E
Tarasovo, Ross.	24	62.49 N	41.10 E
Tarasovo, Ross.	80	58.18 N	48.45 E
Tarasovo, Ross.	88	55.52 N	107.48 E
Tarasovskij	78	48.43 N	40.22 E
Tarasp	58	46.38 N	10.25 E
Tarat	148	26.13 N	9.18 E
Tarat, Oued V	148	26.09 N	9.20 E
Tarata, Bol.	248	17.37 S	66.01 W
Tarata, Perú	248	17.28 S	70.02 W
Taratai	174t	1.32 N	173.00 E
Taratakbuluh	112	0.23 N	101.27 E
Tāratanr	126	23.58 N	86.29 E
Tarauacá	248	8.10 S	70.46 W
Tarauacá ≃	248	7.19 S	70.15 W
Taravao, Baie de c	174s	17.43 S	149.17 W
Taravao, Isthme de ⊥[3]	174s	17.43 S	149.19 W
Taravo ≃	36	41.42 N	8.49 E
Tarawa I[1]	174t	1.25 N	173.00 E
Tarawera	172	39.02 S	176.35 E
Tarawera, Lake ⊜	172	38.12 S	176.27 E
Tarawera, Mount ∧[1]	172	38.14 S	176.30 E
Tarazona	34	41.54 N	1.44 W
Tarazona de la Mancha	34	39.15 N	1.55 W
Tarba	144	0.48 N	42.39 E
Tårbæk	41	55.47 N	12.36 E
Tarbagataj, Ross.	88	51.30 N	107.22 E
Tarbagataj, Ross.	88	52.07 N	109.12 E
Tarbagataj, Ross.	88	51.12 N	109.05 E
Tarbagataj, chrebet ⋏	86	47.12 N	83.00 E
Tarbat Ness ›	46	57.51 N	3.47 W
Tarbela	123	34.08 N	72.49 E
Tarbela Reservoir ⊜[1]	123	34.10 N	72.50 E
Tarbert, Ire.	48	52.32 N	9.23 W
Tarbert, Scot., U.K.	46	55.52 N	5.26 W
Tarbert, Scot., U.K.	46	57.54 N	6.49 W
Tarbert, East Loch c	46	57.52 N	6.45 W
Tarbert, Loch c	46	55.57 N	6.00 W
Tarbert, West Loch c, Scot., U.K.	46	55.48 N	5.32 W
Tarbert, West Loch c, Scot., U.K.	46	57.55 N	6.54 W
Tarbes	32	43.14 N	0.05 E
Tarbet	46	56.12 N	4.43 W
Tarbock Green	262	53.23 N	2.49 W
Tarbolton	46	55.31 N	4.29 W
Tarboro	192	35.53 N	77.32 W
Tarbū	146	26.02 N	15.10 E
Tarcăului, Munții ⋏	38	46.45 N	26.20 E
Tarcento	64	46.13 N	13.13 E
Tarchov Cholm, gora ∧[2]	76	57.11 N	38.25 E
Tarchovka	265a	60.04 N	29.58 E
Tarcoola	162	30.41 S	134.33 E
Tarcoon	166	30.16 S	146.43 E
Tarcutta	171b	35.17 S	147.44 E
Tarcutta Creek ≃	171b	35.08 S	147.36 E
Tārdah	272b	22.27 N	88.31 E
Tardajos	34	42.21 N	3.49 W
Tardoki-Jani, gora ∧	89	48.55 N	138.04 E
Tardun	162	28.48 S	115.45 E
Taredo •[8]	272c	19.58 N	72.49 E
Taree	166	31.54 S	152.28 E
Tareja	74	73.20 N	90.37 E
Taremert-n-Akli, Oued V	148	25.49 N	5.17 E
Tärendö	24	67.10 N	22.38 E
Tarent, Golf von → Taranto, Golfo di c	68	40.10 N	17.20 E
Tarentaise V	62	45.30 N	6.30 E
Tarento, Golfo de → Taranto, Golfo di c	68	40.10 N	17.20 E
Tarentum	214	40.36 N	79.45 W
Tarf, Garaet et ⊜	148	35.40 N	7.10 E
Ṭarfā', Baṭn aṭ- ≋	128	23.50 N	51.27 E
Ṭarfā', Ra's aṭ- ›	144	17.05 N	42.24 E
Ṭarfā', Wādī aṭ- V	142	28.25 N	30.50 E
Ṭarfāwī, Bi'r ⊤[4], Miṣr	140	22.55 N	28.53 E
Tarfawi, Bi'r ⊤[4], Sūd.	140	21.04 N	34.08 E
Tarfaya	148	27.58 N	12.55 W
Tarfside	46	56.54 N	2.50 W
Tarf Water ≃	44	54.55 N	4.35 W
Targa	124	22.27 N	84.40 E
Targan ≃	85	43.38 N	75.58 E
Target Rock National Wildlife Refuge •[4]	276	40.56 N	73.26 W
Targhee Pass)(	202	44.41 N	111.17 W
Targon	32	44.44 N	0.16 W
Tărgovište, Blg.	38	43.15 N	26.34 E
Târgoviște, Rom.	38	44.56 N	25.27 E
Târgu Bujor	38	45.52 N	27.54 E
Târgu Cărbunești	38	44.58 N	23.31 E
Târgu Frumos	38	47.13 N	27.00 E
Targuist	148	34.57 N	4.18 W
Târgu Jiu	38	45.02 N	23.17 E
Târgu Lăpuș	38	47.27 N	23.52 E
Târgu Mureș	38	46.33 N	24.33 E
Târgu-Neamț	38	47.12 N	26.22 E
Târgu Ocna	38	46.15 N	26.37 E
Târgu Secuiesc	38	46.00 N	26.08 E
Târgușor	38	44.28 N	28.25 E
Tarhjijt	148	29.05 N	9.24 W
Tarhu	102	41.09 N	107.58 E
Tarhūnah	146	32.26 N	13.38 E
Tari	164	5.50 S	143.00 E
Tarialan	86	49.47 N	91.55 E
Tariat	88	48.06 N	99.32 E
Táriba	246	7.49 N	72.13 W
Tarifa	34	36.01 N	5.36 W
Tarifa, Punta de ›	34	36.00 N	5.37 W
Tariffville	207	41.54 N	72.45 W
Tarija	248	21.31 S	64.45 W
Tarija □[5]	248	21.30 S	64.00 W
Tarikere	122	13.43 N	75.49 E
Tariki	172	39.14 S	174.15 E
Tariku ≃	164	3.04 S	138.09 E
Tarīm	144	16.03 N	48.59 E

Symbols in the index entries represent the broad categories identified in the key at the right. Symbols with superior numbers (⋏[1]) identify subcategories (see complete key on page *I · 1*).

Symbole im Register stellen die rechts im Schlüssel erklärten Kategorien dar. Symbole mit hochgestellten Ziffern (⋏[1]) bezeichnen Unterabteilungen einer Kategorie (vgl. vollständiger Schlüssel auf Seite *I · 1*).

Los símbolos incluídos en el texto del índice representan las grandes categorías identificadas con la clave a la derecha. Los símbolos con numeros en su parte superior (⋏[1]) identifican las subcategorías (véase la clave completa en la página *I · 1*).

Les symboles de l'index représentent les catégories indiquées dans la légende à droite. Les symboles suivis d'un indice (⋏[1]) représentent des sous-catégories (voir légende complète à la page *I · 1*).

Os símbolos incluídos no texto do índice representam as grandes categorias identificadas com a chave à direita. Os símbolos com números em sua parte superior (⋏[1]) identificam as subcategorias (veja-se a chave completa à página *I · 1*).

	English	Deutsch	Español	Français	Português
∧	Mountain	Berg	Montaña	Montagne	Montanha
⋏	Mountains	Gebirge	Montañas	Montagnes	Montanhas
)(	Pass	Paß	Paso	Col	Passo
V	Valley, Canyon	Tal, Cañon	Valle, Cañón	Vallée, Canyon	Vale, Canhão
≚	Plain	Ebene	Llano	Plaine	Planície
›	Cape	Kap	Cabo	Cap	Cabo
I	Island	Insel	Isla	Île	Ilha
II	Islands	Inseln	Islas	Îles	Ilhas
⊥	Other Topographic Features	Andere Topographische Objekte	Otros Elementos Topográficos	Autres données topographiques	Outros acidentes topográficos

ESPAÑOL · FRANÇAIS · PORTUGUÊS

Nombre / Nom / Nome	Página / Page	Lat.°′	Long.°′ W = Oeste / Ouest
Tarim ≃	90	41.05 N	86.40 E
Tarimoro	234	20.17 N	100.45 W
Tarim Pendi ≍ [1]	90	39.00 N	83.00 E
Taring	114	3.50 N	97.33 E
Tarīn Kowt	120	32.52 N	65.38 E
Taritatu ≃	164	2.54 S	138.27 E
Tarituba	256	23.02 S	44.36 W
Tarjannevesi ⊜	26	62.07 N	24.03 E
Tarka	150	14.37 N	7.55 E
Tarka ≃	158	32.18 S	25.44 E
Tarka, Vallée de V	150	14.00 N	6.00 E
Tarkastad	158	32.00 S	26.16 E
Tarkazy	80	53.52 N	53.39 E
Tarkhankut, mys ≻	78	45.21 N	32.30 E
Tarkhūrān	128	34.41 N	50.00 E
Tarki	84	42.56 N	47.30 E
Tarkiln	207	41.57 N	71.36 W
Tarkington Bayou ≃	222	30.10 N	94.59 W
Tarkio	194	40.26 N	95.22 W
Tarkio ≃	198	40.10 N	95.26 W
Tarko-Sale	74	64.55 N	77.49 E
Tarkwa	150	5.19 N	1.59 W
Tarlac	116	15.29 N	120.35 E
Tarlac □ [4]	116	15.30 N	120.25 E
Tarlac ≃	116	15.45 N	120.27 E
Tarland	46	57.08 N	2.52 W
Tarlee	168b	34.16 S	138.46 E
Tarleton	44	53.41 N	2.50 W
T'arlevo	265a	59.42 N	30.27 E
Tarlo ≃	170	34.28 S	150.04 E
Tarlo River National Park ♠	170	34.31 S	149.55 E
Tarlscough	262	53.37 N	2.52 W
Tarm	26	55.55 N	8.32 E
Tarma	248	11.25 S	75.42 W
Tarmstedt	52	53.13 N	9.04 E
Tarn □ [5]	32	43.50 N	2.00 E
Tarn ≃	32	44.05 N	1.06 E
Tarna ≃	30	47.31 N	19.59 E
Tärnaby	24	65.43 N	15.16 E
Tarnak ≃	120	31.26 N	65.31 E
Țarna Mare	38	48.04 N	23.12 E
Târnava Mare ≃	38	46.09 N	23.42 E
Târnava Mică ≃	38	46.11 N	23.55 E
Târnăveni	38	46.20 N	24.17 E
Tårnby	41	55.38 N	12.36 E
Tarneit	274b	37.52 S	144.41 E
Tarn-et-Garonne □ [5]	32	44.05 N	1.20 E
Tarnewitz	54	53.58 N	11.14 E
Tarnobrzeg	30	50.35 N	21.41 E
Tarnobrzeg □ [4]	30	50.45 N	21.50 E
Tarnogród	30	50.23 N	22.45 E
Tarnogskij Gorodok	24	60.29 N	43.33 E
Tarnopol → Ternopil'	78	49.34 N	25.36 E
Târnova	38	48.10 N	27.40 E
Tarnów, Pol.	30	50.01 N	21.00 E
Tarnów, Pol.	54	52.47 N	14.58 E
Tarnów □ [4]	30	50.00 N	21.00 E
Tarnowskie Góry	30	50.27 N	18.52 E
Tärnsjö	40	60.09 N	16.56 E
Tarn Tāran	123	31.27 N	74.55 E
Taro ≃	36	45.00 N	10.15 E
Taron	164	4.25 S	153.05 E
Tarong	166	26.46 S	151.51 E
Taronga Zoo ♠	274a	33.51 S	151.15 E
Taroom	166	25.39 S	149.49 E
Tarouca	34	41.00 N	7.40 W
Taroudant	148	30.31 N	8.55 W
Ta Roun, Co ∧	110	17.17 N	106.18 E
Tarp	41	54.40 N	9.23 E
Tarpey	226	36.47 N	119.41 W
Tarpon, Lake ⊜	220	28.07 N	82.44 W
Tarpon Springs	220	28.08 N	82.45 W
Tarporley	44	53.09 N	2.40 W
Tarqui	246	1.35 S	75.15 W
Tarquinia	66	42.15 N	11.45 E
Tarqūmiyah	132	31.35 N	35.01 E
Tarra ≃	246	9.05 N	72.30 W
Tarrabool Lake ⊜	162	18.15 S	135.04 E
Tarrafal, C.V.	150a	16.58 N	25.19 W
Tarrafal, C.V.	150a	15.17 N	23.46 W
Tarragona	34	41.07 N	1.15 E
Tarragona □ [4]	34	41.00 N	0.45 E
Tarraleah	166	42.18 S	146.27 E
Tarrant □ [6]	222	32.47 N	97.18 W
Tarrant City	194	33.34 N	86.46 W
Tarrant Hinton	42	50.53 N	2.05 W
Tarrara Creek ≃	208	36.33 N	77.10 W
Tarras	172	44.50 S	169.25 E
Tàrrega	34	41.39 N	1.09 E
Tarri	144	0.42 N	41.38 E
Tarrs	214	40.10 N	79.35 W
Tarrtown	214	40.51 N	79.31 W
Tarryall Creek ≃	200	39.05 N	105.19 W
Tarrytown	210	41.04 N	73.51 W
Tarrytown Reservoir ⊜ [1]	276	41.05 N	73.51 W
Tarsus	130	36.55 N	34.53 E
Tarta	128	40.02 N	52.46 E
Tartagal, Arg.	252	22.32 S	63.49 W
Tartagal, Arg.	252	28.40 S	59.52 W
Tärtär	84	40.20 N	46.55 E
Tärtär ≃	84	40.35 N	47.22 E
Tartaro ≃	64	45.02 N	11.30 E
Tartas ≃	86	55.37 N	76.44 E
Tartu	76	58.23 N	26.43 E
Țarțūs	130	34.53 N	35.53 E
Țarțūs □ [8]	130	35.00 N	36.00 E
Taruaçu	256	21.37 S	42.56 W
Tarui	94	35.22 N	136.32 E
Tarum ≃	115a	5.59 S	107.03 E
Tarumi ⬥ [8]	270	34.38 N	135.03 E
Tarumirim	255	19.16 S	41.59 W
Tarumizu	92	31.29 N	130.42 E
Tarumovka	84	44.03 N	46.33 E
Tarusa	82	54.43 N	37.11 E
Tarusa ≃	82	54.44 N	37.11 E
Țārūț	142	30.32 N	31.28 E
Tarutao, Ko I	114	6.35 N	99.40 E
Tarutino	82	55.07 N	36.56 E
Tarutung	114	2.01 N	98.58 E
Tarutyne	78	46.12 N	29.09 E
Tarvagatajn nuruu ⋏	88	48.20 N	99.00 E
Tarves	46	57.22 N	2.13 W
Tarvisio	64	46.30 N	13.35 E
Tarvo ≃	248	14.47 S	61.03 W
Tarwin ≃	169	38.42 S	145.50 E
Tarwin, East Branch ≃	169	38.34 S	146.00 E
Tarwin, West Branch ≃	169	38.34 S	146.00 E
Tarza	24	62.30 N	40.25 E
Tarzan	196	32.18 N	101.58 W
Tarzana ⬥ [8]	280	34.10 N	118.32 W
Tarzo	64	45.58 N	12.14 E
Tas	80	48.27 N	51.02 E
Tas ≃	42	52.36 N	1.18 E
Taşağıl	130	36.55 N	31.14 E
Tašanta	86	49.43 N	89.11 E
Tasaral	86	46.20 N	73.58 E
Tašauz	72	41.50 N	59.58 E
Tašauz □ [8]	128	40.15 N	59.00 E
Tasāwah	146	25.58 N	13.30 E
Tasbuget	86	44.48 N	65.33 E
Taschkent → Taškent	85	41.20 N	69.18 E
Taşçı	130	38.13 N	35.48 E
Taşdelen	130	38.51 N	38.31 E
Tasejeva ≃	86	58.06 N	94.01 E
Tasejevo	86	57.12 N	94.54 E
Taseko ≃	182	52.00 N	123.40 W
Taseko Lakes ⊜	182	51.15 N	123.35 W
Taseko Mountain ∧	182	51.14 N	123.28 W
Tašelan	88	51.45 N	108.55 E
Tasendjanet, Oued V	148	24.36 N	1.07 E
Tāsgaon	122	17.02 N	74.36 E
Tashan, Zhg.	104	40.48 N	122.39 E
Tashan, Zhg.	104	40.51 N	120.56 E
Tashi Gang Dzong	120	27.19 N	91.34 E
Tashimalike	85	39.06 N	75.41 E
Tashiyi	100	29.43 N	112.48 E
Țashk, Daryācheh-ye ⊜	128	29.45 N	53.30 E
Tashkent → Taškent	85	41.20 N	69.18 E
Tāshkurghān → Kholm	120	36.42 N	67.41 E
Tashuik'u	269d	25.13 N	121.30 E
Tasikmalaya	115a	7.20 S	108.12 E
Tasīl	132	32.50 N	35.58 E
Tåsinge I	41	55.00 N	10.36 E
Tašir	84	41.07 N	44.17 E
Taširovo	82	55.25 N	36.39 E
Tasitan	85	39.17 N	76.07 E
Tåsjö	26	64.13 N	15.54 E
Tåsjön ⊜	26	64.15 N	15.47 E
Taskajevo	86	55.06 N	78.36 E
Taşkent, Tür.	130	36.55 N	32.31 E
Taškent (Tashkent), Uzb.	85	41.20 N	69.18 E
Taškent □ [4]	85	41.00 N	69.30 E
Taškepri	128	36.18 N	62.38 E
Taşkesen	130	39.43 N	41.29 E
Taskesken	86	47.15 N	80.44 E
Taşköprü	130	41.30 N	34.14 E
Taskul	164	2.35 S	150.25 E
Taš-Kumyr	85	41.21 N	72.14 E
Taškyja	85	40.16 N	74.19 E
Tašla	80	51.47 N	52.46 E
Taşlı ≃	267b	41.03 N	28.56 E
Tasman, Mount ∧	172	43.34 S	170.09 E
Tasman Basin ✣ [1]	6	43.00 S	158.00 E
Tasman Bay ⊂	172	41.00 S	173.20 E
Tasmania □ [3]	166	43.00 S	147.00 E
Tasmania I	166	42.00 S	147.00 E
Tasmanien → Tasmania I	166	42.00 S	147.00 E
Tasman Mountains ⋏	172	41.07 S	172.33 E
Tasman Peninsula ≻ [1]	166	43.05 S	147.50 E
Tasman Sea ⊤ [2]	14	40.00 S	163.00 E
Tășnad	38	47.29 N	22.35 E
Tasoba	80	49.47 N	49.52 E
Taşova	130	40.46 N	36.20 E
Tasrār Sharīf	123	33.52 N	74.46 E
Taşrumi	84	38.48 N	44.04 E
Tassajara Creek ≃	282	37.41 N	121.53 W
Tassara	150	16.48 N	5.39 E
Tassdorf	264a	52.30 N	13.47 E
Tassialouc, Lac ⊜	176	59.03 N	74.00 W
Tassin-la-Demi-Lune	62	45.46 N	4.47 E
Tasso Lake ⊜	212	45.27 N	78.56 W
Tassu, Serra di lu ∧	71	41.01 N	9.08 E
Taštagol	86	52.47 N	87.53 E
Tastiota	232	28.22 N	111.23 W
Tåstrup	41	55.39 N	12.19 E
Taštyp	86	52.48 N	89.54 E
Taşucu	130	36.19 N	33.53 E
Tasutkol'skoje vodochranilišče ⊜ [1]	85	43.22 N	74.00 E
Tata, Magreb	148	29.44 N	7.56 W
Tata, Magy.	30	47.39 N	18.18 E
Tata □ [4]	148	29.40 N	7.45 W
T'at'a, vulkan ∧ [1]	92a	44.21 N	146.15 E
Tataa, Pointe ≻	174s	17.34 S	149.37 W
Tatabánya	30	47.34 N	18.26 E
Tatahuicapan	234	18.14 N	94.45 W
Tatal	80	47.17 N	46.16 E
Tatalin ≃	102	37.30 N	95.28 E
Tata Mailau ∧	112	8.55 S	125.30 E
Tatamy	208	40.44 N	75.15 W
Tataouine	148	32.56 N	10.27 E
Tata Raphael, Camp ■	273b	4.18 S	15.17 E
Tatarbunary	78	45.49 N	29.36 E
Tatarija □ [3]	80	55.00 N	51.00 E
Tatarinka	76	55.58 N	33.54 E
Tatarino	78	50.36 N	39.07 E
Tatarinovo, Ross.	82	55.13 N	37.56 E
Tatarinovo, Ross.	82	56.34 N	38.25 E
Tatarischer Sund → Tatarskij proliv ʊ	89	50.00 N	141.15 E
Tatarka, Bela.	76	53.16 N	28.48 E
Tatarka, Ross.	86	53.58 N	75.05 E
Tatarlar	130	41.46 N	26.55 E
Tatarovo ⬥ [8]	265b	55.46 N	37.26 E
Tātārpur ⬥ [8]	272a	28.39 N	77.07 E
Tatarsk	86	55.13 N	75.58 E
Tatarskij Kandyz	80	54.07 N	53.07 E
Tatarskij proliv (Tatar Strait) ʊ	89	50.00 N	141.15 E
Tatarskij Sajman	80	53.18 N	47.07 E
Tatarskoje-Maklakovo	80	55.48 N	45.34 E
Tatarstan → Tatarija □ [3]	80	55.00 N	51.00 E
Tatar Strait → Tatarskij proliv ʊ	89	50.00 N	141.15 E
Tatau ≃	112	3.07 N	112.49 E
Tatau Island I	164	2.50 S	152.00 E
Tataurovo, Ross.	76	58.44 N	43.20 E
Tataurovo, Ross.	80	57.48 N	49.34 E
Tataurovo, Ross.	88	51.37 N	112.56 E
Tate	192	34.25 N	84.22 W
Tate ≃	166	17.22 S	143.44 E
Tatebayashi	94	36.15 N	139.32 E
Tate Gallery ⱴ	260	51.29 N	0.08 W
Tateishi-misaki ≻	94	35.46 N	136.01 E
Tateiwa	94	37.05 N	139.32 E
Tateiwa-chosuichi ⊜ [1]	96	34.33 N	132.10 E
Tateshina	94	36.16 N	138.19 E
Tateyama, Nihon	94	34.59 N	139.52 E
Tateyama, Nihon	94	36.40 N	137.19 E
Tate-yama ∧	94	36.35 N	137.37 E
Tathlina Lake ⊜	176	60.32 N	117.32 W
Tathlīth, Wādī V	144	20.44 N	44.17 E
Tathong Point ≻	271d	22.14 N	114.17 E
Tathra	166	36.44 S	149.59 E
Tatikawa → Tachikawa	94	35.42 N	139.25 E
Tatiščevo, Ross.	80	51.40 N	45.35 E
Tatiščevo, Ross.	82	56.24 N	37.31 E
Tatitlek	180	60.52 N	146.41 W
Tatla Lake	182	51.55 N	124.36 W
Tatla Lake ⊜	182	52.00 N	124.25 W
Tatlayoko Lake	182	51.39 N	124.24 W
Tatlayoko Lake ⊜	182	51.30 N	124.25 W
Tatlow, Mount ∧	182	51.23 N	123.52 W
Tatnam, Cape ≻	176	57.16 N	91.00 W
Tatomi	94	35.36 N	138.31 E
Tatoosh Island I	224	48.24 N	124.44 W
Tatrang	120	38.28 N	85.35 E
Tatranský národní park ♠	30	49.10 N	20.05 E
Tatrzański Park Narodowy ♠	30	49.15 N	20.00 E
Tatsfield	260	51.18 N	0.02 E
Tatsuno, Nihon	94	35.59 N	137.59 E
Tatsuno, Nihon	96	34.52 N	134.33 E
Tatsunokuchi	94	36.27 N	136.35 E
Tatsuruhama	94	37.04 N	136.53 E
Tatsuyama	94	34.58 N	137.49 E
Tatta	120	24.45 N	67.55 E
Tattenhall	44	53.06 N	2.46 W
Tatton Hall ⊥	262	53.20 N	2.23 W
Tatton Mere ⊜	262	53.19 N	2.22 W
Tatton Park ♠	262	53.20 N	2.22 W
Tatty	85	43.12 N	73.19 E
Tatu ≃	100	24.12 N	120.29 E
Tatuapé ⬥ [8]	287b	23.32 S	46.34 W
Tatuk Lake ⊜	182	53.32 N	124.15 W
Tatum, N.M., U.S.	196	33.15 N	103.19 W
Tatum, Tx., U.S.	222	32.19 N	94.31 W
Tat'ung → Datong	102	40.05 N	113.18 E
Tat'un Shan ∧	269d	25.11 N	121.31 E
Tatvan	130	38.30 N	42.16 E
Tatzuli ≃	100	24.08 N	121.39 E
Tau, Am. Sam.	174y	14.14 S	169.32 W
Tau, Kaz.	80	49.40 N	47.17 E
Tau, Nor.	26	59.04 N	5.54 E
Tau I	174y	14.15 S	169.30 W
Tauá	250	6.01 S	40.26 W
Taualap Pass ʊ	175c	7.28 N	151.36 E
Taubaté	256	23.02 S	45.33 W
Tauber ≃	56	49.46 N	9.31 E
Tauberbischofsheim	56	49.37 N	9.40 E
Taucha	54	51.23 N	12.30 E
Taučik	72	44.21 N	51.19 E
Tauern-Tunnel ⬥ [5]	64	47.05 N	13.05 E
Täuffelen	58	47.04 N	7.12 E
Taufkirchen	60	48.21 N	12.08 E
Taufstein ∧	56	50.31 N	9.14 E
Taughannock Creek ≃	210	42.33 N	76.36 W
Taughannock Falls State Park ♠	210	42.32 N	76.35 W
Tauini ≃	246	0.30 N	58.22 W
Taujskaja guba ⊂	74	59.20 N	150.20 E
Taukum ⬥ [2]	86	44.50 N	75.30 E
Taulabé	236	14.38 N	87.59 W
Taulihawā	124	27.32 N	83.03 E
Taulov	41	55.33 N	9.37 E
Taumarunui	172	38.52 S	175.17 E
Taum Sauk Mountain ∧	194	37.34 N	90.44 W
Taunay	248	20.18 S	56.05 W
Taunay, Cascatinha ∟	287a	22.57 S	43.17 W
Taung	158	27.33 S	24.47 E
Taungbon	110	15.25 N	97.50 E
Taungdwingyi	110	20.01 N	95.33 E
Taunggon	110	23.38 N	96.32 E
Taunggyi	110	20.47 N	97.02 E
Taungnyo Range ⋏	110	15.38 N	97.56 E
Taungup	110	18.51 N	94.14 E
Taungup Pass)(	110	18.40 N	94.45 E
Taunsa	123	30.42 N	70.39 E
Taunsa Barrage ⬥ [6]	123	30.31 N	70.51 E
Taunton, Eng., U.K.	42	51.01 N	3.06 W
Taunton, Ma., U.S.	207	41.54 N	71.05 W
Taunton, N.Y., U.S.	210	43.01 N	76.13 W
Taunton ≃	207	41.42 N	71.10 W
Taunton, Vale of V	42	51.02 N	3.08 W
Taunton Lake ⊜	285	39.51 N	74.51 W
Taunton Lakes	285	39.51 N	74.51 W
Taunus ⋏	56	50.10 N	8.15 E
Taunusstein	56	50.08 N	8.08 E
Taupiri	172	37.37 S	175.11 E
Tauplitz	61	47.33 N	14.00 E
Taupo	172	38.41 S	176.05 E
Taupo, Lake ⊜	172	38.49 S	175.55 E
Tauragė	76	55.15 N	22.17 E
Taurak	86	51.35 N	85.01 E
Tauranga	172	37.42 S	176.10 E
Taurasi	68	41.00 N	14.57 E
Taureau, Réservoir ⊜ [1]	206	46.46 N	73.50 W
Tauri ≃	164	8.08 S	146.06 E
Taurianova	68	38.21 N	16.01 E
Tauripampa	248	12.35 S	76.07 W
Taurisano	68	39.57 N	18.13 E
Taurisma	248	15.10 S	72.51 W
Tauroa Point ≻	172	35.10 S	173.04 E
Taurovo	86	59.36 N	73.18 E
Taurus Mountains → Toros Dağları ⋏	130	37.00 N	33.00 E
Tauste	34	41.55 N	1.15 W
Tautira	174s	17.44 S	149.09 W
Tauxigny	50	47.13 N	0.50 E
Tavaí	252	26.07 S	55.32 W
Tavajvaam ≃	180	64.56 N	177.30 E
Tavajza	89	45.12 N	136.44 E
Țavālesh, Kūhhā-ye → Talish Mountains ⋏	128	38.42 N	48.18 E
Tavanasa	58	46.45 N	9.04 E
Tavannes	58	47.13 N	7.12 E
Tavant	50	47.07 N	0.23 E
Tavares, Bra.	250	7.38 S	37.54 W
Tavares, Fl., U.S.	220	28.48 N	81.43 W
Tavares, Ilha dos I	287a	22.49 S	43.06 W
Tavarnelle Val di Pesa	66	43.33 N	11.10 E
Tavas	130	37.34 N	29.04 E
Tavastehus → Hämeenlinna	26	61.00 N	24.27 E
Tavaux	58	47.02 N	5.24 E
Tavda	86	58.03 N	65.15 E
Tavda ≃	72	57.47 N	67.16 E
Tave ≃	62	44.07 N	4.42 E
Tavera ≃	64	46.29 N	11.21 E
Taverham	42	52.41 N	1.12 E
Taverna	68	39.01 N	16.35 E
Tavern Creek ≃	194	38.19 N	92.18 W
Tavernelle, It.	64	44.18 N	10.04 E
Tavernelle, It.	66	43.00 N	12.09 E
Tavernes	62	43.36 N	6.01 E
Tavernes de Valldigna	34	39.04 N	0.16 W
Tavernier	220	25.00 N	80.30 W
Tavernole sul Mella	64	45.45 N	10.14 E
Taverny	50	49.02 N	2.13 E
Taveta, Kenya	154	3.24 S	37.41 E
Taveta, Tan.	154	9.01 S	35.37 E
Taveuni I	175g	16.51 S	179.58 W
Taviano	68	39.59 N	18.05 E
Tavil'dara	85	38.43 N	70.28 E
Tavira	34	37.07 N	7.39 W
Tavistock, On., Can.	212	43.19 N	80.50 W
Tavistock, Eng., U.K.	42	50.33 N	4.08 W
Tavn-Gašun	80	46.01 N	45.55 E
Tavolara, Isola I	71	40.54 N	9.42 E
Tavoliere ⬥ [1]	68	41.35 N	15.25 E
Tavolžan	86	52.44 N	77.27 E
Tavor, Har (Mount Tabor) ∧	132	32.41 N	35.23 E
Távora ≃	34	41.09 N	7.35 W
Tavoy → Dawei	110	14.05 N	98.12 E
Tavoy Point ≻	110	13.32 N	98.10 E
Tavričanka	89	43.22 N	131.52 E
Tavričeskoje	86	54.35 N	73.38 E
Tavry	265a	59.55 N	30.42 E
Tavsalayihüseynan	130	38.38 N	40.32 E
Tavşanlı	130	39.33 N	29.30 E
Tavua	175g	17.27 S	177.51 E
Tavy ≃	42	50.16 N	4.10 W
Taw ≃	42	51.04 N	4.11 W
Tawa	172	41.10 S	174.51 E
Tawa ≃	124	22.48 N	77.48 E
Tawaeli	112	0.43 S	119.51 E
Tawakoni, Lake ⊜ [1]	222	32.55 N	96.00 W
Tawara	270	34.27 N	135.57 E
Tawarada	268	35.19 N	140.04 E
Tawaramoto	96	34.33 N	135.48 E
Tawas City	190	44.16 N	83.30 W
Tawau	112	4.15 N	117.54 E
Tawd ≃	262	53.36 N	2.48 W
Tāwi ≃	123	32.40 N	74.41 E
Țawīlah, Juzur II	140	27.35 N	33.46 E
Tawi-Tawi □ [4]	116	5.20 N	120.00 E
Tawi-Tawi Group II	116	5.10 N	120.15 E
Tawi-Tawi Island I	116	5.10 N	120.00 E
Țawkar	140	18.26 N	37.44 E
Tawu	100	22.22 N	120.54 E
Țāwūq	128	35.08 N	44.27 E
Tāwurghā'	146	32.02 N	15.09 E
Țawwah Banī Ibrāhīm	142	28.05 N	30.41 E
Taxco de Alarcón	234	18.33 N	99.36 W
Taxenbach	64	47.17 N	12.58 E
Taxi	89	49.26 N	126.08 E
Taxila	123	33.44 N	72.49 E
Taxisco	236	14.04 N	90.28 W
Taxkorgan Tajik Zizhixian	120	37.49 N	75.14 E
Taxusi	102	32.58 N	98.10 E
Tay ≃, On., Can.	212	44.53 N	76.07 W
Tay ≃, Yk., Can.	180	62.34 N	134.22 W
Tay ≃, Scot., U.K.	46	56.22 N	3.21 W
Tay, Firth of ⊂ [1]	46	56.26 N	3.00 W
Tay, Lake ⊜	162	32.55 S	120.48 E
Tay, Loch ⊜	46	56.31 N	4.10 W
Tayabamba	248	8.17 S	77.18 W
Tayabas	116	14.01 N	121.35 E
Tayabas Bay ⊂	116	13.45 N	121.45 E
Tayan	112	0.02 S	110.07 E
Tayandu, Kepulauan II	164	5.30 S	132.15 E
Tayayi	105	39.25 N	115.03 E
Tayeegle	144	4.02 N	44.31 E
Taylor, B.C., Can.	182	56.10 N	120.41 W
Taylor, Az., U.S.	200	34.27 N	110.05 W
Taylor, Ar., U.S.	194	33.06 N	93.27 W
Taylor, Mi., U.S.	216	42.14 N	83.16 W
Taylor, Mo., U.S.	219	39.56 N	91.32 W
Taylor, Ne., U.S.	198	41.46 N	99.22 W
Taylor, Pa., U.S.	210	41.23 N	75.42 W
Taylor, Tx., U.S.	222	30.34 N	97.24 W
Taylor ≃	200	38.40 N	106.51 W
Taylor, Mount ∧, N.Z.	172	43.30 S	171.19 E
Taylor, Mount ∧, N.M., U.S.	200	35.14 N	107.37 W
Taylor Creek ≃, On., Can.	275b	43.42 N	79.20 W
Taylor Creek ≃, Il., U.S.	219	39.13 N	90.18 W
Taylor Lake Village	222	29.36 N	95.03 W
Taylor Mountain ∧	202	44.53 N	114.13 W
Taylor Mountains ⋏	180	60.50 N	157.20 W
Taylor Run ≃	285	39.57 N	75.39 W
Taylors	192	34.55 N	82.17 W
Taylors Bush Park ♠	275b	43.42 N	79.19 W
Taylors Island	208	38.28 N	76.17 W
Taylor Springs	219	39.08 N	89.30 W
Taylors Run ≃	279b	40.11 N	79.57 W
Taylorstown	214	40.10 N	80.23 W
Taylorsville, In., U.S.	218	39.17 N	85.57 W
Taylorsville, Ky., U.S.	194	38.01 N	85.20 W
Taylorsville, Ms., U.S.	194	31.49 N	89.25 W
Taylorsville, N.C., U.S.	192	35.55 N	81.10 W
Taylorsville Dam ⬥ [6]	218	39.53 N	84.10 W
Taylortown, N.J., U.S.	276	40.56 N	74.24 W
Taylortown, Oh., U.S.	214	40.28 N	80.40 W
Taylortown Reservoir ⊜ [1]	276	40.58 N	74.22 W
Taylorville	219	39.32 N	89.17 W
Taylorville, Lake ⊜ [1]	219	39.30 N	89.15 W
Taymā'	128	27.38 N	38.29 E
Taymouth	186	46.11 N	66.37 W
Taymyr Peninsula → Tajmyr, poluostrov ≻ [1]	74	76.00 N	104.00 E
Tay Ninh	110	11.18 N	106.06 E
Taynuilt	46	56.25 N	5.14 W
Tayoltita	232	24.05 N	105.56 W
Tayport	46	56.27 N	2.53 W
Táyros	267c	37.58 N	23.42 E
Tayside □ [4]	46	56.30 N	3.30 W
Taytay, Pil.	116	10.49 N	119.31 E
Taytay, Pil.	116	14.34 N	121.08 E
Taytay Bay ⊂	116	10.55 N	119.35 E
Tayu	115a	6.32 S	111.02 E
Tayüan, T'aiwan	100	25.04 N	121.11 E
Tayuan, Zhg.	89	51.27 N	124.16 E
Tayyārah	140	13.12 N	30.47 E
Țayyebāt	128	34.44 N	60.45 E
Taz ≃	72	67.32 N	78.40 E
Taza	148	34.16 N	4.01 W
Taza □ [4]	148	34.05 N	3.45 W
Tazawa-ko ⊜	92	39.43 N	140.40 E
Tazenakht	148	30.35 N	7.12 W
Tazewell, Tn., U.S.	192	36.27 N	83.34 W
Tazewell, Va., U.S.	192	37.06 N	81.31 W
Tazhuang	105	39.55 N	117.13 E
Tazicheng	89	46.35 N	123.06 E
Tazigou ≃	104	41.44 N	121.30 E
Tazin ≃	176	60.26 N	110.45 W
Tazin Lake ⊜	176	59.47 N	109.03 W
T'ažinskij	86	56.07 N	88.31 E
Tāzirbū ⊤ [4]	146	25.45 N	21.00 E
Tazishan	107	29.28 N	104.14 E
Tazlina	180	62.04 N	145.25 W
Tazlina Lake ⊜	180	61.50 N	146.30 W
Tazoult-Lambese	34	35.29 N	6.15 E
Tazovskaja guba ⊂	74	69.05 N	76.00 E
Tazovskij	74	67.28 N	78.42 E
Tazovskij poluostrov ≻ [1]	72	68.35 N	76.00 E
Tazrouk	148	23.25 N	6.16 E
Tazumal ⊥	236	13.59 N	89.41 W
Tāzumuddin	126	22.29 N	90.53 E
Tazungdām	102	28.02 N	97.35 E
Tbessa	148	35.28 N	8.09 E
Tbessa □ [5]	148	35.10 N	8.00 E
Tbilisi	84	41.43 N	44.49 E
Tbilisskaja	78	45.23 N	40.12 E
Tchad → Chad □ [1]	146	15.00 N	19.00 E
Tchad, Lac (Lake Chad) ⊜	146	13.20 N	14.00 E
Tchaguine Golo	146	10.03 N	16.19 E
Tchamba	150	9.02 N	1.25 E
Tch'ang-Cha → Changsha	100	28.12 N	112.58 E
Tchaourou	150	8.53 N	2.36 E
Tchefuncta ≃	194	30.22 N	90.10 W
Tchékapika	152	1.17 S	16.11 E
Tcheliabinsk → Čel'abinsk	86	55.10 N	61.24 E
Tcheng-Tcheou → Zhengzhou	102	34.48 N	113.39 E
Tchentlo Lake ⊜	182	55.11 N	125.00 W
Tchériba	150	12.16 N	3.05 W
Tchesinkut Lake ⊜	182	54.05 N	125.40 W
Tchetti	150	7.50 N	1.40 E
Tchibanga	152	2.51 S	11.02 E
Tchigaï, Plateau du ⋏ [1]	146	21.30 N	14.50 E
Tchikala-Tcholohanga	152	12.38 S	16.03 E
Tchin-Tabáradene	150	15.58 N	5.50 E
Tchitondi	152	4.33 S	12.08 E
Tchollire	146	8.24 N	14.10 E
Tchong-K'ing → Chongqing	107	29.34 N	106.35 E
Tchořovice	60	49.27 N	13.48 E
Tchula	194	33.10 N	90.13 W
T.C. Steele State Memorial ⊥	218	39.08 N	86.20 W
Tczew	30	54.06 N	18.47 E
Té ≃	110	12.27 N	106.02 E
Te, Kinh ≊	269c	10.45 N	106.42 E
Teá ≃	246	0.30 S	65.09 W
Teaca	38	46.55 N	24.31 E
Teacapan	234	22.33 N	105.45 W
Tea Creek ≃	284a	43.02 N	79.06 W
Teaehoa, Pointe ≻	174x	9.51 S	139.01 W
Teague	222	31.37 N	96.17 W
Teahupoo	174s	17.51 S	149.13 W
Te Anau	172	45.25 S	167.43 E
Te Anau, Lake ⊜	172	45.12 S	167.48 E
Teanaway ≃	224	47.10 N	120.50 W
Teanaway, Middle Fork ≃	224	47.15 N	120.53 W
Teanaway, North Fork ≃	224	47.22 N	120.53 W
Teaneck	210	40.53 N	74.00 W
Teangue	46	57.07 N	5.50 W
Teano	68	41.15 N	14.04 E
Teapa	234	17.33 N	92.57 W
Teapa ≃	234	17.58 N	92.54 W
Te Araroa	172	37.38 S	178.22 E
Tearinibai	174t	1.35 N	172.58 E
Te Aroha	172	37.33 S	175.43 E
Teaticket	207	41.33 N	70.35 W
Tea Tree	162	22.11 S	133.17 E
Tea Tree Gully	168b	34.49 S	138.44 E
Te Atukura ∧	174k	21.14 S	159.45 W
Te Awamutu	172	38.01 S	175.19 E
Teba, Esp.	34	36.58 N	4.56 W
Teba, Indon.	164	1.29 S	137.54 E
Tebakang	112	1.06 N	110.30 E
Tebas	256	21.35 S	42.44 W
Tebay	44	54.26 N	2.35 W
Tebbetts	219	38.37 N	91.57 W
Teberda	84	43.28 N	41.45 E
Teberdinskij zapovednik ♠	84	43.20 N	41.45 E
Tebicuary ≃	252	26.36 S	58.16 W
Tebicuary-Mí ≃	252	26.26 S	56.51 W
Tebingbulan	112	3.03 S	103.44 E
Tebingtinggi, Indon.	112	0.36 N	101.36 E
Tebingtinggi, Indon.	112	3.36 S	103.05 E
Tebingtinggi, Indon.	114	3.20 N	99.09 E
Tebingtinggi, Pulau I	114	0.54 N	102.45 E
Tébourba	36	36.49 N	9.51 E
Téboursouk	148	36.28 N	9.15 E
Téboursouk, Monts de ⋏	36	36.30 N	9.10 E
Tebra ≃	76	56.51 N	21.12 E
Tebstrup	41	55.59 N	9.53 E
Tebulosmta, gora ∧	84	42.33 N	45.19 E
Tebza ≃	80	58.23 N	41.19 E
Tecalitlán	234	19.26 N	103.15 W
Tecamachalco	234	18.53 N	97.44 W
Tecate	232	32.34 N	116.38 W
Tech ≃	32	42.36 N	3.03 E
Teche, Bayou ≃	194	29.43 N	91.13 W
Techendorf	64	46.43 N	13.17 E
Techiman	150	7.35 N	1.56 W
Techimentia	150	7.11 N	2.02 W
Techirghiol	38	44.03 N	28.36 E
Techlé	148	21.35 N	14.58 W
Techou → Dezhou	98	37.27 N	116.18 E
Techtin	76	53.51 N	29.44 E
Tecka	254	43.29 S	70.48 W
Tecka ≃	254	42.37 S	70.25 W
Tecklenburg	52	52.13 N	7.48 E
Teckomatorp	41	55.52 N	13.05 E
Tecolote Creek ≃	200	35.22 N	105.15 W
Tecolotlán	234	20.13 N	104.03 W
Tecolutla ≃	234	20.29 N	97.00 W
Tecomán	234	18.55 N	103.53 W
Tecomate, Laguna ⊂	234	16.35 N	99.25 W
Tecominoacán	234	17.53 N	93.37 W
Tecopa	204	35.50 N	116.13 W
Tecozautla	234	20.32 N	99.38 W
Tecpan ≃	234	17.25 N	100.40 W
Tecpan de Galeana	234	17.15 N	100.41 W
Tecpán Guatemala	236	14.46 N	91.00 W
Tecpatan	234	17.08 N	93.18 W
Tecuala	234	22.23 N	105.27 W
Tecuamburro, Volcán ∧ [1]	236	14.09 N	90.24 W
Tecuautzi, Cerro ∧	286a	19.19 N	99.00 W
Tecuci	38	45.50 N	27.26 E
Tecumseh, On., Can.	214	42.19 N	82.54 W
Tecumseh, Mi., U.S.	216	42.00 N	83.56 W
Tecumseh, Ne., U.S.	198	40.22 N	96.11 W
Tecumseh, Ok., U.S.	196	35.15 N	96.56 W
Ted Ceidaar Dabole	144	4.24 N	43.55 E
Teddington ⬥ [8]	260	51.25 N	0.20 W
Tédji	146	11.46 N	21.19 E
Tedori ≃	94	36.29 N	136.28 E
Tedrow	216	41.37 N	84.13 W
Tedžen	128	37.23 N	60.31 E
Tedžen (Harīrūd) ≃	128	37.24 N	60.38 E
Tedženstroj	128	36.55 N	60.53 E
Teec Nos Pos	200	36.56 N	109.42 W
Teeli	86	51.07 N	90.14 E
Teels Marsh ⁝	204	38.12 N	118.21 W
Teen ⊜	40	59.07 N	14.40 E
Teerijärvi → Terjärv	26	63.32 N	23.30 E
Tees ≃	44	54.34 N	1.16 W
Tees Bay ⊂	44	54.39 N	1.07 W
Teesdale V	44	54.38 N	2.07 W
Teesside → Middlesbrough	44	54.35 N	1.14 W
Tees-Side Airport ⊠	44	54.31 N	1.25 W
Teeswater	212	44.00 N	81.17 W
Teeswater ≃	212	44.18 N	81.17 W
Tefé	246	3.22 S	64.42 W
Tefé ≃	242	3.35 S	64.47 W
Tefé, Lago ⊜	246	3.27 S	64.47 W
Tefenni	130	37.18 N	29.47 E
Tefft	216	41.12 N	86.58 W
Tefle	150	5.59 N	0.35 E
Tegal	115a	6.52 S	109.08 E
Tegalombo	115a	8.04 S	111.17 E
Tégama ⬥ [1]	150	15.50 N	8.12 E
Tega-numa ⊜	268	35.51 N	140.04 E
Tegel ⬥ [8]	54	52.35 N	13.17 E
Tegel, Berliner Forst ⬥ [3]	264a	52.37 N	13.16 E
Tegelen	52	51.21 N	6.09 E
Tegeler See ⊜	264a	52.35 N	13.15 E
Tegernsee	64	47.43 N	11.45 E
Tegernsee ⊜	64	47.42 N	11.45 E
Teggiano	68	40.23 N	15.32 E
Teghra	124	25.29 N	85.57 E
Tegid, Llyn ⊜	42	52.53 N	3.36 W
Tegina	150	10.05 N	6.14 E
Tegineneng	112	5.12 S	105.10 E
Tegistyk	85	44.02 N	68.22 E
Teglio	64	46.10 N	10.04 E
Tégua I	175f	13.15 S	166.37 E
Tegualda	254	41.02 S	73.26 W
Tegucigalpa	236	14.06 N	87.13 W
Tegul'det	86	57.19 N	88.10 E
Tehachapi	228	35.07 N	118.26 W
Tehachapi Creek ≃	228	35.17 N	118.38 W
Tehachapi Mountains ⋏	228	35.00 N	118.40 W
Tehachapi Pass)(	228	35.06 N	118.18 W
Tehamiyam	140	18.20 N	36.32 E
Te Hapua	172	34.31 S	172.54 E
Tehar ⬥ [8]	272a	28.38 N	77.07 E
Te Haroto	172	39.08 S	176.36 E
Tehata	126	23.43 N	88.32 E
Tehek Lake ⊜	176	64.55 N	95.38 W
Teheran → Tehrān	128	35.40 N	51.26 E
Téhini	150	9.36 N	3.40 W
Tehoohaivei, Cap ≻	174x	9.49 S	138.54 W
Te Hope O Te Keho, Cap ≻	174x	10.02 S	139.06 W
Tehoru	164	3.23 S	129.30 E
Tehrān, Īrān	128	35.40 N	51.26 E
Tehrān, Īrān	267d	35.40 N	51.26 E
Tehrān □ [4]	128	35.30 N	51.30 E
Tehrān, University of ⱴ [2]	267d	35.42 N	51.24 E
Tehran International Airport ⊠	267d	35.41 N	51.19 E
Tehrān Pārs ⬥ [8]	267d	35.44 N	51.32 E
Tehrathum	124	27.07 N	87.32 E
Tehri	124	30.23 N	78.29 E
Tehuacán	234	18.27 N	97.23 W
Tehuacana	222	31.44 N	96.33 W
Tehuacana Creek ≃, Tx., U.S.	222	31.31 N	97.02 W
Tehuacana Creek ≃, Tx., U.S.	222	31.50 N	95.59 W
Tehuantepec	234	18.41 N	103.17 W
Tehuantepec ≃	234	16.10 N	95.07 W
Tehuantepec, Golfo de ⊂	234	16.00 N	94.50 W
Tehuantepec, Istmo de ⊥ [3]	234	17.00 N	95.00 W
Tehuantepec Ridge ✣ [3]	16	13.30 N	98.00 W
Tehuelches	254	46.56 S	67.27 W
Tehuipango	234	18.31 N	97.04 W
Tehuitzingo	234	18.21 N	98.17 W
Teià	266d	41.30 N	2.19 E
Teichl ≃	61	47.46 N	14.10 E
Teichröda	54	50.45 N	11.18 E
Teichwolframsdorf	54	50.43 N	12.14 E
Teide, Parque Nacional del ♠	148	28.15 N	16.30 W
Teide, Pico de ∧	148	28.16 N	16.38 W
Teifi ≃	42	52.07 N	4.42 W
Teifiside ⬥ [1]	42	52.02 N	4.22 W
Teiga Plateau ⋏ [1]	140	15.38 N	25.40 E
Teign ≃	42	50.33 N	3.29 W
Teignmouth	42	50.33 N	3.30 W
Teise ≃	260	51.13 N	0.25 E
Teisendorf	64	47.51 N	12.49 E
Teisnach	60	49.02 N	13.00 E
Teith ≃	46	56.08 N	3.59 W
Teixeira	250	7.13 S	37.15 W
Teixeira Pinto	150	12.10 N	13.55 W
Teixeira Soares	252	25.22 S	50.27 W
Tejakula	115b	8.08 S	115.20 E
Tejamén	232	24.48 N	105.07 W
Tejkovo	80	56.52 N	40.34 E
Tejo → Tagus ≃	34	38.40 N	9.24 W
Tejon Creek ≃	228	35.08 N	118.53 W
Tejon Pass)(	228	34.48 N	118.52 W
Tejupan, Punta ≻	234	18.20 N	103.32 W
Tejupilco de Hidalgo	234	18.54 N	100.09 W
Te Kaha	172	37.44 S	177.41 E
Tekai ≃	114	4.14 N	102.23 E
Tékakwitha, Île I	275a	45.25 N	73.42 W
Tekam ≃	114	3.52 N	102.27 E
Tekamah	198	41.46 N	96.13 W
Te Kao	172	34.39 S	172.57 E
Tekapo, Lake ⊜	172	43.53 S	170.31 E
Te Karaka	172	38.28 S	177.52 E
Tekāri	124	24.56 N	84.50 E
Te Kauwhata	172	37.24 S	175.09 E
Tekax	232	20.12 N	89.17 W
Teke	130	41.04 N	29.39 E
Teke, ozero ⊜	86	53.48 N	73.00 E
Teke Burnu ≻	130	38.05 N	26.36 E
Tekeli	86	44.48 N	78.57 E
Tekeli Dağı ∧	130	40.09 N	37.28 E
Tekes	86	43.10 N	81.43 E
Tekes ≃	86	43.36 N	82.32 E
Tekeze (Satīt) ≃	140	14.20 N	35.50 E
Tekirdağ	130	40.59 N	27.31 E
Tekirdağ □ [4]	130	41.00 N	27.30 E
Tekkali	122	18.37 N	84.14 E
Tekke	130	40.43 N	36.12 E
Tekke Burnu ≻	130	40.02 N	26.10 E
Tekkiraz	130	40.59 N	37.08 E
Tekman	130	39.38 N	41.31 E
Tekoa	202	47.13 N	117.04 W
Tekong, Pulau I	271c	1.24 N	104.03 E
Tekong Kechil, Pulau I	271c	1.25 N	104.01 E
Tekonsha	216	42.05 N	84.59 W
Te Kopuru	172	36.02 S	173.56 E
Tekouiat, Oued V	148	22.25 N	2.35 E
Tékro ⊤ [4]	146	19.30 N	20.58 E
Tekstil'ščiki	82	55.57 N	37.49 E
Tekstil'ščiki ⬥ [8]	265b	55.42 N	37.44 E
Teku	112	0.46 S	123.26 E
Te Kuiti	172	38.20 S	175.10 E
Tekukor, Pulau I	271c	1.14 N	103.50 E
Tel ≃	122	20.50 N	83.54 E
Tela, Hond.	236	15.44 N	87.27 W
Tela, India	272a	28.44 N	77.20 E
Tela, Bahía de ⊂	236	15.48 N	87.30 W
Telaga	116	6.51 N	117.03 E
Telaga, Teluk ⊂	114	2.10 N	98.00 E
Telaga-kulon	115a	6.58 S	108.18 E
Télagh	148	34.47 N	0.34 W
Telaopengsha Shan ∧	120	30.33 N	86.25 E
Tel Ashqelon ⊥	132	31.39 N	34.32 E
Telavåg	26	60.16 N	4.49 E
Telavi	84	41.55 N	45.28 E
Tel Aviv □ [5]	132	32.05 N	34.48 E
Tel Aviv-Yafo	132	32.03 N	34.46 E
Telč	30	49.11 N	15.27 E
Tel'čje	76	53.21 N	36.20 E
Telde	148	28.00 N	15.25 W
Tele ≃, Afr.	158	30.26 S	27.33 E
Tele ≃, Zaïre	152	2.48 N	23.54 E
Telechany	76	52.31 N	25.51 E
Teleckoje, ozero ⊜	86	51.35 N	87.40 E
Telefomin	164	5.10 S	141.35 E
Telegapulang	112	2.55 S	112.25 E
Telegino	80	52.55 N	44.34 E
Telegrafo, Pizzo ∧	70	37.37 N	13.10 E
Telegraph Canyon V	280	33.55 N	117.45 W
Telegraph Cove	182	50.33 N	126.50 W
Telegraph Creek	180	57.55 N	131.10 W
Telêmaco Borba	252	24.20 S	50.40 W
Telemark □ [6]	26	59.30 N	8.40 E
Telemba	88	52.43 N	113.16 E
Telembí ≃	246	1.50 N	78.16 W
Telén	252	36.16 S	65.30 W
Telen ≃	112	0.26 S	116.42 E
Telenești	38	47.30 N	28.22 E
Teleno ∧	34	42.21 N	6.23 W
Teleorman □ [6]	38	44.00 N	25.15 E
Teleorman ≃	38	43.52 N	25.26 E
Téléphone, Île du I	273b	4.20 S	15.12 E
Telerig	38	43.51 N	27.40 E
Telertheba, Djebel ∧	148	24.10 N	6.51 E
Telescope Peak ∧	204	36.10 N	117.05 W
Telescope Point ≻	241k	12.08 N	61.36 W
Telese	68	41.13 N	14.32 E
Telesterion ⊥	267c	38.02 N	23.32 E
Telferner	222	28.51 N	96.53 W
Telfes	64	47.10 N	11.22 E
Telford, Eng., U.K.	42	52.40 N	2.28 W
Telford, Pa., U.S.	208	40.19 N	75.19 W
Telfs	64	47.18 N	11.04 E
Telgte	52	51.59 N	7.47 E
Telica ≃	236	14.43 N	86.08 W
Telica, Volcán ∧ [1]	236	12.36 N	86.50 W
Telida	180	63.23 N	153.16 W
Telikovka	80	52.35 N	48.17 E
Télimélé	150	10.54 N	13.02 W
Telixtlahuaca	234	17.18 N	96.54 W
Telizi	265a	59.42 N	29.59 E
Teljo, Jabal ∧	140	14.42 N	25.56 E
Telkwa	182	54.42 N	127.03 W
Telkwa ≃	182	54.41 N	127.02 W
Tel Lakhish ⊥	132	31.34 N	34.51 E
Tellaro ≃	70	36.50 N	15.06 E
Tell City	194	37.57 N	86.46 W
Teller	180	65.16 N	166.22 W
Tellicherry	122	11.45 N	75.32 E
Tellico ≃	192	35.36 N	84.13 W
Tellico Plains	192	35.21 N	84.17 W
Tellier	254	47.39 S	66.03 W
Tellier, Lac ⊜	206	46.23 N	74.00 W
Tello	246	3.04 N	75.08 W
Telluride	200	37.56 N	107.48 W
Tel'ma	88	52.43 N	103.41 E
Tel'manove	83	47.24 N	38.02 E
Tel Megiddo (Armageddon) ⊥	132	32.35 N	35.11 E
Telmen	88	48.38 N	97.37 E
Telmen nuur ⊜	88	48.50 N	97.18 E
Tel Mond	132	32.15 N	34.56 E
Tel'novskij	89	49.22 N	142.05 E
Telo	110	0.03 N	98.16 E
Teloekbetoeng → Tanjungkarang-Telukbetung	115a	5.27 S	105.16 E
Telogia Creek ≃	192	30.16 N	84.44 W
Telok Anson	114	4.02 N	101.01 E
Telok Datok	114	2.49 N	101.31 E
Teloloapan	234	18.21 N	99.51 W
Telpaneca	236	13.32 N	86.17 W
Telsen	254	42.24 S	66.57 W
Telsen, Arroyo ≃	254	42.51 S	66.48 W
Telšiai	76	55.59 N	22.15 E

≃ River	Fluß	Río	Rivière	Rio
≊ Canal	Kanal	Canal	Canal	Canal
∟ Waterfall, Rapids	Wasserfall, Stromschnellen	Cascada, Rápidos	Chute d'eau, Rapides	Cascata, Rápidos
ʊ Strait	Meeresstraße	Estrecho	Détroit	Estreito
⊂ Bay, Gulf	Bucht, Golf	Bahía, Golfo	Baie, Golfe	Baía, Golfo
⊜ Lake, Lakes	See, Seen	Lago, Lagos	Lac, Lacs	Lago, Lagos
⁝ Swamp	Sumpf	Pantano	Marais	Pântano
⊓ Ice Features, Glacier	Eis- und Gletscherformen	Accidentes Glaciales	Formes glaciaires	Acidentes glaciares
⊤ Other Hydrographic Features	Andere Hydrographische Objekte	Otros Elementos Hidrográficos	Autres données hydrographiques	Outros acidentes hidrográficos

✣ Submarine Features	Untermeerische Objekte	Accidentes Submarinos	Formes de relief sous-marin	Acidentes submarinos
□ Political Unit	Politische Einheit	Unidad Politica	Entité politique	Unidade política
ⱴ Cultural Institution	Kulturelle Institution	Institución Cultural	Institution culturelle	Instituição cultural
⊥ Historical Site	Historische Stätte	Sitio Histórico	Site historique	Sitio histórico
♠ Recreational Site	Erholungs- und Ferienort	Sitio de Recreo	Centre de loisirs	Area de Lazer
⊠ Airport	Flughafen	Aeropuerto	Aéroport	Aeroporto
■ Military Installation	Militäranlage	Instalación Militar	Installation militaire	Instalação militar
⬥ Miscellaneous	Verschiedenes	Misceláneo	Divers	Diversos

ENGLISH | DEUTSCH

Name / Name	Page / Seite	Lat.°′ / Breite°′	Long.°′ / Länge°′ E = Ost
Telti	71	40.52 N	9.21 E
Teltow	54	52.23 N	13.16 E
Teltow -●-[1]	264a	52.18 N	13.25 E
Teltower Hochfläche ⋌[1]	264a	52.22 N	13.20 E
Teltowkanal ≋	264a	52.26 N	13.35 E
Telukbatang	112	1.00 S	109.46 E
Telukbayur, Indon.	112	2.09 N	117.24 E
Telukbayur, Indon.	112	1.00 S	100.22 E
Telukbrombang	114	2.03 N	100.52 E
Telukbutun	112	4.13 N	108.12 E
Telukdalem	114	0.34 N	97.49 E
Teluklanjut	112	0.09 N	103.29 E
Teluklecak	114	1.51 N	101.44 E
Telukmerbau	114	2.04 N	100.38 E
Telukpambang	114	1.28 N	102.28 E
Teluk Punggur, Ujung >	112	3.53 S	102.17 E
Telumengtang Shan ∧	120	30.33 N	86.27 E
Teluša	76	53.03 N	29.31 E
Tem'	88	55.21 N	100.44 E
Tema	150	5.38 N	0.01 E
Temae	174s	17.29 S	149.46 W
Temagami, Lake ⊜	190	47.00 N	80.05 W
Temaju, Pulau I	112	0.29 N	108.52 E
Temalacacingo	234	17.52 N	98.41 W
Temalı Bendi -●-[6]	267b	41.04 N	29.06 E
Te Manga ∧	174k	21.13 S	159.45 W
Temangan Baharu	114	5.42 N	102.09 E
Temangga	112	0.27 N	111.21 E
Temanggung	115a	7.18 S	110.10 E
Temascal, Méx.	234	23.24 N	104.14 W
Temascal, Méx.	234	18.15 N	96.20 W
Tem'asovo	86	52.59 N	58.06 E
Temastián	234	21.53 N	103.28 W
Tematangi I[1]	14	21.41 S	140.40 W
Temax	232	21.09 N	88.56 W
Tembakul, Pulau I	271c	1.14 N	103.52 E
Tembe	154	0.16 S	28.14 E
Tembe ≃	158	26.03 S	32.26 E
Tembeling	114	4.04 N	102.19 E
Tembeling ≃	114	4.04 N	102.20 E
Tembenči ≃	74	64.36 N	99.58 E
Tembesi ≃	112	1.43 S	103.06 E
Tembilahan	112	0.19 S	103.09 E
Tembisa	158	25.58 S	28.14 E
Temblador	246	8.59 N	62.44 W
Tembleque	34	39.42 N	3.30 W
Temblor Range ⋌	226	35.20 N	119.55 W
Tembo Aluma	152	7.42 S	17.17 E
Tembuè	154	14.52 S	32.58 E
Tembuland □[9]	158	31.30 S	27.40 E
Teme ≃	42	52.09 N	2.18 W
Temecula	228	33.29 N	117.08 W
Temecula Creek ≃	228	33.28 N	117.08 W
Temelli	130	39.44 N	32.22 E
Temengor	114	5.19 N	101.22 E
Temengor, Tasek ⊜[1]	114	5.30 N	101.20 E
Temerin	38	45.24 N	19.53 E
Temerloh	114	3.27 N	102.25 E
Temescal Canyon V	280	34.04 N	118.32 W
Temescal Wash V	228	33.40 N	117.20 W
Temesvár → Timişoara	38	45.45 N	21.13 E
Temiang, Pulau I	112	0.19 N	104.23 E
Teminaabuan	164	1.26 S	132.01 E
Temir	86	49.08 N	57.06 E
Temir ≃	86	48.31 N	57.27 E
Temirgojevskaja	78	45.07 N	40.16 E
Temirlanovka	85	42.36 N	69.17 E
Temirtau, Kaz.	86	50.05 N	72.56 E
Temirtau, Ross.	86	53.08 N	87.28 E
Témiscamie, Lac ⊜	186	51.11 N	72.12 W
Témiscaming	190	46.43 N	79.06 W
Témiscouata, Lac ⊜	186	47.41 N	68.47 W
Temixco	234	18.50 N	99.14 W
Temnik ≃	88	51.00 N	106.18 E
Temnikov	80	54.38 N	43.12 E
Temnikovo	265b	55.43 N	38.01 E
Temo ≃	71	40.17 N	8.28 E
Temoaya	234	19.28 N	99.35 W
Temora	166	34.26 S	147.32 E
Temosachic	232	28.57 N	107.51 W
Tempe	200	33.24 N	111.54 W
Tempe, Danau ⊜	112	4.06 S	119.57 E
Tempelfelde	264a	52.43 N	13.43 E
Tempelhof -●-[8]	264a	52.28 N	13.23 E
Temperance	216	41.46 N	83.34 W
Temperanceville	208	37.53 N	75.32 W
Temperley -●-[8]	258	34.47 S	58.24 W
Tempest, Mount ∧[2]	171a	27.10 S	153.26 E
Tempilang	112	2.07 S	105.40 E
Tempino	112	1.44 S	103.29 E
Tempio di Clitunno ⊥	66	42.48 N	12.45 E
Tempio Pausania	71	40.54 N	9.06 E
Tempisque ≃	236	10.12 N	85.14 W
Temple, Ok., U.S.	196	34.16 N	98.14 W
Temple, Pa., U.S.	208	40.24 N	75.55 W
Temple, Tx., U.S.	222	31.05 N	97.20 W
Temple City	228	34.06 N	118.03 W
Templecombe	42	51.00 N	2.25 W
Temple Ewell	42	51.09 N	1.16 E
Temple Hills Park	284c	38.48 N	76.57 W
Templemore	48	52.48 N	7.50 W
Templers	168b	34.28 S	138.45 E
Temple Sowerby	44	54.39 N	2.35 W
Templestowe	169	37.45 S	145.07 E
Temple Terrace	220	28.02 N	82.23 W
Templeton, P.Q., Can.	212	45.29 N	75.36 W
Templeton, Ca., U.S.	226	35.33 N	120.42 W
Templeton, In., U.S.	216	40.31 N	87.12 W
Templeton, Ma., U.S.	207	42.33 N	72.04 W
Templeton, Pa., U.S.	214	40.55 N	79.27 W
Templeton ≃	166	21.14 S	138.13 E
Temple University ʊ[2]	285	39.59 N	75.09 W
Templeuve	50	50.32 N	3.10 E
Templi, Valle dei ⊥	70	37.17 N	13.35 E
Templin	54	53.07 N	13.30 E
Templiner See ⊜	264a	52.22 N	13.01 E
Templo Island I	116	13.09 N	122.52 E
Tempoal ≃	234	21.47 N	98.27 W
Tempoal de Sánchez	234	21.31 N	98.23 W
Tempy	82	56.38 N	37.18 E
Temr'uk	78	45.17 N	37.23 E
Temr'ukskij zaliv c	78	45.24 N	37.20 E
Temse	50	51.08 N	4.13 E
Temù	64	46.15 N	10.28 E
Temuco	252	38.44 S	72.36 W
Temuka	172	44.15 S	171.17 E
Temwen I	174r	6.52 N	158.19 E
Tena	246	0.59 S	77.49 W
Tenabo	232	20.03 N	90.14 W
Tenafly	210	40.55 N	73.57 W
Tenaha	194	31.57 N	94.15 W
Tenakee Springs	180	57.47 N	135.13 W
Tenakill Brook ≃	276	40.59 N	73.58 W
Tena Kourou ∧[2]	150	10.45 N	5.25 W
Tenāli	122	16.15 N	80.35 E
Tenamaxtlán	234	20.13 N	104.10 W
Tenancingo [de Degollado]	234	18.58 N	99.36 W
Tenango de Arista	234	19.07 N	99.33 W
Tenantongo, Presa ⊜[1]	286a	19.28 N	99.16 W
Tenasillahe Island I	224	46.14 N	123.27 W
Tenasserim	110	12.05 N	99.01 E
Tenay	58	45.55 N	5.30 E
Tenaya Creek ≃	226	37.44 N	119.35 W
Tenbury Wells	42	52.19 N	2.35 W
Tenby	42	51.41 N	4.43 W
Tence	62	45.07 N	4.17 E
Tench Island I	164	1.40 S	150.40 E
Tencin	62	45.19 N	5.58 E
Tenda, Colle di (Col de Tende))(	62	44.09 N	7.34 E
Tendaho	144	11.48 N	40.52 E
Tendai-san ∧	270	34.55 N	135.28 E
Tende	62	44.05 N	7.36 E
Tende, Col de (Colle di Tenda))(	62	44.09 N	7.34 E
Tende, Tunnel de -●-[5]	62	44.09 N	7.34 E
Ten Degree Channel ʯ	110	10.00 N	93.00 E
Tendeka	158	27.44 S	30.54 E
Tendō	92	38.21 N	140.22 E
Tendrara	148	33.04 N	1.59 W
Tendrivs'ka Kosa, ostriv >[2]	78	46.12 N	31.50 E
Tendrivs'ka zatoka c	78	46.15 N	31.55 E
Tendürek Dağı ∧	84	39.22 N	43.52 E
Ténenkou	150	14.28 N	4.55 W
Tenente Marques ≃	248	11.10 S	59.56 W
Tenente Portela	252	27.22 S	53.45 W
Ténéré -●-[2]	146	19.00 N	10.30 E
Ténéré, Erg du ⊥[8]	146	17.35 N	10.55 E
Tenerife I	148	28.19 N	16.34 W
Ténès	148	36.31 N	1.14 E
Ténès, Cap >	34	36.33 N	1.21 E
Tenexpa	234	17.11 N	100.43 W
Tenextepango	234	18.43 N	98.57 W
Teng ≃	110	19.52 N	97.45 E
Tengah, Kepulauan II	112	7.30 S	117.30 E
Teng'aopu	104	41.05 N	122.49 E
Tengchong	102	25.04 N	98.29 E
Tengeh Reservoir ⊜[1]	271c	1.21 N	103.39 E
Tengen	58	47.49 N	8.40 E
Tenggara, Nusa (Lesser Sunda Islands) II	108	9.00 S	120.00 E
Tenggarong	112	0.24 S	116.58 E
Tengger Shamo -●-[2]	102	38.00 N	104.40 E
Tenggol, Pulau I	114	4.48 N	103.38 E
Tenghilan	112	6.14 N	116.19 E
Tengi ≃	114	3.24 N	101.10 E
Tengiz, ozero ⊜	86	50.24 N	68.57 E
Tengjiabao	100	31.10 N	115.29 E
Tengqiao	110	18.22 N	109.46 E
Tengra	272b	22.48 N	88.32 E
Tengréla	150	10.29 N	6.24 W
Tengtian	100	27.04 N	115.40 E
Tengtiao (Na) ≃	110	22.05 N	103.09 E
Ten'guševo	80	54.46 N	42.44 E
Tengxian, Zhg.	98	35.08 N	117.10 E
Tengxian, Zhg.	102	23.21 N	110.53 E
Teniente Rodolfo Marsh ʊ[3]	9	62.12 S	58.54 W
Tenigerbad	58	46.42 N	8.57 E
Tenino	224	46.51 N	122.51 W
Tenis, ozero ⊜	86	56.09 N	71.56 E
Teniya-zaki >	174m	26.33 N	128.09 E
Teniz, ozero ⊜	86	54.08 N	64.34 E
Tenjin ≃	96	35.30 N	133.53 E
Tenjo, Mount ∧[2]	174p	13.25 N	144.42 E
Tenkāsi	122	8.58 N	77.18 E
Tenke, Zaïre	154	10.35 S	26.07 E
Tenke, Zaïre	154	11.26 S	26.45 E
Tenkeli	74	70.01 N	140.58 E
Tenkergynpil'gyn, laguna c	180	68.30 N	178.00 W
Ten'ki	80	55.26 N	49.00 E
Tenkiller Ferry Lake ⊜[1]	196	35.43 N	95.00 W
Tenkodogo	150	11.47 N	0.22 W
Tenmile ≃, Ma., U.S.	283	41.58 N	71.20 W
Tenmile ≃, N.Y., U.S.	210	41.40 N	73.31 W
Ten Mile Creek ≃, On., Can.	284a	43.07 N	79.11 W
Ten Mile Creek ≃, Ky., U.S.	218	38.43 N	84.46 W
Tenmile Creek ≃, Oh., U.S.	216	41.42 N	83.33 W
Tenmile Creek ≃, Pa., U.S.	188	40.08 N	80.22 W
Tenmile Creek ≃, Tx., U.S.	222	32.34 N	96.34 W
Ten Mile Lake ⊜	186	51.06 N	56.41 W
Tenmile Run ≃	276	40.27 N	74.35 W
Tenmile Wash V	200	32.52 N	113.28 W
Tenmoku-san ∧	94	35.52 N	139.03 E
Tenna ≃	66	43.14 N	13.47 E
Tennant Creek	162	19.40 S	134.10 E
Tennenbronn	58	48.11 N	8.20 E
Tennengau -●-[1]	64	47.40 N	13.15 E
Tennengebirge ⋌	64	47.30 N	13.15 E
Tennent	208	40.16 N	74.20 W
Tennent Pond ⊜	276	40.26 N	74.20 W
Tennessee □[3]	178	35.50 N	85.30 W
Tennessee ≃	178	37.04 N	88.33 W
Tennessee Colony	222	31.50 N	95.50 W
Tenneville	56	50.06 N	5.32 E
Tennille	192	32.56 N	82.48 W
Tenno	64	45.55 N	10.49 E
Tennōji -●-[8]	270	34.39 N	135.31 E
Teno	252	34.52 S	71.11 W
Tenom	112	5.08 N	115.57 E
Ténos, Pointe >	240e	14.48 N	61.00 W
Tenosique	232	17.29 N	91.26 W
Tenri	96	34.36 N	135.51 E
Tenryū, Nihon	94	35.16 N	137.51 E
Tenryū, Nihon	94	34.52 N	137.49 E
Tenryū ≃	94	34.39 N	137.47 E
Tensas ≃	194	31.38 N	91.49 W
Tensed	202	47.09 N	116.55 W
Tensift, Oued ≃	148	32.02 N	9.22 W
Ten Sleep	202	44.02 N	107.27 W
Tensta	40	60.02 N	17.40 E
Tente -●-[8]	263	51.18 N	7.14 E
Tenteksor ≍	80	47.18 N	53.24 E
Tentena	112	1.47 S	120.39 E
Tenterden	42	51.05 N	0.42 E
Tenterfield	166	29.03 S	152.01 E
Tent Hill	171a	27.36 S	152.14 E
Tenthill Creek ≃	171a	27.34 S	152.14 E
Ten Thousand Islands II	220	25.50 N	81.33 W
Tentolomatinan, Gunung ∧	112	0.56 N	121.48 E
Tentugal	250	1.19 S	46.59 W
Tentulia	272b	22.50 N	88.28 E
Teocaltiche	234	21.26 N	102.35 W
Teocelo	234	19.23 N	96.58 W
Teocuitatlán de Corona	234	20.07 N	103.24 W
Teodelina	252	34.11 S	61.32 W
Teófilo Cunha	287a	22.39 S	43.34 W
Teófilo Otoni	255	17.51 S	41.30 W
Teofipol'	78	49.50 N	26.25 E
Teohotepapa, Pointe >	174x	9.46 S	138.48 W
Teohotupa, Pointe >	174x	9.46 S	138.50 W
Teo Lakes ⊜	184	51.30 N	109.21 W
Teolo	64	45.21 N	11.40 E
Teomabal Island I	116	6.20 N	120.51 E
Teor	64	45.51 N	13.03 E
Teora	68	40.51 N	15.15 E
Teotihuacán ⊥	234	19.44 N	98.50 W
Teotitlán de Flores Magón	234	18.08 N	97.05 W
Teotitlán del Valle	234	17.02 N	96.30 W
Tepa, Ghana	150	7.00 N	2.10 W
Tepa, Indon.	164	7.52 S	129.31 E
Tepalcatepec	234	19.11 N	102.51 W
Tepalcingo	234	18.36 N	98.51 W
Tepa Point >	174v	19.07 S	169.56 W
Tepatitlán de Morelos	234	20.49 N	102.44 W
Tepatlaxco [de Hidalgo]	234	19.04 N	97.58 W
Tepe	130	37.48 N	40.47 E
Tepeaca	234	18.58 N	97.54 W
Tepeapulco	234	19.47 N	98.33 W
Tepebaşı	130	36.40 N	32.45 E
Tepechitlán	234	21.40 N	103.20 W
Tepeguaje	196	25.40 N	99.50 W
Tepeguajes	234	23.30 N	97.50 W
Tepehan	130	38.06 N	38.45 E
Tepehuanes	232	25.20 N	105.44 W
Tepehuanes ≃	232	25.10 N	105.25 W
Tepeji de Ocampo	234	19.54 N	99.21 W
Tepelenë	38	40.18 N	20.01 E
Tepelmeme de Morelos	234	17.51 N	97.21 W
Tepelská vrchovina ⋌[1]	60	50.00 N	13.00 E
Tepeören	130	41.04 N	35.30 E
Tepepan -●-[8]	286a	19.16 N	99.08 W
Tepe Saif	267d	35.36 N	51.18 E
Tepetiltic, Volcán ∧[1]	234	21.15 N	104.43 W
Tepetixtla	234	17.13 N	100.08 W
Tepetlixpa	234	19.02 N	98.49 W
Tepi	144	7.10 N	35.23 E
Tepic	234	21.30 N	104.54 W
Tepko	168b	34.58 S	139.11 E
Teplá	60	49.59 N	12.52 E
Teplá ≃	54	50.14 N	12.52 E
Teple ≃	83	48.47 N	39.19 E
Teplice	54	50.39 N	13.48 E
Teplitz → Teplice	54	50.39 N	13.48 E
Teplooz'orsk	89	49.00 N	131.48 E
Teplovka	80	51.33 N	51.33 E
Teplovo	80	55.25 N	42.56 E
Teplyk	78	48.40 N	29.44 E
Tepoca, Bahía c	232	30.15 N	112.50 W
Tepoca, Punta >	232	29.55 N	112.46 W
Te Pohue	172	39.15 S	176.41 E
Tepopa, Cabo >	232	29.22 N	112.27 W
Te Puia	172	38.04 S	178.18 E
Te Puke	172	37.47 S	176.20 E
Tepuxtepec, Presa ⊜[1]	234	20.02 N	100.13 W
Tepuzhuacán	234	20.53 N	104.33 W
Tequila	234	20.54 N	103.47 W
Tequisquita Slough ≃	226	36.58 N	121.27 W
Tequixquitla	234	19.19 N	97.40 W
Tequma	132	31.27 N	34.35 E
Ter ≃, Esp.	34	42.01 N	3.12 E
Ter ≃, Ityo.	144	7.20 N	42.11 E
Ter ≃, Eng., U.K.	42	51.50 N	0.36 E
Téra	150	14.01 N	0.45 E
Tera ≃	34	41.54 N	5.44 W
Teradomari	92	37.38 N	138.46 E
Terai	94	36.26 N	136.30 E
Teraina I	14	4.43 N	160.24 W
Ter'ajevo	82	56.11 N	36.07 E
Terakhāda	126	22.56 N	89.40 E
Teralba	170	32.58 S	151.37 E
Teramo	66	42.39 N	13.42 E
Teramo □[4]	66	42.39 N	13.41 E
Terán	234	16.45 N	93.10 W
Terang	169	38.14 S	142.55 E
Teranum	114	3.44 N	101.49 E
Ter Apel	52	52.53 N	7.04 E
Teraruma	164	8.00 S	141.50 E
Teras	114	3.45 N	101.49 E
Teratak	112	0.46 S	110.32 E
Terborg	52	51.55 N	6.21 E
Terbuny	76	52.08 N	38.17 E
Tercan	130	39.47 N	40.24 E
Terceira I	148a	38.43 N	24.13 W
Tercero ≃	252	32.55 S	62.19 W
Tercero de Febrero, Parque ♠	288	34.34 S	58.25 W
Terdal	122	16.30 N	75.03 E
Terdoppio, Torrente ≃	266b	45.23 N	8.50 E
Terebovlya	78	49.18 N	25.43 E
Terebuš	82	54.16 N	38.09 E
Terebutinec	76	59.01 N	33.39 E
Terechovka	76	52.13 N	31.27 E
Terechovo	82	55.50 N	35.45 E
Te Rehunga	172	40.13 S	176.01 E
Tereida	140	10.35 N	31.17 E
Terek, Kyrg.	85	40.01 N	73.33 E
Terek, Ross.	84	43.29 N	44.08 E
Terek ≃	84	43.44 N	46.33 E
Terekli-Mekteb	84	44.10 N	45.53 E
Terek-Saj	85	41.32 N	71.09 E
Terektinskij chrebet ⋌	86	50.30 N	86.00 E
Terekty	80	48.34 N	49.02 E
Terempa	112	3.14 N	106.14 E
Terence Bay	186	44.28 N	63.43 W
Teren'ga	80	53.42 N	48.24 E
Terengganu □[3]	114	5.00 N	103.00 E
Terengganu ≃	114	5.17 N	103.05 E
Terenino	76	54.31 N	33.35 E
Terenkuduk	80	48.24 N	47.11 E
Terenni ⊥	150	16.30 N	9.35 W
Terenos	255	20.26 S	54.50 W
Terensaj	86	51.36 N	59.31 E
Terenuzek	86	45.05 N	64.59 E
Teresina	250	5.05 S	42.49 W
Tereška ≃	80	51.48 N	46.26 E
Teresópolis	256	22.26 S	42.59 W
Terespol	30	52.05 N	23.36 E
Teresva	78	48.01 N	23.42 E
Terevaka, Cerro ∧	174z	27.05 S	109.23 W
Terezín	54	50.31 N	14.08 E
Tergauči	85	41.11 N	71.30 E
Tergnier	50	49.39 N	3.18 E
Tergun Daba Shan ⋌	102	38.25 N	95.55 E
Terhorne	52	53.02 N	5.46 E
Teriang	114	3.14 N	102.25 E
Teriang ≃	114	3.19 N	102.31 E
Teribe ≃	236	9.22 N	82.32 W
Terib'orka	24	69.08 N	35.08 E
Terihi I	174x	10.02 S	138.49 W
Terio	164	8.25 S	143.00 E
Terjärv (Teerijärvi)	26	63.32 N	23.30 E
Terlago	64	46.06 N	11.02 E
Terlano	64	46.32 N	11.15 E
Terlingua	196	29.19 N	103.37 W
Terlingua Creek ≃	196	29.10 N	103.36 W
Terlizzi	68	41.08 N	16.32 E
Termas de Río Hondo	252	27.29 S	64.52 W
Terme	130	41.12 N	36.59 E
Terme del Brennero (Brennerbad)	64	46.58 N	11.29 E
Terme di Stigliano	66	42.09 N	12.01 E
Terme di Suio	68	41.18 N	13.51 E
Terme di Valdieri	62	44.12 N	7.16 E
Termeno (Tramin)	64	46.20 N	11.14 E
Termez	72	37.14 N	67.16 E
Termignon	62	45.17 N	6.49 E
Terminal	258	34.09 S	57.31 W
Terminal Island I	280	33.45 N	118.15 W
Terminal Island Coast Guard Base ■	280	33.43 N	118.17 W
Termini Imerese	70	37.59 N	13.42 E
Termini Imerese, Golfo di c	70	38.01 N	13.45 E
Terminillo, Monte ∧	66	42.28 N	13.00 E
Términos, Laguna de c	232	18.37 N	91.33 W
Termit, Massif de ⋌	146	16.15 N	11.17 E
Termoli	66	42.00 N	15.00 E
Termonde → Dendermonde	50	51.02 N	4.07 E
Termsdorf	264a	52.16 N	13.07 E
Tern ≃	42	52.47 N	2.32 W
Ternate, Indon.	108	0.48 N	127.24 E
Ternate, Pil.	116	14.17 N	120.43 E
Ternberg	61	47.58 N	14.22 E
Ternej	89	45.03 N	136.37 E
Terneuzen	52	51.20 N	3.50 E
Terni	66	42.34 N	12.37 E
Terni □[4]	66	42.41 N	12.19 E
Ternitz	61	47.44 N	16.03 E
Ternivka, Ukr.	78	47.02 N	32.01 E
Ternivka, Ukr.	78	48.32 N	29.58 E
Ternoise ≃	50	50.23 N	2.01 E
Ternopil'	78	49.34 N	25.36 E
Ternopil' □[4]	78	49.30 N	25.30 E
Ternovka, Ross.	80	51.41 N	41.37 E
Ternovka, Ross.	89	53.09 N	45.02 E
Ternovka, Ross.	80	51.19 N	42.56 E
Ternovoje	89	45.11 N	133.45 E
Ternovskaja	78	45.53 N	40.42 E
Ternuvate	78	47.50 N	36.09 E
Terny, Ukr.	78	48.09 N	33.33 E
Terny, Ukr.	78	50.59 N	33.59 E
Terny, Ukr.	83	49.05 N	37.57 E
Terolak	114	3.53 N	101.23 E
Terong	114	4.43 N	100.44 E
Terontola	66	43.13 N	12.02 E
Terpe	54	51.32 N	14.19 E
Terpenija, mys >	89	48.39 N	144.44 E
Terpenija, zaliv c	89	49.00 N	143.30 E
Terra Alta	188	39.26 N	79.32 W
Terra Bella	204	35.58 N	119.03 W
Terrace	182	54.31 N	128.35 W
Terrace Bay	190	48.47 N	87.06 W
Terracina	66	41.17 N	13.15 E
Terra del Sole	66	44.11 N	11.57 E
Terral	196	33.53 N	97.56 W
Terralba	71	39.43 N	8.39 E
Terra Linda	226	38.01 N	122.32 W
Terranova → Newfoundland □[4]	176	52.00 N	56.00 W
Terra Nova Bay c	9	74.45 S	164.30 E
Terranova da Sibari	68	39.39 N	16.20 E
Terranova di Pollino	68	39.59 N	16.18 E
Terranova di Sicilia → Gela	70	37.04 N	14.15 E
Terra Nova Lake ⊜	186	48.30 N	54.20 W
Terra Nova National Park ♠	186	48.37 N	53.56 W
Terranuova Bracciolini	66	43.33 N	11.35 E
Terra Rica	255	22.43 S	52.38 W
Terrarossa, Foce di)(	64	44.12 N	10.26 E
Terra Roxa	252	24.08 S	53.59 W
Terras, Pinhal do -●-[3]	266c	38.39 N	9.02 W
Terra Santa	250	2.06 S	56.29 W
Terrasini	70	38.09 N	13.05 E
Terrassa	34	41.34 N	2.01 E
Terrasse-Vaudreuil	206	45.24 N	73.59 W
Terrasson-la-Villedieu	32	45.08 N	1.18 E
Terravecchia	68	39.29 N	16.58 E
Terrebonne	206	45.42 N	73.38 W
Terrebonne □[6]	206	46.00 N	74.10 W
Terrebonne Bay c	194	29.09 N	90.35 W
Terre Ceia	220	27.35 N	82.35 W
Terre-de-Bas	241o	15.51 N	61.39 W
Terre-de-Bas I	241o	15.52 N	61.38 W
Terre de Feu → Tierra del Fuego, Isla Grande de I	254	54.00 S	69.00 W
Terre-de-Haut	241o	15.58 N	61.35 W
Terre-de-Haut I	241o	15.52 N	61.35 W
Terre des Hommes ♠	275a	45.31 N	73.32 W
Terre Haute	194	39.28 N	87.24 W
Terre Hill	208	40.09 N	76.03 W
Terrell	222	32.44 N	96.16 W
Terrell, Lake ⊜	224	48.52 N	122.41 W
Terrell Hills	196	29.28 N	98.27 W
Terrenceville	186	47.40 N	54.44 W
Terre-Neuve → Newfoundland □[4]	176	52.00 N	56.00 W
Terre Noire Creek ≃	194	33.49 N	92.55 W
Terre Rouge Creek ≃	194	33.49 N	93.11 W
Terres australes et antarctiques françaises → French Southern and Antarctic □[2]	6	49.30 S	69.30 E
Terrey Hills	170	33.41 S	151.14 E
Terrigal	170	33.27 S	151.27 E
Terrington Saint Clement	42	52.45 N	0.18 E
Territoires du Nord-Ouest → Northwest Territories □[4]	176	70.00 N	100.00 W
Territorio Antártico Británico → British Antarctic Territory □[2]	9	60.00 S	45.00 W
Territorio Británico del Océano Índico → British Indian Ocean Territory □[2]	12	7.00 S	72.00 E
Territorios del Noroeste → Northwest Territories □[4]	176	70.00 N	100.00 W
Terror Point >	182	53.10 N	129.56 W
Terrugem	266c	38.51 N	9.20 W
Terry, Ms., U.S.	194	32.05 N	90.17 W
Terry, Mt., U.S.	198	46.47 N	105.18 W
Terry Peak ∧	198	44.19 N	103.50 W
Terryville, Ct., U.S.	207	41.40 N	73.00 W
Terryville, N.Y., U.S.	210	40.54 N	73.03 W
Tersa, Ross.	80	52.05 N	47.32 E
Tersa, Ross.	80	50.53 N	43.48 E
Tersa ≃	80	50.46 N	44.40 E
Tersakan Gölü ⊜	130	38.35 N	33.06 E
Tersakkan ≃	86	51.15 N	67.10 E
Terschelling I	52	53.24 N	5.20 E
Tersiva, Punta ∧	62	45.37 N	7.28 E
Terskej-Alatau, chrebet ⋌	85	41.55 N	77.00 E
Terskij chrebet ⋌	84	43.32 N	45.00 E
Terslev	41	55.22 N	11.59 E
Tersløse	41	55.31 N	11.30 E
Tertenia	71	39.42 N	9.34 E
Teru	123	36.11 N	72.45 E
Teruel, Col.	246	2.44 N	75.33 W
Teruel, Esp.	34	40.21 N	1.06 W
Teruel □[4]	34	40.35 N	0.45 W
Terujak	114	4.23 N	97.31 E
Tervakoski	26	60.48 N	24.37 E
Tervel	38	43.45 N	27.24 E
Tervola	26	66.05 N	24.48 E
Tervuren	56	50.49 N	4.31 E
Terwagne	56	50.27 N	5.20 E
Terwolde	52	52.16 N	6.06 E
Terzaghi Dam -●-[6]	182	50.49 N	122.12 W
Terzigno	68	40.48 N	14.29 E
Teržola	84	42.12 N	42.59 E
Tes	88	50.27 N	93.30 E
Teša	80	55.30 N	42.50 E
Tesalia	246	2.29 N	75.44 W
Tešanj	38	44.37 N	18.00 E
Tes-Chem (Tesijn) ≃	88	50.28 N	93.04 E
Teschendorf	54	52.51 N	13.10 E
Tescott	198	39.00 N	97.52 W
Tesechoacán ≃	234	18.31 N	95.42 W
Teseney	144	15.07 N	36.41 E
Tesero	64	46.17 N	11.31 E
Teshekpuk Lake ⊜	180	70.35 N	153.30 W
Teshikaga	92a	43.29 N	144.28 E
Te-shima I, Nihon	96	34.29 N	134.05 E
Te-shima I, Nihon	96	34.24 N	133.40 E
Teshio	92a	44.53 N	141.44 E
Teshio ≃	92a	44.53 N	141.44 E
Teshio-sanchi ⋌	92a	44.15 N	142.05 E
Tešig	88	49.56 N	102.34 E
Tesijn (Tes-Chem) ≃	88	50.28 N	93.04 E
Tesimo (Tisens)	64	46.34 N	11.10 E
Teslić	38	44.37 N	17.51 E
Teslin	180	60.09 N	132.45 W
Teslin ≃	180	61.34 N	134.54 W
Teslin Lake ⊜	180	60.15 N	132.57 W
Tesouras ≃	255	14.36 S	50.51 W
Tesouro	255	16.04 S	53.34 W
Tesperhude	54	53.24 N	10.26 E
Tessa, Oued ≃	36	[illegible]	8.54 E
Tessa-Araal, Oued V	148	26.18 N	1.58 E
Tessala, Djebel ∧	34	35.17 N	0.49 W
Tessala, Monts du ∧	34	35.25 N	0.45 W
Tessalit	150	20.12 N	1.00 E
Tessancourt-sur-Aubette	261	49.02 N	1.55 E
Tessaoua	150	13.45 N	7.59 E
Tessei	96	34.56 N	133.20 E
Tessenderlo	56	51.04 N	5.05 E
Tesserete	58	46.04 N	8.58 E
Tessin	54	54.01 N	12.28 E
Tessin → Ticino □[3]	58	46.20 N	8.45 E
Tessy-sur-Vire	32	48.58 N	1.04 W
Test ≃	42	50.55 N	1.29 W
Testa, Capo >	71	41.14 N	9.08 E
Teston, On., Can.	275b	43.52 N	79.32 W
Teston, Eng., U.K.	260	51.15 N	0.26 E
Testour	36	36.33 N	9.27 E
Tesuque	200	35.45 N	105.55 W
Têt ≃	32	42.44 N	3.02 E
Tetachuck Lake ⊜	182	53.20 N	125.50 W
Tetagouche ≃	186	47.38 N	65.41 W
Tetas, Punta >	252	23.31 S	70.38 W
Tetbury	42	51.39 N	2.10 W
Tete	154	16.13 S	33.35 E
Tete □[5]	154	15.15 S	32.40 E
Tété ≃	146	9.12 N	20.29 E
Tête-à-la-Baleine	186	50.41 N	59.20 W
Tête du Parmelan ∧	58	45.57 N	6.14 E
Tête-Jaune-Cache	182	52.57 N	119.26 W
Te Teko	172	38.02 S	176.48 E
Tetepare Island I	175e	8.43 S	157.33 E
Tétépisca, Lac ⊜	186	51.00 N	69.25 W
Teterboro	276	40.52 N	74.03 W
Teterboro Airport ⊠	276	40.51 N	74.04 W
Téterchen	56	49.14 N	6.34 E
Tetere ≃	88	59.30 N	105.00 E
Teteriv ≃	78	51.01 N	30.05 E
Teterow	54	53.46 N	12.34 E
Teteven	38	42.55 N	24.16 E
Tetiaroa I[1]	14	17.05 S	149.32 W
Tetica ∧	34	37.15 N	2.25 W
Tetiyiv	78	49.23 N	29.41 E
Tetla	234	19.26 N	98.06 W
Tetlin	180	63.08 N	142.31 W
Tetlin Lake ⊜	180	63.05 N	142.45 W
Teton	202	43.53 N	111.40 W
Teton ≃, Id., U.S.	202	43.54 N	111.51 W
Teton ≃, Mt., U.S.	202	47.56 N	110.31 W
Tetonia	202	43.49 N	111.09 W
Teton Range ⋌	202	43.45 N	110.50 W
Tétouan	148	35.34 N	5.23 W
Tétouan □[4]	148	35.30 N	5.30 W
Tetovo	38	42.01 N	20.58 E
Tétreauville -●-[8]	275a	45.36 N	73.32 W
Tetri-Ckaro	84	41.34 N	44.28 E
Tetschen → Děčín	54	50.48 N	14.13 E
Tetsuta	96	34.56 N	133.28 E
Tettau	54	50.28 N	11.15 E
Tettens	52	53.38 N	7.53 E
Tettnang	58	47.40 N	9.35 E
Tetuán → Tétouan	148	35.34 N	5.23 W
Tetufera, Mont ∧	174s	17.40 S	149.26 W
Tetulbāria	126	21.58 N	90.03 E
Tetulia ≃[1]	126	22.15 N	90.37 E
Teturi	154	1.04 N	29.08 E
Tet'uši	80	54.57 N	48.50 E
Tet'ušskoje	80	54.18 N	48.03 E
Teublitz	60	49.13 N	12.05 E
Teuchern	54	51.07 N	12.01 E
Teuco ≃	252	25.38 S	60.12 W
Teufelshöhle ⊥[5]	60	49.45 N	11.25 E
Teufels-Insel → Diable, Île du I	250	5.17 N	52.35 W
Teufelsmoor -●-[3]	52	53.15 N	8.50 E
Teufen	58	47.23 N	9.23 E
Teufenbach	61	47.08 N	14.21 E
Teuhtli, Volcán ∧[1]	286a	19.14 N	99.01 W
Teulada	71	38.58 N	8.46 E
Teulada, Capo >	71	38.52 N	8.38 E
Teúl de González Ortega	234	21.28 N	103.29 W
Teulon	184	50.23 N	97.16 W
Teun, Pulau I	164	6.59 S	129.08 E
Teunom ≃	114	4.26 N	95.48 E
Teunz	60	49.29 N	12.23 E
Teupitz	54	52.08 N	13.36 E
Teureubangan-cut	114	3.12 N	97.18 E
Teuri-tō I	92a	44.25 N	141.19 E
Teuschnitz	54	50.24 N	11.23 E
Teutleben	54	50.57 N	10.33 E
Teutoburger Wald -●-[3]	52	52.10 N	8.15 E
Teutopolis	194	39.07 N	88.28 W
Teutschenthal	54	51.27 N	11.46 E
Teuva	26	62.29 N	21.44 E
Tevere (Tiber) ≃	66	41.44 N	12.14 E
Teverya (Tiberias)	132	32.47 N	35.32 E
Teviot ≃	44	55.36 N	2.26 W
Teviot Brook ≃	171a	27.51 S	152.57 E
Teviotdale V	44	55.25 N	2.50 W
Teviothead	44	55.21 N	2.56 W
Tevli	76	52.20 N	24.15 E
Tevriz	86	57.34 N	72.24 E
Te Waewae Bay c	172	46.15 S	167.30 E
Tewah	112	1.05 S	113.42 E
Te Whaiti	172	38.35 S	176.47 E
Tewkesbury	42	51.59 N	2.09 W
Tewksbury	207	42.36 N	71.14 W
Tew-Mac Airport ⊠	283	42.36 N	71.12 W
Têwo	102	34.02 N	103.05 E
Texada Island I	182	49.40 N	124.24 W
Texana, Lake ⊜[1]	222	28.58 N	96.32 W
Texarkana, Ar., U.S.	194	33.26 N	94.02 W
Texarkana, Tx., U.S.	194	33.25 N	94.02 W
Texas, Austl.	166	28.51 S	151.11 E
Texas, Oh., U.S.	216	41.26 N	83.57 W
Texas □[3], U.S.	178	31.30 N	99.00 W
Texas □[3], U.S.	196	31.30 N	99.00 W
Texas City	222	29.23 N	94.54 W
Texcaltitlán	234	18.54 N	99.55 W
Texcoco, Lago de ⊜	234	19.30 N	99.00 W
Texel I	52	53.05 N	4.45 E
Texhoma	196	36.30 N	101.46 W
Texico	196	34.23 N	103.03 W
Texline	196	36.23 N	103.01 W
Texoma, Lake ⊜[1]	196	33.55 N	96.37 W
Teyateyaneng	158	29.07 S	27.34 E
Teyéa ⊥	38	37.29 N	22.24 E
Teylān	120	35.32 N	64.47 E
Teynham	42	51.20 N	0.50 E
Teywarah	120	33.21 N	64.25 E
Teza ≃	80	56.32 N	41.53 E
Teziutlán	234	19.49 N	97.21 W
Težler, gora ∧	84	40.42 N	44.37 E
Tezoatlán de Segura y Luna	234	17.42 N	97.49 W
Tezpur	120	26.37 N	92.48 E
Tezu	120	27.53 N	96.11 E
Tezzeron Lake ⊜	182	54.41 N	124.25 W
Tha ≃	110	20.07 N	100.36 E
Tha-anne ≃	176	60.31 N	94.37 W
Thabana-Ntlenyana ∧	158	29.28 S	29.16 E
Thaba Nchu	158	29.17 S	26.52 E
Thabankulu ∧	158	27.30 S	30.20 E
Thaba-Putsoa Range ⋌	158	29.45 S	27.55 E
Thabaung	110	17.02 N	94.48 E
Thabawleikkyi	110	12.01 N	99.12 E
Thabazimbi	156	24.41 S	27.21 E
Thabor, Mont ∧	62	45.07 N	6.34 E
Thabyu	110	15.36 N	98.29 E
Thacher Island I	207	42.38 N	70.35 W
Thādiq	128	25.18 N	45.52 E
Thagyettaw	110	13.45 N	98.09 E
Thai Binh	110	20.27 N	106.20 E
Thailand (Prathet Thai) □[1], Asia	108	15.00 N	100.00 E
Thailand (Prathet Thai) □[1], Asia	110	15.00 N	100.00 E
Thailand, Gulf of c	110	10.00 N	101.00 E
Thaïlande → Thailand □[1]	110	15.00 N	100.00 E
Thailandia → Thailand □[1]	110	15.00 N	100.00 E
Thai Muang	110	8.24 N	98.16 E
Thai Nguyen	110	21.36 N	105.50 E
Thak	120	30.32 N	70.13 E
Thakhek → Muang Khammouan	110	17.24 N	104.48 E
Thākurdwāra	124	29.12 N	78.51 E
Thākurdwāri	272b	22.34 N	88.28 E
Thākurgaon	124	26.02 N	88.28 E
Thākurpukur	272b	22.28 N	88.19 E
Thākurvādi	272c	18.54 N	73.04 E
Thal, Dtsch.	54	50.55 N	10.23 E
Thal, Pāk.	123	33.22 N	70.33 E
Tha'l, Jabal ∧	140	14.13 N	24.14 E
Thala	36	35.35 N	8.40 E
Thalang	110	8.01 N	98.19 E
Thal-Assling	64	46.47 N	12.38 E
Thalāthah	142	30.35 N	32.20 E
Thal Desert -●-[2]	123	31.30 N	71.40 E
Thale	54	51.45 N	11.02 E
Thalfang	56	49.45 N	6.59 E
Thalgau	64	47.50 N	13.15 E
Thalheim	54	50.42 N	12.51 E
Thalheim bei Wels	61	48.09 N	14.02 E
Tha Li	110	17.37 N	101.25 E
Thalia	196	33.59 N	99.32 W
Thālith, Ash-Shallāl ath- (Third Cataract) ∟	140	19.49 N	30.19 E
Thalitter	56	51.13 N	8.53 E
Thalkirch	58	46.38 N	9.16 E
Thallon	166	28.38 S	148.52 E
Thallwitz	54	51.26 N	12.40 E
Thalmah, Marsā c	142	29.03 N	32.38 E
Thalmässing	60	49.05 N	11.13 E
Thalwil	58	47.17 N	8.34 E
Thamar, Jabal ∧	144	13.53 N	45.12 E
Thame	42	51.45 N	0.59 W
Thames	172	37.08 S	175.33 E
Thames ≃, On., Can.	190	42.19 N	82.27 W
Thames ≃, Eng., U.K.	42	51.28 N	0.43 E
Thames ≃, Ct., U.S.	207	41.18 N	72.05 W
Thames, Firth of c	172	37.00 S	175.25 E
Thames Barrier -●-[6]	260	51.29 N	0.03 E
Thames Ditton	260	51.23 N	0.21 W
Thames Estuary c[1]	260	51.30 N	0.40 W
Thamesford	212	43.04 N	81.00 W
Thames Haven	260	51.30 N	0.31 E
Thamesville	214	42.33 N	81.59 W
Thāmit, Wādī V	146	31.15 N	16.06 E
Thammasat University ʊ[2]	269a	13.45 N	100.30 E
Thamūd, Bi'r ⊤[4]	144	17.17 N	49.56 E
Thāna, India	122	19.12 N	72.58 E
Thāna, Pāk.	128	28.55 N	63.45 E
Thāna Creek c	272c	19.00 N	72.57 E
Thāna Gāzi	124	27.25 N	76.19 E
Thāna Kasba	124	25.13 N	77.20 E
Thanbyuzayat	110	15.58 N	97.44 E
Thandaung	110	19.04 N	96.41 E
Thānedārwāla	123	32.36 N	71.07 E
Thānesar	124	29.59 N	76.49 E
Thanet, Isle of I	42	51.22 N	1.20 E
Thanet Lake ⊜	212	44.47 N	77.46 W
Thang Binh	110	15.44 N	108.22 E
Thangoo	162	18.10 S	122.22 E
Thangool	166	24.29 S	150.35 E
Thanh Hoa	110	19.48 N	105.46 E
Thanh My Tay	269c	10.49 N	106.46 E
Thanh Pho Ho Chi Minh (Saigon), Viet	110	10.45 N	106.40 E
Thanh Pho Ho Chi Minh (Saigon), Viet	269c	10.45 N	106.40 E
Thanjāvūr	122	10.48 N	79.09 E
Thann	58	47.49 N	7.05 E
Thannhausen	58	48.17 N	10.28 E
Thāno Bula Khān	120	25.22 N	67.50 E
Than Uyen	110	22.00 N	103.54 E
Thaoge ≃	156	20.27 S	22.36 E
Thaon-les-Vosges	58	48.15 N	6.25 E
Tha Pla	110	17.48 N	100.32 E
Thap Than ≃	110	15.21 N	104.06 E
Tharabwin West	110	12.17 N	99.03 E
Tharād	120	24.24 N	71.38 E
Tharandt	54	50.59 N	13.35 E
't Harde	52	52.25 N	5.53 E
Thar Desert (Great Indian Desert) -●-[2]	120	27.00 N	71.00 E
Thargomindah	166	28.00 S	143.49 E
Thāri Pātan ∧	124	28.58 N	82.04 E
Thar Nhom	140	7.26 N	30.29 E
Tharptown	210	40.48 N	76.34 W
Tharr, Wüste → Thar Desert -●-[2]	120	27.00 N	71.00 E
Tharrawaddy	110	17.39 N	95.48 E
Tharrawaw	110	17.41 N	95.28 E
Tharros ⊥	71	39.52 N	8.26 E
Tharsuinn, Beinn ∧	46	57.47 N	4.21 W
Tharthār, Buḥayrat ath- ⊜	128	34.00 N	43.05 E
Tharthār, Wādī ath- V	128	33.59 N	43.12 E
Tharwa	171b	35.31 S	149.04 E
Tha Sala	110	8.40 N	99.56 E
Thásos	38	40.47 N	24.42 E
Thásos I	38	40.41 N	24.47 E
Thásos ⊥	38	40.46 N	24.33 E
Tha Tako	110	15.38 N	100.29 E
Thatcham	42	51.25 N	1.15 W
Thatch Cay I	240m	18.22 N	64.52 W
Thatcher	200	32.50 N	109.45 W
Thatch Island I	276	40.38 N	73.23 W
That Khe	110	22.16 N	106.28 E
Thaton	110	16.55 N	97.22 E
That Phanom	110	16.57 N	104.44 E
Thatto Heath	262	53.26 N	2.45 W
Tha Tum	110	15.19 N	103.41 E
Thau, Bassin de c	32	43.23 N	3.36 E
Thaungdut	110	24.26 N	94.42 E
Thaungyin ≃	110	17.50 N	97.42 E
Tha Uthen	110	17.34 N	104.36 E
Thawville	216	40.41 N	88.07 W
Thaxted	42	51.57 N	0.20 E
Thaya (Dyje) ≃	61	48.37 N	16.56 E
Thayawthadangyi Kyun I	110	12.20 N	98.00 E
Thayer, Il., U.S.	219	39.32 N	89.46 W
Thayer, In., U.S.	216	41.10 N	87.20 W
Thayer, Ks., U.S.	198	37.29 N	95.28 W
Thayer, Mo., U.S.	194	36.31 N	91.32 W
Thayetchaung	110	13.52 N	98.16 E
Thayetmyo	110	19.19 N	95.11 E
Thayngen	58	47.45 N	8.42 E
Thazi	110	20.51 N	96.05 E
The Aldermen Islands II	172	36.58 S	176.05 E
Theale	42	51.27 N	1.04 W
Thealka	192	37.49 N	82.47 W
The Basin	274b	37.51 S	145.19 E
Thebes → Thívai, Ellás	38	38.21 N	23.19 E
Thebes, Il., U.S.	194	37.13 N	89.28 W
Thebes ⊥	140	25.42 N	32.37 E
The Birket ≃	262	53.24 N	3.01 W
The Bluffs ⊥[4]	210	43.22 N	76.40 W
The Bourne ≃	260	51.22 N	0.29 W
The Calvados Chain II	164	11.10 S	152.40 E
The Camels Hump ∧	169	37.23 S	144.35 E
The Capital ʊ	284c	38.53 N	77.00 W
The Cheviot ∧	44	55.28 N	2.09 W
The Citadel ⊥, Magy.	264c	47.29 N	19.03 E
The Citadel ⊥, Mişr	273c	30.02 N	31.15 E
The Cloisters ʊ	276	40.52 N	73.56 W
The Colony	222	33.05 N	96.52 W
The Coorong c	168b	35.40 S	139.15 E
The Coteau ∧[2]	184	51.10 N	107.30 W
The Curragh ♠	48	53.10 N	6.52 W

Symbols in the index entries represent the broad categories identified in the key at the right. Symbols with superior numbers (⋌[1]) identify subcategories (see complete key on page I · 1).

Symbole im Register stellen die rechts im Schlüssel erklärten Kategorien dar. Symbole mit hochgestellten Ziffern (⋌[1]) bezeichnen Unterabteilungen einer Kategorie (vgl. vollständiger Schlüssel auf Seite I · 1).

Los símbolos incluidos en el texto del índice representan las grandes categorías identificadas con la clave a la derecha. Los símbolos con numeros en su parte superior (⋌[1]) identifican las subcategorías (véase la clave completa en la página I · 1).

Les symboles de l'index représentent les catégories indiquées dans la légende à droite. Les symboles suivis d'un indice (⋌[1]) représentent des sous-catégories (voir légende complète à la page I · 1).

Os símbolos incluídos no texto do índice representam as grandes categorias identificadas com a chave à direita. Os símbolos com números em sua parte superior (⋌[1]) identificam as subcategorias (veja-se a chave completa à página I · 1).

English	Deutsch	Español	Français	Português
∧ Mountain	Berg	Montaña	Montagne	Montanha
⋌ Mountains	Gebirge	Montañas	Montagnes	Montanhas
)(Pass	Paß	Paso	Col	Passo
V Valley, Canyon	Tal, Cañon	Valle, Cañón	Vallée, Canyon	Vale, Canhão
≍ Plain	Ebene	Llano	Plaine	Planície
> Cape	Kap	Cabo	Cap	Cabo
I Island	Insel	Isla	Île	Ilha
II Islands	Inseln	Islas	Îles	Ilhas
⊥ Other Topographic Features	Andere Topographische Objekte	Otros Elementos Topográficos	Autres données topographiques	Outros acidentes topográficos

ESPAÑOL Nombre / FRANÇAIS Nom / PORTUGUÊS Nome	Página / Page / Página	Lat.°′	Long.°′ W = Oeste / W = Ouest
The Dalles	224	45.35 N	121.10 W
The Dalles Dam ◆[6]	224	45.37 N	121.08 W
The Deeps ⊂	46a	60.09 N	1.23 W
Thedford	198	41.58 N	100.34 W
Thedinghausen	52	52.58 N	9.01 E
The Downs ⊤[3]	42	51.13 N	1.27 E
Theebine	166	25.57 S	152.33 E
The English Companys Islands II	164	11.50 S	136.32 E
The Entrance	170	33.21 S	151.30 E
Theessen	54	52.14 N	12.02 E
The Fens ◆[1]	42	52.38 N	0.02 E
The Fishing Lakes ⊜	184	50.45 N	103.51 W
The Flash ⊜	262	53.29 N	2.33 W
The Flat Tops ⋏	200	40.00 N	107.10 W
The Forest of Nisene Marks State Park ♠	226	37.03 N	121.53 W
The Glenkens ◆[1]	44	55.10 N	4.15 W
Thègon	110	18.39 N	95.25 E
The Granites	162	20.35 S	130.21 E
The Granites ∧	162	20.35 S	130.20 E
The Graves II	283	42.22 N	70.52 W
The Grove	222	31.16 N	97.32 W
The Hague → 's-Gravenhage	52	52.06 N	4.18 E
The Heads >	202	42.44 N	124.31 W
The Hermitage ʊ	265a	59.56 N	30.20 E
The Home Park ♠	260	51.28 N	0.36 W
The Hunters Hills ⋏[2]	172	44.30 S	170.50 E
Theinkun	110	11.53 N	99.09 E
The Isles Lagoon ⊂	174o	1.50 N	157.23 W
Theiss → Tisa ≃	38	45.15 N	20.17 E
Theissen	54	51.05 N	12.06 E
The Key Indian Reserve ◆[4]	184	51.45 N	102.08 W
The Lake Fleet Islands II	212	44.18 N	76.07 W
The Lakes National Park ♠	166	38.05 S	147.40 E
The Little Minch ⋓	46	57.35 N	6.55 W
Thelon ≃	176	64.16 N	96.05 W
The Long Mynd ∧	42	52.35 N	2.48 W
The Lower Hope ≃[1]	260	51.28 N	0.28 E
Thelwall	262	53.23 N	2.32 W
The Lynd	166	18.56 S	144.30 E
Them	41	56.06 N	9.33 E
The Machars ◆[1]	44	54.50 N	4.33 W
The Mall in Columbia ◆[9]	284b	39.13 N	76.52 W
Themar	54	50.30 N	10.37 E
The Meadows Race Track ♠	279b	40.13 N	80.12 W
The Mere ⊜	262	53.20 N	2.24 W
Théméricourt	261	49.05 N	1.54 E
The Minch ⋓	46	58.10 N	5.50 W
The Mumbles	42	51.34 N	4.00 W
Then	123	32.26 N	75.44 E
The Narrows ⋓	276	40.37 N	74.03 W
The Navy Islands II	212	44.21 N	76.03 W
The Naze >	42	51.53 N	1.16 E
The Needles >	42	50.39 N	1.34 W
Thénezay	32	46.43 N	0.02 W
Thenia	148	36.43 N	3.34 E
Theniet el Hadd	148	35.47 N	2.01 E
The Oa >[1]	46	55.37 N	6.16 W
The Oaks, Austl.	170	34.04 S	150.34 E
The Oaks, Ca., U.S.	226	39.13 N	121.05 W
Theodore, Austl.	166	24.57 S	150.05 E
Theodore, Sk., Can.	184	51.25 N	102.54 W
Theodore, Al., U.S.	194	30.32 N	88.10 W
Theodore Francis Green Airport ⊠	207	41.44 N	71.26 W
Theodore Roosevelt Inaugural National Historic Site ⊥	284a	42.54 N	78.52 W
Theodore Roosevelt Island I	284c	38.54 N	77.03 W
Theodore Roosevelt Lake ⊜[1]	200	33.42 N	111.07 W
Theodore Roosevelt National Park (South Unit) ♠, N.D., U.S.	198	46.55 N	103.26 W
Theodore Roosevelt National Park (North Unit) ♠, N.D., U.S.	198	47.34 N	103.24 W
Theodor-Heuss-Brücke ◆[5]	263	51.15 N	6.45 E
Theog	123	31.07 N	77.21 E
Theólogos	38	40.39 N	24.41 E
The Orchards	284b	39.18 N	76.50 W
Théoule-sur-Mer	62	43.31 N	6.57 E
The Oval ⊥	260	51.29 N	0.07 W
The Pages II	168b	35.47 S	138.17 E
The Paps ∧	48	52.00 N	9.17 W
The Pas	184	53.50 N	101.15 W
The Peak ∧	192	36.24 N	81.39 W
Thepha	110	6.52 N	100.58 E
The Pinnacle ∧[2]	219	39.22 N	90.55 W
Thérain ≃	50	49.15 N	2.27 E
The Rajah ∧	182	53.15 N	118.31 W
The Rand → Witwatersrant ◆[1]	158	26.00 S	27.00 E
The Range	154	19.00 S	31.04 E
Theresa	212	44.12 N	75.47 W
Theresa Creek ≃	166	23.26 S	148.09 E
Theresa Park	274a	34.01 S	150.39 E
Theresienstadt → Terezín	54	50.31 N	14.08 E
The Rhins >[1]	44	54.50 N	5.00 W
The Rip ⊂	169	38.17 S	144.37 E
Thermaïkós Kólpos ⊂	38	40.23 N	22.47 E
Thermalito	226	39.31 N	121.36 W
Thermopílai (Thermopylae) ⊥	38	38.48 N	22.33 E
Thermopolis	200	43.38 N	108.12 W
Thermopylae → Thermopílai ⊥	38	38.48 N	22.33 E
The Road ⊂	42a	49.56 N	6.20 W
The Rock	166	35.16 S	147.07 E
The Rockies ∧	224	46.39 N	122.22 W
Theron Mountains ⋏	9	79.05 S	28.15 W
The Rope ⫫[4]	174e	25.04 S	130.05 W
Thérouanne	50	50.38 N	2.15 E
The Savannahs ⊜	220	27.19 N	80.17 W
Theseion ⊥	267c	37.58 N	23.43 E
Thesiger Bay ⊂	176	71.30 N	124.05 W
The Sisters ∧[2]	162	26.17 S	126.40 E
The Slot → New Georgia Sound ⋓	175e	8.00 S	158.10 E
The Sluice ≊	262	53.41 N	2.57 W
The Sny ≃	219	39.16 N	90.44 W
The Solent ⋓	42	50.46 N	1.20 W
The Sound (Øresund) ⋓	41	55.50 N	12.40 E
The Springs	207	40.52 N	72.32 W
Thesprotikón	38	39.15 N	20.47 E
Thessalía □[4]	38	39.30 N	22.30 E
Thessalía □[9]	38	39.30 N	22.15 E
Thessalon	190	46.15 N	83.34 W
Thessaloníki (Salonika)	38	40.38 N	22.56 E
Thessalonique → Thessaloníki	38	40.38 N	22.56 E
The Storr ∧	46	57.31 N	6.12 W
The Swale ⋓	42	51.22 N	0.56 E
Thet ≃	42	52.24 N	0.45 E
The Tauride Palace ʊ	265a	59.57 N	30.23 E
The Terraces ⫫[4]	162	28.40 S	121.30 E
Thetford	42	52.25 N	0.45 E
Thetford-Mines	206	46.05 N	71.18 W
The Thorofare ⋓	208	37.15 N	75.54 W
The Thumbs ∧	172	43.36 S	170.44 E
Thetis Island	224	49.59 N	123.40 W
Thetis Island I	224	49.00 N	123.41 W
The Twelve Pins ∧	48	53.31 N	9.50 W
The Twins ∧	172	41.14 S	172.39 E
Theunissen	158	28.30 S	26.41 E
Theux	56	50.32 N	5.49 E
The Valley	238	18.13 N	63.04 W
Thevenard	162	32.09 S	133.38 E
Thevenard Island I	162	21.27 S	115.00 E
The Wash ⊂	42	52.55 N	0.15 E
The Weald ◆[1]	42	51.05 N	0.05 E
The Whirlpool ≃	284a	43.07 N	79.04 W
The Winehead ∧	210	40.58 N	77.28 W
The Wolds ⋏[2]	44	53.20 N	0.10 W
The Woodlands	222	30.09 N	95.27 W
The Wrekin ∧[2]	42	52.41 N	2.34 W
Theydon Bois	260	51.40 N	0.06 E
Theys	62	45.18 N	6.00 E
Thiais	261	48.46 N	2.23 E
Thiant	50	50.18 N	3.27 E
Thiaucourt-Regniéville	56	48.57 N	5.52 E
Thibaudeau	184	57.05 N	94.08 W
Thiberville	50	49.08 N	0.27 E
Thibodaux	194	29.47 N	90.49 W
Thicket	222	30.24 N	94.38 W
Thicket Portage	184	55.19 N	97.42 W
Thiéblemont-Farémont	58	48.41 N	4.44 E
Thief ≃	198	48.08 N	96.10 W
Thief Lake ⊜	198	48.30 N	95.55 W
Thief River Falls	198	48.07 N	96.10 W
Thiéle ≃	58	47.03 N	7.05 E
Thiel Mountains ⋏	9	85.15 S	91.00 W
Thielsen, Mount ∧	202	43.09 N	122.04 W
Thiendorf	54	51.17 N	13.44 E
Thiene	64	45.42 N	11.29 E
Thiensville	216	43.14 N	87.58 W
Thiérache, Collines de la ⋏[2]	50	49.50 N	3.50 E
Thierhaupten	56	48.34 N	10.54 E
Thiers	62	45.51 N	3.34 E
Thiersheim	54	50.04 N	12.07 E
Thierville-sur-Meuse	56	49.10 N	5.21 E
Thiès	150	14.48 N	16.56 W
Thiès □[4]	150	14.45 N	16.50 W
Thiesi	71	40.31 N	8.43 E
Thiessow	54	54.16 N	13.43 E
Thieux	261	49.01 N	2.40 E
Thieveley Pike ∧[2]	262	53.45 N	2.12 W
Thika	154	1.03 S	37.05 E
Thikombia Island I	175g	15.44 S	179.55 W
Thilay	56	49.52 N	4.49 E
Thilenius, Cape >	164	1.35 S	149.57 E
Thimphu	124	27.28 N	89.39 E
Thines	62	44.29 N	4.03 E
Thingvallavatn ⊜	24a	64.12 N	21.10 W
Thingvellir	24a	64.17 N	21.07 W
Thingvellir National Park ♠	24a	64.17 N	21.06 W
Thio	175f	21.37 S	166.14 E
Thionville	56	49.22 N	6.10 E
Thiou	150	13.48 N	2.40 W
Thíra	38	36.25 N	25.26 E
Thíra (Santorini) I	38	36.24 N	25.29 E
Third ≃	276	40.49 N	74.08 W
Third Cataract → Thālith, Ash-Shallāl ath- ∟	140	19.49 N	30.19 E
Third Cliff ⫫[4]	283	42.11 N	70.43 W
Third Creek ≃, Mo., U.S.	219	38.26 N	91.40 W
Third Creek ≃, N.C., U.S.	192	35.47 N	80.31 W
Third Han-gang Bridge ◆[5]	271b	37.32 N	127.00 E
Third Herring Brook ≃	283	42.07 N	70.48 W
Third Lake ⊜	206	45.14 N	71.12 W
Third Street Station ◆[5]	282	37.46 N	122.23 W
Thirlmere	170	34.12 S	150.34 E
Thirlmere ⊜	44	54.33 N	3.04 W
Thirlmere Lakes National Park ♠	170	34.14 S	150.32 E
Thiron	50	48.19 N	0.59 E
Thironne ≃	50	48.17 N	1.15 E
Thirroul	170	34.19 S	150.56 E
Thirsk	44	54.14 N	1.20 W
Thirtieth Street Station ◆[5]	285	39.57 N	75.11 W
Thirtymile Creek ≃	198	46.22 N	102.03 W
Thirtymile Point >	210	43.22 N	78.29 W
Thiruvārūr	122	10.46 N	79.39 E
Thisted	26	56.57 N	8.42 E
Thistilfjörður ⊂	24a	66.20 N	15.25 W
Thistledown Race Track ♠	279a	41.26 N	81.32 W
Thistle Island I	166	35.00 S	136.09 E
Thistletown ◆[8]	275b	43.44 N	79.33 W
Thithia Island I	175g	17.45 S	179.18 W
Thívai (Thebes)	38	38.21 N	23.19 E
Thiverval-Grignon	261	48.51 N	1.55 E
Thiviers	32	45.25 N	0.56 E
Thizy	32	46.02 N	4.19 E
Thjórsá ≃	24a	63.47 N	20.48 W
Thlewiaza ≃	176	60.28 N	94.45 W
Thoa ≃	176	60.30 N	109.47 W
Tho Chu, Dao II	110	9.20 N	103.28 E
Thoen	110	17.36 N	99.12 E
Thohoyandou	156	23.00 S	30.29 E
Thoi Binh	110	9.21 N	105.05 E
Thoirette	58	46.16 N	5.32 E
Thoiry	261	48.52 N	1.48 E
Thoissey	58	46.10 N	4.48 E
Tholen	52	51.32 N	4.12 E
Tholen I	52	51.35 N	4.05 E
Tholey	56	49.29 N	7.02 E
Thollon	58	46.23 N	6.43 E
Thomas, Ok., U.S.	196	35.44 N	98.44 W
Thomas, Pa., U.S.	279b	40.15 N	80.06 W
Thomas, Wa., U.S.	224	47.21 N	122.13 W
Thomas, W.V., U.S.	188	39.08 N	79.29 W
Thomasboro	216	40.15 N	88.11 W
Thomas Creek ≃	202	44.40 N	122.56 W
Thomas Hill Reservoir ⊜[1]	194	39.40 N	92.40 W
Thomas J. O'Brien Lock and Dam ◆[5]	278	41.39 N	87.35 W
Thomas Lake ⊜	184	57.00 N	96.43 W
Thomas Mountains ⋏	9	75.32 S	70.57 W
Thomas Point >	208	38.54 N	76.28 W
Thomaston, Al., U.S.	194	32.15 N	87.37 W
Thomaston, Ct., U.S.	207	41.40 N	73.04 W
Thomaston, Ga., U.S.	192	32.53 N	84.19 W
Thomaston, Me., U.S.	188	44.04 N	69.10 W
Thomaston, N.Y., U.S.	276	40.47 N	73.43 W
Thomaston, Tx., U.S.	222	29.00 N	97.09 W
Thomastown, Austl.	274b	37.41 S	145.01 E
Thomastown, Ire.	48	52.31 N	7.08 W
Thomasville, Al., U.S.	194	31.54 N	87.44 W
Thomasville, Ga., U.S.	192	30.50 N	83.58 W
Thomasville, N.C., U.S.	192	35.52 N	80.04 W
Thomasville, Pa., U.S.	208	39.56 N	76.51 W
Thomes Creek ≃	204	39.59 N	122.06 W
Thom Lake ⊜	184	55.24 N	96.08 W
Thomlinson, Mount ∧	182	55.33 N	127.29 W
Thompson, Mb., Can.	184	55.45 N	97.45 W
Thompson, Ct., U.S.	207	41.57 N	71.51 W
Thompson, Ia., U.S.	190	43.22 N	93.46 W
Thompson, Mo., U.S.	219	39.11 N	91.59 W
Thompson, N.D., U.S.	198	47.46 N	97.06 W
Thompson, Oh., U.S.	214	41.41 N	81.03 W
Thompson, Pa., U.S.	210	41.52 N	75.31 W
Thompson ≃, B.C., Can.	182	50.15 N	121.33 W
Thompson ≃, U.S.	194	39.45 N	93.36 W
Thompson Creek ≃, U.S.	198	45.04 N	104.25 W
Thompson Creek ≃, Ms., U.S.	194	31.10 N	88.54 W
Thompson Falls	202	47.35 N	115.20 W
Thompson Island I	283	42.23 N	71.01 W
Thompson Pass)(	180	61.08 N	145.45 W
Thompson Peak ∧	204	41.00 N	123.03 W
Thompson Place	224	47.03 N	122.45 W
Thompson Ridge	210	41.34 N	74.20 W
Thompson Run ≃	279b	40.24 N	79.50 W
Thompsons	222	29.30 N	95.36 W
Thompsons Creek ≃	284a	43.03 N	79.08 W
Thompson Sound ⋓	172	45.09 S	166.57 E
Thompsontown	208	40.33 N	77.14 W
Thompsonville	190	44.31 N	85.56 W
Thomsen ≃	176	74.08 N	119.35 W
Thomson, Ga., U.S.	192	33.28 N	82.30 W
Thomson, Il., U.S.	190	41.58 N	90.06 W
Thomson, N.Y., U.S.	210	43.07 N	73.35 W
Thomson ≃, Austl.	166	25.11 S	142.53 E
Thomson ≃, Austl.	169	37.58 S	146.32 E
Thomson, Lake ⊜[1]	169	37.45 S	146.22 E
Thomson Lake ⊜[1]	184	49.45 N	106.35 W
Thon ≃	50	49.53 N	3.55 E
Thon Buri	110	13.43 N	100.29 E
Thônes	62	45.53 N	6.20 E
Thong	260	51.24 N	0.24 E
Thong Hoe	271c	1.25 N	103.42 E
Thong Tay Hoi	269c	10.50 N	106.39 E
Thongwa	110	16.46 N	96.32 E
Thon Lac Nghiep	110	11.20 N	108.54 E
Thonnance-lès-Joinville	58	48.27 N	5.10 E
Thonon-les-Bains	58	46.22 N	6.29 E
Thonotosassa	220	28.03 N	82.18 W
Thonze	110	17.38 N	95.47 E
Thorah Island I	212	44.27 N	79.14 W
Thorame-Haute	62	44.06 N	6.33 E
Thorburn	186	45.34 N	62.33 W
Thoreau	200	35.24 N	108.13 W
Thorembais-les-Béguines	56	50.40 N	4.49 E
Thorenc	62	43.48 N	6.49 E
Thorens-Glières	58	45.59 N	6.15 E
Thorhild	182	54.10 N	113.07 W
Thorial	140	8.40 N	29.56 E
Thorigny-sur-Marne	261	48.53 N	2.42 E
Thorigny-sur-Oreuse	50	48.17 N	3.24 E
Thórisvatn ⊜	24a	64.16 N	18.54 W
Thörl	61	47.31 N	15.13 E
Thorlákshöfn	24a	63.53 N	21.18 W
Thormanby	44	54.10 N	1.14 W
Thorn, Ned.	52	51.10 N	5.50 E
Thorn → Toruń, Pol.	30	53.02 N	18.35 E
Thornaby-on-Tees	44	54.34 N	1.18 W
Thornapple ≃, Mi., U.S.	216	42.56 N	85.28 W
Thornapple ≃, Wi., U.S.	190	45.28 N	91.16 W
Thornapple Lake ⊜	216	42.37 N	85.11 W
Thornburg	279b	40.26 N	80.05 W
Thornbury, Austl.	274b	37.45 S	145.00 E
Thornbury, On., Can.	212	44.34 N	80.26 W
Thornbury, N.Z.	172	46.17 S	168.06 E
Thornbury, Eng., U.K.	42	51.37 N	2.32 W
Thorn Creek ≃	278	41.36 N	87.35 W
Thorndale, On., Can.	212	43.06 N	81.08 W
Thorndale, Tx., U.S.	222	30.36 N	97.12 W
Thorndike	207	42.11 N	72.20 W
Thorndon	42	52.17 N	1.08 E
Thorne	44	53.37 N	0.58 W
Thorne ≃	184	54.56 N	90.35 W
Thorne Bay	182	55.44 N	132.32 W
Thorney	42	52.37 N	0.07 W
Thorngumbald	44	53.43 N	0.10 W
Thornhill, On., Can.	275b	43.48 N	79.25 W
Thornhill, S. Afr.	273d	26.07 S	28.09 E
Thornhill, Scot., U.K.	44	55.15 N	3.46 W
Thornhurst	210	41.11 N	75.35 W
Thornleigh	274a	33.44 S	151.05 E
Thornton, Austl.	171a	27.49 S	152.23 E
Thornton, Eng., U.K.	44	53.53 N	3.02 W
Thornton, Eng., U.K.	262	53.30 N	3.00 W
Thornton, Eng., U.K.	262	53.47 N	1.51 W
Thornton, Scot., U.K.	46	56.10 N	3.09 W
Thornton, Ar., U.S.	194	33.46 N	92.29 W
Thornton, Ca., U.S.	226	38.14 N	121.25 W
Thornton, Co., U.S.	200	39.52 N	104.58 W
Thornton, Il., U.S.	278	41.35 N	87.37 W
Thornton, Pa., U.S.	285	39.54 N	75.32 W
Thornton, Tx., U.S.	222	31.24 N	96.34 W
Thornton Beach ♠	282	37.42 N	122.30 W
Thornton Dale	44	54.14 N	0.43 W
Thornton Hough	262	53.19 N	3.03 W
Thornton-le-Moors	262	53.16 N	2.50 W
Thornton Moor Reservoir ⊜[1]	262	53.47 N	1.55 W
Thorntonville	196	31.34 N	102.55 W
Thornwood	210	41.07 N	73.46 W
Thornwood Common	260	51.43 N	0.08 E
Thorny Mountain ∧[2]	194	37.06 N	91.10 W
Thorofare	285	39.50 N	75.11 W
Thorold	212	43.07 N	79.12 W
Thorold South	284a	43.06 N	79.12 W
Thoronet, Abbaye du ʊ[1]	62	43.28 N	6.16 E
Thorp, Wa., U.S.	224	47.04 N	120.40 W
Thorp, Wi., U.S.	190	44.57 N	90.47 W
Thorpe	260	51.24 N	0.32 W
Thorpe-le-Soken	42	51.52 N	1.10 E
Thorp Spring	222	32.28 N	97.49 W
Thorsby, Ab., Can.	182	53.14 N	114.03 W
Thorsby, Al., U.S.	194	32.54 N	86.42 W
Thorshavn → Tórshavn	22	62.01 N	6.46 W
Thórshöfn	24a	66.13 N	15.17 W
Thorsø	41	56.18 N	9.48 E
Thorsteinson Lake ⊜	184	57.15 N	97.30 W
Thot Not	110	10.16 N	105.32 E
Thouars	32	46.59 N	0.13 W
Thouin, Cape >	162	20.20 S	118.12 E
Thoune → Thun	58	46.45 N	7.37 E
Thourotte	50	49.29 N	2.53 E
Thousand Islands II	212	44.15 N	76.12 W
Thousand Islands International Bridge ◆[5]	212	44.20 N	75.58 W
Thousand Lake Mountain ∧	200	38.25 N	111.29 W
Thousand Oaks	228	34.10 N	118.50 W
Thousand Ships Bay ⊂	175e	8.25 S	159.40 E
Thousand Springs Creek ≃	200	41.17 N	113.51 W
Thowa ≃	154	1.33 S	40.03 E
Thowgla Creek ≃	171b	36.10 S	147.57 E
Thrace □[9]	38	41.20 N	26.45 E
Thrakikón Pélagos ⊤[2]	38	40.15 N	24.28 E
Thrall	222	30.35 N	97.18 W
Thrapston	42	52.24 N	0.32 W
Thrasher Lake ⊜	212	44.55 N	78.58 W
Thread Creek ≃	216	43.01 N	83.42 W
Thredbo Village	171b	36.29 S	148.19 E
Three Bridges	208	40.31 N	74.47 W
Three Brothers ∧	224	47.23 N	120.45 W
Three Brothers Mountain ∧	224	49.10 N	120.46 W
Three Creek ≃	208	36.47 N	77.10 W
Three Fathoms Cove ⊂	271d	22.26 N	114.17 E
Three Fingered Jack ∧	202	44.29 N	121.50 W
Three Fingers ∧	224	48.10 N	121.41 W
Three Fools Creek ≃	224	48.53 N	120.57 W
Three Forks	202	45.53 N	111.33 W
Three Hills	182	51.42 N	113.16 W
Three Hummock Island I	166	40.26 S	144.55 E
Three Kings Islands II	172	34.10 S	172.05 E
Three Lakes	190	45.47 N	89.09 W
Three M Airport ⊠	285	40.08 N	74.51 W
Three Mile Bay	212	44.04 N	76.11 W
Three Mile Plains	186	44.58 N	64.07 W
Three Oaks	216	41.47 N	86.36 W
Three Pagodas Pass)(	110	15.18 N	98.23 E
Threepoint Lake ⊜	184	55.41 N	98.56 W
Three Points, Cape >	150	4.45 N	2.06 W
Three Rivers, Austl.	162	25.07 S	119.09 E
Three Rivers → Trois-Rivières, P.Q., Can.	206	46.21 N	72.33 W
Three Rivers, Ma., U.S.	207	42.10 N	72.21 W
Three Rivers, Mi., U.S.	216	41.56 N	85.37 W
Three Rivers, Tx., U.S.	196	28.27 N	98.10 W
Three Rivers □[8]	260	51.40 N	0.27 W
Three Sisters	158	31.54 S	23.06 E
Three Sisters ∧	202	44.10 N	121.46 W
Three Sisters Islands II	175e	10.10 S	161.57 E
Three Springs, Austl.	162	29.32 S	115.45 E
Three Springs, Pa., U.S.	214	40.12 N	77.59 W
Threlkeld	44	54.38 N	3.03 W
Throat ≃	184	51.48 N	93.30 W
Throckmorton	196	33.10 N	99.10 W
Throgs Neck ◆[8]	276	40.49 N	73.49 W
Throgs Neck Bridge ◆[5]	276	40.48 N	73.48 W
Throgs Point >	276	40.48 N	73.48 W
Throop	210	41.27 N	75.36 W
Throssel, Lake ⊜	162	27.27 S	124.16 E
Throssell Range ⋏	162	22.03 S	121.43 E
Thrushel ≃	42	50.39 N	4.15 W
Thruway Mall ◆[9]	284a	42.55 N	78.46 W
Thu, Cu Lao I	110	10.33 N	108.57 E
Thuan Chau	110	21.26 N	103.41 E
Thu Dau Mot	110	10.58 N	106.39 E
Thu Duc	269c	10.51 N	106.45 E
Thueyts	62	44.41 N	4.13 E
Thuilley-aux-Groseilles	58	48.34 N	5.58 E
Thuin	50	50.20 N	4.17 E
Thul	120	28.14 N	68.46 E
Thulaythiwāt, Tilāl ath- ∧	132	30.58 N	36.40 E
Thulba ≃	56	50.11 N	9.52 E
Thule	16	76.34 N	68.47 W
Thulī Bherī ≃	124	28.42 N	82.16 E
Thum	54	50.40 N	12.57 E
Thumb Peak ∧	116	9.48 N	118.36 E
Thumby	41	54.35 N	9.54 E
Thun	58	46.45 N	7.37 E
Thun Chang	110	19.25 N	100.53 E
Thunder Bay	190	48.23 N	89.15 W
Thunder Bay ⊂, On., Can.	190	48.24 N	89.00 W
Thunder Bay ⊂, On., Can.	212	44.48 N	80.03 W
Thunder Bay ⊂, Mi., U.S.	190	45.00 N	83.22 W
Thunder Bay ≃	190	45.04 N	83.25 W
Thunder Bay, North Branch ≃	190	45.08 N	83.35 W
Thunderbird, Lake ⊜[1]	196	35.15 N	97.20 W
Thunderbolt	192	32.02 N	81.03 W
Thunder Butte ∧	198	45.19 N	101.53 W
Thunder Butte Creek ≃	198	45.13 N	101.42 W
Thunder Creek ≃, Sk., Can.	184	50.23 N	105.32 W
Thunder Creek ≃, Wa., U.S.	224	48.40 N	121.05 W
Thunder Hills ⋏[2]	184	54.30 N	106.00 W
Thunder Mountain ∧[2]	216	42.16 N	86.20 W
Thundersley	260	51.34 N	0.35 E
Thunersee ⊜	58	46.40 N	7.45 E
Thüngen	56	49.56 N	9.51 E
Thung Song	110	8.09 N	99.41 E
Thung Wa	110	7.06 N	99.46 E
Thur ≃, Fr.	58	48.05 N	7.23 E
Thur ≃, Schw.	58	47.36 N	8.35 E
Thurcroft	44	53.24 N	1.16 W
Thurgau □[3]	58	47.35 N	9.00 E
Thurgovie → Thurgau □[3]	58	47.35 N	9.00 E
Thüringen	58	47.12 N	9.45 E
Thüringen □[3]	30	51.00 N	11.00 E
Thüringer Wald ⋏	30	50.40 N	10.50 E
Thürkow	54	53.50 N	12.33 E
Thurles	48	52.41 N	7.49 W
Thurmont	208	39.37 N	77.24 W
Thurn, Pass)(	64	47.19 N	12.24 E
Thurnau	60	50.01 N	11.23 E
Thurnham	260	51.17 N	0.36 E
Thurnscoe	44	53.31 N	1.19 W
Thurnwald Range ⋏	164	4.45 S	141.15 E
Thurø	41	55.03 N	10.40 E
Thurrock □[8]	260	51.30 N	0.21 E
Thursby	44	54.51 N	3.03 W
Thursday Island	164	10.35 S	142.13 E
Thurso, P.Q., Can.	206	45.36 N	75.15 W
Thurso, Scot., U.K.	46	58.35 N	3.32 W
Thurso ≃	46	58.36 N	3.30 W
Thurstaston	262	53.21 N	3.08 W
Thurston	42	52.15 N	0.49 E
Thurston □[6]	224	46.59 N	122.42 W
Thurston Island I	9	72.20 S	99.00 W
Thusis	58	46.42 N	9.26 E
Thwaites Iceberg Tongue ⍓	9	74.45 S	106.30 W
Thy ◆[1]	26	57.00 N	8.30 E
Thyborøn	26	56.42 N	8.13 E
Thylungra	166	26.04 S	143.28 E
Thyolo	154	16.10 S	35.10 E
Thyregod	41	55.54 N	9.16 E
Thysville → Mbanza-Ngungu	152	5.15 S	14.52 E
Tiadiaye	150	14.25 N	16.42 W
Tía Juana	246	10.16 N	71.22 W
Tian ≃	105	40.42 N	116.33 E
Tiana, Esp.	266d	44.29 N	2.16 E
Tiana, It.	71	40.04 N	9.08 E
Tian'anmen Square ⊥	271a	39.55 N	116.23 E
Tianbao	100	24.36 N	117.35 E
Tianchang	100	32.41 N	119.01 E
Tiancunpu	105	39.06 N	115.41 E
Tiandeng	102	23.09 N	107.10 E
Tiandong	102	23.36 N	107.08 E
Tian'e	102	25.01 N	107.20 E
Tianeti	84	42.07 N	44.59 E
Tianfanjie	100	29.20 N	116.50 E
Tiangang, Zhg.	89	43.24 N	125.54 E
Tiangang, Zhg.	89	43.55 N	127.00 E
Tiangongsi	105	39.14 N	115.53 E
Tianguá	250	3.44 S	40.59 W
Tianhe	100	27.01 N	114.30 E
Tianhekou	100	32.08 N	113.25 E
Tianhelong	89	43.56 N	120.39 E
Tianhuang	98	35.29 N	117.18 E
Tianjara, Mount ∧	170	35.11 S	150.18 E
Tianjia, Zhg.	104	41.07 N	122.03 E
Tianjia, Zhg.	107	29.40 N	105.08 E
Tianjiaba	102	32.08 N	110.03 E
Tianjiatun	104	41.39 N	123.44 E
Tianjiawopu	104	42.28 N	122.38 E
Tianjiazhen	100	29.56 N	115.26 E
Tianjin (Tientsin)	105	39.08 N	117.12 E
Tianjing	106	31.27 N	120.46 E
Tianjin Shi (Tientsin Shih) □[7]	98	39.30 N	117.15 E
Tianjun	102	37.25 N	98.58 E
Tiankai	105	39.38 N	115.51 E
Tiankoura	150	10.46 N	3.16 W
Tiankoye	150	12.35 N	12.40 W
Tianlin, Zhg.	102	24.14 N	106.03 E
Tianlin, Zhg.	107	29.49 N	105.19 E
Tian Ling ∧	89	44.22 N	129.52 E
Tianmashan	106	31.04 N	121.08 E
Tianmen	100	30.39 N	113.06 E
Tianmu Shan ⋏	100	30.25 N	119.30 E
Tianpu	106	31.56 N	121.07 E
Tianqiaochang	104	40.52 N	121.02 E
Tianqiaoling	89	43.26 N	129.38 E
Tianquan	102	30.10 N	102.48 E
Tian Shan → Tien Shan ⋏	90	42.00 N	80.00 E
Tianshenggang	106	32.03 N	120.45 E
Tianshifu	98	41.17 N	124.21 E
Tianshui	102	34.30 N	105.58 E
Tianshuijing, Zhg.	102	40.17 N	95.21 E
Tianshuijing, Zhg.	104	41.19 N	121.48 E
Tianshuituo	105	39.20 N	118.12 E
Tianshuizhan	104	41.00 N	123.34 E
Tiantai	100	29.09 N	121.02 E
Tiantang	102	22.32 N	111.55 E
Tiantou, Zhg.	100	28.48 N	120.39 E
Tiantou, Zhg.	100	26.19 N	115.57 E
Tianwangsi	106	31.45 N	119.12 E
Tianxin, Zhg.	100	27.53 N	113.06 E
Tianxin, Zhg.	100	28.11 N	114.35 E
Tianxin, Zhg.	102	27.21 N	111.00 E
Tianxingqiao	106	32.05 N	119.57 E
Tianxiyang	100	26.31 N	118.33 E
Tianyang	102	23.51 N	106.34 E
Tianyangping	107	29.11 N	105.16 E
Tianyar	115b	8.12 S	115.30 E
Tianzhen	98	40.28 N	114.06 E
Tianzhongying	100	33.13 N	115.22 E
Tianzhu, Zhg.	102	37.14 N	102.59 E
Tianzhu, Zhg.	102	26.50 N	109.00 E
Tianzhuang, Zhg.	100	25.43 N	113.40 E
Tianzhuang, Zhg.	105	39.25 N	117.54 E
Tianzhuangtai	104	40.50 N	122.08 E
Tiao ≃	106	30.56 N	120.11 E
Tiaodengchang	107	30.47 N	106.22 E
Tiarel	174s	17.32 S	149.20 W
Tiarno	64	45.53 N	10.40 E
Tiaro	166	25.44 S	152.35 E
Tiassalé	150	5.54 N	4.50 W
Tiati ∧	154	1.19 N	35.56 E
Ti'avea	175a	13.57 S	171.24 W
Tiawichi Creek ≃	222	32.19 N	94.44 W
Tiba → Chiba	94	35.36 N	140.07 E
Tibaji	252	24.30 S	50.24 W
Tibaji ≃	252	22.47 S	51.01 W
Tibari	154	5.01 N	31.43 E
Tibasti, Sarīr ◆[2]	146	24.00 N	17.00 E
Tibati	152	6.27 N	12.38 E
Tibbermore	46	56.22 N	3.32 W
Tibbie	194	31.21 N	88.14 W
Tibe	144	9.03 N	37.08 E
Tibel'ti	88	51.46 N	103.11 E
Tiber → Tevere ≃	66	41.44 N	12.14 E
Tiberias → Teverya	132	32.47 N	35.32 E
Tiberias, Lake → Kinneret, Yam ⊜	132	32.48 N	35.35 E
Tiberina, Val V	66	43.31 N	12.10 E
Tibesti ⋏	146	21.30 N	17.30 E
Tibet → Xizang Zizhiqu □[4]	90	32.00 N	88.00 E
Tibet, Lake ⊜	220	28.27 N	81.31 W
Tibet, Plateau of → Qing Zang Gaoyuan ⋏[1]	12	33.00 N	92.00 E
Tibiao	116	11.17 N	122.02 E
Tibiao Point >	116	11.18 N	122.02 E
Tibidabo ∧	266d	41.25 N	2.07 E
Tibiri, Niger	150	13.34 N	7.04 E
Tibiri, Niger	150	13.06 N	4.00 E
Tibirke	41	56.03 N	12.07 E
Tiblawan	116	6.29 N	126.06 E
Tiblemont, Lac ⊜	190	48.14 N	77.18 W
Tibnah	132	32.59 N	36.13 E
Tibnīn	132	33.12 N	35.25 E
Tibooburra	166	29.26 S	142.01 E
Tibro	26	58.26 N	14.10 E
Tiburon	226	37.52 N	122.27 W
Tiburón, Cabo >	246	8.42 N	77.24 W
Tiburón, Isla I	232	29.00 N	112.23 W
Tiburon Peninsula >[1]	282	37.53 N	122.28 W
Tiča, Jazovir ⊜[1]	38	43.05 N	26.45 E
Ticao Island I	116	12.31 N	123.42 E
Ticao Pass ⋓	116	12.38 N	123.47 E
Tice	220	26.40 N	81.48 W
Tice Creek ≃	282	37.53 N	122.03 W
Ticehurst	42	51.03 N	0.25 E
Tichigan	216	42.50 N	88.12 W
Tichigan Lake ⊜	216	42.49 N	88.13 W
Tîchît	150	18.28 N	9.30 W
Tîchît, Dahr ⫫[4]	150	18.30 N	9.25 W
Tichmenevo, Ross.	76	58.00 N	38.36 E
Tichmenevo, Ross.	89	49.12 N	142.54 E
Ticho	144	7.50 N	39.32 E
Tichon	24	59.23 N	46.38 E
Tichonova Pustyn'	82	54.38 N	36.09 E
Tichonovka	88	53.13 N	104.13 E
Tichookeanskij	89	43.00 N	132.24 E
Tichoreck	78	45.51 N	40.09 E
Tichtozero	24	65.35 N	30.27 E
Tichvin	76	59.39 N	33.31 E
Tichvinskaja gr'ada ∧	76	59.30 N	34.30 E
Ticino □[3]	58	46.20 N	8.45 E
Ticino ≃	36	45.09 N	9.14 E
Tickfaw	194	30.34 N	90.28 W
Tickfaw ≃	194	30.20 N	90.28 W
Tickhill	44	53.26 N	1.06 W
Ticomán ◆[8]	286a	19.31 N	99.08 W
Ticonderoga	188	43.50 N	73.25 W
Ticul	232	20.24 N	89.32 W
Tīdah	142	31.15 N	30.50 E
Tidaholm	26	58.11 N	13.57 E
Tidan ≃	40	58.42 N	13.58 E
Tiddim	110	23.23 N	93.39 E
Tide Lake ⊜	184	50.33 N	111.20 W
Tideswell	44	53.16 N	1.46 W
Tidewater	208	37.51 N	76.42 W
Tidewater ◆[1]	208	37.45 N	77.00 W
Tidikelt ≚	148	26.54 N	1.20 E
Tidioute	214	41.41 N	79.24 W
Tidirhine, Jebel ∧	148	34.50 N	4.30 W
Tidjikja	150	18.33 N	11.25 W
Tidö	40	59.30 N	16.28 E
Tidone ≃	62	45.04 N	9.32 E
Tidore	108	0.40 N	127.26 E
Tiébissou	150	7.10 N	5.13 W
Tiechang, Zhg.	98	41.44 N	126.11 E
Tiechang, Zhg.	100	24.10 N	115.30 E
Tiechang, Zhg.	102	26.34 N	103.58 E
Tiechang, Zhg.	105	40.04 N	118.12 E
Tiechangpu	107	29.29 N	104.20 E
Tiefenbach	60	49.26 N	12.35 E
Tiefenbroich	263	51.18 N	6.49 E
Tiefencastel	58	46.40 N	9.35 E
Tiefensee	54	52.41 N	13.50 E
Tiefo	107	29.45 N	104.33 E
T'iehling → Tieling	104	42.18 N	123.49 E
Tiekou	98	37.16 N	121.13 E
Tiel	52	51.54 N	5.25 E
Tieli	89	46.59 N	128.02 E
Tieling	104	42.18 N	123.49 E
Tielt	50	51.00 N	3.19 E
Tielutou	100	27.49 N	115.48 E
Tiémé	150	9.33 N	7.19 W
T'ienching → Tianjin	105	39.08 N	117.12 E
T'ienchung	100	23.52 N	120.35 E
Tienen	56	50.48 N	4.57 E
Tiengen	58	47.38 N	8.16 E
Tiénigboué	150	8.11 N	5.43 W
Tienko	150	10.14 N	7.29 W
Tien Shan ⋏	90	42.00 N	80.00 E
T'ienshui → Tianshui	102	34.30 N	105.58 E
Tientsin → Tianjin	105	39.08 N	117.12 E
Tien Yen	110	21.20 N	107.24 E
Tiepido ≃	64	44.37 N	10.59 E
Tie Plant	194	33.44 N	89.47 W
Tierga	34	41.37 N	1.36 W
Tiergarten ◆[8]	264a	52.31 N	13.21 E
Tiergarten ♠	264a	52.31 N	13.21 E
Tieroko, Tarso ∧	146	20.45 N	17.52 E
Tierp	40	60.20 N	17.30 E
Tierpark ♠	264a	52.30 N	13.32 E
Tierra Amarilla, Chile	252	27.29 S	70.17 W
Tierra Amarilla, N.M., U.S.	200	36.42 N	106.32 W
Tierra Blanca, Méx.	196	27.12 N	104.53 W
Tierra Blanca, Méx.	234	18.25 N	96.20 W
Tierra Blanca Creek ≃	196	35.00 N	101.54 W
Tierra Buena	226	39.09 N	121.40 W
Tierra Colorada, Méx.	234	17.10 N	99.35 W
Tierra Colorada, Méx.	234	17.56 N	92.39 W
Tierra Colorada, Bajo de la ≚[1]	254	42.52 S	66.48 W
Tierra de Campos ◆[1]	34	42.10 N	4.50 W
Tierra del Fuego □[8]	254	54.00 S	67.00 W
Tierra del Fuego, Isla Grande de I	254	54.00 S	69.00 W
Tierra del Fuego, Parque Nacional ♠	254	54.39 S	68.30 W
Tierra del Norte → Severnaja Zeml'a II	74	79.30 N	98.00 E
Tierralta	246	8.11 N	76.04 W
Tierra Redonda Mountain ∧	226	35.47 N	120.59 W
Tierras Australes y Antárticas Francesas → French Southern and Antarctic Terr □[2]	6	49.30 S	69.30 E
Tieshan	100	30.14 N	114.52 E
Tieshanguan	100	23.30 N	113.54 E
Tiétar ≃	34	39.50 N	6.01 W
Tietê	255	23.07 S	47.43 W
Tietê ≃	255	20.40 S	51.35 W
Tiéti	175f	20.57 S	165.19 E
Tieton	224	46.42 N	120.45 W
Tieton ≃	224	46.45 N	120.45 W
Tieton, South Fork ≃	224	46.38 N	121.08 W
Tietzow	264a	52.43 N	12.56 E
Tif	148	27.00 N	1.37 E
Tiffany Mountain ∧	202	48.40 N	119.56 W
Tiffin	214	41.07 N	83.11 W
Tiffin ≃	216	41.17 N	84.23 W
Tiflis → Tbilisi	84	41.43 N	44.49 E
Tifton	192	31.27 N	83.30 W
Tiftona	192	35.05 N	85.10 W
Tiga, Île I	175f	21.07 S	167.49 E
Tiga, Pulau I	112	5.43 N	115.39 E
Tigalda Island I	180	54.05 N	165.05 W
Tigapuluh, Pegunungan ⋏	112	1.05 S	102.30 E
Tigard	224	45.25 N	122.46 W
Tigasaki → Chigasaki	94	35.19 N	139.24 E
Tigbauan	116	10.41 N	122.22 E
Tigeaux	261	48.50 N	2.54 E
Tiger Lake ⊜	220	27.53 N	81.22 W
Tiger Stadium ♠	281	42.20 N	83.04 W
Tigery	261	48.38 N	2.31 E
Tighennif	148	35.20 N	0.21 E
Tighina (Bender)	38	46.48 N	29.29 E
Tighvein ∧[2]	46	55.30 N	5.10 W
Tigil'	74	57.48 N	158.40 E
Tiglid	148	28.31 N	10.15 W
Tiglione ≃	62	44.48 N	8.27 E
Tignale	64	45.44 N	10.44 E
Tignall	192	33.52 N	82.44 W
Tignère	152	7.22 N	12.39 E
Tignes	62	45.30 N	6.55 E
Tignish	186	46.57 N	64.02 W
Tignousti, Jebel ∧	148	31.31 N	6.44 W
Tigoda ≃	76	59.22 N	31.54 E
Tigray □[4]	144	13.40 N	40.00 E
Tigre, Arg.	258	34.25 S	58.34 W
Tigre, Col.	246	2.28 N	68.15 W
Tigre □[5]	288	34.24 S	58.37 W
Tigre ≃, Arg.	288	34.25 S	58.35 W
Tigre → Tigris ≃, Asia	128	31.00 N	47.25 E
Tigre ≃, Méx.	234	22.43 N	97.51 W
Tigre ≃, Perú	246	4.26 S	74.05 W
Tigre ≃, Ven.	246	9.20 N	62.30 W
Tigre, Cerro ∧	236	8.31 N	83.28 W
Tigre, Isla del I	258	34.47 S	56.23 W
Tigre, Punta del >	258	34.46 S	56.33 W
Tigres, Baía dos ⊂	152	16.38 S	11.46 E
Tigris (Dicle) (Dijlah) ≃	128	31.00 N	47.25 E
Tiguabos	240p	20.14 N	75.21 W
Tiguentourine	148	27.50 N	9.18 E
Tiguesmat ⋏[2]	148	24.54 N	8.14 W
Tigy	50	47.48 N	2.12 E
Tigyaing	110	23.46 N	96.08 E
Tigzert, Oued V	148	28.20 N	9.35 W
Tigzirt	34	36.54 N	4.08 E
Tīh, Jabal at- ⋏[1]	140	29.30 N	34.00 E
Tihāmah ≚	128	26.00 N	36.30 E
Tihany ⊥	30	46.54 N	17.53 E
Tihert	148	35.28 N	1.21 E
Tihert □[5]	148	35.00 N	1.45 E
Ṭihnāwī, Wādī aṭ- V	142	28.11 N	30.46 E
Tihua → Ürümqi	86	43.48 N	87.35 E
Tihuatlán	234	20.43 N	97.32 W
Tiilikkajärven kansallispuisto ♠	26	63.38 N	28.20 E
Tijamuchi ≃	248	14.10 S	64.58 W
Tijesno	36	43.48 N	15.39 E
Tījī	146	32.01 N	11.22 E
Tijuana	232	32.32 N	117.01 W
Tijuana ≃	204	32.33 N	117.07 W
Tijuca ◆[8]	287a	22.56 S	43.14 W
Tijuca, Barra da ⋓	287a	23.01 S	43.18 W
Tijuca, Lagoa da ⊂	287a	22.59 S	43.20 W
Tijuca, Parque Nacional da ♠	287a	22.58 S	43.15 W
Tijuca, Pico da ∧	287a	22.56 S	43.17 W
Tijucas	252	27.14 S	48.38 W
Tijucas do Sul	252	25.55 S	49.12 W
Tijuco ≃	255	18.40 S	50.05 W
Tikal ⊥	232	17.20 N	89.39 W
Tīkamgarh	124	24.44 N	78.50 E
Tikaré	150	13.17 N	1.43 W
Tikchik Lakes ⊜	180	60.07 N	158.35 W
Tikei, Île I	14	14.58 S	144.32 W
Tikhand ◆[8]	272a	28.31 N	77.17 E
Tikhoretsk → Tichoreck	78	45.51 N	40.09 E
Tikitiki	172	37.48 S	178.24 E
Tiko	152	4.05 N	9.22 E
Tikokino	172	39.49 S	176.27 E
Tikrīt	128	34.36 N	43.42 E
Tikša	24	64.07 N	32.27 E
Tikšeozero, ozero ⊜	24	66.16 N	31.53 E
Tiksi	74	71.36 N	128.48 E
Tiku	112	0.24 S	99.56 E
Til	130	38.44 N	41.49 E
Tiladummati Atoll I[1]	122	6.50 N	73.05 E
Tilamuta	112	0.30 N	122.20 E
Tilarán	236	10.28 N	84.59 W

Symbol	English	Deutsch	Español	Français	Português
≃	River	Fluß	Río	Rivière	Rio
≊	Canal	Kanal	Canal	Canal	Canal
∟	Waterfall, Rapids	Wasserfall, Stromschnellen	Cascada, Rápidos	Chute d'eau, Rapides	Cascata, Rápidos
⋓	Strait	Meeresstraße	Estrecho	Détroit	Estreito
⊂	Bay, Gulf	Bucht, Golf	Bahía, Golfo	Baie, Golfe	Baía, Golfo
⊜	Lake, Lakes	See, Seen	Lago, Lagos	Lac, Lacs	Lago, Lagos
⩸	Swamp	Sumpf	Pantano	Marais	Pântano
⍓	Ice Features, Glacier	Eis- und Gletscherformen	Accidentes Glaciales	Formes glaciaires	Acidentes glaciares
⊤	Other Hydrographic Features	Andere Hydrographische Objekte	Otros Elementos Hidrográficos	Autres données hydrographiques	Outros acidentes hidrográficos
✣	Submarine Features	Untermeerische Objekte	Accidentes Submarinos	Formes de relief sous-marin	Acidentes submarinos
□	Political Unit	Politische Einheit	Unidad Politica	Entité politique	Unidade política
ʊ	Cultural Institution	Kulturelle Institution	Institución Cultural	Institution culturelle	Instituição cultural
⊥	Historical Site	Historische Stätte	Sitio Histórico	Site historique	Sitio histórico
♠	Recreational Site	Erholungs- und Ferienort	Sitio de Recreo	Centre de loisirs	Area de Lazer
⊠	Airport	Flughafen	Aeropuerto	Aéroport	Aeroporto
■	Military Installation	Militäranlage	Instalación Militar	Installation militaire	Instalação militar
◆	Miscellaneous	Verschiedenes	Misceláneo	Divers	Diversos

ENGLISH / DEUTSCH

Name	Page	Lat.°′	Long.°′
Tilbalakan, Laguna ⊂	236	15.30 N	84.17 W
Tilbānah	142	30.59 N	31.27 E
Tilburg	52	51.34 N	5.05 E
Tilbury, On., Can.	214	42.16 N	82.26 W
Tilbury, Eng., U.K.	42	51.28 N	0.23 E
Tilcara	252	23.34 S	65.22 W
Tilcha	166	29.36 S	140.54 E
Til-Châtel	58	47.31 N	5.10 E
Tilden, Il., U.S.	219	38.12 N	89.40 W
Tilden, Ne., U.S.	198	42.02 N	97.50 W
Tilden, Tx., U.S.	196	28.28 N	98.33 W
Tilden Lake ⊜	226	38.07 N	119.36 W
Tilden Woods	284c	39.03 N	77.09 W
Tilemsès	150	15.37 N	4.44 E
Tilemsi, Vallée du V	150	16.15 N	0.02 E
Tilff	56	50.34 N	5.35 E
Tilghman Island I	208	38.42 N	76.20 W
Tilhar	124	27.59 N	79.44 E
Tilia, Oued V	148	27.27 N	0.01 W
Tiliktino	82	56.06 N	36.36 E
Tilimsen	148	34.52 N	1.15 W
Tilimsen □[5]	148	35.00 N	2.00 W
Tilin	110	21.42 N	94.04 E
Tilisarao	252	32.44 S	65.18 W
Till ≃, Eng., U.K.	44	55.41 N	2.12 W
Till ≃, Eng., U.K.	44	53.16 N	0.37 W
Tillaberi	150	14.13 N	1.27 E
Tillamook	202	45.27 N	123.50 W
Tillamook □[6]	224	45.25 N	123.39 W
Tillamook ≃	224	45.28 N	123.53 W
Tillamook Bay ⊂	224	45.30 N	123.53 W
Tillamook Head ›	224	45.57 N	124.00 W
Tillanchāng Dwīp I	110	8.30 N	93.37 E
Tillberga	40	59.41 N	16.37 E
Tille ≃	58	47.07 N	5.21 E
Tillery, Lake ⊜[1]	192	35.17 N	80.05 W
Tilley	182	50.27 N	111.39 W
Tilli	126	23.57 N	89.57 E
Tillia	150	16.08 N	4.47 E
Tillicoultry	46	56.09 N	3.45 W
Tillicum	224	47.08 N	122.33 W
Tillières-sur-Avre	50	48.46 N	1.04 E
Tilling Bourne ≃	260	51.13 N	0.34 W
Tillmans Corner	194	30.43 N	88.05 W
Tillson	210	41.49 N	74.04 W
Tillsonburg	212	42.51 N	80.44 W
Tillyfourie	46	57.11 N	2.35 W
Tilogne	150	15.58 N	13.36 W
Tilomar	112	9.21 S	125.08 E
Tílos I	38	36.25 N	27.25 E
Tilpa	166	30.57 S	144.24 E
Tilrhemt	148	33.10 N	3.21 E
Tilsit → Sovetsk	76	55.05 N	21.53 E
Tilt ≃	46	56.46 N	3.50 W
Tilton, Il., U.S.	194	40.05 N	87.38 W
Tilton, Ky., U.S.	218	38.22 N	83.45 W
Tilton, N.H., U.S.	188	43.26 N	71.35 W
Tilton ≃	224	46.33 N	122.33 W
Tiltonsville	214	40.10 N	80.41 W
Tilzapotla	234	18.29 N	99.16 W
Tim	78	51.37 N	37.07 E
Tim ≃	76	52.15 N	37.22 E
Tīmā	140	26.54 N	31.26 E
Timah, Bukit ∧[2]	271c	1.21 N	103.47 E
Timahoe	48	53.20 N	6.49 W
Timaná	246	1.58 N	75.56 W
Timane ≃	248	20.34 S	59.15 W
Timanskij kr'až ∧	24	65.00 N	51.00 E
Timar	84	38.49 N	43.27 E
Timaricha	80	57.33 N	44.47 E
Timaru	172	44.24 S	171.15 E
Timaševo, Ross.	80	53.21 N	51.12 E
Timaševo, Ross.	82	55.08 N	36.29 E
Timaševsk	78	45.37 N	38.57 E
Timau, It.	64	46.35 N	13.00 E
Timau, Kenya	154	0.05 N	37.14 E
Timavo San Giovanni	64	45.48 N	13.37 E
Timay al-Amdīd	142	30.57 N	31.32 E
Timbákion	38	35.04 N	24.46 E
Timbalier Bay ⊂	194	29.10 N	90.20 W
Timbaúba	250	7.31 S	35.19 W
Timbavati Game Reserve ◆[4]	156	24.27 S	31.27 E
Timbedgha	150	16.15 N	8.10 W
Timber	224	45.43 N	123.17 W
Timber Creek	164	15.39 S	130.29 E
Timber Creek ≃	198	44.49 N	98.17 W
Timber Lake, Il., U.S.	278	42.14 N	88.07 W
Timberlake, Oh., U.S.	214	41.41 N	81.25 W
Timber Lake, S.D., U.S.	198	45.26 N	101.04 W
Timber Run ≃	284b	39.27 N	76.52 W
Timber Trails	278	41.52 N	87.57 W
Timberview	284b	39.13 N	76.45 W
Timbío	246	2.20 N	76.40 W
Timbiras	250	4.15 S	43.57 W
Timblin	214	40.58 N	79.12 W
Timbó, Bra.	252	26.50 S	49.18 W
Timbo, Guinée	150	10.38 N	11.50 W
Timbo, Liber.	150	5.37 N	9.43 W
Timbó ≃	287a	22.52 S	43.16 W
Timboon	169	38.29 S	142.59 E
Timbuctoo	285	40.00 N	74.49 W
Timbuktu → Tombouctou	150	16.46 N	3.01 W
Timbun Mata, Pulau I	112	4.39 N	118.28 E
Timel'ga	86	58.53 N	76.42 E
Timelkam	60	48.00 N	13.36 E
Times Square ⊥	276	40.45 N	74.00 W
Timétrine	150	19.27 N	0.26 W
Timétrine ⩘	150	19.20 N	0.42 W
Timeu Creek ≃	182	54.28 N	114.27 W
Timewell	219	40.00 N	90.52 W
Timgad ⊥	148	35.29 N	6.28 E
Timimoun	148	29.14 N	0.16 E
Timimoun, Sebkha de ⊜	148	29.00 N	0.05 E
Timinar	140	19.02 N	30.29 E
Timi Ouli, Ehi ∧	146	21.08 N	16.31 E
Timir'azevo	76	55.05 N	21.37 E
Timir'azevskij	86	56.29 N	84.54 E
Timirevo	82	55.08 N	39.10 E
Timirist, Râs ›	150	19.23 N	16.32 W
Timiș □[6]	38	45.40 N	21.20 E
Timiș (Tamiš) ≃	38	44.51 N	20.39 E
Timiskaming, Lake ⊜	190	47.10 N	79.25 W
Timișoara	38	45.45 N	21.13 E
Timkoviči	76	53.03 N	27.00 E
Timkovo	82	55.56 N	38.37 E
Timmendorfer Strand	54	54.00 N	10.46 E
Timmernabben	26	56.58 N	16.26 E
Timmins	190	48.28 N	81.20 W
Timmonsville	192	34.08 N	79.56 W
Timms Hill ∧[2]	190	45.27 N	90.11 W
Timok ≃	38	44.13 N	22.40 E
Timon	250	5.06 S	42.49 W
Timonovo	82	56.13 N	37.02 E
Timor I	112	9.00 S	125.00 E
Timor Sea ⊤[2]	14	11.00 S	128.00 E
Timor Timur □[4]	112	8.35 S	126.00 E
Timor Trough ✧[1]	14	9.50 S	126.00 E
Timošino, Ross.	76	60.05 N	36.10 E
Timošino, Ross.	80	57.50 N	44.25 E
Timotes	246	8.59 N	70.44 W
Timothy Lake ⊜[1]	224	45.07 N	121.47 W
Timoudi	148	29.19 N	1.09 W
Timousserarène ≃	150	16.21 N	8.07 E
Timpanogos Cave National Monument ♦	200	40.18 N	111.52 W
Timpas Creek ≃	198	38.02 N	103.38 W
Timpaus, Pulau I	112	1.51 S	124.01 E
Timperley	262	53.24 N	2.19 W
Timpson	194	31.54 N	94.23 W
Timpton ≃	74	58.43 N	127.12 E
Timra	26	62.31 N	17.22 E
Timsāh, Buḥayrat at- (Lake Timsah) ⊜	142	30.34 N	32.17 E
Timsah, Lake → Timsāh, Buḥayrat at- ⊜	142	30.34 N	32.17 E
Timšer	24	62.06 N	54.40 E
Tims Ford Lake ⊜[1]	194	35.15 N	86.10 W
Timun	114	0.50 N	103.22 E
Timur	85	42.50 N	68.26 E
Timur, Banjaran ⩘	114	5.00 N	102.30 E
Timurni	124	22.22 N	77.22 E
Tīn, Ra's at- ›	146	32.37 N	23.08 E
Tina ≃	158	31.18 S	29.14 E
Tinaca Point ›	116	5.33 N	125.20 E
Tinaco	246	9.42 N	68.26 W
Tinaga Island I	116	14.28 N	122.56 E
Tīnah, Khalīj aṭ- ⊂	140	31.08 N	32.40 E
Tinahely	48	52.48 N	6.28 W
Tinaja, Punta ›	248	16.14 S	73.39 W
Tinalmud	116	13.36 N	122.53 E
Tinambac	116	13.49 N	123.19 E
Tinambung	112	3.31 S	119.01 E
Ti-n-Amzi V	150	18.20 N	4.32 E
Tinapagee	166	29.28 S	144.23 E
Tinaquillo	246	9.55 N	68.18 W
Tindari, Capo ›	70	38.10 N	15.03 E
Tinderry Peak ∧	171b	35.42 S	149.16 E
Tindila	150	10.16 N	8.15 W
Tindis	126	21.35 N	86.44 E
Tindivanam	122	12.15 N	79.39 E
Tindouf	148	27.50 N	8.04 W
Tindouf, Hamada de ◆[1]	148	27.30 N	9.00 W
Tindouf, Sebkha de ≚	148	27.45 N	7.15 W
Tineba, Pegunungan ⩘	112	1.40 S	120.25 E
Tinée ≃	62	43.55 N	7.11 E
Tineg ≃	116	17.38 N	120.37 E
Tineo	34	43.20 N	6.25 W
Ting ≃	100	24.24 N	116.35 E
Tinga ∧	146	9.21 N	23.38 E
Tingambato	234	19.30 N	101.52 W
Tinggi, Pulau I	114	2.18 N	104.07 E
Tingha	166	29.57 S	151.13 E
Tinghert, Ḥamādat (Plateau du Tinghert) ⩘[1]	148	29.00 N	9.00 E
Tinghert, Plateau du (Ḥamādat Tinghert) ⩘[1]	148	29.00 N	9.00 E
Tinghsien → Dingxian	98	38.32 N	114.59 E
Tingkar ∧	116	5.20 N	117.06 E
Ting Kau	271d	22.22 N	114.05 E
Tingkawk Sakan	110	26.04 N	96.44 E
Tingkou	98	36.34 N	119.46 E
Tinglev	41	54.56 N	9.15 E
Tinglin	106	30.53 N	121.17 E
Tingliuhe	98	39.34 N	118.49 E
Tingloy	116	13.40 N	120.52 E
Tingmerkpuk Mountain ∧	180	68.34 N	162.28 W
Tingo de Saposoa	248	7.07 S	76.38 W
Tingo María	248	9.09 S	75.56 W
Tingo María, Parque Nacional ♦	248	9.15 S	76.05 W
Tingqian	100	30.10 N	115.54 E
Tingri, Zhg.	120	28.35 N	86.38 E
Tingri, Zhg.	120	28.38 N	87.04 E
Tingsiqiao	100	29.50 N	114.12 E
Tingsryd	26	56.32 N	14.59 E
Tingstäde	26	57.44 N	18.36 E
Tingsted	41	54.49 N	11.56 E
Tinguá	256	22.36 S	43.26 W
Tingüindín	234	19.45 N	102.29 W
Tinguiririca, Volcán ∧[1]	252	34.49 S	70.21 W
Tingvoll	26	62.54 N	8.12 E
Tingvollfjorden ⊂[2]	26	62.50 N	8.11 E
Tingwick	206	45.50 N	71.58 W
Tingwon Group II	164	2.35 S	149.45 E
Tingzitou	106	30.12 N	119.46 E
Tinharé, Ilha de I	255	13.30 S	38.58 W
Tinh Bien	110	10.36 N	104.57 E
Tinian	174n	14.58 N	145.38 E
Tinian I	174n	15.00 N	145.38 E
Tinian Harbor ⊂	174n	14.57 N	145.36 E
Tinié	150	14.20 N	1.28 W
Tiniguiban	116	11.22 N	119.30 E
Tinitian	116	10.04 N	119.12 E
Tinjar ≃	112	4.04 N	114.18 E
Tinjil, Pulau I	115a	6.58 S	105.47 E
Tinker Air Force Base ■	196	35.25 N	97.24 W
Tinkers Creek ≃, Md., U.S.	284c	38.46 N	76.57 W
Tinkers Creek ≃, Oh., U.S.	214	41.22 N	81.37 W
Tinkertown	283	42.01 N	70.44 W
Tinkisso ≃	150	11.21 N	9.10 W
Tinley Creek ≃	278	41.39 N	87.45 W
Tinley Creek Woods ♦	278	41.39 N	87.47 W
Tinley Park	216	41.34 N	87.47 W
Tinniswood, Mount ∧	182	50.19 N	123.50 W
Tinnoset	26	59.43 N	9.02 E
Tinnsjø ⊜	26	59.54 N	8.55 E
Tinogasta	252	28.04 S	67.34 W
Tinompo	112	2.09 S	121.17 E
Tínos	38	37.32 N	25.10 E
Tínos I	38	37.38 N	25.10 E
Tinquipaya	248	19.11 S	65.51 W
Tin Rerhoh, Tassili ⩘	150	19.40 N	4.00 E
Tinrhir	148	31.28 N	5.30 W
Tin Sam	271d	22.22 N	114.11 E
Tinskoj	88	56.10 N	96.55 E
Tinsley	194	32.43 N	90.27 W
Tinsukia	120	27.30 N	95.22 E
Tintagel, B.C., Can.	182	54.12 N	125.35 W
Tintagel, Eng., U.K.	42	50.40 N	4.45 W
Tintagel Head ›	42	50.41 N	4.46 W
Tintaldra	171b	36.03 S	147.56 E
Tintas, Rio das ≃	287a	22.52 S	43.28 W
Tinte, Cerro ∧	248	22.40 S	67.02 W
Tintern Abbey ⊍[1]	42	51.41 N	2.40 W
Tintern Parva	42	51.42 N	2.40 W
Tintigny	56	49.41 N	5.31 E
Tintina	252	27.02 S	62.43 W
Tintinara	166	35.54 S	140.03 E
Tintioulé	150	10.13 N	9.12 W
Tinto ∧	46	55.36 N	3.39 W
Tinto ≃	34	37.12 N	6.55 W
Tinton Falls	276	40.19 N	74.04 W
Ti-n-Toumma ◆[1]	146	16.04 N	12.40 E
Tintwistle	262	53.28 N	1.58 W
Tinui	172	40.53 S	176.04 E
Tinwald	172	43.55 S	171.43 E
Ti-n-Zaouatene	150	19.55 N	2.52 E
Tinzap ≃	120	38.23 N	77.24 E
Tio	144	14.42 N	40.58 E
Tioga, Il., U.S.	219	40.13 N	91.21 W
Tioga, N.D., U.S.	198	48.23 N	102.56 W
Tioga, Pa., U.S.	210	41.55 N	77.08 W
Tioga □[6], N.Y., U.S.	210	42.06 N	76.16 W
Tioga □[6], Pa., U.S.	210	41.45 N	77.17 W
Tioga ◆[8]	285	40.00 N	75.10 W
Tioga ≃	210	42.09 N	77.05 W
Tioga Center	210	42.04 N	76.21 W
Tioga Pass)(	226	37.54 N	119.16 W
Tioga Terrace	210	42.03 N	76.07 W
Tiojala	24	61.10 N	23.52 E
Tioman, Pulau I	114	2.48 N	104.10 E
Tiona	214	41.45 N	79.03 W
Tione di Trento	64	46.02 N	10.43 E
Tionesta	214	41.30 N	79.27 W
Tionesta Creek ≃	214	41.28 N	79.22 W
Tionesta Lake ⊜[1]	214	41.28 N	79.28 W
Tioor, Pulau I	164	4.45 S	131.45 E
Tior	140	6.23 N	31.11 E
Tioro	112	4.41 S	122.36 E
Tioro, Selat ʊ	112	4.40 S	122.20 E
Tioroniaradougou	150	9.21 N	5.38 W
Tioughnioga ≃	210	42.14 N	75.51 W
Tioughnioga, East Branch ≃	210	42.36 N	76.10 W
Tipasa	34	36.35 N	2.27 E
Tipitapa	236	12.12 N	86.06 W
Tipoca, Monte ∧[2]	250	3.34 N	51.20 W
Tipp City	218	39.57 N	84.10 W
Tippecanoe, In., U.S.	216	41.12 N	86.06 W
Tippecanoe, Oh., U.S.	214	40.16 N	81.17 W
Tippecanoe □[6]	216	40.25 N	86.53 W
Tippecanoe ≃	216	40.31 N	86.47 W
Tippecanoe, Lake ⊜	216	41.20 N	85.46 W
Tippecanoe Battlefield State Memorial ⊥	216	40.31 N	86.52 W
Tippecanoe River State Park ♦	216	41.07 N	86.36 W
Tipperary, Austl.	164	13.44 S	131.02 E
Tipperary, Ire.	48	52.29 N	8.10 W
Tipperary □[6]	48	52.40 N	8.20 W
Tipton, Eng., U.K.	42	52.32 N	2.05 W
Tipton, Ca., U.S.	226	36.03 N	119.18 W
Tipton, In., U.S.	216	40.16 N	86.02 W
Tipton, Ia., U.S.	190	41.46 N	91.07 W
Tipton, Mi., U.S.	216	42.01 N	84.04 W
Tipton, Mo., U.S.	194	38.39 N	92.46 W
Tipton, Ok., U.S.	196	34.30 N	99.08 W
Tipton, Pa., U.S.	214	40.38 N	78.18 W
Tipton □[6]	216	40.17 N	86.02 W
Tipton, Mount ∧	200	35.32 N	114.12 W
Tiptonville	194	36.22 N	89.28 W
Tip Top Mountain ∧	190	48.16 N	85.59 W
Tiptree	42	51.49 N	0.45 E
Tiptūr	122	13.16 N	76.29 E
Tiputini ≃	246	0.47 S	75.32 W
Tiquicheo	234	18.53 N	100.44 W
Tīra	132	32.14 N	34.57 E
Tira Chapéu, Morro ∧	256	22.45 S	44.39 W
Tiradentes	255	21.07 S	44.11 W
Tīrah, Baḥr ≊	142	31.03 N	31.15 E
Tīrān I	128	27.56 N	34.34 E
Tīrān, Maḍīq ʊ	140	27.58 N	34.28 E
Tiran, Strait of → Tīrān, Maḍīq ʊ	140	27.58 N	34.28 E
Tirana → Tiranë	38	41.20 N	19.50 E
Tiranë	38	41.20 N	19.50 E
Tirano	64	46.13 N	10.10 E
Tiraque	248	17.37 S	65.04 W
Tirari Desert ◆[2]	162	28.00 S	138.20 E
Tiraspol	38	46.51 N	29.38 E
Tirat Karmel	132	32.46 N	34.58 E
Tirat Ẓevi	132	32.25 N	35.32 E
Tirau	172	37.59 S	175.45 E
Tire	130	38.04 N	27.45 E
Tirebolu	130	41.00 N	38.48 E
Tiree I	46	56.31 N	6.49 W
Tire Hill	214	40.16 N	78.55 W
Tires (Tiers), It.	64	46.28 N	11.31 E
Tires, Port.	266c	38.43 N	9.21 W
Tires ◆[1]	148	23.30 N	13.10 W
Tirhahart, Oued V	148	23.45 N	3.10 E
Tiria, Monte ∧	71	40.23 N	9.16 E
Tirich Mīr ∧	123	36.15 N	71.50 E
Tiriro	150	10.27 N	8.39 W
Tiris Zemmour □[4]	148	24.10 N	9.30 W
Tirl'anskij	86	54.14 N	58.35 E
Tirna ≃	122	18.04 N	76.57 E
Tírnavos	38	39.45 N	22.17 E
Tirnovo → Veliko Târnovo	38	43.04 N	25.39 E
Tiro	214	40.54 N	82.46 W
Tirodi	120	21.41 N	79.42 E
Tirol □[3]	64	47.15 N	11.20 E
Tiroler Ache (Grossache) ≃	60	47.51 N	12.30 E
Tirolo (Tirol)	64	46.42 N	11.10 E
Tiros	255	19.00 S	45.58 W
Tiroungoulou	146	9.34 N	22.09 E
Tīr Pol	128	34.36 N	61.15 E
Tirrenia	66	43.38 N	10.17 E
Tirreno, Mare → Tyrrhenian Sea ⊤[2]	36	40.00 N	12.00 E
Tirry ≃	46	58.02 N	4.26 W
Tirsā, Miṣr	142	29.25 N	30.49 E
Tirsā, Miṣr	273c	29.58 N	31.12 E
Tirschenreuth	60	49.53 N	12.21 E
Tirso ≃	71	39.53 N	8.32 E
Tirsted	41	54.44 N	11.21 E
Tirstrup	41	56.18 N	10.42 E
Tīrthahalli	122	13.42 N	75.14 E
Tirua Point ›	172	38.23 S	174.38 E
Tiruchchirāppalli	122	10.49 N	78.41 E
Tiruchengodu	122	11.23 N	77.56 E
Tirukkalukkunram	122	12.37 N	80.04 E
Tirukkovilūr	122	11.57 N	79.12 E
Tiruliai	76	55.47 N	23.22 E
Tirumangalam	122	9.50 N	77.59 E
Tirunelveli	122	8.44 N	77.42 E
Tirupati	122	13.39 N	79.25 E
Tiruppattūr, India	122	12.30 N	78.34 E
Tiruppattūr, India	122	10.08 N	78.37 E
Tiruppur	122	11.06 N	77.21 E
Tirūr	122	10.54 N	75.55 E
Tiruttani	122	13.11 N	79.38 E
Tirutturaippūndi	122	10.32 N	79.39 E
Tiruvalla	122	9.23 N	76.34 E
Tiruvallūr	122	13.09 N	79.55 E
Tiruvannāmalai	122	12.13 N	79.04 E
Tiruvettipuram	122	12.40 N	79.33 E
Tirūvottiyūr	122	13.09 N	80.18 E
Tiruvur	122	17.06 N	80.38 E
Tisa (Tisza) (Tysa) ≃	38	45.15 N	20.17 E
Tis'ah	142	30.02 N	32.35 E
Tisaiyanvilai	122	8.20 N	77.53 E
Tisaren ⊜	40	59.00 N	15.08 E
Tisbury	42	51.04 N	2.03 W
Tisdale	184	52.51 N	104.04 W
Tishomingo, Ms., U.S.	194	34.38 N	88.13 W
Tishomingo, Ok., U.S.	196	34.14 N	96.40 W
Tisisat Falls ∟	144	11.29 N	37.35 E
Ṭīsīyah	132	32.24 N	36.27 E
Tisjön ⊜	26	60.55 N	12.58 E
Tiskilwa	190	41.17 N	89.30 W
Tiskino	86	58.05 N	83.10 E
Tiškovo, Ross.	80	46.02 N	48.36 E
Tiškovo, Ross.	82	56.05 N	37.44 E
Tisma	236	12.05 N	86.01 W
Tisnaren ⊜	40	58.57 N	15.57 E
Tišnevo	82	55.10 N	36.17 E
Tišnov	30	49.21 N	16.25 E
Tisovec	30	48.43 N	19.57 E
Tissa	146	7.26 N	10.16 E
Tissemsilt	148	35.35 N	1.50 E
Tissø ⊜	41	55.35 N	11.18 E
Tīsta ≃	124	25.23 N	89.43 E
Tisul'	86	55.45 N	88.19 E
Tisvildeleje	41	56.03 N	12.05 E
Tisza (Tisa) (Tysa) ≃	38	45.15 N	20.17 E
Tiszaföldvár	30	46.59 N	20.15 E
Tiszafüred	30	47.37 N	20.46 E
Tiszavasvári	30	47.58 N	21.22 E
Tit	148	23.00 N	5.10 E
Titaf	148	27.26 N	0.13 W
Titāgarh	126	22.45 N	88.22 E
Titano, Monte ∧	66	43.55 N	12.28 E
Titao	150	13.46 N	2.04 W
Tit-Ary	74	71.58 N	127.01 E
Titel	38	45.12 N	20.18 E
Tithwāl	123	34.24 N	73.47 E
Titicaca, Lago ⊜	248	15.50 S	69.20 W
Titicus	207	41.18 N	73.30 W
Titi Karangan	114	5.31 N	100.37 E
Titikaveka	174k	21.15 S	159.45 W
Titilāgarh	122	20.18 N	83.09 E
Titisee-Neustadt	58	47.54 N	8.13 E
Titlis ∧	58	46.47 N	8.25 E
Tito	68	40.35 N	15.40 E
Titonka	190	43.14 N	94.02 W
Titou	100	29.52 N	112.42 E
Titova Korenica	36	44.45 N	15.43 E
Titovka	83	48.59 N	39.44 E
Titovo, Ross.	80	53.17 N	43.41 E
Titovo, Ross.	82	54.19 N	36.56 E
Titovo, Ross.	82	55.35 N	39.07 E
Titovo Velenje	61	46.22 N	15.07 E
Titov Veles	38	41.41 N	21.48 E
Titov vrh ∧	38	42.00 N	20.51 E
Titran	26	63.40 N	8.18 E
Tittabawassee ≃	190	43.23 N	83.59 W
Titteri ⩘	34	36.00 N	3.30 E
Titterstone Clee Hill ∧[2]	42	52.23 N	2.35 W
Titting	60	49.00 N	11.13 E
Tittling	60	48.44 N	13.23 E
Tittmoning	60	48.04 N	12.46 E
Titu	38	44.41 N	25.32 E
Titule	154	3.17 N	25.32 E
Titus □[6]	222	33.05 N	94.58 W
Titusville, Fl., U.S.	220	28.36 N	80.48 W
Titusville, N.J., U.S.	208	40.18 N	74.52 W
Titusville, Pa., U.S.	214	41.37 N	79.40 W
Titz	56	51.01 N	6.25 E
Tiu Chung Chau I	271d	22.20 N	114.19 E
Tiumpan Head ›	46	58.16 N	6.09 W
Tiuni	120	30.57 N	77.51 E
Tiva ≃	154	2.20 S	38.48 E
Tivaouane	150	14.57 N	16.49 W
Tiveden ⩘[2]	40	58.45 N	14.40 E
Tiverton, Eng., U.K.	42	50.55 N	3.29 W
Tiverton, R.I., U.S.	207	41.37 N	71.12 W
Tivoli, Gren.	241k	12.10 N	61.37 W
Tivoli, It.	66	41.58 N	12.48 E
Tivoli, N.Y., U.S.	210	42.03 N	73.54 W
Tivoli, Tx., U.S.	196	28.27 N	96.53 W
Tivoli ♦	41	55.40 N	12.34 E
Ṭiwāl, Wādī V	146	10.22 N	22.43 E
Ṭiwāl al-'Abā ∧	130	36.20 N	39.22 E
Tiwi, Pil.	116	13.27 N	123.41 E
Ṭīwī, 'Umān	128	22.49 N	59.16 E
Tiwuronto	115b	8.48 S	120.09 E
Tixtla de Guerrero	234	17.35 N	99.26 W
Tiyās	130	34.33 N	37.40 E
Tiyo, Pegunungan ⩘	164	4.00 S	135.30 E
Tizapán ◆[8]	286a	19.20 N	99.13 W
Tizapán El Alto	234	20.10 N	103.04 W
Tizimín	232	21.10 N	88.10 W
Tizi-Ouzou	148	36.48 N	4.02 E
Tizi Ouzou □[5]	148	36.40 N	4.10 E
Tizmant ash-Sharqīyah	142	29.03 N	31.03 E
Tiznados ≃	246	8.16 N	67.47 W
Tiznit	148	29.43 N	9.44 W
Tiznit □[4]	148	29.40 N	9.45 W
Tizoc	196	25.41 N	101.59 W
Tjällmo	40	58.43 N	15.21 E
Tjeukemeer ⊜	52	52.54 N	5.50 E
Tjilatjap → Cilacap	115a	7.44 S	109.00 E
Tjirebon → Cirebon	115a	6.44 S	108.34 E
Tjolotjo	154	19.47 S	27.46 E
Tjøme I	26	59.07 N	10.24 E
Tjörn I	26	58.00 N	11.38 E
Tjörnarp	41	56.00 N	13.37 E
Tkibuli	84	42.21 N	42.59 E
Tkvarčeli	84	42.51 N	41.41 E
Tlachichuca	234	19.06 N	97.25 W
Tlacoapa	234	17.09 N	98.52 W
Tlacotalpan	234	18.37 N	95.40 W
Tlacotepec	234	17.46 N	99.59 W
Tlacuitapan	234	21.14 N	102.12 W
Tláhuac ◆[8]	286a	19.16 N	99.00 W
Tlahualilo de Zaragoza	232	26.07 N	103.27 W
Tlahuelilpan	234	20.08 N	99.14 W
Tlahuitoltepec	234	17.04 N	95.59 W
Tlajomulco de Zúñiga	234	20.28 N	103.27 W
Tlalchapa	234	18.24 N	100.28 W
Tlalcozotitlán	234	17.54 N	99.15 W
Tlalixtac de Cabrera	234	17.04 N	96.39 W
Tlalixtaquilla	234	17.21 N	98.28 W
Tlalnepantla	234	19.33 N	99.12 W
Tlalnepantla ≃	286a	19.31 N	99.16 W
Tlalpan ◆[8]	286a	19.17 N	99.10 W
Tlalpujahua	234	19.48 N	100.10 W
Tlaltenango de Sánchez Román	234	21.47 N	103.19 W
Tl'ančetamak	80	55.28 N	52.37 E
Tlapacoyan	234	19.58 N	97.13 W
Tlapa de Comonfort	234	17.33 N	98.33 W
Tlapaneco ≃	234	18.05 N	98.48 W
Tlapehuala	234	18.13 N	100.31 W
Tlapeng	156	23.15 S	21.49 E
Tlaquepaque	234	20.39 N	103.19 W
Tl'arata	84	42.07 N	46.22 E
Tlatlauquitepec	234	19.51 N	97.29 W
Tlaxcala □[3]	234	19.25 N	98.10 W
Tlaxcala [de Xicoténcatl]	234	19.19 N	98.14 W
Tlaxcoapan	234	20.05 N	99.13 W
Tlaxco [de Morelos]	234	19.37 N	98.07 W
Tlaxmalac	234	18.21 N	99.25 W
Tlazazalca	234	19.58 N	102.04 W
Tletat ed Douair	34	35.59 N	2.55 E
Tlētē Ouāte Gharbī, Jabal ∧	130	35.20 N	39.13 E
Tlevak Strait ʊ	182	55.03 N	132.58 W
Tlhakgameng	158	26.27 S	24.21 E
Tloch	84	42.38 N	46.28 E
Tlučiná	60	49.44 N	13.14 E
Tlumach	78	48.52 N	25.01 E
Tłuszcz	30	52.26 N	21.26 E
Tmassah	146	26.22 N	15.47 E
Tmīsān	146	27.32 N	13.19 E
Tnâot ≃	110	11.29 N	104.57 E
Tnekvejem ≃	180	65.50 N	177.31 E
Toa ≃	240p	20.23 N	74.32 W
Toa Alta	240m	18.23 N	66.15 W
Toab	46a	59.53 N	1.19 W
Toa Baja	240m	18.27 N	66.15 W
Toabré ≃	236	8.56 N	80.33 W
Toachi ≃	246	0.08 N	79.18 W
Toahayaná	232	26.08 N	107.44 W
Toamasina	157b	18.10 S	49.23 E
Toamasina □[4]	157b	18.00 S	48.40 E
Toandonggu	98	40.33 N	127.35 E
Toandos Peninsula ›[1]	224	47.43 N	122.47 W
Toano, It.	64	44.23 N	10.34 E
Toano, Va., U.S.	208	37.22 N	76.48 W
Toano Draw V	204	41.27 N	114.35 W
Toano Range ⩘	204	40.50 N	114.20 W
Toast	192	36.30 N	80.37 W
Toa Vaca, Embalse ⊜[1]	240m	18.06 N	66.28 W
Toay	252	36.40 S	64.21 W
Toba, Mali	150	11.52 N	7.28 W
Toba, Nihon	94	34.29 N	136.51 E
Toba, Zhg.	102	31.18 N	97.40 E
Toba ≃	182	50.30 N	124.15 W
Toba, Danau ⊜	114	2.35 N	98.50 E
Tobacco ≃	190	43.49 N	84.24 W
Tobacco Plains Indian Reserve ◆[4]	182	49.04 N	115.06 W
Tobacco Root Mountains ⩘	202	45.35 N	112.00 W
Tobago I	241r	11.15 N	60.40 W
Toba Inlet ⊂	182	50.20 N	124.50 W
Toba Kākar Range ⩘	120	31.15 N	68.00 E
Tobalaba Eulogio Sánchez, Aeródromo ⊠	286e	33.27 S	70.33 W
Tobalai, Pulau I	164	1.37 S	128.20 E
Tobarra	34	38.35 N	1.41 W
Tobas	252	28.08 S	62.42 W
Tobašino	80	56.56 N	47.40 E
Toba Tek Singh	123	30.58 N	72.29 E
Tobe	96	33.44 N	132.47 E
Tobejuba, Isla I	246	9.20 N	60.52 W
Tobekuduk	86	49.50 N	54.15 E
Tobelo	108	1.44 N	128.01 E
Tobelombang	112	0.57 S	122.00 E
Tobercurry	48	54.03 N	8.43 W
Tobermorey	166	22.15 S	138.00 E
Tobermory, Austl.	166	27.17 S	143.41 E
Tobermory, On., Can.	190	45.15 N	81.40 W
Tobermory, Scot., U.K.	46	56.37 N	6.05 W
Toberonochy	46	56.13 N	5.38 W
Tōbetsu	92a	43.13 N	141.31 E
Tobi I	108	3.00 N	131.10 E
Tobias	198	40.25 N	97.20 W
Tobias Barreto	250	11.11 S	38.01 W
Tobiishi-bana ›	174f	24.45 N	141.17 E
Tobin, Mount ∧	204	40.22 N	117.32 W
Tobin Lake ⊜, Austl.	162	21.45 S	125.49 E
Tobin Lake ⊜, Sk., Can.	184	53.40 N	103.35 W
Tobique ≃	186	46.46 N	67.42 W
Tobi-shima I	92	39.12 N	139.34 E
Toblach → Dobbiaco	64	46.44 N	12.14 E
Tobo, Indon.	164	3.34 S	130.11 E
Tobo, Sve.	40	60.16 N	17.39 E
Toboali	112	3.00 S	106.30 E
Tobol	86	52.40 N	62.39 E
Tobol ≃	86	58.10 N	68.12 E
Toboli	112	0.43 S	120.05 E
Tobol'sk	86	58.12 N	68.16 E
Tobong-san ∧	271b	37.42 N	127.01 E
Tobor	150	12.39 N	16.16 W
Toboso	116	10.43 N	123.31 E
Tobré	150	10.12 N	2.08 E
Tobruk → Ṭubruq	146	32.05 N	23.59 E
Tobseda	24	68.36 N	52.14 E
Tōbu	94	36.21 N	138.20 E
Toburdanovo	80	55.22 N	47.38 E
Toby, Mount ∧	207	42.29 N	72.32 W
Tobyhanna	210	41.10 N	75.25 W
Tobyhanna Creek ≃	210	41.07 N	75.39 W
Tobyhanna State Park ♦	210	41.13 N	75.25 W
Tobyš ≃	24	65.30 N	51.00 E
Toca Grande, Morro da ∧	287a	22.58 S	43.31 W
Tocantínia	250	9.33 S	48.22 W
Tocantinópolis	250	6.20 S	47.25 W
Tocantins □[3]	250	10.00 S	48.00 W
Tocantins ≃, Bra.	242	1.45 S	49.10 W
Tocantins ≃, Bra.	250	5.21 S	55.58 W
Tocantinzinho ≃	255	13.57 S	48.20 W
Toccoa	192	34.34 N	83.19 W
Toccoa (Ocoee) ≃	192	35.12 N	84.40 W
Toce ≃	58	45.56 N	8.29 E
Tochapan	234	18.54 N	97.37 W
Tochcha Lake ⊜	182	54.56 N	125.54 W
Tochigi	94	36.23 N	139.44 E
Tochigi □[5]	94	36.45 N	139.45 E
Tochimilco	234	18.54 N	98.34 W
Tochio	92	37.28 N	139.00 E
Tochoj	88	50.30 N	105.00 E
Tochta	24	62.14 N	48.48 E
Tochtamyš	120	37.50 N	74.39 E
Tockholes	262	53.42 N	2.31 W
Tockoje	80	52.32 N	52.45 E
Töcksfors	26	59.30 N	11.50 E
Točnik	60	49.27 N	13.19 E
Toco, Chile	252	22.05 S	69.35 W
Toco, Trin.	241r	10.50 N	60.57 W
Tocoa	236	15.41 N	86.03 W
Tócome ≃	286c	10.29 N	66.49 W
Toconao	252	23.11 S	68.01 W
Tocopilla	252	22.05 S	70.12 W
Tocos do Moji	256	22.22 S	46.06 W
Tocuco ≃	246	9.36 N	72.15 W
Tocumwal	166	35.49 S	145.34 E
Tocuyo ≃	246	11.03 N	68.23 W
Tocuyo de la Costa	246	11.02 N	68.23 W
Toda	94	35.48 N	139.41 E
Toda Bhīm	124	26.55 N	76.49 E
Todaiji Temple ⊍[1]	270	34.42 N	135.51 E
Todang-ni	271b	37.37 N	126.50 E
Toda Rāisingh	120	26.01 N	75.29 E
Todd	214	40.16 N	78.04 W
Todd ≃	162	24.52 S	135.48 E
Todd Estates	285	39.40 N	75.43 W
Todd Fork ≃	218	39.21 N	84.08 W
Todd Fork, East Fork ≃	218	39.24 N	84.00 W
Toddington	42	51.57 N	0.32 W
Todd Point ›	284b	39.15 N	76.27 W
Toddville, Md., U.S.	208	38.17 N	76.04 W
Toddville, N.Y., U.S.	210	41.17 N	73.53 W
Todeli	112	1.40 S	124.29 E
Todenyang	154	4.32 N	35.56 E
Todi	66	42.47 N	12.24 E
Tödi ∧	58	46.49 N	8.56 E
Todmorden, Austl.	162	27.08 S	134.48 E
Todmorden, Eng., U.K.	44	53.43 N	2.05 W
Todoga-saki ›	92	39.33 N	142.05 E
Todoromi	270	34.53 N	135.28 E
Todos Santos, Bol.	248	16.48 S	65.08 W
Todos Santos, Méx.	232	23.27 N	110.13 W
Todos Santos, Bahía ⊂	232	31.48 N	116.42 W
Todro	154	3.21 N	30.14 E
Todtenhausen	52	52.20 N	8.56 E
Todtmoos	58	47.44 N	8.00 E
Todtmoos Au	58	47.42 N	7.58 E
Todtnau	58	47.50 N	7.56 E
Toe Head ›	46	57.50 N	7.08 W
Tōei	94	35.04 N	137.41 E
T'oejo	98	39.54 N	127.46 E
Toéssé	150	11.50 N	1.16 W
Toetoes Bay ⊂	172	46.38 S	168.43 E
Tofield	182	53.22 N	112.40 W
Tofino	182	49.09 N	125.54 W
Töfsingdalens Nationalpark ♦	26	62.09 N	12.30 E
Tofte	26	59.33 N	10.34 E
Toften ⊜	40	59.03 N	14.36 E
Tofterup	41	55.39 N	8.50 E
Toftlund	41	55.11 N	9.04 E
Toga	94	36.27 N	137.02 E
Toga I	175f	13.26 S	166.42 E
Togakushi	94	36.44 N	138.05 E
Togakushi-yama ∧	94	36.46 N	138.04 E
Toganas	80	50.49 N	52.02 E
Tōgane	94	35.33 N	140.22 E
Togano, Monte ∧	58	46.06 N	8.25 E
Togauchi	96	34.34 N	132.13 E
Togdheer □[4]	144	9.00 N	46.00 E
Toggenburg V	58	47.15 N	9.10 E
Togho	152	6.01 N	17.26 E
Togi	94	37.08 N	136.44 E
Togiak	180	59.04 N	160.24 W
Togiak Bay ⊂	180	59.00 N	160.30 W
Togian, Kepulauan II	112	0.20 S	122.00 E
Togian, Pulau I	112	0.22 S	121.56 E
Töging am Inn	60	48.15 N	12.35 E
Togliatti → Toljatti	80	53.31 N	49.26 E
Togni	140	18.04 N	35.13 E
Tōgō, Nihon	94	35.05 N	137.03 E
Tōgō, Nihon	96	35.28 N	133.53 E
Togo □[1], Afr.	134	8.00 N	1.10 E
Togo □[1], Afr.	150	8.00 N	1.10 E
Togochale	144	9.33 N	43.18 E
Tōgō-ike ⊜	96	35.28 N	133.54 E
Togoron	116	12.35 N	123.37 E
Tögrög, Mong.	102	45.46 N	94.48 E
Tögrög, Mong.	102	45.32 N	102.59 E
Togtoh	102	40.22 N	111.11 E
Togučin	86	55.16 N	84.23 E
Togur	86	58.24 N	82.49 E
Togura	94	36.29 N	138.09 E
Toguzak ≃	86	54.06 N	62.50 E
Toguzbulak	85	42.06 N	76.44 E
Togwotee Pass)(	202	43.45 N	110.04 W
Tōgyu-san ∧	98	35.46 N	127.40 E
Tōgyu-san Kukrip Kongwŏn ♦	98	35.52 N	127.45 E
Togyz	86	47.34 N	60.33 E
Tōhaku	96	35.30 N	133.40 E
Tohakum Peak ∧	204	40.11 N	119.27 W
Tohāna	124	29.42 N	75.54 E
Tohiea, Mont ∧	174s	17.33 S	149.49 W
Tohma ≃	130	38.31 N	38.25 E
Toholampi	26	63.46 N	24.15 E
Tohopekaliga, Lake ⊜	220	28.12 N	81.23 W
Tohor, Tanjong ›	114	1.51 N	102.42 E
T'ohyŏn-ni	98	39.53 N	124.52 E
Toi, Nihon	94	34.54 N	138.47 E
Toi, Niue	174v	18.57 S	169.51 W
Toijala	26	61.10 N	23.52 E
Toili	112	1.27 S	122.24 E
Toi-misaki ›	92	31.20 N	131.22 E
Tōin	94	35.05 N	136.35 E
Toinya	140	6.17 N	29.44 E
Toi Sar	120	31.06 N	69.54 E
Toiyabe Range ⩘	204	39.10 N	117.10 W
Tojg	128	32.04 N	61.48 E
To-jima I	96	33.12 N	132.22 E
Tojo, Indon.	112	1.17 S	121.11 E
Tōjō, Nihon	96	34.53 N	133.16 E
Tōjō, Nihon	270	34.55 N	135.04 E
Tojtepa	85	41.03 N	69.22 E
Tōju-in ⊍[1]	94	35.19 N	136.04 E
Tok	180	63.19 N	142.59 W
Tok ≃	80	52.46 N	52.22 E
Tokaanu	172	38.58 S	175.46 E
Tokachi ≃	92a	42.44 N	143.42 E
Tokachi-dake ∧	92a	43.25 N	142.41 E
Tokachi-heiya ≚	92a	43.00 N	143.30 E
Tōkagi	268	35.42 N	139.56 E
Tokai, Malay.	114	6.01 N	100.24 E
Tōkai, Nihon	94	36.27 N	140.34 E
Tōkai, Nihon	94	35.00 N	136.53 E
Tokaj ≃	78	51.18 N	41.04 E
Tokala	112	1.47 S	121.43 E
Tōkamachi	94	37.08 N	138.46 E
Tokanui	172	46.34 S	168.56 E
Tokara-kaikyō ʊ	93b	30.10 N	130.10 E
Tokara-rettō II	93b	29.36 N	129.43 E
Tokarevka	86	50.08 N	73.12 E
Tokar Game Reserve ◆[4]	140	18.15 N	37.45 E
Tokar'ovka	80	51.59 N	41.09 E
Tokar'ovo, Ross.	76	55.17 N	35.04 E
Tokar'ovo, Ross.	265b	55.38 N	37.55 E
Tokashiki-jima I	93b	26.11 N	127.21 E
Tokat	130	40.19 N	36.34 E
Tokat □[4]	130	40.25 N	36.30 E
Tŏkchŏk-kundo II	98	37.14 N	126.07 E
Tŏkch'ŏn	98	39.46 N	126.19 E
Tokeland	224	46.42 N	123.58 W
Tokelau □[2]	14	9.00 S	171.45 W
Tokelau-Inseln → Tokelau □[2]	14	9.00 S	171.45 W
Tokeneke Brook ≃	276	41.03 N	73.28 W
Tŏkhŭng-ni	98	40.02 N	127.08 E
Toki	94	35.21 N	137.11 E
Toki ≃	94	35.12 N	136.52 E
Tokio → Tōkyō	94	35.42 N	139.46 E
Toki Point ›	174a	19.19 N	166.35 E
Tokiwadaira	268	35.48 N	139.57 E
Tokke ⊜	26	59.01 N	9.15 E
Tokko	74	59.59 N	119.52 E
Tokko ≃	88	58.42 N	119.50 E
Toklar	130	38.26 N	36.01 E
Toklat ≃	180	64.27 N	150.17 W
Tokma	88	58.13 N	105.42 E
Tokmak, Kyrg.	85	42.55 N	75.18 E
Tokmak, Ukr.	78	47.15 N	35.43 E
Toko	172	39.20 S	174.24 E
Tököl	264c	47.19 N	18.58 E
Tokolimbu	112	2.48 S	121.34 E
Tokomaru	172	40.28 S	175.30 E
Tokomaru Bay	172	38.08 S	178.18 E
Tokoname	94	34.53 N	136.51 E
Toko Range ⩘	166	23.05 S	138.20 E
Tokoro ≃	92a	44.07 N	144.05 E
Tokoroa	172	38.14 S	175.52 E
Tokorozawa	94	35.47 N	139.28 E
Tokovs'ke	78	47.38 N	33.59 E
Tokrau ≃	86	46.48 N	75.24 E
Toksook Bay	180	60.32 N	165.06 W
Toksovo	76	60.09 N	30.31 E
Tok-to (Take-shima) II	92	37.17 N	131.53 E
Toktogul	85	41.50 N	72.50 E
Toktogul'skoje vodochranilišče ⊜[1]	85	41.50 N	72.55 E
Toku Island I	14	18.10 S	174.11 W
Tokuji	96	34.11 N	131.40 E
Tokul Creek ≃	224	47.35 N	121.50 W
Tokung	112	0.18 S	114.28 E
Tokuno-shima I	93b	27.45 N	128.58 E
Tokur	89	53.10 N	132.53 E
Tokura	270	34.58 N	135.18 E
Tokura-tōge)(	96	35.17 N	134.31 E
Tokusaga-mine ∧	96	34.26 N	131.41 E
Tokushima	96	34.04 N	134.34 E
Tokushima □[5]	96	33.45 N	134.00 E
Tokuyama, Nihon	94	35.42 N	136.29 E
Tokuyama, Nihon	96	34.03 N	131.49 E
Tokwe ≃	154	21.09 S	31.30 E
Tōkyō, Nihon	94	35.42 N	139.46 E
Tōkyō, Nihon	268	35.42 N	139.46 E
Tōkyō □[5]	94	35.45 N	139.30 E
Tokyo Bay → Tōkyō-wan ⊂	94	35.25 N	139.47 E
Tōkyō-daigaku-uchūkūkan-kenkyūsho ⊍[3]	92	31.17 N	131.05 E
Tokyo Disneyland ♦	268	35.37 N	139.53 E
Tōkyō-kō ⊂	268	35.37 N	139.47 E
Tōkyō-kokusai-kūkō ⊠	94	35.45 N	140.21 E
Tokyo Station ◆[5]	268	35.41 N	139.46 E
Tokyo Tower ⊍	268	35.39 N	139.45 E
Tokyo University ⊍[2]	268	35.42 N	139.46 E
Tokyo University of Education ⊍[2]	268	35.43 N	139.44 E
Tōkyō-wan (Tokyo Bay) ⊂	94	35.25 N	139.47 E
Tokzār	120	35.52 N	66.26 E
Tol I	175c	7.22 N	151.37 E
Tolaga Bay	172	38.22 S	178.18 E
Tolala	112	2.56 S	121.06 E
Tolang	114	1.56 N	99.26 E
Tolbert	52	53.10 N	6.21 E
Tolbo Nuur	86	48.25 N	90.17 E
Tolbuchino	80	57.51 N	40.03 E
Tolderol Point ›	168b	35.22 S	139.10 E
Toldo, Pico del ∧	240p	20.30 N	74.54 W
Tole, Kaz.	85	42.40 N	70.08 E
Tolé, Pan.	236	8.14 N	81.41 W
Toledo, Bol.	248	18.10 S	67.25 W
Toledo, Bra.	252	24.44 S	53.45 W
Toledo, Bra.	256	22.44 S	46.23 W
Toledo, Col.	246	7.19 N	72.28 W
Toledo, Esp.	34	39.52 N	4.01 W
Toledo, Pil.	116	10.23 N	123.38 E
Toledo, Il., U.S.	194	39.16 N	88.14 W
Toledo, Ia., U.S.	190	41.59 N	92.34 W
Toledo, Oh., U.S.	214	41.39 N	83.33 W
Toledo, Or., U.S.	202	44.37 N	123.56 W
Toledo, Wa., U.S.	224	46.26 N	122.50 W
Toledo, Ur.	258	34.45 S	56.05 W
Toledo □[4]	34	39.45 N	4.00 W
Toledo □[5]	236	16.20 N	88.55 W
Toledo, Montes de ⩘	34	39.33 N	4.20 W
Toledo Bend Reservoir ⊜[1]	194	31.30 N	93.45 W
Toledo Express Airport ⊠	216	41.35 N	83.49 W

Symbols in the index entries represent the broad categories identified in the key at the right. Symbols with superior numbers (⩘[1]) identify subcategories (see complete key on page *I · 1).*

Symbole im Register stellen die rechts im Schlüssel erklärten Kategorien dar. Symbole mit hochgestellten Ziffern (⩘[1]) bezeichnen Unterabteilungen einer Kategorie (vgl. vollständiger Schlüssel auf Seite *I · 1).*

Los símbolos incluídos en el texto del índice representan las grandes categorías identificadas con la clave a la derecha. Los símbolos con numeros en su parte superior (⩘[1]) identifican las subcategorías (véase la clave completa en la página *I · 1).*

Les symboles de l'index représentent les catégories indiquées dans la légende à droite. Les symboles suivis d'un indice (⩘[1]) représentent des sous-catégories (voir légende complète à la page *I · 1).*

Os símbolos incluídos no texto do índice representam as grandes categorias identificadas com a chave à direita. Os símbolos com números em sua parte superior (⩘[1]) identificam as subcategorias (veja-se a chave completa à página *I · 1).*

∧ Mountain	Berg	Montaña	Montagne	Montanha
⩘ Mountains	Gebirge	Montañas	Montagnes	Montanhas
)(Pass	Paß	Paso	Col	Passo
V Valley, Canyon	Tal, Cañon	Valle, Cañón	Vallée, Canyon	Vale, Canhão
≚ Plain	Ebene	Llano	Plaine	Planície
› Cape	Kap	Cabo	Cap	Cabo
I Island	Insel	Isla	Île	Ilha
II Islands	Inseln	Islas	Îles	Ilhas
⊥ Other Topographic Features	Andere Topographische Objekte	Otros Elementos Topográficos	Autres données topographiques	Outros acidentes topográficos

ESPAÑOL

Nombre	Página	Lat.°'	Long.°' W = Oeste
Tolentino	66	43.12 N	13.17 E
Tolfa	66	42.09 N	11.56 E
Tolfa, Monti della ⋏	66	42.08 N	11.54 E
Tolga, Alg.	148	34.46 N	5.22 E
Tolga, Nor.	26	62.25 N	11.00 E
Toli	86	45.57 N	83.37 E
Toliara	157b	23.21 S	43.40 E
Toliara □[4]	157b	24.00 S	45.00 E
Tolima □[5]	246	3.45 N	75.15 W
Tolima, Nevado del ∧	246	4.40 N	75.19 W
Tolimán, Méx.	234	19.36 N	103.55 W
Tolimán, Méx.	234	20.55 N	99.56 W
Tolitoli	112	1.02 N	120.49 E
Toljatti (Togliatti)	80	53.31 N	49.26 E
Tol'ka	74	64.02 N	81.55 E
Tolkmicko	30	54.20 N	19.31 E
Tolland	207	41.52 N	72.22 W
Tolland □[6]	207	41.52 N	72.22 W
Tollarp	26	55.56 N	13.59 E
Tollense ≃	54	53.54 N	13.02 E
Tollensesee ⊜	54	53.30 N	13.11 E
Tollesboro	218	38.33 N	83.34 W
Tollesbury	42	51.46 N	0.50 E
Tolleson	200	33.27 N	112.15 W
Tollhouse	226	37.01 N	119.23 W
Tolloche	252	25.30 S	63.32 W
Tølløse	41	55.37 N	11.45 E
Tollygunge ◆[8]	272b	22.30 N	88.21 E
Tolmači	76	57.26 N	35.41 E
Tolmačovo	76	58.52 N	29.55 E
Tolmezzo	64	46.24 N	13.01 E
Tolmin	36	46.11 N	13.44 E
Tolna	30	46.26 N	18.46 E
Tolna □[6]	30	46.30 N	18.35 E
Tolo	152	2.56 S	18.34 E
Tolo, Teluk c	112	2.00 S	122.30 E
Toloa, Houma ›	174w	21.17 S	175.08 W
Toločin	76	54.25 N	29.42 E
Tolokiwa Island I	164	5.20 S	147.40 E
Tolomo	89	50.03 N	137.45 E
Tolong Bay c	116	9.20 N	122.49 E
Tolongoina	157b	21.33 S	47.31 E
Tolono	194	39.59 N	88.15 W
Tolosa	34	43.08 N	2.04 W
Tolosa, Aeródromo ⊠	288	34.53 S	57.58 W
Tolovana ≃	180	64.51 N	149.45 W
Tolpuddle	42	50.45 N	2.18 W
Tolsan-do I	98	34.38 N	127.45 E
Tol'skij Majdan	80	54.57 N	44.39 E
Tolsta Head ›	46	58.20 N	6.10 W
Tolstoj, mys ›	74	59.10 N	155.12 E
Tolstopal'cevo	265b	55.38 N	37.13 E
Tolt, North Fork ≃	224	47.42 N	121.49 W
Toltén	254	39.13 S	73.14 W
Tolten ≃	254	39.15 S	73.14 W
Tolti	123	35.02 N	76.06 E
Tolt-Seattle Water Supply Reservoir ⊜[1]	224	47.42 N	121.39 W
Tolú	246	9.31 N	75.35 W
Toluca	216	41.00 N	89.08 W
Toluca, Nevado de ∧[1]	234	19.08 N	99.44 W
Toluca [de Lerdo]	234	19.17 N	99.40 W
Tolvajarvi	24	62.17 N	31.27 E
Tolvdalselva ≃	26	58.10 N	8.00 E
Tolve	68	40.42 N	16.01 E
Tolwa	140	6.38 N	32.37 E
Tolworth ◆[8]	260	51.23 N	0.17 W
Tolyatti → Toljatti	80	53.31 N	49.26 E
Tolybaj	86	50.31 N	62.19 E
Tom' ≃, Ross.	86	56.50 N	84.27 E
Tom' ≃, Ross.	89	51.00 N	127.54 E
Toma	150	12.46 N	2.53 W
Tomago	170	32.50 S	151.44 E
Tomah	190	43.58 N	90.30 W
Tomahawk	190	45.28 N	89.43 W
Tomakivka	78	47.48 N	34.44 E
Tomakomai	92a	42.38 N	141.36 E
Tomani	112	4.50 N	115.55 E
Tomanivi ∧	175g	17.37 S	178.01 E
Tomar, Kaz.	86	46.24 N	75.03 E
Tomar, Port.	34	39.36 N	8.25 W
Tomari	89	47.47 N	142.03 E
Tomarovka	78	50.41 N	36.14 E
Tomarza	130	38.27 N	35.49 E
Tomás Barrón (Eucaliptus)	248	17.35 S	67.31 W
Tomasboda ∧[2]	40	59.24 N	14.58 E
Tomás Gomensoro	252	30.26 S	57.26 W
Tomashhorod	78	51.19 N	27.02 E
Tomashpil'	78	48.33 N	28.31 E
Tomasine ≃	190	46.40 N	76.16 W
Tomás Jofré	258	34.43 S	59.19 W
Tomášov	61	48.09 N	17.16 E
Tomaszów Lubelski	30	50.28 N	23.25 E
Tomaszów Mazowiecki	30	51.32 N	20.01 E
Tomatin	46	57.20 N	3.59 W
Tomatlán	234	19.56 N	105.15 W
Tomatlán ≃	234	19.50 N	105.23 W
Tomave	248	20.06 S	66.35 W
Tomazina	255	23.46 S	49.58 W
Tomba di Nerone ◆[8]	267a	41.57 N	12.27 E
Tombadonkéa	150	11.00 N	14.23 W
Tombador, Serra do ⋏[1]	248	12.00 S	57.40 W
Tomball	222	30.06 N	95.37 W
Tombe	140	5.49 N	31.41 E
Tombigbee ≃	194	31.04 N	87.58 W
Tombo, Punta ›	254	44.03 S	65.11 W
Tombôco	152	6.48 S	13.18 E
Tombolo	64	45.38 N	11.50 E
Tombos	255	20.55 S	42.02 W
Tombouctou (Timbuktu)	150	16.46 N	3.01 W
Tombouctou □[4]	150	18.20 N	3.50 W
Tombs of the Caliphs ⊥	273c	30.03 N	31.17 E
Tombstone	200	31.42 N	110.04 W
Tombstone Mountain ∧	180	64.25 N	138.30 W
Tombua	152	15.49 S	11.53 E
Tom Burke	156	23.05 S	28.00 E
Tomdoun	46	57.04 N	5.03 W
Tomé	252	36.37 S	72.57 W
Tomea, Pulau I	112	5.45 S	123.56 E
Tomé-Açu	250	2.25 S	48.09 W
Tömek	130	38.02 N	32.41 E
Tomelilla	26	55.33 N	13.57 E
Tomelloso	34	39.10 N	3.01 W
Tomerong	170	35.04 S	150.35 E
Tomhannock Reservoir ⊜[1]	210	42.51 N	73.33 W
Tomi ≃	152	5.07 N	19.19 E
Tomich	46	57.18 N	4.48 W
Tomichi Creek ≃	200	38.31 N	106.58 W
Tomifobia ≃	206	45.11 N	72.02 W
Tomiko Lake ⊜	190	46.32 N	79.49 W
Tomilino	265b	55.39 N	37.57 E
Tomini	112	0.30 N	120.32 E
Tomini, Teluk c	112	0.20 S	121.00 E
Tominian	150	13.17 N	4.35 W
Tomintoul	46	57.14 N	3.22 W
Tomio ≃	270	34.35 N	135.44 E
Tomioka	94	36.15 N	138.54 E
Tomisato	94	35.44 N	140.19 E
Tomiura	94	35.03 N	139.50 E
Tomiyama, Nihon	94	35.11 N	137.48 E
Tomiyama, Nihon	94	35.05 N	139.51 E
Tomizawa	94	35.14 N	138.29 E
T'omkino	76	55.05 N	35.01 E
Tomkins Cove	210	41.15 N	73.59 W
Tomkinson Ranges ⋏	162	26.11 S	129.05 E
Tomkinsville	208	38.19 N	76.53 W
Tomlinson Run State Park ♠	214	40.33 N	80.34 W
Tommerup Stationsby	41	55.19 N	10.13 E

FRANÇAIS

Nom	Page	Lat.°'	Long.°' W = Ouest
Tommot	74	58.58 N	126.19 E
Tomnavoulin	46	57.18 N	3.19 W
T'omnyj	88	53.24 N	118.31 E
Tomo ≃	246	5.20 N	67.48 W
Tomobe	94	36.20 N	140.20 E
Tomogashima-suidō ʯ	96	34.17 N	135.00 E
Tomohon	112	1.19 N	124.49 E
Tömör Bulag	88	49.16 N	100.15 E
Tomori	174m	26.08 N	127.44 E
Tomori, Teluk c	112	1.58 S	121.28 E
Tompa	88	55.08 N	109.47 E
Tompkins, Nf., Can.	186	47.48 N	59.13 W
Tompkins, Sk., Can.	184	50.04 N	108.47 W
Tompkins □[6]	210	42.27 N	76.30 W
Tompkins County Airport ⊠	210	42.29 N	76.57 W
Tompkinsville	194	36.42 N	85.41 W
Tompo	112	0.56 N	120.20 E
Tom Price	162	22.41 S	117.43 E
Tom Price, Mount ∧	162	22.39 S	117.40 E
Tomptokan	74	57.06 N	133.59 E
Tomra	26	62.35 N	6.56 E
Toms ≃	208	39.57 N	74.07 W
Toms, Ridgeway Branch ≃	208	40.00 N	74.14 W
Toms Cove c	208	37.53 N	75.22 W
Toms Creek ≃	208	39.38 N	77.17 W
Tomsk	86	56.30 N	84.58 E
Tomsk Oblast' □[4]	86	58.00 N	82.00 E
Toms River	208	39.58 N	74.12 W
Tom Steed Reservoir ⊜[1]	196	34.45 N	99.00 W
Tomtabacken ∧[2]	26	57.30 N	14.28 E
Tömük	130	36.41 N	34.22 E
Tomuzlovka ≃	84	44.46 N	44.10 E
Ton	64	46.15 N	11.04 E
Tonadico	64	46.11 N	11.50 E
Tonaki-shima I	93b	26.21 N	127.09 E
Tonalá, Méx.	234	16.04 N	93.45 W
Tonalá, Méx.	234	20.37 N	103.14 W
Tonalá ≃	234	18.13 N	94.11 W
Tonale, Passo del)(	64	46.16 N	10.35 E
Tonami	94	36.38 N	136.54 E
Tonantins	246	2.47 S	67.47 W
Tonantins ≃	246	2.47 S	67.47 W
Tonara	71	40.02 N	9.10 E
Tonasket	202	48.42 N	119.26 W
Tonate	250	4.55 N	52.22 W
Tonatico	234	18.47 N	99.41 W
Tonawanda, N.Y., U.S.	210	43.01 N	78.52 W
Tonawanda, N.Y., U.S.	210	42.59 N	78.52 W
Tonawanda Channel ≃[1]	284a	43.04 N	79.00 W
Tonawanda Creek ≃	210	43.02 N	78.53 W
Tonawanda Indian Reservation ◆[4]	210	43.05 N	78.27 W
Tonawanda Island I	284a	43.02 N	78.53 W
Tonbara	96	35.05 N	132.47 E
Tonbo	110	18.31 N	95.05 E
Tonbridge	42	51.12 N	0.16 E
Tonbridge and Malling □[8]	260	51.16 N	0.20 E
Tonda	270	34.50 N	135.36 E
Tonda ≃	96	33.38 N	135.24 E
Tondabayashi	96	34.30 N	135.36 E
Tondano	112	1.19 N	124.54 E
Tønder	41	54.56 N	8.54 E
Tondhre	272c	19.05 N	73.08 E
Tondi	122	9.44 N	79.01 E
Tondibi	150	16.39 N	0.14 W
Tondidji	150	13.06 N	10.20 W
Tondi Kiwindi	150	14.28 N	2.02 E
Tondoro	156	17.45 S	18.50 E
Tone, Nihon	94	36.42 N	139.13 E
Tone, Nihon	94	35.51 N	140.09 E
Tone ≃	94	35.44 N	140.51 E
Tonekābon	128	36.49 N	50.53 E
Tone-unga ≊	268	35.54 N	139.53 E
Tonež	78	51.49 N	27.48 E
Tonga, Cam.	152	4.58 N	10.42 E
Tonga, Sūd.	140	9.28 N	31.03 E
Tonga □[1]	14	20.00 S	175.00 W
Tongaat	158	29.37 S	31.03 E
Tonga Islands II	14	20.00 S	175.00 W
Tong'an	100	24.46 N	118.08 E
Tonganoxie	198	39.06 N	95.05 W
Tong'anqiao	106	31.22 N	120.27 E
Tonga Ridge ✢[3]	14	21.00 S	175.00 W
Tongariro, Mount ∧	172	39.08 S	175.38 E
Tongariro National Park ♠	172	39.15 S	175.30 E
Tongas	115a	7.44 S	113.06 E
Tongatapu □[8]	174w	21.10 S	175.10 W
Tongatapu I	174w	21.10 S	175.10 W
Tongatapu Group II	14	21.10 S	175.10 W
Tonga Trench ✢[1]	14	20.00 S	173.00 W
Tongbai, Zhg.	100	32.22 N	113.24 E
Tongbai, Zhg.	105	39.35 N	116.44 E
Tongbai Shan ∧	100	32.20 N	113.14 E
Tongbai Shan ⋏	100	32.20 N	113.15 E
Tongbei	89	47.45 N	126.46 E
Tongcheng, Zhg.	100	31.03 N	116.58 E
Tongcheng, Zhg.	100	32.53 N	118.58 E
Tongcheng, Zhg.	100	29.11 N	113.49 E
Tongchengzha	100	31.30 N	118.07 E
Tongchengzhuang	105	39.22 N	117.36 E
T'ongch'ŏn	98	38.54 N	127.54 E
Tongchuan	102	35.01 N	109.01 E
Tongdao	102	26.23 N	109.23 E
Tongde	102	35.17 N	100.42 E
Tongerbao	104	41.26 N	123.02 E
Tongeren	56	50.47 N	5.28 E
Tongerlo	56	51.07 N	4.54 E
Tonggou	98	41.53 N	125.46 E
Tonggu, Zhg.	100	28.33 N	114.21 E
Tonggu, Zhg.	100	21.53 N	112.55 E
Tongguan, Zhg.	100	28.29 N	112.48 E
Tongguan, Zhg.	102	34.38 N	110.20 E
Tongguan, Zhg.	102	23.18 N	101.23 E
Tongguanyi	107	29.20 N	106.23 E
Tonghai	102	24.07 N	102.49 E
Tonghaikou	100	30.14 N	113.08 E
Tonghe, Zhg.	89	45.59 N	128.45 E
Tonghe, Zhg.	100	32.56 N	112.45 E
Tongho-ri	98	35.49 N	127.54 E
Tonghua, Zhg.	98	41.41 N	125.55 E
Tonghua (Kuaidamao), Zhg.	98	41.40 N	125.44 E
Tonghui ≃	271a	39.53 N	116.41 E
Tongi	126	23.53 N	90.24 E
Tong Island I	164	2.05 S	147.50 E
Tongjiang, Zhg.	89	47.40 N	132.30 E
Tongjiang, Zhg.	102	31.58 N	107.14 E
Tongjiangchang	107	29.37 N	103.43 E
Tongjiangkou	104	42.37 N	123.41 E
Tongjing	100	31.47 N	118.33 E
Tongjosŏn-man c	98	39.30 N	128.00 E
Tongjuzhen	98	38.36 N	117.11 E
Tongken ≃	89	46.31 N	126.22 E
Tongli	106	31.10 N	120.43 E
Tongliang	107	29.51 N	106.03 E
Tongliao	89	43.39 N	122.14 E
Tongling, Zhg.	100	30.53 N	117.46 E
Tongling, Zhg.	102	23.28 N	109.40 E
Tonglu	100	29.48 N	119.40 E
Tonglü Yunhe ≊	106	32.04 N	121.40 E
Tongmang-ni	98	37.37 N	126.26 E
Tongmu, Zhg.	100	27.57 N	113.55 E
Tongmu, Zhg.	102	24.09 N	110.04 E
Tongnae	98	35.12 N	129.05 E
Tongnan	107	30.11 N	105.48 E
Tongno-gang ≃	98	40.58 N	126.04 E
Tongo	166	30.30 S	143.45 E
Tongoa I	175f	16.54 S	168.34 E
Tongobory	157b	23.32 S	44.20 E
Tongololo Creek ≃	162	22.06 S	121.08 E
Tongoy	252	30.15 S	71.30 W

PORTUGUÊS

Nome	Página	Lat.°'	Long.°' W = Oeste
Tongqin	100	28.52 N	119.56 E
Tongquansi	107	30.23 N	104.50 E
Tongquil Island I	116	6.02 N	121.51 E
Tongren, Zhg.	102	27.38 N	109.03 E
Tongren, Zhg.	102	35.32 N	101.54 E
Tongrengchang	107	30.02 N	106.42 E
Tongsa ≃	124	26.52 N	90.57 E
Tongsa Dzong	124	27.31 N	90.30 E
Tongsan-ni	271b	37.38 N	126.53 E
Tongshan	100	29.38 N	114.29 E
Tongshi	98	35.26 N	117.43 E
Tongshuping	100	27.17 N	114.54 E
Tongta	110	21.20 N	99.16 E
Tongtai	100	32.38 N	120.47 E
Tongtan	107	28.56 N	105.17 E
Tongtian ≃	102	33.25 N	96.32 E
Tongue	46	58.28 N	4.25 W
Tongue ≃, U.S.	202	46.24 N	105.52 W
Tongue ≃, N.D., U.S.	198	48.56 N	97.18 W
Tongue ≃, Tx., U.S.	196	34.07 N	100.25 W
Tongue, Kyle of c	46	58.30 N	4.26 W
Tongue of the Ocean ✢[1]	238	24.30 N	77.30 W
Tongue River Reservoir ⊜[1]	202	45.06 N	106.47 W
Tongwei	102	35.07 N	105.27 E
Tongxi	107	29.59 N	106.08 E
Tongxian	105	39.55 N	116.39 E
Tongxianchang	107	30.14 N	105.24 E
Tongxiang	106	30.38 N	120.32 E
Tongxin	102	37.02 N	106.09 E
Tongxinchang	107	29.42 N	106.26 E
Tongxing	107	30.35 N	106.12 E
Tongxu	98	34.29 N	114.28 E
Tongyang-ni	98	39.08 N	126.52 E
Tongyang Yunhe ≊	106	32.02 N	120.48 E
Tongyu	89	44.48 N	123.05 E
Tongyuan, Zhg.	100	28.04 N	116.08 E
Tongyuan, Zhg.	106	30.28 N	120.52 E
Tongyuanpu	104	40.49 N	123.54 E
Tongzhaipu	100	32.48 N	112.44 E
Tongzi	102	28.08 N	106.49 E
Tongzidixia	104	41.08 N	120.34 E
Tonica	216	41.12 N	89.04 W
Tonila	234	19.26 N	103.31 W
Tönisberg	263	51.25 N	6.30 E
Tönisheide	263	51.19 N	7.03 E
Tönisvorst	56	51.19 N	6.29 E
Tonj	140	7.17 N	28.45 E
Tonk	120	26.10 N	75.47 E
Tonkawa	196	36.40 N	97.18 W
Tonkin → Bac Phan □[9]	110	22.00 N	105.00 E
Tonkin, Gulf of c	110	20.00 N	108.00 E
Tonkino	80	57.23 N	46.28 E
Tonkou, Mont ∧	150	7.27 N	7.39 W
Tonkwa	110	23.36 N	96.58 E
Tônlé Sab, Bœng ⊜	110	13.00 N	104.00 E
Tonle Sap → Tônlé Sab, Bœng ⊜	110	13.00 N	104.00 E
Tonnay-Boutonne	32	45.58 N	0.42 W
Tonneins	32	44.23 N	0.19 E
Tonner Canyon V	280	33.58 N	117.48 W
Tonnerre	50	47.51 N	3.58 E
Tönnet	40	60.14 N	13.30 E
Tönning	41	54.19 N	8.56 E
Tōno	92	39.19 N	141.32 E
Tonogaya	268	35.46 N	139.22 E
Tonopah	204	38.04 N	117.13 W
Tōnoshō, Nihon	94	35.49 N	140.42 E
Tonoshō, Nihon	96	34.29 N	134.11 E
Tonosí	246	7.24 N	80.27 W
Tonota	156	21.29 S	27.29 E
Tonquish Creek ≃	281	42.21 N	83.22 W
Tons ≃	124	25.17 N	82.04 E
Tonšajevo	80	57.44 N	47.00 E
Tønsberg	26	59.17 N	10.25 E
Tönsholt	263	51.38 N	6.58 E
Tonstad	26	58.40 N	6.43 E
Tonto Creek ≃	200	33.46 N	111.15 W
Tontogany	216	41.25 N	83.44 W
Tonto National Monument ♠	200	33.34 N	111.02 W
Tonya	130	40.53 N	39.16 E
Tonypandy	42	51.38 N	3.27 W
Tonyrefail	42	51.36 N	3.25 W
Toobeah	166	28.25 S	149.52 E
Toodyay	168a	31.33 S	116.28 E
Tooele	200	40.31 N	112.17 W
Toogoolawah	171a	27.06 S	152.23 E
Tool	222	32.16 N	96.10 W
Toolik ≃	180	69.55 N	149.30 W
Tooma	171b	35.58 S	148.03 E
Tooma ≃	171b	36.04 S	148.00 E
Tooma Reservoir ⊜[1]	171b	36.04 S	148.16 E
Toomebridge	48	54.45 N	6.27 W
Toompine	166	27.13 S	144.22 E
Toomsboro	192	32.49 N	83.04 W
Toomyvara	48	52.50 N	8.02 W
Toongabbie	274a	33.47 S	150.57 E
Toora	169	38.40 S	146.20 E
Toora-Chem	88	52.28 N	96.17 E
Toorak	274b	37.51 S	145.01 E
Toormakeady	48	53.39 N	9.24 W
Toosey Indian Reserve ◆[4]	182	51.56 N	122.29 W
Toot Hill	260	51.42 N	0.12 E
Tootias	144	3.57 N	43.57 E
Tootie, Mount ∧	170	33.28 S	150.30 E
Tootsi	76	58.34 N	24.47 E
Toowoomba	171a	27.33 S	151.57 E
Topanga	228	34.06 N	118.36 W
Topanga Canyon V	280	34.05 N	118.36 W
Topanga State Park ♠	280	34.06 N	118.33 W
Topar	86	49.32 N	72.50 E
Topawa	200	31.48 N	111.49 W
Topaz Lake ⊜	226	38.41 N	119.32 W
Topçam	130	40.38 N	37.48 E
Topchānchi	126	23.54 N	86.12 E
Töpchin	54	52.10 N	13.34 E
Topčicha	86	52.49 N	83.10 E
Topeka, In., U.S.	216	41.32 N	85.32 W
Topeka, Ks., U.S.	198	39.02 N	95.40 W
Töpen	54	50.23 N	11.52 E
Topia	232	25.13 N	106.34 W
Topilejo ◆[8]	286a	19.12 N	99.09 W
Topino ≃	66	43.02 N	12.30 E
Topkanovo	82	54.43 N	38.29 E
Topkapı ◆[8]	267b	41.02 N	28.54 E
Topkapi Palace ⊥	267b	41.00 N	28.59 E
Topki	86	55.16 N	85.36 E
Topko, gora ∧	74	57.08 N	137.24 E
Topl'a ≃	30	48.45 N	21.45 E
Topley	182	54.30 N	126.18 W
Toplica ≃	38	43.13 N	21.49 E
Toplița	38	46.55 N	25.21 E
T'oploje, Ross.	76	53.13 N	38.53 E
T'oploje, Ross.	76	53.37 N	37.36 E
T'oplyj Stan	80	53.58 N	50.10 E
T'oplyj Stan ◆[8]	265b	55.37 N	37.30 E
Topo ≃	286c	10.33 N	67.00 W
Topocalma, Punta ›	252	34.08 S	72.01 W
Top of Hebers	262	53.34 N	2.12 W
Topo Infiernito ∧	286c	10.33 N	66.55 W
Topol'čany	30	48.34 N	18.10 E
Topoli	80	47.59 N	51.36 E
Topolobampo	232	25.36 N	109.03 W
Topolog	38	44.53 N	28.22 E
Topolovățu Mare	38	45.46 N	21.37 E
Topolovgrad	38	42.05 N	26.20 E
Toporok	76	58.33 N	33.28 E
Topozero, ozero ⊜	24	65.40 N	32.00 E
Toppenish	202	46.22 N	120.18 W
Toppenish Creek ≃	202	46.20 N	120.11 W
Toppenish Ridge ∧	224	46.18 N	120.40 W
Toppings	262	53.37 N	2.25 W
Toprakkale	130	37.06 N	36.07 E
Tops, Mount ∧	162	21.50 S	134.00 E

Topsa	24	62.39 N	43.34 E
Topsfield	207	42.38 N	70.57 W
Topsham, Eng., U.K.	42	50.41 N	3.27 W
Topsham, Me., U.S.	188	43.55 N	69.58 W
Top Springs	164	16.38 S	131.50 E
Topton	208	40.30 N	75.42 W
Toquima Range ⋏	204	38.45 N	116.55 W
Toquop Wash V	204	36.45 N	114.11 W
Tor	144	7.51 N	33.35 E
Torahime	94	35.25 N	136.16 E
Torano Castello	68	39.30 N	16.08 E
Torawitan, Tanjung ›	112	1.46 N	124.58 E
Toraya	248	14.03 S	73.18 W
Torbalı	130	38.10 N	27.21 E
Torbat-e Ḥeydarīyeh	128	35.16 N	59.13 E
Torbat-e Jām	128	35.14 N	60.36 E
Torbay	186	47.40 N	52.44 W
Torbay □[9]	42	50.26 N	3.34 W
Tor Bay c	42	50.25 N	3.30 W
Torbejevo, Ross.	80	54.05 N	43.15 E
Torbejevo, Ross.	82	54.44 N	36.11 E
Torbert, Mount ∧	180	61.25 N	152.24 W
Torbino	76	58.35 N	32.53 E
Torbole	64	45.52 N	10.52 E
Torbreck, Mount ∧	169	37.21 S	145.57 E
Torbrook	186	44.55 N	64.59 W
Torch ≃	184	53.50 N	103.05 W
Torchany	80	55.34 N	46.36 E
Torchiarolo	68	40.29 N	18.03 E
Torch Lake ⊜	190	45.00 N	85.19 W
Torchyn	78	50.46 N	24.59 E
Torcy	261	48.51 N	2.39 E
Torda → Turda	38	46.34 N	23.47 E
Tordera ≃	34	41.39 N	2.47 E
Tordesillas	34	41.30 N	5.00 W
Tordino ≃	66	42.44 N	13.59 E
Tor di Quinto ◆[8]	267a	41.56 N	12.28 E
Töre	26	65.54 N	22.39 E
Töreboda	40	58.43 N	14.08 E
Torej	88	50.33 N	104.50 E
Torekov	26	56.26 N	12.37 E
Toreno	34	42.42 N	6.30 W
Torez	83	48.01 N	38.37 E
Torfou	261	48.32 N	2.14 E
Torgau	54	51.34 N	13.00 E
Torgelow	54	53.37 N	14.00 E
Torgelower See ⊜	54	53.34 N	12.47 E
Torgo	88	58.28 N	119.50 E
Torgun ≃	80	50.15 N	46.18 E
Torhamn	26	56.05 N	15.50 E
Torhout	50	51.04 N	3.06 E
Toribulu	112	0.19 S	120.01 E
Toride	94	35.53 N	140.04 E
Torigakubi-misaki ›	94	37.10 N	138.06 E
Torigoe	94	36.21 N	136.36 E
Toriido	270	34.25 N	135.43 E
Torii-tōge)(	94	36.29 N	138.24 E
Toriki	265a	59.47 N	30.07 E
Torino (Turin)	62	45.03 N	7.40 E
Torino □[4]	62	45.08 N	7.22 E
Torino di Sangro Marina	66	42.11 N	14.32 E
Torío ≃	34	42.35 N	5.34 W
Toriparu	255	16.20 S	53.55 W
Torit	154	4.24 N	32.34 E
Toritto	68	41.00 N	16.41 E
Toriya	94	36.59 N	136.54 E
Torjun	115a	7.10 S	113.13 E
Torkestān, Selseleh-ye Band-e ⋏	128	35.25 N	64.15 E
Torkoviči	76	58.52 N	30.20 E
Torlino	86	58.53 N	63.46 E
Torment, Point ›	162	17.02 S	123.36 E
Tormentine, Cape ›	186	46.07 N	63.47 W
Tormes ≃	34	41.18 N	6.29 W
Tormestorp	41	56.07 N	13.44 E
Tormey	282	38.03 N	122.15 W
Tormini	64	45.36 N	10.29 E
Tormosin	80	48.12 N	42.42 E
Torna	24	68.04 N	44.10 E
Torna ∧	122	18.16 N	73.37 E
Tornado Mountain ∧	182	49.58 N	114.39 W
Tornal'a	30	48.27 N	20.20 E
Tornareccio	66	42.02 N	14.24 E
Tornberget ∧[2]	40	59.08 N	18.01 E
Torne ≃	44	53.36 N	0.44 W
Torneälven (Tornionjoki) ≃	24	65.48 N	24.08 E
Torne Brook ≃	276	41.08 N	74.10 W
Tornesch	52	53.41 N	9.43 E
Torneträsk ⊜	24	68.20 N	19.10 E
Torngat Mountains ⋏	176	59.00 N	64.00 W
Tornillo	200	31.27 N	106.05 W
Tornillo Creek ≃	196	29.11 N	103.00 W
Tornimparte	66	42.17 N	13.18 E
Torning	41	56.17 N	9.20 E
Tornio	26	65.51 N	24.08 E
Tornionjoki (Torneälven) ≃	24	65.48 N	24.08 E
Tornquist	252	38.06 S	62.14 W
Tornyiszentmiklós	61	46.31 N	16.34 E
Toro	34	41.31 N	5.24 W
Torö I	40	58.50 N	17.50 E
Toro, Arroyo ≃	288	34.27 S	58.52 W
Toro, Cañada del ≃	258	35.16 S	59.05 W
Toro, Cerro ∧	234	19.10 N	104.27 W
Toro, Lago del ⊜	254	51.14 S	72.45 W
Toro, Punta ›	252	33.47 S	71.49 W
Torobuku	112	4.25 S	122.26 E
Torodi	150	13.18 N	1.40 E
Toro-iseki ⊥	94	34.57 N	138.24 E
Torok	146	10.03 N	14.33 E
Torokina	175e	6.14 S	155.03 E
Törökszentmiklós	30	47.11 N	20.25 E
Torola ≃	236	13.52 N	88.30 W
Torom	89	54.32 N	135.50 E
Torom ≃	89	54.36 N	135.46 E
Toroni, Nevado ∧	248	19.43 S	68.41 W
Toronto, Austl.	170	33.01 S	151.36 E
Toronto, On., Can.	212	43.39 N	79.23 W
Toronto, On., Can.	275b	43.39 N	79.23 W
Toronto, Ks., U.S.	198	37.47 N	95.56 W
Toronto, Oh., U.S.	214	40.27 N	80.36 W
Toronto, S.D., U.S.	198	44.34 N	96.38 W
Toronto □[6]	275b	43.44 N	79.24 W
Toronto, Canadian Forces Base ■	212	43.45 N	79.28 W
Toronto, University of ʊ[2]	275b	43.40 N	79.24 W
Toronto Harbour c	275b	43.38 N	79.22 W
Toronto Island Airport ⊠	275b	43.38 N	79.24 W
Toronto Lake ⊜[1]	198	37.46 N	95.57 W
Toronto Reservoir ⊜[1]	210	41.38 N	74.51 W
Toronto Zoo, Metro ♠	275b	43.49 N	79.11 W
Toro Peak ∧	204	33.32 N	116.25 W
Toropec	76	56.30 N	31.39 E
Toropovo	82	54.21 N	36.07 E
Tororo	154	0.42 N	34.11 E
Toros (Acho), Plaza de ♠	286d	12.02 S	77.02 W
Toros Dağları (Taurus Mountains) ⋏	130	37.00 N	33.00 E
Torošino	76	57.56 N	28.36 E
Torosozero	24	62.30 N	38.10 E
Torotoro	248	18.07 S	65.46 W
Toroume ∧[2]	174k	21.15 S	159.45 W
Torpa ⊥	26	57.39 N	13.16 E
Torpè	71	40.38 N	9.40 E
Torphins	46	57.06 N	2.37 W
Tor Pignatara ◆[8]	267a	41.52 N	12.32 E
Torpo	26	60.40 N	8.43 E
Torpoint	42	50.22 N	4.11 W
Torpy ≃	182	53.44 N	120.55 W
Torquay, Austl.	169	38.21 S	144.19 E
Torquay, Sk., Can.	184	49.08 N	103.31 W
Torquay, Eng., U.K.	42	50.28 N	3.30 W
Torquemada	34	42.02 N	4.19 W
Torraca	68	40.07 N	15.38 E

Torrance, Ca., U.S.	228	33.50 N	118.20 W
Torrance, Pa., U.S.	214	40.25 N	79.14 W
Torrance Lake ⊜	184	57.04 N	98.12 W
Torrance Municipal Airport ⊠	280	33.48 N	118.20 W
Torrão	34	38.18 N	8.13 W
Torre Annunziata	68	40.45 N	14.27 E
Torre Baja	34	40.07 N	1.15 W
Torrebelvicino	64	45.43 N	11.18 E
Torre Beretti	62	45.04 N	8.40 E
Torreblanca	34	40.13 N	0.12 E
Torrebruna	66	41.52 N	14.33 E
Torrecilla ∧	34	37.36 N	2.31 W
Torrecilla en Cameros	34	42.16 N	2.37 W
Torre del Campo	34	37.46 N	3.53 W
Torre del Greco	68	40.47 N	14.22 E
Torre del Lago Puccini	66	43.50 N	10.17 E
Torre de Moncorvo	34	41.10 N	7.03 W
Torre de'Passeri	66	42.14 N	13.56 E
Torre di Mosto	64	45.41 N	12.43 E
Torre di Santa Maria	64	46.14 N	9.51 E
Torredonjimeno	34	37.46 N	3.57 W
Torre Faro ◆[8]	70	38.16 N	15.39 E
Torre Gaia ◆[8]	267a	41.51 N	12.39 E
Torregrotta	70	38.11 N	15.21 E
Torrejon Air Base ■	266a	40.28 N	3.28 W
Torrejoncillo	34	39.54 N	6.28 W
Torrejón de Ardoz	34	40.27 N	3.29 W
Torrejón-Tajo, Embalse de ⊜[1]	34	39.50 N	5.50 W
Torrelaguna	34	40.50 N	3.32 W
Torrelavega	34	43.21 N	4.03 W
Torrellas, Riera de ≃	266d	41.23 N	2.01 E
Torrelles de Llobregat	266d	41.21 N	1.59 E
Torrelletes	266d	41.21 N	1.57 E
Torremaggiore	68	41.41 N	15.17 E
Torremolinos	34	36.37 N	4.30 W
Torrenieri	66	43.05 N	11.33 E
Torrens ≃	168b	34.56 S	138.30 E
Torrens, Lake ⊜	166	31.00 S	137.50 E
Torrens, Mount ∧	168b	34.52 S	138.56 E
Torrens Creek	166	20.46 S	145.02 E
Torrens Creek ≃	166	22.22 S	145.09 E
Torrens Island I	168b	34.48 S	138.32 E
Torrent, Arg.	252	28.50 S	56.28 W
Torrent, Esp.	34	39.26 N	0.28 W
Torreões	256	21.52 S	43.33 W
Torreón	232	25.33 N	103.26 W
Torre Orsaia	68	40.08 N	15.28 E
Torre Pedrera	66	44.06 N	12.31 E
Torre Pellice	62	44.49 N	7.13 E
Torreperogil	34	38.02 N	3.17 W
Torres, Arg.	258	34.26 S	59.08 W
Torres, Bra.	252	29.21 S	49.44 W
Torres, Arroyo ≃	288	34.39 S	58.45 W
Torres, Îles II	175f	13.15 S	166.37 E
Torre Santa Susanna	68	40.28 N	17.44 E
Torresdale ◆[8]	285	40.03 N	75.00 W
Torres de Alcalá	34	35.10 N	4.16 W
Torres Martinez Indian Reservation ◆[4]	204	33.35 N	116.02 W
Torres Novas	34	39.29 N	8.32 W
Torres Strait ʯ	164	10.25 S	142.10 E
Torres Vedras	34	39.06 N	9.16 W
Torretta	70	38.08 N	13.14 E
Torrette di Fano	66	43.47 N	13.07 E
Torrevella	34	37.59 N	0.41 W
Torricella	68	40.21 N	17.29 E
Torricella in Sabina	66	42.16 N	12.52 E
Torricella Peligna	66	42.01 N	14.15 E
Torricella Sicura	66	42.39 N	13.39 E
Torricelli Mountains ⋏	164	3.25 S	142.20 E
Torridge ≃	42	51.03 N	4.11 W
Torridon	46	57.33 N	5.31 W
Torridon, Loch c	46	57.35 N	5.46 W
Torriglia	62	44.31 N	9.10 E
Torrijos, Esp.	34	39.59 N	4.17 W
Torrijos, Pil.	116	13.19 N	122.05 E
Torrild	41	55.59 N	10.04 E
Torrimpietra ◆[8]	267a	41.56 N	12.13 E
Torrin	46	57.12 N	6.02 W
Tørring	41	55.51 N	9.29 E
Torrington, Ct., U.S.	207	41.48 N	73.07 W
Torrington, Wy., U.S.	198	42.03 N	104.10 W
Torrinha	255	22.26 S	48.09 W
Torrita di Siena	66	43.10 N	11.46 E
Torröjen ⊜	26	63.55 N	12.56 E
Torrox	34	36.46 N	3.58 W
Torrvarpen ⊜	40	59.42 N	14.30 E
Torsåker	40	60.31 N	16.29 E
Tor Sapienza ◆[8]	267a	41.54 N	12.35 E
Torsås	26	56.24 N	16.00 E
Torsburgen ⊥	26	57.25 N	18.43 E
Torsby	26	60.08 N	13.00 E
Tors Cove	186	47.13 N	52.51 W
Torshälla	40	59.25 N	16.28 E
Tórshavn	22	62.01 N	6.46 W
Torside Reservoir ⊜[1]	262	53.29 N	1.54 W
Torsö	40	58.47 N	13.48 E
Torsö I	40	58.48 N	13.50 E
Torteval	43b	49.27 N	2.38 W
Torto ≃	70	37.58 N	13.46 E
Tortola I	240m	18.27 N	64.36 W
Tórtolas, Cerro de las ∧	252	29.56 S	69.54 W
Tortolì	71	39.55 N	9.39 E
Tortona	62	44.54 N	8.52 E
Tortora	68	39.56 N	15.48 E
Tortoreto	66	42.48 N	13.55 E
Tortorici	70	38.02 N	14.49 E
Tortosa	34	40.48 N	0.31 E
Tortosa, Cap de ›	34	40.43 N	0.55 E
Tortue ≃	186	50.18 N	65.23 W
Tortue, Île de la I	238	20.04 N	72.49 W
Tortue, Rivière de la ≃	206	45.24 N	73.32 W
Tortuguero ≃	236	10.34 N	83.31 W
Tortuguero, Laguna c	240m	18.28 N	66.26 W
Tortuguero, Parque Nacional ♠	236	10.25 N	83.55 W
Tortuguitas	288	34.28 S	58.46 W
Tortum	130	40.19 N	41.35 E
Toru ≃	114	1.26 N	98.46 E
Toruajgyr	85	42.32 N	76.26 E
Torue	112	0.58 S	120.18 E
Torugart, pereval)(	85	40.33 N	75.20 E
Torul	130	40.35 N	39.18 E
Toruń	30	53.02 N	18.35 E
Toruń □[4]	30	53.20 N	19.00 E
Torunos	246	8.30 N	70.04 W
Torup, Sve.	26	56.58 N	13.05 E
Torup, Sve.	41	55.34 N	13.12 E
Tõrva	76	58.00 N	25.56 E
Tory	88	51.47 N	103.00 E
Tory Island I	48	55.16 N	8.14 W
Torysa ≃	30	48.39 N	21.21 E
Tory Sound ʯ	48	55.14 N	8.14 W
Toržok	76	57.03 N	34.58 E
Torzym	30	52.20 N	15.04 E
Tosa, Nihon	96	33.29 N	133.25 E
Tosa, Nihon	96	33.44 N	133.32 E
T'oša ≃	80	55.38 N	42.09 E
T'osan	98	38.18 N	126.43 E
Tosari	115a	7.53 S	112.54 E
Tosa-shimizu	92	32.46 N	132.57 E
Tosa-wan c	96	33.20 N	133.40 E
Tosayama	96	33.38 N	133.32 E
Tosa-yamada	96	33.36 N	133.41 E
Tosca	156	25.53 S	23.58 E
Toscaig	46	57.24 N	5.50 W
Toscana (Tuscany) □[4]	36	43.25 N	11.00 E
Toscano ≃	234	18.01 N	102.32 W
Toscolano	64	45.38 N	10.37 E
Tösens	58	47.01 N	10.36 E

Toses, Collada de)(	34	42.19 N	2.01 E
Tōshi-jima I	94	34.31 N	136.53 E
Toshima ◆[8]	268	35.44 N	139.43 E
To-shima I	94	34.31 N	139.17 E
Toshkivka	83	48.46 N	38.34 E
Tōshō-gū ʊ[1]	94	36.46 N	139.36 E
Tosi, Indon.	115b	9.35 S	118.57 E
Tosi, It.	66	43.45 N	11.31 E
Tosilei	144	1.25 N	41.24 E
Toškalykaja, gora ∧	86	50.38 N	89.30 E
Tosna ≃	265a	59.46 N	30.46 E
Tosno	76	59.33 N	30.53 E
Toson Cengel	88	48.47 N	98.15 E
Toson Hu ⊜	102	35.18 N	98.54 E
T'osovo	76	55.37 N	34.30 E
T'osovo-Netyl'skij	76	58.57 N	31.04 E
T'osovskij	76	58.48 N	30.52 E
Töss ≃	58	47.33 N	8.33 E
Tossens	52	53.34 N	8.16 E
Tossicia	66	42.33 N	13.39 E
Tostado	252	29.14 S	61.46 W
Tõstamaa	76	58.20 N	24.00 E
Tostedt	52	53.17 N	9.42 E
Tosterön I	40	59.25 N	17.00 E
Tostu	85	41.34 N	71.34 E
Tost uul ⋏	102	43.15 N	100.30 E
Tosu	96	33.22 N	130.31 E
Tosya	130	41.01 N	34.02 E
Totagatic ≃	190	46.05 N	92.11 W
Totak ⊜	26	59.42 N	7.57 E
Totana	34	37.46 N	1.30 W
Totānāla	126	22.05 N	87.40 E
Totatiche	234	21.56 N	103.27 W
Totban	80	46.47 N	49.06 E
Toteng	156	20.22 S	22.58 E
Tôtes	50	49.41 N	1.03 E
Totes Gebirge ⋏	30	47.42 N	13.55 E
T'otkino	78	51.17 N	34.16 E
Tot'ma	76	59.57 N	42.45 E
Totnes	42	50.25 N	3.41 W
Totness	250	5.53 N	56.19 W
Toto	152	7.08 S	14.16 E
Totonicapán	236	14.55 N	91.22 W
Totonicapán □[5]	236	15.00 N	91.20 W
Totopotomoy Creek ≃	208	37.41 N	77.13 W
Totora, Bol.	248	17.42 S	65.09 W
Totora, Bol.	248	17.49 S	68.07 W
Totoras	252	32.35 S	61.11 W
Totos	248	13.31 S	74.30 W
Tototlán	234	20.33 N	102.48 W
Totowa	210	40.54 N	74.12 W
Totoya Island I	175g	18.57 S	179.50 W
Totson Mountain ∧	180	64.26 N	157.15 W
Totsuka ◆[8]	268	35.24 N	139.32 E
Tottenham, Austl.	166	32.14 S	147.21 E
Tottenham, On., Can.	212	44.01 N	79.49 W
Tottenham ◆[8]	260	51.35 N	0.04 W
Tottenham Hotspur Football Ground ♠	260	51.36 N	0.04 W
Totten Inlet c	224	47.07 N	123.02 W
Tottenville ◆[8]	276	40.31 N	74.15 W
Totteridge ◆[8]	260	51.38 N	0.12 W
Tottington	44	53.37 N	2.20 W
Totton	42	50.56 N	1.29 W
Tottori	96	35.30 N	134.14 E
Tottori □[5]	96	35.30 N	134.00 E
Tottori-sakyū ∧[2]	96	35.31 N	134.15 E
Totuskey Creek ≃	208	37.52 N	76.45 W
Tou, Motu I	174k	21.11 S	159.48 W
Touba, C. Iv.	150	8.17 N	7.41 W
Touba, Sén.	150	14.51 N	15.53 W
Toubei	100	26.44 N	116.05 E
Toubéré Bafal	150	14.23 N	13.32 W
Toubkal, Jebel ∧	148	31.05 N	7.55 W
Toubkal, Parc National du ♠	148	31.05 N	7.55 W
Toubori	146	13.59 N	12.18 E
Touboro	152	7.43 N	15.12 E
T'ouch'eng	100	24.52 N	121.49 E
Touchet ≃	202	46.02 N	118.41 W
Touchwood Hills ⋏[2]	184	51.35 N	104.17 W
Touchwood Lake ⊜, Ab., Can.	182	54.50 N	111.23 W
Touchwood Lake ⊜, Mb., Can.	184	54.29 N	95.00 W
Toucy	50	47.44 N	3.18 E
Toudao ≃	98	42.36 N	127.11 E
Toudaogou, Zhg.	98	42.46 N	129.12 E
Toudaogou, Zhg.	104	41.37 N	121.40 E
Toudaogou, Zhg.	105	40.58 N	117.59 E
Touët-sur-Var	62	43.57 N	7.00 E
Tougan	150	13.04 N	3.04 W
Touggourt	148	33.10 N	6.00 E
Toughkenamon	285	39.50 N	75.46 W
Tougouri	150	13.19 N	0.31 W
Tougué	150	11.27 N	11.41 W
Touho	175f	20.47 S	165.14 E
Touiel, Oued V	148	31.30 N	4.46 E
Touil, Oued V	148	35.30 N	2.33 E
Touisset	207	41.43 N	71.13 W
Toukansi	100	29.22 N	119.06 E
Toukley	170	33.16 S	151.33 E
Toukoto	150	13.27 N	9.53 W
Toul	58	48.41 N	5.54 E
Toulépleu	150	6.35 N	8.25 W
Touliu	100	23.43 N	120.32 E
Toulnustouc ≃	186	49.35 N	68.24 W
Toulnustouc Nord-Est ≃	186	50.56 N	67.44 W
Toulon, Fr.	62	43.07 N	5.56 E
Toulon, Il., U.S.	190	41.05 N	89.51 W
Toulon Lake ⊜	204	40.01 N	118.40 W
Toulon-sur-Arroux	32	46.42 N	4.08 E
Touloubre ≃	62	43.33 N	5.02 E
Toulourenc ≃	62	44.14 N	5.09 E
Toulouse	32	43.36 N	1.26 E
Toumen Shan I	100	28.41 N	121.46 E
Toumfafi	150	15.02 N	5.38 E
Toumodi	150	6.33 N	5.01 W
Tounan	100	23.41 N	120.28 E
Tounassine, Hamada ◆[2]	148	28.30 N	5.00 W
Toungo	146	8.07 N	12.03 E
Toungoo	110	18.56 N	96.26 E
Toupeng	106	30.19 N	120.31 E
Touques	50	49.22 N	0.06 E
Touques ≃	50	49.22 N	0.06 E
Tour, Étang de la ⊜	261	48.40 N	1.53 E
Toura, Monts du ⋏	150	7.40 N	7.25 W
Touraine	188	45.34 N	75.47 W
Touraine □[9]	32	47.12 N	0.40 E
Tourakom	110	18.26 N	102.32 E
Tourane → Da Nang	108	16.04 N	108.13 E
Tourassine ⍑[4]	148	24.37 N	11.23 W
Tourbe ≃	56	49.10 N	4.52 E
Tourcoing	50	50.43 N	3.09 E
Touriñan, Cabo ›	34	43.03 N	9.18 W
Tournai	50	50.36 N	3.23 E
Tournan-en-Brie	50	48.44 N	2.46 E
Tourndo, Oued V	148	22.15 N	10.28 E
Tournesac ≃	50	47.27 N	4.01 E
Tournon	62	45.04 N	4.50 E
Tournus	58	46.34 N	4.54 E
Touros	250	5.12 S	35.28 W
Tou Rout	110	16.24 N	107.00 E
Tourouvre	50	48.35 N	0.40 E
Tourrette-Levens	62	43.47 N	7.16 E
Tours	50	47.23 N	0.41 E
Tours-sur-Marne	50	49.03 N	4.07 E
Tours-sur-Meymont	62	45.40 N	3.35 E
Tourteron	56	49.32 N	4.39 E
Tourves	62	43.24 N	5.56 E
Toury	50	48.12 N	1.56 E
Toussaint Creek ≃	214	41.35 N	83.04 W
Tousside, Pic ∧	146	21.02 N	16.25 E
Toussoro, Mont ∧	146	9.18 N	23.28 E
Toussus-le-Noble	261	48.45 N	2.07 E

	English	Deutsch	Español	Français	Português
≃	River	Fluß	Río	Rivière	Rio
≊	Canal	Kanal	Canal	Canal	Canal
ʟ	Waterfall, Rapids	Wasserfall, Stromschnellen	Cascada, Rápidos	Chute d'eau, Rapides	Cascata, Rápidos
ʯ	Strait	Meeresstraße	Estrecho	Détroit	Estreito
c	Bay, Gulf	Bucht, Golf	Bahía, Golfo	Baie, Golfe	Baía, Golfo
⊜	Lake, Lakes	See, Seen	Lago, Lagos	Lac, Lacs	Lago, Lagos
⁝⁝	Swamp	Sumpf	Pantano	Marais	Pântano
⌂	Ice Features, Glacier	Eis- und Gletscherformen	Accidentes Glaciales	Formes glaciaires	Acidentes glaciares
⍑	Other Hydrographic Features	Andere Hydrographische Objekte	Otros Elementos Hidrográficos	Autres données hydrographiques	Outros acidentes hidrográficos
✢	Submarine Features	Untermeerische Objekte	Accidentes Submarinos	Formes de relief sous-marin	Acidentes submarinos
□	Political Unit	Politische Einheit	Unidad Politica	Entité politique	Unidade política
ʊ	Cultural Institution	Kulturelle Institution	Institución Cultural	Institution culturelle	Instituição cultural
⊥	Historical Site	Historische Stätte	Sitio Histórico	Site historique	Sitio histórico
♠	Recreational Site	Erholungs- und Ferienort	Sitio de Recreo	Centre de loisirs	Area de Lazer
⊠	Airport	Flughafen	Aeropuerto	Aéroport	Aeroporto
■	Military Installation	Militäranlage	Instalación Militar	Installation militaire	Instalação militar
◆	Miscellaneous	Verschiedenes	Misceláneo	Divers	Diversos

ENGLISH: Name, Page, Lat.°', Long.°' — DEUTSCH: Name, Seite, Breite°', Länge°' E = Ost

Name	Page	Lat.°'	Long.°'
Toussus-le-Noble, Aéroport de ⊠	261	48.45 N	2.06 E
Toustain	36	36.40 N	8.15 E
Toutai, Zhg.	89	45.40 N	124.50 E
Toutai, Zhg.	104	41.41 N	121.11 E
Toutaizi	104	42.19 N	122.49 E
Toutle	224	46.20 N	122.41 W
Toutle ≃	224	46.17 N	122.55 W
Toutle, North Fork ≃	224	46.23 N	122.34 W
Toutle, South Fork ≃	224	46.20 N	122.44 W
Toutle Mountain Range ⋀	224	46.20 N	122.30 W
Toutuohe	100	31.06 N	116.25 E
Touws ≃	158	33.45 S	21.11 E
Touwsrivier	158	33.20 S	20.00 E
Touzhan	89	49.27 N	119.41 E
Toužim	60	50.04 N	13.00 E
Töv □[4]	88	47.30 N	106.30 E
Tova	24	65.58 N	40.45 E
Tovar	246	8.20 N	71.46 W
Tovarkovo	82	54.42 N	35.57 E
Tovarkovskij	76	53.40 N	38.14 E
Tove ≃	42	52.05 N	0.38 W
Tovey	219	39.35 N	89.27 W
Tovste	78	48.50 N	25.44 E
Tovtry ⋀[1]	78	49.00 N	26.10 E
Tovuz	84	41.00 N	45.38 E
Tow	196	30.53 N	98.28 W
Tōwa	96	33.13 N	132.53 E
Towaco	210	40.55 N	74.20 W
Towada	92	40.37 N	141.13 E
Towada-Hachimantai-kokuritsu-kōen ♦	92	40.35 N	140.53 E
Towada-ko ⊜	92	40.28 N	140.55 E
Towai	172	35.29 S	174.08 E
Towamencin Creek ≃	285	40.13 N	75.23 W
Towanda, Il., U.S.	216	40.34 N	88.54 W
Towanda, Ks., U.S.	198	37.47 N	96.59 W
Towanda, Pa., U.S.	210	41.46 N	76.26 W
Towanda Creek ≃	210	41.45 N	76.26 W
Towan Head ›	42	50.25 N	5.07 W
Towar Gardens	216	42.45 N	84.28 W
Towari	112	4.36 S	121.29 E
Towcester	42	52.08 N	1.00 W
Tower	190	47.48 N	92.16 W
Tower City, N.D., U.S.	198	46.55 N	97.40 W
Tower City, Pa., U.S.	208	40.35 N	76.33 W
Tower Hamlets ⊸[8]	260	51.32 N	0.03 W
Tower Hill, Austl.	166	22.03 S	144.36 E
Tower Hill, Il., U.S.	219	39.23 N	88.57 W
Towerhill Creek ≃	166	22.29 S	144.39 E
Tower of London ⊥	260	51.30 N	0.05 W
Tower Peak ∧	226	38.09 N	119.33 W
Towers of Silence ⊻[1]	272c	18.58 N	72.48 E
Tower Soudan State Park ♦	190	47.50 N	92.15 W
Towla, Mount ∧	154	21.22 S	29.52 E
Tow Law	44	54.44 N	1.49 W
Towlī	84	39.11 N	47.32 E
Town ≃	283	42.00 N	70.57 W
Town and Country	202	47.42 N	117.23 W
Town Bank	208	39.00 N	74.56 W
Town Creek ≃, Al., U.S.	194	34.46 N	87.25 W
Town Creek ≃, Al., U.S.	194	34.24 N	86.11 W
Town Creek ≃, Oh., U.S.	216	41.05 N	84.25 W
Town Creek Manor	208	38.19 N	76.27 W
Towneley Hall ⊥	262	53.46 N	2.13 W
Towner	198	48.20 N	100.24 W
Town Estates	285	40.04 N	74.52 W
Town Hill ∧[2]	240a	32.19 N	64.44 W
Townline Tunnel ⊸[5]	284a	42.57 N	79.15 W
Town of Niagara	284a	43.06 N	78.59 W
Town of Pines	216	41.41 N	86.58 W
Townsend, On., Can.	212	42.54 N	80.07 W
Townsend, De., U.S.	208	39.23 N	75.41 W
Townsend, Ma., U.S.	207	42.40 N	71.42 W
Townsend, Mt., U.S.	202	46.19 N	111.31 W
Townsend, Va., U.S.	208	37.11 N	75.57 W
Townsend, Mount ∧	171b	36.25 S	148.15 E
Townsend Island I	276	40.38 N	73.26 W
Townsends Inlet c	208	39.07 N	74.43 W
Townshend Island I	166	22.15 S	150.30 E
Township Line Run ≃	279b	40.13 N	79.33 W
Townsville	166	19.16 S	146.48 E
Townville	214	41.41 N	79.53 W
Towrang	170	34.42 S	149.51 E
Towrang, Mount ∧	170	34.46 S	149.51 E
Towra Point ›	274a	34.00 S	151.10 E
Towr Kham	123	34.08 N	71.05 E
Towrzī, Afg.	120	30.11 N	65.59 E
Towrzī, Afg.	128	32.38 N	65.53 E
Towson	208	39.24 N	76.36 W
Towson State College ⊻[2]	284b	39.24 N	76.37 W
Towuti, Danau ⊜	112	2.45 S	121.32 E
Toxkan (Aksaj) ≃, Asia	85	40.55 N	78.16 E
Toxkan ≃, Zhg.	90	41.08 N	80.11 E
Toyah	196	31.19 N	103.47 W
Toyah Creek ≃	196	31.18 N	103.27 W
Tōya-ko ⊜	92a	42.35 N	140.51 E
Toyama	94	36.41 N	137.13 E
Toyama □[5]	94	36.30 N	137.30 E
Toyama-heiya ≚	94	36.40 N	137.15 E
Toyama-wan c	94	36.50 N	137.10 E
Toyapakeh	115b	8.41 S	115.29 E
Tōyo, Nihon	96	33.55 N	133.05 E
Tōyō, Nihon	96	33.30 N	134.16 E
Toyo ≃	94	34.47 N	137.20 E
Toyoake	94	35.03 N	137.01 E
Toyoda, Nihon	94	34.45 N	137.49 E
Toyoda, Nihon	268	35.39 N	139.23 E
Toyofuta	268	35.53 N	139.57 E
Toyohama	96	34.04 N	133.38 E
Toyohara	175d	24.15 N	123.48 E
Toyohashi	94	34.46 N	137.23 E
Toyohira	96	34.40 N	132.24 E
Toyokawa	94	34.49 N	137.24 E
Toyo-kawa-yōsui ≋	94	34.35 N	137.03 E
Toyonaka, Nihon	96	34.09 N	133.42 E
Toyonaka, Nihon	96	34.47 N	135.28 E
Toyone	94	35.09 N	137.43 E
Toyono	94	36.43 N	138.16 E
Toyooka, Nihon	94	35.33 N	137.54 E
Toyooka, Nihon	94	34.50 N	137.52 E
Toyooka, Nihon	96	35.32 N	134.50 E
Toyooka, Nihon	268	35.11 N	139.58 E
Toyosaka, Nihon	92	37.56 N	139.13 E
Toyosaka, Nihon	96	34.34 N	132.50 E
Toyosato	94	36.06 N	140.02 E
Toyoshina	94	36.18 N	137.54 E
Toyota, Nihon	94	35.05 N	137.09 E
Toyota, Nihon	94	36.46 N	138.19 E
Toyota, Nihon	96	34.12 N	131.04 E
Toyota-ko ⊜	96	34.14 N	131.08 E
Toyotomi	94	35.34 N	138.33 E
Toyotsu	96	33.40 N	130.58 E
Toyoura	96	34.08 N	130.58 E
Toy's Hill	260	51.14 N	0.06 E
Tozer, Mount ∧	164	12.45 S	143.13 E
Tozeur	148	33.55 N	8.08 E
Tozi, Mount ∧	180	65.41 N	150.58 W
Tozitna ≃	180	65.08 N	152.23 W
Tpig	84	41.47 N	47.36 E
Traar ⊸[8]	263	51.23 N	6.36 E
Trabaria, Bocca)(	66	43.36 N	12.14 E
Traben-Trarbach	56	49.57 N	7.06 E
Trabia	70	37.59 N	13.39 E
Trabiju	255	22.03 S	48.18 W
Trabuco, Arroyo ≃	228	33.31 N	117.40 W
Trabzon	130	41.00 N	39.43 E
Trabzon □[4]	130	40.50 N	39.50 E
Tracadie	186	47.31 N	64.54 W
Trachselwald	58	47.01 N	7.45 E
Tra Cu	110	9.42 N	106.16 E
Tracy, P.Q., Can.	206	46.01 N	73.09 W
Tracy, Ca., U.S.	226	37.44 N	121.25 W
Tracy, Mn., U.S.	198	44.14 N	95.37 W
Tracy City	194	35.15 N	85.44 W
Tracyton	224	47.36 N	122.39 W
Tradate	62	45.43 N	8.54 E
Trade Lake ⊜	184	55.22 N	103.44 W
Tradewater ≃	194	37.31 N	88.03 W
Trading Bay c	212	45.15 N	78.55 W
Tradinghouse Creek Reservoir ⊜[1]	222	31.35 N	96.55 W
Traditional Cultures, Museum of ⊻	269f	14.31 N	121.00 E
Trælleborg ⊥	41	55.23 N	11.17 E
Traer	190	42.11 N	92.27 W
Traessu, Monte ∧	71	40.28 N	8.40 E
Trafalgar, Austl.	169	38.12 S	146.09 E
Trafalgar, On., Can.	275b	43.29 N	79.43 W
Trafalgar, In., U.S.	218	39.24 N	86.09 W
Trafalgar, Cabo ›	34	36.11 N	6.02 W
Trafaria	266c	38.40 N	9.14 W
Trafford	214	40.23 N	79.45 W
Trafford □[8]	262	53.24 N	2.21 W
Trafford, Lake ⊜	220	26.25 N	81.30 W
Trafford Park	262	53.28 N	2.20 W
Trafoi	64	46.33 N	10.31 E
Tragacete	34	40.21 N	1.51 W
Tragliata ⊸[8]	267a	41.58 N	12.15 E
Tragwein	61	48.20 N	14.37 E
Traição, Córrego ≃	287b	23.36 S	46.41 W
Traid	34	40.40 N	1.49 W
Traiguén	252	38.15 S	72.41 W
Traiguén, Isla I	254	45.35 S	73.42 W
Trail	182	49.06 N	117.42 W
Trail Creek	216	41.41 N	86.51 W
Trailer Estates	220	27.24 N	82.34 W
Trail Ridge ∧	192	30.35 N	82.05 W
Traînel	50	48.25 N	3.27 E
Trainer	285	39.50 N	75.25 W
Traipu	250	9.58 S	37.01 W
Traíra (Taraira) ≃	246	1.04 S	69.26 W
Trairão ≃	250	7.20 S	51.14 W
Traíras ≃	255	14.07 S	48.31 W
Trairi	250	3.17 S	39.15 W
Traisen	61	48.02 N	15.37 E
Traisen ≃	61	48.22 N	15.46 E
Traiskirchen	61	48.01 N	16.18 E
Traismauer	61	48.21 N	15.44 E
Traîtres, Baie des c	174x	9.50 S	139.02 W
Trajouce	266c	38.44 N	9.20 W
Trakai	76	54.38 N	24.56 E
Trakt	24	62.44 N	51.11 E
Träkvista	40	59.16 N	17.47 E
Tralee	48	52.16 N	9.42 W
Tralee Bay c	48	52.15 N	9.59 W
Trá Lí → Tralee	48	52.16 N	9.42 W
Tramatza	71	40.00 N	8.39 E
Tramayes	58	46.18 N	4.36 E
Tramelan	58	47.13 N	7.06 E
Tra Mi	110	15.20 N	108.13 E
Tramin → Termeno	64	46.20 N	11.14 E
Trammel	192	37.00 N	82.17 W
Trammel Creek ≃	194	36.52 N	86.23 W
Tramonti di sopra	64	46.18 N	12.47 E
Tramore	48	52.10 N	7.10 W
Tramperos Creek (Punta de Agua Creek) ≃	196	35.32 N	102.27 W
Tramping Lake ⊜	184	52.08 N	108.49 W
Tramutola	68	40.19 N	15.47 E
Trăn	38	42.50 N	22.39 E
Tranås	26	58.03 N	14.59 E
Trancão ≃	266c	38.48 N	9.06 W
Trancas	252	26.13 S	65.17 W
Trancoso	34	40.47 N	7.21 W
Trand	123	34.38 N	72.59 E
Tranderup	41	54.52 N	10.22 E
Tranebjerg	41	55.50 N	10.36 E
Tranekær	41	55.00 N	10.51 E
Tranemo	26	57.29 N	13.21 E
Tranent	46	55.57 N	2.58 W
Tränental	158	27.09 S	19.33 E
Trang	110	7.33 N	99.36 E
Trangahy	157b	19.07 S	44.43 E
Trangan, Pulau I	164	6.35 S	134.20 E
Trangie	166	32.02 S	147.59 E
Tran Grande ≃	116	6.43 N	124.01 E
Trängslet	26	61.25 N	13.40 E
Trani	68	41.17 N	16.26 E
Tranmere	262	53.23 N	3.01 W
Trannon ≃	42	52.31 N	3.25 W
Tranoroa	157b	24.42 S	45.04 E
Tranquebar	122	11.02 N	79.51 E
Tranqueras	252	31.12 S	55.45 W
Tranquility	218	38.58 N	83.32 W
Tranquillity	226	36.38 N	120.15 W
Transantarctic Mountains ⋀	9	85.00 S	175.00 W
Trans-en-Provence	62	43.30 N	6.29 E
Transfer	214	41.20 N	80.26 W
Transit Airpark ⊠	284a	43.06 N	78.44 W
Transkei □[9]	158	31.20 S	29.00 E
Transquaking ≃	208	38.22 N	76.00 W
Transsylvanische Alpen → Carpații Meridionali ⋀	38	45.30 N	24.15 E
Transtrand	26	61.05 N	13.19 E
Transtrandsfjällen ∧	26	61.17 N	13.00 E
Transylvania □[9]	38	46.30 N	24.00 E
Transylvanian Alps → Carpații Meridionali ⋀	38	45.30 N	24.15 E
Tranters Creek ≃	192	35.33 N	77.05 W
Traona	58	46.09 N	9.31 E
Trapalcó, Salinas de ≚	254	39.45 S	66.45 W
Trapani	70	38.01 N	12.31 E
Trapani □[4]	70	37.50 N	12.40 E
Traphole Brook ≃	283	42.10 N	71.11 W
Trappe, Md., U.S.	208	38.39 N	76.03 W
Trappe, Pa., U.S.	208	40.12 N	75.29 W
Trappenkamp	54	54.03 N	10.16 E
Trapper Peak ∧	202	45.54 N	114.18 W
Trappes	50	48.47 N	2.00 E
Trappeto	70	38.04 N	13.03 E
Trapuá ≃	287b	23.36 S	46.17 W
Traralgon	169	38.12 S	146.32 E
Traralgon Creek ≃	169	38.10 S	146.31 E
Traras, Monts des ⋀	34	35.10 N	1.40 W
Trarza □[4]	150	17.45 N	15.45 W
Trârza ⊸[1]	150	18.00 N	15.00 W
Trasacco	66	41.57 N	13.32 E
Trasadingen	58	47.40 N	8.26 E
Trascău, Munții ⋀	38	46.23 N	23.33 E
Trasimeno, Lago ⊜	66	43.08 N	12.06 E
Trask ≃	224	45.28 N	123.53 W
Träslövsläge	26	57.04 N	12.16 E
Trasna	82	54.45 N	38.42 E
Trás-os-Montes □[9]	34	41.30 N	7.15 W
Trassem	56	49.34 N	6.31 E
Trăstenik	38	43.31 N	24.28 E
Trat	110	12.14 N	102.30 E
Tratalias	71	39.06 N	8.34 E
Tratzberg, Schloss ⊥	64	47.23 N	11.44 E
Trauchgau	58	47.38 N	10.49 E
Traun	61	48.13 N	14.14 E
Traun ≃, Dtsch.	60	48.00 N	12.32 E
Traun ≃, Öst.	30	48.16 N	14.22 E
Traunkirchen	64	47.50 N	13.47 E
Traunreut	64	47.56 N	12.35 E
Traunsee ⊜	64	47.51 N	13.48 E
Traunstein, Dtsch.	64	47.52 N	12.38 E
Traunstein, Öst.	61	48.26 N	15.07 E
Traunstein ∧	64	47.52 N	13.50 E
Trautenstein	54	51.41 N	10.43 E
Travagliato	64	45.31 N	10.05 E
Trave ≃	54	53.54 N	10.50 E
Travedona	62	45.48 N	8.40 E
Travellers Lake ⊜	166	33.18 S	142.00 E
Travemünde ⊸[8]	54	53.57 N	10.52 E
Traver	226	36.27 N	119.29 W
Travers, Mount ∧	172	42.01 S	172.44 E
Travers, Val de V	58	46.57 N	6.38 E
Traverse, Lake ⊜	198	45.43 N	96.40 W
Traverse Bay c	184	50.40 N	96.25 W
Traverse City	190	44.45 N	85.37 W
Traversella	62	45.30 N	7.45 E
Traverse Peak ∧	180	65.10 N	159.12 W
Traversetolo	64	44.38 N	10.23 E
Travers Reservoir ⊜[1]	182	50.14 N	112.51 W
Tra Vinh	110	9.56 N	106.20 E
Travis	222	31.08 N	97.00 W
Travis □[6]	222	30.18 N	97.40 W
Travis, Lake ⊜[1]	196	30.27 N	98.00 W
Travis Air Force Base ■	226	38.16 N	121.55 W
Travnik	36	44.14 N	17.40 E
Trawalla	169	37.26 S	143.29 E
Trawbreaga Bay c	48	55.17 N	7.18 W
Trawick	222	31.46 N	94.45 W
Trawsfynydd	42	52.54 N	3.55 W
Trayning	162	31.07 S	117.48 E
Trazegnies	50	50.28 N	4.19 E
Trbovlje	36	46.10 N	15.03 E
Treadwell	210	42.21 N	75.03 W
Treales	262	53.47 N	2.51 W
Treasure Island	220	27.46 N	82.46 W
Treasure Island I	226	37.48 N	122.22 W
Treasure Island Naval Station ■	282	37.49 N	122.22 W
Trebatsch	54	52.05 N	14.09 E
Trebbia ≃	62	45.04 N	9.41 E
Trebbin	54	52.13 N	13.13 E
Třebechovice pod Orebem	30	50.12 N	16.00 E
Trebel	54	52.59 N	11.20 E
Trebel ≃	54	53.55 N	13.01 E
Trebelsee ⊜	54	52.28 N	12.47 E
Třebenice	54	50.29 N	14.00 E
Trebgast	60	50.04 N	11.33 E
Třebíč	30	49.13 N	15.53 E
Trebinje	38	42.43 N	18.20 E
Trebisacce	68	39.52 N	16.32 E
Trebišov	30	48.40 N	21.47 E
Trebitz	54	51.45 N	12.44 E
Trebizond → Trabzon	130	41.00 N	39.43 E
Trebjerg ∧[2]	41	55.10 N	10.14 E
Třebkov	60	49.22 N	14.04 E
Treble Mountain ∧	182	55.50 N	129.51 W
Treblinka	30	52.39 N	22.03 E
Třeboň	61	49.00 N	14.47 E
Třebouň ∧	60	50.01 N	12.59 E
Trebsen	54	51.17 N	12.45 E
Trebur	56	49.56 N	8.25 E
Trecastagni	70	37.37 N	15.05 E
Trecate	62	45.26 N	8.44 E
Trecchina	68	40.02 N	15.46 E
Trece Martires	116	14.16 N	120.50 E
Trecenta	64	45.02 N	11.28 E
Tred Avon River c	208	38.42 N	76.08 W
Tredegar	42	51.47 N	3.16 W
Tredici Archi, Ponte ⊸[5]	66	41.32 N	14.57 E
Treene ≃	41	54.22 N	9.05 E
Trees Mills	279b	40.23 N	80.13 W
Treffen	64	46.40 N	13.52 E
Treffort	58	46.16 N	5.22 E
Treffurt	56	51.08 N	10.14 E
Trèfle, Lac du ⊜	206	46.36 N	73.55 W
Tregaron	42	52.13 N	3.55 W
Tregnago	64	45.31 N	11.10 E
Tregosse Islets II	166	17.41 S	150.43 E
Tregubovo	76	58.59 N	31.33 E
Tréguier	32	48.47 N	3.14 W
Treharris	42	51.41 N	3.16 W
Treherne	184	49.38 N	98.41 W
Trehörningsjö	26	63.42 N	18.48 E
Treia, Dtsch.	41	54.30 N	9.17 E
Treia, It.	66	43.19 N	13.19 E
Treig, Loch ⊜	46	56.50 N	4.44 W
Treinta y Tres	252	33.14 S	54.23 W
Treis	56	50.10 N	7.17 E
Trekkopje	156	22.18 S	14.53 E
Trélazé	32	47.27 N	0.28 W
Trelde Næs ›	41	55.37 N	9.52 E
Trelew	254	43.15 S	65.18 W
Trelleborg	41	55.22 N	13.10 E
Treloar	219	38.39 N	91.10 W
Tremadog	42	52.56 N	4.09 W
Tremblant, Lac ⊜	206	46.15 N	74.38 W
Tremblant, Mont ∧	206	46.16 N	74.35 W
Tremblay, Hippodrome du ♦	261	48.50 N	2.29 E
Tremblay-lès-Gonesse	261	48.59 N	2.34 E
Trembleur Lake ⊜	182	54.51 N	125.07 W
Tremedal	255	14.58 S	41.24 W
Tremembé	256	22.58 S	45.33 W
Tremezzo	58	45.59 N	9.15 E
Tremino	88	56.42 N	98.04 E
Tremiti, Isole II	66	42.07 N	15.30 E
Tremo La)(	124	27.44 N	89.12 E
Tremont, Il., U.S.	190	40.31 N	89.29 W
Tremont, In., U.S.	216	41.39 N	87.02 W
Tremont, Pa., U.S.	208	40.37 N	76.23 W
Tremont ⊸[8]	276	40.51 N	73.55 W
Tremont City	218	40.00 N	83.50 W
Tremonton	200	41.42 N	112.09 W
Třemošna	60	49.49 N	13.20 E
Třemošná ≃	60	49.52 N	13.32 E
Tremp	34	42.10 N	0.54 E
Trempealeau	190	44.00 N	91.26 W
Trempealeau ≃	190	44.02 N	91.32 W
Tremsbüttel	52	53.44 N	10.18 E
Trena	144	10.45 N	40.38 E
Trenčín	30	48.54 N	18.04 E
Trendelburg	52	51.34 N	9.25 E
Trenel	252	35.42 S	64.08 W
Trêng	110	12.49 N	102.54 E
Trenggalek	115a	8.03 S	111.43 E
Trenque Lauquen	252	35.58 S	62.42 W
Trent, Dtsch.	54	54.31 N	13.15 E
Trent → Trento, It.	64	46.04 N	11.08 E
Trent ≃, On., Can.	212	44.06 N	77.34 W
Trent ≃, Eng., U.K.	28	53.42 N	0.41 W
Trent ≃, N.C., U.S.	192	35.05 N	77.02 W
Trent, Vale of V	42	52.44 N	1.50 W
Trent and Mersey Canal ≋	262	53.19 N	2.39 W
Trente et un Milles, Lac des ⊜	188	46.12 N	75.49 W
Trentham	169	37.23 S	144.19 E
Trentino-Alto Adige □[4]	64	46.30 N	11.20 E
Trento	64	46.04 N	11.08 E
Trento □[4]	64	46.08 N	11.07 E
Trentola-Ducenta	68	40.59 N	14.10 E
Trenton, N.S., Can.	186	45.37 N	62.38 W
Trenton, On., Can.	212	44.06 N	77.35 W
Trenton, Fl., U.S.	192	29.36 N	82.49 W
Trenton, Ga., U.S.	192	34.52 N	85.30 W
Trenton, Il., U.S.	219	38.36 N	89.40 W
Trenton, Ky., U.S.	194	36.43 N	87.15 W
Trenton, Mi., U.S.	216	42.08 N	83.10 W
Trenton, Mo., U.S.	194	40.04 N	93.36 W
Trenton, Ne., U.S.	198	40.10 N	101.00 W
Trenton, N.J., U.S.	208	40.13 N	74.44 W
Trenton, N.C., U.S.	192	35.04 N	77.21 W
Trenton, Oh., U.S.	218	39.29 N	84.28 W
Trenton, Tn., U.S.	194	35.58 N	88.56 W
Trenton, Tx., U.S.	196	33.26 N	96.20 W
Trenton, Canadian Forces Base ■	190	44.07 N	77.33 W
Trenton Channel ≃[1]	281	42.06 N	83.11 W
Trentwood	202	47.42 N	117.13 W
Trepalade	64	45.34 N	12.24 E
Trepassey	186	46.44 N	53.22 W
Trepassey Bay c	186	46.37 N	53.20 W
Treptow ⊸[8]	54	52.29 N	13.29 E
Trepuzzi	68	40.24 N	18.05 E
Trequanda	66	43.11 N	11.40 E
Tresa ≃	58	46.00 N	8.43 E
Tres Algarrobos	252	35.12 S	62.46 W
Tres Árboles	252	32.24 S	56.43 W
Tres Arroyos	252	38.23 S	60.17 W
Tres Cerros	254	48.13 S	67.33 W
Treščevo	82	54.11 N	37.55 E
Tresckow	210	40.54 N	75.58 W
Tresco I	42a	49.57 N	6.19 W
Três Corações	256	21.42 S	45.16 W
Trescore Balneario	62	45.41 N	9.50 E
Três Coroas	252	29.32 S	50.48 W
Tres de Febrero → Caseros	258	34.36 S	58.33 W
Tres de Febrero □[5]	288	34.36 S	58.35 W
Três de Maio	252	27.47 S	54.14 W
Tresenda	64	46.10 N	10.05 E
Tres Esquinas	246	0.43 N	75.16 W
Três Fronteiras	255	20.13 S	50.55 W
Treshnish Isles II	46	56.30 N	6.24 W
Treshnish Point ›	46	56.33 N	6.21 W
Três Ilhas	256	22.04 S	43.29 W
Tresinaro ≃	64	44.39 N	10.47 E
Tres Isletas	252	26.21 S	60.26 W
Treskino	80	52.40 N	44.40 E
Três Lagoas	255	20.48 S	51.43 W
Tres Lagos	254	49.37 S	71.30 W
Tres Lomas	252	36.27 S	62.51 W
Três Marias	255	18.12 S	45.14 W
Três Marias, Represa de ⊜[1]	255	18.12 S	45.15 W
Tres Montes, Golfo c	254	46.54 S	75.00 W
Tres Montes, Península ›[1]	254	46.50 S	75.30 W
Tres Montosas ∧	200	34.06 N	107.28 W
Tres Morros, Alto de ∧	246	7.08 N	76.11 W
Tresnuraghes	71	40.15 N	8.31 E
Tres Padres, Pico ∧	286a	19.35 N	99.08 W
Tres Palacios ≃	196	28.45 N	96.09 W
Tres Palos, Laguna c	234	16.46 N	99.44 W
Três Passos	252	27.27 S	53.56 W
Tres Picos	234	15.52 N	93.32 W
Tres Picos, Cerro ∧, Arg.	252	38.09 S	61.57 W
Tres Picos, Cerro ∧, Méx.	234	16.12 N	93.37 W
Tres Pinos	226	36.48 N	121.19 W
Tres Pinos Creek ≃	226	36.47 N	121.21 W
Três Pontas	256	21.22 S	45.31 W
Três Pontas, Cabo das ›	152	10.23 S	13.32 E
Tres Puntas, Cabo ›, Arg.	254	47.06 S	65.53 W
Tres Puntas, Cabo ›, Guat.	236	15.56 N	88.37 W
Três Ranchos	255	18.22 S	47.47 W
Tres Reyes Islands II	116	13.14 N	121.51 E
Três Rios, Bra.	256	22.07 S	43.12 W
Tres Ríos, C.R.	236	9.54 N	83.58 W
Tressancourt	261	48.55 N	2.00 E
Třešť	30	49.18 N	15.30 E
Tresta	46a	60.14 N	1.21 W
Tres Valles	234	18.15 N	96.08 W
Tres Vírgenes, Volcán de las ∧[1]	232	27.27 N	112.34 W
Tres Zapotes ⊥	234	18.28 N	95.24 W
Tret'akovskaja Galereja ⊻	265b	55.45 N	37.37 E
Tretet	114	4.40 N	96.51 E
Trets	62	43.27 N	5.41 E
Tretten	26	61.19 N	10.19 E
Treuchtlingen	56	48.57 N	10.54 E
Treuen	54	50.32 N	12.18 E
Treuenbrietzen	54	52.06 N	12.52 E
Treuhandgebiet Pazifische Inseln → Trust Territory of the Pacific Islands □[2]	14	5.00 N	137.00 E
Trevelín	254	43.04 S	71.28 W
Trèves → Trier	56	49.45 N	6.38 E
Trevi	66	42.52 N	12.45 E
Treviglio	62	45.31 N	9.35 E
Trevignano Romano	66	42.09 N	12.15 E
Treviño	34	42.44 N	2.45 W
Treviso	64	45.40 N	12.15 E
Treviso □[4]	64	45.50 N	12.13 E
Trevor	216	42.30 N	88.07 W
Trevorton	208	40.46 N	76.40 W
Trevose	208	40.08 N	74.58 W
Trevose Head ›	42	50.33 N	5.01 W
Trevose Heights	285	40.09 N	74.59 W
Trévoux	58	45.56 N	4.46 E
Trexlertown	208	40.33 N	75.36 W
Trezevant	194	36.00 N	88.37 W
Trezzano sul Naviglio	266b	45.25 N	9.04 E
Trezzo sull'Adda	62	45.36 N	9.31 E
Trgovište	38	42.21 N	22.05 E
Trhomné	60	49.55 N	13.05 E
Trhové Sviny	61	48.51 N	14.39 E
Triabunna	166	42.30 S	147.55 E
Triadelphia Reservoir ⊜[1]	208	39.13 N	77.01 W
Trialeti	84	41.33 N	44.07 E
Trialetskij chrebet ⋀	84	41.45 N	43.50 E
Triana	66	42.47 N	11.33 E
Triánda	38	36.24 N	28.10 E
Triangle, Eng., U.K.	262	53.42 N	1.56 W
Triangle, Va., U.S.	208	38.32 N	77.20 W
Triangle Lake	210	42.32 N	74.13 W
Triangul'atorov, pik ∧	88	53.45 N	97.00 E
Triángulos, Arrecífes ✣[2]	232	20.57 N	92.16 W
Triaucourt-en-Argonne	56	48.59 N	5.04 E
Tribeni	126	22.59 N	88.24 E
Triberg	58	48.08 N	8.13 E
Tribes Hill	210	42.57 N	74.17 W
Tribobó	287a	22.52 S	43.01 W
Triborough Bridge ⊸[5]	276	40.47 N	73.55 W
Tri Brata, porog ⌊	86	57.25 N	95.39 E
Tribsees	54	54.05 N	12.45 E
Tribugá, Ensenada de c	246	5.45 N	77.20 W
Tribune, Sk., Can.	184	49.15 N	103.50 W
Tribune, Ks., U.S.	198	38.28 N	101.45 W
Tribune Channel ʉ	182	50.50 N	126.16 W
Tribuswinkel	264b	48.00 N	16.16 E
Tricarico	68	40.37 N	16.09 E
Tricase	68	39.56 N	18.22 E
Tricesimo	64	46.10 N	13.13 E
Trichardt	158	26.28 S	29.13 E
Trichiana	64	46.05 N	12.07 E
Trichinopoly → Tiruchchirāppalli	122	10.49 N	78.41 E
Trichūr	122	10.31 N	76.13 E
Tri Cities	222	32.09 N	95.56 W
Tricot	50	49.34 N	2.35 E
Tri County Supply Canal ≋	198	40.49 N	100.06 W
Trida	166	33.01 S	145.01 E
Trident Peak ∧	204	41.54 N	118.25 W
Trieben	61	47.29 N	14.30 E
Triebes	54	50.41 N	12.01 E
Triel-sur-Seine	261	48.59 N	2.00 E
Trient → Trento	64	46.04 N	11.08 E
Triepkendorf	54	53.17 N	13.20 E
Trier	56	49.45 N	6.38 E
Trier □[5]	56	50.00 N	6.40 E
Triesen	58	47.06 N	9.31 E
Trieste (Triest) (Trst)	64	45.40 N	13.46 E
Trieste □[4]	64	45.40 N	13.50 E
Trieste, Gulf of c	64	45.40 N	13.35 E
Triesting ≃	61	48.05 N	16.24 E
Trieux	56	49.20 N	5.56 E
Triftern	60	48.24 N	13.01 E
Trigal	248	18.17 S	64.08 W
Triggiano	68	41.04 N	16.55 E
Triglav ∧	64	46.23 N	13.50 E
Triglitz	54	53.12 N	12.05 E
Trigna, Pizzo ∧	70	37.58 N	13.34 E
Trigno ≃	66	42.04 N	14.48 E
Trigueros	34	37.23 N	6.50 W
Tríkala	38	39.34 N	21.46 E
Trikhonís, Límni ⊜	38	38.34 N	21.28 E
Trikora, Puncak (Wilhelmina Peak) ∧	164	4.15 S	138.45 E
Tri-Lakes	216	41.14 N	85.26 W
Trilbardou	261	48.57 N	2.48 E
Trilby	220	28.27 N	82.11 W
Trillick	48	54.27 N	7.30 W
Trilport	50	48.57 N	2.57 E
Trim	48	53.34 N	6.47 W
Triman	120	29.38 N	69.05 E
Trimbach	58	47.22 N	7.54 E
Trimble □[6]	218	38.37 N	85.20 W
Trim Creek ≃	216	41.10 N	87.38 W
Trimdon	44	54.42 N	1.25 W
Trimont	198	43.45 N	94.42 W
Trimonte	256	21.43 S	42.35 W
Trin	58	46.50 N	9.22 E
Trinchera Creek ≃	200	37.19 N	105.45 W
Trincheras, Méx.	196	25.37 N	101.55 W
Trincheras, Méx.	232	30.24 N	111.32 W
Trincomalee	122	8.34 N	81.14 E
Trincomali Channel ʉ	224	48.02 N	123.30 W
Trindade	255	16.40 S	49.30 W
Trindade I	244	20.31 S	29.19 W
Třinec	30	49.41 N	18.40 E
Tring	42	51.48 N	0.40 W
Trinidad, Bol.	248	14.47 S	64.47 W
Trinidad, Col.	246	5.25 N	71.40 W
Trinidad, Cuba	240p	21.48 N	79.59 W
Trinidad, Hond.	236	14.57 N	88.45 W
Trinidad, Co., U.S.	198	37.10 N	104.30 W
Trinidad, Tx., U.S.	222	32.08 N	96.05 W
Trinidad, Ur.	252	33.32 S	56.54 W
Trinidad I	241r	10.30 N	61.15 W
Trinidad ≃	234	17.49 N	95.09 W
Trinidad, Golfo c	254	49.55 S	75.25 W
Trinidad, Isla I	252	39.08 S	61.58 W
Trinidad and Tobago □[1], N.A.	230	11.00 N	61.00 W
Trinidad and Tobago □[1], N.A.	241r	11.00 N	61.00 W
Trinità	62	44.30 N	7.45 E
Trinità, Lago della ⊜	70	37.43 N	12.46 E
Trinità d'Agultu	71	40.59 N	8.54 E
Trinitapoli	68	41.21 N	16.05 E
Trinité, Havre de la c	240e	14.44 N	60.58 W
Trinity, Nf., Can.	186	48.59 N	53.55 W
Trinity, Tx., U.S.	222	30.56 N	95.22 W
Trinity □[6]	222	31.07 N	95.10 W
Trinity ≃, Ca., U.S.	204	41.11 N	123.42 W
Trinity ≃, Tx., U.S.	222	29.47 N	94.42 W
Trinity, Clear Fork ≃	196	32.46 N	97.21 W
Trinity, East Fork ≃	222	32.30 N	96.30 W
Trinity, Elm Fork ≃	222	32.47 N	96.54 W
Trinity, South Fork ≃	204	40.54 N	123.35 W
Trinity, West Fork ≃	196	32.48 N	96.51 W
Trinity Bay c, Nf., Can.	186	48.00 N	53.40 W
Trinity Bay c, Tx., U.S.	222	29.40 N	94.45 W
Trinity Islands II	180	56.33 N	154.25 W
Trinity Mountain ∧	202	43.36 N	115.26 W
Trinity Mountains ⋀	204	41.00 N	122.30 W
Trinity Park ♦	275b	43.39 N	79.25 W
Trinity Peak ∧	204	40.14 N	118.45 W
Trinity Site ⊥	200	33.41 N	106.28 W
Trinkat Island I	110	8.05 N	93.30 E
Trinkitat	140	18.41 N	37.43 E
Trino	62	45.12 N	8.18 E
Trins	64	47.05 N	11.25 E
Trinway	214	40.08 N	82.00 W
Triolet	157c	20.03 S	57.32 E
Triolo ≃	66	41.40 N	15.34 E
Trion	192	34.32 N	85.18 W
Trionto ≃	68	39.37 N	16.45 E
Trionto, Capo ›	68	39.37 N	16.45 E
Triora	62	43.59 N	7.46 E
Tripa ≃	114	3.53 N	96.23 E
Tripi	70	38.03 N	15.06 E
Triplett Creek ≃	218	38.10 N	83.27 W
Triplett Creek, North Fork ≃	218	38.10 N	83.31 W
Tripoli → Ṭarābulus, Lībiyā	146	32.54 N	13.11 E
Tripoli → Ṭarābulus, Lubnān	130	34.26 N	35.51 E
Tripoli, Ia., U.S.	190	42.48 N	92.15 W
Trípolis, Ellás	38	37.31 N	22.21 E
Tripolis → Ṭarābulus, Lībiyā	146	32.54 N	13.11 E
Tripolis ⊥	130	37.58 N	28.59 E
Tripolitania → Ṭarābulus □[9]	146	31.00 N	15.00 E
Triponzo	66	42.50 N	12.56 E
Tripp	198	43.13 N	97.57 W
Trips Subdivision	281	42.34 N	83.25 W
Triptis	54	50.44 N	11.52 E
Tripura □[3]	120	24.00 N	92.00 E
Triquet, Lac ⊜	186	50.42 N	59.47 W
Trisanna ≃	58	47.07 N	10.30 E
Tristan da Cunha Group II	10	37.15 S	12.30 W
Tristan Island I	10	37.05 S	12.17 W
Tristán Suárez	258	34.53 S	58.34 W
Tristao, Îles II	150	10.53 N	14.58 W
Tristate Village	278	41.44 N	87.57 W
Triste	34	42.23 N	0.43 W
Triste, Golfo c	246	10.40 N	68.10 W
Triśuli Gaṅggā ≃	124	27.49 N	84.47 E
Tri Ton	110	10.25 N	105.00 E
Tritriva	157b	22.46 S	46.07 E
Trittau	52	53.37 N	10.25 E
Trittenheim	56	49.49 N	6.54 E
Triuggio	266b	45.40 N	9.16 E
Triumph	194	29.20 N	89.28 W
Triunfo, Igarapé ≃	250	6.22 S	52.25 W
Trivandrum	122	8.29 N	76.55 E
Trivento	66	41.47 N	14.33 E
Trivero	62	45.40 N	8.10 E
Trivigno	68	40.35 N	15.59 E
Trnava	30	48.23 N	17.35 E
Trnovo → Veliko Târnovo	38	43.04 N	25.39 E
Tr'ochgolovyj Golec, gora ∧	88	53.22 N	107.03 E
Tr'ochsv'atskoje	82	56.29 N	37.03 E
Trochtelfingen	58	48.18 N	9.14 E
Trochu	182	51.50 N	113.13 W
Troense	41	55.02 N	10.39 E
Trofa, Arroyo de ≃	266a	40.30 N	3.45 W
Trofaiach	61	47.25 N	15.00 E
Trofarello	62	44.59 N	7.44 E
Trögd ›[1]	40	59.31 N	17.15 E
Trogen	58	47.24 N	9.28 E
Trogir	36	43.31 N	16.15 E
Troglav ∧	36	43.57 N	16.36 E
Tröglitz	54	51.04 N	12.11 E
Troia	68	41.22 N	15.18 E
Troica	76	54.24 N	40.14 E
Troice-Lykovo ⊸[8]	265b	55.47 N	37.24 E
Troick, Ross.	86	54.06 N	61.35 E
Troick, Ross.	88	57.25 N	94.50 E
Troickaja	78	45.08 N	38.07 E
Troickij, Ross.	80	50.14 N	43.03 E
Troickij, Ross.	80	50.14 N	43.05 E
Troickij, Ross.	86	50.41 N	54.38 E
Troickij, Ross.	86	57.03 N	63.43 E
Troickij, Ross.	88	54.36 N	113.09 E
Troickije Rosl'ai	80	53.21 N	41.24 E
Troickij Sungur	80	53.17 N	47.37 E
Troickij Zavod	88	53.27 N	102.09 E
Troickoje, Ross.	78	51.17 N	41.28 E
Troickoje, Ross.	80	46.26 N	44.15 E
Troickoje, Ross.	80	53.22 N	48.23 E
Troickoje, Ross.	80	53.06 N	52.32 E
Troickoje, Ross.	80	53.23 N	52.48 E
Troickoje, Ross.	82	55.23 N	37.25 E
Troickoje, Ross.	82	54.52 N	37.07 E
Troickoje, Ross.	83	47.22 N	38.53 E
Troickoje, Ross.	86	52.19 N	56.23 E
Troickoje, Ross.	86	59.07 N	58.25 E
Troickoje, Ross.	86	52.58 N	84.40 E
Troickoje, Ross.	89	49.27 N	136.36 E
Troicko-Pečorsk	24	62.44 N	56.06 E
Troina	70	37.47 N	14.36 E
Troina ≃	70	37.49 N	14.46 E
Troisdorf	56	50.49 N	7.08 E
Trois Fourches, Cap des ›	148	35.26 N	2.58 W
Trois-Pistoles	186	48.07 N	69.10 W
Trois Pitons, Morne ∧	240d	15.22 N	61.20 W
Trois Ponts	56	50.22 N	5.52 E
Trois-Rivières, P.Q., Can.	206	46.21 N	72.33 W
Trois-Rivières, Guad.	241o	15.59 N	61.39 W
Trois-Rivières-Ouest	206	46.19 N	72.35 W
Troisvierges	56	50.08 N	6.00 E
Trojan	38	42.51 N	24.43 E
Trojanova Tabla ⊥	38	44.37 N	22.20 E
Trojebratskij	86	54.28 N	66.01 E
Trojekurovo, Ross.	76	53.00 N	38.58 E
Trojekurovo, Ross.	76	53.25 N	39.43 E
Tr'okhizdenka	83	48.45 N	38.58 E
Troldhede	41	55.59 N	8.45 E
Trolleholm	41	55.54 N	13.15 E
Trollhättan	26	58.16 N	12.18 E
Trollheimen ∧	26	62.51 N	9.05 E
Trombay ⊸[8]	272c	19.02 N	72.57 E
Trombetas ≃	250	1.55 S	55.35 W
Tromelin, Île I	138	15.52 S	54.25 E
Tromello	62	45.12 N	8.52 E
Tromper Wiek c	54	54.37 N	13.24 E
Trompia, Val V	64	45.44 N	10.12 E
Trompsburg	158	30.01 S	25.46 E
Troms □[6]	24	69.15 N	19.40 E
Tromsø	24	69.40 N	18.58 E
Trona	204	35.45 N	117.22 W
Tronador, Monte ∧	254	41.10 S	71.54 W
Troncoso	234	22.44 N	102.22 W
Trondheim	26	63.25 N	10.25 E
Trondheimsfjorden c[2]	26	63.39 N	10.49 E
Trondheimsleia ʉ	26	63.30 N	9.00 E
Tronto ≃	66	42.54 N	13.55 E
Tronville-en-Barrois	56	48.43 N	5.17 E
Tronzano Vercellese	62	45.21 N	8.10 E
Troo	50	47.47 N	0.47 E
Troödos	130	34.55 N	32.53 E
Trooilapspan	158	28.40 S	21.25 E
Troon, Eng., U.K.	42	50.12 N	5.16 W
Troon, Scot., U.K.	46	55.32 N	4.40 W
Trooper	285	40.09 N	75.24 W
Troparevo	82	55.23 N	35.54 E
Tropar'ovo ⊸[8]	265b	55.39 N	37.29 E
Tropas, Rio das ≃	250	6.07 S	57.28 W
Tropea	68	38.41 N	15.54 E
Trophy Mountain ∧	182	51.47 N	119.48 W
Tropic	200	37.37 N	112.04 W
Tropojë	38	42.24 N	20.10 E
Troppau → Opava	30	49.56 N	17.54 E
Trosa	40	58.54 N	17.33 E
Troškovo	80	57.19 N	46.05 E
Troškūnai	76	55.36 N	24.51 E
Trosna	76	52.26 N	35.46 E
Trossingen	58	48.04 N	8.38 E
Trostan ∧	48	55.03 N	6.09 W
Tröstau	60	50.01 N	11.57 E
Trostberg	60	48.01 N	12.32 E
Trostenskoje, ozero ⊜	82	55.52 N	36.29 E
Trostyanets', Ukr.	78	50.28 N	34.59 E
Trostyanets', Ukr.	78	48.31 N	29.12 E
Trotha ⊸[8]	54	51.31 N	11.58 E
Trottiscliffe	260	51.19 N	0.21 E
Trotuș ≃	38	46.03 N	27.14 E
Trotwood	218	39.47 N	84.18 W
Troublesome Creek ≃	219	39.54 N	91.37 W
Troubridge Point ›	168b	35.11 S	137.41 E
Trou-du-Nord	238	19.38 N	72.01 W
Troup	222	32.08 N	95.07 W
Troup Head ›	46	57.41 N	2.18 W
Troupsburg	210	42.03 N	77.33 W
Trout	194	31.41 N	92.10 W
Trout ≃, N.T., Can.	176	61.19 N	119.51 W
Trout ≃, N.A.	206	45.05 N	74.10 W
Trout Brook ≃, Ma., U.S.	283	42.16 N	71.18 W
Trout Brook ≃, Ma., U.S.	283	42.39 N	71.16 W
Trout Creek, Mi., U.S.	190	46.28 N	89.00 W
Trout Creek, Mt., U.S.	182	47.50 N	115.35 W
Trout Creek, N.Y., U.S.	210	42.12 N	75.17 W
Trout Creek ≃, Az., U.S.	200	34.56 N	113.36 W
Trout Creek ≃, Or., U.S.	202	44.48 N	121.03 W
Trout Creek ≃, Or., U.S.	202	42.23 N	118.36 W
Trout Creek ≃, Pa., U.S.	285	40.07 N	75.24 W
Trout Creek ≃, Wa., U.S.	224	46.02 N	121.12 W
Trout Creek Pass)(	200	38.54 N	105.58 W
Troutdale	224	45.32 N	122.23 W
Trout Lake	224	45.59 N	121.31 W
Trout Lake ⊜, B.C., Can.	182	50.35 N	117.26 W
Trout Lake ⊜, N.T., Can.	176	60.35 N	121.10 W
Trout Lake ⊜, On., Can.	184	51.13 N	93.20 W
Trout Lake ⊜, On., Can.	190	46.18 N	79.20 W
Trout Lake ⊜, On., Can.	190	46.13 N	80.35 W
Trout Lake Creek ≃	224	46.00 N	121.30 W
Trout Peak ∧	202	44.36 N	109.32 W
Trout River	186	49.29 N	58.08 W
Trout Run	210	41.23 N	77.03 W
Troutville, Pa., U.S.	214	41.02 N	78.47 W
Troutville, Va., U.S.	192	37.25 N	79.52 W
Trouville-sur-Mer	50	49.22 N	0.05 E
Trowbridge	42	51.20 N	2.13 W
Troxelville	210	40.48 N	77.12 W
Troy, Al., U.S.	194	31.48 N	85.58 W
Troy, Id., U.S.	202	46.44 N	116.46 W
Troy, Il., U.S.	219	38.43 N	89.52 W
Troy, In., U.S.	194	37.59 N	86.47 W
Troy, Ks., U.S.	198	39.46 N	95.05 W
Troy, Mi., U.S.	214	42.34 N	83.09 W
Troy, Mo., U.S.	219	38.58 N	90.58 W
Troy, Mt., U.S.	202	48.27 N	115.53 W
Troy, N.H., U.S.	207	42.49 N	72.10 W
Troy, N.Y., U.S.	210	42.43 N	73.41 W
Troy, N.C., U.S.	192	35.21 N	79.53 W
Troy, Oh., U.S.	218	40.02 N	84.12 W
Troy, Pa., U.S.	210	41.47 N	76.47 W
Troy, Tn., U.S.	194	36.20 N	89.09 W
Troy, Tx., U.S.	222	31.12 N	97.18 W
Troy → Truva ⊥	130	39.57 N	26.15 E
Troyaniv	78	50.07 N	28.31 E

Symbols in the index entries represent the broad categories identified in the key at the right. Symbols with superior numbers (⋀[1]) identify subcategories (see complete key on page *I · 1*).

Symbole im Register stellen die rechts im Schlüssel erklärten Kategorien dar. Symbole mit hochgestellten Ziffern (⋀[1]) bezeichnen Unterabteilungen einer Kategorie (vgl. vollständiger Schlüssel auf Seite *I · 1*).

Los símbolos incluídos en el texto del índice representan las grandes categorías identificadas con la clave a la derecha. Los símbolos con numeros en su parte superior (⋀[1]) identifican las subcategorías (véase la clave completa en la página *I · 1*).

Les symboles de l'index représentent les catégories indiquées dans la légende à droite. Les symboles suivis d'un indice (⋀[1]) représentent des sous-catégories (voir légende complète à la page *I · 1*).

Os símbolos incluídos no texto do índice representam as grandes categorias identificadas com a chave à direita. Os símbolos com números em sua parte superior (⋀[1]) identificam as subcategorias (veja-se a chave completa à página *I · 1*).

∧	Mountain	Berg	Montaña	Montagne	Montanha
⋀	Mountains	Gebirge	Montañas	Montagnes	Montanhas
)(	Pass	Paß	Paso	Col	Passo
V	Valley, Canyon	Tal, Cañon	Valle, Cañón	Vallée, Canyon	Vale, Canhão
≚	Plain	Ebene	Llano	Plaine	Planície
›	Cape	Kap	Cabo	Cap	Cabo
I	Island	Insel	Isla	Île	Ilha
II	Islands	Inseln	Islas	Îles	Ilhas
⊥	Other Topographic Features	Andere Topographische Objekte	Otros Elementos Topográficos	Autres données topographiques	Outros acidentes topográficos

ESPAÑOL · FRANÇAIS · PORTUGUÊS

Nombre / Nom / Nome	Página / Page / Página	Lat.°′	Long.°′ W = Oeste / W = Ouest / W = Oeste
Troyanivka	78	51.20 N	25.17 E
Troy Brook ≃	276	40.50 N	74.22 W
Troyes	50	48.18 N	4.05 E
Troy Grove	216	41.28 N	89.05 W
Troy Hills	210	40.51 N	74.23 W
Troyits'ke, Ukr.	78	49.55 N	38.19 E
Troyits'ke, Ukr.	78	47.38 N	30.19 E
Troyits'ke, Ukr.	83	48.32 N	38.23 E
Troyits'ko-Khartsyz'k	83	47.58 N	38.16 E
Troy Lake ⊜	204	34.49 N	116.33 W
Troy Meadows ⩩	276	40.50 N	74.22 W
Troy Peak ∧	204	38.19 N	115.30 W
Trpanj	36	43.00 N	17.17 E
Trst			
→ Trieste	64	45.40 N	13.46 E
Trstená	30	49.22 N	19.37 E
Trstenik	38	43.37 N	21.00 E
Truax	184	49.55 N	104.58 W
Trubč'ovsk	76	52.37 N	33.44 E
Trubetčino	76	52.53 N	39.33 E
Trubino, Ross.	82	54.58 N	36.42 E
Trubino, Ross.	82	55.59 N	38.08 E
Trub'ož ≃	82	56.44 N	38.51 E
Truchas	200	36.02 N	105.48 W
Truchas Peak ∧	200	35.58 N	105.39 W
Truchtersheim	58	48.40 N	7.36 E
Trucial States			
→ United Arab			
Emirates □[1]	128	24.00 N	54.00 E
Truckee	226	39.19 N	120.10 W
Truckee ≃	204	39.51 N	119.24 W
Trucksville	210	41.18 N	75.56 W
Trud	76	57.37 N	33.58 E
Trudfront	80	45.56 N	47.41 E
Trudnovo	86	56.39 N	91.30 E
Trudovoj	80	51.42 N	52.43 E
Trues Creek ≃	276	40.41 N	73.17 W
Truganina	274b	37.49 S	144.43 E
Truim ≃	46	57.02 N	4.10 W
Truite, Lac à la ⊜	190	47.16 N	78.17 W
Trujillo, Col.	246	4.10 N	76.19 W
Trujillo, Esp.	34	39.28 N	5.53 W
Trujillo, Hond.	236	15.55 N	86.00 W
Trujillo, Méx.	234	23.10 N	103.13 W
Trujillo, Perú	248	8.07 S	79.02 W
Trujillo, Ven.	246	9.22 N	70.26 W
Trujillo □[3]	246	9.25 N	70.30 W
Trujillo Alto	240m	18.22 N	66.01 W
Trujillo Creek ≃	196	35.28 N	102.52 W
Truk Islands ‖	175c	7.25 N	151.47 E
Truk Lagoon ⊂	175c	7.25 N	151.45 E
Trull Brook ≃	283	42.39 N	71.15 W
Truman	198	43.49 N	94.26 W
Trumann	194	35.40 N	90.30 W
Trumansburg	210	42.32 N	76.39 W
Trumbauersville	208	40.25 N	75.23 W
Trumbull	207	41.14 N	73.12 W
Trumbull □[6]	214	41.14 N	80.52 W
Trumbull, Mount ∧	200	36.25 N	113.10 W
Trumon	114	2.49 N	97.38 E
Trun, Fr.	50	48.51 N	0.02 E
Trun, Schw.	58	46.45 N	8.58 E
Trundle	166	32.55 S	147.43 E
Trung Luong	110	13.57 N	109.15 E
Trung Phan □[9]	110	15.00 N	108.00 E
Trunovskoje	80	45.29 N	42.08 E
Truro, Austl.	168b	34.25 S	139.07 E
Truro, N.S., Can.	186	45.22 N	63.16 W
Truro, Eng., U.K.	42	50.16 N	5.03 W
Truro, Ma., U.S.	207	41.59 N	70.03 W
Trusan ≃	112	4.58 N	115.11 E
Truscott	196	33.45 N	99.49 W
Trușeni	38	47.04 N	28.41 E
Trușești	38	47.46 N	27.01 E
Trusetal	54	50.47 N	10.25 E
Truskavets'	78	49.16 N	23.33 E
Truslejka	80	53.54 N	46.24 E
Trus Madi, Gunong ∧	112	5.33 N	116.31 E
Trust Territory of the			
Pacific Islands □[2]	14	5.00 N	137.00 E
Truth or			
Consequences			
(Hot Springs)	200	33.07 N	107.15 W
Trutnov	30	50.34 N	15.55 E
Truva (Troy) ⊥	130	39.57 N	26.15 E
Truxall	279b	40.33 N	79.33 W
Truxton, Mo., U.S.	219	39.00 N	91.14 W
Truxton, N.Y., U.S.	210	42.43 N	76.02 W
Truxton Wash V	200	35.38 N	114.04 W
Truyère ≃	32	44.39 N	2.34 E
Trwyn Cilan ›	42	52.46 N	4.30 W
Tryduby	78	48.06 N	30.24 E
Trylisy	78	49.59 N	29.50 E
Tryon, Ne., U.S.	198	41.33 N	100.57 W
Tryon, N.C., U.S.	192	35.12 N	82.14 W
Tryonville	214	41.42 N	79.47 W
Trypillya	78	50.07 N	30.46 E
Trysil	26	61.19 N	12.16 E
Trysilelva (Klarälven)			
≃	26	59.23 N	13.32 E
Tryškiai	76	56.04 N	22.35 E
Tryweryn ≃	42	52.55 N	3.35 W
Trzcianka	30	53.03 N	16.28 E
Trzciel	30	52.23 N	15.52 E
Trzcińsko-Zdrój	30	52.58 N	14.35 E
Trzebiatów	30	54.04 N	15.14 E
Trzebiel	54	51.37 N	14.50 E
Trzebież	30	53.42 N	14.31 E
Trzebinia	30	50.10 N	19.18 E
Trzebnica	30	51.19 N	17.03 E
Trzemeszno	30	52.35 N	17.50 E
Trzęsacz	54	54.05 N	14.58 E
Tržič	36	46.22 N	14.19 E
Tsacha Lake ⊜	182	53.05 N	124.40 W
Tsala Apopka Lake ⊜	220	28.52 N	82.20 W
Tsamkong			
→ Zhanjiang	102	21.16 N	110.28 E
Tsandi	156	17.42 S	14.50 E
Tsangano	154	15.08 S	34.32 E
Ts'anghsien			
→ Cangzhou	98	38.19 N	116.51 E
T'sangwu			
→ Wuzhou	102	23.30 N	111.27 E
Ts'aot'un	100	23.59 N	120.41 E
Tsarabaria	157b	13.46 S	49.58 E
Tsaramandroso	157b	16.22 S	47.02 E
Tsaratanana	157b	16.47 S	47.39 E
Tsaratanana, Massif			
du ⩕	157b	14.00 S	49.00 E
Tsaraxaibis	158	27.25 S	19.22 E
Tsaritsyn			
→ Volgograd	80	48.44 N	44.25 E
Tsarychanka	78	48.57 N	34.29 E
Tsau	156	20.12 S	22.22 E
Tsaukaib	156	26.37 S	15.31 E
Tsavo	154	2.59 S	38.28 E
Tsavo East National			
Park ♠	154	2.11 S	38.25 E
Tsavo West National			
Park ♠	154	2.55 S	37.55 E
Tsawwassen	224	49.01 N	123.06 W
Tsaydaychuz Peak ∧	182	53.02 N	126.35 W
Tsayta Lake ⊜	182	55.25 N	125.30 W
Tschad			
→ Chad □[1]	146	15.00 N	19.00 E
Tschad-See			
→ Chad, Lake ⊜	146	13.20 N	14.00 E
Tschagguns	58	47.05 N	9.54 E
Tschamut	58	46.40 N	8.42 E
Tschangscha			
→ Changsha	100	28.12 N	112.58 E
Tschangtschun			
→ Changchun	89	43.53 N	125.19 E
Tscheljuskin, Kap			
→ Čel'uskin, mys ›	74	77.45 N	104.20 E
Tschengtu			
→ Chengdu	107	30.39 N	104.04 E
Tschenstochau			
→ Częstochowa	30	50.49 N	19.06 E
Tschernitz	54	51.35 N	14.37 E
Tscheschkaja-Bucht			
→ Češskaja guba			
⊂	24	67.30 N	46.30 E
Tschida, Lake ⊜[1]	198	46.36 N	101.54 W
Tschingtau			
→ Qingdao	98	36.06 N	120.19 E
Tschittagong			
→ Chittagong	120	22.20 N	91.50 E
Tschuktschen-Meer			
→ Chukchi Sea ⍑[2]	16	69.00 N	171.00 W
Tschungking			
→ Chongqing	107	29.34 N	106.35 E
Tsebrykove	78	47.09 N	30.06 E
Tsekanyani	156	19.52 S	26.39 E
Tsembeyi	158	31.36 S	27.03 E
Ts'engwen ≃	100	23.03 N	120.03 E
Tsenke ≃	273b	4.24 S	15.26 E
Tses	156	25.58 S	18.08 E
Tsévié	150	6.25 N	1.13 E
Tshabong	156	26.03 S	22.29 E
Tshabuta	152	7.47 S	23.16 E
Tshane	156	24.05 S	21.54 E
Tshaneni	158	26.00 S	31.47 E
Tshangalele, Lac ⊜	154	10.55 S	27.03 E
Tshangu ≃	273b	4.25 S	15.23 E
Tshela	152	4.59 S	12.56 E
Tshesebe	156	21.51 S	27.35 E
Tshibeke	154	2.44 S	28.36 E
Tshibinda	154	2.19 S	28.45 E
Tshibomba	152	9.02 S	22.34 E
Tshidilamolomo	156	25.50 S	24.41 E
Tshikapa	152	6.25 S	20.48 E
Tshilenge	152	6.15 S	23.46 E
Tshimbulu	152	6.29 S	22.51 E
Tshindjamba	152	10.54 S	22.41 E
Tshinota	152	7.01 S	20.57 E
Tshinsenda	154	12.18 S	27.58 E
Tshisuku	152	6.26 S	19.55 E
Tshitadi	152	6.45 S	21.45 E
Tshoa	152	5.34 S	12.41 E
Tshofa	154	5.14 S	25.15 E
Tshopo ≃	154	0.33 N	25.07 E
Tshuapa ≃	152	0.14 S	20.42 E
Tshukudu	156	22.30 S	23.22 E
Tshumbiri	152	2.39 S	16.14 E
Tshwaane	156	22.29 S	22.03 E
Tsiafajavona ∧	157b	19.21 S	47.15 E
Tsianaloka	157b	18.08 S	44.50 E
Tsiémé ≃	273b	4.15 S	15.18 E
Tsiga	152	1.32 S	10.11 E
Tsihombe	157b	25.18 S	45.29 E
Tsilmamo	144	6.01 N	35.17 E
Tsimanampetsotsa,			
Lac ⊜	157b	24.08 S	43.46 E
Tsimilofo	157b	24.59 S	45.10 E
Tsimpsean Indian			
Reserve ◆[4]	182	54.30 N	130.22 W
Tsinan			
→ Jinan	98	36.40 N	116.57 E
Tsineng	158	27.06 S	23.04 E
Tsinghai			
→ Qinghai □[4]	90	36.00 N	96.00 E
Tsingkiang			
→ Qingjiang	100	33.35 N	119.02 E
Tsingtao			
→ Qingdao	98	36.06 N	120.19 E
Tsing Yi I	271d	22.21 N	114.05 E
Tsingyuan			
→ Baoding	105	38.52 N	115.29 E
Tsining			
→ Jining	98	35.25 N	116.36 E
Tsinjoarivo	157b	19.37 S	47.40 E
Tsinjomitondraka	157b	15.36 S	47.08 E
Tsinling Shan			
→ Qin Ling ⩕	102	34.00 N	108.00 E
Tsintsabis	156	18.45 S	17.51 E
Tsiribihina ≃	157b	19.42 S	44.31 E
Tsiroanomandidy	157b	18.46 S	46.02 E
Tsitondroina	157b	21.19 S	46.00 E
Tsitsihar			
→ Qiqihar	89	47.19 N	123.55 E
Tsitsikama Forest			
and Coastal			
National Park ♠	158	33.57 S	23.53 E
Tsitsutl Peak ∧	182	52.44 N	125.47 W
Tsivory	157b	24.04 S	46.05 E
Tskhinvali			
→ Cchinvali	84	42.13 N	43.56 E
Tsna			
→ Cna ≃	80	54.32 N	42.05 E
Tsobis	156	19.27 S	17.30 E
Tsolo	158	31.18 S	28.37 E
Tsomo	158	32.00 S	27.42 E
Tsomo ≃	158	32.25 S	27.50 E
Tsoying	100	22.41 N	120.17 E
Tsu	94	34.43 N	136.31 E
Tsubakuro-dake ∧	94	36.24 N	137.42 E
Tsubame	92	37.39 N	138.56 E
Tsubata	94	36.40 N	136.44 E
Tsuboro-suigenchi ⊜[1]	270	34.24 N	135.54 E
Tsuchiura	94	36.05 N	140.12 E
Tsuchiyama	94	34.56 N	136.17 E
Tsuda, Nihon	96	34.17 N	134.15 E
Tsuda, Nihon	270	34.49 N	135.43 E
Tsuen Wan			
(Quanwan)	271d	22.22 N	114.07 E
Tsugaru-hantō ›[1]	92	41.00 N	140.30 E
Tsugaru-heiya ≚	92	40.49 N	140.27 E
Tsugaru-kaikyō ɰ	92a	41.35 N	141.00 E
Tsuge	94	34.37 N	135.57 E
Tsugu	94	35.10 N	137.37 E
Tsuha	174m	26.14 N	127.47 E
Tsuiki	96	33.40 N	131.03 E
Tsujidō	268	35.20 N	139.27 E
Tsukahara	268	35.18 N	139.58 E
Tsukechi	94	35.38 N	137.26 E
Tsuken-jima I	174m	26.15 N	127.57 E
Tsukigase	94	34.42 N	136.02 E
Tsukinowa-kofun ⊥	96	34.55 N	134.11 E
Tsukiyono	94	36.41 N	138.59 E
Tsukuba	94	36.13 N	140.06 E
Tsukuba-san ∧	94	36.13 N	140.06 E
Tsukude	94	34.59 N	137.25 E
Tsukui	94	35.35 N	139.16 E
Tsukumi	96	33.04 N	131.52 E
Tsukumono ◆[8]	270	34.50 N	135.11 E
Tsukuryne	83	48.05 N	37.18 E
Tsukushi-heiya ≚	96	33.20 N	130.30 E
Tsukushi-sanchi ⩕	92	33.30 N	130.30 E
Tsumagoi	94	36.31 N	138.32 E
Tsuman'	78	50.49 N	25.53 E
Tsumeb	156	19.13 S	17.42 E
Tsumeb □[5]	156	19.00 S	17.30 E
Tsumeki-zaki ›	94	34.39 N	138.59 E
Tsumis Park	156	23.43 S	17.28 E
Tsumkwe	156	19.41 S	20.30 E
Tsuna	96	34.26 N	134.54 E
Tsunan	94	37.01 N	138.39 E
Tsunashima ◆[8]	268	35.32 N	139.38 E
Tsunekami-misaki ›	94	35.38 N	135.49 E
Tsuni			
→ Zunyi	102	27.39 N	106.57 E
Tsuno-shima I	96	34.21 N	130.51 E
Tsuru	94	35.33 N	138.55 E
Tsuruga	94	35.39 N	136.04 E
Tsurugaoka-			
hachimangu Shrine			
Ʊ[1]	268	35.19 N	139.33 E
Tsurugashima	268	35.56 N	139.24 E
Tsuruga-wan ⊂	94	35.45 N	136.04 E
Tsurugi	94	36.27 N	136.38 E
Tsurugi-dake ∧	94	36.37 N	137.37 E
Tsurugi-san ∧	96	33.51 N	134.06 E
Tsurugi-san-kokutei-			
kōen ♠	96	33.50 N	134.06 E
Tsuruhara	270	34.26 N	135.20 E
Tsuruma	268	35.51 N	139.33 E
Tsurumi ◆[8]	268	35.30 N	139.41 E
Tsurumi ≃	94	35.29 N	139.41 E
Tsurumi-dake ∧	96	33.17 N	131.26 E
Tsuruoka	92	38.44 N	139.50 E
Tsushima, Nihon	94	35.10 N	136.43 E
Tsushima, Nihon	96	33.05 N	132.30 E
Tsushima ‖	92	34.30 N	129.22 E
Tsushima-kaikyō			
(Eastern Channel)			
ɰ	92	34.00 N	129.00 E
Tsuwano	96	34.28 N	131.46 E
Tsuyama	96	35.03 N	134.00 E
Tsuyazaki	96	33.47 N	130.28 E
Tsvitkove	78	49.11 N	31.33 E
Tsvitne	78	48.57 N	32.29 E
Tsybuliv	78	49.06 N	29.50 E
Tsyurupyns'k	78	46.37 N	32.43 E
Ttruchchendūr	122	8.29 N	78.07 E
Tu			
→ Tsu	94	34.43 N	136.31 E
Tua	152	3.38 S	16.36 E
Tua ≃	34	41.13 N	7.26 W
Tua, Tanjung ›	115a	5.54 S	105.44 E
Tua Chau	110	21.55 N	103.21 E
Tuakau	172	37.16 S	174.57 E
Tual	164	5.40 S	132.45 E
Tualatin	224	45.23 N	122.45 W
Tualatin ≃	224	45.20 N	122.39 W
Tuam	48	53.31 N	8.50 W
Tuamarina	172	41.26 S	173.57 E
Tuamotu, Îles			
(Tuamotu			
Archipelago) ‖	14	19.00 S	142.00 W
Tuamotu Ridge ✣[3]	14	17.00 S	145.00 W
Tuan, Tanjong ›	114	2.23 N	101.52 E
Tuanan	112	2.07 S	114.24 E
Tuanfeng	100	30.38 N	114.51 E
Tuan Giao	110	21.35 N	103.25 E
Tuangku, Pulau I	114	2.10 N	97.16 E
Tuanlin	98	39.35 N	119.15 E
Tuannian	107	29.55 N	106.03 E
Tuanpi	100	30.44 N	115.13 E
Tuanshan	98	40.02 N	123.34 E
Tuanwang	98	36.45 N	120.38 E
Tuanxi	102	27.28 N	107.08 E
Tuapa	174v	18.57 S	169.54 W
Tuapeka Mouth	172	46.01 S	169.31 E
Tuapse	84	44.07 N	39.05 E
Tuaran	112	6.11 N	116.14 E
Tuas	114	1.19 N	103.38 E
Tuasivi	175a	13.40 S	172.07 W
Tuasivi, Cape ›	175a	13.40 S	172.07 W
Tuatapere	172	46.08 S	167.41 E
Tuath, Loch ɰ	46	56.30 N	6.12 W
Tuba	88	57.24 N	102.48 E
Tuba ≃	86	53.57 N	91.31 E
Tubac	200	31.36 N	111.02 W
Tuba City	200	36.08 N	111.14 W
T'ub'ak-Čekurča	80	56.05 N	49.56 E
Tubalan Head ›	116	6.30 N	125.35 E
Tuban	115a	6.54 S	112.03 E
Tubarão	252	28.30 S	49.01 W
Ṭūbās	132	32.19 N	35.22 E
Tubau	112	3.08 N	113.42 E
Tubbataha Reefs ✣[2]	116	8.51 N	119.56 E
Tubbergen	52	52.25 N	6.46 E
Tubbs Island I	282	38.08 N	122.26 W
Ṭubhār	142	29.19 N	30.42 E
Tubig ≃	116	11.54 N	125.25 E
Tubigan Island I	116	6.26 N	120.47 E
Tubingantan Point ›	116	5.54 N	120.55 E
Tübingen	58	48.31 N	9.02 E
Tübingen □[5]	58	48.10 N	9.30 E
Tubinskij	86	52.53 N	58.13 E
Tubize	50	50.41 N	4.12 E
T'ub-Karagan, mys ›	84	44.39 N	50.18 E
T'ub-Karagan,			
poluostrov ›[1]	84	44.30 N	50.30 E
Tubli	116	13.56 N	124.09 E
Tubod	116	8.03 N	123.48 E
Tubre	64	46.39 N	10.27 E
Ṭubruq (Tobruk)	146	32.05 N	23.59 E
Tubuai I	14	23.18 S	149.30 W
Tuburan, Pil.	116	10.44 N	123.49 W
Tuburan, Pil.	116	6.39 N	122.16 E
Tubusereia	164	9.33 S	147.18 E
Tubutama	200	30.53 N	111.29 W
Tucacas	246	10.48 N	68.19 W
Tucacas, Punta ›	246	10.50 N	68.14 W
Tucalota Creek ≃	228	33.32 N	117.10 W
Tucannon ≃	202	46.33 N	118.11 W
Tucano	250	10.58 S	38.48 W
Tucava ≃	248	18.37 S	58.59 W
T'uch'ang	100	24.35 N	121.29 E
Tucheim	54	52.17 N	12.11 E
Tüchen	54	53.04 N	12.05 E
T'uch'eng, T'aiwan	269d	24.59 N	121.26 E
Tucheng, Zhg.	98	38.53 N	121.15 E
Tucheng, Zhg.	102	28.12 N	105.58 E
Tuchengzi, Zhg.	98	41.20 N	116.29 E
Tuchengzi, Zhg.	98	40.29 N	124.24 E
Tuchengzi, Zhg.	104	42.27 N	122.44 E
Tuchengzicun	104	41.52 N	120.41 E
Tuchengziwuhao	98	40.56 N	113.58 E
Tuchlovice	54	50.06 N	14.00 E
Tuchola	30	53.35 N	17.50 E
Tuchów	30	49.54 N	21.03 E
T'uchtet	86	56.32 N	89.19 E
Tuckahoe, N.J., U.S.	208	39.17 N	74.45 W
Tuckahoe, N.Y., U.S.	276	40.57 N	73.49 W
Tuckahoe ≃	208	39.17 N	74.39 W
Tuckahoe Creek ≃	208	38.49 N	75.53 W
Tuckanarra	162	27.07 S	118.05 E
Tucker Heights	210	42.55 N	73.55 W
Tuckerman	194	35.43 N	91.11 W
Tuckernuck Island I	207	41.18 N	70.15 W
Tuckerton, N.J., U.S.	208	39.36 N	74.20 W
Tuckerton, Pa., U.S.	208	40.25 N	75.57 W
Tuckfield, Mount ∧	162	18.44 S	124.54 E
Tučkovo	82	55.36 N	36.28 E
Tucson	200	32.13 N	110.55 W
Tucumã ≃[1]	246	3.58 S	66.26 W
Tucumán			
→ San Miguel de			
Tucumán	252	26.49 S	65.13 W
Tucumán □[4]	252	27.00 S	65.30 W
Tucumcari	196	35.10 N	103.43 W
Tucumcari Mountain			
∧	196	35.08 N	103.42 W
Tucunuco	252	30.36 S	68.38 W
Tucupido	246	9.17 N	65.47 W
Tucupita	246	9.04 N	62.03 W
Tucuruí	250	3.42 S	49.27 W
Tucuruí, Represa de			
⊜[1]	250	4.40 S	49.20 W
Tucuruvi ◆[8]	287b	23.28 S	46.35 W
Tuczna	30	51.54 N	23.26 E
Tud ≃	42	52.38 N	1.15 E
Tudameda	112	10.52 S	122.55 E
Tudcum	252	30.14 S	69.15 W
Tudeå ≃	41	55.23 N	11.13 E
Tudela, Esp.	34	42.05 N	1.36 W
Tudela, Pil.	116	8.15 N	123.50 E
Tudela de Duero	34	41.35 N	4.35 W
Tudian	106	30.35 N	120.37 E
Tudichang	107	30.06 N	103.56 E
Tuditang	100	30.12 N	114.18 E
Tudmur (Palmyra)	130	34.33 N	38.17 E
Tudu	76	59.11 N	26.51 E
Tudweiliog	42	52.54 N	4.35 W
Tuela ≃	34	41.30 N	7.12 W
Tuen Mun	271d	22.24 N	113.58 E
Tuenno	64	46.20 N	11.01 E
Tueré ≃	250	2.48 S	50.59 W
Tuergate	85	40.28 N	75.21 E
Tufanbeyli	130	38.16 N	36.13 E
Tufānganj	124	26.19 N	89.40 E
Tuffé	50	48.07 N	0.31 E
Tufi	164	9.05 S	149.20 E
Tufo	68	41.00 N	14.47 E
Tufts University Ʊ[2]	283	42.24 N	71.07 W
Tufu Point ›	174y	14.13 S	169.32 W
Tugaske	184	50.53 N	106.16 W
Tugela	158	29.09 S	31.29 E
Tugela ≃	158	29.14 S	31.30 E
Tugela Falls ∟	158	28.45 S	28.58 E
Tugela Ferry	158	28.44 S	30.27 E
Tug Fork ≃	192	38.06 N	82.36 W
Tuggerah Lake ⊂	170	33.18 S	151.30 E
Tughlakābād ◆[8]	272a	28.31 N	77.16 E
Tugidak Island I	180	56.30 N	154.36 W
Tuğköyü	130	38.27 N	42.16 E
Tuglie	68	40.04 N	18.05 E
Tugnug Point ›	116	11.21 N	125.38 E
Tugolesskij Bor	80	55.33 N	39.49 E
Tugolukovo	80	51.56 N	41.40 E
Tugubun Point ›	116	7.00 N	126.27 E
Tuguegarao	116	17.37 N	121.44 E
Tugulym	86	57.04 N	64.39 E
Tugun	171a	28.09 S	153.30 E
Tugur	89	53.48 N	136.48 E
Tugur ≃	89	53.48 N	136.44 E
Tugurskij poluostrov			
›[1]	89	54.00 N	137.24 E
Tuguša	88	55.57 N	96.26 E
Tugutuj	88	52.40 N	104.50 E
Tuhai ≃	98	37.55 N	118.05 E
Tuhepu	104	40.54 N	122.49 E
Tuhuangba	102	31.40 N	108.21 E
Tuibo	89	44.01 N	127.47 E
Tuichi ≃	248	14.36 S	67.35 W
Tuim	86	54.20 N	89.55 E
Tuineje	148	28.19 N	14.03 W
Tuira ≃	246	8.21 N	78.03 W
Tuirc, Beinn an ∧[2]	46	55.34 N	5.34 W
Tuitán	234	21.08 N	103.48 W
Tuitui	256	22.47 S	46.42 W
Tuj ≃	86	57.33 N	72.31 E
T'ujabuguz	85	40.58 N	69.15 E
Tujemojnak	86	49.20 N	62.55 E
Tuji-ri	98	41.31 N	127.12 E
Tujmazy	80	54.36 N	53.42 E
Tüjn Gol ≃	102	45.04 N	100.46 E
Tujunga ◆[8]	280	34.15 N	118.17 W
Tujunga Valley V	280	34.17 N	118.20 W
Tujunga Wash V	280	34.09 N	118.24 W
Tukaj	86	55.24 N	90.49 E
T'ukalinsk	86	55.52 N	72.12 E
Tukan	86	53.50 N	57.26 E
Tukan ≃	86	60.02 N	71.36 E
Tukangbesi,			
Kepulauan ‖	112	5.40 S	123.50 E
Tukayel	144	8.08 N	45.22 E
Ṭūkh, Miṣr	142	30.21 N	31.12 E
Ṭūkh, Miṣr	142	27.41 N	30.49 E
Ṭūkh al-Aqlām	142	30.52 N	31.26 E
Ṭūkh al-Khayl	142	28.06 N	30.40 E
Tukituki ≃	172	39.36 S	176.57 E
Tuk Méas	110	10.40 N	104.34 E
Tukolon'	88	55.24 N	107.42 E
Tukosméra, Mont ∧	175f	19.35 S	169.22 E
Tukpo	154	4.25 N	25.52 E
Tūkrah	146	32.32 N	20.34 E
Tuktoyaktuk	180	69.27 N	133.02 W
Tuktoyaktuk			
Peninsula ›[1]	180	69.45 N	131.20 W
Tukuj-Mekteb	84	44.20 N	45.11 E
Tukums	76	57.00 N	23.10 E
Tukuran	116	7.51 N	123.35 E
Tukuringra, chrebet ⩕	89	54.20 N	126.20 E
Tukuyu	154	9.15 S	33.39 E
T'uk'u Yüeh ∧	269d	25.02 N	121.38 E
Tukwila	224	47.28 N	122.15 W
Tula, Am. Sam.	174u	14.15 S	170.34 W
Tula, It.	71	40.44 N	8.59 E
Tula, Méx.	234	23.00 N	99.43 W
Tula, Nig.	146	9.50 N	11.28 E
Tula, Ross.	82	54.12 N	37.37 E
Tula ≃, Kenya	154	0.50 S	39.51 E
Tula ≃, Méx.	234	20.40 N	99.30 W
Tula ⊥	234	20.06 N	99.19 W
Tula de Allende	234	20.03 N	99.21 W
Tulaghi	175e	9.06 S	160.09 E
Tulagt Ar ≃	120	36.35 N	92.20 E
Tulai Nanshan ⩕	102	38.44 N	98.20 E
Tūlak	128	33.58 N	63.44 E
Tulalip Indian			
Reservation ◆[4]	224	48.06 N	122.15 W
Tulancingo	234	20.05 N	98.22 W
Tulangbawang ≃	112	4.24 S	105.52 E
Tula Oblast' □[4]	76	54.00 N	37.30 E
Tulaodian	104	41.13 N	121.27 E
T'ul'apsy	86	57.28 N	89.38 E
Tulare, Ca., U.S.	226	36.12 N	119.20 W
Tulare, S.D., U.S.	198	44.44 N	98.30 W
Tulare □[6]	226	36.20 N	119.18 W
Tulare Canal ≊	226	36.08 N	119.25 W
Tulare Lake Bed ⊜	226	36.03 N	119.49 W
Tulare Lake Canal ≊	226	36.04 N	119.39 W
Tularosa	200	33.04 N	106.01 W
Tularosa ≃	200	33.41 N	108.46 W
Tularosa Valley ≚[1]	200	32.45 N	106.10 W
Tulbagh	158	33.17 S	19.09 E
Tulbing	264b	48.16 N	16.09 E
Tulbinger Kogel ∧[2]	264b	48.17 N	16.09 E
Tulcán	246	0.48 N	77.43 W
Tulcea	38	45.11 N	28.48 E
Tulcea □[6]	38	45.00 N	29.00 E
Tul'chyn	78	48.39 N	28.52 E
Tulcingo de Valle	234	18.03 N	98.26 W
Tule ≃, Nic.	236	11.20 N	84.52 W
Tule ≃, Ca., U.S.	226	36.03 N	119.50 W
Tule, North Branch ≃	226	36.06 N	119.22 W
Tule, South Branch			
≃	226	36.05 N	119.29 W
Tule Canal ≊	226	38.37 N	121.35 W
Tule Creek ≃	196	34.40 N	101.14 W
T'ulek	85	41.56 N	75.41 E
Tulelake	204	41.57 N	121.29 W
Tule Lake Sump ⊜[1]	204	41.54 N	121.32 W
Tulemalu Lake ⊜	176	62.58 N	99.25 W
T'ulenij, ostrov I	84	44.28 N	47.30 E
Tule River Indian			
Reservation ◆[4]	204	36.02 N	118.42 W
Tulette	62	44.17 N	4.56 E
Tule Valley V	200	39.20 N	113.25 W
T'ul'gan	86	52.22 N	56.12 E
Tul'govičі	78	51.47 N	29.38 E
Tuli	154	21.59 S	29.15 E
Tuli ≃	154	21.48 S	29.04 E
Tulia	196	34.32 N	101.45 W
Tuliahan ≃	269f	14.41 N	120.58 E
Tulica ≃	82	54.12 N	37.37 E
Tulik Volcano ∧[1]	180	53.22 N	168.03 W
Tuling	100	25.11 N	118.50 E
Tuliszków	30	52.05 N	18.17 E
Ṭūlkarm	132	32.19 N	35.02 E
T'ul'kino	86	59.49 N	56.30 E
T'ul'kubas	85	42.28 N	70.02 E
Tulla	48	52.52 N	8.45 W
Tullahoma	194	35.21 N	86.12 W
Tullamarine	274b	37.41 S	144.52 E
Tullamarine			
International			
Airport ⊠, Austl.	169	37.40 S	144.50 E
Tullamarine			
International			
Airport ⊠, Austl.	274b	37.40 S	144.50 E
Tullamore, Austl.	166	32.38 S	147.34 E
Tullamore, On., Can.	275b	43.47 N	79.46 W
Tullamore, Ire.	48	53.16 N	7.30 W
Tullaroop Creek ≃	169	36.53 S	143.53 E
Tullaroop Reservoir			
⊜[1]	169	37.07 S	143.52 E
Tull Bay ⊂	208	36.30 N	76.04 W
Tulle	32	45.16 N	1.46 E
Tullgarn	40	58.57 N	17.35 E
Tullibigeal	166	33.25 S	146.44 E
Tullinge	40	59.12 N	17.53 E
Tullins	62	45.18 N	5.29 E
Tulln	61	48.20 N	16.03 E
Tullner Feld ◆[1]	264b	48.19 N	16.10 E
Tulloch Reservoir ⊜[1]	226	37.53 N	120.35 W
Tullock Creek ≃	202	46.08 N	107.27 W
Tullos	194	31.49 N	92.19 W
Tullow	48	52.48 N	6.44 W
Tullus	140	11.03 N	24.33 E
Tully, Austl.	166	17.56 S	145.56 E
Tully, N.Y., U.S.	210	42.47 N	76.06 W
Tully Dam ◆[6]	207	42.39 N	72.11 W
Tullytown	208	40.09 N	74.49 W
Ṭulmaythah	146	32.43 N	20.57 E
Tuloma ≃	24	68.52 N	32.49 E
Tulpfontein	158	32.44 S	19.43 E
Tulsa	196	36.09 N	95.59 W
Tulsequah	176	58.35 N	133.35 W
Tulsī Lake ⊜	272c	19.11 N	72.55 E
Tulsīpur	124	28.07 N	82.18 E
Tulsk	48	53.47 N	8.16 W
Tul'skij	84	44.31 N	40.10 E
Tulstrup	41	56.07 N	9.46 E
Tultepec	234	19.41 N	99.08 W
Tultitlán	286a	19.39 N	99.09 W
Tuluá	246	4.06 N	76.11 W
Tuluksak	180	61.06 N	160.58 W
Tulum	232	20.13 N	87.28 W
Tulum ⊥	232	20.12 N	87.26 W
Tulumayo ≃	248	11.10 S	75.16 W
Tulun	88	54.35 N	100.33 E
Tulungagung	115a	8.04 S	111.54 E
Tulungselapan	112	3.15 S	105.19 E
Tuluran Island I	116	10.59 N	119.17 E
Tulu Welel ∧	144	8.53 N	34.47 E
Tulyehualco ◆[8]	286a	19.15 N	99.01 W
Tum	164	3.38 S	130.23 E
Tuma	80	55.09 N	40.34 E
Tuma ≃	236	13.03 N	84.44 W
Tumacacori National			
Monument ♠	200	31.25 N	111.01 W
Tumaco	246	1.49 N	78.46 W
Tumaco, Rada de ⊂	246	1.55 N	78.45 W
Tumak	80	46.14 N	48.31 E
Tumalykol'	86	48.21 N	60.03 E
Tuman'an	84	41.00 N	44.40 E
Tuman-gang (Tumen)			
≃	98	42.18 N	130.41 E
Tumannaja, gora ∧	180	66.33 N	179.43 E
Tumanovo	76	55.25 N	34.39 E
Tumanšet ≃	88	55.53 N	97.30 E
Tumanskij	180	63.58 N	178.12 E
Tumany	74	60.56 N	155.56 E
Tumarbong	116	10.23 N	119.27 E
T'um'ati			
→ Sklad	74	71.55 N	123.33 E
Tumatumari	246	5.22 N	59.00 W
Tumauini	116	17.17 N	121.49 E
Tumba	40	59.12 N	17.49 E
Tumba, Lac ⊜	152	0.48 S	18.03 E
Tumbarumba	171b	35.47 S	148.01 E
Tumbarumba Creek			
≃	171b	35.58 S	148.03 E
Tumbes	246	3.34 S	80.28 W
Tumbes □[5]	246	3.50 N	80.30 W
Tumbes (Puyango) ≃	246	3.30 S	80.27 W
Tumbes, Punta ›	252	36.37 S	73.07 W
Tumbiscatio de Ruiz	234	18.31 N	102.21 W
Tumble Mountain ∧	202	45.19 N	110.02 W
Tumbler Ridge	182	55.07 N	120.55 W
Tumblong	171b	35.09 S	148.00 E
Tumbotino	80	55.59 N	43.02 E
Tumbur	154	4.20 N	31.34 E
Tumby Bay	166	34.22 S	136.06 E
Tumča ≃	24	66.36 N	30.48 E
Tŭmch'on-ni ◆[8]	271b	37.34 N	126.51 E
T'umen', Ross.	86	57.09 N	65.32 E
Tumen, Zhg.	98	42.58 N	129.49 E
Tumen (Tuman-gang)			
≃	98	42.18 N	130.41 E
T'umen'-Aryk	86	44.02 N	67.01 E
T'umencevo	86	53.20 N	81.31 E
T'umenec, porog ∟	88	56.38 N	99.00 E
T'umen' Oblast' □[4]	86	58.00 N	69.00 E
Tumenpu	107	29.49 N	103.39 E
Tumenskoje	82	55.00 N	38.32 E
Tumenzi	102	37.43 N	103.09 E
Tumeremo	246	7.18 N	61.30 W
Tumiritinga	255	18.58 S	41.38 W
Tumkūr	122	13.21 N	77.05 E
Tummel ≃	46	56.38 N	3.40 W
Tumnin ≃	89	49.18 N	140.22 E
Tumon Bay ⊂	174p	13.31 N	144.48 E
Tumos ≃	156	22.55 S	14.37 E
Tumoteqi	102	40.52 N	111.28 E
Tumpang	115a	8.00 S	112.46 E
Tumpat	114	6.12 N	102.10 E
Tumsar	120	21.23 N	79.44 E
Tumtum	182	47.53 N	117.40 W
Tumu, Ghana	150	10.52 N	1.59 W
Tumu, Zhg.	105	40.23 N	115.36 E
Tumuc-Humac			
Mountains ⩕	250	2.20 N	55.00 W
Tumut	171b	35.18 S	148.13 E
Tumut ≃	171b	35.07 S	148.13 E
Tumut Pond			
Reservoir ⊜[1]	171b	35.59 S	148.25 E
Tumutuk	80	55.02 N	53.19 E
Tumwater	224	47.00 N	122.54 W
Tun ≃	110	17.25 N	98.42 E
Tuna Canyon V	280	34.03 N	118.36 W
Tunago Lake ⊜	180	66.18 N	125.50 W
Tuna-Hästberg	40	60.20 N	15.11 E
Tunapuna	241r	10.38 N	61.23 W
Tunari, Cerro ∧	248	17.18 S	66.22 W
Tunas Creek ≃	196	31.01 N	102.11 W
Tunas de Zaza	240p	21.38 N	79.33 W
Tūnat al-Jabal, Miṣr	142	27.46 N	30.44 E
Tūnat al-Jabal, Miṣr	142	28.13 N	30.43 E
Tunaydah	140	25.31 N	29.21 E
Tunbridge Wells			
→ Royal Tunbridge			
Wells	42	51.08 N	0.16 E
Tunçbilek	130	39.37 N	29.29 E
Tunceli	130	39.07 N	39.32 E
Tunceli □[4]	130	39.10 N	39.30 E
Tunchang	110	19.28 N	110.08 E
T'unch'i			
→ Tunxi	100	29.44 N	118.18 E
Tunda, Pulau I	115a	5.49 S	106.16 E
Tundazi ∧	154	17.33 S	28.05 E
Tündern	52	52.04 N	9.22 E
Tūndla	124	27.12 N	78.17 E
Tundubai ⍑[4]	140	18.31 N	28.33 E
Tunduru	154	11.07 S	37.21 E
Tundyk ≃	86	51.04 N	77.24 E
Tundža ≃	38	41.40 N	26.34 E
Tune	41	55.36 N	12.11 E
Tunesien			
→ Tunisia □[1]	148	34.00 N	9.00 E
T'unež, Ross.	82	54.37 N	38.29 E
Túnez			
→ Tunis, Tun.	148	36.48 N	10.11 E
Túnez			
→ Tunisia □[1]	148	34.00 N	9.00 E
T'ung ≃	74	63.46 N	121.35 E
Tunga	150	8.00 N	9.19 E
Tunga ≃	122	14.00 N	75.41 E
Tungabhadra ≃	122	15.57 N	78.15 E
Tungabhadra			
Reservoir ⊜[1]	122	15.16 N	76.21 E
Tungaru	140	10.14 N	30.42 E
Tungauan Bay ⊂	116	7.28 N	122.21 E
Tungchi University Ʊ[2]	269b	31.18 N	121.29 E
Tungchi Yü I	100	23.15 N	119.40 E
T'ungchou			
→ Tongxian	105	39.55 N	116.39 E
T'ungch'uan			
→ Tongchuan	102	35.01 N	109.01 E
Tungch'üan Tao I	100	25.58 N	119.58 E
Tungelsta	40	59.06 N	18.02 E
Tung Hai			
→ East China Sea			
⍑[2]	90	30.00 N	126.00 E
Tungho	100	22.58 N	121.18 E
T'unghsien			
→ Tongxian	105	39.55 N	116.39 E
T'unghua			
→ Tonghua	98	41.41 N	125.55 E
Tunghwa			
→ Tonghua	98	41.41 N	125.55 E
Tungir ≃	88	55.24 N	120.32 E
Tungirskij chrebet ⩕	88	54.40 N	119.40 E
Tungkal ≃	112	0.49 S	103.29 E
Tungkang	100	22.28 N	120.26 E
Tungkillo	168b	34.49 S	139.04 E
Tungku	112	5.01 N	118.53 E
Tungla	236	13.18 N	84.26 W
T'ungliao			
→ Tongliao	89	43.39 N	122.14 E
Tung Lung Island I	271d	22.15 N	114.17 E
Tung O	271d	22.12 N	114.08 E
Tungokočen	88	53.33 N	115.36 E
Tungsha Tao (Pratas			
Island) I	90	20.42 N	116.43 E
Tungshih	100	24.15 N	120.49 E
Tungsten	180	61.57 N	128.16 W
Tungsunga, Jabal ∧	140	11.29 N	23.21 E
Tungting Tao I	100	24.10 N	118.14 E
Tungurahua □[4]	246	1.15 S	78.35 W
Tungurahua ∧[1]	246	1.27 S	78.26 W
Tungyin Tao I	100	26.22 N	120.30 E
Tuni	122	17.21 N	82.33 E
Tunia ≃	246	1.13 N	72.44 W
Tunica	194	34.41 N	90.22 W
Tunis	148	36.48 N	10.11 E
Tunis □[8]	148	36.50 N	10.15 E
Tūnis			
→ Tunisia □[1]	148	34.00 N	9.00 E
Tunis, Golfe de ⊂	36	37.00 N	10.30 E
Tunis et Banlieue □[8]	36	36.48 N	10.10 E
Tunisia (Tunisie) □[1],			
Afr.	134	34.00 N	9.00 E
Tunisia (Tunisie) □[1],			
Afr.	148	34.00 N	9.00 E
Tunisie			
→ Tunisia □[1]	148	34.00 N	9.00 E
Tunis Sud □[8]	148	36.30 N	10.00 E
Tunitas Creek ≃	282	37.21 N	122.24 W
Tunja	246	5.31 N	73.22 W
Tunjang	114	6.16 N	100.21 E
Tunka	88	51.45 N	102.32 E
Tunkás	232	20.54 N	88.45 W
Tunkhannock	210	41.32 N	75.56 W
Tunkhannock Creek			
≃	210	41.32 N	75.57 W
Tunkhannock Creek,			
East Branch ≃	210	41.38 N	75.43 W
Tunliu	102	36.19 N	112.54 E
Tunnel	210	42.13 N	75.44 W
Tunnel Hill, Ga., U.S.	192	34.50 N	85.02 W
Tunnelhill, Pa., U.S.	214	40.29 N	78.33 W
Tunnelton, In., U.S.	218	38.46 N	86.21 W
Tunnelton, W.V., U.S.	188	39.23 N	79.44 W
Tunnsjøen ⊜	24	64.43 N	13.24 E
Tunø I	41	55.57 N	10.26 E
Tuntenhausen	64	47.56 N	12.01 E
Tuntum	250	5.14 S	44.39 W
Tuntutuliak	180	60.22 N	162.38 W
Tununak	180	60.35 N	165.16 W
Tunungayualok Island			
I	176	56.05 N	61.05 W
Tunuyán	252	33.34 S	69.01 W
Tunuyán ≃	252	34.03 S	66.45 W
Tunxi	100	29.44 N	118.18 E
Tuo ≃, Zhg.	100	33.16 N	117.45 E
Tuo ≃, Zhg.	102	28.57 N	105.27 E
Tuobalage	120	31.37 N	88.10 E
Tuobuja	74	62.00 N	122.02 E
Tuocheng	100	24.05 N	115.13 E
Tuoe Shan ∧	102	24.20 N	103.32 E
Tuoheji	100	33.26 N	117.26 E
Tuoj-Chaja	74	62.32 N	111.18 E
Tuoji Dao I	98	38.09 N	120.14 E
Tuokedingling	120	32.45 N	84.55 E
Tuokusidawan Ling ∧	120	37.14 N	85.47 E
Tuoli	105	39.46 N	116.01 E
Tuolumne	226	37.57 N	120.14 W
Tuolumne □[6]	226	37.59 N	120.23 W
Tuolumne ≃	226	37.36 N	121.10 W
Tuolumne, Lyell Fork			
≃	226	37.53 N	119.23 W
Tuolumne, North			
Fork ≃	226	37.54 N	120.15 W
Tuolumne, South			
Fork ≃	226	37.50 N	120.03 W
Tuolunduo	89	50.35 N	120.05 E
Tuong Duong	110	19.16 N	104.27 E
Tuotuo ≃	120	34.15 N	93.11 E
Tuowu	102	28.58 N	102.13 E
T'up	85	42.44 N	78.22 E
Tupã	255	21.56 S	50.30 W
Tupaciguara	255	18.35 S	48.42 W
Tupana ≃	246	4.25 S	60.05 W
Tupanciretã	252	29.05 S	53.51 W
Tuparro ≃	246	5.13 N	67.50 W
Tupelo, Ms., U.S.	194	34.15 N	88.42 W
Tupelo, Ok., U.S.	196	34.36 N	96.25 W
Tupelo National			
Battlefield ⊥	194	34.13 N	88.44 W
Tupi	116	6.19 N	124.57 E
Tupik	88	54.26 N	119.57 E
Tupilac	116	7.40 N	122.30 E
Tupinambarana, Ilha I	246	3.00 S	58.00 W
Tupi Paulista	255	21.24 S	51.34 W
Tupiraçaba	255	14.29 S	48.34 W
Tupiza	248	21.27 S	65.43 W
Tuplice	30	51.41 N	14.50 E
Tupman	226	35.17 N	119.21 W
Tupper	182	55.31 N	120.02 W
Tupper Lake	188	44.13 N	74.29 W
Tupperville	214	42.36 N	82.16 W
Tupungato	252	33.22 S	69.08 W
Tupungato, Cerro ∧	252	33.22 S	69.47 W
Tupychiv	78	51.46 N	31.26 E
Tuqiao, Zhg.	106	31.56 N	119.03 E
Tuqiao, Zhg.	106	31.39 N	120.24 E
Tuqiao, Zhg.	107	30.24 N	105.28 E
Tuqiaozhen	107	30.32 N	104.50 E
Tuquan	89	45.26 N	121.50 E
Túquerres	246	1.05 N	77.37 W
Tuquiaochang	107	29.47 N	106.01 E
Tura, India	124	25.31 N	90.13 E
Ṭurā, Miṣr	142	29.56 N	31.16 E
Tura, Ross.	74	64.17 N	100.15 E
Tura ≃, Ross.	86	57.12 N	66.56 E
Tura ≃, Ross.	88	51.36 N	114.09 E
Turabah	144	21.13 N	41.39 E
Turabah ⍑[4]	128	28.15 N	42.55 E
Turābah, 'Ayn at- ⍑[4]	132	31.36 N	35.25 E
Turāg ≃	126	23.45 N	90.21 E
Turaiyūr	122	11.10 N	78.37 E
Turakina	172	40.02 S	175.13 E
Turakina ≃	172	40.04 S	175.08 E
Turama ≃	164	6.50 S	143.05 E
Turambhe	272c	19.04 N	73.01 E
Turan, Ross.	88	51.38 N	101.40 E
Turan, Ross.	88	52.08 N	93.55 E
Turangi	172	39.00 S	175.49 E
Turano ≃	66	42.26 N	12.47 E
Turanskaja			
nizmennost' ≚	86	44.30 N	63.00 E
Ṭurāq al-'Ilab ⩕[2]	130	33.55 N	38.18 E
Turate	266b	45.39 N	9.00 E
Tur'at Ghunaym	142	31.16 N	31.29 E
Ṭurayf	128	31.44 N	38.33 E
Turbaco	246	10.20 N	75.25 W
Turbacz ∧	30	49.33 N	20.08 E
Turbat	128	25.59 N	63.04 E
Turbenthal	58	47.27 N	8.51 E
Turbigo	62	45.32 N	8.44 E
Turbio ≃	234	20.19 N	101.37 W
Turbiv	78	49.21 N	28.44 E
Turbo	246	8.06 N	76.43 W
Turbotville	210	41.06 N	76.46 W

	English	Deutsch	Español	Français	Português
≃	River	Fluß	Río	Rivière	Rio
≊	Canal	Kanal	Canal	Canal	Canal
∟	Waterfall, Rapids	Wasserfall, Stromschnellen	Cascada, Rápidos	Chute d'eau, Rapides	Cascata, Rápidos
ɰ	Strait	Meeresstraße	Estrecho	Détroit	Estreito
⊂	Bay, Gulf	Bucht, Golf	Bahía, Golfo	Baie, Golfe	Baía, Golfo
⊜	Lake, Lakes	See, Seen	Lago, Lagos	Lac, Lacs	Lago, Lagos
⩩	Swamp	Sumpf	Pantano	Marais	Pântano
⍓	Ice Features, Glacier	Eis- und Gletscherformen	Accidentes Glaciales	Formes glaciaires	Acidentes glaciares
⍑	Other Hydrographic Features	Andere Hydrographische Objekte	Otros Elementos Hidrográficos	Autres données hydrographiques	Outros acidentes hidrográficos
✣	Submarine Features	Untermeerische Objekte	Accidentes Submarinos	Formes de relief sous-marin	Acidentes submarinos
□	Political Unit	Politische Einheit	Unidad Politica	Entité politique	Unidade política
Ʊ	Cultural Institution	Kulturelle Institution	Institución Cultural	Institution culturelle	Institução cultural
⊥	Historical Site	Historische Stätte	Sitio Histórico	Site historique	Sitio histórico
♠	Recreational Site	Erholungs- und Ferienort	Sitio de Recreo	Centre de loisirs	Area de Lazer
⊠	Airport	Flughafen	Aeropuerto	Aéroport	Aeroporto
■	Military Installation	Militäranlage	Instalación Militar	Installation militaire	Instalação militar
◆	Miscellaneous	Verschiedenes	Misceláneo	Divers	Diversos

ENGLISH / DEUTSCH

Name	Page	Lat.°′	Long.°′
Turčasovo	24	63.06 N	39.12 E
Turchi, Balata dei >	70	36.43 N	12.02 E
Turčiansky Svätý Martin → Martin	30	49.05 N	18.55 E
Turckheim	58	48.05 N	7.17 E
Turda	38	46.34 N	23.47 E
Turdej	76	53.22 N	38.01 E
Turee Creek	162	23.37 S	118.39 E
Turee Creek ≃	162	23.35 S	117.25 E
Turek	30	52.02 N	18.30 E
Turen	115a	8.10 S	112.41 E
Turenki	26	60.55 N	24.38 E
Turfan → Turpan	86	42.56 N	89.10 E
Turfan Depression → Turpan Pendi ⊥[7]	86	42.40 N	89.10 E
Turffontein ◆[8]	273d	26.15 S	28.02 E
Turffontein Race Course ♦	273d	26.14 S	28.03 E
Turgaj, Kaz.	86	49.38 N	63.28 E
Turgaj, Kaz.	86	51.46 N	72.44 E
Turgaj □[8]	86	50.00 N	65.20 E
Turgaj ≃	86	48.01 N	62.45 E
Turgajskaja ložbina V	86	51.00 N	64.30 E
Turgajskoje plato ⋏[1]	86	51.00 N	64.00 E
Turgen', Kaz.	85	43.24 N	77.36 E
Türgen, Mong.	86	50.04 N	91.36 E
Turgen' ≃	85	43.50 N	77.38 E
Turgenevka	88	53.02 N	105.41 E
Turgenevo	80	54.50 N	46.19 E
Turginovo	82	56.30 N	36.00 E
Turgojak	86	55.10 N	60.07 E
Turgoš	76	59.18 N	35.10 E
Tŭrgovishte → Târgovište	38	43.15 N	26.34 E
Turgut, Tür.	130	38.37 N	31.49 E
Turgut, Tür.	130	37.22 N	28.02 E
Turgutlu	130	38.30 N	27.43 E
Turgwi ≃	154	20.28 S	32.18 E
Turhal	130	40.24 N	36.06 E
Türi, Eesti	76	58.48 N	25.26 E
Turi, It.	68	40.55 N	17.01 E
Turia ≃	34	39.27 N	0.19 W
Turiaçu	250	1.41 S	45.21 W
Turiaçu ≃	250	1.36 S	45.19 W
Turij Rog	89	45.14 N	131.58 E
Turilovka	83	49.06 N	40.13 E
Turimetta Head >	274a	33.42 S	151.19 E
Turimiquire, Cerro ∧	246	10.07 N	63.53 W
Turin, Ab., Can.	182	49.58 N	112.31 W
Turin → Torino, It.	62	45.03 N	7.40 E
Turin, N.Y., U.S.	212	43.38 N	75.25 W
Turinge	40	59.12 N	17.27 E
Turinsk	86	58.03 N	63.42 E
Turinskaja Sloboda	86	57.37 N	64.25 E
Turiya ≃	78	51.48 N	24.52 E
Turiys'k	78	51.07 N	24.31 E
Turka, Ross.	88	52.57 N	108.13 E
Turka, Ukr.	78	49.10 N	23.02 E
Turka ≃	88	52.56 N	108.13 E
Turkana, Lake → Rudolf, Lake ⊜	144	3.30 N	36.05 E
Türkei → Turkey □[1]	22	39.00 N	35.00 E
Türkeli Adası I	130	40.30 N	27.30 E
Turkestan	85	43.18 N	68.15 E
Turkestanskij chrebet ⋏	85	39.35 N	69.15 E
Turkestanskij kanal ≊	85	42.44 N	69.00 E
Túrkeve	30	47.06 N	20.45 E
Turkey	196	34.23 N	100.53 W
Turkey (Türkiye) □[1], Asia	22	39.00 N	35.00 E
Turkey (Türkiye) □[1], Asia	130	39.00 N	35.00 E
Turkey ≃	190	42.43 N	91.01 W
Turkey Branch ≃	284c	38.52 N	76.48 W
Turkey City	214	41.11 N	79.37 W
Turkey Creek	164	17.02 S	128.12 E
Turkey Creek ≃, On., Can.	281	42.14 N	83.06 W
Turkey Creek ≃, U.S.	198	39.58 N	96.02 W
Turkey Creek ≃, In., U.S.	278	41.31 N	87.18 W
Turkey Creek ≃, Ia., U.S.	198	41.20 N	95.05 W
Turkey Creek ≃, Ks., U.S.	198	38.53 N	97.11 W
Turkey Creek ≃, Ne., U.S.	198	40.23 N	96.53 W
Turkey Creek ≃, Ok., U.S.	196	35.58 N	97.56 W
Turkey Creek ≃, Tx., U.S.	222	30.39 N	97.05 W
Turkey Island I	284c	38.58 N	77.12 W
Turkey Point >, On., Can.	212	42.40 N	80.21 W
Turkey Point >, Fl., U.S.	220	25.26 N	80.19 W
Turkey Point Provincial Park ♦	212	42.40 N	80.22 W
Turkey Run State Park ♦	194	39.54 N	87.13 W
Turkeytown	279b	40.12 N	79.44 W
Türkheim	58	48.03 N	10.38 E
Turki	80	51.59 N	43.16 E
Turkish Republic of Northern Cyprus → Cyprus, North □[1]	130	35.15 N	33.40 E
Türkiye → Turkey □[1]	22	39.00 N	35.00 E
Turkmān Deh	267d	35.40 N	51.36 E
Turkmenia → Turkmenistan □[1]	72	40.00 N	60.00 E
Turkmenija → Turkmenistan □[1]	72	40.00 N	60.00 E
Turkmenistan □[1], Asia	72	40.00 N	60.00 E
Turkmenistan □[1], Asia	128	39.00 N	60.00 E
Turkmeniya → Turkmenistan □[1]	72	40.00 N	60.00 E
Turkmen-Kala	128	37.26 N	62.20 E
Turkmenskij zaliv c	128	38.54 N	53.48 E
Turk Mine	154	19.45 S	28.50 E
Türkoğlu	130	37.31 N	36.49 E
Turks and Caicos Islands □[2], N.A.	230	21.45 N	71.35 W
Turks and Caicos Islands □[2], N.A.	238	21.45 N	71.35 W
Turks Island Passage ʊ	238	21.25 N	71.19 W
Turks Islands II	238	21.24 N	71.07 W
Turks-und Caicos-Inseln → Turks and Caicos Islands □[2]	238	21.45 N	71.35 W
Turku (Åbo)	26	60.27 N	22.17 E
Turkwel ≃	154	3.06 N	36.06 E
Turlan	85	43.36 N	69.03 E
Turley	196	36.14 N	95.58 W
Turlock	226	37.29 N	120.50 W
Turlock Lake ⊜[1]	226	42.17 N	73.21 W
Turmalina	255	17.17 S	42.45 W
Turmantas	76	55.42 N	26.27 E
Turmerito, Quebrada ≃	286c	10.26 N	66.55 W
Turnagain ≃	180	59.06 N	127.35 W
Turnagain, Cape >	172	40.29 S	176.37 E
Turnagain Arm c	180	61.00 N	150.00 W
Turnagain Island I	164	9.34 S	142.18 E
Turnau	61	47.33 N	15.20 E
Turnbull, Mount ∧	200	33.04 N	110.16 W
Turnbull, Mount ∧[2]	162	21.03 S	131.57 E
Turneffe Islands II	232	17.22 N	87.51 W
Turner, Austl.	162	17.50 S	128.17 E
Turner, Mt., U.S.	202	48.50 N	108.24 W
Turner, Or., U.S.	202	44.50 N	122.57 W
Turner ≃	162	20.21 S	118.25 E
Turner Field ⊠	285	40.13 N	75.13 W
Turners Falls	207	42.36 N	72.33 W
Turners Peninsula >[1]	150	7.22 N	12.22 W
Turnersville, N.J., U.S.	285	39.46 N	75.03 W
Turnersville, Tx., U.S.	222	31.37 N	97.44 W
Turner Valley	182	50.40 N	114.17 W
Turnhout	56	51.19 N	4.57 E
Türnitz	61	47.57 N	15.30 E
Turnor Lake ⊜	184	56.32 N	108.38 W
Turnov	30	50.35 N	15.10 E
Tŭrnovo → Veliko Târnovo	38	43.04 N	25.39 E
Turnpike Lake ⊜	283	42.01 N	71.19 W
Turnu Măgurele	38	43.45 N	24.53 E
Turnu Roşu, Pasul)(	38	45.33 N	24.16 E
Turnu-Severin → Drobeta-Turnu Severin	38	44.38 N	22.39 E
Turobin	30	50.50 N	22.45 E
Turočak	86	52.16 N	87.08 E
Turon	198	37.48 N	98.25 W
Turon ≃	170	33.03 S	149.43 E
Turopolje ≚	36	45.40 N	16.05 E
Turopyn	78	51.00 N	24.27 E
Tuross ≃	171b	36.09 S	149.39 E
Turov	76	52.04 N	27.44 E
Turovo	82	54.52 N	37.49 E
Turpan	86	42.56 N	89.10 E
Turpan Pendi (Turfan Depression) ⊥[7]	86	42.40 N	89.10 E
Turques et Caicos, Îles → Turks and Caicos Islands □[2]	238	21.45 N	71.35 W
Turquía → Turkey □[1]	22	39.00 N	35.00 E
Turquie → Turkey □[1]	22	39.00 N	35.00 E
Turquino, Pico ∧	240p	19.59 N	76.50 W
Turrach	64	46.57 N	13.52 E
Turramurra	274a	33.44 S	151.08 E
Turrell	194	35.22 N	90.15 W
Turret Peak ∧	200	34.15 N	111.53 W
Turriaco	64	45.49 N	13.26 E
Turrialba	236	9.54 N	83.41 W
Turrialba, Volcán ∧[1]	236	10.02 N	83.46 W
Turriers	62	44.24 N	6.10 E
Turriff	46	57.32 N	2.28 W
Turritano ◆[1]	71	40.45 N	8.35 E
Turrubares, Cerro ∧	236	9.47 N	84.28 W
Tursi	68	40.15 N	16.28 E
Tursunzade	85	38.32 N	68.13 E
Turtas ≃	86	59.06 N	68.52 E
Turtipār	124	26.10 N	83.54 E
Turtle ≃, Mb., Can.	184	51.07 N	99.39 W
Turtle ≃, On., Can.	184	48.51 N	92.45 W
Turtle, North Branch ≃	198	47.57 N	97.35 W
Turtle Creek, N.B., Can.	186	45.58 N	64.53 W
Turtle Creek, Pa., U.S.	214	40.24 N	79.49 W
Turtle Creek ≃, Pa., U.S.	279b	40.23 N	79.51 W
Turtle Creek ≃, S.D., U.S.	198	44.55 N	98.29 W
Turtle Creek ≃, Wi., U.S.	216	42.29 N	89.03 W
Turtle-Flambeau Flowage ⊜[1]	190	46.05 N	90.11 W
Turtleford	184	53.23 N	108.56 W
Turtle Harbor Channel ʊ	220	25.15 N	80.18 W
Turtle Islands II	150	7.37 N	13.02 W
Turtle Lake, N.D., U.S.	198	47.31 N	100.53 W
Turtle Lake, Wi., U.S.	190	45.23 N	92.08 W
Turtle Lake ⊜	184	53.35 N	108.40 W
Turtle Mountain ∧[2]	184	49.00 N	100.15 W
Turtle Mountain Indian Reservation ◆[4]	198	48.51 N	99.45 W
Turtle Mountain Provincial Park ♦	184	49.03 N	100.15 W
Turtmann	58	46.18 N	7.41 E
Turton and Entwistle Reservoir ⊜[1]	262	53.39 N	2.25 W
Turton Bottoms	262	53.38 N	2.24 W
Turton Moor ◆[3]	262	53.40 N	2.29 W
Turton Tower ʋ	262	53.38 N	2.25 W
Turu ≃	74	64.38 N	100.00 E
Turua	172	37.14 S	175.34 E
Turuchan ≃	74	65.56 N	87.42 E
Turuchansk	74	65.49 N	87.59 E
Turun-Porin lääni □[4]	26	61.20 N	22.30 E
Turuntajevo, Ross.	86	56.38 N	85.59 E
Turuntajevo, Ross.	88	52.12 N	107.37 E
Turusele ∧	71	40.09 N	9.34 E
Turvo	252	28.56 S	49.41 W
Turvo ≃, Bra.	255	17.46 S	50.12 W
Turvo ≃, Bra.	255	19.56 S	49.55 W
Turvo ≃, Bra.	256	22.04 S	45.42 W
Turvo ≃, Bra.	256	22.29 S	44.15 W
Turvo Grande ≃	256	21.42 S	44.22 W
Turvolândia	256	21.47 S	45.47 W
Turvo Pequeno ≃	256	21.42 S	44.22 W
Turyu-san ∧	98	41.10 N	128.47 E
Turzovka	30	49.25 N	18.39 E
Tusa	70	37.59 N	14.14 E
Tusa ≃	70	38.01 N	14.16 E
Tusas, Rio ≃	200	36.23 N	106.03 W
Tuscaloosa	194	33.12 N	87.34 W
Tuscaloosa, Lake ⊜[1]	194	33.20 N	87.35 W
Tuscania	66	42.25 N	11.52 E
Tuscany → Toscana □[4]	36	43.25 N	11.00 E
Tuscarawas	214	40.24 N	81.25 W
Tuscarawas □[6]	214	40.30 N	81.27 W
Tuscarawas ≃	214	40.17 N	81.52 W
Tuscarora, N.Y., U.S.	210	42.38 N	77.52 W
Tuscarora, Pa., U.S.	208	40.46 N	76.02 W
Tuscarora Creek ≃, N.Y., U.S.	210	42.07 N	77.14 W
Tuscarora Creek ≃, Pa., U.S.	208	40.32 N	77.23 W
Tuscarora Creek, North Branch ≃	210	42.05 N	77.18 W
Tuscarora Indian Reservation ◆[4]	210	43.09 N	78.57 W
Tuscarora Mountain ∧	188	40.10 N	77.45 W
Tuscarora Mountains ⋏	204	41.00 N	116.20 W
Tuscarora State Park ♦	208	40.48 N	76.01 W
Tuscarora Tunnel ◆[5]	214	40.05 N	77.50 W
Tuscola, Il., U.S.	194	39.47 N	88.16 W
Tuscola, Tx., U.S.	196	32.12 N	99.48 W
Tuscolo ⊥	267a	41.48 N	12.42 E
Tuscumbia, Al., U.S.	194	34.43 N	87.42 W
Tuscumbia, Mo., U.S.	194	38.13 N	92.27 W
Tuse	41	55.43 N	11.37 E
Tushan	98	34.14 N	117.51 E
Tušino ◆[8]	265b	55.50 N	37.26 E
Tuskegee	194	32.25 N	85.41 W
Tusker Rock II[1]	42	51.27 N	3.40 W
Tussey Mountain ∧	214	40.25 N	78.07 W
Tüssling	60	48.13 N	12.36 E
Tustin	228	33.44 N	117.49 W
Tustin Marine Corps Air Station (Helicopter) ■	280	33.43 N	117.50 W
Tustumena Lake ⊜	180	60.12 N	150.50 W
Tuszyn	30	51.37 N	19.34 E
Tut	130	37.48 N	37.55 E
Tuta	152	14.37 S	20.45 E
Tutaekuri ≃	172	39.30 S	176.54 E
Tutaizi	104	41.01 N	122.38 E
Tutajev	80	57.53 N	39.32 E
Tutak	84	39.32 N	42.46 E
Tutang	100	29.21 N	116.24 E
Tutbury	42	52.51 N	1.41 W
Tuthills Creek ≃	276	40.45 N	73.02 W
Tuticorin	122	8.47 N	78.08 E
Tutin	38	42.59 N	20.20 E
T'ut'kovo	82	54.37 N	38.32 E
Tutóia	250	2.45 S	42.16 W
Tutoko, Mount ∧	172	44.36 S	168.00 E
Tutong	112	4.50 N	114.40 E
Tutova ≃	38	46.06 N	27.32 E
Tutrakan	38	44.03 N	26.37 E
Tuttle, N.D., U.S.	198	47.08 N	99.59 W
Tuttle, Ok., U.S.	196	35.17 N	97.48 W
Tuttle Creek Lake ⊜[1]	198	39.22 N	96.40 W
Tuttlingen	58	47.59 N	8.49 E
Tutuala	112	8.24 S	127.15 E
Tutuban Station ◆[5]	269f	14.37 N	120.58 E
Tutu Bay c	116	5.55 N	121.12 E
Tutubu	154	5.30 S	32.41 E
Tutuí ≃	250	2.39 S	54.10 W
Tutuila I	174u	14.18 S	170.42 W
Tuṭūn	142	29.09 N	30.46 E
Tütüncü	130	40.04 N	27.43 E
Tutupaca, Volcán ∧[1]	248	17.01 S	70.22 W
Tutura	88	54.46 N	105.15 E
Tututalak Mountain ∧	180	67.46 N	161.10 W
Tutwiler	194	34.00 N	90.25 W
Tutzing	64	47.54 N	11.17 E
Tuul ≃	90	48.57 N	104.48 E
Tuupovaara	26	62.29 N	30.36 E
Tuusniemi	26	62.49 N	28.30 E
Tuutapu, Cerro ∧	174z	27.08 S	109.24 W
Tuva □[3]	72	52.00 N	95.00 E
T'uva-Guba	24	69.08 N	33.32 E
Tuvalu □[1]	14	8.00 S	178.00 E
Tuvutha Island I	175g	17.40 S	178.48 W
Tuwang	107	29.06 N	105.48 E
Ṭuwayq, Jabal ⋏	118	23.00 N	46.00 E
Ṭuwayyil ash-Shihāq ∧[2]	132	30.36 N	36.08 E
Tuxedo Park, De., U.S.	285	39.43 N	75.37 W
Tuxedo Park, N.Y., U.S.	210	41.11 N	74.11 W
Tuxer Alpen ⋏	64	47.10 N	11.45 E
Tuxford, Sk., Can.	184	50.35 N	105.35 W
Tuxford, Eng., U.K.	44	53.13 N	0.53 W
Tuxiaqiao	100	28.47 N	121.29 E
Tuxpan, Méx.	234	19.33 N	103.24 W
Tuxpan, Méx.	234	19.34 N	100.28 W
Tuxpan, Méx.	234	21.57 N	105.18 W
Tuxpan, Méx.	234	20.57 N	97.24 W
Tuxpan ≃	234	20.59 N	97.18 W
Tuxsun	86	42.47 N	88.38 E
Tuxtepec	234	18.06 N	96.07 W
Tuxtla Gutiérrez	234	16.45 N	93.07 W
Tuy	34	42.03 N	8.38 W
Tuy ≃	246	10.24 N	65.59 W
Tuy An	110	13.17 N	109.16 E
Tuyen Hoa	110	17.50 N	106.10 E
Tuyen Quang	110	21.49 N	105.13 E
Tuy Hoa	110	13.05 N	109.18 E
Tūysarkān	128	34.33 N	48.27 E
Tuyün → Duyun	102	26.12 N	107.31 E
Ṭuyūr, Burj aṭ- ∧[2]	140	20.55 N	27.55 E
Tuža	80	57.37 N	47.57 E
T'uzašu, pereval)(	85	42.21 N	73.48 E
T'uzbel'	85	40.34 N	73.21 E
Tuzdykol', ozero ⊜	80	49.36 N	52.20 E
Tuz Gölü ⊜	130	38.45 N	33.25 E
Tuzigoot National Monument ♦	200	34.49 N	112.01 W
Ṭūz Khurmātū	128	34.53 N	44.38 E
Tuzla, Bos.	38	44.32 N	18.41 E
Tuzla, Tür.	130	36.42 N	35.05 E
Tuzla ≃	130	39.43 N	40.16 E
Tuzla Gölü ⊜	130	39.02 N	35.50 E
Tuzlagözü	130	38.11 N	41.34 E
Tuzlov ≃	83	47.23 N	40.08 E
Tuzluca	84	40.03 N	43.40 E
Tuzlukçu	130	38.28 N	31.38 E
Tuzly	78	45.52 N	30.05 E
Tuzuntla ≃	234	18.51 N	100.44 W
Tvărdica	38	42.42 N	25.52 E
Tvardiţa	38	46.09 N	28.58 E
Tvedestrand	26	58.37 N	8.55 E
Tveitsund	26	59.01 N	8.32 E
Tver' (Kalinin)	82	56.52 N	35.55 E
Tverca ≃	76	56.52 N	35.55 E
Tver' Oblast' □[4]	76	57.00 N	34.00 E
Twain Harte	226	38.02 N	120.14 W
Twann	58	47.06 N	7.10 E
Twardogóra	30	51.22 N	17.28 E
Tweed	212	44.29 N	77.19 W
Tweed ≃	44	55.46 N	2.00 W
Tweeddale V	46	55.40 N	3.10 W
Tweede Exloërmond	52	52.55 N	6.58 E
Tweed Heads	171a	28.10 S	153.31 E
Tweedmouth	44	55.45 N	2.01 W
Tweedsmuir Provincial Park ♦	182	52.55 N	126.05 W
Tweedy Mountain ∧	202	45.29 N	112.58 W
Tweeling	158	27.38 S	28.31 E
Twee Rivieren	158	26.27 S	20.37 E
Tweespruit	158	29.11 S	27.01 E
Twello	52	52.14 N	6.06 E
Twelve Mile	216	40.52 N	86.13 W
Twelve Mile Creek ≃, On., Can.	212	43.11 N	79.16 W
Twelvemile Creek ≃, N.Y., U.S.	210	43.18 N	78.51 W
Twelvemile Island I	279b	40.32 N	79.51 W
Twelve Mile Lake ⊜, On., Can.	212	45.02 N	78.43 W
Twelve Mile Lake ⊜, Sk., Can.	184	49.29 N	106.14 W
Tweng	64	47.11 N	13.36 E
Twente ◆[1]	52	52.17 N	6.40 E
Twentekanaal ≊	52	52.15 N	6.40 E
Twentieth Century Fox Studios ʋ[3]	280	34.03 N	118.25 W
Twentyfive Mile Wash V	200	37.33 N	111.07 W
Twenty Mile Creek ≃	212	43.10 N	79.22 W
Twentynine Palms	204	34.08 N	116.03 W
Twentynine Palms Marine Corps Center ■	204	34.25 N	116.10 W
Tweya	152	0.54 S	19.05 E
Twickenham ◆[8]	260	51.27 N	0.20 W
Twilight Cove c	162	32.16 S	126.03 E
Twilight Park	210	42.11 N	74.05 W
Twillingate	186	49.39 N	54.46 W
Twimberg	61	46.55 N	14.50 E
Twin Beach	216	42.34 N	83.24 W
Twin Bridge Farm	285	39.57 N	75.33 W
Twin Bridges	202	45.32 N	112.19 W
Twin Butte Creek ≃	198	38.46 N	100.56 W
Twin Buttes ∧	202	44.20 N	122.15 W
Twin Buttes Reservoir ⊜[1]	196	31.20 N	100.35 W
Twin City	192	32.34 N	82.09 W
Twin Creek ≃	218	39.33 N	84.21 W
Twin Falls	202	42.33 N	114.27 W
Twin Heads ⋏	162	20.13 S	126.30 E
Twin Hills	180	59.23 N	159.58 W
Twin Lakes, Ca., U.S.	226	36.58 N	122.00 W
Twin Lakes, Ga., U.S.	192	30.42 N	83.12 W
Twin Lakes, In., U.S.	216	41.19 N	86.23 W
Twin Lakes, Mi., U.S.	216	42.02 N	86.04 W
Twin Lakes, Oh., U.S.	214	41.11 N	81.21 W
Twin Lakes, Pa., U.S.	210	41.24 N	74.54 W
Twin Lakes, Wi., U.S.	216	42.31 N	88.14 W
Twin Lakes ⊜, Ca., U.S.	226	38.09 N	119.21 W
Twin Lakes ⊜, Ct., U.S.	207	42.02 N	73.26 W
Twin Lakes ⊜, Wa., U.S.	224	47.55 N	120.51 W
Twin Oaks	208	39.51 N	75.26 W
Twin Peak Islands II	162	34.00 S	122.50 E
Twin Peaks	228	34.12 N	117.12 W
Twin Peaks ⋏, Ca., U.S.	282	37.45 N	122.27 W
Twin Peaks ⋏, Id., U.S.	202	44.35 N	114.29 W
Twin Rocks, Or., U.S.	224	45.36 N	123.57 W
Twin Rocks, Pa., U.S.	214	40.29 N	78.51 W
Twinsburg	214	41.18 N	81.26 W
Twin Valley	198	47.15 N	96.15 W
Twisp	202	48.21 N	120.07 W
Twiss Green	262	53.27 N	2.32 W
Twist	52	52.38 N	7.03 E
Twiste ≃	52	51.29 N	9.09 E
Twistringen	52	52.48 N	8.38 E
Twitchell Reservoir ⊜[1]	204	35.00 N	120.19 W
Twitya ≃	180	64.10 N	128.12 W
Two, Channel ʊ	220	24.50 N	80.45 W
Two Butte Creek ≃	198	38.02 N	102.08 W
Twofold Bay c	166	37.06 S	149.55 E
Two Harbors	190	47.01 N	91.40 W
Two Hills	182	53.43 N	111.45 W
Two Lakes ⊜	224	46.22 N	121.27 W
Two Medicine ≃	202	48.29 N	112.14 W
Two Mile Creek ≃, On., Can.	284a	43.16 N	79.06 W
Twomile Creek ≃, N.Y., U.S.	284a	43.01 N	78.55 W
Twong	140	8.18 N	28.20 E
Two Penny Run ≃	285	39.41 N	75.26 W
Two River Lake ⊜	184	53.52 N	91.27 W
Two Rivers	190	44.09 N	87.34 W
Two Rivers Reservoir ⊜[1]	196	33.17 N	104.45 W
Two Thumb Range ⋏	172	43.45 S	170.43 E
Two Wells	168b	34.36 S	138.30 E
Twrch ≃, Wales, U.K.	42	52.42 N	3.29 W
Twrch ≃, Wales, U.K.	42	51.46 N	3.46 W
Twyford, Eng., U.K.	42	51.29 N	0.53 W
Twyford, Eng., U.K.	42	51.01 N	1.19 W
Twymyn ≃	42	52.38 N	3.44 W
Tyabb	169	38.16 S	145.11 E
Tyachiv	78	48.02 N	23.34 E
Tyahynka	78	46.47 N	33.04 E
Tyasmyn ≃	78	49.05 N	32.48 E
Tybee Island	192	32.01 N	80.51 W
Tybju	24	60.37 N	50.20 E
Tychy	30	50.09 N	18.59 E
Tyczyn	30	49.58 N	22.02 E
Tydal	26	63.04 N	11.34 E
Tye	196	32.27 N	99.52 W
Tyende Creek ≃	200	36.50 N	109.43 W
Tyendinaga Indian Reserve ◆[4]	212	44.11 N	77.07 W
Tyers ≃	169	38.10 S	146.26 E
Tyfors	40	60.09 N	14.12 E
Tygarts Creek ≃	218	38.43 N	82.57 W
Tygda	89	53.07 N	126.20 E
Tygda ≃	89	52.35 N	127.55 E
Tygelsjö	41	55.31 N	13.00 E
Tygh Valley	224	45.14 N	121.10 W
Tyin ⊜	26	61.17 N	8.13 E
Tyja ≃	88	55.36 N	109.20 E
Tykhonovychi	78	51.56 N	32.09 E
Tylden	158	32.07 S	27.05 E
Tyldesley	44	53.31 N	2.28 W
Tyler, Mn., U.S.	198	44.16 N	96.08 W
Tyler, Pa., U.S.	214	41.14 N	78.32 W
Tyler, Tx., U.S.	222	32.21 N	95.18 W
Tyler □[6]	222	30.47 N	94.32 W
Tyler, Lake ⊜[1]	222	32.13 N	95.10 W
Tyler East, Lake ⊜[1]	222	32.15 N	95.10 W
Tyler Park	284c	38.52 N	77.12 W
Tylersburg	214	41.23 N	79.19 W
Tyler State Park ♦, Pa., U.S.	208	40.14 N	74.59 W
Tyler State Park ♦, Tx., U.S.	222	32.29 N	95.14 W
Tylersville	210	41.00 N	77.25 W
Tylerton	208	37.58 N	76.01 W
Tylertown	194	31.06 N	90.08 W
Tylihul ≃	78	47.04 N	30.57 E
Tylihul's'kyy lyman ⊜	78	46.48 N	31.08 E
Tylla	40	60.28 N	15.33 E
Tylösand	26	56.39 N	12.44 E
Tylöskog ⋏[2]	40	58.45 N	15.20 E
Tylovaj	80	57.30 N	53.47 E
Tylyhulo-Berezhanka	78	46.52 N	31.24 E
Tym ≃, Ross.	74	59.25 N	80.04 E
Tym' ≃, Ross.	89	51.51 N	143.10 E
Tymna, laguna c	180	64.00 N	178.30 E
Tymochtee Creek ≃	214	40.57 N	83.16 W
Tymovskoje	89	50.51 N	142.39 E
Tymsk	86	59.24 N	80.18 E
Tynagh	48	53.09 N	8.22 W
Tyndall	198	42.59 N	97.51 W
Tyndall Air Force Base ■	194	30.04 N	85.35 W
Tyndaris ⊥	70	38.09 N	15.03 E
Tyndinskij	74	55.10 N	124.43 E
Tyndrum	46	56.27 N	4.44 W
Tyne ≃, Eng., U.K.	44	55.01 N	1.26 W
Tyne ≃, Scot., U.K.	46	56.01 N	2.37 W
Tyne and Wear □[6]	44	54.55 N	1.35 W
Tynemouth	44	55.01 N	1.24 W
Tyner	216	41.24 N	86.24 W
Tyngsboro	283	42.40 N	71.25 W
Tyngsjö	40	60.18 N	13.53 E
Týn nad Vltavou	30	49.14 N	14.26 E
Tynnelsö	40	59.25 N	17.06 E
Tynset	26	62.17 N	10.47 E
Tynytsya	78	51.08 N	32.54 E
Tyonek	180	61.02 N	151.17 W
Typta	88	54.35 N	104.31 E
Tyr	89	52.57 N	139.48 E
Tyre → Şūr, Lubnān	132	33.16 N	35.11 E
Tyre, Pa., U.S.	214	40.26 N	80.16 W
Tyresö	40	59.14 N	18.18 E
Tyret'	88	53.41 N	102.19 E
Tyrgetuj	88	51.27 N	113.46 E
Tyrifjorden ⊜	26	60.02 N	10.08 E
Tyringe	41	56.10 N	13.35 E
Tyringham	207	42.14 N	73.12 W
Tyrka	88	54.30 N	107.09 E
Tyrma	89	50.03 N	132.12 E
Tyrma ≃	89	50.29 N	131.18 E
Tyrnyauz	84	43.23 N	42.56 E
Tyrone, Ky., U.S.	218	38.01 N	84.50 W
Tyrone, N.Y., U.S.	210	42.25 N	77.03 W
Tyrone, Ok., U.S.	196	36.57 N	101.03 W
Tyrone, Pa., U.S.	214	40.40 N	78.14 W
Tyrone Lake ⊜	281	42.42 N	83.43 W
Tyrrell, Lake ⊜	166	35.21 S	142.50 E
Tyrrellspass	48	53.23 N	7.22 W
Tyrrhenian Sea (Mare Tirreno) ⊤[2]	36	40.00 N	12.00 E
Tyrrhenisches Meer → Tyrrhenian Sea ⊤[2]	36	40.00 N	12.00 E
Tysa (Tisa) (Tisza) ≃	38	45.15 N	20.17 E
Tyshkivka	78	48.29 N	30.56 E
Tysmenytsya	78	48.54 N	24.49 E
Tysnesøy I	26	60.00 N	5.35 E
Tysons Corner	284c	38.55 N	77.14 W
Tysons Corner Center ◆[9]	284c	38.55 N	77.13 W
Tysons Green	284c	38.55 N	77.15 W
Tysse	26	60.22 N	5.45 E
Tyssedal	26	60.07 N	6.34 E
Tysslingen ⊜	40	59.19 N	15.02 E
Tystberga	40	58.52 N	17.15 E
Tystrup Sø ⊜	41	55.22 N	11.35 E
Tytherington	262	53.17 N	2.08 W
Tytuvėnai	76	55.36 N	23.12 E
Ty Ty	192	31.28 N	83.38 W
Tyumen' → T'umen'	86	57.09 N	65.32 E
Tyvriv	78	49.01 N	28.30 E
Tywa ≃	54	53.13 N	14.29 E
Tywardreath	42	50.22 N	4.41 W
Tywi ≃	42	51.46 N	4.22 W
Tywyn	42	52.35 N	4.05 W
Tzaneen	156	23.50 S	30.09 E
Tzekung → Zigong	107	29.24 N	104.47 E
Tzeliutsing → Zigong	107	29.24 N	104.47 E
Tzucacab	232	20.04 N	89.03 W
Tzukung → Zigong	107	29.24 N	104.47 E
Tzupo → Boshan, Zhg.	98	36.29 N	117.50 E
Tzupo → Zibo, Zhg.	98	36.47 N	118.01 E
U			
Uaboe	174b	0.31 S	166.55 E
Uac, Mount ∧	116	12.12 N	123.40 E
Uaçá ≃	250	4.13 N	51.32 W
Uagadugu → Ouagadougou	150	12.22 N	1.31 W
Uamba	152	7.12 S	16.25 E
Uamba (Wamba) ≃, Afr.	152	3.56 S	17.12 E
Uamba ≃, Ang.	152	7.58 S	17.09 E
Uampochane	158	26.23 S	32.41 E
Uaoa Bay c	229a	20.56 N	156.16 W
Uaran → Ouarâne ◆[1]	134	21.00 N	10.30 W
Uato-Lari	112	8.45 S	126.34 E
Uatumã ≃	246	2.26 S	57.37 W
Uauá	250	9.50 S	39.28 W
Uaupés (Vaupés) ≃	246	0.02 N	67.16 W
Uaxactún ⊥	232	17.24 N	89.39 W
Ubá	255	21.07 S	42.56 W
Uba ≃	86	50.15 N	81.41 E
Übach-Palenberg	56	50.55 N	6.07 E
Ubagan ≃	86	54.24 N	64.45 E
Ubai	164	5.40 S	150.40 E
Ubaidullaganj	124	22.59 N	77.36 E
Ubaitaba	255	14.18 S	39.20 W
Ubajara	250	3.51 S	40.56 W
Ubajara, Parque Nacional de ♦	250	3.47 S	40.56 W
Ubangi (Oubangui) ≃	152	0.30 S	17.42 E
Ubatã	255	14.12 S	39.31 W
Ubaté	246	5.19 N	73.49 W
Ubatuba	256	23.26 S	45.04 W
Ubatuba, Baía de c	256	23.27 S	45.02 W
Ubauro	120	28.10 N	69.44 E
Ubay	116	10.03 N	124.28 E
Ubaye	62	44.28 N	6.22 E
Ubaye ≃	62	44.28 N	6.18 E
Ubayyiḍ, Wādī al- V	128	32.34 N	43.48 E
Ubby	41	55.37 N	11.13 E
Ube	96	33.56 N	131.15 E
Úbeda	34	38.01 N	3.22 W
Uberaba	255	19.45 S	47.55 W
Uberaba ≃	255	20.07 S	48.31 W
Uberaba, Lagoa ⊜	248	17.30 S	57.45 W
Überackern	60	48.11 N	12.52 E
Über dem Wind, Inseln → Leeward Islands II	238	17.00 N	63.00 W
Uberlândia	255	18.56 S	48.18 W
Überlingen	58	47.46 N	9.10 E
Überlinger See c	58	47.45 N	9.09 E
Übersee	64	47.49 N	12.28 E
Ubiaja	150	6.38 N	6.21 E
Ubid' ≃	78	51.27 N	32.29 E
Ubili	154	1.07 S	26.55 E
Ubin, Pulau I	271c	1.24 N	103.58 E
Ubinskoje	86	55.19 N	79.41 E
Ubinskoje, ozero ⊜	86	55.30 N	80.05 E
Ubl'a	30	48.55 N	22.23 E
Ubly	190	43.42 N	82.55 W
Uboldo	266b	45.37 N	9.00 E
Ubombo	158	27.33 S	32.00 E
Ubondo	154	0.52 S	25.37 E
Ubon Ratchathani	110	15.14 N	104.54 E
Úborsko	60	49.20 N	13.09 E
Ubort' ≃	78	52.06 N	28.28 E
Ubrique	34	36.41 N	5.27 W
Ubudiah, Masjid ʋ[1]	114	4.46 N	100.56 E
Ubundu (Ponthierville)	154	0.21 S	25.29 E
Ubur-Tochtor	88	50.06 N	113.37 E
Uča ≃, Ross.	82	56.02 N	37.37 E
Uča ≃, Ross.	265b	55.56 N	37.57 E
Ucacha	252	33.02 S	63.31 W
Uč-Adži	128	38.05 N	62.48 E
Učaly	86	54.19 N	59.27 E
Učami	74	63.50 N	96.29 E
Ucar	84	40.31 N	47.39 E
Učaral	86	46.10 N	80.56 E
Ucayali □[5]	248	9.00 S	74.00 W
Ucayali ≃	242	4.30 S	73.27 W
Uccellina, Monti dell' ⋏	66	42.38 N	11.05 E
Uccle	50	50.48 N	4.19 E
Uch	123	29.14 N	71.03 E
Uchab	156	19.47 S	17.42 E
Uchāna	124	29.28 N	76.10 E
Uchaud	62	43.45 N	4.16 E
Uchee Creek ≃	192	32.18 N	84.57 W
Uchihara	94	36.22 N	140.21 E
Uchihata	270	34.25 N	135.27 E
Uchiko	96	33.33 N	132.39 E
Uchi Lake	184	51.05 N	92.35 W
Uchinada	94	36.39 N	136.39 E
Uchinomi	96	34.30 N	134.20 E
Uchinoura	92	31.16 N	131.05 E
Uchiumi	96	33.01 N	132.30 E
Uchiura-wan c	92a	42.20 N	140.40 E
Uchiza	248	8.29 S	76.23 W
Uchoa	255	20.56 S	49.13 W
Ucholovo	80	53.47 N	40.29 E
Uchra ≃	80	58.20 N	39.00 E
Uchta, Ross.	24	61.12 N	38.32 E
Uchta, Ross.	24	63.33 N	53.38 E
Uchte	52	52.30 N	8.54 E
Uchte ≃	54	52.46 N	11.45 E
Uchtoma	76	60.10 N	38.02 E
Uchtspringe	54	52.32 N	11.36 E
Učinskij Ryboučastok	86	60.02 N	65.10 E
Učinskoje vodochranilišče ⊜[1]	82	56.02 N	37.45 E
Uckange	56	49.18 N	6.09 E
Ückendorf ◆[8]	263	51.30 N	7.07 E
Uckermark ◆[1]	54	53.10 N	13.35 E
Uckfield	42	50.58 N	0.06 E
Üçköşe	130	40.13 N	41.00 E
Uckro	54	51.51 N	13.37 E
Učkupr'uk	85	40.33 N	71.04 E
Učkurgan	85	41.07 N	72.05 E
Ucluelet	182	48.57 N	125.33 W
Ucon	202	43.35 N	111.57 W
Üçpınar	130	37.08 N	32.16 E
Ucria	70	38.03 N	14.53 E
Üçtepeler ∧	130	39.39 N	42.41 E
Učterek	85	41.45 N	73.12 E
Úcua ≃	152	8.35 S	13.40 E
Učujevskij Majdan	80	54.33 N	44.30 E
Učur ≃	74	58.48 N	130.35 E
Uda ≃, Ross.	88	56.05 N	99.34 E
Uda ≃, Ross.	88	51.47 N	107.33 E
Uda ≃, Ross.	89	54.42 N	135.14 E
Udagamandalam	122	11.24 N	76.42 E
Udaipur	120	24.35 N	73.41 E
Udala	126	21.35 N	86.34 E
Udalguri	120	26.46 N	92.08 E
Udall	198	37.23 N	97.06 W
Udamalpet	122	10.35 N	77.15 E
Udankudi	122	8.26 N	78.01 E
Udaquiola	252	36.34 S	58.31 W
Udarnyj	89	49.07 N	142.09 E
Uday ≃	78	50.05 N	33.07 E
Udaypur	124	26.56 N	86.31 E
Udbina	36	44.32 N	15.46 E
Udby	41	55.05 N	11.57 E
Uddeholm	40	60.01 N	13.37 E
Uddel	52	52.15 N	5.46 E
Uddevalla	26	58.21 N	11.55 E
Uddingston	46	55.50 N	4.06 W
Uddjaure ⊜	24	65.55 N	17.49 E
Udel'naja	82	55.38 N	38.03 E
Udel'naja ◆[8]	265a	60.01 N	30.19 E
Uden	52	51.40 N	5.36 E
Udenhout	52	51.37 N	5.08 E
Uder	56	51.22 N	10.05 E
Üdersdorf	56	50.09 N	6.49 E
Udgīr	122	18.23 N	77.07 E
Udhampur	123	32.56 N	75.08 E
Udhruḥ	132	30.20 N	35.36 E
Udi	150	6.19 N	7.25 E
Udimskij	24	61.09 N	45.52 E
Udine	64	46.03 N	13.14 E
Udine □[4]	64	46.10 N	13.00 E
Udmurtia → Udmurtija □[3]	80	57.00 N	53.00 E
Udmurtija □[3]	80	57.00 N	53.00 E
Udokan, chrebet ⋏	88	56.20 N	118.10 E
Udoml'a	76	57.52 N	35.01 E
Udone-jima I	94	34.28 N	139.18 E
Udono	92	33.44 N	136.01 E
Udon Thani	110	17.26 N	102.46 E
Udor, Mount ∧	162	23.30 S	131.01 E
Udot I	175c	7.23 N	151.43 E
Udskaja guba c	89	54.50 N	135.45 E
Udskoje	89	54.32 N	134.26 E
Udubo	146	11.57 N	10.38 E
Udupi	122	13.21 N	74.45 E
Udy	78	50.24 N	36.03 E
Udyl', ozero ⊜	89	52.06 N	139.48 E
Udža	74	71.14 N	117.10 E
Uebigau	54	51.35 N	13.18 E
Uebonti	112	0.55 S	121.38 E
Uebonti, Teluk c	112	0.50 S	121.45 E
Uecker ≃	54	53.45 N	14.04 E
Ueckeritz	54	54.00 N	14.02 E
Ueckermünde	54	53.44 N	14.03 E
Ueckermünder Heide ◆[3]	54	53.40 N	14.10 E
Ueda	94	36.24 N	138.16 E
Uedem	52	51.40 N	6.16 E
Uedesheim	263	51.10 N	6.48 E
Uegō	268	35.13 N	139.56 E
Ueharu	175d	24.25 N	123.46 E
Uehlfeld	56	49.40 N	10.43 E
Uele ≃	136	4.09 N	22.26 E
Uelen	180	66.10 N	169.48 W
Uel'kal'	180	65.32 N	179.17 W
Uelsen	52	52.30 N	6.53 E
Uelzen, Dtsch.	52	52.58 N	10.33 E
Uelzen, Dtsch.	263	51.33 N	7.44 E
Ueno, Nihon	94	36.05 N	138.47 E
Ueno, Nihon	94	34.45 N	136.08 E
Ueno, Nihon	270	34.53 N	135.14 E
Uenohara	94	35.37 N	139.07 E
Ueno Park ♦	268	35.43 N	139.46 E
Uenoshiba	270	34.33 N	135.28 E
Uerdingen ◆[8]	263	51.21 N	6.39 E
Uere ≃	154	3.42 N	25.24 E
Uetersen	52	53.41 N	9.39 E
Uettingen	56	49.48 N	9.43 E
Uetz	264a	52.28 N	12.56 E
Uetze	52	52.28 N	10.11 E
Ufa	86	54.44 N	55.56 E
Ufa ≃	86	54.40 N	56.00 E
Ufala, Punta >	70	38.22 N	14.59 E
Uffculme	42	50.54 N	3.20 W
Uffenheim	56	49.32 N	10.14 E
Ufita ≃	68	41.09 N	14.56 E
Ufra	128	40.00 N	53.02 E
Uft'uga ≃	76	59.46 N	39.21 E
Ugab ≃	156	21.08 S	13.40 E
Ugak Bay c	180	57.25 N	152.45 W
Ugāle	76	57.16 N	22.02 E
Ugalla ≃	154	5.08 S	30.42 E
Ugamskij chrebet ⋏	85	42.00 N	70.20 E
Uganda □[1]	154	1.00 N	32.00 E
Uganik Island I	180	57.53 N	153.28 W
Ugărčin	38	43.06 N	24.25 E
Ugarit ⊥	130	35.35 N	35.45 E
Ugashik	180	57.32 N	157.25 W
Ugashik Bay c	180	57.34 N	157.38 W
Ugatkyn ≃	180	68.24 N	171.30 E
Ugento	68	39.56 N	18.10 E
Ugep	150	5.48 N	8.05 E
Ugerløse	41	55.35 N	11.40 E
Uggiano la Chiesa	68	40.06 N	18.27 E
Ughaybish	140	10.52 N	31.05 E
Ughelli	150	5.29 N	5.59 E
Ugie	158	31.10 S	28.13 E
Ugie ≃	46	57.30 N	1.47 W
Ugíjar	34	36.57 N	3.03 W
Ugine	62	45.45 N	6.25 E
Uglegorsk	89	49.02 N	142.03 E
Uglekamensk	89	43.13 N	133.11 E
Uglezavodsk	89	47.21 N	142.38 E
Uglič	76	57.32 N	38.19 E
Ugljan, Otok I	36	44.05 N	15.10 E
Uglovaja	80	57.01 N	52.57 E
Uglovka	76	58.14 N	33.31 E
Uglovoje	89	43.20 N	132.06 E
Uglovskoje	86	51.23 N	80.12 E
Ugodiči	80	57.10 N	39.30 E
Ugodskij Zavod	82	55.02 N	36.45 E
Ugol'naja, buchta c	180	63.00 N	179.20 E
Ugolnyy	180	62.58 N	179.17 E
Ugoma ∧	154	4.00 S	28.45 E
Ugovizza	64	46.31 N	13.29 E
Ugra	76	54.47 N	34.17 E
Ugra ≃	82	54.30 N	36.07 E
Ugr'umovo	82	55.09 N	37.40 E
Ugtaal Cajdam	88	48.17 N	105.25 E
Uguj	86	56.02 N	76.03 E
Uğurludağ	130	40.27 N	34.28 E
Ug'ut	85	41.24 N	74.50 E
Ugyak, Cape >	180	58.17 N	154.04 W
Uh ≃	30	48.34 N	22.00 E
Uha-dong	98	40.41 N	125.38 E
Uḥayjibah, Jabal al- ∧	132	30.11 N	34.33 E
Uherčice	61	48.55 N	15.38 E
Uherské Hradiště	30	49.05 N	17.28 E
Uherský Brod	30	49.02 N	17.39 E
Uhingen	56	48.42 N	9.35 E
Úhlava ≃	60	49.43 N	13.23 E
Uhlenhorst	156	23.45 S	17.55 E
Ühlingen	58	47.43 N	8.19 E
Uhlman Lake ⊜	184	56.40 N	98.23 W
Uhlstädt	54	50.44 N	11.28 E
Uhniv	78	50.23 N	23.44 E
Uhrichsville	214	40.23 N	81.20 W
Uhroyidi	78	50.52 N	35.17 E
Uhyst, Dtsch.	54	51.11 N	14.13 E
Uhyst, Dtsch.	54	51.24 N	14.30 E
Uiche	152	12.03 S	21.02 E
Ui-do I	98	34.37 N	125.51 E
Uig	46	57.35 N	6.22 W
Uíge	152	7.37 S	15.03 E
Uíge □[5]	152	7.00 S	15.30 E

Symbols in the index entries represent the broad categories identified in the key at the right. Symbols with superior numbers (⋏[1]) identify subcategories (see complete key on page *I · 1).*

Symbole im Register stellen die rechts im Schlüssel erklärten Kategorien dar. Symbole mit hochgestellten Ziffern (⋏[1]) bezeichnen Unterabteilungen einer Kategorie (vgl. vollständiger Schlüssel auf Seite *I · 1).*

Los símbolos incluídos en el texto del índice representan las grandes categorías identificadas con la clave a la derecha. Los símbolos con numeros en su parte superior (⋏[1]) identifican las subcategorías (véase la clave completa en la página *I · 1).*

Les symboles de l'index représentent les catégories indiquées dans la légende à droite. Les symboles suivis d'un indice (⋏[1]) représentent des sous-catégories (voir légende complète à la page *I · 1).*

Os símbolos incluídos no texto do índice representam as grandes categorias identificadas com a chave à direita. Os símbolos com números em sua parte superior (⋏[1]) identificam as subcategorias (veja-se a chave completa à página *I · 1).*

	English	Deutsch	Español	Français	Português
∧	Mountain	Berg	Montaña	Montagne	Montanha
⋏	Mountains	Gebirge	Montañas	Montagnes	Montanhas
)(	Pass	Paß	Paso	Col	Passo
V	Valley, Canyon	Tal, Cañon	Valle, Cañón	Vallée, Canyon	Vale, Canhão
≚	Plain	Ebene	Llano	Plaine	Planície
>	Cape	Kap	Cabo	Cap	Cabo
I	Island	Insel	Isla	Île	Ilha
II	Islands	Inseln	Islas	Îles	Ilhas
⊥	Other Topographic Features	Andere Topographische Objekte	Otros Elementos Topográficos	Autres données topographiques	Outros acidentes topográficos

ESPAÑOL

Nombre	Página	Lat.°′	Long.°′ W = Oeste
Ŭijŏngbu	98	37.44 N	127.03 E
Ŭiju	98	40.12 N	124.32 E
Uil	86	49.05 N	54.40 E
Uil ≃	80	48.36 N	52.30 E
Uilpata, gora ∧	84	42.48 N	43.48 E
Uimaharju	26	62.55 N	30.15 E
Uinebona ≃	246	5.04 N	63.01 W
Uinskoje	86	56.53 N	56.35 E
Uinta ≃	200	40.14 N	109.51 W
Uintah and Ouray Indian Reservation ➛[4]	200	40.20 N	110.20 W
Uinta Mountains ∧∧	200	40.45 N	110.05 W
Uiraúna	250	6.31 S	38.25 W
Uis	156	21.08 S	14.49 E
Ŭisŏng	98	36.22 N	128.41 E
Uitenhage	158	33.40 S	25.28 E
Uitgeest	52	52.32 N	4.43 E
Uithoorn	52	52.14 N	4.50 E
Uithuizen	52	53.24 N	6.40 E
Uithuizermeeden	52	53.24 N	6.42 E
Uitspanning	158	26.46 S	29.56 E
Uj ≃, Asia	86	54.17 N	64.58 E
Uj ≃, Ross.	86	57.06 N	74.12 E
Ujae I[1]	14	9.05 N	165.40 E
Ujaly	86	44.37 N	60.57 E
Ujandina ≃	74	68.23 N	145.50 E
Ujar	86	55.48 N	94.20 E
Ujarrás ⊥	236	9.51 N	83.50 W
Ujedinenija, ostrov I	72	77.28 N	82.28 E
Ujelang I[1]	14	9.49 N	160.55 E
Ujemskij	24	64.29 N	40.50 E
Újezd, Česká Rep.	54	50.03 N	14.44 E
Újezd, Česká Rep.	60	49.26 N	13.27 E
Újezd u Brna	61	49.06 N	16.45 E
Újfehértó	30	47.48 N	21.40 E
Ujgursaj	85	40.53 N	71.03 E
Ujhāni	124	28.01 N	79.01 E
Uji	96	34.53 N	135.48 E
Uji ≃	96	34.53 N	135.42 E
Uji-guntō II	92	31.11 N	129.27 E
Ujiie	94	36.41 N	139.58 E
Ujiji	154	4.55 S	29.41 E
Uji-tawara	96	34.51 N	135.52 E
Uji-yamada → Ise	94	34.29 N	136.42 E
Ujjain	120	23.11 N	75.46 E
Újkér	61	47.28 N	16.49 E
ʿUjmān	128	25.25 N	55.27 E
Újpest ➛[8]	264c	47.34 N	19.06 E
Ujście	30	53.04 N	16.43 E
Ujskoje	86	54.22 N	60.00 E
Ujum	85	38.22 N	70.51 E
Ujung	112	7.04 S	120.46 E
Ujungbatu	114	0.43 N	100.31 E
Ujungbatu, Pulau I	114	2.20 N	97.24 E
Ujungberung	115a	6.55 S	107.42 E
Ujunggading	110	0.16 N	99.33 E
Ujunggenteng	115a	7.22 S	106.24 E
Ujungkulon, Semenanjung ≻[1]	115a	6.45 S	105.20 E
Ujungkulon National Park ♠	115a	6.40 S	105.20 E
Ujunglamuru	112	4.40 S	119.58 E
Ujungpandang (Makasar)	112	5.07 S	119.24 E
Újvidék → Novi Sad	38	45.15 N	19.50 E
Uk	88	55.04 N	98.52 E
Uka, Nihon	174m	26.48 N	128.14 E
Uka, Ross.	74	57.50 N	162.06 E
Ukamas	158	28.02 S	19.45 E
Ukara Island I	154	1.50 S	33.03 E
Ukerewe Island I	154	2.03 S	33.00 E
Ukhayḍir, Wādī V	132	30.55 N	37.01 E
Ukhra	126	23.39 N	87.14 E
Ukhrul	120	25.07 N	94.22 E
Ukhta → Uchta	24	63.33 N	53.38 E
Ukiah, Ca., U.S.	204	39.09 N	123.12 W
Ukiah, Or., U.S.	202	45.08 N	118.55 W
Ukibaru-jima I	174m	26.18 N	128.00 E
Ukiha	96	33.19 N	130.47 E
Uki Ni Masi Island I	175e	10.15 S	161.45 E
Ukmergė	76	55.15 N	24.45 E
Ukolnoi Island I	180	55.14 N	161.34 W
Ukraina → Ukraine □[1]	22	49.00 N	32.00 E
Ukraine □[1], Europe	22	49.00 N	32.00 E
Ukraine (Ukrayina) □[1], Europe	78	49.00 N	32.00 E
Ukrainka	86	54.39 N	71.20 E
Ukrayins'k	83	48.06 N	37.18 E
Ukrina ≃	36	45.05 N	17.56 E
Uks'anskoje	86	55.57 N	63.01 E
Uktuz	86	55.38 N	68.30 E
Uktym	24	62.38 N	48.52 E
Uku	152	11.24 S	14.15 E
Ukui	112	0.09 S	102.11 E
Ukurejskij	88	52.24 N	116.49 E
Ukuti	154	3.39 N	33.32 E
Ukyō ➛[8]	270	35.03 N	135.42 E
Ukyr	88	49.28 N	108.52 E
Ula, India	272b	22.43 N	88.33 E
Ula, Tür.	130	37.05 N	28.26 E
Ulaanbaatar	88	47.55 N	106.53 E
Ulaanbaatar □[8]	88	47.55 N	106.53 E
Ulaanbadrach	102	44.07 N	110.11 E
Ulaan Chus	86	49.02 N	89.23 E
Ulaangom	86	49.58 N	92.02 E
Ulaan nuur ⊜	102	44.30 N	103.35 E
Ulaan Tajga ∧∧	88	50.45 N	98.30 E
Ula-Chuduk	80	47.39 N	45.34 E
Ulak Island I	181a	51.22 N	179.00 W
Ulakmedan	114	2.43 N	99.38 E
Ulamba	152	9.07 S	23.40 E
Ulamona	164	5.00 S	151.15 E
Ulan, Austl.	166	32.17 S	149.44 E
Ulan, Zhg.	102	36.59 N	98.26 E
Ulan Bator → Ulaanbaatar	88	47.55 N	106.53 E
Ulanbel'	86	44.48 N	71.10 E
Ulan Buh Shamo ➛[2]	102	40.00 N	106.30 E
Ulan-Burgasy, chrebet ∧∧	88	52.45 N	109.00 E
Ulan-Erge	80	46.19 N	44.53 E
Ulang ≃	236	14.27 N	83.14 W
Ulanhot → Horqin Youyi Qianqi	89	46.05 N	122.05 E
Ulānia	126	22.12 N	90.29 E
Ulaniv	78	49.42 N	28.08 E
Ulanove	78	51.46 N	34.18 E
Ulanovskij	82	54.04 N	37.51 E
Ulanów	30	50.30 N	22.16 E
Ulansuhai Nur ⊜	102	40.56 N	108.49 E
Ulan-Ude	88	51.50 N	107.37 E
Ulan Ul Hu ⊜	120	34.45 N	90.25 E
Ulan-Ušotej	88	50.45 N	105.29 E
Ular, Pulau I	271c	1.14 N	103.45 E
Ulaş	130	39.27 N	37.03 E
Ul'ašovo	24	65.27 N	56.57 E
Ulatis Creek ≃	226	38.18 N	121.00 W
Ul'atuj	88	51.09 N	116.14 E
Ulawa Island I	175e	9.46 S	161.57 E
Ulawun, Mount ∧	164	5.03 S	151.20 E
Ulaya	154	7.04 S	36.54 E
Ułazów	30	50.17 N	23.00 E
Ul'ba	86	50.16 N	83.22 E
Ul'banskij zaliv ⊂	89	53.45 N	137.50 E
Ulchin	98	36.59 N	129.23 E
Ul'chun-Partija	88	49.56 N	112.46 E
Ulcinj	38	41.55 N	19.11 E
Ulco	158	28.21 S	24.15 E
Ulcombe	260	51.12 N	0.39 E
Ulcumayo	248	11.01 S	75.55 W
Uldum	41	55.51 N	9.36 E
Uldz ≃	88	49.56 N	115.31 E
Uleåborg → Oulu	26	65.01 N	25.28 E

FRANÇAIS

Nom	Page	Lat.°′	Long.°′ W = Ouest
Ulefoss	26	59.17 N	9.16 E
Ulen	198	47.04 N	96.15 W
Ulety	88	51.22 N	112.29 E
Ulfborg	26	56.16 N	8.20 E
Ulft	52	51.54 N	6.23 E
Ulgueira	266c	38.47 N	9.28 W
Ulhās ≃	272c	19.13 N	73.01 E
Ulhāsnagar	122	19.13 N	73.07 E
Uliast	86	48.57 N	91.17 E
Uliastaj (Džavchlant)	88	47.45 N	96.49 E
Úlice	60	49.45 N	13.09 E
Ulindi ≃	154	1.40 S	25.52 E
Ulingan	164	4.30 S	145.25 E
Ulithi I[1]	108	9.58 N	139.40 E
Ulja	74	58.51 N	141.50 E
Uljanino	82	55.21 N	38.26 E
Uljanovka	76	59.38 N	30.46 E
Uljanovo, Ross.	76	53.43 N	35.32 E
Uljanovo, Uzb.	85	40.07 N	68.30 E
Uljanovsk	80	54.20 N	48.24 E
Uljanovsk Oblast' □[4]	80	53.30 N	47.30 E
Uljanovskoje, Kaz.	86	50.02 N	73.42 E
Uljanovskoje, Ross.	89	46.17 N	142.13 E
Uljuan tekojärvi ⊜	26	64.19 N	25.57 E
Ul'kajak ≃	86	48.54 N	62.00 E
Ul'kan	88	57.14 N	107.19 E
Ul'kan ≃	88	55.53 N	107.45 E
Ul'ken-Karoj, ozero ⊜	86	54.00 N	71.58 E
Ulla	76	55.14 N	29.15 E
Ulla ≃, Bela.	76	55.14 N	29.14 E
Ulla ≃, Esp.	34	42.39 N	8.44 W
Ulladulla	170	35.21 S	150.29 E
Ulladulla Head ≻	170	35.22 S	150.30 E
Ullāpāra	126	24.19 N	89.34 E
Ullapool	46	57.54 N	5.10 W
Ullastrell	266d	41.31 N	1.58 E
Üllendahl ➛[8]	263	51.17 N	7.11 E
Ullerslev	41	55.22 N	10.40 E
Ullervad	40	58.40 N	13.52 E
Ullin	194	37.17 N	89.11 W
Üllő	264c	47.23 N	19.21 E
Ullswater ⊜	44	54.34 N	2.54 W
Ullučaj ≃	84	42.18 N	48.08 E
Ullŭng-do I	92	37.29 N	130.52 E
Ullvettern ⊜	40	59.27 N	14.16 E
Ullvi	40	59.42 N	16.37 E
Ulm, Dtsch.	58	48.24 N	10.00 E
Ulm, Mt., U.S.	202	47.25 N	111.30 W
Ul'ma ≃	89	51.54 N	129.18 E
Ulmarra	166	29.37 S	153.02 E
Ulmen	56	50.13 N	6.59 E
Ulmeni	38	45.04 N	26.39 E
Ulmer, Mount ∧	9	77.35 S	86.09 W
Ulongué	154	14.37 S	34.19 E
Ulpur	126	23.04 N	89.50 E
Ulricehamn	26	57.47 N	13.25 E
Ulrichskirchen	61	48.24 N	16.29 E
Ulrichstein	56	50.34 N	9.11 E
Ulrum	52	53.22 N	6.20 E
Ulsan	98	35.34 N	129.19 E
Ulsta	46a	60.30 N	1.09 W
Ulsteinvik	26	62.20 N	5.53 E
Ulster	210	41.51 N	76.30 W
Ulster □[6]	210	41.56 N	74.00 W
Ulster □[9]	48	54.35 N	7.00 W
Ulster ≃	56	50.51 N	9.59 E
Ulster Canal ≍	48	54.08 N	7.22 W
Ultimo, Val d' V	64	46.35 N	11.00 E
Ultraoriental, Cordillera (Serra do Divisor) ∧∧	248	8.20 S	73.30 W
Ulu, Indon.	112	2.45 N	125.24 E
Ulu, Ross.	74	60.19 N	127.24 E
Ulu, Sūd.	140	10.43 N	33.29 E
Ulúa ≃	236	15.53 N	87.44 W
Ulubāria	126	22.28 N	88.06 E
Ulubat Gölü ⊜	130	40.10 N	28.35 E
Ulubey, Tür.	130	38.25 N	29.18 E
Ulubey, Tür.	130	40.53 N	37.43 E
Uluborlu	130	38.05 N	30.28 E
Uluçınar	130	36.27 N	35.51 E
Uludağ ∧	130	40.04 N	29.13 E
Uludāngar	272b	22.51 N	88.31 E
Uludere	128	37.27 N	42.51 E
Ulugan Bay ⊂	116	10.07 N	118.47 E
Ulugqat	85	39.48 N	74.21 E
Uluinggalau ∧	175g	16.54 S	179.59 E
Ulujul ≃	86	57.46 N	85.30 E
Ulukışla, Kıbrıs	130	35.13 N	33.37 E
Ulukışla, Tür.	130	37.33 N	34.30 E
Ulul I	14	8.35 N	149.40 E
Ulu Laho, Bukit ∧	114	5.43 N	101.27 E
Ulunchan	88	54.51 N	111.02 E
Ulundi	158	28.17 S	31.26 E
Ulunga	89	46.31 N	136.56 E
Ulungur ≃	86	46.59 N	87.27 E
Ulungur Hu ⊜	86	47.15 N	87.20 E
Ulurijskij Golec, gora ∧	88	50.12 N	111.45 E
Uluru National Park ♠	162	25.20 S	131.00 E
Ulus	130	41.35 N	32.39 E
Ulusara	126	24.16 N	90.36 E
Ulut ≃	116	12.00 N	125.27 E
Ulutau	86	48.39 N	67.01 E
Ulutau, gora ∧	86	48.39 N	66.56 E
Ulutau, gory ∧∧	86	49.00 N	67.00 E
Ulu Tiram	114	1.36 N	103.49 E
Ulu Yam	114	3.27 N	101.38 E
Ulva	272c	18.59 N	73.02 E
Ulva I	46	56.29 N	6.14 W
Ulvenhout	52	51.34 N	4.48 E
Ulverston	44	54.12 N	3.06 W
Ulverstone	166	41.09 S	146.10 E
Ulvöarna II	26	63.01 N	18.40 E
Ulvshale ≻[1]	41	55.02 N	12.16 E
Ulvshyttan	40	60.18 N	15.22 E
Ulvsund ⋈	41	54.59 N	12.11 E
Ulyanivka	78	50.58 N	34.18 E
Ul'yanovka	78	48.20 N	30.13 E
Ulyanovsk → Uljanovsk	80	54.20 N	48.24 E
Ulysses, Ks., U.S.	198	37.34 N	101.21 W
Ulysses, Ne., U.S.	198	41.04 N	97.12 W
Ulysses, Pa., U.S.	214	41.54 N	77.46 W
Uly-Žilanšik ≃	86	48.51 N	63.47 E
Ulzë	38	41.41 N	19.54 E
Uma	89	52.36 N	120.37 E
Umag	36	45.25 N	13.32 E
Umaji	96	33.33 N	134.03 E
Umal'tinskij	89	51.56 N	133.36 E
Umán, Méx.	232	20.53 N	89.45 W
Uman', Ukr.	78	48.44 N	30.14 E
ʿUmān → Oman □[1]	118	22.00 N	58.00 E
Uman I	175c	7.18 N	151.53 E
Umanak	176	70.40 N	52.07 W
Umanak Fjord ⊂[2]	176	70.55 N	53.00 W
Umancevo	80	47.44 N	44.16 E
Umargāon	122	20.12 N	72.45 E
Umari	250	6.38 S	38.42 W
Umari ≃	248	7.05 S	64.34 W
ʿUmarī, Qāʿ al- ⊜	132	31.42 N	36.57 E
Umaria	124	23.32 N	80.50 E
Umarizal	250	5.59 S	37.49 W
Umarkot	120	25.22 N	69.44 E
Umatac	174p	13.18 N	144.39 E
Umatilla, Fl., U.S.	220	28.55 N	81.39 W
Umatilla, Or., U.S.	202	45.55 N	119.20 W
Umatilla ≃	202	45.55 N	119.20 W
Umatilla, Lake ⊜[1]	202	45.44 N	120.35 W
Umatilla Indian Reservation ➛[4]	202	45.41 N	118.31 W
Umayan ≃	116	8.13 N	125.50 E
Umaze	270	34.57 N	135.03 E
Umba	24	66.41 N	34.15 E
Umbagog Lake ⊜	188	44.45 N	71.05 W
Umbai	114	2.10 N	102.20 E
Umbaúba	250	11.22 S	37.39 W
Umbelasha ≃	140	9.51 N	24.50 E
Umbertide	66	43.18 N	12.20 E

PORTUGUÊS

Nome	Página	Lat.°′	Long.°′ W = Oeste
Umbogintwini	158	30.00 S	30.58 E
Umboi Island I	164	5.36 S	148.00 E
Umbrail, Pass (Giogo di Santa Maria))(	64	46.34 N	10.25 E
Umbria □[4]	66	43.00 N	12.30 E
Umbriatico	68	39.21 N	16.55 E
Umbroli	272c	19.11 N	73.06 E
Umbukul	164	2.30 S	150.00 E
Umbuzero, ozero ⊜	24	67.43 N	34.25 E
Ume ≃	154	16.40 S	28.26 E
Umeå	26	63.50 N	20.15 E
Umeälven ≃	24	63.47 N	20.16 E
Umedani	270	34.44 N	135.51 E
Umedpur	126	22.31 N	89.59 E
Umfolozi Game Reserve ➛[4]	158	28.19 S	31.50 E
Umfors	24	65.56 N	15.00 E
Umfreville Lake ⊜	184	50.18 N	94.45 W
Umfuli ≃	154	17.30 S	29.23 E
Umgungundhlovu ⊥	158	28.27 S	31.28 E
Umguza	154	19.25 S	27.51 E
Umhausen	64	47.08 N	10.56 E
Umhlanga Rocks	158	29.43 S	31.06 E
Umi	96	33.34 N	130.30 E
Umingan	116	15.56 N	120.50 E
Umkomaas	158	30.15 S	30.42 E
Umm ad-Daraj, Jabal ∧	132	32.19 N	35.48 E
Umm ʿAjārim ⊥[8]	142	30.50 N	32.49 E
Umm al-Abīd	146	27.31 N	15.02 E
Umm al-ʿArāʾis, Wādī V	146	26.26 N	13.55 E
Umm al-Arānib	146	26.08 N	14.45 E
Umm al-Birak	128	23.25 N	39.13 E
Umm al-Ḥawāyā, Jabal ∧	142	28.41 N	31.06 E
Umm al-Jimāl, Khirbat ⊥	132	32.20 N	36.22 E
Umm al-Khashab	144	17.21 N	42.32 E
Umm al-Qaywayn	128	25.35 N	55.34 E
Umm al-Qiṭṭayn	132	32.19 N	36.38 E
Umm al-Quṣūr	142	27.23 N	30.54 E
Ummanz	54	54.28 N	13.10 E
Umm Artah, Wādī V	142	28.41 N	32.37 E
Umm as-Saʿd ⊥	132	33.16 N	36.47 E
Umm Badr	140	14.14 N	27.57 E
Umm Balad, Wādī V	142	27.40 N	32.39 E
Umm Bayyūʿd	140	12.05 N	31.40 E
Umm Bel	140	13.32 N	28.04 E
Umm Boim	140	11.43 N	25.57 E
Umm Dabbī	140	14.37 N	30.23 E
Umm Dam	140	13.45 N	30.59 E
Umm Dhibbān, Sūd.	140	14.14 N	29.37 E
Umm Dhibbān, Sūd.	140	15.26 N	32.51 E
Umm Digulgulaya	140	10.29 N	24.57 E
Umm Dīnār	142	30.12 N	31.04 E
Umm Durmān (Omdurman)	140	15.38 N	32.30 E
Umm el Faḥm	132	32.31 N	35.09 E
Ummeln	52	51.58 N	8.27 E
Ummendorf	54	52.09 N	11.11 E
Umm Habwah, Jabal ∧[2]	142	27.23 N	31.29 E
Umm Ḥamāṭ	132	31.02 N	35.46 E
Umm Jamālah	140	11.27 N	28.12 E
Umm Kaddādah	140	13.36 N	26.42 E
Umm Khunān	273c	29.55 N	31.15 E
Umm Khushayb, Wādī V	142	30.24 N	32.43 E
Umm Kuwaykah	140	13.00 N	32.17 E
Umm Lajj	128	25.04 N	37.13 E
Umm Marahik, Jabal ∧[2]	140	13.40 N	26.53 E
Umm Mirdi	140	18.59 N	33.32 E
Umm Mitmān ⊥[8]	142	30.41 N	32.30 E
Umm Qantur	140	14.17 N	31.22 E
Umm Qaṣr	128	30.02 N	47.56 E
Umm Qurayn	140	9.58 N	28.55 E
Umm Quṣayr	132	31.40 N	35.53 E
Umm Raqm, Jabal ∧	142	30.14 N	31.52 E
Umm Rīshah, Birkat ⊜	142	30.21 N	30.22 E
Umm Rumaylah ⊤[4]	140	16.55 N	31.40 E
Umm Ruwābah	140	12.54 N	31.13 E
Umm Saggāt, Wādī V	140	15.15 N	23.12 E
Umm Saysabān, Jabal ∧	132	29.45 N	35.10 E
Umm Sayyālah	140	14.25 N	31.10 E
Umm Shalīl	140	10.51 N	23.42 E
Umm Shanqah	140	13.14 N	27.14 E
Umm Shuṭūr	140	7.17 N	33.14 E
Umm Sidr, Wādī V	142	27.54 N	32.33 E
Umm Sughra ⊤[4]	140	15.03 N	27.12 E
Umm ʿUmayd, Raʾs ∧	142	27.50 N	32.19 E
Umm ʿUmayyid, Biʾr ⊤[4]	142	27.53 N	32.30 E
Umm ʿUmayyid, Wādī V	142	27.37 N	32.41 E
Umm Urūmah I	128	25.46 N	36.32 E
Umm Walad	132	32.39 N	36.26 E
Umm Zaytah, Jabal ∧[2]	142	29.49 N	32.16 E
Umnak	180	53.17 N	168.20 W
Umnak Island I	180	53.25 N	168.10 W
Umnak Pass ⋈	180	53.20 N	167.45 W
Umnäs	24	65.24 N	16.10 E
Umniati	154	18.39 S	29.49 E
Umniati ≃	154	17.30 S	29.23 E
Um'ot, Ross.	80	54.08 N	42.42 E
Um'ot, Ross.	80	52.31 N	42.58 E
Umpferstedt	54	50.59 N	11.25 E
Umpqua ≃	202	43.42 N	124.03 W
Umpulo	152	12.38 S	17.42 E
ʿUmrān	144	15.50 N	43.56 E
ʿUmrānī, Wādī al- V	142	27.37 N	30.53 E
Umraniye	130	39.10 N	31.15 E
Umraniye ➛[8]	267b	41.01 N	29.05 E
Umred	122	20.51 N	79.20 E
Umreth	120	22.42 N	73.07 E
Umsini, Gunung ∧	164	1.22 S	133.45 E
Ŭmsŏng	98	36.56 N	127.41 E
Umstead State Park ♠	192	35.52 N	78.47 W
Umtanum Creek ≃	224	46.52 N	120.35 W
Umtata	158	31.35 S	28.47 E
Umtentweni	158	30.42 S	30.28 E
Umuahia	150	5.33 N	7.29 E
Umuarama	255	23.45 S	53.20 W
Umurbey	130	40.14 N	26.36 E
Umurlu	130	37.50 N	27.58 E
Umzimkulu	158	30.16 S	29.56 E
Umzingwani ≃	154	22.12 S	29.56 E
Umzinto	158	30.22 S	30.33 E
Una, Bra.	255	15.18 S	39.04 W
Una, India	120	20.49 N	71.02 E
Una, India	123	31.29 N	76.17 E
Una ≃	36	45.16 N	16.55 E
Una, Mount ∧	172	42.13 S	172.35 E
Una, Ribeirão ≃	287b	23.31 S	46.18 W
Unac ≃	36	44.30 N	16.09 E
Uña de Gato	196	25.58 N	99.41 W
Unadilla, Ga., U.S.	192	32.15 N	83.44 W
Unadilla, N.Y., U.S.	210	42.19 N	75.18 W
Unadilla ≃	210	42.20 N	75.25 W
Unaí	255	16.23 S	46.53 W
Unakami	94	35.46 N	140.45 E
Unalakleet	180	63.53 N	160.47 W
Unalaska	180	53.52 N	166.32 W
Unalaska Island I	180	53.45 N	166.45 W
Unanderra	170	34.27 S	150.52 E
Unango	154	12.50 S	35.20 E
Únanov	61	48.54 N	16.04 E
Unao	124	25.35 N	78.36 E
Unare ≃	246	10.03 N	65.14 W
Unauna, Pulau I	112	0.10 S	121.35 E
Unayyir, Ḥarrat al- ⊥[9]	128	25.20 N	37.45 E
ʿUnayzah, Ar. Su.	128	26.06 N	43.56 E
ʿUnayzah, Urd.	132	30.29 N	35.48 E

ʿUnayzah, Jabal ∧, Asia	128	32.12 N	39.18 E
ʿUnayzah, Jabal ∧, Urd.	132	30.30 N	35.47 E
Unazuki	94	36.49 N	137.35 E
Uncasville	207	41.26 N	72.06 W
Unchahra	124	24.23 N	80.47 E
Ŭnch'ŏn	98	38.34 N	125.26 E
Uncia	248	18.27 S	66.37 W
Uncompahgre ≃	200	38.45 N	108.06 W
Uncompahgre Peak ∧	200	38.04 N	107.28 W
Uncompahgre Plateau ∧∧[1]	200	38.30 N	108.25 W
Uncukul'	84	42.42 N	46.48 E
Uncular	130	40.28 N	41.28 E
Unda	88	51.42 N	116.56 E
Unda ≃	88	51.25 N	116.05 E
Unden ⊜	40	58.47 N	14.26 E
Undenäs	40	58.39 N	14.25 E
Underberg	158	29.50 S	29.22 E
Under River	260	51.15 N	0.14 E
Undersåker	26	63.20 N	13.23 E
Underwood, In., U.S.	218	38.36 N	85.46 W
Underwood, N.D., U.S.	198	47.27 N	101.08 W
Underwood, Wa., U.S.	224	45.43 N	121.31 W
Undløse	41	55.36 N	11.35 E
Undory	80	54.37 N	48.25 E
Undu, Tanjung ≻	115b	10.05 S	120.51 E
Undu Point ≻	175g	16.08 S	179.57 W
Undva nina ≻	76	58.32 N	21.55 E
Unea Island I	164	4.55 S	149.10 E
Uneča	76	52.50 N	32.40 E
Uneča ≃	76	52.50 N	31.56 E
Uneiuxi ≃	246	0.34 S	64.58 W
Úněšov	60	49.53 N	13.09 E
Unga Island I	180	55.15 N	160.45 W
Ungama Bay ⊂	154	2.45 S	40.20 E
Ungaran	115a	7.07 S	110.24 E
Ungarie	166	33.38 S	146.58 E
Ungarn → Hungary □[1]	30	47.00 N	20.00 E
Ungava, Péninsule d' ≻[1]	176	60.00 N	74.00 W
Ungava Bay ⊂	176	59.30 N	67.30 W
Ungch'ŏn	98	35.07 N	128.44 E
Unggi	98	42.20 N	130.24 E
Ungheni	38	47.12 N	27.48 E
Ungurkuj	88	50.27 N	106.58 E
Ungvár → Uzhhorod	78	48.37 N	22.18 E
Unhos	266c	38.50 N	9.07 W
Unhošt'	54	50.04 N	14.08 E
Uni	80	57.46 N	51.30 E
União	250	4.35 S	42.52 W
União da Vitória	252	26.13 S	51.05 W
União dos Palmares	250	9.10 S	36.02 W
Unica	24	62.38 N	34.38 E
Unicoi	192	36.11 N	82.20 W
Unicorn Branch ≃	208	39.15 N	75.52 W
Unidad Santa Fe ➛[8]	286a	19.23 N	99.15 W
Uniejów	30	51.58 N	18.49 E
Unieux	62	45.24 N	4.16 E
Unije, Otok I	36	44.38 N	14.15 E
Unimak Island I	180	54.50 N	164.00 W
Unimak Pass ⋈	180	54.35 N	164.43 W
Unini ≃	246	1.41 S	61.31 W
Unión, Arg.	252	35.09 S	65.57 W
Union, On., Can.	212	42.42 N	81.12 W
Unión, C.R.	236	8.36 N	83.03 W
Unión, Para.	252	24.48 S	56.33 W
Union, Il., U.S.	216	42.14 N	88.33 W
Union, Ia., U.S.	190	42.14 N	93.03 W
Union, Ky., U.S.	218	38.56 N	84.40 W
Union, La., U.S.	194	30.06 N	90.54 W
Union, Ms., U.S.	194	32.34 N	89.07 W
Union, Mo., U.S.	219	38.26 N	91.00 W
Union, N.J., U.S.	210	40.41 N	74.15 W
Union, Oh., U.S.	218	39.53 N	84.18 W
Union, Or., U.S.	202	45.12 N	117.51 W
Union, S.C., U.S.	192	34.42 N	81.37 W
Union, Wa., U.S.	224	47.21 N	123.06 W
Union, W.V., U.S.	192	37.35 N	80.32 W
Union □[6], In., U.S.	218	39.38 N	84.56 W
Union □[6], N.J., U.S.	208	40.40 N	74.11 W
Union □[6], Oh., U.S.	214	40.18 N	83.19 W
Union □[6], Pa., U.S.	210	40.58 N	76.54 W
Unión ➛[8]	258	34.53 S	56.08 W
Union Bay	182	49.35 N	124.53 W
Union Beach	208	40.26 N	74.10 W
Union Bridge	208	39.34 N	77.10 W
Union Center	210	42.09 N	76.04 W
Union City, Ca., U.S.	226	37.35 N	122.04 W
Union City, Ga., U.S.	192	33.35 N	84.32 W
Union City, In., U.S.	194	40.07 N	85.05 W
Union City, Mi., U.S.	216	42.04 N	85.09 W
Union City, N.J., U.S.	276	40.46 N	74.01 W
Union City, Oh., U.S.	216	40.11 N	84.48 W
Union City, Pa., U.S.	214	41.53 N	79.50 W
Union City, Tn., U.S.	194	36.25 N	89.03 W
Union City Dam ➛[6]	214	41.55 N	79.54 W
Uniondale, S. Afr.	158	33.40 S	23.08 E
Uniondale, In., U.S.	216	40.50 N	85.15 W
Uniondale, N.Y., U.S.	276	40.42 N	73.35 W
Union Dale, Pa., U.S.	210	41.43 N	75.30 W
Unión de Reyes	240p	22.48 N	81.32 W
Unión de San Antonio	234	21.06 N	101.58 W
Union des Émirats Arabes → United Arab Emirates □[1]	128	24.00 N	54.00 E
Unión de Tula	234	19.58 N	104.16 W
Union Flat Creek ≃	202	46.50 N	117.59 W
Union Gap	202	46.33 N	120.28 W
Union Grove, Tx., U.S.	222	32.34 N	94.55 W
Union Grove, Wi., U.S.	216	42.41 N	88.03 W
Unión Hidalgo	234	16.28 N	94.50 W
Union Hill	210	43.13 N	77.23 W
Union Lake	216	42.36 N	83.26 W
Union Lake ⊜, Mi., U.S.	216	42.03 N	85.11 W
Union Lake ⊜, Mi., U.S.	281	42.37 N	83.26 W
Union Lake ⊜, N.J., U.S.	208	39.25 N	75.03 W
Union Mills	216	41.29 N	86.46 W
Union Park	220	28.30 N	81.15 W
Union Pier	216	41.49 N	86.41 W
Union Point	192	33.36 N	83.04 W
Unionport, In., U.S.	218	40.07 N	85.06 W
Unionport, Oh., U.S.	214	40.21 N	80.51 W
Union Seamount ✢[3]	16	49.35 N	132.45 W
Union Springs, Al., U.S.	194	32.08 N	85.42 W
Union Springs, N.Y., U.S.	210	42.50 N	76.41 W
Union Station ➛[5], On., Can.	275b	43.39 N	79.23 W
Union Station ➛[5], Ca., U.S.	280	34.04 N	118.14 W
Union Station ➛[5], D.C., U.S.	284c	38.54 N	77.00 W
Union Station ➛[5], Il., U.S.	278	41.53 N	87.38 W
Uniontown, Al., U.S.	194	32.26 N	87.30 W
Uniontown, Ky., U.S.	194	37.46 N	87.55 W
Uniontown, Md., U.S.	208	39.35 N	77.06 W
Uniontown, Oh., U.S.	214	40.58 N	81.24 W
Uniontown, Pa., U.S.	188	39.54 N	79.44 W
Union Valley Reservoir ⊜[1]	226	38.50 N	120.26 W
Union Village	207	41.59 N	71.32 W
Unionville, On., Can.	275b	43.52 N	79.18 W
Unionville, Ct., U.S.	207	41.45 N	72.53 W
Unionville, In., U.S.	218	39.14 N	86.25 W
Unionville, Mi., U.S.	190	43.39 N	83.27 W
Unionville, Mo., U.S.	194	40.28 N	93.00 W
Unionville, N.J., U.S.	285	40.01 N	74.46 W
Unionville, N.Y., U.S.	210	41.18 N	74.34 W
Unionville, Oh., U.S.	214	41.47 N	81.00 W
Unionville, Pa., U.S.	285	39.54 N	75.44 W
Unionville Center	214	40.08 N	83.21 W
Uniopolis	216	40.36 N	84.05 W
Unipouheos Indian Reserve ➛[4]	184	53.52 N	110.21 W
Unisan	116	13.51 N	121.59 E
United	214	40.13 N	79.29 W
United Arab Emirates (Al-Imārāt al-ʿArabīyah al-Muttaḥidah) □[1], Asia	118	24.00 N	54.00 E
United Arab Emirates (Al-Imārāt al-ʿArabīyah al-Muttaḥidah) □[1], Asia	128	24.00 N	54.00 E
United Arab Republic → Egypt □[1]	140	27.00 N	30.00 E
United Kingdom □[1], Europe	22	54.00 N	2.00 W
United Kingdom □[1], Europe	28	54.00 N	2.00 W
United Kingdom Sovereign Base Area ■	130	35.00 N	33.45 E
United Nations Headquarters ⛉	276	40.45 N	73.58 W
United States □[1]	178	38.00 N	97.00 W
United States Air Force Academy ■	200	39.00 N	104.55 W
United States Coast Guard Academy ■	207	41.22 N	72.06 W
United States Merchant Marine Academy ⛉[2]	276	40.48 N	73.46 W
United States Military Academy ■	210	41.23 N	73.58 W
United States Naval Academy ■	208	38.59 N	76.30 W
United States Steel Corporation (Lorain Plant) ⛉[3], Oh., U.S.	279a	41.27 N	82.07 W
United States Steel Corporation ⛉[3], Pa., U.S.	279b	40.20 N	79.54 W
United States Steel Corporation Fairless Works ⛉[3]	285	40.09 N	74.45 W
Unity	184	52.27 N	109.10 W
Unity Reservoir ⊜[1]	279b	40.17 N	79.30 W
Universal City	196	29.32 N	98.17 W
Universal City ⛉[3]	280	34.09 N	118.21 W
Universal Mall ➛[9]	281	42.30 N	83.05 W
Universitaria, Ciudad ⛉[2]	266d	41.23 N	2.08 E
University	194	34.21 N	89.32 W
University City	219	38.39 N	90.19 W
University Gardens	276	40.46 N	73.43 W
University Heights, Ca., U.S.	226	37.26 N	122.12 W
University Heights, Oh., U.S.	279a	41.29 N	81.32 W
University Park, Il., U.S.	216	41.36 N	87.39 W
University Park, Md., U.S.	284c	38.58 N	76.57 W
University Park, N.M., U.S.	200	32.06 N	106.39 W
University Park, Tx., U.S.	222	32.52 N	96.47 W
University Place	224	47.14 N	122.32 W
University View	218	40.00 N	83.03 W
Unjha	120	23.48 N	72.24 E
Unkel	56	50.35 N	7.13 E
Unken	64	47.39 N	12.43 E
Unkurda	86	55.48 N	59.24 E
Unley	168b	34.57 S	138.35 E
Unna	52	51.32 N	7.41 E
ʿUnnāb, Jabal al- ∧	132	29.57 N	36.55 E
ʿUnnāb, Wādī al- V	132	30.11 N	36.39 E
Unnão	124	26.32 N	80.30 E
Uno, Canal Numero ≍	252	36.17 S	57.08 W
Uno, Ilha I	150	11.12 N	16.15 W
Unoke	94	36.43 N	136.42 E
Ŭnp'a	98	38.26 N	125.45 E
Unpenji-san ∧	96	34.02 N	133.44 E
Unqua Point ≻	276	40.39 N	73.26 W
Unquillo	252	31.14 S	64.19 W
Ŭnsan	98	39.25 N	126.01 E
Unseburg	54	51.56 N	11.30 E
Unserfrau → Madonna	64	46.43 N	10.52 E
Unsleben	56	50.22 N	10.15 E
Unst I	46a	60.45 N	0.53 W
Unstrut ≃	54	51.10 N	11.48 E
Un't	88	49.07 N	102.50 E
Unten	174m	26.41 N	128.00 E
Unterägeri	58	47.08 N	8.35 E
Unterbach, Dtsch.	263	51.12 N	6.54 E
Unterbäch, Schw.	58	46.17 N	7.48 E
Unter dem Wind, Inseln → Windward Islands II	238	13.00 N	61.00 W
Unterelchingen	58	48.27 N	10.07 E
Unterföhring	60	48.12 N	11.38 E
Unterfranken □[5]	56	50.10 N	10.00 E
Untergermaringen	58	47.56 N	10.40 E
Unterglottertal	58	48.03 N	7.56 E
Untergriesbach	60	48.35 N	13.40 E
Untergröningen	56	48.55 N	9.53 E
Untergrüne	263	51.22 N	7.39 E
Unterhaching	60	48.04 N	11.38 E
Unterhausen	58	48.26 N	9.16 E
Unterinntal V	64	47.24 N	11.47 E
Unterjettenberg	64	47.41 N	12.49 E
Unterlaa ➛[8]	264b	48.08 N	16.25 E
Unterlüss	52	52.50 N	10.17 E
Untermauerbach	264b	48.14 N	16.12 E
Untermünkheim	56	49.09 N	9.44 E
Untermünstertal	58	47.51 N	7.46 E
Unteröwisheim	56	49.08 N	8.40 E
Unterrath ➛[8]	263	51.16 N	6.47 E
Unterschächen	58	46.52 N	8.47 E
Unterschwaningen	56	49.04 N	10.37 E
Unterseen	58	46.41 N	7.51 E
Untertauern	64	47.18 N	13.30 E
Unterterzen	58	47.07 N	9.15 E
Unterthingau	58	47.46 N	10.31 E
Unterueckersee ⊜	54	53.17 N	13.51 E
Unteruhldingen	58	47.43 N	9.14 E
Unterwasser	58	47.12 N	9.19 E
Unterweissbach	54	50.37 N	11.10 E
Unterwellenborn	54	50.39 N	11.26 E
Unterwössen	64	47.44 N	12.27 E
Unterzeiring	61	47.15 N	14.31 E
Untraverket	40	60.25 N	17.18 E
Unuli Horog	120	35.06 N	91.51 E
Ünye	130	41.08 N	37.17 E
Unža	80	58.01 N	44.01 E
Unža ≃	80	57.20 N	43.08 E
Unzen-Amakusa-kokuritsu-kōen ♠	92	32.45 N	130.17 E
Unzen-dake ∧	92	32.45 N	130.17 E
Unže-Pavinskaja	86	58.53 N	64.02 E
Uojan	88	56.07 N	111.38 E
Uono ≃	94	37.15 N	138.53 E
Uo-shima I	96	34.11 N	133.19 E
Uozu	94	36.48 N	137.24 E
Upa ≃	76	54.02 N	36.15 E
Upala	236	10.47 N	85.02 W
Upanema	250	5.38 S	37.15 W
Upano ≃	246	2.45 S	78.12 W
Upata	246	8.01 N	62.24 W
Upatoi Creek ≃	192	32.22 N	84.58 W
Upavon	42	51.18 N	1.49 W
Ŭpchŏ-ri	98	37.53 N	125.09 E
Upchurch	260	51.23 N	0.39 E
Upemba, Lac ⊜	154	8.36 S	26.26 E
Upemba, Parc National de l' ♠	154	9.10 S	26.35 E
Upernavik	176	72.47 N	56.10 W
Upgant-Schott	52	53.30 N	7.16 E
Uphal	140	6.58 N	34.16 E
Upham	198	48.34 N	100.43 W
Up Holland	262	53.33 N	2.44 W
Uphusen	52	53.01 N	8.58 E
Upi	116	6.57 N	124.09 E
Upía ≃	246	4.18 N	72.45 W
Upington	158	28.25 S	21.15 E
Upire ≃	246	11.27 N	68.58 W
Upland, Ca., U.S.	228	34.05 N	117.38 W
Upland, In., U.S.	216	40.28 N	85.29 W
Upland, Ne., U.S.	198	40.19 N	98.54 W
Upland, Pa., U.S.	285	39.51 N	75.23 W
Upleta	120	21.44 N	70.17 E
Upnuk Lake ⊜	180	60.21 N	158.58 W
Upolu I	175a	13.55 S	171.45 W
Upolu Point ≻	229d	20.16 N	155.51 W
Uporovo	86	56.18 N	66.17 E
Upper □[4]	150	10.30 N	1.30 W
Upper Arlington	218	40.00 N	83.03 W
Upper Arrow Lake ⊜	182	50.30 N	117.55 W
Upper Artichoke Reservoir ⊜[1]	283	42.48 N	70.57 W
Upper Bay ⊂	276	40.41 N	74.03 W
Upper Beaconsfield	274b	38.01 S	145.25 E
Upper Berkshire Valley	276	40.56 N	74.35 W
Upper Beverley Lake ⊜	212	44.37 N	76.05 W
Upper Black Eddy	210	40.35 N	75.07 W
Upper Blackville	186	46.39 N	65.52 W
Upper Brookville	276	40.51 N	73.34 W
Upper Canada Village ⊥	206	44.57 N	75.03 W
Upper Castlereagh	274a	33.43 S	150.40 E
Upperco	208	39.33 N	76.50 W
Upper Coliban Reservoir ⊜[1]	169	37.18 S	144.23 E
Upper Crystal Springs Reservoir ⊜[1]	282	37.30 N	122.20 W
Upper Darby	208	39.55 N	75.16 W
Upper Demerara-Berbice □[4]	246	5.30 N	58.20 W
Upper des Lacs Lake ⊜[1]	198	48.50 N	102.07 W
Upper Egypt → Aṣ-Ṣaʿīd □[9]	140	26.00 N	32.00 E
Upper End	262	53.17 N	1.52 W
Upper Erskine Lake ⊜	276	41.06 N	74.15 W
Upper Fairmount	208	38.06 N	75.47 W
Upper Falls	284b	39.26 N	76.24 W
Upper Ferntree Gully	274b	37.54 S	145.19 E
Upper Fraser	182	54.07 N	121.56 W
Upper Ganga Canal ≍	124	29.57 N	78.12 E
Upper Gap ⋈	212	44.06 N	76.50 W
Upper Goose Lake ⊜	184	51.44 N	92.44 W
Upper Greenwood Lake	276	41.10 N	74.22 W
Upper Greenwood Lake ⊜	276	41.11 N	74.23 W
Upper Hat Creek	182	50.38 N	121.35 W
Upper Humber ≃	186	49.10 N	57.28 W
Upper Hutt	172	41.08 S	175.04 E
Upper Iowa ≃	190	43.29 N	91.14 W
Upper Island Cove	186	47.39 N	53.12 W
Upper Keechi Creek ≃	222	31.23 N	95.42 W
Upper Klamath Lake ⊜	202	42.23 N	122.55 W
Upper Lake	204	39.10 N	122.54 W
Upper Lake ⊜	204	41.44 N	120.08 W
Upper Lehigh	210	41.02 N	75.55 W
Upper Liard	180	60.02 N	128.55 W
Upper Machodoc Creek ≃	208	38.18 N	77.02 W
Upper Manitou Lake ⊜	184	49.24 N	92.48 W
Upper Marlboro	208	38.48 N	76.45 W
Upper Matecumbe Key I	220	24.55 N	80.39 W
Upper Moutere	172	41.16 S	173.00 E
Upper Musquodoboit	186	45.08 N	62.57 W
Upper Mystic Lake ⊜	283	42.27 N	71.09 W
Upper Nyack	210	41.07 N	73.55 W
Upper Peirce Reservoir ⊜[1]	271c	1.22 N	103.48 E
Upper Red Lake ⊜	198	48.10 N	94.40 W
Upper Rideau Lake ⊜	212	44.41 N	76.20 W
Upper River Rouge ≃	281	42.23 N	83.16 W
Upper Saddle River	276	41.03 N	74.05 W
Upper Saint Clair	279b	40.21 N	80.05 W
Upper Sandusky	214	40.49 N	83.16 W
Upper San Leandro Reservoir ⊜[1]	226	37.47 N	122.07 W
Upper Sheila	186	47.28 N	64.56 W
Upper Straits Lake ⊜	281	42.35 N	83.24 W
Upper Sumas	224	49.01 N	122.12 W
Upper Swan	168a	31.46 S	116.01 E
Upper Takaka	172	41.02 S	172.50 E
Upper Takutu-Upper Essequibo □[4]	246	3.00 N	59.00 W
Upper Tean	42	52.57 N	1.58 W
Upper Tooting ➛[8]	260	51.26 N	0.10 W
Upper Trajan's Wall ⊥	38	46.35 N	29.00 E
Upper Ugashik Lake ⊜	180	57.40 N	156.43 W
Upper Volta → Burkina Faso □[1]	150	13.00 N	1.30 W
Upper Windigo Lake ⊜	184	52.30 N	91.35 W
Upper Yarra Reservoir ⊜[1]	169	37.41 S	145.56 E
Upper Yosemite Fall ⌞	226	37.45 N	119.36 W
Uppingham	42	52.35 N	0.43 W
Uppland □[9]	40	59.59 N	17.48 E
Upplanda	40	60.14 N	17.44 E
Upplands Väsby	40	59.31 N	17.54 E
Uppsala	40	59.52 N	17.38 E
Uppsala Län □[6]	40	60.00 N	17.45 E
Upright, Cape ≻	180	60.17 N	172.15 W
Upsala → Uppsala	40	59.52 N	17.38 E
Upshi	120	33.50 N	77.49 E
Upshur □[6]	222	32.45 N	94.55 W
Upstart, Cape ≻	166	19.42 S	147.45 E
Upton, P.Q., Can.	206	45.39 N	72.41 W
Upton, Eng., U.K.	44	53.13 N	2.52 W
Upton, Eng., U.K.	44	53.37 N	1.17 W
Upton, Eng., U.K.	260	51.30 N	0.35 W
Upton, Eng., U.K.	262	53.23 N	3.06 W
Upton, Ky., U.S.	194	37.27 N	85.53 W
Upton, Ma., U.S.	207	42.10 N	71.36 W
Upton, Wy., U.S.	198	44.05 N	104.37 W
Upton Hill ∧[2]	169	36.52 S	145.27 E
Upton upon Severn	42	52.04 N	2.13 W
Uptown ➛[8]	278	41.58 N	87.40 W
Upwell	42	52.36 N	0.12 E
Upwey	274b	37.54 S	145.20 E
Uquía, Cerro ∧	246	4.22 N	63.46 W
Ur → Tall al-Muqayyar ⊥	128	30.57 N	46.09 E
Urabá, Golfo de ⊂	246	8.25 N	76.53 W
Urachi	84	42.21 N	47.36 E
Uracoa	246	9.00 N	62.21 W
Urad	54	52.15 N	14.45 E
Uradome-kaigan ♠	96	35.35 N	134.21 E

≃	River	Fluß	Río	Rivière	Rio
≍	Canal	Kanal	Canal	Canal	Canal
⌞	Waterfall, Rapids	Wasserfall, Stromschnellen	Cascada, Rápidos	Chute d'eau, Rapides	Cascata, Rápidos
⋈	Strait	Meeresstraße	Estrecho	Détroit	Estreito
⊂	Bay, Gulf	Bucht, Golf	Bahía, Golfo	Baie, Golfe	Baía, Golfo
⊜	Lake, Lakes	See, Seen	Lago, Lagos	Lac, Lacs	Lago, Lagos
≋	Swamp	Sumpf	Pantano	Marais	Pântano
⊓	Ice Features, Glacier	Eis- und Gletscherformen	Accidentes Glaciales	Formes glaciaires	Acidentes glaciares
⊤	Other Hydrographic Features	Andere Hydrographische Objekte	Otros Elementos Hidrográficos	Autres données hydrographiques	Outros acidentes hidrográficos
✢	Submarine Features	Untermeerische Objekte	Accidentes Submarinos	Formes de relief sous-marin	Acidentes submarinos
□	Political Unit	Politische Einheit	Unidad Politica	Entité politique	Unidade política
⛉	Cultural Institution	Kulturelle Institution	Institución Cultural	Institution culturelle	Institução cultural
⊥	Historical Site	Historische Stätte	Sitio Histórico	Site historique	Sitio histórico
♠	Recreational Site	Erholungs- und Ferienort	Sitio de Recreo	Centre de loisirs	Area de Lazer
⊠	Airport	Flughafen	Aeropuerto	Aéroport	Aeroporto
■	Military Installation	Militäranlage	Instalación Militar	Installation militaire	Instalação militar
➛	Miscellaneous	Verschiedenes	Misceláneo	Divers	Diversos

ENGLISH: Name Page Lat.°′ Long.°′

DEUTSCH: Name Seite Breite°′ Länge°′ E = Ost

Urad Zhonghou Lianheqi 102 41.42 N 108.49 E
Uraga 268 35.15 N 139.43 E
Uraga-kō c 268 35.14 N 139.44 E
Uraga-suidō ʊ 94 35.13 N 139.45 E
Uragawara 94 37.09 N 138.26 E
Urahoro 92a 42.48 N 143.39 E
Uraj 86 60.08 N 64.48 E
Urakan 88 58.38 N 106.01 E
Urakawa 92a 42.09 N 142.47 E
Ural ≃ 72 47.00 N 51.48 E
Uralla 166 30.39 S 151.30 E
Ural Mountains
→ Ural'skije gory ⋏ 72 60.00 N 60.00 E
Uralo-Kl'uči 88 56.03 N 97.28 E
Uralove 78 52.11 N 33.34 E
Ural'sk 80 51.14 N 51.22 E
Ural'sk □[8] 80 50.00 N 51.00 E
Ural'skij 80 51.36 N 51.40 E
Ural'skije gory (Ural Mountains) ⋏ 72 60.00 N 60.00 E
Urambo 154 5.04 S 32.03 E
Uran 272c 18.52 N 72.56 E
Urana 166 35.20 S 146.16 E
Urandangi 166 21.36 S 138.18 E
Urandi 255 14.46 S 42.38 W
Urangan 166 25.18 S 152.54 E
Urania, Austl. 168b 34.31 S 137.36 E
Urania, La., U.S. 194 31.51 N 92.17 W
Uranium City 176 59.34 N 108.36 W
Uranquinty 171b 35.12 S 147.15 E
Urarey 162 27.26 S 122.18 E
Urariá, Paraná ≃[1] 246 3.03 S 57.43 W
Uraricaá ≃ 246 3.20 N 61.56 W
Uraricoera 246 3.27 N 60.59 W
Uraricoera ≃ 246 3.02 N 60.30 W
Uras 71 39.42 N 8.42 E
Urasaki 174m 26.40 N 127.53 E
Urasoe 174m 26.15 N 127.43 E
Ura-T'ube 85 39.55 N 68.59 E
Uravakonda 122 14.57 N 77.16 E
Uravan 200 38.22 N 108.44 W
Urawa 94 35.51 N 139.39 E
Urayasu 94 35.39 N 139.54 E
'Urayfan Nāqah, Jabal ∧ 132 30.22 N 34.27 E
'Urayyidah, Bi'r ⫪[4] 142 29.00 N 31.58 E
Urazmetovo 86 53.49 N 55.25 E
Urazovka 80 55.24 N 45.38 E
Urazovo 78 50.07 N 38.04 E
Urbach 56 50.53 N 7.05 E
Urban 224 48.38 N 122.40 W
Urbana, Ar., U.S. 194 33.09 N 92.26 W
Urbana, Il., U.S. 194 40.06 N 88.12 W
Urbana, In., U.S. 216 40.53 N 85.47 W
Urbana, Mo., U.S. 194 37.50 N 93.10 W
Urbana, Oh., U.S. 218 40.06 N 83.45 W
Urbancrest 218 39.53 N 83.05 W
Urbandale, Ia., U.S. 190 41.37 N 93.42 W
Urbandale, Mi., U.S. 216 44.09 N 85.11 W
Urbania 66 43.40 N 12.31 E
Urbanna 208 37.38 N 76.34 W
Urbano Noris 240p 20.36 N 76.08 W
Urbano Santos 250 3.12 S 43.23 W
Urbe 62 44.29 N 8.36 E
Urbe, Aeroporto dell' ⊠ 267a 41.57 N 12.30 E
Urbiña, Peña ∧ 34 43.01 N 5.57 W
Urbino 66 43.43 N 12.38 E
Urbisaglia 66 43.12 N 13.23 E
Urcos 248 13.42 S 71.38 W
Urda 80 48.47 N 47.26 E
Urdaneta 116 15.59 N 120.34 E
Urdenbach ◆[8] 263 51.09 N 6.53 E
Urdinarrain 252 32.41 S 58.53 W
Urdoma 24 61.47 N 48.32 E
Urdžar 86 47.05 N 81.38 E
Uré 246 7.46 N 75.31 W
Ure ≃, Fr. 50 48.45 N 0.11 E
Ure ≃, Eng., U.K. 44 54.01 N 1.12 W
Urečje 76 52.57 N 27.54 E
Ûrein 142 30.58 N 30.42 E
Ureki 84 41.59 N 41.46 E
Ureliki 180 64.23 N 173.15 W
Uren' 80 57.28 N 45.49 E
Uren ⊜ 40 58.59 N 16.44 E
Urén ≃ 236 9.33 N 82.55 W
Ureña 246 7.55 N 72.28 W
Urenui 172 39.00 S 174.23 E
Uréparapara I 175f 13.32 S 167.20 E
Ures 232 29.26 N 110.24 W
Ureshino, Nihon 92 33.06 N 129.59 E
Ureshino, Nihon 94 34.37 N 136.29 E
Ureterp 52 53.05 N 6.10 E
Urewera National Park ♠ 172 38.40 S 177.00 E
Urft ≃ 56 50.35 N 6.30 E
Urga
→ Ulaanbaatar, Mong. 88 47.55 N 106.53 E
Urga, Uzb. 86 43.35 N 58.30 E
Urgamal 88 48.29 N 94.20 E
Urgenč 72 41.33 N 60.38 E
Urgnano 62 45.35 N 9.41 E
Urgučenskij Golec, gora ∧ 88 53.30 N 118.08 E
Ürgüp 130 38.38 N 34.56 E
Urgut 85 39.23 N 67.15 E
Urho 86 46.48 N 89.45 E
Urho Kekkosen kansallispuisto ♠ 24 68.10 N 28.30 E
Uri, India 123 34.05 N 74.02 E
Uri, It. 71 40.38 N 8.29 E
Uri □[3] 58 46.50 N 8.40 E
Uriah 194 31.18 N 87.30 W
Uriangato 234 20.09 N 101.11 W
Uribante ≃ 246 7.18 N 70.44 W
Uribe 246 3.13 N 74.24 W
Uribelarrea 258 35.09 S 58.54 W
Uribia 246 11.43 N 72.16 W
Urich 194 38.27 N 94.00 W
Urick ◆[8] 265a 59.50 N 30.11 E
Urickij 86 53.19 N 65.34 E
Urickoje 78 52.02 N 38.11 E
Urie ≃ 46 57.19 N 2.30 W
Urimba 152 10.56 S 16.32 E
Urión ≃[1] 288 34.24 S 58.31 W
Urique 232 27.13 N 107.55 W
Urique ≃ 232 26.29 N 107.58 W
Uri-Rotstock ∧ 58 46.52 N 8.33 E
Urituyacu ≃ 246 4.45 S 75.28 W
Uriuaná ≃ 250 2.47 S 50.29 W
Urizura 94 36.30 N 140.27 E
Urjala 26 61.05 N 23.32 E
Urk 52 52.39 N 5.36 E
Urkan ≃ 89 53.27 N 126.56 E
Urkarach 84 42.11 N 47.38 E
Urla 130 38.18 N 26.46 E
Urlați 38 44.59 N 26.14 E
Urlingford 48 52.42 N 7.35 W
Urlings 240c 17.02 N 61.52 W
Urluk 88 50.03 N 107.55 E
Urma 126 23.10 N 86.15 E
Urman, Ross. 86 54.52 N 56.52 E
'Urmān, Sūrīy. 132 32.30 N 36.45 E
Urmary 80 55.42 N 47.57 E
Urmetan 85 39.27 N 68.17 E
Urmi ≃ 89 48.44 N 134.16 E
Urmia
→ Orūmīyeh 128 37.33 N 45.04 E
Urmia, Lake
→ Orūmīyeh, Daryācheh-ye ⊜ 128 37.40 N 45.30 E
Urmston 44 53.27 N 2.21 W
Urnäsch 58 47.19 N 9.17 E
Urnersee ⊜ 58 46.55 N 8.37 E
Uroindo 248 21.41 S 64.41 W
Üröm 264c 47.36 N 19.01 E
Uromi 150 6.44 N 6.18 E
Uroševac 38 42.22 N 21.09 E
Uroyán, Montañas de ⋏ 240m 18.14 N 67.02 W
Urožajnoje, Ross. 84 43.42 N 44.13 E
Urožajnoje, Ross. 84 44.47 N 44.55 E
Urquhart, Glen V 46 57.20 N 4.35 W
Urrao 246 6.20 N 76.11 W
Urr Water ≃ 44 54.53 N 3.49 W
Ursa 219 40.04 N 91.22 W
Uršel'skij 80 55.41 N 40.13 E
Ursensollen 60 49.24 N 11.46 E
Ursk 86 54.27 N 85.24 E
Urspring 56 48.33 N 9.53 E
Urtazym 86 52.12 N 58.50 E
Urtigueira 252 24.12 S 50.55 W
Urt Moron 120 37.00 N 93.18 E
Uru ≃ 255 15.24 S 49.36 W
Uruaçu 255 14.30 S 49.10 W
Uruana 255 15.30 S 49.41 W
Uruapan 204 31.38 N 116.15 W
Uruapan del Progreso 234 19.25 N 102.04 W
Urubamba 248 13.18 S 72.07 W
Urubamba ≃ 248 10.44 S 73.45 W
Urubaxi ≃ 246 0.31 S 64.50 W
Urubu ≃, Bra. 246 2.55 S 58.25 W
Urubu ≃, Bra. 250 10.51 S 49.47 W
Uruburetama 250 3.38 S 39.30 W
Urucará 250 2.32 S 57.45 W
Uruch ≃ 84 43.28 N 44.06 E
Urucu ≃ 246 4.11 S 63.36 W
Uruçuca 255 14.35 S 39.16 W
Uruçuí 250 7.14 S 44.33 W
Uruçuí, Serra da ⋏[2] 250 9.00 S 44.45 W
Urucuia ≃ 255 16.08 S 45.05 W
Uruçui-preto ≃ 250 7.20 S 44.38 W
Urucurituba 250 2.41 S 57.40 W
Urugi 94 35.16 N 137.42 E
Uruguaiana 252 29.45 S 57.05 W
Uruguay □[1], S.A. 244 33.00 S 56.00 W
Uruguay □[1], S.A. 252 33.00 S 56.00 W
Uruguay (Uruguai) ≃ 252 34.12 S 58.18 W
Urugudejevskij Golec, gora ∧ 88 51.25 N 102.09 E
Urul'ga 88 51.45 N 114.47 E
Urul'unguj ≃ 88 50.24 N 119.08 E
Ur'um, ozero ⊜ 86 54.33 N 78.30 E
Urumchi
→ Ürümqi 90 43.48 N 87.35 E
Ur'umkan ≃ 88 52.35 N 120.08 E
Ürümqi 90 43.48 N 87.35 E
Urundel 252 23.33 S 64.25 W
Ur'ung-Chaja 74 72.48 N 113.23 E
Uruoca 250 3.20 S 40.32 W
Urup 84 43.52 N 41.09 E
Urup ≃ 84 44.49 N 41.10 E
Urup, gora ∧ 84 43.38 N 40.58 E
Urup, ostrov I 74 46.00 N 150.00 E
Urupá ≃ 248 10.54 S 61.57 W
Urupadi ≃ 250 3.51 S 57.21 W
Urupês 255 21.13 S 49.17 W
Ur'upino 88 52.46 N 120.00 E
Ur'upinsk 80 50.47 N 41.59 E
Ururicaia, Ilha I 250 1.30 S 52.05 W
Uruša 89 54.03 N 122.54 E
Urus-Martan 84 43.08 N 45.32 E
Urusovo 82 54.15 N 38.26 E
Urussanga 252 28.31 S 49.19 W
Urussu 80 54.36 N 53.24 E
Urutaí 255 17.28 S 48.12 W
Urutaí, Ilha I 250 1.07 S 51.17 W
Urutaú 252 25.42 S 63.04 W
Uruti 172 38.57 S 174.32 E
Uru Uru, Lago ⊜ 248 18.10 S 67.10 W
Uruwira 154 6.27 S 31.21 E
Uryl' 86 49.15 N 86.20 E
Uryū-yama ∧ 270 35.03 N 135.48 E
Uryv 78 51.07 N 39.10 E
Urzajbaš 80 54.43 N 54.23 E
Urziceni 38 44.43 N 26.38 E
Ürzig 56 49.59 N 7.01 E
Urzulei 71 40.06 N 9.30 E
Uržum 80 57.08 N 50.00 E
Us 261 49.06 N 1.58 E
Us ≃ 86 52.07 N 92.15 E
Usa, Nihon 96 33.31 N 131.22 E
Usa, Ross. 86 54.03 N 88.45 E
Uša ≃, Bela. 76 54.00 N 28.55 E
Usa ≃, Ross. 24 65.57 N 56.55 E
Ušač' ≃ 76 55.32 N 28.30 E
Ušači 76 55.11 N 28.37 E
Usada Island I 116 6.08 N 120.33 E
Usadel 54 53.26 N 13.11 E
Uşak 130 38.41 N 29.25 E
Uşak □[4] 130 38.35 N 29.20 E
Ušaki 76 59.29 N 30.59 E
Usakos 156 22.01 S 15.32 E
Ušakovka 83 48.48 N 39.48 E
Ušakovo, Ross. 86 56.22 N 75.41 E
Ušakovo, Ross. 89 51.55 N 126.34 E
Usambara Mountains ⋏ 154 4.45 S 38.30 E
Usangu Flats ≚ 154 8.30 S 34.15 E
Usanovy 86 59.28 N 73.24 E
Ušaral 85 43.54 N 70.42 E
Usarp Mountains ⋏ 9 71.10 S 160.00 E
Úšava 60 49.46 N 12.40 E
Usaymir, Wādī al- V 273c 30.04 N 31.23 E
Ušba, gora ∧ 84 43.08 N 42.40 E
Ušbas ≃ 85 43.55 N 69.39 E
Usborne, Mount ∧ 254 51.41 S 58.50 W
Ušće 38 43.28 N 20.37 E
Uščerpje 76 52.43 N 31.53 E
Uscio 62 44.25 N 9.10 E
Usedom 54 53.52 N 13.55 E
Usedom (Uznam) I 54 54.00 N 14.00 E
Useldange 56 49.47 N 5.59 E
Usellus 71 39.48 N 8.51 E
Usen' ≃ 80 54.44 N 53.38 E
'Usfān 144 21.55 N 39.21 E
Ushaa 152 14.55 S 23.18 E
Ushant
→ Ouessant, Île d' I 32 48.28 N 5.05 W
Ushashi 154 2.00 S 33.57 E
'Ushayrah 144 21.46 N 40.38 E
Ushetu 154 4.10 S 32.16 E
Ushibuka 92 32.11 N 130.01 E
Ushiku 94 35.58 N 140.08 E
Ushimado 96 34.37 N 134.10 E
Ushuaia 254 54.48 S 68.18 W
Ushytsya ≃ 78 48.35 N 27.08 E
Usibelli 180 63.51 N 148.47 W
Usingen 56 50.20 N 8.32 E
Usini 71 40.40 N 8.32 E
Usinsk 24 65.58 N 56.39 E
Usisya 154 11.09 S 34.11 E
Usk, B.C., Can. 182 54.38 N 128.25 W
Usk, Wales, U.K. 42 51.43 N 2.54 W
Usk, Wa., U.S. 202 48.18 N 117.16 W
Usk ≃ 42 51.36 N 2.58 W
Uškanij kr'až ∧ 180 65.15 N 178.35 E
Uskedal 26 59.56 N 5.52 E
Usken ⊜ 40 59.39 N 15.01 E
Uskovo 265b 55.56 N 37.19 E
Üsküb
→ Skopje 38 41.59 N 21.26 E
Uskumru ◆[8] 267b 41.12 N 29.01 E
Uslar 52 51.39 N 9.38 E
Úslava ≃ 60 49.45 N 13.24 E
Usmajac 234 19.52 N 103.34 W
Usman', Ross. 76 52.02 N 39.44 E
Usman', Ross. 89 51.29 N 134.00 E
Usmanka 80 52.49 N 51.42 E
Usmānpur ◆[8] 272a 28.41 N 77.15 E
Usmas ezers ⊜ 76 57.11 N 22.10 E
Usmat 85 39.44 N 67.40 E
Usmate Velate 62 45.39 N 9.21 E
Ušmunskij Golec, gora ∧ 89 51.40 N 118.35 E
Usmyn' 76 55.52 N 31.09 E
Ušna ≃ 80 55.43 N 42.12 E
Usoke 154 5.06 S 32.20 E
Usolje, Ross. 80 53.23 N 49.05 E
Usolje, Ross. 82 56.49 N 38.40 E
Usolje, Ross. 86 59.25 N 56.41 E
Usolje-Sibirskoje 88 52.47 N 103.38 E
Usolka ≃ 86 57.47 N 94.35 E
Uson 116 12.13 N 123.47 E
Usoro 150 5.34 N 6.13 E
Usovo 265b 55.44 N 37.13 E
Uspallata 252 32.35 S 69.20 W
Uspanapa ≃ 234 17.58 N 94.29 W
Uspenka, Kaz. 86 52.54 N 77.25 E
Uspenka, Ross. 80 50.38 N 41.28 E
Uspenka, Ukr. 83 48.23 N 39.10 E
Uspenka, Ukr. 83 47.43 N 38.42 E
Uspenovka 80 51.16 N 53.36 E
Uspenskij 86 48.42 N 72.40 E
Uspenskoje 82 55.43 N 37.04 E
Usri ≃ 126 24.03 N 86.23 E
Uššaj 86 43.50 N 58.53 E
Ussassai 71 39.49 N 9.23 E
Usseglio 62 45.14 N 7.13 E
Ussel 32 45.33 N 2.18 E
Ussel ≃ 56 48.44 N 11.04 E
Usshers Creek ≃ 284a 43.03 N 79.02 W
Usson-en-Forez 62 45.23 N 3.56 E
Ussure 154 4.39 S 34.23 E
Ussuri (Wusuli) ≃ 89 48.27 N 135.04 E
Ussurijsk 89 43.48 N 131.59 E
Ūst 123 36.56 N 72.53 E
Usta 80 57.26 N 45.40 E
Usta ≃ 80 56.53 N 45.28 E
Ust'-Ajsk 86 56.07 N 57.40 E
Ustaoset 26 60.30 N 8.04 E
Ustaritz 32 43.24 N 1.27 W
Ust'-Bagar'ak 86 56.08 N 61.52 E
Ust'-Barguzin 88 53.27 N 108.59 E
Ust'-Belaja 74 65.30 N 173.20 E
Ust'-Bol'šereck 74 52.48 N 156.14 E
Ust'-B'ur' 86 53.49 N 90.15 E
Ust'-Buzulukskaja 80 50.12 N 42.10 E
Ust'-Bystr'anskaja 80 47.49 N 41.03 E
Ust'-Čaja 86 58.17 N 82.38 E
Ust'-Čaryšskaja Pristan' 86 52.24 N 83.39 E
Ust'-Čaun 74 68.47 N 170.30 E
Ust'-Choperskaja 80 49.36 N 42.24 E
Ust'-Chorna 78 48.18 N 23.56 E
Ust'-Cil'ma 24 65.27 N 52.06 E
Ust'-Čižapka 86 59.02 N 79.37 E
Ust'-Čornaja 88 52.57 N 119.02 E
Ust'-Dolyssy 76 56.09 N 29.39 E
Ust'-Doneckij 80 47.39 N 40.52 E
Ust'-Džegutinskaja 84 44.05 N 41.58 E
Úštěk 54 50.36 N 14.20 E
Ust'-Elegest 88 51.32 N 94.05 E
Uster 58 47.21 N 8.43 E
Ust'-Gr'aznucha 80 50.28 N 45.26 E
Ustica 70 38.42 N 13.11 E
Ustica, Isola di I 70 38.42 N 13.11 E
Ust'-Il'a 88 50.25 N 113.41 E
Ust'-Ilga 88 55.00 N 105.02 E
Ust'-Ilimsk 88 58.00 N 102.39 E
Ust'-Ilimskoje vodochranilišče ⊜[1] 88 57.00 N 102.15 E
Ust'-Ilyč 24 62.32 N 56.41 E
Ústí nad Labem 54 50.40 N 14.02 E
Ústí nad Orlicí 30 49.58 N 16.24 E
Ust'-Išim 86 57.44 N 71.10 E
Ust'-Izes 86 55.56 N 76.56 E
Ust'-Ižora 265a 59.48 N 30.36 E
Ustja ≃ 24 61.30 N 42.36 E
Ust'-Javron'ga 24 63.25 N 44.21 E
Ustje, Ross. 76 60.49 N 32.49 E
Ustje, Ross. 76 59.38 N 39.43 E
Ustje, Ross. 80 57.47 N 39.47 E
Ustje, Ross. 82 55.16 N 36.20 E
Ustje, Ross. 86 57.46 N 94.42 E
Ustje-Kirovskoje 76 58.45 N 35.55 E
Ustka 30 54.35 N 16.50 E
Ust'-K'achta 88 50.32 N 106.16 E
Ust'-Kajtym 86 57.23 N 95.28 E
Ust'-Kalmanka 86 52.07 N 83.19 E
Ust'-Kamčatsk 74 56.15 N 162.30 E
Ust'-Kamenogorsk 86 49.58 N 82.38 E
Ust'-Kan, Ross. 86 50.57 N 84.45 E
Ust'-Kan, Ross. 86 56.31 N 93.48 E
Ust'-Karenga 88 54.26 N 116.30 E
Ust'-Karsk 88 52.43 N 118.48 E
Ust'-Katav 86 54.56 N 58.10 E
Ust'-Kemčug 86 57.13 N 90.30 E
Ust'-Kil'mez' 80 56.57 N 50.30 E
Ust'-Kišert' 86 57.22 N 57.15 E
Ust'-Koksa 86 50.18 N 85.36 E
Ust'-Kujda 74 70.01 N 135.36 E
Ust'-Kulom 24 61.42 N 53.40 E
Ust'-Kurd'um 80 51.39 N 46.12 E
Ust'-Kurenga 86 57.27 N 75.34 E
Ust'-Kut 88 56.46 N 105.40 E
Ust'-Labinsk 78 45.13 N 39.42 E
Ust'-Lubija 88 52.36 N 120.16 E
Ust'-Luga 76 59.40 N 28.15 E
Ust'-Lyža 24 65.44 N 56.36 E
Ust'-Maja 74 60.25 N 134.32 E
Ust'-Manja 72 62.11 N 60.20 E
Ust'-Naryk 86 54.20 N 87.25 E
Ust'-Nemda 80 57.03 N 50.22 E
Ust'-Nera 74 64.34 N 143.12 E
Ust'-Niman 89 51.23 N 132.42 E
Ust'-N'ukža 88 56.34 N 121.37 E
Uštobe 86 45.16 N 78.00 E
Ust'-Omčug 74 61.09 N 149.38 E
Ust'-Ordynskij 88 52.48 N 104.45 E
Ust'-Ordynskij Burjatskij Avtonomnyj Okrug □[8] 88 53.30 N 104.00 E
Ust'-Oz'ornaja 88 50.42 N 117.06 E
Ust'-Oz'ornoje 86 58.54 N 87.48 E
Ust'-Paden'ga 24 61.53 N 42.36 E
Ust'-Pečengskoje 76 59.47 N 42.37 E
Ust'-Pinega 24 64.11 N 41.56 E
Ust'-Pit 86 58.59 N 91.44 E
Ust'-Pogožje 80 49.28 N 44.38 E
Ustreka 76 58.38 N 34.33 E
Ust'-Reki 24 62.12 N 46.45 E
Ustroń 30 49.43 N 18.49 E
Ustrzyki Dolne 30 49.26 N 22.37 E
Ust'-Šara 76 60.13 N 33.57 E
Ust'-Ščerbedino 80 51.53 N 42.52 E
Ust'-Slav'anka ◆[8] 265a 59.50 N 30.32 E
Ust'-Šonoša 24 61.10 N 41.18 E
Ust'-Sumy 86 54.48 N 80.26 E
Ust'-Tara 86 56.41 N 74.39 E
Ust'-Tarka 86 55.34 N 75.42 E
Ust'-Tašino 89 51.07 N 129.35 E
Ust'-Tygda 89 52.35 N 127.53 E
Ust'-Tym 86 59.26 N 80.08 E
Ust'-Tyrma 89 50.29 N 131.18 E
Ust'uckoje 76 58.32 N 35.20 E
Ust'-Uda 88 54.10 N 103.03 E
Üstükran 130 39.16 N 41.17 E
Ust'-Ulagan 86 50.38 N 87.58 E
Ust'-Umal'ta 89 51.39 N 133.18 E
Ust'-Undurga 89 53.07 N 118.04 E
Ust'-Unja 24 61.48 N 57.48 E
Ust'-Urgal 89 51.09 N 132.33 E
Ust'urt, plato ⋏[1] 72 43.00 N 56.00 E
Ust'-Us 86 52.07 N 92.17 E
Ust'-Usa 24 65.59 N 56.54 E
Ust'-Uza 80 52.58 N 45.17 E
Ust'užna 76 58.51 N 36.26 E
Ust'-Vichoreva 88 56.47 N 101.24 E
Ust'-Voja 24 64.27 N 57.40 E
Ust'-Vyjskaja 24 62.57 N 46.41 E
Ust'-Vym' 24 62.14 N 50.24 E
Ustylyh 78 50.51 N 24.09 E
Ustynivka 78 47.57 N 32.32 E
Ust'-Zaza 88 53.10 N 111.40 E
Ust'-Žuja 88 58.48 N 118.12 E
Usu 86 44.27 N 84.37 E
Usuchčaj 84 41.25 N 47.53 E
Usuda 94 36.12 N 138.29 E
Usugli 88 52.39 N 115.16 E
Usui 96 33.34 N 130.42 E
Usuki 96 33.08 N 131.49 E
Usuki-wan c 96 33.10 N 131.52 E
Usulután 236 13.21 N 88.27 W
Usumacinta ≃ 232 18.24 N 92.38 W
Usumbura
→ Bujumbura 154 3.23 S 29.22 E
Ušumun 89 52.49 N 126.27 E
Ušur 80 57.47 N 52.58 E
Usuyŏng 98 34.35 N 126.18 E
Usu-zan ∧ 92a 42.32 N 140.51 E
Usv'aty 76 55.45 N 30.45 E
Uta 71 39.17 N 8.57 E
Utah □[3], U.S. 178 39.30 N 111.30 W
Utah □[3], U.S. 200 39.30 N 111.30 W
Utah Lake ⊜ 200 40.13 N 111.49 W
Utajärvi 26 64.45 N 26.23 E
Utamba 154 1.06 S 26.50 E
Utamboni ≃ 152 1.00 N 9.48 E
Utan 115b 8.24 S 117.07 E
Utano 94 34.28 N 135.59 E
Utapi 156 17.31 S 15.08 E
Utashinai 92a 43.31 N 142.03 E
Utata 88 50.51 N 102.45 E
'Utaybah, Buḥayrat al- ⊜ 132 33.32 N 36.37 E
Ute 198 42.03 N 95.42 W
Ute ≃ 248 15.28 S 65.05 W
Ute Creek ≃ 196 35.21 N 103.50 W
Utegi 154 1.20 S 34.35 E
Utelle 62 43.55 N 7.15 E
Utembo ≃ 152 17.06 S 22.01 E
Ute Mountain Indian Reservation ◆[4] 200 37.10 N 108.35 W
Utena 76 55.30 N 25.36 E
Utengule 154 8.57 S 35.50 E
Ute Reservoir ⊜[1] 196 36.21 N 103.31 W
Úterský potok ≃ 60 49.48 N 13.06 E
Utersum 30 54.43 N 8.24 E
Utete 154 7.59 S 38.47 E
Utevka 80 52.57 N 50.58 E
Utfort 263 51.28 N 6.38 E
Uthai Thani 110 15.22 N 100.03 E
Uthal 120 25.48 N 66.37 E
U Thong 110 14.22 N 99.54 E
Uthumphon Phisai 110 15.05 N 104.08 E
Utiariti 248 13.02 S 58.17 W
Utica, Il., U.S. 216 41.20 N 89.00 W
Utica, In., U.S. 218 38.20 N 85.39 W
Utica, Ks., U.S. 198 38.38 N 100.10 W
Utica, Mi., U.S. 214 42.37 N 83.02 W
Utica, Ms., U.S. 194 32.06 N 90.37 W
Utica, Ne., U.S. 198 40.54 N 97.21 W
Utica, N.Y., U.S. 210 43.06 N 75.13 W
Utica, Oh., U.S. 214 40.14 N 82.27 W
Utica, Pa., U.S. 214 41.26 N 79.58 W
Utica
→ Utique ⊥ 36 37.03 N 10.03 E
Utiel 34 39.34 N 1.12 W
Utikoomak Lake Indian Reserve ◆[4] 182 55.57 N 115.30 W
Utikuma Lake ⊜ 182 55.50 N 115.25 W
Utila 236 16.06 N 86.54 W
Utila, Isla de I 236 16.06 N 86.56 W
Utinga 287b 23.38 S 46.32 W
Utinga ≃ 255 12.34 S 41.20 W
Utique 36 37.03 N 10.03 E
Utique ⊥ 36 37.03 N 10.03 E
Utirik I[1] 14 11.15 N 169.48 E
Utlängan I 26 56.01 N 15.47 E
Utlyuts'kyy lyman c[1] 78 46.15 N 35.12 E
Ut'ma 86 57.35 N 71.45 E
Utmānzai 123 34.11 N 71.46 E
Uto 92 32.41 N 130.40 E
Utö I 40 58.56 N 18.16 E
Utokota 156 17.50 S 20.22 E
Utonde 152 1.56 N 9.49 E
Utopia, Austl. 162 22.14 S 134.33 E
Utopia, Tx., U.S. 196 29.37 N 99.32 W
Utorgoš 76 58.17 N 30.15 E
Utraula 124 27.19 N 82.25 E
Utrecht, Ned. 52 52.05 N 5.08 E
Utrecht, S. Afr. 158 27.38 S 30.20 E
Utrecht □[4] 52 52.05 N 5.08 E
Utrera 34 37.11 N 5.47 W
Utroja ≃ 76 57.23 N 28.09 E
Utsaladdy 224 48.15 N 122.30 W
Utsira 26 59.18 N 4.54 E
Utsjoki 24 69.53 N 27.00 E
Utsumi 96 34.21 N 133.17 E
Utsunomiya 94 36.33 N 139.52 E
Utta 80 46.23 N 46.01 E
Uttamapālāiyam 122 9.48 N 77.20 E
Uttaradit 110 17.38 N 100.06 E
Uttarkāshi 120 30.44 N 78.27 E
Uttarpara-Kotrung 272b 22.40 N 88.21 E
Uttar Pradesh □[3] 120 27.00 N 80.00 E
Uttendorf, Öst. 60 48.09 N 13.07 E
Uttendorf, Öst. 64 47.17 N 12.34 E
Uttenweiler 58 48.09 N 9.36 E
Ütterlingsen 263 51.15 N 7.45 E
Utting 60 48.02 N 11.05 E
Uttlesford □[8] 260 51.47 N 0.19 E
Uttoxeter 42 52.54 N 1.51 W
Utu 154 1.45 S 27.54 E
Utuado 240m 18.16 N 66.42 W
Utukok ≃ 180 70.04 N 162.18 W
Utulei 174u 14.17 S 170.40 W
Utunomiya
→ Utsunomiya 94 36.33 N 139.52 E
Utupua I 14 11.16 S 166.29 E
Utva ≃ 86 51.28 N 52.40 E
Utzenstorf 58 47.08 N 7.33 E
Uudenmaan lääni □[4] 26 60.30 N 25.00 E
Uulu 76 58.17 N 24.35 E
Üür ≃ 88 50.18 N 101.54 E
Uurainen 26 62.30 N 25.27 E
Uusikaarlepyy (Nykarleby) 26 63.32 N 22.32 E
Uusikaupunki (Nystad) 26 60.48 N 21.25 E
Uusimaa ◆[1] 26 60.30 N 25.00 E
Uvá, Bra. 255 15.53 S 50.25 W
Uva, Ross. 80 56.59 N 52.13 E
Uvá ≃ 246 3.57 N 68.24 W
Uvalda 192 33.41 N 83.25 W
Uvalde 196 29.12 N 99.47 W
Úvaly 54 50.03 N 14.47 E
Uvån ≃ 40 60.01 N 13.37 E
Uvarovići 76 52.36 N 30.44 E
Uvarovka 76 55.32 N 35.37 E
Uvarovo 80 51.59 N 42.15 E
Uvas Creek ≃ 226 36.58 N 121.33 W
Uvas Reservoir ⊜[1] 226 37.05 N 121.42 W
Uvat 86 59.09 N 68.54 E
'Uvda, Biq'at V 132 29.57 N 34.57 E
Uvdal 26 60.16 N 8.44 E
Uvel'skij 86 54.26 N 61.22 E
Uvernet 62 44.22 N 6.38 E
Uvero, Punta › 241s 11.21 N 68.41 W
Uvinza 154 5.06 S 30.22 E
Uvira 154 3.24 S 29.08 E
Uvod' ≃ 80 56.26 N 41.26 E
Uvongo Beach 158 30.51 S 30.23 E
Uvs □[4] 86 50.00 N 92.00 E
Uvs nuur ⊜ 74 50.20 N 92.45 E
Uvworé › 175f 18.47 S 169.16 E
Uwa 96 33.20 N 132.30 E
Uwajima 96 33.13 N 132.34 E
Uwa-kai ⫪[2] 96 33.15 N 132.15 E
'Uwaybid, Jabal ∧ 142 30.06 N 32.09 E
Uwayl 140 8.46 N 27.24 E
'Uwaynāt 130 35.43 N 36.05 E
'Uwaynāt, Jabal al- ∧ 140 21.54 N 24.58 E
'Uwayriḍ, Ḥarrat al- ⊥[9] 128 27.00 N 37.30 E
Uwchland 285 40.05 N 75.42 W
Uwi, Pulau I 112 1.05 N 107.24 E
Uxbridge, On., Can. 212 44.06 N 79.07 W
Uxbridge, Ma., U.S. 207 42.04 N 71.37 W
Uxbridge ◆[8] 260 51.33 N 0.29 W
Uxmal ⊥ 232 20.22 N 89.46 W
Uyak Bay c 180 57.36 N 153.57 W
Uyama 270 34.50 N 135.41 E
U-yin 110 22.53 N 95.13 E
Uyo 150 5.03 N 7.56 E
Uyu ≃ 110 24.51 N 94.57 E
Uyuni 248 20.28 S 66.50 W
Uyuni, Salar de ≚ 248 20.20 S 67.42 W
Uza ≃, Ross. 76 57.48 N 29.31 E
Uza ≃, Ross. 80 53.02 N 45.18 E
Užanicha 86 54.41 N 81.02 E
Uzas 86 57.04 N 76.55 E
Užava 76 57.14 N 21.27 E
'Uzaym, Nahr al- ≃ 128 34.01 N 44.19 E
Uzbekistan □[1] 72 41.00 N 64.00 E
Uzboj ≃ 128 39.30 N 55.00 E
Uzda 76 53.27 N 27.13 E
Uzdin 38 45.12 N 20.38 E
Uzerche 32 45.26 N 1.34 E
Uzès 62 44.01 N 4.25 E
Uzgen 85 40.46 N 73.18 E
Uzh ≃ 78 51.15 N 30.12 E
Uzhhorod 78 48.37 N 22.18 E
Užice 38 43.51 N 19.51 E
Uzkij Lug 88 50.42 N 108.01 E
Uzkoje ◆[8] 265b 55.37 N 37.32 E
Uzlovaja 76 53.59 N 38.10 E
Uzmorje 80 51.15 N 45.55 E
Uznach 58 47.14 N 9.00 E
Uznam (Usedom) I 54 54.00 N 14.00 E
Uzola ≃ 80 56.32 N 43.38 E
Uz'ukovo 80 53.38 N 49.43 E
Üzümlü, Tür. 130 37.32 N 31.37 E
Üzümlü, Tür. 130 36.44 N 29.14 E
Uzun 85 38.22 N 68.03 E
Uzun Ada I 130 38.28 N 26.42 E
Uzunagač, Kaz. 85 43.13 N 76.20 E
Uzunagač, Kaz. 85 43.36 N 76.19 E
Uzunbulak 86 45.23 N 84.06 E
Uzunca ≃ 267b 40.58 N 28.50 E
Uzunköprü 130 41.16 N 26.41 E
Uzunkuduk 85 40.33 N 67.11 E
Uzunkuyu 130 38.17 N 26.33 E
Uzunovo 82 54.32 N 38.37 E
Užur 86 55.20 N 89.50 E
Užventis 76 55.47 N 22.39 E
Uzyn 78 49.50 N 30.24 E

V

Vä 26 55.59 N 14.05 E
Vaajakoski 26 62.16 N 25.54 E
Vääksy 26 61.11 N 25.33 E
Vaal ≃ 158 29.04 S 23.38 E
Vaala 26 64.26 N 26.48 E
Vaaldam ⊜[1] 158 26.55 S 28.12 E
Vaalhartsdam ⊜[1] 158 28.06 S 24.55 E
Vaalkop ∧ 158 31.21 S 26.31 E
Vaals 56 50.46 N 6.01 E
Vaalserberg ∧[2] 56 50.45 N 6.01 E
Vaalwater 156 24.20 S 28.03 E
Vaasa (Vasa) 26 63.06 N 21.36 E
Vaasan lääni □[4] 26 63.00 N 23.00 E
Vaassen 52 52.17 N 5.57 E
Vabalninkas 76 55.58 N 24.45 E
Vabkent 128 40.02 N 64.30 E
Vác 30 47.47 N 19.08 E
Vaca, Bol. 248 19.54 S 63.48 W
Vača, Ross. 80 55.48 N 42.46 E
Vaca, Mount ∧ 226 38.24 N 122.06 W
Vacacaí ≃ 252 29.55 S 53.06 W
Vaca Key I 220 24.43 N 81.04 W
Vacaria 252 28.30 S 50.56 W
Vacaria ≃, Bra. 255 16.39 S 42.45 W
Vacaria ≃, Bra. 255 21.55 S 53.59 W
Vacas, Arroyo de las ≃ 258 34.00 S 58.18 W
Vacaville 226 38.21 N 121.59 W
Vacca, Kaap › 158 34.21 S 21.53 E
Vaccarès, Étang de c 62 43.32 N 4.34 E
Vach ≃ 74 60.45 N 76.45 E
Vacha 56 50.50 N 10.01 E
Vache, Île à I 238 18.05 N 73.38 W
Vaches, Île aux I 275a 45.41 N 73.40 W
Vaches, Rivière aux ≃ 206 46.02 N 72.46 W
Vachrušev 89 48.59 N 142.58 E
Vachš ≃ 72 37.06 N 68.18 E
Vachšskij chrebet ⋏ 85 38.35 N 69.45 E
Vachtan 80 57.58 N 46.42 E
Vači 84 42.05 N 47.13 E
Vacía Talega, Punta › 240m 18.27 N 65.54 W
Vacoas 157c 20.18 S 57.29 E
Vad, Ross. 80 55.32 N 44.12 E
Vad, Sve. 40 60.02 N 15.39 E
Vad ≃ 80 54.33 N 42.37 E
Väddö I 40 60.00 N 18.50 E
Vădeni 38 45.22 N 27.56 E
Vader 224 46.24 N 122.57 W
Vadheim 26 61.13 N 5.49 E
Vādi 272c 18.56 N 73.06 E
Vadino 76 55.16 N 33.16 E
Vadinsk 80 53.43 N 43.04 E
Vadnagar 120 23.47 N 72.38 E
Vadodara 122 22.18 N 73.12 E
Vado de Cedillos 200 31.05 N 105.50 W
Vado de Piedra 196 29.50 N 104.40 W
Vado Hondo 200 31.09 N 111.22 W
Vado Ligure 62 44.17 N 8.27 E
Vadret, Piz ∧ 58 46.41 N 9.57 E
Vadsbro 40 58.58 N 16.36 E
Vadsø 24 70.05 N 29.46 E
Vadstena 26 58.27 N 14.54 E
Vaduz 58 47.09 N 9.31 E
Vadvetjåkko Nationalpark ♠ 24 68.35 N 18.20 E
Væggerløse 41 54.42 N 11.56 E
Værøy I 24 67.40 N 12.39 E
Vaga ≃ 24 62.48 N 42.56 E
Vagaj 86 57.56 N 69.01 E
Vagaj ≃ 86 57.59 N 69.01 E
Vågåmo 26 61.53 N 9.06 E
Vaganski Vrh ∧ 36 44.22 N 15.31 E
Vaggeryd 26 57.30 N 14.07 E
Vaghena Island I 175e 7.26 S 157.46 E
Vaglia 66 43.54 N 11.17 E
Vaglio Basilicata 68 40.40 N 15.55 E
Vagney 58 48.01 N 6.43 E
Vagnhärad 40 58.55 N 17.30 E
Vagues 258 34.19 S 59.26 W
Váh ≃ 30 47.55 N 18.00 E
Vahrn
→ Varna 64 46.44 N 11.38 E
Vaiano 66 43.58 N 11.07 E
Vaich, Loch ⊜ 46 57.43 N 4.46 W
Vaiden 194 33.19 N 89.44 W
Vaigai ≃ 122 9.21 N 79.00 E
Vaigat ʊ 176 70.11 N 53.00 W
Vaihingen an der Enz 56 48.56 N 8.58 E
Vaijāpur 122 19.55 N 74.44 E
Vaikam 122 9.46 N 76.24 E
Väike-Maarja 76 59.08 N 26.15 E
Väike Pakri I 76 59.20 N 24.00 E
Vail, Co., U.S. 200 39.38 N 106.22 W
Vail, Ia., U.S. 198 42.03 N 95.11 W
Vaila I 46a 60.12 N 1.37 W
Vailala ≃ 164 7.25 S 145.25 E
Vaileka 175g 17.23 S 178.09 E
Vail Lake ⊜[1] 228 33.29 N 116.58 W
Vailly-sur-Aisne 50 49.25 N 3.31 E
Vailly-sur-Sauldre 50 47.27 N 2.39 E
Vail Mills 210 43.03 N 74.13 W
Vailoatai 174u 14.22 S 170.47 W
Vail Point › 212 44.43 N 80.45 W
Vails Gate 210 41.27 N 74.04 W
Vaimali 175f 16.34 S 168.11 E
Vaiņode 76 56.26 N 21.50 E
Vaiont, Lago di ⊜ 64 46.16 N 12.22 E
Vaippār ≃ 122 9.01 N 78.17 E
Vair ≃ 58 48.27 N 5.42 E
Vairano Scalo 68 41.20 N 14.08 E
Vairao 174s 17.47 S 149.17 W
Vaires-sur-Marne 261 48.52 N 2.39 E
Vaison-la-Romaine 62 44.14 N 5.04 E
Vaitahu 174x 9.56 S 139.06 W
Vaîte 58 47.35 N 5.44 E
Vaitogi 174u 14.21 S 170.44 W
Vaitown 150 6.52 N 10.52 W
Vaitupu I 14 7.28 S 178.41 E
Vaja ≃ 80 57.27 N 46.00 E
Vajgač 72 70.25 N 58.46 E
Vajgač, ostrov I 72 70.00 N 59.30 E
Vajk' 84 39.40 N 45.30 E
Vakaga □[5] 146 10.00 N 22.30 E
Vakaga ≃ 146 9.48 N 21.32 E
Vākhān ≃ 120 37.00 N 72.40 E
Vākhān ◆[1] 120 37.00 N 73.00 E
Vakhrusheve 83 48.10 N 38.46 E
Vaklan 272c 19.07 N 73.06 E
Vaksdal 26 60.29 N 5.44 E
Vala ≃ 80 56.59 N 51.16 E
Valaam 24 61.23 N 30.57 E
Valaam, ostrov I 26 61.22 N 30.57 E
Vålådalen 26 63.10 N 12.57 E
Valadeces 196 26.14 N 98.40 W
Valadim 154 12.22 S 36.10 E
Valais (Wallis) □[3] 58 46.10 N 7.30 E
Val-Alain 206 46.24 N 71.45 W
Valamaz 80 57.32 N 52.05 E
Valandovo 38 41.19 N 22.34 E
Valangin 58 47.01 N 6.54 E
Valap 272c 19.03 N 73.08 E
Valare, Baie c 174s 17.31 S 149.46 W
Valašské Klobouky 30 49.08 N 18.01 E
Valašské Meziříčí 30 49.28 N 17.58 E
Valatie 210 42.24 N 73.40 W
Vala Ull 272c 19.02 N 73.07 E
Val-Bélair 206 46.51 N 71.26 W
Valbella 58 46.45 N 9.33 E
Vålberg 26 59.24 N 13.12 E
Valbert 56 51.07 N 7.44 E
Valbo 40 60.40 N 17.04 E
Valbondione 64 46.02 N 10.00 E
Valbonnais 62 44.54 N 5.54 E
Valbrona 58 45.53 N 9.18 E
Valcanuta ◆[8] 267a 41.53 N 12.25 E
Vâlcea □[6] 38 45.19 N 24.00 E
Vălčedrăm 38 43.42 N 23.27 E
Valcheta 254 40.42 S 66.09 W
Valchetta ≃ 267a 41.58 N 12.30 E
Valchiusella 62 45.32 N 7.42 E
Valcivières 62 45.35 N 3.48 E
Valcourt 206 45.29 N 72.18 W
Valdagno 64 45.39 N 11.18 E
Valdahon 58 47.09 N 6.21 E
Valdai Hills
→ Valdajskaja vozvyšennost' ⋏[2] 76 57.00 N 33.30 E
Valdaj, Ross. 24 63.26 N 35.30 E
Valdaj, Ross. 76 57.59 N 33.14 E
Valdajskaja vozvyšennost' ⋏[2] 24 57.00 N 33.30 E
Valdarno V 66 43.35 N 11.30 E
Valdavia ≃ 34 42.24 N 4.16 W
Val-David 206 46.01 N 74.12 W
Valdebeba, Arroyo de ≃ 266a 41.23 N 2.10 E
Valdeblore 62 44.04 N 7.12 E
Val-de-Cães 250 1.23 S 48.29 W
Valdecañas, Embalse de ⊜[1] 34 39.45 N 5.30 W
Valdelândia 255 15.11 S 50.02 W
Val-de-Marne □[5] 261 48.47 N 2.29 E
Valdemārpils 76 57.22 N 22.35 E
Valdemarsvik 26 58.12 N 16.36 E
Valdepeñas 34 38.46 N 3.23 W
Valderaduey ≃ 34 41.31 N 5.42 W
Valderas 34 42.05 N 5.27 W
Valderice 70 38.03 N 12.38 E
Valderrama 116 11.00 N 122.08 E
Valderrobres 34 40.53 N 0.09 E
Valders 190 44.03 N 87.53 W
Valdés, Península ›[1] 254 42.30 S 64.00 W
Val-des-Bois 188 45.54 N 75.35 W
Valdese 192 35.44 N 81.33 W
Valdes Island I 224 49.04 N 123.38 W
Valdéz, Ec. 246 1.15 N 79.00 W
Valdez, Ak., U.S. 180 61.07 N 146.16 W
Valdieri 62 44.17 N 7.24 E
Val-d'Isère 62 45.27 N 6.59 E
Valdivia, Chile 254 39.48 S 73.14 W
Valdivia, Col. 246 7.11 N 75.27 W
Valdobbiadene 64 45.54 N 12.00 E
Valdoie 58 47.40 N 6.51 E
Val-d'Oise □[5] 50 49.10 N 2.10 E
Val-d'Or 190 48.07 N 77.47 W
Valdorf 52 52.09 N 8.51 E
Valdosta 192 30.49 N 83.16 W
Valdoviño 34 43.36 N 8.08 W
Valdres V 26 60.55 N 9.10 E
Valdurna (Durnholz) 64 46.44 N 11.26 E
Vale, Guernsey 43b 49.29 N 2.31 W
Vale, Or., U.S. 202 43.58 N 117.14 W
Valea lui Mihai 38 47.31 N 22.09 E
Vale de Lobos 266c 38.49 N 9.17 W
Valeene 218 38.26 N 86.24 W
Valeggio sul Mincio 64 45.21 N 10.44 E
Valehouse Reservoir ⊜[1] 262 53.29 N 1.57 W
Valemount 182 52.50 N 119.15 W
Valença, Bra. 255 13.22 S 39.05 W
Valença, Bra. 256 22.15 S 43.43 W
Valença, Port. 34 42.02 N 8.38 W
Valença do Piauí 250 6.24 S 41.45 W
Valençay 50 47.09 N 1.34 E
Valence
→ València, Esp. 34 39.28 N 0.22 W
Valence, Fr. 62 44.56 N 4.54 E
València, Esp. 34 39.28 N 0.22 W
Valencia, Hond. 236 14.47 N 85.18 W
Valencia, Pil. 116 7.57 N 125.03 E
Valencia, Ca., U.S. 228 34.26 N 118.36 W
Valencia, Pa., U.S. 214 40.40 N 79.59 W
Valencia, Ven. 246 10.11 N 68.00 W
València □[4] 34 39.30 N 0.45 W
València, Golf de c 34 39.50 N 0.30 E
Valencia, Lago de ⊜ 246 10.15 N 67.45 W
Valencia, Quebrada ≃ 286c 10.30 N 66.46 W
Valencia de Alcántata 34 39.25 N 7.14 W
Valencia de Don Juan 34 42.18 N 5.31 W
Valencia Island I 48 51.52 N 10.20 W
Valenciennes 50 50.21 N 3.32 E
Vălenii de Munte 38 45.12 N 26.03 E
Valensole 62 43.50 N 5.59 E
Valentano 66 42.34 N 11.49 E
Valente 250 11.34 S 39.27 W
Valentigney 58 47.28 N 6.50 E
Valentin 89 43.08 N 134.17 E
Valentín Alsina ◆[8] 288 34.40 S 58.25 W
Valentine, Ne., U.S. 198 42.52 N 100.33 W
Valentine, Tx., U.S. 196 30.34 N 104.29 W
Valentine Mountain ∧ 224 48.32 N 123.56 W
Valentinovka 265b 55.55 N 37.56 E
Valenton 261 48.45 N 2.28 E
Valenza 62 45.01 N 8.38 E
Valenzano 68 41.02 N 16.53 E
Valenzuela 269f 14.42 N 120.58 E
Våler 26 60.40 N 11.50 E
Valera 246 9.19 N 70.37 W
Valérien, Mont ∧[2] 261 48.53 N 2.13 E
Vale Royal □[8] 262 53.17 N 2.37 W
Valets, Lac ⊜ 190 48.32 N 76.30 W

Symbols in the index entries represent the broad categories identified in the key at the right. Symbols with superior numbers (⋏[1]) identify subcategories (see complete key on page *I · 1*).

Symbole im Register stellen die rechts im Schlüssel erklärten Kategorien dar. Symbole mit hochgestellten Ziffern (⋏[1]) bezeichnen Unterabteilungen einer Kategorie (vgl. vollständiger Schlüssel auf Seite *I · 1*).

Los símbolos incluídos en el texto del índice representan las grandes categorías identificadas con la clave a la derecha. Los símbolos con numeros en su parte superior (⋏[1]) identifican las subcategorías (véase la clave completa en la página *I · 1*).

Les symboles de l'index représentent les catégories indiquées dans la légende à droite. Les symboles suivis d'un indice (⋏[1]) représentent des sous-catégories (voir légende complète à la page *I · 1*).

Os símbolos incluídos no texto do índice representam as grandes categorias identificadas com a chave à direita. Os símbolos com números em sua parte superior (⋏[1]) identificam as subcategorias (veja-se a chave completa à página *I · 1*).

	English	Deutsch	Español	Français	Português
∧	Mountain	Berg	Montaña	Montagne	Montanha
⋏	Mountains	Gebirge	Montañas	Montagnes	Montanhas
)(	Pass	Paß	Paso	Col	Passo
V	Valley, Canyon	Tal, Cañon	Valle, Cañón	Vallée, Canyon	Vale, Canhão
≚	Plain	Ebene	Llano	Plaine	Planície
›	Cape	Kap	Cabo	Cap	Cabo
I	Island	Insel	Isla	Île	Ilha
II	Islands	Inseln	Islas	Îles	Ilhas
⊥	Other Topographic Features	Andere Topographische Objekte	Otros Elementos Topográficos	Autres données topographiques	Outros acidentes topográficos

ESPAÑOL · FRANÇAIS · PORTUGUÊS

Nombre / Nom / Nome	Página / Page	Lat. °′	Long. °′ W = Oeste / Ouest
Valette, La → Valletta	36	35.54 N	14.31 E
Valfabbrica	66	43.09 N	12.36 E
Valflaunès	62	43.48 N	3.52 E
Valfurva	64	46.27 N	10.25 E
Valfurva V	64	46.26 N	10.26 E
Valga	76	57.47 N	26.02 E
Valge ≏	76	59.35 N	25.42 E
Valgorge	62	44.35 N	4.07 E
Valgrisanche	62	45.38 N	7.04 E
Valguarnera Caropepe	70	37.30 N	14.23 E
Valhalla, S. Afr.	158	25.49 S	28.08 E
Valhalla, N.Y., U.S.	210	41.04 N	73.46 W
Valhalla, Lake ⊜	276	40.56 N	74.22 W
Valiente, Península ›[1]	236	9.05 N	81.51 W
Valiente, Punta ›	236	9.11 N	81.55 W
Valier, Il., U.S.	194	38.01 N	89.03 W
Valier, Mt., U.S.	202	48.18 N	112.14 W
Valier, Pa., U.S.	214	40.55 N	79.03 W
Valili ∧	175g	16.39 S	179.10 E
Valinda	280	34.02 N	117.56 W
Valinhos	256	22.57 S	47.01 W
Valjevo	38	44.16 N	19.53 E
Valka	76	57.46 N	26.00 E
Valkeakoski	26	61.16 N	24.02 E
Valkenburg	56	50.52 N	5.50 E
Valkenswaard	52	51.21 N	5.28 E
V'alki	82	55.39 N	38.05 E
Valkininkas	76	54.21 N	24.50 E
Valky	78	49.50 N	35.37 E
Valla	40	59.02 N	16.23 E
Valladares	196	26.53 N	100.37 W
Valladolid, Ec.	246	4.33 S	79.08 W
Valladolid, Esp.	34	41.39 N	4.43 W
Valladolid, Méx.	232	20.41 N	88.12 W
Valladolid □[4]	34	41.40 N	4.50 W
Vallage ✦[1]	58	48.24 N	5.00 E
Vallåkra	41	55.58 N	12.52 E
Vallarsa	64	45.47 N	11.07 E
Vallata	68	41.02 N	15.15 E
Vallauris	62	43.35 N	7.03 E
Vallco Fashion Park ✦[9]	282	37.19 N	122.01 W
Valldal	26	62.20 N	7.21 E
Valldoreix	266d	41.28 N	2.04 E
Valle, Esp.	34	43.14 N	4.18 W
Valle, Lat.	76	56.30 N	24.44 E
Valle □[5]	236	13.30 N	87.35 W
Valle, Arroyo ≏	226	37.39 N	121.54 W
Vallecas ✦[8]	266a	40.23 N	3.37 W
Valle Castellana	66	42.44 N	13.29 E
Vallecillo	196	26.40 N	99.58 W
Vallecito	226	38.07 N	120.27 W
Vallecitos	200	36.05 N	106.20 W
Vallecitos Creek ≏	282	37.36 N	121.53 W
Vallecorsa	66	41.27 N	13.24 E
Valle Crucis Abbey ⚘[1]	42	52.59 N	3.12 W
Valle d'Aosta □[4]	36	45.45 N	7.25 E
Valle de Bravo	234	19.11 N	100.08 W
Valle de Guadalupe	234	21.00 N	102.37 W
Valle de Guanape	246	9.54 N	65.41 W
Valle de Juárez	234	19.53 N	102.51 W
Valle de la Pascua	246	9.13 N	66.00 W
Valle del Cauca □[5]	246	3.45 N	76.30 W
Valle de Olivos	232	27.12 N	106.17 W
Valle de Santiago	234	20.23 N	101.12 W
Valle de Zaragoza	232	27.28 N	105.49 W
Valle di Cadore	64	46.24 N	12.20 E
Valle di Sotto	64	46.25 N	10.21 E
Valledolmo	70	37.45 N	13.49 E
Valledupar	246	10.29 N	73.15 W
Valle Edén	252	31.50 S	56.09 W
Vallefiorita	68	38.46 N	16.27 E
Vallegrande	248	18.29 S	64.06 W
Valle Hermoso, Arg.	252	31.07 S	64.29 W
Valle Hermoso, Méx.	196	25.39 N	97.52 W
Vallehermoso, Pil.	116	10.20 N	123.19 E
Vallejo	226	38.06 N	122.15 W
Valle Lomellina	62	45.09 N	8.40 E
Vallelunga Pratameno	70	37.41 N	13.50 E
Valle Mosso	62	45.38 N	8.09 E
Vällen ⊜	40	60.03 N	18.20 E
Vallenar	252	28.35 S	70.46 W
Vallendar	56	50.24 N	7.37 E
Vallensbæk	41	55.38 N	12.22 E
Vallentuna	40	59.32 N	18.05 E
Vallepietra	66	41.55 N	13.14 E
Valleraugue	62	44.05 N	3.38 E
Valle Redondo	204	32.31 N	116.46 W
Vallermosa	71	39.22 N	8.48 E
Vallerotonda	66	41.33 N	13.55 E
Valleroy	56	49.12 N	5.55 E
Valles → Ciudad de Valles	234	21.59 N	99.01 W
Valles Caldera ▲[6]	200	35.52 N	106.33 W
Vallet	32	47.10 N	1.16 W
Valletta	36	35.54 N	14.31 E
Valley, Al., U.S.	194	32.49 N	85.10 W
Valley, Ne., U.S.	198	41.18 N	96.20 W
Valley, Wa., U.S.	182	48.10 N	117.43 W
Valley ≏	184	51.21 N	99.55 W
Valley Bend	188	38.46 N	79.56 W
Valley Center, Ca., U.S.	228	33.13 N	117.02 W
Valley Center, Ks., U.S.	198	37.50 N	97.22 W
Valley City, N.D., U.S.	198	46.55 N	97.59 W
Valley City, Oh., U.S.	214	41.14 N	81.56 W
Valley Cottage	210	41.07 N	73.57 W
Valley Creek ≏, Pa., U.S.	285	39.58 N	75.40 W
Valley Creek ≏, Pa., U.S.	285	40.06 N	75.28 W
Valley Creek ≏, Tx., U.S.	196	31.43 N	100.02 W
Valleydale	280	34.06 N	117.56 W
Valley Falls, Ks., U.S.	198	39.20 N	95.27 W
Valley Falls, N.Y., U.S.	210	42.54 N	73.34 W
Valley Falls, R.I., U.S.	207	41.54 N	71.23 W
Valley Farms	200	32.59 N	111.26 W
Valleyfield	186	49.08 N	53.37 W
Valley Forge	208	40.05 N	75.28 W
Valley Forge Estates	285	40.05 N	75.26 W
Valley Forge National Historical Park ♠	208	40.06 N	75.27 W
Valley Grove	214	40.05 N	80.34 W
Valley Head, Al., U.S.	194	34.34 N	85.36 W
Valley Head, W.V., U.S.	188	38.32 N	80.02 W
Valley Home	226	37.50 N	120.55 W
Valley Mede	284b	39.17 N	76.50 W
Valley Mills	222	31.39 N	97.28 W
Valley of Desolation National Monument ♠	158	32.17 S	24.30 E
Valley of Fire State Park ♠	204	36.26 N	114.30 W
Valley of the Kings ⊥	140	25.45 N	32.37 E
Valley Park	219	38.32 N	90.29 W
Valley Plaza ✦[9]	280	34.11 N	118.24 W
Valley Springs, Ca., U.S.	226	38.12 N	120.50 W
Valley Springs, S.D., U.S.	198	43.34 N	96.28 W
Valley Station	194	38.06 N	85.52 W
Valley Stream	210	40.39 N	73.42 W
Valley Stream ≏	276	40.39 N	73.45 W
Valley Stream State Park ♠	276	40.41 N	73.42 W
Valleyview, Ab., Can.	182	55.04 N	117.17 W
Valley View, Il., U.S.	216	41.50 N	88.03 W
Valley View, Oh., U.S.	279a	41.23 N	81.37 W
Valley View, Pa., U.S.	210	40.38 N	76.32 W
Valley View, Tx., U.S.	196	33.29 N	97.10 W
Valley View Park	228	34.13 N	117.20 W
Vallgrund I	26	63.12 N	21.14 E
Valliant	196	34.00 N	95.05 W
Valli del Pasubio	64	45.41 N	11.15 E
Vallières	58	45.54 N	5.56 E
Vallimanca, Arroyo ≏	252	35.40 S	60.02 W
Vallio	64	45.38 N	10.23 E
Vallirana	266d	41.23 N	1.56 E
Vallø	41	55.24 N	12.15 E
Vallo della Lucania	68	40.14 N	15.17 E
Valloire	62	45.10 N	6.26 E
Vallombrosa	66	43.44 N	11.32 E
Vallonia	218	38.50 N	86.05 W
Vallon-Pont-d'Arc	62	44.24 N	4.24 E
Vallorbe	58	46.43 N	6.22 E
Vallorcine	58	46.02 N	6.56 E
Vallouise	62	44.51 N	6.29 E
Vallromanes	266d	41.32 N	2.18 E
Valls	34	41.17 N	1.15 E
Valluga ∧	58	47.09 N	10.12 E
Vallvidrera ✦[8]	266d	41.25 N	2.07 E
Vallvidrera, Riera de ≏	266d	41.25 N	2.01 E
Val-Marie	184	49.14 N	107.44 W
Valmaseda	34	43.12 N	3.12 W
Valmeyer	219	38.17 N	90.18 W
Valmiera	76	57.33 N	25.24 E
Valmondois	261	49.06 N	2.12 E
Valmont	50	49.44 N	0.31 E
Valmontone	66	41.46 N	12.57 E
Valmy	56	49.05 N	4.46 E
Valognes	32	49.31 N	1.28 W
Valois	210	42.32 N	76.53 W
Valois, Baie de ⊂	275a	45.26 N	73.47 W
Valok	78	45.47 N	34.57 E
Valona → Vlorë	38	40.27 N	19.30 E
Valongo	34	41.11 N	8.30 W
Valoria la Buena	34	41.48 N	4.32 W
Vālpārai	122	10.22 N	76.58 E
Valparaíso, Bra.	255	21.13 S	50.51 W
Valparaíso, Chile	252	33.02 S	71.38 W
Valparaíso, Méx.	234	22.46 N	103.34 W
Valparaiso, Fl., U.S.	194	30.29 N	86.29 W
Valparaiso, In., U.S.	216	41.28 N	87.03 W
Valparaiso, Ne., U.S.	198	41.04 N	96.49 W
Valparaíso □[4]	252	32.45 S	71.20 W
Valparaíso ≏	234	22.33 N	103.39 W
Valpelline V	62	45.50 N	7.25 E
Valpovo	38	45.39 N	18.26 E
Valprato Soana	62	45.31 N	7.33 E
Valréas	62	44.23 N	4.59 E
Valrico	220	27.57 N	82.16 W
Val Roveto V	66	41.52 N	13.30 E
Vals ≏	158	27.23 S	26.30 E
Vals, Tanjung ›	164	8.26 S	137.38 E
Val-Saint-Michel	206	46.52 N	71.27 W
Valsbaai ⊂	158	34.12 S	18.40 E
Valserine ≏	58	46.06 N	5.50 E
Valserrhein ≏	58	46.42 N	9.10 E
Valsertal V	58	46.37 N	9.10 E
Valsetz	202	44.50 N	123.39 W
Valsinni	68	40.10 N	16.26 E
Valsjöbyn	26	64.04 N	14.08 E
Valskog	40	59.27 N	15.57 E
Vals-les-Bains	62	44.40 N	4.22 E
Vals Platz	58	46.37 N	9.11 E
Vals-Près-le-Puy	62	45.01 N	3.52 E
Valstagna	64	45.51 N	11.39 E
Val-Suzon	58	47.25 N	4.54 E
Valtellina V	58	46.11 N	9.55 E
Valthermond	52	52.53 N	6.59 E
Valtice	61	48.44 N	16.45 E
Valtierrilla	234	20.32 N	101.08 W
Valtimo	26	63.40 N	28.48 E
Valtorta	58	45.59 N	9.32 E
Valtournanche	62	45.53 N	7.37 E
Valujec	76	52.46 N	33.23 E
Valujevka	80	46.44 N	43.43 E
Valujevo	265b	55.35 N	37.21 E
Valujki	78	50.13 N	38.08 E
Valvasone	64	45.59 N	12.52 E
Valverde	148	27.48 N	17.55 W
Valverde del Camino	34	37.34 N	6.45 W
Val Verde Park	228	34.27 N	118.40 W
Valyermo	228	34.26 N	117.50 W
Vamba ≏	152	7.27 S	14.17 E
Vamdrup	41	55.25 N	9.17 E
Våmhus	26	61.08 N	14.28 E
Vamizi, Ilha I	154	11.02 S	40.40 E
Vammala	26	61.20 N	22.54 E
Vamori Wash V	200	31.57 N	112.21 W
Van, Tür.	128	38.28 N	43.20 E
Van, Pa., U.S.	214	41.19 N	79.40 W
Van, Tx., U.S.	222	32.31 N	95.38 W
Van □[4]	128	39.00 N	43.45 E
Vanajavesi ⊜	26	61.09 N	24.15 E
Vanak ✦[8]	267d	35.45 N	51.23 E
Van Alstyne	196	33.25 N	96.34 W
Vanån ≏	40	60.31 N	14.14 E
Vananda	182	49.45 N	124.33 W
Vanapa ≏	164	9.05 S	147.10 E
Vanault-les-Dames	56	48.51 N	4.46 E
Vanavana I[1]	14	20.47 S	139.09 W
Vanavara	74	60.22 N	102.16 E
Van Buren, Ar., U.S.	194	35.26 N	94.20 W
Van Buren, In., U.S.	216	40.37 N	85.30 W
Van Buren, Me., U.S.	186	47.09 N	67.56 W
Van Buren, Mo., U.S.	194	36.59 N	91.00 W
Van Buren, Oh., U.S.	216	41.08 N	83.38 W
Van Buren □[6]	216	42.14 N	86.04 W
Van Buren Point	214	42.27 N	79.25 W
Vanč	85	38.23 N	71.26 E
Vanč ≏	85	38.18 N	71.19 E
Vance Air Force Base ■	196	36.21 N	97.55 W
Vanceboro	188	45.33 N	67.25 W
Vanceburg	218	38.35 N	83.19 W
Vancleave	194	30.32 N	88.41 W
Van Cortlandt Park ♠	276	40.54 N	73.53 W
Van Cortlandtville	210	41.19 N	73.54 W
Vancouver, B.C., Can.	224	49.16 N	123.07 W
Vancouver, Wa., U.S.	224	45.38 N	122.39 W
Vancouver, Cape ›, Austl.	162	35.01 S	118.12 E
Vancouver, Cape ›, Ak., U.S.	180	60.33 N	165.27 W
Vancouver, Mount ∧	180	60.20 N	139.40 W
Vancouver International Airport ⊠	224	48.39 N	123.26 W
Vancouver Island I	182	49.45 N	126.00 W
Vancouver Island Ranges ⋏	182	49.25 N	125.25 W
Vancouver Lake ⊜	224	45.41 N	122.44 W
Van Daalen ≏	164	3.05 S	138.09 E
Vandalia, Il., U.S.	219	38.57 N	89.05 W
Vandalia, Mi., U.S.	216	41.55 N	85.55 W
Vandalia, Mo., U.S.	219	39.18 N	91.29 W
Vandalia, Oh., U.S.	218	39.53 N	84.11 W
Vandalia Lake ⊜[1]	219	39.01 N	89.09 W
Vändam	84	40.57 N	47.57 E
Vandavāsi	122	12.30 N	79.37 E
Vandekerckhove Lake ⊜	184	57.02 N	101.25 W
Vandel	41	55.42 N	9.13 E
Vandenberg Air Force Base ■	204	34.43 N	120.33 W
Van den Bosch, Tanjung ›	164	4.06 S	132.55 E
Vandenesse	58	47.13 N	4.37 E
Vanderbijlpark	158	26.42 S	27.54 E
Vanderbilt, Mi., U.S.	190	45.08 N	84.39 W
Vanderbilt, Tx., U.S.	196	28.49 N	96.37 W
Vanderbilt Mansion National Historic Site ⊥	210	41.47 N	73.56 W
Vanderbilt Museum ⚘	276	40.54 N	73.22 W
Vandercook Lake	216	42.11 N	84.23 W
Vandergrift	214	40.36 N	79.33 W
Vanderhoof	182	54.01 N	124.01 W
Vanderlin Island I	164	15.44 S	137.02 E
Vandervoort	194	34.22 N	94.21 W
Van Diemen, Cape ›, Austl.	164	11.10 S	130.23 E
Van Diemen, Cape ›, Austl.	164	16.31 S	139.41 E
Van Diemen Gulf ⊂	164	11.50 S	132.00 E
Vandling	210	41.38 N	75.29 W
Vandoeuvre-lès-Nancy	58	48.39 N	6.11 E
Vandoies (Vintl)	64	46.49 N	11.43 E
Vändra	76	58.39 N	25.02 E
Van Duzen ≏	204	40.33 N	124.08 W
Vandúzi ≏	154	18.56 S	34.01 E
Vandykpark	273d	26.16 S	28.19 E
Vandžiogala	76	55.07 N	23.58 E
Vanegas	234	23.51 N	100.52 W
Vänern ⊜	26	58.55 N	13.30 E
Vänersborg	26	58.22 N	12.19 E
Van Etten	210	42.11 N	76.33 W
Vang, Mount ∧	9	73.56 S	68.39 W
Vanga	154	4.39 S	39.13 E
Vangaindrano	157b	23.21 S	47.36 E
Vängelälven ≏	26	63.41 N	16.25 E
Van Gölü ⊜	128	38.33 N	42.46 E
Vangsnes	26	61.11 N	6.38 E
Vanguard	184	49.55 N	107.20 W
Vangunu, Mount ∧	175e	8.42 S	158.00 E
Vangunu Island I	175e	8.38 S	158.00 E
Van Hook Arm ⊂	198	47.50 N	102.25 W
Van Horn	196	31.02 N	104.49 W
Van Horne	190	42.00 N	92.05 W
Van Hornesville	210	42.54 N	74.50 W
Vani	84	42.06 N	42.30 E
Vanier	212	45.26 N	75.40 W
Vanikolo I	14	11.39 S	166.54 E
Vaniköy ✦[8]	267b	41.04 N	29.04 E
Vanimo	164	2.40 S	141.20 E
Vanino	89	49.05 N	140.15 E
Vānīvilāsa Sāgara ⊜[1]	122	13.52 N	76.26 E
Vāniyambādi	122	12.41 N	78.37 E
Vânju Mare	38	44.26 N	22.52 E
Vankarem	180	67.51 N	175.50 W
Vankarem ≏	180	67.42 N	176.17 W
Vankarem, laguna ⊂	180	67.40 N	176.00 W
Vankaremskaja nizmennost' ◡	180	67.30 N	176.00 W
Van Kleef Aquarium ♠	271c	1.18 N	103.51 E
Vankleek Hill	206	45.31 N	74.39 W
Vanlay	50	48.02 N	4.01 E
Van Lear	192	37.46 N	82.45 W
Vanlue	216	40.58 N	83.28 W
Vanna I	24	70.09 N	19.51 E
Vännäs	26	63.55 N	19.45 E
Vanndale	194	35.18 N	90.46 W
Vanne ≏	50	48.12 N	3.16 E
Vanne et du Loing, Aqueduc de ≊[1]	261	48.36 N	2.26 E
Vannes	32	47.39 N	2.46 W
Vannes-sur-Cosson	50	47.43 N	2.13 E
Van Ninh	110	12.42 N	109.14 E
Van Norman Lakes ⊜[1]	228	34.18 N	118.28 W
Vannovka	85	42.32 N	70.21 E
Van Nuys ✦[8]	228	34.11 N	118.26 W
Van Nuys Airport ⊠	280	34.12 N	118.29 W
Van Nuys-Sherman Oaks War Memorial Park ♠	280	34.10 N	118.27 W
Vanoi ≏	64	46.06 N	11.45 E
Vanoise, Massif de la ⋏	62	45.20 N	6.40 E
Vanoise, Parc National de la ♠	62	45.20 N	6.45 E
Van Ormer	214	40.41 N	78.30 W
Van Phong, Vung ⊂	110	12.33 N	109.18 E
Vanport	214	40.41 N	80.20 W
Van Reenen	158	28.22 S	29.24 E
Van Reenen's Plaats	158	30.55 S	21.14 E
Van Rees, Pegunungan ⋏	164	2.35 S	138.15 E
Vanrhynsdorp	158	31.36 S	18.44 E
Vanrook	166	16.57 S	141.57 E
Vanryndam ⊜[1]	273d	26.09 S	28.21 E
Vansant	192	37.13 N	82.05 W
Van Saun Mill Brook ≏	276	40.55 N	74.03 W
Vansbro	40	60.31 N	14.13 E
Van Sciver Lake ⊜	285	40.09 N	74.48 W
Van Sickle Island I	282	38.04 N	121.53 W
Vansittart Island I	176	65.50 N	84.00 W
Vansjön ⊜	40	59.59 N	16.57 E
Vanskoje	76	58.56 N	36.52 E
Vanstadensrus	158	29.59 S	27.02 E
Vantaa (Vanda)	26	60.16 N	25.03 E
Vantaa ≏	26	60.13 N	24.59 E
Vanthali	120	21.29 N	70.20 E
Vanua Lava I	175f	13.48 S	167.28 E
Vanua Levu I	175g	16.33 S	179.15 E
Vanua Mbalavu Island I	175g	17.40 S	178.57 W
Vanuatu □[1], Oc.	14	16.00 S	167.00 E
Vanuatu □[1], Oc.	175f	16.00 S	167.00 E
Vanves	261	48.50 N	2.18 E
Van Vleck	222	29.01 N	95.53 W
Van Voorhis	279b	40.10 N	79.58 W
Van Wert	216	40.52 N	84.35 W
Van Wert □[6]	216	40.52 N	84.35 W
Vanwyksdorp	158	33.46 S	21.28 E
Vanwyksvlei	158	30.18 S	21.49 E
Vanzaghello	266b	45.35 N	8.47 E
Vanzago	266b	45.32 N	9.00 E
Van Zandt □[6]	222	32.35 N	95.50 W
Vanzylsrus	158	26.52 S	22.04 E
Vao	175f	22.39 S	167.32 E
Vapnyarka	78	48.32 N	28.44 E
Vaqueros Creek ≏	226	36.16 N	121.20 W
Var □[5]	62	43.30 N	6.20 E
Var ≏	62	43.39 N	7.12 E
Vara	26	58.16 N	12.57 E
Vara ≏	64	44.09 N	9.53 E
Varada ≏	122	14.55 N	75.40 E
Varadero	240p	23.09 N	81.16 W
Varades	32	47.23 N	1.02 W
Varages	62	43.36 N	5.58 E
Varaita ≏	62	44.49 N	7.36 E
Varaita, Valle V	62	44.35 N	7.10 E
Varakļāni	76	56.37 N	26.44 E
Varallo, It.	62	45.49 N	8.15 E
Varallo, It.	266b	45.40 N	8.38 E
Varāmīn	128	35.20 N	51.39 E
Vārānasi (Benares)	124	25.20 N	83.00 E
Varandej	24	68.48 N	58.00 E
Varangerfjorden ⊂[2]	24	70.00 N	30.00 E
Varangerhalvøya ›[1]	24	70.25 N	29.30 E
Varangéville	56	48.38 N	6.19 E
Varano, Lago Di ⊂	68	41.53 N	15.45 E
Varano de'Melegari	64	44.41 N	10.01 E
Varapodio	68	38.19 N	15.59 E
Varaždin	36	46.19 N	16.20 E
Varazze	62	44.22 N	8.34 E
Varberg	26	57.06 N	12.15 E
Varces	62	45.05 N	5.41 E
Varciche	84	42.08 N	42.43 E
Vardak □[4]	120	34.15 N	68.00 E
Vardaman	194	33.52 N	89.10 W
Vardar (Axiós) ≏	38	40.35 N	22.50 E
Varde	26	55.38 N	8.29 E
Vardenik	84	40.08 N	45.27 E
Vardenis	84	40.11 N	45.43 E
Vardenskij chrebet ⋏	84	39.58 N	45.25 E
Vardhoúsia Óri ⋏	38	38.44 N	22.07 E
Vardø	24	70.21 N	31.02 E
Vardūj ≏	123	37.01 N	70.47 E
Varedo	266b	45.36 N	9.09 E
Varegovo	80	57.47 N	39.17 E
Varel	52	53.22 N	8.10 E
Varela	252	34.07 S	66.27 W
Varėna	76	54.13 N	24.34 E
Varengeville-sur-Mer	50	49.55 N	0.59 E
Varenikovskaja	78	45.07 N	37.37 E
Varenna	58	46.01 N	9.17 E
Varenne ≏	50	49.53 N	1.08 E
Varennes	206	45.41 N	73.26 W
Varennes, Îles de II	275a	45.40 N	73.27 W
Varennes-en-Argonne	56	49.14 N	5.02 E
Varennes-Jarcy	261	48.41 N	2.34 E
Varennes-Saint-Sauveur	58	46.29 N	5.15 E
Varennes-sur-Allier	32	46.19 N	3.24 E
Varennes-sur-Amance	58	47.54 N	5.37 E
Varenovka	83	47.18 N	39.02 E
Vareš	38	44.09 N	18.19 E
Varese	62	45.48 N	8.48 E
Varese □[4]	62	45.48 N	8.40 E
Varese, Lago di ⊜	62	45.49 N	8.45 E
Varese Ligure	62	44.22 N	9.37 E
Varèze ≏	62	45.25 N	4.45 E
Varfolomejevka	80	50.01 N	48.12 E
Vârfurile	38	46.19 N	22.31 E
Vårgårda	26	58.02 N	12.48 E
Vargas □[5]	286c	10.34 N	66.52 W
Vargaši	86	55.23 N	65.48 E
Vargem	256	22.53 S	46.25 W
Vargem, Riacho da ≏	250	8.42 S	39.09 W
Vargem Alegre	256	22.30 S	43.55 W
Vargem do Laje	256	22.08 S	44.49 W
Vargem Grande	250	3.33 S	43.56 W
Vargem Grande ✦[8]	287a	22.59 S	43.29 W
Vargem Grande, Ribeirão da ≏	256	22.17 S	45.40 W
Vargem Grande do Sul	256	21.50 S	46.53 W
Vargem Grande Paulista	256	23.36 S	47.01 W
Varginha	256	21.33 S	45.26 W
Vargön	26	58.22 N	12.22 E
Varigotti	62	44.11 N	8.24 E
Väringen ⊜	40	59.26 N	15.23 E
Varirata National Park ♠	164	9.20 S	147.20 E
Varjão	255	17.03 S	49.37 W
Varkallai	122	8.40 N	76.50 E
Varkaus	26	62.19 N	27.55 E
Varkhān ≏	128	32.55 N	65.30 E
Varlamovo	86	54.38 N	60.40 E
Värmdölandet I	40	59.20 N	18.33 E
Värmeln ⊜	26	59.32 N	12.54 E
Värmland □[9]	26	59.48 N	13.03 E
Värmlands Län □[6]	26	59.45 N	13.15 E
Värmlandsnäs ›[1]	26	59.00 N	13.10 E
Varna, Blg.	38	43.13 N	27.55 E
Varna (Vahrn), It.	64	46.44 N	11.38 E
Varna, Ross.	86	53.24 N	60.58 E
Varna, N.Y., U.S.	210	42.27 N	76.26 W
Varna □[4]	38	43.24 N	27.33 E
Värnamo	26	57.11 N	14.02 E
Varnavino	80	57.24 N	45.04 E
Varnenski Zaliv ⊂	38	43.11 N	27.56 E
Varner-Hogg Plantation State Historic Park ♠	222	29.09 N	95.37 W
Varnhem	26	58.23 N	13.39 E
Varniai	76	55.45 N	22.22 E
Varnsdorf	54	50.52 N	14.40 E
Varnville	192	32.51 N	81.04 W
Värö	26	57.16 N	12.11 E
Városliget ♠	264c	47.31 N	19.06 E
Varpaisjärvi	26	63.22 N	27.45 E
Várpalota	30	47.12 N	18.09 E
Varpan ⊜	40	60.38 N	15.36 E
Varresbeck ✦[8]	263	51.15 N	7.06 E
Vars, On., Can.	212	45.21 N	75.21 W
Vars, Fr.	62	44.37 N	6.41 E
Vars, Col de)(	62	44.32 N	6.42 E
Vărșec	38	43.12 N	23.17 E
Varsi	62	44.40 N	9.51 E
Varsinais-Suomi ✦[1]	26	60.40 N	22.30 E
Värska	76	57.58 N	27.38 E
Varsovie → Warszawa	30	52.15 N	21.00 E
Varsseveld	52	51.57 N	6.28 E
Vårsta	40	59.10 N	17.48 E
Varto	130	39.10 N	41.28 E
Vârtopu	38	44.12 N	23.21 E
V'artsil'a	24	62.11 N	30.41 E
Varty Lake ⊜	212	44.23 N	76.48 W
Varuna ≏	124	25.21 N	83.03 E
Varva	78	50.31 N	32.41 E
Varvarin	38	43.43 N	21.19 E
Varvarivka, Ukr.	78	48.42 N	36.02 E
Varvarivka, Ukr.	78	49.33 N	35.12 E
Varvarivka, Ukr.	83	49.05 N	38.24 E
Varysburg	210	42.46 N	78.19 W
Várzea	256	22.30 S	44.46 W
Várzea, Rio da ≏	252	27.13 S	53.19 W
Várzea Alegre	250	6.47 S	39.17 W
Várzea da Palma	255	17.36 S	44.44 W
Varzea de Sintra	266c	38.49 N	9.24 W
Várzea Grande	248	15.39 S	56.08 W
Varzeão	252	24.34 S	49.26 W
Várzea Paulista	256	23.12 S	46.50 W
Varzi, It.	62	44.49 N	9.12 E
Varzi, Ross.	80	56.03 N	52.50 E
Varzino	24	68.19 N	38.19 E
Varzo	58	46.12 N	8.15 E
Varzob	85	38.46 N	68.49 E
Varzob ≏	85	38.30 N	68.45 E
Varzuga	24	67.24 N	36.32 E
Varzy	50	47.22 N	3.23 E
Varzyk	85	41.07 N	71.14 E
Vas	64	45.56 N	11.56 E
Vas □[6]	30	47.05 N	16.45 E
Vasa → Vaasa	26	63.06 N	21.36 E
Vasai (Bassein)	122	19.21 N	72.48 E
Vasalemma	76	59.14 N	24.18 E
Vašana ≏	82	54.36 N	37.10 E
Vasar	272c	19.11 N	73.09 E
Vascão, Ribeirão do ≏	34	37.31 N	7.31 W
Vașcău	38	46.28 N	22.28 E
Väse	40	59.23 N	13.57 E
Vāshi	272c	19.04 N	72.59 E
Vashkivtsi, Ukr.	78	48.24 N	27.08 E
Vashkivtsi, Ukr.	78	48.23 N	25.30 E
Vashon	224	47.26 N	122.27 W
Vashon Heights	224	47.30 N	122.28 W
Vashon Island I	224	47.24 N	122.27 W
Vasilevići	76	52.14 N	29.49 E
Vasilija, mys ›	180	64.34 N	178.33 E
Vasiliká	38	40.28 N	23.08 E
Vasiliški	76	53.47 N	24.51 E
Vasiljevka, Bela.	76	52.15 N	31.31 E
Vasiljevka, Ross.	89	46.52 N	134.03 E
Vasiljevo, Ross.	24	60.46 N	38.59 E
Vasiljevo, Ross.	80	55.52 N	48.42 E
Vasiljevskij, ostrov I	265a	59.56 N	30.15 E
Vasiljevskij Moch	76	57.01 N	35.55 E
Vasiljevskoje, Ross.	80	56.56 N	41.40 E
Vasiljevskoje, Ross.	80	56.31 N	45.49 E
Vasiljevskoje, Ross.	82	55.00 N	37.25 E
Vasiljevskoje, Ross.	82	56.20 N	37.54 E
Vasil'sursk	80	56.08 N	46.01 E
Vasis	86	57.22 N	74.44 E
Vaška ≏	24	64.53 N	45.47 E
Vaskelovo	76	60.22 N	30.22 E
Vaskess Bay ⊂	174o	1.51 N	157.31 W
Vaslui	38	46.38 N	27.44 E
Vaslui □[6]	38	46.30 N	27.45 E
Väsman ⊜	40	60.11 N	15.04 E
Vass	192	35.15 N	79.16 W
Vassako-Bolo, Réserve Naturelle Intégrale de la ✦[4]	146	8.10 N	19.45 E
Vassar	190	43.22 N	83.35 W
Vassdalseggi ∧	26	59.46 N	7.10 E
Vassieux-en-Vercors	62	44.53 N	5.22 E
Vassouras	256	22.25 S	43.40 W
Vassy	50	47.34 N	4.10 E
Västanfors	40	59.59 N	15.49 E
Västerås	40	59.37 N	16.33 E
Västeråsfjärden ⊂	40	59.34 N	16.34 E
Västerbotten □[9]	26	64.36 N	20.04 E
Västerbottens Län □[6]	24	64.00 N	17.30 E
Västerby	40	60.19 N	15.55 E
Västerdalälven ≏	40	60.33 N	15.08 E
Västerfärnebo	40	59.57 N	16.17 E
Västergötland □[9]	26	58.01 N	13.03 E
Västerhaninge	40	59.07 N	18.06 E
Västernorrlands Län □[6]	26	63.00 N	17.30 E
Västervik	26	57.45 N	16.38 E
Västmanland □[9]	40	59.38 N	15.15 E
Västmanlands Län □[6]	40	59.45 N	16.20 E
Vasto	66	42.07 N	14.42 E
Västra Laxsjön ⊜	40	58.54 N	14.38 E
Västra Ringsjön ⊜	41	55.53 N	13.28 E
Västra Torup	41	56.09 N	13.29 E
Vastseliina	76	57.44 N	27.17 E
Vas'ugan ≏	86	59.07 N	80.46 E
Vas'uganje ⩸	86	58.00 N	77.00 E
Vas'unino	82	55.15 N	37.01 E
Vašutino	265b	55.56 N	37.26 E
Vašutkiny ozera ⊜	24	68.06 N	61.18 E
Vasvár	30	47.03 N	16.49 E
Vasylivka	78	47.26 N	35.16 E
Vasyl'kiv	78	50.12 N	30.19 E
Vasyl'kivka	78	48.13 N	36.02 E
Vát	61	47.17 N	16.47 E
Vața de Jos	38	46.10 N	22.35 E
Vatan	32	47.05 N	1.48 E
Vaternish Point ›	46	57.36 N	6.38 W
Vatersay I	46	56.55 N	7.32 W
Vaterstetten	60	48.07 N	11.47 E
Vatican (Cité du) → Vatican City □[1]	267a	41.54 N	12.27 E
Vatican City (Città del Vaticano) □[1], Europe	66	41.54 N	12.27 E
Vatican City (Città del Vaticano) □[1], Europe	267a	41.54 N	12.27 E
Vaticano, Capo ›	68	38.38 N	15.50 E
Vatikanstadt → Vatican City □[1]	66	41.54 N	12.27 E
V'atka → Kirov	80	58.38 N	49.42 E
V'atka ≏	80	55.36 N	51.30 E
Vatlirchvin, gora ∧	180	68.08 N	179.52 W
Vatnajökull ⊓	24a	64.25 N	16.50 W
Vatneyri	24a	65.38 N	23.57 W
Vätö I	40	59.49 N	18.57 E
Vatoa Island I	175g	19.50 S	178.13 W
Vatoloha ∧	157b	17.52 S	47.48 E
Vatomandry	157b	19.20 S	48.59 E
Vatra Dornei	38	47.21 N	25.21 E
V'atskije Pol'any	80	56.14 N	51.04 E
V'atskij uval ⋏[2]	80	57.20 N	49.10 E
V'atskoje, Ross.	80	57.52 N	40.16 E
V'atskoje, Ross.	89	48.44 N	135.43 E
Vattalkundu	122	10.10 N	77.46 E
Vättern ⊜	26	58.24 N	14.36 E
Vättersee → Vättern ⊜	26	58.24 N	14.36 E
Vattholma	40	60.01 N	17.44 E
Vättis	58	46.55 N	9.27 E
Vatu Ira Channel ⊔	175g	17.17 S	178.31 E
Vatukoula	175g	17.31 S	177.51 E
Vatulele I	175g	18.33 S	177.37 E
Vatulino	82	55.39 N	36.09 E
Vatutine	78	49.02 N	31.04 E
Vaubecourt	56	48.56 N	5.07 E
Vauclaix	50	47.14 N	3.49 E
Vauclin, Montagne du ∧	240e	14.33 N	60.53 W
Vaucluse	274a	33.51 S	151.17 E
Vaucluse □[5]	62	44.00 N	5.10 E
Vaucluse, Fontaine de ⊥	62	43.55 N	5.08 E
Vaucluse, Plateau de ⋏[1]	62	44.00 N	5.22 E
Vaucouleurs	58	48.36 N	5.40 E
Vaucouleurs ≏	261	48.59 N	1.44 E
Vaud □[3]	58	46.40 N	6.30 E
Vaudherland	261	49.00 N	2.29 E
Vaudoy-en-Brie	50	48.41 N	3.05 E
Vaudreuil (Saint-Michel-de-Vaudreuil)	206	45.24 N	74.01 W
Vaudreuil □[6]	206	45.26 N	74.15 W
Vaudreuil, Baie de ⊂	275a	45.24 N	74.00 W
Vaufrey	58	47.21 N	6.55 E
Vaughan	212	43.47 N	79.36 W
Vaughn, N.M., U.S.	200	34.36 N	105.12 W
Vaughn, Wa., U.S.	224	47.21 N	122.46 W
Vaughnsville	216	40.53 N	84.09 W
Vaugneray	62	45.44 N	4.39 E
Vaugrigneuse	261	48.36 N	2.07 E
Vauhallan	261	48.44 N	2.12 E
Vaujours	261	48.56 N	2.35 E
Vaulovo	82	56.09 N	39.17 E
Vaulruz	58	46.37 N	6.59 E
Vaulx-en-Velin	62	45.47 N	4.56 E
Vaupés □[8]	246	0.45 N	70.30 W
Vaupés (Uaupés) ≏	246	0.02 N	67.16 W
Vauréal	261	49.02 N	2.02 E
Vauréal, Chute ∟	186	49.34 N	62.42 W
Vauvenargues	62	43.33 N	5.36 E
Vauvert	62	43.42 N	4.17 E
Vauvillers	58	47.55 N	6.06 E
Vauvise ≏	50	47.18 N	2.57 E
Vaux ≏	50	49.33 N	4.17 E
Vaux, Ru des ≏	261	48.42 N	2.00 E
Vauxhall	182	50.04 N	112.07 W
Vaux-le-Compte, Château de ⊥	50	48.36 N	2.43 E
Vaux-le-Pénil	261	48.32 N	2.41 E
Vaux-lès-Saint-Claude	58	46.22 N	5.44 E
Vaux-le-Vicomte, Château de ⊥	261	48.36 N	2.43 E
Vaux-Sous-Aubigny	58	47.39 N	5.17 E
Vaux-sur-Seine	261	49.00 N	1.58 E
Vavatenina	157b	17.28 S	49.12 E
Vava'u I	14	18.36 S	174.00 W
Vava'u Group II	14	18.40 S	174.00 W
Vavincourt	56	48.49 N	5.13 E
Vavoua	150	7.23 N	6.29 W
Vavož	80	56.47 N	51.55 E
Vavuniya	122	8.45 N	80.30 E
Vaxholm	40	59.24 N	18.20 E
Växjö	26	56.52 N	14.49 E
V'aža	78	49.16 N	41.01 E
Vaza-barris ≏	250	11.10 S	37.10 W
Vazante	255	18.00 S	46.54 W
Vazante Grande ≏	248	19.21 S	56.53 W
V'azemskij	89	47.32 N	134.48 E
Važgort	24	64.01 N	47.02 E
V'az'ma	76	55.13 N	34.18 E
V'az'ma ≏, Ross.	76	55.28 N	33.34 E
V'az'ma ≏, Ross.	82	56.29 N	35.49 E
V'azniki	80	56.15 N	42.10 E
Vazobe ∧	157b	18.25 S	47.18 E
V'azovaja	80	57.39 N	45.44 E
V'azovka, Ross.	80	48.19 N	45.36 E
V'azovka, Ross.	80	51.48 N	45.47 E
V'azovka, Ross.	80	52.52 N	48.24 E
V'azovka, Ross.	80	50.52 N	43.57 E
V'azovoje, Ross.	78	51.54 N	36.59 E
V'azovoje, Ross.	78	51.09 N	37.01 E
Vazuza ≏	76	56.10 N	34.35 E
Vazuzskoje vodochranilišče ⊜[1]	76	56.00 N	34.28 E
V'azyn'	76	54.25 N	27.10 E
Vazzola	64	45.50 N	12.23 E
Veachland	218	38.12 N	85.11 W
Veado, Ilha do I	287a	22.57 S	43.06 W
Veazie	188	44.50 N	68.42 W
Veberöd	41	55.38 N	13.29 E
Veblen	198	45.51 N	97.17 W
Vecchiano	66	43.47 N	10.23 E
Vechelde	52	52.16 N	10.22 E
Vecht (Vechte) ≏	52	52.35 N	6.05 E
Vechta	52	52.43 N	8.16 E
Vechte (Vecht) ≏	52	52.35 N	6.05 E
Veckerhagen	52	51.30 N	9.35 E
Vecpiebalga	76	57.08 N	25.50 E
Vecsés	30	47.25 N	19.16 E
Vecumnieki	76	56.36 N	24.31 E
Vedado ✦[8]	286b	23.08 N	82.24 W
Vedano al Lambro	266b	45.37 N	9.16 E
Vedano Olona	62	45.46 N	8.53 E
Vedāranniyam	122	10.22 N	79.51 E
Vedbæk	41	55.51 N	12.34 E
Vedder Crossing	224	49.06 N	121.57 W
Veddige	26	57.16 N	12.19 E
Vedea	38	44.47 N	24.37 E
Vedea ≏	38	43.43 N	25.32 E
Vedelago	64	45.41 N	12.01 E
Vedène	62	43.59 N	4.54 E
Vedeno	84	42.58 N	46.05 E
Vedeseta	58	45.53 N	9.32 E
Vedevåg	40	59.32 N	15.17 E
Vedi	84	39.56 N	44.42 E
Vedia	252	34.30 S	61.32 W
Vednoje	76	57.08 N	36.10 E
Vedomša	82	56.44 N	38.21 E
Vedrovo	80	57.33 N	42.52 E
Veedersburg	194	40.06 N	87.15 W
Veen	263	51.37 N	6.27 E
Veendam	52	53.06 N	6.58 E
Veenendaal	52	52.02 N	5.34 E
Veenhuizen	52	53.03 N	6.24 E
Veenoord	52	52.43 N	6.50 E
Veere	52	51.34 N	3.40 E
Veert	52	51.33 N	6.17 E
Vefsna ≏	24	65.50 N	13.12 E
Vega	196	35.15 N	102.26 W
Vega I	24	65.39 N	11.50 E
Vega, Arroyo de la ≏	266a	40.31 N	3.33 W
Vega Alta	240m	18.25 N	66.20 W
Vega Baja	240m	18.27 N	66.23 W
Vega Point ›	181a	51.49 N	177.16 E
Vegår ⊜	26	58.48 N	8.47 E
Vegesack ✦[8]	52	53.10 N	8.37 E
Veghel	52	51.37 N	5.33 E
Veglie	68	40.20 N	17.58 E
Vegreville	182	53.30 N	112.03 W
Veguita	200	34.30 N	106.46 W
Vehār Lake ⊜	272c	19.09 N	72.55 E
Vehlefanz	264a	52.43 N	13.06 E
Vehnemoor ✦[3]	52	53.05 N	8.00 E
Veigné	50	47.17 N	0.44 E
Veil, Loch ⊜	46	56.20 N	4.25 W
Veilsdorf	54	50.24 N	10.48 E
Veinte de Noviembre	196	25.47 N	97.33 W
Veinticinco de Agosto	258	34.24 S	56.25 W
Veinticinco de Mayo, Arg.	252	35.26 S	60.10 W
Veinticinco de Mayo, Arg.	252	34.35 S	68.33 W
Veinticinco de Mayo, Ur.	258	34.12 S	56.22 W
Veintiocho de Mayo	246	3.50 S	78.52 W
Veintiocho de Noviembre	254	51.39 S	72.18 W
Veintisiete de Abril	236	10.15 N	85.45 W
Veio ⊥	66	42.02 N	12.24 E
Veiros	250	2.05 S	52.10 W
Veisiejai	76	54.06 N	23.42 E
Veitsbronn	56	49.31 N	10.53 E
Veitsch	61	47.35 N	15.30 E
Veitschalpe ⋏	61	47.39 N	15.30 E
Veitshöchheim	56	49.50 N	9.52 E
Vejbystrand	41	56.19 N	12.45 E
Vejdelevka	78	50.09 N	38.27 E
Vejen	41	55.29 N	9.09 E
Vejer de la Frontera	34	36.15 N	5.58 W
Vejlby	41	56.12 N	10.13 E
Vejle	41	55.42 N	9.32 E
Vejle □[6]	41	55.45 N	9.30 E
Vejle Fjord ⊂	41	55.40 N	9.50 E
Vejprty	54	50.30 N	13.02 E
Vejrhøj ∧[2]	41	55.47 N	11.24 E
Vejrø I	41	55.02 N	11.22 E
Vekšor	24	60.33 N	49.26 E
Vel'a ≏	82	56.31 N	37.41 E
Vela Luka	36	42.58 N	16.43 E
Velapāda	272c	18.59 N	73.04 E
Velardeña	232	25.04 N	103.44 W
Velas	148a	38.41 N	28.13 W
Velas, Cabo ›	236	10.22 N	85.53 W
Velázquez	252	34.02 S	54.17 W
Velbert	56	51.20 N	7.02 E
Velburg	60	49.14 N	11.41 E
Velddrif	158	32.47 S	18.11 E
Velden, Dtsch.	60	48.19 N	12.16 E
Velden, Dtsch.	60	49.37 N	11.31 E
Velden, Öst.	61	46.37 N	14.03 E
Veldhoven	52	51.24 N	5.24 E
Velebit ⋏	36	44.38 N	15.03 E
Velebitski Kanal ⊔	36	45.00 N	14.50 E
Velegož	82	54.42 N	37.16 E
Veleka ≏	38	42.04 N	27.58 E
Velemín	54	50.33 N	13.59 E
Velen	52	51.53 N	6.59 E
Velencei-tó ⊜	30	47.12 N	18.35 E
Velesa ≏	76	56.03 N	31.58 E
Velešín	61	48.50 N	14.28 E
Velestínon	38	39.23 N	22.45 E
Velet'ma	80	55.20 N	42.25 E
Velevščina	76	54.44 N	28.35 E
Vélez	246	6.01 N	73.41 W
Velez de la Gomera, Peñón de I	34	35.11 N	4.21 W
Vélez-Málaga	34	36.47 N	4.06 W
Vélez Rubio	34	37.39 N	2.04 W
Velgast	54	54.16 N	12.48 E
Vel'gija	76	58.23 N	33.59 E
Velhas, Canal do ≊	287a	22.42 S	43.22 W
Velhas, Rio das ≏	255	17.13 S	44.49 W
Veličkovo	82	54.59 N	36.46 E
Velika Gorica	36	45.43 N	16.05 E
Velikaja, Ross.	24	59.13 N	49.04 E
Velikaja, Ross.	180	64.04 N	176.12 E
Velikaja ≏, Ross.	74	64.40 N	176.20 E
Velikaja ≏, Ross.	76	57.48 N	28.20 E
Velikaja Kema	89	45.30 N	137.12 E
Velika Kapela ⋏	36	45.15 N	15.00 E
Velika Morava ≏	38	44.43 N	21.03 E
Velika Plana	38	44.20 N	21.04 E
Velike Lašče	36	45.50 N	14.38 E
Veliki Bečkerek → Zrenjanin	38	45.23 N	20.24 E
Velikij Bor	78	52.02 N	29.56 E
Velikij Dvor	82	56.46 N	37.25 E
Velikije Luki	76	56.20 N	30.32 E
Velikij Ust'ug	24	60.48 N	46.18 E
Veliki kanal ≊	38	45.45 N	18.50 E
Veliki Stol (Hochstuhl) ∧	61	46.26 N	14.10 E
Veliki Vitorog ∧	36	44.07 N	17.03 E
Velikoarch-angel'skoje	78	50.51 N	40.46 E
Velikodvorskaja	76	60.18 N	41.58 E
Velikodvorskij	80	55.15 N	40.41 E
Veliko Gradište	38	44.45 N	21.32 E
Velikoje, Ross.	76	59.32 N	36.59 E
Velikoje, Ross.	80	57.21 N	39.47 E
Velikoje, ozero ⊜, Ross.	76	57.02 N	36.34 E
Velikoje, ozero ⊜, Ross.	80	55.13 N	40.10 E
Velikonda Hills ⋏[2]	122	14.45 N	79.10 E

Symbol	English	Deutsch	Español	Français	Português
≏	River	Fluß	Río	Rivière	Rio
≊	Canal	Kanal	Canal	Canal	Canal
∟	Waterfall, Rapids	Wasserfall, Stromschnellen	Cascada, Rápidos	Chute d'eau, Rapides	Cascata, Rápidos
⊔	Strait	Meeresstraße	Estrecho	Détroit	Estreito
⊂	Bay, Gulf	Bucht, Golf	Bahía, Golfo	Baie, Golfe	Baía, Golfo
⊜	Lake, Lakes	See, Seen	Lago, Lagos	Lac, Lacs	Lago, Lagos
⩸	Swamp	Sumpf	Pantano	Marais	Pântano
⊓	Ice Features, Glacier	Eis- und Gletscherformen	Accidentes Glaciales	Formes glaciaires	Acidentes glaciares
	Other Hydrographic Features	Andere Hydrographische Objekte	Otros Elementos Hidrográficos	Autres données hydrographiques	Outros acidentes hidrográficos
✣	Submarine Features	Untermeerische Objekte	Accidentes Submarinos	Formes de relief sous-marin	Acidentes submarinos
□	Political Unit	Politische Einheit	Unidad Politica	Entité politique	Unidade política
⚘	Cultural Institution	Kulturelle Institution	Institución Cultural	Institution culturelle	Institução cultural
⊥	Historical Site	Historische Stätte	Sitio Histórico	Site historique	Sitio histórico
♠	Recreational Site	Erholungs- und Ferienort	Sitio de Recreo	Centre de loisirs	Area de Lazer
⊠	Airport	Flughafen	Aeropuerto	Aéroport	Aeroporto
■	Military Installation	Militäranlage	Instalación Militar	Installation militaire	Instalação militar
✦	Miscellaneous	Verschiedenes	Misceláneo	Divers	Diversos

ENGLISH | DEUTSCH

Name (Name)	Page (Seite)	Lat.°′ (Breite°′)	Long.°′ (Länge°′ E = Ost)
Velikookt'abr'skij	76	57.26 N	33.49 E
Velikorusskoje	86	54.39 N	74.38 E
Veliko Tărnovo	38	43.04 N	25.39 E
Velikovisočnoje	24	67.16 N	52.01 E
Velikovo	76	59.18 N	42.08 E
Velilla de San Antonio	266a	40.22 N	3.29 W
Veli Lošinj	36	44.31 N	14.30 E
Vélingara, Sén.	150	15.00 N	14.40 W
Vélingara, Sén.	150	13.09 N	14.07 W
Velingrad	38	42.04 N	24.00 E
Velino ≐	66	42.33 N	12.43 E
Velino, Monte ∧	66	42.09 N	13.23 E
Veliž	76	55.38 N	31.12 E
Veližany	86	57.34 N	65.49 E
Vélizy-Villacoublay	261	48.47 N	2.10 E
Veljaminovo, Ross.	82	55.12 N	37.52 E
Veljaminovo, Ross.	82	55.53 N	36.52 E
Velká Bíteš	30	49.17 N	16.13 E
Vel'ké Kapušany	30	48.33 N	22.04 E
Velké Meziříčí	30	49.21 N	16.00 E
Velké Němčie	61	48.59 N	16.40 E
Velké Pavlovice	61	48.54 N	16.49 E
Velký Bor	60	49.22 N	13.42 E
Velký Šenov	54	51.00 N	14.25 E
Vellach ≐	61	46.35 N	14.29 E
Vella Gulf ᴗ	175e	8.00 S	156.50 E
Vella Lavella I	175e	7.45 S	156.40 E
Vellano	66	43.57 N	10.43 E
Vellār ≐	122	11.29 N	79.46 E
Vellberg	56	49.05 N	9.53 E
Vellechevreux-et-Courbenans	58	47.33 N	6.32 E
Velletri	66	41.41 N	12.47 E
Vellinge	41	55.28 N	13.01 E
Vellmar	56	51.21 N	9.28 E
Vellore, On., Can.	275b	43.50 N	79.34 W
Vellore, India	122	12.56 N	79.08 E
Velm	264b	48.03 N	16.27 E
Velma	196	34.27 N	97.40 W
Vel'maj ≐	180	67.26 N	175.28 W
Velmede	56	51.21 N	8.22 E
Velo d'Astico	64	45.43 N	11.23 E
Velp	52	52.00 N	5.59 E
Velp ≐	56	50.58 N	5.05 E
Velpke	54	52.24 N	10.56 E
Velsen	52	52.27 N	4.39 E
Vel'sk	24	61.05 N	42.05 E
Vel't	24	68.03 N	49.55 E
Velten	54	52.41 N	13.10 E
Veltheim	52	52.11 N	8.58 E
Veltrusy	54	50.14 N	14.18 E
Veluwe ◆[1]	52	52.12 N	5.45 E
Veluwemeer ◎	52	52.22 N	5.38 E
Velva, It.	62	44.16 N	9.33 E
Velva, N.D., U.S.	198	48.03 N	100.55 W
Velvary	54	50.15 N	14.15 E
Velyka Bahachka	78	49.47 N	33.43 E
Velyka Bilozerka	78	47.16 N	34.42 E
Velyka Blahovishchenka	78	46.51 N	34.03 E
Velyka Chernihivka	83	48.57 N	39.25 E
Velyka Danylivka	78	50.04 N	36.19 E
Velyka Dymerka	78	50.36 N	30.55 E
Velyka Hlusha	78	51.49 N	25.02 E
Velyka Korenykha	78	46.57 N	31.54 E
Velyka Koshnytsya	78	48.09 N	28.27 E
Velyka Lepetykha	78	47.11 N	33.56 E
Velyka Mykhaylivka	78	47.04 N	29.52 E
Velyka Novosilka	78	47.50 N	36.50 E
Velyka Oleksandrivka	78	47.20 N	33.18 E
Velyka Rublivka	78	49.53 N	34.49 E
Velyka Vradyyivka	78	47.52 N	30.35 E
Velyki Birky	78	49.32 N	25.45 E
Velyki Dederkaly	78	50.02 N	26.07 E
Velyki Kopani	78	46.29 N	32.59 E
Velyki Korovyntsi	78	49.59 N	28.17 E
Velyki Krynky	78	49.27 N	33.29 E
Velyki Luchky	78	48.26 N	22.35 E
Velyki Mosty	78	50.14 N	24.06 E
Velyki Sorochyntsi	78	50.03 N	33.56 E
Velykoanadol's'kyy lis ♦	83	47.42 N	37.23 E
Velykodolyns'ke	78	46.21 N	30.35 E
Velykoplos'ke	78	47.01 N	29.40 E
Velykots'k	83	49.21 N	40.02 E
Velykyy Bereznyy	78	48.53 N	22.27 E
Velykyy Burluk	78	50.05 N	37.24 E
Velykyy Bychkiv	78	47.58 N	24.03 E
Velykyy Hlubochyk	78	49.37 N	25.32 E
Velykyy Khutir	78	49.52 N	32.06 E
Velykyy Kuyal'nyk ≐	78	46.46 N	30.36 E
Velykyy Loh	83	48.15 N	39.33 E
Velykyy Sukhodil	83	48.25 N	39.53 E
Velykyy Vys' ≐	78	48.45 N	30.54 E
Velykyy Zhvanchyk	78	48.46 N	26.59 E
Velymche	78	51.36 N	24.44 E
Vémars	261	49.04 N	2.34 E
Vemdalen	26	62.27 N	13.52 E
Vemmenæs	41	54.59 N	10.40 E
Ven I	41	55.54 N	12.41 E
Venachar, Loch ◎	46	56.13 N	4.19 W
Venaco	36	42.14 N	9.10 E
Venadillo	246	4.43 N	74.55 W
Venado	234	22.56 N	101.05 W
Venado, Isla I	241r	10.00 N	62.25 W
Venado, Isla del I	236	11.57 N	83.44 W
Venado Tuerto	252	33.45 S	61.58 W
Venafiorita, Aeroporto di ⊠	71	40.53 N	9.30 E
Venafro	66	41.29 N	14.02 E
Venâncio Aires	252	29.36 S	52.11 W
Venango	214	41.46 N	80.07 W
Venango ▫[6]	214	41.24 N	79.50 W
Venanson	62	44.03 N	7.15 E
Venant	261	48.30 N	2.06 E
Venarey-les-Laumes	58	47.32 N	4.26 E
Venaria	62	45.08 N	7.38 E
Venasca	62	44.33 N	7.24 E
Venasque	62	43.59 N	5.09 E
Vence	62	43.43 N	7.07 E
Venceslau Brás	256	22.31 S	45.21 W
Venceslau Braz	255	23.51 S	49.48 W
Vencimont	56	50.02 N	4.55 E
Venda ▫[9]	156	23.00 S	30.30 E
Venda Nova	34	41.40 N	7.58 W
Vendargues	62	43.39 N	3.58 E
Vendas Novas	34	38.41 N	8.28 W
Vendée ▫[5]	32	46.40 N	1.20 W
Vendéen, Bocage ◆[1]	32	46.40 N	1.30 W
Vendel	40	60.10 N	17.36 E
Vendelsö	40	59.12 N	18.12 E
Vendeuvre-sur-Barse	58	48.14 N	4.28 E
Vendin-lès-Béthune	50	50.32 N	2.37 E
Vendin-le-Vieil	50	50.28 N	2.52 E
Vendôme	50	47.48 N	1.04 E
Vendsyssel ◆[1]	26	57.20 N	10.00 E
Vendychany	78	48.37 N	27.48 E
Venecia, C.R.	236	10.22 N	84.17 W
Venecia → Venezia, It.	64	45.27 N	12.21 E
Venedig → Venezia	64	45.27 N	12.21 E
Venedocia	216	40.44 N	84.25 W
Venedy	219	38.24 N	89.39 W
Veneta, Laguna c	64	45.25 N	12.19 E
Venetia	214	40.15 N	80.03 W
Venetian Village	216	42.24 N	88.02 W
Venetie	180	67.01 N	146.25 W
Veneto ▫[4]	64	45.30 N	11.45 E
Venev	82	54.21 N	38.16 E
Venezia (Venice)	64	45.27 N	12.21 E
Venezia ▫[4]	64	45.35 N	12.34 E
Venezuela ▫[1], S.A.	242	8.00 N	66.00 W
Venezuela ▫[1], S.A.	246	8.00 N	66.00 W
Venezuela, Golfo de c	246	11.30 N	71.00 W
Venezuelan Basin ◆[1]	16	15.00 N	68.00 W
Veng	41	56.07 N	9.53 E
Vengerovo	86	55.41 N	76.45 E
Vengurla	122	15.52 N	73.38 E
Veniaminof, Mount ∧	180	56.13 N	159.18 W
Venice → Venezia, It.	64	45.27 N	12.21 E
Venice, Fl., U.S.	220	27.05 N	82.27 W
Venice, Il., U.S.	219	38.40 N	90.10 W
Venice, La., U.S.	194	29.16 N	89.21 W
Venice, Oh., U.S.	214	41.27 N	82.46 W
Venice, Pa., U.S.	279b	40.19 N	80.14 W
Venice ◆[8]	228	34.00 N	118.29 W
Venice, Gulf of c	64	45.15 N	13.00 E
Venice Gardens	220	27.04 N	82.26 W
Venise → Venezia	64	45.27 N	12.21 E
Vénissieux	62	45.41 N	4.53 E
Venjan	26	60.57 N	13.55 E
Venjansjön ◎	26	60.54 N	14.00 E
Venkatagiri	122	13.58 N	79.35 E
Venlo	52	51.24 N	6.10 E
Vennesla	26	58.17 N	7.59 E
Vennhausen ◆[8]	263	51.13 N	6.51 E
Venosa	68	40.57 N	15.49 E
Vénosc	62	44.59 N	6.07 E
Venosta, Val V	64	46.40 N	10.35 E
Venoste, Alpi (Ötztaler Alpen) ⋀	64	46.45 N	10.55 E
Venray	52	51.32 N	5.59 E
Vent	64	46.52 N	10.56 E
Vent, Îles du → Windward Islands II	238	13.00 N	61.00 W
Venta ≐	76	57.24 N	21.33 E
Ventanas	246	1.23 S	79.25 W
Ventasso, Monte ∧	64	44.23 N	10.17 E
Ventersburg	158	28.09 S	27.08 E
Ventersdorp	158	26.17 S	26.48 E
Venterspos	273d	26.18 S	27.39 E
Venterstad	158	30.47 S	25.48 E
Venticano	68	41.05 N	14.50 E
Ventimiglia	62	43.47 N	7.36 E
Ventimiglia di Sicilia	70	37.55 N	13.34 E
Ventnor	42	50.36 N	1.11 W
Ventnor City	208	39.20 N	74.28 W
Ventotene	66	40.48 N	13.26 E
Ventotene, Isola I	66	40.47 N	13.25 E
Ventoux, Mont ∧	62	44.10 N	5.17 E
Ventry	48	52.08 N	10.22 W
Ventspils	76	57.24 N	21.36 E
Ventuari ≐	246	3.58 N	67.02 W
Ventura (San Buenaventura)	228	34.16 N	119.17 W
Ventura ▫[6]	228	34.30 N	119.00 W
Ventura ≐	228	34.16 N	119.18 W
Venturina	66	43.02 N	10.36 E
Venus, Fl., U.S.	220	27.04 N	81.21 W
Venus, Pa., U.S.	214	41.22 N	79.29 W
Venus, Tx., U.S.	222	32.26 N	97.06 W
Vénus, Pointe >	174s	17.29 S	149.29 W
Venus Bay c	169	38.40 S	145.43 E
Venustiano Carranza, Méx.	232	16.21 N	92.33 W
Venustiano Carranza, Méx.	234	20.31 N	97.38 W
Venustiano Carranza, Méx.	234	19.44 N	103.47 W
Venustiano Carranza, Bahía c	232	19.20 N	87.35 W
Venustiano Carranza, Presa ◎[1]	232	27.30 N	100.40 W
Venzone	64	46.20 N	13.09 E
Véore ≐	62	44.49 N	4.49 E
Vép	61	47.14 N	16.44 E
Vepryk	78	50.23 N	34.11 E
Vepsovskaja vozvyšennost' ⋀[1]	76	60.20 N	35.15 E
Ver ≐	42	51.42 N	0.20 W
Vera, Arg.	252	29.28 S	60.13 W
Vera, Esp.	34	37.15 N	1.52 W
Vera, Il., U.S.	219	39.02 N	89.07 W
Veracruz, Méx.	200	32.25 N	115.05 W
Vera Cruz, Pa., U.S.	208	40.30 N	75.30 W
Veracruz ▫[3]	234	19.20 N	96.40 W
Veracruz [Llave]	234	19.12 N	96.08 W
Veraguas ▫[4]	236	8.30 N	81.00 W
Verano Brianza	266b	45.41 N	9.14 E
Veranópolis	252	28.57 S	51.33 W
Verāval	120	20.54 N	70.22 E
Verba	78	50.17 N	25.37 E
Verbania	58	45.56 N	8.33 E
Verbank	210	41.44 N	73.43 W
Verbeek, Pegunungan ⋀	112	2.35 S	121.25 E
Verberg ◆[8]	263	51.22 N	6.36 E
Verberie	50	49.19 N	2.44 E
Verbicaro	68	39.45 N	15.55 E
Verbier	58	46.06 N	7.13 E
Verbilki	82	56.32 N	37.36 E
Verbinskij	83	47.53 N	40.02 E
Verblyuzhka	78	48.23 N	32.54 E
Verbovskij	80	55.32 N	42.00 E
Vercelli	62	45.19 N	8.25 E
Vercelli ▫[4]	62	45.37 N	8.10 E
Vercel-Villedieu-le-Camp	58	47.11 N	6.24 E
Verch'aja Irmen'	86	54.35 N	82.14 E
Verchazovka	80	50.56 N	48.46 E
Vercheje Talyzino	80	55.06 N	45.49 E
Verchères	206	45.47 N	73.21 W
Verchères ▫[6]	206	45.45 N	73.20 W
Verchn'aja Amga	74	59.30 N	126.08 E
Verchn'aja Angara ≐	88	55.42 N	109.54 E
Verchn'aja Balkarija	84	43.06 N	43.24 E
Verchn'aja Buzinovka	80	49.04 N	43.12 E
Verchn'aja Čebula	86	56.02 N	87.36 E
Verchn'aja Chava	78	51.50 N	39.56 E
Verchn'aja Chila	88	52.06 N	115.54 E
Verchn'aja Dobrinka	80	50.46 N	45.03 E
Verchn'aja Gniluša	78	50.16 N	40.23 E
Verchn'aja Grajvoronka	78	51.41 N	37.46 E
Verchn'aja Inta	24	66.00 N	60.20 E
Verchn'aja Maza	80	52.58 N	47.56 E
Verchn'aja Orl'anka	80	53.44 N	51.04 E
Verchn'aja Pyšma	86	56.55 N	60.37 E
Verchn'aja Salda	86	58.02 N	60.33 E
Verchn'aja Serebr'akovka	80	47.21 N	42.14 E
Verchn'aja Sin'ačicha	86	57.59 N	61.40 E
Verchn'aja Sysert'	86	56.26 N	60.46 E
Verchn'aja Tajmyra ≐	74	74.15 N	99.48 E
Verchn'aja Tarka	86	56.37 N	77.30 E
Verchnaja Tereška	80	52.54 N	47.24 E
Verchn'aja Tišanka	78	51.19 N	40.32 E
Verchn'aja Tojma	24	62.13 N	45.00 E
Verchn'aja Troica	76	57.15 N	37.08 E
Verchn'aja Tura	86	58.22 N	59.49 E
Verchn'aja Zaimka	88	55.51 N	110.09 E
Verchn'aja Zima	88	53.48 N	101.47 E
Verchneaks'onovskij	80	48.21 N	42.38 E
Verchneangarskij chrebet ⋀	88	56.20 N	111.30 E
Verchne-Anikin	83	48.09 N	39.59 E
Verchnebakanskij	78	44.52 N	37.39 E
Verchneber'ozovskij	86	50.17 N	82.13 E
Verchnebuzanskij	80	46.38 N	48.02 E
Verchnecaricynskij	80	48.23 N	43.57 E
Verchnedneprovskij	76	54.59 N	33.21 E
Verchnedvinsk	76	55.47 N	27.56 E
Verchneimbatskoje	74	63.11 N	87.58 E
Verchnejarkejevo	80	55.27 N	54.19 E
Verchneje Šachlovo	82	55.02 N	37.15 E
Verchnemakejevka	78	49.10 N	41.03 E
Verchnemulomskoje vodochranilišče ◎[1]	24	68.30 N	31.05 E
Verchnesjezžeje	80	52.44 N	51.15 E
Verchnespasskoje	80	52.39 N	41.47 E
Verchnetulomskij	24	68.38 N	31.45 E
Verchneural'sk	86	53.53 N	59.13 E
Verchneusinskoje	86	52.14 N	93.01 E
Verchnevil'ujsk	74	63.27 N	120.18 E
Verchnevolynskoje	85	40.43 N	68.51 E
Verchnij Amyl	88	53.08 N	94.30 E
Verchnij Avz'an	86	53.32 N	57.33 E
Verchnij Balyklej	80	49.34 N	45.10 E
Verchnij Baskunčak	80	48.14 N	46.44 E
Verchnij Byk	78	50.43 N	41.14 E
Verchnije Dvoriki	82	56.28 N	38.22 E
Verchnije Kigi	86	55.25 N	58.37 E
Verchnije Korobki	80	50.19 N	44.38 E
Verchnije Lipki	80	49.38 N	43.51 E
Verchnije Tatyšly	86	56.17 N	55.52 E
Verchnij Ikorec	78	51.11 N	39.46 E
Verchnij Karačan	80	51.24 N	41.46 E
Verchnij Krasnyj Pereval	89	46.33 N	134.37 E
Verchnij Kužebar	86	53.22 N	93.15 E
Verchnij Landech	80	56.51 N	42.36 E
Verchnij Leb'ažinskij	80	46.45 N	47.50 E
Verchnij Lomov	80	53.28 N	43.34 E
Verchnij Lomovec	76	52.13 N	38.37 E
Verchnij Mamon	78	50.10 N	40.23 E
Verchnij Most	76	57.31 N	28.50 E
Verchnij Nejvinskij	86	57.17 N	60.09 E
Verchnij Petr'ak	86	57.29 N	77.30 E
Verchnij Šergol'džin	88	50.12 N	108.20 E
Verchnij Tagil	86	57.22 N	59.56 E
Verchnij Takermen'	80	55.39 N	52.43 E
Verchnij Ufalej	86	56.04 N	60.14 E
Verchnij Ul'chun	88	49.34 N	112.32 E
Verchnij Uslon	80	55.47 N	48.57 E
Verchnij Zub, gora ∧	86	53.45 N	89.15 E
Verchnyje Nikul'asy	76	60.25 N	30.45 E
Verchnyj Jenisej (Ulug-Chem) ≐	88	51.47 N	92.00 E
Verchojansk	74	67.35 N	133.27 E
Verchojanskij chrebet ⋀	74	67.00 N	129.00 E
Vercholensk	88	54.06 N	105.35 E
Verchopuja	24	61.34 N	41.31 E
Verchošižemje	80	58.01 N	49.07 E
Verchososna	78	50.44 N	38.14 E
Verchoturje	86	58.52 N	60.48 E
Verchoturovo	86	58.22 N	95.21 E
Verchovažje	24	60.45 N	42.00 E
Verchovino	76	59.33 N	43.19 E
Verchovje	76	52.49 N	37.14 E
Verchovl'an'	82	55.03 N	38.21 E
Verchozim	80	52.56 N	46.23 E
Verchubinka	86	50.29 N	82.26 E
Verclause	62	44.23 N	5.26 E
Vercors ◆[1]	62	44.57 N	5.25 E
Verdalsøra	26	63.48 N	11.29 E
Verde ≐, Bra.	248	11.54 S	55.48 W
Verde ≐, Bra.	248	13.33 S	58.01 W
Verde ≐, Bra.	250	10.27 S	42.16 W
Verde ≐, Bra.	255	15.07 S	48.40 W
Verde ≐, Bra.	255	17.05 S	46.05 W
Verde ≐, Bra.	255	18.01 S	50.14 W
Verde ≐, Bra.	255	19.11 S	50.44 W
Verde ≐, Bra.	255	19.55 S	49.45 W
Verde ≐, Bra.	255	21.12 S	51.53 W
Verde ≐, Bra.	256	21.34 S	45.31 W
Verde ≐, Bra.	256	21.38 S	47.03 W
Verde ≐, Méx.	234	21.37 N	99.15 W
Verde ≐, Méx.	234	20.42 N	103.14 W
Verde ≐, Méx.	234	16.45 N	98.07 W
Verde ≐, Méx.	234	15.59 N	97.47 W
Verde ≐, Para.	252	23.09 S	57.37 W
Verde ≐, S.A.	248	13.59 S	60.24 W
Verde ≐, Az., U.S.	200	33.33 N	111.40 W
Verde, Arroyo ≐, Arg.	254	41.56 S	65.03 W
Verde, Arroyo ≐, Bol.	248	11.25 S	66.20 W
Verde, Cape >	238	22.50 N	74.52 W
Verde, Cerro ∧	234	20.30 N	104.36 W
Verde, Costa ⊥[2]	71	39.34 N	8.28 E
Verde Grande ≐	255	14.35 S	43.53 W
Verde Island I	116	13.33 N	121.05 E
Verde Island Passage ᴗ	116	13.34 N	120.51 E
Verdello	62	45.36 N	9.37 E
Verden, Dtsch.	52	52.55 N	9.13 E
Verden, Ok., U.S.	196	35.05 N	98.05 W
Verde Pequeno ≐	255	14.48 S	43.31 W
Verdesela, Pinhal da ♦	266c	38.37 N	9.08 W
Verdi	226	39.31 N	119.59 W
Verdigre	198	42.35 N	98.02 W
Verdigre Creek ≐	198	42.42 N	98.03 W
Verdigris ≐	196	35.48 N	95.19 W
Verdinho ≐	255	17.29 S	50.27 W
Verdon	198	40.08 N	95.42 W
Verdon ≐	62	43.43 N	5.46 E
Verdon, Canal du ≅	62	43.43 N	5.57 E
Verdoy	210	42.46 N	73.48 W
Verduga	76	58.46 N	29.12 E
Verdugo Mountains ⋀	280	34.13 N	118.18 W
Verdun, P.Q., Can.	206	45.27 N	73.34 W
Verdun, Fr.	32	43.52 N	1.14 E
Verdun-sur-le-Doubs	58	46.54 N	5.01 E
Verdun-sur-Meuse	56	49.10 N	5.23 E
Verdura ≐	70	37.28 N	13.12 E
Vereb'jo	76	58.41 N	32.42 E
Vereeniging	158	26.38 S	27.57 E
Veregin	184	51.35 N	102.05 W
Vereinigte Arabische Emirate → United Arab Emirates ▫[1]	128	24.00 N	54.00 E
Vereinigte Königreich → United Kingdom ▫[1]	28	54.00 N	2.00 W
Vereinigte Staaten → United States ▫[1]	178	38.00 N	97.00 W
Vereja, Ross.	82	55.46 N	39.06 E
Vereja, Ross.	82	55.21 N	36.11 E
Vereja, Ross.	265b	55.37 N	38.02 E
Veremejki	76	53.46 N	31.15 E
Vereščagino, Ross.	74	64.14 N	87.37 E
Vereščagino, Ross.	80	58.05 N	54.40 E
Veresegyház	264c	47.39 N	19.17 E
Veresoch	78	51.19 N	31.46 E
Veretje	82	54.08 N	36.17 E
Véretz	50	47.22 N	0.48 E
Verga	285	39.52 N	75.10 W
Verga, Cap >	150	10.12 N	14.27 W
Vergara	252	32.56 S	53.57 W
Vergato	64	44.17 N	11.07 E
Vergel	196	25.39 N	103.32 W
Vergeletto	58	46.14 N	8.36 E
Vergemont Creek ≐	166	24.12 S	143.17 E
Vergennes	188	44.10 N	73.15 W
Verghereto	66	43.47 N	12.00 E
Vergiate	62	45.43 N	8.42 E
Vergons	62	43.55 N	6.35 E
Vergt	32	45.02 N	0.43 E
Verigino	82	56.42 N	38.08 E
Verín	34	41.56 N	7.26 W
Veringenstadt	58	48.11 N	9.12 E
Verin Talin	84	40.23 N	43.53 E
Veriora	76	58.00 N	27.21 E
Veríssimo	255	19.42 S	48.18 W
Verkeerdevlei	158	28.48 S	26.48 E
Verkhivtseve	78	48.29 N	34.14 E
Verkhna Khortytsya	78	47.51 N	35.01 E
Verkhne Syn'ovydne	78	49.06 N	23.34 E
Verkhneudinsk → Ulan-Ude	88	51.50 N	107.37 E
Verkhniy Rohachyk	78	47.14 N	34.21 E
Verkhniy Ufaley → Verchnij Ufalej	86	56.04 N	60.14 E
Verkhn'odniprovs'k	78	48.39 N	34.21 E
Verkhn'osadove	78	44.42 N	33.42 E
Verkhnyachka	78	48.49 N	30.02 E
Verkhnyaya Salda → Verchn'aja Salda	86	58.02 N	60.33 E
Verkhnye	78	48.53 N	38.28 E
Verkhnye ◆[8]	83	48.53 N	38.28 E
Verkhnyeduvannyy	78	48.20 N	39.48 E
Verkhovyna	78	48.09 N	24.47 E
Verkhoyansk → Verchojansk	74	67.35 N	133.27 E
Verkykerskop	158	27.54 S	29.17 E
Verl (Senne I)	52	51.53 N	8.31 E
Vermaaklikheid	158	34.19 S	21.01 E
Vermaas	158	26.30 S	25.59 E
Vermand	50	49.52 N	3.09 E
Vermejo ≐	196	36.30 N	104.33 W
Vermelho ≐, Bra.	250	9.16 S	47.23 W
Vermelho ≐, Bra.	250	7.44 S	47.17 W
Vermelho ≐, Bra.	250	5.33 S	49.14 W
Vermelho ≐, Bra.	255	14.54 S	51.06 W
Vermenton	50	47.40 N	3.44 E
Vermette Lake ◎	184	55.40 N	109.05 W
Vermezzo	266b	45.24 N	8.59 E
Vermiglio	64	46.18 N	10.42 E
Vermilion, Ab., Can.	182	53.22 N	110.51 W
Vermilion, Oh., U.S.	214	41.25 N	82.21 W
Vermilion ▫[6]	216	40.08 N	87.37 W
Vermilion ≐, Ab., Can.	184	53.44 N	110.18 W
Vermilion ≐, On., Can.	190	46.16 N	81.41 W
Vermilion ≐, Il., U.S.	216	41.19 N	89.04 W
Vermilion ≐, La., U.S.	194	29.46 N	92.09 W
Vermilion ≐, Mn., U.S.	190	48.16 N	92.30 W
Vermilion ≐, Oh., U.S.	214	41.26 N	82.22 W
Vermilion, Middle Fork ≐	216	40.12 N	87.45 W
Vermilion, North Fork ≐, Il., U.S.	216	40.49 N	88.30 W
Vermilion, North Fork ≐, Il., U.S.	216	40.13 N	87.39 W
Vermilion, South Fork ≐	216	40.49 N	88.30 W
Vermilion Bay	184	49.51 N	93.24 W
Vermilion Bay c	194	29.40 N	92.00 W
Vermilion Lake ◎, On., Can.	184	50.03 N	92.13 W
Vermilion Lake ◎, Mn., U.S.	190	47.53 N	92.25 W
Vermilion Pass)(	182	51.14 N	116.03 W
Vermillion	198	42.46 N	96.55 W
Vermillion ≐	198	42.44 N	96.53 W
Vermillion, East Fork ≐	198	43.44 N	97.03 W
Vermillion, West Fork ≐	198	43.44 N	97.03 W
Vermillion Bluffs ⊥[4]	200	40.50 N	108.30 W
Vermillion Creek ≐, U.S.	200	40.46 N	108.53 W
Vermillion Creek ≐, Ks., U.S.	198	39.12 N	96.13 W
Vermont, Austl.	274b	37.50 S	145.12 E
Vermont, Il., U.S.	194	40.17 N	90.25 W
Vermont ▫[3], U.S.	178	43.50 N	72.45 W
Vermont ▫[3], U.S.	188	43.50 N	72.45 W
Vermontville	216	42.37 N	85.01 W
Vernà, Pizzo di ∧	70	38.01 N	15.15 E
Vernaison	62	45.39 N	4.49 E
Vernal	200	40.27 N	109.31 W
Vernalis	226	37.37 N	121.17 W
Vernante	62	44.15 N	7.32 E
Vernayaz	58	46.08 N	7.02 E
Vernazza	62	44.08 N	9.41 E
Verndale	198	46.24 N	95.01 W
Verne	52	51.41 N	8.34 E
Verner	190	46.25 N	80.07 W
Verneuil	32	48.44 N	0.56 E
Verneuil-L'Étang	261	48.39 N	2.50 E
Verneuil-sur-Avre	50	48.44 N	0.56 E
Verneuil-sur-Seine	261	48.59 N	1.59 E
Verneukpan	158	30.00 S	21.00 E
Verneukpan ≚	158	30.00 S	21.10 E
Vernier	58	46.13 N	6.06 E
Verninge	41	55.18 N	10.13 E
Vernio	66	44.03 N	11.09 E
Vernole	68	40.17 N	18.18 E
Vernon, B.C., Can.	182	50.16 N	119.16 W
Vernon, On., Can.	212	45.10 N	75.28 W
Vernon, Fr.	50	49.05 N	1.29 E
Vernon, Al., U.S.	194	33.45 N	88.06 W
Vernon, Ca., U.S.	280	34.01 N	118.13 W
Vernon, Ct., U.S.	207	41.49 N	72.28 W
Vernon, Fl., U.S.	194	30.37 N	85.42 W
Vernon, Il., U.S.	219	38.48 N	89.05 W
Vernon, In., U.S.	218	38.59 N	85.36 W
Vernon, Mi., U.S.	216	42.56 N	84.02 W
Vernon, N.J., U.S.	210	41.11 N	74.29 W
Vernon, N.Y., U.S.	210	43.05 N	75.32 W
Vernon, Oh., U.S.	214	41.23 N	80.34 W
Vernon, Tx., U.S.	196	34.09 N	99.15 W
Vernon, Ut,. U.S.	200	40.05 N	112.25 W
Vernon, Lake ◎	212	45.20 N	79.17 W
Vernon Dam ◆[6]	207	42.46 N	72.31 W
Vernon Hills	278	42.13 N	87.58 W
Vernonia	224	45.51 N	123.11 W
Vernon Lake ◎[1]	194	31.15 N	93.25 W
Vernon River	186	46.12 N	62.50 W
Vernouillet	261	48.58 N	1.59 E
Vernoux-en-Vivarais	62	44.54 N	4.39 E
Verny	56	49.01 N	6.12 E
Vero ≐	34	42.00 N	0.10 E
Vero Beach	220	27.38 N	80.23 W
Véroia	38	40.31 N	22.12 E
Verolanuova	64	45.19 N	10.04 E
Verolavecchia	64	45.19 N	10.03 E
Veroli	66	41.41 N	13.25 E
Verona, On., Can.	212	44.29 N	76.42 W
Verona, It.	64	45.27 N	11.00 E
Verona, Ky., U.S.	218	38.49 N	84.39 W
Verona, Ms., U.S.	194	34.11 N	88.43 W
Verona, N.J., U.S.	276	40.49 N	74.14 W
Verona, N.Y., U.S.	210	43.08 N	75.34 W
Verona, Oh., U.S.	218	39.54 N	84.29 W
Verona, Pa., U.S.	279b	40.30 N	79.50 W
Verona, Wi., U.S.	216	42.59 N	89.31 W
Verona ▫[4]	64	45.25 N	11.02 E
Verona Beach	210	43.12 N	75.44 W
Verona Beach State Park ♦	210	43.14 N	75.44 W
Verona Park	216	42.21 N	85.09 W
Verónica	258	35.22 S	57.20 W
Verperluda, ostrov I	265a	59.59 N	30.01 E
Verplanck	210	41.15 N	73.58 W
Verran	166	33.51 S	136.18 E
Verrazano-Narrows Bridge ◆[5]	210	40.36 N	74.03 W
Verrès	62	45.40 N	7.42 E
Verrettes	238	19.03 N	72.28 W
Verrey-sous-Salmaise	58	47.26 N	4.40 E
Verrières, Bois de ♦	261	48.45 N	2.15 E
Verrières-le-Buisson	261	48.45 N	2.16 E
Versa ≐	62	44.54 N	8.16 E
Versailles, Fr.	50	48.48 N	2.08 E
Versailles, Il., U.S.	194	39.53 N	90.39 W
Versailles, In., U.S.	218	39.04 N	85.15 W
Versailles, Ky., U.S.	218	38.03 N	84.43 W
Versailles, Mo., U.S.	194	38.25 N	92.50 W
Versailles, N.Y., U.S.	210	42.31 N	78.59 W
Versailles, Oh., U.S.	216	40.13 N	84.29 W
Versailles, Pa., U.S.	279b	40.21 N	79.51 W
Versailles, Château de ⊥	261	48.48 N	2.07 E
Versailles, Parc de ♦	261	48.49 N	2.06 E
Versailles State Park ♦	218	39.04 N	85.13 W
Verse ≐	263	51.15 N	7.46 E
Versec → Vršac	38	45.07 N	21.18 E
Versestausee ◎[1]	263	51.11 N	7.41 E
Versien	158	27.05 S	27.52 E
Veršina Tei	86	53.20 N	89.36 E
Veršino-Darasunskij	88	52.20 N	115.32 E
Veršino-Šachtaminskij	88	51.21 N	117.50 E
Versmold	52	52.02 N	8.09 E
Versoix	58	46.16 N	6.10 E
Ver-sur-Launette	261	49.06 N	2.41 E
Vert	261	48.57 N	1.41 E
Vert, Cap >	150	14.43 N	17.30 W
Vert'ačij	80	48.57 N	43.53 E
Verte, Île I, P.Q., Can.	186	48.02 N	69.26 W
Verte, Île I, P.Q., Can.	275a	45.34 N	73.30 W
Vertedero	240m	18.05 N	66.15 W
Verteillac	32	45.21 N	0.22 E
Vertientes	240p	21.16 N	78.09 W
Vertiyivka	78	51.10 N	31.51 E
Vertkovo	82	56.07 N	36.25 E
Vert-le-Grand	261	48.34 N	2.22 E
Vert-le-Petit	261	48.33 N	2.22 E
Vertlinskoje	82	56.14 N	36.58 E
Vertou	32	47.10 N	1.29 W
Vertova	62	45.48 N	9.50 E
Vert-Saint-Denis	261	48.34 N	2.37 E
Vertus	50	48.54 N	4.00 E
Verucchio	66	43.59 N	12.25 E
Verulam	158	29.45 S	31.02 E
Verulamium ⊥	42	51.45 N	0.22 W
Verviers	56	50.35 N	5.52 E
Vervins	50	49.50 N	3.54 E
Verwall Gruppe ⋀	58	47.02 N	10.10 E
Verwood	42	50.53 N	1.52 W
Veryan	42	50.13 N	4.54 W
Verzasca ≐	58	46.09 N	8.52 E
Verzegnis	64	46.25 N	12.59 E
Verzenay	50	49.10 N	4.09 E
Verzino	68	39.19 N	16.51 E
Verzuolo	62	44.36 N	7.29 E
Verzy	50	49.09 N	4.10 E
Vesanto	26	62.56 N	26.25 E
Vesava ◆[8]	272c	19.08 N	72.48 E
Vescovato, Fr.	36	42.30 N	9.26 E
Vescovato, It.	64	45.10 N	10.10 E
Vescovo di Squillace, Roccelletta del ⊥	68	38.48 N	16.35 E
Vesdre ≐	56	50.37 N	5.37 E
Veseja	76	53.04 N	27.41 E
Vesela Hora	83	48.43 N	39.16 E
Vesele	78	47.01 N	34.55 E
Veselí nad Lužnicí	30	49.11 N	14.43 E
Veselí nad Moravou	30	48.58 N	17.22 E
Veseli Terny	78	48.07 N	33.32 E
Veselovskoje	86	54.00 N	78.43 E
Veselovskoje vodochranilišče ◎[1]	80	47.00 N	41.18 E
Veselynove	78	47.21 N	31.14 E
Veselyy Podil	78	49.36 N	33.16 E
Vésenaz	58	46.14 N	6.12 E
Vešenskaja	80	49.38 N	41.43 E
Vesgre ≐	50	48.48 N	1.36 E
Vesijärvi ◎	26	61.06 N	25.32 E
Vesjegonsk	76	58.40 N	37.16 E
Veškajma, Ross.	80	54.04 N	47.02 E
Veškajma, Ross.	80	54.03 N	47.08 E
Veški	265b	55.56 N	37.37 E
Vesle ≐	50	49.23 N	3.38 E
Vešn'aki ◆[8]	265b	55.44 N	37.49 E
Ves'olaja Rošča	86	53.47 N	76.22 E
Vesole, Monte ∧	68	40.24 N	15.10 E
Ves'oloje, Kaz.	85	43.19 N	77.06 E
Ves'oloje, Ross.	80	50.17 N	45.15 E
Ves'oloje, Ross.	83	47.10 N	38.45 E
Ves'olo-Voznesenka	83	47.09 N	38.20 E
Ves'olyj, Ross.	80	47.06 N	40.45 E
Ves'olyj, Ross.	83	47.20 N	39.18 E
Ves'olyj Jar, Ross.	86	51.18 N	81.07 E
Ves'olyj Jar, Ross.	89	43.57 N	135.28 E
Ves'olyj Podol	86	53.31 N	65.54 E
Ves'olyj Pos'olok ◆[8]	265a	59.54 N	30.28 E
Vesoul	58	47.38 N	6.10 E
Vespasiano	255	19.40 S	43.55 W
Vespolate	62	45.21 N	8.40 E
Vesta	236	9.43 N	83.03 W
Vest-Agder ▫[6]	26	58.30 N	7.10 E
Vestal	210	42.05 N	76.03 W
Vestal Center	210	42.02 N	76.01 W
Vestavia Hills	194	33.26 N	86.46 W
Vestbygd	26	58.06 N	6.35 E
Vesterålen II	24	68.45 N	15.00 E
Vester Egede	41	55.16 N	11.59 E
Vesterø Havn	26	57.18 N	10.56 E
Vester Skerninge	41	55.03 N	10.28 E
Vester Sottrup	41	54.57 N	9.43 E
Vestfjorden c[2]	24	68.08 N	15.00 E
Vestfold ▫[6]	26	59.15 N	10.10 E
Vestmannaeyjar	24a	63.26 N	20.12 W
Vestone	64	45.42 N	10.24 E
Vestreno	58	46.06 N	9.18 E
Vestsjælland ▫[6]	41	55.35 N	11.30 E
Vestvågøya I	24	68.15 N	13.50 E
Vésubie ≐	62	43.52 N	7.12 E
Vesubio → Vesuvio ∧[1]	68	40.49 N	14.26 E
Vesuv → Vesuvio ∧[1]	68	40.49 N	14.26 E
Vesuvio (Vesuvius) ∧[1]	68	40.49 N	14.26 E
Vesuvius → Vesuvio ∧[1]	68	40.49 N	14.26 E
Vesuvius Bay	224	48.53 N	123.35 W
Veszprém	30	47.06 N	17.55 E
Veszprém ▫[6]	30	47.10 N	17.40 E
Vésztő	30	46.55 N	21.16 E
Vet ≐	158	27.40 S	25.40 E
Vetapālem	122	15.47 N	80.19 E
Vetčin	76	52.27 N	28.10 E
Veterans Stadium ♦	285	39.54 N	75.10 W
Vétheuil	50	49.04 N	1.42 E
Vetju	24	62.57 N	50.44 E
Vetka	76	52.33 N	31.10 E
Vetlanda	26	57.26 N	15.04 E
Vetl'anka	80	52.52 N	51.09 E
Vetluga	80	57.51 N	45.47 E
Vetluga ≐	80	56.18 N	46.24 E
Vetlužskij, Ross.	80	57.11 N	45.07 E
Vetlužskij, Ross.	80	58.23 N	45.26 E
Vetoškino	80	57.18 N	49.44 E
Vetovo	38	43.42 N	26.16 E
Vetralla	66	42.19 N	12.03 E
Vetren	38	42.16 N	24.03 E
Vetrino	76	55.25 N	28.28 E
Vetriolo	64	46.02 N	11.18 E
Vetrișoaia	38	46.26 N	28.13 E
Větřni	61	48.46 N	14.17 E
Vetschau	54	51.47 N	14.04 E
Vettisfossen L	26	61.22 N	7.55 E
Vetto	64	44.29 N	10.20 E
Vettore, Monte ∧	66	42.49 N	13.16 E
Vetulonia	66	42.51 N	10.58 E
Veules-les-Roses	50	49.52 N	0.48 E
Veulettes-sur-Mer	50	49.51 N	0.36 E
Veurne (Furnes)	50	51.04 N	2.40 E
Vevay	218	38.44 N	85.04 W
Vevelstad	24	65.43 N	12.30 E
Veveno, Khawr V	140	6.40 N	32.58 E
Vevey	58	46.28 N	6.51 E
Vex	58	46.13 N	7.24 E
Veyle ≐	58	46.18 N	4.50 E
Veynes	62	44.32 N	5.49 E
Veyrier	62	45.53 N	6.10 E
Vézelay	50	47.28 N	3.44 E
Vézelise	58	48.29 N	6.05 E
Vézénobres	62	44.03 N	4.09 E
Vézère ≐	32	44.53 N	0.53 E
Vezirköprü	130	41.09 N	35.28 E
Vezouze ≐	58	48.35 N	6.29 E
Vezza d'Oglio	64	46.14 N	10.24 E
Vezzana, Cima della ∧	64	46.17 N	11.50 E
Vezzano	64	46.05 N	11.00 E
Vezzano Ligure	64	44.09 N	9.52 E
Viacha	248	16.39 S	68.18 W
Viadana	64	44.56 N	10.31 E
Viadutos	252	27.34 S	52.01 W
Viale	252	31.53 S	60.01 W
Vialonga	266c	38.52 N	9.05 W
Via Mala V	58	46.40 N	9.26 E
Viamão	252	30.05 S	51.02 W
Viamonte	252	33.44 S	63.06 W
Vian	196	35.29 N	94.58 W
Viana	250	3.13 S	45.00 W
Viana, Ilha do I	287a	22.52 S	43.08 W
Viana del Bollo	34	42.11 N	7.06 W
Viana do Alentejo	34	38.20 N	8.00 W
Viana do Castelo	34	41.42 N	8.50 W
Vianden	56	49.57 N	6.11 E
Vianen	52	52.00 N	5.05 E
Viangchan (Vientiane)	110	17.58 N	102.36 E
Viangphoukha	110	20.41 N	101.04 E
Viar ≐	34	37.36 N	5.50 W
Viareggio	64	43.52 N	10.14 E
Viarmes	50	49.08 N	2.22 E
Viatka → Kirov	80	58.38 N	49.42 E
Viaur ≐	32	44.08 N	2.23 E
Vibank	184	50.20 N	103.55 W
Víboras, Arroyo de las ≐	258	33.57 S	58.21 W
Viborg, Dan.	26	56.26 N	9.24 E
Viborg → Vyborg, Ross.	76	60.42 N	28.45 E
Viborg, S.D., U.S.	198	43.10 N	97.04 W
Viborg ▫[6]	41	56.18 N	9.27 E
Vibo Valentia	68	38.40 N	16.06 E
Vibraye	50	48.03 N	0.44 E
Viburnum	194	37.42 N	91.08 W
Viby	41	55.33 N	12.02 E
Viby ◆[8]	41	56.07 N	10.10 E
Vic (Vich)	34	41.56 N	2.15 E
Vic, Étang de c	62	43.29 N	3.50 E
Vicálvaro ◆[8]	266a	40.24 N	3.36 W
Vícam	232	27.35 N	110.20 W
Vicarello	66	42.10 N	12.12 E
Vicari	70	37.49 N	13.34 E
Vicchio	66	43.56 N	11.28 E
Vicco	192	37.12 N	83.03 W
Vic-en-Bigorre	32	43.23 N	0.03 E
Vicente, Point >	280	33.44 N	118.25 W
Vicente Casares	258	34.57 S	58.38 W
Vicente de Carvalho	256	23.56 S	46.19 W
Vicente Guerrero, Méx.	234	23.45 N	103.59 W
Vicente Guerrero, Méx.	234	18.24 N	92.53 W
Vicente Guerrero, Méx.	234	19.08 N	98.10 W
Vicente Guerrero, Presa ◎[1]	234	24.00 N	98.45 W
Vicente López	258	34.32 S	58.28 W
Vicente López ▫[5]	288	34.32 S	58.30 W
Vicente Noble	238	18.23 N	71.11 W
Vicenza	64	45.33 N	11.33 E
Vicenza ▫[4]	64	45.40 N	11.27 E
Viceroy	184	49.27 N	105.22 W
Vichada ▫[5]	246	5.00 N	69.30 W
Vichada ≐	246	4.55 N	67.50 W
Vichadero	252	31.48 S	54.43 W
Vichigasta	252	29.29 S	67.31 W
Vichoreva ≐	88	56.47 N	101.22 E
Vichorevka	88	56.12 N	101.09 E
Vichra ≐	76	54.01 N	31.52 E
Vichuga → Vičuga	80	57.13 N	41.56 E
Vichuquén	252	34.53 S	72.00 W
Vichy	32	46.08 N	3.26 E
Vici	196	36.08 N	99.17 W
Vickery	214	41.23 N	82.56 W
Vicksburg, Mi., U.S.	216	42.07 N	85.31 W
Vicksburg, Ms., U.S.	194	32.21 N	90.52 W
Vicksburg, Pa., U.S.	210	40.56 N	76.59 W
Vicksburg National Military Park ♦	194	32.24 N	90.52 W
Vico	36	42.10 N	8.48 E
Vico, Lago di ◎	66	42.19 N	12.10 E
Vico Canavese	62	45.30 N	7.47 E
Vico del Gargano	68	41.54 N	15.57 E
Vico Equense	68	40.40 N	14.25 E
Vicoforte	62	44.21 N	7.54 E
Vicopisano	66	43.42 N	10.35 E
Viçosa, Bra.	250	9.24 S	36.14 W
Viçosa, Bra.	255	20.45 S	42.53 W
Viçosa do Ceará	250	3.34 S	41.05 W
Vicosoprano	58	46.22 N	9.37 E
Vicovaro	66	42.01 N	12.54 E
Vicq	261	48.49 N	1.50 E
Vic-sur-Aisne	50	49.24 N	3.07 E
Vic-sur-Cère	32	44.59 N	2.37 E
Vic-sur-Seille	56	48.47 N	6.32 E
Victor, Ca., U.S.	226	38.08 N	121.12 W
Victor, Id., U.S.	202	43.36 N	111.06 W
Victor, Ia., U.S.	190	41.43 N	92.17 W
Victor, Mt., U.S.	202	46.25 N	114.08 W
Victor, N.Y., U.S.	210	42.58 N	77.24 W
Victor, Lac ◎	186	50.35 N	61.50 W
Victorbur	52	53.29 N	7.20 E
Victor Harbor	168b	35.34 S	138.37 E
Victoria, Arg.	252	32.37 S	60.10 W
Victoria → Vitória, Bra.	255	20.19 S	40.21 W
Victoria, Cam.	152	4.01 N	9.12 E
Victoria, B.C., Can.	224	48.25 N	123.22 W
Victoria, P.E., Can.	186	46.13 N	63.29 W
Victoria, Chile	252	38.13 S	72.20 W
Victoria, Gren.	241k	12.12 N	61.42 W
Victoria, Guinée	150	10.50 N	14.33 W
Victoria (Xianggang), H.K.	271d	22.17 N	114.09 E
Victoria, Malay.	112	5.17 N	115.15 E
Victoria → Ciudad Victoria, Méx.	234	23.44 N	99.08 W
Victoria, Pil.	116	13.12 N	121.15 E
Victoria, Pil.	116	15.35 N	120.41 E
Victoria, Rom.	38	45.45 N	24.41 E
Victoria, Sey.	138	4.38 S	55.27 E
Victoria, Ks., U.S.	198	38.51 N	99.08 W
Victoria, Tx., U.S.	196	28.48 N	97.00 W
Victoria, Va., U.S.	192	36.59 N	78.13 W
Victoria ▫[3]	166	38.00 S	145.00 E
Victoria ▫[4]	154	20.54 S	31.21 E
Victoria ▫[6], On., Can.	212	44.35 N	78.50 W
Victoria ▫[6], Tx., U.S.	222	28.55 N	97.00 W
Victoria ◆[8]	288	34.28 S	58.31 W
Victoria ≐, Austl.	160	15.12 S	129.43 E
Victoria ≐, Nf., Can.	186	48.45 N	56.40 W
Victoria ≐, Méx.	234	21.02 N	99.50 W
Victoria, Isla I	254	45.18 S	73.58 W
Victoria, Lake ◎, Afr.	154	1.00 S	33.00 E
Victoria, Lake ◎, Austl.	166	34.00 S	141.16 E
Victoria, Mount ∧, Mya.	110	21.14 N	93.55 E
Victoria, Mount ∧, Pap. N. Gui.	164	8.55 S	147.35 E
Victoria, Pont ◆[5]	275a	45.29 N	73.32 W
Victoria and Albert Museum ⊡	272c	18.59 N	72.50 E
Victoria Beach	184	50.43 N	96.33 W
Victoria Beach ⊥[2]	273a	6.25 N	3.25 E
Victoria de Durango → Durango	234	24.02 N	104.40 W
Victoria Falls	154	17.56 S	25.50 E
Victoria Falls L	154	17.55 S	25.51 E
Victoria Falls National Park ♦	154	17.55 S	25.40 E
Victoria Gardens ♦	272c	18.59 N	72.50 E
Victoria Harbour	212	44.45 N	79.46 W
Victoria International Airport ⊠	224	48.39 N	123.26 W
Victoria Island I, N.T., Can.	176	71.00 N	110.00 W
Victoria Island I, Nig.	273a	6.26 N	3.26 E
Victoria Lake ◎	273d	26.14 S	28.09 E
Victoria Lake ◎[1]	186	48.18 N	57.30 W
Victoria Land ◆[1]	9	75.00 S	163.00 E

Symbols in the index entries represent the broad categories identified in the key at the right. Symbols with superior numbers (⋀[1]) identify subcategories (see complete key on page *I · 1).*

Symbole im Register stellen die rechts im Schlüssel erklärten Kategorien dar. Symbole mit hochgestellten Ziffern (⋀[1]) bezeichnen Unterabteilungen einer Kategorie (vgl. vollständiger Schlüssel auf Seite *I · 1).*

Los símbolos incluídos en el texto del índice representan las grandes categorías identificadas con la clave a la derecha. Los símbolos con numeros en su parte superior (⋀[1]) identifican las subcategorías (véase la clave completa en la página *I · 1).*

Les symboles de l'index représentent les catégories indiquées dans la légende à droite. Les symboles suivis d'un indice (⋀[1]) représentent des sous-catégories (voir légende complète à la page *I · 1).*

Os símbolos incluídos no texto do índice representam as grandes categorias identificadas com a chave à direita. Os símbolos com números em sua parte superior (⋀[1]) identificam as subcategorias (veja-se a chave completa à página *I · 1).*

∧ Mountain	Berg	Montaña	Montagne	Montanha
⋀ Mountains	Gebirge	Montañas	Montagnes	Montanhas
)(Pass	Paß	Paso	Col	Passo
V Valley, Canyon	Tal, Cañon	Valle, Cañón	Vallée, Canyon	Vale, Canhão
≚ Plain	Ebene	Llano	Plaine	Planície
> Cape	Kap	Cabo	Cap	Cabo
I Island	Insel	Isla	Île	Ilha
II Islands	Inseln	Islas	Îles	Ilhas
⊥ Other Topographic Features	Andere Topographische Objekte	Otros Elementos Topográficos	Autres données topographiques	Outros acidentes topográficos

ESPAÑOL

Nombre	Página	Lat.°′	Long.°′ W = Oeste
Victoria Lawn Tennis Association Courts ♠	274b	37.51 S	145.02 E
Victoria Memorial Hall ʋ	271c	1.17 N	103.51 E
Victoria Memorial Museum ʋ	272b	22.33 N	88.21 E
Victoria Nile ≏	154	2.14 N	31.26 E
Victoria Park	168a	31.58 S	115.55 E
Victoria Park ♠, H.K.	271d	22.17 N	114.11 E
Victoria Park ♠, Eng., U.K.	262	53.23 N	2.34 W
Victoria Peak ʌ, Belize	232	16.48 N	88.37 W
Victoria Peak ʌ, B.C., Can.	182	50.03 N	126.06 W
Victoria Peak ʌ, H.K.	271d	22.17 N	114.08 E
Victoria Peaks ⋌	116	9.22 N	118.20 E
Victoria Point	171a	27.35 S	153.18 E
Victoria Range ⋌, N.Z.	172	42.09 S	172.08 E
Victoria Range ⋌, Pil.	116	9.32 N	118.23 E
Victoria River	164	15.37 S	131.08 E
Victoria River Downs	164	16.24 S	131.00 E
Victorias	116	10.54 N	123.05 E
Victoria State Car Club Race Circuit ♠	274b	37.45 S	145.11 E
Victoria Station ◆[5]	262	53.29 N	2.15 W
Victoria Strait ʮ	176	69.15 N	100.30 W
Victoria Terminus ◆[5]	272c	18.57 N	72.50 E
Victoria University of Manchester ʋ[2]	262	53.28 N	2.14 W
Victoriaville	206	46.03 N	71.57 W
Victoria West	158	31.25 S	23.04 E
Victorica	252	36.13 S	65.27 W
Victorino	246	2.48 N	67.50 W
Victorino de la Plaza	252	36.36 S	62.40 W
Víctor Rosales	234	22.57 N	102.42 W
Victorville	228	34.32 N	117.17 W
Victory, Mount ʌ	164	9.10 S	149.05 E
Victory Gardens	276	40.52 N	74.32 W
Victory Heights	214	41.22 N	79.46 W
Victory Hills	279b	40.11 N	79.53 W
Victory Mills	210	43.05 N	73.36 W
Victory Monument ⊥	269a	13.46 N	100.33 E
Vičuga	80	57.13 N	41.56 E
Vicuña	252	30.02 S	70.44 W
Vicuña Mackenna	252	33.54 S	64.23 W
Vidal, Kaap ›	158	28.09 S	32.33 E
Vidal Gormaz, Isla I	254	52.00 S	74.45 W
Vidalia, Ga., U.S.	192	32.13 N	82.24 W
Vidalia, La., U.S.	194	31.33 N	91.25 W
Vidal Ramos	252	27.23 S	49.22 W
Vidauban	62	43.26 N	6.26 E
Videbæk	26	56.05 N	8.38 E
Videira	252	27.00 S	51.08 W
Videle	38	44.16 N	25.31 E
Vidigueira	34	38.13 N	7.48 W
Vidim, Česká Rep.	54	50.28 N	14.31 E
Vidim, Ross.	88	56.29 N	103.09 E
Vidin	38	43.59 N	22.52 E
Vidisha	124	23.32 N	77.49 E
Vidlica	24	61.10 N	32.21 E
Vidnoje	82	55.34 N	37.41 E
Vidogošči	82	56.42 N	36.23 E
Vidor	194	30.07 N	94.00 W
Vidos ≏	267b	40.58 N	28.53 E
Vidöstern ⊜	26	57.04 N	14.01 E
Vidourle ≏	62	43.32 N	4.08 E
Vidra, Rom.	38	44.16 N	26.11 E
Vidra, Rom.	38	45.55 N	26.54 E
Vidsel	24	65.51 N	20.24 E
Vidzeme □[9]	76	57.10 N	25.30 E
Vidzy	76	55.24 N	26.38 E
Vie ≏	50	49.05 N	0.04 E
Viecht	60	48.30 N	12.04 E
Viechtach	60	49.05 N	12.53 E
Viechtwang	61	47.55 N	13.57 E
Viedma	254	40.48 S	63.00 W
Viedma, Lago ⊜	254	49.35 S	72.35 W
Viehberg ʌ	61	48.33 N	14.37 E
Viehhausen	60	48.59 N	11.58 E
Vieil Armand ⊥	58	47.52 N	7.10 E
Vieillard, Lac du ⊜	190	47.23 N	78.02 W
Vieille Case	240d	15.36 N	61.24 W
Vieira do Minho	34	41.39 N	8.09 W
Viejo, Cerro ʌ	248	4.49 S	79.27 W
Viekšniai	76	56.16 N	22.31 E
Vielank	54	53.15 N	11.08 E
Viella	34	42.42 N	0.48 E
Vielle-Eglise-en-Yvelines	261	48.40 N	1.53 E
Vielsalm	56	50.17 N	5.55 E
Viels-Maisons	50	48.54 N	3.24 E
Viena → Vienne ≏	32	47.13 N	0.05 E
Vienenburg	54	51.57 N	10.34 E
Vienna, On., Can.	212	42.41 N	80.48 W
Vienna → Wien, Öst.	61	48.13 N	16.20 E
Vienna, Ga., U.S.	192	32.05 N	83.47 W
Vienna, Il., U.S.	194	37.25 N	88.54 W
Vienna, In., U.S.	218	38.39 N	85.46 W
Vienna, Md., U.S.	208	38.29 N	75.49 W
Vienna, Mo., U.S.	194	38.11 N	91.56 W
Vienna, N.J., U.S.	210	40.52 N	74.53 W
Vienna, Oh., U.S.	214	41.14 N	80.40 W
Vienna, S.D., U.S.	198	44.42 N	97.30 W
Vienna, Va., U.S.	208	38.29 N	75.49 W
Vienna, Va., U.S.	208	38.54 N	77.15 W
Vienna, W.V., U.S.	188	39.19 N	81.32 W
Vienne, Fr.	62	45.31 N	4.52 E
Vienne → Wien, Öst.	61	48.13 N	16.20 E
Vienne □[5]	32	46.35 N	0.30 E
Vienne ≏	32	47.13 N	0.05 E
Vienne-en-Arthies	261	49.04 N	1.44 E
Vienne-le-Château	56	49.11 N	4.53 E
Vientiane → Viangchan	110	17.58 N	102.36 E
Vientos, Paso de los → Windward Passage ʮ	238	20.00 N	73.50 W
Vieques	240m	18.09 N	65.27 W
Vieques, Aeropuerto ⊠	240m	18.07 N	65.30 W
Vieques, Isla de I	240m	18.08 N	65.25 W
Vieques, Pasaje de ʮ	240m	18.11 N	65.37 W
Vieques, Sonda de ʮ	240m	18.15 N	65.23 W
Vière ≏	56	48.46 N	4.41 E
Viereck	54	53.32 N	14.02 E
Vieremä	26	63.45 N	27.01 E
Vierfontein	158	27.03 S	26.46 E
Vierhouten	52	52.20 N	5.50 E
Vieringhausen ◆[8]	263	51.11 N	7.10 E
Vierlande ◆[1]	52	53.26 N	10.14 E
Viernau	54	50.40 N	10.32 E
Viernheim	56	49.32 N	8.34 E
Vierraden	54	53.06 N	14.17 E
Viersen	56	51.15 N	6.23 E
Vierumäki	26	61.06 N	25.57 E
Vierwaldstättersee ⊜	58	47.00 N	8.28 E
Vierzehnheiligen ʋ[1]	56	50.08 N	11.02 E
Vierzon	50	47.13 N	2.05 E
Viesca	232	25.21 N	102.48 W
Viesecke	54	53.01 N	12.01 E
Vieselbach	54	51.00 N	11.08 E
Viesīte	76	56.21 N	25.33 E
Vieste	68	41.53 N	16.10 E
Vietgest	54	53.45 N	12.20 E
Vietnam □[1], Asia	108	16.00 N	108.00 E
Vietnam □[1], Asia	110	16.00 N	108.00 E
Vietnam Veterans Memorial ⊥	284c	38.53 N	77.03 W
Vietri di Potenza	68	40.36 N	15.30 E
Vietri sul Mare	68	40.40 N	14.44 E
Viet Tri	110	21.18 N	105.26 E
Vieux-Condé	50	50.27 N	3.34 E
Vieux-Ferette	58	47.30 N	7.18 E

FRANÇAIS

Nom	Page	Lat.°′	Long.°′ W = Ouest
Vieux-Fort, P.Q., Can.	186	51.26 N	57.49 W
Vieux-Fort, Guad.	241o	15.57 N	61.43 W
Vieux Fort, St. Luc.	241f	13.44 N	60.57 W
Vieux-Fort, Pointe du ›	241o	15.57 N	61.43 W
Vieux Fort Bay c	241f	13.44 N	60.58 W
Vieux-Habitants	241o	16.04 N	61.46 W
Vieux-Thann	58	47.48 N	7.08 E
Vievis	76	54.46 N	24.48 E
View Park	280	34.00 N	118.20 W
Vieytes	258	35.16 S	57.35 W
Vif	62	45.03 N	5.40 E
Vig	41	55.51 N	11.36 E
Viga ≏	76	59.14 N	43.41 E
Vigala	76	58.43 N	24.22 E
Vigan	116	17.34 N	120.23 E
Vigarano Mainarda	64	44.50 N	11.30 E
Vigatto	64	44.43 N	10.20 E
Vigeland	26	58.05 N	7.18 E
Vigentino ◆[8]	266b	45.25 N	9.11 E
Vigersted	41	55.29 N	11.54 E
Vigese, Monte ʌ	64	44.12 N	11.06 E
Vigésima Quinta de Abril, Ponte ◆[5]	266c	38.41 N	9.11 W
Vigevano	62	45.19 N	8.51 E
Viggianello	68	39.58 N	16.05 E
Viggiano	68	40.20 N	15.54 E
Viggiù	62	45.52 N	8.54 E
Vigia	250	0.48 S	48.08 W
Vigie Airport ⊠	241f	14.01 N	60.59 W
Vignacourt	50	50.01 N	2.12 E
Vignale	266b	45.29 N	8.36 E
Vignanello	66	42.23 N	12.17 E
Vigneulles-lès-Hattonchâtel	56	48.59 N	5.43 E
Vigneux-sur-Seine	261	48.42 N	2.25 E
Vignola	64	44.29 N	11.00 E
Vignory	58	48.17 N	5.06 E
Vignot	56	48.46 N	5.36 E
Vigny	261	49.05 N	1.56 E
Vigo	34	42.14 N	8.43 W
Vigo, Ría de c[1]	34	42.15 N	8.45 W
Vigodarzere	64	45.27 N	11.53 E
Vigo di Fassa	64	46.25 N	11.40 E
Vigolzone	62	44.55 N	9.40 E
Vigone	62	44.51 N	7.30 E
Vigonovo	64	45.23 N	12.00 E
Vigo-Rendena	64	46.05 N	10.43 E
Vigrestad	26	58.34 N	5.42 E
Viguzzolo	62	44.54 N	8.55 E
Vigy	56	49.12 N	6.18 E
Vihanti	26	64.29 N	25.00 E
Vihāri	123	30.02 N	72.21 E
Vihiers	32	47.09 N	0.32 W
Vihowa	123	31.08 N	70.30 E
Vihren ʌ	38	41.46 N	23.24 E
Vihti	26	60.25 N	24.20 E
Viiala	26	61.13 N	23.47 E
Viinijärvi	26	62.39 N	29.14 E
Viinijärvi ⊜	26	62.44 N	29.17 E
Viipuri → Vyborg	76	60.42 N	28.45 E
Viișoara	38	46.20 N	28.26 E
Viitasaari	26	63.04 N	25.52 E
Viivikonna	76	59.19 N	27.42 E
Vijāpur	120	23.34 N	72.45 E
Vijayawāda	122	16.31 N	80.37 E
Vijosë (Aóös) ≏	38	40.37 N	19.20 E
Vik	40	59.44 N	17.28 E
Vik ⊥	40	59.44 N	17.27 E
Vika	40	60.31 N	15.42 E
Vikajärvi	24	66.37 N	26.12 E
Vikārābād	122	17.20 N	77.54 E
Vikbolandet ›[1]	40	58.32 N	16.40 E
Vikeke	112	8.52 S	126.22 E
Viken	41	56.09 N	12.34 E
Viken ⊜	26	58.39 N	14.20 E
Vikern ⊜	40	59.30 N	14.55 E
Vikersund	26	59.59 N	10.02 E
Vikhroli ◆[8]	272c	19.07 N	72.56 E
Viking	182	53.06 N	111.46 W
Viking Village	218	39.05 N	84.18 W
Vikmanshyttan	40	60.17 N	15.49 E
Vikna	24	64.57 N	10.58 E
Vikna I	24	64.57 N	10.58 E
Vikno	78	48.34 N	25.58 E
Vikramasingapuram	122	8.43 N	77.24 E
Viksøyri	26	61.05 N	6.35 E
Viktor	24	66.09 N	58.07 E
Viktorovka	86	52.51 N	62.32 E
Viktring	61	46.35 N	14.16 E
Vikulovo	86	56.49 N	70.37 E
Vil'a	80	55.15 N	42.13 E
Vila Alferes Chamusca	156	24.29 S	33.00 E
Vila Augusta	287b	23.28 S	46.32 W
Vila Babi	287a	22.42 S	43.23 W
Vila Boacaya ◆[8]	287b	23.29 S	46.44 W
Vila Caldas Xavier	154	15.59 S	34.12 E
Vila da Maganja	154	17.18 S	37.30 E
Vila da Ribeira Brava	150a	16.37 N	24.18 W
Viladecans	266d	41.19 N	2.00 E
Viladecavalls del Vallès	266d	41.33 N	1.58 E
Vila de Manica	156	18.56 S	32.53 E
Vila de Rei	34	39.40 N	8.09 W
Vila Dirce	287b	23.35 S	46.48 W
Vila do Bispo	34	37.05 N	8.55 W
Vila do Conde	34	41.21 N	8.45 W
Vila do Porto	148a	36.56 N	25.09 W
Vila Embaú	256	22.37 S	45.02 W
Vila Flor	34	41.18 N	7.09 W
Vila Fontes	156	17.50 S	35.21 E
Vila Formosa ◆[8]	287b	23.34 S	46.33 W
Vilafranca del Penedès	34	41.21 N	1.42 E
Vila Franca de Xira	34	38.57 N	8.59 W
Vila Galvão	287b	23.27 S	46.33 W
Vila Gamito	154	14.12 S	33.00 E
Vila Gomes da Costa	156	24.19 S	33.38 E
Vila Gouveia	156	18.03 S	33.11 E
Vila Guilherme ◆[8]	287b	23.30 S	46.36 W
Vilaine ≏	32	47.30 N	2.27 W
Vila Isabel ◆[8]	287a	22.55 S	43.15 W
Vila Jaguára ◆[8]	287b	23.31 S	46.45 W
Viļaka	76	57.11 N	27.41 E
Vila Luísa	156	25.44 S	32.40 E
Vilama, Laguna de ⊜	252	22.36 S	66.55 W
Vila Machado	156	19.18 S	34.11 E
Vila Madalena ◆[8]	287b	23.33 S	46.42 W
Vila Maria ◆[8]	287b	23.31 S	46.34 W
Vila Mariana ◆[8]	287b	23.35 S	46.38 W
Vila Matilde ◆[8]	287b	23.32 S	46.31 W
Vilanculos	156	22.01 S	35.19 E
Viļāni	76	56.33 N	26.57 E
Vila Nova ≏	250	0.04 S	51.13 W
Vila Nova de Famalicão	34	41.25 N	8.32 W
Vila Nova de Foz Côa	34	41.05 N	7.12 W
Vila Nova de Gaia	34	41.08 N	8.37 W
Vilanova de la Roca	266d	41.33 N	2.17 E
Vilanova i la Geltrú	34	41.14 N	1.44 E
Vila Novo de Ourém	34	39.39 N	8.35 W
Vila Paiva de Andrada	156	18.44 S	34.03 E
Vila Progresso	287a	22.55 S	43.03 W
Vila Prudente ◆[8]	287b	23.35 S	46.33 W
Vila-real, Esp.	34	39.56 N	0.06 W
Vila Real, Port.	34	41.18 N	7.45 W
Vila Real de Santo António	34	37.12 N	7.25 W
Vilar Formoso	34	40.37 N	6.50 W
Vilarinho do Monte	250	1.37 S	52.01 W
Vilassar de Dalt	266d	41.31 N	2.22 E
Vilassar de Mar	266d	41.30 N	2.24 E
Vila Vasco da Gama	154	14.54 S	32.14 E
Vila Velha, Bra.	250	3.13 N	51.13 W
Vila Velha, Bra.	255	20.20 S	40.17 W

PORTUGUÊS

Nome	Página	Lat.°′	Long.°′ W = Oeste
Vila Velha de Ródão	34	39.38 N	7.40 W
Vila Verde, Port.	34	41.39 N	8.26 W
Vila Verde, Port.	266c	38.50 N	9.22 W
Vila Viçosa	34	38.47 N	8.13 W
Vilcabamba, Cordillera de ⋌	248	12.45 S	73.20 W
Vil'cha	78	51.22 N	29.24 E
Vil'che	78	49.14 N	22.53 E
Vildbjerg	41	56.12 N	8.46 E
Vilejka	76	54.30 N	26.53 E
Vilelas	252	27.57 S	62.38 W
Vilenki	82	54.16 N	38.55 E
Vil'gort, Ross.	24	61.35 N	50.40 E
Vil'gort, Ross.	24	60.34 N	56.24 E
Vilhelmina	26	64.37 N	16.39 E
Vilhena	248	12.43 S	60.07 W
Vilija (Neris) ≏	76	54.54 N	23.53 E
Viljandi	76	58.22 N	25.36 E
Viljoensdrif	158	26.44 S	27.55 E
Viljoenshof	158	34.40 S	19.42 E
Viljoenskroon	158	27.12 S	27.00 E
Viljoenspos	158	27.35 S	30.30 E
Vilkaviškis	76	54.39 N	23.02 E
Vil'khova ≏	83	48.35 N	39.17 E
Vil'kickogo, ostrov I, Ross.	72	73.29 N	75.50 E
Vil'kickogo, ostrov I, Ross.	74	75.44 N	152.20 E
Vil'kickogo, proliv ʮ	74	77.55 N	103.00 E
Vilkija	76	55.03 N	23.35 E
Villa Abecia	248	21.00 S	65.23 W
Villa Aberastain	252	31.39 S	68.35 W
Villa Acuña → Ciudad Acuña	232	29.18 N	100.55 W
Villa Adelina ◆[8]	288	34.31 S	58.32 W
Villa Adriana ⊥	66	41.56 N	12.45 E
Villa Alejandrina	258	33.46 S	58.21 W
Villa Alemana	252	33.03 S	71.23 W
Villa Álvarez	234	19.14 N	103.43 W
Villa Ana	252	28.29 S	59.37 W
Villa Ángela	252	27.35 S	60.43 W
Villa Atamisqui	252	28.29 S	63.48 W
Villa Atuel	252	34.50 S	67.54 W
Villaba	116	11.13 N	124.23 E
Villa Ballester ◆[8]	258	34.32 S	58.33 W
Villabassa (Niederdorf)	64	46.44 N	12.10 E
Villabate	70	38.04 N	13.26 E
Villabé	261	48.35 N	2.27 E
Villa Bella	248	10.23 S	65.24 W
Villa Berthet	252	27.17 S	60.25 W
Villablino	34	42.56 N	6.19 W
Villa Borghese ʋ	267a	41.55 N	12.29 E
Villa Bosch ◆[8]	288	34.35 S	58.34 W
Villa Bruzual	246	9.20 N	69.06 W
Villa Cañás, Arg.	252	34.00 S	61.36 W
Villacañas, Esp.	34	39.38 N	3.20 W
Villa Carlos Paz	252	31.24 S	64.31 W
Villacarriedo	34	43.14 N	3.48 W
Villacarrillo	34	38.07 N	3.05 W
Villa Castelli, Arg.	252	29.00 S	68.11 W
Villa Castelli, It.	68	40.35 N	17.28 E
Villacastín	34	40.47 N	4.25 W
Villach	64	46.36 N	13.50 E
Villacidro	71	39.27 N	8.44 E
Villa Ciudadela ◆[8]	258	34.38 S	58.34 W
Villa Clara □[4]	240p	22.30 N	80.00 W
Villa Comaltitlan	236	15.13 N	92.35 W
Villa Concepción del Tío	252	31.19 S	62.50 W
Villa Constitución	252	33.14 S	60.20 W
Villa Cortese	266b	45.34 N	8.53 E
Villa Corzo	234	16.10 N	93.15 W
Villacoublay, Aérodrome de ⊠	261	48.45 N	2.10 E
Villa Creek ≏	226	35.27 N	120.58 W
Villa Cuauhtémoc, Méx.	234	19.24 N	99.34 W
Villa Cuauhtémoc, Méx.	234	22.11 N	97.50 W
Villada	34	42.15 N	4.58 W
Villa de Apaseo El Alto	234	20.27 N	100.37 W
Villa de Arista	234	22.39 N	100.50 W
Villa de Arriaga	234	21.54 N	101.23 W
Villadeati	62	45.04 N	8.10 E
Villa de Cos	234	23.17 N	102.21 W
Villa de Cura	246	10.02 N	67.29 W
Villa de Guadalupe	234	23.22 N	100.46 W
Villa del Carmen	252	32.57 S	65.03 W
Villa del Pueblito	234	20.32 N	100.27 W
Villa del Río	34	37.59 N	4.17 W
Villa del Rosario, Arg.	252	31.35 S	63.32 W
Villa del Rosario, Arg.	252	30.47 S	57.55 W
Villa de María	252	29.54 S	63.43 W
Villa de Mayo	258	34.30 S	58.41 W
Villa de Nova Sintra	150a	14.52 N	24.43 W
Villa de Reyes	234	21.48 N	100.56 W
Villa de San Antonio	236	14.16 N	87.36 W
Villa de San Francisco	236	14.10 N	86.58 W
Villa de Soto	252	30.51 S	64.59 W
Villa d'Este ⊥	267a	41.57 N	12.48 E
Villa Devoto ◆[8]	288	34.36 S	58.31 W
Villa Diamante ◆[8]	288	34.41 S	58.26 W
Villa di Chiavenna	58	46.20 N	9.29 E
Villadiego	34	42.31 N	4.00 W
Villa Dolores	252	31.56 S	65.12 W
Villa Domínico ◆[8]	258	34.41 S	58.19 W
Villadose	64	45.04 N	11.53 E
Villadossola	58	46.04 N	8.16 E
Villa Elisa	252	32.10 S	58.24 W
Villa Elisa ◆[8]	258	34.50 S	58.05 W
Villa Escalante	234	19.24 N	101.39 W
Villa Flores	234	16.14 N	93.14 W
Villa Florida	252	26.23 S	57.09 W
Villafranca d'Asti	62	44.55 N	8.02 E
Villafranca del Bierzo	34	42.36 N	6.48 W
Villafranca de los Barros	34	38.34 N	6.20 W
Villafranca di Verona	64	45.21 N	10.50 E
Villafranca in Lunigiana	64	44.17 N	9.57 E
Villafranca Piemonte	62	44.47 N	7.33 E
Villafranca Sicula	70	37.35 N	13.17 E
Villafranca Tirrena	70	38.14 N	15.26 E
Villafrati	70	37.54 N	13.29 E
Villagarcía, Esp.	34	42.36 N	8.45 W
Villa García, Méx.	234	22.10 N	101.57 W
Village	196	35.33 N	97.33 W
Village Creek ≏	194	35.28 N	91.19 W
Village Green	285	39.52 N	75.26 W
Villa General Roca	252	32.39 S	66.28 W
Village of Drummond Hill	285	39.43 N	75.42 W
Village of the Branch	276	40.51 N	73.11 W
Villa Gesell	252	37.15 S	56.55 W
Villa Giambruno	288	34.48 S	58.13 W
Villa González Ortega	234	22.30 N	101.55 W
Villagrán, Méx.	232	24.29 N	99.29 W
Villagrán, Méx.	234	20.31 N	100.59 W
Villagrande Strisaili	71	39.58 N	9.30 E
Villa Grazia	70	38.09 N	13.10 E
Villa Grove	194	39.51 N	88.09 W
Villaguay	252	31.51 S	59.01 W
Villa Guerrero, Méx.	234	21.59 N	103.36 W
Villa Guerrero, Méx.	234	18.52 N	99.39 W
Villa Guillermina	252	28.14 S	59.28 W
Villa Hayes	252	25.06 S	57.34 W
Villahermosa	234	17.59 N	92.55 W
Villa Hernandarias	252	31.13 S	59.59 W
Villa Hidalgo, Méx.	204	30.59 N	116.10 W
Villa Hidalgo, Méx.	234	21.40 N	102.36 W
Villa Hidalgo, Méx.	234	21.44 N	105.15 W
Villa Hidalgo Yalalag	234	17.11 N	96.11 W
Villa Huidobro	252	34.50 S	64.35 W
Villaines-la-Juhel	32	48.21 N	0.17 W
Villa Insurgentes	232	25.12 N	111.44 W
Villa Iris	252	38.10 S	63.15 W
Villa Jiménez	234	19.55 N	101.35 W

Villa José L. Suárez ◆[8]	288	34.32 S	58.35 W
Villa Juanita	234	17.47 N	95.09 W
Villa Juárez, Méx.	232	27.10 N	109.50 W
Villa Juárez, Méx.	234	22.20 N	100.17 W
Villa Krause	252	31.34 S	68.32 W
Villa La Angostura	254	40.47 S	71.40 W
Villalago	66	41.56 N	13.50 E
Villa Larca	252	32.37 S	64.59 W
Villa La Venta	234	18.10 N	94.07 W
Villalba, Esp.	34	43.18 N	7.41 W
Villalba, It.	70	37.39 N	13.50 E
Villalba, P.R.	240m	18.08 N	66.30 W
Villaldama	232	26.30 N	100.26 W
Villa Lia	258	34.07 S	59.26 W
Villalon	116	11.31 N	124.22 E
Villalón de Campos	34	42.06 N	5.02 W
Villalonga	254	39.53 S	62.35 W
Villalpando	34	41.52 N	5.24 W
Villa Lugano ◆[8]	288	34.41 S	58.28 W
Villalvernia	62	44.49 N	8.51 E
Villa Lynch ◆[8]	288	34.36 S	58.31 W
Villa Madero, Arg.	288	34.42 S	58.30 W
Villa Madero, Méx.	234	19.24 N	101.16 W
Villa Mainero	232	24.32 N	99.38 W
Villamar	71	39.37 N	8.59 E
Villa María, Arg.	252	32.25 S	63.15 W
Villa Maria, Pa., U.S.	214	41.05 N	80.30 W
Villa Maria del Triunfo	286d	12.10 S	76.56 W
Villa María Grande	252	31.39 S	59.54 W
Villa Martín, Bol.	248	20.46 S	67.47 W
Villamartín, Esp.	34	36.52 N	5.38 W
Villamarzana	64	45.01 N	11.41 E
Villamassargia	71	39.16 N	8.38 E
Villa Matoque	252	25.49 S	63.49 W
Villa Mazán	252	28.40 S	66.34 W
Villa Media Agua	252	31.59 S	68.25 W
Villa Mercedes	252	30.07 S	68.42 W
Villa Minozzo	64	44.22 N	10.28 E
Villamontes	248	21.15 S	63.30 W
Villa Morelos	234	20.00 N	101.25 W
Villandraut	32	44.28 N	0.23 W
Villa Nova, Md., U.S.	284b	39.21 N	76.44 W
Villa Nova, Oh., U.S.	216	40.33 N	84.26 W
Villanova, Pa., U.S.	208	40.02 N	75.20 W
Villanova d'Asti	62	44.57 N	7.56 E
Villanova Mondovì	62	44.21 N	7.45 E
Villanova Monferrato	62	45.11 N	8.28 E
Villanova Monteleone	71	40.30 N	8.28 E
Villanova sull'Arda	64	45.01 N	10.00 E
Villanova Tulo	71	39.47 N	9.13 E
Villanova University ʋ[2]	285	40.02 N	75.21 W
Villa Nueva, Arg.	252	32.26 S	63.15 W
Villa Nueva, Arg.	252	32.54 S	68.47 W
Villanueva, Col.	246	10.37 N	72.59 W
Villa Nueva, Guat.	236	14.31 N	90.35 W
Villanueva, Hond.	236	15.17 N	88.00 W
Villanueva, Méx.	234	22.21 N	102.53 W
Villa Nueva, Nic.	236	12.58 N	86.49 W
Villanueva, N.M., U.S.	200	35.16 N	105.21 W
Villanueva de Córdoba	34	38.20 N	4.37 W
Villanueva de la Serana	34	38.58 N	5.48 W
Villanueva de la Sierra	34	40.12 N	6.24 W
Villanueva de los Infantes	34	38.44 N	2.59 W
Villanueva del Río y Minas	34	37.39 N	5.42 W
Villa Numancia	288	34.55 S	58.24 W
Villa Obregón	234	21.07 N	102.42 W
Villa Ocampo	252	28.28 S	59.22 W
Villa Ojo de Agua	252	29.31 S	63.42 W
Villa Oliva	252	26.01 S	57.53 W
Villa Opicina	64	45.40 N	13.49 E
Villa Oropeza	248	19.10 S	65.17 W
Villa Ottone (Uttenheim)	64	46.52 N	11.57 E
Villa Papale ʋ	267a	41.45 N	12.39 E
Villa Park, Ca., U.S.	228	33.48 N	117.48 W
Villa Park, Il., U.S.	278	41.53 N	87.59 W
Villa Park Dam ◆[6]	280	33.48 N	117.46 W
Villa Pérez	240m	18.12 N	66.47 W
Villapiana	68	39.51 N	16.28 E
Villapiana Lido	68	39.48 N	16.29 E
Villapinzón	246	5.13 N	73.36 W
Villa Potenza	66	43.19 N	13.25 E
Villaputzu	71	39.26 N	9.34 E
Villa Quinteros	252	27.14 S	65.33 W
Villa Quintilio Varo ⊥	267a	41.58 N	12.47 E
Villa Ramírez	252	32.11 S	60.12 W
Villarcayo	34	42.56 N	3.34 W
Villar-d'Arène	62	45.02 N	6.20 E
Villard-Bonnot	62	45.14 N	5.53 E
Villard-de-Lans	62	45.04 N	5.33 E
Villardefrades	34	41.43 N	5.15 W
Villar del Arzobispo	34	39.44 N	0.49 W
Villareal	116	11.34 N	124.56 E
Villa Real ◆[8]	288	34.37 S	58.31 W
Villa Regina	252	39.06 S	67.04 W
Villa Reynolds	252	33.43 S	65.23 W
Villa Rica	192	33.43 N	84.55 W
Villa Rivero	248	17.37 S	65.48 W
Villaroche	261	48.37 N	2.39 E
Villaroche ■	261	48.37 N	2.40 E
Villa Romana del Casale ⊥	70	37.22 N	14.20 E
Villa Rosa, Arg.	258	34.25 S	58.52 W
Villarosa, It.	70	37.35 N	14.10 E
Villar Pellice	62	44.48 N	7.09 E
Villar Perosa	62	44.56 N	7.15 E
Villarreales	196	26.07 N	100.20 W
Villarrica, Chile	254	39.16 S	72.13 W
Villarrica, Col.	246	3.58 N	74.37 W
Villarrica, Para.	252	25.45 S	56.26 W
Villarrica, Lago ⊜	254	39.15 S	72.06 W
Villarrobledo	34	39.16 N	2.36 W
Villarrubia de los Ojos	34	39.13 N	3.36 W
Villars, Arg.	258	34.50 S	58.56 W
Villars, Schw.	58	46.18 N	7.04 E
Villars-Colmars	62	44.10 N	6.36 E
Villars-en-Azois	58	48.04 N	4.45 E
Villars-les-Dombes	58	46.00 N	5.01 E
Villars-sur-Var	62	43.56 N	7.06 E
Villa Ruiz	258	34.25 S	59.15 W
Villas	208	39.01 N	74.56 W
Villa Sáenz Peña ◆[8]	288	34.36 S	58.31 W
Villa San Andrés ◆[8]	288	34.33 S	58.32 W
Villa Sandino	236	12.03 N	84.59 W
Villa San Giovanni	68	38.13 N	15.38 E
Villa San José	252	32.12 S	58.13 W
Villa San Martín	252	28.18 S	64.12 W
Villasanta	62	45.37 N	9.18 E
Villa Santa, Montaña ʌ	236	14.12 N	86.27 W
Villa Santa Maria	66	41.57 N	14.21 E
Villa Santina	64	46.24 N	12.55 E
Villa Santo Domingo	234	23.20 N	101.44 W
Villa Santos Lugares ◆[8]	288	34.36 S	58.32 W
Villasayas	34	41.21 N	2.37 W
Villa Serrano	248	19.06 S	64.22 W
Villasimius	71	39.08 N	9.31 E
Villasis	116	15.54 N	120.35 E
Villasor	71	39.23 N	8.56 E
Villa Talavera	248	19.49 S	65.25 W
Villa Tunari	248	16.55 S	65.25 W
Villa Turdera ◆[8]	288	34.48 S	58.25 W
Villa Unión, Arg.	252	29.18 S	68.12 W
Villa Unión, Arg.	252	29.24 S	62.47 W
Villa Unión, Méx.	232	28.15 N	100.43 W
Villa Unión, Méx.	234	23.58 N	104.02 W
Villa Unión, Méx.	234	23.12 N	106.14 W
Villa Urquiza ◆[8]	288	34.34 S	58.29 W
Villa Valeria	252	34.20 S	64.55 W
Villa Vallelonga	66	41.52 N	13.37 E
Villaverde ◆[8]	266a	40.21 N	3.42 W

Villaverla	64	45.39 N	11.29 E
Villa Verona	226	39.28 N	121.33 W
Villavicencio	246	4.09 N	73.37 W
Villaviciosa	34	43.29 N	5.26 W
Villaviciosa de Córdoba	34	38.05 N	5.01 W
Villa Victoria	234	18.47 N	103.24 W
Villa Viscarra	248	17.59 S	65.36 W
Villa Vomano	66	42.37 N	13.46 E
Villazón	248	22.06 S	65.36 W
Villa Zorraquín	252	31.19 S	58.02 W
Villé	58	48.20 N	7.18 E
Villebon, Lac ⊜	190	47.58 N	77.17 W
Villebon-sur-Yvette	261	48.42 N	2.15 E
Villeconin	261	48.31 N	2.08 E
Villecresnes	261	48.43 N	2.32 E
Villecroze	62	43.35 N	6.16 E
Ville-d'Avray	261	48.50 N	2.11 E
Ville-de-Laval → Laval	206	45.35 N	73.45 W
Villedieu	32	48.50 N	1.13 W
Ville-en-Tardenois	50	49.11 N	3.48 E
Villefort	62	44.26 N	3.56 E
Villefranche	58	45.59 N	4.43 E
Villefranche-de-Rouergue	32	44.21 N	2.02 E
Villefranche-sur-Cher	50	47.18 N	1.46 E
Villefranche-sur-Mer	62	43.42 N	7.19 E
Villejuif	50	48.48 N	2.22 E
Villejust	261	48.41 N	2.14 E
Ville-Marie	190	47.19 N	79.26 W
Villemaur-sur-Vanne	50	48.15 N	3.44 E
Villemeux-sur-Eure	50	48.40 N	1.28 E
Villemoisson-sur-Orge	261	48.40 N	2.19 E
Villemomble	261	48.53 N	2.31 E
Villena	34	38.38 N	0.51 W
Ville Nacional	234	17.50 N	96.14 W
Villenauxe-la-Grande	50	48.35 N	3.33 E
Villeneuve, It.	62	45.42 N	7.14 E
Villeneuve, Schw.	58	46.24 N	6.55 E
Villeneuve-d'Ascq	50	50.37 N	3.10 E
Villeneuve-d'Aveyron	32	44.26 N	2.02 E
Villeneuve-de-Berg	62	44.33 N	4.30 E
Villeneuve-la-Garenne	261	48.56 N	2.20 E
Villeneuve-la-Guyard	50	48.20 N	3.04 E
Villeneuve-l'Archevêque	50	48.14 N	3.33 E
Villeneuve-le-Comte	261	48.49 N	2.50 E
Villeneuve-le-Roi	50	48.44 N	2.25 E
Villeneuve-lès-Avignon	62	43.58 N	4.48 E
Villeneuve-lès-Maguelonne	62	43.32 N	3.52 E
Villeneuve-Saint-Denis	261	48.49 N	2.48 E
Villeneuve-Saint-Georges	50	48.44 N	2.27 E
Villeneuve-sous-Dammartin	261	49.02 N	2.39 E
Villeneuve-sur-Lot	32	44.25 N	0.42 E
Villeneuve-sur-Yonne	50	48.05 N	3.18 E
Villennes-sur-Seine	261	48.56 N	2.00 E
Villenoy	50	48.57 N	2.52 E
Villeny	50	47.37 N	1.45 E
Villeparisis	50	48.56 N	2.37 E
Villepinte	261	48.58 N	2.32 E
Ville Platte	194	30.41 N	92.16 W
Villepreux	261	48.50 N	2.01 E
Villequier	50	49.31 N	0.40 E
Villeron	261	49.03 N	2.33 E
Villeroy	50	48.59 N	2.47 E
Villers-Bocage, Fr.	32	49.05 N	0.39 W
Villers-Bocage, Fr.	50	49.59 N	2.20 E
Villers-Bretonneux	50	49.52 N	2.31 E
Villers-Carbonnel	50	49.52 N	2.54 E
Villers-Cotterêts	50	49.15 N	3.05 E
Villers-devant-Orval	56	49.37 N	5.19 E
Villers-en-Arthies	261	49.05 N	1.44 E
Villersexel	58	47.33 N	6.26 E
Villers-Farlay	58	47.00 N	5.45 E
Villers-la-Ville	50	50.35 N	4.32 E
Villers-le-Lac	58	47.04 N	6.40 E
Villers-lès-Nancy	58	48.40 N	6.09 E
Villers-lès-Pots	58	47.13 N	5.21 E
Villers-Outréaux	50	50.02 N	3.18 E
Villers-Saint-Paul	50	49.17 N	2.29 E
Villers-Semeuse	56	49.44 N	4.45 E
Villerupt	56	49.28 N	5.56 E
Villerville	50	49.24 N	0.08 E
Ville-Saint-Georges → Saint-Georges	188	46.07 N	70.40 W
Villes-sur-Auzon	62	44.03 N	5.14 E
Ville-sur-Tourbe	56	49.11 N	4.47 E
Villeta	246	5.01 N	74.28 W
Villetta Barrea	66	41.47 N	13.56 E
Villeurbanne	62	45.46 N	4.53 E
Villevaudé	261	48.55 N	2.39 E
Villeziers	261	48.40 N	2.10 E
Villiers	158	27.03 S	28.35 E
Villiers-Adam	261	49.04 N	2.14 E
Villiersdorp	158	34.00 S	19.19 E
Villiers-le-Bâcle	261	48.44 N	2.08 E
Villiers-le-Bel	261	49.00 N	2.23 E
Villiers-le-Sec	261	49.04 N	2.23 E
Villiers-Saint-Frédéric	261	48.49 N	1.54 E
Villiers-Saint-Georges	50	48.39 N	3.25 E
Villiers-sur-Marne	261	48.50 N	2.33 E
Villiers-sur-Morin	261	48.52 N	2.53 E
Villigst	263	51.26 N	7.35 E
Villingen-Schwenningen	58	48.04 N	8.28 E
Villisca	198	40.55 N	94.58 W
Villmanstrand → Lappeenranta	26	61.04 N	28.11 E
Villmergen	58	47.21 N	8.15 E
Villorba	64	45.44 N	12.14 E
Villoresi, Canale ≆	266b	45.33 N	9.19 E
Villotta	64	45.52 N	12.45 E
Vilm I	54	54.19 N	13.32 E
Vilmnitz	54	54.21 N	13.31 E
Vilna, Ab., Can.	182	54.07 N	111.55 W
Vilna → Vilnius, Liet.	76	54.41 N	25.19 E
Vilnius	76	54.41 N	25.19 E
Vil'nohirs'k	78	48.29 N	34.01 E
Vilosnes-sur-Meuse	56	49.20 N	5.14 E
Vilppula	26	62.01 N	24.31 E
Vils	58	47.33 N	10.38 E
Vils ≏, Dtsch.	60	49.09 N	11.58 E
Vils ≏, Dtsch.	60	48.37 N	13.11 E
Vils ≏, Europe	58	47.33 N	10.40 E
Vilsandi saar I	76	58.23 N	21.52 E
Vilsbiburg	60	48.27 N	12.12 E
Vilseck	60	49.37 N	11.48 E
Vil'shana	78	49.13 N	31.13 E
Vil'shanka	78	48.14 N	30.52 E
Vil'shany, Ukr.	78	50.03 N	35.53 E
Vil'shany, Ukr.	78	49.47 N	37.46 E
Vilsheim	60	48.27 N	12.07 E
Vilshofen	60	48.39 N	13.12 E
Vil'uj ≏	74	64.24 N	126.26 E
Vil'ujsk	74	63.45 N	121.35 E
Vil'ujskoje vodochranilišče ⊜[1]	74	62.30 N	111.00 E
Viluppuram	122	11.56 N	79.29 E
Vil'va	86	58.37 N	56.52 E
Vilvoorde	50	50.56 N	4.26 E
Vimercate	62	45.37 N	9.22 E
Vimianzo	34	43.07 N	9.02 W
Vimmerby	26	57.40 N	15.51 E
Vimodrone	266b	45.31 N	9.17 E
Vimoutiers	50	48.55 N	0.12 E
Vimpeli	26	63.09 N	23.48 E
Vimperk	60	49.03 N	13.47 E
Vimy	50	50.22 N	2.49 E
Vina	204	39.55 N	122.03 W
Vina ≏	146	7.45 N	15.36 E
Viñac	248	12.56 S	75.47 W
Viña del Mar	252	33.02 S	71.34 W
Vinadi	58	46.55 N	10.29 E

Vinadio	62	44.18 N	7.10 E
Viñales	240p	22.37 N	83.43 W
Vinalhaven	188	44.02 N	68.49 W
Vinalhaven Island I	188	44.05 N	68.52 W
Vinantes	261	49.01 N	2.44 E
Vina Roni, Mount ʌ	175e	8.10 S	157.28 E
Vinaròs	34	40.28 N	0.29 E
Vinay	62	45.13 N	5.24 E
Vinazco ≏	234	20.56 N	97.44 W
Vincennes, Fr.	50	48.51 N	2.26 E
Vincennes, In., U.S.	194	38.40 N	87.31 W
Vincennes, Bois de ♠	261	48.50 N	2.25 E
Vincennes, Château de ⊥	261	48.51 N	2.26 E
Vincennes, Étang de ⊜	261	48.47 N	2.45 E
Vincennes Bay c	9	66.30 S	109.30 E
Vincent	194	33.22 N	86.22 W
Vincent, Point ›	174c	29.00 S	167.55 E
Vincentown	208	39.56 N	74.44 W
Vinces	246	1.32 S	79.45 W
Vincey	58	48.20 N	6.20 E
Vinchiaturo	66	41.29 N	14.35 E
Vinchina	252	28.46 S	68.10 W
Vinchos	248	13.16 S	74.21 W
Vinci	66	43.47 N	10.55 E
Vinco	214	40.25 N	78.52 W
Vindeby	41	55.03 N	10.38 E
Vindelälven ≏	24	63.54 N	19.52 E
Vindeln	26	64.12 N	19.44 E
Vinden, Mount ʌ	162	27.01 S	115.38 E
Vinderslev	41	56.15 N	9.26 E
Vinderup	26	56.29 N	8.47 E
Vindhya Range ⋌	120	23.00 N	77.00 E
Vinding	41	55.41 N	9.35 E
Vindinge	41	55.19 N	10.45 E
Vine Brook ≏	283	42.27 N	71.13 W
Vinegar Hill ʌ	202	44.43 N	118.34 W
Vine Grove	194	37.48 N	85.58 W
Vine Hill	282	38.00 N	122.06 W
Vineland, Mi., U.S.	216	42.03 N	86.30 W
Vineland, N.J., U.S.	208	39.29 N	75.01 W
Vinemont	194	34.14 N	86.51 W
Vine Valley	210	42.43 N	77.20 W
Vineyard Canyon V	226	35.46 N	120.41 W
Vineyard Haven	207	41.27 N	70.36 W
Vineyard Lake ⊜	216	42.05 N	84.13 W
Vineyard Sound ʮ	207	41.25 N	70.46 W
Vingåker	40	59.02 N	15.52 E
Vingeanne ≏	58	47.21 N	5.29 E
Ving Ngün	110	22.37 N	99.16 E
Vinh	110	18.40 N	105.40 E
Vinhais	34	41.50 N	7.00 W
Vinhas, Ribeira das ≏	266c	38.42 N	9.25 W
Vinh Chau	110	9.19 N	105.59 E
Vinhedo	256	23.01 S	46.59 W
Vinh Loc	269c	10.49 N	106.34 E
Vinh Long	110	10.15 N	105.58 E
Vinh Tuy, Viet	110	9.37 N	105.22 E
Vinh Tuy, Viet	110	17.24 N	106.36 E
Vinica	36	45.28 N	15.15 E
Vinita	196	36.38 N	95.09 W
Vinkekuil	158	32.42 S	20.27 E
Vinkeveen	52	52.13 N	4.54 E
Vin'kivtsi	78	49.02 N	27.14 E
Vinkovci	38	45.17 N	18.49 E
Vinnhorst	52	52.25 N	9.43 E
Vinnitsa → Vinnytsya	78	49.14 N	28.29 E
Vinnum	263	51.41 N	7.24 E
Vinnytsya	78	49.14 N	28.29 E
Vinnytsya □[4]	78	49.00 N	28.45 E
Vinogradovo, Ross.	82	55.25 N	38.32 E
Vinogradovo, Ross.	82	55.57 N	37.32 E
Vinogrobol'	78	51.51 N	36.26 E
Vinön I	40	59.12 N	15.43 E
Vinon-sur-Verdon	62	43.43 N	5.48 E
Vinovo	62	44.57 N	7.38 E
Vinslöv	26	56.06 N	13.55 E
Vinson Massif ʌ	9	78.35 S	85.25 W
Vinstra	26	61.36 N	9.45 E
Vintilă Vodă	38	45.28 N	26.44 E
Vinto	248	17.58 S	67.04 W
Vinton, Ia., U.S.	190	42.10 N	92.01 W
Vinton, La., U.S.	194	30.11 N	93.34 W
Vinton, Va., U.S.	192	37.16 N	79.53 W
Vintondale	214	40.28 N	78.55 W
Vintrosa	40	59.15 N	14.57 E
Viñuelas, Arroyo de ≏	266a	40.33 N	3.33 W
Viny	76	58.22 N	32.13 E
Vinzelberg	54	52.33 N	11.40 E
Vinzili	86	56.58 N	65.46 E
Viola, Il., U.S.	190	41.12 N	90.35 W
Viola, N.Y., U.S.	276	41.08 N	74.05 W
Viola, Wi., U.S.	190	43.30 N	90.40 W
Viola, Val V	64	46.27 N	10.15 E
Violín, Isla I	236	8.51 N	83.39 W
Viols-le-Fort	62	43.45 N	3.42 E
Viosne ≏	50	49.03 N	2.06 E
Vipava	36	45.51 N	13.58 E
Vipava ≏	64	45.54 N	13.33 E
Vipiteno (Sterzing)	64	46.54 N	11.26 E
Vipos	252	26.29 S	65.22 W
Vipperow	54	53.19 N	12.41 E
Vir, Otok I	36	44.18 N	15.04 E
Vira	58	46.08 N	8.51 E
Virac	116	13.35 N	124.15 E
Viracopos, Aeroporto de ⊠	256	23.00 S	47.08 W
Virac Point ›	116	13.31 N	124.13 E
Viradouro	255	20.53 S	48.18 W
Virago Sound ʮ	182	54.00 N	132.36 W
Viramgām	120	23.07 N	72.02 E
Virandozero	24	64.05 N	35.58 E
Viranşehir	130	37.13 N	39.45 E
Vīrarājendrapet	122	12.12 N	75.48 E
Virbalis	76	54.38 N	22.49 E
Virden, Mb., Can.	184	49.51 N	100.55 W
Virden, Il., U.S.	219	39.30 N	89.46 W
Virden, N.M., U.S.	200	32.41 N	109.00 W
Vire	32	48.50 N	0.53 W
Vire ≏	32	49.20 N	1.07 W
Virelles	50	50.04 N	4.20 E
Virelles, Étang de ⊜	50	50.04 N	4.21 E
Vireux-Molhain	56	50.05 N	4.43 E
Virgem da Lapa	255	16.49 S	42.21 W
Virgen	64	47.00 N	12.27 E
Vírgen del San Cristóbal ʋ[1]	286e	33.26 S	70.39 W
Vírgenes, Cabo ›	254	52.22 S	68.20 W
Vírgenes, Islas → British Virgin Islands □[2], N.A.	240m	18.30 N	64.30 W
Vírgenes, Islas → Virgin Islands □[2], N.A.	240m	18.20 N	64.50 W
Virgen Tal V	64	47.00 N	12.25 E
Virgil, On., Can.	284a	43.13 N	79.08 W
Virgil, Ks., U.S.	198	37.58 N	96.00 W
Virgil, N.Y., U.S.	210	42.31 N	76.12 W
Virgilina	192	36.33 N	78.52 W
Virgilio	64	45.07 N	10.47 E
Virgin ≏	200	36.31 N	114.20 W
Virgin, North Fork ≏	200	37.10 N	113.01 W
Virginal-Samme	50	50.38 N	4.12 E
Virgin Gorda I	240m	18.30 N	64.24 W
Virgin Gorda Peak ʌ	240m	18.30 N	64.24 W
Virginia, Austl.	168b	34.40 S	138.34 E
Virgínia, Bra.	256	22.20 S	45.06 W
Virginia, Ire.	48	53.49 N	7.04 W
Virginia, S. Afr.	158	28.12 S	26.49 E
Virginia, Il., U.S.	219	39.57 N	90.12 W
Virginia, Mn., U.S.	190	47.31 N	92.32 W
Virginia □[3]	178	37.30 N	78.45 W
Virginia Beach	208	36.51 N	75.58 W
Virginia City, Mt., U.S.	202	45.17 N	111.56 W

Symbol	English	Deutsch	Español	Français	Português
≏	River	Fluß	Río	Rivière	Rio
≆	Canal	Kanal	Canal	Canal	Canal
ᒪ	Waterfall, Rapids	Wasserfall, Stromschnellen	Cascada, Rápidos	Chute d'eau, Rapides	Cascata, Rápidos
ʮ	Strait	Meeresstraße	Estrecho	Détroit	Estreito
c	Bay, Gulf	Bucht, Golf	Bahía, Golfo	Baie, Golfe	Baía, Golfo
⊜	Lake, Lakes	See, Seen	Lago, Lagos	Lac, Lacs	Lago, Lagos
⩸	Swamp	Sumpf	Pantano	Marais	Pântano
⊡	Ice Features, Glacier	Eis- und Gletscherformen	Accidentes Glaciales	Formes glaciaires	Acidentes glaciares
⩚	Other Hydrographic Features	Andere Hydrographische Objekte	Otros Elementos Hidrográficos	Autres données hydrographiques	Outros acidentes hidrográficos

Symbol	English	Deutsch	Español	Français	Português
✣	Submarine Features	Untermeerische Objekte	Accidentes Submarinos	Formes de relief sous-marin	Acidentes submarinos
□	Political Unit	Politische Einheit	Unidad Politica	Entité politique	Unidade política
ʋ	Cultural Institution	Kulturelle Institution	Institución Cultural	Institution culturelle	Instituição cultural
⊥	Historical Site	Historische Stätte	Sitio Histórico	Site historique	Sitio histórico
♠	Recreational Site	Erholungs- und Ferienort	Sitio de Recreo	Centre de loisirs	Area de Lazer
⊠	Airport	Flughafen	Aeropuerto	Aéroport	Aeroporto
■	Military Installation	Militäranlage	Instalación Militar	Installation militaire	Instalação militar
◆	Miscellaneous	Verschiedenes	Misceláneo	Divers	Diversos

ENGLISH: Name | Page | Lat.°′ | Long.°′

DEUTSCH: Name | Seite | Breite°′ | Länge°′ E = Ost

Virginia City, Nv., U.S. **226** 39.18 N 119.38 W
Virginia Creek ≃ **226** 38.13 N 119.14 W
Virginia Falls ⌞ **180** 61.38 N 125.42 W
Virginia Gardens **220** 25.49 N 80.17 W
Virginia Hills **208** 38.47 N 77.06 W
Virginia Key I **220** 25.44 N 80.09 W
Virginia Peak ∧ **204** 39.45 N 119.28 W
Virginia Ranch Reservoir ⊜[1] **226** 39.20 N 121.19 W
Virginia Range ⋏ **226** 39.18 N 119.30 W
Virginiatown **190** 48.08 N 79.35 W
Virginia Water **260** 51.24 N 0.34 W
Virginia Water ⊜[1] **260** 51.24 N 0.37 W
Virginie occidentale → West Virginia □[3] **188** 38.45 N 80.30 W
Virgin Islands □[2], N.A. **230** 18.20 N 64.50 W
Virgin Islands □[2], N.A. **240m** 18.20 N 64.50 W
Virgin Islands II **240m** 18.00 N 64.40 W
Virgin Islands National Park ♦ **240m** 18.20 N 64.45 W
Virginópolis **255** 18.45 S 42.45 W
Virgin Passage ⊔ **240m** 18.20 N 65.10 W
Virginville **208** 40.31 N 75.52 W
Virgolândia **255** 18.27 S 42.18 W
Virieu **62** 45.29 N 5.28 E
Virieu-le-Grand **62** 45.51 N 5.39 E
Virihaure ⊜ **24** 67.20 N 16.35 E
Virje **36** 46.04 N 16.59 E
Virkkala **26** 60.12 N 24.01 E
Virklund **41** 56.07 N 9.34 E
Virneburg **56** 50.20 N 7.04 E
Virôchey **110** 13.59 N 106.49 E
Viroflay **50** 48.48 N 2.10 E
Viroin ≃ **56** 50.05 N 4.43 E
Virojoki **26** 60.35 N 27.42 E
Víron **267c** 37.57 N 23.45 E
Vironvay **50** 49.12 N 1.13 E
Viroqua **190** 43.33 N 90.53 W
Virovitica **36** 45.50 N 17.23 E
Virpazar **38** 42.15 N 19.05 E
Virrat **26** 62.14 N 23.47 E
Virsbo **40** 59.52 N 16.02 E
Virserum **26** 57.19 N 15.35 E
Virtaniemi **24** 68.53 N 28.27 E
Virton **56** 49.34 N 5.32 E
Virtsu **76** 58.34 N 23.31 E
Virú **248** 8.25 S 78.45 W
Virudunagar **122** 9.36 N 77.58 E
Viru-Jaagupi **76** 59.15 N 26.28 E
Virulento **196** 28.52 N 104.21 W
Virunga, Parc National de ♦ **154** 1.00 S 29.15 E
Virungu **154** 7.04 S 29.46 E
Viru-Nigula **76** 59.27 N 26.41 E
Virvyčia ≃ **76** 56.13 N 22.34 E
Viry-Châtillon **50** 48.40 N 2.23 E
Vis **36** 43.03 N 16.12 E
Vis ≃, Fr. **62** 43.56 N 3.42 E
Vis (Fish) ≃, Namibia **156** 28.07 S 17.45 E
Vis ≃, S. Afr. **158** 30.53 S 20.23 E
Vis, Otok I **36** 43.02 N 16.11 E
Visale **175e** 9.15 S 159.42 E
Visalia **226** 36.19 N 119.17 W
Visalia Airport ⊠ **226** 36.19 N 119.23 W
Visayan Islands II **12** 11.00 N 123.30 E
Visayan Sea ⊤[2] **116** 11.35 N 123.51 E
Visbek **52** 52.48 N 8.19 E
Visby **26** 57.38 N 18.18 E
Viscaya, Bahía de → Biscay, Bay of ⊂ **32** 44.00 N 4.00 W
Viscount **184** 51.57 N 105.39 W
Viscount Melville Sound ⊔ **176** 74.10 N 108.00 W
Visé **56** 50.44 N 5.42 E
Višegrad **38** 43.47 N 19.17 E
Vis-en-Artois **50** 50.15 N 2.56 E
Višera ≃ **76** 58.34 N 31.24 E
Viserba **66** 44.05 N 12.32 E
Viseu, Bra. **250** 1.12 S 46.07 W
Viseu, Port. **34** 40.39 N 7.55 W
Vișeu ≃ **38** 47.55 N 24.09 E
Vișeu de Sus **38** 47.44 N 24.22 E
Vishākhapatnam **122** 17.42 N 83.18 E
Vishoek **158** 34.08 S 18.26 E
Visim **86** 57.39 N 59.30 E
Visingsö I **26** 58.03 N 14.20 E
Visitation, Île de la I **275a** 45.35 N 73.40 W
Viskafors **26** 57.38 N 12.50 E
Viskan ≃ **26** 57.14 N 12.12 E
Viškil' **80** 58.05 N 48.19 E
Viskinge **41** 55.40 N 11.16 E
Visl'ajevo **82** 54.25 N 36.43 E
Vislanda **26** 56.47 N 14.27 E
Vislinskij zaliv ⊂ **30** 54.27 N 19.40 E
Vismen ⊜ **40** 59.17 N 14.17 E
Visnagar **120** 23.42 N 72.33 E
Višn'aki **265b** 55.47 N 37.54 E
Višn'akovo **82** 55.45 N 38.10 E
Visnevo **76** 54.08 N 26.14 E
Višnevoje **80** 52.38 N 43.26 E
Višňové **61** 48.59 N 16.09 E
Višn'ovka **86** 50.49 N 72.12 E
Viso, Monte ∧ **62** 44.40 N 7.07 E
Visoki Dečani, Manastir ⊍[1] **38** 42.30 N 20.31 E
Visoko **38** 43.59 N 18.11 E
Visokoi Island I **18** 56.42 S 27.12 W
Visp **58** 46.18 N 7.53 E
Vispa ≃ **58** 46.18 N 7.52 E
Visrivier **158** 31.55 S 25.25 E
Vissefjärda **26** 56.32 N 15.35 E
Visselhövede **52** 52.59 N 9.35 E
Vissenbjerg **41** 55.23 N 10.08 E
Visso **66** 42.56 N 13.05 E
Vissoie **58** 46.13 N 7.36 E
Vista, Ca., U.S. **228** 33.12 N 117.14 W
Vista, N.Y., U.S. **210** 41.12 N 73.31 W
Vista Alegre, Arg. **252** 38.45 S 68.11 W
Vista Alegre, Bra. **256** 21.27 S 42.35 W
Vista Alegre, Chile **286e** 33.30 S 70.43 W
Vista Alegre, Perú **286d** 12.09 S 77.00 W
Vista Flores **252** 33.38 S 69.09 W
Vistahermosa de Negrete **234** 20.16 N 102.29 W
Vista La Mesa **228** 32.35 N 117.01 W
Vista Park **228** 35.21 N 118.55 W
Vistina **76** 59.47 N 28.29 E
Vistre ≃ **62** 43.40 N 4.15 E
Vistula → Wisła ≃ **30** 54.22 N 18.55 E
Vit ≃ **38** 43.41 N 24.45 E
Vita, Mb., Can. **184** 49.08 N 96.34 W
Vita, It. **70** 37.52 N 12.49 E
Vita ≃ **246** 6.11 N 67.31 W
Vitacura **286e** 33.24 S 70.36 W
Vitali **116** 7.22 N 122.18 E
Vitanje **36** 46.23 N 15.18 E
Vitarte **248** 12.02 S 76.56 W
Vite **122** 17.17 N 74.33 E
Vitebsk **76** 55.12 N 30.11 E
Vitebsk □[8] **76** 55.20 N 29.00 E
Vitebsk Station ⊸[5] **265a** 59.55 N 30.21 E
Vitel, Laguna ⊜ **258** 35.32 S 58.07 W
Viterbo **66** 42.25 N 12.06 E
Viterbo □[4] **66** 42.25 N 12.05 E
Vitiaz Strait ⊔ **164** 5.50 S 147.20 E
Vitichi **248** 20.13 S 65.29 W
Vitigudino **34** 41.01 N 6.26 W
Viti Levu I **175g** 18.00 S 178.00 E
Vitim **74** 59.28 N 112.34 E
Vitim ≃ **74** 59.26 N 112.34 E
Vitimskij **88** 58.14 N 113.18 E
Vitimskoje ploskogorje ⋏[1] **88** 54.00 N 113.30 E
Vitinia ⊸[8] **267a** 41.47 N 12.24 E
Vitinja)(**38** 42.47 N 23.49 E
Vitis **61** 48.45 N 15.10 E
Vítkov **30** 49.46 N 17.45 E
Vito **175e** 6.02 S 155.24 E
Vítor **248** 16.26 S 71.49 W
Vitor ≃ **248** 16.37 S 72.19 W
Vitória, Bra. **250** 2.54 S 52.01 W
Vitória, Bra. **255** 20.19 S 40.21 W
Vitoria (Gasteiz), Esp. **34** 42.51 N 2.40 W
Vitória, Ilha da I **256** 23.45 S 45.01 W
Vitória da Conquista **255** 14.51 S 40.51 W
Vitória de Santo Antão **250** 8.07 S 35.18 W
Vitória do Mearim **250** 3.28 S 44.53 W
Vitorino Freire **250** 4.04 S 45.10 W
Vitravo ≃ **68** 39.11 N 17.05 E
Vitré **32** 48.08 N 1.12 W
Vitrey-sur-Mance **58** 47.49 N 5.45 E
Vitry-aux-Loges **50** 47.56 N 2.16 E
Vitry-en-Artois **50** 50.20 N 2.59 E
Vitry-la-Ville **50** 48.50 N 4.28 E
Vitry-le-François **56** 48.44 N 4.35 E
Vitry [-sur-Seine] **50** 48.48 N 2.24 E
Vitshumbi **154** 0.41 S 29.23 E
Vittangi **24** 67.41 N 21.36 E
Vitte **54** 54.34 N 13.06 E
Vitteaux **58** 47.24 N 4.32 E
Vittel **58** 48.12 N 5.57 E
Vittinge **40** 59.54 N 17.04 E
Vittoria, On., Can. **212** 42.46 N 80.19 W
Vittoria, It. **70** 36.57 N 14.32 E
Vittorio Veneto **64** 45.59 N 12.18 E
Vittsjö **26** 56.20 N 13.40 E
Vitulano **68** 41.10 N 14.38 E
Vitznau **58** 47.01 N 8.29 E
Viù **62** 45.14 N 7.22 E
Vivarais □[9] **62** 44.40 N 4.30 E
Vivarais, Monts du ⋏ **62** 44.55 N 4.15 E
Viver **34** 39.55 N 0.36 W
Vivero **34** 43.40 N 7.35 W
Viverols **62** 45.26 N 3.53 E
Viverone, Lago di ⊜ **62** 45.25 N 8.02 E
Vivi ≃ **74** 63.52 N 97.50 E
Vivian **194** 32.52 N 93.59 W
Viviers **62** 44.29 N 4.41 E
Viviers-du-Lac **62** 45.39 N 5.54 E
Vivione, Passo del)(**64** 46.02 N 10.12 E
Vivonne **32** 46.26 N 0.16 E
Vivoratá **252** 37.40 S 57.39 W
Vivorillo, Cayos II **236** 15.50 N 83.18 W
Viwa I **175g** 17.08 S 176.54 E
Vizagapatam → Vishākhapatnam **122** 17.42 N 83.18 E
Vizcaíno, Desierto de ⊸[2] **232** 27.40 N 113.40 W
Vizcaíno, Isla I **258** 33.47 S 59.15 W
Vize **130** 41.34 N 27.45 E
Vize, ostrov I **72** 79.30 N 77.00 E
Vizianagaram **122** 18.07 N 83.25 E
Vizille **62** 45.05 N 5.46 E
Vižinada **36** 45.20 N 13.46 E
Vizinga **24** 61.05 N 50.04 E
Vizzini **70** 37.10 N 14.53 E
Vizzola **266b** 45.38 N 8.42 E
Vjulka ≃ **82** 56.53 N 37.57 E
Vjunka ≃ **265b** 55.42 N 38.01 E
Vjuny **86** 55.31 N 82.55 E
Vlaanderen → Flanders □[9] **50** 51.00 N 3.00 E
Vlaardingen **52** 51.54 N 4.21 E
Vlachovo Březí **60** 49.05 N 13.57 E
Vladař ∧ **54** 50.05 N 13.14 E
Vlădeasa, Vârful ∧ **38** 46.45 N 22.48 E
Vlădeni **38** 47.25 N 27.20 E
Vladičin Han **38** 42.42 N 22.04 E
Vladikavkaz **84** 43.03 N 44.40 E
Vladimir **80** 56.10 N 40.25 E
Vladimir Oblast' □[4] **76** 56.00 N 40.30 E
Vladimirovka, Kaz. **80** 50.51 N 51.08 E
Vladimirovka, Kaz. **86** 53.28 N 64.02 E
Vladimirskij Tupik **76** 55.42 N 33.18 E
Vladimirskoje **80** 56.49 N 45.07 E
Vladivostok **89** 43.10 N 131.56 E
Vladyčnoje **76** 58.49 N 39.29 E
Vladykino ⊸[8] **265b** 55.52 N 37.36 E
Vlasenica **38** 44.11 N 18.56 E
Vlašim **30** 49.42 N 14.54 E
Vlaskovo **82** 56.11 N 36.31 E
Vlasotince **38** 42.58 N 22.08 E
Vlasovo, Ross. **74** 70.48 N 135.00 E
Vlasovo, Ross. **82** 56.38 N 38.14 E
Vlazoviči **76** 53.01 N 32.18 E
Vledder **52** 52.52 N 6.12 E
Vleesbaai ⊂ **158** 34.16 S 21.57 E
Vleikolk **158** 29.43 S 20.50 E
Vleuten **52** 52.05 N 5.02 E
Vlieland I **52** 53.15 N 5.00 E
Vlijmen **52** 51.42 N 5.15 E
Vlissingen (Flushing) **52** 51.26 N 3.35 E
Vlodrop **52** 51.08 N 6.05 E
Vloesberg → Flobecq **50** 50.44 N 3.44 E
Vlonë → Vlorë **38** 40.27 N 19.30 E
Vlorë **38** 40.27 N 19.30 E
Vlorës, Gji i ⊂ **38** 40.25 N 19.25 E
Vlotho **52** 52.10 N 8.51 E
Vltava ≃ **30** 50.21 N 14.30 E
Vnukovo **82** 55.38 N 37.16 E
Vnukovo Airport ⊠ **265b** 55.37 N 37.17 E
Voca **196** 31.01 N 99.11 W
Vochrinka **82** 55.24 N 38.18 E
Vochtoga **76** 58.47 N 41.07 E
Voćin **36** 45.37 N 17.32 E
Vöckla ≃ **64** 48.00 N 13.36 E
Vöcklabruck **60** 48.01 N 13.39 E
Vöcklamarkt **60** 48.00 N 13.29 E
Vodla ≃ **24** 61.49 N 36.00 E
Vodlozero, ozero ⊜ **24** 62.20 N 36.55 E
Vodňany **30** 49.09 N 14.11 E
Vodnjan **36** 44.57 N 13.51 E
Vodnyj **24** 63.32 N 53.18 E
Vodo **64** 46.25 N 12.14 E
Vodosalma **24** 64.29 N 30.44 E
Vodovatovo **80** 55.24 N 43.34 E
Vodzimonje **80** 56.49 N 51.38 E
Voël ≃ **158** 33.07 S 25.07 E
Voerde, Dtsch. **52** 51.35 N 6.41 E
Voerde, Dtsch. **263** 51.18 N 7.24 E
Vogelenzang **52** 52.19 N 4.35 E
Vogelheim ⊸[8] **263** 51.29 N 6.59 E
Vogelkop → Doberai, Jazirah ›[1] **164** 1.30 S 132.30 E
Vogel Peak → Dimlang ∧ **146** 8.24 N 11.47 E
Vogelsang, Dtsch. **54** 53.43 N 14.09 E
Vogelsang, Dtsch. **56** 50.35 N 6.27 E
Vogelsberg ⋏ **56** 50.30 N 9.15 E
Vogesen → Vosges ⋏ **58** 48.30 N 7.10 E
Voghera **62** 44.59 N 9.01 E
Vognema **76** 59.59 N 38.10 E
Vogogna **58** 46.01 N 8.17 E
Vogtland ⊸[1] **54** 50.30 N 12.05 E
Voh **175f** 20.58 S 164.42 E
Vohburg an der Donau **60** 48.46 N 11.37 E
Vohenstrauss **60** 49.37 N 12.21 E
Vohibinany **157b** 18.49 S 49.04 E
Vohilava **157b** 21.04 S 48.00 E
Vohimarina **157b** 13.21 S 50.02 E
Vohipeno **157b** 22.22 S 47.51 E
Vohitsora **157b** 23.54 S 44.17 E
Võhma **76** 58.38 N 25.33 E
Vöhrenbach **58** 48.02 N 8.18 E
Vöhringen, Dtsch. **58** 48.16 N 10.04 E
Vöhringen, Dtsch. **58** 48.20 N 8.40 E
Vöhrum **52** 52.20 N 10.10 E
Vohwinkel ⊸[8] **263** 51.14 N 7.09 E
Voi **154** 3.23 S 38.34 E
Void **58** 48.41 N 5.37 E
Voight Creek ≃ **224** 47.06 N 122.10 W
Voikkaa **26** 60.56 N 26.37 E
Voinești **38** 47.05 N 27.26 E
Voinjama **150** 8.25 N 9.45 W
Voire ≃ **58** 48.27 N 4.25 E
Voiron **62** 45.22 N 5.35 E
Voise **50** 48.24 N 1.43 E
Voise ≃ **50** 48.35 N 1.35 E
Voisenon **261** 48.34 N 2.40 E
Voisins-le-Bretonneux **50** 48.45 N 2.03 E
Voiteur **58** 46.45 N 5.37 E
Voitsberg **61** 47.03 N 15.10 E
Voja ≃ **80** 57.23 N 49.55 E
Vojens **41** 55.15 N 9.19 E
Vojevodskoje **86** 52.47 N 85.35 E
Vojkovice **54** 50.15 N 13.02 E
Vojmsjön ⊜ **26** 64.55 N 16.40 E
Vojnić **36** 45.19 N 15.42 E
Vojnica **24** 65.12 N 30.15 E
Vojtanov **54** 50.06 N 12.19 E
Vojvodina □[4] **38** 45.00 N 20.00 E
Voj-Vož, Ross. **24** 64.20 N 55.03 E
Voj-Vož, Ross. **24** 62.56 N 54.56 E
Vokeo Island I **164** 3.10 S 144.05 E
Volano **66** 44.48 N 12.15 E
Volant **214** 41.07 N 80.16 W
Volary **60** 48.55 N 13.54 E
Volcán, Arg. **252** 23.54 S 65.27 W
Volcán, Pan. **236** 8.46 N 82.38 W
Volcán Isluga, Parque Nacional ♦ **248** 19.30 S 68.30 W
Volčanka **80** 52.33 N 49.59 E
Volcano, Ca., U.S. **226** 38.26 N 120.37 W
Volcano, Hi., U.S. **229d** 19.25 N 155.14 W
Volcano Island I **116** 14.00 N 121.00 E
Volcano Islands → Kazan-rettō II **14** 25.00 N 141.00 E
Volcán Poás, Parque Nacional ♦ **236** 10.10 N 84.15 W
Volčansk **86** 59.56 N 60.04 E
Volčenskij **83** 48.14 N 40.07 E
Volchonka-Zil ⊸[8] **265b** 55.40 N 37.37 E
Volchov **76** 59.55 N 32.20 E
Volchov ≃ **76** 60.08 N 32.20 E
Volčicha **86** 52.02 N 80.23 E
Volčij Nos, mys › **76** 60.31 N 32.35 E
Volčki **80** 52.29 N 40.42 E
Volda **26** 62.09 N 6.06 E
Volders **64** 47.17 N 11.34 E
Volendam **52** 52.30 N 5.04 E
Volga, Ross. **76** 57.57 N 38.24 E
Volga, Ia., U.S. **190** 42.48 N 91.32 W
Volga, S.D., U.S. **198** 44.19 N 96.55 W
Volga ≃, Ross. **72** 45.55 N 47.52 E
Volga ≃, Ia., U.S. **190** 42.45 N 91.17 W
Volga-Baltic Canal → Volgo-Baltijskij kanal ≋ **24** 59.00 N 38.00 E
Volgino **76** 58.27 N 33.52 E
Volgo, ozero ⊜ **76** 56.55 N 33.10 E
Volgo-Baltijskij kanal ≋ **24** 59.00 N 38.00 E
Volgodonsk **80** 47.33 N 42.08 E
Volgo-Donskoj sudochodnyj kanal imeni V.I. Lenina ≋ **80** 48.40 N 43.37 E
Volgograd (Stalingrad) **80** 48.44 N 44.25 E
Volgograd Oblast' □[4] **80** 49.30 N 44.00 E
Volgogradskoje vodochranilišče ⊜[1] **80** 49.20 N 45.00 E
Volgorečensk **76** 57.30 N 41.02 E
Volintiri **38** 46.26 N 29.37 E
Volissós **38** 38.29 N 25.58 E
Vol'ka **76** 52.47 N 25.39 E
Volkach **56** 49.52 N 10.13 E
Volkel **52** 51.38 N 5.40 E
Völkermarkt **61** 46.39 N 14.38 E
Völkermarkter Stausee ⊜[1] **61** 46.39 N 14.38 E
Völkerschlacht-Denkmal ⊥ **54** 51.18 N 12.24 E
Völklingen **56** 49.15 N 6.50 E
Volkmarsen **56** 51.24 N 9.07 E
Volkovo, Ross. **76** 59.15 N 41.27 E
Volkovo, Ross. **82** 55.46 N 36.15 E
Volkovo Cemetery ⊸ **265a** 59.54 N 30.22 E
Volkovskoje **82** 54.49 N 37.13 E
Volkovysk **76** 53.10 N 24.28 E
Volksdorf ⊸[8] **52** 53.39 N 10.10 E
Völksen **52** 52.13 N 9.37 E
Volksrust **158** 27.24 S 29.53 E
Vollenhove **52** 52.41 N 5.58 E
Vollersode **52** 53.18 N 8.56 E
Vollme **263** 51.10 N 7.36 E
Vollore-Montagne **62** 45.47 N 3.41 E
Vollore-Ville **62** 45.47 N 3.36 E
Vollsjö **41** 55.42 N 13.46 E
Volma ≃ **76** 53.35 N 28.19 E
Volmarstein **56** 51.22 N 7.23 E
Volme ≃ **263** 51.24 N 7.27 E
Volmerange-les-Mines **56** 49.27 N 6.05 E
Volmerswerth ⊸[8] **263** 51.11 N 6.46 E
Volmunster **56** 49.07 N 7.21 E
Vol'naja Gorka **76** 58.43 N 30.51 E
Volnay **58** 47.00 N 4.47 E
Vol'noje, Ross. **80** 47.09 N 47.38 E
Vol'noje, Ross. **86** 54.17 N 71.21 E
Volnovakha **83** 47.36 N 37.31 E
Vol'nyj **80** 45.55 N 45.14 E
Vol'nyj, ostrov I **265a** 59.58 N 30.14 E
Voločajevka Vtoraja **89** 48.34 N 134.34 E
Voločanka **74** 71.00 N 94.28 E
Volochys'k **78** 49.32 N 26.11 E
Volockaja **76** 60.17 N 42.59 E
Volodarka, Ross. **86** 52.43 N 83.38 E
Volodarka, Ukr. **78** 49.31 N 29.55 E
Volodarsk, Ross. **76** 56.13 N 43.10 E
Volodars'k, Ukr. **83** 48.06 N 39.35 E
Volodars'ke **83** 47.12 N 37.20 E
Volodarskij, Ross. **80** 46.24 N 48.32 E
Volodarskij, Ross. **82** 55.30 N 37.57 E
Volodarskij ⊸[8] **265a** 59.49 N 30.05 E
Volodarskoje **86** 53.18 N 68.08 E
Volodars'k-Volyns'kyy **78** 50.37 N 28.25 E
Volodino **86** 57.06 N 83.54 E
Volodymyrets' **78** 51.25 N 26.08 E
Volodymyrivka, Ukr. **78** 47.32 N 32.55 E
Volodymyrivka, Ukr. **83** 47.44 N 37.23 E
Volodymyr-Volyns'kyy **78** 50.51 N 24.20 E
Vologda **76** 59.12 N 39.55 E
Vologda ≃ **76** 59.17 N 40.13 E
Vologda Oblast' □[4] **24** 60.00 N 40.00 E
Voloje **76** 54.09 N 34.35 E
Volokolamsk **82** 56.02 N 35.57 E
Volokonovka **78** 50.29 N 37.51 E
Volokovaja **24** 66.28 N 48.10 E
Volonga **24** 67.07 N 47.41 E
Volonne **62** 44.07 N 6.01 E
Vólos **38** 39.21 N 22.56 E
Vološino, Ross. **83** 48.55 N 39.56 E
Vološino, Ross. **83** 47.31 N 39.40 E
Vološka **24** 61.20 N 40.06 E
Volos'ka Balakliya **83** 49.37 N 37.20 E
Vološn'a ≃ **82** 55.51 N 35.54 E
Vološno **76** 58.29 N 28.29 E
Volosoviči **76** 54.46 N 28.50 E
Volosovo **76** 59.26 N 29.29 E
Volot **76** 57.56 N 30.42 E
Volovets' **78** 48.43 N 23.11 E
Volovo, Ross. **76** 53.35 N 38.02 E
Volovo, Ross. **78** 52.03 N 37.53 E
Vložin **76** 54.05 N 26.32 E
Volpago del Montello **64** 45.47 N 12.07 E
Volpedo **62** 44.53 N 8.59 E
Volpiano **62** 45.12 N 7.46 E
Völpke **54** 52.08 N 11.09 E
Völs → Fiè **64** 46.31 N 11.30 E
Volsini, Monti ⋏ **66** 42.40 N 11.55 E
Vol'sk **80** 52.02 N 47.23 E
Volstruisleegte **158** 33.05 S 23.28 E
Volta □[4] **150** 7.00 N 0.30 E
Volta ≃ **150** 5.46 N 0.41 E
Volta, Lake ⊜[1] **150** 7.30 N 0.15 E
Volta Blanche (White Volta) ≃ **150** 9.10 N 1.15 W
Voltaggio **62** 44.37 N 8.50 E
Voltago **64** 46.16 N 12.00 E
Volta Grande **256** 21.46 S 42.32 W
Voltaire, Cape › **164** 14.16 S 125.35 E
Volta Mantovana **64** 45.19 N 10.39 E
Volta Noire (Black Volta) ≃ **150** 8.41 N 1.33 W
Volta Redonda **256** 22.32 S 44.07 W
Volta Rouge ≃ **150** 10.34 N 0.30 W
Volterra **66** 43.24 N 10.51 E
Vol'teva **24** 64.30 N 44.12 E
Voltri **62** 44.26 N 8.45 E
Volturara Appula **68** 41.30 N 15.03 E
Volturara Irpina **68** 40.53 N 14.55 E
Volturino **68** 41.28 N 15.07 E
Volturino, Monte ∧ **68** 40.25 N 15.49 E
Volturno ≃ **66** 41.01 N 13.55 E
Volubilis ⊥ **148** 34.00 N 5.30 W
Voluntown **207** 41.34 N 71.52 W
Volusia □[6] **220** 28.51 N 81.05 W
Vólvi, Límni ⊜ **38** 40.41 N 23.23 E
Volx **62** 43.53 N 5.51 E
Volyn' □[4] **78** 51.00 N 25.00 E
Volyn' □[9] **78** 50.50 N 27.00 E
Volyncy, Bela. **76** 55.42 N 28.11 E
Volyncy, Ross. **80** 57.48 N 45.28 E
Volyně **60** 49.10 N 13.53 E
Volynka **78** 51.37 N 32.26 E
Volyňka ≃ **60** 49.16 N 13.54 E
Volyns'ka vysochyna ⋏[1] **78** 50.30 N 25.30 E
Volzhskiy → Volžskij **80** 48.50 N 44.44 E
Volžsk **80** 55.53 N 48.21 E
Volžskij, Ross. **80** 53.27 N 50.07 E
Volžskij, Ross. **80** 48.50 N 44.44 E
Vom **150** 9.41 N 8.42 E
Vomano ≃ **66** 42.39 N 14.02 E
Vombsjön ⊜ **41** 55.41 N 13.36 E
Vomp **64** 47.20 N 11.41 E
Vonavona Island I **175e** 8.15 S 157.05 E
Vonda **184** 52.19 N 106.06 W
Vondanka **24** 59.07 N 47.49 E
Vondrozo **157b** 22.49 S 47.20 E
Von Frank Mountain ∧ **180** 63.33 N 154.20 W
Võnnu **76** 58.17 N 27.05 E
Vonozero **76** 60.22 N 34.26 E
Vonsild **41** 55.27 N 9.29 E
Von Treuer Tableland ⋏[1] **162** 26.38 S 122.53 E
Voorburg **52** 52.05 N 4.23 E
Voordeelspan **158** 29.05 S 21.32 E
Voorheesville **210** 42.39 N 73.56 W
Voorne I **52** 51.54 N 4.08 E
Voorschoten **52** 52.07 N 4.27 E
Voorst **52** 52.10 N 6.09 E
Voorthuizen **52** 52.12 N 5.35 E
Vop' ≃ **76** 54.56 N 32.44 E
Vopnafjörður **24a** 65.47 N 14.44 W
Vopnafjörður ⊂ **24a** 65.52 N 14.40 W
Vörå (Vöyri) **26** 63.09 N 22.15 E
Vor'a ≃, Ross. **76** 54.54 N 35.01 E
Vor'a ≃, Ross. **82** 55.52 N 38.13 E
Vorarlberg □[3] **58** 47.15 N 9.55 E
Vorau **61** 47.25 N 15.54 E
Vorbach **60** 49.49 N 11.45 E
Vorbasse **41** 55.38 N 9.05 E
Vorbjovo **88** 57.23 N 102.18 E
Vorchdorf **60** 48.00 N 13.55 E
Vörden, Dtsch. **52** 52.28 N 8.05 E
Vorden, Ned. **52** 52.07 N 6.18 E
Vorder-Grauspitz ∧ **58** 47.03 N 9.36 E
Vorderkrimmi **64** 47.14 N 12.12 E
Vordernberg **61** 47.28 N 15.00 E
Vorderrhein ≃ **58** 46.49 N 9.25 E
Vorderriss **64** 47.33 N 11.26 E
Vordingborg **41** 55.01 N 11.55 E
Voreifel ⋏ **56** 50.15 N 7.10 E
Vóreion Aiyaíon □[4] **38** 38.30 N 26.00 E
Voreppe **62** 45.18 N 5.38 E
Vorey **62** 45.11 N 3.54 E
Vorga **76** 53.45 N 32.45 E
Vorhalle ⊸[8] **263** 51.23 N 7.28 E
Vorhelm **52** 51.48 N 7.56 E
Vøringsfossen ⌞ **26** 60.26 N 7.15 E
Vórioi Sporádhes II **38** 39.15 N 23.55 E
Vórios Evvoïkós Kólpos ⊂ **38** 38.40 N 23.15 E
Vorkuta **24** 67.27 N 63.58 E
Vorlich, Ben ∧, Scot., U.K. **46** 56.17 N 4.46 W
Vorlich, Ben ∧, Scot., U.K. **46** 56.20 N 4.14 W
Vorma ≃ **26** 60.09 N 11.27 E
Vormholz **263** 51.24 N 7.18 E
Vormsi I **76** 59.00 N 23.20 E
Vorn'any **76** 54.44 N 26.01 E
Vorobjevo, Ross. **82** 56.11 N 35.45 E
Vorobjevo, Ross. **86** 56.08 N 76.32 E
Vorobji **82** 55.09 N 36.48 E
Vorobjovka **80** 50.38 N 40.56 E
Vorob'jovo **76** 59.38 N 40.55 E
Vorobyove **78** 45.20 N 33.15 E
Vorokhta **78** 48.18 N 24.36 E
Voron' **76** 55.00 N 28.39 E
Voron, porog ⌞ **88** 57.05 N 98.40 E
Vorona ≃ **80** 51.22 N 42.03 E
Voroncov **38** 47.43 N 29.08 E
Voroncovka, Kaz. **86** 48.49 N 81.32 E
Voroncovka, Ross. **78** 50.37 N 40.21 E
Voroncovka, Ross. **86** 59.39 N 60.14 E
Voroncovka, Ross. **88** 58.51 N 112.56 E
Voroncovo, Ross. **76** 57.18 N 28.42 E
Voroncovo, Ross. **80** 55.16 N 40.27 E
Voronej → Voronež **78** 51.40 N 39.10 E
Voronež **78** 51.40 N 39.10 E
Voronež ≃ **76** 51.56 N 39.25 E
Voronezh → Voronež **78** 51.40 N 39.10 E
Voronež Oblast' □[4] **78** 51.00 N 40.00 E
Voronežskij zapovednik ⊸[4] **76** 51.56 N 39.37 E
Voronino **82** 56.24 N 36.52 E
Voronizh **78** 51.46 N 33.28 E
Voronja ≃ **24** 69.10 N 35.50 E
Voronjo, Ross. **24** 68.27 N 35.21 E
Voronjo, Ross. **80** 58.00 N 42.01 E
Voronki **82** 55.48 N 37.16 E
Voron'ky **78** 50.14 N 33.02 E
Voronok **76** 52.23 N 32.40 E
Voronov, mys › **76** 60.15 N 32.05 E
Voronovkova Niva **76** 57.04 N 29.16 E
Voronovo, Bela. **76** 54.09 N 25.19 E
Voronovo, Ross. **82** 55.19 N 37.10 E
Voronovo, Ross. **86** 56.01 N 83.52 E
Voronovytsya **78** 49.06 N 28.41 E
Vorontsivka **78** 45.51 N 33.47 E
Voropajevo **76** 55.09 N 27.13 E
Voroshilov → Ussurijsk **89** 43.48 N 131.59 E
Voroshilovsk → Stavropol' **72** 45.02 N 41.59 E
Vorošilovgrad → Luhans'k **83** 48.34 N 39.20 E
Vorotajevka **80** 51.56 N 47.16 E
Vorotynec **80** 56.04 N 45.52 E
Vorotynsk **82** 54.25 N 36.05 E
Vorovskolesskaja **84** 44.23 N 42.25 E
Vorožejka **86** 58.12 N 90.02 E
Vorozhba **78** 51.12 N 34.14 E
Vorpommern □[9] **54** 53.40 N 13.45 E
Vorra **60** 49.33 N 11.30 E
Vorsfelde **54** 52.26 N 10.49 E
Vorskla ≃ **78** 48.53 N 34.06 E
Vorsma **80** 55.59 N 43.16 E
Vorst, Bel. **56** 51.04 N 5.01 E
Vorst, Dtsch. **56** 51.18 N 6.25 E
Vørterkaka Nunatak ∧ **9** 72.20 S 27.29 E
Võrtsjärv ⊜ **76** 58.16 N 26.03 E
Võru **76** 57.50 N 27.01 E
Voruch **85** 39.52 N 70.35 E
Vorzel' **78** 50.33 N 30.09 E
Vosburg **158** 30.33 S 22.52 E
Voschod **80** 47.24 N 41.50 E
Vösendorf **61** 48.07 N 16.20 E
Vosges □[5] **58** 48.10 N 6.20 E
Vosges ⋏ **58** 48.30 N 7.10 E
Vosja **76** 59.01 N 41.11 E
Voskresenka, Ross. **80** 51.01 N 46.28 E
Voskresenka, Ross. **88** 53.15 N 119.31 E
Voskresenki **82** 54.57 N 38.04 E
Voskresenovskoje **265a** 59.43 N 30.47 E
Voskresensk **82** 55.19 N 38.42 E
Voskresens'ke **78** 47.02 N 32.09 E
Voskresenskoje, Ross. **76** 53.12 N 38.43 E
Voskresenskoje, Ross. **76** 58.54 N 38.36 E
Voskresenskoje, Ross. **76** 59.26 N 37.56 E
Voskresenskoje, Ross. **76** 57.49 N 37.40 E
Voskresenskoje, Ross. **80** 56.51 N 45.26 E
Voskresenskoje, Ross. **80** 51.51 N 46.56 E
Voskresenskoje, Ross. **82** 54.07 N 37.07 E
Voskresenskoje, Ross. **82** 56.20 N 38.29 E
Voskresenskoje, Ross. **86** 53.08 N 56.10 E
Voslapp **52** 53.36 N 8.05 E
Voss **26** 60.39 N 6.26 E
Vosselaar **56** 51.19 N 4.53 E
Vossman's Beacon **158** 26.11 S 30.40 E
Vostočnaja Kambal'nica **24** 68.18 N 46.00 E
Vostočno-Kazachstan □[8] **86** 49.00 N 84.00 E
Vostočno-Kounradskij **86** 47.02 N 75.07 E
Vostočno-Sibirskoje more (East Siberian Sea) ⊤[2] **12** 74.00 N 166.00 E
Vostočnyj, Ross. **82** 55.47 N 37.52 E
Vostočnyj, Ross. **86** 58.48 N 61.52 E
Vostočnyj, Ross. **89** 53.29 N 143.03 E
Vostočnyj, Ross. **89** 48.17 N 142.34 E
Vostočnyj Sajan ⋏ **88** 53.00 N 97.00 E
Vostok I **14** 10.06 S 152.23 W
Vostok ⊍[3] **9** 78.30 S 106.50 E
Vostr'akovo **82** 55.23 N 37.49 E
Vostrecovo **89** 45.53 N 134.58 E
Vostrovo **86** 52.09 N 80.38 E
Vosves **261** 48.31 N 2.36 E
Votaw **222** 30.26 N 94.41 W
Votice **30** 49.38 N 14.39 E
Votkinsk **80** 57.03 N 53.59 E
Votkinskoje vodochranilišče ⊜[1] **86** 57.00 N 54.30 E
Vot'pa **86** 60.13 N 62.57 E
Votuporanga **255** 20.24 S 49.59 W
Voué **50** 48.28 N 4.07 E
Vouga ≃ **34** 40.41 N 8.40 W
Vougba **152** 5.10 N 23.06 E
Vougeot **58** 47.10 N 4.58 E
Vouillé **32** 46.39 N 0.10 E
Voujeaucourt **58** 47.28 N 6.46 E
Voulangis **261** 48.51 N 2.54 E
Voulou **146** 8.33 N 22.36 E
Voulx **50** 48.17 N 2.58 E
Voulzie ≃ **50** 48.25 N 3.12 E
Voutenay-sur-Cure **50** 47.33 N 3.47 E
Vouvray **50** 47.25 N 0.48 E
Vouvry **58** 46.20 N 6.53 E
Vouziers **56** 49.24 N 4.42 E
Vovcha ≃ **78** 48.00 N 36.08 E
Vovchans'k **78** 50.18 N 36.57 E
Vovchoyarivka **83** 48.50 N 38.22 E
Voves **50** 48.16 N 1.38 E
Vovkovyntsi **78** 49.13 N 27.39 E
Vovodo ≃ **140** 5.40 N 24.21 E
Vowinckel **214** 41.25 N 79.14 W
Voxnan ≃ **26** 61.17 N 16.26 E
Voyageurs National Park ♦ **190** 48.30 N 93.00 W
Voyinka **78** 45.52 N 33.59 E
Voykove **78** 45.31 N 33.52 E
Voykovs'kyy **83** 47.46 N 38.20 E
Voynyliv **78** 49.08 N 24.30 E
Vöyri → Vörå **26** 63.09 N 22.15 E
Voža ≃ **82** 54.38 N 39.10 E
Vožajol' **24** 62.50 N 51.17 E
Vožd' Proletariata **76** 55.26 N 39.19 E
Vozdviženka **80** 53.10 N 54.14 E
Vozdviženskoje, Ross. **80** 56.58 N 45.37 E
Vozdviženskoje, Ross. **80** 45.50 N 43.40 E
Vozdviženskoje, Ross. **82** 56.12 N 38.04 E
Vozdvyzhivka **78** 47.46 N 36.05 E
Vože, ozero ⊜ **24** 60.30 N 39.00 E
Vožega **76** 60.29 N 40.12 E
Vožega ≃ **76** 60.33 N 39.11 E
Vožgaly **80** 58.09 N 50.11 E
Vožgora **24** 64.32 N 48.25 E
Voznesenje **24** 61.01 N 35.27 E
Voznesenka, Kaz. **86** 52.24 N 70.12 E
Voznesenka, Ukr. **78** 46.51 N 35.26 E
Voznesenovka **80** 46.16 N 44.21 E
Voznesens'k **78** 47.34 N 31.20 E
Voznesenskoje, Ross. **80** 54.54 N 42.46 E
Voznesenskoje, Ross. **80** 45.49 N 43.25 E
Vozroždenija, ostrov I **86** 45.03 N 59.12 E
Vozroždenije **80** 52.42 N 48.12 E
Vozsiyats'ke **78** 47.41 N 32.07 E
Vozžajevka **89** 50.44 N 128.41 E
Vrå **26** 57.21 N 9.57 E
Vráble **30** 48.15 N 18.19 E
Vraca **38** 43.12 N 23.33 E
Vračevo **82** 54.53 N 39.10 E
Vrådal **26** 59.20 N 8.25 E
Vrancea □[6] **38** 45.45 N 27.00 E
Vrancei, Munții ⋏ **38** 46.00 N 26.30 E
Vrangel'a, mys › **89** 54.17 N 138.39 E
Vrangel'a, ostrov I **74** 71.00 N 179.30 W
Vranje **38** 42.33 N 21.54 E
Vranov **61** 48.54 N 15.49 E
Vranov [nad Topl'ou] **30** 48.54 N 21.41 E
Vrbas **38** 45.35 N 19.39 E
Vrbas ≃ **36** 45.06 N 17.31 E
Vrbovec **36** 45.53 N 16.25 E
Vrbovsko **36** 45.23 N 15.05 E
Vrchlabí **30** 50.38 N 15.37 E
Vrede **158** 27.30 S 29.06 E
Vredefort **158** 27.05 S 27.16 E
Vreden **52** 52.02 N 6.52 E
Vredenburg **158** 32.54 S 17.59 E
Vredenburgh **194** 31.49 N 87.19 W
Vredendal **158** 31.41 S 18.35 E
Vreed en Hoop **246** 6.48 N 58.11 W
Vreeswijk **52** 52.01 N 5.05 E
Vrena **40** 58.52 N 16.41 E
Vresse **56** 49.52 N 4.56 E
Vreta kloster ⊍[1] **26** 58.28 N 15.29 E
Vretstorp **40** 59.02 N 14.52 E
Vrginmost **36** 45.21 N 15.52 E
Vrhnika **36** 45.58 N 14.18 E
Vriddhāchalam **122** 11.30 N 79.20 E
Vriendschaps ≃ **164** 5.28 S 138.53 E
Vries **52** 53.04 N 6.35 E
Vriezenveen **52** 52.25 N 6.38 E
Vrigne-Meuse **56** 49.42 N 4.51 E
Vrigstad **26** 57.21 N 14.28 E
Vrilissia **267c** 38.02 N 23.50 E
Vrille ≃ **50** 47.31 N 2.52 E
Vrin **58** 46.39 N 9.06 E
Vrin ≃ **50** 48.00 N 3.20 E
Vrindāvan **124** 27.35 N 77.42 E
Vrlika **36** 43.55 N 16.24 E
Vrnograč **36** 45.10 N 15.57 E
Vroeggedeel **158** 28.02 S 22.32 E
Vron **50** 50.19 N 1.45 E
Vrondádhes **38** 38.24 N 26.08 E
Vroomshoop **52** 52.27 N 6.34 E
Vrouenspan **158** 27.50 S 20.24 E
Vroutek **54** 50.08 N 13.24 E
Vršac **38** 45.07 N 21.18 E
Vrsar **64** 45.08 N 13.37 E
Vršič)(**64** 46.26 N 13.44 E
Vrubivs'kyy **83** 48.26 N 39.07 E
Vrútky **30** 49.07 N 18.55 E
Vryburg **158** 26.55 S 24.45 E
Vryheid **158** 27.46 S 30.48 E
Vschody **76** 54.42 N 34.06 E
Vselug, ozero ⊜ **76** 57.03 N 32.42 E
Všepadly **60** 49.28 N 13.06 E
Všeruby **60** 49.50 N 13.15 E
Vsetín **30** 49.21 N 17.59 E
Vsevidof, Mount ∧ **180** 53.07 N 168.43 W
Vsevoložsk **265a** 60.01 N 30.40 E
Vtoroje Potapovo **265b** 55.56 N 37.58 E
Vtoryje Levyje Lamki **80** 53.17 N 41.04 E
Vuadil' **85** 40.11 N 71.43 E
Vuanggava Island I **175g** 18.52 S 178.54 W
Vučitrn **38** 42.49 N 20.58 E
Vudor, gora ∧ **85** 38.13 N 71.49 E
Vue-des-Alpes)(**58** 47.04 N 6.53 E
Vught **52** 51.40 N 5.17 E
Vuhlehirs'k **83** 48.19 N 38.17 E
Vuhle-Zavod **78** 52.11 N 32.53 E
Vuillafans **58** 47.04 N 6.13 E
Vuitebœuf **58** 46.37 N 6.34 E
Vukovar **38** 45.21 N 19.00 E
Vulcan, Ab., Can. **182** 50.24 N 113.15 W
Vulcan, Rom. **38** 45.23 N 23.17 E
Vulcan, Mi., U.S. **190** 45.46 N 87.51 W
Vulcănești **38** 45.41 N 28.24 E
Vulcano, Bocche di ⊔ **70** 38.26 N 14.57 E
Vulcano, Isola I **70** 38.24 N 14.58 E
Vulcano, Monte ∧[2] **70a** 35.51 N 12.52 E
Vulci ⊥ **66** 42.25 N 11.35 E
Vulkanichnyy khrebet ⋏ **78** 48.30 N 23.00 E
Vulture, Monte ∧ **68** 40.57 N 15.38 E
Vul'vyvejem ≃ **180** 66.58 N 179.10 W
Vung Tau **110** 10.21 N 107.04 E
Vunindawa **175g** 17.49 S 178.19 E
Vunisea Station **175g** 19.03 S 178.09 E
Vuoggatjålme **24** 66.36 N 16.22 E
Vuohijärvi **26** 61.05 N 26.48 E
Vuohijärvi ⊜ **26** 61.12 N 26.42 E
Vuokatti ∧[2] **26** 64.07 N 28.14 E
Vuoksa ≃ **26** 61.03 N 30.11 E
Vuoksa, ozero ⊜ **76** 60.40 N 29.50 E
Vuoksenniska **26** 61.13 N 28.49 E
Vurnary **80** 55.29 N 46.58 E
Vuturu, Pizzo ∧ **70** 37.56 N 14.13 E
Vuya **154** 5.21 N 29.40 E
Vuyyūru **122** 16.22 N 80.51 E
Vuzenica **61** 46.36 N 15.10 E
Vvedenka **86** 54.03 N 63.45 E
Vvedenovka **89** 51.19 N 128.12 E
Vvedenskoje **82** 55.42 N 36.54 E
Vyāra **120** 21.07 N 73.24 E
Vyatka → Kirov **80** 58.38 N 49.42 E
V'yazivok **78** 49.11 N 31.25 E
Vyaz'ma → V'az'ma **76** 55.13 N 34.18 E
Vyazniki → V'azniki **80** 56.15 N 42.10 E
Vyborg **76** 60.42 N 28.45 E
Vyborgskij zaliv ⊂ **76** 60.35 N 28.24 E
Výčapy **61** 49.09 N 15.53 E
Vyčegda ≃ **24** 61.18 N 46.36 E
Vyčegodskij **24** 61.16 N 46.48 E
Vychino ⊸[8] **265b** 55.43 N 37.48 E
Východočeský Kraj □[4] **30** 50.10 N 16.00 E
Východoslovenský Kraj □[4] **30** 49.00 N 21.15 E
Vydrino, Ross. **88** 51.27 N 104.39 E
Vydrino, Ross. **88** 56.50 N 99.02 E
Vygoda **78** 48.56 N 23.55 E
Vygoniči **76** 53.08 N 34.05 E
Vygonišči **76** 52.37 N 25.55 E
Vygozero, ozero ⊜ **24** 63.35 N 34.42 E
Vyjezdnoje **80** 55.23 N 43.47 E
Vyjezžij Log **86** 54.58 N 93.57 E
Vyksa **80** 55.18 N 42.11 E
Vylkove **78** 45.25 N 29.35 E
Vylkovo **86** 53.05 N 81.26 E
Vym' ≃ **24** 62.13 N 50.25 E
Vynnyky **78** 49.48 N 24.08 E
Vynohradiv **78** 48.09 N 23.02 E
Vyntja **86** 60.31 N 67.18 E
Vypolzovo **76** 57.53 N 33.42 E
Vyrica **76** 59.25 N 30.21 E
Vyrnwy ≃ **42** 52.46 N 3.00 W
Vyrnwy, Lake ⊜ **42** 52.47 N 3.30 W
Vyša **80** 53.52 N 42.24 E
Vyša ≃ **80** 54.02 N 42.06 E
Vyšehrad ⊸[8] **54** 50.01 N 14.27 E
Vyšelej **80** 53.26 N 45.29 E
Vyselki **78** 45.35 N 39.38 E
Vyšesteblijevskaja **78** 45.12 N 37.00 E
Vyšgorodok **76** 57.02 N 28.01 E
Vyshcha Dubechna **78** 50.44 N 30.40 E
Vyshkivs'kyi, pereval)(**78** 48.42 N 23.38 E
Vyshneve **78** 48.27 N 33.56 E
Vyshnivchyk **78** 49.02 N 26.28 E
Vyshnivets' **78** 49.54 N 25.45 E
Vyška, Ross. **76** 57.31 N 35.57 E
Vyška, Turk. **128** 39.20 N 54.08 E
Vyskod' **76** 57.46 N 30.04 E
Vyškov, Česká Rep. **30** 49.16 N 17.00 E
Vyškov, Ross. **76** 52.29 N 31.41 E
Vyšná Radvaň **30** 49.07 N 21.56 E
Vyšneol'šanoje **76** 52.08 N 37.39 E
Vyšnevolockoje vodochranilišče ⊜[1] **76** 57.35 N 34.28 E
Vyšnij Voločok **76** 57.35 N 34.34 E
Vysočany ⊸[8] **54** 50.05 N 14.31 E
Vysock **76** 60.36 N 28.34 E
Vysokaja, gora ∧ **89** 45.59 N 136.35 E
Vysokaja Gora **80** 55.56 N 49.19 E
Vysoké Mýto **30** 49.57 N 16.10 E
Vysoké Tatry ⋏ **30** 49.12 N 20.05 E
Vysokiniči **82** 54.54 N 36.55 E
Vysokogornyj **89** 50.09 N 139.09 E
Vysokogorsk **89** 44.23 N 135.23 E
Vysokoje, Bela. **76** 52.22 N 23.22 E
Vysokoje, Kaz. **85** 42.30 N 70.32 E
Vysokoje, Ross. **76** 56.43 N 34.55 E
Vysokoje, Ross. **76** 54.02 N 33.44 E
Vysokoje, Ross. **82** 54.30 N 37.03 E
Vysokoje, Ross. **265b** 55.59 N 37.09 E
Vysokopillya **78** 47.29 N 33.32 E
Vysokovsk **82** 56.19 N 36.33 E
Vysoký kámen ∧ **61** 49.06 N 15.13 E
Vysots'k **78** 51.43 N 26.39 E
Vyšší Brod **61** 48.37 N 14.19 E
Vystupovychi **78** 51.34 N 29.04 E
Vysun' ≃ **78** 47.07 N 32.53 E
Vytebet' ≃ **76** 53.53 N 35.38 E
Vytegra **24** 61.00 N 36.24 E

Symbols in the index entries represent the broad categories identified in the key at the right. Symbols with superior numbers (⋏[1]) identify subcategories (see complete key on page *I · 1)*.

Symbole im Register stellen die rechts im Schlüssel erklärten Kategorien dar. Symbole mit hochgestellten Ziffern (⋏[1]) bezeichnen Unterabteilungen einer Kategorie (vgl. vollständiger Schlüssel auf Seite *I · 1)*.

Los símbolos incluídos en el texto del índice representan las grandes categorías identificadas con la clave a la derecha. Los símbolos con numeros en su parte superior (⋏[1]) identifican las subcategorías (véase la clave completa en la página *I · 1)*.

Les symboles de l'index représentent les catégories indiquées dans la légende à droite. Les symboles suivis d'un indice (⋏[1]) représentent des sous-catégories (voir légende complète à la page *I · 1)*.

Os símbolos incluídos no texto do índice representam as grandes categorias identificadas com a chave à direita. Os símbolos com números em sua parte superior (⋏[1]) identificam as subcategorias (veja-se a chave completa à página *I · 1)*.

	English	Deutsch	Español	Français	Português
∧	Mountain	Berg	Montaña	Montagne	Montanha
⋏	Mountains	Gebirge	Montañas	Montagnes	Montanhas
)(	Pass	Paß	Paso	Col	Passo
V	Valley, Canyon	Tal, Cañon	Valle, Cañón	Vallée, Canyon	Vale, Canhão
≍	Plain	Ebene	Llano	Plaine	Planície
›	Cape	Kap	Cabo	Cap	Cabo
I	Island	Insel	Isla	Île	Ilha
II	Islands	Inseln	Islas	Îles	Ilhas
⊥	Other Topographic Features	Andere Topographische Objekte	Otros Elementos Topográficos	Autres données topographiques	Outros acidentes topográficos

ESPAÑOL — Nombre | Página | Lat.°′ | Long.°′ W = Oeste
FRANÇAIS — Nom | Page | Lat.°′ | Long.°′ W = Ouest
PORTUGUÊS — Nome | Página | Lat.°′ | Long.°′ W = Oeste

Vytyazivka 78 48.01 N 31.53 E
Vyzhivka ≃ 78 51.41 N 24.35 E
Vyzhnytsya 78 48.15 N 25.12 E
Vzmorje 89 47.51 N 142.31 E
Vzvad 76 58.10 N 31.29 E

W

W, Parc National du ♠ 150 12.50 N 2.30 E
Wa 150 10.04 N 2.29 W
Waabs 41 54.32 N 9.58 E
Waackaack Creek ≃ 276 40.27 N 74.08 W
Waadt → Vaud □[3] 58 46.40 N 6.30 E
Waajid 144 3.48 N 43.15 E
Waakirchen 64 47.46 N 11.40 E
Waal 58 48.00 N 10.46 E
Waal ≃ 52 51.49 N 4.58 E
Waalre 52 51.24 N 5.26 E
Waalwijk 52 51.42 N 5.04 E
Waao 102 24.20 N 104.40 E
Waar, Meos I 164 2.05 S 134.23 E
Waarschoot 50 51.09 N 3.36 E
Waasmunster 50 51.06 N 4.05 E
Wabag 164 5.30 S 143.40 E
Wabamun 182 53.33 N 114.28 W
Wabamun Indian Reserve ◆[4] 182 53.30 N 114.30 W
Wabamun Lake ⊜ 182 53.33 N 114.35 W
Waban 283 42.20 N 71.14 W
Waban, Lake ⊜ 283 42.17 N 71.17 W
Wabana 186 47.38 N 52.57 W
Wabasca 182 56.00 N 113.53 W
Wabasca ≃ 176 58.22 N 115.20 W
Wabasca Indian Reserve ◆[4] 182 55.53 N 113.32 W
Wabash, In., U.S. 216 40.47 N 85.49 W
Wabash, Oh., U.S. 216 40.33 N 84.45 W
Wabash □[6] 216 40.48 N 85.49 W
Wabash ≃ 194 37.46 N 88.02 W
Wabasha 190 44.23 N 92.01 W
Wabasso, Fl., U.S. 220 27.44 N 80.26 W
Wabasso, Mn., U.S. 198 44.24 N 95.15 W
Wabatongushi Lake ⊜ 190 48.26 N 84.15 W
Wabe Gestro ≃ 144 4.17 N 42.02 E
Wabe Mena ≃ 144 5.32 N 41.11 E
Wabeno 190 45.26 N 88.39 W
Wabera 144 6.26 N 40.42 E
Wabern 56 51.06 N 9.20 E
Wabigoon Lake ⊜ 184 49.44 N 92.44 W
Wabowden 184 54.55 N 98.38 W
Wabrah ⍑[4] 128 27.26 N 47.22 E
Wąbrzeźno 30 53.17 N 18.57 E
Wabu 100 32.17 N 116.55 E
Wabu Hu ⊜ 100 32.23 N 116.54 E
Wabuska 226 39.08 N 119.10 W
W.A.C. Bennett Dam ◆[6] 182 56.01 N 122.10 W
Waccamaw ≃ 192 33.21 N 79.16 W
Waccamaw, Lake ⊜ 192 34.17 N 78.30 W
Waccasassa Bay c 192 29.06 N 82.52 W
Wachapreague 208 37.36 N 75.41 W
Wachapreague Inlet c 208 37.35 N 75.36 W
Wachau ◆[1] 61 48.18 N 15.24 E
Wachenheim 56 49.26 N 8.10 E
Wachi 96 35.15 N 135.24 E
Wąchock, Klasztory ⛉[1] 30 51.05 N 21.01 E
Wachtberg 56 50.37 N 7.11 E
Wachtendonk 56 51.24 N 6.20 E
Wächtersbach 56 50.15 N 9.17 E
Wachusett Mountain ∧ 207 42.29 N 71.53 W
Wachusett Reservoir ⊜[1] 207 42.23 N 71.43 W
Wacissa 192 30.21 N 83.59 W
Wackersdorf 60 49.19 N 12.11 E
Waco 222 31.32 N 97.08 W
Waco Lake ⊜[1] 222 31.34 N 97.13 W
Waconda Lake ⊜[1] 198 39.30 N 98.24 W
Waconia 190 44.51 N 93.47 W
Wacouno ≃ 186 50.54 N 65.57 W
Wacousta 216 42.49 N 84.42 W
Wad 120 27.21 N 66.22 E
Wada, Nihon 94 35.02 N 140.01 E
Wada, Nihon 94 36.12 N 138.13 E
Wada, Nihon 268 35.12 N 139.38 E
Wada, Nihon 270 34.33 N 135.55 E
Wadagou 104 42.27 N 120.58 E
Wad Al-Ḥaddād 140 13.49 N 33.32 E
Wadamago 144 8.55 N 46.17 E
Wada-misaki › 96 34.39 N 135.11 E
Wādat Ga 120 26.57 N 97.37 E
Wadayama 96 35.19 N 134.52 E
Wad Bandah 140 13.06 N 27.57 E
Wad Ban Naqa 140 16.30 N 33.08 E
Wadbilliga National Park ♠ 166 36.20 S 149.35 E
Waddān 146 29.10 N 16.08 E
Waddān, Jabal ⋀[2] 146 29.20 N 16.20 E
Waddeneilanden II 52 53.26 N 5.30 E
Waddenzee ⍑[2] 52 53.15 N 5.15 E
Wadderin 162 32.00 S 118.27 E
Waddesdon 42 51.51 N 0.56 W
Waddingham 44 53.27 N 0.31 W
Waddington, Eng., U.K. 44 53.10 N 0.32 W
Waddington, N.Y., U.S. 212 44.51 N 75.12 W
Waddington, Mount ∧ 182 51.23 N 125.15 W
Waddinxveen 52 52.03 N 4.40 E
Waddy 218 38.08 N 85.04 W
Wade, Mount ∧ 9 84.51 S 174.15 W
Wadebridge 42 50.32 N 4.50 W
Wadena, Sk., Can. 184 51.57 N 103.47 W
Wadena, In., U.S. 216 40.43 N 87.16 W
Wadena, Mn., U.S. 198 46.26 N 95.08 W
Wädenswil 58 47.14 N 8.40 E
Wadern 56 49.32 N 6.53 E
Wadersloh 52 51.44 N 8.15 E
Wadesboro 192 34.58 N 80.04 W
Wadeville 273d 26.16 S 28.11 E
Wadeye 164 14.13 S 129.32 E
Wadgassen 56 49.16 N 6.47 E
Wad Ḥāmid 140 16.30 N 32.48 E
Wadham Islands II 186 49.34 N 53.50 W
Wadhams 182 51.30 N 127.31 W
Wadhurst 42 51.04 N 0.21 E
Wadian 100 32.48 N 112.30 E
Wādī as-Sīr 132 31.57 N 35.49 E
Wādī Ḥalfā' 140 21.56 N 31.20 E
Wādī Jimāl, Jazīrat I 140 24.40 N 35.10 E
Wādī Mūsā 132 30.19 N 35.29 E
Wading ≃, Ma., U.S. 283 41.56 N 71.13 W
Wading ≃, N.J., U.S. 208 39.33 N 74.28 W
Wading, West Branch ≃ 208 39.40 N 74.32 W
Wading River 207 40.57 N 72.50 W
Wādī Rashrāsh, Bi'r ⍑[4] 142 29.26 N 31.31 E
Wadley, Al., U.S. 194 33.07 N 85.33 W
Wadley, Ga., U.S. 192 32.52 N 82.24 W
Wad Madanī 140 14.25 N 33.28 E
Wadowice 30 49.53 N 19.30 E
Wadsworth, Il., U.S. 216 42.26 N 87.56 W
Wadsworth, Nv., U.S. 204 39.38 N 119.17 W
Wadsworth, N.Y., U.S. 210 42.49 N 77.54 W
Wadsworth, Oh., U.S. 214 41.01 N 81.43 W
Wadsworth Moor ◆[3] 262 53.48 N 2.02 W
Wadu I 122 5.51 N 72.58 E
Waegwan 98 35.58 N 128.24 E
Waelder 222 29.42 N 97.18 W
Waenhuiskrans 158 34.41 S 20.14 E
Wafang 98 41.44 N 118.54 E
Wafania 152 1.21 S 20.20 E
Wafrah 128 28.33 N 48.02 E
Wagadugu → Ouagadougou 150 12.22 N 1.31 W
Wāgah 123 31.36 N 74.33 E
Wagait Aboriginal Reserve ◆[4] 164 13.00 S 130.20 E
Wagang 102 28.04 N 103.10 E
Wagenborgen 52 53.15 N 6.56 E
Wagenfeld-Hasslingen 52 52.33 N 8.34 E
Wageningen, Ned. 52 51.58 N 5.40 E
Wageningen, Sur. 250 5.46 N 56.41 W
Wager Bay c 176 65.26 N 88.40 W
Wagerup 168a 32.55 S 115.54 E
Waggaman Heights 284c 38.49 N 76.57 W
Wagga Wagga 171b 35.07 S 147.22 E
Waggoner 219 39.23 N 89.39 W
Waghäusel 56 49.14 N 8.31 E
Wagin 162 33.18 S 117.21 E
Waging am See 64 47.56 N 12.43 E
Waginger See ⊜ 64 47.56 N 12.47 E
Wägitaler See ⊜ 58 47.06 N 8.55 E
Waglan Island I 271d 22.11 N 114.18 E
Wagna 61 46.46 N 15.34 E
Wagner 198 43.04 N 98.17 W
Wagner College ⛉[2] 276 40.37 N 74.07 W
Wagoner 196 35.57 N 95.22 W
Wagon Mound 196 36.00 N 104.42 W
Wagontire Mountain ∧ 202 43.21 N 119.53 W
Wagontown 208 40.01 N 75.51 W
Wagrain 64 47.20 N 13.18 E
Wagram → Deutsch Wagram 61 48.18 N 16.34 E
Wagrien ◆[1] 54 54.15 N 10.45 E
Wągrowiec 30 52.49 N 17.11 E
Waha 146 28.16 N 19.54 E
Wahādurgañj 124 27.32 N 82.50 E
Wahai 164 2.48 S 129.30 E
Waharoa 172 37.46 S 175.46 E
Wāh Cantonment 123 33.48 N 72.42 E
Wahiawa 229c 21.30 N 158.01 W
Wāḥid 142 30.49 N 32.20 E
Wahkiakum □[6] 224 46.16 N 123.28 W
Wahlen 56 49.37 N 8.51 E
Wahlstedt 54 53.57 N 10.12 E
Wahnbachstausee ⊜[1] 56 50.48 N 7.19 E
Wahneta 220 27.57 N 81.44 W
Wahoo 198 41.12 N 96.37 W
Wahpeton 198 46.15 N 96.36 W
Wahran (Oran) 148 35.43 N 0.43 W
Wahran □[5] 148 35.30 N 0.30 E
Wahrenbrück 54 51.33 N 13.22 E
Wahrenholz 54 52.36 N 10.36 E
Währing ◆[8] 264b 48.14 N 16.21 E
Wahroonga 274a 33.43 S 151.07 E
Wahweap Creek ≃ 200 37.02 N 111.35 W
Wai, India 122 17.56 N 73.54 E
Wai, Indon. 164 1.42 S 127.59 E
Waialeale ∧ 229b 22.04 N 159.30 W
Waialua 229c 21.34 N 158.07 W
Waialua Bay c 229c 21.36 N 158.07 W
Waianae 229c 21.26 N 158.11 W
Waianae Range ⋀ 229c 21.30 N 158.10 W
Waianapanapa State Park ♠ 229a 20.47 N 156.01 W
Waiapu ≃ 172 37.47 S 178.29 E
Waiatoto ≃ 172 43.59 S 168.47 E
Waiau 172 42.39 S 173.03 E
Waiau ≃, N.Z. 172 42.47 S 173.22 E
Waiau ≃, N.Z. 172 46.12 S 167.38 E
Waiau ≃, N.Z. 172 38.58 S 177.24 E
Waibakul 115b 9.36 S 119.35 E
Waibeem 164 0.28 S 132.58 E
Waiblingen 56 48.50 N 9.19 E
Waibstadt 56 49.18 N 8.54 E
Waichagoumen 98 40.54 N 125.45 E
Waidbruck → Ponte Gardena 64 46.36 N 11.32 E
Waidhān 124 24.04 N 82.20 E
Waidhofen an der Thaya 61 48.49 N 15.18 E
Waidhofen an der Ybbs 61 47.58 N 14.47 E
Waidmannslust ◆[8] 264a 52.36 N 13.20 E
Waidring 64 47.35 N 12.34 E
Waiehu 229a 20.55 N 156.30 W
Waigang 106 31.22 N 121.11 E
Waigatsch → Vajgač, ostrov I 72 70.00 N 59.30 E
Waigeo, Pulau I 164 0.14 S 130.45 E
Waigoumen 98 41.24 N 116.13 E
Waihao Downs 172 44.48 S 170.55 E
Waihau Bay 172 37.37 S 177.55 E
Waihee 229a 20.56 N 156.30 W
Waihee Point › 229a 20.57 N 156.31 W
Waiheke Island I 172 36.48 S 175.06 E
Waihi 172 37.24 S 175.51 E
Waihola 172 46.02 S 170.06 E
Waihopai ≃ 172 41.31 S 173.44 E
Waihou ≃ 172 37.10 S 175.32 E
Waihuantan 106 30.25 N 118.40 E
Waika 154 2.21 S 25.43 E
Waikabubak 115b 9.38 S 119.25 E
Waikaia 172 45.44 S 168.51 E
Waikaia ≃ 172 45.53 S 168.48 E
Waikanae 172 40.53 S 175.04 E
Waikane 229c 21.30 N 157.51 W
Waikapu 229a 20.51 N 156.30 W
Waikare, Lake ⊜ 172 37.26 S 175.13 E
Waikaremoana, Lake ⊜ 172 38.46 S 177.07 E
Waikari 172 42.58 S 172.41 E
Waikato ≃ 172 37.23 S 174.43 E
Waikelo 115b 9.24 S 119.14 E
Waikerie 166 34.11 S 139.59 E
Waikiki Beach ♠ 229c 21.17 N 157.50 W
Waikino 172 37.25 S 175.46 E
Waikouaiti 172 45.36 S 170.41 E
Waikuatang 106 31.20 N 120.41 E
Wailo 144 9.25 N 48.55 E
Wailua 229b 22.03 N 159.20 W
Wailua River State Park ♠ 229b 22.02 N 159.21 W
Wailuku 229a 20.53 N 156.30 W
Waimahaka 172 46.31 S 168.49 E
Waimakariri ≃ 172 43.24 S 172.42 E
Waimamaku 172 35.33 S 173.29 E
Waimana 172 38.09 S 177.05 E
Waimana ≃ 172 38.04 S 177.00 E
Waimanalo 229c 21.21 N 157.43 W
Waimangaroa 172 41.43 S 171.46 E
Waimangura 115b 9.30 S 119.14 E
Waimarama 172 39.48 S 176.59 E
Waimate 172 44.44 S 171.02 E
Waimea, Hi., U.S. 229c 21.38 N 158.03 W
Waimea, Hi., U.S. 229d 21.57 N 159.40 W
Waimea Canyon V 229b 22.04 N 159.39 W
Waimea Canyon State Park ♠ 229b 22.04 N 159.40 W
Waimes 56 50.25 N 6.07 E
Wainfleet All Saints 44 53.07 N 0.14 E
Wainganga ≃ 122 18.50 N 79.55 E
Waingapu 115b 9.39 S 120.16 E
Waini ≃ 246 8.24 N 59.51 W
Wainscott 260 51.25 N 0.31 E
Wainstalls 262 53.45 N 1.56 W
Wainuiomata 172 41.16 S 174.57 E
Wainunu Bay c 175g 16.55 S 178.53 E
Wainwright, Ab., Can. 182 52.49 N 110.52 W
Wainwright, Ak., U.S. 180 70.38 N 160.01 W
Wainwright, Oh., U.S. 214 40.25 N 81.25 W
Waiohau 172 38.14 S 176.51 E
Waiotira 172 35.56 S 174.12 E
Waiouru 172 39.29 S 175.40 E
Waipa ≃ 172 37.41 S 175.09 E
Waipahi 172 46.07 S 169.15 E
Waipahu 229c 21.23 N 158.00 W
Waipaoa 172 38.32 S 177.54 E
Waipara 172 43.04 S 172.45 E
Waipara ≃ 172 43.09 S 172.48 E
Waipawa 172 39.56 S 176.36 E
Waipiata 172 45.11 S 170.10 E
Waipio Acres 229c 21.28 N 158.00 W
Waipio Bay c 229a 20.55 N 156.13 W
Waipiro • 172 38.01 S 178.20 E
Waipu 172 35.59 S 174.27 E
Waipukurau 172 40.00 S 176.34 E
Wairakei 172 38.38 S 176.06 E
Wairarapa, Lake ⊜ 172 41.13 S 175.15 E
Wairau ≃ 172 41.30 S 174.04 E
Wairau Valley 172 41.34 S 173.32 E
Wairio 172 46.00 S 168.02 E
Wairoa 172 39.02 S 177.25 E
Wairoa ≃ 172 39.04 S 177.26 E
Waisanzao 106 30.57 N 121.52 E
Waischenfeld 60 49.51 N 11.21 E
Waïsisi 175f 19.30 S 169.22 E
Waitahanui 172 38.47 S 176.05 E
Waitahuna 172 45.59 S 169.46 E
Waitakaruru 172 37.15 S 175.23 E
Waitaki ≃ 172 44.57 S 171.09 E
Waitara, Austl. 274a 33.43 S 151.07 E
Waitara, N.Z. 172 39.00 S 174.13 E
Waitara ≃ 172 38.59 S 174.14 E
Waitarere 172 40.33 S 175.12 E
Waita Reservoir ⊜[1] 229b 21.55 N 159.27 W
Waitati 172 45.45 S 170.34 E
Waita-zan ∧ 96 33.08 N 131.10 E
Waite Hill 214 41.37 N 81.22 W
Waitemata 172 36.56 S 174.42 E
Waite Park 190 45.33 N 94.13 W
Waitoa 172 37.37 S 175.38 E
Waitotara 172 39.48 S 174.44 E
Waitotara ≃ 172 39.51 S 174.41 E
Waitpinga 168b 35.37 S 138.29 E
Waitsburg 202 46.16 N 118.09 W
Waitzen → Vác 30 47.47 N 19.08 E
Waiuku 172 37.15 S 174.45 E
Waiuta 172 42.18 S 171.49 E
Waiwera South 172 46.13 S 169.30 E
Waiwo 164 0.56 S 131.03 E
Waiya 164 3.13 S 128.55 E
Waizenkirchen 60 48.20 N 13.52 E
Wajiki 96 33.51 N 134.30 E
Wajima 92 37.24 N 136.54 E
Wajir 154 1.45 N 40.04 E
Waka, Ityo. 144 7.07 N 37.26 E
Waka, Tx., U.S. 196 36.17 N 101.03 W
Waka, Zaïre 152 1.01 N 20.13 E
Wakajabi 164 5.38 S 134.24 E
Wakakusa 94 35.36 N 138.29 E
Wakakusa-yama ∧[2] 270 34.42 N 135.52 E
Wakamatsu → Aizu-wakamatsu 92 37.30 N 139.56 E
Wakami ≃ 190 47.43 N 82.22 W
Wakami Lake ⊜ 190 47.29 N 82.51 W
Wakamiya 96 33.44 N 130.37 E
Wakano-ura ♠ 96 34.11 N 135.11 E
Wakarusa 216 41.32 N 86.03 W
Wakarusa ≃ 198 38.57 N 95.05 W
Wakasa 96 35.20 N 134.24 E
Wakasa-wan c 92 35.45 N 135.40 E
Wakasa-wan-kokutei-kōen ♠ 96 35.35 N 135.30 E
Wakatipu, Lake ⊜ 172 45.05 S 168.34 E
Wakatomika Creek ≃ 214 40.07 N 82.00 W
Wakato-ōhashi ◆[5] 96 33.54 N 130.49 E
Wakaw 184 52.39 N 105.44 W
Wakaw Lake ⊜ 184 52.40 N 105.35 W
Wakayama 96 34.13 N 135.11 E
Wakayama □[5] 96 34.00 N 135.20 E
Wakayanagi 92 38.46 N 141.08 E
Wake, Nihon 96 34.48 N 134.08 E
Wake, Zaïre 152 0.48 S 20.10 E
WaKeeney 198 39.01 N 99.53 W
Wakefield, N.Z. 172 41.24 S 173.03 E
Wakefield, Eng., U.K. 44 53.42 N 1.29 W
Wakefield, Ks., U.S. 198 39.12 N 97.00 W
Wakefield, Ma., U.S. 207 42.30 N 71.04 W
Wakefield, Ne., U.S. 198 42.16 N 96.51 W
Wakefield, Oh., U.S. 218 38.59 N 83.01 W
Wakefield, R.I., U.S. 207 41.26 N 71.30 W
Wakefield, Va., U.S. 192 36.58 N 76.59 W
Wakefield ≃ 168b 34.10 S 138.10 E
Wakefield Forest 284c 38.50 N 77.14 W
Wake Forest 192 35.58 N 78.30 W
Wake Island □[2], Oc. 14 19.17 N 166.36 E
Wake Island □[2], Oc. 174a 19.17 N 166.36 E
Wake Island I[1] 174a 19.18 N 166.38 E
Wake Island Air Force Base ■ 174a 19.17 N 166.37 E
Wake Lagoon c 174a 19.18 N 166.36 E
Wakema 110 16.36 N 95.11 E
Wakeman 214 41.15 N 82.23 W
Wakeman ≃ 182 51.00 N 126.30 W
Wakenda Creek ≃ 194 39.19 N 93.16 W
Wake Village 194 33.26 N 94.07 W
Wakhān → Vākhān ◆[1] 120 37.00 N 73.00 E
Waki 96 34.04 N 134.09 E
Wakis 164 6.13 S 150.17 E
Wakita 196 36.53 N 97.55 W
Wakkanai 92a 45.25 N 141.40 E
Wakkerstroom 158 27.24 S 30.10 E
Wakō, Nihon 268 35.47 N 139.37 E
Wako, Pap. N. Gui. 164 6.05 S 149.05 E
Wakomata Lake ⊜ 190 46.34 N 83.22 W
Wakonassin ≃ 190 46.28 N 81.51 W
Wakonda 198 43.00 N 97.06 W
Wakre 164 0.19 S 131.09 E
Waku Kundo 152 11.25 S 15.07 E
Wakunai 175e 5.52 S 155.13 E
Wakusimi ≃ 190 49.08 N 82.17 W
Wala ≃ 154 5.46 S 32.04 E
Walachia □[9] 38 44.00 N 25.00 E
Walamba 154 13.29 S 28.45 E
Walanae ≃ 112 4.08 S 119.58 E
Walang 102 28.33 N 100.54 E
Wal Athiang 140 7.42 N 29.40 E
Walawe ≃ 122 6.06 N 81.01 E
Walbeck 52 51.30 N 6.15 E
Walberswick 42 52.19 N 1.39 E
Walbran Creek ≃ 224 48.34 N 124.40 W
Walbridge 214 41.35 N 83.29 W
Wałbrzych (Waldenburg) 30 50.46 N 16.17 E
Walburg 222 30.44 N 97.35 W
Walbury Hill ∧[2] 42 51.21 N 1.30 W
Walcha 166 30.59 S 151.36 E
Walchensee ⊜ 64 47.36 N 11.20 E
Walcheren I 52 51.33 N 3.35 E
Walchsee 64 47.39 N 12.19 E
Walcott, B.C., Can. 182 54.31 N 126.51 W
Walcott, Ia., U.S. 190 41.35 N 90.46 W
Walcott, N.D., U.S. 198 46.32 N 96.56 W
Walcott, Lake ⊜[1] 202 42.40 N 113.23 W
Walcourt 50 50.15 N 4.25 E
Wałcz 30 53.17 N 16.28 E
Wald 58 47.17 N 8.55 E
Wald ◆[8] 263 51.11 N 7.03 E
Waldai → Valdajskaja vozvyšennost' ⋀[2] 24 57.00 N 33.30 E
Waldaist ≃ 61 48.19 N 14.34 E
Wald am Schoberpass 61 47.27 N 14.40 E
Waldbauer ◆[8] 263 51.18 N 7.28 E
Waldbillig 56 49.47 N 6.18 E
Waldböckelheim 56 49.49 N 7.43 E
Waldbröl 56 50.53 N 7.37 E
Waldbronn 56 48.56 N 8.29 E
Waldburg 58 47.45 N 9.43 E
Waldeck, Dtsch. 56 51.12 N 9.04 E
Waldeck, Dtsch. 60 49.52 N 11.57 E
Walden, Co., U.S. 200 40.43 N 106.16 W
Walden, N.Y., U.S. 210 41.33 N 74.11 W
Walden, Lake ⊜ 281 42.39 N 83.46 W
Waldenbuch 56 48.38 N 9.07 E
Waldenburg, Dtsch. 54 50.52 N 12.36 E
Waldenburg, Dtsch. 56 49.11 N 9.38 E
Waldenburg → Wałbrzych, Pol. 30 50.46 N 16.17 E
Waldenburg, Schw. 58 47.23 N 7.45 E
Walden Pond ⊜, Ma., U.S. 283 42.26 N 71.20 W
Walden Pond ⊜, Ma., U.S. 283 42.28 N 71.00 W
Walden Ridge ∧ 194 35.30 N 85.15 W
Waldershof 60 49.59 N 12.04 E
Walderslade 260 51.21 N 0.32 E
Waldfischbach 56 49.17 N 7.40 E
Waldheim, Sk., Can. 184 52.37 N 106.38 W
Waldheim, Dtsch. 54 51.04 N 13.01 E
Waldighoffen 58 47.33 N 7.19 E
Wald im Pinzgau 64 47.15 N 12.14 E
Waldkappel 56 51.08 N 9.52 E
Waldkirch 58 48.05 N 7.57 E
Waldkirchen 60 48.44 N 13.37 E
Waldkirchen am Wesen 60 48.26 N 13.49 E
Waldkraiburg 60 48.12 N 12.28 E
Waldmohr 56 49.23 N 7.20 E
Waldmünchen 60 49.23 N 12.43 E
Waldnaab ≃ 60 49.36 N 12.08 E
Waldo, B.C., Can. 182 49.13 N 115.13 W
Waldo, Ar., U.S. 194 33.21 N 93.17 W
Waldo, Oh., U.S. 214 40.27 N 83.04 W
Waldoboro 188 44.05 N 69.22 W
Waldo Lake ⊜ 283 42.07 N 71.03 W
Waldo Lake ⊜[1] 202 43.44 N 122.03 W
Waldon ≃ 42 50.51 N 4.15 W
Waldorf 208 38.37 N 76.56 W
Waldport 202 44.25 N 124.04 W
Waldron, Sk., Can. 184 50.51 N 102.30 W
Waldron, Ar., U.S. 194 34.53 N 94.05 W
Waldron, In., U.S. 218 39.27 N 85.40 W
Waldron, Mi., U.S. 216 41.43 N 84.25 W
Waldron Island I 224 48.43 N 123.02 W
Waldsassen 60 50.00 N 12.18 E
Waldshut 58 47.37 N 8.13 E
Waldstatt 58 47.21 N 9.17 E
Waldthurn 60 49.40 N 12.20 E
Waldviertel ◆[1] 61 48.40 N 15.15 E
Waldwick 276 41.00 N 74.07 W
Walea, Selat ⊻ 112 0.40 S 122.00 E
Walembele 150 10.30 N 1.58 W
Walensee ⊜ 58 47.07 N 9.12 E
Walenstadt 58 47.07 N 9.19 E
Wales, Ak., U.S. 180 65.36 N 168.05 W
Wales, Ma., U.S. 207 42.04 N 72.13 W
Wales, Wi., U.S. 216 43.00 N 88.23 W
Wales □[8] 28 52.30 N 3.30 W
Wales Center 210 42.46 N 78.32 W
Wales Island I, B.C., Can. 182 54.45 N 130.30 W
Wales Island I, N.T., Can. 176 68.00 N 86.43 W
Walewale 150 10.21 N 0.48 W
Walgett 166 30.01 S 148.07 E
Walgreen Coast ▬[2] 9 75.15 S 105.00 W
Walhachin 182 50.45 N 120.59 W
Walhalla, N.D., U.S. 198 48.55 N 97.55 W
Walhalla, S.C., U.S. 192 34.45 N 83.03 W
Walhalla ⊥ 60 49.03 N 12.14 E
Walheim 56 50.42 N 6.10 E
Walhonding 214 40.22 N 82.09 W
Walhonding ≃ 214 40.18 N 81.53 W
Wali 105 39.42 N 118.20 E
Walia 164 3.47 S 138.32 E
Walikale 154 1.25 S 28.03 E
Walincourt 50 50.04 N 3.20 E
Walis Island I 164 3.15 S 143.20 E
Walkaway 162 28.57 S 114.48 E
Walkden 44 53.32 N 2.24 W
Walkenried 54 51.35 N 10.37 E
Walker, Ia., U.S. 190 42.17 N 91.46 W
Walker, Mi., U.S. 216 43.00 N 85.46 W
Walker, Mn., U.S. 190 47.06 N 94.35 W
Walker, N.Y., U.S. 210 43.18 N 77.52 W
Walker □[6] 222 30.42 N 95.35 W
Walker ≃ 204 38.54 N 118.47 W
Walker, Lac ⊜ 186 50.16 N 67.09 W
Walker, Mount ∧[2] 171a 27.48 S 152.34 E
Walker Basin Creek ≃ 228 35.20 N 118.47 W
Walker Bay c 158 34.30 S 19.20 E
Walker Creek ≃, Az., U.S. 200 36.58 N 109.42 W
Walker Creek ≃, Ma., U.S. 283 42.38 N 70.44 W
Walker Creek ≃, Wy., U.S. 198 43.09 N 104.52 W
Walker Lake ⊜, Mb., Can. 184 54.42 N 96.57 W
Walker Lake ⊜, Ak., U.S. 180 67.10 N 154.26 W
Walker Lake ⊜, Nv., U.S. 204 38.44 N 118.43 W
Walker Lake ⊜[1] 210 40.48 N 77.11 W
Walker Point › 158 34.05 S 22.57 E
Walker River Indian Reservation ◆[4] 204 39.00 N 118.40 W
Walkers Mill 279b 40.24 N 80.08 W
Walkersville 208 39.29 N 77.21 W
Walkerton, On., Can. 212 44.07 N 81.09 W
Walkerton, In., U.S. 216 41.28 N 86.28 W
Walkerton, Va., U.S. 208 37.43 N 77.01 W
Walkertown 192 36.10 N 80.09 W
Walker Valley 210 41.38 N 74.23 W
Walkerville 202 46.02 N 112.32 W
Walk Mill 262 53.46 N 2.12 W
Wall, Pa., U.S. 279b 40.24 N 79.47 W
Wall, S.D., U.S. 198 43.59 N 102.14 W
Wallace, Ca., U.S. 226 38.12 N 120.59 W
Wallace, Id., U.S. 202 47.28 N 115.55 W
Wallace, Ne., U.S. 198 40.50 N 101.09 W
Wallace, N.Y., U.S. 210 42.26 N 77.28 W
Wallace, N.C., U.S. 192 34.44 N 77.59 W
Wallaceburg 214 42.36 N 82.23 W
Wallace Lake ⊜ 279a 41.22 N 81.52 W
Wallaceton 214 40.57 N 78.17 W
Wallacetown 214 42.38 N 81.28 W
Wallach 263 51.35 N 6.34 E
Wallacia 170 33.52 S 150.39 E
Wallal Downs 162 19.47 S 120.40 E
Wallam Creek ≃ 166 28.40 S 147.20 E
Wallan 169 37.25 S 144.59 E
Wallangarra 166 28.56 S 151.56 E
Wallaroo 168b 33.56 S 137.38 E
Wallaroo Mines 168b 33.57 S 137.41 E
Wallasey 44 53.26 N 3.03 W
Wallau 56 50.56 N 8.28 E
Walla Walla 202 46.03 N 118.20 W
Walldorf, Dtsch. 54 50.36 N 10.23 E
Walldorf, Dtsch. 56 49.18 N 8.38 E
Walldürn 56 49.35 N 9.22 E
Walled Lake 216 42.32 N 83.28 W
Walled Lake ⊜ 281 42.31 N 83.29 W
Wallen 216 41.09 N 85.09 W
Wallend 260 51.27 N 0.42 E
Wallenfels 54 50.16 N 11.28 E
Wallenhorst 52 52.21 N 8.01 E
Wallenpaupack, Lake ⊜ 210 41.25 N 75.12 W
Waller 222 30.04 N 95.56 W
Waller □[6] 222 30.00 N 96.00 W
Wallerawang 170 33.25 S 150.04 E
Wallern im Burgenland 61 47.43 N 16.56 E
Wallers 50 50.22 N 3.24 E
Wallersdorf 60 48.44 N 12.45 E
Wallersee ⊜ 64 47.55 N 13.11 E
Wallerstein 56 48.53 N 10.28 E
Wallgau 64 47.31 N 11.16 E
Wallgrove 274a 33.47 S 150.51 E
Wallhead Airport ⊠ 279a 41.21 N 82.09 W
Wallingford, Eng., U.K. 42 51.37 N 1.08 W
Wallingford, Ct., U.S. 207 41.27 N 72.49 W
Wallingford, Pa., U.S. 285 39.54 N 75.22 W
Wallingford, Vt., U.S. 188 43.28 N 72.58 W
Wallington 276 40.51 N 74.06 W
Wallington ◆[8] 260 51.21 N 0.09 W
Wallis 222 29.37 N 96.03 W
Wallis → Valais □[3] 58 46.10 N 7.30 E
Wallis, Îles II 14 13.18 S 176.10 W
Wallis and Futuna □[2] 14 14.00 S 177.00 W
Wallisellen 58 47.25 N 8.36 E
Wallisville 222 29.50 N 94.44 W
Wallisville Lake ⊜[1] 222 29.50 N 94.45 W
Wallkill 210 41.36 N 74.11 W
Wallkill ≃, U.S. 210 41.51 N 74.03 W
Wallkill ≃, U.S. 276 41.11 N 74.35 W
Wallkill, Wildcat Branch ≃ 276 41.07 N 74.36 W
Wall Lake, Ia., U.S. 198 42.16 N 95.05 W
Wall Lake, Mi., U.S. 216 42.31 N 85.24 W
Wall Lake ⊜ 216 42.31 N 85.23 W
Wallmer Bridge 262 53.43 N 2.48 W
Wallmerod 56 50.29 N 7.56 E
Wallops Island I 208 37.52 N 75.27 W
Wallowa 202 45.34 N 117.31 W
Wallowa ≃ 202 45.43 N 117.47 W
Wallowa Mountains ⋀ 202 45.10 N 117.30 W
Walls, Scot., U.K. 46a 60.14 N 1.35 W
Walls, Ms., U.S. 194 34.57 N 90.09 W
Wallsbüll 41 54.47 N 9.14 E
Wallsend, Austl. 170 32.55 S 151.40 E
Wallsend, Eng., U.K. 44 55.00 N 1.31 W
Wallstawe 54 52.47 N 11.01 E
Wall Town Drainage Ditch ≊ 216 40.26 N 88.10 W
Wallula, Lake ⊜[1] 202 46.00 N 119.00 W
Walmer, S. Afr. 158 33.59 S 25.36 E
Walmer, Eng., U.K. 42 51.13 N 1.24 E
Walmersley 262 53.37 N 2.18 W
Walney, Isle of I 44 54.07 N 3.15 W
Walnut, Ca., U.S. 228 34.01 N 117.51 W
Walnut, Il., U.S. 190 41.33 N 89.35 W
Walnut, Ia., U.S. 198 41.28 N 95.13 W
Walnut, Ks., U.S. 198 37.36 N 95.04 W
Walnut, Ms., U.S. 194 34.56 N 88.53 W
Walnut, N.C., U.S. 192 35.50 N 82.44 W
Walnut ≃ 198 37.03 N 97.00 W
Walnut Canyon National Monument ♠ 200 35.10 N 111.31 W
Walnut Canyon Reservoir ⊜[1] 280 33.50 N 117.45 W
Walnut Cove 192 36.17 N 80.08 W
Walnut Creek, Ca., U.S. 226 37.54 N 122.03 W
Walnut Creek, Oh., U.S. 214 40.33 N 81.43 W
Walnut Creek ≃, Ca., U.S. 280 34.03 N 118.01 W
Walnut Creek ≃, Ca., U.S. 282 37.54 N 122.03 W
Walnut Creek ≃, Ks., U.S. 198 38.21 N 98.41 W
Walnut Creek ≃, Oh., U.S. 188 39.41 N 82.59 W
Walnut Creek ≃, Tx., U.S. 222 32.38 N 97.00 W
Walnut Creek, Middle Fork ≃ 198 38.32 N 100.08 W
Walnut Creek, South Fork ≃ 198 38.25 N 99.53 W
Walnut Grove, B.C., Can. 224 49.11 N 122.39 W
Walnut Grove, Ca., U.S. 226 38.15 N 121.31 W
Walnut Grove, Mn., U.S. 198 44.13 N 95.28 W
Walnut Grove, Ms., U.S. 194 32.35 N 89.27 W
Walnut Heights 282 37.53 N 122.08 W
Walnut Hill 219 38.29 N 89.03 W
Walnut Lake 281 42.33 N 83.19 W
Walnut Lake ⊜ 281 42.33 N 83.20 W
Walnut Park 280 33.58 N 118.13 W
Walnutport 208 40.45 N 75.35 W
Walnut Ridge 194 36.04 N 90.57 W
Walnut Springs 222 32.03 N 97.45 W
Walpert Ridge ∧ 282 37.38 N 122.00 W
Walpeup 166 35.08 S 142.02 E
Walpole, Austl. 162 34.57 S 116.44 E
Walpole, Ma., U.S. 207 42.08 N 71.15 W
Walpole, N.H., U.S. 188 43.04 N 72.25 W
Walpole Island I 214 42.34 N 82.30 W
Walpole Island Indian Reserve ◆[4] 214 42.32 N 82.37 W
Walpole Saint Peter 42 52.42 N 0.15 E
Walsall 42 52.35 N 1.58 W
Walschleben 54 51.04 N 10.56 E
Walsden 262 53.42 N 2.06 W
Walsenburg 200 37.37 N 104.46 W
Walsh, Austl. 164 16.39 S 143.54 E
Walsh, Ab., Can. 184 49.57 N 110.03 W
Walsh, Co., U.S. 198 37.23 N 102.16 W
Walsh, Ky., U.S. 218 38.41 N 82.58 W
Walsh ≃ 164 16.31 S 143.42 E
Walshaw Dean Reservoirs ⊜[1] 262 53.48 N 2.03 W
Walshville 219 39.04 N 89.37 W
Walsingham 212 42.41 N 80.32 W
Walsoorden 52 51.23 N 4.02 E
Walsrode 52 52.52 N 9.35 E
Walston 214 40.58 N 79.01 W
Walsum 52 51.32 N 6.41 E
Walt Disney World ♠ 220 28.26 N 81.35 W
Waltenhofen 64 47.40 N 10.17 E
Walterboro 192 32.54 N 80.40 W
Walter F. George Lake ⊜[1] 192 31.49 N 85.08 W
Walter Reed Army Medical Center ⛉ 284c 38.58 N 77.02 W
Walters 196 34.21 N 98.18 W
Waltersdorf, Dtsch. 54 50.52 N 14.38 E
Waltersdorf, Dtsch. 264a 52.22 N 13.35 E
Waltershausen 54 50.53 N 10.33 E
Waltershofen 58 47.46 N 9.55 E
Waltersville 194 32.22 N 90.52 W
Walthall 194 33.36 N 89.16 W
Waltham, Eng., U.K. 44 53.31 N 0.06 W
Waltham, Ma., U.S. 207 42.22 N 71.14 W
Waltham Abbey 42 51.42 N 0.01 E
Waltham Forest ◆[8] 42 51.35 N 0.01 W
Waltham on the Wolds 42 52.49 N 0.49 W
Walthamstow ◆[8] 260 51.35 N 0.01 W
Walthill 198 42.08 N 96.29 W
Walton, N.S., Can. 186 45.14 N 64.00 W
Walton, Eng., U.K. 42 51.24 N 0.25 W
Walton, Eng., U.K. 42 51.58 N 1.21 E
Walton, Fl., U.S. 220 27.17 N 80.15 W
Walton, In., U.S. 216 40.39 N 86.14 W
Walton, Ky., U.S. 218 38.52 N 84.36 W
Walton, N.Y., U.S. 210 42.10 N 75.07 W
Walton Hills 214 41.22 N 81.32 W
Walton-le-Dale 44 53.45 N 2.39 W
Walton on the Hill 260 51.17 N 0.15 W
Walton-on-the-Naze 42 51.51 N 1.16 E
Walton Run ≃ 285 40.05 N 74.59 W
Waltonville 219 38.13 N 89.02 W
Waltrop 52 51.37 N 7.23 E
Walt Whitman Bridge ◆[5] 285 39.54 N 75.08 W
Walt Whitman Homes 285 39.52 N 75.11 W
Walt Whitman House State Historic Site ⊥ 276 40.49 N 73.25 W
Walt Whitman Mall ◆[9] 276 40.50 N 73.25 W
Waltz 216 42.06 N 83.23 W
Walupt Lake ⊜ 224 46.25 N 121.28 W
Walvis Bay 156 22.59 S 14.31 E
Walvis Bay □[5] 156 22.59 S 14.31 E
Walvis Bay c 156 22.57 S 14.30 E
Walvis Ridge ✢[3] 10 28.00 S 3.00 E
Walwa 171b 35.58 S 147.45 E
Walwen 262 53.14 N 3.15 W
Walworth, N.Y., U.S. 210 43.08 N 77.17 W
Walworth, Wi., U.S. 216 42.31 N 88.35 W
Walworth □[6] 216 42.41 N 88.32 W
Walyunga National Park ♠ 168a 31.44 S 116.04 E
Walyungup, Lake ⊜ 168a 32.21 S 115.47 E
Walze 263 51.16 N 7.31 E
Walzin, Château de ⊥ 56 50.13 N 4.55 E
Wama 152 12.14 S 15.33 E
Wamac 219 38.31 N 89.08 W
Wamba, Kenya 154 0.59 N 37.19 E
Wamba, Nig. 150 8.58 N 8.36 E
Wamba, Zaïre 154 2.09 N 28.00 E
Wamba (Uamba) ≃ 152 3.56 S 17.12 E
Wambel ◆[8] 263 51.32 N 7.32 E
Wamego 198 39.12 N 96.18 W
Wamel 52 51.53 N 5.28 E
Wamesit 283 42.37 N 71.15 W
Wami ≃ 154 6.08 S 38.49 E
Wamiao 100 30.49 N 113.02 E
Wamic 224 45.13 N 121.16 W
Wamma ≃ 164 3.23 S 135.13 E
Wamme ≃ 56 50.10 N 5.16 E
Wamplers Lake ⊜ 216 42.05 N 84.09 W
Wampool ≃ 44 54.54 N 3.14 W
Wampsville 210 43.04 N 75.42 W
Wampú 236 15.01 N 85.02 W
Wampú ≃ 236 14.59 N 85.03 W
Wampum 214 40.53 N 80.20 W
Wampus ≃ 276 41.07 N 73.43 W
Wampus Lake Reservoir ⊜[1] 276 41.09 N 73.43 W
Wamsasi 112 3.33 S 126.10 E
Wamsutter 200 41.40 N 107.58 W
Wamuran 171a 27.02 S 152.52 E
Wanaaring 166 29.42 S 144.09 E
Wanaka 172 44.42 S 169.09 E
Wanaka, Lake ⊜ 172 44.30 S 169.08 E
Wanakah 210 42.45 N 78.54 W
Wanamassa 208 40.14 N 74.02 W
Wanamie 210 41.10 N 76.02 W
Wanamingo 190 44.18 N 92.47 W
Wan'an, Zhg. 100 26.56 N 117.22 E
Wan'an, Zhg. 100 26.30 N 114.49 E
Wan'an ≃ 100 25.20 N 117.21 E
Wan'anchang 107 30.39 N 104.25 E
Wanapiri 164 4.33 S 135.59 E
Wanapitei ≃ 190 46.02 N 80.51 W
Wanapitei Lake ⊜ 190 46.45 N 80.45 W
Wanapum Lake ⊜[1] 202 47.00 N 120.00 W
Wanaque 210 41.02 N 74.17 W
Wanaque ≃ 276 40.58 N 74.17 W
Wanaque Reservoir ⊜[1] 210 41.05 N 74.17 W
Wanatah 216 41.25 N 86.53 W
Wanau 164 1.22 S 132.42 E
Wanbaoshan 89 44.12 N 125.11 E
Wanbi 166 34.46 S 140.19 E
Wanblee 198 43.34 N 101.40 W
Wanborough 42 51.33 N 1.42 W
Wanchangchang 107 29.43 N 104.19 E
Wanchese 192 35.50 N 75.38 W
Wanda 158 29.36 S 24.28 E
Wandai 164 3.41 S 136.41 E
Wandana 162 32.04 S 133.49 E
Wandawega 216 42.45 N 88.40 W
Wande 98 36.21 N 116.56 E
Wanderer 154 19.37 S 29.59 E
Wandering 168a 32.40 S 116.40 E
Wandering ≃ 182 55.05 N 112.30 W
Wanderup 41 54.41 N 9.20 E
Wandhofen 263 51.26 N 7.33 E
Wandingzhen 102 24.05 N 98.04 E
Wandlitz 54 52.45 N 13.26 E
Wandlitzer See ⊜ 264a 52.46 N 13.27 E
Wando 98 34.18 N 126.47 E
Wan-do I 98 34.21 N 126.42 E
Wandoan 166 26.08 S 149.57 E
Wandsbek ◆[8] 52 53.34 N 10.04 E
Wandsworth ◆[8] 42 51.27 N 0.11 W
Waneta Lake ⊜ 210 42.27 N 77.06 W
Wanette 196 34.57 N 97.01 W
Wanfang 104 41.57 N 122.52 E
Wanfoxia 102 40.04 N 95.55 E
Wanfried 56 51.10 N 10.10 E
Wanfu ≃ 98 35.10 N 116.35 E
Wang ≃ 110 17.08 N 99.02 E
Wanga 154 2.58 N 29.13 E
Wangal 164 6.10 S 134.12 E
Wanganderry, Mount ∧ 170 34.20 S 150.15 E
Wanganui 172 39.56 S 175.03 E
Wanganui ≃ 172 39.56 S 175.00 E
Wang'anzhen 105 39.19 N 114.54 E
Wangaratta 166 36.22 S 146.20 E
Wangary 166 34.33 S 135.29 E
Wangbaotaicun 104 41.10 N 123.18 E
Wangbenying 105 40.28 N 116.06 E
Wangbintun 104 41.58 N 123.43 E
Wangchang, Zhg. 107 28.52 N 105.55 E
Wangchang, Zhg. 107 29.05 N 104.40 E
Wangchangtuizigou 104 41.14 N 120.32 E
Wangcheng 100 28.23 N 112.48 E
Wang Chin 110 17.53 N 99.37 E
Wangcun 98 36.41 N 117.41 E
Wangcunkou 100 28.22 N 118.59 E
Wangdain 124 29.02 N 89.15 E
Wangdalong 102 29.25 N 99.03 E
Wangdian 106 30.37 N 120.44 E
Wangdu 98 38.43 N 115.09 E
Wangdu Phodrang 124 27.29 N 89.54 E
Wange 154 2.00 S 40.55 E
Wangels 54 54.16 N 10.45 E
Wangen an der Aare 58 47.14 N 7.39 E
Wangenbourg 58 48.37 N 7.19 E
Wangen im Allgäu 58 47.41 N 9.50 E
Wangerooge 52 53.48 N 7.54 E
Wangerooge I 52 53.46 N 7.55 E
Wangersen 52 53.22 N 9.25 E
Wangfu 104 42.05 N 121.29 E
Wanggameti, Gunung ∧ 115b 10.07 S 120.14 E
Wanggangpu 104 41.38 N 123.09 E
Wanggao 102 24.38 N 111.30 E
Wanggezhuang 105 40.00 N 117.52 E
Wanggil-li 271b 37.36 N 126.39 E
Wanggoutun 104 41.40 N 121.53 E
Wanghai 98 40.26 N 120.30 E
Wanghai Shan ∧ 104 41.37 N 121.41 E
Wanghechenggou 104 41.52 N 121.13 E
Wang Hin, Khlong ≊ 269a 13.48 N 100.35 E
Wanghu 98 39.47 N 113.54 E
Wanghuzhuang 105 38.50 N 117.05 E
Wängi 58 47.30 N 8.57 E
Wangingsha 100 22.44 N 113.33 E
Wangi Wangi 170 33.04 S 151.35 E
Wangiwangi, Pulau I 112 5.20 S 123.35 E
Wangji, Zhg. 100 33.52 N 118.44 E
Wangji, Zhg. 100 34.00 N 117.46 E
Wangjia, Zhg. 106 31.59 N 121.13 E
Wangjia, Zhg. 106 32.07 N 120.59 E
Wangjiadian, Zhg. 100 31.26 N 113.58 E
Wangjiadian, Zhg. 105 40.03 N 117.29 E
Wangjiagou 104 42.33 N 123.16 E
Wangjiajing, Zhg. 98 37.49 N 115.23 E
Wangjiajing, Zhg. 98 39.56 N 122.11 E
Wangjiang 100 30.09 N 116.41 E

≃ River	Fluß	Río	Rivière	Rio	✢ Submarine Features	Untermeerische Objekte	Accidentes Submarinos	Formes de relief sous-marin	Acidentes submarinos
≊ Canal	Kanal	Canal	Canal	Canal	□ Political Unit	Politische Einheit	Unidad Politica	Entité politique	Unidade política
∟ Waterfall, Rapids	Wasserfall, Stromschnellen	Cascada, Rápidos	Chute d'eau, Rapides	Cascata, Rápidos	⛉ Cultural Institution	Kulturelle Institution	Institución Cultural	Institution culturelle	Institução cultural
⊻ Strait	Meeresstraße	Estrecho	Détroit	Estreito	⊥ Historical Site	Historische Stätte	Sitio Histórico	Site historique	Sitio histórico
c Bay, Gulf	Bucht, Golf	Bahía, Golfo	Baie, Golfe	Baía, Golfo	♠ Recreational Site	Erholungs- und Ferienort	Sitio de Recreo	Centre de loisirs	Area de Lazer
⊜ Lake, Lakes	See, Seen	Lago, Lagos	Lac, Lacs	Lago, Lagos	⊠ Airport	Flughafen	Aeropuerto	Aéroport	Aeroporto
≡ Swamp	Sumpf	Pantano	Marais	Pântano	■ Military Installation	Militäranlage	Instalación Militar	Installation militaire	Instalação militar
⍓ Ice Features, Glacier	Eis- und Gletscherformen	Accidentes Glaciales	Formes glaciaires	Acidentes glaciares	◆ Miscellaneous	Verschiedenes	Misceláneo	Divers	Diversos
⍑ Other Hydrographic Features	Andere Hydrographische Objekte	Otros Elementos Hidrográficos	Autres données hydrographiques	Outros acidentes hidrográficos					

ENGLISH — DEUTSCH

Name (Name)	Page (Seite)	Lat.°′ (Breite°′)	Long.°′ (Länge°′ E = Ost)
Wangjiangjing	106	30.53 N	120.43 E
Wang Jian Mu (Tomb of Wang Jian) ⊥	107	30.38 N	104.04 E
Wangjiaputun	104	40.39 N	122.50 E
Wangjiapuzi, Zhg.	104	40.41 N	122.24 E
Wangjiapuzi, Zhg.	104	41.05 N	123.34 E
Wangjiaqiao	106	30.50 N	119.18 E
Wangjiashan	105	40.19 N	114.45 E
Wangjiashao	102	23.57 N	102.18 E
Wangjiatai	105	39.17 N	117.29 E
Wangjiaying, Zhg.	105	40.36 N	116.34 E
Wangjiaying, Zhg.	105	39.06 N	115.59 E
Wangjiazhai	106	31.21 N	121.37 E
Wangjiazui	106	31.16 N	120.18 E
Wangkantou	100	29.12 N	120.09 E
Wangkou	105	38.56 N	116.44 E
Wangkui	89	46.50 N	126.30 E
Wanglanzhuang	105	39.26 N	118.01 E
Wangling	100	27.13 N	113.26 E
Wangliu	100	32.25 N	115.40 E
Wangmiao	100	26.50 N	112.52 E
Wangmulazi	104	41.42 N	124.02 E
Wang Noi	110	14.13 N	100.44 E
Wangong	89	49.10 N	118.53 E
Wangpan Shan II	106	30.30 N	121.15 E
Wangpan Yang C	100	30.30 N	121.46 E
Wangpingchang	107	29.17 N	105.45 E
Wangqing	89	43.20 N	129.48 E
Wangqingmen	98	41.42 N	125.23 E
Wangqingtuo	105	39.11 N	116.53 E
Wangqinzhuang	105	39.15 N	117.05 E
Wangqucun	106	31.22 N	120.19 E
Wangs	58	47.02 N	9.26 E
Wang Saphung	110	17.18 N	101.46 E
Wangshanhutun	104	42.03 N	122.37 E
Wangshi	100	33.11 N	116.04 E
Wangsi	98	38.00 N	116.55 E
Wangsim-ni ⊶[8]	271b	37.36 N	127.03 E
Wangsiying	107	30.34 N	103.29 E
Wangtai, Zhg.	98	36.05 N	119.59 E
Wangtai, Zhg.	100	26.39 N	117.57 E
Wangtan	100	29.45 N	120.40 E
Wang Thong	110	16.50 N	100.26 E
Wangtian	100	25.59 N	116.04 E
Wangting	106	31.26 N	120.26 E
Wangtongshitai	104	42.05 N	123.11 E
Wangtuan, Zhg.	98	37.32 N	116.08 E
Wangtuan, Zhg.	98	37.17 N	122.04 E
Wangtuanji	100	33.12 N	116.21 E
Wangu	107	30.19 N	106.05 E
Wanguzhen	107	29.41 N	105.57 E
Wangwenzhuang	105	38.53 N	117.15 E
Wangxiangshang	106	31.29 N	120.15 E
Wangxiangtai	105	40.02 N	115.09 E
Wangxiuqiao	106	31.38 N	121.03 E
Wangyangzhen	107	29.44 N	104.14 E
Wangyedian	98	41.36 N	118.17 E
Wangyefu	98	41.50 N	118.23 E
Wangyehmiao → Horqin Youyi Qianqi	89	46.05 N	122.05 E
Wangyiguantun	104	42.36 N	123.19 E
Wangzhai	98	34.09 N	116.47 E
Wangzhimawo	105	39.39 N	117.40 E
Wangzhong	98	35.08 N	116.58 E
Wangzhuang	100	33.07 N	117.29 E
Wangzhuangbu	98	39.27 N	113.56 E
Wangzhuangji	98	34.09 N	118.23 E
Wangzhuangzi	105	39.17 N	118.14 E
Wanham	182	55.44 N	118.24 W
Wanhedian	100	32.16 N	113.16 E
Wanheimerort ⊶[8]	263	51.24 N	6.46 E
Wanhsien → Wanxian	102	30.52 N	108.22 E
Wanhuyu	102	38.24 N	110.40 E
Wani	122	20.04 N	78.57 E
Wani, Gunung ∧	112	4.29 S	123.01 E
Wanica □[5]	250	5.50 N	55.10 W
Wanie-Rukula	154	0.15 N	25.32 E
Wanigela	164	9.22 S	149.10 E
Wanipigow ≃	184	51.11 N	96.18 W
Wanjiabu	100	28.51 N	115.39 E
Wanjiaqiao	106	30.25 N	119.07 E
Wanjiatun	98	40.03 N	119.51 E
Wanjindian	100	32.50 N	114.46 E
Wānkāner	120	22.37 N	70.56 E
Wankendorf	54	54.07 N	10.13 E
Wanle Weyne	144	2.37 N	44.54 E
Wanli, T'aiwan	269d	25.11 N	121.41 E
Wanli, Zhg.	106	31.06 N	120.16 E
Wanna	52	53.44 N	8.46 E
Wanna Lakes ⊜	162	28.30 S	128.27 E
Wān Namton	110	22.03 N	99.33 E
Wanne-Eickel	52	51.32 N	7.09 E
Wanneroo	168a	31.45 S	115.48 E
Wannery Creek ≃	162	22.47 S	115.43 E
Wannian	100	28.42 N	117.03 E
Wanning	110	18.53 N	110.26 E
Wannsee ⊶[8]	54	52.25 N	13.09 E
Wanon Niwat	110	17.38 N	103.46 E
Wanouchi	94	35.17 N	136.38 E
Wānow	120	32.38 N	65.54 E
Wanparti	122	16.22 N	78.04 E
Wanquan	98	40.52 N	114.45 E
Wansbeck ≃	44	55.10 N	1.34 W
Wansdorf	264a	52.38 N	13.05 E
Wan-See → Van Gölü ⊜	128	38.33 N	42.46 E
Wanshan	107	30.23 N	106.06 E
Wanshouchang	107	29.26 N	105.55 E
Wanstead	172	40.08 S	176.32 E
Wanstead ⊶[8]	260	51.34 N	0.02 E
Wantage	42	51.36 N	1.25 W
Wantagh	210	40.41 N	73.30 W
Wantan	102	30.03 N	110.18 E
Wantirna	274b	37.51 S	145.14 E
Wantirna South	274b	37.52 S	145.14 E
Wanxian, Zhg.	102	30.52 N	108.22 E
Wanxian, Zhg.	105	38.50 N	115.09 E
Wanyuan	102	32.04 N	108.02 E
Wanzai	100	28.06 N	114.27 E
Wanzarīk	146	27.31 N	13.29 E
Wanzhuang	105	39.34 N	116.36 E
Wanzleben	54	52.03 N	11.26 E
Wapack Range ⩙	207	42.48 N	71.52 W
Wapakoneta	216	40.34 N	84.11 W
Wapanucka	196	34.22 N	96.25 W
Wapato	202	46.26 N	120.25 W
Wapawekka Hills ⩙[2]	184	54.45 N	104.20 W
Wapawekka Lake ⊜	184	54.55 N	104.40 W
Wapella, Sk., Can.	184	50.15 N	102.00 W
Wapella, Il., U.S.	219	40.13 N	88.58 W
Wapello	190	41.10 N	91.11 W
Wapenamanda	164	5.35 S	143.55 E
Wapesi Lake ⊜	184	50.34 N	92.21 W
Wāpi	122	20.22 N	72.54 E
Wapinda	152	3.41 N	22.48 E
Wapinitia Pass)(	224	45.14 N	121.42 W
Wapisu Lake ⊜	184	55.47 N	99.11 W
Wapiti ≃	182	55.08 N	118.18 W
Wapizagonke, Lac ⊜	206	46.43 N	73.02 W
Waples	222	32.29 N	97.43 W
Wapoga ≃	164	2.42 S	136.06 E
Wappapello, Lake ⊜[1]	194	36.58 N	90.20 W
Wapping	207	41.50 N	72.33 W
Wappinger Creek ≃	210	41.35 N	73.57 W
Wappingers Falls	210	41.35 N	73.54 W
Wapsipinicon ≃	190	41.44 N	90.20 W
Waptus Lake ⊜	224	47.30 N	121.10 W
Wapus ≃	190	47.11 N	76.06 W
Wapus Lake ⊜	184	56.27 N	102.12 W
Waqf aṣ-Ṣawwān, Jibāl ⩙	132	30.53 N	36.48 E
Wāqid	142	30.42 N	30.44 E
Waqqāṣ	132	32.33 N	35.36 E
War	192	37.18 N	81.41 W
Wara	94	35.45 N	137.05 E
Warabi	94	35.49 N	139.41 E
Wārāh	120	27.27 N	67.48 E
Warakaraket I	164	2.15 S	130.36 E
Waramaug, Lake ⊜	207	41.42 N	73.22 W
Warangal	122	18.00 N	79.35 E
Wararisbari, Tanjung ⩥	164	1.05 S	136.23 E
Wārāseoni	120	21.45 N	80.02 E
Waratah, Austl.	166	41.27 S	145.32 E
Waratah, Austl.	170	32.54 S	151.44 E
Waratah Bay C	166	38.51 S	146.04 E
Warboys	42	52.24 N	0.04 W
Warbreccan	166	24.18 S	142.51 E
Warburg	52	51.29 N	9.08 E
Warburton, Austl.	162	26.07 S	126.35 E
Warburton, Austl.	169	37.46 S	145.41 E
Warburton, Pāk.	123	31.33 N	73.50 E
Warburton, Eng., U.K.	262	53.24 N	2.27 W
Warburton Aboriginal Reserve ⊶[4]	162	24.00 S	128.15 E
Warburton Bay C	176	63.50 N	111.30 W
Warburton Creek ≃	166	27.55 S	137.28 E
Warchha	123	32.25 N	71.59 E
Ward, N.Z.	172	41.50 S	174.08 E
Ward, Pa., U.S.	285	39.53 N	75.31 W
Ward ≃	166	26.32 S	146.06 E
Ward, Mount ∧	172	43.52 S	169.50 E
Warda	222	30.03 N	96.55 W
Wardcliff	216	42.43 N	84.28 W
Ward Cove	182	55.24 N	131.44 W
Warden, S. Afr.	158	27.56 S	29.00 E
Warden, Wa., U.S.	202	46.58 N	119.02 W
Wardenburg	52	53.04 N	8.11 E
Warder	54	53.59 N	10.22 E
Wardersee ⊜	54	53.58 N	10.26 E
Wardha	122	20.45 N	78.37 E
Wardha ≃	122	19.38 N	79.48 E
Ward Hill ∧[2], Scot., U.K.	46	58.54 N	3.20 W
Ward Hill ∧[2], Scot., U.K.	46	58.57 N	3.09 W
Ward Hunt, Cape ⩥	164	8.05 S	149.55 E
Ward Hunt Strait ⋓	164	9.25 S	149.55 E
Wardle	44	53.39 N	2.08 W
Wardlow	182	50.54 N	111.33 W
Ward Mountain ∧	202	46.10 N	114.17 W
Wardner	182	49.25 N	115.26 W
Wardour, Vale of V	42	51.05 N	2.00 W
Wards Chapel	284b	39.24 N	76.52 W
Wards Island I	276	40.47 N	73.56 W
Ward's Stone ∧	44	54.02 N	2.38 W
Wardsville, On., Can.	214	42.39 N	81.45 W
Wardsville, Mo., U.S.	219	38.29 N	92.10 W
Wardswell Draw V	196	32.39 N	102.35 W
Wardt	52	51.41 N	6.25 E
Ware, Eng., U.K.	42	51.49 N	0.02 W
Ware, Ma., U.S.	207	42.15 N	72.14 W
Ware ≃	207	42.11 N	72.22 W
War Eagle Creek ≃	194	36.14 N	94.00 W
Waregem	50	50.53 N	3.25 E
Wareham, Eng., U.K.	42	50.41 N	2.07 W
Wareham, Ma., U.S.	207	41.45 N	70.43 W
Warehouse Point	207	41.55 N	72.37 W
Waremme	56	50.41 N	5.15 E
Waren, Dtsch.	54	53.31 N	12.40 E
Waren, Indon.	164	2.16 S	136.20 E
Warenai ≃	164	2.52 S	135.55 E
Warenda	166	22.37 S	140.32 E
Warendorf	52	51.57 N	7.59 E
Ware River C	208	37.23 N	76.27 W
Ware Shoals	192	34.23 N	82.14 W
Waretown	208	39.47 N	74.11 W
Warffum	52	53.23 N	6.34 E
Warfusée-Abancourt	50	49.52 N	2.35 E
Warga	52	53.08 N	5.51 E
Wargalo	144	6.17 N	47.31 E
Wargla	148	31.59 N	5.25 E
Wargla □[5]	148	29.00 N	8.00 E
Warialda	166	29.32 S	150.34 E
Wariap	164	1.34 S	134.11 E
Warilau	164	5.24 S	134.30 E
Warilau, Pulau I	164	5.23 S	134.33 E
Warin	54	53.48 N	11.42 E
Warinanco Park ♦	276	40.39 N	74.14 W
Warin Chamrap	110	15.12 N	104.53 E
Waring Mountains ⩙	180	66.50 N	159.00 W
Wāris Alīganj	124	25.01 N	85.38 E
Warka	30	51.47 N	21.10 E
Warkopi	164	1.08 S	134.07 E
Warks Burn ≃	44	55.03 N	2.08 W
Warkworth, On., Can.	212	44.12 N	77.53 W
Warkworth, N.Z.	172	36.24 S	174.40 E
Warkworth, Eng., U.K.	44	55.21 N	1.36 W
Warland, Eng., U.K.	262	53.41 N	2.05 W
Warland, Mt., U.S.	182	48.30 N	115.17 W
Warland Reservoir ⊜[1]	262	53.41 N	2.04 W
Warley → Smethwick	42	52.30 N	1.58 W
Warley Moor Reservoir ⊜[1]	262	53.47 N	1.57 W
Warlingham	42	51.19 N	0.04 W
Warlington	42	51.39 N	1.01 W
Warman	184	52.20 N	106.34 W
Warmandi	164	0.22 S	132.39 E
Warmbad, Namibia	156	28.29 S	18.41 E
Warmbad, S. Afr.	156	24.55 S	28.15 E
Warm Baths → Warmbad	156	24.55 S	28.15 E
Warm Beach	224	48.10 N	122.21 W
War Memorial Cross ⊥	169	37.20 S	144.36 E
Warmenhuizen	52	52.43 N	4.44 E
Warmensteinach	60	49.59 N	11.47 E
Warmeriville	50	49.21 N	4.13 E
Warmington	42	52.08 N	1.24 W
Warminster, Eng., U.K.	42	51.13 N	2.12 W
Warminster, Pa., U.S.	208	40.12 N	75.06 W
Warminster Naval Air Development Center ■	285	40.12 N	75.09 W
Warm Springs, Ga., U.S.	192	32.53 N	84.40 W
Warm Springs, Mt., U.S.	202	46.11 N	112.48 W
Warm Springs, Or., U.S.	202	44.45 N	121.15 W
Warm Springs, Va., U.S.	192	38.02 N	79.47 W
Warm Springs ≃	202	44.52 N	121.04 W
Warm Springs Indian Reservation ⊶[4]	224	45.00 N	121.25 W
Warm Springs Reservoir ⊜[1]	202	43.37 N	118.14 W
Warnbro Sound ⋓	168a	32.20 S	115.40 E
Warnemünde ⊶[8]	54	54.10 N	12.04 E
Warner, Ab., Can.	182	49.17 N	112.12 W
Warner, N.H., U.S.	188	43.16 N	71.49 W
Warner, Ok., U.S.	196	35.29 N	95.18 W
Warner Lakes ⊜	202	42.25 N	119.50 W
Warner Mountains ⩙	204	41.40 N	120.20 W
Warner Peak ∧	202	42.27 N	119.44 W
Warner Ranch	228	33.56 N	117.13 W
Warner Robins	192	32.37 N	83.36 W
Warners	210	43.05 N	76.20 W
Warners Pond ⊜	283	42.28 N	71.24 W
Warnerville	210	42.34 N	74.30 W
Warnes, Arg.	252	34.55 S	60.31 W
Warnes, Bol.	248	17.30 S	63.10 W
Warnes Brook ≃	276	40.25 N	74.18 W
Warneton	50	50.45 N	2.57 E
Warngau	64	47.50 N	11.41 E
Warnicken → Primorje	76	54.57 N	20.02 E
Warnkenhagen	54	54.00 N	11.04 E
Warnow ≃	54	54.06 N	12.09 E
Warns	52	52.52 N	5.25 E
Warnsveld	52	52.08 N	6.13 E
Waroona	168a	32.50 S	115.55 E
Warpath ≃	184	52.21 N	98.26 W
Warra	166	26.56 S	150.55 E
Warrabri Aboriginal Reserve ⊶[4]	162	21.00 S	134.20 E
Warracknabeal	166	36.15 S	142.24 E
Warr Acres	196	35.31 N	97.37 W
Warragamba Dam ⊶[6]	170	33.54 S	150.36 E
Warragul	169	38.10 S	145.56 E
Warrandyte	274b	37.45 S	145.13 E
Warrandyte South	274b	37.46 S	145.14 E
Warrāq al-ʿArab	273c	30.06 N	31.12 E
Warrāq al-Ḥaḍar, Jazīrat I	273c	30.07 N	31.13 E
Warrāq al-Hadar wa Ambūtbah wa Mīt an-Naṣārā	273c	30.06 N	31.13 E
Warrawagine	162	20.51 S	120.42 E
Warrawee	274a	33.44 S	151.07 E
Warrawolong, Mount ∧	170	33.03 S	151.15 E
Warrawong	170	34.29 S	150.53 E
Warrego ≃	166	30.24 S	145.21 E
Warrego Range ⩙	166	25.00 S	146.30 E
Warren, Austl.	166	31.42 S	147.50 E
Warren, Eng., U.K.	262	53.14 N	2.10 W
Warren, Ar., U.S.	194	33.36 N	92.03 W
Warren, Il., U.S.	190	42.29 N	89.59 W
Warren, In., U.S.	216	40.40 N	85.25 W
Warren, Ma., U.S.	207	42.12 N	72.11 W
Warren, Mi., U.S.	216	42.28 N	83.01 W
Warren, Mn., U.S.	198	48.11 N	96.46 W
Warren, Mo., U.S.	219	39.47 N	91.45 W
Warren, N.J., U.S.	276	40.37 N	74.30 W
Warren, Oh., U.S.	214	41.14 N	80.49 W
Warren, Or., U.S.	224	45.49 N	122.50 W
Warren, Pa., U.S.	214	41.50 N	79.08 W
Warren, R.I., U.S.	207	41.43 N	71.16 W
Warren □[6], In., U.S.	216	40.21 N	87.17 W
Warren □[6], Mo., U.S.	219	38.45 N	91.09 W
Warren □[6], N.J., U.S.	210	40.49 N	75.05 W
Warren □[6], N.Y., U.S.	210	43.26 N	73.43 W
Warren □[6], Oh., U.S.	218	39.26 N	84.13 W
Warren □[6], Pa., U.S.	214	41.51 N	79.08 W
Warren ≃	162	34.35 S	115.50 E
Warren City	222	32.33 N	94.54 W
Warrendale	214	40.39 N	80.04 W
Warren Dunes State Park ♦	216	41.56 N	86.36 W
Warren H. Manning State Park ♦	283	42.34 N	71.18 W
Warren Park	218	39.46 N	86.03 W
Warren Peaks ⩙	198	44.29 N	104.28 W
Warrenpoint	48	54.06 N	6.15 W
Warren Point ⩥	180	69.44 N	132.30 W
Warrens	190	44.07 N	90.29 W
Warrensburg, Il., U.S.	219	39.56 N	89.04 W
Warrensburg, Mo., U.S.	194	38.45 N	93.44 W
Warrensburg, N.Y., U.S.	188	43.29 N	73.46 W
Warrensville	210	41.19 N	76.57 W
Warrensville Heights	214	41.26 N	81.32 W
Warrenton, S. Afr.	158	28.09 S	24.47 E
Warrenton, Ga., U.S.	192	33.24 N	82.39 W
Warrenton, Mo., U.S.	219	38.48 N	91.08 W
Warrenton, N.C., U.S.	192	36.23 N	78.09 W
Warrenton, Or., U.S.	224	46.09 N	123.55 W
Warrenton, Tx., U.S.	222	30.01 N	96.44 W
Warrenton, Va., U.S.	188	38.42 N	77.47 W
Warrenville	216	41.49 N	88.10 W
Warrenzin	54	53.54 N	12.57 E
Warri	150	5.31 N	5.45 E
Warriedar Hill ∧[2]	162	29.06 S	117.06 E
Warriewood	274a	33.42 S	151.18 E
Warrill Creek ≃	171a	27.39 S	152.44 E
Warrington, N.Z.	172	45.43 S	170.35 E
Warrington, Eng., U.K.	44	53.24 N	2.37 W
Warrington, Fl., U.S.	194	30.23 N	87.16 W
Warrington, Pa., U.S.	285	40.15 N	75.08 W
Warrington □[8]	262	53.24 N	2.33 W
Warrington Airport ⊠	285	40.16 N	75.09 W
Warrior	194	33.48 N	86.48 W
Warrior Creek ≃	192	31.15 N	83.34 W
Warrior Reefs ✢[2]	164	9.35 S	143.10 E
Warriors Mark	214	40.42 N	78.08 W
Warrnambool	166	38.23 S	142.29 E
Warroad	198	48.54 N	95.18 W
Warrumbungle National Park ♦	166	31.20 S	149.00 E
Warsak	123	34.10 N	71.25 E
Warsaw → Warszawa, Pol.	30	52.15 N	21.00 E
Warsaw, Il., U.S.	190	40.21 N	91.26 W
Warsaw, In., U.S.	216	41.14 N	85.51 W
Warsaw, Ky., U.S.	218	38.47 N	84.54 W
Warsaw, Mo., U.S.	194	38.14 N	93.22 W
Warsaw, N.Y., U.S.	210	42.44 N	78.07 W
Warsaw, N.C., U.S.	192	34.59 N	78.05 W
Warsaw, Oh., U.S.	214	40.20 N	82.00 W
Warsaw, Va., U.S.	208	37.57 N	76.45 W
Warsaw Station ⊶[5]	265a	59.54 N	30.19 E
Warschau → Warszawa	30	52.15 N	21.00 E
Warscheneck ∧	61	47.39 N	14.14 E
Warshiikh	144	2.18 N	45.48 E
Warsop	44	53.13 N	1.09 W
Warspite	182	54.06 N	112.37 W
Warstein	56	51.26 N	8.21 E
Warszawa (Warsaw)	30	52.15 N	21.00 E
Warszawa □[4]	30	52.15 N	21.00 E
Warta	30	51.42 N	18.38 E
Warta ≃	30	52.35 N	14.39 E
Wartburg, S. Afr.	158	29.25 S	30.35 E
Wartburg, Tn., U.S.	192	36.06 N	84.35 W
Wartburg ⊥	54	50.58 N	10.18 E
Wartenberg	60	48.24 N	11.59 E
Wartenberg ⊶[8]	264a	52.34 N	13.31 E
Warth	58	47.15 N	10.11 E
Warthan Creek ≃	226	36.08 N	120.20 W
Warthe → Warta ≃	30	52.35 N	14.39 E
Wartin	54	53.15 N	14.09 E
Warton, Eng., U.K.	44	54.09 N	2.47 W
Warton, Eng., U.K.	44	53.45 N	2.54 W
Warton Aerodrome ⊠	262	53.45 N	2.54 W
Wartrace	194	35.31 N	86.20 W
Wartsberg ∧[2]	263	51.25 N	6.29 E
Waru	164	3.24 S	130.40 E
Warud	120	21.28 N	78.16 E
Warunta, Laguna de ⊜	236	15.23 N	84.05 W
Waruta ≃	164	3.18 S	140.08 E
Warwick, Austl.	171a	28.13 S	152.02 E
Warwick, P.Q., Can.	206	45.56 N	71.59 W
Warwick, Eng., U.K.	42	52.17 N	1.34 W
Warwick, Md., U.S.	208	39.25 N	75.46 W
Warwick, N.Y., U.S.	210	41.15 N	74.21 W
Warwick, R.I., U.S.	207	41.41 N	71.22 W
Warwick ≃	208	37.05 N	76.33 W
Warwick Castle ⊥	42	52.17 N	1.34 W
Warwick Channel ⋓	164	13.51 S	136.16 E
Warwick Farm Racecourse and Motor Race Track ♦	274a	33.55 S	150.57 E
Warwickshire □[6]	42	52.13 N	1.37 W
Warza	54	51.00 N	10.41 E
Wasaga Beach	212	44.31 N	80.01 W
Wasagu	150	11.25 N	5.49 E
Wasatch Mountain State Park ♦	200	40.33 N	111.31 W
Wasatch Plateau ⩙[1]	200	39.20 N	111.30 W
Wasatch Range ⩙	200	40.40 N	111.35 W
Wasāwewāla	123	30.28 N	73.40 E
Wasbank	158	28.24 S	30.05 E
Wasbister	46	59.10 N	3.07 W
Wascana Creek ≃	184	50.39 N	104.55 W
Wäschenbeuren	56	48.46 N	9.41 E
Wasco, Ca., U.S.	226	35.35 N	119.20 W
Wasco, Or., U.S.	224	45.35 N	120.41 W
Wasco □[6]	224	45.10 N	121.12 W
Wase	150	9.06 N	9.59 E
Wase ≃	146	8.27 N	10.06 E
Waseca	190	44.04 N	93.30 W
Waseda University ✠[2]	268	35.42 N	139.43 E
Wasekamio Lake ⊜	184	56.45 N	108.45 W
Wasen	58	47.03 N	7.48 E
Wasgomuwa National Park ♦	122	7.40 N	80.45 E
Washademoak Lake ⊜	186	45.48 N	65.58 W
Washago	212	44.45 N	79.20 W
Washburn, Il., U.S.	190	40.55 N	89.17 W
Washburn, Me., U.S.	186	46.47 N	68.09 W
Washburn, N.D., U.S.	198	47.17 N	101.01 W
Washburn, Wi., U.S.	190	46.40 N	90.53 W
Washburn ≃	44	53.54 N	1.39 W
Washburn, Mount ∧	202	44.48 N	110.25 W
Washburn Lake ⊜	176	70.03 N	106.50 W
Washdyke	172	44.21 S	171.14 E
Washicoutai	186	50.17 N	60.42 W
Washiga-take ∧	94	35.56 N	136.58 E
Wāshīm	122	20.06 N	77.09 E
Washimiya	94	36.06 N	139.40 E
Washington, Eng., U.K.	44	54.55 N	1.30 W
Washington, Ca., U.S.	226	39.22 N	120.48 W
Washington, Ct., U.S.	207	41.37 N	73.18 W
Washington, D.C., U.S.	208	38.53 N	77.02 W
Washington, D.C., U.S.	284c	38.53 N	77.02 W
Washington, Ga., U.S.	192	33.44 N	82.44 W
Washington, Il., U.S.	190	40.42 N	89.24 W
Washington, In., U.S.	194	38.39 N	87.10 W
Washington, Ia., U.S.	190	41.17 N	91.41 W
Washington, Ks., U.S.	198	39.49 N	97.03 W
Washington, Ky., U.S.	218	38.36 N	83.48 W
Washington, La., U.S.	194	30.36 N	92.03 W
Washington, Mi., U.S.	214	42.44 N	83.02 W
Washington, Mo., U.S.	219	38.33 N	91.01 W
Washington, N.J., U.S.	210	40.45 N	74.58 W
Washington, N.C., U.S.	192	35.31 N	77.01 W
Washington, Pa., U.S.	214	40.10 N	80.14 W
Washington, Tx., U.S.	222	30.20 N	96.10 W
Washington, Ut,. U.S.	200	37.07 N	113.30 W
Washington, Va., U.S.	188	38.42 N	78.09 W
Washington □[6], Il., U.S.	219	38.21 N	89.23 W
Washington □[6], In., U.S.	218	38.36 N	86.06 W
Washington □[6], N.Y., U.S.	210	43.15 N	73.27 W
Washington □[6], Or., U.S.	224	45.33 N	123.07 W
Washington □[6], Pa., U.S.	214	40.10 N	80.15 W
Washington □[6], R.I., U.S.	207	41.28 N	71.35 W
Washington □[6], Tx., U.S.	222	30.15 N	96.20 W
Washington □[6], Wi., U.S.	216	43.14 N	88.15 W
Washington □[3], U.S.	178	47.30 N	120.30 W
Washington □[3], U.S.	202	47.30 N	120.30 W
Washington, Lake ⊜, Fl., U.S.	220	28.07 N	80.45 W
Washington, Lake ⊜, Wa., U.S.	224	47.37 N	122.15 W
Washington, Mount ∧	188	44.15 N	71.15 W
Washington Court House	218	39.32 N	83.26 W
Washington Crossing	208	40.17 N	74.52 W
Washington Crossing State Historic Site ⊥	208	40.17 N	74.53 W
Washington Depot	207	41.38 N	73.18 W
Washington Heights ⊶[8]	276	40.52 N	73.56 W
Washington Island	190	45.23 N	86.55 W
Washington Island I	190	45.23 N	86.55 W
Washington Memorial Chapel ✠[1]	285	40.06 N	75.26 W
Washington Mills	210	43.03 N	75.16 W
Washington Monument ♦	284c	38.53 N	77.03 W
Washington Monument State Park ♦	208	39.30 N	77.38 W
Washington National Airport ⊠	208	38.51 N	77.02 W
Washington-on-the-Brazos State Historic Park ♦	222	30.20 N	96.09 W
Washington Park	219	38.38 N	90.05 W
Washington Park ♦, Il., U.S.	278	41.48 N	87.37 W
Washington Park ♦, Oh., U.S.	279a	41.27 N	81.40 W
Washington Pass)(	224	48.32 N	120.39 W
Washington Place	218	39.47 N	86.01 W
Washington Rock State Park ♦	276	40.37 N	74.28 W
Washington's Headquarters ⊥	285	40.06 N	75.28 W
Washington Terrace	200	41.10 N	111.58 W
Washington Township	276	40.54 N	74.00 W
Washington Valley	276	40.48 N	74.32 W
Washington Valley Reservoir ⊜[1]	276	40.36 N	74.34 W
Washingtonville, N.Y., U.S.	210	41.26 N	74.10 W
Washingtonville, Oh., U.S.	214	40.54 N	80.46 W
Washingtonville, Pa., U.S.	210	41.03 N	76.40 W
Washita ≃	196	34.12 N	96.50 W
Washoe □[6]	226	39.22 N	119.43 W
Washoe Lake ⊜	226	39.16 N	119.48 W
Washougal	224	45.34 N	122.21 W
Washougal ≃	224	45.35 N	122.23 W
Washow Bay C	184	51.22 N	96.47 W
Washtenaw □[6]	216	42.15 N	83.50 W
Washtucna	202	46.45 N	118.18 W
Wāshuk	128	27.44 N	64.48 E
Wasian	164	1.54 S	133.17 E
Wasilków	30	53.12 N	23.12 E
Wasilla	180	61.35 N	149.26 W
Wasior	164	2.43 S	134.30 E
Wasiri	112	7.35 S	126.38 E
Wāsiṭ □[4]	128	32.45 N	45.25 E
Waskada	184	49.06 N	100.46 W
Waskaganish	176	51.30 N	78.45 W
Waskahigan ≃	182	54.45 N	117.12 W
Waskaiowaka Lake ⊜	184	56.30 N	96.20 W
Waskatenau	182	54.07 N	112.47 W
Waskesiu Lake ⊜	184	53.56 N	106.10 W
Waskom	194	32.29 N	94.04 W
Wąsosz	30	51.34 N	16.42 E
Waspam	236	14.44 N	83.58 W
Waspuk ≃	236	14.38 N	84.26 W
Wasquehal	50	50.40 N	3.09 E
Wassaic	210	41.48 N	73.35 W
Wasselonne	58	48.38 N	7.27 E
Wassen	58	46.42 N	8.36 E
Wassenaar	52	52.07 N	4.24 E
Wassenberg	56	51.06 N	6.08 E
Wasseralfingen	56	48.52 N	10.06 E
Wasserbillig	56	49.44 N	6.30 E
Wasserburg am Inn	60	48.04 N	12.13 E
Wasserkuppe ∧	56	50.30 N	9.56 E
Wasserkurl	263	51.33 N	7.38 E
Wasserleben	54	51.55 N	10.44 E
Wassertrüdingen	56	49.02 N	10.35 E
Wassigny	50	50.01 N	3.36 E
Wass Lake ⊜	184	53.40 N	95.25 W
Wassmannsdorf	264a	52.22 N	13.28 E
Wassou	150	10.02 N	13.39 W
Wassy	58	48.30 N	4.57 E
Wast Water ⊜	44	54.26 N	3.18 W
Wasu	164	6.00 S	147.15 E
Wasum	164	6.05 S	149.20 E
Wasungen	54	50.40 N	10.22 E
Watabeag Lake ⊜	190	48.14 N	80.32 W
Watampone (Bone)	112	4.32 S	120.20 E
Watamu Marine National Park ♦	154	3.23 S	40.00 E
Waṭan, Wādī al- V	142	30.26 N	31.49 E
Watansopeng	112	4.21 S	119.53 E
Watapi Lake ⊜	184	55.18 N	109.35 W
Watarai	94	34.26 N	136.37 E
Watarase ≃	94	36.13 N	139.42 E
Wataru I	122	5.43 N	73.23 E
Watatic, Mount ∧	207	42.42 N	71.53 W
Watauga	222	32.51 N	97.15 W
Watchet	42	51.12 N	3.20 W
Watch Hill	207	41.18 N	71.51 W
Watchung	276	40.38 N	74.27 W
Watchung Reservation ♦	276	40.41 N	74.23 W
Water	262	53.44 N	2.14 W
Waterbeach	42	52.16 N	0.11 E
Waterberg	156	20.28 S	17.13 E
Waterberge ⩙	156	24.30 S	28.00 E
Waterberg Plateau Park ♦	156	20.30 S	17.00 E
Waterbury, Ct., U.S.	207	41.33 N	73.02 W
Waterbury, Vt., U.S.	188	44.20 N	72.45 W
Waterdale	158	30.40 S	24.02 E
Wateree ≃	192	33.45 N	80.37 W
Wateree Lake ⊜[1]	192	34.25 N	80.50 W
Waterend, Eng., U.K.	260	51.47 N	0.30 W
Water End, Eng., U.K.	262	53.41 N	2.15 W
Waterfall, Austl.	170	34.08 S	151.00 E
Waterfall, Pa., U.S.	214	40.08 N	78.04 W
Waterford, On., Can.	212	42.56 N	80.17 W
Waterford (Port Láirge), Ire.	48	52.15 N	7.06 W
Waterford, S. Afr.	158	33.05 S	25.00 E
Waterford, Ca., U.S.	226	37.38 N	120.46 W
Waterford, Ct., U.S.	207	41.20 N	72.09 W
Waterford, In., U.S.	216	41.40 N	86.50 W
Waterford, Mi., U.S.	216	42.42 N	83.24 W
Waterford, N.Y., U.S.	210	42.47 N	73.40 W
Waterford, Pa., U.S.	214	41.56 N	79.59 W
Waterford, Wi., U.S.	216	42.45 N	88.12 W
Waterford □[6]	48	52.10 N	7.40 W
Waterford Harbour C	48	52.10 N	6.55 W
Waterford Mills	216	41.33 N	85.50 W
Waterford Works	208	39.43 N	74.50 W
Watergate Bay C	42	50.27 N	5.05 W
Watergrasshill	48	52.01 N	8.21 W
Watergrove Reservoir ⊜[1]	262	53.39 N	2.08 W
Waterhen ≃	184	54.38 N	107.47 W
Waterhen Lake ⊜, Mb., Can.	184	52.06 N	99.34 W
Waterhen Lake ⊜, Sk., Can.	184	54.28 N	108.25 W
Waterhouse Range ⩙	162	24.01 S	133.25 E
Wateringbury	260	51.15 N	0.25 E
Wateringen	52	52.02 N	4.16 E
Water Island	276	40.41 N	73.02 W
Waterkloof	158	30.19 S	25.18 E
Waterloo, Austl.	164	16.38 S	129.18 E
Waterloo, Austl.	168a	33.20 S	115.47 E
Waterloo, Austl.	168b	33.59 S	138.53 E
Waterloo, Bel.	50	50.43 N	4.23 E
Waterloo, On., Can.	212	43.28 N	80.31 W
Waterloo, P.Q., Can.	206	45.21 N	72.31 W
Waterloo, S.L.	150	8.20 N	13.04 W
Waterloo, Eng., U.K.	44	53.28 N	3.02 W
Waterloo, Al., U.S.	194	34.55 N	88.03 W
Waterloo, Il., U.S.	219	38.20 N	90.08 W
Waterloo, In., U.S.	216	41.25 N	85.01 W
Waterloo, Ia., U.S.	190	42.29 N	92.20 W
Waterloo, N.Y., U.S.	210	42.54 N	76.51 W
Waterloo, Wi., U.S.	216	43.11 N	88.59 W
Waterloo □[6]	212	43.30 N	80.30 W
Waterloo Bay C	168b	35.08 S	137.26 E
Waterloo State Recreation Area ♦	216	42.22 N	84.20 W
Waterlooville	42	50.53 N	1.02 W
Waterman, Il., U.S.	216	41.46 N	88.46 W
Waterman, Wa., U.S.	224	47.34 N	122.35 W
Waterman Mountain ∧	228	34.20 N	117.56 W
Waterman Wash V	200	33.21 N	112.31 W
Water Mill	207	40.55 N	72.21 W
Waterport	210	43.20 N	78.16 W
Waterport Pond ⊜[1]	212	43.19 N	78.16 W
Waterproof	194	31.48 N	91.23 W
Waterside	214	40.11 N	78.23 W
Waterside Park	276	40.56 N	73.20 W
Watersmeet	190	46.16 N	89.10 W
Waterton ≃	182	49.32 N	113.16 W
Waterton-Glacier International Peace Park ♦	202	48.47 N	113.45 W
Waterton Lakes National Park ♦	182	49.05 N	113.50 W
Watertown, Ct., U.S.	207	41.36 N	73.07 W
Watertown, Ma., U.S.	207	42.22 N	71.11 W
Watertown, N.Y., U.S.	212	43.58 N	75.54 W
Watertown, S.D., U.S.	198	44.53 N	97.06 W
Watertown, Wi., U.S.	216	43.11 N	88.43 W
Waterval-Boven	156	25.40 S	30.20 E
Watervale	168b	33.57 S	138.38 E
Water Valley, Ms., U.S.	194	34.09 N	89.37 W
Water Valley, N.Y., U.S.	284a	42.42 N	78.51 W
Water View	208	37.43 N	76.36 W
Waterville, N.S., Can.	186	45.03 N	64.41 W
Waterville, P.Q., Can.	206	45.16 N	71.54 W
Waterville, Ire.	48	51.49 N	10.13 W
Waterville, Ks., U.S.	198	39.41 N	96.44 W
Waterville, Me., U.S.	188	44.33 N	69.37 W
Waterville, Ma., U.S.	207	42.40 N	72.04 W
Waterville, Mn., U.S.	190	44.13 N	93.34 W
Waterville, N.Y., U.S.	210	42.55 N	75.22 W
Waterville, Oh., U.S.	216	41.30 N	83.43 W
Waterville, Pa., U.S.	210	41.19 N	77.22 W
Waterville, Wa., U.S.	202	47.38 N	120.04 W
Watervliet, Mi., U.S.	216	42.11 N	86.15 W
Watervliet, N.Y., U.S.	210	42.43 N	73.42 W
Watervliet Reservoir ⊜[1]	210	42.43 N	73.58 W
Wates, Indon.	114	1.00 N	100.16 E
Wates, Indon.	115a	7.55 S	112.07 E
Wates, Indon.	115a	7.51 S	110.10 E
Watford, On., Can.	214	42.57 N	81.53 W
Watford, Eng., U.K.	42	51.40 N	0.25 W
Watford □[8]	260	51.40 N	0.25 W
Watford City	198	47.48 N	103.16 W
Wa'th	140	8.10 N	32.07 E
Wathaman ≃	184	57.16 N	102.52 W
Wathaman Lake ⊜	184	56.55 N	103.43 W
Wathena	198	39.45 N	94.56 W
Watheroo	162	30.17 S	116.04 E
Watheroo National Park ♦	162	30.14 S	115.52 E
Wathlingen	52	52.32 N	10.09 E
Wath upon Dearne	44	53.29 N	1.20 W
Wati	120	28.02 N	96.59 E
Watino	182	55.43 N	117.37 W
Watkins Glen	210	42.22 N	76.52 W
Watkins Glen International Raceway ♦	210	42.20 N	76.55 W
Watkins Glen State Park ♦	210	42.22 N	76.55 W
Watkins Island I	284c	39.02 N	77.17 W
Watkins Lake ⊜	281	42.40 N	83.22 W
Watkinsville	192	33.51 N	83.24 W
Watlaar	164	5.28 S	133.07 E
Watling Island → San Salvador I	238	24.02 N	74.28 W
Watlington	42	51.37 N	1.00 W
Watoga State Park ♦	188	38.07 N	80.05 W
Watonga	196	35.50 N	98.24 W
Watonwan ≃	198	44.04 N	94.07 W
Watopeka ≃	206	45.34 N	72.00 W
Watou	50	50.51 N	2.37 E
Wat Phai Tan, Khlong ≊	269a	13.48 N	100.33 E
Watrous, Sk., Can.	184	51.40 N	105.28 W
Watrous, N.M., U.S.	200	35.47 N	104.58 W
Watsa	154	3.03 N	29.32 E
Watseka	216	40.46 N	87.44 W
Watsi Kengo	152	0.48 S	20.33 E
Watson, Austl.	162	30.29 S	131.31 E
Watson, Sk., Can.	184	52.07 N	104.31 W
Watson, In., U.S.	218	38.22 N	85.41 W
Watsonia	274b	37.43 S	145.05 E
Watson Lake	180	60.07 N	128.48 W
Watsons Bay	274a	33.51 S	151.17 E
Watsons Creek	274b	37.40 S	145.13 E
Watsons Creek ≃	274b	37.43 S	145.16 E
Watsontown	210	41.05 N	76.51 W
Watsonville	226	36.54 N	121.45 W
Watt	222	31.39 N	96.51 W
Watten	50	50.50 N	2.13 E
Watten, Loch ⊜	46	58.29 N	3.19 W
Wattens	64	47.17 N	11.36 E
Wattenscheid	56	51.29 N	7.08 E
Wattenwil	58	46.46 N	7.30 E
Wattignies	50	50.35 N	3.03 E
Wattiwarriganna ≃	162	28.57 S	136.10 E
Wattle Flat	170	33.08 S	149.41 E
Wattle Glen	274b	37.40 S	145.11 E
Wattle Park ♦	274b	37.50 S	145.07 E
Watt Mountain ∧	240d	15.19 N	61.19 W
Watton	42	52.35 N	0.48 E
Wattrelos	50	50.42 N	3.13 E
Watts ⊶[8]	280	33.56 N	118.15 W
Watts Bar Lake ⊜[1]	192	35.48 N	84.39 W
Watts Branch ≃	284c	39.03 N	77.15 W
Wattsburg	214	42.00 N	79.49 W
Watts Island I	208	37.48 N	75.53 W
Watts Mills	192	34.31 N	82.02 W
Wattville	273d	26.13 S	28.18 E
Wattwil	58	47.18 N	9.06 E
Watu	152	3.18 S	20.03 E
Watubela, Kepulauan II	164	4.35 S	131.40 E
Wat Wat	164	4.29 S	152.21 E
Watzekopf ∧	58	46.59 N	10.48 E
Watzmann ∧	64	47.33 N	12.55 E
Wau	164	7.20 S	146.45 E
Waubach	56	50.55 N	6.03 E
Waubaushene	212	44.45 N	79.42 W
Waubaushene Channel ⋓	212	44.46 N	79.45 W
Waubay	198	45.19 N	97.18 W
Waubay Lake ⊜	198	45.25 N	97.25 W
Waubesa, Lake ⊜	216	43.01 N	89.20 W
Waubra	169	37.21 S	143.39 E
Waubuno Creek ≃	212	42.58 N	81.08 W
Wauchope, Austl.	162	20.36 S	134.15 E
Wauchope, Austl.	166	31.27 S	152.44 E
Wauchula	220	27.32 N	81.48 W
Wauconda, Il., U.S.	216	42.15 N	88.08 W
Wauconda, Wa., U.S.	182	48.43 N	119.00 W
Wauconda, Wa., U.S.	202	48.43 N	119.00 W
Waugh	184	49.40 N	95.13 W
Waugh Mountain ∧	202	45.29 N	114.47 W
Waukara, Bukit ∧	112	1.15 S	119.42 E
Waukaringa	166	32.18 S	139.26 E
Waukarlycarly, Lake ⊜	162	21.25 S	121.50 E
Waukegan	216	42.21 N	87.50 W
Waukena	226	36.08 N	119.31 W
Waukesha	216	43.00 N	88.13 W
Waukesha □[6]	216	43.02 N	88.20 W
Waukomis	196	36.16 N	97.53 W
Waukon	190	43.16 N	91.28 W
Waulsort	56	50.13 N	4.52 E
Wauna	224	47.22 N	122.38 W
Waunakee	216	43.11 N	89.27 W
Wauneta	198	40.25 N	101.22 W
Waupaca	190	44.21 N	89.05 W
Waupecan Creek ≃	216	41.20 N	88.28 W
Waupoos Island I	212	43.59 N	76.58 W
Waupun	190	43.38 N	88.43 W
Wauregan	207	41.44 N	71.54 W
Waurika	196	34.10 N	97.59 W
Waurika Lake ⊜[1]	196	34.15 N	98.05 W
Wausa	198	42.29 N	97.32 W
Wausau	190	44.57 N	89.37 W
Wausaukee	190	45.22 N	87.57 W
Wauseon	216	41.32 N	84.08 W
Waushakum Pond ⊜	283	42.16 N	71.26 W
Wautoma	190	44.04 N	89.17 W
Wauwa	154	3.27 N	27.21 E
Wauwatosa	216	43.02 N	88.00 W
Wauzeka	190	43.05 N	90.52 W
Wave Hill	162	17.29 S	130.57 E
Waveland, Ma., U.S.	283	42.17 N	70.53 W
Waveland, Ms., U.S.	194	30.17 N	89.22 W
Waveney ≃	42	52.28 N	1.45 E
Waver ≃	44	54.52 N	3.17 W
Waverley, Austl.	169	37.53 S	145.10 E
Waverley, Austl.	274a	33.54 S	151.16 E
Waverley, N.Z.	172	39.46 S	174.38 E
Waverley, S. Afr.	158	31.58 S	26.28 E
Waverley, Ma., U.S.	283	42.23 N	71.11 W
Waverley ⊶[8]	273d	26.08 S	28.04 E
Waverly, Al., U.S.	194	32.44 N	85.35 W
Waverly, Fl., U.S.	220	27.59 N	81.37 W
Waverly, Il., U.S.	219	39.35 N	89.57 W
Waverly, Ia., U.S.	190	42.43 N	92.28 W
Waverly, Ks., U.S.	198	38.23 N	95.36 W
Waverly, Mi., U.S.	216	42.44 N	84.33 W
Waverly, Mn., U.S.	190	45.04 N	93.57 W
Waverly, Mo., U.S.	194	39.12 N	93.31 W
Waverly, Ne., U.S.	198	40.55 N	96.31 W
Waverly, N.Y., U.S.	210	42.00 N	76.31 W
Waverly, Oh., U.S.	218	39.07 N	82.59 W
Waverly, Pa., U.S.	210	41.32 N	75.42 W
Waverly, Tn., U.S.	194	36.05 N	87.47 W
Waverly, Va., U.S.	208	37.02 N	77.05 W
Waverly Hall	192	32.41 N	84.44 W
Wavre	56	50.43 N	4.37 E
Wavrin	50	50.34 N	2.55 E
Wāw	140	7.42 N	28.00 E
Wāw ≃	140	7.03 N	27.13 E
Wawa, On., Can.	190	47.59 N	84.47 W
Wawa, Nig.	150	9.55 N	4.25 E
Wawa, Sūd.	140	20.26 N	30.21 E
Wawa ≃	236	13.53 N	83.28 W
Wawaka	216	41.27 N	85.28 W
Wāw al-Kabīr	146	25.20 N	16.43 E
Wawanesa	184	49.36 N	99.41 W
Wawarsing	210	41.46 N	74.21 W
Wawasee, Lake ⊜	216	41.24 N	85.41 W
Wawayanda State Park ♦	276	41.11 N	74.26 W
Wawiag ≃	190	48.25 N	91.07 W
Wawoi ≃	164	8.01 S	143.33 E
Waworada, Teluk C	115b	8.44 S	118.51 E
Wawota	184	49.55 N	102.00 W
Waxahachie	222	32.23 N	96.50 W
Waxahachie, Lake ⊜[1]	222	32.20 N	96.49 W
Waxhaw	192	34.55 N	80.44 W
Waxuecun	106	31.07 N	121.38 E
Waxweiler	56	50.05 N	6.22 E

Symbols in the index entries represent the broad categories identified in the key at the right. Symbols with superior numbers (⩙[1]) identify subcategories (see complete key on page *I · 1).*

Symbole im Register stellen die rechts im Schlüssel erklärten Kategorien dar. Symbole mit hochgestellten Ziffern (⩙[1]) bezeichnen Unterabteilungen einer Kategorie (vgl. vollständiger Schlüssel auf Seite *I · 1).*

Los símbolos incluídos en el texto del índice representan las grandes categorías identificadas con la clave a la derecha. Los símbolos con numeros en su parte superior (⩙[1]) identifican las subcategorías (véase la clave completa en la página *I · 1).*

Les symboles de l'index représentent les catégories indiquées dans la légende à droite. Les symboles suivis d'un indice (⩙[1]) représentent des sous-catégories (voir légende complète à la page *I · 1).*

Os símbolos incluídos no texto do índice representam as grandes categorias identificadas com a chave à direita. Os símbolos com números em sua parte superior (⩙[1]) identificam as subcategorias (veja-se a chave completa à página *I · 1).*

∧	Mountain	Berg	Montaña	Montagne	Montanha
⩙	Mountains	Gebirge	Montañas	Montagnes	Montanhas
)(	Pass	Paß	Paso	Col	Passo
V	Valley, Canyon	Tal, Cañon	Valle, Cañón	Vallée, Canyon	Vale, Canhão
≚	Plain	Ebene	Llano	Plaine	Planície
⩥	Cape	Kap	Cabo	Cap	Cabo
I	Island	Insel	Isla	Île	Ilha
II	Islands	Inseln	Islas	Îles	Ilhas
⊥	Other Topographic Features	Andere Topographische Objekte	Otros Elementos Topográficos	Autres données topographiques	Outros acidentes topográficos

ESPAÑOL

Nombre	Página	Lat.°′	Long.°′ W = Oeste
Way, Lake ⊜	162	26.48 S	120.18 E
Waya I	175g	17.18 S	177.08 E
Wayabula	108	2.17 N	128.12 E
Wayaopu	106	30.33 N	118.53 E
Waycross	192	31.12 N	82.21 W
Wayi	154	5.11 N	30.10 E
Wayland, Ia., U.S.	190	41.08 N	91.39 W
Wayland, Ky., U.S.	192	37.26 N	82.48 W
Wayland, Ma., U.S.	283	42.21 N	71.21 W
Wayland, Mi., U.S.	216	42.40 N	85.38 W
Wayland, N.Y., U.S.	210	42.34 N	77.35 W
Wayland, Oh., U.S.	214	41.10 N	81.04 W
Waylyn	192	32.51 N	79.59 W
Waymansville	218	39.04 N	86.03 W
Waymart	210	41.34 N	75.24 W
Wayne, Ab., Can.	182	51.23 N	112.39 W
Wayne, Mi., U.S.	216	42.16 N	83.23 W
Wayne, Ne., U.S.	198	42.13 N	97.01 W
Wayne, N.J., U.S.	210	40.55 N	74.16 W
Wayne, N.Y., U.S.	210	42.28 N	77.06 W
Wayne, Oh., U.S.	214	41.18 N	83.28 W
Wayne, Ok., U.S.	196	34.55 N	97.18 W
Wayne, Pa., U.S.	208	40.02 N	75.23 W
Wayne, W.V., U.S.	188	38.13 N	82.26 W
Wayne □[6], Il., U.S.	219	38.25 N	88.40 W
Wayne □[6], In., U.S.	218	39.50 N	84.54 W
Wayne □[6], Mi., U.S.	216	42.14 N	83.12 W
Wayne □[6], N.Y., U.S.	210	43.04 N	77.00 W
Wayne □[6], Oh., U.S.	214	40.48 N	81.56 W
Wayne □[6], Pa., U.S.	210	41.34 N	75.16 W
Wayne City	194	38.20 N	88.35 W
Wayne Lakes	218	40.01 N	84.39 W
Waynesboro, Ga., U.S.	192	33.05 N	82.00 W
Waynesboro, Ms., U.S.	194	31.40 N	88.38 W
Waynesboro, Pa., U.S.	208	39.45 N	77.34 W
Waynesboro, Tn., U.S.	194	35.19 N	87.45 W
Waynesboro, Va., U.S.	192	38.04 N	78.53 W
Waynesburg, Oh., U.S.	214	40.40 N	81.15 W
Waynesburg, Pa., U.S.	188	39.53 N	80.10 W
Waynesfield	216	40.36 N	83.59 W
Wayne State University ⊍[2]	281	42.21 N	83.04 W
Waynesville, Il., U.S.	194	40.15 N	89.08 W
Waynesville, Mo., U.S.	194	37.49 N	92.12 W
Waynesville, N.C., U.S.	192	35.29 N	82.59 W
Waynesville, Oh., U.S.	218	39.32 N	84.05 W
Waynoka	196	36.34 N	98.52 W
Waynoka, Lake ⊜[1]	218	38.55 N	83.47 W
Wayoh Reservoir ⊜[1]	262	53.39 N	2.24 W
Waza	146	11.25 N	14.34 E
Waza, Parc National de ♠	146	11.20 N	13.40 E
Wazah	120	33.22 N	69.26 E
Wāzah Khwāh	120	32.12 N	68.21 E
Waziers	50	50.23 N	3.07 E
Wāzin	146	31.57 N	10.40 E
Wazīrābād	123	32.27 N	74.07 E
Wazirābād ➜[8]	272a	28.43 N	77.14 E
Wāzirpur ➜[8]	272a	28.41 N	77.10 E
Wazuka	96	34.47 N	135.55 E
Wazuka ≃	270	34.45 N	135.53 E
Wda ≃	30	53.25 N	18.29 E
We, Pulau I	114	5.51 N	95.18 E
Wea Creek ≃	216	40.24 N	86.57 W
Weagamow Lake ⊜	184	52.53 N	91.22 W
Weald Park ♠	260	51.38 N	0.14 E
Wealdstone ➜[8]	260	51.36 N	0.20 W
Weam	164	8.40 S	141.08 E
Wear ≃	44	54.55 N	1.22 W
Wearhead	44	54.45 N	2.13 W
Wearyan ≃	164	15.57 S	136.51 E
Weatherford, Ok., U.S.	196	35.31 N	98.42 W
Weatherford, Tx., U.S.	222	32.45 N	97.47 W
Weatherford, Lake ⊜[1]	222	32.47 N	97.41 W
Weatherly	210	40.56 N	75.50 W
Weatogue	207	41.51 N	72.49 W
Weaubleau	194	37.53 N	93.32 W
Weaver, Austl.	168b	34.56 S	137.40 E
Weaver, Al., U.S.	194	33.45 N	85.48 W
Weaver, Tx., U.S.	222	33.10 N	95.25 W
Weaver ≃	44	53.18 N	2.43 W
Weaverham	44	53.16 N	2.35 W
Weaver Lake ⊜	184	52.45 N	96.35 W
Weavertown	279b	40.16 N	80.11 W
Weaverville, Ca., U.S.	204	40.43 N	122.56 W
Weaverville, N.C., U.S.	192	35.41 N	82.33 W
Webau	54	51.10 N	12.04 E
Webb, Sk., Can.	184	50.11 N	108.12 W
Webb, Ms., U.S.	194	33.56 N	90.20 W
Webb Brook ≃	283	42.32 N	71.14 W
Webb City	194	37.08 N	94.27 W
Webber Lake ⊜	184	54.28 N	94.00 W
Webberville	216	42.40 N	84.10 W
Webbwood	190	46.16 N	81.53 W
Weber ≃	200	41.13 N	112.16 W
Weber, Mount ∧	182	55.32 N	128.31 W
Weber City	192	36.37 N	82.33 W
Weber Creek ≃	226	38.46 N	121.00 W
Weber Hill	219	38.27 N	90.34 W
Weberi Bekera	144	9.39 N	39.03 E
Webster, Ab., Can.	182	55.26 N	118.42 W
Webster, Fl., U.S.	220	28.36 N	82.03 W
Webster, In., U.S.	218	39.54 N	84.57 W
Webster, Ma., U.S.	207	42.03 N	71.52 W
Webster, N.Y., U.S.	210	43.12 N	77.25 W
Webster, Pa., U.S.	214	40.11 N	79.50 W
Webster, S.D., U.S.	198	45.19 N	97.31 W
Webster, Wi., U.S.	190	45.52 N	92.22 W
Webster City	190	42.28 N	93.48 W
Webster Crossing	210	42.40 N	77.38 W
Webster Groves	219	38.35 N	90.21 W
Webster Lake ⊜	216	41.19 N	85.41 W
Websters Corners, B.C., Can.	224	49.13 N	122.30 W
Websters Corners, N.Y., U.S.	284a	41.47 N	78.45 W
Webster Springs	188	38.28 N	80.24 W
Weches	222	31.33 N	95.14 W
Wechmar	54	50.53 N	10.47 E
Wechselburg	54	51.00 N	12.47 E
Weda	108	0.21 N	127.52 E
Wedau ➜[8]	263	51.24 N	6.48 E
Wedau, Sportpark ♠	263	51.25 N	6.47 E
Weddell Island I	254	51.55 S	61.00 W
Weddell Sea ⊤[2]	9	72.00 S	45.00 W
Wedderburn	166	36.25 S	143.37 E
Wedding ➜[8]	54	52.33 N	13.22 E
Weddinghofen	263	51.36 N	7.37 E
Wedel	52	53.35 N	9.41 E
Wedemark	52	52.33 N	9.44 E
Wedge, Central Mount ∧	162	22.51 S	131.50 E
Wedge Mountain ∧	182	50.10 N	122.50 W
Wedgeport	186	43.44 N	65.59 W
Wedgewood	219	38.47 N	90.17 W
Wedmore	42	51.14 N	2.49 W
Wedowee	194	33.18 N	85.29 W
Wedron	216	41.26 N	88.46 W
Weduar, Tanjung ›	164	6.00 S	132.50 E
Wedweil	140	9.00 N	27.12 E
Wedza	154	18.35 S	31.35 E
Weebo	162	28.01 S	121.03 E
Weed	204	41.25 N	122.23 W
Weed Heights	226	38.59 N	119.12 W
Weedon	206	45.42 N	71.28 W
Weedon Beck	42	52.14 N	1.05 W

FRANÇAIS

Nom	Page	Lat.°′	Long.°′ W = Ouest
Weedon Island I	220	27.51 N	82.36 W
Weed Patch	228	35.19 N	118.55 W
Weed Patch Hill ∧[2]	218	39.10 N	86.13 W
Weedsport	210	43.02 N	76.33 W
Weedville	214	41.17 N	78.30 W
Weehawken	276	40.46 N	74.01 W
Weeim, Pulau I	164	1.29 S	130.14 E
Wee Jasper	171b	35.09 S	148.41 E
Weekapauq	207	41.20 N	71.45 W
Weeki Wachee Spring ♠	220	28.32 N	82.35 W
Weeki Wachee Swamp ≡	220	28.31 N	82.37 W
Weeks Point ›	276	40.53 N	73.39 W
Weekstown	208	39.35 N	74.36 W
Weelde	56	51.25 N	5.00 E
Weeley	42	51.51 N	1.07 E
Weel Shimbirro	144	2.23 N	44.16 E
Weems	208	37.39 N	76.26 W
Weende	52	51.33 N	9.55 E
Weenen	158	28.57 S	30.03 E
Weener	52	53.10 N	7.21 E
Weeney Bay ⊂	274a	34.01 S	151.10 E
Weeping Water	198	40.52 N	96.08 W
Weequahic Lake ⊜	276	40.42 N	74.12 W
Weert	52	51.15 N	5.43 E
Weesatche	222	28.51 N	97.27 W
Weesby	41	54.50 N	9.08 E
Weesow	264a	52.39 N	13.43 E
Weesp	52	52.17 N	5.02 E
Weetfeld ➜[8]	263	51.38 N	7.49 E
Weethalle	166	33.53 S	146.38 E
Weeting	42	52.27 N	0.37 E
Weeton	262	53.48 N	2.56 W
Weetulta	168b	34.15 S	137.38 E
Wee Waa	166	30.14 S	149.26 E
Weeze	52	51.37 N	6.12 E
Wefensleben	54	52.11 N	11.09 E
Weferlingen	54	52.19 N	11.02 E
Wegberg	56	51.08 N	6.16 E
Wegdraai	158	28.50 S	21.52 E
Wegeleben	54	51.53 N	11.10 E
Wegendorf	264a	52.36 N	13.45 E
Wegenstedt	54	52.23 N	11.11 E
Wegeringhausen	56	51.02 N	7.45 E
Weggis	58	47.02 N	8.26 E
Węgliniec	30	51.17 N	15.13 E
Węgorzewo	30	54.14 N	21.44 E
Węgorzyno	30	53.32 N	15.33 E
Węgrów	30	52.25 N	22.01 E
Wegscheid	60	48.36 N	13.48 E
Wehdel	52	53.30 N	8.48 E
Wehebach Stausee ⊜[1]	56	50.45 N	6.20 E
Wehingen	58	48.08 N	8.47 E
Wehofen ➜[8]	263	51.32 N	6.46 E
Wehr	58	47.37 N	7.54 E
Wehringhausen ➜[8]	263	51.21 N	7.27 E
Wehrsdorf	54	51.03 N	14.22 E
Wei ≃, Zhg.	98	36.51 N	115.43 E
Wei ≃, Zhg.	98	37.05 N	119.28 E
Wei ≃, Zhg.	102	34.30 N	110.20 E
Weichang (Zhuizishan)	98	42.00 N	117.32 E
Weichsel → Wisła ≃	30	54.22 N	18.55 E
Weichselboden	61	47.40 N	15.10 E
Weichuan	98	34.17 N	113.58 E
Weicun	106	31.59 N	119.55 E
Weida	54	50.45 N	12.04 E
Weida ≃	54	50.47 N	12.06 E
Weiden am See	61	47.55 N	16.52 E
Weidenberg	60	49.57 N	11.43 E
Weiden in der Oberpfalz	60	49.41 N	12.10 E
Weidenstetten	56	48.33 N	9.59 E
Weidhausen	54	50.12 N	11.08 E
Weiding	60	49.16 N	12.46 E
Weidling	264b	48.17 N	16.19 E
Weidlingau ➜[8]	264b	48.13 N	16.13 E
Weidlingbach	264b	48.16 N	16.15 E
Weidlingerbach ≃	264b	48.18 N	16.20 E
Weifang	98	36.42 N	119.04 E
Weigelstown	208	39.59 N	76.49 W
Weihai	98	37.28 N	122.07 E
Weihaiwei → Weihai	98	37.28 N	122.07 E
Weihmichl	60	48.36 N	12.03 E
Weihnachtsinsel → Christmas Island □[2]	112	10.30 S	105.40 E
Wei Island I	164	3.20 S	144.25 E
Weijiagou	105	40.28 N	115.08 E
Weijiatang	106	31.25 N	118.55 E
Weijiazhuang	105	39.37 N	116.22 E
Weijiazui	100	30.29 N	117.20 E
Weijingtang	106	31.27 N	120.39 E
Weikersheim	56	49.29 N	9.54 E
Weil ≃	56	50.28 N	8.16 E
Weil am Rhein	58	47.37 N	7.38 E
Weilburg	56	50.29 N	8.15 E
Weil der Stadt	56	48.45 N	8.52 E
Weiler	58	47.36 N	9.55 E
Weilerbach	56	49.29 N	7.37 E
Weilerswist	56	50.45 N	6.50 E
Weilheim	64	47.50 N	11.08 E
Weilheim an der Teck	56	48.37 N	9.32 E
Weilmoringle	166	29.15 S	146.51 E
Weilmünster	56	50.26 N	8.22 E
Weimar, Dtsch.	54	50.59 N	11.19 E
Weimar, Dtsch.	56	51.22 N	9.23 E
Weimar, Ca., U.S.	226	39.02 N	120.58 W
Weimar, Tx., U.S.	222	29.42 N	96.46 W
Weinan	102	34.29 N	109.29 E
Weinböhla	54	51.10 N	13.34 E
Weinel Cross Roads	279b	40.37 N	79.37 W
Weiner	194	35.37 N	90.53 W
Weinfelden	58	47.34 N	9.06 E
Weingarten, Dtsch.	56	49.05 N	8.31 E
Weingarten, Dtsch.	58	47.48 N	9.38 E
Weinheim	56	49.33 N	8.39 E
Weining, Zhg.	102	26.43 N	104.18 E
Weining, Zhg.	104	41.21 N	123.49 E
Weinsberg	56	49.10 N	9.17 E
Weinsberger Wald ➜[3]	61	48.30 N	14.50 E
Weinviertel ➜[1]	61	48.38 N	16.25 E
Weipa	164	12.41 S	141.52 E
Weippe	202	46.22 N	115.56 W
Weir, India	124	27.01 N	77.11 E
Weir, Ks., U.S.	198	37.18 N	94.46 W
Weir, Ms., U.S.	194	33.16 N	89.17 W
Weir ≃, Austl.	166	28.50 S	149.06 E
Weir ≃, Mb., Can.	184	56.54 N	93.21 W
Weir ≃, Ma., U.S.	283	42.16 N	70.53 W
Weir, Lake ⊜	220	29.00 N	81.57 W
Weir River	184	56.49 N	94.04 W
Weirsdale	220	28.58 N	81.55 W
Weirton	214	40.25 N	80.35 W
Weisburd	252	27.18 S	62.36 W
Weisburg	218	39.13 N	85.03 W
Weischlitz	54	50.26 N	12.02 E
Weisendorf	56	49.37 N	10.49 E
Weiser	202	44.15 N	116.58 W
Weiser ≃	202	44.15 N	116.59 W
Weishan (Xiazhen), Zhg.	98	34.52 N	117.09 E
Weishan, Zhg.	100	29.20 N	120.25 E
Weishan, Zhg.	100	29.41 N	120.48 E
Weishan, Zhg.	102	25.15 N	100.20 E
Weishancheng	100	32.34 N	113.24 E
Weishanhe	104	40.47 N	123.31 E
Weishan Hu ⊜	98	34.40 N	117.15 E
Weishanzhuang	105	39.40 N	116.25 E
Weishi	98	34.25 N	114.11 E
Weismain	54	50.05 N	11.14 E
Weisner Mountain ∧	194	34.02 N	85.40 W
Weissach	56	48.50 N	8.55 E
Weissbriach	64	46.41 N	13.15 E
Weisse Elster ≃	54	51.26 N	11.57 E

PORTUGUÊS

Nome	Página	Lat.°′	Long.°′ W = Oeste
Weissenbach	264b	48.05 N	16.13 E
Weissenbach am Lech	58	47.26 N	10.39 E
Weissenberg	54	51.11 N	14.40 E
Weissenborn	54	50.52 N	13.25 E
Weissenbrunn	54	50.12 N	11.20 E
Weissenburg	58	46.39 N	7.28 E
Weissenburg in Bayern	56	49.01 N	10.58 E
Weissenfels	54	51.12 N	11.58 E
Weissenhorn	58	48.18 N	10.09 E
Weissensee	54	51.11 N	11.04 E
Weissensee ➜[8]	264a	52.33 N	13.27 E
Weissensee ⊜	64	46.42 N	13.22 E
Weissenstadt	54	50.06 N	11.53 E
Weissenstein, Dtsch.	56	48.42 N	9.53 E
Weissenstein, Öst.	64	46.41 N	13.44 E
Weissenstein ∧	58	47.15 N	7.31 E
Weissenstein Tunnel ➜[5]	58	47.12 N	7.23 E
Weissenthurm	56	50.24 N	7.27 E
Weisser Main ≃	60	50.04 N	11.24 E
Weisser Nil → White Nile ≃	140	15.38 N	32.31 E
Weisser See → Beloje, ozero ⊜	76	60.11 N	37.37 E
Weisser Stein ∧	56	50.23 N	6.20 E
Weisses Meer → Beloje more ⊤[2]	24	65.30 N	38.00 E
Weisse Spitze ∧	64	46.52 N	12.21 E
Weissfluh ∧	58	46.50 N	9.48 E
Weisshorn ∧	58	46.06 N	7.42 E
Weissig	54	51.05 N	13.52 E
Weisskugel (Palla Bianca) ∧	64	46.48 N	10.44 E
Weiss Lake ⊜[1]	192	34.15 N	85.35 W
Weissmeer-Ostsee Kanal → Belomorsko-Baltijskij kanal ≋	24	62.48 N	34.48 E
Weissport	210	40.50 N	75.42 W
Weisstannen	58	46.59 N	9.21 E
Weisswasser	54	51.30 N	14.38 E
Weisweiler	56	50.50 N	6.19 E
Weitang	105	40.24 N	117.24 E
Weitang ≃	104	42.19 N	122.18 E
Weitendorf	54	53.54 N	12.16 E
Weitensfeld	61	46.51 N	14.11 E
Weiterstadt	56	49.54 N	8.35 E
Weitian	100	27.43 N	118.46 E
Weitin	54	53.34 N	13.12 E
Weiting	106	31.22 N	120.47 E
Weitmar ➜[8]	263	51.27 N	7.12 E
Weitnau	58	47.38 N	10.07 E
Weitou	100	24.34 N	118.34 E
Weitra	61	48.42 N	14.54 E
Weituo	107	30.03 N	106.08 E
Weitzgrund	54	52.11 N	12.32 E
Weiwan	98	36.43 N	115.54 E
Weixdorf	54	51.09 N	13.48 E
Weixi, Zhg.	102	27.14 N	99.12 E
Weixi, Zhg.	107	30.12 N	106.39 E
Weixian, Zhg.	98	36.57 N	115.15 E
Weixian, Zhg.	98	36.22 N	114.56 E
Weixian (Hanting), Zhg.	98	36.52 N	119.07 E
Weixin	102	27.48 N	105.06 E
Weiyuan	107	29.33 N	104.39 E
Weiyuan ≃	102	22.50 N	100.20 E
Weiyuankou	100	30.09 N	115.15 E
Weiyuanpu	98	42.39 N	124.16 E
Weiz	61	47.13 N	15.37 E
Weizhen	98	37.17 N	114.44 E
Weizhou Dao I	102	21.03 N	109.04 E
Weizhou Wan ⊂	100	24.34 N	118.30 E
Weizhuang	105	39.02 N	115.20 E
Weizi	98	40.04 N	123.10 E
Weizigou, Zhg.	104	42.25 N	122.47 E
Weizigou, Zhg.	104	41.05 N	120.38 E
Weizigou, Zhg.	104	42.05 N	120.34 E
Weizigoumen	98	41.58 N	116.49 E
Weiziyu	98	41.29 N	124.31 E
Wejherowo	30	54.37 N	18.15 E
Wekiva ≃	220	28.52 N	81.23 W
Wekiwa Springs State Park ♠	220	28.43 N	81.27 W
Wekoewa Punt ›	241s	12.14 N	68.24 W
Wekusko Lake ⊜	184	54.45 N	99.50 W
Welaka	192	29.28 N	81.40 W
Welbourn Hill	162	27.21 S	134.06 E
Welch, Ok., U.S.	196	36.52 N	95.05 W
Welch, Tx., U.S.	196	32.56 N	102.08 W
Welch, W.V., U.S.	192	37.25 N	81.35 W
Welch Creek ≃	282	37.32 N	121.51 W
Welches	224	45.19 N	121.57 W
Welch Peak ∧	224	49.10 N	121.36 W
Welcome, On., Can.	212	43.58 N	78.21 W
Welcome, Mn., U.S.	198	43.40 N	94.37 W
Welcome, S.C., U.S.	192	34.49 N	82.26 W
Welcome Lake ⊜	212	45.25 N	78.25 W
Welcome Monument ⊥	269e	6.11 S	106.49 E
Welden	58	48.27 N	10.40 E
Weldiya	144	11.50 N	39.41 E
Weldon, Sk., Can.	184	53.00 N	105.08 W
Weldon, Il., U.S.	219	40.07 N	88.45 W
Weldon, N.C., U.S.	192	36.25 N	77.35 W
Weldon, Tx., U.S.	222	31.01 N	95.34 W
Weldon ≃	194	40.06 N	93.38 W
Weldona	198	40.20 N	103.58 W
Weldon Brook ≃	276	40.58 N	74.35 W
Weleetka	196	35.20 N	96.08 W
Welega □[4]	144	9.40 N	35.50 E
Weleri	115a	6.58 S	110.04 E
Welfare Island I	276	40.45 N	73.57 W
Welgedag	273d	26.12 S	28.30 E
Welhamgreen	260	51.44 N	0.13 W
Welheim ➜[8]	263	51.32 N	6.59 E
Weligama	122	5.58 N	80.25 E
Welikaja → Velikaja ≃	76	57.48 N	28.20 E
Welkenraedt	56	50.40 N	5.59 E
Welker Seamount ✣[3]	16	55.07 N	140.20 W
Welkite	144	8.15 N	37.50 E
Welkom	158	27.59 S	26.45 E
Well	52	51.34 N	6.06 E
Welland	212	42.59 N	79.15 W
Welland ≃, On., Can.	212	43.04 N	79.03 W
Welland ≃, Eng., U.K.	42	52.52 N	0.03 W
Welland Canal ≋	212	43.03 N	79.13 W
Welland Junction	284a	42.57 N	79.14 W
Wellard	168a	32.19 S	115.50 E
Wellaune	54	51.34 N	12.33 E
Wellborn, Fl., U.S.	192	30.13 N	82.49 W
Wellborn, Tx., U.S.	222	30.32 N	96.18 W
Wellerode	56	51.14 N	9.34 E
Wellers Bay ⊂	212	44.00 N	77.34 W
Wellers Creek ≃	278	42.03 N	87.53 W
Wellesbourne	42	52.12 N	1.35 W
Welles Harbor ⊂	174g	28.12 N	177.26 W
Wellesley, On., Can.	212	43.28 N	80.45 W
Wellesley, Ma., U.S.	207	42.17 N	71.17 W
Wellesley ≃	168a	33.17 S	115.44 E
Wellesley College ⊍[2]	283	42.18 N	71.19 W
Wellesley Hills	283	42.19 N	71.17 W
Wellesley Island I	212	44.19 N	75.58 W
Wellesley Islands II	164	16.42 S	139.30 E
Wellesley Island State Park ♠	212	44.19 N	76.01 W
Wellesley Lake ⊜	180	62.30 N	139.50 W
Wellfleet	207	41.56 N	70.02 W
Well Hill	260	51.21 N	0.09 E
Wellin	56	50.05 N	5.07 E
Welling ➜[8]	260	51.28 N	0.07 E
Wellingborough	42	52.19 N	0.42 W
Wellinghofen ➜[8]	263	51.28 N	7.29 E
Wellington, Austl.	166	32.33 S	148.57 E

Wellington, B.C., Can.	224	49.13 N	124.01 W
Wellington, On., Can.	212	43.57 N	77.21 W
Wellington, N.Z.	172	41.18 S	174.47 E
Wellington, S. Afr.	158	33.38 S	18.57 E
Wellington, Eng., U.K.	42	52.43 N	2.31 W
Wellington, Eng., U.K.	42	50.59 N	3.14 W
Wellington, Co., U.S.	200	40.42 N	105.00 W
Wellington, Il., U.S.	216	40.32 N	87.41 W
Wellington, Ks., U.S.	198	37.15 N	97.22 W
Wellington, Mo., U.S.	194	39.08 N	93.58 W
Wellington, Nv., U.S.	226	38.45 N	119.22 W
Wellington, Oh., U.S.	214	41.10 N	82.13 W
Wellington, Tx., U.S.	196	34.51 N	100.12 W
Wellington, Ut,. U.S.	200	39.32 N	110.44 W
Wellington □[6]	212	43.50 N	80.30 W
Wellington, Isla I	254	49.20 S	74.40 W
Wellington Bay ⊂, N.T., Can.	176	69.30 N	106.30 W
Wellington Bay ⊂, On., Can.	212	43.56 N	77.21 W
Wellington Channel ⋓	176	75.00 N	93.00 W
Wellington Point	171a	27.29 S	153.15 E
Wellington Reservoir ⊜[1]	168a	33.24 S	116.01 E
Wellington Station	186	46.27 N	64.00 W
Wellman, Ia., U.S.	190	41.27 N	91.50 W
Wellman, Tx., U.S.	196	33.03 N	102.26 W
Wells, B.C., Can.	182	53.06 N	121.34 W
Wells, Eng., U.K.	42	51.13 N	2.39 W
Wells, Mi., U.S.	190	45.47 N	87.04 W
Wells, Mn., U.S.	190	43.44 N	93.43 W
Wells, Nv., U.S.	204	41.06 N	114.57 W
Wells, N.Y., U.S.	210	43.24 N	74.17 W
Wells, Tx., U.S.	222	31.29 N	94.56 W
Wells □[6]	216	40.44 N	85.11 W
Wells, Lake ⊜	162	26.43 S	123.10 E
Wells, Mount ∧	168a	32.42 S	116.20 E
Wells, Mount ∧[2]	162	17.26 S	127.14 E
Wellsboro	210	41.44 N	77.18 W
Wells Bridge	210	42.22 N	75.15 W
Wellsburg, Ia., U.S.	190	42.27 N	92.56 W
Wellsburg, N.Y., U.S.	210	42.00 N	76.43 W
Wellsburg, W.V., U.S.	214	40.16 N	80.36 W
Wells Cathedral ⊍[1]	42	51.13 N	2.39 W
Wellsford	172	36.17 S	174.31 E
Wells Gray Provincial Park ♠	182	52.20 N	120.00 W
Wells Lake ⊜	184	57.15 N	101.00 W
Wells-next-the-Sea	42	52.58 N	0.51 E
Wells Point ›	284b	39.17 N	76.23 W
Wells State Park ♠	207	42.09 N	72.05 W
Wells Tannery	214	40.05 N	78.10 W
Wellston, Oh., U.S.	188	39.07 N	82.31 W
Wellston, Ok., U.S.	196	35.41 N	97.03 W
Wellsville, Ks., U.S.	198	38.43 N	95.04 W
Wellsville, Mo., U.S.	219	39.04 N	91.34 W
Wellsville, N.Y., U.S.	210	42.07 N	77.56 W
Wellsville, Oh., U.S.	214	40.36 N	80.38 W
Wellsville, Pa., U.S.	208	40.03 N	76.56 W
Wellsville, Ut,. U.S.	200	41.38 N	111.55 W
Wellton	200	32.40 N	114.08 W
Welmel ≃	144	5.38 N	40.47 E
Welmen	263	51.39 N	6.41 E
Welney	42	52.31 N	0.15 E
Welo □[4]	144	11.50 N	40.20 E
Welper	263	51.25 N	7.12 E
Wels	61	48.10 N	14.02 E
Welsberg → Monguelfo	64	46.45 N	12.06 E
Welschbillig	56	49.51 N	6.34 E
Welse ≃	54	53.10 N	14.18 E
Welsford	186	45.27 N	66.20 W
Welsh	194	30.14 N	92.49 W
Welshpool, Austl.	169	38.39 S	146.26 E
Welshpool, Wales, U.K.	42	52.40 N	3.09 W
Welsickendorf	54	51.54 N	13.08 E
Welsleben	54	52.00 N	11.38 E
Weltenburg	60	48.54 N	11.50 E
Welver	52	51.38 N	7.57 E
Welverdiend	158	26.23 S	27.16 E
Welwitschia	156	20.21 S	14.57 E
Welwyn Garden City	42	51.50 N	0.13 W
Welwyn Hatfield □[8]	260	51.47 N	0.12 W
Welzheim	56	48.53 N	9.38 E
Welzow	54	51.34 N	14.10 E
Wem	42	52.51 N	2.44 W
Wema	152	0.26 S	21.38 E
Wembere ≃	154	4.10 S	34.11 E
Wembley	182	55.09 N	119.08 W
Wembley ➜[8]	260	51.33 N	0.18 W
Wembley Stadium ♠, S. Afr.	273d	26.14 S	28.03 E
Wembley Stadium ♠, Eng., U.K.	260	51.33 N	0.17 W
Wembury	42	50.19 N	4.05 W
Wemding	56	48.52 N	10.43 E
Wemeldinge	52	51.31 N	4.00 E
Wemme	224	45.20 N	121.57 W
Wemperhardt	56	50.09 N	6.05 E
Wemyss Bay	46	55.53 N	4.54 W
Wen ≃, Zhg.	98	35.28 N	118.32 E
Wen ≃, Zhg.	98	36.38 N	119.22 E
Wen'an	105	38.52 N	116.28 E
Wen'an Wa ≡	105	38.54 N	116.37 E
Wenas Creek ≃	224	46.42 N	120.35 W
Wenatchee	202	47.25 N	120.18 W
Wenatchee ≃	202	47.27 N	120.19 W
Wenatchee, Lake ⊜	224	47.49 N	120.47 W
Wenatchee Mountains ⋀	202	47.20 N	120.45 W
Wenchang	110	19.41 N	110.48 E
Wencheng	100	27.50 N	120.05 E
Wenchi	150	7.42 N	2.07 W
Wenchow → Wenzhou	100	28.01 N	120.39 E
Wendaohezi	104	41.46 N	124.09 E
Wendel	279b	40.18 N	79.41 W
Wendell, Id., U.S.	202	42.46 N	114.42 W
Wendell, N.C., U.S.	192	35.46 N	78.22 W
Wendelsheim	56	49.46 N	7.59 E
Wendelstein	60	49.21 N	11.08 E
Wendelstein ∧	64	47.42 N	12.00 E
Wendelville	284a	43.04 N	78.47 W
Wenden, Dtsch.	52	52.19 N	10.30 E
Wenden, Dtsch.	56	50.57 N	7.51 E
Wenden, Az., U.S.	200	33.49 N	113.32 W
Wendeng	98	37.12 N	122.04 E
Wendesi	164	2.25 S	134.13 E
Wendilou	104	41.13 N	121.08 E
Wendisch Rietz	54	52.13 N	14.01 E
Wendish Baggendorf	54	54.04 N	12.56 E
Wendji	152	0.04 S	18.10 E
Wendland ➜[1]	54	53.00 N	11.10 E
Wendo	144	6.38 N	38.27 E
Wendover, Eng., U.K.	42	51.46 N	0.46 W
Wendover, Ut,. U.S.	200	40.44 N	114.02 W
Wenduine	50	51.18 N	3.05 E
Wenebegon ≃	190	46.53 N	83.12 W
Wenebegon Lake ⊜	190	47.24 N	83.08 W
Wenfang	100	28.02 N	117.19 E
Weng	60	48.40 N	12.23 E
Weng ≃	100	24.10 N	113.24 E
Weng'an	102	26.53 N	107.22 E
Wengbo	120	31.23 N	86.40 E
Wengcheng	100	24.23 N	113.51 E
Wengdang	124	28.50 N	90.03 E
Wenge	152	0.03 N	24.01 E
Wengen, Dtsch.	58	47.41 N	10.09 E
Wengen, Schw.	58	46.36 N	7.56 E
Wengern	263	51.24 N	7.21 E
Wengjiabu	106	30.23 N	120.21 E
Wengong	107	30.11 N	104.09 E
Wenguantun	104	41.53 N	123.30 E
Wengyang	100	28.03 N	120.58 E
Wengyuan	100	24.21 N	114.08 E
Wenham	207	42.36 N	70.53 W

Wenham Lake ⊜	283	42.35 N	70.53 W
Wenham Swamp ≡	283	42.37 N	70.55 W
Wenheng	100	25.42 N	116.45 E
Wenī	124	28.21 N	83.34 E
Wenigzell	61	47.26 N	15.47 E
Wenjiachang	107	30.41 N	103.55 E
Wenjiang	107	30.42 N	103.49 E
Wenjiangban	100	26.01 N	117.51 E
Wenjiazhen	100	28.20 N	116.05 E
Wenling	100	28.22 N	121.20 E
Wenlock	164	13.06 S	142.58 E
Wenlock ≃	164	12.02 S	141.55 E
Wenlock Edge ⌓[4]	42	52.30 N	2.40 W
Wenlong	100	24.48 N	114.54 E
Wenmingsi	100	25.33 N	113.20 E
Wennigsen	52	52.16 N	9.34 E
Wenning ≃	44	54.07 N	2.39 W
Wennington ➜[8]	260	51.30 N	0.13 E
Wenniu	102	24.18 N	104.31 E
Wenns	58	47.10 N	10.44 E
Wenona, Il., U.S.	216	41.03 N	89.03 W
Wenona, Md., U.S.	208	38.08 N	75.57 W
Wenonah	208	39.47 N	75.08 W
Wenquan, Zhg.	86	44.59 N	81.04 E
Wenquan, Zhg.	100	23.37 N	113.43 E
Wenquansi	104	41.20 N	124.04 E
Wenshan	102	23.30 N	104.20 E
Wenshang	98	35.44 N	116.29 E
Wenshui, Zhg.	102	28.28 N	106.30 E
Wenshui, Zhg.	102	37.28 N	112.01 E
Wensickendorf	264a	52.45 N	13.23 E
Wensleydale V	44	54.19 N	2.00 W
Wensum ≃	42	52.37 N	1.19 E
Went ≃	44	53.39 N	0.59 W
Wentorf	52	53.30 N	10.15 E
Wentworth, Austl.	166	34.07 S	141.55 E
Wentworth, N.C., U.S.	192	36.24 N	79.46 W
Wentworth, S.D., U.S.	198	43.59 N	96.57 W
Wentworth Falls	170	33.43 S	150.22 E
Wentworth Park	273d	26.07 S	27.48 E
Wentworthville	274a	33.48 S	150.58 E
Wentzville	219	38.48 N	90.51 W
Wenxi	102	35.26 N	111.11 E
Wenxian	102	32.58 N	104.46 E
Wenxingchang	107	29.52 N	106.29 E
Wenyu ≃	105	39.56 N	116.40 E
Wenzenbach	60	49.05 N	12.12 E
Wenzhou	100	28.01 N	120.39 E
Wenzhu	100	27.01 N	113.58 E
Wenzhuangzicun	104	42.16 N	123.51 E
Weobley	42	52.09 N	2.51 W
Weohyakapka, Lake ⊜	220	27.49 N	81.25 W
Wepener	158	29.46 S	27.00 E
Wépion	56	50.25 N	4.52 E
Weppersdorf	61	47.35 N	16.26 E
Wequetequock	207	41.21 N	71.52 W
Wera ≃	115b	8.20 S	120.43 E
Werbellin	54	52.53 N	13.41 E
Werbellinsee ⊜	54	52.54 N	13.40 E
Werben	54	52.52 N	11.58 E
Werbomont	56	50.23 N	5.41 E
Werchojansker Gebirge → Verchojanskij chrebet ⋀	74	67.00 N	129.00 E
Werda	156	25.15 S	23.16 E
Werdau	54	50.44 N	12.22 E
Werden ➜[8]	263	51.23 N	7.00 E
Werder, Dtsch.	54	52.23 N	12.56 E
Werder, Ityo.	144	6.58 N	45.20 E
Werder ➜[1]	54	53.40 N	13.25 E
Werdohl	56	51.15 N	7.45 E
Were Ilu	144	10.37 N	39.28 E
Werfen	64	47.28 N	13.11 E
Weri	164	3.12 S	132.38 E
Werkel	56	51.09 N	9.18 E
Werkendam	52	51.49 N	4.53 E
Werl	52	51.33 N	7.54 E
Werlaburgdorf	54	52.04 N	10.31 E
Werl-Aspe	52	52.04 N	8.43 E
Werleshausen	56	51.19 N	9.54 E
Werlte	52	52.51 N	7.41 E
Wermelskirchen	56	51.08 N	7.13 E
Wermsdorf	54	51.17 N	12.56 E
Wern ≃	56	50.02 N	9.44 E
Wernadinga	166	18.07 S	139.58 E
Wernberg, Dtsch.	60	49.32 N	12.10 E
Wernberg, Öst.	64	46.37 N	13.56 E
Werne	52	51.40 N	7.38 E
Werne ➜[8]	263	51.29 N	7.18 E
Werneck, Bra.	256	22.13 S	43.19 W
Werneck, Dtsch.	56	49.59 N	10.05 E
Werneuchen	54	52.38 N	13.44 E
Wernigerode	54	51.50 N	10.47 E
Wernitz	264a	52.34 N	12.55 E
Wernsdorf	264a	52.22 N	13.43 E
Wernsdorfer See ⊜	264a	52.23 N	13.42 E
Wernshausen	54	50.43 N	10.21 E
Wernstein	60	48.30 N	13.28 E
Werra ≃	30	51.26 N	9.39 E
Werribee	169	37.54 S	144.40 E
Werribee ≃	169	37.59 S	144.41 E
Werribee Gorge State Park ♠	169	37.40 S	144.21 E
Werribee South	169	37.56 S	144.42 E
Werries	52	51.41 N	7.53 E
Werrington	274a	33.45 S	150.46 E
Werris Creek	166	31.21 S	150.39 E
Werschweiler	56	49.27 N	7.13 E
Wersten ➜[8]	263	51.11 N	6.49 E
Wertach	58	47.36 N	10.25 E
Wertach ≃	58	48.24 N	10.53 E
Wertheim	56	49.46 N	9.31 E
Werther, Dtsch.	52	52.04 N	8.24 E
Werther, Dtsch.	54	51.29 N	10.46 E
Wertingen	56	48.34 N	10.41 E
Wervershoof	52	52.44 N	5.09 E
Wervik	50	50.47 N	3.02 E
Wervin	262	53.15 N	2.52 W
Werwaru	164	8.13 S	128.11 E
Weschnitz ≃	56	49.43 N	8.24 E
Weseke	52	51.54 N	6.51 E
Wesel	52	51.40 N	6.38 E
Wesel-Datteln-Kanal ≋	263	51.38 N	6.36 E
Wesenberg	54	53.17 N	12.58 E
Wesendahl	264a	52.36 N	13.49 E
Wesendorf	52	52.35 N	10.31 E
Weser ≃	52	53.32 N	8.34 E
Weser-Elbe-Kanal (Mittellandkanal) ≋	54	52.16 N	11.41 E
Weser-Ems □[5]	52	52.45 N	8.00 E
Wesergebirge ⋀	52	52.15 N	9.10 E
Wesham	262	53.48 N	2.53 W
Wesickaman Creek ≃	285	39.44 N	74.43 W
Wesī Śahar	124	28.15 N	84.23 E
Weskan	198	38.52 N	101.57 W
Weslaco	196	26.09 N	97.59 W
Weslemkoon Lake ⊜	212	45.02 N	77.25 W
Wesley, Dom.	240d	15.34 N	61.19 W
Wesley, Ia., U.S.	190	43.05 N	93.59 W
Wesleyville, Nf., Can.	186	49.09 N	53.34 W
Wesleyville, Pa., U.S.	214	42.08 N	80.00 W
Wessel, Cape ›	164	10.59 S	136.46 E
Wesseling	56	50.49 N	6.58 E
Wessel Islands II	164	11.30 S	136.25 E
Wesselsbron	158	27.50 S	25.23 E
Wesselsvlei	158	27.23 S	23.47 E
Wessington	198	44.27 N	98.41 W
Wessington Springs	198	44.04 N	98.34 W
Wessobrunn	64	47.52 N	11.01 E
Wesson	194	31.42 N	90.23 W
Wessum	52	52.05 N	6.58 E
West, Ms., U.S.	194	33.11 N	89.46 W
West, Tx., U.S.	222	31.48 N	97.05 W
West ≃, N.Y., U.S.	210	42.41 N	77.22 W

West ≃, Vt., U.S.	188	42.52 N	72.33 W
West Abington	207	42.05 N	70.58 W
Westacres	216	42.35 N	83.26 W
West Acton	207	42.28 N	71.28 W
West Alexander	214	40.06 N	80.31 W
West Alexandria	218	39.44 N	84.31 W
Westall, Point ›	162	32.55 S	134.04 E
West Allen ≃	44	54.55 N	2.19 W
West Allis	216	43.01 N	88.00 W
Westalton	219	38.51 N	90.13 W
West Amityville	276	40.41 N	73.26 W
West Andover	207	42.39 N	71.09 W
West Athens	280	33.55 N	118.18 W
West Atlantic City	208	39.23 N	74.28 W
West Babylon	210	40.43 N	73.21 W
Westbahnhof ➜[5]	264b	48.11 N	16.20 E
West Baines ≃	164	15.36 S	129.58 E
West Bangor	210	40.52 N	75.14 W
Westbank	182	49.50 N	119.38 W
West Bank □[9]	132	31.40 N	35.15 E
West Barnstable	207	41.42 N	70.22 W
West Barrington	207	41.44 N	71.20 W
West Bay, N.S., Can.	186	45.43 N	61.10 W
Westbay, Fl., U.S.	194	30.17 N	85.52 W
West Bay ⊂, Fl., U.S.	194	30.16 N	85.47 W
West Bay ⊂, Tx., U.S.	222	29.15 N	94.57 W
West Bay Shore	276	40.42 N	73.16 W
West Belmar	208	40.10 N	74.02 W
West Bend, Ia., U.S.	198	42.57 N	94.26 W
West Bend, Wi., U.S.	190	43.25 N	88.11 W
West Bengal □[3]	124	24.00 N	88.00 E
West Bergholt	42	51.55 N	0.51 E
West Berlin	208	39.48 N	74.56 W
West Bernard Creek ≃	222	29.23 N	95.58 W
Westbevern	52	52.01 N	7.47 E
West Bhāgīrath Plain ⊻	126	23.30 N	88.00 E
West Bijou Creek ≃	198	39.51 N	104.08 W
West Billerica	283	42.33 N	71.19 W
West Blocton	194	33.07 N	87.07 W
West Bloomfield	210	42.54 N	77.32 W
West Bolivar	214	40.23 N	79.10 W
Westborough	207	42.16 N	71.37 W
Westbourne	184	50.09 N	98.35 W
West Bow Creek ≃	198	42.46 N	97.08 W
West Boxford	283	42.42 N	71.04 W
West Boylston	207	42.22 N	71.47 W
West Bradenton	220	27.30 N	82.37 W
West Branch, Ia., U.S.	190	41.40 N	91.20 W
West Branch, Mi., U.S.	190	44.16 N	84.14 W
West Branch Reservoir ⊜[1]	210	41.25 N	73.42 W
West Branch State Park ♠	214	41.07 N	81.05 W
Westbridge	182	49.10 N	118.59 W
West Bridgewater	207	42.01 N	71.00 W
West Bridgford	42	52.56 N	1.08 W
West Bristol	285	40.06 N	74.53 W
West Bromwich	42	52.31 N	1.56 W
Westbrook, Austl.	171a	27.36 S	151.52 E
Westbrook, On., Can.	212	44.16 N	76.38 W
Westbrook, Ct., U.S.	207	41.17 N	72.26 W
Westbrook, Me., U.S.	188	43.40 N	70.22 W
Westbrook, Mn., U.S.	198	44.02 N	95.26 W
Westbrook, Tx., U.S.	196	32.21 N	101.01 W
West Brook ≃	276	41.04 N	74.18 W
West Brookfield	207	42.14 N	72.08 W
Westbrookville	210	41.30 N	74.34 W
West Burlington, Ia., U.S.	190	40.49 N	91.09 W
West Burlington, N.Y., U.S.	210	42.42 N	75.11 W
West Burra I	46a	60.05 N	1.21 W
Westbury, Eng., U.K.	42	52.41 N	2.57 W
Westbury, Eng., U.K.	42	51.16 N	2.11 W
Westbury, N.Y., U.S.	276	40.45 N	73.35 W
Westbury-on-Severn	42	51.50 N	2.24 W
West Butte ∧	202	48.57 N	111.32 W
Westby, Austl.	171b	35.30 S	147.25 E
Westby, Mt., U.S.	198	48.52 N	104.03 W
Westby, Wi., U.S.	190	43.39 N	90.51 W
West Cache Creek ≃	196	34.13 N	98.23 W
West Caicos I	238	21.39 N	72.28 W
West Calder	46	55.52 N	3.35 W
West Caldwell	276	40.50 N	74.18 W
West Cameron	208	40.45 N	76.41 W
West Camp	210	42.07 N	73.56 W
West Canada Creek ≃	188	43.01 N	74.58 W
West Cape ›	172	45.54 S	166.26 E
West Cape Howe ›	162	35.08 S	117.36 E
West Cape May	208	38.56 N	74.56 W
West Carlisle	196	33.35 N	101.56 W
West Caroline Basin ✣[1]	14	4.00 N	138.00 E
West Carrollton	218	39.40 N	84.15 W
West Carson	280	33.57 N	118.23 W
West Carthage	212	43.58 N	75.36 W
West Catfish Creek ≃	212	42.46 N	81.04 W
West Channel ≃[1]	180	68.51 N	136.10 W
West Chelmsford	283	42.37 N	71.23 W
Westchester, Il., U.S.	216	41.51 N	87.52 W
West Chester, Pa., U.S.	208	39.57 N	75.36 W
Westchester, Va., U.S.	284c	38.51 N	77.16 W
Westchester □[6]	210	41.02 N	73.46 W
Westchester ➜[8], Ca., U.S.	280	33.55 N	118.25 W
Westchester ➜[8], N.Y., U.S.	276	40.51 N	73.52 W
West Chester Airport ⊠	285	39.59 N	75.35 W
Westchester County Airport ⊠	207	41.04 N	73.43 W
Westchester Creek ≃	276	40.48 N	73.51 W
Westchester Estates	284c	38.47 N	76.55 W
Westchester Station	186	45.37 N	63.40 W
West Chester University of Pennsylvania ⊍[2]	285	39.57 N	75.36 W
West Chicago	216	41.53 N	88.12 W
West Clandon	260	51.15 N	0.30 W
West Clarksville	210	42.08 N	78.15 W
West Clear Creek ≃	200	34.34 N	111.51 W
West Cleddau ≃	42	51.46 N	4.54 W
Westcliffe	200	38.08 N	105.27 W
Westcliffe ➜[8]	273d	26.11 S	28.02 E
Westcliff-on-Sea	260	51.32 N	0.41 E
West College Corner	218	39.34 N	84.48 W
West Collingswood Heights	285	39.59 N	75.07 W
West Columbia, S.C., U.S.	192	33.59 N	81.04 W
West Columbia, Tx., U.S.	222	29.08 N	95.38 W
West Concord, Ma., U.S.	207	42.27 N	71.23 W
West Concord, Mn., U.S.	190	44.09 N	92.53 W
West Conshohocken	285	40.04 N	75.19 W
West Cote Blanche Bay ⊂	194	29.40 N	91.45 W
Westcott	260	51.13 N	0.22 W
Westcott Cove ⊂	276	41.02 N	73.30 W
West Covina	228	34.04 N	117.56 W
West Creek	208	39.38 N	74.18 W
West Creek ≃, In., U.S.	216	41.12 N	87.30 W
West Creek ≃, Pa., U.S.	214	41.30 N	78.15 W
Westdale, Ma., U.S.	283	42.01 N	70.59 W
Westdale, N.Y., U.S.	210	43.23 N	75.49 W
West Danby	210	42.19 N	76.32 W

Symbol	English	Deutsch	Español	Français	Português
≃	River	Fluß	Río	Rivière	Rio
≋	Canal	Kanal	Canal	Canal	Canal
⌊	Waterfall, Rapids	Wasserfall, Stromschnellen	Cascada, Rápidos	Chute d'eau, Rapides	Cascata, Rápidos
⋓	Strait	Meeresstraße	Estrecho	Détroit	Estreito
⊂	Bay, Gulf	Bucht, Golf	Bahía, Golfo	Baie, Golfe	Baía, Golfo
⊜	Lake, Lakes	See, Seen	Lago, Lagos	Lac, Lacs	Lago, Lagos
≡	Swamp	Sumpf	Pantano	Marais	Pântano
⊓	Ice Features, Glacier	Eis- und Gletscherformen	Accidentes Glaciales	Formes glaciaires	Acidentes glaciares
⊤	Other Hydrographic Features	Andere Hydrographische Objekte	Otros Elementos Hidrográficos	Autres données hydrographiques	Outros acidentes hidrográficos
✣	Submarine Features	Untermeerische Objekte	Accidentes Submarinos	Formes de relief sous-marin	Acidentes submarinos
□	Political Unit	Politische Einheit	Unidad Politica	Entité politique	Unidade política
⊍	Cultural Institution	Kulturelle Institution	Institución Cultural	Institution culturelle	Instituição cultural
⊥	Historical Site	Historische Stätte	Sitio Histórico	Site historique	Sitio histórico
♠	Recreational Site	Erholungs- und Ferienort	Sitio de Recreo	Centre de loisirs	Area de Lazer
⊠	Airport	Flughafen	Aeropuerto	Aéroport	Aeroporto
■	Military Installation	Militäranlage	Instalación Militar	Installation militaire	Instalação militar
➜	Miscellaneous	Verschiedenes	Misceláneo	Divers	Diversos

ENGLISH — DEUTSCH

Name	Page	Lat.°′	Long.°′
West Davenport	210	42.27 N	74.58 W
West Deane Park ♠	275b	43.40 N	79.34 W
West Decatur	214	40.56 N	78.17 W
West Delaware Aqueduct ≋[1]	210	41.52 N	74.31 W
Westdene ➛[8]	273d	26.11 S	27.59 E
West Dennis	207	41.39 N	70.10 W
West Derby ➛[8]	262	53.26 N	2.54 W
West Derry	214	40.20 N	79.20 W
West Des Moines	190	41.34 N	93.42 W
West Ditch ≋	276	40.56 N	74.19 W
West Dolores ≃	200	37.35 N	108.21 W
West Drayton ➛[8]	260	51.30 N	0.29 W
West Duffins Creek ≃	212	43.51 N	79.04 W
West Duxbury	283	42.03 N	70.47 W
West Easton	210	40.41 N	75.14 W
West Eaton	210	42.51 N	75.39 W
Westecunk Creek ≃	208	39.37 N	74.16 W
West Edmeston	210	42.46 N	75.17 W
West Edmondale	284b	39.18 N	76.43 W
West Elizabeth	279b	40.17 N	79.54 W
West Elk Mountains ⛏	200	38.40 N	107.15 W
West Elk Peak ∧	200	38.43 N	107.13 W
West Elkton	218	39.35 N	84.33 W
West Ellicott	214	42.05 N	79.16 W
West Elmira	210	42.04 N	76.50 W
West End, Ba.	238	26.41 N	78.58 W
West End, Eng., U.K.	260	51.44 N	0.04 W
West End, Eng., U.K.	260	51.20 N	0.38 W
West End, Ar., U.S.	194	34.13 N	92.03 W
West End, Il., U.S.	216	42.17 N	89.09 W
West End, N.Y., U.S.	210	42.28 N	75.05 W
West End, N.C., U.S.	192	35.14 N	79.34 W
West End ➛[8], Eng., U.K.	260	51.32 N	0.24 W
West End ➛[8], Pa., U.S.	279b	40.27 N	80.02 W
Westende, Bel.	50	51.10 N	2.46 E
Westende, Dtsch.	263	51.25 N	7.24 E
Westendorf	64	47.26 N	12.13 E
Westenfeld ➛[8]	263	51.28 N	7.09 E
Westenholz	52	51.45 N	8.28 E
Westenschouwen	52	51.41 N	3.42 E
Westerbauer ➛[8]	263	51.20 N	7.23 E
Westerblokker	52	52.39 N	5.08 E
Westerbönen	263	51.36 N	7.46 E
Westerbork	52	52.51 N	6.37 E
Westerburg	56	50.33 N	7.58 E
Westercelle	52	52.36 N	10.05 E
Westerdale	46	58.27 N	3.30 W
Westeregeln	54	51.57 N	11.23 E
Westerham	42	51.16 N	0.05 E
Westerhausen	54	51.48 N	11.03 E
Westerholt	52	51.36 N	7.05 E
Westerholz ➛[3]	263	51.32 N	7.28 E
Westerkappeln	52	52.18 N	7.52 E
Westerland	30	54.54 N	8.18 E
Westerlo, Bel.	56	51.05 N	4.55 E
Westerlo, N.Y., U.S.	210	42.31 N	74.03 W
Westerly	207	41.22 N	71.49 W
Western	198	40.23 N	97.11 W
Western □[4], Ghana	150	5.30 N	2.30 W
Western □[4], Kenya	154	0.30 N	34.35 E
Western □[4], Sol.Is.	175e	8.00 S	157.00 E
Western □[4], Zam.	152	16.00 S	24.00 E
Western □[5], Pap. N. Gui.	164	7.00 S	142.00 E
Western □[5], Ug.	154	1.00 N	31.00 E
Western ≃	166	22.22 S	142.25 E
Western Area □[4]	150	8.20 N	13.00 W
Western Australia □[3]	160	25.00 S	122.00 E
Western Branch ≃	284c	38.55 N	76.48 W
Western Canal ≋	226	39.28 N	121.35 W
Western Cape □[4]	158	33.30 S	20.00 E
Western Channel ʊ	98	34.40 N	129.00 E
Western Cove c	168b	35.43 S	137.38 E
Western Desert → Gharbīyah, Aṣ-Ṣaḥrā' al- ➛[2]	140	27.00 N	27.00 E
Western Division □[5]	175g	18.00 S	177.30 E
Western Ghāts ⛏	122	14.00 N	75.00 E
Western Highlands □[5]	164	5.45 S	144.30 E
Western Isles □[4]	46	57.40 N	7.00 W
Westernport	188	39.29 N	79.02 W
Western Port c	169	38.22 N	145.20 E
Western Port Bay c	169	38.15 S	145.20 E
Western Sahara □[2], Afr.	134	24.30 N	13.00 W
Western Sahara □[2], Afr.	148	24.30 N	13.00 W
Western Samoa □[1], Oc.	14	13.55 S	172.00 W
Western Samoa □[1], Oc.	175a	13.55 S	172.00 W
Western Sayans → Zapadnyj Sajan ⛏	74	53.00 N	94.00 E
Western Shore	186	44.32 N	64.19 W
Western Springs	278	41.48 N	87.54 W
Westernville	210	43.18 N	75.23 W
Westerschelde c[1]	52	51.25 N	3.45 E
Westerstede	52	53.15 N	7.55 E
Westervelt	219	39.29 N	88.52 W
Westerville	214	40.07 N	82.55 W
Westerwald ⛏	56	50.40 N	7.55 E
West European Basin ✤[1]	10	47.00 N	15.00 W
West Exeter	210	42.48 N	75.09 W
West Fairview	208	40.16 N	76.54 W
Westfalen □[9]	52	51.50 N	7.30 E
Westfalenhalle ʋ	263	51.30 N	7.27 E
West Falkland I	254	51.50 S	60.00 W
West Falls	210	42.42 N	78.41 W
West Falmouth	207	41.36 N	70.38 W
West Fargo	198	46.52 N	96.54 W
West Farleigh	260	51.15 N	0.27 E
West Farmington	214	41.23 N	80.58 W
Westfield, Eng., U.K.	42	50.55 N	0.35 E
Westfield, Il., U.S.	194	39.27 N	88.01 W
Westfield, In., U.S.	218	40.02 N	86.07 W
Westfield, Ma., U.S.	207	42.07 N	72.45 W
Westfield, N.J., U.S.	210	40.39 N	74.20 W
Westfield, N.Y., U.S.	214	42.19 N	79.34 W
Westfield, Pa., U.S.	210	41.55 N	77.32 W
Westfield, Tx., U.S.	222	30.01 N	95.24 W
Westfield, Wi., U.S.	190	43.53 N	89.29 W
Westfield ≃	207	42.05 N	72.35 W
Westfield, Middle Branch ≃	207	42.16 N	72.52 W
Westfield, West Branch ≃	207	42.13 N	72.52 W
Westfield Center	214	41.01 N	81.55 W
West Fiord c[2]	176	76.02 N	90.00 W
Westford, Ma., U.S.	283	42.34 N	71.26 W
Westford, N.Y., U.S.	210	42.39 N	74.48 W
West Fork	194	35.55 N	94.11 W
West Foxboro	283	42.05 N	71.17 W
West Frankfort	194	37.53 N	88.55 W
West Friesland ➛[1]	52	52.45 N	4.50 E
West Frisian Islands → Waddeneilanden II	52	53.26 N	5.30 E
West Fulton	210	42.34 N	74.28 W
Westgate, Austl.	166	26.35 S	146.12 E
Westgate, Mi., U.S.	216	43.03 N	85.42 W
Westgate on Sea	42	51.23 N	1.21 E
West Genesee Terrace	210	43.03 N	76.16 W
West-Ghats → Western Ghāts ⛏	122	14.00 N	75.00 E
West Gilgo Beach	276	40.37 N	73.25 W
West Glacier	202	48.29 N	113.58 W
West Glamorgan □[6]	42	51.35 N	3.35 W
West Glens Falls	210	43.18 N	73.43 W
West Glenville	210	42.56 N	74.04 W
West Goshen	207	41.49 N	73.15 W
West Granby	207	41.57 N	72.50 W
West Grand Lake ⊜	188	45.15 N	67.50 W
West Groton	207	42.36 N	71.37 W
West Grove	208	39.49 N	75.49 W
Westham	208	37.35 N	77.32 W
West Ham ➛[8]	260	51.31 N	0.01 E
West Hamburg	208	40.33 N	76.00 W
West Ham Football Club ♠	260	51.32 N	0.02 E
Westham Island I	224	49.05 N	123.10 W
West Hamlin	188	38.17 N	82.11 W
Westhampton, N.Y., U.S.	207	40.49 N	72.39 W
Westhampton, Va., U.S.	284c	38.54 N	77.11 W
West Hanningfield	260	51.40 N	0.30 E
West Hanover	283	42.07 N	70.53 W
West Harbor c	276	40.54 N	73.32 W
West Harrison	218	39.15 N	84.49 W
West Hartford	207	41.45 N	72.44 W
West Hartland	207	42.00 N	72.58 W
Westhausen	56	48.53 N	10.11 E
Westhaven, Ca., U.S.	204	41.03 N	124.06 W
West Haven, Ct., U.S.	207	41.16 N	72.57 W
Westhaven, Il., U.S.	278	41.35 N	87.51 W
West Haverstraw	210	41.12 N	73.59 W
West Hazleton	210	40.57 N	75.59 W
Westhead	262	53.34 N	2.51 W
West Hebron	210	43.14 N	73.22 W
West Heidelberg	274b	37.45 S	145.02 E
Westheim	56	49.03 N	9.44 E
West Helena	194	34.33 N	90.38 W
Westhemmerde	263	51.33 N	7.47 E
West Hempstead	276	40.42 N	73.39 W
West Henrietta	210	43.02 N	77.40 W
West Hickory	214	41.34 N	79.25 W
Westhill	46	57.09 N	2.17 W
West Hill ➛[8]	275b	43.46 N	79.11 W
Westhofen	263	51.25 N	7.31 E
Westhoff	222	29.12 N	97.28 W
Westhoffen	58	48.36 N	7.26 E
West Hollywood, Ca., U.S.	228	34.05 N	118.21 W
West Hollywood, Fl., U.S.	220	26.01 N	80.10 W
Westholme	224	49.52 N	123.42 W
West Homestead	279b	40.24 N	79.55 W
Westhope, N.D., U.S.	198	48.54 N	101.01 W
Westhope, Oh., U.S.	216	41.18 N	83.57 W
West Horndon	260	51.34 N	0.21 E
West Horsley	260	51.16 N	0.27 W
Westhoughton	262	53.33 N	2.32 W
West Hoxton	274a	33.55 S	150.49 E
West Humber ≃	212	43.44 N	79.33 W
West Humble	260	51.15 N	0.20 W
West Huntington	276	40.42 N	73.18 W
West Hurley	210	42.00 N	74.06 W
Westhuyzen	158	27.30 S	25.27 E
West Hyde	260	51.37 N	0.30 W
West Ice Shelf ⩍	9	67.00 S	85.00 E
Westick	263	51.35 N	7.38 E
Westig	263	51.22 N	7.45 E
West Indies II	230	19.00 N	70.00 W
Westindische Inseln → West Indies II	230	19.00 N	70.00 W
West Irian → Irian Jaya □[4]	164	5.00 S	138.00 E
West Island I, Austl.	164	15.36 S	136.34 E
West Island I, Ma., U.S.	207	41.36 N	70.50 W
West Islip	210	40.42 N	73.18 W
West Jan Mayen Ridge ✤[3]	10	71.00 N	13.00 W
West Jefferson, N.C., U.S.	192	36.24 N	81.29 W
West Jefferson, Oh., U.S.	218	39.56 N	83.16 W
West Jordan	200	40.36 N	111.56 W
Westkapelle, Bel.	50	51.19 N	3.18 E
Westkapelle, Ned.	52	51.32 N	3.27 E
West Keansburg	276	40.27 N	74.09 W
West Kettle ≃	182	49.07 N	119.00 W
West Kilbride	46	55.42 N	4.51 W
West Kill	210	42.13 N	74.31 W
West Kingsdown	42	51.21 N	0.17 E
West Kingston	207	41.28 N	71.33 W
West Kirby	44	53.22 N	3.10 W
Westkirchen	52	51.53 N	8.02 E
West Kittanning	214	40.49 N	79.32 W
West Lafayette, In., U.S.	216	40.25 N	86.54 W
West Lafayette, Oh., U.S.	214	40.16 N	81.45 W
Westlake, La., U.S.	194	30.15 N	93.15 W
Westlake, Oh., U.S.	214	41.27 N	81.55 W
Westlake, Tx., U.S.	222	32.59 N	97.12 W
West Lake ⊜, On., Can.	212	43.56 N	77.17 W
West Lake ⊜, Fl., U.S.	220	25.12 N	80.49 W
West Lake ⊜, N.J., U.S.	276	40.58 N	74.22 W
West Lamma Channel ʊ	271d	22.13 N	114.04 E
West Lancashire □[8]	262	53.35 N	2.50 W
Westland, Mi., U.S.	216	42.19 N	83.24 W
Westland, Pa., U.S.	214	40.17 N	80.16 W
Westland Center ➛[9]	281	42.20 N	83.23 W
Westland National Park ♠	172	43.30 S	170.10 E
Westlands	207	42.37 N	71.20 W
West Lanham Hills	284c	38.57 N	76.53 W
West Laramie	200	41.18 N	105.37 W
West Lawn	284c	38.52 N	77.11 W
West Lebanon, In., U.S.	216	40.16 N	87.23 W
West Lebanon, Pa., U.S.	214	40.35 N	79.22 W
West Leechburg	214	40.37 N	79.37 W
Westleigh, S. Afr.	158	27.31 S	27.21 E
Westleigh, Eng., U.K.	262	53.30 N	2.31 W
West Leipsic	216	41.07 N	84.00 W
Westley	226	37.33 N	121.12 W
West Leyden	212	43.28 N	75.28 W
West Liberty, Ia., U.S.	190	41.34 N	91.15 W
West Liberty, Ky., U.S.	192	37.55 N	83.15 W
West Liberty, Oh., U.S.	216	40.15 N	83.45 W
West Liberty, Pa., U.S.	214	41.00 N	80.03 W
West Liberty, W.V., U.S.	214	40.10 N	80.35 W
West Liberty ➛[8]	279b	40.24 N	80.01 W
Westliche Sahara → Western Sahara □[2]	148	24.30 N	13.00 W
Westliche Sierra Madre → Madre Occidental, Sierra ⛏	232	25.00 N	105.00 W
Westline	214	41.47 N	78.46 W
West Linn	224	45.21 N	122.36 W
West Linton	46	55.46 N	3.22 W
West Little Owyhee ≃	202	42.28 N	117.15 W
Westlock	182	54.09 N	113.52 W
West Lorne	214	42.36 N	81.36 W
West Los Angeles ➛[8]	280	34.03 N	118.28 W
West Lulworth	42	50.38 N	2.15 W
West Lunga ≃	154	13.06 S	24.39 E
West Lunga National Park ♠	154	12.55 S	25.10 E
Westmalle	52	51.18 N	4.41 E
West Malling	42	51.18 N	0.25 E
West Malling Aerodrome ⊠	260	51.16 N	0.24 E
West Manayunk	285	40.01 N	75.14 W
West Manchester	218	39.54 N	84.37 W
West Mansfield, Ma., U.S.	207	41.59 N	71.14 W
West Mansfield, Oh., U.S.	216	40.24 N	83.32 W
West Mariana Basin ✤[1]	14	15.00 N	137.00 E
West Mayfield	214	40.47 N	80.20 W
West Meadowview	216	41.08 N	87.52 W
Westmeath □[6]	48	53.30 N	7.30 W
West Medway	207	42.08 N	71.25 W
West Melbourne	220	28.04 N	80.39 W
West Memphis	194	35.08 N	90.11 W
West Meon	42	51.01 N	1.05 W
Westmere	210	42.41 N	73.52 W
West Mersea	42	51.47 N	0.55 E
West Miami	220	25.45 N	80.17 W
West Middlesex	214	41.10 N	80.27 W
West Middletown	214	40.15 N	80.25 W
West Midlands □[6]	42	52.30 N	2.00 W
West Mifflin	214	40.22 N	79.52 W
West Milford	210	41.07 N	74.22 W
West Millbury	207	42.11 N	71.48 W
West Mill Creek ≃	222	29.55 N	96.17 W
West Milton, Oh., U.S.	218	39.57 N	84.19 W
West Milton, Pa., U.S.	210	41.01 N	76.52 W
West Milwaukee	216	43.00 N	87.58 W
West Mineola	222	32.41 N	95.31 W
Westminster, Ca., U.S.	228	33.45 N	118.02 W
Westminster, Co., U.S.	200	39.50 N	105.02 W
Westminster, Md., U.S.	208	39.34 N	76.59 W
Westminster, Ma., U.S.	207	42.32 N	71.54 W
Westminster, Oh., U.S.	216	40.42 N	83.58 W
Westminster, S.C., U.S.	192	34.39 N	83.05 W
Westminster ➛[8]	260	51.30 N	0.09 W
Westminster Abbey ʋ[1]	260	51.30 N	0.07 W
Westminster Mall ➛[9]	280	33.45 N	118.01 W
West Modesto	226	37.37 N	121.02 W
West Monroe	194	32.31 N	92.08 W
Westmont, Ca., U.S.	280	33.56 N	118.18 W
Westmont, Il., U.S.	278	41.47 N	87.58 W
Westmont, N.J., U.S.	285	39.54 N	75.02 W
Westmont, Pa., U.S.	214	40.18 N	78.57 W
West Monterey	214	41.03 N	79.39 W
West Montreal ≃	190	47.56 N	80.39 W
West Moors	42	50.49 N	1.55 W
Westmoreland, Ks., U.S.	198	39.23 N	96.24 W
Westmoreland, N.Y., U.S.	210	43.07 N	75.24 W
Westmoreland, Tn., U.S.	194	36.33 N	86.14 W
Westmoreland, Va., U.S.	208	38.04 N	76.34 W
Westmoreland □[6], Pa., U.S.	214	40.18 N	79.33 W
Westmoreland □[6], Va., U.S.	208	38.10 N	76.50 W
Westmoreland City	214	40.20 N	79.41 W
Westmoreland State Park ♠	208	38.09 N	76.50 W
Westmorland	204	33.02 N	115.37 W
Westmount	206	45.29 N	73.36 W
West Mountain ∧	188	43.51 N	74.43 W
West Mud Creek ≃	222	32.07 N	95.10 W
West Mustang Creek ≃	222	29.04 N	96.26 W
West Nab ∧	262	53.35 N	1.53 W
West Nanticoke	210	40.13 N	76.01 W
West New Britain □[5]	164	5.45 S	149.30 E
West Newbury	207	42.48 N	70.59 W
West Newton, Ma., U.S.	283	42.21 N	71.14 W
West Newton, Pa., U.S.	214	40.12 N	79.46 W
West New York	276	40.47 N	74.00 W
West Nicholson	154	21.06 S	29.25 E
West Nishnabotna ≃	198	40.39 N	95.37 W
West Nodaway ≃	194	40.38 N	95.01 W
West Norriton	208	40.08 N	75.22 W
West Norwood ➛[8]	260	51.26 N	0.06 W
West Novaya Zemlya Trough ✤[1]	10	73.30 N	50.00 E
West Nueces ≃	196	29.16 N	99.56 W
West Nyack	210	41.06 N	73.58 W
West Okaw ≃	219	39.32 N	88.42 W
Weston, Austl.	170	32.49 S	151.28 E
Weston, Malay.	112	5.13 N	115.36 E
Weston, Eng., U.K.	262	53.19 N	2.44 W
Weston, Co., U.S.	200	37.07 N	104.50 W
Weston, Ct., U.S.	207	41.12 N	73.22 W
Weston, Id., U.S.	202	42.02 N	111.58 W
Weston, Ma., U.S.	207	42.22 N	71.18 W
Weston, Mi., U.S.	216	41.46 N	84.06 W
Weston, Mo., U.S.	194	39.24 N	94.54 W
Weston, Ne., U.S.	198	41.11 N	96.44 W
Weston, Oh., U.S.	216	41.20 N	83.47 W
Weston, Or., U.S.	202	45.48 N	118.25 W
Weston, Pa., U.S.	210	40.57 N	76.09 W
Weston, W.V., U.S.	188	39.02 N	80.28 W
Weston □[8]	275b	43.43 N	79.31 W
Westonaria	273d	26.19 S	27.39 E
West Oneonta	210	42.28 N	75.07 W
Westönnen	52	51.33 N	7.58 E
Weston Reservoir ⊜[1]	283	42.21 N	71.18 W
Westons Mill Pond ⊜	276	40.28 N	74.25 W
Westons Mills	210	42.04 N	78.23 W
Weston-super-Mare	42	51.21 N	2.59 W
Weston upon Trent	42	52.45 N	2.02 W
West Orange, N.J., U.S.	276	40.47 N	74.14 W
West Orange, Tx., U.S.	194	30.05 N	93.46 W
Westover, Md., U.S.	208	38.07 N	75.42 W
Westover, Pa., U.S.	214	40.45 N	78.40 W
Westover, Tn., U.S.	194	35.36 N	88.52 W
Westover, W.V., U.S.	188	39.38 N	79.58 W
Westover Air Force Base ■	207	42.12 N	72.33 W
Westoverledingen	52	53.10 N	7.28 E
Westowne	284b	39.17 N	76.43 W
West Palm Beach	220	26.42 N	80.03 W
West Palm Beach Canal ≋	220	26.38 N	80.03 W
West Paris	188	44.19 N	70.34 W
West Park	210	41.48 N	73.58 W
West Paterson	276	40.53 N	74.11 W
West Pawlet	210	43.21 N	73.15 W
West Peckham	260	51.15 N	0.22 E
West Pensacola	194	30.25 N	87.16 W
Westphalia, Ks., U.S.	198	38.10 N	95.29 W
Westphalia, Mi., U.S.	216	42.55 N	84.47 W
Westphalia, Mo., U.S.	219	38.26 N	91.59 W
West Pittsburg, Ca., U.S.	226	38.01 N	121.56 W
West Pittsburg, Pa., U.S.	214	40.55 N	80.21 W
West Pittston	210	41.19 N	75.47 W
West Plains	194	36.43 N	91.51 W
West Point, Ca., U.S.	226	38.23 N	120.31 W
West Point, Ga., U.S.	192	32.52 N	85.11 W
Westpoint, In., U.S.	216	40.21 N	87.03 W
West Point, Ia., U.S.	190	40.43 N	91.27 W
West Point, Ky., U.S.	194	37.59 N	85.56 W
West Point, Ms., U.S.	194	33.36 N	88.39 W
West Point, Ne., U.S.	198	41.50 N	96.42 W
West Point, N.Y., U.S.	210	41.23 N	73.57 W
West Point, Oh., U.S.	214	40.43 N	80.42 W
West Point, Pa., U.S.	285	40.12 N	75.18 W
West Point, Va., U.S.	208	37.31 N	76.47 W
West Point ∧	180	64.57 N	144.40 W
West Point ≻, Austl.	166	35.01 S	135.57 E
West Point ≻, P.E., Can.	186	46.37 N	64.25 W
West Point Lake ⊜[1]	192	33.00 N	85.10 W
West Pond ⊜	276	40.53 N	73.38 W
Westport, Nf., Can.	186	49.47 N	56.38 W
Westport, N.S., Can.	186	44.16 N	66.21 W
Westport, On., Can.	212	44.41 N	76.26 W
Westport, Ire.	48	53.48 N	9.32 W
Westport, N.Z.	172	41.45 S	171.36 E
Westport, Ct., U.S.	207	41.08 N	73.21 W
Westport, In., U.S.	218	39.10 N	85.34 W
Westport, Ky., U.S.	218	38.28 N	85.28 W
Westport, Ma., U.S.	207	41.37 N	71.04 W
Westport, Or., U.S.	224	46.07 N	123.22 W
Westport, Pa., U.S.	214	41.18 N	77.51 W
Westport, Wa., U.S.	224	46.53 N	124.06 W
West Portland	224	45.25 N	122.45 W
West Portland Park	224	45.21 N	122.37 W
Westport Point	207	41.31 N	71.04 W
West Portsmouth	218	38.45 N	83.01 W
West Prairie ≃	182	55.30 N	116.31 W
West Puente Valley	280	34.04 N	117.59 W
West Pullman ➛[8]	278	41.41 N	87.39 W
Westpunt ≻	241s	12.37 N	70.03 W
West Pymble	274a	33.46 S	151.08 E
West Quoddy Head ≻	188	44.49 N	66.57 W
West Rand	273d	26.07 S	27.45 E
Westray I	46	59.18 N	3.00 W
Westray Firth ʊ	46	59.12 N	2.55 W
West Redding	207	41.19 N	73.26 W
Westrem	50	50.58 N	3.52 E
Westrich ➛[1]	56	49.15 N	7.20 E
West Richfield	214	41.14 N	81.39 W
West Richland	202	46.18 N	119.20 W
West River ⊥	208	38.52 N	76.31 W
West Road ≃	182	53.19 N	122.52 W
West Rosebud Creek ≃	202	45.29 N	109.27 W
West Roxbury ➛[8]	283	42.17 N	71.09 W
West Rupert	210	43.14 N	73.14 W
West Rutland	188	43.35 N	73.02 W
West Ryde	274a	33.48 S	151.05 E
West Sacramento	226	38.34 N	121.31 W
West Saint Marys ≃	186	45.15 N	62.04 W
West Saint Modeste	186	51.36 N	56.42 W
West Salem, Il., U.S.	194	38.31 N	88.00 W
West Salem, Oh., U.S.	214	40.58 N	82.06 W
West Salem, Wi., U.S.	190	43.53 N	91.04 W
West Salt Creek ≃	200	39.13 N	108.54 W
Westsamoa → Western Samoa □[1]	175a	13.55 S	172.00 W
West Sand Lake	210	42.39 N	73.37 W
West Saugerties	210	42.07 N	74.03 W
West Sayville	276	40.43 N	73.05 W
West Sayville County Park ♠	276	40.43 N	73.06 W
West Scenic Park	220	27.55 N	81.39 W
West Scotia Basin ✤[1]	18	57.00 S	53.00 W
West Seneca	210	42.50 N	78.45 W
West Sepik □[5]	164	4.00 S	141.30 E
West Shoal Lake ⊜	184	50.20 N	97.41 W
West Siberian Plain → Zapadno-Sibirskaja ravnina ≚	72	60.00 N	75.00 E
Westsibirisches Flachland → Zapadno-Sibirskaja ravnina ≚	72	60.00 N	75.00 E
West Side Canal ≋	226	35.19 N	119.23 W
West Side Tennis Club ♠	276	40.43 N	73.51 W
West Simsbury	207	41.52 N	72.51 W
West Slope	224	45.29 N	122.45 W
West Spanish Peak ∧	200	37.23 N	104.59 W
West Springfield, Ma., U.S.	207	42.06 N	72.37 W
West Springfield, Pa., U.S.	214	41.57 N	80.29 W
West Springfield, Va., U.S.	208	38.46 N	77.13 W
West Stewartstown	206	44.59 N	71.31 W
West Stockbridge	207	42.20 N	73.22 W
West Stony Creek ≃	210	43.15 N	74.13 W
West Suffield	207	41.59 N	72.41 W
West Sunbury	214	41.00 N	79.54 W
West Sussex □[6]	42	50.55 N	0.35 W
West Swanzey	207	42.52 N	72.20 W
West Terre Haute	194	39.27 N	87.27 W
West-Terschelling	52	53.21 N	5.13 E
West Thompson Lake ⊜[1]	207	41.57 N	71.54 W
West Thurrock	260	51.29 N	0.16 E
West Tiana	207	40.52 N	72.33 W
West Tilbury	260	51.29 N	0.24 E
West Tisbury	207	41.22 N	70.40 W
West Toodyay	168a	31.33 S	116.27 E
West Torrens	168b	34.56 S	138.32 E
Westtown, N.Y., U.S.	210	41.20 N	74.32 W
Westtown, Pa., U.S.	285	39.56 N	75.33 W
West Townsend	207	42.40 N	71.44 W
West Turffontein ➛[8]	273d	26.16 S	28.02 E
West Union, Ia., U.S.	190	42.57 N	91.48 W
West Union, Oh., U.S.	218	38.47 N	83.32 W
West Union, W.V., U.S.	188	39.17 N	80.46 W
West Union Creek ≃	282	37.25 N	122.16 W
West Unity	216	41.35 N	84.26 W
West University Place	222	29.43 N	95.26 W
West Upton	207	42.10 N	71.37 W
Westvale	210	43.02 N	76.13 W
West Valley, Mt., U.S.	202	46.08 N	113.01 W
West Valley, N.Y., U.S.	210	42.24 N	78.37 W
West Valley City	200	40.42 N	111.57 W
West Vancouver	182	49.22 N	123.12 W
West View	214	40.31 N	80.02 W
West View Amusement Park ♠	279b	40.31 N	80.02 W
Westview Heights	207	41.33 N	73.05 W
Westville, N.S., Can.	186	45.34 N	62.43 W
Westville, In., U.S.	216	41.32 N	86.54 W
Westville, N.H., U.S.	207	42.49 N	71.07 W
Westville, N.J., U.S.	285	39.52 N	75.07 W
Westville, Oh., U.S.	218	40.07 N	83.51 W
Westville, Ok., U.S.	194	35.59 N	94.34 W
Westville, Pa., U.S.	214	41.13 N	78.50 W
Westville Center	206	44.57 N	74.24 W
Westville Grove	285	39.51 N	75.07 W
Westville Lake ⊜[1]	207	42.05 N	72.05 W
Westville Oaks	285	39.51 N	75.08 W
West Virginia □[3], U.S.	178	38.45 N	80.30 W
West Virginia □[3], U.S.	188	38.45 N	80.30 W
West-Vlaanderen □[4]	50	51.00 N	3.00 E
West Walker ≃	226	38.53 N	119.10 W
West Wallsend	170	32.54 S	151.35 E
Westward Ho!	42	51.02 N	4.15 W
West Wareham	207	41.47 N	70.45 W
West Warren	207	42.12 N	72.14 W
West Warwick	207	41.42 N	71.31 W
West Water ≃	46	56.47 N	2.38 W
West Webster	210	43.12 N	77.29 W
Westwego	194	29.54 N	90.08 W
West Wellow	42	50.58 N	1.35 W
West Whittier	280	33.59 N	118.03 W
West Wickham ➛[8]	260	51.22 N	0.01 W
West Willington	207	41.52 N	72.18 W
West Willow	216	42.14 N	83.34 W
West Windsor	210	42.06 N	74.46 W
West Winfield, N.Y., U.S.	210	42.53 N	75.11 W
West Winfield, Pa., U.S.	214	40.48 N	79.42 W
Westwold	182	50.28 N	119.45 W
Westwood, Ca., U.S.	204	40.18 N	121.00 W
Westwood, In., U.S.	218	39.55 N	85.25 W
Westwood, Ma., U.S.	207	42.12 N	71.14 W
Westwood, Mi., U.S.	216	42.18 N	85.38 W
Westwood, N.J., U.S.	210	40.59 N	74.01 W
Westwood, Pa., U.S.	214	40.18 N	78.56 W
Westwood ➛[8]	280	34.04 N	118.27 W
Westwood Lakes	220	25.44 N	80.22 W
Westworth Village	222	32.45 N	97.25 W
West Wyalong	166	33.55 S	147.13 E
West Wycombe	42	51.39 N	0.49 W
West Yarmouth	207	41.39 N	70.14 W
West Yegua Creek ≃	222	30.20 N	96.52 W
West Yellow Creek ≃	194	39.38 N	93.04 W
West Yellowstone	202	44.39 N	111.06 W
West York	208	39.57 N	76.45 W
West Yorkshire □[6]	44	53.45 N	1.40 W
Wetan, Pulau I	164	7.54 S	129.32 E
Wetar, Pulau I	112	7.48 S	126.18 E
Wetar, Selat ʊ	112	8.20 S	126.30 E
Wetaskiwin	182	52.58 N	113.22 W
Wete	154	5.04 S	39.43 E
Wethau	54	51.08 N	11.52 E
Wetherby	44	53.56 N	1.23 W
Wetherill Park	274a	33.51 S	150.54 E
Wethersfield	207	41.43 N	72.40 W
Wethmar	263	51.37 N	7.33 E
Wetiko Hills ⛏[2]	184	54.30 N	92.20 W
Wetluga → Vetluga ≃	80	56.18 N	46.24 E
Wetmore	198	39.38 N	95.48 W
Wet Mountains ⛏	200	38.00 N	105.10 W
Weto	152	7.57 N	7.50 E
Wetten	52	51.34 N	6.17 E
Wetter, Dtsch.	56	50.54 N	8.43 E
Wetter, Dtsch.	56	51.23 N	7.23 E
Wetter ≃	56	50.18 N	8.49 E
Wetterau ➛[1]	56	50.15 N	8.50 E
Wetteren	50	51.00 N	3.53 E
Wetterhorn ∧	58	46.39 N	8.08 E
Wetterstein Gebirge ⛏	64	47.25 N	11.05 E
Wettigan	110	18.57 N	95.21 E
Wettin	54	51.35 N	11.48 E
Wettingen	58	47.28 N	8.19 E
Wettringen	52	52.12 N	7.19 E
Wetumka	196	35.14 N	96.14 W
Wetumpka	194	32.32 N	86.12 W
Wetwang	44	54.01 N	0.34 W
Wetzikon	58	47.19 N	8.47 E
Wetzlar	56	50.33 N	8.29 E
Wetzstein ∧[2]	54	50.27 N	11.27 E
Wevelgem	50	50.48 N	3.10 E
Wevelinghoven	56	51.06 N	6.37 E
Wewahitchka	192	30.06 N	85.12 W
Wewak	164	3.35 S	143.40 E
Wewelsfleth	52	53.50 N	9.24 E
Wewer	52	51.41 N	8.42 E
Wewoka	196	35.09 N	96.29 W
Wexford, Ire.	48	52.20 N	6.27 W
Wexford, Pa., U.S.	214	40.38 N	80.03 W
Wexford □[6]	48	52.20 N	6.40 W
Wexford ➛[8]	275b	43.45 N	79.18 W
Wexford Harbour c	48	52.20 N	6.24 W
Wey ≃	42	51.23 N	0.28 W
Weyakwin Lake ⊜	184	54.30 N	106.00 W
Weyanoke	284c	38.48 N	77.09 W
Weyarn	64	47.51 N	11.48 E
Weyauwega	190	44.19 N	88.56 W
Weybridge	42	51.23 N	0.28 W
Weyburn	184	49.41 N	103.52 W
Weyer ➛[8]	263	51.10 N	7.01 E
Weyer Markt	61	47.52 N	14.41 E
Weyersheim	56	48.43 N	7.48 E
Weyhausen	52	52.47 N	10.23 E
Weyhe	52	52.59 N	8.52 E
Weymouth, N.S., Can.	186	44.25 N	66.00 W
Weymouth, Eng., U.K.	42	50.36 N	2.28 W
Weymouth, Ma., U.S.	207	42.13 N	70.56 W
Weymouth, N.J., U.S.	208	39.30 N	74.46 W
Weymouth, Cape ≻	164	12.37 S	143.27 E
Weymouth Back ≃	283	42.15 N	70.55 W
Weymouth Fore ≃	283	42.16 N	70.56 W
Weymouth Great Pond ⊜	283	42.12 N	71.02 W
Wezemaal	56	50.57 N	4.46 E
Wezep	52	52.27 N	6.00 E
Whakatane	172	37.58 S	177.00 E
Whakatane ≃	172	37.57 S	177.00 E
Whalan	274a	33.45 S	150.49 E
Whale Creek ≃	276	40.27 N	74.13 W
Whaley Bridge	44	53.20 N	1.59 W
Whaley Lake	210	41.33 N	73.40 W
Whaleysville	208	38.23 N	75.18 W
Whaleyville	208	36.37 N	76.41 W
Whalley	44	53.50 N	2.24 W
Whalom	207	42.34 N	71.44 W
Whalsay I	46a	60.20 N	0.59 W
Whangaehu ≃	172	40.03 S	175.06 E
Whangamata	172	37.12 S	175.52 E
Whangamomona	172	39.09 S	174.44 E
Whanganui National Park ♠	172	39.20 S	175.00 E
Whangara	172	38.34 S	178.13 E
Whangarei	172	35.43 S	174.19 E
Whangaruru Harbour c	172	35.22 S	174.21 E
Whaplode	42	52.48 N	0.02 W
Wharfe ≃	44	53.51 N	1.07 W
Wharfedale V	44	54.01 N	1.56 W
Wharles	262	53.49 N	2.50 W
Wharton, N.J., U.S.	210	40.53 N	74.34 W
Wharton, Oh., U.S.	214	40.52 N	83.21 W
Wharton, Tx., U.S.	222	29.18 N	96.06 W
Wharton, W.V., U.S.	188	37.54 N	81.40 W
Wharton □[6]	222	29.17 N	96.13 W
Wharton Basin ✤[1]	12	21.00 S	100.00 E
Wharton Lake ⊜	176	64.00 N	99.55 W
Wharton State Forest ♠	285	39.45 N	74.40 W
Whataroa	172	43.17 S	170.25 E
Whatatutu	172	38.23 S	177.50 E
What Cheer	190	41.24 N	92.21 W
Whatcom □[6]	224	48.48 N	121.59 W
Whatcom, Lake ⊜	224	48.43 N	122.20 W
Whately	207	42.26 N	72.38 W
Whatley	194	31.39 N	87.42 W
Whatshan Lake ⊜	182	50.00 N	118.03 W
Whauphill	44	54.49 N	4.29 W
Wheao ≃	172	38.34 S	176.39 E
Wheatfield	216	40.33 N	87.06 W
Wheatland, Ca., U.S.	226	39.00 N	121.25 W
Wheatland, Ia., U.S.	190	41.49 N	90.50 W
Wheatland, Pa., U.S.	214	41.12 N	80.28 W
Wheatland, Wy., U.S.	200	42.03 N	104.57 W
Wheatland Hills	208	40.02 N	76.21 W
Wheatland Reservoir ⊜[1]	200	41.52 N	105.36 W
Wheatley, On., Can.	214	42.06 N	82.27 W
Wheatley, Eng., U.K.	42	51.44 N	1.08 W
Wheatley, Ar., U.S.	194	34.54 N	91.06 W
Wheatley Hill	44	54.45 N	1.23 W
Wheaton, Il., U.S.	216	41.51 N	88.06 W
Wheaton, Md., U.S.	208	39.02 N	77.03 W
Wheaton, Mn., U.S.	198	45.48 N	96.29 W
Wheaton Plaza ➛[9]	284c	39.02 N	77.03 W
Wheaton Regional Park ♠	284c	39.03 N	77.02 W
Wheat Ridge	200	39.45 N	105.04 W
Wheelbarrow Peak ∧	204	37.27 N	116.05 W
Wheeler, In., U.S.	216	41.30 N	87.10 W
Wheeler, Ms., U.S.	194	34.34 N	88.36 W
Wheeler, Tx., U.S.	196	35.26 N	100.16 W
Wheeler ≃, P.Q., Can.	176	57.02 N	67.13 W
Wheeler ≃, Sk., Can.	184	57.20 N	105.30 W
Wheeler Air Force Base ■	229c	21.29 N	158.03 W
Wheeler Dam ➛[6]	283	42.48 N	71.12 W
Wheeler Island I	282	38.05 N	121.56 W
Wheeler Lake ⊜[1]	194	34.40 N	87.05 W
Wheeler Peak ∧, Ca., U.S.	226	38.25 N	119.17 W
Wheeler Peak ∧, Nv., U.S.	204	38.59 N	114.19 W
Wheeler Peak ∧, N.M., U.S.	200	36.34 N	105.25 W
Wheeler Ridge	228	35.06 N	119.01 W
Wheelersburg	218	38.43 N	82.51 W
Wheelers Hill	274b	37.55 S	145.11 E
Wheeling, Il., U.S.	216	42.08 N	87.55 W
Wheeling, W.V., U.S.	214	40.03 N	80.43 W
Wheeling Creek ≃	214	40.03 N	80.41 W
Wheelock	222	30.54 N	96.24 W
Wheelock ≃	44	53.12 N	2.26 W
Wheelton	262	53.41 N	2.36 W
Wheelwright, Arg.	252	33.47 S	61.13 W
Wheelwright, Ky., U.S.	192	37.19 N	82.43 W
Wheelwright Park ♠	283	42.15 N	70.49 W
Wheeny Creek ≃	170	33.26 S	150.50 E
Whela Creek ≃	162	26.17 S	116.50 E
Whelan, Mount ∧[2]	166	23.25 S	138.54 E
Whelpleyhill	260	51.44 N	0.33 W
Whernside ∧	44	54.14 N	2.23 W
Whetstone Creek ≃	214	40.23 N	83.03 W
Whetstone Gulf State Park ♠	212	43.44 N	75.27 W
Whickham	44	54.56 N	1.41 W
Whidbey Island I	224	48.15 N	122.40 W
Whidbey Island Naval Air Station ■	224	48.17 N	122.37 W
Whiddon Down	42	50.43 N	3.51 W
Whigham	192	30.52 N	84.19 W
Whigville	207	41.43 N	72.56 W
Whim Creek	162	20.50 S	117.50 E
Whinham, Mount ∧	162	26.04 S	130.15 E
Whippany	210	40.49 N	74.25 W
Whippany ≃	276	40.51 N	74.21 W
Whirl Creek ≃	212	43.28 N	81.12 W
Whirlwind Reefs ✤[2]	164	4.42 S	148.16 E
Whiskey Peak ∧	200	42.18 N	107.35 W
Whiskeytown-Shasta-Trinity National Recreation Area ♠	204	40.45 N	122.15 W
Whisky Chitto Creek ≃	194	30.31 N	92.55 W
Whiston	262	53.25 N	2.50 W
Whitacres	207	41.48 N	72.39 W
Whitaker	279b	40.24 N	79.53 W
Whitakers	192	36.06 N	77.42 W
Whitbourne	186	47.25 N	53.32 W
Whitburn, Eng., U.K.	44	54.57 N	1.22 W
Whitburn, Scot., U.K.	46	55.52 N	3.42 W
Whitby, On., Can.	212	43.52 N	78.56 W
Whitby, Eng., U.K.	44	54.29 N	0.37 W
Whitby, Eng., U.K.	262	53.17 N	2.54 W
Whitby Abbey ʋ[1]	44	54.28 N	0.38 W
Whitchurch, Eng., U.K.	42	51.53 N	0.51 W
Whitchurch, Eng., U.K.	42	51.14 N	1.20 W
Whitchurch, Eng., U.K.	42	51.52 N	2.39 W
Whitchurch, Eng., U.K.	42	52.58 N	2.41 W
Whitchurch-Stouffville	212	43.58 N	79.15 W
Whitcombe, Mount ∧	172	43.13 S	170.55 E
White, Ga., U.S.	192	34.16 N	84.44 W
White, S.D., U.S.	198	44.26 N	96.38 W
White □[6]	216	40.45 N	86.46 W
White ≃, B.C., Can.	182	50.23 N	115.35 W
White ≃, On., Can.	190	48.33 N	86.16 W
White ≃, N.A.	180	63.11 N	139.36 W
White ≃, U.S.	194	33.53 N	91.03 W
White ≃, U.S.	198	43.45 N	99.30 W
White ≃, U.S.	200	40.04 N	109.41 W
White ≃, Az., U.S.	200	33.44 N	110.13 W
White ≃, In., U.S.	194	38.25 N	87.44 W
White ≃, Mi., U.S.	190	43.25 N	86.21 W
White ≃, Nv., U.S.	204	37.42 N	115.10 W
White ≃, Or., U.S.	224	45.14 N	121.04 W
White ≃, Tx., U.S.	196	33.14 N	100.56 W
White ≃, Vt., U.S.	188	43.37 N	72.20 W
White ≃, Wa., U.S.	224	47.12 N	122.15 W
White ≃, Wa., U.S.	224	47.50 N	120.49 W
White ≃, Wi., U.S.	190	46.36 N	90.42 W
White ≃, Wi., U.S.	216	42.41 N	88.17 W
White, East Fork ≃, Az., U.S.	200	33.47 N	110.00 W
White, East Fork ≃, In., U.S.	194	38.33 N	87.14 W
White, Lake ⊜	162	21.05 S	129.00 E
White, Lake ⊜[1]	218	39.07 N	83.02 W
White, North Fork ≃, Az., U.S.	200	33.47 N	110.00 W
White, North Fork ≃, Co., U.S.	200	39.58 N	107.38 W
White, South Fork ≃	200	39.58 N	107.38 W
White, West Fork ≃	224	47.07 N	121.37 W
White Bay c	186	50.00 N	56.30 W
White Bear Indian Reserve ➛[4]	184	49.45 N	102.15 W
White Bear Lake	190	45.03 N	93.00 W
Whitebear Lake ⊜	184	51.05 N	108.05 W
White Bluff	194	36.06 N	87.13 W
White Breast Creek ≃	190	41.24 N	93.02 W
White Butte ∧	198	46.23 N	103.19 W
Whitecap Lake ⊜	184	56.54 N	95.14 W
White Cap Mountain ∧	188	45.35 N	69.13 W
White Castle	194	30.10 N	91.08 W
White Center	224	47.31 N	122.21 W
White Chuck ≃	224	48.11 N	121.27 W
White City, Fl., U.S.	220	29.53 N	85.13 W
White City, Ks., U.S.	198	38.47 N	96.44 W
White City Stadium ♠	260	51.31 N	0.14 W
White Clay Creek ≃, U.S.	198	43.12 N	102.48 W
White Clay Creek ≃, U.S.	285	39.42 N	75.37 W
White Cliffs, Austl.	162	28.26 S	122.57 E
White Cliffs, Austl.	166	30.51 S	143.05 E
White Cloud	190	43.33 N	85.46 W
White Cloud Island I	212	44.50 N	80.58 W
Whitecoomb ∧, N.Z.	172	45.36 S	169.05 E
White Coomb ∧, Scot., U.K.	44	55.26 N	3.20 W
Whitecourt	182	54.09 N	115.41 W
White Creek	210	42.58 N	73.18 W
White Creek ≃, In., U.S.	218	38.58 N	86.01 W
White Creek ≃, Wa., U.S.	224	46.01 N	121.08 W
White Deer, Pa., U.S.	210	41.05 N	76.52 W
White Deer, Tx., U.S.	196	35.26 N	101.10 W
White Deer Creek ≃	210	41.05 N	76.53 W
White Earth ≃	198	48.09 N	102.42 W
White Earth Indian Reservation ➛[4]	198	47.18 N	95.50 W
White Esk ≃	44	55.12 N	3.10 W
Whiteface	196	33.36 N	102.37 W
Whiteface ≃	190	46.58 N	92.48 W
Whiteface Mountain ∧	188	44.22 N	73.54 W
Whitefield, Eng., U.K.	44	53.33 N	2.18 W
Whitefield, N.H., U.S.	188	44.22 N	71.36 W
Whitefish	202	48.24 N	114.20 W
Whitefish ≃	190	45.55 N	86.57 W
Whitefish Bay	216	43.06 N	87.54 W
Whitefish Bay c, On., Can.	184	49.26 N	94.14 W
Whitefish Bay c, N.A.	190	46.40 N	84.50 W
Whitefish Lake ⊜, Ab., Can.	182	54.22 N	111.55 W

DEUTSCH: Name — Seite — Breite°′ — Länge°′ E = Ost

Symbols in the index entries represent the broad categories identified in the key at the right. Symbols with superior numbers (⛏[1]) identify subcategories (see complete key on page I · 1).

Symbole im Register stellen die rechts im Schlüssel erklärten Kategorien dar. Symbole mit hochgestellten Ziffern (⛏[1]) bezeichnen Unterabteilungen einer Kategorie (vgl. vollständiger Schlüssel auf Seite I · 1).

Los símbolos incluídos en el texto del índice representan las grandes categorías identificadas con la clave a la derecha. Los símbolos con numeros en su parte superior (⛏[1]) identifican las subcategorías (véase la clave completa en la página I · 1).

Les symboles de l'index représentent les catégories indiquées dans la légende à droite. Les symboles suivis d'un indice (⛏[1]) représentent des sous-catégories (voir légende complète à la page I · 1).

Os símbolos incluídos no texto do índice representam as grandes categorias identificadas com a chave à direita. Os símbolos com números em sua parte superior (⛏[1]) identificam as subcategorias (veja-se a chave completa à página I · 1).

∧ Mountain	Berg	Montaña	Montagne	Montanha
⛏ Mountains	Gebirge	Montañas	Montagnes	Montanhas
)(Pass	Paß	Paso	Col	Passo
V Valley, Canyon	Tal, Cañon	Valle, Cañón	Vallée, Canyon	Vale, Canhão
≚ Plain	Ebene	Llano	Plaine	Planície
≻ Cape	Kap	Cabo	Cap	Cabo
I Island	Insel	Isla	Île	Ilha
II Islands	Inseln	Islas	Îles	Ilhas
⊥ Other Topographic Features	Andere Topographische Objekte	Otros Elementos Topográficos	Autres données topographiques	Outros acidentes topográficos

ESPAÑOL — Nombre | Página | Lat.°′ | Long.°′ W = Oeste
FRANÇAIS — Nom | Page | Lat.°′ | Long.°′ W = Ouest
PORTUGUÊS — Nome | Página | Lat.°′ | Long.°′ W = Oeste

Whitefish Lake ⊜, Mb., Can. 184 55.34 N 93.13 W
Whitefish Lake ⊜, N.T., Can. 176 62.41 N 106.48 W
Whitefish Lake ⊜, On., Can. 190 48.03 N 84.29 W
Whitefish Lake ⊜, On., Can. 212 45.18 N 79.47 W
Whitefish Lake ⊜, On., Can. 212 44.31 N 76.14 W
Whitefish Lake ⊜, Ak., U.S. 180 61.21 N 160.00 W
Whitefish Lake ⊜, Mt., U.S. 202 48.27 N 114.22 W
White Fish Lake Indian Reserve ◆[4] 182 54.20 N 111.45 W
Whitefish Point 190 46.45 N 84.59 W
Whitefish Point › 190 46.45 N 85.00 W
Whitefish Range ∧ 202 48.40 N 114.26 W
Whiteford 208 39.42 N 76.20 W
Whiteford Point › 42 51.38 N 4.14 W
White Fox 184 53.27 N 104.05 W
White Fox ≃ 184 53.32 N 104.00 W
Whitegate 48 51.50 N 8.14 W
White Gull Creek ≃ 184 53.44 N 104.20 W
Whitehall (Paulstown), Ire. 48 52.41 N 7.01 W
Whitehall, Scot., U.K. 46 59.07 N 2.37 W
White Hall, Ar., U.S. 194 34.16 N 92.05 W
White Hall, Il., U.S. 219 39.26 N 90.24 W
White Hall, Md., U.S. 208 39.37 N 76.37 W
Whitehall, Mi., U.S. 190 43.24 N 86.20 W
Whitehall, Mt., U.S. 202 45.52 N 112.05 W
Whitehall, N.Y., U.S. 188 43.33 N 73.24 W
Whitehall, Oh., U.S. 218 39.58 N 82.53 W
Whitehall, Pa., U.S. 214 40.21 N 79.59 W
Whitehall, Wi., U.S. 190 44.22 N 91.18 W
Whitehaven, Eng., U.K. 44 54.33 N 3.35 W
White Haven, Pa., U.S. 210 41.03 N 75.46 W
Whitehead 48 54.46 N 5.43 W
White Holme Reservoir ⊜[1] 262 53.41 N 2.02 W
Whitehorse, Yk., Can. 180 60.43 N 135.03 W
White Horse, N.J., U.S. 208 40.11 N 74.42 W
White Horse, Vale of ∨ 42 51.37 N 1.37 W
Whitehorse Hill ∧[2] 42 51.34 N 1.34 W
Whitehouse, Scot., U.K. 46 57.13 N 2.37 W
Whitehouse, N.J., U.S. 210 40.37 N 74.46 W
Whitehouse, Oh., U.S. 216 41.31 N 83.48 W
White House, Tn., U.S. 194 36.35 N 86.49 W
Whitehouse, Tx., U.S. 222 32.13 N 95.14 W
White House ⅰ[2] 284c 38.54 N 77.02 W
White House Station 210 40.36 N 74.46 W
White Island ⅰ, Ant. 9 66.44 S 48.35 E
White Island ⅰ, N.T., Can. 176 65.50 N 84.50 W
White Island ⅰ, N.Z. 172 37.31 S 177.11 E
White Lake, Mi., U.S. 281 42.41 N 83.33 W
White Lake, N.Y., U.S. 210 41.40 N 74.50 W
White Lake, S.D., U.S. 198 43.43 N 98.42 W
White Lake, Wi., U.S. 190 45.09 N 88.45 W
White Lake ⊜, On., Can. 190 48.48 N 85.36 W
White Lake ⊜, On., Can. 212 44.47 N 76.45 W
White Lake ⊜, On., Can. 212 45.18 N 76.31 W
White Lake ⊜, On., Can. 212 44.27 N 77.03 W
White Lake ⊜, La., U.S. 194 29.45 N 92.30 W
White Lake ⊜, Mi., U.S. 281 42.40 N 83.34 W
Whiteland 218 39.33 N 86.05 W
Whitelaw 182 56.07 N 118.04 W
Whiteley Village 260 51.21 N 0.26 W
White Lick Creek ≃ 218 39.30 N 86.23 W
White Lick Creek, East Fork ≃ 218 39.35 N 86.22 W
White Lick Creek, West Fork ≃ 218 39.38 N 86.23 W
Whiteman Air Force Base ■ 194 38.44 N 93.34 W
Whiteman Airpark ⊠ 280 34.15 N 118.25 W
Whiteman Range ∧ 164 5.50 S 149.55 E
Whitemans Creek ≃ 212 43.10 N 80.21 W
Whitemark 166 40.07 S 148.01 E
White Marsh 284b 39.23 N 76.26 W
Whitemarsh Run ≃ 284b 39.22 N 76.25 W
White Meadow Lake 210 40.55 N 74.31 W
White Meadow Lake ⊜ 276 40.55 N 74.31 W
White Mills 210 41.32 N 75.12 W
White Mountain 180 64.41 N 163.24 W
White Mountain Peak ∧ 204 37.38 N 118.15 W
White Mountains ∧, U.S. 204 37.30 N 118.15 W
White Mountains ∧, Az., U.S. 200 33.45 N 109.40 W
White Mountains ∧, N.H., U.S. 188 44.10 N 71.35 W
Whitemouth 184 49.57 N 95.59 W
Whitemouth ≃ 184 50.07 N 96.02 W
Whitemouth Lake ⊜ 184 49.14 N 95.40 W
Whitemud ≃ 184 50.15 N 98.37 W
Whiten Head › 46 58.34 N 4.36 W
White Nile (Al-Bahr al-Abyad) ≃ 140 15.38 N 32.31 E
White Nile Dam — Jabal al-Awliyā', Khazzān ◆[6] 140 15.14 N 32.29 E
White Oak, Md., U.S. 284c 39.02 N 77.00 W
White Oak, Pa., U.S. 279b 40.20 N 79.48 W
White Oak, Tx., U.S. 222 32.32 N 94.52 W
White Oak ≃ 192 34.40 N 77.07 W
White Oak Creek ≃, Oh., U.S. 218 38.47 N 83.57 W
White Oak Creek ≃, Tx., U.S. 194 33.16 N 94.39 W
White Oak Creek, East Fork ≃ 218 39.00 N 83.53 W
White Oak Creek, North Fork ≃ 218 39.00 N 83.53 W
White Oak Lake ⊜[1] 194 33.40 N 93.10 W
White Oak Regional Park ♦ 279a 40.21 N 79.47 W
White Pass ⋈, N.A. 180 59.38 N 135.05 W
White Pass ⋈, Wa., U.S. 224 46.38 N 121.24 W
White Pigeon 216 41.47 N 85.38 W
White Pine, Mi., U.S. 190 46.45 N 89.35 W
Whitepine, Mt., U.S. 182 47.45 N 115.29 W
White Pine, Tn., U.S. 192 36.06 N 83.17 W
White Pines, Ca., U.S. 226 38.18 N 120.21 W
White Pines, Il., U.S. 278 41.57 N 87.57 W
White Plains, Md., U.S. 208 38.35 N 76.56 W
White Plains, N.Y., U.S. 210 41.02 N 73.45 W
White Plains, N.C., U.S. 192 36.26 N 80.38 W
White Pond ⊜ 283 42.26 N 71.23 W
White River, On., Can. 190 48.35 N 85.15 W
Whiteriver, Az., U.S. 200 33.50 N 109.57 W
White River, S.D., U.S. 198 43.34 N 100.44 W
White River Junction 188 43.38 N 72.19 W
White Rock 224 49.02 N 122.49 W
White Rock Creek ≃, Ks., U.S. 198 39.55 N 97.51 W
White Rock Creek ≃, Tx., U.S. 222 30.54 N 95.16 W
White Rock Creek ≃, Tx., U.S. 222 32.43 N 96.44 W
White Rock Lake ⊜[1] 222 32.50 N 96.44 W
White Rocks ∧ 192 36.40 N 83.27 W
Whiterocks ≃ 200 40.26 N 109.55 W
White Roding 260 51.48 N 0.16 E
White Russia — Belarus □[1] 22 53.50 N 28.00 E
Whitesail Lake ⊜ 182 53.30 N 127.00 W
White Salmon 224 45.43 N 121.29 W
White Salmon ≃ 224 45.43 N 121.31 W
Whitesand ≃ 184 51.34 N 101.55 W
White Sands Beach 207 41.18 N 72.09 W
White Sands Missile Range ■ 200 32.23 N 106.28 W
White Sands National Monument ♦ 200 32.46 N 106.20 W
Whitesboro, N.J., U.S. 208 39.02 N 74.51 W
Whitesboro, N.Y., U.S. 210 43.07 N 75.17 W
Whitesboro, Tx., U.S. 196 33.39 N 96.54 W
Whitesburg 192 37.07 N 82.49 W
White Sea — Beloje more ⊤[2] 24 65.30 N 38.00 E
White Settlement 222 32.45 N 97.27 W
Whiteshell Provincial Park ♦ 184 50.00 N 95.25 W
Whiteside 219 39.11 N 91.01 W
Whiteside, Canal ♮ 254 53.55 S 70.15 W
White's Landing 214 41.25 N 82.54 W
White Springs 192 30.19 N 82.45 W
White Stone 208 37.38 N 76.23 W
Whitestone ◆[8] 276 40.47 N 73.49 W
White Stone Lake ⊜ 184 56.25 N 97.31 W
Whitestown 218 39.59 N 86.20 W
White Sulphur Springs, Mt., U.S. 202 46.32 N 110.54 W
White Sulphur Springs, N.Y., U.S. 210 41.48 N 74.50 W
White Sulphur Springs, W.V., U.S. 192 37.47 N 80.17 W
Whites Valley 210 41.42 N 75.22 W
Whitesville, Ky., U.S. 194 37.40 N 86.52 W
Whitesville, N.Y., U.S. 210 42.02 N 77.45 W
Whitesville, W.V., U.S. 188 37.58 N 81.31 W
White Swan 224 46.22 N 120.43 W
Whiteswan Lakes ⊜ 184 54.05 N 105.10 W
Whitevale 212 43.53 N 79.09 W
White Valley 214 40.25 N 79.36 W
Whiteville, N.C., U.S. 192 34.20 N 78.42 W
Whiteville, Tn., U.S. 194 35.19 N 89.08 W
White Volta (Volta Blanche) ≃ 150 9.10 N 1.15 W
Whitewater, Ks., U.S. 198 37.57 N 97.08 W
Whitewater, Mt., U.S. 202 48.45 N 107.37 W
Whitewater, Wi., U.S. 216 42.50 N 88.43 W
Whitewater ≃, U.S. 218 39.10 N 84.47 W
Whitewater ≃, Ca., U.S. 204 33.30 N 116.03 W
Whitewater ≃, Mo., U.S. 194 37.01 N 89.43 W
Whitewater, Dry Fork ≃ 218 39.11 N 84.47 W
Whitewater, East Fork ≃ 218 39.24 N 85.01 W
Whitewater Baldy ∧[2] 200 33.20 N 108.39 W
Whitewater Bay ⊂ 220 25.16 N 81.00 W
Whitewater Creek ≃, N.A. 202 48.30 N 107.11 W
Whitewater Creek ≃, Ga., U.S. 192 32.21 N 84.03 W
Whitewater Creek ≃, Wi., U.S. 216 42.52 N 88.45 W
Whitewater Lake ⊜, Mb., Can. 184 49.15 N 100.20 W
Whitewater Lake ⊜, Wi., U.S. 216 42.47 N 88.42 W
Whitewater State Park ♦ 218 39.36 N 84.58 W
White Woman Creek ≃ 198 38.25 N 100.54 W
Whitewood, Austl. 166 21.28 S 143.36 E
Whitewood, Sk., Can. 184 50.20 N 102.15 W
Whitewood, S.D., U.S. 198 44.27 N 103.38 W
Whitewood, Lake ⊜ 198 44.20 N 97.18 W
Whitewright 196 33.30 N 96.23 W
Whitfield 42 51.09 N 1.18 E
Whithorn, Jam. 241q 18.15 N 78.02 W
Whithorn, Scot., U.K. 44 54.44 N 4.25 W
Whitianga 172 36.50 S 175.42 E
Whiting, In., U.S. 216 41.40 N 87.29 W
Whiting, Ia., U.S. 198 42.07 N 96.08 W
Whiting, Ks., U.S. 198 39.35 N 95.36 W
Whiting, N.J., U.S. 208 39.57 N 74.22 W
Whiting, Wi., U.S. 190 44.29 N 89.33 W
Whiting Bay 46 55.29 N 5.06 W
Whiting Field Naval Air Station ■ 194 30.43 N 87.02 W
Whitingham 207 42.47 N 72.53 W
Whitinsville 207 42.06 N 71.40 W
Whitland 42 51.50 N 4.37 W
Whitley Bay 44 55.03 N 1.25 W
Whitley City 192 36.43 N 84.28 W
Whitley Row 260 51.15 N 0.09 E
Whitman 207 42.04 N 70.56 W
Whitman Mission National Historic Site ⅰ 202 46.01 N 118.30 W
Whitmans Pond ⊜ 283 42.12 N 70.57 W
Whitman Square 208 39.45 N 75.03 W
Whitmire 192 34.30 N 81.36 W
Whitmore Lake 216 42.25 N 83.46 W
Whitmore Lake ⊜ 281 42.26 N 83.45 W
Whitmore Mountains ∧ 9 82.35 S 104.30 W
Whitmore Village 229c 21.30 N 158.01 W
Whitner Heights 226 36.37 N 119.32 W
Whitney, On., Can. 212 45.30 N 78.14 W
Whitney, Pa., U.S. 214 40.15 N 79.24 W
Whitney, Tx., U.S. 222 31.57 N 97.19 W
Whitney, Lake ⊜[1] 222 31.55 N 97.23 W
Whitney, Mount ∧ 204 36.35 N 118.18 W
Whitney Point 210 42.19 N 75.58 W
Whitney Point Lake ⊜[1] 210 42.25 N 75.55 W
Whitney Woods Reservation ♦ 283 42.13 N 70.51 W
Whitstable 42 51.22 N 1.02 E
Whitsunday Island ⅰ 166 20.17 S 148.59 E
Whittaker 216 42.08 N 83.36 W
Whittemore, Ia., U.S. 198 43.03 N 94.25 W
Whittemore, Mi., U.S. 190 44.14 N 83.48 W
Whittier, Ak., U.S. 180 60.47 N 148.42 W
Whittier, Ca., U.S. 228 33.58 N 118.01 W
Whittier, N.C., U.S. 192 35.26 N 83.22 W
Whittier Narrows Dam ◆[6] 280 34.01 N 118.04 W
Whittier Narrows Flood Control Basin ⊜[1] 280 34.02 N 118.04 W
Whittingham 44 55.24 N 1.54 W
Whittington 42 52.52 N 3.00 W
Whittle, Cap › 186 50.11 N 60.08 W
Whittle Hill ∧[2] 262 53.40 N 2.16 W
Whittle-le-Woods 262 53.41 N 2.38 W
Whittlesea, Austl. 169 37.31 S 145.07 E
Whittlesea, S. Afr. 158 32.10 S 26.50 E
Whittlesey 42 52.34 N 0.08 W
Whittlesey, Mount ∧[2] 190 46.18 N 90.37 W
Whitwell 194 35.12 N 85.31 W
Whitwick 42 52.44 N 1.21 W
Whitworth 44 53.40 N 2.10 W
Whitworth Peak ∧ 224 49.05 N 121.13 W
Wholdaia Lake ⊜ 176 60.43 N 104.10 W
Whonock 224 49.11 N 122.28 W
W. Howard Frankland Bridge ◆[5] 220 27.56 N 82.35 W
Whyalla 166 33.02 S 137.35 E
Whycocomagh 186 45.59 N 61.07 W
Whymper, Mount ∧ 224 48.57 N 124.10 W
Wiang Pa Pao 110 19.22 N 99.30 E
Wiang Phan 110 20.26 N 99.53 E
Wiarton 212 44.45 N 81.09 W
Wiasi 150 10.21 N 1.20 W
Wiau Lake ⊜ 182 55.23 N 111.18 W
Wiawso 150 6.12 N 2.29 W
Wiay ⅰ 46 57.23 N 7.13 W
Wiązów 30 50.49 N 17.11 E
Wibaux 198 46.59 N 104.11 W
Wiblingen ◆[8] 58 48.21 N 9.58 E
Wiblingwerde 263 51.18 N 7.37 E
Wichian Buri 110 15.39 N 101.07 E
Wichita 198 37.41 N 97.20 W
Wichita ≃ 196 34.07 N 98.10 W
Wichita Falls 196 33.54 N 98.29 W
Wichita Mountains ∧ 196 34.45 N 98.40 W
Wichlinghofen ◆[8] 263 51.27 N 7.30 E
Wick 46 58.26 N 3.06 W
Wick ≃ 46 58.27 N 3.05 W
Wickatunk 276 40.21 N 74.14 W
Wickede 52 51.29 N 7.52 E
Wickede ◆[8] 263 51.32 N 7.37 E
Wickenburg 200 33.58 N 112.43 W
Wickepin 162 32.46 S 117.30 E
Wicker Memorial Park ♦ 278 41.34 N 87.28 W
Wickett 196 31.34 N 102.59 W
Wickford 42 51.38 N 0.31 E
Wickham, Austl. 162 20.31 S 117.08 E
Wickham, P.Q., Can. 206 45.45 N 72.30 W
Wickham, Eng., U.K. 42 50.54 N 1.10 W
Wickham ≃ 164 16.22 S 131.06 E
Wickham, Cape › 166 39.36 S 143.57 E
Wickham Bishops 260 51.47 N 0.40 E
Wickham Market 42 52.09 N 1.22 E
Wickiup Reservoir ⊜[1] 202 43.40 N 121.43 W
Wickliffe, Ky., U.S. 194 36.58 N 89.05 W
Wickliffe, Oh., U.S. 214 41.06 N 80.43 W
Wickliffe, Oh., U.S. 214 41.36 N 81.27 W
Wicklow 48 52.59 N 6.03 W
Wicklow □[6] 48 53.00 N 6.30 W
Wicklow Head › 48 52.58 N 6.00 W
Wicklow Mountains ∧ 48 53.02 N 6.24 W
Wickrath 56 51.07 N 6.24 E
Wicksteed Lake ⊜ 190 46.46 N 79.40 W
Wicomico 208 37.17 N 76.31 W
Wicomico □[6] 208 38.22 N 75.36 W
Wicomico ≃ 208 38.13 N 75.55 W
Wicomico Church 208 37.49 N 76.23 W
Wiconisco 208 40.34 N 76.41 W
Wiconisco Creek ≃ 208 40.32 N 76.58 W
Wid ≃ 260 51.45 N 0.27 E
Widas ≃ 115a 7.30 S 112.08 E
Widden Brook ≃ 170 32.32 S 150.22 E
Widdern 56 49.19 N 9.25 E
Widdert ◆[8] 263 51.08 N 7.04 E
Widdop Reservoir ⊜[1] 262 53.48 N 2.06 W
Widdrington Station 44 55.15 N 1.36 W
Wide Bay ⊂, Pap. N. Gui. 164 5.05 S 152.05 E
Wide Bay ⊂, Ak., U.S. 180 57.20 N 156.25 W
Widecombe in the Moor 42 50.35 N 3.48 W
Widemouth Bay 42 50.47 N 4.32 W
Widen 188 38.27 N 80.51 W
Widener College ⅴ[2] 285 39.52 N 75.21 W
Wide Open 44 55.03 N 1.38 W
Widerøe, Mount ∧ 9 72.08 S 23.30 E
Wide Ruin Wash ∨ 200 35.13 N 109.52 W
Widford 260 51.43 N 0.27 E
Widgeegoara Creek ≃ 166 27.30 S 145.55 E
Widgiemooltha 162 31.30 S 121.34 E
Widnes 44 53.22 N 2.44 W
Wi-do ⅰ 98 35.36 N 126.17 E
Widodaren 115a 7.25 S 111.14 E
Widuchowa 54 53.10 N 14.25 E
Widur 124 27.55 N 85.10 E
Wiebelskirchen 56 49.22 N 7.11 E
Wiecbork 30 53.22 N 17.30 E
Wieck 54 54.06 N 13.26 E
Wied ≃ 56 50.26 N 7.27 E
Wieda 54 51.38 N 10.34 E
Wiederitzsch 54 51.24 N 12.22 E
Wiedlisbach 58 47.15 N 7.39 E
Wiefelstede 52 53.15 N 8.07 E
Wiehe 54 51.16 N 11.25 E
Wiehengebirge ∧ 52 52.20 N 8.40 E
Wiehl 56 50.57 N 7.31 E
Wiek 54 54.37 N 13.17 E
Wieleń 30 52.54 N 16.10 E
Wielichowo 30 52.08 N 16.21 E
Wieliczka 30 49.59 N 20.04 E
Wielkopolska ◆[1] 30 51.50 N 17.20 E
Wielkopolski Park Narodowy ♦ 30 52.15 N 16.50 E
Wieluń 30 51.14 N 18.34 E
Wiemelhausen ◆[8] 263 51.28 N 7.13 E
Wien (Vienna), Öst. 61 48.13 N 16.20 E
Wien (Vienna), Öst. 264b 48.13 N 16.22 E
Wien □[3] 61 48.12 N 16.22 E
Wien ≃ 264b 48.13 N 16.22 E
Wien, Universität ⅴ[2] 264b 48.13 N 16.22 E
Wiener Berg ∧[2] 264b 48.10 N 16.22 E
Wienerherberg 264b 48.03 N 16.33 E
Wiener Neudorf 61 48.05 N 16.19 E
Wiener Neustadt 61 47.49 N 16.15 E
Wiener Neustädter Kanal ≚ 61 48.05 N 16.22 E
Wienerwald ∧ 61 48.10 N 16.00 E
Wienhausen 52 52.35 N 10.11 E
Wien-Schwechat, Flughafen ⊠ 61 48.07 N 16.33 E
Wiepke 54 52.36 N 11.20 E
Wieprz ≃ 30 51.34 N 21.49 E
Wieprza ≃ 30 54.26 N 16.22 E
Wieprz-Krzna, Kanał ≚ 30 51.56 N 22.56 E
Wiera ≃ 56 50.55 N 9.10 E
Wierden 52 52.22 N 6.35 E
Wieren 54 52.53 N 10.39 E
Wiergate 194 31.00 N 93.42 W
Wieringermeer ◆[1] 52 52.45 N 5.00 E
Wieringerwerf 52 52.51 N 5.02 E
Wieruszów 30 51.18 N 18.08 E
Wierzyca ≃ 30 53.51 N 18.50 E
Wies ⅰ[1] 58 47.43 N 10.53 E
Wies ⅴ[1] 58 47.40 N 10.53 E
Wiesa 54 50.36 N 13.01 E
Wiesau 60 49.55 N 12.11 E
Wiesbaden 56 50.05 N 8.14 E
Wiescheid ◆[8] 263 51.08 N 6.59 E
Wischerhöfen ◆[8] 263 51.39 N 7.46 E
Wiese ≃ 58 47.35 N 7.35 E
Wiesede 52 53.27 N 7.46 E
Wieselburg 61 48.08 N 15.09 E
Wiesen 58 46.43 N 9.43 E
Wiesenburg 54 52.07 N 12.26 E
Wiesenfeld 56 51.16 N 10.06 E
Wiesensteig 58 48.34 N 9.37 E
Wiesent ≃ 60 49.42 N 11.05 E
Wiesentheid 56 49.47 N 10.20 E
Wieseth ≃ 56 49.10 N 10.39 E
Wiesloch 56 49.17 N 8.42 E
Wiesmoor 52 53.25 N 7.43 E
Wieting 61 46.52 N 14.32 E
Wietmarschen 52 52.31 N 7.07 E
Wietze 52 52.39 N 9.50 E
Wietzen 52 52.43 N 9.04 E
Wigan 44 53.33 N 2.38 W
Wigan □[8] 262 53.32 N 2.35 W
Wiggensbach 58 47.44 N 10.14 E
Wigger ≃ 58 47.18 N 7.53 E
Wiggington 260 51.47 N 0.38 W
Wiggins, Co., U.S. 198 40.13 N 104.04 W
Wiggins, Ms., U.S. 194 30.51 N 89.08 W
Wiggins Fork ≃ 202 43.27 N 109.28 W
Wigglesworth 44 54.01 N 2.17 W
Wight, Isle of ⅰ 42 50.40 N 1.20 W
Wigmore, Eng., U.K. 42 52.19 N 2.51 W
Wigmore, Eng., U.K. 260 51.21 N 0.35 E
Wignehies 50 50.01 N 4.00 E
Wigston 42 52.36 N 1.05 W
Wigton 44 54.49 N 3.09 W
Wigtown 44 54.52 N 4.26 W
Wigtown Bay ⊂ 44 54.46 N 4.15 W
Wijalpurā 124 26.55 N 85.51 E
Wijchen 52 51.48 N 5.43 E
Wijhe 52 52.24 N 6.07 E
Wijk aan Zee 52 52.29 N 4.35 E
Wijk bij Duurstede 52 51.58 N 5.20 E
Wil 58 47.27 N 9.03 E
Wilbarger Creek ≃ 222 30.11 N 97.23 W
Wilber 198 40.28 N 96.57 W
Wilberforce, Austl. 170 33.33 S 150.50 E
Wilberforce, Oh., U.S. 218 39.42 N 83.52 W
Wilberforce Falls ⌞ 176 67.07 N 108.47 W
Wilbraham 207 42.07 N 72.25 W
Wilbur 202 47.45 N 118.42 W
Wilburton 196 34.55 N 95.18 W
Wilcannia 166 31.34 S 143.23 E
Wilcock, Península ›[1] 254 50.40 S 74.00 W
Wilcox, Sk., Can. 184 50.07 N 104.44 W
Wilcox, Ne., U.S. 198 40.21 N 99.10 W
Wilcox, Pa., U.S. 214 41.34 N 78.41 W
Wilcox, Tx., U.S. 222 30.27 N 96.22 W
Wilcox, Mount ∧ 207 42.13 N 73.16 W
Wildalpen 61 47.39 N 14.59 E
Wildau 54 52.19 N 13.38 E
Wildbad im Schwarzwald 56 48.45 N 8.32 E
Wildberg, Dtsch. 54 52.52 N 12.37 E
Wildberg, Dtsch. 56 48.37 N 8.44 E
Wildboarclough 262 53.13 N 2.02 W
Wildcat Canyon Regional Park ♦ 282 37.56 N 122.17 W
Wildcat Creek ≃, Ca., U.S. 282 37.57 N 122.23 W
Wildcat Creek ≃, In., U.S. 216 40.28 N 86.52 W
Wildcat Creek, Middle Fork ≃ 216 40.25 N 86.46 W
Wildcat Creek, South Fork ≃ 216 40.26 N 86.48 W
Wildcat Hill ∧[2] 184 53.17 N 102.30 W
Wild Coast ≃[2] 158 32.30 S 28.45 E
Wilde ◆[8] 288 34.42 S 58.20 W
Wildegg 58 47.25 N 8.11 E
Wildeman ≃ 164 5.33 S 139.13 E
Wildemann 52 51.49 N 10.17 E
Wildenbruch 264a 52.17 N 13.04 E
Wildenfels 54 50.40 N 12.35 E
Wildenstein 58 47.59 N 6.58 E
Wildenthal 54 50.27 N 12.37 E
Wilder 202 43.40 N 116.54 W
Wilderness 158 34.00 S 22.36 E
Wilderness of Judaea (Midbar Yehuda) ◆[2] 132 31.30 N 35.18 E
Wilderness State Park ♦ 190 45.42 N 84.57 W
Wildersville 194 35.46 N 88.21 W
Wildervank 52 53.04 N 6.51 E
Wildeshausen 52 52.54 N 8.26 E
Wildfield 212 43.49 N 79.44 W
Wildflecken 56 50.23 N 9.54 E
Wildfontein 158 31.04 S 24.50 E
Wildhaus 58 47.12 N 9.22 E
Wildhay ≃ 182 54.02 N 117.20 W
Wildhorn ∧ 58 46.21 N 7.22 E
Wildhorse Creek ≃, U.S. 198 40.36 N 102.00 W
Wildhorse Creek ≃, Ok., U.S. 196 34.32 N 97.10 W
Wild Horse Creek ≃, Wy., U.S. 198 44.39 N 106.08 W
Wild Horse Draw ∨ 196 31.11 N 104.50 W
Wild Horse Hill ∧[2] 168a 33.12 S 116.40 E
Wild Horse Lake ⊜ 202 48.58 N 110.00 W
Wild Horse Plains 168b 34.22 S 138.17 E
Wildnest Lake ⊜ 184 55.00 N 102.20 W
Wildon 61 46.53 N 15.31 E
Wild Rice ≃, Mn., U.S. 198 47.20 N 96.50 W
Wild Rice ≃, N.D., U.S. 198 46.45 N 96.47 W
Wild Rice, South Branch ≃ 198 47.12 N 96.38 W
Wildrose, N.D., U.S. 198 48.37 N 103.11 W
Wild Rose, Wi., U.S. 190 44.10 N 89.14 W
Wildseeloder ∧ 64 47.26 N 12.32 E
Wildspitze ∧ 64 46.53 N 10.52 E
Wildstrubel ∧ 58 46.24 N 7.32 E
Wildwood, Ab., Can. 182 53.37 N 115.14 W
Wildwood, Fl., U.S. 220 28.51 N 82.02 W
Wildwood, Il., U.S. 216 42.21 N 88.00 W
Wildwood, N.J., U.S. 208 38.59 N 74.48 W
Wildwood, Pa., U.S. 214 40.36 N 79.58 W
Wildwood, Lake ⊜ 276 41.09 N 74.32 W
Wild Wood Beach 284b 39.15 N 76.25 W
Wildwood Canyon Park ♦ 280 34.13 N 118.17 W
Wildwood Crest 208 38.58 N 74.50 W
Wiley 224 46.33 N 120.39 W
Wilfersdorf 61 48.35 N 16.38 E
Wilge ≃, S. Afr. 158 27.03 S 28.20 E
Wilge ≃, S. Afr. 158 25.34 S 29.10 E
Wilgena 162 30.46 S 134.44 E
Wilgespruit ≃ 273d 26.07 S 27.52 E
Wilhelm, Lake ⊜[1] 214 41.23 N 80.08 W
Wilhelm, Mount ∧ 164 5.45 S 145.05 E
Wilhelmina Gebergte ∧ 250 3.45 N 56.30 W
Wilhelminakanaal ≚ 52 51.47 N 4.51 E
Wilhelminaoord 52 52.53 N 6.10 E
Wilhelmina Peak — Trikora, Puncak ∧ 164 4.15 S 138.45 E
Wilhelmsburg 61 48.06 N 15.36 E
Wilhelmsburg ◆[8] 52 53.30 N 10.00 E
Wilhelmshaven 52 53.31 N 8.08 E
Wilhelmshöhe, Schloss ⅰ 56 51.21 N 9.22 E
Wilhelmshorst 54 52.19 N 13.03 E
Wilhelmstadt ◆[8] 264a 52.31 N 13.11 E
Wilhelmstal 156 21.54 S 16.19 E
Wilhelmstein, Schloss ⅰ 52 52.28 N 9.18 E
Wilis, Gunung ∧ 115a 7.52 S 111.48 E
Wilkau-Hasslau 54 50.40 N 12.31 E
Wilkerson Pass ⋈ 200 39.02 N 105.32 W
Wilkes-Barre 210 41.14 N 75.52 W
Wilkes-Barre Scranton Airport ⊠ 210 41.20 N 75.45 W
Wilkesboro 192 36.08 N 81.09 W
Wilkes Island ⅰ 174a 19.18 N 166.34 E
Wilkes Land ◆[1] 9 69.00 S 120.00 E
Wilkeson 224 47.06 N 122.02 W
Wilket Creek ≃ 275b 43.43 N 79.21 W
Wilket Creek Park ♦ 275b 43.43 N 79.22 W
Wilkhaven 46 57.52 N 3.45 W
Wilkie 184 52.25 N 108.43 W
Wilkinsburg 214 40.26 N 79.51 W
Wilkinson 218 39.53 N 85.36 W
Wilkinson Lakes ⊜ 162 29.40 S 132.39 E
Wilkins Sound ♮ 9 70.15 S 73.00 W
Wilkins Township 279b 40.25 N 79.50 W
Will □[6] 216 41.32 N 88.05 W
Will, Mount ∧ 180 57.31 N 128.46 W
Willacoochee 192 31.20 N 83.02 W
Willamette ≃ 202 45.39 N 122.46 W
Willamette, Middle Fork ≃ 202 44.01 N 123.01 W
Willamette, North Fork ≃ 202 43.46 N 122.32 W
Willamina 224 45.04 N 123.29 W
Willamina Creek ≃ 224 45.05 N 123.28 W
Willandra Billabong Creek ≃ 166 33.08 S 144.06 E
Willapa 224 46.40 N 123.39 W
Willapa ≃ 224 46.42 N 123.50 W
Willapa Bay ⊂ 224 46.37 N 124.00 W
Willard, Mo., U.S. 194 37.18 N 93.25 W
Willard, N.M., U.S. 200 34.35 N 106.01 W
Willard, N.Y., U.S. 210 42.40 N 76.52 W
Willard, Oh., U.S. 214 41.03 N 82.44 W
Willard, Ut., U.S. 200 41.24 N 112.02 W
Willard, Wa., U.S. 224 45.48 N 121.38 W
Willard, Punta › 232 28.50 N 113.15 W
Willards 208 38.23 N 75.20 W
Willaston, Austl. 168b 34.36 S 138.45 E
Willaston, Eng., U.K. 262 53.18 N 3.00 W
Willaumez Peninsula ›[1] 164 5.05 S 150.05 E
Willcox 200 32.15 N 109.49 W
Willcox Playa ⊜ 200 32.08 N 109.51 W
Willebadessen 52 51.37 N 9.02 E
Willebroek 50 51.04 N 4.22 E
Willem Pretorius Game Reserve ◆[4] 158 28.16 S 27.13 E
Willemsoord 52 52.49 N 6.05 E
Willemstad, Ned. 52 51.42 N 4.26 E
Willemstad, Ned. Ant. 241s 12.06 N 68.56 W
Willerburn Acres 284c 39.03 N 77.10 W
Willeroo 164 15.17 S 131.35 E
Willer-sur-Thur 58 47.51 N 7.05 E
Willerswalde 54 54.07 N 13.08 E
Willesden ◆[8] 260 51.33 N 0.14 W
Willet 210 42.28 N 75.55 W
Willett Pond ⊜ 283 42.11 N 71.14 W
Willey Creek ≃ 279a 41.25 N 81.25 W
William, Lac ⊜ 206 46.07 N 71.34 W
William, Mount ∧, Austl. 166 37.17 S 142.36 E
William, Mount ∧, Austl. 169 37.13 S 144.47 E
William, Mount ∧[2] 168a 32.57 S 116.07 E
William Bill Dannelly Reservoir ⊜[1] 194 32.10 N 87.10 W
William Boyce Regional Park ♦ 279b 40.28 N 79.45 W
William Girling Reservoir ⊜[1] 260 51.37 N 0.02 W
William H. Harsha Lake ⊜[1] 218 39.02 N 84.07 W
William Lake ⊜ 184 53.50 N 99.25 W
Williamnagar 124 25.30 N 90.35 E
William Patterson College ⅴ[2] 276 40.56 N 74.12 W
William P. Gleason Park ♦ 278 41.33 N 87.21 W
William Preston Lane Jr. Memorial Bridge ◆[5] 208 39.00 N 76.28 W
Williams, Austl. 168a 33.01 S 116.52 E
Williams, Az., U.S. 200 35.14 N 112.11 W
Williams, Ca., U.S. 226 39.09 N 122.08 W
Williams, Ia., U.S. 190 42.29 N 93.32 W
Williams, Mn., U.S. 198 48.46 N 94.57 W
Williams □[6] 216 41.35 N 84.33 W
Williams ≃, Austl. 166 20.04 S 141.08 E
Williams ≃, Austl. 168a 32.59 S 116.24 E
Williams ≃, Austl. 170 32.45 S 151.45 E
Williams, Cape › 9 70.29 S 164.05 E
Williams Air Force Base ■ 200 33.18 N 111.40 W
Williams Bay 216 42.34 N 88.32 W
Williamsburg, On., Can. 212 44.58 N 75.15 W
Williamsburg, In., U.S. 218 39.57 N 84.59 W
Williamsburg, Ia., U.S. 190 41.39 N 92.00 W
Williamsburg, Ky., U.S. 192 36.44 N 84.09 W
Williamsburg, Ma., U.S. 207 42.23 N 72.43 W
Williamsburg, Mo., U.S. 219 38.55 N 91.42 W
Williamsburg, Oh., U.S. 218 39.03 N 84.03 W
Williamsburg, Pa., U.S. 214 40.27 N 78.12 W
Williamsburg, Va., U.S. 208 37.16 N 76.42 W
Williamsburg ◆[8] 276 40.42 N 73.57 W
Williamsburg Bridge ◆[5] 276 40.43 N 73.58 W
Williams Center 216 41.26 N 84.36 W
Williams Creek ≃, Austl. 274a 33.57 S 150.58 E
Williams Creek ≃, In., U.S. 218 39.36 N 85.09 W
Williamsdale 171b 35.35 S 149.09 E
Williamsfield 214 41.32 N 80.32 W
Williams Fork ≃ 200 40.26 N 107.39 W
Williams Lake 182 52.08 N 122.09 W
Williams Lake Indian Reserve ◆[4] 182 52.07 N 122.00 W
Williams Mountain ∧[2] 194 34.15 N 94.33 W
Williamson, N.Y., U.S. 210 43.13 N 77.11 W
Williamson, W.V., U.S. 192 37.40 N 82.16 W
Williamson □[6] 222 30.40 N 97.32 W
Williamson ≃ 202 42.28 N 121.57 W
Williamson, Mount ∧ 204 36.39 N 118.18 W
Williamson Head › 9 69.09 S 157.49 E
Williamsport, Nf., Can. 186 50.32 N 56.19 W
Williamsport, In., U.S. 216 40.17 N 87.17 W
Williamsport, Oh., U.S. 214 39.35 N 83.07 W
Williamsport, Pa., U.S. 210 41.14 N 77.00 W
Williamston, Mi., U.S. 216 42.41 N 84.16 W
Williamston, N.C., U.S. 192 35.51 N 77.03 W
Williamston, S.C., U.S. 192 34.37 N 82.28 W
Williamstown, Austl. 168b 34.40 S 138.53 E
Williamstown, Austl. 169 37.52 S 144.54 E
Williamstown, On., Can. 206 45.08 N 74.35 W
Williamstown, Ky., U.S. 218 38.38 N 84.33 W
Williamstown, Ma., U.S. 207 42.42 N 73.12 W
Williamstown, N.J., U.S. 208 39.41 N 74.59 W
Williamstown, N.Y., U.S. 212 43.26 N 75.54 W
Williamstown, Pa., U.S. 208 40.34 N 76.37 W
Williamstown, Vt., U.S. 188 44.07 N 72.32 W
Williamstown, W.V., U.S. 188 39.24 N 81.27 W
Williamstown Junction 285 39.45 N 74.56 W
Williamstown Lake ⊜[1] 218 38.41 N 84.32 W
Williamsville, Il., U.S. 219 39.57 N 89.32 W
Williamsville, N.Y., U.S. 210 42.57 N 78.44 W
Williamtown 170 32.49 S 151.50 E
Willich 56 51.16 N 6.33 E
Willikies 240c 17.05 N 61.42 W
Willimantic 207 41.42 N 72.12 W
Willimantic ≃ 207 41.43 N 72.12 W
Willingale 260 51.44 N 0.19 E
Willingboro 208 40.01 N 74.52 W
Willingdon, Ab., Can. 182 53.50 N 112.08 W
Willingdon, Eng., U.K. 42 50.47 N 0.15 E
Willingdon, Mount ∧ 182 51.45 N 116.15 W
Willingen 56 51.17 N 8.37 E
Willingham 42 52.19 N 0.04 E
Willington, Eng., U.K. 42 52.50 N 1.33 W
Willington, Eng., U.K. 44 54.43 N 1.41 W
Willis, Mi., U.S. 216 42.09 N 83.33 W
Willis, Tx., U.S. 222 30.25 N 95.28 W
Willis ≃ 192 37.41 N 78.07 W
Willisau 58 47.07 N 8.00 E
Willis Group ⅱ 164 16.18 S 150.00 E
Willis Island ⅰ 186 48.48 N 53.42 W
Williston, S. Afr. 158 31.20 S 20.53 E
Williston, Fl., U.S. 192 29.23 N 82.26 W
Williston, N.D., U.S. 198 48.08 N 103.38 W
Williston, Oh., U.S. 214 41.36 N 83.20 W
Williston, S.C., U.S. 192 33.24 N 81.25 W
Williston Lake ⊜[1] 176 55.40 N 123.40 W
Williston Park 276 40.45 N 73.38 W
Willisville 194 37.59 N 89.35 W
Willis Wharf 208 37.30 N 75.48 W
Williton 42 51.10 N 3.20 W
Willits 204 39.24 N 123.21 W
Willmar 198 45.07 N 95.02 W
Willmersdorf 264a 52.40 N 13.41 E
Willmore Wilderness Provincial Park ♦ 182 53.45 N 119.00 W
Willoughby, Austl. 170 33.48 S 151.12 E
Willoughby, Oh., U.S. 214 41.38 N 81.25 W
Willoughby, Cape › 166 35.51 S 138.07 E
Willoughby Bay ⊂ 240c 17.02 N 61.44 W
Willoughby Hills 214 41.35 N 81.25 W
Willow, Ak., U.S. 180 61.45 N 150.03 W
Willow, Mi., U.S. 216 42.07 N 83.24 W
Willow, N.Y., U.S. 210 42.05 N 74.14 W
Willow ≃, Ab., Can. 182 55.58 N 113.55 W
Willow ≃, B.C., Can. 182 54.03 N 122.21 W
Willow ≃, Mn., U.S. 198 46.40 N 93.35 W
Willow ≃, Wi., U.S. 190 44.59 N 92.46 W
Willowbrook, Sk., Can. 184 51.13 N 102.47 W
Willow Brook, Ca., U.S. 280 33.54 N 118.13 W
Willowbrook, Il., U.S. 278 41.46 N 87.56 W
Willowbrook, Md., U.S. 284c 39.02 N 77.11 W
Willow Brook ≃, On., Can. 212 43.53 N 80.16 W
Willow Brook ≃, Eng., U.K. 42 52.32 N 0.24 W
Willow Brook ≃, N.J., U.S. 276 40.20 N 74.10 W
Willowbrook Mall ◆[9] 276 40.53 N 74.15 W
Willowbrook Park ♦ 276 40.36 N 74.09 W
Willow Bunch 184 49.24 N 105.37 W
Willow Bunch Lake ⊜ 184 49.27 N 105.28 W
Willow City 198 48.36 N 100.17 W
Willow Creek, Ca., U.S. 204 40.56 N 123.38 W
Willow Creek, Mt., U.S. 202 45.49 N 111.38 W
Willow Creek ≃, Ab., Can. 182 49.46 N 113.21 W
Willow Creek ≃, On., Can. 212 44.25 N 79.53 W
Willow Creek ≃, Ca., U.S. 226 37.09 N 119.27 W
Willow Creek ≃, Ca., U.S. 226 39.22 N 122.05 W
Willow Creek ≃, Il., U.S. 216 41.42 N 89.10 W
Willow Creek ≃, In., U.S. 216 41.15 N 85.08 W
Willow Creek ≃, Mi., U.S. 281 42.20 N 83.25 W
Willow Creek ≃, Mt., U.S. 202 48.10 N 111.11 W
Willow Creek ≃, Mt., U.S. 202 48.09 N 106.38 W
Willow Creek ≃, Mt., U.S. 202 46.28 N 108.28 W
Willow Creek ≃, Nv., U.S. 204 38.10 N 116.35 W
Willow Creek ≃, N.D., U.S. 198 48.34 N 100.27 W
Willow Creek ≃, Oh., U.S. 279a 41.20 N 82.03 W
Willow Creek ≃, Or., U.S. 202 44.00 N 117.13 W
Willow Creek ≃, Or., U.S. 202 45.48 N 120.01 W
Willow Creek ≃, Ut., U.S. 200 40.02 N 109.45 W
Willow Creek, North Fork ≃ 226 37.13 N 119.30 W
Willow Creek, South Fork ≃ 226 39.32 N 122.10 W
Willowdale ◆[8] 275b 43.47 N 79.26 W
Willowdale State Forest ♦ 283 42.40 N 70.54 W
Willowdene 273d 26.18 S 27.56 E
Willowemac 210 41.55 N 74.41 W
Willowemoc Creek ≃ 210 41.53 N 74.48 W
Willow Glen ◆[8] 282 37.18 N 121.53 W
Willow Grove 208 40.08 N 75.06 W
Willow Grove Naval Air Station ■ 208 40.12 N 75.08 W
Willow Grove Park ♦ 285 40.08 N 75.08 W
Willow Hill 214 40.06 N 77.48 W
Willowick 214 41.37 N 81.28 W
Willow Lake 198 44.37 N 97.38 W
Willow Lake ⊜, N.T., Can. 176 62.11 N 119.10 W
Willow Lake ⊜, N.Y., U.S. 276 40.43 N 73.50 W
Willowlake ≃ 176 62.52 N 123.08 W
Willow Metropolitan Park ♦ 281 42.08 N 83.22 W
Willowmore 158 33.17 S 23.29 E
Willow Park 222 32.45 N 97.39 W
Willowra 162 21.15 S 132.35 E
Willowra Aboriginal Reserve ◆[4] 162 21.15 S 132.35 E
Willow Reservoir ⊜[1] 190 45.45 N 89.50 W
Willow Ridge Estates 284a 43.01 N 78.49 W
Willow River 182 54.04 N 122.28 W
Willow Run, De., U.S. 285 39.44 N 75.37 W
Willow Run, Mi., U.S. 216 42.14 N 83.35 W
Willow Run, Va., U.S. 284c 38.49 N 77.10 W
Willow Run Airport ⊠ 281 42.14 N 83.32 W
Willows 226 39.31 N 122.11 W
Willow Springs, Ca., U.S. 228 34.53 N 118.18 W
Willow Springs, Il., U.S. 278 41.44 N 87.51 W
Willow Springs, Mo., U.S. 194 36.59 N 91.58 W
Willow Springs, Pa., U.S. 279b 40.19 N 79.44 W
Willow Street 208 39.59 N 76.17 W
Willowvale 158 32.16 S 28.30 E
Willow Woods 284c 38.50 N 77.16 W
Will Rogers Beach State Park ♦ 280 34.01 N 118.30 W
Will Rogers State Park ♦ 280 34.03 N 118.31 W
Willroth 56 50.34 N 7.31 E
Wills, Lake ⊜ 162 21.25 S 128.51 E
Wills Creek ≃, Austl. 166 22.43 S 140.02 E

Symbol	English	Deutsch	Español	Français	Português
≃	River	Fluß	Río	Rivière	Rio
≚	Canal	Kanal	Canal	Canal	Canal
⌞	Waterfall, Rapids	Wasserfall, Stromschnellen	Cascada, Rápidos	Chute d'eau, Rapides	Cascata, Rápidos
♮	Strait	Meeresstraße	Estrecho	Détroit	Estreito
⊂	Bay, Gulf	Bucht, Golf	Bahía, Golfo	Baie, Golfe	Baía, Golfo
⊜	Lake, Lakes	See, Seen	Lago, Lagos	Lac, Lacs	Lago, Lagos
⩸	Swamp	Sumpf	Pantano	Marais	Pântano
⍓	Ice Features, Glacier	Eis- und Gletscherformen	Accidentes Glaciales	Formes glaciaires	Acidentes glaciares
⊤	Other Hydrographic Features	Andere Hydrographische Objekte	Otros Elementos Hidrográficos	Autres données hydrographiques	Outros acidentes hidrográficos
✢	Submarine Features	Untermeerische Objekte	Accidentes Submarinos	Formes de relief sous-marin	Acidentes submarinos
□	Political Unit	Politische Einheit	Unidad Política	Entité politique	Unidade política
ⅴ	Cultural Institution	Kulturelle Institution	Institución Cultural	Institution culturelle	Instituição cultural
ⅰ	Historical Site	Historische Stätte	Sitio Histórico	Site historique	Sitio histórico
♦	Recreational Site	Erholungs- und Ferienort	Sitio de Recreo	Centre de loisirs	Área de Lazer
⊠	Airport	Flughafen	Aeropuerto	Aéroport	Aeroporto
■	Military Installation	Militäranlage	Instalación Militar	Installation militaire	Instalação militar
◆	Miscellaneous	Verschiedenes	Misceláneo	Divers	Diversos

Wills Creek ≐, Oh., U.S. 188 40.09 N 81.55 W
Wills Creek Lake ⊜¹ 214 40.08 N 81.45 W
Willseyville 210 42.17 N 76.23 W
Willshire 216 40.45 N 84.48 W
Wills Point 222 32.43 N 96.01 W
Willston 284c 38.52 N 77.09 W
Willunga 168b 35.17 S 138.33 E
Wilmar 194 33.37 N 91.55 W
Wilmer, Al., U.S. 194 30.49 N 88.21 W
Wilmer, Pa., U.S. 285 40.07 N 75.32 W
Wilmer, Tx., U.S. 222 32.35 N 96.41 W
Wilmerding 279b 40.23 N 79.48 W
Wilmersdorf ◆⁸ 264a 52.30 N 13.19 E
Wilmette 216 42.04 N 87.43 W
Wilmington, Austl. 166 32.39 S 138.07 E
Wilmington, Eng., U.K. 260 51.26 N 0.12 E
Wilmington, De., U.S. 208 39.44 N 75.32 W
Wilmington, Il., U.S. 216 41.18 N 88.08 W
Wilmington, Ma., U.S. 207 42.32 N 71.10 W
Wilmington, N.C., U.S. 192 34.13 N 77.56 W
Wilmington, Oh., U.S. 218 39.26 N 83.49 W
Wilmington, Vt., U.S. 188 42.52 N 72.52 W
Wilmington ◆⁸ 280 33.47 N 118.16 W
Wilmington Manor 285 39.41 N 75.35 W
Wilmington Manor Gardens 285 39.40 N 75.34 W
Wilmore, Ky., U.S. 192 37.51 N 84.39 W
Wilmore, Pa., U.S. 214 40.23 N 78.43 W
Wilmot, Ar., U.S. 194 33.03 N 91.34 W
Wilmot, Oh., U.S. 214 40.39 N 81.38 W
Wilmot, S.D., U.S. 198 45.24 N 96.51 W
Wilmot, Wi., U.S. 216 42.31 N 88.11 W
Wilmot Woods ♦ 278 42.18 N 87.56 W
Wilmslow 44 53.20 N 2.15 W
Wilna → Vilnius 76 54.41 N 25.19 E
Wilnecote 42 52.36 N 1.40 W
Wilnsdorf 56 50.49 N 8.09 E
Wilpattu National Park ♦ 122 8.20 N 80.00 E
Wilpen 214 40.17 N 79.12 W
Wilpshire 262 53.47 N 2.28 W
Wilsall 202 45.59 N 110.39 W
Wilsdruff 54 51.05 N 13.32 E
Wilseder Berg ∧² 52 53.10 N 9.56 E
Wilseyville 226 38.23 N 120.31 W
Wilshamstead 42 52.05 N 0.27 W
Wilson, Austl. 166 32.00 S 138.22 E
Wilson, Ar., U.S. 194 35.34 N 90.02 W
Wilson, Ct., U.S. 207 41.48 N 72.38 W
Wilson, Il., U.S. 278 42.21 N 87.54 W
Wilson, Ks., U.S. 198 38.49 N 98.28 W
Wilson, La., U.S. 194 30.55 N 91.06 W
Wilson, N.Y., U.S. 210 43.18 N 78.49 W
Wilson, N.C., U.S. 192 35.43 N 77.54 W
Wilson, Ok., U.S. 196 34.09 N 97.25 W
Wilson, Pa., U.S. 208 40.41 N 75.14 W
Wilson, Tx., U.S. 196 33.19 N 101.44 W
Wilson ≐, Austl. 164 16.47 S 128.17 E
Wilson ≐, Austl. 166 27.38 S 141.24 E
Wilson ≐, Or., U.S. 224 45.28 N 123.53 W
Wilson, Cape ≻ 176 66.59 N 81.28 W
Wilson, Mount ∧, Az., U.S. 200 35.59 N 114.37 W
Wilson, Mount ∧, Ca., U.S. 280 34.13 N 118.04 W
Wilson, Mount ∧, Co., U.S. 200 37.51 N 107.59 W
Wilson, Mount ∧, Nv., U.S. 204 38.15 N 114.23 W
Wilson, Mount ∧, Or., U.S. 224 45.04 N 121.39 W
Wilson, Mount ∧², Austl. 162 20.14 S 127.39 E
Wilson, Mount ∧², Austl. 168b 35.13 S 138.38 E
Wilson, Point ≻, Austl. 169 38.05 S 144.30 E
Wilson, Point ≻, Wa., U.S. 224 48.08 N 122.45 W
Wilson Cliffs ≗⁴ 162 22.03 S 127.09 E
Wilson Creek ≐, Tx., U.S. 222 33.07 N 96.35 W
Wilson Creek ≐, Wa., U.S. 202 47.25 N 119.07 W
Wilson Lake ⊜¹, Al., U.S. 194 34.49 N 87.30 W
Wilson Lake ⊜¹, Ks., U.S. 198 38.57 N 98.40 W
Wilson Range ⋏ 162 28.50 S 124.25 E
Wilson Run ≐, De., U.S. 285 39.48 N 75.35 W
Wilson Run ≐, Pa., U.S. 279b 40.13 N 79.37 W
Wilsons Beach 186 44.56 N 66.56 W
Wilson's Creek National Battlefield ♦ 194 37.06 N 93.27 W
Wilsons Promontory ≻ 166 38.55 S 146.20 E
Wilsons Promontory National Park ♦ 166 39.00 S 146.25 E
Wilsonville, Il., U.S. 219 39.04 N 89.51 W
Wilsonville, Ne., U.S. 198 40.06 N 100.06 W
Wilsonville, Or., U.S. 224 45.18 N 122.46 W
Wilster 52 53.55 N 9.22 E
Wilthen 54 51.06 N 14.24 E
Wilton, Eng., U.K. 42 51.05 N 1.52 W
Wilton, Ct., U.S. 207 41.11 N 73.26 W
Wilton, Me., U.S. 188 44.35 N 70.13 W
Wilton, N.H., U.S. 207 42.50 N 71.44 W
Wilton, N.Y., U.S. 210 43.11 N 73.45 W
Wilton, N.D., U.S. 198 47.09 N 100.46 W
Wilton, Wi., U.S. 190 43.48 N 90.31 W
Wilton ≐ 164 14.45 S 134.33 E
Wilton Creek ≐ 212 44.12 N 76.56 W
Wilton Farm Acres 284b 39.18 N 76.50 W
Wilton Manors 220 26.09 N 80.08 W
Wiltshire □⁶ 42 51.15 N 1.50 W
Wiltz 56 49.57 N 5.55 E
Wiluna 162 26.36 S 120.13 E
Wimapedi ≐ 184 55.27 N 99.07 W
Wimauma 220 27.42 N 82.17 W
Wimberley 196 30.00 N 98.06 W
Wimbleball Reservoir ⊜¹ 42 51.04 N 3.28 W
Wimbledon 198 47.10 N 98.27 W
Wimbledon ◆⁸ 260 51.25 N 0.12 W
Wimbledon Common ♦ 260 51.26 N 0.14 W
Wimborne Minster 42 50.48 N 1.59 W
Wimereux 50 50.46 N 1.37 E
Wimmelburg 54 51.31 N 11.30 E
Wimmenau 56 48.55 N 7.25 E
Wimmera ≐ 169 36.55 S 142.56 E
Wimmis 58 46.41 N 7.38 E
Winagami Lake ⊜ 182 55.38 N 116.45 W
Winam c 154 0.15 S 34.35 E
Winamac 216 41.03 N 86.36 W
Winburg 158 28.37 S 27.00 E
Winburne 214 40.57 N 78.08 W
Wincanton 42 51.04 N 2.25 W
Wincham 262 53.16 N 2.29 W
Winchcombe 42 51.57 N 1.58 W
Winchelsea, Austl. 169 38.15 S 143.59 E
Winchelsea, Eng., U.K. 42 50.55 N 0.42 E
Winchendon 207 42.41 N 72.02 W
Winchester, On., Can. 212 45.06 N 75.21 W
Winchester, N.Z. 172 44.12 S 171.17 E
Winchester, Eng., U.K. 42 51.04 N 1.19 W
Winchester, Ca., U.S. 228 33.42 N 117.05 W
Winchester, Id., U.S. 202 46.14 N 116.37 W
Winchester, Il., U.S. 219 39.37 N 90.27 W
Winchester, In., U.S. 218 40.10 N 84.58 W
Winchester, Ky., U.S. 192 37.59 N 84.10 W
Winchester, Ma., U.S. 283 42.27 N 71.08 W
Winchester, N.H., U.S. 207 42.46 N 72.23 W
Winchester, Oh., U.S. 218 38.56 N 83.39 W
Winchester, Tn., U.S. 194 35.11 N 86.06 W
Winchester, Tx., U.S. 222 30.01 N 97.01 W
Winchester, Va., U.S. 188 39.11 N 78.10 W
Winchester Cathedral ᵾ¹ 42 51.04 N 1.19 W
Winchmore Hill 260 51.39 N 0.39 W
Winchmore Hill ◆⁸ 260 51.38 N 0.06 W
Wind ≐, Yk., Can. 180 65.49 N 135.18 W
Wind ≐, Wa., U.S. 224 45.43 N 121.47 W
Wind ≐, Wy., U.S. 202 43.35 N 108.13 W
Windang 170 34.32 S 150.53 E
Windau → Ventspils 76 57.24 N 21.36 E
Windber 214 40.14 N 78.50 W
Wind Cave National Park ♦ 198 43.32 N 103.25 W
Windeck 56 50.48 N 7.37 E
Winder 192 33.59 N 83.43 W
Winder, Lake ⊜ 220 28.15 N 80.51 W
Windera 166 26.03 S 151.50 E
Windermere, B.C., Can. 182 50.30 N 115.58 W
Windermere, Eng., U.K. 44 54.23 N 2.54 W
Windermere, Fl., U.S. 220 28.30 N 81.32 W
Windermere ⊜ 44 54.22 N 2.56 W
Windermere Lake ⊜ 190 47.56 N 83.47 W
Winder Village 285 40.06 N 74.52 W
Windfall, Ab., Can. 182 54.11 N 116.15 W
Windfall, In., U.S. 216 40.21 N 85.57 W
Windgap 210 40.51 N 75.18 W
Windham, Ct., U.S. 207 41.41 N 72.09 W
Windham, N.H., U.S. 283 42.48 N 71.18 W
Windham, N.Y., U.S. 210 42.19 N 74.15 W
Windham, Oh., U.S. 214 41.14 N 81.02 W
Windham □⁶, Ct., U.S. 207 41.55 N 71.55 W
Windham □⁶, Vt., U.S. 207 42.50 N 72.43 W
Windham Manor 284c 39.04 N 77.00 W
Windhoek 156 22.34 S 17.06 E
Windhoek □⁵ 156 22.30 S 17.00 E
Windigo ≐ 184 53.22 N 91.48 W
Windigo Lake ⊜ 184 52.35 N 91.32 W
Windisch 58 47.29 N 8.13 E
Windischeschenbach 60 49.48 N 12.09 E
Windischgarsten 61 47.44 N 14.20 E
Wind Lake 216 42.49 N 88.09 W
Wind Lake ⊜ 216 42.50 N 88.09 W
Windlass Run ≐ 284b 39.24 N 76.24 W
Windleite ∧ 54 51.22 N 10.56 E
Windlesham 260 51.22 N 0.40 W
Windley Key I 220 24.57 N 80.35 W
Windmill Point ≻, On., Can. 284a 42.52 N 79.01 W
Windmill Point ≻, Mi., U.S. 281 42.22 N 82.55 W
Windmill Point ≻, Va., U.S. 208 37.37 N 76.17 W
Windom, Mn., U.S. 198 43.51 N 95.07 W
Windom, N.Y., U.S. 210 42.47 N 78.48 W
Windom Peak ∧ 200 37.37 N 107.35 W
Windorah 166 25.26 S 142.39 E
Windorf, Dtsch. 60 48.37 N 13.13 E
Windorf, Öst. 61 48.27 N 14.02 E
Window Rock 200 35.40 N 109.03 W
Wind Point 216 42.47 N 87.45 W
Wind River Indian Reservation ◆⁴ 202 43.26 N 109.00 W
Wind River Peak ∧ 200 42.42 N 109.07 W
Wind River Range ⋏ 200 43.05 N 109.25 W
Windrush ≐ 42 51.42 N 1.25 W
Windsbach 56 49.14 N 10.50 E
Windsor, Austl. 168b 34.25 S 138.20 E
Windsor, Austl. 170 33.37 S 150.49 E
Windsor, Nf., Can. 186 48.57 N 55.40 W
Windsor, N.S., Can. 186 44.59 N 64.08 W
Windsor, On., Can. 214 42.18 N 83.01 W
Windsor, On., Can. 281 42.18 N 83.01 W
Windsor, P.Q., Can. 206 45.34 N 72.00 W
Windsor, Eng., U.K. 42 51.29 N 0.38 W
Windsor, Ca., U.S. 204 38.33 N 122.49 W
Windsor, Co., U.S. 200 40.28 N 104.54 W
Windsor, Ct., U.S. 207 41.51 N 72.38 W
Windsor, Il., U.S. 194 39.26 N 88.35 W
Windsor, In., U.S. 218 40.09 N 85.12 W
Windsor, Mo., U.S. 194 38.31 N 93.31 W
Windsor, N.J., U.S. 208 40.15 N 74.35 W
Windsor, N.Y., U.S. 210 42.05 N 75.39 W
Windsor, N.C., U.S. 192 35.59 N 76.56 W
Windsor, Oh., U.S. 214 41.32 N 80.56 W
Windsor, Pa., U.S. 208 39.54 N 76.35 W
Windsor, Vt., U.S. 188 43.29 N 72.23 W
Windsor, Va., U.S. 208 36.48 N 76.44 W
Windsor, Wi., U.S. 216 43.13 N 89.20 W
Windsor, Gare ◆⁵ 275a 45.30 N 73.34 W
Windsor, University of ᵾ² 281 42.18 N 83.04 W
Windsor Airport ✈ 214 42.17 N 82.58 W
Windsor and Maidenhead □⁸ 260 51.28 N 0.37 W
Windsor Castle ⊥ 42 51.29 N 0.36 W
Windsor Forest 192 31.58 N 81.07 W
Windsor Forest ◆³ 42 51.27 N 0.43 W
Windsor Great Park ♦ 260 51.27 N 0.37 W
Windsor Heights 214 40.12 N 80.40 W
Windsor Hills 280 33.59 N 118.21 W
Windsor Locks 207 41.55 N 72.37 W
Windsor Race Course ♦ 260 51.29 N 0.39 W
Windsor Raceway ♦ 281 42.15 N 83.05 W
Windsor Terrace 284b 39.19 N 76.43 W
Windsorton 158 28.16 S 24.44 E
Windsorville 207 41.53 N 72.32 W
Windthorst 196 33.34 N 98.26 W
Windward Islands II 238 13.00 N 61.00 W
Windward Passage ʯ 238 20.00 N 73.50 W
Windy Hills 285 39.48 N 75.35 W
Windy Lake ⊜ 184 54.22 N 102.35 W
Windy Peak ∧, Co., U.S. 200 38.21 N 106.16 W
Windy Peak ∧, Wa., U.S. 202 48.56 N 119.58 W
Windy Run ≐ 284c 38.54 N 77.05 W
Winefred ≐ 184 56.02 N 110.36 W
Winefred Lake ⊜ 182 55.30 N 110.35 W
Winejok 140 9.01 N 27.34 E
Winesburg 214 40.37 N 81.42 W
Winfield, Ab., Can. 182 52.58 N 114.26 W
Winfield, Al., U.S. 194 33.55 N 87.49 W
Winfield, Il., U.S. 216 41.52 N 88.10 W
Winfield, Ia., U.S. 190 41.07 N 91.26 W
Winfield, Ks., U.S. 198 37.14 N 96.59 W
Winfield, Mo., U.S. 219 38.59 N 90.44 W
Winfield, N.J., U.S. 276 40.38 N 74.17 W
Winfield, Tx., U.S. 222 33.10 N 95.07 W
Winfield, W.V., U.S. 188 38.31 N 81.53 W
Wing 198 47.08 N 100.16 W
Wing ≐ 198 46.29 N 94.58 W
Wingate, Eng., U.K. 44 54.44 N 1.23 W
Wingate, Md., U.S. 208 38.16 N 76.04 W
Wingate, N.C., U.S. 192 34.59 N 80.26 W
Wingate Mountains ⋏ 164 14.29 S 130.42 E
Wingates 262 53.34 N 2.32 W
Wingdale 210 41.39 N 73.34 W
Wingecarribee ≐ 170 34.23 S 150.07 E
Wingecarribee Reservoir ⊜¹ 170 34.34 S 150.30 E
Wingello 170 34.42 S 150.09 E
Wingene 50 51.04 N 3.16 E
Wingen-sur-Moder 56 48.55 N 7.22 E
Wingerworth 44 53.12 N 1.26 W
Wingham, Austl. 166 31.52 S 152.22 E
Wingham, On., Can. 212 43.53 N 81.19 W
Wingham, Eng., U.K. 42 51.17 N 1.13 E
Wing Lake Shores 281 42.33 N 83.17 W
Wingles 50 50.29 N 2.51 E
Wingo 194 36.38 N 88.44 W
Wings Field ✈ 285 40.08 N 75.16 W
Wingst 52 53.43 N 9.03 E
Winhole Channel ʯ 276 43.37 N 73.48 W
Winhöring 60 48.16 N 12.39 E
Winifred 202 47.33 N 109.22 W
Winifreda 252 36.15 S 64.14 W
Winisk 176 55.15 N 85.12 W
Winisk ≐ 176 55.17 N 85.05 W
Winisk Lake ⊜ 176 52.55 N 87.22 W
Wink 196 31.45 N 103.06 W
Winkana 110 15.44 N 98.01 E
Winkelman 200 32.59 N 110.46 W
Winkelpos 158 27.35 S 26.49 E
Winkler, Mb., Can. 184 49.11 N 97.56 W
Winkler, Tx., U.S. 222 31.56 N 96.13 W
Winklern 64 46.52 N 12.52 E
Winlaw 182 49.37 N 117.34 W
Winlock 224 46.29 N 122.56 W
Winneba 150 5.25 N 0.36 W
Winnebago, Il., U.S. 190 42.15 N 89.14 W
Winnebago, Mn., U.S. 190 43.46 N 94.09 W
Winnebago, Ne., U.S. 198 42.14 N 96.28 W
Winnebago □⁶ 216 42.17 N 89.06 W
Winnebago ≐ 190 43.03 N 92.57 W
Winnebago, Lake ⊜ 190 44.00 N 88.25 W
Winnebago Indian Reservation ◆⁴, Ne., U.S. 198 42.15 N 96.31 W
Winnebago Indian Reservation ◆⁴, Wi., U.S. 190 44.15 N 90.38 W
Winnecke, Mount ∧² 162 18.47 S 130.20 E
Winnecke Creek ≐ 162 18.35 S 131.34 E
Winneconne 190 44.06 N 88.42 W
Winneconnet 283 41.59 N 71.08 W
Winneconnet Pond ⊜ 283 41.58 N 71.08 W
Winnekendonk 52 51.36 N 6.17 E
Winnekenni Park ♦ 283 42.47 N 71.04 W
Winnemucca 204 40.58 N 117.44 W
Winnemucca Lake ⊜ 204 40.09 N 119.20 W
Winnenden 56 48.53 N 9.24 E
Winner 198 43.22 N 99.51 W
Winnetka 216 42.06 N 87.44 W
Winnetka ◆⁸ 280 34.13 N 118.35 W
Winnett 202 47.00 N 108.21 W
Winnfield 194 31.55 N 92.38 W
Winnibigoshish, Lake ⊜ 190 47.27 N 94.12 W
Winnie 194 29.49 N 94.23 W
Winning 162 23.09 S 114.32 E
Winningen, Dtsch. 54 51.49 N 11.26 E
Winningen, Dtsch. 56 50.18 N 7.31 E
Winnipeg 184 49.53 N 97.09 W
Winnipeg ≐ 184 50.38 N 96.19 W
Winnipeg, Lake ⊜ 184 52.00 N 97.00 W
Winnipeg Beach 184 50.31 N 96.58 W
Winnipegosis 184 51.39 N 99.56 W
Winnipegosis, Lake ⊜ 184 52.30 N 100.00 W
Winnipesaukee, Lake ⊜ 188 43.35 N 71.20 W
Winnsboro, La., U.S. 194 32.09 N 91.43 W
Winnsboro, S.C., U.S. 192 34.22 N 81.05 W
Winnsboro, Tx., U.S. 222 32.57 N 95.17 W
Winnsboro, Lake ⊜¹ 222 32.55 N 95.21 W
Winnsboro Mills 192 34.21 N 81.05 W
Winnweiler 56 49.34 N 7.51 E
Winona, Ks., U.S. 198 39.03 N 101.14 W
Winona, Mi., U.S. 190 46.52 N 88.55 W
Winona, Mn., U.S. 190 44.03 N 91.38 W
Winona, Ms., U.S. 194 33.28 N 89.43 W
Winona, Mo., U.S. 194 37.00 N 91.19 W
Winona, Oh., U.S. 214 40.50 N 80.54 W
Winona, Tx., U.S. 222 32.29 N 95.10 W
Winona Lake, In., U.S. 216 41.13 N 85.49 W
Winona Lake, N.Y., U.S. 210 41.31 N 74.03 W
Winona Lake ⊜ 216 41.13 N 85.50 W
Winooski 188 44.29 N 73.11 W
Winooski ≐ 188 44.30 N 73.15 W
Winooski, North Branch ≐ 188 44.15 N 72.35 W
Winschoten 52 53.08 N 7.02 E
Winscombe 42 51.18 N 2.50 W
Winsen, Dtsch. 52 52.41 N 9.54 E
Winsen, Dtsch. 52 53.22 N 10.12 E
Winsford, Eng., U.K. 42 51.06 N 3.33 W
Winsford, Eng., U.K. 44 53.12 N 2.32 W
Winshill 42 52.48 N 1.36 W
Winside 198 42.10 N 97.10 W
Winslow, Eng., U.K. 42 51.57 N 0.54 W
Winslow, Az., U.S. 200 35.01 N 110.41 W
Winslow, Me., U.S. 188 44.32 N 69.37 W
Winslow, N.J., U.S. 285 39.39 N 74.52 W
Winslow Reef ◆² 14 1.36 S 174.57 W
Winsted, Ct., U.S. 207 41.55 N 73.03 W
Winsted, Mn., U.S. 190 44.57 N 94.02 W
Winston, Fl., U.S. 220 28.01 N 82.00 W
Winston, Or., U.S. 202 43.07 N 123.24 W
Winston Churchill Memorial ᵾ 219 38.52 N 91.58 W
Winston Creek ≐ 224 46.30 N 122.40 W
Winston-Salem 192 36.05 N 80.14 W
Winsum 52 53.19 N 6.31 E
Wintego Lake ⊜ 184 55.33 N 102.52 W
Winter 190 45.49 N 91.00 W
Winter Beach 220 27.43 N 80.25 W
Winterberg, Dtsch. 56 51.11 N 8.32 E
Winterberg, Dtsch. 263 51.17 N 7.18 E
Winterberg ∧² 263 51.20 N 7.13 E
Winterberge ⋏ 158 32.28 S 26.15 E
Winterbourne Abbas 42 50.43 N 2.34 W
Winter Creek ≐ 280 34.12 N 118.02 W
Winterfeld 54 52.44 N 11.14 E
Winter Garden 220 28.33 N 81.35 W
Winter Gardens 228 32.50 N 116.56 W
Winter Harbor 188 44.23 N 68.05 W
Winter Harbour 182 50.31 N 128.02 W
Winterhaven, Ca., U.S. 204 32.44 N 114.38 W
Winter Haven, Fl., U.S. 220 28.01 N 81.43 W
Winter Hill ∧² 262 53.38 N 2.31 W
Wintering ≐ 198 48.12 N 100.34 W
Wintering Lake ⊜ 184 55.24 N 97.42 W
Winter Island I, N.T., Can. 176 66.14 N 83.04 W
Winter Island I, Ca., U.S. 282 38.03 N 121.51 W
Winter Island I, Ma., U.S. 283 42.32 N 70.52 W
Winterlingen 58 48.11 N 9.07 E
Winter Park, Fl., U.S. 220 28.35 N 81.20 W
Winter Park, N.C., U.S. 192 34.12 N 77.53 W
Winterport 188 44.38 N 68.51 W
Winters, Ca., U.S. 226 38.31 N 121.58 W
Winters, Tx., U.S. 196 31.57 N 99.57 W
Winters Bayou ≐ 222 30.22 N 95.06 W
Winters Canal ≊ 226 38.32 N 121.58 W
Wintersdorf 54 51.03 N 12.21 E
Winterset, Ia., U.S. 190 41.19 N 94.00 W
Winterset, Oh., U.S. 214 40.06 N 81.25 W
Winter Springs 220 28.41 N 81.18 W
Winters Run ≐ 208 39.26 N 76.18 W
Winterstown 208 39.50 N 76.37 W
Wintersville 214 40.22 N 80.42 W
Winterswijk 52 51.58 N 6.44 E
Winterthur, Schw. 58 47.30 N 8.43 E
Winterthur, De., U.S. 285 39.48 N 75.35 W
Winterthur Museum ᵾ 285 39.48 N 75.36 W
Winterton, Nf., Can. 186 47.58 N 53.20 W
Winterton, S. Afr. 158 28.46 S 29.35 E
Winterton, Eng., U.K. 44 53.39 N 0.36 W
Winterton-on-Sea 42 52.43 N 1.42 E
Winterville, Ga., U.S. 192 33.58 N 83.16 W
Winterville, Ms., U.S. 194 33.30 N 91.03 W
Winterville, N.C., U.S. 192 35.31 N 77.24 W
Winthrop, Ct., U.S. 207 41.21 N 72.29 W
Winthrop, Ia., U.S. 190 42.28 N 91.44 W
Winthrop, Me., U.S. 188 44.18 N 69.58 W
Winthrop, Ma., U.S. 283 42.22 N 70.59 W
Winthrop, Mn., U.S. 190 44.32 N 94.21 W
Winthrop, Wa., U.S. 182 48.28 N 120.11 W
Winthrop, Lake ⊜ 283 42.11 N 71.25 W
Winthrop Harbor 216 42.28 N 87.49 W
Wintinna 162 27.44 S 134.07 E
Wintinna Creek ≐ 162 27.47 S 134.14 E
Winton, Austl. 166 22.23 S 143.02 E
Winton, N.Z. 172 46.09 S 168.20 E
Winton, S. Afr. 158 27.29 S 22.34 E
Winton, Ca., U.S. 226 37.23 N 120.37 W
Winton, N.C., U.S. 192 36.23 N 76.55 W
Winton, Wa., U.S. 224 47.44 N 120.44 W
Wintzenheim 58 48.04 N 7.17 E
Winwick 262 53.26 N 2.36 W
Winz 263 51.23 N 7.09 E
Winzenberg 263 51.06 N 7.38 E
Winzer 60 48.44 N 13.04 E
Winzermark 263 51.23 N 7.08 E
Wipper ≐, Dtsch. 54 51.17 N 11.10 E
Wipper ≐, Dtsch. 54 51.47 N 11.42 E
Wipper ≐, Dtsch. 263 51.07 N 7.24 E
Wipperdorf 54 51.28 N 10.42 E
Wipperfeld 263 51.05 N 7.19 E
Wipperfürth 56 51.07 N 7.23 E
Wippra 54 51.34 N 11.16 E
Wirātnagar 124 26.29 N 87.17 E
Wīrendranagar 124 28.35 N 81.38 E
Wireton, Il., U.S. 278 41.40 N 87.42 W
Wireton, Pa., U.S. 279b 40.34 N 80.14 W
Wīrgañj 124 27.00 N 84.52 E
Wiriagar ≐ 164 2.17 S 132.52 E
Wirksworth 44 53.05 N 1.34 W
Wirosari 115a 7.05 S 111.05 E
Wirral □⁸ 262 53.22 N 3.05 W
Wirral ≻¹ 44 53.20 N 3.03 W
Wirraminna 166 31.12 S 136.15 E
Wirrulla 162 32.24 S 134.31 E
Wisbech 42 52.40 N 0.10 E
Wisby → Visby 26 57.38 N 18.18 E
Wiscasset 188 44.00 N 69.39 W
Wischhafen 52 53.46 N 9.19 E
Wisconsin □³, U.S. 178 44.45 N 89.30 W
Wisconsin □³, U.S. 190 44.45 N 89.30 W
Wisconsin ≐ 190 43.00 N 91.10 W
Wisconsin, Lake ⊜¹ 190 43.24 N 89.43 W
Wisconsin Dells 190 43.37 N 89.46 W
Wisconsin Dells V 190 43.41 N 89.49 W
Wisconsin Rapids 190 44.23 N 89.49 W
Wiscoy 210 42.30 N 78.05 W
Wisdom 202 45.37 N 113.27 W
Wisdom, Lake ⊜ 164 5.20 S 147.05 E
Wise 192 36.58 N 82.34 W
Wise □⁶ 222 33.07 N 97.40 W
Wise ≐ 202 45.48 N 112.57 W
Wiseman 180 67.25 N 150.06 W
Wisemans Ferry 170 33.24 S 150.59 E
Wises Landing 218 38.35 N 85.25 W
Wishart 184 51.34 N 104.00 W
Wishaw 46 55.47 N 3.56 W
Wishek 198 46.16 N 99.33 W
Wishkah ≐ 224 46.58 N 123.45 W
Wishram 224 45.39 N 120.57 W
Wiske ≐ 44 54.15 N 1.26 W
Wisła 30 49.40 N 18.52 E
Wisła ≐ 30 54.22 N 18.55 E
Wisley Aerodrome ✈ 260 51.18 N 0.28 W
Wisley Gardens ♦ 260 51.19 N 0.29 W
Wisłok ≐ 30 50.13 N 22.32 E
Wisłoka ≐ 30 50.27 N 21.23 E
Wismar, Dtsch. 54 53.53 N 11.28 E
Wismar, Guy. 246 6.00 N 58.18 W
Wismarbucht c 54 53.57 N 11.25 E
Wisner, La., U.S. 194 31.58 N 91.39 W
Wisner, Ne., U.S. 198 41.59 N 96.54 W
Wissahickon Creek ≐ 285 40.01 N 75.12 W
Wissant 50 50.53 N 1.40 E
Wissembourg 56 49.02 N 7.57 E
Wissen 56 50.47 N 7.43 E
Wissenkerke 52 51.35 N 3.45 E
Wissey ≐ 42 52.33 N 0.21 E
Wissinoming ◆⁸ 285 40.01 N 75.04 W
Wissmar 56 50.38 N 8.41 E
Wissous 261 48.44 N 2.20 E
Wister 194 34.58 N 94.43 W
Wisznice 30 51.48 N 23.12 E
Witbank 158 25.56 S 29.07 E
Witberge ⋏ 158 30.45 S 27.32 E
Witbooisvlei 156 25.04 S 18.27 E
Witchekan Lake ⊜ 184 53.25 N 107.35 W
Witches Falls National Park ♦ 171a 27.56 S 153.10 E
Witch Hazel 224 45.30 N 122.46 W
Witdraai 158 26.58 S 20.45 E
Witfield 273d 26.11 S 28.12 E
Witham 42 51.48 N 0.38 E
Witham ≐ 44 53.06 N 0.13 W
Withamsville 218 39.03 N 84.16 W
Withens Clough Reservoir ⊜¹ 262 53.42 N 2.02 W
Witheridge 42 50.55 N 3.42 W
Withernsea 44 53.44 N 0.02 E
Witherspoon, Mount ∧ 180 61.23 N 147.12 W
Withington ◆⁸ 262 53.26 N 2.14 W
Withington Green 262 53.14 N 2.18 W
Withlacoochee ≐, U.S. 192 30.24 N 83.10 W
Withlacoochee ≐, Fl., U.S. 192 29.00 N 82.45 W
Withnell 262 53.42 N 2.34 W
Withokspruit ≐ 273d 26.19 S 28.21 E
Witjira National Park ♦ 162 26.25 S 135.40 E
Wit-Kei ≐ 158 32.09 S 27.24 E
Witkoppies ∧ 158 27.44 S 29.20 E
Witkowo 30 52.27 N 17.47 E
Witless Bay 186 47.16 N 52.50 W
Witley 42 51.09 N 0.38 W
Wit-Mfolozi ≐ 158 28.22 S 31.58 E
Witney 42 51.48 N 1.29 W
Witnica 30 52.40 N 14.55 E
Wit Nossob ≐ 156 23.05 S 18.45 E
Witpoort 158 27.10 S 26.08 E
Witrivier 156 24.40 S 31.00 E
Witry-lès-Reims 50 49.18 N 4.07 E
Witsand 158 34.24 S 20.50 E
Witt 219 39.15 N 89.20 W
Wittabrenna Creek ≐ 166 29.20 S 142.43 E
Witteberg ⋏ 158 28.40 S 28.02 E
Witteberge ⋏ 158 33.18 S 20.36 E
Wittelsheim 58 47.49 N 7.15 E
Witten 56 51.26 N 7.20 E
Wittenau ◆⁸ 264a 52.35 N 13.20 E
Wittenberg, Dtsch. 54 51.52 N 12.39 E
Wittenberg, Wi., U.S. 190 44.49 N 89.10 W
Wittenberge 54 53.00 N 11.44 E
Wittenburg 54 53.31 N 11.04 E
Wittenheim 58 47.49 N 7.20 E
Wittenoom 162 22.17 S 118.19 E
Wittensee ⊜ 41 54.23 N 9.45 E
Wittering 42 52.37 N 0.27 W
Wittgensdorf 54 50.53 N 12.52 E
Wittichenau 54 51.23 N 14.14 E
Wittingen 54 52.43 N 10.44 E
Wittislingen 56 48.37 N 10.25 E
Wittlaer 56 51.19 N 6.44 E
Wittlich 56 49.59 N 6.53 E
Wittman 208 38.47 N 76.17 W
Wittmar 54 52.07 N 10.38 E
Wittmund 52 53.34 N 7.47 E
Witton Park ♦ 262 53.45 N 2.31 W
Wittow ≻¹ 54 54.38 N 13.19 E
Wittstock 54 53.10 N 12.29 E
Witu 154 2.23 S 40.26 E
Witu Islands II 164 4.40 S 149.25 E

ENGLISH

Name Page Lat.°′ Long.°′

Witvlai 156 22.23 S 18.32 E
Witwatersrand, University of the ᵾ² 273d 26.12 S 28.02 E
Witwatersrand Gold Mine ◆⁷ 273d 26.12 S 28.11 E
Witwatersrant ◆¹ 158 26.00 S 27.00 E
Witzenhausen 56 51.20 N 9.51 E
Witzhelden 263 51.07 N 7.06 E
Witzputz 156 27.25 S 17.43 E
Wiveliscombe 42 51.03 N 3.19 W
Wivenhoe 42 51.52 N 0.58 E
Wivenhoe Reservoir ⊜¹ 171a 27.20 S 152.35 E
Wiwa Creek ≐ 184 50.02 N 106.31 W
Wixom 216 42.31 N 83.32 W
Wiżajny 30 54.23 N 22.51 E
Wizernes 50 50.43 N 2.14 E
Wjatka → V'atka ≐ 80 55.36 N 51.30 E
W. Kerr Scott Reservoir ⊜¹ 192 36.07 N 81.15 W
Wkra ≐ 30 52.27 N 20.44 E
Wladiwostok → Vladivostok 89 43.10 N 131.56 E
Władysławowo 30 54.49 N 18.25 E
Wleń 30 51.01 N 15.40 E
Wlingi 115a 8.05 S 112.19 E
Włocławek 30 52.39 N 19.02 E
Włocławek □⁴ 30 52.30 N 19.05 E
Włodawa 30 51.34 N 23.32 E
Włoszczowa 30 50.52 N 19.59 E
Wnion ≐ 42 52.45 N 3.54 W
Woady Yaloak ≐ 169 38.06 S 143.33 E
Wobaer 85 39.19 N 75.32 E
Wöbbelin 54 53.24 N 11.30 E
Woburn 207 42.28 N 71.09 W
Woburn ◆⁸ 275b 43.46 N 79.13 W
Woburn Sands 42 52.01 N 0.39 W
Woden, Austl. 171b 35.22 S 149.08 E
Woden, Tx., U.S. 222 31.30 N 94.32 W
Wodgina 162 21.11 S 118.40 E
Wodonga 166 36.07 S 146.54 E
Wodzisław Śląski 30 50.00 N 18.28 E
Woensdrecht 52 51.26 N 4.18 E
Woerdeke 85 39.41 N 77.53 E
Woerden 52 52.05 N 4.54 E
Woerth 56 48.56 N 7.45 E
Woëvre ◆¹ 56 49.05 N 5.40 E
Wofosi 105 40.09 N 115.18 E
Wo Fo Si (Temple of the Sleeping Buddha) ᵾ¹ 105 40.01 N 116.12 E
Wognum 52 52.41 N 5.01 E
Wohlde 41 54.24 N 9.17 E
Wohlen 58 47.21 N 8.17 E
Wohlensee ⊜ 58 46.58 N 7.20 E
Wohlford, Lake ⊜¹ 228 33.10 N 116.59 W
Wohlthat Mountains ⋏ 9 71.35 S 12.20 E
Wohra ≐ 56 50.49 N 8.55 E
Woi 140 7.53 N 31.10 E
Woincourt 50 50.04 N 1.32 E
Woippy, Dtsch. 56 49.09 N 6.09 E
Woippy, Fr. 56 49.09 N 6.09 E
Wojcieszów 30 50.58 N 15.56 E
Wokalup 168a 33.06 S 115.53 E
Wokam, Pulau I 164 5.37 S 134.30 E
Wokha 120 26.06 N 94.16 E
Woking, Ab., Can. 182 55.35 N 118.46 W
Woking, Eng., U.K. 42 51.20 N 0.34 W
Woking □⁸ 260 51.19 N 0.32 W
Wokingham 42 51.25 N 0.51 W
Wokingham Creek ≐ 166 22.19 S 142.30 E
Wolbach 198 41.24 N 98.24 W
Wolbeck 52 51.55 N 7.43 E
Wolbrom 30 50.24 N 19.46 E
Wolcott, Ct., U.S. 207 41.36 N 72.59 W
Wolcott, In., U.S. 216 40.45 N 87.02 W
Wolcott, N.Y., U.S. 210 43.13 N 76.48 W
Wolcott Creek ≐ 210 43.17 N 76.50 W
Wolcottsburg 210 43.04 N 78.38 W
Wolcottsville 210 43.07 N 78.31 W
Wolcottville 216 41.32 N 85.22 W
Wołcza ≐ 54 53.58 N 14.53 E
Wołczenica ≐ 54 53.52 N 14.44 E
Wołczyn 30 51.01 N 18.03 E
Woldberg ⋏¹ 52 52.25 N 5.55 E
Woldegk 54 53.27 N 13.35 E
Woldingham 260 51.17 N 0.02 W
Woleai I¹ 108 7.21 N 143.52 E
Woleu-Ntem □⁴ 152 1.30 N 12.00 E
Wolf ≐, On., Can. 190 48.49 N 88.30 W
Wolf ≐, U.S. 194 35.09 N 90.04 W
Wolf ≐, Ks., U.S. 198 39.54 N 95.11 W
Wolf ≐, Ms., U.S. 194 30.21 N 89.18 W
Wolf ≐, Wi., U.S. 190 44.11 N 88.48 W
Wolf, Isla I 246a 1.23 N 91.49 W
Wolf, Volcán ∧¹ 246a 0.02 N 91.20 W
Wolfach 58 48.17 N 8.13 E
Wolf-Bay 186 50.16 N 60.08 W
Wolf Creek, Mt., U.S. 202 47.00 N 112.04 W
Wolf Creek, Or., U.S. 202 42.41 N 123.23 W
Wolf Creek ≐, U.S. 196 36.35 N 99.30 W
Wolf Creek ≐, Ca., U.S. 226 39.02 N 121.08 W
Wolf Creek ≐, Co., U.S. 200 40.12 N 108.29 W
Wolf Creek ≐, In., U.S. 216 41.15 N 87.07 W
Wolf Creek ≐, Ia., U.S. 190 42.20 N 92.09 W
Wolf Creek ≐, Mt., U.S. 198 48.05 N 105.40 W
Wolf Creek ≐, Mt., U.S. 202 47.37 N 109.38 W
Wolf Creek ≐, Oh., U.S. 214 41.16 N 83.11 W
Wolf Creek ≐, Pa., U.S. 214 41.03 N 80.07 W
Wolf Creek ≐, S.D., U.S. 198 43.21 N 97.37 W
Wolf Creek ≐, S.D., U.S. 198 44.42 N 98.40 W
Wolf Creek Lake ⊜¹ 198 38.14 N 95.41 W
Wolf Creek Pass)(200 37.29 N 106.48 W
Wolf Creek State Park ♦ 219 39.30 N 88.41 W
Wolfdale 214 40.12 N 80.17 W
Wolfe □⁶ 206 45.45 N 71.30 W
Wolfeboro 188 43.35 N 71.12 W
Wolfe City 196 33.22 N 96.04 W
Wolfegg 58 47.49 N 9.47 E
Wolfe Island 212 44.12 N 76.26 W
Wolfe Island I 212 44.12 N 76.20 W
Wolfe Lake ⊜ 212 44.40 N 76.30 W
Wolfen 54 51.40 N 12.16 E
Wolfenbüttel 52 52.10 N 10.32 E
Wolfenden, Mount ∧ 182 50.26 N 127.33 W
Wolfenschiessen 58 46.55 N 8.24 E
Wolfertschwenden 58 47.53 N 10.16 E
Wolfforth 196 33.30 N 102.01 W
Wolfgangsee ⊜ 64 47.44 N 13.26 E
Wolfhagen 56 51.19 N 9.10 E
Wölfis 54 50.48 N 10.46 E
Wolf Island I 212 44.33 N 78.15 W
Wolflake, In., U.S. 216 41.20 N 85.30 W
Wolf Lake, Mi., U.S. 216 43.15 N 86.06 W
Wolf Lake ⊜, Ab., Can. 182 54.42 N 110.59 W
Wolf Lake ⊜, On., Can. 212 44.44 N 78.11 W
Wolf Lake ⊜, Yk., Can. 180 60.40 N 131.40 W
Wolf Lake ⊜, U.S. 278 41.40 N 87.31 W
Wolf Lake ⊜, N.J., U.S. 276 40.57 N 74.42 W
Wolf Mountain ∧ 180 65.17 N 154.02 W
Wolfpassing 264b 48.19 N 16.11 E
Wolf Point 202 48.05 N 105.38 W
Wolframs-Eschenbach 56 49.14 N 10.43 E

DEUTSCH

Name Seite Breite°′ Länge°′ E = Ost

Wolfratshausen 64 47.54 N 11.25 E
Wolf Rock I² 28 49.57 N 5.49 W
Wolf Run 214 40.30 N 80.54 W
Wolfsberg 61 46.51 N 14.51 E
Wolfsberg ∧² 263 51.38 N 6.27 E
Wolfsburg 54 52.25 N 10.47 E
Wolf's Castle 42 51.54 N 4.58 W
Wolfsegg am Hausruck 60 48.06 N 13.40 E
Wolfstein 56 49.35 N 7.36 E
Wolftrap Creek ≐ 284c 38.58 N 77.17 W
Wolf Trap Farms for the Performing Arts ♦ 284c 38.56 N 77.16 W
Wolfurt 58 47.28 N 9.45 E
Wolfville 186 45.05 N 64.22 W
Wolga → Volga ≐ 72 45.55 N 47.52 E
Wolgan ≐ 170 33.12 S 150.28 E
Wolgast 54 54.03 N 13.46 E
Wolgograd → Volgograd 80 48.44 N 44.25 E
Wolgograder Stausee → Volgogradskoje vodochranilišče ⊜¹ 80 49.20 N 45.00 E
Wolhusen 58 47.04 N 8.04 E
Wolin 30 53.50 N 14.35 E
Wolin I 54 53.55 N 14.31 E
Woliński Park Narodowy ♦ 30 53.55 N 14.30 E
Wolkenstein 54 50.39 N 13.04 E
Wolkersdorf 61 48.23 N 16.31 E
Wölkisch 54 51.13 N 13.21 E
Wolkramshausen 54 51.25 N 10.44 E
Wollangambe ≐ 170 33.21 S 150.35 E
Wollaston 42 52.15 N 0.40 W
Wollaston, Islas II 254 55.40 S 67.30 W
Wollaston Beach ≗² 283 42.17 N 71.01 W
Wollaston Lake ⊜, On., Can. 212 44.50 N 77.50 W
Wollaston Lake ⊜, Sk., Can. 176 58.15 N 103.20 W
Wollaston Peninsula ≻¹ 176 70.00 N 115.00 W
Wollemi Creek ≐ 170 33.13 S 150.31 E
Wollemi National Park ♦ 166 32.50 S 150.30 E
Wollogorang 166 17.13 S 137.57 E
Wollombi 170 32.56 S 151.09 E
Wollombi Brook ≐ 170 32.33 S 151.04 E
Wollondilly ≐ 170 33.57 S 150.26 E
Wollongong 170 34.25 S 150.54 E
Wöllstein 56 49.49 N 7.58 E
Wolmaransstad 158 27.12 S 26.13 E
Wolmirsleben 54 51.57 N 11.29 E
Wolmirstedt 54 52.15 N 11.37 E
Wolnzach 60 48.36 N 11.37 E
Wołomin 30 52.21 N 21.14 E
Wołów 30 51.21 N 16.39 E
Wolowaru 115b 8.46 S 121.54 E
Wolseley, Sk., Can. 184 50.25 N 103.19 W
Wolseley, S. Afr. 158 33.26 S 19.12 E
Wolsey 198 44.24 N 98.28 W
Wolsingham 44 54.44 N 1.52 W
Wolsztyn 30 52.08 N 16.06 E
Wolterdingen 52 53.02 N 9.50 E
Woltersdorf, Dtsch. 54 52.24 N 12.22 E
Woltersdorf, Dtsch. 54 52.26 N 13.45 E
Woluogu 105 39.40 N 117.46 E
Woluwe-Saint-Lambert (Sint-Lambrechts-Woluwe) 56 50.51 N 4.24 E
Wolvega 52 52.53 N 6.00 E
Wolverhampton 42 52.36 N 2.08 W
Wolverine 190 45.16 N 84.36 W
Wolverine Lake 281 42.33 N 83.29 W
Wolverine Loon Lake ⊜ 281 42.33 N 83.30 W
Wolverine Mountain ∧ 180 65.20 N 149.51 W
Wolvertem 50 50.57 N 4.18 E
Wolverton 42 52.04 N 0.50 W
Wolwehoek 158 26.55 S 27.48 E
Wölzerbach ≐ 61 47.08 N 14.23 E
Wolziger See ⊜ 54 52.16 N 13.50 E
Woman ≐ 190 47.57 N 82.19 W
Wombarra 170 34.16 S 150.58 E
Wombat, Mount ∧ 169 36.51 S 145.40 E
Wombeyan Caves ≗⁵ 170 34.18 S 149.56 E
Wombourne 42 52.32 N 2.11 W
Wombwell 44 53.31 N 1.24 W
Womelsdorf 208 40.22 N 76.11 W
Women's Rights National Historical Park ♦ 210 42.54 N 76.47 W
Wommels 52 53.06 N 5.36 E
Wompatuck State Park ♦ 283 42.13 N 70.51 W
Wonarah 162 19.55 S 136.20 E
Wondai 166 26.19 S 151.52 E
Wondelgem 50 51.05 N 3.43 E
Wonderfonteinspruit ≐ 273d 26.16 S 27.42 E
Wonderkop 158 27.50 S 27.26 E
Wonder Lake 216 42.25 N 88.21 W
Wonderland 204 40.24 N 121.19 W
Wonderland Center ◆⁹ 281 42.22 N 83.20 W
Wondinong 162 27.52 S 118.25 E
Wŏndong-ni 98 34.23 N 126.40 E
Wonersh 260 51.12 N 0.33 W
Wonewoc 190 43.39 N 90.13 W
Wong ≐ 124 27.10 N 89.30 E
Wongan Hills 162 30.53 S 116.42 E
Wonga Park 274b 37.44 S 145.16 E
Wonga-Wongué, Parc National de ♦ 152 0.30 S 9.30 E
Wonggarasi 112 0.33 N 121.36 E
Wong Ka Wai 271d 22.24 N 113.58 E
Woniushi 104 42.31 N 123.03 E
Wŏnjang-ni 98 39.05 N 125.32 E
Wŏnju 98 37.22 N 127.58 E
Wonogiri 115a 7.49 S 110.55 E
Wonokromo 115a 7.18 S 112.44 E
Wonosari 115a 7.58 S 110.35 E
Wonosegoro 115a 7.18 S 110.39 E
Wonosobo 115a 7.22 S 109.54 E
Wonotobo Vallen ∟ 250 4.22 N 57.58 W
Wonreli 112 8.05 S 127.09 E
Wŏnsan 98 39.09 N 127.25 E
Wonthaggi 169 38.36 S 145.35 E
Woocalla 166 31.42 S 137.13 E
Wood, Pa., U.S. 214 40.10 N 78.08 W
Wood, S.D., U.S. 198 43.29 N 100.28 W
Wood □⁶, Oh., U.S. 216 41.22 N 83.39 W
Wood □⁶, Tx., U.S. 222 32.48 N 95.20 W
Wood ≐, B.C., Can. 182 52.10 N 118.30 W
Wood ≐, Sk., Can. 184 50.08 N 106.10 W
Wood ≐, U.S. 207 41.26 N 71.43 W
Wood ≐, Ak., U.S. 180 64.35 N 148.41 W
Wood ≐, Ne., U.S. 198 41.02 N 98.05 W
Wood ≐, Wy., U.S. 202 44.07 N 108.58 W
Wood, Mount ∧, Yk., Can. 180 61.14 N 140.31 W
Wood, Mount ∧, Mt., U.S. 202 45.17 N 109.49 W
Woodacre 226 38.05 N 122.36 W
Woodall Mountain ∧² 194 34.45 N 88.11 W
Wood Bay c 180 69.45 N 129.00 W
Woodberry Forest 284c 38.48 N 76.56 W
Woodbine, Ga., U.S. 192 30.57 N 81.43 W
Woodbine, Ia., U.S. 198 41.44 N 95.42 W
Woodbine, Md., U.S. 208 39.21 N 77.03 W
Woodbine, N.J., U.S. 208 39.14 N 74.48 W
Woodbourne, N.Y., U.S. 210 41.45 N 74.35 W
Woodbourne, Oh., U.S. 218 39.38 N 84.10 W

Symbols in the index entries represent the broad categories identified in the key at the right. Symbols with superior numbers (⋏¹) identify subcategories (see complete key on page *I · 1).*

Symbole im Register stellen die rechts im Schlüssel erklärten Kategorien dar. Symbole mit hochgestellten Ziffern (⋏¹) bezeichnen Unterabteilungen einer Kategorie (vgl. vollständiger Schlüssel auf Seite *I · 1).*

Los símbolos incluídos en el texto del índice representan las grandes categorías identificadas con la clave a la derecha. Los símbolos con numeros en su parte superior (⋏¹) identifican las subcategorías (véase la clave completa en la página *I · 1).*

Les symboles de l'index représentent les catégories indiquées dans la légende à droite. Les symboles suivis d'un indice (⋏¹) représentent des sous-catégories (voir légende complète à la page *I · 1).*

Os símbolos incluídos no texto do índice representam as grandes categorias identificadas com a chave à direita. Os símbolos com números em sua parte superior (⋏¹) identificam as subcategorias (veja-se a chave completa à página *I · 1).*

∧ Mountain	Berg	Montaña	Montagne	Montanha
⋏ Mountains	Gebirge	Montañas	Montagnes	Montanhas
)(Pass	Paß	Paso	Col	Passo
V Valley, Canyon	Tal, Cañon	Valle, Cañón	Vallée, Canyon	Vale, Canhão
≚ Plain	Ebene	Llano	Plaine	Planície
≻ Cape	Kap	Cabo	Cap	Cabo
I Island	Insel	Isla	Île	Ilha
II Islands	Inseln	Islas	Îles	Ilhas
≗ Other Topographic Features	Andere Topographische Objekte	Otros Elementos Topográficos	Autres données topographiques	Outros acidentes topográficos

ESPAÑOL

Nombre	Página	Lat. °′	Long. °′ W = Oeste
Woodbourne, Pa., U.S.	285	40.12 N	74.53 W
Woodbridge, Eng., U.K.	42	52.06 N	1.19 E
Woodbridge, Ca., U.S.	226	38.09 N	121.18 W
Woodbridge, Ct., U.S.	207	41.21 N	73.00 W
Woodbridge, N.J., U.S.	210	40.33 N	74.17 W
Woodbridge, Va., U.S.	208	38.39 N	77.15 W
Woodbridge Center ◆[9]	276	40.33 N	74.18 W
Woodbridge Creek ≃	276	40.32 N	74.15 W
Woodbridge Island I	283	42.48 N	70.50 W
Woodburn, Il., U.S.	219	39.03 N	90.00 W
Woodburn, In., U.S.	216	41.07 N	84.51 W
Woodburn, Or., U.S.	224	45.08 N	122.51 W
Woodbury, Eng., U.K.	42	50.41 N	3.24 W
Woodbury, Ct., U.S.	207	41.32 N	73.12 W
Woodbury, Ga., U.S.	192	32.59 N	84.34 W
Woodbury, Mi., U.S.	216	42.46 N	85.05 W
Woodbury, N.J., U.S.	208	39.50 N	75.09 W
Woodbury, N.Y., U.S.	276	40.49 N	73.28 W
Woodbury, Pa., U.S.	214	40.14 N	78.22 W
Woodbury, Tn., U.S.	194	35.49 N	86.04 W
Woodbury Creek ≃	285	39.52 N	75.11 W
Woodbury Heights	285	39.49 N	75.09 W
Woodchester	168b	35.13 S	138.57 E
Woodchopper	180	65.18 N	143.25 W
Woodchurch	42	51.05 N	0.46 E
Woodcliff Lake	276	41.01 N	74.04 W
Woodcliff Lake ⊜	276	41.01 N	74.03 W
Woodcock	214	41.45 N	80.05 W
Woodcock, Mount ∧	162	19.16 S	134.02 E
Woodcrest, Ca., U.S.	228	33.52 N	117.21 W
Woodcrest, Pa., U.S.	285	39.59 N	75.35 W
Wood Dale	278	41.57 N	87.58 W
Woodenbong	166	28.23 S	152.37 E
Woodend	169	37.22 S	144.32 E
Woodfibre	182	49.40 N	123.15 W
Woodfield ◆[9]	278	42.03 N	88.03 W
Woodford, Austl.	171a	26.57 S	152.47 E
Woodford, Ire.	48	53.03 N	8.23 W
Woodford, Eng., U.K.	262	53.21 N	2.10 W
Woodford □[6], Il., U.S.	216	40.43 N	89.16 W
Woodford □[6], Ky., U.S.	218	38.06 N	84.15 W
Woodford ◆[8]	260	51.36 N	0.02 E
Woodford Aerodrome ⊠	262	53.20 N	2.09 W
Woodford Bridge ◆[8]	260	51.36 N	0.04 E
Woodford Halse	42	52.10 N	1.12 W
Wood Green ◆[8]	260	51.36 N	0.07 W
Woodhall Spa	44	53.09 N	0.13 W
Woodham	260	51.21 N	0.30 W
Woodham Ferrers	260	51.40 N	0.36 E
Woodham Mortimer	260	51.43 N	0.37 E
Woodham Walter	260	51.44 N	0.37 E
Woodhaven	216	42.08 N	83.14 W
Woodhaven ◆[8]	276	40.41 N	73.51 W
Woodhead Reservoir ⊜[1]	262	53.30 N	1.52 W
Woodhill	275b	43.45 N	79.41 W
Wood Hill ∧[2]	283	42.39 N	71.13 W
Woodhull, Il., U.S.	190	41.10 N	90.18 W
Woodhull, N.Y., U.S.	210	42.05 N	77.25 W
Woodinville	224	47.45 N	122.09 W
Wood Islands	186	45.58 N	62.45 W
Woodlake, Ca., U.S.	204	36.25 N	119.06 W
Wood Lake, Ne., U.S.	198	42.38 N	100.14 W
Woodlake, Tx., U.S.	222	31.01 N	95.02 W
Wood Lake ⊜, On., Can.	212	45.01 N	79.05 W
Wood Lake ⊜, Sk., Can.	184	55.17 N	103.17 W
Woodland, Ca., U.S.	226	38.40 N	121.46 W
Woodland, Ga., U.S.	192	32.47 N	84.33 W
Woodland, Il., U.S.	216	40.43 N	87.44 W
Woodland, Me., U.S.	188	45.09 N	67.24 W
Woodland, Mi., U.S.	216	42.43 N	85.08 W
Woodland, N.C., U.S.	192	36.19 N	77.12 W
Woodland, Pa., U.S.	214	40.59 N	78.20 W
Woodland, Wa., U.S.	224	45.54 N	122.44 W
Woodland Beach	216	41.57 N	83.19 W
Woodland Heights	214	41.25 N	79.43 W
Woodland Hills ◆[8]	280	34.11 N	118.35 W
Woodland Hills Park ♦	279a	41.28 N	81.36 W
Woodland Park, Co., U.S.	200	38.59 N	105.03 W
Woodland Park, Pa., U.S.	210	41.18 N	77.03 W
Woodlands, N.Z.	172	46.22 S	168.33 E
Woodlands, Sing.	271c	1.27 N	103.46 E
Woodlands, N.Y., U.S.	276	41.01 N	73.50 W
Woodlawn, Il., U.S.	219	38.20 N	89.02 W
Woodlawn, Ky., U.S.	194	37.02 N	88.34 W
Woodlawn, Md., U.S.	284b	39.19 N	76.43 W
Woodlawn, Md., U.S.	284c	38.57 N	76.53 W
Woodlawn, Wa., U.S.	224	47.01 N	123.48 W
Woodlawn ◆[8]	278	41.47 N	87.36 W
Woodlawn Beach	210	42.48 N	78.51 W
Woodlawn Heights	284b	39.11 N	76.39 W
Woodley	42	51.28 N	0.54 W
Woodlyn	285	39.52 N	75.20 W
Woodlynne	285	39.55 N	75.05 W
Woodmansey	44	53.50 N	0.29 W
Woodmansterne	260	51.19 N	0.10 W
Woodmere, N.Y., U.S.	210	40.37 N	73.42 W
Woodmere, Oh., U.S.	279a	41.28 N	81.29 W
Woodmoor	284b	39.20 N	76.44 W
Wood Mountain ∧	184	49.14 N	106.20 W
Wood Mountain Indian Reserve ◆[4]	184	49.21 N	106.24 W
Woodplumpton	262	53.48 N	2.47 W
Woodport	276	40.59 N	74.36 W
Woodrarung Range ϰ	162	27.10 S	115.30 E
Woodridge, Austl.	171a	27.38 S	153.06 E
Woodridge, Mb., Can.	184	49.17 N	96.09 W
Woodridge, Il., U.S.	216	41.44 N	88.03 W
Wood-Ridge, N.J., U.S.	276	40.50 N	74.05 W
Woodridge, N.Y., U.S.	210	41.43 N	74.34 W
Wood River, Ak., U.S.	180	59.04 N	158.26 W
Wood River, Il., U.S.	219	38.51 N	90.05 W
Wood River, Ne., U.S.	198	40.49 N	98.35 W
Wood River Lakes ⊜	180	59.30 N	158.45 W
Wood River Mountains ϰ	180	59.32 N	159.30 W
Woodroffe ≃	166	21.28 S	137.58 E
Woodroffe, Mount ∧	162	26.20 S	131.45 E
Woodrow	192	35.08 N	77.05 W
Woodrow Wilson Memorial Bridge ◆[5]	284c	38.48 N	77.02 W
Woodruff, Az., U.S.	200	34.46 N	110.02 W
Woodruff, S.C., U.S.	192	34.44 N	82.02 W
Woodruff, Wi., U.S.	190	45.53 N	89.41 W
Woodruff Creek ≃	281	42.21 N	83.43 W
Woods	168b	34.15 S	138.31 E
Woods, Lake ⊜	162	17.50 S	133.30 E
Woods, Lake of the ⊜	184	49.15 N	94.45 W
Woods Bay ⊂	212	45.08 N	80.00 W
Woodsboro, Md., U.S.	208	39.31 N	77.18 W
Woodsboro, Tx., U.S.	196	28.14 N	97.19 W
Woodsburgh	276	40.37 N	73.42 W
Woods Creek ≃, N.Y., U.S.	276	40.39 N	73.24 W

FRANÇAIS

Nom	Page	Lat. °′	Long. °′ W = Ouest
Woods Creek ≃, N.Y., U.S.	284a	43.04 N	78.58 W
Woodsfield	188	39.45 N	81.06 W
Woods Hole	207	41.31 N	70.40 W
Woodside, Austl.	166	38.31 S	146.52 E
Woodside, Austl.	168b	34.57 S	138.52 E
Woodside, Eng., U.K.	260	51.45 N	0.11 W
Woodside, Ca., U.S.	226	37.25 N	122.15 W
Woodside, De., U.S.	208	39.04 N	75.34 W
Woodside, Pa., U.S.	285	40.13 N	74.53 W
Woodside ◆[8]	276	40.45 N	73.55 W
Woodside National Historic Park ♦	212	43.26 N	80.08 W
Woodson, Il., U.S.	219	39.38 N	90.13 W
Woodson, Tx., U.S.	196	33.01 N	99.03 W
Woods Point	169	37.35 S	146.15 E
Woods Reservoir ⊜[1]	194	35.20 N	86.00 W
Woodstock, Austl.	166	22.15 S	141.57 E
Woodstock, N.B., Can.	186	46.09 N	67.34 W
Woodstock, On., Can.	212	43.08 N	80.45 W
Woodstock, Eng., U.K.	42	51.52 N	1.21 W
Woodstock, Ct., U.S.	207	41.56 N	71.58 W
Woodstock, Il., U.S.	216	42.18 N	88.26 W
Woodstock, Md., U.S.	284b	39.19 N	76.52 W
Woodstock, N.Y., U.S.	210	42.02 N	74.07 W
Woodstock, Oh., U.S.	218	40.10 N	83.32 W
Woodstock, Vt., U.S.	188	43.37 N	72.31 W
Woodstock, Va., U.S.	188	38.52 N	78.30 W
Woodstown	208	39.39 N	75.19 W
Wood Street	260	51.15 N	0.38 W
Woodsville	188	44.09 N	72.02 W
Woodvale Airfield ⊠	262	53.35 N	3.03 W
Wood Village	224	45.32 N	122.19 W
Woodville, Austl.	168b	34.53 S	138.32 E
Woodville, On., Can.	212	44.24 N	78.59 W
Woodville, N.Z.	172	40.20 S	175.52 E
Woodville, Al., U.S.	194	34.38 N	86.16 W
Woodville, Ca., U.S.	226	36.06 N	119.12 W
Woodville, Fl., U.S.	192	30.20 N	84.15 W
Woodville, Ga., U.S.	192	33.40 N	83.06 W
Woodville, Ma., U.S.	207	42.14 N	71.33 W
Woodville, Mi., U.S.	216	43.39 N	85.40 W
Woodville, Ms., U.S.	194	31.06 N	91.17 W
Woodville, N.Y., U.S.	210	42.40 N	77.22 W
Woodville, Oh., U.S.	214	41.27 N	83.21 W
Woodville, Tx., U.S.	194	30.46 N	94.24 W
Woodward, Ia., U.S.	190	41.51 N	93.55 W
Woodward, Ok., U.S.	196	36.26 N	99.23 W
Woodward, Pa., U.S.	210	40.54 N	77.21 W
Woodward Reservoir ⊜[1]	226	37.51 N	120.52 W
Woodway, Tx., U.S.	222	31.30 N	97.12 W
Woodway, Wa., U.S.	224	47.47 N	122.23 W
Woodworth, Oh., U.S.	214	40.59 N	80.40 W
Woodworth, Wi., U.S.	216	42.34 N	88.00 W
Woody ≃	184	52.30 N	100.51 W
Woody Creek ≃	202	47.27 N	106.21 W
Woody Head >	166	29.22 S	153.22 E
Woody Island	180	57.47 N	152.22 W
Wool	42	50.41 N	2.14 W
Woolacombe	42	51.10 N	4.13 W
Woolamai, Cape >	169	38.34 S	145.21 E
Wool Bay	168b	35.00 S	137.45 E
Wooldridge	158	33.13 S	27.15 E
Wooler	44	55.33 N	2.01 W
Woolford	208	38.30 N	76.11 W
Woolgangie	162	31.10 S	120.32 E
Woolgoolga	166	30.07 S	153.12 E
Woollahra	274a	33.53 S	151.15 E
Woolmarket	194	30.28 N	88.59 W
Woolooware Bay ⊂	274a	34.02 S	151.09 E
Woolpit	42	52.13 N	0.54 E
Woolrich	210	41.12 N	77.23 W
Woolsey Peak ∧	200	33.10 N	112.53 W
Woolston	262	53.24 N	2.32 W
Woolton ◆[8]	262	53.23 N	2.52 W
Woolwich ◆[8]	260	51.29 N	0.04 E
Woomargama	171b	35.50 S	147.15 E
Woomera	166	31.31 S	137.10 E
Woomera Prohibited Area ◆[4]	162	29.45 S	134.30 E
Woonona	170	34.21 S	150.55 E
Woonsocket, R.I., U.S.	207	42.00 N	71.30 W
Woonsocket, S.D., U.S.	198	44.03 N	98.16 W
Woorabinda	166	24.08 S	149.28 E
Wooramel	162	25.44 S	114.17 E
Wooramel ≃	162	25.47 S	114.10 E
Woorim	171a	27.08 S	153.12 E
Wooroloo	168a	31.48 S	116.19 E
Wooster	214	40.48 N	81.56 W
Wootton	42	52.11 N	0.53 W
Wootton Bassett	42	51.33 N	1.54 W
Wootton Wawen	42	52.16 N	1.47 W
Woqooyi Gelbeed □[4]	144	10.00 N	44.00 E
Worb	58	46.56 N	7.34 E
Worbis	54	51.25 N	10.21 E
Worcester, S. Afr.	158	33.39 S	19.27 E
Worcester, Eng., U.K.	42	52.11 N	2.13 W
Worcester, Ma., U.S.	207	42.15 N	71.48 W
Worcester, N.Y., U.S.	210	42.35 N	74.45 W
Worcester, Pa., U.S.	285	40.12 N	75.21 W
Worcester □[6], Md., U.S.	208	38.11 N	75.24 W
Worcester □[6], Ma., U.S.	207	42.16 N	71.48 W
Worcester Municipal Airport ⊠	207	42.16 N	71.52 W
Worden, Il., U.S.	219	38.55 N	89.50 W
Worden, Mt., U.S.	202	45.57 N	108.09 W
Worden Pond ⊜	207	41.26 N	71.35 W
Wördern	61	48.20 N	16.13 E
Wörgl	64	47.29 N	12.04 E
Workai, Pulau I	164	6.40 S	134.40 E
Work Channel ⋓	182	54.30 N	130.15 W
Workers' Stadium ♦	271a	39.55 N	116.27 E
Workington	44	54.39 N	3.35 W
Worksop	44	53.18 N	1.07 W
Workum	52	52.57 N	5.26 E
Worland	202	44.01 N	107.57 W
World End Pond ⊜	283	42.45 N	71.12 W
Worli ◆[8]	272c	19.01 N	72.50 E
Wörlitz	54	51.50 N	12.25 E
Wormerveer	52	52.28 N	4.46 E
Wormhoudt	50	50.53 N	2.28 E
Wormit	46	56.25 N	2.59 W
Wormley	260	51.44 N	0.01 W
Worms	56	49.38 N	8.22 E
Worms Head >	42	51.34 N	4.20 W
Wormshill	260	51.17 N	0.42 E
Wörnitz ≃	56	48.42 N	10.45 E
Woronesch → Voronež	78	51.40 N	39.10 E
Woronoco	207	42.09 N	72.49 W
Woronora	274a	34.01 S	151.03 E
Woronora ≃	274a	34.00 S	151.04 E
Woronora Reservoir ⊜[1]	170	34.08 S	150.56 E
Worplesdon	260	51.16 N	0.37 W
Worpswede	52	53.13 N	8.56 E
Wörrstadt	56	49.50 N	8.07 E
Wörsbach ≃	56	50.22 N	8.09 E
Worsbrough	44	53.31 N	1.29 W
Worsley	262	53.30 N	2.23 W
Worsthorne	262	53.47 N	2.11 W
Wörth, Dtsch.	56	49.48 N	9.09 E
Worth, Dtsch.	263	51.13 N	7.39 E
Worth, Il., U.S.	216	41.41 N	87.47 W
Worth, Lake ⊜[1]	222	32.48 N	97.28 W
Wortham	222	31.47 N	96.27 W
Wörth am Rhein	56	49.03 N	8.16 E

PORTUGUÊS

Nome	Página	Lat. °′	Long. °′ W = Oeste
Wörth an der Donau	60	49.00 N	12.25 E
Wörth an der Isar	60	48.37 N	12.24 E
Worthen	42	52.38 N	3.00 W
Wörther See ⊜	61	46.37 N	14.10 E
Worthing	42	50.48 N	0.23 W
Worthington, In., U.S.	194	39.07 N	86.58 W
Worthington, Md., U.S.	284b	39.14 N	76.47 W
Worthington, Mn., U.S.	198	43.37 N	95.35 W
Worthington, N.Y., U.S.	276	41.02 N	73.50 W
Worthington, Oh., U.S.	214	40.05 N	83.01 W
Worthington, Pa., U.S.	214	40.50 N	79.37 W
Worthington Peak ∧	204	37.55 N	115.37 W
Wörthsee ⊜	60	48.03 N	11.10 E
Worthville, Ky., U.S.	218	38.36 N	85.04 W
Worthville, Pa., U.S.	214	41.02 N	79.08 W
Worton	208	39.16 N	76.05 W
Wŏrun-dong	98	39.36 N	125.20 E
Wosimi	164	2.54 S	134.31 E
Wostok → Vostok ♉[3]	9	78.30 S	106.50 E
Wosu	112	2.21 S	121.50 E
Wotap, Pulau I	164	7.21 S	131.16 E
Wotho I[1]	14	10.06 N	165.59 E
Wotje I[1]	14	9.27 N	170.02 E
Wotton, P.Q., Can.	206	45.44 N	71.48 W
Wotton, Eng., U.K.	260	51.13 N	0.23 W
Wotton-under-Edge	42	51.39 N	2.21 W
Wotu	112	2.35 S	120.48 E
Woudenberg	52	52.05 N	5.25 E
Woudrichem	52	51.49 N	5.00 E
Woudsend	52	52.56 N	5.36 E
Wouldham	260	51.21 N	0.28 E
Wounded Knee	198	43.08 N	102.21 W
Wounded Knee Creek ≃	198	43.26 N	102.32 W
Wounta	236	13.33 N	83.32 W
Wounta, Laguna de ⊂	236	13.38 N	83.34 W
Wour	146	21.21 N	15.57 E
Wouri ≃	152	4.06 N	9.43 E
Woutchaba	152	5.13 N	13.05 E
Wouw	52	51.32 N	4.24 E
Wowan	166	23.55 S	150.12 E
Wowoni, Pulau I	112	4.08 S	123.06 E
Woyla ≃	114	4.18 N	95.56 E
Woy Woy	170	33.30 S	151.20 E
Woźniki	30	50.36 N	19.03 E
Wragby	44	53.18 N	0.19 W
Wrangel Island → Vrangel'a, ostrov I	74	71.00 N	179.30 W
Wrangell	180	56.28 N	132.23 W
Wrangell, Cape >	181a	52.50 N	172.26 E
Wrangell, Mount ∧	180	62.00 N	144.06 W
Wrangell Island I	180	56.15 N	132.10 W
Wrangell Mountains ϰ	180	62.00 N	143.00 W
Wrangell-Saint Elias National Park ♦	180	61.00 N	142.00 W
Wrath, Cape >	46	58.37 N	5.01 W
Wray	198	40.04 N	102.13 W
Wraysbury	260	51.27 N	0.33 W
Wrea Green	262	53.46 N	2.55 W
Wreck Bay ⊂	170	35.11 S	150.40 E
Wreck Island I	208	37.16 N	75.48 W
Wreck Reef ✣[2]	166	22.13 S	155.17 E
Wrecks, Bay of ⊂	174a	1.52 N	157.17 W
Wredenhagen	54	53.17 N	12.31 E
Wremen	52	53.39 N	8.30 E
Wren	216	40.48 N	84.46 W
Wrens	192	33.12 N	82.23 W
Wrentham, Ab., Can.	182	49.32 N	112.10 W
Wrentham, Eng., U.K.	42	52.23 N	1.40 E
Wrentham, Ma., U.S.	207	42.04 N	71.19 W
Wrentham State Forest ♦	283	42.02 N	71.20 W
Wrexham	44	53.03 N	3.00 W
Wriezen	54	52.43 N	14.08 E
Wright, Mount ∧, Austl.	166	31.12 S	142.26 E
Wright, Mount ∧, Mt., U.S.	202	47.58 N	112.49 W
Wright Brothers National Memorial ⊥	192	35.55 N	75.50 W
Wright City, Mo., U.S.	219	38.49 N	91.01 W
Wright City, Ok., U.S.	194	34.03 N	95.00 W
Wright City, Tx., U.S.	222	32.12 N	94.59 W
Wrightington Bar	262	53.37 N	2.42 W
Wright Patman Lake ⊜[1]	194	33.16 N	94.14 W
Wright-Patterson Air Force Base ■	218	39.49 N	84.03 W
Wright Peak ∧	204	38.59 N	122.46 W
Wrights	219	39.23 N	90.18 W
Wrightsboro	222	29.22 N	97.34 W
Wrights Corners	210	43.13 N	78.46 W
Wrightson, Mount ∧	200	31.42 N	110.50 W
Wrightstown, N.J., U.S.	208	40.02 N	74.37 W
Wrightstown, Pa., U.S.	208	40.17 N	74.58 W
Wrightstown, Wi., U.S.	190	44.19 N	88.09 W
Wrightsville, Ga., U.S.	192	32.43 N	82.43 W
Wrightsville, Pa., U.S.	214	40.01 N	76.31 W
Wrightsville Beach	192	34.12 N	77.47 W
Wrightwood	228	34.21 N	117.37 W
Wrigley, N.T., Can.	180	63.16 N	123.37 W
Wrigley, Tn., U.S.	194	35.54 N	87.20 W
Wrigley Field ♦	278	41.57 N	87.39 W
Wrigley Gulf ⊂	9	74.00 S	129.00 W
Writtle	42	51.44 N	0.26 E
Wrocław (Breslau)	30	51.06 N	17.00 E
Wrocław □[4]	30	51.15 N	17.00 E
Wrong Lake ⊜	184	52.38 N	96.10 W
Wronki	30	52.43 N	16.23 E
Wrotham	42	51.19 N	0.19 E
Wrotham Heath	260	51.18 N	0.21 E
Wrottesley, Cape >	176	74.33 N	121.32 W
Wroughton	42	51.31 N	1.46 W
Wroxham	42	52.42 N	1.24 E
Wroxton	184	51.14 N	101.53 W
Września	30	52.20 N	17.34 E
Wschowa	30	51.48 N	16.19 E
Wu ≃, Zhg.	98	34.25 N	117.55 E
Wu ≃, Zhg.	100	28.57 N	116.39 E
Wu ≃, Zhg.	100	24.48 N	113.35 E
Wu ≃, Zhg.	102	27.12 N	109.48 E
Wu ≃, Zhg.	102	29.43 N	107.24 E
Wu ≃, Zhg.	102	27.03 N	109.53 E
Wu'an	98	36.40 N	114.12 E
Wubaozhen	107	29.14 N	104.29 E
Wubin	162	30.06 S	116.38 E
Wubu	102	37.33 N	110.39 E
Wuchagou	89	46.46 N	120.16 E
Wuchang, Zhg.	89	44.54 N	127.08 E
Wuchang → Wuhan, Zhg.	100	30.36 N	114.17 E
Wuchang Hu ⊜	100	30.17 N	116.47 E
Wucheng, Zhg.	98	37.09 N	115.53 E
Wucheng (Jiucheng), Zhg.	98	37.13 N	116.02 E
Wucheng, Zhg.	100	29.36 N	118.10 E
Wucheng, Zhg.	100	33.28 N	113.44 E
Wucheng, Zhg.	100	29.10 N	115.59 E
Wuch'i	100	24.16 N	120.31 E
Wuchin → Changzhou	106	31.47 N	119.57 E
Wuch'iu Yü I	100	25.00 N	119.27 E
Wuchow → Wuzhou	102	23.30 N	111.27 E
Wuchuan, Zhg.	102	21.25 N	110.40 E

Wuchuan, Zhg.	102	28.25 N	107.56 E
Wuchuan, Zhg.	102	41.05 N	111.23 E
Wuchung → Wuzhong	102	37.57 N	106.10 E
Wucun	105	38.57 N	115.19 E
Wuda	102	39.30 N	106.40 E
Wudao	98	39.28 N	121.28 E
Wudaogou, Zhg.	98	41.43 N	127.05 E
Wudaogou, Zhg.	98	42.08 N	125.51 E
Wudaoliang	120	35.11 N	93.35 E
Wudaolianggou	104	40.59 N	120.35 E
Wudi	98	37.44 N	117.35 E
Wudian, Zhg.	100	32.42 N	117.18 E
Wudian, Zhg.	100	31.57 N	112.46 E
Wuding	102	25.32 N	102.23 E
Wuding ≃	102	37.05 N	110.20 E
Wudinna	166	33.03 S	135.28 E
Wudu, Zhg.	100	28.23 N	118.14 E
Wudu, Zhg.	100	27.37 N	119.00 E
Wudu, Zhg.	102	33.24 N	104.50 E
Wuduhe	102	31.03 N	111.03 E
Wuerqihan	89	49.37 N	121.45 E
Wufeng	102	30.11 N	110.33 E
Wufeng Shan I	106	31.07 N	120.16 E
Wufengxi	107	30.37 N	104.29 E
Wufu	100	30.06 N	120.58 E
Wugang	102	26.44 N	110.38 E
Wugong	102	34.20 N	108.04 E
Wugong Shan ∧	100	27.35 N	114.18 E
Wugong Shan ϰ	100	27.21 N	113.50 E
Wugouying	100	33.28 N	114.08 E
Wugunuoer	89	49.10 N	119.19 E
Wuhai	102	39.39 N	106.41 E
Wuhan	100	30.36 N	114.17 E
Wuhe, Zhg.	100	33.10 N	117.54 E
Wuhe, Zhg.	100	24.26 N	115.25 E
Wuhle ≃	264a	52.29 N	13.34 E
Wuhsi → Wuxi	106	31.35 N	120.18 E
Wuhsing → Huzhou	106	30.52 N	120.06 E
Wuhu, Zhg.	100	31.21 N	118.22 E
Wuhu, Zhg.	100	31.11 N	118.35 E
Wuhua	100	23.57 N	115.48 E
Wuhuanchi	104	42.20 N	121.51 E
Wuhuang	107	29.58 N	104.46 E
Wuhudongmiao	102	38.19 N	107.20 E
Wüjang	120	33.38 N	79.50 E
Wuji, Zhg.	98	38.13 N	114.57 E
Wuji, Zhg.	98	34.12 N	119.02 E
Wujia ≃	102	41.10 N	108.45 E
Wujiabeigou	104	40.57 N	123.50 E
Wujiang, Zhg.	100	31.52 N	118.28 E
Wujiang, Zhg.	100	27.14 N	115.15 E
Wujiang, Zhg.	106	31.10 N	120.38 E
Wujiangdu	102	27.16 N	106.48 E
Wujianpu	107	29.10 N	105.50 E
Wujiapai	105	39.32 N	117.18 E
Wujiapu	105	38.52 N	117.07 E
Wujiazhen	107	29.38 N	105.24 E
Wujiazhuang, Zhg.	105	40.35 N	115.20 E
Wujiazhuang, Zhg.	106	32.18 N	120.10 E
Wujiazi, Zhg.	89	46.27 N	123.34 E
Wujiazi, Zhg.	104	42.13 N	122.08 E
Wujiazi, Zhg.	104	42.30 N	121.10 E
Wujing	100	25.16 N	114.36 E
Wukang	106	30.33 N	119.58 E
Wukari	150	7.51 N	9.47 E
Wukeshu, Zhg.	89	46.02 N	123.45 E
Wukeshu, Zhg.	89	44.48 N	126.08 E
Wulai	100	24.52 N	121.33 E
Wulajia	89	48.23 N	129.58 E
Wulanheduojia	102	42.40 N	113.20 E
Wulanhutong	98	41.44 N	114.49 E
Wulanmutou	104	42.23 N	121.21 E
Wulanwusu, Zhg.	86	44.20 N	85.50 E
Wulanwusu, Zhg.	102	41.39 N	107.48 E
Wular Lake ⊜	123	34.20 N	74.33 E
Wulasitai, Zhg.	89	43.15 N	121.27 E
Wulasitai, Zhg.	89	43.28 N	122.44 E
Wulateqianqi	102	40.39 N	109.05 E
Wulaxi	102	28.38 N	101.40 E
Wuleidao Wan ⊂	98	36.55 N	122.00 E
Wulfen	52	51.43 N	7.00 E
Wülfrath	56	51.17 N	7.02 E
Wulfsen	52	53.18 N	10.08 E
Wulfsode	52	53.04 N	10.13 E
Wulften	52	51.40 N	10.10 E
Wulian (Hongning)	98	35.47 N	119.15 E
Wulian Feng ϰ	102	28.03 N	103.57 E
Wuliangdian	104	41.52 N	122.16 E
Wuliang Shan ϰ	102	24.30 N	100.45 E
Wuliaru, Pulau I	164	7.27 S	131.04 E
Wulichuan	102	33.49 N	111.08 E
Wulie ≃	105	40.54 N	117.55 E
Wuling	98	35.53 N	114.36 E
Wuling Shan ∧	105	40.36 N	117.29 E
Wulitaizi	104	41.28 N	123.21 E
Wulizhuang	100	33.49 N	118.57 E
Wulka ≃	61	47.52 N	16.40 E
Wüllen	52	52.04 N	6.58 E
Wullwye Creek ≃	171b	36.30 S	148.49 E
Wulong, Zhg.	102	29.20 N	107.43 E
Wulong, Zhg.	104	41.39 N	124.13 E
Wulong ≃	98	36.35 N	120.56 E
Wulongbei	98	40.21 N	124.16 E
Wulsdorf ◆[8]	52	53.30 N	8.35 E
Wultschau	61	48.42 N	14.50 E
Wulu ≃	85	39.38 N	74.38 E
Wuluhan	115a	8.21 S	113.33 E
Wuluhayingzi	104	42.20 N	121.34 E
Wulumuch'i → Ürümqi	90	43.48 N	87.35 E
Wulumuqi → Ürümqi	90	43.48 N	87.35 E
Wuluo	102	26.09 N	108.15 E
Wulur	164	7.09 S	128.39 E
Wulu Station ◆[5]	271a	39.56 N	116.16 E
Wum	152	6.23 N	10.04 E
Wumang Dao I	98	39.14 N	123.03 E
Wumiaoxiang	107	30.23 N	104.17 E
Wuming	102	23.10 N	108.18 E
Wümme ≃	52	53.10 N	8.44 E
Wunamu	86	46.06 N	85.44 E
Wundowie	168a	31.46 S	116.22 E
Wundwin	110	21.05 N	96.02 E
Wuneba	154	4.50 N	30.20 E
Wungong Brook ≃	168a	32.06 S	115.59 E
Wuning	100	29.17 N	115.06 E
Wünnenberg	52	51.31 N	8.42 E
Wunnummin Lake ⊜	176	52.55 N	89.10 W
Wun Rog	140	9.00 N	28.21 E
Wünschendorf	54	50.48 N	12.05 E
Wünsdorf	54	52.10 N	13.28 E
Wunsiedel	60	50.02 N	12.01 E
Wunstorf	52	52.25 N	9.26 E
Wuntho	110	23.54 N	95.41 E
Wunuer	89	48.53 N	121.15 E
Wupaowan	107	29.50 N	103.59 E
Wupatki National Monument ♦	200	35.24 N	111.14 W
Wuping	100	25.08 N	116.06 E
Wupper ≃	263	51.05 N	7.00 E
Wuppertal, Dtsch.	56	51.16 N	7.11 E
Wuppertal, Dtsch.	263	51.16 N	7.11 E
Wuppertal, S. Afr.	158	32.15 S	19.15 E
Wuqi, Zhg.	100	27.10 N	120.23 E
Wuqi, Zhg.	102	37.08 N	108.10 E
Wuqia	85	39.42 N	75.13 E
Wuqiang (Xiaofan)	98	38.03 N	115.58 E
Wuqing (Yangcun)	105	39.23 N	117.04 E
Wuraming	168a	32.48 S	116.16 E
Wurarga	162	28.25 S	116.17 E
Würenlingen	58	47.32 N	8.16 E
Wurgwitz	54	51.01 N	13.37 E
Wurm ≃, Dtsch.	56	51.08 N	6.10 E
Würm ≃, Dtsch.	56	48.53 N	8.42 E
Würm ≃, Dtsch.	60	48.10 N	11.28 E
Wurmannsquick	60	48.21 N	12.47 E
Wurmberg ∧	54	51.45 N	10.37 E

Wurno	150	13.17 N	5.24 E
Wurong	164	6.07 S	140.47 E
Würselen	56	50.49 N	6.08 E
Wursten, Land ◆[1]	52	53.40 N	8.35 E
Wurtsboro	210	41.35 N	74.29 W
Wurtsboro Hills	210	41.36 N	74.30 W
Wurtsmith Air Force Base ■	190	44.27 N	83.23 W
Wuruf	164	6.43 S	146.25 E
Wuryantoro	115a	7.54 S	110.51 E
Wurzbach	54	50.28 N	11.32 E
Würzburg	56	49.48 N	9.56 E
Wurzen	54	51.22 N	12.44 E
Wusanga	152	3.22 S	22.50 E
Wusha	100	30.39 N	117.18 E
Wushan, Zhg.	100	32.04 N	117.03 E
Wushan, Zhg.	102	34.38 N	105.04 E
Wushan, Zhg.	102	31.05 N	109.48 E
Wushan, Zhg.	106	31.44 N	118.58 E
Wusheng, Zhg.	100	29.56 N	119.25 E
Wusheng, Zhg.	107	30.21 N	106.17 E
Wushengchang	107	29.00 N	103.43 E
Wushenqi	102	38.58 N	109.01 E
Wushi, Zhg.	102	22.11 N	110.11 E
Wushi, Zhg.	106	31.44 N	120.59 E
Wushishi	150	9.46 N	6.07 E
Wushu	100	26.20 N	114.56 E
Wusi	175f	15.22 S	166.36 E
Wusih → Wuxi	106	31.35 N	120.18 E
Wuskwatim Lake ⊜	184	55.32 N	98.32 W
Wusong	106	31.23 N	121.29 E
Wusong ≃	106	31.15 N	121.29 E
Wust	54	52.33 N	12.07 E
Wüsten	52	52.06 N	8.47 E
Wüstensachsen	56	50.30 N	10.00 E
Wusterhausen	54	52.54 N	12.28 E
Wusterhusen	54	54.07 N	13.37 E
Wustermark	54	52.33 N	12.56 E
Wüstermarke	54	51.49 N	13.36 E
Wusterwitz	54	52.22 N	12.18 E
Wüsting	52	53.07 N	8.20 E
Wustrow, Dtsch.	54	54.05 N	11.34 E
Wustrow, Dtsch.	54	52.55 N	11.07 E
Wustrow >[1]	54	54.05 N	11.34 E
Wusuli (Ussuri) ≃	89	48.27 N	135.04 E
Wusuo	100	25.02 N	116.02 E
Wuta	106	31.31 N	120.39 E
Wutach ≃	58	47.37 N	8.15 E
Wutai, Zhg.	85	39.28 N	78.09 E
Wutai, Zhg.	86	44.36 N	82.06 E
Wutai, Zhg.	98	41.18 N	113.59 E
Wutai, Zhg.	102	38.44 N	113.17 E
Wutai Shan ∧	98	39.04 N	113.35 E
Wutai Shan ϰ	98	39.13 N	113.45 E
Wutaizi	104	42.27 N	123.17 E
Wutan	102	28.29 N	111.40 E
Wutanchang	107	29.15 N	106.04 E
Wutang	106	31.31 N	119.10 E
Wutangdun	106	30.38 N	120.08 E
Wutangjie	100	29.59 N	122.22 E
Wuteve, Mount ∧	150	8.09 N	9.56 W
Wutianzhen	100	30.23 N	117.12 E
Wutong	102	25.18 N	110.01 E
Wutonghaolai	89	42.55 N	120.15 E
Wutongqiao	107	29.26 N	103.51 E
Wutongwozi	102	42.27 N	95.17 E
Wutsin → Changzhou	106	31.47 N	119.57 E
Wutun	100	27.51 N	118.04 E
Wut'ungch'iao → Wutongqiao	107	29.26 N	103.51 E
Wutungkiao → Wutongqiao	107	29.26 N	103.51 E
Wutuohuo	102	40.51 N	101.48 E
Wuustwezel	50	51.23 N	4.36 E
Wuvulu Island I	164	1.45 S	142.50 E
Wuwei, Zhg.	100	31.18 N	117.54 E
Wuwei (Liangzhou), Zhg.	102	37.58 N	102.49 E
Wuxi, Zhg.	102	31.25 N	109.34 E
Wuxi, Zhg.	106	31.20 N	118.39 E
Wuxi (Wuhsi), Zhg.	106	31.35 N	120.18 E
Wuxi ≃	100	29.00 N	118.56 E
Wuxiang	102	36.51 N	113.00 E
Wuxingchang	106	31.13 N	119.23 E
Wuxuan	102	23.36 N	109.42 E
Wuyang, Zhg.	100	33.26 N	113.34 E
Wuyang, Zhg.	100	25.41 N	115.55 E
Wuyang, Zhg.	102	26.41 N	110.20 E
Wuyi, Zhg.	98	37.49 N	115.54 E
Wuyi, Zhg.	100	32.13 N	118.26 E
Wuyi, Zhg.	100	28.54 N	119.48 E
Wuying	89	48.05 N	129.15 E
Wuyi Shan ϰ	90	27.52 N	117.40 E
Wuyuan, Zhg.	100	29.15 N	117.49 E
Wuyuan, Zhg.	102	41.06 N	108.29 E
Wuyun	89	49.16 N	129.37 E
Wuyunqiao	100	26.02 N	114.52 E
Wuyur ≃	89	47.00 N	124.10 E
Wuzaizi	104	42.28 N	123.57 E
Wuzhai	102	38.58 N	111.55 E
Wuzhan	89	45.51 N	126.17 E
Wuzhen	106	30.46 N	120.29 E
Wuzhi Shan ∧, Zhg.	105	40.29 N	118.00 E
Wuzhi Shan ∧, Zhg.	110	18.57 N	109.43 E
Wuzhong	102	38.00 N	106.10 E
Wuzhou (Wuchow)	102	23.30 N	111.27 E
Wuzong	106	32.14 N	121.03 E
Wyaaba Creek ≃	164	16.27 S	141.35 E
Wyaconda	194	40.23 N	91.55 W
Wyaconda ≃	194	40.04 N	91.30 W
Wyalkatchem	162	31.10 S	117.22 E
Wyalusing	210	41.40 N	76.15 W
Wyalusing Creek ≃	210	41.40 N	76.16 W
Wyandanch	276	40.45 N	73.21 W
Wyandot	214	40.44 N	83.08 W
Wyandot □[6]	214	40.50 N	83.17 W
Wyandotte	216	42.12 N	83.09 W
Wyandotte Cave ⩡[5]	218	38.14 N	86.18 W
Wyandotte National Wildlife Refuge ◆[4]	281	42.14 N	83.08 W
Wyandra	166	27.15 S	145.59 E
Wyangala, Lake ⊜[1]	166	33.58 S	148.55 E
Wyano	214	40.12 N	79.42 W
Wyatt, In., U.S.	216	41.31 N	86.10 W
Wyatt, Mo., U.S.	194	36.54 N	89.13 W
Wycheproof	166	36.05 S	143.14 E
Wychwood	273d	26.12 S	28.08 E
Wyckoff	210	41.00 N	74.10 W
Wydgee	162	28.51 S	117.49 E
Wydgelee	158	34.23 S	20.26 E
Wy-Dit-Joli-Village	261	49.06 N	1.50 E
Wye	42	51.11 N	0.56 E
Wye ≃, On., Can.	212	44.44 N	79.52 W
Wye ≃, U.K.	42	51.37 N	2.39 W
Wye ≃, Eng., U.K.	44	53.12 N	1.37 W
Wyee	170	33.11 S	151.29 E
Wye Lake ⊜	212	44.43 N	79.52 W
Wyemandoo ∧	162	28.31 S	118.32 E
Wyeville	190	44.01 N	90.23 W
Wyhl	58	48.09 N	7.39 E
Wyhra ≃	54	51.09 N	12.27 E
Wyk	30	54.42 N	8.34 E
Wyke Regis	42	50.36 N	2.29 W
Wykoff	190	43.42 N	92.16 W
Wylandville	279b	40.12 N	80.08 W
Wyleswood Lake ⊜	279a	41.20 N	81.55 W
Wylie, Pa., U.S.	279b	40.27 N	79.59 W
Wylie, Tx., U.S.	222	33.01 N	96.32 W
Wylie, Lake ⊜[1]	192	35.07 N	81.02 W
Wylye ≃	42	51.04 N	1.52 W
Wymah	171b	36.02 S	147.17 E
Wymark	184	50.07 N	107.44 W
Wymeswold	42	52.47 N	1.06 W
Wymondham	42	52.34 N	1.07 E
Wymore	198	40.07 N	96.39 W
Wynantskill	210	42.42 N	73.39 W
Wynberg	158	34.02 S	18.28 E
Wynbring	162	30.33 S	133.32 E

Wyncote	285	40.05 N	75.08 W
Wyndham, Austl.	164	15.28 S	128.06 E
Wyndham, N.Z.	172	46.20 S	168.51 E
Wyndmere	198	46.16 N	97.07 W
Wyndmoor	285	40.04 N	75.11 W
Wynigen	58	47.06 N	7.40 E
Wynndel	182	49.11 N	116.33 W
Wynne	194	35.13 N	90.47 W
Wynnewood, Ok., U.S.	196	34.38 N	97.09 W
Wynnewood, Pa., U.S.	285	40.00 N	75.16 W
Wynniatt Bay ⊂	176	72.55 N	110.30 W
Wynnum	171a	27.27 S	153.10 E
Wynona	196	36.32 N	96.19 W
Wynoochee ≃	224	46.58 N	123.35 W
Wynoochee Lake ⊜[1]	224	47.25 N	123.35 W
Wynot	198	42.44 N	97.10 W
Wynyard, Austl.	166	40.59 S	145.41 E
Wynyard, Sk., Can.	184	51.47 N	104.10 W
Wyocena	190	43.29 N	89.18 W
Wyodak	198	44.17 N	105.22 W
Wyola Lake ⊜	162	29.08 S	130.17 E
Wyoming, On., Can.	190	42.57 N	82.07 W
Wyoming, De., U.S.	208	39.07 N	75.33 W
Wyoming, Il., U.S.	190	41.03 N	89.46 W
Wyoming, Ia., U.S.	190	42.03 N	91.00 W
Wyoming, Mi., U.S.	216	42.54 N	85.42 W
Wyoming, N.Y., U.S.	210	42.49 N	78.05 W
Wyoming, Oh., U.S.	218	39.13 N	84.27 W
Wyoming, Pa., U.S.	210	41.18 N	75.50 W
Wyoming, R.I., U.S.	207	41.30 N	71.42 W
Wyoming □[6], N.Y., U.S.	210	42.44 N	78.08 W
Wyoming □[6], Pa., U.S.	210	41.32 N	75.57 W
Wyoming □[3]	178	43.00 N	107.30 W
Wyoming Peak ∧	200	42.36 N	110.37 W
Wyomissing	208	40.19 N	75.57 W
Wyong	170	33.17 S	151.25 E
Wyong ≃	170	33.18 S	151.28 E
Wyperfield National Park ♦	166	35.30 S	142.00 E
Wyre ≃	44	53.55 N	3.00 W
Wyreema	171a	27.39 S	151.52 E
Wyre Forest ◆[3]	42	52.23 N	2.23 W
Wyrzysk	30	53.10 N	17.15 E
Wyśmierzyce	30	51.38 N	20.49 E
Wysoka	30	53.11 N	17.05 E
Wysokie Mazowieckie	30	52.56 N	22.32 E
Wysox	210	41.46 N	76.24 W
Wyszków	30	52.36 N	21.28 E
Wyszogród	30	52.23 N	20.11 E
Wythenshawe ◆[8]	262	53.24 N	2.17 W
Wythenshawe Hall ⊥	262	53.24 N	2.17 W
Wytheville	192	36.56 N	81.05 W
Wytschegda → Vyčegda ≃	24	61.18 N	46.36 E
Wyvis, Ben ∧	46	57.42 N	4.35 W

X

Xaafuun	144	10.25 N	51.16 E
Xàbia	34	38.47 N	0.10 E
Xabregas ◆[8]	266c	38.44 N	9.07 W
Xá-Cassau	152	9.02 S	20.14 E
Xaçınçay ≃	84	40.13 N	47.18 E
Xaclbal ≃	236	16.06 N	90.58 W
Xaçmaz	84	41.28 N	48.48 E
Xaidulla	120	36.21 N	78.02 E
Xainza	120	30.57 N	88.38 E
Xaitongmoin	124	29.22 N	88.15 E
Xai-Xai	156	25.02 S	33.34 E
Xalapa	234	19.32 N	96.55 W
Xaldan	84	40.43 N	47.15 E
Xalin	144	9.06 N	48.37 E
Xalisco	234	21.27 N	104.54 W
Xalostoc	234	19.24 N	98.03 W
Xalpatlahuac	234	17.01 N	99.18 W
Xaltianguis	234	17.04 N	99.50 W
Xam (Chu) ≃	110	19.53 N	105.45 E
Xambioá	250	6.25 S	48.40 W
Xambrê ≃	255	24.02 S	53.59 W
Xam Nua	110	20.25 N	104.02 E
Xá-Muteba	152	9.34 S	17.50 E
Xan (San) ≃	110	13.32 N	105.58 E
Xang ≃	124	29.22 N	89.09 E
Xangongo	152	16.43 S	15.01 E
Xankändi (Stepanakert)	84	39.49 N	46.44 E
Xanlar	84	40.34 N	46.20 E
Xanten	52	51.39 N	6.26 E
Xánthi	38	41.08 N	24.53 E
Xanxerê	252	26.53 S	52.23 W
Xapecó ≃	252	27.06 S	53.01 W
Xapuri	248	10.39 S	68.31 W
Xapuri ≃	248	10.39 S	68.30 W
Xarardheere	144	4.39 N	47.51 E
Xar Moron ≃, Zhg.	90	43.25 N	121.41 E
Xar Moron ≃, Zhg.	102	43.02 N	111.20 E
Xarrama ≃	34	38.14 N	8.20 W
Xàtiva (Játiva)	34	38.59 N	0.31 W
Xau, Lake ≚	156	21.15 S	24.38 E
Xauen → Chaouen	148	35.10 N	5.16 W
Xavante ≃	250	11.23 S	49.41 W
Xavantes ≃	250	10.40 S	50.41 W
Xavantina	255	21.15 S	52.48 W
Xa Vo Dat	110	11.09 N	107.31 E
Xaxim	252	26.56 S	52.31 W
Xcalak	232	18.16 N	87.50 W
X-Can	232	20.50 N	87.43 W
Xelva	34	39.45 N	0.59 W
Xenia, Il., U.S.	219	38.38 N	88.38 W
Xenia, Oh., U.S.	218	39.41 N	83.55 W
Xénô	110	16.35 N	104.50 E
Xercavins, Arroyo de ≃	266d	41.30 N	2.02 E
Xerém	256	22.33 S	43.18 W
Xeres → Jerez de la Frontera	34	36.41 N	6.08 W
Xertigny	58	48.03 N	6.24 E
Xeruã ≃	248	6.03 S	67.50 W
Xhumo	156	21.07 S	24.42 E
Xi ≃, Zhg.	100	25.14 N	118.03 E
Xi ≃, Zhg.	100	30.21 N	115.06 E
Xi ≃, Zhg.	100	24.34 N	117.30 E
Xi ≃, Zhg.	102	22.25 N	113.23 E
Xi ≃, Zhg.	102	42.20 N	100.20 E
Xi ≃, Zhg.	104	41.15 N	123.32 E
Xi ≃, Zhg.	104	41.30 N	121.26 E
Xi ≃, Zhg.	107	30.26 N	103.48 E
Xiaang	106	30.45 N	120.07 E
Xiaba	100	24.54 N	116.06 E
Xiabai, Zhg.	106	31.12 N	119.50 E
Xiabai, Zhg.	106	30.29 N	120.00 E
Xiabanghu	100	30.31 N	112.38 E
Xiabian	104	40.51 N	120.30 E
Xiabuji	100	28.19 N	116.20 E
Xiacang	105	39.47 N	117.24 E
Xiache	100	24.40 N	115.08 E
Xiachengzi	89	44.41 N	130.27 E
Xiachuan Dao I	102	21.40 N	112.37 E
Xiacun	105	40.21 N	116.14 E
Xiadao	100	26.34 N	118.16 E
Xiadian, Zhg.	98	37.06 N	120.19 E
Xiadian, Zhg.	100	31.26 N	114.17 E
Xiadian, Zhg.	105	39.57 N	116.55 E
Xiadianjie	100	25.13 N	118.27 E
Xiafeidi	98	42.18 N	124.21 E
Xiafu, Zhg.	100	25.01 N	113.41 E
Xiafu, Zhg.	100	23.52 N	115.45 E
Xiagaixin	102	22.36 N	99.59 E
Xiagang	106	31.55 N	120.13 E
Xiagezhuang	98	36.41 N	120.25 E

≃	River	Fluß	Río	Rivière	Rio
≊	Canal	Kanal	Canal	Canal	Canal
∟	Waterfall, Rapids	Wasserfall, Stromschnellen	Cascada, Rápidos	Chute d'eau, Rapides	Cascata, Rápidos
⋓	Strait	Meeresstraße	Estrecho	Détroit	Estreito
⊂	Bay, Gulf	Bucht, Golf	Bahía, Golfo	Baie, Golfe	Baía, Golfo
⊜	Lake, Lakes	See, Seen	Lago, Lagos	Lac, Lacs	Lago, Lagos
≣	Swamp	Sumpf	Pantano	Marais	Pântano
⍓	Ice Features, Glacier	Eis- und Gletscherformen	Accidentes Glaciales	Formes glaciaires	Acidentes glaciares
⍑	Other Hydrographic Features	Andere Hydrographische Objekte	Otros Elementos Hidrográficos	Autres données hydrographiques	Outros acidentes hidrográficos

✣	Submarine Features	Untermeerische Objekte	Accidentes Submarinos	Formes de relief sous-marin	Acidentes submarinos
□	Political Unit	Politische Einheit	Unidad Política	Entité politique	Unidade política
♉	Cultural Institution	Kulturelle Institution	Institución Cultural	Institution culturelle	Institução cultural
⊥	Historical Site	Historische Stätte	Sitio Histórico	Site historique	Sitio histórico
♦	Recreational Site	Erholungs- und Ferienort	Sitio de Recreo	Centre de loisirs	Area de Lazer
⊠	Airport	Flughafen	Aeropuerto	Aéroport	Aeroporto
■	Military Installation	Militäranlage	Instalación Militar	Installation militaire	Instalação militar
◆	Miscellaneous	Verschiedenes	Misceláneo	Divers	Diversos

Xiaguan, Zhg. 98 39.07 N 114.09 E
Xiaguan, Zhg. 102 25.34 N 100.14 E
Xiaguan, Zhg. 106 32.06 N 118.44 E
Xiaguanjunchang 104 41.28 N 121.40 E
Xiaguanpi 100 24.04 N 117.06 E
Xiagucheng 102 36.47 N 102.53 E
Xiagucun 106 30.56 N 119.09 E
Xiahada 104 41.58 N 124.08 E
Xiahailangzhai 104 41.35 N 123.46 E
Xiahe 102 35.18 N 102.30 E
Xiahuangjintun 104 41.57 N 123.48 E
Xiahuayuan 105 40.29 N 115.17 E
Xiajiabaozi 98 42.16 N 124.37 E
Xiajialou 104 42.25 N 123.39 E
Xiajiang 100 27.32 N 115.08 E
Xiajiangdun 106 31.14 N 120.24 E
Xiajiangwu 106 30.29 N 119.00 E
Xiajiayuan 106 32.13 N 120.38 E
Xiajiezi 102 27.28 N 101.35 E
Xiajin 98 36.55 N 115.57 E
Xiakou 100 28.28 N 118.31 E
Xialianggang 105 39.14 N 115.07 E
Xialufang 102 31.11 N 103.38 E
Xiamaguan 102 37.14 N 106.28 E
Xiamen (Amoy) 100 24.28 N 118.07 E
Xiamen Gang c 100 24.19 N 118.10 E
Xiamianzhen 107 30.08 N 106.32 E
Xiamin'ansutai 104 41.54 N 120.53 E
Xiamocun 106 31.09 N 119.22 E
Xi'an (Sian) 102 34.15 N 108.52 E
Xian ≐ 107 29.22 N 104.44 E
Xianchenggu 98 36.53 N 115.17 E
Xiandu 100 25.04 N 117.44 E
Xianfeng, Zhg. 100 25.42 N 117.53 E
Xianfeng, Zhg. 102 29.41 N 109.02 E
Xiang ≐, Zhg. 100 25.35 N 115.49 E
Xiang ≐, Zhg. 102 29.00 N 112.56 E
Xiang'an 100 31.12 N 117.46 E
Xiangcheng, Zhg. 100 33.28 N 114.53 E
Xiangcheng, Zhg. 100 33.53 N 113.29 E
Xiangcheng, Zhg. 102 28.59 N 99.45 E
Xiangcheng, Zhg. 106 31.29 N 120.44 E
Xiangfan 102 32.03 N 112.01 E
Xiangfuguan 100 28.30 N 115.26 E
Xiangfusi 107 30.06 N 104.24 E
Xianggang
→ Victoria 271d 22.17 N 114.09 E
Xianggongshi 100 28.25 N 113.32 E
Xianggongzhuang 105 39.48 N 118.19 E
Xianghe 105 39.46 N 116.59 E
Xiangheguan 100 33.08 N 113.26 E
Xianghuazhen 106 31.31 N 121.43 E
Xiangjia, Zhg. 106 31.20 N 120.31 E
Xiangjia, Zhg. 106 31.19 N 120.23 E
Xiangjiachang 107 30.08 N 104.18 E
Xiangkhoang 110 19.20 N 103.22 E
Xiangkhoang, Plateau de ⋌[1] 110 19.30 N 103.10 E
Xiangning 102 36.01 N 110.45 E
Xiangride 102 36.02 N 98.08 E
Xiangshan, Zhg. 100 29.28 N 121.51 E
Xiangshan, Zhg. 105 39.59 N 116.12 E
Xiangshan Gang c 100 29.38 N 121.48 E
Xiangshizhen 107 29.17 N 105.09 E
Xiangshui, Zhg. 100 23.15 N 114.10 E
Xiangshui, Zhg. 100 34.12 N 119.34 E
Xiangtan 100 27.51 N 112.54 E
Xiangtang 100 28.26 N 115.58 E
Xiangxiang 102 27.43 N 112.27 E
Xiangyang 105 39.13 N 115.25 E
Xiangyangkou 105 40.06 N 115.47 E
Xiangyin 100 28.40 N 112.53 E
Xiangyuan 102 36.32 N 113.00 E
Xiangyun 102 25.30 N 100.30 E
Xiangzhenpu 100 30.52 N 117.21 E
Xiangzhou, Zhg. 98 36.12 N 119.24 E
Xiangzhou, Zhg. 102 23.55 N 109.49 E
Xiangzhu 100 29.02 N 120.04 E
Xianinggang 100 28.20 N 112.56 E
Xianjiang 100 27.48 N 120.30 E
Xianju 100 28.51 N 120.44 E
Xianning 100 29.53 N 114.13 E
Xiannongtan Stadium ♦ 271a 39.52 N 116.23 E
Xiannübu 100 25.36 N 114.40 E
Xianru 89 43.11 N 128.02 E
Xianshichang 107 28.43 N 105.44 E
Xianshui ≐ 102 30.05 N 110.59 E
Xianshuigu 105 38.59 N 117.23 E
Xiantan, Zhg. 107 29.21 N 104.53 E
Xiantan, Zhg. 107 28.50 N 106.12 E
Xiantang 100 23.48 N 114.46 E
Xianxia Ling ⋌ 100 28.30 N 118.46 E
Xianxian 98 38.13 N 116.06 E
Xianyang, Zhg. 100 28.02 N 118.30 E
Xianyang, Zhg. 102 34.22 N 108.42 E
Xianyou 100 25.23 N 118.40 E
Xianzhong 100 28.36 N 113.48 E
Xiao ≐ 100 28.11 N 120.14 E
Xiao'an ≐ 107 29.59 N 106.13 E
Xiao'ao 100 26.14 N 119.39 E
Xiaoazhang 102 23.42 N 104.58 E
Xiaobangniulu 104 41.34 N 122.46 E
Xiaobeigou 104 41.55 N 120.46 E
Xiaobeihe, Zhg. 104 42.39 N 123.58 E
Xiaobeihe, Zhg. 104 41.22 N 122.50 E
Xiaocaohu 86 43.06 N 88.30 E
Xiaochangshan Dao I 98 39.12 N 122.41 E
Xiaocheng 100 26.20 N 119.47 E
Xiaochengdu 106 30.59 N 120.04 E
Xiaochengzi, Zhg. 89 46.33 N 122.54 E
Xiaochengzi, Zhg. 89 42.56 N 123.12 E
Xiaochi 100 30.33 N 116.23 E
Xiaochikou 100 29.46 N 115.59 E
Xiaodanyang 106 31.38 N 118.43 E
Xiaodong 102 22.14 N 108.39 E
Xiao'ergou 89 49.12 N 123.42 E
Xiaofangshen 104 42.13 N 123.54 E
Xiaofanshan 105 40.16 N 115.19 E
Xiaofen 106 31.45 N 119.39 E
Xiaofeng 106 30.36 N 119.32 E
Xiaogan 100 30.55 N 113.54 E
Xiaogangkou 100 28.14 N 115.50 E
Xiaogaojiatun 104 41.02 N 121.59 E
Xiaogencaigangzi 104 41.48 N 122.42 E
Xiaogu 107 29.08 N 104.01 E
Xiaoguai 86 45.13 N 85.02 E
Xiaogushan 98 39.49 N 123.12 E
Xiaohaizhen 106 31.58 N 120.59 E
Xiaohaladaokou 98 42.37 N 119.32 E
Xiaohan 98 35.48 N 114.52 E
Xiaohe 106 32.01 N 119.52 E
Xiaohei Shan ∧ 102 24.42 N 98.55 E
Xiaohekou 102 33.19 N 107.25 E
Xiaoheyan 98 42.26 N 119.38 E
Xiaoheying 102 32.37 N 104.23 E
Xiao Hinggan Ling (Lesser Khingan Range) ⋌ 89 48.45 N 127.00 E
Xiaohongmen 271a 39.49 N 116.26 E
Xiaohu 100 27.20 N 118.14 E
Xiaohuying 98 41.09 N 117.13 E
Xiaoji, Zhg. 98 36.45 N 121.01 E
Xiaoji, Zhg. 100 27.08 N 113.15 E
Xiaoji, Zhg. 100 32.38 N 119.48 E
Xiaojiachang 107 30.18 N 106.28 E
Xiaojiagang 100 31.06 N 113.55 E
Xiaojialing 100 29.35 N 116.32 E
Xiaojiang 100 25.08 N 114.59 E
Xiaojianji 100 33.23 N 116.29 E
Xiaojiawu 105 39.36 N 116.36 E
Xiaojiayingzi 98 40.17 N 118.47 E
Xiaojieling 100 31.36 N 115.09 E
Xiaojin 102 31.00 N 102.21 E
Xiaojingfang 105 39.22 N 116.34 E
Xiaojiu 89 45.15 N 127.47 E
Xiaokaoshantun 104 42.10 N 123.53 E
Xiaokuli 89 50.18 N 120.20 E
Xiaokunshan 106 31.02 N 121.07 E
Xiaolan 100 22.41 N 113.14 E
Xiaoliangshan 104 42.05 N 122.32 E
Xiaoling, Zhg. 89 45.20 N 127.18 E
Xiaoling, Zhg. 104 42.18 N 123.23 E
Xiaoling ≐ 104 41.06 N 121.07 E
Xiaolingzi 104 41.07 N 123.19 E
Xiaolinzhuang 104 41.36 N 124.01 E
Xiaolipu 98 36.24 N 116.35 E
Xiaolongtan 102 23.51 N 103.10 E
Xiaoluan ≐ 98 41.36 N 117.05 E
Xiaolüzhuang 106 31.57 N 119.25 E
Xiaomei 100 27.50 N 118.58 E
Xiaomei Guan)(100 25.17 N 114.17 E
Xiaomiaozi 98 41.24 N 114.25 E
Xiaonanhai 107 29.23 N 106.27 E
Xiaopikou 98 35.47 N 115.53 E
Xiaopingyang 102 23.22 N 109.13 E
Xiao Qaidam He ⊜ 102 37.30 N 95.12 E
Xiaoqiao 100 26.57 N 118.30 E
Xiaoqiaotou 106 30.43 N 119.27 E
Xiaoqing ≐ 98 37.17 N 118.52 E
Xiaoqingchuizi 104 42.30 N 123.39 E
Xiaoquandong 102 41.14 N 95.26 E
Xiaosanjiazi 104 42.34 N 123.23 E
Xiaosha ≐ 104 41.13 N 122.45 E
Xiaoshakou 100 29.58 N 113.16 E
Xiaoshan 106 30.10 N 120.15 E
Xiaoshangqiao 100 33.43 N 113.58 E
Xiaoshi 100 27.27 N 116.49 E
Xiaoshixiang 100 30.36 N 116.38 E
Xiaoshu 106 30.48 N 119.46 E
Xiaoshun 100 29.11 N 119.51 E
Xiaosigou 98 40.53 N 118.33 E
Xiaosijia 104 42.24 N 120.46 E
Xiaotang 98 41.38 N 119.33 E
Xiaotanghe 98 42.04 N 127.10 E
Xiaotao 100 25.46 N 117.08 E
Xiaotazi 104 42.17 N 123.08 E
Xiaotian 100 31.12 N 116.33 E
Xiaotianji 100 32.45 N 115.36 E
Xiaotun 104 42.24 N 123.44 E
Xiaotunzicun 104 41.14 N 123.20 E
Xiaowa 104 41.03 N 122.04 E
Xiaowan 100 26.53 N 116.36 E
Xiaowangmiao 100 29.41 N 121.21 E
Xiaowutai Shan ∧ 105 39.51 N 115.09 E
Xiaowutai Shan ⋌ 105 39.50 N 115.00 E
Xiaoxi 100 25.48 N 115.21 E
Xiaoxi ≐ 106 32.15 N 120.24 E
Xiaoxian 98 34.11 N 116.56 E
Xiaoxincheng 105 39.24 N 115.11 E
Xiaoxintian 271a 39.58 N 116.22 E
Xiaoxizhen 106 30.51 N 119.50 E
Xiaoyangjiadian 104 42.23 N 122.24 E
Xiaoyangqi 89 50.48 N 124.12 E
Xiaoyantai 104 41.26 N 123.10 E
Xiaoyaozhen 100 33.46 N 114.16 E
Xiaoyi 102 37.10 N 111.46 E
Xiaoying, Zhg. 98 37.18 N 118.04 E
Xiaoying, Zhg. 105 40.12 N 116.33 E
Xiaoyingcun 105 39.28 N 116.41 E
Xiaoyuan 107 30.00 N 104.56 E
Xiaozhan 105 38.55 N 117.25 E
Xiaozhang ≐ 105 39.47 N 117.22 E
Xiaozhongdian 102 27.40 N 99.46 E
Xiaozhuang 104 41.30 N 121.27 E
Xiaozhujiawan 106 31.24 N 121.01 E
Xiapu, Zhg. 100 26.52 N 120.01 E
Xiapu, Zhg. 100 27.49 N 114.26 E
Xiaqialafangzi 104 41.48 N 121.44 E
Xiaqi Dao I 100 29.42 N 122.15 E
Xiaqiubao 98 37.01 N 119.54 E
Xiasantumen 105 38.50 N 114.48 E
Xiashe 106 30.33 N 120.11 E
Xiashesi 100 27.46 N 112.57 E
Xiashi
→ Haining 106 30.32 N 120.41 E
Xiashu 106 32.11 N 119.10 E
Xiashuerfowei 89 50.23 N 120.47 E
Xiashuiquan 104 41.52 N 123.38 E
Xiataizi 105 40.37 N 117.45 E
Xiatang, Zhg. 100 33.45 N 112.39 E
Xiatang, Zhg. 106 31.29 N 118.41 E
Xiatangtian 106 30.55 N 120.12 E
Xiataohuatu 104 41.42 N 120.36 E
Xiawa 98 42.39 N 120.35 E
Xiawajiang 106 30.59 N 121.51 E
Xiawaziyu 104 41.15 N 123.38 E
Xiaxi 106 31.43 N 119.45 E
Xiaxian 102 35.11 N 111.15 E
Xiaxiangcheng 102 28.42 N 99.59 E
Xiaxikou 100 26.15 N 118.59 E
Xiaxinhe 106 31.40 N 119.31 E
Xiayang, Zhg. 100 28.48 N 119.41 E
Xiayang, Zhg. 100 26.46 N 117.59 E
Xiayang, Zhg. 100 24.39 N 116.52 E
Xiayi 98 34.14 N 116.06 E
Xiaying, Zhg. 98 37.03 N 119.25 E
Xiaying, Zhg. 105 40.10 N 117.25 E
Xiayunling 105 39.43 N 115.44 E
Xiazhang 98 36.08 N 116.57 E
Xiazhen 100 28.39 N 118.21 E
Xiazhuang, Zhg. 98 35.28 N 118.43 E
Xiazhuang, Zhg. 100 27.22 N 119.01 E
Xiazhuang, Zhg. 105 39.54 N 117.01 E
Xiazhuang, Zhg. 105 39.38 N 115.26 E
Xiazikou 105 39.01 N 115.25 E
Xiban 107 30.32 N 106.12 E
Xibaqianmou 104 40.59 N 121.35 E
Xibeiyingzi 104 41.55 N 121.38 E
Xibo ≐ 98 42.17 N 118.57 E
Xibu 100 31.46 N 118.17 E
Xicang 106 31.34 N 120.29 E
Xichang, Zhg. 102 27.58 N 102.13 E
Xichang, Zhg. 104 42.15 N 124.12 E
Xicheng 89 48.10 N 125.29 E
Xichong 102 31.00 N 105.52 E
Xicicun 105 39.29 N 116.08 E
Xico 234 19.25 N 97.00 W
Xicoténcatl 234 23.00 N 98.56 W
Xicotepec de Juárez 234 20.17 N 97.57 W
Xictle, Volcán ∧[1] 286a 19.14 N 99.14 W
Xicun 100 27.46 N 114.14 E
Xidachuan 98 41.46 N 127.34 E
Xidapo 89 43.12 N 130.02 E
Xidaying 105 39.41 N 116.14 E
Xidian 100 29.32 N 121.26 E
Xiditou 105 39.16 N 117.23 E
Xidongting Shan ∧ 106 31.07 N 120.16 E
Xié ≐ 246 0.54 N 67.11 W
Xiecun 105 39.00 N 115.31 E
Xiedian 100 33.27 N 113.28 E
Xiefang 100 26.12 N 116.41 E
Xieji 98 34.32 N 115.29 E
Xiejia 98 42.24 N 125.42 E
Xiejiagangzi 104 41.55 N 122.20 E
Xiejiapu 106 31.15 N 119.09 E
Xiejunmiao 107 30.15 N 103.40 E
Xielipuke 120 31.30 N 82.45 E
Xiemachang 107 29.46 N 106.22 E
Xiemata Shan ∧ 89 50.28 N 120.47 E
Xiepu 100 30.02 N 121.37 E
Xieqiao, Zhg. 106 32.03 N 120.22 E
Xieqiao, Zhg. 106 30.29 N 120.34 E
Xietang 106 31.18 N 120.44 E
Xiexi 106 31.54 N 118.54 E
Xiexinggou 104 41.51 N 121.05 E
Xifei ≐ 100 32.38 N 116.39 E
Xifeng, Zhg. 98 42.43 N 124.40 E
Xifeng, Zhg. 102 27.02 N 106.30 E
Xifengkou 105 40.24 N 118.19 E
Xifocun 104 41.26 N 122.33 E
Xigangzi 89 49.58 N 127.20 E
Xigaolizhuangzi 104 41.40 N 122.55 E
Xigaotan 98 38.18 N 116.13 E
Xigaotun 98 40.27 N 122.36 E
Xigazê 120 29.17 N 88.53 E
Xiguanjiatun 104 42.35 N 123.10 E
Xiguanyingzi 104 41.50 N 120.37 E
Xihaikou 104 40.50 N 121.05 E
Xihan ≐ 102 33.30 N 106.02 E
Xihe, Zhg. 100 31.01 N 118.28 E
Xihe, Zhg. 100 31.41 N 113.27 E
Xihe, Zhg. 102 34.01 N 105.17 E
Xiheying 105 39.53 N 114.42 E
Xihezhuang 105 39.20 N 118.02 E
Xi Hu ⊜ 106 30.15 N 120.08 E
Xihua 100 33.47 N 114.31 E
Xihuangcang 106 31.43 N 121.40 E
Xihuanzidong 104 41.31 N 122.28 E
Xihuashan, Zhg. 100 25.28 N 114.20 E
Xihuashan, Zhg. 105 40.07 N 116.54 E
Xihuishan 104 41.41 N 122.38 E
Xiis 144 10.53 N 46.54 E
Xiji, Zhg. 102 35.58 N 105.44 E
Xiji, Zhg. 105 39.49 N 116.52 E
Xijialong 102 23.31 N 103.51 E
Xijiang 100 25.50 N 115.49 E
Xijianshanzi 104 40.47 N 120.48 E
Xi Jiao Airfield ⊠ 271a 39.58 N 116.15 E
Xijiapuzitun 104 41.26 N 123.50 E
Xijir Ulan Hu ⊜ 120 35.12 N 90.18 E
Xikou, Zhg. 89 46.40 N 120.40 E
Xikou, Zhg. 100 28.52 N 119.11 E
Xikou, Zhg. 100 25.26 N 118.45 E
Xikou, Zhg. 100 29.44 N 118.02 E
Xikou, Zhg. 100 29.11 N 114.23 E
Xikou, Zhg. 100 29.14 N 114.24 E
Xikou, Zhg. 106 30.40 N 118.41 E
Xikouxu 100 25.24 N 117.03 E
Xikouzi 89 53.06 N 120.40 E
Xilai 107 30.20 N 103.29 E
Xilaiqiao 106 32.03 N 119.54 E
Xilaizhen 106 32.07 N 120.25 E
Xilin 120 28.33 N 87.48 E
Xi Ling (Western Tombs) ⊥ 105 39.24 N 115.18 E
Xilintuo 120 30.08 N 88.04 E
Xilitla 234 21.20 N 98.58 W
Xiliuhe 105 38.58 N 116.32 E
Xiliushuyingzi 104 42.25 N 121.54 E
Xıllı 84 39.25 N 49.05 E
Xilókastron 38 38.05 N 22.38 E
Xiluga ≐ 98 42.21 N 118.38 E
Xiluncun 89 47.08 N 126.26 E
Ximagou 105 40.16 N 117.50 E
Ximakou 100 30.33 N 113.47 E
Ximalatu 89 47.00 N 122.01 E
Ximalin 98 40.48 N 114.29 E
Ximiao 102 41.09 N 100.17 E
Ximucheng 104 40.42 N 122.54 E
Xin ≐ 100 28.37 N 116.40 E
Xin'an, Zhg. 89 43.46 N 125.40 E
Xin'an, Zhg. 100 23.02 N 114.56 E
Xinan, Zhg. 100 25.26 N 117.35 E
Xin'an, Zhg. 100 26.44 N 116.13 E
Xin'an, Zhg. 105 39.09 N 116.38 E
Xin'an, Zhg. 106 31.47 N 120.09 E
Xin'an, Zhg. 106 31.30 N 120.22 E
Xin'an ≐ 100 29.33 N 118.58 E
Xin'andian 100 32.37 N 114.03 E
Xin'andu 100 30.52 N 116.53 E
Xin'anji 100 33.22 N 115.13 E
Xin'anjiang Shuiku ⊜[1] 100 29.27 N 119.06 E
Xin'anpu 104 42.39 N 123.27 E
Xin'anqiao 106 32.16 N 121.07 E
Xin'ansuo 102 23.16 N 103.27 E
Xin'anzhen, Zhg. 89 44.06 N 123.46 E
Xin'anzhen, Zhg. 105 39.45 N 117.32 E
Xi'nanzhuang 105 40.48 N 118.23 E
Xinavane 156 25.02 S 32.47 E
Xinba, Zhg. 98 34.27 N 119.09 E
Xinba, Zhg. 100 30.24 N 116.52 E
Xinba, Zhg. 106 32.08 N 120.39 E
Xinba, Zhg. 106 32.16 N 119.45 E
Xinbao'an 105 40.27 N 115.24 E
Xin Barag Youqi (Altan Emel) 88 48.41 N 116.53 E
Xin Barag Zuoqi (Amgalang) 88 48.14 N 118.18 E
Xinbin, Zhg. 98 41.42 N 125.02 E
Xinbin, Zhg. 106 30.56 N 121.04 E
Xinbo 98 42.19 N 117.44 E
Xincai 100 32.44 N 114.59 E
Xincang, Zhg. 106 30.25 N 120.42 E
Xincang, Zhg. 106 30.44 N 121.11 E
Xinchang, Zhg. 100 29.30 N 120.53 E
Xinchang, Zhg. 102 28.03 N 103.46 E
Xinchang, Zhg. 102 25.10 N 104.18 E
Xinchang, Zhg. 106 31.42 N 121.46 E
Xinchang, Zhg. 106 31.02 N 121.38 E
Xinchang, Zhg. 107 30.29 N 106.21 E
Xinchang, Zhg. 107 30.16 N 104.29 E
Xinchang, Zhg. 107 29.20 N 104.15 E
Xinchang, Zhg. 107 29.38 N 104.33 E
Xinchangzi 107 29.40 N 103.46 E
Xincheng, Zhg. 100 25.34 N 114.36 E
Xincheng, Zhg. 102 24.09 N 108.46 E
Xincheng (Gaobeidian), Zhg. 105 39.20 N 115.51 E
Xincheng, Zhg. 105 38.59 N 117.33 E
Xincheng, Zhg. 106 32.17 N 119.14 E
Xincheng, Zhg. 106 30.48 N 120.36 E
Xinchengzi 104 42.03 N 123.30 E
Xinchepaizi 86 44.55 N 84.30 E
Xincunji 100 32.53 N 115.31 E
Xindai 106 30.49 N 121.05 E
Xindi 104 42.21 N 120.31 E
Xindian, Zhg. 89 45.55 N 127.50 E
Xindian, Zhg. 98 37.07 N 114.49 E
Xindian, Zhg. 98 37.29 N 118.28 E
Xindian, Zhg. 100 33.07 N 112.38 E
Xindian, Zhg. 100 31.33 N 115.16 E
Xindian, Zhg. 100 33.38 N 113.51 E
Xindian, Zhg. 100 29.40 N 113.40 E
Xindian, Zhg. 105 40.11 N 116.11 E
Xindian, Zhg. 105 40.47 N 116.49 E
Xindian, Zhg. 105 39.10 N 116.27 E
Xindian, Zhg. 107 29.19 N 105.40 E
Xindianbu 100 32.24 N 116.22 E
Xindianzi, Zhg. 105 40.04 N 118.01 E
Xindianzi, Zhg. 107 28.49 N 103.35 E
Xindianzi, Zhg. 107 29.03 N 103.46 E
Xindianzi, Zhg. 107 29.52 N 106.06 E
Xindianzi, Zhg. 107 29.46 N 105.11 E
Xindianzi, Zhg. 107 29.43 N 104.01 E
Xindu 102 23.59 N 111.46 E
Xinfatuncun 104 41.13 N 122.28 E
Xinfeng, Zhg. 100 25.24 N 114.56 E
Xinfeng, Zhg. 100 27.26 N 116.40 E
Xinfeng, Zhg. 100 33.19 N 120.30 E
Xinfeng, Zhg. 100 24.04 N 114.12 E
Xinfeng, Zhg. 100 24.05 N 116.53 E
Xinfeng, Zhg. 106 31.09 N 118.40 E
Xinfeng, Zhg. 106 32.05 N 119.34 E
Xinfeng, Zhg. 106 30.43 N 120.55 E
Xinfeng ≐ 100 23.42 N 114.42 E
Xinfeng Shuiku ⊜[1] 100 23.52 N 114.30 E
Xing'an, Zhg. 89 48.49 N 121.45 E
Xing'an, Zhg. 102 25.37 N 110.31 E
Xin'gang, Zhg. 106 31.56 N 120.57 E
Xingang, Zhg. 106 32.03 N 120.25 E
Xing'antun 89 51.31 N 120.08 E
Xingcheng 104 40.37 N 120.43 E
Xingguo 100 26.21 N 115.19 E
Xinghai 102 35.31 N 99.36 E
Xinghe 98 40.48 N 113.58 E
Xinghua 100 32.57 N 119.50 E
Xinghua Wan c 100 25.20 N 119.20 E
Xingjing 102 29.43 N 102.59 E
Xingkai Hu (ozero Chanka) ⊜ 89 45.00 N 132.24 E
Xingliu 100 33.04 N 115.41 E
Xinglong, Zhg. 100 32.05 N 112.51 E
Xinglong, Zhg. 102 35.38 N 106.08 E
Xinglong, Zhg. 105 40.26 N 117.34 E
Xinglong, Zhg. 107 30.20 N 106.07 E
Xinglong, Zhg. 107 30.36 N 106.20 E
Xinglongchang, Zhg. 107 29.34 N 106.09 E
Xinglongchang, Zhg. 107 29.54 N 105.26 E
Xinglongchang, Zhg. 107 30.25 N 104.06 E
Xinglongcun 89 49.50 N 125.12 E
Xinglongdian, Zhg. 104 42.16 N 124.00 E
Xinglongdian, Zhg. 104 41.59 N 123.03 E
Xinglonggou, Zhg. 104 41.46 N 120.38 E
Xinglonggou, Zhg. 104 40.45 N 123.08 E
Xinglongpao 89 46.27 N 125.47 E
Xinglongtai 104 42.30 N 123.48 E
Xingning 100 24.09 N 115.45 E
Xingou, Zhg. 100 30.41 N 113.57 E
Xingou, Zhg. 100 30.08 N 112.56 E
Xingren 102 25.27 N 105.13 E
Xingrenbu 102 37.06 N 105.12 E
Xingshanbao 89 45.30 N 125.45 E
Xingtai 98 37.04 N 114.29 E
Xingtan 100 22.46 N 113.07 E
Xingtang 98 38.26 N 114.33 E
Xingtian 100 27.30 N 118.02 E
Xingu ≐ 242 1.30 S 51.53 W
Xinguan 100 33.38 N 118.05 E
Xingwenping 102 29.24 N 103.23 E
Xingxian 102 38.36 N 111.15 E
Xingxing 106 30.39 N 121.09 E
Xingyi, Zhg. 98 38.18 N 115.01 E
Xingyi, Zhg. 102 25.06 N 104.58 E
Xingzhuangzi 105 40.34 N 115.00 E
Xingzi 100 29.28 N 116.01 E
Xinhe, Zhg. 98 37.32 N 115.14 E
Xinhe, Zhg. 100 28.30 N 121.27 E
Xinhe, Zhg. 105 39.03 N 117.37 E
Xinhe, Zhg. 106 31.59 N 121.21 E
Xinhekou 89 48.22 N 130.45 E
Xinheng 100 23.38 N 116.18 E
Xinhezhen 106 31.35 N 121.31 E
Xinhezhuang 106 31.10 N 118.46 E
Xinhua 102 27.37 N 111.02 E
Xinhuai ≐ 100 34.23 N 120.05 E
Xinhuang 106 30.37 N 120.55 E
Xinhui 100 22.32 N 113.02 E
Xining (Sining) 102 36.38 N 101.55 E
Xiniu, Zhg. 100 24.10 N 113.07 E
Xiniu, Zhg. 106 31.25 N 120.07 E
Xiniuguchengzi 104 41.01 N 122.24 E
Xinji, Zhg. 98 35.19 N 115.36 E
Xinji, Zhg. 100 33.24 N 114.44 E
Xinji, Zhg. 105 39.52 N 117.10 E
Xinji, Zhg. 105 40.04 N 118.21 E
Xinjiaji 98 36.56 N 116.59 E
Xinjian, Zhg. 100 28.46 N 120.02 E
Xinjian, Zhg. 100 28.34 N 115.47 E
Xinjian, Zhg. 106 31.33 N 119.39 E
Xinjiang, Zhg. 100 24.29 N 113.52 E
Xinjiang, Zhg. 102 35.40 N 111.11 E
Xinjiang, Zhg. 106 32.05 N 120.40 E
Xinjianglang 106 30.58 N 120.54 E
Xinjiang Uygur Zizhiqu (Sinkiang) □[4] 90 40.00 N 85.00 E
Xinjiapu 105 40.32 N 115.57 E
Xinjiazhuang 105 40.31 N 114.58 E
Xinjie 102 26.48 N 101.15 E
Xinjieji 89 52.08 N 126.24 E
Xinjin (Pulandian), Zhg. 98 39.24 N 121.58 E
Xinjin, Zhg. 107 30.25 N 103.49 E
Xinjingzi 86 42.13 N 87.36 E
Xinjuntun 105 39.39 N 117.57 E
Xinkai ≐ 89 43.37 N 123.36 E
Xinkaigang 106 31.55 N 120.56 E
Xinkengdong 100 26.09 N 113.46 E
Xinle (Dongchangshou) 98 38.24 N 114.47 E
Xinli 89 44.41 N 126.45 E
Xinlitun, Zhg. 89 43.34 N 125.18 E
Xinlitun, Zhg. 104 42.00 N 122.09 E
Xinlitun, Zhg. 104 42.15 N 122.51 E
Xinlizhuang 105 39.17 N 116.10 E
Xinmin 104 42.00 N 122.48 E
Xinmintun 104 41.39 N 123.02 E
Xinning 102 26.19 N 110.45 E
Xinping 102 24.06 N 101.58 E
Xinpu 100 24.31 N 116.08 E
Xinqianhu 98 37.59 N 118.15 E
Xinqiao, Zhg. 106 31.32 N 119.04 E
Xinqiao, Zhg. 106 31.04 N 121.18 E
Xinqiao, Zhg. 107 29.32 N 106.28 E
Xinqiao, Zhg. 107 30.10 N 103.50 E
Xinqiao, Zhg. 107 30.33 N 105.33 E
Xinqiaotou 106 31.00 N 119.24 E
Xinqiaozhen 107 29.36 N 103.39 E
Xinqiu 98 41.53 N 119.41 E
Xinqizhou 100 28.56 N 115.50 E
Xinqu 86 44.57 N 85.15 E
Xinquan 100 25.23 N 116.38 E
Xinsanyu 106 31.58 N 120.07 E
Xinshao 102 27.11 N 111.20 E
Xinshengzhen 107 29.29 N 104.39 E
Xinshi, Zhg. 106 30.37 N 120.19 E
Xinshi, Zhg. 106 32.04 N 120.02 E
Xinshizhen, Zhg. 102 28.39 N 104.02 E
Xinshizhen, Zhg. 107 30.20 N 104.35 E
Xinshu ≐ 98 34.41 N 119.12 E
Xintai 98 35.54 N 117.44 E
Xintaimen 98 40.50 N 120.23 E
Xintaizi, Zhg. 104 41.06 N 122.42 E
Xintaizi, Zhg. 104 42.07 N 123.36 E
Xintang, Zhg. 100 23.08 N 113.36 E
Xintang, Zhg. 102 30.13 N 109.30 E
Xintang, Zhg. 106 31.02 N 119.59 E
Xintangcun 106 31.53 N 119.31 E
Xintanpu 100 29.43 N 114.54 E
Xintian 102 25.53 N 112.05 E
Xintun 104 42.11 N 123.45 E
Xinvi 105 40.04 N 118.21 E
Xinwei 100 25.21 N 115.48 E
Xinwen (Suncun) 98 35.53 N 117.40 E
Xinxian, Zhg. 100 31.38 N 114.51 E
Xinxian, Zhg. 102 38.25 N 112.48 E
Xinxiang 98 35.20 N 113.51 E
Xinxim ≐ 250 7.57 S 53.20 W
Xinxing, Zhg. 89 43.16 N 129.48 E
Xinxing, Zhg. 100 22.40 N 112.52 E
Xinxing, Zhg. 102 19.57 N 109.32 E
Xinxu, Zhg. 100 22.52 N 114.20 E
Xinxu, Zhg. 100 24.57 N 117.34 E
Xinyang 100 32.08 N 114.04 E
Xinyao 100 27.39 N 118.52 E
Xinye 100 32.33 N 112.21 E
Xinyi (Xin'anzhen), Zhg. 98 34.22 N 118.21 E
Xinyi (Dongzhen), Zhg. 102 22.13 N 110.50 E
Xinyi ≐ 100 34.29 N 119.49 E
Xinying 102 36.03 N 105.35 E
Xinyu 100 27.49 N 114.57 E
Xinyuan 86 43.08 N 82.31 E
Xinzao 100 23.02 N 113.26 E
Xinzha 102 23.41 N 101.09 E
Xinzhai, Zhg. 98 39.24 N 118.46 E
Xinzhai, Zhg. 98 36.24 N 118.37 E
Xinzhai, Zhg. 102 24.33 N 99.08 E
Xinzhan 100 33.33 N 114.50 E
Xinzhang 105 39.05 N 116.46 E
Xinzhangzi 105 40.45 N 117.50 E
Xinzhao 102 39.32 N 107.52 E
Xinzhazhen 106 31.50 N 119.52 E
Xinzhen, Zhg. 98 35.37 N 114.03 E
Xinzhen, Zhg. 105 39.01 N 116.22 E
Xinzhen, Zhg. 106 31.24 N 121.24 E
Xinzheng 100 34.25 N 113.43 E
Xinzhou, Zhg. 100 30.50 N 114.47 E
Xinzhou, Zhg. 102 19.48 N 109.18 E
Xinzhuang, Zhg. 98 35.05 N 117.56 E
Xinzhuang, Zhg. 271a 39.56 N 116.31 E
Xinzhuangtou 105 39.25 N 115.45 E
Xinzhuangzi, Zhg. 104 41.05 N 121.23 E
Xinzhuangzi, Zhg. 105 40.14 N 116.59 E
Xinzhuangzi, Zhg. 105 40.32 N 115.10 E
Xinzhuangzi, Zhg. 105 38.52 N 117.21 E
Xinzhuangzi, Zhg. 105 39.20 N 118.25 E
Xinzo de Limia 34 42.03 N 7.43 W
Xiongdi Yu II 100 23.33 N 117.40 E
Xiongjiachang 102 26.31 N 105.39 E
Xiongxian 105 38.59 N 116.05 E
Xiongyuecheng 98 40.10 N 122.08 E
Xipamanu (Chipamanu) ≐ 248 10.43 S 67.50 W
Xiping, Zhg. 100 33.23 N 114.02 E
Xiping, Zhg. 100 28.27 N 119.29 E
Xiping'anhe 104 40.47 N 122.01 E
Xiqia 106 31.03 N 119.37 E
Xiqilichiquan 89 49.59 N 119.27 E
Xiqin 100 26.33 N 118.06 E
Xiqing Shan ⋌ 102 35.30 N 101.30 E
Xique-Xique 250 10.50 S 42.44 W
Xırdalan 84 40.26 N 49.51 E
Xisanshilipu 100 32.40 N 117.31 E
Xisantai 98 39.38 N 121.37 E
Xishan, Zhg. 100 28.34 N 115.37 E
Xishan, Zhg. 105 39.38 N 118.10 E
Xishanqiao 106 31.57 N 118.43 E
Xishanxicun 105 40.01 N 116.50 E
Xisha Qundao (Paracel Islands) II 108 16.30 N 112.15 E
Xishijiazi 104 41.46 N 120.55 E
Xishiqiao 106 31.53 N 120.06 E
Xishu 98 36.41 N 113.49 E
Xishui 100 30.27 N 115.13 E
Xishuiyu 105 40.25 N 116.16 E
Xisuhupu 104 41.41 N 123.14 E
Xitai 98 40.37 N 120.12 E
Xitan 100 23.47 N 117.08 E
Xitang 106 30.57 N 120.53 E
Xitangqiao, Zhg. 106 31.49 N 120.38 E
Xitangqiao, Zhg. 106 30.37 N 121.01 E
Xitaoyuan 104 40.57 N 122.11 E
Xiti 120 33.27 N 82.48 E
Xitianmu Shan ∧ 106 30.21 N 119.25 E
Xitiao ≐ 106 30.57 N 120.10 E
Xiting 106 32.07 N 121.00 E
Xitole 150 11.43 N 14.50 W
Xituan 105 39.29 N 115.47 E
Xiu ≐ 100 29.13 N 115.56 E
Xiujiangpu 104 41.17 N 123.02 E
Xiuning 100 29.47 N 118.10 E
Xiushan 102 28.29 N 108.52 E
Xiushui 100 29.04 N 114.33 E
Xiushui ≐ 104 42.03 N 122.58 E
Xiushuihe 104 42.22 N 123.01 E
Xiuyan 98 40.17 N 123.18 E
Xiva 34 39.28 N 0.43 W
Xiwei 100 25.22 N 117.46 E
Xiweizigou 104 42.01 N 121.59 E
Xiwenquan 107 29.42 N 106.07 E
Xiwu 100 29.40 N 121.30 E
Xiwukou 106 30.24 N 118.54 E
Xixabangma Feng ∧ 124 28.22 N 85.50 E
Xixi 100 26.45 N 118.42 E
Xixia 102 33.22 N 111.28 E
Xixian, Zhg. 100 32.21 N 114.44 E
Xixian, Zhg. 102 36.43 N 110.52 E
Xixiang 102 32.48 N 107.55 E
Xixiangyang 105 39.33 N 116.02 E
Xixiaojie 104 40.42 N 122.12 E
Xixiashu 106 31.57 N 119.49 E
Xixing 106 30.11 N 120.13 E
Xixona 34 38.32 N 0.30 W
Xiyang, Zhg. 98 37.37 N 113.42 E
Xiyang, Zhg. 100 25.50 N 117.25 E
Xiyang, Zhg. 106 31.49 N 120.43 E
Xiyang, Zhg. 106 31.52 N 119.23 E
Xiyang Dao I 100 26.32 N 120.04 E
Xiyangji 100 33.25 N 116.22 E
Xiyangjiao 106 31.43 N 120.23 E
Xiyangshugou 104 40.41 N 122.44 E
Xiyangzhuang 106 31.50 N 119.22 E
Xiyingzi 104 41.55 N 122.34 E
Xiyou 98 37.24 N 119.56 E
Xiyushi 106 30.36 N 119.26 E
Xizang Zizhiqu (Tibet) □[4] 90 32.00 N 88.00 E
Xizhi ≐ 100 23.04 N 114.31 E
Xizhimen Station ◆[5] 271a 39.56 N 116.21 E
Xizhong Dao I 98 39.26 N 121.17 E
Xizhou 100 29.29 N 121.39 E
Xizi 98 41.48 N 119.16 E
Xocaväند 84 39.48 N 47.06 E
Xochiapa 234 17.39 N 95.46 W
Xochicalco ⊥ 234 18.48 N 99.19 W
Xochimilco ◆[8] 286a 19.16 N 99.06 W
Xochimilco, Lago de ⊜ 286a 19.16 N 99.06 W
Xochipala 234 17.48 N 99.39 W
Xochistlahuaca 234 16.47 N 98.15 W
Xochitlán 234 19.59 N 97.36 W
Xoka 120 29.58 N 93.48 E
Xom Binh Phuoc 269c 10.40 N 106.47 E
Xom Xoai Minh 269c 10.42 N 106.50 E
Xu ≐ 100 28.17 N 116.05 E
Xuancheng 106 30.58 N 118.45 E
Xuan'en 102 30.00 N 109.20 E
Xuanfeng 100 27.42 N 114.08 E
Xuang ≐ 110 19.58 N 102.15 E
Xuanhan 102 31.24 N 107.43 E
Xuanhua 105 40.37 N 115.03 E
Xuanhuadian 100 31.42 N 114.29 E
Xuanhui ≐ 98 38.07 N 117.45 E
Xuanjiabao 106 32.17 N 120.01 E
Xuanjiangying 98 41.25 N 116.45 E
Xuan Loc 110 10.56 N 107.14 E
Xuantan 107 29.12 N 105.34 E
Xuan Thoi Thuong 269c 10.52 N 106.34 E
Xuanwei 102 26.07 N 104.05 E
Xuanzhuang 105 39.29 N 118.07 E
Xubu 98 40.02 N 113.43 E
Xuchang, Zhg. 100 34.03 N 113.49 E
Xuchang, Zhg. 107 29.06 N 104.31 E
Xucheng 98 35.56 N 116.27 E
Xuchilquitongo 234 17.15 N 96.53 W
Xucun 106 30.27 N 120.22 E
Xudat 84 41.38 N 48.42 E
Xudazhuang 100 33.44 N 117.53 E
Xuddun 144 9.09 N 47.28 E
Xuddur 144 4.07 N 43.54 E
Xueao 100 29.27 N 121.30 E
Xuebu 106 31.43 N 119.22 E
Xuecheng 98 34.50 N 117.16 E
Xuedian, Zhg. 100 34.04 N 113.04 E
Xuedian, Zhg. 100 34.30 N 113.44 E
Xuefanggou 104 41.57 N 121.01 E
Xuefeng 100 33.21 N 118.22 E
Xuehu 98 34.08 N 116.27 E
Xueshan Zhang ∧ 100 24.24 N 113.37 E
Xueshuiwen 89 49.10 N 129.45 E
Xuetangpuzi 104 40.38 N 123.53 E
Xueyanqiao 106 31.30 N 120.06 E
Xuezhen 106 31.35 N 118.38 E
Xuguanzhen 106 31.23 N 120.30 E
Xuguichenxiaodian 106 32.07 N 121.20 E
Xuguit Qi (Yakeshi) 89 49.17 N 120.41 E
Xuji 100 31.50 N 116.22 E
Xujiabu 100 29.27 N 116.18 E
Xujiadong 100 25.54 N 113.02 E
Xujiadu 100 28.18 N 114.44 E
Xujiagou 104 42.17 N 124.04 E
Xujiapuzi 104 40.44 N 123.18 E
Xujiatou 106 31.19 N 119.25 E
Xujiazhai, Zhg. 106 31.11 N 121.46 E
Xujiazhai, Zhg. 269b 31.23 N 121.17 E
Xuliying 105 39.28 N 116.02 E
Xun ≐, Zhg. 89 49.27 N 128.55 E
Xun ≐, Zhg. 102 23.28 N 111.18 E
Xungru 120 29.15 N 84.49 E
Xunhe 89 49.18 N 128.04 E
Xunhua 102 35.49 N 102.26 E
Xunjiansi 105 40.50 N 116.04 E
Xunke 89 49.35 N 128.25 E
Xunle 102 25.17 N 108.12 E
Xunmukou 98 34.03 N 114.42 E
Xunshansuo 98 37.10 N 122.29 E
Xunwu 100 24.58 N 115.38 E
Xunwu ≐ 100 24.28 N 115.26 E
Xunxian 98 35.43 N 114.31 E
Xupu, Zhg. 102 27.44 N 110.24 E
Xupu, Zhg. 106 31.45 N 120.54 E
Xushe 106 31.24 N 119.39 E
Xushi 106 31.40 N 120.57 E
Xushui 105 39.02 N 115.39 E
Xutian 98 34.10 N 114.03 E
Xuwan 100 27.55 N 116.31 E
Xuwen 102 20.21 N 110.11 E
Xuxiandai 106 30.40 N 120.47 E
Xuxiang 106 31.33 N 120.13 E
Xuyen Moc 110 10.34 N 107.25 E
Xuyi 100 33.01 N 118.29 E
Xuyong 102 28.10 N 105.24 E
Xuzhou (Süchow) 98 34.16 N 117.11 E
Xuzhuang 106 31.09 N 120.32 E

Y

Yaak 182 48.50 N 115.42 W
Yaan 102 30.03 N 103.02 E
Yaapeet 166 35.46 S 142.03 E
Yaaq-Baraawe 144 1.57 N 43.11 E
Yaba ◆[8] 273a 6.30 N 3.23 E
Yaba College of Technology ⊍[2] 273a 6.32 N 3.23 E
Ya'bad 132 32.27 N 35.10 E
Yabakei 96 33.27 N 131.07 E
Yabassi 152 4.28 N 9.58 E
Yabe 96 33.09 N 130.49 E
Yabe ≐ 96 33.06 N 130.26 E
Yabelo 144 4.54 N 38.05 E
Yablis 236 14.10 N 83.49 W
Yablonovy Range
→ Jablonovyj chrebet ⋌ 88 53.30 N 115.00 E
Yabluniv 78 48.24 N 24.57 E
Yablychne 78 50.18 N 35.14 E
Yabrīn ⊤[4] 128 23.17 N 48.58 E
Yabrūd 130 33.58 N 36.40 E
Yabu, Nihon 96 35.22 N 134.47 E
Yabu, Nihon 174m 26.36 N 127.57 E
Yabucoa 240m 18.03 N 65.53 W
Yabuki 94 37.12 N 140.19 E
Yabuli 89 44.55 N 128.35 E
Yacambu, Parque Nacional ♦ 246 9.40 N 69.42 W
Yacaré Norte, Riacho ≐ 252 22.43 S 58.14 W
Yacheng 110 18.25 N 109.11 E
Yachi ≐ 102 27.18 N 107.15 E
Yachimata 94 35.39 N 140.19 E
Yachiyo, Nihon 94 35.43 N 140.07 E
Yachiyo, Nihon 94 36.10 N 139.53 E
Yacimiento Río Turbio 254 51.32 S 72.18 W
Yaco 248 17.09 S 67.24 W
Yaco (Iaco) ≐ 248 9.03 S 68.34 W
Yacolt 224 45.51 N 122.24 W
Yacuiba 248 22.02 S 63.45 W
Yacuma ≐ 248 13.38 S 65.23 W
Yacyretá, Isla I 252 27.25 S 56.30 W
Yada ≐ 96 35.38 N 134.37 E
Yādgīr 122 16.46 N 77.08 E
Yadkin ≐ 192 35.23 N 80.03 W
Yadkinville 192 36.08 N 80.39 W
Yad Mordekhay 132 31.35 N 34.34 E
Yadong 124 27.29 N 88.55 E
Yādūdah 132 32.40 N 36.04 E
Yaduty 78 51.22 N 32.19 E
Yaenengu 152 2.28 N 23.15 E
Yaeyama-rettō II 175d 24.20 N 124.00 E
Yāfā 132 32.41 N 35.17 E
Yafran 146 32.04 N 12.31 E
Yaftābād 267d 35.39 N 51.19 E
Yafuquan 85 39.12 N 76.09 E
Yagachi-shima I 174m 26.40 N 128.01 E
Yağcılar 130 39.25 N 28.23 E
Yageg 144 3.16 N 44.00 E
Yagi 96 35.04 N 135.32 E
Yagishiri-tō I 92a 44.26 N 141.25 E
Yağlıca Dağı ∧ 84 40.18 N 43.18 E
Yago 234 21.50 N 105.04 W
Yagonde 152 0.02 N 22.41 E
Yagoona 274a 33.55 S 151.02 E
Yagoua 146 10.20 N 15.14 E
Yagradagzê Shan ∧ 120 35.12 N 95.20 E
Yaguachi Nuevo 246 2.07 S 79.41 W
Yaguajay 240p 22.19 N 79.14 W
Yaguala ≐ 236 15.25 N 86.40 W
Yaguará 246 2.40 N 75.31 W
Yaguaraparo 246 10.34 N 62.49 W
Yaguarí 252 31.31 S 54.58 W
Yaguarón (Jaguarão) ≐ 252 32.39 S 53.12 W
Yaguas ≐ 246 2.45 S 70.04 W
Yagur 132 32.44 N 35.04 E
Yahagi ≐ 94 34.50 N 136.59 E
Yahagong 102 28.24 N 99.11 E
Yahara ≐ 190 42.48 N 89.07 W
Yahata
→ Kitakyūshū 96 33.53 N 130.50 E
Yahe, Zhg. 89 45.24 N 130.24 E
Yahe, Zhg. 106 31.44 N 119.52 E
Yahila 152 0.13 N 24.28 E
Yahk 182 49.05 N 116.05 W
Yahmūm al-Asmar, Jabal ∧ 142 29.56 N 31.38 E
Yaho 268 35.41 N 139.27 E
Yahōga-take ∧ 96 33.04 N 130.50 E
Yahongqiao 105 39.45 N 117.51 E
Yahorlyts'kyy lyman c 78 46.24 N 31.50 E
Yahotyn 78 50.17 N 31.46 E
Yahualica 234 21.08 N 102.51 W
Yahuma 152 1.05 N 23.13 E
Yahyalı 130 38.07 N 35.22 E
Yai ≐ 114 5.02 N 101.47 E
Yai, Khao ∧, Asia 110 12.27 N 99.26 E
Yai, Khao ∧, Thai 110 15.25 N 99.20 E
Yainax Butte ∧ 202 42.20 N 121.16 W
Yaita, Nihon 94 36.48 N 139.56 E
Yaita, Nihon 268 35.57 N 140.03 E
Yaitopya
→ Ethiopia □[1] 144 9.00 N 39.00 E
Yaizu 94 34.52 N 138.20 E
Yajiang 102 30.02 N 101.05 E
Yaka 130 41.15 N 34.01 E
Yakacık 130 36.47 N 36.10 E
Yakacık ◆[8] 267b 40.55 N 29.13 E
Yakage 96 34.37 N 133.35 E
Yakak, Cape › 180 51.38 N 177.00 W
Yakapınar 130 37.00 N 35.36 E
Yakarta
→ Jakarta 115a 6.10 S 106.48 E
Yake-dake ∧ 94 36.14 N 137.35 E
Yake-yama ∧ 94 36.55 N 138.03 E
Yakhchāl, Afg. 120 31.47 N 64.41 E
Yakhchāl, Afg. 128 31.47 N 64.41 E
Yakhnyky 78 50.26 N 33.10 E
Yakima 202 46.36 N 120.30 W
Yakima □[6] 224 46.34 N 121.03 W
Yakima ≐ 202 46.15 N 119.02 W
Yakima Firing Center ▪ 202 46.44 N 120.10 W
Yakima Indian Reservation ◆[4] 224 46.16 N 121.03 W
Yakkan ≐ 96 33.34 N 131.22 E
Yakmach 128 28.45 N 63.51 E
Yako 150 12.58 N 2.16 W
Yakō ◆[8] 268 35.32 N 139.41 E
Yakobi Island I 180 58.00 N 136.30 W
Yakoma 152 4.05 N 22.27 E
Yakou 100 24.46 N 118.46 E
Yakuendai 268 35.43 N 140.03 E
Yakuluku 154 4.20 N 28.48 E
Yakumo 92a 42.15 N 140.16 E
Yakuno 96 35.19 N 135.00 E
Yakushi-dake ∧ 94 36.28 N 137.33 E
Yakushi-ji ⊍[1] 94 36.25 N 139.53 E
Yaku-shima I 93b 30.20 N 130.30 E

Symbols in the index entries represent the broad categories identified in the key at the right. Symbols with superior numbers (⋌[1]) identify subcategories (see complete key on page *I · 1).*

Symbole im Register stellen die rechts im Schlüssel erklärten Kategorien dar. Symbole mit hochgestellten Ziffern (⋌[1]) bezeichnen Unterabteilungen einer Kategorie (vgl. vollständiger Schlüssel auf Seite *I · 1).*

Los símbolos incluídos en el texto del índice representan las grandes categorías identificadas con la clave a la derecha. Los símbolos con numeros en su parte superior (⋌[1]) identifican las subcategorías (véase la clave completa en la página *I · 1).*

Les symboles de l'index représentent les catégories indiquées dans la légende à droite. Les symboles suivis d'un indice (⋌[1]) représentent des souscatégories (voir légende complète à la page *I · 1).*

Os símbolos incluídos no texto do índice representam as grandes categorias identificadas com a chave à direita. Os símbolos com números em sua parte superior (⋌[1]) identificam as subcategorias (veja-se a chave completa à página *I · 1).*

∧ Mountain	Berg	Montaña	Montagne	Montanha
⋌ Mountains	Gebirge	Montañas	Montagnes	Montanhas
)(Pass	Paß	Paso	Col	Passo
V Valley, Canyon	Tal, Cañon	Valle, Cañón	Vallée, Canyon	Vale, Canhão
≚ Plain	Ebene	Llano	Plaine	Planície
› Cape	Kap	Cabo	Cap	Cabo
I Island	Insel	Isla	Île	Ilha
II Islands	Inseln	Islas	Îles	Ilhas
⩡ Other Topographic Features	Andere Topographische Objekte	Otros Elementos Topográficos	Autres données topographiques	Outros acidentes topográficos

ESPAÑOL — FRANÇAIS — PORTUGUÊS

Nombre / Nom / Nome	Página / Page	Lat.°′	Long.°′ W = Oeste / W = Ouest
Yakutat	180	59.33 N	139.44 W
Yakutat Bay ⊂	180	59.40 N	140.00 W
Yakutat Seamount ✣[3]	16	35.15 N	48.00 W
Yakutia → Jakutija □[3]	74	67.00 N	125.00 E
Yakutsk → Jakutsk	74	62.00 N	129.40 E
Yakymivka	78	46.42 N	35.09 E
Yala, Ghana	150	10.07 N	1.52 W
Yala, Thai	110	6.33 N	101.18 E
Yalaha	220	28.44 N	81.48 W
Yalahau, Laguna ⊂	232	21.30 N	87.15 W
Yalakdere	130	40.36 N	29.33 E
Yalama	84	41.44 N	48.34 E
Yalata	162	31.29 S	131.52 E
Yalata Aboriginal Reserve ◆[4]	162	31.30 S	131.45 E
Yalca, Laguna ⊜	258	35.34 S	57.55 W
Yalding	260	51.13 N	0.26 E
Yale, B.C., Can.	182	49.34 N	121.26 W
Yale, Mi., U.S.	190	43.07 N	82.47 W
Yale, Ok., U.S.	196	36.06 N	96.41 W
Yale, Va., U.S.	208	36.50 N	77.17 W
Yale, Lake ⊜	220	28.54 N	81.45 W
Yale, Mount ∧	200	38.51 N	106.18 W
Yale Lake ⊜[1]	224	46.00 N	122.12 W
Yalgar ≃	162	26.09 S	117.57 E
Yalgoo	162	28.20 S	116.41 E
Yalgorup National Park ♠	168a	32.55 S	115.41 E
Yali	152	0.04 N	21.03 E
Yaliji	98	36.06 N	114.56 E
Yalikamba	152	1.17 S	22.30 E
Yalinga	152	6.31 N	23.15 E
Yalisere	152	0.11 N	22.33 E
Yalleroi	166	24.04 S	145.45 E
Yallourn	169	38.11 S	146.21 E
Yallourn North	169	38.09 S	146.22 E
Yalnızçam Dağları ⋏	84	41.10 N	42.25 E
Yalobusha ≃	194	33.33 N	90.10 W
Yaloká	152	5.19 N	17.05 E
Yalong ≃	102	26.37 N	101.48 E
Yaloupi ≃	250	2.47 N	52.28 W
Yalova	130	40.39 N	29.15 E
Yalpuh, ozero ⊜	78	45.25 N	28.37 E
Yalta, Ukr.	78	44.30 N	34.10 E
Yalta, Ukr.	83	46.58 N	37.16 E
Yaltushkiv	78	48.58 N	27.30 E
Yalu	89	48.34 N	122.09 E
Yalu (Amnok-kang) ≃, Asia	98	39.55 N	124.22 E
Yalu ≃, Zhg.	89	46.56 N	123.30 E
Yalufi	152	0.45 N	24.26 E
Yalvaç	130	38.17 N	31.11 E
Yalwal Creek ≃	170	34.50 S	150.23 E
Yamachiche	206	46.16 N	72.50 W
Yamachiche ≃	206	46.16 N	72.48 W
Yamada, Nihon	92	39.28 N	141.57 E
Yamada, Nihon	94	35.49 N	140.36 E
Yamada, Nihon	94	36.34 N	137.05 E
Yamada, Nihon	96	33.33 N	130.47 E
Yamada → Tosa-yamada, Nihon	96	33.36 N	133.41 E
Yamada, Nihon	174m	26.26 N	127.47 E
Yamada, Nihon	270	34.31 N	135.39 E
Yamada, Nihon	270	34.48 N	135.32 E
Yamada ≃	270	34.47 N	135.04 E
Yamaga, Nihon	96	33.01 N	130.41 E
Yamaga, Nihon	96	33.27 N	131.30 E
Yamagata, Nihon	92	38.15 N	140.20 E
Yamagata, Nihon	94	36.38 N	140.24 E
Yamagata, Nihon	94	36.10 N	137.52 E
Yamagawa	92	31.12 N	130.39 E
Yamaguchi, Nihon	94	35.33 N	137.33 E
Yamaguchi, Nihon	96	34.10 N	131.29 E
Yamaguchi, Nihon	270	34.50 N	135.15 E
Yamaguchi □[5]	96	34.20 N	131.30 E
Yamaguchi-chosuichi ⊜[1]	268	35.46 N	139.25 E
Yama-Hita-Hiko-san-kokutei-kōen ♠	96	33.25 N	131.02 E
Yamakawa	96	34.04 N	134.15 E
Yamakita	94	35.21 N	139.05 E
Yamakuni	96	33.24 N	131.02 E
Yamakuni ≃	96	33.37 N	131.12 E
Yamalia → Jamalo-Neneckij □[3]	72	67.00 N	75.00 E
Yamām, Jabal al- ∧	132	30.02 N	35.28 E
Yamamoto, Nihon	96	34.07 N	133.44 E
Yamamoto, Nihon	270	34.38 N	135.38 E
Yamanaka	94	36.15 N	136.22 E
Yamanakako	94	35.24 N	138.52 E
Yamanaka-ko ⊜	94	35.25 N	138.52 E
Yamanashi	94	35.40 N	138.40 E
Yamanashi □[5]	94	35.30 N	138.30 E
Yamanouchi	94	36.44 N	138.25 E
Yamasaki	96	35.00 N	134.33 E
Yamashina ◆[8]	270	34.58 N	135.49 E
Yamashiro, Nihon	94	34.45 N	135.49 E
Yamashiro, Nihon	96	33.57 N	133.45 E
Yamaska (Saint-Michel)	206	46.00 N	72.55 W
Yamaska □[6]	206	46.00 N	72.45 W
Yamaska ≃	206	46.06 N	72.56 W
Yamaska, Mont ∧[2]	206	45.27 N	72.52 W
Yamaska Nord ≃	206	45.17 N	72.51 W
Yamaska Sud-Est ≃	206	45.17 N	72.55 W
Yamate	270	34.30 N	135.27 E
Yamatengwumulu	102	38.38 N	97.05 E
Yamato, Nihon	94	35.48 N	136.54 E
Yamato, Nihon	94	35.29 N	139.29 E
Yamato, Nihon	94	37.10 N	138.56 E
Yamato, Nihon	96	33.08 N	130.26 E
Yamato ≃	96	34.36 N	135.26 E
Yamato-Aogaki-kokutei-kōen ♠	94	34.40 N	135.50 E
Yamato-kōriyama	96	34.38 N	135.47 E
Yamato-takada	96	34.31 N	135.45 E
Yamatsuri	94	36.52 N	140.25 E
Yamazaki	268	35.56 N	139.54 E
Yamba	166	29.26 S	153.22 E
Yambata	152	2.26 N	21.58 E
Yambéring	150	11.49 N	12.21 W
Yambio	154	4.34 N	28.23 E
Yambol → Jambol	38	42.29 N	26.30 E
Yamboyo	152	0.40 N	22.18 E
Yambrasbamba	248	5.45 S	77.54 W
Yambuya	154	1.16 N	24.33 E
Yamdena, Pulau ▮	164	7.36 S	131.25 E
Yame	96	33.28 N	130.34 E
Ya Men ⊂	100	22.09 N	113.05 E
Yamenkou	105	39.53 N	116.12 E
Yamenying	89	43.25 N	122.19 E
Yamethin	110	20.26 N	96.09 E
Yamhill	224	45.21 N	123.11 W
Yamhill □[6]	224	45.15 N	123.20 W
Yamhill ≃	224	45.14 N	123.00 W
Yamia	150	13.24 N	10.18 E
Yamizo-san ∧	94	36.56 N	140.17 E
Yamma Yamma, Lake ⊜	166	26.20 S	141.25 E
Yamoussoukro	150	6.49 N	5.17 W
Yampa	200	40.09 N	106.54 W
Yampa ≃	200	40.32 N	108.59 W
Yampa Plateau ⋏[1]	200	40.25 N	109.00 W
Yamparaez	248	19.10 S	65.10 W
Yampil', Ukr.	78	49.58 N	26.14 E
Yampil', Ukr.	78	51.57 N	33.46 E
Yampil', Ukr.	78	48.16 N	28.17 E
Yampil', Ukr.	83	48.56 N	37.58 E
Yamsay Mountain ∧	202	42.56 N	121.22 W
Yamu	102	43.48 N	94.48 E
Yamuna ≃	120	25.25 N	81.50 E
Yamuna Bridge ◆[5]	272a	28.40 N	77.14 E
Yamunānagar	124	30.07 N	77.18 E
Yamzho Yumco ⊜	120	28.58 N	90.44 E
Yan	114	5.48 N	100.22 E
Yan ≃, S. Lan.	122	8.55 N	81.01 E
Yan ≃, Zhg.	102	36.24 N	110.28 E
Yanac	166	36.08 S	141.26 E
Yanacachi	248	16.23 S	67.43 W
Yanachaga-Chemillen, Parque Nacional ♠	248	10.10 S	75.20 W
Yanadani	96	33.32 N	133.01 E
Yanagawa	96	33.10 N	130.24 E
Yanagi	270	34.25 N	135.56 E
Yanagimoto	270	34.34 N	135.51 E
Yanahara	96	34.55 N	134.05 E
Yanaha-shima ▮	174m	26.54 N	127.56 E
Yanahuara	248	16.24 S	71.33 W
Yanai	96	33.58 N	132.07 E
Yanaka	268	35.24 N	140.01 E
Yanam	122	16.44 N	82.13 E
Yan'an	102	36.36 N	109.28 E
Yanaoca	248	14.13 S	71.26 W
Yanarsu	130	38.02 N	41.33 E
Yanbian	102	26.55 N	101.30 E
Yanbu	100	23.05 N	113.10 E
Yanbu' al-Baḥr	128	24.05 N	38.03 E
Yanbutou	100	29.52 N	115.04 E
Yanceyville	192	36.24 N	79.20 W
Yanchang	102	36.31 N	110.08 E
Yancheng, Zhg.	100	33.36 N	113.57 E
Yancheng, Zhg.	100	33.24 N	120.09 E
Yanchep	168a	31.33 S	115.41 E
Yanchep National Park ♠	168a	31.32 S	115.40 E
Yanchi, Zhg.	102	37.52 N	107.22 E
Yanchi, Zhg.	105	40.02 N	115.53 E
Yanchuan	102	36.56 N	110.05 E
Yanco	166	34.36 S	146.25 E
Yanco Creek ≃	166	35.16 S	145.07 E
Yanda Creek ≃	166	30.28 S	145.45 E
Yandal	162	27.33 S	121.07 E
Yandama Creek ≃	166	30.00 S	140.10 E
Yandé, Île ▮	175f	20.03 S	163.49 E
Yande Aboriginal Reserve ◆[4]	162	21.35 S	118.45 E
Yandev	150	7.20 N	9.01 E
Yandina	175e	9.07 S	159.13 E
Yandja	152	1.41 S	17.43 E
Yandongi	152	2.51 N	22.16 E
Yandoon	110	17.02 N	95.39 E
Yandua Island ▮	175g	16.49 S	178.18 E
Yandun	102	42.20 N	94.09 E
Yanfeng	102	25.53 N	101.01 E
Yanfolila	150	11.11 N	8.09 W
Yang ≃, Thai	110	15.44 N	104.00 E
Yang ≃, Zhg.	105	40.24 N	115.20 E
Yangambi	154	0.47 N	24.28 E
Yangan, Austl.	171a	28.12 S	152.13 E
Yang'an, Zhg.	98	37.38 N	117.09 E
Yan'gang	100	26.02 N	116.22 E
Yangarakata	154	3.01 N	30.28 E
Yangasa Levu ▮	175g	18.57 S	178.26 W
Yangbajain	120	30.06 N	90.33 E
Yangce	100	32.58 N	113.14 E
Yangcha	98	41.11 N	126.15 E
Yangchang	107	30.22 N	103.42 E
Yangcheng, Zhg.	102	35.29 N	112.25 E
Yangcheng, Zhg.	106	31.24 N	120.47 E
Yangcheng Hu ⊜	106	31.26 N	120.47 E
Yangchiang → Yangjiang	102	21.51 N	111.56 E
Yangch'ŏn ◆[8]	271b	37.34 N	126.51 E
Yangchow → Yangzhou	100	32.24 N	119.26 E
Yangchu	98	37.11 N	120.47 E
Yangch'üan → Yangquan	98	37.52 N	113.36 E
Yangchun	102	22.10 N	111.46 E
Yangcun, Zhg.	100	28.07 N	117.40 E
Yangcun, Zhg.	100	23.26 N	114.30 E
Yangcun, Zhg.	105	39.09 N	115.50 E
Yangcunqiao	100	29.36 N	119.28 E
Yangdachengzi	89	43.59 N	124.25 E
Yangdalinzi	98	42.38 N	125.07 E
Yangdang	100	32.23 N	112.39 E
Yangdian	106	31.08 N	119.45 E
Yang'erzhuang	98	38.18 N	117.30 E
Yangfang	105	40.07 N	116.07 E
Yangfangpu	105	40.48 N	115.01 E
Yangfengang	105	39.07 N	116.52 E
Yangfenzhen	106	30.28 N	120.03 E
Yanggang Do □[4]	98	41.15 N	128.00 E
Yangganzhen	106	31.00 N	119.15 E
Yanggao	98	40.25 N	113.44 E
Yanggezhuang	105	40.09 N	116.48 E
Yanggong-ni	271b	37.39 N	126.37 E
Yanggu, Taehan	98	38.06 N	127.59 E
Yanggu, Zhg.	98	34.44 N	114.48 E
Yanggu, Zhg.	98	36.08 N	115.48 E
Yangguanpu	100	32.13 N	115.31 E
Yanghang	106	31.22 N	121.26 E
Yanghe	100	33.47 N	118.23 E
Yanghexi	102	29.39 N	108.40 E
Yanghu	100	32.34 N	116.30 E
Yanghua	107	30.11 N	104.45 E
Yanghua ≃	107	30.09 N	104.42 E
Yangi-Yul' → Jangijul'	85	41.07 N	69.03 E
Yangji, Zhg.	98	36.44 N	113.56 E
Yangji, Zhg.	98	34.25 N	116.06 E
Yangji, Zhg.	100	34.19 N	119.28 E
Yangjia, Zhg.	98	34.19 N	119.28 E
Yangjia, Zhg.	106	30.41 N	120.15 E
Yangjiachang, Zhg.	107	29.23 N	104.21 E
Yangjiachang, Zhg.	107	29.45 N	105.21 E
Yangjiafeng	100	30.49 N	112.47 E
Yangjiagou	105	39.18 N	117.54 E
Yangjiajie	107	30.18 N	104.39 E
Yangjian	106	31.39 N	120.33 E
Yangjiang	102	21.51 N	111.56 E
Yangjiaogou	98	37.16 N	118.50 E
Yangjiaqiao, Zhg.	100	27.44 N	112.46 E
Yangjiaqiao, Zhg.	106	31.53 N	121.42 E
Yangjiaqiao, Zhg.	106	32.02 N	121.26 E
Yangjiatao	105	39.49 N	117.51 E
Yangjiawopu	104	42.21 N	122.57 E
Yangjiazeng	105	40.12 N	117.04 E
Yangjiazhangzi	104	40.48 N	120.33 E
Yangjie	102	24.49 N	100.22 E
Yangjishi	100	26.39 N	113.14 E
Yangkou	100	26.47 N	117.51 E
Yangkoushi	100	28.39 N	118.53 E
Yanglinjie	100	29.07 N	113.27 E
Yangliupu, Zhg.	100	30.52 N	118.37 E
Yangliupu, Zhg.	107	30.09 N	104.03 E
Yangliuqing	105	39.08 N	117.01 E
Yangloudong	100	29.31 N	113.44 E
Yanglousi	100	29.30 N	113.38 E
Yangluo	100	30.41 N	114.34 E
Yangluomayu	104	40.47 N	122.54 E
Yangmachang	107	30.39 N	103.45 E
Yangma Dao ▮	98	37.28 N	121.37 E
Yangmahe	107	30.29 N	104.31 E
Yangmeisi	100	25.42 N	114.30 E
Yangmiao, Zhg.	98	34.11 N	114.53 E
Yangmiao, Zhg.	106	30.51 N	120.49 E
Yangmingshan ◆[8]	269d	25.09 N	121.33 E
Yangming Shan ∧	102	26.03 N	111.56 E
Yangmugou, Zhg.	98	40.36 N	124.28 E
Yangmugou, Zhg.	104	41.11 N	123.50 E
Yangmulin	105	40.06 N	115.12 E
Yangon (Rangoon)	110	16.47 N	96.10 E
Yangon □[8]	110	16.50 N	96.10 E
Yangor	174b	0.31 S	166.54 E
Yangpingguan	102	32.51 N	106.09 E
Yangpu	100	27.14 N	119.08 E
Yangp'yŏng	98	37.30 N	127.29 E
Yangp'yŏng-ni	98	40.53 N	127.58 E
Yangqi	106	31.23 N	119.57 E
Yangquan	98	37.52 N	113.36 E
Yangriwan	102	31.37 N	110.49 E
Yangsan	98	35.21 N	129.03 E
Yangshan, Zhg.	98	41.13 N	120.24 E
Yangshan, Zhg.	98	35.13 N	116.13 E
Yangshan, Zhg.	102	24.28 N	112.38 E
Yangshigangzi	104	41.42 N	122.59 E
Yangshitun	104	42.06 N	123.44 E
Yangshu	106	31.39 N	120.08 E
Yangshugemen	105	40.55 N	118.18 E
Yangshugoudonggou	104	41.43 N	120.41 E
Yangshuling	98	41.02 N	118.47 E
Yangshuo	102	24.45 N	110.24 E
Yangtan	106	30.42 N	119.11 E
Yangtian Zhang ∧	100	24.37 N	115.38 E
Yangting	98	37.24 N	122.07 E
Yangtou	100	23.26 N	115.24 E
Yangtze → Chang ≃	90	31.48 N	121.10 E
Yanguan	106	30.26 N	120.32 E
Yangwan, Zhg.	100	28.22 N	116.46 E
Yangwan, Zhg.	106	31.03 N	120.22 E
Yangxi, Zhg.	100	30.11 N	118.39 E
Yangxi, Zhg.	100	27.18 N	114.10 E
Yangxian	102	33.03 N	107.47 E
Yangxiang, Zhg.	106	31.29 N	119.35 E
Yangxiang, Zhg.	106	31.12 N	121.01 E
Yangxiangtun	104	40.58 N	122.48 E
Yangxiaodian	100	31.46 N	116.45 E
Yangximu ≃	104	42.04 N	123.00 E
Yangxin, Zhg.	98	37.39 N	117.34 E
Yangxin, Zhg.	100	29.51 N	115.12 E
Yangxiudian	271a	39.44 N	116.32 E
Yangyang	98	38.04 N	128.36 E
Yangyuan (Xicheng)	98	40.01 N	114.10 E
Yangze	100	26.57 N	118.23 E
Yangzhong	106	32.16 N	119.49 E
Yangzhou	100	32.24 N	119.26 E
Yangzhuang	100	33.36 N	118.58 E
Yangzhujuanzi	104	41.38 N	122.46 E
Yangzi	100	31.19 N	112.36 E
Yangzishao	98	42.28 N	126.09 E
Yanhaiyingzi	104	41.52 N	123.05 E
Yanhe, Zhg.	100	31.16 N	115.07 E
Yanhe, Zhg.	102	28.37 N	108.35 E
Yanhecheng	105	40.04 N	115.43 E
Yanheying	98	40.02 N	119.03 E
Yanhui	98	37.54 N	113.51 E
Yanina → Ioánnina	38	39.40 N	20.50 E
Yanji, Zhg.	98	34.41 N	115.27 E
Yanji, Zhg.	98	42.57 N	129.32 E
Yanji (Longjing), Zhg.	98	42.47 N	129.26 E
Yanji, Zhg.	98	34.17 N	115.39 E
Yanjia	104	40.57 N	121.41 E
Yanjiabao	106	32.19 N	120.07 E
Yanjiadian	98	39.48 N	121.49 E
Yanjiahe	100	31.48 N	114.50 E
Yanjiajie	104	41.02 N	121.32 E
Yanjiao	105	39.56 N	116.48 E
Yanjiapu	105	39.52 N	118.00 E
Yanjiatuozi	104	42.27 N	123.47 E
Yanjiawopeng	104	40.59 N	121.17 E
Yanjin	98	35.11 N	114.11 E
Yanjing, Zhg.	102	29.00 N	98.34 E
Yanjing, Zhg.	107	29.56 N	106.21 E
Yankalilla	168b	35.28 S	138.21 E
Yankalilla Bay ⊂	168b	35.28 S	138.15 E
Yankari Game Reserve ◆[4]	146	9.45 N	10.30 E
Yankdŏk	98	39.14 N	126.41 E
Yankee Lake	210	41.35 N	74.33 W
Yankee Springs State Recreation Area ♠	216	42.38 N	85.30 W
Yankee Stadium ♠	276	40.50 N	73.56 W
Yankeetown	220	29.01 N	82.42 W
Yankton	198	42.52 N	97.23 W
Yankton Indian Reservation ◆[4]	198	43.10 N	98.22 W
Yanling, Zhg.	98	34.07 N	114.11 E
Yanling, Zhg.	106	31.54 N	119.30 E
Yanliumiao	100	32.01 N	116.52 E
Yanmeimeizi	105	39.42 N	115.03 E
Yanna	166	26.56 S	146.03 E
Yannarie ≃	162	22.28 S	114.48 E
Yanqi	90	42.00 N	86.15 E
Yanqian, Zhg.	100	24.54 N	116.14 E
Yanqian, Zhg.	100	26.15 N	117.28 E
Yanqianhu	104	42.16 N	123.12 E
Yanqiao	106	31.41 N	120.17 E
Yanqidoumen	106	31.17 N	118.42 E
Yanqing	105	40.28 N	115.58 E
Yanque	248	15.39 S	71.39 W
Yanrey	162	22.31 S	114.48 E
Yanshan, Zhg.	98	38.05 N	117.13 E
Yanshan, Zhg.	100	28.18 N	117.41 E
Yanshan, Zhg.	102	23.41 N	104.21 E
Yan Shan ⋏	105	40.20 N	117.40 E
Yanshankou	105	39.59 N	117.42 E
Yanshi	100	25.17 N	117.10 E
Yanshi ≃	100	25.20 N	117.17 E
Yanshou	89	45.28 N	128.20 E
Yansi	100	29.48 N	118.20 E
Yanṭā	132	33.36 N	35.57 E
Yantabulla	166	29.21 S	145.00 E
Yantai (Chefoo), Zhg.	98	37.33 N	121.20 E
Yantai, Zhg.	105	39.47 N	116.38 E
Yantan, Zhg.	100	28.28 N	120.44 E
Yantan, Zhg.	100	28.55 N	120.11 E
Yantan, Zhg.	107	29.17 N	104.52 E
Yantian, Zhg.	100	26.53 N	119.53 E
Yantian, Zhg.	100	27.21 N	114.22 E
Yantic ≃	207	41.31 N	72.05 W
Yantietang ≅	106	31.49 N	120.46 E
Yanting	102	31.19 N	105.23 E
Yantis	222	32.56 N	95.35 W
Yantongshan, Zhg.	89	43.17 N	126.00 E
Yantongshan, Zhg.	105	40.42 N	115.06 E
Yanu	164	9.57 S	148.25 E
Yanwangshan	104	41.36 N	123.57 E
Yanweigang	98	34.30 N	119.48 E
Yanxi	100	24.46 N	117.47 E
Yanxia	100	29.34 N	114.50 E
Yanxidu	100	26.51 N	114.58 E
Yanxing	102	25.23 N	101.42 E
Yan Yean Reservoir ⊜[1]	169	37.33 S	145.08 E
Yanyegongsi	106	32.02 N	121.41 E
Yanyuan	102	27.29 N	101.32 E
Yanzhou	98	35.33 N	116.50 E
Yanziji	106	32.09 N	118.49 E
Yanzijiao	102	23.38 N	100.12 E
Yanzikou	102	27.31 N	105.21 E
Yao, Centraf.	152	5.19 N	19.36 E
Yao, Nihon	96	34.37 N	135.36 E
Yao, Tchad	146	12.51 N	17.34 E
Yao Airport ⊠	270	34.36 N	135.36 E
Yao'an	102	25.32 N	101.12 E
Yaoba	107	28.45 N	105.39 E
Yaocun, Zhg.	98	36.12 N	113.50 E
Yaocun, Zhg.	98	35.41 N	116.57 E
Yaocun, Zhg.	105	39.09 N	115.32 E
Yaodafangshen	104	42.27 N	122.59 E
Yaoerwan	105	40.49 N	115.27 E
Yaogongbu	100	29.51 N	120.18 E
Yaohongcaopao	104	40.55 N	122.26 E
Yaohuamen	106	32.08 N	118.52 E
Yaohuangdi	104	41.32 N	122.48 E
Yaojiaji	100	31.14 N	114.22 E
Yaojiaqiao	106	32.10 N	119.46 E
Yaojiatun	104	41.18 N	121.57 E
Yaojiawopeng	104	41.47 N	122.25 E
Yaojie	102	36.26 N	102.59 E
Yaoling	100	24.49 N	113.58 E
Yaolugou	98	40.34 N	119.24 E
Yaoluzi	104	41.26 N	121.34 E
Yaopi	100	26.52 N	113.38 E
Yaopu	100	32.14 N	118.20 E
Yaoqianhutun	104	41.32 N	123.36 E
Yaoshizhen	107	30.11 N	105.30 E
Yaotou	100	26.38 N	114.48 E
Yaotsu	94	35.28 N	137.09 E
Yaotun, Zhg.	89	49.28 N	127.30 E
Yaotun, Zhg.	104	40.59 N	122.18 E
Yaotutun	104	42.06 N	123.29 E
Yaoundé	152	3.52 N	11.31 E
Yaowan	98	34.12 N	118.03 E
Yaowangmiao	98	40.47 N	120.10 E
Yaoxian	102	34.56 N	108.53 E
Yaoya ≃	236	13.28 N	84.14 W
Yao Yai, Ko ▮	110	8.00 N	98.35 E
Yaozhan	89	52.53 N	125.13 E
Yap ▮	174q	9.31 N	138.06 E
Yapacaní	248	16.45 S	64.18 W
Yapacani ≃	248	16.00 S	64.25 W
Yapakopra	164	4.24 S	135.05 E
Yapehe	152	0.13 S	24.27 E
Yapei (Tamale Port)	150	9.10 N	1.10 W
Yapen, Pulau ▮	164	1.45 S	136.15 E
Yapen, Selat ʯ	164	1.30 S	136.10 E
Yapero	164	4.59 S	137.11 E
Yapeyú	252	29.28 S	56.49 W
Yaphank	207	40.50 N	72.56 W
Yappar ≃	166	18.22 S	141.16 E
Yapraklı	130	40.46 N	33.47 E
Yap Trench ✣[1]	14	8.30 N	138.00 E
Yaqian	100	26.38 N	114.30 E
Ya'qūb	140	12.29 N	25.11 E
Yaque del Norte ≃	238	19.51 N	71.41 W
Yaqui ≃	232	27.37 N	110.39 W
Yaquina ≃	202	44.37 N	124.04 W
Yara	240p	20.16 N	76.57 W
Yaracuy □[3]	246	10.20 N	69.10 W
Yaraka	166	24.53 S	144.04 E
Yaratuar	164	2.58 S	134.40 E
Yarbasan	130	38.59 N	28.49 E
Yarcombe	42	50.52 N	3.05 W
Yardea	166	32.23 S	135.32 E
Yardımcı	130	37.00 N	38.59 E
Yardımcı Burnu ›	130	36.13 N	30.25 E
Yardımlı	84	38.55 N	48.15 E
Yardley	208	40.14 N	74.50 W
Yardville	208	40.10 N	74.39 W
Yare ≃	42	52.35 N	1.44 E
Yaremcha	78	48.27 N	24.33 E
Yarí ≃	246	0.23 S	72.16 W
Yariga-take ∧	94	36.20 N	137.39 E
Yārik	123	32.06 N	70.47 E
Yarīm	144	14.29 N	44.21 E
Yaring	110	6.52 N	101.22 E
Yaritagua	246	10.05 N	69.08 W
Yarkand → Shache	120	38.25 N	77.16 E
Yarkand → Yarkant ≃	90	40.28 N	80.52 E
Yarkant (Yarkand) ≃	90	40.28 N	80.52 E
Yarker	212	44.23 N	76.46 W
Yarkhūn ≃	123	36.17 N	72.30 E
Yarlarweelor	162	25.35 S	117.59 E
Yarle Lakes ⊜	162	30.15 S	131.27 E
Yarloop	168a	32.57 S	115.54 E
Yarlung → Brahmaputra ≃	120	24.02 N	90.59 E
Yarma	130	37.49 N	32.54 E
Yarmolyntsi	78	49.12 N	26.50 E
Yarmouth, N.S., Can.	186	43.50 N	66.07 W
Yarmouth, Eng., U.K.	42	50.42 N	1.29 W
Yarmouth → Great Yarmouth, Eng., U.K.	42	52.37 N	1.44 E
Yarmouth, Me., U.S.	188	43.48 N	70.11 W
Yarmouth, Ma., U.S.	207	41.42 N	70.13 W
Yarmu	164	4.18 S	142.17 E
Yarmūk, Nahr al- ≃	132	32.38 N	35.34 E
Yaroslavets'	78	51.33 N	33.40 E
Yarova	83	49.03 N	37.37 E
Yarra ≃	169	37.51 S	144.54 E
Yarra Bend Park ♠	274b	37.48 S	145.01 E
Yarra Glen	169	37.40 S	145.23 E
Yarragon	169	38.12 S	146.04 E
Yarra Junction	169	37.47 S	145.37 E
Yarraloola	162	21.34 S	115.52 E
Yarram	166	38.33 S	146.41 E
Yarraman	171a	26.50 S	151.59 E
Yarrangobilly	171b	35.39 S	148.28 E
Yarrangobilly ≃	171b	35.48 N	148.23 E
Yarrangobilly Caves ⍛[5]	171b	35.44 S	148.29 E
Yarraville	274b	37.49 S	144.53 E
Yarrawonga	166	36.01 S	146.00 E
Yarra Yarra Lakes ⊜	162	29.40 S	115.47 E
Yarrow, B.C., Can.	224	49.05 N	122.02 W
Yarrow, Scot., U.K.	46	55.32 N	3.01 W
Yarrow ≃	262	53.40 N	2.49 W
Yarrowee ≃	169	37.48 S	143.56 E
Yarrow Point	224	47.39 N	122.13 W
Yarrow Reservoir ⊜[1]	262	53.38 N	2.34 W
Yarrow Water ≃	46	55.34 N	2.51 W
Yarrunga, Lake ⊜[1]	170	34.45 S	150.20 E
Yarty ≃	42	50.47 N	3.01 W
Yarumal	246	6.58 N	75.24 W
Yasa	152	3.42 S	21.24 E
Yasaka, Nihon	96	35.39 N	135.07 E
Yasaka, Nihon	96	34.46 N	132.04 E
Yasa-Lokwa	152	5.15 S	19.24 E
Yasato	94	36.14 N	140.12 E
Yasawa ▮	175g	16.47 S	177.31 E
Yasawa Group ▮▮	175g	17.00 S	177.23 E
Yasendu	152	0.27 N	24.20 E
Yasenivs'kyy	83	48.10 N	39.10 E
Yashanjie	106	30.51 N	119.03 E
Yashbum	144	14.19 N	46.56 E
Yashi	150	12.23 N	7.54 E
Yashikera	150	9.46 N	3.28 E
Ya-shima ▮	96	33.44 N	132.09 E
Yashima ♠	96	34.23 N	134.08 E
Yashio	268	35.49 N	139.51 E
Yashiro	96	34.55 N	134.58 E
Yashiro-jima ▮	96	33.55 N	132.15 E
Yāsīn	123	36.21 N	73.19 E
Yasinya	78	48.16 N	24.20 E
Yasku	146	12.20 N	12.30 E
Yasnohirka	83	48.47 N	37.33 E
Yasothon	110	15.45 N	104.08 E
Yass	166	34.50 S	148.55 E
Yassıada ▮	267b	40.51 N	29.00 E
Yassy → Iași	38	47.10 N	27.35 E
Yasu, Nihon	94	35.03 N	136.01 E
Yasu, Nihon	96	33.32 N	133.45 E
Yasuda	96	33.26 N	133.59 E
Yasugi	96	35.26 N	133.15 E
Yāsūj	128	30.40 N	51.36 E
Yasun Burnu ›	130	41.08 N	37.41 E
Yasuní ≃	246	0.56 S	75.23 W
Yasuni, Parque Nacional ♠	246	0.50 S	76.15 W
Yasuoka	94	35.22 N	137.50 E
Yasuura	96	34.17 N	132.45 E
Yasuzuka	94	37.08 N	138.28 E
Yasynivka	83	48.08 N	37.57 E
Yasynuvata	83	48.08 N	37.51 E
Yata	248	13.20 S	66.35 W
Yata ≃, Bol.	248	10.29 S	65.26 W
Yata ≃, Centraf.	146	10.23 N	22.45 E
Yatabe	94	36.02 N	140.04 E
Yatağan	130	37.20 N	28.09 E
Yatakala	150	14.48 N	0.22 E
Yata-Ngaya, Réserve de Faune de la ◆[4]	146	9.15 N	23.30 W
Yāṭar	132	33.09 N	35.20 E
Yatate-yama ∧	92	34.10 N	129.10 E
Yaté	175f	22.09 S	166.57 E
Yates □[6]	210	42.40 N	77.03 W
Yatesboro	214	40.48 N	79.20 W
Yates Center	198	37.52 N	95.43 W
Yates City	190	40.46 N	90.00 W
Yathata Island ▮	175g	17.15 S	179.32 W
Yathkyed Lake ⊜	176	62.41 N	98.00 W
Yating	102	25.03 N	106.05 E
Yatomi	94	35.06 N	136.43 E
Yatsuga-take ∧	94	35.59 N	138.23 E
Yatsuga-take-chūshin-kōgen-kokutei-kōen ♠	94	36.03 N	138.20 E
Yatsuka	96	35.17 N	133.42 E
Yatsuo	94	36.34 N	137.08 E
Yatsushiro	92	32.30 N	130.36 E
Yatsushiro-kai ⊂	92	32.20 N	130.25 E
Yaṭṭah	132	31.27 N	35.05 E
Yatta Plateau ⋏[1]	154	2.00 S	38.00 E
Yatton	42	51.24 N	2.49 W
Yatuá ≃	246	1.43 N	66.30 W
Yatusiro → Yatsushiro	92	32.30 N	130.36 E
Yauca	248	15.40 S	74.32 W
Yauca ≃	248	15.41 S	74.31 W
Yauco	240m	18.02 N	66.51 W
Yauco ≃	240m	17.59 N	66.48 W
Yauco, Embalse de ⊜[1]	240m	18.07 N	66.50 W
Yauli	248	11.41 S	76.06 W
Yaundé → Yaoundé	152	3.52 N	11.31 E
Yaupi	246	2.59 S	77.50 W
Yauri	248	14.47 S	71.29 W
Yautepec	234	18.53 N	99.04 W
Yau Tong	271d	22.18 N	114.13 E
Yauyos	248	12.24 S	75.57 W
Yāval	120	21.10 N	75.42 E
Yavarí (Javari) ≃	242	4.21 S	70.02 W
Yavarí Mirim ≃	246	4.31 S	71.44 W
Yavaros	232	26.42 N	109.31 W
Yavatmāl	122	20.24 N	78.08 E
Yaven Yaven Creek ≃	171b	35.06 S	147.46 E
Yavero ≃	248	12.06 S	72.57 W
Yavi	130	39.48 N	36.13 E
Yaví, Cerro ∧	246	5.32 N	65.59 W
Yavita	246	2.55 N	67.26 W
Yaviza	246	8.11 N	77.41 W
Yavkine	78	47.16 N	32.37 E
Yavne	132	31.53 N	34.45 E
Yavoriv	78	49.56 N	23.23 E
Yavuzeli	130	37.20 N	37.33 E
Yavuzkemal	130	40.43 N	38.21 E
Yaw ≃	110	20.55 N	94.49 E
Yawahara	268	35.59 N	140.01 E
Yawata, Nihon	96	34.52 N	135.42 E
Yawata → Kitakyūshū, Nihon	96	33.53 N	130.50 E
Yawata, Nihon	268	35.32 N	140.08 E
Yawatahama	96	33.27 N	132.24 E
Yaxchilán ⊥	232	16.54 N	90.58 W
Yaxi	102	27.32 N	106.45 E
Yaxian	110	18.20 N	109.30 E
Yaxigang	106	31.23 N	119.10 E
Yaxley	42	52.31 N	0.16 W
Yayama	152	1.16 S	23.07 E
Yayladağı	130	35.56 N	36.01 E
Yayladere	130	39.14 N	40.03 E
Yaylak	130	37.23 N	38.20 E
Yayouta	150	8.11 N	8.30 W
Yayuan	98	41.47 N	126.11 E
Yazd	128	31.53 N	54.25 E
Yazd □[4]	128	32.00 N	54.30 E
Yazi	98	37.04 N	121.17 E
Yazichangcun	104	41.16 N	122.26 E
Yazıhan	130	38.36 N	38.11 E
Yazmān	123	29.08 N	71.45 E
Yazoo ≃	194	32.22 N	91.00 W
Yazoo City	194	32.51 N	90.24 W
Ybbs ≃	61	48.10 N	15.06 E
Ybbs an der Donau	61	48.11 N	15.05 E
Ybbsitz	61	47.56 N	14.53 E
Ybor City	220	27.57 N	82.27 W
Ybycuí	252	26.01 S	57.03 W
Yding Skovhøj ∧[2]	41	56.00 N	9.48 E
Ydstebøhavn	26	59.08 N	5.15 E
Ydžid Parma ⋏	24	63.06 N	58.15 E
Ye	110	15.15 N	97.51 E
Yea	169	37.13 S	145.26 E
Yea ≃	169	37.11 S	145.23 E
Yeading ◆[8]	260	51.32 N	0.24 W
Yeadon, Eng., U.K.	44	53.52 N	1.41 W
Yeadon, Pa., U.S.	285	39.56 N	75.15 W
Yeagertown	208	40.38 N	77.34 W
Yealm ≃	42	50.18 N	4.03 W
Yealmpton	42	50.21 N	3.59 W
Yebawgyi	110	18.40 N	94.35 E
Yebbi-Bou	146	20.58 N	18.04 E
Yébigué, Enneri ∨	146	22.04 N	17.49 E
Yèbles	261	48.38 N	2.46 E
Yebyu	110	14.15 N	98.12 E
Yecapixtla	234	18.53 N	98.52 W
Yecheng	120	37.54 N	77.25 E
Yech'ŏn	98	36.40 N	128.26 E
Yecla	34	38.37 N	1.07 W
Yécora	232	28.20 N	108.58 W
Yedashe	110	19.09 N	96.21 E
Yedi Göller Milli Parkı ♠	130	40.50 N	31.30 E
Yedikule ◆[8]	267b	40.59 N	28.55 E
Yedikule ⊥	267b	40.59 N	28.55 E
Yédinga, Ouadi ∨	146	15.46 N	20.05 E
Yedseram ≃	146	12.30 N	14.05 E
Yeed	144	4.33 N	43.02 E
Yeeda	162	17.36 S	123.39 E
Yeelanna	166	34.09 S	135.45 E
Yeelirrie	162	27.17 S	120.06 E
Yeernuozha Hu ⊜	120	32.30 N	89.30 E
Yegor'yevsk → Jegorjevsk	82	55.23 N	39.02 E
Yegros	252	26.24 S	56.25 W
Yegua Creek ≃	222	30.23 N	96.18 W
Yeguas, Punta ›	258	34.55 S	56.19 W
Yeguas, Río de las ≃	34	37.22 N	4.45 W
Yehliu	269d	25.12 N	121.41 E
Yehliu Chia ›	269d	25.13 N	121.42 E
Yehud	132	32.02 N	34.53 E
Yei	154	4.05 N	30.40 E
Yei ≃	140	6.15 N	30.13 E
Yeji, Ghana	150	8.13 N	0.39 W
Yeji, Zhg.	100	31.52 N	115.55 E
Yekaterinburg → Jekaterinburg	86	56.51 N	60.36 E
Yekaterinodar → Krasnodar	78	45.02 N	39.00 E
Yekaterinoslav → Dnipropetrovs'k	78	48.27 N	34.59 E
Yekokora ≃	152	1.20 N	20.21 E
Yekumbo	152	1.02 S	23.27 E
Ye Kyun ▮	110	18.37 N	93.47 E
Yela Island ▮	160	11.21 S	154.09 E
Yelanets'	78	47.42 N	31.51 E
Yelarbon	166	28.34 S	150.45 E
Yelcho, Lago ⊜	254	43.18 S	72.18 W
Yele	150	8.25 N	11.50 W
Yelets → Jelec	76	52.37 N	38.30 E
Yélimané	150	15.08 N	10.34 W
Yelizarove	78	48.12 N	34.33 E
Yelizavethradka	78	48.48 N	32.24 E
Yell ▮	46a	60.36 N	1.06 W
Yellandu	122	17.36 N	80.20 E
Yellow ≃, U.S.	194	30.33 N	87.00 W
Yellow ≃, In., U.S.	216	41.16 N	86.50 W
Yellow ≃, Ia., U.S.	190	43.05 N	91.11 W
Yellow ≃, Wi., U.S.	190	44.58 N	91.18 W
Yellow ≃, Wi., U.S.	190	43.59 N	90.03 W
Yellow ≃, Wi., U.S.	190	46.01 N	92.22 W
Yellow → Huang ≃, Zhg.	90	37.32 N	118.19 E
Yellow Breeches Creek ≃	208	40.13 N	76.51 W
Yellow Creek ≃, U.S.	194	33.34 N	88.20 W
Yellow Creek ≃, Co., U.S.	200	40.10 N	108.24 W
Yellow Creek ≃, Oh., U.S.	214	40.34 N	80.40 W
Yellow Creek ≃, Tn., U.S.	194	36.26 N	87.34 W
Yellow Creek, North Fork ≃	214	40.33 N	80.42 W
Yellow Creek State Park ♠	214	40.35 N	79.02 W
Yellowdine	162	31.18 S	119.39 E
Yellow Grass	184	49.49 N	104.08 W
Yellowhead Pass)(	182	52.53 N	118.28 W
Yellow House Draw ∨	196	33.35 N	101.50 W
Yellowknife	176	62.27 N	114.21 W
Yellowknife ≃	176	62.31 N	114.19 W
Yellow Lake ⊜	212	44.20 N	75.36 W
Yellow Medicine ≃	198	44.44 N	95.25 W
Yellow Mountain ∧	166	32.30 S	146.51 E
Yellow Sea ⊤[2]	90	36.00 N	123.00 E
Yellow Springs	218	39.48 N	83.53 W
Yellowstone ≃	178	47.58 N	103.59 W
Yellowstone, Clarks Fork ≃	202	45.39 N	108.43 W
Yellowstone Falls ∟	202	44.43 N	110.30 W
Yellowstone Lake ⊜	202	44.25 N	110.22 W
Yellowstone National Park	202	44.59 N	110.42 W
Yellowstone National Park ♠	202	44.30 N	110.35 W
Yellowtail Dam ◆[6]	202	45.12 N	107.57 W
Yell Sound ʯ	46a	60.32 N	1.15 W
Yellville	194	36.13 N	92.41 W
Yelm	224	46.56 N	122.36 W
Yelma	162	26.30 S	121.40 E
Yelvertoft	166	20.13 S	138.53 E
Yelverton	42	50.30 N	4.05 W
Yelwa	150	10.51 N	4.46 E
Yelyseyivka	78	47.02 N	36.24 E
Yema ≃	102	41.25 N	95.10 E
Yemadu	86	43.36 N	81.50 E
Yemagong	124	29.28 N	89.06 E
Yemaotai	104	42.20 N	122.53 E
Yemassee	192	32.41 N	80.51 W
Yematan	102	34.40 N	98.16 E
Yemen (Al-Yaman) □[1], Asia	118	15.00 N	47.00 E
Yemen (Al-Yaman) □[1], Asia	144	15.00 N	47.00 E
Yemen, People's Democratic Republic of → Yemen □[1]	144	15.00 N	47.00 E
Yemen, República Popular Democrática del → Yemen □[1]	144	15.00 N	47.00 E
Yémen, République démocratique populaire du → Yemen □[1]	144	15.00 N	47.00 E
Yemil'chyne	78	50.52 N	27.48 E
Yen	152	2.27 N	12.41 E
Yenagoa	150	4.55 N	6.19 E
Yenakiyeve	83	48.14 N	38.13 E
Yenangyaung	110	20.28 N	94.52 E
Yenanma	110	19.46 N	94.48 E
Yen Bai	110	21.42 N	104.52 E
Yen Chau	110	21.03 N	104.18 E
Yench'eng → Yancheng	100	33.24 N	120.09 E
Yenchi → Yanji	98	42.57 N	129.32 E
Yenda	166	34.15 S	146.11 E
Yende Millimou	150	8.53 N	10.11 W
Yendéré	150	10.12 N	4.58 W
Yendi	150	9.26 N	0.01 W
Ye-ngan	110	21.09 N	96.27 E
Yenge ≃	152	0.55 S	20.40 E
Yengema	150	8.43 N	11.10 W
Yengisar	85	38.57 N	76.03 E
Yengo	152	0.22 N	15.29 E
Yengo, Mount ∧	170	32.59 S	150.51 E
Yéni	150	13.26 N	2.59 E
Yeniçağa	130	40.46 N	32.02 E
Yenice, Tür.	130	39.45 N	28.55 E
Yenice, Tür.	130	39.55 N	27.18 E
Yenice, Tür.	130	36.59 N	35.03 E
Yenice, Tür.	130	41.11 N	32.19 E
Yenice ≃	130	41.35 N	32.03 E
Yenicekale	130	37.37 N	36.37 E
Yeniceoba	130	38.53 N	32.48 E
Yenierenköy	130	35.32 N	34.11 E
Yenifoça	130	38.44 N	26.51 E
Yenikapı ◆[8]	267b	41.00 N	28.57 E
Yeniköy	130	39.46 N	28.00 E
Yeniköy ◆[8]	267b	40.59 N	28.53 E
Yenimehmetli	130	39.26 N	32.10 E
Yenipazar, Tür.	130	37.48 N	28.12 E
Yenipazar, Tür.	130	40.11 N	30.31 E
Yenişehir	130	40.16 N	29.39 E
Yenisey → Jenisej ≃	72	71.50 N	82.40 E
Yennadon	224	49.14 N	122.34 W
Yenne	62	45.42 N	5.46 E
Yennora	274a	33.52 S	150.58 E
Yenshuichen	100	23.20 N	120.16 E
Yentna ≃	180	61.34 N	150.28 W
Yeo ≃, Eng., U.K.	42	50.45 N	3.36 W
Yeo ≃, Eng., U.K.	42	51.02 N	2.49 W
Yeo ≃, Eng., U.K.	42	51.01 N	3.50 W
Yeola	122	20.02 N	74.29 E
Yeo Lake ⊜	162	28.04 S	124.23 E
Yeoman	216	40.40 N	86.43 W
Yeoval	166	32.45 S	148.40 E
Yeovil	42	50.57 N	2.39 W
Yeoville ◆[8]	273d	26.12 S	28.04 E
Yepachic	232	28.26 N	108.23 W
Yeppoon	166	23.08 S	150.45 E
Yerba Buena, Montaña ∧	236	14.05 N	87.26 W
Yerba Buena Island ▮	282	37.48 N	122.22 W
Yères ≃	50	50.02 N	1.19 E
Yerevan → Jerevan	84	40.11 N	44.30 E
Yerilla	162	29.28 S	121.49 E
Yering	274b	37.41 S	145.23 E
Yerington	226	38.59 N	119.09 W
Yerington Indian Reservation ◆[4]	226	39.05 N	119.12 W
Yerkes	285	40.10 N	75.27 W
Yerkes Astronomical Observatory ᵿ[3]	216	42.34 N	88.34 W
Yerkesik	130	37.07 N	28.17 E
Yerköy	130	39.38 N	34.29 E
Yerky	78	48.59 N	31.00 E
Yerlisu	130	40.46 N	26.39 E
Yermasóyia	130	34.43 N	33.05 E
Yermenonville	261	48.33 N	1.37 E
Yermo	204	34.54 N	116.49 W
Yeroḥam	132	31.00 N	34.55 E
Yerolimín	38	36.28 N	22.24 E
Yèrre ≃	50	48.01 N	1.16 E
Yerres	50	48.43 N	2.30 E
Yerres ≃	50	48.43 N	2.27 E
Yerseke	52	51.29 N	4.02 E
Yerupaja, Nevado ∧	248	10.16 S	76.54 W
Yerushalayim (Al-Quds) (Jerusalem)	132	31.46 N	35.14 E
Yerushalayim □[5]	132	31.45 N	35.00 E
Yerville	50	49.40 N	0.54 E
Yeryk ≃	83	48.59 N	38.30 E
Yesa, Embalse de ⊜[1]	34	42.36 N	1.09 W
Yesan	98	36.41 N	126.50 E
Yeshenpu	104	40.51 N	122.32 E
Yeshiva University ᵿ[2]	276	40.51 N	73.55 W
Yeshvi	272c	18.55 N	73.03 E
Yeşil ≃	130	41.24 N	36.35 E
Yeşilçonlu	130	40.13 N	28.06 E
Yeşildere	130	37.09 N	33.31 E
Yeşilhisar	130	38.21 N	35.06 E
Yeşilkent	130	36.59 N	36.10 E
Yeşilköy	130	40.57 N	28.49 E

Symbol	English	Deutsch	Español	Français	Português
≃	River	Fluß	Río	Rivière	Rio
≅	Canal	Kanal	Canal	Canal	Canal
∟	Waterfall, Rapids	Wasserfall, Stromschnellen	Cascada, Rápidos	Chute d'eau, Rapides	Cascata, Rápidos
ʯ	Strait	Meeresstraße	Estrecho	Détroit	Estreito
⊂	Bay, Gulf	Bucht, Golf	Bahía, Golfo	Baie, Golfe	Baía, Golfo
⊜	Lake, Lakes	See, Seen	Lago, Lagos	Lac, Lacs	Lago, Lagos
≡	Swamp	Sumpf	Pantano	Marais	Pântano
⊓	Ice Features, Glacier	Eis- und Gletscherformen	Accidentes Glaciales	Formes glaciaires	Acidentes glaciares
⊤	Other Hydrographic Features	Andere Hydrographische Objekte	Otros Elementos Hidrográficos	Autres données hydrographiques	Outros acidentes hidrográficos
✣	Submarine Features	Untermeerische Objekte	Accidentes Submarinos	Formes de relief sous-marin	Acidentes submarinos
□	Political Unit	Politische Einheit	Unidad Politica	Entité politique	Unidade política
ᵿ	Cultural Institution	Kulturelle Institution	Institución Cultural	Institution culturelle	Instituição cultural
⊥	Historical Site	Historische Stätte	Sitio Histórico	Site historique	Sitio histórico
♠	Recreational Site	Erholungs- und Ferienort	Sitio de Recreo	Centre de loisirs	Area de Lazer
⊠	Airport	Flughafen	Aeropuerto	Aéroport	Aeroporto
■	Military Installation	Militäranlage	Instalación Militar	Installation militaire	Instalação militar
◆	Miscellaneous	Verschiedenes	Misceláneo	Divers	Diversos

Yeşilköy Burnu > 267b 40.57 N 28.50 E
Yeşilova 130 37.30 N 29.46 E
Yeşiltepe 130 37.12 N 33.02 E
Yeşilyazı 130 39.20 N 39.05 E
Yeşilyurt 130 38.18 N 38.15 E
Yeso 196 34.26 N 104.36 W
Yeso Creek ≃ 196 34.13 N 104.15 W
Yesŏng-gang ≃ 98 37.53 N 126.24 E
Yessentuki
— Jessentuki 84 44.03 N 42.51 E
Yeste 34 38.22 N 2.18 W
Yes Tor ∧ 42 50.42 N 4.00 W
Yesud HaMa'ala 132 33.03 N 35.36 E
Yetholme 170 33.27 S 149.49 E
Yetman 166 28.54 S 150.46 E
Yetminster 42 50.53 N 2.33 W
Yetsou I 152 2.08 S 10.42 E
Yettem 226 36.29 N 119.16 W
Yetti 164 3.00 S 140.53 E
Yetti •[1] 148 26.10 N 7.50 W
Ye-u 110 22.46 N 95.26 E
Yeu, Île d' I 32 46.42 N 2.20 W
Yevlax 84 40.36 N 47.09 E
Yevpatoriya, Ukr. 78 45.12 N 33.22 E
Yevpatoriya
— Yevpatoriya, Ukr. 78 45.12 N 33.22 E
Yevsuh 83 49.13 N 39.18 E
Yevsuh ≃ 83 48.47 N 39.19 E
Yexian, Zhg. 98 37.13 N 119.54 E
Yexian, Zhg. 100 33.37 N 113.20 E
Yexie 106 30.56 N 121.19 E
Yextla ≃ 234 18.00 N 100.06 W
Yeysk
— Jejsk 78 46.42 N 38.16 E
Yeyuan 98 36.22 N 118.27 E
Yeywa 110 21.41 N 96.24 E
Yezd
— Yazd 128 31.53 N 54.25 E
Yeze Hu ⊜ 106 31.08 N 120.40 E
Yezhuang 105 39.10 N 116.18 E
Yezhuhe 105 40.53 N 118.13 E
Ygatimí 252 24.05 S 55.30 W
Ygnacio Canal ≅ 282 37.55 N 122.03 W
Yguazú ≃ 252 25.20 S 55.00 W
Yhú 252 24.59 S 55.59 W
Yi 98 42.08 N 118.48 E
Yi ≃, Ur. 252 33.07 S 57.08 W
Yi ≃, Zhg. 98 34.07 N 118.15 E
Yi ≃, Zhg. 100 34.10 N 112.10 E
Yi ≃, Zhg. 105 39.14 N 115.46 E
Yi'an 89 47.55 N 125.20 E
Yiannitsá 38 40.48 N 22.25 E
Yíaros I 38 37.37 N 24.43 E
Yibao 106 30.25 N 119.53 E
Yibin (Ipin) 107 28.47 N 104.38 E
Yibug Caka ⊜ 120 33.00 N 86.25 E
Yibutan 107 28.54 N 104.40 E
Yicanghe 100 32.47 N 120.43 E
Yichang (Ichang) 102 30.42 N 111.17 E
Yicheng, Zhg. 98 34.46 N 117.37 E
Yicheng, Zhg. 98 36.48 N 114.17 E
Yicheng, Zhg. 102 31.43 N 112.07 E
Yichexun 102 26.50 N 103.28 E
Yichuan, Zhg. 100 34.26 N 112.24 E
Yichuan, Zhg. 102 36.04 N 110.06 E
Yichun, Zhg. 90 47.42 N 128.55 E
Yichun, Zhg. 100 27.50 N 114.23 E
Yicun 105 38.57 N 115.37 E
Yidan 89 43.24 N 125.25 E
Yidie 102 37.08 N 110.30 E
Yidu, Zhg. 98 36.41 N 118.28 E
Yidu, Zhg. 102 30.22 N 111.22 E
Yidun 102 29.56 N 99.22 E
Yiewsley •[8] 260 51.31 N 0.28 W
Yifag 144 12.02 N 37.44 E
Yifeng, Zhg. 100 33.19 N 113.47 E
Yifeng, Zhg. 100 28.26 N 114.46 E
Yigaolou 106 30.56 N 120.20 E
Yığılca 130 40.58 N 31.27 E
Yiğitler 130 39.52 N 26.37 E
Yigou 98 35.51 N 114.20 E
Yihe 100 23.50 N 114.53 E
Yihechang 107 30.23 N 106.24 E
Yi He Yuan (Summer Palace) ⊕ 105 40.00 N 116.16 E
Yihezhuang, Zhg. 98 37.53 N 118.23 E
Yihezhuang, Zhg. 104 41.15 N 122.57 E
Yihuang 100 27.34 N 116.10 E
Yihuang ≃ 100 28.05 N 116.18 E
Yijiangzhen 100 30.55 N 118.28 E
Yijiawan 100 27.58 N 113.01 E
Yijiazi 104 42.29 N 122.41 E
Yijingpu 105 40.08 N 117.47 E
Yijinqiao 100 30.54 N 117.12 E
Yijun 102 35.24 N 109.00 E
Yikengaolu 102 42.17 N 98.19 E
Yikou 100 26.45 N 117.00 E
Yilaha 89 48.50 N 125.10 E
Yilan 89 46.19 N 129.34 E
Yilaxi 89 43.47 N 126.08 E
Yıldız Dağı ∧ 130 40.08 N 36.56 E
Yıldız Dağları ⋏ 38 41.50 N 27.30 E
Yıldızeli 130 39.52 N 36.38 E
Yilehuli Shan ⋏ 89 51.20 N 124.30 E
Yili 107 30.45 N 105.58 E
Yiliang, Zhg. 102 24.58 N 103.07 E
Yiliang, Zhg. 102 27.35 N 104.01 E
Yiliekede 89 48.51 N 121.37 E
Yilin 100 33.36 N 119.37 E
Yiling 100 32.30 N 119.46 E
Yiliping 120 37.55 N 93.30 E
Yilliminning 162 32.54 S 117.22 E
Yilong, Zhg. 89 47.28 N 125.23 E
Yilong, Zhg. 102 31.34 N 106.19 E
Yilong, Zhg. 102 25.20 N 103.14 E
Yimachi 104 42.11 N 122.15 E
Yimatu 104 41.55 N 121.25 E
Yimen, Zhg. 100 33.39 N 116.02 E
Yimen, Zhg. 102 24.43 N 102.10 E
Yimuhe 89 52.45 N 120.07 E
Yin ≃, Mya. 110 20.04 N 95.01 E
Yin ≃, Zhg. 98 42.19 N 118.37 E
Yinan (Jiehu) 98 35.37 N 118.30 E
Yinbaing 110 17.25 N 97.46 E
Yinchuan 102 38.30 N 106.18 E
Yindarlgooda, Lake ⊜ 162 30.45 S 121.55 E
Yindi 154 1.35 N 27.40 E
Yinfang 105 39.07 N 114.52 E
Ying ≃ 100 32.30 N 116.32 E
Yingcheng 100 30.57 N 113.32 E
Yingchengzi, Zhg. 89 44.08 N 125.56 E
Yingchengzi, Zhg. 98 38.58 N 121.23 E
Yingchengzi, Zhg. 104 41.50 N 124.04 E
Yingchengzi, Zhg. 104 42.22 N 124.14 E
Yingde 100 24.12 N 113.24 E
Yingen 102 41.09 N 104.45 E
Yingfang 105 40.14 N 116.17 E
Yinggehai 110 18.31 N 108.44 E
Yinghe 100 32.16 N 116.31 E
Yingjin ≃ 98 42.20 N 119.19 E
Yingkoshih ≃ 269d 25.06 N 121.43 E
Yingkou, Zhg. 104 40.40 N 122.14 E
Yingkou (Dashiqiao), Zhg. 104 40.38 N 122.30 E
Yingpan, Zhg. 102 25.48 N 106.18 E
Yingpan, Zhg. 102 24.44 N 99.38 E
Yingpanjie 102 25.27 N 98.24 E
Yingqiao 100 33.58 N 113.39 E
Yingshan, Zhg. 100 30.45 N 115.39 E
Yingshan, Zhg. 100 31.38 N 113.50 E
Yingshan, Zhg. 102 31.08 N 106.31 E
Yingshang 100 32.38 N 116.15 E
Yingshouyingzi, Zhg. 105 40.33 N 117.38 E
Yingshouyingzi, Zhg. 105 40.49 N 117.55 E
Yingtan 100 28.14 N 117.00 E
Yingtaogou 104 42.08 N 121.57 E
Yingtaoyuan 104 41.10 N 123.05 E
Yingtian 100 28.50 N 112.56 E
Yingxiangjie 107 29.24 N 105.11 E
Yingxianpu 104 41.20 N 121.31 E
Yining (Kuldja) 86 43.54 N 81.21 E
Yinjiadai 106 32.03 N 120.07 E
Yinjiang 102 28.02 N 108.28 E
Yinjiawopeng 104 42.34 N 121.01 E
Yinkeng 100 26.14 N 115.34 E
Yinliu 105 39.59 N 117.23 E
Yinmabin 110 22.05 N 94.54 E
Yinmahe 89 44.07 N 125.44 E
Yinmatu ≃ 98 40.57 N 117.43 E
Yinnietharra 162 24.39 S 116.11 E
Yinnyein 110 16.48 N 97.23 E
Yinong 102 30.19 N 101.01 E
Yinping 98 34.15 N 118.39 E
Yinqiaotou 106 31.52 N 119.13 E
Yin Shan ⋏ 102 41.48 N 109.00 E
Yinshanzhen 107 29.41 N 104.58 E
Yinwogou 98 41.55 N 117.55 E
Yinxian 100 29.50 N 121.38 E
Yinxiang 106 31.55 N 118.49 E
Yinxianji 100 32.07 N 116.32 E
Yinyangjie 104 42.16 N 121.23 E
Yinyuan 102 23.26 N 101.54 E
Yinzhan'ao 100 23.33 N 113.07 E
Yio Chu Kang 271c 1.23 N 103.51 E
Yi'ong 102 30.17 N 94.51 E
Yi'ong ≃ 120 29.56 N 95.10 E
Yi Pak 271d 22.19 N 114.00 E
Yipinchang 107 29.17 N 106.34 E
Yipinglang 102 25.11 N 101.51 E
Yiqian 100 26.34 N 116.11 E
Yirba Muda 144 6.12 N 38.42 E
Yirga Alem 144 6.52 N 38.22 E
Yirkā 132 32.57 N 35.13 E
Yirol 140 6.33 N 30.30 E
Yirrkala 164 12.14 S 136.56 E
Yirshi 89 47.20 N 119.45 E
Yirwa 140 7.47 N 27.15 E
Yisaduo 102 28.50 N 96.44 E
Yishan, Zhg. 100 27.32 N 120.32 E
Yishan, Zhg. 102 24.40 N 108.35 E
Yishui 98 35.50 N 118.41 E
Yishun 271c 1.26 N 103.50 E
Yisikan 89 49.09 N 124.47 E
Yisra'el
— Israel □[1] 132 31.30 N 35.00 E
Yisuhe 100 27.46 N 112.54 E
Yitajing 102 42.32 N 94.12 E
Yitang, Zhg. 98 35.10 N 118.16 E
Yitang, Zhg. 100 31.06 N 113.42 E
Yíthion 38 36.45 N 22.34 E
Yiting 100 29.15 N 119.57 E
Yitm, Wādī al- V 132 29.34 N 35.01 E
Yitong 89 43.20 N 125.17 E
Yitong ≃ 98 42.40 N 125.58 E
Yitulihe 89 50.38 N 121.34 E
Yiwu, Zhg. 100 29.18 N 120.04 E
Yiwu, Zhg. 102 43.15 N 94.45 E
Yiwu, Zhg. 102 22.00 N 101.28 E
Yiwulü Shan ⋏ 104 41.42 N 121.42 E
Yixi 100 23.45 N 116.38 E
Yixian, Zhg. 100 29.55 N 117.56 E
Yixian, Zhg. 104 41.32 N 121.15 E
Yixian, Zhg. 105 39.21 N 115.29 E
Yixiken 89 52.57 N 125.40 E
Yixing 106 31.22 N 119.50 E
Yixingbu 105 39.12 N 117.12 E
Yixingchang 107 30.37 N 106.38 E
Yixu 100 26.02 N 119.16 E
Yixun ≃ 98 41.16 N 117.35 E
Yiyang, Zhg. 100 28.23 N 117.25 E
Yiyang, Zhg. 102 28.36 N 112.20 E
Yiyang, Zhg. 102 34.30 N 112.10 E
Yiyuan (Nanma) 98 36.11 N 118.08 E
Yiyuankou 98 40.10 N 119.35 E
Yizhang 100 25.26 N 112.56 E
Yizheng 106 32.16 N 119.12 E
Yizikong 102 25.38 N 104.28 E
Yizre'él 132 32.33 N 35.20 E
Yizre'el, 'Émeq ⩦ 132 32.36 N 35.14 E
Ylakiai 76 56.17 N 21.51 E
Yläne 26 60.53 N 22.55 E
Ylihärmä 26 63.09 N 22.47 E
Yli-Kitka ⊜ 26 66.08 N 28.30 E
Ylimarkku
— Övermark 26 62.38 N 21.30 E
Ylistaro 26 62.57 N 22.31 E
Ylivieska 26 64.05 N 24.33 E
Ylöjärvi 26 61.33 N 23.36 E
Ymeray 261 48.31 N 1.42 E
Ymir 182 49.17 N 117.13 W
Yndin 24 61.24 N 55.10 E
Yngaren ⊜ 40 58.52 N 16.35 E
Yngen ⊜ 40 59.44 N 14.18 E
Yntaly 86 48.58 N 70.55 E
Ynykčanskij 74 60.15 N 137.43 E
Yoakum 222 29.17 N 97.09 W
Yobi, Indon. 164 1.43 S 138.04 E
Yobi, Indon. 164 1.42 S 136.27 E
Yockanookany ≃ 194 32.40 N 89.40 W
Yoco 246 10.36 N 62.24 W
Yocona ≃ 194 34.11 N 90.11 W
Yōda 268 35.24 N 139.25 E
Yoder 216 40.55 N 85.10 W
Yodo ≃ 96 34.41 N 135.25 E
Yodoe 96 35.28 N 133.26 E
Yodogawa •[8] 270 34.42 N 135.28 E
Yoe 208 39.55 N 76.39 W
Yōga •[8] 268 35.38 N 139.38 E
Yogo 94 35.33 N 136.12 E
Yog Point > 116 14.06 N 124.12 E
Yoğuntaş 130 41.50 N 27.04 E
Yogyakarta 115a 7.48 S 110.22 E
Yogyakarta □[4] 115a 7.45 S 110.30 E
Yoho National Park ♦ 182 51.26 N 116.30 W
Yoichi 92a 43.12 N 140.41 E
Yojoa, Lago de ⊜ 236 14.50 N 88.00 W
Yŏju 98 37.18 N 127.37 E
Yōka 96 35.24 N 134.46 E
Yokadouma 152 3.31 N 15.03 E
Yōkaichi 94 35.06 N 136.12 E
Yōkaichiba 94 35.42 N 140.33 E
Yokamba 152 0.01 N 22.17 E
Yokana 152 0.45 N 22.53 E
Yokawa 96 34.52 N 135.06 E
Yokchi-do I 98 34.38 N 128.15 E
Yokkaichi, Nihon 94 34.58 N 136.37 E
Yokkaichi, Nihon 96 33.32 N 131.20 E
Yoko 152 2.36 S 20.06 E
Yokoate-jima I 93b 28.48 N 129.00 E
Yokohama, Nihon 94 35.27 N 139.39 E
Yokohama, Nihon 268 35.27 N 139.39 E
Yokohama-kō ⊂ 268 35.27 N 139.39 E
Yokohama National University ⊕[2] 268 35.25 N 139.36 E
Yokohama Park Baseball Ground ♦ 268 35.26 N 139.39 E
Yokolo 152 0.36 S 23.04 E
Yokonuma 268 35.58 N 139.27 E
Yokoshiba 94 35.40 N 140.28 E
Yokosuka 94 35.18 N 139.40 E
Yokosuka District Naval Headquarters ■ 268 35.17 N 139.39 E
Yokosuka-kō ⊂ 268 35.18 N 139.39 E
Yokosuka Naval Base ■ 94 35.18 N 139.41 E
Yokota, Nihon 96 35.10 N 133.06 E
Yokota, Nihon 268 35.23 N 140.01 E
Yokota, Nihon 270 34.40 N 135.55 E
Yokota Air Base ■ 268 35.45 N 139.21 E
Yokote 92 39.18 N 140.34 E
Yola 146 9.12 N 12.29 E
Yolaina, Serranías de ⋏ 236 11.40 N 84.20 W
Yolboyu 130 37.55 N 40.00 E
Yolo 226 38.44 N 121.48 W
Yolo □[6] 226 38.41 N 121.46 W
Yolo ≃ 273b 4.19 S 15.20 E
Yolo Bypass ≃ 226 38.25 N 121.40 W
Yolombó, Col. 246 6.36 N 75.01 W
Yolombo, Zaïre 152 1.32 S 23.15 E
Yolonga 152 1.36 S 23.12 E
Yom ≃ 110 15.52 N 100.16 E
Yombi 152 1.26 S 10.37 E
Yomou 150 7.34 N 9.16 W
Yona 174p 13.25 N 144.47 E
Yonabaru 174m 26.12 N 127.45 E
Yonago 96 35.26 N 133.20 E
Yonaguni 175d 24.27 N 122.57 E
Yonaguni-shima I 175d 24.27 N 123.00 E
Yonaha-dake ∧[2] 174m 26.43 N 128.13 E
Yŏnan 98 37.55 N 126.10 E
Yoncalı 130 39.01 N 38.15 E
Yoncalla 202 43.35 N 123.16 W
Yŏnch'on •[8] 271b 37.38 N 127.04 E
Yoneshiro ≃ 92 40.13 N 140.01 E
Yonezawa 92 37.55 N 140.07 E
Yŏngam 98 34.48 N 126.40 E
Yongamp'o 98 39.55 N 124.24 E
Yŏngan, C.M.I.K. 98 41.15 N 129.30 E
Yong'an, Zhg. 100 25.58 N 117.22 E
Yongan, Zhg. 107 30.44 N 106.16 E
Yong'an, Zhg. 107 29.13 N 104.46 E
Yong'an ≃ 100 28.52 N 121.04 E
Yonganbao 98 40.15 N 119.52 E
Yong'anchang 107 30.24 N 103.58 E
Yong'anshi 100 28.13 N 113.19 E
Yŏngbyŏn 98 39.49 N 125.48 E
Yongchang, Zhg. 100 29.13 N 119.20 E
Yongchang, Zhg. 102 38.17 N 101.59 E
Yongchangzhen 106 31.42 N 121.44 E
Yongcheng 100 33.58 N 116.21 E
Yongch'ŏn, C.M.I.K. 98 39.59 N 124.28 E
Yŏngch'ŏn, Taehan 98 38.07 N 127.05 E
Yŏngch'ŏn, Taehan 98 35.58 N 128.56 E
Yongch'ŏn-dong 98 41.18 N 129.40 E
Yongchuan 107 29.21 N 105.54 E
Yongchun 100 25.21 N 118.21 E
Yongdeng 102 36.48 N 103.14 E
Yongdian 98 40.34 N 124.48 E
Yongding 100 24.46 N 116.43 E
Yongding ≃, Zhg. 100 24.42 N 116.34 E
Yongding ≃, Zhg. 105 39.20 N 117.04 E
Yongdingmen Station •[5] 271a 39.52 N 116.23 E
Yŏngdŏk 98 36.26 N 129.23 E
Yŏngdong 98 36.10 N 127.48 E
Yŏngdŭngp'o •[8] 271b 37.32 N 126.54 E
Yongfeng, Zhg. 100 29.44 N 116.49 E
Yongfeng, Zhg. 100 27.19 N 115.24 E
Yongfengchang 107 30.33 N 105.05 E
Yongfu 100 25.05 N 117.20 E
Yonggang 98 38.52 N 125.21 E
Yonggangonch'ŏn 98 38.53 N 125.14 E
Yonggi 98 36.24 N 128.24 E
Yongguzhai 98 34.05 N 116.50 E
Yonghe 100 28.18 N 113.51 E
Yongheshi 100 28.18 N 113.51 E
Yonghŭng 98 39.32 N 127.13 E
Yŏnghŭng-do I 98 37.16 N 126.28 E
Yŏnghŭng-man ⊂ 98 39.15 N 127.30 E
Yongi 89 43.40 N 126.30 E
Yŏngil-man ⊂ 98 36.02 N 129.26 E
Yongji 102 34.51 N 110.29 E
Yongjia, Zhg. 100 28.11 N 120.42 E
Yongjia, Zhg. 107 29.34 N 106.01 E
Yŏngjong-do I 98 37.30 N 126.31 E
Yŏngju 98 36.50 N 128.37 E
Yongkang, Zhg. 100 32.32 N 117.24 E
Yongkang, Zhg. 100 28.53 N 120.02 E
Yongkou 100 26.16 N 118.19 E
Yongle, Zhg. 89 45.45 N 125.12 E
Yongle, Zhg. 105 39.32 N 115.59 E
Yongle ≃ 100 26.54 N 113.12 E
Yongledian 105 39.43 N 116.46 E
Yonglong 106 31.34 N 121.48 E
Yonglonghe 100 30.46 N 112.48 E
Yŏngmi-dong 98 39.40 N 125.31 E
Yongnian (Linmingguan) 98 36.47 N 114.30 E
Yongnianchang 107 29.08 N 104.51 E
Yongning, Zhg. 100 24.43 N 118.42 E
Yongning, Zhg. 102 22.42 N 108.50 E
Yongning, Zhg. 102 27.47 N 100.38 E
Yongning, Zhg. 102 38.20 N 106.17 E
Yongningcheng 105 40.34 N 116.11 E
Yongningjian 98 39.56 N 121.48 E
Yong Peng 114 2.01 N 103.04 E
Yongping, Zhg. 100 28.12 N 117.45 E
Yongping, Zhg. 102 25.28 N 99.33 E
Yongqing, Zhg. 105 39.19 N 116.29 E
Yongqing, Zhg. 107 30.00 N 105.27 E
Yongquan 100 28.46 N 121.19 E
Yongren 102 26.08 N 101.40 E
Yŏngsan-gang ≃ 98 34.54 N 126.32 E
Yongsan-ni 98 38.52 N 125.56 E
Yŏngsanp'o 98 34.58 N 126.44 E
Yongshan 102 28.15 N 103.24 E
Yongshanqiao 100 29.06 N 117.17 E
Yongsheng 102 26.42 N 100.43 E
Yongshou 102 34.43 N 108.05 E
Yongshun 102 28.57 N 109.41 E
Yongshunchang 107 30.06 N 105.26 E
Yongtai 100 25.54 N 118.58 E
Yŏngwŏl 98 37.12 N 128.28 E
Yŏngwŏn 98 39.49 N 126.32 E
Yongwŏn-ni 98 40.41 N 128.42 E
Yongxin, Zhg. 100 26.56 N 114.18 E
Yongxin, Zhg. 107 28.59 N 106.32 E
Yongxing, Zhg. 98 40.11 N 123.52 E
Yongxing, Zhg. 100 26.08 N 113.06 E
Yongxing, Zhg. 102 39.08 N 110.31 E
Yongxing, Zhg. 106 31.56 N 120.55 E
Yongxing, Zhg. 107 30.34 N 105.35 E
Yongxing, Zhg. 107 30.13 N 105.06 E
Yongxingchang, Zhg. 107 29.02 N 104.34 E
Yongxingchang, Zhg. 107 29.37 N 106.23 E
Yongxingchang, Zhg. 107 30.20 N 103.44 E
Yongxiu 100 29.04 N 115.49 E
Yŏngyang, Taehan 98 36.40 N 129.07 E
Yongyang, Zhg. 100 26.57 N 114.46 E
Yŏngyn 98 39.18 N 125.34 E
Yongyŏn-ni 98 40.44 N 126.09 E
Yongzhai 100 27.59 N 115.26 E
Yŏnhŭi-ri 271b 37.33 N 126.41 E
Yŏnhwa-san ∧ 98 40.46 N 127.23 E
Yonibana 150 8.26 N 12.14 W
Yonkers 210 40.55 N 73.53 W
Yonkers Raceway ♦ 276 40.55 N 73.52 W
Yonne □[5] 50 47.55 N 3.45 E
Yonne ≃ 32 48.23 N 2.58 E
Yono 94 35.53 N 139.38 E
Yŏnp'yŏng-yŏlto II 98 37.38 N 125.40 E
Yonsei University ⊕[2] 271b 37.34 N 126.56 E
Yoo, Enneri V 146 19.24 N 16.38 E
Yoontow 144 0.08 S 42.34 E
Yopal 246 5.21 N 72.23 W
Yop'o-ri 98 38.50 N 125.33 E
Yopurga 85 39.15 N 76.45 E
Yoqne'am 132 32.39 N 35.07 E
Yorba Linda 228 33.53 N 117.48 W
Yorii 94 36.07 N 139.12 E
Yorishima 96 34.29 N 133.35 E
York, Austl. 168a 31.53 S 116.46 E
York, On., Can. 212 43.41 N 79.29 W
York, S.L. 150 8.17 N 13.11 W
York, Eng., U.K. 44 53.58 N 1.05 W
York, Al., U.S. 194 32.29 N 88.17 W
York, In., U.S. 216 41.41 N 84.49 W
York, Ne., U.S. 198 40.52 N 97.35 W
York, N.Y., U.S. 210 42.52 N 77.53 W
York, N.D., U.S. 198 48.18 N 99.34 W
York, Pa., U.S. 208 39.57 N 76.43 W
York, S.C., U.S. 192 34.59 N 81.14 W
York □[6], On., Can. 212 43.55 N 79.25 W
York □[6], Pa., U.S. 208 39.58 N 76.44 W
York □[6], Va., U.S. 208 37.15 N 76.40 W
York ≃, On., Can. 212 45.20 N 77.35 W
York ≃, P.Q., Can. 186 48.49 N 64.34 W
York ≃, Va., U.S. 208 37.15 N 76.23 W
York, Cape > 164 10.42 S 142.31 E
York, Kap > 16 75.53 N 66.12 W
York, Vale of V 44 54.10 N 1.20 W
Yorkana 208 39.59 N 76.35 W
York Center, Il., U.S. 278 41.52 N 87.59 W
York Center, Oh., U.S. 216 40.24 N 83.27 W
Yorkdale Centre •[9] 275b 43.44 N 79.27 W
Yorke Peninsula >[1] 166 35.00 S 137.30 E
Yorketown 168b 35.02 S 137.36 E
York Factory 184 57.00 N 92.18 W
Yorkfield 278 41.52 N 87.56 W
York Haven 208 40.06 N 76.42 W
Yorklyn 285 39.48 N 75.40 W
York Minster ⊕[1] 44 53.57 N 1.04 W
York New Salem 208 39.54 N 76.47 W
Yorkshire, N.Y., U.S. 210 42.31 N 78.28 W
Yorkshire, Pa., U.S. 208 39.59 N 76.41 W
Yorkshire, Va., U.S. 208 38.47 N 77.27 W
Yorkshire Dales National Park ♦ 44 54.13 N 2.10 W
Yorkshire Wolds ⋏[2] 44 54.00 N 0.40 W
York Sound ⊔ 160 14.50 S 125.05 E
York Springs 208 40.00 N 77.07 W
Yorkton 184 51.13 N 102.28 W
Yorktown, In., U.S. 218 40.10 N 85.29 W
Yorktown, Tx., U.S. 222 28.58 N 97.30 W
Yorktown, Va., U.S. 208 37.14 N 76.30 W
Yorktown •[9] 278 41.51 N 88.01 W
Yorktown Battlefield ⊥ 208 37.13 N 76.31 W
Yorktown Heights 210 41.16 N 73.46 W
Yorktown Manor 207 41.38 N 71.26 W
York Township Airport ⊠ 278 41.51 N 88.02 W
York University ⊕[2] 275b 43.47 N 79.30 W
Yorkville, Il., U.S. 216 41.38 N 88.26 W
Yorkville, Mi., U.S. 216 42.23 N 85.24 W
Yorkville, N.Y., U.S. 210 43.06 N 75.16 W
Yorkville, Oh., U.S. 214 40.09 N 80.43 W
Yorkville •[8] 275b 43.40 N 79.24 W
Yoro, Hond. 236 15.09 N 87.07 W
Yoro, Mali 150 14.17 N 2.08 W
Yōrō, Nihon 94 35.18 N 136.33 E
Yoro □[5] 236 15.15 N 87.15 W
Yōrō ≃ 94 35.32 N 140.04 E
Yoroi-zaki > 94 34.24 N 136.55 E
Yoron-jima I 93b 27.02 N 128.26 E
Yōrō-no-taki ∟ 94 35.17 N 136.32 E
Yorosso 150 12.22 N 4.47 W
Yosemite Creek ≃ 226 37.44 N 119.36 W
Yosemite National Park 226 37.45 N 119.35 W
Yosemite National Park ♦ 226 37.51 N 119.33 W
Yoshida, Nihon 94 36.02 N 139.02 E
Yoshida, Nihon 94 34.46 N 138.15 E
Yoshida, Nihon 96 33.16 N 132.33 E
Yoshida, Nihon 96 34.40 N 132.42 E
Yoshida, Nihon 96 35.10 N 132.51 E
Yoshida ≃ 96 34.03 N 131.02 E
Yoshii, Nihon 94 36.15 N 138.59 E
Yoshii, Nihon 96 33.20 N 130.45 E
Yoshii, Nihon 96 34.38 N 133.26 E
Yoshii, Nihon 96 34.55 N 134.06 E
Yoshii, Nihon 270 34.53 N 135.03 E
Yoshii ≃ 96 34.36 N 134.03 E
Yoshikawa, Nihon 94 37.13 N 138.25 E
Yoshikawa, Nihon 94 35.53 N 139.51 E
Yoshikawa, Nihon 270 34.55 N 135.28 E
Yoshimi 94 36.02 N 139.27 E
Yoshino, Nihon 96 34.21 N 135.51 E
Yoshino, Nihon 96 34.06 N 134.23 E
Yoshino ≃, Nihon 94 34.22 N 135.40 E
Yoshino ≃, Nihon 96 34.05 N 134.36 E
Yoshinodani 94 36.17 N 136.39 E
Yoshino-Kumano-kokuritsu-kōen ♦ 92 34.07 N 135.55 E
Yoshioka 94 36.27 N 139.01 E
Yoshiumi 96 34.09 N 133.03 E
Yoshiwa 96 34.29 N 132.09 E
Yoshkar-Ola
— Joškar-Ola 80 56.38 N 47.52 E
Yosowilangun 115a 8.15 S 113.18 E
Yos Sudarso, Pulau (Frederik Hendrikeiland) I 164 7.50 S 138.30 E
Yŏsu 98 34.46 N 127.44 E
Yotausito 248 16.03 S 63.03 W
Yōtei-zan ∧ 92a 42.49 N 140.49 E
Yotsukaidō 94 35.39 N 140.10 E
Yotvata 132 29.53 N 35.03 E
You ≃, Zhg. 100 26.23 N 118.27 E
You ≃, Zhg. 102 22.50 N 108.06 E
You ≃, Zhg. 102 28.27 N 110.24 E
Youanmi 162 28.37 S 118.49 E
Youbou 224 48.53 N 124.13 W
Youcheng 100 29.14 N 116.48 E
Youfang 106 32.09 N 119.50 E
Youghal 48 51.57 N 7.51 W
Youghal Bay ⊂ 48 51.52 N 7.50 W
Youghiogheny ≃ 214 40.22 N 79.52 W
Yougoslavie
— Yugoslavia □[1] 22 44.00 N 21.00 E
Youhe 100 32.19 N 113.50 E
Youjidong 104 42.12 N 121.07 E
Youkounkoun 150 12.32 N 13.08 W
Youlan 100 28.34 N 116.10 E
Young, Austl. 166 34.19 S 148.18 E
Young, Sk., Can. 184 51.47 N 105.46 W
Young, Az., U.S. 200 34.06 N 110.57 W
Young, Ur. 252 32.41 S 57.38 W
Young America 216 40.34 N 86.20 W
Younghusband Peninsula >[1] 166 36.00 S 139.30 E
Youngs ≃ 224 46.10 N 123.49 W
Youngs, Lake ⊜ 224 47.25 N 122.07 W
Youngs Creek 218 38.29 N 86.30 W
Youngs Creek ≃ 219 39.21 N 91.51 W
Youngs Rock I[2] 174e 25.03 S 130.07 W
Youngstown, Ab., Can. 182 51.32 N 111.13 W
Youngstown, Fl., U.S. 192 30.21 N 85.26 W
Youngstown, N.Y., U.S. 210 43.14 N 79.03 W
Youngstown, Oh., U.S. 214 41.05 N 80.38 W
Youngstown Municipal Airport ⊠ 214 41.15 N 80.41 W
Youngsville, La., U.S. 194 30.05 N 91.59 W
Youngsville, N.Y., U.S. 210 41.48 N 74.54 W
Youngsville, N.C., U.S. 192 36.01 N 78.28 W
Youngsville, Pa., U.S. 214 41.51 N 79.19 W
Youngwood 214 40.14 N 79.34 W
Youngwood Park ♦ 279b 40.14 N 79.36 W
Yountville 226 38.24 N 122.22 W
Youshashan 120 38.08 N 91.10 E
Youssoufia 148 32.16 N 8.33 W
Youtingpu 107 29.26 N 105.45 E
Youville •[8] 275a 45.33 N 73.39 W
Youxi, Zhg. 100 28.45 N 121.06 E
Youxi, Zhg. 100 26.11 N 118.09 E
Youxi, Zhg. 107 29.12 N 106.09 E
Youxian 100 27.00 N 113.21 E
Youxizhen 107 30.35 N 106.18 E
Youyang 102 28.58 N 108.41 E
Youyi 89 46.44 N 131.44 E
Youyu 102 40.09 N 112.32 E
Youzhagou 106 31.04 N 118.46 E
Youzhou 105 40.09 N 115.42 E
Yoweragabbie 162 28.13 S 117.39 E
Yŏyang-ni 98 37.30 N 128.43 E
Yozgat 130 39.50 N 34.48 E
Yozgat □[4] 130 39.40 N 35.10 E
Ypacaraí 252 25.23 S 57.16 W
Ypané ≃ 252 23.29 S 57.19 W
Ypé Jhú 252 23.54 S 55.20 W
Yport 50 49.44 N 0.19 E
Ypres
— Ieper 50 50.51 N 2.53 E

ENGLISH Name	Page	Lat.°′	Long.°′

Ypsilanti 216 42.14 N 83.36 W
Ypsilanti East 216 42.15 N 83.35 W
Yreka 204 41.44 N 122.38 W
Yrgajty ≃ 85 43.03 N 74.43 E
Yron ≃ 56 49.10 N 5.52 E
Ysabel Channel ⊔ 164 2.00 S 150.00 E
Ysbyty Ystwyth 42 52.20 N 3.48 W
Yser (IJzer) ≃ 50 51.09 N 2.43 E
Ysieux, Ruisseau l' ≃ 261 49.09 N 2.22 E
Yssche ≃ 56 50.49 N 4.38 E
Yssel
— IJssel ≃ 52 52.35 N 5.50 E
Ysselmeer
— IJsselmeer ⊽[2] 52 52.45 N 5.25 E
Yssingeaux 62 45.08 N 4.07 E
Ystad 41 55.25 N 13.49 E
Ystalyfera 42 51.47 N 3.47 W
Ysterfonteinpunt > 158 33.22 S 18.09 E
Ystrad ≃ 44 53.13 N 3.20 W
Ystrad Aeron 42 52.11 N 4.11 W
Ystradfellte 42 51.48 N 3.34 W
Ystradgynlais 42 51.47 N 3.45 W
Ystwyth ≃ 42 52.24 N 4.05 W
Ytambey ≃ 252 24.46 S 54.24 W
Ythan ≃ 46 57.18 N 2.00 W
Ytre Arna 26 60.26 N 5.30 E
Ytterharnäs 40 60.39 N 17.21 E
Ytterhogdal 26 62.12 N 14.51 E
Yttermalung 40 60.35 N 13.50 E
Ytterselö 40 59.23 N 17.15 E
Yttre Hållsfjärden ⊂[2] 40 59.08 N 17.40 E
Yttygran, ostrov I 180 64.36 N 172.40 W
Yū 96 34.02 N 132.13 E
Yu ≃ 102 23.24 N 110.05 E
Yu, Pulau I 164 0.03 S 129.36 E
Yu'alliq, Jabal ∧ 140 30.22 N 33.31 E
Yuam ≃ 110 17.47 N 97.45 E
Yuan
— Red ≃, Asia 110 20.17 N 106.34 E
Yuan ≃, Zhg. 100 28.09 N 115.34 E
Yuan ≃, Zhg. 102 28.58 N 111.49 E
Yuan'an 102 31.04 N 111.26 E
Yuanao 100 26.29 N 119.48 E
Yuanbachang 107 29.44 N 105.27 E
Yuanhua 106 30.25 N 120.46 E
Yuanjiang 102 23.34 N 102.03 E
Yuankeng 100 26.48 N 117.44 E
Yüanli 100 24.27 N 120.39 E
Yüanlin 100 23.58 N 120.34 E
Yuanling 102 28.20 N 110.16 E
Yuanmou 102 25.38 N 101.54 E
Yuanshancun 106 31.08 N 120.20 E
Yuanshi 98 37.45 N 114.32 E
Yuantan, Zhg. 100 32.47 N 112.53 E
Yuantan, Zhg. 100 23.39 N 113.12 E
Yuantongsi 107 30.13 N 104.15 E
Yuantouzhu 106 31.32 N 120.14 E
Yuanxiang 98 34.14 N 115.19 E
Yuanxiangzhen 106 31.39 N 119.15 E
Yuanxing 107 30.36 N 104.59 E
Yuanyang (Yangwu), Zhg. 98 35.04 N 113.57 E
Yuanyang, Zhg. 102 23.12 N 102.52 E
Yuanyangpu 107 30.10 N 105.15 E
Yuanyangqiao 107 29.41 N 106.33 E
Yuasa 96 34.02 N 135.11 E
Yuat ≃ 164 4.25 S 143.55 E
Yuba 102 29.27 N 97.42 E
Yuba □[6] 226 39.16 N 121.17 W
Yuba ≃ 226 39.07 N 121.36 W
Yuba City 226 39.08 N 121.36 W
Yubara 96 35.12 N 133.45 E
Yubara-chosuichi ⊜ 96 35.13 N 133.43 E
Yūbari 92a 43.04 N 141.59 E
Yūbari-sanchi ⋏ 92a 43.15 N 142.20 E
Yubdo 144 9.00 N 35.22 E
Yūbetsu 92a 44.14 N 143.37 E
Yūbetsu ≃ 92a 44.14 N 143.37 E
Yucaipa 228 34.02 N 117.02 W
Yucatán □[3] 232 20.50 N 89.00 W
Yucatán, Canal de ⊔ 238 21.45 N 85.45 W
Yucatan Peninsula (Península de Yucatán) >[1] 232 19.30 N 89.00 W
Yucca 200 34.52 N 114.08 W
Yucca Lake ⊜ 204 36.59 N 116.01 W
Yucca Mountain ∧ 204 36.56 N 116.29 W
Yucca Valley 204 34.07 N 116.35 W
Yuchaozhuang 105 39.35 N 117.50 E
Yucheng, Zhg. 98 36.56 N 116.39 E
Yucheng, Zhg. 106 30.32 N 120.51 E
Yuci 102 37.45 N 112.41 E
Yuda 92 39.20 N 140.50 E
Yudaokou 98 42.14 N 116.48 E
Yudi Shan ∧ 89 52.17 N 121.52 E
Yudong 106 32.02 N 121.22 E
Yudu 100 25.59 N 115.24 E
Yue ≃ 107 28.50 N 104.21 E
Yuebo 107 29.03 N 104.12 E
Yuecheng 100 32.39 N 114.49 E
Yuechi 107 30.33 N 106.26 E
Yuejiatun 104 41.10 N 120.43 E
Yuejiawopeng 104 41.35 N 122.20 E
Yuekou 100 30.32 N 113.03 E
Yuelai 106 31.56 N 121.27 E
Yuelaichang, Zhg. 107 29.44 N 106.32 E
Yuelaichang, Zhg. 107 28.53 N 106.22 E
Yuemenpu 107 30.28 N 106.34 E
Yuendumu 162 22.16 S 131.49 E
Yuendumu Aboriginal Reserve •[4] 162 22.20 S 131.47 E
Yuen Long 271d 22.26 N 114.02 E
Yuepu 106 31.25 N 121.26 E
Yueqing 100 28.08 N 120.58 E
Yuewang 106 31.33 N 121.09 E
Yuexi, Zhg. 100 30.50 N 116.24 E
Yuexi, Zhg. 102 28.42 N 102.28 E
Yueyang 100 29.23 N 113.06 E
Yuezi 100 24.54 N 115.02 E
Yufa 105 39.31 N 116.19 E
Yufeng 107 30.37 N 105.11 E
Yufu-dake ∧ 96 33.17 N 131.24 E
Yufuin 96 33.15 N 131.20 E
Yugan 100 28.41 N 116.41 E
Yugawara 94 35.09 N 139.04 E
Yuge 96 34.15 N 133.12 E
Yugoslavia (Jugoslavija) □[1], Europe 22 44.00 N 21.00 E
Yugoslavia (Jugoslavija) □[1], Europe 38 44.00 N 21.00 E
Yugou 100 33.42 N 118.55 E
Yuguan 98 39.56 N 119.22 E
Yuguo 104 41.52 N 123.15 E
Yuhang (Linping) 106 30.25 N 120.18 E
Yuhebu 102 38.01 N 109.37 E
Yuhu 100 27.53 N 120.08 E
Yuhuaizhuang 105 39.24 N 117.40 E
Yuhuan 100 28.10 N 121.12 E
Yuhuan Dao I 100 28.08 N 121.12 E
Yuhuang Ding ∧ 98 36.50 N 121.21 E
Yui 94 35.06 N 138.34 E
Yuin 162 27.58 S 116.02 E
Yujiachang 107 29.57 N 104.04 E
Yujiacun 106 31.45 N 121.48 E
Yujiang 100 28.11 N 116.47 E
Yujiaqiao 106 31.30 N 119.25 E
Yujiawan 86 44.32 N 86.45 E
Yukarıbey 130 39.15 N 27.06 E
Yukarıdudullu •[8] 267b 41.02 N 29.09 E
Yuke 98 37.58 N 115.39 E
Yūki, Nihon 94 36.18 N 139.53 E
Yuki, Nihon 96 34.29 N 132.16 E
Yuki, Nihon 96 34.46 N 133.17 E
Yuki, Nihon 96 33.46 N 134.36 E
Yukon, Ok., U.S. 196 35.30 N 97.45 W
Yukon, Pa., U.S. 214 40.13 N 79.41 W
Yukon □[4], Can. 176 64.00 N 135.00 W
Yukon □[4], Can. 180 64.00 N 135.00 W
Yukon ≃ 180 62.33 N 163.59 W

DEUTSCH Name	Seite	Breite°′	Länge°′ E = Ost

Yukon Flats ≡ 180 66.30 N 146.00 W
Yukou 105 40.12 N 117.00 E
Yukuhashi 96 33.44 N 130.59 E
Yulan 210 41.31 N 74.56 W
Yulao 102 23.31 N 111.46 E
Yulara 162 25.14 S 131.04 E
Yule ≃ 162 20.41 S 118.17 E
Yule Bay ⊂ 9 70.44 S 166.40 E
Yule Island I 164 8.50 S 146.30 E
Yuli, Nig. 146 9.42 N 10.17 E
Yüli, T'aiwan 100 23.20 N 121.18 E
Yuli, Zhg. 98 37.00 N 121.25 E
Yuliang 100 29.52 N 118.30 E
Yuliangpu 89 43.26 N 121.55 E
Yulin, Zhg. 102 22.36 N 110.07 E
Yulin, Zhg. 102 38.20 N 109.29 E
Yulin, Zhg. 110 18.16 N 109.32 E
Yulincun 105 40.12 N 116.42 E
Yul-li 98 38.52 N 126.13 E
Yulong 107 29.58 N 104.22 E
Yuma, Az., U.S. 200 32.43 N 114.37 W
Yuma, Co., U.S. 198 40.08 N 102.43 W
Yuma, Bahía de ⊂ 238 18.21 N 68.35 W
Yuma Marine Corps Air Station ■ 200 32.40 N 114.38 W
Yuma Proving Ground ■ 204 33.05 N 114.25 W
Yumare 246 10.37 N 68.41 W
Yumbel 252 37.08 S 72.32 W
Yumbi, Zaïre 152 1.53 S 16.32 E
Yumbi, Zaïre 154 1.14 S 26.14 E
Yumbo 246 3.35 N 76.28 W
Yumen (Laojunmiao) 102 39.56 N 97.51 E
Yumenzhen 102 40.17 N 97.07 E
Yumesaki 96 34.58 N 134.42 E
Yumezaki ≃ 96 34.47 N 134.39 E
Yumin 86 46.02 N 82.37 E
Yumurtalık 130 36.49 N 35.45 E
Yun ≃ 100 30.43 N 114.04 E
Yuna, Austl. 162 28.20 S 115.00 E
Yuna, Nihon 174m 26.46 N 128.12 E
Yuna ≃ 238 19.12 N 69.37 W
Yunak 130 38.49 N 31.45 E
Yunan (Ducheng) 102 23.11 N 111.29 E
Yunaska Island I 180 52.40 N 170.50 W
Yuncao 100 31.26 N 118.04 E
Yuncheng, Zhg. 98 35.35 N 115.54 E
Yuncheng, Zhg. 102 35.00 N 110.59 E
Yundamindra 162 29.07 S 122.02 E
Yundanyingzi 104 42.00 N 121.34 E
Yunderup 168a 32.35 S 115.46 E
Yunfeng Ding ∧ 106 30.56 N 120.02 E
Yungas •[1] 248 16.00 S 67.45 W
Yungay, Chile 252 37.07 S 72.01 W
Yungay, Perú 248 9.09 S 77.44 W
Yungchi
— Jilin 89 43.51 N 126.33 E
Yungchia
— Wenzhou 100 28.01 N 120.39 E
Yungho 269d 25.01 N 121.31 E
Yungning
— Nanning 102 22.48 N 108.20 E
Yung Shue Wan 271d 22.14 N 114.06 E
Yunhe
— Peixian, Zhg. 98 34.21 N 117.59 E
Yunhe, Zhg. 100 28.06 N 119.34 E
Yunjin 107 29.06 N 105.40 E
Yunkai Dashan ⋏ 102 22.30 N 111.00 E
Yun Ling ⋏ 102 27.20 N 99.20 E
Yunlong, Zhg. 102 25.50 N 99.17 E
Yunlong, Zhg. 107 30.31 N 104.46 E
Yunluchang 107 29.45 N 105.57 E
Yunmeng 100 31.02 N 113.41 E
Yunmenling 100 25.15 N 115.49 E
Yunmenzhen 107 30.06 N 106.20 E
Yunnan □[4] 102 24.00 N 101.00 E
Yunnanfu
— Kunming 102 25.05 N 102.40 E
Yunotani 94 37.14 N 139.01 E
Yunotsu 96 35.05 N 132.21 E
Yunta 166 32.35 S 139.33 E
Yunting 106 31.53 N 120.19 E
Yunwu Shan ∧ 98 41.07 N 116.34 E
Yunxi, Zhg. 100 29.28 N 113.16 E
Yunxi, Zhg. 102 32.49 N 110.13 E
Yunxian, Zhg. 102 24.30 N 100.03 E
Yunxian (Yunyang), Zhg. 102 32.49 N 110.49 E
Yunxiao 100 24.04 N 117.20 E
Yunyan ≃ 100 34.39 N 119.18 E
Yunyang, Zhg. 100 33.28 N 112.42 E
Yunyang, Zhg. 102 30.58 N 109.05 E
Yunzalin ≃ 110 17.23 N 97.40 E
Yunzhong 100 29.13 N 117.40 E
Yunzhou 98 41.01 N 115.44 E
Yuping 102 27.07 N 108.47 E
Yuqi 106 31.43 N 120.11 E
Yuqia 102 38.07 N 94.35 E
Yuqian'gou 104 41.41 N 121.28 E
Yuqiao Shuiku ⊜[1] 105 40.02 N 117.33 E
Yuqing 102 27.05 N 107.44 E
Yura, Nihon 96 33.57 N 135.07 E
Yura, Perú 248 16.11 S 71.40 W
Yura ≃ 96 35.31 N 135.17 E
Yurano-hana > 96 33.01 N 132.23 E
Yurécuaro 234 20.20 N 102.18 W
Yurga
— Jurga 86 55.42 N 84.51 E
Yuri-jima I 96 33.51 N 132.32 E
Yurimaguas 248 5.54 S 76.05 W
Yuriria 234 20.12 N 101.09 W
Yuriria, Laguna de ⊜ 234 20.15 N 101.06 W
Yur'iyivka 83 48.30 N 39.00 E
Yurove 78 51.22 N 27.50 E
Yuruarí ≃ 246 6.44 N 61.40 W
Yurubi, Parque Nacional ♦ 246 10.25 N 68.42 W
Yürük 130 40.56 N 27.04 E
Yurumanguí ≃ 246 3.27 N 77.21 W
Yurungkax ≃ 120 37.00 N 79.55 E
Yuryev
— Tartu 76 58.23 N 26.43 E
Yuryivka 78 48.44 N 36.02 E
Yusala, Laguna ⊜ 248 14.05 S 67.12 W
Yuşa Tepesi ∧[2] 267b 41.09 N 29.05 E
Yuscarán 236 13.55 N 86.51 W
Yushan, Zhg. 100 26.54 N 118.36 E
Yushan, Zhg. 100 28.41 N 118.15 E
Yushan, Zhg. 100 33.19 N 113.41 E
Yü Shan ∧, T'aiwan 100 23.28 N 120.57 E
Yu Shan ∧, Zhg. 100 26.06 N 115.20 E
Yushanzhen 102 29.38 N 108.19 E
Yushu, Zhg. 89 44.46 N 126.34 E
Yushu (Jiegu), Zhg. 102 33.01 N 97.00 E
Yushugou 86 44.07 N 87.05 E
Yushulinzi, Zhg. 98 41.30 N 119.07 E
Yushulinzi, Zhg. 98 40.59 N 125.57 E
Yushupu 104 41.10 N 122.08 E
Yushutai, Zhg. 89 43.30 N 124.17 E
Yushutai, Zhg. 104 41.42 N 123.26 E
Yushuwan 105 40.04 N 115.35 E
Yusichang 107 29.14 N 105.25 E
Yūsofābād •[8] 267d 35.44 N 51.25 E
Yuste, Monasterio de ⊕[1] 34 40.08 N 5.45 W
Yūsuf, Baḥr ≅ 142 29.18 N 30.50 E
Yusufeli 130 40.50 N 41.33 E
Yusuhara 96 33.23 N 132.55 E
Yusuhara ≃ 96 33.11 N 132.58 E
Yutai (Guting) 98 35.02 N 116.40 E
Yutian, Zhg. 100 26.27 N 114.36 E
Yutian, Zhg. 105 39.53 N 117.45 E
Yutian, Zhg. 120 36.51 N 81.40 E
Yuting 100 29.50 N 117.57 E
Yūtō 94 34.42 N 137.38 E
Yutou 100 28.36 N 118.30 E
Yuty 252 26.32 S 56.18 W
Yutz 56 49.21 N 6.11 E
Yütz'u
— Yuci 102 37.45 N 112.41 E
Yūwan-dake ∧ 93b 28.18 N 129.21 E

Symbols in the index entries represent the broad categories identified in the key at the right. Symbols with superior numbers (⋏[1]) identify subcategories (see complete key on page I · 1).

Symbole im Register stellen die rechts im Schlüssel erklärten Kategorien dar. Symbole mit hochgestellten Ziffern (⋏[1]) bezeichnen Unterabteilungen einer Kategorie (vgl. vollständiger Schlüssel auf Seite I · 1).

Los símbolos incluídos en el texto del índice representan las grandes categorías identificadas con la clave a la derecha. Los símbolos con numeros en su parte superior (⋏[1]) identifican las subcategorías (véase la clave completa en la página I · 1).

Les symboles de l'index représentent les catégories indiquées dans la légende à droite. Les symboles suivis d'un indice (⋏[1]) représentent des sous-catégories (voir légende complète à la page I · 1).

Os símbolos incluídos no texto do índice representam as grandes categorias identificadas com a chave à direita. Os símbolos com números em sua parte superior (⋏[1]) identificam as subcategorias (veja-se a chave completa à página I · 1).

English	Deutsch	Español	Français	Português
∧ Mountain	Berg	Montaña	Montagne	Montanha
⋏ Mountains	Gebirge	Montañas	Montagnes	Montanhas
)(Pass	Paß	Paso	Col	Passo
V Valley, Canyon	Tal, Cañon	Valle, Cañón	Vallée, Canyon	Vale, Canhão
⩦ Plain	Ebene	Llano	Plaine	Planície
> Cape	Kap	Cabo	Cap	Cabo
I Island	Insel	Isla	Île	Ilha
II Islands	Inseln	Islas	Îles	Ilhas
⊥ Other Topographic Features	Andere Topographische Objekte	Otros Elementos Topográficos	Autres données topographiques	Outros acidentes topográficos

ESPAÑOL

Nombre | Página | Lat.°′ | Long.°′ W = Oeste

Yuwangcheng 100 31.31 N 114.29 E
Yüweng Tao I 100 23.36 N 119.30 E
Yuwŏnjin 98 40.18 N 126.37 E
Yuxarı Garabağ kanalı ≍ 84 39.44 N 47.57 E
Yuxi, Zhg. 100 25.36 N 119.18 E
Yuxi, Zhg. 102 24.23 N 102.34 E
Yuxi, Zhg. 106 32.03 N 121.11 E
Yuxi, Zhg. 107 30.19 N 105.47 E
Yuxian, Zhg. 98 39.48 N 114.33 E
Yuxian, Zhg. 100 34.10 N 113.28 E
Yuxian, Zhg. 102 38.09 N 113.25 E
Yuxiangpu 98 34.27 N 114.57 E
Yuxiangtou 106 31.14 N 120.53 E
Yuxikou 100 31.26 N 118.17 E
Yuyao 100 30.04 N 121.10 E
Yuya-wan c 96 34.23 N 130.56 E
Yuyŏn-ni 98 38.42 N 127.10 E
Yuyuan Tan ⊜ 271a 39.55 N 116.18 E
Yuza 92 39.01 N 139.54 E
Yuzawa, Nihon 92 39.10 N 140.30 E
Yuzawa, Nihon 94 36.56 N 138.49 E
Yuzhno-Sakhalinsk → Južno-Sachalinsk 89 46.58 N 142.42 E
Yuzovka → Donets'k 83 48.00 N 37.48 E
Yuzuruha-san ∧ 96 34.14 N 134.49 E
Yvelines □[5] 50 48.50 N 1.50 E
Yvelines, Forêt des ♦ 261 48.40 N 1.55 E
Yverdon 58 46.47 N 6.39 E
Yvetot 50 49.37 N 0.46 E
Yvette 261 48.43 N 1.55 E
Yvette ≃ 50 48.40 N 2.20 E
Yvoir 56 50.20 N 4.53 E
Yvoire 58 46.22 N 6.20 E
Yvonand 58 46.48 N 6.45 E
Yvron ≃ 50 48.39 N 2.56 E
Ywamun 110 20.31 N 95.25 E
Ywathagyi 110 22.18 N 95.42 E
Ywathit 110 19.10 N 97.30 E
Yxlan I 40 59.38 N 18.52 E
Yxsjöberg 40 60.03 N 14.46 E
Yzeron 62 45.42 N 4.35 E
Yzeure 32 46.34 N 3.21 E

Z

Za ≃ 102 32.00 N 96.55 E
Za, Oued ≃ 148 34.34 N 3.03 W
Zaachila 234 16.57 N 96.45 W
Zaaimansdal 158 33.35 S 23.22 E
Zaajatskaja 86 52.53 N 61.35 E
Zaalajskij chrebet ⋏ 85 39.20 N 72.30 E
Zaamin 85 39.58 N 68.24 E
Zaanstad 52 52.26 N 4.49 E
Žabaj ≃ 86 51.42 N 68.22 E
Zabajkal'sk 88 49.38 N 117.19 E
Zăbala ≃ 38 45.51 N 26.46 E
Žabalj 38 46.01 N 21.55 E
Žabari 38 44.21 N 21.13 E
Zabarjad, Jazīrat I 140 23.37 N 36.12 E
Žabasak 86 50.21 N 61.40 E
Zāb-e Kūchek → Little Zab ≃ 128 35.12 N 43.25 E
Zaberfeld 56 49.03 N 8.55 E
Zabīd 144 14.10 N 43.17 E
Zabīd, Wādī V 144 14.07 N 43.06 E
Žabinka 76 52.12 N 24.01 E
Zabituj 88 53.16 N 102.50 E
Ząbkowice Śląskie 30 50.36 N 16.53 E
Žabljak 38 43.09 N 19.07 E
Zabłudów 30 53.01 N 23.20 E
Żabno 30 50.09 N 20.53 E
Zābol 128 31.02 N 61.30 E
Zābol □[4] 120 32.00 N 67.15 E
Zābolī 128 27.07 N 61.40 E
Zabolotiv 78 48.29 N 25.16 E
Zabolotje, Bela. 76 52.40 N 28.34 E
Zabolotje, Bela. 76 53.56 N 24.46 E
Zabolotje, Ross. 82 54.24 N 38.54 E
Zabolotje, Ross. 82 55.32 N 38.12 E
Zabolotje, Ross. 82 56.40 N 38.06 E
Zabolottya 78 51.38 N 24.15 E
Zaborje, Bela. 76 55.55 N 29.19 E
Zaborje, Ross. 76 53.06 N 31.42 E
Zaborje, Ross. 76 54.51 N 32.41 E
Zaborje, Ross. 76 55.24 N 31.34 E
Zaborje, Ross. 82 55.23 N 37.47 E
Zabory 76 55.58 N 32.17 E
Zabré 150 11.10 N 0.38 W
Zábřeh 30 49.53 N 16.52 E
Zabrze (Hindenburg) 30 50.18 N 18.46 E
Zaburunje 80 46.44 N 50.09 E
Zabyčanje 76 53.25 N 31.52 E
Zabzugu 150 9.17 N 0.22 E
Zacapa 236 14.58 N 89.32 W
Zacapa □[5] 236 15.00 N 89.30 W
Zacapoaxtla 234 19.53 N 97.35 W
Zacapu 234 19.50 N 101.43 W
Zacata 208 38.07 N 76.47 W
Zacatecas 234 22.47 N 102.35 W
Zacatecas □[3] 232 23.00 N 103.00 W
Zacatecoluca 236 13.30 N 88.52 W
Zacatepec 234 18.39 N 99.12 W
Zacatlán 234 19.56 N 97.58 W
Zacatongo 234 20.49 N 104.33 W
Zacharias Creek ≃ 285 40.11 N 75.23 W
Zacharkovo 265b 55.47 N 37.19 E
Zacharovo, Ross. 76 54.22 N 39.17 E
Zacharovo, Ross. 82 56.31 N 36.44 E
Zacharvan' 24 66.21 N 55.48 E
Zachary 194 30.38 N 91.09 W
Zachepylivka 78 49.12 N 35.14 E
Zachmet 128 37.43 N 62.30 E
Zachožje 265a 59.44 N 30.51 E
Zachrebetnoje 24 69.00 N 36.25 E
Začistje 76 54.24 N 28.45 E
Zacks Bay c 276 40.36 N 73.29 W
Zacoalco de Torres 234 20.14 N 103.35 W
Zacualpa 236 15.05 N 90.50 W
Zacualpan, Méx. 234 21.15 N 105.10 W
Zacualpan, Méx. 234 20.28 N 98.22 W
Zacualtipan 234 20.39 N 98.36 W
Zaculeu ⊥ 236 15.21 N 91.29 W
Zadar 36 44.07 N 15.14 E
Zadetkale Kyun I 110 10.08 N 98.12 E
Zadetkyi Kyun I 110 9.58 N 98.13 E
Zadi (Inkisi) ≃ 152 4.46 S 14.52 E
Zadní Chodov 60 49.54 N 12.44 E
Zadoi 120 33.10 N 95.05 E
Zadonsk 76 52.23 N 38.57 E
Zadorra ≃ 34 42.40 N 2.54 W
Zaerap 76 59.18 N 36.37 E
Zafarabad 85 40.11 N 68.51 E
Zafar al-Qadīmah 142 30.58 N 31.37 E
Za'farānah, Bi'r ⊤[4] 142 29.07 N 32.33 E
Za'farānah, Ra's › 142 29.06 N 32.40 E
Zafarwāl 123 32.21 N 74.54 E
Zafer Burnu › 130 35.42 N 34.35 E
Zafferana Etnea 70 37.41 N 15.06 E
Zafferano, Capo › 70 38.06 N 13.30 E
Zafirovo 38 44.00 N 26.50 E
Zafra 34 38.25 N 6.25 W
Žaga 64 46.18 N 13.29 E
Zagabria → Zagreb 36 45.48 N 15.58 E
Żagań 30 51.37 N 15.19 E
Žagare 76 56.21 N 23.15 E
Zagarise 68 39.00 N 16.39 E
Zagarolo 66 41.50 N 12.50 E
Zagazig → Az-Zaqāzīq 142 30.35 N 31.31 E
Zaghouan 148 36.24 N 10.09 E
Zaghouan, Jebel ∧ 36 36.21 N 10.08 E
Zagnanado 150 7.16 N 2.21 E
Zagora 148 30.22 N 5.50 W

FRANÇAIS

Nom | Page | Lat.°′ | Long.°′ W = Ouest

Zagora ⋏ 36 43.40 N 16.15 E
Zagor'anskij 265b 55.55 N 37.55 E
Zagórów 30 52.11 N 17.55 E
Zagorskij 89 47.19 N 142.28 E
Zagórz 30 49.31 N 22.17 E
Zagreb 36 45.48 N 15.58 E
Zāgros, Kūhhā-ye ⋏ 128 33.40 N 47.00 E
Zagros Mountains → Zāgros, Kūhhā-ye ⋏ 128 33.40 N 47.00 E
Žagubica 38 44.13 N 21.48 E
Zagustaj 88 51.58 N 110.45 E
Za'gya ≃ 120 31.55 N 88.58 E
Zagyva ≃ 30 47.10 N 20.13 E
Zahana 34 35.32 N 0.25 W
Zāhedān 128 29.30 N 60.52 E
Zahīrābād 122 17.41 N 77.37 E
Zahlah 130 33.51 N 35.53 E
Zahna 54 51.54 N 12.47 E
Zahnitkiv 78 48.03 N 28.54 E
Zahns Airport ⊠ 276 40.42 N 73.24 W
Záhony 30 48.25 N 22.11 E
Záhorská Ves 61 48.23 N 16.51 E
Zahrān 144 17.40 N 43.30 E
Zahrensdorf, Dtsch. 54 53.45 N 11.40 E
Zahrensdorf, Dtsch. 54 53.24 N 10.48 E
Zahryzove 83 49.31 N 37.43 E
Zăicani 38 47.59 N 27.22 E
Zaidpur 124 26.50 N 81.20 E
Zaigrajevo 88 51.50 N 108.16 E
Zaijiafangzi 104 41.17 N 122.39 E
Zailijskij-Alatau, chrebet ⋏ 85 43.00 N 77.00 E
Žailma, Kaz. 85 43.46 N 69.47 E
Žailma, Kaz. 86 51.32 N 61.37 E
Zaimka 88 58.41 N 100.40 E
Zaimokuza 268 35.18 N 139.33 E
Zainsk 80 55.18 N 52.06 E
Zaire □[5] 152 7.00 S 13.30 E
Zaire (Zaïre) □[1] 138 4.00 S 25.00 E
Zaïre → Congo ≃ 138 6.04 S 12.24 E
Zaizhuangzi 105 40.02 N 117.43 E
Zaj ≃ 80 55.36 N 51.40 E
Zajarsk 88 56.10 N 102.52 E
Zajcevka 83 49.41 N 40.00 E
Zajcevo, Ross. 82 54.08 N 37.26 E
Zajcevo, Ross. 265b 55.39 N 37.11 E
Zaječar 38 43.54 N 22.17 E
Zaj-Karataj 80 54.42 N 52.22 E
Zajmo-Obryv 83 47.02 N 39.19 E
Zajsan 86 47.28 N 84.55 E
Zajsan, ozero ⊜ 86 48.00 N 84.00 E
Žajsk 80 55.54 N 42.32 E
Zajukovo 84 43.37 N 43.19 E
Zaka 154 20.20 S 31.29 E
Zakamensk 88 50.23 N 103.17 E
Zakarpattya □[4] 78 48.30 N 23.00 E
Zákas 38 40.02 N 21.16 E
Zakatnyj 80 46.32 N 44.04 E
Zakfero 140 12.10 N 27.35 E
Zakhidne 78 51.29 N 31.15 E
Zākhū 128 37.08 N 42.41 E
Zákinthos 38 37.47 N 20.53 E
Zákinthos I 38 37.52 N 20.44 E
Zakínthou, Porthmós ⋓ 38 37.50 N 21.00 E
Zakitne 83 48.54 N 37.58 E
Zakīyah 132 33.20 N 36.08 E
Zakliczyn 30 49.51 N 20.48 E
Zaklików 30 50.47 N 22.06 E
Zákolany 54 50.10 N 14.14 E
Zakopane 30 49.19 N 19.57 E
Zakotne 83 49.28 N 38.58 E
Zakouma 146 10.54 N 19.49 E
Zakouma, Parc National de ♦ 146 10.45 N 19.30 E
Zakroczym 30 52.26 N 20.37 E
Žaksy 86 51.55 N 67.20 E
Žaksybaj ≃ 80 49.24 N 53.18 E
Zákupy 54 50.42 N 14.40 E
Zala 144 6.28 N 37.20 E
Zala □[6] 30 46.45 N 16.50 E
Zala ≃ 30 46.43 N 17.16 E
Zalaegerszeg 30 46.51 N 16.51 E
Zalai-dombság ⋏[2] 61 46.37 N 16.48 E
Zalalövő 30 46.51 N 16.35 E
Zalamea de la Serena 34 38.39 N 5.39 W
Žalanaš 86 51.12 N 65.02 E
Zalanga 150 10.37 N 10.10 E
Žalany 54 50.35 N 13.55 E
Zalari 88 53.34 N 102.32 E
Zalaszentgrót 30 46.59 N 17.02 E
Zalatárnok 61 46.42 N 16.46 E
Zalau, Nig. 150 10.20 N 9.00 E
Zalău, Rom. 38 47.11 N 23.03 E
Žalauly, ozero ⊜ 86 52.53 N 74.10 E
Zaldívar, Laguna ⊜ 286b 22.58 N 82.27 W
Žalec 36 46.15 N 15.10 E
Zalegošč' 76 52.56 N 36.53 E
Zalesje, Ross. 76 54.51 N 21.32 E
Zalesje, Ross. 76 58.42 N 36.10 E
Zalesovo 86 54.00 N 84.47 E
Zalingei 140 12.54 N 23.29 E
Zalishchyky 78 48.38 N 25.44 E
Zaliznychne 78 47.53 N 33.29 E
Zalozhtsi 78 49.48 N 25.24 E
Zaltan 146 32.57 N 11.52 E
Zaltbommel 52 51.48 N 5.15 E
Žaltyr 86 51.40 N 69.50 E
Žaltyr, ozero ⊜ 80 47.24 N 51.07 E
Zalučje 76 57.40 N 31.46 E
Zalukokoaže 84 43.54 N 43.13 E
Zalun 110 17.29 N 95.34 E
Zama, Nihon 268 35.29 N 139.24 E
Zama, Ms., U.S. 194 32.58 N 89.22 W
Zama, Camp ■ 268 35.30 N 139.24 E
Zama-iriya 268 35.29 N 139.24 E
Zamakh 144 16.30 N 47.35 E
Zamālik, Jazīrat az- I 273c 30.03 N 31.13 E
Žaman-Akkol', ozero ⊜ 86 48.58 N 63.30 E
Žamankak 80 48.56 N 48.45 E
Žamantau, gora ∧[2] 80 48.20 N 51.50 E
Zamantı ≃ 130 37.36 N 35.35 E
Zamarino 82 54.18 N 37.11 E
Žambaj 80 47.11 N 50.34 E
Zambales □[4] 116 15.20 N 120.05 E
Zambales Mountains ⋏ 116 15.45 N 120.05 E
Žamberk 30 50.05 N 16.28 E
Zambezi 152 13.33 S 23.06 E
Zambezi (Zambeze) ≃ 138 18.55 S 36.04 E
Zambézia □[5] 154 16.15 S 37.30 E
Zambezi Escarpment ⊥[4] 154 16.10 S 30.30 E
Zambia □[1], Afr. 138 14.30 S 27.30 E
Zambia □[1], Afr. 154 14.30 S 29.00 E
Zambie → Zambia □[1] 154 14.30 S 27.30 E
Zamboanga 116 6.54 N 122.04 E
Zamboanga del Norte □[4] 116 8.15 N 123.00 E
Zamboanga del Sur □[4] 116 7.50 N 123.00 E
Zamboanga Peninsula ›[1] 116 7.32 N 122.16 E
Zamboanguita 116 9.06 N 123.12 E
Zambrano 246 9.45 N 74.49 W
Zambrone 68 38.42 N 15.59 E
Zambrów 30 53.00 N 22.15 E
Zâmbuè 154 15.10 S 30.50 E
Zambujal 266c 38.52 N 9.07 W
Zamch 30 50.20 N 23.00 E
Zamežnaja 24 65.02 N 51.50 E
Zamfara ≃ 150 12.05 N 4.02 E
Zamhlay 78 51.49 N 31.13 E
Zami ≃ 110 16.09 N 97.58 E

PORTUGUÊS

Nome | Página | Lat.°′ | Long.°′ W = Oeste

Zamjany 80 46.50 N 47.40 E
Zamkova, gora ∧[2] 76 53.30 N 25.43 E
Zamora, Ec. 246 4.04 S 78.58 W
Zamora, Esp. 34 41.30 N 5.45 W
Zamora, Ca., U.S. 226 38.48 N 121.53 W
Zamora □[4] 34 41.45 N 6.00 W
Zamora ≃ 246 2.59 S 78.13 W
Zamora-Chinchipe □[4] 246 4.15 S 78.50 W
Zamora de Hidalgo 234 19.59 N 102.16 W
Zamość 30 50.44 N 23.15 E
Zamość □[4] 30 50.35 N 23.20 E
Zamozhne 83 47.19 N 37.49 E
Zams 58 47.09 N 10.35 E
Zamševa 86 59.07 N 89.14 E
Zamuro, Punta › 246 11.26 N 68.50 W
Zamzam, Wādī V 146 31.26 N 15.27 E
Zamzor 88 55.21 N 98.35 E
Zana ⊥ 34 35.45 N 6.05 E
Žanadarja 86 44.45 N 64.40 E
Zanaga 152 2.51 S 13.50 E
Zanapa ≃ 234 17.58 N 94.06 W
Žanašu 80 47.27 N 48.31 E
Žanatalap, Kaz. 86 47.11 N 61.52 E
Žanatalap, Kaz. 86 47.06 N 84.13 E
Žanatarlyk 86 44.16 N 73.12 E
Žanatas 85 43.34 N 69.45 E
Záncara ≃ 34 39.18 N 3.18 W
Zanda 120 31.30 N 79.30 E
Žandov 54 50.44 N 14.24 E
Zandvoort 52 52.22 N 4.32 E
Zandvoort, Circuit Autorace ♦ 52 52.24 N 4.32 E
Zane Hills ⋏[2] 180 66.10 N 156.00 W
Zanesfield 216 40.20 N 83.41 W
Zanesville, In., U.S. 216 41.02 N 85.00 W
Zanesville, Oh., U.S. 188 39.56 N 82.00 W
Zanevka 265a 59.56 N 30.31 E
Zangakatun 84 39.50 N 45.03 E
Zangasso 150 12.09 N 5.37 W
Zängäzur silsiläsi ⋏ 84 39.30 N 45.54 E
Zangenstein 60 49.24 N 12.19 E
Zanggezhuang 98 37.28 N 120.57 E
Zangguy 120 37.22 N 78.48 E
Zängilan 84 39.06 N 46.39 E
Žangiztobe 86 49.16 N 81.18 E
Zangji 100 33.01 N 113.52 E
Zangmār ≃ 84 39.17 N 44.50 E
Zânguè ≃ 154 17.52 S 35.20 E
Zangwan 100 29.27 N 117.23 E
Zanhuang 98 37.38 N 114.26 E
Zanjān 128 36.40 N 48.29 E
Zanjān □[4] 128 36.30 N 49.00 E
Zanjān ≃ 128 37.08 N 47.47 E
Zanjón 252 27.55 S 64.15 W
Zanjón ≃ 252 31.16 S 67.41 W
Žankala ⊥ 86 44.29 N 64.05 E
Žannetty, ostrov I 74 76.43 N 158.00 E
Zannone, Isola I 66 40.58 N 13.03 E
Zanpa-misaki › 174m 26.26 N 127.43 E
Zanri 102 28.58 N 100.50 E
Zante → Zákinthos I 38 37.52 N 20.44 E
Žanterek 86 47.57 N 54.21 E
Zanthus 162 31.02 S 123.34 E
Zantiébougou 150 11.24 N 7.15 W
Zanyang 98 34.00 N 116.13 E
Zanzibar 154 6.10 S 39.11 E
Zanzibar I 154 6.10 S 39.20 E
Zanzibar Channel ⋓ 154 6.00 S 39.00 E
Zaohe 98 34.03 N 118.07 E
Zaoheshi 100 26.53 N 114.41 E
Zaojiang 98 37.30 N 115.43 E
Zaojiaochang 107 29.58 N 106.11 E
Zaojiatuo 105 39.23 N 118.11 E
Zaokskij 82 54.44 N 37.24 E
Zaolin 100 26.24 N 114.24 E
Zaorosongou 152 5.02 N 16.13 E
Zaoshi, Zhg. 100 26.22 N 112.50 E
Zaoshi, Zhg. 100 30.51 N 113.20 E
Zaostroviči 76 52.54 N 26.47 E
Zaostrovje, Ross. 24 60.50 N 30.22 E
Zaostrovje, Ross. 76 60.38 N 33.16 E
Zaouiet Azmour 36 36.55 N 11.01 E
Zaouiet el Mgaïz 36 36.56 N 10.50 E
Zaoxi 100 30.13 N 119.30 E
Zaoyang 100 32.10 N 112.43 E
Zaō-zan ∧ 92 38.08 N 140.26 E
Zaozhuang 98 34.53 N 117.34 E
Zaoz'orje, Ross. 76 57.12 N 38.15 E
Zaoz'orje, Ross. 265b 55.34 N 38.02 E
Zaoz'ornyj 86 55.58 N 94.42 E
Zap 198 47.17 N 101.55 W
Zapadnaja Dvina 76 56.16 N 32.04 E
Zapadnaja Dvina (Daugava) ≃ 76 57.04 N 24.03 E
Zapadna Morava ≃ 38 43.42 N 21.23 E
Zapadno-Sibirskaja ravnina ≚ 72 60.00 N 75.00 E
Zapadnyj Alamedin, pik ∧ 85 42.32 N 74.34 E
Zapadnyj chrebet ⋏ 89 50.00 N 142.25 E
Zapadnyj Karakol ≃ 85 42.08 N 74.05 E
Zapadnyj Sajan ⋏ 74 53.00 N 94.00 E
Západočeský Kraj □[4] 30 49.45 N 13.00 E
Západoslovenský Kraj □[4] 30 48.20 N 18.00 E
Zapala 252 38.54 S 70.04 W
Zapaleri, Cerro ∧ 252 22.49 S 67.11 W
Zapardiel ≃ 34 41.29 N 5.02 W
Zapata 196 26.54 N 99.16 W
Zapata, Península de ›[1] 240p 22.20 N 81.35 W
Zapatera, Isla I 236 11.45 N 85.50 W
Zapatoca 246 6.49 N 73.17 W
Zapato Chino Creek ≃ 226 36.09 N 120.11 W
Zapatosa, Ciénaga de ⊜ 246 9.05 N 73.50 W
Zapfendorf 56 50.01 N 10.56 E
Zapiola 258 35.03 S 59.03 W
Zaplavnoje, Ross. 80 52.58 N 51.44 E
Zaplavnoje, Ross. 80 48.43 N 45.01 E
Zapl'usje 76 58.26 N 29.43 E
Zapokrovskij 88 50.50 N 119.05 E
Zapol'arnyj, Ross. 24 69.26 N 30.48 E
Zapol'arnyj, Ross. 24 67.30 N 63.42 E
Zapolje 76 58.23 N 29.41 E
Zapopan 234 20.43 N 103.24 W
Zaporizhzhya, Ukr. 78 47.50 N 35.10 E
Zaporizhzhya, Ukr. 83 48.14 N 38.41 E
Zaporizhzhya □[4] 78 47.30 N 35.30 E
Zaporojie → Zaporizhzhya 78 47.50 N 35.10 E
Zaporozh'ye → Zaporizhzhya 78 47.50 N 35.10 E
Zaporožskaja 78 45.23 N 36.52 E
Zapotán 234 18.41 N 103.39 W
Zapotillo 246 4.25 S 80.31 W
Zapotiltic 234 19.37 N 103.26 W
Zapotitlán 234 19.31 N 103.44 W
Zapotlán, Laguna ⊜ 234 19.45 N 103.30 W
Zapotlanejo 234 20.38 N 103.04 W
Zapovednoje 76 55.04 N 21.24 E
Zapovednyj 89 42.52 N 133.45 E
Zaprudn'a 82 56.34 N 37.26 E
Zaqatala 84 41.38 N 46.39 E
Zaqqūt 146 28.29 N 19.37 E
Zara → Zadar, Hrv. 36 44.07 N 15.14 E
Zara, Tür. 130 39.55 N 37.46 E
Zarāf, Bahr az- ≃ 140 9.25 N 31.10 E
Zaragoza, Col. 246 7.30 N 74.52 W
Zaragoza, Esp. 34 41.38 N 0.53 W
Zaragoza, Méx. 232 31.39 N 106.20 W
Zaragoza, Méx. 232 28.29 N 100.55 W
Zaragoza, Méx. 234 23.58 N 99.46 W
Zaragoza, Méx. 234 19.46 N 97.33 W
Zaragoza, Méx. 234 22.02 N 100.44 W
Zaragoza □[4] 34 42.30 N 1.00 W
Zarajsk 82 54.46 N 38.53 E

Zaramag 84 42.43 N 43.57 E
Zarand 128 30.48 N 56.35 E
Zarand, Munții ⋏ 38 46.10 N 22.15 E
Zaranda Hill ∧[2] 150 10.15 N 9.35 E
Zarand-e Kohneh 128 35.17 N 50.30 E
Zaranj 128 31.06 N 61.53 E
Zarasai 76 55.44 N 26.15 E
Zárate 258 34.06 S 59.02 W
Zarautz 34 43.17 N 2.10 W
Zaraza 246 9.21 N 65.19 W
Žarbulak 86 46.05 N 82.04 E
Zarcero 236 10.11 N 84.23 W
Zärdab 84 40.13 N 47.43 E
Zardaly 85 39.38 N 70.57 E
Zard Kūh ∧ 128 32.22 N 50.04 E
Zarečensk 24 66.40 N 31.23 E
Zarečje, Ross. 24 63.08 N 44.46 E
Zarečje, Ross. 76 56.52 N 33.50 E
Zarečje, Ross. 76 58.56 N 39.40 E
Zarečje, Ross. 265b 55.41 N 37.23 E
Zarečnyj, Ross. 76 53.45 N 39.35 E
Zarečnyj, Ross. 80 57.28 N 42.18 E
Zarečnyj, Ross. 80 53.13 N 45.13 E
Zarembo Island I 180 56.20 N 132.50 W
Zarephath 276 40.32 N 74.35 W
Zaresskoje, ozero ⊜ 85 38.13 N 72.45 E
Zargān 128 29.46 N 52.43 E
Zarghūn Shahr 120 32.51 N 68.25 E
Zari 146 13.04 N 12.43 E
Zaria 150 11.07 N 7.44 E
Zarichne 78 51.48 N 26.06 E
Zarinskaja 86 53.43 N 84.58 E
Žarkamys 86 47.56 N 56.26 E
Żarki 30 50.38 N 19.22 E
Žarkova 86 58.00 N 87.17 E
Žarkovskij 76 55.52 N 32.17 E
Žarma 86 48.48 N 80.50 E
Zarnān 267d 35.41 N 51.09 E
Zărnești 38 45.34 N 25.19 E
Zarow ≃ 54 53.46 N 14.02 E
Zarqā', Nahr az- ≃ 132 32.07 N 35.33 E
Zarqā', Raqabat az- V 140 9.14 N 29.44 E
Zarqā' Mā'īn, Wādī V 132 31.37 N 35.34 E
Zarqūn 142 31.07 N 30.28 E
Zarrentin 54 53.35 N 10.55 E
Zarrīneh ≃ 128 37.05 N 45.54 E
Zarrīn Shahr 128 32.32 N 51.23 E
Žarsuat 86 46.27 N 80.48 E
Zarten 58 47.58 N 7.56 E
Zarubino, Ross. 76 58.44 N 33.28 E
Zarubino, Ross. 89 42.40 N 131.04 E
Zaruma 246 3.41 S 79.37 W
Zarumilla 246 3.30 S 80.16 W
Żary (Sorau) 30 51.38 N 15.09 E
Žaryk 86 48.52 N 72.51 E
Žaryn' 76 53.47 N 33.04 E
Zarzaïtine 148 28.18 N 9.48 E
Zarzal 246 4.24 N 76.04 W
Zarzis 148 33.30 N 11.07 E
Zarzuela, Arroyo de la ≃ 266a 40.29 N 3.45 W
Zarzuela, Hipodromo de la ♦ 266a 40.28 N 3.45 W
Zasa 76 56.17 N 25.58 E
Zaschwitz 54 51.10 N 13.02 E
Zašejek 24 67.25 N 32.28 E
Zasenbeck 54 52.40 N 10.51 E
Zasieki 54 51.43 N 14.43 E
Zāskār ≃ 123 34.10 N 77.20 E
Zāskār Mountains ⋏ 120 33.00 N 78.00 E
Zaslavl' 76 54.01 N 27.15 E
Zaslavl'skoje vodochranilišče ⊜[1] 76 53.58 N 27.22 E
Zasosna 78 50.37 N 38.23 E
Žastalap 80 49.11 N 50.24 E
Zastava 24 59.12 N 46.46 E
Zastávka 61 49.11 N 16.23 E
Zastavna 78 48.31 N 25.50 E
Zastron 158 30.18 S 27.07 E
Zasulje, Bela. 76 53.34 N 26.50 E
Zasulje, Ross. 24 64.41 N 47.48 E
Za'tarī, Wādī az- V 132 32.09 N 36.15 E
Žatec 54 50.18 N 13.32 E
Zaterečnyj 84 44.48 N 45.11 E
Z'at'kovo 86 53.36 N 80.20 E
Zatobol'sk 86 53.12 N 63.43 E
Zaton 86 53.18 N 83.49 E
Zatyshshya, Ukr. 38 47.19 N 29.51 E
Zatyshshya, Ukr. 78 47.19 N 29.51 E
Zauche ◆[1] 54 52.15 N 12.35 E
Zauchwitz 54 52.12 N 13.02 E
Zauel 144 3.33 N 43.45 E
Zaural'skoje plato ⋏[1] 86 53.00 N 62.00 E
Zavalla 194 31.09 N 94.26 W
Zavallya 78 48.13 N 30.01 E
Zaval'noje 76 52.02 N 39.51 E
Zave 154 17.13 S 30.02 E
Zaventem 50 50.53 N 4.28 E
Zavet 38 43.46 N 26.40 E
Zavetnoje 80 47.07 N 43.52 E
Zavety Iljiča 89 49.02 N 140.17 E
Zavidovići 38 44.27 N 18.09 E
Zavidovka 82 54.16 N 38.49 E
Zavidovo 82 56.32 N 36.32 E
Zavitinsk 89 50.07 N 129.27 E
Zavjalovo, Ross. 80 56.47 N 53.23 E
Zavjalovo, Ross. 86 54.30 N 82.27 E
Zavlekov 60 49.20 N 13.30 E
Zavod Michajlovskij 80 56.32 N 54.17 E
Zavodo-Petrovskij 86 56.50 N 66.45 E
Zavodoukovsk 86 56.33 N 66.32 E
Zavodouspenskoje 86 56.51 N 65.00 E
Zavodovski Island I 18 56.20 S 27.35 W
Zavodskoj, Ross. 78 48.24 N 40.19 E
Zavodskoj, Ross. 86 53.04 N 84.25 E
Zavolžje 80 56.37 N 43.26 E
Zavolžsk 80 57.30 N 42.10 E
Zavolžskoje 80 46.59 N 47.37 E
Zavoronežskoje 80 52.53 N 40.33 E
Zavorovo 82 55.20 N 38.13 E
Zāwa 120 28.04 N 66.23 E
Zawadzkie 30 50.37 N 18.29 E
Zawichost 30 50.49 N 21.52 E
Zawiercie 30 50.30 N 19.25 E
Zawīlah 146 26.10 N 15.07 E
Zāwiyat 'Abd al-Qādir 142 31.02 N 29.49 E
Zāwiyat Abū Musallum 273c 29.56 N 31.10 E
Zāwiyat al-Amwāt 142 28.04 N 30.50 E
Zawiyat al-Judhāmī 142 28.42 N 30.54 E
Zāwiyat al-Mukhaylā 146 32.09 N 22.17 E
Zāwiyat Masūs 146 31.33 N 21.03 E
Zāwiyat Nābit 273c 30.07 N 31.09 E
Zāwiyat Razīn 142 30.25 N 30.51 E
Zāwiyat Saqr 142 30.56 N 30.12 E
Zawiyat Shammās 140 31.31 N 26.24 E
Zāwiyat Sīdī Ghāzī 142 31.03 N 30.05 E
Zāwiyet an-Najjār 273c 30.11 N 31.17 E
Zawr, Ra's az- ›, Ar. Su. 128 27.25 N 49.20 E
Zawr, Ra's az- ›, Kuwayt 128 28.44 N 48.24 E
Zäyämçay ≃ 84 41.00 N 45.59 E
Zāyandeh ≃ 128 32.16 N 52.53 E
Zaydābād 120 34.17 N 69.07 E
Zaytseve, Ukr. 83 48.32 N 38.04 E
Zaytseve, Ukr. 83 48.24 N 38.02 E
Zayü 102 28.48 N 97.27 E
Zayü ≃ 102 28.28 N 97.03 E
Zaza ≃ 240p 21.37 N 79.32 W
Zaza, Presa ⊜[1] 240p 21.50 N 79.23 W
Zaza del Medio 240p 22.00 N 79.23 W
Zazafotsy 157b 22.13 S 46.26 E
Zāzamt, Wādī V 146 30.58 N 14.49 E
Zazir, Oued V 148 20.25 N 5.30 E
Zban 86 48.53 N 63.58 E
Zbarazh 78 49.39 N 25.47 E

Zbąszyń 30 52.16 N 15.55 E
Zbąszynek 30 52.15 N 15.50 E
Zbečno 60 50.03 N 13.56 E
Zbiroh 60 49.52 N 13.47 E
Zboriv 78 49.39 N 25.08 E
Zborovy 60 49.23 N 13.31 E
Zbraslav 30 49.59 N 14.24 E
Zbruch ≃ 78 48.32 N 26.26 E
Zbůch 60 49.41 N 13.14 E
Ždanov → Mariupol' 83 47.06 N 37.33 E
Ždanova 86 58.37 N 88.58 E
Žd'ár 60 50.03 N 13.28 E
Žd'ár nad Sazavou 30 49.34 N 15.57 E
Ždiar 30 49.17 N 20.16 E
Zdice 60 49.55 N 13.59 E
Zdikovec 60 49.05 N 13.42 E
Zdolbuniv 78 50.31 N 26.15 E
Zdroje ◆[8] 54 53.20 N 14.40 E
Zduńska Wola 30 51.36 N 18.57 E
Zduny 30 51.39 N 17.24 E
Zdvyzh ≃ 78 51.01 N 30.02 E
Ze ≃ 105 38.50 N 115.13 E
Zealandia 184 51.37 N 107.45 W
Zearing 190 42.09 N 93.17 W
Zēbāk 120 36.32 N 71.21 E
Zeballos 182 49.59 N 126.51 W
Zeballos, Monte ∧ 254 47.01 S 71.42 W
Zebediela 156 24.19 S 29.21 E
Zebila 150 10.56 N 0.29 W
Zebl'aki 80 58.23 N 45.45 E
Žebrák 60 49.52 N 13.56 E
Zebulon, Ga., U.S. 192 33.06 N 84.20 W
Zebulon, N.C., U.S. 192 35.49 N 78.18 W
Zechlinerhütte 54 53.09 N 12.51 E
Zeda, Monte ∧ 58 46.03 N 8.32 E
Zedang 120 29.16 N 91.46 E
Zeddine, Oued ≃ 34 36.15 N 1.48 E
Zedelgem 50 51.09 N 3.08 E
Zederhaus 64 47.09 N 13.30 E
Zeebrugge 50 51.20 N 3.12 E
Zeehan 166 41.53 S 145.20 E
Zeeland, Ned. 52 51.42 N 5.40 E
Zeeland, Mi., U.S. 216 42.48 N 86.01 W
Zeeland, N.D., U.S. 198 45.58 N 99.49 W
Zeeland □[4] 52 51.27 N 3.45 E
Zeelandbrug ◆[5] 52 51.37 N 3.53 E
Zeerust 156 25.33 S 26.06 E
Zeesen 54 52.16 N 13.38 E
Zeestow 264a 52.34 N 12.58 E
Zeeuws-Vlaanderen □[9] 52 51.19 N 3.45 E
Zefat (Safad) 132 32.58 N 35.30 E
Žegalovo, Ross. 80 54.43 N 43.25 E
Žegalovo, Ross. 265b 55.54 N 37.59 E
Žegdoči 89 53.20 N 120.49 E
Zege 144 11.42 N 37.23 E
Zegher, Ḥamādat ≚ 146 27.18 N 11.30 E
Zégoua 150 10.30 N 5.40 W
Zegrir, Oued V 148 32.43 N 5.00 E
Zeguo 100 28.32 N 121.20 E
Zehdenick 54 52.59 N 13.20 E
Zehlendorf 54 52.47 N 13.23 E
Zehlendorf ◆[8] 54 52.26 N 13.15 E
Zeigler 194 37.53 N 89.03 W
Zeil 56 50.01 N 10.35 E
Zeil, Mount ∧ 162 23.24 S 132.23 E
Zeiselmauer 264b 48.20 N 16.11 E
Zeist 52 52.05 N 5.15 E
Zeithain 54 51.19 N 13.19 E
Zeitlarn 60 49.05 N 12.06 E
Zeitz 54 51.03 N 12.08 E
Zeja 89 53.45 N 127.15 E
Zeja ≃ 89 50.13 N 127.35 E
Zejskoje vodochranilišče ⊜[1] 89 54.28 N 127.45 E
Zekeriyaköy ◆[8] 267b 41.11 N 29.01 E
Zekiah Swamp Run ≃ 208 38.25 N 76.57 W
Žel'abino 265b 55.52 N 37.11 E
Žel'abužskaja 82 54.36 N 36.32 E
Zelaya 258 34.21 S 58.52 W
Zelaya □[5] 236 13.00 N 84.00 W
Želča ≃ 76 58.19 N 27.40 E
Žel'dyadyr ◆[1] 86 49.30 N 68.30 E
Želdybino 82 56.14 N 39.02 E
Zele 50 51.04 N 4.02 E
Żelechów 30 51.49 N 21.54 E
Zelee, Cape › 175e 9.45 S 161.34 E
Zelená Lhota 60 49.14 N 13.10 E
Zelencovo 76 59.52 N 44.59 E
Zelenčukskaja 84 43.52 N 41.36 E
Zelene 78 47.43 N 33.12 E
Zelenec 24 62.29 N 55.16 E
Zelenga 80 46.11 N 48.37 E
Zelengora ⋏ 38 43.15 N 18.45 E
Zelenivka 78 46.59 N 36.14 E
Zelenoborskij 24 66.49 N 32.18 E
Zelenogorsk 76 60.12 N 29.42 E
Zelenograd 82 56.01 N 37.11 E
Zelenogradsk 76 54.58 N 20.29 E
Zelenokumsk 84 44.24 N 43.53 E
Želetava 61 49.09 N 15.38 E
Zeletin ≃ 38 46.03 N 27.23 E
Železinka 86 53.32 N 75.18 E
Železn'a 82 54.31 N 37.28 E
Železná Ruda 60 49.09 N 13.14 E
Železnik 38 44.43 N 20.23 E
Železnodorožnyj, Ross. 24 62.35 N 50.55 E
Železnodorožnyj, Ross. 76 54.22 N 21.19 E
Železnodorožnyj, Ross. 82 55.45 N 38.01 E
Železnodorožnyj, Uzb. 86 43.04 N 58.50 E
Železnogorsk 76 52.22 N 35.23 E
Železnogorsk-Ilimskij 88 56.37 N 104.08 E
Železnovodsk 84 44.08 N 43.02 E
Zelienople 214 40.47 N 80.08 W
Zelina 36 45.58 N 16.15 E
Zell, Dtsch. 56 50.01 N 7.10 E
Zell, Dtsch. 58 47.42 N 7.51 E
Zell, Schw. 58 47.09 N 7.55 E
Zella-Mehlis 54 50.39 N 10.39 E
Zell am Harmersbach 58 48.21 N 8.04 E
Zell am Moos 64 47.54 N 13.19 E
Zell am See 64 47.19 N 12.47 E
Zell am Ziller 64 47.14 N 11.53 E
Zellersee c 58 47.42 N 9.03 E
Zeller See ⊜ 64 47.19 N 12.48 E
Zellingen 56 49.53 N 9.43 E
Zellwood 220 28.44 N 81.36 W
Želnava 61 48.50 N 13.57 E
Želon' ≃ 78 51.33 N 29.51 E
Zel'onaja Rošča, Ross. 76 60.10 N 29.08 E
Zel'onaja Rošča, Ross. 80 54.29 N 52.02 E
Zel'onaja Rošča, Ross. 83 47.07 N 40.13 E
Zel'onodol'sk 80 55.51 N 48.33 E
Zel'onoje Ozero 88 53.40 N 116.36 E
Zel'onyj, Kaz. 80 48.07 N 51.31 E
Zel'onyj, Kaz. 80 51.10 N 50.41 E
Zel'onyj, ostrov (Shibotsu-Tō) I 92a 43.30 N 146.09 E
Zel'onyj Bor 76 54.01 N 28.28 E
Zelo Surrigone 266b 45.23 N 8.59 E
Zelów 30 51.28 N 19.13 E
Žel'tau Ajtau ⋏ 86 44.30 N 74.00 E
Zeltweg 61 47.11 N 14.45 E
Želudok 76 53.36 N 24.59 E
Zel'va, Bela. 76 53.09 N 24.49 E
Želva, Liet. 76 55.13 N 25.06 E
Zel'v'anka ≃ 76 53.24 N 24.32 E
Zelzate 50 51.12 N 3.49 E
Žemaičių Naumiestis 76 55.22 N 21.42 E
Žemaitija □[9] 76 55.45 N 23.00 E
Žembejtinskij 80 50.30 N 52.39 E

Zembin 76 54.22 N 28.13 E
Zembla Septentrional → Severnaja Zeml'a II 74 79.30 N 98.00 E
Zembra, Île I 36 37.08 N 10.48 E
Žemčug 88 51.41 N 102.24 E
Zemcy 76 56.15 N 32.23 E
Zemetčino 80 53.30 N 42.38 E
Zemgale □[9] 76 56.30 N 25.00 E
Zémio 154 5.02 N 25.08 E
Zeml'ansk 78 51.54 N 38.44 E
Zemmer 56 49.53 N 6.41 E
Zemmora 34 35.44 N 0.45 E
Zemmour ◆[1] 148 24.50 N 12.15 W
Zemo-Kedi 84 41.26 N 46.24 E
Zémongo, Réserve de Faune de ◆[4] 140 6.45 N 25.15 E
Zemoul, Oued V 148 29.12 N 7.52 W
Žemovo 82 54.45 N 38.49 E
Zempin 54 54.04 N 13.57 E
Zempoala 234 19.24 N 96.24 W
Zempoala ≃ 234 20.16 N 97.27 W
Zempoala ⊥ 234 19.27 N 96.23 W
Zempoala, Punta › 234 19.28 N 96.19 W
Zemst 50 50.59 N 4.28 E
Zemun 38 44.50 N 20.24 E
Zenas 218 39.07 N 85.29 W
Zendeh Jān 128 34.21 N 61.45 E
Zeneta 184 50.44 N 102.02 W
Zeng ≃ 100 23.09 N 113.46 E
Zengcheng 100 23.19 N 113.49 E
Zengjiawan 105 39.22 N 118.24 E
Zengkou ≃ 105 39.19 N 117.37 E
Zenica 38 44.12 N 17.55 E
Zenifim, Har ∧[2] 132 30.06 N 34.51 E
Zenith 224 47.23 N 122.19 W
Zenn ≃ 56 49.31 N 10.58 E
Zenne (Senne) ≃ 50 51.04 N 4.26 E
Zenon Park 184 53.04 N 103.45 W
Zenon Videla Dorna 258 35.33 S 58.53 W
Zenson di Piave 64 45.41 N 12.29 E
Zentralafrikanische Republik → Central African Republic □[1] 136 7.00 N 21.00 E
Zentral-Friedhof ◆ 264b 48.09 N 16.27 E
Zentral-Massiv → Central, Massif ⋏ 32 45.00 N 3.10 E
Zentsūji 96 34.14 N 133.47 E
Zenza do Itombe 152 9.16 S 14.13 E
Zenzeli 80 45.56 N 47.03 E
Zepernick 54 52.39 N 13.32 E
Zephyr 196 31.41 N 98.48 W
Zephyr Cove 226 39.00 N 119.57 W
Zephyrhills 220 28.14 N 82.10 W
Zepu 120 38.13 N 77.16 E
Zérab, Ouadi V 146 11.03 N 19.47 E
Zeralda 34 36.41 N 2.53 E
Zeravšan 85 39.11 N 68.40 E
Zeravšan ≃ 72 39.22 N 63.45 E
Zeravšanskij chrebet ⋏ 85 39.15 N 68.30 E
Zerbst 54 51.58 N 12.04 E
Žerdevka 80 51.51 N 41.28 E
Zereh, Gowd-e ⊥[7] 128 29.45 N 61.50 E
Zerenda 86 52.55 N 69.10 E
Zerf 56 49.36 N 6.41 E
Zerga, Merja c 34 34.51 N 6.17 W
Zergenta 80 47.42 N 45.12 E
Zeri 62 44.21 N 9.46 E
Zerind 38 46.37 N 21.31 E
Żerków 30 52.05 N 17.34 E
Zermatt 58 46.02 N 7.45 E
Zernez 58 46.43 N 10.05 E
Zernograd 78 46.50 N 40.19 E
Žernovka 82 54.49 N 37.46 E
Zernsdorf 54 52.18 N 13.41 E
Zero ≃ 64 45.32 N 12.22 E
Zeroud, Oued V 36 35.50 N 10.13 E
Zerqan 38 41.30 N 20.21 E
Žešart 24 62.05 N 49.34 E
Zestafoni 84 42.07 N 43.02 E
Žest'anka 80 51.36 N 49.24 E
Žestoki 82 56.19 N 36.22 E
Žestylevo 82 56.24 N 37.39 E
Zetel 52 53.25 N 7.58 E
Žetybaj 80 48.51 N 48.04 E
Žetykol', ozero ⊜ 86 51.02 N 60.54 E
Zeulenroda 54 50.39 N 11.58 E
Zeuthen 54 52.20 N 13.37 E
Zeuthener See ⊜ 264a 52.21 N 13.39 E
Zeven 52 53.18 N 9.16 E
Zevenaar 52 51.56 N 6.05 E
Zevenbergen 52 51.38 N 4.36 E
Zevenbergschen Hoek 52 51.41 N 4.40 E
Zevenwouden ◆[1] 52 52.57 N 6.00 E
Zevio 64 45.22 N 11.08 E
Zeyādah Kot 272b 22.27 N 88.20 E
Zeyawadi 110 18.33 N 96.26 E
Zeytinbağı 130 40.23 N 28.47 E
Zeytinburnu ◆[8] 267b 40.59 N 28.54 E
Zeytindağ 130 38.58 N 27.04 E
Zeyveh 84 39.07 N 47.42 E
Zeze 270 35.00 N 135.54 E
Zêzere ≃ 34 39.28 N 8.20 W
Zghartā 130 34.24 N 35.54 E
Zgierz 30 51.52 N 19.25 E
Zgornje Hoče 61 46.29 N 15.38 E
Zgorzelec 30 51.12 N 15.01 E
Zhabuchaka Hu ⊜ 120 31.30 N 84.00 E
Zhadove 78 52.03 N 32.39 E
Zhage 102 26.20 N 103.51 E
Zhagenasongduo 102 33.12 N 94.33 E
Zhag'yab 102 30.32 N 98.00 E
Zhahasutai 86 42.58 N 85.20 E
Zhai ≃ 100 32.19 N 115.02 E
Zhaihe 100 32.08 N 114.54 E
Zhaili 100 27.42 N 117.22 E
Zhailing 98 41.00 N 116.53 E
Zhaiqiao 106 31.35 N 119.55 E
Zhaitang 105 39.57 N 115.42 E
Zhaitun 104 41.46 N 122.06 E
Zhakou, Zhg. 102 29.59 N 112.10 E
Zhakou, Zhg. 106 30.23 N 120.47 E
Zhakou, Zhg. 106 30.13 N 120.08 E
Zhalantun → Butha Qi 89 48.02 N 122.43 E
Zhalanyingzi 104 41.29 N 120.37 E
Zhalun 120 32.25 N 81.35 E
Zhaluomude 89 49.13 N 120.22 E
Zhancheng 98 37.41 N 117.46 E
Zhang ≃, Zhg. 100 31.05 N 113.11 E
Zhang ≃, Zhg. 100 25.51 N 114.46 E
Zhang ≃, Zhg. 102 36.10 N 115.05 E
Zhangbei 98 41.04 N 114.48 E
Zhangcang 98 35.54 N 119.57 E
Zhangcun, Zhg. 100 33.20 N 115.59 E
Zhangcun, Zhg. 100 28.50 N 117.57 E
Zhangcun, Zhg. 106 30.28 N 119.22 E
Zhangcun, Zhg. 106 30.40 N 119.57 E
Zhangdang 104 41.54 N 124.05 E
Zhangde 100 34.07 N 113.27 E
Zhangdiyingzi 89 50.30 N 127.16 E
Zhangdu 100 30.38 N 118.13 E
Zhangdu Hu ⊜ 100 30.40 N 114.42 E
Zhangfang 105 39.35 N 115.41 E
Zhangfengji 98 35.14 N 116.01 E
Zhanggang 100 30.34 N 112.51 E
Zhanggezhuang, Zhg. 98 36.47 N 119.47 E
Zhanggezhuang, Zhg. 105 40.08 N 116.56 E
Zhanggou 104 42.07 N 124.06 E
Zhangguangcai Ling ⋏ 89 45.25 N 129.20 E
Zhangguizhuang 105 39.07 N 117.18 E
Zhanggutai 98 42.40 N 122.28 E
Zhanghezhuang 105 38.56 N 114.56 E

≃ River	Fluß	Río	Rivière	Rio
≍ Canal	Kanal	Canal	Canal	Canal
⌊ Waterfall, Rapids	Wasserfall, Stromschnellen	Cascada, Rápidos	Chute d'eau, Rapides	Cascata, Rápidos
⋓ Strait	Meeresstraße	Estrecho	Détroit	Estreito
c Bay, Gulf	Bucht, Golf	Bahía, Golfo	Baie, Golfe	Baía, Golfo
⊜ Lake, Lakes	See, Seen	Lago, Lagos	Lac, Lacs	Lago, Lagos
≚ Swamp	Sumpf	Pantano	Marais	Pântano
⊓ Ice Features, Glacier	Eis- und Gletscherformen	Accidentes Glaciales	Formes glaciaires	Acidentes glaciares
⊤ Other Hydrographic Features	Andere Hydrographische Objekte	Otros Elementos Hidrográficos	Autres données hydrographiques	Outros acidentes hidrográficos

✢ Submarine Features	Untermeerische Objekte	Accidentes Submarinos	Formes de relief sous-marin	Acidentes submarinos
□ Political Unit	Politische Einheit	Unidad Politica	Entité politique	Unidade política
ʊ Cultural Institution	Kulturelle Institution	Institución Cultural	Institution culturelle	Instituição cultural
⊥ Historical Site	Historische Stätte	Sitio Histórico	Site historique	Sitio histórico
♦ Recreational Site	Erholungs- und Ferienort	Sitio de Recreo	Centre de loisirs	Area de Lazer
⊠ Airport	Flughafen	Aeropuerto	Aéroport	Aeroporto
■ Military Installation	Militäranlage	Instalación Militar	Installation militaire	Instalação militar
◆ Miscellaneous	Verschiedenes	Misceláneo	Divers	Diversos

Zhanghuang 102 22.01 N 109.27 E
Zhanghuanggang 106 32.07 N 120.30 E
Zhanghuban 100 26.23 N 118.29 E
Zhangji 98 34.08 N 117.24 E
Zhangjiachang, Zhg. 107 29.26 N 104.34 E
Zhangjiachang, Zhg. 107 29.33 N 104.54 E
Zhangjiachang, Zhg. 107 29.57 N 103.48 E
Zhangjiadian 105 39.44 N 114.54 E
Zhangjiagou 100 30.18 N 113.22 E
Zhangjiaji 100 32.09 N 112.23 E
Zhangjiajie 104 41.28 N 124.08 E
Zhangjiakou (Kalgan) 105 40.50 N 114.53 E
Zhangjiapang 100 30.25 N 115.47 E
Zhangjiapu 104 41.18 N 122.02 E
Zhangjiaqiao, Zhg. 106 31.36 N 120.36 E
Zhangjiaqiao, Zhg. 107 30.02 N 104.15 E
Zhangjiatou 106 31.38 N 119.05 E
Zhangjiatun, Zhg. 104 41.05 N 121.44 E
Zhangjiatun, Zhg. 105 40.37 N 114.57 E
Zhangjiawa 105 40.10 N 117.52 E
Zhangjiawan 105 39.51 N 116.41 E
Zhangjiawopu 104 41.10 N 122.17 E
Zhangjiayingzi 104 42.04 N 120.57 E
Zhangjingqiao 106 31.39 N 120.27 E
Zhangjinhe 100 30.14 N 112.35 E
Zhangliangdian 100 33.42 N 113.02 E
Zhangliantang 106 31.01 N 121.02 E
Zhangling 98 36.32 N 119.29 E
Zhanglu 98 36.16 N 115.33 E
Zhangmang 100 32.03 N 114.32 E
Zhangming 102 31.49 N 104.51 E
Zhangmuqiao 100 31.26 N 116.44 E
Zhangmushi 100 27.01 N 112.38 E
Zhangmutou 100 22.55 N 114.05 E
Zhangping 100 25.19 N 117.25 E
Zhangpu, Zhg. 100 24.09 N 117.36 E
Zhangpu, Zhg. 106 31.17 N 120.57 E
Zhangqiangzhen 98 42.39 N 122.59 E
Zhangqiao 100 32.21 N 117.38 E
Zhangqiu (Mingshui) 98 36.43 N 117.30 E
Zhangsanta 102 39.37 N 110.14 E
Zhangsanying 98 41.34 N 117.39 E
Zhangshitai 104 41.50 N 122.51 E
Zhangshuping 102 31.20 N 111.02 E
Zhangshuxia 100 25.54 N 112.45 E
Zhangtaitai 104 40.59 N 121.05 E
Zhangtaizi 104 41.22 N 123.16 E
Zhangting 100 30.02 N 121.19 E
Zhangwan 100 26.43 N 119.36 E
Zhangwenpu 105 40.26 N 116.04 E
Zhangwu, Zhg. 104 42.22 N 122.31 E
Zhangwu, Zhg. 106 30.47 N 119.33 E
Zhangwutaimen 104 42.16 N 122.42 E
Zhangxinliuji 100 33.43 N 115.48 E
Zhangyan, Zhg. 106 31.48 N 119.44 E
Zhangyan, Zhg. 106 30.48 N 121.16 E
Zhangyangongtun 104 40.58 N 120.46 E
Zhangye 102 38.56 N 100.27 E
Zhangze 106 30.55 N 121.15 E
Zhangzhishan 106 31.56 N 121.01 E
Zhangzhou (Longxi) 100 24.33 N 117.39 E
Zhangzhu 106 31.16 N 119.37 E
Zhangzhuang, Zhg. 98 37.03 N 116.32 E
Zhangzhuang, Zhg. 98 36.02 N 118.01 E
Zhangzhuang, Zhg. 106 31.57 N 119.52 E
Zhangzi Dao I 98 39.00 N 122.44 E
Zhanhua (Fuguo) 98 37.42 N 118.08 E
Zhanji 98 34.14 N 115.52 E
Zhanjiajing 107 29.15 N 104.55 E
Zhanjiang 102 21.16 N 110.28 E
Zhanjiaqiao, Zhg. 100 29.19 N 113.34 E
Zhanjiaqiao, Zhg. 106 30.25 N 120.08 E
Zhanyang 100 25.30 N 119.28 E
Zhanyi 102 25.38 N 103.43 E
Zhanyu 89 44.31 N 122.37 E
Zhao'an 100 23.47 N 117.12 E
Zhao'an Wan C 100 23.38 N 117.19 E
Zhaobeikou 105 38.55 N 116.06 E
Zhaochuan 105 40.41 N 115.18 E
Zhaocun 105 39.35 N 116.14 E
Zhaodong 89 46.05 N 125.59 E
Zhaogezhuang, Zhg. 98 37.27 N 120.37 E
Zhaogezhuang, Zhg. 105 39.45 N 118.24 E
Zhaoguang 89 48.07 N 126.43 E
Zhaohe 100 33.12 N 112.49 E
Zhaohuazhen 107 29.02 N 105.08 E
Zhaojiagou 104 40.47 N 123.27 E
Zhaojiapuzi 104 40.51 N 123.49 E
Zhaojiaqiao 106 30.44 N 121.12 E
Zhaojiatangfang 104 42.07 N 122.57 E
Zhaojiatun 104 41.24 N 121.53 E
Zhaojiawopeng 104 42.30 N 123.06 E
Zhaojiaying 105 38.58 N 116.42 E
Zhaojue 102 28.15 N 102.50 E
Zhaomaozhuang 105 39.28 N 117.59 E
Zhaomutun 104 41.10 N 121.38 E
Zhaoping 102 24.03 N 110.52 E
Zhaoqiao 100 28.42 N 114.45 E
Zhaoqing (Gaoyao) 102 23.03 N 112.27 E
Zhaosu 86 43.06 N 81.08 E
Zhaotan 100 29.42 N 116.48 E
Zhaotong 102 27.19 N 103.48 E
Zhaotun 104 41.54 N 121.59 E
Zhaoxian, Zhg. 98 37.45 N 114.46 E
Zhaoxian, Zhg. 98 35.44 N 118.55 E
Zhaoxing 89 47.43 N 131.19 E
Zhaoya 107 29.00 N 105.35 E
Zhaoyi 105 39.55 N 116.43 E
Zhaoyuan, Zhg. 89 45.31 N 125.09 E
Zhaoyuan, Zhg. 98 37.22 N 120.24 E
Zhaozhou 89 45.41 N 125.21 E
Zhaozhuang, Zhg. 98 34.45 N 116.27 E
Zhaozhuang, Zhg. 98 34.14 N 116.38 E
Zhaozhuangzi 105 39.10 N 117.20 E
Zhapu 106 30.36 N 121.05 E
Zhari Namco ⊜ 120 31.05 N 85.35 E
Zhashkiv 78 49.15 N 30.06 E
Zhashui 102 33.40 N 109.01 E
Zhaxi Co ⊜ 120 32.10 N 85.05 E
Zhaxigang 120 32.32 N 79.41 E
Zhayi 102 28.34 N 99.09 E
Zhaze 106 32.09 N 119.29 E
Zhdanivka 83 48.10 N 38.15 E
Zhdanov
— Mariupol' 83 47.06 N 37.33 E
Zhdany 78 50.12 N 33.13 E
Zhecheng 98 34.06 N 115.19 E
Zhegao 100 31.46 N 117.45 E
Zhegu 120 28.43 N 91.43 E
Zhêhor 102 31.41 N 100.24 E
Zhejiang (Chekiang) □[4] 100 29.00 N 120.00 E
Zhelang 100 22.43 N 115.32 E
Zhelanne 83 48.13 N 37.25 E
Zhelin, Zhg. 100 29.14 N 115.30 E
Zhelin, Zhg. 100 23.36 N 117.06 E
Zhelin, Zhg. 106 30.50 N 121.29 E
Zhen ≐ 100 24.55 N 113.44 E
Zhen'an 102 33.27 N 109.01 E
Zhenbeikou 102 39.15 N 106.17 E
Zhenbiancheng 105 40.10 N 115.49 E
Zhenchang, Zhg. 105 39.47 N 115.24 E
Zhenchang, Zhg. 106 32.04 N 121.02 E
Zhenfeng 102 25.23 N 105.41 E
Zheng'an 102 28.31 N 107.29 E
Zheng'anpu 104 41.43 N 121.56 E
Zhengcun 105 39.13 N 115.40 E
Zhengding 98 38.10 N 114.34 E
Zhengdongyu 106 31.59 N 120.10 E
Zhengfang 100 28.42 N 117.53 E
Zhengguanchang 107 29.54 N 106.35 E
Zhengguo 100 23.25 N 113.53 E
Zhenghe 100 27.22 N 118.50 E
Zhengji 98 34.26 N 117.01 E
Zhengjiadiancun 104 41.05 N 122.20 E
Zhengjiawu 100 29.29 N 120.05 E
Zhenglan Qi (Dund Hot) 98 42.16 N 115.49 E
Zhengning 102 35.22 N 108.24 E
Zhengping 100 25.22 N 114.46 E
Zhen'guosi 271a 39.51 N 116.21 E
Zhengxiangbai Qi (Qagan Nur) 98 42.16 N 114.52 E
Zhengyang 100 32.37 N 114.23 E
Zhengyangguan 100 32.28 N 116.32 E
Zhengyi 106 31.23 N 120.52 E
Zhengzhou (Chengchow) 102 34.48 N 113.39 E
Zhengzhuang 100 28.11 N 119.01 E
Zhengzi 107 29.22 N 104.16 E
Zhengzichang 107 29.08 N 106.38 E
Zhenhai, Zhg. 100 29.57 N 121.42 E
Zhenhai, Zhg. 100 24.16 N 118.06 E
Zhenhai, Zhg. 102 21.53 N 112.25 E
Zhenjiang, Zhg. 98 40.44 N 125.28 E
Zhenjiang, Zhg. 106 32.13 N 119.26 E
Zhenjiangguan 102 32.25 N 103.35 E
Zhenjiaqiao 106 32.08 N 120.49 E
Zhenjinqiao 107 30.12 N 104.22 E
Zhenkang 102 24.06 N 99.16 E
Zhenlai 89 45.52 N 123.14 E
Zhenning 102 26.05 N 105.46 E
Zhenping 102 33.08 N 112.19 E
Zhenru 106 31.15 N 121.24 E
Zhentou 100 27.04 N 114.56 E
Zhentou ≐ 100 32.58 N 114.24 E
Zhentoudian 100 29.10 N 117.29 E
Zhentoushi 100 28.01 N 113.20 E
Zhenxi 107 29.29 N 104.33 E
Zhenxiaguan 100 27.12 N 120.28 E
Zhenxing 98 42.38 N 124.53 E
Zhenxiong 102 27.27 N 104.50 E
Zhenyu 100 27.08 N 120.18 E
Zhenyuan, Zhg. 102 35.46 N 107.18 E
Zhenyuan, Zhg. 102 26.53 N 108.19 E
Zhenze 106 30.55 N 120.30 E
Zhenzhumen 98 41.53 N 126.45 E
Zhenzichang, Zhg. 107 29.59 N 105.11 E
Zhenzichang, Zhg. 107 29.52 N 104.12 E
Zhenzichang, Zhg. 107 30.38 N 104.20 E
Zhenzijie 107 28.48 N 106.40 E
Zhenziling 104 42.10 N 124.12 E
Zhenzizhen 105 39.50 N 118.20 E
Zheqiao 100 26.27 N 112.48 E
Zherebets' ≐ 83 48.57 N 38.03 E
Zheriv ≐ 78 51.12 N 29.04 E
Zherong 100 27.16 N 119.54 E
Zheshan 106 30.15 N 120.24 E
Zhetang 106 31.45 N 118.55 E
Zhidan 102 37.00 N 108.40 E
Zhidoi 102 33.08 N 94.50 E
Zhierling 98 40.26 N 114.16 E
Zhigou 98 35.55 N 119.13 E
Zhijiang 102 27.27 N 109.41 E
Zhijin 102 26.41 N 105.37 E
Zhili 106 30.52 N 120.16 E
Zhitan 100 29.35 N 117.16 E
Zhitang, Zhg. 106 31.33 N 121.01 E
Zhitang, Zhg. 106 31.36 N 120.58 E
Zhitomir
— Zhytomyr 78 50.16 N 28.40 E
Zhitouji 100 33.28 N 118.18 E
Zhiwucun 106 30.38 N 119.47 E
Zhixi 100 23.57 N 114.33 E
Zhixia 100 29.42 N 119.36 E
Zhixiqiao 106 31.49 N 119.29 E
Zhiyang 100 33.47 N 113.07 E
Zhizushan 104 41.50 N 121.24 E
Zhmerynka 78 49.02 N 28.06 E
Zhob 120 31.20 N 69.27 E
Zhob ≐ 120 32.04 N 69.50 E
Zhonganpu 104 41.37 N 121.58 E
Zhong'aozhen 107 29.46 N 105.41 E
Zhongba, Zhg. 100 23.43 N 115.22 E
Zhongba, Zhg. 120 29.38 N 84.13 E
Zhongbu, Zhg. 100 31.25 N 117.45 E
Zhongbu, Zhg. 100 31.40 N 117.45 E
Zhongbu, Zhg. 100 28.50 N 117.16 E
Zhongchuan 100 26.58 N 119.27 E
Zhongcun 102 33.27 N 110.05 E
Zhongdai 106 30.46 N 120.59 E
Zhongdian 102 27.50 N 99.40 E
Zhongdu, Zhg. 100 24.56 N 116.26 E
Zhongdu, Zhg. 100 33.04 N 118.46 E
Zhongdu, Zhg. 107 28.46 N 103.58 E
Zhongduan 100 25.17 N 116.41 E
Zhongerchong 104 41.58 N 123.58 E
Zhonggang 100 32.38 N 115.45 E
Zhonggong 98 36.30 N 117.01 E
Zhonggoumen 98 41.00 N 116.26 E
Zhonggu 104 42.27 N 124.00 E
Zhongguan 106 30.39 N 120.11 E
Zhongguo
— China □[1] 90 35.00 N 105.00 E
Zhonghe 102 27.11 N 103.52 E
Zhonghechang 107 30.12 N 104.49 E
Zhongheying 102 23.48 N 103.36 E
Zhonghezhen 107 30.34 N 104.06 E
Zhonghuamen 106 32.01 N 118.46 E
Zhonghuopu 100 29.44 N 113.59 E
Zhongjianchang 107 28.46 N 106.13 E
Zhongjiang 102 31.00 N 104.18 E
Zhongjiatai 104 40.48 N 122.46 E
Zhonglou 98 35.24 N 119.02 E
Zhongluotan 100 23.23 N 113.23 E
Zhongluyantai 104 41.32 N 123.17 E
Zhongmeihe 100 31.19 N 116.45 E
Zhongmou 98 34.46 N 114.01 E
Zhongning 102 37.27 N 105.38 E
Zhongpingchang 102 31.15 N 110.10 E
Zhongqiao 106 31.11 N 119.11 E
Zhongsha 100 26.24 N 116.36 E
Zhongshan, Zhg. 100 26.12 N 117.26 E
Zhongshan (Shiqizhen), Zhg. 100 22.31 N 113.22 E
Zhongshan ʊ[3] 9 69.22 S 76.23 E
Zhongshan Park ♠ 269b 31.13 N 121.25 E
Zhongtiao Shan ⋏ 102 35.12 N 111.35 E
Zhongting ≐ 105 39.03 N 116.46 E
Zhongtou 100 34.00 N 113.21 E
Zhongwei 102 37.33 N 105.10 E
Zhongwopu 102 38.30 N 102.59 E
Zhongxian, Zhg. 100 27.17 N 116.47 E
Zhongxian, Zhg. 102 30.29 N 108.05 E
Zhongxiang 100 31.11 N 112.33 E
Zhongxiangzhen 107 29.50 N 104.08 E
Zhongxin, Zhg. 100 23.16 N 113.38 E
Zhongxin, Zhg. 100 24.14 N 114.44 E
Zhongxin, Zhg. 104 40.47 N 124.08 E
Zhongxing, Zhg. 106 32.17 N 119.34 E
Zhongxing, Zhg. 107 30.12 N 103.32 E
Zhongxingchang 107 29.07 N 105.18 E
Zhongxinzhen, Zhg. 107 30.16 N 106.15 E
Zhongxinzhen, Zhg. 107 30.30 N 104.03 E
Zhongyangqu 104 40.47 N 122.05 E
Zhongyaozhan 89 50.46 N 125.54 E
Zhongyi 100 31.08 N 114.52 E
Zhongying 105 39.38 N 117.06 E
Zhongzangcun 105 38.52 N 115.38 E
Zhongzhan 100 25.16 N 114.24 E
Zhongzhuang 105 39.25 N 114.47 E
Zhou ≐ 105 39.47 N 117.23 E
Zhouba 107 29.06 N 103.43 E
Zhoubachang 107 28.59 N 103.52 E
Zhoucun 98 36.47 N 117.48 E
Zhoudangfan 100 31.54 N 114.31 E
Zhoujiachang 107 30.33 N 104.25 E
Zhoujiadai 106 32.12 N 120.26 E
Zhoujiadu 106 31.11 N 121.29 E
Zhoujiagou 107 30.08 N 104.30 E
Zhoujiatun, Zhg. 104 41.29 N 121.50 E
Zhoujiatun, Zhg. 104 41.04 N 120.47 E
Zhoujiatun, Zhg. 104 41.16 N 120.58 E
Zhoujiatun, Zhg. 104 41.34 N 121.05 E
Zhoujiawopu 104 42.31 N 122.45 E
Zhoujiayao 104 41.19 N 122.48 E
Zhoujingxiang 106 31.32 N 120.23 E
Zhoukoudianzhen 105 39.41 N 115.56 E
Zhoulichang 107 29.55 N 105.09 E
Zhouning 100 27.16 N 119.12 E
Zhoupo 107 29.48 N 104.01 E
Zhoupu 106 31.07 N 121.34 E
Zhouqu 102 33.43 N 104.10 E
Zhouquan 106 30.35 N 120.21 E
Zhoushan Dao I 100 30.05 N 122.10 E
Zhoushan Qundao II 100 30.00 N 122.00 E
Zhoushu 106 31.28 N 120.59 E
Zhoushuizi 98 38.57 N 121.34 E
Zhoutieqiao 106 31.26 N 120.00 E
Zhouwangmiao 106 30.28 N 120.29 E
Zhouxi 100 29.13 N 116.20 E
Zhouxiang 100 30.10 N 121.08 E
Zhouxinzhen 106 31.30 N 120.18 E
Zhouzhai 106 32.02 N 121.31 E
Zhouzhi 102 34.12 N 108.10 E
Zhouzhuang, Zhg. 105 39.09 N 115.18 E
Zhouzhuang, Zhg. 106 31.06 N 120.51 E
Zhouzhuang, Zhg. 106 32.15 N 120.08 E
Zhovkva 78 50.04 N 23.58 E
Zhovnyne 78 49.23 N 32.41 E
Zhovte, Ukr. 78 47.47 N 33.50 E
Zhovte, Ukr. 78 48.30 N 33.31 E
Zhovten', Ukr. 78 49.03 N 24.45 E
Zhovten', Ukr. 78 47.14 N 30.20 E
Zhovti Vody 78 48.21 N 33.31 E
Zhovtneve, Ukr. 78 46.52 N 32.02 E
Zhovtneve, Ukr. 78 49.39 N 34.09 E
Zhovtneve, Ukr. 78 50.57 N 34.22 E
Zhovtneve, Ukr. 78 51.15 N 28.07 E
Zhovtneve, Ukr. 78 48.38 N 33.04 E
Zhuanghang 106 30.54 N 121.23 E
Zhuanghe 98 39.43 N 123.01 E
Zhuangji 98 34.20 N 115.15 E
Zhuanglang 102 34.58 N 106.07 E
Zhuangtou 105 40.55 N 117.57 E
Zhuangtouyingzi, Zhg. 104 41.43 N 120.32 E
Zhuangtouyingzi, Zhg. 104 41.50 N 120.43 E
Zhuangxi 107 30.33 N 104.31 E
Zhuangyuanqiao 100 27.54 N 120.48 E
Zhuanping Shan ∧ 107 29.07 N 103.37 E
Zhuanqiao 106 31.04 N 121.23 E
Zhuantouwan 100 31.29 N 112.24 E
Zhuanwantai 104 41.20 N 122.22 E
Zhuao 100 29.05 N 121.16 E
Zhucang 102 27.18 N 107.26 E
Zhucheng 98 36.00 N 119.24 E
Zhudi 269b 31.12 N 121.18 E
Zhudian 100 30.33 N 115.12 E
Zhuergan 89 52.04 N 120.48 E
Zhufengzhen 106 30.35 N 118.56 E
Zhufuo 107 29.02 N 105.51 E
Zhugan ≐ 100 32.18 N 114.42 E
Zhuganpu 100 32.13 N 114.39 E
Zhugao 107 30.37 N 104.40 E
Zhuge, Zhg. 98 36.00 N 118.32 E
Zhuge, Zhg. 100 29.15 N 119.18 E
Zhugentan 107 29.25 N 103.50 E
Zhugou 98 36.52 N 120.15 E
Zhugouzhen 100 32.47 N 113.42 E
Zhugusi 102 37.01 N 102.27 E
Zhuhai 100 22.16 N 113.33 E
Zhuhe 100 29.44 N 113.06 E
Zhuhongyu 104 40.48 N 123.00 E
Zhuji 100 29.43 N 120.14 E
Zhujiabeng 106 31.21 N 120.41 E
Zhujiabian 106 31.38 N 119.11 E
Zhujiachang, Zhg. 107 29.48 N 104.20 E
Zhujiachang, Zhg. 107 30.03 N 104.13 E
Zhujiafang 104 41.20 N 122.40 E
Zhujiahang 106 30.51 N 121.19 E
Zhujiahe 106 31.08 N 120.53 E
Zhujia Jian I 100 29.54 N 122.24 E
Zhujiajiao 106 31.06 N 121.02 E
Zhujiajiaotou 106 31.24 N 121.11 E
Zhujiang Kou C[1] 100 22.36 N 113.44 E
Zhujiangqing 100 27.18 N 114.44 E
Zhujiaqiao 106 30.26 N 119.03 E
Zhujiawan, Zhg. 100 32.28 N 117.29 E
Zhujiawan, Zhg. 100 30.56 N 114.10 E
Zhujiawan, Zhg. 105 40.08 N 114.56 E
Zhujiawopeng 104 42.27 N 122.13 E
Zhujiesi 102 33.34 N 97.21 E
Zhukeng 100 23.49 N 112.55 E
Zhukou, Zhg. 98 34.07 N 115.04 E
Zhukou, Zhg. 100 27.41 N 118.53 E
Zhukou, Zhg. 100 26.58 N 117.16 E
Zhukovskiy
— Žukovskij 82 55.35 N 38.08 E
Zhulanbu 100 25.36 N 115.46 E
Zhulin, Zhg. 100 32.20 N 113.38 E
Zhulin, Zhg. 106 31.45 N 119.27 E
Zhulong ≐ 98 38.47 N 115.59 E
Zhulongqiao 100 32.21 N 118.09 E
Zhuluke 98 41.36 N 119.54 E
Zhumadian 100 32.58 N 114.03 E
Zhuolu 105 40.22 N 115.12 E
Zhuoni 102 34.32 N 103.24 E
Zhuotian 100 25.38 N 116.13 E
Zhuoxian 105 39.30 N 115.58 E
Zhuozi 102 40.52 N 112.33 E
Zhuqianzongpuzi 104 42.17 N 123.18 E
Zhuqiao, Zhg. 98 37.22 N 120.05 E
Zhuqiao, Zhg. 106 31.07 N 121.44 E
Zhuqiao, Zhg. 106 30.26 N 120.36 E
Zhuravychi 78 50.59 N 25.43 E
Zhurivka 78 50.31 N 31.46 E
Zhurushan 100 30.26 N 113.48 E
Zhushan 102 32.10 N 110.19 E
Zhusigang 100 31.14 N 118.23 E
Zhutan 100 28.04 N 114.10 E
Zhutang, Zhg. 106 31.06 N 118.39 E
Zhutang, Zhg. 106 31.47 N 120.24 E
Zhutian 100 28.43 N 117.01 E
Zhuting, Zhg. 100 27.24 N 113.04 E
Zhuting, Zhg. 100 27.48 N 114.02 E
Zhuwo 105 40.02 N 115.48 E
Zhuwotuo 107 30.31 N 104.34 E
Zhuwumiao 100 30.54 N 116.19 E
Zhuxi, Zhg. 100 28.10 N 118.53 E
Zhuxi, Zhg. 102 32.09 N 109.42 E
Zhuxi, Zhg. 107 29.32 N 105.40 E
Zhuxianzhen 98 34.37 N 114.16 E
Zhuxichang 100 28.58 N 114.06 E
Zhuya 98 36.38 N 118.12 E
Zhuyang 98 36.16 N 117.22 E
Zhuyangxi 107 29.03 N 105.57 E
Zhuyangzhen 102 34.20 N 110.44 E
Zhuyivka 83 48.04 N 38.15 E
Zhuyuan 107 29.34 N 104.08 E
Zhuzeqiao 106 31.34 N 119.20 E
Zhuzhenji 100 32.31 N 118.42 E
Zhuzhou (Chuchow) 100 27.50 N 113.09 E
Zhuzikou 100 29.17 N 112.41 E
Zhydachiv 78 49.23 N 24.08 E
Zhyhaylivka 78 50.38 N 35.07 E
Zhytomyr 78 50.16 N 28.40 E
Zhytomyr □[4] 78 50.30 N 28.30 E
Zi ≐, Zhg. 98 37.12 N 118.34 E
Zi ≐, Zhg. 102 28.41 N 112.43 E
Zi ≐, Zhg. 102 31.59 N 96.53 E
Zia Indian Reservation ◆[4] 200 35.30 N 106.43 W
Zia International Airport ⊠ 126 23.46 N 90.23 E
Ziama Mansouria 34 36.40 N 5.29 E
Ziano 64 46.17 N 11.34 E
Ziārat 120 30.23 N 67.43 E
Zīārat-e Shāh Maqṣūd 120 31.59 N 65.30 E
Ziārat Gali Chāh ⊤[4] 128 28.20 N 63.38 E
Žiar nad Hronom 30 48.36 N 18.52 E
Zibdīn 132 33.22 N 35.28 E
Zibo (Zhangdian) 98 36.47 N 118.01 E
Zicapa 234 17.57 N 99.02 W
Zicavo 36 41.54 N 9.08 E
Zichang 102 37.19 N 109.33 E
Žichovice 60 49.16 N 13.37 E
Zichuan 98 36.38 N 117.55 E
Žičicy 76 55.07 N 31.17 E
Zickhusen 54 53.45 N 11.25 E
Ziddi 85 39.03 N 68.48 E
Žideli 86 48.40 N 70.29 E
Zid'ky 78 49.42 N 36.21 E
Židlochovice 61 49.02 N 16.37 E
Ziębice 30 50.37 N 17.00 E
Ziegelroda 54 51.20 N 11.28 E
Ziegendorf 54 53.18 N 11.49 E
Ziegenhain 56 50.55 N 9.15 E
Ziegenhals 264a 52.21 N 13.40 E
Ziegenrück 54 50.37 N 11.38 E
Zielona Góra (Grünberg) 30 51.56 N 15.31 E
Zielona Góra □[4] 30 52.00 N 15.20 E
Ziemetshausen 58 48.18 N 10.31 E
Zierenberg 56 51.22 N 9.18 E
Zierikzee 52 51.38 N 3.55 E
Ziersdorf 61 48.31 N 15.55 E
Ziesar 54 52.16 N 12.17 E
Ziesendorf 54 54.00 N 12.02 E
Ziethen 54 53.53 N 13.40 E
Žiežmariai 76 54.48 N 24.27 E
Ziftā 142 30.43 N 31.15 E
Žigalgan 84 44.36 N 50.46 E
Žigalovo 88 54.48 N 105.08 E
Žigansk 74 66.45 N 123.20 E
Zigazinskij 86 53.50 N 57.20 E
Zigong (Tzukung) 107 29.24 N 104.47 E
Ziguéy 146 14.43 N 15.47 E
Zigui 102 31.00 N 110.31 E
Ziguinchor 150 12.35 N 16.16 W
Ziguinchor □[4] 150 12.45 N 16.20 W
Žigulevsk 80 53.25 N 49.27 E
Žiguli 80 53.22 N 49.19 E
Žiguli ⋏ 80 53.20 N 49.40 E
Zigutaicun 104 42.01 N 121.16 E
Zig Zag, Cerro ∧[2] 286d 12.12 S 76.59 W
Zihedian 98 36.48 N 118.22 E
Zihuatanejo 234 17.38 N 101.33 W
Zihukou, Zhg. 100 28.44 N 112.33 E
Zihukou, Zhg. 100 28.55 N 118.08 E
Ziiyang 102 32.31 N 108.48 E
Žijančurino 86 51.33 N 56.55 E
Žijenkum 85 42.50 N 69.00 E
Zijiao 98 37.21 N 117.25 E
Zijin 100 23.40 N 115.11 E
Zijingguan 105 39.23 N 115.12 E
Zijin Shan ∧[2] 106 32.04 N 118.51 E
Zikejevo 76 53.44 N 34.52 E
Zikhron Ya'aqov 132 32.34 N 34.57 E
Zikoufang 100 26.22 N 117.24 E
Zilair 86 52.14 N 57.30 E
Žilaja Kosa 80 46.49 N 53.12 E
Žilaja Tambica 24 62.32 N 36.09 E
Zile 130 40.18 N 35.54 E
Zili 102 26.50 N 100.27 E
Žilina 30 49.14 N 18.46 E
Žilino 76 54.54 N 21.56 E
Zillah, Lībiyā 146 28.33 N 17.35 E
Zillah, Wa., U.S. 202 46.24 N 120.15 W
Ziller ≐ 64 47.24 N 11.50 E
Zillertal V 64 47.20 N 11.50 E
Zillertaler Alpen (Alpi Aurine) ⋏ 64 47.00 N 11.55 E
Zillis 58 46.38 N 9.27 E
Zillisheim 58 47.41 N 7.16 E
Zilly 54 51.56 N 10.49 E
Zilme 144 16.25 N 43.49 E
Žiloj Bor 76 59.06 N 34.37 E
Žil'ovo 82 54.59 N 38.02 E
Ziltendorf 54 52.12 N 14.37 E
Zilupe 76 56.23 N 28.07 E
Zilwaukee 190 43.28 N 83.55 W
Zima 88 53.55 N 102.04 E
Zima ≐ 88 53.52 N 102.02 E
Žima, gora ∧ 88 53.18 N 107.38 E
Zimapán 234 20.45 N 99.21 W
Zimatlán 234 16.52 N 96.47 W
Zimba 154 17.19 S 26.13 E
Zimbabwe □[1], Afr. 138 20.00 S 30.00 E
Zimbabwe □[1], Afr. 154 20.00 S 30.00 E
Zimbor 38 47.00 N 23.16 E
Zimella 64 45.20 N 11.22 E
Zimi 150 7.19 N 11.18 W
Zimljansker-Stausee
— Ciml'anskoje vodochranilišče ⊜[1] 80 48.00 N 43.00 E
Zimmara, Monte ∧ 70 37.45 N 14.16 E
Zimn'ackij 80 49.44 N 42.53 E
Zimnicea 38 43.39 N 25.21 E
Zimonino 76 53.47 N 31.52 E
Zimovniki 80 47.08 N 42.28 E
Zimovskoje 86 57.31 N 86.52 E
Zin, Naḥal V 132 30.57 N 35.19 E
Zinal 58 46.08 N 7.38 E
Zinapécuaro [de Figueroa] 234 19.52 N 100.49 W
Zinave, Parque Nacional de ♠ 156 21.35 S 33.35 E
Zinder 150 13.48 N 8.59 E
Zinder □[5] 146 15.00 N 10.30 E
Zinga 152 3.43 N 18.35 E
Zinga Mulike 154 9.09 S 38.44 E
Zingaro, Passo dello)(70 37.43 N 14.50 E
Zingst 54 54.26 N 12.41 E
Zingst ≻[1] 54 54.25 N 12.50 E
Zingwanda 140 7.10 N 27.56 E
Ziniaré 150 12.35 N 1.18 W
Žiniške ≐ 85 43.14 N 78.30 E
Zinkgruvan 40 58.49 N 15.05 E
Zin'kiv, Ukr. 78 49.04 N 27.04 E
Zin'kiv, Ukr. 78 50.13 N 34.22 E
Zinnik
— Soignies 50 50.35 N 4.04 E
Zinnowitz 54 54.04 N 13.55 E
Zinswiller 56 48.55 N 7.35 E
Zion, Il., U.S. 216 42.26 N 87.49 W
Zion, Md., U.S. 208 39.40 N 75.57 W
Zionhill 208 40.29 N 75.24 W
Zion National Park ♠ 200 37.10 N 113.00 W
Zionsville 218 39.57 N 86.15 W
Zionz Lake ⊜ 184 51.25 N 91.52 W
Zipaquirá 246 5.02 N 74.00 W
Žipkovšino 88 51.52 N 112.59 E
Zippori 132 32.45 N 35.17 E
Zipsendorf 54 51.02 N 12.16 E
Ziqlāb, Wādī V 132 32.30 N 35.34 E
Zir 130 39.59 N 32.31 E
Zīra 123 30.58 N 74.59 E
Žir'akovo 86 57.53 N 65.37 E
Zirándaro 234 18.27 N 100.59 W
Zirāpur 124 24.01 N 76.22 E
Žir'atino 76 53.15 N 33.44 E
Zirbitzkogel ∧ 61 47.04 N 14.34 E
Zirchow 54 53.53 N 14.08 E
Zirgan 86 53.14 N 55.55 E
Žirje, Otok I 36 43.40 N 15.39 E
Zirl 64 47.17 N 11.14 E
Zirndorf 56 49.26 N 10.58 E
Žirnov 80 48.13 N 41.06 E
Žirnovsk 80 51.00 N 44.46 E
Ziro 120 27.38 N 93.42 E
Žiroškino 82 55.22 N 38.03 E
Žirovnice 30 49.15 N 15.11 E
Zishan 100 25.57 N 115.35 E
Zistersdorf 61 48.32 N 16.45 E
Zisterzienserabtei ʊ[1] 56 49.01 N 8.47 E
Zisuntang 106 30.38 N 118.42 E
Zitadelle ⊥ 264a 52.33 N 13.13 E
Žiteli 24 65.04 N 47.26 E
Žitenice 54 50.35 N 14.08 E
Žitjevo 76 59.54 N 41.06 E
Žitkoviči 76 52.14 N 27.54 E
Žitkovo 76 60.42 N 29.20 E
Žitkur 80 48.57 N 46.17 E
Zitlala 234 17.38 N 99.05 W
Zitlaltepec 234 19.12 N 97.54 W
Žitnoje 80 45.49 N 47.41 E
Zitong 102 31.43 N 105.10 E
Zittau 54 50.54 N 14.47 E
Zitundo 156 26.45 S 32.50 E
Ziwa Magharibi □[4] 154 2.00 S 31.30 E
Ziway, Lake ⊜ 144 8.00 N 38.50 E
Ziwuji 100 32.55 N 115.58 E
Zixi, Zhg. 100 27.42 N 117.02 E
Zixi, Zhg. 100 28.01 N 117.46 E
Zixing 100 25.58 N 113.24 E
Ziya ≐ 105 39.09 N 117.10 E
Ziyamet 130 35.28 N 34.08 E
Ziyang 107 30.07 N 104.39 E
Ziyuan 102 26.01 N 110.31 E
Ziyun 102 25.43 N 106.05 E
Ziz, Oued V 148 30.39 N 4.26 W
Žizdra 76 53.45 N 34.44 E
Žizdra ≐ 82 54.14 N 36.12 E
Zizers 58 46.56 N 9.34 E
Zizhong 107 29.48 N 104.50 E
Zizhou 102 37.37 N 109.41 E
Žižica 76 56.17 N 31.21 E
Žižickoje, ozero ⊜ 76 56.14 N 31.15 E
Žižma ≐ 76 53.54 N 25.36 E
Zlarin 36 43.42 N 15.50 E
Zlatá Koruna ʊ[1] 61 48.52 N 14.22 E
Zlatar 36 46.06 N 16.05 E
Zlaté Moravce 30 48.25 N 18.24 E
Zlatograd 38 41.23 N 25.06 E
Zlatoust 86 55.10 N 59.40 E
Zlatoustovsk 89 52.58 N 133.38 E
Zlín 30 49.13 N 17.41 E
Zlītan 146 32.28 N 14.34 E
Žlobin 76 52.54 N 30.03 E
Złocieniec 30 53.33 N 16.01 E
Złoczew 30 51.25 N 18.36 E
Zlonice 54 50.15 N 14.07 E
Złotoryja 30 51.08 N 15.55 E
Złotów 30 53.22 N 17.02 E
Žlutice 54 50.03 N 13.10 E
Zlydnev 80 48.46 N 45.48 E
Zlynka, Ross. 76 52.25 N 31.44 E
Zlynka, Ukr. 78 48.28 N 31.32 E
Zmeinogorsk 86 51.10 N 82.13 E
Żmigród 30 51.29 N 16.55 E
Žminj 36 45.09 N 13.55 E
Zmi'ovka 76 52.40 N 36.23 E
Zmiyinyy, ostriv I 78 45.15 N 30.12 E
Zmiyiv 78 49.40 N 36.19 E
Zna
— Cna ≐ 80 54.32 N 42.05 E
Znaim
— Znojmo 61 48.52 N 16.02 E
Znamenka, Kaz. 86 50.05 N 79.32 E
Znamenka, Ross. 76 54.54 N 34.34 E
Znamenka, Ross. 80 52.24 N 41.26 E
Znamenka, Ross. 86 53.10 N 79.30 E
Znamenka, Ross. 86 53.32 N 91.54 E
Znamenka, Ross. 88 54.42 N 104.50 E
Znamensk 76 54.37 N 21.13 E
Znamenskoje, Ross. 76 53.17 N 35.41 E
Znamenskoje, Ross. 80 53.19 N 42.57 E
Znamenskoje, Ross. 86 57.08 N 73.55 E
Znamenskoje, Ross. 265b 55.45 N 37.09 E
Znam'yanka 78 48.43 N 32.40 E
Znam'yanka Druha 78 48.43 N 32.35 E
Żnin 30 52.52 N 17.43 E
Znob-Novhorods'ke 78 52.16 N 33.36 E
Znojmo 61 48.52 N 16.02 E
Zoagli 62 44.20 N 9.16 E
Zoar 158 33.30 S 21.28 E
Zoar Village State Memorial ⊥ 214 40.36 N 81.27 W
Zoarville 214 40.35 N 81.24 W
Zobia 154 2.58 N 25.56 E
Zöblitz 54 50.39 N 13.14 E
Zóbuè 154 15.38 S 34.26 E
Zocca 64 44.21 N 10.59 E
Žochova, ostrov I 74 76.04 N 152.40 E
Zod 84 40.12 N 45.52 E
Žodino 76 54.06 N 28.21 E
Žodiški 76 54.38 N 26.26 E
Zoétélé 152 3.15 N 11.53 E
Zoetermeer 52 52.03 N 4.30 E
Zofingen 58 47.18 N 7.57 E
Zogang 102 29.55 N 97.44 E
Zogno 62 45.48 N 9.40 E
Zográfos 267c 37.59 N 23.46 E
Zohar 132 31.36 N 34.42 E
Zohar, Mizpé ∧[2] 132 31.13 N 35.14 E
Zohreh ≐ 128 30.04 N 49.31 E
Zola Predosa 64 44.29 N 11.12 E
Zolder 56 51.01 N 5.18 E
Zoldo Alto 64 46.22 N 12.06 E
Zolfo Springs 220 27.29 N 81.47 W
Zolka ≐ 84 44.17 N 43.51 E
Żółkiewka 30 50.55 N 22.51 E
Zollhaus 56 50.17 N 8.04 E
Zollikofen 58 47.00 N 7.28 E
Zollikon 58 47.20 N 8.35 E
Zolling 60 48.27 N 11.46 E
Zol'noje 80 53.27 N 49.48 E
Zolochiv, Ukr. 78 50.17 N 35.59 E
Zolochiv, Ukr. 78 49.47 N 24.52 E
Zolotaja Gora 89 54.16 N 126.36 E
Zolota Lypa ≐ 78 48.59 N 25.04 E
Zolotari 80 49.46 N 46.21 E
Zolotar'ovka 80 53.04 N 45.20 E
Zolote 83 48.41 N 38.31 E
Zolotkovo 80 55.32 N 41.06 E
Zolotnyky 78 49.17 N 25.23 E
Zolotoje 80 50.51 N 45.53 E
Zolotonosha 78 49.40 N 32.02 E
Zolotucha 80 47.49 N 46.44 E
Zolotuchino 78 52.05 N 36.23 E
Zolotyy Potik 78 48.54 N 25.20 E
Žolymbet 86 51.45 N 71.44 E
Zomba 154 15.23 S 35.18 E
Zomergem 50 51.07 N 3.33 E
Zone Point ≻ 42 50.08 N 5.00 W
Zongchang 107 28.52 N 104.36 E
Zongjiaxiang 269b 31.12 N 121.22 E
Zongo 152 4.21 N 18.36 E
Zonguldak 130 41.27 N 31.49 E
Zonguldak □[4] 130 41.30 N 32.15 E
Zongwe 154 5.05 S 27.55 E
Zongyang 100 30.42 N 117.12 E
Zonhoven 56 50.59 N 5.21 E
Zonnebeke 50 50.52 N 2.59 E
Zons 56 51.07 N 6.50 E
Zonza 36 41.45 N 9.10 E
Zoo, Bahnhof ◆[5] 264a 52.30 N 13.20 E
Zooafskolk 158 29.56 S 20.24 E
Zoom ≐ 52 51.30 N 4.14 E
Zoppot
— Sopot 30 54.28 N 18.34 E
Zopui 120 23.39 N 92.14 E
Zörbig 54 51.37 N 12.07 E
Zorge 54 51.38 N 10.38 E
Zorge ≐ 54 51.27 N 10.54 E
Zorgo 150 12.15 N 0.36 W
Zorgongo 150 12.16 N 0.48 W
Zorita 34 39.17 N 5.42 W
Zorkul', ozero ⊜ 120 37.27 N 73.40 E
Zorn ≐ 56 48.45 N 7.55 E
Zorneding 60 48.05 N 11.49 E
Zornica 38 42.23 N 26.56 E
Zorra, Arroyo de la ≐ 196 29.31 N 101.13 W
Zorritos 246 3.40 S 80.40 W
Zorykivka 83 49.24 N 39.51 E
Zoryns'k 83 48.25 N 38.34 E
Zorzor 150 7.46 N 9.28 W
Zöschen 54 51.21 N 12.07 E
Zossen 54 52.13 N 13.27 E
Zoti 84 41.53 N 42.28 E
Zottegem 50 50.52 N 3.48 E
Zou □[5] 150 8.00 N 2.15 E
Zou ≐ 150 6.28 N 2.25 E
Zouan-Hounien 150 6.55 N 8.13 W
Zouar 146 20.27 N 16.32 E
Zouérat 148 22.42 N 12.30 W
Zoug
— Zug 58 47.10 N 8.31 E
Zoulabot 152 3.17 N 14.02 E
Zoumagang 107 29.28 N 106.18 E
Zoumayi 98 39.07 N 114.34 E
Zouping 98 36.53 N 117.42 E
Zourma 150 11.22 N 0.49 W
Zousfana, Oued V 148 30.29 N 2.17 W
Zoutelande 52 51.30 N 3.30 E
Zoutkamp 52 53.20 N 6.18 E
Zouxian 98 35.24 N 117.00 E
Zova 132 31.48 N 35.06 E
Zovka 76 58.26 N 28.52 E
Zoziv 78 49.19 N 29.01 E
Zrenjanin 38 45.23 N 20.24 E
Zriba 36 36.20 N 10.16 E
Zrmanja ≐ 36 44.15 N 15.32 E
Zruč nad Sázavou 30 49.45 N 15.07 E
Zscherndorf 54 51.36 N 12.15 E
Zschieren ◆[8] 54 51.00 N 13.52 E
Zschopau 54 50.44 N 13.04 E
Zschopau ≐ 54 51.08 N 13.03 E
Zschorlau 54 50.34 N 12.38 E
Zschornewitz 54 51.43 N 12.25 E
Zschortau 54 51.28 N 12.21 E
Žuanbalyk 86 45.04 N 61.51 E
Žuantobe 86 44.45 N 68.54 E
Zuarungu 150 10.47 N 0.48 W
Zuata ≐ 246 7.52 N 65.22 W
Zubaydīyah, Jabal az- ∧ 132 33.48 N 37.02 E
Zubayr, Jazā'ir az- II 144 15.05 N 42.08 E
Zubayr, Wādī V 142 27.27 N 32.41 E
Zubcov 76 56.10 N 34.34 E
Zubkovychi 78 51.02 N 27.41 E
Zubova Pol'ana 80 54.04 N 42.51 E
Zubovka 80 54.16 N 51.06 E
Zubovo, Ross. 76 54.33 N 35.29 E
Zubovo, Ross. 76 60.19 N 36.57 E
Zubovo, Ross. 80 56.52 N 44.08 E
Zuccarello 62 44.07 N 8.07 E
Zuccone, Monte ∧ 62 44.26 N 9.37 E
Zuchwil 58 47.12 N 7.33 E
Zuckerhütl ∧ 64 46.58 N 11.09 E
Zudar 54 54.15 N 13.20 E
Z'udev, ostrov I 80 45.35 N 47.58 E
Zuel 64 46.31 N 12.08 E
Zuénoula 150 7.26 N 6.03 W
Zuera 34 41.52 N 0.47 W
Zufār ◆[1] 118 17.00 N 54.10 E
Zufaytat Mashtūl 142 30.20 N 31.21 E
Zug 58 47.10 N 8.31 E
Zug □[3] 58 47.00 N 8.30 E
Zugdeli 88 55.03 N 111.10 E
Zugdidi 84 42.30 N 41.53 E
Zugersee ⊜ 58 47.08 N 8.30 E
Zug Island I 281 42.17 N 83.07 W
Zugló ◆[8] 264c 47.31 N 19.08 E
Zugspitze ∧ 64 47.25 N 10.59 E
Zugurma Game Reserve ◆[4] 150 9.55 N 5.00 E
Zühlsdorf 264a 52.44 N 13.24 E
Zuhres 83 48.01 N 38.15 E
Zui 76 57.06 N 31.37 E
Zuid-Beijerland 52 51.45 N 4.22 E
Zuid-Beveland I 52 51.25 N 3.45 E
Zuidbroek 52 53.10 N 6.52 E
Zuidelijk Flevoland ◆[1] 52 52.22 N 5.20 E
Zuiderzee
— IJsselmeer ⊤[2] 52 52.45 N 5.25 E
Zuid-Holland □[4] 52 52.00 N 4.30 E
Zuidhorn 52 53.14 N 6.24 E
Zuidlaren 52 53.05 N 6.41 E
Zuid-Willemsvaart ≊ 52 51.12 N 5.52 E
Zuidwolde 52 53.15 N 6.35 E
Žuja ≐ 88 58.45 N 118.11 E
Zújar ≐ 34 39.01 N 5.47 W
Zújar, Embalse del ⊜[1] 34 38.50 N 5.20 W
Zujevka 80 58.25 N 51.10 E
Z'ukajka 80 58.12 N 54.43 E
Žukopa 76 56.33 N 32.42 E
Žukopa ≐ 76 56.54 N 32.46 E
Žukovka, Ross. 76 53.32 N 33.44 E
Žukovka, Ross. 86 56.05 N 91.42 E
Žukovka, Ross. 265b 55.44 N 37.15 E
Žukovskaja 80 47.37 N 42.28 E
Žukovskij 82 55.35 N 38.08 E
Žukovskoje 80 46.05 N 41.21 E
Żukowo 30 54.21 N 18.22 E
Zula 144 15.11 N 39.41 E
Zula ≐ 234 20.21 N 102.46 W
Žulanka 86 54.22 N 80.36 E
Zulayl, Wādī az- V 132 32.09 N 36.03 E
Žuldyz 80 49.16 N 49.30 E
Žulebino 265b 55.42 N 37.51 E
Zuli ≐ 102 36.35 N 104.35 E
Zulia □[3] 246 10.00 N 72.10 W
Zulia ∧ 154 4.07 N 33.58 E
Zulia ≐ 246 9.04 N 72.18 W
Zülpich 56 50.41 N 6.39 E
Zulueta 240p 22.22 N 79.34 W
Zululand □[9] 158 28.10 S 32.00 E
Z'ul'z'a 88 52.33 N 116.13 E
Žumala 80 50.29 N 49.47 E
Zumar, Tur'at az- ≊ 273c 29.58 N 31.15 E
Zumarraga 116 11.38 N 124.50 E
Zumba 246 4.52 S 79.09 W
Zumbo 154 15.36 S 30.25 E
Zumbro ≐ 190 44.18 N 91.56 W
Zumbro, North Fork ≐ 190 44.15 N 92.29 W
Zumbro, South Fork ≐ 190 44.15 N 92.29 W
Zumbrota 190 44.17 N 92.40 W
Zumpango del Río 234 17.39 N 99.30 W
Zumpango de Ocampo 234 19.48 N 99.06 W
Zundert 52 51.28 N 4.40 E
Zundi 152 10.28 S 16.48 E
Zune 156 18.59 S 35.18 E
Zungeru 150 9.48 N 6.09 E
Zungri 68 38.39 N 15.59 E
Zungur 150 9.58 N 9.47 E
Zungwini 158 27.34 S 30.53 E
Zunhua 105 40.12 N 117.58 E
Zuni, N.M., U.S. 200 35.04 N 108.51 W
Zuni, Va., U.S. 208 36.51 N 76.49 W
Zuni ≐ 200 34.39 N 109.40 W
Zuni Indian Reservation ◆[4] 200 35.15 N 108.20 W
Zunsuzhi 102 44.40 N 112.50 E
Zunyi 102 27.39 N 106.57 E
Zuo ≐ 102 22.50 N 108.06 E
Zuo'an 100 26.10 N 114.16 E
Zuodeng 102 23.27 N 106.57 E
Zuogezhuang 105 39.01 N 116.37 E
Zuomaozigou 104 42.12 N 120.41 E
Zuomuchedong Hu ⊜ 120 28.25 N 88.15 E
Zuoquan 102 37.03 N 113.30 E
Zuosuo 102 27.45 N 100.54 E
Zuotema 120 35.50 N 80.45 E
Zuowei 105 40.41 N 114.43 E
Zuoxiunulemiao 88 48.08 N 115.38 E
Zuoyun 102 40.02 N 112.54 E
Zuoz 58 46.36 N 9.58 E
Županja 38 45.04 N 18.42 E
Zūq Muṣbīḥ 132 33.58 N 35.37 E
Zura 80 57.37 N 53.26 E
Zūrābād 128 38.49 N 44.35 E
Žuraviči 76 53.15 N 30.33 E
Žuravl'ovka 86 51.57 N 69.56 E
Zurayghiṭ 128 26.29 N 40.33 E
Žurban 89 54.12 N 127.56 E
Zurich, On., Can. 190 43.26 N 81.37 W
Zurich, Ned. 52 53.06 N 5.23 E
Zürich, Schw. 58 47.23 N 8.32 E
Zürich □[3] 58 47.25 N 8.40 E
Zürich, Flughafen ⊠ 58 47.27 N 8.33 E
Zurich, Lake ⊜ 278 42.12 N 88.06 W
Zürichsee ⊜ 58 47.13 N 8.45 E
Zurigo
— Zürich 58 47.23 N 8.32 E
Zurmi 150 12.46 N 6.48 E
Żuromin 30 53.04 N 19.55 E

Symbols in the index entries represent the broad categories identified in the key at the right. Symbols with superior numbers (⋏[1]) identify subcategories (see complete key on page *I · 1*).

Symbole im Register stellen die rechts im Schlüssel erklärten Kategorien dar. Symbole mit hochgestellten Ziffern (⋏[1]) bezeichnen Unterabteilungen einer Kategorie (vgl. vollständiger Schlüssel auf Seite *I · 1*).

Los símbolos incluídos en el texto del índice representan las grandes categorías identificadas con la clave a la derecha. Los símbolos con numeros en su parte superior (⋏[1]) identifican las subcategorías (véase la clave completa en la página *I · 1*).

Les symboles de l'index représentent les catégories indiquées dans la légende à droite. Les symboles suivis d'un indice (⋏[1]) représentent des sous-catégories (voir légende complète à la page *I · 1*).

Os símbolos incluídos no texto do índice representam as grandes categorias identificadas com a chave à direita. Os símbolos com números em sua parte superior (⋏[1]) identificam as subcategorias (veja-se a chave completa à página *I · 1*).

∧ Mountain	Berg	Montaña	Montagne	Montanha
⋏ Mountains	Gebirge	Montañas	Montagnes	Montanhas
)(Pass	Paß	Paso	Col	Passo
V Valley, Canyon	Tal, Cañon	Valle, Cañón	Vallée, Canyon	Vale, Canhão
≐ Plain	Ebene	Llano	Plaine	Planície
≻ Cape	Kap	Cabo	Cap	Cabo
I Island	Insel	Isla	Île	Ilha
II Islands	Inseln	Islas	Îles	Ilhas
⊥ Other Topographic Features	Andere Topographische Objekte	Otros Elementos Topográficos	Autres données topographiques	Outros acidentes topográficos

ESPAÑOL

Nombre	Página	Lat.°′	Long.°′ W = Oeste
Zurq, Al-Qārāt az- ∧[2]	**142**	29.00 N	29.55 E
Zürs	**58**	47.10 N	10.10 E
Zuru	**150**	11.27 N	5.12 E
Zurzach	**58**	47.35 N	8.18 E
Zuša ≏	**76**	53.27 N	36.23 E
Zusam ≏	**56**	48.42 N	10.45 E
Žusandala ◆[2]	**86**	44.20 N	75.00 E
Zushi	**94**	35.18 N	139.35 E
Zusmarshausen	**58**	48.24 N	10.35 E
Züssow	**54**	53.59 N	13.32 E
Žut, Otok I	**36**	43.52 N	15.19 E
Zutiua ≏	**250**	3.43 S	45.29 W
Žutovo Vtoroje	**80**	47.49 N	43.51 E
Zutphen	**52**	52.08 N	6.12 E
Zützen	**54**	51.57 N	13.38 E

FRANÇAIS

Nom	Page	Lat.°′	Long.°′ W = Ouest
Zuwārah	**146**	32.56 N	12.06 E
Zuwayzā	**132**	31.42 N	35.55 E
Zuya	**78**	45.03 N	34.20 E
Z'uzel'skij	**86**	56.29 N	60.07 E
Žužemberk	**36**	45.50 N	14.56 E
Z'uzino	**265b**	55.40 N	38.07 E
Z'uzino ◆[8]	**265b**	55.39 N	37.35 E
Žuzymdyk	**85**	43.05 N	69.08 E
Zv'agino	**265b**	55.59 N	37.48 E
Zvannoje	**78**	51.23 N	34.33 E
Zvenigorod	**82**	55.44 N	36.51 E
Zvenigovo	**80**	55.58 N	48.02 E
Zvenyhorodka	**78**	49.04 N	30.57 E
Zverevo	**83**	48.01 N	40.07 E
Zverinogolovskoje	**86**	54.28 N	64.50 E

PORTUGUÊS

Nome	Página	Lat.°′	Long.°′ W = Oeste
Zvezdec	**38**	42.07 N	27.25 E
Zvezdnyj	**88**	56.49 N	106.27 E
Zvíkovec	**60**	49.56 N	13.42 E
Zvishavane	**154**	20.20 S	30.02 E
Zvolen	**30**	48.35 N	19.08 E
Zvon ∧	**60**	49.33 N	12.39 E
Zvornik	**38**	44.23 N	19.06 E
Zwaag	**52**	52.40 N	5.05 E
Zwaagwesteinde	**52**	53.15 N	6.04 E
Zwadība	**152**	3.04 N	14.02 E
Zwanenburg	**52**	52.23 N	4.45 E
Zwartemeer	**52**	52.43 N	7.03 E
Zwarte Meer ⊜	**52**	52.37 N	5.57 E
Zwartsluis	**52**	52.37 N	6.04 E
Zweckel ◆[8]	**263**	51.36 N	6.59 E

Zwedru	**150**	6.04 N	8.08 W
Zweibrücken	**56**	49.15 N	7.21 E
Zweifall	**56**	50.43 N	6.15 E
Zweisimmen	**58**	46.33 N	7.22 E
Zweite Wiener Hochquellenleitung ≡[1]	**61**	48.10 N	16.14 E
Zwenkau	**54**	51.13 N	12.19 E
Zwentendorf	**61**	48.21 N	15.55 E
Zwesten	**56**	51.03 N	9.10 E
Zwettl	**61**	48.37 N	15.10 E
Zwevegem	**50**	50.48 N	3.20 E
Zwevezele	**50**	51.02 N	3.12 E
Zwickau	**54**	50.44 N	12.29 E
Zwickauer Mulde ≏	**54**	51.10 N	12.48 E

Zwiefalten	**58**	48.14 N	9.28 E
Zwiefaltendorf	**58**	48.13 N	9.31 E
Zwierzyniec	**30**	50.37 N	22.58 E
Zwiesel	**60**	49.01 N	13.14 E
Zwieselstein	**64**	46.56 N	11.02 E
Zwijndrecht	**52**	51.49 N	4.39 E
Zwillbrock	**52**	52.04 N	6.42 E
Zwingenberg, Dtsch.	**56**	49.25 N	9.02 E
Zwingenberg, Dtsch.	**56**	49.43 N	8.37 E
Zwischenahner Meer ⊜	**52**	53.12 N	8.01 E
Zwochau	**54**	51.28 N	12.16 E
Zwoleń	**30**	51.22 N	21.35 E
Zwölfaxing	**264b**	48.06 N	16.28 E
Zwolle, Ned.	**52**	52.30 N	6.05 E

Zwolle, La., U.S.	**194**	31.37 N	93.38 W
Zwönitz	**54**	50.38 N	12.49 E
Zwota	**54**	50.21 N	12.25 E
Żychlin	**30**	52.15 N	19.39 E
Zymoetz ≏	**182**	54.33 N	128.26 W
Zymohir'ya	**83**	48.35 N	38.56 E
Zyr'anka	**74**	65.45 N	150.51 E
Zyr'anovsk	**86**	49.43 N	84.20 E
Zyr'anovskij	**86**	57.46 N	61.42 E
Zyr'anskoje	**86**	56.50 N	86.38 E
Żyrardów	**30**	52.04 N	20.25 E
Zyryanovsk → Zyr'anovsk	**86**	49.43 N	84.20 E
Żyrzyn	**30**	51.30 N	22.07 E
Żywiec	**30**	49.41 N	19.12 E

≏ River	Fluß	Río	Rivière	Rio
≡ Canal	Kanal	Canal	Canal	Canal
Waterfall, Rapids	Wasserfall, Stromschnellen	Cascada, Rápidos	Chute d'eau, Rapides	Cascata, Rápidos
Strait	Meeresstraße	Estrecho	Détroit	Estreito
Bay, Gulf	Bucht, Golf	Bahía, Golfo	Baie, Golfe	Baía, Golfo
⊜ Lake, Lakes	See, Seen	Lago, Lagos	Lac, Lacs	Lago, Lagos
Swamp	Sumpf	Pantano	Marais	Pântano
Ice Features, Glacier	Eis- und Gletscherformen	Accidentes Glaciales	Formes glaciaires	Acidentes glaciares
Other Hydrographic Features	Andere Hydrographische Objekte	Otros Elementos Hidrográficos	Autres données hydrographiques	Outros acidentes hidrográficos

Submarine Features	Untermeerische Objekte	Accidentes Submarinos	Formes de relief sous-marin	Acidentes submarinos
□ Political Unit	Politische Einheit	Unidad Politica	Entité politique	Unidade política
Cultural Institution	Kulturelle Institution	Institución Cultural	Institution culturelle	Instituição cultural
Historical Site	Historische Stätte	Sitio Histórico	Site historique	Sitio histórico
Recreational Site	Erholungs- und Ferienort	Sitio de Recreo	Centre de loisirs	Area de Lazer
Airport	Flughafen	Aeropuerto	Aéroport	Aeroporto
■ Military Installation	Militäranlage	Instalación Militar	Installation militaire	Instalação militar
◆ Miscellaneous	Verschiedenes	Misceláneo	Divers	Diversos

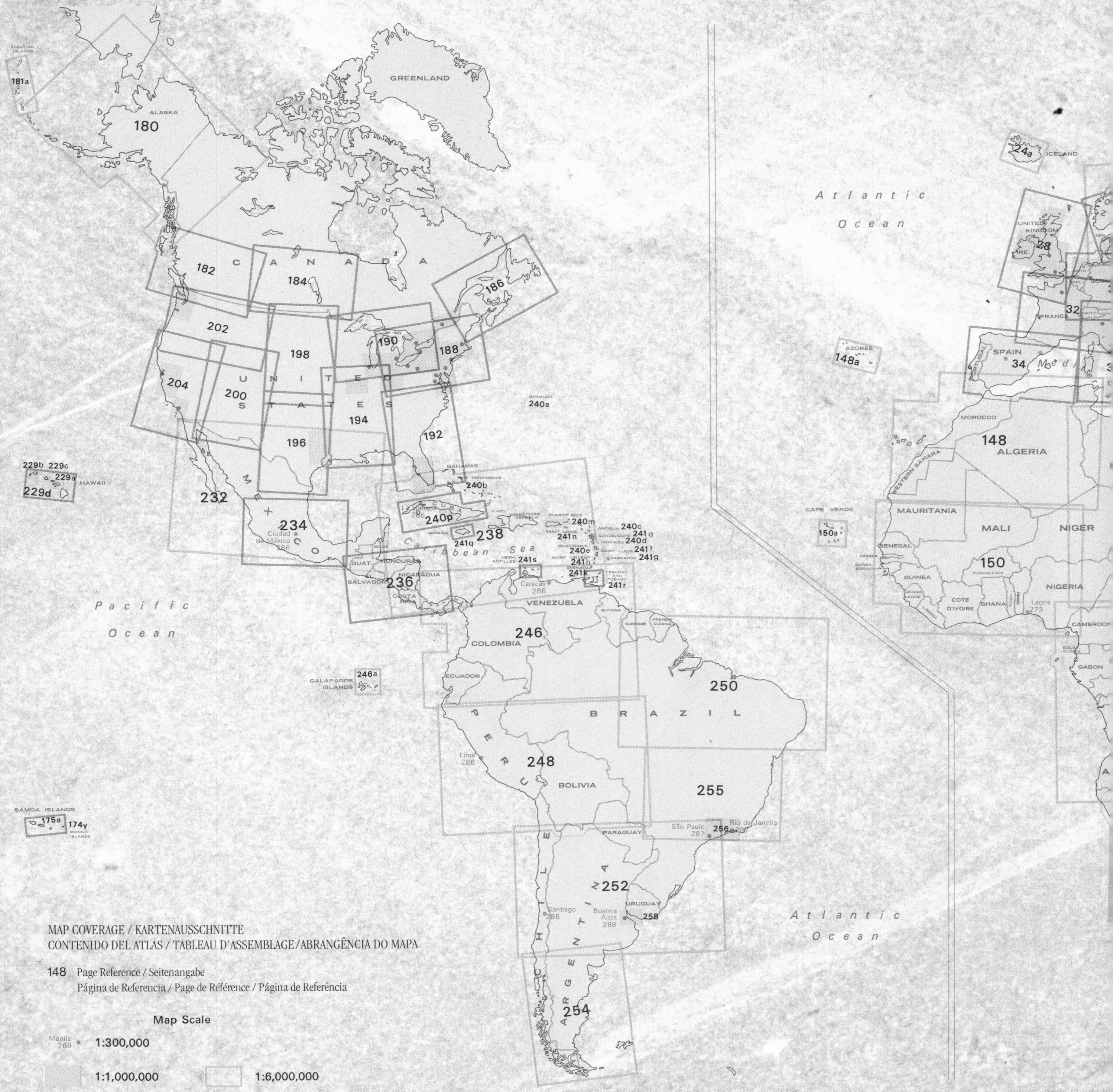
GREENLAND
ALASKA
180
181a
C A N A D A
182
184
186
188
190
192
194
196
198
200
202
204
U N I T E D S T A T E S
M E X I C O
232
234
236
238
240a
240b
240p
241q
BERMUDA
BAHAMAS
Ciudad de México 286
Caribbean Sea
Pacific Ocean
Atlantic Ocean
HAWAII
229a
229b
229c
229d
GALAPAGOS ISLANDS
246a
SAMOA ISLANDS
175a
174y
VENEZUELA
Caracas 286
COLOMBIA
246
ECUADOR
PERU
Lima 286
248
BOLIVIA
B R A Z I L
250
255
São Paulo 287
Rio de Janeiro
256
PARAGUAY
URUGUAY
258
CHILE
Santiago 286
Buenos Aires 288
ARGENTINA
252
254
AZORES
148a
ICELAND
24a
UNITED KINGDOM
28
FRANCE
32
SPAIN
34
MOROCCO
148
ALGERIA
CAPE VERDE
150a
MAURITANIA
MALI
NIGER
150
NIGERIA
Lagos 273
GABON

MAP COVERAGE / KARTENAUSSCHNITTE
CONTENIDO DEL ATLAS / TABLEAU D'ASSEMBLAGE / ABRANGÊNCIA DO MAPA

148 Page Reference / Seitenangabe
Página de Referencia / Page de Référence / Página de Referência

Map Scale

Manila 289 • 1:300,000

1:1,000,000 1:6,000,000

1:3,000,000 1:12,000,000

Enlarged maps of Anglo-America and Europe on page XIII.
Vergrösserte Karten von Anglo-Amerika und Europa auf Seite XIII.
Mapas aumentados de América Anglosajona y Europa, página XIII.
Cartes à grande échelle de l'Amérique anglo-saxonne et de l'Europe à la page XIII.
Mapas ampliados da América Anglo-saxônica e da Europa, página XIII.

World, Ocean, and Continent maps on page 2-19.
Weltkarten, Karten der Ozeane und Erdteile auf Seiten 2-19.
Mapas del Mundo, Océanos y Continentes, páginas 2-19.
Cartes du Monde, des Océans et des Continents aux pages 2-19.
Mapas do Mundo, dos Oceanos e dos Continentes, páginas 2-19.

Additional Pacific Ocean Island maps on pages 174-175.
Zusätzliche Karten der Inseln des Pazifischen Ozeans auf Seite 174 175.
Mapas adicionales de las Islas del Océano Pacífico, páginas 174-175.
Cartes supplémentaires des Îles de l'Océan Pacifique aux pages 174-175.
Mapas suplementares das ilhas do Oceano Pacífico, páginas 174-175.